Income
Tax
Regulations

Including
Proposed
Regulations

As of November 10, 2011

Volume 4

§ 1.970-1–§ 25.2704-3

CCH Editorial Staff Publication

.CCH

a Wolters Kluwer business

ISBN 978-0-8080-2737-9 (Set)
ISBN 978-0-8080-2768-3 (Volume 1)
ISBN 978-0-8080-2769-0 (Volume 2)
ISBN 978-0-8080-2770-6 (Volume 3)
ISBN 978-0-8080-2771-3 (Volume 4)
ISBN 978-0-8080-2772-0 (Volume 5)
ISBN 978-0-8080-2773-7 (Volume 6)

4025 W. Peterson Ave.
Chicago, IL 60646-6085
800 248 3248
CCHGroup.com

Printed in the United States of America

SUSTAINABLE FORESTRY INITIATIVE

Certified Fiber Sourcing

www.sfiprogram.org

Income from Sources Without the United States

See p. 20,601 for regulations not amended to reflect law changes

[Reg. §1.970-1]

§1.970-1. Export trade corporations.—(a) *In general.*—Sections 970 through 972 provide in general that if a controlled foreign corporation is an export trade corporation for any taxable year, the subpart F income of such corporation shall, subject to limitations provided by section 970(a) and paragraph (b) of this section, be reduced by so much of such corporation's export trade income as constitutes foreign base company income. To the extent subpart F income of an export trade corporation is reduced under section 970 and this section, an amount is required by section 970(b) and paragraph (c) of this section to be included in gross income of United States shareholders of the corporation if there is a subsequent decrease in such corporation's investments in export trade assets. See section 971(a) and paragraph (a) of §1.971-1 for definition of the term "export trade corporation", section 971(b) and paragraph (b) of §1.971-1 for definition of the term "export trade income", and section 971(c) and paragraph (c) of §1.971-1 for definition of the term "export trade assets".

(b) *Amount by which export trade income shall reduce subpart F income.*—(1) *Deductible amount.*—The subpart F income, determined as provided in section 952 and the regulations thereunder but without regard to section 970 and this paragraph, of a controlled foreign corporation which is an export trade corporation for its taxable year shall be reduced by an amount equal to so much of its export trade income as constitutes foreign base company income for such taxable year, but only to the extent that such amount of export trade income does not exceed the limitation determined under subparagraph (2) of this paragraph for such taxable year. See section 972 and §1.972-1 for rules relating to the consolidation of export trade corporations for purposes of determining the limitations described in subparagraph (2) of this paragraph.

(2) *Limitation on the amount of export trade income deductible from subpart F income.*—The amount by which subpart F income of an export trade corporation may be reduced for any taxable year under subparagraph (1) of this paragraph may not exceed whichever of the following limitations is the smallest:

(i) The amount which is equal to 150 percent of the export promotion expenses, as defined in section 971(d) and paragraph (d) of §1.971-1, of the export trade corporation paid or incurred during the taxable year which are properly allocable to the receipt or the production of so much of its export trade income as constitutes foreign base company income for such taxable year;

(ii) The amount which is equal to 10 percent of the gross receipts (other than from commissions, fees, or other compensation for services), plus 10 percent of the gross amount upon the basis of which are computed commissions, fees, or other compensation for services included in gross receipts, of the export trade corporation received or accrued during the taxable year from, or in connection with, the sale, installation, operation, maintenance, or use of property in respect of which such corporation derives export trade income which constitutes foreign base company income for such taxable year; or

(iii) The amount which bears the same ratio to the increase in investments in export trade assets, as defined in section 970(c)(2) and paragraph (d)(2) of this section, of the export trade corporation for its taxable year as the export trade income which constitutes foreign base company income of such corporation for such taxable year bears to the entire export trade income of the corporation for such year.

Under subdivision (ii) of this subparagraph, in the case of minimum or maximum fee arrangements, the determination shall be made on the basis of the actual gross amounts with respect to which such fees are paid, rather than on the basis of the amounts upon which such minimum or maximum fees are computed. All determinations of limitations under this subparagraph shall be made on an aggregate basis and not with respect to separate items or categories of income described in paragraph (b)(1) of §1.971-1.

(3) *Determination of export promotion expense limitation.*—For purposes of determining the limitation contained in subparagraph (2)(i) of this paragraph for any taxable year of the export trade corporation, there shall be taken into account with respect to those items or categories of export trade income which constitute foreign base company income the entire amount of those export promotion expenses which are directly related to such items or categories of income and a ratable part of any other export promotion expenses which are indirectly related to such items or categories of income, except that no export promotion expense shall be allocated to an item or category of income to which it clearly does not apply and no deduction allowable to such corporation under section 882(c) and the regulations thereunder shall be taken into account.

(4) *Application of section 482.*—The limitations provided in section 970(a) and subparagraph (2) of this paragraph shall not affect the authority of the district director to apply the provisions of section 482 and the regulations

thereunder, relating to allocation of income and deductions among taxpayers.

(5) *Illustrations.*—The application of this paragraph may be illustrated by the following examples:

Example (1). Foreign corporation A is a wholly owned subsidiary of domestic corporation M. Both corporations use the calendar year as the taxable year. For 1963, A Corporation's subpart F income determined under section 952 and the regulations thereunder is $35, the total of its gross receipts and gross amounts referred to in subparagraph (2)(ii) of this paragraph is $310, its export promotion expenses properly allocable to its export trade income which constitutes foreign base company income are $18, its increase in investments in export trade assets is $32, and its export trade income is $40, of which $30 constitutes foreign base company income and $10 does not constitute foreign base company income. The subpart F income of A Corporation for 1963 as reduced under section 970(a) is $11, determined as follows:

(i)	Subpart F income	$35
(ii)	Less: $30 export trade income which constitutes foreign base company income, but deduction not to exceed the smallest of the following limitations (smallest of *(a)*, *(b)*, or *(c)*):	
(a)	150 percent of allocable export promotion expenses referred to in subparagraph (2)(i) of this paragraph (150% of $18)	$27
(b)	10 percent of gross receipts and gross amounts referred to in subparagraph (2)(ii) of this paragraph (10% of $310)	31
(c)	Amount which bears to the increase in investments in export trade assets ($32) the same ratio as the export trade income which constitutes foreign base company income ($30) bears to total export trade income ($40) (75% [$30/$40] of $32)	24 $24
(iii)	Subpart F income as reduced under sec. 970(a)	11

Example (2). The facts are the same as in example (1), except that A Corporation's export promotion expenses properly allocable to export trade income which constitutes foreign base company income are $14 instead of $18. The applicable limitation on the amount deductible from A Corporation's subpart F income for 1963 is $21 (150% of $14) instead of $24. The subpart F income as reduced under section 970(a) is $14 ($35 less $21).

Example (3). The facts are the same as in example (1), except that the total amount of A Corporation's gross receipts and gross amounts referred to in subparagraph (2)(ii) of this paragraph is $200 instead of $310. The applicable limitation on the amount deductible from A Corporation's subpart F income for 1963 is $20 (10 percent of $200) instead of $24. The subpart F income as reduced under section 970(a) is $15 ($35 less $20).

Example (4). The facts are the same as in example (1), except that A Corporation derives its export trade income which constitutes foreign base company income of $30 in a service arrangement with M Corporation under which it receives as a fee 5 percent of the gross receipts from M Corporation's sales or a minimum fee of $30. Such gross receipts are $220. The gross amounts taken into account in determining the limitation under subparagraph (2)(ii) of this paragraph are $220. The applicable limitation on the amount deductible from A Corporation's subpart F income for 1963 is $22 (10 percent of $220) instead of $24. The subpart F income as reduced under section 970(a) is $13 ($35 minus $22).

Example (5). The facts are the same as in example (1), except that A Corporation derives its export trade income which constitutes foreign base company income of $30 in a service arrangement with M Corporation under which it receives as a fee 9 percent of the gross receipts from M Corporation's sales or a maximum fee of $30. Such gross receipts are $400. In such instance, the limitation under (ii)*(b)* of example (1) is $40 (10 percent of $400 instead of $31. The applicable limitation on the amount deductible from A Corporation's subpart F income for 1963 is $24, the smallest of the three limitations. The subpart F income as reduced under section 970(a) is $11 ($35 less $24).

(c) *Withdrawal of previously excluded export trade income.*—(1) *Inclusion of withdrawal in income of United States shareholders.*—If—

(i) a controlled foreign corporation was an export trade corporation for any taxable year,

(ii) such corporation in any such taxable year derived subpart F income which, under the provisions of section 970(a) and paragraph (b) of this section, was reduced, and

(iii) such corporation has in a subsequent taxable year a decrease in investments in export trade assets,

every person who is a United States shareholder, as defined in section 951(b), of such corporation on the last day of such subsequent taxable year on which such corporation is a controlled foreign corporation shall include in his gross income, under section 951(a)(1)(A)(ii) and the regulations thereunder as an amount to which section 955 (as in effect before the enactment of the Tax Reduction Act of 1975) applies, his pro rata share of the amount of such decrease in investments but only to the extent that such pro rata share does not exceed the limitations determined under subparagraph (2) of this paragraph. A United States shareholder's pro rata share of a controlled foreign corporation's decrease for any taxable year in investments in export trade assets shall be his pro rata share of such corporation's decrease for such year determined under section 970(c)(3) and paragraph (d)(3) of this section.

(2) *Limitations applicable in determining amount includible in income.*—(i) *General.*—A United States shareholder's pro rata share of a controlled foreign corporation's decrease in investments in export trade assets for any taxable year of such corporation shall, for purposes of determining an amount to be included in the gross income for any taxable year of such shareholder, not exceed the lesser of the limitations determined under *(a)* and *(b)* of this subdivision:

(a) Such shareholder's pro rata share of the sum of the controlled foreign corporation's earnings and profits (or deficit in earnings and profits) for the taxable year, computed as of the close of the taxable year without diminution by reason of any distributions made during the taxable year, plus his pro rata share of the sum of its earnings and profits (or deficits in earnings and profits) accumulated for prior taxable years beginning after December 31, 1962, or

(b)(1) Such shareholder's pro rata share of the sum of the amounts by which the subpart F income of such controlled foreign corporation for prior taxable years was reduced under section 970(a) and paragraph (b) of this section, plus

(2) Such shareholder's pro rata share of the sum of the amounts which were not included in the subpart F income of such controlled foreign corporation for such prior taxable years by reason of the application of section 972 and § 1.972-1, minus

(3) Such shareholder's pro rata share of the sum of the amounts which were previously included in his gross income for prior taxable years under section 951(a)(1)(A)(ii) by reason of the application of section 970(b) and this paragraph with respect to such controlled foreign corporation. The net amount determined under *(b)* of this subdivision with respect to any stock owned by the United States shareholder shall be determined without taking into account any amount attributable to a period prior to the date on which such shareholder acquired such stock. See section 1248 and the regulations thereunder for rules governing the treatment of gain from sales or exchanges of stock in certain foreign corporations.

(ii) *Treatment of earnings and profits.*—For purposes of determining earnings and profits of a controlled foreign corporation under subdivision (i)*(a)* of this subparagraph, such earnings and profits shall be considered not to include any amounts which are attributable to—

(a) Amounts which are, or have been, included in the gross income of a United States shareholder of such controlled foreign corporation under section 951(a) (other than an amount included in the gross income of a United States shareholder under section 951(a)(1)(A)(ii) or section 951 (a)(1)(B) for the taxable year) and have not been distributed, or

(b)(1) Amounts which, for the current taxable year, are included in the gross income of a United States shareholder of such controlled foreign corporation under section 551(b) or would be so included under such section but for the fact that such amounts were distributed to such shareholder during the taxable year, or

(2) Amounts which, for any prior taxable year, have been included in the gross income of a United States shareholder of such controlled foreign corporation under section 551(b) and have not been distributed. The rules of this subdivision apply only in determining the limitation on a United States shareholder's pro rata share of a controlled foreign corporation's decrease in investments in export trade assets. See section 959 and the regulations thereunder for limitations on the exclusion of previously taxed earnings and profits.

(iii) *Rules of application.*—The determinations made under subdivision (i) of this subparagraph for purposes of determining the United States shareholder's pro rata share of a controlled foreign corporation's decrease in investments in export trade assets for any taxable year shall be made on the basis of the stock such shareholder owns, within the meaning of section 958(a) and the regulations thereunder, in the controlled foreign corporation on the last day in the taxable year on which such corporation is a controlled foreign corporation even though such shareholder owned more or less stock in such corporation prior to that date. See section 972 and paragraph (b)(3) of § 1.972-1 for rules relating to the allocation of a decrease in investments in export trade assets of export trade corporations in a consolidated chain of such corporations. See section 951(a)(3) and the regulations thereunder for an additional limitation upon the amount of a United States shareholder's pro rata share determined under this paragraph.

(3) *Illustrations.*—The application of this paragraph may be illustrated by the following examples:

Example (1). Foreign corporation A, which has one class of stock outstanding, is a wholly owned subsidiary of domestic corporation M throughout 1963 and 1964. Both corporations use the calendar year as the taxable year. For 1963, A Corporation qualifies as an export trade corporation and its subpart F income, determined in accordance with the provisions of section 952 and the regulations thereunder, is reduced by $20 under the provisions of section 970(a) and paragraph (b) of this section. Section 972 is assumed not to apply to A Corporation. For 1964, A Corporation has a decrease of $8 in investments in export trade assets. For 1963 and 1964, A Corporation has earnings and profits of $30 (determined under the provisions of subparagraph (2) of this paragraph). Corporation M's pro rata share of A Corporation's decrease in investments in export trade assets for 1964 which is includible in M Corporation's gross income for 1964 under section 951(a)(1)(A)(ii) by reason of the application of section 970(b) is $8, determined as follows:

(i) Corporation M's pro rata share of A Corporation's decrease in investments in export trade assets for 1964 (100% of $8)		$8
(ii) Limitation on amount includible in gross income of M Corporation for 1964 (smaller of (a) or (b)):		
(a) Corporation M's pro rata share of A Corporation's earnings and profits for 1963 and 1964 determined under subparagraph (2) of this paragraph (100% of $30)		$30
(b) Corporation M's pro rata share of amounts by which the subpart F income of A Corporation for 1963 was reduced under sec. 970(a)(100% of $20)	$20	
Plus: Corporation M's pro rata share of amounts which were not included in subpart F income of A Corporation for 1963 by reason of the application of sec. 972	0	
Total	$20	
Less: Corporation M's pro rata share of the sum of amounts which were previously included in gross income of M Corporation under sec. 951(a)(1)(A)(ii) by reason of the application of sec. 970(b) with respect to A Corporation	0	20
(iii) Corporation M's pro rata share includible in gross income for 1964 under sec. 951(a)(1)(A)(ii) by reason of the application of sec. 970(b) (smaller of (i) or (ii))		$8

Example (2). Assume the same facts as in example (1), except that on February 14, 1965, M Corporation sells 25 percent of its stock in A Corporation to N Corporation. Corporation N is a domestic corporation which also uses the calendar year as a taxable year. For 1965, A Corporation has a decrease of $16 in investments in

export trade assets. Corporation A's earnings and profits for 1963 and 1964 (determined under the provisions of subparagraph (2) of this paragraph) are $22 ($30 minus $8). Corporation A's earnings and profits for 1965 are $6 (determined under the provisions of subparagraph (2) of this paragraph). For 1965, M Corporation's pro rata share of A Corporation's decrease in investments in export trade assets which is includible in M Corporation's gross income under section 951(a)(1)(A)(ii) is $9, and N Corporation's pro rata share includible in gross income under such section is $0, determined as follows:

M CORPORATION

(i) Corporation M's pro rata share of A Corporation's decrease in investments in export trade assets for 1965 (75% of $16)		$12
(ii) Limitation on amount includible in gross income of M Corporation for 1965 (smaller of (a) or (b)):		
(a) Corporation M's pro rata share of A Corporation's earnings and profits for 1963, 1964, and 1965 determined under subparagraph (2) of this paragraph (75% of $28) .		$21
(b) Corporation M's pro rata share of amounts by which the subpart F income of A Corporation for 1963 was reduced under sec. 970(a) (75% of $20)	$15	
Plus: Corporation M's pro rata share of amounts which were not included in subpart F income of A Corporation for 1963 and 1964 by reason of the application of sec. 972 . .	$0	
Total	$15	
Less: Corporation M's pro rata share of the sum of amounts which were previously included in gross income of M Corporation under sec. 951(a)(1)(A)(ii) by reason of the application of sec. 970(b) with respect to A Corporation (75% of $8) .	$6	$9
(iii) Corporation M's pro rata share includible in gross income for 1965 under sec. 951(a)(1)(A)(ii) by reason of the application of sec. 970(b) (smaller of (i) or (ii))		$9

N CORPORATION

(i) Corporation N's pro rata share of A Corporation's decrease in investments in export trade assets for 1965 (25% of $16) $4

(ii) Limitation on amount includible in gross income of N Corporation for 1965 (smaller of (a) or (b)):

(a) Corporation N's pro rata share of A Corporation's earnings and profits for 1963, 1964, and 1965 determined under subparagraph (2) of this paragraph (25% of $28) . $7

(b) Corporation N's pro rata share of amounts by which the subpart F income of A Corporation for 1963 was reduced under sec. 970(a) (amounts prior to 2/14/65 not being taken into account)

. . . . $0

Plus: Corporation N's pro rata share of amounts which were not included in subpart F income of A Corporation for 1963 and 1964 by reason of the application of sec. 972 (amounts prior to 2/14/65 not being taken into account) $0

Total $0

Less: Corporation N's pro rata share of the sum of amounts which were previously included in gross income of N Corporation under sec. 951(a)(1)(A)(ii) by reason of the application of sec. 970(b) with respect to A Corporation (amounts prior to 2/14/65 not being taken into account) $0 $0

(iii) Corporation N's pro rata share includible in gross income for 1965 under sec. 951(a)(1)(A)(ii) by reason of the application of sec. 970(b) (smaller of (i) or (ii)) $0

(d) *Investments in export trade assets.*—(1) *Amount of investments.*—For purposes of sections 970 through 972 and §§ 1.970-1 to 1.972-1, inclusive, export trade assets shall be taken into account on the following bases:

(i) *Working capital.*—Working capital to which section 971(c)(1) applies shall be taken into account at the adjusted basis of current assets, determined as of the applicable determina-tion date, less any current liabilities (except as provided in subdivision (iii) of this subparagraph).

(ii) *Other export trade assets.*—Inventory to which section 971(c)(2) applies, facilities to which section 971(c)(3) applies, and evidences of indebtedness to which section 971(c)(4) applies, shall be taken into account at their adjusted bases as of the applicable determination date, reduced by any liabilities (except as provided in subdivision (iii) of this subparagraph) to which such property is subject on such date. To be taken into account under this subparagraph, a liability must constitute a specific charge against the property involved. Thus, a liability evidenced by an open account or a liability secured only by the general credit of the controlled foreign corporation will not be taken into account. On the other hand, if a liability constitutes a specific charge against several items of property and cannot definitely be allocated to any single item of property, the liability shall be apportioned against each of such items of property in that ratio which the adjusted basis of such item on the applicable determination date bears to the adjusted basis of all such items on such date. A liability in excess of the adjusted basis of the property which is subject to such liability will not be taken into account for the purpose of reducing the adjusted basis of other property which is not subject to such liability. See paragraph (c)(6) of § 1.971-1 for treatment of export trade assets which constitute working capital to which section 971(c)(1) applies and which also constitute inventory to which section 971(c)(2) applies or evidences of indebtedness to which section 971(c)(4) applies.

(iii) *Treatment of certain liabilities.*—For purposes of subdivisions (i) and (ii) of this subparagraph, a current liability, or a specific charge created with respect to any item of property, principally for the purpose of artificially increasing or decreasing the amount of a controlled foreign corporation's investments in export trade assets shall be taken into account in such a manner as to properly reflect the controlled foreign corporation's investments in export trade assets; whether a specific charge or current liability is created principally for such purpose will depend upon all the facts and circumstances of each case. One of the factors that will be considered in making such a determination with respect to a loan is whether the loan is from a related person, as defined in section 954(d)(3) and paragraph (e) of § 1.954-1.

(iv) *Statement required.*—If for purposes of this section a United States shareholder of a controlled foreign corporation reduces the adjusted basis of property which constitutes an export trade asset on the ground that such property is subject to a liability, he shall attach to his return a statement setting forth the adjusted basis of the property before the reduction and the amount and nature of the reduction.

(2) *Increase in investments in export trade assets.*—For purposes of section 970(a) and paragraph (b) of this section, the amount of increase in investments in export trade assets of a controlled foreign corporation for a taxable year shall be, except as provided in §1.970-2, the amount by which—

(i) The amount of its investments in export trade assets at the close of such taxable year, exceeds

(ii) The amount of its investments in export trade assets at the close of the preceding taxable year.

(3) *Decrease in investments in export trade assets.*—For purposes of section 970(b) and paragraph (c) of this section, the amount of the decrease in investments in export trade assets of a controlled foreign corporation for a taxable year shall be, except as provided in §1.970-2, the amount by which—

(i) The amount of its investments in export trade assets at the close of the preceding taxable year, minus

(ii) An amount equal to the excess of recognized losses over recognized gains on sales, exchanges, involuntary conversions, or other dispositions, of export trade assets during the taxable year, exceeds

(iii) The amount of its investments in export trade assets at the close of the taxable year.
For purposes of subdivision (ii) of this subparagraph, recognized losses include a write-down of inventory to lower of cost or market in accordance with a method of inventory valuation established or adopted by or on behalf of such foreign corporation under paragraph (c) of §1.964-1. [Reg. §1.970-1.]

☐ [*T.D. 6755, 9-8-64. Amended by T.D. 6795, 1-28-65, T.D. 6892, 8-22-66, T.D. 7293, 11-27-73 and T.D. 7893, 5-11-83.*]

[Reg. §1.970-2]

§1.970-2. Elections as to date of determining investments in export trade assets.—(a) *Nature of elections.*—(1) *In general.*—In lieu of determining the increase under the provisions of paragraph (d)(2) of §1.970-1, or the decrease under the provisions of paragraph (d)(3) of §1.970-1, in a controlled foreign corporation's investments in export trade assets for a taxable year in the manner provided in such provisions, a United States shareholder of such corporation may elect, under the provisions of section 970(c)(4) and this section, to determine such increase or decrease in accordance with the provisions of subparagraph (2) of this paragraph or, in the case of export trade assets which are facilities described in section 971(c)(3), in accordance with the provisions of subparagraph (3) of this paragraph. Separate elections may be made under subparagraph (2)

and/or (3) of this paragraph with respect to each controlled foreign corporation with respect to which a person is a United States shareholder, within the meaning of section 951(b).

(2) *Election of 75-day rule.*—A United States shareholder of a controlled foreign corporation may elect with respect to a taxable year of such corporation to make the determinations under subparagraphs (2)(i) and (3)(iii) of paragraph (d) of §1.970-1 of the amount of such corporation's investments in export trade assets as of the 75th day after the close of the taxable year referred to in such subparagraphs of paragraph (d) of §1.970-1. The election provided by this subparagraph may be made with respect to export trade assets other than facilities described in section 971(c)(3) or with respect to export trade assets which are facilities or with respect to both types of export trade assets (but the election under this paragraph with respect to export trade assets which are facilities or with respect to both types of export trade assets may be made only if the election provided by subparagraph (3) of this paragraph is not made). If the election provided by this subparagraph is made, the amount of export trade assets with respect to which such election is made at the close of the preceding taxable year which is described in subparagraphs (2)(ii) and (3)(i) of paragraph (d) of §1.970-1 shall be the amount of export trade assets which was considered by application of the 75-day rule to be the amount of export trade assets at the close of such preceding taxable year; except that for the first taxable year of the controlled foreign corporation for which the 75-day rule is elected the amount of investments in export trade assets with respect to which such election is made at the close of such preceding year described in subparagraphs (2)(ii) and (3)(i) of paragraph (d) of §1.970-1 shall be the amount of investments in export trade assets at the actual close of such preceding year. In the case of a taxable year of such corporation beginning after December 31, 1962, and before December 31, 1963, the amount of investments in export trade assets with respect to which such election is made alternatively may be determined by the United States shareholder as of the 75th day after the close of the preceding taxable year referred to in subparagraphs (2)(ii) and (3)(i) of paragraph (d) of §1.970-1 rather than as of the close of such preceding taxable year.

(3) *Election for export trade assets which are facilities.*—A United States shareholder of a controlled foreign corporation may elect with respect to a taxable year of such corporation to make the determinations under subparagraphs (2)(i) and (3)(iii) of paragraph (d) of §1.970-1 of the amount of such corporation's investments in export trade assets which are facilities described in section 971(c)(3) as of the close of such corporation's taxable year following the taxable year referred to in such subparagraphs of paragraph

(d) of §1.970-1. The election provided by this subparagraph may be made only if the United States shareholder does not elect the 75-day rule of subparagraph (2) of this paragraph with respect to export trade assets which are facilities. If the election provided by this subparagraph is made, the amount of investments in export trade assets which are facilities at the close of the preceding taxable year which is described in subparagraphs (2)(ii) and (3)(i) of paragraph (d) of §1.970-1 shall be the amount of export trade assets which are facilities which was considered, by reason of the application of the following-year rule provided in this subparagraph with respect to such preceding taxable year, to be the amount of export trade assets which are facilities at the close of such preceding taxable year; except that for the first taxable year of the controlled foreign corporation for which such following-year rule is elected the amount of investments in export trade assets which are facilities at the close of the preceding taxable year described in subparagraphs (2)(ii) and (3)(i) of paragraph (d) of §1.970-1 shall be the amount of investments in export trade assets which are facilities at the actual close of such preceding taxable year.

(b) *Time and manner of making elections.*— (1) *Without consent.*—A United States shareholder may, with respect to any controlled foreign corporation, make one or both of the elections described in paragraph (a)(2) or (3) of this section without the consent of the Commissioner by filing a statement to such effect with his return for his taxable year in which or with which ends the first taxable year of such corporation in which—

(i) Such shareholder owns, within the meaning of section 958(a), or is considered as owning, by applying the rules of section 958(b), 10 percent or more of the total combined voting power of all classes of stock entitled to vote of such corporation, and

(ii) Such corporation realizes subpart F income which is reduced under section 970(a) and paragraph (b) of §1.970-1.

The statement shall contain the name and address of the controlled foreign corporation, identification of such first taxable year of such corporation, and an indication as to which election or elections described in paragraph (a) of this section the United States shareholder is making. If such return has been filed on or before the 90th day after the date these regulations are published in the Federal Register, such United States shareholder shall file such statement with the district director with which the return was filed on or before such 90th day.

(2) *With consent.*—A United States shareholder may make one or both of the elections described in paragraph (a)(2) or (3) of this section with respect to any controlled foreign corpo-

ration at any time with the consent of the Commissioner. Consent will not be granted unless the shareholder and the Commissioner agree to the terms, conditions, and adjustments under which the election will be effected. The application for consent to elect shall be made by the shareholder's mailing a letter for such purpose to the Commissioner of Internal Revenue, Washington, D.C. 20224. The application shall be mailed before the close of the first taxable year of the controlled foreign corporation with respect to which the shareholder desires to determine an exclusion under section 970(a) in accordance with one or both of the elections provided in paragraph (a) of this section. The application shall include the following information:

(i) The name, address, and taxable year of the United States shareholder;

(ii) The name, address, and taxable year of the controlled foreign corporation;

(iii) A statement indicating which of the elections the shareholder desires to make;

(iv) The amount of the foreign corporation's investments in export trade assets (by a category which includes export trade assets other than facilities and a category which includes only export trade assets which are facilities) at the close of its preceding taxable year;

(v) The shareholder's pro rata share of the sum of the amounts by which the subpart F income of the foreign corporation, for all prior taxable years during which such shareholder was a United States shareholder of such corporation, was reduced under section 970(a) and paragraph (b) of §1.970-1;

(vi) The shareholder's pro rata share of the sum of the amounts which were not included in the subpart F income of the foreign corporation, for all prior taxable years during which such shareholder was a United States shareholder of such corporation, by reason of the application of section 972 and §1.972-1; and

(vii) The shareholder's pro rata share of the sum of the amounts which were previously included in his gross income, for all prior taxable years during which such shareholder was a United States shareholder of such corporation, under section 951(a)(1)(A)(ii) by reason of the application of section 970(b) and paragraph (b) of §1.970-1 to the foreign corporation.

(c) *Effect of elections.*—(1) *General.*—Except as provided in subparagraphs (3) and (4) of this paragraph, an election made under paragraph (a) of this section with respect to a controlled foreign corporation shall be binding on the United States shareholder and—

(i) In the case of the election described in paragraph (a)(2) of this section, shall apply to all investments in export trade assets with respect to which such election is made, acquired, or disposed of, by such corporation during the 75-day period following its taxable year for which subpart F income is first computed under

Reg. §1.970-2(c)(1)(i)

the election and during all succeeding corresponding 75-day periods of such corporation, or

(ii) In the case of the election described in paragraph (a)(3) of this section, shall apply to all investments in export trade assets which are facilities acquired, or disposed of, by such corporation during the taxable year following its taxable year for which subpart F income is first computed under the election and during all succeeding corresponding taxable years of such corporation.

(2) *Returns.*—Any return of a United States shareholder required to be filed before the completion of a period with respect to which determinations are to be made as to a controlled foreign corporation's investments in export trade assets for purposes of computing such shareholder's taxable income shall be filed on the basis of an estimate of the amount of such corporation's investments in export trade assets at the close of the period. If the actual amount of such investments is not the same as the amount of the estimate, the shareholder shall immediately notify the Commissioner. The Commissioner will thereupon redetermine the amount of such shareholder's tax for the year or years with respect to which the incorrect amount was taken into account. The amount of tax, if any, due upon such redetermination shall be paid by the shareholder upon notice and demand by the district director. The amount of tax, if any, shown by such redetermination to have been overpaid shall be credited or refunded to the shareholder in accordance with the provisions of sections 6402 and 6511 and the regulations thereunder.

(3) *Revocation.*—(i) *In general.*—(a) *Consent required.*—Upon application by the United States shareholder, an election made under paragraph (a) of this section may, subject to the approval of the Commissioner, be revoked. Approval will not be granted unless the shareholder and the Commissioner agree to the terms, conditions, and adjustments under which the revocation will be effected.

(b) *Revocation of 75-day rule.*—In the case of the revocation of an election described in paragraph (a)(2) of this section, the change in the controlled foreign corporation's investments in export trade assets with respect to which such election was made for its first taxable year for which subpart F income or a decrease in investments in export trade assets is computed without regard to the election previously made shall, unless the agreement with the Commissioner provides otherwise, be considered to be the amount by which—

(1) Such corporation's investments in export trade assets with respect to which such election was made at the close of such taxable year exceeds or, if applicable, is exceeded by

(2) Such corporation's investments in export trade assets with respect to which such

election was made at the close of the 75th day after the close of the preceding taxable year of such corporation.

(c) *Revocation of following-year rule.*—In the case of the revocation of an election described in paragraph (a)(3) of this section, the change in the controlled foreign corporation's investments in export trade assets which are facilities for its first taxable year for which subpart F income or a decrease in investments in export trade assets is computed without regard to the election previously made shall, unless the agreement with the Commissioner provides otherwise, be considered to be zero.

(ii) *Time and manner of applying for consent to revocation.*—(a) *Application to Commissioner.*—The application for consent to revocation of an election shall be made by the United States shareholder's mailing a letter for such purpose to the Commissioner of Internal Revenue, Washington, D.C., 20224. The application shall be mailed before the close of the first taxable year of the controlled foreign corporation with respect to which the shareholder desires to determine an exclusion under section 970(a) or an inclusion under section 970(b) without regard to such election.

(b) *Information required.*—The application shall include the following information:

(1) The name, address, and taxable year of the United States shareholder;

(2) The name, address, and taxable year of the controlled foreign corporation;

(3) A statement indicating the election the shareholder desires to revoke under this subparagraph;

(4) The information required under subdivisions (iv) through (vii) of paragraph (b)(2) of this section;

(5) In the case of an application for consent to revocation of an election made under paragraph (a)(2) of this section, the amount of the foreign corporation's investments in export trade assets with respect to which such election was made at the close of the 75th day after the close of such corporation's taxable year immediately preceding the taxable year of such corporation; and

(6) The reason for the request for consent to revocation.

(4) *Transfer of stock.*—(i) *Election of 75-day rule in force.*—(a) If during any taxable year of a controlled foreign corporation—

(1) A United States shareholder who has made the election described in paragraph (a)(2) of this section with respect to such corporation sells, exchanges, or otherwise disposes of all or part of his stock in such corporation, and

(2) The foreign corporation is a controlled foreign corporation immediately after the sale, exchange, or other disposition,

then, with respect to the stock so sold, exchanged, or disposed of, the successor in interest shall consider the controlled foreign corporation's change during the first 75 days of such taxable year in investments in export trade assets with respect to which such election is made to be zero.

(b) If the United States shareholder's successor in interest makes an election under paragraph (a)(2) of this section in order to determine an exclusion under section 970(a) for the taxable year of such corporation in which he acquires such stock, the amount of the controlled foreign corporation's investments in export trade assets with respect to which such election is made at the close of its preceding taxable year shall be considered, with respect to the stock so acquired, to be the amount of such corporation's investments in export trade assets with respect to which such election is made at the close of the 75th day after the close of such preceding taxable year.

(c) If the United States shareholder's successor in interest makes an election under paragraph (a)(2) of this section in order to determine an exclusion under section 970(a) for a taxable year of such corporation subsequent to the taxable year in which he acquired the stock, the amount of the controlled foreign corporation's investments in export trade assets with respect to which such election is made at the close of its taxable year immediately preceding such subsequent taxable year shall, with respect to the stock so acquired, be the amount of such corporation's investments in such assets at the actual close of such preceding taxable year.

(ii) *Election in force with respect to export trade assets which are facilities.*—(a) If during any taxable year of a controlled foreign corporation—

(1) A United States shareholder who has made the election described in paragraph (a)(3) of this section with respect to such corporation sells, exchanges, or otherwise disposes of all or part of his stock in such corporation, and

(2) The foreign corporation is a controlled foreign corporation immediately after the sale, exchange or other disposition,

then, with respect to the stock so sold, exchanged, or disposed of, the successor in interest shall consider the controlled foreign corporation's change for such taxable year in investments in export trade assets which are facilities to be zero.

(b) If the United States shareholder's successor in interest makes an election under paragraph (a)(3) of this section in order to determine an exclusion under section 970(a) for the taxable year of such corporation in which he acquires such stock, the amount of the controlled foreign corporation's investments in export trade assets which are facilities at the close of its preceding taxable year shall be considered, with

respect to the stock so acquired, to be the amount of such corporation's investments in export trade assets which are facilities at the close of the taxable year in which such stock is acquired.

(c) If the United States shareholder's successor in interest makes an election under paragraph (a)(3) of this section in order to determine an exclusion under section 970(a) for a taxable year of such corporation subsequent to the taxable year in which he acquired the stock, the amount of the controlled foreign corporation's investments in export trade assets which are facilities at the close of its taxable year immediately preceding such subsequent taxable year shall, with respect to the stock so acquired, be the amount of such corporation's investments in such assets at the actual close of such preceding taxable year.

(d) *Illustrations.*—The principles contained in this section are illustrated by the examples set forth in paragraph (d) of § 1.955-3. [Reg. § 1.970-2.]

☐ [*T.D. 6755, 9-8-64.*]

[Reg. § 1.970-3]

§ 1.970-3. Effective date of subpart G.—Sections 970 through 972 and §§ 1.970-1 through 1.972-1 shall apply with respect to taxable years of foreign corporations beginning after December 31, 1962, and to taxable years of United States shareholders within which or with which such taxable years of such corporations end. [Reg. § 1.970-3.]

☐ [*T.D. 6755, 9-8-64.*]

[Reg. § 1.971-1]

§ 1.971-1. Definitions with respect to export trade corporations.—(a) *Export trade corporations.*—(1) *In general.*—For purposes of sections 970 through 972 and §§ 1.970-1 to 1.972-1, inclusive, the term "export trade corporation" means a controlled foreign corporation which for the period specified in subparagraph (2) of this paragraph satisfies the conditions specified in subparagraph (3) of this paragraph. However, no controlled foreign corporation may qualify as an export trade corporation for any taxable year beginning after October 31, 1971, unless it qualified as an export trade corporation for any taxable year beginning before such date. In addition, if a corporation fails to qualify as an export trade corporation for a period of any 3 consecutive taxable years beginning after October 31, 1971, then for any taxable year beginning after such 3 year period, such corporation shall not be included within the term "export trade corporation".

(2) *Three-year period.*—The period referred to in subparagraph (1) of this paragraph is the 3-year period ending with the close of the controlled foreign corporation's current taxable

year, or such part of such 3-year period as occurs on and after the beginning of the corporation's first taxable year beginning after December 31, 1962, whichever period is shorter.

(3) *Gross income requirements.*—The conditions referred to in subparagraph (1) of this paragraph are that the controlled foreign corporation derives—

(i) 90 percent or more of its gross income from sources without the United States, and

(ii)(*a*) 75 percent or more of its gross income from transactions, activities, or interest described in section 971(b) and paragraph (b) of this section, or

(*b*) 50 percent or more of its gross income from transactions, activities, or interest described in section 971(b) and paragraph (b) of this section in respect of agricultural products grown in the United States.

(4) *Determination of sources of gross income.*—The sources of gross income of a controlled foreign corporation shall be determined for purposes of subparagraph (3)(i) of this paragraph in accordance with the rules for determining sources of gross income set forth in sections 861 through 864 and the regulations thereunder.

(b) *Export trade income.*—(1) *General rule.*—For purposes of sections 970 through 972 and §§1.970-1 to 1.972-1, inclusive, the term "export trade income" means the gross export trade income of a controlled foreign corporation derived from transactions, activities, or interest described in subdivisions (i) through (vii) of this subparagraph, less deductions allowed under subdivision (viii) of this subparagraph.

(i) *Sale of export property.*—Gross export trade income of a controlled foreign corporation includes gross income it derives from the sale of export property (as defined in paragraph (e) of this section) which it purchases, if the sale is made to an unrelated person for use, consumption, or disposition outside the United States. See section 971(b)(1). As a general rule, property will be presumed to have been sold for use, consumption, or disposition in the country of destination of the sale. However, if at the time of the sale the controlled foreign corporation knows, or should have known from the facts and circumstances surrounding the sales transaction, that the property will probably be used, consumed, or disposed of in the United States, such property will be presumed to have been sold for use, consumption, or disposition in the United States unless the controlled foreign corporation establishes that such property was used, consumed, or disposed of outside the United States. For purposes of this subdivision, export property must be sold by a controlled foreign corporation in essentially the same form in which such property is purchased. Whether export property sold is in essentially the same form in which such

property is purchased shall be determined on the basis of all the facts and circumstances in each case. Storage, handling, transportation, packaging, or servicing of property will be considered not to alter the form in which property is purchased. However, manufacture or production, within the meaning of paragraph (a)(4) of §1.954-3, will be considered to alter the form in which property is purchased and no part of the gross income from the sale of such property will be treated as export trade income. The application of this subdivision may be illustrated by the following example:

Example. Controlled foreign corporation A, incorporated under the laws of foreign country Y, purchases articles manufactured in the United States from domestic corporation M and sells them in the form in which purchased to foreign corporation B, unrelated to A corporation, for use in foreign countries X, Y, and Z. The gross income of A Corporation from the purchase and sale of the articles constitutes gross export trade income.

(ii) *Commissions and other income derived in connection with the sale of export property.*—Gross export trade income of a controlled foreign corporation includes gross commissions, fees, compensation, or other income derived by such corporation from the performance for any person of commercial, industrial, financial, technical, scientific, managerial, engineering, architectural, skilled, or other services in respect of a sale by such corporation in a transaction described in subdivision (i) of this subparagraph or in respect of the sale by any other person of export property to a person unrelated to the controlled foreign corporation for use, consumption, or disposition outside the United States. Such gross export trade income includes payments received for surveys made prior to, and in connection with, the sale of such export property (whether or not such sales are ultimately consummated). See section 971(b)(1). The term "any person" or "any other person" as used in this subdivision includes a related person as defined in section 954(d)(3) and paragraph (e) of §1.954-1. The application of this subdivision may be illustrated by the following examples:

Example (1). Controlled foreign corporation A, incorporated under the laws of foreign country X, receives from M Corporation a commission equal to 6 percent of the gross selling price of all personal property shipped by M Corporation as a result of services performed by A Corporation in soliciting orders in foreign countries X, Y, and Z. In fulfillment of such orders, M Corporation ships products manufactured by it in the United States. Corporation A does not assume title to the property sold. Gross commissions received by A Corporation from M Corporation in connection with the sale of such property to persons unrelated to A Corporation for use, consumption, or disposition outside the

United States constitute gross export trade income.

Example (2). Foreign corporation B, incorporated under the laws of foreign country X, is a wholly owned subsidiary of domestic corporation N. Corporation N is engaged in the business of manufacturing heavy duty electrical equipment in the United States. By contract, N Corporation engages B Corporation for the purpose of conducting engineering, technical, and financial studies required by N Corporation in the preparation of bids to supply foreign country Y with electrical equipment for a construction project to be undertaken by such country. Corporation N pays B Corporation a fee for the services, all of which are performed in country Y, which is based upon the number of hours of work performed without regard to whether a sale is ultimately consummated. Corporation N does not receive a contract from country Y on its bid to supply equipment. Income derived by B Corporation from performance of the service contract constitutes gross export trade income.

(iii) *Commissions and other income derived in connection with the installation or maintenance of export property.*—Gross export trade income of a controlled foreign corporation includes gross commissions, fees, compensation, or other income derived by such corporation from the performance for any person or commercial, industrial, financial, technical, scientific, managerial, engineering, architectural, skilled, or other services in respect of the installation or maintenance of export property which has been sold by such corporation in a transaction described in subdivision (i) of this subparagraph or by any other person to a person unrelated to the controlled foreign corporation for use, consumption, or disposition outside the United States. See section 971(b)(1). The term "any person" or "any other person" as used in this subdivision includes a related person as defined in section 954(d)(3) and paragraph (e) of § 1.954-1.

(iv) *Commissions and other income derived in connection with the use of patents, copyrights, and other like property.*—Gross export trade income of a controlled foreign corporation includes gross commissions, fees, compensation, or other income derived by such corporation from the performance for any person of commercial, industrial, financial, technical, scientific, managerial, engineering, architectural, skilled, or other services in connection with the use outside of the United States by an unrelated person of patents, copyrights, secret processes and formulas, goodwill, trademarks, trade brands, franchises, and other like property, including gross income derived from obtaining licensees for patents, but only if the patent, copyright, or other like property is acquired, or developed, and owned by the manufacturer, producer, grower, or extractor of any export property, in respect of which the controlled foreign corpora-

tion also derives gross export trade income within the meaning of subdivision (i), (ii), or (iii) of this subparagraph. See section 971(b)(2). The application of this subdivision may be illustrated by the following example:

Example. Foreign corporation A incorporated under the laws of foreign country X, is a wholly owned subsidiary of domestic corporation M. Corporation M, the owner of a patent registered in foreign country X, grants B Corporation, a corporation unrelated to A Corporation, the right to use such patent in foreign country Y in exchange for payment of a royalty. By a separate contract with B Corporation, A Corporation agrees for a gross fee of $100,000 to furnish, by maintaining a staff of technical representatives at the offices of B Corporation, technical services to B Corporation in connection with B Corporation's use of the patent. Corporation A also derives export trade income from the sale of export property which it purchases from M Corporation, the manufacturer of such property, and sells to C Corporation, an unrelated person, for use in country Y by C Corporation. The gross fee of $100,000 received by A Corporation for the furnishing of technical services in connection with B Corporation's use of M Corporation's patent constitutes gross export trade income since the service for which the fee is paid is performed in connection with the use outside the United States by an unrelated person (B Corporation) of a patent owned by a manufacturer (M Corporation) of export property in respect of which the controlled foreign corporation (A Corporation) derives gross export trade income from the sale to an unrelated person (C Corporation) for use outside the United States of export property purchased by it from the manufacturer (M Corporation).

(v) *Income attributable to use of export property by an unrelated person.*—Gross export trade income of a controlled foreign corporation includes gross commissions, fees, rents, compensation, or other income which is received by such corporation from an unrelated person and is attributable to the use of export property by such unrelated person. See section 971(b)(3). The application of this subdivision may be illustrated by the following example:

Example. Foreign corporation A, incorporated under the laws of foreign country X, is a wholly owned subsidiary of domestic corporation M. Corporation A acquires by purchase bottling machines manufactured in the United States and leases the machines to B Corporation, a corporation unrelated to A Corporation, for use by B Corporation in foreign country Y. Gross rental income of A Corporation from the lease of the machines to B Corporation constitutes gross export trade income.

(vi) *Income attributable to the use of export property in the rendition of technical, scientific, or engineering services.*—(a) *General.*—Gross export

Reg. § 1.971-1(b)(1)(vi)(a)

trade income of a controlled foreign corporation includes gross commissions, fees, compensation, or other income which is received by such corporation from an unrelated person and is attributable to the use of export property in the performance of technical, scientific, or engineering services to such unrelated person. See section 971(b)(3).

(b) *Rule of apportionment.*—If a commission, fee, or other income received by a controlled foreign corporation from an unrelated person under a contract or arrangement for the performance of technical, scientific, or engineering services is not solely attributable to the use of export property in the performance of such services and the amount of the gross income attributable to such use of export property cannot be established by reference to transactions between other unrelated persons, such gross income shall be an amount which bears the same ratio to total gross income from the contract or arrangement as the cost of the export property consumed in the performance of such services, including a reasonable allowance for depreciation with respect to the export property so used, bears to the total costs and expenses attributable to the production of income under the contract or arrangement.

(c) *Illustration.*—The application of this subdivision may be illustrated by the following example:

Example. Foreign corporation A, incorporated under the laws of foreign country X, is a wholly owned subsidiary of domestic corporation M. Corporation A is engaged in the seismograph service business in foreign country X. In an effort to establish the probable existence of oil in a concession area it owns in foreign country Y, B Corporation which is unrelated to A Corporation enters into a contract with A Corporation whereby A Corporation is required to make seismographic tests of the area in country Y for a fixed fee of $100,000. In performance of the contract, A Corporation hires a skilled crew to carry out the contract and utilizes equipment and supplies (for example, trucks, seismographic equipment, etc.) which constitute export property. Corporation A cannot establish by reference to transactions between other unrelated persons, the income attributable to the use of the export property in the performance of the contract. Corporation A's total costs and expenses (for example, salaries of the crew, administrative expenses, all supplies, total depreciation on property used in performance of the contract, etc.) incurred in performance of the contract are $80,000. The cost of export property consumed in performance of the contract (for example, dynamite, motor oil, and other supplies which were produced in the United States, reasonable depreciation on trucks and seismographic equipment manufactured in the United States and used in performance of the contract, etc.) is $30,000. Cor-

poration A's gross export trade income from the contract is $37,500, that is, the amount which bears the same ratio to total gross income from the contract ($100,000) as the cost of the export property consumed in the rendition of the services ($30,000) bears to total costs and expenses attributable to the contract ($80,000).

(vii) *Interest from export trade assets.*—Gross export trade income of a controlled foreign corporation includes interest derived by it from export trade assets described in section 971(c)(4) and paragraph (c)(5) of this section. See section 971(b)(4).

(viii) *Deductions to be taken into account.*—Export trade income of a controlled foreign corporation for any taxable year shall be the amount determined by deducting from the items or categories of gross income described in subdivisions (i) through (vii) of this subparagraph the entire amount of those expenses, taxes, and other deductions properly allocable to such items or categories of income. For purposes of this section, expenses, taxes, and other deductions shall first be allocated to items or categories of gross income to which they directly relate; then, expenses, taxes, and other deductions which cannot definitely be allocated to some item or category of gross income shall be ratably apportioned among all items or categories of gross income, except that no expense, tax, or other deduction shall be allocated to an item or category of income to which it clearly does not apply and no deduction allowable to such controlled foreign corporation under section 882(c) and the regulations thereunder shall be taken into account.

(2) *Cross reference.*—For rules governing the determination of gross income and taxable income of a foreign corporation, see § 1.952-2.

(c) *Export trade assets.*—(1) *In general.*—For purposes of sections 970 through 972 and §§ 1.970-1 to 1.972-1, inclusive, the term "export trade assets" means—

(i) Working capital reasonably necessary for the production of export trade income,

(ii) Inventory of export property held for use, consumption, or disposition outside the United States,

(iii) Facilities located outside the United States for the storage, handling, transportation, packaging, servicing, sale, or distribution of export property, and

(iv) Evidences of indebtedness executed by unrelated persons in connection with payment for purchases of export property for use, consumption, or disposition outside the United States, or in connection with the payment for services described in section 971(b)(2) or (3) and paragraph (b)(1)(iv), (v), or (vi) of this section.

(2) *Working capital.*—For purposes of subparagraph (1)(i) of this paragraph, working capi-

tal of a controlled foreign corporation is the excess of its current assets over its current liabilities. Liabilities maturing in one year or less shall be considered current liabilities. A determination of the amount of working capital of a controlled foreign corporation which is reasonably necessary for the production of export trade income will depend upon the nature and volume of the activities of the controlled foreign corporation which produce export trade income as they exist on the applicable determination date. In determining working capital which is reasonably necessary for the production of export trade income, the anticipated future needs of the business will be taken into account to the extent that such needs relate to the year of the controlled foreign corporation following the applicable determination date; anticipated future needs relating to a later period will not be taken into account unless it is clearly established that such needs are reasonably related to the production of export trade income as of the applicable determination date.

(3) *Inventory of export property.*—For purposes of subparagraph (1)(ii) of this paragraph, the inclusion of items in inventory shall be determined in accordance with rules applicable to domestic corporations. See §§ 1.471-1 through 1.471-9. Inventory of export property of a controlled foreign corporation includes export property held for use, consumption, or disposition outside the United States regardless of where it is located on the applicable determination date. Thus, such property may be physically located in the United States on such date. However, for property physically located in the United States to constitute export property, it must have been acquired by the controlled foreign corporation with a clear intent that it would dispose of the property for use, consumption, or disposition outside the United States. As a general rule, if during the year following the applicable determination date export property which was physically located in the United States on such date is actually exported for use, consumption, or disposition outside the United States, such property will be deemed held for such purpose on the applicable determination date. On the other hand, the indefinite warehousing of export property in the United States by the controlled foreign corporation, or the subsequent sale of export property by such corporation for use, consumption, or disposition in the United States, will evidence a lack of intent by such corporation on the applicable determination date to hold such property for use, consumption, or disposition outside the United States.

(4) *Facilities located outside the United States.*—(i) *In general.*—For purposes of subparagraph (1)(iii) of this paragraph, a facility, as defined in subdivision (ii)(a) of this subparagraph, will be considered an export trade asset only—

(a) If such facility is located outside the United States, and

(b) To the extent that such facility is used, within the meaning of subdivision (ii)(c) of this subparagraph, by the controlled foreign corporation for the storage, handling, transportation, packaging, servicing, sale, or distribution of export property in essentially the same form in which such property is acquired by such corporation.

Thus, a facility in which property is manufactured or produced, even though export property is used or consumed in the production or becomes a component part of the manufactured article, will not qualify as an export trade asset.

(ii) *Special rules.*—(a) *Facility defined.*—For purposes of subdivision (i) of this subparagraph, the term "facility" includes any asset or group of assets used for the storage, handling, transportation, packaging, servicing, sale, or distribution of export property. Thus, such term includes warehouse, storage, or sales facilities (for example, sales office equipment), transportation equipment (for example, motor trucks, vessels, etc.), and machinery and equipment (for example, packaging equipment, servicing equipment, cranes, fork lift trucks used in warehouses, etc.).

(b) *Determination of location of transportation facilities.*—A transportation facility shall be considered to be located outside the United States for purposes of subdivision (i)(a) of this subparagraph if such property is predominantly located outside the United States. As a general rule, on an applicable determination date a transportation facility will be considered to be predominantly located outside the United States if 70 percent or more of the miles traversed (during the 12-month period immediately preceding such determination date or for such part of such period as such facility is owned by the controlled foreign corporation) in the use of such facility are traversed outside the United States or if such facility is located outside the United States at least 70 percent of the time during such period or such part thereof.

(c) *Determination of use.*—For purposes of subdivision (i)(b) of this subparagraph, the extent to which a facility is used in carrying on the activities described in such subdivision depends on the use made of the facility for the 12-month period immediately preceding the applicable determination date or for such part of such period as such facility is owned by the controlled foreign corporation. The method of measuring such use will depend upon the facts and circumstances in each case. However, such determinations of use will generally be made for a facility as a whole and not on the basis of individual items used in the operation of a facility. Thus, a determination as to the use of a warehouse facility will generally be made with respect to the entire facility and not separately for the items used in such warehouse, such as fork lift trucks, storage bins, etc.

Reg. §1.971-1(c)(4)(ii)(c)

(5) *Evidences of indebtedness.*—For purposes of subparagraph (1)(iv) of this paragraph, the term "evidence of indebtedness" shall mean a note, installment sales contract, a time bill of exchange evidencing a sale on credit, or similar written instrument executed by an unrelated person which evidences the obligation of an unrelated person to pay for export property which an unrelated person purchases for use, consumption, or disposition outside the United States or to pay for services described in section 971(b)(2) or (3) and paragraph (b)(1)(iv), (v), or (vi) of this section which are performed for an unrelated person. Receivables which arise out of the delivery of export property, or the performance of services, which are evidenced by invoices, bills of lading, bills of exchange which do not evidence a sale on credit, sales slips, and similar documents created by the unilateral act of a creditor shall not be considered evidences of indebtedness for purposes of section 971(c)(4).

(6) *Duplication of treatment and priority of application.*—No asset which constitutes an export trade asset shall be taken into account more than once in determining the investments in export trade assets of a controlled foreign corporation. Assets which constitute working capital and also constitute inventory to which section 971(c)(2) applies or evidences of indebtedness to which section 971(c)(4) applies shall be taken into account in determining whether the amount of working capital of the controlled foreign corporation is reasonably necessary for the production of export trade income. However, to the extent that the amount of inventory to which section 971(c)(2) applies or evidences of indebtedness to which section 971(c)(4) applies is not included in working capital to which section 971(c)(1) applies on the ground that such amount is not reasonably necessary for the production of export trade income, the amount shall be included under section 971(c)(2) or 971(c)(4), as the case may be, in a controlled foreign corporation's investments in export trade assets.

(d) *Export promotion expenses.*—(1) *In general.*—For purposes of sections 970 through 972, and § § 1.970-1 to 1.972-1, inclusive, the term "export promotion expenses" means, subject to the provisions of subparagraph (2) of this paragraph, all the ordinary and necessary expenses paid or incurred during the taxable year by the controlled foreign corporation which are reasonably allocable to the receipt or production of export trade income including—

(i) A reasonable allowance for salaries or other compensation for personal services actually rendered for such purpose,

(ii) Rentals or other payments for the use of property actually used for such purpose, and

(iii) A reasonable allowance for the exhaustion, wear and tear, or obsolescence of property actually used for such purpose.

In determining for purposes of this subparagraph whether expenses are reasonably allocable to the receipt or production of export trade income, consideration shall be given to the facts and circumstances of each case. As a general rule, if export trade income results from the sale of export property, export promotion expenses allocable to such income shall include warehousing, advertising, selling, billing, collection, other administrative, and similar costs properly allocable to the marketing activity, but shall not include cost of goods sold, income or similar tax, any expense which does not advance the distribution or sale of export property for use, consumption, or disposition outside the United States, or any expense for which the controlled foreign corporation is reimbursed. If export trade income results from the rental of export property, export promotion expenses allocable to such income shall include a reasonable allowance for depreciation and servicing of such property, and the administrative and similar costs properly allocable to the rental activity. If export trade income results from the performance of services, export promotion expenses shall include a reasonable allowance for compensation of the persons performing services for the controlled foreign corporation in the execution of the service contract or arrangement and administrative expenses reasonably allocable to the service activity. In no case shall income taxes be included in export promotion expenses.

(2) *Expenses incurred within the United States.*—No expense incurred within the United States shall be treated as an export promotion expense for purposes of section 971(d) and subparagraph (1) of this paragraph unless at least—

(i) 90 percent of all salaries and other personal service compensation incurred in the receipt or the production of export trade income,

(ii) 90 percent of rents and other payments for the use of property used in the receipt or the production of export trade income,

(iii) 90 percent of the allowances for the exhaustion, wear and tear, or obsolescence of property used in the receipt or the production of export trade income, and

(iv) 90 percent of all other ordinary and necessary expenses reasonably allocable to the receipt or the production of export trade income, is incurred outside the United States. For this purpose, personal service compensation will be considered incurred at the place where the service is performed (for example, salaries will be considered incurred at the place where the employee works; payments for art work will be considered incurred at the place where the art work is prepared, etc.); rent, depreciation, and other expenses related to real or personal property will be considered incurred at the place where the property is located; and expenses for media advertising will be considered incurred at the place where the advertising is consumed. For

Reg. § 1.971-1(c)(5)

such purpose, newspaper or periodical advertising will be considered consumed where the newspaper or periodical is principally distributed, and television and radio advertising will be considered consumed at the place where the audience is primarily located. Technicalities of contract or payment, for example, the place where a contract is executed or the location of a bank account from which payment is made, shall not be determinative of the place where an expense is incurred.

(e) *Export property.*—For purposes of sections 970 through 972 and §§ 1.970-1 to 1.972-1, inclusive, the term "export property" means property, or any interest in property, which is manufactured, produced, grown, or extracted in the United States. Whether property will be considered manufactured or produced in the United States will depend on the facts and circumstances of each case. As a general rule, if—

(1) The property sold, serviced, used, or rented by the controlled foreign corporation is substantially transformed in the United States prior to its export from the United States, or

(2) The operations conducted in the United States with respect to the property sold, serviced, used, or rented by the controlled foreign corporation, whether performed in the United States by one person or a series of persons in a chain of distribution, are substantial in nature and are generally considered to constitute the manufacture or production of property,

then the property sold, serviced, used, or rented will be considered to have been manufactured or produced in the United States. The rules under paragraph (a)(4)(ii) of § 1.954-3, relating to the substantial transformation of property, and paragraph (a)(4)(iii) of such section, dealing with a substantive test for determining whether property will be treated as having been manufactured or produced, shall apply for purposes of making determinations under this paragraph.

(f) *Unrelated person.*—For purposes of sections 970 through 972 and §§ 1.970-1 to 1.972-1, inclusive, the term "unrelated person" means a person other than a related person as defined in section 954(d)(3) and paragraph (e) of § 1.954-1. [Reg. § 1.971-1.]

☐ [T.D. 6755, 9-8-64. *Amended by T.D. 7293, 11-27-73 and T.D. 7533, 2-14-78.*]

[Reg. § 1.985-0]

§ 1.985-0. Outline of regulations.—This section lists the paragraphs contained in §§ 1.985-1 through 1.985-6.

§ 1.985-1. Functional currency.

(a) Applicability and effective date.

(b) Dollar functional currency.

(c) Functional currency of a QBU that is not required to use the dollar.

(d) Single functional currency for a foreign corporation.

(e) Translation of nonfunctional currency transactions.

(f) Examples.

§ 1.985-2. Election to use the United States dollar as the functional currency of a QBU.

(a) Background and scope.

(b) Eligible QBU.

(c) Time and manner for dollar election.

(d) Effect of dollar election.

§ 1.985-3. United States dollar approximate separate transactions method.

(a) Scope and effective date.

(b) Statement of method.

(c) Translation into United States dollars.

(d) Computation of DASTM gain or loss.

(e) Effect of DASTM gain or loss on gross income, taxable income, or earnings and profits.

§ 1.985-4. Method of accounting.

(a) Adoption or election.

(b) Condition for changing functional currencies.

(c) Relationship to certain other sections of the Code.

§ 1.985-5. Adjustments required upon change in functional currency.

(a) In general.

(b) Step 1—Taking into account exchange gain or loss on certain section 988 transactions.

(c) Step 2—Determining the new functional currency basis of property and the new functional currency amount of liabilities and any other relevant items.

(d) Step 3A—Additional adjustments that are necessary when a branch changes functional currency.

(e) Step 3B—Additional adjustments that are necessary when a taxpayer changes functional currency.

(f) Examples.

§ 1.985-6. Transition rules for a QBU that uses the dollar approximate separate transactions method for its first taxable year beginning in 1987.

(a) In general.

(b) Certain controlled foreign corporations.

(c) All other foreign corporations.

(d) Pre-1987 section 902 amounts.

(e) Net worth branch.

(f) Profit and loss branch.

[Reg. § 1.985-0.]

☐ [T.D. 8263, 9-19-89. *Amended by T.D. 8464, 12-31-92 and T.D. 8556, 7-22-94.*]

[Reg. § 1.985-1]

§ 1.985-1. Functional currency.—(a) *Applicability and effective date.*—(1) *Purpose* *and scope.*—These regulations provide guidance with respect to defining the functional currency of a taxpayer and each qualified business unit (QBU), as defined in section 989 (a). Generally, a taxpayer and each QBU must make all determinations under subtitle A of the Code (relating to income taxes) in its respective functional currency. This section sets forth rules for determining when the functional currency is the United States dollar (dollar) or a currency other than the dollar. Section 1.985-2 provides an election to use the dollar as the functional currency for certain QBUs that absent the election would have a functional currency that is a hyperinflationary currency, and explains the effect of making the election. Section 1.985-3 sets forth the dollar approximate separate transactions method that certain QBUs must use to compute their income or loss or earnings and profits. Section 1.985-4 provides that the adoption of a functional currency is a method of accounting and sets forth conditions for a change in functional currency. Section 1.985-5 provides adjustments that are required to be made upon a change in functional currency. Finally, § 1.985-6 provides transition rules for a QBU that uses the dollar approximate separate transactions method for its first taxable year beginning after December 31, 1986.

(2) *Effective date.*—These regulations apply to taxable years beginning after December 31, 1986. However, any taxpayer desiring to apply temporary Income Tax Regulations § 1.985-0T through § 1.985-4T in lieu of these regulations to all taxable years beginning after December 31, 1986, and on or before OCT. 20, 1989 may (on a consistent basis) so choose. For the text of the temporary regulations, see 53 Fed. Reg. 20308 (1988).

(b) *Dollar functional currency.*.—(1) *In general.*—The dollar shall be the functional currency of a taxpayer or QBU described in paragraph (b)(1)(i) through (v) of this section regardless of the currency used in keeping its books and records (as defined in § 1.989(a)-1(d)). The dollar shall be the functional currency of—

(i) A taxpayer that is not a QBU (e.g., an individual);

(ii) A QBU that conducts its activities primarily in dollars. A QBU conducts its activities primarily in dollars if the currency of the economic environment in which the QBU conducts its activities is primarily the dollar. The facts and circumstances test set forth in paragraph (c)(2) of this section shall apply in making this determination;

(iii) Except as otherwise provided by ruling or administrative pronouncement, a QBU that has the United States, or any possession or territory of the United States where the dollar is the standard currency, as its residence (as defined in section 988(a)(3)(B));

(iv) A QBU that does not keep books and records in the currency of any economic environ-

ment in which a significant part of its activities is conducted. Whether a QBU keeps such books and records is determined in accordance with paragraph (c)(3) of this section; or

(v) A QBU that produces income or loss that is, or is treated as, effectively connected with the conduct of a trade or business within the United States.

(2) *QBUs operating in a hyperinflationary environment.*—(i) *Taxable years beginning on or before August 24, 1994.*—For taxable years beginning on or before August 24, 1994, see § 1.985-2 with respect to a QBU that elects to use, or is otherwise required to use, the dollar as its functional currency.

(ii) *Taxable years beginning after August 24, 1994.*—(A) *In general.*—For taxable years beginning after August 24, 1994, except as otherwise provided in paragraph (b)(2)(ii)(B) of this section, any QBU that otherwise would be required to use a hyperinflationary currency as its functional currency must use the dollar as its functional currency and compute income or loss or earnings and profits under the rules of § 1.985-3.

(B) *Exceptions.*—(1) *Certain QBU branches.*—The functional currency of a QBU that otherwise would be required to use a hyperinflationary currency as its functional currency and that is a branch of a foreign corporation having a non-dollar functional currency that is not hyperinflationary shall be the functional currency of the foreign corporation. Such QBU's income or loss or earnings and profits shall be determined under § 1.985-3 by substituting the functional currency of the foreign corporation for the dollar.

(2) *Corporation that is not a controlled foreign corporation.*—A foreign corporation (or its QBU branch) operating in a hyperinflationary environment is not required to use the dollar as its functional currency pursuant to paragraph (b)(2)(ii)(A) of this section if that foreign corporation is not a controlled foreign corporation as defined in section 957 or 953(c)(1)(B). However, a noncontrolled section 902 corporation, as defined in section 904(d)(2)(E), may elect to use the dollar (or, if appropriate, the currency specified in paragraph (b)(2)(ii)(B)(1) of this section) as its (or its QBU branch's) functional currency under the procedures set forth in § 1.985-2(c)(3).

(C) *Change in functional currency.*—(1) *In general.*—If a QBU is required to change its functional currency to the dollar under paragraph (b)(2)(ii)(A) of this section, or chooses or is required to change its functional currency to the dollar for any open taxable year (and all subsequent taxable years) under § 1.985-3(a)(2)(ii), the change is considered to be made with the consent of the Commissioner for purposes of § 1.985-4. A QBU changing functional currency must make adjustments described in § 1.985-7 if the year of change (as defined in §1.481-1(a)(1)) begins after 1987, or the adjustments described in §1.985-6 if the year of change begins in 1987. No adjustments under section 481 are required solely because of a change in functional currency described in this paragraph (b)(2)(ii)(C).

(2) *Effective date.*—This paragraph (b)(2)(ii)(C) applies to taxable years beginning after April 6, 1998. However, a taxpayer may choose to apply this paragraph (b)(2)(ii)(C) to all open years after December 31, 1986, provided each person, and each QBU branch of a person, that is related (within the meaning of §1.985-2(d)(3)) also applies to this paragraph (b)(2)(ii)(C).

(D) *Hyperinflationary currency.*—For purposes of sections 985 through 989, the term hyperinflationary currency means the currency of a country in which there is cumulative inflation during the base period of at least 100 percent as determined by reference to the consumer price index of the country listed in the monthly issues of the "International Financial Statistics" or a successor publication of the International Monetary Fund. If a country's currency is not listed in the monthly issues of "International Financial Statistics," a QBU may use any other reasonable method consistently applied for determining the country's consumer price index. Base period means, with respect to any taxable year, the thirty-six calendar months immediately preceding the first day of the current calendar year. For this purpose, the cumulative inflation rate for the base period is based on compounded inflation rates. Thus, if for 1991, 1992, and 1993, a country's annual inflation rates are 29 percent, 25 percent, and 30 percent, respectively, the cumulative inflation rate for the three-year base period is 110 percent $[((1.29 \times 1.25 \times 1.3) - 1.0 = 1.10) \times 100 = 110\%]$ and the currency of the country for the QBU's 1994 year is considered hyperinflationary. In making the determination whether a currency is hyperinflationary, the determination for purposes of United States generally accepted accounting principles may be used for income tax purposes provided the determination is based on criteria that is substantially similar to the rules previously set forth in this paragraph (b)(2)(ii)(D), the method of determination is applied consistently from year to year, and the same method is applied to all related persons as defined in §1.985-3(e)(2)(vi).

(E) *Change in functional currency when currency ceases to be hyperinflationary.*—(1) *In general.*—A QBU that has been required to use the dollar as its functional currency under paragraph (b)(2) of this section, or has elected to use the dollar as its functional currency under paragraph (b)(2)(ii)(B)(2) of this section or §1.985-2, must change its functional currency as of the first day of the first taxable year that follows three consecutive taxable years in which the cur-

rency of its economic environment, determined under paragraph (c)(2) of this section, is not a hyperinflationary currency. The functional currency of the QBU for such year shall be determined in accordance with paragraph (c) of this section. For purposes of §1.985-4, the change is considered to be made with the consent of the Commissioner. See §1.985-5 for adjustments that are required upon a change in functional currency.

(2) *Effective date.*—This paragraph (b)(2)(ii)(E) of this section applies to taxable years beginning after April 6, 1998.

(c) *Functional currency of a QBU that is not required to use the dollar.*—(1) *General rule.*—The functional currency of a QBU that is not required to use the dollar under paragraph (b) of this section shall be the currency of the economic environment in which a significant part of the QBU's activities is conducted, if the QBU keeps, or is presumed under paragraph (c) (3) of this section to keep, its books and records in such currency.

(2) *Economic environment.*—For purposes of section 985 and the regulations thereunder, the economic environment in which a significant part of a QBU's activities is conducted shall be determined by taking into account all the facts and circumstances.

(i) *Facts and circumstances.*—The facts and circumstances that are considered in determining the economic environment in which a significant part of a QBU's activities is conducted include, but are not limited to, the following:

(A) The currency of the country in which the QBU is a resident as determined under section 988 (a)(3)(B);

(B) The currencies of the QBU's cash flows;

(C) The currencies in which the QBU generates revenues and incurs expenses;

(D) The currencies in which the QBU borrows and lends;

(E) The currencies of the QBU's sales markets;

(F) The currencies in which pricing and other financial decisions are made;

(G) The duration of the QBU's business operations; and

(H) The significance and/or volume of the QBU's independent activities.

(ii) *Rate of inflation.*—The rate of inflation (regardless of how it is determined) shall not be a factor used to determine a QBU's economic environment.

(iii) *Consistency.*—A taxpayer must consistently apply the facts and circumstances test set forth in this paragraph (c) (2) in evaluating the economic environment of its QBUs, *e.g.*, its branches, that engage in the same or similar trades or businesses.

(3) *Books and records presumption.*—A QBU shall be presumed to keep books and records in the currency of the economic environment in which a significant part of its activities are conducted. The presumption may be overcome only if the QBU can demonstrate to the satisfaction of the district director that a substantial nontax purpose exists for not keeping any books and records in such currency. A taxpayer may not use this presumption affirmatively in determining a QBU's functional currency.

(4) *Multiple currencies.*—If a QBU has more than one currency that satisfies the requirements of paragraph (c) (1) of this section, the QBU may choose any such currency as its functional currency.

(5) *Relationship of United States accounting principles.*—In making the functional currency determination under this paragraph (c), the currency of the QBU for purposes of United States generally accepted accounting principles (GAAP) will ordinarily be accepted as the functional currency of the QBU for income tax purposes, provided that the GAAP determination is based on facts and circumstances substantially similar to those set forth in paragraph (c) (2) of this section.

(6) *Effect of changed circumstances.*—Regardless of any change in circumstances, a QBU may change its functional currency determined under this paragraph (c) only if the QBU complies with § 1.985-4 or the Commissioner's consent is considered to have been granted under § 1.985-2(d)(4) or § 1.985-3a(2)(ii). For special rules relating to the conversion to the euro, see § 1.985-8.

(d) *Single functional currency for a foreign corporation.*—(1) *General rule.*—This paragraph (d) applies to a foreign corporation that has two or more QBUs that do not have the same functional currency. The foreign corporation shall be treated as having a single functional currency for the corporation as a whole that is different from the functional currency of one or more of its QBUs. The determination of a foreign corporation's functional currency shall be made by first applying paragraph (d) (1) (i) and then paragraph (d) (1) (ii) of this section.

(i) *Step 1.*—Each QBU of the foreign corporation determines its functional currency in accordance with the rules set forth in paragraphs (b) and (c) of this section and § 1.985-2.

(ii) *Step 2.*—The foreign corporation determines its functional currency applying the principles of paragraphs (b) and (c) of this section to the corporation's activities as a whole. Thus, if a foreign corporation has two branches, the corporation shall determine its functional

currency by applying the principles of paragraphs (b) and (c) of this section to the combined activities of the corporation and the branches.

For purposes of this paragraph (d)(1), if a QBU of a foreign corporation has the dollar as its functional currency under paragraph (b)(2) of this section, the QBU's activities shall be considered dollar activities of the corporation.

(2) *Translation of income or loss of QBUs having different functional currencies than the foreign corporation as a whole.*—Where the functional currency of a foreign corporation as a whole differs from the functional currency of one or more of its QBUs, each such QBU shall determine the amount of its income or loss or earnings and profits (or deficit in earnings and profits) in its functional currency under the principles of section 987 (relating to branch transactions). The amount of income or loss or earnings and profits (or deficit in earnings and profits) of each QBU in its functional currency shall then be translated into the foreign corporation's functional currency using the appropriate exchange rate as defined in section 989 (b) (4) for purposes of determining the corporation's income or loss or earnings and profits (or deficit in earnings and profits).

(e) *Translation of nonfunctional currency transactions.*—Except for a QBU using the dollar approximate separate transactions method described in § 1.985-3, *see* section 988 and the regulations thereunder for the treatment of nonfunctional currency transactions.

(f) *Examples.*—The provisions of this section are illustrated by the following examples:

Example (1). P, a domestic corporation, operates exclusively through foreign branch X in Country A. X is a QBU within the meaning of section 989 (a) and its residence is Country A as determined under section 988 (a) (3) (B). The currency of Country A is the LC. All of X's purchases, sales, and expenses are in the LC. The laws of A require X to keep books and records in the LC. It is determined that the LC is the currency of X under United States generally accepted accounting principles. This determination is based on facts and circumstances substantially similar to those set forth in paragraph (c) (2) of this section. Under these facts, while the functional currency of P is the dollar since its residence is the United States, the functional currency of X is the LC.

Example (2). P, a publicly-held domestic regulated investment company (as defined under section 851), operates exclusively through foreign branch B in Country R. B is a QBU within the meaning of section 989 (a) and its residence is Country R as determined under section 988 (a) (3) (B). The currency of Country R is the LC. B's principal activities consist of purchasing and selling stock and securities of Country R companies and securities issued by Country R. It is determined that the dollar is the currency of B under United States generally accepted accounting principles. This determination is not based on facts and circumstances substantially similar to those set forth in paragraph (c) (2) of this section. Under these facts, while the functional currency of P is the dollar since its residence is the United States, B may choose the LC as its functional currency because it has significant activities in the LC provided it keeps books and records in the LC. The fact that the dollar is the currency of B under generally accepted accounting principles is irrelevant for purposes of determining B's functional currency because the GAAP determination was not based on factors similar to those set forth in paragraph (c) (2) of this section.

Example (3). P, a domestic bank, operates through foreign branch X in Country R. X is a QBU within the meaning of section 989 (a) and its residence is Country R as determined under section 988 (a) (3) (B). The currency of Country R is the LC. The laws of R require X to keep books and records in the LC. The branch customarily loans dollars and LCs. In the case of its LC loans, X ordinarily fixes the terms of the loans by reference to a contemporary London Inter-Bank Offered Rate (LIBOR) on dollar deposits. For instance, the interest on the amount of the outstanding LC loan principal might equal LIBOR plus 2 percent and the amount of the outstanding LC loan principal would be adjusted to reflect changes in the dollar value of the LC. X is primarily funded with dollar-denominated funds borrowed from related and unrelated parties. X's only LC activities are paying local taxes, employee wages, and local expenses such as rent and electricity. Under these facts, X's activities are primarily conducted in dollars. Thus, although X keeps its books and records in LCs, X's functional currency is the dollar.

Example (4). S, a foreign corporation organized in Country U, is wholly-owned by P, a domestic corporation. The currency of Country U is the LC. S's sole function is acting as a financing vehicle for P and domestic corporations that are affiliated with P. All borrowing and lending transactions between S and P and its domestic affiliates are in dollars. Furthermore, primarily all of S's other borrowings are dollar-denominated or based on a dollar index. S's only LC activities are paying local taxes, employee wages, and local expenses such as rent and electricity. S keeps its books and records in the LC. Under these facts, S's activities are primarily conducted in dollars. Thus, although S keeps its books and records in LCs, S's functional currency is the dollar.

Example (5). D is a domestic corporation whose primary activity is the extraction of natural gas and oil through foreign branch X in Country Y. X is a QBU within the meaning of section 989 (a) and its residence is Country Y as determined

under section 988 (a) (3) (B). The currency of Country Y is the LC. X bills a significant amount of its natural gas and oil sales in dollars and a significant amount in LCs. X also incurs significant LC and dollar expenses and liabilities. The laws of Country Y require X to keep its books and records in the LC. It is determined that the LC is the currency of X under United States generally accepted accounting principles. This determination is based on facts and circumstances substantially similar to those set forth in paragraph (c) (2) of this section. Absent other factors indicating that K primarily conducts its activities in the dollar, D could choose either the dollar or the LC as X's functional currency because X has significant activities in both the dollar and the LC, provided the books and records requirement is satisfied. If, instead, X's activities were determined to be primarily in the dollar, then X would have to use the dollar as its functional currency.

Example (6). S, a foreign corporation organized in Country U, is wholly-owned by P, a domestic corporation. The currency of U is the LC. S purchases the products it sells from related and unrelated parties, including P. These purchases are made in the LC. In addition, most of S's gross receipts are generated by transactions denominated in the LC. S attempts to determine its LC price for goods sold in such a manner as to obtain an LC equivalent of a certain dollar amount after reduction for all LC costs. However, local market conditions sometimes result in pricing adjustments. Thus, changes in the LC-dollar exchange rate from period to period generally result in corresponding changes in the LC price of S's products. S pays local taxes, employee wages, and other local expenses in the LC. It is determined that the dollar is the currency of S under United States generally accepted accounting principles. This determination is not based on facts and circumstances substantially similar to those set forth in paragraph (c) (2) of this section. Under these facts, S could choose either the dollar or the LC as its functional currency because S has significant activities in both the dollar and the LC, provided that the books and records requirement is satisfied.

Example (7). S, a foreign corporation organized in Country X, is wholly-owned by P, a domestic corporation. S conducts all of its operations through two branches. Branch A is located in Country F and branch B is located in Country G. S, A, and B are QBUs within the meaning of section 989 (a). Branch A's and branch B's residences are Country F and Country G respectively as determined under section 988 (a) (3) (B). The currency of Country F is the FC and the currency of Country G is the LC. The functional currencies of S, A, and B are determined in a two step procedure.

Step 1: The functional currency of branches A and B. Branch A and branch B both conduct all activities in their respective local currencies. The FC is the currency of branch A and the LC is the currency of branch B under United States generally accepted accounting principles. This determination is based on facts and circumstances substantially similar to those set forth in paragraph (c) (2) of this section. Under these facts, the functional currency of branch A is the FC and the functional currency of branch B is the LC.

Step 2: The functional currency of S. S's functional currency is determined by disregarding the fact that A and B are branches. When A's activities and B's activities are viewed as a whole, S determines that it only conducts significant activities in the LC. Therefore, S's functional currency is the LC. See Examples (9), (10), and (11) for how the earnings and profits of a foreign corporation, which has branches with different functional currencies, are determined.

Example (8). Assume the same facts as in Example (7), except that S does not exist and P conducts all of its operations through branch A and branch B. In this instance P's functional currency in Step 2 is the dollar, regardless of the fact that its branches' activities viewed as a whole are in the LC, because P is a taxpayer whose residence is the United States under section 988 (a) (3) (B) (i). Therefore, while the functional currency of branch A is the FC and the functional currency of branch B is the LC, the functional currency of P is the dollar because its residence is the United States.

Example (9). The facts are the same as in Example (7). In addition, assume that in 1987 branch A has earnings of 100 FC and branch B has earnings of 100 LC as determined under section 987. The weighted average exchange rate for the year is 1 FC/2 LC. Branch A's earnings are translated into 200 LC for purposes of computing S's earnings and profits in 1987. Thus, the total earnings and profits of S from branch A and branch B for 1987 is 300 LC.

Example (10). (i) X, a foreign corporation organized in Country W, is wholly-owned by P, a domestic corporation. Both X and P are calendar year taxpayers that began business during 1987. X operates exclusively through two branches, A and B both of which are located outside of Country W. The functional currency of X and A is the LC, while the functional currency of B is the DC as determined under section 985 and § 1.985-1. The earnings of B must be computed under section 987, relating to branch transactions. In 1987, A earns 900 LCs of nonsubpart F income and B earns 200 DCs of nonsubpart F income. Under section 904 (d) (2), A's income is financial service income and B's income is general limitation income. In order to determine X's earnings and profits, B's income must be translated into LCs (the functional currency of X). The weighted average exchange rate for 1987 is 1 LC/2 DC. Thus, in 1987 X's current earnings and profits (and its post-1986 undistributed earnings) are 1000 LCs consisting of 900 LCs of financial services in-

come earned by A and 100 LCs (200 DC/2) of general limitation income earned by B. Neither A nor B makes any remittances during 1987.

(ii) In 1988, neither A nor B earns any income or generates any loss. On December 31, 1988, A remits 50 LCs directly to P. The remittance to P is considered to be remitted by A to X and then immediately distributed by X as a dividend. The 50 LC remittance does not result in an exchange gain or loss under section 987 to X because the functional currency of X and A is the LC. See section 987 (3). Under section 904 (d) (3) (D), the 50 LC dividend is treated as income in a separate category to the extent of the dividend's pro rata share of X's earnings and profits in each separate limitation category. Thus, 90 percent, or 45 LCs, is treated as financial services income, and 10 percent, or 5 LCs, is treated as general limitation income. After the dividend distribution, X has 950 LCs of accumulated earnings and profits (and post-1986 undistributed earnings) consisting of 855 LCs of financial service limitation income and 95 LCs of general limitation income.

Example (11). The facts are the same as in Example (10), except that A makes no remittance during 1988 but B remits 120 DCs to X on December 31, 1988, which X immediately converts into LCs, and X makes no dividend distribution during 1988. Assume that the appropriate exchange rate for the remittance is 1 LC/3 DCs. B's remittance triggers exchange loss to X. See section 987 (3). Under section 987, the exchange loss on the remittance is 20 LCs calculated as follows: 40 LCs, which is the LC value of the 120 DC remittance (120 DCs/3), less 60 LCs, their LC basis (120 DCs/2). This loss is sourced and characterized under section 987 and regulations thereunder.

Example (12). F, a foreign corporation, has gain from the disposition of a United States real property interest (as defined in section 897 (c)). The gain is taken into account as if F were engaged in a trade or business within the United States during the taxable year and as if such gain were effectively connected with such trade or business. F's disposition activity shall be treated as a separate QBU with a dollar functional currency because such activity produced income that is treated as effectively connected with a trade or business within the United States. Therefore, F must compute its gain from the disposition by giving the United States real property interest an historic dollar basis. [Reg. § 1.985-1.]

☐ [*T.D. 8263, 9-19-89. Amended by T.D. 8556, 7-22-94; T.D. 8765, 3-4-98 (corrected 3-31-98); T.D. 8776, 7-28-98 and T.D. 8927, 1-10-2001.*]

[Reg. § 1.985-2]

§ 1.985-2. Election to use the United States dollar as the functional currency of a QBU.— (a) *Background and scope.*—(1) *In general.*—This section permits an eligible QBU to elect to use the dollar as its functional currency for taxable years beginning on or before August 24, 1994. An election to use a dollar functional currency is not permitted for a QBU other than an eligible QBU. Paragraph (b) of this section defines an eligible QBU. Paragraph (c) of this section describes the time and manner for making the dollar election and paragraph (d) of this section describes the effect of making the election. For the definition of a QBU, see section 989(a). See § 1.985-1(b)(2)(ii) for rules requiring a QBU to use the dollar as its functional currency in taxable years beginning after August 24, 1994.

(2) *Exception.*—Pursuant to § 1.985-1(b)(2)(ii)(B)(2), the rules of paragraph (c)(3) of this section shall apply with respect to the procedure required to be followed by a noncontrolled section 902 corporation as defined in section 904(d)(2)(E) to elect the dollar as its (or its QBU branch's) functional currency and the application of § 1.985-3.

(b) *Eligible QBU.*—(1) *In general.*—The term "eligible QBU" means a QBU that could have used a hyperinflationary currency as its functional currency absent the dollar election. *See* § 1.985-1 for how a QBU determines its functional currency absent the dollar election.

(2) *Hyperinflationary currency.*—See § 1.985-1(b)(2)(ii)(D) for the definition of hyperinflationary currency.

(c) *Time and manner for dollar election.*— (1) *QBUs that are branches of United States persons.*—(i) *Rule.*—If an eligible QBU is a branch of a United States person, the dollar election shall be made by attaching a completed Form 8819 to the United States person's timely filed (taking extensions into account) tax return for the first taxable year for which the election is to be effective.

(ii) *Procedure prior to the issuance of Form 8819.*—In the absence of Form 8819, the election shall be made in accordance with § 1.985-2T(c)(1). Failure to file an amended return within the time period prescribed in § 1.985-2T(c)(1) shall not invalidate the dollar election if it is established to the satisfaction of the district director that reasonable cause existed for such failure. A subsequent election for 1988 will not prejudice the taxpayer with respect to such reasonable cause determination. Nevertheless, each United States person making an election under the § 1.985-2T(c)(1) must file a Form 8819 in the time and manner provided in the Form's instructions.

(2) *Eligible QBUs that are controlled foreign corporations or branches of controlled foreign corporations.*—(i) *Rule.*—If an eligible QBU is a controlled foreign corporation (as described in section 957), or a branch of a controlled foreign corporation, the election may be made either by the foreign corporation or by the controlling

United States shareholders on behalf of the foreign corporation by—

(A) Filing a completed Form 8819 in the time and manner provided in the Form's instructions, and

(B) Providing the written notice required by paragraph (c)(2)(ii) of this section at the time and in the manner prescribed therein.

The term "controlling United States shareholders" means those United States shareholders (as defined in section 951(b)) who, in the aggregate, own (within the meaning of section 958(a)) greater than 50 percent of the total combined voting power of all classes of stock of the foreign corporation entitled to vote. If the foreign corporation is a controlled foreign corporation (as described in section 957) but the United States shareholders do not, in the aggregate, own the requisite voting power, the term "controlling United States shareholders" means all the United States shareholders (as defined in section 951(b)) who own (within the meaning of section 958(a)) stock of the controlled foreign corporation.

(ii) *Notice.*—Prior to filing Form 8819, the controlling United States shareholders (or the foreign corporation, if the dollar election is made by the corporation) shall provide written notice that the dollar election will be made to all United States persons known to be shareholders who own (within the meaning of section 958(a)) stock of the foreign corporation. Such notice shall also include all information required in Form 8819.

(iii) *Reasonable cause exception.*—Failure of the controlling United States shareholders (or the foreign corporation, if the dollar election is made by the corporation) to timely file Form 8819 or provide written notice to a United States person required to be notified by paragraph (c)(2)(ii) of this section shall not invalidate the dollar election, if it is established to the satisfaction of the district director that reasonable cause existed for such failure.

(iv) *Procedure prior to the issuance of Form 8819.*—In the absence of Form 8819, an eligible QBU described in paragraph (c)(2)(i) of this section shall make the dollar election in accordance with § 1.985-2T(c)(2). Nevertheless, the person or persons that made such election must file a Form 8819 in the time and manner provided in the Form's instructions.

(3) *Eligible QBUs that are noncontrolled foreign corporations or branches of noncontrolled foreign corporations.*—(i) *Rule.*—If an eligible QBU is a noncontrolled foreign corporation (a foreign corporation not described in section 957), or a branch of a noncontrolled foreign corporation, the dollar election must be made by the corporation or the majority domestic corporate shareholders on behalf of the corporation by applying the rules provided in paragraph (c)(2)(i)(A) and (B), (ii), (iii), and (iv) of this section substituting

"majority domestic corporate shareholders" for "controlling United States shareholders" wherever it appears therein. The term "majority domestic corporate shareholders" means those domestic corporate shareholders (as described in section 902(a)) who, in the aggregate, own (within the meaning of section 958(a) greater than 50 percent of the total combined voting stock of all classes of stock of the noncontrolled foreign corporation entitled to vote that is owned (within the meaning of section 958(a)) by all the domestic corporate shareholders.

(ii) *Procedure prior to the issuance of Form 8819.* In the absence of Form 8819, an eligible QBU described in paragraph (c)(3)(i) of this section shall make the dollar election in accordance with §1.985-2T(c)(3). Nevertheless, the person or persons that made such election must file a Form 8819 in the time and manner provided in the Form's instructions.

(4) *Others.*—Any other person making a dollar election under this section shall elect by filing Form 8819 and fulfilling any other notice requirements that may be required by the Commissioner.

(d) *Effect of dollar election.*—(1) *General rule.*—If a dollar election is made (or considered made under paragraph (d)(3) of this section) by or on behalf of an eligible QBU, the QBU shall be deemed to have the dollar as its functional currency. Each United States person that owns (within the meaning of section 958(a)) stock of a foreign corporation which has the dollar as its functional currency under §1.985-2 must make all of its federal income tax calculations with respect to the foreign corporation using the dollar as the corporation's functional currency (regardless of when ownership was acquired or whether the United States person received the written notice required by paragraph (c)(2)(i)(B) of this section).

(2) *Computation.*—(i) *In general.*—Except as provided in paragraph (d)(2)(ii) of this section, any eligible QBU that pursuant to this §1.985-2 has a dollar functional currency must compute income or loss or earnings and profits (or deficit in earnings and profits) in dollars using the dollar approximate separate transactions method described in §1.985-3.

(ii) *Alternative method.*—An eligible QBU that has a dollar functional currency pursuant to this §1.985-2 may use a method other than the dollar approximate separate transactions method described in §1.985-3 only if the QBU demonstrates to the satisfaction of the Commissioner that it can properly employ such method. Generally, the QBU must show that it could compute foreign currency gain or loss under the principles of section 988 with respect to each of its section 988 transactions. If subsequently the QBU can no longer demonstrate to the satisfac-

tion of the district director that it can properly employ such an alternative method, then the QBU will be deemed to have changed its method of accounting to the dollar approximate separate transactions method described in §1.985-3. This change in accounting will be treated as having been made with the consent of the Commissioner. No adjustments under either §1.985-5T (or any succeeding final regulation) or section 481(a) shall be required solely because of the change. Rather the QBU shall begin accounting for its operations under §1.985-3 based on its dollar books and records as of the time of the change.

(3) *Conformity.*—(i) *General rule.*—If a dollar election is made under this §1.985-2 for an eligible QBU ("electing QBU"), then the dollar shall be the functional currency of any related person (regardless of when such person became related to the electing QBU) that is an eligible QBU, or any branch of any such related person that is an eligible QBU. For purposes of the preceding sentence, the term "related person" means any person with a relationship defined in section 267(b) to the electing QBU (or to the United States or foreign person of which the electing QBU is a part). In determining whether two or more corporations are members of the same controlled group under section 267(b)(3), a person is considered to own stock owned directly by such person, stock owned with the application of section 1563(e)(1), and stock owned with the application of section 267(c).

(ii) *Branches of United States and foreign persons.*—If a dollar election is made for a QBU branch of any person, each eligible QBU branch of such person shall have the dollar as its functional currency.

(4) *Required adjustments.*—If an eligible QBU's functional currency changes due to a dollar election, or due to the conformity requirements of paragraph (d)(3) of this section, such change shall be deemed for purposes of §1.985-4 to be consented to by the Commissioner. No adjustments under section 481(a) shall be required solely because of the change. However, the QBU must make those adjustments required by §1.985-5T (or any succeeding final regulation).

(5) *Taxable year conformity required.*—Generally, the adjustments required by paragraph (d)(4) of this section shall be made for a related person's taxable year—

(i) that includes the date in which the electing QBU made the dollar election if the person was related to such electing QBU at any time during the QBU's taxable year that includes such date, or

(ii) during which the person first becomes related to any electing QBU, in all other cases.

Reg. §1.985-2(c)(3)(ii)

For purposes of this paragraph (d)(5), the date in which the electing QBU makes the dollar election shall be the last day of the electing QBU's taxable year. The district director may permit the related party to make such adjustments beginning one taxable year later if, in the district director's sole judgment, reasonable cause exists for the related party not being able to make the required adjustments for the earlier year.

(6) *Availability of election.*—A dollar election may be made by or on behalf of a QBU, or considered made under the conformity rule of paragraph (d)(3), in any year in which the QBU is an eligible QBU. If a dollar election is not made by or on behalf of a QBU for its first taxable year beginning after December 31, 1986 in which it is an eligible QBU, then any dollar election made by or on behalf of the QBU, or considered made under the conformity rules of paragraph (d)(3) of this section, that results in a change in the QBU's functional currency shall be treated as having been made with the consent of the Commissioner. In such a case, however, the taxpayer must make those adjustments required by § 1.985-5T (or any succeeding final regulation).

(7) *Effect of changed circumstances.*—Regardless of any change in circumstances (e.g., a currency ceases to qualify as hyperinflationary), a QBU whose functional currency is the dollar under this section may change its functional currency only if the QBU complies with § 1.985-4.

(8) *Examples.*—The provisions of this section are illustrated by the following examples.

Example (1). X is a calendar year domestic corporation that in 1987 establishes a branch, A, in Country Z. A's functional currency under section 985(b)(1) and (2) and § 1.985-1 is the "h", the currency of Country Z. The cumulative inflation in Country Z exceeds 100 percent for the thirty-six months prior to January 1987, as measured by the consumer price index of Country Z listed in the monthly issues of the "International Financial Statistics". Accordingly, A is an eligible QBU in 1987 because the h is a hyperinflationary currency. Thus, X may elect the dollar as the functional currency of A for 1987.

Example (2). The facts are the same as in Example (1). X does not elect the dollar as the functional currency of A for 1987. Rather, X elects the dollar as the functional currency of A for 1991, a year A is an eligible QBU. The election constitutes a change in A's functional currency that is made with the consent of the Commissioner. However, A must make the adjustments required under § 1.985-5T (or any succeeding final regulation).

Example (3). X is a domestic corporation that establishes A, an eligible QBU branch. X is wholly owned by domestic corporation Y. Y has an eligible QBU branch, B. Both X and Y are calendar year taxpayers. X makes a dollar elec-

tion for A in 1987. Thus, A is an electing QBU. X and Y are related persons as defined in section 267(b) (*i.e.*, Y has a relationship under section 267(b)(3) to X, the corporation of which A is a part). Therefore, the dollar election by X for A in 1987 results in B, the eligible QBU branch of Y, also having the dollar as its functional currency for 1987.

Example (4). The facts are the same as in Example (3), except that Y does not have an eligible QBU branch but owns all the stock of C, a calendar year controlled foreign corporation, which is not itself an eligible QBU but which has an eligible QBU branch, D. X and C are related persons as defined in section 267(b) (*i.e.*, C has a relationship under section 267(b)(3) to X, the corporation of which A is a part). Therefore, the dollar election by X for A in 1987 results in D, the eligible QBU branch of C, also having the dollar as its functional currency for 1987.

Example (5). X, whose taxable year ends September 30, is an eligible QBU that does not use the dollar as its functional currency. X is wholly-owned by domestic corporation W. On January 1, 1989, X acquires all the stock of Y, an unrelated eligible QBU that made the dollar election under § 1.985-2. Y is a calendar year taxpayer. After the stock purchase, X and Y are related persons as defined in section 267(b). Under § 1.985-2(d)(3) and (5), the dollar shall be the functional currency of X, any person related to X, and any branch of such related person that is an eligible QBU beginning with the taxable year that includes December 31, 1989. Thus, X must change to the dollar for its taxable year beginning October 1, 1988. However, the district director may allow X to change to the dollar for its taxable year beginning October 1, 1989, provided reasonable cause exists. Those QBUs changing to the dollar as their functional currency as the result of the conformity requirements must make the adjustments required under § 1.985-5T (or any succeeding final regulation).

Example (6). The facts are the same as in Example (5), except that before X purchased the Y stock, X made the dollar election under § 1.985-2 but Y did not use the dollar as its functional currency. Under § 1.985-2(d)(3) and (5) the dollar shall be the functional currency of Y, any person related to Y, and any branch of such related person that is an eligible QBU beginning with the taxable year that includes September 30, 1989. Thus, Y must change to the dollar for its taxable year beginning January 1, 1989. However the district director may allow Y to change to the dollar for its taxable year beginning January 1, 1990, provided reasonable cause exists. Those QBUs changing to the dollar as their functional currency as the result of the conformity requirements must make the adjustments required under § 1.985-5T (or any succeeding final regulation). [Reg. § 1.985-2.]

☐ [*T.D.* 8263, 9-19-89. *Amended by T.D.* 8556, 7-22-94.]

Reg. § 1.985-2(d)(8)

[Reg. § 1.985-3]

§1.985-3. United States dollar approximate separate transactions method.—(a) *Scope and effective date.*—(1) *Scope.*—This section describes the United States dollar (dollar) approximate separate transactions method of accounting (DASTM). For all purposes of subtitle A, this method of accounting must be used to compute the gross income, taxable income or loss, or earnings and profits (or deficit in earnings and profits) of a QBU (as defined in section 989(a)) that has the dollar as its functional currency pursuant to §1.985-1(b)(2).

(2) *Effective date.*—(i) *In general.*—This section is effective for taxable years beginning after August 24, 1994.

(ii) *DASTM prior-year election.*—A taxpayer may elect to apply this section to any open taxable year beginning after December 31, 1986 (whether or not DASTM has been previously elected for some or all of those years). In order to make this election, the taxpayer must apply §1.985-3 to that year and all subsequent years. In addition, each person that is related (within the meaning of §1.985-3(e)(2)(vi)) to the taxpayer on the last day of any taxable year for which the election is effective and that would have been eligible to elect DASTM must also apply these rules to that year and all subsequent years. A taxpayer that has not previously elected to apply DASTM to its prior taxable years may make the DASTM election for the pertinent years by filing amended returns and complying with the applicable election procedures of §1.985-2. Form 8819 shall be attached to the return for the first year for which the election is to be effective. A taxpayer that has elected DASTM for prior taxable years and applied the rules under §1.985-3 (as contained in the April 1, 1994 edition of 26 CFR part 1 (1.908 to 1.1000)) may amend its returns to apply the rules of this §1.985-3. In either case, the DASTM election for prior taxable years shall be deemed to be made with the consent of the Commissioner.

(b) *Statement of method.*—Under DASTM, income or loss or earnings and profits (or a deficit in earnings and profits) of a QBU for its taxable year shall be determined in dollars by—

(1) Preparing an income or loss statement from the QBU's books and records (within the meaning of §1.989(a)-1(d)) as recorded in QBU's hyperinflationary currency (as defined in §1.985-1(b)(2)(ii)(D));

(2) Making the adjustments necessary to conform such statement to United States generally accepted accounting principles and tax accounting principles (including reversing monetary correction adjustments required by local accounting principles);

(3) Translating the amounts of hyperinflationary currency as shown on such adjusted statement into dollars in accordance with paragraph (c) of this section; and

(4) Adjusting the resulting dollar income or loss or earnings and profits (or deficit in earnings and profits) and, where necessary, particular items of gross income, deductible expense or other amounts, in accordance with paragraph (e) of this section to reflect the amount of DASTM gain or loss as determined under paragraph (d) of this section.

(c) *Translation into United States dollars.*—(1) *In general.*—Except as otherwise provided in this paragraph (c), the amounts shown on the income or loss statement, as adjusted under paragraph (b)(2) of this section, shall be translated into dollars at the exchange rate (as defined in paragraph (c)(6) of this section) for the translation period (as defined in paragraph (c)(7) of this section) to which they relate. However, if the QBU previously changed its functional currency to the dollar, and the rules of §1.985-5 (or, if applicable, §1.985-5T, as contained in the April 1, 1993 edition of 26 CFR part 1 (1.908 to 1.1000)) applied in translating its balance sheet amounts into dollars, then the spot exchange rate applied under those rules shall be used to translate any amount that would otherwise be translated at a rate determined by reference to a translation period prior to the change in functional currency. For example, depreciation with respect to an asset acquired while the QBU had a nondollar functional currency shall be translated into dollars at the spot rate on the last day of the taxable year before the year of change to a dollar functional currency, rather than at the rate for the period in which the asset was acquired.

(2) *Cost of goods sold.*—The dollar value of cost of goods sold shall equal the sum of the dollar values of beginning inventory and purchases less the dollar value of closing inventory as these amounts are determined under paragraph (c)(3) of this section.

(3) *Beginning inventory, purchases, and closing inventory.*—(i) *Beginning inventory.*—Amounts representing beginning inventory shall be translated so as to obtain the same amount of dollars which represented such items in the closing inventory balance for the preceding taxable year.

(ii) *Purchases.*—Amounts representing items purchased or otherwise first included in inventory during the taxable year shall be translated at the exchange rate for the translation period in which the cost of such items was incurred.

(iii) *Closing inventory.*—(A) *In general.*—Amounts representing items included in the closing inventory balance shall be translated at the exchange rate for the translation period in which the cost of such items was incurred. However, if amounts representing items included in the closing inventory balance are either valued at market or written down to market value, they shall be translated at the exchange rate existing on the last day of the taxable year. For purposes of determining lower of cost or market, items of inventory included in the closing inventory balance shall be translated into dollars at the exchange rate for the translation period in which the cost of such items was incurred and compared with market as determined in the QBU's hyperinflationary currency translated into dollars at the exchange rate existing on the last day of the taxable year.

(B) *Determination of translation period.*— The method used to determine the translation period of amounts representing items of closing inventory for purposes of paragraph (c)(3)(iii)(A) of this section may be based upon reasonable approximations and averages, including rates of turnover, provided that the method is used consistently from year to year.

(4) *Depreciation, depletion, and amortization.*— Amounts representing allowances for depreciation, depletion, or amortization shall be translated at the exchange rate for the translation period in which the cost of the underlying asset was incurred, except as provided in paragraph (c)(1) of this section.

(5) *Prepaid expenses or income.*—Amounts representing expense or income paid or received in a prior taxable year shall be translated at the exchange rate for the translation period during which they were paid or received.

(6) *Exchange rate.*—The exchange rate for a translation period may be determined under any reasonable method, provided that the method is consistently applied to all translation periods and conforms to the taxpayer's method of financial accounting. Reasonable methods include the average of beginning and ending exchange rates for the translation period and the spot rate on the last day of the translation period. Once chosen, a method for determining an exchange rate can be changed only with the consent of the district director.

(7) *Translation period.*—(i) *In general.*—Except as provided in paragraphs (c)(3)(iii)(B) and (c)(7)(ii) of this section, a translation period shall be each month within a QBU's taxable year.

(ii) *Exception.*—A taxpayer may divide its taxable year into translation periods of equal length (with not more than one short period annually) that are less than one month. Once such a translation period is established, it may not be changed without the consent of the district director.

(8) *Dollar transactions.*—(i) *In general.*—Except as provided in paragraph (c)(8)(ii) of this section, no DASTM gain or loss is realized with respect to dollar transactions since the dollar is

the functional currency of the QBU. Thus, the amount of any payment or receipt of dollars shall be reflected in the income or loss statement by the amount of such dollars. Also, the income or loss attributable to any transaction in which the amount that a QBU is entitled to receive (or is required to pay) by reason of such transaction is denominated in terms of the dollar, or is determined by reference to the value of the dollar, must be computed transaction by transaction. For example, if a foreign corporation lends 20 LC when 20 LC = $20 and is entitled to receive the LC equivalent of $20 at maturity plus a market rate of interest in dollars (or its LC equivalent), the loan is a dollar transaction. Similarly, this paragraph applies to any transaction that is determined to be a dollar transaction under section 988.

(ii) *Non-dollar functional currency.*—If pursuant to § 1.985-1(b)(2)(ii)(B)(*1*), a QBU is required to use a functional currency other than the dollar, then that currency shall be substituted for the dollar in applying paragraph (c)(8)(i) of this section.

(9) *Third currency transactions.*—A taxpayer may use any reasonable method of accounting for transactions described in section 988(c)(1)(B) and (C) that are denominated in, or determined by reference to, a currency other than the QBU's hyperinflationary currency or the dollar (third currency transactions) so long as such method is consistent with its method of financial accounting.

(10) *Examples.*—The provisions of this paragraph (c) are illustrated by the following examples:

Example 1. S is an accrual basis QBU that is required to use the dollar as its functional currency for its first taxable year beginning in 1994. S's hyperinflationary currency is the "h." During 1994, S accrues 100 dollars attributable to dollar-denominated sales. Because this is a dollar transaction under paragraph (c)(8) of this section, S's income or loss for 1994 shall reflect the 100 dollars (not the hyperinflationary value of such dollars when accrued).

Example 2. (i) S is an accrual basis QBU that is required to use the dollar as its functional currency for its first taxable year beginning in 1994. S's hyperinflationary currency is the "h." During 1994, S's sales amounted to 240,000,000h, its currently deductible expenses were 26,000,000h, and its total inventory purchases amounted to 100,000,000h. During January and February of 1994, S purchased depreciable assets for 80,000,000h and was allowed depreciation of 4,000,000h. At the end of 1994, S's closing inventory was 23,000,000h. No election to use a translation period other than the month is made, S had no transactions described in paragraph (c)(8) or (c)(9) of this section, and S's closing inventory was computed on the first-in, first-out inventory

Reg. §1.985-3(c)(10)

method. S's adjusted income or loss statement
for 1994 is translated into dollars as follows:

	Hyperinflationary Currency	Exchange Rate	United States Dollars
Sales			
(Jan-Feb)	10,000,000 h	20:1 [1]	$ 500,000
(Mar-Apr)	20,000,000	21:1	952,381
(May-June)	50,000,000	22:1	2,272,727
(July)	50,000,000	23:1	2,173,913
(August)	20,000,000	26:1	769,231
(Sept.)	20,000,000	28:1	714,286
(Oct.)	20,000,000	29:1	689,655
(Nov.)	20,000,000	30:1	666,667
(Dec.)	30,000,000	31:1	967,742
Total	240,000,000 h		$9,706,602
Cost of Goods Sold:			
Opening Inventory	-0-		-0-
Purchases:			
(Jan-Feb)	15,000,000h	20:1	$ 750,000
(Mar-Apr)	10,000,000	21:1	476,190
(May-June)	30,000,000	22:1	1,363,636
(July)	20,000,000	23:1	869,565
(August)	10,000,000	26:1	384,615
(Sept.)	5,000,000	28:1	178,571
(Oct.)	5,000,000	29:1	172,414
(Nov.)	2,500,000	30:1	83,333
(Dec.)	2,500,000	31:1	80,645
Less Closing Inventory	(23,000,000)	[2]	(822,655)
	77,000,000 h		$3,536,314

[1] Where multiple months are indicated, the exchange rate applies for all months.
[2] See paragraph (ii) for this *Example.*

(ii) Since S uses the first-in, first-out inventory method, the closing inventory is assumed to consist of purchases made during the most recent translation period as follows:

	Hyperinflationary Currency	Exchange Rate	United States Dollars
December	2,500,000 h	31:1	$80,645
November	2,500,000	30:1	83,333
October	5,000,000	29:1	172,414
September	5,000,000	28:1	178,571
August	8,000,000	26:1	307,692
Total	23,000,000 h		$822,655
Non-Capitalized Expenses:			
(Jan-Feb)	4,000,000 h	20:1	$200,000
(Mar-Apr)	2,500,000	21:1	119,048
(May-June)	2,500,000	22:1	113,636
(July)	2,000,000	23:1	86,957
(August)	3,000,000	26:1	115,385
(Sept.)	3,000,000	28:1	107,143
(Oct.)	2,000,000	29:1	68,966
(Nov.)	3,000,000	30:1	100,000
(Dec.)	4,000,000	31:1	129,032
Total	26,000,000 h		$1,040,167
Depreciation	4,000,000 h	20:1	$200,000
Total Cost & Expenses	107,000,000 h		$4,776,481
Operating Profit	133,000,000 h		$4,930,121

Reg. §1.985-3(c)(10)

(d) *Computation of DASTM gain or loss.*—(1) *Rule.*—DASTM gain or loss of a QBU equals—

(i) The net worth of the QBU (as determined under paragraph (d)(2) of this section) at the end of the taxable year minus the net worth of the QBU at the end of the preceding taxable year; plus

(ii) The dollar amount of the items described in paragraph (d)(3) of this section and minus the dollar amount of the items described in paragraph (d)(4) of this section; minus

(iii) The amount of dollar income or earnings and profits (or plus the amount of any dollar loss or deficit in earnings and profits) as determined for the taxable year pursuant to paragraphs (b)(1) through (b)(3) of this section.

(2) *Net worth.*—Net worth of a QBU at the end of any taxable year equals the aggregate dollar amount representing assets on the QBU's balance sheet at the end of the taxable year less the aggregate dollar amount representing liabilities on the balance sheet. Notwithstanding any other provision in this paragraph (d)(2), the district director may adjust the amount of any asset or liability if a purpose for acquiring (or disposing of) the asset or incurring (or discharging) the liability is to manipulate the composition of the balance sheet for any period during the taxable year in order to avoid tax. The taxpayer shall determine net worth by—

(i) Preparing a balance sheet as of the end of the taxable year from the QBU's books and records (within the meaning of § 1.989(a)-1(d)) as recorded in the QBU's hyperinflationary currency;

(ii) Making adjustments necessary to conform such balance sheet to United States generally accepted accounting principles and tax accounting principles (including reversing monetary correction adjustments required by local accounting principles); and

(iii) Translating the asset and liability amounts shown on the balance sheet into United States dollars in accordance with paragraph (d)(5) of this section.

(3) *Positive adjustments.*—(i) *In general.*—The items described in this paragraph (d)(3) are dividend distributions for the taxable year and any items that decrease net worth for the taxable year but that generally do not affect income or loss or earnings and profits (or a deficit in earnings and profits). Such items include a transfer to the home office of a QBU branch and a return of capital.

(ii) *Translation.*—Except as provided by ruling or administrative pronouncement, items described in paragraph (d)(3)(i) of this section shall be translated into dollars as follows:

(A) (A) If the item giving rise to the adjustment would be translated under paragraph (d)(5) of this section at the exchange rate for the last translation period of the taxable year if it were shown on the QBU's year-end balance sheet, such item shall be translated at the exchange rate on the date the item is transferred.

(B) (B) If the item giving rise to the adjustment would be translated under paragraph (d)(5) of this section at the exchange rate for the translation period in which the cost of the item was incurred if it were shown on the QBU's year-end balance sheet, such item shall be translated at the same historical rate.

(iii) *Effective date.*—Paragraph (d)(3)(ii) of this section is applicable for any transfer, dividend, or distribution that is a return of capital that is made after March 8, 2005, and that gives rise to an adjustment under this paragraph (d)(3).

(4) *Negative adjustments.*—The items described in this paragraph (d)(4) are items that increase net worth for the taxable year but that generally do not affect income or loss or earnings and profits (or a deficit in earnings and profits). Such items include a capital contribution or a transfer from a home office to a QBU branch. Except as otherwise provided by ruling or administrative pronouncement, if the contribution or transfer is not in dollars, the amount of a capital contribution or transfer shall be translated into dollars at the exchange rate on the date made.

(5) *Translation of balance sheet.*—Asset and liability amounts shown on the balance sheet in hyperinflationary currency (adjusted pursuant to paragraph (d)(2)(ii) of this section) shall be translated into dollars as provided in this paragraph (d)(5). However, if the QBU previously changed its functional currency to the dollar and the rules of § 1.985-5 (or, if applicable, § 1.985-5T, as contained in the April 1, 1993 edition of 26 CFR part 1 (1.908 to 1.1000)) applied in translating its balance sheet amounts into dollars, then the spot exchange rate applied under those rules shall be used to translate any amount that would otherwise be translated at a rate determined by reference to a translation period prior to the change in functional currency. For example, the basis of real property acquired while the QBU had a nondollar functional currency shall be translated into dollars at the spot rate on the last day of the taxable year before the year of change to a dollar functional currency, rather than at the rate for the period in which the cost was incurred.

(i) *Closing inventory.*—Amounts representing items of inventory included in the closing inventory balance shall be translated in accordance with paragraph (c)(3)(iii) of this section.

(ii) *Bad debt reserves.*—Amounts representing bad debt reserves shall be translated at the exchange rate for the last translation period for the taxable year.

(iii) *Prepaid income or expense.*—Amounts representing expenses or income paid or received in a prior taxable year shall be translated in accordance with paragraph (c)(5) of this section.

(iv) *Hyperinflationary currency.*—Amounts of the hyperinflationary currency and hyperinflationary demand deposit balances shall be translated at the exchange rate for the last translation period of the taxable year.

(v) *Certain assets.*—(A) *In general.*—Amounts representing plant, real property, equipment, goodwill, and patents and other intangibles shall be translated at the exchange rate for the translation period in which the cost of the asset was incurred.

(B) *Adjustment to certain assets.*—Amounts representing depreciation, depletion, and amortization reserves shall be translated in accordance with paragraph (c)(4) of this section.

(vi) *Hyperinflationary debt obligations.*—Except as provided in paragraph (d)(5)(vii) of this section, amounts representing a hyperinflationary debt obligation (including accounts receivable and payable) shall be translated at the exchange rate for the last translation period for the taxable year.

(vii) *Accrued foreign income taxes.*—Amounts representing an accrued but unpaid foreign income tax shall be translated at the exchange rate on the last day of the last translation period of the taxable year of accrual.

(viii) *Certain hyperinflationary financial instruments.*—Amounts representing any item described in section 988(c)(1)(B)(iii) (relating to forward contracts, futures contracts, options, or similar financial instruments) denominated in or determined by reference to the hyperinflationary currency shall be translated at the exchange rate for the last translation period for the taxable year.

(ix) *Other assets and liabilities.*—Amounts representing assets and liabilities, other than those described in paragraphs (d)(5)(i) through (viii) of this section, shall be translated at the exchange rate for the translation period in which the cost of the asset or the amount of the liability was incurred.

(6) *Dollar transactions.*—Notwithstanding any other provisions of this paragraph (d), where the amount representing an item shown on the balance sheet reflects a dollar transaction (described in paragraph (c)(8) of this section), the transaction shall be taken into account in accordance with that paragraph.

(7) *Third currency transactions.*—A taxpayer may use any reasonable method of accounting for transactions described in section 988(c)(1)(B) and (C) that are denominated in, or determined by reference to, a currency other than the QBU's hyperinflationary currency or the dollar (third currency transactions), so long as such method is consistent with its method of financial accounting.

(8) *Character.*—The amount of DASTM gain or loss determined under paragraph (d)(1) of this section shall be ordinary income or loss.

(9) *Example.*—The provisions of this paragraph (d) are illustrated by the following example:

Example. (i) S, an accrual method calendar year foreign corporation, uses DASTM. S's hyperinflationary currency is the "h." S's net worth at December 31, 1993 was $3,246,495. For 1994, S's operating profit is 81,340,000h, or $2,038,200. S made a 5,000,000h distribution in April and again in December of 1994. S's translation period is the month. None of S's assets or liabilities reflect a dollar or third currency transaction described in paragraph (c)(8) or (c)(9) of this section, respectively. The exchange rate for each month in 1994 is as follows:

January	32h:$1
Feb.-Mar.	33:1
April-May	34:1
June	35:1
July	36:1
Aug.-Sept.	37:1
Oct.	38:1
Nov.	39:1
Dec.	40:1

(ii) At the end of 1994, S's assets and liabilities, as adjusted and translated pursuant to paragraphs (d)(2) and (d)(5) of this section, are as follows:

	Hyper-inflationary	Exchange Rate	U.S.-Dollar
Hyperinflationary cash on hand	40,000 h	40:1	$ 1,000
Checking account	400,000	40:1	10,000
Accounts Receivable- 30 Day Accounts	20,000,000	40:1 [1]	500,000

	Hyper-inflationary	Exchange Rate	U.S.-Dollar
60 Day Accounts	25,000,000	40:1	625,000
Inventory	65,000,000	2	2,500,000
Fixed assets—Property	90,000,000	27:1	3,333,333
Plant	190,000,000	3	6,785,714
Accumulated Depreciation	(600,000)	4	(21,428)
Equipment	10,000,000	4	340,000
Accumulated Depreciation	(400,000)	4	(13,333)
Common Stock—Stock A	500,000	34:1	14,706
Stock B	400,000	26:1	15,385
Preferred Stock	1,000,000	32:1	31,250
C.D.s	5,000,000	40:1	125,000
Total Assets	406,340,000		14,246,627
Accounts Payable	35,000,000	40:1	875,000
Long-term liabilities:			
Liability A	150,000,000	40:1	3,750,000
Liability B	80,000,000	40:1	2,000,000
Liability C	30,000,000	40:1	750,000
Total Liabilities	295,000,000 h		$7,375,000

[1] S ages its accounts receivable and groups them into two categories - those outstanding for 30 days and those outstanding for 60 days.

[2] Translated the same as closing inventory under paragraph (c)(3)(iii).

[3] The cost of S's plant was incurred in several translation periods. Therefore, the dollar cost and dollar depreciation reflect several translation rates.

[4] S has a variety of equipment.

(iii) The DASTM gain of S for 1994 is computed as follows:

Net worth—1994			$6,871,627
Less—Net worth—1993			$3,246,495
Plus—1994 Dividends:	April	$149,254	
	December	126,582 [1]	275,836
Less Operating Profit—1994			2,038,200
DASTM Gain			$1,862,768

[1] The exchange rates on the date of the April and December dividends were 33.5h:$1 and 39.5h:$1, respectively.

(iv) Thus, total profit = $2,038,200 + $1,862,768 = $3,900,968

(e) *Effect of DASTM gain or loss on gross income, taxable income, or earnings and profits.*—(1) *In general.*—For all purposes of subtitle A, the amount of DASTM gain or loss of a QBU determined under paragraph (d) of this section is taken into account by the QBU for purposes of determining the amount of its gross income, taxable income or loss, earnings and profits (or deficit in earnings and profits), and, where necessary, particular items of income, expense or other amounts. DASTM gain or loss is allocated under one of two methods. Certain small QBUs may elect the small QBU DASTM allocation described in paragraph (e)(2) of this section. All other QBUs must use the 9-step procedure described in paragraph (e)(3) of this section.

(2) *Small QBU DASTM allocation.*—(i) *Election threshold.*—A taxpayer may elect to use the small QBU DASTM allocation described in paragraph (e)(2)(iv) of this section with respect to a QBU that has an adjusted basis in assets (translated as provided in paragraph (d)(5) of this section) of $10 million or less at the end of any taxable year. In calculating the $10 million threshold, a QBU shall be treated as owning all of the assets of each related QBU (as defined in paragraph (e)(2)(vi) of this section) having its residence (as defined in section 988(a)(3)(B)) in the QBU's country of residence (related same-country QBU). For this purpose, appropriate adjustment shall be made to eliminate the double counting of assets created in transactions between related QBUs resident in the same country. For example, assume QBU-1, resident in country X, sells inventory to related QBU-2, also resident in country X, in exchange for an account receivable. For purposes of determining the assets of QBU-1 under this paragraph (e)(2)(i), the taxpayer shall take into account either the inventory shown on the books of QBU-2 or QBU-1's receivable from QBU-2 (but not both).

(ii) *Consent to election.*—The election of the small QBU DASTM allocation or subsequent application of the rules of paragraph (e)(3) of this section due to an increase in the adjusted basis of the QBU's assets shall be deemed to have been made with the consent of the Commissioner. Once the election under paragraph (e)(2)(iii) of this section is made, it shall apply for all years in which the adjusted basis of the assets of the QBU (and any related same-country QBU) is $10 million or less, unless revoked with the Commissioner's consent. If the adjusted basis of the assets of the QBU (and any related same-country QBU) exceeds $10 million at the end of any taxable year, the rules of paragraph (e)(3) of this section shall apply to that QBU (and any related same-country QBU) for such year and each subsequent year unless such QBU again qualifies, and applies for and obtains the Commissioner's consent, to use the small QBU DASTM allocation. However, if a QBU acquires assets with a principal purpose of avoiding the application of paragraph (e)(2)(iv) of this section, the Commissioner may disregard the acquisition of such assets.

(iii) *Manner of making election.*—(A) *QBUs that are branches of United States persons.*—For the first year in which this election is effective, in the case of a QBU branch of a United States person, a statement shall be attached to the United States person's timely filed Federal income tax return (taking extensions into account). The statement shall identify the QBU (or QBUs) for which the election is being made by describing its business and its country of residence, state the adjusted basis of the assets of the QBU (and any related same-country QBUs) to which the election applies, and include a statement that the election is being made pursuant to § 1.985-3(e)(2).

(B) *Other QBUs.*—In the case of a QBU other than one described in paragraph (e)(2)(iii)(A) of this section, an election must be made in the manner prescribed in § 1.964-1. The statement filed with the Internal Revenue Service as required under § 1.964-1 must include the information required under paragraph (e)(2)(iii)(A) of this section.

(iv) *Effect of election.*—If a taxpayer elects under this paragraph (e)(2) to use the small QBU DASTM allocation, DASTM gain or loss, as determined under paragraph (d) of this section, of a small QBU shall be allocated ratably to all items of the QBU's gross income (determined prior to adjustment for DASTM gain or loss). Therefore, for purposes of the foreign tax credit, DASTM gain or loss shall be allocated on the basis of the relative amounts of gross income in each separate category as defined in § 1.904-5(a)(1). In the case of a controlled foreign corporation (within the meaning of section 957 or 953(c)(1)(B)), for purposes of section 952, DASTM gain or loss shall be allocated to subpart

F income in a separate category in the same ratio that the gross subpart F income in that category for the taxable year bears to its total gross income in that category for the taxable year.

(v) *Conformity.*—If a person (or a QBU of such person) makes an election under this paragraph (e)(2) to use the small QBU DASTM allocation, then each QBU of any related person (as defined in paragraph (e)(2)(vi) of this section) that satisfies the threshold requirement of paragraph (e)(2)(i) of this section (after application of the aggregation rule of paragraph (e)(2)(i) of this section) shall be deemed to have made the election.

(vi) *Related person.*—The term related person means any person with a relationship to the QBU (or to the United States or foreign person of which the electing QBU is a part) that is defined in section 267(b) or section 707(b).

(3) *DASTM 9-step procedure.*—(i) *Step 1— prepare balance sheets.*—The taxpayer shall prepare an opening and a closing balance sheet for the QBU for each balance sheet period during the taxable year. The balance sheet period is the most frequent period for which balance sheet data are reasonably available (but in no event less frequently than quarterly). The balance sheet period may not be changed without the consent of the district director. The balance sheets must be prepared under the principles of paragraph (d)(2) of this section.

(ii) *Step 2—identify certain assets and liabilities.*—The taxpayer shall identify each item on the balance sheet that is described in section 988(c)(1)(B) or (C) and that would have been translated under paragraph (d)(5) of this section into dollars at the exchange rate for the last translation period for the taxable year (or the exchange rate on the last day of the last translation period of the taxable year in the case of an accrued foreign income tax liability).

(iii) *Step 3—characterize the assets.*—The taxpayer shall characterize and group the assets identified in paragraph (e)(3)(ii) of this section (Step 2) according to the source and the type of income that they generate, have generated, or may reasonably be expected to generate by applying the principles of § 1.861-9T(g)(3) or its successor regulation (relating to characterization of assets for purposes of interest expense allocation). If a purpose for a taxpayer's business practices is to manipulate asset characterization or groupings, the district director may allocate or apportion DASTM gain or loss attributable to the assets. Thus, if a taxpayer that previously did not separately state interest on accounts receivable begins to impose an interest charge and a purpose for the change was to manipulate tax characterizations or groupings, then the district director may require that none of the DASTM gain or loss attributable to those receivables be allocated or apportioned to interest income.

(iv) *Step 4—determine DASTM gain or loss attributable to certain assets.—(A) General rule.—* The taxpayer shall determine the dollar amount of DASTM gain or loss attributable to assets in each group identified in paragraph (e)(3)(iii) of this section (Step 3) as follows:

$[(bb + eb) \div 2] \times [er - br]$

where

     bb = the hyperinflationary currency adjusted basis of the assets in the group at the beginning of the balance sheet period.

     eb = the hyperinflationary currency adjusted basis of the assets in the group at the end of the balance sheet period.

     er = one dollar divided by the number of hyperinflationary currency units that equal one dollar at the end of the balance sheet period.

     br = one dollar divided by the number of hyperinflationary currency units that equal one dollar at the beginning of the balance sheet period.

(B) *Weighting to prevent distortion.—* If averaging the adjusted basis of assets in a group at the beginning and end of a balance sheet period results in an allocation of DASTM gain or loss that does not clearly reflect income, as might be the case in the event of a purchase or disposition of an asset that is not in the normal course of business, the taxpayer must use a weighting method that reflects the time the assets are held by the QBU during the translation period.

(C) *Example.—* The provisions of this paragraph (e)(3)(iv) are illustrated by the following example:

Example. S is a foreign corporation that operates in the hyperinflationary currency "h" and computes its income or loss or earnings and profits under DASTM. S's adjusted basis in a group of assets described in section 988(c)(1)(B) or (C) that generate general limitation foreign source income (as characterized under paragraph (e)(3)(iii) of this section) at the beginning of the balance sheet period is 750,000h. S's basis in such assets at the end of the balance sheet period is 1,250,000h. The exchange rate at the beginning of the balance sheet period is $1 = 200h. The exchange rate at the end of the balance sheet period is $1 = 500h. The DASTM loss attributable to the assets described above is $3,000, determined as follows:

$[(750,000h + 1,250,000h) \div 2] \times$
$[(\$1 \div 500h) - (\$1 \div 200h)] = (\$3000)$

(v) *Step 5—adjust dollar gross income by DASTM gain or loss from assets.—* The taxpayer shall adjust the dollar amount of the QBU's gross income (computed under paragraphs (b)(1) through (b)(3) of this section) generated by each group of assets characterized in paragraph (e)(3)(iii) of this section (Step 3) by the amount of DASTM gain or loss attributable to those assets computed under paragraph (e)(3)(iv) of this section (Step 4). Thus, if a group of assets, such as accounts receivable, generates both a category of income described in section 904(d)(1)(I) (relating to general limitation income) that is not foreign base company income as defined in section 954 and a DASTM loss under paragraph (e)(3)(iv) of this section (Step 4), the amount of the DASTM loss would reduce the amount of the QBU's gross income in that category. Similarly, if a group of assets, such as short-term bank deposits, generates both foreign personal holding company income that is passive income (described in sections 954(c)(1)(A) and 904(d)(1)(A)) and a DASTM loss under paragraph (e)(3)(iv) of this section (Step 4), the amount of the DASTM loss would reduce the amount of the QBU's foreign personal holding company income and passive income. See section 904(f) and the regulations thereunder in the case where that section would apply and DASTM loss attributable to a group of assets exceeds the income generated by such assets.

(vi) *Step 6—determine DASTM gain or loss attributable to liabilities.—(A) General rule.—* The taxpayer shall determine the dollar amount of DASTM gain or loss attributable to liabilities identified in paragraph (e)(3)(ii) of this section (Step 2), and described in paragraph (e)(3)(vi)(B) of this section as follows:

$[(bl + el) \div 2] \times [br - er]$

where

     bl = the hyperinflationary currency amount of liabilities at the beginning of the balance sheet period.

     el = the hyperinflationary currency amount of liabilities at the end of the balance sheet translation period.

     br = one dollar divided by the number of hyperinflationary currency units that equal one dollar at the beginning of the balance sheet period.

     er = one dollar divided by the number of hyperinflationary currency units that equal one dollar at the end of the balance sheet period.

(B) *Separate calculation.—* The calculation shall be made separately for interest-bearing liabilities described in paragraph (e)(3)(vii) of this section (Step 7) and for each of the classes of non-interest-bearing liabilities described in paragraph (e)(3)(viii) of this section (Step 8).

(C) *Weighting to prevent distortion.—* Where a distortion would result from averaging the amount of liabilities at the beginning and end of a balance sheet period, as might be the case where a taxpayer incurs or retires a substantial liability, the taxpayer must use a different method that more clearly reflects the average amount of liabilities weighted to reflect the time the liability was outstanding during the balance sheet period.

　　(vii) Step 7—adjust dollar income and expense by DASTM gain or loss from interest-bearing liabilities.—(A) In general.—The taxpayer shall apply the amount of DASTM gain on interest-bearing liabilities computed under paragraph (e)(3)(vi) of this section (Step 6) to reduce interest expense generated by such liabilities (*e.g.*, prior to the application of §1.861-9T or its successor regulation). To the extent DASTM gain on such liabilities exceeds interest expense, it shall be sourced or otherwise classified in the same manner that interest expense is allocated and apportioned under §1.861-9T or its successor regulation. The amount of DASTM loss on interest-bearing liabilities computed under paragraph (e)(3)(vi) of this section (Step 6) shall be allocated and apportioned in the same manner that interest expense is allocated and apportioned under §1.861-9T or its successor regulation (without regard to the exceptions to fungibility in §1.861-10T or its successor regulation). For purposes of this section, an interest-bearing liability is a liability that requires payment of periodic interest (whether fixed or variable), has original issue discount, or would have interest imputed under subtitle A.

　　(B) Allocation of DASTM gain or loss from interest-bearing liabilities that generate related person interest expense.—DASTM gain or loss from interest-bearing liabilities that generate related person interest expense (as provided in section 954(b)(5)) shall be allocated for purposes of subtitle A (including sections 904 and 952) in the same manner that the related person interest expense of that debt is required to be allocated under the rules of section 954(b)(5) and §1.904-5(c)(2).

　　(C) Modified gross income method.—In applying the modified gross income method described in §1.861-9T(j) or its successor regulation, gross income shall be adjusted for any DASTM gain or loss from assets as provided in paragraph (e)(3)(v) of this section (Step 5) and any DASTM gain or loss with respect to short-term, non-interest-bearing trade payables as provided in paragraph (e)(3)(viii)(A) of this section.

　　(viii) Step 8—adjust dollar income and expense by DASTM gain or loss from non-interest bearing liabilities.—(A) Short-term, non-interest-bearing trade payables.—The taxpayer shall allocate DASTM gain or loss on short-term non-interest-bearing trade payables for purposes of subtitle A (including sections 904 and 952) to the same category or type of gross income as the cost or expense to which the trade payable relates. For this purpose, a short-term, non-interest-bearing trade payable is a non-interest-bearing liability with a term of 183 days or less that is incurred to purchase property or services to be used by the obligor in an active trade or business.

　　(B) Excise tax payables.—The taxpayer shall allocate DASTM gain or loss on excise tax payables for purposes of subtitle A (including sections 904 and 952) to the same category or type of gross income as would be derived from the activity to which the excise tax relates.

　　(C) Other non-interest-bearing liabilities.—(1) In general.—Except as provided in paragraphs (e)(3)(viii)(A), (e)(3)(viii)(B), and (e)(3)(viii)(C)(2) of this section, DASTM gain or loss on non-interest-bearing liabilities shall be allocated under paragraph (e)(3)(ix) of this section (Step 9).

　　(2) Tracing if substantial distortion of income.—DASTM gains and losses on liabilities described in paragraph (e)(3)(viii)(C)(1) of this section may be attributed to the same section 904(d) separate category or subpart F category as the transaction to which the liability relates if the taxpayer demonstrates to the satisfaction of the district director, or it is determined by the district director, that application of paragraph (e)(3)(viii)(C)(1) of this section results in a substantial distortion of income.

　　(ix) Step 9—allocate residual DASTM gain or loss.—If there is a difference between the net DASTM gain or loss determined under paragraphs (e)(3)(i) through (viii) of this section (Steps 1 through 8) and the DASTM gain or loss determined under paragraph (d) of this section, the amount of the difference must be allocated for purposes of subtitle A (including sections 904 and 952) to the QBU's gross income (computed under paragraphs (b)(1) through (3) of this section, as adjusted under paragraphs (e)(3)(i) through (viii) of this section (Steps 1 through 8)) on the basis of the relative amounts of each category or type of gross income. [Reg. §1.985-3.]

　　☐ [T.D.8263, 9-19-89. *Amended by T.D. 8556, 7-22-94 and T.D. 9320, 3-29-2007.*]

[Reg. §1.985-4]

§1.985-4. Method of accounting.—(a) *Adoption or election.*—The adoption of, or the election to use, a functional currency shall be treated as a method of accounting. The functional currency shall be used for the year of adoption (or election) and for all subsequent taxable years unless permission to change is granted, or considered to be granted under §1.985-2 or 1.985-8, by the Commissioner.

　　(b) *Condition for changing functional currencies.*—Generally, permission to change functional currencies shall not be granted unless significant changes in the facts and circumstances of the QBU's economic environment occur. If the determination of the functional currency of the QBU for purposes of United States generally accepted accounting principles (GAAP) is based on facts and circumstances substantially similar to those set forth in § 1.985-1(c)(2), then ordinarily the Commissioner will grant a taxpayer's request to change its functional currency (or the functional currency of its branch that is a QBU) to a new functional currency only if the taxpayer (or its QBU) also changes to the new functional currency for purposes of GAAP. However, permission to change will not necessarily be granted merely because the new functional currency will conform to the taxpayer's GAAP functional currency.

(c) *Relationship to certain other sections of the Code.*—Nothing in this section shall be construed to override the provisions of any other sections of the Code or regulations that require the use of consistent accounting methods. Such provisions must be independently satisfied separate and apart from the identification of a functional currency. For instance, while separate geographical divisions of a taxpayer's trade or business may have different functional currencies, such geographical divisions may nevertheless be required to consistently use other methods of accounting. [Reg. § 1.985-4.]

☐ [*T.D. 8263, 9-19-89. Amended by T.D. 8776, 7-28-98 and T.D. 8927, 1-10-2001.*]

[Reg. § 1.985-5]

§ 1.985-5. Adjustments required upon change in functional currency.—(a) *In general.*—This section applies in the case of a QBU that changes from one functional currency (old functional currency) to another functional currency (new functional currency). A taxpayer or QBU subject to the rules of this section shall make the adjustments set forth in the 3-step procedure described in paragraphs (b) through (e) of this section. The adjustments shall be made on the last day of the taxable year ending before the year of change as defined in § 1.481-1(a)(1). Gain or loss required to be recognized under paragraphs (b), (d)(2), and (e)(2) of this section is not subject to section 481 and, therefore, the full amount of the gain or loss must be included in income or earnings and profits on the last day of the taxable year ending before the year of change. Except as provided in § 1.985-6, a QBU with a functional currency for its first taxable year beginning in 1987 that is different from the currency in which it had kept its books and records for United States accounting and tax accounting purposes for its prior taxable year shall apply the principles of this § 1.985-5 for purposes of computing the relevant functional currency items, such as earnings and profits, basis of an asset, and amount of a liability, as of the first day of a taxpayer's first taxable year beginning in 1987. However, a QBU that changes to the dollar pursuant to § 1.985-1(b)(2) after 1987 shall apply § 1.985-7.

(b) *Step 1—Taking into account exchange gain or loss on certain section 988 transactions.*—The QBU shall recognize or otherwise take into account for all purposes of the Code the amount of any unrealized exchange gain or loss attributable to a section 988 transaction (as defined in section 988(c)(1)(A), (B), and (C)) that, after applying section 988(d), is denominated in terms of or determined by reference to the new functional currency. The amount of such gain or loss shall be determined without regard to the limitations of section 988(b) (*i.e.*, whether any gain or loss would be realized on the transaction as a whole). The character and source of such gain or loss shall be determined under section 988.

(c) *Step 2—Determining the new functional currency basis of property and the new functional currency amount of liabilities and any other relevant items.*—The new functional currency adjusted basis of property and the new functional currency amount of liabilities and any other relevant items (*e.g.*, items described in section 988(c)(1)(B)(iii)) shall equal the product of the amount of the old functional currency adjusted basis or amount multiplied by the new functional currency/old functional currency spot exchange rate on the last day of the taxable year ending before the year of change (spot rate).

(d) *Step 3A—Additional adjustments that are necessary when a branch changes functional currency.*—(1) *Branch changing to a functional currency other than the taxpayer's functional currency.*—(i) *Rule.*—If a QBU that is a branch of a taxpayer changes to a functional currency other than the taxpayer's functional currency, the branch shall make the adjustments set forth in either paragraph (d)(1)(ii) or (d)(1)(iii) of this section for purposes of section 987. See § 1.987-5(d) for rules for computing the branch's equity pool and basis pool.

(ii) *Where prior to the change the branch and taxpayer had different functional currencies.*—If the branch and the taxpayer had different functional currencies prior to the change, the branch's new functional currency equity pool shall equal the product of the old functional currency amount of the equity pool multiplied by the spot rate. No adjustment to the basis pool is necessary.

(iii) *Where prior to the change the branch and taxpayer had the same functional currency.*—If the branch and the taxpayer had the same functional currency prior to the change, the branch's basis pool shall equal the difference between the branch's total old functional currency basis of its assets and its total old functional currency amount of its liabilities. The branch's equity pool shall equal the product of the basis pool multiplied by the spot rate.

(2) *Branch changing to the taxpayer's functional currency.*—If a branch changes its functional currency to the taxpayer's functional

currency, the branch shall be treated as if it terminated on the last day of the taxable year ending before the year of change. In such a case, the taxpayer shall realize gain or loss attributable to the branch's equity pool under the principles of section 987.

(e) *Step 3B—Additional adjustments that are necessary when a taxpayer changes functional currency.*—(1) *Corporations.*—The amount of a corporation's new functional currency earnings and profits and the amount of its new functional currency paid-in capital shall equal the product of the old functional currency amounts of such items multiplied by the spot rate. The foreign income taxes and accumulated profits or deficits in accumulated profits of a foreign corporation that were maintained in foreign currency for purposes of section 902 and that are attributable to taxable years of the foreign corporation beginning before January 1, 1987, also shall be translated into the new functional currency at the spot rate.

(2) *Collateral consequences to a United States shareholder of a corporation changing to the United States dollar as its functional currency.*—A United States shareholder (within the meaning of section 951(b) or section 953(c)(1)(A)) of a controlled foreign corporation (within the meaning of section 957 or section 953(c)(1)(B)) changing its functional currency to the dollar shall recognize foreign currency gain or loss computed under section 986(c) as if all previously taxed earnings and profits, if any, (including amounts attributable to pre-1987 taxable years that were translated from dollars into functional currency in the foreign corporation's first post-1986 taxable year) were distributed immediately prior to the change. Such a shareholder shall also recognize gain or loss attributable to the corporation's paid-in capital to the same extent, if any, that such gain or loss would be recognized under the regulations under section 367(b) if the corporation was liquidated completely.

(3) *Taxpayers that are not corporations.*—[Reserved]

(4) *Adjustments to a branch's accounts when a taxpayer changes functional currency.*—(i) *Taxpayer changing to a functional currency other than the branch's functional currency.*—If a taxpayer changes to a functional currency that differs from the functional currency of a branch of the taxpayer, the branch shall adjust its basis pool in the manner prescribed in paragraph (d)(1)(ii) of this section for adjusting the equity pool, if the taxpayer's old functional currency was different from the branch's functional currency. If the taxpayer's old functional currency was the same as the branch's functional currency, the branch shall determine its equity pool and basis pool in the manner set forth in paragraph (d)(1)(iii) of

this section for determining the basis pool and equity pool, respectively.

(ii) *Taxpayer changing to the same functional currency as the branch.*—If a taxpayer changes to the same functional currency as a branch of the taxpayer, the taxpayer shall realize gain or loss as set forth in paragraph (d)(2) of this section.

(f) *Examples.*—The provisions of this section are illustrated by the following examples.

Example 1. S, a calendar year foreign corporation, is wholly owned by domestic corporation P. The Commissioner granted permission to change S's functional currency from the LC to the FC beginning January 1, 1993. The LC/FC exchange rate on December 31, 1992 is 1 LC/2 FC. The following shows how S must convert the items on its balance sheet from the LC to the FC.

LC	1:2	FC
Assets:		
Cash on hand	40,000	80,000
Accounts Receivable	10,000	20,000
Inventory	100,000	200,000
100,000 FC Bond		
(100,000 LC historical		
basis)	50,000 [1]	100,000
Fixed assets:		
Property	200,000	400,000
Plant	500,000	1,000,000
Accumulated		
Depreciation	(200,000)	(400,000)
Equipment	1,000,000	2,000,000
Accumulated		
Depreciation	(400,000)	(800,000)
Total Assets	1,300,000	2,600,000
Liabilities:		
Accounts Payable . .	50,000	100,000
Long-term Liabilities	400,000	800,000
Paid-in-Capital	800,000	1,600,000
Retained Earnings . .	50,000 [2]	100,000
Total Liabilities and		
Equity	1,300,000	2,600,000

[1] Under § 1.985-5(b), S will recognize a 50,000 LC loss (100,000 LC basis – 50,000 LC value) on the bond resulting from the change in functional currency. Thus, immediately before the change, S's basis in the PC bond (taking into account the loss) is 50,000 LC.

[2] The amount of S's LC retained earnings reflects the 50,000 LC loss on the bond.

Example 2. P, a domestic corporation, operates a foreign branch, S. The Commissioner granted permission to change S's functional currency from the LC to the FC beginning January 1, 1993. As of December 31, 1992, S's equity pool was 2,000 LC and its basis pool was $4,000. The LC/FC exchange rate on December 31, 1992 is 1 LC/2 FC. On January 1, 1993, the new functional currency amount of S's equity pool is 4,000 FC. The basis pool is not affected. [Reg. § 1.985-5.]

☐ [*T.D.* 8464, 12-31-92. *Amended by T.D.* 8765, 3-4-98.]

Reg. § 1.985-5(e)

[Reg. §1.985-6]

§1.985-6. Transition rules for a QBU that uses the dollar approximate separate transactions method for its first taxable year beginning in 1987.—(a) *In general.*—This section sets forth transition rules for a QBU that used the dollar approximate separate transactions method of accounting set forth in §1.985-3 or §1.985-3T (as contained in the April 1, 1989 edition of 26 CFR part 1 (1.908 to 1.1000)) for its first taxable year beginning in 1987 (DASTM QBU). A DASTM QBU must determine the dollar and hyperinflationary currency basis of its assets and the dollar and hyperinflationary currency amount of its liabilities that were acquired or incurred in taxable years beginning before January 1, 1987. In addition, a DASTM QBU must determine its net worth, including its retained earnings, at the end of the QBU's last taxable year beginning before January 1, 1987. This section provides rules for controlled foreign corporations (as defined in section 957 or section 953(c)(1)(B)), other foreign corporations, and branches of United States persons that must make these determinations.

(b) *Certain controlled foreign corporations.*—If a DASTM QBU was a controlled foreign corporation for its last taxable year beginning before January 1, 1987, and it had a significant event as described in §1.964-1(c)(6) in a taxable year beginning before January 1, 1987, then the rules of this paragraph (b) shall apply.

(1) *Basis in assets and amount of liabilities.*—The hyperinflationary currency adjusted basis of the QBU's assets and the hyperinflationary currency amount of the QBU's liabilities acquired or incurred by the QBU in a taxable year beginning before January 1, 1987, shall be the basis or the amount as determined under §1.964-1(e) prior to translation under §1.964-1(e)(4). The dollar adjusted basis of such assets and the dollar amount of such liabilities shall be the adjusted basis or the amount as determined under the rules of §1.964-1(e) after translation under §1.964-1(e)(4).

(2) *Retained earnings.*—The dollar amount of the QBU's retained earnings at the end of its last taxable year beginning before January 1, 1987, shall be the dollar amount determined under §1.964-1(e)(3).

(c) *All other foreign corporations.*—If a foreign corporation is a DASTM QBU that is not described in paragraph (b) of this section, then the hyperinflationary currency and dollar adjusted basis in the QBU's assets acquired in taxable years beginning before January 1, 1987, the hyperinflationary currency and dollar amount of the QBU's liabilities acquired or incurred in taxable years beginning before January 1, 1987, and the dollar amount of the QBU's net worth, including its retained earnings, at the end of its last taxable year beginning before January 1, 1987,

shall be determined by applying the principles of §1.985-3T or §1.985-3. Thus, for example, the dollar basis of plant and equipment shall be determined using the appropriate historical exchange rate.

(d) *Pre-1987 section 902 amounts.*—(1) *Translation of pre-1987 section 902 accumulated profits and taxes into United States dollars.*—The foreign income taxes and accumulated profits or deficits in accumulated profits of a foreign corporation that were maintained in foreign currency for purposes of section 902 and that are attributable to taxable years of the foreign corporation beginning before January 1, 1987, shall be translated into dollars at the spot exchange rate on the first day of its first taxable year beginning after December 31, 1986. Once translated into dollars, these accumulated profits and taxes shall (absent a change in functional currency) remain in dollars for all federal income tax purposes.

(2) *Carryforward of accumulated deficits in accumulated profits from pre-1987 taxable years to post-1986 taxable years.*—For purposes of sections 902 and 960, the post-1986 undistributed earnings of a foreign corporation that is subject to the rules of this section shall be reduced by the dollar amount of the corporation's deficit in accumulated profits, if any, determined under section 902 and the regulations thereunder, that was accumulated at the end of the corporation's last taxable year beginning before January 1, 1987. The dollar amount of the accumulated deficit shall be determined by multiplying the foreign currency amount of such deficit by the spot exchange rate on the last day of the corporation's last taxable year beginning before January 1, 1987, and shall be taken into account on the first day of the corporation's first taxable year beginning after December 31, 1986. Post-1986 undistributed earnings may not be reduced by the dollar amount of a pre-1987 deficit in retained earnings determined under §1.964-1(e).

(e) *Net worth branch.*—If a DASTM QBU is a branch of a United States person and the QBU used a net worth method of accounting for its last taxable year beginning before January 1, 1987, then the rules of this paragraph (e) shall apply. A net worth method of accounting is any method of accounting under which the taxpayer calculates the taxable income of a QBU based on the net change in the dollar value of the QBU's equity (assets minus liabilities) during the course of a taxable year, taking into account any contributions or remittances made during the year. *See, e.g.,* Rev. Rul. 75-106, 1975-1 C.B. 31. (See §601.601(d)(2)(ii)(b) of this chapter).

(1) *Basis in assets and amount of liabilities.*—(i) *Hyperinflationary amounts.*—For the first taxable year beginning in 1987, the hyperinflationary currency adjusted basis of a QBU's assets or the hyperinflationary currency amounts of its liabilities acquired or incurred in a taxable year begin-

Reg. §1.985-6(e)(1)(i)

ning before January 1, 1987 is the hyperinflationary currency basis or amount at the date when acquired or incurred, as adjusted according to United States generally accepted accounting and tax accounting principles. If a hyperinflationary currency basis or amount was not determined at such date, the dollar basis or amount, as adjusted according to United States generally accepted accounting and tax accounting principles, shall be translated into hyperinflationary currency at the spot exchange rate on the date when the asset or liability was acquired or incurred.

(ii) *Dollar amounts.*—For the first taxable year beginning in 1987, the dollar adjusted basis of the QBU's assets and the amounts of its liabilities shall be those amounts reflected on the QBU's dollar books and records at the end of the taxpayer's last taxable year beginning before January 1, 1987, after adjusting the books and records according to United States generally accepted accounting and tax accounting principles.

(2) *Ending net worth.*—The dollar amount of the QBU's net worth at the end of its last taxable year beginning before January 1, 1987 shall equal the QBU's net worth at that date as determined under paragraph (e)(1)(ii) of this section.

(f) *Profit and loss branch.*—If a DASTM QBU is a branch of a United States person and the QBU used a profit and loss method of accounting for its last taxable year beginning before January 1, 1987, then the United States person shall first apply the transition rules of § 1.987-5 in order to determine the beginning amount and dollar basis of the branch's EQ pool, the hyperinflationary currency basis of the branch's assets, and the hyperinflationary currency amounts of its liabilities. A profit and loss method of accounting is any method of accounting under which the taxpayer calculates the profits of a QBU by computing the QBU's profits in its functional currency and translating the net result into dollars. *See, e.g.,* Rev. Rul. 75-107, 1975-1 C.B. 32. (See § 601.601(d)(2)(ii)(*b*) of this chapter). The QBU and the taxpayer must then make the adjustments required by § 1.985-5, *e.g.,* the QBU must take into account unrealized exchange gain or loss on dollar-denominated section 988 transactions, the taxpayer must account for the deemed termination of the branch, and the taxpayer must translate the QBU's balance sheet items from hyperinflationary currency into dollars at the spot rate. [Reg. § 1.985-6.]

☐ [*T.D.* 8464, 12-31-92.]

[Reg. § 1.985-7]

§ 1.985-7. Adjustments required in connection with a change to DASTM.—(a) *In general.*—If a QBU begins to use the dollar approximate separate transactions method of accounting set forth in § 1.985-3 (DASTM) in a taxable year beginning after April 6, 1998, adjust-

ments shall be made as provided by this section. For the rules with respect to foreign corporations, see paragraph (b) of this section. For the rules with respect to adjustments to the income of United States shareholders of controlled foreign corporations, see paragraph (c) of this section. For the rules with respect to adjustments relating to QBU branches, see paragraph (d) of this section. For the effective date of this section, see paragraph (e). For purposes of applying this section, the look-back period shall be the period beginning with the first taxable year after the transition date and ending on the last day prior to the taxable year of change. The term transition date means the later of the last day of the last taxable year ending before the base period as defined in § 1.985-1(b)(2)(ii)(D) or the last day of the taxable year in which the QBU last applied DASTM. The taxable year of change shall mean the taxable year of change as defined in § 1.481-1(a)(1). The application of this paragraph may be illustrated by the following examples:

Example 1. A calendar year QBU that has not previously used DASTM operates in a country in which the functional currency of the country is hyperinflationary as defined under § 1.985-1(b)(2)(ii)(D) for the QBU's 1999 tax year. The look-back period is the period from January 1, 1996 through December 31, 1998, the transition date is December 31, 1995, and the taxable year of change is the taxable year beginning January 1, 1999.

Example 2. A QBU that has not previously used DASTM with a taxable year ending June 30, operates in a country in which the functional currency of the country is hyperinflationary for the QBU's tax year beginning July 1, 1999 as defined under § 1.985-1(b)(2)(ii)(D) (where the base period is the thirty-six calendar months immediately preceding the first day of the current calendar year 1999). The look-back period is the period from July 1, 1995 through June 30, 1999, the transition date is June 30, 1995, and the taxable year of change is the taxable year beginning July 1, 1999.

(b) *Adjustments to foreign corporations.*—(1) *In general.*—In the case of a foreign corporation, the corporation shall make the adjustments set forth in paragraphs (b)(2) through (4) of this section. The adjustments shall be made on the first day of the taxable year of change.

(2) *Treatment of certain section 988 transactions.*—(i) *Exchange gain or loss from section 988 transactions unrealized as of the transition date.*—A foreign corporation shall adjust earnings and profits by the amount of any unrealized exchange gain or loss that was attributable to a section 988 transaction (as defined in sections 988(c)(1)(A), (B), and (C)) that was denominated in terms of (or determined by reference to) the dollar and was held by the corporation on the transition date. Such gain or loss shall be computed as if recognized on the transition date and

shall be reduced by any gain and increased by any loss recognized by the corporation with respect to such transaction during the look-back period. The amount of such gain or loss shall be determined without regard to the limitations of section 988(b) (i.e., whether any gain or loss would be realized on the transaction as a whole). The character and source of such gain or loss shall be determined under section 988. Proper adjustments shall be made to account for gain or loss taken into account by reason of this paragraph (b)(2). See § 1.985-5(f) *Example 1, footnote 1.*

(ii) *Treatment of a section 988 transaction entered into and terminated during the look-back period.*—A foreign corporation shall reduce earnings and profits by the amount of any gain, and increase earnings and profits by the amount of any loss, that was recognized with respect to any dollar denominated section 988 transactions entered into and terminated during the look-back period.

(3) *Opening balance sheet.*—The opening balance sheet of a foreign corporation for the taxable year of change shall be determined as if the corporation had changed its functional currency to the dollar by applying § 1.985-5(c) on the transition date and had translated its assets and liabilities acquired and incurred during the look-back period under § 1.985-3.

(4) *Earnings and profits adjustments.*— (i) *Pre-1987 accumulated profits.*—The foreign income taxes and accumulated profits or deficits in accumulated profits of a foreign corporation that are attributable to taxable years beginning before January 1, 1987, as stated on the transition date, and that were maintained for purposes of section 902 in the old functional currency, shall be translated into dollars at the spot rate in effect on the transition date. The applicable accumulated profits shall be reduced on a last-in, first-out basis by the aggregate dollar amount (translated from functional currency in accordance with the rules of section 989(b)) attributable to earnings and profits that were distributed (or treated as distributed) during the look-back period to the extent such amounts distributed exceed the earnings and profits calculated under (b)(4)(ii) or (b)(4)(iii), as applicable. See § 1.902-1(b)(2)(ii). Once translated into dollars, these pre-1987 taxes and accumulated profits or deficits in accumulated profits shall (absent a change in functional currency) remain in dollars for all federal income tax purposes.

(ii) *Post-1986 undistributed earnings of a CFC.*—In the case of a controlled foreign corporation (within the meaning of section 957 or section 953(c)(1)(B)) (CFC) or a foreign corporation subject to the rules of § 1.904-6(a)(2), the corporation's post-1986 undistributed earnings in each separate category as defined in § 1.904-5(a)(1) as of the first day of the taxable year of change (and prior to adjustment under

paragraph (c)(1) of this section) shall equal the sum of—

(A) The corporation's post-1986 undistributed earnings and profits (or deficit in earnings and profits) in each separate category as defined in § 1.904-5(a)(1) as stated on the transition date translated into dollars at the spot rate in effect on the transition date; and

(B) The sum of the earnings and profits (or deficit in earnings and profits) in each separate category determined under § 1.985-3 for each post-transition date taxable year prior to the taxable year of change.

Such amount shall be reduced by the aggregate dollar amount (translated from functional currency in accordance with the rules of section 989(b)) attributable to earnings and profits that were distributed (or treated as distributed) during the look-back period out of post-1986 earnings and profits in such separate category. For purposes of applying this paragraph (b)(4)(ii)(B), the opening balance sheet for calculating earnings and profits under § 1.985-3 for the first post-transition year shall be translated into dollars pursuant to § 1.985-5(c).

(iii) *Post-1986 undistributed earnings of other foreign corporations.*—In the case of a foreign corporation that is not a CFC or subject to the rules of § 1.904-6(a)(2), the corporation's post-1986 undistributed earnings shall equal the sum of—

(A) The corporation's post-1986 undistributed earnings (or deficit) on the transition date translated into dollars at the spot rate in effect on the transition date; and

(B) The sum of the earnings and profits (or deficit in earnings and profits) determined under § 1.985-3 for each post-transition date taxable year (or such later year determined under section 902(c)(3)(A)) prior to the taxable year of change.

Such amount shall be reduced by the aggregate dollar amount (translated from functional currency in accordance with the rules of section 989(b)) that was distributed (or treated as distributed) during the look-back period out of post-1986 earnings and profits. For purposes of applying this paragraph (b)(4)(iii)(B), the opening balance sheet for calculating earnings and profits under § 1.985-3 for the first post-transition year shall be translated into dollars pursuant to § 1.985-5(c).

(c) *United States shareholders of controlled foreign corporations.*—(1) *In general.*—A United States shareholder (within the meaning of section 951(b) or section 953(c)(1)(B)) of a CFC that changes to DASTM shall make the adjustments set forth in paragraphs (c)(2) through (5) of this section on the first day of the taxable year of change. Adjustments under this section shall be taken into account by the shareholder (or such shareholder's successor in interest) ratably over four taxable years beginning with the taxable year of change. Similar rules shall apply in determining adjustments to income of United States persons who have made an election under section 1295 to treat a passive foreign investment company as a qualified electing fund.

(2) *Treatment under subpart F of income recognized on section 988 transactions.*—The character of amounts taken into account under paragraph (b)(2) of this section for purposes of sections 951 through 964, shall be determined on the transition date and to the extent characterized as subpart F income shall be taken into account in accordance with the rules of paragraph (c)(1) of this section. Such amounts shall retain their character for all federal income tax purposes (including sections 902, 959, 960, 961, 1248, and 6038).

(3) *Recognition of foreign currency gain or loss on previously taxed earnings and profits on the transition date.*—Gain or loss is recognized under section 986(c) as if all previously taxed earnings and profits as determined on the transition date, if any, were distributed on such date. Such gain or loss shall be reduced by any foreign currency gain and increased by any foreign currency loss that was recognized under section 986(c) with respect to distributions of previously taxed earnings and profits during the look-back period. Such amount shall be characterized in accordance with section 986(c) and taken into account in accordance with the rules of paragraph (c)(1) of this section.

(4) *Subpart F income adjustment.*—Subpart F income in a separate category shall be determined under §1.985-3 for each look-back year. For this purpose, the opening DASTM balance sheet shall be determined under §1.985-5. The sum of the difference (positive or negative) between the amount computed pursuant to §1.985-3 and amount that was included in income for each year shall be taken into account in the taxable year of change pursuant to paragraph (c)(1) of this section. Such amounts shall retain their character for all federal income tax purposes (including sections 902, 959, 960, 961, 1248, and 6038). For rules applicable if an adjustment under this section results in a loss for the taxable year in a separate category, see section 904(f) and the regulations thereunder. The amount of previously taxed earnings and profits as determined under section 959(c)(2) shall be adjusted (positively or negatively) by the amount taken into account under this paragraph (c)(4) as of the first day of the taxable year of change.

(5) *Foreign tax credit.*—A United States shareholder of a CFC shall compute an amount of foreign taxes deemed paid under section 960 with respect to any positive adjustments determined under paragraph (c) of this section. The amount of foreign tax deemed paid shall be computed with reference to the full amount of the adjustment and to the post-1986 undistributed earnings determined under paragraph (b)(4)(i) and (ii) of this section and the post-1986 foreign income taxes of the CFC on the first day of the taxable year of change (i.e., without taking into account earnings and taxes for the taxable year of change). For purposes of section 960, the associated taxes in each separate category shall be allocated pro rata among, and deemed paid in, the shareholder's taxable years in which the income is taken into account. (No adjustment to foreign taxes deemed paid in prior years is required solely by reason of a negative adjustment to income under paragraph (c)(1) of this section).

(d) *QBU branches.*—(1) *In general.*—In the case of a QBU branch, the taxpayer shall make the adjustments set forth in paragraphs (d)(2) through (d)(4) of this section. Adjustments under this section shall be taken into account by the taxpayer ratably over four taxable years beginning with the taxable year of change.

(2) *Treatment of certain section 988 transactions.*—(i) *Exchange gain or loss from section 988 transactions unrealized as of the transition date.*—A QBU branch shall adjust income by the amount of any unrealized exchange gain or loss that was attributable to a section 988 transaction (as defined in sections 988(c)(1)(A), (B), and (C)) that was denominated in terms of (or determined by reference to) the dollar and was held by the QBU branch on the transition date. Such gain or loss shall be computed as if recognized on the transition date and shall be reduced by any gain and increased by any loss recognized by the QBU branch with respect to such transaction during the look-back period. The amount of such gain or loss shall be determined without regard to the limitations of section 988(b) (i.e., whether any gain or loss would be realized on the transaction as a whole). The character and source of such gain or loss shall be determined under section 988. Proper adjustments shall be made to account for gain or loss taken into account by reason of this paragraph (d)(2). See §1.985-5(f) *Example 1, footnote 1.*

(ii) *Treatment of a section 988 transaction entered into and terminated during the look-back period.*—A QBU branch shall reduce income by the amount of any gain, and increase income by the amount of any loss, that was recognized with respect to any dollar denominated section 988 transactions entered into and terminated during the look-back period.

(3) *Deemed termination income adjustment.*— The taxpayer shall realize gain or loss attributable to the QBU branch's equity pool (as stated on the transition date) under the principles of section 987, computed as if the branch terminated on the transition date. Such amount shall be reduced by section 987 gain and increased by section 987 loss that was recognized by such

taxpayer with respect to remittances during the look-back period.

(4) *Branch income adjustment.*—Branch income in a separate category shall be determined under § 1.985-3 for each look-back year. For this purpose, the opening DASTM balance sheet shall be determined under § 1.985-5. The sum of the difference (positive or negative) between the amount computed pursuant to § 1.985-3 and amount taken into account for each year shall be taken into account in the taxable year of change pursuant to paragraph (d)(1) of this section. Such amounts shall retain their character for all federal income tax purposes.

(5) *Opening balance sheet.*—The opening balance sheet of a QBU branch for the taxable year of change shall be determined as if the branch had changed its functional currency to the dollar by applying § 1.985-5(c) on the transition date and had translated its assets and liabilities acquired and incurred during the look-back period under § 1.985-3.

(e) *Effective date.*—This section is effective for taxable years beginning after April 6, 1998. However, a taxpayer may choose to apply this section to all open taxable years beginning after December 31, 1986, provided each person, and each QBU branch of a person, that is related (within the meaning of § 1.985-2(d)(3)) to the taxpayer also applies this section. [Reg. § 1.985-7.]

☐ [*T.D.* 8765, 3-4-98 (*corrected* 3-31-98).]

[Reg. § 1.985-8]

§ 1.985-8. Special rules applicable to the European Monetary Union (conversion to euro).—
(a) *Definitions.*—(1) *Legacy currency.*—A legacy currency is the former currency of a Member State of the European Community which is substituted for the euro in accordance with the Treaty establishing the European Community signed February 7, 1992. The term legacy currency shall also include the European Currency Unit.

(2) *Conversion rate.*—The conversion rate is the rate at which the euro is substituted for a legacy currency.

(b) *Operative rules.*—(1) *Initial adoption.*—A QBU (as defined in § 1.989(a)-1(b)) whose first taxable year begins after the euro has been substituted for a legacy currency may not adopt a legacy currency as its functional currency.

(2) *QBU with a legacy currency as its functional currency.*—(i) *Required change.*—A QBU with a legacy currency as its functional currency is required to change its functional currency to the euro beginning the first day of the first taxable year—

(A) That begins on or after the day that the euro is substituted for that legacy currency

(in accordance with the Treaty on European Union); and

(B) In which the QBU begins to maintain its books and records (as described in § 1.989(a)-1(d)) in the euro.

(ii) Notwithstanding paragraph (b)(2)(i) of this section, a QBU with a legacy currency as its functional currency is required to change its functional currency to the euro no later than the last taxable year beginning on or before the first day such legacy currency is no longer valid legal tender.

(3) *QBU with a non-legacy currency as its functional currency.*—(i) *In general.*—A QBU with a non-legacy currency as its functional currency may change its functional currency to the euro pursuant to this § 1.985-8 if—

(A) Under the rules set forth in § 1.985-1(c), the euro is the currency of the economic environment in which a significant part of the QBU's activities are conducted;

(B) After conversion, the QBU maintains its books and records (as described in § 1.989(a)-1(d)) in the euro; and

(C) The QBU is not required to use the dollar as its functional currency under § 1.985-1(b).

(ii) *Time period for change.*—A QBU with a non-legacy currency as its functional currency may change its functional currency to the euro under this section only if it does so within the period set forth in paragraph (b)(2) of this section as if the functional currency of the QBU was a legacy currency.

(4) *Consent of Commissioner.*—A change made pursuant to paragraph (b) of this section shall be deemed to be made with the consent of the Commissioner for purposes of § 1.985-4. A QBU changing its functional currency to the euro pursuant to paragraph (b)(2) of this section must make adjustments as provided in paragraph (c) of this section. A QBU changing its functional currency to the euro pursuant to paragraph (b)(3) must make adjustments as provided in § 1.985-5.

(5) *Statement to file upon change.*—With respect to a QBU that changes its functional currency to the euro under paragraph (b) of this section, an affected taxpayer shall attach to its return for the taxable year of change a statement that includes the following: "TAXPAYER CERTIFIES THAT A QBU OF THE TAXPAYER HAS CHANGED ITS FUNCTIONAL CURRENCY TO THE EURO PURSUANT TO TREAS. REG. § 1.985-8." For purposes of this paragraph (b)(5), an affected taxpayer shall be in the case where the QBU is: a QBU of an individual U.S. resident (as a result of the activities of such individual), the individual; a QBU branch of a U.S. corporation, the corporation; a controlled foreign corporation (as described in section 957) (or QBU

branch thereof), each United States shareholder (as described in section 951(b)); a partnership, each partner separately; a noncontrolled section 902 corporation (as described in section 904(d)(2)(E)) (or branch thereof), each domestic shareholder as described in § 1.902-1(a)(1); or a trust or estate, the fiduciary of such trust or estate.

(c) *Adjustments required when a QBU changes its functional currency from a legacy currency to the euro pursuant to paragraph (b)(2) of this section.*— (1) *In general.*—A QBU that changes its functional currency from a legacy currency to the euro pursuant to paragraph (b)(2) of this section must make the adjustments described in paragraphs (c)(2) through (5) of this section. Section 1.985-5 shall not apply.

(2) *Determining the euro basis of property and the euro amount of liabilities and other relevant items.*—The euro basis in property and the euro amount of liabilities and other relevant items shall equal the product of the legacy functional currency adjusted basis or amount of liabilities multiplied by the applicable conversion rate.

(3) *Taking into account exchange gain or loss on legacy currency section 988 transactions.*—(i) *In general.*—Except as provided in paragraphs (c)(3)(iii) and (iv) of this section, a legacy currency denominated section 988 transaction (determined after applying section 988(d)) outstanding on the last day of the taxable year immediately prior to the year of change shall continue to be treated as a section 988 transaction after the change and the principles of section 988 shall apply.

(ii) *Examples.*—The application of this paragraph (c)(3) may be illustrated by the following examples:

Example 1. X, a calendar year QBU on the cash method of accounting, uses the deutschmark as its functional currency. X is not described in section 1281(b). On July 1, 1998, X converts 10,000 deutschmarks (DM) into Dutch guilders (fl) at the spot rate of fl1 = DM1 and loans the 10,000 guilders to Y (an unrelated party) for one year at a rate of 10% with principal and interest to be paid on June 30, 1999. On January 1, 1999, X changes its functional currency to the euro pursuant to this section. Assume that the euro/deutschmark conversion rate is set by the European Council at €1 = DM2. Assume further that the euro/guilder conversion rate is set at €1 = fl2.25. Accordingly, under the terms of the note, on June 30, 1999, X will receive €4444.44 (fl10,000/2.25) of principal and €4444.44 (fl1,000/2.25) of interest. Pursuant to this paragraph (c)(3), X will realize an exchange loss on the principal computed under the principles of § 1.988-2(b)(5). For this purpose, the exchange rate used under § 1.988-2(b)(5)(i) shall be the guilder/euro conversion rate. The amount

under § 1.988-2(b)(5)(ii) is determined by translating the fl10,000 at the guilder/deutschmark spot rate on July 1, 1998, and translating that deutschmark amount into euros at the deutschmark/euro conversion rate. Thus, X will compute an exchange loss for 1999 of €555.56 determined as follows: [€4444.44 (fl10,000/2.25) − €5000 ((fl10,000/1) /2) = -€555.56]. Pursuant to this paragraph (c)(3), the character and source of the loss are determined pursuant to section 988 and regulations thereunder. Because X uses the cash method of accounting for the interest on this debt instrument, X does not realize exchange gain or loss on the receipt of that interest.

Example 2. (i) X, a calendar year QBU on the accrual method of accounting, uses the deutschmark as its functional currency. On February 1, 1998, X converts 12,000 deutschmarks into Dutch guilders at the spot rate of fl1 = DM1 and loans the 12,000 guilders to Y (an unrelated party) for one year at a rate of 10% with principal and interest to be paid on January 31, 1999. In addition, assume the average rate (deutschmark/guilder) for the period from February 1, 1998, through December 31, 1998 is fl1.07 = DM1. Pursuant to § 1.988-2(b)(2)(ii)(C), X will accrue eleven months of interest on the note and recognize interest income of DM1028.04 (fl1100/1.07) in the 1998 taxable year.

(ii) On January 1, 1999, the euro will replace the deutschmark as the national currency of Germany pursuant to the Treaty on European Union signed February 7, 1992. Assume that on January 1, 1999, X changes its functional currency to the euro pursuant to this section. Assume that the euro/deutschmark conversion rate is set by the European Council at €1 = DM2. Assume further that the euro/guilder conversion rate is set at €1 = fl2.25. In 1999, X will accrue one month of interest equal to €44.44 (fl100/2.25). On January 31, 1999, pursuant to the note, X will receive interest denominated in euros of €533.33 (fl1200/2.25). Pursuant to this paragraph (c)(3), X will realize an exchange loss in the 1999 taxable year with respect to accrued interest computed under the principles of § 1.988-2(b)(3). For this purpose, the exchange rate used under § 1.988-2(b)(3)(i) is the guilder/euro conversion rate and the exchange rate used under § 1.988-2(b)(3)(ii) is the deutschmark/euro conversion rate. Thus, with respect to the interest accrued in 1998, X will realize exchange loss of €25.13 under § 1.988-2(b), (3) as follows: [€488.89 (fl1100/2.25) − €514.02 (DM1028.04/2) = -€25.13]. With respect to the one month of interest accrued in 1999, X will realize no exchange gain or loss since the exchange rate when the interest accrued and the spot rate on the payment date are the same.

(iii) X will realize exchange loss of €666.67 on repayment of the loan principal computed in the same manner as in Example 1 [€5333.33 (fl12,000/2.25) − €6000 fl12,000/1) /2)]. The losses with respect to accrued interest and principal are characterized and sourced under the rules of section 988.

(iii) *Special rule for legacy nonfunctional currency.*—The QBU shall realize or otherwise take into account for all purposes of the Internal Revenue Code the amount of any unrealized exchange gain or loss attributable to nonfunctional currency (as described in section 988(c)(1)(C)(ii)) that is denominated in a legacy currency as if the currency were disposed of on the last day of the taxable year immediately prior to the year of change. The character and source of the gain or loss are determined under section 988.

(iv) *Legacy currency denominated accounts receivable and payable.*—(A) *In general.*—A QBU may elect to realize or otherwise take into account for all purposes of the Internal Revenue Code the amount of any unrealized exchange gain or loss attributable to a legacy currency denominated item described in section 988(c)(1)(B)(ii) as if the item were terminated on the last day of the taxable year ending prior to the year of change.

(B) *Time and manner of election.*—With respect to a QBU that makes an election described in paragraph (c)(3)(iv)(A) of this section, an affected taxpayer (as described in paragraph (b)(5) of this section) shall attach a statement to its tax return for the taxable year ending immediately prior to the year of change which includes the following: "TAXPAYER CERTIFIES THAT A QBU OF THE TAXPAYER HAS ELECTED TO REALIZE CURRENCY GAIN OR LOSS ON LEGACY CURRENCY DENOMINATED ACCOUNTS RECEIVABLE AND PAYABLE UPON CHANGE OF FUNCTIONAL CURRENCY TO THE EURO." A QBU making the election must do so for all legacy currency denominated items described in section 988(c)(1)(B)(ii).

(4) *Adjustments when a branch changes its functional currency to the euro.*—(i) *Branch changing from a legacy currency to the euro in a taxable year during which taxpayer's functional currency is other than the euro.*—If a branch changes its functional currency from a legacy currency to the euro for a taxable year during which the taxpayer's functional currency is other than the euro, the branch's euro equity pool shall equal the product of the legacy currency amount of the equity pool multiplied by the applicable conversion rate. No adjustment to the basis pool is required.

(ii) *Branch changing from a legacy currency to the euro in a taxable year during which taxpayer's functional currency is the euro.*—If a branch changes its functional currency from a legacy currency to the euro for a taxable year during which the taxpayer's functional currency is the euro, the taxpayer shall realize gain or loss attributable to the branch's equity pool under the principles of section 987, computed as if the branch terminated on the last day prior to the year of change. Adjustments under this paragraph (c)(4)(ii) shall be taken into account by the taxpayer ratably over four taxable years beginning with the taxable year of change.

(5) *Adjustments to a branch's accounts when a taxpayer changes to the euro.*—(i) *Taxpayer changing from a legacy currency to the euro in a taxable year during which a branch's functional currency is other than the euro.*—If a taxpayer changes its functional currency to the euro for a taxable year during which the functional currency of a branch of the taxpayer is other than the euro, the basis pool shall equal the product of the legacy currency amount of the basis pool multiplied by the applicable conversion rate. No adjustment to the equity pool is required.

(ii) *Taxpayer changing from a legacy currency to the euro in a taxable year during which a branch's functional currency is the euro.*—If a taxpayer changes its functional currency from a legacy currency to the euro for a taxable year during which the functional currency of a branch of the taxpayer is the euro, the taxpayer shall take into account gain or loss as determined under paragraph (c)(4)(ii) of this section.

(6) *Additional adjustments that are necessary when a corporation changes its functional currency to the euro.*—The amount of a corporation's euro currency earnings and profits and the amount of its euro paid-in capital shall equal the product of the legacy currency amounts of these items multiplied by the applicable conversion rate. The foreign income taxes and accumulated profits or deficits in accumulated profits of a foreign corporation that were maintained in foreign currency for purposes of section 902 and that are attributable to taxable years of the foreign corporation beginning before January 1, 1987, also shall be translated into the euro at the conversion rate.

(d) *Treatment of legacy currency section 988 transactions with respect to a QBU that has the euro as its functional currency.*—(1) *In general.*—This §1.985-8(d) applies to a QBU that has the euro as its functional currency and that holds a section 988 transaction denominated in, or determined by reference to, a currency that is substituted by the euro. For example, this paragraph (d) will apply to a German QBU with the euro as its functional currency if the QBU is holding Country X currency or other section 988 transactions denominated in such currency on the day in the year 2005 when the euro is substituted for the Country X currency.

(2) *Principles of paragraph (c)(3) of this section shall apply.*—With respect to a QBU described in paragraph (d) of this section, the principles of paragraph (c)(3) of this section shall apply. For

example, if a German QBU with the euro as its functional currency is holding a Country X currency denominated debt instrument on the day in the year 2005 when the euro is substituted for the Country X currency, the instrument shall continue to be treated as a section 988 transaction pursuant to the principles of paragraph (c)(3)(i) of this section. However, if such QBU holds Country X currency, the QBU shall take into account any unrealized exchange gain or loss pursuant to the principles of paragraph (c)(3)(iii) of this section as if the currency was disposed of on the day prior to the day the euro is substituted for the Country X currency. Similarly, if the QBU makes an election under the principles of paragraph (c)(3)(iv) of this section, the QBU shall take into account for all purposes of the Internal Revenue Code the amount of any unrealized exchange gain or loss attributable to a legacy currency denominated item described in section 988(c)(1)(B)(ii) as if the item were terminated on the day prior to the day the euro is substituted for the Country X currency.

(e) *Effective date.*—This section applies to tax years ending after July 29, 1998. [Reg. §1.985-8.]

☐ [*T.D.* 8927, 1-10-2001.]

[Reg. §1.987-1]

§1.987-1. Profit and loss method of accounting for a qualified business unit of a taxpayer having a different functional currency from the taxpayer.—[RESERVED]

[Reg. §1.987-2]

§1.987-2. Accounting for gain or loss on certain transfers of property.—[RESERVED]

[Reg. §1.987-3]

§1.987-3. Termination.—[RESERVED]

[Reg. §1.987-4]

§1.987-4. Special rules relating to QBU branches of foreign taxpayers.—[RESERVED]

[Reg. §1.987-5]

§1.987-5. Transition rules for certain qualified business units using a profit and loss method of accounting for taxable years beginning before January 1, 1987.—(a) *Applicability.*—(1) *In general.*—This section applies to qualified business unit (QBU) branches of United States persons, whose functional currency (as defined in section 985 of the Code and the regulations thereunder) is other than the United States dollar (dollar) and that used a profit and loss method of accounting for their last taxable year beginning before January l, 1987. Generally, a profit and loss method of accounting is any method of accounting under which the taxpayer calculates the profits of a QBU branch in its functional currency and trans-

lates the net result into dollars. For all taxable years beginning after December 31, 1986, such QBU branches must use the profit and loss method of accounting as described in section 987, except to the extent otherwise provided in regulations under section 985 or any other provision of the Code. *See* §1.989(c)-1 regarding transition rules for QBU branches of United States persons that have a nondollar functional currency and that used a net worth method of accounting for their last taxable year beginning before January 1, 1987.

(2) *Insolvent QBU branches.*—A taxpayer may apply the principles of this section to a QBU branch that used a profit and loss method of accounting for its last taxable year beginning before January 1, 1987, whose $E pool (as defined in paragraph (d)(3)(i) of this section) is negative. For taxable years beginning on or after October 25, 1991, the principles of this section shall apply to insolvent QBU branches.

(b) *General rules.*—Generally, section 987 gain or loss occurs when a QBU branch makes a remittance. A remittance is considered to be made from one or more functional currency pools under rules provided in paragraph (c) of this section. In general, the amount of section 987 gain or loss from a remittance equals the difference between the dollar value of the functional currency adjusted basis of the property remitted and the portion of the dollar basis in the applicable pool. Section 987 gain or loss is calculated under a 4-step procedure described in paragraph (d) of this section. Section 987 gain or loss attributable to a remittance is realized and must be recognized in the taxable year of the remittance except to the extent otherwise provided in regulations.

(c) *Determining the pool(s) from which a remittance is made.*—(1) *Remittances made during taxable years beginning after December 31, 1986, and before October 25, 1991.*—A remittance made during taxable years beginning after December 31, 1986 and before October 25, 1991, first represents an amount of the QBU branch's post-86 profits pool (including functional currency profits for the current taxable year determined without regard to remittances made during the current year). To the extent the functional currency amount of the remittance exceeds the post-86 profits pool, it is considered to come out of the EQ pool. Paragraph (d)(2) of this section describes the EQ pool and the post-86 profits pool.

(2) *Remittances made in taxable years beginning on or after October 25, 1991.*—For remittances made in taxable years beginning on or after October 25, 1991, the post-86 profits and EQ pools are combined into one pool called the equity pool. Therefore, remittances made during those taxable years will only come from the equity pool. The dollar basis of, and section 987 gain or loss on, such remittances shall be calculated

utilizing the principles set forth in paragraph (d)(4) and (5) of this section.

(d) *Calculation of section 987 gain or loss.*— (1) *In general.*—This paragraph (d) describes the 4-step procedure for calculating section 987 gain or loss.

(2) *Step 1—Calculate the amount of the functional currency pools.*—(i) *EQ pool.*—(A) *Begin*ning *pool.*—The beginning amount of the EQ pool is equal to the functional currency adjusted bases of a QBU branch's assets less the functional currency amount of the QBU branch's liabilities at the end of the taxpayer's last taxable year beginning before January 1, 1987, as these amounts are determined under the rules of paragraphs (e) and (f) of this section. The district director may allow for additional adjustments to the beginning amount of the EQ pool to prevent the recognition of section 987 gain or loss due to factors unrelated to the movement of exchange rates.

(B) *Adjusting the EQ pool.*—The EQ pool is increased by the functional currency amount of any transfer (as determined under section 987) to the QBU branch made during the current taxable year or any prior taxable year beginning after December 31, 1986. If the transfer is made in a nonfunctional currency, this amount is translated into the QBU branch's functional currency at the spot rate (determined under the principles of section 988 and the regulations thereunder) on the date of the transfer. The method for determining the rate must be applied consistently each quarter. The EQ pool is decreased by the functional currency amount of any remittance (as determined under section 987) made during a prior taxable year beginning after December 31, 1986, that is considered remitted from the EQ pool under paragraph (c) of this section. The EQ pool must also be decreased by any transfer from the QBU branch that is not a remittance.

(ii) *Post-86 profits pool.*—The amount of a QBU branch's post-86 profits pool is calculated at the end of each taxable year beginning after December 31, 1986. The opening balance of the post-86 profits pool at the beginning of the first taxable year beginning after December 31, 1986, is zero. The post-86 profits pool is increased by the functional currency amount of the QBU branch's profits (determined under section 987) for the taxable year. The post-86 profits pool is decreased by the functional currency amount of the QBU branch's losses (determined under section 987) for the taxable year and the amount of any remittances by the QBU branch during the taxable year from the post-86 profits pool as provided under paragraph (c) of this section.

(iii) *Adjustments to the equity pool.*—For remittances made in taxable years beginning on or after October 25, 1991 under paragraph (c)(2) of this section, the post-86 profits and EQ pools are combined into one pool called the equity pool. Additions to and subtractions from the equity pool shall be made utilizing the principles of paragraphs (d)(2)(i)(B) and (ii) of this section. For example, remittances shall reduce the equity pool.

(3) *Step 2—Calculate the dollar basis of the pools.*—(i) *Dollar basis of the EQ pool.*— (A) *Beginning dollar basis.*—The beginning dollar basis of the EQ pool (hereinafter referred to as the $E pool) equals:

(1) The dollar amount of all the QBU branch's profits reported on the taxpayer's income tax returns for taxable years beginning before January 1, 1987, plus the total dollar amount of all transfers to the QBU branch during that period (properly reflected on the taxpayer's books), less

(2) The dollar amount of all the QBU branch's losses reported on the taxpayer's income tax returns for such years, and the total dollar basis of all remittances and all transfers made by the QBU branch during that period (properly reflected on the taxpayer's books).

A QBU branch's profits and losses shall be properly adjusted for foreign taxes of the QBU branch.

(B) *Adjusting the $E pool.*—The $E pool is increased by the dollar amount of any transfers to the QBU branch made during the current taxable year or any prior taxable year beginning after December 31, 1986. If a transfer is made in a currency other than the dollar, the amount of the currency is translated into dollars at the spot rate (determined under the principles of section 988 and the regulations thereunder) on the date of the transfer. The $E pool is decreased by the dollar basis of any remittance made during a prior taxable year beginning after December 31, 1986, that is considered remitted from the $E pool under paragraphs (c) and (d)(4) of this section. The $E pool is also reduced by the amount of a transfer (other than a remittance) from the QBU branch translated into dollars at the spot rate (determined under the principles of section 988 and the regulations thereunder) on the date of the transfer. The method for determining the spot rate must be applied consistently to all transfers to and from a QBU branch.

(ii) *Dollar basis of the post-86 profits pool.*— The amount of a QBU branch's dollar basis in the post-86 profits pool (the $P pool) is calculated at the end of each taxable year beginning after December 31, 1986. The opening balance of the $P pool at the beginning of the first taxable year beginning after December 31, 1986, is zero. The $P pool is increased by the functional currency amount of the QBU branch's profits (determined under section 987) for the taxable year translated into dollars at the weighted average exchange rate (as defined in § 1.989(b)-1) for the year. The $P pool is decreased by the functional currency amount of the QBU branch's losses (determined under section 987) for the taxable year translated into dollars at the weighted average exchange rate for the year and by the dollar basis of any remittances made by the QBU branch during the taxable year from the post-86 profits pool under paragraph (c)(1) of this section.

(iii) *Combination of the $E and the $P pools.*—For taxable years beginning on or after

$$\frac{\text{amount of remittance (in QBU branch's functional currency) from the applicable pool (EQ, post-86 profits, or equity pool)}}{\text{Balance of the applicable pool (EQ, post-86 profits, or equity pool) reduced by prior remittances}} \times \frac{\text{The dollar basis of the applicable pool ($E, $P, or basis pool) reduced by prior remittances}}{}$$

(5) *Step 4—Calculation of the section 987 gain or loss on a remittance.*—Section 987 gain or loss equals the difference between—

(i) The dollar amount of the remittance, and

(ii) The dollar basis of the remittance as calculated under paragraph (d)(4) of this section.

(e) *Functional currency adjusted basis of QBU branch assets acquired in taxable years beginning before January 1, 1987.*—(1) *Basis of asset.*—For taxable years beginning after December 31, 1986, the functional currency adjusted basis of a QBU branch asset acquired in a taxable year beginning before January 1, 1987, is the functional currency basis of the asset at the date of acquisition, as adjusted according to United States tax principles. The functional currency adjusted basis of an asset for which a functional currency basis was not determined at the date of acquisition is the nonfunctional currency basis of the asset at the date of acquisition multiplied by the spot exchange rate on the date of acquisition, as adjusted according to United States tax principles.

(2) *Adjustment to basis of asset.*—Any future adjustments to the functional currency adjusted basis of such an asset are determined with respect to the appropriate functional currency adjusted basis of the asset as determined under this paragraph (e).

(f) *Functional currency amount of QBU branch liabilities acquired in taxable years beginning before January 1, 1987.*—For the first taxable year beginning after December 31, 1986, the amount of a QBU branch liability incurred in a taxable year beginning before January 1, 1987, is the functional currency amount of the liability at the date incurred, as adjusted according to United States

October 25, 1991 the $P and the $E pools are combined into one pool called the basis pool. Additions to and subtractions from the basis pool shall be made utilizing the principles set forth in paragraph (d)(3)(i) and (ii) of this section.

(4) *Step 3—Calculation of the dollar basis of a remittance.*—For all taxable years beginning after December 31, 1986, the dollar basis of a remittance is calculated using the following formula:

tax principles. The functional currency amount of a liability for which a functional currency amount was not determined at the date incurred is the nonfunctional currency amount of the liability at the date incurred multiplied by the spot exchange rate on the date incurred, as adjusted according to United States tax principles.

(g) *Examples.*—The provisions of this section are illustrated by the following examples.

Example 1—(i) *Facts.* U.S. is a domestic corporation. B, a QBU branch of U.S., operates in country X and was established in 1985. B's functional currency is the FC. U.S. is on a calendar taxable year and, prior to January 1, 1987, accounted for the operations of B by the profit and loss method of accounting as set forth in Rev. Rul. 75-107, 1975-1 C.B. 32. B's books and records were kept according to United States tax principles. B received a transfer of $2,000 in 1985, and had profits of $3,000 in 1985 and $5,000 in 1986. B made a remittance in 1986, the dollar basis of which was $1,000. As of December 31, 1986, the adjusted basis of B's functional currency assets exceeded the functional currency amount of its liabilities by 15,000 FC (the beginning pool of EQ). Under section 987, B has profits of 8,000 FC in 1987, which are worth $1,000 when translated at the weighted average exchange rate for 1987 as required by sections 987(2) and 989(b)(4). B has no profits or loss in 1988. There are no transfers to B in 1987 and 1988. B remits 18,000 FC in 1988. Under section 987, the appropriate exchange rate for the 1988 remittance is 10 FC/$1.

(ii) *Calculation of section 987 loss on remittance*—(A) *Post-86 profits.* Under paragraph (c)(i) of this section, the 18,000 FC remittance comes first out of the post-86 profits pool (8,000 FC) and second out of EQ (10,000 FC). The loss on the 1988 remittance out of the post-86 profits pool equals:

Reg. §1.987-5(d)(3)(iii)

$$\text{Dollar value of post-86 profits remitted} - \text{Dollar basis of post-86 profit remitted}$$

$$= (8{,}000 \text{ FC} \times 10 \text{ FC}/\$1) - \$1{,}000$$
$$= \$800 - \$1{,}000$$
$$= <\$200> \text{ loss}$$

(B) *EQ*. Under paragraph (d) of this section, U.S. calculates 987 gain or loss on the 10,000 FC remittance of EQ from B as follows:

Step 1. The total EQ pool equals 15,000 FC (the functional currency adjusted bases of its assets less the functional currency amount of its liabilities as of December 31, 1986). There are no adjustments necessary under paragraph (d)(2)(i)(B) of this section.

Step 2. The \$E pool is \$9,000 (the \$2,000 transfer in 1985 plus profits of \$3,000 in 1985 and \$5,000 in 1986 less the \$1,000 basis of the 1986 remittance). There are no adjustments necessary under paragraph (d)(3)(i)(B) of this section.

Step 3. The entire 10,000 FC remittance is deemed to come out of EQ.

Step 4. The dollar basis of the EQ remitted equals:

$$= \frac{N \times \$E \text{ determined under paragraph (d)(3)(i)}}{15{,}000 \text{ FC}} \times \$9{,}000$$
$$\frac{10{,}000 \text{ FC}}{15{,}000 \text{ FC}}$$
$$= \$6{,}000$$

Where:

$$N = \frac{\text{Portion of remittance out of EQ}}{\text{EQ balance determined under paragraph (d)(2)(i) of this section}}$$

Step 5. Section 987 loss of U.S. on remittance equals:

$$\text{Dollar value of the EQ remitted} - \text{Dollar basis of the EQ remitted}$$

$$= (10{,}000 \text{ FC} \times 10 \text{ FC}/\$1) - \$6{,}000$$
$$= \$1{,}000 - \$6{,}000$$
$$= <\$5{,}000> \text{ loss}$$

(C) *Total loss on remittance.* The total combined loss on the remittance is <\$5,200>. The total of amounts determined in paragraphs (ii)(A) and (B) of this Example 1.

Example 2—(i) *Facts.* D is a domestic corporation. B, a QBU branch of D, operates in country X. B's functional currency is the FC. At the end of B's last taxable year beginning before October 25, 1991 B's EQ pool equals 15,000 FC and B's post-86 profits pool equals 8,000 FC. B's \$E amount equals \$9,000, and the \$P pool equals \$1,000. In B's first taxable year beginning on or after October 25, 1991 B remits 18,000 FC. Under section 987, the appropriate exchange rate for this remittance is 10FC:\$1.

(ii) *Computation of the equity pool.*

$$\underset{\text{(EQ pool)}}{15{,}000 \text{ FC}} + \underset{\text{(post-86 profits pool)}}{8{,}000 \text{ FC}} = \underset{\text{(equity pool)}}{23{,}000 \text{ FC}}$$

(iii) *Computation of the basis pool.*

$$\underset{\text{(\$E amount)}}{\$9{,}000} + \underset{\text{(\$P amount)}}{\$1{,}000} = \$10{,}000$$

(iv) *Dollar basis in remittance.*

$$\frac{\underset{\text{(amount of remittance)}}{18{,}000 \text{ FC}}}{\underset{\text{(equity pool)}}{23{,}000 \text{ FC}}} \times \$10{,}000 = \$7{,}826$$

(v) *Computation of section 987 loss by U.S. on remittance.*

$$\underset{\text{(dollar value of remittance)}}{\$1,800} - \underset{\text{(dollar basis in remittance)}}{\$7,826} = \underset{\text{(loss on remittance)}}{<\$6,026>}$$

(h) *Character and source of section 987 gain or loss.*—Section 987 gain or loss is sourced and characterized as provided by section 987 and regulations issued under that section. [Reg. §1.987-5.]

□ [T.D. 8367, 9-24-91.]

[Reg. §1.988-0T]

§1.988-0T. Taxation of gain or loss from a section 988 transaction; Table of Contents (Temporary regulations).—[This section listed captioned paragraphs contained in §§1.988-0T through 1.988-5T, temporary regulations under section 988 of the Internal Revenue Code. T.D. 8400 removed Temporary Reg. §§1.988-1T through 1.988-5T, but did not officially remove §1.988-0T. The text of Temporary Reg. §1.988-0T has been removed to conform to T.D. 8400 and the addition of Reg. §1.988-0.—CCH.]

[Reg. §1.988-0]

§1.988-0. Taxation of gain or loss from a section 988 transaction; Table of contents.—This section lists captioned paragraphs contained in §§1.988-1 through 1.988-6.

§1.988-1. Certain definitions and special rules.
(a) Section 988 transaction.
  (1) In general.
  (2) Description of transactions.
  (3)-(5) [Reserved]
  (6) Examples.
  (7) Special rules for regulated futures contracts and non-equity options.
  (8) Special rules for qualified funds.
  (9) Exception for certain transactions entered into by an individual.
  (10) Intra-taxpayer transactions.
  (11) Authority of Commissioner to include or exclude transactions from section 988.
(b) Spot contract.
(c) Nonfunctional currency.
(d) Spot rate.
  (1) In general.
  (2) Consistency required in valuing transactions subject to section 988.
  (3) Use of certain spot rate conventions for payables and receivables denominated in nonfunctional currency.
  (4) Currency where an official government established rate differs from a free market rate.
(e) Exchange gain or loss.
(f) Hyperinflationary currency.
(g) Fair market value.
(h) Interaction with sections 1092 and 1256 in examples.

(i) Effective date.

§1.988-2. Recognition and computation of exchange gain or loss.
(a) Disposition of nonfunctional currency.
  (1) Recognition of exchange gain or loss.
  (2) Computation of exchange gain or loss.
(b) Translation of interest income or expense and determination of exchange gain or loss with respect to debt instruments.
  (1) Translation of interest income received with respect to a nonfunctional currency demand account.
  (2) Translation of nonfunctional currency interest income or expense received or paid with respect to a debt instrument described in §1.988-1(a)(1)(ii) and (2)(i).
  (3) Exchange gain or loss recognized by the holder with respect to accrued interest income.
  (4) Exchange gain or loss recognized by the obligor with respect to accrued interest expense.
  (5) Exchange gain or loss recognized by the holder of a debt instrument with respect to principal.
  (6) Exchange gain or loss recognized by the obligor of a debt instrument with respect to principal.
  (7) Payment ordering rules.
  (8) Limitation of exchange gain or loss on payment or disposition of a debt instrument.
  (9) Examples.
  (10) Treatment of bond premium.
  (11) Market discount.
  (12) Tax exempt bonds.
  (13) Nonfunctional currency debt exchanged for stock of obligor.
  (14) [Reserved]
  (15) Debt instruments and deposits denominated in hyperinflationary currencies.
  (16) Coordination with section 267 regarding debt instruments.
  (17) Coordination with installment method under section 453.
  (18) Interaction of section 988 and §1.1275-2(g).
(c) Item of expense or gross income or receipts which is to be paid or received after the date accrued.
  (1) In general.
  (2) Determination of exchange gain or loss with respect to an item of gross income or receipts.
  (3) Determination of exchange gain or loss with respect to an item of expense.
  (4) Examples.

(d) Exchange gain or loss with respect to forward contracts, futures contracts and option contracts.

(1) Scope.

(2) Realization of exchange gain or loss.

(3) Recognition of exchange gain or loss.

(4) Determination of exchange gain or loss.

(5) Hyperinflationary contracts.

(e) Currency swaps and notional principal contracts.

(1) Notional principal contract denominated in a single nonfunctional currency.

(2) Special rules for currency swaps.

(3) Amortization of swap premium or discount in the case of off market swaps.

(4) Treatment of taxpayer disposing of a currency swap.

(5) Examples.

(6) Special effective date for rules regarding currency swaps.

(7) Special rules for currency swap contracts in hyperinflationary currencies.

(f) Substance over form.

(1) In general.

(2) Example.

(g) Effective date.

(h) Timing of income and deductions from notional principal contracts.

§ 1.988-3. Character of exchange gain or loss.

(a) In general.

(b) Election to characterize exchange gain or loss on certain identified forward contracts, futures contracts and option contracts as capital gain or loss.

(1) In general.

(2) Special rule for contracts that become part of a straddle after the election is made.

(3) Requirements for making the election.

(4) Verification.

(5) Independent verification.

(6) Effective date.

(c) Exchange gain or loss treated as interest.

(1) In general.

(2) Exchange loss realized by the holder on nonfunctional currency tax exempt bonds.

(d) Effective date.

§ 1.988-4. Source of gain of [or] loss realized on a section 988 transaction.

(a) In general.

(b) Qualified business unit.

(1) In general.

(2) Proper reflection on the books of the taxpayer or qualified business unit.

(c) Effectively connected exchange gain or loss.

(d) Residence.

(1) In general.

(2) Exception.

(3) Partner in a partnership not engaged in a U.S. trade or business under section 864(b)(2).

(e) Special rule for certain related party loans.

(1) In general.

(2) United States person.

(3) Loans by related person.

(4) 10 percent owned foreign corporation.

(f) Exchange gain or loss treated as interest under § 1.988-3.

(g) Exchange gain or loss allocated in the same manner as interest under § 1.861-9T.

(h) Effective date.

§ 1.988-5. Section 988(d) hedging transactions.

(a) Integration of a nonfunctional currency debt instrument and a § 1.988-5(a) hedge.

(1) In general.

(2) Exception.

(3) Qualifying debt instrument.

(4) Section 1.988-5(a) hedge.

(5) Definition of integrated economic transaction.

(6) Special rules for legging in and legging out of integrated treatment.

(7) Transactions part of a straddle.

(8) Identification requirements.

(9) Taxation of qualified hedging transactions.

(10) Transition rules and effective dates.

(b) Hedged executory contracts.

(1) In general.

(2) Definitions.

(3) Identification rules.

(4) Effect of hedged executory contract.

(5) References to this paragraph (b).

(c) Hedges of period between trade date and settlement date on purchase or sale of publicly traded stock or security.

(d) [Reserved]

(e) Advance rulings regarding net hedging and anticipatory hedging systems.

(f) [Reserved]

(g) General effective date.

§ 1.988-6 Nonfunctional currency contingent payment debt instruments.

(a) In general.

(1) Scope.

(2) Exception for hyperinflationary currencies.

(b) Instruments described in paragraph (a)(1)(i) of this section.

(1) In general.

(2) Application of noncontingent bond method.

(3) Treatment and translation of amounts determined under noncontingent bond method.

(4) Determination of gain or loss not attributable to foreign currency.

(5) Determination of foreign currency gain or loss.

(6) Source of gain or loss.

(7) Basis different from adjusted issue price.

(8) Fixed but deferred contingent payments.

(c) Examples.

(d) Multicurrency debt instruments.

(1) In general.

(2) Determination of denomination currency.

(3) Issuer/holder consistency.

(4) Treatment of payments in currencies other than the denomination currency.

(e) Instruments issued for nonpublicly traded property.

(1) Applicability.

(2) Separation into components.

(3) Treatment of components consisting of one or more noncontingent payments in the same currency.

(4) Treatment of components consisting of contingent payments.

(5) Basis different from adjusted issue price.

(6) Treatment of holder on sale, exchange, or retirement.

(f) Rules for nonfunctional currency tax exempt obligations described in § 1.1275-4(d).

(g) Effective date.

[Reg. § 1.988-0.]

☐ [*T.D. 8400, 3-16-92. Amended by T.D. 8860, 1-12-2000 and T.D. 9157, 8-27-2004.*]

[Reg. § 1.988-1]

§ 1.988-1. Certain definitions and special rules.—(a) *Section 988 transaction.*—(1) *In general.*—The term "section 988 transaction" means any of the following transactions—

(i) A disposition of nonfunctional currency as defined in paragraph (c) of this section;

(ii) Any transaction described in paragraph (a)(2) of this section if any amount which the taxpayer is entitled to receive or is required to pay by reason of such transaction is denominated in terms of a nonfunctional currency or is determined by reference to the value of one or more nonfunctional currencies.

A transaction described in this paragraph (a) need not require or permit payment with a nonfunctional currency as long as any amount paid or received is determined by reference to the value of one or more nonfunctional currencies. The acquisition of nonfunctional currency is treated as a section 988 transaction for purposes of establishing the taxpayer's basis in such currency and determining exchange gain or loss thereon.

(2) *Description of transactions.*—The following transactions are described in this paragraph (a)(2).

(i) *Debt instruments.*—Acquiring a debt instrument or becoming an obligor under a debt instrument. The term "debt instrument" means a bond, debenture, note, certificate or other evidence of indebtedness.

(ii) *Payables, receivables, etc.*—Accruing, or otherwise taking into account, for purposes of subtitle A of the Internal Revenue Code, any item of expense or gross income or receipts which is to be paid or received after the date on which so accrued or taken into account. A payable relating to cost of goods sold, or a payable or receivable relating to a capital expenditure or receipt, is within the meaning of this paragraph (a)(2)(ii). Generally, a payable relating to foreign taxes (whether or not claimed as a credit under section 901) is within the meaning of this paragraph (a)(2)(ii). However, a payable of a domestic person relating to accrued foreign taxes of its qualified business unit (QBU branch) is not within the meaning of this paragraph (a)(2)(ii) if the QBU branch's functional currency is the U.S. dollar and the foreign taxes are claimed as a credit under section 901.

(iii) *Forward contract, futures contract, option contract, or similar financial instrument.*—Except as otherwise provided in this paragraph (a)(2)(iii) and paragraph (a)(4)(i) of this section, entering into or acquiring any forward contract, futures contract, option, warrant, or similar financial instrument.

(A) *Limitation for certain derivative instruments.*—A forward contract, futures contract, option, warrant, or similar financial instrument is within this paragraph (a)(2)(iii) only if the underlying property to which the instrument ultimately relates is a nonfunctional currency or is otherwise described in paragraph (a)(1)(ii) of this section. Thus, if the underlying property of an instrument is another financial instrument (*e.g.,* an option on a futures contract), then the underlying property to which such other instrument (*e.g.,* the futures contract) ultimately relates must be a nonfunctional currency. For example, a forward contract to purchase wheat denominated in a nonfunctional currency, an option to enter into a forward contract to purchase wheat denominated in a nonfunctional currency, or a warrant to purchase stock denominated in a nonfunctional currency is not described in this paragraph (a)(2)(iii). On the other hand, a forward contract to purchase a nonfunctional currency, an option to enter into a forward contract to purchase a nonfunctional currency, an option to purchase a bond denominated in or the payments of which are determined by reference to the value of a nonfunctional currency, or a warrant to purchase nonfunctional currency is described in this paragraph (a)(2)(iii).

(B) *Nonfunctional currency notional principal contracts.*—(1) *In general.*—The term "similar financial instrument" includes a notional principal contract only if the payments required to be made or received under the contract are

Income from Sources Without the United States
See p. 20,601 for regulations not amended to reflect law changes
50,849

determined with reference to a nonfunctional currency.

(2) *Definition of notional principal contract.*—The term "notional principal contract" means a contract (*e.g.*, a swap, cap, floor or collar) that provides for the payment of amounts by one party to another at specified intervals calculated by reference to a specified index upon a notional principal amount in exchange for specified consideration or a promise to pay similar amounts. For this purpose, a "notional principal contract" shall only include an instrument where the underlying property to which the instrument ultimately relates is money (*e.g.*, functional currency), nonfunctional currency, or property the value of which is determined by reference to an interest rate. Thus, the term "notional principal contract" includes a currency swap as defined in § 1.988-2(e)(2)(ii), but does not include a swap referenced to a commodity or equity index.

(C) *Effective date with respect to certain contracts.*—This paragraph (a)(2)(iii) does not apply to any forward contract, futures contract, option, warrant, or similar financial instrument entered into or acquired on or before October 21, 1988, if such instrument would have been marked to market under section 1256 if held on the last day of the taxable year.

(3)-(5) [Reserved]

(6) *Examples.*—The following examples illustrate the application of paragraph (a) of this section. The examples assume that X is a U.S. corporation on an accrual method with the calendar year as its taxable year. Because X is a U.S. corporation the U.S. dollar is its functional currency under section 985. The examples also assume that section 988(d) does not apply.

Example 1. On January 1, 1989, X acquires 10,000 Canadian dollars. On January 15, 1989, X uses the 10,000 Canadian dollars to purchase inventory. The acquisition of the 10,000 Canadian dollars is a section 988 transaction for purposes of establishing X's basis in such Canadian dollars. The disposition of the 10,000 Canadian dollars is a section 988 transaction pursuant to paragraph (a)(1) of this section.

Example 2. On January 1, 1989, X acquires 10,000 Canadian dollars. On January 15, 1989, X converts the 10,000 Canadian dollars to U.S. dollars. The acquisition of the 10,000 Canadian dollars is a section 988 transaction for purposes of establishing X's basis in such Canadian dollars. The conversion of the 10,000 Canadian dollars to U.S. dollars is a section 988 transaction pursuant to paragraph (a)(1) of this section.

Example 3. On January 1, 1989, X borrows 100,000 British pounds (£) for a period of 10 years and issues a note to the lender with a face amount of £100,000. The note provides for payments of interest at an annual rate of 10% paid quarterly in pounds and has a stated redemption

price at maturity of £100,000. X's becoming the obligor under the note is a section 988 transaction pursuant to paragraphs (a)(1)(ii) and (2)(i) of this section. Because X is an accrual basis taxpayer, the accrual of interest expense under X's note is a section 988 transaction pursuant to paragraphs (a)(1)(ii) and (2)(ii) of this section. In addition, the acquisition of the British pounds to make payments under the note is a section 988 transaction for purposes of establishing X's basis in such pounds, and the disposition of such pounds is a section 988 transaction under paragraph (a)(1)(i) of this section. See § 1.988-2(b) with respect to the translation of accrued interest expense and the determination of exchange gain or loss upon payment of accrued interest expense.

Example 4. On January 1, 1989, X purchases at original issue for 74,621.54 British pounds (£) a 3-year bond maturing on December 31, 1991, at a stated redemption price of £100,000. The bond provides for no stated interest. The bond has a yield to maturity of 10% compounded semiannually and has £25,378.46 of original issue discount. The acquisition of the bond is a section 988 transaction as provided in paragraphs (a)(1)(ii) and (2)(i) of this section. The accrual of original issue discount with respect to the bond is a section 988 transaction under paragraphs (a)(1)(ii) and (2)(ii) of this section. See § 1.988-2(b) with respect to the translation of original issue discount and the determination of exchange gain or loss upon receipt of such amounts.

Example 5. On January 1, 1989, X sells and delivers inventory to Y for 10,000,000 Italian lira for payment on April 1, 1989. Under X's method of accounting, January 1, 1989 is the accrual date. Because X is an accrual basis taxpayer, the accrual of a nonfunctional currency denominated item of gross receipts on January 1, 1989, for payment after the date of accrual is a section 988 transaction under paragraphs (a)(1)(ii) and (2)(ii) of this section.

Example 6. On January 1, 1989, X agrees to purchase a machine from Y for delivery on March 1, 1990 for 1,000,000 yen. The agreement calls for X to pay Y for the machine on June 1, 1990. Under X's method of accounting, the expenditure for the machine does not accrue until delivery on March 1, 1990. The agreement to purchase the machine is not a section 988 transaction. In particular, the agreement to purchase the machine is not described in paragraph (a)(2)(ii) of this section because the agreement is not an item of expense taken into account under subtitle A (but rather is an agreement to purchase a capital asset in the future). However, the payable that will arise on the delivery date is a section 988 transaction under paragraphs (a)(1)(ii) and (2)(ii) of this section even though the payable relates to a capital expenditure. In addition, the disposition of yen to satisfy the payable on June 1, 1990, is a section 988 transaction under paragraph (a)(1)(i) of this section.

Example 7. On January 1, 1989, X purchases and takes delivery of inventory for 10,000 French francs with payment to be made on April 1, 1989. Under X's method of accounting, the expense accrues on January 1, 1989. On January 1, 1989, X also enters into a forward contract with a bank to purchase 10,000 French francs for $2,000 on April 1, 1989. Because X is an accrual basis taxpayer, the accrual of a nonfunctional currency denominated item of expense on January 1, 1989, for payment after the date of accrual is a section 988 transaction under paragraphs (a)(1)(ii) and (2)(ii) of this section. Entering into the forward contract to purchase the 10,000 French francs is a section 988 transaction under paragraphs (a)(1)(ii) and (2)(iii) of this section.

Example 8. On January 1, 1989, X acquires 100,000 Norwegian krone. On January 15, 1989, X purchases and takes delivery of 1,000 shares of common stock with the 100,000 krone acquired on January 1, 1989. On August 1, 1989, X sells the 1,000 shares of common stock and receives 120,000 krone in payment. On August 30, 1989, X converts the 120,000 krone to U.S. dollars. The acquisition of the 100,000 krone on January 1, 1989, and the acquisition of the 120,000 krone on August 1, 1989, are section 988 transactions for purposes of establishing the basis of such krone. The disposition of the 100,000 krone on January 15, 1989, and the 120,000 krone on August 30, 1989, are section 988 transactions as provided in paragraph (a)(1)(i) of this section. Neither the acquisition on January 15, 1989, nor the disposition on August 1, 1989, of the stock is a section 988 transaction.

Example 9. On May 11, 1989, X purchases a one year note at original issue for its issue price of $1,000. The note pays interest in dollars at the rate of 4 percent compounded semiannually. The amount of principal received by X upon maturity is equal to $1,000 plus the equivalent of the excess, if any, of (a) the Financial Times One Hundred Stock Index (an index of stocks traded on the London Stock Exchange hereafter referred to as the FT100) determined and translated into dollars on the last business day prior to the maturity date, over (b) £2,150, the "stated value" of the FT100, which is equal to 110% of the average value of the index for the six months prior to the issue date, translated at the exchange rate of £1 = $1.50. The purchase by X of the instrument described above is not a section 988 transaction because the index used to compute the principal amount received upon maturity is determined with reference to the value of stock and not nonfunctional currency.

Example 10. On April 9, 1989, X enters into an interest rate swap that provides for the payment of amounts by X to its counterparty based on 4% of a 10,000 yen principal amount in exchange for amounts based on yen LIBOR rates. Pursuant to paragraphs (a)(1)(ii) and (2)(iii) of this section, this yen for yen interest rate swap is a section 988 transaction.

Example 11. On August 11, 1989, X enters into an option contract for sale of a group of stocks traded on the Japanese Nikkei exchange. The contract is not a section 988 transaction within the meaning of §1.988-1(a)(2)(iii) because the underlying property to which the option relates is a group of stocks and not nonfunctional currency.

(7) *Special rules for regulated futures contracts and non-equity options.*—(i) *In general.*—Except as provided in paragraph (a)(7)(ii) of this section, paragraph (a)(2)(iii) of this section shall not apply to any regulated futures contract or non-equity option which would be marked to market under section 1256 if held on the last day of the taxable year.

(ii) *Election to have paragraph (a)(2)(iii) of this section apply.*—Notwithstanding paragraph (a)(7)(i) of this section, a taxpayer may elect to have paragraph (a)(2)(iii) of this section apply to regulated futures contracts and non-equity options as provided in paragraph (a)(7)(iii) and (iv) of this section.

(iii) *Procedure for making the election.*—A taxpayer shall make the election provided in paragraph (a)(7)(ii) of this section by sending to the Internal Revenue Service Center, Examination Branch, Stop Number 92, Kansas City, MO 64999 a statement titled "ELECTION TO TREAT REGULATED FUTURES CONTRACTS AND NON-EQUITY OPTIONS AS SECTION 988 TRANSACTIONS UNDER SECTION 988(c)(1)(D)(ii)" that contains the following:

(A) The taxpayer's name, address, and taxpayer identification number;

(B) The date the notice is mailed or otherwise delivered to the Internal Revenue Service Center;

(C) A statement that the taxpayer (including all members of such person's affiliated group as defined in section 1504 or in the case of an individual all persons filing a joint return with such individual) elects to have section 988(c)(1)(D)(i) and §1.988-1(a)(7)(i) not apply;

(D) The date of the beginning of the taxable year for which the election is being made;

(E) If the election is filed after the first day of the taxable year, a statement regarding whether the taxpayer has previously held a contract described in section 988(c)(1)(D)(i) or §1.988-1(a)(7)(i) during such taxable year, and if so, the first date during the taxable year on which such contract was held; and

(F) The signature of the person making the election (in the case of individuals filing a joint return, the signature of all persons filing such return).

The election shall be made by the following persons: in the case of an individual, by such individual; in the case of a partnership, by each partner separately; effective for taxable years be-

Reg. §1.988-1(a)(7)

ginning after March 17, 1992, in the case of tiered partnerships, each ultimate partner; in the case of an S corporation, by each shareholder separately; in the case of a trust (other than a grantor trust) or estate, by the fiduciary of such trust or estate; in the case of any corporation other than an S corporation, by such corporation (in the case of a corporation that is a member of an affiliated group that files a consolidated return, such election shall be valid and binding only if made by the common parent, as that term is used in § 1.1502-77(a)); in the case of a controlled foreign corporation, by its controlling United States shareholders under § 1.964-1(c)(3). With respect to a corporation (other than an S corporation), the election, when made by the common parent, shall be binding on all members of such corporation's affiliated group as defined in section 1504 that file a consolidated return. The election shall be binding on any income or loss derived from the partner's share (determined under the principles of section 702(a)) of all contracts described in section 988(c)(1)(D)(i) or paragraph (a)(7)(i) of this section in which the taxpayer holds a direct interest or indirect interest through a partnership or S corporation; however, the election shall not apply to any income or loss of a partnership for any taxable year if such partnership made an election under section 988(c)(1)(E)(iii)(V) for such year or any preceding year. Generally, a copy of the election must be attached to the taxpayer's income tax return for the first year it is effective. It is not required to be attached to subsequent returns. However, in the case of a partner, a copy of the election must be attached to the taxpayer's income tax return for every year during which the taxpayer is a partner in a partnership that engages in a transaction that is subject to the election.

(iv) *Time for making the election.*—(A) *In general.*—Unless the requirements for making a late election described in paragraph (a)(7)(iv)(B) of this section are satisfied, an election under section 988(c)(1)(D)(ii) and paragraph (a)(7)(ii) of this section for any taxable year shall be made on or before the first day of the taxable year or, if later, on or before the first day during such taxable year on which the taxpayer holds a contract described in section 988(c)(1)(D)(ii) and paragraph (a)(7)(ii) of this section. The election under section 988(c)(1)(D)(ii) and paragraph (a)(7)(ii) of this section shall apply to contracts entered into or acquired after October 21, 1988, and held on or after the effective date of the election. The election shall be effective as of the beginning of the taxable year and shall be binding with respect to all succeeding taxable years unless revoked with the prior consent of the Commissioner. In determining whether to grant revocation of the election, recapture of the tax benefit derived from the election in previous taxable years will be considered.

(B) *Late elections.*—A taxpayer may make an election under section 988(c)(1)(D)(ii) and paragraph (a)(7)(ii) of this section within 30 days after the time prescribed in the first sentence of paragraph (a)(7)(iv)(A) of this section. Such a late election shall be effective as of the beginning of the taxable year; however, any losses recognized during the taxable year with respect to contracts described in section 988(c)(1)(D)(ii) or paragraph (a)(7)(ii) of this section which were entered into or acquired after October 21, 1988, and held on or before the date on which the late election is mailed or otherwise delivered to the Internal Revenue Service Center shall not be treated as derived from a section 988 transaction. A late election must comply with the procedures set forth in paragraph (a)(7)(iii) of this section.

(v) *Transition rule.*—An election made prior to September 21, 1989 which satisfied the requirements of Notice 88-124, 1988-51 I.R.B. 6, shall be deemed to satisfy the requirements of paragraphs (a)(7)(iii) and (iv) of this section.

(vi) *General effective date provision.*—This paragraph (a)(7) shall apply with respect to futures contracts and options entered into or acquired after October 21, 1988.

(8) *Special rules for qualified funds.*—(i) *Definition of qualified fund.*—The term "qualified fund" means any partnership if—

(A) At all times during the taxable year (and during each preceding taxable year to which an election under section 988(c)(1)(E)(iii)(V) applied) such partnership has at least 20 partners and no single partner owns more than 20 percent of the interests in the capital or profits of the partnership;

(B) The principal activity of such partnership for such taxable year (and each such preceding taxable year) consists of buying and selling options, futures, or forwards with respect to commodities;

(C) At least 90 percent of the gross income of the partnership for the taxable year (and each such preceding year) consists of income or gains described in subparagraph (A), (B), or (G) of section 7704(d)(1) or gain from the sale or disposition of capital assets held for the production of interest or dividends;

(D) No more than a de minimis amount of the gross income of the partnership for the taxable year (and each such preceding taxable year) was derived from buying and selling commodities; and

(E) An election under section 988(c)(1)(E)(iii)(V) as provided in paragraph (a)(8)(iv) of this section applies to the taxable year.

(ii) *Special rules relating to paragraph (a)(8)(i)(A) of this section.*—(A) *Certain general partners.*—The interest of a general partner in the

Reg. § 1.988-1(a)(8)(ii)(A)

partnership shall not be treated as failing to meet the 20 percent ownership requirement of paragraph (a)(8)(i)(A) of this section for any taxable year of the partnership if, for the taxable year of the partner in which such partnership's taxable year ends, such partner (and each corporation filing a consolidated return with such partner) had no ordinary income or loss from a section 988 transaction (other than income from the partnership) which is exchange gain or loss (as the case may be).

(B) *Treatment of incentive compensation.*—For purposes of paragraph (a)(8)(i)(A) of this section, any income allocable to a general partner as incentive compensation based on profits rather than capital shall not be taken into account in determining such partner's interest in the profits of the partnership.

(C) *Treatment of tax exempt partners.*—The interest of a partner in the partnership shall not be treated as failing to meet the 20 percent ownership requirements of paragraph (a)(5)(8)(A) of this section if none of the income of such partner from such partnership is subject to tax under chapter 1 of subtitle A of the Internal Revenue Code (whether directly or through one or more pass-through entities).

(D) *Look-through rule.*—In determining whether the 20% ownership requirement of paragraph (a)(8)(i)(A) of this section is met with respect to any partnership, any interest in such partnership held by another partnership shall be treated as held proportionately by the partners in such other partnership.

(iii) *Other special rules.*—(A) *Related persons.*—Interests in the partnership held by persons related to each other (within the meaning of section 267(b) or 707(b)) shall be treated as held by one person.

(B) *Predecessors.*—Reference to any partnership shall include a reference to any predecessor thereof.

(C) *Treatment of certain debt instruments.*—Solely for purposes of paragraph (a)(8)(i)(D) of this section, any debt instrument which is described in both paragraph (a)(1)(ii) and (2)(i) of this section shall be treated as a commodity.

(iv) *Procedure for making the election provided in section 988(c)(1)(E)(iii)(V).*—A partnership shall make the election provided in section 988(c)(1)(E)(iii)(V) by sending to the Internal Revenue Service Center, Examination Branch, Stop Number 92, Kansas City, MO 64999 a statement titled "QUALIFIED FUND ELECTION UNDER SECTION 988(c)(1)(E)(iii)(V)" that contains the following:

(A) The partnership's name, address, and taxpayer identification number;

(B) The name, address and taxpayer identification number of the general partner making the election on behalf of the partnership;

(C) The date the notice is mailed or otherwise delivered to the Internal Revenue Service Center;

(D) A brief description of the activity of the partnership;

(E) A statement that the partnership is making the election provided in section 988(c)(1)(E)(iii)(V);

(F) The date of the beginning of the taxable year for which the election is being made;

(G) If the election is filed after the first day of the taxable year, then a statement regarding whether the partnership previously held an instrument referred to in section 988(c)(1)(E)(i) during such taxable year and, if so, the first date during the taxable year on which such contract was held; and

(H) The signature of the general partner making the election.

The election shall be made by a general partner with management responsibility of the partnership's activities and a copy of such election shall be attached to the partnership's income tax return (Form 1065) for the first taxable year it is effective. It is not required to be attached to subsequent returns.

(v) *Time for making the election.*—The election under section 988(c)(1)(E)(iii)(V) for any taxable year shall be made on or before the first day of the taxable year or, if later, on or before the first day during such year on which the partnership holds an instrument described in section 988(c)(1)(E)(i). The election under section 988(c)(1)(E)(iii)(V) shall apply to the taxable year for which made and all succeeding taxable years. Such election may only be revoked with the consent of the Commissioner. In determining whether to grant revocation of the election, recapture by the partners of the tax benefit derived from the election in previous taxable years will be considered.

(vi) *Operative rules applicable to qualified funds.*—(A) *In general.*—In the case of a qualified fund, any bank forward contract or any foreign currency futures contract traded on a foreign exchange which is not otherwise a section 1256 contract shall be treated as a section 1256 contract for purposes of section 1256.

(B) *Gains and losses treated as short-term.*—In the case of any instrument treated as a section 1256 contract under paragraph (a)(8)(vi)(A) of this section, subparagraph (A) of section 1256(a)(3) shall be applied by substituting "100 percent" for "40 percent" (and subparagraph (B) of such section shall not apply).

(vii) *Transition rule.*—An election made prior to September 21, 1989, which satisfied the requirements of Notice 88-124, 1988-51 I.R.B. 6, shall be deemed to satisfy the requirements of § 1.988-1(a)(8)(iv) and (v).

(viii) *General effective date rules.*—(A) The requirements of subclause (IV) of section 988(c)(1)(E)(iii) shall not apply to contracts entered into or acquired on or before October 21, 1988.

(B) In the case of any partner in an existing partnership, the 20 percent ownership requirements of subclause (I) of section 988(c)(1)(E)(iii) shall be treated as met during any period during which such partner does not own a percentage interest in the capital or profits of such partnership greater than 33 1/3 percent (or, if lower, the lowest such percentage interest of such partner during any period after October 21, 1988, during which such partnership is in existence). For purposes of the preceding sentence, the term "existing partnership" means any partnership if—

(1) such partnership was in existence on October 21, 1988, and principally engaged on such date in buying and selling options, futures, or forwards with respect to commodities; or

(2) a registration statement was filed with respect to such partnership with the Securities and Exchange Commission on or before such date and such registration statement indicated that the principal activity of such partnership will consist of buying and selling instruments referred to in paragraph (a)(8)(viii)(B)(1) of this section.

(9) *Exception for certain transactions entered into by an individual.*—(i) *In general.*—A transaction entered into by an individual which otherwise qualifies as a section 988 transaction shall be considered a section 988 transaction only to the extent expenses properly allocable to such transaction meet the requirements of section 162 or 212 (other than the part of section 212 dealing with expenses incurred in connection with taxes).

(ii) *Examples.*—The following examples illustrate the application of paragraph (a)(9) of this section.

Example 1. X is a U.S. citizen who therefore has the U.S. dollar as his functional currency. On January 1, 1990, X enters into a spot contract to purchase 10,000 British pounds (£) for $15,000 for delivery on January 3, 1990. Immediately upon delivery, X acquires at original issue a pound denominated bond with an issue price of £ 10,000. The bond matures on January 3, 1993, pays interest in pounds at a rate of 10% compounded semiannually, and has no original issue discount. Assume that all expenses properly allocable to these transactions would meet the requirements of section 212. Under § 1.988-2(d)(1)(ii), entering into the spot contract on January 1, 1990, is not a section 988 transaction. The acquisition of the pounds on January 3,

1990, under the spot contract is a section 988 transaction for purposes of establishing X's basis in the pounds. The disposition of the pounds and the acquisition of the bond by X are section 988 transactions. These transactions are not excluded from the definition of a section 988 transaction under paragraph (a)(9) of this section because expenses properly allocable to such transactions meet the requirements of section 212.

Example 2. X is a U.S. citizen who therefore has the dollar as his functional currency. In preparation for X's vacation, X purchases 1,000 British pounds (£) from a bank on June 1, 1989. During the period of X's vacation in the United Kingdom beginning June 10, 1989, and ending June 20, 1989, X spends £500 for hotel rooms, £ 300 for food and £200 for miscellaneous vacation expenses. The expenses properly allocable to such dispositions do not meet the requirements of section 162 or 212. Thus, the disposition of the pounds by X on his vacation are not section 988 transactions.

(10) *Intra-taxpayer transactions.*—(i) *In general.*—Except as provided in paragraph (a)(10)(ii) of this section, transactions between or among the taxpayer and/or qualified business units of that taxpayer ("intra-taxpayer transactions") are not section 988 transactions. See section 987 and the regulations thereunder.

(ii) *Certain transfers.*—Exchange gain or loss with respect to nonfunctional currency or any item described in paragraph (a)(2) of this section entered into with another taxpayer shall be realized upon an intra-taxpayer transfer of such currency or item where as the result of the transfer the currency or other such item—

(A) Loses its character as nonfunctional currency or an item described in paragraph (a)(2) of this section; or

(B) Where the source of the exchange gain or loss could be altered absent the application of this paragraph (a)(10)(ii). Such exchange gain or loss shall be computed in accordance with § 1.988-2 (without regard to § 1.988-2(b)(8)) as if the nonfunctional currency or item described in paragraph (a)(2) of this section had been sold or otherwise transferred at fair market value between unrelated taxpayers. For purposes of the preceding sentence, a taxpayer must use the translation rate that it uses for purposes of computing section 987 gain or loss with respect to the QBU branch that makes the transfer. In the case of a gain or loss incurred in a transaction described in this paragraph (a)(10)(ii) that does not have a significant business purpose, the Commissioner, may defer such gain or loss.

(iii) *Example.*—The following example illustrates the provisions of this paragraph (a)(10).

Example. (A) X, a corporation with the U.S. dollar as its functional currency, operates through foreign branches Y and Z. Y and Z are qualified business units as defined in section 989(a) with the LC as their functional currency. X computes Y's and Z's income under section 987 (relating to branch transactions). On November 12, 1988, Y transfers $25 to the home office of X when the fair market value of such amount equals LC120. Y has a basis of LC100 in the $25. Under paragraph (a)(10)(ii) of this section, Y realizes foreign source exchange gain of LC20 (LC120 – LC100) as the result of the $25 transfer. For purposes of determining whether the transfer is a remittance resulting in additional gain or loss, see section 987 and the regulations thereunder.

(B) If instead Y transfers the $25 to Z, exchange gain is not realized because the $25 is nonfunctional currency with respect to Z and if Z were to immediately convert the $25 into LCs, the gain would be foreign source. For purposes of determining whether the transfer is a remittance resulting in additional gain or loss, see section 987 and the regulations thereunder.

(11) *Authority to include or exclude transactions from section 988.*—(i) *In general.*—The Commissioner may recharacterize a transaction (or series of transactions) in whole or in part as a section 988 transaction if the effect of such transaction (or series of transactions) is to avoid section 988. In addition, the Commissioner may exclude a transaction (or series of transactions) which in form is a section 988 transaction from the provisions of section 988 if the substance of the transaction (or series of transactions) indicates that it is not properly considered a section 988 transaction.

(ii) *Example.*—The following example illustrates the provisions of this paragraph (a)(11).

Example. B is an individual with the U.S. dollar as its functional currency. B holds 500,000 Swiss francs which have a basis of $100,000 and a fair market value of $400,000 as of October 15, 1989. On October 16, 1989, B transfers the 500,000 Swiss francs to a newly formed U.S. corporation, X, with the dollar as its functional currency. On October 16, 1989, B sells the stock of X for $400,000. Assume the transfer to X qualified for nonrecognition under section 351. Because the sale of the stock of X is a substitute for the disposition of an asset subject to section 988, the Commissioner may recharacterize the sale of the stock as a section 988 transaction. The same result would obtain if B transferred the Swiss francs to a partnership and then sold the partnership interest.

(b) *Spot contract.*—A spot contract is a contract to buy or sell nonfunctional currency on or before two business days following the date of the execution of the contract. See § 1.988-2(d)(1)(ii) for operative rules regarding spot contracts.

(c) *Nonfunctional currency.*—The term "nonfunctional currency" means with respect to a taxpayer or a qualified business unit (as defined in section 989(a)) a currency (including the European Currency Unit) other than the taxpayer's or the qualified business unit's functional currency as defined in section 985 and the regulations thereunder. For rules relating to nonrecognition of exchange gain or loss with respect to certain dispositions of nonfunctional currency, see § 1.988-2(a)(1)(iii).

(d) *Spot rate.*—(1) *In general.*—Except as otherwise provided in this paragraph, the term "spot rate" means a rate demonstrated to the satisfaction of the District Director or the Assistant Commissioner (International) to reflect a fair market rate of exchange available to the public for currency under a spot contract in a free market and involving representative amounts. In the absence of such a demonstration, the District Director or the Assistant Commissioner (International), in his or her sole discretion, shall determine the spot rate from a source of exchange rate information reflecting actual transactions conducted in a free market. For example, the taxpayer or the District Director or the Assistant Commissioner (International) may determine the spot rate by reference to exchange rates published in the pertinent monthly issue of "International Financial Statistics" or a successor publication of the International Monetary Fund; exchange rates published by the Board of Governors of the Federal Reserve System pursuant to 31 U.S.C. section 5151; exchange rates published in newspapers, financial journals or other daily financial news sources; or exchange rates quoted by electronic financial news services.

(2) *Consistency required in valuing transactions subject to section 988.*—If the use of inconsistent sources of spot rate quotations results in the distortion of income, the District Director or the Assistant Commissioner (International) may determine the appropriate spot rate.

(3) *Use of certain spot rate conventions for payables and receivables denominated in nonfunctional currency.*—If consistent with the taxpayer's financial accounting, a taxpayer may utilize a spot rate convention determined at intervals of one quarter year or less for purposes of computing exchange gain or loss with respect to payables and receivables denominated in a nonfunctional currency that are incurred in the ordinary course of business with respect to the acquisition or sale of goods or the obtaining or performance of services. For example, if consistent with the taxpayer's financial accounting, a taxpayer may accrue all payables and receivables incurred during the month of January at the spot rate on December 31 or January 31 (or at an average of any spot rates occurring between these two dates) and record the payment or receipt of amounts in satisfaction of such payables and

receivables consistent with such convention. The use of a spot rate convention cannot be changed without the consent of the Commissioner.

(4) *Currency where an official government established rate differs from a free market rate.*—(i) *In general.*—If a currency has an official government established rate that differs from a free market rate, the spot rate shall be the rate which most clearly reflects the taxpayer's income. Generally, this shall be the free market rate.

(ii) *Examples.*—The following examples illustrate the application of this paragraph (d)(4).

Example 1. X is an accrual method U.S. corporation with the dollar as its functional currency. X owns all the stock of a Country L subsidiary, CFC. CFC has the currency of Country L, the LC, as its functional currency. Country L imposes restrictions on the remittance of dividends. On April 1, 1990, CFC pays a dividend to X in the amount of LC100. Assume that the official government established rate is $1 = LC1 and the free market rate, which takes into account the remittance restrictions and which is the rate that most clearly reflects income, is $1 = LC4. On April 1, 1990, X donates the LC100 in a transaction that otherwise qualifies as a charitable contribution under section 170(c). Both the amount of the dividend income and the deduction under section 170 is $25 (LC100 × the free market rate, $.25).

Example 2. X, a corporation with the U.S. dollar as its functional currency, operates in foreign country L through branch Y. Y is a qualified business unit as defined in section 989(a). X computes Y's income under the dollar approximate separate transactions method as described in §1.985-3. The currency of L is the LC. X can purchase legally United States dollars ($) in L only from the L government. In order to take advantage of an arbitrage between the official and secondary dollar to LC exchange rates in L:

(i) X purchases LC100 for $60 in L on the secondary market when the official exchange rate is $1 = LC1;

(ii) X transfers the LC100 to Y;

(iii) Y purchases $100 for LC100; and

(iv) Y transfers $65 ($100 less an L tax withheld of $35 on the transfer) to the home office of X.

Under paragraph (a)(7) of this section, the transfer of the LC100 by X to Y is a realization event. X has a basis of $60 in the LC100. Under these facts, the appropriate dollar to LC exchange rate for computing the amount realized by X is the official exchange rate. Therefore, X realizes $40 ($100 – $60) of U.S. source gain from the transfer to Y. The same result would obtain if Y rather than X purchased the LC100 on the secondary market in L with $60 supplied by X, because the substance of this transaction is that X is performing the arbitrage.

(e) *Exchange gain or loss.*—The term "exchange gain or loss" means the amount of gain or loss realized as determined in §1.988-2 with respect to a section 988 transaction. Except as otherwise provided in these regulations (*e.g.,* §1.988-5), the amount of exchange gain or loss from a section 988 transaction shall be separately computed for each section 988 transaction, and such amount shall not be integrated with gain or loss recognized on another transaction (whether or not such transaction is economically related to the section 988 transaction). See §1.988-2(b)(8) for a special rule with respect to debt instruments.

(f) *Hyperinflationary currency.*—(1) *Definition.*—(i) *General rule.*—For purposes of section 988, a hyperinflationary currency means a currency described in §1.985-1(b)(2)(ii)(D). Unless otherwise provided, the currency in any example used in §§1.988-1 through 1.988-5 is not a hyperinflationary currency.

(ii) *Special rules for determining base period.*—In determining whether a currency is hyperinflationary under §1.985-1(b)(2)(ii)(D) for purposes of this paragraph (f), the following rules will apply:

(A) The base period means the thirty-six calendar month period ending on the last day of the taxpayer's (or qualified business unit's) current taxable year. Thus, for example, if for 1996, 1997, and 1998, a country's annual inflation rates are 6 percent, 11 percent, and 90 percent, respectively, the cumulative inflation rate for the three-year base period is 124% [((1.06 × 1.11 × 1.90) – 1.0 = 1.24) × 100 = 124%]. Accordingly, assuming the QBU has a calendar year as its taxable year, the currency of the country is hyperinflationary for the 1998 taxable year. This change in the §1.985-1(b)(2)(ii)(D) base period shall not apply to any section 988 transaction of an entity described in section 851 (regulated investment company (RIC)) or section 856 (real estate investment trust (REIT)). The Service may, by notice, provide that the foregoing change in the §1.985-1(b)(2)(ii)(D) base period does not apply to any section 988 transaction of an entity with distribution requirements similar to a RIC or REIT.

(B) The last sentence of §1.985-1(b)(2)(ii)(D) shall not apply to alter the base period for purposes of this paragraph (f) in determining whether a currency is hyperinflationary for purposes of section 988. Accordingly, generally accepted accounting principles may not apply to alter the base period for purposes of this paragraph (f).

(2) *Effective date.*—Paragraph (f)(1) of this section shall apply to transactions entered into after February 14, 2000.

(g) *Fair market value.*—The fair market value of an item shall, where relevant, reflect an appropriate premium or discount for the time value of money (*e.g.*, the fair market value of a forward contract to buy or sell nonfunctional currency shall reflect the present value of the difference between the units of nonfunctional currency times the market forward rate at the time of valuation and the units of nonfunctional currency times the forward rate set forth in the contract). However, if consistent with the taxpayer's method of financial accounting (and consistently applied from year to year), the preceding sentence shall not apply to a financial instrument that matures within one year from the date of issuance or acquisition. Unless otherwise provided, the fair market value given in any example used in §§1.988-1 through 1.988-5 is deemed to reflect appropriately the time value of money. If the use of inconsistent sources of forward or other market rate quotations results in the distortion of income, the District Director or the Assistant Commissioner (International) may determine the appropriate rate.

(h) *Interaction with sections 1092 and 1256.*—Unless otherwise provided, it is assumed for purposes of §§1.988-1 through 1.988-5 that any contract used in any example is not a section 1256 contract and is not part of a straddle as defined in section 1092. No inference is intended regarding the application of section 1092 or 1256 unless expressly stated.

(i) *Effective date.*—Except as otherwise provided in this section, this section shall be effective for taxable years beginning after December 31, 1986. Thus, except as otherwise provided in this section, any payments made or received with respect to a section 988 transaction in taxable years beginning after December 31, 1986, are subject to this section. [Reg. §1.988-1.]

☐ [*T.D. 8400, 3-16-92. Amended by T.D. 8914, 12-29-2000.*]

[Reg. §1.988-2]

§1.988-2. Recognition and computation of exchange gain or loss.—(a) *Disposition of nonfunctional currency*—.—(1) *Recognition of exchange gain or loss.*—(i) *In general.*—Except as otherwise provided in this section, §1.988-1(a)(7)(ii), and §1.988-5, the recognition of exchange gain or loss upon the sale or other disposition of nonfunctional currency shall be governed by the recognition provisions of the Internal Revenue Code which apply to the sale or disposition of property (*e.g.*, section 1001 or, to the extent provided in regulations, section 1092). The disposition of nonfunctional currency in settlement of a forward contract, futures contract, option contract, or similar financial instrument is considered to be a sale or disposition of the nonfunctional currency for purposes of the preceding sentence.

(ii) *Clarification of section 1031.*—An amount of one nonfunctional currency is not "property of like kind" with respect to an amount of a different nonfunctional currency.

(iii) *Coordination with section 988(c)(1)(C)(ii).*—No exchange gain or loss is recognized with respect to the following transactions—

(A) An exchange of units of nonfunctional currency for different units of the same nonfunctional currency;

(B) The deposit of nonfunctional currency in a demand or time deposit or similar instrument (including a certificate of deposit) issued by a bank or other financial institution if such instrument is denominated in such currency;

(C) The withdrawal of nonfunctional currency from a demand or time deposit or similar instrument issued by a bank or other financial institution if such instrument is denominated in such currency;

(D) The receipt of nonfunctional currency from a bank or other financial institution from which the taxpayer purchased a certificate of deposit or similar instrument denominated in such currency by reason of the maturing or other termination of such instrument; and

(E) The transfer of nonfunctional currency from a demand or time deposit or similar instrument issued by a bank or other financial institution to another demand or time deposit or similar instrument denominated in the same nonfunctional currency issued by a bank or other financial institution.

The taxpayer's basis in the units of nonfunctional currency or other property received in the transaction shall be the adjusted basis of the units of nonfunctional currency or other property transferred. See paragraph (b) of this section with respect to the timing of interest income or expense and the determination of exchange gain or loss thereon.

(iv) *Example.*—The following example illustrates the provisions of paragraph (a)(1)(iii) of this section.

Example. X is a corporation on the accrual method of accounting with the U.S. dollar as its functional currency. On January 1, 1989, X acquires 1,500 British pounds (£) for $2,250 (£1 = $1.50). On January 3, 1989, when the spot rate is £1 = $1.49, X deposits the £1,500 with a British financial institution in a non-interest bearing demand account. On February 1, 1989, when the spot rate is £1 = $1.45, X withdraws the £1,500. On February 5, 1989, when the spot rate is £1 = $1.42, X purchases inventory in the amount of £1,500. Pursuant to paragraph (a)(1)(iii) of this section, no exchange loss is realized until February 5, 1989, when X disposes of the £1,500 for inventory. At that time, X realizes exchange loss in the amount of $120 computed under paragraph (a)(2) of this section. The loss is not an adjustment to the cost of the inventory.

(2) *Computation of gain or loss.*—(i) *In general.*—Exchange gain realized from the sale or other disposition of nonfunctional currency shall be the excess of the amount realized over the adjusted basis of such currency, and exchange loss realized shall be the excess of the adjusted basis of such currency over the amount realized.

(ii) *Amount realized.*—(A) *In general.*—The amount realized from the disposition of nonfunctional currency shall be determined under section 1001(b). A taxpayer that uses a spot rate convention under § 1.988-1(d)(3) to determine exchange gain or loss with respect to a payable shall determine the amount realized upon the disposition of nonfunctional currency paid in satisfaction of the payable in a manner consistent with such convention.

(B) *Exchange of nonfunctional currency for property.*—For purpose of paragraph (a)(2) of this section, the exchange of nonfunctional currency for property (other than nonfunctional currency) shall be treated as—

(1) An exchange of the units of nonfunctional currency for units of functional currency at the spot rate on the date of the exchange, and

(2) The purchase or sale of the property for such units of functional currency.

(C) *Example.*—The following example illustrates the provisions of paragraph (a)(2)(ii)(B) of this section.

Example. G is a U.S. corporation with the U.S. dollar as its functional currency. On January 1, 1989, G enters into a contract to purchase a paper manufacturing machine for 10,000,000 British pounds (£) for delivery on January 1, 1991. On January 1, 1991, when G exchanges £10,000,000 (which G purchased for $12,000,000) for the machine, the fair market value of the machine is £17,000,000. On January 1, 1991, the spot exchange rate is £1 = $1.50. Under paragraph (a)(2)(ii)(B) of this section, the transaction is treated as an exchange of £ 10,000,000 for $15,000,000 and the purchase of the machine for $15,000,000. Accordingly, in computing G's exchange gain of $3,000,000 on the disposition of the £10,000,000, the amount realized is $15,000,000. G's basis in the machine is $15,000,000. No gain is recognized on the bargain purchase of the machine.

(iii) *Adjusted basis.*—(A) *In general.*—Except as provided in paragraph (a)(2)(iii)(B) of this section, the adjusted basis of nonfunctional currency is determined under the applicable provisions of the Internal Revenue Code (*e.g.*, sections 1011 through 1023). A taxpayer that uses a spot rate convention under § 1.988-1(d)(3) to determine exchange gain or loss with respect to a receivable shall determine the basis of nonfunctional currency received in satisfaction of such

receivable in a manner consistent with such convention.

(B) *Determination of the basis of nonfunctional currency withdrawn from an account with a bank or other financial institution.*—(1) *In general.*—The basis of nonfunctional currency withdrawn from an account with a bank or other financial institution shall be determined under any reasonable method that is consistently applied from year to year by the taxpayer to all accounts denominated in a nonfunctional currency. For example, a taxpayer may use a first in first out method, a last in first out method, a prorata method (as illustrated in the example below), or any other reasonable method that is consistently applied. However, a method that consistently results in units of nonfunctional currency with the highest basis being withdrawn first shall not be considered reasonable.

(2) *Example.*—The following example illustrates the provisions of this paragraph (a)(2)(iii)(B).

Example. (i) X, a cash basis individual with the dollar as his functional currency, opens a demand account with a Swiss bank. Assume expenses associated with the demand account are deductible under section 212. The following chart indicates Swiss franc deposits to the account, Swiss franc interest credited to the account, the dollar basis of each deposit, and the determination of the aggregate dollar basis of all Swiss francs in the account. Assume that the taxpayer has properly translated all the amounts specified in the chart and that all transactions are subject to section 988.

Date	Swiss francs Deposited	Interest Received	U.S. dollar Basis	Aggregate U.S. dollar Basis
1/01/89	1000 Sf		$500	$500
3/31/89		50 Sf	$25	$525
6/30/89		50 Sf	$24	$549
9/30/89		50 Sf	$25	$574
12/31/89		50 Sf	$26	$600

(ii) On January 1, 1990, X withdraws 500 Swiss francs from the account. X may determine his basis in the Swiss francs by multiplying the aggregate U.S. dollar basis of Swiss francs in the account by a fraction the numerator of which is the number of Swiss francs withdrawn from the account and the denominator is the total number of Swiss francs in the account. Under this method, X's basis in the 500 Swiss francs is $250 computed as follows:

$$\frac{500 \text{ Sf}}{1200 \text{ Sf}} \times \$600 = \$250$$

(iii) X's basis in the Swiss francs remaining in the account is $350 ($600 − $250). X must use this method consistently from year to year with respect to withdrawals of nonfunctional currency from all of X's accounts.

Reg. § 1.988-2(a)(2)(iii)(B)(2)

(iv) *Purchase and sale of stock or securities traded on an established securities market by cash basis taxpayer.*—(A) *Amount realized.*—If stock or securities traded on an established securities market are sold by a cash basis taxpayer for nonfunctional currency, the amount realized with respect to the stock or securities (as determined on the trade date) shall be computed by translating the units of nonfunctional currency received into functional currency at the spot rate on the settlement date of the sale. This rule applies notwithstanding that the stock or securities are treated as disposed of on a date other than the settlement date under another section of the Code. See section 453(k).

(B) *Basis.*—If stock or securities traded on an established securities market are purchased by a cash basis taxpayer for nonfunctional currency, the basis of the stock or securities shall be determined by translating the units of nonfunctional currency paid into functional currency at the spot rate on the settlement date of the purchase.

(C) *Example.*—The following example illustrates the provisions of this paragraph (a)(2)(iv).

Example. On November 1, 1989 (the trade date), X, a calendar year cash basis U.S. individual, purchases stock for £100 for settlement on November 5, 1989. On November 1, 1989, the spot value of the £100 is $140. On November 5, 1989, X purchases £100 for $141 which X uses to pay for the stock. X's basis in the stock is $141. On December 30, 1990 (the trade date), X sells the stock for £110 for settlement on January 5, 1991. On December 30, 1990, the spot value of £110 is $165. On January 5, 1991, X transfers the stock and receives £110 which, translated at the spot rate, equal $166. Under section 453(k), the stock is considered disposed of on December 30, 1990. The amount realized with respect to such disposition is the value of the £110 on January 5, 1991 ($166). Accordingly, X's gain realized on December 30, 1990, from the disposition of the stock is $25 ($166 amount realized less $141 basis). X's basis in the £110 received from the sale of the stock is $166.

(v) *Purchase and sale of stock or securities traded on an established securities market by accrual basis taxpayer.*—For taxable years beginning after March 17, 1992, an accrual basis taxpayer may elect to apply the rules of paragraph (a)(2)(iv) of this section. The election shall be made by filing a statement with the taxpayer's first return in which the election is effective clearly indicating that the election has been made. A method so elected must be applied consistently from year to year and cannot be changed without the consent of the Commissioner.

(b) *Translation of interest income or expense and determination of exchange gain or loss with respect to debt instruments.*—(1) *Translation of interest income received with respect to a nonfunctional currency demand account.*—Interest income received with respect to a demand account with a bank or other financial institution which is denominated in (or the payments of which are determined by reference to) a nonfunctional currency shall be translated into functional currency at the spot rate on the date received or accrued or pursuant to any reasonable spot rate convention consistently applied by the taxpayer to all taxable years and to all accounts denominated in nonfunctional currency in the same financial institution. For example, a taxpayer may translate interest income received with respect to a demand account on the last day of each month of the taxable year, on the last day of each quarter of the taxable year, on the last day of each half of the taxable year, or on the last day of the taxable year. No exchange gain or loss is realized upon the receipt or accrual of interest income with respect to a demand account subject to this paragraph (b)(1).

(2) *Translation of nonfunctional currency interest income or expense received or paid with respect to a debt instrument described in §1.988-1(a)(1)(ii) and (2)(i).*—(i) *Scope.*—(A) *In general.*—Paragraph (b) of this section only applies to debt instruments described in §1.988-1(a) (1)(ii) and (2)(i) where all payments are denominated in, or determined with reference to, a single nonfunctional currency. Except as provided in paragraph (b)(2)(i)(B) of this section, this paragraph (b) shall not apply to contingent payment debt instruments.

(B) *Nonfunctional currency contingent payment debt instruments.*—(1) *Operative rules.*—See §1.988-6 for rules applicable to contingent payment debt instruments for which one or more payments are denominated in, or determined by reference to, a nonfunctional currency.

(2) *Certain instruments are not contingent payment debt instruments.*—For purposes of sections 163(e) and 1271 through 1275 and the regulations thereunder, a debt instrument does not provide for contingent payments merely because the instrument is denominated in, or all payments of which are determined with reference to, a single nonfunctional currency. See §1.988-6 for the treatment of nonfunctional currency contingent payment debt instruments.

(ii) *Determination and translation of interest income or expense.*—(A) *In general.*—Interest income or expense on a debt instrument described in paragraph (b)(2)(i) of this section (including original issue discount determined in accordance with sections 1271 through 1275 and 163(e) as adjusted for acquisition premium under section 1272(a)(7), and acquisition discount determined in accordance with sections 1281 through 1283) shall be determined in units of nonfunctional currency and translated into functional currency as provided in paragraphs (b)(2)(ii)(B) and (C) of this section. For purposes of sections 483, 1273(b)(5) and 1274, the nonfunctional currency in which an instrument is denominated (or by reference to which payments are determined) shall be considered money.

(B) *Translation of interest income or expense that is not required to be accrued prior to receipt or payment.*—With respect to an instrument described in paragraph (b)(2)(i) of this section, interest income or expense received or paid that is not required to be accrued by the taxpayer prior to receipt or payment shall be translated at the spot rate on the date of receipt or payment. No exchange gain or loss is realized with respect to the receipt or payment of such interest income or expense (other than the exchange gain or loss that might be realized under paragraph (a) of this section upon the disposition of the nonfunctional currency so received or paid).

(C) *Translation of interest income or expense that is required to be accrued prior to receipt or payment.*—With respect to an instrument described in paragraph (b)(2)(i) of this section, interest income or expense that is required to be accrued prior to receipt or payment (*e.g.,* under section 1272, 1281 or 163(e) or because the taxpayer uses an accrual method of accounting) shall be translated at the average rate (or other rate specified in paragraph (b)(2) (iii)(B) of this section) for the interest accrual period or, with respect to an interest accrual period that spans two taxable years, at the average rate (or other rate specified in paragraph (b)(2)(iii)(B) of this section) for the partial period within the taxable year. See paragraphs (b)(3) and (4) of this section for the determination of exchange gain or loss on the receipt or payment of accrued interest income or expense.

(iii) *Determination of average rate or other accrual convention.*—(A) *In general.*—For purposes of this paragraph (b), the average rate for an accrual period (or partial period) shall be a simple average of the spot exchange rates for each business day of such period or other average exchange rate for the period reasonably derived and consistently applied by the taxpayer.

(B) *Election to use spot accrual convention.*—For taxable years beginning after March 17, 1992, a taxpayer may elect to translate interest income and expense at the spot rate on the last day of the interest accrual period (and in the case of a partial accrual period, the spot rate on the last day of the taxable year). If the last day of the interest accrual period is within five business days of the date of receipt or payment, the taxpayer may translate interest income or expense at the spot rate on the date of receipt or payment. The election shall be made by filing a statement with the taxpayer's first return in which the election is effective clearly indicating that the election has been made. A method so elected must be applied consistently to all debt instruments

from year to year and cannot be changed without the consent of the Commissioner.

(3) *Exchange gain or loss recognized by the holder with respect to accrued interest income.*—The holder of a debt instrument described in paragraph (b)(2)(i) of this section shall realize exchange gain or loss with respect to accrued interest income on the date such accrued interest income is received or the instrument is disposed of (including a deemed disposition under section 1001 that results from a material change in terms of the instrument). Except as otherwise provided in this paragraph (b) (*e.g.,* paragraph (b)(8) of this section), exchange gain or loss realized with respect to accrued interest income shall be recognized in accordance with the applicable recognition provisions of the Internal Revenue Code. The amount of exchange gain or loss so realized with respect to accrued interest income is determined for each accrual period by—

(i) Translating the units of nonfunctional currency interest income received with respect to such accrual period (as determined under the ordering rules of paragraph (b)(7) of this section) into functional currency at the spot rate on the date the interest income is received or the instrument is disposed of (or deemed disposed of), and

(ii) Subtracting from such amount the amount computed by translating the units of nonfunctional currency interest income accrued with respect to such income received at the average rate (or other rate specified in paragraph (b)(2) (iii)(B) of this section) for the accrual period.

(4) *Exchange gain or loss recognized by the obligor with respect to accrued interest expense.*—The obligor under a debt instrument described in paragraph (b)(2)(i) of this section shall realize exchange gain or loss with respect to accrued interest expense on the date such accrued interest expense is paid or the obligation to make payments is transferred or extinguished (including a deemed disposition under section 1001 that results from a material change in terms of the instrument). Except as otherwise provided in this paragraph (b) (*e.g.,* paragraph (b)(8) of this section), exchange gain or loss realized with respect to accrued interest expense shall be recognized in accordance with the applicable recognition provisions of the Internal Revenue Code. The amount of exchange gain or loss so realized with respect to accrued interest expense is determined for each accrual period by—

(i) Translating the units of nonfunctional currency interest expense accrued with respect to the amount of interest paid into functional currency at the average rate (or other rate specified in paragraph (b)(2)(iii)(B) of this section) for such accrual period; and

(ii) Subtracting from such amount the amount computed by translating the units of nonfunctional currency interest paid (or, if the obligation to make payments is extinguished or transferred, the units accrued) with respect to such accrual period (as determined under the ordering rules in paragraph (b)(7) of this section) into functional currency at the spot rate on the date payment is made or the obligation is transferred or extinguished (or deemed extinguished).

(5) *Exchange gain or loss recognized by the holder of a debt instrument with respect to principal.*—The holder of a debt instrument described in paragraph (b)(2)(i) of this section shall realize exchange gain or loss with respect to the principal amount of such instrument on the date principal (determined under the ordering rules of paragraph (b)(7) of this section) is received from the obligor or the instrument is disposed of (including a deemed disposition under section 1001 that results from a material change in terms of the instrument). For purposes of computing exchange gain or loss, the principal amount of a debt instrument is the holder's purchase price in units of nonfunctional currency. See paragraph (b)(10) of this section for rules regarding the amortization of that part of the principal amount that represents bond premium and the computation of exchange gain or loss thereon. If, however, the holder acquired the instrument in a transaction in which exchange gain or loss was realized but not recognized by the transferor, the nonfunctional currency principal amount of the instrument with respect to the holder shall be the same as that of the transferor. Except as otherwise provided in this paragraph (b) (*e.g.*, paragraph (b)(8) of this section), exchange gain or loss realized with respect to such principal amount shall be recognized in accordance with the applicable recognition provisions of the Internal Revenue Code. The amount of exchange gain or loss so realized by the holder with respect to principal is determined by—

(i) Translating the units of nonfunctional currency principal at the spot rate on the date payment is received or the instrument is disposed of (or deemed disposed of); and

(ii) Subtracting from such amount the amount computed by translating the units of nonfunctional currency principal at the spot rate on the date the holder (or a transferor from whom the nonfunctional principal amount is carried over) acquired the instrument (is deemed to acquire the instrument).

(6) *Exchange gain or loss recognized by the obligor of a debt instrument with respect to principal.*— The obligor under a debt instrument described in paragraph (b)(2)(i) of this section shall realize exchange gain or loss with respect to the principal amount of such instrument on the date principal (determined under the ordering rules of paragraph (b)(7) of this section) is paid or the obligation to make payments is transferred or extinguished (including a deemed disposition under section 1001 that results from a material change in terms of the instrument). For purposes

of computing exchange gain or loss, the principal amount of a debt instrument is the amount received by the obligor for the debt instrument in units of nonfunctional currency. See paragraph (b)(10) of this section for rules regarding the amortization of that part of the principal amount that represents bond premium and the computation of exchange gain or loss thereon. If, however, the obligor became the obligor in a transaction in which exchange gain or loss was realized but not recognized by the transferor, the nonfunctional currency principal amount of the instrument with respect to such obligor shall be the same as that of the transferor. Except as otherwise provided in this paragraph (b) (*e.g.*, paragraph (b)(8) of this section), exchange gain or loss realized with respect to such principal shall be recognized in accordance with the applicable recognition provisions of the Internal Revenue Code. The amount of exchange gain or loss so realized by the obligor is determined by—

(i) Translating the units of nonfunctional currency principal at the spot rate on the date the obligor (or a transferor from whom the principal amount is carried over) became the obligor (or is deemed to have become the obligor); and

(ii) Subtracting from such amount the amount computed by translating the units of nonfunctional currency principal at the spot rate on the date payment is made or the obligation is transferred or extinguished (or deemed extinguished).

(7) *Payment ordering rules.*—(i) *Debt instruments subject to the rules of sections 163(e), or 1271 through 1288.*—In the case of a debt instrument described in paragraph (b)(2)(i) of this section that is subject to the rules of sections 163(e), or 1272 through 1288, units of nonfunctional currency (or an amount determined with reference to nonfunctional currency) received or paid with respect to such debt instrument shall be treated first as a receipt or payment of periodic interest under the principles of section 1273 and the regulations thereunder, second as a receipt or payment of original issue discount to the extent accrued as of the date of the receipt or payment, and finally as a receipt or payment of principal. Units of nonfunctional currency (or an amount determined with reference to nonfunctional currency) treated as a receipt or payment of original issue discount under the preceding sentence are attributed to the earliest accrual period in which original issue discount has accrued and to which prior receipts or payments have not been attributed. No portion thereof shall be treated as prepaid interest. These rules are illustrated by *Example 10* of paragraph (b)(9) of this section.

(ii) *Other debt instruments.*—In the case of a debt instrument described in paragraph (b)(2)(i) of this section that is not subject to the rules of section 163(e) or 1272 through 1288, whether units of nonfunctional currency (or an amount determined with reference to nonfunctional currency) received or paid with respect to such debt instrument are treated as interest or principal shall be determined under section 163 or other applicable section of the Code.

(8) *Limitation of exchange gain or loss on payment or disposition of a debt instrument.*—When a debt instrument described in paragraph (b)(2)(i) of this section is paid or disposed of, or when the obligation to make payments thereunder is satisfied by another person, or extinguished or assumed by another person, exchange gain or loss is computed with respect to both principal and any accrued interest (including original issue discount), as provided in paragraph (b)(3) through (7) of this section. However, pursuant to section 988(b)(1) and (2), the sum of any exchange gain or loss with respect to the principal and interest of any such debt instrument shall be realized only to the extent of the total gain or loss realized on the transaction. The gain or loss realized shall be recognized in accordance with the general principles of the Code. See *Examples 3, 4* and *6* of paragraph (b)(9) of this section.

(9) *Examples.*—The preceding provisions are illustrated in the following examples. The examples assume that any transaction involving an individual is a section 988 transaction.

Example 1. (i) X is an individual on the cash method of accounting with the dollar as his functional currency. On January 1, 1992, X converts $13,000 to 10,000 British pounds (£) at the spot rate of £1 = $1.30 and loans the £10,000 to Y for 3 years. The terms of the loan provide that Y will make interest payments of £1,000 on December 31 of 1992, 1993, and 1994, and will repay X's £10,000 principal on December 31, 1994. Assume the spot rates for the pertinent dates are as follows:

Date	Spot rate (pounds to dollars)
January 1, 1992	£1 = $1.30
December 31, 1992	£1 = $1.35
December 31, 1993	£1 = $1.40
December 31, 1994	£1 = $1.45

(ii) Under paragraph (b)(2)(ii)(B) of this section, X will translate the £1,000 interest payments at the spot rate on the date received. Accordingly, X will have interest income of $1,350 in 1992, $1,400 in 1993, and $1,450 in 1994. Because X is a cash basis taxpayer, X does not realize exchange gain or loss on the receipt of interest income.

(iii) Under paragraph (b)(5) of this section, X will realize exchange gain upon repayment of the £10,000 principal amount determined by translating the £10,000 at the spot rate on the date it is received (£10,000 × $1.45 = $14,500) and subtracting from such amount, the amount determined by translating the £10,000 at the spot rate on the date the loan was made (£10,000 ×

$1.30 = $13,000). Accordingly, X will realize an exchange gain of $1,500 on the repayment of the loan on December 31, 1994.

Example 2. (i) Assume the same facts as in *Example 1* except that X is an accrual method taxpayer and that average rates are as follows:

Accrual Period	Average rate (pounds to dollars)
1992	£1 = $1.32
1993	£1 = $1.37
1994	£1 = $1.42

(ii) Under paragraph (b)(2)(ii)(C) of this section, X will accrue the £1,000 interest payments at the average rate for the accrual period. Accordingly, X will have interest income of $1,320 in 1992, $1,370 in 1993, and $1,420 in 1994. Because X is an accrual basis taxpayer, X determines exchange gain or loss for each interest accrual period by translating the units of nonfunctional currency interest income received with respect to such accrual period at the spot rate on the date received and subtracting the amounts of interest income accrued for such period. Thus, X will realize $90 of exchange gain with respect to interest received under the loan, computed as follows:

Year	Spot Value Interest Received	Accrued Interest @ Avg. Rate	Exch. Gain
1992	$1,350	$1,320	$30
1993	$1,400	$1,370	$30
1994	$1,450	$1,420	$30
TOTAL			$90

(iii) Under paragraph (b)(5) of this section, X will realize exchange gain upon repayment of the £10,000 loan principal determined in the same manner as in *Example 1.* Accordingly, X will realize an exchange gain of $1,500 on the repayment of the loan principal on December 31, 1994.

Example 3. Assume the same facts as in *Example 1* except that X is a calendar year taxpayer on the accrual method of accounting that elects to use a spot rate convention to translate interest income as provided in § 1.988-2(b)(2)(iii)(B). Interest income is received by X on the last day of each accrual period. Under paragraph (b)(2)(ii)(C), X will translate the interest income at the spot rate on the last day of each interest accrual period. Accordingly, X will have interest income of $1,350 in 1992, and $1,400 in 1993, $1,450 in 1994. Because the rate at which the interest income is translated is the same as the rate on the day of receipt, X will not realize any exchange gain or loss with respect to the interest income. Under paragraph (b)(5) of this section, X will realize exchange gain upon repayment of the £10,000 loan principal determined in the same manner as in *Example 1.* Accordingly, X will realize an exchange gain of $1,500 on the repayment of the loan principal on December 31, 1994.

Example 4. Assume the same facts as in *Example 1* except that on December 31, 1993, X sells Y's note for 9,821.13 British pounds (£) after the interest payment. Under paragraph (b)(8) of this section, X will compute exchange gain on the £10,000 principal. The exchange gain is $1,000 [(£10,000 × $1.40) – (£10,000 × $1.30)]. This exchange gain, however, is only realized to the extent of the total gain on the disposition. X's total gain is $749.58 [(£9,821.13 × $1.40) – (£10,000 × $1.30)]. Thus, X will realize $749.58 of exchange gain (and will realize no market loss).

Example 5. (i) The facts are the same as in *Example 1* except that Y becomes insolvent and fails to repay the full £10,000 principal when due. Instead, X and Y agree to compromise the debt for a payment of £8,000 on December 31, 1994. Under paragraph (b)(8) of this section, X will compute exchange gain on the £10,000 originally booked. The exchange gain is $1,500 [(£10,000 × $1.45) – (£10,000 × $1.30) = $1,500]. This exchange gain, however, is only realized to the extent of the total gain on the disposition. X realizes an overall loss on the disposition of $1,400 [(£8,000 × $1.45) – (£10,000 × $1.30) = ($1,400)]. Thus, X will realize no exchange gain (and a $1400 market loss).

(ii) If the exchange rate on December 31, 1994, were £1 = $1.25, rather than £1 = $1.45, X would compute exchange loss under paragraph (b)(8) of this section, on the £10,000 originally booked. The exchange loss would be $500 [(£10,000 × $1.25) – (£10,000 × $1.30) = ($500)]. X's total loss on the disposition would be $3,000 [(£8,000 × $1.25) – £10,000 × $1.30) = ($3,000)]. Thus, X would realize $500 of exchange loss and a $2,500 market loss on the disposition.

Example 6. (i) X is an individual with the dollar as his functional currency. X is on the cash method of accounting. On January 1, 1989, X borrows 10,000 British pounds (£) from Y, an unrelated person. The terms of the loan provide that X will make interest payments of £1,200 on December 31 of 1989 and 1990 and will repay Y's £10,000 principal on December 31, 1990. The spot rates for the pertinent dates are as follows:

DATE	SPOT RATE (pounds to dollars)
January 1, 1989	1 = $1.50
December 31, 1989	1 = $1.60
December 31, 1990	1 = $1.70

Assume that the basis of the £1,200 paid as interest by X on December 31, 1989 is $2,000, the basis of the £1,200 paid as interest by X on December 31, 1990, is $2,020 and the basis of the £10,000 principal paid by X on December 31, 1990 is $16,000.

(ii) Under paragraph (b)(2)(ii)(B) of this section, X translates the £1,200 interest payments at the spot rate on the day paid. Thus, X paid $1,920 (£1,200 × $1.60) of interest on December 31, 1989 and $2,040 (£1,200 × $1.70) of interest on

December 31, 1990. In addition, X will realize exchange gain or loss on the disposition of the £1,200 on December 31, 1989 and 1990, under paragraph (a) of this section. Pursuant to paragraph (a)(2) of this section, X will realize an exchange loss of $80 [(£1,200 × $1.60) – $2,000] on December 31, 1989 and exchange gain of $20 [(£1,200 × $1.70) – $2,020] on December 31, 1990.

(iii) Under paragraph (b)(6) of this section, X will realize exchange loss on December 31, 1990 upon repayment of the £10,000 principal amount determined by translating the £10,000 received at the spot rate on January 1, 1989 (£10,000 × $1.50 = $15,000) and subtracting from such amount, the amount determined by translating the £ 10,000 paid at the spot rate on December 31, 1990 (£10,000 × $1.70 = $17,000). Thus, under paragraph (b)(6) of this section, X has an exchange loss with respect to the £10,000 principal of $2,000. Further, under paragraph (a)(2) of this section, X will realize an exchange gain upon disposition of the £10,000 on December 31, 1990. Under paragraph (a)(2) of this section, X will subtract his adjusted basis in the £10,000 ($16,000) from the amount realized upon the disposition of the £10,000 (£10,000 × $1.70 = $17,000) resulting in a gain of $1,000. Accordingly, X's combined exchange gain and loss realized on December 31, 1990 with respect to the repayment of the £10,000 is a $1,000 exchange loss.

Example 7. (i) X is a calendar year corporation on the accrual method of accounting and with the dollar as its functional currency. On January 1, 1989, X purchases at original issue for 82.64 Canadian dollars (C$) M corporation's 2 year note maturing on December 31, 1990, at a stated redemption price of C$ 100. The yield to maturity in Canadian dollars is 10 percent and the accrual period is the one year period beginning January 1 and ending December 31. The note has C$17.36 of original issue discount. Assume that the spot rates are as follows: C$1 = U.S.$.72 on January 1, 1989; C$1 = U.S.$.80 on January 1, 1990; C$1 = U.S.$.82 on December 31, 1990. Assume further that the average rate for 1989 is C$1 = U.S.$.76 and for 1990 is C$1 = U.S.$.81.

(ii) Under paragraph (b)(2)(ii)(A) of this section, X will determine its interest income in Canadian dollars. Accordingly, under section 1272, X must take into account original issue discount in the amount of C$8.26 on December 31, 1989 and C$9.10 on December 31, 1990. Pursuant to paragraph (b)(2)(ii)(C) of this section, X will translate these amounts into U.S. dollars at the average exchange rate for the relevant accrual period. Thus, the amount of interest income taken into account in 1989 is U.S.$6.28 (C$8.26 × U.S.$.76) and in 1990 is U.S.$7.37 (C$9.10 × U.S.$.81). Pursuant to paragraph (b)(3)(ii) of this section, X will realize exchange gain or loss with respect to the accrued interest determined for each accrual period by translating the Canadian dollars received with respect to such accrual period into U.S. dollars at the spot rate on the date the interest is received and subtracting from that amount the amount accrued in U.S. dollars. Thus, the amount of exchange gain realized on December 31, 1990, is U.S.$.58 (U.S.$.49 from 1989 + U.S.$.09 from 1990). Pursuant to paragraph (b)(5) of this section, X shall realize exchange gain or loss with respect to the principal (C$82.64) on December 31, 1990, computed by translating the C$82.64 at the spot rate on December 31, 1990 (U.S.$67.76) and subtracting the C$82.64 translated at the spot rate on January 1, 1989 (U.S.$59.50) for an exchange gain of U.S.$8.26. Thus, X's combined exchange gain is U.S.$8.84 (U.S.$.49 + U.S.$.09 + U.S.$8.26).

(iii) Assume instead that on January 1, 1990, X sells the note for C$86.95, which it immediately converts to U.S. dollars. X's exchange gain is computed under paragraph (b)(8) of this section with reference to the nonfunctional currency denominated principal amount (C$82.64) and the nonfunctional currency denominated accrued original issue discount (C$8.26). X will compute an exchange gain of U.S.$6.61 with respect to the issue price [(C$82.64 × U.S.$.80) − (C$82.64 × U.S.$.72)] and an exchange gain of U.S.$.33 with respect to the accrued original issue discount [(C$8.26 × U.S.$.80) − (C$8.26 × U.S.$.76)]. Accordingly, prior to the application of paragraph (b)(8) of this section, X's total exchange gain is U.S.$6.94 (U.S.$6.61 + U.S.$.33), and X's market loss is U.S.$3.16 [(C$90.90 − C$86.95) × U.S.$.80]. Pursuant to paragraph (b)(8) of this section, however, X's market loss on the note of U.S.$3.16 is netted against X's exchange gain of U.S.$6.94, resulting in a realized exchange gain of U.S.$3.78 and no market loss.

Example 8. (i) The facts are the same as in *Example 7* (i) except that on January 1, 1990, X contributes the M corporation note to Y, a wholly-owned U.S. subsidiary of X with the dollar as its functional currency, and Y collects C$100 from M corporation at maturity on December 31, 1990, when the spot rate is C$1= U.S.$.82. The transfer of the note from X to Y qualifies for nonrecognition of gain under section 351(a). On December 31, 1990, Y includes C$9.10 of accrued interest in income which translated at the average exchange rate of C$1 = U.S.$.81 for the year results in U.S.$7.37 of interest income.

(ii) Y's exchange gain is computed under paragraph (b)(3) of this section with respect to accrued interest income and paragraph (b)(5) of this section with respect to the nonfunctional currency principal amount. Under paragraph (b)(3) of this section, Y will realize exchange gain or loss for each accrual period computed by translating the units of nonfunctional currency interest income received with respect to such accrual period at the spot rate on the day received and subtracting the amounts of interest income accrued for such period. Thus, Y will realize $.49 of exchange gain with respect to original issue discount accrued in 1989 [(C$8.26 × U.S.$.82) − (C$8.26 × U.S.$.76) = U.S.$.49] and

$.09 of exchange gain with respect to original issue discount accrued in 1990 [(C$9.10 × U.S.$.82) − (C$9.10 × U.S.$.81) = $.09].

(iii) Pursuant to paragraph (b)(5) of this section, the nonfunctional currency principal amount of the M bond in the hands of Y is C$82.64, the amount carried over from X, the transferor. Y's exchange gain with respect to the nonfunctional currency principal amount is $8.26 [(C$82.64 × U.S.$.82) − (C$82.64 × U.S.$.72) = U.S.$8.26]. Accordingly, Y's combined exchange gain is U.S.$8.84 (U.S.$.49 + U.S.$.09 + $8.26). Because the amount realized in Canadian dollars equals the adjusted issue price (C$100) on retirement of the M note, there is no market loss, and the netting rule of paragraph (b)(8) of this section does not limit realization of the exchange gain.

Example 9. (i) X is a calendar year corporation on the accrual method of accounting and with the dollar as its functional currency. X elects to use the spot rate convention to translate interest income as provided in paragraph (b)(2)(iii)(B) of this section. On January 31, 1992, X loans £1000 to Y, an unrelated person. Under the terms of the loan, Y will pay X interest of £50 on July 31, 1992, and January 31, 1993, and will repay the £ 1000 principal on January 31, 1993. Assume the following spot exchange rates:

DATE	SPOT RATE (pounds to dollars)
January 31, 1992	£1 = $1.50
July 31, 1992	£1 = $1.55
December 31, 1992	£1 = $1.60
January 31, 1993	£1 = $1.61

(ii) Under paragraph (b)(2)(ii)(C) of this section, X will translate the interest income at the spot rate on the last day of each interest accrual period (and in the case of a partial accrual period, at the spot rate on the last day of the taxable year). Accordingly, X will have interest income of $77.50 (£50 × $1.55) on July 31, 1992. Assuming under X's method of accounting that interest is accrued daily, X will accrue $66.50 (153/184 × £ 50) × $1.60) of interest income on December 31, 1992. On January 31, 1993, X will have interest income of $13.60 ((31/184 × £50) × $1.61). Because the rate at which the interest income is translated is the same as the rate on the day of receipt, X will not realize any exchange gain or loss with respect to the interest income received on July 31, 1992. However, X will realize exchange gain on the £41.50 (153/184 ×£50) of accrued interest income of $.41 [(£41.50 ×$1.61) − (£41.50 × $1.60) = $.41].

(iii) Under paragraph (b)(5) of this section, X will realize exchange gain upon repayment of the £ 100 principal amount determined by translating the £100 at the spot rate on the date it is received (£100 × $1.61 = $161.00) and subtracting from such amount, the amount determined by translating the £100 at the spot rate on the date the loan was made (£100 × $1.50 = $150.00). Accordingly, X will realize an exchange gain of $11 on the repayment of the loan on January 31, 1993.

Reg. § 1.988-2(b)(9)

Example 10. (i) X, a cash basis taxpayer with the dollar as its functional currency, has the calendar year as its taxable year. On January 1, 1992, X purchases at original issue for 65.88 British pounds (£) M corporation's 5-year bond maturing on December 31, 1996, having a stated redemption price at maturity of £100. The bond provides for annual payments of interest in pounds of 1 pound per year on December 31 of each year. The bond has 34.12 British pounds of original issue discount. The yield to maturity is 10 percent in British pounds and the accrual period is the one year period beginning January 1 and ending December 31 of each calendar year.

The amount of original issue discount is determined in pounds for each accrual period by multiplying the adjusted issue price expressed in pounds by the yield and subtracting from such amount the periodic interest payments expressed in pounds for such period. The periodic interest payments are translated at the spot rate on the payment date (December 31 of each year). The original issue discount is translated at the average rate for the accrual period (January 1 through December 31). The following chart describes the determination of interest income with respect to the facts presented and provides other pertinent information.

Table 1

1 Year (Dec. 31)	2 Periodic interest payments in pounds for the accrual period	3 Original issue discount in pounds for the accrual period	4 Issue price or adjusted issue price in pounds	5 Assumed spot rate on Dec. 31 (pounds to dollars)	6 Assumed average rate for accrual period (pounds to dollars)	7 Periodic interest payments in pounds multiplied by spot rate on the date of payment (column 2 times column 5)	8 Original issue discount in pounds multiplied by the average rate for the accrual period (column 3 times column 6)	9 Total interest income in dollars (column 7 plus column 8)	10 Adjusted issue price in dollars
Issue Date			65.88	1 = $1.20					$79.06
1992	1	5.59	71.47	1 = $1.30	1 = $1.25	$1.30	$6.99	$8.29	$86.05
1993	1	6.15	77.62	1 = $1.40	1 = $1.35	$1.40	$8.30	$9.70	$94.35
1994	1	6.76	84.38	1 = $1.50	1 = $1.45	$1.50	$9.80	$11.30	$104.15
1995	1	7.44	91.82	1 = $1.60	1 = $1.55	$1.60	$11.53	$13.13	$115.68
1996	1	8.18	100.00	1 = $1.70	1 = $1.65	$1.70	$13.50	$15.20	$129.18

(ii) Because X is a cash basis taxpayer, X does not realize exchange gain or loss on the receipt of the £1 periodic interest payments. However, X will realize exchange gain on December 31, 1996 totaling $7.88 with respect to the original issue discount. Exchange gain is determined for each interest accrual period by translating the units of nonfunctional currency interest income received with respect to such accrual period at the spot rate on the date received and subtracting from such amount, the amount computed by translating the units of nonfunctional currency interest income accrued for such period at the average rate for the period. The following chart illustrates this computation:

Table 2

1 Year	2 OID accrued in pounds for each accrual period	3 Assumed spot rate on date payment received (pounds to dollars)	4 Interest received times spot rate on the date received (col. 2 times col. 3)	5 Assumed average rate for accrual period (pounds to dollars)	6 OID in pounds times the average rate for the accrual period (col. 2 times col. 5)	7 Exchange gain or loss (col. 4 less col. 6)
1992	5.59	1 = $1.70	$9.50	1 = $1.25	$6.99	$2.51
1993	6.15	1 = $1.70	$10.46	1 = $1.35	$8.30	$2.16
1994	6.76	1 = $1.70	$11.49	1 = $1.45	$9.80	$1.69
1995	7.44	1 = $1.70	$12.65	1 = $1.55	$11.53	$1.12
1996	8.18	1 = $1.70	$13.90	1 = $1.65	$13.50	$.40
					TOTAL	$7.88

Reg. § 1.988-2(b)(9)

(iii) X will also realize exchange gain with respect to the principal of the loan (*i.e.*, the issue price of 65.88 British pounds) on December 31, 1996 computed by translating the units of nonfunctional currency principal received at the spot rate on the date principal is received (65.88 British pounds × $1.70 = $112.00) and subtracting from such amount, the units of nonfunctional currency principal received translated at the spot rate on the date the instrument was acquired (65.88 British pounds × $1.20 = $79.06). Accordingly, X's exchange gain on the principal is $32.94 and X's total exchange gain with respect to the accrued interest and principal is $40.82. It should be noted that, under this fact pattern, the total exchange gain may be determined in an alternative fashion. Exchange gain may be computed by subtracting the adjusted issue price in dollars at maturity ($129.18—see column 10 of Table 1) from the amount computed by multiplying the stated redemption price at maturity in pounds times the spot rate on the maturity date (£100 × $1.70 = $170), which equals $40.82.

Example 11. (i) The facts are the same as in *Example 10* except that X makes an election under paragraph (b)(2)(iii) of this section to translate accrued interest on the last day of the accrual period. Accordingly, columns 8, 9 and 10 in Table 1 would change as follows:

1	8	9	10
Year (Dec. 31)	Original issue discount in pounds multiplied by the spot rate on last day of accrual period (Dec. 31)	Total interest income in dollars (column 7 plus column 8)	Adjusted issue price in dollars
			$79.06
1992	$7.27	$8.57	$87.63
1993	$8.61	$10.01	$97.64
1994	$10.14	$11.64	$109.28
1995	$11.90	$13.50	$122.78
1996	$13.91	$15.61	$138.39

(ii) Because X is a cash basis taxpayer, X does not realize exchange gain or loss on the receipt of the £1 periodic interest payments. However, X will realize exchange gain on December 31, 1993 totaling $6.18 with respect to the original issue discount. Exchange gain is determined for each interest accrual period by translating the units of nonfunctional currency interest income received with respect to such accrual period at the spot rate on the date received and subtracting from such amount, the amount computed by translating the units of nonfunctional currency interest income accrued for such period at the spot rate on the last day of the accrual period. Accordingly, columns 5, 6 and 7 of Table 2 would change as follows:

1	5	6	7
Year	Spot rate on last day of accrual period	OID in pounds times the spot rate on the last day of the accrual period (col. 2 times col. 3)	Exchange gain or loss (col. 4 less col. 6)
1992	$1.30	$7.27	$2.23
1993	$1.40	$8.61	$1.85
1994	$1.50	$10.14	$1.35
1995	$1.60	$11.90	$0.75
1996	$1.70	$13.90	$0.00
			$6.18

(iii) X will realize exchange gain with respect to the principal amount of the loan as provided in the preceding example.

Example 12. (i) C is a corporation that is a calendar year accrual method taxpayer with the dollar as its functional currency. On January 1, 1989, C lends 100 British pounds (£) in exchange for a note under the terms of which C will receive two equal payments of £57.62 on December 31, 1989, and December 31, 1990. Each payment of £57.62 represents the annual payment necessary to amortize the £100 principal amount at a rate of 10% compounded annually over a two year period. The following tables reflect the amounts of principal and interest that compose each payment and assumptions as to the relevant exchange rates:

Date	Principal	Interest
12/31/89	£47.62	£10.00
12/31/90	£52.38	£5.24

Date	Spot Rate £1 =	Average Rate for Year Ending
1/01/89	$1.30	
12/31/89	$1.40	$1.35
12/31/90	$1.50	$1.45

(ii) Because each interest payment is equal to the product of the outstanding principal balance of the obligation and a single fixed rate of interest, each stated interest payment constitutes periodic interest under the principles of section 1273. Accordingly, there is no original issue discount.

(iii) Because C is an accrual basis taxpayer, C will translate the interest income at the average rate for the annual accrual period pursuant to paragraph (b)(2)(ii)(C) of this section. Thus, C's interest income is $13.50 (£10.00 × $1.35) in 1989, and $7.60 (£5.24 × $1.45) in 1990. C will realize exchange gain or loss upon receipt of accrued interest computed in accordance with paragraph (b)(3) of this section. Thus, C will realize exchange gain in the amount of $ .50 [(£10.00 × $1.40) – $13.50] in 1989, and $ .26 [(£5.24 × $1.50) – $7.60] in 1990.

(iv) In addition, C will realize exchange gain or loss upon the receipt of principal each year computed under paragraph (b)(5) of this section. Thus, C will realize exchange gain in the amount of $4.76 [(£47.62 × $1.40) – (£47.62 × $1.30)] in 1989, and $10.48 [(£52.38 × $1.50) – (£52.38 × $1.30)] in 1990.

(10) *Treatment of bond premium.*—(i) *In general.*—Amortizable bond premium on a bond described in paragraph (b)(2)(i) of this section shall be computed in the units of nonfunctional currency in which the bond is denominated (or in which the payments are determined). Amortizable bond premium properly taken into account under section 171 or §1.61-12 (or the successor provision thereof) shall reduce interest income or expense in units of nonfunctional currency. Exchange gain or loss is realized with respect to bond premium described in the preceding sentence by treating the portion of premium amortized with respect to any period as a return of principal. With respect to a holder that does not elect to amortize bond premium under section 171, the amount of bond premium will constitute a market loss when the bond matures. See paragraph (b)(8) of this section. The principles set forth in this paragraph (b)(10) shall apply to determine the treatment of acquisition premium described in section 1272(a)(7).

(ii) *Example.*—The following example illustrates the provisions of this paragraph (b)(10).

Example. (A) X is an individual on the cash method of accounting with the dollar as his functional currency. On January 1, 1989, X purchases Y corporation's note for 107.99 British pounds (£) from Z, an unrelated party. The note has an issue price of £100, a stated redemption price at maturity of £100, pays interest in pounds at the rate of 10% compounded annually, and matures on December 31, 1993. X elects to amortize the bond premium of £7.99 under the rules of section 171. Pursuant to paragraph (b)(10)(i) of

this section, bond premium is determined and amortized in British pounds. Assume the amortization schedule is as follows:

Year Ending 12/31	Bond Premium Amortized	Unamortized Premium Plus Principal £107.99	Interest
1989	£1.36	£106.63	£8.64
1990	£1.47	£105.16	£8.53
1991	£1.59	£103.57	£8.41
1992	£1.71	£101.86	£8.29
1993	£1.85	£100.00	£8.25

(B) The bond premium reduces X's pound interest income under the note. For example, the £10 stated interest payment made in 1989 is reduced by £1.36 of bond premium, and the resulting £8.64 interest income is translated into dollars at the spot rate on December 31, 1989. Exchange gain or loss is realized on the £1.36 bond premium based on the difference between the spot rates on January 1, 1989, the date the premium is paid to acquire the bond, and December 31, 1989, the date the bond premium is returned as part of the stated interest. The £1.36 bond premium reduces the unamortized premium plus principal to £106.63 (£107.99 – £1.36). On December 31, 1993, when the bond matures and the £7.99 of bond premium has been fully amortized, X will realize exchange gain or loss with respect to the remaining purchase price of £100.

(11) *Market discount.*—(i) *In general.*—Market discount as defined in section 1278(a)(2) shall be determined in units of nonfunctional currency in which the market discount bond is denominated (or in which the payments are determined). Accrued market discount (other than market discount currently included in income pursuant to section 1278(b)) shall be translated into functional currency at the spot rate on the date the market discount bond is disposed of. No part of such accrued market discount is treated as exchange gain or loss. Accrued market discount currently includible in income pursuant to section 1278(b) shall be translated into functional currency at the average exchange rate for the accrual period. Exchange gain or loss with respect to accrued market discount currently includible in income under section 1278(b) shall be determined in accordance with paragraph (b)(3) of this section relating to accrued interest income.

(ii) *Example.*—The following example illustrates the provisions of this paragraph (b)(11).

Example—(A) X is a calendar year corporation with the U.S. dollar as its functional currency. On January 1, 1990, X purchases a bond of M corporation for 96,530 British pounds (£). The bond, which was issued on January 1, 1989, has an issue price of £100,000, a stated redemption price at maturity of £100,000, and provides for annual pound payments of interest at 8 percent. The bond matures on December 31, 1991. X purchased the bond at a market discount of 3,470 pounds and did not elect to include the market discount currently in income under section 1278(b). X holds the bond to maturity and on December 31, 1991, receives payment of £100,000 (plus £8,000 interest) when the exchange rate is £1 = $1.50.

(B) Pursuant to paragraph (b)(11) of this section, X computes market discount in units of nonfunctional currency. Thus, the market discount as defined under section 1278(a)(2) is £ 3,470. Accrued market discount (other than market discount currently included in income pursuant to section 1278(b)) is translated at the spot rate on the date the market discount bond is disposed of. Accordingly, X will translate the accrued market discount of £3,470 at the spot rate on December 31, 1991 (£3,470 × $1.50 = $5,205). No exchange gain or loss is realized with respect to the £3,470 of accrued market discount. See paragraphs (b)(3) and (5) of this section for the realization and recognition of exchange gain or loss with respect to accrued interest and principal.

(12) *Tax exempt bonds.*—See § 1.988-3(c)(2), which characterizes exchange loss realized with respect to a nonfunctional currency tax exempt bond as a reduction of interest income.

(13) *Nonfunctional currency debt exchanged for stock of obligor.*—(i) *In general.*—Notwithstanding any other section of the Code other than section 267, 1091 or 1092, exchange gain or loss shall be realized and recognized by the holder and the obligor in accordance with the rules of paragraphs (b)(3) through (7) of this section with respect to the principal and accrued interest of a debt instrument described in paragraph (b)(2)(i) of this section that is acquired by the obligor in exchange for its stock, provided however, that such gain or loss shall be recognized only to the extent of the total gain or loss on the exchange (regardless of whether such gain or loss would otherwise be recognized). This rule shall apply whether the debt instrument is converted into stock according to its terms or exchanged pursuant to a separate agreement between the obligor and the holder. A debt instrument that is acquired by the obligor from a shareholder as a contribution to capital shall be treated for purposes of this section as exchanged for stock, whether or not additional stock is issued.

(ii) *Coordination with section 108.*—Section 988 and this section shall apply before section 108. Exchange gain realized by the obligor on an exchange described in paragraph (b)(13)(i) of this section shall not be treated as discharge of indebtedness income, but shall be considered to reduce the amount of the liability for purposes of computing the obligor's income on the exchange under section 108(e)(4), section 108(e)(6) or section 108(e)(10).

(iii) *Effective date.*—This paragraph (b)(13) shall be effective for exchanges of debt for stock effected after September 21, 1989.

(iv) *Examples.*—The following examples illustrate the operation of this paragraph (b)(13). In each such example, assume that sections 267, 1091 and 1092 do not apply.

Example 1. (i) X is a calendar year U.S. corporation with the U.S. dollar as its functional currency. On January 1, 1990 (the issue date), X acquired a convertible bond maturing on December 31, 1998, issued by Y corporation, a U.K. corporation with the British pound (£) as its functional currency. The issue price of the bond is £ 100,000, the stated redemption price at maturity is £100,000, and the bond provides for annual pound interest payments at the rate of 10%. The terms of the bond also provide that at any time prior to December 31, 1998, the holder may surrender all of his interest in the bond in exchange for 20 shares of Y common stock. On January 1, 1994, X surrenders his interest in the bond for 20 shares of Y common stock. Assume the following: (a) The spot rate on January 1, 1990, is £1 = $1.30, (b) The spot rate on January 1, 1994, is £1 = $1.50, and (c) The 20 shares of Y common stock have a market value of £200,000 on January 1, 1994.

(ii) Pursuant to paragraph (b)(13) of this section, X will realize and recognize exchange gain with respect to the issue price (£100,000) of the bond on January 1, 1994, when the bond is converted to stock. X will compute exchange gain pursuant to paragraph (b)(5) of this section by translating the issue price at the spot rate on the conversion date (£100,000 × $1.50 = $150,000) and subtracting from such amount the issue price translated at the spot rate on the date X acquired the bond (£100,000 × $1.30 = $130,000). Thus, X will realize and recognize $20,000 of exchange gain. X's basis in the 20 shares of Y common stock is $150,000 ($130,000 substituted basis + $20,000 recognized gain).

Example 2. (i) X, a foreign corporation with the British pound (£) as its functional currency, lends £100 at a market rate of interest to Y, its wholly-owned U.S. subsidiary, on January 1, 1990, on which date the spot exchange rate is £1 = $1. Y's functional currency is the U.S. dollar. On January 1, 1992, when the spot exchange rate is £1 = $.50, X cancels the debt as a contribution to capital. Pursuant to paragraph (b)(13) of this section, Y will realize and recognize exchange gain with respect to the £100 issue price of the debt instrument on January 1, 1992. Y will compute exchange gain pursuant to paragraph (b)(6) of this section by translating the issue price at the spot rate on the date Y became the obligor (£100 × $1 = $100) and subtracting from such amount the issue price translated at the spot rate on the date of extinguishment (£100 × $.50 = $50). Thus, Y will realize and recognize $50 of exchange gain.

(ii) Under section 108(e)(6), on the acquisition of its indebtedness from X as a contribution to capital Y is treated as having satisfied the debt with an amount of money equal to X's adjusted basis in the debt (£100). For purposes of section 108(e)(6), X's adjusted basis is translated into United States dollars at the spot rate on the date Y acquires the debt (£1 = $.50). Therefore, Y is treated as having satisfied the debt for $50. Pursuant to paragraph (b)(13) of this section, for purposes of section 108 the amount of the indebtedness is considered to be reduced by the exchange gain from $100 to $50. Accordingly, Y recognizes $50 of exchange gain and no discharge of indebtedness income on the extinguishment of its debt to X.

(iii) If X were a United States taxpayer with a dollar functional currency and a $100 basis in Y's obligation, X would realize and recognize an exchange loss of $50 under paragraph (b)(5) of this section on the contribution of the debt to Y. The recognized loss would reduce X's adjusted basis in the debt from $100 to $50, so that for purposes of applying section 108(e)(6) Y is treated as having satisfied the debt for $50. Accordingly, under these facts as well Y would recognize $50 of exchange gain and no discharge of indebtedness income.

Example 3. (i) X and Y are unrelated calendar year U.S. corporations with the U.S. dollar as their functional currency. On January 1, 1990 (the issue date), X acquires Y's bond maturing on December 31, 1999. The issue price of the bond is £100,000, the stated redemption price at maturity is £100,000, and the bond provides for annual pound interest payments at the rate of 10%. On January 1, 1994, X and Y agree that Y will redeem its bond from X in exchange for 20 shares of Y common stock. Assume the following:

(a) The spot rate on January 1, 1990, is £1 = $1.00,

(b) The spot rate on January 1, 1994, is £1 = $.50,

(c) Interest rates on equivalent bonds have increased so that as of January 1, 1994, the value of Y's bond has declined to £90,000, and

(d) The 20 shares of Y common stock have a market value of £90,000 as of January 1, 1994.

(ii) Pursuant to paragraph (b)(13) of this section, X will realize and recognize exchange loss with respect to the issue price (£100,000) of the bond on January 1, 1994, when the bond is exchanged for stock. X will compute exchange loss pursuant to paragraph (b)(5) of this section

by translating the issue price at the spot rate on the exchange date (£100,000 × $.50 = $50,000) and subtracting from such amount the issue price translated at the spot rate on the date X acquired the bond (£100,000 × $1.00 = $100,000). Thus, X will compute $50,000 of exchange loss, all of which will be realized and recognized because it does not exceed the total $55,000 realized loss on the exchange ($45,000 worth of stock received less $100,000 basis in the exchanged bond).

(iii) Pursuant to paragraph (b)(13) of this section, Y will realize and recognize exchange gain with respect to the issue price, computed under paragraph (b)(6) of this section by translating the issue price at the spot rate on the date Y became the obligor (£100,000 × $1.00 = $100,000) and subtracting from such amount the issue price translated at the spot rate on the exchange date (£100,000 × $.50 = $50,000). Thus, Y will realize and recognize $50,000 of exchange gain. Under section 108(e)(10), on the transfer of stock to X in satisfaction of its indebtedness Y is treated as having satisfied the indebtedness with an amount of money equal to the fair market value of the stock (£90,000 × $.50 = $45,000). Pursuant to paragraph (b)(13) of this section, for purposes of section 108 the amount of the indebtedness is considered to be reduced by the recognized exchange gain from $100,000 to $50,000. Accordingly, Y recognizes an additional $5,000 of discharge of indebtedness income on the exchange.

Example 4. (i) The facts are the same as in *Example 3* except that interest rates on equivalent bonds have declined, rather than increased, so that the value of Y's bond on January 1, 1994, has risen to £112,500; and X and Y agree that Y will redeem its bond from X on that date in exchange for 25 shares of Y common stock worth £112,500. Pursuant to paragraphs (b)(13) and (b)(5) of this section, X will compute $50,000 of exchange loss on the exchange with respect to the £100,000 issue price of the bond. See Example 3. However, because X's total loss on the exchange is only $43,750 ($56,250 worth of stock received less $100,000 basis in the exchanged bond), under the netting rule of paragraph (b)(13) of this section the realized exchange loss is limited to $43,750.

(ii) Pursuant to paragraphs (b)(13) and (b)(6) of this section, Y will compute $50,000 of exchange gain with respect to the issue price. See *Example 3.* Under section 108(e)(10), Y is treated as having satisfied the $100,000 indebtedness with an amount of money equal to the fair market value of the stock (£112,500 × $.50 = $56,250), resulting in a total gain on the exchange of $43,750. Accordingly, under paragraph (b)(13) of this section Y's realized (and recognized) exchange gain on the exchange is limited to $43,750. Also pursuant to paragraph (b)(13) of this section, for purposes of section 108 the amount of the indebtedness is considered to be reduced by the recognized exchange gain from $100,000 to $56,250. Accordingly, Y recognizes no discharge of indebtedness income on the exchange.

(14) [Reserved]

(15) *Debt instruments and deposits denominated in hyperinflationary currencies.*—(i) *In general.*—If a taxpayer issues, acquires, or otherwise enters into or holds a hyperinflationary debt instrument (as defined in paragraph (b)(15)(vi)(A) of this section) or a hyperinflationary deposit (as defined in paragraph (b)(15)(vi)(B) of this section) on which interest is paid or accrued that is denominated in (or determined by reference to) a nonfunctional currency of the taxpayer, then the taxpayer shall realize exchange gain or loss with respect to such instrument or deposit for its taxable year determined by reference to the change in exchange rates between—

(A) The later of the first day of the taxable year, or the date the instrument was entered into (or an amount deposited); and

(B) The earlier of the last day of the taxable year, or the date the instrument (or deposit) is disposed of or otherwise terminated.

(ii) *Only exchange gain or loss is realized.*—No gain or loss is realized under paragraph (b)(15)(i) by reason of factors other than movement in exchange rates, such as the creditworthiness of the debtor.

(iii) *Special rule for synthetic, non-hyperinflationary currency debt instruments.*—(A) *General rule.*—Paragraph (b)(15)(i) does not apply to a debt instrument that has interest and principal payments that are to be made by reference to a currency or item that does not reflect hyperinflationary conditions in a country (within the meaning of § 1.988-1(f)).

(B) *Example.*—Paragraph (b)(15)(iii)(A) is illustrated by the following example:

Example. When the Turkish lira (TL) is a hyperinflationary currency, A, a U.S. corporation with the U.S. dollar as its functional currency, makes a 5 year, 100,000 TL-denominated loan to B, an unrelated corporation, at a 10% interest rate when 1,000 TL equals $1. Under the terms of the debt instrument, B must pay interest annually to A in amount of Turkish lira that is equal to $100. Also under the terms of the debt instrument, B must pay A upon maturity of the debt instrument an amount of Turkish lira that is equal to $1,000. Although the principal and interest are payable in a hyperinflationary currency, the debt instrument is a synthetic dollar debt instrument and is not subject to paragraph (b)(15)(i) of this section.

(iv) *Source and character of gain or loss.*—(A) *General rule for hyperinflationary conditions.*—The rules of this paragraph (b)(15)(iv)(A) shall

apply to any taxpayer that is either an issuer of (or obligor under) a hyperinflationary debt instrument or deposit and has currency gain on such debt instrument or deposit, or a holder of a hyperinflationary debt instrument or deposit and has currency loss on such debt instrument or deposit. For purposes of subtitle A of the Internal Revenue Code, any exchange gain or loss realized under paragraph (b)(15)(i) of this section is directly allocable to the interest expense or interest income, respectively, from the debt instrument or deposit (computed under this paragraph (b)), and therefore reduces or increases the amount of interest income or interest expense paid or accrued during that year with respect to that instrument or deposit. With respect to a debt instrument or deposit during a taxable year, to the extent exchange gain realized under paragraph (b)(15)(i) of this section exceeds interest expense of an issuer, or exchange loss realized under paragraph (b)(15)(i) of this section exceeds interest income of a holder or depositor, the character and source of such excess amount shall be determined under §§ 1.988-3 and 1.988-4.

(B) *Special rule for subsiding hyperinflationary conditions.*—If the taxpayer is an issuer of (or obligor under) a hyperinflationary debt instrument or deposit and has currency loss, or if the taxpayer is a holder of a hyperinflationary debt instrument or deposit and has currency gain, then for purposes of subtitle A of the Internal Revenue Code, the character and source of the currency gain or loss is determined under §§ 1.988-3 and 1.988-4. Thus, if an issuer has both interest expense and currency loss, the currency loss is sourced and characterized under section 988, and does not affect the determination of interest expense.

(v) *Adjustment to principal or basis.*—Any exchange gain or loss realized under paragraph (b)(15)(i) of this section is an adjustment to the functional currency principal amount of the issuer, functional currency basis of the holder, or the functional currency amount of the deposit. This adjusted amount or basis is used in making subsequent computations of exchange gain or loss, computing the basis of assets for purposes of allocating interest under §§ 1.861-9T through 1.861-12T and 1.882-5, or making other determinations that may be relevant for computing taxable income or loss.

(vi) *Definitions.*—(A) *Hyperinflationary debt instrument.*—A hyperinflationary debt instrument is a debt instrument that provides for—

(1) Payments denominated in or determined by reference to a currency that is hyperinflationary (as defined in § 1.988-1(f)) at the time the taxpayer enters into or otherwise acquires the debt instrument; or

(2) Payments denominated in or determined by reference to a currency that is hyperinflationary (as defined in § 1.988-1(f)) dur-

ing the taxable year, and the terms of the instrument provide for the adjustment of principal or interest payments in a manner that reflects hyperinflation. For example, a debt instrument providing for a variable interest rate based on local conditions and generally responding to changes in the local consumer price index will reflect hyperinflation.

(B) *Hyperinflationary deposit.*—A hyperinflationary deposit is a demand or time deposit or similar instrument issued by a bank or other financial institution that provides for—

(1) Payments denominated in or determined by reference to a currency that is hyperinflationary (as defined in § 1.988-1(f)) at the time the taxpayer enters into or otherwise acquires the deposit; or

(2) Payments denominated in or determined by reference to a currency that is hyperinflationary (as defined in § 1.988-1(f)) during the taxable year, and the terms of the deposit provide for the adjustment of the deposit amount or interest payments in a manner that reflects hyperinflation.

(vii) *Interaction with other provisions.*—(A) *Interest allocation rules.*—In determining the amount of interest expense, this paragraph (b)(15) applies before §§ 1.861-9T through 1.861-12T, and 1.882-5.

(B) *DASTM.*—With respect to a qualified business unit that uses the United States dollar approximate separate transactions method of accounting described in § 1.985-3, paragraph (b)(15)(i) of this section does not apply.

(C) *Interaction with section 988(a)(3)(C).*—Section 988(a)(3)(C) does not apply to a debt instrument subject to the rules of paragraph (b)(15)(i) of this section.

(D) *Hedging rules.*—To the extent § 1.446-4 or 1.988-5 apply, the rules of paragraph (b)(15)(i) of this section will not apply. This paragraph (b)(15)(vii)(D) does not apply if the application of § 1.988-5 results in hyperinflationary debt instrument or deposit described in paragraph (b)(15)(vi)(A) or (B) of this section.

(viii) *Effective date.*—This paragraph (b)(15) applies to transactions entered into after February 14, 2000.

(16) *Coordination with section 267 regarding debt instruments.*—(i) *Treatment of a creditor.*—For rules applicable to a corporation included in a controlled group that is a creditor under a debt instrument see § 1.267(f)-1(h).

(ii) *Treatment of a debtor.*—[Reserved]

(17) *Coordination with installment method under section 453.*—[Reserved]

(18) *Interaction of section 988 and § 1.1275-2(g).*—(i) *In general.*—If a principal purpose of structuring a debt instrument subject to section 988 and any related hedges is to achieve a result that is unreasonable in light of the purposes of section 163(e), section 988, sections 1271 through 1275, or any related section of the Internal Revenue Code, the Commissioner can apply or depart from the regulations under the applicable sections as necessary or appropriate to achieve a reasonable result. For example, if this paragraph (b)(18) applies to a multicurrency debt instrument and a hedge or hedges, the Commissioner can wholly or partially integrate transactions or treat portions of the debt instrument as separate instruments where appropriate. See also § 1.1275-2(g).

(ii) *Unreasonable result.*—Whether a result is unreasonable is determined based on all the facts and circumstances. In making this determination, a significant fact is whether the treatment of the debt instrument is expected to have a substantial effect on the issuer's or a holder's U.S. tax liability. Another significant fact is whether the result is obtainable without the application of § 1.988-6 and any related provisions (e.g., if the debt instrument and the contingency were entered into separately). A result will not be considered unreasonable, however, in the absence of an expected substantial effect on the present value of a taxpayer's tax liability.

(iii) *Effective date.*—This paragraph (b)(18) shall apply to debt instruments issued on or after October 29, 2004.

(c) *Item of expense or gross income or receipts which is to be paid or received after the date accrued.*—(1) *In general.*—Except as provided in § 1.988-5, exchange gain or loss with respect to an item described in § 1.988-1(a)(1)(ii) and (2)(ii) (other than accrued interest income or expense subject to paragraph (b) of this section) shall be realized on the date payment is made or received. Except as provided in the succeeding sentence, such exchange gain or loss shall be recognized in accordance with the applicable recognition provisions of the Internal Revenue Code. If the taxpayer's right to receive income, or obligation to pay an expense, is transferred or modified in a transaction in which gain or loss would otherwise be recognized, exchange gain or loss shall be realized and recognized only to the extent of the total gain or loss on the transaction.

(2) *Determination of exchange gain or loss with respect to an item of gross income or receipts.*—Exchange gain or loss realized on an item of gross income or receipts described in paragraph (c)(1) of this section shall be determined by multiplying the units of nonfunctional currency received by the spot rate on the payment date, and subtracting from such amount the amount determined by multiplying the units of nonfunctional

currency received by the spot rate on the booking date. The term "spot rate on the payment date" means the spot rate determined under § 1.988-1(d) on the date payment is received or otherwise taken into account. Pursuant to § 1.988-1(d)(3), a taxpayer may use a spot rate convention for purposes of determining the spot rate on the payment date. The term "spot rate on the booking date" means the spot rate determined under § 1.988-1(d) on the date the item of gross income or receipts is accrued or otherwise taken into account. Pursuant to § 1.988-1(d)(3), a taxpayer may use a spot rate convention for purposes of determining the spot rate on the booking date.

(3) *Determination of exchange gain or loss with respect to an item of expense.*—Exchange gain or loss realized on an item of expense described in paragraph (c)(1) of this section shall be determined by multiplying the units of nonfunctional currency paid by the spot rate on the booking date and subtracting from such amount the amount determined by multiplying the units of nonfunctional currency paid by the spot rate on the payment date. The term "spot rate on the booking date" means the spot rate determined under § 1.988-1(d) on the date the item of expense is accrued or otherwise taken into account. Pursuant to § 1.988-1(d)(3), a taxpayer may use a spot rate convention for purposes of determining the spot rate on the booking date. The term "spot rate on the payment date" means the spot rate determined under § 1.988-1(d) on the date payment is made or otherwise taken into account. Pursuant to § 1.988-1(d)(3), a taxpayer may use a spot rate convention for purposes of determining the spot rate on the payment date.

(4) *Examples.*—The following examples illustrate the application of paragraph (c) of this section.

Example 1. X is a calendar year corporation with the dollar as its functional currency. X is on the accrual method of accounting. On January 15, 1989, X sells inventory for 10,000 Canadian dollars (C$). The spot rate on January 15, 1989, is C$1 = U.S. $.55. On February 23, 1989, when X receives payment of the C$10,000, the spot rate is C$1 = U.S. $.50. On February 23, 1989, X will realize exchange loss. X's loss is computed by multiplying the C$10,000 by the spot rate on the date the C$10,000 are received (C$10,000 × .50 = U.S. $5,000) and subtracting from such amount, the amount computed by multiplying the C$10,000 by the spot rate on the booking date (C$10,000 × .55 = U.S. $5,500). Thus, X's exchange loss on the transaction is U.S. $500 (U.S. $5,000 − U.S. $5,500).

Example 2. The facts are the same as in *Example 1* except that X uses a spot rate convention to determine the spot rate as provided in § 1.988-1(d)(3). Pursuant to X's spot rate convention, the spot rate at which a payable or receivable is booked is determined monthly for each nonfunctional currency payable or receivable by adding the spot rate at the beginning of the month and the spot rate at the end of the month and dividing by two. All payables and receivables in a nonfunctional currency booked during the month are translated into functional currency at the rate described in the preceding sentence. Further, the translation of nonfunctional currency paid with respect to a payable, and nonfunctional currency received with respect to a receivable, is also performed pursuant to the spot rate convention. Assume the spot rate determined under the spot rate convention for the month of January is C$1 = U.S. $.54 and for the month of February is C$1 = U.S. $.51. On the last date in February, X will realize exchange loss. X's loss is computed by multiplying the C$10,000 by the spot rate convention for the month of February (C$10,000 × U.S. $.51 = U.S. $5,100) and subtracting from such amount, the amount computed by multiplying the C$10,000 by the spot rate convention for the month of January (C$10,000 × U.S. $.54 = $5,400). Thus, X's exchange loss on the transaction is U.S. $300 (U.S. $5,100 − U.S. $5,400). X's basis in the C$10,000 is U.S. $5,400.

Example 3. The facts are the same as in *Example 2* except that X has a standing order with X's bank for the bank to convert any nonfunctional currency received in satisfaction of a receivable into U.S. dollars on the day received and to deposit those U.S. dollars in X's U.S. dollar bank account. X may use its convention to translate the amount booked into U.S. dollars, but must use the U.S. dollar amounts received from the bank with respect to such receivables to determine X's exchange gain or loss. Thus, if X receives payment of the C$10,000 on February 23, 1989, when the spot rate is C$1 = U.S.$ .50, X determines exchange gain or loss by subtracting the amount booked under X's convention (U.S.$5,400) from the amount of U.S. dollars received from the bank under the standing conversion order (assume $5,000). X's exchange loss is U.S.$400.

(d) *Exchange gain or loss with respect to forward contracts, futures contracts and option contracts.*—(1) *Scope.*—(i) *In general.*—This paragraph (d) applies to forward contracts, futures contracts and option contracts described in § 1.988-1(a)(1)(ii) and (2)(iii). For rules applicable to currency swaps and notional principal contracts described in § 1.988-1(a)(1)(ii) and (2)(iii), see paragraph (e) of this section.

(ii) *Treatment of spot contracts.*—Solely for purposes of this paragraph (d), a spot contract as defined in § 1.988-1(b) to buy or sell nonfunctional currency is not considered a forward contract or similar transaction described in § 1.988-1(a)(2)(iii) unless such spot contract is disposed of (or otherwise terminated) prior to making or taking delivery of the currency. For example, if a taxpayer with the dollar as its

Reg. § 1.988-2(d)(1)(ii)

functional currency enters into a spot contract to purchase British pounds, and takes delivery of such pounds under the contract, the delivery of the pounds is not a realization event under section 988(c)(5) and paragraph (e)(4)(ii) of this section because the contract is not considered a forward contract or similar transaction described in § 1.988-1(a)(2)(iii). However, if the taxpayer sells or otherwise terminates the contract before taking delivery of the pounds, exchange gain or loss shall be realized and recognized in accordance with paragraphs (d)(2) and (3) of this section.

(2) *Realization of exchange gain or loss.*—(i) *In general.*—Except as provided in § 1.988-5, exchange gain or loss on a contract described in § 1.988-2(d)(1) shall be realized in accordance with the applicable realization section of the Internal Revenue Code (*e.g.*, sections 1001, 1092, and 1256). See also section 988(c)(5). For purposes of determining the timing of the realization of exchange gain or loss, sections 1092 and 1256 shall take precedence over section 988(c)(5).

(ii) *Realization by offset.*—(A) *In general.*—Except as provided in paragraphs (d)(2)(ii)(B) and (C) of this section, exchange gain or loss with respect to a transaction described in § 1.988-1(a)(1)(ii) and (2)(iii) shall not be realized solely because such transaction is offset by another transaction (or transactions).

(B) *Exception where economic benefit is derived.*—If a transaction described in § 1.988-1(a)(1)(ii) and (2)(iii) is offset by another transaction or transactions, exchange gain shall be realized to the extent the taxpayer derives, by pledge or otherwise, an economic benefit (*e.g.*, cash, property or the proceeds from a borrowing) from any gain inherent in such offsetting positions. Proper adjustment shall be made in the amount of any gain or loss subsequently realized for gain taken into account by reason of the preceding sentence. This paragraph (d)(2)(ii)(B) shall apply to transactions creating an offset after September 21, 1989.

(C) *Certain contracts traded on an exchange.*—If a transaction described in § 1.988-1(a)(1)(ii) and (2)(iii) is traded on an exchange and it is the general practice of the exchange to terminate offsetting contracts, entering into an offsetting contract shall be considered a termination of the contract being offset.

(iii) *Clarification of section 988(c)(5).*—If the delivery date of a contract subject to section 988(c)(5) and paragraph (d)(4)(ii) of this section is different than the date the contract expires, then for purposes of determining the date exchange gain or loss is realized, the term delivery date shall mean expiration date.

(iv) *Examples.*—The following examples illustrate the rules of this paragraph (d)(1) and (2).

Example 1. On August 1, 1989, X, a calendar year corporation with the dollar as its functional currency, enters into a forward contract with Bank A to buy 100 New Zealand dollars for $80 for delivery on January 31, 1990. (The forward purchase contract is not a section 1256 contract.) On November 1, 1989, the market price for the purchase of 100 New Zealand dollars for delivery on January 31, 1990, is $76. On November 1, 1989, X cancels its obligation under the forward purchase contract and pays Bank A $3.95 (the present value of $4 discounted at 12% for the period) in cancellation of such contract. Under section 1001(a), X realizes an exchange loss of $3.95 on November 1, 1989, because cancellation of the forward purchase contract for cash results in the termination of X's contract.

Example 2. X is a corporation with the dollar as its functional currency. On January 1, 1989, X enters into a currency swap contract with Bank A under which X is obligated to make a series of Japanese yen payments in exchange for a series of dollar payments. On February 21, 1992, X has a gain of $100,000 inherent in such contract as a result of interest rate and exchange rate movements. Also on February 21, 1992, X enters into an offsetting swap with Bank A to lock in such gain. If on February 21, 1992, X pledges the gain inherent in such offsetting positions as collateral for a loan, X's initial swap contract is treated as being terminated on February 21, 1992, under paragraph (d)(2)(ii)(B) of this section. Proper adjustment is made in the amount of any gain or loss subsequently realized for the gain taken into account by reason of paragraph (d)(2)(ii)(B) of this section.

Example 3. X is a calendar year corporation with the dollar as its functional currency. On October 1, 1989, X enters into a forward contract to buy 100,000 Swiss francs (Sf) for delivery on March 1, 1990, for $51,220. Assume that the contract is a section 1256 contract under section 1256(g)(2) and that section 1256(e) does not apply. Pursuant to section 1256(a)(1), the forward contract is treated as sold for its fair market value on December 31, 1989. Assume that the fair market value of the contract is $1,000 determined under § 1.988-1(g). Thus X will realize an exchange gain of $1,000 on December 31, 1989. Such gain is subject to the character rules of § 1.988-3 and the source rules of § 1.988-4.

(v) *Extension of the maturity date of certain contracts.*—An extension of time for making or taking delivery under a contract described in paragraph (d)(1) of this section (*e.g.*, a historical rate rollover as defined in § 1.988-5(b)(2)(iii)(C)) shall be considered a sale or exchange of the contract for its fair market value on the date of the extension and the establishment of a new contract on such date. If, under the terms of the extension, the time value of any gain or loss recognized pursuant to the preceding sentence adjusts the price of the currency to be bought or sold under the new contract, the amount attributable to such time value shall be treated as interest income or expense for all purposes of the Code. However, the preceding sentence shall not apply and the amount attributable to the time value of any gain or loss recognized shall be treated as exchange gain or loss if the period beginning on the first date the contract is rolled over and ending on the date payment is ultimately made or received with respect to such contract does not exceed 183 days.

(3) *Recognition of exchange gain or loss.*—Except as provided in §1.988-5 (relating to section 988 hedging transactions), exchange gain or loss realized with respect to a contract described in paragraph (d)(1) of this section shall be recognized in accordance with the applicable recognition provisions of the Internal Revenue Code. For example, a loss realized with respect to a contract described in paragraph (d)(1) of this section which is part of a straddle shall be recognized in accordance with the provisions of section 1092 to the extent such section is applicable.

(4) *Determination of exchange gain or loss.*— (i) *In general.*—Exchange gain or loss with respect to a contract described in §1.988-2(d)(1) shall be determined by subtracting the amount paid (or deemed paid), if any, for or with respect to the contract (including any amount paid upon termination of the contract) from the amount received (or deemed received), if any, for or with respect to the contract (including any amount received upon termination of the contract). Any gain or loss determined according to the preceding sentence shall be treated as exchange gain or loss.

(ii) *Special rules where taxpayer makes or takes delivery.*—If the taxpayer makes or takes delivery in connection with a contract described in paragraph (d)(1) of this section, any gain or loss shall be realized and recognized in the same manner as if the taxpayer sold the contract (or paid another person to assume the contract) on the date on which he took or made delivery for its fair market value on such date. See paragraph (d)(2)(iii) of this section regarding the definition of the term "delivery date." This paragraph (d)(4)(ii) shall not apply in any case in which the taxpayer makes or takes delivery before June 11, 1987.

(iii) *Examples.*—The following examples illustrate the application of paragraph (d)(4) of this section.

Example 1. X is a calendar year corporation with the dollar as its functional currency. On October 1, 1989, when the six month forward rate is $.4907, X enters into a forward contract to buy 100,000 New Zealand dollars (NZD) for delivery on March 1, 1990. On March 1, 1990, when

X takes delivery of the 100,000 NZD, the spot rate is 1NZD equals $.48. Pursuant to section 988(c)(5) and paragraph (d)(4)(ii) of this section, a taxpayer that takes delivery of nonfunctional currency under a forward contract that is subject to section 988 is treated as if the taxpayer sold the contract for its fair market value on the date delivery is taken. If X sold the contract on March 1, 1990, the transferee would require a payment of $1,070 [($.48 × 100,000NZD) − ($.4907 × 100,000NZD)]to compensate him for the loss in value of the 100,000NZD. Therefore, X realizes an exchange loss of $1,070. X has a basis in the 100,000NZD of $48,000.

Example 2. Assume the same facts as in *Example 1* except that the contract is for Swiss francs and is a section 1256 contract. Assume further that on December 31, 1989, the value to X of the contract as marked to market is $1,000. Pursuant to section 1256(a), X realizes an exchange gain of $1,000. Such gain, however, is characterized as ordinary income under §1.988-3 and will be sourced under §1.988-4.

Example 3. X is a calendar year corporation with the dollar as its functional currency. On May 2, 1989, X enters into an option contract with Bank A to purchase 50,000 Canadian dollars (C$) for U.S. $42,500 (C$1 = U.S. $.85) for delivery on or before September 18, 1989. X pays a $285 premium to Bank A to obtain the option contract. On September 18, 1989, when X exercises the option and takes delivery of the C$50,000, the spot rate is C$1 equals U.S. $.90. Pursuant to section 988(c)(5) and paragraph (d)(4)(ii) of this section, a taxpayer that takes delivery under an option contract that is subject to section 988 is treated as if the taxpayer sold the contract for its fair market value on the date delivery is taken. If X sold the contract for its fair market value on September 18, 1989, X would receive U.S. $2,500 [(C$50,000 × U.S. $.90) − (C$50,000 × U.S. $.85)]. Accordingly, X is deemed to have received U.S. $2,500 on the sale of the contract at its fair market value. X will realize U.S. $2,215 ($2,500 deemed received less $285 paid) of exchange gain with respect to the delivery of Canadian dollars under the option contract. X's basis in the 50,000 Canadian dollars is U.S. $45,000.

(5) *Hyperinflationary contracts.*—(i) *In general.*—If a taxpayer acquires or otherwise enters into a hyperinflationary contract (as defined in paragraph (d)(5)(ii) of this section) that has payments to be made or received that are denominated in (or determined by reference to) a nonfunctional currency of the taxpayer, then the taxpayer shall realize exchange gain or loss with respect to such contract for its taxable year determined by reference to the change in exchange rates between—

(A) The later of the first day of the taxable year, or the date the contract was acquired or entered into; and

(B) The earlier of the last day of the taxable year, or the date the contract is disposed of or otherwise terminated.

(ii) *Definition of hyperinflationary contract.*—A hyperinflationary contract is a contract described in paragraph (d)(1) of this section that provides for payments denominated in or determined by reference to a currency that is hyperinflationary (as defined in § 1.988-1(f)) at the time the taxpayer acquires or otherwise enters into the contract.

(iii) *Interaction with other provisions.*—(A) *DASTM.*—With respect to a qualified business unit that uses the United States dollar approximate separate transactions method of accounting described in § 1.985-3, this paragraph (d)(5) does not apply.

(B) *Hedging rules.*—To the extent § 1.446-4 or 1.988-5 apply, this paragraph (d)(5) does not apply.

(C) *Adjustment for subsequent transactions.*—Proper adjustments must be made in the amount of any gain or loss subsequently realized for gain or loss taken into account by reason of this paragraph (d)(5).

(iv) *Effective date.*—This paragraph (d)(5) is applicable to transactions acquired or otherwise entered into after February 14, 2000.

(e) *Currency swaps and other notional principal contracts.*—(1) *In general.*—Except as provided in paragraph (e)(2) of this section or in § 1.988-5, the timing of income, deduction and loss with respect to a notional principal contract that is a section 988 transaction shall be governed by section 446 and the regulations thereunder. Such income, deduction and loss is characterized as exchange gain or loss (except as provided in another section of the Internal Revenue Code (or regulations thereunder), § 1.988-5, or in paragraph (f) of this section).

(2) *Special rules for currency swaps.*—(i) *In general.*—Except as provided in paragraph (e)(2)(iii)(B) of this section, the provisions of this paragraph (e)(2) shall apply solely for purposes of determining the realization, recognition and amount of exchange gain or loss with respect to a currency swap contract, and not for purposes of determining the source of such gain or loss, or characterizing such gain or loss as interest. Except as provided in § 1.988-3(c), any income or loss realized with respect to a currency swap contract shall be characterized as exchange gain or loss (and not as interest income or expense). Any exchange gain or loss realized in accordance with this paragraph (e)(2) shall be recognized unless otherwise provided in an applicable section of the Code. For purposes of this paragraph (e)(2), a currency swap contract is a contract defined in paragraph (e)(2)(ii) of this section. With respect to a contract which requires the

payment of swap principal prior to maturity of such contract, see paragraph (f) of this section. For purposes of this paragraph (e), the rules of paragraph (d)(2)(ii) of this section (regarding realization by offset) apply. See Example 2 of paragraph (d)(2)(iv) of this section.

(ii) *Definition of currency swap contract.*—(A) *In general.*—A currency swap contract is a contract involving different currencies between two or more parties to—

(1) Exchange periodic interim payments, as defined in paragraph (e)(2)(ii)(C) of this section, on or prior to maturity of the contract; and

(2) Exchange the swap principal amount upon maturity of the contract.
A currency swap contract may also require an exchange of the swap principal amount upon commencement of the agreement.

(B) *Swap principal amount.*—The swap principal amount is an amount of two different currencies which, under the terms of the currency swap contract, is used to determine the periodic interim payments in each currency and which is exchanged upon maturity of the contract. If such amount is not clearly set forth in the contract, the Commissioner may determine the swap principal amount.

(C) *Exchange of periodic interim payments.*—An exchange of periodic interim payments is an exchange of one or more payments in one currency specified by the contract for one or more payments in a different currency specified by the contract where the payments in each currency are computed by reference to an interest index applied to the swap principal amount. A currency swap contract must clearly indicate the periodic interim payments, or the interest index used to compute the periodic interim payments, in each currency.

(iii) *Timing and computation of periodic interim payments.*—(A) *In general.*—Except as provided in paragraph (e)(2)(iii)(B) of this section and § 1.988-5, the timing and computation of the periodic interim payments provided in a currency swap agreement shall be determined by treating—

(1) Payments made under the swap as payments made pursuant to a hypothetical borrowing that is denominated in the currency in which payments are required to be made (or are determined with reference to) under the swap, and

(2) Payments received under the swap as payments received pursuant to a hypothetical loan that is denominated in the currency in which payments are received (or are determined with reference to) under the swap.
Except as provided in paragraph (e)(2)(v) of this section, the hypothetical issue price of such hypothetical borrowing and loan shall be the swap

principal amount. The hypothetical stated redemption price at maturity is the total of all payments (excluding any exchange of the swap principal amount at the inception of the contract) provided under the hypothetical borrowing or loan other than periodic interest payments under the principles of section 1273. For purposes of determining economic accrual under the currency swap, the number of hypothetical interest compounding periods of such hypothetical borrowing and loan shall be determined pursuant to a semiannual compounding convention unless the currency swap contract indicates otherwise. For purposes of determining the timing and amount of the periodic interim payments, the principles regarding the amortization of interest (see generally, sections 1272 through 1275 and 163(e)) shall apply to the hypothetical interest expense and income of such hypothetical borrowing and loan. However, such principles shall not apply to determine the time when principal is deemed to be paid on the hypothetical borrowing and loan. See paragraph (d)(2)(iii) of this section and *Example 2* of paragraph (d)(5) of this section with respect to the time when principal is deemed to be paid. With respect to the translation and computation of exchange gain or loss on any hypothetical interest income or expense, see §1.988-2(b). The amount treated as exchange gain or loss by the taxpayer with respect to the periodic interim payments for the taxable year shall be the amount of hypothetical interest income and exchange gain or loss attributable to such interest income from the hypothetical borrowing and loan for such year less the amount of hypothetical interest expense and exchange gain or loss attributable to the interest expense from such hypothetical borrowing and loan for such year.

(B) *Effect of prepayment for purposes of section 956.*—For purposes of section 956, the Commissioner may treat any prepayment of a currency swap as a loan.

(iv) *Timing and determination of exchange gain or loss with respect to the swap principal amount.*—Exchange gain or loss with respect to the swap principal amount shall be realized on the day the units of swap principal in each currency are exchanged. (See paragraph (e)(2)(ii)(A)(2) of this section which requires that the entire swap principal amount be exchanged upon maturity of the contract.) Such gain or loss shall be determined on the date of the exchange by subtracting the value (on such date) of the units of swap principal paid from the value of the units of swap principal received. This paragraph (e)(2)(iv) does not apply to an equal exchange of the swap principal amount at the commencement of the agreement at a market exchange rate.

(v) *Anti-abuse rules.*—(A) *Method of accounting does not clearly reflect income.*—If the taxpayer's method of accounting for income, expense, gain or loss attributable to a currency swap does not clearly reflect income, or if the present value of the payments to be made is not equivalent to that of the payments to be received (including the swap premium or discount, as defined in paragraph (e)(3)(ii) of this section) on the day the taxpayer enters into or acquires the contract, the Commissioner may apply principles analogous to those of section 1274 or such other rules as the Commissioner deems appropriate to clearly reflect income. For example, in order to clearly reflect income the Commissioner may determine the hypothetical issue price, the hypothetical stated redemption price at maturity, and the amounts required to be taken into account within a taxable year. Further, if the present value of the payments to be made is not equivalent to that of the payments to be received (including the swap premium or discount, as defined in paragraph (e)(3)(ii) of this section) on the day the taxpayer enters into or acquires the contract, the Commissioner may integrate the swap with another transaction (or transactions) in order to clearly reflect income.

(B) *Terms must be clearly stated.*—If the currency swap contract does not clearly set forth the swap principal amount in each currency, and the periodic interim payments in each currency (or the interest index used to compute the periodic interim payments in each currency), the Commissioner may defer any income, deduction, gain or loss with respect to such contract until termination of the contract.

(3) *Amortization of swap premium or discount in the case of off-market currency swaps.*—(i) *In general.*—An "off-market currency swap" is a currency swap contract under which the present value of the payments to be made is not equal to that of the payments to be received on the day the taxpayer enters into or acquires the contract (absent the swap premium or discount, as defined in paragraph (e)(3)(ii) of this section). Generally, such present values may not be equal if the swap exchange rate (as defined in paragraph (e)(3)(iii) of this section) is not the spot rate, or the interest indices used to compute the periodic interim payments do not reflect current values, on the day the taxpayer enters into or acquires the currency swap.

(ii) *Treatment of taxpayer entering into or acquiring an off-market currency swap.*—If a taxpayer that enters into or acquires a currency swap makes a payment (that is, the taxpayer pays a premium, "swap premium," to enter into or acquire the currency swap) or receives a payment (that is, the taxpayer enters into or acquires the currency swap at a discount, "swap discount") in order to make the present value of the amounts to be paid equal the amounts to be received, such payment shall be amortized in a manner which places the taxpayer in the same position it would have been in had the taxpayer entered into a currency swap contract under which the present value of the amounts to be paid equal the amounts to be received (absent any swap premium or discount). Thus, swap premium or discount shall be amortized as follows—

(A) The amount of swap premium or discount that is attributable to the difference between the swap exchange rate (as defined in paragraph (e)(3)(iii) of this section) and the spot rate on the date the contract is entered into or acquired shall be taken into account as income or expense on the date the swap principal amounts are taken into account; and

(B) The amount of swap premium or discount attributable to the difference in values of the periodic interim payments shall be amortized in a manner consistent with the principles of economic accrual. *Cf.*, section 171.

Any amount taken into account pursuant to this paragraph (e)(3)(ii) shall be treated as exchange gain or loss.

(iii) *Definition of swap exchange rate.*—The swap exchange rate is the single exchange rate set forth in the contract at which the swap principal amounts are determined. If the swap exchange rate is not clearly set forth in the contract, the Commissioner may determine such rate.

(iv) *Coordination with § 1.446-3(g)(4) regarding swaps with significant nonperiodic payments.*—The rules of § 1.446-3(g)(4) apply to any currency swap with a significant nonperiodic payment. Section 1.446-3(g)(4) applies before this paragraph (e)(3). Thus, if § 1.446-3(g)(4) applies, currency gain or loss may be realized on the loan. This paragraph (e)(3)(iv) applies to transactions entered into after February 14, 2000.

(4) *Treatment of taxpayer disposing of a currency swap.*—Any gain or loss realized on the disposition or the termination of a currency swap is exchange gain or loss.

(5) *Examples.*—The following examples illustrate the application of this paragraph (e).

Example 1. (i) C is an accrual method calendar year corporation with the dollar as its functional currency. On January 1, 1989, C enters into a currency swap with J with the following terms:

(1) the principal amount is $150 and 100 British pounds (£) (the equivalent of $150 on the effective date of the contract assuming a spot rate of £1 = $1.50 on January 1, 1989);

(2) C will make payments equal to 10% of the dollar principal amount on December 31, 1989, and December 31, 1990;

(3) J will make payments equal to 12% of the pound principal amount on December 31, 1989, and December 31, 1990; and

(4) on December 31, 1990, C will pay to J the $150 principal amount and J will pay to C the £100 principal amount.

Assume that the spot rate is £1 = $1.50 on January 1, 1989, £1 = $1.40 on December 31, 1989, and £1 = $1.30 on December 31, 1990. Assume further that the average rate for 1989 is £1 = $1.45 and for 1990 is £1 = $1.35.

(ii) Solely for determining the realization of gain or loss in accordance with paragraph (e)(2) of this section (and not for purposes of determining whether any payments are treated as interest), C will treat the dollar payments made by C as payments made pursuant to a dollar borrowing with an issue price of $150, a stated redemption price at maturity of $150, and yield to maturity of 10%. C will treat the pound payments received as payments received pursuant to a pound loan with an issue price of £100, a stated redemption price at maturity of £100, and a yield of 12% to maturity. Pursuant to § 1.988-2(b), C is required to compute hypothetical accrued pound interest income at the average rate for the accrual period and then determine exchange gain or loss on the day payment is received with respect to such accrued amount. Accordingly, C will accrue $17.40 (£12 × $1.45) in 1989 and $16.20 (£12 × $1.35) in 1990. C also will compute hypothetical exchange loss of $.60 on December 31, 1989 [(£12 × $1.40) – (£12 × $1.45)] and hypothetical exchange loss of $.60 on December 31, 1990 [£12 × $1.30) – (£12 × $1.35)]. All such hypothetical interest income and exchange loss are characterized and sourced as exchange gain and loss. Further, C is treated as having paid $15 ($150 × 10%) of hypothetical interest on December 31, 1989, and again on December 31, 1990. Such hypothetical interest expense is characterized and sourced as exchange loss. Thus, C will have a net exchange gain of $1.80 ($17.40 – $.60 – $15.00) with respect to the periodic interim payments in 1989 and a net exchange gain of $.60 ($16.20 – $.60 – $15.00) with respect to the periodic interim payments in 1990. Finally, C will realize an exchange loss on December 31, 1990 with respect to the exchange of the swap principal amount. This loss is determined by subtracting the value of the units of swap principal paid ($150) from the value of the units of swap principal received (£100 × $1.30 = $130) resulting in a $20 exchange loss.

Example 2. (i) C is an accrual method calendar year corporation with the dollar as its functional currency. On January 1, 1989, when the spot rate is £1 = $1.50, C enters into a currency swap contract with J under which C agrees to make and receive the following payments:

Date	C Pays	J Pays
December 31, 1989	$15.00	£12.00
December 31, 1990	$41.04	£12.00

Date	C Pays	J Pays
December 31, 1991	$0.00	£12.00
December 31, 1992	$150.00	£112.00

(ii) Under paragraph (e)(2)(iii) of this section, C must treat the dollar periodic interim payments under the swap as made pursuant to a hypothetical dollar borrowing. The hypothetical issue price is $150 and the stated redemption price at maturity is $206.04. The amount of hypothetical interest expense must be amortized in accordance with economic accrual. Thus J must include and C must deduct periodic interim payment amounts as follows:

	Amount Taken into Account	Adjusted Issue Price
December 31, 1989	$15.00	150.00
December 31, 1990	$15.00	123.96
December 31, 1991	$12.40	136.36
December 31, 1992	$13.64	

(iii) Gain or loss with respect to the periodic interim payments of the currency swap is determined under paragraph (e)(2)(iii)(A) of this section with respect to the dollar cash flow amortized as set forth above and the corresponding pound cash flow as stated in the currency swap contract. Gain or loss with respect to the principal payments (i.e., $150 and £100) exchanged on December 31, 1992, is determined under paragraph (e)(2)(iv) of this section on December 31, 1992, notwithstanding that under the principles regarding amortization of interest $26.04 would have been regarded as a payment of principal on December 31, 1990.

Example 3. (i) X is a corporation on the accrual method of accounting with the dollar as its functional currency and the calendar year as its taxable year. On January 1, 1989, X enters into a three year currency swap contract with Y with the following terms. The swap principal amount is $100 and the Swiss franc (Sf) equivalent of such amount which equals Sf200 translated at the swap exchange rate of $1 = Sf2. There is no initial exchange of the swap principal amount. The interest rates used to compute the periodic interim payments are 10% compounded annually for U.S. dollar payments and 5% compounded annually for Swiss franc payments. Thus, under the currency swap, X agrees to pay Y $10 (10% × $100) on December 31st of 1989, 1990 and 1991 and to pay Y the swap principal amount of $100 on December 31, 1991. Y agrees to pay X Sf10 (5% × Sf200) on December 31st of 1989, 1990 and 1991 and to pay X the swap principal amount of Sf200 on December 31, 1991. Assume that the average rate for 1989 and the spot rate on December 31, 1989, is $1 = Sf2.5.

(ii) Under paragraph (e)(2)(iii) of this section, on December 31, 1989, X will realize an exchange loss of $6 (the sum of $10 of loss paid to Y and $4.00 of gain, the value of Sf10 on December 31, 1989, from the receipt of Sf10 on such date).

(iii) On January 1, 1990, X transfers its rights and obligations under the swap contract to Z, an unrelated corporation. Z has the dollar as its functional currency, is on the accrual method of accounting, and has the calendar year as its taxable year. On January 1, 1990, the exchange rate is $1 = Sf2.50. The relevant dollar interest rate is 8% compounded annually and the relevant Swiss franc interest rate is 5% compounded annually. Because of the movement in exchange and interest rates, the agreement between X and Z to transfer the currency swap requires X to pay Z $23.56 (the swap discount as determined under paragraph (e)(3) of this section).

(iv) Pursuant to paragraph (e)(4) of this section, X may deduct the loss of $23.56 in 1990. The loss is characterized under § 1.988-3 and sourced under § 1.988-4.

(v) Pursuant to paragraph (e)(3)(ii) of this section, Z is required to amortize the $23.56 received as follows. The amount of the $23.56 payment that is attributable to movements in exchange rates ($20) is taken into account on December 31, 1991, the date the swap principal amounts are exchanged, under paragraph (e)(3)(ii)(A) of this section. This amount is the present value (discounted at 10%, the rate under the currency swap contract used to compute the dollar periodic interim payments) of the financial asset required to compensate Z for the loss in value of the hypothetical Swiss franc loan resulting from movements in exchange rates between January 1, 1989 and January 1, 1990. This amount is determined by assuming that interest rates did not change from the date the swap originally was entered into (January 1, 1989), but that the exchange rate is $1 = Sf2.50. Under this assumption, a taxpayer undertaking the obligation to pay dollars under the currency swap on January 1, 1990, would only agree to pay $8 for Sf10 on December 31, 1990 and $88 for Sf210 on December 31, 1991, because the exchange rates have moved from $1 = Sf2 to $1 = Sf2.50. Thus, Z requires $2 on December 31, 1990 and $22 on December 31, 1991 to compensate for the amount of dollar payments Z is required to make in exchange for the Swiss francs received on December 31, 1990 and 1991. The present value of $2 on December 31, 1990 and $22 on December 31, 1991 discounted at the rate for U.S. dollar payments of 10% is $20 ($1.82 + $18.18). This amount is discounted at the rate for U.S. dollar payments (i.e., at the historic rate) because the amount of the $23.56 payment received by Z that is attributable to movements in interest rates is computed and amortized separately as provided in the following paragraph.

(vi) Pursuant to paragraph (e)(3)(ii)(B) of this section, Z is required to amortize the portion of the $23.56 payment attributable to movements in interest rates under principles of economic accrual over the term of the currency swap agreement. The amount of the $23.56 payment that is attributable to movements in interest rates (assuming that exchange rates have not changed) is the present value ($3.56) of the excess ($2.00 in 1990 and $2.00 in 1991) of the periodic interim payments Z is required to pay under the currency swap agreement ($10 in 1990 and $10 in 1991) over the amount Z would be required to pay if the currency swap agreement reflected current interest rates on the day Z acquired the swap contract ($8 in 1990 and $8 in 1991) discounted at the appropriate dollar interest rate on January 1, 1990. Thus, under principles of economic accrual (e.g., see section 171 of the Code), Z will include in income $1.72 on December 31, 1990, the amount that, when added to the interest ($.28) on the $3.56 computed at the 8% rate on the date Z acquired the currency swap contract, will equal the $2.00 needed to compensate Z for the movement in interest rates between January 1, 1989 and January 1, 1990. Z also will include in income $1.85 on December 31, 1991, the amount that, when added to the interest ($.15) on the $1.85 (the remaining balance of the $3.56 payment) computed at the 8% rate on the date Z acquired the currency swap contract, will equal the $2.00 needed to compensate Z for the movement in interest rates between January 1, 1990 and January 1, 1991. This amount is computed assuming exchange rates have not changed because the amount attributable to movements in exchange rates is computed and amortized separately under the preceding paragraph.

(6) *Special effective date for rules regarding currency swaps.*—Paragraph (e)(3) of this section regarding amortization of swap premium or discount in the case of off-market currency swaps shall be effective for transactions entered into after September 21, 1989, unless such swap premium or discount was paid or received pursuant to a binding contract with an unrelated party that was entered into prior to such date. For transactions entered into prior to this date, see Notice 89-21, 1989-8 I.R.B. 23.

(7) *Special rules for currency swap contracts in hyperinflationary currencies.*—(i) *In general.*—If a taxpayer enters into a hyperinflationary currency swap (as defined in paragraph (e)(7)(iv) of this section), then the taxpayer realizes exchange gain or loss for its taxable year with respect to such instrument determined by reference to the change in exchange rates between—

(A) The later of the first day of the taxable year, or the date the instrument was entered into (by the taxpayer); and

(B) The earlier of the last day of the taxable year, or the date the instrument is disposed of or otherwise terminated.

(ii) *Adjustment to principal or basis.*—Proper adjustments are made in the amount of any gain or loss subsequently realized for gain or loss taken into account by reason of this paragraph (e)(7).

(iii) *Interaction with DASTM.*—With respect to a qualified business unit that uses the United States dollar approximate separate transactions method of accounting described in § 1.985-3, this paragraph (e)(7) does not apply.

(iv) *Definition of hyperinflationary currency swap contract.*—A hyperinflationary currency swap contract is a currency swap contract that provides for—

(A) Payments denominated in or determined by reference to a currency that is hyperinflationary (as defined in § 1.988-1(f)) at the time the taxpayer enters into or otherwise acquires the currency swap; or

(B) Payments that are adjusted to take into account the fact that the currency is hyperinflationary (as defined in § 1.988-1(f)) during the current taxable year. A currency swap contract that provides for periodic payments determined by reference to a variable interest rate based on local conditions and generally responding to changes in the local consumer price index is an example of this latter type of currency swap contract.

(v) *Special effective date for nonfunctional hyperinflationary currency swap contracts.*—This paragraph (e)(7) applies to transactions entered into after February 14, 2000.

(f) *Substance over form.*—(1) *In general.*—If the substance of a transaction described in § 1.988-1(a)(1) differs from its form, the timing, source, and character of gains or losses with respect to such transaction may be recharacterized by the Commissioner in accordance with its substance. For example, if a taxpayer enters into a transaction that it designates a "currency swap contract" that requires the prepayment of all payments to be made or to be received (but not both), the Commissioner may recharacterize the contract as a loan. In applying the substance over form principle, separate transactions may be integrated where appropriate. See also § 1.861-9T(b)(1).

(2) *Example.*—The following example illustrates the provisions of this paragraph (f).

Example. (i) On January 1, 1990, X, a U.S. corporation with the dollar as its functional currency, enters into a contract with Y under which X will pay Y $100 and Y will pay X LC100 on

January 1, 1990, and X will pay Y LC109.3 and Y will pay X $133 on December 31, 1992. On January 1, 1990, the spot exchange rate is LC1 = $1

Date		
1/1/90		
12/31/90		
12/31/91		
12/31/92		

(ii) X and Y designate this contract as a "currency swap." Notwithstanding this designation, for purposes of determining the timing, source, and character with respect to the transaction, the transaction is characterized by the Commissioner in accordance with its substance. Thus, the January 1, 1990, exchange by X of $100 for LC 100 is treated as a spot purchase of LCs by X and the December 31, 1992, exchange by X at 109.3 LC for $133 is treated as a forward sale of LCs by X. Under such treatment there would be no tax consequences to X under paragraph (e)(2) of this section in 1990, 1991, and 1992 with respect to this transaction other than the realization of exchange gain or loss on the sale of the LC109.3 on December 31, 1992. Calculation of such gain or loss would be governed by the rules of paragraph (d) of this section.

(g) *Effective date.*—Except as otherwise provided in this section, this section shall be effective for taxable years beginning after December 31, 1986. Thus, except as otherwise provided in this section, any payments made or received with respect to a section 988 transaction in taxable years beginning after December 31, 1986, are subject to this section.

(h) *Timing of income and deductions from notional principal contracts.*—Except as otherwise provided (e.g., in § 1.988-5 or 1.446-3(g)), income or loss from a notional principal contract described in § 1.988-1(a)(2)(iii)(B) (other than a currency swap) is exchange gain or loss. For the rules governing the timing of income and deductions with respect to notional principal contracts, see § 1.446-3. See paragraph (e)(2) of this section with respect to currency swaps. [Reg. § 1.988-2.]

☐ [*T.D.* 8400, 3-16-92. *Amended by T.D.* 8491, 10-8-93; *T.D.* 8860, 1-12-2000 *and T.D.* 9157, 8-27-2004.]

[Reg. § 1.988-3]

§ 1.988-3. Character of exchange gain or loss.—(a) *In general.*—The character of exchange gain or loss recognized on a section 988 transaction is governed by section 988 and this section. Except as otherwise provided in section 988(c)(1)(E), section 1092, § 1.988-5 and this section, exchange gain or loss realized with respect to a section 988 transaction (including a section 1256 contract that is also a section 988 transaction) shall be characterized as ordinary gain or loss. Accordingly, unless a valid election is made under paragraph (b) of this section, any section

and the 3 year forward rate is LC1 = $.8218. X's cash flows are summarized below:

	Dollar	LC
	(100)	100
	0	0
	0	0
	133	(109.3)

providing special rules for capital gain or loss treatment, such as sections 1233, 1234, 1234A, 1236 and 1256(f)(3), shall not apply.

(b) *Election to characterize exchange gain or loss on certain identified forward contracts, futures contracts and option contracts as capital gain or loss.*—(1) *In general.*—Except as provided in paragraph (b)(2) of this section, a taxpayer may elect, subject to the requirements of paragraph (b)(3) of this section, to treat any gain or loss recognized on a contract described in § 1.988-2(d)(1) as capital gain or loss, but only if the contract—

(i) Is a capital asset in the hands of the taxpayer;

(ii) Is not part of a straddle within the meaning of section 1092(c) (without regard to subsections (c) (4) or (e)); and

(iii) Is not a regulated futures contract or nonequity option with respect to which an election under section 988(c)(1)(D)(ii) is in effect.

If a valid election under this paragraph (b) is made with respect to a section 1256 contract, section 1256 shall govern the character of any gain or loss recognized on such contract.

(2) *Special rule for contracts that become part of a straddle after an election is made.*—If a contract which is the subject of an election under paragraph (b)(1) of this section becomes part of a straddle within the meaning of section 1092(c) (without regard to subsections (c)(4) or (e)) after the date of the election, the election shall be invalid with respect to gains from such contract and the Commissioner, in his sole discretion, may invalidate the election with respect to losses.

(3) *Requirements for making the election.*—A taxpayer elects to treat gain or loss on a transaction described in paragraph (b)(1) of this section as capital gain or loss by clearly identifying such transaction on its books and records on the date the transaction is entered into. No specific language or account is necessary for identifying a transaction referred to in the preceding sentence. However, the method of identification must be consistently applied and must clearly identify the pertinent transaction as subject to the section 988(a)(1)(B) election. The Commissioner, in his sole discretion, may invalidate any purported election that does not comply with the preceding sentence.

(4) *Verification.*—A taxpayer that has made an election under § 1.988-3(b)(3) must attach to

his income tax return a statement which sets forth the following:

(i) A description and the date of each election made by the taxpayer during the taxpayer's taxable year;

(ii) A statement that each election made during the taxable year was made before the close of the date the transaction was entered into;

(iii) A description of any contract for which an election was in effect and the date such contract expired or was otherwise sold or exchanged during the taxable year;

(iv) A statement that the contract was never part of a straddle as defined in section 1092; and

(v) A statement that all transactions subject to the election are included on the statement attached to the taxpayer's income tax return.

In addition to any penalty that may otherwise apply, the Commissioner, in his sole discretion, may invalidate any or all elections made during the taxable year under § 1.988-3(b)(1) if the taxpayer fails to verify each election as provided in this § 1.988-3(b)(4). The preceding sentence shall not apply if the taxpayer's failure to verify each election was due to reasonable cause or bona fide mistake. The burden of proof to show reasonable cause or bona fide mistake made in good faith is on the taxpayer.

(5) *Independent verification.*—(i) *Effect of independent verification.*—If the taxpayer receives independent verification of the election in paragraph (b)(3) of this section, the taxpayer shall be presumed to have satisfied the requirements of paragraphs (b)(3) and (4) of this section. A contract that is a part of a straddle as defined in section 1092 may not be independently verified and shall be subject to the rules of paragraph (b)(2) of this section.

(ii) *Requirements for independent verification.*—A taxpayer receives independent verification of the election in paragraph (b)(3) of this section if—

(A) The taxpayer establishes a separate account(s) with an unrelated broker(s) or dealer(s) through which all transactions to be independently verified pursuant to this paragraph (b)(5) are conducted and reported.

(B) Only transactions entered into on or after the date the taxpayer establishes such account may be recorded in the account.

(C) Transactions subject to the election of paragraph (b)(3) of this section are entered into such account on the date such transactions are entered into.

(D) The broker or dealer provides the taxpayer a statement detailing the transactions conducted through such account and includes on such statement the following: "Each transaction identified in this account is subject to the election set forth in section 988(a)(1)(B)."

(iii) *Special effective date for independent verification.*—The rules of this paragraph (b)(5) shall be effective for transactions entered into after March 17, 1992.

(6) *Effective date.*—Except as otherwise provided, this paragraph (b) is effective for taxable years beginning on or after September 21, 1989. For prior taxable years, any reasonable contemporaneous election meeting the requirements of section 988(a)(1)(B) shall satisfy this paragraph (b).

(c) *Exchange gain or loss treated as interest.*—(1) *In general.*—Except as provided in this paragraph (c)(1), exchange gain or loss realized on a section 988 transaction shall not be treated as interest income or expense. Exchange gain or loss realized on a section 988 transaction shall be treated as interest income or expense as provided in paragraph (c)(2) of this section with regard to tax exempt bonds, § 1.988-2(e)(2)(ii)(B), § 1.988-5, and in administrative pronouncements. See § 1.861-9T(b), providing rules for the allocation of certain items of exchange gain or loss in the same manner as interest expense.

(2) *Exchange loss realized by the holder on nonfunctional currency tax exempt bonds.*—Exchange loss realized by the holder of a debt instrument the interest on which is excluded from gross income under section 103(a) or any similar provision of law shall be treated as an offset to and reduce total interest income received or accrued with respect to such instrument. Therefore, to the extent of total interest income, no exchange loss shall be recognized. This paragraph (c)(2) shall be effective with respect to debt instruments acquired on or after June 24, 1987.

(d) *Effective date.*—Except as otherwise provided in this section, this section shall be effective for taxable years beginning after December 31, 1986. Thus, except as otherwise provided in this section, any payments made or received with respect to a section 988 transaction in taxable years beginning after December 31, 1986, are subject to this section. Thus, for example, a payment made prior to January 1, 1987, under a forward contract that results in the deferral of a loss under section 1092 to a taxable year beginning after December 31, 1986, is not characterized as an ordinary loss by virtue of paragraph (a) of this section because payment was made prior to January 1, 1987. [Reg. § 1.988-3.]

☐ [T.D. 8400, 3-16-92.]

[Reg. § 1.988-4]

§ 1.988-4. Source of gain or loss realized on a section 988 transfer.—(a) *In general.*—Except as otherwise provided in § 1.988-5 and this section, the source of exchange gain or loss shall be determined by reference to the residence of the taxpayer. This rule applies even if the taxpayer has made an election under § 1.988-3(b) to characterize exchange gain or loss as capital gain or loss. This section takes precedence over section 865.

(b) *Qualified business unit.*—(1) *In general.*—The source of exchange gain or loss shall be determined by reference to the residence of the qualified business unit of the taxpayer on whose books the asset, liability, or item of income or expense giving rise to such gain or loss is properly reflected.

(2) *Proper reflection on the books of the taxpayer or qualified business unit.*—(i) *In general.*—Whether an asset, liability, or item of income or expense is properly reflected on the books of a qualified business unit is a question of fact.

(ii) *Presumption if booking practices are inconsistent.*—It shall be presumed that an asset, liability, or item of income or expense is not properly reflected on the books of the qualified business unit if the taxpayer and its qualified business units employ inconsistent booking practices with respect to the same or similar assets, liabilities, or items of income or expense. If not properly reflected on the books, the Commissioner may allocate any asset, liability, or item of income or expense between or among the taxpayer and its qualified business units to properly reflect the source (or realization) of exchange gain or loss.

(c) *Effectively connected exchange gain or loss.*—Notwithstanding paragraphs (a) and (b) of this section, exchange gain or loss that under principles similar to those set forth in §1.864-4(c) arises from the conduct of a United States trade or business shall be sourced in the United States and such gain or loss shall be treated as effectively connected to the conduct of a United States trade or business for purposes of sections 871(b) and 882(a)(1).

(d) *Residence.*—(1) *In general.*—Except as otherwise provided in this paragraph (d), for purposes of sections 985 through 989, the residence of any person shall be—

(i) In the case of an individual, the country in which such individual's tax home (as defined in section 911(d)(3)) is located;

(ii) In the case of a corporation, partnership, trust or estate which is a United States person (as defined in section 7701(a)(30)), the United States; and

(iii) In the case of a corporation, partnership, trust or estate which is not a United States person, a country other than the United States.

If an individual does not have a tax home (as defined in section 911(d)(3)), the residence of such individual shall be the United States if such individual is a United States citizen or a resident alien and shall be a country other than the United States if such individual is not a United States citizen or resident alien. If the taxpayer is a U.S. person and has no principal place of business outside the United States, the residence of the taxpayer is the United States. Notwithstanding paragraph (d)(1)(ii) of this section, if a partnership is formed or availed of to avoid tax by altering the source of exchange gain or loss, the source of such gain or loss shall be determined by reference to the residence of the partners rather than the partnership.

(2) *Exception.*—In the case of a qualified business unit of any taxpayer (including an individual), the residence of such unit shall be the country in which the principal place of business of such qualified business unit is located.

(3) *Partner in a partnership not engaged in a U.S. trade or business under section 864(b)(2).*—The determination of residence shall be made at the partner level (without regard to whether the partnership is a qualified business unit of the partners) in the case of partners in a partnership that are not engaged in a U.S. trade or business by reason of section 864(b)(2).

(e) *Special rule for certain related party loans.*—(1) *In general.*—In the case of a loan by a United States person or a related person to a 10 percent owned foreign corporation, or a corporation that meets the 80 percent foreign business requirements test of section 861(c)(1), other than a corporation subject to §1.861-11T(e)(2)(i), which is denominated in, or determined by reference to, a currency other than the U.S. dollar and bears interest at a rate at least 10 percentage points higher than the Federal mid-term rate (as determined under section 1274(d)) at the time such loan is entered into, the following rules shall apply—

(i) For purposes of section 904 only, such loan shall be marked to market annually on the earlier of the last business day of the United States person's (or related person's) taxable year or the date the loan matures; and

(ii) Any interest income earned with respect to such loan for the taxable year shall be treated as income from sources within the United States to the extent of any notional loss attributable to such loan under paragraph (d)(1)(i) of this section.

(2) *United States person.*—For purposes of this paragraph (e), the term "United States person" means a person described in section 7701(a)(30).

(3) *Loans by related foreign persons.*—(i) *In general.*—[Reserved]

(ii) *Definition of related person.*—For purposes of this paragraph (e), the term "related person" has the meaning given such term by section 954(d)(3) except that such section shall be applied by substituting "United States person" for "controlled foreign corporation" each place such term appears.

(4) *10 percent owned foreign corporation.*—For purposes of this paragraph (e), the term "10 percent owned foreign corporation" means any foreign corporation in which the United States person owns directly or indirectly (within the meaning of section 318(a)) at least 10 percent of the voting stock.

(f) *Exchange gain or loss treated as interest under §1.988-3.*—Notwithstanding the provisions of this section, any gain or loss realized on a section 988 transaction that is treated as interest income or expense under §1.988-3(c)(1) shall be sourced or allocated and apportioned pursuant to section 861(a)(1), 862(a)(1), or 864(e) as the case may be.

(g) *Exchange gain or loss allocated in the same manner as interest under §1.861-9T.*—The allocation and apportionment of exchange gain or loss under §1.861-9T shall not affect the source of exchange gain or loss for purposes of sections 871(a), 881, 1441, 1442 and 6049.

(h) *Effective date.*—This section shall be effective for taxable years beginning after December 31, 1986. Thus, any payments made or received with respect to a section 988 transaction in taxable years beginning after December 31, 1986, are subject to this section. [Reg. §1.988-4.]

☐ [T.D. 8400, 3-16-92.]

[Reg. §1.988-5]

§1.988-5. Section 988(d) hedging transactions.—(a) *Integration of a nonfunctional currency debt instrument and a §1.988-5(a) hedge.*—(1) *In general.*—This paragraph (a) applies to a qualified hedging transaction as defined in this paragraph (a)(1). A qualified hedging transaction is an integrated economic transaction, as provided in paragraph (a)(5) of this section, consisting of a qualifying debt instrument as defined in paragraph (a)(3) of this section and a §1.988-5(a) hedge as defined in paragraph (a)(4) of this section. If a taxpayer enters into a transaction that is a qualified hedging transaction, no exchange gain or loss is recognized by the taxpayer on the qualifying debt instrument or on the §1.988-5(a) hedge for the period that either is part of a qualified hedging transaction, and the transactions shall be integrated as provided in paragraph (a)(9) of this section. However, if the qualified hedging transaction results in a synthetic nonfunctional currency denominated debt instrument, such instrument shall be subject to the rules of §1.988-2(b).

(2) *Exception.*—This paragraph (a) does not apply with respect to a qualified hedging transaction that creates a synthetic asset or liability denominated in, or determined by reference to, a currency other than the U.S. dollar if the rate that approximates the Federal short-term rate in such currency is at least 20 percentage points higher than the Federal short term rate (determined under section 1274(d)) on the date the taxpayer

identifies the transaction as a qualified hedging transaction.

(3) *Qualifying debt instrument.*—(i) *In general.*—A qualifying debt instrument is a debt instrument described in §1.988-1(a)(2)(i), regardless of whether denominated in, or determined by reference to, nonfunctional currency (including dual currency debt instruments, multi-currency debt instruments and contingent payment debt instruments). A qualifying debt instrument does not include accounts payable, accounts receivable or similar items of expense or income.

(ii) *Special rule for debt instrument of which all payments are proportionately hedged.*—If a debt instrument satisfies the requirements of paragraph (a)(3)(i) of this section, and all principal and interest payments under the instrument are hedged in the same proportion, then for purposes of this paragraph (a), that portion of the instrument that is hedged is eligible to be treated as a qualifying debt instrument, and the rules of this paragraph (a) shall apply separately to such qualifying debt instrument. See Example 8 in paragraph (a)(9)(iv) of this section.

(4) *Section 1.988-5(a) hedge.*—(i) *In general.*—A §1.988-5(a) hedge (hereinafter referred to in this paragraph (a) as a "hedge") is a spot contract, futures contract, forward contract, option contract, notional principal contract, currency swap contract, similar financial instrument, or series or combination thereof, that when integrated with a qualifying debt instrument permits the calculation of a yield to maturity (under principles of section 1272) in the currency in which the synthetic debt instrument is denominated (as determined under paragraph (a)(9)(ii)(A) of this section).

(ii) *Retroactive application of definition of currency swap contract.*—A taxpayer may apply the definition of currency swap contract set forth in §1.988-2(e)(2)(ii) in lieu of the definition of swap agreement in section 2(e)(5) of Notice 87-11, 1987-1 C.B. 423 to transactions entered into after December 31, 1986 and before September 21, 1989.

(5) *Definition of integrated economic transaction.*—A qualifying debt instrument and a hedge are an integrated economic transaction if all of the following requirements are satisfied—

(i) All payments to be made or received under the qualifying debt instrument (or amounts determined by reference to a nonfunctional currency) are fully hedged on the date the taxpayer identifies the transaction under paragraph (a) of this section as a qualified hedging transaction such that a yield to maturity (under principles of section 1272) in the currency in which the synthetic debt instrument is denominated (as determined under paragraph (a)(9)(ii)(A) of this section) can be calculated.

Any contingent payment features of the qualifying debt instrument must be fully offset by the hedge such that the synthetic debt instrument is not classified as a contingent payment debt instrument. See *Examples 6* and *7* of paragraph (a)(9)(iv) of this section.

(ii) The hedge is identified in accordance with paragraph (a)(8) of this section on or before the date the acquisition of the financial instrument (or instruments) constituting the hedge is settled or closed.

(iii) None of the parties to the hedge are related. The term "related" means the relationships defined in section 267(b) or section 707(b).

(iv) In the case of a qualified business unit with a residence, as defined in section 988(a)(3)(B), outside of the United States, both the qualifying debt instrument and the hedge are properly reflected on the books of such qualified business unit throughout the term of the qualified hedging transaction.

(v) Subject to the limitations of paragraph (a)(5) of this section, both the qualifying debt instrument and the hedge are entered into by the same individual, partnership, trust, estate, or corporation. With respect to a corporation, the same corporation must enter into both the qualifying debt instrument and the hedge whether or not such corporation is a member of an affiliated group of corporations that files a consolidated return.

(vi) With respect to a foreign person engaged in a U.S. trade or business that enters into a qualifying debt instrument or hedge through such trade or business, all items of income and expense associated with the qualifying debt instrument and the hedge (other than interest expense that is subject to § 1.882-5), would have been effectively connected with such U.S. trade or business throughout the term of the qualified hedging transaction had this paragraph (a) not applied.

(6) *Special rules for legging in and legging out of integrated treatment.*—(i) *Legging in.*—"Legging in" to integrated treatment under this paragraph (a) means that a hedge is entered into after the date the qualifying debt instrument is entered into or acquired, and the requirements of this paragraph (a) are satisfied on the date the hedge is entered into ("leg in date"). If a taxpayer legs into integrated treatment, the following rules shall apply—

(A) Exchange gain or loss shall be realized with respect to the qualifying debt instrument determined solely by reference to changes in exchange rates between—

(1) The date the instrument was acquired by the holder, or the date the obligor assumed the obligation to make payments under the instrument; and

(2) The leg in date.

(B) The recognition of such gain or loss will be deferred until the date the qualifying debt instrument matures or is otherwise disposed of.

(C) The source and character of such gain or loss shall be determined on the leg in date as if the qualifying debt instrument was actually sold or otherwise terminated by the taxpayer.

(ii) *Legging out.*—With respect to a qualifying debt instrument and hedge that are properly identified as a qualified hedging transaction, "legging out" of integrated treatment under this paragraph (a) means that the taxpayer disposes of or otherwise terminates all or a part of the qualifying debt instrument or hedge prior to maturity of the qualified hedging transaction, or the taxpayer changes a material term of the qualifying debt instrument (*e.g.*, exercises an option to change the interest rate or index, or the maturity date) or hedge (*e.g.*, changes the interest or exchange rates underlying the hedge, or the expiration date) prior to maturity of the qualified hedging transaction. A taxpayer that disposes of or terminates a qualified hedging transaction (*i.e.*, disposes of or terminates both the qualifying transaction and the hedge on the same day) shall be considered to have disposed of or otherwise terminated the synthetic debt instrument rather than as legging out. If a taxpayer legs out of integrated treatment, the following rules shall apply—

(A) The transaction will be treated as a qualified hedging transaction during the time the requirements of this paragraph (a) were satisfied.

(B) If the hedge is disposed of or otherwise terminated, the qualifying debt instrument shall be treated as sold for its fair market value on the date the hedge is disposed of or otherwise terminated (the "leg-out date"), and any gain or loss (including gain or loss resulting from factors other than movements in exchange rates) from the identification date to the leg-out date is realized and recognized on the leg-out date. The spot rate on the leg-out date shall be used to determine exchange gain or loss on the debt instrument for the period beginning on the leg-out date and ending on the date such instrument matures or is disposed of or otherwise terminated. Proper adjustment to the principal amount of the debt instrument must be made to reflect any gain or loss taken into account. The netting rule of § 1.988-2(b)(8) shall apply.

(C) If the qualifying debt instrument is disposed of or otherwise terminated, the hedge shall be treated as sold for its fair market value on the date the qualifying debt instrument is disposed of or otherwise terminated (the "leg-out date"), and any gain or loss from the identification date to the leg-out date is realized and recognized on the leg-out date. The spot rate on the leg-out date shall be used to determine exchange gain or loss on the hedge for the period beginning on the leg-out date and ending on the

Reg. § 1.988-5(a)(6)(ii)(C)

date such hedge is disposed of or otherwise terminated.

(D) Except as provided in paragraph (a)(8)(iii) of this section (regarding identification by the Commissioner), that part of the qualified hedging transaction that has not been terminated (*i.e.*, the remaining debt instrument in its entirety even if partially hedged, or hedge) cannot be part of a qualified hedging transaction for any period subsequent to the leg out date.

(E) If a taxpayer legs out of a qualified hedging transaction and realizes a gain with respect to the terminated instrument, then paragraph (a)(6)(ii)(B) or (C) of this section, as appropriate, shall not apply if during the period beginning 30 days before the leg-out date and ending 30 days after that date the taxpayer enters into another transaction that hedges at least 50% of the remaining currency flow with respect to the qualifying debt instrument which was part of the qualified hedging transaction (or, if appropriate, an equivalent amount under the §1.988-5 hedge which was part of the qualified hedging transaction).

(7) *Transactions part of a straddle.*—At the discretion of the Commissioner, a transaction shall not satisfy the requirements of paragraph (a)(5) of this section if the debt instrument making up the qualified hedging transaction is part of a straddle as defined in section 1092(c) prior to the time the qualified hedging transaction is identified.

(8) *Identification requirements.*— (i) *Identification by the taxpayer.*—A taxpayer must establish a record and before the close of the date the hedge is entered into, the taxpayer must enter into the record for each qualified hedging transaction the following information—

(A) The date the qualifying debt instrument and hedge were entered into;

(B) The date the qualifying debt instrument and the hedge are identified as constituting a qualified hedging transaction;

(C) The amount that must be deferred, if any, under paragraph (a)(6) of this section and the source and character of such deferred amount;

(D) A description of the qualifying debt instrument and the hedge; and

(E) A summary of the cash flow resulting from treating the qualifying debt instrument and the hedge as a qualified hedging transaction.

(ii) *Identification by trustee on behalf of beneficiary.*—A trustee of a trust that enters into a qualified hedging transaction may satisfy the identification requirements described in paragraph (a)(8)(i) of this section on behalf of a beneficiary of such trust.

(iii) *Identification by the Commissioner.*—If—

(A) A taxpayer enters into a qualifying debt instrument and a hedge but fails to comply with one or more of the requirements of this paragraph (a), and

(B) On the basis of all the facts and circumstances, the Commissioner concludes that the qualifying debt instrument and the hedge are, in substance, a qualified hedging transaction,

then the Commissioner may treat the qualifying debt instrument and the hedge as a qualified hedging transaction. The Commissioner may identify a qualifying debt instrument and a hedge as a qualified hedging transaction regardless of whether the qualifying debt instrument and the hedge are held by the same taxpayer.

(9) *Taxation of qualified hedging transactions.*—(i) *In general.*—(A) *General rule.*—If a transaction constitutes a qualified hedging transaction, the qualifying debt instrument and the hedge are integrated and treated as a single transaction with respect to the taxpayer that has entered into the qualified hedging transaction during the period that the transaction qualifies as a qualified hedging transaction. Neither the qualifying debt instrument nor the hedge that makes up the qualified hedging transaction shall be subject to section 263(g), 1092 or 1256 for the period such transactions are integrated. However, the qualified hedging transaction may be subject to section 263(g) or 1092 if such transaction is part of a straddle.

(B) *Special rule for income or expense of foreign persons effectively connected with a U.S. trade or business.*—Interest income of a foreign person resulting from a qualified hedging transaction entered into by such foreign person that satisfies the requirements of paragraph (a)(5)(vii) of this section shall be treated as effectively connected with a U.S. trade or business. Interest expense of a foreign person resulting from a qualified hedging transaction entered into by such foreign person that satisfies the requirements of paragraph (a)(5)(vii) of this section shall be allocated and apportioned under §1.882-5 of the regulations.

(C) *Special rule for foreign persons that enter into qualified hedging transactions giving rise to U.S. source income not effectively connected with a U.S. trade or business.*—If a foreign person enters into a qualified hedging transaction that gives rise to U.S. source interest income (determined under the source rules for synthetic asset transactions as provided in this section) not effectively connected with a U.S. trade or business of such foreign person, for purposes of sections 871(a), 881, 1441, 1442 and 6049, the provisions of this paragraph (a) shall not apply and such sections of the Internal Revenue Code shall be applied separately to the qualifying debt instrument and the hedge. To the extent relevant to any foreign person, if the requirements of this paragraph (a) are otherwise met, the provisions of this paragraph (a) shall apply for all other purposes of the Internal Revenue Code (*e.g.,* for purposes of calculating the earnings and profits of a controlled foreign corporation that enters into a qualified hedging transaction through a qualified business unit resident outside the United States, income or expense with respect to such qualified hedging transaction shall be calculated under the provisions of this paragraph (a)).

(ii) *Income tax effects of integration.*—The effect of integrating and treating a transaction as a single transaction is to create a synthetic debt instrument for income tax purposes, which is subject to the original issue discount provisions of sections 1272 through 1288 and 163(e), the terms of which are determined as follows:

(A) *Denomination of synthetic debt instrument.*—In the case where the qualifying debt instrument is a borrowing, the denomination of the synthetic debt instrument is the same as the currency paid under the terms of the hedge to acquire the currency used to make payments under the qualifying debt instrument. In the case where the qualifying debt instrument is a lending, the denomination of the synthetic debt instrument is the same as the currency received under the terms of the hedge in exchange for amounts received under the qualifying debt instrument. For example, if the hedge is a forward contract to acquire British pounds for dollars, and the qualifying debt instrument is a borrowing denominated in British pounds, the synthetic debt instrument is considered a borrowing in dollars.

(B) *Term and accrual periods.*—The term of the synthetic debt instrument shall be the period beginning on the identification date and ending on the date the qualifying debt instrument matures or such earlier date that the qualifying debt instrument or hedge is disposed of or otherwise terminated. Unless otherwise clearly indicated by the payment interval under the hedge, the accrual period shall be a six month period which ends on the dates determined under section 1272(a)(5).

(C) *Issue price.*—The issue price of the synthetic debt instrument is the adjusted issue price of the qualifying debt instrument translated into the currency in which the synthetic debt instrument is denominated at the spot rate on the identification date.

(D) *Stated redemption price at maturity.*—In the case where the qualifying debt instrument is a borrowing, the stated redemption price at maturity shall be determined under section 1273(a)(2) on the identification date by reference to the amounts to be paid under the hedge to acquire the currency necessary to make interest and principal payments on the qualifying debt instrument. In the case where the qualifying debt instrument is a lending, the stated redemption price at maturity shall be determined under section 1273(a)(2) on the identification date by reference to the amounts to be received under the hedge in exchange for the interest and principal payments received pursuant to the terms of the qualifying debt instrument.

(iii) *Source of interest income and allocation of expense.*—Interest income from a synthetic debt instrument described in paragraph (a)(9)(ii) of this section shall be sourced by reference to the source of income under sections 861(a)(1) and 862(a)(1) of the qualifying debt instrument. The character for purposes of section 904 of interest income from a synthetic debt instrument shall be determined by reference to the character of the interest income from qualifying debt instrument. Interest expense from a synthetic debt instrument described in paragraph (a)(9)(ii) of this section shall be allocated and apportioned under §§1.861-8T through 1.861-12T or the successor sections thereof or under §1.882-5.

(iv) *Examples.*—The following examples illustrate the application of this paragraph (a)(9).

Example 1. (i) K is a U.S. corporation with the U.S. dollar as its functional currency. On December 24, 1989, K agrees to close the following transaction on December 31, 1989. K will borrow from an unrelated party on December 31, 1989, 100 British pounds (£) for 3 years at a 10 percent rate of interest, payable annually, with no principal payment due until the final installment. K will also enter into a currency swap contract with an unrelated counterparty under the terms of which—

(a) K will swap, on December 31, 1989, the £100 obtained from the borrowing for $100; and

(b) K will exchange dollars for pounds pursuant to the following table in order to obtain the pounds necessary to make payments on the pound borrowing:

DATE	U.S. Dollars	Pounds
December 31, 1990	8	10
December 31, 1991	8	10
December 31, 1992	108	110

(ii) The interest rate on the borrowing is set and the exchange rates on the swap are fixed on December 24, 1989. On December 31, 1989, K borrows the £100 and swaps such pounds for $100. Assume K has satisfied the identification requirements of paragraph (a)(8) of this section.

(iii) The pound borrowing (which constitutes a qualifying debt instrument under paragraph (a)(3) of this section) and the currency swap contract (which constitutes a hedge under paragraph (a)(4) of this section) are a qualified hedging transaction as defined in paragraph (a)(1) of this section. Accordingly, the pound borrowing and the swap are integrated and treated as one transaction with the following consequences:

(A) The integration of the pound borrowing and the swap results in a synthetic dollar borrowing with an issue price of $100 under section 1273(b)(2).

(B) The total amount of interest and principal of the synthetic dollar borrowing is equal to the dollar payments made by K under the currency swap contract (i.e., $8 in 1990, $8 in 1991, and $108 in 1992).

(C) The stated redemption price at maturity (defined in section 1273(a)(2)) is $100. Because the stated redemption price equals the issue price, there is no OID on the synthetic dollar borrowing.

(D) K may deduct the annual interest payments of $8 under section 163(a) (subject to any limitations on deductibility imposed by other provisions of the Code) according to its regular method of accounting. K has also paid $100 as a return of principal in 1992.

(E) K must allocate and apportion its interest expense with respect to the synthetic dollar borrowing under the rules of §§1.861-8T through 1.861-12T.

Example 2. (i) K, a U.S. corporation, has the U.S. dollar as its functional currency. On December 24, 1989, when the spot rate for Swiss francs (Sf) is Sf1 = $1, K enters into a forward contract to purchase Sf100 in exchange for $100.04 for delivery on December 31, 1989. The Sf100 are to be used for the purchase of a franc denominated debt instrument on December 31, 1989. The instrument will have a term of 3 years, an issue price of Sf100, and will bear interest at 6 percent, payable annually, with no repayment of principal until the final installment. On December 24, 1989, K also enters into a series of forward contracts to sell the franc interest and principal payments that will be received under the terms of the franc denominated debt instrument for dollars according to the following schedule:

Date	U.S. Dollars	Francs
December 31, 1990	6.12	6
December 31, 1991	6.23	6
December 31, 1992	112.16	106

(ii) On December 31, 1989, K takes delivery of the Sf100 and purchases the franc denominated debt instrument. Assume K satisfies the identification requirements of paragraph (a)(8) of this section. The purchase of the franc debt instrument (which constitutes a qualifying debt instrument under paragraph (a)(3) of this section) and the series of forward contracts (which constitute a hedge under paragraph (a)(4) of this section) are a qualified hedging transaction under paragraph (a)(1) of this section. Accordingly, the franc debt instrument and all the forward contracts are integrated and treated as one transaction with the following consequences:

(A) The integration of the franc debt instrument and the forward contracts results in a synthetic dollar debt instrument in an amount equal to the dollars exchanged under the forward contract to purchase the francs necessary to acquire the franc debt instrument. Accordingly, the issue price is $100.04 (section 1273(b)(2) of the Code).

(B) The total amount of interest and principal received by K with respect to the synthetic dollar debt instrument is equal to the dollars received under the forward sales contracts (i.e., $6.12 in 1990, $6.23 in 1991, and $112.16 in 1992).

(C) The synthetic dollar debt instrument is an installment obligation and its stated redemption price at maturity is $106.15 (i.e., $6.12 of the payments in 1990, 1991, and 1992 are treated as periodic interest payments under the principles of section 1273). Because the stated redemption price at maturity exceeds the issue price, under section 1273(a)(1) the synthetic dollar debt instrument has OID of $6.11.

(D) The yield to maturity of the synthetic dollar debt instrument is 8.00 percent, compounded annually. Assuming K is a calendar year taxpayer, it must include interest income of $8.00 in 1990 (of which $1.88 constitutes OID), $8.15 in 1991 (of which $2.03 constitutes OID), and $8.32 in 1992 (of which $2.20 constitutes OID). The amount of the final payment received by K in excess of the interest income includible is a return of principal and a payment of previously accrued OID.

(E) The source of the interest income shall be determined by applying sections 861(a)(1) and 862(a)(1) with reference to the franc interest income that would have been received had the transaction not been integrated.

Example 3. (i) K is an accrual method U.S. corporation with the U.S. dollar as its functional currency. On January 1, 1992, K borrows 100 British pounds (£) for 3 years at a 10% rate of interest payable on December 31 of each year with no principal payment due until the final installment. The spot rate on January 1, 1992, is £ 1 = $1.50. On January 1, 1993, when the spot rate is £1 = $1.60, K enters into a currency swap contract with an unrelated counterparty under the terms of which K will exchange dollars for pounds pursuant to the following table in order to obtain the pounds necessary to make the remaining payments on the pound borrowing:

Reg. §1.988-5(a)(9)(iv)

DATE	U.S. Dollars	Pounds
December 31, 1993	12.80	10
December 31, 1994	12.80	10
December 31, 1994	160.00	100

(ii) Assume that British pound interest rates are still 10% and that K properly identifies the pound borrowing and the currency swap contract as a qualified hedging transaction as provided in paragraph (a)(8) of this section. Under paragraph (a)(6)(i) of this section, K must realize exchange gain or loss with respect to the pound borrowing determined solely by reference to changes in exchange rates between January 1, 1992 and January 1, 1993. (Thus, gain or loss from other factors such as movements in interest rates or changes in credit quality of K are not taken into account). Recognition of such gain or loss is deferred until K terminates its pound borrowing. Accordingly, K must defer exchange loss in the amount of $10 [(£100 × 1.50) – (£100 × 1.60)].

(iii) Additionally, the qualified hedging transaction is treated as a synthetic U.S. dollar debt instrument with an issue date of January 1, 1993, and a maturity date of December 31, 1994. The issue price of the synthetic debt instrument is $160 (£100 × 1.60, the spot rate on January 1, 1993) and the total amount of interest and principal is $185.60. The accrual period is the one year period beginning on January 1 and ending December 31 of each year. The stated redemption price at maturity is $160. Thus, K is treated as paying $12.80 of interest in 1993, $12.80 of interest in 1994, and $160 of principal in 1994. The interest expense from the synthetic instrument is allocated and apportioned in accordance with the rules of §§1.861-8T through 1.861-12T. Sections 263(g), 1092, and 1256 do not apply to the positions comprising the synthetic dollar borrowing.

Example 4. (i) K is an accrual method U.S. corporation with the U.S. dollar as its functional currency. On January 1, 1990, K borrows 100 British pounds (£) for 3 years at a 10% rate of interest payable on December 31 of each year with no principal payment due until the final installment. The spot rate on January 1, 1990, is £ 1 = $1.50. Also on January 1, 1990, K enters into a currency swap contract with an unrelated counterparty under the terms of which K will exchange dollars for pounds pursuant to the following table in order to obtain the pounds necessary to make the remaining payments on the pound borrowing:

DATE	U.S. Dollars	Pounds
December 31, 1990	12.00	10
December 31, 1991	12.00	10
December 31, 1992	162.00	110

(ii) Assume that K properly identifies the pound borrowing and the currency swap contract as a qualified hedging transaction as provided in paragraph (a)(1) of this section.

(iii) The pound borrowing (which constitutes a qualifying debt instrument under paragraph (a)(3) of this section) and the currency swap contract (which constitutes a hedge under paragraph (a)(4) of this section) are a qualified hedging transaction as defined in paragraph (a)(1) of this section. Accordingly, the pound borrowing and the swap are integrated and treated as one transaction with the following consequences:

(A) The integration of the pound borrowing and the swap results in a synthetic dollar borrowing with an issue price of $150 under section 1273(b)(2).

(B) The total amount of interest and principal of the synthetic dollar borrowing is equal to the dollar payments made by K under the currency swap contract (i.e., $12 in 1990, $12 in 1991, and $162 in 1992).

(C) The stated redemption price at maturity (defined in section 1273(a)(2)) is $150. Because the stated redemption price equals the issue price, there is no OID on the synthetic dollar borrowing.

(D) K may deduct the annual interest payments of $12 under section 163(a) (subject to any limitations on deductibility imposed by other provisions of the Code) according to its regular method of accounting. K has also paid $150 as a return of principal in 1992.

(E) K must allocate and apportion its interest expense from the synthetic instrument under the rules of §§1.861-8T through 1.861-12T.

(iv) Assume that on January 1, 1991, the spot exchange rate is £1 = $1.60, interest rates have not changed since January 1, 1990, (accordingly, assume that the market value of K's bond in pounds has not changed) and that K transfers its rights and obligations under the currency swap contract in exchange for $10. Under §1.988-2(e)(3)(iii), K will include in income as exchange gain $10 on January 1, 1991. Pursuant to paragraph (a)(6)(ii) of this section, the pound borrowing and the currency swap contract are treated as a qualified hedging transaction for 1990. The loss inherent in the pound borrowing from January 1, 1990, to January 1, 1991, is realized and recognized on January 1, 1991. Such loss is exchange loss in the amount of $10.00 [(£100 × $1.50, the spot rate on January 1, 1990) – (£100 × $1.60, the spot rate on January 1, 1991)]. For purposes of determining exchange gain or loss on the £100 principal amount of the debt instrument for the period January 1, 1991, to December 31, 1992, the spot rate on January 1, 1991 is used rather than the spot rate on the issue date. Thus, assuming that the spot rate on December 31, 1992, the maturity date, is £1 = $1.80, K realizes exchange loss in the amount of $20 [(£100 × $1.60) − (£100 × $1.80)]. Except as provided in paragraph (a)(8)(iii) (regarding identification by the Commissioner), the pound borrowing cannot be part of a qualified hedging transaction for any period subsequent to the leg out date.

Example 5. (i) K, a U.S. corporation, has the U.S. dollar as its functional currency. On

DATE		
December 31, 1990		
December 31, 1991		
December 31, 1992		

(ii) Assume K satisfies the identification requirements of paragraph (a)(8) of this section. Assume further that on January 1, 1991, the spot exchange rate is Sf1 = U.S.$ .5143, the U.S. dollar interest rate is 10%, compounded annually, and the Swiss franc interest rate is the same as on January 1, 1990 (5%, compounded annually). On January 1, 1991, K disposes of the forward contracts that were to mature on December 31, 1991, and December 31, 1992 and incurs a loss of $3.62 (the present value of $.10 with respect to the 1991 contract and $4.27 with respect to the 1992 contract).

(iii) The purchase of the franc debt instrument (which constitutes a qualifying debt instrument under paragraph (a)(3) of this section) and the series of forward contracts (which constitute a hedge under paragraph (a)(4) of this section) are a qualified hedging transaction under paragraph (a)(1) of this section. Accordingly, the franc debt instrument and all the forward contracts are integrated for the period beginning January 1, 1990, and ending January 1, 1991.

(A) The integration of the franc debt instrument and the forward contracts results in a synthetic dollar debt instrument with an issue price of $100.

(B) The total amount of interest and principal to be received by K with respect to the synthetic dollar debt instrument is equal to the dollars to be received under the forward sales contracts (i.e., $5.14 in 1990, $5.29 in 1991, and $114.26 in 1992).

(C) The synthetic dollar debt instrument is an installment obligation and its stated redemption price at maturity is $109.27 (i.e., $5.14 of the payments in 1990, 1991, and 1992 is treated as periodic interest payments under the principles of section 1273). Because the stated redemption price at maturity exceeds the issue price, under section 1273(a)(1) the synthetic dollar debt instrument has OID of $9.27.

January 1, 1990, when the spot rate for Swiss francs (Sf) is Sf1 = $.50, K converts $100 to Sf200 and purchases a franc denominated debt instrument. The instrument has a term of 3 years, an adjusted issue price of Sf200, and will bear interest at 5 percent, payable annually, with no repayment of principal until the final installment. The U.S. dollar interest rate on an equivalent instrument is 8% on January 1, 1990, compounded annually. On January 1, 1990, K also enters into a series of forward contracts to sell the franc interest and principal payments that will be received under the terms of the franc denominated debt instrument for dollars according to the following schedule:

	U.S. Dollars	*Francs*
	5.14	10
	5.29	10
	114.26	210

(D) The yield to maturity of the synthetic dollar debt instrument is 8.00 percent, compounded annually. Assuming K is a calendar year taxpayer, it must include interest income of $8.00 in 1990 (of which $2.86 constitutes OID).

(E) The source of the interest income is determined by applying sections 861(a)(1) and 862(a)(1) with reference to the franc interest income that would have been received had the transaction not been integrated.

(iv) Because K disposed of the forward contracts on January 1, 1991, the rules of paragraph (a)(6)(ii) of this section shall apply. Accordingly, the $3.62 loss from the disposition of the forward contracts is realized and recognized on January 1, 1991. Additionally, K is deemed to have sold the franc debt instrument for $102.86, its fair market value in dollars on January 1, 1991. K will compute gain or loss with respect to the deemed sale of the franc debt instrument by subtracting its adjusted basis in the instrument ($102.86—the value of the Sf200 issue price at the spot rate on the identification date plus $2.86 of original issue discount accrued on the synthetic dollar debt instrument for 1990) from the amount realized on the deemed sale of $102.86. Thus K realizes and recognizes no gain or loss from the deemed sale of the debt instrument. The dollar amount used to determine exchange gain or loss with respect to the franc debt instrument is the Sf200 issue price on January 1, 1991, translated into dollars at the spot rate on January 1, 1991, of Sf1 = U.S.$ .5143. Except as provided in paragraph (a)(8)(iii) of this section (regarding identification by the Commissioner), the franc borrowing cannot be part of a qualified hedging transaction for any period subsequent to the leg out date.

Example 6. (i) K is a U.S. corporation with the dollar as its functional currency. On January 1, 1992, K issues a debt instrument with the following terms: the issue price is $1,000, the instrument pays interest annually at a rate of 8% on the $1,000 principal amount, the instrument matures on December 31, 1996, and the amount paid at maturity is the greater of zero or $2,000 less the U.S. dollar value (determined on December 31, 1996) of 150,000 Japanese yen.

(ii) Also on January 1, 1992, K enters into the following hedges with respect to the instrument described in the preceding paragraph: a forward contract under which K will sell 150,000 yen for $1,000 on December 31, 1996 (note that this forward rate assumes that interest rates in yen and dollars are equal); and an option contract that expires on December 31, 1996, under which K has the right (but not the obligation) to acquire 150,000 yen for $2,000. K will pay for the option by making payments to the writer of the option equal to $5 each December 31 from 1992 through 1996.

(iii) The net economic effect of these transactions is that K has created a liability with a principal amount and amount paid at maturity of $1,000, with an interest cost of 8.5% (8% on debt instrument, 0.5% option price) compounded annually. For example, if on December 31, 1996, the spot exchange rate is $1 = 100 yen, K pays $500 on the bond [$2,000 − (150,000 yen/ $100)], and $500 in satisfaction of the forward contract [$1,000 − (150,000 yen/$100)]. If instead the spot exchange rate on December 31, 1996 is $1 = 200 yen, K pays $1,250 on the bond [$2,000 − (150,000 yen/$200)] and K receives $250 in satisfaction of the forward contract [$1,000 − (150,000 yen/$200)]. Finally, if the spot exchange rate on December 31, 1996 is $1 = 50 yen, K pays $0 on the bond [$2,000 − (150,000 yen/$50), but the bond holder is not required under the terms of the instrument to pay additional principal]; K exercises the option to buy 150,000 yen for $2,000; and K then delivers the 150,000 yen as required by the forward contract in exchange for $1,000.

(iv) Assume K satisfies the identification requirements of paragraph (a)(8) of this section. The debt instrument described in paragraph (i) of this *Example 6* (which constitutes a qualifying debt instrument under paragraph (a)(3) of this section) and the forward contract and option contract described in paragraph (ii) of this example (which constitute a hedge under paragraph (a)(4) of this section and are collectively referred to hereafter as "the contracts") together are a qualified hedging transaction under paragraph (a)(1) of this section. Accordingly, with respect to K, the debt instrument and the contracts are integrated, resulting in a synthetic dollar debt instrument with an issue price of $1000, a stated redemption price at maturity of $1000 and a yield to maturity of 8.5% compounded annually (with no original issue discount). K must allocate and apportion its annual interest expense of $85 under the rules of §§ 1.861-8T through 1.861-12T.

Example 7: (i) R is a U.S. corporation with the dollar as its functional currency. On January 1, 1995, R issues a debt instrument with the following terms: the issue price is 504 British pounds (£), the instrument pays interest at a rate of 3.7% (compounded semi-annually) on the £504 principal amount, the instrument matures on December 31, 1999, with a repayment at maturity of the £ 504 principal plus the proportional gain, if any, in the "Financial Times" 100 Stock Exchange (FTSE) index (determined by the excess of the value of the FTSE index on the maturity date over the value of the FTSE on the issue date, divided by the value of the FTSE index on the issue date, multiplied by the number of FTSE index contracts that could be purchased on the issue date for £504).

(ii) Also on January 1, 1995, R enters into a contract with a bank under which on January 1, 1995, R will swap the £504 for $1,000 (at the current spot rate). R will make U.S. dollar payments to the bank equal to 8.15% on the notional principal amount of $1,000 (compounded semi-annually) for the period beginning January 1, 1995 and ending December 31, 1999. R will receive pound payments from the bank equal to 3.7% on the notional principal amount of £504 (compounded semi-annually) for the period beginning January 1, 1995 and ending December 31, 1999. On December 31, 1999, R will swap with the bank $1,000 for £504 plus the proportional gain, if any, in the FTSE index (computed as provided above).

(iii) Economically, both the indexed debt instrument and the hedging contract are hybrid instruments with the following components. The indexed debt instrument is composed of a par pound debt instrument that is assumed to have a 10.85% coupon (compounded semi-annually) plus an embedded FTSE equity index option for which the investor pays a premium of 7.15% (amortized semi-annually) on the pound principal amount. The combined effect is that the premium paid by the investor partially offsets the coupon payments resulting in a return of 3.7% (10.85% − 7.15%). Similarly, the dollar payments under the hedging contract to be made by R are computed by multiplying the dollar notional principal amount by an 8.00% rate (compounded semi-annually) which the facts assume would be the rate paid on a conventional currency swap plus a premium of 0.15% (amortized semi-annually) on the dollar notional principal amount for an embedded FTSE equity index option.

(iv) Assume R satisfies the identification requirements of paragraph (a)(8) of this section. The indexed debt instrument described in paragraph (i) of this *Example 7* constitutes a qualifying debt instrument under paragraph (a)(3) of this section. The hedging contract described in paragraph (ii) of this *Example 7* constitutes a hedge under paragraph (a)(4) of this section. Since both the pound exposure of the indexed debt instrument and the exposure to movements of the FTSE embedded in the indexed debt instrument are hedged such that a yield to maturity can be determined in dollars, the transaction satisfies the requirement of paragraph (a)(5)(i) of this section. Assuming the transactions satisfy the other requirements of paragraph (a)(5) of this section, the indexed debt instrument and hedge are a qualified hedging transaction under paragraph (a)(1) of this section. Accordingly, with respect to R, the debt instrument and the contracts are integrated, resulting in a synthetic dollar debt instrument with an issue price of $1000, a stated redemption price at maturity of $1000 and a yield to maturity of 8.15% compounded semi-annually (with no original issue discount). K must allocate and apportion its interest expense from the synthetic instrument under the rules § § 1.861-8T through 1.861-12T.

DATE	U.S. Dollars	Pounds
December 31, 1993	8	10
December 31, 1994	8	10
December 31, 1995	108	110

(ii) The interest rate on the borrowing is set and the exchange rates on the swap are fixed on December 24, 1992. On December 31, 1992, K borrows the £200 and swaps £100 for $100. Assume K has satisfied the identification requirements of paragraph (a)(8) of this section.

(iii) The £200 debt instrument satisfies the requirements of paragraph (a)(3)(i) of this section. Because all principal and interest payments under the instrument are hedged in the same proportion (50% of all interest and principal payments are hedged), 50% of the payments under the £200 instrument (principal amount of £100 and annual interest of £10) are treated as a qualifying debt instrument for purposes of paragraph (a) of this section. Thus, the distinct £100 borrowing and the currency swap contract (which constitutes a hedge under paragraph (a)(4) of this section) are a qualified hedging transaction as defined in paragraph (a)(1) of this section. Accordingly, £100 of the pound borrowing and the swap are integrated and treated as one synthetic dollar transaction with the following consequences:

(A) The integration of £100 of the pound borrowing and the swap results in a synthetic dollar borrowing with an issue price of $100 under section 1273(b)(2).

(B) The total amount of interest and principal of the synthetic dollar borrowing is equal to the dollar payments made by K under the currency swap contract (i.e., $8 in 1993, $8 in 1994, and $108 in 1995).

(C) The stated redemption price at maturity (defined in section 1273(a)(2)) is $100. Because the stated redemption price equals the issue price, there is no OID on the synthetic dollar borrowing.

(D) K may deduct the annual interest payments of $8 under section 163(a) (subject to any limitations on deductibility imposed by other provisions of the Code) according to its regular

Example 8. (i) K is a U.S. corporation with the U.S. dollar as its functional currency. On December 24, 1992, K agrees to close the following transaction on December 31, 1992. K will borrow from an unrelated party on December 31, 1992, 200 British pounds (£) for 3 years at a 10 percent rate of interest, payable annually, with no principal payment due until the final installment. K will also enter into a currency swap contract with an unrelated counterparty under the terms of which—

(A) K will swap, on December 31, 1992, £ 100 obtained from the borrowing for $100; and

(B) K will exchange dollars for pounds pursuant to the following table:

method of accounting. K has also paid $100 as a return of principal in 1995.

(E) K must allocate and apportion its interest expense from the synthetic instrument under the rules of § § 1.861-8T through 1.861-12T. That portion of the £200 pound debt instrument that is not hedged (*i.e.,* £100) is treated as a separate debt instrument subject to the rules of § 1.988-2(b) and § § 1.861-8T through 1.861-12T.

Example 9. (i) K is an accrual method U.S. corporation with the U.S. dollar as its functional currency. On January 1, 1992, K borrows 100 British pounds (£) for 3 years at a 10% rate of interest payable on December 31 of each year with no principal payment due until the final installment. On the same day, K enters into a currency swap agreement with an unrelated bank under which K agrees to the following:

(A) On January 1, 1992, K will exchange the £100 borrowed for $150.

(B) For the period beginning January 1, 1992 and ending December 31, 1994, K will pay at the end of each month an amount determined by multiplying $150 by one month LIBOR less 65 basis points and receive from the bank on December 31st of 1992, 1993, and 1994, £10.

(C) On December 31, 1994, K will exchange $150 for £100.

Assume K satisfies the identification requirements of paragraph (a)(8) of this section.

(ii) The pound borrowing (which constitutes a qualifying debt instrument under paragraph (a)(3) of this section) and the currency swap contract (which constitutes a hedge under paragraph (a)(4) of this section) are a qualified hedging transaction as defined in paragraph (a)(1) of this section. Accordingly, the pound borrowing and the swap are integrated and treated as one transaction with the following consequences:

(A) The integration of the pound borrowing and the swap results in a synthetic dollar borrowing with an issue price of $150 under section 1273(b)(2).

(B) The total amount of interest and principal of the synthetic dollar borrowing is equal to the dollar payments made by K under the currency swap contract.

(C) The stated redemption price at maturity (defined in section 1273(a)(2)) is $150. Because the stated redemption price equals the issue price, there is no OID on the synthetic dollar borrowing.

(D) K may deduct the monthly variable interest payments under section 163(a) (subject to any limitations on deductibility imposed by other provisions of the Code) according to its

DATE		Pounds	Dollars
December 31, 1992		10	12
December 31, 1993		10	12
December 31, 1994		110	162

(ii) Assume that K properly identifies the pound borrowing and the currency swap contract as a qualified hedging transaction as provided in paragraph (a)(1) of this section.

(iii) The pound loan (which constitutes a qualifying debt instrument under paragraph (a)(3) of this section) and the currency swap contract (which constitutes a hedge under paragraph (a)(4) of this section) are a qualified hedging transaction as defined in paragraph (a)(1) of this section. Accordingly, the pound loan and the swap are integrated and treated as one transaction with the following consequences:

(A) The integration of the pound loan and the swap results in a synthetic dollar loan with an issue price of $150 under section 1273(b)(2).

(B) The total amount of interest and principal of the synthetic dollar loan is equal to the dollar payments received by K under the currency swap contract (i.e., $12 in 1992, $12 in 1993, and $162 in 1994).

(C) The stated redemption price at maturity (defined in section 1273(a)(2)) is $150. Because the stated redemption price equals the issue price, there is no OID on the synthetic dollar loan.

(D) K must include in income as interest $12 in 1992, 1993, and 1994.

(E) The source of the interest income shall be determined by applying sections 861(a)(1) and 862(a)(1) with reference to the pound interest income that would have been received had the transaction not been integrated.

(iv) On January 1, 1993, K transfers both the pound loan and the currency swap to B, its wholly owned U.S. subsidiary, in exchange for B stock in a transfer that satisfies the requirements of section 351. Under paragraph (a)(6) of this section, the transfer of both instruments is not "legging out." Rather, K is considered to have transferred the synthetic dollar loan to B in a

regular method of accounting. K has also paid $150 as a return of principal in 1994.

(E) K must allocate and apportion its interest expense from the synthetic instrument under the rules of §§ 1.861-8T through 1.861-12T.

Example 10. (i) K is an accrual method U.S. corporation with the U.S. dollar as its functional currency. On January 1, 1992, K loans 100 British pounds (£) for 3 years at a 10% rate of interest payable on December 31 of each year with no principal payment due until the final installment. The spot rate on January 1, 1992, is £ 1 = $1.50. Also on January 1, 1992, K enters into a currency swap contract with an unrelated counterparty under the terms of which K will exchange pounds for dollars pursuant to the following table:

transaction in which gain or loss is not recognized. B's basis in the loan under section 362 is $100.

(10) *Transition rules and effective dates for certain provisions.*—(i) *Coordination with Notice 87-11.*—Any transaction entered into prior to September 21, 1989 which satisfied the requirements of Notice 87-11, 1987-1 C.B. 423, shall be deemed to satisfy the requirements of paragraph (a) of this section.

(ii) *Prospective application to contingent payment debt instruments.*—In the case of a contingent payment debt instrument, the definition of qualifying debt instrument set forth in paragraph (a)(3)(i) of this section applies to transactions entered into after March 17, 1992.

(iii) *Prospective application of partial hedging rule.*—Paragraph (a)(3)(ii) of this section is effective for transactions entered into after March 17, 1992.

(iv) *Effective date for paragraph (a)(6)(i) of this section.*—The rules of paragraph (a)(6)(i) of this section are effective for qualified hedging transactions that are legged into after March 17, 1992.

(b) *Hedged executory contracts.*—(1) *In general.*—If the taxpayer enters into a hedged executory contract as defined in paragraph (b)(2) of this section, the executory contract and the hedge shall be integrated as provided in paragraph (b)(4) of this section.

(2) *Definitions.*—(i) *Hedged executory contract.*—A hedged executory contract is an executory contract as defined in paragraph (b)(2)(ii) of this section that is the subject of a hedge as defined in paragraph (b)(2)(iii) of this section, provided that the following requirements are satisfied—

(A) The executory contract and the hedge are identified as a hedged executory contract as provided in paragraph (b)(3) of this section.

(B) The hedge is entered into (*i.e.*, settled or closed, or in the case of nonfunctional currency deposited in an account with a bank or other financial institution, such currency is acquired and deposited) on or after the date the executory contract is entered into and before the accrual date as defined in paragraph (b)(2)(iv) of this section.

(C) The executory contract is hedged in whole or in part throughout the period beginning with the date the hedge is identified in accordance with paragraph (b)(3) of this section and ending on or after the accrual date.

(D) None of the parties to the hedge are related. The term related means the relationships defined in section 267(b) and section 707(c)(1).

(E) In the case of a qualified business unit with a residence, as defined in section 988(a)(3)(B), outside of the United States, both the executory contract and the hedge are properly reflected on the books of the same qualified business unit.

(F) Subject to the limitations of paragraph (b)(2)(i)(E) of this section, both the executory contract and the hedge are entered into by the same individual, partnership, trust, estate, or corporation. With respect to a corporation, the same corporation must enter into both the executory contract and the hedge whether or not such corporation is a member of an affiliated group of corporations that files a consolidated return.

(G) With respect to a foreign person engaged in a U.S. trade or business that enters into an executory contract or hedge through such trade or business, all items of income and expense associated with the executory contract and the hedge would have been effectively connected with such U.S. trade or business throughout the term of the hedged executory contract had this paragraph (b) not applied.

(ii) *Executory contract.*—(A) *In general.*—Except as provided in paragraph (b)(2)(ii)(B) of this section, an executory contract is an agreement entered into before the accrual date to pay nonfunctional currency (or an amount determined with reference thereto) in the future with respect to the purchase of property used in the ordinary course of the taxpayer's business, or the acquisition of a service (or services), in the future, or to receive nonfunctional currency (or an amount determined with reference thereto) in the future with respect to the sale of property used or held for sale in the ordinary course of the taxpayer's business, or the performance of a service (or services), in the future. Notwithstanding the preceding sentence, a contract to buy or sell stock shall be considered an executory contract. (Thus, for example, a contract to sell stock

of an affiliate is an executory contract for this purpose.) On the accrual date, such agreement ceases to be considered an executory contract and is treated as an account payable or receivable.

(B) *Exceptions.*—An executory contract does not include a section 988 transaction. For example, a forward contract to purchase nonfunctional currency is not an executory contract. An executory contract also does not include a transaction described in paragraph (c) of this section.

(C) *Effective date for contracts to buy or sell stock.*—That part of paragraph (b)(2)(ii)(A) of this section which provides that a contract to buy or sell stock shall be considered an executory contract applies to contracts to buy or sell stock entered into on or after March 17, 1992.

(iii) *Hedge.*—(A) *In general.*—For purposes of this paragraph (b), the term hedge means a deposit of nonfunctional currency in a hedging account (as defined in paragraph (b)(3)(iii)(D) of this section), a forward or futures contract described in § 1.988-1(a)(1)(ii) and (2)(iii), or combination thereof, which reduces the risk of exchange rate fluctuations by reference to the taxpayer's functional currency with respect to nonfunctional currency payments made or received under an executory contract. The term hedge also includes an option contract described in § 1.988-1(a)(1)(ii) and (2)(iii), but only if the option's expiration date is on or before the accrual date. The premium paid for an option that lapses shall be integrated with the executory contract.

(B) *Special rule for series of hedges.*—A series of hedges as defined in paragraph (b)(3)(iii)(A) of this section shall be considered a hedge if the executory contract is hedged in whole or in part throughout the period beginning with the date the hedge is identified in accordance with paragraph (b)(3)(i) of this section and ending on or after the accrual date. A taxpayer that enters into a series of hedges will be deemed to have satisfied the preceding sentence if the hedge that succeeds a hedge that has been terminated is entered into no later than the business day following such termination.

(C) *Special rules for historical rate rollovers.*—(1) *Definition.*—A historical rate rollover is an extension of the maturity date of a forward contract where the new forward rate is adjusted on the rollover date to reflect the taxpayer's gain or loss on the contract as of the rollover date plus the time value of such gain or loss through the new maturity date.

(2) *Certain historical rate rollovers considered a hedge.*—A historical rate rollover is considered a hedge if the rollover date is before the accrual date.

(3) Treatment of time value component of certain historical rate rollovers that are hedges.—Interest income or expense determined under § 1.988-2(d)(2)(v) with respect to a historical rate rollover shall be considered part of a hedge if the period beginning on the first date a hedging contract is rolled over and ending on the date payment is made or received under the executory contract does not exceed 183 days. Such interest income or expense shall not be recognized and shall be an adjustment to the income from, or expense of, the services performed or received under the executory contract, or to the amount realized or basis of the property sold or purchased under the executory contract. For the treatment of such interest income or expense that is not considered part of a hedge, see § 1.988-2(d)(2)(v).

(D) Special rules regarding deposits of nonfunctional currency in a hedging account.—A hedging account is an account with a bank or other financial institution used exclusively for deposits of nonfunctional currency used to hedge executory contracts. For purposes of determining the basis of units in such account that comprise the hedge, only those units in the account as of the accrual date shall be taken into consideration. A taxpayer may adopt any reasonable convention (consistently applied to all hedging accounts) to determine which units comprise the hedge as of the accrual date and the basis of the units as of such date.

(E) Interest income on deposit of nonfunctional currency in a hedging account.—Interest income on a deposit of nonfunctional currency in a hedging account may be taken into account for purposes of determining the amount of a hedge if such interest is accrued on or before the accrual date. However, such interest income shall be included in income as provided in section 61. For example, if a taxpayer with the dollar as its functional currency enters into an executory contract for the purchase and delivery of a machine in one year for 100 British pounds (£), and on such date deposits £90.91 in a properly identified bank account that bears interest at the rate of 10%, the interest that accrues prior to the accrual date shall be included in income and may be considered a hedge.

(iv) Accrual date.—The accrual date is the date when the item of income or expense (including a capital expenditure) that relates to an executory contract is required to be accrued under the taxpayer's method of accounting.

(v) Payment date.—The payment date is the date when payment is made or received with respect to an executory contract or the subsequent corresponding account payable or receivable.

(3) Identification rules.—(i) *Identification by the taxpayer.*—A taxpayer must establish a record and before the close of the date the hedge is entered into, the taxpayer must enter into the record a clear description of the executory contract and the hedge and indicate that the transaction is being identified in accordance with paragraph (b)(3) of this section.

(ii) Identification by the Commissioner.—If a taxpayer enters into an executory contract and a hedge but fails to satisfy one or more of the requirements of paragraph (b) of this section and, based on the facts and circumstances, the Commissioner concludes that the executory contract in substance is hedged, then the Commissioner may apply the provisions of paragraph (b) of this section as if the taxpayer had satisfied all of the requirements therein, and may make appropriate adjustments. The Commissioner may apply the provisions of paragraph (b) of this section regardless of whether the executory contract and the hedge are held by the same taxpayer.

(4) Effect of hedged executory contract.—(i) *In general.*—If a taxpayer enters into a hedged executory contract, amounts paid or received under the hedge by the taxpayer are treated as paid or received by the taxpayer under the executory contract, or any subsequent account payable or receivable, or that portion to which the hedge relates. Also, the taxpayer recognizes no exchange gain or loss on the hedge. If an executory contract, on the accrual date, becomes an account payable or receivable, the taxpayer recognizes no exchange gain or loss on such payable or receivable for the period covered by the hedge.

(ii) Partially hedged executory contracts.—The effect of integrating an executory contract and a hedge that partially hedges such contract is to treat the amounts paid or received under the hedge as paid or received under the portion of the executory contract being hedged, or any subsequent account payable or receivable. The income or expense of services performed or received under the executory contract, or the amount realized or basis of property sold or purchased under the executory contract, that is attributable to that portion of the executory contract that is not hedged shall be translated into functional currency on the accrual date. Exchange gain or loss shall be realized when payment is made or received with respect to any payable or receivable arising on the accrual date with respect to such unhedged amount.

(iii) Disposition of a hedge or executory contract prior to the accrual date.—(A) *In general.*—If a taxpayer identifies an executory contract as part of a hedged executory contract as defined in paragraph (b)(2) of this section, and disposes of (or otherwise terminates) the executory contract prior to the accrual date, the hedge shall be treated as sold for its fair market value on the date the executory contract is disposed of and any gain or loss shall be realized and recognized

on such date. Such gain or loss shall be an adjustment to the amount received or expended with respect to the disposition or termination, if any. The spot rate on the date the hedge is treated as sold shall be used to determine subsequent exchange gain or loss on the hedge. If a taxpayer identifies a hedge as part of a hedged executory contract as defined in paragraph (b)(2) of this section, and disposes of the hedge prior to the accrual date, any gain or loss realized on such disposition shall not be recognized and shall be an adjustment to the income from, or expense of, the services performed or received under the executory contract, or to the amount realized or basis of the property sold or purchased under the executory contract.

(B) *Certain events in a series of hedges treated as a termination of the hedged executory contract.*—If the rules of paragraph (b)(2)(iii)(B) of this section are not satisfied, the hedged executory contract shall be terminated and the provisions of paragraph (b)(4)(iii)(A) of this section shall apply to any gain or loss previously realized with respect to such hedge. Any subsequent hedging contracts entered into to reduce the risk of exchange rate movements with respect to such executory contract shall not be considered a hedge as defined in paragraph (b)(2)(iii) of this section.

(C) *Executory contracts between related persons.*—If an executory contract is between related persons as defined in section 267(b) and 707(b), and the taxpayer disposes of the hedge or terminates the executory contract prior to the accrual date, the Commissioner may redetermine the timing, source, and character of gain or loss from the hedge or the executory contract if he determines that a significant purpose for disposing of the hedge or terminating the executory contract prior to the accrual date was to affect the timing, source, or character of income, gain, expense, or loss for Federal income tax purposes.

(iv) *Disposition of a hedge on or after the accrual date.*—If a taxpayer identifies a hedge as part of a hedged executory contract as defined in paragraph (b)(2) of this section, and disposes of the hedge on or after the accrual date, no gain or loss is recognized on the hedge and the booking date as defined in § 1.988-2(c)(2) of the payable or receivable for purposes of computing exchange gain or loss shall be the date such hedge is disposed of. See *Example 3* of paragraph (b)(4)(iv) of this section.

(v) *Sections 263(g), 1092, and 1256 do not apply.*—Sections 263(g), 1092, and 1256 do not apply with respect to an executory contract or hedge which comprise a hedged executory contract as defined in paragraph (b)(2) of this section. However, sections 263(g), 1092 and 1256 may apply to the hedged executory contract if such transaction is part of a straddle.

(vi) *Examples.*—The principles set forth in paragraph (b) of this section are illustrated in the following examples. The examples assume that K is an accrual method, calendar year U.S. corporation with the dollar as its functional currency.

Example 1. (i) On January 1, 1992, K enters into a contract with JPF, a Swiss machine manufacturer, to pay 500,000 Swiss francs for delivery of a machine on June 1, 1993. Also on January 1, 1992, K enters into a foreign currency forward agreement to purchase 500,000 Swiss francs for $250,000 for delivery on June 1, 1993. K properly identifies the executory contract and the hedge in accordance with paragraph (b)(3)(i) of this section. On June 1, 1993, K takes delivery of the 500,000 Swiss francs (in exchange for $250,000) under the forward contract and makes payment of 500,000 Swiss francs to JPF in exchange for the machine. Assume that the accrual date is June 1, 1993.

(ii) Under paragraph (b)(1) of this section, the hedge is integrated with the executory contract. Therefore, K is deemed to have paid $250,000 for the machine and there is no exchange gain or loss on the foreign currency forward contract. K's basis in the machine is $250,000. Section 1256 does not apply to the forward contract.

Example 2. (i) On January 1, 1992, K enters into a contract with S, a Swiss machine manufacturer, to pay 500,000 Swiss francs for delivery of a machine on June 1, 1993. Under the contract, K is not obligated to pay for the machine until September 1, 1993. On February 1, 1992, K enters into a foreign currency forward agreement to purchase 500,000 Swiss francs for $250,000 for delivery on September 1, 1993. K properly identifies the executory contract and the hedge in accordance with paragraph (b)(3) of this section. On June 1, 1993, K takes delivery of [the] machine. Assume that under K's method of accounting the delivery date is the accrual date. On September 1, 1993, K takes delivery of the 500,000 Swiss francs (in exchange for $250,000) under the forward contract and makes payment of 500,000 Swiss francs to S.

(ii) Under paragraph (b)(1) of this section, the hedge is integrated with the executory contract. Therefore K is deemed to have paid $250,000 for the machine and there is no exchange gain or loss on the foreign currency forward contract. Thus K's basis in the machine is $250,000. In addition, no exchange gain or loss is recognized on the payable in existence from June 1, 1993, to September 1, 1993. Section 1256 does not apply to the forward contract.

Example 3. The facts are the same as in *Example 2* except that K disposed of the forward contract on August 1, 1993 for $10,000. Pursuant to paragraph (b)(4)(iv) of this section, K does not recognize the $10,000 gain. K's basis in the machine is $250,000 (the amount fixed by the forward contract), regardless of the amount in dollars that K actually pays to acquire the Sf500,000 when K pays for the machine. K has a payable with a booking date of August 1, 1993, payable on September 1, 1993 for 500,000 Swiss francs. Thus, K will realize exchange gain or loss on the difference between the amount booked on August 1, 1993 and the amount paid on September 1, 1993 under § 1.988-2(c).

Example 4. (i) On January 1, 1992, K enters into a contract with S, a Swiss machine repair firm, to pay 500,000 Swiss francs for repairs to be performed on June 1, 1992. Under the contract, K is not obligated to pay for the repairs until September 1, 1992. On February 1, 1992, K enters into a foreign currency forward agreement to purchase 500,000 Swiss francs for $250,000 for delivery on August 1, 1992. K properly identifies the executory contract and the hedge in accordance with paragraph (b)(3) of this section. On June 1, 1992, S performs the repair services. Assume that under K's method of accounting this date is the accrual date. On August 1, 1992, K takes delivery of the 500,000 Swiss francs (in exchange for $250,000) under the forward contract. On the same day, K deposits the Sf500,000 in a separate account with a bank and properly identifies the transaction as a continuation of the hedged executory contract. On September 1, 1992, K makes payment of the Sf500,000 in the account to S.

(ii) Under paragraph (b)(1) of this section, the hedge is integrated with the executory contract. Therefore K is deemed to have paid $250,000 for the services and there is no exchange gain or loss on the foreign currency forward contract or on the disposition of Sf500,000 in the account. Any interest on the Swiss francs in the account is included in income but is not considered part of the hedge (because the amount paid for the services must be set on or before the accrual date). In addition, no exchange gain or loss is recognized on the payable in existence from June 1, 1992, to September 1, 1992. Section 1256 does not apply to the forward contract.

Example 5. (i) On January 1, 1992, K enters into a contract with S, a Swiss machine manufacturer, to pay 500,000 Swiss francs for delivery of a machine on June 1, 1993. Under the contract, K is not obligated to pay for the machine until September 1, 1993. On February 1, 1992, K enters into a foreign currency forward agreement to purchase 250,000 Swiss francs for $125,000 for delivery on September 1, 1993. K properly identifies the executory contract and the hedge in accordance with paragraph (b)(3) of this section. On June 1, 1993, K takes delivery of the machine. Assume that under K's method of accounting the delivery date is the accrual date. Assume further that the exchange rate is Sf1 = $.50 on June 1, 1993. On August 30, 1993, K purchases Sf250,000 for $135,000. On September 1, 1993, K takes delivery of the 250,000 Swiss francs (in exchange for $125,000) under the forward contract and

makes payment of 500,000 Swiss francs (the Sf250,000 received under the contract plus the Sf250,000 purchased on August 30, 1993) to S. Assume the spot rate on September 1, 1993, is 1 Sf1 = $.5420 (Sf250,000 equal $135,500).

(ii) Under paragraph (b)(1) of this section, the partial hedge is integrated with the executory contract. K is deemed to have paid $250,000 for the machine [$125,000 on the hedged portion of the Sf500,000 and $125,000 ($.50, the spot rate on June 1, 1993, times Sf250,000) on the unhedged portion of the Sf500,000]. K's basis in the machine therefore is $250,000. K recognizes no exchange gain or loss on the foreign currency forward contract but K will realize exchange gain of $500 on the disposition of the Sf250,000 purchased on August 30, 1993 under § 1.988-2(a). In addition, exchange loss is realized on the unhedged portion of the payable in existence from June 1, 1993, to September 1, 1993. Thus, K will realize exchange loss of $10,500 ($125,000 booked less $135,500 paid) under § 1.988-2 (c) on the payable. Section 1256 does not apply to the forward contract.

Example 6. (i) On January 1, 1990, K enters into a contract with S, a Swiss steel manufacturer, to buy steel for 1,000,000 Swiss francs (Sf) for delivery and payment on December 31, 1990. On January 1, 1990, the spot rate is Sf1 = $.50, the U.S. dollar interest rate is 10% compounded annually, and the Swiss franc rate is 5% compounded annually. Under K's method of accounting, the delivery date is the accrual date.

(ii) Assume that on January 1, 1990, K enters into a foreign currency forward contract to buy Sf1,000,000 for $523,800 for delivery on December 31, 1990. K properly identifies the executory contract and the hedge in accordance with paragraph (b)(3) of this section. Pursuant to paragraph (b)(2)(iii) of this section, the forward contract constitutes a hedge. Assuming that the requirements of paragraph (b)(2)(i) of this section are satisfied, the executory contract to buy steel and the forward contract are integrated under paragraph (b)(1) of this section. Thus, K is deemed to have paid $523,800 for the steel and will have a basis in the steel of $523,800. No gain or loss is realized with respect to the forward contract and section 1256 does not apply to such contract.

(iii) Assume instead that on January 1, 1990, K enters into a foreign currency forward contract to buy Sf1,000,000 for $512,200 for delivery on July 1, 1990. K properly identifies the executory contract and the hedge in accordance with paragraph (b)(3) of this section. On July 1, 1990, when the spot rate is Sf1 = $.53, K cancels the forward contract in exchange for $17,800 ($530,000 – $512,200). On July 1, 1990, K enters into a second forward agreement to buy Sf1,000,000 for $542,900 for delivery on December 31, 1990. K properly identifies the second forward agreement as a hedge in accordance with paragraph (b)(3) of this section. Pursuant to

Reg. § 1.988-5(b)(4)(vi)

paragraph (b)(2)(iii) of this section, the forward contract entered into on January 1, 1990, and the forward contract entered into on July 1, 1990, constitute a hedge. Assuming that the requirements of paragraph (b)(2)(i) of this section are satisfied, the executory contract to buy steel and the forward agreements are integrated under paragraph (b)(1) of this section. Thus, K is deemed to have paid $525,100 for the steel (the forward price in the second forward agreement of $542,900 less the gain on the first forward agreement of $17,800) and will have a basis in the steel of $525,100. No gain is realized with respect to the forward contracts and section 1256 does not apply to such contracts.

(iv) Assume instead that on January 1, 1990, K enters into a foreign currency forward contract to buy Sf1,000,000 for $512,200 for delivery on July 1, 1990. K properly identifies the executory contract and the hedge in accordance with paragraph (b)(3) of this section. On July 1, 1990, when the spot rate is Sf1 = $.53, K enters into a historical rate rollover of its $17,800 gain ($530,000 − $512,200) on the forward agreement. Thus, K enters into a second foreign currency forward agreement to buy Sf1,000,000 for $524,210 for delivery on December 31, 1990. (The forward price of $524,210 is the market forward price on July 1, 1990 for the purchase of Sf1,000,000 for delivery on December 31, 1990 of $542,900 less the $17,800 gain on January 1, 1990 contract and less the time value of such gain of $890.) K properly identifies the second forward agreement as a hedge in accordance with paragraph (b)(3) of this section. On December 31, 1990, when the spot rate is Sf1 = $.54, K takes delivery of the Sf1,000,000 (in exchange for $524,210) and purchases the steel for Sf1,000,000. Pursuant to paragraph (b)(2)(iii) of this section, the forward contract entered into on January 1, 1990, and the forward contract entered into on July 1, 1990, which incorporates the rollover of K's gain on the January 1, 1990 contract, constitute a hedge. Assuming that the requirements of paragraph (b)(2)(i) of this section are satisfied, the executory contract to buy steel and the forward agreements are integrated under paragraph (b)(1) of this section. Because the period from the rollover date to the date payment is made under the executory contract does not exceed 183 days, the $890 of interest income is considered part of the hedge and is not recognized. Thus, K is deemed to have paid $524,210 for the steel and will have a basis in the steel of $524,210. No gain is realized with respect to the forward contracts and section 1256 does not apply to such contracts.

(v) Assume instead that on January 1, 1990, K purchases Sf952,380.95 (the present value of Sf1,000,000 to be paid on December 31, 1990) for $476,190.48 and on the same day deposits the Swiss francs in a separate bank account that bears interest at a rate of 5%, compounded annually. K properly identifies the transaction as a hedged executory contract. Over the period beginning January 1, 1990, and ending December 31, 1990, K receives Sf47,619.05 in interest on the account that is included in income and that has a basis of $25,714.29. (Assume that under § 1.988-2(b)(1), K uses the spot rate of Sf1 = $.54 to translate the interest income). On December 31, 1990, K makes payment of the Sf1,000,000 principal and accrued interest in the account to S. Pursuant to paragraph (b)(2)(iii) of this section, the principal in the bank account and the interest constitute a hedge. Under paragraph (b)(1) of this section, the hedge is integrated with the executory contract. Therefore K is deemed to have paid $501,904.77 (the basis of the principal deposited plus the basis of the interest) for the steel and there is no exchange gain or loss on the disposition of the Sf1,000,000. K's basis in the steel therefore is $501,904.77.

(5) *References to this paragraph (b).*—If the rules of this paragraph (b) are referred to in another paragraph of this section (*e.g.*, paragraph (c) of this section), then the rules of this paragraph (b) shall be applied for purposes of such other paragraph by substituting terms appropriate for such other paragraph. For example, paragraph (c)(2) of this section refers to the identification rules of paragraph (b)(3) of this section. Accordingly, for purposes of paragraph (c)(2), the rules of paragraph (b)(3) will be applied by substituting the term "stock or security" for "executory contract".

(c) *Hedges of period between trade date and settlement date on purchase or sale of publicly traded stock or security.*—If a taxpayer purchases or sells stocks or securities which are traded on an established securities market and—

(1) Hedges all or part of such purchase or sale for any part of the period beginning on the trade date and ending on the settlement date; and

(2) Identifies the hedge and the underlying stock or securities as an integrated transaction under the rules of paragraph (b)(3) of this section;

then any gain or loss on the hedge shall be an adjustment to the amount realized or the adjusted basis of the stock or securities sold or purchased (and shall not be taken into account as exchange gain or loss). The term hedge means a deposit of nonfunctional currency in a hedging account (within the meaning of paragraph (b)(2)(iii)(D) of this section), or a forward or futures contract described in § 1.988-1(a)(1)(ii) and (2)(iii), or combination thereof, which reduces the risk of exchange rate fluctuations for any portion of the period beginning on the trade date and ending on the settlement date. The provisions of paragraphs (b)(2)(i)(D) through (G), and (b)(2)(iii)(D) and (E) of this section shall apply. Sections 263(g), 1092, and 1256 do not apply with respect to stock or securities and a hedge which are subject to this paragraph (c).

(d) [Reserved]

(e) *Advance rulings regarding net hedging and anticipatory hedging systems.*—In his sole discretion, the Commissioner may issue an advance ruling addressing the income tax consequences of a taxpayer's system of hedging either its net nonfunctional currency exposure or anticipated nonfunctional currency exposure. The ruling may address the character, source, and timing of both the section 988 transaction(s) making up the hedge and the underlying transactions being hedged. The procedures for obtaining a ruling shall be governed by such pertinent revenue procedures and revenue rulings as the Commissioner may provide. The Commissioner will not issue a ruling regarding hedges of a taxpayer's investment in a foreign subsidiary.

(f) [Reserved]

(g) *General effective date.*—Except as otherwise provided in this section, the rules of this section shall apply to qualified hedging transactions, hedged executory contracts and transactions described in paragraph (c) of this section entered into on or after September 21, 1989. This section shall apply even if the transaction being hedged (*e.g.*, the debt instrument) was entered into or acquired prior to such date. The effective date regarding advance rulings for net and anticipatory hedging shall be governed by such revenue procedures that the Commissioner may publish. [Reg. § 1.988-5.]

☐ *[T.D. 8400, 3-16-92.]*

[Reg. § 1.988-6]

§ 1.988-6. Nonfunctional currency contingent payment debt instruments.—(a) *In general.*—(1) *Scope.*—This section determines the accrual of interest and the amount, timing, source, and character of any gain or loss on nonfunctional currency contingent payment debt instruments described in this paragraph (a)(1) and to which § 1.1275-4(a) would otherwise apply if the debt instrument were denominated in the taxpayer's functional currency. Except as provided by the rules in this section, the rules in § 1.1275-4 (relating to contingent payment debt instruments) apply to the following instruments—

(i) A debt instrument described in § 1.1275-4(b)(1) for which all payments of principal and interest are denominated in, or determined by reference to, a single nonfunctional currency and which has one or more non-currency related contingencies;

(ii) A debt instrument described in § 1.1275-4(b)(1) for which payments of principal or interest are denominated in, or determined by reference to, more than one currency and which has no non-currency related contingencies;

(iii) A debt instrument described in § 1.1275-4(b)(1) for which payments of principal or interest are denominated in, or determined by reference to, more than one currency and which

has one or more non-currency related contingencies; and

(iv) A debt instrument otherwise described in paragraph (a)(1)(i), (ii) or (iii) of this section, except that the debt instrument is described in § 1.1275-4(c)(1) rather than § 1.1275-4(b)(1) (e.g., the instrument is issued for non-publicly traded property).

(2) *Exception for hyperinflationary currencies.*—(i) *In general.*—Except as provided in paragraph (a)(2)(ii) of this section, this section shall not apply to an instrument described in paragraph (a)(1) of this section if any payment made under such instrument is determined by reference to a hyperinflationary currency, as defined in § 1.985-1(b)(2)(ii)(D). In such case, the amount, timing, source and character of interest, principal, foreign currency gain or loss, and gain or loss relating to a non-currency contingency shall be determined under the method that reflects the instrument's economic substance.

(ii) *Discretion as to method.*—If a taxpayer does not account for an instrument described in paragraph (a)(2)(i) of this section in a manner that reflects the instrument's economic substance, the Commissioner may apply the rules of this section to such an instrument or apply the principles of § 1.988-2(b)(15), reasonably taking into account the contingent feature or features of the instrument.

(b) *Instruments described in paragraph (a)(1)(i) of this section.*—(1) *In general.*—Paragraph (b)(2) of this section provides rules for applying the noncontingent bond method (as set forth in § 1.1275-4(b)) in the nonfunctional currency in which a debt instrument described in paragraph (a)(1)(i) of this section is denominated, or by reference to which its payments are determined (the denomination currency). Paragraph (b)(3) of this section describes how amounts determined in paragraph (b)(2) of this section shall be translated from the denomination currency of the instrument into the taxpayer's functional currency. Paragraph (b)(4) of this section describes how gain or loss (other than foreign currency gain or loss) shall be determined and characterized with respect to the instrument. Paragraph (b)(5) of this section describes how foreign currency gain or loss shall be determined with respect to accrued interest and principal on the instrument. Paragraph (b)(6) of this section provides rules for determining the source and character of any gain or loss with respect to the instrument. Paragraph (b)(7) of this section provides rules for subsequent holders of an instrument who purchase the instrument for an amount other than the adjusted issue price of the instrument. Paragraph (c) of this section provides examples of the application of paragraph (b) of this section. See paragraph (d) of this section for the determination of the denomination currency of an instrument described in paragraph (a)(1)(ii) or (iii) of this section. See paragraph (e) of this section for the treatment of an instrument described in paragraph (a)(1)(iv) of this section.

(2) *Application of noncontingent bond method.*—(i) *Accrued interest.*—Interest accruals on an instrument described in paragraph (a)(1)(i) of this section are initially determined in the denomination currency of the instrument by applying the noncontingent bond method, set forth in § 1.1275-4(b), to the instrument in its denomination currency. Accordingly, the comparable yield, projected payment schedule, and comparable fixed rate debt instrument, described in § 1.1275-4(b)(4), are determined in the denomination currency. For purposes of applying the noncontingent bond method to instruments described in this paragraph, the applicable Federal rate described in § 1.1275-4(b)(4)(i) shall be the rate described in § 1.1274-4(d) with respect to the denomination currency.

(ii) *Net positive and negative adjustments.*—Positive and negative adjustments, and net positive and net negative adjustments, with respect to an instrument described in paragraph (a)(1)(i) of this section are determined by applying the rules of § 1.1275-4(b)(6) (and § 1.1275-4(b)(9)(i) and (ii), if applicable) in the denomination currency. Accordingly, a net positive adjustment is treated as additional interest (in the denomination currency) on the instrument. A net negative adjustment first reduces interest that otherwise would be accrued by the taxpayer during the current tax year in the denomination currency. If a net negative adjustment exceeds the interest that would otherwise be accrued by the taxpayer during the current tax year in the denomination currency, the excess is treated as ordinary loss (if the taxpayer is a holder of the instrument) or ordinary income (if the taxpayer is the issuer of the instrument). The amount treated as ordinary loss by a holder with respect to a net negative adjustment is limited, however, to the amount by which the holder's total interest inclusions on the debt instrument (determined in the denomination currency) exceed the total amount of the holder's net negative adjustments treated as ordinary loss on the debt instrument in prior taxable years (determined in the denomination currency). Similarly, the amount treated as ordinary income by an issuer with respect to a net negative adjustment is limited to the amount by which the issuer's total interest deductions on the debt instrument (determined in the denomination currency) exceed the total amount of the issuer's net negative adjustments treated as ordinary income on the debt instrument in prior taxable years (determined in the denomination currency). To the extent a net negative adjustment exceeds the current year's interest accrual and the amount treated as ordinary loss to a holder (or ordinary income to the issuer), the excess is treated as a negative adjustment carryforward, within the meaning of

§ 1.1275-4(b)(6)(iii)(C), in the denomination currency.

(iii) *Adjusted issue price.*—The adjusted issue price of an instrument described in paragraph (a)(1)(i) of this section is determined by applying the rules of § 1.1275-4(b)(7) in the denomination currency. Accordingly, the adjusted issue price is equal to the debt instrument's issue price in the denomination currency, increased by the interest previously accrued on the debt instrument (determined without regard to any net positive or net negative adjustments on the instrument) and decreased by the amount of any noncontingent payment and the projected amount of any contingent payment previously made on the instrument. All adjustments to the adjusted issue price are calculated in the denomination currency.

(iv) *Adjusted basis.*—The adjusted basis of an instrument described in paragraph (a)(1)(i) of this section is determined by applying the rules of § 1.1275-4(b)(7) in the taxpayer's functional currency. In accordance with those rules, a holder's basis in the debt instrument is increased by the interest previously accrued on the debt instrument (translated into functional currency), without regard to any net positive or net negative adjustments on the instrument (except as provided in paragraph (b)(7) or (8) of this section, if applicable), and decreased by the amount of any noncontingent payment and the projected amount of any contingent payment previously made on the instrument to the holder (translated into functional currency). See paragraph (b)(3)(iii) of this section for translation rules.

(v) *Amount realized.*—The amount realized by a holder and the repurchase price paid by the issuer on the scheduled or unscheduled retirement of a debt instrument described in paragraph (a)(1)(i) of this section are determined by applying the rules of § 1.1275-4(b)(7) in the denomination currency. For example, with regard to a scheduled retirement at maturity, the holder is treated as receiving the projected amount of any contingent payment due at maturity, reduced by the amount of any negative adjustment carryforward. For purposes of translating the amount realized by the holder into functional currency, the rules of paragraph (b)(3)(iv) of this section shall apply.

(3) *Treatment and translation of amounts determined under noncontingent bond method.*—(i) *Accrued interest.*—The amount of accrued interest, determined under paragraph (b)(2)(i) of this section, is translated into the taxpayer's functional currency at the average exchange rate, as described in § 1.988-2(b)(2)(iii)(A), or, at the taxpayer's election, at the appropriate spot rate, as described in § 1.988-2(b)(2)(iii)(B).

(ii) *Net positive and negative adjustments.*—(A) *Net positive adjustments.*—A net positive adjustment, as referenced in paragraph (b)(2)(ii) of this section, is translated into the taxpayer's functional currency at the spot rate on the last day of the taxable year in which the adjustment is taken into account under § 1.1275-4(b)(6), or, if earlier, the date the instrument is disposed of or otherwise terminated.

(B) *Net negative adjustments.*—A net negative adjustment is treated and, where necessary, is translated from the denomination currency into the taxpayer's functional currency under the following rules:

(1) The amount of a net negative adjustment determined in the denomination currency that reduces the current year's interest in that currency shall first reduce the current year's accrued but unpaid interest, and then shall reduce the current year's interest which was accrued and paid. No translation is required.

(2) The amount of a net negative adjustment treated as ordinary income or loss under § 1.1275-4(b)(6)(iii)(B) first is attributable to accrued but unpaid interest accrued in prior taxable years. For this purpose, the net negative adjustment shall be treated as attributable to any unpaid interest accrued in the immediately preceding taxable year, and thereafter to unpaid interest accrued in each preceding taxable year. The amount of the net negative adjustment applied to accrued but unpaid interest is translated into functional currency at the same rate used, in each of the respective prior taxable years, to translate the accrued interest.

(3) Any amount of the net negative adjustment remaining after the application of paragraphs (b)(3)(ii)(B)(1) and (2) of this section is attributable to interest accrued and paid in prior taxable years. The amount of the net negative adjustment applied to such amounts is translated into functional currency at the spot rate on the date the debt instrument was issued or, if later, acquired.

(4) Any amount of the net negative adjustment remaining after application of paragraphs (b)(3)(ii)(B)(1), (2) and (3) of this section is a negative adjustment carryforward, within the meaning of § 1.1275-4(b)(6)(iii)(C). A negative adjustment carryforward is carried forward in the denomination currency and is applied to reduce interest accruals in subsequent years. In the year in which the instrument is sold, exchanged or retired, any negative adjustment carryforward not applied to interest reduces the holder's amount realized on the instrument (in the denomination currency). An issuer of a debt instrument described in paragraph (a)(1)(i) of this section who takes into income a negative adjustment carryforward (that is not applied to interest) in the year the instrument is retired, as described in § 1.1275-4(b)(6)(iii)(C), translates such income into functional currency at the spot rate on the date the instrument was issued.

(iii) *Adjusted basis.*—(A) *In general.*—Except as otherwise provided in this paragraph and paragraph (b)(7) or (8) of this section, a holder determines and maintains adjusted basis by translating the denomination currency amounts determined under § 1.1275-4(b)(7)(iii) into functional currency as follows:

(1) The holder's initial basis in the instrument is determined by translating the amount paid by the holder to acquire the instrument (in the denomination currency) into functional currency at the spot rate on the date the instrument was issued or, if later, acquired.

(2) An increase in basis attributable to interest accrued on the instrument is translated at the rate applicable to such interest under paragraph (b)(3)(i) of this section.

(3) Any noncontingent payment and the projected amount of any contingent payments determined in the denomination currency that decrease the holder's basis in the instrument under § 1.1275-4(b)(7)(iii) are translated as follows:

(i) The payment first is attributable to the most recently accrued interest to which prior amounts have not already been attributed. The payment is translated into functional currency at the rate at which the interest was accrued.

(ii) Any amount remaining after the application of paragraph (b)(3)(iii)(A)(3)(i) of this section is attributable to principal. Such amounts are translated into functional currency at the spot rate on the date the instrument was issued or, if later, acquired.

(B) *Exception for interest reduced by a negative adjustment carryforward.*—Solely for purposes of this § 1.988-6, any amounts of accrued interest income that are reduced as a result of a negative adjustment carryforward shall be treated as principal and translated at the spot rate on the date the instrument was issued or, if later, acquired.

(iv) *Amount realized.*—(A) *Instrument held to maturity.*—(1) *In general.*—With respect to an instrument held to maturity, a holder translates the amount realized by separating such amount in the denomination currency into the component parts of interest and principal that make up adjusted basis prior to translation under paragraph (b)(3)(iii) of this section, and translating each of those component parts of the amount realized at the same rate used to translate the respective component parts of basis under paragraph (b)(3)(iii) of this section. The amount realized first shall be translated by reference to the component parts of basis consisting of accrued interest during the taxpayer's holding period as determined under paragraph (b)(3)(iii) of this section and ordering such amounts on a last in first out basis. Any remaining portion of the amount realized shall be translated by reference to the rate used to translate the component of basis consisting of principal as determined under paragraph (b)(3)(iii) of this section.

(2) *Subsequent purchases at discount and fixed but deferred contingent payments.*—For purposes of this paragraph (b)(3)(iv) of this section, any amount which is required to be added to adjusted basis under paragraph (b)(7) or (8) of this section shall be treated as additional interest which was accrued on the date the amount was added to adjusted basis. To the extent included in amount realized, such amounts shall be translated into functional currency at the same rates at which they were translated for purposes of determining adjusted basis. See paragraphs (b)(7)(iv) and (b)(8) of this section for rules governing the rates at which the amounts are translated for purposes of determining adjusted basis.

(B) *Sale, exchange, or unscheduled retirement.*—(1) *Holder.*—In the case of a sale, exchange, or unscheduled retirement, application of the rule stated in paragraph (b)(3)(iv)(A) of this section shall be as follows. The holder's amount realized first shall be translated by reference to the principal component of basis as determined under paragraph (b)(3)(iii) of this section, and then to the component of basis consisting of accrued interest as determined under paragraph (b)(3)(iii) of this section and ordering such amounts on a first in first out basis. Any gain recognized by the holder (i.e., any excess of the sale price over the holder's basis, both expressed in the denomination currency) is translated into functional currency at the spot rate on the payment date.

(2) *Issuer.*—In the case of an unscheduled retirement of the debt instrument, any excess of the adjusted issue price of the debt instrument over the amount paid by the issuer (expressed in denomination currency) shall first be attributable to accrued unpaid interest, to the extent the accrued unpaid interest had not been previously offset by a negative adjustment, on a last-in-first-out basis, and then to principal. The accrued unpaid interest shall be translated into functional currency at the rate at which the interest was accrued. The principal shall be translated at the spot rate on the date the debt instrument was issued.

(C) *Effect of negative adjustment carryforward with respect to the issuer.*—Any amount of negative adjustment carryforward treated as ordinary income under § 1.1275-4(b)(6)(iii)(C) shall be translated at the exchange rate on the day the debt instrument was issued.

(4) *Determination of gain or loss not attributable to foreign currency.*—A holder of a debt instrument described in paragraph (a)(1)(i) of this section shall recognize gain or loss upon sale, exchange, or retirement of the instrument equal to the difference between the amount realized with respect to the instrument, translated into

functional currency as described in paragraph (b)(3)(iv) of this section, and the adjusted basis in the instrument, determined and maintained in functional currency as described in paragraph (b)(3)(iii) of this section. The amount of any gain or loss so determined is characterized as provided in § 1.1275-4(b)(8), and sourced as provided in paragraph (b)(6) of this section.

(5) *Determination of foreign currency gain or loss.*—(i) *In general.*—Other than in a taxable disposition of the debt instrument, foreign currency gain or loss is recognized with respect to a debt instrument described in paragraph (a)(1)(i) of this section only when payments are made or received. No foreign currency gain or loss is recognized with respect to a net positive or negative adjustment, as determined under paragraph (b)(2)(ii) of this section (except with respect to a positive adjustment described in paragraph (b)(8) of this section). As described in this paragraph (b)(5), foreign currency gain or loss is determined in accordance with the rules of § 1.988-2(b).

(ii) *Foreign currency gain or loss attributable to accrued interest.*—The amount of foreign currency gain or loss recognized with respect to payments of interest previously accrued on the instrument is determined by translating the amount of interest paid or received into functional currency at the spot rate on the date of payment and subtracting from such amount the amount determined by translating the interest paid or received into functional currency at the rate at which such interest was accrued under the rules of paragraph (b)(3)(i) of this section. For purposes of this paragraph, the amount of any payment that is treated as accrued interest shall be reduced by the amount of any net negative adjustment treated as ordinary loss (to the holder) or ordinary income (to the issuer), as provided in paragraph (b)(2)(ii) of this section. For purposes of determining whether the payment consists of interest or principal, see the payment ordering rules in paragraph (b)(5)(iv) of this section.

(iii) *Principal.*—The amount of foreign currency gain or loss recognized with respect to payment or receipt of principal is determined by translating the amount paid or received into functional currency at the spot rate on the date of payment or receipt and subtracting from such amount the amount determined by translating the principal into functional currency at the spot rate on the date the instrument was issued or, in case of the holder, if later, acquired. For purposes of determining whether the payment consists of interest or principal, see the payment ordering rules in paragraph (b)(5)(iv) of this section.

(iv) *Payment ordering rules.*—(A) *In general.*—Except as provided in paragraph (b)(5)(iv)(B) of this section, payments with respect to an instrument described in paragraph (a)(1)(i) of this section shall be treated as follows:

(1) A payment shall first be attributable to any net positive adjustment on the instrument that has not previously been taken into account.

(2) Any amount remaining after applying paragraph (b)(5)(iv)(A)*(1)* of this section shall be attributable to accrued but unpaid interest, remaining after reduction by any net negative adjustment, and shall be attributable to the most recent accrual period to the extent prior amounts have not already been attributed to such period.

(3) Any amount remaining after applying paragraphs (b)(5)(iv)(A)*(1)* and *(2)* of this section shall be attributable to principal. Any interest paid in the current year that is reduced by a net negative adjustment shall be considered a payment of principal for purposes of determining foreign currency gain or loss.

(B) *Special rule for sale or exchange or unscheduled retirement.*—Payments made or received upon a sale or exchange or unscheduled retirement shall first be applied against the principal of the debt instrument (or in the case of a subsequent purchaser, the purchase price of the instrument in denomination currency) and then against accrued unpaid interest (in the case of a holder, accrued while the holder held the instrument).

(C) *Subsequent purchaser that has a positive adjustment allocated to a daily portion of interest.*—A positive adjustment that is allocated to a daily portion of interest pursuant to paragraph (b)(7)(iv) of this section shall be treated as interest for purposes of applying the payment ordering rule of this paragraph (b)(5)(iv).

(6) *Source of gain or loss.*—The source of foreign currency gain or loss recognized with respect to an instrument described in paragraph (a)(1)(i) of this section shall be determined pursuant to § 1.988-4. Consistent with the rules of § 1.1275-4(b)(8), all gain (other than foreign currency gain) on an instrument described in paragraph (a)(1)(i) of this section is treated as interest income for all purposes. The source of an ordinary loss (other than foreign currency loss) with respect to an instrument described in paragraph (a)(1)(i) of this section shall be determined pursuant to § 1.1275-4(b)(9)(iv). The source of a capital loss with respect to an instrument described in paragraph (a)(1)(i) of this section shall be determined pursuant to § 1.865-1(b)(2).

(7) *Basis different from adjusted issue price.*—(i) *In general.*—The rules of § 1.1275-4(b)(9)(i), except as set forth in this paragraph (b)(7), shall apply to an instrument described in paragraph (a)(1)(i) of this section purchased by a subsequent holder for more or less than the instrument's adjusted issue price.

(ii) *Determination of basis.*—If an instrument described in paragraph (a)(1)(i) of this section is purchased by a subsequent holder, the subsequent holder's initial basis in the instrument shall equal the amount paid by the holder to acquire the instrument, translated into functional currency at the spot rate on the date of acquisition.

(iii) *Purchase price greater than adjusted issue price.*—If the purchase price of the instrument (determined in the denomination currency) exceeds the adjusted issue price of the instrument, the holder shall, consistent with the rules of § 1.1275-4(b)(9)(i)(B), reasonably allocate such excess to the daily portions of interest accrued on the instrument or to a projected payment on the instrument. To the extent attributable to interest, the excess shall be reasonably allocated over the remaining term of the instrument to the daily portions of interest accrued and shall be a negative adjustment on the dates the daily portions accrue. On the date of such adjustment, the holder's adjusted basis in the instrument is reduced by the amount treated as a negative adjustment under this paragraph (b)(7)(iii), translated into functional currency at the rate used to translate the interest which is offset by the negative adjustment. To the extent related to a projected payment, such excess shall be treated as a negative adjustment on the date the payment is made. On the date of such adjustment, the holder's adjusted basis in the instrument is reduced by the amount treated as a negative adjustment under this paragraph (b)(7)(iii), translated into functional currency at the spot rate on the date the instrument was acquired.

(iv) *Purchase price less than adjusted issue price.*—If the purchase price of the instrument (determined in the denomination currency) is less than the adjusted issue price of the instrument, the holder shall, consistent with the rules of § 1.1275-4(b)(9)(i)(C), reasonably allocate the difference to the daily portions of interest accrued on the instrument or to a projected payment on the instrument. To the extent attributable to interest, the difference shall be reasonably allocated over the remaining term of the instrument to the daily portions of interest accrued and shall be a positive adjustment on the dates the daily portions accrue. On the date of such adjustment, the holder's adjusted basis in the instrument is increased by the amount treated as a positive adjustment under this paragraph (b)(7)(iv), translated into functional currency at the rate used to translate the interest to which it relates. For purposes of determining adjusted basis under paragraph (b)(3)(iii) of this section, such increase in adjusted basis shall be treated as an additional accrual of interest during the period to which the positive adjustment relates. To the extent related to a projected payment, such difference shall be treated as a positive adjustment on the date the payment is

Reg. § 1.988-6(b)(7)(iv)

made. On the date of such adjustment, the holder's adjusted basis in the instrument is increased by the amount treated as a positive adjustment under this paragraph (b)(7)(iv), translated into functional currency at the spot rate on the date the adjustment is taken into account. For purposes of determining the amount realized on the instrument in functional currency under paragraph (b)(3)(iv) of this section, amounts attributable to the excess of the adjusted issue price of the instrument over the purchase price of the instrument shall be translated into functional currency at the same rate at which the corresponding adjustments are taken into account under this paragraph (b)(7)(iv) for purposes of determining the adjusted basis of the instrument.

(8) *Fixed but deferred contingent payments.*— In the case of an instrument with a contingent payment that becomes fixed as to amount before the payment is due, the rules of § 1.1275-4(b)(9)(ii) shall be applied in the denomination currency of the instrument. For this purpose, foreign currency gain or loss shall be recognized on the date payment is made or received with respect to the instrument under the principles of paragraph (b)(5) of this section. Any increase or decrease in basis required under § 1.1275-4(b)(9)(ii)(D) shall be taken into account at the same exchange rate as the corresponding net positive or negative adjustment is taken into account.

(c) *Examples.*—The provisions of paragraph (b) of this section may be illustrated by the following examples. In each example, assume that the instrument described is a debt instrument for federal income tax purposes. No inference is intended, however, as to whether the instrument is a debt instrument for federal income tax purposes. The examples are as follows:

Example 1. Treatment of net positive adjustment— (i) *Facts.* On December 31, 2004, Z, a calendar year U.S. resident taxpayer whose functional currency is the U.S. dollar, purchases from a foreign corporation, at original issue, a zero-coupon debt instrument with a non-currency contingency for £1000. All payments of principal and interest with respect to the instrument are denominated in, or determined by reference to, a single nonfunctional currency (the British pound). The debt instrument would be subject to § 1.1275-4(b) if it were denominated in dollars. The debt instrument's comparable yield, determined in British pounds under paragraph (b)(2)(i) of this section and § 1.1275-4(b), is 10 percent, compounded annually, and the projected payment schedule, as constructed under the rules of § 1.1275-4(b), provides for a single payment of £1210 on December 31, 2006 (consisting of a noncontingent payment of £975 and a projected payment of £235). The debt instrument is a capital asset in the hands of Z. Z does not elect to use the spot-rate convention described in

§ 1.988-2(b)(2)(iii)(B). The payment actually made on December 31, 2006, is £1300. The relevant pound/dollar spot rates over the term of the instrument are as follows:

Date	Spot rate (pounds to dollars)
Dec. 31, 2004	£1.00 = $1.00
Dec. 31, 2005	£1.00 = $1.10
Dec. 31, 2006	£1.00 = $1.20

Accrual period	Average rate (pounds to dollars)
2005	£1.00 = $1.05
2006	£1.00 = $1.15

(ii) *Treatment in 2005*—(A) *Determination of accrued interest.* Under paragraph (b)(2)(i) of this section, and based on the comparable yield, Z accrues £100 of interest on the debt instrument for 2005 (issue price of £1000 × 10 percent). Under paragraph (b)(3)(i) of this section, Z translates the £100 at the average exchange rate for the accrual period ($1.05 × £100 = $105). Accordingly, Z has interest income in 2005 of $105.

(B) *Adjusted issue price and basis.* Under paragraphs (b)(2)(iii) and (iv) of this section, the adjusted issue price of the debt instrument determined in pounds and Z's adjusted basis in dollars in the debt instrument are increased by the interest accrued in 2005. Thus, on January 1, 2006, the adjusted issue price of the debt instrument is £1100. For purposes of determining Z's dollar basis in the debt instrument, the $1000 basis ($1.00 × £1000 original cost basis) is increased by the £100 of accrued interest, translated at the rate at which interest was accrued for 2005. See paragraph (b)(3)(iii) of this section. Accordingly, Z's adjusted basis in the debt instrument as of January 1, 2006, is $1105.

(iii) *Treatment in 2006*—(A) *Determination of accrued interest.* Under paragraph (b)(2)(i) of this section, and based on the comparable yield, Z accrues £110 of interest on the debt instrument for 2006 (adjusted issue price of £1100 × 10 percent). Under paragraph (b)(3)(i) of this section, Z translates the £110 at the average exchange rate for the accrual period ($1.15 × £110 = $126.50). Accordingly, Z has interest income in 2006 of $126.50.

(B) *Effect of net positive adjustment.* The payment actually made on December 31, 2006, is £1300, rather than the projected £1210. Under paragraph (b)(2)(ii) of this section, Z has a net positive adjustment of £90 on December 31, 2006, attributable to the difference between the amount of the actual payment and the amount of the projected payment. Under paragraph (b)(3)(ii)(A) of this section, the £90 net positive adjustment is treated as additional interest income and is translated into dollars at the spot rate on the last day of the year ($1.20 × £90 =

$108). Accordingly, Z has a net positive adjustment of $108 resulting in a total interest inclusion for 2006 of $234.50 ($126.50 + $108 = $234.50).

(C) *Adjusted issue price and basis.* Based on the projected payment schedule, the adjusted issue price of the debt instrument immediately before the payment at maturity is £1210 (£1100 plus £110 of accrued interest for 2006). Z's adjusted basis in dollars, based only on the noncontingent payment and the projected amount of the contingent payment to be received, is $1231.50 ($1105 plus $126.50 of accrued interest for 2006).

(D) *Amount realized.* Even though Z receives £1300 at maturity, for purposes of determining the amount realized, Z is treated under paragraph (b)(2)(v) of this section as receiving the projected amount of the contingent payment on December 31, 2006. Therefore, Z is treated as receiving £1210 on December 31, 2006. Under paragraph (b)(3)(iv) of this section, Z translates its amount realized into dollars and computes its gain or loss on the instrument (other than foreign currency gain or loss) by breaking the amount realized into its component parts. Accordingly, £100 of the £1210 (representing the interest accrued in 2005) is translated at the rate at which it was accrued (£1 = $1.05), resulting in an amount realized of $105; £110 of the £1210 (representing the interest accrued in 2006) is translated into dollars at the rate at which it was accrued (£1 = $1.15), resulting in an amount realized of $126.50; and £1000 of the £1210 (representing a return of principal) is translated into dollars at the spot rate on the date the instrument was purchased (£1 = $1), resulting in an amount realized of $1000. Z's total amount realized is $1231.50, the same as its basis, and Z recognizes no gain or loss (before consideration of foreign currency gain or loss) on retirement of the instrument.

(E) *Foreign currency gain or loss.* Under paragraph (b)(5) of this section Z recognizes foreign currency gain under section 988 on the instrument with respect to the consideration actually received at maturity (except for the net positive adjustment), £1210. The amount of recognized foreign currency gain is determined based on the difference between the spot rate on the date the instrument matures and the rates at which the principal and interest were taken into account. With respect to the portion of the payment attributable to interest accrued in 2005, the foreign currency gain is $15 [£100 × ($1.20 – $1.05)]. With respect to interest accrued in 2006, the foreign currency gain equals $5.50 [£110 × ($1.20 – $1.15)]. With respect to principal, the foreign currency gain is $200 [£1000 × ($1.20 – $1.00)]. Thus, Z recognizes a total foreign currency gain on December 31, 2006, of $220.50.

(F) *Source.* Z has interest income of $105 in 2005, interest income of $234.50 in 2006 (attributable to £110 of accrued interest and the £90 net positive adjustment), and a foreign currency gain

of $220.50 in 2006. Under paragraph (b)(6) of this section and section 862(a)(1), the interest income is sourced by reference to the residence of the payor and is therefore from sources without the United States. Under paragraph (b)(6) of this section and § 1.988-4, Z's foreign currency gain of $220.50 is sourced by reference to Z's residence and is therefore from sources within the United States.

Example 2. Treatment of net negative adjustment—(i) *Facts.* Assume the same facts as in *Example 1*, except that Z receives £975 at maturity instead of £1300.

(ii) *Treatment in 2005.* The treatment of the debt instrument in 2005 is the same as in Example 1. Thus, Z has interest income in 2005 of $105. On January 1, 2006, the adjusted issue price of the debt instrument is £1100, and Z's adjusted basis in the instrument is $1105.

(iii) *Treatment in 2006*—(A) *Determination of accrued interest.* Under paragraph (b)(2)(i) of this section and based on the comparable yield, Z's accrued interest for 2006 is £110 (adjusted issue price of £1100 × 10 percent). Under paragraph (b)(3)(i) of this section, the £110 of accrued interest is translated at the average exchange rate for the accrual period ($1.15 × £110 = $126.50).

(B) *Effect of net negative adjustment.* The payment actually made on December 31, 2006, is £975, rather than the projected £1210. Under paragraph (b)(2)(ii) of this section, Z has a net negative adjustment of £235 on December 31, 2006, attributable to the difference between the amount of the actual payment and the amount of the projected payment. Z's accrued interest income of £110 in 2006 is reduced to zero by the net negative adjustment. Under paragraph (b)(3)(ii)(B)(1) of this section the net negative adjustment which reduces the current year's interest is not translated into functional currency. Under paragraph (b)(2)(ii) of this section, Z treats the remaining £125 net negative adjustment as an ordinary loss to the extent of the £100 previously accrued interest in 2005. This £100 ordinary loss is attributable to interest accrued but not paid in the preceding year. Therefore, under paragraph (b)(3)(ii)(B)(2) of this section, Z translates the loss into dollars at the average rate for such year (£1 = $1.05). Accordingly, Z has an ordinary loss of $105 in 2006. The remaining £25 of net negative adjustment is a negative adjustment carryforward under paragraph (b)(2)(ii) of this section.

(C) *Adjusted issue price and basis.* Based on the projected payment schedule, the adjusted issue price of the debt instrument immediately before the payment at maturity is £1210 (£1100 plus £110 of accrued interest for 2006). Z's adjusted basis in dollars, based only on the noncontingent payments and the projected amount of the contingent payments to be received, is $1231.50 ($1105 plus $126.50 of accrued interest for 2006).

(D) *Amount realized.* Even though Z receives £975 at maturity, for purposes of determining

Reg. § 1.988-6(c)

the amount realized, Z is treated under paragraph (b)(2)(v) of this section as receiving the projected amount of the contingent payment on December 31, 2006, reduced by the amount of Z's negative adjustment carryforward of £25. Therefore, Z is treated as receiving £1185 (£1210 – £25) on December 31, 2006. Under paragraph (b)(3)(iv) of this section, Z translates its amount realized into dollars and computes its gain or loss on the instrument (other than foreign currency gain or loss) by breaking the amount realized into its component parts. Accordingly, £100 of the £1185 (representing the interest accrued in 2005) is translated at the rate at which it was accrued (£1 = $1.05), resulting in an amount realized of $105; £110 of the £1185 (representing the interest accrued in 2006) is translated into dollars at the rate at which it was accrued (£1 = $1.15), resulting in an amount realized of $126.50; and £975 of the £1185 (representing a return of principal) is translated into dollars at the spot rate on the date the instrument was purchased (£1 = $1), resulting in an amount realized of $975. Z's amount realized is $1206.50 ($105 + $126.50 + $975 = $1206.50), and Z recognizes a capital loss (before consideration of foreign currency gain or loss) of $25 on retirement of the instrument ($1206.50 – $1231.50 = –$25).

(E) *Foreign currency gain or loss.* Z recognizes foreign currency gain with respect to the consideration actually received at maturity, £975. Under paragraph (b)(5)(ii) of this section, no foreign currency gain or loss is recognized with respect to unpaid accrued interest reduced to zero by the net negative adjustment resulting in 2006. In addition, no foreign currency gain or loss is recognized with respect to unpaid accrued interest from 2005, also reduced to zero by the ordinary loss. Accordingly, Z recognizes foreign currency gain with respect to principal only. Thus, Z recognizes a total foreign currency gain on December 31, 2006, of $195 [£975 × ($1.20 – $1.00)].

(F) *Source.* In 2006, Z has an ordinary loss of $105, a capital loss of $25, and a foreign currency gain of $195. Under paragraph (b)(6) of this section and § 1.1275-4(b)(9)(iv), the $105 ordinary loss generally reduces Z's foreign source passive income under section 904(d) and the regulations thereunder. Under paragraph (b)(6) of this section and § 1.865-1(b)(2), the $25 capital loss is sourced by reference to how interest income on the instrument would have been sourced. Therefore, the $25 capital loss generally reduces Z's foreign source passive income under section 904(d) and the regulations thereunder. Under paragraph (b)(6) of this section and § 1.988-4, Z's foreign currency gain of $195 is sourced by reference to Z's residence and is therefore from sources within the United States.

Example 3. Negative adjustment and periodic interest payments—(i) *Facts.* On December 31, 2004, Z, a calendar year U.S. resident taxpayer whose functional currency is the U.S. dollar, purchases

from a foreign corporation, at original issue, a two-year debt instrument with a non-currency contingency for £1000. All payments of principal and interest with respect to the instrument are denominated in, or determined by reference to, a single nonfunctional currency (the British pound). The debt instrument would be subject to § 1.1275-4(b) if it were denominated in dollars. The debt instrument's comparable yield, determined in British pounds under §§ 1.988-2(b)(2) and 1.1275-4(b), is 10 percent, compounded semiannually. The debt instrument provides for semiannual interest payments of £30 payable each June 30, and December 31, and a contingent payment at maturity on December 31, 2006, which is projected to equal £1086.20 (consisting of a noncontingent payment of £980 and a projected payment of £106.20) in addition to the interest payable at maturity. The debt instrument is a capital asset in the hands of Z. Z does not elect to use the spot-rate convention described in § 1.988-2(b)(2)(iii)(B). The payment actually made on December 31, 2006, is £981.00. The relevant pound/dollar spot rates over the term of the instrument are as follows:

Date	Spot rate (pounds to dollars)
Dec. 31, 2004	£1.00 = $1.00
June 30, 2005	£1.00 = $1.20
Dec. 31, 2005	£1.00 = $1.40
June 30, 2006	£1.00 = $1.60
Dec. 31, 2006	£1.00 = $1.80

Accrual period	Average rate (pounds to dollars)
Jan. – June 2005	£1.00 = $1.10
July – Dec. 2005	£1.00 = $1.30
Jan. – June 2006	£1.00 = $1.50
July – Dec. 2006	£1.00 = $1.70

(ii) *Treatment in 2005*—(A) *Determination of accrued interest.* Under paragraph (b)(2)(i) of this section, and based on the comparable yield, Z accrues £50 of interest on the debt instrument for the January-June accrual period (issue price of £1000 × 10 percent/2). Under paragraph (b)(3)(i) of this section, Z translates the £50 at the average exchange rate for the accrual period ($1.10 × £50 = $55.00). Similarly, Z accrues £51 of interest in the July-December accrual period [(£1000 + £50 – £30) × 10 percent/2], which is translated at the average exchange rate for the accrual period ($1.30 × £51 = $66.30). Accordingly, Z accrues $121.30 of interest income in 2005.

(B) *Adjusted issue price and basis*—(1) *January-June accrual period.* Under paragraphs (b)(2)(iii) and (iv) of this section, the adjusted issue price of the debt instrument determined in pounds and Z's adjusted basis in dollars in the debt instrument are increased by the interest accrued, and decreased by the interest payment made, in the January-June accrual period. Thus, on July 1, 2005, the adjusted issue price of the debt instrument is £1020 (£1000 + £50 − £30 = £1020). For purposes of determining Z's dollar basis in the debt instrument, the $1000 basis is increased by the £50 of accrued interest, translated, under paragraph (b)(3)(iii) of this section, at the rate at which interest was accrued for the January-June accrual period ($1.10 × £50 = $55). The resulting amount is reduced by the £30 payment of interest made during the accrual period, translated, under paragraph (b)(3)(iii) of this section and § 1.988-2(b)(7), at the rate applicable to accrued interest ($1.10 × £30 = $33). Accordingly, Z's adjusted basis as of July 1, 2005, is $1022 ($1000 + $55 − $33).

(2) *July-December accrual period.* Under paragraphs (b)(2)(iii) and (iv) of this section, the adjusted issue price of the debt instrument determined in pounds and Z's adjusted basis in dollars in the debt instrument are increased by the interest accrued, and decreased by the interest payment made, in the July-December accrual period. Thus, on January 1, 2006, the adjusted issue price of the instrument is £1041 (£1020 + £51 − £30 = £1041). For purposes of determining Z's dollar basis in the debt instrument, the $1022 basis is increased by the £51 of accrued interest, translated, under paragraph (b)(3)(iii) of this section, at the rate at which interest was accrued for the July-December accrual period ($1.30 × £51 = $66.30). The resulting amount is reduced by the £30 payment of interest made during the accrual period, translated, under paragraph (b)(3)(iii) of this section and § 1.988-2(b)(7), at the rate applicable to accrued interest ($1.30 × £30 = $39). Accordingly, Z's adjusted basis as of January 1, 2006, is $1049.30 ($1022 + $66.30 − $39).

(C) *Foreign currency gain or loss.* Z will recognize foreign currency gain on the receipt of each £30 payment of interest actually received during 2005. The amount of foreign currency gain in each case is determined, under paragraph (b)(5)(ii) of this section, by reference to the difference between the spot rate on the date the £30 payment was made and the average exchange rate for the accrual period during which the interest accrued. Accordingly, Z recognizes $3 of foreign currency gain on the January-June interest payment [£30 × ($1.20 − $1.10)], and $3 of foreign currency gain on the July-December interest payment [£30 × ($1.40 − $1.30)]. Z recognizes in 2005 a total of $6 of foreign currency gain.

(D) *Source.* Z has interest income of $121.30 and a foreign currency gain of $6. Under paragraph (b)(6) of this section and section 862(a)(1), the interest income is sourced by reference to the residence of the payor and is therefore from sources without the United States. Under paragraph (b)(6) of this section and § 1.988-4, Z's foreign currency gain of $6 is sourced by reference to Z's residence and is therefore from sources within the United States.

(iii) *Treatment in 2006*—(A) *Determination of accrued interest.* Under paragraph (b)(2)(i) of this section, and based on the comparable yield, Z's accrued interest for the January-June accrual period is £52.05 (adjusted issue price of £1041 × 10 percent/2). Under paragraph (b)(3)(i) of this section, Z translates the £52.05 at the average exchange rate for the accrual period ($1.50 × £52.05 = $78.08). Similarly, Z accrues £53.15 of interest in the July-December accrual period [(£1041 + £52.05 − £30) × 10 percent/2], which is translated at the average exchange rate for the accrual period ($1.70 × £53.15 = $90.35). Accordingly, Z accrues £105.20, or $168.43, of interest income in 2006.

(B) *Effect of net negative adjustment.* The payment actually made on December 31, 2006, is £981.00, rather than the projected £1086.20. Under paragraph (b)(2)(ii)(B) of this section, Z has a net negative adjustment of £105.20 on December 31, 2006, attributable to the difference between the amount of the actual payment and the amount of the projected payment. Z's accrued interest income of £105.20 in 2006 is reduced to zero by the net negative adjustment. Elimination of the 2006 accrued interest fully utilizes the net negative adjustment.

(C) *Adjusted issue price and basis*—(1) *January-June accrual period.* Under paragraphs (b)(2)(iii) and (iv) of this section, the adjusted issue price of the debt instrument determined in pounds and Z's adjusted basis in dollars in the debt instrument are increased by the interest accrued, and decreased by the interest payment made, in the January-June accrual period. Thus, on July 1, 2006, the adjusted issue price of the debt instrument is £1063.05 (£1041 + £52.05 − £30 = £1063.05). For purposes of determining Z's dollar basis in the debt instrument, the $1049.30 adjusted basis is increased by the £52.05 of accrued interest, translated, under paragraph (b)(3)(iii) of this section, at the rate at which interest was accrued for the January-June accrual period ($1.50 × £52.05 = $78.08). The resulting amount is reduced by the £30 payment of interest made during the accrual period, translated, under paragraph (b)(3)(iii) of this section and § 1.988-2(b)(7), at the rate applicable to accrued interest ($1.50 × £30 = $45). Accordingly, Z's adjusted basis as of July 1, 2006, is $1082.38 ($1049.30 + $78.08 − $45).

(2) *July-December accrual period.* Under paragraphs (b)(2)(iii) and (iv) of this section, the adjusted issue price of the debt instrument determined in pounds and Z's adjusted basis in dollars in the debt instrument are increased by the interest accrued, and decreased by the interest payment made, in the July-December accrual period. Thus, immediately before maturity on December 31, 2006, the adjusted issue price of the instrument is £1086.20 (£1063.05 + £53.15 − £30 = £1086.20). For purposes of determining Z's dollar basis in the debt instrument, the $1082.38 adjusted basis is increased by the £53.15 of ac-

crued interest, translated, under paragraph (b)(3)(iii) of this section, at the rate at which interest was accrued for the July-December accrual period ($1.70 × £53.15 = $90.36). The resulting amount is reduced by the £30 payment of interest made during the accrual period, translated, under paragraph (b)(3)(iii) of this section and § 1.988-2(b)(7), at the rate applicable to accrued interest ($1.70 × £30 = $51). Accordingly, Z's adjusted basis on December 31, 2006, immediately prior to maturity is $1121.74 ($1082.38 + $90.36 − $51).

(D) *Amount realized.* Even though Z receives £981.00 at maturity, for purposes of determining the amount realized, Z is treated under paragraph (b)(2)(v) of this section as receiving the projected amount of the contingent payment on December 31, 2006. Therefore, Z is treated as receiving £1086.20 on December 31, 2006. Under paragraph (b)(3)(iv) of this section, Z translates its amount realized into dollars and computes its gain or loss on the instrument (other than foreign currency gain or loss) by breaking the amount realized into its component parts. Accordingly, £20 of the £1086.20 (representing the interest accrued in the January-June 2005 accrual period, less £30 interest paid) is translated into dollars at the rate at which it was accrued (£1 = $1.10), resulting in an amount realized of $22; £21 of the £1086.20 (representing the interest accrued in the July-December 2005 accrual period, less £30 interest paid) is translated into dollars at the rate at which it was accrued (£1 = $1.30), resulting in an amount realized of $27.30; £22.05 of the £1086.20 (representing the interest accrued in the January-June 2006 accrual period, less £30 interest paid) is translated into dollars at the rate at which it was accrued (£1 = $1.50), resulting in an amount realized of $33.08; £23.15 of the £1086.20 (representing the interest accrued in the July 1-December 31, 2006 accrual period, less the £30 interest payment) is translated into dollars at the rate at which it was accrued (£1 = $1.70), resulting in an amount realized of $39.36; and £1000 (representing principal) is translated into dollars at the spot rate on the date the instrument was purchased (£1 = $1), resulting in an amount realized of $1000. Accordingly, Z's total amount realized is $1121.74 ($22 + $27.30 + $33.08 + $39.36 + $1000), the same as its basis, and Z recognizes no gain or loss (before consideration of foreign currency gain or loss) on retirement of the instrument.

(E) *Foreign currency gain or loss.* Z recognizes foreign currency gain with respect to each £30 payment actually received during 2006. These payments, however, are treated as payments of principal for this purpose because all 2006 accrued interest is reduced to zero by the net negative adjustment. See paragraph (b)(5)(iv)(A)(3) of this section. The amount of foreign currency gain in each case is determined, under paragraph (b)(5)(iii) of this section, by reference to the difference between the spot rate on the date the £30

payment is made and the spot rate on the date the debt instrument was issued. Accordingly, Z recognizes $18 of foreign currency gain on the January-June 2006 interest payment [£30 × ($1.60 − $1.00)], and $24 of foreign currency gain on the July-December 2006 interest payment [£30 × ($1.80 − $1.00)]. Z separately recognizes foreign currency gain with respect to the consideration actually received at maturity, £981.00. The amount of such gain is determined based on the difference between the spot rate on the date the instrument matures and the rates at which the principal and interest were taken into account. With respect to the portion of the payment attributable to interest accrued in January-June 2005 (other than the £30 payments), the foreign currency gain is $14 [£20 × ($1.80 − $1.10)]. With respect to the portion of the payment attributable to interest accrued in July-December 2005 (other than the £30 payments), the foreign currency gain is $10.50 [£21 × ($1.80 − $1.30)]. With respect to the portion of the payment attributable to interest accrued in 2006 (other than the £30 payments), no foreign currency gain or loss is recognized under paragraph (b)(5)(ii) of this section because such interest was reduced to zero by the net negative adjustment. With respect to the portion of the payment attributable to principal, the foreign currency gain is $752 [£940 × ($1.80 − $1.00)]. Thus, Z recognizes a foreign currency gain of $42 on receipt of the two £30 payments in 2006, and $776.50 ($14 + $10.50 + $752) on receipt of the payment at maturity, for a total 2006 foreign currency gain of $818.50.

(F) *Source.* Under paragraph (b)(6) of this section and § 1.988-4, Z's foreign currency gain of $818.50 is sourced by reference to Z's residence and is therefore from sources within the United States.

Example 4. Purchase price greater than adjusted issue price—(i) *Facts.* On July 1, 2005, Z, a calendar year U.S. resident taxpayer whose functional currency is the U.S. dollar, purchases a debt instrument with a non-currency contingency for £1405. All payments of principal and interest with respect to the instrument are denominated in, or determined by reference to, a single nonfunctional currency (the British pound). The debt instrument would be subject to § 1.1275-4(b) if it were denominated in dollars. The debt instrument was originally issued by a foreign corporation on December 31, 2003, for an issue price of £1000, and matures on December 31, 2006. The debt instrument's comparable yield, determined in British pounds under §§ 1.988-2(b)(2) and 1.1275-4(b), is 10.25 percent, compounded semiannually, and the projected payment schedule for the debt instrument (determined as of the issue date under the rules of § 1.1275-4(b)) provides for a single payment at maturity of £1349.70 (consisting of a noncontingent payment of £1000 and a projected payment of £349.70). At the time of the purchase, the adjusted issue price of the debt instrument is £1161.76, assuming semiannual accrual periods ending on June 30 and December 31 of each year. The increase in the value of the debt instrument over its adjusted issue price is due to an increase in the expected amount of the contingent payment. The debt instrument is a capital asset in the hands of Z. Z does not elect to use the spot-rate convention described in § 1.988-2(b)(2)(iii)(B). The payment actually made on December 31, 2006, is £1400. The relevant pound/dollar spot rates over the term of the instrument are as follows:

Date	Spot rate (pounds to dollars)
July 1, 2005	£1.00 = $1.00
Dec. 31, 2006	£1.00 = $2.00

Accrual period	Average rate (pounds to dollars)
July 1 – December 31, 2005	£1.00 = $1.50
January 1 – June 30, 2006	£1.00 = $1.50
July 1 – December 31, 2006	£1.00 = $1.50

(ii) *Initial basis.* Under paragraph (b)(7)(ii) of this section, Z's initial basis in the debt instrument is $1405, Z's purchase price of £1405, translated into functional currency at the spot rate on the date the debt instrument was purchased (£1 = $1).

(iii) *Allocation of purchase price differential.* Z purchased the debt instrument for £1405 when its adjusted issue price was £1161.76. Under paragraph (b)(7)(iii) of this section, Z allocates the £243.24 excess of purchase price over adjusted issue price to the contingent payment at maturity. This allocation is reasonable because the excess is due to an increase in the expected amount of the contingent payment and not, for example, to a decrease in prevailing interest rates.

(iv) *Treatment in 2005*—(A) *Determination of accrued interest.* Under paragraph (b)(2)(i) of this section, and based on the comparable yield, Z accrues £59.54 of interest on the debt instrument for the July-December 2005 accrual period (issue price of £1161.76 × 10.25 percent/2). Under paragraph (b)(3)(i) of this section, Z translates the £59.54 of interest at the average exchange rate for the accrual period ($1.50 × £59.54 = $89.31). Accordingly, Z has interest income in 2005 of $89.31.

(B) *Adjusted issue price and basis.* Under paragraphs (b)(2)(iii) and (iv) of this section, the adjusted issue price of the debt instrument determined in pounds and Z's adjusted basis in dollars in the debt instrument are increased by the interest accrued in July-December 2005. Thus, on January 1, 2006, the adjusted issue price of the debt instrument is £1221.30 (£1161.76 + £59.54). For purposes of determining Z's dollar basis in the debt instrument on January 1, 2006, the $1405 basis is increased by the £59.54 of accrued interest, translated at the rate at which interest was accrued for the July-December 2005 accrual period. Paragraph (b)(3)(iii) of this section. Accord-

ingly, Z's adjusted basis in the instrument, as of January 1, 2006, is $1494.31 [$1405 + (£59.54 × $1.50)].

(v) *Treatment in 2006*—(A) *Determination of accrued interest.* Under paragraph (b)(2)(i) of this section, and based on the comparable yield, Z accrues £62.59 of interest on the debt instrument for the January-June 2006 accrual period (issue price of £1221.30 × 10.25 percent/2). Under paragraph (b)(3)(i) of this section, Z translates the £62.59 of accrued interest at the average exchange rate for the accrual period ($1.50 × £62.59 = $93.89). Similarly, Z accrues £65.80 of interest in the July-December 2006 accrual period [(£1221.30 + £62.59) × 10.25 percent/2], which is translated at the average exchange rate for the accrual period ($1.50 × £65.80 = $98.70). Accordingly, Z accrues £128.39, or $192.59, of interest income in 2006.

(B) *Effect of positive and negative adjustments*—(1) *Offset of positive adjustment.* The payment actually made on December 31, 2006, is £1400, rather than the projected £1349.70. Under paragraph (b)(2)(ii) of this section, Z has a positive adjustment of £50.30 on December 31, 2006, attributable to the difference between the amount of the actual payment and the amount of the projected payment. Under paragraph (b)(7)(iii) of this section, however, Z also has a negative adjustment of £243.24, attributable to the excess of Z's purchase price for the debt instrument over its adjusted issue price. Accordingly, Z will have a net negative adjustment of £192.94 (£50.30 – £243.24 = –£192.94) for 2006.

(2) *Offset of accrued interest.* Z's accrued interest income of £128.39 in 2006 is reduced to zero by the net negative adjustment. The net negative adjustment which reduces the current year's interest is not translated into functional currency. Under paragraph (b)(2)(ii) of this section, Z treats the remaining £64.55 net negative adjustment as an ordinary loss to the extent of the £59.54 previously accrued interest in 2005. This £59.54 ordinary loss is attributable to interest accrued but not paid in the preceding year. Therefore, under paragraph (b)(3)(ii)(B)(2) of this section, Z translates the loss into dollars at the average rate for such year (£1 = $1.50). Accordingly, Z has an ordinary loss of $89.31 in 2006. The remaining £5.01 of net negative adjustment is a negative adjustment carryforward under paragraph (b)(2)(ii) of this section.

(C) *Adjusted issue price and basis*—(1) *January-June accrual period.* Under paragraph (b)(2)(iii) of this section, the adjusted issue price of the debt instrument on July 1, 2006, is £1283.89 (£1221.30 + £62.59 = £1283.89). Under paragraphs (b)(2)(iv) and (b)(3)(iii) of this section, Z's adjusted basis as of July 1, 2006, is $1588.20 ($1494.31 + $93.89).

(2) *July-December accrual period.* Based on the projected payment schedule, the adjusted issue price of the debt instrument immediately before the payment at maturity is £1349.70 (£1283.89 + £65.80 accrued interest for July-December). Z's

Reg. § 1.988-6(c)

adjusted basis in dollars, based only on the non-contingent payments and the projected amount of the contingent payments to be received, is $1686.90 ($1588.20 plus $98.70 of accrued interest for July-December).

(3) *Adjustment to basis upon contingent payment.* Under paragraph (b)(7)(iii) of this section, Z's adjusted basis in the debt instrument is reduced at maturity by £243.24, the excess of Z's purchase price for the debt instrument over its adjusted issue price. For this purpose, the adjustment is translated into functional currency at the spot rate on the date the instrument was acquired (£1 = $1). Accordingly, Z's adjusted basis in the debt instrument at maturity is $1443.66 ($1686.90 – $243.24).

(D) *Amount realized.* Even though Z receives £1400 at maturity, for purposes of determining the amount realized, Z is treated under paragraph (b)(2)(v) of this section as receiving the projected amount of the contingent payment on December 31, 2006, reduced by the amount of Z's negative adjustment carryforward of £5.01. Therefore, Z is treated as receiving £1344.69 (£1349.70 – £5.01) on December 31, 2006. Under paragraph (b)(3)(iv) of this section, Z translates its amount realized into dollars and computes its gain or loss on the instrument (other than foreign currency gain or loss) by breaking the amount realized into its component parts. Accordingly, £59.54 of the £1344.69 (representing the interest accrued in 2005) is translated at the rate at which it was accrued (£1 = $1.50), resulting in an amount realized of $89.31; £62.59 of the £1344.69 (representing the interest accrued in January-June 2006) is translated into dollars at the rate at which it was accrued (£1 = $1.50), resulting in an amount realized of $93.89; £65.80 of the £1344.69 (representing the interest accrued in July-December 2006) is translated into dollars at the rate at which it was accrued (£1 = $1.50), resulting in an amount realized of $98.70; and £1156.76 of the £1344.69 (representing a return of principal) is translated into dollars at the spot rate on the date the instrument was purchased (£1 = $1), resulting in an amount realized of $1156.76. Z's amount realized is $1438.66 ($89.31 + $93.89 + $98.70 + $1156.76), and Z recognizes a capital loss (before consideration of foreign currency gain or loss) of $5 on retirement of the instrument ($1438.66 - $1443.66 = –$5).

(E) *Foreign currency gain or loss.* Z recognizes foreign currency gain under section 988 on the instrument with respect to the entire consideration actually received at maturity, £1400. While foreign currency gain or loss ordinarily would not have arisen with respect to £50.30 of the £1400, which was initially treated as a positive adjustment in 2006, the larger negative adjustment in 2006 reduced this positive adjustment to zero. Accordingly, foreign currency gain or loss is recognized with respect to the entire £1400. Under paragraph (b)(5)(ii) of this section, how-

ever, no foreign currency gain or loss is recognized with respect to unpaid accrued interest reduced to zero by the net negative adjustment resulting in 2006, and no foreign currency gain or loss is recognized with respect to unpaid accrued interest from 2005, also reduced to zero by the ordinary loss. Therefore, the entire £1400 is treated as a return of principal for the purpose of determining foreign currency gain or loss, and Z recognizes a total foreign currency gain on December 31, 2001, of $1400 [£1400 × ($2.00 – $1.00)].

(F) *Source.* Z has an ordinary loss of $89.31, a capital loss of $5, and a foreign currency gain of $1400. Under paragraph (b)(6) of this section and § 1.1275-4(b)(9)(iv), the $89.31 ordinary loss generally reduces Z's foreign source passive income under section 904(d) and the regulations thereunder. Under paragraph (b)(6) of this section and § 1.865-1(b)(2), the $5 capital loss is sourced by reference to how interest income on the instrument would have been sourced. Therefore, the $5 capital loss generally reduces Z's foreign source passive income under section 904(d) and the regulations thereunder. Under paragraph (b)(6) of this section and § 1.988-4, Z's foreign currency gain of $1400 is sourced by reference to Z's residence and is therefore from sources within the United States.

Example 5. Sale of an instrument with a negative adjustment carryforward—(i) *Facts.* On December 31, 2003, Z, a calendar year U.S. resident taxpayer whose functional currency is the U.S. dollar, purchases at original issue a debt instrument with non-currency contingencies for £1000. All payments of principal and interest with respect to the instrument are denominated in, or determined by reference to, a single nonfunctional currency (the British pound). The debt instrument would be subject to § 1.1275-4(b) if it were denominated in dollars. The debt instrument's comparable yield, determined in British pounds under §§ 1.988-2(b)(2) and 1.1275-4(b), is 10 percent, compounded annually, and the projected payment schedule for the debt instrument provides for payments of £310 on December 31, 2005 (consisting of a noncontingent payment of £50 and a projected amount of £260) and £990 on December 31, 2006 (consisting of a noncontingent payment of £940 and a projected amount of £50). The debt instrument is a capital asset in the hands of Z. Z does not elect to use the spot-rate convention described in § 1.988-2(b)(2)(iii)(B). The payment actually made on December 31, 2005, is £50. On December 30, 2006, Z sells the debt instrument for £940. The relevant pound/dollar spot rates over the term of the instrument are as follows:

Date	Spot rate (pounds to dollars)
Dec. 31, 2003	£1.00 = $1.00
Dec. 31, 2005	£1.00 = $2.00
Dec. 30, 2006	£1.00 = $2.00

Accrual period	Average rate (pounds to dollars)
January 1 – December 31, 2004	£1.00 = $2.00
January 1 – December 31, 2005	£1.00 = $2.00
January 1 – December 31, 2006	£1.00 = $2.00

(ii) *Treatment in 2004*—(A) *Determination of accrued interest.* Under paragraph (b)(2)(i) of this section, and based on the comparable yield, Z accrues £100 of interest on the debt instrument for 2004 (issue price of £1000 × 10 percent). Under paragraph (b)(3)(i) of this section, Z translates the £100 at the average exchange rate for the accrual period ($2.00 × £100 = $200). Accordingly, Z has interest income in 2004 of $200.

(B) *Adjusted issue price and basis.* Under paragraphs (b)(2)(iii) and (iv) of this section, the adjusted issue price of the debt instrument determined in pounds and Z's adjusted basis in dollars in the debt instrument are increased by the interest accrued in 2004. Thus, on January 1, 2005, the adjusted issue price of the debt instrument is £1100. For purposes of determining Z's dollar basis in the debt instrument, the $1000 basis ($1.00 × £1000 original cost basis) is increased by the £100 of accrued interest, translated at the rate at which interest was accrued for 2004. See paragraph (b)(3)(iii) of this section. Accordingly, Z's adjusted basis in the debt instrument as of January 1, 2005, is $1200 ($1000 + $200).

(iii) *Treatment in 2005*—(A) *Determination of accrued interest.* Under paragraph (b)(2)(i) of this section, and based on the comparable yield, Z's accrued interest for 2005 is £110 (adjusted issue price of £1100 × 10 percent). Under paragraph (b)(3)(i) of this section, the £110 of accrued interest is translated at the average exchange rate for the accrual period ($2.00 × £110 = $220).

(B) *Effect of net negative adjustment.* The payment actually made on December 31, 2005, is £50, rather than the projected £310. Under paragraph (b)(2)(ii) of this section, Z has a net negative adjustment of £260 on December 31, 2005, attributable to the difference between the amount of the actual payment and the amount of the projected payment. Z's accrued interest income of £110 in 2005 is reduced to zero by the net negative adjustment. Under paragraph (b)(3)(ii)(B)(1) of this section, the net negative adjustment which reduces the current year's interest is not translated into functional currency. Under paragraph (b)(2)(ii) of this section, Z treats the remaining £150 net negative adjustment as an ordinary loss to the extent of the £100 previously accrued interest in 2004. This £100 ordinary loss is attributable to interest accrued but not paid in the preceding year. Therefore, under paragraph (b)(3)(ii)(B)(2) of this section, Z translates the loss into dollars at the average rate

for such year (£1 = $2.00). Accordingly, Z has an ordinary loss of $200 in 2005. The remaining £50 of net negative adjustment is a negative adjustment carryforward under paragraph (b)(2)(ii) of this section.

(C) *Adjusted issue price and basis.* Based on the projected payment schedule, the adjusted issue price of the debt instrument on January 1, 2006 is £900, i.e., the adjusted issue price of the debt instrument on January 1, 2005 (£1100), increased by the interest accrued in 2005 (£110), and decreased by the projected amount of the December 31, 2005, payment (£310). See paragraph (b)(2)(iii) of this section. Z's adjusted basis on January 1, 2006 is Z's adjusted basis on January 1, 2005 ($1200), increased by the functional currency amount of interest accrued in 2005 ($220), and decreased by the amount of the payments made in 2005, based solely on the projected payment schedule, (£310). The amount of the projected payment is first attributable to the interest accrued in 2005 (£110), and then to the interest accrued in 2004 (£100), and the remaining amount to principal (£100). The interest component of the projected payment is translated into functional currency at the rates at which it was accrued, and the principal component of the projected payment is translated into functional currency at the spot rate on the date the instrument was issued. See paragraph (b)(3)(iii) of this section. Accordingly, Z's adjusted basis in the debt instrument, following the increase of adjusted basis for interest accrued in 2005 ($1200 + $220 = $1420), is decreased by $520 ($220 + $200 + $100 = $520). Z's adjusted basis on January 1, 2006 is therefore, $900.

(D) *Foreign currency gain or loss.* Z will recognize foreign currency gain on the receipt of the £50 payment actually received on December 31, 2005. Based on paragraph (b)(5)(iv) of this section, the £50 payment is attributable to principal since the accrued unpaid interest was completely eliminated by the net negative adjustment. The amount of foreign currency gain is determined, under paragraph (b)(5)(iii) of this section, by reference to the difference between the spot rate on the date the £50 payment was made and the spot rate on the date the debt instrument was issued. Accordingly, Z recognizes $50 of foreign currency gain on the £50 payment. [($2.00 − $1.00) × £50 = $50]. Under paragraph (b)(6) of this section and §1.988-4, Z's foreign currency gain of $50 is sourced by reference to Z's residence and is therefore from sources within the United States.

(iv) *Treatment in 2006*—(A) *Determination of accrued interest.* Under paragraph (b)(2)(i) of this section, and based on the comparable yield, Z accrues £90 of interest on the debt instrument for 2006 (adjusted issue price of £900 × 10 percent). Under paragraph (b)(3)(i) of this section, Z translates the £90 at the average exchange rate for the accrual period ($2.00 × £90 = $180). Accordingly, prior to taking into account the 2005 negative adjustment carryforward, Z has interest income in 2006 of $180.

(B) *Effect of net negative adjustment.* The £50 negative adjustment carryforward from 2005 is a negative adjustment for 2006. Since there are no other positive or negative adjustments, there is a £50 negative adjustment in 2006 which reduces Z's accrued interest income by £50. Accordingly, after giving effect to the £50 negative adjustment carryforward, Z will accrue $80 of interest income. [(£90 − £50) × $2.00 = $80].

(C) *Adjusted issue price.* Under paragraph (b)(2)(iii) of this section, the adjusted issue price of the debt instrument determined in pounds is increased by the interest accrued in 2006 (prior to taking into account the negative adjustment carryforward). Thus, on December 30, 2006, the adjusted issue price of the debt instrument is £990.

(D) *Adjusted basis.* For purposes of determining Z's dollar basis in the debt instrument, Z's $900 adjusted basis on January 1, 2006, is increased by the accrued interest, translated at the rate at which interest was accrued for 2006. See paragraph (b)(3)(iii)(A) of this section. Note, however, that under paragraph (b)(3)(iii)(B) of this section the amount of accrued interest which is reduced as a result of the negative adjustment carryforward, i.e., £50, is treated for purposes of this section as principal, and is translated at the spot rate on the date the instrument was issued, i.e., £1.00 = $1.00. Accordingly, Z's adjusted basis in the debt instrument as of December 30, 2006, is $1030 ($900 + $50 + $80).

(E) *Amount realized.* Z's amount realized in denomination currency is £940, i.e., the amount of pounds Z received on the sale of the debt instrument. Under paragraph (b)(3)(iv)(B)(1) of this section, Z's amount realized is first translated by reference to the principal component of basis (including the amount which is treated as principal under paragraph (b)(3)(iii)(B) of this section) and then the remaining amount realized, if any, is translated by reference to the accrued unpaid interest component of adjusted basis. Thus, £900 of Z's amount realized is translated by reference to the principal component of adjusted basis. The remaining £40 of Z's amount realized is treated as principal under paragraph (b)(3)(iii)(B) of this section, and is also is translated by reference to the principal component of adjusted basis. Accordingly, Z's amount realized in functional currency is $940. (No part of Z's amount realized is attributable to the interest accrued on the debt instrument.) Z realizes a loss of $90 on the sale of the debt instrument ($1030 basis − $940 amount realized). Under paragraph (b)(4) of this section and §1.1275-4(b)(8), $80 of the loss is characterized as ordinary loss, and the remaining $10 of loss is characterized as capital loss. Under §§1.988-6(b)(6) and 1.1275-4(b)(9)(iv) the $80 ordinary loss is treated as a deduction that is definitely related to the interest income accrued on the debt instrument. Similarly, under §§1.988-6(b)(6) and

1.865-1(b)(2) the $10 capital loss is also allocated to the interest income from the debt instrument.

(F) *Foreign currency gain or loss.* Z recognizes foreign currency gain with respect to the £940 he received on the sale of the debt instrument. Under paragraph (b)(5)(iv) of this section, the £940 Z received is attributable to principal (and the amount which is treated as principal under paragraph (b)(3)(iii)(B) of this section). Thus, Z recognizes foreign currency gain on December 31, 2006, of $940. [($2.00 − $1.00) × £940]. Under paragraph (b)(6) of this section and §1.988-4, Z's foreign currency gain of $940 is sourced by reference to Z's residence and is therefore from sources within the United States.

(d) *Multicurrency debt instruments.*—(1) *In general.*—Except as provided in this paragraph (d), a multicurrency debt instrument described in paragraph (a)(1)(ii) or (iii) of this section shall be treated as an instrument described in paragraph (a)(1)(i) of this section and shall be accounted for under the rules of paragraph (b) of this section. Because payments on an instrument described in paragraph (a)(1)(ii) or (iii) of this section are denominated in, or determined by reference to, more than one currency, the issuer and holder or holders of the instrument are required to determine the denomination currency of the instrument under paragraph (d)(2) of this section before applying the rules of paragraph (b) of this section.

(2) *Determination of denomination currency.*—(i) *In general.*—The denomination currency of an instrument described in paragraph (a)(1)(ii) or (iii) of this section shall be the predominant currency of the instrument. Except as otherwise provided in paragraph (d)(2)(ii) of this section, the predominant currency of the instrument shall be the currency with the greatest value determined by comparing the functional currency value of the noncontingent and projected payments denominated in, or determined by reference to, each currency on the issue date, discounted to present value (in each relevant currency) and translated (if necessary) into functional currency at the spot rate on the issue date. For this purpose, the applicable discount rate may be determined using any method, consistently applied, that reasonably reflects the instrument's economic substance. If a taxpayer does not determine a discount rate using such a method, the Commissioner may choose a method for determining the discount rate that does reflect the instrument's economic substance. The predominant currency is determined as of the issue date and does not change based on subsequent events (e.g., changes in value of one or more currencies).

(ii) *Difference in discount rate of greater than 10 percentage points.*—This §1.988-6(d)(2)(ii) applies if no currency has a value determined under paragraph (d)(2)(i) of this section that is greater than 50% of the total value of all payments. In such a case, if the difference between the discount rate in the denomination currency otherwise determined under (d)(2)(i) of this section and the discount rate determined under paragraph (d)(2)(i) of this section with respect to any other currency in which payments are made (or determined by reference to) pursuant to the instrument is greater than 10 percentage points, then the Commissioner may determine the predominant currency under any reasonable method.

(3) *Issuer/holder consistency.*—The issuer determines the denomination currency under the rules of paragraph (d)(2) of this section and provides this information to the holders of the instrument in a manner consistent with the issuer disclosure rules of § 1.1275-2(e). If the issuer does not determine the denomination currency of the instrument, or if the issuer's determination is unreasonable, the holder of the instrument must determine the denomination currency under the rules of paragraph (d)(2) of this section. A holder that determines the denomination currency itself must explicitly disclose this fact on a statement attached to the holder's timely filed federal income tax return for the taxable year that includes the acquisition date of the instrument.

(4) *Treatment of payments in currencies other than the denomination currency.*—For purposes of applying the rules of paragraph (b) of this section to debt instruments described in paragraph (a)(1)(ii) or (iii) of this section, payments not denominated in (or determined by reference to) the denomination currency shall be treated as non-currency-related contingent payments. Accordingly, if the denomination currency of the instrument is determined to be the taxpayer's functional currency, the instrument shall be accounted for under § 1.1275-4(b) rather than under this section.

(e) *Instruments issued for nonpublicly traded property.*—(1) *Applicability.*—This paragraph (e) applies to debt instruments issued for nonpublicly traded property that would be described in paragraph (a)(1)(i), (ii), or (iii) of this section, but for the fact that such instruments are described in § 1.1275-4(c)(1) rather than § 1.1275-4(b)(1). For example, this paragraph (e) generally applies to a contingent payment debt instrument denominated in a nonfunctional currency that is issued for non-publicly traded property. Generally the rules of § 1.1275-4(c) apply except as set forth by the rules of this paragraph (e).

(2) *Separation into components.*—An instrument described in this paragraph (e) is not accounted for using the noncontingent bond method of § 1.1275-4(b) and paragraph (b) of this section. Rather, the instrument is separated into its component payments. Each noncontingent payment or group of noncontingent payments which is denominated in a single currency shall

be considered a single component treated as a separate debt instrument denominated in the currency of the payment or group of payments. Each contingent payment shall be treated separately as provided in paragraph (e)(4) of this section.

(3) *Treatment of components consisting of one or more noncontingent payments in the same currency.*—The issue price of each component treated as a separate debt instrument which consists of one or more noncontingent payments is the sum of the present values of the noncontingent payments contained in the separate instrument. The present value of any noncontingent payment shall be determined under § 1.1274-2(c)(2), and the test rate shall be determined under § 1.1274-4 with respect to the currency in which each separate instrument is considered denominated. No interest payments on the separate debt instrument are qualified stated interest payments (within the meaning of § 1.1273-1(c)) and the de minimis rules of section 1273(a)(3) and § 1.1273-1(d) do not apply to the separate debt instrument. Interest income or expense is translated, and exchange gain or loss is recognized on the separate debt instrument as provided in § 1.988-2(b)(2), if the instrument is denominated in a nonfunctional currency.

(4) *Treatment of components consisting of contingent payments.*—(i) *General rule.*—A component consisting of a contingent payment shall generally be treated in the manner provided in § 1.1275-4(c)(4). However, except as provided in paragraph (e)(4)(ii) of this section, the test rate shall be determined by reference to the U.S. dollar unless the dollar does not reasonably reflect the economic substance of the contingent component. In such case, the test rate shall be determined by reference to the currency which most reasonably reflects the economic substance of the contingent component. Any amount received in nonfunctional currency from a component consisting of a contingent payment shall be translated into functional currency at the spot rate on the date of receipt. Except in the case when the payment becomes fixed more than six months before the payment is due, no foreign currency gain or loss shall be recognized on a contingent payment component.

(ii) *Certain delayed contingent payments.*—(A) *Separate debt instrument relating to the fixed component.*—The rules of § 1.1275-4(c)(4)(iii) shall apply to a contingent component the payment of which becomes fixed more than 6 months before the payment is due. For this purpose, the denomination currency of the separate debt instrument relating to the fixed payment shall be the currency in which payment is to be made and the test rate for such separate debt instrument shall be determined in the currency of that instrument. If the separate debt instrument relating to the fixed payment is denominated in

Reg. § 1.988-6(e)(4)(ii)(A)

nonfunctional currency, the rules of § 1.988-2(b)(2) shall apply to that instrument for the period beginning on the date the payment is fixed and ending on the payment date.

(B) *Contingent component.*—With respect to the contingent component, the issue price considered to have been paid by the issuer to the holder under § 1.1275-4(c)(4)(iii)(A) shall be translated, if necessary, into the functional currency of the issuer or holder at the spot rate on the date the payment becomes fixed.

(5) *Basis different from adjusted issue price.*—The rules of § 1.1275-4(c)(5) shall apply to an instrument subject to this paragraph (e).

(6) *Treatment of a holder on sale, exchange, or retirement.*—The rules of § 1.1275-4(c)(6) shall apply to an instrument subject to this paragraph (e).

(f) *Rules for nonfunctional currency tax exempt obligations described in § 1.1275-4(d).*—(1) *In general.*—Except as provided in paragraph (f)(2) of this section, section 1.988-6 shall not apply to a debt instrument the interest on which is excluded from gross income under section 103(a).

(2) *Operative rules.*—[RESERVED].

(g) *Effective date.*—This section shall apply to debt instruments issued on or after October 29, 2004. [Reg. § 1.988-6.]

☐ [*T.D.* 9157, 8-27-2004.]

[Reg. § 1.989(a)-1]

§ 1.989(a)-1. Definition of a Qualified Business Unit.—(a) *Applicability.*—(1) *In general.*—This section provides rules relating to the definition of the term "qualified business unit" (QBU) within the meaning of section 989.

(2) *Effective date.*—These rules shall apply to taxable years beginning after December 31, 1986. However, any person may apply on a consistent basis § 1.989(a)-1T(c) of the Temporary Income Tax Regulations in lieu of § 1.989(a)-1(c) to all taxable years beginning after December 31, 1986, and on or before February 3, 1990. For the text of the temporary regulation, see 53 FR 20612 (June 8, 1988).

(b) *Definition of a qualified business unit.*—(1) *In general.*—A QBU is any separate and clearly identified unit of a trade or business of a taxpayer provided that separate books and records are maintained.

(2) *Application of the QBU definition.*—(i) *Persons.*—A corporation is a QBU. An individual is not a QBU. A partnership, trust, or estate is a QBU of a partner or beneficiary.

(ii) *Activities.*—Activities of a corporation, partnership, trust, estate, or individual qualify as a QBU if—

(A) The activities constitute a trade or business; and

(B) A separate set of books and records is maintained with respect to the activities.

(3) *Special rule.*—Any activity (wherever conducted and regardless of its frequency) that produces income or loss that is, or is treated as, effectively connected with the conduct of a trade or business within the United States shall be treated as a separate QBU, provided the books and records requirement of paragraph (d)(2) of this section is satisfied.

(c) *Trade or business.*—The determination as to whether activities constitute a trade or business is ultimately dependent upon an examination of all the facts and circumstances. Generally, a trade or business for purposes of section 989(a) is a specific unified group of activities that constitutes (or could constitute) an independent economic enterprise carried on for profit, the expenses related to which are deductible under section 162 or 212 (other than that part of section 212 dealing with expenses incurred in connection with taxes). To constitute a trade or business, a group of activities must ordinarily include every operation which forms a part of, or a step in, a process by which an enterprise may earn income or profit. Such group of activities must ordinarily include the collection of income and the payment of expenses. It is not necessary that the activities carried out by a QBU constitute a different trade or business from those carried out by other QBUs of the taxpayer. A vertical, functional, or geographic division of the same trade or business may be a trade or business for this purpose provided that the activities otherwise qualify as a trade or business under this paragraph (c). However, activities that are merely ancillary to a trade or business will not constitute a trade or business under this paragraph (c). Activities of an individual as an employee are not considered by themselves to constitute a trade or business under this paragraph (c).

(d) *Separate books and records.*—(1) *General rule.*—Except as provided in paragraph (d)(2) of this section, a separate set of books and records shall include books of original entry and ledger accounts, both general and subsidiary, or similar records. For example, in the case of a taxpayer using the cash receipts and disbursements method of accounting, the books of original entry include a cash receipts and disbursements journal where each receipt and each disbursement is recorded. Similarly, in the case of a taxpayer using an accrual method of accounting, the books of original entry include a journal to record sales (accounts receivable) and a journal to record expenses incurred (accounts payable). In general, a journal represents a chronological account of all transactions entered into by an entity for an accounting period. A ledger account, on the other hand, chronicles the impact during an accounting period of the specific transactions recorded in the journal for that period upon the various items shown on the entity's balance sheet (*i.e.*, assets, liabilities, and capital accounts) and income statement (*i.e.*, revenues and expenses).

(2) *Special rule.*—For purposes of paragraph (b)(3) of this section, books and records include books and records used to determine income or loss that is, or is treated as, effectively connected with the conduct of a trade or business within the United States.

(e) *Examples.*—The provisions of this section may be illustrated by the following examples:

Example (1). Corporation X is a domestic corporation. Corporation X manufactures widgets in the U.S. for export. Corporation X sells widgets in the United Kingdom through a branch office in London. The London office has its own employees and solicits and processes orders. Corporation X maintains in the U.S. a separate set of books and records for all transactions conducted by the London office. Corporation X is a QBU under paragraph (b)(2)(i) of this section because of its corporate status. The London branch office is a QBU under paragraph (b)(2)(ii) of this section because (1) the sale of widgets is a trade or business as defined in paragraph (c) of this section; and (2) a complete and separate set of books and records (as described in paragraph (d) of this section) is maintained with respect to its sales operations.

Example (2). A domestic corporation incorporates a wholly-owned subsidiary in Switzerland. The domestic corporation is a manufacturer that markets its product abroad primarily through the Swiss subsidiary. To facilitate sales of the parent's product in Europe, the Swiss subsidiary has branch offices in France and West Germany that are responsible for all marketing operations in those countries. Each branch has its own employees, solicits and processes orders, and maintains a separate set of books and records. The domestic corporation and the Swiss subsidiary are both QBUs under paragraph (b)(2)(i) of this section because of their corporate status. The French and West German branches are QBUs of the Swiss subsidiary. They satisfy paragraph (b)(2)(ii) because each constitutes a trade or business (as defined in paragraph (c) of this section) and because separate sets of books and records (as described in paragraph (d) of this section) of their respective operations is maintained. Each branch is considered to have a trade or business although each is a geographical division of the same trade or business.

Example (3). W is a domestic corporation that manufactures product X in the United States for sale worldwide. All of W's sales functions are conducted exclusively in the United States. W employs individual Q to work in France. Q's sole function is to act as a courier to deliver sales documents to customers in France. With respect to Q's activities in France, a separate set of books and records as described in paragraph (d) is maintained. Under paragraph (c) of this section, Q's activities in France do not constitute a QBU since they are merely ancillary to W's manufacturing and selling business. Q is not considered to have a QBU because an individual's activities as an employee are not considered to constitute a trade or business of the individual under paragraph (c).

Example (4). The facts are the same as in example (3) except that the courier function is the sole activity of a wholly-owned French subsidiary of W. Under paragraph (b)(2)(i) of this section, the French subsidiary is considered to be a QBU.

Example (5). A corporation incorporated in the Netherlands is a subsidiary of a domestic corporation and a holding company for the stock of one or more subsidiaries incorporated in other countries. The Dutch corporation's activities are limited to paying its directors and its administrative expenses, receiving capital contributions from its United States parent corporation, contributing capital to its subsidiaries, receiving dividend distributions from its subsidiaries, and distributing dividends to its domestic parent corporation. Under paragraph (b)(2)(i) of this section, the Netherlands corporation is considered to be a QBU.

Example (6). Taxpayer A, an individual resident of the United States, is engaged in a trade or business wholly unrelated to any type of investment activity. A also maintains a portfolio of foreign currency-denominated investments through a foreign broker. The broker is responsible for all activities necessary to the management of A's investments and maintains books and records as described in paragraph (d) of this section, with respect to all investment activities of A. A's investment activities qualify as a QBU under paragraph (b)(2)(ii) of this section to the extent the activities engaged in by A generate expenses that are deductible under section 212 (other than that part of section 212 dealing with expenses incurred in connection with taxes).

Example (7). Taxpayer A, an individual resident of the United States, is the sole shareholder of foreign corporation (FC) whose activities are limited to trading in stocks and securities. FC is a QBU under paragraph (b)(2)(i) of this section.

Example (8). Taxpayer A, an individual resident of the United States, markets and sells in Spain and in the United States various products produced by other United States manufacturers. A has an office and employs a salesman to manage A's activities in Spain, maintains a separate set of books and records with respect to his activities in Spain, and is engaged in a trade or business as defined in paragraph (c) of this section. Therefore, under paragraph (b)(2)(ii) of this section, the activities of A in Spain are considered to be a QBU.

Reg. §1.989(a)-1(e)

Example (9). Foreign corporation FX is incorporated in Mexico and is wholly owned by a domestic corporation. The domestic corporation elects to treat FX as a domestic corporation under section 1504(d). FX operates entirely in Mexico and maintains a separate set of books and records with respect to its activities in Mexico. FX is a QBU under paragraph (b)(2)(i) of this section. The activities of FX in Mexico also constitute a QBU under paragraph (b)(2)(ii) of this section.

Example (10). F, a foreign corporation, computes a gain of $100 from the disposition of a United States real property interest (as defined in section 897(c)). The gain is taken into account as if F were engaged in a trade or business in the United States and as if such gain were effectively connected with such trade or business. F is a QBU under paragraph (b)(2)(i) of this section because of its corporate status. F's disposition activity constitutes a separate QBU under paragraph (b)(3) of this section. [Reg. § 1.989(a)-1.]

☐ [T.D. 8279, 1-3-90.]

[Reg. § 1.989(b)-1]

§ 1.989(b)-1. Definition of weighted average exchange rate.—For purposes of section 989(b)(3) and (4), the term "weighted average exchange rate" means the simple average of the daily exchange rates (determined by reference to a qualified source of exchange rates described in § 1.988-1(d)(1)), excluding weekends, holidays and any other nonbusiness days for the taxable year. [Reg. § 1.989(b)-1.]

☐ [T.D. 8263, 9-19-89. *Amended by T.D. 8367*, 9-24-91 *and T.D. 9452, 6-10-2009.*]

[Reg. § 1.989(c)-1]

§ 1.989(c)-1. Transition rules for certain branches of United States persons using a net worth method of accounting for taxable years beginning before January 1, 1987.—(a) *Applicability.*—(1) *In general.*—This section applies to qualified business units (QBU) branches of United States persons, whose functional currency (as defined in section 985 of the Code and regulations issued thereunder) is other than the United States dollar (dollar) and that used a net worth method of accounting for their last taxable year beginning before January 1, 1987. Generally, a net worth method of accounting is any method of accounting under which the taxpayer calculates the taxable income of a QBU branch based on the net change in the dollar value of the QBU branch's equity over the course of a taxable year, taking into account any remittance made during the year. QBU branch equity is the excess of QBU branch assets over QBU branch liabilities. For all taxable years beginning after December 31, 1986, such QBU branches must use the profit and loss method of accounting as described in section 987, except to the

extent otherwise provided in regulations under section 985 or any other provision of the Code.

(2) *Insolvent QBU branches.*—A taxpayer may apply the principles of this section to a QBU branch that used a net worth method of accounting for its last taxable year beginning before January 1, 1987, whose $E pool (as defined in paragraph (d)(3)(i) of this section) is negative. For taxable years beginning on or after October 25, 1991 the principles of this section shall apply to insolvent QBU branches.

(b) *General rules.*—For the general rules, see § 1.987-5(b).

(c) *Determining the pool(s) from which a remittance is made.*—To determine from which pool(s) a remittance is made, see § 1.987-5(c).

(d) *Calculation of Section 987 gain or loss.*—(1) *In general.*—See § 1.987-5(d)(1) for rules to make this calculation.

(2) *Step 1—Calculate the amount of the functional currency pools.*—For calculation of the amount of the functional currency pools, see § 1.987-5(d)(2).

(3) *Step 2—Calculate the dollar basis pools.*—(i) *Dollar basis of the EQ pool.*—(A) *Beginning dollar basis.*—The beginning dollar basis of the EQ pool (hereinafter referred to as the $E pool) equals the final net worth of the QBU branch. Final net worth of the QBU branch equals the QBU branch's equity value (assets less liabilities) measured in dollars at the end of the taxpayer's last taxable year beginning before January 1, 1987, determined on the basis of the QBU branch's books and records as adjusted according to United States tax principles.

(B) *Adjusting the $E pool.*—For adjustments to be made to the $E pool, see § 1.987-5(d)(3)(i)(B).

(ii) *Dollar basis of the post-86 profits pool.*—To calculate the dollar basis of the post-86 profits pool, see § 1.987-5(d)(3)(ii).

(iii) *Dollar basis of the equity pool.*—To calculate the dollar basis of the equity pool, see § 1.987-5(d)(3)(iii).

(4) *Step 3—Calculation of the dollar basis of a remittance.*—To calculate the dollar basis of the EQ remitted, see § 1.987-5(d)(4).

(5) *Step 4—Calculation of the section 987 gain or loss on a remittance.*—To calculate 987 gain or loss determined on a remittance, see § 1.987-5(d)(5).

(e) *Functional currency adjusted basis of QBU branch assets acquired in taxable years beginning before January 1, 1987.*—To determine the functional currency adjusted basis of QBU branch assets acquired in taxable years beginning before January 1, 1987, see § 1.987-5(e).

(f) *Functional currency amount of QBU branch liabilities acquired in taxable years beginning before*

January 1, 1987.—To determine the functional currency amount of QBU branch liabilities acquired in taxable years beginning before January 1, 1987, see § 1.987-5(f). [Reg. § 1.989(c)-1.]

☐ [T.D. 8367, 9-24-91.]

Domestic International Sales Corporation

[Reg. § 1.991-1]

§ 1.991-1. Taxation of a domestic international sales corporation.—(a) *In general.*—A corporation which is a DISC for a taxable year is not subject to any tax imposed by subtitle A of the Code (sections 1 through 1564) for such taxable year, except for the tax imposed by chapter 5 thereof (sections 1491 through 1494) on certain transfers to avoid tax. Thus, for example, a corporation which is a DISC for a taxable year is not subject for such year to the corporate income tax (section 11), the minimum tax on tax preferences (sections 56 through 58), or the accumulated earnings tax (sections 531 through 537). A DISC is liable for the payment of all taxes payable by corporations under other subtitles of the Code, such as, for example, income taxes withheld at the source and other employment taxes under subtitle C and the interest equalization tax and other miscellaneous excise taxes imposed by subtitle D. In addition, a DISC is subject to the provisions of chapter 3 of subtitle A (including section 1461), relating to withholding of tax on nonresident aliens and foreign corporations and tax-free covenant bonds. See § 1.992-1 for the definition of the term "DISC".

(b) *Determination of taxable income.*—(1) *In general.*—Although a DISC is not subject to tax under subtitle A of the Code (other than chapter 5 thereof), a DISC's taxable income shall be determined for each taxable year in order to determine, for example, the amount deemed distributed for that taxable year to its shareholders pursuant to § 1.995-2. Except as otherwise provided in the Code and the regulations thereunder, the taxable income of a DISC shall be determined in the same manner as if the DISC were a domestic corporation which had not elected to be treated as a DISC. Thus, for example, a DISC chooses its method of depreciation, inventory method, and annual accounting period in the same manner as if it were a corporation which had not elected to be treated as a DISC. Any elections affecting the determination of taxable income shall be made by the DISC. Thus, as a further example, a DISC which makes an installment sale described in section 453 is able to avail itself of the benefits of section 453: *Provided,* The DISC complies with the election requirements of such section. See § 1.995-2(e) and § 1.996-8 and the regulations thereunder for rules relating to the application for a taxable year of a DISC of a deduction under section 172 for a net operating loss carryback or carryover or of a

capital loss carryback or carryover under section 1212.

(2) *Choice of method of accounting.*—A DISC may, generally, choose any method of accounting permissible under section 446(c) and the regulations thereunder. However, if a DISC is a member of a controlled group (as defined in § 1.993-1(k)), the DISC may not choose a method of accounting which, when applied to transactions between the DISC and other members of the controlled group, will result in a material distortion of the income of the DISC or any other member of the controlled group. Such a material distortion of income would occur, for example, if a DISC chooses to use the cash method of accounting where the DISC acts as commission agent in a substantial volume of sales of property by a related corporation which uses the accrual method of accounting and which customarily pays commissions to the DISC more than 2 months after such sales. As a further example, a material distortion of income would occur if a DISC chooses to use the accrual method of accounting where the DISC leases a substantial amount of property from a related corporation which uses the cash method of accounting, if the DISC customarily accrues any portion of the rent on such property more than 2 months before the rent is paid. Changes in the method of accounting of a DISC are subject to the requirements of section 446(e) and the regulations thereunder.

(3) *Choice of annual accounting period.*—(i) *In general.*—A DISC may choose its annual accounting period without regard to the annual accounting period of any of its stockholders. In general, changes in the annual accounting period of a DISC are subject to the requirements of section 442 and the regulations thereunder.

(ii) *Transition rule for change in taxable year in order to become a DISC.*—A corporation may, without the consent of the Commissioner, change its annual accounting period and adopt a new taxable year beginning on the first day of any month in 1972, provided that—

(a) Such change has the effect of accelerating the time as of which such corporation can become a DISC,

(b) The Commissioner is notified of such change by means of a statement filed (with the regional service center with which such corporation files its election to be treated as a DISC) not later than the end of the period during which

Reg. § 1.991-1(b)(3)(ii)(b)

such corporation may file an election to be treated as a DISC for such new taxable year, and

(c) The short period required to effect such change is not a taxable year in which such corporation has a net operating loss as defined in section 172.

Thus, for example, if a corporation which uses the calendar year for its taxable year does not complete arrangements to become a DISC until May 15, 1972, such corporation can, pursuant to this subdivision, change its annual accounting period and adopt a taxable year beginning on the first day of any month in 1972 after May. A change to a new annual accounting period made pursuant to this subdivision is effective only if the corporation which makes such change qualifies as a DISC for such new period. A corporation may change its annual accounting period and adopt a new taxable year pursuant to this subdivision without regard to the provisions of § 1.1502-76 (relating to the taxable year of members of a group). A copy of the statement described in (b) of this subdivision shall be attached to the return of a corporation for the new taxable year to which such corporation changes pursuant to this subdivision. A corporation which changes its annual accounting period pursuant to this subparagraph will not be permitted under section 442 to change its annual accounting period at any time before 1982, except with the consent of the Commissioner as provided in § 1.442-1(b)(1) or pursuant to subparagraph (4) of this paragraph.

(4) *Transition rule for change of taxable year of certain DISC's.*—In the case of a DISC all of the shares of which are held by a single shareholder or by members of a group who file a consolidated return, such DISC may (without the consent of the Commissioner) change its annual accounting period and adopt a taxable year beginning in 1972 which is the same as the taxable year of such shareholder or the members of such group. A change to a new annual accounting period may be made by a DISC pursuant to this subparagraph even if such DISC has changed its annual accounting period pursuant to subparagraph (3)(ii) of this paragraph.

(5) *Transition rule for beginning of first taxable year of certain corporations.*—If a corporation organized before January 1, 1972, neither acquires assets (other than cash or other property acquired as consideration for the issuance of stock) nor begins doing business prior to January 1, 1972, the first taxable year of such corporation is deemed to begin at the time such corporation acquires any asset (other than cash or other property acquired as consideration for the issuance of stock) or begins doing business, whichever is earlier: *Provided,* That such corporation is a DISC for such first taxable year. For purposes of § 1.6012-2(a), such corporation is treated as not coming into existence until the beginning of such first taxable year.

(c) *Effective date.*—The provisions of this section and the regulations under sections 992 through 997 apply with respect to taxable years ending after December 31, 1971, except that a corporation may not be a DISC for any taxable year beginning before January 1, 1972.

(d) *Related statutes.*—For rules relating to the transfer, during a taxable year beginning before January 1, 1976, to a DISC of assets of an export trade corporation (as defined in section 971), where a parent owns all the outstanding stock of both such DISC and such export trade corporation, see section 505(b) of the Revenue Act of 1971 (85 Stat. 551). For rules regarding limitations on the qualification of a corporation as an export trade corporation for any taxable year beginning after October 31, 1971, see section 971(a)(3). [Reg. § 1.991-1.]

□ [*T.D. 7323, 9-24-74. Amended by T.D. 7854, 11-15-82.*]

[Reg. § 1.992-1]

§ 1.992-1. Requirements of a DISC.— (a) *"DISC" defined.*—The term "DISC" refers to a domestic international sales corporation. The term "DISC" means a corporation which, for a taxable year—

(1) Is duly incorporated and existing under the laws of any State or the District of Columbia,

(2) Satisfies the gross receipts test described in paragraph (b) of this section,

(3) Satisfies the assets test described in paragraph (c) of this section,

(4) Satisfies the capitalization requirement described in paragraph (d) of this section,

(5) Satisfies the requirement that an election to be treated as a DISC be in effect for such year, as described in paragraph (e) of this section,

(6) [Reserved],

(7) Maintains separate books and records, and

(8) Is not an ineligible corporation described in paragraph (f) of this section.

A corporation which satisfies the requirements described in subparagraphs (1) through (8) of this paragraph for a taxable year is treated as a separate corporation for Federal tax purposes and qualifies as a DISC, even though such corporation would not be treated (if it were not a DISC) as a corporate entity for Federal income tax purposes. An association cannot qualify as a DISC even if such association is taxable as a corporation pursuant to section 7701(a)(3). In addition, a corporation created or organized in, or under the law of, a possession of the United States cannot qualify as a DISC. The rules contained in this paragraph constitute a relaxation of the general rules of corporate substance otherwise applicable under the Code. The separate incorporation of a DISC is required under section 992(a)(1) to make it possible to keep a better record of the income which is subject to the special treatment provided by sections 991 through 996, but this does not necessitate in all other respects the separate relationships which otherwise would be required between a parent corporation and its subsidiary. However, this relaxation of the general rules of corporate substance does not apply with respect to other corporations in other contexts. In the case of a transaction between a DISC and a person related to such DISC for purposes of section 482, see § 1.993-1(l) for rules for determining whether income is income of a DISC to which the intercompany pricing rules authorized by section 994 apply.

(b) *Gross receipts test.*—In order for a corporation described in paragraph (a)(1) of this section to be a DISC for a taxable year, 95 percent or more of its gross receipts (as defined in § 1.993-6) for such year must consist of qualified export receipts (as defined in § 1.993-1). Gross receipts for a taxable year are determined in accordance with the method of accounting adopted by the corporation pursuant to § 1.991-1(b)(2). However, for rules regarding gross receipts in the case of a commission sale by such corporation, see § 1.993-6. See § 1.992-3 with respect to distributions to meet qualification requirements in the event the requirements of this paragraph are not satisfied for the taxable year.

(c) *Assets test.*—(1) *In general.*—In order for a corporation described in paragraph (a)(1) of this section to be a DISC for a taxable year, the adjusted basis (determined under section 1011) of its qualified export assets (as defined in § 1.993-2) at the close of such year must equal or exceed 95 percent of the sum of the adjusted bases (determined under section 1011) of all assets of such corporation at the close of such year. See § 1.992-3 with respect to distributions to meet qualification requirements in the event the requirements of this paragraph are not satisfied for the taxable year.

(2) *Assets acquired to meet assets test.*—For purposes of determining whether the requirements of subparagraph (1) of this paragraph are satisfied by a corporation at the end of a taxable year, an asset which is a qualified export asset (as defined in § 1.993-2) is treated as not being an asset of such corporation at such time if such asset is held for a total of 60 days or less and is acquired directly or indirectly through borrowing, unless the acquisition of such asset is established to the satisfaction of the Commissioner or his delegate to have been for bona fide purposes. Such acquisition is deemed to have been for bona fide purposes if, for example, it is made in the usual course of the corporation's trade or business.

(d) *Capitalization requirement.*—(1) *In general.*—To qualify as a DISC for a taxable year, a corporation must have, on each day of that taxable year, only one class of stock. The par value

(or, in the case of stock without par value, the stated value) of the corporation's outstanding stock must be on each day of the taxable year at least $2,500. In the case of a corporation which elects to be treated as a DISC for its first taxable year, the requirements of this paragraph (d)(1) are satisfied if the corporation has no more than one class of stock at any time during the year and if the par value (or, in the case of stock without par value, the stated value) of the corporation's outstanding stock is at least $2,500 on the last day of the period within which the election must be made and on each succeeding day of the year. For purposes of this paragraph (d)(1), the stated value of shares is the aggregate amount of the consideration paid for such shares which is not allotted to paid in surplus, or other surplus. The law of the State of incorporation of the DISC determines what consideration may be used to capitalize the DISC. A corporation will not be a qualified DISC unless at least $2,500 of valid consideration was used for this purpose. If a corporation has a realized or unrealized loss during a taxable year which results in the impairment of all or part of the capital required under this paragraph (d)(1), that impairment does not result in disqualification under this paragraph (d)(1), provided that the corporation does not take any legal or formal action under State law to reduce capital for that year below the amount required under this paragraph (d)(1).

(2) *Treatment of debt payable to shareholders.*—(i) *In general.*—Purported debt of a DISC payable to any person, whether or not such person is a shareholder or a member of a controlled group (as defined in § 1.993-1(k)) of which such DISC is a member, is treated as debt for all purposes of the Code, provided that such purported debt—

(a) Would qualify as debt for purposes of the Code if the DISC were a corporation which did not qualify as a DISC.

(b) Qualifies under subdivision (ii) of this subparagraph, or

(c) Are trade accounts payable described in subdivision (iii) of this subparagraph. Such debt is not treated as stock, and interest payable by the DISC on such debt is treated as interest by both the DISC and the holder of such debt. Payment of the principal of such debt by a DISC does not constitute the payment of a dividend by such DISC. The provisions of this subparagraph apply for a taxable year of a DISC, even though debt described in this subparagraph would be treated as stock of the corporation if such corporation did not qualify as a DISC for such year.

(ii) *Safe harbor rule.*—Purported debt of a DISC will in no event be treated as other than debt for purposes of subdivision (i) of this subparagraph if—

(a) It is a written obligation to pay a sum certain on or before a fixed maturity date,

(b) Interest is payable on such purported debt at an arm's length interest rate (as determined under §1.482-2(a)(2)), expressed as a fixed dollar amount or a fixed percentage of principal,

(c) Such purported debt is not convertible into stock or into other purported debt unless such purported debt qualifies under this subparagraph as debt of the DISC,

(d) Such purported debt does not confer voting rights upon its holder, except in the event of default thereon, and

(e) Interest and principal are paid in accordance with the terms of such purported debt or with any modification of such terms consistent with (a) through (d) of this subdivision.

The determination of whether purported debt of a DISC constitutes debt described in this subdivision is made without regard to the proportion of debt of the DISC held by any of its shareholders, to the ratio of the outstanding debt of the DISC to its equity, or to the amount of outstanding debt of such DISC. The provisions of (e) of this subdivision do not prevent the modification of the terms of debt of a DISC where, for example, a DISC becomes unable to make timely payments of principal required under such terms, provided that such modification is consistent with (a) through (d) of this subdivision.

(iii) *Trade accounts payable.*—Trade accounts payable of a DISC which arise in the normal course of its trade or business (such as in consideration for inventory or supplies) constitute debt of the DISC (whether or not such accounts payable are debt described in subdivision (i)(a) or (b) of this subparagraph), provided that such accounts are payable within 15 months after they arise. If such accounts are payable more than 15 months after they arise, they are debt of such DISC only if they are debt described in subdivision (i)(a) or (b) of this subparagraph.

(iv) *Relation of subparagraph to other corporations.*—The provisions of this subparagraph generally constitute a relaxation of the ordinary rules used in determining whether purported debt of a corporation is debt or equity. This relaxation is in recognition of the principle that a corporation may qualify as a DISC even though it has relatively little capital. This relaxation does not apply with respect to purported debt of other corporations in other contexts. The provisions of subdivisions (i), (ii), and (iii) of this subparagraph apply only for taxable years for which a corporation qualifies (or is treated as) a DISC.

(3) *Classes of stock.*—[Reserved]

(e) *Election in effect.*—In order for a corporation to be a DISC for a taxable year, an election to be treated as a DISC must be made by such corporation pursuant to §1.992-2 and must be in effect for such taxable year. A corporation does not become or remain a DISC solely by making such an election. A corporation is a DISC for a taxable year only if such an election is in effect for that year and the corporation also satisfies the requirements of paragraphs (a) through (d) of this section. See §1.992-2 for rules regarding the time and manner of making such an election.

(f) *Ineligible corporations.*—The following corporations shall not be eligible to be treated as a DISC—

(1) A corporation exempt from tax by reason of section 501,

(2) A personal holding company (as defined in section 542),

(3) A financial institution to which section 581 or 593 applies,

(4) An insurance company subject to the tax imposed by Subchapter L,

(5) A regulated investment company (as defined in section 851(a)),

(6) A China Trade Act corporation receiving the special deduction provided in section 941(a), or

(7) An electing small business corporation (as defined in section 1371(b)).

(g) *Status as DISC after having filed return as a DISC.*—Under section 992(a)(2), notwithstanding the failure of a corporation to meet the requirements of paragraph (a) of this section for a taxable year, such corporation will be treated as a DISC for purposes of the Code for such taxable year (and thus, will not be able to claim that it is not eligible to be a DISC) if—

(1) Such corporation files a return as a DISC for such taxable year,

(2) Such corporation does not notify the district director, more than 30 days before the expiration of the period of limitation (including extensions thereof) on assessment for underpayment of tax for such taxable year (as determined under section 6501 and the regulations thereunder), that it is not a DISC for such taxable year, and

(3) The Internal Revenue Service has not issued, within such period of limitation (including extensions thereof) on assessment for underpayment of tax for such taxable year, a notice of deficiency based on a determination that such corporation is not a DISC for such taxable year.

A corporation is treated as a DISC, for all purposes, pursuant to the provisions of this paragraph for any taxable year for which it meets the requirements of this paragraph, even if such corporation is an ineligible corporation described in paragraph (f) of this section for such taxable year. Thus, for example, a corporation which is treated as a DISC for a taxable year pursuant to this paragraph is treated as a DISC for that taxable year for purposes of §1.992-2(e)(3) (relating to the termination of a DISC election if a corporation is not a DISC for each of any 5 consecutive taxable years). If a corporation is treated as a DISC for a taxable year pursuant to this paragraph, persons who held stock of such corporation at any time during such taxable year are treated, with respect to such stock, as holders of stock in a DISC for the period or periods during which they held such stock within such taxable year.

(h) *Definition of "former DISC".*—Under section 992(a)(3), the term "former DISC" refers to a corporation which is not a DISC for a taxable year but which was (or was treated as) a DISC for a prior taxable year. However, a corporation is not a former DISC for a taxable year unless such corporation has, at the beginning of such taxable year, undistributed previously taxed income (as defined in §1.996-3(c)) or accumulated DISC income (as defined in §1.996-3(b)). A corporation which is a former DISC for a taxable year is a former DISC for all purposes of the Code. [Reg. §1.992-1].

☐ [*T.D. 7323, 9-24-74. Amended by T.D. 7420, 5-19-76; T.D. 7747, 12-29-80; T.D. 7920, 11-3-83 and T.D. 8371, 10-24-91.*]

[Reg. §1.992-2]

§1.992-2. Election to be treated as a DISC.— (a) *Manner and time of election.*—(1) *Manner.*— (i) *In general.*—A corporation can elect to be treated as a DISC for a taxable year beginning after December 31, 1971. Except as provided in subdivision (ii) of this subparagraph, the election is made by the corporation filing Form 4876 with the service center with which it would file its income tax return if it were subject for such taxable year to all the taxes imposed by subtitle A of the Internal Revenue Code of 1954. The form shall be signed by any person authorized to sign a corporation return under section 6062, and shall contain the information required by such form. Except as provided in paragraphs (b)(3) and (c) of this section, such election to be treated as a DISC shall be valid only if the consent of every person who is a shareholder of the corporation as of the beginning of the first taxable year for which such election is effective is on or attached to such Form 4876 when filed with the service center.

(ii) *Transitional rule for corporations electing during 1972.*—If the first taxable year for which an election by a corporation to be treated as a DISC is a taxable year beginning after December 31, 1971, and on or before December 31, 1972, such election may be made either in the manner prescribed in subdivision (i) of this subparagraph or by filing, at the place prescribed in subdivision (i) of this subparagraph, a statement captioned "Election to be Treated as a DISC." Such statement of election shall be valid only if the consent of each shareholder is filed with the service center in the form, and at the time, pre-

scribed in paragraph (b) of this section. Such statement shall be signed by any person authorized to sign a corporation return under section 6062 and shall include the name, address, and employer identification number (if known) of the corporation, the beginning date of the first taxable year for which the election is effective, the number of shares of stock of the corporation issued and outstanding as of the earlier of the beginning of the first taxable year for which the election is effective or the time the statement is filed, the number of shares held by each shareholder as of the earlier of such dates, and the date and place of incorporation. As a condition of the election being effective, a corporation which elects to become a DISC by filing a statement in accordance with this subdivision must furnish (to the service center with which the statement was filed) such additional information as is required by Form 4876 by March 31, 1973.

(2) *Time of making election.*—(i) *In general.*— In the case of a corporation making an election to be treated as a DISC for its first taxable year, such election shall be made within 90 days after the beginning of such taxable year. In the case of a corporation which makes an election to be treated as a DISC for any taxable year beginning after March 31, 1972 (other than the first taxable year of such corporation), the election shall be made during the 90-day period immediately preceding the first day of such taxable year.

(ii) *Transitional rules for certain corporations electing during 1972.*—In the case of a corporation which makes an election to be treated as a DISC for a taxable year beginning after December 31, 1971, and on or before March 31, 1972 (other than its first taxable year), the election shall be made within 90 days after the beginning of such taxable year.

(b) *Consent by shareholders.*—(1) *In general.*— (i) *Time and manner of consent.*—Under paragraph (a)(1)(i) of this section, subject to certain exceptions, the election to be treated as a DISC is not valid unless each person who is a shareholder as of the beginning of the first taxable year for which the election is effective signs either the statement of consent on Form 4876 or a separate statement of consent attached to such form. A shareholder's consent is binding on such shareholder and all transferees of his shares and may not be withdrawn after a valid election is made by the corporation. In the case of a corporation which files an election to become a DISC for a taxable year beginning after December 31, 1972, if a person who is a shareholder as of the beginning of the first taxable year for which the election is effective does not consent by signing the statement of consent set forth on Form 4876, such election shall be valid (except in the case of an extension of the time for filing granted under the provisions of subparagraph (3) of this paragraph or paragraph (c) of this section) only if the consent of such shareholder is attached to the Form 4876 upon which such election is made.

(ii) *Form of consent.*—A consent other than the statement of consent set forth on Form 4876 shall be in the form of a statement which is signed by the shareholder and which sets forth (*a*) the name and address of the corporation and of the shareholder and (*b*) the number of shares held by each such shareholder as of the time the consent is made and (if the consent is made after the beginning of the corporation's taxable year for which the election is effective) as of the beginning of such year. If the consent is made by a recipient of transferred shares pursuant to paragraph (c) of this section, the statement of consent shall also set forth the name and address of the person who held such shares as of the beginning of such taxable year and the number of such shares. Consent shall be made in the following form: "I (insert name of shareholder), a shareholder of (insert name of corporation seeking to make the election) consent to the election of (insert name of corporation seeking to make the election) to be treated as a DISC under section 992(b) of the Internal Revenue Code. The consent so made by me is irrevocable and is binding upon all transferees of my shares in (insert name of corporation seeking to make the election)." The consents of all shareholders may be incorporated in one statement.

(iii) *Who may consent.*—Where stock of the corporation is owned by a husband and wife as community property (or the income from such stock is community property), or is owned by tenants in common, joint tenants, or tenants by the entirety, each person having a community interest in such stock or the income therefrom and each tenant in common, joint tenant, and tenant by the entirety must consent to the election. The consent of a minor shall be made by his legal guardian or by his natural guardian if no legal guardian has been appointed. The consent of an estate shall be made by the executor or administrator thereof. The consent of a trust shall be made by the trustee thereof. The consent of an estate or trust having more than one executor, administrator, or trustee, may be made by any executor, administrator, or trustee, authorized to make a return of such estate or trust pursuant to section 6012(b)(5). The consent of a corporation or partnership shall be made by an officer or partner authorized pursuant to section 6062 or 6063, as the case may be, to sign the return of such corporation or partnership. In the case of a foreign person, the consent may be signed by any individual (whether or not a U.S. person) who would be authorized under sections 6061 through 6063 to sign the return of such foreign person if he were a U.S. person.

(2) *Transitional rule for corporations electing during 1972.*—In the case of a corporation which files an election to be treated as a DISC for a taxable year beginning after December 31, 1971, and on or before December 31, 1972, such election shall be valid only if the consent of each person who is a shareholder as of the beginning of the first taxable year for which such election is effective is filed with the service center with which the election was filed within 90 days after the first day of such taxable year or within the time granted for an extension of time for filing such consent. The form of such consent shall be the same as that prescribed in subparagraph (1) of this paragraph. Such consent shall be attached to the statement of election or shall be filed separately (with such service center) with a copy of the statement of election. An extension of time for filing a consent may be granted in the manner, and subject to the conditions, described in subparagraph (3) of this paragraph.

(3) *Extension of time to consent.*—An election which is timely filed and would be valid except for the failure to attach the consent of any shareholder to the Form 4876 upon which the election was made or to comply with the 90-day requirement in subparagraph (2) of this paragraph or paragraph (c)(1) of this section, as the case may be, will not be invalid for such reason if it is shown to the satisfaction of the service center that there was reasonable cause for the failure to file such consent, and if such shareholder files a proper consent to the election within such extended period of time as may be granted by the Internal Revenue Service. In the case of a late filing of a consent, a copy of the Form 4876 or statement of election shall be attached to such consent and shall be filed with the same service center as the election. The form of such consent shall be the same as that set forth in paragraph (b)(1)(ii) of this section. In no event can any consent be made pursuant to this paragraph on or after the last day of the first taxable year for which a corporation elects to be treated as a DISC.

(c) *Consent by holder of transferred shares.*—(1) *In general.*—If a shareholder of a corporation transfers—

(i) Prior to the first day of the first taxable year for which such corporation elects to be treated as a DISC, some or all of the shares held by him without having consented to such election, or

(ii) On or before the 90th day after the first day of the first taxable year for which such corporation elects to be treated as a DISC, some or all of the shares held by him as of the first day of such year (or if later, held by him as of the time such shares are issued) without having consented to such election, then consent may be made by any recipient of such shares on or before the 90th day after the first day of such first taxable year. If such recipient fails to file his consent on or before such 90th day, an extension of time for filing such consent may be granted in the manner, and subject to the conditions, described in paragraph (b)(3) of this section. In addition, if the transfer occurs more than 90 days after the first day of such taxable year, an extension of time for filing such consent may be granted to such recipient only if it is determined under paragraph (b)(3) of this section that an extension of time would have been granted the transferor for the filing of such consent if the transfer had not occurred. A consent which is not attached to the original Form 4876 or statement of election (as the case may be) shall be filed with the same service center as the original Form 4876 or statement of election and shall have attached a copy of such original form or statement of election. The form of such consent shall be the same as that set forth in paragraph (b)(1)(ii) of this section. For the purposes of this paragraph, a transfer of shares includes any sale, exchange, or other disposition, including a transfer by gift or at death.

(2) *Requirement for the filing of an amended Form 4876 or statement of election.*—In any case in which a consent to a corporation's election to be treated as a DISC is made pursuant to subparagraph (1) of this paragraph, such corporation must file an amended Form 4876 or statement of election (as the case may be) reflecting all changes in ownership of shares. Such form must be filed with the same service center with which the original Form 4876 or statement of election was filed by such corporation.

(d) *Effect of election.*—(1) *Effect on corporation.*—A valid election to be treated as a DISC remains in effect (without regard to whether the electing corporation qualifies as a DISC for a particular year) until terminated by any of the methods provided in paragraph (e) of this section. While such election is in effect, the electing corporation is subject to sections 991 through 997 and other provisions of the Code applicable to DISC's for any taxable year for which it qualifies as a DISC (or is treated as qualifying as a DISC pursuant to §1.992-1(g)). Such corporation is also subject to such provisions for any taxable year for which it is treated as a former DISC as a result of qualifying or being treated as a DISC for any taxable year for which such election was in effect.

(2) *Effect on shareholders.*—A valid election by a corporation to be treated as a DISC subjects the shareholders of such corporation to the provisions of section 995 (relating to the taxation of the shareholders of a DISC or former DISC) and to all other provisions of the Code relating to the shareholders of a DISC or former DISC. Such provisions of the Code apply to any person who is a shareholder of a DISC or former DISC whether or not such person was a shareholder at the time the corporation elected to become a DISC.

(e) *Termination of election.*—(1) *In general.*—An election to be treated as a DISC is terminated only as provided in subparagraph (2) or (3) of this paragraph.

(2) *Revocation of election.*—(i) *Manner of revocation.*—An election by a corporation to be treated as a DISC may be revoked by the corporation for any taxable year of the corporation after the first taxable year for which the election is effective. Such revocation shall be made by the corporation filing a statement that the corporation revokes its election under section 992(b) to be treated as a DISC. Such statement shall indicate the corporation's name, address, employer identification number, and the first taxable year of the corporation for which the revocation is to be effective. The statement shall be signed by any person authorized to sign a corporation return under section 6062. Such revocation shall be filed with the service center with which the corporation filed its election, except that, if it filed an annual information return under section 6011(e)(2), the revocation shall be filed with the service center with which it filed its last such return.

(ii) *Years for which revocation is effective.*—If a corporation files a statement revoking its election to be treated as a DISC during the first 90 days of a taxable year (other than the first taxable year for which such election is effective), such revocation will be effective for such taxable year and all taxable years thereafter. If the corporation files a statement revoking its election to be treated as a DISC after the first 90 days of a taxable year, the revocation will be effective for all taxable years following such taxable year.

(3) *Continued failure to be a DISC.*—If a corporation which has elected to be treated as a DISC does not qualify as a DISC (and is not treated as a DISC pursuant to §1.992-1(g)) for each of any 5 consecutive taxable years, such election terminates and will not be effective for any taxable year after such fifth taxable year. Such termination will be effective automatically, without notice to such corporation or to the Internal Revenue Service. If, during any 5-year period for which an election is effective, the corporation should qualify as a DISC (or be treated as a DISC pursuant to §1.992-1(g)) for a taxable year, a new 5-year period shall automatically start at the beginning of the following taxable year.

(4) *Election after termination.*—If a corporation has made a valid election to be treated as a DISC and such election terminates in either manner described in subparagraph (2) or (3) of this paragraph, such corporation is eligible to reelect to be treated as a DISC at any time by following the procedures described in paragraphs (a) through (c) of this section. If a corporation terminates its election and subsequently reelects to be treated as a DISC, the corporation and its shareholders continue to be subject to sections 995 and 996 with respect to the period during which its

first election was in effect. Thus, for example, distributions upon disqualification includible in the gross incomes of shareholders of a corporation pursuant to section 995(b)(2) continue to be so includible for taxable years for which a second election of such corporation is in effect without regard to the second election. [Reg. § 1.992-2.]

☐ [*T.D. 7323, 9-24-74. Amended by T.D. 7420, 5-19-76.*]

[Reg. § 1.992-3]

§1.992-3. Deficiency distributions to meet qualification requirements.—(a) *In general.*—A corporation which meets the requirements described in § 1.992-1 for treatment as a DISC for a taxable year, other than the 95 percent of gross receipts test described in § 1.992-1(b) or the 95-percent assets test described in § 1.992-1(c), or both tests, may nevertheless qualify as a DISC for such year by making deficiency distributions (attributable to its gross receipts other than qualified export receipts and its assets other than qualified export assets) if all of the following requirements are satisfied:

(1) The corporation distributes the amount determined under paragraph (b) of this section as a deficiency distribution. The amount of a deficiency distribution is determined without regard to the amount by which the corporation fails to meet either test.

(2) The reasonable cause requirements prescribed in paragraph (c)(1) of this section are satisfied with respect to both the corporation's failure to meet either test and its failure to make a deficiency distribution prior to the time the distribution is made.

(3) The corporation makes such deficiency distribution pro rata to all its shareholders.

(4) The corporation designates the distribution, at the time of the distribution, as a deficiency distribution, pursuant to section 992(c), to meet the qualification requirements to be a DISC. Such designation shall be in the form of a communication sent at the time of such distribution to each shareholder and to the service center with which the corporation has filed or will file its return for the taxable year to which the distribution relates. A corporation may not retroactively designate a prior distribution as a deficiency distribution to meet qualification requirements. Subject to the limitation described in paragraph (c)(3) of this section, a corporation may make a deficiency distribution with respect to a taxable year at any time after the close of such taxable year or, in the case of a deficiency distribution made on or before September 29, 1975, at any time during or after such taxable year.

See sections 246(d), 904(f), 995, and 996 for rules regarding the treatment of a deficiency distribution to meet qualification requirements by the shareholders and the corporation.

(b) *Amount of deficiency distribution.*—(1) *In general.*—In order to meet the requirements of paragraph (a) of this section, the amount of a deficiency distribution must be, if the corporation fails to meet—

(i) The 95 percent of gross receipts test, the amount determined in subparagraph (2) of this paragraph,

(ii) The 95-percent assets test, the amount determined in subparagraph (3) of this paragraph, and

(iii) Both such tests, except as provided in subparagraph (4) of this paragraph, the sum of the amounts determined in subparagraphs (2) and (3) of this paragraph.

(2) *Computation of deficiency distribution to meet 95 percent of gross receipts test.*—(i) *In general.*—If a corporation fails to meet the 95 percent of gross receipts test described in § 1.992-1(b) for its taxable year, the amount of the deficiency distribution required by this subparagraph is an amount equal to the sum of its taxable income (if any) from each transaction giving rise to gross receipts (as defined in § 1.993-6) which are not qualified export receipts (as defined in § 1.993-1). A corporation's taxable income from a transaction shall be the amount of such gross receipts from such transaction reduced only by (a) its cost of goods sold attributable to such gross receipts, and by (b) its expenses, losses, and other deductions properly apportioned or allocated thereto in a manner consistent with the rules set forth in § 1.861-8. For purposes of this subdivision, however, any expenses, losses, or other deductions which cannot definitely be allocated to some item or class of gross income in such manner shall not reduce such gross receipts. If the corporation is a commission agent for a principal in a transaction, the corporation's taxable income is the amount of the commission from such transaction reduced only by the amounts described in (b) of this subdivision.

(ii) *Example.*—The provisions of this subparagraph may be illustrated by the following example:

Example. (a) X and Y are calendar year taxpayers. X, a domestic manufacturing company, owns all the stock of Y, which seeks to qualify as a DISC for 1973. During 1973, X manufactures a machine which is eligible to be export property as defined in § 1.993-3. Y is made a commission agent with respect to exporting such machine. Thereafter, during 1973 Y is considered to receive gross receipts of $100,000, as determined under section 993(f), attributable to X's sale of the machine in a manner which causes the gross receipts to be excluded receipts pursuant to section 993(a)(2) and, therefore, not qualified export receipts. Y's total gross receipts for 1973 are $1 million of which $900,000 (i.e., 90 percent) are qualified export receipts. Therefore, Y does not satisfy the 95 percent of gross receipts test for 1973 because less than 95 percent of its gross receipts are qualified export receipts. Y has $9,000 of expenses properly apportioned or allocated to its gross income from such sale and $1,000 of other expenses which cannot definitely be allocated to some item or class of gross income, determined in a manner consistent with the rules set forth in § 1.861-8. In order to satisfy the 95 percent of gross receipts test for 1973, if the commission due from X to Y were $15,000, Y must make a deficiency distribution of $6,000 computed as follows:

Y's commission (gross income) from the transaction	$15,000
Less: Y's expenses apportioned or allocated to its gross income from the transaction	9,000
Required deficiency distribution by reason of $100,000 of gross receipts which are not qualified export receipts	6,000

(b) If the commission due from X to Y were $9,400, resulting in a net loss of $600 to Y ($9,400 to $10,000), Y must make a deficiency distribution of $400 computed as follows:

Y's commissions (gross income) from the transaction	$9,400
Less: Y's expenses apportioned or allocated to its gross income from the transaction	9,000
Required deficiency distribution by reason of $100,000 of gross receipts which are not qualified export receipts	400

(c) If the commission due from X to Y were $8,500, Y would not be required to make a deficiency distribution since, under this subparagraph, there would be no taxable income attributable to gross receipts from the sale.

(3) *Computation of deficiency distribution to meet 95 percent assets test.*—(i) *In general.*—If a corporation fails to meet the 95 percent assets test described in § 1.992-1(c) for its taxable year, the amount of the deficiency distribution required by this subparagraph is an amount equal to the fair market value as of the last day of such taxable year of the assets which are not qualified export assets held by such corporation on such last day.

(ii) *Asset held for more than 1 year.*—In the case of a corporation which holds continuously an asset which is not a qualified export asset at the close of more than 1 taxable year, it must distribute an amount equal to its fair market value (or, if greater, the amount determined under subparagraph (4) of this paragraph) only once if, at the close of the first such taxable year, such corporation reasonably believed that such asset was a qualified export asset. This subdivision shall not apply for any taxable year beginning after the date the corporation knows (or a reasonable man would have known) that an asset is not a qualified export asset and in order to qualify for each such year, the corporation must distribute the fair market value of such asset for each such year.

(4) *Computation in the case of a failure to meet both tests as a result of a single transaction.*—If a corporation fails to meet both the 95 percent of gross receipts test and the 95 percent assets test for a taxable year, and if the corporation holds at the end of such year assets (other than cash or qualified export assets) which were received as proceeds of a sale or exchange during such year which resulted in gross receipts other than qualified export receipts, then the amount of the deficiency distribution required by this paragraph with respect to such sale or exchange and assets held is the larger of the amount required by subparagraph (2) of this paragraph with respect to the sale or exchange or the amount required by subparagraph (3) of this paragraph with respect to such assets held. Thus, for example, if a corporation sells property which is not a qualified export asset for $100, receives $85 in cash and a note for $15, and derives $25 of taxable income from the sale as determined under subparagraph (2) of this paragraph, it must distribute $25. If the provisions of this subparagraph are applied with respect to assets of a DISC, (other than qualified export assets), such provisions do not apply to any property received as proceeds from a sale or exchange of such assets.

(c) *Reasonable cause for failure.*—(1) *In general.*—If for a taxable year, a corporation has failed to meet the 95 percent of gross receipts test, the 95 percent assets test, or both tests, such corporation may satisfy any such test for such year by means of a deficiency distribution in the amount determined under paragraph (b) of this section only if the reasonable cause requirements of this subparagraph are satisfied. Such reasonable cause requirements are satisfied if—

(i) There is reasonable cause (as determined in accordance with subparagraph (2) of this paragraph) for such corporation's failure to satisfy such test and to make such distribution prior to the date on which it was made, the time limit in subparagraph (3) of this paragraph for making the distribution is satisfied, and interest (if required) is paid in the amount and in the manner prescribed by subparagraph (4) of this paragraph, or

(ii) The time and "70-percent" requirements of the reasonable cause test of paragraph (d) of this section are satisfied.

(2) *Determination of reasonable cause.*—In general, whether a corporation's failure to meet the 95 percent of gross receipts test, the 95 percent assets test, or both tests for a taxable year and its failure to make a pro rata distribution prior to the date on which it was made will be

considered for reasonable cause where the action or inaction which resulted in such failure occurred in good faith, such as failure to meet the 95 percent assets test resulting from blocked currency or expropriation, or failure to meet either test because of reasonable uncertainty as to what constitutes a qualified export receipt or a qualified export asset. For further examples, if a corporation's reasonable determination of the percentage of its total gross receipts that are qualified export receipts is subsequently redetermined to be less than 95 percent as a result of a price adjustment by the Internal Revenue Service under section 482, or if the corporation has a casualty loss for which it receives an unanticipated insurance recovery which causes its qualified export receipts to be less than 95 percent of its gross receipts, then the failure to satisfy the 95 percent of gross receipts test is considered to be due to reasonable cause.

(3) *Time limit for deficiency distribution.*—Except as otherwise provided in this subparagraph, the time limit prescribed by this subparagraph for making a deficiency distribution is satisfied if the amount of the distribution required by paragraph (b) of this section is made within 90 days from the date of the first written notification to the corporation by the Internal Revenue Service that it had not satisfied the 95 percent of gross receipts test or the 95 percent assets test or both tests, for a taxable year. Upon a showing by the corporation that an extension of the 90-day time limit is reasonable and necessary, the Commissioner may grant such extension of such time limit. In any case in which a corporation contests the decision of the Internal Revenue Service that such corporation has not met the 95 percent of gross receipts test, the 95 percent assets test, or both tests, an extension of the 90-day time limit will be allowed until 30 days after the final determination of such contest. The date of the final determination of such contest shall, for purposes of section 992(c), be established in the manner specified in subdivisions (i) through (iv) of this subparagraph:

(i) The date of final determination by a decision of the United States Tax Court is the date upon which such decision becomes final, as prescribed in section 7481.

(ii) The date of final determination in a case which is contested in a court (and upon which there is a judgment) other than the Tax Court is the date upon which the judgment becomes final and will be determined on the basis of the facts and circumstances of each particular case. For example, ordinarily a judgment of a United States district court becomes final upon the expiration of the time allowed for taking an appeal, if no such appeal is duly taken within such time; and a judgment of the United States Court of Claims becomes final upon the expiration of the time allowed for filing a petition for certiorari if no such petition is duly filed within such time.

(iii) The date of a final determination by a closing agreement, made under section 7121, is the date such agreement is approved by the Commissioner.

(iv) A final determination under section 992(c) may be made by an agreement signed by the district director or director of the service center with which the corporation files its annual return or by such other official to which authority to sign has been delegated, and by or on behalf of the taxpayer. The agreement shall set forth the total amount of the deficiency distribution to be paid to the shareholders of the DISC for the taxable year or years. An agreement under this subdivision shall be sent to the taxpayer at his last known address by either registered or certified mail. For further guidance regarding the definition of last known address, see § 301.6212-2 of this chapter. If registered mail is used for such purpose, the date of registration is considered the date of final determination; if certified mail is used for such purpose, the date of postmark on the sender's receipt for such mail is considered the date of final determination. If the corporation makes a deficiency distribution before such registration or postmark date but on or after the date the district director or director of the service center or other official has signed the agreement, the date of signature by the district director or director of the service center or other official is considered the date of final determination. If the corporation makes a deficiency distribution before the district director or director of the service center or other official signs the agreement, the date of final determination is considered to be the date of the making of the deficiency distribution. During any extension of time the interest charge provided in subparagraph (4) of this paragraph will continue to accrue at the rate provided for in such subparagraph.

(4) *Payment of interest for delayed distribution.*—(i) *In general.*—If a corporation makes a deficiency distribution after the 15th day of the ninth month after the close of the taxable year with respect to which such distribution is made, such distribution will not be deemed to satisfy the 95 percent of gross receipts test or the 95 percent assets test for such year unless such corporation pays to the Internal Revenue Service a charge determined by multiplying (a) an amount equal to $4\frac{1}{2}$ percent of such distribution by (b) the number of its taxable years which begin (1) after the taxable year with respect to which the distribution is made and (2) before such distribution is made. Such charge must be paid, within the 30-day period beginning with the day on which such distribution is made, to the service center with which the corporation files its annual information return for its taxable year in which the distribution is made. For purposes of the Internal Revenue Code, such charge is considered interest.

(ii) *Example.*—The provisions of subdivision (i) of this subparagraph may be illustrated by the following example:

Example. X corporation, which uses the calendar year as its taxable year, meets the 95 percent assets test but fails to meet the 95 percent of gross receipts test for 1972 and does not by September 15, 1973, make the deficiency distribution required by reason of its failure to meet such test. Assume that reasonable cause exists for the corporation's failure to meet the 95 percent of gross receipts test and failure to make the required deficiency distribution. If X makes the required deficiency distribution, in the amount of $10,000, on April 1, 1976, X must pay on or before April 30, 1976, to the service center with which it files its annual information return a charge of $1,800, computed as follows:

Deficiency distribution made by X . .	$10,000
Multiplied by 4½ percent	.045
Intermediate product	450
Multiplied by: Number of X's taxable years beginning after 1972 and before April 1, 1976	4
Charge to be paid service center because of late deficiency distribution (which is considered interest)	1,800

(d) *Certain distributions deemed for reasonable cause.*—If a corporation makes a distribution in the amount required by paragraph (b) of this section with respect to a taxable year on or before the 15th day of the ninth month after the close of such year, it will be deemed to have acted with reasonable cause with respect to its failure to satisfy the 95 percent of gross receipts test, the 95 percent assets test, or both tests, for such year and its failure to make such distribution prior to the date on which the distribution was made if—

(1) At least 70 percent of the gross receipts of such corporation for such taxable year consist of qualified export receipts; and

(2) The sum of the adjusted bases of the qualified export assets held by such corporation on the last day of each month of the taxable year equals or exceeds 70 percent of the sum of the adjusted bases of all assets held by the corporation on each such day. [Reg. § 1.992-3.]

☐ [*T.D.* 7323, 9-24-74. *Amended by T.D.* 7420, 5-19-76; *T.D.* 7854, 11-15-82 *and T.D.* 8939, 1-11-2001.]

[Reg. § 1.992-4]

§ 1.992-4. Coordination with personal holding company provisions in case of certain produced film rents.—(a) *In general.*—Section 992(d)(2) provides that a personal holding company is not eligible to be treated as a DISC. Section 543(a)(5)(B) provides that, for purposes of section 543, the term "produced film rents" means payments received with respect to an interest in a film for the use of, or the right to use, such film, but only to the extent that such interest was acquired before substantial completion of production of such film. Under section 992(e), if such produced film rents are included in the ordinary gross income (as defined in section 543(b)(1)) of a qualified subsidiary for a taxable year of such subsidiary, and such interest was acquired by such subsidiary from its parent, such interest is deemed (for purposes of the application of sections 541, 543(b)(1), and 992(d)(2), and § 1.992-1(f) for such taxable year) to have been acquired by such subsidiary at the time such interest was acquired by such parent. Thus, for example, if a parent acquires an interest in a film before it is substantially completed, then substantially completes such film prior to transferring an interest in such motion picture to a qualified subsidiary, the qualified subsidiary is considered as having acquired such interest prior to substantial completion of such motion picture for purposes of determining whether payments from the rental of such motion picture will be classified as produced film rents of such subsidiary. The provisions of section 992(e) and this section are not applicable in determining whether payments received with respect to an interest in a film are included in the ordinary gross income of a parent or a qualified subsidiary. Thus, even though a qualified subsidiary is treated pursuant to this section as having acquired an interest in a film at the time such interest was acquired by such subsidiary's parent, payments received by such parent with respect to such interest prior to the transfer of such interest to such subsidiary are includible in the ordinary gross income of such parent and not includible in the ordinary gross income of such subsidiary.

(b) *Definitions.*—(1) *"Qualified subsidiary".*—For purposes of this section, a corporation is a qualified subsidiary for a taxable year if—

(i) Such corporation was established for the purpose of becoming a DISC,

(ii) Such corporation would qualify (or be treated) as a DISC for such taxable year if it is not a personal holding company, and

(iii) On every day of such taxable year on which shares of such corporation are outstanding, at least 80 percent of such shares are held directly by a second corporation.

(2) *"Parent".*—For purposes of this section, the term "parent" means a second corporation referred to in subparagraph (1)(iii) of this paragraph. [Reg. § 1.992-4.]

☐ [*T.D.* 7323, 9-24-74.]

[Reg. § 1.993-1]

§ 1.993-1. Definition of qualified export receipts.—(a) *In general.*—For a corporation to qualify as a DISC, at least 95 percent of its gross receipts for a taxable year must consist of qualified export receipts. Under section 993(a), the term "qualified export receipts" means any of the eight amounts described in paragraphs (b) through (i) of this section, except to the extent that any of the eight amounts is an excluded receipt within the meaning of paragraph (j) of this section. For purposes of this section and §§ 1.993-2 through 1.993-6—

(1) *DISC.*—All references to a DISC mean a DISC, except when the context indicates that such term means a corporation in the process of meeting the conditions necessary for that corporation to become a DISC, or a corporation being tested as to whether it qualifies as a DISC.

(2) *Sale, lease, and license.*—The term "sale" includes an exchange or other disposition and the term "lease" includes a rental or a sublease. The term "license" includes a sublicense. All rules under this section and §§ 1.993-2 through 1.993-6 applicable to leases of export property apply in the same manner to licenses of export property. See § 1.993-3(f)(3) for a description of intangible property which cannot be export property.

(3) *Gross receipts.*—The term "gross receipts" is defined by section 993(f) and § 1.993-6.

(4) *Qualified export assets.*—The term "qualified export assets" is defined by section 993(b) and § 1.993-2.

(5) *Export property.*—The term "export property" is defined by section 993(c) and § 1.993-3.

(6) *Related person.*—The term "related person" means a person who is related to another person if either immediately before or after a transaction—

(i) The relationship between such persons would result in a disallowance of losses under section 267 (relating to disallowance of losses, etc., between related taxpayers), or section 707(b) (relating to losses disallowed, etc., between partners and controlled partnerships), and the regulations thereunder, or

(ii) Such persons are members of the same controlled group of corporations, as defined in section 1563(a) (relating to definition of controlled group of corporations), except that (*a*) "more than 50 percent" shall be substituted for "at lease 80 percent" each place it appears in section 1563(a) and the regulations thereunder, and (*b*) the provisions of section 1563(b) shall not apply in determining whether such persons are members of the same controlled group.

(7) *Related supplier.*—The term "related supplier" is defined by § 1.994-1(a)(3)(ii).

(8) *Controlled group.*—The term "controlled group" is defined by paragraph (k) of this section.

(b) *Sales of export property.*—Qualified export receipts of a DISC include gross receipts from the sale of export property by such DISC, or by any principal for whom such DISC acts as a commission agent (whether or not such principal is a related supplier), pursuant to the terms of a contract entered into with a purchaser by such DISC or by such principal at any time or by any other person and assigned to such DISC or such principal at any time prior to the shipment of such property to the purchaser. Any agreement, oral or written, which constitutes a contract at law, satisfies the contractual requirement of this paragraph. Gross receipts from the sale of export property, whenever received, do not constitute qualified export receipts unless the seller (or the corporation acting as commission agent for the seller) is a DISC at the time of the shipment of such property to the purchaser. For example, if a corporation which sells export property under the installment method is not a DISC for the taxable year in which the property is shipped to the purchaser, gross receipts from such sale do not constitute qualified export receipts for any taxable year of the corporation.

(c) *Leases of export property.*—(1) *In general.*—Qualified export receipts of a DISC include gross receipts from the lease of export property provided that—

(i) Such property is held by such DISC (or by a principal for whom such DISC acts as commission agent with respect to the lease) either as an owner or lessee at the beginning of the term of such lease, and

(ii) Such DISC qualified (or was treated) as a DISC for its taxable year in which the term of such lease began.

(2) *Prepayment of lease receipts.*—If part or all of the gross receipts from a lease of property are prepaid, then—

(i) All such prepaid gross receipts are qualified export receipts of a DISC if it is reasonably expected at the time of such prepayment that throughout the term of such lease they would be qualified export receipts if received not as a prepayment; or

(ii) If it is reasonably expected at the time of such prepayment that throughout the term of such lease they would not be qualified export receipts if received not as a prepayment, then only those prepaid receipts, for the taxable years of the DISC for which they would be qualified export receipts, are qualified export receipts.

Thus, for example, if a lessee makes a prepayment of the first and last years' rent, and it is reasonably expected that the leased property will be export property for the first half of the lease period but not the second half of such period, the amount of the prepayment which represents the first year's rent will be considered qualified export receipts if it would otherwise qualify, whereas the amount of the prepayment which represents the last year's rent will not be considered qualified export receipts.

(d) *Related and subsidiary services.*—(1) *In general.*—Qualified export receipts of a DISC include gross receipts from services furnished by such DISC which are related and subsidiary to any sale or lease (as described in paragraph (b) or (c) of this section) of export property by such DISC or with respect to which such DISC acts as a commission agent, provided that such DISC derives qualified export receipts from such sale or lease. Such services may be performed within or without the United States.

(2) *Services furnished by DISC.*—Services are considered to be furnished by a DISC for purposes of this paragraph if such services are provided by—

(i) The person who sold or leased the export property to which such services are related and subsidiary, provided that the DISC acts as a commission agent with respect to the sale or lease of such property and with respect to such services,

(ii) The DISC as principal, or any other person pursuant to a contract between such person and such DISC, provided the DISC acted as principal or commission agent with respect to the sale or lease of such property, or

(iii) A member of the same controlled group as the DISC where the sale or lease of the export property is made by another member of such controlled group provided, however, that the DISC act as principal or commission agent with respect to such sale or lease and as commission agent with respect to such services.

(3) *Related services.*—A service is related to a sale or lease of export property if—

(i) Such service is of the type customarily and usually furnished with the type of transaction in the trade or business in which such sale or lease arose and

(ii) The contract to furnish such service—

(*a*) Is expressly provided for in or is provided for by implied warranty under the contract of sale or lease,

(*b*) Is entered into on or before the date which is 2 years after the date on which the contract under which such sale or lease was entered into, provided that the person described in subparagraph (2) of this paragraph which is to furnish such service delivers to the purchaser or lessor a written offer or option to furnish such services on or before the date on which the first shipment of goods with respect to which the service is to be performed is delivered, or

(*c*) Is a renewal of the services contract described in (*a*) or (*b*) of this subdivision. Services which may be related to a sale or lease of export property include but are not limited to warranty service, maintenance service, repair service, and installation service. Transportation (including insurance related to such transportation) may be related to a sale or lease of export property, provided that the cost of such transportation is included in the sale price or rental of the property or, if such cost is separately stated, is paid by the DISC (or its principal) which sold or leased the property to the person furnishing the transportation service. Financing or the obtaining of financing for a sale or lease is not a related service for purposes of this paragraph.

(4) *Subsidiary services.*—(i) *In general.*—Services related to a sale or lease of export property are subsidiary to such sale or lease only if it is reasonably expected at the time of such sale or lease that the gross receipts from all related services furnished by the DISC (as defined in subparagraphs (2) and (3) of this paragraph) will not exceed 50 percent of the sum of (a) the gross receipts from such sale or lease and (b) the gross receipts from related services furnished by the DISC (as described in subparagraph (2) of this paragraph). In the case of a sale, reasonable expectations at the time of the sale are based on the gross receipts from all related services which may reasonably be expected to be performed at any time before the end of the 10-year period following the date of such sale. In the case of a lease, reasonable expectations at the time of the lease are based on the gross receipts from all related services which may reasonably be expected to be performed at any time before the end of the term of such lease (determined without regard to renewal options).

(ii) *Allocation of gross receipts from services.*—In determining whether the services related to a sale or lease of export property are subsidiary to such sale or lease, the gross receipts to be treated as derived from the furnishing of services may not be less than the amount of gross receipts reasonably allocated to such services as determined under the facts and circumstances of each case without regard to whether—

(*a*) Such services are furnished under a separate contract or under the same contract pursuant to which such sale or lease occurs or

(*b*) The cost of such services is specified in the contract of sale or lease.

(iii) *Transactions involving more than one item of export property.*—If more than one item of export property is sold or leased in a single transaction pursuant to one contract, the total gross receipts from such transaction and the total gross receipts from all services related to such transaction are each taken into account in determining whether such services are subsidiary to such transaction. However, the provisions of this subdivision apply only if such items could be included in the same product line, as determined under § 1.994-1(c)(7).

Reg. § 1.993-1(d)(4)(iii)

(iv) *Renewed service contracts.*—If under the terms of a contract for related services, such contract is renewable within 10 years after a sale of export property, or during the term of a lease of export property, related services to be performed under the renewed contract are subsidiary to such sale or lease if it is reasonably expected at the time of such renewal that the gross receipts from all related services which have been and which are to be furnished by the DISC (as described in subparagraph (2) of this paragraph) will not exceed 50 percent of the sum of (*a*) the gross receipts from such sale or lease and (*b*) the gross receipts from related services furnished by the DISC (as so described). Reasonable expectations are determined as provided in subdivision (i) of this subparagraph.

(v) *Parts used in services.*—If a services contract described in subparagraph (3) of this paragraph provides for the furnishing of parts in connection with the furnishing of related services, gross receipts from the furnishing of such parts are not taken into account in determining whether under this subparagraph the services are subsidiary. See paragraph (b) or (c) of this section to determine whether the gross receipts from the furnishing of parts constitute qualified export receipts. See § 1.993-3(c)(2)(iv) and (e)(3) for rules regarding the treatment of such parts with respect to the manufacture of export property and the foreign content of such property, respectively.

(5) *Relation to leases.*—If the gross receipts for services which are related and subsidiary to a lease of property have been prepaid at any time for all such services which are to be performed before the end of the term of such lease, then as of the time of the prepayment the rules in paragraph (c)(2) of this section (relating to prepayment of lease receipts) will determine whether prepaid services under this subdivision are qualified export receipts. Thus, for example, if it is reasonably expected that leased property will be export property for the first year of the term of the lease but will not be export property for the second year of the term, prepaid gross receipts for related and subsidiary services to be furnished in the first year may be qualified export receipts. However, any prepaid gross receipts for such services to be furnished in the second year cannot be qualified export receipts.

(6) *Relation with export property determination.*—The determination as to whether gross receipts from the sale or lease of export property constitute qualified export receipts does not depend upon whether services connected with such sale or lease are related and subsidiary to such sale or lease. Thus, for example, assume that a DISC receives gross receipts of $1,000 from the sale of export property and gross receipts of $1,100 from installation and maintenance ser-vices which are to be furnished by such DISC within 10 years after the sale and which are related to such sale. The $1,100 which the DISC receives for such services would not be qualified export receipts since the gross receipts from the services exceed 50 percent of the sum of the gross receipts from the sale and the gross receipts from the related services furnished by such DISC. The $1,000 which the DISC receives from the sale of export property would, however, be a qualified export receipt if the sale met the requirements of paragraph (b) of this section.

(e) *Gains from sales of certain qualified export assets.*—Qualified export receipts of a DISC include gross receipts from the sale by such DISC of any assets (wherever located) which, as of the date of such sale, are qualified export assets as defined in § 1.993-2 even though such assets are not export property (as defined in § 1.993-3). Gross receipts are derived from the sale of such assets only where such sale results in recognized gain (see § 1.993-6(a)). For purposes of this paragraph, losses from the sale of such qualified export assets shall not be taken into account for purposes of determining the DISC's qualified export receipts.

(f) *Dividends.*—Qualified export receipts of a DISC for a taxable year include all dividends includible in the gross income of such DISC for such taxable year with respect to the stock of related foreign export corporations (as defined in § 1.993-5) and all amounts includible in the gross income of such DISC with respect to such corporations pursuant to section 951 (relating to amounts included in the gross income of U.S. shareholders of controlled foreign corporations).

(g) *Interest on obligations which are qualified export assets.*—Qualified export receipts of a DISC include interest on any obligation which is a qualified export asset of such DISC, including any amount includible in gross income as interest (such as, for example, an amount treated as original issue discount pursuant to section 1232) or as imputed interest under section 483. Gain from the sale of obligations described in this paragraph is treated (to the extent such gain is not treated as interest on such obligations) as qualified export receipts pursuant to paragraph (e) of this section.

(h) *Engineering and architectural services.*— (1) *In general.*—Qualified export receipts of a DISC include gross receipts from engineering services (as described in subparagraph (5) of this paragraph) or architectural services (as described in subparagraph (6) of this paragraph) furnished by such DISC (as described in subparagraph (7) of this paragraph) for a construction project (as defined in subparagraph (8) of this paragraph) located, or proposed for location, outside the United States. Such services may be performed within or without the United States.

(2) *Services included.*—Engineering and architectural services include feasibility studies for a proposed construction project whether or not such project is ultimately initiated.

(3) *Excluded services.*—Engineering and architectural services do not include—

(i) Services connected with the exploration for minerals or

(ii) Technical assistance or know-how.

For purposes of this paragraph, the term "technical assistance or know-how" includes activities or programs designed to enable business, commerce, industrial establishments, and governmental organizations to acquire or use scientific, architectural, or engineering information.

(4) *Other services.*—Receipts from the performance of construction activities other than engineering and architectural services constitute qualified export receipts to the extent that such activities are related and subsidiary services (within the meaning of paragraph (d) of this section) with respect to a sale or lease of export property.

(5) *Engineering services.*—For purposes of this paragraph, engineering services in connection with any construction project (within the meaning of subparagraph (8) of this paragraph) include any professional services requiring engineering education, training, and experience and the application of special knowledge of the mathematical, physical, or engineering sciences to such professional services as consultation, investigation, evaluation, planning, design, or responsible supervision of construction for the purpose of assuring compliance with plans, specifications, and design.

(6) *Architectural services.*—For purposes of this paragraph, architectural services include the offering or furnishing of any professional services such as consultation, planning, aesthetic, and structural design, drawings and specifications, or responsible supervision of construction (for the purpose of assuring compliance with plans, specifications, and design) or erection, in connection with any construction project (within the meaning of subparagraph (8) of this paragraph).

(7) *Definition of "furnished by such DISC".*—For purposes of this paragraph, architectural and engineering services are considered furnished by a DISC if such services are provided—

(i) By the DISC,

(ii) By another person (whether or not a United States person) pursuant to a contract entered into by such person with the DISC at any time prior to the furnishing of such services, provided that the DISC acts as principal with respect to the furnishing of such services, or

(iii) By another person (whether or not a United States person) pursuant to a contract for the furnishing of such services entered into at any time prior to the furnishing of such services provided that the DISC acts as commission agent with respect to such services.

(8) *Definition of "construction project".*—For purposes of this paragraph, the term "construction project" includes the erection, expansion, or repair (but not including minor remodeling or minor repairs) of new or existing buildings or other physical facilities including, for example, roads, dams, canals, bridges, tunnels, railroad tracks, and pipelines. The term also includes site grading and improvement and installation of equipment necessary for the construction. Gross receipts from the sale or lease of construction equipment are not qualified export receipts unless such equipment is export property (as defined in § 1.993-3).

(i) *Managerial services.*—(1) *In general.*—Qualified export receipts of a first DISC for its taxable year include gross receipts from the furnishing of managerial services provided for another DISC, which is not a related person, to aid such unrelated DISC in deriving qualified export receipts, provided that at least 50 percent of the gross receipts of the first DISC for such year consists of qualified export receipts derived from the sale or lease of export property and the furnishing of related and subsidiary services, as described in paragraphs (b), (c), and (d) of this section, respectively. For purposes of this paragraph, managerial services are considered furnished by a DISC if such services are provided—

(i) By the first DISC,

(ii) By another person (whether or not a United States person) pursuant to a contract entered into by such person with the first DISC at any time prior to the furnishing of such services, provided that the first DISC acts as principal with respect to the furnishing of such services, or

(iii) By another person (whether or not a United States person) pursuant to a contract for the furnishing of such services entered into at any time prior to the furnishing of such services provided that the DISC acts as commission agent with respect to such services.

(2) *Definition of "managerial services".*—The term "managerial services" as used in this paragraph means activities relating to the operation of another unrelated DISC which derives qualified export receipts from the sale or lease of export property and from the furnishing of services related and subsidiary to such sales or leases. Such term includes staffing and operational services necessary to operate such other DISC, but does not include legal, accounting, scientific, or technical services. Examples of managerial services are: (i) Export market studies, (ii) making shipping arrangements, and (iii) contacting potential foreign purchasers.

(3) *Status of recipient of managerial services.*— (i) *In general.*—Qualified export receipts of a first DISC include receipts from the furnishing of managerial services during any taxable year of a recipient if such recipient qualifies as a DISC (within the meaning of § 1.992-1(a)) for such taxable year.

(ii) *Recipient deemed to qualify as a DISC.*— For purposes of subdivision (i) of this subparagraph, a recipient is deemed to qualify as a DISC for its taxable year if the first DISC obtains from such recipient a copy of such recipient's election to be treated as a DISC as described in § 1.992-2(a) together with such recipient's sworn statement that such election has been filed with the Internal Revenue Service Center. The recipient may mark out the names of its shareholders on a copy of its election to be treated as a DISC before submitting it to the first DISC. The copy of the election and the sworn statement of such recipient must be received by the first DISC within 6 months after the beginning of the first taxable year of the recipient during which such first DISC furnishes managerial services for such recipient. The copy of the election and the sworn statement of the recipient need not be obtained by the first DISC for subsequent taxable years of the recipient.

(iii) *Recipient not treated as a DISC.*—For purposes of subdivision (i) of this subparagraph, a recipient of managerial services is not treated as a DISC with respect to such services performed during a taxable year for which such recipient does not qualify as a DISC if the DISC performing such services does not believe or if a reasonable person would not believe (taking into account the furnishing DISC's managerial relationship with such recipient DISC) at the beginning of such taxable year that the recipient will qualify as a DISC for such taxable year.

(j) *Excluded receipts.*—(1) *In general.*—Notwithstanding the provisions of paragraphs (b) through (i) of this section, qualified export receipts of a DISC do not include any of the five amounts described in subparagraphs (2) through (6) of this paragraph.

(2) *Sales and leases of property for ultimate use in the United States.*—Property which is sold or leased for ultimate use in the United States does not constitute export property (relating to determination of where the ultimate use of the property occurs). See § 1.993-3(d)(4). Thus, qualified export receipts of a DISC described in paragraph (b) or (c) of this section do not include gross receipts of the DISC from the sale or lease of such property.

(3) *Sales of export property accomplished by subsidy.*—Qualified export receipts of a DISC do not include gross receipts described in paragraph (b) of this section if the sale of export property (whether or not such property consists of agricultural products) is pursuant to any of the following:

(i) The development loan program, or grants under the technical cooperation and development grants program of the Agency for International Development, or grants under the military assistance program administered by the Department of Defense, pursuant to the Foreign Assistance Act of 1961, as amended (22 U.S.C. 2151), unless the DISC shows to the satisfaction of the district director that, under the conditions existing at the time of the sale, the purchaser had a reasonable opportunity to purchase, on competitive terms and from a seller who was not a U.S. person, goods which were substantially identical to such property and which were not manufactured, produced, grown, or extracted (as described in § 1.993-3(c)) in the United States,

(ii) The Public Law 480 program authorized under Title I of the Agricultural Trade Development and Assistance Act of 1954, as amended (7 U.S.C. 1691, 1701-1710).

(iii) For taxable years ending before January 1, 1974, the Barter program of the Commodity Credit Corporation authorized by section 4(h) of the Commodity Credit Corporation Charter Act, as amended (15 U.S.C. 714b(h)), and section 303 of the Agricultural Trade Development and Assistance Act of 1954, as amended (7 U.S.C. 1692) but only if the taxpayer treats such sales as sales giving rise to excluded receipts,

(iv) The Export Payment Program of the Commodity Credit Corporation authorized by sections 5(d) and (f) of the Commodity Credit Corporation Charter Act, as amended (15 U.S.C. 714c(d) and (f)),

(v) The section 32 export payment programs authorized by section 32 of the Act of August 24, 1935, as amended (7 U.S.C. 612c), and

(vi) For taxable years beginning after November 3, 1972, the Export Sales program of the Commodity Credit Corporation authorized by sections 5(d) and (f) of the Commodity Credit Corporation Charter Act, as amended (15 U.S.C. 714c(d) and (f)), other than the GSM-4 program provided under 7 CFR 1488, and section 407 of the Agricultural Act of 1949, as amended (7 U.S.C. 1427), for the purpose of disposing of surplus agricultural commodities and exporting or causing to be exported agricultural commodities, except that for taxable years beginning on or before November 3, 1972, the taxpayer may treat such sales as sales giving rise to excluded receipts.

(4) *Sales or leases of export property and furnishing of engineering or architectural services for use by the United States.*—(i) *In general.*—Qualified export receipts of a DISC do not include gross receipts described in paragraph (b), (c), or (h) of this section if a sale or lease of export property, or the furnishing of engineering or architectural services, is for use by the United States or an instrumentality thereof in any case

in which any law or regulation requires in any manner the purchase or lease of property manufactured, produced, grown, or extracted in the United States or requires the use of engineering or architectural services performed by a U.S. person. For example, a sale by a DISC of export property to the Department of Defense for use outside the United States would not produce qualified export receipts for such DISC if the Department of Defense purchased such property from appropriated funds subject to any provisions of the Armed Forces Procurement Regulations (32 CFR Subchapter A, Part 6, Subpart A) or any appropriations act for the Department of Defense for the applicable year which restricts the availability of such appropriated funds to the procurement of items which are grown, reprocessed, reused, or produced in the United States.

(ii) *Direct or indirect sales or leases.*—Any sale or lease of export property is for use by the United States or an instrumentality thereof if such property is sold or leased by a DISC (or by a principal for whom such DISC acts as commission agent) to—

(a) A person who is a related person with respect to such DISC or such principal and who sells or leases such property for use by the United States or an instrumentality thereof or

(b) A person who is not a related person with respect to such DISC or such principal if, at the time of such sale or lease, there is an agreement or understanding that such property will be sold or leased for use by the United States or an instrumentality thereof (or if a reasonable person would have known at the time of such sale or lease that such property would be sold or leased for use by the United States or an instrumentality thereof) within 3 years after such sale or lease.

(iii) *Excluded programs.*—The provisions of subdivisions (i) and (ii) of this subparagraph do not apply in the case of a purchase by the United States or an instrumentality thereof if such purchase is pursuant to—

(a) The Foreign Military Sales Act, as amended (22 U.S.C. §2751 *et seq.*), or a program under which the U.S. Government purchases property for resale, on commercial terms, to a foreign government or agency or instrumentality thereof, or

(b) A program (whether bilateral or multi-lateral) under which sales to the U.S. Government are open to international competitive bidding.

(5) *Services.*—Qualified export receipts of a DISC do not include gross receipts described in paragraph (d) of this section (concerning related and subsidiary services) if the services from which such gross receipts are derived are related and subsidiary to the sale or lease of property

which results in excluded receipts pursuant to this paragraph.

(6) *Receipts within controlled group.*—(i) *In general.*—Gross receipts of a corporation do not constitute qualified export receipts for any taxable year of such corporation if—

(a) At the time of the sale, lease, or other transaction resulting in such gross receipts, such corporation and the person from whom such receipts are directly or indirectly derived (whether or not such corporation and such person are the same person) are members of the same controlled group (as defined in paragraph (k) of this section) and

(b) Such corporation and such person each qualifies (or is treated under section 992(a)(2)) as a DISC for its taxable year in which its receipts arise.

Thus, for example, assume that R, S, X, and Y are members of the same controlled group and that X and Y are DISC's. If R sells property to S and pays X a commission relating to that sale and if S sells the same property to an unrelated foreign party and pays Y a commission relating to that sale, the receipts received by X from the sale of such property by R to S will be considered to be derived from Y, a DISC which is a member of the same controlled group as X, and thus will not result in qualified export receipts to X. The receipts received by Y from the sale to an unrelated foreign party may, however, result in qualified export receipts to Y. For another example, if R and S both assign the commissions to X, receipts derived from the sale from R to S will be considered to be derived from X acting as commission agent for S and will not result in qualified export receipts to X. Receipts derived by X from the sale of property by S to an unrelated foreign party, may, however, constitute qualified export receipts.

(ii) *Leased property.*—See §1.993-3(f)(2) regarding property not constituting export property in certain cases where such property is leased to any corporation which is a member of the same controlled group as the lessor.

(k) *Definition of "controlled group.".*—For purposes of sections 991 through 996 and the regulations thereunder, the term "controlled group" has the same meaning as is assigned to the term "controlled group of corporations" by section 1563(a), except that (1) the phrase "more than 50 percent" is substituted for the phrase "at least 80 percent" each place the latter phrase appears in section 1563(a), and (2) section 1563(b) shall not apply. Thus, for example, a foreign corporation subject to tax under section 881 may be a member of a controlled group. Furthermore, two or more corporations (including a foreign corporation) are members of a controlled group at any time such corporations meet the requirements of section 1563(a) (as modified by this paragraph).

Reg. §1.993-1(k)

(l) *DISC's entitlement to income.*—(1) *Application of section 994.*—A corporation which meets the requirements of §1.992-1(a) to be treated as a DISC for a taxable year is entitled to income, and the intercompany pricing rules of section 994(a)(1) or (2) apply, in the case of any transactions described in §1.994-1(b) between such DISC and its related supplier (as defined in §1.994-1(a)(3)). For purposes of this subparagraph, such DISC need not have employees or perform any specific function.

(2) *Other transactions.*—In the case of a transaction to which the provisions of subparagraph (1) of this paragraph do not apply but from which a DISC derives gross receipts, the income to which the DISC is entitled as a result of the transaction is determined pursuant to the terms of the contract for such transaction and, if applicable, section 482 and the regulations thereunder.

(3) *Examples.*—The provisions of this paragraph may be illustrated by the following examples:

Example (1). P Corporation forms S Corporation as a wholly-owned subsidiary. S qualifies as a DISC for its taxable year. S has no employees on its payroll. S is granted a franchise with respect to specified exports of P. P will sell such exports to S for resale by S. Such exports are of a type which produce qualified export receipts as defined in paragraph (b) of this section. P's sales force will solicit orders in the name of S using S's order forms. S places orders with P only when S itself has received orders. No inventory is maintained by S. P makes shipments directly to customers of S. Employees of P will act for S and billings and collections will be handled by P in the name of S. Under these facts, the income derived by S for such taxable year from the purchase and resale of the specified export is treated for Federal income tax purposes as the income of S, and the amount of income allocable to S will be determined under section 994 of the Code.

Example (2). P Corporation forms S Corporation as a wholly-owned subsidiary. S qualifies as a DISC for its taxable year. S has no employees on its payroll. S is granted a sales franchise with respect to specified exports of P and will receive commissions with respect to such exports. Such exports are of a type which will produce gross receipts for S which are qualified export receipts as defined in paragraph (b) of this section. P's sales force will solicit orders in the name of P. Billings and collections are handled directly by P. Under these facts, the commissions paid to S for such taxable year with respect to the specified exports shall be treated for Federal income tax purposes as the income of S, and the amount of income allocable to S is determined under section 994 of the Code. [Reg. § 1.993-1.]

☐ [T.D. 7514, 10-14-77. *Amended by* T.D. 7854, 11-15-82.]

[Reg. §1.993-2]

§1.993-2. Definition of qualified export assets.—(a) *In general.*—For a corporation to qualify as a DISC, at the close of its taxable year it must have qualified export assets with adjusted bases equal to at least 95 percent of the sum of the adjusted bases of all its assets. An asset which is a qualified export asset under more than one paragraph of this section shall be taken into account only once in determining the sum of the adjusted bases of all qualified export assets. Under section 993(b), the qualified export assets held by a corporation are—

(1) Export property as defined in §1.993-3 (see paragraph (b) of this section),

(2) Business assets described in paragraph (c) of this section,

(3) Trade receivables described in paragraph (d) of this section,

(4) Temporary investments to the extent described in paragraph (e) of this section,

(5) Producer's loans as defined in §1.993-4 (see paragraph (f) of this section),

(6) Stock or securities (described in paragraph (g) of this section) of related foreign export corporations as defined in §1.993-5,

(7) Export-Import Bank and other obligations described in paragraph (h) of this section,

(8) Financing obligations described in paragraph (i) of this section, and

(9) Funds awaiting investment described in paragraph (j) of this section.

(b) *Export property.*—In general, export property is certain property held for sale or lease which meets the requirements of §1.993-3.

(c) *Business assets.*—For purposes of this section, business assets are assets used by a DISC (other than as a lessor) primarily in connection with—

(1) The sale, lease, storage, handling, transportation, packaging, assembly, or servicing of export property, or

(2) The performance of engineering or architectural services (described in §1.993-1(h)) or managerial services (described in §1.993-1(i)) in furtherance of the production of qualified export receipts.

Assets used primarily in the manufacture, production, growth, or extraction (within the meaning of §1.993-3(c)) of property are not business assets.

(d) *Trade receivables.*—(1) *In general.*—For purposes of this section, trade receivables are accounts receivable and evidences of indebtedness which arise by reason of transactions of such corporation or of another corporation which is a DISC and which is a member of a controlled group which includes such corporation described in subparagraph (A), (B), (C), (D), (G), or (H), of section 993(a)(1) and which are due the

DISC (or, if it acts as an agent, due its principal) and held by the DISC.

(2) *Trade receivables representing commissions.*—If a DISC acts as commission agent for a principal in a transaction described in § 1.993-1(b), (c), (d), (e), (h), or (i) which results in qualified export receipts for the DISC, and if an account receivable or evidence of indebtedness held by the DISC and representing the commission payable to the DISC as a result of the transaction arises (and, in the case of an evidence of indebtedness, designated on its face as representing such commission), such account receivable or evidence of indebtedness shall be treated as a trade receivable. If, however, the principal is a related supplier (as defined in § 1.994-1(a)(3)) with respect to the DISC, such account receivable or evidence of indebtedness will not be treated as a trade receivable unless it is payable and paid in a time and manner which satisfy the requirements of § 1.994-1(e)(3) or (5) (relating to initial payment of transfer price or commission and procedure for adjustments to transfer price or commission, respectively), as the case may be. However, see subparagraph (3) of this paragraph for rules regarding certain accounts receivable representing commissions payable to a DISC by its related supplier.

(3) *Indebtedness arising under § 1.994-1(e).*— An indebtedness arising under § 1.994-1(e)(3)(iii) (relating to initial payment of transfer price of commission) in favor of a DISC is not a qualified export asset. An indebtedness arising under § 1.994-1(e)(5)(i) (relating to procedure for adjustments to transfer price or commission) in favor of a DISC is a trade receivable if it is paid in the time and manner described in § 1.994-1(e)(5)(i) and (ii) and if it otherwise satisfies the requirements of subparagraph (2) of this paragraph. If such an indebtedness is not paid in the time and manner described in § 1.994-1(e)(5)(i) and (ii), it is not a qualified export asset.

(e) *Temporary investments.*—(1) *In general.*— For purposes of this section, temporary investments are money, bank deposits (not including time deposits of more than 1 year), and other similar temporary investments to the extent maintained by a DISC as reasonably necessary to meet its requirements for working capital. For purposes of this paragraph, a temporary investment is an obligation, including an evidence of indebtedness as defined in paragraph (d)(1) of this section, which is a demand obligation or has a period remaining to maturity of not more than 1 year at the date it is acquired by the DISC. A temporary investment does not include trade receivables.

(2) *Determination of amount of working capital maintained.*—For purposes of this paragraph—

(i) The working capital of a DISC is the excess of its current assets over current liabilities,

(ii) Current assets are cash and other assets (other than trade receivables) which may reasonably be expected to be converted into cash or sold or consumed during the current normal operating cycle of the DISC's trade or business,

(iii) Current liabilities are obligations (or portions of obligations) due within the current normal operating cycle of the trade or business of the DISC whose satisfaction when due is reasonably expected to require the use of current assets,

(iv) Generally accepted financial accounting treatments will be accepted, and

(v) Current assets (other than temporary investments) are taken into account before temporary investments, and trade receivables are never taken into account, in determining whether such temporary investments are maintained by the DISC as reasonably necessary to meet its current liabilities and its requirements for working capital.

(3) *Determination of amount of working capital reasonably required.*—For purposes of this paragraph, a determination of the amount of money, bank deposits, and other similar temporary investments reasonably necessary to meet the requirements of the DISC for working capital will depend upon the nature and volume of the activities of the DISC existing at the end of the DISC's taxable year for which such determination is made, such as, for example—

(i) In the case of a DISC which purchases and sells inventory, the amount of working capital reasonably required is limited to an amount reasonably necessary to meet the ordinary operating expenses during the current normal operating cycle of the trade or business of the DISC, an amount reasonably needed to meet specific and definite plans for expansion and any amounts necessary for reasonably anticipated extraordinary business expenses.

(ii) In the case of a DISC which actively conducts a trade or business (including the employment of a sales force) and receives commissions in respect of goods to which such DISC does not have title, the amount of working capital required will depend upon the nature and volume of the activities of the DISC which produce such income as they exist on the applicable determination date. In determining the amount of working capital which is reasonably required for the production of such income, the anticipated future needs of the business will be taken into account to the extent that such needs relate to the year of the DISC following the applicable determination date. Anticipated future needs relating to a later period will not be taken into account unless it is clearly established that such needs are reasonably related to the production of such income as of the applicable determination date.

(iii) In the case of a DISC which does not actively conduct a trade or business, and which receives commissions solely by reason of section 994(a)(1), (a)(2), or (b) with respect to goods to which such DISC does not have title, no working capital would be required beyond a *de minimis* amount unless it appears from the facts and circumstances that additional working capital will be required.

(iv) In the case of a DISC deriving income from the leasing of property, the amount of working capital required will be determined on the basis of the facts and circumstances in such case.

(4) *Relationship of working capital to other qualified export assets.*—If a temporary investment is a qualified export asset under any provisions of this section (other than this paragraph), this paragraph shall not affect its status as a qualified export asset. However, any such temporary investment is taken into account before other temporary investments in determining whether such other temporary investments are maintained by a DISC as reasonably necessary to meet its requirements for working capital. Current assets (other than temporary investments) are taken into account before temporary investments, and trade receivables are never taken into account, in determining whether such temporary investments are maintained by the DISC as reasonably necessary requirements for working capital. An obligation issued or incurred by a member of a controlled group (as defined in § 1.993-1(k)) of which the DISC is a member is not a qualified export asset under this paragraph. For rules regarding working capital as of the end of each month of a taxable year for purposes of the 70-percent reasonableness standard with respect to certain deficiency distributions, see paragraph (j)(3) of this section.

(f) *Producer's loans.*—For purposes of this section, a producer's loan is an evidence of indebtedness arising in connection with producer's loans which are made by a DISC and which meet the requirements of § 1.993-4. If a producer's loan is a qualified export asset, interest accrued with respect to the producer's loan will also be treated as a qualified export asset provided that payment is made in the form of money, property (valued at its fair market value on its date of transfer and including accounts receivable for sales by or through a DISC), a written obligation which qualifies as a debt under the safe harbor rule of § 1.992-1(d)(2)(ii), or an accounting entry offsetting the account receivable against an existing debt owed by the person in whose favor the account receivable was established to the person with whom it engaged in the transaction and that payment is made no later than 60 days following the close of the taxable year of accrual of the interest. This paragraph (f) is effective for taxable years beginning after January 10, 1985 except that the taxpayer may at its option apply the provisions of this paragraph to taxable years ending after December 31, 1971.

(g) *Stock or securities of related foreign export corporations.*—For purposes of this section, the term "stock or securities", with respect to a related foreign export corporation (as defined in § 1.993-5), has the same meaning of such term has as used in section 351 (relating to transfers to controlled corporations), except that the term "securities" does not include obligations which are repaid, in whole or in part, at any time during the taxable year of the DISC following the taxable year of the DISC during which such obligations were acquired by the DISC or were issued, unless the DISC demonstrates to the satisfaction of the district director that the repayment was for bona fide business purposes and not for the purpose of avoidance of Federal income taxes.

(h) *Export-Import Bank obligations.*—For purposes of this section, the term "Export-Import Bank obligations" means obligations issued, guaranteed, insured, or reinsured (in whole or in part) by the Export-Import Bank of the United States or by the Foreign Credit Insurance Association, but only if such obligations are acquired by the DISC—

(1) From the Export-Import Bank of the United States,

(2) From the Foreign Credit Insurance Association, or

(3) From the person selling or purchasing the goods or services by reason of which such obligations arose, or from any corporation which is a member of the same controlled group (as defined in § 1.993-1(k)) as such person.

For purposes of this paragraph, obligations issued by a person described in subparagraphs (1), (2), and (3) of this paragraph are treated as acquired from such person by the DISC if acquired from any person not more than 90 days after the date of original issue (as defined in § 1.1232-3(b)(3)). Examples of specific types of Export-Import Bank obligations include debentures issued by such bank and certificates of loan participation.

(i) *Financing obligations.*—For purposes of this section, financing obligations are obligations (held by a DISC) of a domestic corporation organized solely for the purpose of financing sales of export property pursuant to an agreement with the Export-Import Bank of the United States under which such corporation makes export loans guaranteed by such Bank.

(j) *Funds awaiting investment.*—(1) *In general.*—For purposes of this section, subject to the limitation described in subparagraph (2) of this paragraph, if, at the close of a DISC's taxable year, the sum of the DISC's money, bank deposits, and other similar temporary investments is determined under paragraph (e) of this section to exceed an amount reasonably necessary to meet the DISC's requirements for working capital, the amount of the DISC's bank deposits in the United States to the extent of the amount of this excess are funds awaiting investments at the close of such taxable year.

(2) *Limitation.*—Bank deposits described in subparagraph (1) of this paragraph are funds awaiting investment only if, by the last day of each of the sixth, seventh, and eighth months after the close of such taxable year, the sum of the adjusted bases of the qualified export assets of the DISC (other than such bank deposits) equals or exceeds 95 percent of the sum of the adjusted bases of all assets of the DISC (including such bank deposits) it held on the last day of such taxable year. For purposes of this subparagraph, the adjusted bases of assets of a DISC are determined as of the end of each of the months referred to in this subparagraph. Funds awaiting investment as described in this paragraph need not be traceable to any of the qualified export assets held by the DISC at the end of any of the months referred to in this subparagraph.

(3) *Coordination with certain deficiency distribution provisions.*—Under section 992(c)(3) and §1.992-3(d), a deficiency distribution made on or before the 15th day of the ninth month after the end of a corporation's taxable year is deemed to be for reasonable cause if certain requirements are met, including the requirement (described in section 992(c)(3)(B) and §1.992-3(d)(2)) that the sum of the adjusted bases of the qualified export assets held by the corporation on the last day of each month of such year equals or exceeds 70 percent of the sum of the adjusted bases of all assets held by the corporation on each such last day. If, on any such last day, the sum of a DISC's money, bank deposits, and other similar temporary investments is determined under paragraph (e) of this section to exceed an amount reasonably necessary to meet the DISC's requirements for working capital, the amount of the DISC's bank deposits to the extent of the amount of this excess are funds awaiting investment on such last day, if either—

(i) The requirements of subparagraph (2) of this paragraph are satisfied with respect to the taxable year of the DISC which includes such month or

(ii) At the close of such taxable year the sum of the DISC's money, bank deposits, and other similar temporary investments is determined under paragraph (e) of this section not to exceed an amount reasonably necessary to meet the DISC's requirements for working capital. [Reg. §1.993-2.]

☐ [*T.D. 7514, 10-14-77. Amended by T.D. 7854, 11-15-82 and T.D. 7984, 10-11-84.*]

[Reg. §1.993-3]

§1.993-3. Definition of export property.—(a) *General rule.*—Under section 993(c), except as otherwise provided with respect to excluded property in paragraph (f) of this section and with respect to certain short supply property in paragraph (i) of this section, export property is property in the hands of any person (whether or not a DISC)—

(1) Manufactured, produced, grown, or extracted in the United States by any person or persons other than a DISC (see paragraph (c) of this section),

(2) Held primarily for sale or lease in the ordinary course of a trade or business to any person for direct use, consumption, or disposition outside the United States (see paragraph (d) of this section),

(3) Not more than 50 percent of the fair market value of which is attributable to articles imported into the United States (see paragraph (e) of this section), and

(4) Which is not sold or leased by a DISC, or with a DISC as commission agent, to another DISC which is a member of the same controlled group (as defined in §1.993-1(k)) as the DISC.

(b) *Services.*—For purposes of this section, services (including the written communication of services in any form) are not export property. Whether an item is property or services shall be determined on the basis of the facts and circumstances attending the development and disposition of the item. Thus, for example, the preparation of a map of a particular construction site would constitute services and not export property, but standard maps prepared for sale to customers generally would not constitute services and would be export property if the requirements of this section were otherwise met.

(c) *Manufacture, production, growth, or extraction of property.*—(1) *By a person other than a DISC.*—Export property may be manufactured, produced, grown, or extracted in the United States by any person, provided that such person does not qualify (and is not treated) as a DISC. Property held by a DISC which was manufactured, produced, grown, or extracted by it at a time when it did not qualify (and was not treated) as a DISC is not export property of the DISC. Property which sustains further manufacture or production outside the United States prior to sale or lease by a person but after manufacture or production in the United States will not be considered as manufactured, produced, grown, or extracted in the United States by such person.

(2) *Manufactured or produced.*—(i) *In general.*—For purposes of this section, property which is sold or leased by a person is considered to be manufactured or produced by such person if such property is manufactured or produced (within the meaning of either subdivision (ii), (iii), or (iv) of this subparagraph) by such person or by another person pursuant to a contract with such person. Except as provided in subdivision (iv) of this subparagraph, manufacture or production of property does not include assembly

or packaging operations with respect to property.

(ii) *Substantial transformation.*—Property is manufactured or produced by a person if such property is substantially transformed by such person. Examples of substantial transformation of property would include the conversion of woodpulp to paper, steel rods to screws and bolts, and the canning of fish.

(iii) *Operations generally considered to constitute manufacturing.*—Property is manufactured or produced by a person if the operations performed by such person in connection with such property are substantial in nature and are generally considered to constitute the manufacture or production of property.

(iv) *Value added to property.*—Property is manufactured or produced by a person if with respect to such property conversion costs (direct labor and factory burden including packaging or assembly) of such person account for 20 percent or more of—

(a) The cost of goods sold or inventory amount of such person for such property if such property is sold or held for sale, or

(b) The adjusted basis of such person for such property, as determined in accordance with the provisions of section 1011, if such property is held for lease or leased.

The value of parts provided pursuant to a services contract, as described in § 1.993-1(d)(4)(v), is not taken into account in applying this subdivision.

(d) *Primary purpose for which property is held.*—(1) *In general.*—(i) *General rule.*—Under paragraph (a)(2) of this section, export property (a) must be held primarily for the purpose of sale or lease in the ordinary course of a trade or business to a DISC, or to any other person, and (b) such sale or lease must be for direct use, consumption, or disposition outside the United States. Thus, property cannot qualify as export property unless it is sold or leased for direct use, consumption, or disposition outside the United States. Property is sold or leased for direct use, consumption, or disposition outside the United States if such sale or lease satisfies the destination test described in subparagraph (2) of this paragraph, the proof of compliance requirements described in subparagraph (3) of this paragraph, and the use-outside-the-United-States test described in subparagraph (4) of this paragraph.

(ii) *Factors not taken into account.*—In determining whether property which is sold or leased to a DISC is sold or leased for direct use, consumption, or disposition outside the United States, the fact that the acquiring DISC holds the property in inventory or for lease prior to the time it sells or leases it for direct use, consumption, or disposition outside the United States will not affect the characterization of the property as export property. Export property need not be physically segregated from other property.

(2) *Destination test.*—(i) For purposes of subparagraph (1) of this paragraph, the destination test in this subparagraph is satisfied with respect to property sold or leased by a seller or lessor only if it is delivered by such seller or lessor (or an agent of such seller or lessor) regardless of the F.O.B. point or the place at which title passes or risk of loss shifts from the seller or lessor—

(a) Within the United States to a carrier or freight forwarder for ultimate delivery outside the United States to a purchaser or lessee (or to a subsequent purchaser or sublessee),

(b) Within the United States to a purchaser or lessee, if such property is ultimately delivered, directly used, or directly consumed outside the United States (including delivery to a carrier or freight forwarder for delivery outside the United States) by the purchaser or lessee (or a subsequent purchaser or sublessee) within 1 year after such sale or lease,

(c) Within or outside the United States to a purchaser or lessee which, at the time of the sale or lease, is a DISC and is not a member of the same controlled group (as defined in § 1.993-1(k)) as the seller or lessor,

(d) From the United States to the purchaser or lessee (or a subsequent purchaser or sublessee) at a point outside the United States by means of a ship, aircraft, or other delivery vehicle, owned, leased, or chartered by the seller or lessor,

(e) Outside the United States to a purchaser or lessee from a warehouse, a storage facility, or assembly site located outside the United States, if such property was previously shipped by such seller or lessor from the United States, or

(f) Outside the United States to a purchaser or lessee if such property was previously shipped by such seller or lessor from the United States and if such property is located outside the United States pursuant to a prior lease by the seller or lessor, and either

(1) Such prior lease terminated at the expiration of its term (or by the action of the prior lessee acting alone),

(2) The sale occurred or the term of the subsequent lease began after the time at which the term of the prior lease would have expired, or

(3) The lessee under the subsequent lease is not a related person (as defined in § 1.993-1(a)(6)) with respect to the lessor and the prior lease was terminated by the action of the lessor (acting alone or together with the lessee).

(ii) For purposes of this subparagraph (other than (c) and (f) (3) of subdivision (i) thereof), any relationship between the seller or lessor and any purchaser, subsequent purchaser, lessee, or sublessee is immaterial.

(iii) In no event is the destination test of this subparagraph satisfied with respect to property which is subject to any use (other than a resale or sublease), manufacture, assembly, or other processing (other than packaging) by any person between the time of the sale or lease by such seller or lessor and the delivery or ultimate delivery outside the United States described in this subparagraph.

(iv) If property is located outside the United States at the time it is purchased by a person or leased by a person as lessee, such property may be export property in the hands of such purchaser or lessee only if it is imported into the United States prior to its further sale or lease (including a sublease) outside the United States. Paragraphs (a)(3) and (e) of this section (relating to 50 percent foreign content test) are applicable in determining whether such property is export property. Thus, for example, if such property is not subjected to manufacturing or production (as defined in paragraph (c) of this section) within the United States after such importation, it does not qualify as export property.

(3) *Proof of compliance with destination test.*— (i) *Delivery outside the United States.*—For purposes of subparagraph (2) of this paragraph (other than subdivision (i)(c) thereof), a seller or lessor shall establish ultimate delivery, use, or consumption of property outside the United States by providing—

(a) A facsimile or carbon copy of the export bill of lading issued by the carrier who delivers the property,

(b) A certificate of an agent or representative of the carrier disclosing delivery of the property outside the United States,

(c) A facsimile or carbon copy of the certificate of lading for the property executed by a customs officer of the country to which the property is delivered,

(d) If such contract has no customs administration, a written statement by the person to whom delivery outside the United States was made,

(e) A facsimile or carbon copy of the shipper's export declaration, a monthly shipper's summary declaration filed with the Bureau of Customs, or a magnetic tape filed in lieu of the Shipper's Export Declaration, covering the property, or

(f) Any other proof (including evidence as to the nature of the property or the nature of the transaction) which establishes to the satisfaction of the Commissioner that the property was ultimately delivered, or directly sold, or directly consumed outside the United States within 1 year after the sale or lease.

(ii) The requirements of subdivision (i) (a), (b), (c), or (e) of this subparagraph will be considered satisfied even though the name of the ultimate consignee and the price paid for the goods is marked out provided that, in the case of a Shipper's Export Declaration or other document listed in such subdivision (e) or a document such as an export bill of lading such document still indicates the country in which delivery to the ultimate consignee is to be made and, in the case of a certificate of an agent or representative of the carrier, that such document indicates that the property was delivered outside the United States.

(iii) A seller or lessor shall also establish the meeting of the requirement of subparagraph (2)(i) of this paragraph (other than subdivision (c) thereof), that the property was delivered outside the United States without further use, manufacture, assembly, or other processing within the United States.

(iv) *Sale or lease to an unrelated DISC.*—For purposes of subparagraph (2)(i)(c) of this paragraph, a purchaser or lessee of property is deemed to qualify as a DISC for its taxable year if the seller or lessor obtains from such purchaser or lessee a copy of such purchaser's or lessee's election to be treated as a DISC as described in § 1.992-2(a) together with such purchaser's or lessee's sworn statement that such election has been filed with the Internal Revenue Service Center. The copy of the election and the sworn statement of such purchaser or lessee must be received by the seller or lessor within 6 months after the sale or lease. A purchaser or lessee is not treated as a DISC with respect to a sale or lease during a taxable year for which such purchaser or lessee does not qualify as a DISC if the seller or lessor does not believe or if a reasonable person would not believe at the time such sale or lease is made that the purchaser or lessee will qualify as a DISC for such taxable year.

(v) *Failure of proof.*—If a seller or lessor fails to provide proof of compliance with the destination test as required by this subparagraph, the property sold or leased is not export property.

(4) *Sales and leases of property for ultimate use in the United States.*—(i) *In general.*—For purposes of subparagraph (1) of this paragraph, the use test in this subparagraph is satisfied with respect to property which—

(a) Under subdivisions (ii) through (iv) of this subparagraph is not sold for ultimate use in the United States or

(b) Under subdivision (v) of this subparagraph is leased for ultimate use outside the United States.

(ii) *Sales of property for ultimate use in the United States.*—For purposes of subdivision (i) of this subparagraph, a purchaser of property (including components, as defined in subdivision (vii) of this subparagraph) is deemed to use such property ultimately in the United States if any of the following conditions exists:

(a) Such purchaser is a related person (as defined in § 1.993-1(a)(6)) with respect to the seller and such purchaser ultimately uses such property, or a second product into which such property is incorporated as a component, in the United States.

(b) At the time of the sale, there is an agreement or understanding that such property, or a second product into which such property is incorporated as a component, will be ultimately used by the purchaser in the United States.

(c) At the time of the sale, a reasonable person would have believed that such property or such second product would be ultimately used by such purchaser in the United States unless, in the case of a sale of components, the fair market value of such components at the time of delivery to the purchaser constitutes less than 20 percent of the fair market value of the second product into which such components are incorporated (determined at the time of completion of the production, manufacture, or assembly of such second product).

For purposes of (b) of this subdivision, there is an agreement or understanding that property will ultimately be used in the United States if, for example, a component is sold abroad under an express agreement with the foreign purchaser that the component is to be incorporated into a product to be sold back to the United States. As a further example, there would also be such an agreement or understanding if the foreign purchaser indicated at the time of the sale or previously that the component is to be incorporated into a product which is designed principally for the United States market. However, such an agreement or understanding does not result from the mere fact that a second product, into which components exported from the United States have been incorporated and which is sold on the world market, is sold in substantial quantities in the United States.

(iii) *Use in the United States.*—For purposes of subdivision (ii) of this subparagraph, property (including components incorporated into a second product) is or would be ultimately used in the United States by such purchaser if, at any time within 3 years after the purchase of such property or components, either such property or components (or the second product into which such components are incorporated) is resold by such purchaser for use by a subsequent purchaser within the United States or such purchaser or subsequent purchaser fails, for any period of 365 consecutive days, to use such property or second product predominantly outside the United States as defined in subdivision (vi) of this subparagraph).

(iv) *Sales to retailers.*—For purposes of subdivision (ii)(c) of this subparagraph property sold to any person whose principal business consists of selling from inventory to retail customers at retail outlets outside the United States will be considered as property for ultimate use outside the United States.

(v) *Leases of property for ultimate use outside the United States.*—For purposes of subdivision (i) of this subparagraph, a lessee of property is deemed to use such property ultimately outside the United States during a taxable year of the lessor if such property is used predominantly outside the United States (as defined in subdivision (vi) of this subparagraph) by the lessee during the portion of the lessor's taxable year which is included within the term of the lease. A determination as to whether the ultimate use of leased property satisifes the requirements of this subdivision is made for each taxable year of the lessor. Thus, leased property may be used predominantly outside the United States for a taxable year of the lessor (and thus, constitute export property if the remaining requirements of this section are met) even if the property is not used predominantly outside the United States in earlier taxable years or later taxable years of the lessor.

(vi) *Predominant use outside the United States.*—For purposes of this subparagraph, property is used predominantly outside the United States for any period if, during such period, such property is located outside the United States more than 50 percent of the time. An aircraft, railroad rolling stock, vessel, motor vehicle, container, or other property used for transportation purposes is deemed to be used predominantly outside the United States for any period if, during such period, either such property is located outside the United States more than 50 percent of the time or more than 50 percent of the miles traversed in the use of such property are traversed outside the United States. However, any such property is deemed to be within the United States at all times during which it is engaged in transport between any two points within the United States except where such transport constitutes uninterrupted international air transportation within the meaning of section 4262(c)(3) and the regulations thereunder (relating to tax on air transportation of persons). For purposes of applying section 4262(c)(3) to this subdivision, the term "United States" has the same meaning as in § 1.993-7.

(vii) *Component.*—For purposes of this subparagraph, a component is property which is (or is reasonably expected to be) incorporated into a second product by the purchaser of such component by means of production, manufacture, or assembly.

(e) *Foreign content of property.*—(1) *The 50 percent test.*—Under paragraph (a)(3) of this section, no more than 50 percent of the fair market value of export property may be attributable to the fair market value of articles which were imported into the United States. For purposes of this paragraph, articles imported into the United States are referred to as "foreign content." The fair market value of the foreign content of export property is computed in accordance with subparagraph (4) of this paragraph. The fair market value of export property which is sold to a person who is not a related person with respect to the seller is the sale price for such property (not including interest, finance or carrying charges, or similar charges).

(2) *Application of 50 percent test.*—The 50 percent test described in subparagraph (1) of this paragraph is applied on an item-by-item basis. If, however, a person sells or leases a substantial volume of substantially identical export property in a taxable year and if all of such property contains substantially identical foreign content in substantially the same proportion, such person may determine the portion of foreign content contained in such property on an aggregate basis.

(3) *Parts and services.*—If, at the time property is sold or leased the seller or lessor agrees to furnish parts pursuant to a services contract (as provided in § 1.993-1(d)(4)(v)) and the price for the parts is not separately stated, the 50 percent test described in subparagraph (1) of this paragraph is applied on an aggregate basis to the property and parts. If the price for the parts is separately stated, the 50 percent test described in subparagraph (1) of this paragraph is applied separately to the property and to the parts.

(4) *Computation of foreign content.*— (i) *Valuation.*—For purposes of applying the 50 percent test described in subparagraph (1) of this paragraph, it is necessary to determine the fair market value of all articles which constitute foreign content of the property being tested to determine if it is export property. The fair market value of such imported articles is determined as of the time such articles are imported into the United States. With respect to articles imported into the United States before July 1, 1980, the fair market value of such articles is their appraised value as determined under section 402 or 402a of the Tariff Act of 1930 (19 U.S.C. 1401a or 1402) in connection with their importation. With respect to articles imported into the United States on or after July 1, 1980, the fair market value of such articles in their appraised value as determined under section 402 of the Tariff Act of 1930 (19 U.S.C. 1401a) in connection with their importation. The appraised value of such articles is the full dutiable value of such articles, determined, however, without regard to any special provision in the United States tariff laws which would result in a lower dutiable value. Thus, an article which is imported into the United States is treated as entirely imported even if all or a portion of such article was originally manufactured, produced, grown, or extracted in the United States.

(ii) *Evidence of fair market value.*—For purposes of subdivision (i) of this subparagraph, the fair market value of imported articles constituting foreign content may be evidenced by the customs invoice issued on the importation of such articles into the United States. If the holder of such articles is not the importer (or a related person with respect to the importer), the fair market value of such articles may be evidenced by a certificate based upon information contained in the customs invoice and furnished to the holder by the person from whom such articles (or property incorporating such articles) were purchased. If a customs invoice or certificate described in the preceding sentence is not available to a person purchasing property, such person shall establish that no more than 50 percent of the fair market value of such property is attributable to the fair market value of articles which were imported into the United States.

(iii) *Interchangeable component articles.*— (*a*) Where identical or similar component articles can be incorporated interchangeably into property and a person acquires some such component articles that are imported into the United States and other such component articles that are not imported into the United States, the determination whether imported component articles were incorporated in such property as is exported from the United States shall be made on a substitution basis as in the case of the rules relating to drawback accounts under the customs laws. See section 313(b) of the Tariff Act of 1930, as amended (19 U.S.C. 1313(b)).

(*b*) The provisions of (*a*) of this subdivision may be illustrated by the following example:

Example. Assume that a manufacturer produces a total of 20,000 electronic devices. The manufacturer exports 5,000 of the devices and subsequently sells 11,000 of the devices to a DISC which exports the 11,000 devices. The major single component article in each device is a tube which represents 60 percent of the fair market value of the device at the time the device is sold by the manufacturer. The manufacturer imports 8,000 of the tubes and produces the remaining 12,000 tubes. For purposes of this subdivision, in accordance with the substitution principle used in the customs drawback laws, the 5,000 devices exported by the manufacturer are each treated as containing an imported tube because the devices were exported prior to the sale to the DISC. The remaining 3,000 imported tubes are treated as being contained in the first 3,000 devices purchased and exported by the DISC. Thus, since the 50 percent test is not met with respect to the first 3,000 devices purchased and exported by the DISC, those devices are not export property. The remaining 8,000 devices purchased and exported by the DISC are treated as containing tubes produced in the United States, and those devices are export property (if they otherwise meet the requirements of this section).

(f) *Excluded property.*—(1) *In general.*—Notwithstanding any other provision of this section, the following property is not export property—

(i) Property described in subparagraph (2) of this paragraph (relating to property leased to a member of a controlled group),

(ii) Property described in subparagraph (3) of this paragraph (relating to certain types of intangible property),

(iii) Products described in paragraph (g) of this section (relating to depletable products), and

(iv) Products described in paragraph (h) of this section (relating to certain export controlled products).

(2) *Property leased to member of controlled group.*—(i) *In general.*—Property leased to a person (whether or not a DISC) which is a member of the same controlled group (as defined in § 1.993-1(k)) as the lessor constitutes export property for any period of time only if during the period—

(a) Such property is held for sublease, or is subleased, by such person to a third person for the ultimate use of such third person;

(b) Such third person is not a member of the same controlled group; and

(c) Such property is used predominantly outside the United States by such third person.

(ii) *Predominant use.*—The provisions of paragraph (d)(4)(vi) of this section apply in determining under subdivision (i)(c) of this subparagraph whether such property is used predominantly outside the United States by such third person.

(iii) *Leasing rule.*—For purposes of this subparagraph, leased property is deemed to be ultimately used by a member of the same controlled group as the lessor if such property is leased to a person which is not a member of such controlled group but which subleases such property to a person which is a member of such controlled group. Thus, for example, if X, a DISC for the taxable year, leases a movie film to Y, a foreign corporation which is not a member of the same controlled group as X, and Y then subleases the film to persons which are members of such group for showing to the general public, the film is not export property. On the other hand, if X, a DISC for the taxable year, leases a movie film to Z, a foreign corporation which is a member of the same controlled group as X, and Z then subleases the film to Y, another foreign corporation, which is not a member of the same controlled group for showing to the general public, the film is not disqualified under this subparagraph from being export property.

(iv) *Certain copyrights.*—With respect to a copyright which is not excluded by subparagraph (3) of this paragraph from being export property, the ultimate use of such property is the sale or exhibition of such property to the general public. Thus, if A, a DISC for the taxable year, leases recording tapes to B, a foreign corporation which is a member of the same controlled group as A, and if B makes records from the recording tape and sells the records to C, another foreign corporation, which is not a member of the same controlled group, for sale by C to the general public, the recording tape is not disqualified under this subparagraph from being export property, notwithstanding the leasing of the recording tape by A to a member of the same controlled group, since the ultimate use of the tape is the sale of the records (*i.e.*, property produced from the recording tape).

(3) *Intangible property.*—Export property does not include any patent, invention, model, design, formula, or process, whether or not patented, or any copyright (other than films, tapes, records, or similar reproductions, for commercial or home use), goodwill, trademark, tradebrand, franchise, or other like property. Although a copyright such as a copyright on a book does not constitute export property, a copyrighted article (such as a book) if not accompanied by a right to reproduce it is export property if the requirements of this section are otherwise satisfied. However, a license of a master recording tape for reproduction outside the United States is not disqualified under this subparagraph from being export property.

(g) *Depletable products.*—(1) *In general.*—Under section 993(c)(2)(C), a product or commodity which is a depletable product (as defined in subparagraph (2) of this paragraph) or contains a depletable product is not export property if—

(i) It is a primary product from oil, gas, coal, or uranium (as described in subparagraph (3) of this paragraph), or

(ii) It does not qualify as a 50-percent manufactured or processed product (as described in subparagraph (4) of this paragraph).

(2) *Definition of "depletable product".*—For purposes of this paragraph, the term "depletable product" means any product or commodity of a character with respect to which a deduction for depletion is allowable under section 613 or 613A. Thus, the term depletable product includes any mineral extracted from a mine, an oil or gas well, or any other natural deposit, whether or not the DISC or related supplier is allowed a deduction, or is eligible to take a deduction, for depletion with respect to the mineral in computing its taxable income. Thus, for example, iron ore purchased by a DISC from a broker is a depletable product in the hands of the DISC for purposes of this paragraph even though the DISC is not eligi-

ble to take a deduction for depletion under section 613 or 613A.

(3) *Primary product from oil, gas, coal, or uranium.*—A primary product from oil, gas, coal, or uranium is not export property. For purposes of this paragraph—

(i) *Primary product from oil.*—The term "primary product from oil" means crude oil and all products derived from the destructive distillation of crude oil, including—

(A) Volatile products,

(B) Light oils such as motor fuel and kerosene,

(C) Distillates such as naphtha,

(D) Lubricating oils,

(E) Greases and waves, and

(F) Residues such as fuel oil.

For purposes of this paragraph, a product or commodity derived from shale oil which would be a primary product from oil if derived from crude oil is considered a primary product from oil.

(ii) *Primary product from gas.*—The term "primary product from gas" means all gas and associated hydrocarbon components from gas wells or oil wells, whether recovered at the lease or upon further processing, including—

(A) Natural gas,

(B) Condensates,

(C) Liquefied petroleum gases such as ethane, propane, and butane, and

(D) Liquid products such as natural gasoline.

(iii) *Primary product from coal.*—The term "primary product from coal" means coal and all products recovered from the carbonization of coal including—

(a) Coke,

(b) Coke-oven gas,

(c) Gas liquor,

(d) Crude light oil, and

(e) Coal tar.

(iv) *Primary product from uranium.*—The term "primary product from uranium" means uranium ore and uranium concentrates (known in the industry as "yellow cake"), and nuclear materials derived from the refining of uranium ore and uranium concentrates, or produced in a nuclear reaction, including—

(A) Uranium hexafluoride,

(B) Enriched uranium hexafluoride,

(C) Uranium metal,

(D) Uranium compounds, such as uranium carbide,

(E) Uranium dioxide, and

(F) Plutonium fuels.

(v) *Primary products and changing technology.*—The primary products from oil, gas, coal,

or uranium described in paragraphs (g)(3)(i) through (iv) of this section and the processes described in those subdivisions are not intended to represent either the only primary products from oil, gas, coal, or uranium, or the only processes from which primary products may be derived under existing and future technologies, such as the gasification and liquefaction of coal.

(vi) *Petrochemicals.*—For purposes of this paragraph, petrochemicals are not considered primary products from oil, gas, or coal.

(4) *50-percent manufactured or processed product.*—(i) *In general.*—A product or commodity (other than a primary product from oil, gas, coal, or uranium) which is or contains a depletable product is not excluded from the term "export property" by reason of section 993(c)(2)(C) if it is a 50-percent manufactured or processed product. Such a product or commodity is a "50-percent manufactured or processed product" if, after the cutoff point of the depletable product, it is manufactured or processed (as defined in paragraph (g)(4)(ii) of this section) and either the cost test described in paragraph (g)(4)(iv) of this section or the fair market value test described in paragraph (g)(4)(v) of this section is satisfied. To determine cutoff point, see paragraphs (g)(4)(vi) and (vii) of this section.

(ii) *Manufactured or processed.*—A product is manufactured or processed if it is manufactured or produced within the meaning of paragraph (c)(2) of this section, except that for purposes of this subparagraph the term manufacturing or processing does not include any excluded process (as defined in paragraph (g)(4)(iii) of this section) and the term conversion costs (as used in subparagraph (iv) of such paragraph (c)(2)) does not include any costs attributable to any excluded process.

(iii) *Excluded processes.*—For purposes of this paragraph, excluded processes are extracting (*i.e.,* all processes which are applied before the cutoff point of the mineral to which such processes are applied), and handling, packing, packaging, grading, storing, and transporting.

(iv) *Cost test.*—A product or commodity will qualify as a 50-percent manufactured or processed product if—

(A) Its manufacturing and processing costs (that is, the portion of the cost of goods sold or inventory amount of the product or commodity attributable to the aggregate cost of manufacturing or processing each mineral contained therein) equal or exceed

(B) An amount equal to either of the following:

(1) 50 percent of its cost of goods sold or inventory amount (decreased, at the DISC's option, by the portion of such cost or amount the DISC establishes is allocable to the difference between each prior owner's selling

Reg. §1.993-3(g)(4)(iv)(B)(1)

price for each depletable product contained in such product or commodity and such prior owner's cost of goods sold with respect thereto).

(2) The aggregate of the cost at the cutoff point (see paragraphs (9)(4)(vi) and (vii) of this section) properly attributable to each mineral contained in such product or commodity. However, if this subparagraph (2) is applied, then the amount in (A) of this subparagraph (iv) shall be decreased and the amount in this subparagraph (2) shall be increased, by so much of the cost of goods sold or inventory amount of the product or commodity as is properly allocable to any process other than transportation applied after the cutoff point of such mineral which would be a mining process (within the meaning of §1.613-4) were it applied before such point.

(v) *Fair market value test.*—A product or commodity will qualify as a 50-percent manufactured or processed product if—

(A) The excess of its fair market value on the date it is sold, exchanged, or otherwise disposed of (or, if not sold, exchanged, or otherwise disposed of, the last day of the DISC's taxable year) over the portion thereof properly allocable to excluded processes other than extracting is equal to or greater than

(B) Twice the aggregate of the fair market value at the cutoff point for each mineral contained in such product or commodity.

For purposes of this subparagraph (v), the fair market value of a product or commodity on the date it is sold, exchanged, or otherwise disposed of is the price at which it is disposed of, subject to any adjustment that may be required under the arm's length standard of section 482 and the regulations thereunder. If such product or commodity is not sold, exchanged, or otherwise disposed of, then, for purposes of section 992(a)(1)(B) (relating to the 95-percent test with respect to qualified export assets), the fair market value of a product or commodity on the last day of the DISC's taxable year is the arm's length price at which such product or commodity would have been sold on such date, determined by applying the principles of section 482 and the regulations thereunder.

(vi) *Cutoff point of a mineral.*—For purposes of this subparagraph—

(A) The cutoff point is the point at which gross income from the property (within the meaning of section 613(a)) was in fact determined.

(B) The cost at the cutoff point is deemed to be the amount of the gross income from the property of the taxpayer eligible for a depletion deduction with respect to the mineral.

(C) The fair market value at the cutoff point is deemed to be the amount of the gross income from the property of the taxpayer eligible for a depletion deduction with respect to the mineral, except that, if (1) the fair market value

of a product or commodity on the date specified in paragraph (g)(4)(v)(A) of this section exceeds the aggregate of the fair market value at the cutoff point for each mineral contained therein and (2) 10 percent or more of such excess is attributable to a net increase in the fair market values of such minerals by reason of factors other than manufacturing or processing or the application of excluded processes (such as, for example, increases in the fair market values of some minerals by reason of inflation or speculation exceed decreases in such values of other minerals by reason of deflation or speculation), then the aggregate of the fair market value at the cutoff point for each such mineral shall be increased to reflect the net excess so attributable.

(D) The provisions of this subparagraph (vi) are illustrated by the following example.

Example. An integrated manufacturer, X, on February 1, 1976, had gross income from the property (within the meaning of section 613(a)) of $50 with respect to a specified volume of a mineral. Thus, the cost at the cutoff point of the mineral was $50. X converted the mineral into a product which it sold on July 15, 1976, for $75. Of the $25 excess of the selling price over the gross income from the property, $23 was attributable to manufacturing, processing, and the application of excluded processes, and $2 was attributable to an increase in the fair market value of the mineral due to inflation between February 1 and July 15, 1976. Since only 8 percent of such excess ($2/$25) was attributable to factors other than manufacturing, processing, and the application of excluded processes, the fair market value at the cutoff point of the mineral is $50. However, had $3 of the $25 excess, or 12 percent, been attributable to an increase in fair market value of the mineral due to inflation, then the fair market value at the cutoff point of the mineral would be $53.

(vii) *Cutoff point of timber.*—[Reserved.]

(viii) *Special rule for certain used products, and scrap products.*—If a product or commodity is a used 50-percent manufactured or processed product, or is recovered as scrap from a 50-percent manufactured or processed product, such product or commodity will be treated as a 50-percent manufactured or processed product.

(ix) *Special rule for byproducts and waste products.*—For purposes of applying the cost test or fair market value test of paragraphs (g)(4)(iv) or (v) of this section if a depletable product is recovered from a manufacturing process as a byproduct or waste product, then the cost and fair market value at the cutoff point are each deemed to be the lesser of—

(A) The fair market value of the waste product or byproduct containing the depletable product, determined as of the date the byproduct or waste product is recovered, or

(B) The amount the cost at the cutoff point would be for a depletable product of like kind and grade which is extracted, determined as of the date the byproduct or waste product is recovered.

For purposes of (B) of this subparagraph, the cutoff point for the depletable product of like kind and grade is deemed to be the point at which gross income from the property would be determined if such depletable product were sold by the taxpayer eligible to take a deduction for depletion after the completion of all mining processes applied to the depletable product and before the application of any nonmining process.

(x) *Proof of satisfaction of 50-percent manufactured or processed test.*—(A) No substantiation is required to establish that either the cost test or the fair market value test of paragraphs (g)(4)(iv) or (v) of this section is satisfied or that a product or commodity qualifies under paragraph (g)(4)(viii) of this section as either a used 50-percent manufactured or processed product or as scrap from a 50-percent manufactured or processed product as long as it is reasonably obvious, on the basis of all relevant facts and circumstances, that either the cost test or fair market value test is satisfied, or that the product or commodity qualifies either as used 50-percent manufactured or processed product or as scrap from a 50-percent manufactured or processed product. Thus, for example, in the case of a DISC exporting a high precision lens at least 50 percent of the fair market value of which is obviously attributable to grinding, no substantiation of gross income from the property properly allocable to the depletable products contained in the lens, costs, or fair market values will be required.

(B) In cases in which satisfaction of either the cost test or the fair market value test is not reasonably obvious, a DISC will be required to substantiate the gross income from the property properly allocable to each depletable product in a product or commodity and either all costs or fair market values relied upon the DISC.

(C) For purposes of substantiating (1) gross income from the property properly allocable to a depletable product, (2) costs, and (3) fair market values, the DISC and related supplier shall each identify items in (or that were in) inventory in the same manner each used to identify items in inventory for purposes of computing Federal income tax.

(xi) *Application of 50-percent test.*—The 50-percent test described in this subparagraph is applied on an item-by-item basis. If, however, a DISC sells a substantial volume of substantially identical products or commodities and if all or a group of such products or commodities contain substantially identical depletable products in substantially the same proportions and have cost or fair market value relationships (as the case may be) that are in substantially the same proportions, such DISC may apply the 50-percent

test on an aggregate basis with respect to all such products or commodities, or group, as the case may be.

(5) *Effective dates.* Except as provided in subparagraph (6) of this paragraph, section 993(c)(2)(C) applies—

(i) With respect to any product or commodity not owned by a DISC, to sales, exchanges, or other dispositions made after March 18, 1975, with respect to which the DISC derives gross receipts.

(ii) With respect to any product or commodity acquired by a DISC after March 18, 1975.

(iii) With respect to any product or commodity owned by a DISC on March 18, 1975, to sales, exchanges, or other dispositions made after March 18, 1976, and to owning such product or commodity after such date.

For purposes of this subparagraph and subparagraph (6) of this paragraph, the date of a sale, exchange, or other disposition of a product or commodity is the date as of which title to such product or commodity passes. The accounting method of a person is not determinative of the date of a sale, exchange, or other disposition.

(6) *Fixed contracts.*—Section 1101(f) of the Tax Reform Act of 1976 provides an exception to the effective date rules in this paragraph and in paragraph (h) of this section. Section 1101(f)(2) of the Act provides that section 993(c)(2)(C) and (D) shall not apply to sales, exchanges, and other dispositions made after March 18, 1975, but before March 19, 1980, if they are made pursuant to a fixed contract. Section 1101(f)(2) also defines fixed contract. Under that definition, if the seller can vary the price of the product for unspecified cost increases (which could include tax cost increases), or if the quantity of products or commodities to be sold can be increased or decreased under the contract by the seller without penalty, the contract is not to be considered a fixed contract with respect to the amount over which the seller has discretion. For example, if a contract calls for a minimum delivery of *x* amount of a product but allows the seller to refuse to deliver goods beyond that minimum amount (or allows a renegotiation of the sales price of goods beyond that amount), then with respect to the amount above the minimum the contract is not a fixed quantity contract.

(h) *Export controlled products.*—(1) *In general.*—An export controlled product is not export property. A product or commodity may be an export controlled product at one time but not an export controlled product at another time. For purposes of this paragraph, a product or commodity is an "export controlled product" at a particular time if at that time the export of such product or commodity is prohibited or curtailed under section 4(b) of the Export Administration Act of 1969 or section 7(a) of the Export Administration Act of 1979, to effectuate the policy relating to the protection of the domestic econ-

Reg. §1.993-3(h)(1)

omy set forth in such Acts (paragraph (2)(A) of section 3 of the Export Administration Act of 1969 and paragraph (2)(C) of section 3 of the Export Administration Act of 1979). Such policy is to use export controls to the extent necessary "to protect the domestic economy from the excessive drain of scarce materials and to reduce the serious inflationary impact of foreign demand."

(2) *Products considered export controlled products.*—(i) *In general.*—For purposes of this paragraph, an export controlled product is a product or commodity which is subject to short supply export controls under 15 CFR Part 377. A product or commodity is considered an export controlled product for the duration of each control period which applies to such product or commodity. A control period of a product or commodity begins on and includes the initial control date (as defined in paragraph (o)(2)(ii) of this section) and ends on and includes the final control date (as defined in paragraph (n)(2)(iii) of this section).

(ii) *Initial control date.*—The initial control date of a product or commodity which was subject to short supply export controls on March 19, 1975, is March 19, 1975. The initial control date of a product or commodity which is subject to short supply export controls after March 19, 1975, is the effective date stated in the regulations to 15 CFR Part 377 which subjects such product or commodity to short supply export controls. If there is no effective date stated in such regulations, the initial control date of such product or commodity is the date on which such regulations are filed for publication in the FEDERAL REGISTER.

(iii) *Final control date.*—The final control date of a product or commodity is the effective date stated in the regulations to 15 CFR Part 377 which removes such product or commodity from short supply export controls. If there is no effective date stated in such regulations, then the final control date of such product or commodity is the date on which such regulations are filed for publication in the FEDERAL REGISTER.

(iv) *Expiration of Export Administration Act.*—An initial control date and a final control date cannot occur after the expiration date of the export administration act under the authority of which the short supply export controls were issued.

(3) *Effective dates.*—(i) *Products controlled on March 19, 1975.*—Except as provided in paragraph (g)(6) of this section, if a product or commodity was subject to short supply export controls on March 19, 1975, this paragraph applies—

(A) With respect to any such product or commodity not owned by a DISC, to sales, exchanges, other dispositions, or leases made after March 18, 1975, with respect to which the DISC derives gross receipts.

(B) With respect to any such product or commodity acquired by a DISC after March 18, 1975, and

(C) With respect to any such product or commodity owned by a DISC on March 18, 1975, to sales, exchanges, other dispositions, and leases made after March 18, 1976, and to owning such product or commodity after such date.

(ii) *Products first controlled after March 19, 1975.*—If a product or commodity becomes subject to short supply export controls after March 19, 1975, this paragraph applies to sales, exchanges, other dispositions, or leases of such product or commodity made on or after the initial control date of such product or commodity, and to owning such product or commodity on or after such date.

(iii) *Date of sale, exchange, lease, or other disposition.*—For purposes of this subparagraph, the date of sale, exchange, or other disposition of a product or commodity is the date as of which title to such product or commodity passes. The date of a lease is the date as of which the lessee takes possession of a product or commodity. The accounting method of a person is not determinative of the date of sale, exchange, other disposition, or lease.

(i) *Property in short supply.*—Except as provided in paragraph (g)(6) of this section, if the President determines that the supply of any property which is otherwise export property as defined in this section is insufficient to meet the requirements of the domestic economy, he may by Executive order designate such property as in short supply. Any property so designated will be treated as property which is not export property during the period beginning with the date specified in such Executive order and ending with the date specified in an Executive order setting forth the President's determination that such property is no longer in short supply. [Reg. §1.993-3.]

☐ [*T.D.* 7514, 10-14-77. *Amended by T.D.* 7513, 10-14-77 *and T.D.* 7854, 11-15-82.]

[Reg. §1.993-4]

§1.993-4. Definition of producer's loans.—(a) *General rule.*—(1) *Definition.*—Under section 993(d), a loan made by a DISC to a person, referred to in this section as the "borrower," is a producer's loan if—

(i) The loan is made out of accumulated DISC income within the meaning of subparagraph (3) of this paragraph,

(ii) The loan is evidenced by an obligation described in subparagraph (4) of this paragraph,

(iii) The requirement as to the trade or business of the borrower described in subparagraph (5) of this paragraph is satisfied.

(iv) At the time the loan is made, the obligation referred to in subdivision (ii) of this subparagraph bears a legend stating "This Obligation Is Designated A Producer's Loan Within The Meaning of Section 993(d) of the Internal Revenue Code" or words of substantially the same meaning,

(v) The limitation as to the export-related assets of the borrower described in paragraph (b) of this section is satisfied,

(vi) The requirement as to the increased investment of the borrower in export-related assets described in paragraph (c) of this section is satisfied, and

(vii) The requirement of paragraph (d) of this section as to proof of compliance with paragraphs (b) and (c) of this section is satisfied.

(2) *Application of this section.*—(i) *In general.*—A loan which is a producer's loan is a qualified export asset of the DISC (see § 1.993-2(a)(5) and (f)). The interest on a producer's loan is a qualified export receipt of the DISC (see § 1.993-1(g)). A producer's loan is not a dividend to a borrower which is also a shareholder of the DISC making the loan. For rules with respect to deemed distributions by reason of the amount of foreign investment attributable to producer's loans, see section 995(b)(1)(G) and (d) and the regulations thereunder.

(ii) *No tracing of loan proceeds.*—For purposes of applying this section, in order to qualify as a producer's loan, the proceeds of the loan need not be traced to an investment in any specific asset.

(iii) *Unrelated borrower.*—For purposes of applying this section, it is not necessary for a borrower to be a related person with respect to the DISC from which it receives a producer's loan or a member of the same controlled group as the DISC.

(iv) *Unpaid balance of producer's loans.*— For purposes of applying this section, the unpaid balance of producer's loans does not include the unpaid balance of any producer's loan to the extent the loan has been deducted or charged off by the DISC as totally or partially worthless under section 165 or 166.

(v) *Refinancing, renewal, and extension.*— For purposes of applying this section, the refinancing, renewal, or extension of a producer's loan shall be treated as the making of a new loan which may qualify as a producer's loan only if the requirements of subparagraph (1) of this paragraph are met.

(vi) *Events subsequent to time loan is made.*—The determination as to whether a loan qualifies as a producer's loan is made on the basis of the relevant facts taken into account for purposes of determining whether the loan was a producer's loan when made. Thus, for example,

if the accumulated DISC income of the lender is later reduced below the unpaid balance of all producer's loans previously made by the DISC, such subsequent decrease in the amount of accumulated DISC income will not result in later disqualification of such loan (or part thereof) as a producer's loan. Similarly, if a loan (or part of a loan) does not qualify as a producer's loan because of an insufficient amount of accumulated DISC income at the time the loan is made, a subsequent increase in the amount of accumulated DISC income will not result in later qualification of such loan (or part thereof) as a producer's loan. As a further example, for purposes of applying the borrower's export related assets limitation described in paragraph (b) of this section, a loan which qualifies as a producer's loan when made will not later be disqualified if property, the gross receipts from the sale or lease of which were includible in the numerator of the fraction described in paragraph (b)(3)(i) of this section at the time of sale or lease by the borrower, is later characterized as excluded property (as defined in § 1.993-3(f)).

(vii) *Application of tests under paragraphs (b) and (c) on controlled group bases.*—If the borrower is a member of a controlled group (as defined in § 1.993-1(k)) at the time a loan is made, all amounts that must be determined for purposes of applying the limitation and increased investment requirement with respect to the export-related assets of the borrower (described in paragraphs (b) and (c), respectively, of this section) may be determined at the election of the borrower by aggregating such amounts for all members of the controlled group, determined for the taxable year of each member of the controlled group during which the loan is made, excluding only such members of the group as are DISC's or foreign corporations for such year. However, such amounts may be included only to the extent that such amounts have not already been taken into account in applying the limitation and increased investment requirement with respect to any other borrower. The borrower may make such election by causing its written statement of election to be attached to the lending DISC's return under section 6011(e)(2) for the first taxable year of the lending DISC within which or with which the borrower's taxable year for which the election is to apply ends. An election once made is binding on all members of the controlled group which includes the borrower with respect to all taxable years of the borrower beginning with its first taxable year for which the election is made. A borrower who makes such election may revoke it only if it secures the consent of the Commissioner to such revocation upon application made through the lending DISC.

(3) *Loan out of accumulated DISC income.*— (i) *In general.*—A loan is a producer's loan only to the extent that it is made out of accumulated

DISC income. A loan is made out of accumulated DISC income only if the amount of the loan, when added to the unpaid balance at the time such loan is made of all other producer's loans made by a DISC, does not exceed the amount of accumulated DISC income of the DISC at the beginning of the month in which the loan is made. The amount of accumulated DISC income at the beginning of any month is determined as if the DISC's taxable year closed at the end of the immediately preceding month.

(ii) *Presumption.*—A loan made during a taxable year shall be deemed under subdivision (i) of this subparagraph to have been made out of accumulated DISC income if the balance of producer's loans at the beginning of the year and those made during the year do not exceed accumulated DISC income at the end of the year.

(iii) *Deemed distributions.*—For purposes of this subparagraph, accumulated DISC income as of the end of any taxable year (or month) shall be determined without regard to deemed distributions under section 995(b)(1)(G) for the amount of foreign investment attributable to producer's loans for such year (or for the taxable year for which such month is a part) but actual distributions shall be taken into account.

(4) *Evidence and terms of obligation.*—A loan is a producer's loan only if the loan is evidenced by a note or other evidence of indebtedness which is made by the borrower and which has a stated maturity date not more than 5 years from the date the loan is made. Accordingly, a loan which does not have a stated maturity date or which has a stated maturity date more than 5 years from the date such loan is made can never meet the 5-year requirement of this subparagraph. Thus, for example, even if there is a period of less than 5 years remaining to the stated maturity date of a loan, the loan can never be a producer's loan if it had a stated maturity date more than 5 years from the date it was made. For a further example, if a loan having a period remaining to maturity of 2 years is extended for a further period of 3 years (making a total of 5 years to maturity from the date of the extension), the extension of the loan would under subparagraph (2)(v) of this paragraph constitute the making of a new producer's loan and the original producer's loan would terminate. If, however, a loan having a period remaining to maturity of 2 years is extended for a further period of 4 years (making a total of 6 years to maturity from the date of the extension), the original producer's loan will terminate and the new loan will not be a producer's loan. If a producer's loan is not paid in full at its maturity date and is not formally refinanced, renewed, or extended, such loan shall be deemed to be a new loan which does not have a stated maturity date and, thus, will not be a producer's loan. For purposes of this subparagraph, an evidence of

indebtedness is a written instrument of indebtedness. Section 482 and the regulations thereunder are applicable to determine in the case of a loan by the DISC to a borrower which is owned or controlled directly or indirectly by the same interests as the DISC within the meaning of section 482, whether the interest charged on such loan is at an arm's length rate.

(5) *Borrower's trade or business.*—A loan is a producer's loan only if the loan is made to a person engaged in the United States in the manufacture, production, growth, or extraction (within the meaning of § 1.993-3(c)) of export property determined without regard to § 1.993-3(f)(1)(iii) and (iv). The borrower may also be engaged in other trades or businesses and the loan need not be traceable to specific investments in export property.

(b) *Borrower's export related assets limitation.*— (1) *General rule.*—A loan to a borrower is a producer's loan only to the extent that the amount of the loan, when added to the unpaid balance of all other producer's loans made by all DISC's to the borrower which are outstanding at the time the loan is made, does not exceed an amount equal to the amount of the borrower's export-related assets (determined under subparagraph (2) of this paragraph) multiplied by the fraction set forth in subparagraph (3) of this paragraph.

(2) *Amount of export-related assets.*—(i) *In general.*—For purposes of subparagraph (1) of this paragraph, the amount of the borrower's export-related assets is the sum of the amounts described in subdivisions (ii), (iii) and (iv) of this subparagraph.

(ii) *Borrower's plant and equipment.*—The amount described in this subdivision is the sum of the borrower's adjusted bases (determined as of the beginning of the borrower's taxable year in which a loan is made to it) for plant, machinery, equipment, and supporting production facilities, which are located in the United States. Supporting production facilities are all property used primarily in connection with the manufacture, production, growth, or extraction (within the meaning of § 1.993-3(c)) or storage, handling, transportation, or assembly of property by the borrower.

(iii) *Borrower's property held primarily for sale or lease.*—The amount described in this subdivision is the amount of the borrower's property (at the beginning of the taxable year of the borrower in which a loan is made to it) held primarily for sale or lease to customers in the ordinary course of its trade or business. The amount of such property held for sale is determined under the methods of identifying and valuing inventory normally used by the borrower. The amount of such property held for lease or leased is the borrower's adjusted basis, determined under section 1011, for such property.

(iv) *Borrower's research and experimental expenditures.*—The amount described in this subdivision is the aggregate amount, whether or not charged to capital account, of research and experimental expenditures (within the meaning of section 174) incurred in the United States by the borrower during each of its taxable years which begin after December 31, 1971, and precede the taxable year in which the loan is made to the borrower. Such research and experimental expenditures need bear no relationship to export property (as defined in §1.993-3) of the borrower. The aggregate amount of all such expenditures for each of such preceding taxable years is taken into account for purposes of this subparagraph, regardless of whether all or any portion of the aggregate amount has been taken into account with respect to producer's loans made to the borrower by any DISC in preceding taxable years. The aggregate amount of all such expenditures shall include such expenditures of a corporation, the assets of which were acquired by the borrower in a distribution or a transfer described in section 381(a)(1) or (2) (relating to carryovers in certain corporate acquisitions).

(3) *Fraction referred to in subparagraph (1) of this paragraph.*—(i) *Numerator of fraction.*—The numerator of the fraction set forth in this subparagraph is the sum of the borrower's gross receipts for each of its 3 taxable years immediately preceding the taxable year in which the loan is made (but not including any taxable year beginning before January 1, 1972) from the sale or lease of export property (determined without regard to §1.993-3(f)(1)(iii) and (iv)) which is manufactured, produced, grown, or extracted (within the meaning of §1.993-3(c)) by the borrower whether or not sold or leased directly or through a related domestic person (notwithstanding §1.993-3(a)(4) and (f)(2)). For purposes of the preceding sentence, with respect to a sale or lease to a related DISC in which the transfer price is determined under section 994(a)(1) or (2), the rules under §1.994-1(c)(5) (relating to incomplete transactions) shall be applied, and with respect to all other sales and leases the rules under §1.994-1(c)(5) other than subdivision (i)(d) thereof shall be applied.

(ii) *Denominator of fraction.*—The denominator of the fraction set forth in this subparagraph is the sum of the amount included in the numerator and all other gross receipts of the borrower, for each of its taxable years for which gross receipts are included in the numerator of the fraction, from all sales or leases of all property held by the borrower primarily for sale or lease to customers in the ordinary course of its trade or business.

For purposes of subdivision (i) of this subparagraph and this subdivision, if such property is sold or leased to a domestic related person which resells or subleases such property, the borrower's gross receipts shall be the gross receipts derived by the domestic related person from the resale or sublease of the export property.

(iii) *Taxable years.*—If the borrower has not engaged in the sale or lease of property (as described in this subparagraph) for the 3 immediately preceding taxable years, or if 3 taxable years beginning after December 31, 1971, have not elapsed, the fraction will be computed on the basis of such gross receipts for its taxable years immediately preceding the loan and beginning after December 31, 1971, during which the borrower has so engaged. No producer's loans can be made to a borrower until after the end of the first taxable year of the borrower beginning after December 31, 1971.

(c) *Requirement for increased investment in export-related assets.*—(1) *In general.*—A loan to a borrower is a producer's loan only to the extent that the amount of the loan, when added to the unpaid balance of all other producer's loans made by all DISC's to the borrower during the borrower's taxable year during which such loan is made, does not exceed the amount of the borrower's increase for the year in investment in export-related assets. Such increase for any taxable year is the sum of—

(i) The increase (if any) in the borrower's adjusted basis of certain types of assets as determined under subparagraph (2) of this paragraph and

(ii) The amount (if any) during the year of its research and experimental expenditures as determined under paragraph (b)(2)(iv) of this section.

(2) *Increase in adjusted basis.*—The amount under this subparagraph is the amount (not less than zero) by which—

(i) The borrower's adjusted basis (determined as of the end of its taxable year in which the producer's loan is made) in all of its property which is described in paragraph (b)(2)(ii) (plant and equipment), and (iii) (property held primarily for sale or lease) of this section, including any such property acquired by it during such taxable year, exceeds

(ii) Its adjusted bases in all such property (determined as of the beginning of such year).

(3) *Ordering rule.*—If during the borrower's taxable year the amount of increase in investment in export-related assets determined under this subparagraph is exceeded by amounts loaned to the borrower during such year that would otherwise qualify as producer's loans such loans shall be applied in the order made against the amount of such increase in order to determine which loans qualify as producer's loans.

Reg. §1.993-4(c)(3)

(d) *Proof of borrower's compliance with paragraphs (b) and (c) of this section.*—For purposes of paragraphs (b) and (c) of this section, a DISC shall be prepared to establish initially the compliance of the borrower with the requirements of such paragraphs by providing the written statement of the borrower, certified by a certified public accountant, stating that the borrower has complied with the limitation and increased investment requirement in section 993(d)(2) and (3) of the Internal Revenue Code of 1954. In lieu of certification by a certified public accountant, the DISC may attach to its return a statement signed by the borrower under penalties of perjury on a form provided by the Internal Revenue Service certifying that the borrower has complied with the limitation and increased investment requirement in section 993(d)(2) and (3) of the Internal Revenue Code of 1954. For taxable years ending after October 17, 1977 the DISC must attach either the certification by the certified public accountant or the certification by the borrower to its return. Additional full substantiation of the borrower's compliance with the requirements of such paragraphs may be required by the district director. If full substantiation of such compliance is not provided by the DISC (or the borrower) when required, the loan shall be deemed not to be a producer's loan.

(e) *Special limitation in the case of domestic film maker.*—(1) *General rule.*—The limitation of paragraph (b) of this section as to the export-related assets of the borrower will be considered satisfied if the DISC—

(i) Is engaged in the trade or business of selling or leasing films which are export property, or is acting as a commission agent for a person who is so engaged.

(ii) Makes a loan to a borrower which is a domestic film maker (as defined in subparagraph (5) of this paragraph) for the purpose of making a film, and

(iii) The amount of such loan, when added to the unpaid balance of all other producer's loans made by all DISC's to the borrower which are outstanding at the time the loan is made, does not exceed an amount determined by multiplying—

(a) The sum of (1) the amount of the export-related assets of the borrower (determined under paragraph (b)(2)(i) of this section as of the beginning of the borrower's taxable year in which the loan is made), plus (2) the amount of a reasonable estimate of the amount of such export-related assets obtained or to be obtained by the borrower during such year and subsequent years with respect to films as to which filming begins within such year by

(b) The percentage which, based on the experience of other film makers of similar films for the 5 calendar years preceding the calendar year in which the loan is made, the annual gross receipts (as described in § 1.993-6(a)(1), whether or not such films constitute property described therein) of such other film makers from the sale or lease of such films outside the United States is of the annual gross receipts of such other film makers from all sales or leases of such films.

(2) *Purpose of loan.*—A loan by a DISC will be deemed to be for the making of a film if there exists a written agreement between the DISC and the borrower, executed at or before the time the loan is made, stating that the loan is made or to be made to enable the borrower to make such film.

(3) *Reasonable estimate of amounts.*—For purposes of subparagraph (1)(iii) (a)(2) of this paragraph, a reasonable estimate shall be based on the conditions known by the DISC and borrower to exist at the time a loan is made (or which the DISC and borrower have reason to know to exist at such time).

(4) *Experience of film makers.*—For purposes of subparagraph (1)(iii)(b) of this paragraph, the experience of other film makers of similar films for the 5 calendar years preceding the calendar year in which the loan is made shall be derived from such records and statistics as are acknowledged in the trade as reasonably reliable.

(5) *Domestic film maker.*—For purposes of this section, a borrower is a domestic film maker with respect to a film if—

(i) The borrower is a U.S. person within the meaning of section 7701(a)(30), except that (a) with respect to a partnership all of the partners must be U.S. persons and (b) with respect to a corporation all of its officers and at least a majority of its directors must be U.S. persons,

(ii) The borrower is engaged in the trade or business of making the film with respect to which the loan is made,

(iii) Each studio, if any, used or to be used for filming or for recording sound incorporated into such film is located in the United States (as defined in section 7701(a)(9)),

(iv) At least 80 percent of the aggregate playing time of the film is or will be photographed within the United States (as defined in section 7701(a)(9)), and

(v) At least 80 percent of the total amount (not including any amount which is contingent upon receipts or profits of such film and which is fully taxable by the United States) paid or to be paid for services performed in the making of the film is either paid or to be paid to persons who are U.S. persons at the time such services are performed or consists of amounts which are fully taxable by the United States.

(6) *Amounts as fully taxable.*—For purposes of subparagraph (5)(v) of this paragraph, an amount is considered fully taxable by the United States if the entire amount is included in gross income under section 61 or is subject to with-

Reg. § 1.993-4(d)

holding under any provision of U.S. law or treaty to which the United States is a party and is not exempt from taxation under any provision of such law or treaty. Where a nonresident alien individual is engaged for the making of a film or where a foreign corporation is engaged to furnish the services of one of its officers or employees for the making of a film, the amount paid such individual or corporation will be considered as fully taxable by the United States only if it meets the test of this subparagraph. [Reg. §1.993-4.]

☐ [T.D. 7513, 10-14-77. *Amended by T.D. 7513, 10-14-77 and T.D. 7854, 11-15-82.*]

[Reg. §1.993-5]

§1.993-5. Definition of related foreign export corporation.—(a) *General rule.*—(1) *Definition.*— Under section 993(e), a foreign corporation is a related foreign export corporation with respect to a DISC if—

(i) It is a foreign international sales corporation described in paragraph (b) of this section,

(ii) It is a real property holding company described in paragraph (c) of this section, or

(iii) It is an associated foreign corporation described in paragraph (d) of this section.

(2) *Application of this section.*—It is necessary to determine whether a foreign corporation is a related foreign export corporation with respect to a DISC for the following two purposes:

(i) *Qualified export assets.*—Under §1.993-2(g), the stock or securities of a related foreign export corporation held by the DISC are qualified export assets.

(ii) *Qualified export receipts.*—Under §1.993-1(e), (f), and (g), certain receipts of the DISC with respect to stock or securities of a related foreign export corporation held by the DISC are qualified export receipts.

(b) *Foreign international sales corporation.*— (1) *In general.*—A foreign corporation is a foreign international sales corporation with respect to a taxable year of a DISC if—

(i) On each day during such taxable year of the DISC on which the foreign corporation has stock issued and outstanding, the DISC owns directly stock of the foreign corporation possessing more than 50 percent of the total combined voting power of all classes of stock of the foreign corporation entitled to vote as determined under the principles of §1.957-1(b) (relating to definition of controlled foreign corporation),

(ii) 95 percent or more of such foreign corporation's gross receipts (as defined in §1.993-6) for its taxable year ending with or within such taxable year of the DISC consists of qualified export receipts described in §1.993-1(b) through (e) or interest described in §1.993-1(g)

derived from any obligations described in §1.993-2(d) or (e), and

(iii) The sum of the adjusted bases of the assets of the foreign corporation which are qualified export assets described in §1.993-2(b) through (e) and which are held by the foreign corporation at the close of its taxable year which ends with or within such taxable year of the DISC equals or exceeds 95 percent of the sum of the adjusted bases of all assets held by the foreign corporation at the close of such taxable year.

(2) *Certain determinations.*—The determinations as to whether gross receipts are qualified export receipts described in subparagraph (1)(ii) of this paragraph and as to whether assets are qualified export assets described in subparagraph (1)(iii) of this paragraph are made by applying the requirements of §§1.993-1 and 1.993-2 to the foreign corporation as if it were a domestic corporation being tested to determine whether it is a DISC. For purposes of making either of such determinations, the principles of accounting applicable for purposes of computing earnings and profits under §1.964-1 (relating to a controlled foreign corporation's earnings and profits) shall apply.

(c) *Real property holding company.*—(1) *In general.*—A foreign corporation is a real property holding company with respect to a taxable year of a DISC if—

(i) On each day during such taxable year of the DISC on which the foreign corporation has stock issued and outstanding, the DISC owns directly stock of the foreign corporation possessing more than 50 percent of the total combined voting power of all classes of stock of the foreign corporation entitled to vote as determined under the principles of §1.957-1(b) and

(ii) The sole function of the foreign corporation is to hold title to real property situated outside the United States for the exclusive use of the DISC, title to which may not be held by the DISC (and, if the DISC subleases such property to a related supplier, as described in subparagraph (3) of this paragraph, by such related supplier) under the law of the country in which such property is situated.

(2) *Activities of the foreign corporation.*—For purposes of subparagraph (1)(ii) of this paragraph, a foreign corporation which holds title to real property situated outside the United States may also perform activities with respect to such property (such as management, maintenance, and payment of taxes) which are ancillary to its function of holding title to such property.

(3) *Exclusive use by the DISC.*—Real property held by the foreign corporation must be used exclusively by the DISC whether under a lease or any other arrangement. Real property is not so used by the DISC if the DISC subleases such

property to any other person. If, however, during a taxable year of the DISC—

(i) 90 percent or more of the qualified export receipts of the DISC for such year are derived from transactions with respect to which it is a commission agent for a related supplier (as defined in §1.994-1(a)(3)(ii), and

(ii) The DISC subleases such property to such related supplier then such property will be considered as used exclusively by the DISC during such year if such related supplier does not sublease such property.

(d) *Associated foreign corporation.*—(1) *In general.*—A foreign corporation is an associated foreign corporation with respect to a taxable year of the DISC if—

(i) On each day during such taxable year of the DISC on which the foreign corporation has stock issued and outstanding, the DISC, or one or more members of the same controlled group of corporations (as defined in subparagraph (2) of this paragraph) as the DISC, owns (within the meaning of sec. 1563 (d) and (e)) stock of the foreign corporation possessing less than 10 percent of the total combined voting power of all classes of stock of the foreign corporation entitled to vote, as determined under the principles of §1.957-1(b), or owns no stock of such corporation, and

(ii) The ownership of stock, or of securities (as defined in §1.993-2(g)), of the foreign corporation by the DISC or by one or more members of such controlled group of corporations reasonably furthers a transaction or transactions giving rise to qualified export receipts for the DISC.

(2) *Controlled group of corporations.*—For purposes of this paragraph, the term "controlled group of corporations" has the same meaning assigned to the term in section 1563(a) and not section 993(a)(3) and §1.993-1(k). Thus, for purposes of this paragraph, the test of control is 80 percent control and, since the rules of section 1563(b) apply, only domestic members are considered to be members of the controlled group.

(3) *Furtherance of qualified export receipts.*—Ownership of stock or securities of a foreign corporation will be considered as reasonably furthering a transaction or transactions giving rise to qualified export receipts for a DISC if—

(i) The ownership is necessary to obtain or maintain the foreign corporation as a customer of the DISC or of a related supplier, as defined in §1.994-1(a)(3)(ii) of the DISC or to aid the sales distribution system of the DISC or of such related supplier, and

(ii) The amount of the investment in the foreign corporation bears a reasonable relationship to the amount of the DISC's annual net profit from transactions in its trade or business which it may reasonably expect to derive on account of such ownership.

In determining whether the amount of the investment is reasonable, there shall be taken into account any stock or securities of the foreign corporation owned by any other foreign corporation which, if it were a domestic corporation, would be a member of the same controlled group of corporations as the DISC. [Reg. §1.993-5.]

☐ [T.D. 7514, 10-14-77.]

[Reg. §1.993-6]

§1.993-6. Definition of gross receipts.—(a) *General rule.*—Under section 993(f), for purposes of sections 991 through 996, the gross receipts of a person for a taxable year are—

(1) The total amounts received or accrued by the person from the sale or lease of property held primarily for sale or lease in the ordinary course of a trade or business, and

(2) Gross income recognized from all other sources, such as, for example, from—

(i) The furnishing of services (whether or not related to the sale or lease of property described in subparagraph (1) of this paragraph),

(ii) Dividends and interest,

(iii) The sale at a gain of any property not described in subparagraph (1) of this paragraph, and

(iv) Commission transactions as and to the extent described in paragraph (e) of this section.

(b) *Nongross receipts items.*—For purposes of paragraph (a) of this section, gross receipts do not include amounts received or accrued by a person from—

(1) The proceeds of a loan or of the repayment of a loan, or

(2) A receipt of property in a transaction to which section 118 (relating to contribution to capital) or 1032 (relating to exchange of stock for property) applies.

(c) *Nonreduction of total amounts.*—For purposes of paragraph (a) of this section, the total amounts received or accrued by a person are not reduced by returns and allowances, costs of goods sold, expenses, losses, a deduction for dividends received under section 243, or any other deductible amounts.

(d) *Method of accounting.*—For purposes of paragraph (a) of this section, the total amounts received or accrued by a person shall be determined under the method of accounting used in computing its taxable income. If, for example, a DISC receives advance or installment payments for the sale or lease of property described in paragraph (a)(1) of this section, for the furnishing of services, or which represent recognized gain from the sale of property not described in paragraph (a)(1) of this section, any amount of such advance payments is considered to be gross receipts of the DISC for the taxable year for which such amount is included in the gross income of the DISC.

(e) *Commission transactions.*—(1) In the case of transactions which give rise to a commission on the sale or lease of property or the furnishing of services by a principal, the amount recognized by the commission agent as gross income from all such transactions shall be the gross receipts derived by the principal from the sale or lease of the property, or the gross income derived by the principal from the furnishing of services, with respect to which the commissions are derived. In the case of a commission agent for a related supplier (as defined in § 1.994-1(a)(3)(ii)), the gross receipts or gross income of such agent shall be determined as if it used the same method of accounting as its related supplier. In the case of a commission agent for a principal other than a related supplier, the gross receipts or gross income of such principal shall be determined as if such principal used the same method of accounting as its agent.

(2) If the commission arrangement provides that the commission agent will receive a commission only with respect to sales or leases of export property, or the furnishing of services, which result in qualified export receipts, the commission agent will not take into account the gross receipts or gross income, as the case may be, derived by the principal from any transaction for which the commission agent would not be entitled to a commission under the commission arrangement.

(f) *Example.*—The provisions of this section may be illustrated by the following example:

Example. During 1973, M, a related supplier (as defined in § 1.994-1(a)(3)(ii)) of N, is engaged in the manufacture of machines in the United States. N, a calendar year taxpayer, is engaged in the sale and lease of such machines in foreign countries. N furnishes services which are related and subsidiary to its sale and lease of such machines. N also acts as a commission agent in foreign countries for Z, an unrelated supplier, with respect to Z's sale of products. N receives dividends on stock owned by it in a related foreign export corporation (as defined in § 1.993-5), interest on producer's loans made to M, and proceeds from sales of business assets located outside the United States resulting in a recognized gains and losses. N's gross receipts for 1973 are $3,550, computed on the basis of the additional facts assumed in the table below:

(1) N's sales receipts for machines manufactured by M (without reduction for cost of goods sold and selling expenses)	$1,500
(2) N's lease receipts for machines manufactured by M (without reduction for depreciation and leasing expenses)	500
(3) N's gross income from services for machines manufactured by M (without reduction for service expenses)	400
(4) Z's sale receipts for products manufactured by Z (without reduction for Z's cost of goods sold, commissions on sales, and commission sales expenses)	550
(5) Dividends received by N . . .	150
(6) Interest received by N on producer's loans	200
(7) Proceeds received by N representing recognized gain (but not losses) from sales of business assets located outside the United States	250
(8) N's gross receipts	$3,550

[Reg. § 1.993-6.]

[Reg. § 1.993-7]

§ 1.993-7. Definition of United States.—Under section 993(g), the term "United States" includes the States, the District of Columbia, the Commonwealth of Puerto Rico, and possessions of the United States. For the requirement that a DISC must be incorporated and existing under the laws of a State or the District of Columbia, see § 1.992-1(a)(1). [Reg. § 1.993-7.]

☐ [*T.D.* 7514, 10-14-77.]

[Reg. § 1.994-1]

§ 1.994-1. Inter-company pricing rules for DISC's.—(a) *In general.*—(1) *Scope.*—In the case of a transaction described in paragraph (b) of this section, section 994 permits a person related to a DISC to determine the allowable transfer price charged the DISC (or commission paid the DISC) by its choice of three methods described in paragraph (c)(2), (3), and (4) of this section: The "4 percent" gross receipts method, the "50-50" combined taxable income method, and the section 482 method. Under the first two methods, the DISC is entitled to 10 percent of its export promotion expenses as additional taxable income. When the gross receipts method or combined taxable income method is applied to a transaction, the Commissioner may not make distributions, apportionments, or allocations as provided by section 482 and the regulations thereunder. For rules as to certain "incomplete transactions" and for computing combined taxable income, see paragraphs (c)(5) and (6) of this section. Grouping of transactions for purposes of applying the method chosen is provided by paragraph (c)(7) of this section. The rules in paragraph (c) of this section are directly applicable only in the case of sales or exchanges of export property to a DISC for resale, and are applicable by analogy to leases, commissions, and services as provided in paragraph (d) of this section. For rules limiting the application of the gross receipts method and combined taxable income method so that the supplier related to the DISC will not incur a loss on transactions, see paragraph (e)(1) of this section. Paragraph (e)(2) of this section provides for the applicability of section 482 to resales by the DISC to related persons. Paragraph (e)(3) of this section provides for the time by which a reasonable estimate of the transfer price (including commissions and other payments) should be paid. The subsequent determination and further adjustments to transfer prices are set forth in paragraph (e)(4) of this section. Export promotion expenses are defined in paragraph (f) of this section. Paragraph (g) of this section has several examples illustrating the provisions of this section. Section 1.994-2 prescribes the marginal costing rules authorized by section 994(b)(2).

(2) *Performance of substantial economic functions.*—The application of section 994(a)(1) or (2) does not depend on the extent to which the DISC performs substantial economic functions (except with respect to export promotion expenses). See paragraph (1) of § 1.993-1.

(3) *Related party and related supplier.*—For the purposes of this section—

(i) The term "related party" means a person which is owned or controlled directly or indirectly by the same interests as the DISC within the meaning of section 482 and § 1.482-1(a).

(ii) The term "related supplier" means a related party which singly engages in a transaction directly with the DISC which is subject to the rules of section 994 and this section. However, a DISC may have different related suppliers with respect to different transactions. If, for example, X owns all the stock of Y, a corporation, and of Z, a DISC, and sells a product to Y which is resold to Z, only Y is the related supplier of Z, and, thus, only the resale from Y to Z is subject to section 994 and this section. If, however, X sells directly to Z and Y also sells directly to Z, then, as to the transactions involving direct sales to Z, each of X and Y is a related supplier of Z.

(b) *Transactions to which section 994 applies.*—Section 994(a)(3) may be applied, as described in paragraph (a) of this section, to any transaction between a related supplier and a DISC. Sections 994(a)(1) or (2) may be applied, as described in paragraph (a) of this section, to a transaction between a related supplier and a DISC only in the following cases:

(1) Where the related supplier sells export property to the DISC for resale or where the DISC is commission agent for the related supplier on sales by the related supplier of export property to third parties whether or not related parties. For purposes of this section, references to sales include exchanges.

(2) Where the related supplier leases export property to the DISC for sublease for a comparable period with comparable terms of payment or where the DISC is commission agent for the related supplier on leases by the related supplier of export property to third parties whether or not related parties.

(3) Where services are furnished by a related supplier which are related and subsidiary to any sale or lease by the DISC, acting as principal or commission agent, of export property under subparagraph (1) or (2) of this paragraph.

(4) Where engineering or architectural services for construction projects located (or proposed for location) outside of the United States are furnished by a related supplier where the DISC is acting as principal or commission agent with respect to the furnishing of such services to a third party whether or not a related party.

(5) Where the related supplier furnishes managerial services in furtherance of the production of qualified export receipts of an unrelated DISC where the related DISC is acting as principal or commission agent with respect to the furnishing of such services to an unrelated DISC.

Transactions are included, for purposes of this paragraph, only if they give rise to qualified export receipts (within the meaning of section 993(a)) in the hands of the related DISC. If a transaction is not included in subparagraph (1), (2), (3), (4), or (5) of this paragraph, the rules of section 994(a)(1) or (2) do not apply. Thus, for example, the rules of section 994(a)(1) or (2) would not apply if a DISC purchased export property from its related supplier and leased such property to a third party.

(c) *Transfer price for sales of export property.*—(1) *In general.*—Under this paragraph, rules are prescribed for computing the allowable price for the transfer from a related supplier to a DISC in the case of a sale of export property described in paragraph (b)(1) of this section.

(2) *The "4-percent" gross receipts method.*—Under the gross receipts method of pricing, the transfer price for a sale by the related supplier to the DISC is the price as a result of which the taxable income derived by the DISC from the sale will not exceed the sum of (i) 4 percent of the qualified export receipts of the DISC derived from the sale of the export property (as defined in section 993(c)) and (ii) 10 percent of the export promotion expenses (as defined in paragraph (f) of this section) of the DISC attributable to such qualified export receipts.

(3) *The "50-50" combined taxable income method.*—Under the combined taxable income method of pricing, the transfer price for a sale by the related supplier to the DISC is the price as a result of which the taxable income derived by the DISC from the sale will not exceed the sum of (i) 50 percent of the combined taxable income (as defined in subparagraph (6) of this para-

graph) of the DISC and its related supplier attributable to the qualified export receipts from such sale and (ii) 10 percent of the export promotion expenses (as defined in paragraph (f) of this section) of the DISC attributable to such qualified export receipts.

(4) *Section 482 method.*—If the rules of subparagraphs (2) and (3) of this paragraph are inapplicable to a sale or a taxpayer does not choose to use them, the transfer price for a sale by the related supplier to the DISC is to be determined on the basis of the sale price actually charged but subject to the rules provided by section 482 and the regulations thereunder.

(5) *Incomplete transactions.*—(i) For purposes of the gross receipts and combined taxable income methods, where property encompassed within a transaction or group chosen under subparagraph (7) of this paragraph is transferred by a related supplier to a DISC during a taxable year of either the DISC or related supplier, but some or all of such property is not sold by the DISC during such year—

(a) The transfer price of such property sold by the DISC during such year shall be computed separately from the transfer price of the property not sold by the DISC during such year.

(b) With respect to such property not sold by the DISC during such year, the transfer price paid by the DISC for such year shall be the related supplier's cost of goods sold (see subparagraph (6)(ii) of this paragraph) with respect to the property, except that, with respect to such taxable years ending on or before [date which is 30 days after publication of this Treasury decision], the transfer price paid by the DISC shall be at least (but need not exceed) the related supplier's cost of goods sold with respect to the property.

(c) For the subsequent taxable year during which such property is resold by the DISC, an additional amount shall be paid by the DISC (to be treated as income for such year by the related supplier) equal to the excess of the amount which would have been the transfer price under this section had the transfer to the DISC by the related supplier and the resale by the DISC taken place during the taxable year of the DISC during which it resold the property over the amount already paid under (b) of this subdivision.

(d) The time and manner of payment of transfer prices required by (b) and (c) of this subdivision shall be determined under paragraph (e)(3), (4), and (5) of this section.

(ii) For purposes of this paragraph, a DISC may determine the year in which it receives property from a related supplier and the year in which it sells property in accordance with the method of identifying goods in its inventory properly used under section 471 or 472 (relating respectively to general rule for invento-

ries and to LIFO inventories). Transportation expense of the related supplier in connection with a transaction to which this subparagraph applies shall be treated as an item of cost of goods sold with respect to the property if the related supplier includes the cost of intracompany transportation between its branches, divisions, plants, or other units in its cost of goods sold (see subparagraph (6)(ii) of this paragraph).

(6) *Combined taxable income.*—For purposes of this section, the combined taxable income of a DISC and its related supplier from a sale of export property is the excess of the gross receipts (as defined in section 993(f)) of the DISC from such sale over the total costs of the DISC and related supplier which relate to such gross receipts. Gross receipts from a sale do not include interest with respect to the sale. Combined taxable income under this paragraph shall be determined after taking into account under paragraph (e)(2) of this section all adjustments required by section 482 with respect to transactions to which such section is applicable. In determining the gross receipts of the DISC and the total costs of the DISC and related supplier which relate to such gross receipts, the following rules shall be applied:

(i) Subject to subdivisions (ii) through (v) of this subparagraph, the taxpayer's method of accounting used in computing taxable income will be accepted for purposes of determining amounts and the taxable year for which items of income and expense (including depreciation) are taken into account. See § 1.991-1(b)(2) with respect to the method of accounting which may be used by a DISC.

(ii) Cost of goods sold shall be determined in accordance with the provisions of § 1.61-3. See sections 471 and 472 and the regulations thereunder with respect to inventories. With respect to property to which an election under section 631 applies (relating to cutting of timber considered as a sale or exchange), cost of goods sold shall be determined by applying § 1.631-1(d)(3) and (e) (relating to fair market value as of the beginning of the taxable year of the standing timber cut during the year considered as its cost).

(iii) Costs (other than cost of goods sold) which shall be treated as relating to gross receipts from sales of export property are (a) the expenses, losses, and other deductions definitely related, and therefore allocated and apportioned, thereto, and (b) a ratable part of any other expenses, losses, or other deductions which are not definitely related to a class of gross income, determined in a manner consistent with the rules set forth in § 1.861-8.

(iv) The taxpayer's choice in accordance with subparagraph (7) of this paragraph as to the grouping of transactions shall be controlling, and costs deductible in a taxable year shall be allocated and apportioned to the items or classes of gross income of such taxable year resulting from such grouping.

(v) If an account receivable arising with respect to a sale of export property is transferred by the related supplier to a DISC which is a member of the same controlled group within the meaning of § 1.993-1(k) for an amount reflecting a discount from the selling price taken into account in computing (without regard to this subdivision) combined taxable income of the DISC and its related supplier, then the combined taxable income from such sale shall be reduced by the amount of the discount.

(7) *Grouping transactions.*—(i) Generally, the determinations under this section are to be made on a transaction-by-transaction basis. However, at the annual choice of the taxpayer some or all of these determinations may be made on the basis of groups consisting of products or product lines.

(ii) A determination by a taxpayer as to a product or a product line will be accepted by a district director if such determination conforms to any one of the following standards: (*a*) a recognized industry or trade usage, or (*b*) the two-digit major groups (or any inferior classifications or combinations thereof, with a major group) of the Standard Industrial Classification as prepared by the Statistical Policy Division of the Office of Management and Budget, Executive Office of the President.

(iii) A choice by the taxpayer to group transactions for a taxable year on a product or product line basis shall apply to all transactions with respect to that product or product line consummated during the taxable year. However, the choice of a product or product line grouping applies only to transactions covered by the grouping and, as to transactions not encompassed by the grouping, the determinations are made on a transaction-by-transaction basis. For example, the taxpayer may choose a product grouping with respect to one product and use the transaction-by-transaction method for another product within the same taxable year.

(iv) For rules as to grouping certain related and subsidiary services, see paragraph (d)(3)(ii) of this section.

(d) *Rules under section 994(a)(1) and (2) for transactions other than sales.*—The following rules are prescribed for purposes of applying the gross receipts method or combined taxable income method to transactions other than sales:

(1) *Leases.*—In the case of a lease of export property by a related supplier to a DISC for sublease by the DISC to produce gross receipts, for any taxable year the amount of rent the DISC must pay to the related supplier shall be determined under the DISC's lease with its related supplier but must be computed in a manner consistent with the rules in paragraph (c) of this section for computing the transfer price in the

case of sales and resales of export property under the gross receipts method or combined taxable income method. For purposes of applying this subparagraph, transactions may not be so grouped on a product or product line basis under the rules of paragraph (c)(7) of this section as to combine in any one group of transactions both lease transactions and sale transactions involving the same product or product line.

(2) *Commissions.*—If any transaction to which section 994 applies is handled on a commission basis for a related supplier by a DISC and such commissions give rise to qualified export receipts under section 993(a)—

(i) The amount of the income that may be earned by the DISC in any year is the amount, computed in a manner consistent with paragraph (c) of this section, which the DISC would have been permitted to earn under the gross receipts method, the combined taxable income method, or section 482 method if the related supplier had sold (or leased) the property or service to the DISC and the DISC in turn sold (or subleased) to a third party, whether or not a related party, and

(ii) The maximum commission the DISC may charge the related supplier is the sum of the amount of income determined under subdivision (i) of this subparagraph plus the DISC's total costs for the transaction as determined under paragraph (c)(6) of this section.

(3) *Receipts from services.*—(i) *Related and subsidiary services attributable to the year of the export transaction.*—The gross receipts for related and subsidiary services described in paragraph (b)(3) of this section shall be treated as part of the receipts from the export transaction to which such services are related and subsidiary, but only if, under the arrangement between the DISC and its related supplier and the accounting method otherwise employed by the DISC, the income from such services is includible for the same taxable year as income from such export transaction.

(ii) *Other services.*—In the case of related and subsidiary services to which subdivision (i) of this subparagraph does not apply and other services described in paragraph (b)(4) or (5) of this section performed by a related supplier (relating respectively to engineering and architectural services and certain managerial services), the amount of taxable income which the DISC may derive for any taxable year shall be determined under the arrangement between the DISC and its related supplier and shall be computed in a manner consistent with the rules in paragraph (c) of this section for computing the transfer price in the case of sales for resale of export property under the gross receipts method or combined taxable income method. Related and subsidiary services to which subdivision (i) of this subparagraph does not apply may be grouped, under the rules for grouping of transactions in paragraph (c)(7) of this section, with the products or product lines to which they are related and subsidiary, so long as the grouping of services chosen is consistent with the grouping of products or product lines chosen for the taxable year in which either the products or product lines were sold or in which payment for such services is received or accrued. The rules for grouping of transaction in paragraph (c)(7) of this section shall not apply with respect to the determination of taxable income which the DISC may derive from other services described in paragraph (b)(4) or (5) of this section performed by a related supplier or commissions on such services, and such determination shall be made only on a transaction-by-transaction basis.

(e) *Methods of applying paragraphs (c) and (d) of this section.*—(1) *Limitation on DISC income ("no loss" rule).*—(i) *In general.*—Except as otherwise provided in this subparagraph, neither the gross receipts method nor the combined taxable income method may be applied to cause in any taxable year a loss to the related supplier, but either method may be applied to the extent it does not cause a loss. A loss to a related supplier would result if the taxable income of the DISC would exceed the combined taxable income of the related supplier and the DISC. If, however, there is no combined taxable income of the DISC and the related supplier (because, for example, a combined loss is incurred), a transfer price (or commission) will not be deemed to cause a loss to the related supplier if it allows the DISC to recover an amount not in excess of its costs (if any).

(ii) *Special rule for applying "4 percent" gross receipts method to sales.*—A transfer price or commission, determined under the "4 percent" gross receipts method (determined without regard to subdivision (i) of this subparagraph), for a sale of export property referred to in paragraph (b)(1) of this section, will not be considered to cause a loss for the related supplier if for the DISC's taxable year, the ratio that (a) the taxable income of the DISC derived from such sale by using such price or commission bears to (b) the DISC's gross receipts from such sale is not greater than the ratio that (c) all of the taxable income of the related supplier and the DISC from all sales of the same product or product line (domestic and foreign) to third parties whether or not related parties bears to (d) the total gross receipts of the related supplier and the DISC from such sales. For purposes of the preceding sentence, sales between the DISC and its related suppliers shall not be taken into account under (c) or (d) of this subdivision. For example, assume that for a taxable year of a DISC the total costs of the related supplier and the DISC with respect to all sales ($150 for domestic and $44 for foreign) of a product line are $194 and the total gross receipts of the related supplier and the

DISC with respect to such sales are $200 so that the total taxable income of the related supplier and the DISC with respect to such sales is $6. The parties would thus be entitled to compute a transfer price determined under the gross receipts method on any given sale of product A of such product line by the related supplier to the DISC which would allocate to the DISC taxable income equal to not more than 3 percent (i.e., $6/$200) of its gross receipts derived from its resale of such product. If the DISC were to resell an item of product A for $10, the transfer price paid by the DISC to the related supplier determined under the gross receipts method could be as low as $9.70.

(iii) *Grouping transactions.*—For purposes of subdivision (i) of this subparagraph, the basis for grouping transactions chosen by the taxpayer under paragraph (c)(7) of this section for the taxable year shall be applied. For purposes of making the computations of subdivision (ii)(c) and (d) of this subparagraph, however, the taxpayer may choose any basis for grouping transactions permissible under paragraph (c)(7) of this section, even though it may not be the same basis as that already chosen under paragraph (c)(7) of this section for computing transfer prices or commissions to a DISC. If, for example, the taxpayer has chosen to group transactions on a product basis for computing transfer prices or commissions to a DISC for a taxable year, the taxpayer may still group transactions on a product line basis for purposes of computing taxable income and total gross receipts under subdivision (ii)(c) and (d) of this subparagraph. For a further example, if the taxpayer computes taxable income for one group of transactions under the gross receipts method and computes taxable income for a second group of transactions under the combined taxable income method, the taxpayer may aggregate these transactions for purposes of computing taxable income and total gross receipts under subdivision (ii)(c) and (d) of this subparagraph.

(2) *Relationship to section 482.*—In applying the rules under section 994, it may be necessary to first take into account the price of a transfer (or other transaction) between the DISC (or related supplier), and a related party which is subject to the arm's length standard of section 482. Thus, for example, where a related supplier sells export property to a DISC which the related supplier purchased from related parties, the costs taken into account in computing the combined taxable income of the DISC and the related supplier are determined after any necessary adjustment under section 482 of the price paid by the related supplier to the related parties. In applying section 482 to a transfer by a DISC, however, the DISC and its related supplier are treated as if they were a single entity carrying on all the functions performed by the DISC and the related supplier with respect to the transaction

and the DISC shall be allowed to receive under the section 482 standard the amount the related supplier would have received had there been no DISC.

(3) *Initial payment of transfer price or commission.*—(i) The amount of a transfer price (or reasonable estimate thereof) actually charged by a related supplier to a DISC or a sales commission (or reasonable estimate thereof) actually charged by a DISC to a related supplier, in a transaction to which section 994 applies must be paid no later than 60 days following the close of the taxable year of the DISC during which the transaction occurred.

(ii) Payment must be in the form of money, property (including accounts receivable from sales by or through the DISC), a written obligation which qualifies as debt under the safe harbor rule of § 1.992-1(d)(2)(ii), or an accounting entry offsetting the account receivable against an existing debt owed by the person in whose favor the account receivable was established to the person with whom it engaged in the transaction. The form of the payment to a DISC need not be a qualified export asset under § 1.993-2. However, for the requirement that the adjusted basis of the qualified export assets of the DISC at the close of its taxable year must equal or exceed 95 percent of the sum of the adjusted bases of all assets of the DISC at the close of its taxable year, see section 992(a)(1)(B).

(iii) If the district director can demonstrate, based upon the data available as of the 60th day after the close of such taxable year, that the amount actually paid did not represent a reasonable estimate of the transfer price or commission (as the case may be) to be determined under section 994 and this section, an indebtedness will be deemed to arise, from the person required to make the payment in favor of the person to whom the payment is required to be made, in an amount equal to the difference between the amount of the transfer price or commission determined under section 994 and this section and the amount (if any) actually paid and received. Such indebtedness will be deemed to arise as of the date the transaction occurred which gave rise to the indebtedness, except that, if such transaction occurred in a taxable year of the DISC ending on or before August 15, 1975, at the taxpayer's option, the indebtedness will be deemed to arise as of the date by which payment was required under subdivision (i) of this paragraph (e)(3). Such indebtedness owed to a DISC shall be treated as an asset but shall not be treated as a trade receivable or other qualified export asset (see § 1.993-2(d)(3)) as of the end of the taxable year of the DISC in which the indebtedness is deemed to arise.

(iv)(a) Except with respect to incomplete transactions to which paragraph (c)(5)(i)(b) of this section applies, if the amount actually paid results in the DISC realizing at least 50 percent of

the DISC's taxable income from the transaction as reported in its tax return for the taxable year the transaction is completed, then the amount actually paid shall be deemed to be a reasonable estimate of such transfer price or commission.

(b) With respect to incomplete transactions to which paragraph (c)(5)(i)(b) of this section applies and which were initiated during a taxable year ending after August 15, 1975, the amount actually paid shall be deemed to be a reasonable estimate of such transfer price if any one of the following three tests is met:

(1) The amount actually paid by the DISC to the related supplier in respect to the property does not exceed the related supplier's cost of goods sold (see paragraph (c)(6)(ii) of this section) with respect to the property.

(2) If the transaction is completed by the date on which the DISC's return is required to be filed for the year in which the transaction was initiated, the amount actually paid by the DISC to the related supplier in respect of the property results in the DISC realizing at least 50 percent of the DISC's taxable income from the transaction when completed.

(3) The percentage that (i) an amount equal to (a) the amount actually paid by the DISC to the related supplier in respect of the property minus (b) the related supplier's cost of goods sold with respect to the property, bears to (ii) the related supplier's cost of goods sold in respect of the property, is not greater than 50 percent of the percentage that (iii) the combined taxable income for completed transactions of the same group as the property during the DISC's taxable year in which the incomplete transaction was initiated, bears to (iv) the cost of goods sold of the related supplier and DISC with respect to such transactions.

(c) For purposes of this subdivision (iv), whether the transfer price or commission actually paid is deemed a reasonable estimate may be determined on the basis of grouping transactions chosen by the taxpayer under paragraph (c)(5) and (7) of this section.

(v) An indebtedness arising under subdivision (iii) of this subparagraph shall bear interest at an arm's length rate, computed in the manner provided by § 1.482-2(a)(2) from the 61st day after the close of the DISC's taxable year in which the transaction occurred which gave rise to the indebtedness to the date of payment. The interest so computed shall be accrued and included in the taxable income of the person to whom the indebtedness is owed for each taxable year during which the indebtedness is unpaid.

(4) *Subsequent determination of transfer price or commission.*—The DISC and its related supplier would ordinarily determine under section 994 and this section the transfer price payable by the DISC (or the commission payable to the DISC) for a transaction before the DISC files its return for the taxable year of the transaction.

After the DISC has filed its return, a redetermination of the transfer price (or commission) may only be made if permitted by the Code and regulations thereunder. Such a redetermination would include a redetermination by reason of an adjustment under section 482 and the regulations thereunder or section 861 and § 1.861-8 which affects the amounts which entered into the determination of the transfer price or commission.

(5) *Procedure for adjustments to transfer price or commission.*—(i)(a) If the transfer price (or commission) for a transaction determined under section 994 is different from the price (or commission) actually charged, the person who received too small a transfer price (or commission) or paid too large a transfer price (or commission) shall establish (or be deemed to have established), at the date of the determination or redetermination under subparagraph (4) of this paragraph of the transfer price (or commission) under section 994, an account receivable from the person with whom it engaged in the transaction equal to the difference in amount between the transfer price (or commission) so determined and the transfer price (or commission) previously paid and received. If the account receivable due the DISC is paid within 90 days after the date it is established (or deemed established), then as of the end of the taxable year of the DISC in which the transaction occurred which gave rise to the indebtedness, the account receivable shall be treated as an asset and, under § 1.993-2(d)(3) as a trade receivable, and thus as a qualified export asset.

(b) If, for example, during 1972, a DISC which uses the calendar year as its taxable year sold a product which it purchased that year from its related supplier and paid a price of $10,000 which price is a reasonable estimate under subparagraph (3)(iii) of this paragraph but is later determined under section 994 to be $8,000 immediately before the DISC filed its return for 1972, the DISC must be paid $2,000 (*i.e.*, $10,000–$8,000) by its related supplier or establish an account receivable from its related supplier of $2,000. The account receivable may be paid without tax consequences, provided that such account receivable is paid within 90 days after the date it is established (or deemed established). Such account receivable paid within such 90 days will be considered to relate to the taxable year in which the transaction occurred which gave rise thereto rather than the taxable year during which it is established or paid.

(ii) Payment must be in a form specified in subparagraph (3) of this paragraph.

(iii) If an account receivable of a DISC described in subdivision (i) of this paragraph (e)(5) is not paid within 90 days of the date it is established (or deemed established), then, as of the end of the taxable year of the DISC in which the transaction occurred which gives rise to the

indebtedness, the account receivable shall be treated as an asset except that, if the account receivable is established (or deemed established) in a taxable year of the DISC ending on or before August 15, 1975, at the taxpayer's option, the account receivable shall be treated as an asset as of the end of such taxable year. However, under § 1.993-2(d)(3), an account receivable referred to in the preceding sentence shall not be treated as a trade receivable or other qualified export asset.

(iv) An account receivable established in accordance with subdivision (i) of this subparagraph shall bear interest at an arm's length rate, computed in the manner provided by § 1.482-2(a)(2) from the day after the date the account receivable is deemed established to the date of payment. The interest so computed shall be accrued and included in the taxpayer's taxable income for each taxable year during which the account receivable is outstanding.

(v)(a) In lieu of establishing an account receivable in accordance with subdivision (i) of this subparagraph for all or part of an amount due a related supplier, the related supplier and DISC are permitted to treat all or part of any distribution which was made by the DISC out of its previously taxed income with respect to the year to which the determination or redetermination relates as an additional payment of transfer price or repayment of commission (and not as a distribution) made as of the date the distribution was made. Any additional amount arising on the determination or redetermination due the related supplier after this treatment shall be represented by an account receivable established under subdivision (i) of this subparagraph. To the extent that a distribution is so treated under this subdivision (v), it shall cease to qualify as distribution for any Federal income tax purpose, and the DISC's account for previously taxed income shall be adjusted accordingly. If all or part of any distribution made to a shareholder other than the related supplier is recharacterized under this subdivision (v), the related supplier shall establish an account receivable from that shareholder for the amount so recharacterized. Such account receivable shall be paid in the time and manner set forth in this paragraph (e)(5). In order to obtain the relief provided by this subdivision (v), the conditions and procedures prescribed by Revenue Procedure 84-3 must be met. The provisions of this paragraph (e)(5)(v) shall apply to all open taxable years ending after December 31, 1971.

(b) If, for example, during 1982, a DISC commission from a related supplier with respect to a transaction completed in 1980 was redetermined to be $1,000 less than the commission actually charged by, and paid to, the DISC, the amount of any distribution previously made by the DISC from its 1980 previously taxed income to the related supplier as a shareholder may, to the extent of $1,000, be treated not as a distribution but as a repayment of commission.

(vi) The procedure for adjustments to transfer price provided by this subparagraph does not apply to incomplete transactions described in paragraph (c)(5)(i)(b) of this section. Such procedure will, however, be applied to any such transaction with respect to the taxable year in which the transaction is completed.

(6) *Examples.*—The provisions of this paragraph may be illustrated by the following examples:

Example (1). (i) During 1975, a DISC which uses the calendar year as its taxable year purchased a product from its related supplier and made an initial payment of $8,500. If $8,500 were determined to be the transfer price under section 994, the DISC's taxable income from the transaction would be $1,000. Immediately before the DISC filed its return for 1975, under section 994 it is determined that the transfer price is $8,000 and the DISC's taxable income is $1,500. Thus, the requirement of a reasonable estimate under subparagraph (3) of this paragraph was met because the amount ($8,500) actually paid resulted in the DISC realizing taxable income of $1,000 which is not less than 50 percent of the DISC's taxable income ($1,500) from the transaction as determined under section 994.

(ii) Pursuant to subparagraph (5) of this paragraph, an account receivable due the DISC for $500, *i.e.,* $8,500-$8,000, is established on September 15, 1976, the date the DISC files its return for 1975, and is paid on December 1, 1976. The account receivable for $500 will be considered to relate to the taxable year (1975) in which the transaction occurred which gave rise thereto and will be a qualified export asset under § 1.993-2(d)(3) for the last day of such year.

Example (2). Assume the same facts as in example (1) except that the account receivable for $500 is paid on January 1, 1977. The account receivable for $500 will still be considered to relate to the taxable year (1975) in which the transaction occurred which gave rise thereto. However, such account receivable will be treated as an asset which is not a qualified export asset under § 1.993-2(d)(3) for the last day of such year.

(f) *Export promotion expenses.*—(1) *Purpose of expense.*—(i) In order for an expense or cost of a type described in subparagraph (2) of this paragraph to be an export promotion expense, the expense or cost must be incurred or treated as incurred by the DISC (under subparagraph (7) of this paragraph) to advance the sale, lease, or other distribution of export property for use, consumption, or distribution outside the United States. Costs of services in performing installation (but not assembly) on the site and for meeting warranty commitments if such services are related and subsidiary (within the meaning of § 1.993-1(d)) to any qualified sale, lease, or other distribution of export property by the DISC (or with respect to which the DISC received a com-

mission) will be considered to advance the sale, lease, or other distribution of export property. General and administrative expenses attributable to billing customers, other clerical functions of the DISC, or generally operating the DISC, will also be considered to advance the sale, lease, or other distribution of export property.

(ii) Where an expense or cost incurred or treated as incurred by the DISC qualifies only in part as an export promotion expense, such expense or cost must be allocated between the qualified portion and such other portion on a reasonable basis. See § 1.994-2(b)(2) for the option of the related supplier not to claim expenses as export promotion expenses.

(2) *Types of expenses.*—The only expenses or costs which may be export promotion expenses are those expenses or costs meeting the test of subparagraph (1) of this paragraph which constitute—

(i) Ordinary and necessary expenses of the DISC paid or incurred during the DISC's taxable year in carrying on any trade or business, allowable as deductions under section 162, such as expenses for market studies, advertising, salaries and wages (including contributions or compensations deductible under section 404) of sales, clerical, and other personnel, rentals on property, sales commissions, warehousing, and other selling expenses,

(ii) A reasonable allowance under section 167 for exhaustion, wear and tear, or obsolescence of the property of the DISC,

(iii) Costs of freight (subject to the limitations of subparagraph (4) of this paragraph),

(iv) Costs of packaging for export (as defined in subparagraph (5) of this paragraph), or

(v) Costs of designing and labeling packages exclusively for export markets (under subparagraph (6) of this paragraph).

(3) *Ineligible expenses.*—Items ineligible to be export promotion expenses include, for example, interest expenses, bad debt expenses, freight insurance, State and local income and franchise taxes, the cost of manufacture or assembly operations, and items of cost of goods sold (except as otherwise provided in this paragraph in the case of certain freight, packaging, and designing and labeling expenses). Income or similar taxes eligible for a foreign tax credit under sections 901 and 903 are also not eligible to be export promotion expenses.

(4) *Freight expenses.*—(i) *In general.*—Export promotion expenses include one-half of the freight expense (not including insurance) for shipping export property aboard a United States flag carrier in those cases where law or regulation of the United States or of any State or political subdivision thereof or of any agency or instrumentality of any of these does not require that the export property be shipped aboard a United States flag carrier. For purposes of this

paragraph, the term "freight expense" includes charges paid for C.O.D. service, miscellaneous ground charges, such as charges incurred for services normally performed by United States flag carriers, charges for services of loading aboard United States flag carriers normally performed by such carriers, freight forwarders, or independent contractors engaged in loading property, and charges attributable to a freight consolidation function normally performed by freight forwarders. In order for one-half of freight expenses paid to the owner (or the agent of the owner) of a United States flag carrier to be claimed as an export promotion expense, the DISC must obtain a written statement (such as, for example, a bill of lading) from the owner (or the agent) disclosing that the export property was shipped aboard the owner's United States flag carrier or another United States flag carrier, and the DISC must have no reasonable basis for disbelieving such statement of the owner (or the agent). For the requirement of a written statement from a freight forwarder, see subdivision (iv) of this subparagraph.

(ii) *U.S.-flag carrier defined.*—For purposes of this paragraph, the term "U.S.-flag carrier" is an airplane owned and operated by a U.S. person or persons (as defined in section 7701(a)(30)) or a ship documented under the laws of the United States. Shipment initiated by delivery to the U.S. Postal Service shall be considered shipment aboard a U.S.-flag carrier, but not if shipped to a place to which mail shipments from the United States are ordinarily accomplished by land transportation, such as to Canada or Mexico, unless airmail is specified.

(iii) *Shipment pursuant to law or regulation.*—Shipment pursuant to law or regulation includes instances where a U.S.-flag carrier must be used in order to obtain permission from the Government to make the export. If the law or regulation requires a fixed portion of the export property to be shipped aboard a U.S.-flag carrier, the freight expense on that portion of such export property that was so shipped in order to satisfy such requirement cannot qualify as an export promotion expense.

(iv) *Freight forwarders.*—A payment to a freight forwarder shall be considered freight expense within the meaning of this paragraph to the extent the forwarder utilizes a United States flag carrier. For purposes of this paragraph, the term "freight forwarder" includes air freight consolidators and carriers owned and operated by United States persons utilizing United States flag carriers such as non-vessel-owning common carriers. In order for one-half of freight expenses paid to a freight forwarder to be claimed as export promotion expenses, the DISC must obtain a written statement (such as, for example, a bill of lading) from the freight forwarder that the export property was shipped aboard a United States flag carrier, and the DISC must have no reasonable basis for disbelieving such statements of the freight forwarder.

(v) *Freight within the United States.*—A DISC may not claim as export promotion expense any amount that is attributable to carriage of export property between points within the United States. If, however, export property is carried from the United States to a foreign country on a through shipment pursuant to a single bill of lading or similar document aboard one or more United States flag carriers, the freight expense of such carriage shall not be apportioned between the domestic and foreign portions of such carriage, even though a carrier may stop en route within the United States or the export property may be shifted from one carrier to another, and one-half of such freight expense may be claimed as an export promotion expense. Freight expense does not include the cost of transporting the export property to the depot of the United States flag carrier or freight forwarder for shipment abroad. The expense of shipment of export property initiated by delivery to the United States Postal Service for ultimate delivery outside the United States shall be considered as attributable entirely to carriage of such property outside the United States.

(5) *Packaging for export.*—(i) Export promotion expenses include the direct and indirect cost of packaging export property (including the cost of the package) for export whether or not the packaging is the same as domestic packaging. Such packaging costs do not include costs of manufacturing (as defined in the regulations under section 993) and assembly. Thus, if a DISC buys and packages export property for resale, its costs of packaging the export property are export promotion expenses. If, however, the process of such packaging by the DISC is physically integrated with the process of manufacturing the export property by the related supplier, the costs of such packaging are not export promotion expenses.

(ii) The cost of containers leased from a shipping company to which the DISC also pays freight for the property packaged is not a cost of packaging. However, in such circumstances, one-half of the rental charge may be allowable as a freight expense if permitted under subparagraph (4) of this paragraph.

(6) *Designing and labeling packages.*—Export promotion expenses include the direct and indirect costs of designing and labeling packages, including bottles, cans, jars, boxes, cartons, or containers, to the extent incurred for export markets. Thus, for example, to the extent incurred for supplying export markets, the cost of designing labels in a foreign language and the cost of printing such labels are export promotion expenses.

Reg. § 1.994-1(f)(6)

(7) *DISC must incur export promotion expenses.*—(i) *In general.*—In order for an expense to be an export promotion expense it must be incurred or treated as incurred under this subparagraph by the DISC. For example, an expense is incurred by a DISC if the expense results from (*a*) the DISC incurring an obligation to pay compensation to its employees, (*b*) depreciation of property owned by the DISC and used by its employees, (*c*) the DISC incurring an obligation to pay for office supplies used by its employees, (*d*) the DISC incurring an obligation to pay space costs for use by its employees, or (*e*) the DISC incurring an obligation to pay other costs supporting efforts by its employees.

(ii) *Payments to independent contractors.*— A payment to an independent contractor, directly or indirectly, is treated as incurred by the DISC if the cost of performing the function performed by the independent contractor would be considered an export promotion expense described in subparagraphs (1) and (2) of this paragraph if performed by the DISC, and if, in a case where the services of the independent contractor were engaged by a party related to the DISC, such related party and such DISC agreed in writing before the contract was entered into that a specified portion or all of the contract was for the benefit of the DISC and that all of the expenses of the contract (eligible to be considered as export promotion expenses) with respect to such portion would be borne by the DISC.

(iii) *Expenses incurred by related parties.*— Reimbursements or other payments by a DISC to a related party are export promotion expenses only if the expenses of the related person for which reimbursement is made are for space in a building actually used by employees of the DISC or for export property owned by the DISC. Except as otherwise provided in the preceding sentence, expenses incurred by a foreign international sales corporation (FISC) or a real property holding company (as defined in section 993(e)(1) and (2), respectively) shall not be treated as export promotion expenses of its DISC.

(iv) *Selling commissions paid by a DISC.*—A commission paid by a DISC to a person other than a related person, with respect to a transaction which gives rise to qualified export receipts of the DISC, is an export promotion expense of the DISC. A commission paid by a DISC to a related person is not an export promotion expense.

(v) *Sales of promotional material.*—If a DISC sells promotional material to a buyer of export property from the DISC at a price which is greater than the costs of the DISC for such material, such costs are not export promotion expenses. If, however, the DISC sells promotional material at a price which is less than its costs for such material, the excess of such costs over such price is an export promotion expense. For rules relating to the status of promotional material as qualified export assets and export property, see § 1.993-2 and § 1.993-3, respectively.

(vi) An expense may be incurred by the DISC under subdivisions (i) through (v) of this subparagraph even if the accounting for and payment of such expense is handled by a related party and the DISC reimburses the related party for such expenses.

(8) *Incomplete transactions.*—Expenses eligible to be treated as export promotion expenses which are attributable to the sale, lease, or other distribution of export property and which are incurred prior to the taxable year of sale, lease, or other distribution by the DISC are not treated as export promotion expenses until the taxable year of sale, lease, or other distribution or until the taxable year in which it is first determined that no transaction is reasonably expected to result from the expense incurred (whether or not a transaction subsequently results). Thus, for example, if a DISC incurs a packaging cost which is otherwise eligible to be treated as an export promotion expense, the DISC may not include such charge as an export promotion expense until the year in which the export property with respect to which the packaging cost was incurred is actually sold by the DISC. If no transaction is reasonably expected to result from the packaging cost, such cost should be allocated as an export promotion expense to the group of transactions to which such cost is most closely related.

(g) *Examples.*—The provisions of this section may be illustrated by the following examples:

Example (1). J and K are calendar year taxpayers. J, a domestic manufacturing company, owns all the stock of K, a DISC for the taxable year. During 1972, J manufactures only 100 units of a product (which is eligible to be export property as defined in section 993(c)). J enters into a written agreement with K whereby K is granted a sales franchise with respect to exporting such property and K will receive commissions with respect to such exports equal to the maximum amount permitted to be received under the intercompany pricing rules of section 994. Thereafter, the 100 units are sold for $1,000. J's cost of goods sold attributable to the 100 units is $650. J's direct selling expenses so attributable are $100. Although J has other deductible expenses, for purposes of this example assume that J has no other deductible expenses. K pays $230 to independent contractors which qualify as export promotion expenses under paragraph (f)(7)(ii) of this section. K does not perform functions substantial enough to entitle it to an allocation of income which meets the arm's length standard of section 482. The income which K may earn under section 994 under the franchise is $20, computed as follows:

(1) Combined taxable income:

(a) K's sales price	$1,000

(b) Less deductions:

J's cost of goods sold	$650
J's direct selling expenses	100
K's export promotion expenses .	230
Total deductions	980
(c) Combined taxable income	20

(2) K's profit under combined taxable income method (before application of loss limitation):

(a) 50 percent of combined taxable income	$10
(b) Plus: 10 percent of K's export promotion expenses (10% of $230) .	23
(c) K's profit.	33

(3) K's profit under gross receipts method (before application of loss limitation):

(a) 4 percent of K's sales price (4% of $1,000)	$40
(b) Plus: 10 percent of K's export promotion expenses (10% of $230) .	23
(c) K's profit.	63

Since combined taxable income ($20) is lower than both K's profit under the combined taxable income method ($33) and under the gross receipts method ($63), the maximum income K may earn is $20. Accordingly, the commissions K may receive from J are $250, i.e., K's expenses ($230) plus K's profit ($20).

Example (2). M and N are calendar year taxpayers. M, a domestic manufacturing company, owns all the stock of N, a DISC for the taxable year. During 1972, M produces and sells a particular product line of export property to N for $75, a price which can be justified as satisfying the standard of arm's length price of section 482. N performs substantial functions with respect to the transaction and resells the export property for $100. M's cost of goods sold attributable to the export property is $60. M's direct selling expenses so attributable (relating to advertising of the product line in foreign markets) are $12. Although M has other deductible expenses, for purposes of this example, assume that M has no other deductible expenses. N's expenses attributable to resale of the export property are $22 of which $20 are export promotion expenses. The maximum profit which N may earn with respect to the product line is $6, computed as follows:

(1) Combined taxable income:

(a) N's sales price	$100

(b) Less deductions:

M's cost of goods sold	60
M's direct selling expenses	12
N's expenses	22
Total deductions	94
(c) Combined taxable income	6

(2) N's profit under combined taxable income method (before application of loss limitation):

(a) 50 percent of combined taxable income	3
(b) Plus: 10 percent of N's export promotion expenses (10% of $20)	2
(c) N's profit	5

(3) N's profit under gross receipts method (before application of loss limitation):

(a) 4 percent of N's sales price (4% of $100)	4
(b) Plus: 10 percent of N's export promotion expenses (10% of $20)	2
(c) N's profit	6

(4) N's profit under section 482 method:

(a) N's sales price	100

(b) Less deductions:

N's cost of goods sold (price paid by N to M)	75
N's expenses	22
Total deductions	97
(c) N's profit	3

Since the gross receipts method results in greater profit to N ($6) than does the combined taxable income method ($5) or section 482 method ($3), and does not exceed combined taxable income ($6), N may earn a maximum profit of $6. Accordingly, the transfer price from M to

N may be readjusted as long as the transfer price is not readjusted below $72, computed as follows:

(5) Transfer price from M to N:

(a) N's sales price	$100
(b) Less:	
N's expenses	22
N's profit	6
Total subtractions	28
(c) Transfer price	72

Example (3). Q and R are calendar year taxpayers. Q, a domestic manufacturing company, owns all the stock of R, a DISC for the taxable year. During 1972, Q produces and sells a product line of export property to R for $170, a price which can be justified as satisfying the standards of arm's length price of section 482, and R resells the export property for $200. Q's cost of goods sold attributable to the export property is $115 so that the combined gross income from the sale of the export property is $85 (*i.e.*, $200 minus $115). Q's expenses incurred in connection with the property sold are $35. Q's deductible overhead and other supportive expenses allocable to all gross income are $6. Apportionment of these supportive expenses on the basis of gross income does not result in a material distortion of income and is a reasonable method of apportionment. Q's gross income from sources other than the transaction is $170 making total gross income of Q and R (excluding the transfer price paid by R) $255 (*i.e.*, $85 plus $170). R's expenses attributable to resale of the export property are $20, all of which are export promotion expenses. The maximum profit which R may earn with respect to the product line is $16, computed as follows:

(1) Combined taxable income:

(a) R's sales price		$200
(b) Less deductions:		
(i) Q's cost of goods sold	$115	
(ii) Q's expenses incurred in connection with the property sold	35	
(iii) Apportionment of Q's supportive expenses:		
Q's supportive expenses	$6	
Combined gross income from sale of export property	85	
Total gross income of Q and R	255	
Apportionment	(6×85)/255	2
(iv) R's expenses		20
Total deductions		172
(c) Combined taxable income		$28

(2) R's profit under combined taxable income method (before application of loss limitation):

(a) 50 percent of combined taxable income	$14
(b) Plus: 10 percent of R's export promotion expenses (10% of $20)	2
(c) R's profit	$16

(3) R's profit under gross receipts method (before application of loss limitation):

(a) 4 percent of R's sales price (4% of $200)	$8
(b) Plus: 10 percent of R's export promotion expenses (10% of $20)	2
(c) R's profit	$10

(4) R's profit under section 482 method:

(a) R's sales price		$200
(b) Less deductions:		
R's cost of goods sold (price paid by R to Q)	$170	
R's expenses	20	
Total deductions		$190
(c) R's profit		$10

Since the combined taxable income method results in greater profit to R ($16) than does the gross receipts method ($10) or section 482 method ($10), and does not exceed combined taxable income ($28), R may earn a maximum profit of $16. Accordingly, the transfer price from Q to R may be readjusted as long as the transfer price is not readjusted below $164 computed as follows:

(5) Transfer price from Q to R:

(a) R's sales price		$200
(b) Less: R's expenses	$20	
R's profit	16	
		36
(c) Transfer price		$164

Example (4). S and T are calendar year taxpayers. S, a domestic manufacturing company, owns all the stock of T, a DISC for the taxable year. During 1972, S produces and sells 100 units of a particular product to T under a written agreement which provides that the transfer price between S and T shall be that price which allocates to T the maximum permitted to be received under the intercompany pricing rules of section 994. Thereafter, the 100 units are sold by T for $950. S's cost of goods sold attributable to the 100 units is $650. S's other deductible expenses so attributable are $300. Although S has other deductible expenses, for purposes of this example, assume that S has no deductible expenses not definitely allocable to any item of gross income. T's expenses attributable to the resale of the 100 units are $50. S chooses not to apply the section 482 method. T may not earn any income under the gross receipts or combined taxable income method with respect to resale of the 100 units because combined taxable income is a negative figure, computed as follows:

(1) Combined taxable income:

(a) T's sales price		$950
(b) Less deductions:		
S's cost of goods sold	$650	
S's expenses	300	
T's expenses	50	
Total deductions		1,000
(c) Combined taxable income (loss)		($50)

Under paragraph (e)(1)(i) of this section, T is permitted to recover its expenses attributable to the 100 units ($50) even though such recovery results in a loss or increased loss to the related supplier. Accordingly, the transfer price from S to T may be readjusted as long as the transfer price is not readjusted below $900, computed as follows:

(2) Transfer price from S to T:

(a) T's sales price		$950
(b) Less: T's expenses		50
(c) Transfer price		$900

Example (5). Assume the same facts as in example (4) except that S chooses to apply the section 482 method and that under arm's length dealings T would have derived $10 of income. Accordingly, the transfer price from S to T may be set at an amount not less than $890, computed as follows:

(1) Transfer price from S to T:

(a) T's sales price		$950
(b) Less: T's expenses	$50	
T's profit	10	
Total deductions		60
(c) Transfer price		$890

Example (6). X and Y are calendar year taxpayers. X, a domestic manufacturing company, owns all the stock of Y, a DISC for the taxable year. During March 1972, X manufactures a particular product of export property which it leases on April 1, 1972, to Y for a term of 1 year at a monthly rental of $1,000, a rent which satisfies the standard of arm's length rental under section 482. Y subleases the product on April 1, 1972, for a term of 1 year at a monthly rental of $1,200. X's cost for the product leased is $40,000. X's other deductible expenses attributable to the product are $900, all of which are incurred in 1972. Although X has other deductible expenses, for purposes of this example, assume that X has no other deductible expenses. Y's expenses attributable to sublease of the export property are $450, all of which are incurred in 1972 and are export promotion expenses. X depreciates the property on a straight line basis without the use of an averaging convention, assuming a useful life of 8 years and no salvage value. The profit which Y may earn with respect to the transaction is $2,895 for 1972 and $1,175 for 1973, computed as follows:

COMPUTATION FOR 1972

(1) Combined taxable income:

(a) Y's sublease rental receipts for year ($1,200 × 9 months) $10,800

(b) Less deductions:

X's depreciation ($40,000 × $\frac{1}{8}$ × 9/12)	3,750
X's other expenses	900
Y's expenses	450
Total deductions	5,100
(c) Combined taxable income	$ 5,700

(2) Y's profit under combined taxable income method (before application of loss limitation):

(a) 50 percent of combined taxable income	$ 2,850
(b) Plus: 10 percent of Y's export promotion expenses (10% of $450)	45
(c) Y's profit	2,895

(3) Y's profit under gross receipts method (before application of loss limitation):

(a) 4 percent of Y's sublease rental receipts for year (4% of $10,800)	$ 432
(b) Plus: 10 percent of Y's export promotion expenses (10% of $450)	45
(c) Y's profit	477

(4) Y's profit under section 482 method:

(a) Y's sublease rental receipts for year $10,800

(b) Less deductions:

Y's lease rental payments for year	9,000
Y's expenses	450
Total deductions	9,450
(c) Y's profit	1,350

Since the combined taxable income method results in greater profit to Y ($2,895) than does the gross receipts method ($477) or section 482 method ($1,350), Y may earn a profit of $2,895 for 1971. Accordingly, the monthly rental payable by Y to X for 1972 may be readjusted as long as the monthly rental payable is not readjusted below $828.33, computed as follows:

(5) Monthly rental payable by Y to X for 1972:

(a) Y's sublease rental receipts for year $10,800.00

(b) Less:

Y's expenses	450.00
Y's profit	2,895.00
Total	3,345.00
(c) Rental payable for 1972	7,455.00
(d) Rental payable each month ($7,455 ÷ 9 months)	828.33

COMPUTATION FOR 1973

(1) Combined taxable income:

(a) Y's sublease rental receipts for year ($1,200 × 3 months)	$3,600
(b) Less: X's depreciation ($40,000 × $\frac{1}{8}$ × 3/12)	1,250
(c) Combined taxable income	2,350

(2) Y's profit under combined taxable income method (before application of loss limitation):

(a) 50 percent of combined taxable income	$1,175
(b) Y's profit	1,175

(3) Y's profit under gross receipts method (before application of loss limitation):

(a) 4 percent of Y's sublease rental receipts for year (4% of $3,600)	144
(b) Y's profit	$144

(4) Y's profit under section 482 method:

(a) Y's sublease rental receipts for year	$3,600
(b) Less: Y's lease rental payments for year	3,000
(c) Y's profit	$600

Since the combined taxable income method results in greater profit to Y ($1,175) than does the gross receipts method ($144) or section 482 method ($600), Y may earn a profit of $1,175 for 1973. Accordingly, the monthly rental payable by Y to X for 1973 may be readjusted as long as the monthly rental payable is not readjusted below $808.33, computed as follows:

(5) Monthly rental payable by Y to X for 1973:

(a) Y's sublease rental receipts for year	$3,600.00
(b) Less: Y's profit	1,175.00
(c) Rental payable for 1973	2,425.00
(d) Rental payable for each month ($2,425 ÷ 3 months)	$808.33

[Reg. § 1.994-1.]

☐ [*T.D. 7364, 7-15-75. Amended by T.D. 7435, 9-29-76, T.D. 7854, 11-6-82 and T.D. 7984, 10-11-84.*]

[Reg. § 1.994-2]

§ 1.994-2. Marginal costing rules.—(a) *In general.*—This section prescribes the marginal costing rules authorized by section 994(b)(2). If under paragraph (c)(1) of this section a DISC is treated for its taxable year as seeking to establish or maintain a foreign market for sales of an item, product, or product line of export property (as defined in § 1.993-3) from which qualified export receipts are derived, the marginal costing rules prescribed in paragraph (b) of this section may be applied to allocate costs between gross receipts derived from such sales and other gross receipts for purposes of computing, under the "50-50" combined taxable income method of § 1.994-1(c)(3), the combined taxable income of the DISC and related supplier derived from such sales. Such marginal costing rules may be applied whether or not the related supplier manufactures, produces, grows, or extracts (within the meaning of § 1.993-3(c)) the export property sold. Such marginal costing rules do not apply to sales of export property which in the hands of a purchaser related under section 954(d)(3) to the seller give rise to foreign base company sales income as described in section 954(d) unless, for the purchaser's year in which it resells the export property, section 954(b)(3)(A) is applicable or such income is under the exceptions in section 954(b)(4). Such marginal costing rules do not apply to leases of property or the performance of any services whether or not related and subsidiary services (as defined in § 1.994-1(b)(3)).

(b) *Marginal costing rules for allocations of costs.*—(1) *In general.*—Marginal costing is a method under which only marginal or variable costs of producing and selling a particular item, product, or product line are taken into account for purposes of section 994. Where this section is applicable, costs attributable to deriving qualified export receipts for the DISC's taxable year from sales of an item, product, or product line may be determined in any manner the related supplier (as defined in § 1.994-1(a)(3)(ii)) chooses, provided that the requirements of both subparagraphs (2) and (3) of this paragraph are met.

(2) *Variable costs taken into account.*—There are taken into account in computing the combined taxable income of the DISC and its related supplier from sales of an item, product, or product line the following costs: (i) Direct production costs (as defined in § 1.471-11(b)(2)(i)) and (ii) costs which are export promotion expenses, but only if they are claimed as export promotion expenses in determining taxable income derived by the DISC under the combined taxable income method of § 1.994-1(c)(3). At the taxpayer's option, all, a part, or none of the costs which qualify as export promotion expenses may be so claimed as export promotion expenses.

(3) *Overall profit percentage limitation.*—As a result of such determination of costs attributable to such qualified export receipts for the DISC's taxable year, the combined taxable income of the DISC and its related supplier from sales of such item, product, or product line for the DISC's taxable year does not exceed gross receipts (determined under § 1.993-6) of the DISC derived from such sales, multiplied by the overall profit percentage (determined under paragraph (c)(2) of this section).

(c) *Definitions.*—(1) *Establishing or maintaining a foreign market.*—A DISC shall be treated for its taxable year as seeking to establish or maintain a foreign market with respect to sales of an item, product, or product line of export property from which qualified export receipts are derived if the combined taxable income computed under paragraph (b) of this section is greater than the combined taxable income computed under § 1.994-1(c)(6).

(2) *Overall profit percentage.*—(i) For purposes of this section, the overall profit percentage for a taxable year of the DISC for a product or product line is the percentage which—

(a) The combined taxable income of the DISC and its related supplier plus all other taxable income of its related supplier from all sales (domestic and foreign) of such product or product line during the DISC's taxable year, computed under the full costing method, is of

(b) The total gross receipts (determined under § 1.993-6) from all such sales.

(ii) At the annual option of the related supplier, the overall profit percentage for the DISC's taxable year for all products and product lines may be determined by aggregating the amounts described in subdivision (i)(a) and (b) of this subparagraph of the DISC, and all domestic members of the controlled group (as defined in § 1.993-1(k)) of which the DISC is a member, for the DISC's taxable year and for taxable years of such members ending with or within the DISC's taxable year.

(iii) For purposes of determining the amounts in subdivisions (i)(b) and (ii) of this subparagraph, a sale of property between a DISC and its related supplier or between domestic members of the controlled group shall be taken into account only during the DISC's taxable year (or taxable year of the member ending within the DISC's taxable year) during which the property is ultimately sold to a person which is neither the DISC nor such a domestic member.

(3) *Grouping of transactions.*—(i) In general, for purposes of this section, an item, product, or product line is the item or group consisting of the product or product line pursuant to § 1.994-1(c)(7) used by the taxpayer for purposes of applying the intercompany pricing rules of § 1.994-1.

(ii) However, for purposes of determining the overall profit percentage under subparagraph (2) of this paragraph, any product or product line grouping permissible under § 1.994-1(c)(7) may be used at the annual choice of the taxpayer, even though it may not be the same item or grouping referred to in subdivision (i) of this subparagraph, as long as the grouping chosen for determining the overall profit percentage is at least as broad as the grouping referred to in such subdivision (i).

(4) *Full costing method.*—For purposes of this section, the term "full costing method" is the method for determining combined taxable income set forth in § 1.994-1(c)(6).

(d) *Application of limitation on DISC income ("no loss" rule).*—If the marginal costing rules of this section are applied, the combined taxable income method of § 1.994-1(c)(3) may not be applied to cause in any taxable year a loss to the related supplier, but such method may be applied to the extent it does not cause a loss. For purposes of the preceding sentence, a loss to a related supplier would result if the taxable income of the DISC would exceed the combined taxable income of the related supplier and the DISC determined in accordance with paragraph (b) of this section. If, however, there is no combined taxable income (so determined), see the last sentence of § 1.994-1(e)(1)(i).

(e) *Examples.*—The provisions of this section may be illustrated by the following examples:

Example (1). X and Y are calendar year taxpayers. X, a domestic manufacturing company, owns all the stock of Y, a DISC for the taxable year. During 1973, X manufactures a product line which is eligible to be export property (as defined in § 1.993-3). X enters into a written agreement with Y whereby Y is granted a sales franchise with respect to exporting such product line from which qualified export receipts will be derived and Y will receive commissions with respect to such exports equal to the maximum amount permitted to be received under the intercompany pricing rules of section 994. Commissions are computed using the combined taxable income method under § 1.994-1(c)(3). For purposes of applying the combined taxable income method, X and Y compute their combined taxable income attributable to the product line of export property under the marginal costing rules in accordance with the additional facts assumed in the table below:

(1) Maximum combined taxable income (determined under paragraph (b)(2) of this section):

(a) Y's gross receipts from export sales	$95.00
(b) Less:	
(i) Direct materials	40.00
(ii) Direct labor	20.00
(iii) Y's export promotion expenses claimed in determining Y's DISC taxable income	$ 5.00
(iv) Total deductions	65.00
(c) Maximum combined taxable income	30.00

(2) Overall profit percentage limitation (determined under paragraph (b)(3) of this section):

(a) Gross receipts of X and Y from all domestic and foreign sales	400.00
(b) Less deductions:	
(i) Direct materials	160.00
(ii) Direct labor	80.00

(iii) Other costs (of which $8 are costs of the DISC including $5 of export promotion expenses claimed in determining Y's taxable income) 40.00

(c) Total deductions 280.00

(d) Total taxable income from all sales computed on a full costing method . 120.00

(e) Overall profit percentage (line (d) ($120) divided by line (a) ($400)) (percent) 30

(f) Multiply by gross receipts from Y's export sales (line (1)(a)) .... $ 95.00

(g) Overall profit percentage limitation 28.50

Since the overall profit percentage limitation under line (2)(g) ($28.50) is less than the maximum combined taxable income under line (1)(c) ($30), combined taxable income under marginal costing is limited to $28.50. Since under the franchise agreement Y is to earn the maximum commission permitted under the intercompany pricing rules of section 994, combined taxable income on the transactions is $28.50. Accordingly, the costs attributable to export sales (other than for direct material, direct labor, and export promotion expenses) are $1.50, i.e., line (1)(c) ($30) minus line (2)(g) ($28.50). Under the combined taxable income method of § 1.994-1(c)(3), Y will have taxable income attributable to the sales of $14.75, i.e., the sum of $1/2$ of combined taxable income ($1/2$ of $28.50) and 10 percent of Y's export promotion expenses claimed in determining Y's taxable income (10 percent of $5). Accordingly, the commissions Y receives from X are $22.75, i.e., Y's costs ($8, see line (2)(b)(iii)) plus Y's profit ($14.75).

Example (2). (1) Assume the same facts as in example (1), except that gross receipts from export sales are only $85 and gross receipts from all sales remain at $400. For purposes of applying the combined taxable income method, X and Y may compute their combined taxable income attributable to the product line of export property under the marginal costing rules as follows:

(1) Maximum combined taxable income (determined under paragraph (b)(2) of this section):

(a) Y's gross receipts from export sales $85.00

(b) Less:
  (i) Direct materials $40.00
  (ii) Direct labor 20.00
  (iii) Y's export promotion expenses claimed in determining Y's taxable income 5.00
  (iv) Total deductions 65.00

(c) Maximum combined taxable income 20.00

(2) Overall profit percentage limitation (determined under paragraph (b)(3) of this section):

(a) Gross receipts from Y's export sales (line (1)(a)) 85.00

(b) Multiply by overall profit percentage (as determined in example (1)) (percent) 30

(c) Overall profit percentage limitation 25.50

Since maximum combined taxable income under line (1)(c) ($20) is less than the overall profit percentage limitation under line (2)(c) ($25.50), combined taxable income under marginal costing is limited to $20. Since under the franchise agreement Y is to earn the maximum commission permitted under the intercompany pricing rules of section 994, combined taxable income on the transactions is $20. Accordingly, no costs (other than for direct material, direct labor, and export promotion expenses) will be attributed to export sales. Under the combined taxable income method of § 1.994-1(c)(3), Y will have taxable income attributable to the sales of $10.50, i.e., the sum of $1/2$ of combined taxable income ($1/2$ of $20) and 10 percent of Y's export promotion expenses claimed in determining Y's taxable income (10 percent of $5). Accordingly, the Commissions Y receives from X are $18.50, i.e., Y's costs ($8, see line (2)(b)(iii) of example (1)) plus Y's profit ($10.50).

(2) If export promotion expenses are not claimed in determining taxable income of Y under the combined taxable income method, the taxable income of Y would be increased to $12.50 and commissions payable to Y would be increased to $20.50, computed as follows:

(3) Maximum combined taxable income (determined under paragraph (b)(2) of this section):

(a) Y's gross receipts from export sales $85.00

(b) Less:
  (i) Direct materials 40.00
  (ii) Direct labor 20.00
  (iii) Total deductions 60.00

(c) Maximum combined taxable income 25.00

(4) Overall profit percentage limitation (line (2)(c)) 25.50

Since maximum combined taxable income under line (3)(c) ($25) is less than the overall profit percentage under line (4) ($25.50), combined taxable income under marginal costing is limited to $25. Since under the franchise agreement Y is to earn the maximum commission permitted under the intercompany pricing rules of section 994, combined taxable income on the transactions is $25. Accordingly, no costs (other than for direct material and direct labor) will be attributed to export sales. Under the combined taxable income method of § 1.994-1(c)(3), Y will have taxable income attributable to the sales of $12.50, i.e., $1/2$ of combined taxable income ($1/2$ of $25). Accordingly, the commissions Y receives from X are $20.50, i.e., Y's costs ($8, see line (2)(b)(iii) of example (1)) plus Y's profit ($12.50).

Example (3). (1) Assume the same facts as in example (1), except that gross receipts from export sales are only $85, gross receipts from all sales remain at $400, and Y has costs of $40 consisting of Y's export promotion expenses of $35 and costs of $5 other than for direct material, direct labor, or export promotion expenses. For purposes of applying the combined taxable income method, X and Y may compute their combined taxable income attributable to the product line of export property under the marginal costing rules as follows:

(1) Maximum combined taxable income (determined under paragraph (b)(2) of this section):

(a) Y's gross receipts from export sales		$85.00
(b) Less:		
(i) Direct materials	40.00	
(ii) Direct labor	20.00	
(iii) Y's export promotion expenses claimed in determining Y's taxable income	35.00	
(iv) Total deductions	95.00	
(c) Maximum combined taxable income (loss)		(10.00
(2) Overall profit percentage limitation (as determined in example (2))		25.50

Since maximum combined taxable income under line (1)(c) (which is a loss of $10) is less than the overall profit percentage limitation under line (2)(c) ($25.50), combined taxable income under marginal costing is a loss of $10 and under the combined taxable income method of §1.994-1(c)(3), Y will have no taxable income or loss attributable to the sales. Accordingly, the commissions Y receives from X are $40, i.e., Y's costs ($40).

(2) If export promotion expenses are not claimed in determining Y's taxable income under the combined taxable income method, the taxable income of Y would be increased to $12.50 and commissions payable to Y would be increased to $52.50 computed as follows:

(3) Maximum combined taxable income (determined under paragraph (b)(2) of this section) (line (3)(c) of example (2))	$25.00
(4) Overall profit percentage limitation (as determined in example (2))	25.50

The results would be the same as in part (2) of example (2), except that the commissions Y receives from X are $52.50, i.e., Y's cost ($40) plus Y's profit ($12.50). [Reg. §1.994-2.]

☐ [T.D. 7364, 7-15-75.]

Reg. §1.995-1

[Reg. §1.995-1]

§1.995-1. Taxation of DISC income to shareholders.—(a) *In general.*—(1) Under §1.991-1(a), a corporation which is a DISC for a taxable year is not subject to any tax imposed by subtitle A of the Code (sections 1 through 1564) for the taxable year, except for the tax imposed by chapter 5 thereof (sections 1491 through 1494) on certain transfers to avoid tax.

(2) Under section 995(a), the shareholders of a DISC, or a former DISC, are subject to taxation on the earnings and profits of the DISC in accordance with the provisions of chapter 1 of the Code generally applicable to shareholders, but subject to the modifications provided in sections 995, 996, and 997.

(3) Under §1.996-3, three divisions of earnings and profits of a DISC, or former DISC, are defined: "accumulated DISC income", "previously taxed income", and "other earnings and profits". Under §1.995-2, certain amounts of the DISC's earnings and profits are deemed to be distributed as dividends to shareholders of the DISC at the close of the DISC's taxable year in which such earnings were derived. Such deemed distributions do not cause a reduction in the DISC's earnings and profits, but are taken into account in §1.996-3(c) as an increase in previously taxed income. To the extent the DISC's earnings and profits are paid out in a subsequent distribution which is, under §1.996-1, treated as made out of such "previously taxed income," they will not be taxable to the shareholders a second time.

(4) In general, "accumulated DISC income" is the earnings and profits of the DISC which have not been deemed distributed and which may be deferred from taxation so long as they are not actually distributed with respect to its stock. However, deferral of taxation on "accumulated DISC income" may be terminated, in whole or in part, in the event of: (i) Certain foreign investment attributable to producer's loans (see §1.995-2(a)(5) and §1.995-5); (ii) revocation of the election to be treated as a DISC or other disqualification (see §1.995-3); and (iii) certain dispositions of DISC stock in which gain is realized (see §1.995-4).

(5) Since a DISC is not taxed on its taxable income, section 246(d) and §1.246-4 provide that the deduction otherwise allowed under section 243 shall not be allowed with respect to a dividend from a DISC, or former DISC, paid or treated as paid out of accumulated DISC income or previously taxed income or with respect to a deemed distribution in a qualified year under §1.995-2(a).

(b) *Amounts and character of amounts includible in shareholder's gross income.*—Each shareholder of a corporation which is a DISC, or former DISC, shall include in his gross income—

(1) Amounts actually distributed to him that are includible in his gross income in accordance with paragraph (c) of this section,

(2) Amounts which, pursuant to §1.995-2, he is deemed to receive as a distribution taxable as a dividend on the last day of each of the corporation's taxable years for which it qualifies as a DISC,

(3) Amounts which, pursuant to §1.995-3, he is deemed to receive as a distribution taxable as a dividend in the event the corporation revokes its election to be treated as a DISC or otherwise is disqualified as a DISC, and

(4) Gain realized on certain dispositions of stock in the corporation which, under §1.995-4, is includible in his gross income as a dividend.

(c) *Treatment of actual distributions.*—(1) Except as provided in subparagraph (3) of this paragraph, amounts actually distributed to a shareholder of a DISC, or former DISC, with respect to his stock are includible in his gross income in accordance with section 301.

(2) Since a deemed distribution does not reduce the earnings and profits of a DISC, it does not affect the determination as to whether a subsequent actual distribution is a "dividend" under section 316(a). Since, however, the amount of a deemed distribution increases "previously taxed income", it does affect the determination as to whether a subsequent actual distribution is excluded (as described in subparagraph (3) of this paragraph) from gross income.

(3) Under §1.996-1(c), the amount of any actual distribution (including a deficiency distribution made pursuant to §1.992-3), with respect to stock in a DISC, or former DISC, which is treated under §1.996-1 as made out of previously taxed income, is excluded by the distributee from gross income, but only to the extent that such amount does not exceed the adjusted basis of the distributee's stock. Under §1.996-5(b), that portion of any actual distribution which is treated as made out of previously taxed income shall be applied against and reduce the adjusted basis of the stock and, to the extent that it exceeds the adjusted basis of the stock, it shall be treated as gain from the sale or exchange of property.

(4) A deficiency distribution pursuant to §1.992-3 may be made after the close of the DISC's taxable year with respect to which it is made. The determinations as to whether such deficiency distribution is a dividend under section 301 and as to which division of earnings and profits is the source thereof depend upon the status of the DISC's earnings and profits account and divisions thereof at the time the distribution is actually made. See §1.996-1(d) for the priority of such deficiency distribution over other actual distributions made during the same taxable year.

(d) *Personal holding company income.*—(1) Any amount includible in a shareholder's gross income as a dividend with respect to the stock of a DISC, or former DISC, pursuant to paragraph (b) of this section shall be treated as a dividend for all purposes of the Code, except that for purposes of determining whether such shareholder is a personal holding company within the meaning of section 542 any amount deemed distributed for qualified years under §1.995-2 or upon disqualification under §1.995-3, any amount of gain on certain dispositions of DISC stock to which §1.995-4 applies, and any amount treated under §1.996-1 as distributed out of accumulated DISC income or previously taxed income shall not be treated as a dividend or any other kind of income described in section 543(a).

(2) Notwithstanding subparagraph (1) of this paragraph, the shareholder may treat as an item of income described under section 543 (for example, rents) any amount to which the exception in such subparagraph (1) applies, if it establishes to the satisfaction of the district director that such amount is attributable to earnings and profits derived from such item of income. [Reg. §1.995-1.]

☐ [T.D. 7324, 9-27-74.]

[Reg. §1.995-2]

§1.995-2. Deemed distributions in qualified years.—(a) *General rule.*—Under section 995(b)(1), each shareholder of a DISC shall be treated as having received a distribution taxable as a dividend with respect to his stock on the last day of each taxable year of the DISC, in an amount which is equal to his pro rata share of the sum (as limited by paragraph (b) of this section), of the following seven items:

(1) An amount equal to the gross interest derived by the DISC during such year from producer's loans (as defined in §1.993-4).

(2) An amount equal to the lower of—

(i) Any gain recognized by the DISC during such year on the sale or exchange of property (other than property which in the hands of the DISC is a qualified export asset) which was previously transferred to it in a transaction in which the transferor realized gain which was not recognized in whole or in part, or

(ii) The amount of the transferor's gain which was not recognized on the previous transfer of the property to the DISC.

For purposes of this subparagraph, each item of property shall be considered separately. See paragraph (d) of this section for special rules with respect to certain tax-free acquisitions of property by the DISC.

(3) An amount equal to the lower of—

(i) Any gain recognized by the DISC during such year on the sale or exchange of property which in the hands of the DISC is a qualified export asset (other than stock in trade or property described in section 1221(1)) and which was previously transferred to the DISC in a transaction in which the transferor realized gain which was not recognized in whole or in part, or

(ii) The amount of the transferor's gain which was not recognized on the previous transfer of the property to the DISC and which would have been includible in the transferor's gross income as ordinary income if its entire realized gain had been recognized upon the transfer.

For purposes of this subparagraph, each item of property shall be considered separately. See paragraph (d) of this section for special rules with respect to certain tax-free acquisitions of property by the DISC.

(4) For taxable years beginning after December 31, 1975, an amount equal to 50 percent of the taxable income of the DISC for the taxable years attributable to military property (as defined in §1.995-6).

(5) For taxable years beginning after December 31, 1975, the taxable income for the taxable year attributable to base period export gross receipts (as defined in §1.995-7).

(6) The sum of—

(i)(A) In the case of a corporate shareholder, an amount equal to 57.5 percent of the excess (if any) (one-half for DISCs' taxable years beginning before January 1, 1983) of the taxable income of the DISC for such year (computed as provided in §1.991-1(b)(1)) over the sum of the amounts deemed distributed for the taxable year in accordance with subparagraph (1), (2), (3), (4) and (5) of this paragraph, or

(B) In the case of a non-corporate shareholder, an amount equal to one-half of the excess (if any) of the taxable income of the DISC for such year (computed as provided in §1.991-1(b)(1)) over the sum of the amounts deemed distributed for the taxable year in accordance with subparagraphs (1), (2), (3), (4), and (5) of this paragraph.

(ii)(A) An amount equal to the amount under subdivision (i) of paragraph (a)(6) of this section multiplied by the international boycott factor as determined under section 999(c)(1), or

(B) In lieu of the amount determined under subdivision (ii)(A) of paragraph (a)(6) of this section, the amount described under section 999(c)(2) of such international boycott income, and

(iii) An amount equal to the sum of any illegal bribes, kickbacks, or other payments paid by or on behalf of the DISC directly or indirectly to an official, employee, or agent in fact of a government. An amount is paid by a DISC where it is paid by any officer, director, employee, shareholder, or agent of the DISC for the benefit of such DISC. For purposes of this section, the principles of section 162(c) and the regulations thereunder shall apply. The fair market value of an illegal payment made in the form of property or services shall be considered the amount of such illegal payment.

(7) The amount of foreign investment attributable to producer's loans of the DISC, as of the close of the "group taxable year" ending with such taxable year of the DISC, determined in accordance with §1.995-5. The amount of such foreign investment attributable to producer's loans so determined for any taxable year of a former DISC shall be deemed distributed as a dividend to the shareholders of such former DISC on the last day of such taxable year. See §1.995-3(e) for the effect that such deemed distribution has on scheduled installments of deemed distributions of accumulated DISC income under §1.995-3(a) upon disqualification.

(b) *Limitation on amount of deemed distributions under section 995(b)(1).*—(1) The sum of the amounts described in paragraph (a)(1) through (a)(6) of this section which is deemed distributed pro rata to the DISC's shareholders a dividend for any taxable year of the corporation shall not exceed the DISC's earnings and profits for such year.

(2) The amount of foreign investment attributable to producer's loans of the DISC (as described in paragraph (a)(7) of this section) which is deemed to be distributed pro rata to the DISC's shareholders as dividends for any taxable year of the corporation shall not exceed the lower of the corporation's accumulated DISC income at the beginning of such year or the corporation's accumulated earnings and profits at the beginning of such year (but not less than zero)—

(i) Increased by any DISC income of the corporation for such year as defined in §1.996-3(b)(2) (*i.e.,* any excess of the DISC's earnings and profits for such year over the sum of the amounts described in paragraph (a)(1) through (a)(6) of this section), or

(ii) Decreased by any deficit in the corporation's earnings and profits for such year.

Thus, for example, if a DISC has a deficit in accumulated earnings and profits at the beginning of a taxable year of $10,000, current earnings and profits of $12,000, no amounts described in paragraph (a)(1) through (a)(6) of this section for the year, and foreign investment attributable to producer's loans for the taxable year of $5,000, the DISC would have a deemed distribution described in paragraph (a)(7) of this section of $5,000 for the taxable year. On the other hand, suppose the DISC had accumulated earnings and profits of $13,000 at the beginning of the taxable year, accumulated DISC income of $10,000 at the beginning of the taxable year, a deficit in earnings and profits for the taxable year of $12,000, no amounts described in paragraph (a)(1) through (a)(6) of this section for the taxable year, and foreign investment attributable to producer's loans for the taxable year of $5,000. Under these facts the DISC would have no deemed distribution described in paragraph (a)(7) of this section because the corporation had no DISC income for the taxable year and the

Reg. §1.995-2(a)(3)(ii)

current year's deficit in earnings and profits subtracted from the DISC's accumulated DISC income at the beginning of the year produces a negative amount. For rules relating to the carryover to a subsequent year of the $5,000 of foreign investment attributable to producer's loans, see § 1.995-5(a)(6).

(3) If, by reason of the limitation in subparagraph (1) of this paragraph, less than the sum of the amounts described in paragraph (a)(1) through (a)(6) of this section is deemed distributed, then the portion of such sum which is deemed distributed shall be attributed first to the amount described in subparagraph (1) of such paragraph, to the extent thereof; second to the amount described in subparagraph (2) of such paragraph, to the extent thereof; third to the amount described in subparagraph (3) of such paragraph, to the extent thereof; and so forth, and finally to the amount described in paragraph (b)(6) of this paragraph.

(c) *Examples.*—Paragraphs (a) and (b) of this section may be illustrated by the following examples:

Example (1). Y is a corporation which uses the calendar year as its taxable year and which elects to be treated as a DISC beginning with 1972. X is its sole shareholder. In 1972, X transfers certain property to Y in exchange for Y's stock in a transaction in which X does not recognize gain or loss by reason of the application of section 351(a). Included in the property transferred to Y is depreciable property described in paragraph (a)(3) of this section on which X realizes, but does not recognize by reason of the application of section 1245(b)(3), a gain of $20,000. If X had sold such property for cash, the $20,000 gain would have been recognized as ordinary income under section 1245. Also included in the transfer of Y is 100 shares of stock in a third corporation (which is not a related foreign export corporation) on which X realizes, but does not recognize, a gain of $5,000. In 1973, Y sells such property and recognizes a gain of $25,000 on the depreciable property and $8,000 on the 100 shares of stock. Y has accumulated earnings and profits at the beginning of 1973 of $5,000, earnings and profits for 1973 of $72,000, and taxable income for 1973 of $100,000. At the beginning of 1973, Y has $6,000 of accumulated DISC income, no previously taxed income, and a deficit of $1,000 of other earnings and profits. Under these facts and the additional facts assumed in the table below, X is treated as having received a deemed distribution taxable as a dividend of $76,000 on December 31, 1973, determined as follows:

(1)	Gross interest derived by Y in 1973 from producer's loans	$7,000
(2)	Amount of gain on depreciable property (lower of Y's recognized gain ($25,000) or X's gain not recognized on section 1245 property ($20,000))	20,000
(3)	Amount of gain on stock (lower of X's gain not recognized ($5,000) or Y's recognized gain ($8,000))	5,000
(4)	One-half excess of taxable income for 1973 over the sum of lines (1), (2), and (3) (½ of ($100,000 minus $32,000))	34,000
(5)	Limitation on lines (1) through (4):	
(a)	Sum of lines (1) through (4) .	66,000
(b)	Earnings and profits for 1973	72,000
(c)	Lower of lines (a) and (b) . .	$66,000
(6)	Amount under paragraph (a)(5) of this section:	
(a)	Foreign investment attributable to producer's loans under § 1.995-5	10,000
(b)	Sum of the lower of accumulated earnings and profits at beginning of 1973 ($5,000) or accumulated DISC income at beginning of 1973 ($6,000) and excess of earnings and profits for 1973 over line (5)(c) ($72,000 minus $66,000)	11,000
(c)	Lower of lines (a) and (b) . .	10,000
(7)	Total deemed distribution (sum of lines (5)(c) and (6)(c))	76,000

Example (2). Assume the facts are the same as in example (1), except that earnings and profits for 1973 amount to only $60,000. Under these facts, X is treated as receiving a deemed distribution taxable as a dividend of $65,000 on December 31, 1973, determined as follows:

(5)	Limitation on lines (1) through (4):	
(a)	Line (5)(a) of example (1) .	$66,000
(b)	Earnings and profits for 1973	60,000
(c)	Lower of lines (a) and (b)	60,000
(6)	Amount under paragraph (a)(5) of this section:	
(a)	Line (6)(a) of example (1) .	10,000

(b) Sum of the lower of accumulated earnings and profits at beginning of 1973 ($5,000) or accumulated DISC income at beginning of 1973 ($6,000) plus excess of earnings and profits for 1973 over line (5)(c) ($60,000 minus $60,000) . .   5,000

(c) Lower of lines (a) and (b)   5,000

(7) Total deemed distribution (sum of lines (5)(c) and (6)(c))   65,000

Example (3). Assume the facts are the same as in example (1), except that Y has a deficit in accumulated earnings and profits at the beginning of 1973 of $4,000. Such deficit is comprised of accumulated DISC income of $1,000, no previously taxed income, and a deficit in other earnings and profits of $5,000. Under these facts, X is treated as receiving a deemed distribution taxable as a dividend in the amount of $72,000 on December 31, 1973, determined as follows:

(5) Limitation on lines (1) through (4):
  (a) Line (5)(a) of example (1) . . $66,000
  (b) Earnings and profits for 1973   72,000
  (c) Lower of lines (a) and (b) . .   66,000

(6) Amount under paragraph (a)(5) of this section:
  (a) Line (6)(a) of example (1) . .   10,000
  (b) Sum of accumulated earnings and profits at beginning of 1973 (not less than $0), and excess of earnings and profits for 1973 over amount in line (5)(c) ($72,000 minus $66,000)   6,000
  (c) Lower of lines (a) and (b) . .   6,000

(7) Total deemed distribution (sum of lines (5)(c) and (6)(c))   72,000

(d) *Special rules for certain tax-free acquisitions of property by the DISC.*—(1) For purposes of paragraph (a)(2)(i) and (3)(i) of this section, if—

(i) A DISC acquires property in a first transaction and in a second transaction it disposes of such property in exchange for other property, and

(ii) By reason of the application of section 1031 (relating to like-kind exchanges) or section 1033 (relating to involuntary conversions), the basis in the DISC's hands of the other property acquired in such second transaction is determined in whole or in part with reference to the basis of the property acquired in the first transaction,

then upon a disposition of such other property in a third transaction by the DISC such other property shall be treated as though it had been transferred to the DISC in the first transaction. Thus, if the first transaction is a purchase of the property for cash, then paragraph (a)(2) and (3) of this section will not apply to a sale by the DISC of the other property acquired in the second transaction.

(2) For purposes of paragraph (a)(2)(i) and (3)(i) of this section, if a DISC acquires property in a first transaction and it transfers such property to a transferee DISC in a second transaction in which the transferor DISC's gain is not recognized in whole or in part, then such property shall be treated as though it had been transferred to the transferee DISC in the same manner in which it was acquired in the first transaction by the transferor DISC. For example, if X and Y both qualify as DISC's and X transfers property to Y in a second transaction in which gain or loss is not recognized, paragraph (a)(2) or (3) of this section does not apply to a sale of such property by Y in a third transaction if X had acquired the property in a first transaction by a purchase for cash. If, however, X acquired the property from a transferor other than a DISC in the first transaction in which the transferor's realized gain was not recognized, then paragraph (a)(2) or (3) of this section may apply to the sale by Y if the other conditions of such paragraph (a)(2) or (3) are met.

(3) If a DISC acquires property in a second transaction described in subparagraph (1) or (2) of this paragraph in which it (or, in the case of a second transaction described in subparagraph (2) of this paragraph, the transferor DISC) recognizes a portion (but not all) of the realized gain, then the amount described in paragraph (a)(2)(ii) or (a)(3)(ii) of this section with respect to a disposition by the DISC of such acquired property in a third transaction shall not exceed the transferor's gain which was not recognized on the first transaction minus the amount of gain recognized by the DISC (or transferor DISC) on the second transaction.

(4) The provisions of this paragraph may be illustrated by the following examples:

Example (1). X and Y are corporations each of which qualifies as a DISC and uses the calendar year as its taxable year. In 1972, X acquires section 1245 property in a first transaction in which the transferor's entire realized gain of $17 is not recognized. In 1973, X transfers such property to Y in a second transaction in which X realizes a gain of $20 of which only $4 is recognized. (On December 31, 1973, X's shareholders are treated as having received a deemed distribution of a dividend which includes such $4 under paragraph (a)(3) of this section, provided the limitation in paragraph (b) of this section is met.) In a third transaction in 1974, Y sells such property and recognizes a gain of $25. With respect to Y's shareholders on December 31, 1974, the amount described in paragraph (a)(3)(ii) of this section would be limited to $13, which is the amount of the transferor's gain which was not recognized on the first transaction ($17) minus the amount of gain recognized by X on the second transaction ($4).

Example (2). Z is a DISC using the calendar year as its taxable year. In a first transaction in 1972, in exchange for its stock, Z acquires section 1245 property from A, an individual who is its sole shareholder, in a transaction in which A's realized gain of $30 is not recognized by reason of the application of section 351(a). In a second transaction in 1973, Z exchanges such property for other property in a like-kind exchange to which section 1031 (b) applies and recognizes $10 of a realized gain of $35. (On December 31, 1973, A is treated as having received a deemed distribution of a dividend which includes such $10 under paragraph (a)(3) of this section, provided the limitation in paragraph (b) of this section is met.) In a third transaction in 1974, Z sells the property acquired in the like-kind exchange and recognizes a gain of $25. With respect to A on December 31, 1974, the amount described in paragraph (a)(3)(ii) of this section is limited to $20, which is the amount of A's gain which was not recognized on the first transaction ($30) minus the amount of gain recognized by Z on the second transaction ($10).

(e) *Carryback of net operating loss and capital loss to prior DISC taxable year.*—For purposes of sections 991, 995, and 996, the amount of the deduction for the taxable year under section 172 for a net operating loss carryback or carryover or under section 1212 for a capital loss carryback or carryover shall be determined in the same manner as if the DISC were a domestic corporation which had not elected to be treated as a DISC. Thus, the amount of the deduction will be the same whether or not the corporation was a DISC in the year of the loss or in the year to which the loss is carried. For provisions setting forth adjustments to the DISC's, or former DISC's, deemed distributions, adjustments to its divisions of earnings and profits, and other tax consequences arising from such carrybacks, see § 1.996-8. [Reg. § 1.995-2.]

☐ [T.D. 7324, 9-27-74. *Amended by T.D. 7862,* 12-16-82 *and T.D. 7984, 10-11-84.*]

[Reg. § 1.995-3]

§ 1.995-3. Distributions upon disqualification.—(a) *General rule.*—Under section 995(b)(2), a shareholder of a corporation which is disqualified from being a DISC, either because pursuant to § 1.992-2(e)(2) it revoked its election to be treated as a DISC or because it has failed to satisfy the requirements as set forth in § 1.992-1 to be a DISC for a taxable year, shall be deemed to have received (at the times specified in paragraph (b) of this section) distributions taxable as dividends aggregating an amount equal to his pro rata share of the accumulated DISC income (as defined in § 1.996-3(b)) of such corporation which was accumulated during the immediately

preceding consecutive taxable years for which the corporation was a DISC. The pro rata share referred to in the preceding sentence shall be determined as of the close of the last of such consecutive taxable years for which the corporation was a DISC. See § 1.996-7(c) for rules relating to the carryover of, and maintaining a separate account for, such accumulated DISC income in certain reorganizations.

(b) *Time of receipt of deemed distributions.*—Distributions described in paragraph (a) of this section shall be deemed to be received in equal installments on the last day of each of the 10 taxable years of the corporation following the year of the disqualification described in paragraph (a) of this section, except that in no case may the number of equal installments exceed the number of the immediately preceding consecutive taxable years for which the corporation was a DISC.

(c) *Transfer of shares.*—Deemed distributions are includible under paragraphs (a) and (b) of this section in a shareholder's gross income as a dividend only so long as he continues to hold the shares with respect to which the distribution is deemed made. Thus, the transferee of such shareholder will include in his gross income under paragraphs (a) and (b) of this section the remaining installments of the deemed distribution which the transferor would have included in his gross income as a dividend had he not transferred the shares. However, if the transferee acquires the shares in a transaction in which the transferor's gain is treated under § 1.995-4 in whole or in part as a dividend, then under § 1.996-4(a) such transferee does not include subsequent installments in his gross income to the extent that the transferee treats such subsequent installments as made out of previously taxed income.

(d) *Effect of requalification.*—Deemed distributions under paragraphs (a) and (b) of this section continue and are includible in gross income as dividends by the shareholders whether or not the corporation subsequently requalifies and is treated as a DISC.

(e) *Effect of actual distributions and deemed distributions under section 995(b)(1)(G).*—If, during the period a shareholder of a DISC, or former DISC, is taking into account deemed distributions under paragraphs (a) and (b) of this section, an actual distribution is made to him out of accumulated DISC income or a deemed distribution because of foreign investment attributable to producer's loans is made under § 1.995-2(a)(5) out of accumulated DISC income, such actual or deemed distribution shall first reduce the last installment of the deemed distributions scheduled to be included in the shareholder's gross income as a dividend, and then the preceding scheduled installments in reverse order. If deemed distributions are scheduled to be included in gross income for two or more disqualifications, an actual distribution or a deemed distribution under §1.995-2(a)(5) which is treated as made out of accumulated DISC income reduces the deemed distributions resulting from the earlier disqualification first.

(f) *Examples.*—This section may be illustrated by the following examples:

Example (1). X Corporation, which uses the calendar year as its taxable year, elects to be treated as a DISC beginning with 1972. X qualifies as a DISC for taxable years 1972 through 1975, but, pursuant to §1.992-2(e)(2), revokes its election as of January 1, 1976, and is disqualified as a DISC. On that date, X has $24,000 of accumulated DISC income. X's shareholders will be deemed to receive $6,000 in distributions taxable as a dividend on the last day of each of X's four succeeding taxable years (1977, 1978, 1979, and 1980).

Example (2). Assume the same facts as in example (1), except that in 1978 X makes an actual distribution of $22,000 to its shareholders of which $10,000 is treated under §1.996-1 as made out of accumulated DISC income. (The remaining $12,000 of such distribution is treated as made out of previously taxed income.) The actual distribution would first reduce the $6,000 deemed distribution scheduled for 1980 to zero and then reduce the $6,000 deemed distribution scheduled for 1979 to $2,000. Thus, X's shareholders include in 1978 $16,000 in gross income as dividends ($10,000 of actual distributions and the $6,000 deemed distribution scheduled for that year) and $2,000 as a dividend in 1979.

Example (3). Assume the same facts as in example (2), except that X requalifies as a DISC for taxable year 1977 during which it derives $7,000 of DISC income (computed after taking into account a deemed distribution under §1.995-2(a)(4) of $7,000), but is again disqualified in 1978. In addition, X makes an actual distribution in 1977 equal to the deemed distribution of $7,000. Such actual distribution is excluded from gross income under §1.996-1(c). In 1977, X's shareholders include in gross income as dividends the $6,000 deemed distribution upon disqualification (in addition to the deemed distributions of $7,000 under §1.995-2 for 1977 when it was treated as a DISC). The actual distribution in 1978 still reduces the installments resulting from the earlier disqualification. Thus, in 1978, X's shareholders include $16,000 in gross income as dividends. In 1979, X's shareholders include $9,000 in gross income as dividends (the final installment of $2,000 from the earlier disqualification plus the single deemed distribution of $7,000 resulting from the later disqualification). [Reg. §1.995-3.]

☐ [*T.D. 7324, 9-27-74. Amended by T.D. 7854, 11-15-82.*]

§1.995-4. Gain on certain dispositions of stock in a DISC.—(a) *Disposition in which gain is recognized.*—(1) *In general.*—If a shareholder disposes, or is treated as disposing, of stock in a DISC, or former DISC, then any gain recognized on such disposition shall be included in the shareholder's gross income as a dividend, notwithstanding any other provision of the Code, to the extent of the accumulated DISC income amount (described in paragraph (d) of this section). To the extent the recognized gain exceeds the accumulated DISC income amount, it is taxable as gain from the sale or exchange of the stock.

(2) *Nonapplication of subparagraph (1).*—The provisions of subparagraph (1) of this paragraph do not apply (i) to the extent gain is not recognized (such as, for example, in the case of a gift or an exchange of stock to which section 354 applies) and (ii) to the amount of any recognized gain which is taxable as a dividend (such as, for example, under section 301 or 356(a)(2)) or as gain from the sale or exchange of property which is not a capital asset. The amount taxable as a dividend under section 301 or 356(a)(2) is subject to the rules provided in §1.995-1(c) for the treatment of actual distributions by a DISC.

(b) *Disposition in which separate corporate existence of DISC is terminated.*—(1) *General.*—If stock in a corporation that is a DISC, or former DISC, is disposed of in a transaction in which its separate corporate existence as a DISC, or former DISC, is terminated, then, notwithstanding any other provision of the Code, an amount of realized gain shall be recognized and included in the transferor's gross income as a dividend. The realized gain shall be recognized to the extent that such gain—

(i) Would not have been recognized but for the provisions of this paragraph, and

(ii) Does not exceed the accumulated DISC income amount (described in paragraph (d) of this section).

(2) *Cessation of separate corporate existence as a DISC, or former DISC.*—For purposes of subparagraph (1) of this paragraph, separate corporate existence as a DISC, or former DISC, will be treated as having ceased if, as a result of the transaction, there is no separate entity which is a DISC and to which is carried over the accumulated DISC income and other tax attributes of the DISC, or former DISC, the stock of which is disposed of. Thus, for example, if stock in a DISC, or former DISC, is exchanged in a transaction described in section 381(a) (relating to carryovers in certain corporate acquisitions), the gain realized on the transfer of such stock will not be recognized under subparagraph (1) of this paragraph if the assets of such DISC, or former DISC, are acquired by a corporation which immedi-

ately after the acquisition qualifies as a DISC. For a further example, if a DISC, or former DISC, is liquidated in a transaction to which section 332 (relating to complete liquidations of subsidiaries) applies, the transaction will be subject to subparagraph (1) of this paragraph if the basis to the transferee corporation of the assets acquired on the liquidation is determined under section 334(b)(2) (as in effect prior to amendment by the Tax Equity and Fiscal Responsibility Act of 1982) or if immediately after such liquidation the transferee of such assets does not qualify as a DISC. However, separate corporate existence as a DISC, or former DISC, will not be treated as having ceased in the case of a mere change in place of organization, however effected. See § 1.996-7 for rules for the carryover of the divisions of a DISC's earnings and profits to one or more DISC's.

(c) *Disposition to which section 311, 336, or 337 applies.*—(1) *In general.*—If, after December 31, 1976, a shareholder distributes, sells, or exchanges stock in a DISC, or former DISC, in a transaction to which section 311, 336, or 337 applies, then an amount equal to the excess of the fair market value of such stock over its adjusted basis in the hands of the shareholder shall, notwithstanding any other provision of the Code, be included in gross income of the shareholder as a dividend to the extent of the accumulated DISC income amount (described in paragraph (d) of this section).

(2) *Nonapplication of subparagraph (1).*—Subparagraph (1) shall not apply if the person receiving the stock in the disposition has a holding period for the stock which includes the period for which the stock was held by the shareholder disposing of such stock.

(d) *Accumulated DISC income amount.*—(1) *General.*—For purposes of this section, the accumulated DISC income amount is the accumulated DISC income of the DISC or former DISC which is attributable to the stock disposed of and which was accumulated in taxable years of such DISC or former DISC during the period or periods such stock was held by the shareholder who disposed of such stock.

(2) *Period during which a shareholder has held stock.*—For purposes of this section, the period during which a shareholder has held stock includes the period he is considered to have held it by reason of the application of section 1223 and, if his basis is determined in whole or in part under the provisions of section 1014(d) (relating to special rule for DISC stock acquired from decedent), the holding period of the decedent. Such holding period is to exclude the day of acquisition but include the day of disposition. Thus, for example, if A purchases stock in a DISC on December 31, 1972, and makes a gift of such stock to B on June 30, 1973, then on December 31, 1974, B will be treated as having held the

stock for 2 full years. If the basis of the stock in C's hands is determined under section 1014(d) upon a transfer from B's estate on December 31, 1976 by reason of B's death on June 30, 1974, then on December 31, 1976, C will be treated as having held the stock for 4 full years.

(e) *Accumulated DISC income allocable to shareholder under section 995(c)(2).*—(1) *In general.*— Under this paragraph, rules are prescribed for purposes of paragraph (d) of this section as to the manner of determining, with respect to the stock of a DISC, a former DISC, disposed of, the amount of accumulated DISC income which is attributable to such stock and which was accumulated in taxable years of the corporation during the period or periods the stock disposed of was held or treated under paragraph (d)(2) of this section as held by the transferor. Subparagraphs (2), (3), and (4) of this paragraph set forth a method of computation which may be employed to determine such amount. Any other method may be employed so long as the result obtained would be the same as the result obtained under such method.

(2) *Step 1.*—Determine the increase (or decrease) in accumulated DISC income for each taxable year of the DISC, or former DISC, by subtracting from the amount of accumulated DISC income (as defined in § 1.996-3(b)) at the close of each taxable year the amount thereof as of the close of the immediately preceding taxable year.

(3) *Step 2.*—(i) Determine for each taxable year of the DISC, or former DISC, the increase (or decrease) in accumulated DISC income per share by dividing such increase (or decrease) for the year by the number of shares outstanding or deemed outstanding on each day of such year.

(ii) If the number of shares of stock in the corporation outstanding on each day of a taxable year of the DISC, or former DISC, is not constant, then the number of such shares deemed outstanding on each day of such year shall be the sum of the fractional amounts in respect of each share which was outstanding on any day of the taxable year. The fractional amount in respect of a share shall be determined by dividing the number of days in the taxable year on which such share was outstanding (excluding the day the share became outstanding, but including the day the share ceased to be outstanding), by the total number of days in such taxable year.

(iii) If for any taxable year of a DISC, or former DISC, the share disposed of was not held (or treated under paragraph (d)(2) of this section as held) by the disposing shareholder for the entire year, then the amount of increase (or decrease) in accumulated DISC income attributable to such share for such year is the amount determined as if he held the share until the end of such year multiplied by a fraction the numerator of which is the number of days in the taxable

Reg. § 1.995-4(e)(3)(iii)

year on which the shareholder held (or under paragraph (d)(2) of this section is treated as having held) such share and the denominator of which is the total number of days in the taxable year.

(4) *Step 3.*—Add the amounts computed in step 2 for each taxable year of the DISC, or former DISC, in which the shareholder held such share of stock.

(5) *Examples.*—This paragraph may be illustrated by the following examples:

Example (1). X Corporation uses the calendar year as its taxable year and elects to be a DISC for the first time for 1973. On January 1, 1973, X has 20 shares issued and outstanding. A and B each own 10 shares. On July 1, 1976, X issues 10 shares to C. On December 31, 1977, A sells his 10 shares to D and recognizes a gain of $120. Under these facts and other facts assumed in the table below, A includes in his gross income for 1977 a dividend under paragraph (b) of this section of $61.30 and long-term capital gain of $58.70.

Year	(a) Year end accumulated DISC income	(b) Increase (decrease) in accumulated DISC income	(c) Shares outstanding	(d) Increase (decrease) per share (column (b) ÷ column (c))
1973	$80	$80	20	$4.00
1974	50	(30)	20	(1.50)
1975	80	30	20	1.50
1976	100	20	25 [1]	.80
1977	140	40	30	1.33

[1] Under subparagraph (3)(ii) of this paragraph, the aggregate fractional amount of the 10 shares issued on July 1, 1976, is 5 shares, *i.e.*, 10 shares, multiplied by (183 days/366 days). Thus, the number of shares deemed outstanding for 1976 is 25 shares, *i.e.*, 20 shares plus 5 shares.

(1)	Total increase in accumulated DISC income for each share disposed of (sum of amounts in column (d))	$6.13
	Multiply by number of shares disposed of	10
(2)	Total amount of accumulated DISC income attributable to A's shares disposed of	$61.30
(3)	A's gain	120.00
(4)	Portion of A's gain taxable as a dividend (lower of lines (2) and (3))	61.30
(5)	Portion of A's gain taxable as long-term capital gain (line (3) minus line (4))	$58.70

Example (2). Assume the same facts as in example (1), except that A sells his 10 shares to D on July 1, 1977. Under subparagraph (3)(iii) of this paragraph, the amount of increase in accumulated DISC income for 1977 which is attributable to each share disposed of is limited to $.67, *i.e.*, $1.33 multiplied by 182 days/365 days. Therefore, the sum of the yearly increases (and decreases) in accumulated DISC income for each share is reduced by $.66 (*i.e.*, $1.33 minus $.67). The total increase in accumulated DISC income for each share disposed of is $5.47 (*i.e.*, $6.13 minus $.66). Under these facts, A would include in his gross income for 1977 a dividend of $54.70 and long-term capital gain of $65.30 determined as follows:

(1)	Total increase in accumulated DISC income for each share disposed of	$5.47
	Multiplied by number of shares disposed of	10
(2)	Total amount of accumulated DISC income attributable to all shares disposed of	54.70
(3)	A's gain	120.00
(4)	Portion of A's gain taxable as a dividend (lower of lines (2) and (3))	54.70
(5)	Portion of A's gain taxable as long-term capital gain (line (3) minus line (4))	65.30

[Reg. § 1.995-4.]

☐ [*T.D. 7324, 9-27-74. Amended by T.D. 7854,* 11-15-82.]

[Reg. § 1.995-5]

§ 1.995-5. Foreign investment attributable to producer's loans.—(a) *In general.*—(1) *Limitation.*—Under section 995(d), the amount as of the close of a "group taxable year" (as defined in

subparagraph (3) of this paragraph) of foreign investment attributable to producer's loans of a DISC for purposes of section 995(b)(1)(G) shall be the excess (as of the close of such year) of—

(i) The smallest of—

(a) The amount of the net increase in foreign assets (as defined in paragraph (b) of this section) by domestic and foreign members of the controlled group which includes the DISC, *(b)* The amount of the actual foreign investment by the domestic members of such group (as determined under paragraph (c) of this section), or

(c) The amount of outstanding producer's loans (as determined under § 1.993-4) by such DISC to members of such controlled group, over

(ii) The amount (determined under § 1.995-2(a)(5) and (b)(2)) of foreign investment attributable to producer's loans treated under section 995(b)(1)(G) as deemed distributions by the particular DISC taxable as dividends for prior taxable years of that particular DISC.

Thus, for example, if the shareholders of a DISC which uses the calendar year as its taxable year (and which is a member of a controlled group in which all of the members use the calendar year as their taxable year) are treated under section 995(b)(1)(G) as receiving foreign investment attributable to producer's loans of a DISC of $0 in 1972, $10 in 1973, and $30 in 1974, or a total of $40, and if the smallest of the amounts described in subdivision (i) of this subparagraph at the end of 1975 is $90, then the amount of the foreign investment attributable to producer's loans of a DISC at the end of 1975 is $50, *i.e.,* the excess (as of the close of 1975) of the smallest of the amounts described in subdivision (i) of this subparagraph ($90) over the sum of the amounts of foreign investment attributable to producer's loans treated under section 995(b)(1)(G) as deemed distributions by the DISC taxable as dividends for prior taxable years of the DISC ($40). If the separate corporate existence of the DISC as to which the amount described in subdivision (ii) of this subparagraph relates ceases to exist within the meaning of § 1.995-4(c)(2), then such amount shall no longer be taken into account by the group for any purpose. For inclusion of amounts because of certain corporate acquisitions, see paragraph (d) of this section.

(2) *Controlled group; domestic and foreign member.*—For purposes of this section—

(i) The term "controlled group" has the meaning assigned to such term by § 1.993-1(k).

(ii) The term "domestic member" means a domestic corporation which is a member of a controlled group, and the term "foreign member" means a foreign corporation which is a member of a controlled group.

(3) *Group taxable year.*—(i) The term "group taxable year" refers collectively to the taxable year of the DISC and to the taxable year of each corporation in the controlled group which includes the DISC ending with or within the taxable year of the DISC. Thus, for example, if a corporation has a subsidiary which uses the calendar year as its taxable year and which elects to be treated as a DISC, and if the parent has a taxable year ending on October 31, the "group taxable year" for 1973 would refer to calendar

year 1973 for the DISC and to the parent's taxable year ending October 31, 1973.

(ii) In cases in which the DISC makes a return for a short taxable year, that is, for a taxable year consisting of a period of less than 12 months, pursuant to section 443 and the regulations thereunder, or § 1.991-1(b)(3), the following rules shall apply—

(a) In the case of a change in the annual accounting period of the DISC resulting in a short taxable year, the "group taxable year" refers collectively to the short taxable year and to the taxable year of each corporation in the controlled group which includes the DISC ending with or within the short taxable year.

(b) In the case of a DISC which is in existence during only part of what would otherwise be its taxable year, the "group taxable year" refers collectively to the short period during which the DISC was in existence and to the taxable year of each corporation in the controlled group which includes the DISC ending with or within the 12-month period ending on the last day of the short period.

(iii) With respect to periods prior to the first taxable year for which a member of the group qualified (or is treated) as a DISC, each group taxable year shall be determined under subdivision (i) of this subparagraph as if such member was in existence, it qualified as a DISC, and its taxable year ended on that date corresponding to the date such member's first taxable year ended after it qualified (or is treated) as a DISC whether or not the corporation which qualifies (or is treated) as a DISC used the same taxable year before it so qualified (or is so treated). Thus, for example, if a corporation which is organized on March 3, 1975, uses the calendar year as its taxable year, and is a member of a controlled group which does not include a DISC, first qualifies (or is treated) as a DISC for calendar year 1975, then the term "group taxable year" with respect to years prior to 1975 refers collectively to such prior calendar years and to the taxable year of each corporation in the group ending with or within such prior calendar years.

(iv) For special rules in the case of a group which includes more than one DISC, see paragraph (g) of this section.

(4) *Amounts determined for prior years.*—Unless the 3-year limitation is properly elected under subparagraph (5) of this paragraph, the amounts described in paragraphs (b) (relating to net increase in foreign assets) and (c) (relating to actual foreign investments by domestic members) of this section reflect, as of the close of a group taxable year, amounts for all taxable years of members of the group beginning after December 31, 1971 (and amounts arising after December 31, 1971, or such other date prescribed in paragraph (b)(7) of this section), provided that such amounts relate to such group taxable year and preceding group taxable years. Thus, for

example, if all members of a controlled group use the calendar year as the taxable year, and 1980 is the first taxable year for which any member of the group qualifies (or is treated) as a DISC, then, unless the 3-year limitation is elected under subparagraph (5) of this paragraph, the amounts described in paragraphs (b) and (c) of this section will be taken into account beginning with the dates specified in the preceding sentence. For rules as to carryovers on certain corporate acquisitions and reorganizations, see paragraph (d) of this section.

(5) *Three-year elective limitation.*—(i) A DISC may elect to take into account only amounts described in paragraphs (b) (relating to net increase in foreign assets) and (c) (relating to actual foreign investment by domestic members) of this section for the 3 taxable years of each member immediately preceding its taxable year included in that first group taxable year which includes a member's first taxable year during which it qualifies (or is treated) as a DISC. For purposes of the preceding sentence, determinations shall be made by reference to the taxable year of the issuer or transferor (as the case may be). If an election is made under this subdivision, the offset for uncommitted transitional funds under paragraph (b)(7) of this section is not allowed. If an election is made under this subdivision, the 3-year limitation applies to amounts described in paragraphs (b)(4) and (c)(1) and (2) of this section.

(ii) An election under subdivision (i) of this subparagraph shall not apply with respect to amounts which must be carried over under paragraph (d) of this section in the case of certain corporate acquisitions and reorganizations.

(iii) An election under subdivision (i) of this subparagraph shall be made by the DISC attaching to its first return, filed under section 6011(e)(2), a statement to the effect that the 3-year limitation is being elected under §1.995-5(a)(5)(i).

(6) *Cumulative basis.*—Pursuant to section 995(d)(5), all determinations of amounts specified in this section are to be made on a cumulative basis from the 1st year (or date) provided for in this section. Thus, each such determination shall take into account a net increase or a net decrease during the year, as the case may be. However, if the 3-year limitation is elected under subparagraph (5) of this paragraph, then only amounts with respect to periods specified in such subparagraph (5) are amounts taken into account for years before a member of the group qualifies (or is treated) as a DISC. The computations described in this section may be made in any way chosen by the DISC (including a corporation being tested as to whether it qualifies as a DISC), provided such method results in the amount prescribed by this section.

(7) *Example.*—The provisions of this paragraph may be illustrated by the following example:

Example. X Corporation, which uses the calendar year as its taxable year, is a member of a controlled group (within the meaning of subparagraph (2) of this paragraph). X elects to be treated as a DISC beginning with 1972. The amount of foreign investment attributable to X's producer's loans treated under section 995(b)(1)(G) as a distribution taxable as a dividend as of the close of each group taxable year with respect to each taxable year of X from 1972 through 1975 are set forth in the table below, computed on the basis of the facts assumed (the amounts on lines (1), (2), (3), and (5) being running balances):

	Taxable year of X	1972	1973	1974	1975
(1)	Net increase (or decrease) in foreign assets since January 1, 1972, at close of group taxable year	$(30)	$10	$100	$150
(2)	Actual foreign investment at close of group taxable year	20	60	80	140
(3)	Outstanding producer's loans of X (the DISC) as of the close of group taxable year	0	40	90	120
(4)	Smallest of lines (1), (2), or (3) (not less than zero)	0	10	80	120
(5)	Less section 995(b)(1)(G) deemed distributions for prior taxable years (sum of lines (5) and (6) from prior year)	0	0	10	80
(6)	Section 995(b)(1)(G) deemed distribution as of close of taxable year	0	10	70	40

(b) *Net increase in foreign assets.*—(1) *In general.*—(i) The term "net increase in foreign assets" when used in this section means the excess for the controlled group (as of the close of the group taxable year) of (a) the investment in foreign assets to be taken into account under subparagraph (2) of this paragraph over (b) the aggregate of the five offsets allowed by subparagraphs (3) through (7) of this paragraph.

Reg. §1.995-5(a)(5)(i)

(ii) No amount described in this paragraph (other than amounts described in subparagraphs (4) and (7) of this paragraph) with respect to a member of the group (or foreign branch of a member) shall be taken into account unless it is attributable to a taxable year of such member beginning after December 31, 1971. For a 3-year elective limitation with respect to the first taxable year for which a member qualifies (or is treated) as a DISC, see paragraph (a)(5) of this section. For manner of determining amounts on a cumulative basis, see paragraph (a)(6) of this section.

(2) *Investments made in foreign assets.*—(i) For purposes of subparagraph (1) of this paragraph, there shall be taken into account as investment in foreign assets the aggregate of the amounts expended (within the meaning of subdivision (ii) of this subparagraph) during the period described in subparagraph (1)(ii) of this paragraph by all members of the controlled group which includes the DISC to acquire assets described in section 1231(b) (determined without regard to any holding period therein provided) which are located outside the United States (as defined in § 1.993-7) reduced by the aggregate of the amounts received by all such members of the controlled group from the sale, exchange, or involuntary conversion of such assets described in section 1231(b) which are located outside the United States. For purposes of this section, amounts expended for assets which are qualified export assets (as defined in § 1.993-2) of a DISC (or which would be qualified export assets if owned by a DISC) shall not be taken into account. Thus, for example, if a DISC acquires a qualified export asset located outside the United States, the asset is not to be taken into account for purposes of determining the net increase in foreign assets.

(ii) As used in subdivision (i) of this subparagraph, the term "amounts expended" (or amounts received) means the amount of any money or the fair market value (on the date of acquisition, sale, exchange, or involuntary conversion) of any property (other than money) used to acquire (or received for) the assets described in such subdivision (i).

(iii) For purposes of this subparagraph, an asset (other than an aircraft or vessel) is considered as located outside the United States if it was used predominantly outside the United States during the group taxable year. The determination as to whether such an asset is used predominantly outside the United States during the group taxable year in which it was acquired or sold, exchanged, or involuntarily converted shall be made by applying the rules of § 1.993-3(d) except that an aircraft described in section 48(a)(2)(B)(i) or a vessel described in section 48(a)(2)(B)(iii) shall be considered located in the United States and all other aircraft or vessels shall be considered located outside the United

States. Thus, for example, if a member of a controlled group which includes a DISC acquires a vessel which is documented under the laws of a foreign country, the amount expended to acquire that vessel is an amount described in subdivision (i) of this subparagraph.

(iv) *Examples.*—The provisions of this subparagraph may be illustrated by the following examples:

Example (1). X Corporation, which uses the calendar year as its taxable year, is a domestic member of a controlled group (within the meaning of paragraph (a)(2) of this section). During 1972, in a transaction to which section 1031 applies, X acquires a warehouse located outside the United States and having a fair market value of $100. As consideration, X transfers $20 in cash and a warehouse located within the United States and having a fair market value of $80. Under these facts, $100 will be taken into account as investment in foreign assets.

Example (2). The facts are the same as in example (1), except that the warehouse transferred by X as consideration is located outside the United States. Under these facts, only $20 will be taken into account as investment in foreign assets because the amount expended for such assets (*i.e.*, $100) is reduced by the fair market value of any property located outside the United States received in exchange for such assets (*i.e.*, $80).

(3) *Depreciation with respect to all foreign assets of a controlled group.*—(i) An offset allowed by this subparagraph is the depreciation (determined under subdivision (ii) of this subparagraph) or depletion (determined under subdivision (iii) of this subparagraph) attributable to taxable years of the member beginning after December 31, 1971, with respect to all of the group's foreign assets described in subparagraph (2) of this paragraph including such assets acquired prior to the date provided in such subparagraph (2), and without regard to whether the 3-year election in paragraph (a)(5) of this section is made. Thus, for example, depreciation for a taxable year of a member beginning after December 31, 1971, with respect to an asset described in section 1231(b) which is located outside of the United States and which was acquired during a taxable year of the member beginning before January 1, 1972, is an offset allowed by this subparagraph. For a further example, depreciation with respect to a qualified export asset is not such an offset.

(ii) The depreciation taken into account under subdivision (i) of this subparagraph shall be—

(a) In the case of an asset owned by a domestic member, only the amount allowed under section 167(b)(1) (relating to the allowance of the straight-line method of depreciation) and § 1.162-11(b) (relating to amortization in lieu of depreciation), but not the amount allowed under

Reg. § 1.995-5(b)(3)(ii)(a)

section 179 (relating to the additional first-year depreciation allowance).

(b) In the case of an asset owned by a foreign member, the depreciation and amortization (referred to in (a) of this subdivision) allowable for purposes of computing earnings and profits under subparagraph (5)(i) of this paragraph.

(iii) The depletion taken into account under subdivision (i) of this subparagraph shall be limited to cost depletion computed under sections 611 and 612 and the regulations thereunder. Thus, percentage depletion is not to be taken into account in computing the offset under this subparagraph.

(4) *Amount of outstanding stock or debt.*— (i) An offset allowed by this subparagraph is the outstanding amount of stock (including treasury stock) or debt obligations of any member of the group issued, sold, or exchanged after December 31, 1971, by any member (whether or not the same member) to persons who (on the date of such issuance, sale, or exchange) were neither United States persons (within the meaning of section 7701(a)(30)) nor members of the group, provided that, in the case of a debt obligation, such obligation is not repaid within 12 months after such issuance, sale, or exchange. Thus, for example, if stock is issued to a member of the group before January 1, 1972, and after December 31, 1971, it is sold to a person who is neither a United States person nor a member of the group, an offset allowed by this subparagraph includes the outstanding amount of such stock. For purposes of this subparagraph, foreign branches of United States banks are not considered to be United States persons.

(ii) The outstanding amount of stock or debt obligations shall be determined in accordance with the following provisions:

(a) The outstanding amount of stock or debt obligations described in subdivision (i) of this subparagraph is equal to the net amount described in (b) of this subdivision reduced (but not below zero) by the amount described in (c) of this subdivision.

(b) The net amount described in this subdivision (b) is the excess of (1) the aggregate of the amount of money and the fair market value of property (other than money) transferred by persons who are not members of the group and who are not U.S. persons as consideration for such stock and debt obligations over (2) fees and commission expenses borne by the issuer or transferor with respect to their issuance, sale, or exchange.

(c) The amount described in this subdivision (c) is the aggregate amount of money and fair market value of property (other than money) distributed to such persons on distributions in respect of such stock from other than earnings and profits or on distributions in redemption of

such stock and the amount of principal paid pursuant to such debt obligations.

(d) For purposes of this subdivision (ii), in the case of a redemption, the stock or debt redeemed shall be charged against the earliest of such stock or debt issued, sold, or exchanged in order to determine the amount by which the balance of outstanding stock or debt is to be reduced. For purposes of this subparagraph, the fair market value of property received as consideration shall be determined as of the date the transaction occurs, and a contribution to capital within the meaning of section 118 shall be treated as the issuance of stock.

(iii) The provisions of subdivision (i) of this subparagraph apply regardless of the treatment under the Code of the transaction in which the stock or debt was issued, sold, or exchanged. Thus, for example, if X Corporation, a member of a controlled group which includes a DISC, acquires from a nonresident alien individual in exchange solely for X's voting stock all of the stock of Y Corporation pursuant to a reorganization as defined in section 368 (a)(1)(B), the fair market value of the Y stock on the date of the exchange would be an offset allowed by this subparagraph.

(iv) The provisions of this subparagraph may be illustrated by the following example:

Example. X Corporation is a member of a controlled group (within a meaning of paragraph (a)(2) of this section) every member of which uses the calendar year as its taxable year. On January 1, 1972, X issues in a public offering its stock to persons described in subdivision (i) of this subparagraph who, in the aggregate, pay $1,000 as consideration. X pays $100 in underwriting fees. On the same date, X receives $425 upon issuing a $500 debt obligation to such persons at a discount of $75 and pays $25 in underwriting fees. On December 31, 1972, the offset allowed under this subparagraph is $1,300 *i.e.,* ($1,000 minus $100) plus ($425 minus $25). If, during 1973, X makes a distribution of $150 (not in redemption) from other than earnings and profits with respect to such stock, then the offset is reduced to $1,150.

(5) *Earnings and profits.*—(i) An offset allowed by this subparagraph is one-half the aggregate of the earnings and profits accumulated for all taxable years beginning after December 31, 1971, computed (without regard to any distributions from earnings and profits by a foreign corporation to a domestic corporation) in accordance with § 1.964-1 (relating to a controlled foreign corporation's earnings and profits), of each foreign member of the group which is controlled directly or indirectly (as determined under the principles of section 958 and the regulations thereunder) by a domestic member of the group and each foreign branch of a domestic member of the group (computed as if the branch were a foreign corporation). The DISC is bound by any

action on behalf of a foreign member that was taken pursuant to § 1.964-1(c)(3) or by any failure to take action by or on behalf of a foreign member within the time specified in § 1.964-1(c)(6). With respect to a foreign member for which action was not previously required under § 1.964-1(c)(6) to be taken, the DISC may take action on behalf of such member by attaching a statement to that effect to the return of the DISC under section 6011(e)(2) for the first taxable year during which it qualifies (or is treated) as a DISC and there is outstanding a producer's loan made by such DISC to a member of the controlled group which includes the DISC.

(ii) If the aggregate of the accumulated earnings and profits described in subdivision (i) of this subparagraph is a deficit, the amount allowable as an offset under this subparagraph is zero.

(6) *Royalties and fees.*—An offset allowed by this subparagraph is one-half the royalties and fees paid by foreign members of the group to domestic members of the group and by foreign branches of domestic members of the group to domestic members of the group during the taxable years of such members beginning after December 31, 1971.

(7) *Uncommitted transitional funds.*—(i) An offset allowed by this subparagraph for the uncommitted transitional funds of the group is the sum described in subdivision (ii) of this subparagraph of the amount of certain capital raised under the foreign direct investment program and the amounts described in subdivision (iv) of this subparagraph of certain foreign excess working capital held on October 31, 1971.

(ii) The amount described in this subdivision of certain capital raised under the foreign direct investment program is the excess (if any) of—

(a) The amount of the offset allowed by subparagraph (4) of this paragraph, determined, however, with respect to the stock and debt obligations of domestic members of the group outstanding on December 31, 1971 (including amounts treated as stock outstanding by reason of a contribution to capital), whether or not outstanding after such date which were issued, sold, or exchanged on or after January 1, 1968, by any member (whether or not the same member) to persons who (on the date of such issuance, sale, or exchange) were neither United States persons (within the meaning of section 7701(a)(30)) nor members of the group, but only to the extent the taxpayer establishes that such amount constitutes a long-term borrowing (see 15 CFR § 1000.324) for purposes of the foreign direct investment program (see 15 CFR Part 1000), over

(b) The amount (determined under paragraph (c) of this section) of actual foreign investment by the domestic members of the group during the portion of the period such stock or debt obligations have been outstanding prior to

January 1, 1972, such determination to be made by substituting January 1, 1968, for the December 31, 1971, date specified in such paragraph (c) and by not taking into account the earnings and profits described in paragraph (c)(3) of this section.

For purposes of this subparagraph, foreign branches of United States banks are not considered to be United States persons.

(iii)(a) A taxpayer may establish that an amount under subdivision (ii)(a) of this subparagraph constitutes a long-term borrowing for purposes of the foreign direct investment program by keeping records sufficient to demonstrate that appropriate reports were filed with the Office of Foreign Direct Investment of the Department of Commerce with respect to the foreign borrowing or by any other method satisfactory to the district director.

(b) The amounts described in subdivision (ii)(a) of this subparagraph include amounts with respect to which an election under section 4912(c), to subject certain obligations of a United States person to the interest equalization tax, has been made, provided that the obligations to which such amounts relate were issued by an "overseas financing subsidiary" described in 15 CFR Part 1000 N and were assumed by a United States person from such overseas financing subsidiary. Thus, for example, if an overseas financing subsidiary issues its notes to a foreign person in 1968, and such notes are assumed by its United States parent in 1973, which parent elects under section 4912(c) to have the notes subject to the interest equalization tax, then the amount of money received by the subsidiary is an amount described in subdivision (ii)(a) of this subparagraph.

(iv) The amount described in this subdivision of foreign excess working capital is the amount of liquid assets held by the foreign members of such group and foreign branches of domestic members of such group on October 31, 1971 (whether or not so held after such date) in excess of their reasonable working capital needs (as defined in § 1.993-2(e)) on that date, but only to the extent not included in subdivision (ii) of this subparagraph. For purposes of this subdivision, the term "liquid assets" means money, bank deposits (not including time deposits), and indebtedness of any kind (including time deposits) which on the day acquired had a maturity of 2 years or less.

(8) *Example.*—The provisions of this paragraph may be illustrated by the following example:

Example. X Corporation, which uses the calendar year as its taxable year is a member of a controlled group (within the meaning of paragraph (a)(2) of this section). X elects to be treated as a DISC beginning with 1972. The amount of net increase in foreign assets of the group at the close of each group taxable year with respect to each taxable year of X from 1972 through 1975 are set forth in the table below, computed on the basis of the facts assumed (the amounts on each line being running balances):

	Taxable Year of X	1972	1973	1974	1975
(1)	Investment in foreign assets	$150	$165	$260	$300
(2)	Depreciation with respect to foreign assets of group	20	40	60	80
(3)	Amount of stock or debt outstanding issued after December 31, 1971	30	30	30	30
(4)	One-half earnings and profits of foreign members..............	40	70	100	130
(5)	Royalties and fees paid by foreign members to domestic members ...	10	15	20	20
(6)	Uncommitted transitional funds ...	10	10	10	10
(7)	Sum of lines (2) through (6)	110	165	220	270
(8)	Net increase in foreign assets (line (1) minus line (6))	$40	$0	$40	$30

(c) *Actual foreign investment by domestic members.*—For purposes of determining the limitation in paragraph (a) of this section, the amount of the actual foreign investment by domestic members of a controlled group is the sum (as of the close of the group taxable year) determined on a cumulative basis (see paragraph (a)(6) of this section) of—

(1) *Outstanding stock or debt (including contributions to capital).*—The outstanding amount (determined in accordance with the principles of paragraph (b)(4)(ii) of this section, applied with respect to stock or debt obligations described in this subparagraph) of stock (including treasury stock) or debt obligations (other than normal trade indebtedness) of foreign members of the group issued, sold, or exchanged after December 31, 1971, by any person (whether or not a member) which is not a domestic member to domestic members of the group, provided that the outstanding amount of debt obligations of any foreign member shall be the greater of such amount outstanding at the close of the taxable year of such member or the highest such amount outstanding at any time during the immediately preceding 90 days,

(2) *Transfers to foreign branches.*—The amount of money or the fair market value of property (other than money) transferred by domestic members of the group after December 31, 1971, to foreign branches of such members in transactions which would, if the branch were a corporation, be in consideration for the sale of stock or debt obligations of (or a contribution of capital to) such foreign branches (as determined under subparagraph (1) of this paragraph), and

(3) *Earnings and profits of foreign members.*—One-half of the earnings and profits (computed in accordance with paragraph (b)(5) of this section for purposes of computing net increase in foreign assets) of foreign members of the group which are controlled directly or indirectly (as determined under the principles of section 958

and the regulations thereunder) by a domestic member of the group and foreign branches (treated for this purpose as a corporation) of domestic members of the group accumulated during the taxable years of such foreign members (or branches) beginning after December 31, 1971, or, if later, the taxable year referred to in paragraph (a)(5)(i) of this section if the 3-year election provided for in such paragraph (a)(5)(i) is made.

(d) *Carryovers on certain corporate acquisitions and reorganizations.*—(1) *Certain corporate acquisitions.*—(i) If—

(a) A member of a controlled group ("first controlled group") acquires in a transaction to which section 381 applies the assets of a corporation which is a member of a second controlled group or acquires stock in such a corporation pursuant to a reorganization as defined in section 368(a)(1)(B) to which section 361 applies, or

(b) A member or combination of members of the first controlled group acquire in a transaction not described in (a) of this subdivision a majority interest (as defined in paragraph (e)(2) of this section) in the stock of a corporation which is a member of a second controlled group which includes a DISC so that such DISC after the acquisition is a member of the new controlled group,

then, for purposes of computing foreign investment attributable to producer's loans with respect to the new controlled group as constituted after such acquisition, all amounts described in paragraphs (a) through (c) of this section, including the amount specified in paragraph (a)(1)(ii) of this section (relating to amounts treated under section 995(b)(1)(G) as deemed distributions by the DISC taxable as dividends for prior taxable years of the DISC), with respect to members of the second controlled group which become members of the new controlled group shall carry over to such new controlled group. For purposes of this subdivision (i), a controlled group may

Reg. § 1.995-5(c)

consist of only one member. With respect to certain transactions involving foreign corporations, see section 367.

(ii) If a member or combination of members of a controlled group, immediately after an acquisition of stock to which subdivision (i) of this subparagraph applies, do not control the total combined voting power (determined under § 1.957-1(b)) of the corporation whose stock was acquired, proper apportionment consistent with the principles of paragraph (e)(5) of this section shall be made with respect to amounts to which paragraphs (a) through (c) of this section apply.

(iii)(a) If subdivision (i) of this subparagraph applies, then for purposes of determining the application of the 3-year elective limitation provided for in paragraph (a)(5) of this section, the rules in (b), (c), and (d) of this subdivision (iii) apply.

(b) If both the "first controlled group" and the "second controlled group" (as those terms are defined in subdivision (i) of this subparagraph) include a DISC, and a DISC in either group has elected the 3-year limitation provided in paragraph (a)(5) of this section, then only those amounts taken into account under such paragraph (a)(5) by the electing DISC or DISC's shall be taken into account.

(c) If one of the groups includes a DISC and the other does not, and if the DISC has elected the 3-year limitation provided in paragraph (a)(5) of this section, then, for purposes of computing foreign investment attributable to producer's loans with respect to the new controlled group as constituted after the acquisition, all amounts described in paragraphs (a) through (c) of this section with respect to members of the controlled group which did not include the DISC shall carry over to such new controlled group, but only to the extent provided in such paragraph (a)(5), computed as if the group taxable year in which the acquisition occurred was the first group taxable year which includes a member's first taxable year during which it qualifies (or is treated) as a DISC.

(d) If (c) of this subdivision (iii) applies, except that the DISC has not elected the 3-year limitation provided in paragraph (a)(5) of this section, then the DISC in the new controlled group as constituted after the acquisition may, with respect to members of the controlled group which did not include the DISC, make the election provided in such paragraph (a)(5), and treat the year in which the acquisition occurred as if it were the first group taxable year which includes a member's first taxable year during which it qualifies (or is treated) as a DISC.

(iv) If a majority interest, or an interest in addition to a majority interest, is acquired in a transaction other than a transaction described in subdivision (i) of this subparagraph, then the rules in paragraph (e) of this section (relating to the acquisition of the foreign assets of a corporation) apply.

(2) *Corporation ceasing to be a member.*—As of the date a corporation which is a member of a controlled group ceases to be a member of such group, the amounts of such group described in paragraphs (a) through (c) of this section will be reduced by such amounts which are attributable to the corporation which is no longer a member of the group.

(e) *Acquisition of a majority interest in a corporation..*—(1) *In general.*—If paragraph (d)(1)(i) of this section (relating to certain corporate acquisitions in which all amounts described in paragraphs (a) through (c) of this section carry over) does not apply, then, for purposes of determining under paragraph (b)(2) of this section the investments made in foreign assets by a controlled group, the acquisition of a majority interest (as defined in subparagraph (2) of this paragraph) or an interest in addition to a majority interest in a corporation by any member or combination of members of the controlled group is considered an acquisition of the assets (to the extent provided in subparagraph (5) of this paragraph) of the acquired corporation by the group, including the assets of any foreign corporation in which the acquired corporation owns a majority interest (to the extent provided in subparagraph (5) of this paragraph). For the rules concerning the date upon which an acquisition of a majority interest is considered to have occurred, see subparagraph (3) of this paragraph.

(2) *Majority interest.*—For purposes of this section, a majority interest is more than 50 percent of the total combined voting power of all classes of a corporation's stock entitled to vote, as determined under § 1.957-1(b).

(3) *Acquisition date.*—For purposes of this paragraph, an acquisition of a majority interest shall be considered to have occurred on the day on which the combined voting power of the group first reached the percentage required in subparagraph (2) of this paragraph.

(4) *Valuation of assets.*—For purposes of this section, the amount of a corporation's assets deemed acquired is the fair market value of the assets on the date of a majority interest, or an interest in addition to a previously held majority interest, is acquired.

(5) *Apportionment in the case of the acquisition of less than all of the voting stock.*—(i) If the acquisition described in subparagraph (1) of this paragraph of a majority interest is of less than 100 percent of the total combined voting power of all classes of stock of the acquired corporation entitled to vote, then for purposes of subparagraph (1) of this paragraph the amount of the foreign assets of the corporation deemed acquired as of the day the majority interest is considered acquired shall be an amount equal to the fair market value of all of the corporation's foreign assets described in paragraph (b)(2) of this section as of

such day multiplied by the percentage of the total combined voting power (determined under §1.957-1(b)) held by members of the group on the day the majority interest is considered acquired.

(ii) If any member or combination of members of the controlled group hold a majority interest in a corporation, then for purposes of subparagraph (1) of this paragraph the acquisition of additional combined voting power by members of the controlled group shall be considered an acquisition of its foreign assets described in paragraph (b)(2) of this section in an amount equal to the fair market value of all such assets held by the foreign corporation on the date of the acquisition, multiplied by the increase (expressed in percentage points) in total combined voting power (as determined under §1.957-1(b)) which occurred.

(6) *Examples.*—The application of this paragraph may be illustrated by the following examples:

Example (1). M Corporation uses the calendar year as its taxable year. On November 18, 1973, M acquires from A, an individual United States person, for $1 million cash all 10,000 shares of the voting stock of N, a foreign corporation. N's only asset is a warehouse located in France with a fair market value on the date of acquisition of $1 million. Under subparagraph (1) of this paragraph, the controlled group of which M is a member is considered to have expended $1 million for the acquisition of foreign assets described in paragraph (b)(2) of this section.

Example (2). The facts are the same as in example (1), except that on November 18, 1973, M acquires only 80 percent of N's voting stock. M is considered to have expended $800,000 for the acquisition of assets described in paragraph (b)(2) of this section, computed as follows:

(1)	Fair market value of N's foreign assets described in paragraph (b)(2) of this section	$1,000,000
(2)	Multiply by percentage of total combined voting power of all classes of N stock entitled to vote acquired by M	.8
(3)	Amount considered expended	$800,000

Example (3). The facts are the same as in example (2), except that individual A is not a United States person, and M acquires the 80 percent of N voting stock in exchange for cash of $100,000 and M stock having a fair market value on the date of the acquisition of $700,000. M is considered to have acquired assets described in paragraph (b)(2) of this section in the amount of $800,000 (see computations in example (2)) and

to have an offset under paragraph (b)(4) of this section (relating to outstanding stock or debt) of $700,000 (the fair market value of the M stock transferred to A who is not a United States person). However, the controlled group of which M is a member is not considered to have acquired any other amounts described in paragraphs (a) through (c) of this section with respect to N for taxable years prior to the taxable year of N during which the acquisition occurred.

Example (4). P Corporation, which uses the calendar year as its taxable year, is a member of a controlled group which includes a DISC. During 1973, P acquires from B, an individual United States person, for cash, 30 percent of the total combined voting power of all classes of stock entitled to vote of Q, a foreign corporation. All of Q's assets are assets described in paragraph (b)(2) of this section. No additional interest in Q is acquired by members of the group during 1973. The controlled group of which Q is a member is not considered to have made any investments in foreign assets described in such paragraph (b)(2) as of the close of 1973.

Example (5). Assume the same facts as in example (4). Assume further that during 1974, R Corporation, a member of the controlled group which includes P, acquires for cash 40 percent of the total combined voting power of all classes of stock of Q entitled to vote as follows: 20 percent on July 31, and 20 percent on December 31. Thus, on December 31, 1974, members of the controlled group own 70 percent of Q's voting power (30 + 20 + 20) and on that date are considered to have acquired a majority interest in Q. The fair market value of Q's assets on December 31, 1974, is $5 million. The group is considered to have expended $3,500,000 for the acquisition of assets described in paragraph (b)(2) of this section computed as follows:

(1)	Fair market value of Q's foreign assets described in paragraph (b)(2) of this section as of the date the acquisition is deemed to have occurred under subparagraph (3) of this paragraph (December 31, 1974)	$5,000,000
(2)	Multiply by percentage of total combined voting power of all classes of Q stock entitled to vote held by members of the group on such date	.7
		3,500,000

Example (6). The facts are the same as in example (5). Assume further that on July 15, 1975, P acquires the remaining 30 percent of the total combined voting power of all classes of Q stock entitled to vote, and on such date the fair market value of Q's assets is $5,500,000. The group is considered to have expended $5,150,000 for the acquisition of assets described in paragraph (b)(2) of this section as of the close of 1975, computed as follows:

(1)	Amount of prior years' investment	$3,500,000
(2)	Investment during 1975:	
	(a) Fair market value of Q's foreign assets described in paragraph (b)(2) of this section on July 15, 1975 . .	$5,500,000
	(b) Multiply by additional percentage acquired of total combined voting power of all classes of Q stock entitled to vote . . .	.3
	(c) Investment during 1975 .	$1,650,000
(3)	Amount considered expended for foreign assets described in paragraph (b)(2) of this section by reason of the acquisition of Q stock	$5,150,000

(f) *Records.*—A DISC shall keep or be readily able to produce such permanent books of account or records as are sufficient to establish the transactions and amounts described in this section. Where applicable, such books of account or records shall be cumulative and shall show transactions and amounts of the members of the controlled group which includes the DISC which occurred prior to the date the DISC qualified (or is treated) as a DISC.

(g) *Multiple DISC's.*—(1) *Allocation amoung DISC's.*—In the case of a controlled group which includes more than one DISC, the amounts described in paragraphs (b) and (c) of this section shall be allocated among the DISC's in order to determine the limitation in paragraph (a) of this section. Each DISC's allocable portion of these amounts shall be equal to the total of such amounts multiplied by a fraction the numerator of which is the individual DISC's outstanding producer's loans to members of the group, and the denominator of which is the aggregate amounts of outstanding producer's loans to members of the group by all DISC's which are members of the group.

(2) *Different taxable years.*—If all of the DISC's which are members of the controlled group do not have the same taxable year, then one such DISC shall on behalf of all such DISC's elect to make all computations under section 995(d) as if all DISC's that are members of the group use the same taxable year as the actual taxable year of any one of the DISC's. The election as to which DISC's taxable year is to be used shall be made by the electing DISC attaching to its first return, filed under section 6011(e)(2), a statement indicating which such taxable year will be used. Once such an election is made it may not be revoked until such time as all of the

DISC's which are members of the group use the same taxable year. If this subparagraph applies, books and records must be kept by the group which are adequate to show the necessary computations under section 995(d).

(3) This paragraph may be illustrated by the following example:

Example. Corporation X and Corporation Y are members of the same controlled group and each has elected to be treated as a DISC. X uses a taxable year ending March 31, and Y uses a taxable year ending November 30. Notwithstanding the fact that all other members of the group use the calendar year as their taxable year, all computations for purposes of determining the amount of foreign investment attributable to producer's loans under section 995(d) must be made as if both DISC's use a taxable year ending either March 31 (X's taxable year) or November 30 (Y's taxable year). [Reg. § 1.995-5.]

☐ [*T.D. 7324, 9-27-74. Amended by T.D. 7420, 5-19-76 and T.D. 7854, 11-6-82.*]

[Reg. § 1.995-6]

§ 1.995-6. Taxable income attributable to military property.—(a) *Gross income attributable to military property.*—For purposes of section 995(b)(3)(A)(i), the term "gross income which is attributable to military property" includes income from the sale, exchange, lease, or rental of military property (as described in paragraph (c) of this section). The term also includes gross income from the performance of services which are related and subsidiary (as defined in § 1.993-1(d)) to any qualified sale, exchange, lease, or rental of military property. Where gross income cannot be determined on an item by item basis, the gross income with respect to those items not so determinable shall be apportioned. Such apportionment shall be accomplished using appropriate facts and circumstances, so that the gross income apportioned to sale of military property bears a reasonably close factual relationship to the actual gross income earned on such sales. The apportionment shall be based on methods which include the fair market value of property sold or exchanged, the fair rental value of any leaseholds granted, the fair market value of any related or subsidiary services performed in connection with such sale or leases or methods based on gross receipts or costs of goods sold, where appropriate.

(b) *Deductions.*—For purposes of section 995(b)(3)(A)(ii), deductions shall be properly allocated and apportioned to gross income, described in paragraph (a) of this section, in accordance with the rules of § 1.861-8. These deductions include all applicable deductions from gross income provided under part VI of subchapter B of chapter 1 of the Code.

(c) *Military property.*—For purposes of this section, the term "military property" means any property which is an arm, ammunition, or implement of war designated in the munitions list published pursuant to section 38 of the International Security Assistance and Arms Export Control Act of 1976 (22 U.S.C. 2778 which superseded 22 U.S.C. 1934) and the regulations thereunder (22 CFR 121.01).

(d) *Illustration.*—The principles of this section may be illustrated by the following example:

Example. X Corporation elects to be a DISC for the first time in 1976. X has taxable income of $50,000, of which $30,000 is attributable to military property and $10,000 to interest on producer's loans. The total deemed distributions with respect to X are as follows:

(1)	Gross interest from Producer's loans in 1976	$10,000
(2)	50 percent of the taxable income of the DISC attributable to military property in 1976	15,000
(3)	One-half of the excess of taxable income for 1976 over the sum of lines (1) and (2) ($\frac{1}{2}$ of ($50,000 minus $25,000))	12,500
(4)	Total deemed distributions (sum of total lines (1), (2), and (3))	37,500

[Reg. §1.995-6.]

☐ [*T.D.* 7984, 10-11-84.]

[Reg. §1.996-1]

§1.996-1. Rules for actual distributions and certain deemed distributions.—(a) *General rule.*—Under section 996(a)(1), any actual distribution (other than a distribution described in paragraph (b) of this section or to which §1.995-4 applies) to a shareholder by a DISC, or former DISC, which is made out of earnings and profits shall be treated as made—

(1) First, out of "previously taxed income" (as defined in §1.996-3(c)) to the extent thereof,

(2) Second, out of "accumulated DISC income" (as defined in §1.996-3(b)) to the extent thereof, and

(3) Third, out of "other earnings and profits" (as defined in §1.996-3(d)) to the extent thereof.

(b) *Rules for qualifying distributions and deemed distributions under section 995(b)(1)(G).*—(1) *In general.*—Except as provided in subparagraph (2), any actual distribution to meet qualification requirements made pursuant to §1.992-3 and any deemed distribution pursuant to §1.995-2(a)(5) (relating to foreign investment attributable to producer's loans) which is made out of earnings and profits shall be treated as made—

(i) First, out of "accumulated DISC income" (as defined in §1.996-3(b)) to the extent thereof,

(ii) Second, out of "other earnings and profits" (as defined in §1.996-3(d)) to the extent thereof, and

(iii) Third, out of "previously taxed income" (as defined in §1.996-3(c)) to the extent thereof.

(2) *Special rule.*—For taxable years beginning after December 31, 1975, paragraph (b)(1) of this section shall apply to one-half of the amount of an actual distribution made pursuant to §1.992-3 to satisfy the condition of §1.992-1(b) (the gross receipts test) and paragraph (a) of this section shall apply to the remaining one-half of such amount.

(c) *Exclusion from gross income.*—Under section 996(a)(3), amounts distributed out of previously taxed income shall be excluded by the distributee from gross income. However, see §1.996-5(b) for treatment as gain from the sale or exchange of property of the portion of an actual distribution out of previously taxed income to the extent it exceeds the adjusted basis of the stock with respect to which the distribution is made.

(d) *Priority of distributions.*—Under section 996(c), for purposes of determining their treatment under paragraphs (a), (b), and (c) of this section, distributions made during a taxable year shall be treated as being made in the following order—

(1) Deemed distributions under §§1.995-2 and 1.995-3.

(2) Actual distributions to meet qualification requirements made pursuant to §1.992-3 in the order in which they are made, and

(3) Other actual distributions in the order in which they are made.

Thus, the treatment of any distribution shall be determined after the divisions of earnings and profits have been properly adjusted by taking into account distributions of higher priority which are made or deemed made during the same taxable year.

(e) *Examples.*—The provisions of this section may be illustrated by the following examples:

Example (1). Y Corporation, which uses the calendar year as its taxable year elects to be treated as a DISC beginning with 1972. During 1973, Y makes a cash distribution of $100 to X Corporation, Y's sole shareholder. For 1973, Y has no earnings and profits. As of the beginning of 1973, Y has $300 of accumulated earnings and profits, which consist of $70 of accumulated DISC income, $40 of previously taxed income, and $190 of other earnings and profits. The entire $100 distribution is a dividend under section 316. However, $40 thereof is treated as made out of previously taxed income and is thus excluded from gross income. Accordingly, only $60 is treated as distributed out of accumulated DISC income and includible in gross income. See §1.246-4 for the inapplicability of the dividend received deduction with respect to the entire distribution of $100.

Example (2). Assume the same facts as in example (1), except that the cash distribution is designated as a distribution to meet qualification requirements made pursuant to §1.992-3. Under these facts, X includes the entire distribution in its gross income as a dividend. Of the $100 distributed, $70 is treated as made out of accumulated DISC income and the remaining $30 is treated as made out of other earnings and profits. The dividend received deduction under section 243 is available only with respect to such $30.

Example (3). Y Corporation, which uses the calendar year as its taxable year, elects to be treated as a DISC beginning with 1972. As of the end of 1975, Y had failed to meet the gross receipts test for that year. In 1975 Y had $100 of taxable income, $80 of which was attributable to qualified export receipts and $20 of which was attributable to receipts that did not qualify as qualified export receipts. As of the beginning of 1976, Y had $300 of accumulated earnings and profits, which consisted of $70 of accumulated DISC income, $40 of previously taxed income, and $190 of other earnings and profits. In 1976 Y makes a cash distribution of $20 pursuant to §1.992-3 in order to satisfy the gross receipts test for 1975. For 1976 Y has no earnings and profits and no deemed distributions. The entire $20 distribution is a dividend under section 316. Under §1.996-1(b)(2), half of the $20 cash distribution is treated pursuant to §1.996-1(b)(1) and half is treated pursuant to §1.996-1(a). Thus, $10 is treated as distributed out of accumulated DISC income and is includible in gross income. The other $10 is treated as made out of previously taxed income and is thus excluded from gross income. As of the beginning of 1977, Y has $280 of accumulated earnings and profits, which consists of $60 of accumulated DISC income, $30 of previously taxed income, and $190 of other earnings and profits. [Reg. §1.996-1.]

☐ [*T.D. 7324, 9-27-74. Amended by T.D. 7854,* 11-6-82.]

[Reg. §1.996-2]

§1.996-2. Ordering rules for losses.—(a) *In general.*—Under section 996(b), if for any taxable year a DISC, or a former DISC, incurs a deficit in earnings and profits, such deficit shall be charged—

(1) First, to other earnings and profits (as defined in §1.996-3(d)) to the extent thereof,

(2) Second, to accumulated DISC income (as defined in §1.996-3(b)) to the extent thereof, subject to the special rule in paragraph (b) of this section,

(3) Third, to previously taxed income (as defined in §1.996-3(c)) to the extent thereof, and

(4) To the extent that the amount of such deficit exceeds the sum of the amounts charged in accordance with subparagraphs (1), (2), and (3) of this paragraph, to other earnings and profits (as defined in §1.996-3(d)). Thus, the excess deficit charged to other earnings and profits under subparagraph (4) of this paragraph will create a deficit therein in the amount of such excess. To determine the amount of any division of earnings and profits for the purpose of determining under §1.996-1 the treatment of any actual and certain deemed distributions, the portion of a deficit in earnings and profits chargeable under this paragraph to such division prior to such distribution shall be determined in a manner consistent with the rules in §1.316-2(b) for determining the amount of earnings and profits available on the date of any distribution.

(b) *Deficits subsequent to a disqualification.*—A deficit in earnings and profits of a DISC, or former DISC, shall not be charged to accumulated DISC income which has been determined is to be deemed distributed to the shareholders pursuant to §1.995-3 as a result of a revocation of election or other disqualification. Thus, in accordance with paragraph (a) of this section as modified by this paragraph, a deficit incurred by a former DISC following such a revocation or disqualification shall be charged first to other earnings and profits and then to previously taxed income with any balance being charged to other earnings and profits and creating a deficit therein. The preceding sentence shall also apply in the case of a deficit incurred by a DISC which has no accumulated DISC income accumulated during its current taxable year and all immediately preceding consecutive taxable years for which it was a DISC. If as a result of the application of this paragraph the amount of a deficit in other earnings and profits exceeds the amount of a deficit in accumulated earnings and profits, then upon any subsequent actual distribution the deficit in other earnings and profits shall be reduced by the lower of (1) the amount of such actual distribution chargeable to accumulated DISC income or previously taxed income or (2) the amount of such excess.

(c) *Examples.*—The provisions of this section may be illustrated by the following examples:

Example (1). X Corporation, which uses the calendar year as its taxable year, becomes a DISC beginning with 1976. In addition to other facts assumed in the table below, X incurs a deficit in earnings and profits for 1979 of $70. Such deficit is charged to the divisions of X's earnings and profits pursuant to paragraph (a) of this section in the manner set forth in such table.

	Accumulated DISC income	Previously taxed income	Other earnings and profits
Balance Jan. 1, 1976	...	...	$50
Increase for 1976	$10	$8	...
Increase for 1977	10	8	...
Increase for 1978	10	8	...
Balance Jan. 1, 1979	30	24	50
Deficit for 1979 of $70:			
Charge No. 1	...	...	(50)
Charge No. 2	(20)	...	...
Balance Jan. 1, 1980	10	24	0

Example (2). Assume the same facts as in example (1), except that effective for taxable years beginning with 1979, X revokes its election to be treated as a DISC. Under §1.995-3, X has $30 of accumulated DISC income which is to be deemed distributed $10 per year in 1980, 1981, and 1982. The deficit in earnings and profits for 1979 is charged to the divisions of X's earnings and profits pursuant to paragraph (b) of this section in the manner set forth in the table below:

	Accumulated DISC income	Previously taxed income	Other earnings and profits
Balance Jan. 1, 1979	$30	$24	$50
Deficit for 1979 of $70:			
Charge No. 1	...	...	(50)
Charge No. 2	...	(20)	...
Balance Jan. 1, 1980	30	4	0

Example (3). Assume the same facts as in example (2), except that the deficit in earnings and profits for 1979 is $120. Assume further that for 1980, 1981, and 1982, during which years X's shareholders are receiving scheduled installments of the deemed distributions of accumulated DISC income under §1.995-3, X, a former DISC, has neither earnings and profits nor a deficit in earnings and profits. The $120 deficit for 1979 is charged to the divisions of X's earnings and profits pursuant to paragraph (b) of this section in the manner set forth in the table below:

	Accumulated DISC income	Previously taxed income	Other earnings and profits	Accumulated earnings and profits
Balance Jan. 1, 1979	$30	$24	$50	$104
Deficit for 1979 of $120	...	...	...	(120)
Charge No. 1	...	...	(50)	...
Charge No. 2	...	(24)	...	...
Charge No. 3	...	...	(46)	...
Balance Jan. 1, 1980	$30	$0	($46)	($16)
Deemed distributions in 1980 under §1.995-3	(10)	10	...	...
Balance Jan. 1, 1981	20	10	(46)	(16)

Example (4). Assume the same facts as in example (3), except that on December 31, 1980, X makes an actual distribution of $10 out of previously taxed income. On January 1, 1981, X has $20 of accumulated DISC income, no previously taxed income, and a deficit of $36 in other earnings and profits. The deficit of $16 in accumulated earnings and profits remains the same. [Reg. §1.996-2.]

☐ [T.D. 7324, 9-27-74.]

[Reg. §1.996-3]

§1.996-3. Divisions of earnings and profits.—(a) *In general.*—For purposes of sections 991 through 997, the earnings and profits of a DISC, or former DISC, shall be treated as composed of the following three divisions:

(1) Accumulated DISC income (as defined in paragraph (b) of this section),

(2) Previously taxed income (as defined in paragraph (c) of this section), and

(3) Other earnings and profits (as defined in paragraph (d) of this section).

(b) *Accumulated DISC income defined.*—(1) Accumulated DISC income is that portion of a corporation's earnings and profits which were derived during taxable years for which it qualified as a DISC and which were deferred from taxation. Accumulated DISC income as of the close of each taxable year of the corporation is—

(i) The amount of accumulated DISC income as of the close of the immediately preceding taxable year increased by

(ii) The amount of DISC income for the year (as determined in subparagraph (2) of this paragraph) and reduced (but not below zero) by

(iii) The items enumerated in subparagraph (3) of this paragraph.

(2) Under section 996(f)(1), DISC income is (i) the earnings and profits derived by the corporation during a taxable year for which such corporation is a DISC minus (ii) amounts deemed distributed under §1.995-2 other than the amount of foreign investment attributable to producer's loans described in §1.995-2(a)(5). For example, the earnings and profits of a DISC for a taxable year include any amounts includible in such DISC's gross income pursuant to section 951(a) (relating to controlled foreign corporations). Deemed distributions under §1.995-2(a)(5) are taken into account under subparagraph (3) of this paragraph as a reduction in computing accumulated DISC income.

(3) The accumulated DISC income (as increased by DISC income for the year determined under subparagraph (2) of this paragraph) is reduced by each of the following items in the following order:

(i) Any amount deemed distributed for such year under §1.995-3 (relating to deemed distributions upon disqualification),

(ii) Any amount of foreign investment attributable to producer's loans deemed distributed for such year under §1.995-2(a)(5) to the extent it is charged to accumulated DISC income under §1.996-1(b)(1)(i),

(iii) The amount of any adjustment to accumulated DISC income for such year under §1.996-4(b)(1), and

(iv) To the extent they are treated, under §1.996-1(a) or (b) (relating to ordering rules for distributions), as made out of accumulated DISC income, the amounts of any actual qualifying distributions pursuant to §1.992-3 in the order in which they are made, and thereafter by the amounts of any other actual distributions in the order in which they are made, except that, prior to each actual distribution, accumulated DISC income shall be reduced by the portion of any deficit in earnings and profits for the taxable year chargeable at that time under §1.996-2(a)(2) to accumulated DISC income.

(4) Every distribution or other reduction in accumulated DISC income pursuant to subparagraph (3) of this paragraph shall be charged to the most recently accumulated DISC income.

(c) *Previously taxed income.*—Under section 996(f)(2), previously taxed income as of the close of each taxable year of the corporation is an amount equal to—

(1) The sum of—

(i) The amount of previously taxed income as of the close of the immediately preceding taxable year,

(ii) Amounts deemed distributed for the current year under §1.995-2 (relating to deemed distributions in qualified years),

(iii) Amounts deemed distributed for the current year under §1.995-3 (relating to deemed distributions upon disqualification),

(iv) With respect to a distribution in redemption to which §1.996-4(b)(1) applies, an amount equal to the excess (if any) of (*a*) the amount of the reduction under §1.996-4(b)(1) in accumulated DISC income over (*b*) the reduction in the corporation's earnings and profits (see section 312(e)), and

(v) Any amount by which accumulated DISC income is reduced under paragraph (b)(3)(ii) of this section by reason of a deemed distribution as a dividend, under §1.995-2(a)(5), of an amount of foreign investment attributable to producer's loans,

(2) Decreased (but not below zero), to the extent they are treated, under §1.996-1(a) or (b) (relating to ordering rules for distributions), as made out of previously taxed income, by the amounts of any actual qualifying distributions pursuant to §1.992-3 in the order in which they are made, and thereafter by the amounts of any other actual distributions in the order in which they are made, except that, prior to any actual distribution, previously taxed income shall be reduced by the portion of any deficit in earnings and profits for the taxable year chargeable at that time under §1.996-2(a)(3) to previously taxed income.

(d) *Other earnings and profits.*—Under section 996(f)(3), other earnings and profits consist of earnings and profits other than accumulated DISC income and previously taxed income described respectively in paragraphs (b) and (c) of this section. Other earnings and profits as of the close of each taxable year of the corporation is (subject to paragraph (e) of this section) an amount equal to the amount of other earnings and profits as of the close of the immediately preceding taxable year decreased (if necessary, below zero) in the following order by—

(1) To the extent they are treated, under §1.996-1(a) or (b) (relating to ordering rules for distributions), as made out of other earnings and profits, the amounts of any actual qualifying distributions pursuant to §1.992-3 in the order in which they are made, and thereafter the amount of any other actual distributions in the order in which they are made, except that, prior to any actual distribution, other earnings and profits shall be reduced by the portion of any deficit in earnings and profits for the taxable year chargeable at that time under §1.996-2(a)(1) to other earnings and profits, and

(2) With respect to a distribution in redemption to which §1.996-4(b)(1) applies, an amount

equal to the excess (if any) of (*a*) the reduction in the corporation's earnings and profits (see section 312(e)) over (*b*) the amount of the reduction under §1.996-4(b)(1) in accumulated DISC income.

(e) *Distributions in kind.*—(1) For purposes of determining, under paragraphs (b), (c), and (d) of this section, the amount by which any division of earnings and profits is reduced by reason of a distribution of property (other than money, or the DISC's, or former DISC's, own obligations), the amount of such distribution is the fair market value of such property at the time of the distribution.

(2) For any taxable year in which the DISC makes a distribution of such property, the amount of other earnings and profits determined under paragraph (d) of this section (without regard to this subparagraph) shall be—

(i) Increased by the excess (if any) of the amount of such distribution treated as a dividend under section 316(a) over the adjusted basis of such property, and

(ii) Decreased by the excess (if any) of the adjusted basis of such property over the amount of such distribution treated as a dividend under section 316(a).

Each item of property shall be considered separately for purposes of making the adjustment under this subparagraph.

(f) *Examples.*—The provisions of §§1.996-1, 1.996-2, and this section may be illustrated by the following examples:

Example (1). M Corporation, which uses the calendar year as its taxable year, elects to be treated as a DISC beginning with 1974. During 1975, M derives no earnings and profits and makes no deemed or actual distributions, except that on December 31, 1975, M's shareholders are treated as having received a dividend distribution of $100 under §1.995-2(a)(5) (relating to foreign investment attributable to producer's loans). M's earnings and profits are adjusted as shown on line (2) of the table below on the basis of facts assumed therein.

		Accumulated earnings and profits	Accumulated DISC income	Previously taxed income	Other earnings and profits
(1)	Balance Jan. 1, 1975	$450	$100	$250	$100
(2)	Adjustments (see paragraphs (b)(3)(ii) and (c)(1)(v) of this section)	0	(100)	100	0
(3)	Balance Jan. 1, 1976	450	0	350	100

Example (2). N Corporation, which uses the calendar year as its taxable year, elects to be treated as a DISC beginning with 1972. During 1973, N derives no earnings and profits for the year and makes no deemed or actual distributions, except that A, a shareholder, realized $200 of gain upon receiving an actual cash distribution of $300 in redemption of N stock having an adjusted basis of $100 in his hands. The redemp-

tion is treated as an exchange under section 302(a) but, under section 995(c), A includes the $200 of gain in his gross income as a dividend. Assuming that, under section 312(e), $240 is properly chargeable to capital account of N and that, under §1.996-4(b), accumulated DISC income is reduced by $200, N's accounts are adjusted on line (2) of the table below on the basis of facts assumed therein.

		Capital	Accumulated earnings and profits	Accumulated DISC income	Previously taxed income	Other earnings and profits
(1)	Balance Jan. 1, 1973 . . .	$2,000	$400	$300	$100	0
(2)	Adjustments (see §1.996-4(b) and paragraph (c)(1)(iv) of this section)	(240)	(60)	(200)	140	0
(3)	Balance Jan. 1, 1974	1,760	340	100	240	0

Example (3). P Corporation, which uses the calendar year as its taxable year, elects to be treated as a DISC beginning with 1973. During 1974, P derives no earnings and profits for the year and makes no deemed or actual distributions, except for a distribution to B, its sole shareholder, of property with a fair market value of $100 and an adjusted basis in P's hands of $40.

Under §1.996-1(a)(1), B treats the entire amount of the distribution as being made out of previously taxed income and, under §1.996-1(c), excludes it from his gross income. P's earnings and profits' divisions are adjusted on lines (2) and (3) of the table below on the basis of facts assumed therein.

Reg. §1.996-3(e)(1)

		Accumulated earnings and profits	Accumulated DISC income	Previously taxed income	Other earnings and profits
(1)	Balance January 1, 1974	$200	$80	$120	$0
(2)	Adjustment under paragraphs (c)(2) and (e)(1) this section	(40)	0	(100)	0
(3)	Adjustment under paragraph (e)(2)(i) of this section	0	0	0	60
(4)	Balance January 1, 1975	160	80	20	60

Example (4). Q Corporation, which uses the calendar year as its taxable year, elects to be treated as a DISC beginning with 1974. On January 1, 1975, Q has accumulated earnings and profits of $1,200 and, during 1975, Q incurs a deficit in earnings and profits of $365. The amount of such deficit incurred as of any date before the close of 1975 cannot be shown. On July 1, 1975, Q makes a cash distribution of $650, with respect to its stock to C, Q's sole shareholder. C subsequently transfers by gift all of his

Q stock to D. On December 31, 1975, Q makes a cash distribution of $650, with respect to its stock, to D. Under these facts and additional facts assumed in the table below, C is treated as having received a dividend of $650 of which $320 is treated as distributed out of previously taxed income and excluded from gross income. D is treated as receiving a dividend of $186. Adjustments to Q's earnings and profits accounts are illustrated in the table below.

		Accumulated earnings and profits	Accumulated DISC income	Previously taxed income	Other earnings and profits
(1)	Balance January 1, 1975	$1,200	$800	$320	$80
(2)	Portion of 1975 deficit of $365 chargeable as of June 30, 1975, pursuant to § 1.996-2(a)	(181)	(101)	0	(80)
(3)	Balance July 1, 1975	1,019	699	320	0
(4)	$650 distributed to C on July 1, 1975	(650)	(330)	(320)	0
(5)	Portion of 1975 deficit of $365 chargeable as of December 30, 1975, pursuant to § 1.996-2(a)	(183)	(183)	0	0
(6)	Balance December 31, 1975	186	186	0	0
(7)	$650 distributed to D on December 31, 1975[1]	(186)	(186)	0	0
(8)	Balance January 1, 1976	0	0	0	0

[1] $60 treated as return of capital pursuant to section 301(c)(2).

Example (5)—(1) *Facts.* R Corporation, which uses the calendar year as its taxable year, elects to be treated as a DISC beginning with 1972. X Corporation is its sole shareholder. At the beginning of 1974, R has a deficit in earnings and profits of $60 all of which is composed of "other earnings and profits". For 1974, R has earnings and profits of $80 before reduction for any distributions and taxable income of $70. On June 15, 1974, R makes a cash distribution to X of $60, with respect to its stock, to which section 301 applies. On August 15, 1974, R makes a cash distribution to X of $30 designated as a distribution to meet qualification requirements pursuant to § 1.992-3. Under § 1.995-2(a), X is deemed to receive, on December 31, 1974, a distribution of a dividend of $35, *i.e.*, one-half of R's taxable income of $70. The tax consequences of these facts to X and their effect on R's earnings and profits are set forth in the subsequent subparagraphs of this example.

(2) *Dividend treatment of actual distributions.* Since R had $80 of earnings and profits for 1974 and a deficit in accumulated earnings and profits at the beginning of 1974, only $80 of the actual distributions ($90) are treated as dividends under sections 301(c)(1) and 316(a)(2). ($10 of the actual distribution, which is not treated as a dividend is treated in the manner specified in section 301(c)(2) and (3).) Thus, under § 1.316-2(b), $26.67 of the actual qualifying distribution made on August 15, 1974 ($30 × $80/$90), and $53.33 of the actual distribution made on June 15, 1974 ($60 × $80/$90), are considered made out of earnings and profits.

(3) *Priority of distributions.* Under § 1.996-1(d), for purposes of adjusting the divisions of R's earnings and profits and determining the treatment of subsequent distributions, the sequence in which each distribution is treated as having been made is—

(i) First, the deemed distribution of $35,

(ii) Second, the actual qualifying distribution of $30 made on August 15, 1974, pursuant to § 1.992-3, and

(iii) Finally, the actual distribution of $60 made on June 15, 1974.

(4) *Treatment and effect of deemed distribution.* Under § 1.995-2(a), on December 31, 1974, X includes the deemed distribution of $35 in its gross income as a dividend. Under paragraph (b)(1)(ii) of this section, R's previously taxed income is increased by $35 as shown on line (3) of the table in subparagraph (7) of this example. Under paragraph (b)(1)(ii) and (2) of this section, accumulated DISC income is increased by $45 of DISC income, *i.e.,* R's earnings and profits for 1974, $80, minus the deemed distribution of $35, as shown on line (4) of the table.

(5) *Treatment and effect of actual qualifying distribution of $30.* As indicated in subparagraph (2) of this example, $26.67 of the $30 qualifying distribution on August 15, 1974, is treated as made out of earnings and profits for 1974. Under § 1.996-1(b)(1)(i), the entire $26.67 is treated as distributed out of accumulated DISC income. Thus, on August 15, 1974, X includes $26.67 in its gross income as a dividend. No deduction is allowable under section 243. Under paragraph (b)(3)(iv) of this section, R's accumulated DISC income is reduced by $26.67 as shown on line (6) of the table in subparagraph (7) of this example.

(6) *Treatment and effect of actual distribution of $60.* As indicated in subparagraph (2) of this example, $53.33 of the $60 distribution on June 15, 1974, is treated as made out of earnings and profits for 1974. Under § 1.996-1(a), the $53.33 is treated as distributed out of previously taxed income to the extent thereof, $35, and then out of accumulated DISC income, $18.33. Thus, on June 15, 1974, X includes $18.33 in its gross income as a dividend. Under § 1.996-1(c), the distribution of $35 out of previously taxed income is excluded from gross income. No deduction is allowable under section 243 with respect to the actual distribution of $53.33. Under paragraph (b)(3)(iv) of this section, accumulated DISC income is reduced by $18.33 and, under paragraph (c)(2) of this section, previously taxed income is reduced by $35, as shown on line (7) of the table in subparagraph (7) of this example.

(7) *Summary.* The effects on earnings and profits and the divisions of earnings and profits are summarized in the following table:

		Earnings and profits for year	Accumulated earnings and profits	Accumulated DISC income	Previously taxed income	Other earnings and profits
(1)	Balance Jan. 1, 1974 .	. . .	($60.00)	. . .	. . .	($60.00)
(2)	Earnings and profits for year before reduction for distributions　.	$80.00	. . .	. . .	. . .	. . .
(3)	Deemed distribution of $35 to X on Dec. 31, 1974, under § 1.995-2(a)	. . .	. . .	. . .	$35.00	. . .
(4)	DISC income for 1974 of $45 as defined in paragraph (b)(2) of this section (line 2 ($80) minus line 3 ($35))	. . .	. . .	$45.00	. . .	. . .
(5)	Balance before actual distributions　.	80.00	(60.00)	45.00	35.00	(60.00)
(6)	Qualifying distribution of $30 to X on Aug. 15, 1974, pursuant to § 1.992-3	(26.67)	. . .	(26.67)	. . .	. . .
(7)	Actual distribution to P of $60 on June 15, 1974	(53.33)	. . .	(18.33)	(35.00)	. . .
(8)	Balance Jan. 1, 1975 .	0	($60.00)	0	. . .	($60.00)

Example (6). Assume the facts are the same as in example (5), except that at the beginning of 1974 R's accumulated earnings and profits amount to $60 consisting of accumulated DISC income of $20, previously taxed income of $10, and other earnings and profits of $30. In addition, on August 1, 1974, X transfers all R's stock to Y Corporation in a reorganization described in section 368(a)(1)(B) in which under section 354 X recognizes no gain or loss. Under these facts, X includes in its gross income for 1974 a dividend of $15 which is attributable to the actual distribution of $60 paid out of earnings and profits on June 15, 1974. X excludes from gross income the balance of the $60 distribution ($45) paid out of earnings and profits because, under § 1.996-1(a), it is treated as paid out of previously taxed income. Y includes in its gross income for 1974 a dividend of $65 of which $35 is attributable to the deemed distribution of a dividend to Y on December 31, 1974, under § 1.995-2(a) and $30 is attributable to the qualifying distribution paid out of earnings and profits to Y on August 15, 1974. The adjustments to R's earnings and profits are summarized in the following table:

		Earnings and profits for year	Accumulated earnings and profits	Accumulated DISC income	Previously taxed income	Other earnings and profits
(1)	Balance Jan. 1, 1974	...	$60.00	$20.00	$10.00	$30.00
(2)	Earnings and profits for year before reduction for distributions	$80.00	...	...	...	...
(3)	Deemed distribution of $35 to Y on Dec. 31, 1974, under § 1.995-2(a)	...	...	...	$35.00	...
(4)	DISC income for 1974 of $45 as defined in paragraph (b)(2) of this section (line 2 ($80) minus line 3 ($35))	...	...	$45.00	...	...
(5)	Balance before actual distributions	$80.00	$60.00	65.00	45.00	$30.00
(6)	Qualifying distribution of $30 to Y on Aug. 15, 1974, pursuant to § 1.992-3	(26.67)	(3.33)	(30.00)	...	...
(7)	Actual distribution to X of $60 on June 15, 1974	(53.33)	(6.67)	(15.00)	(45.00)	...
(8)	Balance Jan. 1, 1975	...	50.00	20.00	0	30.00

(g) *DISCs having corporate and noncorporate shareholders.*—In the case of a DISC having one or more corporate shareholders but less than all of its shareholders subject to the special rules of section 291(a)(4), relating to certain deferred DISC income as a corporate preference item, accumulated DISC income and previously taxed income of the DISC are divided between the corporate shareholders, as a class, and the other shareholders, as a class, in proportion to amounts of DISC income not deemed distributed and amounts deemed distributed to each class. Subsequent taxation of actual and qualifying distributions shall be based upon this division. Thus, if a DISC is owned 50 percent by corporate shareholders and 50 percent by individual shareholders and has undistributed taxable income of $2,000 for its year, the division is made as follows:

Corporate shareholders:
Previously taxed income (57.5% of $2,000 ÷ 2) $575
Accumulated DISC income (42.5% of $2,000 ÷ 2) 425
Individual shareholders:
Previously taxed income (50% of $2,000 ÷ 2) 500
Accumulated DISC income (50% of $2,000 ÷ 2) 500

[Reg. § 1.996-3.]

☐ [*T.D. 7324, 9-27-74. Amended by T.D. 7854, 11-15-82 and T.D. 7984, 10-11-84.*]

[Reg. § 1.996-4]

§ 1.996-4. Subsequent effect of previous disposition of DISC stock.—(a) *Shareholder adjustment for previously taxed income.*—(1) Under section 996(d)(1), except as provided in subparagraph (2) of this paragraph, if—

(i) Gain with respect to a share of stock of a DISC, or former DISC, is treated under § 1.995-4 as a dividend, and

(ii) With respect to such share, any person subsequently receives an actual distribution made out of accumulated DISC income, or a deemed distribution made, pursuant to § 1.995-3, by reason of disqualification, out of accumulated DISC income,

then such person shall treat such distribution in the same manner as a distribution from previously taxed income (and thus excludable from gross income under § 1.996-1(c)) to the extent that the gain referred to in subdivision (i) of this subparagraph exceeds the aggregate amount of any other distributions with respect to such share which were treated under this subparagraph as made from previously taxed income.

Reg. § 1.996-4(a)(1)(ii)

(2) In applying subparagraph (1) of this paragraph with respect to a share of stock in a DISC, or former DISC, the gain referred to in subparagraph (1)(i) of this paragraph does not include any gain to a shareholder on a redemption of such share which qualifies as an exchange under section 302(a) or any gain on a disposition of such share prior to such redemption. Distributions described in subparagraph (1)(ii) of this paragraph do not include a distribution in a redemption which qualifies as an exchange under section 302(a). For adjustments to accumulated DISC income by reason of dividend treatment under §1.995-4 with respect to gain upon a redemption of DISC stock to which section 302(a) applies and upon a prior disposition of such stock, see paragraph (b) of this section.

(3) *Example.*—The provisions of this paragraph may be illustrated by the following example:

Example. In 1974, under §1.995-4, A, a shareholder of a DISC, on the sale of his DISC stock to B, is required to treat $20 of his gain as a dividend. The DISC has no previously taxed income and $40 of accumulated DISC income. Subsequently in the same year, B, the purchaser of the stock, receives an actual dividend distribution of $15 with respect to such stock which, under §1.996-1(a), is treated as made out of accumulated DISC income. The amounts of the DISC's previously taxed income and accumulated DISC income were not adjusted by reason of the $20 treated as a dividend on the prior sale. However, even though the DISC had no previously taxed income, the purchaser would treat the $15 as though it had been paid out of previously taxed income and, therefore would not include the $15 in gross income. If in 1975, B receives another actual distribution of $9 with respect to such stock, $5 (i.e., $20 dividend on A's sale less the $15 distribution to B in 1974 which was treated under subparagraph (1) of this paragraph as made from previously taxed income) is treated as made from previously taxed income and excluded from gross income. The result would be the same if, on January 1, 1975, B had transferred such stock to C by gift and the $9 distribution had been made to C.

(b) *Corporate adjustment upon redemption.*— (1) Under section 996(d)(2), if by reason of §1.995-4 gain on a redemption of stock in a DISC, or former DISC, is included in the shareholder's gross income as a dividend, then the accumulated DISC income shall be reduced by an amount equal to the sum of—

(i) The amount of gain on such redemption which, under §1.995-4, is treated as a dividend, and

(ii) The amount of any gain with respect to such redeemed stock which, under §1.995-4,

was treated as a dividend on a disposition prior to such redemption minus the amount of distributions with respect to such stock which have been treated as made out of previously taxed income by reason of the application of paragraph (a)(1) of this section.

(2) The provisions of this paragraph may be illustrated by the following examples:

Example (1). The entire stock of a DISC, which uses the calendar year as its taxable year, has been owned equally by A, B, C, and D since it was organized. At the close of 1976, when the DISC has $100 of accumulated DISC income, it redeems all of A's shares in a transaction qualifying as an exchange under section 302(a) and A, under §1.995-4, includes $25 in his gross income as a dividend. The redemption has the effect of reducing accumulated DISC income by $25 to $75.

Example (2). Assume the same facts as in example (1) except that the stock of the DISC has not been held equally by A, B, C, and D since its organization. A purchased his shares from X in 1974 in a transaction in which X, under §1.995-4, included in his gross income $30 as a dividend. In 1975, A receives a distribution of $10 out of accumulated DISC income which, under paragraph (a)(1) of this section, is treated as made out of previously taxed income. Under these facts, the redemption of A's stock in 1976 has the effect of reducing accumulated DISC income by $45 to $55 determined as follows:

(a)	Accumulated DISC income		$100
(b)	Minus sum of		
	(1) Dividend on redemption of A's stock	$25	
	Excess of dividend on X's sale ($30) over distribution to A treated as made out of previously taxed		
	(2) income ($10)	20	
	Total		45
(c)	Accumulated DISC income on 12/31/76 . . .		$ 55

[Reg. §1.996-4.]

☐ [T.D. 7324, 9-27-74.]

[Reg. §1.996-5]

§1.996-5. Adjustment to basis.—(a) *Addition to basis.*—Under section 996(e)(1) amounts representing deemed distributions as provided in section 995(b) shall increase the basis of the stock with respect to which the distribution is made.

(b) *Reductions of basis.*—Under section 996(e)(2), the portion of an actual distribution treated as made out of previously taxed income shall reduce the basis of the stock with respect to which it is made and, to the extent that it exceeds the adjusted basis of such stock, shall be treated as gain from the sale or exchange of property. In the case of stock includible in the gross estate of a decedent for which an election is made under section 2032 (relating to alternate valuation), this paragraph shall not apply to any distribution made after the date of the decedent's death and before the alternate valuation date provided by section 2032. See section 1014(d) for a special rule for determining the basis of stock in a DISC, or former DISC, acquired from a decedent. [Reg. § 1.996-5.]

[T.D. 7324, 9-27-74.]

[Reg. § 1.996-6]

§ 1.996-6. Effectively connected income.—In the case of a shareholder who is a nonresident alien individual or a foreign corporation, trust, or estate, amounts taxable as dividends by reason of the application of § 1.995-4 (relating to gain on disposition of stock in a DISC), amounts treated under § 1.996-1 as distributed out of accumulated DISC income, and amounts deemed distributed under § 1.995-2(a)(1) through (4) shall be treated as gains and distributions which are effectively connected with the conduct of a trade or business conducted through a permanent establishment of such shareholder within the United States, and shall be subject to tax in accordance with the provisions of section 871(b) and the regulations thereunder in the case of nonresident alien individuals, trusts, or estates, or section 882 and the regulations thereunder in the case of foreign corporations. In no case, however, shall other income of such shareholder be taxable as effectively connected with the conduct of a trade or business through a permanent establishment in the United States solely because of the application of this section. [Reg. § 1.996-6.]

[T.D. 7324, 9-27-74.]

[Reg. § 1.996-7]

§ 1.996-7. Carryover of DISC tax attributes.— (a) *In general.*—Carryover of a DISC's divisions of earnings and profits to acquiring corporations in nontaxable transactions shall be subject to rules generally applicable to other corporate tax attributes. For example, a DISC which acquires the assets of another DISC in a transaction to which section 381(a) applies shall succeed to, and take into account, the divisions of the earnings and profits of the transferor DISC in accordance with section 381(c)(2).

(b) *Allocation of divisions of earnings and profits in corporate separations.*—(1) If one DISC transfers part of its assets to a controlled DISC in a transaction to which section 368(a)(1)(D) applies and immediately thereafter the stock of the controlled DISC is distributed in a distribution or

exchange to which section 355 (or so much of section 356 as relates to section 355) applies, then—

(i) The earnings and profits of the distributing DISC immediately before the transaction shall be allocated between the distributing DISC and the controlled DISC in accordance with the provisions of § 1.312-10.

(ii) Each of the divisions of such earnings and profits, namely previously taxed income, accumulated DISC income, and other earnings and profits, shall be allocated between the distributing DISC and the controlled DISC on the same basis as the earnings and profits are allocated.

(iii) Any assets of the distributing DISC whose status as qualified export assets is limited by its accumulated DISC income (*e.g.*, producer's loans described in § 1.993-4, Export-Import Bank and other obligations described in § 1.993-2(h), and financing obligations described in § 1.993-2(i)) shall be treated as having been allocated, for the purpose of determining the classification of such assets in the hands of the distributing DISC or the controlled DISC, on the same basis as the earnings and profits are allocated regardless of how such assets are actually allocated.

(2) *Example.*—The provisions of this paragraph may be illustrated by the following example:

Example. On January 1, 1974, P Corporation transfers part of its assets to S Corporation, a newly organized subsidiary of P, in a transaction described in section 368(a)(1)(D) and distributes all the S stock in a transaction which qualifies under section 355. Immediately before such transfer, P had earnings and profits of $120,000 of which $100,000 constitutes accumulated DISC income. The unpaid balance of P's producer's loans is $80,000 all of which is retained by P. Pursuant to § 1.312-10, 25 percent of P's accumulated DISC income is allocated to S (*i.e.*, $25,000). P's producer's loans will be treated as allocated to S in the same proportion. Accordingly, for purposes of determining, under § 1.993-4(a)(3), the amount of producer's loans which S is entitled to make, S is treated as having an unpaid balance of producer's loans of $20,000 (*i.e.*, 25% × $80,000) and P is treated as having an unpaid balance of $60,000 (*i.e.*, 75% × $80,000).

(c) *Accumulated DISC income accounts of separate DISC's maintained after corporate combination.*—If two or more DISC's combine to form a new DISC, or if the assets of one DISC are acquired by another DISC, in a transaction described in section 381(a), accumulated DISC income of the acquired DISC or DISC's shall carry over and be taken into account by the acquiring or new DISC, except that a separate account shall be maintained for the accumulated DISC income of any DISC scheduled to be received as a deemed distribution by its shareholders under § 1.995-3 (relating to deemed distributions upon disqualification). If, as a part of such transaction, the stock of the DISC which has accumulated DISC income scheduled to be deemed distributed is exchanged for stock of the acquiring or new DISC to which such accumulated DISC income is carried over and which maintains a separate account, then such accumulated DISC income shall be deemed distributed pro rata to shareholders of the acquiring or new DISC on the basis of stock ownership immediately after the exchange. [Reg. § 1.996-7.]

☐ [T.D. 7324, 9-27-74.]

[Reg. § 1.996-8]

§ 1.996-8. Effect of carryback of capital loss or net operating loss to prior DISC taxable year.—(a) Under § 1.995-2(e), the deduction under section 172 for a net operating loss carryback or under section 1212 for a capital loss carryback is determined as if the DISC were a domestic corporation which had not elected to be treated as a DISC. A carryback of a net operating loss or of a capital loss of any corporation which reduces its taxable income for a preceding taxable year for which it qualified as a DISC will have the consequences enumerated in paragraphs (b) through (e) of this section.

(b) For such preceding taxable year, the amount of a deemed distribution of one-half of certain taxable income described in § 1.995-2(a)(4) will ordinarily be reduced in effect (but not below zero) by one-half of the sum of the amount of the deduction under section 172 for such year for net operating loss carrybacks and the amount of the deduction under section 1212 for such year for capital loss carrybacks.

(c) The amount of reduction in the deemed distribution under paragraph (b) of this section will have the effect of increasing the limitation, provided in § 1.995-2(b)(2), on the amount of foreign investment attributable to producer's loans which is deemed distributed under § 1.995-2(a)(5).

(d) If the amount of a deemed distribution for a preceding taxable year is reduced as described in paragraph (b) of this section, then for such preceding taxable year the previously taxed income (as defined in § 1.996-3(c)) shall be de-

creased by the amount of such reduction and the accumulated DISC income (as defined in § 1.996-3(b)) shall be increased by the amount of such reduction. Such adjustments shall be made as of the time the deemed distribution for such preceding taxable year is treated as having occurred. See § 1.996-1(d) for the priority of such deemed distribution in relation to other distributions made in that preceding taxable year.

(e) The amount and treatment of any actual distribution made in such preceding taxable year or a year subsequent to such preceding year, and the treatment of gain on a disposition (in any such year) of the DISC's stock to which § 1.995-4 applies, shall be properly adjusted to reflect the adjustments to previously taxed income and accumulated DISC income described in paragraph (d) of this section. [Reg. § 1.996-8.]

☐ [T.D. 7324, 9-27-74.]

[Reg. § 1.997-1]

§ 1.997-1. Special rules for subchapter C of the Code.—(a) For purposes of applying the provisions of sections 301 through 395 of the Code, any distribution in property to a corporation by a DISC, or former DISC, which is made out of previously taxed income or accumulated DISC income shall be treated as a distribution in the same amount as if such distribution of property were made to an individual, and have a basis, in the hands of the recipient corporation, equal to such amount treated as having been distributed.

(b) This section may be illustrated by the following example:

Example. X corporation is the sole shareholder of Y corporation which is a DISC. Y makes an actual distribution of property to X with respect to X's stock in Y. The property has a basis of $50 and a fair market value of $100. The distribution is treated as made out of accumulated DISC income under section 996(a) and is taxable as a dividend under section 301(c)(1). Even though X is a corporation, the amount of the distribution is $100 notwithstanding the provisions of section 301(b)(1)(B) and the basis of the property in X's hands is $100 notwithstanding the provisions of section 301(d)(2). [Reg. § 1.997-1.]

☐ [T.D. 7324, 9-27-74.]

International Boycott Determinations

[Reg. § 7.999-1]

§ 7.999-1. Computation of the international boycott factor (Temporary).—(a) *In general.*— Sections 908(a), 952(a)(3), and 995(b)(1)(F) provide that certain benefits of the foreign tax credit, deferral of earnings of foreign corporations, and DISC are denied if a person or a member of a controlled group (within the meaning of section 993(a)(3)) that includes that person participates in or cooperates with an international boycott

(within the meaning of section 999(b)(3)). The loss of tax benefits may be determined by multiplying the otherwise allowable tax benefits by the "international boycott factor." Section 999(c)(1) provides that the international boycott factor is to be determined under regulations prescribed by the Secretary. The method of computing the international boycott factor is set forth in paragraph (c) of this section. A special rule for computing the international boycott factor of a person that is a member of two or more controlled groups is set forth in paragraph (d). Transitional rules for making adjustments to the international boycott factor for years affected by the effective dates are set forth in paragraph (e). The definitions of the terms used in this section are set forth in paragraph (b).

(b) *Definitions.*—For purposes of this section:

(1) *Boycotting country.*—In respect of a particular international boycott, the term "boycotting country" means any country described in section 999(a)(1)(A) or (B) that requires participation in or cooperation with that particular international boycott.

(2) *Participation in or cooperation with an international boycott.*—For the definition of the term "participation in or cooperation with an international boycott", see section 999(b)(3) and Parts H through M of the Treasury Department's International Boycott Guidelines.

(3) *Operations in or related to a boycotting country.*—For the definitions of the terms "operations", "operations in a boycotting country", "operations related to a boycotting country", and "operations with the government, a company, or a national of a boycotting country", see Part B of the Treasury Department's International Boycott Guidelines.

(4) *Clearly demonstrating clearly separate and identifiable operations.*—For the rules for "clearly demonstrating clearly separate and identifiable operations", see Part D of the Treasury Department's International Boycott Guidelines.

(5) *Purchase made from a country.*—The terms "purchase made from a boycotting country" and "purchases made from any country other than the United States" mean, in respect of any particular country, the gross amount paid in connection with the purchase of, the use of, or the right to use:

(i) Tangible personal property (including money) from a stock of goods located in that country,

(ii) Intangible property (other than securities) in that country,

(iii) Securities by a dealer to a beneficial owner that is a resident of that country (but only if the dealer knows or has reason to know the country of residence of the beneficial owner),

(iv) Real property located in that country, or

(v) Services performed in, and the end product of services performed in, that country (other than payroll paid to a person that is an officer or employee of the payor).

(6) *Sales made to a country.*—The terms "sales made to a boycotting country" and "sales made to any country other than the United States" mean, in respect of any particular coun-try, the gross receipts from the sale, exchange, other disposition, or use of:

(i) Tangible personal property (including money) for direct use, consumption, or disposition in that country,

(ii) Services performed in that country.

(iii) The end product of services (wherever performed) for direct use, consumption, or disposition in that country,

(iv) Intangible property (other than securities) in that country,

(v) Securities by a dealer to a beneficial owner that is a resident of the country (but only if the dealer knows or has reason to know the country of residence of the beneficial owner), or

(vi) Real property located in that country. To determine the country of direct use, consumption, or disposition of tangible personal property and the end product of services, see paragraph (b)(10) of this section.

(7) *Sales made from a country.*—The terms "sales made from a boycotting country" and "sales made from any country other than the United States" mean, in respect of a particular country, the gross receipts from the sale, exchange, other disposition, or use of:

(i) Tangible personal property (including money) from a stock of goods located in that country,

(ii) Intangible property (other than securities) in that country, or

(iii) Services performed in, and the end product of services performed in, that country.

However, gross receipts from any such sale, exchange, other disposition, or use by a person that are included in the numerator of that person's international boycott factor by reason of paragraph (b)(6) of this section shall not again be included in the numerator by reason of this subparagraph.

(8) *Payroll paid or accrued for services performed in a country.*—The terms "payroll paid or accrued for services performed in a boycotting country" and "payroll paid or accrued for services performed in any country other than the United States" mean, in respect of a particular country, the total amount paid or accrued as compensation to officers and employees, including wages, salaries, commissions, and bonuses, for services performed in that country.

(9) *Services performed partly within and partly without a country.*—(i) *In general.*—Except as provided in paragraph (b)(9)(ii) of this section, for purposes of allocating to a particular country:

(A) The gross amount paid in connection with the purchase or use of,

(B) The gross receipts from the sale, exchange, other disposition or use of, and

(C) The payroll paid or accrued
for services performed, or the end product of services performed, partly within and partly

Reg. §7.999-1(b)(9)(i)(C)

without that country, the amount paid, received, or accrued to be allocated to that country, unless the facts and circumstances of a particular case warrant a different amount, will be that amount that bears the same relation to the total amount paid, received, or accrued as the number of days of performance of the services within that country bears to the total number of days of performance of services for which the total amount is paid, received, or accrued.

(ii) *Transportation, telegraph, and cable services.*—Transportation, telegraph, and cable services performed partly within one country and partly within another country are allocated between the two countries as follows:

(A) In the case of a purchase of such services performed from Country A to Country B, fifty percent of the gross amount paid is deemed to be a purchase made from Country A and the remaining fifty percent is deemed to be a purchase made from Country B.

(B) In the case of a sale of such services performed from Country A to Country B, fifty percent of the gross receipts is deemed to be a sale made from Country B and the remaining fifty percent is deemed to be a sale made to Country B.

(10) *Country of use, consumption, or disposition.*—As a general rule, the country of use, consumption, or disposition of tangible personal property (including money) and the end product of services (wherever performed) is deemed to be the country of destination of the tangible personal property or the end product of the services. (Thus, if legal services are performed in one country and an opinion is given for use by a client in a second country, the end product of the legal services is used, consumed, or disposed of in the second country.) The occurrence in a country of a temporary interruption in the shipment of the tangible personal property or the delivery of the end product of services shall not constitute such country the country of destination. However, if at the time of the transaction the person providing the tangible personal property or the end product of services knew, or should have known from the facts and circumstances surrounding the transaction, that the tangible personal property or the end product of services probably would not be used, consumed, or disposed of in the country of destination, that person must determine the country of ultimate use, consumption or disposition of the tangible personal property or the end product of services. Notwithstanding the preceding provisions of this subparagraph, a person that sells, exchanges, otherwise disposes of, or makes available for use, tangible personal property to any person all of whose business except for an insubstantial part consists of selling from inventory to retail customers at retail outlets all within one country may assume at the time of such sale to such person that the tangible personal property will be used, consumed, or disposed of within such country.

(11) *Controlled group taxable year.*—The term "controlled group taxable year" means the taxable year of the controlled group's common parent corporation. In the event that no common parent corporation exists, the members of the group shall elect the taxable year of one of the members of the controlled group to serve as the controlled group taxable year. The taxable year election is a binding election to be changed only with the approval of the Secretary or his delegate. The election is to be made in accordance with the procedures set forth in the instructions to Form 5713, the International Boycott Report.

(c) *Computation of international boycott factor.*—(1) *In general.*—The method of computing the international boycott factor of a person that is not a member of a controlled group is set forth in paragraph (c)(2) of this section. The method of computing the international boycott factor of a person that is a member of a controlled group is set forth in paragraph (c)(3) of this section. For purposes of paragraphs (c)(2) and (3), purchases and sales made by, and payroll paid or accrued by, a partnership are deemed to be made or paid or accrued by a partner in that proportion that the partner's distributive share bears to the purchases and sales made by, and the payroll paid or accrued by, the partnership. Also for purposes of paragraphs (c)(2) and (3), purchases and sales made by, and payroll paid or accrued by, a trust referred to in section 671 are deemed to be made both by the trust (for purposes of determining the trust's international boycott factor), and by a person treated under section 671 as the owner of the trust (but only in that proportion that the portion of the trust that such person is considered as owning under sections 671 through 679 bears to the purchases and sales made by, and the payroll paid and accrued by, the trust).

(2) *International boycott factor of a person that is not a member of a controlled group.*—The international boycott factor to be applied by a person that is not a member of a controlled group (within the meaning of section 993(a)(3)) is a fraction.

(i) The numerator of the fraction is the sum of the—

(A) Purchases made from all boycotting countries associated in carrying out a particular international boycott,

(B) Sales made to or from all boycotting countries associated in carrying out a particular international boycott, and

(C) Payroll paid or accrued for services performed in all boycotting countries associated in carrying out a particular international boycott by that person during that person's taxable year, minus the amount of such purchases, sales, and payroll that is clearly demonstrated to be attributable to clearly separate and identifiable operations in connection with which there was no participation in or cooperation with that international boycott.

(ii) The denominator of the fraction is the sum of the—

(A) Purchases made from any country other than the United States,

(B) Sales made to or from any country other than the United States, and

(C) Payroll paid or accrued for services performed in any country other than the United States

by that person during that person's taxable year.

(3) *International boycott factor of a person that is a member of a controlled group.*—The international boycott factor to be applied by a person that is a member of a controlled group (within the meaning of section 993(a)(3)) shall be computed in the manner described in paragraph (c)(2) of this section, except that there shall be taken into account the purchases and sales made by, and the payroll paid or accrued by, each member of the controlled group during each member's own taxable year that ends with or within the controlled group taxable year that ends with or within that person's taxable year.

(d) *Computation of the international boycott factor of a person that is a member of two or more controlled groups.*—The international boycott factor to be applied under sections 908(a), 953(a)(3), and 995(b)(1)(F) by a person that is a member of two or more controlled groups shall be determined in the manner described in paragraph (c)(3), except that the purchases, sales, and payroll included in the numerator and denominator shall include the purchases, sales, and payroll of that person and of all other members of the two or more controlled groups of which that person is a member.

(e) *Transitional rules.*—(1) *Pre-November 3, 1976 boycotting operations.*—The international boycott factor to be applied under sections 908(a), 952(a)(3), and 995(b)(1)(F) by a person that is not a member of a controlled group, for that person's taxable year that includes November 3, 1976, or a person that is a member of a controlled group, for the controlled group taxable year that includes November 3, 1976, shall be computed in the manner described in paragraphs (c)(2) and (c)(3), respectively, of this section. However, that the following adjustments shall be made:

(i) There shall be excluded from the numerators described in paragraphs (c)(2)(i) and (c)(3)(i) of this section purchases, sales, and payroll clearly demonstrated to be attributable to clearly separate and identifiable operations—

(A) That were completed on or before November 3, 1976, or

(B) In respect of which it is demonstrated that the agreements constituting participation in or cooperation with the international boycott were renounced, the renunciations were communicated on or before November 3, 1976, to the governments or persons with which the agreements were made, and the agreements have not been reaffirmed after November 3, 1976, and

(ii) The international boycott factor resulting after the numerator has been modified in accordance with paragraph (e)(1)(i) of this section shall be further modified by multiplying it by a fraction. The numerator of that fraction shall be the number of days in that person's taxable year (or, if applicable, in that person's controlled group taxable year) remaining after November 3, 1976, and the denominator shall be 366.

The principles of this subparagraph are illustrated in the following example:

Example. Corporation A, a calendar year taxpayer, is not a member of a controlled group. During the 1976 calendar year, Corporation A had three operations in a boycotting country under three separate contracts, each of which contained agreements constituting participation in or cooperation with an international boycott. Each contract was entered into on or after September 2, 1976. Operation (1) was completed on November 1, 1976. The sales made to a boycotting country in connection with Operation (1) amounted to $10. Operation (2) was not completed during the taxable year, but on November 1, 1976, Corporation A communicated a renunciation of the boycott agreement covering that operation to the government of the boycotting country. The sales made to a boycotting country in connection with Operation (2) amounted to $40. Operation (3) was not completed during the taxable year, nor was any renunciation of the boycott agreement made. The sales made to a boycotting country in connection with Operation (3) amounted to $25. Corporation A had no purchases made from, sales made from, or payroll paid or accrued for services performed in, a boycotting country. Corporation A had $500 of purchases made from, sales made from, sales made to, and payroll paid or accrued for services performed in, countries other than the United States. Company A's boycott factor for 1976, computed under paragraph (c)(2) of this section (before the application of this subparagraph) would be:

$$\frac{\$10 + \$40 + \$25}{\$500} = \frac{\$75}{\$500}$$

However, the $10 is eliminated from the numerator by reason of paragraph (e)(j)(1)(A) of this section, and the $40 is eliminated from the numerator by reason of paragraph (e)(j)(1)(B) of this section. Thus, before the application of paragraph (e)(1)(ii) of this section, Corporation A's international boycott factor is $25/$500. After the application of paragraph (e)(1)(ii), Corporation A's international boycott factor is:

$$\frac{\$25}{\$500} \times \frac{58}{366}$$

(2) *Pre-December 31, 1977 boycotting operations.*—The international boycott factor to be applied under sections 908(a), 952(a)(3), and 995(b)(1)(P) by a person that is not a member of a controlled group, for that person's taxable year that includes December 31, 1977, or by a person that is a member of a controlled group, for the controlled group taxable year that includes December 31, 1977, shall be computed in the manner described in paragraphs (c)(2) and (c)(3), respectively, of this section. However, the following adjustments shall be made:

(i) There shall be excluded from the numerators described in paragraphs (c)(2)(i) and (c)(3)(i) of this section purchases, sales, and payroll clearly demonstrated to be attributable to clearly separate and identifiable operations that were carried out in accordance with the terms of binding contracts entered into before September 3, 1976, and—

(A) That were completed on or before December 31, 1977, or

(B) In respect of which it is demonstrated that the agreements constituting participation in or cooperation with the international boycott were renounced, the renunciations were communicated on or before December 31, 1977, to the governments or persons with which the agreements were made, and the agreements were not reaffirmed after December 31, 1977, and

(ii) In the case of clearly separate and identifiable operations that are carried out in accordance with the terms of binding contracts entered into before September 2, 1976, but that do not meet the requirements of paragraph (e)(2)(i) of this section, the numerators described in paragraphs (e)(2)(i) and (e)(3)(i) of this section shall be adjusted by multiplying the purchases, sales, and payroll clearly demonstrated to be attributable to those operations by a fraction, the numerator of which is the number of days in such person's taxable year (or, if applicable, in such person's controlled group taxable year) remaining after December 31, 1977, and the denominator of which is 365.

The principles of this subparagraph are illustrated in the following example:

Example. Corporation A is not a member of a controlled group and reports on the basis of a July 1-June 30 fiscal year. During the 1977-1978 fiscal year, Corporation A had 2 operations carried out pursuant to the terms of separate contracts, each of which had a clause that constituted participation in or cooperation with an international boycott. Neither operation was completed during the fiscal year, nor were either of the boycotting clauses renounced. Operation (1) was carried out in accordance with the terms of a contract entered into on November 15, 1976. Operation (2) was carried out in accordance with the terms of a binding contract entered into before September 2, 1976. Corporation A had sales made to a boycotting country in connection with Operation (1) in the amount of $50, and in connection with Operation (2) in the amount of $100. Corporation A had sales made to countries other than the United States in the amount of $500. Corporation A had no purchases made from, sales made from, or payroll paid or accrued for services performed in, any country other than the United States. In the absence of this subparagraph, Corporation A's international boycott factor would be

$$\frac{\$50 + \$100}{\$500}$$

However, by reason of the application of this subparagraph, Corporation A's international boycott factor is reduced to

$$\frac{[(\$50 + \$100) \, (181 \, / \, 365)]}{500}$$

(3) *Incomplete controlled group taxable year.*—If, at the end of the taxable year of a person that is a member of a controlled group, the controlled group taxable year that includes November 3, 1976 has not ended, or the taxable year of one or more members of the controlled group that includes November 3, 1976 has not ended, then the international boycott factor to be applied under sections 908(a), 952(a)(3) and 955(b)(1)(P) by such person for the taxable year shall be computed in the manner described in paragraph (c)(3) of this section. However, the numerator and the denominator in that paragraph shall include only the purchases, sales, and payroll of those members of the controlled group whose taxable years ending after November 3, 1976 have ended as the end of the taxable year of such person.

(f) *Effective date.*—This section applies to participation in or cooperation with an international boycott after November 3, 1976. In the case of operations which constitute participation in or cooperation with an international boycott and which are carried out in accordance with the terms of a binding contract entered into before September 2, 1976, this section applies to such participation or cooperation after December 31, 1977. [Temporary Reg. §7.999-1.]

☐ [T.D. 7467, 2-24-77.]

[The next page is 51,901.]

GAIN OR LOSS ON DISPOSITION OF PROPERTY

Determination and Recognition of Gain or Loss

See p. 20,601 for regulations not amended to reflect law changes

[Reg. §1.1001-1]

§1.1001-1. Computation of gain or loss.—
(a) *General Rule.*—Except as otherwise provided in subtitle A of the Code, the gain or loss realized from the conversion of property into cash, or from the exchange of property for other property differing materially either in kind or in extent, is treated as income or as loss sustained. The amount realized from a sale or other disposition of property is the sum of any money received plus the fair market value of any property (other than money) received. The fair market value of property is a question of fact, but only in rare and extraordinary cases will property be considered to have no fair market value. The general method of computing such gain or loss is prescribed by section 1001(a) through (d) which contemplates that from the amount realized upon the sale or exchange there shall be withdrawn a sum sufficient to restore the adjusted basis prescribed by section 1011 and the regulations thereunder (i.e., the cost or other basis adjusted for receipts, expenditures, losses, allowances, and other items chargeable against and applicable to such cost or other basis). The amount which remains after the adjusted basis has been restored to the taxpayer constitutes the realized gain. If the amount realized upon the sale or exchange is insufficient to restore to the taxpayer the adjusted basis of the property, a loss is sustained to the extent of the difference between such adjusted basis and the amount realized. The basis may be different depending upon whether gain or loss is being computed. For example, see section 1015(a) and the regulations thereunder. Section 1001(e) and paragraph (f) of this section prescribe the method of computing gain or loss upon the sale or other disposition of a term interest in property the adjusted basis (or a portion) of which is determined pursuant, or by reference, to section 1014 (relating to the basis of property acquired from a decedent) or section 1015 (relating to the basis of property acquired by gift or by a transfer in trust).

(b) *Real estate taxes as amounts received.*—
(1) Section 1001(b) and section 1012 state rules applicable in making an adjustment upon a sale of real property with respect to the real property taxes apportioned between seller and purchaser under section 164(d). Thus, if the seller pays (or agrees to pay) real property taxes attributable to the real property tax year in which the sale occurs, he shall not take into account, in determining the amount realized from the sale under section 1001(b), any amount received as reimbursement for taxes which are treated under section 164(d) as imposed upon the purchaser. Similarly, in computing the cost of the property under section 1012, the purchaser shall not take into account any amount paid to the seller as reimbursement for real property taxes which are treated under section 164(d) as imposed upon the purchaser. These rules apply whether or not the contract of sale calls for the purchaser to reimburse the seller for such real property taxes paid or to be paid by the seller.

(2) On the other hand, if the purchaser pays (or is to pay) an amount representing real property taxes which are treated under section 164(d) as imposed upon the seller, that amount shall be taken into account both in determining the amount realized from the sale under section 1001(b) and in computing the cost of the property under section 1012. It is immaterial whether or not the contract of sale specifies that the sale price has been reduced by, or is in any way intended to reflect, the taxes allocable to the seller. See also paragraph (b) of §1.1012-1.

(3) Subparagraph (1) of this paragraph shall not apply to a seller who, in a taxable year prior to the taxable year of sale, pays an amount representing real property taxes which are treated under section 164(d) as imposed on the purchaser, if such seller has elected to capitalize such amount in accordance with section 266 and the regulations thereunder (relating to election to capitalize certain carrying charges and taxes).

(4) The application of this paragraph may be illustrated by the following examples:

Example (1). Assume that the contract price on the sale of a parcel of real estate is $50,000 and that real property taxes thereon in the amount of $1,000 for the real property tax year in which occurred the date of sale were previously paid by the seller. Assume further that $750 of the taxes are treated under section 164(d) as imposed upon the purchaser and that he reimburses the seller in that amount in addition to the contract price. The amount realized by the seller is $50,000. Similarly, $50,000 is the purchaser's cost. If, in this example, the purchaser made no payment other than the contract price of $50,000, the amount realized by the seller would be $49,250, since the sales price would be deemed to include $750 paid to the seller in reimbursement for real property taxes imposed upon the purchaser. Similarly, $49,250 would be the purchaser's cost.

Example (2). Assume that the purchaser in example (1) above, paid all of the real property taxes. Assume further that $250 of the taxes are treated under section 164(d) as imposed upon the seller. The amount realized by the seller is $50,250. Similarly, $50,250 is the purchaser's cost, regardless of the taxable year in which the purchaser makes actual payment of the taxes.

Example (3). Assume that the seller described in the first part of example (1), above, paid the real property taxes of $1,000 in the taxable year prior to the taxable year of sale and elected under section 266 to capitalize the $1,000 of taxes. In such a case, the amount realized is $50,750. Moreover, regardless of whether the seller elected to capitalize the real property taxes, the purchaser in that case could elect under section 266 to capitalize the $750 of taxes treated under section 164(d) as imposed upon him, in which case his adjusted basis would be $50,750 (cost of $50,000 plus capitalized taxes of $570 [$750]).

(c) *Other rules.*—(1) Even though property is not sold or otherwise disposed of, gain is realized if the sum of all the amounts received which are required by section 1016 and other applicable provisions of subtitle A of the Code to be applied against the basis of the property exceeds such basis. Except as otherwise provided in section 301(c)(3)(B) with respect to distributions out of increase in value of property accrued prior to March 1, 1913, such gain is includible in gross income under section 61 as "income from whatever source derived". On the other hand, a loss is not ordinarily sustained prior to the sale or other disposition of the property, for the reason that until such sale or other disposition occurs there remains the possibility that the taxpayer may recover or recoup the adjusted basis of the property. Until some identifiable event fixes the actual sustaining of a loss and the amount thereof, it is not taken into account.

(2) The provisions of subparagraph (1) of this paragraph may be illustrated by the following example:

Example. A, an individual on a calendar year basis, purchased certain shares of stock subsequent to February 28, 1913, for $10,000. On January 1, 1954, A's adjusted basis for the stock had been reduced to $1,000 by reason of receipts and distributions described in sections 1016(a)(1) and 1016(a)(4). He received in 1954 a further distribution of $5,000, being a distribution covered by section 1016(a)(4), other than a distribution out of increase of value of property accrued prior to March 1, 1913. This distribution applied against the adjusted basis as required by section 1016(a)(4) exceeds that basis by $4,000. The $4,000 excess is a gain realized by A in 1954 and is includible in gross income in his return for that calendar year. In computing gain from the stock, as in adjusting basis, no distinction is made between items of receipts or distributions described in section 1016. If A sells the stock in 1955 for $5,000, he realizes in 1955 a gain of $5,000, since the adjusted basis of the stock for the purpose of computing gain or loss from the sale is zero.

(d) *Installment sales.*—In the case of property sold on the installment plan, special rules for the taxation of the gain are prescribed in section 453.

(e) *Transfers in part a sale and in part a gift.*—(1) Where a transfer of property is in part a sale and in part a gift, the transferor has a gain to the extent that the amount realized by him exceeds his adjusted basis in the property. However, no loss is sustained on such a transfer if the amount realized is less than the adjusted basis. For determination of basis of the property in the hands of the transferee, see § 1.1015-4. For the allocation of the adjusted basis of property in the case of a bargain sale to a charitable organization, see § 1.1011-2.

(2) *Examples.*—The provisions of subparagraph (1) may be illustrated by the following examples:

Example (1). A transfers property to his son for $60,000. Such property in the hands of A has an adjusted basis of $30,000 (and a fair market value of $90,000). A's gain is $30,000, the excess of $60,000, the amount realized, over the adjusted basis, $30,000. He has made a gift of $30,000, the excess of $90,000, the fair market value, over the amount realized, $60,000.

Example (2). A transfers property to his son for $30,000. Such property in the hands of A has an adjusted basis of $60,000 (and a fair market value of $90,000). A has no gain or loss, and has made a gift of $60,000, the excess of $90,000, the fair market value, over the amount realized, $30,000.

Example (3). A transfers property to his son for $30,000. Such property in A's hands has an adjusted basis of $30,000 (and a fair market value of $60,000). A has no gain and has made a gift of $30,000, the excess of $60,000, the fair market value, over the amount realized, $30,000.

Example (4). A transfers property to his son for $30,000. Such property in A's hands has an adjusted basis of $90,000 (and a fair market value of $60,000). A has sustained no loss, and has made a gift of $30,000, the excess of $60,000, the fair market value, over the amount realized, $30,000.

(f) *Sale or other disposition of a term interest in property.*—(1) *General rule.*—Except as otherwise provided in subparagraph (3) of this paragraph, for purposes of determining gain or loss from the sale or other disposition after October 9, 1969, of a term interest in property (as defined in subparagraph (2) of this paragraph), a taxpayer shall not take into account that portion of the adjusted basis of such interest which is determined pursuant, or by reference, to section 1014 (relating to the basis of property acquired from a decedent) or section 1015 (relating to the basis of property acquired by gift or by a transfer in trust) to the extent that such adjusted basis is a portion of the adjusted uniform basis of the entire property (as defined in § 1.1014-5). Where a term interest in property is transferred to a corporation in connection with a transaction to which section 351 applies and the adjusted basis of the term interest (i) is determined pursuant to section 1014 or 1015 and (ii) is also a portion of the adjusted uniform basis of the entire property, a subsequent sale or other disposition of such term interest by the corporation will be subject to the provisions of section 1001(e) and this paragraph to the extent that the basis of the term interest so sold or otherwise disposed of is determined by reference to its basis in the hands of the transferor as provided by section 362(a). See subparagraph (2) of this paragraph for rules relating to the characterization of stock received by the transferor of a term interest in property in connection with a transaction to which section 351 applies. That portion of the adjusted uniform basis of the entire property which is assignable to such interest at the time of its sale or other disposition shall be determined under the rules provided in § 1.1014-5. Thus, gain or loss realized from a sale or other disposition of a term interest in property shall be determined by comparing the amount of the proceeds of such sale with that part of the adjusted basis of such interest which is not a portion of the adjusted uniform basis of the entire property.

(2) *Term interest defined.*—For purposes of section 1001(e) and this paragraph, a "term interest in property" means—

    (i) A life interest in property,

    (ii) An interest in property for a term of years, or

    (iii) An income interest in a trust.

Generally subdivisions (i), (ii), and (iii) refer to an interest, present or future, in the income from property or the right to use property which will terminate or fail on the lapse of time, on the occurrence of an event or contingency, or on the failure of an event or contingency to occur. Such divisions do not refer to remainder or reversionary interests in the property itself or other interests in the property which will ripen into ownership of the entire property upon termination or failure of a preceding term interest. A "term interest in property" also includes any property received upon a sale or other disposition of a life interest in property, an interest in property for a term of years, or an income interest in a trust by the original holder of such interest, but only to the extent that the adjusted basis of the property received is determined by reference to the adjusted basis of the term interest so transferred.

(3) *Exception.*—Paragraph (1) of section 1001(e) and subparagraph (1) of this paragraph shall not apply to a sale or other disposition of a term interest in property as a part of a single transaction in which the entire interest in the property is transferred to a third person or to two or more other persons, including persons who acquire such entire interest as joint tenants, tenants by the entirety, or tenants in common. See § 1.1014-5 for computation of gain or loss upon such a sale or other disposition where the property has been acquired from a decedent or by gift or transfer in trust.

(4) *Illustrations.*—For examples illustrating the application of this paragraph, see paragraph (c) of § 1.1014-5.

(g) *Debt instruments issued in exchange for property.*—(1) *In general.*—If a debt instrument is issued in exchange for property, the amount realized attributable to the debt instrument is the issue price of the debt instrument as determined under § 1.1273-2 or § 1.1274-2; whichever is applicable. If, however, the issue price of the debt instrument is determined under section 1273(b)(4), the amount realized attributable to the debt instrument is its stated principal amount reduced by any unstated interest (as determined under section 483).

(2) *Certain debt instruments that provide for contingent payments.*—(i) *In general.*—Paragraph (g)(1) of this section does not apply to a debt instrument subject to either § 1.483-4 or § 1.1275-4(c) (certain contingent payment debt instruments issued for nonpublicly traded property).

    (ii) *Special rule to determine amount realized.*—If a debt instrument subject to § 1.1275-4(c) is issued in exchange for property, and the income from the exchange is not reported under the installment method of section 453, the amount realized attributable to the debt instrument is the issue price of the debt instrument as determined under § 1.1274-2(g), increased by the fair market value of the contingent payments payable on the debt instrument. If a debt instrument subject to § 1.483-4 is issued in exchange for property, and the income from the exchange is not reported under the installment method of section 453, the amount realized attributable to the debt instrument is its stated principal amount, reduced by any unstated interest (as determined under section 483), and increased by the fair market value of the contingent payments payable on the debt instrument. This paragraph (g)(2)(ii), however, does not apply to a debt instrument if the fair market value of the contingent payments is not reasonably ascertainable. Only in rare and extraordinary cases will the fair market value of the contingent payments be treated as not reasonably ascertainable.

(3) *Coordination with section 453.*—If a debt instrument is issued in exchange for property, and the income from the exchange is not reported under the installment method of section 453, this paragraph (g) applies rather than § 15a.453-1(d)(2) to determine the taxpayer's amount realized attributable to the debt instrument.

(4) *Effective date.*—This paragraph (g) applies to sales or exchanges that occur on or after August 13, 1996.

(h) *Severances of trusts.*—(1) *In general.*—The severance of a trust (including without limitation a severance that meets the requirements of

Reg. § 1.1001-1(h)(1)

§26.2642-6 or of §26.2654-1(b) of this chapter) is not an exchange of property for other property differing materially either in kind or in extent if—

(i) An applicable state statute or the governing instrument authorizes or directs the trustee to sever the trust; and

(ii) Any non-pro rata funding of the separate trusts resulting from the severance (including non-pro rata funding as described in §26.2642-6(d)(4) or §26.2654-1(b)(1)(ii)(C) of this chapter), whether mandatory or in the discretion of the trustee, is authorized by an applicable state statute or the governing instrument.

(2) *Effective/applicability date.*—This paragraph (h) applies to severances occurring on or after August 2, 2007. Taxpayers may apply this paragraph (h) to severances occurring on or after August 24, 2004, and before August 2, 2007. [Reg. §1.1001-1.]

☐ [*T.D. 6265, 11-6-57. Amended by T.D. 7142, 9-23-71; T.D. 7207, 10-3-72; T.D. 7213, 10-17-72; T.D. 8517, 1-27-94; T.D. 8674, 6-11-96 and T.D. 9348, 8-1-2007.*]

[Reg. §1.1001-2]

§1.1001-2. Discharge of liabilities.—
(a) *Inclusion in amount realized.*—(1) *In general.*—Except as provided in paragraph (a)(2) and (3) of this section, the amount realized from a sale or other disposition of property includes the amount of liabilities from which the transferor is discharged as a result of the sale or disposition.

(2) *Discharge of indebtedness.*—The amount realized on a sale or other disposition of property that secures a recourse liability does not include amounts that are (or would be if realized and recognized) income from the discharge of indebtedness under section 61(a)(12). For situations where amounts arising from the discharge of indebtedness are not realized and recognized, see section 108 and §1.61-12(b)(1).

(3) *Liability incurred on acquisition.*—In the case of a liability incurred by reason of the acquisition of the property, this section does not apply to the extent that such liability was not taken into account in determining the transferor's basis for such property.

(4) *Special rules.*—For purposes of this section—

(i) The sale or other disposition of property that secures a nonrecourse liability discharges the transferor from the liability;

(ii) The sale or other disposition of property that secures a recourse liability discharges the transferor from the liability if another person agrees to pay the liability (whether or not the transferor is in fact released from liability);

(iii) A disposition of property includes a gift of the property or a transfer of the property in satisfaction of liabilities to which it is subject;

(iv) Contributions and distributions of property between a partner and a partnership are not sales or other dispositions of property; and

(v) The liabilities from which a transferor is discharged as a result of the sale or disposition of a partnership interest include the transferor's share of the liabilities of the partnership.

(b) *Effect of fair market value of security.*—The fair market value of the security at the time of sale or disposition is not relevant for purposes of determining under paragraph (a) of this section the amount of liabilities from which the taxpayer is discharged or treated as discharged. Thus, the fact that the fair market value of the property is less than the amount of the liabilities it secures does not prevent the full amount of those liabilities from being treated as money received from the sale or other disposition of the property. However, see paragraph (a)(2) of this section for a rule relating to certain income from discharge of indebtedness.

(c) *Examples.*—The provisions of this section may be illustrated by the following examples. In each example assume the taxpayer uses the cash receipts and disbursements method of accounting, makes a return on the basis of the calendar year, and sells or disposes of all property which is security for a given liability.

Example (1). In 1976 A purchases an asset for $10,000. A pays the seller $1,000 in cash and signs a note payable to the seller for $9,000. A is personally liable for repayment with the seller having full recourse in the event of default. In addition, the asset which was purchased is pledged as security. During the years 1976 and 1977, A takes depreciation deductions on the asset in the amount of $3,100. During this same time period A reduces the outstanding principal on the note to $7,600. At the beginning of 1978 A sells the asset. The buyer pays A $1,600 in cash and assumes personal liability for the $7,600 outstanding liability. A becomes secondarily liable for repayment of the liability. A's amount realized is $9,200 ($1,600 + $7,600). Since A's adjusted basis in the asset is $6,900 ($10,000 – $3,100) A realizes a gain of $2,300 ($9,200 – $6,900).

Example (2). Assume the same facts as in example (1) except that A is not personally liable on the $9,000 note given to the seller and in the event of default the seller's only recourse is to the asset. In addition, on the sale of the asset by A, the purchaser takes the asset subject to the liability. Nevertheless, A's amount realized is $9,200 and A's gain realized is $2,300 on the sale.

Example (3). In 1975 L becomes a limited partner in partnership GL. L contributes $10,000 in cash to GL and L's distributive share of partnership income and loss is 10 percent. L is not entitled to receive any guaranteed payments. In 1978 M purchases L's entire interest in partnership GL. At the time of the sale L's adjusted basis in the partnership interest is $20,000. At that time L's proportionate share of liabilities, of which no partner has assumed personal liability, is $15,000. M pays $10,000 in cash for L's interest in the partnership. Under section 752(d) and this section, L's share of partnership liabilities, $15,000, is treated as money received. Accordingly, L's amount realized on the sale of the partnership interest is $25,000 ($10,000 + $15,000). L's gain realized on the sale is $5,000 ($25,000 – $20,000).

Example (4). In 1976 B becomes a limited partner in partnership BG. In 1978 B contributes B's entire interest in BG to a charitable organization described in section 170(c). At the time of the contribution all of the partnership liabilities are liabilities for which neither B nor G has assumed any personal liability and B's proportionate share of which is $9,000. The charitable organization does not pay any cash or other property to B, but takes the partnership interest subject to the $9,000 of liabilities. Assume that the contribution is treated as a bargain sale to a charitable organization and that under section 1011 (b) $3,000 is determined to be the portion of B's basis in the partnership interest allocable to the sale. Under section 752(d) and this section, the $9,000 of liabilities is treated by B as money received, thereby making B's amount realized $9,000. B's gain realized is $6,000 ($9,000 – $3,000).

Example (5). In 1975 C, an individual, creates T, an irrevocable trust. Due to certain powers expressly retained by C, T is a "grantor trust" for purposes of subpart E of part 1 of subchapter J of the Code and therefore C is treated as the owner of the entire trust. T purchases an interest in P, a partnership. C, as owner of T, deducts the distributive share of partnership losses attributable to the partnership interest held by T. In 1978, when the adjusted basis of the partnership interest held by T is $1,200, C renounces the powers previously and expressly retained that initially resulted in T being classified as a grantor trust. Consequently, T ceases to be a grantor trust and C is no longer considered to be the owner of the trust. At the time of the renunciation all of J's liabilities are liabilities on which none of the partners have assumed any personal liability and the proportionate share of which of the interest held by T is $11,000. Since prior to the renunciation C was the owner of the entire trust, C was considered the owner of all the trust property for Federal income tax purposes, including the partnership interest. Since C was considered to be the owner of the partnership interest, C not T, was considered to be the partner in P during the time T was a "grantor trust." However, at the time C renounced the powers that gave rise to T's classification as a grantor trust, T no longer qualified as a grantor trust with the result that C was no longer considered to be the owner of the trust and trust property for Federal income tax purposes. Consequently, at that time, C is considered to have transferred ownership of the interest in P to T, now a separate taxable entity, independent of its grantor C. On the transfer, C's share of partnership liabilities ($11,000) is treated as money received. Accordingly, C's amount realized is $11,000 and C's gain realized is $9,800 ($11,000 – $1,200).

Example (6). In 1977 D purchases an asset for $7,500. D pays the seller $1,500 in cash and signs a note payable to the seller for $6,000. D is not personally liable for repayment but pledges as security the newly purchased asset. In the event of default, the seller's only recourse is to the asset. During the years 1977 and 1978 D takes depreciation deductions on the asset totaling $4,200 thereby reducing D's basis in the asset to $3,300 ($7,500 – $4,200). In 1979 D transfers the asset to a trust which is not a "grantor trust" for purposes of subpart E of part 1 of subchapter J of the Code. Therefore D is not treated as the owner of the trust. The trust takes the asset subject to the liability and in addition pays D $750 in cash. Prior to the transfer D had reduced the amount outstanding on the liability to $4,700. D's amount realized on the transfer is $5,450 ($4,700 + $750). Since D's adjusted basis is $3,300, D's gain realized is $2,150 ($5,450 – $3,300).

Example (7). In 1974 E purchases a herd of cattle for breeding purposes. The purchase price is $20,000 consisting of $1,000 cash and a $19,000 note. E is not personally liable for repayment of the liability and the seller's only recourse in the event of default is to the herd of cattle. In 1977 E transfers the herd back to the original seller thereby satisfying the indebtedness pursuant to a provision in the original sales agreement. At the time of the transfer the fair market value of the herd is $15,000 and the remaining principal balance on the note is $19,000. At the time E's adjusted basis in the herd is $16,500 due to a deductible loss incurred when a portion of the herd died as a result of a disease. As a result of the indebtedness being satisfied, E's amount realized is $19,000 notwithstanding the fact that the fair market value of the herd was less than $19,000. E's realized gain is $2,500 ($19,000 – $16,500).

Example (8). In 1980, F transfers to a creditor an asset with a fair market value of $6,000 and the creditor discharges $7,500 of indebtedness for which F is personally liable. The amount realized on the disposition of the asset is its fair market value ($6,000). In addition, F has income from the discharge of indebtedness of $1,500 ($7,500 – $6,000). [Reg. § 1.1001-2.]

☐ [T.D. 7741, 12-11-80.]

[Reg. § 1.1001-3]

§ 1.1001-3. Modifications of debt instruments.—(a) *Scope.*—(1) *In general.*—This section provides rules for determining whether a modification of the terms of a debt instrument results in an exchange for purposes of § 1.1001-1(a). This section applies to any modification of a debt instrument, regardless of the form of the modification. For example, this section applies to an exchange of a new instrument for an existing debt instrument, or to an amendment of an existing debt instrument. This section also applies to a modification of a debt instrument that the issuer and holder accomplish indirectly through one or more transactions with third parties. This section, however, does not apply to exchanges of debt instruments between holders.

(2) *Qualified tender bonds.*—This section does not apply for purposes of determining whether tax-exempt bonds that are qualified tender bonds are reissued for purposes of sections 103 and 141 through 150.

(b) *General rule.*—For purposes of § 1.1001-1(a), a significant modification of a debt instrument, within the meaning of this section, results in an exchange of the original debt instrument for a modified instrument that differs materially either in kind or in extent. A modification that is not a significant modification is not an exchange for purposes of § 1.1001-1(a). Paragraphs (c) and (d) of this section define the term *modification* and contain examples illustrating the application of the rule. Paragraphs (e) and (f) of this section provide rules for determining when a modification is a significant modification. Paragraph (f) of this section also provides rules for determining whether the modified instrument received in an exchange will be classified as an instrument or property right that is not debt for federal income tax purposes. Paragraph (g) of this section contains examples illustrating the application of the rules in paragraphs (e) and (f) of this section.

(c) *Modification defined.*—(1) *In general.*—(i) *Alteration of terms.*—A *modification* means any alteration, including any deletion or addition, in whole or in part, of a legal right or obligation of the issuer or a holder of a debt instrument, whether the alteration is evidenced by an express agreement (oral or written), conduct of the parties, or otherwise.

(ii) *Alterations occurring by operation of the terms of a debt instrument.*—Except as provided in paragraph (c)(2) of this section, an alteration of a legal right or obligation that occurs by operation of the terms of a debt instrument is not a modification. An alteration that occurs by operation of the terms may occur automatically (for example, an annual resetting of the interest rate based on the value of an index or a specified increase in the interest rate if the value of the collateral declines from a specified level) or may occur as a result of the exercise of an option provided to an issuer or a holder to change a term of a debt instrument.

(2) *Exceptions.*—The alterations described in this paragraph (c)(2) are modifications, even if the alterations occur by operation of the terms of a debt instrument.

(i) *Change in obligor or nature of instrument.*—An alteration that results in the substitution of a new obligor, the addition or deletion of a co-obligor, or a change (in whole or in part) in the recourse nature of the instrument (from recourse to nonrecourse or from nonrecourse to recourse) is a modification.

(ii) *Property that is not debt.*—An alteration that results in an instrument or property right that is not debt for Federal income tax purposes is a modification unless the alteration occurs pursuant to a holder's option under the terms of the instrument to convert the instrument into equity of the issuer (notwithstanding paragraph (c)(2)(iii) of this section). The rules of paragraph (f)(7) of this section apply to determine whether an alteration or modification results in an instrument or property right that is not debt.

(iii) *Certain alterations resulting from the exercise of an option.*—An alteration that results from the exercise of an option provided to an issuer or a holder to change a term of a debt instrument is a modification unless—

(A) The option is unilateral (as defined in paragraph (c)(3) of this section); and

(B) In the case of an option exercisable by a holder, the exercise of the option does not result in (or, in the case of a variable or contingent payment, is not reasonably expected to result in) a deferral of, or a reduction in, any scheduled payment of interest or principal.

(3) *Unilateral option.*—For purposes of this section, an option is unilateral only if, under the terms of an instrument or under applicable law—

(i) There does not exist at the time the option is exercised, or as a result of the exercise, a right of the other party to alter or terminate the instrument or put the instrument to a person who is related (within the meaning of section 267(b) or section 707(b)(1)) to the issuer;

(ii) The exercise of the option does not require the consent or approval of—

(A) The other party;

(B) A person who is related to that party (within the meaning of section 267(b) or section 707(b)(1)), whether or not that person is a party to the instrument; or

(C) A court or arbitrator; and

(iii) The exercise of the option does not require consideration (other than incidental costs and expenses relating to the exercise of the option), unless, on the issue date of the instrument, the consideration is a de minimis amount, a specified amount, or an amount that is based on a formula that uses objective financial information (as defined in § 1.446-3(c)(4)(ii)).

(4) *Failure to perform.*—(i) *In general.*—The failure of an issuer to perform its obligations under a debt instrument is not itself an alteration of a legal right or obligation and is not a modification.

Reg. § 1.1001-3(a)(2)

(ii) *Holder's temporary forbearance.*—Notwithstanding paragraph (c)(1) of this section, absent a written or oral agreement to alter other terms of the debt instrument, an agreement by the holder to stay collection or temporarily waive an acceleration clause or similar default right (including such a waiver following the exercise of a right to demand payment in full) is not a modification unless and until the forbearance remains in effect for a period that exceeds—

(A) Two years following the issuer's initial failure to perform; and

(B) Any additional period during which the parties conduct good faith negotiations or during which the issuer is in a title 11 or similar case (as defined in section 368(a)(3)(A)).

(5) *Failure to exercise an option.*—If a party to a debt instrument has an option to change a term of an instrument, the failure of the party to exercise that option is not a modification.

(6) *Time of modification.*—(i) *In general.*—Except as provided in this paragraph (c)(6), an agreement to change a term of a debt instrument is a modification at the time the issuer and holder enter into the agreement, even if the change in the term is not immediately effective.

(ii) *Closing conditions.*—If the parties condition a change in a term of a debt instrument on reasonable closing conditions (for example, shareholder, regulatory, or senior creditor approval, or additional financing), a modification occurs on the closing date of the agreement. Thus, if the reasonable closing conditions do not occur so that the change in the term does not become effective, a modification does not occur.

(iii) *Bankruptcy proceedings.*—If a change in a term of a debt instrument occurs pursuant to a plan of reorganization in a title 11 or similar case (within the meaning of section 368(a)(3)(A)), a modification occurs upon the effective date of the plan. Thus, unless the plan becomes effective, a modification does not occur.

(d) *Examples.*—The following examples illustrate the provisions of paragraph (c) of this section:

Example 1. Reset bond. A bond provides for the interest rate to be reset every 49 days through an auction by a remarketing agent. The reset of the interest rate occurs by operation of the terms of the bond and is not an alteration described in paragraph (c)(2) of this section. Thus, the reset of the interest rate is not a modification.

Example 2. Obligation to maintain collateral. The original terms of a bond provide that the bond must be secured by a certain type of collateral having a specified value. The terms also require the issuer to substitute collateral if the value of the original collateral decreases. Any substitution of collateral that is required to maintain the value of the collateral occurs by operation of the terms of the bond and is not an alteration described in paragraph (c)(2) of this section. Thus, such a substitution of collateral is not a modification.

Example 3. Alteration contingent on an act of a party. The original terms of a bond provide that the interest rate is 9 percent. The terms also provide that, if the issuer files an effective registration statement covering the bonds with the Securities and Exchange Commission, the interest rate will decrease to 8 percent. If the issuer registers the bond, the resulting decrease in the interest rate occurs by operation of the terms of the bond and is not an alteration described in paragraph (c)(2) of this section. Thus, such a decrease in the interest rate is not a modification.

Example 4. Substitution of a new obligor occurring by operation of the terms of the debt instrument. Under the original terms of a bond issued by a corporation, an acquirer of substantially all of the corporation's assets may assume the corporation's obligations under the bond. Substantially all of the corporation's assets are acquired by another corporation and the acquiring corporation becomes the new obligor on the bond. Under paragraph (c)(2)(i) of this section, the substitution of a new obligor, even though it occurs by operation of the terms of the bond, is a modification.

Example 5. Defeasance with release of covenants. (i) A corporation issues a 30-year, recourse bond. Under the terms of the bond, the corporation may secure a release of the financial and restrictive covenants by placing in trust government securities as collateral that will provide interest and principal payments sufficient to satisfy all scheduled payments on the bond. The corporation remains obligated for all payments, including the contribution of additional securities to the trust if necessary to provide sufficient amounts to satisfy the payment obligations. Under paragraph (c)(3) of this section, the option to defease the bond is a unilateral option.

(ii) The alterations occur by operation of the terms of the debt instrument and are not described in paragraph (c)(2) of this section. Thus, such a release of the covenants is not a modification.

Example 6. Legal defeasance. Under the terms of a recourse bond, the issuer may secure a release of the financial and restrictive covenants by placing in trust government securities that will provide interest and principal payments sufficient to satisfy all scheduled payments on the bond. Upon the creation of the trust, the issuer is released from any recourse liability on the bond and has no obligation to contribute additional securities to the trust if the trust funds are not sufficient to satisfy the scheduled payments on the bond. The release of the issuer is an alteration described in paragraph (c)(2)(i) of this section, and thus is a modification.

Example 7. Exercise of an option by a holder that reduces amounts payable. (i) A financial institution holds a residential mortgage. Under the original terms of the mortgage, the financial institution has an option to decrease the interest rate. The financial institution anticipates that, if market interest rates decline, it may exercise this option in lieu of the mortgagor refinancing with another lender.

(ii) The financial institution exercises the option to reduce the interest rate. The exercise of the option results in a reduction in scheduled payments and is an alteration described in paragraph (c)(2)(iii) of this section. Thus, the change in interest rate is a modification.

Example 8. Conversion of adjustable rate to fixed rate mortgage. (i) The original terms of a mortgage provide for a variable interest rate, reset annually based on the value of an objective index. Under the terms of the mortgage, the mortgagor may, upon the payment of a fee equal to a specified percentage of the outstanding principal amount of the mortgage, convert to a fixed rate of interest as determined based on the value of a second objective index. The exercise of the option does not require the consent or approval of any person or create a right of the holder to alter the terms of, or to put, the instrument.

(ii) Because the required consideration to exercise the option is a specified amount fixed on the issue date, the exercise of the option is unilateral as defined in paragraph (c)(3) of this section. The conversion to a fixed rate of interest is not an alteration described in paragraph (c)(2) of this section. Thus, the change in the type of interest rate occurs by operation of the terms of the instrument and is not a modification.

Example 9. [Reserved]. For further guidance, see § 1.1001-3T(d) *Example 9.*

Example 10. Issuer's right to defer payment of interest. A corporation issues a 5-year note. Under the terms of the note, interest is payable annually at the rate of 10 percent. The corporation, however, has an option to defer any payment of interest until maturity. For any payments that are deferred, interest will compound at a rate of 12 percent. The exercise of the option, which results in the deferral of payments, does not result from the exercise of an option by the holder. The exercise of the option occurs by operation of the terms of the debt instrument and is not a modification.

Example 11. Holder's option to grant deferral of payment. (i) A corporation issues a 10-year note to a bank in exchange for cash. Interest on the note is payable semi-annually. Under the terms of the note, the bank may grant the corporation the right to defer all or part of the interest payments. For any payments that are deferred, interest will compound at a rate 150 basis points greater than the stated rate of interest.

(ii) The corporation encounters financial difficulty and is unable to satisfy its obligations under the note. The bank exercises its option under the note and grants the corporation the right to defer payments. The exercise of the option results in a right of the corporation to defer scheduled payments and, under paragraph (c)(3)(i) of this section, is not a unilateral option. Thus, the alteration is described in paragraph (c)(2)(iii) of this section and is a modification.

Example 12. Alteration requiring consent. The original terms of a bond include a provision that the issuer may extend the maturity of the bond with the consent of the holder. Because any extension pursuant to this term requires the consent of both parties, such an extension does not occur by the exercise of a unilateral option (as defined in paragraph (c)(3) of this section) and is a modification.

Example 13. Waiver of an acceleration clause. Under the terms of a bond, if the issuer fails to make a scheduled payment, the full principal amount of the bond is due and payable immediately. Following the issuer's failure to make a scheduled payment, the holder temporarily waives its right to receive the full principal for a period ending one year from the date of the issuer's default to allow the issuer to obtain additional financial resources. Under paragraph (c)(4)(ii) of this section, the temporary waiver in this situation is not a modification. The result would be the same if the terms provided the holder with the right to demand the full principal amount upon the failure of the issuer to make a scheduled payment and, upon such a failure, the holder exercised that right and then waived the right to receive the payment for one year.

(e) *Significant modifications.*—Whether the modification of a debt instrument is a significant modification is determined under the rules of this paragraph (e). Paragraph (e)(1) of this section provides a general rule for determining the significance of modifications not otherwise addressed in this paragraph (e). Paragraphs (e)(2) through (6) of this section provide specific rules for determining the significance of certain types of modifications. Paragraph (f) of this section provides rules of application, including rules for modifications that are effective on a deferred basis or upon the occurrence of a contingency.

(1) *General rule.*—Except as otherwise provided in paragraphs (e)(2) through (e)(6) of this section, a modification is a significant modification only if, based on all facts and circumstances, the legal rights or obligations that are altered and the degree to which they are altered are economically significant. In making a determination under this paragraph (e)(1), all modifications to the debt instrument (other than modifications subject to paragraphs (e)(2) through (6) of this section) are considered collectively, so that a series of such modifications may be significant when considered together although each modification, if considered alone, would not be significant.

(2) *Change in yield.*—(i) *Scope of rule.*—This paragraph (e)(2) applies to debt instruments that provide for only fixed payments, debt instruments with alternative payment schedules sub-

ject to § 1.1272-1(c), debt instruments that provide for a fixed yield subject to § 1.1272-1(d) (such as certain demand loans), and variable rate debt instruments. Whether a change in the yield of other debt instruments (for example, a contingent payment debt instrument) is a significant modification is determined under paragraph (e)(1) of this section.

     (ii) *In general.*—A change in the yield of a debt instrument is a significant modification if the yield computed under paragraph (e)(2)(iii) of this section varies from the annual yield on the unmodified instrument (determined as of the date of the modification) by more than the greater of—

     (A) 1/4 of one percent (25 basis points); or

     (B) 5 percent of the annual yield of the unmodified instrument (.05 x annual yield).

     (iii) *Yield of the modified instrument.*— (A) *In general.*—The yield computed under this paragraph (e)(2)(iii) is the annual yield of a debt instrument with—

     (1) an issue price equal to the adjusted issue price of the unmodified instrument on the date of the modification (increased by any accrued but unpaid interest and decreased by any accrued bond issuance premium not yet taken into account, and increased or decreased, respectively, to reflect payments made to the issuer or to the holder as consideration for the modification); and

     (2) payments equal to the payments on the modified debt instrument from the date of the modification.

     (B) *Prepayment penalty.*—For purposes of this paragraph (e)(2)(iii), a commercially reasonable prepayment penalty for a pro rata prepayment (as defined in § 1.1275-2(f)) is not consideration for a modification of a debt instrument and is not taken into account in determining the yield of the modified instrument.

     (iv) *Variable rate debt instruments.*—For purposes of this paragraph (e)(2), the annual yield of a variable rate debt instrument is the annual yield of the equivalent fixed rate debt instrument (as defined in § 1.1275-5(e)) which is constructed based on the terms of the instrument (either modified or unmodified, whichever is applicable) as of the date of the modification.

     (3) *Changes in timing of payments.*—(i) *In general.*—A modification that changes the timing of payments (including any resulting change in the amount of payments) due under a debt instrument is a significant modification if it results in the material deferral of scheduled payments. The deferral may occur either through an extension of the final maturity date of an instrument or through a deferral of payments due prior to maturity. The materiality of the deferral depends on all the facts and circumstances, including the length of the deferral, the original term of the instrument, the amounts of the payments that are deferred, and the time period between the modification and the actual deferral of payments.

     (ii) *Safe-harbor period.*—The deferral of one or more scheduled payments within the safe-harbor period is not a material deferral if the deferred payments are unconditionally payable no later than at the end of the safe-harbor period. The safe-harbor period begins on the original due date of the first scheduled payment that is deferred and extends for a period equal to the lesser of five years or 50 percent of the original term of the instrument. For purposes of this paragraph (e)(3)(ii), the term of an instrument is determined without regard to any option to extend the original maturity and deferrals of de minimis payments are ignored. If the period during which payments are deferred is less than the full safe-harbor period, the unused portion of the period remains a safe-harbor period for any subsequent deferral of payments on the instrument.

     (4) *Change in obligor or security.*— (i) *Substitution of a new obligor on recourse debt instruments.*—(A) *In general.*—Except as provided in paragraph (e)(4)(i)(B), (C), or (D) of this section, the substitution of a new obligor on a recourse debt instrument is a significant modification.

     (B) *Section 381(a) transaction.*—The substitution of a new obligor is not a significant modification if the acquiring corporation (within the meaning of section 381) becomes the new obligor pursuant to a transaction to which section 381(a) applies, the transaction does not result in a change in payment expectations, and the transaction (other than a reorganization within the meaning of section 368(a)(1)(F)) does not result in a significant alteration.

     (C) *Certain asset acquisitions.*—The substitution of a new obligor is not a significant modification if the new obligor acquires substantially all of the assets of the original obligor, the transaction does not result in a change in payment expectations, and the transaction does not result in a significant alteration.

     (D) *Tax-exempt bonds.*—The substitution of a new obligor on a tax-exempt bond is not a significant modification if the new obligor is a related entity to the original obligor as defined in section 168(h)(4)(A) and the collateral securing the instrument continues to include the original collateral.

     (E) *Significant alteration.*—For purposes of this paragraph (e)(4), a significant alteration is an alteration that would be a significant modification but for the fact that the alteration occurs by operation of the terms of the instrument.

     (F) *Section 338 election.*—For purposes of this section, an election under section 338 following a qualified stock purchase of an issuer's stock does not result in the substitution of a new obligor.

(G) *Bankruptcy proceedings.*—For purposes of this section, the filing of a petition in a title 11 or similar case (as defined in section 368(a)(3)(A)) by itself does not result in the substitution of a new obligor.

(ii) *Substitution of a new obligor on nonrecourse debt instruments.*—The substitution of a new obligor on a nonrecourse debt instrument is not a significant modification.

(iii) *Addition or deletion of co-obligor.*—The addition or deletion of a co-obligor on a debt instrument is a significant modification if the addition or deletion of the co-obligor results in a change in payment expectations. If the addition or deletion of a co-obligor is part of a transaction or series of related transactions that results in the substitution of a new obligor, however, the transaction is treated as a substitution of a new obligor (and is tested under paragraph (e)(4)(i)) of this section rather than as an addition or deletion of a co-obligor.

(iv) *Change in security or credit enhancement.*—(A) *Recourse debt instruments.*—A modification that releases, substitutes, adds or otherwise alters the collateral for, a guarantee on, or other form of credit enhancement for a recourse debt instrument is a significant modification if the modification results in a change in payment expectations.

(B) [Reserved]. For further guidance, see § 1.1001-3T(e)(4)(iv)(B).

(v) *Change in priority of debt.*—A change in the priority of a debt instrument relative to other debt of the issuer is a significant modification if it results in a change in payment expectations.

(vi) *Change in payment expectations.*—(A) *In general.*—For purposes of this section, a change in payment expectations occurs if, as a result of a transaction—

(1) There is a substantial enhancement of the obligor's capacity to meet the payment obligations under a debt instrument and that capacity was primarily speculative prior to the modification and is adequate after the modification; or

(2) There is a substantial impairment of the obligor's capacity to meet the payment obligations under a debt instrument and that capacity was adequate prior to the modification and is primarily speculative after the modification.

(B) *Obligor's capacity.*—The obligor's capacity includes any source for payment, including collateral, guarantees, or other credit enhancement.

(5) *Changes in the nature of a debt instrument.*—(i) *Property that is not debt.*—A modification of a debt instrument that results in an instrument or property right that is not debt for Federal income tax purposes is a significant modification. The rules of paragraph (f)(7) of this section apply to determine whether a modification results in an instrument or property right that is not debt.

(ii) *Change in recourse nature.*—(A) *In general.*—Except as provided in paragraph (e)(5)(ii)(B) of this section, a change in the nature of a debt instrument from recourse (or substantially all recourse) to nonrecourse (or substantially all nonrecourse) is a significant modification. Thus, for example, a legal defeasance of a debt instrument in which the issuer is released from all liability to make payments on the debt instrument (including an obligation to contribute additional securities to a trust if necessary to provide sufficient funds to meet all scheduled payments on the instrument) is a significant modification. Similarly, a change in the nature of the debt instrument from nonrecourse (or substantially all nonrecourse) to recourse (or substantially all recourse) is a significant modification. If an instrument is not substantially all recourse or not substantially all nonrecourse either before or after a modification, the significance of the modification is determined under paragraph (e)(1) of this section.

(B) *Exceptions.*—(1) *Defeasance of tax-exempt bonds.*—A defeasance of a tax-exempt bond is not a significant modification even if the issuer is released from any liability to make payments under the instrument if the defeasance occurs by operation of the terms of the original bond and the issuer places in trust government securities or tax-exempt government bonds that are reasonably expected to provide interest and principal payments sufficient to satisfy the payment obligations under the bond.

(2) [Reserved]. For further guidance, see § 1.1001-3T(e)(5)(ii)(B)(2).

(6) *Accounting or financial covenants.*—A modification that adds, deletes, or alters customary accounting or financial covenants is not a significant modification.

(f) *Rules of application.*—(1) *Testing for significance.*—(i) *In general.*—Whether a modification of any term is a significant modification is determined under each applicable rule in paragraphs (e)(2) through (6) of this section and, if not specifically addressed in those rules, under the general rule in paragraph (e)(1) of this section. For example, a deferral of payments that changes the yield of a fixed rate debt instrument must be tested under both paragraphs (e)(2) and (3) of this section.

(ii) *Contingent modifications.*—If a modification described in paragraphs (e)(2) through (5) of this section is effective only upon the occurrence of a substantial contingency, whether or not the change is a significant modification is determined under paragraph (e)(1) of this section rather than under paragraphs (e)(2) through (5) of this section.

(iii) *Deferred modifications.*—If a modification described in paragraphs (e)(4) and (5) of this section is effective on a substantially deferred basis, whether or not the change is a significant modification is determined under paragraph (e)(1) of this section rather than under paragraphs (e)(4) and (5) of this section.

(2) *Modifications that are not significant.*—If a rule in paragraphs (e)(2) through (4) of this section prescribes a degree of change in a term of a debt instrument that is a significant modification, a change of the same type but of a lesser degree is not a significant modification under that rule. For example, a 20 basis point change in the yield of a fixed rate debt instrument is not a significant modification under paragraph (e)(2) of this section. Likewise, if a rule in paragraph (e)(4) of this section requires a change in payment expectations for a modification to be significant, a modification of the same type that does not result in a change in payment expectations is not a significant modification under that rule.

(3) *Cumulative effect of modifications.*—Two or more modifications of a debt instrument over any period of time constitute a significant modification if, had they been done as a single change, the change would have resulted in a significant modification under paragraph (e) of this section. Thus, for example, a series of changes in the maturity of a debt instrument constitutes a significant modification if, combined as a single change, the change would have resulted in a significant modification. The significant modification occurs at the time that the cumulative modification would be significant under paragraph (e) of this section. In testing for a change of yield under paragraph (e)(2) of this section, however, any prior modification occurring more than 5 years before the date of the modification being tested is disregarded.

(4) *Modifications of different terms.*—Modifications of different terms of a debt instrument, none of which separately would be a significant modification under paragraphs (e)(2) through (6) of this section, do not collectively constitute a significant modification. For example, a change in yield that is not a significant modification under paragraph (e)(2) of this section and a substitution of collateral that is not a significant modification under paragraph (e)(4)(iv) of this section do not together result in a significant modification. Although the significance of each modification is determined independently, in testing a particular modification it is assumed that all other simultaneous modifications have already occurred.

(5) *Definitions.*—For purposes of this section:

(i) *Issuer* and *obligor* are used interchangeably and mean the issuer of a debt instrument or a successor obligor.

(ii) *Variable rate debt instrument* and *contingent payment debt instrument* have the meanings given those terms in section 1275 and the regulations thereunder.

(iii) *Tax-exempt bond* means a state or local bond that satisfies the requirements of section 103(a).

(iv) *Conduit loan* and *conduit borrower* have the same meanings as in § 1.150-1(b).

(6) *Certain rules for tax-exempt bonds.*—(i) *Conduit loans.*—For purposes of this section, the obligor of a tax-exempt bond is the entity that actually issues the bond and not a conduit borrower of bond proceeds. In determining whether there is a significant modification of a tax-exempt bond, however, transactions between holders of the tax-exempt bond and a borrower of a conduit loan may be an indirect modification under paragraph (a)(1) of this section. For example, a payment by the holder of a tax-exempt bond to a conduit borrower to waive a call right may result in an indirect modification of the tax-exempt bond by changing the yield on that bond.

(ii) *Recourse nature.*—(A) *In general.*—For purposes of this section, a tax-exempt bond that does not finance a conduit loan is a recourse debt instrument.

(B) *Proceeds used for conduit loans.*—For purposes of this section, a tax-exempt bond that finances a conduit loan is a recourse debt instrument unless both the bond and the conduit loan are nonrecourse instruments.

(C) *Government securities as collateral.*—Notwithstanding paragraphs (f)(6)(ii)(A) and (B) of this section, for purposes of this section a tax-exempt bond that is secured only by a trust holding government securities or tax-exempt government bonds that are reasonably expected to provide interest and principal payments sufficient to satisfy the payment obligations under the bond is a nonrecourse instrument.

(7) *Rules for determining whether an alteration or modification results in an instrument or property right that is not debt.*—(i) *In general.*—Except as provided in paragraph (f)(7)(ii) of this section, the determination of whether an instrument resulting from an alteration or modification of a debt instrument will be recharacterized as an instrument or property right that is not debt for Federal income tax purposes shall take into account all of the factors relevant to such a determination.

(ii) *Financial condition of the obligor.*—(A) *Deterioration in financial condition of the obligor generally disregarded.*—Except as provided in

Reg. § 1.1001-3(f)(7)(ii)(A)

paragraph (f)(7)(ii)(B) of this section, in making a determination as to whether an instrument resulting from an alteration or modification of a debt instrument will be recharacterized as an instrument or property right that is not debt, any deterioration in the financial condition of the obligor between the issue date of the debt instrument and the date of the alteration or modification (as it relates to the obligor's ability to repay the debt instrument) is not taken into account. For example, any decrease in the fair market value of a debt instrument (whether or not the debt instrument is publicly traded) between the issue date of the debt instrument and the date of the alteration or modification is not taken into account to the extent that the decrease in fair market value is attributable to the deterioration in the financial condition of the obligor and not to a modification of the terms of the instrument.

(B) *Substitution of a new obligor; addition or deletion of co-obligor.*—If there is a substitution of a new obligor or the addition or deletion of a co-obligor, the rules in paragraph (f)(7)(ii)(A) of this section do not apply.

(g) *Examples.*—The following examples illustrate the provisions of paragraphs (e) and (f) of this section:

Example 1. [Reserved]. For further guidance, see § 1.1001-3T(g) *Example 1.*

Example 2. Extension of maturity and change in yield. (i) A zero-coupon bond has an original maturity of ten years. At the end of the fifth year, the parties agree to extend the maturity for a period of two years without increasing the stated redemption price at maturity (i.e., there are no additional payments due between the original and extended maturity dates, and the amount due at the extended maturity date is equal to the amount due at the original maturity date).

(ii) The deferral of the scheduled payment at maturity is tested under paragraph (e)(3) of this section. The safe-harbor period under paragraph (e)(3)(ii) of this section starts with the date the payment that is being deferred is due. For this modification, the safe-harbor period starts on the original maturity date, and ends five years from this date. All payments deferred within this period are unconditionally payable before the end of the safe-harbor period. Thus, the deferral of the payment at maturity for a period of two years is not a material deferral under the safe-harbor rule of paragraph (e)(3)(ii) of this section and thus is not a significant modification.

(iii) Even though the extension of maturity is not a significant modification under paragraph (e)(3)(ii) of this section, the modification also decreases the yield of the bond. The change in yield must be tested under paragraph (e)(2) of this section.

Example 3. Change in yield resulting from reduction of principal. (i) A debt instrument issued at par has an original maturity of ten years and provides for the payment of $100,000 at maturity

with interest payments at the rate of 10 percent payable at the end of each year. At the end of the fifth year, and after the annual payment of interest, the issuer and holder agree to reduce the amount payable at maturity to $80,000. The annual interest rate remains at 10 percent but is payable on the reduced principal.

(ii) In applying the change in yield rule of paragraph (e)(2) of this section, the yield of the instrument after the modification (measured from the date that the parties agree to the modification to its final maturity date) is computed using the adjusted issue price of $100,000. With four annual payments of $8,000, and a payment of $88,000 at maturity, the yield on the instrument after the modification for purposes of determining if there has been a significant modification under paragraph (e)(2)(i) of this section is 4.332 percent. Thus, the reduction in principal is a significant modification.

Example 4. Deferral of scheduled interest payments. (i) A 20-year debt instrument issued at par provides for the payment of $100,000 at maturity with annual interest payments at the rate of 10 percent. At the beginning of the eleventh year, the issuer and holder agree to defer all remaining interest payments until maturity with compounding. The yield of the modified instrument remains at 10 percent.

(ii) The safe-harbor period of paragraph (e)(3)(ii) of this section begins at the end of the eleventh year, when the interest payment for that year is deferred, and ends at the end of the sixteenth year. However, the payments deferred during this period are not unconditionally payable by the end of that 5-year period. Thus, the deferral of the interest payments is not within the safe-harbor period.

(iii) This modification materially defers the payments due under the instrument and is a significant modification under paragraph (e)(3)(i) of this section.

Example 5. [Reserved]. For further guidance, see § 1.1001-3T(g) *Example 5.*

Example 6. Assumption of mortgage. (i) A recourse debt instrument is secured by a building. In connection with the sale of the building, the purchaser of the building assumes the debt and is substituted as the new obligor on the debt instrument. The purchaser does not acquire substantially all of the assets of the original obligor.

(ii) The transaction does not satisfy any of the exceptions set forth in paragraph (e)(4)(i)(B) or (C) of this section. Thus, the substitution of the purchaser as the obligor is a significant modification under paragraph (e)(4)(i)(A) of this section.

(iii) Section 1274(c)(4), however, provides that if a debt instrument is assumed in connection with the sale or exchange of property, the assumption is not taken into account in determining if section 1274 applies to the debt instrument unless the terms and conditions of the debt instrument are modified in connection with the sale or exchange. Because the purchaser assumed the debt instrument in connection with the sale of property and the debt instrument was not otherwise modified, the debt instrument is not retested to determine whether it provides for adequate stated interest.

Example 7. Substitution of a new obligor in section 381(a) transaction. (i) The interest rate on a 30-year debt instrument issued by a corporation provides for a variable rate of interest that is reset annually on June 1st based on an objective index.

(ii) In the tenth year, the issuer merges (in a transaction to which section 381(a) applies) into another corporation that becomes the new obligor on the debt instrument. The merger occurs on June 1st, at which time the interest rate is also reset by operation of the terms of the instrument. The new interest rate varies from the previous interest rate by more than the greater of 25 basis points and 5 percent of the annual yield of the unmodified instrument. The substitution of a new obligor does not result in a change in payment expectations.

(iii) The substitution of the new obligor occurs in a section 381(a) transaction and does not result in a change in payment expectations. Although the interest rate changed by more than the greater of 25 basis points and 5 percent of the annual yield of the unmodified instrument, this alteration did not occur as a result of the transaction and is not a significant alteration under paragraph (e)(4)(i)(E) of this section. Thus, the substitution meets the requirements of paragraph (e)(4)(i)(B) of this section and is not a significant modification.

Example 8. [Reserved]. For further guidance, see § 1.1001-3T(g) *Example 8.*

Example 9. Improvement to collateral securing nonrecourse debt. A parcel of land and its improvements, a shopping center, secure a nonrecourse debt instrument. The obligor expands the shopping center with the construction of an additional building on the same parcel of land. After the construction, the improvements that secure the nonrecourse debt include the new building. The building is an improvement to the property securing the nonrecourse debt instrument and its inclusion in the collateral securing the debt is not a significant modification under paragraph (e)(4)(iv)(B) of this section.

(h) *Effective/applicability date.*—(1) *In general.*— Except as otherwise provided in paragraph (h)(2) of this section, this section applies to alterations of the terms of a debt instrument on or after September 24, 1996. Taxpayers, however, may rely on this section for alterations of the terms of a debt instrument after December 2, 1992, and before September 24, 1996.

(2) *Exception.*—Paragraph (f)(7) of this section applies to an alteration of the terms of a debt instrument on or after January 7, 2011. A taxpayer, however, may rely on paragraph (f)(7) of this section for alterations of the terms of a debt

instrument occurring before that date. [Reg. § 1.1001-3.]

☐ [*T.D.* 8675, 6-25-96. *Amended by T.D.* 9513, 1-6-2011 *and T.D.* 9533, 7-1-2011.]

[Reg. § 1.1001-3T]

§ 1.1001-3T. Modifications of debt instruments (temporary).—(a) through (d) *Example 8* [Reserved]. For further guidance, see § 1.1001-3(a) through (d) *Example 8.*

Example 9. Holder's option to increase interest rate. (i) A corporation issues an 8-year note to a bank in exchange for cash. Under the terms of the note, the bank has the option to increase the rate of interest by a specified amount if certain covenants in the note are breached. The bank's right to increase the interest rate is a unilateral option as described in § 1.1001-3(c)(3).

(ii) A covenant in the note is breached. The bank exercises its option to increase the rate of interest. The increase in the rate of interest occurs by operation of the terms of the note and does not result in a deferral or a reduction in the scheduled payments or any other alteration described in § 1.1001-3(c)(2). Thus, the change in interest rate is not a modification.

(iii) *Effective/applicability date.* This *Example 9* applies to modifications occurring on or after July 6, 2011.

(d) *Example 10* through (e)(4)(iv)(A) [Reserved]. For further guidance, see § 1.1001-3(d) *Example 10* through (e)(4)(iv)(A).

(B) *Nonrecourse debt instruments.*—(1) A modification that releases, substitutes, adds or otherwise alters a substantial amount of the collateral for, a guarantee on, or other form of credit enhancement for a nonrecourse debt instrument is a significant modification. A substitution of collateral is not a significant modification, however, if the collateral is fungible or otherwise of a type where the particular units pledged are unimportant (for example, government securities or financial instruments of a particular type and credit quality). In addition, the substitution of a similar commercially available credit enhancement contract is not a significant modification, and an improvement to the property securing a nonrecourse debt instrument does not result in a significant modification.

(2) *Effective/applicability date.*—This paragraph (e)(4)(iv)(B) applies to modifications occurring on or after July 6, 2011.

(e)(4)(v) through (e)(5)(ii)(B)(1) [Reserved]. For further guidance, see § 1.1001-3(e)(4)(v) through (e)(5)(ii)(B)(1).

(2) *Original collateral.*—(i) A modification that changes a recourse debt instrument to a nonrecourse debt instrument is not a significant modification if the instrument continues to be secured only by the original collateral and the modification does not result in a change in payment expectations. For this purpose, if the origi-

nal collateral is fungible or otherwise of a type where the particular units pledged are unimportant (for example, government securities or financial instruments of a particular type and credit quality), replacement of some or all units of the original collateral with other units of the same or similar type and aggregate value is not considered a change in the original collateral.

(ii) *Effective/applicability date.*—This paragraph (e)(5)(ii)(B)(2) applies to modifications occurring on or after July 6, 2011.

(e)(6) through (g) introductory text [Reserved]. For further guidance, see § 1.1001-3(e)(6) through (g) introductory text.

Example 1. Modification of call right. (i) Under the terms of a 30-year, fixed-rate bond, the issuer can call the bond for 102 percent of par at the end of ten years or for 101 percent of par at the end of 20 years. At the end of the eighth year, the holder of the bond pays the issuer to waive the issuer's right to call the bond at the end of the tenth year. On the date of the modification, the issuer's credit quality is approximately the same as when the bond was issued, but market rates of interest have declined from that date.

(ii) The holder's payment to the issuer changes the yield on the bond. Whether the change in yield is a significant modification depends on whether the yield on the modified bond varies from the yield on the original bond by more than the change in yield as described in § 1.1001-3(e)(2)(ii).

(iii) If the change in yield is not a significant modification, the elimination of the issuer's call right must also be tested for significance. Because the specific rules of § 1.1001-3(e)(2) through (e)(6) do not address this modification, the significance of the modification must be determined under the general rule of § 1.1001-3(e)(1).

(iv) *Effective/applicability date.* This *Example 1* applies to modifications occurring on or after July 6, 2011.

Example 2 through *Example 4* [Reserved]. For further guidance, see § 1.1001-3(g) *Example 2* through *Example 4.*

Example 5. Assumption of mortgage with increase in interest rate. (i) A recourse debt instrument with a 9 percent annual yield is secured by an office building. Under the terms of the instrument, a purchaser of the building may assume the debt and be substituted for the original obligor if the purchaser is equally or more creditworthy than the original obligor and if the interest rate on the instrument is increased by one-half percent (50 basis points). The building is sold, the purchaser assumes the debt, and the interest rate increases by 50 basis points.

(ii) If the purchaser's acquisition of the building does not satisfy the requirements of § 1.1001-3(e)(4)(i)(B) or (C), the substitution of the purchaser as the obligor is a significant modification under § 1.1001-3(e)(4)(i)(A).

(iii) If the purchaser acquires substantially all of the assets of the original obligor, the assumption of the debt instrument will not result in a significant modification if there is not a change in payment expectations and the assumption does not result in a significant alteration.

(iv) The change in the interest rate, if tested under the rules of § 1.1001-3(e)(2), would result in a significant modification. The change in interest rate that results from the transaction is a significant alteration. Thus, the transaction does not meet the requirements of § 1.1001-3(e)(4)(i)(C) and is a significant modification under § 1.1001-3 (e)(4)(i)(A).

(v) *Effective/applicability date.* Notwithstanding § 1.1001-3(h), this *Example 5* applies to modifications occurring on or after July 6, 2011.

Example 6 through *Example 7* [Reserved]. For further guidance, see § 1.1001-3(g) *Example 6* through *Example 7.*

Example 8. Substitution of credit enhancement contract. (i) Under the terms of a recourse debt instrument, the issuer's obligations are secured by a letter of credit from a specified bank. The debt instrument does not contain any provision allowing a substitution of a letter of credit from a different bank. The specified bank, however, encounters financial difficulty. The issuer and holder agree that the issuer will substitute a letter of credit from another bank.

(ii) Under § 1.1001-3(e)(4)(iv)(A), the substitution of a different credit enhancement contract is not a significant modification of a recourse debt instrument unless the substitution results in a change in payment expectations. While the substitution of a new letter of credit by a different bank does not itself result in a change in payment expectations, such a substitution may result in a change in payment expectations under certain circumstances (for example, if the obligor's capacity to meet payment obligations is dependent on the letter of credit and the substitution substantially enhances that capacity from primarily speculative to adequate).

(iii) *Effective/applicability date.* This *Example 8* applies to modifications occurring on or after July 6, 2011.

Example 9 through (h) [Reserved]. For further guidance, see § 1.1001-3(g) *Example 9* through (h).

(i) *Expiration date.*—The applicability of this section expires on or before July 1, 2014. [Temporary Reg. § 1.1001-3T.]

☐ [*T.D.* 9533, 7-1-2011.]

[Reg. § 1.1001-4]

§ 1.1001-4. Modifications of certain derivative contracts.—(a) through (d) [Reserved]. For further guidance, see § 1.1001-4T(a) through (d). [Reg. § 1.1001-4.]

☐ [*T.D.* 9538, 7-21-2011.]

[Reg. §1.1001-4T]

§1.1001-4T. Modifications of certain derivative contracts (temporary).—(a) *Certain assignments.*—For purposes of §1.1001-1(a), the transfer or assignment of a derivative contract is not treated by the nonassigning counterparty as a deemed exchange of the original contract for a modified contract that differs materially either in kind or in extent if—

(1) Both the party transferring or assigning its rights and obligations under the derivative contract and the party to which the rights and obligations are transferred or assigned are either a dealer or a clearinghouse;

(2) The terms of the derivative contract permit the transfer or assignment of the contract, whether or not the consent of the nonassigning counterparty is required for the transfer or assignment to be effective; and

(3) The terms of the derivative contract are not otherwise modified in a manner that results in a taxable exchange under section 1001.

(b) *Definitions.*—(1) *Dealer.*—For purposes of this section, a *dealer* is a taxpayer who meets the definition of a dealer in securities in section 475(c)(1) or is a dealer in commodities derivative contracts.

(2) *Clearinghouse.*—For purposes of this section, a *clearinghouse* is a derivatives clearing organization (as such term is defined in section 1a of the Commodity Exchange Act (7 U.S.C. 1a)) or a clearing agency (as such term is defined in section 3 of the Securities Exchange Act of 1934 (15 U.S.C. 78c(a))) that is registered, or exempt from registration, under each respective Act.

(3) *Derivative contract.*—For purposes of this section, a *derivative contract* is a contract described in—

(i) Section 475(c)(2)(D), 475(c)(2)(E), or 475(c)(2)(F) without regard to the last sentence of section 475(c)(2) referencing section 1256;

(ii) Section 475(e)(2)(B), 475(e)(2)(C), or 475(e)(2)(D); or

(iii) Section 1.446-3(c)(1).

(c) *Consideration for the assignment.*—Any consideration for the transfer or assignment that passes between the party transferring or assigning its rights and obligations under the contract and the party to which the rights and obligations are transferred or assigned will not affect the treatment of the nonassigning counterparty for purposes of this section.

(d) *Effective/applicability date.*—This section applies to transfers or assignments of derivative contracts on or after July 22, 2011.

(e) *Expiration date.*—The applicability of this section expires on or before July 21, 2014. [Temporary Reg. §1.1001-4T.]

☐ [*T.D.* 9538, 7-21-2011 (*corrected* 8-18-2011).]

[Reg. §1.1001-5]

§1.1001-5. European Monetary Union (conversion to the euro).—(a) *Conversion of currencies.*—For purposes of §1.1001-1(a), the conversion to the euro of legacy currencies (as defined in §1.985-8(a)(1)) is not the exchange of property for other property differing materially in kind or extent.

(b) *Effect of currency conversion on other rights and obligations.*—For purposes of §1.1001-1(a), if, solely as the result of the conversion of legacy currencies to the euro, rights or obligations denominated in a legacy currency become rights or obligations denominated in the euro, that event is not the exchange of property for other property differing materially in kind or extent. Thus, for example, when a debt instrument that requires payments of amounts denominated in a legacy currency becomes a debt instrument requiring payments of euros, that alteration is not a modification within the meaning of §1.1001-3(c).

(c) *Effective date.*—This section applies to tax years ending after July 29, 1998. [Reg. §1.1001-5.]

☐ [*T.D.* 8927, 1-10-2001.]

[Reg. §1.1002-1]

§1.1002-1. Sales or exchanges.—(a) *General rule.*—The general rule with respect to gain or loss realized upon the sale or exchange of property as determined under section 1001 is that the entire amount of such gain or loss is recognized except in cases where specific provisions of subtitle A of the Code provide otherwise.

(b) *Strict construction of exceptions from general rule.*—The exceptions from the general rule requiring the recognition of all gains and losses, like other exceptions from a rule of taxation of general and uniform application, are strictly construed and do not extend either beyond the words or the underlying assumptions and purposes of the exception. Nonrecognition is accorded by the Code only if the exchange is one which satisfies both (1) the specific description in the Code of an excepted exchange, and (2) the underlying purpose for which such exchange is excepted from the general rule. The exchange must be germane to, and a necessary incident of, the investment or enterprise in hand. The relationship of the exchange to the venture or enterprise is always material, and the surrounding facts and circumstances must be shown. As elsewhere, the taxpayer claiming the benefit of the exception must﹣show himself within the exception.

(c) *Certain exceptions to general rule.*—Exceptions to the general rule are made, for example, by sections 351(a), 354, 361(a), 371(a)(1), 371(b)(1), 721, 1031, 1035 and 1036. These sections describe certain specific exchanges of property in which at the time of the exchange particular differences exist between the property parted with and the property acquired, but such differences are more formal than substantial. As to these, the Code provides that such differences shall not be deemed controlling, and that gain or loss shall not be recognized at the time of the exchange. The underlying assumption of these exceptions is that the new property is substantially a continuation of the old investment still unliquidated; and, in the case of reorganizations, that the new enterprise, the new corporate structure, and the new property are substantially continuations of the old still unliquidated.

(d) *Exchange.*—Ordinarily, to constitute an exchange, the transaction must be a reciprocal transfer of property, as distinguished from a transfer of property for a money consideration only. [Reg. § 1.1002-1.]

☐ [*T.D.* 6265, 11-6-57.]

Basis Rules of General Application

[Reg. § 1.1011-1]

§ 1.1011-1. Adjusted basis.—The adjusted basis for determining the gain or loss from the sale or other disposition of property is the cost or other basis prescribed in section 1012 or other applicable provisions of subtitle A of the Code, adjusted to the extent provided in sections 1016, 1017, and 1018 or as otherwise specifically provided for under applicable provisions of internal revenue laws. [Reg. § 1.1011-1.]

☐ [*T.D.* 6265, 11-6-57.]

[Reg. § 1.1011-2]

§ 1.1011-2. Bargain sale to a charitable organization.—(a) *In general.*—(1) If for the taxable year a charitable contributions deduction is allowable under section 170 by reason of a sale or exchange of property, the taxpayer's adjusted basis of such property for purposes of determining gain from such sale or exchange must be computed as provided in section 1011(b) and paragraph (b) of this section. If after applying the provisions of section 170 for the taxable year, including the percentage limitations of section 170(b), no deduction is allowable under that section by reason of the sale or exchange of the property, section 1011(b) does not apply and the adjusted basis of the property is not required to be apportioned pursuant to paragraph (b) of this section. In such case the entire adjusted basis of the property is to be taken into account in determining gain from the sale or exchange, as provided in § 1.1011-1(e). In ascertaining whether or not a charitable contributions deduction is allowable under section 170 for the taxable year for such purposes, that section is to be applied without regard to this section and the amount by which the contributed portion of the property must be reduced under section 170(e)(1) is the amount determined by taking into account the amount of gain which would have been ordinary income or long-term capital gain if the contributed portion of the property had been sold by the donor at its fair market value at the time of the sale or exchange.

(2) If in the taxable year there is a sale or exchange of property which gives rise to a charitable contribution which is carried over under section 170(b)(1)(D)(ii) or section 170(d) to a subsequent taxable year or is postponed under section 170(a)(3) to a subsequent taxable year, section 1011(b) and paragraph (b) of this section must be applied for purposes of apportioning the adjusted basis of the property for the year of the sale or exchange, whether or not such contribution is allowable as a deduction under section 170 in such subsequent year.

(3) If property is transferred subject to an indebtedness, the amount of the indebtedness must be treated as an amount realized for purposes of determining whether there is a sale or exchange to which section 1011(b) and this section apply, even though the transferee does not agree to assume or pay the indebtedness.

(4)(i) Section 1011(b) and this section apply where property is sold or exchanged in return for an obligation to pay an annuity and a charitable contributions deduction is allowable under section 170 by reason of such sale or exchange.

(ii) If in such case the annuity received in exchange for the property is nonassignable, or is assignable but only to the charitable organization to which the property is sold or exchanged, and if the transferor is the only annuitant or the transferor and a designated survivor annuitant or annuitants are the only annuitants, any gain on such exchange is to be reported as provided in example (8) in paragraph (c) of this section. In determining the period over which gain may be reported as provided in such example, the life expectancy of the survivor annuitant may not be taken into account. The fact that the transferor may retain the right to revoke the survivor's annuity or relinquish his own right to the annuity will not be considered, for purposes of this subdivision, to make the annuity assignable to someone other than the charitable organization. Gain on an exchange of the type described in this subdivision pursuant to an agreement which is entered into after December 19, 1969, and before May 3, 1971, may be reported as provided in example (8) in paragraph (c) of this section, even though the annuity is assignable.

(iii) In the case of an annuity to which subdivision (ii) of this subparagraph applies, the gain unreported by the transferor with respect to annuity payments not yet due when the following events occur is not required to be included in gross income of any person where—

(a) The transferor dies before the entire amount of gain has been reported and there is no surviving annuitant, or

(b) The transferor relinquishes the annuity to the charitable organization. If the transferor dies before the entire amount of gain on a two-life annuity has been reported, the unreported gain is required to be reported by the surviving annuitant or annuitants with respect to the annuity payments received by them.

(b) *Apportionment of adjusted basis.*—For purposes of determining gain on a sale or exchange to which this paragraph applies, the adjusted basis of the property which is sold or exchanged shall be that portion of the adjusted basis of the entire property which bears the same ratio to the adjusted basis as the amount realized bears to the fair market value of the entire property. The amount of such gain which shall be treated as ordinary income (or long-term capital gain) shall be that amount which bears the same ratio to the ordinary income (or long-term capital gain) which would have been recognized if the entire property had been sold by the donor at its fair market value at the time of the sale or exchange as the amount realized on the sale or exchange bears to the fair market value of the entire property at such time. The terms "ordinary income" and "long-term capital gain", as used in this section, have the same meaning as they have in paragraph (a) of § 1.170A-4. For determining the portion of the adjusted basis, ordinary income, and long-term capital gain allocated to the contributed portion of the property for purposes of applying section 170(e)(1) and paragraph (a) of § 1.170A-4 to the contributed portion of the property, and for determining the donee's basis in such contributed portion, see paragraph (c)(2) and (4) of § 1.170A-4. For determining the holding period of such contributed portion, see section 1223(2) and the regulations thereunder.

(c) *Illustrations.*—The application of this section may be illustrated by the following examples, which are supplemented by other examples in paragraph (d) of § 1.170A-4:

Example (1). In 1970, a calendar-year individual taxpayer, sells to a church for $4,000 stock held for more than 6 months which has an adjusted basis of $4,000 and a fair market value of $10,000. A's contribution base for 1970, as defined in section 170(b)(1)(F), is $100,000, and during that year he makes no other charitable contributions. Thus, A makes a charitable contribution to the church of $6,000 ($10,000 value – $4,000 amount realized). Without regard to this section, A is allowed a deduction under section 170 of $6,000 for his charitable contribution to the church, since there is no reduction under section 170(e)(1) with respect to the long-term capital gain. Accordingly, under paragraph (b) of this section the adjusted basis for determining gain on the bargain sale is $1,600 ($4,000 adjusted basis × $4,000 amount realized/$10,000 value of property). A has recognized long-term capital gain of $2,400 ($4,000 amount realized – $1,600 adjusted basis) on the bargain sale.

Example (2). The facts are the same as in Example (1) except that A also makes a charitable contribution in 1970 of $50,000 cash to the church. By reason of section 170(b)(1)(A), the deduction allowed under section 170 for 1970 is $50,000 for the amount of cash contributed to the church; however, the $6,000 contribution of property is carried over to 1971 under section 170(d). Under paragraphs (a)(2) and (b) of this section the adjusted basis for determining gain for 1970 on the bargain sale in that year is $1,600 ($4,000 × $4,000/$10,000). A has a recognized long-term capital gain for 1970 of $2,400 ($4,000 – $1,600) on the sale.

Example (3). In 1970, C, a calendar-year individual taxpayer, makes a charitable contribution of $50,000 cash to a church. In addition, he sells for $4,000 to a private foundation not described in section 170(b)(1)(E) stock held for more than 6 months which has an adjusted basis of $4,000 and a fair market value of $10,000. Thus, C makes a charitable contribution of $6,000 of such property to the private foundation ($10,000 value – $4,000 amount realized). C's contribution base for 1970, as defined in section 170(b)(1)(F), is $100,000, and during that year he makes no other charitable contributions. By reason of section 170(b)(1)(A), the deduction allowed under section 170 for 1970 is $50,000 for the amount of cash contributed to the church. Under section 170(e)(1)(B)(ii) and paragraphs (a)(1) and (c)(2)(i) of § 1.170A-4, the $6,000 contribution of stock is reduced to $4,800 ($6,000 – [50% × ($6,000 value of contributed portion of stock – $3,600 adjusted basis)]). However, by reason of section 170(b)(1)(B)(ii), applied without regard to section 1011(b), no deduction is allowed under section 170 for 1970 or any other year for the reduced contribution of $4,800 to the private foundation. Accordingly, paragraph (b) of this section does not apply for purposes of apportioning the adjusted basis of the stock sold to the private foundation, and under section 1.1011-1(e) the recognized gain on the bargain sale is $0 ($4,000 amount realized – $4,000 adjusted basis).

Example (4). In 1970, B, a calendar-year individual taxpayer, sells to a church for $2,000 stock held for not more than 6 months which has an adjusted basis of $4,000 and a fair market value of $10,000. B's contribution base for 1970, as defined in section 170(b)(1)(F), is $20,000 and during such year B makes no other charitable contributions. Thus, he makes a charitable contribution to the church of $8,000 ($10,000 value – $2,000 amount realized). Under paragraph (b) of this section the adjusted basis for determining gain on the bargain sale is $800 ($4,000 adjusted basis × $2,000 amount realized/$10,000 value of stock). Accordingly, B has a recognized short-term capital gain of $1,200 ($2,000 amount realized – $800 adjusted basis) on the bargain sale. After applying section 1011(b) and paragraphs (a)(1) and (c)(2)(i) of § 1.170A-4, B is allowed a charitable contributions deduction for 1970 of $3,200 ($8,000 value of gift – [$8,000 – ($4,000 adjusted basis of property × $8,000 value of gift/ $10,000 value of property)]).

Example (5). The facts are the same as in Example (4) except that B sells the property to the church for $4,000. Thus, B makes a charitable contribution to the church of $6,000 ($10,000 value – $4,000 amount realized). Under paragraph (b) of this section the adjusted basis for determining gain on the bargain sale is $1,600 ($4,000 adjusted basis × $4,000 amount realized/ $10,000 value of stock). Accordingly, B has a recognized short-term capital gain of $2,400 ($4,000 amount realized – $1,600 adjusted basis) on the bargain sale. After applying section 1011(b) and paragraphs (a)(1) and (c)(2)(i) of § 1.170A-4, B is allowed a charitable contributions deduction for 1970 of $2,400 ($6,000 value of gift – [$6,000 – ($4,000 adjusted basis of property × $6,000 value of gift/$10,000 value of property)]).

Example (6). The facts are the same as in Example (4) except that B sells the property to the church for $6,000. Thus, B makes a charitable contribution to the church of $4,000 ($10,000 value – $6,000 amount realized). Under paragraph (b) of this section the adjusted basis for determining gain on the bargain sale is $2,400 ($4,000 adjusted basis × $6,000 amount realized/ $10,000 value of stock). Accordingly, B has a recognized short-term capital gain of $3,600 ($6,000 amount realized – $2,400 adjusted basis) on the bargain sale. After applying section 1011(b) and paragraphs (a)(1) and (c)(2)(i) of § 1.170A-4, B is allowed a charitable contributions deduction for 1970 of $1,600 ($4,000 value of gift – [$4,000 – ($4,000 adjusted basis of property × $4,000 value of gift/$10,000 value of property)]).

Example (7). In 1970, C, a calendar-year individual taxpayer, sells to a church for $4,000 tangible personal property used in his business for more than 6 months which has an adjusted basis of $4,000 and a fair market value of $10,000. Thus, C makes a charitable contribution to the church of $6,000 ($10,000 value – $4,000 adjusted basis). C's contribution base for 1970, as defined in section 170(b)(1)(F), is $100,000 and during such year he makes no other charitable contributions. If C had sold the property at its fair market value at the time of its contribution, it is assumed that under section 1245 $4,000 of the gain of $6,000 ($10,000 value – $4,000 adjusted basis) would have been treated as ordinary income. Thus, there would have been long-term capital gain of $2,000. It is also assumed that the church does not put the property to an unrelated use, as defined in paragraph (b)(3) of § 1.170A-4. Under paragraph (b) of this section the adjusted basis for determining gain on the bargain sale is $1,600 ($4,000 adjusted basis × $4,000 amount realized/ $10,000 value of property). Accordingly, C has a recognized gain of $2,400 ($4,000 amount realized – $1,600 adjusted basis) on the bargain sale, consisting of ordinary income of $1,600 ($4,000 ordinary income × $4,000 amount realized/

$10,000 value of property) and of long-term capital gain of $800 ($2,000 long-term gain × $4,000 amount realized/$10,000 value of property). After applying section 1011(b) and paragraphs (a) and (c)(2)(i) of § 1.170A-4, C is allowed a charitable contributions deduction for 1970 of $3,600 ($6,000 gift – [$4,000 ordinary income × $6,000 value of gift/$10,000 value of property]).

Example (8). (a) On January 1, 1970, A, a male of age 65, transfers capital assets consisting of securities held for more than 6 months to a church in exchange for a promise by the church to pay A a nonassignable annuity of $5,000 per year for life. The annuity is payable monthly with the first payment to be made on February 1, 1970. A's contribution base for 1970, as defined in section 170(b)(1)(F), is $200,000, and during that year he makes no other charitable contributions. On the date of transfer the securities have a fair market value of $100,000 and an adjusted basis to A of $20,000.

(b) The present value of the right of a male age 65 to receive a life annuity of $5,000 per annum, payable in equal installments at the end of each monthly period, is $59,755 ($5,000 × [11.469 + 0.482]), determined in accordance with section 101(b) of the Code, paragraph (e)(1)(iii)(b)(2) of § 1.101-2, and section 3 of Rev. Rul. 62-216, C.B. 1962-2, 30. Thus, A makes a charitable contribution to the church of $40,245 ($100,000 – $59,755). See Rev. Rul. 84-162, 1984-2 C.B. 200, for transfers for which the valuation date falls after November 23, 1984. (See § 601.601(d)(2)(ii)(b) of this chapter). For the applicable valuation tables in connection therewith, see § 20.2031-7(d)(6) of this chapter. See, however, § 1.7520-3(b) (relating to exceptions to the use of standard actuarial factors in certain circumstances).

(c) Under paragraph (b) of this section, the adjusted basis for determining gain on the bargain sale is $11,951 ($20,000 × $59,775/$100,000). Accordingly, A has a recognized long-term capital gain of $47,804 ($59,755 – $11,951) on the bargain sale. Such gain is to be reported by A ratably over the period of years measured by the expected return multiple under the contract but only from that portion of the annual payments which is a return of his investment in the contract under section 72 of the Code. For such purposes, the investment in the contract is $59,755, that is, the present value of the annuity.

(d) The computation and application of the exclusion ratio, the gain, and the ordinary annuity income are as follows, determined by using the expected return multiple of 15.0 applicable under Table I of § 1.72-9:

A's expected return (annual payments of $5,000 × 15)	$75,000.00
Exclusion ratio ($59,755 investment in contract divided by expected return of $75,000)	79.7%
Annual exclusion (annual payments of $5,000 × 79.7%)	3,985.00

Reg. §1.1011-2(c)

Ordinary annuity income
($5,000 – $3,985) 1,015.00
Long-term capital gain per year
($47,804/15) with respect to the annual
exclusion 3,186.93

(e) The exclusion ratio of 79.7 percent applies throughout the life of the contract. During the first 15 years of the annuity, A is required to report ordinary income of $1,015 and long-term capital gain of $3,186.93 with respect to the annuity payments he receives. After the total long-term capital gain of $47,804 has been reported by A, he is required to report only ordinary income of $1,015.00 per annum with respect to the annuity payments he receives.

(d) *Effective date.*—This section applies only to sales and exchanges made after December 19, 1969.

(e) *Cross reference.*—For rules relating to the treatment of liabilities in a bargain sale transaction, see § 1.1001-2. [Reg. § 1.1011-2.]

☐ [T.D. 7207, 10-3-72. *Amended by T.D. 7741,* 12-11-80, T.D. 8176, 2-24-88 *and T.D.* 8540, 6-9-94.]

[Reg. § 1.1012-1]

§ 1.1012-1. Basis of property.—(a) *General rule.*—In general, the basis of property is the cost thereof. The cost is the amount paid for such property in cash or other property. This general rule is subject to exceptions stated in subchapter O (relating to gain or loss on the disposition of property), subchapter C (relating to corporate distributions and adjustments), subchapter K (relating to partners and partnerships), and subchapter P (relating to capital gains and losses), chapter 1 of the Code.

(b) *Real estate taxes as part of cost.*—In computing the cost of real property, the purchaser shall not take into account any amount paid to the seller as reimbursement for real property taxes which are treated under section 164(d) as imposed upon the purchaser. This rule applies whether or not the contract of sale calls for the purchaser to reimburse the seller for such real estate taxes paid or to be paid by the seller. On the other hand, where the purchaser pays (or assumes liability for) real estate taxes which are treated under section 164(d) as imposed upon the seller, such taxes shall be considered part of the cost of the property. It is immaterial whether or not the contract of sale specifies that the sale price has been reduced by, or is in any way intended to reflect, real estate taxes allocable to the seller under section 164(d). For illustrations of the application of the paragraph, see paragraph (b) of § 1.1001-1.

(c) *Sale of stock.*—(1) *In general.*—(i) Except as provided in paragraph (e)(2) of this section (dealing with stock for which the average basis method is permitted), if a taxpayer sells or transfers shares of stock in a corporation that the taxpayer purchased or acquired on different dates or at different prices and the taxpayer does not adequately identify the lot from which the stock is sold or transferred, the stock sold or transferred is charged against the earliest lot the taxpayer purchased or acquired to determine the basis and holding period of the stock. If the earliest lot purchased or acquired is held in a stock certificate that represents multiple lots of stock, and the taxpayer does not adequately identify the lot from which the stock is sold or transferred, the stock sold or transferred is charged against the earliest lot included in the certificate. See paragraphs (c)(2), (c)(3), and (c)(4) of this section for rules on what constitutes an adequate identification.

(ii) A taxpayer must determine the basis of identical stock (within the meaning of paragraph (e)(4) of this section) by averaging the cost of each share if the stock is purchased at separate times on the same calendar day in executing a single trade order and the broker executing the trade provides a single confirmation that reports an aggregate total cost or an average cost per share. However, the taxpayer may determine the basis of the stock by the actual cost per share if the taxpayer notifies the broker in writing of this intent. The taxpayer must notify the broker by the earlier of the date of the sale of any of the stock for which the taxpayer received the confirmation or one year after the date of the confirmation. A broker may extend the one-year period but the taxpayer must notify the broker no later than the date of sale of any of the stock.

(2) *Identification of stock.*—An adequate identification is made if it is shown that certificates representing shares of stock from a lot which was purchased or acquired on a certain date or for a certain price were delivered to the taxpayer's transferee. Except as otherwise provided in subparagraph (3) or (4) of this paragraph, such stock certificates delivered to the transferee constitute the stock sold or transferred by the taxpayer. Thus, unless the requirements of subparagraph (3) or (4) of this paragraph are met, the stock sold or transferred is charged to the lot to which the certificates delivered to the transferee belong, whether or not the taxpayer intends, or instructs his broker or other agent, to sell or transfer stock from a lot purchased or acquired on a different date or for a different price.

(3) *Identification on confirmation document.*—(i) Where the stock is left in the custody of a broker or other agent, an adequate identification is made if—

(a) At the time of the sale or transfer, the taxpayer specifies to such broker or other agent having custody of the stock the particular stock to be sold or transferred, and

(b) Within a reasonable time thereafter, confirmation of such specification is set forth in a written document from such broker or other agent.

Stock identified pursuant to this subdivision is the stock sold or transferred by the taxpayer, even though stock certificates from a different lot are delivered to the taxpayer's transferee.

(ii) Where a single stock certificate represents stock from different lots, where such certificate is held by the taxpayer rather than his broker or other agent, and where the taxpayer sells a part of the stock represented by such certificate through a broker or other agent, an adequate identification is made if—

(a) At the time of the delivery of the certificate to the broker or other agent, the taxpayer specifies to such broker or other agent the particular stock to be sold or transferred, and

(b) Within a reasonable time thereafter, confirmation of such specification is set forth in a written document from such broker or agent. Where part of stock represented by a single certificate is sold or transferred directly by the taxpayer to the purchaser or transferee instead of through a broker or other agent, an adequate identification is made if the taxpayer maintains a written record of the particular stock which he intended to sell or transfer.

(4) *Stock held by a trustee, executor, or administrator.*—(i) A trustee or executor or administrator of an estate holding stock (not left in the custody of a broker) makes an adequate identification if the trustee, executor, or administrator—

(a) Specifies in writing in the books and records of the trust or estate the particular stock to be sold, transferred, or distributed;

(b) In the case of a distribution, furnishes the distributee with a written document identifying the particular stock distributed; and

(c) In the case of a sale or transfer through a broker or other agent, specifies to the broker or agent the particular stock to be sold or transferred, and within a reasonable time thereafter the broker or agent confirms the specification in a written document.

(ii) The stock the trust or estate identifies under paragraph (c)(4)(i) of this section is the stock treated as sold, transferred, or distributed, even if the trustee, executor, or administrator delivers stock certificates from a different lot.

(5) *Subsequent sales.*—If stock identified under subparagraph (3) or (4) of this paragraph as belonging to a particular lot is sold, transferred, or distributed, the stock so identified shall be deemed to have been sold, transferred, or distributed, and such sale, transfer, or distribution will be taken into consideration in identifying the taxpayer's remaining stock for purposes of subsequent sales, transfers, or distributions.

(6) *Bonds.*—Paragraphs (1) through (5), (8), and (9) of this section apply to the sale or transfer of bonds.

(7) *Book-entry securities.*—(i) In applying the provisions of subparagraph (3)(i)(a) of this paragraph in the case of a sale or transfer of a book-entry security (as defined in subdivision (iii)(a) of this subparagraph) which is made after December 31, 1970, pursuant to a written instruction by the taxpayer, a specification by the taxpayer of the unique lot number which he has assigned to the lot which contains the securities being sold or transferred shall constitute specification as required by such subparagraph. The specification of the lot number shall be made either—

(a) In such written instruction, or

(b) In the case of a taxpayer in whose name the book entry by the Reserve Bank is made, in a list of lot numbers with respect to all book-entry securities on the books of the Reserve Bank sold or transferred on that date by the taxpayer, provided such list is mailed to or received by the Reserve Bank on or before the Reserve Bank's next business day.

This subdivision shall apply only if the taxpayer assigns lot numbers in numerical sequence to successive purchases of securities of the same loan title (series) and maturity date, except that securities of the same loan title (series) and maturity date which are purchased at the same price on the same date may be included within the same lot.

(ii) In applying paragraph (c)(3)(i)(b) of this section to a sale or transfer of a book-entry security pursuant to a taxpayer's written instruction, a confirmation is made by furnishing to the taxpayer a written advice of transaction from the Reserve Bank or other person through whom the taxpayer sells or transfers the securities. The confirmation document must describe the securities and specify the date of the transaction and amount of securities sold or transferred.

(iii) For purposes of this paragraph (c)(7):

(a) The term *book-entry security* means a transferable Treasury bond, note, certificate of indebtedness, or bill issued under the Second Liberty Bond Act (31 U.S.C. 774(2)), as amended, or other security of the United States (as defined in paragraph (c)(7)(iii)(b) of this section) in the form of an entry made as prescribed in 31 CFR Part 306, or other comparable Federal regulations, on the records of a Reserve Bank.

(b) The term "other security of the United States" means a bond, note, certificate of indebtedness, bill, debenture, or similar obligation which is subject to the provisions of 31 CFR Part 306 or other comparable Federal regulations and which is issued by (1) any department or agency of the Government of the United States, or (2) the Federal National Mortgage Association, the Federal Home Loan Banks, the Federal Home Loan Mortgage Corporation, the Federal Land Banks, the Federal Intermediate Credit Banks, the Banks for Cooperatives, or the Tennessee Valley Authority;

(c) The term "serially-numbered advice of transaction" means the confirmation (prescribed in 31 CFR 306.116) issued by the Reserve

Bank which is identifiable by a unique number and indicates that a particular written instruction to the Reserve Bank with respect to the deposit or withdrawal of a specified book-entry security (or securities) has been executed; and

(d) The term "Reserve Bank" means a Federal Reserve Bank and its branches acting as Fiscal Agent of the United States.

(8) *Time for making identification.*—For purposes of this paragraph (c), an adequate identification of stock is made at the time of sale, transfer, delivery, or distribution if the identification is made no later than the earlier of the settlement date or the time for settlement required by Rule 15c6-1 under the Securities Exchange Act of 1934, 17 CFR 240.15c6-1 (or its successor). A standing order or instruction for the specific identification of stock is treated as an adequate identification made at the time of sale, transfer, delivery, or distribution.

(9) *Method of writing.*—(i) A written confirmation, record, document, instruction, notification, or advice includes a writing in electronic format.

(ii) A broker or agent may include the written confirmation required under this paragraph (c) in an account statement or other document the broker or agent periodically provides to the taxpayer if the broker or agent provides the statement or other document within a reasonable time after the sale or transfer.

(10) *Method for determining basis of stock.*—A method of determining the basis of stock, including a method of identifying stock sold under this paragraph (c) and the average basis method described in paragraph (e) of this section, is not a method of accounting. Therefore, a change in a method of determining the basis of stock is not a change in method of accounting to which sections 446 and 481 apply.

(11) *Effective/applicability date.*—Paragraphs (c)(1), (c)(4), (c)(6), (c)(7)(ii), (c)(7)(iii)(*a*), (c)(8), (c)(9), and (c)(10) of this section apply for taxable years beginning after October 18, 2010.

(d) *Obligations issued as part of an investment unit.*—For purposes of determining the basis of the individual elements of an investment unit (as defined in paragraph (b)(2)(ii)(*a*) of § 1.1232-3) consisting of an obligation and an option (which is not an excluded option under paragraph (b)(1)(iii)(*c*) of § 1.1232-3), security, or other property, the cost of such investment unit shall be allocated to such individual elements on the basis of their respective fair market values. In the case of the initial issuance of an investment unit consisting of an obligation and an option, security, or other property, where neither the obligation nor the option, security, or other property has a readily ascertainable fair market value, the portion of the cost of the unit which is allocable to the obligation shall be an amount equal to the

issue price of the obligation as determined under paragraph (b)(2)(ii)(*a*) of § 1.1232-3.

(e) *Election to use average basis method.*—(1) *In general.*—Notwithstanding paragraph (c) of this section, and except as provided in paragraph (e)(8) of this section, a taxpayer may use the average basis method described in paragraph (e)(7) of this section to determine the cost or other basis of identical shares of stock if—

(i) The taxpayer leaves shares of stock in a regulated investment company (as defined in paragraph (e)(5) of this section) or shares of stock acquired after December 31, 2010, in connection with a dividend reinvestment plan (as defined in paragraph (e)(6) of this section) with a custodian or agent in an account maintained for the acquisition or redemption, sale, or other disposition of shares of the stock; and

(ii) The taxpayer acquires identical shares of stock at different prices or bases in the account.

(2) *Determination of method.*—(i) If a taxpayer places shares of stock described in paragraph (e)(1)(i) of this section acquired on or after January 1, 2012, in the custody of a broker (as defined by section 6045(c)(1)), including by transfer from an account with another broker, the basis of the shares is determined in accordance with the broker's default method, unless the taxpayer notifies the broker that the taxpayer elects another permitted method. The taxpayer must report gain or loss using the method the taxpayer elects or, if the taxpayer fails to make an election, the broker's default method. *See* paragraphs (e)(9)(i) and (e)(9)(v), *Example 2,* of this section.

(ii) The provisions of this paragraph (e)(2) are illustrated by the following example:

Example. (i) In connection with a dividend reinvestment plan, Taxpayer B acquires 100 shares of G Company in 2012 and 100 shares of G Company in 2013, in an account B maintains with R Broker. B notifies R in writing that B elects to use the average basis method to compute the basis of the shares of G Company. In 2014, B transfers the shares of G Company to an account with S Broker. B does not notify S of the basis determination method B chooses to use for the shares of G Company, and S's default method is first-in, first-out. In 2015, B purchases 200 shares of G Company in the account with S. In 2016, B instructs S to sell 150 shares of G Company.

(ii) Because B does not notify S of a basis determination method for the shares of G Company, under paragraph (e)(2)(i) of this section, the basis of the 150 shares of G Company S sells for B in 2016 must be determined under S's default method, first-in, first-out.

(3) *Shares of stock.*—For purposes of this paragraph (e), securities issued by unit investment trusts described in paragraph (e)(5) of this sec-

Reg. §1.1012-1(e)(3)

tion are treated as shares of stock and the term *share* or *shares* includes fractions of a share.

(4) *Identical stock.*—For purposes of this paragraph (e), *identical shares of stock* means stock with the same Committee on Uniform Security Identification Procedures (CUSIP) number or other security identifier number as permitted in published guidance of general applicability, *see* § 601.601(d)(2) of this chapter.

(5) *Regulated investment company.*—(i) For purposes of this paragraph, a "regulated investment company" means any domestic corporation (other than a personal holding company as defined in section 542) which meets the limitations of section 851(b) and § 1.851-2, and which is registered at all times during the taxable year under the Investment Company Act of 1940, as amended (15 U.S.C. 80a-1 to 80b-2), either as a management company, or as a unit investment trust.

(ii) Notwithstanding subdivision (i), this paragraph shall not apply in the case of a unit investment trust unless it is one—

(a) Substantially all of the assets of which consist (1) of securities issued by a single management company (as defined in such Act) and securities acquired pursuant to subdivision (b) of this subdivision (ii), or (2) securities issued by a single other corporation, and

(b) Which has no power to invest in any other securities except securities issued by a single other management company, when permitted by such Act or the rules and regulations of the Securities and Exchange Commission.

(6) *Dividend reinvestment plan.*—(i) *In general.*—For purposes of this paragraph (e), the term *dividend reinvestment plan* means any written plan, arrangement, or program under which at least 10 percent of every dividend (within the meaning of section 316) on any share of stock is reinvested in stock identical to the stock on which the dividend is paid. A plan is a dividend reinvestment plan if the plan documents require that at least 10 percent of any dividend paid is reinvested in identical stock even if the plan includes stock on which no dividends have ever been declared or paid or on which an issuer ceases paying dividends. A plan that holds one or more different stocks may permit a taxpayer to reinvest a different percentage of dividends in the stocks held. A dividend reinvestment plan may reinvest other distributions on stock, such as capital gain distributions, non-taxable returns of capital, and cash in lieu of fractional shares. The term dividend reinvestment plan includes both issuer administered dividend reinvestment plans and non-issuer administered dividend reinvestment plans.

(ii) *Acquisition of stock.*—Stock is acquired in connection with a dividend reinvestment plan if the stock is acquired under that plan, arrangement, or program, or if the dividends and other distributions paid on the stock are subject to that plan, arrangement, or program. Shares of stock acquired in connection with a dividend reinvestment plan include the initial purchase of stock in the dividend reinvestment plan, transfers of identical stock into the dividend reinvestment plan, additional periodic purchases of identical stock in the dividend reinvestment plan, and identical stock acquired through reinvestment of the dividends or other distributions paid on the stock held in the plan.

(iii) *Dividends and other distributions paid after reorganization.*—For purposes of this paragraph (e)(6), dividends and other distributions declared or announced before or pending a corporate action (such as a merger, consolidation, acquisition, split-off, or spin-off) involving the issuer and subsequently paid and reinvested in shares of stock in the successor entity or entities are treated as reinvested in shares of stock identical to the shares of stock of the issuer.

(iv) *Withdrawal from or termination of plan.*—If a taxpayer withdraws stock from a dividend reinvestment plan or the plan administrator terminates the dividend reinvestment plan, the shares of identical stock the taxpayer acquires after the withdrawal or termination are not acquired in connection with a dividend reinvestment plan. The taxpayer may not use the average basis method after the withdrawal or termination but may use any other permissible basis determination method. See paragraph (e)(7)(v) of this section for the basis of the shares after withdrawal or termination.

(7) *Computation of average basis.*—(i) *In general.*—Average basis is determined by averaging the basis of all shares of identical stock in an account regardless of holding period. However, for this purpose, shares of stock in a dividend reinvestment plan are not identical to shares of stock with the same CUSIP number that are not in a dividend reinvestment plan. The basis of each share of identical stock in the account is the aggregate basis of all shares of that stock in the account divided by the aggregate number of shares. Unless a single-account election is in effect, see paragraph (e)(11) of this section, a taxpayer may not average together the basis of identical stock held in separate accounts that the taxpayer sells, exchanges, or otherwise disposes of on or after January 1, 2012.

(ii) *Order of disposition of shares sold or transferred.*—In the case of the sale or transfer of shares of stock to which the average basis method election applies, shares sold or transferred are deemed to be the shares first acquired. Thus, the first shares sold or transferred are those with a holding period of more than 1 year (long-term shares) to the extent that the account contains long-term shares. If the number of shares sold or transferred exceeds the number of long-term shares in the account, the excess shares sold or transferred are deemed to be shares with a holding period of 1 year or less (short-term shares). Any gain or loss attributable to shares held for more than 1 year constitutes long-term gain or loss, and any gain or loss attributable to shares held for 1 year or less constitutes short-term gain or loss. For example, if a taxpayer sells 50 shares from an account containing 100 long-term shares and 100 short-term shares, the shares sold or transferred are all long-term shares. If, however, the account contains 40 long-term shares and 100 short-term shares, the taxpayer has sold 40 long-term shares and 10 short-term shares.

(iii) *Transition rule from double-category method.*—This paragraph (e)(7)(iii) applies to stock for which a taxpayer uses the double-category method under § 1.1012-1(e)(3) (April 1, 2010), that the taxpayer acquired before April 1, 2011, and that the taxpayer sells, exchanges, or otherwise disposes of on or after that date. The taxpayer must calculate the average basis of this stock by averaging together all identical shares of stock in the account on April 1, 2011, regardless of holding period.

(iv) *Wash sales.*—A taxpayer must apply section 1091 and the associated regulations (dealing with wash sales of substantially identical securities) in computing average basis regardless of whether the stock or security sold or otherwise disposed of and the stock acquired are in the same account or in different accounts.

(v) *Basis after change from average basis method.*—Unless a taxpayer revokes an average basis method election under paragraph (e)(9)(iii) of this section, if a taxpayer changes from the average basis method to another basis determi-

nation method (including a change resulting from a withdrawal from or termination of a dividend reinvestment plan), the basis of each share of stock immediately after the change is the same as the basis immediately before the change. *See* paragraph (e)(9)(iv) of this section for rules for changing from the average basis method.

(vi) The provisions of this paragraph (e)(7) are illustrated by the following examples:

Example 1. (i) In 2011, Taxpayer C acquires 100 shares of H Company and enrolls them in a dividend reinvestment plan administered by T Custodian. C elects to use the average basis method for the shares of H Company enrolled in the dividend reinvestment plan. T also acquires for C's account 50 shares of H Company and does not enroll these shares in the dividend reinvestment plan.

(ii) Under paragraph (e)(7)(i) of this section, the 50 shares of H Company not in the dividend reinvestment plan are not identical to the 100 shares of H Company enrolled in the dividend reinvestment plan, even if they have the same CUSIP number. Accordingly, under paragraphs (e)(1) and (e)(7)(i) of this section, C may not average the basis of the 50 shares of H Company with the basis of the 100 shares of H Company. Under paragraph (e)(1)(i) of this section, C may not use the average basis method for the 50 shares of H Company because the shares are not acquired in connection with a dividend reinvestment plan.

Example 2. (i) Taxpayer D enters into an agreement with W Custodian establishing an account for the periodic acquisition of shares of L Company, a regulated investment company. W acquires for D's account shares of L Company stock on the following dates and amounts:

Date	Number of shares	Cost
January 8, 2010	25 shares	$200
February 8, 2010	24 shares	200
March 8, 2010	20 shares	200
April 8, 2010	20 shares	200

(ii) At D's direction, W sells 40 shares from the account on January 15, 2011, for $10 per share or a total of $400. D elects to use the average basis method for the shares of L Company. The average basis for the shares sold on January 15, 2011, is $8.99 (total cost of shares, $800, divided by the total number of shares, 89).

(iii) Under paragraph (e)(7)(ii) of this section, the shares sold are the shares first acquired. Thus, D realizes $25.25 ($1.01 * 25) long-term capital gain for the 25 shares acquired on January 8, 2010, and $15.15 ($1.01 * 15) short-term capital gain for 15 of the shares acquired on February 8, 2010.

Example 3. (i) The facts are the same as in *Example 2*, except that on February 8, 2011, D changes to the first-in, first-out basis determination method. W purchases 25 shares of L Company for D on March 8, 2011, at $12 per share. D

sells 40 shares on May 8, 2011, and 34 shares on July 8, 2012.

(ii) Because D uses the first-in, first-out method, the 40 shares sold on May 8, 2011 are 9 shares purchased on February 8, 2010, 20 shares purchased on March 8, 2010, and 11 shares purchased on April 8, 2010. Because, under paragraph (e)(7)(v) of this section, the basis of the shares D owns when D changes from the average basis method remains the same, the basis of the shares sold on May 8, 2011, is $8.99 per share, not the original cost of $8.33 per share for the shares purchased on February 8, 2010, or $10 per share for the shares purchased on March 8, 2010, and April 8, 2010. The basis of the shares sold on July 8, 2012, is $8.99 per share for 9 shares purchased on April 8, 2010, and $12 per share for 25 shares purchased on March 8, 2011.

Example 4. (i) The facts are the same as in *Example 2*, except that D uses the first-in, first-out method for the 40 shares sold on January 15, 2011. W purchases 25 shares of L Company for D on March 8, 2011, at $12 per share. D sells 40 shares on May 8, 2011, and elects the average basis method.

(ii) Because D uses the first-in, first-out method for the sale on January 15, 2011, the 40 shares sold are the 25 shares acquired on January 8, 2010, for $200 (basis $8 per share) and 15 of the 24 shares purchased on February 8, 2010, for $200 (basis $8.33 per share).

(iii) Under paragraph (e)(7)(i) of this section, under the average basis method, the basis of all of the shares of identical stock in D's account is averaged. Thus, the basis of each share D sells on May 8, 2011, after electing the average basis method, is $10.47. This figure is the total cost of the shares in D's account ($74.97 for the 9 shares acquired on February 8, 2010, $200 for the 20 shares acquired on March 8, 2010, $200 for the 20 shares acquired on April 8, 2010, and $300 for the 25 shares acquired on March 8, 2011) divided by 74, the total number of shares ($774.97/74).

(8) *Limitation on use of average basis method for certain gift shares.*—(i) Except as provided in paragraph (e)(8)(ii) of this section, a taxpayer may not use the average basis method for shares of stock a taxpayer acquires by gift after December 31, 1920, if the basis of the shares (adjusted for the period before the date of the gift as provided in section 1016) in the hands of the donor or the last preceding owner by whom the shares were not acquired by gift was greater than the fair market value of the shares at the time of the gift. This paragraph (e)(8)(i) does not apply to shares the taxpayer acquires as a result of a taxable dividend or capital gain distribution on the gift shares.

(ii) Notwithstanding paragraph (e)(8)(i) of this section, a taxpayer may use the average basis method if the taxpayer states in writing that the taxpayer will treat the basis of the gift shares as the fair market value of the shares at the time the taxpayer acquires the shares. The taxpayer must provide this statement when the taxpayer makes the election under paragraph (e)(9) of this section or when transferring the shares to an account for which the taxpayer has made this election, whichever occurs later. The statement must be effective for any gift shares identical to the gift shares to which the average basis method election applies that the taxpayer acquires at any time and must remain in effect as long as the election remains in effect.

(iii) The provisions of this paragraph (e)(8) are illustrated by the following examples:

Example 1. (i) Taxpayer E owns an account for the periodic acquisition of shares of M Company, a regulated investment company. On April 15, 2010, E acquires identical shares of M Company by gift and transfers those shares into the account. These shares had an adjusted basis in the hands of the donor that was greater than the

fair market value of the shares on that date. On June 15, 2010, E sells shares from the account and elects to use the average basis method.

(ii) Under paragraph (e)(8)(ii) of this section, E may elect to use the average basis method for shares sold or transferred from the account if E includes a statement with E's election that E will treat the basis of the gift shares in the account as the fair market value of the shares at the time E acquired them. *See* paragraph (e)(9)(ii) of this section.

Example 2. (i) The facts are the same as in *Example 1*, except E acquires the gift shares on April 15, 2012, transfers those shares into the account, and used the average basis method for sales of shares of M Company before acquiring the gift shares. E sells shares of M Company on June 15, 2012.

(ii) Under paragraph (e)(8)(ii) of this section, the basis of the gift shares may be averaged with the basis of the other shares of M Company in E's account if, when E transfers the gift shares to the account, E provides a statement to E's broker that E will treat the basis of the gift shares in the account as the fair market value of the shares at the time E acquired them. *See* paragraph (e)(9)(i) of this section.

(9) *Time and manner for making the average basis method election.*—(i) *In general.*—A taxpayer makes an election to use the average basis method for shares of stock described in paragraph (e)(1)(i) of this section that are covered securities (within the meaning of section 6045(g)(3)) by notifying the custodian or agent in writing by any reasonable means. For purposes of this paragraph (e), a writing may be in electronic format. A taxpayer has not made an election within the meaning of this section if the taxpayer fails to notify a broker of the taxpayer's basis determination method and basis is determined by the broker's default method under paragraph (e)(2) of this section. A taxpayer may make the average basis method election at any time, effective for sales or other dispositions of stock occurring after the taxpayer notifies the custodian or agent. The election must identify each account with that custodian or agent and each stock in that account to which the election applies. The election may specify that it applies to all accounts with a custodian or agent, including accounts the taxpayer later establishes with the custodian or agent. If the election applies to gift shares, the taxpayer must provide the statement required by paragraph (e)(8)(ii) of this section, if applicable, to the custodian or agent with the taxpayer's election.

(ii) *Average basis method election for securities that are noncovered securities.*—A taxpayer makes an election to use the average basis method for shares of stock described in paragraph (e)(1)(i) of this section that are noncovered securities (as described in § 1.6045-1(a)(16) on the taxpayer's income tax return for the first taxable year for which the election applies. A taxpayer may make the election on an amended return filed no later than the time prescribed (including extensions) for filing the original return for the taxable year for which the election applies. The taxpayer must indicate on the return that the taxpayer used the average basis method in reporting gain or loss on the sale or other disposition. A taxpayer must attach to the return the statement described in paragraph (e)(8)(ii) of this section, if applicable. A taxpayer making the election must maintain records necessary to substantiate the average basis reported.

(iii) *Revocation of election.*—A taxpayer may revoke an election under paragraph (e)(9)(i) of this section by the earlier of one year after the taxpayer makes the election or the date of the first sale, transfer, or disposition of that stock following the election. A custodian or agent may extend the one-year period but a taxpayer may not revoke an election after the first sale, transfer, or disposition of the stock. A revocation applies to all stock the taxpayer holds in an account that is identical to the shares of stock for which the taxpayer revokes the election. A revocation is effective when the taxpayer notifies, in writing by any reasonable means, the custodian or agent holding the stock to which the revocation applies. After revocation, the taxpayer's basis in the shares of stock to which the revocation applies is the basis before averaging.

Date	Number of shares	Cost
January 8, 2012	25 shares	$200
February 8, 2012	24 shares	200
March 8, 2012	20 shares	200

(ii) F notifies W that F elects, under paragraph (e)(9)(i) of this section, to use the average basis method for the shares of N Company. On May 8, 2012, under paragraph (e)(9)(iii) of this section, F notifies W that F revokes the average basis method election. On June 1, 2012, F sells 60 shares of N Company using the first-in, first-out basis determination method.

(iii) Under paragraph (e)(9)(iii) of this section, the basis of the N Company shares upon revocation, and for purposes of determining gain on the sale, is $8.00 per share for each of the 25 shares purchased on January 8, 2012, $8.34 per share for each of the 24 shares purchased on February 8, 2012, and $10 per share for the remaining 11 shares purchased on March 8, 2012.

Example 2. (i) The facts are the same as in *Example 1*, except that F does not notify W that F elects a basis determination method. W's default basis determination method is the average basis method and W maintains an averaged basis for F's shares of N Company on W's books and records.

(ii) F has not elected the average basis method under paragraph (e)(9)(i) of this section. Therefore, F's notification to W on May 8, 2012, is not an effective revocation under paragraph (e)(9)(iii) of this section. F's attempted revocation is, instead, notification of a change from the av-

(iv) *Change from average basis method.*—A taxpayer may change basis determination methods from the average basis method to another method prospectively at any time. A change from the average basis method applies to all identical stock the taxpayer sells or otherwise disposes of before January 1, 2012, that was held in any account. A change from the average basis method applies on an account by account basis (within the meaning of paragraph (e)(10) of this section) to all identical stock the taxpayer sells or otherwise disposes of on or after January 1, 2012. The taxpayer must notify, in writing by any reasonable means, the custodian or agent holding the stock to which the change applies. Unless paragraph (e)(9)(iii) of this section applies, the basis of each share of stock to which the change applies remains the same as the basis immediately before the change. *See* paragraph (e)(7)(v) of this section.

(v) *Examples.*—The provisions of this paragraph (e)(9) are illustrated by the following examples:

Example 1. (i) Taxpayer F enters into an agreement with W Custodian establishing an account for the periodic acquisition of shares of N Company, a regulated investment company. W acquires for F's account shares of N Company on the following dates and amounts:

erage basis method under paragraph (e)(9)(iv) of this section. Accordingly, the basis of each share of stock F sells on June 1, 2012, is the basis immediately before the change, $8.70 (total cost of shares, $600, divided by the total number of shares, 69).

(10) *Application of average basis method account by account.*—(i) *In general.*—For sales, exchanges, or other dispositions on or after January 1, 2012, of stock described in paragraph (e)(1)(i) of this section, the average basis method applies on an account by account basis. A taxpayer may use the average basis method for stock in a regulated investment company or stock acquired in connection with a dividend reinvestment plan in one account but use a different basis determination method for identical stock in a different account. If a taxpayer uses the average basis method for a stock described in paragraph (e)(1)(i) of this section, the taxpayer must use the average basis method for all identical stock within that account. The taxpayer may use different basis determination methods for stock within an account that is not identical. Except as provided in paragraph (e)(10)(ii) of this section, a taxpayer must make separate elections to use the average basis method for stock held in separate accounts.

Reg. §1.1012-1(e)(10)(i)

(ii) *Account rule for stock sold before 2012.*—A taxpayer's election to use the average basis method for shares of stock described in paragraph (e)(1)(i) of this section that a taxpayer sells, exchanges, or otherwise disposes of before January 1, 2012, applies to all identical shares of stock the taxpayer holds in any account.

(iii) *Separate account.*—Unless the single-account election described in paragraph (e)(11)(i) of this section applies, stock described in paragraph (e)(1)(i) of this section that is a covered security (within the meaning of section 6045(g)(3)) is treated as held in a separate account from stock that is a noncovered security (as described in §1.6045-1(a)(16), regardless of when acquired.

(iv) *Examples.*—The provisions of this paragraph (e)(10) are illustrated by the following examples:

Example 1. (i) In 2012, Taxpayer G enters into an agreement with Y Broker establishing three accounts (G-1, G-2, and G-3) for the periodic acquisition of shares of P Company, a regulated investment company. Y makes periodic purchases of P Company for each of G's accounts. G elects to use the average basis method for account G-1. On July 1, 2013, G sells shares of P Company from account G-1.

(ii) G is not required to use the average basis method for the shares of P Company that G holds in accounts G-2 and G-3 because, under paragraph (e)(10)(i) of this section, the average basis method election applies to shares sold after 2011 on an account by account basis.

Example 2. The facts are the same as in *Example 1,* except that G also instructs Y to acquire shares of Q Company, a regulated investment company, for account G-1. Under paragraph (e)(10)(i) of this section, G may use any permissible basis determination method for the shares of Q Company because, under paragraph (e)(4) of this section, the shares of Q Company are not identical to the shares of P Company.

Example 3. (i) The facts are the same as in *Example 1,* except that G establishes the accounts in 2011 and Y sells shares of P Company from account G-1 on July 1, 2011.

(ii) For sales before 2012, under paragraph (e)(10)(ii) of this section, G's election applies to all accounts in which G holds identical stock. G must average together the basis of the shares in all accounts to determine the basis of the shares sold from account G-1.

Example 4. (i) In 2011, Taxpayer H acquires 80 shares of R Company and enrolls them in R Company's dividend reinvestment plan. In 2012, H acquires 50 shares of R Company in the dividend reinvestment plan. H elects to use the average basis method for the shares of R Company in the dividend reinvestment plan. R Company does not make the single-account election under paragraph (e)(11)(i) of this section.

(ii) Under section 6045(g)(3) and §1.6045-1(a)(16), the 80 shares acquired in 2011 are noncovered securities and the 50 shares acquired in 2012 are covered securities. Therefore, under paragraph (e)(10)(iii) of this section, the 80 shares are treated as held in a separate account from the 50 shares. H must make a separate average basis method election for each account and must average the basis of the shares in each account separately from the shares in the other account.

Example 5. (i) B Broker maintains an account for Taxpayer J for the periodic acquisition of shares of S Company, a regulated investment company. In 2013, B purchases shares of S Company for J's account that are covered securities within the meaning of section 6045(g)(3). On April 15, 2014, J inherits shares of S Company that are noncovered securities and transfers the shares into the account with B.

(ii) Under paragraph (e)(10)(iii) of this section, J must treat the purchased shares and the inherited shares of S Company as held in separate accounts. J may elect to apply the average basis method to all the shares of S Company, but must make a separate election for each account, and must average the basis of the shares in each account separately from the shares in the other account.

Example 6. (i) In 2010, Taxpayer K purchases stock in T Company in an account with C Broker. In 2012, K purchases additional T Company stock and enrolls that stock in a dividend reinvestment plan maintained by C. K elects the average basis method for the T Company stock. In 2013, K transfers the T Company stock purchased in 2010 into the dividend reinvestment plan.

(ii) Under paragraphs (e)(1)(i) and (e)(6)(ii) of this section, the stock purchased in 2010 is not stock acquired after December 31, 2010, in connection with a dividend reinvestment plan before transfer into the dividend reinvestment plan. Therefore, the stock is not eligible for the average basis method at that time.

(iii) Once transferred into the dividend reinvestment plan in 2013, the stock K purchased in 2010 is acquired after December 31, 2010, in connection with a dividend reinvestment plan within the meaning of paragraph (e)(6)(ii) of this section and is eligible for the average basis method. Because stock purchased in 2010 is a noncovered security under §1.6045-1(a)(16), under paragraph (e)(10)(iii) of this section, the 2010 stock and the 2012 stock must be treated as held in separate accounts. Under paragraph (e)(7)(i) of this section, the basis of the 2010 shares may not be averaged with the basis of the 2012 shares.

Example 7. The facts are the same as in *Example 6,* except that K purchases the initial T Company stock in January 2011. Because this stock is a covered security under section 6045(g)(3) and §1.6045-1(a)(15)(iv)(A), the 2011 stock and the 2012 stock are not required under paragraph (e)(10)(iii) of this section to be treated as held in separate accounts. Under paragraph (e)(7)(i) of this section, the basis of the 2011 shares must be averaged with the basis of the 2012 shares.

Example 8. (i) The facts are the same as in *Example 7,* except that K purchases the additional T Company stock and enrolls in the dividend reinvestment plan in March 2011. In September 2011, K transfers the T Company stock purchased in January 2011 into the dividend reinvestment plan. K sells some of the T Company stock in 2012.

(ii) Under section 6045(g)(3) and § 1.6045-1(a)(16), the stock K purchases in January 2011 is a covered security at the time of purchase but the stock K purchases and enrolls in the dividend reinvestment plan in March 2011 is a noncovered security. However, under § 1.6045-1(a)(15)(iv)(A), the stock purchased in January 2011 becomes a noncovered security after it is transferred to the dividend reinvestment plan. Because all the shares in the dividend reinvestment plan in September 2011 are noncovered securities, when K sells stock in 2012, the January 2011 stock and the March 2011 stock are not required under paragraph (e)(10)(iii) of this section to be treated as held in separate accounts. Under paragraph (e)(7)(i) of this section, the basis of the January 2011 shares must be averaged with the basis of the March 2011 shares.

(11) *Single-account election.*—(i) *In general.*—Paragraph (e)(10)(iii) of this section does not apply if a regulated investment company or dividend reinvestment plan elects to treat all identical shares of stock described in paragraph (e)(1)(i) of this section as held in a single account (single-account election). The single-account election applies only to stock for which a taxpayer elects to use the average basis method that is held in separate accounts or treated as held in separate accounts maintained for the taxpayer and only to accounts with the same ownership. If a broker (as defined by section 6045(c)(1)) holds the stock as a nominee, the broker, and not the regulated investment company or dividend reinvestment plan, makes the election. The single-account election is irrevocable, but is void if the taxpayer revokes the average basis election under paragraph (e)(9)(iii) of this section.

(ii) *Scope of election.*—A company, plan, or broker may make a single-account election for one or more taxpayers for which it maintains an account, and for one or more stocks it holds for a taxpayer. The company, plan, or broker may make the election only for the shares of stock for which it has accurate basis information. A company, plan, or broker has accurate basis information if the company, plan, or broker neither knows nor has reason to know that the basis information is inaccurate. *See* also section 6724 and the associated regulations regarding standards for relief from information reporting penalties. Stock for which accurate basis information is unavailable may not be included in the single-account election and must be treated as held in a separate account.

(iii) *Effect of single-account election.*—If a company, plan, or broker makes the single-account election, the basis of all identical shares of stock to which the election applies must be averaged together regardless of when the taxpayer acquires the shares, and all the shares are treated as covered securities. The single-account election applies to all identical stock a taxpayer later acquires in the account that is a covered security (within the meaning of section 6045(g)(3)). A company, plan, or broker may make another single-account election if, for example, the broker later acquires accurate basis information for a stock, or a taxpayer acquires identical stock in the account that is a noncovered security (as described in § 1.6045-1(a)(16) for which the company, plan, or broker has accurate basis information.

(iv) *Time and manner for making the single-account election.*—A company, plan, or broker makes the single-account election by clearly noting it on its books and records. The books and records must reflect the date of the election; the taxpayer's name, account number, and taxpayer identification number; the stock subject to the election; and the taxpayer's basis in the stock. The company, plan, or broker must provide copies of the books and records regarding the election to the taxpayer upon request. A company, plan, or broker may make the single-account election at any time.

(v) *Notification to taxpayer.*—A company, plan, or broker making the single-account election must use reasonable means to notify the taxpayer of the election. Reasonable means include mailings, circulars, or electronic mail sent separately to the taxpayer or included with the taxpayer's account statement, or other means reasonably calculated to provide actual notice to the taxpayer. The notice must identify the securities subject to the election and advise the taxpayer that the securities will be treated as covered securities regardless of when acquired.

(vi) *Examples.*—The provisions of this paragraph (e)(11) are illustrated by the following examples:

Example 1. (i) E Broker maintains Accounts A and B for Taxpayer M for the acquisition and disposition of shares of T Company, a regulated investment company. In 2011, E purchases 100 shares of T Company for M's Account A. E has accurate basis information for these shares. In 2012, E purchases 150 shares of T Company for M's Account A and 80 shares of T Company for M's Account B. M elects to use the average basis method for all shares of T Company. E makes a single-account election for M's T Company stock.

(ii) The shares of T Company in Accounts A and B are held in separate accounts. Under section 6045(g)(3) and §1.6045-1(a)(16), of the shares purchased in Account A, the 100 shares purchased in 2011 are noncovered securities and the 150 shares purchased in 2012 are covered securities. Under paragraph (e)(10)(iii) of this section, the 100 shares are treated as held in a separate account from the 150 shares. Under paragraph (e)(11)(i) of this section, the single-account election applies to all 330 shares of T Company in Accounts A and B. Thus, under paragraph (e)(11)(iii) of this section, the basis of the 330 shares of stock is averaged together and all the shares are treated as covered securities.

Example 2. The facts are the same as in *Example 1*, except that M owns Account B jointly with Taxpayer N. E may make a single-account election for the 250 shares of stock in M's Account A. However, under paragraph (e)(11)(i) of this section, E may not make a single-account election for Accounts A and B because the accounts do not have the same ownership.

Example 3. (i) C Broker maintains an account for Taxpayer K for the acquisition and disposition of shares of T Company, a regulated investment company, and shares of V Company that K enrolls in C's dividend reinvestment plan. In 2011, C purchases for K's account 100 shares of T Company in multiple lots and 80 shares of V Company in multiple lots that are enrolled in the dividend reinvestment plan. C has accurate basis information for all 100 shares of T Company and 80 shares of V Company. In 2012, C acquires for K's account 150 shares of T Company and 160 shares of V Company that are enrolled in the dividend reinvestment plan. K elects to use the average basis method for all the shares of T Company and V Company.

(ii) Under paragraphs (e)(11)(i) and (ii) of this section, C may make a singleaccount election for the T Company stock or the V Company stock, or both. After making a single-account election for each stock, under paragraph (e)(11)(iii) of this section, the basis of all T Company stock is averaged together and the basis of all V Company stock is averaged together, regardless of when acquired, and all the shares of T Company and V Company are treated as covered securities.

Example 4. The facts are the same as in *Example 3*, except that K transfers the 100 shares of T Company acquired in 2011 from an account with another broker into K's account with C. C does not have accurate basis information for 30 of the 100 shares of T Company, which K had acquired in two lots. Under paragraph (e)(11)(ii) of this section, C may make the single-account election only for the 70 shares of T Company stock for which C has accurate basis information. C must treat the 30 shares of T Company for which C does not have accurate basis information as held in a separate account. K may use the average basis method for the 30 shares of T Company, but must make a separate average

basis method election for these shares and must average the basis of these shares separately from the 70 shares subject to C's single-account election.

Example 5. The facts are the same as in *Example 3*, except that C has made the single-account election and in 2013 K acquires additional shares of T Company that are covered securities in K's account with C. Under paragraph (e)(11)(iii) of this section, these shares of T Company are subject to C's single-account election.

Example 6. The facts are the same as in *Example 3*, except that C has made the single-account election and in 2013 K inherits shares of T Company that are noncovered securities and transfers the shares into the account with C. C has accurate basis information for these shares. Under paragraph (e)(11)(iii) of this section, C may make a second single-account election to include the inherited T Company shares.

Example 7. (i) Between 2002 and 2011, Taxpayer L acquires 1500 shares of W Company, a regulated investment company, in an account with D Broker, for which L uses the average basis method, and sells 500 shares. On January 5, 2012, based on accurate basis information, the averaged basis of L's remaining 1000 shares of W Company is $24 per share. On January 5, 2012, L acquires 100 shares of W Company for $28 per share and makes an average basis election for those shares under paragraph (e)(9)(i) of this section.

(ii) On February 1, 2012, D makes a single-account election that includes all 1100 of L's shares in W Company. Thereafter, the basis of L's shares of W Company is $24.36 per share (($24,000 + $2,800) / 1100). On September 12, 2012, under paragraph (e)(9)(iii) of this section, L revokes the average basis election for the 100 shares acquired on January 5, 2012.

(iii) Under paragraph (e)(11)(i) of this section, D's single-account election is void. Therefore, the basis of the 1000 shares of W Company that L acquires before 2012 is $24 per share and the basis of the 100 shares of W Company that L acquires in 2012 is $28 per share.

(12) *Effective/applicability date.*—Except as otherwise provided in paragraphs (e)(1), (e)(2), (e)(7), (e)(9), and (e)(10) of this section, this paragraph (e) applies for taxable years beginning after October 18, 2010.

(f) *Special rules.*—For special rules for determining the basis for gain or loss in the case of certain vessels acquired through the Maritime Commission (or its successors) or pursuant to an agreement with the Secretary of Commerce, see sections 510, 511, and 607 of the Merchant Marine Act, 1936, as amended (46 U.S.C. 1160, 1161) and 26 CFR Parts 2 and 3. For special rules for determining the unadjusted basis of property recovered in respect of war losses, see section 1336. For special rules with respect to taxable years beginning before January 1, 1964, for determining the basis for gain or loss in the case of a disposition of a share of stock acquired pursuant to the timely exercise of a restricted stock option where the option price was between 85 percent and 95 percent of the fair market value of the stock at the time the option was granted, see paragraph (b) of § 1.421-5. See sections 423(c)(1) or 424(c)(1), whichever is applicable, for special rules with respect to taxable years ending after December 31, 1963, for determining the basis for gain or loss in the case of the disposition of a share of stock acquired pursuant to the timely exercise of a stock option described in such sections. See section 422(c)(1) for special rules with respect to taxable years ending after December 31, 1963, for determining the basis for gain or loss in the case of an exercise of a qualified stock option.

(g) *Debt instruments issued in exchange for property.*—(1) *In general.*—For purposes of paragraph (a) of this section, if a debt instrument is issued in exchange for property, the cost of the property that is attributable to the debt instrument is the issue price of the debt instrument as determined under § 1.1273-2 or § 1.1274-2, whichever is applicable. If, however, the issue price of the debt instrument is determined under section 1273(b)(4), the cost of the property attributable to the debt instrument is its stated principal amount reduced by any unstated interest (as determined under section 483).

(2) *Certain tax-exempt obligations.*—This paragraph (g)(2) applies to a tax-exempt obligation (as defined in section 1275(a)(3)) that is issued in exchange for property and that has an issue price determined under § 1.1274-2(j) (concerning tax-exempt contingent payment obligations and certain tax-exempt variable rate debt instruments subject to section 1274). Notwithstanding paragraph (g)(1) of this section, if this paragraph (g)(2) applies to a tax-exempt obligation, for purposes of paragraph (a) of this section, the cost of the property that is attributable to the obligation is the sum of the present values of the noncontingent payments (as determined under § 1.1274-2(c)).

(3) *Effective date.*—This paragraph (g) applies to sales or exchanges that occur on or after August 13, 1996. [Reg. § 1.1012-1.]

☐ [*T.D.* 6265, 11-6-57. *Amended by T.D.* 6311, 9-10-58; *T.D.* 6837, 7-12-65; *T.D.* 6887, 6-23-66; *T.D.* 6934, 11-13-67; *T.D.* 6984, 12-23-68; *T.D.* 7015, 6-19-69; *T.D.* 7081, 12-30-70; *T.D.* 7129, 7-6-71; *T.D.* 7154, 12-27-71; *T.D.* 7213, 10-17-72; *T.D.* 7568, 10-11-78; *T.D.* 7728, 10-31-80; *T.D.* 8517, 1-27-94; *T.D.* 8674, 6-11-96 *and T.D.* 9504, 10-12-2010.]

[Reg. § 1.1012-2]

§ 1.1012-2. Transfers in part a sale and in part a gift.—For rules relating to basis of property acquired in a transfer which is in part a gift and in part a sale, see § 1.170A-4(c), § 1.1011-2(b), and § 1.1015-4. [Reg. § 1.1012-2.]

☐ [*T.D.* 6265, 11-6-57. *Amended by T.D.* 7207, 10-3-72.]

[Reg. § 1.1013-1]

§ 1.1013-1. Property included in inventory.—The basis of property required to be included in inventory is the last inventory value of such property in the hands of the taxpayer. The requirements with respect to the valuation of an inventory are stated in subpart D (sections 471 and following), part II, or subchapter E, chapter 1 of the Code, and the regulations thereunder. [Reg. § 1.1013-1.]

☐ [*T.D.* 6265, 11-6-57.]

[Reg. § 1.1014-1]

§ 1.1014-1. Basis of property acquired from a decedent.—(a) *General rule.*—The purpose of section 1014 is, in general, to provide a basis for property acquired from a decedent which is equal to the value placed upon such property for purposes of the Federal estate tax. Accordingly, the general rule is that the basis of property acquired from a decedent is the fair market value of such property at the date of the decedent's death, or, if the decedent's executor so elects, at the alternate valuation date prescribed in section 2032, or in section 811(j) of the Internal Revenue Code of 1939. Property acquired from a decedent includes, principally, property acquired by bequest, devise, or inheritance, and, in the case of decedents dying after December 31, 1953, property required to be included in determining the value of the decedent's gross estate under any provision of the Internal Revenue Code of 1954 or the Internal Revenue Code of 1939. The general rule governing basis of property acquired from a decedent, as well as other rules prescribed elsewhere in this section, shall have no application if the property is sold, exchanged, or otherwise disposed of before the decedent's death by the person who acquired the property from the decedent. For general rules on the applicable valuation date where the executor of a decedent's estate elects under section 2032, or under section 811(j) of the Internal Revenue Code of 1939, to value the decedent's gross estate at the alternate valuation date prescribed in such sections, see paragraph (e) of § 1.1014-3.

(b) *Scope and application.*—With certain limitations, the general rule described in paragraph (a) of this section is applicable to the classes of property described in paragraphs (a) and (b) of § 1.1014-2, including stock in a DISC or former DISC. In the case of stock in a DISC or former DISC, the provisions of this section and §§ 1.1014-2 through 1.1014-8 are applicable, except as provided in § 1.1014-9. Special basis rules with respect to the basis of certain other property acquired from a decedent are set forth in paragraph (c) of § 1.1014-2. These special rules concern certain stock or securities of a foreign personal holding company and the surviving spouse's one-half share of community property held with a decedent dying after October 21, 1942, and on or before December 31, 1947. In this section and §§1.1014-2 to 1.1014-6, inclusive, whenever the words "property acquired from a decedent" are used, they shall also mean "property passed from a decedent", and the phrase "person who acquired it from the decedent" shall include the "person to whom it passed from the decedent."

(c) *Property to which section 1014 does not apply.*—Section 1014 shall have no application to the following classes of property:

(1) Property which constitutes a right to receive an item of income in respect of a decedent under section 691; and

(2) Restricted stock options described in section 421 which the employee has not exercised at death if the employee died before January 1, 1957. In the case of employees dying after December 31, 1956, see paragraph (d)(4) of §1.421-5. In the case of employees dying in a taxable year ending after December 31, 1963, see paragraph (c)(4) of §1.421-9 with respect to an option described in part II of subchapter D. [Reg. §1.1014-1.]

☐ [*T.D. 6265, 11-6-57. Amended by T.D. 6527, 1-18-61, T.D. 6887, 6-23-66 and T.D. 7283, 8-2-73.*]

[Reg. §1.1014-2]

§1.1014-2. Property acquired from a decedent.—(a) *In general.*—The following property, except where otherwise indicated, is considered to have been acquired from a decedent and the basis thereof is determined in accordance with the general rule in §1.1014-1:

(1) Without regard to the date of the decedent's death, property acquired by bequest, devise, or inheritance, or by the decedent's estate from the decedent, whether the property was acquired under the decedent's will or under the law governing the descent and distribution of the property of decedents. However, see paragraph (c)(1) of this section if the property was acquired by bequest or inheritance from a decedent dying after August 26, 1937, and if such property consists of stock or securities of a foreign personal holding company.

(2) Without regard to the date of the decedent's death, property transferred by the decedent during his lifetime in trust to pay the income for life to or on the order or direction of the decedent, with the right reserved to the decedent at all times before his death to revoke the trust.

(3) In the case of decedents dying after December 31, 1951, property transferred by the decedent during his lifetime in trust to pay the income for life to or on the order or direction of the decedent with the right reserved to the decedent at all times before his death to make any change in the enjoyment thereof through the exercise of a power to alter, amend, or terminate the trust.

(4) Without regard to the date of the decedent's death, property passing without full and adequate consideration under a general power of appointment exercised by the decedent by will. (See section 2041(b) for definition of general power of appointment.)

(5) In the case of decedents dying after December 31, 1947, property which represents the surviving spouse's one-half share of community property held by the decedent and the surviving spouse under the community property laws of any State, Territory, or possession of the United States or any foreign country, if at least one-half of the whole of the community interest in that property was includible in determining the value of the decedent's gross estate under part III, chapter 11 of the Internal Revenue Code of 1954 (relating to the estate tax) or section 811 of the Internal Revenue Code of 1939. It is not necessary for the application of this subparagraph that an estate tax return be required to be filed for the estate of the decedent or that an estate tax be payable.

(6) In the case of decedents dying after December 31, 1950, and before January 1, 1954, property which represents the survivor's interest in a joint and survivor's annuity if the value of any part of that interest was required to be included in determining the value of the decedent's gross estate under section 811 of the Internal Revenue Code of 1939. It is necessary only that the value of a part of the survivor's interest in the annuity be includible in the gross estate under section 811. It is not necessary for the application of this subparagraph that an estate tax return be required to be filed for the estate of the decedent or that an estate tax be payable.

(b) *Property acquired from a decedent dying after December 31, 1953.*—(1) *In general.*—In addition to the property described in paragraph (a) of this section, and except as otherwise provided in subparagraph (3) of this paragraph, in the case of a decedent dying after December 31, 1953, property shall also be considered to have been acquired from the decedent to the extent that both of the following conditions are met: (i) the property was acquired from the decedent by reason of death, form of ownership, or other conditions (including property acquired through the exercise or non-exercise of a power of appointment), and (ii) the property is includible in the decedent's gross estate under the provisions of the Internal Revenue Code of 1954, or the Internal Revenue Code of 1939, because of such acquisition. The basis of such property in the hands of the person who acquired it from the decedent shall be determined in accordance with the general rule in §1.1014-1. See, however, §1.1014-6 for special adjustments if such property is acquired before the death of the decedent. See also subparagraph (3) of this paragraph for a description of property not within the scope of this paragraph.

(2) *Rules for the application of subparagraph (1) of this paragraph.*—Except as provided in subparagraph (3) of this paragraph, this paragraph generally includes all property acquired from a decedent, which is includible in the gross estate of the decedent if the decedent died after December 31, 1953. It is not necessary for the application of this paragraph that an estate tax return be required to be filed for the estate of the decedent or that an estate tax be payable. Property acquired prior to the death of a decedent which is includible in the decedent's gross estate, such as property transferred by a decedent in contemplation of death, and property held by a taxpayer and the decedent as joint tenants or as tenants by the entireties is within the scope of this paragraph. Also, this paragraph includes property acquired through the exercise or non-exercise of a power of appointment where such property is includible in the decedent's gross estate. It does not include property not includible in the decedent's gross estate such as property not situated in the United States acquired from a nonresident who is not a citizen of the United States.

(3) *Exceptions to application of this paragraph.*—The rules of this paragraph are not applicable to the following property:

(i) Annuities described in section 72;

(ii) Stock or securities of a foreign personal holding company as described in section 1014(b)(5) (see paragraph (c)(1) of this section);

(iii) Property described in any paragraph other than paragraph (9) of section 1014(b). See paragraphs (a) and (c) of this section.
In illustration of subdivision (ii), assume that A acquired by gift stock of a character described in paragraph (c)(1) of this section from a donor and upon the death of the donor the stock was includible in the donor's estate as being a gift in contemplation of death. A's basis in the stock would not be determined by reference to its fair market value at the donor's death under the general rule in section 1014(a). Furthermore, the special basis rules prescribed in paragraph (c)(1) are not applicable to such property acquired by gift in contemplation of death. It will be necessary to refer to the rules in section 1015(a) to determine the basis.

(c) *Special basis rules with respect to certain property acquired from a decedent.*—(1) *Stock or securities of a foreign personal holding company.*—The basis of certain stock or securities of a foreign corporation which was a foreign personal holding company with respect to its taxable year next preceding the date of the decedent's death is governed by a special rule. If such stock was acquired from a decedent dying after August 26, 1937, by bequest or inheritance, or by the decedent's estate from the decedent, the basis of the

property in the hands of the person who so acquired it (notwithstanding any other provision of section 1014) shall be the fair market value of such property at the date of the decedent's death or the adjusted basis of the stock in the hands of the decedent, whichever is lower.

(2) *Spouse's interest in community property of decedent dying after October 21, 1942, and on or before December 31, 1947.*—In the case of a decedent dying after October 21, 1942, and on or before December 31, 1947, a special rule is provided for determining the basis of such part of any property, representing the surviving spouse's one-half share of property held by the decedent and the surviving spouse under the community property laws of any State, Territory, or possession of the United States or any foreign country, as was included in determining the value of the decedent's gross estate, if a tax under chapter 3 of the Internal Revenue Code of 1939 was payable upon the decedent's net estate. In such case the basis shall be the fair market value of such part of the property at the date of death (or the optional valuation elected under section 811(j) of the Internal Revenue Code of 1939) or the adjusted basis of the property determined without regard to this subparagraph, whichever is the higher. [Reg. § 1.1014-2.]

☐ [T.D. 6265, 11-6-57.]

[Reg. § 1.1014-3]

§ 1.1014-3. Other basis rules.—(a) *Fair market value.*—For purposes of this section and § 1.1014-1, the value of property as of the date of the decedent's death as appraised for the purpose of the Federal estate tax or the alternate value as appraised for such purpose, whichever is applicable, shall be deemed to be its fair market value. If no estate tax return is required to be filed under section 6018 (or under section 821 or 864 of the Internal Revenue Code of 1939), the value of the property appraised as of the date of the decedent's death for the purpose of State inheritance or transmission taxes shall be deemed to be its fair market value and no alternative valuation date shall be applicable.

(b) *Property acquired from a decedent dying before March 1, 1913.*—If the decedent died before March 1, 1913, the fair market value on that date is taken in lieu of the fair market value on the date of death, but only to the same extent and for the same purposes as the fair market value on March 1, 1913, is taken under section 1053.

(c) *Reinvestments by a fiduciary.*—The basis of property acquired after the death of the decedent by a fiduciary as an investment is the cost or other basis of such property to the fiduciary, and not the fair market value of such property at the death of the decedent. For example, the executor of an estate purchases stock of X company at a price of $100 per share with the proceeds of the sale of property acquired from a decedent. At the date of the decedent's death the fair market value of such stock was $98 per share. The basis of such stock to the executor or to a legatee, assuming the stock is distributed, is $100 per share.

(d) *Reinvestments of property transferred during life.*—Where property is transferred by a decedent during life and the property is sold, exchanged, or otherwise disposed of before the decedent's death by the person who acquired the property from the decedent, the general rule stated in paragraph (a) of §1.1014-1 shall not apply to such property. However, in such a case, the basis of any property acquired by such donee in exchange for the original property, or of any property acquired by the donee through reinvesting the proceeds of the sale of the original property, shall be the fair market value of the property thus acquired at the date of the decedent's death (or applicable alternate valuation date) if the property thus acquired is properly included in the decedent's gross estate for Federal estate tax purposes. These rules also apply to property acquired by the donee in any further exchanges or in further reinvestments. For example, on January 1, 1956, the decedent made a gift of real property to a trust for the benefit of his children, reserving to himself the power to revoke the trust at will. Prior to the decedent's death, the trustee sold the real property and invested the proceeds in stock of the Y company at $50 per share. At the time of the decedent's death, the value of such stock was $75 per share. The corpus of the trust was required to be included in the decedent's gross estate owing to his reservation of the power of revocation. The basis of the Y company stock following the decedent's death is $75 per share. Moreover, if the trustee sold the Y company stock before the decedent's death for $65 a share and reinvested the proceeds in Z company stock which increased in value to $85 per share at the time of the decedent's death, the basis of the Z company stock following the decedent's death would be $85 per share.

(e) *Alternate valuation dates.*—Section 1014(a) provides a special rule applicable in determining the basis of property described in §1.1014-2 where—

(1) The property is includible in the gross estate of a decedent who died after October 21, 1942, and

(2) The executor elects for estate tax purposes under section 2032, or section 811(j) of the Internal Revenue Code of 1939, to value the decedent's gross estate at the alternate valuation date prescribed in such sections.

In those cases, the value applicable in determining the basis of the property is not the value at the date of the decedent's death but (with certain limitations) the value at the date one year after his death if not distributed, sold, exchanged, or otherwise disposed of in the meantime. If such property was distributed, sold, exchanged, or otherwise disposed of within one year after the date of the decedent's death by the person who acquired it from the decedent, the value applicable in determining the basis is its value as of the date of such distribution, sale, exchange, or other disposition. For illustrations of the operation of this paragraph, see the estate tax regulations under section 2032. [Reg. §1.1014-3.]

☐ [*T.D. 6265, 11-6-57.*]

[Reg. §1.1014-4]

§1.1014-4. Uniformity of basis; adjustment to basis.—(a) *In general.*—(1) The basis of property acquired from a decedent, as determined under section 1014(a), is uniform in the hands of every person having possession or enjoyment of the property at any time under the will or other instrument or under the laws of descent and distribution. The principle of uniform basis means that the basis of the property (to which proper adjustments must, of course, be made) will be the same, or uniform, whether the property is possessed or enjoyed by the executor or administrator, the heir, the legatee or devisee, or the trustee or beneficiary of a trust created by a will or an inter vivos trust. In determining the amount allowed or allowable to a taxpayer in computing taxable income as deductions for depreciation or depletion under section 1016(a)(2), the uniform basis of the property shall at all times be used and adjusted. The sale, exchange, or other disposition by a life tenant or remainderman of his interest in property will, for purposes of this section, have no effect upon the uniform basis of the property in the hands of those who acquired it from the decedent. Thus, gain or loss on sale of trust assets by the trustee will be determined without regard to the prior sale of any interest in the property. Moreover, any adjustment for depreciation shall be made to the uniform basis of the property without regard to such prior sale, exchange, or other disposition.

(2) Under the law governing wills and the distribution of the property of decedents, all titles to property acquired by bequest, devise, or inheritance relate back to the death of the decedent, even though the interest of the person taking the title was, at the date of death of the decedent, legal, equitable, vested, contingent, general, specific, residual, conditional, executory, or otherwise. Accordingly, there is a common acquisition date for all titles to property acquired from a decedent within the meaning of section 1014, and, for this reason, a common or uniform basis for all such interests. For example, if distribution of personal property left by a decedent is not made until one year after his death, the basis of such property in the hands of the legatee is its fair market value at the time when the decedent died, and not when the legatee actually received the property. If the bequest is of the residue to trustees in trust, and the executors do not distribute the residue to such trustees until five years after the death of the decedent, the basis of each piece of property left by the

decedent and thus received, in the hands of the trustees, is its fair market value at the time when the decedent dies. If the bequest is to trustees in trust to pay to A during his lifetime the income of the property bequeathed, and after his death to distribute such property to the survivors of a class, and upon A's death the property is distributed to the taxpayer as the sole survivor, the basis of such property, in the hands of the taxpayer, is its fair market value at the time when the decedent died. The purpose of the Code in prescribing a general uniform basis rule for property acquired from a decedent is, on the one hand, to tax the gain, in respect of such property, to him who realizes it (without regard to the circumstance that at the death of the decedent it may have been quite uncertain whether the taxpayer would take or gain anything); and, on the other hand, not to recognize as gain any element of value resulting solely from the circumstance that the possession or enjoyment of the taxpayer was postponed. Such postponement may be, for example, until the administration of the decedent's estate is completed, until the period of the possession or enjoyment of another has terminated, or until an uncertain event has happened. It is the increase or decrease in the value of property reflected in a sale or other disposition which is recognized as the measure of gain or loss.

(3) The principles stated in subparagraphs (1) and (2) of this paragraph do not apply to property transferred by an executor, administrator or trustee, to an heir, legatee, devisee or beneficiary under circumstances such that the transfer constitutes a sale or exchange. In such a case, gain or loss must be recognized by the transferor to the extent required by the revenue laws, and the transferee acquires a basis equal to the fair market value of the property on the date of the transfer. Thus, for example, if the trustee of a trust created by will transfers to a beneficiary, in satisfaction of a specific bequest of $10,000, securities which had a fair market value of $9,000 on the date of the decedent's death (the applicable valuation date) and $10,000 on the date of the transfer, the trust realizes a taxable gain of $1,000 and the basis of the securities in the hands of the beneficiary would be $10,000. As a further example, if the executor of an estate transfers to a trust property worth $200,000, which had a fair market value of $175,000 on the date of the decedent's death (the applicable valuation date), in satisfaction of the decedent's bequest in trust for the benefit of his wife of cash or securities to be selected by the executor in an amount sufficient to utilize the marital deduction to the maximum extent authorized by law (after taking into consideration any other property qualifying for the marital deduction), capital gain in the amount of $25,000 would be realized by the estate and the basis of the property in the hands of the trustees would be $200,000. If, on the other hand, the decedent bequeathed a fraction of his residuary estate to a trust for the

benefit of his wife, which fraction will not change regardless of any fluctuations in value of property in the decedent's estate after his death, no gain or loss would be realized by the estate upon transfer of property to the trust, and the basis of the property in the hands of the trustee would be its fair market value on the date of the decedent's death or on the alternate valuation date.

(b) *Multiple interests.*—Where more than one person has an interest in property acquired from a decedent, the basis of such property shall be determined and adjusted without regard to the multiple interests. The basis for computing gain or loss on the sale of any one of such multiple interests shall be determined under §1.1014-5. Thus, the deductions for depreciation and for depletion allowed or allowable, under sections 167 and 611, to a legal life tenant as if the life tenant were the absolute owner of the property, constitute an adjustment to the basis of the property not only in the hands of the life tenant, but also in the hands of the remainderman and every other person to whom the same uniform basis is applicable. Similarly, the deductions allowed or allowable under sections 167 and 611, both to the trustee and to the trust beneficiaries, constitute an adjustment to the basis of the property not only in the hands of the trustee, but also in the hands of the trust beneficiaries and every other person to whom the uniform basis is applicable. See, however, section 262. Similarly, adjustments in respect of capital expenditures or losses, tax-free distributions, or other distributions applicable in reduction of basis, or other items for which the basis is adjustable are made without regard to which one of the persons to whom the same uniform basis is applicable makes the capital expenditures or sustains the capital losses, or to whom the tax-free or other distributions are made, or to whom the deductions are allowed or allowable. See §1.1014-6 for adjustments in respect of property acquired from a decedent prior to his death.

(c) *Records.*—The executor or other legal representative of the decedent, the fiduciary of a trust under a will, the life tenant and every other person to whom a uniform basis under this section is applicable, shall maintain records showing in detail all deductions, distributions, or other items for which adjustment to basis is required to be made by sections 1016 and 1017, and shall furnish to the district director such information with respect to those adjustments as he may require. [Reg. §1.1014-4.]

☐ [*T.D.* 6265, 11-6-57.]

[Reg. §1.1014-5]

§1.1014-5. Gain or loss.—(a) *Sale or other disposition of a life interest, remainder interest, or other interest in property acquired from a decedent.*—(1) Except as provided in paragraph (b) of this section with respect to the sale or other disposition after October 9, 1969, of a term interest in property, gain or loss from a sale or other disposition of a life interest, remainder interest, or other interest in property acquired from a decedent is determined by comparing the amount of the proceeds with the amount of that part of the adjusted uniform basis which is assignable to the interest so transferred. The adjusted uniform basis is the uniform basis of the entire property adjusted to the date of sale or other disposition of any such interest as required by sections 1016 and 1017. The uniform basis is the unadjusted basis of the entire property determined immediately after the decedent's death under the applicable sections of part II of subchapter O of chapter 1 of the Code.

(2) Except as provided in paragraph (b) of this section, the proper measure of gain or loss resulting from a sale or other disposition of an interest in property acquired from a decedent is so much of the increase or decrease in the value of the entire property as is reflected in such sale or other disposition. Hence, in ascertaining the basis of a life interest, remainder interest, or other interest which has been so transferred, the uniform basis rule contemplates that proper adjustments will be made to reflect the change in relative value of the interests on account of the passage of time.

(3) The factors set forth in the tables contained in § 20.2031-7 or, for certain prior periods, § 20.2031-7A of Part 20 of this chapter (Estate Tax Regulations) shall be used in the manner provided therein in determining the basis of the life interest, the remainder interest, or the term certain interest in the property on the date such interest is sold. The basis of the life interest, the remainder interest, or the term certain interest is computed by multiplying the uniform basis (adjusted to the time of the sale) by the appropriate factor. In the case of the sale of a life interest or a remainder interest, the factor used is the factor (adjusted where appropriate) which appears in the life interest or the remainder interest column of the table opposite the age (on the date of the sale) of the person at whose death the life interest will terminate. In the case of the sale of a term certain interest, the factor used is the factor (adjusted where appropriate) which appears in the term certain column of the table opposite the number of years remaining (on the date of sale) before the term certain interest will terminate.

(b) *Sale or other disposition of certain term interests.*—In determining gain or loss from the sale or other disposition after October 9, 1969, of a term interest in property (as defined in paragraph (f)(2) of § 1.1001-1) the adjusted basis of which is determined pursuant, or by reference, to section 1014 (relating to the basis of property acquired from a decedent) or section 1015 (relating to the basis of property acquired by gift or by a transfer in trust), that part of the adjusted uniform basis assignable under the rules of paragraph (a) of this section to the interest sold or otherwise disposed of shall be disregarded to the extent and in the manner provided by section 1001(e) and paragraph (f) of § 1.1001-1.

(c) *Illustrations.*—The application of this section may be illustrated by the following examples, in which references are made to the actuarial tables contained in Part 20 of this chapter (Estate Tax Regulations):

Example (1). Securities worth $500,000 at the date of decedent's death on January 1, 1971, are bequeathed to his wife, W, for life, with remainder over to his son, S. W is 48 years of age when the life interest is acquired. The estate does not elect the alternate valuation allowed by section 2032. By reference to § 20.2031-7A(c), the life estate factor for age 48, female, is found to be 0.77488 and the remainder factor for such age is found to be 0.22512. Therefore, the present value of the portion of the uniform basis assigned to W's life interest is $387,440 ($500,000 × 0.77488), and the present value of the portion of the uniform basis assigned to S's remainder interest is $112,560 ($500,000 × 0.22512). W sells her life interest to her nephew, A, on February 1, 1971, for $370,000, at which time W is still 48 years of age. Pursuant to section 1001(e), W realizes no loss; her gain is $370,000, the amount realized from the sale. A has a basis of $370,000 which he can recover by amortization deductions over W's life expectancy.

Example (2). The facts are the same as in example (1) except that W retains the life interest for 12 years, until she is 60 years of age, and then sells it to A on February 1, 1983, when the fair market value of the securities has increased to $650,000. By reference to § 20.2031-7A(c), the life estate factor for age 60, female, is found to be 0.63226 and the remainder factor for such age is found to be 0.36774. Therefore, the present value on February 1, 1983, of the portion of the uniform basis assigned to W's life interest is $316,130 ($500,000 × 0.63226) and the present value on that date of the portion of the uniform basis assigned to S's remainder interest is $183,870 ($500,000 × 0.36774). W sells her life interest for $410,969, that being the commuted value of her remaining life interest in the securities as appreciated ($650,000 × 0.63226). Pursuant to section 1001(e), W's gain is $410,969, the amount realized. A has a basis of $410,969 which he can recover by amortization deductions over W's life expectancy.

Example (3). Unimproved land having a fair market value of $18,800 at the date of the decedent's death on January 1, 1970, is devised to A, a male, for life, with remainder over to B, a female. The estate does not elect the alternate valuation allowed by section 2032. On January 1, 1971, A sells his life interest to S for $12,500. S is not related to A or B. At the time of the sale, A is 39 years of age. By reference to § 20.2031-7A(c), the life estate factor for age 39, male, is found to be 0.79854. Therefore, the present value of the portion of the uniform basis assigned to A's life interest is $15,012.55 ($18,800 × 0.79854). This portion is disregarded under section 1001(e). A realized no loss; his gain is $12,500, the amount realized. S has a basis of $12,500 which he can recover by amortization deductions over A's life expectancy.

Example (4). The facts are the same as in example (3) except that on January 1, 1971, A and B jointly sell the entire property to S for $25,000 and divide the proceeds equally between them. A and B are not related, and there is no element of gift or compensation in the transaction. By reference to § 20.2031-7A(c), the remainder factor for age 39, male, is found to be 0.20146. Therefore, the present value of the uniform basis assigned to B's remainder interest is $3,787.45 ($18,800 × 0.20146). On the sale A realizes a loss of $2,512.55 ($15,012.55 less $12,500), the portion of the uniform basis assigned to his life interest not being disregarded by reason of section 1001(e)(3). B's gain on the sale is $8,712.55 ($12,500 less $3,787.45). S has a basis in the entire property of $25,000, no part of which, however, can be recovered by amortization deductions over A's life expectancy.

Example (5). (a) Nondepreciable property having a fair market value of $54,000 at the date of decedent's death on January 1, 1971, is devised to her husband, H, for life and, after his death, to her daughter, D, for life, with remainder over to her grandson, G. The estate does not elect the alternate valuation allowed by section 2032. On January 1, 1973, H sells his life interest to D for $32,000. At the date of the sale, H is 62 years of age, and D is 45 years of age. By reference to § 20.2031-7A(c), the life estate factor for age 62, male, is found to be 0.52321. Therefore, the present value on January 1, 1973, of the portion of the adjusted uniform basis assigned to H's life interest is $28,253 ($54,000 × 0.52321). Pursuant to section 1001(e), H realizes no loss; his gain is $32,000, the amount realized from the sale. D has a basis of $32,000 which she can recover by amortization deductions over H's life expectancy.

(b) On January 1, 1976, D sells both life estates to G for $40,000. During each of the years 1973 through 1975, D is allowed a deduction for the amortization of H's life interest. At the date of the sale H is 65 years of age, and D is 48 years of age. For purposes of determining gain or loss on the sale by D, the portion of the adjusted uniform basis assigned to H's life interest and the portion assigned to D's life interest are not taken into account under section 1001(e). However, pursuant to § 1.1001-1(f)(1), D's cost basis in H's life interest, minus deductions for the amortization of such interest, is taken into account. On the sale, D realizes gain of $40,000 minus an amount which is equal to the $32,000 cost basis (for H's life estate) reduced by amortization deductions. G is entitled to amortize over H's life expectancy that part of the $40,000 cost which is attributable to H's life interest. That part of the

$40,000 cost which is attributable to D's life interest is not amortizable by G until H dies.

Example (6). Securities worth $1,000,000 at the date of decedent's death on January 1, 1971, are bequeathed to his wife, W, for life, with remainder over to his son, S. W is 48 years of age when the life interest is acquired. The estate does not elect the alternate valuation allowed by section 2032. By reference to § 20.2031-7A(c), the life estate factor for age 48, female, is found to be 0.77488, and the remainder factor for such age is found to be 0.22512. Therefore, the present value of the portion of the uniform basis assigned to W's life interest is $774,880 ($1,000,000 × 0.77488), and the present value of the portion of the uniform basis assigned to S's remainder interest is $225,120 ($1,000,000 × 0.22512). On February 1, 1971, W transfers her life interest to Corporation X in exchange for all of the stock of X pursuant to a transaction in which no gain or loss is recognized by reason of section 351. On February 1, 1972, W sells all of her stock in X to S for $800,000. Pursuant to section 1001(e) and § 1.1001-1(f)(2), W realizes no loss; her gain is $800,000, the amount realized from the sale. On February 1, 1972, X sells to N for $900,000 the life interest transferred to it by W. Pursuant to section 1001(e) and § 1.1001-1(f)(1), X realizes no loss; its gain is $900,000, the amount realized from the sale. N has a basis of $900,000 which it can recover by amortization deductions over W's life expectancy. [Reg. § 1.1014-5.]

☐ *[T.D. 6265, 11-6-57. Amended by T.D. 7142, 9-23-71 and T.D. 8540, 6-9-94.]*

[Reg. § 1.1014-6]

§ 1.1014-6. Special rule for adjustments to basis where property is acquired from a decedent prior to his death.—(a) *In general.*—(1) The basis of property described in section 1014(b)(9) which is acquired from a decedent prior to his death shall be adjusted for depreciation, obsolescence, amortization, and depletion allowed the taxpayer on such property for the period prior to the decedent's death. Thus, in general, the adjusted basis of such property will be its fair market value at the decedent's death, or the applicable alternate valuation date, less the amount allowed (determined with regard to section 1016(a)(2)(B)) to the taxpayer as deductions for exhaustion, wear and tear, obsolescence, amortization and depletion for the period held by the taxpayer prior to the decedent's death. The deduction allowed for a taxable year in which the decedent dies shall be an amount properly allocable to that part of the year prior to his death. For a discussion of the basis adjustment required by section 1014(b)(9) where property is held in trust, see paragraph (c) of this section.

(2) Where property coming within the purview of subparagraph (1) of this paragraph was held by the decedent and his surviving spouse as tenants by the entirety or as joint tenants with

right of survivorship, and joint income tax returns were filed by the decedent and the surviving spouse in which the deductions referred to in subparagraph (1) were taken, there shall be allocated to the surviving spouse's interest in the property that proportion of the deductions allowed for each period for which the joint returns were filed which her income from the property bears to the total income from the property. Each spouse's income from the property shall be determined in accordance with local law.

(3) The application of this paragraph may be illustrated by the following examples:

Example (1). The taxpayer acquired income-producing property by gift on January 1, 1954. The property had a fair market value of $50,000 on the date of the donor's death, January 1, 1956, and was included in his gross estate at that amount for estate tax purposes as a transfer in contemplation of death. Depreciation in the amount of $750 per year was allowable for each of the taxable years 1954 and 1955. However, the taxpayer claimed depreciation in the amount of $500 for each of these years (resulting in a reduction in his taxes) and his income tax returns were accepted as filed. The adjusted basis of the property as of the date of the decedent's death is $49,000 ($50,000, the fair market value at the decedent's death, less $1,000, the total of the amounts actually allowed as deductions).

Example (2). On July 1, 1952, H purchased for $30,000 income-producing property which he conveyed to himself and W, his wife, as tenants by the entirety. Under local law each spouse was entitled to one-half of the income therefrom. H died on January 1, 1955, at which time the fair market value of the property was $40,000. The entire value of the property was included in H's gross estate. H and W filed joint income tax returns for the years 1952, 1953, and 1954. The total depreciation allowance for the year 1952 was $500 and for each of the other years 1953 and 1954 was $1,000. One-half of the $2,500 depreciation will be allocated to W. The adjusted basis of the property in W's hands [as] of January 1, 1955, was $38,750 ($40,000, value on the date of H's death, less $1,250, depreciation allocated to W for periods before H's death). However, if, under local law, all of the income from the property was allocable to H, no adjustment under this paragraph would be required and W's basis for the property as of the date of H's death would be $40,000.

(b) *Multiple interests in property described in section 1014(b)(9) and acquired from a decedent prior to his death.*—(1) Where more than one person has an interest in property described in section 1014(b)(9) which was acquired from a decedent before his death, the basis of such property and of each of the several interests therein shall, in general, be determined and adjusted in accordance with the principles contained in §§ 1.1014-4 and 1.1014-5, relating to the uniformity of basis rule. Application of these principles

to the determination of basis under section 1014(b)(9) is shown in the remaining subparagraphs of this paragraph in connection with certain commonly encountered situations involving multiple interests in property acquired from a decedent before his death.

(2) Where property is acquired from a decedent before his death, and the entire property is subsequently included in the decedent's gross estate for estate tax purposes, the uniform basis of the property, as well as the basis of each of the several interests in the property, shall be determined by taking into account the basis adjustments required by section 1014(a) owing to such inclusion of the entire property in the decedent's gross estate. For example, suppose that the decedent transfers property in trust, with a life estate to A, and the remainder to B or his estate. The transferred property consists of 100 shares of common stock of X Corporation, with a basis of $10,000 at the time of the transfer. At the time of the decedent's death the value of the stock is $20,000. The transfer is held to have been made in contemplation of death and the entire value of the trust is included in the decedent's gross estate. Under section 1014(a), the uniform basis of the property in the hands of the trustee, the life tenant, and the remainderman, is $20,000. If immediately prior to the decedent's death, A's share of the uniform basis of $10,000 was $6,000, and B's share was $4,000, then, immediately after the decedent's death, A's share of the uniform basis of $20,000 is $12,000, and B's share is $8,000.

(3)(i) In cases where, due to the operation of the estate tax, only a portion of property acquired from a decedent before his death is included in the decedent's gross estate, as in cases where the decedent retained a reversion to take effect upon the expiration of a life estate in another, the uniform basis of the entire property shall be determined by taking into account any basis adjustments required by section 1014(a) owing to such inclusion of a portion of the property in the decedent's gross estate. In such cases the uniform basis is the adjusted basis of the entire property immediately prior to the decedent's death increased (or decreased) by an amount which bears the same relation to the total appreciation (or diminution) in value of the entire property (over the adjusted basis of the entire property immediately prior to the decedent's death) as the value of the property included in the decedent's gross estate bears to the value of the entire property. For example, assume that the decedent creates a trust to pay the income to A for life, remainder to B or his estate. The trust instrument further provides that if the decedent should survive A, the income shall be paid to the decedent for life. Assume that the decedent predeceases A, so that, due to the operation of the estate tax, only the present value of the remainder interest is included in the decedent's gross estate. The trust consists of 100 shares of the common stock of X Corporation with an adjusted basis immediately prior to the decedent's death of $10,000 (as determined under section 1015). At the time of the decedent's death the value of the stock is $20,000, and the value of the remainder interest in the hands of B is $8,000. The uniform basis of the entire property following the decedent's death is $14,000, computed as follows:

Uniform basis prior to decedent's death $10,000

plus

Increase in uniform basis (determined by the following formula) 4,000

$$\frac{\text{Increase in uniform basis (to be determined)}}{\$10,000 \text{ (total appreciation)}} = \frac{\$8,000 \text{ (value of property included in gross estate)}}{\$20,000 \text{ (value of entire property)}}$$

Uniform basis under section 1014(a) $14,000

(ii) In cases of the type described in subdivision (i) of this subparagraph, the basis of any interest which is included in the decedent's gross estate may be ascertained by adding to (or subtracting from) the basis of such interest determined immediately prior to the decedent's death the increase (or decrease) in the uniform basis of the property attributable to the inclusion of the interest in the decedent's gross estate. Where the interest is sold or otherwise disposed of at any time after the decedent's death, proper adjustment must be made in order to reflect the change in value of the interest on account of the passage of time, as provided in § 1.1014-5. For an illustration of the operation of this subdivision, see step 6 of the example in § 1.1014-7.

(iii) In cases of the type described in subdivision (i) of this subparagraph (cases where, due to the operation of the estate tax, only a portion of the property is included in the decedent's gross estate), the basis for computing the depreciation, amortization, or depletion allowance shall be the uniform basis of the property determined under section 1014(a). However, the manner of taking into account such allowance computed with respect to such uniform basis is subject to the following limitations:

(a) In cases where the value of the life interest is not included in the decedent's gross estate, the amount of such allowance to the life tenant under section 167(h) (or section 611(b)) shall not exceed (or be less than) the amount which would have been allowable to the life tenant if no portion of the basis of the property was determined under section 1014(a). Proper adjustment shall be made for the amount allowable to the life tenant, as required by section 1016. Thus, an appropriate adjustment shall be made to the uniform basis of the property in the hands of the trustee, to the basis of the life interest in the hands of the life tenant, and to the basis of the remainder in the hands of the remainderman.

(b) Any remaining allowance (that is, the increase in the amount of depreciation, amortization, or depletion allowable resulting from any increase in the uniform basis of the property under section 1014(a)) shall not be allowed to the life tenant. The remaining allowance shall, instead, be allowed to the trustee to the extent that the trustee both (1) is required or permitted, by the governing trust instrument (or under local law), to maintain a reserve for depreciation, amortization, or depletion, and (2) actually maintains such a reserve. If, in accordance with the preceding sentence, the trustee does maintain such a reserve, the remaining allowance shall be taken into account, under section 1016, in adjusting the uniform basis of the property in the hands of the trustee and in adjusting the basis of the remainder interest in the hands of the remainderman, but shall not be taken into account, under section 1016, in determining the basis of the life interest in the hands of the life tenant. For an example of the operation of this subdivision, see paragraph (b) of § 1.1014-7.

(4) In cases where the basis of any interest in property is not determined under section 1014(a), as where such interest (i) is not included in the decedent's gross estate, or (ii) is sold, exchanged or otherwise disposed of before the decedent's death, the basis of such interest shall be determined under other applicable provisions of the Code. To illustrate, in the example shown in subparagraph (3)(i) of this paragraph the basis of the life estate in the hands of A shall be determined under section 1015, relating to the basis of property acquired by gift. If, on the other hand, A had sold his life interest prior to the decedent's death, the basis of the life estate in the hands of A's transferee would be determined under section 1012.

(c) *Adjustments for deductions allowed prior to the decedent's death.*—(1) As stated in paragraph (a) of this section, section 1014(b)(9) requires a reduction in the uniform basis of property acquired from a decedent before his death for certain deductions allowed in respect of such property during the decedent's lifetime. In general, the amount of the reduction in basis required by section 1014(b)(9) shall be the aggregate of the deductions allowed in respect of the property, but shall not include deductions allowed in respect of the property to the decedent himself. In cases where, owing to the operation of the estate tax, only a part of the value of

Reg. § 1.1014-6(c)(1)

the entire property is included in the decedent's gross estate, the amount of the reduction required by section 1014(b)(9) shall be an amount which bears the same relation to the total of all deductions (described in paragraph (a) of this section) allowed in respect of the property as the value of the property included in the decedent's gross estate bears to the value of the entire property.

(2) The application of this paragraph may be illustrated by the following examples:

Example (1). The decedent creates a trust to pay the income to A for life, remainder to B or his estate. The property transferred in trust consists of an apartment building with a basis of $50,000 at the time of the transfer. The decedent dies 2 years after the transfer is made and the gift is held to have been made in contemplation of death. Depreciation on the property was allowed in the amount of $1,000 annually. At the time of the decedent's death the value of the property is $58,000. The uniform basis of the property in the hands of the trustee, the life tenant, and the remainderman, immediately after the decedent's death is $56,000 ($58,000, fair market value of the property immediately after the decedent's death, reduced by $2,000, deductions for depreciation allowed prior to the decedent's death).

Example (2). The decedent creates a trust to pay the income to A for life, remainder to B or his estate. The trust instrument provides that if the decedent should survive A, the income shall be paid to the decedent for life. The decedent predeceases A and the present value of the remainder interest is included in the decedent's gross estate for estate tax purposes. The property transferred consists of an apartment building with a basis of $110,000 at the time of the transfer. Following the creation of the trust and during the balance of the decedent's life, deductions for depreciation were allowed on the property in the amount of $10,000. At the time of decedent's death the value of the entire property is $150,000, and the value of the remainder interest is $100,000. Accordingly, the uniform basis of the property in the hands of the trustee, the life tenant, and the remainderman, as adjusted under section 1014(b)(9), is $126,666, computed as follows:

Uniform basis prior to decedent's death $100,000

plus

Increase in uniform basis—before reduction (determined by the following formula)   33,333

$$\frac{\text{Increase in uniform basis (to be determined)}}{\$50{,}000 \text{ (total appreciation of property since time of transfer)}} = \frac{\$100{,}000 \text{ (value of property included in gross estate)}}{\$150{,}000 \text{ (value of entire property)}}$$

less $133,333

Deductions allowed prior to decedent's death—taken into account under section 1014(b)(9) (determined by the following formula)   6,667

$$\frac{\text{Prior deductions taken into account (to be determined)}}{\$10{,}000 \text{ (total deductions allowed prior to decedent's death)}} = \frac{\$100{,}000 \text{ (value of property included in gross estate)}}{\$150{,}000 \text{ (value of entire property)}}$$

Uniform basis under section 1014 . . . . $126,666

[Reg. § 1.1014-6.]

☐ [*T.D.* 6265, 11-6-57. *Amended by T.D.* 6712, 3-23-64 *and T.D.* 7142, 9-23-71.]

[Reg. § 1.1014-7]

§ 1.1014-7. Example applying rules of §§ 1.1014-4 through 1.1014-6 to case involving multiple interests.—(a) On January 1, 1950, the decedent creates a trust to pay the income to A for life, remainder to B or his estate. The trust instrument provides that if the decedent should survive A, the income shall be paid to the decedent for life. The decedent, who died on January 1, 1955, predeceases A, so that, due to the operation of the estate tax, only the present value of the remainder interest is included in the decedent's gross estate. The trust consists of an apartment building with a basis of $30,000 at the time of transfer. Under the trust instrument the trustee is required to maintain a reserve for depreciation. During the decedent's lifetime depreciation is allowed in the amount of $800 annually. At the time of the decedent's death the value of the apartment building is $45,000. A, the life tenant, is 43 years of age at the time of the decedent's death. Immediately after the decedent's death, the uniform basis of the entire property under section 1014(a) is $32,027; A's basis for the life interest is $15,553; and B's basis for the remainder interest is $16,474, computed as follows:

Step 1. Uniform basis (adjusted) immediately prior to decedent's death:
Basis at time of transfer $30,000
     less
Depreciation allowed under section 1016 before decedent's death
($800 × 5)   4,000

                                                        $26,000

Step 2. Value of property included in decedent's gross estate:
     0.40180 (remainder factor, age 43) × $45,000 (value of entire property)
. . . . $18,081

Step 3. Uniform basis of property under section 1014(a), before reduction
required by section 1014(b)(9):
     Uniform basis (adjusted) prior to decedent's death   26,000
     Increase in uniform basis (determined by the following formula) . .   7,634

$$\frac{\text{Increase in uniform basis (to be determined)}}{\$19{,}000 \text{ (total appreciation, } \$45{,}000 - \$26{,}000)} = \frac{\$18{,}081 \text{ (value of property included in gross estate)}}{\$45{,}000 \text{ (value of entire propery)}}$$

                                                        $33,634

Step 4. Uniform basis reduced as required by section 1014(b)(9) for deductions
allowed prior to death:
     Uniform basis before reduction   33,634
     less
Deductions allowed prior to decedent's death—taken into account
under section 1014(b)(9) (determined by the following formula) . . .   1,607

$$\frac{\text{Prior deductions taken into account (to be determined)}}{\$4{,}000 \text{ (total deductions allowed prior to decedent's death)}} = \frac{\$18{,}081 \text{ (value of property included in gross estate)}}{\$45{,}000 \text{ (value of entire property)}}$$

                                                        $32,027

Step 5. A's basis for the life interest at the time of the decedent's death,
determined under section 1015:
     0.59820 (life factor, age 43) × $26,000   15,553
Step 6. B's basis for the remainder interest, determined under section
1014(a):

     Basis prior to the decedent's death:
     0.40180 (remainder factor, age 43) × $26,000   10,447
     plus
Increase in uniform basis owing to decedent's death:
Increase in uniform basis $7,634
Reduction required by section 1014(b)(9) $1,607 $6,027

                                                        $16,474

(b) Assume the same facts as in (a) of this section. Assume further, that following the decedent's death depreciation is allowed in the amount of $1,000 annually. As of January 1, 1964, when A's age is 52, the adjusted uniform basis of the entire property is $23,027; A's basis for the life interest is $9,323; and B's basis for the remainder interest is $13,704, computed as follows:

Step 7. Uniform basis (adjusted) as of January 1, 1964:
Uniform basis determined under section 1014(a), reduced as required
by section 1014(b)(9) $32,027
Depreciation allowed since decedent's death ($1,000 × 9)   9,000

                                                        $23,027

Step 8. Allocable share of adjustment for depreciation allowable in the nine years since the decedent's death:

A's interest

0.49587 (life factor, age 52) × $7,200 ($800, depreciation attributable to uniform basis before increase under section 1014(a), × 9) 3,570

B's interest

0.50413 (remainder factor, age 52) × $7,200 ($800, depreciation attributable to uniform basis before increase under section 1014(a), × 9) 3,630

plus

$200 (annual depreciation attributable to increase in uniform basis under section 1014(a)) × 9 1,800

$5,430

Step 9. Tentative bases of A's and B's interests as of January 1, 1964 (before adjustment for depreciation).

A's interest

0.49587 (life factor, age 52) × $26,000 (adjusted uniform basis immediately before decedent's death) 12,893

B's interest

0.50413 (remainder factor, age 52) × $26,000 (adjusted uniform basis immediately before decedent's death) 13,107

plus

Increase in uniform basis owing to inclusion of remainder in decedent's gross estate 6,027

$19,134

Step 10. Bases of A's and B's interests as of January 1, 1964

A

Tentative basis (Step 9) $12,893

less

Allocable depreciation (Step 8) 3,570

$9,323

B

Tentative basis (Step 9) $19,134

less

Allocable depreciation (Step 8) 5,430

$13,704

[Reg. § 1.1014-7.]

☐ [T.D. 6265, 11-6-57.]

[Reg. § 1.1014-8]

§ 1.1014-8. Bequest, devise, or inheritance of a remainder interest.—(a)(1) Where property is transferred for life, with remainder in fee, and the remainderman dies before the life tenant, no adjustment is made to the uniform basis of the property on the death of the remainderman (see paragraph (a) of § 1.1014-4). However, the basis of the remainderman's heir, legatee, or devisee for the remainder interest is determined by adding to (or subtracting from) the part of the adjusted uniform basis assigned to the remainder interest (determined in accordance with the principles set forth in § § 1.1014-4 through 1.1014-6) the difference between—

(i) The value of the remainder interest included in the remainderman's estate, and

(ii) The basis of the remainder interest immediately prior to the remainderman's death.

(2) The basis of any property distributed to the heir, legatee, or devisee upon termination of a trust (or legal life estate) or at any other time

(unless included in the gross income of the legatee or devisee) shall be determined by adding to (or subtracting from) the adjusted uniform basis of the property thus distributed the difference between—

(i) The value of the remainder interest in the property included in the remainderman's estate, and

(ii) The basis of the remainder interest in the property immediately prior to the remainderman's death.

(b) The provisions of paragraph (a) of this section are illustrated by the following examples:

Example (1). Assume that, under the will of a decedent, property consisting of common stock with a value of $1,000 at the time of the decedent's death is transferred in trust, to pay the income to A for life, remainder to B or to B's estate. B predeceases A and bequeaths the remainder interest to C. Assume that B dies on January 1, 1956, and that the value of the stock originally transferred is $1,600 at B's death. A's age at that time is 37. The value of the remainder interest included in B's estate is $547 (0.34185, remainder factor age 37, × $1,600), and hence $547 is C's basis for the remainder interest immediately after B's death. Assume that C sells the remainder interest on January 1, 1961, when A's age is 42. C's basis for the remainder interest at the time of such sale is $596, computed as follows:

Basis of remainder interest computed with respect to uniform basis of entire property (0.39131, remainder factor age 42, × $1,000, uniform basis of entire property)		$391
plus		
Value of remainder interest included in B's estate	$547	
less		
Basis of remainder interest immediately prior to B's death (0.34185, remainder factor of age 37, × $1,000)	342	205
Basis of C's remainder interest at the time of sale		$596

Example (2). Assume the same facts as in example (1), except that C does not sell the remainder interest. Upon A's death terminating the trust, C's basis for the stock distributed to him is computed as follows:

Uniform basis of the property, adjusted to date of termination of the trust ..		$1,000
plus		
Value of remainder interest in the property at the time of B's death .	$547	
less		
B's share of uniform basis of the property at the time of his death ..	342	205
C's basis for the stock distributed to him upon the termination of the trust ..		$1,205

Example (3). Assume the same facts as in example (2), except that the property transferred is depreciable. Assume further that $100 of depreciation was allowed prior to B's death and that $50 of depreciation is allowed between the time of B's death and the termination of the trust. Upon A's death terminating the trust, C's basis for the property distributed to him is computed as follows:

Uniform basis of the property, adjusted to date of termination of the trust:		
Uniform basis immediately after decedent's death	$1,000	
Depreciation allowed following decedent's death	150	$850
plus		
Value of remainder interest in the property at the time of B's death .	$547	
less		
B's share of uniform basis of the property at the time of his death (0.34185 × $900, uniform basis at B's death)	$308	$239
C's basis for the property distributed to him upon the termination of the trust .		$1,089

(c) The rules stated in paragraph (a) of this section do not apply where the basis of the remainder interest in the hands of the remainderman's transferee is determined by reference to its cost to such transferee. See, also, paragraph (a) of §1.1014-4. Thus, if, in example *(1)* of paragraph (b) of this section, B sold his remainder interest to C for $547 in cash, C's basis for the stock distributed to him upon the death of A terminating the trust is $547. [Reg. §1.1014-8.]

□ [*T.D. 6265, 11-6-57.*]

[Reg. §1.1014-9]

§1.1014-9. Special rule with respect to DISC stock.—(a) *In general.*—If property consisting of stock of a DISC or former DISC (as defined in section 992(a)(1) or (3) as the case may be) is considered to have been acquired from a decedent (within the meaning of paragraph (a) or (b) of §1.1014-2), the uniform basis of such stock under section 1014, as determined pursuant to §§1.1014-1 through 1.1014-8 shall be reduced as provided in this section. Such uniform basis shall be reduced by the amount (hereinafter referred to in this section as the amount of reduction), if any, which the decedent would have included in his gross income under section 995(c) as a dividend if the decedent had lived and sold such stock at its fair market value on the estate tax valuation date. If the alternate valuation date for Federal estate tax purposes is elected under section 2032, in computing the gain which the decedent would have had if he had lived and sold the stock on the alternate valuation date, the decedent's basis shall be determined with reduction for any distributions with respect to the stock which may have been made, after the date of the decedent's death and on or before the alternate valuation date, from the DISC's previously taxed income (as defined in section 996(f)(2)). For this purpose, the last sentence of section 996(e)(2) (relating to reductions of basis of DISC stock) shall not apply. For purposes of this section, if the corporation is not a DISC or former DISC at the date of the decedent's death but is a DISC for a taxable year which begins after such date and on or before the alternate valuation date, the corporation will be considered to be a DISC or former DISC only if the alternate valuation date is elected. The provisions of this paragraph apply with respect to stock of a DISC or former DISC which is included in the gross estate of the decedent, including but not limited to property which—

(1) Is acquired from the decedent before his death, and the entire property is subsequently included in the decedent's gross estate for estate tax purposes, or

(2) Is acquired property described in paragraph (d) of § 1.1014-3.

(b) *Portion of property acquired from decedent before his death included in decedent's gross estate.*— (1) *In general.*—In cases where, due to the operation of the estate tax, only a portion of property which consists of stock of a DISC or former DISC and which is acquired from a decedent before his death is included in the decedent's gross estate, the uniform basis of such stock under section 1014, as determined pursuant to § 1.1014-1 through § 1.1014-8, shall be reduced by an amount which bears the same ratio to the amount of reduction which would have been determined under paragraph (a) of this section if the entire property consisting of such stock were included in the decedent's gross estate as the value of such property included in the decedent's gross estate bears to the value of the entire property.

(2) *Example.*—The provisions of this paragraph may be illustrated by the following example:

Example. The decedent creates a trust during his lifetime to pay the income to A for life, remainder to B or his estate. The trust instrument further provides that if the decedent should survive A, the income shall be paid to the decedent for life. The decedent predeceases A, so that, due to the operation of the estate tax, only the present value of the remainder interest is included in the decedent's gross estate. The trust consists of 100 shares of the stock of X Corporation (which is a DISC at the time the shares are transferred to the trust and at the time of the decedent's death) with an adjusted basis immediately prior to the decedent's death of $10,000 (as determined under section 1015). At the time of the decedent's death the value of the stock is $20,000, and the value of the remainder interest in the hands of B is $8,000. Applying the principles of paragraph (b)(3)(i) of § 1.1014-6, the uniform basis of the entire property following the decedent's death, prior to reduction pursuant to this paragraph, is $14,000. The amount of reduction which would have been determined under paragraph (a) of this section if the entire property consisting of such stock of X Corporation were included in the decedent's gross estate is

$5,000. The uniform basis of the entire property following the decedent's death, as reduced pursuant to this paragraph, is $12,000, computed as follows:

Uniform basis under section 1014(a), prior
to reduction pursuant to this paragraph
. . . . $14,000
Less decrease in uniform basis
(determined by the following formula) .
. . . . 2,000

$$\frac{\text{Reduction in uniform basis (to be determined)}}{\text{\$5,000 (amount of reduction if paragraph (a) applied)}} = \frac{\text{\$8,000 (value of property included in gross estate)}}{\text{\$20,000 (value of entire property)}}$$

Uniform basis under section 1014(a)
reduced pursuant to this paragraph . $12,000

(c) *Estate tax valuation date.*—For purposes of section 1014(d) and this section, the estate tax valuation date is the date of the decedent's death or, in the case of an election under section 2032, the applicable valuation date prescribed by that section.

(d) *Examples.*—The provisions of this section may be illustrated by the following examples:

Example (1). At the date of A's death, his DISC stock has a fair market value of $100. The estate does not elect the alternate valuation allowed by section 2032, and A's basis in such stock is $60 at the date of his death. The person who acquires such stock from the decedent will take as a basis for such stock its fair market value at A's death ($100), reduced by the amount which would have been included in A's gross income under section 995(c) as a dividend if A had sold stock on the date he died. Thus, if the amount that would have been treated as a dividend under section 995(c) were $30, such person will take a basis of $70 for such stock ($100, reduced by $30). If such person were immediately to sell the DISC stock so received for $100, $30 of the proceeds from the sale would be treated as a dividend by such person under section 995(c).

Example (2). Assume the same facts as in example (1) except that the estate elects the alternate valuation allowed by section 2032, the DISC stock has a fair market value of $140 on the alternate valuation date, the amount that would have been treated as a dividend under section 995(c) in the event of a sale on such date is $50 and the DISC has $20 of previously taxed income which accrued after the date of the decedent's death and before the alternate valuation date. The basis of the person who acquires such stock will be $90 determined as follows:

Reg. § 1.1014-9(a)(1)

(1) Fair market value of DISC stock at
alternate valuation date $140
(2) Less: Amount which would have been
treated as a dividend under section
995(c) 50
(3) Basis of person who acquires DISC stock
. . . . $90

If a distribution of $20 attributable to such previously taxed income had been made by the DISC on or before the alternate valuation date (with the DISC stock having a fair market value of $120 after such distribution), the basis of the person who acquires such stock will be $70 determined as follows:

(1) Fair market value of DISC stock at
alternate valuation date $120
(2) Less: Amount which would have been
treated as a dividend under section
995(c) 50
(3) Basis of person who acquires DISC stock
. . . . $70

[Reg. § 1.1014-9.]

□ [T.D. 7283, 8-2-73.]

[Reg. § 1.1015-1]

§ 1.1015-1. Basis of property acquired by gift after December 31, 1920.—(a) *General rule.*— (1) In the case of property acquired by gift after December 31, 1920 (whether by a transfer in trust or otherwise), the basis of the property for the purpose of determining gain is the same as it would be in the hands of the donor or the last preceding owner by whom it was not acquired by gift. The same rule applies in determining loss unless the basis (adjusted for the period prior to the date of gift in accordance with sections 1016 and 1017) is greater than the fair market value of the property at the time of the gift. In such case, the basis for determining loss is the fair market value at the time of the gift.

(2) The provisions of subparagraph (1) of this paragraph may be illustrated by the following example.

Example. A acquires by gift income-producing property which has an adjusted basis of $100,000 at the date of gift. The fair market value of the property at the date of gift is $90,000. A later sells the property for $95,000. In such case there is neither gain nor loss. The basis for determining loss is $90,000; therefore, there is no loss. Furthermore, there is no gain, since the basis for determining gain is $100,000.

(3) If the facts necessary to determine the basis of property in the hands of the donor or the last preceding owner by whom it was not acquired by gift are unknown to the donee, the district director shall, if possible, obtain such facts from such donor or last preceding owner, or any other person cognizant thereof. If the district director finds it impossible to obtain such

facts, the basis in the hands of such donor or last preceding owner shall be the fair market value of such property as found by the district director as of the date or approximate date at which, according to the best information the district director is able to obtain, such property was acquired by such donor or last preceding owner. See paragraph (e) of this section for rules relating to fair market value.

(b) *Uniform basis; proportionate parts of.*—Property acquired by gift has a single or uniform basis although more than one person may acquire an interest in such property. The uniform basis of the property remains fixed subject to proper adjustment for items under sections 1016 and 1017. However, the value of the proportionate parts of the uniform basis represented, for instance, by the respective interests of the life tenant and remainderman are adjustable to reflect the change in the relative values of such interest on account of the lapse of time. The portion of the basis attributable to an interest at the time of its sale or other disposition shall be determined under the rule provided in § 1.1014-5. In determining gain or loss from the sale or other disposition after October 9, 1969, of a term interest in property (as defined in § 1.1001-1(f)(2)) the adjusted basis of which is determined pursuant, or by reference, to section 1015, that part of the adjusted uniform basis assignable under the rules of § 1.1014-5(a) to the interest sold or otherwise disposed of shall be disregarded to the extent and in the manner provided by section 1001(e) and § 1.1001-1(f).

(c) *Time of acquisition.*—The date that the donee acquires an interest in property by gift is when the donor relinquishes dominion over the property and not necessarily when title to the property is acquired by the donee. Thus, the date that the donee acquires an interest in property by gift where he is a successor in interest, such as in the case of a remainderman of a life estate or a beneficiary of the distribution of the corpus of a trust, is the date such interests are created by the donor and not the date the property is actually acquired.

(d) *Property acquired by gift from a decedent dying after December 31, 1953.*—If an interest in property was acquired by the taxpayer by gift from a donor dying after December 31, 1953, under conditions which require the inclusion of the property in the donor's gross estate for estate tax purposes, and the property had not been sold, exchanged, or otherwise disposed of by the taxpayer before the donor's death, see the rules prescribed in section 1014 and the regulations thereunder.

(e) *Fair market value.*—For the purposes of this section, the value of property as appraised for the purpose of the Federal gift tax, or, if the gift is not subject to such tax, its value as appraised for the purpose of a State gift tax, shall be deemed to be the fair market value of the property at the time of the gift.

(f) *Reinvestments by fiduciary.*—If the property is an investment by the fiduciary under the terms of the gift (as, for example, in the case of a sale by the fiduciary of property transferred under the terms of the gift, and the reinvestment of the proceeds), the cost or other basis to the fiduciary is taken in lieu of the basis specified in paragraph (a) of this section.

(g) *Records.*—To insure a fair and adequate determination of the proper basis under section 1015, persons making or receiving gifts of property should preserve and keep accessible a record of the facts necessary to determine the cost of the property and, if pertinent, its fair market value as of March 1, 1913, or its fair market value as of the date of the gift. [Reg. § 1.1015-1.]

☐ [*T.D. 6265, 11-6-57. Amended by T.D. 6693, 12-2-63 and T.D. 7142, 9-23-71.*]

[Reg. § 1.1015-2]

§ 1.1015-2. Transfer of property in trust after December 31, 1920.—(a) *General rule.*—(1) In the case of property acquired after December 31, 1920, by transfer in trust (other than by a transfer in trust by a gift, bequest, or devise) the basis of property so acquired is the same as it would be in the hands of the grantor increased in the amount of gain or decreased in the amount of loss recognized to the grantor upon such transfer under the law applicable to the year in which the transfer was made. If the taxpayer acquired the property by a transfer in trust, this basis applies whether the property be in the hands of the trustee, or the beneficiary, and whether acquired prior to the termination of the trust and distribution of the property, or thereafter.

(2) The principles stated in paragraph (b) of § 1.1015-1 concerning the uniform basis are applicable in determining the basis of property where more than one person acquires an interest in property by transfer in trust after December 31, 1920.

(b) *Reinvestment by fiduciary.*—If the property is an investment made by the fiduciary (as, for example, in the case of a sale by the fiduciary of property transferred by the grantor, and the reinvestment of the proceeds), the cost or other basis to the fiduciary is taken in lieu of the basis specified in paragraph (a) of this section. [Reg. § 1.1015-2.]

☐ [*T.D. 6265, 11-6-57.*]

[Reg. § 1.1015-3]

§ 1.1015-3. Gift or transfer in trust before January 1, 1921.—(a) In the case of property acquired by gift or transfer in trust before January 1, 1921, the basis of such property is the fair market value thereof at the time of the gift or at the time of the transfer in trust.

(b) The principles stated in paragraph (b) of § 1.1015-1 concerning the uniform basis are applicable in determining the basis of property where more than one person acquires an interest in property by gift or transfer in trust before January 1, 1921. In addition, if an interest in such property was acquired from a decedent and the property had not been sold, exchanged, or otherwise disposed of before the death of the donor, the rules prescribed in section 1014 and the regulations thereunder are applicable in determining the basis of such property in the hands of the taxpayer. [Reg. § 1.1015-3.]

☐ [*T.D. 6265, 11-6-57.*]

[Reg. § 1.1015-4]

§ 1.1015-4. Transfers in part a gift and in part a sale.—(a) *General rule.*—Where a transfer of property is in part a sale and in part a gift, the unadjusted basis of the property in the hands of the transferee is the sum of—

(1) Whichever of the following is the greater:

(i) The amount paid by the transferee for the property, or

(ii) The transferor's adjusted basis for the property at the time of the transfer, and

(2) The amount of increase, if any, in basis authorized by section 1015(d) for gift tax paid (see § 1.1015-5).

For determining loss, the unadjusted basis of the property in the hands of the transferee shall not be greater than the fair market value of the property at the time of such transfer. For determination of gain or loss of the transferor, see § 1.1001-1(e) and § 1.1011-2. For special rule where there has been a charitable contribution of less than a taxpayer's entire interest in property, see section 170(e)(2) and § 1.170A-4(c).

(b) *Examples.*—The rule of paragraph (a) of this section is illustrated by the following examples:

Example (1). If A transfers property to his son for $30,000, and such property at the time of the transfer has an adjusted basis of $30,000 in A's hands (and a fair market value of $60,000), the unadjusted basis of the property in the hands of the son is $30,000.

Example (2). If A transfers property to his son for $60,000, and such property at the time of transfer had an adjusted basis of $30,000 in A's hands (and a fair market value of $90,000), the unadjusted basis of such property in the hands of the son is $60,000.

Example (3). If A transfers property to his son for $30,000, and such property at the time of transfer has an adjusted basis in A's hands of $60,000 (and a fair market value of $90,000), the unadjusted basis of such property in the hands of the son is $60,000.

Example (4). If A transfers property to his son for $30,000 and such property at the time of transfer has an adjusted basis of $90,000 in A's hands (and a fair market value of $60,000), the unadjusted basis of the property in the hands of the son is $90,000. However, since the adjusted basis of the property in A's hands at the time of the transfer was greater than the fair market value at that time, for the purpose of determining any loss on a later sale or other disposition of the property by the son its unadjusted basis in his hands is $60,000. [Reg. § 1.1015-4.]

☐ [*T.D.* 6265, 11-6-57. *Amended by T.D.* 6693, 12-2-63 *and T.D.* 7207, 10-3-72.]

[Reg. § 1.1015-5]

§ 1.1015-5. Increased basis for gift tax paid.—
(a) *General rule in the case of gifts made on or before December 31, 1976.—*(1)(i) Subject to the conditions and limitations provided in section 1015(d), as added by the Technical Amendments Act of 1958, the basis (as determined under section 1015(a) and paragraph (a) of § 1.1015-1) of property acquired by gift is increased by the amount of gift tax paid with respect to the gift of such property. Under section 1015(d)(1)(A), such increase in basis applies to property acquired by gift on or after September 2, 1958 (the date of enactment of the Technical Amendments Act of 1958). Under section 1015(d)(1)(B), such increase in basis applies to property acquired by gift before September 2, 1958, and not sold, exchanged, or otherwise disposed of before such date. If section 1015(d)(1)(A) applies, the basis of the property is increased as of the date of the gift regardless of the date of payment of the gift tax. For example, if the property was acquired by gift on September 8, 1958, and sold by the donee on October 15, 1958, the basis of the property would be increased (subject to the limitation of section 1015(d)) as of September 8, 1958 (the date of the gift), by the amount of gift tax applicable to such gift even though such tax was not paid until March 1, 1959. If section 1015 (d)(1)(B) applies, any increase in the basis of the property due to gift tax paid (regardless of date of payment) with respect to the gift is made as of September 2, 1958. Any increase in basis under section 1015(d) can be no greater than the amount by which the fair market value of the property at the time of the gift exceeds the basis of such property in the hands of the donor at the time of the gift. See paragraph (b) of this section for rules for determining the amount of gift tax paid in respect of property transferred by gift.

(ii) With respect to property acquired by gift before September 2, 1958, the provisions of section 1015(d) and this section do not apply if, before such date, the donee has sold, exchanged, or otherwise disposed of such property. The phrase "sold, exchanged, or otherwise disposed of" includes the surrender of a stock certificate for corporate assets in complete or partial liquidation of a corporation pursuant to section 331. It also includes the exchange of property for property of a like kind such as the exchange of one apartment house for another. The phrase does not, however, extend to transactions which are mere changes in form. Thus, it does not include a transfer of assets to a corporation in exchange for its stock in a transaction with respect to which no gain or loss would be recognizable for income tax purposes under section 351. Nor does it include an exchange of stock or securities in a corporation for stock or securities in the same corporation or another corporation in a transaction such as a merger, recapitalization, reorganization, or other transaction described in section 368(a) or 355, with respect to which no gain or loss is recognizable for income tax purposes under section 354 or 355. If a binding contract for the sale, exchange, or other disposition of property is entered into, the property is considered as sold, exchanged, or otherwise disposed of on the effective date of the contract, unless the contract is not subsequently carried out substantially in accordance with its terms. The effective date of a contract is normally the date it is entered into (and not the date it is consummated, or the date legal title to the property passes) unless the contract specifies a different effective date. For purposes of this subdivision, in determining whether a transaction comes within the phrase "sold, exchanged, or otherwise disposed of", if a transaction would be treated as a mere change in the form of the property if it occurred in a taxable year subject to the Internal Revenue Code of 1954, it will be so treated if the transaction occurred in a taxable year subject to the Internal Revenue Code of 1939 or prior revenue law.

(2) Application of the provisions of subparagraph (1) of this paragraph may be illustrated by the following examples:

Example (1). In 1938, A purchased a business building at a cost of $120,000. On September 2, 1958, at which time the property had an adjusted basis in A's hands of $60,000, he gave the property to his nephew, B. At the time of the gift to B, the property had a fair market value of $65,000 with respect to which A paid a gift tax in the amount of $7,545. The basis of the property in B's hands at the time of the gift, as determined under section 1015(a) and § 1.1015-1, would be the same as the adjusted basis in A's hands at the time of the gift, or $60,000. Under section 1015(d) and this section, the basis of the building in B's hands as of the date of the gift would be increased by the amount of the gift tax paid with respect to such gift, limited to an amount by which the fair market value of the property at the time of the gift exceeded the basis of the property in the hands of A at the time of gift, or $5,000. Therefore, the basis of the property in B's hands immediately after the gift, both for determining gain or loss on the sale of the property, would be $65,000.

Example (2). C purchased property in 1938 at a cost of $100,000. On October 1, 1952, at which time the property had an adjusted basis of $72,000 in C's hands, he gave the property to his daughter, D. At the date of the gift to D, the property had a fair market value of $85,000 with respect to which C paid a gift tax in the amount of $11,745. On September 2, 1958, D still held the property which then had an adjusted basis in her hands of $65,000. Since the excess of the fair market value of the property at the time of the gift to D over the adjusted basis of the property in C's hands at such time is greater than the amount of gift tax paid, the basis of the property in D's hands would be increased as of September 2, 1958, by the amount of the gift tax paid, or $11,745. The adjusted basis of the property in D's hands, both for determining gain or loss on the sale of the property, would then be $76,745 ($65,000 plus $11,745).

Example (3). On December 31, 1951, E gave to his son, F, 500 shares of common stock of the X Corporation which shares had been purchased earlier by E at a cost of $100 per share, or a total cost of $50,000. The basis in E's hands was still $50,000 on the date of the gift to F. On the date of the gift, the fair market value of the 500 shares was $80,000 with respect to which E paid a gift tax in the amount of $10,695. In 1956, the 500 shares of X Corporation stock were exchanged for 500 shares of common stock of the Y Corporation in a reorganization with respect to which no gain or loss was recognized for income tax purposes under section 354. F still held the 500 shares of Y Corporation stock on September 2, 1958. Under such circumstances, the 500 shares of X Corporation stock would not, for purposes of section 1015(d) and this section, be considered as having been "sold, exchanged, or otherwise disposed of" by F before September 2, 1958. Therefore, the basis of the 500 shares of Y Corporation stock held by F as of such date would, by reason of section 1015(d) and this section, be increased by $10,695, the amount of gift tax paid with respect to the gift to F of the X Corporation stock.

Example (4). On November 15, 1953, G gave H property which had a fair market value of $53,000 and a basis in the hands of G of $20,000. G paid gift tax of $5,250 on the transfer. On November 16, 1956, H gave the property to J who still held it on September 2, 1958. The value of the property on the date of the gift to J was $63,000 and H paid gift tax of $7,125 on the transfer. Since the property was not sold, exchanged, or otherwise disposed of by J before September 2, 1958, and the gift tax paid on the transfer to J did not exceed $43,000 ($63,000, fair market value of property at time of gift to J, less $20,000, basis of property in H's hands at that time), the basis of property in his hands is increased on September 2, 1958, by $7,125, the amount of gift tax paid by H on the transfer. No increase in basis is allowed for the $5,250 gift tax paid by G on the transfer to H, since H had sold,

exchanged, or otherwise disposed of the property before September 2, 1958.

(b) *Amount of gift tax paid with respect to gifts made on or before December 31, 1976.*—(1)(i) If only one gift was made during a certain "calendar period" (as defined in § 25.2502-1(c)(1)), the entire amount of the gift tax paid under chapter 12 or the corresponding provisions of prior revenue laws for that calendar period is the amount of the gift tax paid with respect to the gift.

(ii) If more than one gift was made during a certain calendar period, the amount of the gift tax paid under chapter 12 or the corresponding provisions of prior revenue laws with respect to any specified gift made during that calendar period is an amount, A, which bears the same ratio to B (the total gift tax paid for that calendar period) as C (the "amount of the gift," computed as described in this paragraph (b)(1)(ii)) bears to D (the total taxable gifts for the calendar period computed without deduction for the gift tax specific exemption under section 2521 (as in effect prior to its repeal by the Tax Reform Act of 1976) or the corresponding provisions of prior revenue laws).

(iii) If a gift consists of more than one item of property, the gift tax paid with respect to each item shall be computed by allocating to each item a proportionate part of the gift tax paid with respect to the gift, computed in accordance with the provisions of this paragraph.

(2) For purposes of this paragraph, it is immaterial whether the gift tax is paid by the donor or the donee. Where more than one gift of a present interest in property is made to the same donee during a "calendar period" (as defined in § 25.2502-1(c)(1)), the annual exclusion shall apply to the earliest of such gifts in point of time.

(3) Where the donor and his spouse elect under section 2513 or the corresponding provisions of prior law to have any gifts made one-half by each, the amount of gift tax paid with respect to such a gift is the sum of the amounts of tax (computed separately) paid with respect to each half of the gift by the donor and his spouse.

(4) The method described in section 1015(d)(2) and this paragraph for computing the amount of gift tax paid in respect of a gift may be illustrated by the following examples:

Example (1). Prior to 1959 H made no taxable gifts. On July 1, 1959, he made a gift to his wife, W, of land having a value for gift tax purposes of $60,000 and gave to his son, S, certain securities valued at $60,000. During the year 1959, H also contributed $5,000 in cash to a charitable organization described in section 2522. H filed a timely gift tax return for 1959 with respect to which he paid gift tax in the amount of $6,000, computed as follows:

Value of land given to W		$60,000
Less: Annual exclusion	$ 3,000	
Marital deduction	30,000	33,000

Included amount of gift			$27,000
Value of securities given to S		$60,000	
Less: Annual exclusion		3,000	
Included amount of gift			57,000
Gift to charitable organization		$5,000	
Less: Annual exclusion	$3,000		
Charitable deduction	2,000	5,000	
Included amount of gift			None
Total included gifts			84,000
Less: Specific exemption allowed			30,000
Taxable gifts for 1959			54,000
Gift tax on $54,000			$ 6,000

In determining the gift tax paid with respect to the land given to W, amount C of the ratio set forth in subparagraph (1)(ii) of this paragraph is $60,000, value of property given to W, less $33,000 (the sum of $3,000, the amount excluded under section 2503(b), and $30,000, the amount deducted under section 2523), or $27,000. Amount D of the ratio is $84,000 (the amount of taxable gifts, $54,000, plus the gift tax specific exemption, $30,000). The gift tax paid with respect to the land given to W is $1,928.57, computed as follows:

$$\frac{\$27,000 \ (C)}{\$84,000 \ (D)} \times \$6,000 \ (B)$$

Example (2). The facts are the same as in example (1) except that H made his gifts to W and S on July 1, 1971, and that prior to 1971, H made no taxable gifts. Furthermore, H made his charitable contribution on August 12, 1971. These were the only gifts made by H during 1971. H filed his gift tax return for the third quarter of 1971 on November 15, 1971, as required by section 6075(b). With respect to the above gifts, H paid a gift tax in the amount of $6,000, on total taxable gifts of $54,000 for the third quarter of 1971. The gift tax paid with respect to the land given to W is $1,928.57. The computations for these figures are identical to those used in example (1).

Example (3). On January 15, 1956, A made a gift to his nephew, N, of land valued at $86,000, and on June 30, 1956, gave N securities valued at $40,000. On July 1, 1956, A gave to his sister, S, $46,000 in cash. A and his wife, B, were married during the entire calendar year 1956. The amount of A's taxable gifts for prior years was zero although in arriving at that amount A had used in full the specific exemption authorized by section 2521. B did not make any gifts before 1956. A and B elected under section 2513 to have all gifts made by either during 1956 treated as made one-half by A and one-half by B. Pursuant to that election, A and B each filed a gift tax return for 1956. A paid gift tax of $11,325 and B paid gift tax of $5,250, computed as follows:

	A	*B*
Value of land given to N ..	$43,000	$43,000
Less: exclusion	3,000	3,000
Included amount of gift	$40,000	$40,000

Value of securities given to N	$20,000	$20,000
Less: exclusion	none	none
Included amount of gift	20,000	20,000
Cash gift to S	23,000	23,000
Less: exclusion	3,000	3,000
Included amount of gift	20,000	20,000
Total included gifts ...	80,000	80,000
Less: specific exemption ..	none	30,000
Taxable gifts for 1956 ..	80,000	50,000
Gift tax for 1956	11,325	5,250

The amount of the gift tax paid by A with respect to the land given to N is computed as follows:

$$\frac{\$40,000 \ (C)}{\$80,000 \ (D)} \times \$11,325 \ (B) = \$5,662.50$$

The amount of the gift tax paid by B with respect to the land given to N is computed as follows:

$$\frac{\$40,000 \ (C)}{\$80,000 \ (D)} \times \$5,250 \ (B) = \$2,625$$

The amount of the gift tax paid with respect to the land is $5,662.50 plus $2,625, or $8,287.50. Computed in a similar manner, the amount of gift tax paid by A with respect to the securities given to N is $2,831.25, and the amount of gift tax paid by B with respect thereto is $1,312.50, or a total of $4,143.75.

Example (4). The facts are the same as in example (3) except that A gave the land to N on January 15, 1972, the securities to N on February 3, 1972, and the cash to S on March 7, 1972. As in example (3), the amount of A's taxable gifts for taxable years prior to 1972 was zero, although in arriving at that amount A had used in full the specific exemption authorized by section 2521. B did not make any gifts before 1972. Pursuant to the election under section 2513, A and B treated all gifts made by either during 1972 as made one-half by A and one-half by B. A and B each filed a gift tax return for the first quarter of 1972 on May 15, 1972, as required by section 6075(b). A paid gift tax of $11,325 on taxable gifts of $80,000 and B paid gift tax of $5,250 on taxable gifts of $50,000. The amount of the gift tax paid by A and B with respect to the land given to N is

Reg. § 1.1015-5(b)(4)

$5,662.50 and $2,625, respectively. The computations for these figures are identical to those used in example (3).

(c) *Special rule for increased basis for gift tax paid in the case of gifts made after December 31, 1976.*— (1) *In general.*—With respect to gifts made after December 31, 1976 (other than gifts between spouses described in section 1015(e)), the increase in basis for gift tax paid is determined under section 1015(d)(6). Under section 1015(d)(6)(A), the increase in basis with respect to gift tax paid is limited to the amount (not in excess of the amount of gift tax paid) that bears the same ratio to the amount of gift tax paid as the net appreciation in value of the gift bears to the amount of the gift.

(2) *Amount of gift.*—In general, for purposes of section 1015(d)(6)(A)(ii), the amount of the gift is determined in conformance with the provisions of paragraph (b) of this section. Thus, the amount of the gift is the amount included with respect to the gift in determining (for purposes of section 2503(a)) the total amount of gifts made during the calendar year (or calendar quarter in the case of a gift made on or before December 31, 1981), reduced by the amount of any annual exclusion allowable with respect to the gift under section 2503(b), and any deductions allowed with respect to the gift under section 2522 (relating to the charitable deduction) and section 2523 (relating to the marital deduction). Where more than one gift of a present interest in property is made to the same donee during a calendar year, the annual exclusion shall apply to the earliest of such gifts in point of time.

(3) *Amount of gift tax paid with respect to the gift.*—In general, for purposes of section 1015(d)(6), the amount of gift tax paid with respect to the gift is determined in conformance with the provisions of paragraph (b) of this section. Where more than one gift is made by the donor in a calendar year (or quarter in the case of gifts made on or before December 31, 1981), the amount of gift tax paid with respect to any specific gift made during that period is the amount which bears the same ratio to the total gift tax paid for that period (determined after reduction for any gift tax unified credit available under section 2505) as the amount of the gift (computed as described in paragraph (c)(2) of this section) bears to the total taxable gifts for the period.

(4) *Qualified domestic trusts.*—For purposes of section 1015(d)(6), in the case of a qualified domestic trust (QDOT) described in section 2056A(a), any distribution during the noncitizen surviving spouse's lifetime with respect to which a tax is imposed under section 2056A(b)(1)(A) is treated as a transfer by gift, and any estate tax paid on the distribution under section 2056A(b)(1)(A) is treated as a gift tax. The rules under this paragraph apply in determining the extent to which the basis in the assets distributed is increased by the tax imposed under section 2056A(b)(1)(A).

(5) *Examples.*—Application of the provisions of this paragraph (c) may be illustrated by the following examples:

Example 1. (i) Prior to 1995, X exhausts X's gift tax unified credit available under section 2505. In 1995, X makes a gift to X's child Y, of a parcel of real estate having a fair market value of $100,000. X's adjusted basis in the real estate immediately before making the gift was $70,000. Also in 1995, X makes a gift to X's child Z, of a painting having a fair market value of $70,000. X timely files a gift tax return for 1995 and pays gift tax in the amount of $55,500, computed as follows:

Value of real estate transferred to Y	$100,000	. . . . .
Less: Annual exclusion	10,000	. . . . .
Included amount of gift (C)	. . . . .	$90,000
Value of painting transferred to Z	$70,000	. . . . .
Less: annual exclusion	10,000	. . . . .
Included amount of gift	. . . . .	60,000
Total included gifts (D)	. . . . .	$150,000
Total gift tax liability for 1995 gifts (B)	. . . . .	$55,500

(ii) The gift tax paid with respect to the real estate transferred to Y, is determined as follows:

$$\frac{\$90,000 (C)}{\$150,000 (D)} \times \$55,500 = \$33,300$$

(iii) (A) The amount by which Y's basis in the real property is increased is determined as follows:

$$\frac{\$30,000 \text{ (net appreciation)}}{\$90,000 \text{ (amount of gift)}} \times \$33,300 = \$11,000$$

(B) Y's basis in the real property is $70,000 plus $11,100, or $81,100. If X had not exhausted any of X's unified credit, no gift tax would have been paid and, as a result, Y's basis would not be increased.

Reg. §1.1015-5(c)

Example 2. (i) *X* dies in 1995. *X*'s spouse, *Y*, is not a United States citizen. In order to obtain the marital deduction for property passing to *X*'s spouse, *X* established a QDOT in *X*'s will. In 1996, the trustee of the QDOT makes a distribution of principal from the QDOT in the form of shares of stock having a fair market value of $70,000 on the date of distribution. The trustee's basis in the stock (determined under section 1014) is $50,000. An estate tax is imposed on the distribution under section 2056A(b)(1)(A) in the amount $38,500, and is paid. *Y*'s basis in the shares of stock is increased by a portion of the section 2056A estate tax paid determined as follows:

$$\frac{\$20,000 \text{ (net appreciation)}}{\$70,000 \text{ (distribution)}} \times \$38,500 \text{ (section 2056a estate tax)} = \$11,000$$

(ii) *Y*'s basis in the stock is $50,000 plus $11,000, or $61,000.

(6) *Effective date.*—The provisions of this paragraph (c) are effective for gifts made after August 22, 1995.

(d) *Treatment as adjustment to basis.*—Any increase in basis under section 1015(d) and this section shall for purposes of section 1016(b) (relating to adjustments to a substituted basis), be treated as an adjustment under section 1016(a) to the basis of the donee's property to which such increase applies. See paragraph (p) of § 1.1016-5. [Reg. § 1.1015-5.]

☐ [*T.D.* 6693, 12-2-63. *Amended by T.D.* 7238, 12-28-72; *T.D.* 7910, 9-6-83 *and T.D.* 8612, 8-21-95.]

[Reg. § 1.1016-1]

§ 1.1016-1. Adjustments to basis; scope of section.—Section 1016 and §§ 1.1016-2 to 1016-10, inclusive, contain the rules relating to the adjustments to be made to the basis of property to determine the adjusted basis as defined in section 1011. However, if the property was acquired from a decedent before his death, see § 1.1014-6 for adjustments on account of certain deductions allowed the taxpayer for the period between the date of acquisition of the property and the date of death of the decedent. If an election has been made under the Retirement-Straight Line Adjustment Act of 1958 (26 U.S.C. 1016 note), see § 1.9001-1 for special rules for determining adjusted basis in the case of a taxpayer who has changed from the retirement to the straight-line method of computing depreciation allowances. [Reg. § 1.1016-1.]

☐ [*T.D.* 6265, 11-6-57. *Amended by T.D.* 6418, 10-9-59.]

[Reg. § 1.1016-2]

§ 1.1016-2. Items properly chargeable to capital account.—(a) The cost or other basis shall be properly adjusted for any expenditure, receipt, loss, or other item, properly chargeable to capital account, including the cost of improvements and betterments made to the property. No adjustment shall be made in respect of any item which, under any applicable provision of law or regulation, is treated as an item not properly chargeable to capital account but is allowable as a deduction in computing net or taxable income for the taxable year. For example, in the case of oil and gas wells no adjustment may be made in respect of any intangible drilling and development expense allowable as a deduction in computing net or taxable income. See the regulations under section 263(c).

(b) The application of the foregoing provisions may be illustrated by the following example:

Example. A, who makes his returns on the calendar year basis, purchased property in 1941 for $10,000. He subsequently expended $6,000 for improvements. Disregarding, for the purpose of this example, the adjustments required for depreciation, the adjusted basis of the property is $16,000. If A sells the property in 1954 for $20,000, the amount of his gain will be $4,000.

(c) Adjustment to basis shall be made for carrying charges such as taxes and interest, with respect to property (whether real or personal, improved or unimproved, and whether productive or unproductive), which the taxpayer elects to treat as chargeable to capital account under section 266, rather than as an allowable deduction. The term "taxes" for this purpose includes duties and excise taxes but does not include income taxes.

(d) Expenditures described in section 173 to establish, maintain, or increase the circulation of a newspaper, magazine, or other periodical are chargeable to capital account only in accordance with and in the manner provided in the regulations under section 173. [Reg. § 1.1016-2.]

☐ [*T.D.* 6265, 11-6-57.]

[Reg. § 1.1016-3]

§ 1.1016-3. Exhaustion, wear and tear, obsolescence, amortization, and depletion for periods since February 28, 1913.—(a) *In general.*— (1) *Adjustment where deduction is claimed.*— (i) For taxable periods beginning on or after January 1, 1952, the cost or other basis of property shall be decreased for exhaustion, wear and tear, obsolescence, amortization, and depletion by the greater of the following two amounts: (*a*) the amount allowed as deductions in computing taxable income, to the extent resulting in a reduction of the taxpayer's income taxes, or (*b*) the amount allowable for the years involved. See paragraph (b) of this section. Where the taxpayer makes an appropriate election the above rule is applicable for periods since February 28, 1913, and before January 1, 1952. See paragraph (d) of this section. For rule for such periods where no election is made, see paragraph (c) of this section.

(ii) The determination of the amount properly allowable for exhaustion, wear and tear, obsolescence, amortization, and depletion shall be made on the basis of facts reasonably known to exist at the end of the taxable year. A taxpayer is not permitted to take advantage in a later year of his prior failure to take any such allowance or his taking an allowance plainly inadequate under the known facts in prior years. In the case of depreciation, if in prior years the taxpayer has consistently taken proper deductions under one method, the amount allowable for such prior years shall not be increased even though a greater amount would have been allowable under another proper method. For rules governing losses on retirement of depreciable property, including rules for determining basis, see § 1.167(a)-8. This subdivision may be illustrated by the following example:

Example. An asset was purchased January 1, 1950, at a cost of $10,000. The useful life of the asset is 10 years. It has no salvage value. Depreciation was deducted and allowed for 1950 to 1954 as follows:

1950	$500
1951	. . . .
1952	1,000
1953	1,000
1954	1,000
Total amount allowed . .	$3,500

The correct reserve as of December 31, 1954, is computed as follows:

Dec. 31:	
1950 ($10,000 ÷ 10)	$1,000
1951 ($9,000 ÷ 9)	1,000
1952 ($8,000 ÷ 8)	1,000
1953 ($7,000 ÷ 7)	1,000
1954 ($6,000 ÷ 6)	1,000
Reserve Dec. 31, 1954 . . .	$5,000

Depreciation for 1955 is computed as follows:

Cost	$10,000
Reserve as of December 31, 1954	
. . . .	5,000
Unrecovered cost	5,000
Depreciation allowable for 1955	
($5,000 ÷ 5)	1,000

(2) *Adjustment for amount allowable where no depreciation deduction claimed.*—(i) If the taxpayer has not taken a depreciation deduction either in the taxable year or for any prior taxable year, adjustments to basis of the property for depreciation allowable shall be determined by using the

straight-line method of depreciation. (See § 1.1016-4 for adjustments in the case of persons exempt from income taxation.)

(ii) For taxable years beginning after December 31, 1953, and ending after August 16, 1954, if the taxpayer with respect to any property has taken a deduction for depreciation properly under one of the methods provided in section 167(b) for one or more years but has omitted the deduction in other years, the adjustment to basis for the depreciation allowable in such a case will be the deduction under the method which was used by the taxpayer with respect to that property. Thus, if A acquired property in 1954 on which he properly computed his depreciation deduction under the method described in section 167(b)(2) (the declining-balance method) for the first year of its useful life but did not take a deduction in the second and third year of the asset's life, the adjustment to basis for depreciation allowable for the second and third year will be likewise computed under the declining-balance method.

(3) *Adjustment for depletion deductions with respect to taxable years before 1932.*—Where for any taxable year before the taxable year 1932 the depletion allowance was based on discovery value or a percentage of income, then the adjustment for depletion for such year shall not exceed a depletion deduction which would have been allowable for such year if computed without reference to discovery value or a percentage of income.

(b) *Adjustment for periods beginning on or after January 1, 1952.*—The decrease required by paragraph (a) of this section for deductions in respect of any period beginning on or after January 1, 1952, shall be whichever is the greater of the following amounts:

(1) The amount allowed as deductions in computing taxable income under subtitle A of the Code or prior income tax laws and resulting (by reason of the deductions so allowed) in a reduction for any taxable year of the taxpayer's taxes under subtitle A of the Code (other than chapter 2, relating to tax on self-employment income) or prior income, war-profits, or excess-profits tax laws; or

(2) The amount properly allowable as deductions in computing taxable income under subtitle A of the Code or prior income tax laws (whether or not the amount properly allowable would have caused a reduction for any taxable year of the taxpayer's taxes).

(c) *Adjustment for periods since February 28, 1913, and before January 1, 1952, where no election made.*—If no election has been properly made under section 1020, or under section 113(d) of the Internal Revenue Code of 1939 (see paragraph (d) of this section), the decrease required by paragraph (a) of this section for deductions in respect of any period since February 28, 1913, and before January 1, 1952, shall be whichever of the following amounts is the greater:

Reg. § 1.1016-3(a)(1)(ii)

(1) The amount allowed as deductions in computing net income under chapter 1 of the Internal Revenue Code of 1939 or prior income tax laws;

(2) The amount properly allowable in computing net income under chapter 1 of the Internal Revenue Code of 1939 or prior income tax laws.

For the purpose of determining the decrease required by this paragraph, it is immaterial whether or not the amount under subparagraph (1) of this paragraph or the amount under subparagraph (2) of this paragraph would have resulted in a reduction for any taxable year of the taxpayer's taxes.

(d) *Adjustment for periods since February 28, 1913, and before January 1, 1952, where election made.*—If an election has been properly made under section 1020, or under section 113(d) of the Internal Revenue Code of 1939, the decrease required by paragraph (a) of this section for deductions in respect of any period since February 28, 1913, and before January 1, 1952, shall be whichever is the greater of the following amounts:

(1) The amount allowed as deductions in computing net income under chapter 1 of the Internal Revenue Code of 1939 or prior income tax laws and resulting (by reason of the deductions so allowed) in a reduction for any taxable year of the taxpayer's taxes under such chapter 1 (other than subchapter E, relating to tax on self-employment income), subchapter E, chapter 2, of the Internal Revenue Code of 1939, or prior income, war-profits, or excess-profits tax laws;

(2) The amount properly allowable as deductions in computing net income under chapter 1 of the Internal Revenue Code of 1939 or prior income tax laws (whether or not the amount properly allowable would have caused a reduction for any taxable year of the taxpayer's taxes).

(e) *Determination of amount allowed which reduced taxpayer's taxes.*—(1) As indicated in paragraphs (b) and (d) of this section, there are situations in which it is necessary to determine (for the purpose of ascertaining the basis adjustment required by paragraph (a) of this section) the extent to which the amount allowed as deductions resulted in a reduction for any taxable year of the taxpayer's taxes under subtitle A (other than chapter 2 relating to tax on self-employment income) of the Internal Revenue Code of 1954, or prior income, war-profits, or excess-profits tax laws. This amount (amount allowed which resulted in a reduction of the taxpayer's taxes) is hereinafter referred to as the "tax-benefit amount allowed." For the purpose of determining whether the tax-benefit amount allowed exceeded the amount allowable, a determination must be made of that portion of the excess of the amount allowed over the amount allowable which, if disallowed, would not have resulted in an increase in any such tax previously determined. If the entire excess of the amount allowed over the amount allowable could be disallowed without any such increase in tax, the tax-benefit amount allowed shall not be considered to have exceeded the amount allowable. In such a case (if paragraph (b) or (d) of this section is applicable) the reduction in basis required by paragraph (a) of this section would be the amount properly allowable as a deduction. If only part of such excess could be disallowed without any such increase in tax, the tax-benefit amount allowed shall be considered to exceed the amount allowable to the extent of the remainder of such excess. In such a case (if paragraph (b) or (d) of this section is applicable) the reduction in basis required by paragraph (a) of this section would be the amount of the tax-benefit amount allowed.

(2) For the purpose of determining the tax-benefit amount allowed the tax previously determined shall be determined under the principles of section 1314. The only adjustments made in determining whether there would be an increase in tax shall be those resulting from the disallowance of the amount allowed. The taxable years for which the determination is made shall be the taxable year for which the deduction was allowed and any other taxable year which would be affected by the disallowance of such deduction. Examples of such other taxable years are taxable years to which there was a carryover or carryback of a net operating loss from the taxable year for which the deduction was allowed, and taxable years for which a computation under section 111 or section 1333 was made by reference to the taxable year for which the deduction was allowed. In determining whether the disallowance of any part of the deduction would not have resulted in an increase in any tax previously determined, proper adjustment must be made for previous determinations under section 1311, or section 3801 of the Internal Revenue Code of 1939, and for any previous application of section 1016(a)(2)(B), or section 113(b)(1)(B)(ii) of the Internal Revenue Code of 1939.

(3) If a determination under section 1016(a)(2)(B) must be made with respect to several properties for each of which the amount allowed for the taxable year exceeded the amount allowable, the tax-benefit amount allowed with respect to each of such properties shall be an allocated portion of the tax-benefit amount allowed determined by reference to the sum of the amounts allowed and the sum of the amounts allowable with respect to such several properties.

(4) In the case of property held by a partnership or trust, the computation of the tax-benefit amount allowed shall take into account the tax benefit of the partners or beneficiaries, as the case may be, from the deduction by the partnership or trust of the amount allowed to the partnership or the trust. For this purpose, the determination of the amount allowed which resulted in a tax benefit to the partners or benefi-

Reg. § 1.1016-3(e)(4)

ciaries shall be made in the same manner as that provided above with respect to the taxes of the person holding the property.

(5) A taxpayer seeking to limit the adjustment to basis to the tax-benefit amount allowed for any period, in lieu of the amount allowed, must establish the tax-benefit amount allowed. A failure of adequate proof as to the tax-benefit amount allowed with respect to one period does not preclude the taxpayer from limiting the adjustment to basis to the tax-benefit amount allowed with respect to another period for which adequate proof is available.

For example, a corporate transferee may have available adequate records with respect to the tax effect of the deduction of erroneous depreciation for certain taxable years, but may not have available adequate records with respect to the deduction of excessive depreciation for other taxable years during which the property was held by its transferor. In such case the corporate transferee shall not be denied the right to apply this section with respect to the erroneous depreciation for the period for which adequate proof is available.

(f) *Determination of amount allowable in prior taxable years.*—(1) One of the factors in determining the adjustment to basis as of any date is the amount of depreciation, depletion, etc., allowable for periods prior to such date. The amount allowable for such prior periods is determined under the law applicable to such prior periods; all adjustments required by the law applicable to such periods are made in determining the adjusted basis of the property for the purpose of determining the amount allowable. Provisions corresponding to the rules in section 1016(a)(2)(B) described in paragraphs (d) and (e) of this section, which limit adjustments to the "tax-benefit amount allowed" where an election is properly exercised, were first enacted by Act of July 14, 1952 (66 Stat. 629). That law provided that corresponding rules are deemed to be includible in all revenue laws applicable to taxable years ending after December 31, 1931. Accordingly, those rules shall be taken into account in determining the amount of depreciation, etc., allowable for any taxable year ending after December 31, 1931. For example, if the adjusted basis of property held by the taxpayer since January 1, 1930, is determined as of January 1, 1955, and if an election was properly made under section 1020, or section 113(d) of the Internal Revenue Code of 1939, then the amount allowable which is taken into account in computing the adjusted basis as of January 1, 1955, shall be determined by taking those rules into account for all taxable years ending after December 31, 1931. Public Law 539 made no change in the law applicable in determining the amount allowable for taxable years ending before January 1, 1932. If there was a final decision of a court prior to the enactment of the Act of July 14, 1952, deter-

mining the amount allowable for a particular taxable year, such determination shall be adjusted. In such case the adjustment shall be made only for the purpose of taking the provision of that law into account and only to the extent made necessary by such provisions.

(2) Although the Act of July 14, 1952, amended the law applicable to all taxable years ending after December 31, 1931, the amendment does not permit refund, credit, or assessment of a deficiency for any taxable year for which such refund, credit, or assessment was barred by any law or rule of law.

(g) *Property with transferred basis.*—The following rules apply in the determination of the adjustments to basis of property in the hands of a transferee, donee, or grantee which are required by section 1016(b), or section 113(b)(2) of the Internal Revenue Code of 1939, with respect to the period the property was held by the transferor, donor, or grantor:

(1) An election or a revocation of an election under section 1020, or section 113(d) of the Internal Revenue Code of 1939, by a transferor, donor, or grantor, which is made after the date of the transfer, gift, or grant of the property shall not affect the basis of such property in the hands of the transferee, donee, or grantee. An election or a revocation of an election made before the date of the transfer, gift, or grant of the property shall be taken into account in determining under section 1016(b) the adjustments to basis of such property as of the date of the transfer, gift, or grant, whether or not an election or a revocation of an election under section 1020, or section 113(d) of the Internal Revenue Code of 1939, was made by the transferee, donee, or grantee.

(2) An election by the transferee, donee, or grantee, or a revocation of such an election shall be applicable in determining the adjustments to basis for the period during which the property was held by the transferor, donor, or grantor, whether or not the transferor, donor, or grantor had made an election or a revocation of an election, provided that the property was held by the transferee, donee, or grantee at any time on or before the date on which the election or revocation was made.

(h) *Application to a change in method of accounting.*—For purposes of determining whether a change in depreciation or amortization for property subject to section 167, 168, 197, 1400I, 1400L(c), to section 168 prior to its amendment by the Tax Reform Act of 1986 (100 Stat. 2121) (former section 168), or to an additional first year depreciation deduction provision of the Internal Revenue Code (for example, section 168(k), 1400L(b), or 1400N(d)) is a change in method of accounting under section 446(e) and the regulations under section 446(e), section 1016(a)(2) does not permanently affect a taxpayer's lifetime income.

(i) *Examples.*—The application of section 1016(a)(1) and (2) may be illustrated by the following examples:

Example (1). The case of Corporation A discloses the following facts:

(1) Year	(2) Amount allowed	(3) Amount allowed which reduced taxpayer's taxes	(4) Amount allowable	(5) Amount allowable but not less than amount allowed	(6) Amount allowable but not less than amount allowed which reduced taxpayer's taxes
1949	$6,000	$5,500	$5,000	$6,000	$5,500
1950	7,000	7,000	6,500	7,000	7,000
1951	5,000	4,000	6,500	6,500	6,500
Total, 1949-51	...	...	...	19,500	19,000
1952	$6,500	$6,500	$6,000	...	$6,500
1953	5,000	4,000	4,000	...	4,000
1954	4,500	4,500	6,000	...	6,000
Total, 1952-54	...	...	...	...	$16,500

The cost or other basis is to be adjusted by $16,500 with respect to the years 1952-54, that is, by the amount allowable but not less than the amount allowed which reduced the taxpayer's taxes. An adjustment must also be made with respect to the years 1949-1951, the amount of such adjustment depending upon whether an election was properly made under section 1020, or section 113(d) of the Internal Revenue Code of 1939. If no such election was made, the amount of the adjustment with respect to the years 1949-1951 is $19,500, that is, the amount allowed but not less than the amount allowable. If an election was properly made, the amount of the adjustment with respect to the years 1949-1951 is $19,000, that is, the amount allowable but not less than the amount allowed which reduced the taxpayer's taxes.

Example (2). Corporation A, which files its returns on the basis of a calendar year, purchased a building on January 1, 1950, at a cost of $100,000. On the basis of the facts reasonably known to exist at the end of 1950, a period of 50 years should have been used as the correct useful life of the building; nevertheless, depreciation was computed by Corporation A on the basis of a useful life of 25 years, and was allowed for 1950 through 1953 as a deduction in an annual amount of $4,000. The building was sold on January 1, 1954. Corporation A did not make an election under section 1020, or section 113(d) of the Internal Revenue Code of 1939. No part of the amount allowed Corporation A for any of the years 1950 through 1953 resulted in a reduction of Corporation A's taxes. The adjusted basis of the building as of January 1, 1954, is $88,166, computed as follows:

Taxable year	Adjustments to basis as of beginning of taxable year	Adjusted basis on Jan. 1	Remaining life on Jan. 1	Depreciation allowable	Depreciation allowed
1950	...	$100,000	50	$2,000	$4,000
1951	$4,000	96,000	49	1,959	4,000
1952	8,000	92,000	48	1,917	4,000
1953	9,917	90,083	47	1,917	4,000
1954	11,834	88,166	....	.....	.....

Example (3). The facts are the same as in example (2), except that Corporation A made a proper election under section 1020. In such case, the adjusted basis of the building as of January 1, 1954, is $92,000, computed as follows:

Taxable year	Adjustments to basis as of beginning of taxable year	Adjusted basis on Jan. 1	Remaining life on Jan. 1	Depreciation allowable	Depreciation allowed
1950	. . . .	$100,000	50	$2,000	$4,000
1951	$2,000	98,000	49	2,000	4,000
1952	4,000	96,000	48	2,000	4,000
1953	6,000	94,000	47	2,000	4,000
1954	8,000	92,000	. . . .	. . . .	. . . . . .

Example (4). If it is assumed that in example (2), or in example (3), all of the deduction allowed Corporation A for 1953 had resulted in a reduction of A's taxes, the adjustment to the basis of the building for depreciation for 1953 would reflect the entire $4,000 deduction. In such case, the adjusted basis of the building as of January 1, 1954, would be $86,083 in example (2), and $90,000 in example (3).

Example (5). The facts are the same as in example (2), except that for the year 1950 all of the $4,000 amount allowed Corporation A as a de-

duction for depreciation for that year resulted in a reduction of A's taxes. In such case, the adjustments to the basis of the building remain the same as those set forth in example (2).

Example (6). The facts are the same as in example (3) except that for the year 1950 all of the $4,000 amount allowed Corporation A as a deduction for depreciation resulted in a reduction of A's taxes. In such case, the adjusted basis of the building as of January 1, 1954, is $90,123, computed as follows:

Taxable year	Adjustments to basis as of beginning of taxable year	Adjusted basis on Jan. 1	Remaining life on Jan. 1	Depreciation allowable	Depreciation allowed
1950	. . . .	$100,000	50	$2,000	$4,000
1951	$4,000	96,000	49	1,959	4,000
1952	5,959	94,041	48	1,959	4,000
1953	7,918	92,082	47	1,959	4,000
1954	9,877	90,123	. . . . .	. . . . . .	. . . . . .

(j) *Effective date.*—(1) *In general.*—Except as provided in paragraph (j)(2) of this section, this section applies on or after December 30, 2003. For the applicability of regulations before December 30, 2003, see § 1.1016-3 in effect prior to December 30, 2003 (§ 1.1016-3 as contained in 26 CFR part 1 edition revised as of April 1, 2003).

(2) *Depreciation or amortization changes.*— Paragraph (h) of this section applies to a change in depreciation or amortization for property subject to section 167, 168, 197, 1400I, 1400L(c), to former section 168, or to an additional first year depreciation deduction provision of the Internal Revenue Code (for example, section 168(k), 1400L(b), or 1400N(d)) for taxable years ending on or after December 30, 2003. [Reg. § 1.1016-3.]

☐ [T.D. 6265, 11-6-57. *Amended by T.D. 9105, 12-30-2003 and T.D. 9307, 12-22-2006.*]

[Reg. § 1.1016-4]

§ 1.1016-4. Exhaustion, wear and tear, obsolescence, amortization, and depletion; periods during which income was not subject to tax.— (a) Adjustments to basis must be made for exhaustion, wear and tear, obsolescence, amortization, and depletion to the extent actually sustained in respect of:

(1) Any period before March 1, 1913,

(2) Any period since February 28, 1913, during which the property was held by a person or organization not subject to income taxation under chapter 1 of the Code or prior income tax laws,

(3) Any period since February 28, 1913, and before January 1, 1958, during which the property was held by a person subject to tax under part I, subchapter L, chapter 1 of the Code, or prior income tax law, to the extent that section 1016(a)(2) does not apply, or

(4) Any period since February 28, 1913, during which such property was held by a person subject to tax under part II of subchapter L, chapter 1 of the Code, or prior income tax law, to the extent that section 1016(a)(2) does not apply.

(b) The amount of the adjustments described in paragraph (a) of this section actually sustained is that amount charged off on the books of the taxpayer where such amount is considered by the Commissioner to be reasonable. Otherwise, the amount actually sustained will be the amount that would have been allowable as a deduction:

(1) During the period described in paragraph (a)(1) or (2) of this section, had the tax-

payer been subject to income tax during those periods, or

(2) During the period described in paragraph (a)(3) or (4) of this section, with respect to property held by a taxpayer described in that paragraph, to the extent that section 1016(a)(2) was inapplicable to such property during that period.

In the case of a taxpayer subject to the adjustment required by subparagraph (1) or (2) of this paragraph, depreciation shall be determined by using the straight line method. [Reg. § 1.1016-4.]

□ [T.D. 6265, 1-6-57. *Amended by T.D. 6610, 8-30-62 and T.D. 6681, 10-16-63.*]

[Reg. § 1.1016-5]

§ 1.1016-5. **Miscellaneous adjustments to basis.**—(a) *Certain stock distributions.*—(1) In the case of stock, the cost or other basis must be diminished by the amount of distributions previously made which, under the law applicable to the year in which the distribution was made, either were tax free or were applicable in reduction of basis (not including distributions made by a corporation which was classified as a personal service corporation under the provisions of the Revenue Act of 1918 (40 Stat. 1057) or the Revenue Act of 1921 (42 Stat. 227), out of its earnings or profits which were taxable in accordance with the provisions of section 218 of the Revenue Act of 1918 or the Revenue Act of 1921). For adjustments to basis in the case of certain corporate distributions, see section 301 and the regulations thereunder.

(2) The application of subparagraph (1) of this paragraph may be illustrated by the following example:

Example. A, who makes his returns upon the calendar year basis, purchased stock in 1923 for $5,000. He received in 1924 a distribution of $2,000 paid out of earnings and profits of the corporation accumulated before March 1, 1913. The adjusted basis for determining the gain or loss from the sale or other disposition of the stock in 1954 is $5,000 less $2,000, or $3,000, and the amount of the gain or loss from the sale or other disposition of the stock is the difference between $3,000 and the amount realized from the sale or other disposition.

(b) *Amortizable bond premium.*—(1) *In general.*—A holder's basis in a bond is reduced by the amount of bond premium used to offset qualified stated interest income under § 1.171-2. This reduction occurs when the holder takes the qualified stated interest into account under the holder's regular method of accounting.

(2) *Special rules for taxable bonds.*—A holder's basis in a taxable bond is reduced by the amount of bond premium allowed as a deduction under § 1.171-3(c)(5)(ii) (relating to the issuer's call of a taxable bond) or under § 1.171-2(a)(4)(i)(A) (relating to excess bond premium).

(3) *Special rule for tax-exempt obligations.*—A holder's basis in a tax-exempt obligation is reduced by the amount of excess bond premium that is treated as a nondeductible loss under § 1.171-2(a)(4)(ii).

(c) *Municipal bonds.*—In the case of a municipal bond (as defined in section 75(b)), basis shall be adjusted to the extent provided in section 75 or as provided in section 22(o) of the Internal Revenue Code of 1939, and the regulations thereunder.

(d) *Sale or exchange of residence.*—Where the acquisition of a new residence results in the nonrecognition of any part of the gain on the sale, exchange, or involuntary conversion of the old residence, the basis of the new residence shall be reduced by the amount of the gain not so recognized pursuant to section 1034(a), or section 112(n) of the Internal Revenue Code of 1939, and the regulations thereunder. See section 1034(e) and the regulations thereunder.

(e) *Loans from Commodity Credit Corporation.*—In the case of property pledged to the Commodity Credit Corporation, the basis of such property shall be increased by the amount received as a loan from such corporation and treated by the taxpayer as income for the year in which received under section 77, or under section 123 of the Internal Revenue Code of 1939. The basis of such property shall be reduced to the extent of any deficiency on such loan with respect to which the taxpayer has been relieved from liability.

(f) *Deferred development and exploration expenses.*—Expenditures for development and exploration of mines or mineral deposits treated as deferred expenses under sections 615 and 616, or under the corresponding provisions of prior income tax laws, are chargeable to capital account and shall be an adjustment to the basis of the property to which they relate. The basis so adjusted shall be reduced by the amount of such expenditures allowed as deductions which results in a reduction for any taxable year of the taxpayer's taxes under subtitle A (other than chapter 2 relating to tax on self-employment income) of the Code, or prior income, war-profits, or excess-profits tax laws, but not less than the amounts allowable under such provisions for the taxable year and prior years. This amount is considered as the "tax-benefit amount allowed" and shall be determined in accordance with paragraph (e) of § 1.1016-3. For example, if a taxpayer purchases unexplored and undeveloped mining property for $1,000,000 and at the close of the development stage has incurred exploration and development costs of $9,000,000 treated as deferred expenses, the basis of such property at such time for computing gain or loss will be $10,000,000. Assuming that the taxpayer in this example has operated the mine for several years and has deducted allowable percentage depletion in the amount of $2,000,000 and has deducted allowable deferred exploration and development expenditures of $2,000,000, the basis of the property in the taxpayer's hands for purposes of determining gain or loss from a sale will be $6,000,000.

(g) *Sale of land with unharvested crop.*—In the case of an unharvested crop which is sold, exchanged, or involuntarily converted with the land and which is considered as property used in the trade or business under section 1231, the basis of such crop shall be increased by the amount of the items which are attributable to the production of such crop and which are disallowed, under section 268, as deductions in computing taxable income. The basis of any other property shall be decreased by the amount of any such items which are attributable to such other property, notwithstanding any provisions of section 1016 or of this section to the contrary. For example, if the items attributable to the production of an unharvested crop consist only of fertilizer costing $100 and $50 depreciation on a tractor used only to cultivate such crop, and such items are disallowed under section 268, the adjustments to the basis of such crop shall include an increase of $150 for such items and the adjustments to the basis of the tractor shall include a reduction of $50 for depreciation.

(h) *Consent dividends.*—(1) In the case of amounts specified in a shareholder's consent to which section 28 of the Internal Revenue Code of 1939 applies, the basis of the consent stock shall be increased to the extent provided in subsection (h) of such section.

(2) In the case of amounts specified in a shareholder's consent to be treated as a consent dividend to which section 565 applies, the basis of the consent stock shall be increased by the amount which, under section 565(c)(2), is treated as contributed to the capital of the corporation.

(i) *Stock in foreign personal holding company.*— In the case of the stock of a United States shareholder in a foreign personal holding company, basis shall be adjusted to the extent provided in section 551(f) or corresponding provisions of prior income tax laws.

(j) *Research and experimental expenditures.*—Research and experimental expenditures treated as deferred expenses under section 174(b) are chargeable to capital account and shall be an adjustment to the basis of the property to which they relate. The basis so adjusted shall be reduced by the amount of such expenditures allowed as deductions which results in a reduction for any taxable year of the taxpayer's taxes under subtitle A (other than chapter 2 relating to tax on self-employment income) of the Code, or prior income, war-profits, or excess-profits tax laws, but not less than the amounts allowable under such provisions for the taxable year and prior years. This amount is considered as the "tax-benefit amount allowed" and shall be determined in accordance with paragraph (e) of § 1.1016-3.

(k) *Deductions disallowed in connection with disposal of coal or domestic iron ore.*—Basis shall be adjusted by the amount of the deductions disallowed under section 272 with respect to the disposal of coal or domestic iron ore covered by section 631.

(l) *Expenditures attributable to grants or loans covered by section 621.*—In the case of expenditures attributable to a grant or loan made to a taxpayer by the United States for the encouragement of exploration for, or development or mining of, critical and strategic minerals or metals, basis shall be adjusted to the extent provided in section 621, or in section 22(b)(15) of the Internal Revenue Code of 1939.

(m) *Trademark and trade name expenditures.*— Trademark and trade name expenditures treated as deferred expenses under section 177 are chargeable to capital account and shall be an adjustment to the basis of the property to which they relate. The basis so adjusted shall be reduced by the amount of such expenditures allowed as deductions which results in a reduction for any taxable year of the taxpayer's taxes under subtitle A (other than chapter 2, relating to tax on self-employment income) of the Code, but not less than the amounts allowable under such section for the taxable year and prior years. This amount is considered as the "tax-benefit amount allowed" and shall be determined in accordance with paragraph (e) of § 1.1016-3.

(n) *Life insurance companies.*—In the case of any evidence of indebtedness referred to in section 818(b), the basis shall be adjusted to the extent of the adjustments required under section 818(b) (or the corresponding provisions of prior income tax laws) for the taxable year and all prior taxable years. The basis of any such evidence of indebtedness shall be reduced by the amount of the adjustment required under section 818(b) (or the corresponding provision of prior income tax laws) on account of amortizable premium and shall be increased by the amount of the adjustment required under section 818(b) on account of accruable discounts.

(o) *Stock and indebtedness of electing small business corporation.*—In the case of a shareholder of an electing small business corporation, as defined in section 1371(b), the basis of the shareholder's stock in such corporation, and the basis of any indebtedness of such corporation owing to the shareholder, shall be adjusted to the extent provided in § § 1.1375-4, 1.1376-1, and 1.1376-2.

(p) *Gift tax paid on certain property acquired by gift.*—Basis shall be adjusted by that amount of the gift tax paid in respect of property acquired by gift which, under section 1015(d), is an increase in the basis of such property.

(q) *Section 38 property.*—In the case of property which is or has been section 38 property (as defined in section 48(a)), the basis shall be adjusted to the extent provided in section 48(g) and in section 203(a)(2) of the Revenue Act of 1964.

(r) *Stock in controlled foreign corporations and other property.*—In the case of stock in controlled foreign corporations (or foreign corporations which were controlled foreign corporations) and of property by reason of which a person is considered as owning such stock, the basis shall be adjusted to the extent provided in section 961.

(s) *Original issue discount.*—In the case of certain corporate obligations issued at a discount after May 27, 1969, the basis shall be increased under section 1232(a)(3)(E) by the amount of original issue discount included in the holder's gross income pursuant to section 1232(a)(3).

(t) *Section 23 credit.*—In the case of property with respect to which a credit has been allowed under section 23 or former section 44C (relating to residential energy credit), basis shall be adjusted as provided in paragraph (k) of § 1.23-3. [Reg. § 1.1016-5.]

☐ [*T.D.* 6265, 11-6-57. *Amended by T.D.* 6452, 2-3-60, *T.D.* 6610, 9-30-62, *T.D.* 6647, 4-10-63, *T.D.* 6693, 12-2-63, *T.D.* 6795, 1-28-65, *T.D.* 6841, 7-26-65, *T.D.* 7154, 12-27-71, *T.D.* 7717, 8-26-80; *T.D.* 8146, 7-15-87 *and T.D.* 8746, 12-30-97.]

[Reg. § 1.1016-6]

§ 1.1016-6. Other applicable rules.— (a) Adjustments must always be made to eliminate double deductions or their equivalent. Thus, in the case of the stock of a subsidiary company, the basis thereof must be properly adjusted for the amount of the subsidiary company's losses for the years in which consolidated returns were made.

(b) In determining basis, and adjustments to basis, the principles of estoppel apply, as elsewhere under the Code, and prior internal revenue laws. [Reg. § 1.1016-6.]

☐ [*T.D.* 6265, 11-6-57.]

[Reg. § 1.1016-10]

§ 1.1016-10. Substituted basis.— (a) Whenever it appears that the basis of property in the hands of the taxpayer is a substituted basis, as defined in section 1016(b), the adjustments indicated in § § 1.1016-1 to 1.1016-6, inclusive, shall be made after first making in respect of such substituted basis proper adjustments of a similar nature in respect of the period during which the property was held by the transferor, donor, or grantor, or during which the other property was held by the person for whom the basis is to be determined. In addition, whenever it appears that the basis of property in the hands of the taxpayer is a substituted basis, as defined in section 1016(b)(1), the adjustments indicated in § § 1.1016-7 to 1.1016-9, inclusive, and in sec-

tion 1017 shall also be made, whenever necessary, after first making in respect of such substituted basis a proper adjustment of a similar nature in respect of the period during which the property was held by the transferor, donor, or grantor. Similar rules shall also be applied in the case of a series of substituted bases.

(b) The application of this section may be illustrated by the following example:

Example. A, who makes his returns upon the calendar year basis, in 1935 purchased the X Building and subsequently gave it to his son B. B exchanged the X Building for the Y Building in a tax-free exchange, and then gave the Y Building to his wife C. C, in determining the gain from the sale or disposition of the Y Building in 1954, is required to reduce the basis of the building by deductions for depreciation which were successively allowed (but not less than the amount allowable) to A and B upon the X Building and to B upon the Y Building, in addition to the deductions for depreciation allowed (but not less than the amount allowable) to herself during her ownership of the Y Building. [Reg. § 1.1016-10.]

☐ [*T.D.* 6265, 11-6-57.]

[Reg. § 1.1017-1]

§ 1.1017-1. Basis reductions following a discharge of indebtedness.—(a) *General rule for section 108(b)(2)(E).*—This paragraph (a) applies to basis reductions under section 108(b)(2)(E) that are required by section 108(a)(1)(A) or (B) because the taxpayer excluded discharge of indebtedness (COD income) from gross income. A taxpayer must reduce in the following order, to the extent of the excluded COD income (but not below zero), the adjusted bases of property held on the first day of the taxable year following the taxable year that the taxpayer excluded COD income from gross income (in proportion to adjusted basis)—

(1) Real property used in a trade or business or held for investment, other than real property described in section 1221(1), that secured the discharged indebtedness immediately before the discharge;

(2) Personal property used in a trade or business or held for investment, other than inventory, accounts receivable, and notes receivable, that secured the discharged indebtedness immediately before the discharge;

(3) Remaining property used in a trade or business or held for investment, other than inventory, accounts receivable, notes receivable, and real property described in section 1221(1);

(4) Inventory, accounts receivable, notes receivable, and real property described in section 1221(1); and

(5) Property not used in a trade or business nor held for investment.

(b) *Operating rules.*—(1) *Prior tax-attribute reduction.*—The amount of excluded COD income applied to reduce basis does not include any

COD income applied to reduce tax attributes under sections 108(b)(2)(A) through (D) and, if applicable, section 108(b)(5). For example, if a taxpayer excludes $100 of COD income from gross income under section 108(a) and reduces tax attributes by $40 under sections 108(b)(2)(A) through (D), the taxpayer is required to reduce the adjusted bases of property by $60 ($100 – $40) under section 108(b)(2)(E).

(2) *Multiple discharged indebtednesses.*—If a taxpayer has COD income attributable to more than one discharged indebtedness resulting in the reduction of tax attributes under sections 108(b)(2)(A) through (D) and, if applicable, section 108(b)(5), paragraph (b)(1) of this section must be applied by allocating the tax-attribute reductions among the indebtednesses in proportion to the amount of COD income attributable to each discharged indebtedness. For example, if a taxpayer excludes $20 of COD income attributable to secured indebtedness A and excludes $80 of COD income attributable to unsecured indebtedness B (a total exclusion of $100), and if the taxpayer reduces tax attributes by $40 under sections 108(b)(2)(A) through (D), the taxpayer must reduce the amount of COD income attributable to secured indebtedness A to $12 ($20 – ($20 / $100 × $40)) and must reduce the amount of COD income attributable to unsecured indebtedness B to $48 ($80 – ($80 / $100 × $40)).

(3) *Limitation on basis reductions under section 108(b)(2)(E) in bankruptcy or insolvency.*—If COD income arises from a discharge of indebtedness in a title 11 case or while the taxpayer is insolvent, the amount of any basis reduction under section 108(b)(2)(E) shall not exceed the excess of—

(i) The aggregate of the adjusted bases of property and the amount of money held by the taxpayer immediately after the discharge; over

(ii) The aggregate of the liabilities of the taxpayer immediately after the discharge.

(4) *Transactions to which section 381 applies.*.—If a taxpayer realizes COD income that is excluded from gross income under section 108(a) either during or after a taxable year in which the taxpayer is the distributor or transferor of assets in a transaction described in section 381(a), the basis of property acquired by the acquiring corporation in the transaction must reflect the reductions required by section 1017 and this section. For this purpose, the basis of property of the distributor or transferor corporation immediately prior to the transaction described in section 381(a), but after the determination of tax for the year of the distribution or transfer of assets, will be available for reduction under section 108(b)(2). However, the basis of stock or securities of the acquiring corporation, if any, received by the taxpayer in exchange for the transferred assets shall not be available for reduction under section 108(b)(2). See §1.108-7. This paragraph

(b)(4) applies to discharges of indebtedness occurring on or after May 10, 2004.

(c) *Modification of ordering rules for basis reductions under sections 108(b)(5) and 108(c).*—(1) *In general.*—The ordering rules prescribed in paragraph (a) of this section apply, with appropriate modifications, to basis reductions under sections 108(b)(5) and (c). Thus, a taxpayer that elects to reduce basis under section 108(b)(5) may, to the extent that the election applies, reduce only the adjusted basis of property described in paragraphs (a)(1), (2), and (3) of this section and, if an election is made under paragraph (f) of this section, paragraph (a)(4) of this section. Within paragraphs (a)(1),(2), (3) and (4) of this section, such a taxpayer may reduce only the adjusted bases of depreciable property. A taxpayer that elects to apply section 108(c) may reduce only the adjusted basis of property described in paragraphs (a)(1) and (3) of this section and, within paragraphs (a)(1) and (3) of this section, may reduce only the adjusted bases of depreciable real property. Furthermore, for basis reductions under section 108(c), a taxpayer must reduce the adjusted basis of the qualifying real property to the extent of the discharged qualified real property business indebtedness before reducing the adjusted bases of other depreciable real property. The term *qualifying real property* means real property with respect to which the indebtedness is qualified real property business indebtedness within the meaning of section 108(c)(3). See paragraphs (f) and (g) of this section for elections relating to section 1221(1) property and partnership interests.

(2) *Partial basis reductions under section 108(b)(5).*—If the amount of basis reductions under section 108(b)(5) is less than the amount of the COD income excluded from gross income under section 108(a), the taxpayer must reduce the balance of its tax attributes, including any remaining adjusted bases of depreciable and other property, by following the ordering rules under section 108(b)(2). For example, if a taxpayer excludes $100 of COD income from gross income under section 108(a) and elects to reduce the adjusted bases of depreciable property by $10 under section 108(b)(5), the taxpayer must reduce its remaining tax attributes by $90, starting with net operating losses under section 108(b)(2).

(3) *Modification of fresh start rule for prior basis reductions under section 108(b)(5).*—After reducing the adjusted bases of depreciable property under section 108(b)(5), a taxpayer must compute the limitation on basis reductions under section 1017(b)(2) using the aggregate of the remaining adjusted bases of property. For example, if, immediately after the discharge of indebtedness in a title 11 case, a taxpayer's adjusted bases of property is $100 and its undischarged indebtedness is $70, and if the taxpayer elects to reduce the adjusted bases of depreciable

property by $10 under section 108(b)(5); section 1017(b)(2) limits any further basis reductions under section 108(b)(2)(E) to $20 (($100 – $10) – $70).

(d) *Changes in security.*—If any property is added or eliminated as security for an indebtedness during the one-year period preceding the discharge of that indebtedness, such addition or elimination shall be disregarded where a principal purpose of the change is to affect the taxpayer's basis reductions under section 1017.

(e) *Depreciable property.*—For purposes of this section, the term *depreciable property* means any property of a character subject to the allowance for depreciation or amortization, but only if the basis reduction would reduce the amount of depreciation or amortization which otherwise would be allowable for the period immediately following such reduction. Thus, for example, a lessor cannot reduce the basis of leased property where the lessee's obligation in respect of the property will restore to the lessor the loss due to depreciation during the term of the lease, since the lessor cannot take depreciation in respect of such property.

(f) *Election to treat section 1221(1) real property as depreciable.*—(1) *In general.*—For basis reductions under section 108(b)(5) and basis reductions relating to qualified farm indebtedness, a taxpayer may elect under sections 1017(b)(3)(E) and (4)(C), respectively, to treat real property described in section 1221(1) as depreciable property. This election is not available, however, for basis reductions under section 108(c).

(2) *Time and manner.*—To make an election under section 1017(b)(3)(E) or (4)(C), a taxpayer must enter the appropriate information on Form 982, *Reduction of Tax Attributes Due to Discharge of Indebtedness (and Section 1082 Basis Adjustment)*, and attach the form to a timely filed (including extensions) Federal income tax return for the taxable year in which the taxpayer has COD income that is excluded from gross income under section 108(a). An election under this paragraph (f) may be revoked only with the consent of the Commissioner.

(g) *Partnerships.*—(1) *Partnership COD income.*—For purposes of paragraph (a) of this section, a taxpayer must treat a distributive share of a partnership's COD income as attributable to a discharged indebtedness secured by the taxpayer's interest in that partnership.

(2) *Partnership interest treated as depreciable property.*—(i) *In general.*—For purposes of making basis reductions, if a taxpayer makes an election under section 108(b)(5) (or 108(c)), the taxpayer must treat a partnership interest as depreciable property (or depreciable real property) to the extent of the partner's proportionate share of the partnership's basis in depreciable property (or depreciable real property), provided that the partnership consents to a corresponding reduction in the partnership's basis (inside basis) in depreciable property (or depreciable real property) with respect to such partner.

(ii) *Request by partner and consent of partnership.*—(A) *In general.*—Except as otherwise provided in this paragraph (g)(2)(ii), a taxpayer may choose whether or not to request that a partnership reduce the inside basis of its depreciable property (or depreciable real property) with respect to the taxpayer, and the partnership may grant or withhold such consent, in its sole discretion. A request by the taxpayer must be made before the due date (including extensions) for filing the taxpayer's Federal income tax return for the taxable year in which the taxpayer has COD income that is excluded from gross income under section 108(a).

(B) *Request for consent required.*—A taxpayer must request a partnership's consent to reduce inside basis if, at the time of the discharge, the taxpayer owns (directly or indirectly) a greater than 50 percent interest in the capital and profits of the partnership, or if reductions to the basis of the taxpayer's depreciable property (or depreciable real property) are being made with respect to the taxpayer's distributive share of COD income of the partnership.

(C) *Granting of request required.*—A partnership must consent to reduce its partners' shares of inside basis with respect to a discharged indebtedness if consent is requested with respect to that indebtedness by partners owning (directly or indirectly) an aggregate of more than 80 percent of the capital and profits interests of the partnership or five or fewer partners owning (directly or indirectly) an aggregate of more than 50 percent of the capital and profits interests of the partnership. For example, if there is a cancellation of partnership indebtedness that is secured by real property used in a partnership's trade or business, and if partners owning (in the aggregate) 90 percent of the capital and profits interests of the partnership elect to exclude the COD income under section 108(c), the partnership must make the appropriate reductions in those partners' shares of inside basis.

(iii) *Partnership consent statement.*—(A) *Partnership requirement.*—A consenting partnership must include with the Form 1065, U.S. Partnership Return of Income, for the taxable year following the year that ends with or within the taxable year the taxpayer excludes COD income from gross income under section 108(a), and must provide to the taxpayer on or before the due date of the taxpayer's return (including extensions) for the taxable year in which the taxpayer excludes COD income from gross income, a statement that—

(1) Contains the name, address, and taxpayer identification number of the partnership; and

(2) States the amount of the reduction of the partner's proportionate interest in the adjusted bases of the partnership's depreciable property or depreciable real property, whichever is applicable.

(B) Taxpayer's requirement.—For taxable years beginning before January 1, 2003, statements described in § 1.1017-1(g)(2)(iii)(A) must be attached to a taxpayer's timely filed (including extensions) Federal income tax return for the taxable year in which the taxpayer has COD income that is excluded from gross income under section 108(a). For taxable years beginning after December 31, 2002, taxpayers must retain the statements and keep them available for inspection in the manner required by § 1.6001-1(e), but are not required to attach the statements to their returns.

(iv) Partner's share of partnership basis.—(A) *In general.*—For purposes of this paragraph (g), a partner's proportionate share of the partnership's basis in depreciable property (or depreciable real property) is equal to the sum of—

(1) The partner's section 743(b) basis adjustments to items of partnership depreciable property (or depreciable real property); and

(2) The common basis depreciation deductions (but not including remedial allocations of depreciation deductions under § 1.704-3(d)) that, under the terms of the partnership agreement effective for the taxable year in which the discharge of indebtedness occurs, are reasonably expected to be allocated to the partner over the property's remaining useful life. The assumptions made by a partnership in determining the reasonably expected allocation of depreciation deductions must be consistent for each partner. For example, a partnership may not treat the same depreciation deductions as being reasonably expected by more than one partner.

(B) Effective date.—This paragraph (g)(2)(iv) applies to elections made under sections 108(b)(5) and 108(c) on or after December 15, 1999.

(v) Treatment of basis reduction.—(A) *Basis adjustment.*—The amount of the reduction to the basis of depreciable partnership property constitutes an adjustment to the basis of partnership property with respect to the partner only. No adjustment is made to the common basis of partnership property. Thus, for purposes of income, deduction, gain, loss, and distribution, the partner will have a special basis for those partnership properties the bases of which are adjusted under section 1017 and this section.

(B) Recovery of adjustments to basis of partnership property.—Adjustments to the basis of partnership property under this section are recovered in the manner described in § 1.743-1.

(C) Effect of basis reduction.—Adjustments to the basis of partnership property under this section are treated in the same manner and have the same effect as an adjustment to the basis of partnership property under section 743(b). The following example illustrates this paragraph (g)(2)(v):

Example. (i) A, B, and C are equal partners in partnership PRS, which owns (among other things) Asset 1, an item of depreciable property with a basis of $30,000. A's basis in its partnership interest is $20,000. Under the terms of the partnership agreement, A's share of the depreciation deductions from Asset 1 over its remaining useful life will be $10,000. Under section 1017, A requests, and PRS agrees, to decrease the basis of Asset 1 with respect to A by $10,000.

(ii) In the year following the reduction of basis under section 1017, PRS amends its partnership agreement to provide that items of depreciation and loss from Asset 1 will be allocated equally between B and C. In that year, A's distributive share of the partnership's common basis depreciation deductions from Asset 1 is now $0. Under § 1.743-1(j)(4)(ii)(B), the amount of the section 1017 basis adjustment that A recovers during the year is $1,000. A will report $1,000 of ordinary income because A's distributive share of the partnership's common basis depreciation deductions from Asset 1 ($0) is insufficient to offset the amount of the section 1017 basis adjustment recovered by A during the year ($1,000).

(iii) In the following year, PRS sells Asset 1 for $15,000 and recognizes a $12,000 loss. This loss is allocated equally between B and C, and A's share of the loss is $0. Upon the sale of Asset 1, A recovers its entire remaining section 1017 basis adjustment ($9,000). A will report $9,000 of ordinary income.

(D) Effective date.—This paragraph (g)(2)(v) applies to elections made under sections 108(b)(5) and 108(c) on or after December 15, 1999.

(3) Partnership basis reduction.—The rules of this section (including this paragraph (g)) apply in determining the properties to which the partnership's basis reductions must be made.

(h) Special allocation rule for cases to which section 1398 applies.—If a bankruptcy estate and a taxpayer to whom section 1398 applies (concerning only individuals under Chapter 7 or 11 of title 11 of the United States Code) hold property subject to basis reduction under section 108(b)(2)(E) or (5) on the first day of the taxable year following the taxable year of discharge, the bankruptcy estate must reduce all of the adjusted bases of its property before the taxpayer is required to reduce any adjusted bases of property.

(i) Effective date.—This section applies to discharges of indebtedness occurring on or after October 22, 1998. [Reg. § 1.1017-1.]

☐ [*T.D.* 6158, 1-6-56. *Amended by T.D.* 8787, 10-21-98; *T.D.* 8847, 12-14-99; *T.D.* 9080, 7-17-2003; *T.D.* 9100, 12-18-2003 (*corrected* 2-2-2004); *T.D.* 9127, 5-10-2004 *and T.D.* 9300, 12-7-2006.]

[Reg. §1.1019-1]

§1.1019-1. Property on which lessee had made improvements.—In any case in which a lessee of real property has erected buildings or made other improvements upon the leased property and the lease is terminated by forfeiture or otherwise resulting in the realization by such lessor of income which, were it not for the provisions of section 109, would be includible in gross income of the lessor, the amount so excluded from gross income shall not be taken into account in determining the basis or the adjusted basis of such property or any portion thereof in the hands of the lessor. If, however, in any taxable year beginning before January 1, 1942, there has been included in the gross income of the lessor an amount representing any part of the value of such property attributable to such buildings or improvements, the basis of each portion of such property shall be properly adjusted for the amount so included in gross income. For example, A leased in 1930 to B for a period of 25 years unimproved real property and in accordance with the terms of the lease B erected a building on the property. It was estimated that upon expiration of the lease the building would have a depreciated value of $50,000, which value the lessor elected to report (beginning in 1931) as income over the term of the lease. This method of reporting was used until 1942. In 1952 B forfeits the lease. The amount of $22,000 reported as income by A during the years 1931 to 1941, inclusive, shall be added to the basis of the property represented by the improvements in the hands of A. If in such case A did not report during the period of the lease any income attributable to the value of the building erected by the lessee and the lease was forfeited in 1940 when the building was worth $75,000, such amount, having been included in gross income under the law applicable to that year, is added to the basis of the property represented by the improvements in the hands of A. As to treatment of such property for the purposes of capital gains and losses, see subchapter P (sections 1201 and following), chapter 1 of the Code. [Reg. §1.1019-1.]

☐ [*T.D.* 6265, 11-6-57.]

[Reg. §1.1021-1]

§1.1021-1. Sale of annuities.—In the case of a transfer for value of an annuity contract to which section 72(g) and paragraph (a) of §1.72-10 apply, the transferor shall adjust his basis in such contract as of the time immediately prior to such transfer by subtracting from the premiums or other consideration he has paid or is deemed to have paid for such contract all amounts he has received or is deemed to have received under such annuity contract to the extent that such amounts were not includible in the gross income of the transferor or other recipient under the applicable income tax law. In any case where the amounts which were not includible in the gross income of the recipient were received or deemed to have been received by such transferor exceed the amounts paid or deemed paid by him, the adjusted basis of the contract shall be zero. The income realized by the transferor on such a transfer shall not exceed the total of the amounts received as consideration for the transfer. [Reg. §1.1021-1.]

☐ [*T.D.* 6211, 11-14-56.]

Common Nontaxable Exchanges

[Reg. §1.1031-0]

§1.1031-0. Table of contents.

This section lists the captions that appear in the regulations under section 1031.

(c) Computation of basis of properties received.

(d) Examples.

(e) Effective date.

§ 1.1031(k)-1. Treatment of deferred exchanges.

(a) Overview.

(b) Identification and receipt requirements.

(c) Identification of replacement property before the end of the identification period.

(d) Receipt of identified replacement property.

(e) Special rules for identification and receipt of replacement property to be produced.

(f) Receipt of money or other property.

(g) Safe harbors.

(h) Interest and growth factors.

(i) [Reserved]

(j) Determination of gain or loss recognized and the basis of property received in a deferred exchange.

(k) Definition of disqualified person.

(l) [Reserved]

(m) Definition of fair market value.

(n) No inference with respect to actual or constructive receipt rules outside of section 1031.

(o) Effective date. [Reg. § 1.1031-0.]

□ [T.D. 8346, 4-25-91.]

[Reg. § 1.1031(a)-1]

§ 1.1031(a)-1. Property held for productive use in trade or business or for investment.— (a) *In general.*—(1) *Exchanges of property solely for property of a like kind.*—Section 1031(a)(1) provides an exception from the general rule requiring the recognition of gain or loss upon the sale or exchange of property. Under section 1031(a)(1), no gain or loss is recognized if property held for productive use in a trade or business or for investment is exchanged solely for property of a like kind to be held either for productive use in a trade or business or for investment. Under section 1031(a)(1), property held for productive use in trade or business may be exchanged for property held for investment. Similarly, under section 1031(a)(1), property held for investment may be exchanged for property held for productive use in a trade or business. However, section 1031(a)(2) provides that section 1031(a)(1) does not apply to any exchange of—

(i) Stock in trade or other property held primarily for sale;

(ii) Stocks, bonds, or notes;

(iii) Other securities or evidences of indebtedness or interest;

(iv) Interests in a partnership;

(v) Certificates of trust or beneficial interests; or

(vi) Choses in action.

Section 1031(a)(1) does not apply to any exchange of interests in a partnership regardless of whether the interests exchanged are general or limited partnership interests or are interests in the same partnership or in different partnerships. An interest in a partnership that has in effect a valid election under section 761(a) to be excluded from the application of all of subchapter K is treated as an interest in each of the assets of the partnership and not as an interest in a partnership for purposes of section 1031(a)(2)(D) and paragraph (a)(1)(iv) of this section. An exchange of an interest in such a partnership does not qualify for nonrecognition of gain or loss under section 1031 with respect to any asset of the partnership that is described in section 1031(a)(2) or to the extent the exchange of assets of the partnership does not otherwise satisfy the requirements of section 1031(a).

(2) *Exchanges of property not solely for property of a like kind.*—A transfer is not within the provisions of section 1031(a) if, as part of the consideration, the taxpayer receives money or property which does not meet the requirements of section 1031(a), but the transfer, if otherwise qualified, will be within the provisions of either section 1031(b) or (c). Similarly, a transfer is not within the provisions of section 1031(a) if, as part of the consideration, the other party to the exchange assumes a liability of the taxpayer (or acquires property from the taxpayer that is subject to a liability), but the transfer, if otherwise qualified, will be within the provisions of either section 1031(b) or (c). A transfer of property meeting the requirements of section 1031(a) may be within the provisions of section 1031(a) even though the taxpayer transfers in addition property not meeting the requirements of section 1031(a) or money. However, the nonrecognition treatment provided by section 1031(a) does not apply to the property transferred which does not meet the requirements of section 1031(a).

(b) *Definition of "like kind."* .—As used in section 1031(a), the words "like kind" have reference to the nature or character of the property and not to its grade or quality. One kind or class of property may not, under that section, be exchanged for property of a different kind or class. The fact that any real estate involved is improved or unimproved is not material, for that fact relates only to the grade or quality of the property and not to its kind or class. Unproductive real estate held by one other than a dealer for future use or future realization of the increment in value is held for investment and not primarily for sale. For additional rules for exchanges of personal property, see § 1.1031(a)-2.

(c) *Examples of exchanges of property of a "like kind."* .—No gain or loss is recognized if (1) a taxpayer exchanges property held for productive use in his trade or business, together with cash, for other property of like kind for the same use, such as a truck for a new truck or a passenger automobile for a new passenger automobile to be used for a like purpose; or (2) a taxpayer who is not a dealer in real estate exchanges city real estate for a ranch or farm, or exchanges a leasehold of a fee with 30 years or more to run for real estate, or exchanges improved real estate for unimproved real estate; or (3) a taxpayer exchanges investment property and cash for investment property of a like kind.

(d) *Examples of exchanges not solely in kind.*— Gain or loss is recognized if, for instance, a taxpayer exchanges (1) Treasury bonds maturing March 15, 1958, for Treasury bonds maturing December 15, 1968, unless section 1037(a) (or so much of section 1031 as relates to section 1037(a)) applies to such exchange, or (2) a real estate mortgage for consolidated farm loan bonds.

(e) *Effective date relating to exchanges of partnership interests.*—The provisions of paragraph (a)(1) of this section relating to exchanges of partnership interests apply to transfers of property made by taxpayers on or after April 25, 1991. [Reg. § 1.1031(a)-1.]

☐ [*T.D. 6210, 11-6-56. Amended by T.D. 6935, 11-16-67; T.D. 8343, 4-11-91 and T.D. 8346, 4-25-91.*]

[Reg. § 1.1031(a)-2]

§ 1.1031(a)-2. Additional rules for exchanges of personal property.—(a) *Introduction.*—Section 1.1031(a)-1(b) provides that the nonrecognition rules of section 1031 do not apply to an exchange of one kind or class of property for property of a different kind or class. This section contains additional rules for determining whether personal property has been exchanged for property of a like kind or like class. Personal properties of a like class are considered to be of a "like kind" for purposes of section 1031. In addition, an exchange of properties of a like kind may qualify under section 1031 regardless of whether the properties are also of a like class. In determining whether exchanged properties are of a like kind, no inference is to be drawn from the fact that the properties are not of a like class. Under paragraph (b) of this section, depreciable tangible personal properties are of a like class if they are either within the same General Asset Class (as defined in paragraph (b)(2) of this section) or within the same Product Class (as defined in paragraph (b)(3) of this section). Paragraph (c) of this section provides rules for exchanges of intangible personal property and nondepreciable personal property.

(b) *Depreciable tangible personal property.*— (1) *General rule.*—Depreciable tangible personal property is exchanged for property of a "like kind" under section 1031 if the property is exchanged for property of a like kind or like class. Depreciable tangible personal property is of a like class to other depreciable tangible personal property if the exchanged properties are either within the same General Asset Class or within the same Product Class. A single property may not be classified within more than one General

Asset Class or within more than one Product Class. In addition, property classified within any General Asset Class may not be classified within a Product Class. A property's General Asset Class or Product Class is determined as of the date of the exchange.

(2) *General Asset Classes.*—Except as provided in paragraphs (b)(4) and (b)(5) of this section, property within a General Asset Class consists of depreciable tangible personal property described in one of asset classes 00.11 through 00.28 and 00.4 of Rev. Proc. 87-56, 1987-2 C.B. 674. These General Asset Classes describe types of depreciable tangible personal property that frequently are used in many businesses. The General Asset Classes are as follows:

(i) Office furniture, fixtures, and equipment (asset class 00.11),

(ii) Information systems (computers and peripheral equipment) (asset class 00.12),

(iii) Data handling equipment, except computers (asset class 00.13),

(iv) Airplanes (airframes and engines), except those used in commercial or contract carrying of passengers or freight, and all helicopters (airframes and engines) (asset class 00.21),

(v) Automobiles, taxis (asset class 00.22),

(vi) Buses (asset class 00.23),

(vii) Light general purpose trucks (asset class 00.241),

(viii) Heavy general purpose trucks (asset class 00.242),

(ix) Railroad cars and locomotives, except those owned by railroad transportation companies (asset class 00.25),

(x) Tractor units for use over-the-road (asset class 00.26),

(xi) Trailers and trailer-mounted containers (asset class 00.27),

(xii) Vessels, barges, tugs, and similar water-transportation equipment, except those used in marine construction (asset class 00.28), and

(xiii) Industrial steam and electric generation and/or distribution systems (asset class 00.4).

(3) *Product classes.*—Except as provided in paragraphs (b)(4) and (5) of this section, or as provided by the Commissioner in published guidance of general applicability, property within a product class consists of depreciable tangible personal property that is described in a 6-digit product class within Sectors 31, 32, and 33 (pertaining to manufacturing industries) of the North American Industry Classification System (NAICS), set forth in Executive Office of the President, Office of Management and Budget, *North American Industry Classification System*, United States, 2002 (NAICS Manual), as periodically updated. Copies of the NAICS Manual may be obtained from the National Technical Information Service, an agency of the U.S. Depart-

ment of Commerce, and may be accessed on the internet. Sectors 31 through 33 of the NAICS Manual contain listings of specialized industries for the manufacture of described products and equipment. For this purpose, any 6-digit NAICS product class with a last digit of 9 (a miscellaneous category) is not a product class for purposes of this section. If a property is listed in more than one product class, the property is treated as listed in any one of those product classes. A property's 6-digit product class is referred to as the property's NAICS code.

(4) *Modifications of NAICS product classes.*— The product classes of the NAICS Manual may be updated or otherwise modified from time to time as the manual is updated, effective on or after the date of the modification. The NAICS Manual generally is modified every five years, in years ending in a 2 or 7 (such as 2002, 2007, and 2012). The applicability date of the modified NAICS Manual is announced in the Federal Register and generally is January 1 of the year the NAICS Manual is modified. Taxpayers may rely on these modifications as they become effective in structuring exchanges under this section. Taxpayers may rely on the previous NAICS Manual for transfers of property made by a taxpayer during the one-year period following the effective date of the modification. For transfers of property made by a taxpayer on or after January 1, 1997, and on or before January 1, 2003, the NAICS Manual of 1997 may be used for determining product classes of the exchanged property.

(5) *Administrative procedures for revising general asset classes and product classes.*—The Commissioner may, through published guidance of general applicability, supplement, modify, clarify, or update the guidance relating to the classification of properties provided in this paragraph (b). (See § 601.601(d)(2) of this chapter.) For example, the Commissioner may determine not to follow (in whole or in part) a general asset class for purposes of identifying property of like class, may determine not to follow (in whole or in part) any modification of product classes published in the NAICS Manual, or may determine that other properties not listed within the same or in any product class or general asset class nevertheless are of a like class. The Commissioner also may determine that two items of property that are listed in separate product classes or in product classes with a last digit of 9 are of a like class, or that an item of property that has a NAICS code is of a like class to an item of property that does not have a NAICS code.

(6) *No inference outside of section 1031.*—The rules provided in this section concerning the use of general asset classes or product classes are limited to exchanges under section 1031. No inference is intended with respect to the classification of property for other purposes, such as depreciation.

(7) *Examples.*—The application of this paragraph (b) may be illustrated by the following examples:

Example 1. Taxpayer A transfers a personal computer (asset class 00.12) to B in exchange for a printer (asset class 00.12). With respect to A, the properties exchanged are within the same General Asset Class and therefore are of a like class.

Example 2. Taxpayer C transfers an airplane (asset class 00.21) to D in exchange for a heavy general purpose truck (asset class 00.242). The properties exchanged are not of a like class because they are within different General Asset Classes. Because each of the properties is within a General Asset Class, the properties may not be classified within a Product Class. The airplane and heavy general purpose truck are also not of a like kind. Therefore, the exchange does not qualify for nonrecognition of gain or loss under section 1031.

Example 3. Taxpayer E transfers a grader to F in exchange for a scraper. Neither property is within any of the general asset classes. However, both properties are within the same product class (NAICS code 333120). The grader and scraper are of a like class and deemed to be of a like kind for purposes of section 1031.

Example 4. Taxpayer G transfers a personal computer (asset class 00.12), an airplane (asset class 00.21) and a sanding machine (NAICS code 333210), to H in exchange for a printer (asset class 00.12), a heavy general purpose truck (asset class 00.242) and a lathe (NAICS code 333210). The personal computer and the printer are of a like class because they are within the same general asset class. The sanding machine and the lathe are of a like class because they are within the same product class (although neither property is within any of the general asset classes). The airplane and the heavy general purpose truck are neither within the same general asset class nor within the same product class, and are not of a like kind.

(8) *Transition rule.*—Properties within the same product classes based on the 4-digit codes contained in Division D of the Executive Office of the President, Office of Management and Budget, Standard Industrial Classification Manual (1987), will be treated as property of a like class for transfers of property made by taxpayers on or before May 19, 2005.

(c) *Intangible personal property and nondepreciable personal property.*—(1) *General rule.*—An exchange of intangible personal property or nondepreciable personal property qualifies for nonrecognition of gain or loss under section 1031 only if the exchanged properties are of a like kind. No like classes are provided for these properties. Whether intangible personal property is of a like kind to other intangible personal property generally depends on the nature or character of the rights involved (*e.g.,* a patent or a copyright) and also on the nature or character of the underlying property to which the intangible personal property relates.

(2) *Goodwill and going concern value.*—The goodwill or going concern value of a business is not of a like kind to the goodwill or going concern value of another business.

(3) *Examples.*—The application of this paragraph (c) may be illustrated by the following examples:

Example (1). Taxpayer K exchanges a copyright on a novel for a copyright on a different novel. The properties exchanged are of a like kind.

Example (2). Taxpayer J exchanges a copyright on a novel for a copyright on a song. The properties exchanged are not of a like kind.

(d) *Effective date.*—Except as otherwise provided in this paragraph (d), this section applies to exchanges occurring on or after April 11, 1991. Paragraphs (b)(3) through (b)(6), *Example 3* and *Example 4* of paragraph (b)(7), and paragraph (b)(8) of this section apply to transfers of property made by taxpayers on or after August 12, 2004. However, taxpayers may apply paragraphs (b)(3) through (b)(6), and *Example 3* and *Example 4* of paragraph (b)(7) of this section to transfers of property made by taxpayers on or after January 1, 1997, in taxable years for which the period of limitation for filing a claim for refund or credit under section 6511 has not expired. [Reg. §1.1031(a)-2.]

☐ [*T.D.* 8343, 4-11-91. *Amended by T.D.* 9151, 8-12-2004 *and T.D.* 9202, 5-18-2005.]

[Reg. §1.1031(b)-1]

§1.1031(b)-1. Receipt of other property or money in tax-free exchange.—(a) If the taxpayer receives other property (in addition to property permitted to be received without recognition of gain) or money—

(1) In an exchange described in section 1031(a) of property held for investment or productive use in trade or business for property of like kind to be held either for productive use or for investment,

(2) In an exchange described in section 1035(a) of insurance policies or annuity contracts,

(3) In an exchange described in section 1036(a) of common stock for common stock, or preferred stock for preferred stock, in the same

corporation and not in connection with a corporate reorganization, or

(4) In an exchange described in section 1037(a) of obligations of the United States, issued under the Second Liberty Bond Act (31 U.S.C. 774(2)), solely for other obligations issued under such Act,

the gain, if any, to the taxpayer will be recognized under section 1031(b) in an amount not in excess of the sum of the money and the fair market value of the other property, but the loss, if any, to the taxpayer from such an exchange will not be recognized under section 1031(c) to any extent.

(b) The application of this section may be illustrated by the following examples:

Example (1). A, who is not a dealer in real estate, in 1954 exchanges real estate held for investment, which he purchased in 1940 for $5,000, for other real estate (to be held for productive use in trade or business) which has a fair market value of $6,000, and $2,000 in cash. The gain from the transaction is $3,000, but is recognized only to the extent of the cash received of $2,000.

Example (2). (a) B, who uses the cash receipts and disbursements method of accounting and the calendar year as his taxable year, has never elected under section 454(a) to include in gross income currently the annual increase in the redemption price of non-interest-bearing obligations issued at a discount. In 1943, for $750 each, B purchased four $1,000 series E United States savings bonds bearing an issue date of March 1, 1943.

(b) On October 1, 1963, the redemption value of each such bond was $1,396, and the total redemption value of the four bonds was $5,584. On that date B submitted the four $1,000 series E bonds to the United States in a transaction in which one of such $1,000 bonds was reissued by issuing four $100 series E United States savings bonds bearing an issue date of March 1, 1943, and by considering six $100 series E bonds bearing an issue date of March 1, 1943, to have been issued. The redemption value of each such $100 series E bond was $139.60 on October 1, 1963. Then, as part of the transaction, the six $100 series E bonds so considered to have been issued and the three $1,000 series E bonds were exchanged, in an exchange qualifying under section 1037(a), for five $1,000 series H United States savings bonds plus $25.60 in cash.

(c) The gain realized on the exchange qualifying under section 1037(a) is $2,325.60, determined as follows:

Amount realized:

Par value of five series H bonds	$5,000.00
Cash received	25.60
Total realized	5,025.60

Less: Adjusted basis of series E bonds surrendered in
the exchange:

Three $1,000 series E bonds	$2,250	
Six $100 series E bonds at $75 each	450	2,700.00
Gain realized		$2,325.60

(d) Pursuant to section 1031(b), only $25.60 (the money received) of the total gain of $2,325.60 realized on the exchange is recognized at the time of exchange and must be included in B's gross income for 1963. The $2,300 balance of the gain ($2,325.60 less $25.60) must be included in B's gross income for the taxable year in which the series H bonds are redeemed or disposed of, or reach final maturity, whichever is earlier, as provided in paragraph (c) of § 1.454-1.

(e) The gain on the four $100 series E bonds, determined by using $75 as a basis for each such bond, must be included in B's gross income for the taxable year in which such bonds are redeemed or disposed of, or reach final maturity, whichever is earlier.

Example (3). (a) The facts are the same as in example (2), except that, as part of the transaction, the $1,000 series E bond is reissued by considering ten $100 series E bonds bearing an issue date of March 1, 1943, to have been issued. Six of the $100 series E bonds so considered to have been issued are surrendered to the United States as part of the exchange qualifying under section 1037(a) and the other four are immediately redeemed.

(b) Pursuant to section 1031(b), only $25.60 (the money received) of the total gain of $2,325.60 realized on the exchange qualifying under section 1037(a) is recognized at the time of the exchange and must be included in B's gross income for 1963. The $2,300 balance of the gain ($2,325.60 less $25.60) realized on such exchange must be included in B's gross income for the taxable year in which the series H bonds are redeemed or disposed of, or reach final maturity, whichever is earlier, as provided in paragraph (c) of § 1.454-1.

(c) The redemption on October 1, 1963, of the four $100 series E bonds considered to have been issued at such time results in gain of $258.40, which is then recognized and must be included in B's gross income for 1963. This gain of $258.40 is the difference between the $558.40 redemption value of such bonds on the date of the exchange and the $300 (4 × $75) paid for such series E bonds in 1943.

Example (4). On November 1, 1963, C purchased for $91 a marketable United States bond which was originally issued at its par value of $100 under the Second Liberty Bond Act. On February 1, 1964, in an exchange qualifying under section 1037(a), C surrendered the bond to the United States for another marketable United States bond, which then had a fair market value of $92, and $1.85 in cash, $0.85 of which was interest. The $0.85 interest received is includible in gross income for the taxable year of the ex-

change, but the $2 gain ($93 less $91) realized on the exchange is recognized for such year under section 1031(b) to the extent of $1 (the money received). Under section 1031(d), C's basis in the bond received in exchange is $91 (his basis of $91 in the bond surrendered, reduced by the $1 money received and increased by the $1 gain recognized).

(c) Consideration received in the form of an assumption of liabilities (or a transfer subject to a liability) is to be treated as "other property or money" for the purposes of section 1031(b). Where, on an exchange described in section 1031(b), each party to the exchange either assumes a liability of the other party or acquires property subject to a liability, then, in determining the amount of "other property or money" for purposes of section 1031(b), consideration given in the form of an assumption of liabilities (or a receipt of property subject to a liability) shall be offset against consideration received in the form of an assumption of liabilities (or a transfer subject to a liability). See § 1.1031(d)-2, examples (1) and (2). [Reg. § 1.1031(b)-1.]

☐ [*T.D.* 6210, 11-6-56. *Amended by T.D.* 6935, 11-16-67.]

[Reg. § 1.1031(b)-2]

§ 1.1031(b)-2. Safe harbor for qualified intermediaries.—(a) In the case of simultaneous transfers of like-kind properties involving a qualified intermediary (as defined in § 1.1031(k)-1(g)(4)(iii)), the qualified intermediary is not considered the agent of the taxpayer for purposes of section 1031(a). In such a case, the transfer and receipt of property by the taxpayer is treated as an exchange.

(b) In the case of simultaneous exchanges of like-kind properties involving a qualified intermediary (as defined in § 1.1031(k)-1(g)(4)(iii)), the receipt by the taxpayer of an evidence of indebtedness of the transferee of the qualified intermediary is treated as the receipt of an evidence of indebtedness of the person acquiring property from the taxpayer for purposes of section 453 and § 15a.453-1(b)(3)(i) of this chapter.

(c) Paragraph (a) of this section applies to transfers of property made by taxpayers on or after June 10, 1991.

(d) Paragraph (b) of this section applies to transfers of property made by taxpayers on or after April 20, 1994. A taxpayer may choose to apply paragraph (b) of this section to transfers of property made on or after June 10, 1991. [Reg. § 1.1031(b)-2.]

☐ [*T.D.* 8346, 4-25-91. *Amended by T.D.* 8535, 4-19-94.]

[Reg. § 1.1031(c)-1]

§ 1.1031(c)-1. Nonrecognition of loss.—Section 1031(c) provides that a loss shall not be recognized from an exchange of property described in section 1031(a), 1035(a), 1036(a), or 1037(a) where there is received in the exchange other property or money in addition to property permitted to be received without recognition of gain or loss. See example (4) of paragraph (a)(3) of § 1.1037-1 for an illustration of the application of this section in the case of an exchange of United States obligations described in section 1037(a). [Reg. § 1.1031(c)-1.]

□ [*T.D. 6210, 11-6-56. Amended by T.D. 6935, 11-16-67.*]

[Reg. § 1.1031(d)-1]

§ 1.1031(d)-1. Property acquired upon a tax-free exchange.—(a) If, in an exchange of property solely of the type described in section 1031, section 1035(a), section 1036(a), or section 1037(a), no part of the gain or loss was recognized under the law applicable to the year in which the exchange was made, the basis of the property acquired is the same as the basis of the property transferred by the taxpayer with proper adjustments to the date of the exchange. If additional consideration is given by the taxpayer in the exchange, the basis of the property acquired shall be the same as the property transferred increased by the amount of additional consideration given (see section 1016 and the regulations thereunder).

(b) If, in an exchange of properties of the type indicated in section 1031, section 1035(a), section 1036(a), or section 1037(a), gain to the taxpayer was recognized under the provisions of section 1031(b) or a similar provision of a prior revenue law, on account of the receipt of money in the transaction, the basis of the property acquired is the basis of the property transferred (adjusted to the date of the exchange), decreased by the amount of money received and increased by the amount of gain recognized on the exchange. The application of this paragraph may be illustrated by the following example:

Example. A, an individual in the moving and storage business, in 1954 transfers one of his moving trucks with an adjusted basis in his hands of $2,500 to B in exchange for a truck (to be used in A's business) with a fair market value of $2,400 and $200 in cash. A realizes a gain of $100 upon the exchange, all of which is recognized under section 1031(b). The basis of the truck acquired by A is determined as follows:

Adjusted basis of A's former truck	$2,500
Less: Amount of money received	200
Difference	2,300
Plus: Amount of gain recognized	100
Basis of truck acquired by A	$2,400

(c) If, upon an exchange of properties of the type described in section 1031, section 1035(a),

section 1036(a), or section 1037(a), the taxpayer received other property (not permitted to be received without the recognition of gain) and gain from the transaction was recognized as required under section 1031(b), or a similar provision of a prior revenue law, the basis (adjusted to the date of the exchange) of the property transferred by the taxpayer, decreased by the amount of any money received and increased by the amount of gain recognized, must be allocated to and is the basis of the properties (other than money) received on the exchange. For the purpose of the allocation of the basis of the properties received, there must be assigned to such other property an amount equivalent to its fair market value at the date of the exchange. The application of this paragraph may be illustrated by the following example:

Example. A, who is not a dealer in real estate, in 1954 transfers real estate held for investment which he purchased in 1940 for $10,000 in exchange for other real estate (to be held for investment) which has a fair market value of $9,000, an automobile which has a fair market value of $2,000, and $1,500 in cash. A realizes a gain of $2,500, all of which is recognized under section 1031(b). The basis of the property received in exchange is the basis of the real estate A transfers ($10,000) decreased by the amount of money received ($1,500) and increased in the amount of gain that was recognized ($2,500), which results in a basis for the property received of $11,000. This basis of $11,000 is allocated between the automobile and the real estate received by A, the basis of the automobile being its fair market value at the date of the exchange, $2,000, and the basis of the real estate received being the remainder, $9,000.

(d) Section 1031(c) and, with respect to section 1031 and section 1036(a), similar provisions of prior revenue laws provide that no loss may be recognized on an exchange of properties of a type described in section 1031, section 1035(a), section 1036(a), or section 1037(a), although the taxpayer receives other property or money from the transaction. However, the basis of the property or properties (other than money) received by the taxpayer is the basis (adjusted to the date of the exchange) of the property transferred, decreased by the amount of money received. This basis must be allocated to the properties received, and for this purpose there must be allocated to such other property an amount of such basis equivalent to its fair market value at the date of the exchange.

(e) If, upon an exchange of properties of the type described in section 1031, section 1035(a), section 1036(a), or section 1037(a), the taxpayer also exchanged other property (not permitted to be transferred without the recognition of gain or loss) and gain or loss from the transaction is recognized under section 1002 or a similar provision of a prior revenue law, the basis of the property acquired is the total basis of the properties transferred (adjusted to the date of the exchange) increased by the amount of gain and decreased by the amount of loss recognized on the other property. For purposes of this rule, the taxpayer is deemed to have received in exchange for such other property an amount equal to its fair market value on the date of the exchange. The application of this paragraph may be illustrated by the following example:

Example. A exchanges real estate held for investment plus stock for real estate to be held for investment. The real estate transferred has an adjusted basis of $10,000 and a fair market value of $11,000. The stock transferred has an adjusted basis of $4,000 and a fair market value of $2,000. The real estate acquired has a fair market value of $13,000. A is deemed to have received a $2,000 portion of the acquired real estate in exchange for the stock, since $2,000 is the fair market value of the stock at the time of the exchange. A $2,000 loss is recognized under section 1002 on the exchange of the stock for real estate. No gain or loss is recognized on the exchange of the real estate since the property received is of the type permitted to be received without recognition of gain or loss. The basis of the real estate acquired by A is determined as follows:

Adjusted basis of real estate transferred . . .	$10,000
Adjusted basis of stock transferred	4,000
	14,000
Less:	
Loss recognized on transfer of stock	2,000
Basis of real estate acquired upon the exchange	12,000

[Reg. § 1.1031(d)-1.]

☐ [*T.D.* 6210, 11-6-56. *Amended by T.D.* 6453, 2-16-60 *and T.D.* 6935, 11-16-67.]

[Reg. § 1.1031(d)-1T]

§ 1.1031(d)-1T. Coordination of section 1060 with section 1031 (temporary).—If the properties exchanged under section 1031 are part of a group of assets which constitute a trade or business under section 1060, the like-kind property and other property or money which are treated as transferred in exchange for the like-kind property shall be excluded from the allocation rules of section 1060. However, section 1060 shall apply to property which is not like-kind property or other property or money which is treated as transferred in exchange for the like-kind property. For application of the section 1060 allocation rules to property which is not part of the like-kind exchange, see § 1.1060-1(b), (c), and (d) *Example (1).* [Temporary Reg. § 1.1031(d)-1T.]

☐ [*T.D.* 8215, 7-15-88. *Amended by T.D.* 8858, 1-5-2000 *and T.D.* 8940, 2-12-2001.]

[Reg. § 1.1031(d)-2]

§ 1.1031(d)-2. Treatment of assumption of liabilities.—For the purposes of section 1031(d), the amount of any liabilities of the taxpayer assumed by the other party to the exchange (or of any liabilities to which the property exchanged by the taxpayer is subject) is to be treated as money received by the taxpayer upon the exchange, whether or not the assumption resulted in a recognition of gain or loss to the taxpayer under the law applicable to the year in which the exchange was made. The application of this section may be illustrated by the following examples:

Example (1). B, an individual, owns an apartment house which has an adjusted basis in his hands of $500,000, but which is subject to a mortgage of $150,000. On September 1, 1954, he transfers the apartment house to C, receiving in exchange therefor $50,000 in cash and another apartment house with a fair market value on that date of $600,000. The transfer to C is made subject to the $150,000 mortgage. B realizes a gain of $300,000 on the exchange, computed as follows:

Value of property received	$600,000
Cash	50,000
Liabilities subject to which old property was transferred	150,000
Total consideration received	800,000
Less: Adjusted basis of property transferred	500,000
Gain realized	300,000

Under section 1031(b), $200,000 of the $300,000 gain is recognized. The basis of the apartment house acquired by B upon the exchange is $500,000, computed as follows:

Adjusted basis of property transferred		$500,000
Less: Amount of money received:		
Cash	$ 50,000	
Amount of liabilities subject to which property was transferred	150,000	
		200,000
Difference		300,000
Plus: Amount of gain recognized upon the exchange		200,000
Basis of property acquired upon the exchange		$500,000

Example (2). (a) D, an individual, owns an apartment house. On December 1, 1955, the apartment house owned by D has an adjusted basis in his hands of $100,000, a fair market value of $220,000, but is subject to a mortgage of $80,000. E, an individual, also owns an apartment house. On December 1, 1955, the apartment house owned by E has an adjusted basis of $175,000, a fair market value of $250,000, but is subject to a mortgage of $150,000. On December 1, 1955, D transfers his apartment house to E, receiving in exchange therefor $40,000 in cash and the apartment house owned by E. Each apartment house is transferred subject to the mortgage on it.

(b) D realizes a gain of $120,000 on the exchange, computed as follows:

Value of property received	$250,000
Cash	40,000
Liabilities subject to which old property was transferred	80,000
Total consideration received	370,000

Less: Adjusted basis of property		
transferred	$100,000	
Liabilities to which new		
property is subject	150,000	$250,000
Gain realized		$120,000

For purposes of section 1031(b), the amount of "other property or money" received by D is $40,000. (Consideration received by D in the form of a transfer subject to a liability of $80,000 is offset by consideration given in the form of a receipt of property subject to a $150,000 liability. Thus, only the consideration received in the form of cash, $40,000, is treated as "other property or money" for purposes of section 1031(b).) Accordingly, under section 1031(b), $40,000 of the $120,000 gain is recognized. The basis of the apartment house acquired by D is $170,000, computed as follows:

Adjusted basis of property transferred	$100,000
Liabilities to which new property is subject .	150,000
Total	$250,000
Less: Amount of money received:	
Cash $40,000	
Amount of liabilities subject	
to which property was	
transferred 80,000	
	$120,000
Difference	$130,000
Plus: Amount of gain recognized upon the	
exchange	40,000
Basis of property acquired upon the	
exchange	$170,000

(c) E realizes a gain of $75,000 on the exchange, computed as follows:

Value of property received	$220,000
Liabilities subject to which old property was	
transferred	$150,000
Total consideration received	370,000
Less: Adjusted basis of property	
transferred $175,000	
Cash 40,000	
Liabilities to which new	
property is subject 80,000	
	$295,000
Gain realized	$ 75,000

For purposes of section 1031(b), the amount of "other property or money" received by E is $30,000. (Consideration received by E in the form of a transfer subject to a liability of $150,000 is offset by consideration given in the form of a receipt of property subject to an $80,000 liability and by the $40,000 cash paid by E. Although consideration received in the form of cash or other property is not offset by consideration given in the form of an assumption of liabilities or a receipt of property subject to a liability, consideration given in the form of cash or other property is offset against consideration received in the form of an assumption of liabilities or a transfer of property subject to a liability.) Accordingly, under section 1031(b), $30,000 of the

$75,000 gain is recognized. The basis of the apartment house acquired by E is $175,000, computed as follows:

Adjusted basis of property transferred . . .	$175,000
Cash	40,000
Liabilities to which new property is subject	80,000
Total	295,000
Less: Amount of money received:	
Amount of liabilities subject	
to which property was	
transferred $150,000	
	150,000
Difference	$145,000
Plus: Amount of gain recognized upon the	
exchange	30,000
Basis of property acquired upon the	
exchange	$175,000

[Reg. § 1.1031(d)-2.]

☐ [T.D. 6210, 11-6-56.]

[Reg. § 1.1031(e)-1]

§ 1.1031(e)-1. Exchanges of livestock of different sexes.—Section 1031(e) provides that livestock of different sexes are not property of like kind. Section 1031(e) and this section are applicable to taxable years to which the Internal Revenue Code of 1954 applies. [Reg. § 1.1031(e)-1.]

☐ [T.D. 7141, 9-21-71.]

[Reg. § 1.1031(j)-1]

§ 1.1031(j)-1. Exchanges of multiple properties.—(a) *Introduction.*—(1) *Overview.*—As a general rule, the application of section 1031 requires a property-by-property comparison for computing the gain recognized and basis of property received in a like-kind exchange. This section provides an exception to this general rule in the case of an exchange of multiple properties. An exchange is an exchange of multiple properties if, under paragraph (b)(2) of this section, more than one exchange group is created. In addition, an exchange is an exchange of multiple properties if only one exchange group is created but there is more than one property being transferred or received within that exchange group. Paragraph (b) of this section provides rules for computing the amount of gain recognized in an exchange of multiple properties qualifying for nonrecognition of gain or loss under section 1031. Paragraph (c) of this section provides rules for computing the basis of properties received in an exchange of multiple properties qualifying for nonrecognition of gain or loss under section 1031.

(2) *General Approach.*—(i) In general, the amount of gain recognized in an exchange of multiple properties is computed by first separating the properties transferred and the properties received by the taxpayer in the exchange into exchange groups in the manner described in paragraph (b)(2) of this section. The separation of the properties transferred and the properties re-

ceived in the exchange into exchange groups involves matching up properties of a like kind or like class to the extent possible. Next, all liabilities assumed by the taxpayer as part of the transaction are offset by all liabilities of which the taxpayer is relieved as part of the transaction, with the excess liabilities assumed or relieved allocated in accordance with paragraph (b)(2)(ii) of this section. Then, the rules of section 1031 and the regulations thereunder are applied separately to each exchange group to determine the amount of gain recognized in the exchange. See §§ 1.1031(b)-1 and 1.1031(c)-1. Finally, the rules of section 1031 and the regulations thereunder are applied separately to each exchange group to determine the basis of the properties received in the exchange. See §§ 1.1031(d)-1 and 1.1031(d)-2.

(ii) For purposes of this section, the exchanges are assumed to be made at arms' length, so that the aggregate fair market value of the property received in the exchange equals the aggregate fair market value of the property transferred. Thus, the amount realized with respect to the properties transferred in each exchange group is assumed to equal their aggregate fair market value.

(b) *Computation of gain recognized.*—(1) *In general.*—In computing the amount of gain recognized in an exchange of multiple properties, the fair market value must be determined for each property transferred and for each property received by the taxpayer in the exchange. In addition, the adjusted basis must be determined for each property transferred by the taxpayer in the exchange.

(2) *Exchange groups and residual group.*—The properties transferred and the properties received by the taxpayer in the exchange are separated into exchange groups and a residual group to the extent provided in this paragraph (b)(2).

(i) *Exchange groups.*—Each exchange group consists of the properties transferred and received in the exchange, all of which are of a like kind or like class. If a property could be included in more than one exchange group, the taxpayer may include the property in any of those exchange groups. Property eligible for inclusion within an exchange group does not include money or property described in section 1031(a)(2) (*i.e.*, stock in trade or other property held primarily for sale, stocks, bonds, notes, other securities or evidences of indebtedness or interest, interests in a partnership, certificates of trust or beneficial interests, or choses in action). For example, an exchange group may consist of all exchanged properties that are within the same General Asset Class or within the same Product Class (as defined in § 1.1031(a)-2(b)). Each exchange group must consist of at least one property transferred and at least one property received in the exchange.

(ii) *Treatment of liabilities.*—(A) All liabilities assumed by the taxpayer as part of the exchange are offset against all liabilities of which the taxpayer is relieved as part of the exchange, regardless of whether the liabilities are recourse or nonrecourse and regardless of whether the liabilities are secured by or otherwise relate to specific property transferred or received as part of the exchange. See §§ 1.1031(b)-1(c) and 1.1031(d)-2. For purposes of this section, liabilities assumed by the taxpayer as part of the exchange consist of liabilities of the other party to the exchange assumed by the taxpayer and liabilities subject to which the other party's property is transferred in the exchange. Similarly, liabilities of which the taxpayer is relieved as part of the exchange consist of liabilities of the taxpayer assumed by the other party to the exchange and liabilities subject to which the taxpayer's property is transferred.

(B) If there are excess liabilities assumed by the taxpayer as part of the exchange (*i.e.*, the amount of liabilities assumed by the taxpayer exceeds the amount of liabilities of which the taxpayer is relieved), the excess is allocated among the exchange groups (but not to the residual group) in proportion to the aggregate fair market value of the properties received by the taxpayer in the exchange groups. The amount of excess liabilities assumed by the taxpayer that are allocated to each exchange group may not exceed the aggregate fair market value of the properties received in the exchange group.

(C) If there are excess liabilities of which the taxpayer is relieved as part of the exchange (*i.e.*, the amount of liabilities of which the taxpayer is relieved exceeds the amount of liabilities assumed by the taxpayer), the excess is treated as a Class I asset for purposes of making allocations to the residual group under paragraph (b)(2)(iii) of this section.

(D) Paragraphs (b)(2)(ii)(A), (B), and (C) of this section are applied in the same manner even if section 1031 and this section apply to only a portion of a larger transaction (such as a transaction described in section 1060(c) and § 1.1060-1T(b)). In that event, the amount of excess liabilities assumed by the taxpayer or the amount of excess liabilities of which the taxpayer is relieved is determined based on all liabilities assumed by the taxpayer and all liabilities of which the taxpayer is relieved as part of the larger transaction.

(iii) *Residual group.*—If the aggregate fair market value of the properties transferred in all of the exchange groups differs from the aggregate fair market value of the properties received in all of the exchange groups (taking liabilities into account in the manner described in paragraph (b)(2)(ii) of this section), a residual group is created. The residual group consists of an amount of money or other property having an aggregate fair market value equal to that difference. The residual group consists of either money or other property transferred in the exchange or money or other property received in the exchange, but not both. For this purpose, other property includes property described in section 1031(a)(2) (*i.e.*, stock in trade or other property held primarily for sale, stocks, bonds, notes, other securities or evidences of indebtedness or interest, interests in a partnership, certificates of trust or beneficial interests, or choses in action), property transferred that is not of a like kind or like class with any property received, and property received that is not of a like kind or like class with any property transferred. The money and properties that are allocated to the residual group are considered to come from the following assets in the following order: first from Class I assets, then from Class II assets, then from Class III assets, and then from Class IV assets. The terms Class I assets, Class II assets, Class III assets, and Class IV assets have the same meanings as in §1.338-6(b), to which reference is made by §1.1060-1(c)(2). Within each Class, taxpayers may choose which properties are allocated to the residual group.

(iv) *Exchange group surplus and deficiency.*—For each of the exchange groups described in this section, an "exchange group surplus" or "exchange group deficiency," if any, must be determined. An exchange group surplus is the excess of the aggregate fair market value of the properties received (less the amount of any excess liabilities assumed by the taxpayer that are allocated to that exchange group) in an exchange group over the aggregate fair market value of the properties transferred in that exchange group. An exchange group deficiency is the excess of the aggregate fair market value of the properties transferred in an exchange group over the aggregate fair market value of the properties received (less the amount of any excess liabilities assumed by the taxpayer that are allocated to that exchange group) in that exchange group.

(3) *Amount of gain recognized.*—(i) For purposes of this section, the amount of gain or loss realized with respect to each exchange group and the residual group is the difference between the aggregate fair market value of the properties transferred in that exchange group or residual group and the properties' aggregate adjusted basis. The gain realized with respect to each exchange group is recognized to the extent of the lesser of the gain realized and the amount of the exchange group deficiency, if any. Losses realized with respect to an exchange group are not recognized. See section 1031(a) and (c). The total amount of gain recognized under section 1031 in the exchange is the sum of the amount of gain recognized with respect to each exchange group. With respect to the residual group, the gain or loss realized (as determined under this section) is recognized as provided in section 1001 or other applicable provision of the Code.

(ii) The amount of gain or loss realized and recognized with respect to properties transferred by the taxpayer that are not within any exchange group or the residual group is determined under section 1001 and other applicable provisions of the Code, with proper adjustments made for all liabilities not allocated to the exchange groups or the residual group.

(c) *Computation of basis of properties received.*—In an exchange of multiple properties qualifying for nonrecognition of gain or loss under section 1031 and this section, the aggregate basis of properties received in each of the exchange groups is the aggregate adjusted basis of the properties transferred by the taxpayer within that exchange group, increased by the amount of gain recognized by the taxpayer with respect to that exchange group, increased by the amount of the exchange group surplus or decreased by the amount of the exchange group deficiency, and increased by the amount, if any, of excess liabilities assumed by the taxpayer that are allocated to that exchange group. The resulting aggregate basis of each exchange group is allocated proportionately to each property received in the exchange group in accordance with its fair market value. The basis of each property received within the residual group (other than money) is equal to its fair market value.

(d) *Examples.*—The application of this section may be illustrated by the following examples:

Example 1. (i) K exchanges computer A (asset class 00.12) and automobile A (asset class 00.22), both of which were held by K for productive use in its business, with W for printer B (asset class 00.12) and automobile B (asset class 00.22), both of which will be held by K for productive use in its business. K's adjusted basis and the fair market value of the exchanged properties are as follows:

	Adjusted Basis	Fair Market Value
Computer A	$ 375	$1000
Automobile A	1500	4000
Printer B	—	2050
Automobile B	—	2950

(ii) Under paragraph (b)(2) of this section, the properties exchanged are separated into exchange groups as follows:

(A) The first exchange group consists of computer A and printer B (both are within the same General Asset Class) and, as to K, has an exchange group surplus of $1050 because the fair market value of printer B ($2050) exceeds the fair market value of computer A ($1000) by that amount.

(B) The second exchange group consists of automobile A and automobile B (both are within the same General Asset Class) and, as to K, has an exchange group deficiency of $1050 because the fair market value of automobile A ($4000) exceeds the fair market value of automobile B ($2950) by that amount.

(iii) K recognizes gain on the exchange as follows:

(A) With respect to the first exchange group, the amount of gain realized is the excess of the fair market value of computer A ($1000) over its adjusted basis ($375), or $625. The amount of gain recognized is the lesser of the gain realized ($625) and the exchange group deficiency ($0), or $0.

(B) With respect to the second exchange group, the amount of gain realized is the excess of the fair market value of automobile A ($4000) over its adjusted basis ($1500), or $2500. The amount of gain recognized is the lesser of the gain realized ($2500) and the exchange group deficiency ($1050), or $1050.

(iv) The total amount of gain recognized by K in the exchange is the sum of the gains recognized with respect to both exchange groups ($0 + $1050), or $1050.

(v) The basis of the property received by K in the exchange, printer B and automobile B, are determined in the following manner:

(A) The basis of the property received in the first exchange group is the adjusted basis of the property transferred within that exchange group ($375), increased by the amount of gain recognized with respect to that exchange group ($0), increased by the amount of the exchange group surplus ($1050), and increased by the amount of excess liabilities assumed allocated to that exchange group ($0), or $1425. Because printer B was the only property received within the first exchange group, the entire basis of $1425 is allocated to printer B.

(B) The basis of the property received in the second exchange group is the adjusted basis of the property transferred within that exchange group ($1500), increased by the amount of gain recognized with respect to that exchange group ($1050), decreased by the amount of the exchange group deficiency ($1050), and increased by the amount of excess liabilities assumed allocated to that exchange group ($0), or $1500. Because automobile B was the only property received within the second exchange group, the entire basis of $1500 is allocated to automobile B.

Example 2. (i) F exchanges computer A (asset class 00.12) and automobile A (asset class 00.22), both of which were held by F for productive use in its business, with G for printer B (asset class 00.12) and automobile B (asset class 00.22), both of which will be held by F for productive use in its business, and corporate stock and $500 cash. The adjusted basis and fair market value of the properties are as follows:

	Adjusted Basis	Fair Market Value
Computer A	$ 375	$1000
Automobile A	3500	4000
Printer B	—	800

	Adjusted Basis	Fair Market Value
Automobile B	—	2950
Corporate Stock	—	750
Cash	—	500

(ii) Under paragraph (b)(2) of this section, the properties exchanged are separated into exchange groups as follows:

(A) The first exchange group consists of computer A and printer B (both are within the same General Asset Class) and, as to F, has an exchange group deficiency of $200 because the fair market value of computer A ($1000) exceeds the fair market value of printer B ($800) by that amount.

(B) The second exchange group consists of automobile A and automobile B (both are within the same General Asset Class) and, as to F, has an exchange group deficiency of $1050 because the fair market value of automobile A ($4000) exceeds the fair market value of automobile B ($2950) by that amount.

(C) Because the aggregate fair market value of the properties transferred by F in the exchange groups ($5,000) exceeds the aggregate fair market value of the properties received by F in the exchange groups ($3750) by $1250, there is a residual group in that amount consisting of the $500 cash and the $750 worth of corporate stock.

(iii) F recognizes gain on the exchange as follows:

(A) With respect to the first exchange group, the amount of gain realized is the excess of the fair market value of computer A ($1000) over its adjusted basis ($375), or $625. The amount of gain recognized is the lesser of the gain realized ($625) and the exchange group deficiency ($200), or $200.

(B) With respect to the second exchange group, the amount of gain realized is the excess of the fair market value of automobile A ($4000) over its adjusted basis ($3500), or $500. The amount of gain recognized is the lesser of the gain realized ($500) and the exchange group deficiency ($1050), or $500.

(C) No property transferred by F was allocated to the residual group. Therefore, F does not recognize gain or loss with respect to the residual group.

(iv) The total amount of gain recognized by F in the exchange is the sum of the gains recognized with respect to both exchange groups ($200 + $500), or $700.

(v) The bases of the properties received by F in the exchange (printer B, automobile B, and the corporate stock) are determined in the following manner:

(A) The basis of the property received in the first exchange group is the adjusted basis of the property transferred within that exchange group ($375), increased by the amount of gain recognized with respect to that exchange group ($200), decreased by the amount of the exchange group deficiency ($200), and increased by the amount of excess liabilities assumed allocated to that exchange group ($0), or $375. Because printer B was the only property received within the first exchange group, the entire basis of $375 is allocated to printer B.

(B) The basis of the property received in the second exchange group is the adjusted basis of the property transferred within that exchange group ($3500), increased by the amount of gain recognized with respect to that exchange group ($500), decreased by the amount of the exchange group deficiency ($1050), and increased by the amount of excess liabilities assumed allocated to that exchange group ($0), or $2950. Because au-

tomobile B was the only property received within the second exchange group, the entire basis of $2950 is allocated to automobile B.

(C) The basis of the property received within the residual group (the corporate stock) is equal to its fair market value or $750. Cash of $500 is also received within the residual group.

Example 3. (i) J and H enter into an exchange of the following properties. All of the property (except for the inventory) transferred by J was held for productive use in J's business. All of the property received by J will be held by J for productive use in its business.

J Transfers:

	Adjusted Basis	Fair Market Value
Computer A	$1500	$5000
Computer B	500	3000
Printer C	2000	1500
Real Estate D	1200	2000
Real Estate E	0	1800
Scraper F	3300	2500
Inventory	1000	1700
Total	$9500	$17,500

H Transfers:

Property	Fair Market Value
Computer Z	$4500
Printer Y	2500
Real Estate X	1000
Real Estate W	4000
Grader V	2000
Truck T	1700
Cash	1800
Total	$17,500

(ii) Under paragraph (b)(2) of this section, the properties exchanged are separated into exchange groups as follows:

(A) The first exchange group consists of computer A, computer B, printer C, computer Z, and printer Y (all are within the same General Asset Class) and, as to J, has an exchange group deficiency of $2500 (($5000 + $3000 + $1500) – ($4500 + $2500)).

(B) The second exchange group consists of real estate D, E, X and W (all are of a like kind) and, as to J, has an exchange group surplus of $1200 (($1000 + $4000) – ($2000 + $1800)).

(C) The third exchange group consists of scraper F and grader V (both are within the same Product Class (NAICS code 333120)) and, as to J, has an exchange group deficiency of $500 ($2500 – $2000).

(D) Because the aggregate fair market value of the properties transferred by J in the exchange groups ($15,800) exceeds the aggregate fair market value of the properties received by J in the exchange groups ($14,000) by $1800, there is a residual group in that amount consisting of the $1800 cash (a Class I asset).

(E) The transaction also includes a taxable exchange of inventory (which is property described in section 1031(a)(2)) for truck T (which is not of a like kind or like class to any property transferred in the exchange).

(iii) J recognizes gain on the transaction as follows:

(A) With respect to the first exchange group, the amount of gain realized is the excess of the aggregate fair market value of the properties transferred in the exchange group ($9500) over

the aggregate adjusted basis ($4000), or $5500. The amount of gain recognized is the lesser of the gain realized ($5500) and the exchange group deficiency ($2500), or $2500.

(B) With respect to the second exchange group, the amount of gain realized is the excess of the aggregate fair market value of the properties transferred in the exchange group ($3800) over the aggregate adjusted basis ($1200), or $2600. The amount of gain recognized is the lesser of the gain realized ($2600) and the exchange group deficiency ($0), or $0.

(C) With respect to the third exchange group, a loss is realized in the amount of $800 because the fair market value of the property transferred in the exchange group ($2500) is less than its adjusted basis ($3300). Although a loss of $800 was realized, under section 1031(a) and (c) losses are not recognized.

(D) No property transferred by J was allocated to the residual group. Therefore, J does not recognize gain or loss with respect to the residual group.

(E) With respect to the taxable exchange of inventory for truck T, gain of $700 is realized and recognized by J (amount realized of $1700 (the fair market value of truck T) less the adjusted basis of the inventory ($1000)).

(iv) The total amount of gain recognized by J in the transaction is the sum of the gains recognized under section 1031 with respect to each exchange group ($2500 + $0 + $0) and any gain recognized outside of section 1031 ($700), or $3200.

(v) The basis of the property received by J in the exchange are determined in the following manner:

Reg. §1.1031(j)-1(d)

(A) The aggregate basis of the properties received in the first exchange group is the adjusted basis of the properties transferred within that exchange group ($4000), increased by the amount of gain recognized with respect to that exchange group ($2500), decreased by the amount of the exchange group deficiency ($2500), and increased by the amount of excess liabilities assumed allocated to that exchange group ($0), or $4000. This $4000 of basis is allocated proportionately among the assets received within the first exchange group in accordance with their fair market values: computer Z's basis is $2571 ($4000 × $4500/$7000); printer Y's basis is $1429 ($4000 × $2500/$7000).

(B) The aggregate basis of the properties received in the second exchange group is the adjusted basis of the properties transferred within that exchange group ($1200), increased by the amount of gain recognized with respect to that exchange group ($0), increased by the amount of the exchange group surplus ($1200), and increased by the amount of excess liabilities assumed allocated to that exchange group ($0), or $2400. This $2400 of basis is allocated proportionately among the assets received within the second exchange group in accordance with their fair market values: real estate X's basis is $480 ($2400 × $1000/$5000); real estate W's basis is $1920 ($2400 × $4000/$5000).

(C) The basis of the property received in the third exchange group is the adjusted basis of the property transferred within that exchange group ($3300), increased by the amount of gain recognized with respect to that exchange group ($0), decreased by the amount of the exchange group deficiency ($500), and increased by the amount of excess liabilities assumed allocated to that exchange group ($0), or $2800. Because grader V was the only property received within the third exchange group, the entire basis of $2800 is allocated to grader V.

(D) Cash of $1800 is received within the residual group.

(E) The basis of the property received in the taxable exchange (truck T) is equal to its cost of $1700.

Example 4. (i) B exchanges computer A (asset class 00.12), automobile A (asset class 00.22) and truck A (asset class 00.241), with C for computer R (asset class 00.12), automobile R (asset class 00.22), truck R (asset class 00.241) and $400 cash. All properties transferred by either B or C were held for productive use in the respective transferor's business. Similarly, all properties to be received by either B or C will be held for productive use in the respective recipient's business. Automobile A, automobile R and truck R are each secured by a nonrecourse liability and are transferred subject to such liability. The adjusted basis, fair market value, and liability secured by each property, if any, are as follows:

	Adjusted Basis	Fair Market Value	Liability
B Transfers:			
Computer A	$800	$1500	$0
Automobile A	900	2500	500
Truck A	700	2000	0
C Transfers:			
Computer R	$1100	$1600	$0
Automobile R	2100	3100	750
Truck R	600	1400	250
Cash		400	

(ii) The tax treatment to B is as follows:

(A)(1) The first exchange group consists of computers A and R (both are within the same General Asset Class).

(2) The second exchange group consists of automobiles A and R (both are within the same General Asset Class).

(3) The third exchange group consists of trucks A and R (both are in the same General Asset Class).

(B) Under paragraph (b)(2)(ii) of this section, all liabilities assumed by B ($1000) are offset by all liabilities of which B is relieved ($500), resulting in excess liabilities assumed of $500. The excess liabilities assumed of $500 is allocated among the exchange groups in proportion to the fair market value of the properties received by B in the exchange groups as follows:

(1) $131 of excess liabilities assumed ($500 × $1600/$6100) is allocated to the first exchange group. The first exchange group has an exchange group deficiency of $31 because the fair market value of computer A ($1500) exceeds the fair market value of computer R less the excess liabilities assumed allocated to the exchange group ($1600 – $131) by that amount.

(2) $254 of excess liabilities assumed ($500 × $3100/$6100) is allocated to the second exchange group. The second exchange group has an exchange group surplus of $346 because the fair market value of automobile R less the excess liabilities assumed allocated to the exchange group ($3100 – $254) exceeds the fair market value of automobile A ($2500) by that amount.

(3) $115 of excess liabilities assumed ($500 × $1400/$6100) is allocated to the third exchange group. The third exchange group has an exchange group deficiency of $715 because the fair market value of truck A ($2000) exceeds the fair market value of truck R less the excess liabilities assumed allocated to the exchange group ($1400 – $115) by that amount.

(4) The difference between the aggregate fair market value of the properties transferred in all of the exchange groups, $6000, and the aggregate fair market value of the properties received in all of the exchange groups (taking excess liabilities assumed into account), $5600, is $400. Therefore there is a residual group in that amount consisting of $400 cash received.

(C) B recognizes gain on the exchange as follows:

(1) With respect to the first exchange group, the amount of gain realized is the excess of the fair market value of computer A ($1500) over its adjusted basis ($800), or $700. The amount of gain recognized is the lesser of the gain realized ($700) and the exchange group deficiency ($31), or $31.

(2) With respect to the second exchange group, the amount of gain realized is the excess of the fair market value of automobile A ($2500) over its adjusted basis ($900), or $1600. The amount of gain recognized is the lesser of the gain realized ($1600) and the exchange group deficiency ($0), or $0.

(3) With respect to the third exchange group, the amount of gain realized is the excess of the fair market value of truck A ($2000) over its adjusted basis ($700), or $1300. The amount of gain recognized is the lesser of gain realized ($1300) and the exchange group deficiency ($715), or $715.

(4) No property transferred by B was allocated to the residual group. Therefore, B does not recognize gain or loss with respect to the residual group.

(D) The total amount of gain recognized by B in the exchange is the sum of the gains recognized under section 1031 with respect to each exchange group ($31 + $0 + $715), or $746.

(E) The basis of the property received by B in the exchange (computer R, automobile R, and truck R) are determined in the following manner:

(1) The basis of the property received in the first exchange group is the adjusted basis of the property transferred within that exchange group ($800), increased by the amount of gain recognized with respect to that exchange group ($31), decreased by the amount of the exchange group deficiency ($31), and increased by the amount of excess liabilities assumed allocated to that exchange group ($131), or $931. Because computer R was the only property received within the first exchange group, the entire basis of $931 is allocated to computer R.

(2) The basis of the property received in the second exchange group is the adjusted basis of the property transferred within that exchange group ($900), increased by the amount of gain recognized with respect to that exchange group ($0), increased by the amount of the exchange group surplus ($346), and increased by the amount of excess liabilities assumed allocated to that exchange group ($254), or $1500. Because automobile R was the only property received within the second exchange group, the entire basis of $1500 is allocated to automobile R.

(3) The basis of the property received in the third exchange group is the adjusted basis of the property transferred within that exchange group ($700), increased by the amount of gain recognized with respect to that exchange group ($715),

decreased by the amount of the exchange group deficiency ($715), and increased by the amount of excess liabilities assumed allocated to that exchange group ($115), or $815. Because truck R was the only property received within the third exchange group, the entire basis of $815 is allocated to truck R.

(F) Cash of $400 is also received by B.

(iii) The tax treatment to C is as follows:

(A)(1) The first exchange group consists of computers R and A (both are within the same General Asset Class).

(2) The second exchange group consists of automobiles R and A (both are within the same General Asset Class).

(3) The third exchange group consists of trucks R and A (both are in the same General Asset Class).

(B) Under paragraph (b)(2)(ii) of this section, all liabilities of which C is relieved ($1000) are offset by all liabilities assumed by C ($500), resulting in excess liabilities relieved of $500. This excess liabilities relieved is treated as cash received by C.

(1) The first exchange group has an exchange group deficiency of $100 because the fair market value of computer R ($1600) exceeds the fair market value of computer A ($1500) by that amount.

(2) The second exchange group has an exchange group deficiency of $600 because the fair market value of automobile R ($3100) exceeds the fair market value of automobile A ($2500) by that amount.

(3) The third exchange group has an exchange group surplus of $600 because the fair market value of truck A ($2000) exceeds the fair market value of truck R ($1400) by that amount.

(4) The difference between the aggregate fair market value of the properties transferred by C in all of the exchange groups, $6100, and the aggregate fair market value of the properties received by C in all of the exchange groups, $6000, is $100. Therefore, there is a residual group in that amount, consisting of excess liabilities relieved of $100, which is treated as cash received by C.

(5) The $400 cash paid by C and $400 of the excess liabilities relieved which is treated as cash received by C are not within the exchange groups or the residual group.

(C) C recognizes gain on the exchange as follows:

(1) With respect to the first exchange group, the amount of gain realized is the excess of the fair market value of computer R ($1600) over its adjusted basis ($1100), or $500. The amount of gain recognized is the lesser of the gain realized ($500) and the exchange group deficiency ($100), or $100.

(2) With respect to the second exchange group, the amount of gain realized is the excess of the fair market value of automobile R ($3100) over its adjusted basis ($2100), or $1000. The amount

of gain recognized is the lesser of the gain realized ($1000) and the exchange group deficiency ($600), or $600.

(3) With respect to the third exchange group, the amount of gain realized is the excess of the fair market value of truck R ($1400) over its adjusted basis ($600), or $800. The amount of gain recognized is the lesser of gain realized ($800) and the exchange group deficiency ($0), or $0.

(4) No property transferred by C was allocated to the residual group. Therefore, C does not recognize any gain with respect to the residual group.

(D) The total amount of gain recognized by C in the exchange is the sum of the gains recognized under section 1031 with respect to each exchange group ($100 + $600 + $0), or $700.

(E) The basis of the properties received by C in the exchange (computer A, automobile A, and truck A) are determined in the following manner:

(1) The basis of the property received in the first exchange group is the adjusted basis of the property transferred within that exchange group ($1100), increased by the amount of gain recognized with respect to that exchange group ($100), decreased by the amount of the exchange group deficiency ($100), and increased by the amount of excess liabilities assumed allocated to that exchange group ($0), or $1100. Because computer A was the only property received within the first exchange group, the entire basis of $1100 is allocated to computer A.

(2) The basis of the property received in the second exchange group is the adjusted basis of the property transferred within that exchange group ($2100), increased by the amount of gain recognized with respect to that exchange group ($600), decreased by the amount of the exchange group deficiency ($600), and increased by the amount of excess liabilities assumed allocated to that exchange group ($0), or $2100. Because automobile A was the only property received within the second exchange group, the entire basis of $2100 is allocated to automobile A.

(3) The basis of the property received in the third exchange group is the adjusted basis of the property transferred within that exchange group ($600), increased by the amount of gain recognized with respect to that exchange group ($0), increased by the amount of the exchange group surplus ($600), and increased by the amount of excess liabilities assumed allocated to that exchange group ($0), or $1200. Because truck A was the only property received within the third exchange group, the entire basis of $1200 is allocated to truck A.

Example 5. (i) U exchanges real estate A, real estate B, and grader A (NAICS code 333120) with V for real estate R and railroad car R (General Asset Class 00.25). All properties transferred by either U or V were held for productive use in the respective transferor's business. Similarly, all

properties to be received by either U or V will be held for productive use in the respective recipient's business. Real estate R is secured by a recourse liability and is transferred subject to that liability. The adjusted basis, fair market value, and liability secured by each property, if any, are as follows:

	Adjusted Basis	Fair Market Value	Liability
U Transfers:			
Real Estate A	$2000	$5000	
Real Estate B	8000	13,500	
Grader A	500	2000	
V Transfers:			
Real Estate R	$20,000	$26,500	$7000
Railroad Car R	1200	1000	

(ii) The tax treatment to U is as follows:

(A) The exchange group consists of real estate A, real estate B, and real estate R.

(B) Under paragraph (b)(2)(ii) of this section, all liabilities assumed by U ($7000) are excess liabilities assumed. The excess liabilities assumed of $7000 is allocated to the exchange group.

(1) The exchange group has an exchange group surplus of $1000 because the fair market value of real estate R less the excess liabilities assumed allocated to the exchange group ($26,500 − $7000) exceeds the aggregate fair market value of real estate A and B ($18,500) by that amount.

(2) The difference between the aggregate fair market value of the properties received in the exchange group (taking excess liabilities assumed into account), $19,500, and the aggregate fair market value of the properties transferred in the exchange group, $18,500, is $1000. Therefore, there is a residual group in that amount consisting of $1000 (or 50 percent of the fair market value) of grader A.

(3) The transaction also includes a taxable exchange of the 50 percent portion of grader A not allocated to the residual group (which is not of a like kind or like class to any property received by U in the exchange) for railroad car R (which is not of a like kind or like class to any property transferred by U in the exchange).

(C) U recognizes gain on the exchange as follows:

(1) With respect to the exchange group, the amount of the gain realized is the excess of the aggregate fair market value of real estate A and B ($18,500) over the aggregate adjusted basis ($10,000), or $8500. The amount of the gain recognized is the lesser of the gain realized ($8500) and the exchange group deficiency ($0), or $0.

(2) With respect to the residual group, the amount of gain realized and recognized is the excess of the fair market value of the 50 percent portion of grader A that is allocated to the residual group ($1000) over its adjusted basis ($250), or $750.

(3) With respect to the taxable exchange of the 50 percent portion of grader A not allocated to the residual group for railroad car R, gain of $750 is realized and recognized by U (amount realized of $1000 (the fair market value of railroad car R) less the adjusted basis of the 50 percent portion of grader A not allocated to the residual group ($250)).

(D) The total amount of gain recognized by U in the transaction is the sum of the gain recognized under section 1031 with respect to the exchange group ($0), any gain recognized with respect to the residual group ($750), and any gain recognized with respect to property transferred that is not in the exchange group or the residual group ($750), or $1500.

(E) The basis of the property received by U in the exchange (real estate R and railroad car R) are determined in the following manner:

(1) The basis of the property received in the exchange group is the aggregate adjusted basis of the property transferred within that exchange group ($10,000), increased by the amount of gain recognized with respect to that exchange group ($0), increased by the amount of the exchange group surplus ($1000), and increased by the amount of excess liabilities assumed allocated to that exchange group ($7000), or $18,000. Because real estate R is the only property received within the exchange group, the entire basis of $18,000 is allocated to real estate R.

(2) The basis of railroad car R is equal to its cost of $1000.

(iii) The tax treatment to V is as follows:

(A) The exchange group consists of real estate R, real estate A, and real estate B.

(B) Under paragraph (b)(2)(ii) of this section, the liabilities of which V is relieved ($7000) results [sic]in excess liabilities relieved of $7000 and is [sic] treated as cash received by V.

(1) The exchange group has an exchange group deficiency of $8000 because the fair market value of real estate R ($26,500) exceeds the aggregate fair market value of real estate A and B ($18,500) by that amount.

(2) The difference between the aggregate fair market value of the properties transferred by V in the exchange group, $26,500, and the aggregate fair market value of the properties received by V in the exchange group, $18,500, is $8000. Therefore, there is a residual group in that amount, consisting of the excess liabilities relieved of $7000, which is treated as cash received by V, and $1000 (or 50 percent of the fair market value) of grader A.

(3) The transaction also includes a taxable exchange of railroad car R (which is not of a like kind or like class to any property received by V in the exchange) for the 50 percent portion of grader A (which is not of a like kind or like class to any property transferred by V in the exchange) not allocated to the residual group.

(C) V recognizes gain on the exchange as follows:

(1) With respect to the exchange group, the amount of the gain realized is the excess of the fair market value of real estate R ($26,500) over its adjusted basis ($20,000), or $6500. The amount of the gain recognized is the lesser of the gain realized ($6500) and the exchange group deficiency ($8000), or $6500.

(2) No property transferred by V was allocated to the residual group. Therefore, V does not recognize gain or loss with respect to the residual group.

(3) With respect to the taxable exchange of railroad car R for the 50 percent portion of grader A not allocated to the exchange group or the residual group, a loss is realized and recognized in the amount of $200 (the excess of the $1200 adjusted basis of railroad car R over the amount realized of $1000 (fair market value of the 50 percent portion of grader A)).

(D) The basis of the property received by V in the exchange (real estate A, real estate B, and grader A) are determined in the following manner:

(1) The basis of the property received in the exchange group is the adjusted basis of the property transferred within that exchange group ($20,000), increased by the amount of gain recognized with respect to that exchange group ($6500), and decreased by the amount of the exchange group deficiency ($8000), or $18,500. This $18,500 of basis is allocated proportionately among the assets received within the exchange group in accordance with their fair market values: real estate A's basis is $5000 ($18,500 × $5000/$18,500); real estate B's basis is $13,500 ($18,500 × $13,500/$18,500).

(2) The basis of grader A is $2000.

(e) *Effective date.*—Section 1.1031(j)-1 is effective for exchanges occurring on or after April 11, 1991. [Reg. § 1.1031(j)-1.]

☐ [T.D. 8343, 4-11-91. *Amended by T.D.* 8858, 1-5-2000; *T.D.* 8940, 2-12-2001 *and T.D.* 9202, 5-18-2005.]

[Reg. § 1.1031(k)-1]

§ 1.1031(k)-1. Treatment of deferred exchanges.—(a) *Overview.*—This section provides rules for the application of section 1031 and the regulations thereunder in the case of a "deferred exchange." For purposes of section 1031 and this section, a deferred exchange is defined as an exchange in which, pursuant to an agreement, the taxpayer transfers property held for productive use in a trade or business or for investment (the "relinquished property") and subsequently receives property to be held either for productive use in a trade or business or for investment (the "replacement property"). In the case of a deferred exchange, if the requirements set forth in paragraphs (b), (c), and (d) of this section (relating to identification and receipt of replacement property) are not satisfied, the replacement property received by the taxpayer will be treated as property which is not of a like kind to the relinquished property. In order to constitute a deferred exchange, the transaction must be an exchange (i.e., a transfer of property for property, as distinguished from a transfer of property for money). For example, a sale of property followed by a purchase of property of a like kind does not qualify for nonrecognition of gain or loss under section 1031 regardless of whether the identification and receipt requirements of section 1031(a)(3) and paragraphs (b), (c), and (d) of this section are satisfied. The transfer of relinquished property in a deferred exchange is not within the provisions of section 1031(a) if, as part of the consideration, the taxpayer receives money or property which does not meet the requirements of section 1031(a), but the transfer, if otherwise qualified, will be within the provisions of either section 1031(b) or (c). See § 1.1031(a)-1(a)(2). In addition, in the case of a transfer of relinquished property in a deferred exchange, gain or loss may be recognized if the taxpayer actually or constructively receives money or property which does not meet the requirements of section 1031(a) before the taxpayer actually receives like-kind replacement property. If the taxpayer actually or constructively receives money or property which does not meet the requirements of section 1031(a) in the full amount of the consideration for the relinquished property, the transaction will constitute a sale, and not a deferred exchange, even though the taxpayer may ultimately receive like-kind replacement property. For purposes of this section, property which does not meet the requirements of section 1031(a)(whether by being described in section 1031(a)(2) or otherwise) is referred to as "other property." For rules regarding actual and constructive receipt, and safe harbors therefrom, see paragraphs (f) and (g), respectively, of this section. For rules regarding the determination of gain or loss recognized and the basis of property received in a deferred exchange, see paragraph (j) of this section.

(b) *Identification and receipt requirements.*— (1) *In general.*—In the case of a deferred exchange, any replacement property received by the taxpayer will be treated as property which is not of a like kind to the relinquished property if—

(i) The replacement property is not "identified" before the end of the "identification period," or

(ii) The identified replacement property is not received before the end of the "exchange period."

(2) *Identification period and exchange period.*— (i) The identification period begins on the date the taxpayer transfers the relinquished property and ends at midnight on the 45th day thereafter.

(ii) The exchange period begins on the date the taxpayer transfers the relinquished property and ends at midnight on the earlier of the 180th day thereafter or the due date (includ-

ing extensions) for the taxpayer's return of the tax imposed by chapter 1 of subtitle A of the Code for the taxable year in which the transfer of the relinquished property occurs.

(iii) If, as part of the same deferred exchange, the taxpayer transfers more than one relinquished property and the relinquished properties are transferred on different dates, the identification period and the exchange period are determined by reference to the earliest date on which any of the properties are transferred.

(iv) For purposes of this paragraph (b)(2), property is transferred when the property is disposed of within the meaning of section 1001(a).

(3) *Example.*—This paragraph (b) may be illustrated by the following example.

Example. (i) M is a corporation that files its Federal income tax return on a calendar year basis. M and C enter into an agreement for an exchange of property that requires M to transfer property X to C. Under the agreement, M is to identify like-kind replacement property which C is required to purchase and to transfer to M. M transfers property X to C on November 16, 1992.

(ii) The identification period ends at midnight on December 31, 1992, the day which is 45 days after the date of transfer of property X. The exchange period ends at midnight on March 15, 1993, the due date for M's Federal income tax return for the taxable year in which M transferred property X. However, if M is allowed the automatic six-month extension for filing its tax return, the exchange period ends at midnight on May 15, 1993, the day which is 180 days after the date of transfer of property X.

(c) *Identification of replacement property before the end of the identification period.*—(1) *In general.*—For purposes of paragraph (b)(1)(i) of this section (relating to the identification requirement), replacement property is identified before the end of the identification period only if the requirements of this paragraph (c) are satisfied with respect to the replacement property. However, any replacement property that is received by the taxpayer before the end of the identification period will in all events be treated as identified before the end of the identification period.

(2) *Manner of identifying replacement property.*—Replacement property is identified only if it is designated as replacement property in a written document signed by the taxpayer and hand delivered, mailed, telecopied, or otherwise sent before the end of the identification period to either—

(i) The person obligated to transfer the replacement property to the taxpayer (regardless of whether that person is a disqualified person as defined in paragraph (k) of this section); or

(ii) Any other person involved in the exchange other than the taxpayer or a disqualified person (as defined in paragraph (k) of this section).

Reg. § 1.1031(k)-1(b)

Examples of persons involved in the exchange include any of the parties to the exchange, an intermediary, an escrow agent, and a title company. An identification of replacement property made in a written agreement for the exchange of properties signed by all parties thereto before the end of the identification period will be treated as satisfying the requirements of this paragraph (c)(2).

(3) *Description of replacement property.*—Replacement property is identified only if it is unambiguously described in the written document or agreement. Real property generally is unambiguously described if it is described by a legal description, street address, or distinguishable name (e.g., the Mayfair Apartment Building). Personal property generally is unambiguously described if it is described by a specific description of the particular type of property. For example, a truck generally is unambiguously described if it is described by a specific make, model, and year.

(4) *Alternative and multiple properties.*—(i) The taxpayer may identify more than one replacement property. Regardless of the number of relinquished properties transferred by the taxpayer as part of the same deferred exchange, the maximum number of replacement properties that the taxpayer may identify is—

(A) Three properties without regard to the fair market values of the properties (the "3-property rule"), or

(B) Any number of properties as long as their aggregate fair market value as of the end of the identification period does not exceed 200 percent of the aggregate fair market value of all the relinquished properties as of the date the relinquished properties were transferred by the taxpayer (the "200-percent rule").

(ii) If, as of the end of the identification period, the taxpayer has identified more properties as replacement properties than permitted by paragraph (c)(4)(i) of this section, the taxpayer is treated as if no replacement property had been identified. The preceding sentence will not apply, however, and an identification satisfying the requirements of paragraph (c)(4)(i) of this section will be considered made, with respect to—

(A) Any replacement property received by the taxpayer before the end of the identification period, and

(B) Any replacement property identified before the end of the identification period and received before the end of the exchange period, but only if the taxpayer receives before the end of the exchange period identified replacement property the fair market value of which is at least 95 percent of the aggregate fair market value of all identified replacement properties (the "95-percent rule").

For this purpose, the fair market value of each identified replacement property is determined as of the earlier of the date the property is received

by the taxpayer or the last day of the exchange period.

(iii) For purposes of applying the 3-property rule, the 200-percent rule, and the 95-percent rule, all identifications of replacement property, other than identifications of replacement property that have been revoked in the manner provided in paragraph (c)(6) of this section, are taken into account. For example, if, in a deferred exchange, B transfers property X with a fair market value of $100,000 to C and B receives like-kind property Y with a fair market value of $50,000 before the end of the identification period, under paragraph (c)(1) of this section, property Y is treated as identified by reason of being received before the end of the identification period. Thus, under paragraph (c)(4)(i) of this section, B may identify either two additional replacement properties of any fair market value or any number of additional replacement properties as long as the aggregate fair market value of the additional replacement properties does not exceed $150,000.

(5) *Incidental property disregarded.*—(i) Solely for purposes of applying this paragraph (c), property that is incidental to a larger item of property is not treated as property that is separate from the larger item of property. Property is incidental to a larger item of property if—

(A) In standard commercial transactions, the property is typically transferred together with the larger item of property, and

(B) The aggregate fair market value of all of the incidental property does not exceed 15 percent of the aggregate fair market value of the larger item of property.

(ii) This paragraph (c)(5) may be illustrated by the following examples.

Example 1. For purposes of paragraph (c) of this section, a spare tire and tool kit will not be treated as separate property from a truck with a fair market value of $10,000, if the aggregate fair market value of the spare tire and tool kit does not exceed $1,500. For purposes of the 3-property rule, the truck, spare tire, and tool kit are treated as 1 property. Moreover, for purposes of paragraph (c)(3) of this section (relating to the description of replacement property), the truck, spare tire, and tool kit are all considered to be unambiguously described if the make, model, and year of the truck are specified, even if no reference is made to the spare tire and tool kit.

Example 2. For purposes of paragraph (c) of this section, furniture, laundry machines, and other miscellaneous items of personal property will not be treated as separate property from an apartment building with a fair market value of $1,000,000 if the aggregate fair market value of the furniture, laundry machines, and other personal property does not exceed $150,000. For purposes of the 3-property rule, the apartment building, furniture, laundry machines, and other personal property are treated as 1 property. Moreover, for purposes of paragraph (c)(3) of

Reg. §1.1031(k)-1(c)(5)(ii)

this section (relating to the description of replacement property), the apartment building, furniture, laundry machines, and other personal property are all considered to be unambiguously described if the legal description, street address, or distinguishable name of the apartment building is specified, even if no reference is made to the furniture, laundry machines, and other personal property.

(6) *Revocation of identification.*—An identification of replacement property may be revoked at any time before the end of the identification period. An identification of replacement property is revoked only if the revocation is made in a written document signed by the taxpayer and hand delivered, mailed, telecopied, or otherwise sent before the end of the identification period to the person to whom the identification of the replacement property was sent. An identification of replacement property that is made in a written agreement for the exchange of properties is treated as revoked only if the revocation is made in a written amendment to the agreement or in a written document signed by the taxpayer and hand delivered, mailed, telecopied, or otherwise sent before the end of the identification period to all of the parties to the agreement.

(7) *Examples.*—This paragraph (c) may be illustrated by the following examples. Unless otherwise provided in an example, the following facts are assumed: B, a calendar year taxpayer, and C agree to enter into a deferred exchange. Pursuant to their agreement, B transfers real property X to C on May 17, 1991. Real property X, which has been held by B for investment, is unencumbered and has a fair market value on May 17, 1991, of $100,000. On or before July 1, 1991 (the end of the identification period), B is to identify replacement property that is of a like kind to real property X. On or before November 13, 1991 (the end of the exchange period), C is required to purchase the property identified by B and to transfer that property to B. To the extent the fair market value of the replacement property transferred to B is greater or less than the fair market value of real property X, either B or C, as applicable, will make up the difference by paying cash to the other party after the date the replacement property is received by B. No replacement property is identified in the agreement. When subsequently identified, the replacement property is described by legal description and is of a like kind to real property X (determined without regard to section 1031(a)(3) and this section). B intends to hold the replacement property received for investment.

Example 1. (i) On July 2, 1991, B identifies real property E as replacement property by designating real property E as replacement property in a written document signed by B and personally delivered to C.

(ii) Because the identification was made after the end of the identification period, pursuant to paragraph (b)(1)(i) of this section (relating to

the identification requirement), real property E is treated as property which is not of a like kind to real property X.

Example 2. (i) C is a corporation of which 20 percent of the outstanding stock is owned by B. On July 1, 1991, B identifies real property F as replacement property by designating real property F as replacement property in a written document signed by B and mailed to C.

(ii) Because C is the person obligated to transfer the replacement property to B, real property F is identified before the end of the identification period. The fact that C is a "disqualified person" as defined in paragraph (k) of this section does not change this result.

(iii) Real property F would also have been treated as identified before the end of the identification period if, instead of sending the identification to C, B had designated real property F as replacement property in a written agreement for the exchange of properties signed by all parties thereto on or before July 1, 1991.

Example 3. (i) On June 3, 1991, B identifies the replacement property as "unimproved land located in Hood County with a fair market value not to exceed $100,000." The designation is made in a written document signed by B and personally delivered to C. On July 8, 1991, B and C agree that real property G is the property described in the June 3, 1991 document.

(ii) Because real property G was not unambiguously described before the end of the identification period, no replacement property is identified before the end of the identification period.

Example 4. (i) On June 28, 1991, B identifies real properties H, J, and K as replacement properties by designating these properties as replacement properties in a written document signed by B and personally delivered to C. The written document provides that by August 1, 1991, B will orally inform C which of the identified properties C is to transfer to B. As of July 1, 1991, the fair market values of real properties H, J, and K are $75,000, $100,000, and $125,000, respectively.

(ii) Because B did not identify more than three properties as replacement properties, the requirements of the 3-property rule are satisfied, and real properties H, J, and K are all identified before the end of the identification period.

Example 5. (i) On May 17, 1991, B identifies real properties L, M, N, and P as replacement properties by designating these properties as replacement properties in a written document signed by B and personally delivered to C. The written document provides that by July 2, 1991, B will orally inform C which of the identified properties C is to transfer to B. As of July 1, 1991, the fair market values of real properties L, M, N, and P are $30,000, $40,000, $50,000, and $60,000, respectively.

(ii) Although B identified more than three properties as replacement properties, the aggregate fair market value of the identified properties as of the end of the identification period ($180,000) did not exceed 200 percent of the aggregate fair market value of real property X (200% × $100,000 = $200,000). Therefore, the requirements of the 200-percent rule are satisfied, and real properties L, M, N, and P are all identified before the end of the identification period.

Example 6. (i) On June 21, 1991, B identifies real properties Q, R, and S as replacement properties by designating these properties as replacement properties in a written document signed by B and mailed to C. On June 24, 1991, B identifies real properties T and U as replacement properties in a written document signed by B and mailed to C. On June 28, 1991, B revokes the identification of real properties Q and R in a written document signed by B and personally delivered to C.

(ii) B has revoked the identification of real properties Q and R in the manner provided by paragraph (c)(6) of this section. Identifications of replacement property that have been revoked in the manner provided by paragraph (c)(6) of this section are not taken into account for purposes of applying the 3-property rule. Thus, as of June 28, 1991, B has identified only replacement properties S, T, and U for purposes of the 3-property rule. Because B did not identify more than three properties as replacement properties for purposes of the 3-property rule, the requirements of that rule are satisfied, and real properties S, T, and U are all identified before the end of the identification period.

Example 7. (i) On May 20, 1991, B identifies real properties V and W as replacement properties by designating these properties as replacement properties in a written document signed by B and personally delivered to C. On June 4, 1991, B identifies real properties Y and Z as replacement properties in the same manner. On June 5, 1991, B telephones C and orally revokes the identification of real properties V and W. As of July 1, 1991, the fair market values of real properties V, W, Y, and Z are $50,000, $70,000, $90,000, and $100,000, respectively. On July 31, 1991, C purchases real property Y and Z and transfers them to B.

(ii) Pursuant to paragraph (c)(6) of this section (relating to revocation of identification), the oral revocation of the identification of real properties V and W is invalid. Thus, the identification of real properties V and W is taken into account for purposes of determining whether the requirements of paragraph (c)(4) of this section (relating to the identification of alternative and multiple properties) are satisfied. Because B identified more than three properties and the aggregate fair market value of the identified properties as of the end of the identification period ($310,000) exceeds 200 percent of the fair market value of real property X (200% × $100,000 = $200,000), the requirements of paragraph (c)(4) of this section are not satisfied, and B is treated

as if B did not identify any replacement property.

(d) *Receipt of identified replacement property.*— (1) *In general.*—For purposes of paragraph (b)(1)(ii) of this section (relating to the receipt requirement), the identified replacement property is received before the end of the exchange period only if the requirements of this paragraph (d) are satisfied with respect to the replacement property. In the case of a deferred exchange, the identified replacement property is received before the end of the exchange period if—

(i) The taxpayer receives the replacement property before the end of the exchange period, and

(ii) The replacement property received is substantially the same property as identified.

If the taxpayer has identified more than one replacement property, section 1031(a)(3)(B) and this paragraph (d) are applied separately to each replacement property.

(2) *Examples.*—This paragraph (d) may be illustrated by the following examples. The following facts are assumed: B, a calendar year taxpayer, and C agree to enter into a deferred exchange. Pursuant to their agreement, B transfers real property X to C on May 17, 1991. Real property X, which has been held by B for investment, is unencumbered and has a fair market value on May 17, 1991, of $100,000. On or before July 1, 1991 (the end of the identification period), B is to identify replacement property that is of a like kind to real property X. On or before November 13, 1991 (the end of the exchange period), C is required to purchase the property identified by B and to transfer that property to B. To the extent the fair market value of the replacement property transferred to B is greater or less than the fair market value of real property X, either B or C, as applicable, will make up the difference by paying cash to the other party after the date the replacement property is received by B. The replacement property is identified in a manner that satisfies paragraph (c) of this section (relating to identification of replacement property) and is of a like kind to real property X (determined without regard to section 1031(a)(3) and this section). B intends to hold any replacement property received for investment.

Example 1. (i) In the agreement, B identifies real properties J, K, and L as replacement properties. The agreement provides that by July 26, 1991, B will orally inform C which of the properties C is to transfer to B.

(ii) As of July 1, 1991, the fair market values of real properties J, K, and L are $75,000, $100,000, and $125,000, respectively. On July 26, 1991, B instructs C to acquire real property K. On October 31, 1991, C purchases real property K for $100,000 and transfers the property to B.

(iii) Because real property K was identified before the end of the identification period and was received before the end of the exchange

Reg. § 1.1031(k)-1(d)(2)

period, the identification and receipt requirements of section 1031(a)(3) and this section are satisfied with respect to real property K.

Example 2. (i) In the agreement, B identifies real property P as replacement property. Real property P consists of two acres of unimproved land. On October 15, 1991, the owner of real property P erects a fence on the property. On November 1, 1991, C purchases real property P and transfers it to B.

(ii) The erection of the fence on real property P subsequent to its identification did not alter the basic nature or character of real property P as unimproved land. B is considered to have received substantially the same property as identified.

Example 3. (i) In the agreement, B identifies real property Q as replacement property. Real property Q consists of a barn on two acres of land and has a fair market value of $250,000 ($187,500 for the barn and underlying land and $87,500 for the remaining land). As of July 26, 1991, real property Q remains unchanged and has a fair market value of $250,000. On that date, at B's direction, C purchases the barn and underlying land for $187,500 and transfers it to B, and B pays $87,500 to C.

(ii) The barn and underlying land differ in basic nature or character from real property Q as a whole. B is not considered to have received substantially the same property as identified.

Example 4. (i) In the agreement, B identifies real property R as replacement property. Real property R consists of two acres of unimproved land and has a fair market value of $250,000. As of October 3, 1991, real property R remains unimproved and has a fair market value of $250,000. On that date, at B's direction, C purchases 1 1/2 acres of real property R for $187,500 and transfers it to B, and B pays $87,500 to C.

(ii) The portion of real property R that B received does not differ from the basic nature or character of real property R as a whole. Moreover, the fair market value of the portion of real property R that B received ($187,500) is 75 percent of the fair market value of real property R as of the date of receipt. Accordingly, B is considered to have received substantially the same property as identified.

(e) *Special rules for identification and receipt of replacement property to be produced.*—(1) *In general.*—A transfer of relinquished property in a deferred exchange will not fail to qualify for nonrecognition of gain or loss under section 1031 merely because the replacement property is not in existence or is being produced at the time the property is identified as replacement property. For purposes of this paragraph (e), the terms "produced" and "production" have the same meanings as provided in section 263A(g)(1) and the regulations thereunder.

(2) *Identification of replacement property to be produced.*—(i) In the case of replacement property that is to be produced, the replacement property must be identified as provided in paragraph (c) of this section (relating to identification of replacement property). For example, if the identified replacement property consists of improved real property where the improvements are to be constructed, the description of the replacement property satisfies the requirements of paragraph (c)(3) of this section (relating to description of replacement property) if a legal description is provided for the underlying land and as much detail is provided regarding construction of the improvements as is practicable at the time the identification is made.

(ii) For purposes of paragraphs (c)(4)(i)(B) and (c)(5) of this section (relating to the 200-percent rule and incidental property), the fair market value of replacement property that is to be produced is its estimated fair market value as of the date it is expected to be received by the taxpayer.

(3) *Receipt of replacement property to be produced.*—(i) For purposes of paragraph (d)(1)(ii) of this section (relating to receipt of the identified replacement property), in determining whether the replacement property received by the taxpayer is substantially the same property as identified where the identified replacement property is property to be produced, variations due to usual or typical production changes are not taken into account. However, if substantial changes are made in the property to be produced, the replacement property received will not be considered to be substantially the same property as identified.

(ii) If the identified replacement property is personal property to be produced, the replacement property received will not be considered to be substantially the same property as identified unless production of the replacement property received is completed on or before the date the property is received by the taxpayer.

(iii) If the identified replacement property is real property to be produced and the production of the property is not completed on or before the date the taxpayer receives the property, the property received will be considered to be substantially the same property as identified only if, had production been completed on or before the date the taxpayer receives the replacement property, the property received would have been considered to be substantially the same property as identified. Even so, the property received is considered to be substantially the same property as identified only to the extent the property received constitutes real property under local law.

(4) *Additional rules.*—The transfer of relinquished property is not within the provisions of section 1031(a) if the relinquished property is transferred in exchange for services (including production services). Thus, any additional pro-

duction occurring with respect to the replacement property after the property is received by the taxpayer will not be treated as the receipt of property of a like kind.

(5) *Example.*—This paragraph (e) may be illustrated by the following example.

Example. (i) B, a calendar year taxpayer, and C agree to enter into a deferred exchange. Pursuant to their agreement, B transfers improved real property X and personal property Y to C on May 17, 1991. On or before November 13, 1991 (the end of the exchange period), C is required to transfer to B real property M, on which C is constructing improvements, and personal property N, which C is producing. C is obligated to complete the improvements and production regardless of when properties M and N are transferred to B. Properties M and N are identified in a manner that satisfies paragraphs (c)(relating to identification of replacement property) and (e)(2) of this section. In addition, properties M and N are of a like kind, respectively, to real property X and personal property Y (determined without regard to section 1031(a)(3) and this section). On November 13, 1991, when construction of the improvements to property M is 20 percent completed and the production of property N is 90 percent completed, C transfers to B property M and property N. If construction of the improvements had been completed, property M would have been considered to be substantially the same property as identified. Under local law, property M constitutes real property to the extent of the underlying land and the 20 percent of the construction that is completed

(ii) Because property N is personal property to be produced and production of property N is not completed before the date the property is received by B, property N is not considered to be substantially the same property as identified and is treated as property which is not of a like kind to property Y.

(iii) Property M is considered to be substantially the same property as identified to the extent of the underlying land and the 20 percent of the construction that is completed when property M is received by B. However, any additional construction performed by C with respect to property M after November 13, 1991, is not treated as the receipt of property of a like kind.

(f) *Receipt of money or other property.*—(1) *In general.*—A transfer of relinquished property in a deferred exchange is not within the provisions of section 1031(a) if, as part of the consideration, the taxpayer receives money or other property. However, such a transfer, if otherwise qualified, will be within the provisions of either section 1031(b) or (c). See § 1.1031(a)-1(a)(2). In addition, in the case of a transfer of relinquished property in a deferred exchange, gain or loss may be recognized if the taxpayer actually or constructively receives money or other property before the taxpayer actually receives like-kind replacement property. If the taxpayer actually or con-

structively receives money or other property in the full amount of the consideration for the relinquished property before the taxpayer actually receives like-kind replacement property, the transaction will constitute a sale and not a deferred exchange, even though the taxpayer may ultimately receive like-kind replacement property.

(2) *Actual and constructive receipt.*—Except as provided in paragraph (g) of this section (relating to safe harbors), for purposes of section 1031 and this section, the determination of whether (or the extent to which) the taxpayer is in actual or constructive receipt of money or other property before the taxpayer actually receives like-kind replacement property is made under the general rules concerning actual and constructive receipt and without regard to the taxpayer's method of accounting. The taxpayer is in actual receipt of money or property at the time the taxpayer actually receives the money or property or receives the economic benefit of the money or property. The taxpayer is in constructive receipt of money or property at the time the money or property is credited to the taxpayer's account, set apart for the taxpayer, or otherwise made available so that the taxpayer may draw upon it at any time or so that the taxpayer can draw upon it if notice of intention to draw is given. Although the taxpayer is not in constructive receipt of money or property if the taxpayer's control of its receipt is subject to substantial limitations or restrictions, the taxpayer is in constructive receipt of the money or property at the time the limitations or restrictions lapse, expire, or are waived. In addition, actual or constructive receipt of money or property by an agent of the taxpayer (determined without regard to paragraph (k) of this section) is actual or constructive receipt by the taxpayer.

(3) *Example.*—This paragraph (f) may be illustrated by the following example.

Example. (i) B, a calendar year taxpayer, and C agree to enter into a deferred exchange. Pursuant to the agreement, on May 17, 1991, B transfers real property X to C. Real property X, which has been held by B for investment, is unencumbered and has a fair market value on May 17, 1991, of $100,000. On or before July 1, 1991 (the end of the identification period), B is to identify replacement property that is of a like kind to real property X. On or before November 13, 1991 (the end of the exchange period), C is required to purchase the property identified by B and to transfer that property to B. At any time after May 17, 1991, and before C has purchased the replacement property, B has the right, upon notice, to demand that C pay $100,000 in lieu of acquiring and transferring the replacement property. Pursuant to the agreement, B identifies replacement property, and C purchases the replacement property and transfers it to B.

(ii) Under the agreement, B has the unrestricted right to demand the payment of

$100,000 as of May 17, 1991. B is therefore in constructive receipt of $100,000 on that date. Because B is in constructive receipt of money in the full amount of the consideration for the relinquished property before B actually receives the like-kind replacement property, the transaction constitutes a sale, and the transfer of real property X does not qualify for nonrecognition of gain or loss under section 1031. B is treated as if B received the $100,000 in consideration for the sale of real property X and then purchased the like-kind replacement property.

(iii) If B's right to demand payment of the $100,000 were subject to a substantial limitation or restriction (e.g., the agreement provided that B had no right to demand payment before November 14, 1991 (the end of the exchange period)), then, for purposes of this section, B would not be in actual or constructive receipt of the money unless (or until) the limitation or restriction lapsed, expired, or was waived.

(g) *Safe harbors.*—(1) *In general.*—Paragraphs (g)(2) through (g)(5) of this section set forth four safe harbors the use of which will result in a determination that the taxpayer is not in actual or constructive receipt of money or other property for purposes of section 1031 and this section. More than one safe harbor can be used in the same deferred exchange, but the terms and conditions of each must be separately satisfied. For purposes of the safe harbor rules, the term "taxpayer" does not include a person or entity utilized in a safe harbor (e.g., a qualified intermediary). See paragraph (g)(8), *Example 3(v)*, of this section.

(2) *Security or guarantee arrangements.*—(i) In the case of a deferred exchange, the determination of whether the taxpayer is in actual or constructive receipt of money or other property before the taxpayer actually receives like-kind replacement property will be made without regard to the fact that the obligation of the taxpayer's transferee to transfer the replacement property to the taxpayer is or may be secured or guaranteed by one or more of the following—

(A) A mortgage, deed of trust, or other security interest in property (other than cash or a cash equivalent),

(B) A standby letter of credit which satisfies all of the requirements of §15A.453-1(b)(3)(iii) and which may not be drawn upon in the absence of a default of the transferee's obligation to transfer like-kind replacement property to the taxpayer, or

(C) A guarantee of a third party.

(ii) Paragraph (g)(2)(i) of this section ceases to apply at the time the taxpayer has an immediate ability or unrestricted right to receive money or other property pursuant to the security or guarantee arrangement.

(3) *Qualified escrow accounts and qualified trusts.*—(i) In the case of a deferred exchange, the determination of whether the taxpayer is in actual or constructive receipt of money or other property before the taxpayer actually receives like-kind replacement property will be made without regard to the fact that the obligation of the taxpayer's transferee to transfer the replacement property to the taxpayer is or may be secured by cash or a cash equivalent if the cash or cash equivalent is held in a qualified escrow account or in a qualified trust.

(ii) A qualified escrow account is an escrow account wherein—

(A) The escrow holder is not the taxpayer or a disqualified person (as defined in paragraph (k) of this section), and

(B) The escrow agreement expressly limits the taxpayer's rights to receive, pledge, borrow, or otherwise obtain the benefits of the cash or cash equivalent held in the escrow account as provided in paragraph (g)(6) of this section.

(iii) A qualified trust is a trust wherein—

(A) The trustee is not the taxpayer or a disqualified person (as defined in paragraph (k) of this section, except that for this purpose the relationship between the taxpayer and the trustee created by the qualified trust will not be considered a relationship under section 267(b)), and

(B) The trust agreement expressly limits the taxpayer's rights to receive, pledge, borrow, or otherwise obtain the benefits of the cash or cash equivalent held by the trustee as provided in paragraph (g)(6) of this section.

(iv) Paragraph (g)(3)(i) of this section ceases to apply at the time the taxpayer has an immediate ability or unrestricted right to receive, pledge, borrow, or otherwise obtain the benefits of the cash or cash equivalent held in the qualified escrow account or qualified trust. Rights conferred upon the taxpayer under state law to terminate or dismiss the escrow holder of a qualified escrow account or the trustee of a qualified trust are disregarded for this purpose.

(v) A taxpayer may receive money or other property directly from a party to the exchange, but not from a qualified escrow account or a qualified trust, without affecting the application of paragraph (g)(3)(i) of this section.

(4) *Qualified intermediaries.*—(i) In the case of a taxpayer's transfer of relinquished property involving a qualified intermediary, the qualified intermediary is not considered the agent of the taxpayer for purposes of section 1031(a). In such a case, the taxpayer's transfer of relinquished property and subsequent receipt of like-kind replacement property is treated as an exchange, and the determination of whether the taxpayer is in actual or constructive receipt of money or other property before the taxpayer actually receives like-kind replacement property is made as if the qualified intermediary is not the agent of the taxpayer.

(ii) Paragraph (g)(4)(i) of this section applies only if the agreement between the taxpayer and the qualified intermediary expressly limits the taxpayer's rights to receive, pledge, borrow, or otherwise obtain the benefits of money or other property held by the qualified intermediary as provided in paragraph (g)(6) of this section.

(iii) A qualified intermediary is a person who—

(A) Is not the taxpayer or a disqualified person (as defined in paragraph (k) of this section), and

(B) Enters into a written agreement with the taxpayer (the "exchange agreement") and, as required by the exchange agreement, acquires the relinquished property from the taxpayer, transfers the relinquished property, acquires the replacement property, and transfers the replacement property to the taxpayer.

(iv) Regardless of whether an intermediary acquires and transfers property under general tax principals [principles], solely for purposes of paragraph (g)(4)(iii)(B) of this section—

(A) An intermediary is treated as acquiring and transferring property if the intermediary acquires and transfers legal title to that property,

(B) An intermediary is treated as acquiring and transferring the relinquished property if the intermediary (either on its own behalf or as the agent of any party to the transaction) enters into an agreement with a person other than the taxpayer for the transfer of the relinquished property to that person and, pursuant to that agreement, the relinquised property is transferred to that person, and

(C) An intermediary is treated as acquiring and transferring replacement property if the intermediary (either on its own behalf or as the agent of any party to the transaction) enters into an agreement with the owner of the replacement property for the transfer of that property and, pursuant to that agreement, the replacement property is transferred to the taxpayer.

(v) Solely for purposes of paragraphs (g)(4)(iii) and (g)(4)(iv) of this section, an intermediary is treated as entering into an agreement if the rights of a party to the agreement are assigned to the intermediary and all parties to that agreement are notified in writing of the assignment on or before the date of the relevant transfer of property. For example, if a taxpayer enters into an agreement for the transfer of relinquished property and thereafter assigns its rights in that agreement to an intermediary and all parties to that agreement are notified in writing of the assignment on or before the date of the transfer of the relinquished property, the intermediary is treated as entering into that agreement. If the relinquished property is transferred pursuant to that agreement, the intermediary is treated as having acquired and transferred the relinquished property.

(vi) Paragraph (g)(4)(i) of this section ceases to apply at the time the taxpayer has an immediate ability or unrestricted right to receive, pledge, borrow, or otherwise obtain the benefits of money or other property held by the qualified intermediary. Rights conferred upon the taxpayer under state law to terminate or dismiss the qualified intermediary are disregarded for this purpose.

(vii) A taxpayer may receive money or other property directly from a party to the transaction other than the qualified intermediary without affecting the application of paragraph (g)(4)(i) of this section.

(5) *Interest and growth factors.*—In the case of a deferred exchange, the determination of whether the taxpayer is in actual or constructive receipt of money or other property before the taxpayer actually receives the like-kind replacement property will be made without regard to the fact that the taxpayer is or may be entitled to receive any interest or growth factor with respect to the deferred exchange. The preceding sentence applies only if the agreement pursuant to which the taxpayer is or may be entitled to the interest or growth factor expressly limits the taxpayer's rights to receive the interest or growth factor as provided in paragraph (g)(6) of this section. For additional rules concerning interest or growth factors, see paragraph (h) of this section.

(6) *Additional restrictions on safe harbors under paragraphs (g)(3) through (g)(5).*—(i) An agreement limits a taxpayer's rights as provided in this paragraph (g)(6) only if the agreement provides that the taxpayer has no rights, except as provided in paragraphs (g)(6)(ii) and (g)(6)(iii) of this section, to receive, pledge, borrow, or otherwise obtain the benefits of money or other property before the end of the exchange period.

(ii) The agreement may provide that if the taxpayer has not identified replacement property by the end of the identification period, the taxpayer may have rights to receive, pledge, borrow, or otherwise obtain the benefits of money or other property at any time after the end of the identification period.

(iii) The agreement may provide that if the taxpayer has identified replacement property, the taxpayer may have rights to receive, pledge, borrow, or otherwise obtain the benefits of money or other property upon or after—

(A) The receipt by the taxpayer of all of the replacement property to which the taxpayer is entitled under the exchange agreement, or

(B) The occurrence after the end of the identification period of a material and substantial contingency that—

(1) Relates to the deferred exchange,

(2) Is provided for in writing, and

(3) Is beyond the control of the taxpayer and of any disqualified person (as defined in paragraph (k) of this section), other than the

Reg. §1.1031(k)-1(g)(6)(iii)(B)(3)

person obligated to transfer the replacement property to the taxpayer.

(7) *Items disregarded in applying safe harbors under paragraphs (g)(3) through (g)(5).*—In determining whether a safe harbor under paragraphs (g)(3) through (g)(5) of this section ceases to apply and whether the taxpayer's rights to receive, pledge, borrow, or otherwise obtain the benefits of money or other property are expressly limited as provided in paragraph (g)(6) of this section, the taxpayer's receipt of or right to receive any of the following items will be disregarded—

(i) Items that a seller may receive as a consequence of the disposition of property and that are not included in the amount realized from the disposition of property (e.g., prorated rents), and

(ii) Transactional items that relate to the disposition of the relinquished property or to the acquisition of the replacement property and appear under local standards in the typical closing statement as the responsibility of a buyer or seller (e.g., commissions, prorated taxes, recording or transfer taxes, and title company fees).

(8) *Examples.*—This paragraph (g) may be illustrated by the following examples. Unless otherwise provided in an example, the following facts are assumed: B, a calendar year taxpayer, and C agree to enter into a deferred exchange. Pursuant to their agreement, B is to transfer real property X to C on May 17, 1991. Real property X, which has been held by B for investment, is unencumbered and has a fair market value on May 17, 1991, of $100,000. On or before July 1, 1991 (the end of the identification period), B is to identify replacement property that is of a like kind to real property X. On or before November 13, 1991 (the end of the exchange period), C is required to purchase the property identified by B and to transfer that property to B. To the extent the fair market value of the replacement property transferred to B is greater or less than the fair market value of real property X, either B or C, as applicable, will make up the difference by paying cash to the other party after the date the replacement property is received by B. The replacement property is identified as provided in paragraph (c) of this section (relating to identification of replacement property) and is of a like kind to real property X (determined without regard to section 1031(a)(3) and this section). B intends to hold any replacement property received for investment.

Example 1. (i) On May 17, 1991, B transfers real property X to C. On the same day, C pays $10,000 to B and deposits $90,000 in escrow as security for C's obligation to perform under the agreement. The escrow agreement provides that B has no rights to receive, pledge, borrow, or otherwise obtain the benefits of the money in escrow before November 14, 1991, except that:

(A) if B fails to identify replacement property on or before July 1, 1991, B may demand the funds in escrow at any time after July 1, 1991; and

(B) if B identifies and receives replacement property, then B may demand the balance of the remaining funds in escrow at any time after B has received the replacement property.

The funds in escrow may be used to purchase the replacement property. The escrow holder is not a disqualified person as defined in paragraph (k) of this section. Pursuant to the terms of the agreement, B identifies replacement property, and C purchases the replacement property using the funds in escrow and transfers the replacement property to B.

(ii) C's obligation to transfer the replacement property to B was secured by cash held in a qualified escrow account because the escrow holder was not a disqualified person and the escrow agreement expressly limited B's rights to receive, pledge, borrow, or otherwise obtain the benefits of the money in escrow as provided in paragraph (g)(6) of this section. In addition, B did not have the immediate ability or unrestricted right to receive money or other property in escrow before B actually received the like-kind replacement property. Therefore, for purposes of section 1031 and this section, B is determined not to be in actual or constructive receipt of the $90,000 held in escrow before B received the like-kind replacement property. The transfer of real property X by B and B's acquisition of the replacement property qualify as an exchange under section 1031. See paragraph (j) of this section for determining the amount of gain or loss recognized.

Example 2. (i) On May 17, 1991, B transfers real property X to C, and C deposits $100,000 in escrow as security for C's obligation to perform under the agreement. Also on May 17, B identifies real property J as replacement property. The escrow agreement provides that no funds may be paid out without prior written approval of both B and C. The escrow agreement also provides that B has no rights to receive, pledge, borrow, or otherwise obtain the benefits of the money in escrow before November 14, 1991, except that:

(A) B may demand the funds in escrow at any time after the later of July 1, 1991, and [or] the occurrence of any of the following events—

(1) real property J is destroyed, seized, requisitioned, or condemned, or

(2) a determination is made that the regulatory approval necessary for the transfer of real property J cannot be obtained in time for real property J to be transferred to B before the end of the exchange period;

(B) B may demand the funds in escrow at any time after August 14, 1991, if real property J has not been rezoned from residential to commercial use by that date; and

(C) B may demand the funds in escrow at the time B receives real property J or any time thereafter.

Otherwise, B is entitled to all funds in escrow after November 13, 1991. The funds in escrow may be used to purchase the replacement property. The escrow holder is not a disqualified person as described in paragraph (k) of this section. Real property J is not rezoned from residential to commercial use on or before August 14, 1991.

(ii) C's obligation to transfer the replacement property to B was secured by cash held in a qualified escrow account because the escrow holder was not a disqualified person and the escrow agreement expressly limited B's rights to receive, pledge, borrow, or otherwise obtain the benefits of the money in escrow as provided in paragraph (g)(6) of this section. From May 17, 1991, until August 15, 1991, B did not have the immediate ability or unrestricted right to receive money or other property before B actually received the like-kind replacement property. Therefore, for purposes of section 1031 and this section, B is determined not to be in actual or constructive receipt of the $100,000 in escrow from May 17, 1991, until August 15, 1991. However, on August 15, 1991, B had the unrestricted right, upon notice, to draw upon the $100,000 held in escrow. Thus, the safe harbor ceased to apply and B was in constructive receipt of the funds held in escrow. Because B constructively received the full amount of the consideration ($100,000) before B actually received the like-kind replacement property, the transaction is treated as a sale and not as a deferred exchange. The result does not change even if B chose not to demand the funds in escrow and continued to attempt to have real property J rezoned and to receive the property on or before November 13, 1991.

(iii) If real property J had been rezoned on or before August 14, 1991, and C had purchased real property J and transferred it to B on or before November 13, 1991, the transaction would have qualified for nonrecognition of gain or loss under section 1031(a).

Example 3. (i) On May 1, 1991, D offers to purchase real property X for $100,000. However, D is unwilling to participate in a like-kind exchange. B thus enters into an exchange agreement with C whereby B retains C to facilitate an exchange with respect to real property X. C is not a disqualified person as described in paragraph (k) of this section. The exchange agreement between B and C provides that B is to execute and deliver a deed conveying real property X to C who, in turn, is to execute and deliver a deed conveying real property X to D. The exchange agreement expressly limits B's rights to receive, pledge, borrow, or otherwise obtain the benefits of money or other property held by C as provided in paragraph (g)(6) of this section. On May 3, 1991, C enters into an agreement with D to transfer real property X to D for $100,000. On

May 17, 1991, B executes and delivers to C a deed conveying real property X to C. On the same date, C executes and delivers to D a deed conveying real property X to D, and D deposits $100,000 in escrow. The escrow holder is not a disqualified person as defined in paragraph (k) of this section and the escrow agreement expressly limits B's rights to receive, pledge, borrow, or otherwise obtain the benefits of money or other property in escrow as provided in paragraph (g)(6) of this section. However, the escrow agreement provides that the money in escrow may be used to purchase replacement property. On June 3, 1991, B identifies real property K as replacement property. On August 9, 1991, E executes and delivers to C a deed conveying real property K to C and $80,000 is released from the escrow and paid to E. On the same date, C executes and delivers to B a deed conveying real property K to B, and the escrow holder pays B $20,000, the balance of the $100,000 sale price of real property X remaining after the purchase of real property K for $80,000.

(ii) B and C entered into an exchange agreement that satisfied the requirements of paragraph (g)(4)(iii) (B) of this section. Regardless of whether C may have acquired and transferred real property X under general tax principles, C is treated as having acquired and transferred real property X because C acquired and transferred legal title to real property X. Similarly, C is treated as having acquired and transferred real property X because C acquired and transferred legal title to real property K. Thus, C was a qualified intermediary. This result is reached for purposes of this section regardless of whether C was B's agent under state law.

(iii) Because the escrow holder was not a disqualified person and the escrow agreement expressly limited B's rights to receive, pledge, borrow, or otherwise obtain the benefits of money or other property in escrow as provided in paragraph (g)(6) of this section, the escrow account was a qualified escrow account. For purposes of section 1031 and this section, therefore, B is determined not to be in actual or constructive receipt of the funds in escrow before B received real property K.

(iv) The exchange agreement between B and C expressly limited B's rights to receive, pledge, borrow, or otherwise obtain the benefits of any money held by C as provided in paragraph (g)(6) of this section. Because C was a qualified intermediary, for purposes of section 1031 and this section B is determined not to be in actual or constructive receipt of any funds held by C before B received real property K. In addition, B's transfer of real property X and acquisition of real property K qualify as an exchange under section 1031. See paragraph (j) of this section for determining the amount of gain or loss recognized.

(v) If the escrow agreement had expressly limited C's rights to receive, pledge, borrow, or otherwise obtain the benefits of money or other property in escrow as provided in paragraph (g)(6) of this section, but had not expressly limited B's rights to receive, pledge, borrow, or otherwise obtain the benefits of that money or other property, the escrow account would not have been a qualified escrow account. Consequently, paragraph (g)(3)(i) of this section would not have been applicable in determining whether B was in actual or constructive receipt of that money or other property before B received real property X.

Example 4. (i) On May 1, 1991, B enters into an agreement to sell real property X to D for $100,000 on May 17, 1991. However, D is unwilling to participate in a like-kind exchange. B thus enters into an exchange agreement with C whereby B retains C to facilitate an exchange with respect to real property X. C is not a disqualified person as described in paragraph (k) of this section. In the exchange agreement between B and C, B assigns to C all of B's rights in the agreement with D. The exchange agreement expressly limits B's rights to receive, pledge, borrow, or otherwise obtain the benefits of money or other property held by C as provided in paragraph (g)(6) of this section. On May 17, 1991, B notifies D in writing of the assignment. On the same date, B executes and delivers to D a deed conveying real property X to D. D pays $10,000 to B and $90,000 to C. On June 1, 1991, B identifies real property L as replacement property. On July 5, 1991, B enters into an agreement to purchase real property L from E for $90,000, assigns its rights in that agreement to C, and notifies E in writing of the assignment. On August 9, 1991, C pays $90,000 to E, and E executes and delivers to B a deed conveying real property L to B.

(ii) The exchange agreement entered into by B and C satisfied the requirements of paragraph (g)(4)(iii) (B) of this section. Because B's rights in its agreements with D and E were assigned to C, and D and E were notified in writing of the assignment on or before the transfer of real properties X and L, respectively, C is treated as entering into those agreements. Because C is treated as entering into an agreement with D for the transfer of real property X and, pursuant to that agreement, real property X was transferred to D, C is treated as acquiring and transferring real property X. Similarly, because C is treated as entering into an agreement with E for the transfer of real property K and, pursuant to that agreement, real property K was transferred to B, C is treated as acquiring and transferring real property K. This result is reached for purposes of this section regardless of whether C was B's agent under state law and regardless of whether C is considered, under general tax principles, to have acquired title or beneficial ownership of the properties. Thus, C was a qualified intermediary.

(iii) The exchange agreement between B and C expressly limited B's rights to receive, pledge, borrow, or otherwise obtain the benefits of the

money held by C as provided in paragraph (g)(6) of this section. Thus, B did not have the immediate ability or unrestricted right to receive money or other property held by C before B received real property L. For purposes of section 1031 and this section, therefore, B is determined not to be in actual or constructive receipt of the $90,000 held by C before B received real property L. In addition, the transfer of real property X by B and B's acquisition of real property L qualify as an exchange under section 1031. See paragraph (j) of this section for determining the amount of gain or loss recognized.

Example 5. (i) On May 1, 1991, B enters into an agreement to sell real property X to D for $100,000. However, D is unwilling to participate in a like-kind exchange. B thus enters into an agreement with C whereby B retains C to facilitate an exchange with respect to real property X. C is not a disqualified person as described in paragraph (k) of this section. The agreement between B and C expressly limits B's rights to receive, pledge, borrow, or otherwise obtain the benefits of money or other property held by C as provided in paragraph (g)(6) of this section. C neither enters into an agreement with D to transfer real property X to D nor is assigned B's rights in B's agreement to sell real property X to D. On May 17, 1991, B transfers real property X to D and instructs D to transfer the $100,000 to C. On June 1, 1991, B identifies real property M as replacement property. On August 9, 1991, C purchases real property L from E for $100,000, and E executes and delivers to C a deed conveying real property M to C. On the same date, C executes and delivers to B a deed conveying real property M to B.

(ii) Because B transferred real property X directly to D under B's agreement with D, C did not acquire real property X from B and transfer real property X to D. Moreover, because C did not acquire legal title to real property X, did not enter into an agreement with D to transfer real property X to D, and was not assigned B's rights in B's agreement to sell real property X to D, C is not treated as acquiring and transferring real property X. Thus, C was not a qualified intermediary and paragraph (g) (4)(i) of this section does not apply.

(iii) B did not exchange real property X for real property M. Rather, B sold real property X to D and purchased, through C, real property M. Therefore, the transfer of real property X does not qualify for nonrecognition of gain or loss under section 1031.

(h) *Interest and growth factors.*—(1) *In general.*—For purposes of this section, the taxpayer is treated as being entitled to receive interest or a growth factor with respect to a deferred exchange if the amount of money or property the taxpayer is entitled to receive depends upon the length of time elapsed between transfer of the relinquished property and receipt of the replacement property.

(2) *Treatment as interest.*—If, as part of a deferred exchange, the taxpayer receives interest or a growth factor, the interest or growth factor will be treated as interest, regardless of whether it is paid to the taxpayer in cash or in property (including property of a like kind). The taxpayer must include the interest or growth factor in income according to the taxpayer's method of accounting. For rules under section 468B(g) relating to the current taxation of qualified escrow accounts, qualified trusts, and other escrow accounts, trusts, and funds used during deferred exchanges of like-kind property, see § 1.468B-6.

(i) [Reserved]

(j) *Determination of gain or loss recognized and the basis of property received in a deferred exchange.*—(1) In *general.*—Except as otherwise provided, the amount of gain or loss recognized and the basis of property received in a deferred exchange is determined by applying the rules of section 1031 and the regulations thereunder. See §§ 1.1031(b)-1, 1.1031(c)-1, 1.1031(d)-1, 1.1031(d)-1T, 1.1031(d)-2, and 1.1031(j)-1.

(2) *Coordination with section 453.*—(i) *Qualified escrow accounts and qualified trusts.*—Subject to the limitations of paragraphs (j)(2)(iv) and (v) of this section, in the case of a taxpayer's transfer of relinquished property in which the obligation of the taxpayer's transferee to transfer replacement property to the taxpayer is or may be secured by cash or a cash equivalent, the determination of whether the taxpayer has received a payment for purposes of section 453 and § 15a.453-1(b)(3)(i) of this chapter will be made without regard to the fact that the obligation is or may be so secured if the cash or cash equivalent is held in a qualified escrow account or a qualified trust. This paragraph (j)(2)(i) ceases to apply at the earlier of—

(A) The time described in paragraph (g)(3)(iv) of this section; or

(B) The end of the exchange period.

(ii) *Qualified intermediaries.*—Subject to the limitations of paragraphs (j)(2)(iv) and (v) of this section, in the case of a taxpayer's transfer of relinquished property involving a qualified intermediary, the determination of whether the taxpayer has received a payment for purposes of section 453 and § 15a.453-1(b)(3)(i) of this chapter is made as if the qualified intermediary is not the agent of the taxpayer. For purposes of this paragraph (j)(2)(ii), a person who otherwise satisfies the definition of a qualified intermediary is treated as a qualified intermediary even though that person ultimately fails to acquire identified replacement property and transfer it to the taxpayer. This paragraph (j)(2)(ii) ceases to apply at the earlier of—

(A) The time described in paragraph (g)(4)(vi) of this section; or

(B) The end of the exchange period.

(iii) *Transferee indebtedness.*—In the case of a transaction described in paragraph (j)(2)(ii) of this section, the receipt by the taxpayer of an evidence of indebtedness of the transferee of the qualified intermediary is treated as the receipt of an evidence of indebtedness of the person acquiring property from the taxpayer for purposes of section 453 and § 15a.453-1(b)(3)(i) of this chapter.

(iv) *Bona fide intent requirement.*—The provisions of paragraphs (j)(2)(i) and (ii) of this section do not apply unless the taxpayer has a bona fide intent to enter into a deferred exchange at the beginning of the exchange period. A taxpayer will be treated as having a bona fide intent only if it is reasonable to believe, based on all the facts and circumstances as of the beginning of the exchange period, that like-kind replacement property will be acquired before the end of the exchange period.

(v) *Disqualified property.*—The provisions of paragraphs (j)(2)(i) and (ii) of this section do not apply if the relinquished property is disqualified property. For purposes of this paragraph (j)(2), *disqualified property* means property that is not held for productive use in a trade or business or for investment or is property described in section 1031(a)(2).

(vi) *Examples.*—This paragraph (j)(2) may be illustrated by the following examples. Unless otherwise provided in an example, the following facts are assumed: B is a calendar year taxpayer who agrees to enter into a deferred exchange. Pursuant to the agreement, B is to transfer real property X. Real property X, which has been held by B for investment, is unencumbered and has a fair market value of $100,000 at the time of transfer. B's adjusted basis in real property X at that time is $60,000. B identifies a single like-kind replacement property before the end of the identification period, and B receives the replacement property before the end of the exchange period. The transaction qualifies as a like-kind exchange under section 1031.

Example 1. (i) On September 22, 1994, B transfers real property X to C and C agrees to acquire like-kind property and deliver it to B. On that date B has a bona fide intent to enter into a deferred exchange. C's obligation, which is not payable on demand or readily tradable, is secured by $100,000 in cash. The $100,000 is deposited by C in an escrow account that is a qualified escrow account under paragraph (g)(3) of this section. The escrow agreement provides that B has no rights to receive, pledge, borrow, or otherwise obtain the benefits of the cash deposited in the escrow account until the earlier of the date the replacement property is delivered to B or the end of the exchange period. On March 11, 1995, C acquires replacement property having a fair market value of $80,000 and delivers the replacement property to B. The $20,000 in cash remaining in the qualified escrow account is distributed to B at that time.

(ii) Under section 1031(b), B recognizes gain to the extent of the $20,000 in cash that B receives in the exchange. Under paragraph (j)(2)(i) of this section, the qualified escrow account is disregarded for purposes of section 453 and §15a.453-1(b)(3)(i) of this chapter in determining whether B is in receipt of payment. Accordingly, B's receipt of C's obligation on September 22, 1994, does not constitute a payment. Instead, B is treated as receiving payment on March 11, 1995, on receipt of the $20,000 in cash from the qualified escrow account. Subject to the other requirements of sections 453 and 453A, B may report the $20,000 gain in 1995 under the installment method. See section 453(f)(6) for special rules for determining total contract price and gross profit in the case of an exchange described in section 1031(b).

Example 2. (i) D offers to purchase real property X but is unwilling to participate in a like-kind exchange. B thus enters into an exchange agreement with C whereby B retains C to facilitate an exchange with respect to real property X. On September 22, 1994, pursuant to the agreement, B transfers real property X to C who transfers it to D for $100,000 in cash. On that date B has a bona fide intent to enter into a deferred exchange. C is a qualified intermediary under paragraph (g)(4) of this section. The exchange agreement provides that B has no rights to receive, pledge, borrow, or otherwise obtain the benefits of the money held by C until the earlier of the date the replacement property is delivered to B or the end of the exchange period. On March 11, 1995, C acquires replacement property having a fair market value of $80,000 and delivers it, along with the remaining $20,000 from the transfer of real property X, to B.

(ii) Under section 1031(b), B recognizes gain to the extent of the $20,000 cash B receives in the exchange. Under paragraph (j)(2)(ii) of this section, any agency relationship between B and C is disregarded for purposes of section 453 and §15a.453-1(b)(3)(i) of this chapter in determining whether B is in receipt of payment. Accordingly, B is not treated as having received payment on September 22, 1994, on C's receipt of payment from D for the relinquished property. Instead, B is treated as receiving payment on March 11, 1995, on receipt of the $20,000 in cash from C. Subject to the other requirements of sections 453 and 453A, B may report the $20,000 gain in 1995 under the installment method.

Example 3. (i) D offers to purchase real property X but is unwilling to participate in a like-kind exchange. B enters into an exchange agreement with C whereby B retains C as a qualified intermediary to facilitate an exchange with respect to real property X. On December 1, 1994, pursuant to the agreement, B transfers real property X to C who transfers it to D for $100,000 in cash. On that date B has a bona fide intent to enter into a deferred exchange. The exchange

agreement provides that B has no rights to receive, pledge, borrow, or otherwise obtain the benefits of the cash held by C until the earliest of the end of the identification period if B has not identified replacement property, the date the replacement property is delivered to B, or the end of the exchange period. Although B has a bona fide intent to enter into a deferred exchange at the beginning of the exchange period, B does not identify or acquire any replacement property. In 1995, at the end of the identification period, C delivers the entire $100,000 from the sale of real property X to B.

(ii) Under section 1001, B realizes gain to the extent of the amount realized ($100,000) over the adjusted basis in real property X ($60,000), or $40,000. Because B has a bona fide intent at the beginning of the exchange period to enter into a deferred exchange, paragraph (j)(2)(iv) of this section does not make paragraph (j)(2)(ii) of this section inapplicable even though B fails to acquire replacement property. Further, under paragraph (j)(2)(ii) of this section, C is a qualified intermediary even though C does not acquire and transfer replacement property to B. Thus, any agency relationship between B and C is disregarded for purposes of section 453 and §15a.453-1(b)(3)(i) of this chapter in determining whether B is in receipt of payment. Accordingly, B is not treated as having received payment on December 1, 1994, on C's receipt of payment from D for the relinquished property. Instead, B is treated as receiving payment at the end of the identification period in 1995 on receipt of the $100,000 in cash from C. Subject to the other requirements of sections 453 and 453A, B may report the $40,000 gain in 1995 under the installment method.

Example 4. (i) D offers to purchase real property X but is unwilling to participate in a like-kind exchange. B thus enters into an exchange agreement with C whereby B retains C to facilitate an exchange with respect to real property X. C is a qualified intermediary under paragraph (g)(4) of this section. On September 22, 1994, pursuant to the agreement, B transfers real property X to C who then transfers it to D for $80,000 in cash and D's 10-year installment obligation for $20,000. On that date B has a bona fide intent to enter into a deferred exchange. The exchange agreement provides that B has no rights to receive, pledge, borrow, or otherwise obtain the benefits of the money or other property held by C until the earlier of the date the replacement property is delivered to B or the end of the exchange period. D's obligation bears adequate stated interest and is not payable on demand or readily tradable. On March 11, 1995, C acquires replacement property having a fair market value of $80,000 and delivers it, along with the $20,000 installment obligation, to B.

(ii) Under section 1031(b), $20,000 of B's gain (i.e., the amount of the installment obligation B receives in the exchange) does not qualify for nonrecognition under section 1031(a). Under paragraphs (j)(2)(ii) and (iii) of this section, B's receipt of D's obligation is treated as the receipt of an obligation of the person acquiring the property for purposes of section 453 and § 15a.453-1(b)(3)(i) of this chapter in determining whether B is in receipt of payment. Accordingly, B's receipt of the obligation is not treated as a payment. Subject to the other requirements of sections 453 and 453A, B may report the $20,000 gain under the installment method on receiving payments from D on the obligation.

Example 5. (i) B is a corporation that has held real property X to expand its manufacturing operations. However, at a meeting in November 1994, B's directors decide that real property X is not suitable for the planned expansion, and authorize a like-kind exchange of this property for property that would be suitable for the planned expansion. B enters into an exchange agreement with C whereby B retains C as a qualified intermediary to facilitate an exchange with respect to real property X. On November 28, 1994, pursuant to the agreement, B transfers real property X to C, who then transfers it to D for $100,000 in cash. The exchange agreement does not include any limitations or conditions that make it unreasonable to believe that like-kind replacement property will be acquired before the end of the exchange period. The exchange agreement provides that B has no rights to receive, pledge, borrow, or otherwise obtain the benefits of the cash held by C until the earliest of the end of the identification period, if B has not identified replacement property, the date the replacement property is delivered to B, or the end of the exchange period. In early January 1995, B's directors meet and decide that it is not feasible to proceed with the planned expansion due to a business downturn reflected in B's preliminary financial reports for the last quarter of 1994. Thus, B's directors instruct C to stop seeking replacement property. C delivers the $100,000 cash to B on January 12, 1995, at the end of the identification period. Both the decision to exchange real property X for other property and the decision to cease seeking replacement property because of B's business downturn are recorded in the minutes of the directors' meetings. There are no other facts or circumstances that would indicate whether, on November 28, 1994, B had a bona fide intent to enter into a deferred like-kind exchange.

(ii) Under section 1001, B realizes gain to the extent of the amount realized ($100,000) over the adjusted basis of real property X ($60,000), or $40,000. The directors' authorization of a like-kind exchange, the terms of the exchange agreement with C, and the absence of other relevant facts, indicate that B had a bona fide intent at the beginning of the exchange period to enter into a deferred like-kind exchange. Thus, paragraph (j)(2)(iv) of this section does not make paragraph (j)(2)(ii) of this section inapplicable, even though B fails to acquire replacement property. Further, under paragraph (j)(2)(ii) of this section, C is a

qualified intermediary, even though C does not transfer replacement property to B. Thus, any agency relationship between B and C is disregarded for purposes of section 453 and § 15a.453-1(b)(3)(i) of this chapter in determining whether B is in receipt of payment. Accordingly, B is not treated as having received payment until January 12, 1995, on receipt of the $100,000 cash from C. Subject to the other requirements of sections 453 and 453A, B may report the $40,000 gain in 1995 under the installment method.

Example 6. (i) B has held real property X for use in its trade or business, but decides to transfer that property because it is no longer suitable for B's planned expansion of its commercial enterprise. B and D agree to enter into a deferred exchange. Pursuant to their agreement, B transfers real property X to D on September 22, 1994, and D deposits $100,000 cash in a qualified escrow account as security for D's obligation under the agreement to transfer replacement property to B before the end of the exchange period. D's obligation is not payable on demand or readily tradable. The agreement provides that B is not required to accept any property that is not zoned for commercial use. Before the end of the identification period, B identifies real properties J, K, and L, all zoned for residential use, as replacement properties. Any one of these properties, rezoned for commercial use, would be suitable for B's planned expansion. In recent years, the zoning board with jurisdiction over properties J, K, and L has rezoned similar properties for commercial use. The escrow agreement provides that B has no rights to receive, pledge, borrow, or otherwise obtain the benefits of the money in the escrow account until the earlier of the time that the zoning board determines, after the end of the identification period, that it will not rezone the properties for commercial use or the end of the exchange period. On January 5, 1995, the zoning board decides that none of the properties will be rezoned for commercial use. Pursuant to the exchange agreement, B receives the $100,000 cash from the escrow on January 5, 1995. There are no other facts or circumstances that would indicate whether, on September 22, 1994, B had a bona fide intent to enter into a deferred like-kind exchange.

(ii) Under section 1001, B realizes gain to the extent of the amount realized ($100,000) over the adjusted basis of real property X ($60,000), or $40,000. The terms of the exchange agreement with D, the identification of properties J, K, and L, the efforts to have those properties rezoned for commercial purposes, and the absence of other relevant facts, indicate that B had a bona fide intent at the beginning of the exchange period to enter into a deferred exchange. Moreover, the limitations imposed in the exchange agreement on acceptable replacement property do not make it unreasonable to believe that like-kind replacement property would be acquired before the end of the exchange period. Therefore, paragraph (j)(2)(iv) of this section does not make

Reg. § 1.1031(k)-1(j)(2)(vi)

paragraph (j)(2)(i) of this section inapplicable even though B fails to acquire replacement property. Thus, for purposes of section 453 and § 15a.453-1(b)(3)(i) of this chapter, the qualified escrow account is disregarded in determining whether B is in receipt of payment. Accordingly, B is not treated as having received payment on September 22, 1994, on D's deposit of the $100,000 cash into the qualified escrow account. Instead, B is treated as receiving payment on January 5, 1995. Subject to the other requirements of sections 453 and 453A, B may report the $40,000 gain in 1995 under the installment method.

(vii) *Effective date.*—This paragraph (j)(2) is effective for transfers of property occurring on or after April 20, 1994. Taxpayers may apply this paragraph (j)(2) to transfers of property occurring before April 20, 1994 but on or after June 10, 1991, if those transfers otherwise meet the requirements of § 1.1031(k)-1. In addition, taxpayers may apply this paragraph (j)(2) to transfers of property occurring before June 10, 1991, but on or after May 16, 1990, if those transfers otherwise meet the requirements of § 1.1031(k)-1 or follow the guidance of IA-237-84 published in 1990-1, C.B. See § 601.601(d)(2)(ii)(*b*) of this chapter.

(3) *Examples.*—This paragraph (j) may be illustrated by the following examples. Unless otherwise provided in an example, the following facts are assumed: B, a calendar year taxpayer, and C agree to enter into a deferred exchange. Pursuant to their agreement, B is to transfer real property X to C on May 17, 1991. Real property X, which has been held by B for investment, is unencumbered and has a fair market value on May 17, 1991, of $100,000. B's adjusted basis in real property X is $40,000. On or before July 1, 1991 (the end of the identification period), B is to identify replacement property that is of a like kind to real property X. On or before November 13, 1991 (the end of the exchange period), C is required to purchase the property identified by B and to transfer that property to B. To the extent the fair market value of the replacement property transferred to B is greater or less than the fair market value of real property X, either B or C, as applicable, will make up the difference by paying cash to the other party after the date the replacement property is received. The replacement property is identified as provided in paragraph (c) of this section and is of a like kind to real property X (determined without regard to section 1031(a)(3) and this section). B intends to hold any replacement property received for investment.

Example 1. (i) On May 17, 1991, B transfers real property X to C and identifies real property R as replacement property. On June 3, 1991, C transfers $10,000 to B. On September 4, 1991, C purchases real property R for $90,000 and transfers real property R to B.

(ii) The $10,000 received by B is "money or other property" for purposes of section 1031 and

the regulations thereunder. Under section 1031(b), B recognizes gain in the amount of $10,000. Under section 1031(d), B's basis in real property R is $40,000 (i.e., B's basis in real property X ($40,000), decreased in the amount of money received ($10,000), and increased in the amount of gain recognized ($10,000) in the deferred exchange).

Example 2. (i) On May 17, 1991, B transfers real property X to C and identifies real property S as replacement property, and C transfers $10,000 to B. On September 4, 1991, C purchases real property S for $100,000 and transfers real property S to B. On the same day, B transfers $10,000 to C.

(ii) The $10,000 received by B is "money or other property" for purposes of section 1031 and the regulations thereunder. Under section 1031(b), B recognizes gain in the amount of $10,000. Under section 1031 (d), B's basis in real property S is $50,000 (i.e., B's basis in real property X ($40,000), decreased in the amount of money received ($10,000), increased in the amount of gain recognized ($10,000), and increased in the amount of the additional consideration paid by B ($10,000) in the deferred exchange).

Example 3. (i) Under the exchange agreement, B has the right at all times to demand $100,000 in cash in lieu of replacement property. On May 17, 1991, B transfers real property X to C and identifies real property T as replacement property. On September 4, 1991, C purchases real property T for $100,000 and transfers real property T to B.

(ii) Because B has the right on May 17, 1991, to demand $100,000 in cash in lieu of replacement property, B is in constructive receipt of the $100,000 on that date. Thus, the transaction is a sale and not an exchange, and the $60,000 gain realized by B in the transaction (i.e., $100,000 amount realized less $40,000 adjusted basis) is recognized. Under section 1031(d), B's basis in real property T is $100,000.

Example 4. (i) Under the exchange agreement, B has the right at all times to demand up to $30,000 in cash and the balance in replacement property instead of receiving replacement property in the amount of $100,000. On May 17, 1991, B transfers real property X to C and identifies real property U as replacement property. On September 4, 1991, C purchases real property U for $100,000 and transfers real property U to B.

(ii) The transaction qualifies as a deferred exchange under section 1031 and this section. However, because B had the right on May 17, 1991, to demand up to $30,000 in cash, B is in constructive receipt of $30,000 on that date. Under section 1031(b), B recognizes gain in the amount of $30,000. Under section 1031(d), B's basis in real property U is $70,000 (i.e., B's basis in real property X ($40,000), decreased in the amount of money that B received ($30,000), increased in the amount of gain recognized ($30,000), and increased in the amount of additional consideration paid by B ($30,000) in the deferred exchange).

Example 5. (i) Assume real property X is encumbered by a mortgage of $30,000. On May 17, 1991, B transfers real property X to C and identifies real property V as replacement property, and C assumes the $30,000 mortgage on real property X. Real property V is encumbered by a $20,000 mortgage. On July 5, 1991, C purchases real property V for $90,000 by paying $70,000 and assuming the mortgage and transfers real property V to B with B assuming the mortgage.

(ii) The consideration received by B in the form of the liability assumed by C ($30,000) is offset by the consideration given by B in the form of the liability assumed by B ($20,000). The excess of the liability assumed by C over the liability assumed by B, $10,000, is treated as "money or other property." See § 1.1031(b)-1 (c). Thus, B recognizes gain under section 1031(b) in the amount of $10,000. Under section 1031(d), B's basis in real property V is $40,000 (i.e., B's basis in real property X ($40,000), decreased in the amount of money that B is treated as receiving in the form of the liability assumed by C ($30,000), increased in the amount of money that B is treated as paying in the form of the liability assumed by B ($20,000), and increased in the amount of the gain recognized ($10,000) in the deferred exchange).

(k) *Definition of disqualified person.*—(1) For purposes of this section, a disqualified person is a person described in paragraph (k)(2), (k)(3), or (k)(4) of this section.

(2) The person is the agent of the taxpayer at the time of the transaction. For this purpose, a person who has acted as the taxpayer's employee, attorney, accountant, investment banker or broker, or real estate agent or broker within the 2-year period ending on the date of the transfer of the first of the relinquished properties is treated as an agent of the taxpayer at the time of the transaction. Solely for purposes of this paragraph (k)(2), performance of the following services will not be taken into account—

(i) Services for the taxpayer with respect to exchanges of property intended to qualify for nonrecognition of gain or loss under section 1031; and

(ii) Routine financial, title insurance, escrow, or trust services for the taxpayer by a financial institution, title insurance company, or escrow company.

(3) The person and the taxpayer bear a relationship described in either section 267(b) or section 707(b) (determined by substituting in each section "10 percent" for "50 percent" each place it appears).

(4)(i) Except as provided in paragraph (k)(4)(ii) of this section, the person and a person described in paragraph (k)(2) of this section bear a relationship described in either section 267(b) or 707(b) (determined by substituting in each

section "10 percent" for "50 percent" each place it appears).

(ii) In the case of a transfer of relinquished property made by a taxpayer on or after January 17, 2001, paragraph (k)(4)(i) of this section does not apply to a bank (as defined in section 581) or a bank affiliate if, but for this paragraph (k)(4)(ii), the bank or bank affiliate would be a disqualified person under paragraph (k)(4)(i) of this section solely because it is a member of the same controlled group (as determined under section 267(f)(1), substituting "10 percent" for "50 percent" where it appears) as a person that has provided investment banking or brokerage services to the taxpayer within the 2-year period described in paragraph (k)(2) of this section. For purposes of this paragraph (k)(4)(ii), a bank affiliate is a corporation whose principal activity is rendering services to facilitate exchanges of property intended to qualify for nonrecognition of gain under section 1031 and all of whose stock is owned by either a bank or a bank holding company (within the meaning of section 2(a) of the Bank Holding Company Act of 1956 (12 U.S.C. 1841(a)).

(5) This paragraph (k) may be illustrated by the following examples. Unless otherwise provided, the following facts are assumed: On May 1, 1991, B enters into an exchange agreement (as defined in paragraph (g)(4)(iii) (B) of this section) with C whereby B retains C to facilitate an exchange with respect to real property X. On May 17, 1991, pursuant to the agreement, B executes and delivers to C a deed conveying real property X to C. C has no relationship to B described in paragraphs (k)(2), (k) (3), or (k)(4) of this section.

Example 1. (i) C is B's accountant and has rendered accounting services to B within the 2-year period ending on May 17, 1991, other than with respect to exchanges of property intended to qualify for nonrecognition of gain or loss under section 1031.

(ii) C is a disqualified person because C has acted as B's accountant within the 2-year period ending on May 17, 1991.

(iii) If C had not acted as B's accountant within the 2-year period ending on May 17, 1991, or if C had acted as B's accountant within that period only with respect to exchanges intended to qualify for nonrecognition of gain or loss under section 1031, C would not have been a disqualified person.

Example 2. (i) C, which is engaged in the trade or business of acting as an intermediary to facilitate deferred exchanges, is a wholly owned subsidiary of an escrow company that has performed routine escrow services for B in the past. C has previously been retained by B to act as an intermediary in prior section 1031 exchanges.

(ii) C is not a disqualified person notwithstanding the intermediary services previously provided by C to B (see paragraph (k)(2)(i) of this section) and notwithstanding the combination of C's relationship to the escrow company and the escrow services previously provided by the escrow company to B (see paragraph (k)(2)(ii) of this section).

Example 3. (i) C is a corporation that is only engaged in the trade or business of acting as an intermediary to facilitate deferred exchanges. Each of 10 law firms owns 10 percent of the outstanding stock of C. One of the 10 law firms that owns 10 percent of C is M. J is the managing partner of M and is the president of C. J, in his capacity as a partner in M, has also rendered legal advice to B within the 2-year period ending on May 17, 1991, on matters other than exchanges intended to qualify for nonrecognition of gain or loss under section 1031.

(ii) J and M are disqualified persons. C, however, is not a disqualified person because neither J nor M own, directly or indirectly, more than 10 percent of the stock of C. Similarly, J's participation in the management of C does not make C a disqualified person.

(1) [Reserved]

(m) *Definition of fair market value.*—For purposes of this section, the fair market value of property means the fair market value of the property without regard to any liabilities secured by the property.

(n) *No inference with respect to actual or constructive receipt rules outside of section 1031.*—The rules provided in this section relating to actual or constructive receipt are intended to be rules for determining whether there is actual or constructive receipt in the case of a deferred exchange. No inference is intended regarding the application of these rules for purposes of determining whether actual or constructive receipt exists for any other purpose.

(o) *Effective date.*—This section applies to transfers of property made by a taxpayer on or after June 10, 1991. However, a transfer of property made by a taxpayer on or after May 16, 1990, but before June 10, 1991, will be treated as complying with section 1031(a)(3) and this section if the deferred exchange satisfies either the provisions of this section or the provisions of the notice of proposed rulemaking published in the *Federal Register* on May 16, 1990 (55 F.R. 20278). [Reg. § 1.1031(k)-1.]

☐ [T.D. 8346, 4-25-91. *Amended by T.D.* 8535, 4-19-94; *T.D.* 8982, 1-31-2002 *and T.D.* 9413, 7-9-2008.]

[Reg. § 1.1032-1]

§ 1.1032-1. Disposition by a corporation of its own capital stock.—(a) The disposition by a corporation of shares of its own stock (including treasury stock) for money or other property does not give rise to taxable gain or deductible loss to the corporation regardless of the nature of the transaction or the facts and circumstances involved. For example, the receipt by a corporation

of the subscription price of shares of its stock upon their original issuance gives rise to neither taxable gain nor deductible loss, whether the subscription or issue price be equal to, in excess of, or less than, the par or stated value of such stock. Also, the exchange or sale by a corporation of its own shares for money or other property does not result in taxable gain or deductible loss, even though the corporation deals in such shares as it might in the shares of another corporation. A transfer by a corporation of shares of its own stock (including treasury stock) as compensation for services is considered, for purposes of section 1032(a), as a disposition by the corporation of such shares for money or other property.

(b) Section 1032(a) does not apply to the acquisition by a corporation of shares of its own stock except where the corporation acquires such shares in exchange for shares of its own stock (including treasury stock). See paragraph (e) of § 1.311-1, relating to treatment of acquisition of a corporation's own stock. Section 1032(a) also does not relate to the tax treatment of the recipient of a corporation's stock.

(c) Where a corporation acquires shares of its own stock in exchange for shares of its own stock (including treasury stock) the transaction may qualify not only under section 1032(a), but also under section 368(a)(1)(E)(recapitalization) or section 305(a) (distribution of stock and stock rights).

(d) For basis of property acquired by a corporation in connection with a transaction to which section 351 applies or in connection with a reorganization, see section 362. For basis of property acquired by a corporation in a transaction to which section 1032 applies but which does not qualify under any other nonrecognition provision, see section 1012. [Reg. § 1.1032-1.]

☐ [T.D. 6210, 11-6-56.]

[Reg. § 1.1032-2]

§ 1.1032-2. Disposition by a corporation of stock of a controlling corporation in certain triangular reorganizations.—(a) *Scope.*—This section provides rules for certain triangular reorganizations described in § 1.358-6(b) when the acquiring corporation (S) acquires property or stock of another corporation (T) in exchange for stock of the corporation (P) in control of S.

(b) *General nonrecognition of gain or loss.*—For purposes of § 1.1032-1(a), in the case of a forward triangular merger, a triangular C reorganization, or a triangular B reorganization (as described in § 1.358-6(b)), P stock provided by P to S, or directly to T or T's shareholders on behalf of S, pursuant to the plan of reorganization is treated as a disposition by P of shares of its own stock for T's assets or stock, as applicable. For rules governing the use of P stock in a reverse triangular merger, see section 361.

(c) *Treatment of S.*—S must recognize gain or loss on its exchange of P stock as consideration in a forward triangular merger, a triangular C reorganization, or a triangular B reorganization (as described in § 1.358-6(b)), if S did not receive the P stock from P pursuant to the plan of reorganization. See § 1.358-6(d) for the effect on P's basis in its S or T stock, as applicable. For rules governing S's use of P stock in a reverse triangular merger, see section 361.

(d) *Examples.*—The rules of this section are illustrated by the following examples. For purposes of these examples, P, S, and T are domestic corporations, P and S do not file consolidated returns P owns all of the only class of S stock, the P stock exchanged in the transaction satisfies the requirements of the applicable reorganization provisions, and the facts set forth the only corporate activity.

Example 1. Forward triangular merger solely for P stock. (a) *Facts.* T has assets with an aggregate basis of $60 and fair market value of $100 and no liabilities. Pursuant to a plan, P forms S by transferring $100 of P stock to S and T merges into S. In the merger, the T shareholders receive, in exchange for their T stock, the P stock that P transferred to S. The transaction is a reorganization to which sections 368(a)(1)(A) and (a)(2)(D) apply.

(b) *No gain or loss recognized on the use of P stock.* Under paragraph (b) of this section, the P stock provided by P pursuant to the plan of reorganization is treated for purposes of § 1.1032-1 (a) as disposed of by P for the T assets acquired by S in the merger. Consequently, neither P nor S has taxable gain or deductible loss on the exchange.

Example 2. Forward triangular merger solely for P stock provided in part by S. (a) *Facts.* T has assets with an aggregate basis of $60 and fair market value of $100 and no liabilities. S is an operating company with substantial assets that has been in existence for several years. S also owns P stock with a $20 adjusted basis and $30 fair market value. S acquired the P stock in an unrelated transaction several years before the reorganization. Pursuant to a plan, P transfers additional P stock worth $70 to S and T merges into S. In the merger, the T shareholders receive $100 of P stock ($70 of P stock provided by P to S as part of the plan and $30 of P stock held by S previously). The transaction is a reorganization to which sections 368(a)(1)(A) and (a)(2)(D) apply.

(b) *Gain or loss recognized by S on the use of its P stock.* Under paragraph (b) of this section, the $70 of P stock provided by P pursuant to the plan of reorganization is treated as disposed of by P for the T assets acquired by S in the merger. Consequently, neither P nor S has taxable gain or deductible loss on the exchange of those shares. Under paragraph (c) of this section, however, S recognizes $10 of gain on the exchange of its P stock in the reorganization because S did not receive the P stock from P pursuant to the plan of reorganization. See § 1.358-6(d) for the effect on P's basis in its S stock.

(e) *Stock options.*—The rules of this section shall apply to an option to buy or sell P stock issued by P in the same manner as the rules of this section apply to P stock.

(f) *Effective dates.*—This section applies to triangular reorganizations occurring on or after December 23, 1994, except for paragraph (e) of this section, which applies to transfers of stock options occurring on or after May 16, 2000. [Reg. § 1.1032-2.]

☐ [*T.D. 8648, 12-20-95. Amended by T.D. 8883, 5-11-2000.*]

[Reg. § 1.1032-3]

§ 1.1032-3. Disposition of stock or stock options in certain transactions not qualifying under any other nonrecognition provision.— (a) *Scope.*—This section provides rules for certain transactions in which a corporation or a partnership (the acquiring entity) acquires money or other property (as defined in § 1.1032-1) in exchange, in whole or in part, for stock of a corporation (the issuing corporation).

(b) *Nonrecognition of gain or loss.*—(1) *General rule.*—In a transaction to which this section applies; no gain or loss is recognized on the disposition of the issuing corporation's stock by the acquiring entity. The transaction is treated as if, immediately before the acquiring entity disposes of the stock of the issuing corporation, the acquiring entity purchased the issuing corporation's stock from the issuing corporation for fair market value with cash contributed to the acquiring entity by the issuing corporation (or, if necessary, through intermediate corporations or partnerships). For rules that may apply in determining the issuing corporation's adjustment to basis in the acquiring entity (or, if necessary, in determining the adjustment to basis in intermediate entities), see sections 358, 722, and the regulations thereunder.

(2) *Special rule for actual payment for stock of the issuing corporation.*—If the issuing corporation receives money or other property in payment for its stock, the amount of cash deemed contributed under paragraph (b)(1) of this section is the difference between the fair market value of the issuing corporation stock and the amount of money or the fair market value of other property that the issuing corporation receives as payment.

(c) *Applicability.*—The rules of this section apply only if, pursuant to a plan to acquire money or other property—

(1) The acquiring entity acquires stock of the issuing corporation directly or indirectly from the issuing corporation in a transaction in which, but for this section, the basis of the stock of the issuing corporation in the hands of the acquiring entity would be determined, in whole or in part, with respect to the issuing corporation's basis in the issuing corporation's stock under section 362(a) or 723 (provided that, in the

case of an indirect acquisition by the acquiring entity, the transfers of issuing corporation stock through intermediate entities occur immediately after one another);

(2) The acquiring entity immediately transfers the stock of the issuing corporation to acquire money or other property (from a person other than an entity from which the stock was directly or indirectly acquired);

(3) The party receiving stock of the issuing corporation in the exchange specified in paragraph (c)(2) of this section from the acquiring entity does not receive a substituted basis in the stock of the issuing corporation within the meaning of section 7701(a)(42); and

(4) The issuing corporation stock is not exchanged for stock of the issuing corporation.

(d) *Stock options.*—The rules of this section shall apply to an option issued by a corporation to buy or sell its own stock in the same manner as the rules of this section apply to the stock of an issuing corporation.

(e) *Examples.*—The following examples illustrate the application of this section:

Example 1. (i) X, a corporation, owns all of the stock of Y corporation. Y reaches an agreement with C, an individual, to acquire a truck from C in exchange for 10 shares of X stock with a fair market value of $100. To effectuate Y's agreement with C, X transfers to Y the X stock in a transaction in which, but for this section, the basis of the X stock in the hands of Y would be determined with respect to X's basis in the X stock under section 362(a). Y immediately transfers the X stock to C to acquire the truck.

(ii) In this *Example 1*, no gain or loss is recognized on the disposition of the X stock by Y. Immediately before Y's disposition of the X stock, Y is treated as purchasing the X stock from X for $100 of cash contributed to Y by X. Under section 358, X's basis in its Y stock is increased by $100.

Example 2. (i) Assume the same facts as *Example 1*, except that, rather than X stock, X transfers an option with a fair market value of $100 to purchase X stock.

(ii) In this *Example 2*, no gain or loss is recognized on the disposition of the X stock option by Y. Immediately before Y's disposition of the X stock option, Y is treated as purchasing the X stock option from X for $100 of cash contributed to Y by X. Under section 358, X's basis in its Y stock is increased by $100.

Example 3. (i) X, a corporation, owns all of the outstanding stock of Y corporation. Y is a partner in partnership Z. Z reaches an agreement with C, an individual, to acquire a truck from C in exchange for 10 shares of X stock with a fair market value of $100. To effectuate Z's agreement with C, X transfers to Y the X stock in a transaction in which, but for this section, the basis of the X stock in the hands of Y would be determined with respect to X's basis in the X

stock under section 362(a). Y immediately transfers the X stock to Z in a transaction in which, but for this section, the basis of the X stock in the hands of Z would be determined under section 723. Z immediately transfers the X stock to C to acquire the truck.

(ii) In this *Example 3*, no gain or loss is recognized on the disposition of the X stock by Z. Immediately before Z's disposition of the X stock, Z is treated as purchasing the X stock from X for $100 of cash indirectly contributed to Z by X through an intermediate corporation, Y. Under section 722, Y's basis in its Z partnership interest is increased by $100, and, under section 358, X's basis in its Y stock is increased by $100.

Example 4. (i) X, a corporation, owns all of the outstanding stock of Y corporation. B, an individual, is an employee of Y. Pursuant to an agreement between X and Y to compensate B for services provided to Y, X transfers to B 10 shares of X stock with a fair market value of $100. Under § 1.83-6(d), but for this section, the transfer of X stock by X to the would be treated as a contribution of the X stock by X to the capital of Y, and immediately thereafter, a transfer of the X stock by Y to B. But for this section, the basis of the X stock in the hands of Y would be determined with respect to X's basis in the X stock under section 362(a).

(ii) In this *Example 4*, no gain or loss is recognized on the deemed disposition of the X stock by Y. Immediately before Y's deemed disposition of the X stock, Y is treated as purchasing the X stock from X for $100 of cash contributed to Y by X. Under section 358, X's basis in its Y stock is increased by $100.

Example 5. (i) X, a corporation, owns all of the outstanding stock of Y corporation. B, an individual, is an employee of Y. To compensate B for services provided to Y, B is offered the opportunity to purchase 10 shares of X stock with a fair market value of $100 at a reduced price of $80. B transfers $80 and Y transfers $10 to X as partial payment for the X stock.

(ii) In this *Example 5*, no gain or loss is recognized on the deemed disposition of the X stock by Y. Immediately before Y's deemed disposition of the X stock, Y is treated as purchasing the X stock from X for $100, $80 of which Y is deemed to have received from B, $10 of which originated with Y, and $10 of which is deemed to have been contributed to Y by X. Under section 358, X's basis in its Y stock is increased by $10.

Example 6. (i) X, a corporation, owns stock of Y. To compensate Y's employee, B, for services provided to Y, X issues 10 shares of X stock to B, subject to a substantial risk of forfeiture. B does not have an election under section 83(b) in effect with respect to the X stock. X retains the only reversionary interest in the X stock in the event that B forfeits the right to the stock. Several years after X's transfer of the X shares, the stock vests. At the time the stock vests, the 10 shares of X stock have a fair market value of $100. Under § 1.83-6(d), but for this section, the transfer of the

X stock by X to B would be treated, at the time the stock vests, as a contribution of the X stock by X to the capital of Y, and immediately thereafter, a disposition of the X stock by Y to B. The basis of the X stock in the hands of Y, but for this section, would be determined with respect to X's basis in the X stock under section 362(a).

(ii) In this *Example 6*, no gain or loss is recognized on the deemed disposition of X stock by Y when the stock vests Immediately before Y's deemed disposition of the X stock, Y is treated as purchasing X's stock from X for $100 of cash contributed to Y by X. Under section 358, X's basis in its Y stock is increased by $100.

Example 7. (i) Assume the same facts as in *Example 6*, except that Y (rather than X) retains a reversionary interest in the X stock in the event that B forfeits the right to the stock. Several years after X's transfer of the X shares, the stock vests.

(ii) In this *Example 7*, this section does not apply to Y's deemed disposition of the X shares because Y is not deemed to have transferred the X stock to B immediately after receiving the stock from X. For the tax consequences to Y on the deemed disposition of the X stock, see § 1.83-6(b).

Example 8. (i) X, a corporation, owns all of the outstanding stock of Y corporation. In Year 1, X issues to Y's employee, B, a nonstatutory stock option to purchase 10 shares of X stock as compensation for services provided to Y. The option is exercisable against X and does not have a readily ascertainable fair market value (determined under § 1.83-7(b)) at the time the option is granted. In Year 2, B exercises the option by paying X the strike price of $80 for the X stock, which then has a fair market value of $100.

(ii) In this *Example 8*, because, under section 83(e)(3), section 83(a) does not apply to the grant of the option, paragraph (d) of this section also does not apply to the grant of the option. Section 83 and § 1.1032-3 apply in Year 2 when the option is exercised; thus, no gain or loss is recognized on the deemed disposition of X stock by Y in Year 2. Immediately before Y's deemed disposition of the X stock in Year 2, Y is treated as purchasing the X stock from X for $100, $80 of which Y is deemed to have received from B and the remaining $20 of which is deemed to have been contributed to Y by X. Under section 358, X's basis in its Y stock is increased by $20.

Example 9. (i) A, an individual, owns a majority of the stock of X. X owns stock of Y constituting control of Y within the meaning of section 368(c). A transfers 10 shares of its X stock to B, a key employee of Y. The fair market value of the 10 shares on the date of transfer was $100.

(ii) In this *Example 9*, A is treated as making a nondeductible contribution of the 10 shares of X to the capital of X, and no gain or loss is recognized by A as a result of this transfer. See *Commissioner v. Fink*, 483 U.S. 89 (1987). A must allocate his basis in the transferred shares to his remaining shares of X stock. No gain or loss is

recognized on the deemed disposition of the X stock by Y. Immediately before Y's disposition of the X stock, Y is treated as purchasing the X stock from X for $100 of cash contributed to Y by X. Under section 358, X's basis in its Y stock is increased by $100.

Example 10. (i) In Year 1, X, a corporation, forms a trust which will be used to satisfy deferred compensation obligations owed by Y, X's wholly owned subsidiary, to Y's employees. X funds the trust with X stock, which would revert to X upon termination of the trust, subject to the employees' rights to be paid the deferred compensation due to them. The creditors of X can reach all the trust assets upon the insolvency of X. Similarly, Y's creditors can reach all the trust assets upon the insolvency of Y. In Year 5, the trust transfers X stock to the employees of Y in satisfaction of the deferred compensation obligation.

(ii) In this *Example 10*, X is considered to be the grantor of the trust, and, under section 677, X is also the owner of the trust. Any income earned by the trust would be reflected on X's income tax return. Y is not considered a grantor or owner of the trust corpus at the time X transfers X stock to the trust. In Year 5, when employees of Y receive X stock in satisfaction of the deferred compensation obligation, no gain or loss is recognized on the deemed disposition of the X stock by Y. Immediately before Y's deemed disposition of the X stock, Y is treated as purchasing the X stock from X for fair market value using cash contributed to Y by X. Under section 358, X's basis in its Y stock increases by the amount of cash deemed contributed.

(f) *Effective date.*—This section applies to transfers of stock or stock options of the issuing corporation occurring on or after May 16, 2000. [Reg. § 1.1032-3.]

☐ [T.D. 8883, 5-11-2000 (*corrected* 6-14-2000).]

[Reg. § 1.1033(a)-1]

§ 1.1033(a)-1. Involuntary conversion; non-recognition of gain.—(a) *In general.*—Section 1033 applies to cases where property is compulsorily or involuntarily converted. An "involuntary conversion" may be the result of the destruction of property in whole or in part, the theft of property, the seizure of property, the requisition or condemnation of property, or the threat or imminence of requisition or condemnation of property. An "involuntary conversion" may be a conversion into similar property or into money or into dissimilar property. Section 1033 provides that, under certain specified circumstances, any gain which is realized from an involuntary conversion shall not be recognized. In cases where property is converted into other property similar or related in service or use to the converted property, no gain shall be recognized regardless of when the disposition of the converted property occurred and regardless of whether or not the taxpayer elects to have the gain not recognized. In other types of involuntary conversion cases, however, the proceeds arising from the disposition of the converted property must (within the time limits specified) be reinvested in similar property in order to avoid recognition of any gain realized. Section 1033 applies only with respect to gains; losses from involuntary conversions are recognized or not recognized without regard to this section.

(b) *Special rules.*—For rules relating to the application of section 1033 to involuntary conversions of a principal residence with respect to which an election has been made under section 121 (relating to gain from sale or exchange of residence of individual who has attained age 65), see paragraph (g) of § 1.121-5. For rules applicable to involuntary conversions of a principal residence occurring before January 1, 1951, see § 1.1033(a)-3. For rules applicable to involuntary conversions of a principal residence occurring after December 31, 1950, and before January 1, 1954, see paragraph (h)(1) of § 1.1034-1. For rules applicable to involuntary conversions of a personal residence occurring after December 31, 1953, see § 1.1033(a)-3. For special rules relating to the election to have section 1034 apply to certain involuntary conversions of a principal residence occurring after December 31, 1957, see paragraph (h) (2) of § 1.1034-1. For special rules relating to certain involuntary conversions of real property held either for productive use in trade or business or for investment and occurring after December 31, 1957, see § 1.1033(g)-1. See also special rules applicable to involuntary conversions of property sold pursuant to reclamation laws, livestock destroyed by disease, and livestock sold on account of drought provided in §§ 1.1033(c)-1, 1.1033(d)-1, and 1.1033(e)-1, respectively. For rules relating to basis of property acquired through involuntary conversions, see § 1.1033(b)-1. For determination of the period for which the taxpayer has held property acquired as a result of certain involuntary conversions, see section 1223 and regulations issued thereunder. For treatment of gains from involuntary conversions as capital gains in certain cases, see section 1231(a) and regulations issued thereunder. For portion of war loss recoveries treated as gain on involuntary conversion, see section 1332(b)(3) and regulations issued thereunder. [Reg. § 1.1033(a)-1.]

☐ [*T.D. 6222, 1-9-57. Amended by T.D. 6338, 12-11-58, T.D. 6453, 2-6-60, T.D. 6856, 10-19-65, T.D. 7625, 5-29-79 and T.D. 7758, 1-16-81.*]

[Reg. § 1.1033(a)-2]

§ 1.1033(a)-2. Involuntary conversion into similar property, into money or into dissimilar property.—(a) *In general.*—The term "disposition of the converted property" means the destruction, theft, seizure, requisition, or condemnation of the converted property, or the sale or exchange of such property under threat or imminence of requisition or condemnation.

(b) *Conversion into similar property.*—If property (as a result of its destruction in whole or in part, theft, seizure, or requisition or condemnation or threat or imminence thereof) is compulsorily or involuntarily converted only into property similar or related in service or use to the property so converted, no gain shall be recognized. Such nonrecognition of gain is mandatory.

(c) *Conversion into money or into dissimilar property.*—(1) If property (as a result of its destruction in whole or in part, theft, seizure, or requisition or condemnation or threat or imminence thereof) is compulsorily or involuntarily converted into money or into property not similar or related in service or use to the converted property, the gain, if any, shall be recognized, at the election of the taxpayer, only to the extent that the amount realized upon such conversion exceeds the cost of other property purchased by the taxpayer which is similar or related in service or use to the property so converted, or the cost of stock of a corporation owning such other property which is purchased by the taxpayer in the acquisition of control of such corporation, if the taxpayer purchased such other property, or such stock, for the purpose of replacing the property so converted and during the period specified in subparagraph (3) of this paragraph. For the purposes of section 1033 the term "control" means the ownership of stock possessing at least 80 percent of the total combined voting power of all classes of stock entitled to vote and at least 80 percent of the total number of shares of all other classes of stock of the corporation.

(2) All of the details in connection with an involuntary conversion of property at a gain (including those relating to the replacement of the converted property, or a decision not to replace, or the expiration of the period for replacement) shall be reported in the return for the taxable year or years in which any of such gain is realized. An election to have such gain recognized only to the extent provided in subparagraph (1) of this paragraph shall be made by including such gain in gross income for such year or years only to such extent. If, at the time of filing such a return, the period within which the converted property must be replaced has expired, or if such an election is not desired, the gain should be included in gross income for such year or years in the regular manner. A failure to so include such gain in gross income in the regular manner shall be deemed to be an election by the taxpayer to have such gain recognized only to the extent provided in subparagraph (1) of this paragraph even though the details in connection with the conversion are not reported in such return. If, after having made an election under section 1033(a)(2), the converted property is not replaced within the required period of time, or replacement is made at a cost lower than was anticipated at the time of the election, or a decision is made not to replace, the tax liability for the year

or years for which the election was made shall be recomputed. Such recomputation should be in the form of an "amended return". If a decision is made to make an election under section 1033(a)(2) after the filing of the return and the payment of the tax for the year or years in which any of the gain on an involuntary conversion is realized and before the expiration of the period within which the converted property must be replaced, a claim for credit or refund for such year or years should be filed. If the replacement of the converted property occurs in a year or years in which none of the gain on the conversion is realized, all of the details in connection with such replacement shall be reported in the return for such year or years.

(3) The period referred to in subparagraphs (1) and (2) of this paragraph is the period of time commencing with the date of the disposition of the converted property, or the date of the beginning of the threat or imminence of requisition or condemnation of the converted property, whichever is earlier, and ending two years (or, in the case of a disposition occurring before December 31, 1969, one year) after the close of the first taxable year in which any part of the gain upon the conversion is realized, or at the close of such later date as may be designated pursuant to an application of the taxpayer. Such application shall be made prior to the expiration of two years (or, in the case of a disposition occurring before December 31, 1969, one year) after the close of the first taxable year in which any part of the gain from the conversion is realized, unless the taxpayer can show to the satisfaction of the district director—

(i) reasonable cause for not having filed the application within the required period of time, and

(ii) the filing of such application was made within a reasonable time after the expiration of the required period of time.

See section 1033(g)(4) and § 1.1033(g)-1 for the circumstances under which, in the case of the conversion of real property held either for productive use in trade or business or for investment, the 2-year period referred to in this paragraph (c)(3) shall be extended to 3 years.

The application shall contain all of the details in connection with the involuntary conversion. Such application shall be made to the district director for the internal revenue district in which the return is filed for the first taxable year in which any of the gain from the involuntary conversion is realized. No extension of time shall be granted pursuant to such application unless the taxpayer can show reasonable cause for not being able to replace the converted property within the required period of time.

(4) Property or stock purchased before the disposition of the converted property shall be considered to have been purchased for the purpose of replacing the converted property only if such property or stock is held by the taxpayer on the date of the disposition of the converted property. Property or stock shall be considered to have been purchased only if, but for the provisions of section 1033(b), the unadjusted basis of such property or stock would be its cost to the taxpayer within the meaning of section 1012. If the taxpayer's unadjusted basis of the replacement property would be determined, in the absence of section 1033(b), under any of the exceptions referred to in section 1012, the unadjusted basis of the property would not be its cost within the meaning of section 1012. For example, if property similar or related in service or use to the converted property is acquired by gift and its basis is determined under section 1015, such property will not qualify as a replacement for the converted property.

(5) If a taxpayer makes an election under section 1033(a)(2), any deficiency, for any taxable year in which any part of the gain upon the conversion is realized, which is attributable to such gain may be assessed at any time before the expiration of three years from the date the district director with whom the return for such year has been filed is notified by the taxpayer of the replacement of the converted property or of an intention not to replace, or of a failure to replace, within the required period, notwithstanding the provisions of section 6212(c) or the provisions of any other law or rule of law which would otherwise prevent such assessment. If replacement has been made, such notification shall contain all of the details in connection with such replacement. Such notification should be made in the return for the taxable year or years in which the replacement occurs, or the intention not to replace is formed, or the period for replacement expires, if this return is filed with such district director. If this return is not filed with such district director, then such notification shall be made to such district director at the time of filing this return. If the taxpayer so desires, he may, in either event, also notify such district director before the filing of such return.

(6) If a taxpayer makes an election under section 1033(a)(2) and the replacement property or stock was purchased before the beginning of the last taxable year in which any part of the gain upon the conversion is realized, any deficiency, for any taxable year ending before such last taxable year, which is attributable to such election may be assessed at any time before the expiration of the period within which a deficiency for such last taxable year may be assessed, notwithstanding the provisions of section 6212(c) or 6501 or the provisions of any law or rule of law which would otherwise prevent such assessment.

(7) If the taxpayer makes an election under section 1033(a)(2), the gain upon the conversion shall be recognized to the extent that the amount realized upon such conversion exceeds the cost of the replacement property or stock, regardless of whether such amount is realized in one or more taxable years.

(8) The proceeds of a use and occupancy insurance contract, which by its terms insured against actual loss sustained of net profits in the business, are not proceeds of an involuntary conversion but are income in the same manner that the profits for which they are substituted would have been.

(9) There is no investment in property similar in character and devoted to a similar use if—

(i) The proceeds of unimproved real estate, taken upon condemnation proceedings, are invested in improved real estate.

(ii) The proceeds of conversion of real property are applied in reduction of indebtedness previously incurred in the purchase of a leasehold.

(iii) The owner of a requisitioned tug uses the proceeds to buy barges.

(10) If, in a condemnation proceeding, the Government retains out of the award sufficient funds to satisfy special assessments levied against the remaining portion of the plot or parcel of real estate affected for benefits accruing in connection with the condemnation, the amount so retained shall be deducted from the gross award in determining the amount of the net award.

(11) If, in a condemnation proceeding, the Government retains out of the award sufficient funds to satisfy liens (other than liens due to special assessments levied against the remaining portion of the plot or parcel of real estate affected for benefits accruing in connection with the condemnation) and mortgages against the property, and itself pays the same, the amount so retained shall not be deducted from the gross award in determining the amount of the net award. If, in a condemnation proceeding, the Government makes an award to a mortgagee to satisfy a mortgage on the condemned property, the amount of such award shall be considered as a part of the "amount realized" upon the conversion regardless of whether or not the taxpayer was personally liable for the mortgage debt. Thus, if a taxpayer has acquired property worth $100,000 subject to a $50,000 mortgage (regardless of whether or not he was personally liable for the mortgage debt) and, in a condemnation proceeding, the Government awards the taxpayer $60,000 and awards the mortgagee $50,000 in satisfaction of the mortgage, the entire $110,000 is considered to be the "amount realized" by the taxpayer.

(12) An amount expended for replacement of an asset, in excess of the recovery for loss, represents a capital expenditure and is not a deductible loss for income tax purposes. [Reg. §1.1033(a)-2.]

☐ [*T.D.* 6222, 1-9-57. *Amended by T.D.* 6679, 9-30-63, *T.D.* 7075, 11-23-70, *T.D.* 7625, 5-29-79 *and T.D.* 7758, 1-16-81.]

[Reg. §1.1033(a)-3]

§1.1033(a)-3. Involuntary conversion of principal residence.—Section 1033 shall apply in the case of property used by the taxpayer as his principal residence if the destruction, theft, seizure, requisition, or condemnation of such residence, or the sale or exchange of such residence under threat or imminence thereof, occurs before January 1, 1951, or after December 31, 1953. However, section 1033 shall not apply to the seizure, requisition, or condemnation (but not destruction), or the sale or exchange under threat or imminence thereof, of such residence property if the seizure, requisition, condemnation, sale, or exchange occurs after December 31, 1957, and if the taxpayer properly elects under section 1034(i) to treat the transaction as a sale (see paragraph (h)(2)(ii) of §1.1034-1). See section 121 and paragraphs (d) and (g) of §1.121-5 for special rules relating to the involuntary conversion of a principal residence of individuals who have attained age 65. [Reg. §1.1033(a)-3.]

☐ [*T.D.* 6222, 1-9-57. *Amended by T.D.* 6453, 2-16-60, *T.D.* 6856, 10-19-65 *and T.D.* 7625, 5-29-79.]

[Reg. §1.1033(b)-1]

§1.1033(b)-1. Basis of property acquired as a result of an involuntary conversion.—(a) The provisions of the first sentence of section 1033(b) may be illustrated by the following example:

Example. A's vessel which has an adjusted basis of $100,000 is destroyed in 1950 and A receives in 1951 insurance in the amount of $200,000. If A invests $150,000 in a new vessel, taxable gain to the extent of $50,000 would be recognized. The basis of the new vessel is $100,000; that is, the adjusted basis of the old vessel ($100,000) minus the money received by the taxpayer which was not expended in the acquisition of the new vessel ($50,000) plus the amount of gain recognized upon the conversion ($50,000). If any amount in excess of the proceeds of the conversion is expended in the acquisition of the new property, such amount may be added to the basis otherwise determined.

(b) The provisions of the last sentence of section 1033(b) may be illustrated by the following example:

Example. A taxpayer realizes $22,000 from the involuntary conversion of his barn in 1955; the adjusted basis of the barn to him was $10,000, and he spent in the same year $20,000 for a new barn which resulted in the nonrecognition of $10,000 of the $12,000 gain on the conversion. The basis of the new barn to the taxpayer would be $10,000—the cost of the new barn ($20,000) less the amount of the gain not recognized on the conversion ($10,000). The basis of the new barn would not be a substituted basis in the hands of the taxpayer within the meaning of section 1016(b)(2). If the replacement of the converted barn had been made by the purchase of two smaller barns which, together, were similar or related in service or use to the converted barn and which cost $8,000 and $12,000, respectively, then the basis of the two barns would be $4,000 and $6,000, respectively, the total basis of the purchased property ($10,000) allocated in proportion to their respective costs (8,000/20,000 of $10,000 or $4,000; and 12,000/20,000 of $10,000, or $6,000). [Reg. § 1.1033(b)-1.]

☐ [*T.D. 6222, 1-9-57. Amended by T.D. 7625,* 5-29-79.]

[Reg. § 1.1033(c)-1]

§ 1.1033(c)-1. Disposition of excess property within irrigation project deemed to be involuntary conversion.—(a) The sale, exchange, or other disposition occurring in a taxable year to which the Internal Revenue Code of 1954 applies, of excess lands lying within an irrigation project or division in order to conform to acreage limitations of the Federal reclamation laws effective with respect to such project or division shall be treated as an involuntary conversion to which the provisions of section 1033 and the regulations thereunder shall be applicable. The term "excess lands" means irrigable lands within an irrigation project or division held by one owner in excess of the amount of irrigable land held by such owner entitled to receive water under the Federal reclamation laws applicable to such owner in such project or division. Such excess lands may be either (1) lands receiving no water from the project or division, or (2) lands receiving water only because the owner thereof has executed a valid recordable contract agreeing to sell such lands under terms and conditions satisfactory to the Secretary of the Interior.

(b) If a disposition in order to conform to the acreage limitation provisions of Federal reclamation laws includes property other than excess lands (as, for example, where the excess lands alone do not constitute a marketable parcel) the provisions of section 1033(c) shall apply only to the part of the disposition that relates to excess lands.

(c) The provisions of § 1.1033(a)-2 shall be applicable in the case of dispositions treated as involuntary conversions under this section. The details in connection with such a disposition required to be reported under paragraph (c)(2) of § 1.1033(a)-2 shall include the authority whereby the lands disposed of are considered "excess lands", as defined in this section, and a statement that such disposition is not part of a plan contemplating the disposition of all or any nonexcess land within the irrigation project or division.

(d) The term "involuntary conversion," where it appears in subtitle A of the Code or the regulations thereunder, includes dispositions of excess property within irrigation projects described in this section. (See, e.g., section 1231 and the regulations thereunder.) [Reg. § 1.1033(c)-1.]

☐ [*T.D. 6222, 1-9-57. Amended by T.D. 7625,* 5-29-79.]

[Reg. § 1.1033(d)-1]

§ 1.1033(d)-1. Destruction or disposition of livestock because of disease.—(a) The destruction occurring in a taxable year to which the Internal Revenue Code of 1954 applies, of livestock by, or on account of, disease, or the sale or exchange, in such a year, of livestock because of disease, shall be treated as an involuntary conversion to which the provisions of section 1033 and the regulations thereunder shall be applicable. Livestock which are killed either because they are diseased or because of exposure to disease shall be considered destroyed on account of disease. Livestock which are sold or exchanged because they are diseased or have been exposed to disease, and would not otherwise have been sold or exchanged at that particular time shall be considered sold or exchanged because of disease.

(b) The provisions of § 1.1033(a)-2 shall be applicable in the case of a disposition treated as an involuntary conversion under this section. The details in connection with such a disposition required to be reported under paragraph (c)(2) of § 1.1033(a)-2 shall include a recital of the evidence that the livestock were destroyed by or on account of disease, or sold or exchanged because of disease.

(c) The term "involuntary conversion," where it appears in subtitle A of the Code or the regulations thereunder, includes disposition of livestock described in this section. (See, e.g., section 1231 and the regulations thereunder.) [Reg. § 1.1033(d)-1.]

☐ [*T.D. 6222, 1-9-57. Amended by T.D. 7625,* 5-29-79.]

[Reg. § 1.1033(e)-1]

§ 1.1033(e)-1. Sale or exchange of livestock solely on account of drought.—(a) The sale or exchange of livestock (other than poultry) held for draft, breeding, or dairy purposes in excess of the number the taxpayer would sell or exchange during the taxable year if he followed his usual business practices shall be treated as an involuntary conversion to which section 1033 and the regulations thereunder are applicable if the sale or exchange of such livestock by the taxpayer is solely on account of drought. Section 1033(e) and this section shall apply only to sales and exchanges occurring after December 31, 1955.

(b) To qualify under section 1033(e) and this section, the sale or exchange of the livestock need not take place in a drought area. While it is not necessary that the livestock be held in a drought area, the sale or exchange of the livestock must be solely on account of drought conditions the existence of which affected the water, grazing, or other requirements of the livestock so as to necessitate their sale or exchange.

(c) The total sales or exchanges of livestock held for draft, breeding, or dairy purposes occurring in any taxable year which may qualify as an involuntary conversion under section 1033(e)

Reg. § 1.1033(e)-1(c)

and this section is limited to the excess of the total number of such livestock sold or exchanged during the taxable year over the number that the taxpayer would have sold or exchanged if he had followed his usual business practices, that is, the number he would have been expected to sell or exchange under ordinary circumstances if there had been no drought. For example, if in the past it has been a taxpayer's practice to sell or exchange annually one-half his herd of dairy cows, only the number sold or exchanged solely on account of drought conditions which is in excess of one-half of his herd may qualify as an involuntary conversion under section 1033(e) and this section.

(d) The replacement requirements of section 1033 will be satisfied only if the livestock sold or exchanged is replaced within the prescribed period with livestock which is similar or related in service or use to the livestock sold or exchanged because of drought, that is, the new livestock must be the same as the livestock involuntarily converted. This means that the new livestock must be held for the same useful purpose as the old was held. Thus, although dairy cows could be replaced by dairy cows, a taxpayer could not replace draft animals with breeding or dairy animals.

(e) The provisions of § 1.1033(a)-2 shall be applicable in the case of a sale or exchange treated as an involuntary conversion under this section. The details in connection with such a disposition required to be reported under paragraph (c)(2) of § 1.1033(a)-2 shall include:

(1) Evidence of the existence of the drought conditions which forced the sale or exchange of the livestock;

(2) A computation of the amount of gain realized on the sale or exchange;

(3) The number and kind of livestock sold or exchanged; and

(4) The number of livestock of each kind that would have been sold or exchanged under the usual business practice in the absence of the drought.

(f) The term "involuntary conversion", where it appears in subtitle A of the Code or the regulations thereunder, includes the sale or exchange of livestock described in this section.

(g) The provisions of section 1033(e) and this section apply to taxable years ending after December 31, 1955, but only in the case of sales or exchange of livestock after December 31, 1955. [Reg. § 1.1033(e)-1.]

☐ [*T.D. 6338, 12-11-58. Amended by T.D. 7625, 5-29-79.*]

[Reg. § 1.1033(g)-1]

§ 1.1033(g)-1. Condemnation of real property held for productive use in trade or business or for investment.—(a) *Special rule in general.*—This section provides special rules for applying section 1033 with respect to certain dispositions, occurring after December 31, 1957, of real prop-

erty held either for productive use in trade or business or for investment (not including stock in trade or other property held primarily for sale). For this purpose, disposition means the seizure, requisition, or condemnation (but not destruction) of the converted property, or the sale or exchange of such property under threat or imminence of seizure, requisition, or condemnation. In such cases, for purposes of applying section 1033, the replacement of such property with property of like kind to be held either for productive use in trade or business or for investment shall be treated as property similar or related in service or use to the property so converted. For principles in determining whether the replacement property is property of like kind, see paragraph (b) of § 1.1031(a)-1.

(b) *Election to treat outdoor advertising displays as real property.*—(1) *In general.*—Under section 1033(g)(3) of the Code, a taxpayer may elect to treat property which constitutes an outdoor advertising display as real property for purposes of chapter 1 of the Code. The election is available for taxable years beginning after December 31, 1970. In the case of an election made on or before July 21, 1981, the election is available whether or not the period for filing a claim for credit or refund under section 6511 has expired. No election may be made with respect to any property for which (i) the investment credit under section 38 has been claimed, or (ii) an election to expense certain depreciable business assets under section 179(a) is in effect. The election once made applies to all outdoor advertising displays of the taxpayer which may be made the subject of an election under this paragraph, including all outdoor advertising displays acquired or constructed by the taxpayer in a taxable year after the taxable year for which the election is made. The election applies with respect to disposition during the taxable year for which made and all subsequent taxable years (unless an effective revocation is made pursuant to paragraph (b)(2)(ii) or (iii)).

(2) *Election.*—(i) *Time and manner of making election.*—(A) *In general.*—Unless otherwise provided in the return or in the instructions for a return for a taxable year, any election made under section 1033(g)(3) shall be made by attaching a statement to the return (or amended return if filed on or before July 21, 1981) for the first taxable year to which the election is to apply. Any election made under this paragraph must be made not later than the time, including extensions thereof, prescribed by law for filing the income tax return for such taxable year or July 21, 1981, whichever occurs last. If a taxpayer makes an election (or revokes an election under subdivision (ii) or (iii) of this subparagraph (b)(2)) for a taxable year for which he or she has previously filed a return, the return for that taxable year and all other taxable years affected by the election (or revocation) must be amended to reflect any tax consequences of the election (or

revocation). However, no return for a taxable year for which the period for filing a claim for credit or refund under section 6511 has expired may be amended to make any changes other than those resulting from the election (or revocation). In order for the election (or revocation) to be effective, the taxpayer must remit with the amended return any additional tax due resulting from the election (or revocation), notwithstanding the provisions of section 6212(c) or 6501 or the provisions of any other law or rule of law which would prevent assessment or collection of such tax.

(B) *Statement required when making election.*—The statement required when making the election must clearly indicate that the election to treat outdoor advertising displays as real property is being made.

(ii) *Revocation of election by Commissioner's consent.*—Except as otherwise provided in paragraph (b)(2)(iii) of this section, an election under section 1033(g)(3) shall be irrevocable unless consent to revoke is obtained from the Commissioner. In order to secure the Commissioner's consent to revoke an election, the taxpayer must file a request for revocation of election with the Commissioner of Internal Revenue, Washington, D.C. 20224. The request for revocation shall include—

(A) The taxpayer's name, address, and taxpayer identification number,

(B) The date on which and taxable year for which the election was made and the Internal Revenue Service office with which it was filed,

(C) Identification of all outdoor advertising displays of the taxpayer to which the revocation would apply (including the location, date of purchase, and adjusted basis in such property),

(D) The effective date desired for the revocation, and

(E) The reasons for requesting the revocation.

The Commissioner may require such other information as may be necessary in order to determine whether the requested revocation will be permitted. The Commissioner may prescribe administrative procedures (subject to such limitations, terms and conditions as he deems necessary) to obtain his consent to permit the taxpayer to revoke the election. The taxpayer may submit a request for revocation for any taxable year for which the period of limitations for filing a claim for credit or refund for overpayment of tax has not expired.

(iii) *Revocation where election was made on or before December 11, 1979.*—In the case of an election made on or before December 11, 1979, the taxpayer may revoke such election provided such revocation is made not later than March 23, 1981. The request for revocation shall be made in conformity with the requirements of paragraph (b)(2)(ii), except that, in lieu of the information

required by paragraph (b)(2)(ii)(E), the taxpayer shall state that the revocation is being made pursuant to this paragraph. In addition, the taxpayer must forward, with the statement of revocation, copies of his or her tax returns, including both the original return and any amended returns, for the taxable year in which the original election was made and for all subsequent years and must remit any additional tax due as a result of the revocation.

(3) *Definition of outdoor advertising display.*—The term "outdoor advertising display" means a rigidly assembled sign, display, or device that constitutes, or is used to display, a commercial or other advertisement to the public and is permanently affixed to the ground or permanently attached to a building or other inherently permanent structure. The term includes highway billboards affixed to the ground with wood or metal poles, pipes, or beams, with or without concrete footings.

(4) *Character of replacement property.*—For purposes of section 1033(g), an interest in real property purchased as replacement property for a compulsorily or involuntarily converted outdoor advertising display (with respect to which an election under this section is in effect) shall be considered property of a like kind as the property converted even though a taxpayer's interest in the replacement property is different from the interest held in the property converted. Thus, for example, a fee simple interest in real estate acquired to replace a converted billboard and a 5-year leasehold interest in the real property on which the billboard was located qualifies as property of a like kind under this section.

(c) *Special rule for period within which property must be replaced.*—In the case of a disposition described in paragraph (a) of this section, section 1033(a)(2)(B) and §1.1033(a)-2(c)(3) (relating to the period within which the property must be replaced) shall be applied by substituting 3 years for 2 years. This paragraph shall apply to any disposition described in section 1033(f)(1) and paragraph (a) of this section occurring after December 31, 1974, unless a condemnation proceeding with respect to the property was begun before October 4, 1976. Thus, regardless of when the property is disposed of, the taxpayer will not be eligible for the 3-year replacement period if a condemnation proceeding was begun before October 4, 1976. However, if the property is disposed of after December 31, 1974, and the condemnation proceeding was begun (if at all) after October 3, 1976, then the taxpayer is eligible for the 3-year replacement period. For the purposes of this paragraph, whether a condemnation proceeding is considered as having begun is determined under the applicable State or Federal procedural law.

(d) *Limitation on application of special rule.*—This section shall not apply to the purchase of stock in the acquisition of control of a corporation described in section 1033(a)(2)(A). [Reg. §1.1033(g)-1.]

☐ [*T.D. 6453, 2-16-60. Amended by T.D. 7625, 5-29-79, T.D. 7758, 1-16-81 and T.D. 8121, 1-5-87.*]

[Reg. §1.1033(h)-1]

§1.1033(h)-1. Effective date.—Except as provided otherwise in §1.1033(e)-1 and §1.1033(g)-1, the provisions of section 1033 and the regulations thereunder are effective for taxable years beginning after December 31, 1953, and ending after August 16, 1954. [Reg. §1.1033(h)-1.]

☐ [*T.D. 6222, 1-9-57. Amended by T.D. 6338, 12-11-58, T.D. 6453, 1-16-60, T.D. 7625, 5-29-79 and T.D. 7758, 1-16-81.*]

[Reg. §1.1034-1]

§1.1034-1. Sale or exchange of residence.—(a) *Nonrecognition of gain; general statement.*—Section 1034 provides rules for the nonrecognition of gain in certain cases where a taxpayer sells one residence after December 31, 1953, and buys or builds, and uses as his principal residence, another residence within specific time limits before or after such sale. In general, if the taxpayer invests in a new residence an amount at least as large as the adjusted sales price of his old residence, no gain is recognized on the sale of the old residence (see paragraph (b) of this section for definitions of "adjusted sales price", "new residence", and "old residence"). On the other hand, if the new residence costs the taxpayer less than the adjusted sales price of the old residence, gain is recognized to the extent of the difference. Thus, if an amount equal to or greater than the adjusted sales price of an old residence is invested in a new residence, according to the rules stated in section 1034, none of the gain (if any) realized from the sale shall be recognized. If an amount less than such adjusted sales price is so invested, gain shall be recognized, but only to the extent provided in section 1034. If there is no investment in a new residence, section 1034 is inapplicable and all of the gain shall be recognized. Whenever, as a result of the application of section 1034, any or all of the gain realized on the sale of an old residence is not recognized, a corresponding reduction must be made in the basis of the new residence. The provisions of section 1034 are mandatory, so that the taxpayer cannot elect to have gain recognized under circumstances where this section is applicable. Section 1034 applies only to gains; losses are recognized or not recognized without regard to the provisions of this section. Section 1034 affects only the amount of gain recognized, and not the amount of gain realized (see also section 1001 and regulations issued thereunder). Any gain realized upon disposition of other property in exchange for the new residence is not affected by section 1034. For special rules relating to the sale or exchange of a principal residence by a taxpayer who has attained age 65, see section 121

and paragraph (g) of §1.121-5. For special rules relating to a case where real property with respect to the sale of which gain is not recognized under this section is reacquired by the seller in partial or full satisfaction of the indebtedness arising from such sale and resold by him within 1 year after the date of such reacquisition, see §1.1038-2.

(b) *Definitions.*—The following definitions of frequently used terms are applicable for purposes of section 1034 (other definitions and detailed explanations appear in subsequent paragraphs of this regulation):

(1) "Old residence" means property used by the taxpayer as his principal residence which is the subject of a sale by him after December 31, 1953 (section 1034(a); for detailed explanation see paragraph (c)(3) of this section).

(2) "New residence" means property used by the taxpayer as his principal residence which is the subject of a purchase by him (section 1034(a); for detailed explanation and limitations see paragraphs (c)(3) and (d)(1) of this section).

(3) "Adjusted sales price" means the amount realized reduced by the fixing-up expenses (section 1034(b)(1); for special rule applicable in some cases to husband and wife see paragraph (f) of this section).

(4) "Amount realized" is to be computed by subtracting

(i) The amount of the items which, in determining the gain from the sale of the old residence, are properly an offset against the consideration received upon the sale (such as commissions and expenses of advertising the property for sale, of preparing the deed, and of other legal services in connection with the sale); from

(ii) The amount of the consideration so received, determined (in accordance with section 1001(b) and regulations issued thereunder) by adding to the sum of any money so received, the fair market value of the property (other than money) so received. If, as part of the consideration for the sale, the purchaser either assumes a liability of the taxpayer or acquires the old residence subject to a liability (whether or not the taxpayer is personally liable on the debt), such assumption or acquisition, in the amount of the liability, shall be treated as money received by the taxpayer in computing the "amount realized."

(5) "Gain realized" is the excess (if any) of the amount realized over the adjusted basis of the old residence (see also section 1001(a) and regulations issued thereunder).

(6) "Fixing-up expenses" mean the aggregate of the expenses for work performed (in any taxable year, whether beginning before, on, or after January 1, 1954) on the old residence in order to assist in its sale, provided that such expenses (i) are incurred for work performed during the 90-day period ending on the day on which the contract to sell the old residence is

entered into; and (ii) are paid on or before the 30th day after the date of the sale of the old residence; and (iii) are neither (*a*) allowable as deductions in computing taxable income under section 63(a), nor (*b*) taken into account in computing the amount realized from the sale of the old residence (section 1034(b)(2) and (3)). "Fixing-up expenses" does not include expenditures which are properly chargeable to capital account and which would, therefore, constitute adjustments to the basis of the old residence (see section 1016 and regulations issued thereunder).

(7) "Cost of purchasing the new residence" means the total of all amounts which are attributable to the acquisition, construction, reconstruction, and improvements constituting capital expenditures, made during the period beginning 18 months (one year in the case of a sale of an old residence prior to January 1, 1975) before the date of sale of the old residence and ending either (i) 18 months (one year in the case of a sale of an old residence prior to January 1, 1975), after such date in the case of a new residence purchased but not constructed by the taxpayer, or (ii) two years (18 months in the case of a sale of an old residence prior to Janaury 1, 1975) after such date in the case of a new residence the construction of which was commenced by the taxpayer before the expiration of 18 months (one year in the case of a sale of an old residence prior to January 1, 1975) after such date (section 1034(a), (c)(2) and (c)(5); for detailed explanation, see paragraph (c)(4) of this section; for special rule applicable in some cases to husband and wife, see paragraph (f) of this section; see also paragraph (b)(9) of this section for definition of "purchase").

(8) "Sale" (of a residence) means a sale or an exchange (of a residence) for other property which occurs after December 31, 1953, an involuntary conversion (of a residence) which occurs after December 31, 1950, and before January 1, 1954, or certain involuntary conversions where the disposition of the property occurs after December 31, 1957, in respect of which a proper election is made under section 1034(i)(2) (see sections 1034(c)(1), 1034(i)(1)(A), and 1034(i)(2); for detailed explanation concerning involuntary conversions, see paragraph (h) of this section).

(9) "Purchase" (of a residence) means a purchase or an acquisition (of a residence) on the exchange of property or the partial or total construction or reconstruction (of a residence) by the taxpayer (section 1034(c)(1) and (2)). However, the mere improvement of a residence, not amounting to reconstruction, does not constitute "purchase" of a residence.

(c) *Rules for application of section 1034.*— (1) *General rule; limitations on applicability.*—Gain realized from the sale (after December 31, 1953) of an old residence will be recognized only to the extent that the taxpayer's adjusted sales price of the old residence exceeds the taxpayer's cost of purchasing the new residence, provided that the taxpayer either (i) within a period beginning 18 months (one year in the case of a sale of an old residence prior to January 1, 1975) before the date of such sale and ending 18 months (one year in the case of a sale of an old residence prior to January 1, 1975) after such date purchases property and uses it as his principal residence, or (ii) within a period beginning 18 months (one year in the case of a sale of an old residence prior to January 1, 1975) before the date of such sale and ending two years (18 months in the case of a sale of an old residence prior to January 1, 1975) after such date uses as his principal residence a new residence the construction of which was commenced by him at any time before the expiration of 18 months (one year in the case of a sale of an old residence prior to January 1, 1975) after the date of the sale of the old residence (section 1034(a) and (c)(5); for detailed explanation of use as "principal residence" see subparagraph (3) of this paragraph). The rule stated in the preceding sentence applies to a new residence purchased by the taxpayer before the date of sale of the old residence provided the new residence is still owned by him on such date (section 1034(c)(3)). Whether the construction of a new residence was commenced by the taxpayer before the expiration of 18 months (one year in the case of sale of an old residence prior to January 1, 1975) after the date of the sale of the old residence will depend upon the facts and circumstances of each case. Section 1034 is not applicable to the sale of a residence if within the previous 18 months (previous year in the case of a sale of an old residence prior to January 1, 1975) the taxpayer made another sale of residential property on which gain was realized but not recognized (section 1034(d)). For further details concerning limitations on the application of section 1034, see paragraph (d) of this section.

(2) *Computation and examples.*—In applying the general rule stated in subparagraph (1) of this paragraph, the taxpayer should first subtract the commissions and other selling expenses from the selling price of his old residence, to determine the amount realized. A comparison of the amount realized with the cost or other basis of the old residence will then indicate whether there is any gain realized on the sale. Unless the amount realized is greater than the cost or other basis, no gain is realized and section 1034 does not apply. If the amount realized exceeds the cost or other basis, the amount of such excess constitutes the gain realized. The amount realized should then be reduced by the fixing-up expenses (if any), to determine the adjusted sales price. A comparison of the adjusted sales price of the old residence with the cost of purchasing the new residence will indicate how much (if any) of the realized gain is to be recognized. If the cost of purchasing the new residence is the same as, or greater than, the adjusted sales price of the old residence, then none of the realized gain is to be

recognized. On the other hand, if the cost of purchasing the new residence is smaller than the adjusted sales price of the old residence, the gain realized is to be recognized to the extent of the difference. (It should be noted that any amount of gain realized but not recognized is to be applied as a downward adjustment to the basis of the new residence (for details see paragraph (e) of this section).) The application of the general rule stated above may be illustrated by the following examples:

Example (1). A taxpayer decides to sell his residence, which has a basis of $17,500. To make it more attractive to buyers, he paints the outside at a cost of $300 in April, 1954. He pays for the painting when the work is finished. In May, 1954, he sells the house for $20,000. Brokers' commissions and other selling expenses are $1,000. In October, 1954, the taxpayer buys a new residence for $18,000. The amount realized, the gain realized, the adjusted sales price, and the gain to be recognized are computed as follows:

Selling price	$20,000
Less: Commissions and other selling expenses	1,000
Amount realized	19,000
Less: Basis	17,500
Gain realized	1,500
Amount realized	$19,000
Less: Fixing-up expenses	300
Adjusted sales price	18,700
Cost of purchasing new residence	18,000
Gain recognized	700
Gain realized but not recognized	800
Adjusted basis of new residence (see paragraph (e) of this section)	$17,200

Example (2). The facts are the same as in example (1), except that the selling price of the old residence is $18,500. The computations are as follows:

Selling price	$18,500
Less: Commissions and other selling expenses	1,000
Amount realized	17,500
Less: Basis	17,500
Gain realized	0

Note: Since no gain is realized, section 1034 is inapplicable; it is, therefore, unnecessary to compute the adjusted sales price of the old residence and compare it with the cost of purchasing the new residence. No adjustment to the basis of the new residence is to be made.

Example (3). The facts are the same as in example (1), except that the cost of purchasing the new residence is $17,000. The computations are as follows:

Selling price	$20,000
Less: Commissions and other selling expenses	1,000
Amount realized	19,000
Less: Basis	17,500
Gain realized	1,500
Amount realized	$19,000
Less: Fixing-up expenses	300
Adjusted sales price	18,700
Cost of purchasing the new residence	17,000
Gain recognized	1,500

Note: Since the adjusted sales price of the old residence exceeds the cost of purchasing the new residence by $1,700, which is more than the gain realized, all of the gain realized is recognized. No adjustment to the basis of the new residence is to be made.

Gain realized but not recognized	$0

Example (4). The facts are the same as in example (1), except that the fixing-up expenses are $1,100. The computations are as follows:

Selling price	$20,000
Less: Commissions and other selling expenses	1,000
Amount realized	19,000
Less: Basis	17,500
Gain realized	1,500
Amount realized	$19,000
Less: Fixing-up expenses	1,100
Adjusted sales price	17,900
Cost of purchasing the new residence	18,000
Gain recognized	0

Note: Since the cost of purchasing the new residence exceeds the adjusted sales price, none of the gain realized is recognized.

Gain realized but not recognized	$1,500
Adjusted basis of new residence (see paragraph (e) of this section)	16,500

(3) *Property used by the taxpayer as his principal residence.*—(i) Whether or not property is used by the taxpayer as his residence, and whether or not property is used by the taxpayer as his principal residence (in the case of a taxpayer using more than one property as a residence), depends upon all the facts and circumstances in each case, including the good faith of the taxpayer. The mere fact that property is, or has been, rented is not determinative that such property is not used by the taxpayer as his principal residence. For example, if the taxpayer purchases his new residence before he sells his old residence, the fact that he temporarily rents out the new residence during the period before

he vacates the old residence may not, in the light of all the facts and circumstances in the case, prevent the new residence from being considered as property used by the taxpayer as his principal residence. Property used by the taxpayer as his principal residence may include a houseboat, a house trailer, or stock held by a tenant-stockholder in a cooperative housing corporation (as those terms are defined in section 216(b)(1) and (2)), if the dwelling which the taxpayer is entitled to occupy as such stockholder is used by him as his principal residence (section 1034(f)). Property used by the taxpayer as his principal residence does not include personal property such as a piece of furniture, a radio, etc., which, in accordance with the applicable local law, is not a fixture.

(ii) Where part of a property is used by the taxpayer as his principal residence and part is used for other purposes, an allocation must be made to determine the application of this section. If the old residence is used only partially for residential purposes, only that part of the gain allocable to the residential portion is not to be recognized under this section and only an amount allocable to the selling price of such portion need be invested in the new residence in order to have the gain allocable to such portion not recognized under this section. If the new residence is used only partially for residential purposes only so much of its cost as is allocable to the residential portion may be counted as the cost of purchasing the new residence.

(4) *Cost of purchasing new residence.*—(i) The taxpayer's cost of purchasing the new residence includes not only cash but also any indebtedness to which the property purchased is subject at the time of purchase whether or not assumed by the taxpayer (including purchase-money mortgages, etc.) and the face amount of any liabilities of the taxpayer which are part of the consideration for the purchase. Commissions and other purchasing expenses paid or incurred by the taxpayer on the purchase of the new residence are to be included in determining such cost. In the case of an acquisition of a residence upon an exchange which is considered as a "purchase" under this section, the fair market value of the new residence on the date of the exchange shall be considered as the taxpayer's cost of purchasing the new residence. Where any part of the new residence is acquired by the taxpayer other than by "purchase", the value of such part is not to be included in determining the taxpayer's cost of the new residence (see paragraph (b)(9) of this section for definition of "purchase"). For example, if the taxpayer acquires a residence by gift or inheritance, and spends $20,000 in reconstructing such residence, only such $20,000 may be treated as his cost of purchasing the new residence.

(ii) The taxpayer's cost of purchasing the new residence includes only so much of such cost as is attributable to acquisition, construction, reconstruction, or improvements made within the period of three years or 42 months (two years or 30 months in the case of a sale of an old residence prior to January 1, 1975), as the case may be, in which the purchase and use of the new residence must be made in order to have gain on the sale of the old residence not recognized under this section. Thus, if the construction of the new residence is begun three years before the date of sale of the old residence and completed on the date of sale of the old residence, only that portion of the cost which is attributable to the last 18 months (last year in the case of a sale of an old residence prior to January 1, 1975) of such construction constitutes the taxpayer's cost of purchasing the new residence, for purposes of section 1034. Furthermore, the taxpayer's cost of purchasing the new residence includes only such amounts as are properly chargeable to capital account rather than to current expense. As to what constitutes capital expenditures, see section 263.

(iii) The provisions of this subparagraph may be illustrated by the following example:

Example. M began the construction of a new residence on January 15, 1974, and completed it on October 14, 1974. The cost of $45,000 was incurred ratably over the 9-month period of construction. On December 14, 1975, M sold his old residence and realized a gain. In determining the extent to which the realized gain is not to be recognized under section 1034, M's cost of constructing the new residence shall include only the $20,000 which was attributable to the June 15—October 14, 1974, period (4 months at $5,000). The $25,000 balance of the cost of constructing the new residence was not attributable to the period beginning 18 months before the date of the sale of the old residence and ending two years after such date and, under section 1034, is not properly a part of M's cost of constructing the new residence.

(d) *Limitations on application of section 1034.*—(1) If a residence is purchased by the taxpayer prior to the date of the sale of the old residence, the purchased residence shall, in no event, be treated as a new residence if such purchased residence is sold or otherwise disposed of by him prior to the date of the sale of the old residence (section 1034(c)(3)). And, if the taxpayer, during the period within which the purchase and use of the new residence must be made in order to have any gain on the sale of the old residence not recognized under this section, purchases more than one property which is used by him as his principal residence during the 18 months (or two years in the case of the construction of the new residence) succeeding the date of the sale of the old residence, only the last of such properties shall be considered a new residence (section 1034(c)(4)). In the case of a sale of an old residence prior to January 1, 1975, the period of 18 months (or two years) referred to in the preceding sentence shall be one year (or 18 months). If within 18 months (one year in the case of a sale of an old residence prior to January 1, 1975) before the date of the sale of the old residence, the taxpayer sold other property used by him as his principal residence at a gain, and any part of

Reg. § 1.1034-1(d)(1)

such gain was not recognized under this section or section 112(n) of the Internal Revenue Code of 1939, this section shall not apply with respect to the sale of the old residence (section 1034(d)).

(2) The following example will illustrate the rules of subparagraph (1) of this paragraph:

Example. A taxpayer sells his old residence on January 15, 1954, and purchases another residence on February 15, 1954. On March 15, 1954, he sells the residence which he bought on February 15, 1954, and purchases another residence on April 15, 1954. The gain on the sale of the old residence on January 15, 1954, will not be recognized except to the extent to which the taxpayer's adjusted sales price of the old residence exceeds the cost of purchasing the residence which he purchased on April 15, 1954. Gain on the sale of the residence which was bought on February 15, 1954, and sold on March 15, 1954, will be recognized.

(e) *Basis of new residence.*—(1) Where the purchase of a new residence results, under this section, in the nonrecognition of any part of the gain realized upon the sale of an old residence, then, in determining the adjusted basis of the new residence as of any time following the sale of the old residence, the adjustments to basis shall include a reduction by an amount equal to the amount of the gain which was not recognized upon the sale of the old residence (section 1034(e); for special rule applicable in some cases to husband and wife, see paragraph (f) of this section). Such a reduction is not to be made for the purpose of determining the adjusted basis of the new residence as of any time preceding the sale of the old residence. For the purpose of this determination, the amount of the gain not recognized under this section upon the sale of the old residence includes only so much of the gain as is not recognized because of the taxpayer's cost, up to the date of the determination of the adjusted basis, of purchasing the new residence.

(2) The following example will illustrate the rule of subparagraph (1) of this paragraph:

Example. On January 1, 1954, the taxpayer buys a new residence for $10,000. On March 1, 1954, he sells for an adjusted sales price of $15,000 his old residence, which has an adjusted basis to him of $5,000 (no fixing-up expenses are involved, so that $15,000 is the "amount realized" as well as the "adjusted sales price"). Between April 1 and April 15 a wing is constructed on the new house at a cost of $5,000. Between May 1 and May 15 a garage is constructed at a cost of $2,000. The adjusted basis of the new residence is $10,000 during January and February, $5,000 during March, $5,000 following the completion of the construction in April, and $7,000 following the completion of the construction in May. Since the old residence was not sold until March 1, no adjustment to the basis of the new residence is made during January and February. Computations for March, April, and May are as follows:

Amount realized on sale of old residence .	$15,000
Less: Adjusted basis of old residence . . .	5,000
Gain realized on sale of old residence . . .	10,000
March 1, 1954	
Adjusted sales price of old residence	$15,000
Less: Cost of purchasing new residence . .	10,000
Gain recognized	5,000
Gain realized but not recognized	$5,000
Cost of purchasing new residence	$10,000
Less: Gain realized but not recognized . .	5,000
Adjusted basis of new residence	5,000
April 15, 1954	
Gain realized on sale of old residence . . .	$10,000
Adjusted sales price of old residence	15,000
Less: Cost of purchasing new residence . .	15,000
Gain recognized	0
Gain realized but not recognized	10,000
Cost of purchasing new residence	$15,000
Less: Gain realized but not recognized . .	10,000
Adjusted basis of new residence	5,000
May 15, 1954	
Gain realized on sale of old residence . . .	$10,000
Adjusted sales price of old residence	15,000
Less: Cost of purchasing new residence . .	17,000
Gain recognized	0
Gain realized but not recognized	10,000
Cost of purchasing new residence	$17,000
Less: Gain realized but not recognized . .	10,000
Adjusted basis of new residence	7,000

(f) *Husband and wife.*—(1) If the taxpayer and his spouse file the consent referred to in this paragraph, then the "taxpayer's adjusted sales price of the old residence" shall mean the taxpayer's, or the taxpayer's and his spouse's, adjusted sales price of the old residence, and the "taxpayer's cost of purchasing the new residence" shall mean the cost to the taxpayer, or to his spouse, or to both of them, of purchasing the new residence, whether such new residence is held by the taxpayer, or his spouse, or both (section 1034(g)). Such consent may be filed only if the old residence and the new residence are each used by the taxpayer and his same spouse as their principal residence. If the taxpayer and his spouse do not file such a consent, the recognition of gain upon sale of the old residence shall be determined under this section without regard to the foregoing.

(2) The consent referred to in subparagraph (1) of this paragraph is a consent by the taxpayer and his spouse to have the basis of the interest of either of them in the new residence reduced from what it would have been but for the filing of such consent by an amount by which the gain of either of them on the sale of his interest in the old residence is not recognized solely by reason of the filing of such consent. Such reduction in basis is applicable to the basis of the new residence, whether such basis is that of the husband, of the wife, or divided between them. If the basis

is divided between the husband and wife, the reduction in basis shall be divided between them in the same proportion as the basis (determined without regard to such reduction) is divided. Such consent shall be filed with the district director with whom the taxpayer filed the return for the taxable year or years in which the gain from the sale of the old residence was realized.

(3) The following examples will illustrate the application of this rule:

Example (1). A taxpayer, in 1954, sells for an adjusted sales price of $10,000 the principal residence of himself and his wife, which he owns individually and which has an adjusted basis to him of $5,000 (no fixing-up expenses are involved, so that $10,000 is the "amount realized" as well as the "adjusted sales price"). Within a year after such sale he and his wife contribute $5,000 each from their separate funds for the purchase of their new principal residence which they hold as tenants in common, each owning an undivided one-half interest therein. If the taxpayer and his wife file the required consent, the gain of $5,000 upon the sale of the old residence will not be recognized to the taxpayer, and the adjusted basis of the taxpayer's interest in the new residence will be $2,500 and the adjusted basis of his wife's interest in such property will be $2,500.

Example (2). A taxpayer and his wife, in 1954, sell for an adjusted sales price of $10,000 their principal residence, which they own as joint tenants and which has an adjusted basis of $2,500 to each of them ($5,000 together) (no fixing-up expenses are involved, so that $10,000 is the "amount realized" as well as the "adjusted sales price"). Within a year after such sale, the wife spends $10,000 of her own funds in the purchase of a principal residence for herself and the taxpayer and takes title in her name only. If the taxpayer and his wife file the required consent, the adjusted basis to the wife of the new residence will be $5,000, and the gain of the taxpayer of $2,500 upon the sale of the old residence will not be recognized. The wife, as a taxpayer herself, will have her gain of $2,500 on the sale of the old residence not recognized under the general rule.

(g) *Members of Armed Forces.*—(1) Section 1034(h) provides a special rule for members of the Armed Forces with respect to the period after the sale of the old residence within which the acquisition of a new residence may result in a non-recognition of gain on such sale. The running of the period of 18 months (one year in the case of a sale of an old residence prior to January 1, 1975) after the sale of the old residence in the case of the purchase of a new residence, or the period of two years (18 months in the case of a sale of an old residence prior to January 1, 1975) after such sale in the case of the construction of a new residence, is suspended during any time that the taxpayer serves on extended active duty with the Armed Forces of the United States.

(This paragraph applies to time served on extended active duty prior to July 1, 1973, only if such extended active duty occurred during an induction period as defined in section 112(c)(5) as in effect prior to July 1, 1973.) However, in no event may such suspension extend for more than four years after the date of the sale of the old residence the period within which the purchase or construction of a new residence may result in a nonrecognition of gain. For example, if the taxpayer is on extended active duty with the Army from January 1, 1975, to June 30, 1976, and if he sold his old residence on January 10, 1975, the latest date on which the taxpayer may use a new residence constructed by him and have any part of the gain on the sale of his old residence not recognized under this section is June 30, 1978 (the date two years following the taxpayer's termination of active duty). However, if this taxpayer were on extended active duty with the Army from January 1, 1975, to December 31, 1978, the latest date on which he might use a new residence constructed by him and have any part of the gain on the sale of his old residence not recognized under this section would be January 10, 1979 (the date four years following the date of the sale of the old residence).

(2) This suspension covers not only the Armed Forces service of the taxpayer but if the taxpayer and his same spouse used both the old and the new residences as their principal residence, then the extension applies in like manner to the time the taxpayer's spouse is on extended active duty with the Armed Forces of the United States.

(3) The time during which the running of the period is suspended is part of such period. Thus, construction costs during such time are includible in the cost of purchasing the new residence under paragraph (c)(4) of this section.

(4) The running of the period of 18 months (or two years) after the date of sale of the old residence referred to in section 1034(c)(4) and in paragraph (d) of this section is not suspended. The running of the 18-month period prior to the date of the sale of the old residence within which the new residence may be purchased in order to have gain on the sale of the old residence not recognized under this section is also not suspended. In the case of a sale of an old residence prior to January 1, 1975, the periods of 18 months (or two years) referred to in each of the two preceding sentences shall be one year (or 18 months).

(5) The term "extended active duty" means any period of active duty which is served pursuant to a call or order to such duty for a period in excess of 90 days or for an indefinite period. If the call or order is for a period of more than 90 days it is immaterial that the time served pursuant to such call or order is less than 90 days, if the reason for such shorter period of service occurs after the beginning of such duty. As to what constitutes active service as a member of the Armed Forces of the United States, see para-

graph (i) of §1.112-1. As to who are members of the Armed Forces of the United States, see section 7701(a)(15) and the regulations in Part 301 of this chapter (Regulations on Procedure and Administration).

(h) *Special rules for involuntary conversions.*— (1) *In general.*—Except as provided in subparagraph (2) of this paragraph, section 1034 is inapplicable to involuntary conversions of personal residences occurring after December 31, 1953 (section 1034(i)(1)(B)). For purposes of section 1034, an involuntary conversion of a personal residence occurring after December 31, 1950, and before January 1, 1954, is treated as a sale of such residence (section 1034(i)(1)(A); see paragraph (b)(8) of this section). For purposes of this paragraph, an involuntary conversion is defined as the destruction in whole or in part, theft, seizure, requisition, or condemnation of property, or the sale or exchange of property under threat or imminence thereof. See section 1033 and §1.1033(a)-3 for treatment of residences involuntarily converted after December 31, 1953.

(2) *Election to treat condemnation of personal residence as sale.*—(i) Section 1034(i)(2) provides a special rule which permits a taxpayer to elect to treat the seizure, requisition, or condemnation of his principal residence, or the sale or exchange of such residence under threat or imminence thereof, if occurring after December 31, 1957, as the sale of such residence for purposes of section 1034 (relating to sale or exchange of residence). A taxpayer may thus elect to have section 1034 apply, rather than section 1033 (relating to involuntary conversions), in determining the amount of gain realized on the disposition of his old residence that will not be recognized and the extent to which the basis of his new residence acquired in lieu thereof shall be reduced. Once made, the election shall be irrevocable.

(ii) If the taxpayer elects to be governed by the provisions of section 1034, section 1033 will have no application. Thus, a taxpayer who elects under section 1034(i)(2) to treat the seizure, requisition, or condemnation of his principal residence (but not the destruction), or the sale or exchange of such residence under threat or imminence thereof, as a sale for the purposes of section 1034 must satisfy the requirements of section 1034 and this section. For example, under section 1034 a taxpayer generally must replace his old residence with a new residence which he uses as his principal residence, within a period beginning 18 months (one year in the case of a sale of an old residence prior to January 1, 1975) before the date of disposition of his old residence, and ending 18 months (one year in the case of a sale of an old residence prior to January 1, 1975) after such date. However, in the case of a new residence the construction of which was commenced by the taxpayer within such period, the replacement period shall not expire until 2 years (18 months in the case of a sale of an old residence prior to January 1, 1975) after the date of disposition of the old residence.

(iii) *Time and manner of making election.*— The election under section 1034(i)(2) shall be made in a statement attached to the taxpayer's income tax return, when filed, for the taxable year during which the disposition of his old residence occurs. The statement shall indicate that the taxpayer elects under section 1034(i)(2) to treat the disposition of his old residence as a sale for purposes of section 1034, and shall also show—

(a) The basis of the old residence;

(b) The date of its disposition;

(c) The adjusted sales price of the old residence, if known; and

(d) The purchase price, date of purchase, and date of occupancy of the new residence if it has been acquired prior to the time of making the election.

(i) *Statute of limitations.*—(1) Whenever a taxpayer sells property used as his principal residence at a gain, the statutory period prescribed in section 6501(a) for the assessment of a deficiency attributable to any part of such gain shall not expire prior to the expiration of three years from the date of receipt, by the district director with whom the return was filed for the taxable year or years in which the gain from the sale of the old residence was realized (section 1034(j)), of a written notice from the taxpayer of—

(i) The taxpayer's cost of purchasing the new residence which the taxpayer claims results in nonrecognition of any part of such gain,

(ii) The taxpayer's intention not to purchase a new residence within the period when such a purchase will result in nonrecognition of any part of such gain, or

(iii) The taxpayer's failure to make such a purchase within such period.

Any gain from the sale of the old residence which is required to be recognized shall be included in gross income for the taxable year or years in which such gain was realized. Any deficiency attributable to any portion of such gain may be assessed before the expiration of the 3-year period described in this paragraph, notwithstanding the provisions of any law or rule of law which might otherwise bar such assessment.

(2) The notification required by the preceding subparagraph shall contain all pertinent details in connection with the sale of the old residence and, where applicable, the purchase price of the new residence. The notification shall be in the form of a written statement and shall be accompanied, where appropriate, by an amended return for the year in which the gain from the sale of the old residence was realized, in order to reflect the inclusion in gross income for that year of gain required to be recognized in connection with such sale.

(j) *Effective date.*—Pursuant to section 7851(a)(1)(C), paragraphs (a), (b), (c), (d), (f), (g), and (i) of this section apply in the case of any "sale" (as defined in subparagraph (8) of paragraph (b) of this section) made after December 31, 1953, although such sale may occur in a taxable year subject to the Internal Revenue Code of 1939. Similarly, the rule in paragraph (h) of this section that involuntary conversions of personal residences are not to be treated as sales for purposes of section 1034 but are governed by section 1033 applies to any such involuntary conversion made after December 31, 1953, although such involuntary conversion may occur in a taxable year subject to the Internal Revenue Code of 1939. The rule in paragraph (e) of this section requiring an adjustment to the basis of a new residence, the purchase of which results (under section 1034, or section 112(n) of the Internal Revenue Code of 1939) in the nonrecognition of gain on the sale of an old residence, applies in determining the adjusted basis of the new residence at any time following such sale, although such sale may occur in a taxable year subject to the Internal Revenue Code of 1939. [Reg. §1.1034-1.]

□ [*T.D.* 6179, 6-1-56. *Amended by T.D.* 6453, 2-16-60; *T.D.* 6856, 10-19-65; *T.D.* 6916, 4-12-67; *T.D.* 7404, 2-12-76 *and T.D.* 7625, 5-29-79.]

[Reg. §1.1035-1]

§1.1035-1. Certain exchanges of insurance policies.—Under the provisions of section 1035 no gain or loss is recognized on the exchange of:

(a) A contract of life insurance for another contract of life insurance or for an endowment or annuity contract (section 1035 (a)(1));

(b) A contract of endowment insurance for another contract of endowment insurance providing for regular payments beginning at a date not later than the date payments would have begun under the contract exchanged, or an annuity contract (section 1035(a)(2)); or

(c) An annuity contract for another annuity contract (section 1035 (a)(3)),

but section 1035 does not apply to such exchanges if the policies exchanged do not relate to the same insured. The exchange, without recognition of gain or loss, of an annuity contract for another annuity contract under section 1035(a)(3) is limited to cases where the same person or persons are the obligee or obligees under the contract received in exchange as under the original contract. This section and section 1035 do not apply to transactions involving the exchange of an endowment contract or annuity contract for a life insurance contract, nor an annuity contract for an endowment contract. In the case of such exchanges, any gain or loss shall be recognized. In the case of exchanges which would be governed by section 1035 except for the fact that the property received in exchange consists not only of property which could other-wise be received without the recognition of gain or loss, but also of other property or money, see section 1031(b) and (c) and the regulations thereunder. Such an exchange does not come within the provisions of section 1035. Determination of the basis of property acquired in an exchange under section 1035(a) shall be governed by section 1031(d) and the regulations thereunder. [Reg. §1.1035-1.]

□ [*T.D.* 6211, 11-14-56.]

[Reg. §1.1036-1]

§1.1036-1. Stock for stock of the same corporation.—(a) Section 1036 permits the exchange, without the recognition of gain or loss, of common stock for common stock, or of preferred stock for preferred stock, in the same corporation. Section 1036 applies even though voting stock is exchanged for nonvoting stock or nonvoting stock is exchanged for voting stock. It is not limited to an exchange between two individual stockholders; it includes a transaction between a stockholder and the corporation. However, a transaction between a stockholder and the corporation may qualify not only under section 1036(a), but also under section 368(a)(1)(E) (recapitalization) or section 305(a) (distribution of stock and stock rights). The provisions of section 1036(a) do not apply if stock is exchanged for bonds, or preferred stock is exchanged for common stock, or common stock is exchanged for preferred stock, or common stock in one corporation is exchanged for common stock in another corporation. See paragraph (1) of §1.301-1 for certain transactions treated as distributions under section 301. See paragraph (e)(5) of §1.368-2 for certain transactions which result in deemed distributions under section 305(c) to which sections 305(b)(4) and 301 apply.

(b) For rules relating to recognition of gain or loss where an exchange is not wholly in kind, see subsections (b) and (c) of section 1031. For rules relating to the basis of property acquired in an exchange described in paragraph (a) of this section, see subsection (d) of section 1031.

(c) A transfer is not within the provisions of section 1036(a) if as part of the consideration the other party to the exchange assumes a liability of the taxpayer (or if the property transferred is subject to a liability), but the transfer, if otherwise qualified, will be within the provisions of section 1031(b).

(d) *Nonqualified preferred stock.*—See §1.356-7(a) for the applicability of the definition of nonqualified preferred stock in section 351(g)(2) for stock issued prior to June 9, 1997, and for stock issued in transactions occurring after June 8, 1997, that are described in section 1014(f)(2) of the Taxpayer Relief Act of 1997, Public Law 105-34 (111 Stat. 788, 921). [Reg. §1.1036-1.]

□ [*T.D.* 6210, 11-6-56. *Amended by T.D.* 7281, 7-11-73 *and T.D.* 8904, 9-29-2000.]

[Reg. §1.1037-1]

§1.1037-1. Certain exchanges of United States obligations.—(a) *Nonrecognition of gain or loss.*—(1) *In general.*—Section 1037 (a) provides for the nonrecognition of gain or loss on the surrender to the United States of obligations of the United States issued under the Second Liberty Bond Act (31 U.S.C. 774 (2)) when such obligations are exchanged solely for other obligations issued under that Act and the Secretary provides by regulations promulgated in connection with the issue of such other obligations that gain or loss is not to be recognized on such exchange. It is not necessary that at the time of the exchange the obligation which is surrendered to the United States be a capital asset in the hands of the taxpayer. For purposes of section 1037(a) and this subparagraph, a circular of the Treasury Department which offers to exchange obligations of the United States issued under the Second Liberty Bond Act for other obligations issued under that Act shall constitute regulations promulgated by the Secretary in connection with the issue of the obligations offered to be exchanged if such circular contains a declaration by the Secretary that no gain or loss shall be recognized for Federal income tax purposes on the exchange or grants the privilege of continuing to defer the reporting of the income on the bonds exchanged until such time as the bonds received in the exchange are redeemed or disposed of, or have reached final maturity, whichever is earlier. See, for example, regulations of the Bureau of the Public Debt, 31 CFR Part 339, or Treasury Department Circular 1066, 26 F.R. 8647. The application of section 1037(a) and this subparagraph will not be precluded merely because the taxpayer is required to pay money on the exchange. See section 1031 and the regulations thereunder if the taxpayer receives money on the exchange.

(2) *Recognition of gain or loss postponed.*— Gain or loss which has been realized but not recognized on the exchange of a United States obligation for another such obligation because of the provisions of section 1037(a) (or so much of section 1031(b) or (c) as relates to section 1037(a)) shall be recognized at such time as the obligation received in the exchange is disposed of, or redeemed, in a transaction other than an exchange described in section 1037(a) (or so much of section 1031 (b) or (c) as relates to section 1037(a)) or reaches final maturity, whichever is earlier, to the extent gain or loss is realized on such later transaction.

(3) *Illustrations.*—The application of this paragraph may be illustrated by the following examples, in which it is assumed that the taxpayer uses the cash receipts and disbursements method of accounting and has never elected under section 454(a) to include in gross income currently the annual increase in the redemption price of non-interest-bearing obligations issued

at a discount. In addition, it is assumed that the old obligations exchanged are capital assets transferred in an exchange in respect of which regulations are promulgated pursuant to section 1037(a):

Example (1). A, the owner of a $1,000 series E United States savings bond purchased for $750 and bearing an issue date of May 1 1945, surrenders the bond to the United States in exchange solely for series H United States savings bonds on February 1, 1964, when the series E bond has a redemption value of $1,304.80. If in the exchange A pays an additional $195.20 and obtains three $500 series H bonds, none of the $554.80 gain ($1,304.80 less $750) realized by A on the series E bond is recognized at the time of the exchange.

Example (2). In 1963, B purchased for $97 a marketable United States bond which was originally issued at its par value of $100. In 1964 he surrenders the bond to the United States in exchange solely for another marketable United States bond which then has a fair market value of $95. B's loss of $2 on the old bond is not recognized at the time of the exchange, and his basis for the new bond is $97 under section 1031(d). If it had been necessary for B to pay $1 additional consideration in the exchange, his basis in the new bond would be $98.

Example (3). The facts are the same as in example (2) except that B also receives $1 interest on the old bond for the period which has elapsed since the last interest payment date and that B does not pay any additional consideration on the exchange. As in example (2), B has a loss of $2 which is not recognized at the time of the exchange and his basis in the new bond is $97. In addition, the $1 of interest received on the old bond is includible in gross income. B holds the new bond 1 year and sells it in the market for $99 plus interest. At this time he has a gain of $2, the difference between his basis of $97 in the new bond and the sales price of such bond. In addition, the interest received on the new bond is includible in gross income.

Example (4). The facts are the same as in example (2), except that in addition to the new bond B also receives $1.85 in cash, $0.85 of which is interest. The $0.85 interest received is includible in gross income. B's loss of $1 ($97 less $96) on the old bond is not recognized at the time of the exchange by reason of section 1031(c). Under section 1031(d) B's basis in the new bond is $96 (his basis of $97 in the old bond, reduced by the $1 cash received in the exchange.)

Example (5). (a) For $975 D subscribes to a marketable United States obligation which has a face value of $1,000. Thereafter, he surrenders this obligation to the United States in exchange solely for a 10-year marketable $1,000 obligation which at the time of exchange has a fair market value of $930, at which price such obligation is initially offered to the public. At the time of issue of the new obligation there was no intention to call it before maturity. Five years after the exchange D sells the new obligation for $960.

(b) On the exchange of the old obligation for the new obligation D sustains a loss of $45 ($975 less $930), none of which is recognized pursuant to section 1037(a).

(c) The basis of the new obligation in D's hands, determined under section 1031(d), is $975 (the same basis as that of the old obligation).

(d) On the sale of the new obligation D sustains a loss of $15 ($975 less $960), all of which is recognized by reason of section 1002.

Example (6). (a) The facts are the same as in example (5), except that five years after the exchange D sells the new obligation for $1,020.

(b) On the exchange of the old obligation for the new obligation D sustains a loss of $45 ($975 less $930), none of which is recognized pursuant to section 1037(a).

(c) The basis of the new obligation in D's hands, determined under section 1031(d), is $975 (the same basis as that of the old obligation). The issue price of the new obligation under section 1232(b)(2) is $930.

(d) On the sale of the new obligation D realizes a gain of $45 ($1,020 less $975), all of which is recognized by reason of section 1002. Of this gain of $45, the amount of $35 is treated as ordinary income and $10 is treated as long-term capital gain, determined as follows:

(1) Ordinary income under first
sentence of sec. 1232(a)(2)(B) on
sale of new obligation:
Stated redemption price of new
  obligation at maturity $1,000
Less: Issue price of new obligation
  under sec. 1232(b)(2)   930
Original issue discount on new
  obligation   70
Proration under sec. 1232 (a)(2)(B) (ii):
  ($70 × 60 months/120 months)   35
(2) Long-term capital gain ($45 less
  $35) $10

Example (7). (a) The facts are the same as in example (5), except that D retains the new obligation and redeems it at maturity for $1,000.

(b) On the exchange of the old obligation for the new obligation D sustains a loss of $45 ($975 less $930), none of which is recognized pursuant to section 1037(a).

(c) The basis of the new obligation in D's hands, determined under section 1031(d), is $975 (the same basis as that of the old obligation). The issue price of the new obligation is $930 under section 1232(b)(2).

(d) On the redemption of the new obligation D realizes a gain of $25 ($1,000 less $975), all of which is recognized by reason of section 1002. Of this gain of $25, the entire amount is treated as ordinary income, determined as follows:

Ordinary income under first sentence
  of sec. 1232(a)(2)(B) on redemption
  of new obligation:
Stated redemption price of new
  obligation at maturity $1,000
Less: Issue price of new obligation
  under sec. 1232(b)(2)   930
Original issue discount on new
  obligation   70
Proration under sec. 1232(a)(2)(B)(ii):
  ($70 × 120 months/120 months),
  but such amount not to exceed the
  $25 gain recognized on redemption
  . . . . $25

(b) *Application of section 1232 upon disposition or redemption of new obligation.*—(1) *Exchanges involving nonrecognition of gain on obligations issued at a discount.*—If an obligation, the gain on which is subject to the first sentence of section 1232(a)(2)(B) because the obligation was originally issued at a discount, is surrendered to the United States in exchange for another obligation and any part of the gain realized on the exchange is not then recognized because of the provisions of section 1037(a) (or because of so much of section 1031(b) as relates to section 1037(a)), the first sentence of section 1232(a)(2)(B) shall apply to so much of such unrecognized gain as is later recognized upon the disposition or redemption of the obligation which is received in the exchange as though the obligation so disposed of or redeemed were the obligation surrendered, rather than the obligation received, in such exchange. See the first sentence of section 1037(b)(1). Thus, in effect that portion of the gain which is unrecognized on the exchange but is recognized upon the later disposition or redemption of the obligation received from the United States in the exchange shall be considered as ordinary income in an amount which is equal to the gain which, by applying the first sentence of section 1232(a)(2)(B) upon the earlier surrender of the old obligation to the United States, would have been considered as ordinary income if the gain had been recognized upon such earlier exchange. Any portion of the gain which is recognized under section 1031(b) upon the earlier exchange and is treated at such time as ordinary income shall be deducted from the gain which is treated as ordinary income by applying the first sentence of section 1232(a)(2)(B) pursuant to this subparagraph upon the disposition or redemption of the obligation which is received in the earlier exchange. This subparagraph shall apply only in a case where on the exchange of United States obligations there was some gain not recognized by reason of section 1037(a) (or so much of section 1031(b) as relates to section 1037(a)); it shall not apply where only loss was unrecognized by reason of section 1037(a).

(2) *Rules to apply when a nontransferable obligation is surrendered in the exchange.*—For purposes of applying both section 1232(a)(2)(B) and subparagraph (1) of this paragraph to the total gain realized on the obligation which is later disposed of or redeemed, if the obligation surrendered to the United States in the earlier exchange is a nontransferable obligation described in section 454(a) or (c)—

(i) The aggregate amount considered, with respect to the obligation so surrendered in the earlier exchange, as ordinary income shall not exceed the difference between the issue price of the surrendered obligation and the stated redemption price of the surrendered obligation which applied at the time of the earlier exchange, and

(ii) The issue price of the obligation which is received from the United States in the earlier exchange shall be considered to be the stated redemption price of the surrendered obligation which applied at the time of the earlier exchange, increased by the amount of other consideration (if any) paid to the United States as part of the earlier exchange.

If the obligation received in the earlier exchange is a nontransferable obligation described in section 454(c) and such obligation is partially redeemed before final maturity, or partially disposed of by being partially reissued to another owner, the amount determined by applying subdivision (i) of this subparagraph shall be determined on a basis proportional to the total denomination of obligations redeemed or disposed of. See paragraph (c) of § 1.454-1.

(3) *Long-term capital gain.*—If, in a case where both subparagraphs (1) and (2) of this paragraph are applied, the total gain realized on the redemption or disposition of the obligation which is received from the United States in the exchange to which section 1037(a) (or so much of section 1031(b) as relates to section 1037(a)) applies exceeds the amount of gain which, by applying such subparagraphs, is treated as ordinary income, the gain in excess of such amount shall be treated as long-term capital gain.

(4) *Illustrations.*—The application of this paragraph may be illustrated by the following examples, in which it is assumed that the taxpayer uses the cash receipts and disbursements method of accounting and has never elected under section 454(a) to include in gross income currently the annual increase in the redemption price of non-interest-bearing obligations issued at a discount. In addition, it is assumed that the old obligations exchanged are capital assets transferred in an exchange in respect of which regulations are promulgated pursuant to section 1037(a):

Example (1). (a) A purchased a non-interest-bearing nontransferable United States bond for $74 which was issued after December 31, 1954, and redeemable in 10 years for $100. Several years later, when the stated redemption value of such bond is $94.50, A surrenders it to the United States in exchange for $1 in cash and a 10-year marketable bond having a face value of $100. On the date of exchange the bond received in the exchange has a fair market value of $96. Less than one month after the exchange, A sells the new bond for $96.

(b) On the exchange of the old bond for the new bond A realizes a gain of $23, determined as follows:

Amount realized (a new bond worth $96 plus $1 cash)	$97
Less: Adjusted basis of old bond	74
Gain realized	$23

Pursuant to so much of section 1031(b) as applies to section 1037(a), the amount of such gain which is recognized is $1 (the money received). Such recognized gain of $1 is treated as ordinary income. On the exchange of the old bond a gain of $22 ($23 less $1) is not recognized.

(c) The basis of the new bond in A's hands, determined under section 1031(d), is $74 (the basis of the old bond, decreased by the $1 received in cash and increased by the $1 gain recognized on the exchange).

(d) On the sale of the new bond A realizes a gain of $22 ($96 less $74), all of which is recognized by reason of section 1002. Of this gain of $22, the amount of $19.50 is treated as ordinary income and $2.50 is treated as long-term capital gain, determined as follows:

(1) Ordinary income treating sale of new bond as though a sale of old bond and applying sec. 1037(b)(1)(A):	
Stated redemption price of old bond	$94.50
Less: Issue price of old bond	74.00
Aggregate gain under sec. 1037(b)(1)(A) (not to exceed $22 not recognized at time of exchange)	$20.50
Less: Amount of such gain recognized at time of exchange	$ 1.00
Ordinary income	$19.50
(2) Ordinary income under first sentence of sec. 1232(a)(2)(B), applying sec. 1037(b)(1)(B) to sale of new bond:	
Stated redemption price of new bond at maturity	$100.00

Reg. § 1.1037-1(b)(2)

Less: Issue price of new bond under sec. 1037(b)(1)(B) ($94.50
plus $0 additional consideration paid on exchange) 94.50

Original issue discount on new bond . . . . $ 5.50

Proration under sec. 1232(a)(2)(B)(ii): ($5.50 × 0 months/120
months)   0

(3) Total ordinary income (sum of subparagraphs (1) and (2)) $19.50
(4) Long-term capital gain ($22 less $19.50) 2.50

Example (2). (a) The facts are the same as in example (1), except that, less than one month after the exchange of the old bond, the new bond is sold for $92.

(b) On the sale of the new bond A realizes a gain of $18 ($92 less $74), all of which is recognized by reason of section 1002. Of this gain, the entire amount of $18 is treated as ordinary income. This amount is determined as provided in paragraph (d)(1) of example (1) except that the ordinary income of $19.50 is limited to the $18 recognized on the sale of the new bond.

Example (3). (a) The facts are the same as in example (1), except that 2 years after the exchange of the old bond A sells the new bond for $98.

(b) On the sale of the new bond A realizes a gain of $24 ($98 less $74), all of which is recognized by reason of section 1002. Of this gain of $24, the amount of $20.60 is treated as ordinary income and $3.40 is treated as long-term capital gain, determined as follows:

(1) Ordinary income applicable to old
bond (determined as provided in
paragraph (d)(1) of example (1)) . . $19.50
(2) Ordinary income applicable to new
bond (determined as provided in
paragraph (d)(2) of example (1),
except that the proration of the
original issue discount under sec.
1232(a)(2)(B)(ii) amounts to $1.10
($5.50 × 24 months/120 months)) .   1.10
(3) Total ordinary income (sum of
subparagraphs (1) and (2)) $20.60
(4) Long-term capital gain ($24 less
$20.60) 3.40

Example (4). (a) The facts are the same as in example (1), except that A retains the new bond and redeems it at maturity for $100.

(b) On the redemption of the new bond A realizes a gain of $26 ($100 less $74), all of which is recognized by reason by section 1002. Of this gain of $26, the amount of $25 is treated as ordinary income and $1 is treated as long-term capital gain, determined as follows:

(1) Ordinary income applicable to old
bond (determined as provided in
paragraph (d)(1) of example (1)) $19.50
(2) Ordinary income applicable to new
bond (determined as provided in
paragraph (d)(2) of example (1),
except that the proration of the
original issue discount under sec.
1232(a)(2)(B)(ii) amounts to $5.50
($5.50 × 120 months/120 months)) .   5.50
(3) Total ordinary income (sum of
subparagraphs (1) and (2)) 25.00
(4) Long-term capital gain ($26 less $25) .   1.00

Example (5). (a) In 1958 B purchased for $7,500 a series E United States savings bond having a face value of $10,000. In 1965 when the stated redemption value of the series E bond is $9,760, B surrenders it to the United States in exchange solely for a $10,000 series H United States savings bond, after paying $240 additional consideration. B retains the series H bond and redeems it at maturity in 1975 for $10,000, after receiving all the semi-annual interest payments thereon.

(b) On the exchange of the series E bond for the series H bond, B realizes a gain of $2,260 ($9,760 less $7,500), none of which is recognized at such time by reason of section 1037(a).

(c) The basis of the series H bond in B's hands, determined under section 1031(d), is $7,740 (the $7,500 basis of the series E bond, plus $240 additional consideration paid for the series H bond).

(d) On the redemption of the series H bond, B realizes a gain of $2,260 ($10,000 less $7,740), all of which is recognized by reason of section 1002. This entire gain is treated as ordinary income by treating the redemption of the series H bond as though it were a redemption of the series E bond and by applying section 1037(b)(1)(A).

(e) Under section 1037(b)(1)(B) the issue price of the series H bond is $10,000 ($9,760 stated redemption price of the series E bond at time of exchange, plus $240 additional consideration paid). Thus, with respect to the series H bond, there is no original issue discount to which section 1232(a)(2)(B) might apply.

Example (6). (a) The facts are the same as in example (5), except that in 1970 B submits the $10,000 series H bond to the United States for partial redemption in the amount of $3,000 and for reissuance of the remainder in $1,000 series H savings bonds registered in his name. On this transaction B receives $3,000 cash and seven

Reg. §1.1037-1(b)(4)

$1,000 series H bonds bearing the original issue date of the $10,000 bond which is partially redeemed. The $1,000 series H bonds are redeemed at maturity in 1975 for $7,000.

(b) On the partial redemption of the $10,000 series H bond in 1970 B realizes a gain of $678 ($3,000 less $2,322 [$7,740 × $3,000/$10,000]), all of which is recognized at such time by reason of section 1002 and paragraph (c) of § 1.454-1. This entire gain is treated as ordinary income, by treating the partial redemption of the series H bond as though it were a redemption of the relevant denominational portion of the series E bond and by applying section 1037(b)(1)(A).

(c) On the redemption at maturity in 1975 of the seven $1,000 series H bonds B realizes a gain of $1,582 ($7,000 less $5,418 [$7,740 × $7,000/$10,000]), all of which is recognized at such time by reason of section 1002 and paragraph (c) of § 1.454-1. This entire gain is treated as ordinary income, determined in the manner described in paragraph (b) of this example.

Example (7). (a) The facts are the same as in example (5), except that in 1970 B requests the United States to reissue the $10,000 series H bond by issuing two $5,000 series H bonds bearing the original issue date of such $10,000 bond. One of such $5,000 bonds is registered in B's name, and the other is registered in the name of C, who is B's son. Each $5,000 series H bond is redeemed at maturity in 1975 for $5,000.

(b) On the issuing in 1970 of the $5,000 series H bond to C, B realizes a gain of $1,130 ($5,000 less $3,870 [$7,740 × $5,000/$10,000]), all of which is recognized at such time by reason of section 1002 and paragraph (c) of § 1.454-1. This entire gain is treated as ordinary income by treating the transaction as though it were a redemption of the relevant denominational portion of the series E bond and by applying section 1037(b)(1)(A).

(c) On the redemption at maturity in 1975 of the $5,000 series H bond registered in his name B realizes a gain of $1,130 ($5,000 less $3,870 [$7,740 × $5,000/$10,000]), all of which is recognized at such time by reason of section 1002 and paragraph (c) of § 1.454-1. This entire gain is treated as ordinary income, determined in the manner described in paragraph (b) of this example.

(d) On the redemption at maturity in 1975 of the $5,000 series H bond registered in his name C does not realize any gain, since the amount realized on redemption does not exceed his basis in the property, determined as provided in section 1015.

(5) *Exchanges involving nonrecognition of gain or loss on transferable obligations issued at not less than par.*—(i) *In general.*—If a transferable obligation of the United States which was originally issued at not less than par is surrendered to the United States for another transferable obligation in an exchange to which the provisions of section 1037(a) (or so much of section 1031(b) or (c) as relates to section 1037(a)) apply, the issue price of the obligation received from the United States in the exchange shall be considered for purposes of applying section 1232 to gain realized on the disposition or redemption of the obligation so received, to be the same as the issue price of the obligation which is surrendered to the United States in the exchange, increased by the amount of other consideration, if any, paid to the United States as part of the exchange. This subparagraph shall apply irrespective of whether there is gain or loss unrecognized on the exchange and irrespective of the fair market value, at the time of the exchange, of either the obligation surrendered to, or the obligation received from, the United States in the exchange.

(ii) *Illustrations.*—The application of this subparagraph may be illustrated by the following examples, in which it is assumed that the taxpayer uses the cash receipts and disbursements method of accounting and that the old obligations exchanged are capital assets transferred in an exchange in respect of which regulations are promulgated pursuant to section 1037(a):

Example (1). (a) A purchases in the market for $85 a marketable United States bond which was originally issued at its par value of $100. Three months later, A surrenders this bond to the United States in exchange solely for another $100 marketable United States bond which then has a fair market value of $88. He holds the new bond for 5 months and then sells it on the market for $92.

(b) On the exchange of the old bond for the new bond A realizes a gain of $3 ($88 less $85), none of which is recognized by reason of section 1037(a).

(c) The basis of the new bond in A's hands, determined under section 1031(d), is $85 (the same as that of the old bond). The issue price of the new bond for purposes of section 1232(a)(2)(B) is considered under section 1037(b)(2) to be $100 (the same issue price as that of the old bond).

(d)(1) Ordinary income under first sentence of sec. 1232(a)(2)(B), applicable to old bond:

Stated redemption price of old bond at maturity	$100
Less: Issue price of old bond	100
Original issue discount on old bond	0

(2) Ordinary income under first sentence of sec. 1232(a)(2)(B), applying sec. 1037(b)(2) to sale of new bond:

Stated redemption price of new bond at maturity	$100
Less: Issue price of new bond under sec. 1037(b)(2)	100
Original issue discount on new bond	0

Example (2). The facts are the same as in example (1), except that A retains the new bond and redeems it at maturity for $100. On the redemption of the new bond, A realizes a gain of $15 ($100 less $85), all of which is recognized under section 1002. This entire gain is treated as long-term capital gain, determined in the same manner as provided in paragraph (d) of example (1).

Example (3). (a) For $1,000 B subscribes to a marketable United States bond which has a face value of $1,000. Thereafter, he surrenders this bond to the United States in exchange solely for a 10-year marketable $1,000 bond which at the time of exchange has a fair market value of $930, at which price such bond is initially offered to the public. Five years after the exchange, B sells the new bond for $950.

(b) On the exchange of the old bond for the new bond, B sustains a loss of $70 ($1,000 less $930), none of which is recognized pursuant to section 1037(a).

(c) The basis of the new bond in A's hands, determined under section 1031(d), is $1,000 (the same basis as that of the old bond).

(d) On the sale of the new bond B sustains a loss of $50 ($1,000 less $950), all of which is recognized by reason of section 1002.

Example (4). (a) The facts are the same as in example (3), except that five years after the exchange B sells the new bond for $1,020.

(b) On the exchange of the old bond for the new bond B sustains a loss of $70 ($1,000 less $930), none of which is recognized pursuant to section 1037(a).

(c) The basis of the new bond in B's hands, determined under section 1031(d), is $1,000 (the same basis as that of the old bond). The issue price of the new bond for purposes of section 1232(a)(2)(B) is considered under section 1037(b)(2) to be $1,000 (the same issue price as that of the old bond).

(d) On the sale of the new bond B realizes a gain of $20 ($1,020 less $1,000), all of which is recognized by reason of section 1002. This entire gain is treated as long-term capital gain, determined in the same manner as provided in paragraph (d) of example (1).

(6) *Other rules for applying section 1232.*—To the extent not specifically affected by the provisions of section 1037(b) and subparagraphs (1) through (5) of this paragraph, any gain realized on the disposition or redemption of any obligation received from the United States in an exchange to which section 1037(a) (or so much of section 1031(b) or (c) as relates to section 1037(a)) applies shall be treated in the manner provided by section 1232 if the facts and circumstances relating to the acquisition and disposition or redemption of such obligation require the application of section 1232.

(c) *Holding period of obligation received in the exchange.*—The holding period of an obligation received from the United States in an exchange to which the provisions of section 1037(a) (or so much of section 1031(b) or (c) as relates to section 1037(a)) apply shall include the period for which the obligation which was surrendered to the United States in the exchange was held by the taxpayer, but only if the obligation so surrendered was at the time of the exchange a capital asset in the hands of the taxpayer. See section 1223 and the regulations thereunder.

(d) *Basis.*—The basis of an obligation received from the United States in an exchange to which the provisions of section 1037(a) (or so much of section 1031(b) or (c) as relates to section 1037(a)) apply shall be determined as provided in section 1031(d) and the regulations thereunder.

(e) *Effective date.*—Section 1.1037 and this section shall apply only for taxable years ending after September 22, 1959. [Reg. §1.1037-1.]

☐ [*T.D.* 6935, 11-16-67. *Amended by T.D.* 7154, 12-27-71.]

[Reg. §1.1038-1]

§1.1038-1. Reacquisitions of real property in satisfaction of indebtedness.—(a) *Scope of section 1038.*—(1) *General rule on gain or loss.*—If a sale of real property gives rise to indebtedness to the seller which is secured by the real property which is sold, and the seller of such property reacquires such property in a taxable year beginning after September 2, 1964, in partial or full satisfaction of such indebtedness, then, except as provided in paragraphs (b) and (f) of this section, no gain or loss shall result to the seller from such reacquisition. The treatment so provided is mandatory; however, see §1.1038-3 for an election to apply the provisions of this section to certain taxable years beginning after December 31, 1957. It is immaterial, for purposes of applying this subparagraph, whether the seller realized a gain or sustained a loss on the sale of the real property, or whether it can be ascertained at the time of the sale whether gain or loss occurs as a result of the sale. It is also immaterial what method of accounting the seller used in reporting gain or loss from the sale of the real property or whether at the time of reacquisition such property has depreciated or appreciated in value since the time of the original sale. Moreover, the character of the gain realized on the original sale of the property is immaterial for purposes of applying this subparagraph. The provisions of this section shall apply, except as provided in §1.1038-2, to the reacquisition of real property which was used by the seller as his principal residence and with respect to the sale of which an election under section 121 is in effect or with respect to the sale of which gain was not recognized under section 1034.

(2) *Sales giving rise to indebtedness.*—(i) *Sale defined.*—For purposes of this section, it is not necessary for title to the property to have passed to the purchaser in order to have a sale. Ordinarily, a sale of property has occurred in a transaction in which title to the property has not passed to the purchaser, if the purchaser has a contractual right to retain possession of the property so long as he performs his obligations under the

contract and to obtain title to the property upon the completion of the contract. However, a sale may have occurred even if the purchaser does not have the right to possession until he partially or fully satisfies the terms of the contract. For example, if S contracts to sell real property to P, and if S promises to convey title to P upon the completion of all of the payments due under the contract and to allow P to obtain possession of the property after 10 percent of the purchase price has been paid, there has been a sale on the date of the contract for purposes of this section. This section shall not apply to a disposition of real property which constituted an exchange of property or was treated as a sale under section 121(d)(4) or section 1034(i); nor shall it apply to a sale of stock in a cooperative housing corporation described in section 121(d)(3) or section 1034(f).

(ii) *Secured indebtedness defined.*—An indebtedness to the seller is secured by the real property for purposes of this section whenever the seller has the right to take title or possession of the property or both if there is a default with respect to such indebtedness. A sale of real property may give rise to an indebtedness to the seller although the seller is limited in his recourse to the property for payment of the indebtedness in the case of a default.

(3) *Reacquisitions in partial or full satisfaction of indebtedness.*—(i) *Purpose of reacquisition.*—This section applies only where the seller reacquires the real property in partial or full satisfaction of the indebtedness to him that arose from the sale of the real property and was secured by the property. That is, the reacquisition must be in furtherance of the seller's security rights in the property with respect to indebtedness to him that arose at the time of the sale. Accordingly, if the seller in reacquiring the real property does not pay consideration in addition to discharging the purchaser's indebtedness to him that arose from the sale and was secured by such property, this section shall apply to the reacquisition even though the purchaser has not defaulted in his obligations under the contract or such a default is not imminent. If in addition to discharging the purchaser's indebtedness to him that arose from the sale the seller pays consideration in reacquiring the real property, this section shall generally apply to the reacquisition if the reacquisition and the payment of additional consideration is provided for in the original contract for the sale of the property. This section generally shall apply to a reacquisition of real property if the seller reacquires the property either when the purchaser has defaulted in his obligations under the contract or when such a default is imminent. This section generally shall not apply to a reacquisition of real property where the seller pays consideration in addition to discharging the purchaser's indebtedness to him that arose from the sale if the reacquisition and payment of additional consideration was not provided for in the original contract for the sale of the property and

if the purchaser has not defaulted in his obligations under the contract or such a default is not imminent. Thus, for example, if the purchaser is in arrears on the payment of interest or principal or has in any other way defaulted on his contract for the purchase of the property, or if the facts of the case indicate that the purchaser is unable satisfactorily to perform his obligations under the contract, and the seller reacquires the property from the purchaser in a transaction in which the seller pays consideration in addition to discharging the purchaser's indebtedness to him that arose from the sale and was secured by the property, this section shall apply to the reacquisition. Additional consideration paid by the seller includes money and other property paid or transferred by the seller. Also, the reacquisition by the seller of real property subject to an indebtedness (or the assumption, upon the reacquisition, of indebtedness) which arose subsequent to the original sale shall be considered as a payment by the seller of additional consideration. However, the reacquisition by the seller of real property subject to an indebtedness (or the assumption, upon the reacquisition, of an indebtedness) which arose prior to or arose out of the original sale shall not be considered as a payment by the seller of additional consideration.

(ii) *Manner of reacquisition.*—For purposes of applying section 1038 and this section there must be a reacquisition by the seller of the real property itself, but the manner in which the seller so reduces the property to ownership or possession, as the case may be, shall generally be immaterial. Thus, the seller may reduce the real property to ownership or possession or both, as the case may require, by agreement or by process of law. The reduction of the real property to ownership or possession by agreement includes, where valid under local law, such methods as voluntary conveyance from the purchaser and abandonment to the seller. The reduction of the real property to ownership or possession by process of law includes foreclosure proceedings in which a competitive bid is entered, such as foreclosure by judicial sale or by power of sale contained in the loan agreement without recourse to the courts, as well as those types of foreclosure proceedings in which a competitive bid is not entered, such as strict foreclosure and foreclosure by entry and possession, by writ of entry, or by publication or notice.

(4) *Persons from whom real property may be reacquired.*—The real property reacquired in satisfaction of the indebtedness need not be reacquired from the purchaser but may be required from the purchaser's transferee or assignee, or from a trustee holding title to such property pending the purchaser's satisfaction of the terms of the contract, so long as the indebtedness that is partially or completely satisfied in the reacquisition of such property arose in the original sale of the property and was secured by the property so reacquired. In such a case, a reference in this section to the purchaser shall, where appropri-

Reg. §1.1038-1(a)(2)(ii)

ate, include the purchaser's transferee or assignee. Thus, for example, this section will apply if the seller reacquires the property from a purchaser from the original purchaser and either the property is subject to, or the subsequent purchaser assumes, the liability to the seller on the indebtedness.

(5) *Reacquisitions not included.*—This section shall not apply to reacquisitions of real property by mutual savings banks, domestic building and loan associations, and cooperative banks, described in section 593(a). However, for rules respecting the reacquisition of real property by such organizations, see § 1.595-1.

(b) *Amount of gain resulting from a reacquisition.*—(1) *Determination of amount.*—(i) *In general.*—As a result of a reacquisition to which paragraph (a) of this section applies gain shall be derived by the seller to the extent that the amount of money and the fair market value of other property (other than obligations of the purchaser arising with respect to the sale) which are received by the seller, prior to such reacquisition, with respect to the sale of the property exceed the amount of the gain derived by the seller on the sale of such property which is returned as income for periods prior to the reacquisition. However, the amount of gain so determined shall in no case exceed the amount determined under paragraph (c) of this section with respect to such reacquisition.

(ii) *Amount of gain returned as income for prior periods.*—For purposes of this subparagraph and paragraph (c)(1) of this section, the amount of gain on the sale of the property which is returned as income for periods prior to the reacquisition of the real property does not include any amount of income determined under paragraph (f)(2) of this section which is considered to be received at the time of the reacquisition of the property. However, the amount of gain on the sale of the property which is returned as income for such periods does include gain on the sale resulting from payments received in the taxable year in which the date of reacquisition occurs if such payments are received prior to such reacquisition. The application of this subdivision may be illustrated by the following example:

Example. In 1965 S, who uses the calendar year as the taxable year, sells to P for $10,000 real property which has an adjusted basis of $3,000. S properly elects under section 453 to report the income from the sale on the installment method. In 1965 and 1966, S receives a total of $4,000 on the contract. On May 15, 1967, S receives $1,000 on the contract. Because of P's default, S reacquires the property on August 31, 1967. The gain on the sale which is returned as income for periods prior to the reacquisition is $3,500 ($5,000 × $7,000/$10,000).

(2) *Amount of money and other property received with respect to the sale.*—(i) *In general.*— Amounts of money and other property received by the seller with respect to the sale of the prop-

erty include payments made by the purchaser for the seller's benefit, as well as payments made and other property transferred directly to the seller. If the purchaser of the real property makes payments on a mortgage or other indebtedness to which the property is subject at the time of the sale of such property to him, or on which the seller was personally liable at the time of such sale, such payments are considered amounts received by the seller with respect to the sale. However, if after the sale the purchaser borrows money and uses the property as security for the loan, payments by the purchaser in satisfaction of the indebtedness are not considered as amounts received by the seller with respect to the sale, although the seller does in fact receive some indirect benefit when the purchaser makes such payments.

(ii) *Payments by purchaser at time of reacquisition.*—All payments made by the purchaser at the time of the reacquisition of the real property that are with respect to the original sale of the property shall be treated, for purposes of subparagraph (1) of this paragraph, by the seller as having been received prior to the reacquisition with respect to such sale. For example, if the purchaser, at the time of the reacquisition by the seller, pays money or other property to the seller in partial or complete satisfaction of the purchaser's indebtedness on the original sale, the seller shall treat such amounts as having been received prior to the reacquisition with respect to the sale.

(iii) *Interest received.*—For purposes of this subparagraph and paragraph (c)(1) of this section any amounts received by the seller as interest, stated or unstated, are excluded from the computation of gain on the sale of the property and are not considered amounts of money or other property received with respect to the sale.

(iv) *Amounts received on sale of purchaser's indebtedness.*—Money or other property received by the seller on the sale of the purchaser's indebtedness that arose at the time of the sale of the real property are amounts received by the seller with respect to the sale of such real property, except that the amounts so received from the sale of such indebtedness shall be reduced by the amount of money and the fair market value of other property paid or transferred by the seller, before the reacquisition of the real property, to reacquire such indebtedness. For example, if S sells real property to P for $25,000, and under the contract receives $10,000 down and a note from P for $15,000, S would receive $22,000 with respect to the sale if he were to discount the note for $12,000. If before the reacquisition of the real property S were to reacquire the discounted note for $8,000, he would receive $14,000 with respect to the sale.

(3) *Obligations of the purchaser arising with respect to the sale.*—The term "obligations of the purchaser arising with respect to the sale" of the real property includes, for purposes of subpara-

graph (1) of this paragraph, only that indebtedness on which the purchaser is liable to the seller and which arises out of the sale of such property. Thus, the term does not include any indebtedness in respect of the property that the seller owes to a third person which the purchaser assumes, or to which the property is subject, at the time of the sale of the property to the purchaser. Nor does the term include any indebtedness on which the purchaser is liable to the seller if such indebtedness arises subsequent to the sale of such property.

(c) *Limitation upon amount of gain.*—(1) *In general.*—Except as provided by subparagraph (2) of this paragraph, the amount of gain on a reacquisition of real property, as determined under paragraph (b) of this section, shall in no case exceed—

(i) The amount by which the price at which the real property was sold exceeded its adjusted basis at the time of the sale, as determined under §1.1011-1, reduced by

(ii) The amount of gain on the sale of such real property which is returned as income for periods prior to the reacquisition, and by

(iii) The amount of money and the fair market value of other property (other than obligations of the purchaser to the seller which are secured by the real property) paid or transferred by the seller in connection with the reacquisition of such real property.

(2) *Cases where limitation does not apply.*—The limitation provided by subparagraph (1) of this paragraph shall not apply in a case where the selling price of property is indefinite in amount and cannot be ascertained at the time of the reacquisition of such property, as, for example, where the selling price is stated as a percentage of the profits to be realized from the development of the property which is sold. Moreover, the limitation so provided shall not apply to a reacquisition of real property occurring in a taxable year beginning before September 3, 1964, to which the provisions of this section are applied pursuant to an election under §1.1038-3.

(3) *Determination of sales price.*—The price at which the real property was sold shall be, for purposes of subparagraph (1) of this paragraph, the gross sales price reduced by the selling commissions, legal fees, and other expenses incident to the sale of such property which are properly taken into account in determining gain or loss on the sale. For example, the amount of selling commissions paid by a nondealer will be deducted from the gross sales price in determining the price at which the real property was sold; on the other hand, selling commissions paid by a real estate dealer will be deducted as a business expense. Examples of other expenses incident to the sale of the property are expenses for appraisal fees, advertising expense, cost of preparing maps, recording fees, and documentary stamp taxes. Payments on indebtedness to the seller which are for interest, stated or unstated, are not included in determining the price at which the property was sold. See paragraph (b)(2)(iii) of this section.

(4) *Determination of amounts paid or transferred in connection with a reacquisition.*—(i) *In general.*—Amounts of money or property paid or transferred by the seller of the real property in connection with the reacquisition of such property include payments of money, or transfers of property, to persons from whom the real property is reacquired as well as to other persons. Payments or transfers in connection with the reacquisition of the property do not include money or property paid or transferred by the seller to reacquire obligations of the purchaser to the seller which were received by the seller with respect to the sale of the property or which arose subsequent to the sale. Amounts of money or property paid or transferred by the seller in connection with the reacquisition of the property include payments or transfers for such items as court costs and fees for services of an attorney, master, trustee, or auctioneer, or for publication, acquiring title, clearing liens, or filing and recording.

(ii) *Assumption of indebtedness.*—The assumption by the seller, upon reacquisition of the real property, of any indebtedness to another person which at such time is secured by such property will be considered a payment of money by the seller in connection with the reacquisition. Also, if at the time of reacquisition such property is subject to an indebtedness which is not an indebtedness of the purchaser to the seller, the seller shall be considered to have paid money, in an amount equal to such indebtedness, in connection with the reacquisition of the property. Thus, for example, if at the time of the sale the purchaser executes in connection with the sale a first mortgage to a bank and a second mortgage to the seller and at the time of reacquisition the seller reacquires the property subject to the first mortgage which he does not assume, the seller will be considered to have paid money, in an amount equal to the unpaid amount of the first mortgage, in connection with the reacquisition.

(d) *Character of gain resulting from a reacquisition.*—Paragraphs (b) and (c) of this section set forth the extent to which gain shall be derived from a reacquisition to which paragraph (a) of this section applies, but the rules provided by section 1038 and this section do not affect the character of the gain so derived. The character of the gain resulting from such a reacquisition is determined on the basis of whether the gain on the original sale was returned on the installment method or, if not, on the basis of whether title to the real property was transferred to the purchaser; and, if title was transferred to the purchaser in a deferred-payment sale, whether the reconveyance of the property to the seller was voluntary. For example, if the gain on the original sale of the reacquired property was returned on the installment method, the character of the gain on reacquisition by the seller shall be determined in accordance with the rules provided in paragraph (a) of § 1.453-9. If the original sale was not on the installment method but was a deferred-payment sale, as described in § 1.453-6(a), where title to the real property was transferred to the purchaser and the seller accepts a voluntary reconveyance of the property, the gain on the reacquisition shall be ordinary income; however, if the obligations satisfied are securities (as defined in section 165(g)(2)(C)), any gain resulting from the reacquisition is capital gain subject to the provisions of subchapter P of chapter 1 of the Code.

(e) *Recognition of gain.*—The entire amount of the gain determined under paragraphs (b) and (c) of this section with respect to a reacquisition to which paragraph (a) of this section applies shall be recognized notwithstanding any other provision of subtitle A (relating to income taxes) of the Code.

(f) *Special rules applicable to worthless indebtedness.*—(1) *Worthlessness resulting from reacquisition.*—No debt of the purchaser to the seller which was secured by the reacquired real property shall be considered as becoming worthless or partially worthless as a result of a reacquisition of such real property to which paragraph (a) of this section applies. Accordingly, no deduction for a bad debt and no charge against a reserve for bad debts shall be allowed, as a result of the reacquisition, in order to reflect the noncollectibility of any indebtedness of the purchaser to the seller which at the time of reacquisition was secured by such real property.

(2) *Indebtedness treated as worthless prior to reacquisition.*—(i) *Prior taxable years.*—If for any taxable year ending before the taxable year in which occurs a reacquisition of real property to which paragraph (a) of this section applies the seller of such property has treated any indebtedness of the purchaser which is secured by such property as having become worthless or partially worthless by taking a bad debt deduction under section 166(a), he shall be considered as receiving, at the time of such reacquisition, income in an amount equal to the amount of such indebtedness previously treated by him as having become worthless. The amount so treated as income received shall be treated as a recovery of a bad debt previously deducted as worthless or partially worthless. Accordingly, the amount of such income shall be excluded from gross income, as provided in § 1.111-1, to the extent of the "recovery exclusion" with respect to such item. For purposes of § 1.111-1, if the indebtedness was treated as partially worthless in a prior taxable year, the amount treated under this subparagraph as a recovery shall be considered to be with respect to the part of the indebtedness that was previously deducted as worthless. The seller shall not be considered to have treated an indebtedness as worthless in any taxable year for

which he took the standard deduction under section 141 or paid the tax imposed by section 3 if a deduction in respect of such indebtedness was not allowed in determining adjusted gross income for such year under section 62.

(ii) *Current taxable year.*—No deduction shall be allowed under section 166(a), for the taxable year in which occurs a reacquisition of real property to which paragraph (a) of this section applies, in respect of any indebtedness of the purchaser secured by such property which has been treated by the seller as having become worthless or partially worthless in such taxable year but prior to the date of such reacquisition.

(3) *Basis adjustment.*—The basis of any indebtedness described in subparagraph (2)(i) of this paragraph shall be increased (as of the date of the reacquisition) by an amount equal to the amount which, under such subparagraph of this paragraph, is treated as income received by the seller with respect to such indebtedness, but only to the extent the amount so treated as received is not excluded from gross income by reason of the application of § 1.111-1.

(g) *Rules for determining gain or loss on disposition of reacquired property.*—(1) *Basis of reacquired real property.*—The basis of any real property acquired in a reacquisition to which paragraph (a) of this section applies shall be the sum of the following amounts, determined as of the date of such reacquisition:

(i) The amount of the adjusted basis, determined under sections 453 and 1011, and the regulations thereunder, of all indebtedness of the purchaser to the seller which at the time of reacquisition was secured by such property, including any increase by reason of paragraph (f)(3) of this section,

(ii) The amount of gain determined under paragraphs (b) and (c) of this section with respect to such reacquisition, and

(iii) The amount of money and the fair market value of other property (other than obligations of the purchaser to the seller which are secured by the real property) paid or transferred by the seller in connection with the reacquisition of such real property, determined as provided in paragraph (c) of this section even though such paragraph does not apply to the reacquisition.

(2) *Basis of undischarged indebtedness.*—The basis of any indebtedness of the purchaser to the seller which was secured by the reacquired real property described in subparagraph (1) of this paragraph, to the extent that such indebtedness is not discharged upon the reacquisition of such property, shall be zero. Therefore, to the extent not discharged upon the reacquisition of the real property, indebtedness on the original obligation of the purchaser, a substituted obligation of the purchaser, a deficiency judgment entered in a court of law into which the purchaser's obligation has merged, or any other obligation of the purchaser to the seller, shall be zero if such

indebtedness constitutes an indebtedness to the seller which was secured by such property.

(3) *Holding period of reacquired property.*—Since the reacquisition described in subparagraph (1) of this paragraph is in a sense considered a nullification of the original sale of the real property, for purposes of determining gain or loss on a disposition of such property after its reacquisition the period for which the seller has held the real property at the time of such disposition shall include the period for which such property is held by him prior to the original sale. However, the holding period shall not include the period of time commencing with the date following the date on which the property is originally sold to the purchaser and ending with the date on which the property is reacquired by the seller. The period for which the property was held by the seller prior to the original sale shall be determined as provided in § 1.1223-1. For example, if under paragraph (a) of § 1.1223-1 real property, which was acquired as the result of an involuntary conversion, has been held for five months on January 1, 1965, the date of its sale, and such property is reacquired on July 2, 1965,

and resold on July 3, 1965, the seller will be considered to have held such property for five months and one day for purposes of this subparagraph.

(h) *Illustrations.*—The application of this section may be illustrated by the following examples in which it is assumed that the reacquisition is in satisfaction of secured indebtedness arising out of the sale of the real property:

Example (1). (a) S purchases real property for $20 and sells it to P for $100, the property not being mortgaged at the time of sale. Under the contract P pays $10 down and executes a note for $90, with stated interest at 6 percent, to be paid in nine annual installments. S properly elects to report the gain on the installment method. After the second $10 annual payment P defaults and S accepts a voluntary reconveyance of the property in complete satisfaction of the indebtedness. S pays $5 in connection with the reacquisition of the property. The fair market value of the property at the time of the reacquisition is $110.

(b) The gain derived by S on the reacquisition of the property is $6, determined as follows:

Gain before application of limitation:

Money with respect to the sale received by S prior to the reacquisition		$30
Less: Gain returned by S as income for periods to the reacquisition ($30 × [($100 − $20)/$100])		24
Gain before application of limitation		6

Limitation on amount of gain:

Sales price of real property		$100
Less:		
Adjusted basis of the property at the time of sale	$20	
Gain returned by S as income for periods prior to the reacquisition	24	
Amount of money paid by S in connection with the reacquisition	5	49
Limitation on amount of gain		51
Gain resulting from the reacquisition of the property		$6

(c) The basis of the reacquired real property at the date of the reacquisition is $25, determined as follows:

Adjusted basis of P's indebtedness to S ($70 − [$70 × $80/$100])	$14
Gain resulting from the reacquisition of the property	6
Amount of money paid by S in connection with the reacquisition	5
Basis of reacquired property	25

Example (2). (a) The facts are the same as in example (1) except that S purchased the property for $80.

(b) The gain derived by S on the reacquisition of the property is $9, determined as follows:

Gain before application of limitation:

Money with respect to the sale received by S prior to the reacquisition	$30
Less: Gain returned by S as income for periods prior to the reacquisition ($30 × [($100 − $80)/$100])	6
Gain before application of limitation	24

Limitation on amount of gain:

Sales price of real property	$100

Less:

Adjusted basis of the property at the time of sale . .	$80	
Gain returned by S as income for periods prior to the reacquisition	6	
Amount of money paid by S in connection with the reacqusition	5	91
Limitation on amount of gain		9

Gain resulting from the reacquisition of the property $9

(c) The basis of the reacquired real property at the date of reacquisition is $70, determined as follows:

Adjusted basis of P's indebtedness to S ($70 – [$70 × $20/$100])	$56
Gain resulting from the reacquisition of the property	9
Amount of money paid by S in connection with the reacquisition	5
Basis of reacquired property	70

Example (3). (a) S purchases real property for $70 and sells it to P for $100, the property not being mortgaged at the time of sale. Under the contract P pays $10 down and executes a note for $90, with stated interest at 6 percent, to be paid in nine annual installments. S properly elects to report the gain on the installment method. After the first $10 annual payment P defaults and S accepts a voluntary reconveyance of the property in complete satisfaction of the indebtedness. S pays $5 in connection with the reacquisition of the property. The fair market value of the property at the time of the reacquisition is $50.

(b) The gain derived by S on the reacquisition of the property is $14, determined as follows:

Gain before application of limitation:

Money with respect to the sale received by S prior to the reacquisition	$20
Less: Gain returned by S as income for periods prior to the reacquisition ($20 × [($100 – $70)/$100])	6
Gain before application of limitation	14

Limitation on amount of gain:

Sales price of real property		$100
Less:		
Adjusted basis of the property at time of sale	$70	
Gain returned by S as income for periods prior to the reacquisition	6	
Amount paid by S in connection with the reacquisition	5	$81
Limitation on amount of gain		19

Gain resulting from the reacquisition of the property $14

(c) The basis of the reacquired real property at the date of the reacquisition is $75, determined as follows:

Adjusted basis of P's indebtedness to S ($80–[$80 × $30/$100])	$56
Gain resulting from the reacquisition of the property	14
Amount of money paid by S in connection with the reacquisition	5
Basis of reacquired property	75

Example (4). (a) S purchases real property for $20 and sells it to P for $100, the property not being mortgaged at the time of sale. Under the contract P pays $10 down and executes a note for $90, with stated interest at 6 percent, to be paid in nine annual installments. S properly elects to report gain on the installment method. After the second $10 annual payment P defaults and S accepts from P in complete satisfaction of the indebtedness a voluntary reconveyance of the property plus cash in the amount of $20. S does not pay any amount in connection with the reacquisition of the property. The fair market value of the property at the time of the reacquisition is $30.

(b) The gain derived by S on the reacquisition of the property is $10, determined as follows:

Gain before application of the limitation:

Money with respect to the sale received by S prior to the reacquisition ($30 + $20)	$50
Less: Gain returned by S as income for periods prior to the reacquisition ($50 × [($100 – $20)/$100])	40
Gain before application of limitation	10

Limitation on amount of gain:

Sales price of real property		$100
Less:		
Adjusted basis of the property at time of sale	$20	

Gain returned by S as income for periods prior to the reacquisition	40	60
Limitation on amount of gain		40

Gain resulting from the reacquisition of the property $10

(c) The basis of the reacquired real property at the date of the reacquisition is $20, determined as follows:

Adjusted basis of P's indebtedness to S ($50–[$50 × $80/$100])	$ 10
Gain resulting from the reacquisition of the property	10
Basis of reacquired property	20

Example (5). (a) S purchases real property for $80 and sells it to P for $100, the property not being mortgaged at the time of sale. Under the contract P pays $10 down and executes a note for $90, with stated interest at 6 percent, to be paid in nine annual installments. At the time of sale P's note has a fair market value of $90. S does not elect to report the gain on the installment method but treats the transaction as a deferred-payment sale. After the third $10 annual payment P defaults and S forecloses. Under the foreclosure sale S bids in the property at $70, cancels P's obligation of $60, and pays $10 to P. There are no other amounts paid by S in connection with the reacquisition of the property. The fair market value of the property at the time of the reacquisition is $70.

(b) The gain derived by S on the reacquisition of the property is $0, determined as follows:

Gain before application of the limitation:		
Money with respect to the sale received by S prior to the reacquisition		$40
Less: Gain returned by S as income for periods prior to the reacquisition ([$10 + $90] – $80)		$20
Gain before application of limitation		20

Limitation on amount of gain:		
Sales price of real property		$100
Less:		
Adjusted basis of the property at time of sale ...	$80	
Gain returned by S as income for periods prior to the reacquisition	20	
Amount of money paid by S in connection with the reacquisition	10	110
Limitation on amount of gain (not to be less than zero)		0
Gain resulting from the reacquisition of the property ..		0

(c) The basis of the reacquired real property at the date of the reacquisition is $70, determined as follows:

Adjusted basis of P's indebtedness to S (face value at time of reacquisition)		$ 60
Gain resulting from the reacquisition of the property		0
Amount of money paid by S in connection with the reacquisition		10
Basis of reacquired property		70

[Reg. §1.1038-1.]

☐ [*T.D.* 6916, 4-12-67.]

[Reg. §1.1038-2]

§1.1038-2. Reacquisition and resale of property used as a principal residence.— (a) *Application of special rules.*—(1) *In general.*—If paragraph (a) of §1.1038-1 applies to the reacquisition of real property which was used by the seller as his principal residence and with respect to the sale of which an election under section 121 is in effect or with respect to the sale of which gain was not recognized under section 1034, the provisions of §1.1038-1 (other than paragraph (a) thereof) shall not, and this section shall, apply to the reacquisition of such property if the property is resold by the seller within one year after the date of the reacquisition. For purposes of this section an election under section 121 shall be considered to be in effect with respect to the sale of the property if, at the close of the last day for making such an election under section 121(c) with respect to such sale, an election under section 121 has been made and not revoked. Thus, a taxpayer who properly elects, subsequent to the reacquisition, to have section 121 apply to a sale of his residence may be eligible for the treatment provided in this section. The treatment provided by this section is mandatory; however, see §1.1038-3 for an election to apply the provisions of this section to certain taxable years beginning after December 31, 1957.

(2) *Sale and resale treated as one transaction.*— In the case of a reacquisition to which this section applies, the resale of the reacquired property shall be treated, for purposes of applying sections 121 and 1034, as part of the transaction constituting the original sale of such property. In effect, the reacquisition is generally disregarded pursuant to this section and, for purposes of applying sections 121 and 1034, the resale of the property is considered to constitute a sale of such property occurring on the date of the original sale of such property.

(b) *Transactions not included.*—(1) If with respect to the original sale of the property there was no nonrecognition of gain under section 1034 and an election under section 121 is not in effect, the provisions of §1.1038-1, and not this section, shall apply to the reacquisition. Thus, for example, if in the case of a taxpayer not entitled to the benefit of section 121 there is no gain on the original sale of the property, the provisions of §1.1038-1, and not this section, shall apply even though a redetermination of gain under this section would result in the nonrecognition of gain on the sale under section 1034. Also, if in the case of such a taxpayer there was gain on the original sale of the property but after the application of section 1034 all of such gain was recognized, the provisions of § 1.1038-1, and not this section, shall apply to the reacquisition.

(2) If the original sale of the property was not eligible for the treatment provided by section 121 and section 1034, the provisions of § 1.1038-1, and not this section, shall apply to the reacquisition of the property even though the resale of such property is eligible for the treatment provided by either or both of sections 121 and 1034.

(c) *Redetermination of gain required.*—(1) *Sale of old residence.*—The amount of gain excluded under section 121 on the sale of the property and the amount of gain recognized under section 1034 on the sale of the property shall be redetermined under this section by recomputing the adjusted sales price and the adjusted basis of the property, and any adjustments resulting from the redetermination of the gain on the sale of such property shall be reflected in the income of the seller for his taxable year in which the resale of the property occurs.

(2) *Sale of new residence.*—If gain was not recognized under section 1034 on the original sale of the property, the adjusted basis of the new residence shall be redetermined under this section. If the new residence has been sold, the amount of gain returned on such sale of the new residence which is affected by the redetermination of the recognized gain on the sale of the old residence shall be redetermined under this section, and any adjustments resulting from the redetermination of the gain on the sale of the new residence shall be reflected in income of the seller for his taxable year in which the resale of the old residence occurs.

(d) *Redetermination of adjusted sales price.*—For purposes of applying sections 121 and 1034 pursuant to this section, the adjusted sales price of the reacquired real property shall be redetermined by taking into account both the sale and the resale of the property and shall be—

(1) The amount realized, which for purposes of section 1001 shall be—

(i) The amount realized on the resale of the property, as determined under paragraph (b)(4) of § 1.1034-1, plus

(ii) The amount realized on the original sale of the property, determined as provided in paragraph (b)(4) of § 1.1034-1, less that portion of any obligations of the purchaser arising with respect to such sale which at the time of reacquisition is secured by such property and is unpaid, less

(iii) The amount of money and the fair market value of other property (other than obligations of the purchaser to the seller secured by the real property) paid or transferred by the seller in connection with the reacquisition of such real property,

reduced by

(2) The total of the fixing-up expenses (as defined in paragraph (b)(6) of § 1.1034-1) incurred for work performed on such real property to assist in both its original sale and its resale.

For purposes of applying paragraph (b)(6) of § 1.1034-1, there shall be two 90-day periods, the first ending on the day on which the contract to sell is entered into in connection with the original sale of the property, and the second ending on the day on which the contract to sell is entered into in connection with the resale of the property. There shall also be two 30-day periods for such purposes, the first ending on the 30th day after the date of the original sale, and the second ending on the 30th day after the date of the resale. For determination of the obligations of the purchaser arising with respect to the original sale of the property, see paragraph (b)(3) of § 1.1038-1. For determination of amounts paid or transferred by the seller in connection with the reacquisition of the property, see paragraph (c)(4) of § 1.1038-1.

(e) *Determination of adjusted basis at time of resale.*—For purposes of applying sections 121 and 1034 pursuant to this section, the adjusted basis of the reacquired real property at the time of its resale shall be—

(1) The sum of—

(i) The adjusted basis of such property at the time of the original sale, with proper adjustment under section 1016(a) in respect of such property for the period occurring after the reacquisition of such property, and

(ii) Any indebtedness of the purchaser to the seller which arose subsequent to the original sale of such property and which at the time of reacquisition was secured by such property,

reduced by

(2) Any indebtedness of the purchaser to the seller which at the time of reacquisition was secured by the reacquired real property and which, for any taxable year ending before the taxable year in which occurs the reacquisition of such property, was treated by the seller as having become worthless or partially worthless by taking a bad debt deduction under section 166(a). The reduction under the preceding sentence by reason of having treated indebtedness as worthless or partially worthless shall not exceed the amount by which there would be an increase in the basis of such indebtedness under paragraph (f)(3) of § 1.1038-1 if section 1038(d)

Reg. § 1.1038-2(e)(2)

had been applicable to the reacquisition of such property.

(f) *Treatment of indebtedness secured by the property.*—(1) *Year of reacquisition.*—No debt of the purchaser to the seller which was secured by the reacquired real property shall be considered as becoming worthless or partially worthless as a result of a reacquisition of such real property to which this section applies. Accordingly, no deduction for a bad debt shall be allowed, as a result of the reacquisition, in order to reflect the noncollectibility of any indebtedness of the purchaser to the seller which at the time of reacquisition was secured by such real property. In addition, no deduction shall be allowed, for the taxable year in which occurs a reacquisition of real property to which this section applies, in respect of any indebtedness of the purchaser secured by such property which has been treated by the seller as having become worthless or partially worthless in such taxable year but prior to the date of such reacquisition.

(2) *Prior taxable years.*—For reduction of the basis of the real property for indebtedness treated as worthless or partially worthless for taxable years ending before the taxable year in which occurs the reacquisition, see paragraph (e) of this section.

(3) *Basis of indebtedness.*—The basis of any indebtedness of the purchaser to the seller which was secured by the reacquired real property, to the extent that such indebtedness is not discharged upon the reacquisition of such property, shall be zero.

(g) *Date of sale.*—Since the resale of the property, by being treated as part of the transaction constituting the original sale of the property, is treated as having occurred on the date of the original sale, in determining whether any of the time requirements of section 121 or section 1034 are satisfied for purposes of this section the date of the original sale is used, except to the extent provided in paragraph (d)(2) of this section.

(h) *Illustrations.*—The application of this section may be illustrated by the following examples:

Example (1). (a) On June 30, 1964, S, a single individual over 65 years of age, sells his principal residence to P for $25,000, the property not being mortgaged at the time of sale. S properly elects to apply the provisions of section 121 to the sale. Under the contract, P pays $5,000 down and executes a note for $20,000, with stated interest at 6 percent, the principal being payable in installments of $5,000 each on January 1 of each year and the note being secured by the real property which is sold. At the time of sale P's note has a fair market value of $20,000. S does not elect to report the gain on the installment method but treats the transaction as a deferred-payment sale, title to the property being transferred to P at the time of sale. S uses the calendar year as the taxable year and the cash receipts and disbursements method of accounting. After making two annual payments of $5,000 each on the note, P defaults on the contract, and on March 1, 1967, S reacquires the real property in full satisfaction of P's indebtedness, title to the property being voluntarily reconveyed to S. On November 1, 1967, S sells the property to T for $35,000. The assumption is made that no fixing-up expenses are incurred for work performed on the principal residence in order to assist in the sale of the property in 1964 or in the resale of the property in 1967. At the time of sale in 1964 the property has an adjusted basis of $15,000. S does not treat any indebtedness with respect to the sale in 1964 as being worthless or partially worthless or make any capital expenditures with respect to the property after such sale. In his return for 1964, S includes in income $2,000 capital gain from the sale of his residence.

(b) The results obtained before and after the reacquisition of the property are as follows:

	Before Reacquisition	After Reacquisition
Adjusted sales price:		
$5,000 + $20,000	$25,000	. . . .
$15,000 + $35,000	. . . .	$50,000
Less: Adjusted basis of property at time of sale	15,000	15,000
Gain on sale	10,000	35,000
Gain excluded from income under sec. 121:		
$10,000 × $20,000/$25,000	8,000	. . . .
$35,000 × $20,000/$50,000	. . . .	14,000
Gain included in income after applying sec. 121:		
$10,000 − $8,000	$2,000	. . . .
$35,000 − $14,000	. . . .	$21,000

(c) S is required to show the additional inclusion of $19,000 capital gain ($21,000 − $2,000) in income on his return for 1967.

Example (2). (a) The facts are the same as in example (1) except that on April 1, 1965, S purchases a new residence at a cost of $30,000 and qualifies for the nonrecognition of gain under section 1034 in respect of the sale of his principal residence on June 30, 1964. In his return for 1964, S does not include any capital gain in income as a result of the sale of the old residence.

(b) The results obtained before and after the reacquisition of the property are as follows:

	Before Reacquisition	After Reacquisition
Application of sec. 121 (see example (1)):		
Adjusted sales price	$25,000	$50,000
Less: Adjusted basis of property at time of sale	15,000	15,000
Gain on sale	10,000	35,000
Gain excluded from income under sec. 121	8,000	14,000
Gain not excluded from income under sec. 121	2,000	21,000
Application of sec. 1034:		
Adjusted sales price:		
$25,000 – $8,000	$17,000	....
$50,000 – $14,000	...	$36,000
Less: Cost of new residence	30,000	30,000
Gain recognized under sec. 1034 on sale of old residence	0	6,000
Gain not recognized under sec. 1034 on sale of old residence:		
($10,000 – [$8,000 + $0])	$2,000	....
($35,000 – [$14,000 + $6,000])	...	$15,000
Adjusted basis of new residence on April 1, 1965:		
$30,000 – $2,000	28,000	....
$30,000 – $15,000	....	15,000

(c) The $6,000 of capital gain on the sale of the old residence is required to be included in income on the return for 1967. The adjusted basis on April 1, 1965, for determining gain on a sale or exchange of the new residence at any time on or after that date is $15,000, after taking into account the reacquisition and resale of the old residence.

Example (3). The facts are the same as in example (2) except that S sells the new residence on June 20, 1965, for $40,000 and includes $12,000 of capital gain ($40,000 – $28,000) on its sale in his income on the return for 1965. S is required to include the additional capital gain of $13,000 ([$40,000 – $15,000] – $12,000) on the sale of the new residence in his income on the return for 1967. For this purpose, the assumption is also made that there are no additional adjustments to the basis of the new residence after April 1, 1965. [Reg. § 1.1038-2.]

☐ [T.D. 6916, 4-12-67.]

[Reg. § 1.1038-3]

§ 1.1038-3. Election to have section 1038 apply for taxable years beginning after December 31, 1957.—(a) *In general.*—If an election is made in the manner provided by paragraph (b) of this section, the applicable provisions of § 1.1038-1 and § 1.1038-2 shall apply to all reacquisitions of real property occurring in each and every taxable year beginning after December 31, 1957, and before September 3, 1964, for which the assessment of a deficiency, or the credit or refund of an overpayment, is not prevented on September 2, 1964, by the operation of any law or rule of law. The election so made shall apply to all taxable years beginning after December 31, 1957, and before September 3, 1964, for which the assessment of a deficiency, or the credit or refund of an overpayment, is not prevented on September 2, 1964, by the operation of any law or rule of law and shall apply to every reacquisition occurring in such taxable years. The fact that the assessment of a deficiency, or the credit or refund of an overpayment, is prevented for any other taxable year or years affected by the election will not prohibit the making of an election under this section. For example, if an individual who uses the calendar year as the taxable year were to sell in 1960 real property used as his principal residence in respect of the sale of which gain is not recognized under section 1034, and if such property were reacquired by the seller in 1962 and resold within one year, he would be permitted to make an election under this section with respect to such reacquisition even though on September 2, 1964, the period of limitations on assessment or refund has run for 1960. An election under this section shall be deemed a consent to the application of the provisions of this section.

(b) *Time and manner of making election.*—(1) *In general.*—(i) An election to have the provisions of § 1.1038-2 apply to reacquisitions of real property occurring in taxable years beginning after December 31, 1957, and before September 3, 1964, shall be made by filing on or before September 3, 1965, a return, an amended return, or a claim for refund, whichever is proper, for each taxable year in which the resale of such real property occurs. If the return for any such year is not due on or before such date and has not been filed, the election with respect to such taxable year shall be made by filing on or before such date the statement described in subparagraph (2) of this paragraph.

(ii) An election to have the provisions of §1.1038-1 apply to reacquisitions of real property occurring in taxable years beginning after December 31, 1957, and before September 3, 1964, shall be made by filing on or before September 3, 1965, a return, an amended return, or a claim for refund, whichever is proper, for each taxable year in which such reacquisitions occur. If the return for any such year is not due on or before such date and has not been filed, the election with respect to such taxable year shall be made by filing on or before such date the statement described in subparagraph (2) of this paragraph.

(iii) If the facts are such that §1.1038-2 applies to a reacquisition of property except that the reacquisition occurs in a taxable year beginning after December 31, 1957, and before September 3, 1964, an election may not be made under this paragraph to have the provisions of §1.1038-1 apply to such reacquisition.

(iv) Once made, an election under this paragraph may not be revoked after September 3, 1965. To any return, amended return, or claim for refund filed under this subparagraph there shall be attached the statement described in subparagraph (2) of this paragraph.

(2) *Statement to be attached.*—The statement described in subparagraph (1) of this paragraph shall indicate—

(i) The name, address and account number of the taxpayer, and the fact that the taxpayer is electing to have the provisions of section 1038 apply to the reacquisitions of real property,

(ii) The taxable years in which the reacquisitions of property occur and any other taxable year or years the tax for which is affected by the application of section 1038 to such reacquisitions,

(iii) The office of the district director where the return or returns for such taxable year or years were or will be filed,

(iv) The dates on which such return or returns were filed and on which the tax for such taxable year or years was paid,

(v) The type of real property reacquired, the terms under which such property was sold and reacquired, and an indication of whether the taxpayer is applying the provisions of §1.1038-2 to the reacquisition of such property,

(vi) If §1.1038-2 is being applied to the reacquisition, the terms under which the old residence was resold and, if applicable, the terms under which the new residence was sold, and

(vii) The office where, and the date when, the election to apply section 121 in respect of any sale of such property was or will be made.

(3) *Place for filing.*—Any claim for refund, amended return, or statement, filed under this paragraph in respect of any taxable year, whether the taxable year in which occurs the reacquisition of property or the taxable year in which occurs the resale of the old residence, shall be filed in the office of the district director in

which the return for such taxable year was or will be filed.

(c) *Extension of period of limitations on assessment or refund.*—(1) *Assessment of tax.*—If an election is properly made under paragraph (b) of this section and the assessment of a deficiency for the taxable years to which such election applies is not prevented on September 2, 1964, by the operation of any law or rule of law, the period within which a deficiency for such taxable years may be assessed shall, to the extent such deficiency is attributable to the application of section 1038, not expire prior to one year after the date on which such election is made.

(2) *Refund of tax.*—If an election is properly made under paragraph (b) of this section and the credit or refund of any overpayment for the taxable years to which such election applies is not prevented on September 2, 1964, by the operation of any law or rule of law, the period within which a claim for credit or refund of an overpayment for such taxable years may be filed shall, to the extent such overpayment is attributable to the application of section 1038, not expire prior to one year after the date on which such election is made.

(d) *Payment of interest for period prior to September 2, 1964.*—No interest shall be payable with respect to any deficiency attributable to the application of the provisions of section 1038, and no interest shall be allowed with respect to any credit or refund of any overpayment attributable to the application of such section, for any period prior to September 2, 1964. See section 2(c)(3) of the Act of September 2, 1964 (Public Law 88-570, 78 Stat. 856). [Reg. §1.1038-3.]

☐[T.D. 6916, 4-12-67.]

[Reg. §1.1039-1]

§1.1039-1. Certain sales of low-income housing projects.—(a) *Nonrecognition of gain.*—Section 1039 provides rules under which the taxpayer may elect not to recognize gain in certain cases where a qualified housing project is sold or disposed of after October 9, 1969, in an approved disposition and another such qualified housing project or projects (referred to as the "replacement project") is acquired, constructed, or reconstructed within a specified reinvestment period. If the requirements of section 1039 are met, and if the taxpayer makes an election in accordance with the provisions of paragraph (b)(4) of this section, then the gain realized upon the sale or disposition is recognized only to the extent that the net amount realized on such sale or disposition exceeds the cost of the replacement project. However, notwithstanding section 1039, gain may be recognized by reason of the application of section 1245 or 1250 to the sale or disposition. (See §1.1245-6(b) and §1.1250-3(h).) The terms "qualified housing project," "approved disposition," "reinvestment period," and "net amount realized" are defined in paragraph (c) of this section.

(b) *Rules of application.*—(1) *In general.*—The election under section 1039 (a) may be made only by the taxpayer owning the qualified housing project disposed of. Thus, if the qualified housing project disposed of is owned by a partnership, the partnership must make the election. (See section 703(b).) Similarly, if the qualified housing project disposed of is owned by a corporation or trust, the corporation or trust must make the election. In addition, the reinvestment of the taxpayer must be in such a manner that the taxpayer would be entitled to a deduction for depreciation on the replacement project. Thus, if the qualified housing project disposed of is owned by individual A, the purchase by A of stock in a corporation owning or constructing such a project or of an interest in a partnership owning or constructing such a project will not be considered as the purchase or construction by A of such a project.

(2) *Special rules.*—(i) The cost of a replacement project acquired before the approved disposition of a qualified housing project shall be taken into account under section 1039 only if such property is held by the taxpayer on the date of the approved disposition.

(ii) Except as provided in section 1039(d), no property acquired by the taxpayer shall be taken into account for purposes of section 1039(a)(2) unless the unadjusted basis of such property is its cost within the meaning of section 1012. For example, if a qualified housing project is acquired in an exchange under section 1031, relating to exchange of property held for productive use or investment, such property will not be taken into account under section 1039(a)(2) because its basis is determined by reference to the basis of the property exchanged. (See section 1031(d).)

(3) *Cost of replacement project.*—The taxpayer's cost for the replacement project includes only amounts properly treated as capital expenditures by the taxpayer that are attributable to acquisition, construction, or reconstruction made within the reinvestment period (as defined in paragraph (c)(4) of this section). See section 263 for rules as to what constitutes capital expenditures. Thus, assume that a calendar year taxpayer realizes gain in 1970 upon the approved disposition of a qualified housing project occurring on January 1, 1970. If the taxpayer had begun construction of another qualified housing project on January 1, 1969, and completes such construction on June 1, 1972, only that portion of the cost attributable to the period before January 1, 1972, constitutes the cost of the replacement project for purposes of section 1039. For purposes of determining the cost of a replacement project attributable to a particular period, the total cost of the project may be allocated to such period on the basis of the portion of the total project actually constructed during such period.

(4) *Election.*—(i) An election not to recognize the gain realized upon an approved disposition of a qualified housing project to the extent provided in section 1039(a) may be made by attaching a statement to the income tax return filed for the first taxable year in which any portion of the gain on such disposition is realized. Such a statement shall contain the information required by subdivision (iii) of this subparagraph. If the taxpayer does not file such a statement for the first taxable year in which any portion of the gain is realized, but fails to report a portion of the gain realized upon the approved disposition as income for such year or for any subsequent taxable year, then an election shall be deemed to be made under section 1039(a) with respect to that portion of the gain not reported as income.

(ii) An election may be made under section 1039(a) even though the replacement project has not been acquired or constructed at the time of election. However, if an election has been made and *(a)* a replacement project is not constructed, reconstructed, or acquired, *(b)* the cost of the replacement project is lower than the net amount realized from the approved disposition, or *(c)* a decision is made not to construct, reconstruct, or acquire a replacement project, then the tax liability for the year or years for which the election was made shall be recomputed and an amended return filed. An election may be made even though the taxpayer has filed his return and recognized gain upon the disposition provided that the period of limitation on filing claims for credit or refund prescribed by section 6511 has not expired. In such case, a statement containing the information required by subdivision (iii) of this subparagraph should be filed together with a claim for credit or refund for the taxable year or years in which gain was recognized.

(iii) The statement referred to in subdivisions (i) and (ii) of this subparagraph shall contain the following information:

(a) The date of the approved disposition;

(b) If a replacement project has been acquired, the date of acquisition and cost of the project;

(c) If a replacement project has been constructed or reconstructed by or for the taxpayer, the date construction was begun, the date construction was completed, and the percentage of construction completed within the reinvestment period;

(d) If no replacement project has been constructed, reconstructed, or acquired prior to the time of filing of the statement, the estimated cost of such construction, reconstruction, or acquisition;

(e) The adjusted basis of the project disposed of; and

(f) The amount realized upon the approved disposition and a description of the expenses directly connected with the disposition and the taxes (other than income taxes) attributable to the disposition.

(c) *Definitions.*—(1) *General.*—The definitions contained in subparagraphs (2) through (5) of this paragraph shall apply for purposes of this section.

(2) *Qualified housing project.*—The term "qualified housing project" means a rental or cooperative housing project for lower income families that has been constructed, reconstructed, or rehabilitated pursuant to a mortgage which is insured under section 221(d)(3) or 236 of the National Housing Act, provided that with respect to the housing project disposed of and the replacement project constructed, reconstructed, or acquired, the owner of the project at the time of the approved disposition and prior to the close of the reinvestment period is, under such sections or regulations issued thereunder,

(i) Limited as to rate of return on his investment in the project, and

(ii) Limited as to rentals or occupancy charges for units in the project.

If the owner of the project is organized and operated as a nonprofit cooperative or other nonprofit organization, then such owner shall be considered to meet the requirement of subdivision (i) of this subparagraph.

(3) *Approved disposition.*—The term "approved disposition" means a sale or other disposition of a qualified housing project to the tenants or occupants of units in such project, or to a nonprofit cooperative or other nonprofit organization formed and operated solely for the benefit of such tenants or occupants, provided that it is approved by the Secretary of Housing and Urban Development or his delegate under section 221(d)(3) or 236 of the National Housing Act or regulations issued under such sections. Evidence of such approval should be attached to the tax return or statement in which the election under section 1039 is made.

(4) *Reinvestment period.*—(i) The term "reinvestment period" means the period beginning 1 year before the date of the disposition and ending 1 year after the close of the first taxable year in which any part of the gain from such disposition is realized, or at such later date as may be designated pursuant to an application made by the taxpayer. Such application shall be made before the expiration of 1 year after the close of the first taxable year in which any part of the gain from such disposition is realized, unless the taxpayer can show to the satisfaction of the district director that—

(a) Reasonable cause exists for not having filed the application within the required period, and

(b) The filing of such application was made within a reasonable time after the expiration of the required period.

The application shall contain all the information required by paragraph (b)(4) of this section and shall be made to the district director for the internal revenue district in which the return is filed for the first taxable year in which any of the gain from the approved disposition is realized.

(ii) Ordinarily, requests for extension of the reinvestment period will not be granted until near the end of such period and any extension will usually be limited to a period not exceeding 1 year. Although granting of an extension depends upon the facts and circumstances of a particular case, if a predominant portion of the construction of the replacement project has been completed or is reasonably expected to be completed within the reinvestment period (determined without regard to any extension thereof), an extension of the reinvestment period will ordinarily be granted. The fact that there is a scarcity of replacement property for acquisition will not be considered sufficient grounds for granting an extension.

(5) *Net amount realized.*—(i) The "net amount realized" from the approved disposition of a qualified housing project is the amount realized from such disposition, reduced by—

(a) The expenses paid or incurred by the taxpayer which are directly connected with the approved disposition, and

(b) The amount of taxes (other than income taxes) paid or incurred by the taxpayer which are attributable to the approved disposition.

(ii) Examples of expenses directly connected with an approved disposition of a qualified housing project include amounts paid for sales or other commissions, advertising, and for the preparation of a deed or other legal services in connection with the disposition. An amount paid for a repair to the building will be considered as an expense directly connected with the approved disposition under subdivision (i)*(a)* of this subparagraph only if such repair is required as a condition of sale, or is required by the Secretary of Housing and Urban Development or his delegate as a condition of approval of the disposition.

(iii) Examples of taxes that are attributable to the approved disposition include local property transfer taxes and stamp taxes. A local real property tax is not so attributable.

(d) *Basis and holding period of replacement project.*—(1) *Basis.*—If the taxpayer makes an election under section 1039, the basis of the replacement housing project shall be its cost (including costs incurred subsequent to the reinvestment period) reduced by the amount of gain not recognized under section 1039(a). If the replacement consists of more than one housing project, the basis determined under this subparagraph shall be allocated to the properties in proportion to their respective costs.

(2) *Holding period.*—The holding period of the replacement housing project shall begin on the date the taxpayer acquires such project, that is, on the date the taxpayer first acquires possession or control of such project and bears the burdens and enjoys the benefits of ownership of the project. (For special rule regarding the holding period of property for purposes of section 1250, see section 1250(e)(4).)

(e) *Assessment of deficiencies.*—(1) *Deficiency attributable to gain.*—If a taxpayer makes an election under section 1039(a) with respect to an approved disposition, any deficiency attributable to the gain on such disposition, for any taxable year in which any part of such gain is realized, may be assessed at any time before the expiration of 3 years after the date the district director or director of the regional service center with whom the return for such year has been filed is notified by the taxpayer of the acquisition or the completion of construction or reconstruction of the replacement qualified housing project or of the failure to acquire, construct, or reconstruct a replacement qualified housing project, as the case may be. Such a deficiency may be assessed before the expiration of such 3-year period notwithstanding the provisions of section 6212(c) or the provisions of any other law or rule of law which would otherwise prevent such assessment. If replacement has been made, such notification shall contain the information required by paragraph (b)(4)(iii) of this section. Such notification shall be attached to the return filed for the taxable year or years in which the replacement occurs, or in which the period for the replacement expires, and a copy of such notification shall be filed with the district director or director of regional service center with whom the election under section 1039(a) was required to be filed, if the return is not filed with such director.

(2) *Deficiency attributable to election.*—If gain upon an approved disposition is realized in two (or more) taxable years, and the replacement qualified housing project was acquired, constructed, or reconstructed before the beginning of the last such year, any deficiency, for any taxable year before such last year, which is attributable to an election by the taxpayer under section 1039(a) may be assessed at any time before the expiration of the period within which a deficiency for such last taxable year may be assessed, notwithstanding the provisions of section 6212(c) or 6501 or the provisions of any law or rule of law which would otherwise prevent such assessment. Thus, if gain upon an approved disposition is realized in 1971 and 1975, and if a replacement project is purchased in 1971, any deficiency for 1971 may be assessed within the period for assessing a deficiency for 1975. [Reg. § 1.1039-1.]

□ [T.D. 7191, 6-29-72. *Amended by T.D.* 7400, 2-3-76.]

[Reg. § 1.1041-1T]

§ 1.1041-1T. Treatment of transfer of property between spouses or incident to divorce (temporary).—

Q-1. How is the transfer of property between spouses treated under section 1041?

A-1. Generally, no gain or loss is recognized on a transfer of property from an individual to (or in trust for the benefit of) a spouse or, if the transfer is incident to a divorce, a former spouse. The following questions and answers describe more fully the scope, tax consequences and other rules which apply to transfers of property under section 1041.

(a) *Scope of section 1041 in general.*

Q-2. Does section 1041 apply only to transfers of property incident to divorce?

A-2. No. Section 1041 is not limited to transfers of property incident to divorce. Section 1041 applies to any transfer of property between spouses regardless of whether the transfer is a gift or is a sale or exchange between spouses acting at arm's length (including a transfer in exchange for the relinquishment of property or marital rights or an exchange otherwise governed by another nonrecognition provision of the Code). A divorce or legal separation need not be contemplated between the spouses at the time of the transfer nor must a divorce or legal separation ever occur.

Example (1). A and B are married and file a joint return. A is the sole owner of a condominium unit. A sale or gift of the condominium from A to B is a transfer which is subject to the rules of section 1041.

Example (2). A and B are married and file separate returns. A is the owner of an independent sole proprietorship, X Company. In the ordinary course of business, X Company makes a sale of property to B. This sale is a transfer of property between spouses and is subject to the rules of section 1041.

Example (3). Assume the same facts as in example (2), except that X Company is a corporation wholly owned by A. This sale is not a sale between spouses subject to the rules of section 1041. However, in appropriate circumstances, general tax principles, including the step-transaction doctrine, may be applicable in recharacterizing the transaction.

Q-3. Do the rules of section 1041 apply to a transfer between spouses if the transferee spouse is a nonresident alien?

A-3. No. Gain or loss (if any) is recognized (assuming no other nonrecognition provision applies) at the time of a transfer of property if the property is transferred to a spouse who is a nonresident alien.

Q-4. What kinds of transfers are governed by section 1041?

A-4. Only transfers of property (whether real or personal, tangible or intangible) are governed by section 1041. Transfers of services are not subject to the rules of section 1041.

Q-5. Must the property transferred to a former spouse have been owned by the transferor spouse during the marriage?

A-5. No. A transfer of property acquired after the marriage ceases may be governed by section 1041.

(b) *Transfer incident to the divorce.*

Q-6. What is a transfer of property "incident to the divorce"?

A-6. A transfer of property is "incident to the divorce" in either of the following 2 circumstances—

(1) the transfer occurs not more than one year after the date on which the marriage ceases, or

(2) the transfer is related to the cessation of marriage.

Thus, a transfer of property occurring not more than one year after the date on which the marriage ceases need not be related to the cessation of the marriage to qualify for section 1041 treatment. (See A-7 for transfers occurring more than one year after the cessation of the marriage.)

Q-7. When is a transfer of property "related to the cessation of the marriage"?

A-7. A transfer of property is treated as related to the cessation of the marriage if the transfer is pursuant to a divorce or separation instrument, as defined in section 71(b)(2), and the transfer occurs not more than 6 years after the date on which the marriage ceases. A divorce or separation instrument includes a modification or amendment to such decree or instrument. Any transfer not pursuant to a divorce or separation instrument and any transfer occurring more than 6 years after the cessation of the marriage is presumed to be not related to the cessation of the marriage. This presumption may be rebutted only by showing that the transfer was made to effect the division of property owned by the former spouses at the time of the cessation of the marriage. For example, the presumption may be rebutted by showing that (a) the transfer was not made within the one- and six-year periods described above because of factors which hampered an earlier transfer of the property, such as legal or business impediments to transfer or disputes concerning the value of the property owned at the time of the cessation of the marriage, and (b) the transfer is effected promptly after the impediment to transfer is removed.

Q-8. Do annulments and the cessations of marriages that are void *ab initio* due to violations of state law constitute divorces for purposes of section 1041?

A-8. Yes.

(c) *Transfers on behalf of a spouse.*

Q-9. May transfers of property to third parties on behalf of a spouse (or former spouse) qualify under section 1041?

A-9. Yes. There are three situations in which a transfer of property to a third party on behalf of a spouse (or former spouse) will qualify under section 1041, provided all other requirements of the section are satisfied. The first situation is where the transfer to the third party is required by a divorce or separation instrument. The second situation is where the transfer to the third party is pursuant to the written request of the other spouse (or former spouse). The third situation is where the transferor receives from the other spouse (or former spouse) a written consent or ratification of the transfer to the third party. Such consent or ratification must state that the parties intend the transfer to be treated as a transfer to the nontransferring spouse (or former spouse) subject to the rules of section 1041 and must be received by the transferor prior to the date of filing of the transferor's first return of tax for the taxable year in which the transfer was made. In the three situations described above, the transfer of property will be treated as made directly to the nontransferring spouse (or former spouse) and the nontransferring spouse will be treated as immediately transferring the property to the third party. The deemed transfer from the nontransferring spouse (or former spouse) to the third party is not a transaction that qualifies for nonrecognition of gain under section 1041. This A-9 shall not apply to transfers to which § 1.1041-2 applies.

(d) *Tax consequences of transfers subject to section 1041.*

Q-10. How is the transferor of property under section 1041 treated for income tax purposes?

A-10. The transferor of property under section 1041 recognizes no gain or loss on the transfer even if the transfer was in exchange for the release of marital rights or other consideration. This rule applies regardless of whether the transfer is of property separately owned by the transferor or is a division (equal or unequal) of community property. Thus, the result under section 1041 differs from the result in *United States v. Davis*, 370 U.S. 65 (1962).

Q-11. How is the transferee of property under section 1041 treated for income tax purposes?

A-11. The transferee of property under section 1041 recognizes no gain or loss upon receipt of the transferred property. In all cases, the basis of the transferred property in the hands of the transferee is the adjusted basis of such property in the hands of the transferor immediately before the transfer. Even if the transfer is a bona fide sale, the transferee does not acquire a basis in the transferred property equal to the transferee's cost (the fair market value). This carryover basis rule applies whether the adjusted basis of the transferred property is less than, equal to, or greater than its fair market value at the time of transfer (or the value of any consideration provided by the transferee) and applies for purposes of determining loss as well as gain upon the subsequent disposition of the property by the transferee. Thus, this rule is different from the rule applied in section 1015(a) for determining the basis of property acquired by gift.

Q-12. Do the rules described in A-10 and A-11 apply even if the transferred property is subject to liabilities which exceed the adjusted basis of the property?

A-12. Yes. For example, assume A owns property having a fair market value of $10,000 and an adjusted basis of $1,000. In contemplation of making a transfer of this property incident to a divorce from B, A borrows $5,000 from a bank, using the property as security for the borrowing. A then transfers the property to B and B assumes, or takes the property subject to, the liability to pay the $5,000 debt. Under section 1041, A recognizes no gain or loss upon the transfer of the property, and the adjusted basis of the property in the hands of B is $1,000.

Q-13. Will a transfer under section 1041 result in a recapture of investment tax credits with respect to the property transferred?

A-13. In general, no. Property transferred under section 1041 will not be treated as being disposed of by, or ceasing to be section 38 property with respect to, the transferor. However, the transferee will be subject to investment tax credit recapture if, upon or after transfer, the property is disposed of by, or ceases to be section 38 property with respect to, the transferee. For example, as part of a divorce property settlement, B receives a car from A that has been used in A's business for two years and for which an investment tax credit was taken by A. No part of A's business is transferred to B and B's use of the car is solely personal. B is subject to recapture of the investment tax credit previously taken by A.

(e) *Notice and recordkeeping requirement with respect to transactions under section 1041.*

Q-14. Does the transferor of property in a transaction described in section 1041 have to supply, at the time of the transfer, the transferee with records sufficient to determine the adjusted basis and holding period of the property at the time of the transfer and (if applicable) with notice that the property transferred under section 1041 is potentially subject to recapture of the investment tax credit?

A-14. Yes. A transferor of property under section 1041 must, at the time of the transfer, supply the transferee with records sufficient to determine the adjusted basis and holding period of the property as of the date of the transfer. In addition, in the case of a transfer of property which carries with it a potential liability for investment tax credit recapture, the transferor must, at the time of the transfer, supply the transferee with records sufficient to determine the amount and period of such potential liability.

Such records must be preserved and kept accessible by the transferee.

(f) *Property settlements—effective dates, transitional periods and elections.*

Q-15. When does section 1041 become effective?

A-15. Generally, section 1041 applies to all transfers after July 18, 1984. However, it does not apply to transfers after July 18, 1984 pursuant to instruments in effect on or before July 18, 1984. (See A-16 with respect to exceptions to the general rule.)

Q-16. Are there any exceptions to the general rule stated in A-15 above?

A-16. Yes. Two transitional rules provide exceptions to the general rule stated in A-15. First, section 1041 will apply to transfers after July 18, 1984 under instruments that were in effect on or before July 18, 1984 if both spouses (or former spouses) elect to have section 1041 apply to such transfers. Second, section 1041 will apply to all transfers after December 31, 1983 (including transfers under instruments in effect on or before July 18, 1984) if both spouses (or former spouses) elect to have section 1041 apply. (See A-18 relating to the time and manner of making the elections under the first or second transitional rule.)

Q-17. Can an election be made to have section 1041 apply to some, but not all, transfers made after December 31, 1983, or to some, but not all, transfers made after July 18, 1984 under instruments in effect on or before July 18, 1984?

A-17. No. Partial elections are not allowed. An election under either of the two elective transitional rules applies to all transfers governed by that election whether before or after the election is made, and is irrevocable.

(g) *Property settlements—time and manner of making the elections under section 1041.*

Q-18. How do spouses (or former spouses) elect to have section 1041 apply to transfers after December 31, 1983, or to transfers after July 18, 1984 under instruments in effect on or before July 18, 1984?

A-18. In order to make an election under section 1041 for property transfers after December 31, 1983, or property transfers under instruments that were in effect on or before July 18, 1984, both spouses (or former spouses) must elect the application of the rules of section 1041 by attaching to the transferor's first filed income tax return for the taxable year in which the first transfer occurs, a statement signed by both spouses (or former spouses) which includes each spouse's social security number and is in substantially the form set forth at the end of this answer.

In addition, the transferor must attach a copy of such statement to his or her return for each subsequent taxable year in which a transfer is made that is governed by the transitional election. A copy of the signed statement must be kept by both parties.

Reg. §1.1041-1T(g)

The election statements shall be in substantially the following form:

In the case of an election regarding transfers after 1983:

Section 1041 Election

The undersigned hereby elect to have the provisions of section 1041 of the Internal Revenue Code apply to all qualifying transfers of property after December 31, 1983. The undersigned understand that section 1041 applies to all property transferred between spouses, or former spouses incident to divorce. The parties further understand that the effects for Federal income tax purposes of having section 1041 apply are that (1) no gain or loss is recognized by the transferor spouse or former spouse as a result of this transfer; and (2) the basis of the transferred property in the hands of the transferee is the adjusted basis of the property in the hands of the transferor immediately before the transfer, whether or not the adjusted basis of the transferred property is less than, equal to, or greater than its fair market value at the time of the transfer. The undersigned understand that if the transferee spouse or former spouse disposes of the property in a transaction in which gain is recognized, the amount of gain which is taxable may be larger than it would have been if this election had not been made.

In the case of an election regarding preexisting decrees:

Section 1041 Election

The undersigned hereby elect to have the provisions of section 1041 of the Internal Revenue Code apply to all qualifying transfers of property after July 18, 1984 under any instrument in effect on or before July 18, 1984. The undersigned understand that section 1041 applies to all property transferred between spouses, or former spouses incident to the divorce. The parties further understand that the effects for Federal income tax purposes of having section 1041 apply are that (1) no gain or loss is recognized by the transferor spouse or former spouse as a result of this transfer; and (2) the basis of the transferred property in the hands of the transferee is the adjusted basis of the property in the hands of the transferor immediately before the transfer, whether or not the adjusted basis of the transferred property is less than, equal to, or greater than its fair market value at the time of the transfer. The undersigned understand that if the transferee spouse or former spouse disposes of the property in a transaction in which gain is recognized, the amount of gain which is taxable may be larger than it would have been if this election had not been made. [Temp. Reg. §1.1041-1T.]

☐ [*T.D. 7973, 8-30-84. Amended by T.D. 9035, 1-10-2003.*]

[Reg. §1.1041-2]

§1.1041-2. Redemptions of stock.—(a) *In general.*—(1) *Redemptions of stock not resulting in*

constructive distributions.—Notwithstanding Q&A-9 of §1.1041-1T(c), if a corporation redeems stock owned by a spouse or former spouse (transferor spouse), and the transferor spouse's receipt of property in respect of such redeemed stock is not treated, under applicable tax law, as resulting in a constructive distribution to the other spouse or former spouse (nontransferor spouse), then the form of the stock redemption shall be respected for Federal income tax purposes. Therefore, the transferor spouse will be treated as having received a distribution from the corporation in redemption of stock.

(2) *Redemptions of stock resulting in constructive distributions.*—Notwithstanding Q&A-9 of §1.1041-1T(c), if a corporation redeems stock owned by a transferor spouse, and the transferor spouse's receipt of property in respect of such redeemed stock is treated, under applicable tax law, as resulting in a constructive distribution to the nontransferor spouse, then the redeemed stock shall be deemed first to be transferred by the transferor spouse to the nontransferor spouse and then to be transferred by the nontransferor spouse to the redeeming corporation. Any property actually received by the transferor spouse from the redeeming corporation in respect of the redeemed stock shall be deemed first to be transferred by the corporation to the nontransferor spouse in redemption of such spouse's stock and then to be transferred by the nontransferor spouse to the transferor spouse.

(b) *Tax consequences.*—(1) *Transfers described in paragraph (a)(1) of this section.*—Section 1041 will not apply to any of the transfers described in paragraph (a)(1) of this section. See section 302 for rules relating to the tax consequences of certain redemptions; redemptions characterized as distributions under section 302(d) will be subject to section 301 if received from a Subchapter C corporation or section 1368 if received from a Subchapter S corporation.

(2) *Transfers described in paragraph (a)(2) of this section.*—The tax consequences of each deemed transfer described in paragraph (a)(2) of this section are determined under applicable provisions of the Internal Revenue Code as if the spouses had actually made such transfers. Accordingly, section 1041 applies to any deemed transfer of the stock and redemption proceeds between the transferor spouse and the nontransferor spouse, provided the requirements of section 1041 are otherwise satisfied with respect to such deemed transfer. Section 1041, however, will not apply to any deemed transfer of stock by the nontransferor spouse to the redeeming corporation in exchange for the redemption proceeds. See section 302 for rules relating to the tax consequences of certain redemptions; redemptions characterized as distributions under section 302(d) will be subject to section 301 if received

from a Subchapter C corporation or section 1368 if received from a Subchapter S corporation.

(c) *Special rules in case of agreements between spouses or former spouses.*—(1) *Transferor spouse taxable.*—Notwithstanding applicable tax law, a transferor spouse's receipt of property in respect of the redeemed stock shall be treated as a distribution to the transferor spouse in redemption of such stock for purposes of paragraph (a)(1) of this section, and shall not be treated as resulting in a constructive distribution to the nontransferor spouse for purposes of paragraph (a)(2) of this section, if a divorce or separation instrument, or a valid written agreement between the transferor spouse and the nontransferor spouse, expressly provides that—

(i) Both spouses or former spouses intend for the redemption to be treated, for Federal income tax purposes, as a redemption distribution to the transferor spouse; and

(ii) Such instrument or agreement supersedes any other instrument or agreement concerning the purchase, sale, redemption, or other disposition of the stock that is the subject of the redemption.

(2) *Nontransferor spouse taxable.*—Notwithstanding applicable tax law, a transferor spouse's receipt of property in respect of the redeemed stock shall be treated as resulting in a constructive distribution to the nontransferor spouse for purposes of paragraph (a)(2) of this section, and shall not be treated as a distribution to the transferor spouse in redemption of such stock for purposes of paragraph (a)(1) of this section, if a divorce or separation instrument, or a valid written agreement between the transferor spouse and the nontransferor spouse, expressly provides that—

(i) Both spouses or former spouses intend for the redemption to be treated, for Federal income tax purposes, as resulting in a constructive distribution to the nontransferor spouse; and

(ii) Such instrument or agreement supersedes any other instrument or agreement concerning the purchase, sale, redemption, or other disposition of the stock that is the subject of the redemption.

(3) *Execution of agreements.*—For purposes of this paragraph (c), a divorce or separation instrument must be effective, or a valid written agreement must be executed by both spouses or former spouses, prior to the date on which the transferor spouse (in the case of paragraph (c)(1) of this section) or the nontransferor spouse (in the case of paragraph (c)(2) of this section) files such spouse's first timely filed Federal income tax return for the year that includes the date of the stock redemption, but no later than the date such return is due (including extensions).

(d) *Examples.*—The provisions of this section may be illustrated by the following examples:

Example 1. Corporation X has 100 shares outstanding. A and B each own 50 shares. A and B divorce. The divorce instrument requires B to purchase A's shares, and A to sell A's shares to B, in exchange for $100x. Corporation X redeems A's shares for $100x. Assume that, under applicable tax law, B has a primary and unconditional obligation to purchase A's stock, and therefore the stock redemption results in a constructive distribution to B. Also assume that the special rule of paragraph (c)(1) of this section does not apply. Accordingly, under paragraphs (a)(2) and (b)(2) of this section, A shall be treated as transferring A's stock of Corporation X to B in a transfer to which section 1041 applies (assuming the requirements of section 1041 are otherwise satisfied), B shall be treated as transferring the Corporation X stock B is deemed to have received from A to Corporation X in exchange for $100x in an exchange to which section 1041 does not apply and sections 302(d) and 301 apply, and B shall be treated as transferring the $100x to A in a transfer to which section 1041 applies.

Example 2. Assume the same facts as *Example 1*, except that the divorce instrument provides as follows: "A and B agree that the redemption will be treated for Federal income tax purposes as a redemption distribution to A." The divorce instrument further provides that it "supersedes all other instruments or agreements concerning the purchase, sale, redemption, or other disposition of the stock that is the subject of the redemption." By virtue of the special rule of paragraph (c)(1) of this section and under paragraphs (a)(1) and (b)(1) of this section, the tax consequences of the redemption shall be determined in accordance with its form as a redemption of A's shares by Corporation X and shall not be treated as resulting in a constructive distribution to B. See section 302.

Example 3. Assume the same facts as *Example 1*, except that the divorce instrument requires A to sell A's shares to Corporation X in exchange for a note. B guarantees Corporation X's payment of the note. Assume that, under applicable tax law, B does not have a primary and unconditional obligation to purchase A's stock, and therefore the stock redemption does not result in a constructive distribution to B. Also assume that the special rule of paragraph (c)(2) of this section does not apply. Accordingly, under paragraphs (a)(1) and (b)(1) of this section, the tax consequences of the redemption shall be determined in accordance with its form as a redemption of A's shares by Corporation X. See section 302.

Example 4. Assume the same facts as *Example 3*, except that the divorce instrument provides as follows: "A and B agree the redemption shall be treated, for Federal income tax purposes, as resulting in a constructive distribution to B." The divorce instrument further provides that it "supersedes any other instrument or agreement concerning the purchase, sale, redemption, or other disposition of the stock that is the subject of the redemption." By virtue of the special rule of

Reg. §1.1041-2(d)

paragraph (c)(2) of this section, the redemption is treated as resulting in a constructive distribution to B for purposes of paragraph (a)(2) of this section. Accordingly, under paragraphs (a)(2) and (b)(2) of this section, A shall be treated as transferring A's stock of Corporation X to B in a transfer to which section 1041 applies (assuming the requirements of section 1041 are otherwise satisfied), B shall be treated as transferring the Corporation X stock B is deemed to have received from A to Corporation X in exchange for a note in an exchange to which section 1041 does not apply and sections 302(d) and 301 apply, and B shall be treated as transferring the note to A in a transfer to which section 1041 applies.

(e) *Effective date.*—Except as otherwise provided in this paragraph, this section is applicable to redemptions of stock on or after January 13, 2003, except for redemptions of stock that are pursuant to instruments in effect before January 13, 2003. For redemptions of stock before January 13, 2003 and redemptions of stock that are pursuant to instruments in effect before January 13, 2003, see §1.1041-1T(c), A-9. However, these regulations will be applicable to redemptions described in the preceding sentence of this paragraph (e) if the spouses or former spouses execute a written agreement on or after August 3, 2001 that satisfies the requirements of one of the special rules in paragraph (c) of this section with respect to such redemption. A divorce or separation instrument or valid written agreement executed on or after August 3, 2001, and before May 13, 2003 that meets the requirements of the special rule in Regulations Project REG-107151-00 published in 2001-2 C.B. 370 (see §601.601(d)(2) of this chapter) will be treated as also meeting the requirements of the special rule in paragraph (c)(2) of this section. [Reg. §1.1041-2.]

□ [*T.D.* 9035, 1-10-2003.]

[Reg. §1.1042-1T]

§1.1042-1T. Questions and answers relating to the sales of stock to employee stock ownership plans or certain cooperatives (Temporary).—

Q-1: What does section 1042 provide?

A-1: (a) Section 1042 provides rules under which a taxpayer may elect not to recognize gain in certain cases where "qualified securities" are sold to a qualifying employee stock ownership plan or worker-owned cooperative in taxable years of the seller beginning after July 18, 1984, and "qualified replacement property" is purchased by the taxpayer within the "replacement period." If the requirements of Q&A-2 of this section are met, and if the taxpayer makes an election under section 1042(a) in accordance with Q&A-3 of this section, the gain realized by the taxpayer on the sale of the qualified securities is recognized only to the extent that the amount realized on such sale exceeds the cost to the taxpayer of the qualified replacement property.

(b) Under section 1042, the term "qualified securities" means employer securities (as defined in section 409(l)) with respect to which each of the following requirements is satisfied: (1) the employer securities were issued by a domestic corporation; (2) for at least one year before and immediately after the sale, the domestic corporation that issued the employer securities (and each corporation that is a member of a "controlled group of corporations" with such corporation for purposes of section 409(l)) has no stock outstanding that is readily tradable on an established market; (3) as of the time of the sale, the employer securities have been held by the taxpayer for more than 1 year; and (4) the employer securities were not received by the taxpayer in a distribution from a plan described in section 401(a) or in a transfer pursuant to an option or other right to acquire stock to which section 83, 422, 422A, 423, or 424 applies.

(c) The term "replacement period" means the period which begins 3 months before the date on which the sale of qualified securities occurs and which ends 12 months after the date of such sale. A replacement period may include any period which occurs prior to July 19, 1984.

(d) The term "qualified replacement property" means any securities (as defined in section 165(g)(2)) issued by a domestic corporation which does not, for the taxable year of such corporation in which the securities are purchased by the taxpayer, have passive investment income (as defined in section 1362(d)(3)(D)) that exceeds 25 percent of the gross receipts of such corporation for the taxable year preceding the taxable year of purchase. In addition, securities of the domestic corporation that issued the employer securities qualifying under section 1042 (and of any corporation that is a member of a "controlled group of corporations" with such corporation for purposes of section 409(l)) will not qualify as "qualified replacement property."

(e) For purposes of section 1042(a), there is a "purchase" of qualified replacement property only if the basis of such property is determined by reference to its cost to the taxpayer. If the basis of the qualified replacement property is determined by reference to its basis in the hands of the transferor thereof or another person, or by reference to the basis of property (other than cash or its equivalent) exchanged for such property, then the basis of such property is not determined solely by reference to its cost to the taxpayer.

Q-2: What is a sale of qualified securities for purposes of section 1042(b)?

A-2: (a) Under section 1042(b), a sale of qualified securities is one under which all of the following requirements are met:

(1) The qualified securities are sold to an employee stock ownership plan (as defined in section 4975(e)(7)) maintained by the corporation that issued the qualified securities (or by a member of the "controlled group of corporations" with such corporation for purposes of section

409(l)) or to an eligible worker-owned cooperative (as defined in section 1042(c)(2));

(2) The employee stock ownership plan or eligible worker-owned cooperative owns, immediately after the sale, 30 percent or more of the total value of the employer securities (within the meaning of section 409(l)) outstanding as of such time;

(3) No portion of the assets of the employee stock ownership plan or eligible worker-owned cooperative attributable to qualified securities that are sold to the plan or cooperative by the taxpayer or by any other person in a sale with respect to which an election under section 1042(a) is made accrue under the plan or are allocated by the cooperative, either directly or indirectly and either concurrently with or at any time thereafter, for the benefit of (i) the taxpayer; (ii) any person who is a member of the family of the taxpayer (within the meaning of section 267(c)(4)); or (iii) any person who owns (after the application of section 318(a)), at any time after July 18, 1984, and until immediately after the sale, more than 25 percent of in value of the outstanding portion of any class of stock of the corporation that issued the qualified securities (or of any member of the "controlled group of corporations" with such corporation for purposes of section 409(l)). For purposes of this calculation, stock that is owned, directly or indirectly, by or for a qualified plan shall not be treated as outstanding.

(4) The taxpayer files with the Secretary (as part of the required election described in Q&A-3 of this section) a verified written statement of the domestic corporation (or corporations) whose employees are covered by the plan acquiring the qualified securities or of any authorized officer of the eligible worker-owned cooperative, consenting to the application of section 4978(a) with respect to such corporation or cooperative.

(b) For purposes of determining whether paragraph (a)(2) above is satisfied, sales of qualified securities by two or more taxpayers may be treated as a single sale if such sales are made as part of a single, integrated transaction under a prearranged agreement between the taxpayers.

(c) For purposes of determining whether paragraph (a)(3) above is satisfied with respect to the prohibition against an accrual or allocation of qualified securities, the accrual or allocation of any benefits or contributions or other assets that are not attributable to qualified securities sold to the employee stock ownership plan or eligible worker-owned cooperative in a sale with respect to which an election under section 1042(a) is made (including any accrual or allocation under any other plan or arrangement maintained by the corporation or any member of the "the controlled group of corporations" with such corporation for purposes of section 409(l)) must be made without regard to the allocation of such qualified securities. Paragraph (a)(3) above may be illustrated in part by the following example: Individuals A, B, and C own 50, 25, and 25,

respectively, of the 100 outstanding shares of common stock of Corporation X. Such shares constitute qualified securities as defined in Q&A-1 of this section. A and B, but not C, are employees of Corporation X. For the benefit of all its employees, Corporation X establishes an employee stock ownership plan that obtains a loan meeting the exemption requirements of section 4975(d)(3). The loan proceeds are used by the plan to purchase the 100 shares of qualified securities from A, B, and C, all of whom elect nonrecognition treatment under section 1042(a) with respect to the gain realized on their sale of such securities. Under the requirements of paragraph (a)(3) above, no part of the assets of the plan attributable to the 100 shares of qualified securities may accrue under the plan (or under any other plan or arrangement maintained by Corporation X) for the benefit of A or B or any person who is a member of the family of A or B (as determined under section 267(c)(4)). Furthermore, no other assets of the plan or assets of the employer may accrue for the benefit of such individuals in lieu of the receipt of assets attributable to such qualified securities.

(d) A sale under section 1042(a) shall not include any sale of securities by a dealer or underwriter in the ordinary course of its trade or business as a dealer or underwriter, whether or not guaranteed.

Q-3: What is the time and manner for making the election under section 1042(a)?

A-3: (a) The election not to recognize the gain realized upon the sale of qualified securities to the extent provided under section 1042(a) shall be made in a "statement of election" attached to the taxpayer's income tax return filed on or before the due date (including extensions of time) for the taxable year in which the sale occurs. If a taxpayer does not make a timely election under this section to obtain the 1042(a) nonrecognition treatment with respect to the sale of qualified securities, it may not subsequently make an election on an amended return or otherwise. Also, an election once made is irrevocable.

(b) The statement of election shall provide that the taxpayer elects to treat the sale of securities as a sale of qualified securities under section 1042(a), and shall contain the following information:

(1) A description of the qualified securities sold, including the type and number of shares;

(2) The date of the sale of the qualified securities;

(3) The adjusted basis of the qualified securities;

(4) The amount realized upon the sale of the qualified securities;

(5) The identity of the employee stock ownership plan or eligible worker-owned cooperative to which the qualified securities were sold; and

(6) If the sale was part of a single, interrelated transaction under a prearranged agreement between taxpayers involving other sales of quali-

fied securities, the names and taxpayer identification numbers of the other taxpayers under the agreement and the number of shares sold by the other taxpayers. See Q&A-2 of this section.

If the taxpayer has purchased qualified replacement property at the time of the election, the taxpayer must attach as part of the statement of election a "statement of purchase" describing the qualified replacement property, the date of purchase, and the cost of the property, and declaring such property to be the qualifed replacement property with respect to the sale of qualified securities. Such statement of purchase must be notarized by the later of thirty days after the purchase or March 6, 1986. In addition, the statement of election must be accompanied by the verified written statement of consent required under Q&A-2 of this section with respect to the qualified securities sold.

(c) If the taxpayer has not purchased qualified replacement property at the time of the filing of the statement of election, a timely election under this Q&A shall not be considered to have been made unless the taxpayer attaches the notarized statement of purchase described above to the taxpayer's income tax return filed for the taxable year following the year for which the election under section 1042(a) was made. Such notarized statement of purchase shall be filed with the district director or the director of the regional service center with whom such election was originally filed, if the return is not filed with such director.

Q-4: What is the basis of qualified replacement property?

A-4: If a taxpayer makes an election under section 1042(a), the basis of the qualified replacement property purchased by the taxpayer during the replacement period shall be reduced by an amount equal to the amount of gain which was not recognized. If more than one item of qualified replacement property is purchased, the basis of each of such items shall be reduced by an amount determined by multiplying the total gain not recognized by reason of the application of section 1042(a) by a fraction, the numerator of which is the cost of such item of property and the denominator of which is the total cost of all such items of property. For the rule regarding the holding period of qualified replacement property, see section 1223(13).

Q-5: What is the statute of limitations for the assessment of a deficiency relating to the gain on the sale of qualified securities?

A-5: (a) If any gain is realized by the taxpayer on the sale of any qualified securities and such gain has not been recognized under section 1042(a) in accordance with the requirements of this section, the statutory period provided in section 6501(a) for the assessment of any deficiency with respect to such gain shall not expire prior to the expiration of 3 years from the date of receipt, by the district director or director of the

regional service center with whom the statement of election under 1042(a) was originally filed, of:

(1) a notarized statement of purchase as described in Q&A-3;

(2) a written statement of the taxpayer's intention not to purchase qualified replacement property within the replacement period; or

(3) a written statement of the taxpayer's failure to purchase qualified replacement property within the replacement period.

In those situations when a taxpayer is providing a written statement of an intention not to purchase or of a failure to purchase qualified replacement property, the statement shall be accompanied, where appropriate, by an amended return for the taxable year in which the gain from the sale of the qualified securities was realized, in order to reflect the inclusion in gross income for that year of gain required to be recognized in connection with such sale.

(b) Any gain from the sale of qualified securities which is required to be recognized due to a failure to meet the requirements under section 1042 shall be included in the gross income for the taxable year in which the gain was realized. If any gain from the sale of qualified securities is not recognized under section 1042(a) in accordance with the requirements of this section, any deficiency attributable to any portion of such gain may be assessed at any time before the expiration of the 3-year period described in this Q&A, notwithstanding the provision of any law or rule of law which would otherwise prevent such assessment.

Q-6: When does section 1042 become effective?

A-6: Section 1042 applies to sales of qualified securities in taxable years of sellers beginning after July 18, 1984. [Temporary Reg. § 1.1042-1T.]

☐ [*T.D.* 8073, 1-29-86.]

[Reg. § 1.1044(a)-1]

§ 1.1044(a)-1. Time and manner for making election under the Omnibus Budget Reconciliation Act of 1993.—(a) *Description.*—Section 1044(a), as added by section 13114 of the Omnibus Budget Reconciliation Act of 1993 (Public Law 10366, 107 Stat. 430), generally allows individuals and C corporations that sell publicly traded securities after August 9, 1993, to elect not to recognize certain gain from the sale if the taxpayer purchases common stock or a partnership interest in a specialized small business investment company (SSBIC) within the 60-day period beginning on the date the publicly traded securities are sold.

(b) *Time and manner for making the election.*— The election under section 1044(a) must be made on or before the due date (including extensions) for the income tax return for the year in which the publicly traded securities are sold. The election is to be made by reporting the entire gain from the sale of publicly traded securities on Schedule D of the income tax return in accordance with instructions for Schedule D, and by attaching a statement to Schedule D showing—

(1) How the nonrecognized gain was calculated;

(2) The SSBIC in which common stock or a partnership interest was purchased;

(3) The date the SSBIC stock or partnership interest was purchased; and

(4) The basis of the SSBIC stock or partnership interest.

(c) *Revocability of election.*—The election described in this section is revocable with the consent of the Commissioner.

(d) *Effective date.*—The rules set forth in this section are effective December 12, 1996. [Reg. §1.1044(a)-1.]

☐ [*T.D.* 8688, 12-11-96.]

[Reg. §1.1045-1]

§1.1045-1. Application to partnerships.— (a) *Overview of section.*—A partnership that holds qualified small business stock (QSB stock) (as defined in paragraph (g)(1) of this section) for more than 6 months, sells such QSB stock, and purchases replacement QSB stock (as defined in paragraph (g)(2) of this section) may elect to apply section 1045. An eligible partner (as defined in paragraph (g)(3) of this section) of a partnership that sells QSB stock, may elect to apply section 1045 if the eligible partner purchases replacement QSB stock directly or through a purchasing partnership (as defined in paragraph (c)(1)(i) of this section). A taxpayer (other than a C corporation) that holds QSB stock for more than 6 months, sells such QSB stock and purchases replacement QSB stock through a purchasing partnership may elect to apply section 1045. A section 1045 election is revocable only with the prior written consent of the Commissioner. To obtain the Commissioner's prior written consent, the person who made the section 1045 election must submit a request for a private letter ruling. (For further guidance, see Rev. Proc. 2007-1, 2007-1 CB 1 (or any applicable successor) and §601.601(d)(2)(ii)(b) of this chapter.) Paragraph (b) of this section provides rules for partnerships that elect to apply section 1045. Paragraph (c) of this section provides rules for certain taxpayers other than C corporations and for eligible partners that elect to apply section 1045. Paragraph (d) of this section provides a limitation on the amount of gain that an eligible partner does not recognize under section 1045. Paragraph (e) of this section provides rules for partnership distributions of QSB stock to an eligible partner. Paragraph (f) of this section provides rules for contributions of QSB stock or replacement QSB stock to a partnership. Paragraph (g) of this section provides definitions of certain terms used in section 1045 and this section. Paragraph (h) of this section provides reporting rules for partnerships and partners that elect to apply section 1045. Paragraph (i) of this section provides examples illustrating the provisions of this section. Paragraph (j) of this section contains the effective/applicability date.

(b) *Partnership election.*—(1) *Partnership purchase of replacement QSB stock.*—A partnership that holds QSB stock for more than 6 months, sells such QSB stock, and purchases replacement QSB stock may elect in accordance with paragraph (h) of this section to apply section 1045. If the partnership elects to apply section 1045, then, subject to the provisions of paragraphs (b)(4) and (d) of this section, each eligible partner shall not recognize its distributive share of any partnership section 1045 gain (as determined under paragraph (b)(2) of this section). For this purpose, partnership section 1045 gain equals the partnership's gain from the sale of the QSB stock reduced by the greater of—

(i) The amount of the gain from the sale of the QSB stock that is treated as ordinary income; or

(ii) The excess of the amount realized by the partnership on the sale over the total cost of all replacement QSB stock purchased by the partnership (excluding the cost of any replacement QSB stock purchased by the partnership that is otherwise taken into account under section 1045).

(2) *Partner's distributive share of partnership section 1045 gain.*—A partner's distributive share of partnership section 1045 gain shall be in the same proportion as the partner's distributive share of the partnership's gain from the sale of the QSB stock. For this purpose, the partnership's gain from the sale of QSB stock and the partner's distributive share of that gain are determined without regard to basis adjustments under section 743(b) and paragraph (b)(3)(ii) of this section.

(3) *Basis adjustments.*—(i) *Partner's interest in a partnership.*—The adjusted basis of an eligible partner's interest in a partnership shall not be increased under section 705(a)(1) by gain from a partnership's sale of QSB stock that is not recognized by the partner as the result of a partnership election under paragraph (b)(1) of this section.

(ii) *Partnership's replacement QSB stock.*— (A) *Rule.*—The basis of a partnership's replacement QSB stock is reduced (in the order acquired) by the amount of gain from the partnership's sale of QSB stock that is not recognized by an eligible partner as a result of the partnership's election under section 1045. The basis adjustment with respect to any amount described in this paragraph (b)(3)(ii) constitutes an adjustment to the basis of the partnership's replacement QSB stock with respect to that partner only. The effect of such a basis adjustment is determined under the principles of §1.743-1(g), (h), and (j) except as modified in this paragraph (b)(3)(ii)(A). If a partnership sells QSB stock with

Reg. §1.1045-1(b)(3)(ii)(A)

respect to which a basis adjustment has been made under this paragraph (b)(3)(ii), and the partnership makes an election under paragraph (b)(1) of this section with respect to the sale and purchases replacement QSB stock, the basis adjustment shall carry over to the replacement QSB stock except to the extent otherwise provided in this paragraph (b)(3)(ii). The basis adjustment that carries over to the replacement QSB stock shall be reduced (but not below zero) by the eligible partner's distributive share of the excess, if any, of the greater of the amount determined under paragraph (b)(1)(i) or (ii) of this section from the sale of the QSB stock, over the partnership's gain from the sale of the QSB stock (determined without regard to basis adjustments under section 743 or paragraph (b)(3)(ii) of this section). The excess amount that reduces the basis adjustment shall be accounted for as gain in accordance with §1.743-1(j)(3). See *Example 5* of paragraph (i) of this section. For purposes of this paragraph (b)(3)(ii), a partnership must presume that a partner did not recognize that partner's distributive share of the partnership section 1045 gain as a result of the partnership's section 1045 election unless the partner notifies the partnership to the contrary as described in paragraph (b)(5)(ii) of this section. However, if a partnership knows that a particular partner is classified, for Federal tax purposes, as a C corporation, then the partnership may presume that the partner did not defer recognition of its distributive share of the partnership section 1045 gain, even in the absence of a notification by the partner. If a partnership makes an election under section 1045, but an eligible partner opts out of the election under paragraph (b)(4) of this section and provides to the partnership the notification required under paragraph (b)(5)(ii) of this section, no basis adjustments under this paragraph (b)(3)(ii) are required with respect to that partner as a result of the section 1045 election by the partnership.

(B) *Tiered-partnership rule.*—If a partnership (upper-tier partnership) holds an interest in another partnership (lower-tier partnership) that makes an election under section 1045, the portion of the lower-tier partnership's basis adjustment as provided in paragraph (b)(3)(ii)(A) of this section in the replacement QSB stock must be segregated and allocated to the upper-tier partnership and any eligible partner as defined in paragraph (g)(3)(iii) of this section. Similarly, that portion of the basis of the upper-tier partnership's interest in the lower-tier partnership attributable to the basis adjustment as provided in paragraph (b)(3)(ii)(A) of this section in the lower-tier partnership's replacement QSB stock must be segregated and allocated solely to any eligible partner as defined in paragraph (g)(2)(iii) of this section.

(C) *Statement of adjustments.*—A partnership that must adjust the basis of replacement QSB stock under this paragraph (b) must attach a statement to the partnership return for the taxable year in which the partnership purchases replacement QSB stock setting forth the computation of the adjustment, the replacement QSB stock to which the adjustment has been made, the date(s) on which such QSB stock was acquired by the partnership, and the amount of the adjustment that is allocated to each partner.

(4) *Eligible partners may opt out of partnership's section 1045 election.*—An eligible partner may opt out of the partnership's section 1045 election with respect to QSB stock either by recognizing the partner's distributive share of the partnership section 1045 gain, or by making a partner section 1045 election under paragraph (c) of this section with respect to the partner's distributive share of the partnership section 1045 gain. See paragraph (b)(5)(ii) of this section for applicable notification requirements. Opting out of a partnership's section 1045 election under this paragraph (b)(4) does not constitute a revocation of the partnership's election, and such election shall continue to apply to other partners of the partnership.

(5) *Notice requirements.*—(i) *Partnership notification to partners.*—A partnership that makes an election under paragraph (b)(1) of this section must notify all of its partners of the election and the purchase of replacement QSB stock, in accordance with the applicable forms and instructions, and separately state each partner's distributive share of partnership section 1045 gain from the sale of QSB stock under section 702. Each partner shall determine whether the partner is an eligible partner within the meaning of paragraph (g)(3) of this section and report the partner's distributive share of partnership section 1045 gain from the partnership's sale of QSB stock, including gain not recognized, in accordance with the applicable forms and instructions.

(ii) *Partner notification to partnership.*—Any partner that must recognize all or part of the partner's distributive share of partnership section 1045 gain must notify the partnership, in writing, of the amount of partnership section 1045 gain that is recognized by the partner. Similarly, an eligible partner that opts out of a partnership's section 1045 election under paragraph (b)(4) of this section must notify the partnership, in writing, that the partner is opting out of the partnership's section 1045 election.

(c) *Partner election.*—(1) *In general.*—(i) *Rule.*—An eligible partner of a partnership that sells QSB stock (selling partnership) may elect in accordance with paragraph (h) of this section to apply section 1045 if replacement QSB stock is purchased by the eligible partner. An eligible partner of a selling partnership may elect in accordance with paragraph (h) of this section to apply section 1045 if replacement QSB stock is purchased by a partnership in which the taxpayer is a partner (directly or through an upper-tier partnership) on the date on which the partnership acquires the replacement QSB stock (purchasing partnership). A taxpayer other than a C corporation that sells QSB stock held for more than 6 months at the time of the sale may elect in accordance with paragraph (h) of this section to apply section 1045 if replacement QSB stock is purchased by a purchasing partnership (including a selling partnership).

(ii) *Partner purchase of replacement QSB stock.*—Subject to paragraph (d) of this section, an eligible partner of a selling partnership that elects to apply section 1045 with respect to the eligible partner's purchase of replacement QSB stock must recognize its distributive share of gain from the sale of QSB stock by the selling partnership only to the extent of the greater of—

(A) The amount of the eligible partner's distributive share of the selling partnership's gain from the sale of the QSB stock that is treated as ordinary income; or

(B) The excess of the eligible partner's share of the selling partnership's amount realized (as determined under paragraph (c)(2) of this section) on the sale by the selling partnership of the QSB stock (excluding the cost of any replacement QSB stock purchased by the selling partnership) over the cost of any replacement QSB stock purchased by the eligible partner (excluding the cost of any replacement QSB stock that is otherwise taken into account under section 1045).

(iii) *Partnership purchase of replacement QSB stock.*—(A) *Partner of a selling partnership.*— Subject to paragraph (d) of this section, an eligible partner that treats its interest in QSB stock purchased by a purchasing partnership as a purchase of replacement QSB stock by the eligible partner and that elects to apply section 1045 with respect to such purchase must recognize its total gain (the eligible partner's distributive share of gain from the selling partnership's sale of QSB stock and any gain taken into account under paragraph (c)(5) of this section from the sale of replacement QSB stock) only to the extent of the greater of—

(1) The amount of the eligible partner's distributive share of the selling partnership's gain from the sale of the QSB stock that is treated as ordinary income; or

(2) The excess of the eligible partner's share of the selling partnership's amount realized (as determined under paragraph (c)(2) of this section) on the sale by the selling partnership of the QSB stock (excluding the cost of any replacement QSB stock purchased by the selling partnership) over the eligible partner's share of the purchasing partnership's cost of the replacement QSB stock, as determined under paragraph (c)(3) of this section (excluding the cost of any QSB stock that is otherwise taken into account under section 1045).

(B) *Taxpayer other than a C corporation.*— Subject to paragraph (d) of this section, a taxpayer other than a C corporation that treats its interest in QSB stock purchased by a purchasing partnership with respect to which the taxpayer is a partner as a purchase of replacement QSB stock by the taxpayer must recognize its gain from the sale of the QSB stock only to the extent of the greater of—

(1) The amount of gain from the sale of the QSB stock that is treated as ordinary income; or

(2) The excess of the amount realized by the taxpayer on the sale of the QSB stock over the partner's share of the purchasing partnership's cost of the replacement QSB stock, as determined under paragraph (c)(3) of this section (excluding the cost of any QSB stock that is otherwise taken into account under section 1045).

(2) *Eligible partner's share of amount realized by partnership.*—(i) *General rule.*—The eligible partner's share of the amount realized by the selling partnership is the amount realized by the partnership on the sale of the QSB stock (excluding the cost of any replacement QSB stock otherwise taken into account under section 1045) multiplied by the following fraction—

(A) The numerator of which is the eligible partner's distributive share of the partnership's realized gain from the sale of the QSB stock; and

(B) The denominator of which is the partnership's realized gain on the sale of the QSB stock.

(ii) *General rule modified for determining eligible partner's share of amount realized by purchasing partnership upon a sale of replacement QSB stock in certain situations.*—(A) *No gain realized or loss realized on sale of replacement QSB stock.*—If a purchasing partnership does not realize a gain or realizes a loss from the sale of replacement QSB stock for which an election under this section was made for purposes of applying paragraph (c)(1)(iii)(A) of this section, the eligible partner's share of the amount realized is—

(1) The greater of—

(i) The amount determined in paragraph (c)(2)(i) of this section from a prior sale of QSB stock (that is not otherwise taken into account under paragraph (c)(2) of this section) in which the eligible partner had a distributive share of gain allocated to the eligible partner that was not recognized under paragraph (c)(1)(iii)(A) of this section; or

(ii) The amount realized by a taxpayer other than a C corporation from a prior sale of QSB stock (that is not otherwise taken into account under paragraph (c)(2) of this section) in which the taxpayer realized gain that was not recognized under paragraph (c)(1)(iii)(B) of this section; less

Reg. §1.1045-1(c)(2)(ii)(A)(1)(ii)

(2) The eligible partner's distributive share of any loss recognized on the sale of replacement QSB stock, if applicable.

(B) *Eligible partner's interest in purchasing partnership is reduced and gain realized on sale of replacement QSB stock.*—If an eligible partner's interest in a purchasing partnership is reduced subsequent to the sale of QSB stock and the purchasing partnership realizes a gain from the sale of the replacement QSB stock, the eligible partner's share of the amount realized upon a sale of replacement QSB stock must be determined under paragraph (c)(2)(i) of this section based on the distributive share of the partnership's realized gain that would have been allocated to the eligible partner if the eligible partner's interest in the partnership had not been reduced.

(iii) *Eligible partner's share of the amount realized.*—For purposes of determining the eligible partner's share of the amount realized by the partnership, the partnership's realized gain from the sale of QSB stock and the eligible partner's distributive share of that gain are determined without regard to basis adjustments under section 743(b) and paragraphs (b)(3)(ii) and (c) of this section.

(3) *Partner's share of the cost of QSB stock purchased by a purchasing partnership.*—The partner's share of the cost (adjusted basis) of replacement QSB stock purchased by a purchasing partnership is the percentage of the partnership's future income and gain, if any, that is reasonably expected to be allocated to the partner (determined without regard to any adjustment under section 1045) with respect to the replacement QSB stock that was purchased by the partnership, multiplied by the cost of that replacement QSB stock. The assumptions made by a partnership in determining the reasonably expected allocation of income and gain must be consistent for each partner. For example, a partnership may not treat the same item of income or gain as being reasonably expected to be allocated to more than one partner.

(4) *Basis adjustments.*—(i) *Eligible partner's interest in selling partnership.*—Under section 705(a)(1), the adjusted basis of an eligible partner's interest in a selling partnership that sells QSB stock is increased by the partner's distributive share of gain without regard to paragraph (c)(1) of this section. However, if the selling partnership is also a purchasing partnership, the adjusted basis of an eligible partner's interest in a partnership that sells QSB stock may be reduced under paragraph (c)(4)(iii) of this section.

(ii) *Replacement QSB stock.*—A partner's basis in any replacement QSB stock that is purchased by the partner, as well as the adjusted basis of any replacement QSB stock that is purchased by a purchasing partnership and that is treated as the partner's replacement QSB stock

must be reduced (in the order replacement QSB stock is acquired by the partner and purchasing partnership, as applicable) by the partner's distributive share of the gain on the sale of the selling partnership's QSB stock that is not recognized by the partner under paragraph (c)(1) of this section, or by the gain on a sale of QSB stock by the partner that is not recognized by the partner under section 1045, as applicable. If replacement QSB stock is purchased by the purchasing partnership, the purchasing partnership shall maintain its adjusted basis in the replacement QSB stock without regard to any basis adjustments required by this paragraph (c)(4)(ii). The eligible partner, however, shall in computing its distributive share of income, gain, loss and deduction from the purchasing partnership with respect to the replacement QSB stock take into account the variation between the adjusted basis in the QSB stock as determined under this paragraph (c)(4)(ii) and the adjusted basis determined without regard to this paragraph (c)(4)(ii). A partner must retain records setting forth the computation of this basis adjustment, the replacement QSB stock to which the adjustment has been made, and the date(s) on which such stock was acquired. See *Examples 7* and *8* of paragraph (i) of this section.

(iii) *Partner's basis in purchasing partnership interest.*—A partner that treats the partner's interest in QSB stock purchased by a purchasing partnership as the partner's replacement QSB stock must reduce (in the order replacement QSB stock is acquired) the adjusted basis of the partner's interest in the purchasing partnership by the partner's distributive share of the gain on the sale of the selling partnership's QSB stock that is not recognized by the partner pursuant to paragraph (c)(1) of this section, or by the gain on a sale of QSB stock by the partner that is not recognized by the partner under section 1045, as applicable. Similarly, a partner of an upper-tier partnership that treats the partner's interest in QSB stock purchased by a lower-tier purchasing partnership as the partner's replacement QSB stock must reduce (in the order replacement QSB stock is acquired) the adjusted basis of the partner's interest in the upper-tier partnership by the partner's distributive share of the gain on the sale of the selling partnership's QSB stock that is not recognized by the partner pursuant to paragraph (c)(1) of this section, or by the gain on a sale of QSB stock by the partner that is not recognized by the partner under section 1045, as applicable.

(iv) *Increase in basis on sale of QSB stock by purchasing partnership.*—A partner that recognizes gain under paragraph (c)(5) of this section must increase the adjusted basis of the partner's interest in the purchasing partnership under section 705(a)(1) by the amount of the gain recognized by that partner. Similarly, a partner in an upper-tier partnership that recognizes gain under paragraph (c)(5) of this section must increase the adjusted basis of the partner's interest in the upper-tier partnership under section 705(a)(1) by the amount of the gain recognized by that partner.

(5) *Partner recognition of gain.*—At the time that either the partner or the purchasing partnership (whichever applies) sells or exchanges replacement QSB stock, the amount recognized by the partner is determined by taking into account the basis adjustments described in paragraph (c)(4)(ii) of this section. Similarly, a partner of an upper-tier partnership that owns an interest in a lower-tier partnership that holds replacement QSB stock must take into account the basis adjustments described in paragraph (c)(4)(ii) of this section in determining the amount recognized by the partner on a sale of the interest in the lower-tier partnership by the upper-tier partnership or the partner's distributive share of gain from the upper-tier partnership. See paragraph (e)(4) of this section for rules applicable to certain distributions of replacement QSB stock.

(d) *Nonrecognition limitation.*—(1) *In general.*— For purposes of this section, the amount of gain that an eligible partner does not recognize under paragraphs (b)(1) and (c)(1) of this section cannot exceed the nonrecognition limitation. Except as otherwise provided in paragraph (d)(2) of this section, the nonrecognition limitation is equal to the product of—

(i) The partnership's realized gain from the sale of the QSB stock, determined without regard to any basis adjustment under section 734(b) or section 743(b) (other than basis adjustments described in paragraph (b)(3)(ii) of this section); and

(ii) The eligible partner's smallest percentage interest in partnership capital as determined in paragraph (d)(2) of this section. See *Example 9* of paragraph (i) of this section.

(2) *Eligible partner's smallest percentage interest in partnership capital.*—An eligible partner's smallest percentage interest in partnership capital is the eligible partner's percentage share of capital determined at the time of the acquisition of the QSB stock as adjusted prior to the time the QSB stock is sold to reflect any reduction in the capital of the eligible partner including a reduction as a result of a disproportionate capital contribution by other partners, a disproportionate capital distribution to the eligible partner or the transfer of an interest by the eligible partner, but excluding income and loss allocations.

(3) *Special rule for tiered partnerships.*—For purposes of paragraph (d)(1)(ii) of this section, if an eligible partner is treated as owning an interest in a lower-tier purchasing partnership through an upper-tier partnership, the eligible partner's percentage interest in the purchasing partnership shall be proportionately adjusted to reflect the eligible partner's percentage interest in the upper-tier partnership.

(e) *Partnership distribution of QSB stock to a partner.*—(1) *In general.*—Subject to paragraphs (e)(2) and (3) of this section, in the case of a partnership distribution of QSB stock to a partner, the partner shall be treated for purposes of this section as—

(i) Having acquired such stock in the same manner as the partnership; and

(ii) Having held such stock during any continuous period immediately preceding the distribution during which it was held by the partnership. See *Examples 10* and *11* of paragraph (i) of this section.

(2) *Eligibility under section 1202(c).*—Paragraph (e)(1) of this section does not apply unless all eligibility requirements with respect to QSB stock as defined in section 1202(c) are met by the distributing partnership with respect to its investment in QSB stock.

(3) *Distribution nonrecognition limitation.*— (i) *Generally.*—The amount of gain that an eligible partner does not recognize under this section on the sale of QSB stock that was distributed by the partnership to the partner cannot exceed the distribution nonrecognition limitation. For this purpose, the distribution nonrecognition limitation is—

(A) The partner's section 1045 amount realized (determined under paragraph (e)(3)(ii) of this section); reduced by

(B) The partner's section 1045 adjusted basis (determined under paragraph (e)(3)(iii) of this section).

(ii) *Section 1045 amount realized.*— (A) *QSB stock received in liquidation of partner's interest and in certain nonliquidating distributions.*—If a partner receives QSB stock from the partnership in a distribution in liquidation of the partner's interest in the partnership or as part of a series of related distributions by the partnership in which the partnership distributes all of the partnership's QSB stock of a particular type, then the partner's section 1045 amount realized is the partner's amount realized from the sale of the distributed QSB stock, multiplied by a fraction—

(1) The numerator of which is the partner's smallest percentage interest in partnership capital determined under paragraph (e)(3)(ii)(B) of this section; and

(2) The denominator of which is the partner's percentage interest in that type of QSB stock immediately after the distribution (determined under paragraph (e)(3)(iv) of this section).

(B) *Partner's smallest percentage interest in partnership capital.*—A partner's smallest percentage interest in partnership capital is the partner's percentage share of capital determined at the time of the acquisition of the QSB stock as adjusted prior to the time the QSB stock is distributed to the partner to reflect any reduction in the capital of the partner including a reduction

Reg. § 1.1045-1(e)(3)(ii)(B)

as a result of a disproportionate capital contribution by other partners, a disproportionate capital distribution to the partner, or the transfer of a capital interest by the partner, but excluding income and loss allocations.

(C) *QSB stock received in other distributions.*—If a partner receives QSB stock in a distribution from the partnership that is not described in paragraph (e)(3)(ii)(A) of this section, the partner's section 1045 amount realized is the partner's amount realized from the sale of the distributed QSB stock multiplied by the partner's smallest percentage interest in partnership capital determined under paragraph (e)(3)(ii)(B) of this section.

(iii) *Section 1045 adjusted basis.*—(A) *QSB stock received in liquidation of partner's interest and in certain nonliquidating distributions.*—If a partner receives QSB stock from the partnership in a distribution in liquidation of the partner's interest in the partnership or as part of a series of related distributions by the partnership in which the partnership distributes all of the partnership's QSB stock of a particular type, then the partner's section 1045 adjusted basis is the product of—

(1) The partnership's basis in all of the QSB stock of the type distributed (without regard to basis adjustments under section 734(b) or section 743(b), other than basis adjustments described in paragraphs (b)(3)(ii) and (c)(4)(ii) of this section);

(2) The partner's smallest percentage interest in partnership capital determined under paragraph (e)(3)(ii)(B) of this section; and

(3) The proportion of the distributed QSB stock that was sold by the partner.

(B) *QSB stock received in other distributions.*—If a partner receives QSB stock in a distribution from the partnership that is not described in paragraph (e)(3)(iii)(A) of this section, the partner's section 1045 adjusted basis is the product of—

(1) The partnership's basis in the QSB stock sold by the partner (without regard to basis adjustments under section 734(b) or section 743(b), other than basis adjustments described in paragraphs (b)(3)(ii) and (c)(4)(ii) of this section); and

(2) The partner's smallest percentage interest in partnership capital determined under paragraph (e)(3)(ii)(B) of this section.

(iv) *Partner's percentage interest in distributed QSB stock.*—For purposes of this paragraph (e)(3), a partner's percentage interest in a type of QSB stock immediately after a partnership distribution is the value (as of the date of the distribution) of the QSB stock distributed to the partner divided by the value (as of the date of the distribution) of all of that type of QSB stock that was acquired by the partnership.

(v) *QSB stock of the same type.*—For purposes of this paragraph (e)(3), QSB stock will be of the same type as the distributed QSB stock if it has the same issuer and the same rights and preferences as the distributed QSB stock and was acquired by the partnership at original issue.

(4) *Distribution of replacement QSB stock to a partner that reduces another partner's interest in the replacement QSB stock.*—For purposes of this section, a partner must recognize gain upon a distribution of replacement QSB stock to another partner that reduces the partner's share of the replacement QSB stock held by a partnership. The amount of gain that the partner must recognize is determined based on the amount of gain that the partner would recognize upon a sale of the distributed replacement QSB stock for its fair market value on the date of the distribution but not to exceed the amount that was previously not recognized by the partner under section 1045 with respect to the distributed replacement QSB stock. Any gain recognized by a partner whose interest is reduced must be taken into account in determining the adjusted basis of the partner's interest in the partnership and also taken into account in determining the partnership's adjusted basis in the QSB stock distributed to another partner under paragraph (e)(3) of this section.

(f) *Contribution of QSB stock or replacement QSB stock to a partnership.*—Section 721 applies to a contribution of QSB stock to a partnership. Except as provided in section 721(b), any gain that was not recognized by the taxpayer under section 1045 is not recognized when the taxpayer contributes QSB stock to a partnership in exchange for a partnership interest. Stock that is contributed to a partnership is not QSB stock in the hands of the partnership. See *Example 12* of paragraph (i) of this section.

(g) *Definitions.*—For purposes of section 1045 and this section, the following terms are defined as follows:

(1) *Qualified small business stock.*—The term qualified small business stock (QSB stock) has the meaning provided in section 1202(c). The term "QSB stock" does not include an interest in a partnership that purchases or holds QSB stock. See *Example 1* of paragraph (i) of this section.

(2) *Replacement QSB stock.*—The term replacement QSB stock is any QSB stock purchased within 60 days beginning on the date of a sale of QSB stock.

(3) *Eligible partner.*—(i) *In general.*—Except as provided in paragraphs (e)(1), (g)(3)(ii), (iii) and (iv) of this section, an eligible partner with respect to QSB stock is a taxpayer other than a C corporation that holds an interest in a partnership on the date the partnership acquires the QSB stock and at all times thereafter for more

than 6 months until the partnership sells or distributes the QSB stock.

(ii) *Acquisition by gift or at death.*—For purposes of paragraph (g)(3)(i) of this section, a taxpayer who acquires from a partner (other than a C corporation) by gift or at death an interest in a partnership that holds QSB stock is treated as having held the acquired interest in the partnership during the period the partner (other than a C corporation) held the interest in the partnership.

(iii) *Tiered partnership.*—For purposes of paragraph (g)(3)(i) of this section, if a partnership (upper-tier partnership) holds an interest in another partnership (lower-tier partnership) that holds QSB stock, then the upper-tier partnership's ownership of the lower-tier partnership is disregarded and each partner of the upper-tier partnership is treated as owning the interest in the lower-tier partnership directly. The partner of the upper-tier partnership is treated as owning the interest in the lower-tier partnership during the period in which both—

(A) The partner of the upper-tier partnership held an interest in the upper-tier partnership; and

(B) The upper-tier partnership held an interest in the lower-tier partnership. See *Examples 3* and *4* of paragraph (i) of this section.

(iv) Multiple tiers of partnerships. Principles similar to those described in paragraph (g)(3)(iii) of this section apply where a taxpayer holds an interest in a lower-tier partnership through multiple tiers of partnerships.

(4) *Month(s).*—For purposes of this section, the term month(s) means a period commencing on the same numerical day of any calendar month as the day on which the QSB stock is sold and ending with the close of the day preceding the numerically corresponding day of the succeeding calendar month or, if there is no corresponding day, with the last day of the succeeding calendar month.

(h) *Reporting and election rules.*—(1) *Time and manner of making election.*—A partnership making an election under section 1045 (as described under paragraph (b)(1) of this section) must do so on the partnership's timely filed (including extensions) Federal income tax return for the taxable year during which the sale of QSB stock occurs. A partner making an election under section 1045 (as described under paragraph (c)(1) of this section) must do so on the partner's timely filed (including extensions) Federal income tax return for the taxable year during which the partner's distributive share of the partnership's gain from the sale of the QSB stock is taken into account by such partner under section 706. In addition, a partnership or partner making an election under section 1045 must make such election in accordance with the applicable forms and instructions.

(2) *Purchases, distributions, and sales of QSB stock or replacement QSB stock by partnerships.*—A partnership that purchases, distributes to a partner, or sells or exchanges QSB stock or replacement QSB stock must provide information to the Commissioner and to the partnership's partners to the extent provided by the applicable forms and instructions.

(3) *Nonrecognition of gain by eligible partners.*—An eligible partner that does not recognize gain under section 1045 must provide information to the Commissioner to the extent provided by the applicable forms and instructions.

(i) *Examples.*—The provisions of this section are illustrated by the following examples:

Example 1. Sale of a partnership interest. On January 1, 2008, A, an individual, X, a C corporation, and Y, a C corporation, form PRS, a partnership. A, X, and Y each contribute $250 to PRS and agree to share all partnership items equally. PRS purchases QSB stock for $750 on February 1, 2008. On November 4, 2008, A sells A's interest in PRS for $500, realizing $250 of capital gain. Under paragraph (g)(1) of this section, an interest in a partnership that holds QSB stock is not treated as QSB stock. Therefore, the sale of an interest in a partnership that holds QSB stock is not treated as a sale of QSB stock, and A may not elect to apply section 1045 with respect to A's $250 gain from the sale of A's interest in PRS.

Example 2. Election by partner; replacement by partnership. (i) Assume the same facts as in *Example 1,* except that A does not sell A's interest in PRS. Instead, PRS sells the QSB stock (QSB1 stock) for $1,500 on November 3, 2008. PRS realizes $750 of gain from the sale of the QSB1 stock (none of which is treated as ordinary income) and allocates $250 of gain to each of A, X, and Y. PRS does not make a section 1045 election. On November 30, 2008, A contributes $500 to ABC, a partnership, in exchange for a 10 percent interest in ABC. ABC then purchases QSB stock (QSB2 stock) for $5,000 on December 1, 2008. ABC has no other assets. A makes an election under paragraph (c)(1) of this section and treats A's percentage interest in ABC's QSB2 stock as replacement QSB stock under paragraph (c)(1)(iii) of this section with respect to the $250 gain PRS allocated to A. Under paragraph (c)(3) of this section, A's share of the cost of QSB2 stock purchased by ABC is $500 (A's reasonably expected income and gain with respect to QSB2 stock, or 10 percent multiplied by the cost of the QSB2 stock, $5,000). Under paragraph (c)(1)(iii) of this section, A will not recognize the $250 gain PRS allocated to A, because A's share of the amount realized by PRS, $500 (the total amount realized by the partnership on the sale of the QSB1 stock ($1,500) multiplied by A's share of the gain from the sale of the QSB1 stock ($250) over the total gain realized by the partnership on the sale of the QSB1 stock ($750)), does not exceed A's share of ABC's cost of the QSB2 stock acquired by ABC, $500. Under paragraph (c)(4)(ii) of this section, A must reduce A's share of ABC's basis in the QSB2 stock by $250. Under paragraph (c)(4)(iii) of this section, A must reduce A's basis in A's interest in ABC by $250. Under paragraph (c)(4)(i) of this section, A's basis in A's interest in PRS is increased by $250.

(ii) Assume the same facts as in paragraph (i) of this *Example 2*, except that A does not contribute $500 to ABC in exchange for a partnership interest. Instead, on November 30, 2008, EFG, a partnership in which A has an existing 10 percent partnership interest, purchases QSB stock for $5,000. Under paragraph (c)(1) of this section, A may treat A's 10 percent interest in EFG's QSB stock as replacement QSB stock with respect to the $250 of gain PRS allocated to A.

(iii) Assume the same facts as in paragraph (i) of this *Example 2*, except that ABC owns QSB stock that ABC purchased on November 10, 2008, and ABC does not purchase QSB stock on December 1, 2008. Under paragraph (c)(1) of this section, ABC is not a purchasing partnership with respect to A for the QSB stock ABC purchased on November 10, 2008. A may not treat A's percentage interest in ABC's QSB stock as replacement QSB stock to defer the $250 gain PRS allocated to A, because A acquired its interest in ABC after ABC acquired the QSB stock.

(iv) Assume the same facts as in paragraph (i) of this *Example 2*, except that ABC sells QSB2 stock on July 30, 2009, for $5,000. ABC realizes no gain or loss on the sale of QSB2 stock. A desires to continue to rollover the $250 gain from the sale of QSB1 stock. Under paragraph (c)(2)(ii)(A) of this section, A's share of the amount realized is $500, which was A's share of the amount realized on the prior sale of QSB1 stock. Accordingly, A must elect to apply section 1045 and purchase $500 of replacement QSB stock either directly or through a purchasing partnership to continue to defer the $250 gain from the sale of QSB1 stock.

Example 3. Tiered partnerships; partnership election. (i) On January 1, 2008, A, an individual, and B, an individual, each contribute $500 to UTP (upper-tier partnership) for equal partnership interests. On February 1, 2008, UTP and C, an individual, each contribute $1,000 to LTP (lower-tier partnership) for equal partnership interests. On March 1, 2008, LTP purchases QSB stock for $500. On April 1, 2008, D, an individual, joins UTP by contributing $500 to UTP for a 1/3 interest in UTP. On December 1, 2008, LTP sells the QSB stock for $2,000. Under paragraph (g)(3)(iii) of this section, A, B, and D are treated as owning an interest in LTP during the period in which each of the partners held an interest in UTP and UTP held an interest in LTP. Therefore, under paragraphs (g)(3)(i) and (iii) of this section, A and B are eligible partners, and D and UTP are not eligible partners with respect to the QSB stock sold by LTP. Under paragraph (g)(3)(i) of

this section, C is also an eligible partner with respect to the QSB stock sold by LTP.

(ii) Assume the same facts as in paragraph (i) of this *Example 3*. LTP realizes a gain of $1,500 on the December 1, 2008, sale of QSB stock. LTP allocates $750 of gain to each of UTP and C. UTP, in turn, allocates $250 (of the $750 of gain allocated to UTP) to each of A, B, and D. LTP makes a section 1045 election. On January 1, 2009, LTP purchases replacement QSB stock for $2,000. Under paragraph (b)(5)(ii) of this section, D notifies UTP that it recognizes $250 of gain and UTP notifies LTP. Because A, B, and C are eligible partners with respect to the QSB stock sold by LTP, A and B may each defer $250 of LTP's section 1045 gain and C may defer $750 of LTP's section 1045 gain. LTP must decrease its basis in the replacement QSB stock by the $750 of partnership section 1045 gain that was allocated to C and by $500 of the partnership section 1045 gain that was allocated to UTP. These basis reductions are with respect to UTP (A and B) and C only. Under paragraph (b)(3)(ii)(B) of this section, the basis of UTP's interest in LTP attributable to the LTP's replacement QSB stock must be segregated and allocated to A and B. In addition, A and B each have a $250 negative basis adjustment in their respective interests in UTP. If UTP sells its interest in LTP for $1,250, A and B would each recognize $250 of gain from the sale of the LTP interest. D would not recognize any gain or loss from the sale.

Example 4. Tiered partnerships; partner election. (i) On January 1, 2008, A, an individual, and X, a C corporation, form UTP, a partnership. A and X each contribute $250 to UTP and agree to share all partnership items equally. Also, on January 1, 2008, UTP and Y, a C corporation, form LTP, a partnership. UTP and Y contribute $500 and $250, respectively, to LTP. UTP and Y agree to share all partnership items equally. LTP purchases QSB stock for $750 on February 1, 2008. On November 3, 2008, LTP sells the QSB stock for $1,500. LTP realizes $750 of gain from the sale of the QSB stock (none of which is treated as ordinary income) and allocates $250 gain to Y and $500 gain to UTP. Of the $500 gain allocated to UTP from the sale of QSB stock, $250 is allocated to A and $250 is allocated to X. LTP purchases replacement QSB stock (replacement QSB1 stock) for $1,350 on December 15, 2008. LTP does not make an election under section 1045. Under the rules provided in paragraph (c) of this section, A makes an election under section 1045 on its timely filed return for the taxable year for which the distributive share of gain from the sale of QSB stock is taken into account by A under section 706. Under paragraph (c)(1)(iii) of this section, A treats A's interest in replacement QSB1 stock as replacement stock with respect to A's distributive share of LTP's section 1045 gain. On March 30, 2009, LTP sells replacement QSB1 stock for $1,650. LTP realizes $300 of gain from the sale of replacement QSB1 stock (none of which is treated as ordinary income) and allocates $100 to Y and $200 to UTP.

(ii) Under paragraph (c)(1)(iii) of this section, A must recognize its distributive share of gain from LTP's sale of QSB stock ($250) only to the extent of the greater of A's distributive share of LTP's gain from the sale of QSB stock that is treated as ordinary income ($0) or the amount by which A's share of the amount realized by LTP's sale of QSB stock exceeds A's share of LTP's cost of the replacement QSB1 stock, $50 (1/3rd of $1,500, or $500, minus 1/3rd of $1,350, or $450). Because Y is not an eligible partner of LTP under paragraph (g)(3) of this section, Y must recognize its $250 distributive share of partnership gain from the sale of the QSB stock. Also, X is not an eligible partner under paragraph (g)(3) of this section, and it must recognize its $250 distributive share of gain from UTP attributable to UTP's distributive share of $500 of LTP's gain from the sale of QSB stock.

(iii) Under section 705(a)(1), the adjusted basis of Y's interest in LTP is increased by $250, and the adjusted basis of UTP's interest in LTP is increased by $500. Under section 705(a)(1), the adjusted basis of X's interest in UTP is increased by $250, and the adjusted basis of A's interest in UTP is increased by $250. However, under paragraph (c)(4)(iii) of this section, the adjusted basis of A's interest in UTP is reduced by the $200 of partnership section 1045 gain that was not recognized by A.

(iv) Under paragraph (c)(4)(ii) of this section, the LTP's adjusted basis in replacement QSB1 stock is reduced by the $200 of gain from the sale of QSB stock that is not recognized by A, as a result of A's election under section 1045. A must retain records setting forth the computation of this basis adjustment, the replacement QSB stock to which the adjustment is made, and dates the stock was acquired. LTP's adjusted basis in the replacement QSB1 stock is maintained without regard to the eligible partner's adjustment provided in paragraph (c)(4)(ii) of this section.

(v) On the sale of replacement QSB1 stock, LTP realizes a gain of $300, $100 of which is allocated to Y and $200 of which is allocated to UTP. UTP allocates $100 of this gain to A. Under paragraph (c)(5) of this section, in determining A's amount recognized upon the sale of replacement QSB1 stock by LTP, A must take into account A's basis adjustment of $200. Accordingly, A recognizes a total gain of $300 upon the sale of replacement QSB1 stock, absent an additional section 1045 election by A or LTP. Under paragraph (c)(4)(iv) of this section, the adjusted basis of A's interest in UTP is increased by $300 under section 705(a)(1).

(vi) Assume the same facts as in paragraph (i) of this *Example 4*, except that UTP sells its entire interest in LTP on March 30, 2009, for $1,200. UTP realizes a gain of $200 on the sale of its interest in LTP ($1,200 amount realized less $1,000 adjusted basis) and allocates $100 of this

gain to A. Under paragraph (c)(5) of this section, in determining A's amount recognized upon the sale of UTP's interest in LTP, A must take into account A's basis adjustment of $200. Accordingly, A recognizes a total gain of $300 upon the sale of the interest in LTP. Under paragraph (c)(4)(iv) of this section, the adjusted basis in A's interest in UTP is increased by $300 under section 705(a)(1).

Example 5. Partnership sale of QSB stock and purchase and sale of replacement QSB stock. (i) On January 1, 2008, A, an individual, X, a C corporation, and Y, a C corporation, form PRS, a partnership. A, X, and Y each contribute $250 to PRS and agree to share all partnership items equally. PRS purchases QSB stock for $750 on February 1, 2008. On November 3, 2008, PRS sells the QSB stock for $1,500. PRS realizes $750 of gain from the sale of the QSB stock (none of which is treated as ordinary income) and allocates $250 of gain to each of A, X, and Y. PRS purchases replacement QSB stock (replacement QSB1 stock) for $1,350 on December 15, 2008. On its timely filed return for the taxable year during which the sale of the QSB stock occurs, PRS makes an election to apply section 1045. A does not make an election to apply section 1045 with respect to the November 3, 2008, sale of QSB stock. PRS knows that X and Y are C corporations. On March 30, 2009, PRS sells replacement QSB1 stock for $1,650. PRS realizes $300 of gain from the sale of replacement QSB1 stock (none of which is treated as ordinary income) and allocates $100 of gain to each of A, X, and Y. A does not make an election to apply section 1045 with respect to the March 30, 2009, sale of replacement QSB1 stock.

(ii) Under paragraph (b)(1) of this section, the partnership section 1045 gain from the November 3, 2008, sale of QSB stock is $600 ($750 gain less $150 ($1,500 amount realized on the sale of QSB stock less $1,350 cost of replacement QSB1 stock)). This amount must be allocated among the partners in the same proportions as the entire gain from the sale of QSB stock is allocated to the partners, 1/3 ($200) to A, 1/3 ($200) to X, and 1/3 ($200) to Y.

(iii) Because neither X nor Y is an eligible partner under paragraph (g)(3) of this section, X and Y must each recognize its $250 distributive share of partnership gain from the sale of QSB stock. Because A is an eligible partner under paragraph (g)(3) of this section, A may defer recognition of A's $200 distributive share of partnership section 1045 gain. A is not required to separately elect to apply section 1045. A must recognize A's remaining $50 distributive share of the partnership's gain from the sale of QSB stock.

(iv) Under section 705(a)(1), the adjusted bases of X's and Y's interests in PRS are each increased by $250. Under section 705(a)(1) and paragraph (b)(3)(i) of this section, the adjusted basis of A's interest in PRS is not increased by the $200 of partnership section 1045 gain that was not recognized by A, but is increased by A's remaining $50 distributive share of gain.

(v) PRS must decrease its basis in the replacement QSB1 stock by the $200 of partnership section 1045 gain that was allocated to A. This basis reduction is a reduction with respect to A only. PRS then adjusts A's distributive share of gain from the sale of replacement QSB1 stock to reflect the effect of A's basis adjustment under paragraph (b)(3)(ii) of this section. In accordance with the principles of § 1.743-1(j)(3), the amount of A's gain from the March 30, 2009, sale of replacement QSB1 stock in which A has a $200 negative basis adjustment equals $300 (A's share of PRS' gain from the sale of replacement QSB1 stock ($100), increased by the amount of A's negative basis adjustment for replacement QSB1 stock ($200)). Accordingly, upon the sale of replacement QSB1 stock, A recognizes $300 of gain, and X and Y each recognize $100 of gain.

(vi) Assume the same facts as in paragraph (i) of this *Example 5*, except that PRS purchases replacement QSB stock (replacement QSB2 stock) on April 15, 2009, for $1,150 and PRS makes an election to apply section 1045 with respect to the March 30, 2009, sale of replacement QSB1 stock. Under paragraph (b)(3)(ii)(A) of this section, PRS' $200 basis adjustment in QSB1 stock relating to the November 3, 2008, sale of QSB stock carries over to the basis adjustment for QSB2 stock. This basis adjustment is an adjustment with respect to A only. The $200 basis adjustment is reduced by A's distributive share of the excess of $500 (the greater of the amount determined under paragraph (b)(1)(i), $0, or (ii) of this section, $500 ($1,650 amount realized on the sale of QSB1 stock less $1,150 cost of replacement QSB2 stock)) over $300 (PRS' gain from the sale of QSB1 stock), or $67 ($200 ($500 minus $300) divided by 3). Under paragraph (b)(3)(ii)(A), A must account for the $67 excess amount that reduces PRS' basis adjustment in QSB2 stock as gain in accordance with § 1.743-1(j)(3). Therefore, A now has a $133 negative basis adjustment with respect to replacement QSB2 stock (($200) negative basis adjustment from the November 3, 2008, sale of QSB stock plus $67 positive basis adjustment from the March 30, 2009, sale of QSB1 stock). A also recognizes the $100 of gain allocated by PRS to A from the March 30, 2009, sale of replacement QSB1 stock for total gain recognition of $167 ($100 plus $67).

Example 6. Partnership sale of QSB stock; election by eligible partner; replacement QSB stock purchased by purchasing partnership. (i) Assume the same facts as in *Example 5* except that PRS does not make an election under section 1045 with respect to the sale of either the QSB stock on November 3, 2008, or the QSB1 stock on March 30, 2009. However, A makes an election under section 1045 with respect to the sale of QSB stock and treats the purchase of QSB1 stock on December 15, 2008, by PRS, as the purchase of replacement QSB stock. Additionally, A makes an election

under section 1045 with respect to the sale of QSB1 stock and treats the purchase of QSB2 stock on April 15, 2009, by PRS, as the purchase of replacement QSB stock.

(ii) A's distributive share of gain from the November 3, 2008, sale of QSB stock is $250 (A's 1/3 interest in $750 of total PRS gain). Under paragraph (c)(1)(iii) of this section, A must recognize only $50 of A's distributive share of PRS' gain of $250, that is the excess of A's share of the amount realized on the sale of QSB stock, or $500 (the total amount realized by PRS on the sale of QSB stock ($1,500) multiplied by A's share of the gain from the sale of QSB stock ($250) over the total gain realized by PRS on the sale of QSB stock ($750)), minus A's share of PRS' cost of QSB1 stock, or $450 (1/3 of $1,350). Under section 705(a)(1) and paragraph (c)(4)(i) of this section, A's adjusted basis in its interest in PRS is increased by $250. However, under paragraph (c)(4)(iii) of this section, because PRS is a purchasing partnership, A's adjusted basis of its interest in PRS is then reduced by the deferred gain of $200. Also under paragraph (c)(4)(ii) of this section, PRS' adjusted basis in QSB1 stock is reduced by the gain not recognized of $200 and A must take into account such adjusted basis in computing A's income, gain, loss or deduction with respect to QSB1 stock. A must retain records setting forth the computation of this basis adjustment, the replacement QSB stock to which the adjustment is made, and dates the stock was acquired.

(iii) A's distributive share of gain from the March 30, 2009, sale of QSB1 stock is $100 (A's 1/3 interest in $300 of total PRS gain) and under paragraph (c)(5) of this section, A must take into account A's $200 basis adjustment with respect to the QSB1 stock that was sold. Accordingly, A's total gain from the sale of QSB1 stock is $300. Under paragraph (c)(1)(iii) of this section, A must recognize only $167 of A's total gain of $300, that is, the excess of A's share of the amount realized on the sale of QSB1 stock, or $550 (the total amount realized by PRS on the sale of QSB1 stock ($1,650) multiplied by A's share of the gain from the sale of QSB1 stock ($100) over the total gain realized by PRS on the sale of QSB1 stock ($300)) minus A's share of PRS' cost of QSB2 stock, or $383 (1/3 of $1,150). Under section 705(a)(1), A's adjusted basis in A's interest in PRS is increased by A's $100 distributive share of gain from the sale of QSB1 stock. Under paragraph (c)(4)(iv) of this section, A's adjusted basis of A's interest in PRS is increased by the additional $67 of gain recognized under paragraph (c)(5) of this section. Also, under paragraph (c)(4)(ii) of this section, PRS' adjusted basis in QSB2 stock is reduced by the gain not recognized of $133 ($300 minus $167) and A must take into account such adjusted basis in computing A's income, gain, loss or deduction with respect to QSB2 stock. A must retain records setting forth the computation of this basis adjustment, the replacement QSB stock to which the adjustment is made, and dates the stock was acquired.

Example 7. Partnership sale of QSB stock and partner purchase of replacement QSB stock. (i) Assume the same facts as in paragraph (i) of *Example 5*, except that PRS does not make an election under section 1045 with respect to the sale of the QSB stock and does not purchase replacement QSB stock. On November 30, 2008, A, an eligible partner under paragraph (g)(3) of this section, purchases replacement QSB stock for $500. A elects pursuant to paragraph (c) of this section to apply section 1045 on A's timely filed return for the taxable year that A is required to include A's distributive share of PRS' gain from the sale of the QSB stock.

(ii) Under paragraph (c)(2) of this section, A's share of the amount realized from PRS' sale of the QSB stock is $500 (the total amount realized by the partnership on the sale of the QSB stock ($1,500) multiplied by A's share of the gain from the sale of the QSB stock ($250) over the total gain realized by the partnership on the sale of the QSB stock ($750)). Because A purchased, within 60 days of PRS' sale of the QSB stock, replacement QSB stock for a cost equal to A's share of the partnership's amount realized on the sale of the QSB stock, and because A made an election pursuant to paragraph (c) of this section to apply section 1045, A defers recognition of A's $250 distributive share of gain from PRS' sale of the QSB stock. Under section 705(a)(1) and paragraph (c)(4)(i) of this section, the adjusted basis of A's interest in PRS is increased by $250. Under paragraph (c)(4)(ii) of this section, A's adjusted basis in the replacement QSB stock is $250 ($500 cost minus $250 nonrecognition amount).

Example 8. Partial replacement by partnership; partial replacement by partner. (i) On January 1, 2008, A, an individual, and X, a C corporation, form PRS, a partnership. A and X each contribute $500 to PRS and agree to share all partnership items equally. PRS purchases QSB stock on February 1, 2008, for $1,000 and subsequently sells the QSB stock on January 31, 2010, for $3,000. PRS realizes $2,000 of gain from the sale of the QSB stock (none of which is treated as ordinary income) and allocates $1,000 of gain to each of A and X. On February 10, 2010, PRS purchases replacement QSB stock for $2,200. On March 20, 2010, A purchases replacement QSB stock for $400. PRS makes an election to apply section 1045 under paragraph (b)(1) of this section with respect to the partnership section 1045 gain from the sale of QSB stock and A does not opt out of PRS' section 1045 election under paragraph (b)(4) of this section. Also, A makes an election under paragraph (c)(1) of this section with respect to the remaining gain from the sale of the QSB stock.

(ii) Under paragraph (b)(1) of this section, partnership section 1045 gain is $1,200 ($2,000 less $800 ($3,000 amount realized on the sale of the QSB stock minus $2,200 cost of the replacement QSB stock)). This amount is allocated

among the partners in the same proportions as the entire gain from the sale of the QSB stock is allocated to the partners, 1/2 to A ($600), and 1/2 to X ($600). Because A is an eligible partner, A defers recognition of A's $600 distributive share of partnership section 1045 gain.

(iii) A also made an election under section 1045 and purchased, within 60 days of PRS' sale of the QSB stock, replacement QSB stock for $400. Therefore, under paragraph (c)(1) of this section, A may defer a portion of A's distributive share of the remaining gain from the partnership's sale of the QSB stock. A must recognize that remaining gain to the extent that A's share of the amount realized by PRS on the sale of the QSB stock (excluding the cost of the QSB stock that was replaced by PRS) exceeds the cost of the replacement QSB stock purchased by A during the 60-day period following the sale of the QSB stock. The amount realized by PRS on the sale of the QSB stock (excluding the cost of the QSB stock that was replaced by PRS) is $800 ($3,000 minus $2,200). Under paragraph (c)(2) of this section, A's share of that amount realized is $400 ($1,000 (A's share of the realized gain from the sale of the QSB stock) / $2,000 (PRS total realized gain from the sale of the QSB stock) multiplied by $800). Because the replacement QSB stock purchased by A cost $400, A defers recognition of all of the remaining gain from the sale of the QSB stock.

(iv) The adjusted basis of A's interest in PRS is not increased by the $600 gain that was not recognized pursuant to paragraph (b)(1) of this section, but is increased by the $400 gain that was not recognized pursuant to paragraph (c)(1) of this section. See paragraphs (b)(3)(i) and (c)(4)(i) of this section. PRS must decrease its basis in the replacement QSB stock by the $600 of partnership section 1045 gain that was allocated to A. See paragraph (b)(3)(ii) of this section. A must decrease A's basis in the replacement QSB stock purchased by A by the $400 not recognized pursuant to paragraph (c)(1) of this section. See paragraph (c)(4)(ii) of this section.

Example 9. Change in partner's interest in partnership while partnership holds QSB stock. (i) On January 1, 2008, A, an individual, and X, a C corporation, form PRS, a partnership. A and X each contribute $500 to PRS and agree to share all partnership items equally. PRS purchases QSB stock on February 1, 2008, for $1,000. On August 2, 2008, A sells a 25 percent interest in PRS to Z. On July 10, 2009, A repurchases the 25 percent interest from Z for $500. PRS makes a timely election under section 754 for the 2008 taxable year. Under paragraph 743(b), A has a positive basis adjustment of $250. On January 31, 2011, PRS sells the QSB stock for $3,000. PRS realizes $2,000 of gain from the sale of the QSB stock (none of which is treated as ordinary income) and allocates $1,000 of gain to each of A and X. On February 10, 2010, PRS purchases replacement QSB stock for $3,000. PRS makes an election to apply section 1045 under paragraph (b)(1) of this section with respect to the partnership section 1045 gain from the sale of QSB stock.

(ii) Of the $2,000 of realized gain from the sale of the QSB stock, PRS allocates $1,000 to A and $1,000 to X. However, A has a positive basis adjustment of $250 under section 743(b) as a result of the purchase of the 25 percent interest in PRS from Z; therefore, A's share of the gain is reduced to $750. Because A is an eligible partner under paragraph (g)(3) of this section, A may defer recognition of A's distributive share of gain from the sale of the QSB stock subject to the nonrecognition limitation described in paragraph (d) of this section. The smallest percentage interest that A held in PRS capital during the time that PRS held the QSB stock is 25 percent. Under the nonrecognition limitation, A may not defer more than 25 percent of the partnership gain realized from the sale of the QSB stock (determined without regard to any basis adjustment under section 734(b) or section 743(b), other than a basis adjustment described in paragraph (b)(3)(ii) of this section). Because the partnership's realized gain determined without regard to A's basis adjustment under section 743(b) is $2,000, A may defer recognition of $500 (25 percent of $2,000) of the gain from the sale of the QSB stock. A must recognize the remaining $250 of that gain.

Example 10. Sale by partner of QSB stock received in a liquidating distribution. (i) On January 1, 2008, A, an individual, and X, a C corporation, form PRS, a partnership. A and X each contribute $1,500 to PRS and agree to share all partnership items equally. PRS purchases QSB stock on February 1, 2008, for $3,000. On May 1, 2008, when the QSB stock has appreciated in value to $4,000, A contributes $1,000 to PRS, increasing A's interest in PRS capital to 60 percent. On June 1, 2011, when the QSB stock is still worth $4,000, PRS makes a liquidating distribution of $3,000 worth of QSB stock to A. Under section 732, A's basis in the distributed QSB stock is $2,500. A sells the QSB stock on August 4, 2011, for $6,000, realizing a gain of $3,500 (none of which is treated as ordinary income). A purchases replacement QSB stock on August 30, 2011, for $5,500, and makes an election under section 1045 with respect to the August 4, 2011, sale of QSB stock.

(ii) A is an eligible partner under paragraph (g)(3) of this section. Therefore, under paragraph (e)(1) of this section, A is treated as having acquired the distributed QSB stock in the same manner as PRS and as having held the QSB stock since February 1, 2008, its original issue date. Because A purchased, within 60 days of A's sale of the QSB stock, replacement QSB stock, A is eligible to defer a portion of A's gain from the sale of the QSB stock. A must recognize gain, however, to the extent that A's amount realized on the sale of the QSB stock, $6,000, exceeds the cost of the replacement QSB stock purchased by A during the 60-day period beginning on the date of the sale of the QSB stock, $5,500. Accordingly, A must recognize $500 of the gain from

the sale of the QSB stock. A defers recognition of the remaining $3,000 of gain to the extent that such gain does not exceed the distribution nonrecognition limitation under paragraph (e)(3) of this section.

(iii) Under paragraph (e)(3)(i) of this section, A's nonrecognition limitation with respect to the sale of the QSB stock is A's section 1045 amount realized with respect to the stock, reduced by A's section 1045 adjusted basis with respect to the stock. A's amount realized from the sale is the product of A's amount realized from the sale, $6,000; and a fraction—

(1) The numerator of which is A's smallest percentage interest in PRS capital with respect to such stock, 50 percent; and

(2) The denominator of which is A's percentage interest in that type of partnership QSB stock immediately after the distribution, 75 percent (the value of the stock distributed to A, $3,000, divided by the value of all QSB stock of that type acquired by PRS, $4,000).

(iv) Therefore, A's section 1045 amount realized is $4,000 ($6,000 multiplied by 50/75). Because PRS distributed the QSB stock to A in liquidation of A's interest in PRS, A's section 1045 adjusted basis is the product of PRS' basis in all of the QSB stock of the type distributed, $3,000; A's smallest percentage interest in PRS capital with respect to QSB stock of the type distributed, 50 percent; and the percentage of the distributed QSB stock that was sold by A, 100 percent. Therefore, A's section 1045 adjusted basis is $1,500 (the product of $3,000, 50 percent, and 100 percent)) and A's nonrecognition limitation amount on the sale of the QSB stock is $2,500 ($4,000 section 1045 amount realized minus $1,500 section 1045 adjusted basis). Accordingly, A defers recognition of $2,500 of the remaining $3,000 gain from the sale of the QSB stock and must recognize $500 of the remaining $3,000 gain. Accordingly, A's total gain recognized from the sale of the QSB stock is $1,000.

(v) A's basis in the replacement QSB stock is $3,000 (cost of the replacement QSB stock, $5,500, reduced by the gain not recognized under section 1045, $2,500).

Example 11. Sale by partner of QSB stock received in a nonliquidating distribution. (i) The facts are the same as in *Example 10*, except that, on June 1, 2011, PRS distributes only $2,000 of the QSB stock to A, reducing A's interest in PRS capital from 60 percent to 33 percent. PRS' basis in the distributed QSB stock is $1,500. On November 1, 2011, A sells for $2,500 the QSB stock distributed by PRS to A and purchases, within 60 days of the date of sale of the QSB stock, replacement QSB stock for $2,500. A makes a timely election to apply section 1045 with respect to A's sale of the distributed QSB stock.

(ii) Under section 732, A's basis in the distributed QSB stock is $1,500. Therefore, A realizes a gain on the sale of the distributed QSB stock of $1,000. Because A made an election to apply section 1045 to the sale, and because A purchased, within 60 days of A's sale of the QSB stock, replacement QSB stock at a cost equal to the amount realized on the sale of the distributed QSB stock, A defers recognition of the gain from the sale of the QSB stock to the extent that such gain does not exceed the distribution nonrecognition limitation.

(iii) Under paragraph (e)(3) of this section, the nonrecognition limitation with respect to A's sale of the QSB stock is A's section 1045 amount realized reduced by A's section 1045 adjusted basis. Because PRS did not distribute all of the particular type of QSB stock and the distribution of the QSB stock to A was not in liquidation of A's interest in PRS, under paragraph (e)(3)(ii)(C) of this section A's section 1045 amount realized is $1,250 (A's amount realized from the sale of the distributed QSB stock, $2,500, multiplied by A's smallest percentage interest in PRS capital with respect to such stock, 50 percent). Under paragraph (e)(3)(iii)(B) of this section, A's section 1045 adjusted basis is the product of the partnership's basis in the QSB stock sold by the partner, $1,500, and A's smallest percentage interest in the partnership capital with respect to such stock, 50 percent. Therefore, A's section 1045 adjusted basis is $750 (50 percent of $1,500), and A's nonrecognition limitation amount on the sale of the QSB stock is $500 ($1,250 section 1045 amount realized minus $750 section 1045 adjusted basis). As this amount is less than the amount of gain that A is eligible to defer under section 1045, $1,000, A defers recognition of only $500 of the gain from the sale of the QSB stock. A must recognize the remaining $500 of that gain.

(iv) A's basis in the replacement QSB stock is $2,000 (cost of the replacement QSB stock, $2,500, reduced by the gain not recognized under section 1045, $500).

Example 12. Contribution of replacement QSB stock to a partnership. (i) On January 1, 2008, A, an individual, B, an individual, and X, a C corporation, form PRS, a partnership. A, B, and X each contribute $250 to PRS and agree to share all partnership items equally. On February 1, 2008, PRS purchases QSB stock for $750. PRS sells the QSB stock on November 3, 2008, for $1,050. PRS realizes $300 of gain from the sale of the QSB stock (none of which is treated as ordinary income) and allocates $100 of gain to each of its partners. PRS informs the partners that it does not intend to make an election under section 1045 with respect to the sale of the QSB stock. Each partner's share of the amount realized from the sale of the QSB stock is $350. On November 30, 2008, A, an eligible partner within the meaning of paragraph (g)(3) of this section, purchases replacement QSB stock for $350 and makes a section 1045 election under paragraph (c)(1) of this section. Subsequently, A transfers the replacement QSB stock to ABC, a partnership, in exchange for an interest in ABC.

(ii) Because A purchased within 60 days of PRS' sale of the QSB stock, replacement QSB stock for a cost equal to A's share of the partnership's amount realized on the sale of the QSB stock, and because A made a valid election to apply section 1045 with respect to A's share of the gain from PRS' sale of the QSB stock, A does not recognize A's $100 distributive share of the gain from PRS' sale of the QSB stock. Before the contribution of the replacement QSB stock to ABC, A's adjusted basis in the replacement QSB stock is $250 ($350 cost minus $100 nonrecognition amount). A does not recognize gain upon the contribution of QSB stock to ABC under section 721(a). Upon the contribution of the replacement QSB stock to ABC, A's basis in the ABC partnership interest is $250, and ABC's basis in the replacement QSB stock is $250. However, the replacement QSB stock does not qualify as QSB stock in ABC's hands. Neither A nor ABC will be eligible to defer gain under section 1045 on a subsequent sale of the replacement QSB stock.

(j) *Effective date/applicability —In general.*—This section applies to sales of QSB stock on or after August 14, 2007. [Reg. § 1.1045–1.]

☐ [T.D. 9353, 8-13-2007 (*corrected* 10-9-2007).]

Special Rules

[Reg. § 1.1051-1]

§ 1.1051-1. Basis of property acquired during affiliation.—(a)(1) The basis of property acquired by a corporation during a period of affiliation from a corporation with which it was affiliated shall be the same as it would be in the hands of the corporation from which acquired. This rule is applicable if the basis of the property is material in determining tax liability for any year, whether a separate return or a consolidated return is made in respect of such year. For the purpose of this section, the term "period of affiliation" means the period during which such corporations were affiliated (determined in accordance with the law applicable thereto), but does not include any taxable year beginning on or after January 1, 1922, unless a consolidated return was made, nor any taxable year after the taxable year 1928.

(2) The application of subparagraph (1) of this paragraph may be illustrated by the following example:

Example. The X Corporation, the Y Corporation, and the Z Corporation were affiliated for the taxable year 1920. During that year the X Corporation transferred assets to the Y Corporation for $120,000 cash, and the Y Corporation in turn transferred the assets during the same year to the Z Corporation for $130,000 cash. The assets were acquired by the X Corporation in 1916 at a cost of $100,000. The basis of the assets in the hands of the Z Corporation is $100,000.

(b) The basis of property acquired by a corporation during any period, in the taxable year 1929 or any subsequent taxable year, in respect of which a consolidated return was made or was required under the regulations governing the making of consolidated returns, shall be determined in accordance with such regulations. The basis in the case of property held by a corporation during any period, in the taxable year 1929 or any subsequent taxable year, in respect of which a consolidated return is made or is required under the regulations governing the making of consolidated returns, shall be adjusted in respect of any items relating to such period in accordance with such regulations.

(c) Except as otherwise provided in the regulations promulgated under section 141 of the Internal Revenue Code of 1939 or the Revenue Acts of section 1502 of the Internal Revenue Code of 1954 or the regulations under 1938 (52 Stat. 447), 1936 (49 Stat. 1652), 1934 (48 Stat. 683), 1932 (47 Stat. 169), or 1928 (45 Stat. 791), the basis of property after a consolidated return period shall be the same as the basis immediately prior to the close of such period. [Reg. § 1.1051-1.]

☐ [T.D. 6178, 6-1-56.]

[Reg. § 1.1052-1]

§ 1.1052-1. Basis of property established by Revenue Act of 1932.—Section 1052(a) provides that if property was acquired after February 28, 1913, in any taxable year beginning before January 1, 1934, and the basis of the property, for the purposes of the Revenue Act of 1932 (47 Stat. 169), was prescribed by section 113(a)(6), (7), or (9) of that Act, then for purposes of subtitle A of the Code, the basis shall be the same as the basis prescribed in the Revenue Act of 1932. For the rules applicable in determining the basis of stocks or securities under section 113(a)(9) of the Revenue Act of 1932 in case of certain distributions after December 31, 1923, and in any taxable year beginning before January 1, 1934, see 26 CFR (1939) 39.113(a)(12)-1 (Regulations 118). [Reg. § 1.1052-1.]

☐ [T.D. 6178, 6-1-56.]

[Reg. § 1.1052-2]

§ 1.1052-2. Basis of property established by Revenue Act of 1934.—Section 1052(b) provides that if property was acquired after February 28, 1913, in any taxable year beginning before January 1, 1936, and the basis of the property for the purposes of the Revenue Act of 1934 (48 Stat. 683) was prescribed by section 113(a)(6), (7), or (8) of that Act, then for purposes of subtitle A of the Code the basis shall be the same as the basis prescribed in the Revenue Act of 1934. For example, if after December 31, 1920, and in any taxable year beginning before January 1, 1936, property was acquired by a corporation by the issuance of its stock or securities in connection

with a transaction which is not described in section 112(b)(5) of the Internal Revenue Code of 1939 but which is described in section 112(b)(5) of the Revenue Act of 1934, the basis of the property so acquired shall be the same as it would be in the hands of the transferor, with proper adjustments to the date of the exchange. [Reg. § 1.1052-2.]

☐ [T.D. 6178, 6-1-56.]

[Reg. § 1.1052-3]

§ 1.1052-3. Basis of property established by the Internal Revenue Code of 1939.—Section 1052(c) provides that if property was acquired after February 28, 1913, in a transaction to which the Internal Revenue Code of 1939 applied and the basis thereof was prescribed by section 113(a)(6), (7), (8), (13), (15), (18), (19) or (23) of such code, then for purposes of subtitle A the basis shall be the same as the basis prescribed in the Internal Revenue Code of 1939. In such cases see section 113(a) of the Internal Revenue Code of 1939 and the regulations thereunder. [Reg. § 1.1052-3.]

☐ [T.D. 6178, 6-1-56.]

[Reg. § 1.1053-1]

§ 1.1053-1. Property acquired before March 1, 1913.—(a) *Basis for determining gain.*—In the case of property acquired before March 1, 1913, the basis as of March 1, 1913, for determining gain is the cost or other basis, adjusted as provided in section 1016 and other applicable provisions of chapter 1 of the Code, or its fair market value as of March 1, 1913, whichever is greater.

(b) *Basis for determining loss.*—In the case of property acquired before March 1, 1913, the basis as of March 1, 1913, for determining loss is the basis determined in accordance with part II (section 1011 and following), subchapter O, chapter 1 of the Code, or other applicable provisions of chapter 1 of the Code, without reference to the fair market value as of March 1, 1913.

(c) *Example.*—The application of paragraphs (a) and (b) of this section may be illustrated by the following example:

Example. (i) On March 1, 1908, a taxpayer purchased for $100,000, property having a useful life of 50 years. Assuming that there were no capital improvements to the property, the depreciation sustained on the property before March 1, 1913, was $10,000 (5 years @ $2,000), so that the original cost adjusted, as of March 1, 1913, for depreciation sustained prior to that date is $90,000. On that date the property had a fair market value of $94,500 with a remaining life of 45 years.

(ii) For the purpose of determining gain from the sale or other disposition of the property on March 1, 1954, the basis of the property is the fair market value of $94,500 as of March 1, 1913, adjusted for depreciation allowed or allowable after February 28, 1913, computed on $94,500.

Thus, the substituted basis, $94,500, is reduced by the depreciation adjustment from March 1, 1913, to February 28, 1954, in the aggregate of $86,100 (41 years @ $2,100), leaving an adjusted basis for determining gain of $8,400 ($94,500 less $86,100).

(iii) For the purpose of determining loss from the sale or other disposition of such property on March 1, 1954, the basis of the property is its cost, adjusted for depreciation sustained before March 1, 1913, computed on cost, and the amount of depreciation allowed or allowable after February 28, 1913, computed on the fair market value of $94,500 as of March 1, 1913. In this example, the amount of depreciation sustained before March 1, 1913, is $10,000 and the amount of depreciation determined for the period after February 28, 1913, is $86,100. Therefore, the aggregate amount of depreciation for which the cost ($100,000) should be adjusted is $96,100 ($10,000 plus $86,100), and the adjusted basis for determining loss on March 1, 1954, is $3,900 ($100,000 less $96,100).

(d) *Fair market value.*—The determination of the fair market value of property on March 1, 1913, is generally a question of fact and shall be established by competent evidence. In determining the fair market value of stock or other securities, due regard shall be given to the fair market value of the corporate assets as of such date, and other pertinent factors. In the case of property traded in on public exchanges, actual sales on or near the basic date afford evidence of value. In general, the fair market value of a block or aggregate of a particular kind of property is not to be determined by a forced-sale price, or by an estimate of what a whole block or aggregate would bring if placed upon the market at one and the same time. In such a case the value should be determined by ascertaining as the basis the fair market value of each unit of the property. All relevant facts and elements of value as of the basic date should be considered in each case. [Reg. § 1.1053-1.]

☐ [T.D. 6178, 6-1-56.]

[Reg. § 1.1054-1]

§ 1.1054-1. Certain Stock of Federal National Mortgage Association.—(a) *In general.*—The basis in the hands of the initial holder of a share of stock which is issued pursuant to section 303(c) of the Federal National Mortgage Association Charter Act (12 U.S.C., sec. 1718) in a taxable year beginning after December 31, 1959, shall be an amount equal to the issuance price of the stock reduced by the amount, if any, required by section 162(d) to be treated (with respect to such share) as an ordinary and necessary business expense. See section 162(d) and § 1.162-19. For purposes of this section the initial holder is the original purchaser who is issued stock of the Federal National Mortgage Association (FNMA) pursuant to section 303(c) of the Act and who

appears on the books of FNMA as the initial holder. See § 1.162-19.

(b) *Example.*—The provisions of this section may be illustrated by the following example:

Example. Pursuant to section 303(c) of the Federal National Mortgage Association Charter Act a certificate of FNMA stock is issued to A as of January 1, 1961. The issuance price of the stock was $100 and the fair market value of the stock on the date of issue was $69. A was required by section 162(d) to treat $31 as a business expense for the year 1961. The basis of the share of stock in the hands of A, the initial holder, shall be $69, the amount paid for the stock ($100) reduced by $31. [Reg. § 1.1054-1.]

☐ [T.D. 6690, 11-18-83.]

[Reg. § 1.1055-1]

§ 1.1055-1. General rule with respect to redeemable ground rents.—(a) *Character of a redeemable ground rent.*—For purposes of subtitle A of the Code (1) a redeemable ground rent (as defined in section 1055(c) and paragraph (b) of this section) shall be treated as being in the nature of a mortgage, and (2) real property held subject to liabilities under such a redeemable ground rent shall be treated as held subject to liabilities under a mortgage. Thus, under section 1055(a) and this paragraph, the transfer of property subject to a redeemable ground rent has the same effect as the transfer of property subject to a mortgage, the acquisition of property subject to a redeemable ground rent is to be treated the same as the acquisition of property subject to a mortgage, and the holding of property subject to a redeemable ground rent is to be treated in the same manner as the holding of property subject to a mortgage. See section 163(c) for the treatment of any annual or periodic rental payment under a redeemable ground rent as interest.

(b) *Definition of redeemable ground rent.*—For purposes of subtitle A of the Code, the term "redeemable ground rent" means only a ground rent with respect to which all the following conditions are met:

(1) There is a lease of land which is assignable by the lessee without the consent of the lessor.

(2) The term of the lease is for a period in excess of 15 years, taking into account all periods for which the lease may be renewed at the option of the lessee.

(3) The lessee has a present or future right to terminate the lease and to acquire the lessor's interest in the land (*i.e.,* to redeem the ground rent) by the payment of a determined or determinable amount, which amount is referred to in §§ 1.1055-2, 1.1055-3, and 1.1055-4 as a "redemption price". Such right must exist by virtue of State or local law. If the lessee's right to terminate the lease and to acquire the lessor's interest is not granted by State or local law but exists solely by virtue of a private agreement or pri-

vately created condition, the ground rent is not a "redeemable ground rent".

(4) The lessor's interest in the land subject to the lease is primarily a security interest to protect the payment to him of the annual or periodic rental payments due under the lease.

(c) *Effective date.*—In general, the provisions of section 1055 and paragraph (a) of this section take effect on April 11, 1963, and apply with respect to taxable years ending on or after such date. See § 1.1055-3 for rules for determining the basis of real property acquired subject to liabilities under a redeemable ground rent regardless of when such property was acquired. See also § 1.1055-4 for rules for determining the basis of a redeemable ground rent in the hands of a holder who reserved or created such ground rent in connection with a transfer, occurring before April 11, 1963, of the right to hold real property subject to liabilities under such ground rent. [Reg. § 1.1055-1.]

□ [*T.D.* 6821, 5-3-65.]

[Reg. § 1.1055-2]

§ 1.1055-2. Determination of amount realized on the transfer of the right to hold real property subject to liabilities under a redeemable ground rent.—In determining the amount realized from a transfer, occurring on or after April 11, 1963, of the right to hold real property subject to liabilities under a redeemable ground rent, such ground rent shall be accounted for in the same manner as a mortgage for an amount of money equal to the redemption price of the ground rent. The provisions of this section apply in respect of any such transfer even though such ground rent was created prior to April 11, 1963. For provisions relating to the determination of the amount of and recognition of gain or loss from the sale or other disposition of property, see section 1001 and the regulations thereunder. [Reg. § 1.1055-2.]

□ [*T.D.* 6821, 5-3-65.]

[Reg. § 1.1055-3]

§ 1.1055-3. Basis of real property held subject to liabilities under a redeemable ground rent.— (a) *In general.*—The provisions of section 1055(a) and paragraph (a) of § 1.1055-1 are applicable in determining the basis of real property held on or after April 11, 1963, in any case where the property at the time of acquisition was subject to liabilities under a redeemable ground rent. (See section 1055(b)(2).) Thus, if on or after April 11, 1963, a taxpayer holds real property which was subject to liabilities under a redeemable ground rent at the time he acquired it, the basis of such property in the hands of such taxpayer, regardless of when the property was acquired, will include the redeemable ground rent in the same manner as if it were a mortgage in an amount equal to the redemption price of such ground rent. Likewise, if on or after April 11, 1963, a

taxpayer holds real property which was subject to liabilities under a redeemable ground rent at the time he acquired it and which has a substituted basis in his hands, the basis of the property in the hands of the taxpayer's predecessor in interest is to be determined by treating the redeemable ground rent in the same manner as a mortgage in an amount equal to the redemption price of such ground rent.

(b) *Illustrations.*—The provisions of this section may be illustrated by the following examples:

Example (1). On April 11, 1963, taxpayer A held residential property which he acquired on January 15, 1963, for a purchase price of $10,000 and which, at the time he acquired it, was subject to a ground rent redeemable for a redemption price of $1,600. A's basis for the property includes the purchase price ($10,000) plus the redeemable ground rent in the same manner as if it were a mortgage for $1,600.

Example (2). In 1962, taxpayer X, a corporation, acquired real property subject to a redeemable ground rent in a transfer to which section 351 (relating to transfer of property to corporation controlled by transferor) applied and in which the basis of the property to X was the transferor's basis. X still held the property on April 11, 1963. The transferor's basis in the property is to be determined by treating the redeemable ground rent to which it was subject in the transferor's hands as if it were a mortgage. [Reg. § 1.1055-3.]

□ [*T.D.* 6821, 5-3-65.]

[Reg. § 1.1055-4]

§ 1.1055-4. Basis of redeemable ground rent reserved or created in connection with transfers of real property before April 11, 1963.—(a) *In general.*—In the case of a redeemable ground rent created or reserved in connection with a transfer, occurring before April 11, 1963, of the right to hold real property subject to liabilities under such ground rent, the basis of such ground rent on or after April 11, 1963, in the hands of the person who reserved or created the ground rent is the amount which was taken into account in respect of such ground rent in computing the amount realized from the transfer of such real property. Thus, if no such amount was taken into account, such basis shall be determined without regard to section 1055. (See section 1055(b)(3).)

(b) The provisions of this section may be illustrated by the following examples:

Example (1). The taxpayer, who was in the business of building houses, purchased an undeveloped lot of land for $500 and built a house thereon at a cost of $10,000. Subsequently, he transferred the right to hold the lot improved by the house for a consideration of $12,000, and an annual ground rent for such property of $120 which was redeemable for a redemption price of $2,000. The taxpayer reported a $2,000 gain on the transfer, treating the amount realized as $12,000 and his cost allocable to the interest transferred as $10,000. Since the builder did not take the redeemable ground rent into account in computing gain on the transfer, his basis for such ground rent is $500 (the cost of the land not offset against the consideration received for the transfer). Thus, if he subsequently sells the redeemable ground rent (or if it is redeemed from him) for $2,000, he has a gain of $1,500 in the year of sale (or redemption).

Example (2). Assume the same facts as in Example (1) except that the builder reported a gain of $3,500 on the transfer, treating the amount realized as $14,000 ($12,000 cash plus $2,000 for the redeemable ground rent) and his costs as $10,500 ($10,000 for the house and $500 for the lot). Since the taxpayer took the entire amount of the redeemable ground rent into account in computing his gain, his basis for such ground rent is $2,000. Thus, if he subsequently sells the redeemable ground rent (or if it is redeemed from him) for $2,000, he has no gain or loss on the transaction.

Example (3). Assume the same facts as in Example (1) except that the builder reported a gain of $3,000 on the transfer. He computed this gain by treating the amount realized as $12,000 but treating his cost allocable to the interest transferred as $12,000/$14,000ths of his total $10,500 cost, or $9,000. Since the builder still has remaining $1,500 of unallocated cost, his basis for the redeemable ground rent is $1,500. Thus, if he subsequently sells the redeemable ground rent (or if it is redeemed from him) for $2,000, he has a gain of $500 in the year of sale (or redemption). [Reg. § 1.1055-4.]

☐ [T.D. 6821, 5-3-65.]

[Reg. § 1.1059(e)-1]

§ 1.1059(e)-1. Non-pro rata redemptions.— (a) *In general.*—Section 1059(d)(6) (exception where stock held during entire existence of corporation) and section 1059(e)(2) (qualifying dividends) do not apply to any distribution treated as an extraordinary dividend under section 1059(e)(1). For example, if a redemption of stock is not pro rata as to all shareholders, any amount treated as a dividend under section 301 is treated as an extraordinary dividend regardless of whether the dividend is a qualifying dividend.

(b) *Reorganizations.*—For purposes of section 1059(e)(1), any exchange under section 356 is treated as a redemption and, to the extent any amount is treated as a dividend under section 356(a)(2), it is treated as a dividend under section 301.

(c) *Effective date.*—This section applies to distributions announced (within the meaning of section 1059(d)(5)) on or after June 17, 1996. [Reg. § 1.1059(e)-1.]

☐ [T.D. 8724, 7-15-97.]

[Reg. § 1.1059A-1]

§ 1.1059A-1. Limitation on taxpayer's basis or inventory cost in property imported from related persons.—(a) *General rule.*—In the case of property imported into the United States in a transaction (directly or indirectly) by a controlled taxpayer from another member of a controlled group of taxpayers, except for the adjustments permitted by paragraph (c)(2) of this section, the amount of any costs taken into account in computing the basis or inventory cost of the property by the purchasing U.S. taxpayer and which costs are also taken into account in computing the valuation of the property for customs purposes may not, for purposes of the basis or inventory cost, be greater than the amount of the costs used in computing the customs value. For purposes of this section, the terms "controlled taxpayer" and "group of controlled taxpayers" shall have the meaning set forth in § 1.482-1(a).

(b) *Definitions.*—(1) *Import.*—For purposes of section 1059A and this section only, the term "import" means the filing of the entry documentation required by the U.S. Customs Service to secure the release of imported merchandise from custody of the U.S. Customs Service.

(2) *Indirectly.*—For purposes of this section, "indirectly" refers to a transaction between a controlled taxpayer and another member of the controlled group whereby property is imported through a person acting as an agent of, or otherwise on behalf of, either or both related persons, or as a middleman or conduit for transfer of the property between a controlled taxpayer and another member of the controlled group. In the case of the importation of property indirectly, an adjustment shall be permitted under paragraph (c)(2) of this section for a commission or markup paid to the person acting as agent, middleman, or conduit, only to the extent that the commission or markup: is otherwise properly included in cost basis or inventory cost; was actually incurred by the taxpayer and not remitted, directly or indirectly, to the taxpayer or related party; and there is a substantial business reason for the use of a middleman, agent, or conduit.

(c) *Customs value.*—(1) *Definition.*—For purposes of this section only, the term "customs value" means the value required to be taken into account for purposes of determining the amount of any customs duties or any other duties which may be imposed on the importation of any property. Where an item or a portion of an item is not subject to any customs duty or is subject to a free rate of duty, such item or portion of such item shall not be subject to the provisions of section 1059A or this section. Thus, for example, the portion of an item that is an American good returned and not subject to duty (items 806.20 and 806.30, Tariff Schedules of the United States, 19 U.S.C. 1202); imports on which no duty is imposed that are valued by customs for statistical purposes only; and items subject to a zero rate of duty (19 U.S.C. 1202, General Headnote 3) are not subject to section 1059A or this section. Also, items subject only to the user fee under 19 U.S.C. 58(c), or the harbor maintenance tax imposed by 26 U.S.C. 4461, or only to both, are not subject to section 1059A or this section. This section imposes no limitation on a claimed basis or inventory cost in property which is less than the value used to compute the customs duty with respect to the same property. Section 1059A and this section have no application to imported property not subject to any customs duty based on value, including property subject only to a per item duty or a duty based on volume, because there is no customs value, within the meaning of this paragraph, with respect to such property.

(2) *Adjustments to customs value.*—To the extent not otherwise included in customs value, a taxpayer, for purposes of determining the limitation on claimed basis or inventory cost of property under this section, may increase the customs value of imported property by the amounts incurred by it and properly included in inventory cost for—

(i) Freight charges,

(ii) Insurance charges,

(iii) The construction, erection, assembly, or technical assistance provided with respect to, the property after is importation into the United States, and

(iv) Any other amounts which are not taken into account in determining the customs value, which are not properly includible in customs value, and which are appropriately included in the cost basis or inventory cost for income tax purposes. *See* §1.471-11 and section 263A.

Appropriate adjustments may also be made to customs values when the taxpayer has not allocated the value of assists to individual articles but rather has reported the value of assists on a periodic basis in accordance with 19 CFR §152.103(e). When 19 CFR §152.103(e) has been utilized for customs purposes, the taxpayer may adjust his customs values by allocating the value of the assists to all imported articles to which the assists relate. To the extent that an amount attributable to an adjustment permitted by this section is paid by a controlled taxpayer to another member of the group of controlled taxpayers, an adjustment is permitted under this section only to the extent that the amount incurred represents an arm's length charge within the meaning of §1.482-1(d)(3).

(3) *Offsets to adjustments.*—To the extent that a customs value is adjusted under paragraph (c)(2) of this section for purposes of calculating the limitation on claimed cost basis or inventory cost under this section, the amount of the adjustments must be offset (reduced) by amounts that properly reduce the cost basis of inventory and that are not taken into account in determining

customs value, such as rebates and other reductions in the price actually incurred, effected between the purchaser and related seller after the date of importation of the property.

(4) *Application of section 1059A to property having dutiable and nondutiable portions.*—When an item of imported property is subject to a duty upon the full value of the imported article, less the cost or value of American goods returned, and the taxpayer claims a basis or inventory cost greater than the customs value reported for the item, the claimed tax basis or inventory cost in the dutiable portion of the item is limited under section 1059A and this section to the customs value of the dutiable portion under paragraph (c)(1). The claimed tax basis or inventory cost in the nondutiable portion of the item is determined by multiplying the customs value of the nondutiable portion by a fraction the numerator of which is the amount by which the claimed basis or inventory cost of the item exceeds the customs value of the item and the denominator of which is the customs value of the item and adding this amount to the customs value of the nondutiable portion of the item. The claimed tax basis or inventory cost in the dutiable portion is determined by multiplying the customs value of the dutiable portion by a fraction the numerator of which is the amount by which the claimed basis or inventory cost of the item exceeds the customs value of the item and the denominator of which is the customs value of the item and adding this amount to the customs value of the dutiable portion of the item. However, the taxpayer may not claim a tax basis or inventory cost in the dutiable portion greater than the customs value of this portion of the item.

(5) *Allocation of adjustments to property having dutiable and nondutiable portions.*—When an item of imported property is subject to a duty upon the full value of the imported article, less the cost or value of American goods returned, and the taxpayer establishes that the customs value may be increased by adjustments permitted under paragraph (c)(2) of this section for purposes of the section 1059A limitation, the taxpayer's basis or inventory cost of the dutiable portion of the item is determined by multiplying the customs value of the dutiable portion times the percentage that the adjustments represent of the total customs value of the item and adding this amount to the customs value of the dutiable portion of the item. The taxpayer's basis or inventory cost of the nondutiable portion of the item is determined in the same manner. The amount so determined for the dutiable portion of the item is the section 1059A limitation for this portion of the item.

(6) *Alternative method of demonstrating compliance.*—In lieu of calculating all adjustments and offsets to adjustments to customs value for an item of property pursuant to paragraph (c)(2) and (3) of this section, a taxpayer may demon-

strate compliance with this section and section 1059A by comparing costs taken into account in computing basis or inventory costs of the property and the costs taken into account in computing customs value at any time after importation, provided that in any such comparison the same costs are included both in basis or inventory costs and in customs value. If, on the basis of such comparison, the basis or inventory cost is equal to or less than the customs value, the taxpayer shall be deemed to have met the requirements of this section and section 1059A.

(7) *Relationship of section 1059A to section 482.*—Neither this section nor section 1059A limits in any way the authority of the Commissioner to increase or decrease the claimed basis or inventory cost under section 482 or any other appropriate provision of law. Neither does this section or section 1059A permit a taxpayer to adjust upward its cost basis or inventory cost for property appropriately determined under section 482 because such basis or inventory cost is less than the customs value with respect to such property.

(8) *Illustrations.*—The application of this section may be illustrated by the following examples:

Example (1). Corporation X, a United States taxpayer, and Y Corporation are members of a group of controlled corporations. X pays $2,000 to Y for merchandise imported into the United States and an additional $150 for ocean freight and insurance. The customs value of the shipment is determined to be the amount actually paid by X ($2,000) and does not include the charges for ocean freight and insurance. For purposes of computing the limitation on its inventory cost for the merchandise under section 1059A and this section, X is permitted, under paragraph (c)(2) of this section, to increase the customs value ($2,000) by amounts it paid for ocean freight and insurance charges ($150). Thus, the inventory cost claimed by X in the merchandise may not exceed $2,150.

Example (2). Assume the same facts as in Example (1) except that, subsequent to the date of importation of the merchandise, Y grants to X a rebate of $200 of the purchase price. At the time of sale, the rebate was contingent upon the volume of merchandise ultimately bought by X from Y. The value of the merchandise, for customs purposes, is not decreased by the rebate paid to X by Y. Therefore, the customs value, for customs purposes, of the merchandise remains the same ($2,000). For purposes of computing its inventory cost, X was permitted, under paragraph (c)(2) of this section, to increase the customs value for purposes of section 1059A of $2,000 by the amounts it paid for ocean freight and insurance charges ($150). However, under paragraph (c)(3) of this section, X is required to reduce the amount of the customs value by the lesser of the amount of the rebate or the amount of any positive adjustments to the original customs value. The inventory price claimed by X may not exceed $2,000 ($2,000 customs value, plus $150 transportation adjustment, less $150 offsetting rebate adjustment). While X's limitation under section 1059A is $2,000, X may not claim a basis or inventory cost in the merchandise in excess of $1,950. *See* I.R.C. § 1012; and § 1.471-2.

Example (3). Corporation X, a United States taxpayer, and Y Corporation are members of a group of controlled corporations. X pays $10,000 to Y for merchandise imported into the United States. The merchandise is composed, in part, of American goods returned. The customs value of the merchandise, on which a customs duty is imposed, is determined to be $8,000 ($10,000, the amount declared by X, less $2,000, the value of the American goods returned). For income tax purposes, X claims a cost basis in the merchandise of $11,000. None of the adjustments permitted by paragraph (c)(2) of this section is applicable. The portion of the merchandise constituting American goods returned represented 20 percent of the total customs value of the merchandise. Since the cost basis claimed by X for income tax purposes represents a 10 percent increase over the customs valuation (before reduction for American goods returned), the claimed tax basis in the dutiable content is considered to be $8,800 and in the portion constituting American goods returned is $2,200. Since a customs duty was imposed only on the dutiable content of the merchandise, the limitation in section 1059A and this section is applicable only to the claimed tax basis in this portion of the merchandise. Accordingly, under paragraph (a) of this section, X is limited to a cost basis of $10,200 in the merchandise. This amount represents a cost basis of $8,000 in the dutiable content and of $2,200 in the portion of the merchandise constituting American goods returned.

Example (4). Assume the same facts as in Example (3) except that X establishes that it is entitled to increase its customs value by $1,000 in adjustments permitted by paragraph (c)(2) of this section. Since the adjustments to customs value that X is entitled to under paragraph (c)(2) of this section are 10 percent of the customs value, for purposes of determining the limitation under section 1059A and this section, both the dutiable content and the portion of the merchandise constituting American goods returned shall be increased to an amount 10 percent greater than the respective values determined for customs purposes, or $8,800 for the dutiable content and $2,200 for the portion of the merchandise constituting American goods returned. Accordingly, under paragraph (a) of this section, X is limited to a cost basis of $11,000 in the merchandise.

Example (5). Corporation X, a United States taxpayer, and Y Corporation are members of a group of controlled corporations. X pays $10,000 to Y for merchandise imported into the United States. The customs value of the merchandise, on

Reg. § 1.1059A-1(c)(8)

which a customs duty is imposed, is determined to be $10,000. Subsequent to the date of importation of the merchandise, Y grants to X a rebate of $1,000 of the purchase price. The value of the merchandise, for customs purposes, is not decreased by the rebate paid to X by Y. Notwithstanding the fact that X correctly reported and paid customs duty on a value of $10,000 and that its limitation on basis or inventory cost under this section is $10,000, X may not claim a basis or inventory cost in the merchandise in excess of $9,000. *See* I.R.C. § 1012; and § 1.471-2.

Example (6). Corporation X, a United States taxpayer, and Y Corporation are members of a group of controlled corporations. X pays $5,000 to Y for merchandise imported into the United States. The merchandise is not subject to a customs duty or is subject to a free rate of duty and is valued by customs solely for statistical purposes. Accordingly, pursuant to paragraph (c)(1) of this section, the merchandise is not subject to the provisions of section 1059A or this section.

Example (7). Assume the same facts as in Example 6, except that the merchandise is subject to a customs duty based on value and that the customs value (taking into account no costs other than the value of the goods) is determined to be $5,000. Assume further that the $5,000 payment is only for the value of the goods, no other cost is reflected in that payment, and only the $5,000 payment to Y is reflected in X's inventory cost or basis prior to inclusion of any other amounts properly included in inventory or cost basis. Pursuant to paragraph (c)(6) of this section, X, by demonstrating these facts is deemed to meet the requirements of this section and section 1059A.

Example (8). Corporation X, a United States taxpayer, and Y Corporation are members of a group of controlled corporations. X pays $9 to Y for merchandise imported into the United States and an additional $1 for ocean freight. The customs value of the article does not include the $1 paid for ocean freight. Furthermore, for customs purposes the value is calculated pursuant to computed value and is determined to be $8. For purposes of computing the limitation on its inventory cost for the article under section 1059A and this section, X is permitted, under paragraph (c)(2) of this section, to increase the customs value ($8) by the amount it paid for ocean freight ($1). Thus, the inventory cost claimed by X in the article may not exceed $9.

(9) *Averaged customs values.*—In cases of transactions in which (i) an appropriate transfer price is properly determined for tax purposes by reference to events occurring after importation, (ii) the value for customs purposes of one article is higher and of a second article is lower than the actual transaction values, (iii) the relevant articles have been appraised on the basis of a value estimated at the time of importation in accordance with customs regulations, and (iv) the entries have been liquidated upon importation, the

section 1059A limitation on the undervalued article may be increased up to the amount of actual transaction value by the amount of the duty overpaid on the overvalued article times a fraction the numerator of which is "1" and the denominator of which is the rate of duty on the undervalued article. This paragraph (c)(9) applies exclusively to cases of property imported in transactions that are open for tax purposes in which the actual transaction value cannot be determined and the entry has been liquidated for customs purposes on the basis of a value estimated at the time of importation in accordance with customs regulations; in these cases, the property is appropriately valued for tax purposes by reference to a formula, in existence at the time of importation, based on subsequent events and valued for customs purposes by a different formula. This paragraph (c)(9) does not apply where customs value is correctly determined for purposes of liquidating the entry and where the customs value is subsequently adjusted for tax purposes, for example by a rebate, under paragraph (c)(2) of this section. The application of paragraph (c)(9) may be illustrated by the following example:

Example. Corporation X, a United States taxpayer, and Y Corporation are members of a group of controlled corporations. X purchases Articles A and B from Y on consignment and imports the Articles into the United States. The purchase price paid by X will be determined as a percentage of the sale prices that X realizes. Rather than deferring liquidation, customs liquidates the entry on the basis of estimated values and the customs duties are paid by X. Ultimately, it is determined that Article A was undervalued and Article B was overvalued by X for customs purposes. The section 1059A limitation for Article A is computed as follows:

	Article A	Article B
Finally-determined customs value	$9	$9
Transaction value	$10	$5
Duty rate	10 %	5 %
Customs duty paid	$.90	$.45
Duty overpaid or (underpaid)	($.10)	$.20

The section 1059A limitation on Article A may be increased by the amount of the duty over-paid on Article B, $.20, times 1/.10, up to the amount of the transaction value. Therefore, the section 1059A limitation on Article A is $9.00 plus $1.00, or a total of $10.00. The section 1059A limitation on Article B is reduced (but never below transaction value) by $2.00 to $7.00.

(d) *Finality of customs value and of other determinations of the U.S. Customs Service.*—For purposes of section 1059A and this section, a taxpayer is bound by the finally-determined customs value and by every final determination made by the U.S. Customs Service, including, but not limited to, dutiable value, the value attributable to the cost or value of products of the United States, and classification of the product for purposes of imposing any duty. The customs value is considered to be finally determined, and all U.S. Customs Service determinations are considered final, when liquidation of the entry becomes final. For this purpose, the term "liquidation" means the ascertainment of the customs duties occurring on the entry of the property, and liquidation of the entry is considered to become final after 90 days following notice of liquidation to the importer, unless a protest is filed. If the importer files a protest, the customs value will be considered finally determined and all other U.S. Customs Service determinations will be considered final either when a decision by the Customs Service on the protest is not contested after expiration of the period allowed to contest the decision or when a judgment of the Court of International Trade becomes final. For purposes of this section, any adjustments to the customs value resulting from a petition under 19 U.S.C. section 1516 (requests by interested parties unrelated to the importer for redetermination of the appraised value, classification, or the rate of duty imposed on imported merchandise) or reliquidation under 19 U.S.C. section 1521 (reliquidation by the Customs Service upon a finding that fraud was involved in the original liquidation) will not be taken into account. However, reliquidation under 19 U.S.C. section 1501 (voluntary reliquidation by the Customs Service within 90 days of the original liquidation to correct errors in appraisement, classification, or any element entering into a liquidation or reliquidation) or reliquidation under 19 U.S.C. section 1520(c)(1) (to correct a clerical error, mistake of fact, or other inadvertance within one year of a liquidation or reliquidation) will be taken into account in the same manner as, and take the place of, the original liquidation in determining customs value.

(e) *Drawbacks.*—For purposes of this section, a drawback, that is, a refund or remission (in whole or in part) of a customs duty because of a particular use made (or to be made) of the property on which the duty was assessed or collected, shall not affect the determination of the customs value of the property.

(f) *Effective date.*—Property imported by a taxpayer is subject to section 1059A and this section if the entry documentation required to be filed to obtain the release of the property from the custody of the United States Customs Service was filed after March 18, 1986. Section 1059A and this section will not apply to imported property where (1) the entry documentation is filed prior to September 3, 1987; and (2) the importation was liquidated under the circumstances described in paragraph (c)(9) of this section. [Reg. § 1.1059A-1.]

☐ [*T.D.* 8260, 9-7-89.]

[Reg. § 1.1060-1]

§ 1.1060-1. Special allocation rules for certain asset acquisitions.—(a) *Scope.*—(1) *In general.*—This section prescribes rules relating to the requirements of section 1060, which, in the case of an applicable asset acquisition, requires the transferor (the seller) and the transferee (the purchaser) each to allocate the consideration paid or received in the transaction among the assets transferred in the same manner as amounts are allocated under section 338(b)(5) (relating to the allocation of adjusted grossed-up basis among the assets of the target corporation when a section 338 election is made). In the case of an applicable asset acquisition described in paragraph (b)(1) of this section, sellers and purchasers must allocate the consideration under the residual method as described in § § 1.338-6 and 1.338-7 in order to determine, respectively, the amount realized from, and the basis in, each of the transferred assets. For rules relating to distributions of partnership property or transfers of partnership interests which are subject to section 1060(d), see § 1.755-2T.

(2) *Effective dates.*—(i) *In general.*—The provisions of this section apply to any asset acquisition occurring after March 15, 2001. However, paragraphs (b)(9) and (c)(5) of this section apply only to applicable asset acquisitions occurring on or after April 10, 2006. A purchaser or a seller may make an irrevocable election to apply the rules in § 1.338-11 (including the applicable provisions in § § 1.197-2(g)(5), 1.381(c)(22)-1, 846 and 1060) to an applicable asset acquisition occurring before April 10, 2006. Paragraph (a)(2)(ii) of this section describes the time and manner of the election for the purchaser and paragraph (a)(2)(iii) of this section prescribes the time and manner of the election for the seller. The seller may make the election to apply the regulations retroactively without regard to whether the purchaser also makes the election. For rules applicable to asset acquisitions on or before March 15, 2001, see § 1.1060-1T in effect before March 16, 2001 (see 26 CFR part 1 revised April 1, 2000).

(ii) *Time and manner of making the election for the purchaser.*—The purchaser may make an election described in this paragraph (a)(2) by attaching a statement to its original or amended income tax return for the taxable year that includes the applicable asset sale. The statement must be entitled "Election to Retroactively Apply the Rules in § 1.338-11 (Including the Applicable Provisions in § § 1.197-2(g)(5), 1.381(c)(22)-1, 846 and 1060) to an Applicable Asset Acquisition Completed Before April 10, 2006" and must include the following information—

(A) The name and E.I.N. for the purchaser; and

(B) The following declaration (or a substantially similar declaration): The purchaser has amended its income tax returns for the taxable year that includes the applicable asset acquisition and for all affected subsequent years to reflect the rules in §1.338-11 (including the applicable provisions in §§1.197-2(g)(5), 1.381(c)(22)-1, 846 and 1060).

(iii) *Time and manner of making the election for the seller.*—The seller may make an election described in this paragraph (a)(2) by attaching a statement to its original or amended income tax return for the taxable year that includes the applicable asset sale. The statement must be entitled "Election to retroactively apply the rules in §1.338-11 (including the applicable provisions in §§1.197-2(g)(5), 1.381(c)(22)-1, 846 and 1060) to an applicable asset acquisition completed before April 10, 2006" and must include the following information—

(A) The name and E.I.N. for the seller; and

(B) The following declaration (or a substantially similar declaration): The seller has amended its income tax returns for the taxable year that includes the applicable asset acquisition and for all affected subsequent years to reflect the rules in §1.338-11 (including the applicable provisions in §§1.197-2(g)(5), 1.381(c)(22)-1, 846 and 1060).

(3) *Outline of topics.*—In order to facilitate the use of this section, this paragraph (a)(3) lists the major paragraphs in this section as follows:

(a) Scope.

(1) In general.

(2) Effective date.

(3) Outline of topics.

(b) Applicable asset acquisition.

(1) In general.

(2) Assets constituting a trade or business.

(i) In general.

(ii) Goodwill or going concern value.

(iii) Factors indicating goodwill or going concern value.

(3) Examples.

(4) Asymmetrical transfers of assets.

(5) Related transactions.

(6) More than a single trade or business.

(7) Covenant entered into by the seller.

(8) Partial non-recognition exchanges.

(9) Insurance business.

(c) Allocation of consideration among assets under the residual method.

(1) Consideration.

(2) Allocation of consideration among assets.

(3) Certain costs.

(4) Effect of agreement between parties.

(5) Insurance business.

(d) Examples.

(e) Reporting requirements.

(1) Applicable asset acquisitions.

(i) In general.

(ii) Time and manner of reporting.

(A) In general.

(B) Additional reporting requirement.

(C) Election described in §1.338-6(c)(5).

(2) Transfers of interests in partnerships.

(b) *Applicable asset acquisition.*—(1) *In general.*—An applicable asset acquisition is any transfer, whether direct or indirect, of a group of assets if the assets transferred constitute a trade or business in the hands of either the seller or the purchaser and, except as provided in paragraph (b)(8) of this section, the purchaser's basis in the transferred assets is determined wholly by reference to the purchaser's consideration.

(2) *Assets constituting a trade or business.*—(i) *In general.*—For purposes of this section, a group of assets constitutes a trade or business if—

(A) The use of such assets would constitute an active trade or business under section 355; or

(B) Its character is such that goodwill or going concern value could under any circumstances attach to such group.

(ii) *Goodwill or going concern value.*—Goodwill is the value of a trade or business attributable to the expectancy of continued customer patronage. This expectancy may be due to the name or reputation of a trade or business or any other factor. Going concern value is the additional value that attaches to property because of its existence as an integral part of an ongoing business activity. Going concern value includes the value attributable to the ability of a trade or business (or a part of a trade or business) to continue functioning or generating income without interruption notwithstanding a change in ownership. It also includes the value that is attributable to the immediate use or availability of an acquired trade or business, such as, for example, the use of the revenues or net earnings that otherwise would not be received during any period if the acquired trade or business were not available or operational.

(iii) *Factors indicating goodwill or going concern value.*—In making the determination in this paragraph (b)(2), all the facts and circumstances surrounding the transaction are taken into account. Whether sufficient consideration is available to allocate to goodwill or going concern value after the residual method is applied is not relevant in determining whether goodwill or going concern value could attach to a group of assets. Factors to be considered include—

(A) The presence of any intangible assets (whether or not those assets are section 197 intangibles), provided, however, that the transfer of such an asset in the absence of other assets

Reg. §1.1060-1(a)(2)(iii)

will not be a trade or business for purposes of section 1060;

(B) The existence of an excess of the total consideration over the aggregate book value of the tangible and intangible assets purchased (other than goodwill and going concern value) as shown in the financial accounting books and records of the purchaser; and

(C) Related transactions, including lease agreements, licenses, or other similar agreements between the purchaser and seller (or managers, directors, owners, or employees of the seller) in connection with the transfer.

(3) *Examples.*—The following examples illustrate paragraphs (b)(1) and (2) of this section:

Example 1. S is a high grade machine shop that manufactures microwave connectors in limited quantities. It is a successful company with a reputation within the industry and among its customers for manufacturing unique, high quality products. Its tangible assets consist primarily of ordinary machinery for working metal and plating. It has no secret formulas or patented drawings of value. P is a company that designs, manufactures, and markets electronic components. It wants to establish an immediate presence in the microwave industry, an area in which it previously has not been engaged. P is acquiring assets of a number of smaller companies and hopes that these assets will collectively allow it to offer a broad product mix. P acquires the assets of S in order to augment its product mix and to promote its presence in the microwave industry. P will not use the assets acquired from S to manufacture microwave connectors. The assets transferred are assets that constitute a trade or business in the hands of the seller. Thus, P's purchase of S's assets is an applicable asset acquisition. The fact that P will not use the assets acquired from S to continue the business of S does not affect this conclusion.

Example 2. S, a sole proprietor who operates a car wash, both leases the building housing the car wash and sells all of the car wash equipment to P. S's use of the building and the car wash equipment constitute a trade or business. P begins operating a car wash in the building it leases from S. Because the assets transferred together with the asset leased are assets which constitute a trade or business, P's purchase of S's assets is an applicable asset acquisition.

Example 3. S, a corporation, owns a retail store business in State X and conducts activities in connection with that business enterprise that meet the active trade or business requirement of section 355. P is a minority shareholder of S. S distributes to P all the assets of S used in S's retail business in State X in complete redemption of P's stock in S held by P. The distribution of S's assets in redemption of P's stock is treated as a sale or exchange under sections 302(a) and 302(b)(3), and P's basis in the assets distributed to it is determined wholly by reference to the

consideration paid, the S stock. Thus, S's distribution of assets constituting a trade or business to P is an applicable asset acquisition.

Example 4. S is a manufacturing company with an internal financial bookkeeping department. P is in the business of providing a financial bookkeeping service on a contract basis. As part of an agreement for P to begin providing financial bookkeeping services to S, P agrees to buy all of the assets associated with S's internal bookkeeping operations and provide employment to any of S's bookkeeping department employees who choose to accept a position with P. In addition to selling P the assets associated with its bookkeeping operation, S will enter into a long term contract with P for bookkeeping services. Because assets transferred from S to P, along with the related contract for bookkeeping services, are a trade or business in the hands of P, the sale of the bookkeeping assets from S to P is an applicable asset acquisition.

(4) *Asymmetrical transfers of assets.*—A purchaser is subject to section 1060 if—

(i) Under general principles of tax law, the seller is not treated as transferring the same assets as the purchaser is treated as acquiring;

(ii) The assets acquired by the purchaser constitute a trade or business; and

(iii) Except as provided in paragraph (b)(8) of this section, the purchaser's basis in the transferred assets is determined wholly by reference to the purchaser's consideration.

(5) *Related transactions.*—Whether the assets transferred constitute a trade or business is determined by aggregating all transfers from the seller to the purchaser in a series of related transactions. Except as provided in paragraph (b)(8) of this section, all assets transferred from the seller to the purchaser in a series of related transactions are included in the group of assets among which the consideration paid or received in such series is allocated under the residual method. The principles of §1.338-1(c) are also applied in determining which assets are included in the group of assets among which the consideration paid or received is allocated under the residual method.

(6) *More than a single trade or business.*—If the assets transferred from a seller to a purchaser include more than one trade or business, then, in applying this section, all of the assets transferred (whether or not transferred in one transaction or a series of related transactions and whether or not part of a trade or business) are treated as a single trade or business.

(7) *Covenant entered into by the seller.*—If, in connection with an applicable asset acquisition, the seller enters into a covenant (e.g., a covenant not to compete) with the purchaser, that covenant is treated as an asset transferred as part of a trade or business.

Reg. §1.1060-1(b)(7)

(8) *Partial non-recognition exchanges.*—A transfer may constitute an applicable asset acquisition notwithstanding the fact that no gain or loss is recognized with respect to a portion of the group of assets transferred. All of the assets transferred, including the non-recognition assets, are taken into account in determining whether the group of assets constitutes a trade or business. The allocation of consideration under paragraph (c) of this section is done without taking into account either the non-recognition assets or the amount of money or other property that is treated as transferred in exchange for the non-recognition assets (together, the non-recognition exchange property). The basis in and gain or loss recognized with respect to the non-recognition exchange property are determined under such rules as would otherwise apply to an exchange of such property. The amount of the money and other property treated as exchanged for non-recognition assets is the amount by which the fair market value of the non-recognition assets transferred by one party exceeds the fair market value of the non-recognition assets transferred by the other (to the extent of the money and the fair market value of property transferred in the exchange). The money and other property that are treated as transferred in exchange for the non-recognition assets (and which are not included among the assets to which section 1060 applies) are considered to come from the following assets in the following order: first from Class I assets, then from Class II assets, then from Class III assets, then from Class IV assets, then from Class V assets, then from Class VI assets, and then from Class VII assets. For this purpose, liabilities assumed (or to which a non-recognition exchange property is subject) are treated as Class I assets. See *Example 1* in paragraph (d) of this section for an example of the application of section 1060 to a single transaction which is, in part, a non-recognition exchange.

(9) *Insurance business.*—The mere reinsurance of insurance contracts by an insurance company is not an applicable asset acquisition, even if it enables the reinsurer to establish a customer relationship with the owners of the reinsured contracts. However, a transfer of an insurance business is an applicable asset acquisition if the purchaser acquires significant business assets, in addition to insurance contracts, to which goodwill and going concern value could attach. For rules regarding the treatment of an applicable asset acquisition of an insurance business, see paragraph (c)(5) of this section.

(c) *Allocation of consideration among assets under the residual method.*—(1) *Consideration.*—The seller's consideration is the amount, in the aggregate, realized from selling the assets in the applicable asset acquisition under section 1001(b). The purchaser's consideration is the amount, in the aggregate, of its cost of purchasing the assets in the applicable asset acquisition that is properly taken into account in basis.

(2) *Allocation of consideration among assets.*— For purposes of determining the seller's amount realized for each of the assets sold in an applicable asset acquisition, the seller allocates consideration to all the assets sold by using the residual method under § § 1.338-6 and 1.338-7, substituting consideration for ADSP. For purposes of determining the purchaser's basis in each of the assets purchased in an applicable asset acquisition, the purchaser allocates consideration to all the assets purchased by using the residual method under § § 1.338-6 and 1.338-7, substituting consideration for AGUB. In allocating consideration, the rules set forth in paragraphs (c)(3) and (4) of this section apply in addition to the rules in § § 1.338-6 and 1.338-7.

(3) *Certain costs.*—The seller and purchaser each adjusts the amount allocated to an individual asset to take into account the specific identifiable costs incurred in transferring that asset in connection with the applicable asset acquisition (e.g., real estate transfer costs or security interest perfection costs). Costs so allocated increase, or decrease, as appropriate, the total consideration that is allocated under the residual method. No adjustment is made to the amount allocated to an individual asset for general costs associated with the applicable asset acquisition as a whole or with groups of assets included therein (e.g., non-specific appraisal fees or accounting fees). These latter amounts are taken into account only indirectly through their effect on the total consideration to be allocated. If an election described in § 1.338-6(c)(5) is made with respect to an applicable asset acquisition, any allocation of costs pursuant to this paragraph (c)(3) shall be made as if such election had not been made. The preceding sentence applies to applicable asset acquisitions occurring on or after September 11, 2007. For applicable asset acquisitions occurring before September 11, 2007 and on or after September 15, 2004, see § 1.1060-1T as contained in 26 CFR Part 1 in effect on April 1, 2007. For applicable asset acquisitions occurring before September 15, 2004, see § § 1.338-6 and 1.1060-1 as contained in 26 CFR Part 1 in effect on April 1, 2004.

(4) *Effect of agreement between parties.*—If, in connection with an applicable asset acquisition, the seller and purchaser agree in writing as to the allocation of any amount of consideration to, or as to the fair market value of, any of the assets, such agreement is binding on them to the extent provided in this paragraph (c)(4). Nothing in this paragraph (c)(4) restricts the Commissioner's authority to challenge the allocations or values arrived at in an allocation agreement. This paragraph (c)(4) does not apply if the parties are able to refute the allocation or valuation under the standards set forth in *Commissioner v. Danielson*, 378 F.2d 771 (3d Cir.), *cert. denied*, 389 U.S. 858 (1967) (a party wishing to challenge the tax consequences of an agreement as construed by the Commissioner must offer proof that, in an action between the parties to the agreement, would be admissible to alter that construction or

show its unenforceability because of mistake, undue influence, fraud, duress, etc.).

(5) *Insurance business.*—If the trade or business transferred is an insurance business, the rules of this paragraph (c) are modified by the principles of § 1.338-11(a) through (d). However, in transactions governed by section 1060, such principles apply even if the transfer of the trade or business is effected in whole or in part through indemnity reinsurance rather than assumption reinsurance, and, for the insurer or reinsurer, an insurance contract (including an annuity or reinsurance contract) is a Class VI asset regardless of whether it is a section 197 intangible. In addition, the principles of § 1.338-11(f) through (h) apply if the transfer occurs in connection with the complete liquidation of the transferor.

(d) *Examples.*—The following examples illustrate this section:

Example 1. (i) On January 1, 2001, A transfers assets X, Y, and Z to B in exchange for assets D, E, and F plus $1,000 cash.

(ii) Assume the exchange of assets constitutes an exchange of like-kind property to which section 1031 applies. Assume also that goodwill or going concern value could under any circumstances attach to each of the DEF and XYZ groups of assets and, therefore, each group constitutes a trade or business under section 1060.

(iii) Assume the fair market values of the assets and the amount of money transferred are as follows:

By A	Fair Market Value
Asset	
X	$400
Y	400
Z	200
Total	$1,000

By B	Fair Market Value
Asset	
D	$40
E	30
F	30
Cash (amount)	1,000
Total	$1,100

(iv) Under paragraph (b)(8) of this section, for purposes of allocating consideration under paragraph (c) of this section, the like-kind assets exchanged and any money or other property that are treated as transferred in exchange for the like-kind property are excluded from the application of section 1060.

(v) Since assets X, Y, and Z are like-kind property, they are excluded from the application of the section 1060 allocation rules.

(vi) Since assets D, E, and F are like-kind property, they are excluded from the application of the section 1060 allocation rules. Thus, the allocation rules of section 1060 do not apply in determining B's gain or loss with respect to the disposition of assets D, E, and F, and the allocation rules of section 1060 and paragraph (c) of this section are not applied to determine A's bases of assets D, E, and F. In addition, $900 of the $1,000 cash B gave to A for A's like-kind assets (X, Y, and Z) is treated as transferred in exchange for the like-kind property in order to equalize the fair market values of the like-kind assets. Therefore, $900 of the cash is excluded from the application of the section 1060 allocation rules.

(vii) $100 of the cash is allocated under section 1060 and paragraph (c) of this section.

(viii) A received $100 that must be allocated under section 1060 and paragraph (c) of this section. Since A transferred no Class I, II, III, IV, V, or VI assets to which section 1060 applies, in determining its amount realized for the part of the exchange to which section 1031 does not apply, the $100 is allocated to Class VII assets (goodwill and going concern value).

(ix) B gave A $100 that must be allocated under section 1060 and paragraph (c) of this section. Since B received from A no Class I, II, III, IV, V, or VI assets to which section 1060 applies, the $100 consideration is allocated by B to Class VII assets (goodwill and going concern value).

Example 2. (i) On January 1, 2001, S, a sole proprietor, sells to P, a corporation, a group of assets that constitutes a trade or business under paragraph (b)(2) of this section. S, who plans to retire immediately, also executes in P's favor a covenant not to compete. P pays S $3,000 in cash and assumes $1,000 in liabilities. Thus, the total consideration is $4,000.

(ii) On the purchase date, P and S also execute a separate agreement that states that the fair market values of the Class II, Class III, Class V, and Class VI assets S sold to P are as follows:

Asset Class	Asset	Fair Market Value
II	Actively traded securities	$500
	Total Class II	500
III	Accounts receivable	200
	Total Class III	200

Asset Class	Asset	Fair Market Value
V	Furniture and fixtures	800
	Building	800
	Land	200
	Equipment	400
	Total Class V	2,200
VI	Covenant not to compete	900
	Total Class VI	900

(iii) P and S each allocate the consideration in the transaction among the assets transferred under paragraph (c) of this section in accordance with the agreed upon fair market values of the assets, so that $500 is allocated to Class II assets, $200 is allocated to the Class III asset, $2,200 is allocated to Class V assets, $900 is allocated to Class VI assets, and $200 ($4,000 total consideration less $3,800 allocated to assets in Classes II, III, V, and VI) is allocated to the Class VII assets (goodwill and going concern value).

(iv) In connection with the examination of P's return, the Commissioner, in determining the fair market values of the assets transferred, may disregard the parties' agreement. Assume that the Commissioner correctly determines that the fair market value of the covenant not to compete was $500. Since the allocation of consideration among Class II, III, V, and VI assets results in allocation up to the fair market value limitation, the $600 of unallocated consideration resulting from the Commissioner's redetermination of the value of the covenant not to compete is allocated to Class VII assets (goodwill and going concern value).

(e) *Reporting requirements.*—(1) *Applicable asset acquisitions.*—(i) *In general.*—Unless otherwise excluded from this requirement by the Commissioner, the seller and the purchaser in an applicable asset acquisition each must report information concerning the amount of consideration in the transaction and its allocation among the assets transferred. They also must report information concerning subsequent adjustments to consideration.

(ii) *Time and manner of reporting.*—(A) *In general.*—The seller and the purchaser each must file asset acquisition statements on Form 8594, "Asset Allocation Statement," with their income tax returns or returns of income for the taxable year that includes the first date assets are sold pursuant to an applicable asset acquisition. This reporting requirement applies to all asset acquisitions described in this section. For reporting requirements relating to asset acquisitions occurring before March 16, 2001, as described in paragraph (a)(2) of this section, see the temporary regulations under section 1060 in effect prior to March 16, 2001 (see 26 CFR part 1 revised April 1, 2000).

(B) *Additional reporting requirement.*—When an increase or decrease in consideration is taken into account after the close of the first taxable year that includes the first date assets are sold in an applicable asset acquisition, the seller and the purchaser each must file a supplemental asset acquisition statement on Form 8594 with the income tax return or return of income for the taxable year in which the increase (or decrease) is properly taken into account.

(C) *Election described in § 1.338-6(c)(5).*—(1) *Availability.*—The election described in § 1.338-6(c)(5) is available in respect of an applicable asset acquisition provided that the requirements of that section are satisfied. Such election may be made by the seller, regardless of whether the purchaser also makes the election, and may be made by the purchaser, regardless of whether the seller also makes the election.

(2) *Time and manner of making election.*—The election described in § 1.338-6(c)(5) is made by taking a position on a timely filed original tax return for the taxable year of the applicable asset acquisition that is consistent with having made the election.

(3) *Irrevocability of election.*—The election described in § 1.338-6(c)(5) is irrevocable.

(4) *Effective/applicability date.*—This paragraph (e)(1)(ii)(C) applies to applicable asset acquisitions occurring on or after September 11, 2007. For applicable asset acquisitions occurring before September 11, 2007 and on or after September 15, 2004, see § 1.1060-1T as contained in 26 CFR Part 1 in effect on April 1, 2007. For applicable asset acquisitions occurring before September 15, 2004, see § § 1.338-6 and 1.1060-1 as contained in 26 CFR Part 1 in effect on April 1, 2004.

(2) *Transfers of interests in partnerships.*—For reporting requirements relating to the transfer of a partnership interest, see § 1.755-1(d). [Reg. § 1.1060-1.]

☐ [*T.D.* 8940, 2-12-2001. *Amended by T.D.* 9059, 6-6-2003; *T.D.* 9158, 9-15-2004; *T.D.* 9257, 4-7-2006; *T.D.* 9358, 9-10-2007 *and T.D.* 9377, 1-22-2008 (*corrected* 3-17-2008).]

Changes to Effectuate F.C.C. Policy

[Reg. § 1.1071-1]

§ 1.1071-1. Gain from sale or exchange to effectuate policies of Federal Communications Commission.—(a)(1) At the election of the taxpayer, section 1071 postpones the recognition of the gain upon the sale or exchange of property if the Federal Communications Commission grants the taxpayer a certificate with respect to the ownership and control of radio broadcasting stations which is in accordance with subparagraph (2) of this paragraph. Any taxpayer desiring to obtain the benefits of section 1071 shall file such certificate with the Commissioner of Internal Revenue, or the district director for the internal revenue district in which the income tax return of the taxpayer is required to be filed.

(2)(i) In the case of a sale or exchange before January 1, 1958, the certificate from the Federal Communications Commission must clearly identify the property and show that the sale or exchange is necessary or appropriate to effectuate the policies of such Commission with respect to the ownership and control of radio broadcasting stations.

(ii) In the case of a sale or exchange after December 31, 1957, the certificate from the Federal Communications Commission must clearly identify the property and show that the sale or exchange is necessary or appropriate to effectuate a change in a policy of, or the adoption of a new policy by, such Commission with respect to the ownership and control of radio broadcasting stations.

(3) The certificate shall be accompanied by a detailed statement showing the kind of property, the date of acquisition, the cost or other basis of the property, the date of sale or exchange, the name and address of the transferee, and the amount of money and the fair market value of the property other than money received upon such sale or exchange.

(b) Section 1071 applies only in the case of a sale or exchange made necessary by reason of the Federal Communications Commission's policies as to ownership or control of radio facilities. Section 1071 does not apply in the case of a sale or exchange made necessary as a result of other matters, such as the operation of a broadcasting station in a manner determined by the Commission to be not in the public interest or in violation of Federal or State law.

(c) An election to have the benefits of section 1071 shall be made in the manner prescribed in § 1.1071-4.

(d) For purposes of section 1071, the term "radio broadcasting" includes telecasting. [Reg. § 1.1071-1.]

☐ [*T.D. 6178, 6-1-56. Amended by T.D. 6453, 2-16-60.*]

[Reg. § 1.1071-2]

§ 1.1071-2. Nature and effect of election.—(a) *Alternative elections.*—(1) A taxpayer entitled to the benefits of section 1071 in respect of a sale or exchange of property may elect—

(i) To treat such sale or exchange as an involuntary conversion under the provisions of section 1033; or

(ii) To treat such sale or exchange as an involuntary conversion under the provisions of section 1033, and in addition elect to reduce the basis of property, in accordance with the regulations prescribed in § 1.1071-3, by all or part of the gain that would otherwise be recognized under section 1033; or

(iii) To reduce the basis of property, in accordance with the regulations prescribed in § 1.1071-3, by all or part of the gain realized upon the sale or exchange.

(2) The effect of the provisions of subparagraph (1) of this paragraph is, in general, to grant the taxpayer an election to treat the proceeds of the sale or exchange as the proceeds of an involuntary conversion subject to the provisions of section 1033, and a further election to reduce the basis of certain property owned by the taxpayer by the amount of the gain realized upon the sale or exchange to the extent of that portion of the proceeds which is not treated as the proceeds of an involuntary conversion.

(3) An election in respect to a sale or exchange under section 1071 shall be irrevocable and binding for taxable year in which the sale or exchange takes place and for all subsequent taxable years.

(b) *Application of section 1033.*—(1) If the taxpayer elects, under either paragraph (a)(1)(i) or (ii) of this section, to treat the sale or exchange as an involuntary conversion, the provisions of section 1033, as modified by section 1071, together with the regulations prescribed under such sections, shall be applicable in determining the amount of recognized gain and the basis of property acquired as a result of such sale or exchange. For the purposes of section 1071 and the regulations thereunder, stock of a corporation operating a radio broadcasting station shall be treated as property similar or related in service or use to the property sold or exchanged. Securities of such a corporation other than stock, or securities of a corporation not operating a radio broadcasting station, do not constitute property similar or related in service or use to the property sold or exchanged. If the taxpayer exercises the election referred to in paragraph (a)(1)(i) of this section, the gain realized upon such sale or exchange shall be recognized to the extent of that part of the money received upon the sale or exchange which is not expended in the manner prescribed in section 1033 and the regulations thereunder. If, however, the taxpayer exercises the elections referred to in paragraph (a)(1)(ii) of this section, the amount of the gain which would be recognized, determined in the same manner as in the case of an election under paragraph (a)(1)(i) of this section, shall not be recognized but shall be applied to reduce the basis of property, remaining in the hands of the taxpayer after such sale or exchange or acquired by him during the same taxable year, which is of a character subject to the allowance for depreciation under section 167. Such reduction of basis shall be made in accordance with and under the conditions prescribed by § 1.1071-3.

(2) In the application of section 1033 to determine the recognized gain and the basis of property acquired as a result of a sale or exchange pursuant to an election under paragraph (a)(1)(i) or (ii) of this section, the entire amount of the proceeds of such sale or exchange shall be taken into account.

(c) *Example.*—The application of the provisions of section 1071 may be illustrated by the following example:

Example. A, who makes his return on a calendar year basis, sold in 1954, for $100,000 cash, stock of X Corporation, which operates a radio broadcasting station. A's basis of this stock was $75,000. The sale was certified by the Federal Communications Commission as provided in section 1071. Soon after, in the same taxable year, A used $50,000 of the proceeds of the sale to purchase stock in Y Corporation, which operates a radio broadcasting station. A elected in his 1954 return to treat such sale and purchase as an involuntary conversion subject to the provisions of section 1033. He also elected at the same time to reduce the basis of depreciable property by the amount of the gain that otherwise would be recognized under the provisions of section 1033, as made applicable by section 1071. The sale results in a recognized gain of $25,000 under section 1033. However, this gain is not recognized in this case because the taxpayer elected to reduce the basis of other property by the amount of the gain. This may be shown as follows:

(1) Sale price of X Corporation stock	$100,000
Basis for gain or loss	75,000
Gain realized	25,000
Proceeds of sale	$100,000
Amount expended to replace property sold	50,000
Amount not expended in manner prescribed in section 1033	50,000
Realized gain, recognized under section 1033 (not to exceed the unexpended portion of proceeds of sale)	$25,000
Less: Amount applied as a reduction of basis of depreciable property	25,000
Recognized gain for tax purposes	None

(2) The basis of Y Corporation stock in the hands of A is $50,000, computed in accordance with section 1033 and the regulations prescribed

under that section. The $50,000 basis is computed as follows:

Basis of property sold (converted)	$75,000
Less: Amount of proceeds not expended	50,000
Balance	25,000
Plus amount of gain recognized under section 1033	25,000
Basis of Y Corporation stock in A's hands	50,000

[Reg. § 1.1071-2.]

☐ [*T.D.* 6178, 6-1-56.]

[Reg. § 1.1071-3]

§ 1.1071-3. **Reduction of basis of property pursuant to election under section 1071.**—(a) *General rule.*—(1) In addition to the adjustments provided in section 1016 and other applicable provisions of chapter 1 of the Code, which adjustments are required to be made with respect to the cost or other basis of property, a further adjustment shall be made in the amount of the unrecognized gain under section 1071, if the taxpayer so elects. Such further adjustment shall be made only with respect to the cost or other basis of property which is of a character subject to the allowance for depreciation under section 167 (whether or not used in connection with a broadcasting business), and which remains in the hands of the taxpayer immediately after the sale or exchange in respect of which the election is made, or which is acquired by the taxpayer in the same taxable year in which such sale or exchange occurs. If the property is in the hands of the taxpayer immediately after the sale or exchange, the time of reduction of the basis is the date of the sale or exchange; in all other cases the time of reduction of the basis is the date of acquisition.

(2) The reduction of basis under section 1071 in the amount of the unrecognized gain shall be made in respect of the cost or other basis, as of the time prescribed, of all units of property of the specified character. The cost or other basis of each unit shall be decreased in an amount equal to such proportion of the unrecognized gain as the adjusted basis (for determining gain, determined without regard to this section) of such unit bears to the aggregate of such adjusted bases of all units of such property, but the amount of the decrease shall not be more than the amount of such adjusted basis. If in the application of such rule the adjusted basis of any unit is reduced to zero, the process shall be repeated to reduce the adjusted basis of the remaining units of property by the portion of the unrecognized gain which is not absorbed in the first application of the rule. For such purpose the "adjusted basis" of the remaining units shall be the adjusted basis for determining gain reduced by the amount of the adjustment previously

made under this section. The process shall be repeated until the entire amount of the unrecognized gain has been absorbed.

(3) The application of the provisions of this section may be illustrated by the following example:

Example. Using the facts given in the example set forth in § 1.1071-2(c), except that the taxpayer elects to reduce the basis of depreciable property in accordance with paragraph (a)(1)(iii) of § 1.1071-2, the computation may be illustrated as follows:

Sale price of X Corporation stock	$100,000
Basis for gain or loss	75,000
Realized gain (recognized except for the election under § 1.1071-1)	$25,000

Adjusted basis of other depreciable property in hands of A immediately after sale:

Building	$80,000	
Transmitter	16,000	
Fixtures	4,000	
TOTAL	$100,000	

Computation of reduction:

$$\text{Building} \quad \frac{80,000}{100,000} \times \$25,000 \text{ (gain)} \quad \$20,000$$

$$\text{Transmitter} \quad \frac{16,000}{100,000} \times \$25,000 \quad 4,000$$

$$\text{Fixtures} \quad \frac{4,000}{100,000} \times \$25,000 \quad 1,000$$

Total Reduction	$25,000

New basis of assets:

Building ($80,000 minus $20,000)	$60,000
Transmitter ($16,000 minus $4,000)	12,000
Fixtures ($4,000 minus $1,000)	3,000
Total adjusted basis after reduction under section 1071	$75,000
Realized gain upon sale of X Corporation stock	25,000
Less: Amount applied as a reduction to basis of depreciable property	25,000
Recognized gain for tax purposes	None

(b) *Special cases.*—With the consent of the Commissioner, the taxpayer may, however, have the basis of the various units of property of the class specified in section 1071 and this section adjusted in a manner different from the general rule set forth in paragraph (a) above. Variations from such general rule may, for example, involve adjusting the basis of only certain units of such property. The request for variations from such general rule should be filed by the taxpayer with his return for the taxable year in which he elects to have the basis of property reduced under section 1071. Agreement between the taxpayer and the Commissioner as to any variations from such general rule shall be effective only if incorporated in a closing agreement entered into under the provisions of section 7121. [Reg. § 1.1071-3.]

☐ [T.D. 6178, 6-1-56.]

[Reg. § 1.1071-4]

§ 1.1071-4. Manner of election.—(a) An election under the provisions of section 1071 shall be in the form of a written statement and shall be executed and filed in duplicate. Such statement shall be signed by the taxpayer or his authorized representative. In the case of a corporation, the statement shall be signed with the corporate name, followed by the signature and title of an officer of the corporation empowered to sign for the corporation, and the corporate seal must be affixed. An election under section 1071 to reduce the basis of property and an election under such section to treat the sale or exchange as an involuntary conversion under section 1033 may be exercised independently of each other. An election under section 1071 must be filed with the return for the taxable year in which the sale or exchange occurs. Where practicable, the certificate of the Federal Communications Commission required by § 1.1071-1 should be filed with the election.

(b) If, in pursuance of an election to have the basis of its property adjusted under section 1071, the taxpayer desires to have such basis adjusted in any manner different from the general rule set forth in paragraph (a) of §1.1071-3, the precise method (including allocation of amounts) should be set forth in detail on separate sheets accompanying the election. Consent by the Commissioner to any departure from such general rule shall be effected only by a closing agreement entered into under the provisions of section 7121. [Reg. §1.1071-4.]

☐ [T.D. 6178, 6-1-56.]

Exchanges in Obedience to S.E.C. Orders

[Reg. §1.1081-1]

§1.1081-1. Terms used.—The following terms, when used in this section and §§1.1081-2 to 1.1083-1, inclusive, shall have the meanings assigned to them in section 1083: "Order of the Securities and Exchange Commission"; "registered holding company"; "holding company system"; "associate company"; "majority-owned subsidiary company"; "system group"; "nonexempt property"; and "stock or securities". Any other term used in this section and §§1.1081-2 to 1.1083-1, inclusive, which is defined in the Internal Revenue Code of 1954, shall be given the respective definition contained in such Code. [Reg. §1.1081-1.]

☐ [T.D. 6178, 6-1-56.]

[Reg. §1.1081-2]

§1.1081-2. Purpose and scope of exception.— (a) The general rule is that the entire amount of gain or loss from the sale or exchange of property is to be recognized (see section 1002) and that the entire amount received as a dividend is to be included in gross income. (See sections 61 and 301.) Exceptions to the general rule are provided elsewhere in subchapters C and O, chapter 1 of the Code, one of which is that made by section 1081 with respect to exchanges, sales, and distributions specifically described in section 1081. Section 1081 provides the extent to which gain or loss is not to be recognized on (1) the receipt of a distribution described in section 1081(c)(2), or (2) an exchange or sale, or the receipt of a distribution, made in obedience to an order of the Securities and Exchange Commission, which is issued to effectuate the provisions of section 11(b) of the Public Utility Holding Company Act of 1935 (15 U.S.C. 79k(b)). Section 331 provides that a distribution in liquidation of a corporation shall be treated as an exchange. Such distribution is to be treated as an exchange under the provisions of sections 1081 to 1083, inclusive. The order of the Securities and Exchange Commission must be one requiring or approving action which the Commission finds to be necessary or appropriate to effect a simplification or geographical integration of a particular public utility holding company system. For specific requirements with respect to an order of the Securities and Exchange Commission, see section 1081(f).

(b) The requirements for nonrecognition of gain or loss as provided in section 1081 are precisely stated with respect to the following general types of transactions:

(1) The exchange that is provided for in section 1081(a), in which stock or securities in a registered holding company or a majority-owned subsidiary company are exchanged for stock or securities.

(2) The exchange that is provided for in section 1081(b), in which a registered holding company or an associate company of a registered holding company exchanges property for property.

(3) The distribution that is provided for in section 1081(c)(1), in which stock or securities are distributed to a shareholder in a corporation which is a registered holding company or a majority-owned subsidiary company, or the distribution that is provided for in section 1081(c)(2), in which a corporation distributes to a shareholder, rights to acquire common stock in a second corporation.

(4) The transfer that is provided for in section 1081(d), in which a corporation which is a member of a system group transfers property to another member of the same system group.

Certain rules with respect to the receipt of nonexempt property on an exchange described in section 1081(a) are prescribed in section 1081(e).

(c) These exceptions to the general rule are to be strictly construed. Unless both the purpose and the specific requirements of sections 1081 to 1083, inclusive, are clearly met, the recognition of gain or loss upon the exchange, sale, or distribution will not be postponed under those sections. Moreover, even though a taxable transaction occurs in connection or simultaneously with a realization of gain or loss to which nonrecognition is accorded, nevertheless, nonrecognition will not be accorded to such taxable transaction. In other words, the provisions of section 1081 do not extend in any case to gain or loss other than that realized from and directly attributable to a disposition of property as such, or the receipt of a corporate distribution as such, in an exchange, sale, or distribution specifically described in section 1081.

(d) The application of the provisions of part VI (section 1081 and following), subchapter O, chapter 1 of the Code, is intended to result only in postponing the recognition of gain or loss until a disposition of property is made which is not covered by such provisions, and, in the case of an exchange or sale subject to the provisions of section 1081(b), in the reduction of basis of certain property. The provisions of section 1082 with respect to the continuation of basis and the reduction in basis are designed to effect these results. Although the time of recognition may be shifted, there must be a true reflection of income in all cases, and it is intended that the provisions of such part VI, inclusive, shall not be construed or applied in such a way as to defeat this purpose. [Reg. § 1.1081-2.]

☐ [*T.D.* 6178, 6-1-56.]

[Reg. § 1.1081-3]

§ 1.1081-3. Exchanges of stock or securities solely for stock or securities.—The exchange, without the recognition of gain or loss, that is provided for in section 1081(a) must be one in which stock or securities in a corporation which is a registered holding company or a majority-owned subsidiary company are exchanged solely for stock or securities other than stock or securities which constitute nonexempt property. An exchange is not within the provisions of section 1081(a) unless the stock or securities transferred and those received are stock or securities as defined by section 1083(f). The stock or securities which may be received without the recognition or gain or loss are not limited to stock or securities in the corporation from which they are received. An exchange within the provisions of section 1081(a) may be a transaction between the holder of stock or securities and the corporation which issued the stock or securities. Also the exchange may be made by a holder of stock or securities with an associate company (i.e., a corporation in the same holding company system with the issuing corporation) which is a registered holding company or a majority-owned subsidiary company. In either case, the nonrecognition provisions of section 1081(a) apply only to the holder of the stock or securities. However, the transferee corporation must be acting in obedience to an order of the Securities and Exchange Commission directed to such corporation, if no gain or loss is to be recognized to the holder of the stock or securities who makes the exchange with such corporation. See also section 1081(b), in case the holder of the stock or securities is a registered holding company or an associate company of a registered holding company. An exchange is not within the provisions of section 1081(a) if it is within the provisions of section 1081(d), relating to transfers within a system group. For treatment when nonexempt property is received, see section 1081(e); for further limitations, see section 1081(f). [Reg. § 1.1081-3.]

☐ [*T.D.* 6178, 6-1-56.]

[Reg. § 1.1081-4]

§ 1.1081-4. Exchanges of property for property by corporations.—(a) *Application of section 1081(b).*—Section 1081(b) applies only to the transfers specified therein with respect to which section 1081(d) is inapplicable, and deals only with such transfers if gain is realized upon the sale or other disposition effected by such transfers. If loss is realized section 1081(b) is inapplicable and the application of other provisions of subtitle A of the Code must be determined. See

section 1081(g). If section 1081(b) is applicable, the other provisions of subchapters C and O, chapter 1 of the Code, relating to the nonrecognition of gain are inapplicable, and the conditions under which, and the extent to which, the realized gain is not recognized are set forth in paragraphs (b), (c), (d), (e), and (f) of this section.

(b) *Nonrecognition of gain; no nonexempt proceeds.*—No gain is recognized to a transferor corporation upon the sale or other disposition of property transferred by such transferor corporation in exchange solely for property other than nonexempt property, as defined in section 1083(e), but only if all of the following requirements are satisfied:

(1) The transferor corporation is, under the definition in section 1083(b), a registered holding company or an associate company of a registered holding company;

(2) Such transfer is in obedience to an order of the Securities and Exchange Commission (as defined in section 1083(a)) and such order satisfies the requirements of section 1081(f);

(3) The transferor corporation has filed the required consent to the regulations under section 1082(a)(2) (see paragraph (g) of this section); and

(4) The entire amount of the gain, as determined under section 1001, can be applied in reduction of basis under section 1082(a)(2).

(c) *Nonrecognition of gain; nonexempt proceeds.*—If the transaction would be within the provisions of paragraph (b) of this section if it were not for the fact that the property received in exchange consists in whole or in part of nonexempt property (as defined in section 1083(e)), then no gain is recognized if such nonexempt property, or an amount equal to the fair market value of such nonexempt property at the time of the transfer,

(1) Is expended within the required 24-month period for property other than nonexempt property; or

(2) Is invested within the required 24-month period as a contribution to the capital, or as paid-in surplus, of another corporation;

but only if the expenditure or investment is made

(3) In accordance with an order of the Securities and Exchange Commission (as defined in section 1083(a)) which satisfies the requirements of section 1081(f) and which recites that such expenditure or investment by the transferor corporation is necessary or appropriate to the integration or simplification of the holding company system of which the transferor corporation is a member; and

(4) The required consent, waiver, and bond have been executed and filed. See paragraphs (g) and (h) of this section.

(d) *Recognition of gain in part; insufficient expenditure or investment in case of nonexempt proceeds.*—If the transaction would be within the provisions of paragraph (c) of this section if it were not for the fact that the amount expended or invested is less than the fair market value of the nonexempt property received in exchange, then the gain, if any, is recognized, but in an amount not in excess of the amount by which the fair market value of such nonexempt property at the time of the transfer exceeds the amount so expended and invested.

(e) *Items treated as expenditures for the purpose of paragraphs (c) and (d) of this section.*—For the purposes of paragraphs (c) and (d) of this section, the following are treated as expenditures for property other than nonexempt property:

(1) A distribution in cancellation or redemption (except a distribution having the effect of a dividend) of the whole or a part of the transferor's own stock (not acquired on the transfer);

(2) A payment in complete or partial retirement or cancellation of securities representing indebtedness of the transferor or a complete or partial retirement or cancellation of such securities which is a part of the consideration for the transfer; and

(3) If, on the transfer, a liability of the transferor is assumed, or property of the transferor is transferred subject to a liability, the amount of such liability.

(f) *Recognition of gain in part; inability to reduce basis.*—If the transaction would be within the provisions of paragraph (b) or (c) of this section, if it were not for the fact that an amount of gain cannot be applied in reduction of basis under section 1082(a)(2), then the gain, if any, is recognized, but in an amount not in excess of the amount which cannot be so applied in reduction of basis. If the transaction would be within the provisions of paragraph (d) of this section, if it were not for the fact that an amount of gain cannot be applied in reduction of basis under section 1082(a)(2), then the gain, if any, is recognized, but in an amount not in excess of the aggregate of—

(1) The amount of gain which would be recognized under paragraph (d) of this section if there were no inability to reduce basis under section 1082(a)(2); and

(2) The amount of gain which cannot be applied in reduction of basis under section 1082(a)(2).

(g) *Consent to regulations under section 1082(a)(2).*—To be entitled to the benefits of the provisions of section 1081(b), a corporation must file with its return for the taxable year in which the transfer occurs a consent to have the basis of its property adjusted under section 1082(a)(2) (see § 1.1082-3), in accordance with the provisions of the regulations in effect at the time of filing of the return for the taxable year in which the transfer occurs. Such consent shall be made

on Form 982 in accordance with these regulations and instructions on the form or issued therewith.

(h) *Requirements with respect to expenditure or investment.*—If the full amount of the expenditure or investment required for the application of paragraph (c) of this section has not been made by the close of the taxable year in which such transfer occurred, the taxpayer shall file with the return for such year an application for the benefit of the 24-month period for expenditure and investment, reciting the nature and time of the proposed expenditure or investment. When requested by the district director, the taxpayer shall execute and file (at such time and in such form) such waiver of the statute of limitations with respect to the assessment of deficiencies (for the taxable year of the transfer and for all succeeding taxable years in any of which falls any part of the period beginning with the date of the transfer and ending 24 months thereafter) as the district director may specify, and such bond with such surety as the district director may require, in an amount not in excess of double the estimated maximum income tax which would be payable if the corporation does not make the required expenditure or investment within the required 24-month period. [Reg. § 1.1081-4.]

☐ [*T.D. 6178, 6-1-56. Amended by T.D. 6751, 8-5-64 and T.D. 7517, 11-11-77.*]

[Reg. § 1.1081-5]

§ 1.1081-5. Distribution solely of stock or securities.—(a) *In general.*—If, without any surrender of his stock or securities as defined in section 1083(f), a shareholder in a corporation which is a registered holding company or a majority-owned subsidiary company receives stock or securities in such corporation or owned by such corporation, no gain to the shareholder will be recognized with respect to the stock or securities received by such shareholder which do not constitute nonexempt property, if the distribution to such shareholder is made by the distributing corporation in obedience to an order of the Securities and Exchange Commission directed to such corporation. A distribution is not within the provisions of section 1081(c)(1) if it is within the provisions of section 1081(d), relating to transfers within a system group. A distribution is also not within the provisions of section 1081(c)(1) if it involves a surrender by the shareholder of stock or securities or a transfer by the shareholder of property in exchange for the stock or securities received by the shareholder. For further limitations, see section 1081(f).

(b) *Special rule.*—(1) If there is distributed to a shareholder in a corporation rights to acquire common stock in a second corporation, no gain to the shareholder from the receipt of the rights shall be recognized, but only if all the following requirements are met:

(i) The rights are received by the shareholder without the surrender by the shareholder of any stock in the distributing corporation,

(ii) Such distribution is in accordance with an arrangement forming a ground for an order of the Securities and Exchange Commission issued pursuant to section 3 of the Public Utility Holding Company Act of 1935 (15 U.S.C. 79c) that the distributing corporation is exempt from any provision or provisions of such act, and

(iii) Before January 1, 1958, the distributing corporation disposes of all the common stock in the second corporation which it owns.

(2) The distributing corporation shall, as soon as practicable, notify the district director in whose district the corporation's income tax return and supporting data was filed (see paragraph (g) of § 1.1081-11), as to whether or not requirement of subparagraph (1)(iii) of this paragraph has been met. If such requirement has not been met, the periods of limitation (sections 6501 and 6502) with respect to any deficiency, including interest and additions to the tax, resulting solely from the receipt of such rights to acquire stock, shall include one year immediately following the date of such notification; and assessment and collection shall be made notwithstanding any provisions of law or rule of law which would otherwise prevent such assessment and collection. [Reg. § 1.1081-5.]

☐ [T.D. 6178, 6-1-56.]

[Reg. § 1.1081-6]

§ 1.1081-6. Transfers within system group.—
(a) The nonrecognition of gain or loss provided for in section 1081(d)(1) is applicable to an exchange of property for other property (including money and other nonexempt property) between corporations which are all members of the same system group. The term "system group" is defined in section 1083(d).

(b) Section 1081(d)(1) also provides for nonrecognition of gain to a corporation which is a member of a system group if property (including money or other nonexempt property) is distributed to such corporation as a shareholder in a corporation which is a member of the same system group, without the surrender by such shareholder of stock or securities in the distributing corporation.

(c) As stated in § 1.1081-2, nonrecognition of gain or loss will not be accorded to a transaction not clearly provided for in part VI (section 1081 and following), subchapter O, chapter 1 of the Code, even though such transaction occurs simultaneously or in connection with an exchange, sale, or distribution to which nonrecognition is specifically accorded. Therefore, nonrecognition will not be accorded to any gain or loss realized from the discharge, or the removal of the burden, of the pecuniary obligations of a member of a system group, even though such obligations are acquired upon a transfer or distribution specifically described in section 1081(d)(1); but the fact that the acquisition of such obligations was upon a transfer or distribution specifically described in section 1081(d)(1) will, because of the basis provisions of section 1082(d), affect the cost to the member of such discharge or its equivalent. Thus, section 1081(d)(1) does not provide for the nonrecognition of any gain or loss realized from the discharge of the indebtedness of a member of a system group as the result of the acquisition in exchange, sale, or distribution of its own bonds, notes, or other evidences of indebtedness which were acquired by another member of the same system group for a consideration less or more than the issuing price thereof (with proper adjustments for amortization of premiums or discounts).

(d) The provisions of paragraph (c) of this section may be illustrated by the following example:

Example. Suppose that the A Corporation and the B Corporation are both members of the same system group; that the A Corporation holds at a cost of $900 a bond issued by the B Corporation at par, $1,000; and that the A Corporation and the B Corporation enter into an exchange subject to the provisions of section 1081(d)(1) in which the $1,000 bond of the B Corporation is transferred from the A Corporation to the B Corporation. The $900 basis reflecting the cost to the A Corporation which would have been the basis available to the B Corporation if the property transferred to it had been something other than its own securities (see § 1.1082-6) will, in this type of transaction, reflect the cost to the B Corporation of effecting a retirement of its own $1,000 bond. The $100 gain of the B Corporation reflected in the retirement will therefore be recognized.

(e) No exchange or distribution may be made without the recognition of gain or loss as provided for in section 1081(d)(1), unless all the corporations which are parties to such exchange or distribution are acting in obedience to an order of the Securities and Exchange Commission. If an exchange or distribution is within the provisions of section 1081(d)(1) and also may be considered to be within some other provisions of section 1081, it shall be considered that only the provisions of section 1081(d)(1) apply and that the nonrecognition of gain or loss upon such exchange or distribution is by virtue of that section. [Reg. § 1.1081-6.]

☐ [T.D. 6178, 6-1-56.]

[Reg. § 1.1081-7]

§ 1.1081-7. Sale of stock or securities received upon exchange by members of system group.—
(a) Section 1081(d)(2) provides that to the extent that property received upon an exchange by corporations which are members of the same system group consists of stock or securities issued by the corporation from which such property was received, such stock or securities may, under certain specifically described circum-

stances, be sold to a party not a member of the system group, without the recognition of gain or loss to the selling corporation. The nonrecognition of gain or loss is limited, in the case of stock, to a sale of stock which is preferred as to both dividends and assets. The stock or securities must have been received upon an exchange with respect to which section 1081(d)(1) operated to prevent recognition of gain or loss to any party to the exchange. Nonrecognition of gain or loss upon the sale of such stock or securities is permitted only if the proceeds derived from the sale are applied in retirement or cancellation of stock or securities of the selling corporation which were outstanding at the time the exchange was made. It is also essential to nonrecognition of gain or loss upon the sale that both the sale of the stock or securities and the application of the proceeds derived therefrom be made in obedience to an order of the Securities and Exchange Commission. If any part of the proceeds derived from the sale is not applied in making the required retirement or cancellation of stock or securities and if the sale is otherwise within the provisions of section 1081(d)(2), the gain resulting from the sale shall be recognized, but in an amount not in excess of the proceeds which are not so applied. In any event, if the proceeds derived from the sale of the stock or securities exceed the fair market value of such stock or securities at the time of the exchange through which they were acquired by the selling corporation, the gain resulting from the sale is to be recognized to the extent of such excess. Section 1081(d)(2) does not provide for the nonrecognition of any gain resulting from the retirement of bonds, notes, or other evidences of indebtedness for a consideration less than the issuing price thereof. Also, that section does not provide for the nonrecognition of gain or loss upon the sale of any stock or securities received upon a distribution or otherwise than upon an exchange.

(b) The application of paragraph (a) of this section may be illustrated by the following example:

Example. The X Corporation and the Y Corporation, both of which make their income tax returns on a calendar year basis, are members of the same system group. As part of an exchange to which section 1081(d)(1) is applicable the Y Corporation on June 1, 1954, issued to the X Corporation 1,000 shares of class A stock, preferred as to both dividends and assets. The fair market value of such stock at the time of issuance was $90,000 and its basis to the X Corporation was $75,000. On December 1, 1954, in obedience to an appropriate order of the Securities and Exchange Commission, the X Corporation sells all of such stock to the public for $100,000 and applies $95,000 of this amount to the retirement of its own bonds, which are outstanding on June 1, 1954. The remaining $5,000 is not used to retire any of the X Corporation's stock or securities. Of the total gain of $25,000 realized on the disposition of the Y Corporation

stock, only $10,000 is recognized (the difference between the fair market value of the stock when acquired and the amount for which it was sold), since such amount is greater than the portion ($5,000) of the proceeds not applied to the retirement of the X Corporation's stock or securities. If in this example the stock acquired by the X Corporation had not been stock of the Y Corporation issued to the X Corporation or if it had been stock not preferred as to both dividends and assets, the full amount of the gain ($25,000) realized upon its disposition would have been recognized, regardless of what was done with the proceeds. [Reg. § 1.1081-7.]

☐ [*T.D.* 6178, 6-1-56.]

[Reg. § 1.1081-8]

§ 1.1081-8. Exchanges in which money or other nonexempt property is received.— (a) Under section 1081(e)(1), if in any exchange (not within any of the provisions of section 1081(d)), in which stock or securities in a corporation which is a registered holding company or a majority-owned subsidiary are exchanged for stock or securities as provided for in section 1081(a), there is received by the taxpayer money or other nonexempt property (in addition to property permitted to be received without recognition of gain), then—

(1) The gain, if any, to the taxpayer is to be recognized in an amount not in excess of the sum of the money and the fair market value of the other nonexempt property, but

(2) The loss, if any, to the taxpayer from such an exchange is not to be recognized to any extent.

(b) If money or other nonexempt property is received from a corporation in an exchange described in paragraph (a) of this section and if the distribution of such money or other nonexempt property by or on behalf of such corporation has the effect of the distribution of a taxable dividend, then, as provided in section 1081(e)(2), there shall be taxed to each distributee (1) as a dividend, such an amount of the gain recognized on the exchange as is not in excess of the distributee's ratable share of the undistributed earnings and profits of the corporation accumulated after February 28, 1913, and (2) the remainder of the gain so recognized shall be taxed as a gain from the exchange of property. [Reg. § 1.1081-8.]

☐ [*T.D.* 6178, 6-1-56.]

[Reg. § 1.1081-9]

§ 1.1081-9. Requirements with respect to order of Securities and Exchange Commission.— The term "order of the Securities and Exchange Commission" is defined in section 1083(a). In addition to the requirements specified in that definition, section 1081(f) provides that, except in the case of a distribution described in section 1081(c)(2), the provisions of section 1081 shall not apply to an exchange, expenditure, investment, distribution, or sale unless each of the following requirements is met:

(a) The order of the Securities and Exchange Commission must recite that the exchange, expenditure, investment, distribution, or sale is necessary or appropriate to effectuate the provisions of section 11(b) of the Public Utility Holding Company Act of 1935 (15 U.S.C. 79k(b)).

(b) The order shall specify and itemize the stocks and securities and other property (including money) which are ordered to be acquired, transferred, received, or sold upon such exchange, acquisition, expenditure, distribution, or sale and, in the case of an investment, the investment to be made, so as clearly to identify such property.

(c) The exchange, acquisition, expenditure, investment, distribution, or sale shall be made in obedience to such order and shall be completed within the time prescribed in such order.

These requirements were not designed merely to simplify the administration of the provisions of section 1081, and they are not to be considered as pertaining only to administrative matters. Each one of the three requirements is essential and must be met if gain or loss is not to be recognized from the transaction. [Reg. § 1.1081-9.]

☐ [T.D. 6178, 6-1-56.]

[Reg. § 1.1081-10]

§ 1.1081-10. Nonapplication of other provisions of the Internal Revenue Code of 1954.— The effect of section 1081(g) is that an exchange, sale, or distribution which is within section 1081 shall, with respect to the nonrecognition of gain or loss and the determination of basis, be governed only by the provisions of part VI (section 1081 and following), subchapter O, chapter 1 of the Code, the purpose being to prevent overlapping of the provisions of such sections and other provisions of subtitle A of the Code. In other words, if by virtue of section 1081 any portion of a person's gain or loss on any particular exchange, sale, or distribution is not to be recognized, then the gain or loss of such person shall be nonrecognized only to the extent provided in section 1081, regardless of what the result might have been if part VI (section 1081 and following), subchapter O, chapter 1 of the Code, had not been enacted; and similarly, the basis in the hands of such person of the property received by him in such transaction shall be the basis provided by section 1082, regardless of what the basis of such property might have been under section 1011 if such part VI had not been enacted. On the other hand, if section 1081 does not provide for the nonrecognition of any portion of a person's gain or loss (whether or not such person is another party to the same transaction referred to above), then the gain or loss of such person shall be recognized or nonrecognized to the extent provided for by other provisions of subtitle A of the Code as if such part VI had not been enacted; and similarly, the basis in his hands of the property received by him in such transaction shall be the basis provided by other provisions of subtitle A of the Code as if such part VI had not been enacted. [Reg. § 1.1081-10.]

☐ [T.D. 6178, 6-1-56.]

[Reg. § 1.1081-11]

§ 1.1081-11. Records to be kept and information to be filed with returns.—(a) *Distributions and exchanges; significant holders of stock or securities.*—Every significant holder must include a statement entitled, "STATEMENT PURSUANT TO § 1.1081-11(a) BY [INSERT NAME AND TAXPAYER IDENTIFICATION NUMBER (IF ANY) OF TAXPAYER], A SIGNIFICANT HOLDER," on or with such holder's income tax return for the taxable year in which the distribution or exchange occurs. If a significant holder is a controlled foreign corporation (within the meaning of section 957), each United States shareholder (within the meaning of section 951(b)) with respect thereto must include this statement on or with its return. The statement must include—

(1) The name and employer identification number (if any) of the corporation from which the stock, securities, or other property (including money) was received by such significant holder;

(2) The aggregate basis, determined immediately before the exchange, of any stock or securities transferred by the significant holder in the exchange, and the aggregate fair market value, determined immediately before the distribution or exchange, of the stock, securities or other property (including money) received by the significant holder in the distribution or exchange; and

(3) The date of the distribution or exchange.

(b) *Distributions and exchanges; corporations subject to Commission orders.*—Each corporation which is a party to a distribution or exchange made pursuant to an order of the Commission must include on or with its income tax return for its taxable year in which the distribution or exchange takes place a statement entitled, "STATEMENT PURSUANT TO § 1.1081-11(b) BY [INSERT NAME AND EMPLOYER IDENTIFICATION NUMBER (IF ANY) OF TAXPAYER], A DISTRIBUTING OR EXCHANGING CORPORATION." If the distributing or exchanging corporation is a controlled foreign corporation (within the meaning of section 957), each United States shareholder (within the meaning of section 951(b)) with respect thereto must include this statement on or with its return. The statement must include—

(1) The date and control number of the Commission order, pursuant to which the distribution or exchange was made;

(2) The names and taxpayer identification numbers (if any) of the significant holders;

(3) The aggregate fair market value and basis, determined immediately before the distribu-

tion or exchange, of the stock, securities, or other property (including money) transferred in the distribution or exchange; and

(4) The date of the distribution or exchange.

(c) *Sales by members of system groups.*—Each system group member must include a statement entitled, "STATEMENT PURSUANT TO §1.1081-11(c) BY [INSERT NAME AND EMPLOYER IDENTIFICATION NUMBER (IF ANY) OF TAXPAYER], A SYSTEM GROUP MEMBER," on or with its income tax return for the taxable year in which the sale is made. If any system group member is a controlled foreign corporation (within the meaning of section 957), each United States shareholder (within the meaning of section 951(b)) with respect thereto must include this statement on or with its return. The statement must include—

(1) The dates and control numbers of all relevant Commission orders;

(2) The aggregate fair market value and basis, determined immediately before the sale, of all stock or securities sold; and

(3) The date of the sale.

(d) *Definitions.*—(1) For purposes of this section, Commission means the Securities and Exchange Commission.

(2) For purposes of this section, significant holder means a person that receives stock or securities from a corporation (the distributing corporation) pursuant to an order of the Commission, if, immediately before the transaction, such person—

(i) In the case of stock—

(A) Owned at least five percent (by vote or value) of the total outstanding stock of the distributing corporation if the stock owned by such person is publicly traded, or

(B) Owned at least one percent (by vote or value) of the total outstanding stock of the distributing corporation if the stock owned by such person is not publicly traded; or

(ii) In the case of securities, owned securities of the distributing corporation with a basis of $1,000,000 or more.

(3) Publicly traded stock means stock that is listed on—

(i) A national securities exchange registered under section 6 of the Securities Exchange Act of 1934 (15 U.S.C. 78f); or

(ii) An interdealer quotation system sponsored by a national securities association registered under section 15A of the Securities Exchange Act of 1934 (15 U.S.C. 78o-3).

(4) For purposes of paragraph (b) of this section, exchange means exchange, expenditure, or investment.

(5) For purposes of paragraph (c) of this section, system group member means each corporation which is a member of a system group and which, pursuant to an order of the Commission, sells stock or securities received upon an exchange (pursuant to an order of the Commission) and applies the proceeds derived therefrom in retirement or cancellation of its own stock or securities.

(e) *Substantiation information.*—Under §1.6001-1(e), taxpayers are required to retain their permanent records and make such records available to any authorized Internal Revenue Service officers and employees. In connection with the distribution or exchange described in this section, these records should specifically include information regarding the amount, basis, and fair market value of all property distributed or exchanged, and relevant facts regarding any liabilities assumed or extinguished as part of such distribution or exchange.

(f) *Effective/applicability date.*—This section applies to any taxable year beginning on or after May 30, 2006. However, taxpayers may apply this section to any original Federal income tax return (including any amended return filed on or before the due date (including extensions) of such original return) timely filed on or after May 30, 2006. For taxable years beginning before May 30, 2006, see §1.1081-11 as contained in 26 CFR part 1 in effect on April 1, 2006. [Reg. §1.1081-11.]

☐ [*T.D.* 9329, 6-13-2007.]

[Reg. §1.1082-1]

§1.1082-1. Basis for determining gain or loss.—(a) For determining the basis of property acquired in a taxable year beginning before January 1, 1942, in any manner described in section 372 of the Internal Revenue Code of 1939 prior to its amendment by the Revenue Act of 1942 (56 Stat. 798), see such section (before its amendment by such Act).

(b) If the property was acquired in a taxable year beginning after December 31, 1941, in any manner described in section 1082 (other than subsection (a)(2)), or section 372 (other than subsection (a)(2)) of the Internal Revenue Code of 1939 after its amendments, the basis shall be that prescribed in section 1082 with respect to such property. However, in the case of property acquired in a transaction described in section 1081(c)(2), this paragraph is applicable only if the property was acquired in a distribution made in a taxable year subject to the Internal Revenue Code of 1954.

(c) Section 1082 makes provisions with respect to the basis of property acquired in a transfer in connection with which the recognition of gain or loss is prohibited by the provisions of section 1081 with respect to the whole or any part of the property received. In general, and except as provided in §1.1082-3, it is intended that the basis for determining gain or loss pertaining to the property prior to its transfer, as well as the basis for determining the amount of depreciation or depletion deductible and the amount of earnings or profits available for distribution, shall continue notwithstanding the nontaxable conversion of the asset in form or its change in ownership. The continuance of the basis may be reflected in a shift thereof from one asset to another in the hands of the same owner, or in its transfer with the property from one owner into the hands of another. See also § 1.1081-2. [Reg. § 1.1082-1.]

☐ [T.D. 6178, 6-1-56.]

[Reg. § 1.1082-2]

§ 1.1082-2. Basis of property acquired upon exchanges under section 1081(a) or (e).—(a) In the case of an exchange of stock or securities for stock or securities as described in section 1081(a), if no part of the gain or loss upon such exchange was recognized under section 1081, the basis of the property acquired is the same as the basis of the property transferred by the taxpayer with proper adjustments to the date of the exchange.

(b) If, in an exchange of stock or securities as described in section 1081(a), gain to the taxpayer was recognized under section 1081(e) on account of the receipt of money, the basis of the property acquired is the basis of the property transferred (adjusted to the date of the exchange), decreased by the amount of money received and increased by the amount of gain recognized upon the exchange. If, upon such exchange, there were received by the taxpayer money and other nonexempt property (not permitted to be received without the recognition of gain), and gain from the transaction was recognized under section 1081(e), the basis (adjusted to the date of the exchange) of the property transferred by the taxpayer, decreased by the amount of money received and increased by the amount of gain recognized, must be apportioned to and is the basis of the properties (other than money) received on the exchange. For the purpose of the allocation of such basis to the properties received, there must be assigned to the nonexempt property (other than money) an amount equivalent to its fair market value at the date of the exchange.

(c) Section 1081(e) provides that no loss may be recognized on an exchange of stock or securities for stock or securities as described in section 1081(a), although the taxpayer receives money or other nonexempt property from the transaction. However, the basis of the property (other than money) received by the taxpayer is the basis (adjusted to the date of the exchange) of the property transferred, decreased by the amount of money received. This basis must be apportioned to the properties received, and for this purpose there must be allocated to the nonexempt property (other than money) an amount of such basis equivalent to the fair market value of such nonexempt property at the date of the exchange.

(d) Section 1082(a) does not apply in ascertaining the basis of property acquired by a corporation by the issuance of its stock or securities as the consideration in whole or in part for the transfer of the property to it. For the rule in such cases, see section 1082(b).

(e) For purposes of this section, any reference to section 1081 shall be deemed to include a reference to corresponding provisions of prior internal revenue laws. [Reg. § 1.1082-2.]

☐ [T.D. 6178, 6-1-56.]

[Reg. § 1.1082-3]

§ 1.1082-3. Reduction of basis of property by reason of gain not recognized under section 1081(b).—(a) *Introductory.*—In addition to the adjustments provided in section 1016 and other applicable provisions of chapter 1 of the Code, and the regulations relating thereto, which are required to be made with respect to the cost or other basis of property, section 1082(a)(2) provides that a further adjustment shall be made in any case in which there shall have been a nonrecognition of gain under section 1081(b). Such further adjustment shall be made with respect to the basis of the property in the hands of the transferor immediately after the transfer and of the property acquired within 24 months after such transfer by an expenditure or investment to which section 1081(b) relates, and on account of which expenditure or investment gain is not recognized. If the property is in the hands of the transferor immediately after the transfer, the time of reduction is the day of the transfer; in all other cases the time of reduction is the date of acquisition. The effect of applying an amount in reduction of basis of property under section 1081(b) is to reduce by such amount the basis for determining gain upon sale or other disposition, the basis for determining loss upon sale or other disposition, the basis for depreciation and for depletion, and any other amount which the Code prescribes shall be the same as any of such bases. For the purposes of the application of an amount in reduction of basis under section 1081(b), property is not considered as having a basis capable of reduction if—

(1) It is money, or

(2) If its adjusted basis for determining gain at the time the reduction is to be made is zero, or becomes zero at any time in the application of section 1081(b).

(b) *General rule.*—(1) Section 1082(a)(2) sets forth seven categories of property, the basis of which for determining gain or loss shall be reduced in the order stated.

(2) If any of the property in the first category has a basis capable of reduction, the reduction must first be made before applying an amount in reduction of the basis of any property in the second or in a succeeding category, to each of which in turn a similar rule is applied.

(3) In the application of the rule to each category, the amount of the gain not recognized shall be applied to reduce the cost or other basis of all the property in the category as follows: The cost or other basis (at the time immediately after

Reg. § 1.1082-3(b)(3)

the transfer or, if the property is not then held but is thereafter acquired, at the time of such acquisition) of each unit of property in the first category shall be decreased (but the amount of the decrease shall not be more than the amount of the adjusted basis at such time for determining gain, determined without regard to this section) in an amount equal to such proportion of the unrecognized gain as the adjusted basis (for determining gain, determined without regard to this section) at such time of each unit of property of the taxpayer in that category bears to the aggregate of the adjusted basis (for determining gain, computed without regard to this section) at such time of all the property of the taxpayer in that category. When such adjusted basis of the property in the first category has been thus reduced to zero, a similar rule shall be applied, with respect to the portion of such gain which is unabsorbed in such reduction of the basis of the property in such category, in reducing the basis of property in the second category. A similar rule with respect to the remaining unabsorbed gain shall be applied in reducing the basis of the property in the next succeeding category.

(c) *Special cases.*—(1) With the consent of the Commissioner, the taxpayer may, however, have the basis of the various units of property within a particular category specified in section 1082(a)(2) adjusted in a manner different from the general rule set forth in paragraph (b) of this section. Variations from such general rule may, for example, involve adjusting the basis of only certain units of the taxpayer's property within a given category. A request for variations from the general rule should be filed by the taxpayer with its income tax return for the taxable year in which the transfer of property has occurred.

(2) Agreement between the taxpayer and the Commissioner as to any variations from such general rule shall be effective only if incorporated in a closing agreement entered into under the provisions of section 7121. If no such agreement is entered into by the taxpayer and the Commissioner, then the consent filed on Form 982 shall (except as otherwise provided in this subparagraph) be deemed to be a consent to the application of such general rule, and such general rule shall apply in the determination of the basis of the taxpayer's property. If, however, the taxpayer specifically states on such form that it does not consent to the application of the general rule, then, in the absence of a closing agreement, the document filed shall not be deemed a consent within the meaning of section 1081(b)(4). [Reg. § 1.1082-3.]

☐ [*T.D.* 6178, 6-1-56. *Amended by T.D.* 7517, 11-11-77.]

[Reg. § 1.1082-4]

§ 1.1082-4. Basis of property acquired by corporation under section 1081(a), 1081(b) or 1081(e) as contribution of capital or surplus, or in consideration for its own stock or securi-

ties.—If, in connection with an exchange of stock or securities for stock or securities as described in section 1081(a), or an exchange of property for property as described in section 1081(b), or an exchange as described in section 1081(e), property is acquired by a corporation by the issuance of its stock or securities, the basis of such property shall be determined under section 1082(b). If the corporation issued its stock or securities as part or sole consideration for the property acquired, the basis of the property in the hands of the acquiring corporation is the basis (adjusted to the date of the exchange) which the property would have had in the hands of the transferor if the transfer had not been made, increased in the amount of gain or decreased in the amount of loss recognized under section 1081 to the transferor upon the transfer. If any property is acquired by a corporation from a shareholder as paid-in surplus, or from any person as a contribution to capital, the basis of the property to the corporation is the basis (adjusted to the date of acquisition) of the property in the hands of the transferor. [Reg. § 1.1082-4.]

☐ [*T.D.* 6178, 6-1-56.]

[Reg. § 1.1082-5]

§ 1.1082-5. Basis of property acquired by shareholder upon tax-free distribution under section 1081(c)(1) or (2).—(a) *Stock or securities.*—If there was distributed to a shareholder in a corporation which is a registered holding company or a majority-owned subsidiary company, stock or securities (other than stock or securities which are nonexempt property), and if by virtue of section 1081(c)(1) no gain was recognized to the shareholder upon such distribution, then the basis of the stock in respect of which the distribution was made must be apportioned between such stock and the stock or securities so distributed to the shareholder. The basis of the old shares and the stock or securities received upon the distribution shall be determined in accordance with the following rules:

(1) If the stock or securities received upon the distribution consist solely of stock in the distributing corporation and the stock received is all of substantially the same character and preference as the stock in respect of which the distribution is made, the basis of each share will be the quotient of the cost or other basis of the old shares of stock divided by the total number of the old and the new shares.

(2) If the stock or securities received upon the distribution are in whole or in part stock in a corporation other than the distributing corporation, or are in whole or in part stock of a character or preference materially different from the stock in respect of which the distribution is made, or if the distribution consists in whole or in part of securities other than stock, the cost or other basis of the stock in respect of which the distribution is made shall be apportioned between such stock and the stock or securities dis-

Exchanges in Obedience to S.E.C. Orders
52,077
See p. 20,601 for regulations not amended to reflect law changes

tributed in proportion, as nearly as may be, to the respective values of each class of stock or security, old and new, at the time of such distribution, and the basis of each share of stock or unit of security will be the quotient of the cost or other basis of the class of stock or security to which such share or unit belongs, divided by the number of shares or units in the class. Within the meaning of this subparagraph, stocks or securities in one corporation are different in class from stocks or securities in another corporation, and, in general, any material difference in character or preference or terms sufficient to distinguish one stock or security from another stock or security, so that different values may properly be assigned thereto, will constitute a difference in class.

(b) *Stock rights.*—If there was distributed to a shareholder in a corporation rights to acquire common stock in a second corporation, and if by virtue of section 1081(c)(2) no gain was recognized to the shareholder upon such distribution, then the basis of the stock in respect of which the distribution was made must be apportioned between such stock and the stock rights so distributed to the shareholder. The basis of such stock and the stock rights received upon the distribution shall be determined in accordance with the following:

(1) The cost or other basis of the stock in respect of which the distribution is made shall be apportioned between such stock and the stock rights distributed, in proportion to the respective values thereof at the time the rights are issued.

(2) The basis for determining gain or loss from the sale of a right, or from the sale of a share of stock in respect of which the distribution is made, will be the quotient of the cost or other basis, properly adjusted, assigned to the rights or the stock, divided, as the case may be, by the number of rights acquired or by the number of shares of such stock held.

(c) *Cross reference.*—As to the basis of stock or securities distributed by one member of a system group to another member of the same system group, see § 1.1082-6. [Reg. § 1.1082-5.]

☐ [*T.D. 6178, 6-1-56.*]

[Reg. § 1.1082-6]

§ 1.1082-6. Basis of property acquired under section 1081(d) in transactions between corporations of the same system group.—(a) If property was acquired by a corporation which is a member of a system group, from a corporation which is a member of the same system group, upon a transfer or distribution described in section 1081(d)(1), then as a general rule the basis of such property in the hands of the acquiring corporation is the basis which such property would have had in the hands of the transferor if the transfer or distribution had not been made. Except as otherwise indicated in this section, this rule will apply equally to cases in which the

consideration for the property acquired consists of stock or securities, money, and other property, or any of them, but it is contemplated that an ultimate true reflection of income will be obtained in all cases, notwithstanding any peculiarities in form which the various transactions may assume. See the example in § 1.1081-6.

(b) An exception to the general rule is provided for in case the property acquired consists of stock or securities issued by the corporation from which such stock or securities were received. If such stock or securities were the sole consideration for the property transferred to the corporation issuing such stock or securities, then the basis of the stock or securities shall be (1) the same as the basis (adjusted to the time of the transfer) of the property transferred for such stock or securities, or (2) the fair market value of such stock or securities at the time of their receipt, whichever is the lower. If such stock or securities constituted only part consideration for the property transferred to the corporation issuing such stock or securities, then the basis shall be an amount which bears the same ratio to the basis of the property transferred as the fair market value of such stock or securities on their receipt bears to the total fair market value of the entire consideration received, except that the fair market value of such stock or securities at the time of their receipt shall be the basis therefor, if such value is lower than such amount.

(c) The application of paragraph (b) of this section may be illustrated by the following examples:

Example (1). Suppose the A Corporation has property with an adjusted basis of $600,000 and, in an exchange in which section 1081(d)(1) is applicable, transfers such property to the B Corporation in exchange for a total consideration of $1,000,000, consisting of (1) cash in the amount of $100,000, (2) tangible property having a fair market value of $400,000 and an adjusted basis in the hands of the B Corporation of $300,000, and (3) stock or securities issued by the B Corporation with a par value and a fair market value as of the date of their receipt in the amount of $500,000. The basis to the B Corporation of the property received by it is $600,000, which is the adjusted basis of such property in the hands of the A Corporation. The basis to the A Corporation of the assets (other than cash) received by it is as follows: Tangible property, $300,000, the adjusted basis of such property to the B Corporation, the former owner; stock or securities issued by the B Corporation, $300,000, an amount equal to 500,000/1,000,000ths of $600,000.

Example (2). Suppose that in example (1) the property of the A Corporation transferred to the B Corporation had an adjusted basis of $1,100,000 instead of $600,000, and that all other factors in the example remain the same. In such case, the basis to the A Corporation of the stock or securities in the B Corporation is $500,000, which was the fair market value of such stock or securities at the time of their receipt by the A

Corporation, because this amount is less than the amount established as 500,000/1,000,000ths of $1,100,000 or $550,000. [Reg. § 1.1082-6.]

☐ [*T.D.* 6178, 6-1-56.]

[Reg. § 1.1083-1]

§ 1.1083-1. Definitions.—(a) *Order of the Securities and Exchange Commission.*—(1) An order of the Securities and Exchange Commission as defined in section 1083(a) must be issued after May 28, 1938 (the date of the enactment of the Revenue Act of 1938 (52 Stat. 447)), and must be issued under the authority of section 11(b) or 11(e) of the Public Utility Holding Company Act of 1935 (15 U.S.C. 79k(b), (e)), to effectuate the provisions of section 11(b) of such Act. In all cases the order must become or have become final in accordance with law; i.e., it must be valid, outstanding, and not subject to further appeal. See further sections 1083(a) and 1081(f).

(2) Section 11(b) of the Public Utility Holding Company Act of 1935 provides:

Section 11. *Simplification of holding company systems.* * * *

(b) It shall be the duty of the Commission, as soon as practicable after January 1, 1938:

(1) To require by order, after notice and opportunity for hearing, that each registered holding company, and each subsidiary company thereof, shall take such action as the Commission shall find necessary to limit the operations of the holding-company system of which such company is a part to a single integrated public-utility system, and to such other businesses as are reasonably incidental, or economically necessary or appropriate to the operations of such integrated public-utility system: *Provided, however,* That the Commission shall permit a registered holding company to continue to control one or more additional integrated public-utility systems, if, after notice and opportunity for hearing, it finds that—

(A) Each of such additional systems cannot be operated as an independent system without the loss of substantial economies which can be secured by the retention of control by such holding company of such system;

(B) All of such additonal systems are located in one State, or in adjoining States, or in a contiguous foreign country; and

(C) The continued combination of such systems under the control of such holding company is not so large (considering the state of the art and the area or region affected) as to impair the advantages of localized management, efficient operation, or the effectiveness of regulation.

The Commission may permit as reasonably incidental, or economically necessary or appropriate to the operations of one or more integrated public-utility systems the retention of an interest in any business (other than the business of a public-utility company as such) which the Commission shall find necessary or appropriate in the public interest or for the protection of investors or con-

sumers and not detrimental to the proper functioning of such system or systems.

(2) To require by order, after notice and opportunity for hearing, that each registered holding company, and each subsidiary company thereof, shall take such steps as the Commission shall find necessary to ensure that the corporate structure or continued existence of any company in the holding-company system does not unduly or unnecessarily complicate the structure, or unfairly or inequitably distribute voting power among security holders, of such holding-company system. In carrying out the provisions of this paragraph the Commission shall require each registered holding company (and any company in the same holding-company system with such holding company) to take such action as the Commission shall find necessary in order that such holding company shall cease to be a holding company with respect to each of its subsidiary companies which itself has a subsidiary company which is a holding company. Except for the purpose of fairly and equitably distributing voting power among the security holders of such company, nothing in this paragraph shall authorize the Commission to require any change in the corporate structure or existence of any company which is not a holding company, or of any company whose principal business is that of a public-utility company.

The Commission may by order revoke or modify any order previously made under this subsection, if, after notice and opportunity for hearing, it finds that the conditions upon which the order was predicated do not exist. Any order made under this subsection shall be subject to judicial review as provided in section 24.

(3) Section 11(e) of the Public Utility Holding Company Act of 1935 provides:

Sec. 11. *Simplification of holding company systems.* * * *

(e) In accordance with such rules and regulations or order as the Commission may deem necessary or appropriate in the public interest or for the protection of investors or consumers, any registered holding company may, at any time after January 1, 1936, submit a plan to the Commission for the divestment of control, securities, or other assets, or for other action by such company or any subsidiary company of a registered holding company or any subsidiary company thereof for the purpose of enabling such company or any subsidiary company thereof to comply with the provisions of subsection (b). If, after notice and opportunity for hearing, the Commission shall find such plan, as submitted or as modified, necessary to effectuate the provisions of subsection (b) and fair and equitable to the persons affected by such plan, the Commission shall make an order approving such plan; and the Commission, at the request of the company, may apply to a court, in accordance with the provisions of subsection (f) of section 18, to enforce and carry out the terms and provisions of such plan. If, upon any such application, the court, after notice and opportunity for hearing, shall approve such plan as fair and equitable and as appropriate to effectuate the provisions of section 11, the court as a court of equity may, to such extent as it deems necessary for the purpose of carrying out the terms and provisions of such plan, take exclusive jurisdiction and possession of the company or companies and the assets thereof, wherever located; and the court shall have jurisdiction to appoint a trustee, and the court may constitute and appoint the Commission as sole trustee, to hold or administer, under the direction of the court and in accordance with the plan theretofore approved by the court and the Commission, the assets so possessed.

(b) *Registered holding company, holding-company system, and associate company.*—(1) Under section 5 of the Public Utility Holding Company Act of 1935 (15 U.S.C. 79e), any holding company may register by filing with the Securities and Exchange Commission a notification of registration, in such form as the Commission may by rules and regulations prescribe as necessary or appropriate in the public interest or for the protection of investors or consumers. A holding company shall be deemed to be registered upon receipt by the Securities and Exchange Commission of such notification of registration. As used in this part, the term "registered holding company" means a holding company whose notification of registration has been so received and whose registration is still in effect under section 5 of the Public Utility Holding Company Act of 1935. Under section 2(a)(7) of the Public Utility Holding Company Act of 1935 (15 U.S.C. 79b(a)(7)), a corporation is a holding company (unless it is declared not to be such by the Securities and Exchange Commission), if such corporation directly or indirectly owns, controls, or holds with power to vote 10 percent or more of the outstanding voting securities of a public-utility company (i.e., an electric utility company or a gas utility company as defined by such act) or of any other holding company. A corporation is also a holding company if the Securities and Exchange Commission determines, after notice and opportunity for hearing, that such corporation directly or indirectly exercises (either alone or pursuant to an arrangement or understanding with one or more other persons) such a controlling influence over the management or policies of any public-utility company (i.e., an electric utility company or a gas utility company as defined by such act) or holding company as to make it necessary or appropriate in the public interest or for the protection of investors or consumers that such corporation be subject to the obligations, duties and liabilities imposed upon holding companies by the Public Utility Holding Company Act of 1935 (15 U.S.C. ch. 2 C). An electric utility company is defined by section 2(a)(3) of the Public Utility Holding Company Act of 1935 (15 U.S.C. 79b(a)(3)) to mean a company which owns or operates facilities used for the generation, transmission, or distribution of electrical energy for sale, other than sale to tenants or employees of the company operating such facilities for their own use and not for resale; and a gas utility company is defined by section 2(a)(4) of such act (15 U.S.C. 79b(a)(4)), to mean a company which owns or operates facilities used for the distribution at retail (other than distribution only in enclosed portable containers, or distribution to tenants or employees of the company operating such facilities for their own use and not for resale) of natural or manufactured gas for heat, light, or power. However, under certain conditions the Securities and Exchange Commission may declare a company not to be an electric utility company or gas utility company, as the case may be, in which event the company shall not be considered an electric utility company or a gas utility company.

(2) The term "holding company system" has the meaning assigned to it by section 2(a)(9) of the Public Utility Holding Company Act of 1935 (15 U.S.C. 79b(a)(9)), and hence means any holding company, together with all its subsidiary companies (i.e., subsidiary companies within the meaning of section 2(a)(8) of such act (15 U.S.C. 79b(a)(8)), which in general include all companies 10 percent of whose outstanding voting securities is owned directly or indirectly by such holding company) and all mutual service companies of which such holding company or any subsidiary company thereof is a member company. The term "mutual service company" means a company approved as a mutual service company under section 13 of the Public Utility Holding Company Act of 1935 (15 U.S.C. 79m). The term "member company" is defined by section 2(a)(14) of such act (15 U.S.C. 79b(a)(14)), to mean a company which is a member of an association or group of companies mutually served by a mutual service company.

(3) The term "associate company" has the meaning assigned to it by section 2(a)(10) of the Public Utility Holding Company Act of 1935 (15 U.S.C. 79b(a)(10)), and hence an associate company of a company is any company in the same holding-company system with such company.

(c) *Majority-owned subsidiary company.*—The term "majority-owned subsidiary company" is defined in section 1083(c). Direct ownership by a registered holding company of more than 50 percent of the specified stock of another corporation is not necessary to constitute such corporation a majority-owned subsidiary company. To illustrate, if the H Corporation, a registered holding company, owns 51 percent of the common stock of the A Corporation and 31 percent of the common stock of the B Corporation, and the A Corporation owns 20 percent of the common stock of the B Corporation (the common stock in each case being the only stock entitled to vote), both the A Corporation and the B Corporation are majority-owned subsidiary companies.

(d) *System group.*—The term "system group" is defined in section 1083(d) to mean one or more chains of corporations connected through stock ownership with a common parent corporation, if at least 90 percent of each class of stock (other than (1) stock which is preferred as to both dividends and assets, and (2) stock which is limited and preferred as to dividends but which is not preferred as to assets but only if the total value of such stock is less than 1 percent of the aggregate value of all classes of stock which are not preferred as to both dividends and assets) of each of the corporations (except the common parent corporation) is owned directly by one or more of the other corporations, and if the common parent corporation owns directly at least 90 percent of each class of stock (other than stock preferred as to both dividends and assets) of at least one of the other corporations; but no corporation is a member of a system group unless it is either a registered holding company or a majority-owned subsidiary company. While the type of stock which must, for the purpose of this definition, be at least 90 percent owned may be different from the voting stock which must be more than 50 percent owned for the purpose of the definition of a majority-owned subsidiary company under section 1083(c), as a general rule both types of ownership tests must be met under section 1083(d), since a corporation, in order to be a member of a system group, must also be a registered holding company or a majority-owned subsidiary company.

(e) *Nonexempt property.*—The term "nonexempt property" is defined by section 1083(e) to include—

(1) The amount of any consideration in the form of a cancellation or assumption of debts or other liabilities of the transferor (including a continuance of encumbrances subject to which the property was transferred). To illustrate, if in obedience to an order of the Securities and Exchange Commission the X Corporation, a registered holding company, transfers property to the Y Corporation in exchange for property (not nonexempt property) with a fair market value of $500,000, the X Corporation receives $100,000 of nonexempt property, if for example—

(i) The Y Corporation cancels $100,000 of indebtedness owed to it by the X Corporation;

(ii) The Y Corporation assumes an indebtedness of $100,000 owed by the X Corporation to another company, the A Corporation; or

(iii) The Y Corporation takes over the property conveyed to it by the X Corporation subject to a mortgage of $100,000.

(2) Short-term obligations (including notes, drafts, bills of exchange, and bankers' acceptances) having a maturity at the time of issuance of not exceeding 24 months, exclusive of days of grace.

(3) Securities issued or guaranteed as to principal or interest by a government or subdivision thereof (including those issued by a corporation which is an instrumentality of a government or subdivision thereof).

(4) Stock or securities which were acquired from a registered holding company which acquired such stock or securities after February 28, 1938, or an associate company of a registered holding company which acquired such stock or securities after February 28, 1938, unless such stock or securities were acquired in obedience to an order of the Securities and Exchange Commission (as defined in section 1083(a)) or were acquired with the authorization or approval of the Securities and Exchange Commission under any section of the Public Utility Holding Company Act of 1935, and are not nonexempt property within the meaning of section 1083(e)(1), (2), or (3).

(5) Money, and the right to receive money not evidenced by a security other than an obligation described as nonexempt property in section 1083(e)(2) or (3). The term "the right to receive money" includes, among other items, accounts receivable, claims for damages, and rights to refunds of taxes.

(f) *Stock or securities.*—The term "stock or securities" is defined in section 1083(f) for the purposes of part VI (section 1081 and following), subchapter O, chapter 1 of the Code. As therein defined, the term includes voting trust certificates and stock rights or warrants. [Reg. § 1.1083-1.]

☐ [*T.D.* 6178, 6-1-56.]

Wash Sales; Straddles

[Reg. § 1.1091-1]

§ 1.1091-1. **Losses from wash sales of stock or securities.**—(a) A taxpayer cannot deduct any loss claimed to have been sustained from the sale or other disposition of stock or securities if, within a period beginning 30 days before the date of such sale or disposition and ending 30 days after such date (referred to in this section as the 61-day period), he has acquired (by purchase or by an exchange upon which the entire amount of gain or loss was recognized by law), or has entered into a contract or option so to acquire, substantially identical stock or securities. However, this prohibition does not apply (1) in the case of a taxpayer, not a corporation, if the sale or other disposition of stock or securities is made in connection with the taxpayer's trade or business, or (2) in the case of a corporation, a dealer in stock or securities, if the sale or other disposition of stock or securities is made in the ordinary course of its business as such dealer.

(b) Where more than one loss is claimed to have been sustained within the taxable year from the sale or other disposition of stock or securities, the provisions of this section shall be applied to the losses in the order in which the stock or securities the disposition of which resulted in the respective losses were disposed of (beginning with the earliest disposition). If the order of disposition of stock or securities disposed of at a loss on the same day cannot be determined, the stock or securities will be considered to have been disposed of in the order in which they were originally acquired (beginning with the earliest acquisition).

(c) Where the amount of stock or securities acquired within the 61-day period is less than the amount of stock or securities sold or otherwise disposed of, then the particular shares of stock or securities the loss from the sale or other disposition of which is not deductible shall be those with which the stock or securities acquired are matched in accordance with the following rule: The stock or securities acquired will be matched in accordance with the order of their acquisition (beginning with the earliest acquisition) with an equal number of the shares of stock or securities sold or otherwise disposed of.

(d) Where the amount of stock or securities acquired within the 61-day period is not less than the amount of stock or securities sold or otherwise disposed of, then the particular shares of stock or securities the acquisition of which resulted in the nondeductibility of the loss shall be those with which the stock or securities disposed of are matched in accordance with the following rule: The stock or securities sold or otherwise disposed of will be matched with an equal number of the shares of stock or securities acquired in accordance with the order of acquisition (beginning with the earliest acquisition) of the stock or securities acquired.

(e) The acquisition of any share of stock or any security which results in the nondeductibility of a loss under the provisions of this section shall be disregarded in determining the deductibility of any other loss.

(f) The word "acquired" as used in this section means acquired by purchase or by an exchange upon which the entire amount of gain or loss was recognized by law, and comprehends cases where the taxpayer has entered into a contract or option within the 61-day period to acquire by purchase or by such an exchange.

(g) For purposes of determining under this section the 61-day period applicable to a short sale of stock or securities, the principles of paragraph (a) of §1.1233-1 for determining the consummation of a short sale shall generally apply except that the date of entering into the short sale shall be deemed to be the date of sale if, on the date of entering into the short sale, the taxpayer owns (or on or before such date has entered into a contract or option to acquire) stock or securities identical to those sold short and subsequently delivers such stock or securities to close the short sale.

(h) The following examples illustrate the application of this section:

Example (1). A, whose taxable year is the calendar year, on December 1, 1954, purchased 100 shares of common stock in the M Company for $10,000 and on December 15, 1954, purchased 100 additional shares for $9,000. On January 3, 1955, he sold the 100 shares purchased on December 1, 1954, for $9,000. Because of the provisions of section 1091, no loss from the sale is allowable as a deduction.

Example (2). A, whose taxable year is the calendar year, on September 21, 1954, purchased 100 shares of the common stock of the M Company for $5,000. On December 21, 1954, he purchased 50 shares of substantially identical stock for $2,750, and on December 27, 1954, he purchased 25 additional shares of such stock for $1,125. On January 3, 1955, he sold for $4,000 the 100 shares purchased on September 21, 1954. There is an indicated loss of $1,000 on the sale of the 100 shares. Since, within the 61-day period, A purchased 75 shares of substantially identical stock, the loss on the sale of 75 of the shares ($3,750 − $3,000, or $750) is not allowable as a deduction because of the provisions of section 1091. The loss on the sale of the remaining 25 shares ($1,250 − $1,000, or $250) is deductible subject to the limitations provided in sections 267 and 1211. The basis of the 50 shares purchased December 21, 1954, the acquisition of which resulted in the nondeductibility of the loss ($500) sustained on 50 of the 100 shares sold on January 3, 1955, is $2,500 (the cost of 50 of the shares sold on January 3, 1955) + $750 (the difference between the purchase price ($2,750) of 50 of the shares acquired on December 21, 1954, and the selling price ($2,000) of the 50 shares sold on January 3, 1955, or $3,250). Similarly, the basis of the 25 shares purchased on December 27, 1954, the acquisition of which resulted in the nondeductibility of the loss ($250) sustained on 25 of the shares sold on January 3, 1955, is $1,250 + $125, or $1,375. See §1.1091-2.

Example (3). A, whose taxable year is the calendar year, on September 15, 1954, purchased 100 shares of the stock of the M Company for $5,000. He sold these shares on February 1, 1956, for $4,000. On each of the four days from February 15, 1956, to February 18, 1956, inclusive, he purchased 50 shares of substantially identical stock for $2,000. There is an indicated loss of $1,000 from the sale of the 100 shares on February 1, 1956, but, since within the 61-day period A purchased not less than 100 shares of substantially identical stock, the loss is not deductible. The particular shares of stock the purchase of which resulted in the nondeductibility of the loss are the first 100 shares purchased within such period, that is, the 50 shares purchased on February 15, 1956, and the 50 shares purchased on February 16, 1956. In determining the period for which the 50 shares purchased on February 15, 1956, and the 50 shares purchased on February 16, 1956, were held, there is to be included the period for which the 100 shares purchased on September 15, 1954, and sold on February 1, 1956, were held. [Reg. § 1.1091-1.]

☐ [*T.D. 6178, 6-1-56. Amended by T.D. 6926,* 8-8-67.]

[Reg. § 1.1091-2]

§ 1.1091-2. Basis of stock or securities acquired in "wash sales".—(a) *In general.*—The application of section 1091(d) may be illustrated by the following examples:

Example (1). A purchased a share of common stock of the X Corporation for $100 in 1935, which he sold January 15, 1955, for $80. On February 1, 1955, he purchased a share of common stock of the same corporation for $90. No loss from the sale is recognized under section 1091. The basis of the new share is $110; that is, the basis of the old share ($100) increased by $10, the excess of the price at which the new share was acquired ($90) over the price at which the old share was sold ($80).

Example (2). A purchased a share of common stock of the Y Corporation for $100 in 1935, which he sold January 15, 1955, for $80. On February 1, 1955, he purchased a share of common stock of the same corporation for $70. No loss from the sale is recognized under section 1091. The basis of the new share is $90; that is, the basis of the old share ($100) decreased by $10, the excess of the price at which the old share was sold ($80) over the price at which the new share was acquired ($70).

(b) *Special rule.*—For a special rule as to the adjustment to basis required under section 1091(d) in the case of wash sales involving certain regulated investment company stock for which there is an average basis, see paragraph (e)(3)(iii)(*c*) and (*d*) of § 1.1012-1. [Reg. § 1.1091-2.]

☐ [*T.D. 6178, 6-1-56. Amended by T.D. 7129,* 7-6-71.]

[Reg. § 1.1092(b)-1T]

§ 1.1092(b)-1T. Coordination of loss deferral rules and wash sale rules (temporary).—(a) *In general.*—Except as otherwise provided, in the case of the disposition of a position or positions of a straddle, the rules of paragraph (a)(1) of this section apply before the application of the rules of paragraph (a)(2) of this section.

(1) Any loss sustained from the disposition of shares of stock or securities that constitute positions of a straddle shall not be taken into account for purposes of this subtitle if, within a period beginning 30 days before the date of such disposition and ending 30 days after such date, the taxpayer has acquired (by purchase or by an exchange on which the entire amount of gain or loss was recognized by law), or has entered into a contract or option so to acquire, substantially identical stock or securities.

(2) Except as otherwise provided, if a taxpayer disposes of less than all of the positions of a straddle, any loss sustained with respect to the disposition of that position or positions (hereinafter referred to as "loss position") shall not be taken into account for purposes of this subtitle to the extent that the amount of unrecognized gain as of the close of the taxable year in one or more of the following positions—

(i) Successor positions,

(ii) Offsetting positions to the loss position, or

(iii) Offsetting positions to any successor position,

exceeds the amount of loss disallowed under paragraph (a)(1) of this section. See § 1.1092(b)-5T relating to definitions.

(b) *Carryover of disallowed loss.*—Any loss that is disallowed under paragraph (a) of this section shall, subject to any further application of paragraph (a)(1) of this section and the limitations under paragraph (a)(2) of this section, be treated as sustained in the succeeding taxable year. However, a loss disallowed in Year 1, for example, under paragraph (a)(1) of this section will not be allowed in Year 2 unless the substantially identical stock or securities, the acquisition of which caused the loss to be disallowed in Year 1, are disposed of during Year 2 and paragraphs (a)(1) and (a)(2) of this section do not apply in Year 2 to disallow the loss.

(c) *Treatment of disallowed loss.*—(1) *Character.*—If the disposition of a loss position would (but for the application of this section) result in a capital loss, the loss allowed under paragraph (b) of this section with respect to the disposition of the loss position shall be treated as a capital loss. In any other case, a loss allowed under paragraph (b) of this section shall be treated as an ordinary loss. For example, if the disposition of a loss position would, but for the application of paragraph (a) of this section, give rise to a capital loss, that loss when allowed pursuant to paragraph (b) of this section will be treated as a capital loss on the date the loss is allowed regardless of whether any gain or loss with respect to one or more successor positions would be treated as ordinary income or loss.

(2) *Section 1256 contracts.*—If the disposition of a loss position would (but for the application of this section) result in 60 percent long-term capital loss and 40 percent short-term capital loss, the loss allowed under paragraph (b) of this section with respect to the disposition of the loss position shall be treated as 60 percent long-term capital loss and 40 percent short-term capital loss regardless of whether any gain or loss with respect to one or more successor positions would be treated as 100 percent long-term or short-term capital gain or loss.

(d) *Exceptions.*—(1) This section shall not apply to losses sustained—

(i) With respect to the disposition of one or more positions that constitute part of a hedging transaction;

(ii) With respect to the disposition of a loss position included in a mixed straddle account (as defined in paragraph (b) of § 1.1092(b)-4T); and

(iii) With respect to the disposition of a position that is part of a straddle consisting only of section 1256 contracts.

(2) Paragraph (a)(1) of this section shall not apply to losses sustained by a dealer in stock or securities if such losses are sustained in a transaction made in the ordinary course of such business.

(e) *Coordination with section 1091.*—Section 1092(b) applies in lieu of section 1091 to losses sustained from the disposition of positions in a straddle. See example (18) of paragraph (g) of this section.

(f) *Effective date.*—The provisions of this section apply to dispositions of loss positions on or after January 24, 1985.

(g) *Examples.*—This section may be illustrated by the following examples. It is assumed in each example that the following positions are the only positions held directly or indirectly (through a related person or flowthrough entity) by an individual calendar year taxpayer during the taxable year and none of the exceptions contained in paragraph (d) of this section apply.

Example (1). On December 1, 1985, A enters into offsetting long and short positions. On December 10, 1985, A disposes of the short position at an $11 loss, at which time there is $5 of unrealized gain in the offsetting long position. At year-end there is still $5 of unrecognized gain in the offsetting long position. Under these circumstances, $5 of the $11 loss will be disallowed for 1985 because there is $5 of unrecognized gain in the offsetting long position; the remaining $6 of loss, however, will be taken into account in 1985.

Example (2). Assume the facts are the same as in example (1), except that at year-end there is $11 of unrecognized gain in the offsetting long position. Under these circumstances, the entire $11 loss will be disallowed for 1985 because there is $11 of unrecognized gain at year-end in the offsetting long position.

Example (3). Assume the facts are the same as in example (1), except that at year-end there is no unrecognized gain in the offsetting long position. Under these circumstances, the entire $11 loss will be allowed for 1985.

Example (4). On November 1, 1985, A enters into offsetting long and short positions. On November 10, 1985, A disposes of the long position at a $10 loss, at which time there is $10 of unrealized gain in the short position. On November 11, 1985, A enters into a new long position (successor position) that is offsetting with respect to the retained short position but is not substantially

identical to the long position disposed of on November 10, 1985. A holds both positions through year-end, at which time there is $10 of unrecognized gain in the successor long position and no unrecognized gain in the offsetting short position. Under these circumstances, the entire $10 loss will be disallowed for 1985 because there is $10 of unrecognized gain in the successor long position.

Example (5). Assume the facts are the same as in example (4), except that at year-end there is $4 of unrecognized gain in the successor long position and $6 of unrecognized gain in the offsetting short position. Under these circumstances, the entire $10 loss will be disallowed for 1985 because there is a total of $10 of unrecognized gain in both the successor long position and offsetting short position.

Example (6). Assume the facts are the same as in example (4), except that at year-end A disposes of the offsetting short position at a $2 loss. Under these circumstances, $10 of the total $12 loss will be disallowed because there is $10 of unrecognized gain in the successor long position.

Example (7). Assume the facts are the same as in example (4), and on January 10, 1986, A disposes of the successor long position at no gain or loss. A holds the offsetting short position until year-end, at which time there is $10 of unrecognized gain. Under these circumstances, the $10 loss will be disallowed for 1986 because there is $10 of unrecognized gain in an offsetting position at year-end.

Example (8). Assume the facts are the same as in example (4), except at year-end there is $8 of unrecognized gain in the successor long position and $8 of unrecognized loss in the offsetting short position. Under these circumstances, $8 of the total $10 realized loss will be disallowed because there is $8 of unrecognized gain in the successor long position.

Example (9). On October 1, 1985, A enters into offsetting long and short positions. Neither the long nor the short position is stock or securities. On October 2, 1985, A disposes of the short position at a $10 loss and the long position at a $10 gain. On October 3, 1985, A enters into a long position identical to the original long position. At year-end, there is $10 of unrecognized gain in the second long position. Under these circumstances, the $10 loss is allowed because the second long position is not a successor position or offsetting position to the short loss position.

Example (10). On November 1, 1985, A enters into offsetting long and short positions. On November 10, 1985, there is $20 of unrealized gain in the long position and A disposes of the short position at a $20 loss. By November 15, 1985, the value of the long position has declined eliminating all unrealized gain in the position. On November 15, 1985, A establishes a second short position (successor position) that is offsetting with respect to the long position but is not substantially identical to the short position disposed of on November 10, 1985. At year-end there is no unrecognized gain in the offsetting long position or in the successor short position. Under these circumstances, the $20 loss sustained with respect to the short loss position will be allowed for 1985 because at year-end there is no unrecognized gain in the successor short position or the offsetting long position.

Example (11). Assume the facts are the same as in example (10) except that the second short position was established on November 8, 1985, and there is $20 of unrecognized gain in the second short position at year-end. Since the second short position was entered into within 30 days before the disposition of the loss position, the second short position is considered a successor position of the loss position. Under these circumstances, the $20 loss will be disallowed because there is $20 of unrecognized gain in a successor position.

Example (12). Assume the facts are the same as in example (10), except that at year-end there is $18 of unrecognized gain in the offsetting long position and $18 of unrecognized gain in the successor short position. Under these circumstances, the entire loss will be disallowed because there is more than $20 of unrecognized gain in both the successor short position and offsetting long position.

Example (13). Assume the facts are the same as in example (10), except that there is $20 of unrecognized gain in the successor short position and no unrecognized gain in the offsetting long position at year-end. Under these circumstances, the entire $20 loss will be disallowed because there is $20 of unrecognized gain in the successor short position.

Example (14). On January 2, 1986, A enters into offsetting long and short positions. Neither the long nor the short position is stock or securities. On March 3, 1986, A disposes of the long position at a $10 gain. On March 10, 1986, A disposes of the short position at a $10 loss. On March 14, 1986, A enters into a new short position. On April 10, 1986, A enters into an offsetting long position. A holds both positions to year-end, at which time there is $10 of unrecognized gain in the offsetting long position and no unrecognized gain or loss in the short position. Under these circumstances, the $10 loss will be allowed because (1) the rules of paragraph (a)(1) of this section are not applicable; and (2) the rules of paragraph (a)(2) of this section do not apply, since all positions of the straddle that contained the loss position were disposed of.

Example (15). On December 1, 1985, A enters into offsetting long and short positions. On December 4, 1985, A disposes of the short position at a $10 loss. On December 5, 1985, A establishes a new short position that is offsetting to the long position, but is not substantially identical to the short position disposed of on December 4, 1985. On December 6, 1985, A disposes of the long position at a $10 gain. On December 7, 1985, A enters into a second long position that is offset-

ting to the new short position, but is not substantially identical to the long position disposed of on December 6, 1985. A holds both positions to year-end at which time there is no unrecognized gain in the second short position and $10 of unrecognized gain in the offsetting long position. Under these circumstances, the entire $10 loss will be disallowed for the 1985 taxable year because the second long position is an offsetting position with respect to the second short position which is a successor position.

Example (16). On September 1, 1985, A enters into offsetting positions consisting of a long section 1256 contract and short non-section 1256 position. No elections under sections 1256(d)(1) or 1092(b)(2)(A), relating to mixed straddles, are made. On November 1, 1985, at which time there is $20 of unrecognized gain in the short non-section 1256 position, A disposes of the long section 1256 contract at a $20 loss and on the same day acquires a long non-section 1256 position (successor position) that is offsetting with respect to the short non-section 1256 position. But for the application of this section, A's disposition of the section 1256 contract would give rise to a capital loss. At year-end there is $20 of unrecognized gain in the offsetting short non-section 1256 position and no unrecognized gain in the successor long position. Under these circumstances, the entire $20 loss will be disallowed for 1985 because there is $20 unrecognized gain in the offsetting short position. In 1986, A disposes of the successor long non-section 1256 position and there is no unrecognized gain at year-end in the offsetting short position. Under these circumstances, the $20 loss disallowed in 1985 with respect to the section 1256 contract will be treated in 1986 as 60 percent long-term capital loss and 40 percent short-term capital loss.

Example (17). On January 2, 1986, A, not a dealer in stock or securities, acquires stock in X Corporation (X stock) and an offsetting put option. On March 3, 1986, A disposes of the X stock at a $10 loss. On March 10, 1986, A disposes of the put option at a $10 gain. On March 14, 1986, A acquires new X stock that is substantially identical to the X stock disposed of on March 3, 1986. A holds the X stock to year-end. Under these circumstances, the $10 loss will be disallowed for 1986 under paragraph (a)(1) of this section because A, within a period beginning 30 days before March 3, 1986 and ending 30 days after such date, acquired stock substantially identical to the X stock disposed of.

Example (18). On June 2, 1986, A, not a dealer in stock or securities, acquires stock in X Corporation (X stock). On September 2, 1986, A disposes of the X stock at a $100 loss. On September 15, 1986, A acquires new X stock that is substantially identical to the X stock disposed of on September 2, 1986, and an offsetting put option. A holds these straddle positions to year-end. Under these circumstances, section 1091, rather than section 1092(b), will apply to disallow the

$100 loss for 1986 because the loss was not sustained from the disposition of a position that was part of a straddle. See paragraph (e) of this section.

Example (19). On November 1, 1985, A, not a dealer in stock or securities, acquires stock in Y Corporation (Y stock) and an offsetting put option. On November 12, 1985, there is $20 of unrealized gain in the put option and A disposes of the Y stock at a $20 loss. By November 15, 1985, the value of the put option has declined eliminating all unrealized gain in the position. On November 15, 1985, A acquires a second Y stock position that is substantially identical to the Y stock disposed of on November 12, 1985. At year-end there is no unrecognized gain in the put option or in the Y stock. Under these circumstances, the $20 loss will be disallowed for 1985 under paragraph (a)(1) of this section because A, within a period beginning 30 days before November 12, 1985 and ending 30 days after such date, acquired stock substantially identical to the Y stock disposed of.

Example (20). Assume the facts are the same as in example (19), and that on December 31, 1986, A disposes of the put option at a $40 gain and there is $20 of unrecognized loss in the Y stock. Under these circumstances, the $20 loss which was disallowed in 1985 also will be disallowed for 1986 under the rules of paragraph (a)(1) of this section because A has not disposed of the stock substantially identical to the Y stock disposed of on November 12, 1985.

Example (21). Assume the facts are the same as in example (19), except that on December 31, 1986, A disposes of the Y stock at a $20 loss and there is $40 of unrecognized gain in the put option. Under these circumstances, A will not recognize in 1986 either the $20 loss disallowed in 1985 or the $20 loss sustained with respect to the December 31, 1986 disposition of Y stock. Paragraph (a)(1) of this section does not apply to disallow the losses in 1986 since the substantially identical Y stock was disposed of during the year (and no substantially identical stock or securities was acquired by A within the 61 day period). However, paragraph (a)(2) of this section applies to disallow for 1986 the $40 of losses sustained with respect to the dispositions of positions in the straddle because there is $40 of unrecognized gain in the put option, an offsetting position to the loss positions.

Example (22). On January 2, 1986, A, not a dealer in stock or securities, acquires stock in X Corporation (X stock) and an offsetting put option. On March 3, 1986, A disposes of the X stock at a $10 loss. On March 17, 1986, A acquires new X stock that is substantially identical to the X stock disposed of on March 3, 1986. On December 31, 1986, A disposes of the X stock at a $5 gain, at which time there is $5 of unrecognized gain in the put option. Under these circumstances, the $10 loss sustained with respect to the March 3, 1986, disposition of X stock will be allowed under paragraph (a)(1) of this section

since the substantially identical X stock acquired on March 17, 1986, was disposed of by year-end (and no substantially identical stock or securities were acquired by A within the 61 day period). However, $5 of the $10 loss will be disallowed under paragraph (a)(2) of this section because there is $5 of unrecognized gain in the put option, an offsetting position to the loss position.

Example (23). Assume the facts are the same as in example (22), except that on December 31, 1986, A disposes of the offsetting put option at a $5 loss and there is $5 of unrecognized gain in the X stock acquired on March 17, 1986. Under these circumstances, the $10 loss sustained with respect to the X stock disposed of on March 3, 1986, will be disallowed for 1986 under paragraph (a)(1) of this section. The $5 loss sustained upon the disposition of the put option will be allowed because (1) the rules of paragraph (a)(1) of this section are not applicable; and (2) the rules of paragraph (a)(2) of this section allow the loss, since the unrecognized gain in the X stock ($5) is not in excess of the loss ($10) disallowed under paragraph (a)(1) of this section.

Example (24). On January 2, 1986, A, not a dealer in stock or securities, acquires 200 shares of Z Corporation stock (Z stock) and 2 put options on Z stock (giving A the right to sell 200 shares of Z stock). On September 2, 1986, there is $200 of unrealized gain in the put option positions and A disposes of the 200 shares of Z stock at a $200 loss. On September 10, 1986, A acquires 100 shares of Z stock (substantially identical to the Z stock disposed of on September 2, 1986), and a call option that is offsetting to the put options on Z stock and that is not an option to acquire property substantially identical to the Z stock disposed of on September 2, 1986. At year-end, there is $80 of unrecognized gain in the Z stock position, $80 of unrecognized gain in the call option position, and no unrecognized gain or loss in the offsetting put option positions. Under these circumstances, $40 of the $200 loss sustained with respect to the September 2, 1986 disposition of Z stock will be recognized by A in 1986 under paragraph (a) of this section, as set forth below. Paragraph (a)(1) of this section applies first to disallow $100 of the loss ($\frac{1}{2}$ of the loss), since 100 shares of substantially identical Z stock ($\frac{1}{2}$ of the stock) were acquired within the 61 day period. Paragraph (a)(2) of this section then applies to disallow that portion of the loss allowed under paragraph (a)(1) of this section ($200 − $100 = $100) equal to the excess of the total unrecognized gain in the Z stock and call option positions (successor positions to the loss position) ($80 + $80 = $160) over the $100 loss disallowed under paragraph (a)(1) of this section ($160 − $100 = $60; $100 − $60 = $40).

Example (25). Assume the facts are the same as in example (24), except that at year-end there is $110 of unrecognized gain in the Z stock position, $78 of unrecognized gain in the call option position, and $10 of unrecognized gain in the offsetting put option positions. Under these circumstances, $2 of the $200 loss sustained with respect to the September 2, 1986 disposition of Z stock will be allowed in 1986 under paragraph (a) of this section, as set forth below. Paragraph (a)(1) of this section applies first to disallow $100 of the loss ($\frac{1}{2}$ of the loss) since 100 shares of substantially identical Z stock ($\frac{1}{2}$ of the stock) were acquired within the 61 day period. Paragraph (a)(2) of this section then applies to disallow that portion of the loss allowed under paragraph (a)(1) of this section ($200 − $100 = $100) equal to the excess of the total unrecognized gain in the Z stock and call option positions (successor positions to the loss position) and the put option positions (offsetting positions to the loss position) ($110 + $78 + $10 = $198) over the $100 loss disallowed under paragraph (a)(1) of this section ($198 − $100 = $98; $100 − $98 = $2).

Example (26). Assume the facts are the same as in example (24), except that at year-end there is $120 of unrecognized gain in the Z stock position, $88 of unrecognized gain in the call option position, and $10 of unrecognized loss in one of the offsetting put option positions. At year-end A disposes of the other put option position at a $10 loss. Under these circumstances, $2 of the $210 loss sustained with respect to the September 2, 1986 disposition of Z stock ($200) and the year-end disposition of a put option ($10) will be allowed in 1986 under paragraph (a) of this section, as set forth below. Paragraph (a)(1) of this section applies first to disallow $100 of the loss from the disposition of Z stock ($\frac{1}{2}$ of the loss), since 100 shares of substantially identical Z stock ($\frac{1}{2}$ of the stock) were acquired within the 61 day period. Paragraph (a)(2) of this section then applies to disallow that portion of the loss allowed under paragraph (a)(1) of this section ($210 − $100 = $110) equal to the excess of the total unrecognized gain in the Z stock and call option positions (successor positions to the Z stock loss position, and offsetting positions to the put option loss position) ($120 + $88 = $208) over the $100 loss disallowed under paragraph (a)(1) of this section ($208 − $100 = $108; $110 − $108 = $2).

Example (27). On January 27, 1986, A enters into offsetting long (L1) and short (S1) positions. Neither L1 nor S1 nor any other positions entered into by A in 1986 are stock or securities. On February 3, 1986, A disposes of L1 at a $10 loss. On February 5, 1986, A enters into a new long position (L2) that is offsetting to S1. On October 15, 1986, A disposes of S1 at an $11 loss. On October 17, 1986, A enters into a new short position (S2) that is offsetting to L2. On December 30, 1986, A disposes of L2 at a $12 loss. On December 31, 1986, A enters into a new long position (L3) that is offsetting to S2. At year-end, S2 has an unrecognized gain of $33. Paragraph (a)(1) of this section does not apply since none of the positions were shares of stock or securities. However, all $33 ($10 + $11 + $12) of the losses sustained with respect to L1, S1 and L2 will be

disallowed under paragraph (a)(2) because there is $33 of unrecognized gain in S2 at year-end. The $10 loss from the disposition of L1 is disallowed because S2 is or was an offsetting position to a successor long position (L2 or L3). The $11 loss from the disposition of S1 is disallowed because S2 is a successor position to S1. The $12 loss from the disposition of L2 is disallowed because S2 was an offsetting position to L2. [Temporary Reg. § 1.1092(b)-1T.]

☐ [*T.D.* 8007, 1-18-85. *Amended by T.D.* 8070, 1-13-86.]

[Reg. § 1.1092(b)-2T]

§ 1.1092(b)-2T. Treatment of holding periods and losses with respect to straddle positions (Temporary).—(a) *Holding period.*—(1) *In general.*—Except as otherwise provided in this section, the holding period of any position that is part of a straddle shall not begin earlier than the date the taxpayer no longer holds directly or indirectly (through a related person or flow-through entity) an offsetting position with respect to that position. See § 1.1092(b)-5T relating to definitions.

(2) *Positions held for the long-term capital gain holding period (or longer) prior to establishment of the straddle.*—Paragraph (a)(1) of this section shall not apply to a position held by a taxpayer for the long-term capital gain holding period (or longer) before a straddle that includes such position is established. The determination of whether a position has been held by a taxpayer for the long-term capital gain holding period (or longer) shall be made by taking into account the application of paragraph (a)(1) of this section. See section 1222(3) relating to the holding period for long-term capital gains.

(b) *Treatment of loss.*—(1) *In general.*—Except as provided in paragraph (b)(2) of this section, loss on the disposition of one or more positions ("loss position") of a straddle shall be treated as a long-term capital loss if—

(i) On the date the taxpayer entered into the loss position the taxpayer held directly or indirectly (through a related person or flow-through entity) one or more offsetting positions with respect to the loss position; and

(ii) All gain or loss with respect to one or more positions in the straddle would be treated as long-term capital gain or loss if such positions were disposed of on the day the loss position was entered into.

(2) *Special rules for non-section 1256 positions in a mixed straddle.*—Loss on the disposition of one or more positions ("loss position") that are part of a mixed straddle and that are non-section 1256 positions shall be treated as 60 percent long-term capital loss and 40 percent short-term capital loss if—

(i) Gain or loss from the disposition of one or more of the positions of the straddle that are section 1256 contracts would be considered gain or loss from the sale or exchange of a capital asset;

(ii) The disposition of no position in the straddle (other than a section 1256 contract) would result in a long-term capital gain or loss; and

(iii) An election under section 1092(b)(2)(A)(i)(I) (relating to straddle-by-straddle identification) or 1092(b)(2)(A)(i)(II) (relating to mixed straddle accounts) has not been made.

(c) *Exceptions.*—(1) *In general.*—This section shall not apply to positions that—

(i) Constitute part of a hedging transaction;

(ii) Are included in a straddle consisting only of section 1256 contracts; or

(iii) Are included in a mixed straddle account (as defined in paragraph (b) of §1.1092(b)-4T).

(2) *Straddle-by-straddle identification.*— Paragraphs (a)(2) and (b) of this section shall not apply to positions in a section 1092(b)(2) identified mixed straddle. See §1.1092(b)-3T.

(d) *Special rule for positions held by regulated investment companies.*—For purposes of section 851(b)(3) (relating to the definition of a regulated investment company), the holding period rule of paragraph (a) of this section shall not apply to positions of a straddle. However, if section 1233(b) (without regard to sections 1233(e)(2)(A) and 1092(b)) would have applied to such positions, then for purposes of section 851(b)(3) the rules of section 1233(b) shall apply. Similarly, the effect of daily marking-to-market provided under §1.1092(b)-4T(c) will be disregarded for purposes of section 851(b)(3).

(e) *Effective date.*—(1) *In general.*—Except as provided in paragraph (e)(2) of this section, the provisions of this section apply to positions in a straddle established after June 23, 1981, in taxable years ending after such date.

(2) *Special effective date for mixed straddle positions.*—The provisions of paragraph (b)(2) of this section shall apply to positions in a mixed straddle established on or after January 1, 1984.

(f) *Examples.*—Paragraphs (a) through (e) may be illustrated by the following examples. It is assumed in each example that the following positions are the only positions held directly or indirectly (through a related person or flow-through entity) by an individual calendar year taxpayer during the taxable year and none of the exceptions in paragraph (c) of this section apply.

Example (1). On October 1, 1984, A acquires gold. On January 1, 1985, A enters into an offsetting short gold forward contract. On April 1, 1985, A disposes of the short gold forward contract at no gain or loss. On April 10, 1985, A sells the gold at a gain. Since the gold had not been

held for more than 6 months before the offsetting short position was entered into, the holding period for the gold begins no earlier than the time the straddle is terminated. Thus, the holding period of the original gold purchased on October 1, 1984, and sold on April 10, 1985, begins on April 1, 1985, the date the straddle was terminated. Consequently, gain recognized with respect to the gold will be treated as short-term capital gain.

Example (2). On January 1, 1985, A enters into a long gold forward contract. On May 1, 1985, A enters into an offsetting short gold regulated futures contract. A does not make an election under section 1256(d) or 1092(b)(2)(A). On August 1, 1985, A disposes of the gold forward contract at a gain. Since the forward contract had not been held by A for more than 6 months prior to the establishment of the straddle, the holding period for the forward contract begins no earlier than the time the straddle is terminated. Thus, the gain recognized on the closing of the gold forward contract will be treated as short-term capital gain.

Example (3). Assume the facts are the same as in example (2), except that A disposes of the short gold regulated futures contract on July 1, 1985, at no gain or loss and the forward contract on November 1, 1985. Since the forward contract had not been held for more than 6 months before the mixed straddle was established, the holding period for the forward contract begins July 1, 1985, the date the straddle terminated. Thus, the gain recognized on the closing of the forward contract will be treated as short-term capital gain.

Example (4). On January 1, 1985, A enters into a long gold forward contract and on August 4, 1985, A enters into an offsetting short gold forward contract. On September 1, 1985, A disposes of the short position at a loss. Since an offsetting long position had been held by A for more than 6 months prior to the acquisition of the offsetting short position, the loss with respect to the closing of the short position will be treated as long-term capital loss.

Example (5). On March 1, 1985, A enters into a long gold forward contract and on July 17, 1985, A enters into an offsetting short gold regulated futures contract. A does not make an election under section 1256(d) or 1092(b)(2)(A). On August 10, 1985, A disposes of the long gold forward contract at a loss. Since the gold forward contract was part of a mixed straddle, and the disposition of no position in the straddle (other than the regulated futures contract) would give rise to a long-term capital loss, the loss recognized on the termination of the gold forward contract will be treated as 40 percent short-term capital loss and 60 percent long-term capital loss.

Example (6). Assume the facts are the same as in example (5), except that on August 11, 1985, A disposes of the short gold regulated futures contract at a gain. Under these circumstances, the gain will be treated as 60 percent long-term capital gain and 40 percent short-term capital gain since the holding period rules of paragraph (a) of this section are not applicable to section 1256 contracts.

Example (7). Assume the facts are the same as in example (5), except that A enters into the long gold forward contract on January 1, 1985, and does not dispose of the long gold forward contract but instead on August 10, 1985, disposes of the short gold regulated futures contract at a loss. Under these circumstances, the loss will be treated as a long-term capital loss since A held an offsetting non-section 1256 position for more than 6 months prior to the establishment of the straddle. However, such loss may be subject to the rules of §1.1092(b)-1T. [Temporary Reg. §1.1092(b)-2T.]

☐ *[T.D. 8007, 1-18-85. Amended by T.D. 8070, 1-13-86.]*

[Reg. §1.1092(b)-3T]

§1.1092(b)-3T. Mixed straddles; straddle-by-straddle identification under section 1092(b)(2)(A)(i)(I) (Temporary).—(a) *In general.*—Except as otherwise provided, a taxpayer shall treat in accordance with paragraph (b) of this section gains and losses on positions that are part of a mixed straddle for which the taxpayer has made an election under paragraph (d) of this section (hereinafter referred to as a "section 1092(b)(2) identified mixed straddle"). No election may be made under this section for any straddle composed of one or more positions that are includible in a mixed straddle account (as defined in paragraph (b) of §1.1092(b)-4T) or for any straddle for which an election under section 1256(d) has been made. See §1.1092(b)-5T relating to definitions.

(b) *Treatment of gains and losses from positions included in a section 1092(b)(2) identified mixed straddle.*—(1) *In general.*—Gains and losses from positions that are part of a section 1092(b)(2) identified mixed straddle shall be determined and treated in accordance with the rules of paragraph (b)(2) through (7) of this section.

(2) *All positions of a section 1092(b)(2) identified mixed straddle are disposed of on the same day.*—If all positions of a section 1092(b)(2) identified mixed straddle are disposed of (or deemed disposed of) on the same day, gains and losses from section 1256 contracts in the straddle shall be netted, and gains and losses from non-section 1256 positions in the straddle shall be netted. Net gain or loss from the section 1256 contracts shall then be offset against net gain or loss from the non-section 1256 positions to determine the net gain or loss from the straddle. If net gain or loss from the straddle is attributable to the positions of the straddle that are section 1256 contracts, such gain or loss shall be treated as 60 percent long-term capital gain or loss and 40 percent short-term capital gain or loss. If net gain or loss from the straddle is attributable to the positions

of the straddle that are non-section 1256 positions, such gain or loss shall be treated as short-term capital gain or loss. This paragraph (b)(2) may be illustrated by the following examples. It is assumed in each example that the positions are the only positions held directly or indirectly (through a related person or flowthrough entity) by an individual calendar year taxpayer during the taxable year.

Example (1). On April 1, 1985, A enters into a non-section 1256 position and an offsetting section 1256 contract and makes a valid election to treat such straddle as a section 1092(b)(2) identified mixed straddle. On April 10, 1985, A disposes of the non-section 1256 position at a $600 loss and the section 1256 contract at a $600 gain. Under these circumstances, the $600 loss on the non-section 1256 position will be offset against the $600 gain on the section 1256 contract and the net gain or loss from the straddle will be zero.

Example (2). Assume the facts are the same as in example (1), except that the gain on the section 1256 contract is $800. Under these circumstances, the $600 loss on the non-section 1256 position will be offset against the $800 gain on the section 1256 contract. The net gain of $200 from the straddle will be treated as 60 percent long-term capital gain and 40 percent short-term capital gain because it is attributable to the section 1256 contract.

Example (3). Assume the facts are the same as in example (1), except that the loss on the non-section 1256 position is $800. Under these circumstances, the $600 gain on the section 1256 contract will be offset against the $800 loss on the non-section 1256 position. The net loss of $200 from the straddle will be treated as short-term capital loss because it is attributable to the non-section 1256 position.

Example (4). On May 1, 1985, A enters into a straddle consisting of two non-section 1256 positions and two section 1256 contracts and makes a valid election to treat the straddle as a section 1092(b)(2) identified mixed straddle. On May 10, 1985, A disposes of the non-section 1256 positions, one at a $700 loss and the other at a $500 gain, and disposes of the section 1256 contracts, one at a $400 gain and the other at a $300 loss. Under these circumstances, the gain and losses from the section 1256 contracts and non-section 1256 positions will first be netted, resulting in a net gain of $100 ($400 – $300) on the section 1256 contracts and a net loss of $200 ($700 – $500) on the non-section 1256 positions. The net gain of $100 from the section 1256 contracts will then be offset against the $200 net loss on the non-section 1256 positions. The net loss of $100 from the straddle will be treated as short-term capital loss because it is attributable to the non-section 1256 positions.

Example (5). On December 30, 1985, A enters into a section 1256 contract and an offsetting non-section 1256 position and makes a valid election to treat such straddle as a section

1092(b)(2) identified mixed straddle. On December 31, 1985, A disposes of the non-section 1256 position at a $2,000 gain. A also realizes a $2,000 loss on the section 1256 contract because it is deemed disposed of under section 1256(a)(1). Under these circumstances, the $2,000 gain on the non-section 1256 position will be offset against the $2,000 loss on the section 1256 contract, and the net gain or loss from the straddle will be zero.

Example (6). Assume the facts are the same as in example (5), except that the section 1092(b)(2) identified mixed straddle was entered into on November 12, 1985, A realizes a $2,200 loss on the section 1256 contract, and on December 15, 1985, A enters into a non-section 1256 position that is offsetting to the non-section 1256 gain position of the section 1092(b)(2) identified mixed straddle. At year-end there is $200 of unrecognized gain in the non-section 1256 position that was entered into on December 15. Under these circumstances, the $2,200 loss on the section 1256 contract will be offset against the $2,000 gain on the non-section 1256 position. The net $200 loss from the straddle will be treated as 60 percent long-term capital loss and 40 percent short-term capital loss because it is attributable to the section 1256 contract. The net loss of $200 from the straddle will be disallowed in 1985 under the loss deferral rules of section 1092(a) because there is $200 of unrecognized gain in a successor position (as defined in paragraph (n) of § 1.1092(b)-5T) at year-end. See paragraph (c) of this section.

(3) *All of the non-section 1256 positions of a section 1092(b)(2) identified mixed straddle disposed of on the same day.*—This paragraph (b)(3) applies if all of the non-section 1256 positions of a section 1092(b)(2) identified mixed straddle are disposed of on the same day or if this paragraph (b)(3) is made applicable by paragraph (b)(5) of this section. In the case to which this paragraph (b)(3) applies, gain and loss realized from non-section 1256 positions shall be netted. Realized and unrealized gain and loss with respect to the section 1256 contracts of the straddle also shall be netted on that day. Realized net gain or loss from the non-section 1256 positions shall then be offset against net gain or loss from the section 1256 contracts to determine the net gain or loss from the straddle on that day. Net gain or loss from the straddle that is attributable to the non-section 1256 positions shall be realized and treated as short-term capital gain or loss on that day. Net gain or loss from the straddle that is attributable to realized gain or loss with respect to section 1256 contracts shall be realized and treated as 60 percent long-term capital gain or loss and 40 percent short-term capital gain or loss. Any gain or loss subsequently realized on the section 1256 contracts shall be adjusted (through an adjustment to basis or otherwise) to take into account the extent to which gain or loss was offset by unrealized gain or loss on the section 1256 contracts on that day. This paragraph (b)(3) may be illustrated by the following examples. It is assumed in each example that the positions are the only positions held directly or indirectly (through a related person or flow-through entity) by an individual calendar year taxpayer during the taxable year.

Example (1). On July 20, 1985, A enters into a section 1256 contract and an offsetting non-section 1256 position and makes a valid election to treat such straddle as a section 1092(b)(2) identified mixed straddle. On July 27, 1985, A disposes of the non-section 1256 position at a $1,500 loss, at which time there is $1,500 of unrealized gain in the section 1256 contracts. A holds the section 1256 contract at year-end at which time there is $1,800 of gain. Under these circumstances, on July 27, 1985, A offsets the $1,500 loss on the non-section 1256 position against the $1,500 gain on the section 1256 contract and realizes no gain or loss. On December 31, 1985, A realizes a $300 gain on the section 1256 contract because the position is deemed disposed of under section 1256(a)(1). The $300 gain is equal to $1,800 of gain less a $1,500 adjustment for unrealized gain offset against the loss realized on the non-section 1256 position on July 27, 1985, and the gain will be treated as 60 percent long-term capital gain and 40 percent short-term capital gain.

Example (2). Assume the facts are the same as in example (1), except that on July 27, 1985, A realized a $1,700 loss on the non-section 1256 position. Under these circumstances, on July 27, 1985, A offsets the $1,700 loss on the non-section 1256 position against the $1,500 gain on the section 1256 contract. A realizes a $200 loss from the straddle on July 27, 1985, which will be treated as short-term capital loss because it is attributable to the non-section 1256 position. On December 31, 1985, A realizes a $300 gain on the section 1256 contract, computed as in example (1), which will be treated as 60 percent long-term capital gain and 40 percent short-term capital gain.

Example (3). On March 1, 1985, A enters into a straddle consisting of two non-section 1256 positions and two section 1256 contracts and makes a valid election to treat such straddle as a section 1092(b)(2) identified mixed straddle. On March 11, 1985, A disposes of the non-section 1256 positions, one at a $100 loss and the other at a $150 loss, and disposes of one section 1256 contract at a $100 loss. On that day there is $100 of unrealized gain on the section 1256 contract retained by A. A holds the remaining section 1256 contract at year-end, at which time there is $150 of gain. Under these circumstances, on March 11, 1985, A will first net the gains and losses from the section 1256 contracts and net the gains and losses from the non-section 1256 positions resulting in no gain or loss on the section 1256 contracts and a net loss of $250 on the non-section 1256 positions. Since there is no gain or loss to offset against the non-section 1256 positions, the net loss of $250 will be treated as short-term capital loss because it is attributable to the non-section 1256 positions. On December 31, 1985, A realizes a $50 gain on the remaining section 1256 contract because the position is deemed disposed of under section 1256(a)(1). The $50 gain is equal to $150 gain less a $100 adjustment to take into account the $100 unrealized gain that was offset against the $100 loss realized on the section 1256 contract on March 11, 1985.

Example (4). Assume the facts are the same as in example (3), except that A disposes of the section 1256 contract at a $500 gain. As in example (3), A has a net loss of $250 on the non-section 1256 positions disposed of. In this example, however, A has a net gain of $600 ($500 + $100) on the section 1256 contracts on March 11, 1985. Therefore, of the net gain from the straddle of $350 ($600 − $250), $250 ($500 − $250) is treated as 60 percent long-term capital gain and 40 percent short-term capital gain because only $250 is attributable to the realized gain from the section 1256 contract. In addition, because none of the $100 unrealized gain from the remaining section 1256 contract was offset against gain or loss on the non-section 1256 positions, no adjustment is made under paragraph (b)(3) of this section and the entire $150 gain on December 31 with respect to that contract is realized on that date.

(4) *All of the section 1256 contracts of a section 1092(b)(2) identified mixed straddle disposed of on the same day.*—This paragraph (b)(4) applies if all of the section 1256 contracts of a section 1092(b)(2) identified mixed straddle are disposed of (or deemed disposed of) on the same day or if this paragraph (b)(4) is made applicable by paragraph (b)(5) of this section. In the case to which this paragraph (b)(4) applies, gain and loss realized from section 1256 contracts shall be netted. Realized and unrealized gain and loss with respect to the non-section 1256 positions of the straddle also shall be netted on that day. Realized net gain or loss from the section 1256 contracts shall be treated as short-term capital gain or loss to the extent of net gain or loss on the non-section 1256 positions on that day. Net gain or loss with respect to the section 1256 contracts that exceeds the net gain or loss with respect to the non-section 1256 positions of the straddle shall be treated as 60 percent long-term capital gain or loss and 40 percent short-term capital gain or loss. See paragraph (b)(7) of this section relating to the gain or loss on such non-section 1256 positions. This paragraph (b)(4) may be illustrated by the following examples. It is assumed in each example that the positions are the only positions held directly or indirectly (through a related person or flowthrough entity) by an individual calendar year taxpayer during the taxable year.

Example (1). On December 30, 1985, A enters into a section 1256 contract and an offsetting non-section 1256 position and makes a valid election to treat such straddle as a section 1092(b)(2) identified mixed straddle. On December 31, 1985, A disposes of the section 1256 contract at a $1,000 gain, at which time there is $1,000 of unrealized loss in the non-section 1256 position. Under these circumstances, the $1,000 gain realized on the section 1256 contract will be treated as short-term capital gain because there is a $1,000 loss on the non-section 1256 position.

Example (2). Assume the facts are the same as in example (1), except that A realized a $1,500 gain on the disposition of the section 1256 contract. Under these circumstances, $1,000 of the gain realized on the section 1256 contract will be treated as short-term capital gain because there is a $1,000 loss on the non-section 1256 position. The net gain of $500 from the straddle will be treated as 60 percent long-term capital gain and 40 percent short-term capital gain because it is attributable to the section 1256 contract.

Example (3). Assume the facts are the same as in example (1), except that A realized a $1,000 loss on the section 1256 contract and there is $1,000 of unrecognized gain on the non-section 1256 position. Under these circumstances, the $1,000 loss on the section 1256 contract will be treated as short-term capital loss because there is a $1,000 gain on the non-section 1256 position. Such loss, however, will be disallowed in 1985 under the loss deferral rules of section 1092(a) because there is $1,000 of unrecognized gain in an offsetting position at year-end. See paragraph (c) of this section.

Example (4). Assume the facts are the same as in example (1), except that the section 1256 contract and non-section 1256 position were entered into on December 1, 1985, and the section 1256 contract is disposed of, on December 19, 1985, for a $1,000 gain, at which time there is $1,000 of unrealized loss on the non-section 1256 position. At year-end there is only $800 of unrealized loss in the non-section 1256 position. Under these circumstances, the result is the same as in example (1) because there was $1,000 of unrealized loss on the non-section 1256 position at the time of the disposition of the section 1256 contract.

Example (5). On July 15, 1985, A enters into a straddle consisting of two non-section 1256 positions and two section 1256 contracts and makes a valid election to treat such straddle as a section 1092(b)(2) identified mixed straddle. On July 20, 1985, A disposes of one non-section 1256 position at a gain of $1,000 and both section 1256 contracts at a net loss of $1,000. On the same day there is $200 of unrealized loss on the non-section 1256 position retained by A. Under these circumstances, realized and unrealized gain and loss with respect to the non-section 1256 positions is [sic]netted, resulting in a net gain of $800. Thus, $800 of the net loss on the section 1256 contracts disposed of will be treated as short-term capital loss because there is $800 of net gain on the non-section 1256 positions. In addition, the net loss of $200 from the straddle will be treated as 60 percent long-term capital loss and 40 percent short-term capital loss because it is attributable to the section 1256 contract.

(5) *Disposition of one or more, but not all, positions of a section 1092(b)(2) identified mixed straddle on the same day.*—If one or more, but not all, of the positions of a section 1092(b)(2) identified mixed straddle are disposed of on the same day, and paragraph (b)(3) and (4) of this section are not applicable (without regard to this paragraph (b)(5)), the gain and loss from the non-section 1256 positions that are disposed of on that day shall be netted, and the gain and loss from the section 1256 contracts that are disposed of on that day shall be netted. In order to determine whether the rules of paragraph (b)(3) or (b)(4) of this section apply, net gain or loss from the section 1256 contracts disposed of shall then be offset against net gain or loss from the non-section 1256 positions disposed of to determine net gain or loss from such positions of the straddle. If net gain or loss from the disposition of such positions of the straddle is attributable to the non-section 1256 positions disposed of, the rules prescribed in paragraph (b)(3) of this section apply. If net gain or loss from the disposition of such positions is attributable to the section 1256 contracts disposed of, the rules prescribed in paragraph (b)(4) of this section apply. If the net gain or loss from the netting of non-section 1256 positions disposed of and the netting of section 1256 contracts disposed of are either both gains or losses, the rules prescribed in paragraph (b)(3) of this section shall apply to net gain or loss from such non-section 1256 positions, and the rules prescribed in paragraph (b)(4) of this section shall apply to net gain or loss from such section 1256 contracts. However, for purposes of determining the treatment of gain or loss subsequently realized on a position of such straddle, to the extent that unrealized gain or loss on other positions was used to offset realized gain or loss on a non-section 1256 position under paragraph (b)(3) of this section, or was used to treat realized gain or loss on a section 1256 contract as short-term capital gain or loss under paragraph (b)(4) of this section, such amount shall not be used for such purposes again. This paragraph (b)(5) may be illustrated by the following examples. It is assumed that the positions are the only positions held directly or indirectly (through a related person or flow-through entity) by an individual calendar year taxpayer during the taxable year.

Example (1). On July 15, 1985, A enters into a straddle consisting of four non-section 1256 positions and four section 1256 contracts and makes a valid election to treat such straddle as a section 1092(b)(2) identified mixed straddle. On July 20, 1985, A disposes of one non-section 1256 position at a gain of $800 and one section 1256 contract at a loss of $300. On the same day there is $400 of unrealized net loss on the section 1256 contracts retained by A and $100 of unrealized

net loss on the non-section 1256 positions retained by A. Under these circumstances, the loss of $300 on the section 1256 contract disposed of will be offset against the gain of $800 on the non-section 1256 position disposed of. The net gain of $500 is attributable to the non-section 1256 position. Therefore, the rules of paragraph (b)(3) of this section apply. Under the rules of paragraph (b)(3) of this section, the net loss of $700 on the section 1256 contracts is offset against the net gain of $800 attributable to the non-section 1256 position disposed of. The net gain of $100 will be treated as short-term capital gain because it is attributable to the non-section 1256 position disposed of. Gain or loss subsequently realized on the section 1256 contracts will be adjusted to take into account the unrealized loss of $400 that was offset against the $800 gain attributable to the non-section 1256 position disposed of.

Example (2). Assume the facts are the same as in example (1), except that A disposes of the non-section 1256 position at a gain of $300 and the section 1256 contract at a loss of $800, and there is $200 of unrealized net gain in the non-section 1256 positions retained by A. Under these circumstances, the gain of $300 on the non-section 1256 position disposed of will be offset against the loss of $800 on the section 1256 contract disposed of. The net loss of $500 is attributable to the section 1256 contract. Therefore, the rules of paragraph (b)(4) of this section apply. Under the rules of paragraph (b)(4) of this section, $500 of the net loss realized on the section 1256 contract will be treated as short-term capital loss because there is $500 of realized and unrealized gain in the non-section 1256 positions. The remaining net loss of $300 will be treated as 60 percent long-term capital loss and 40 percent short-term capital loss because it is attributable to a section 1256 contract disposed of. In addition, A realizes a $300 short-term capital gain attributable to the disposition of the non-section 1256 position.

Example (3). (i) Assume the facts are the same as in example (1), except that the section 1256 contract was disposed of at a $500 gain. Under these circumstances, there is gain of $500 attributable to the section 1256 contract disposed of and a gain of $800 attributable to the non-section 1256 position. Therefore, the rules of both paragraphs (b)(3) and (4) of this § 1.1092(b)-3T apply.

(ii) Under paragraph (b)(3) of this section, the realized and unrealized gains and losses on the section 1256 contracts are netted, resulting in a net gain of $100 ($500 − $400). The section 1256 contract net gain does not offset the gain on the non-section 1256 position disposed of. Therefore, the gain of $800 on the non-section 1256 position disposed of will be treated as a short-term capital gain because there is no net loss on the section 1256 contracts.

(iii) Under paragraph (b)(4) of this section, the realized and unrealized gains and losses on the non-section 1256 positions are netted, resulting in a non-section 1256 position net gain of $700 ($800 – $100). Because there is no net loss on the non-section 1256 positions, the $500 gain realized on the section 1256 contract will be treated as 60 percent long-term capital gain and 40 percent short-term capital gain.

(6) *Accrued gain and loss with respect to positions of a section 1092(b)(2) identified mixed straddle.*—If one or more positions of a section 1092(b)(2) identified mixed straddle were held by the taxpayer on the day prior to the day the section 1092(b)(2) identified mixed straddle is established, such position or positions shall be deemed sold for their fair market value as of the close of the last business day preceding the day such straddle is established. See §§ 1.1092(b)-1T and 1.1092(b)-2T for application of the loss deferral and wash sale rules and for treatment of holding periods and losses with respect to such positions. An adjustment (through an adjustment to basis or otherwise) shall be made to any subsequent gain or loss realized with respect to such position or positions for any gain or loss recognized under this paragraph (b)(6). This paragraph (b)(6) may be illustrated by the following examples. It is assumed in each example that the positions are the only positions held directly or indirectly (through a related person or flowthrough entity) by an individual calendar year taxpayer during the taxable year.

Example (1). On January 1, 1985, A enters into a non-section 1256 position. As of the close of the day on July 9, 1985, there is $500 of unrealized long-term capital gain in the non-section 1256 position. On July 10, 1985, A enters into an offsetting section 1256 contract and makes a valid election to treat the straddle as a section 1092(b)(2) identified mixed straddle. Under these circumstances, on July 9, 1985, A will recognize $500 of long-term capital gain on the non-section 1256 position.

Example (2). On February 1, 1985, A enters into a section 1256 contract. As of the close of the day on February 4, 1985, there is $500 of unrealized gain on the section 1256 contract. On February 5, 1985, A enters into an offsetting non-section 1256 position and makes a valid election to treat the straddle as a section 1092(b)(2) identified mixed straddle. Under these circumstances, on February 4, 1985, A will recognize a $500 gain on the section 1256 contract, which will be treated as 60 percent long-term capital gain and 40 percent short-term capital gain.

Example (3). Assume the facts are the same as in example (2) and that on February 10, 1985, there is $2,000 of unrealized gain in the section 1256 contract. A disposes of the section 1256 contract at a $2,000 gain and disposes of the offsetting non-section 1256 position at a $1,000 loss. Under these circumstances, the $2,000 gain on the section 1256 contract will be reduced to $1,500 to take into account the $500 gain recognized when the section 1092(b)(2) identified mixed straddle was established. The $1,500 gain

on the section 1256 contract will be offset against the $1,000 loss on the non-section 1256 position. The net $500 gain from the straddle will be treated as 60 percent long-term capital gain and 40 percent short-term capital gain because it is attributable to the section 1256 contract.

Example (4). On March 1, 1985, A enters into a non-section 1256 position. As of the close of the day on March 2, 1985, there is $400 of unrealized short-term capital gain in the non-section 1256 position. On March 3, 1985, A enters into an offsetting section 1256 contract and makes a valid election to treat the straddle as a section 1092(b)(2) identified mixed straddle. On March 10, 1985, A disposes of the section 1256 contract at a $500 loss and the non-section 1256 position at a $500 gain. Under these circumstances, on March 2, 1985, A will recognize $400 of short-term capital gain attributable to the gain accrued on the non-section 1256 position prior to the day the section 1092(b)(2) identified mixed straddle was established. On March 10, 1985, the gain of $500 on the non-section 1256 position will be reduced to $100 to take into account the $400 of gain recognized when the section 1092(b)(2) identified mixed straddle was established. The $100 gain on the non-section 1256 position will be offset against the $500 loss on the section 1256 contract. The net loss of $400 from the straddle will be treated as 60 percent long-term capital loss and 40 percent short-term capital loss because it is attributable to the section 1256 contract.

(7) *Treatment of gain and loss from non-section 1256 positions after disposition of all section 1256 contracts.*—Gain or loss on a non-section 1256 position that is part of a section 1092(b)(2) identified mixed straddle and that is held after all section 1256 contracts in the straddle are disposed of shall be treated as short-term capital gain or loss to the extent attributable to the period when the positions were part of such straddle. See § 1.1092(b)-2T for rules concerning the holding period of such positions. This paragraph (b)(7) may be illustrated by the following example. It is assumed that the positions are the only positions held directly or indirectly (through a related person or flowthrough entity) during the taxable years.

Example. On December 1, 1985, A, an individual calendar year taxpayer, enters into a section 1256 contract and an offsetting non-section 1256 position and makes a valid election to treat such straddle as a section 1092(b)(2) identified mixed straddle. On December 31, 1985, A disposes of the section 1256 contract at a $1,000 loss. On the same day, there is $1,000 of unrecognized gain in the non-section 1256 position. The $1,000 loss on the section 1256 contract is treated as short-term capital loss because there is a $1,000 gain on the non-section 1256 position, but the $1,000 loss is disallowed in 1985 because there is $1,000 of unrecognized gain in the offsetting non-section 1256 position. See section 1092(a) and §1.1092(b)-1T. On July 10, 1986, A disposes of the non-section 1256 position at a $1,500 gain, $500 of which is attributable to the post-straddle period. Under these circumstances, $1,000 of the gain on the non-section 1256 position will be treated as short-term capital gain because that amount of the gain is attributable to the period when the position was part of a section 1092(b)(2) identified mixed straddle. The remaining $500 of the gain will be treated as long-term capital gain because the position was held for more than six months after the straddle was terminated. In addition, the $1,000 short-term capital loss disallowed in 1985 will be taken into account at this time.

(c) *Coordination with loss deferral and wash sale rules of §1.1092(b)-1T.*—This section shall apply prior to the application of the loss deferral and wash sale rules of §1.1092(b)-1T.

(d) *Identification required.*—(1) *In general.*—To elect the provisions of this section, a taxpayer must clearly identify on a reasonable and consistently applied economic basis each position that is part of the section 1092(b)(2) identified mixed straddle before the close of the day on which the section 1092(b)(2) identified mixed straddle is established. If the taxpayer disposes of a position that is part of a section 1092(b)(2) identified mixed straddle before the close of the day on which the straddle is established, such identification must be made at or before the time that the taxpayer disposes of the position. In the case of a taxpayer who is an individual, the close of the day is midnight (local time) in the location of the taxpayer's principal residence. In the case of all other taxpayers, the close of the day is midnight (local time) in the location of the taxpayer's principal place of business. Only the person or entity that directly holds all positions of a straddle may make the election under this section.

(2) *Presumptions.*—A taxpayer is presumed to have identified a section 1092(b)(2) identified mixed straddle by the time prescribed in paragraph (d)(1) of this section if the taxpayer receives independent verification of the identification (within the meaning of paragraph (d)(4) of this section). The presumption referred to in this paragraph (d)(2) may be rebutted by clear and convincing evidence to the contrary.

(3) *Corroborating evidence.*—If the presumption of paragraph (d)(2) of this section does not apply, the burden shall be on the taxpayer to establish that an election under paragraph (d)(1) of this section was made by the time specified in paragraph (d)(1) of this section. If the taxpayer has no evidence of the time when the identification required by paragraph (d)(1) of this section is made, other than the taxpayer's own testimony, the election is invalid unless the taxpayer shows good cause for failure to have evidence other than the taxpayer's own testimony.

(4) *Independent verification.*—For purposes of this section, the following constitute independent verification:

(i) *Separate Account.*—Placement of one or more positions of a section 1092(b)(2) identified mixed straddle in a separate account designated as a "section 1092(b)(2) identified mixed straddle account" that is maintained by a broker (as defined in §1.6045-1(a)(1)), futures commission merchant (as defined in 7 U.S.C. 2 and 17 CFR 1.3 (p)), or similar person and in which notations are made by such person identifying all positions of the section 1092(b)(2) identified mixed straddle and stating the date the straddle is established.

(ii) *Confirmation.*—A written confirmation from a person referred to in paragraph (d)(4)(i) of this section, or from the party from which one or more positions of the section 1092(b)(2) identified mixed straddle are acquired, stating the date the straddle is established and identifying the other positions of the straddle.

(iii) *Other methods.*—Such other methods of independent verification as the Commissioner may approve at the Commissioner's discretion.

(5) *Section 1092(b)(2) identified mixed straddles established before February 25, 1985.*—Notwithstanding the provisions of paragraph (d)(1) of this section, relating to the time of identification of a section 1092(b)(2) identified mixed straddle, a taxpayer may identify straddles that were established before February 25, 1985, as section 1092(b)(2) identified mixed straddles after the time specified in paragraph (d)(1) of this section if the taxpayer adopts a reasonable and consistent economic basis for identifying the positions of such straddles.

(e) *Effective date.*—(1) *In general.*—The provisions of this section shall apply to straddles established on or after January 1, 1984.

(2) *Pre-1984 accrued gain.*—If the last business day referred to in paragraph (b)(6) of this section is contained in a period to which paragraph (b)(6) does not apply, the gains and losses from the deemed sale shall be included in the first period to which paragraph (b)(6) applies. [Temporary Reg. §1.1092(b)-3T.]

☐ [*T.D.* 8008, 1-18-85.]

[Reg. §1.1092(b)-4T]

§1.1092(b)-4T. Mixed straddles; mixed straddle account (Temporary).—(a) *In general.*—A taxpayer may elect (in accordance with paragraph (f) of this section) to establish one or more mixed straddle accounts (as defined in paragraph (b) of this section). Gains and losses from positions includible in a mixed straddle account shall be determined and treated in accordance with the rules set forth in paragraph (c) of this section. A mixed straddle account is treated as established as of the first day of the taxable year for which the taxpayer makes the election or January 1, 1984, whichever is later. See § 1.1092(b)-5T relating to definitions.

(b) *Mixed straddle account defined.*—(1) *In general.*—The term "mixed straddle account" means an account for determining gains and losses from all positions held as capital assets in a designated class of activities by the taxpayer at the time the taxpayer elects to establish a mixed straddle account. A separate mixed straddle account must be established for each separate designated class of activities.

(2) *Permissible designations.*—Except as otherwise provided in this section, a taxpayer may designate as a class of activities the types of positions that a reasonable person, on the basis of all the facts and circumstances, would ordinarily expect to be offsetting positions. This paragraph (b)(2) may be illustrated by the following example. It is assumed in the example that the positions are the only positions held directly or indirectly (through a related person or flowthrough entity) during the taxable year, and that gain or loss from the positions is treated as gain or loss from a capital asset.

Example. B engages in transactions in dealer equity options on XYZ Corporation stock, stock in XYZ Corporation, dealer equity options on UVW Corporation stock, and stock in UVW Corporation. A reasonable person, on the basis of all the facts and circumstances, would not expect dealer equity options on XYZ Corporation stock and stock in XYZ Corporation to offset any dealer equity options on UVW Corporation stock or any stock in UVW Corporation. If B makes the mixed straddle account election under this section for all such positions, B must designate two separate classes of activities, one consisting of transactions in dealer equity options on XYZ Corporation stock and stock in XYZ Corporation, and the other consisting of transactions in dealer equity options on UVW Corporation stock and stock in UVW Corporation, and maintain two separate mixed straddle accounts.

(3) *Positions that offset positions in more than one mixed straddle account.*—Gains and losses from positions that a reasonable person, on the basis of all the facts and circumstances, ordinarily would expect to be offsetting with respect to positions in more than one mixed straddle account shall be allocated among such accounts under a reasonable and consistent method that clearly reflects income. This paragraph (b)(2) may be illustrated by the following example. It is assumed that the positions are the only positions held directly or indirectly (through a related person or flowthrough entity) during the taxable year, and that gain or loss from the positions is treated as gain or loss from a capital asset.

Example. B holds stock in XYZ Corporation, UVW Corporation, and RST Corporation, and options on a broad based stock index future. A

reasonable person, on the basis of all the facts and circumstances, would expect the stock in XYZ Corporation, UVW Corporation, and RST Corporation to be offsetting positions with respect to the options on the broad based stock index future. A reasonable person, on the basis of all the facts and circumstances, would not expect that stock in XYZ Corporation, UVW Corporation, or RST Corporation would be offsetting positions with respect to each other. If B makes the mixed straddle account election under this section for all such positions, B must designate three separate classes of activities: one consisting of stock in XYZ Corporation; one consisting of stock in UVW Corporation; and one consisting of stock in RST Corporation, and maintain three separate mixed straddle accounts. Options on the broad based stock index future must be designated as part of all three classes of activities and gains and losses from such options must be allocated among such accounts under a reasonable and consistent method that clearly reflects income, because such options are a type of position expected to be offsetting with respect to the positions in all three mixed straddle accounts.

(4) *Impermissible designations.*—(i) *Types of positions that are not offsetting included in designated class of activities.*—If the Commissioner determines, on the basis of all the facts and circumstances, that a class of activities designated by a taxpayer includes types of positions that a reasonable person, on the basis of all the facts and circumstances, ordinarily would not expect to be offsetting positions with respect to other types of positions in the account, the Commissioner may—

(A) Amend the class of activities designated by the taxpayer and remove positions from the account that are not within the amended designated class of activities; or

(B) Amend the class of activities designated by the taxpayer to establish two or more mixed straddle accounts.

(ii) *Types of positions that are offsetting not included in designated class of activities.*—If the Commissioner determines, on the basis of all the facts and circumstances, that a designated class of activities does not include types of positions that are offsetting with respect to types of positions within the designated class, the Commissioner may—

(A) Amend the class of activities designated by the taxpayer to include types of positions that are offsetting with respect to the types of positions within the designated class and place such positions in the account; or

(B) Amend the class of activities designated by the taxpayer to exclude types of positions that are offsetting with respect to the types of positions that are not in the account.

(iii) *Treatment of positions removed from or included in the account.*—(A) Positions removed from a mixed straddle account will be subject to the rules of taxation generally applicable to such positions. Thus, for example, if the positions removed from the account are offsetting positions with respect to other positions outside the account, the rules of §§ 1.1092(b)-1T and 1.1092(b)-2T apply.

(B) If the taxpayer acted consistently and in good faith in designating the class of activities of the account and in placing positions in the account, the rules of § 1.1092(b)-2T(b)(2) shall not apply to any mixed straddles resulting from the removal of such positions from the account and the Commissioner, at the Commissioner's discretion, may identify such mixed straddles as section 1092(b)(2) identified mixed straddles and apply the rules of § 1.1092(b)-3T(b) to such straddles.

(C) If positions are placed in a mixed straddle account, such positions shall be treated as if they were originally included in the mixed straddle account in which they are placed.

(5) *Positions included in a mixed straddle account that are not within the designated class of activities.*—The Commissioner may remove one or more positions from a mixed straddle account if, on the basis of all the facts and circumstances, the Commissioner determines that such positions are not within the designated class of activities of the account. See paragraph (b)(4)(iii) of this section for rules concerning the treatment of such positions.

(6) *Positions outside a mixed straddle account that are within the designated class of activities.*—If a taxpayer holds types of positions outside of a mixed straddle account (including positions in another mixed straddle account) that are within the designated class of activities of a mixed straddle account, the Commissioner may require the taxpayer to include such types of positions in the mixed straddle account, move positions from one account to another, or remove from the mixed straddle account types of positions that are offsetting with respect to the types of positions held outside the account. See paragraph (b)(4)(iii) of this section for the treatment of such positions.

(c) *Treatment of gains and losses from positions in a mixed straddle account.*—(1) *Daily account net gain or loss.*—Except as provided in paragraphs (d) and (e) of this section (relating to positions in a mixed straddle account before January 1, 1985) as of the close of each business day of the taxable year, gain or loss shall be determined for each position in a mixed straddle account that is disposed of during the day. Positions in a mixed straddle account that have not been disposed of as of the close of the day shall be treated as if sold for their fair market value at the close of each business day. Gains and losses for each business day from non-section 1256 positions in each mixed straddle account shall be netted to determine "net non-section 1256 position gain or

loss" for the account, and gains and losses for each business day from section 1256 contracts in each mixed straddle account shall be netted to determine "net section 1256 contract gain or loss" for the account. Net non-section 1256 position gain or loss from the account is then offset against net section 1256 contract gain or loss from the same mixed straddle account to determine the "daily account net gain or loss" for the account. If daily account net gain or loss is attributable to the net non-section 1256 position gain or loss, daily account net gain or loss for such account shall be treated as short-term capital gain or loss. If daily account net gain or loss is attributable to the net section 1256 contract gain or loss, daily account net gain or loss for such account shall be treated as 60 percent long-term capital gain or loss and 40 percent short-term capital gain or loss. If net non-section 1256 position gain or loss and net section 1256 contract gain or loss are either both gains or both losses, that portion of the daily account net gain or loss attributable to net non-section 1256 position gain or loss shall be treated as short-term capital gain or loss and that portion of the daily account net gain or loss attributable to net section 1256 contract gain or loss shall be treated as 60 percent long-term capital gain or loss and 40 percent short-term capital gain or loss. An adjustment (through an adjustment to basis or otherwise) shall be made to any subsequent gain or loss determined under this paragraph (c)(1) to take into account any gain or loss determined for prior business days under this paragraph (c)(1).

(2) *Annual account net gain or loss; total annual account net gain or loss.*—On the last business day of the taxable year, the "annual account net gain or loss" for each mixed straddle account established by the taxpayer shall be determined by netting the daily account net gain or loss for each business day in the taxable year for each account. Annual account net gain or loss for each mixed straddle account shall be adjusted pursuant to paragraph (c)(3) of this section. The "total annual account net gain or loss" shall be determined by netting the annual account net gain or loss for all mixed straddle accounts established by the taxpayer, as adjusted pursuant to paragraph (c)(3) of this section. Total annual account net gain or loss is subject to the limitations of paragraph (c)(4) of this section. See paragraphs (d) and (e) of this section for determining the annual account net gain or loss for mixed straddle accounts established for taxable years beginning before January 1, 1985.

(3) *Application of section 263(g) to mixed straddle accounts.*—No deduction shall be allowed for interest and carrying charges (as defined in section 263(g)(2)) properly allocable to a mixed straddle account. Interest and carrying charges properly allocable to a mixed straddle account means the excess of—

(i) The sum of—

Reg. § 1.1092(b)-4T(c)(3)(i)

(A) Interest on indebtedness incurred or continued during the taxable year to purchase or carry any position in the account; and

(B) All other amounts (including charges to insure, store, or transport the personal property) paid or incurred to carry any position in the account; over

(ii) The sum of—

(A) The amount of interest (including original issue discount) includible in gross income for the taxable year with respect to all positions in the account;

(B) Any amount treated as ordinary income under section 1271(a)(3)(A), 1278, or 1281(a) with respect to any position in the account for the taxable year; and

(C) The excess of any dividends includible in gross income with respect to positions in the account for the taxable year over the amount of any deduction allowable with respect to such dividends under section 243, 244, or 245.

For purposes of paragraph (c)(3)(i) of this section, the term "interest" includes any amount paid or incurred in connection with positions in the account used in a short sale. Any interest and carrying charges disallowed under this paragraph (c)(3) shall be capitalized by treating such charges as an adjustment to the annual account net gain or loss and shall be allocated pro rata between net short-term capital gain or loss and net long-term capital gain or loss.

(4) *Limitation on total annual account net gain or loss.*—No more than 50 percent of total annual account net gain for the taxable year shall be treated as long-term capital gain. Any long-term capital gain in excess of the 50 percent limit shall be treated as short-term capital gain. No more than 40 percent of total annual account net loss for the taxable year shall be treated as short-term capital loss. Any short-term capital loss in excess

of the 40 percent limit shall be treated as long-term capital loss.

(5) *Accrued gain and loss with respect to positions includible in a mixed straddle account.*—Positions includible in a mixed straddle account that are held by a taxpayer on the day prior to the day the mixed straddle account is established shall be deemed sold for their fair market value as of the close of the last business day preceding the day such mixed straddle account is established. See §§ 1.1092(b)-1T and 1.1092(b)-2T for application of the loss deferral and wash sale rules and for treatment of holding periods and losses with respect to such positions. An adjustment (through an adjustment to basis or otherwise) shall be made to any subsequent gain or loss realized with respect to such positions for any gain or loss recognized under this paragraph (c)(5).

(6) *Examples.*—This paragraph (c) may be illustrated by the following examples. It is assumed in each example that the positions are the only positions held directly or indirectly (through a related person or flow-through entity) by an individual calendar year taxpayer during the taxable year, and that gain or loss from the positions is treated as gain or loss from a capital asset.

Example (1). A establishes a mixed straddle account for a class of activities consisting of transactions in stock of XYZ Corporation and dealer equity options on XYZ Corporation stock. Assume that A enters into no transactions in XYZ Corporation stock or dealer equity options on XYZ Corporation stock prior to December 26, 1985. Thus, the net non-section 1256 position gain or loss and the net section 1256 contract gain or loss for the account are zero for each business day except the following days:

	Net non-section 1256 position gain or loss (XYZ Corporation stock)	Net section 1256 contract gain or loss (XYZ Corporation dealer equity options)
December 26, 1985	$1,000	$20,000
December 27, 1985	(9,000)	3,000
December 30, 1985	(5,000)	15,000
December 31, 1985	7,000	(2,000)

The daily account net gain or loss is as follows:

	Daily account net gain or loss	Treatment of daily account net gain or loss	Long-term	Short-term
December 26, 1985	$21,000	$1,000 short-term capital gain, $20,000 60 percent long-term capital gain and 40 percent short-term capital gain	$12,000	$9,000
December 27, 1985	(6,000)	short-term capital loss	....	(6,000)

Reg. § 1.1092(b)-4T(c)(3)(i)(A)

	Daily account net gain or loss	Treatment of daily account net gain or loss	Long-term	Short-term
December 30, 1985	10,000	60 percent long-term capital gain and 40 percent short-term capital gain	6,000	4,000
December 31, 1985	5,000	short-term capital gain	. . . . .	5,000

The annual account net gain or loss is $18,000 of long-term capital gain and $12,000 of short-term capital gain. Because A has no other mixed straddle accounts, total annual account net gain or loss is also $18,000 long-term capital gain and $12,000 short-term capital gain. Because more than 50 percent of the total annual account net gain is long-term capital gain, $3,000 of the $18,000 long-term capital gain will be treated as short-term capital gain.

Example (2). Assume the facts are the same as in example (1), except that interest and carrying charges in the amount of $6,000 are allocable to the mixed straddle account and are capitalized under paragraph (c)(3) of this section. Under these circumstances, $3,600 (($18,000/$30,000) × $6,000) of the interest and carrying charges will reduce the $18,000 long-term capital gain to $14,400 long-term capital gain and $2,400 (($12,000/$30,000) × $6,000) of the interest and carrying charges will reduce the $12,000 short-term capital gain to $9,600 short-term capital gain. Because more than 50 percent of the total annual account net gain is long-term capital gain, $2,400 of the $14,400 long-term capital gain will be treated as short-term capital gain.

Example (3). Assume the facts are the same as in example (1), except that A has a second mixed straddle account, which has an annual account net loss of $14,000 of long-term capital loss and $6,000 of short-term capital loss. Under these circumstances, the total annual account net gain is $4,000 ($18,000 − $14,000) of long-term capital gain and $6,000 ($12,000 − $6,000) of short-term capital gain. Because not more than 50 percent of the total annual account net gain is long-term capital gain, none of the long-term capital gain will be treated as short-term capital gain.

Example (4). Assume the facts are the same as in example (3), except that interest and carrying charges in the amount of $4,000 are allocable to the second mixed straddle account and are capitalized under paragraph (c)(3) of this section. Under these circumstances, $2,800 (($14,000/$20,000) × $4,000) of the interest and carrying charges will increase the $14,000 long-term capital loss to $16,800 of long-term capital loss and $1,200 (($6,000/$20,000) × $4,000) of the interest and carrying charges will increase the $6,000 short-term capital loss to $7,200 short-term capital loss. The total annual account net gain is $1,200 of long-term capital gain ($18,000 − $16,800) and $4,800 ($12,000 − $7,200) of short-term capital gain. Because not more than 50 percent of the total annual account net gain is long-term capital gain, none of the $1,200 long-term capital gain will be treated as short-term capital gain.

Example (5). Assume the facts are the same as in example (1), except that A has a second mixed straddle account, which has an annual account net loss of $20,000 of long-term capital loss and $15,000 of short-term capital loss. Under these circumstances, the total annual account net loss is $2,000 ($20,000 − $18,000) of long-term capital loss and $3,000 ($15,000 − $12,000) of short-term capital loss. Because more than 40 percent of the total annual account net loss is short-term capital loss, $1,000 of the short-term capital loss will be treated as long-term capital loss.

Example (6). A establishes two mixed straddle accounts. Account 1 has an annual account net gain of $5,000 short-term capital gain, which results from netting $5,000 of long-term capital loss and $10,000 of short-term capital gain. Account 2 has an annual account net loss of $2,000 long-term capital loss, which results from netting $3,000 of long-term capital loss against $1,000 of short-term capital gain. The total annual account net gain is $3,000 short-term capital gain, which results from netting the annual account net gain of $5,000 short-term capital gain from Account 1 against the annual account net loss of $2,000 long-term capital loss from Account 2.

(d) *Treatment of gains and losses from positions in a mixed straddle account established on or before December 31, 1984, in taxable years ending after December 31, 1984; pre-1985 account net gain or loss.*—For mixed straddle accounts established on or before December 31, 1984, in taxable years ending after December 31, 1984, the taxpayer on December 31, 1984, shall determine gain or loss for each position in the mixed straddle account that has been disposed of on any day during the period beginning on the first day of the taxpayer's taxable year that includes December 31, 1984, and ending on December 31, 1984. Positions in the mixed straddle account that have not been disposed of as of the close of December 31, 1984, shall be treated as if sold for their fair market value as of the close of December 31, 1984. Gains and losses for such period from non-section 1256 positions in each mixed straddle account shall be netted to determine "pre-1985 net non-section 1256 position gain or loss" and gains and losses for such period from section 1256 contracts in each mixed straddle account shall be netted to determine "pre-1985 net section 1256 contract gain or loss." Pre-1985 net non-section 1256 position gain or loss is then offset against pre-1985 net section 1256 contract gain or loss from the same mixed straddle account to determine the "pre-1985 account net gain or loss" for the period. If the pre-1985 account net gain or loss is attributable to pre-1985 net non-section 1256 position gain or loss, the pre-1985 account net gain or loss from such account shall be treated as short-term capital gain or loss. If the pre-1985 account net gain or loss is attributable to pre-1985 net section 1256 contract gain or loss, the pre-1985 account net gain or loss from such account shall be treated as 60 percent long-term capital gain or loss and 40 percent short-term capital gain or loss. If pre-1985 net non-section 1256 position gain or loss and pre-1985 net section 1256 contract gain or loss are either both gains or losses, that portion of the pre-1985 account net gain or loss attributable to pre-1985 net non-section 1256 position gain or loss shall be treated as short-term capital gain or loss and that portion of the pre-1985 account net gain or loss attributable to pre-1985 net section 1256 contract gain or loss shall be treated as 60 percent long-term capital gain or loss and 40 percent short-term capital gain or loss. An adjustment (through an adjustment to basis or otherwise) shall be made to any subsequent gain or loss realized with respect to such positions for any gain or loss recognized under this paragraph (d). To determine the annual account net gain or loss for such account, the pre-1985 account net gain or loss shall be treated as daily account net gain or loss for purposes of paragraph (c)(2) of this section. See paragraph (c)(5) of this section for treatment of accrued gain or loss with respect to positions includible in a mixed straddle account.

(e) *Treatment of gains and losses from positions in a mixed straddle account for taxable years ending on or before December 31, 1984.*—(1) *In general.*—For mixed straddle accounts established on or before December 31, 1984, in taxable years ending on or before December 31, 1984, the taxpayer at the close of the taxable year shall determine gain or loss for each position in the mixed straddle account that has been disposed of on any day during the period beginning on the later of the first day of the taxable year or January 1, 1984, and ending on the last day of the taxable year. Positions in the mixed straddle account that have not been disposed of as of the close of the last business day of the taxable year shall be treated as if sold for their fair market value at the close of such day. Gains and losses from non-section 1256 positions in each mixed straddle account shall be netted to determine "1984 net non-section 1256 position gain or loss" for the account and gains and losses from section 1256 contracts shall be netted to determine "1984 net section 1256 contract gain or loss" for the account. The 1984 net non-section 1256 position gain or loss is then offset against 1984 net section 1256 contract gain or loss from the same mixed straddle account to determine "annual account net gain or loss" for the account. If annual account net gain or loss is attributable to 1984 net non-section 1256 position gain or loss, annual

account net gain or loss shall be treated as short-term capital gain or loss. If annual account net gain or loss is attributable to 1984 net section 1256 contract gain or loss, annual account net gain or loss shall be treated as 60 percent long-term capital gain or loss and 40 percent short-term capital gain or loss. If 1984 net non-section 1256 position gain or loss and 1984 net section 1256 contract gain or loss are either both gains or both losses, that portion of annual account net gain or loss attributable to 1984 net non-section 1256 position gain or loss shall be treated as short-term capital gain or loss and that portion of annual account net gain or loss attributable to 1984 net section 1256 contract gain or loss shall be treated as 60 percent long-term capital gain or loss and 40 percent short-term capital gain or loss. An adjustment (through an adjustment to basis or otherwise) shall be made to any subsequent gain or loss realized with respect to such positions for any gain or loss recognized under this paragraph (e). See paragraph (c)(2) through (5) of this section relating to determining the total annual account net gain or loss, application of section 263(g) to mixed straddle accounts, the limitation on the total annual account net gain or loss, and treatment of accrued gain or loss with respect to positions includible in a mixed straddle account.

(2) *Pre-1984 accrued gain.*—If the last business day referred to in paragraph (c)(5) of this section is contained in a period to which such paragraph (c)(5) does not apply, the gains and losses from the deemed sale shall be included in the first period to which paragraph (c)(5) applies.

(f) *Election.*—(1) *Time for making the election.*—Except as otherwise provided, the election under this section to establish one or more mixed straddle accounts for a taxable year must be made by the due date (without regard to automatic and discretionary extensions) of the taxpayer's income tax return for the immediately preceding taxable year (or part thereof). For example, an individual taxpayer on a calendar year basis must make the election by April 15, 1986, to establish one or more mixed straddle accounts for taxable year 1986. Similarly, a calendar year corporate taxpayer must make its election by March 15, 1986, to establish one or more mixed straddle accounts for 1986. If a taxpayer begins trading or investing in positions in a new class of activities during a taxable year, the election under this seciton with respect to the new class of activities must be made by the taxpayer by the later of the due date of the taxpayer's income tax return for the immediately preceding taxable year (without regard to automatic and discretionary extensions), or 60 days after the first mixed straddle in the new class of activities is entered into. Similarly, if on or after the date the election is made with respect to an account, the taxpayer begins trading or investing in positions that are includible in such account but were not specified in the original election, the taxpayer must make an amended election as prescribed in paragraph (f)(2)(ii) of this section by the later of the due date of the taxpayer's income tax return for the immediately preceding taxable year (without regard to automatic and discretionary extensions), or 60 days after the acquisition of the first of the positions. If an election is made after the times specified in this paragraph (f)(1), the election will be permitted only if the Commissioner concludes that the taxpayer had reasonable cause for failing to make a timely election. For example, if a calendar year taxpayer holds few positions in one class of activities prior to April 15 of a taxable year, and the taxpayer greatly increases trading activity with respect to positions in the class of activities after April 15, then the Commissioner may conclude that the taxpayer had reasonable cause for failing to make a timely election and allow the taxpayer to make a mixed straddle account election for the taxable year. See paragraph (f)(2) of this section for rules relating to the manner for making these elections.

(2) *Manner for making the election.*—(i) *In general.*—A taxpayer must make the election on Form 6781 in the manner prescribed by such Form, and by attaching the Form to the taxpayer's income tax return for the immediately preceding taxable year (or request for an automatic extension). In addition, the taxpayer must attach a statement to Form 6781 designating with specificity the class of activities for which a mixed straddle account is established. The designation must describe the class of activities in sufficient detail so that the Commissioner may determine, on the basis of the designation, whether specific positions are includible in the mixed straddle account. In the case of a taxpayer who elects to establish more than one mixed straddle account, the Commissioner must be able to determine, on the basis of the designations, that specific positions are placed in the appropriate account. The election applies to all positions in the designated class of activities held by the taxpayer during the taxable year.

(ii) *Elections for new classes of activities and expanded elections.*—Amended elections and elections made with respect to a new class of activities that the taxpayer has begun trading or investing in during a taxable year, shall be made on Form 6781 within the times prescribed in paragraph (f)(1) of this section. A statement must be attached to the Form containing the information required in paragraph (f)(2)(i) of this section, with respect to the new or expanded designated class of activities.

(iii) *Special rule.*—The Commissioner may disregard a mixed straddle account election if the Commissioner determines, on the basis of all the facts and circumstances, that the principal purpose for making the mixed straddle account election with respect to a class of activities was to

avoid the rules of § 1.1092(b)-1T(a). For example, if a taxpayer holds stock that is not part of a straddle and that would generate a loss if sold or otherwise disposed of, and the taxpayer both acquires offsetting option positions with respect to the stock and makes a mixed straddle account election with respect to the stock and stock options near the end of a taxable year, the Commissioner may disregard the mixed straddle account election.

(3) *Special rule for taxable years ending after 1983 and before September 1, 1986.*—An election under this section to establish one or more mixed straddle accounts for any taxable year that includes July 17, 1984, and any taxable year that ends before September 1, 1986 (or, in the case of a corporation, October 1, 1986), must be made by the later of—

(i) December 31, 1985, or

(ii) The due date (without regard to automatic and discretionary extensions) of the return for the taxpayer's taxable year that begins in 1984 if the due date of the taxpayer's return for such year (without regard to automatic and discretionary extensions) is after December 31, 1985.

The election shall be made by attaching Form 6781 together with a statement to the taxpayer's income tax return, amended return, or other appropriate form that is filed on or before the deadline determined in the preceding sentence. The attached statement must designate with specificity, in accordance with paragraph (f)(2)(i) of this section, the class of activities for which a mixed straddle account is established. For example, if a fiscal year taxpayer's return (for its taxable year ending September 30, 1985) is due (without regard to extensions) on January 15, 1986, and the taxpayer intends to obtain an automatic extension to file the return, the election under this section for any or all of the fiscal years ending in 1984, 1985 or 1986 must be made on or before January 15, 1986, with the request for an automatic extension. Similarly, a calendar year taxpayer (whether or not such taxpayer has obtained an automatic extension of time to file) who has filed its 1984 income tax return before October 15, 1985, without making a mixed straddle account election for either 1984 or 1985, or both, may make the mixed straddle account election under this section for either or for both of such years with an amended return filed on or before December 31, 1985. The mixed straddle account elected on this amended return will be effective for all positions in the designated class of activities even if the taxpayer had elected straddle-by-straddle identification as provided under § 1.1092(b)-3T for purposes of the previously filed 1984 income tax return. For taxable years beginning in 1984 and 1985, the election under this paragraph (f)(3) is effective for the entire taxable year. For taxable years beginning in 1983, an election shall be effective for that part of the year beginning after December 31, 1983, for which the election under §§ 1.1256(h)-1T or

1.1256(h)-2T is made. See § 1.6081-1T regarding an extension of time to file certain individual income tax returns.

(4) *Period for which election is effective.*—For taxable years beginning on or after January 1, 1984, an election under this section, including an amendment to the election pursuant to paragraph (f)(1) of this section, shall be effective only for the taxable year for which the election is made. This election may be revoked during the taxable year for the remainder of the taxable year only with the consent of the Commissioner. An application for consent to revoke the election shall be filed with the service center with which the election was filed and shall—

(i) Contain the name, address, and taxpayer identification number of the taxpayer;

(ii) Show that the volume or nature of the taxpayer's activities has changed substantially since the election was made, and that the taxpayer's activities no longer warrant the use of such mixed straddle account; and

(iii) Any other relevant information.

If a taxpayer's election for a taxable year is revoked, the taxpayer may not make a new election for the same class of activities under paragraph (f)(1) of this section during the same taxable year.

(g) *Effective date.*—The provisions of this section apply to positions held on or after January 1, 1984. [Temporary Reg. § 1.1092(b)-4T.]

☐ [*T.D.* 8008, 1-18-85. *Amended by T.D.* 8058, 10-11-85.]

[Reg. § 1.1092(b)-5T]

§ 1.1092(b)-5T. Definitions (Temporary).—The following definitions apply for purposes of §§ 1.1092(b)-1T through 1.1092(b)-4T.

(a) *Disposing, disposes, or disposed.*—The term "disposing," "disposes," or "disposed" includes the sale, exchange, cancellation, lapse, expiration, or other termination of a right or obligation with respect to personal property (as defined in section 1092(d)(1)).

(b) *Hedging transaction.*—The term "hedging transaction" means a hedging transaction as defined in section 1256(e).

(c) *Identified straddle.*—The term "identified straddle" means an identified straddle as defined in section 1092(a)(2)(B).

(d) *Loss.*—The term "loss" means a loss otherwise allowable under section 165(a) (without regard to the limitation contained in section 165(f)) and includes a write-down in inventory.

(e) *Mixed straddle.*—The term "mixed straddle" means a straddle—

(1) All of the positions of which are held as capital assets;

(2) At least one (but not all) of the positions of which is a section 1256 contract;

(3) For which an election under section 1256(d) has not been made; and

(4) Which is not part of a larger straddle.

(f) *Non-section 1256 position.*—The term "non-section 1256 position" means a position that is not a section 1256 contract.

(g) *Offsetting position.*—The term "offsetting position" means an offsetting position as defined in section 1092(c)(2).

(h) *Position.*—The term "position" means a position as defined in section 1092(d)(2).

(i) [Reserved]

(j) *Related person or flowthrough entity.*—The term "related person or flowthrough entity" means a related person or flowthrough entity as defined in sections 1092(d)(4)(B) and (C), respectively.

(k) *Section 1256 contract.*—The term "section 1256 contract" means a section 1256 contract as defined in section 1256(b).

(l) [Reserved]

(m) *Straddle.*—The term "straddle" means a straddle as defined in section 1092(c)(1).

(n) *Successor position.*—The term "successor position" means a position ("P") that is or was at any time offsetting to a second position if—

(1) The second position was offsetting to any loss position disposed of; and

(2) P is entered into during a period commencing 30 days prior to, and ending 30 days after, the disposition of the loss position referred to in paragraph (n)(1) of this section.

(3) P is entered into no later than 30 days after the loss position is no longer included in a straddle.

(o) *Unrecognized gain.*—The term "unrecognized gain" means unrecognized gain as defined in section 1092(a)(3)(A).

(p) *Substantially identical.*—The term "substantially identical" has the same meaning as substantially identical in section 1091(a).

(q) *Securities.*—The term "security" means a security as defined in section 1236(c). [Temporary Reg. § 1.1092(b)-5T.]

☐ [*T.D.* 8007, 1-18-85. *Amended by T.D.* 8070, 1-13-86.]

[Reg. § 1.1092(c)-1]

§ 1.1092(c)-1. Qualified covered calls.—(a) *In general.*—Section 1092(c) defines a straddle as offsetting positions with respect to personal property. Under section 1092(d)(3)(B)(i)(I), stock is personal property if the stock is part of a straddle that involves an option on that stock or substantially identical stock or securities. Under section 1092(c)(4), however, writing a qualified covered call option and owning the optioned stock is not treated as a straddle under section 1092 if certain conditions, described in section 1092(c)(4)(B), are satisfied. Section 1092(c)(4)(H) authorizes the Secretary to modify these conditions to carry out the purposes of section 1092(c)(4) in light of changes in the marketplace.

(b) *Term limitation.*—(1) *General rule.*—Except as provided in paragraph (b)(2) of this section, an option is not a qualified covered call unless it is granted not more than 12 months before the day on which the option expires or satisfies term limitation and qualified benchmark requirements established by the Commissioner in guidance published in the Internal Revenue Bulletin (see § 601.601(d)(2)(ii)(*b*) of this chapter).

(2) *Special benchmark rule for an option granted not more than 33 months before the day on which the option expires.*—(i) *In general.*—The 12-month limitation described in paragraph (b)(1) of this section is extended to 33 months provided the lowest qualified benchmark is determined using the adjusted applicable stock price, as defined in § 1.1092(c)-4(e).

(ii) *Examples.*—The following examples illustrate the rules set out in paragraph (b)(2)(i) of this section:

Example 1. Taxpayer owns stock in Corporation X. Taxpayer writes an equity option with standardized terms on Corporation X stock through a national securities exchange with a term of 21 months. The applicable stock price for Corporation X stock is $100. The bench marks for a 21-month equity option with standardized terms with an applicable stock price of $100 will be based upon the adjusted applicable stock price. Using the table at § 1.1092(c)-4(e), the applicable stock price of $100 is multiplied by the adjustment factor 1.12, resulting in an adjusted applicable stock price of $112. Using the bench marks for an equity option with standardized terms with an adjusted applicable stock price of $112, the highest available strike price less than the adjusted applicable stock price is $110, and the second highest strike price less than the adjusted applicable stock price is $105. Therefore, a 21-month equity call option with standardized terms on Corporation X stock will not be deep in the money if the strike price is not less than $105.

Example 2. Taxpayer owns stock in Corporation Y. Taxpayer writes an equity option with standardized terms on Corporation Y stock through a national securities exchange with a term of 21 months. The applicable stock price for Corporation Y stock is $13.25. The bench marks for a 21-month equity option with standardized terms with an applicable stock price of $13.25 will be based upon the adjusted applicable stock price. Using the table at § 1.1092(c)-4(e), the applicable stock price of $13.25 is multiplied by the adjustment factor 1.12, resulting in an adjusted

applicable stock price of $14.84. Using the bench marks for an equity option with standardized terms with an adjusted applicable stock price of $14.84, the highest available strike price less than the adjusted applicable stock price is $12.50. However, under section 1092(c)(4)(D), the lowest qualified bench mark can be no lower than 85% of the applicable stock price, which for Corporation Y stock is $12.61 (85% of the adjusted applicable stock price of $14.84). Thus, because the highest available strike price less than the adjusted applicable stock price for an equity option with standardized terms is lower than the lowest qualified bench mark under section 1092(c)(4)(D), the lowest strike price at which a qualified covered call option can be written is the next higher strike price, or $15.00. Therefore, a 21-month equity call option with standardized terms on Corporation Y stock will not be deep in the money if the strike price is not less than $15.

(c) *Effective date.*—This section applies to qualified covered call options entered into on or after July 29, 2002. [Reg. § 1.1092(c)-1.]

☐ [*T.D.* 8990, 4-26-2002.]

[Reg. § 1.1092(c)-2]

§ 1.1092(c)-2. Equity options with flexible terms.—(a) *In general.*—Section 1092(c)(4) provides an exception to the general rule that a straddle exists if a taxpayer holds stock and writes a call option on that stock. Under section 1092(c)(4), the ownership of stock and the issuance of a call option meeting certain requirements result in a qualified covered call, which is exempted from the general straddle rules of section 1092. This section addresses the consequences of the availability of equity options with flexible terms under the qualified covered call rules.

(b) *No effect on lowest qualified bench mark for standardized options.*—The availability of strike prices for equity options with flexible terms does not affect the determination of the lowest qualified bench mark, as defined in section 1092(c)(4)(D), for an equity option with standardized terms.

(c) *Qualified covered call option status.*—(1) *Requirements.*—An equity option with flexible terms is a qualified covered call option only if—

(i) The option meets the requirements of section 1092(c)(4)(B) and § 1.1092(c)-1 (taking into account paragraph (c)(2) of this section);

(ii) The only payments permitted with respect to the option are a single fixed premium paid not later than 5 business days after the day on which the option is granted, and a single fixed strike price, as defined in § 1.1092(c)-4(d), that is payable entirely at (or within 5 business days of) exercise;

(iii) An equity option with standardized terms is outstanding for the underlying equity; and

(iv) The underlying security is stock in a single corporation.

(2) *Lowest qualified bench mark.*—(i) *In general.*—For purposes of determining whether an equity option with flexible terms is deep in the money within the meaning of section 1092(c)(4)(C), the lowest qualified bench mark under section 1092(c)(4)(D) is the same for an equity option with flexible terms as the lowest qualified bench mark for an equity option with standardized terms on the same stock having the same applicable stock price.

(ii) *Examples.*—The following examples illustrate the rules set out in paragraph (c)(2)(i) of this section:

Example 1. Taxpayer owns stock in Corporation X. Taxpayer writes an equity call option with flexible terms on Corporation X stock through a national securities exchange for a term of not more than 12 months. The applicable stock price for Corporation X stock is $73.75. Using the bench marks for an equity option with standardized terms with an applicable stock price of $73.75, the highest available strike price less than the applicable stock price is $70, and the second highest strike price less than the applicable stock price is $65. Therefore, an equity call option with flexible terms on Corporation X stock with a term of 90 days or less will not be deep in the money if the strike price is not less than $70. If the term is greater than 90 days, an equity call option with flexible terms on Corporation X will not be deep in the money if the strike price is not less than $65.

Example 2. Taxpayer owns stock in Corporation Y. Taxpayer writes a 9-month equity call option with flexible terms on Corporation Y stock through a national securities exchange. The applicable stock price for Corporation Y stock is $14.75. Using the bench marks for an equity option with standardized terms with an applicable stock price of $14.75, the highest available strike price less than the applicable stock price is $12.50. However, under section 1092(c)(4)(D), the lowest qualified bench mark can be no lower than 85% of the applicable stock price, which for Corporation Y stock is $12.54. Thus, because the highest available strike price less than the applicable stock price for an equity option with standardized terms is lower than the lowest qualified bench mark under section 1092(c)(4)(D), the lowest strike price at which a qualified covered call option can be written is the next higher strike price, or $15.00. This $15.00 strike price requirement for a qualified covered call option applies to equity options with flexible terms, equity options with standardized terms, and qualifying over-the-counter options.

Example 3. Taxpayer owns stock in Corporation Z. On May 8, 2003, Taxpayer writes a 21-month equity call option with flexible terms on Corporation Z stock through a national securities exchange. The applicable stock price for

Corporation Z stock is $100. The bench marks for a 21-month equity option with standardized terms with an applicable stock price of $100 will be based upon the adjusted applicable stock price. Using the table at § 1.1092(c)-4(e), the applicable stock price of $100 is multiplied by the adjustment factor 1.12, resulting in an adjusted applicable stock price of $112. The highest available strike price less than the adjusted applicable stock price is $110, and the second highest strike price less than the adjusted applicable stock price is $105. Therefore, a 21-month equity call option with flexible terms on Corporation Z stock will not be deep in the money if the strike price is not less than $105.

(d) *Effective date.*—(1) *In general.*—Except as provided in paragraph (d)(2) of this section, this section applies to equity options with flexible terms entered into on or after January 25, 2000.

(2) *Effective date for paragraphs (b) and (c) of this section.*—Paragraphs (b) and (c) of this section apply to equity options with flexible terms entered into on or after July 29, 2002. [Reg. § 1.1092(c)-2.]

☐ [*T.D. 8866, 1-21-2000. Redesignated and amended by T.D. 8990, 4-26-2002.*]

[Reg. § 1.1092(c)-3]

§ 1.1092(c)-3. Qualifying over-the-counter options.—(a) *In general.*—Under section 1092(c)(4)(B)(i), an equity option is not a qualified covered call option unless it is traded on a national securities exchange that is registered with the Securities and Exchange Commission or other market that the Secretary determines has rules adequate to carry out the purposes of section 1092(c)(4). In accordance with section 1092(c)(4)(H), this requirement is modified as provided in paragraph (b) of this section.

(b) *Qualified covered call option status.*—A qualifying over-the-counter option, as defined in § 1.1092(c)-4(c), is a qualified covered call option if it meets the requirements of § § 1.1092(c)-1 and 1.1092(c)-2(c) after using the language "qualifying over-the-counter option" in place of "equity option with flexible terms". For purposes of this paragraph (b), a qualifying over-the-counter option is deemed to satisfy the requirements of section 1092(c)(4)(B)(i).

(c) *Effective date.*—This section applies to qualifying over-the-counter options entered into on or after July 29, 2002. [Reg. § 1.1092(c)-3.]

☐ [*T.D. 8990, 4-26-2002.*]

[Reg. § 1.1092(c)-4]

§ 1.1092(c)-4. Definitions.—The following definitions apply for purposes of § § 1.1092(c)-1 through 1.1092(c)-3:

(a) *Equity option with flexible terms.*—means an equity option—

(1) That is described in any of the following Securities Exchange Act Releases—

(i) Self-Regulatory Organizations; Order Approving Proposed Rule Changes and Notice of Filing and Order Granting Accelerated Approval of Amendments by the Chicago Board Options Exchange, Inc. and the Pacific Stock Exchange, Inc., Relating to the Listing of Flexible Equity Options on Specified Equity Securities, Securities Exchange Act Release No. 34-36841 (Feb. 21, 1996); or

(ii) Self-Regulatory Organizations; Order Approving Proposed Rule Changes and Notice of Filing and Order Granting Accelerated Approval of Amendment Nos. 2 and 3 to the Proposed Rule Change by the American Stock Exchange, Inc., Relating to the Listing of Flexible Equity Options on Specified Equity Securities, Securities Exchange Act Release No. 34-37336 (June 27, 1996); or

(iii) Self-Regulatory Organizations; Order Approving Proposed Rule Change and Notice of Filing and Order Granting Accelerated Approval of Amendment Nos. 2, 4 and 5 to the Proposed Rule Change by the Philadelphia Stock Exchange, Inc., Relating to the Listing of Flexible Exchange Traded Equity and Index Options, Securities Exchange Act Release No. 34-39549 (Jan. 23, 1998); or

(iv) Any changes to the Security Exchange Act Releases described in paragraphs (a)(1)(i) through (iii) of this section that are approved by the Securities and Exchange Commission; or

(2) That is traded on any national securities exchange that is registered with the Securities and Exchange Commission (other than those described in the Security Exchange Act Releases set forth in paragraph (a)(1) of this section) and is—

(i) Substantially identical to the equity options described in paragraph (a)(1) of this section; and

(ii) Approved by the Securities and Exchange Commission in a Securities Exchange Act Release.

(b) *Equity option with standardized terms.*—means an equity option—

(1) That is traded on a national securities exchange registered with the Securities and Exchange Commission;

(2) That, on the date the option is written, expires on the Saturday following the third Friday of the month of expiration;

(3) That has a strike price that is set at a uniform minimum strike price interval, that is established by the applicable national securities exchange registered with the Securities and Exchange Commission, and that is not less than $1.00; and

(4) That has stock in a single corporation as its underlying security.

(c) *Qualifying over-the-counter option.*—means an equity option that—

(1) Is not traded on a national securities exchange registered with the Securities and Exchange Commission; and

(2) Is entered into with—

(i) A broker-dealer, acting as principal or agent, who is registered with the Securities and Exchange Commission under section 15 of the Securities Act of 1934 (15 U.S.C. 78a through 78mm) and the regulations thereunder and who must comply with the recordkeeping requirements of 17 CFR 240.17a-3; or

(ii) An alternative trading system under 17 CFR 242.300 through 17 CFR 242.303; or

(iii) A person, acting as principal or agent, who must comply with the recordkeeping requirements for securities transactions described in 12 CFR 12.3, 12 CFR 208.34, or 12 CFR 344.4.

(d) *Single fixed strike price.*—means a strike price that is fixed, determinable, and stated as a dollar amount on the date the option is written. An option will not fail to have a single fixed strike price if, after the date the option is written, the strike price is adjusted to account for the effects of a dividend, stock dividend, stock distribution, stock split, reverse stock split, rights offering, distribution, reorganization, recapitalization, or reclassification with respect to the underlying security, or a merger, consolidation, dissolution, or liquidation of the issuer of the underlying security.

(e) *Adjusted applicable stock price.*—means the applicable stock price, as defined in section 1092(C)(4)(G), adjusted for time. To determine the adjusted applicable stock price, the applicable stock price, which is determined in accordance with the rules in section 1092(c)(4)(G), is multiplied by an adjustment factor. The adjustment factor table is as follows:

Option Term		Adjustment Factor
Greater Than	Not More Than	
12 months	15 months	1.08
15 months	18 months	1.10
18 months	21 months	1.12
21 months	24 months	1.14
24 months	27 months	1.16
27 months	30 months	1.18
30 months	33 months	1.20

(f) *Securities Exchange Act Release.*—means a release issued by the Securities and Exchange Commission. To determine identifying information for releases referenced in paragraph (d)(1) of this section, including release titles, identification numbers, and issue dates, contact the Office of the Secretary, Securities and Exchange Commission, 450 5th Street, NW., Washington, DC 20549. To obtain a copy of a Securities Exchange Act Release, submit a written request, including the specific release identification number, title, and issue date, to Securities and Exchange Commission, Attention Public Reference, 450 5th Street, NW., Washington, DC 20549.

(g) *Effective dates.*—(1) Except for paragraph (a)(2) of this section, paragraph (a) of this section applies to equity options with flexible terms entered into on or after January 25, 2000. Paragraph (a)(2) of this section applies to equity options with flexible terms entered into on or after July 29, 2002.

(2) Paragraphs (b), (c), (d), and (e) of this section apply to equity options entered into on or after July 29, 2002.

(3) Paragraph (f) of this section applies to equity options entered into on or after January 25, 2000. [Reg. § 1.1092(c)-4.]

☐ [*T.D.* 8990, 4-26-2002.]

[Reg. § 1.1092(d)-1]

§ 1.1092(d)-1. Definitions and special rules.—(a) *Actively traded.*—Actively traded personal property includes any personal property for which there is an established financial market.

(b) *Established financial market.*—(1) *In general.*—For purposes of this section, an established financial market includes—

(i) A national securities exchange that is registered under section 6 of the Securities Exchange Act of 1934 (15 U.S.C. 78f);

(ii) An interdealer quotation system sponsored by a national securities association registered under section 15A of the Securities Exchange Act of 1934;

(iii) A domestic board of trade designated as a contract market by the Commodities Futures Trading Commission;

(iv) A foreign securities exchange or board of trade that satisfies analogous regulatory requirements under the law of the jurisdiction in which it is organized (such as the London International Financial Futures Exchange, the Marche a Terme International de France, the International Stock Exchange of the United Kingdom and the Republic of Ireland, Limited, the Frankfurt Stock Exchange, and the Tokyo Stock Exchange);

(v) An interbank market;

(vi) An interdealer market (as defined in paragraph (b)(2)(i) of this section); and

(vii) Solely with respect to a debt instrument, a debt market (as defined in paragraph (b)(2)(ii) of this section).

(2) *Definitions.*—(i) *Interdealer market.*—An interdealer market is characterized by a system of general circulation (including a computer listing disseminated to subscribing brokers, dealers, or traders) that provides a reasonable basis to determine fair market value by disseminating either recent price quotations (including rates, yields, or other pricing information) of one or more identified brokers, dealers, or traders or actual prices (including rates, yields, or other

pricing information) of recent transactions. An interdealer market does not include a directory or listing of brokers, dealers, or traders for specific contracts (such as yellow sheets) that provides neither price quotations nor actual prices of recent transactions.

(ii) *Debt market.*—A debt market exists with respect to a debt instrument if price quotations for the instrument are readily available from brokers, dealers, or traders. A debt market does not exist with respect to a debt instrument if—

(A) No other outstanding debt instrument of the issuer (or of any person who guarantees the debt instrument) is traded on an established financial market described in paragraph (b)(1)(i), (ii), (iii), (iv), (v), or (vi) of this section (other traded debt);

(B) The original stated principal amount of the issue that includes the debt instrument does not exceed $25 million;

(C) The conditions and covenants relating to the issuer's performance with respect to the debt instrument are materially less restrictive than the conditions and covenants included in all of the issuer's other traded debt (e.g., the debt instrument is subject to an economically significant subordination provision whereas the issuer's other traded debt is senior); or

(D) The maturity date of the debt instrument is more than 3 years after the latest maturity date of the issuer's other traded debt.

(c) *Notional principal contracts.*—For purposes of section 1092(d)—

(1) A notional principal contract (as defined in § 1.446-3(c)(1)) constitutes personal property of a type that is actively traded if contracts based on the same or substantially similar specified indices are purchased, sold, or entered into on an established financial market within the meaning of paragraph (b) of this section; and

(2) The rights and obligations of a party to a notional principal contract are rights and obligations with respect to personal property and constitute an interest in personal property.

(d) *Effective dates.*—Paragraph (b)(1)(vii) of this section applies to positions entered into on or after October 14, 1993. Paragraph (c) of this section applies to positions entered into on or after July 8, 1991. [Reg. § 1.1092(d)-1.]

☐ [*T.D.* 8491, 10-8-93.]

[Reg. § 1.1092(d)-2]

§ 1.1092(d)-2. Personal property.—(a) *Special rules for stock.*—Under section 1092(d)(3)(B), personal property includes any stock that is part of a straddle, at least one of the offsetting positions of which is a position with respect to substantially similar or related property (other than stock). For purposes of this rule, the term *substantially similar or related property* is defined in § 1.246-5 (other than § 1.246-5(b)(3)). The rule in

§ 1.246-5(c)(6) does not narrow the related party rule in section 1092(d)(4).

(b) *Effective date.*—(1) *In general.*—This section applies to positions established on or after March 17, 1995.

(2) *Special rule for certain straddles.*—This section applies to positions established after March 1, 1984, if the taxpayer substantially diminished its risk of loss by holding substantially similar or related property involving the following types of transactions—

(i) Holding offsetting positions consisting of stock and a convertible debenture of the same corporation where the price movements of the two positions are related; or

(ii) Holding a short position in a stock index regulated futures contract (or alternatively an option on such a regulated futures contract or an option on the stock index) and stock in an investment company whose principal holdings mimic the performance of the stocks included in the stock index (or alternatively a portfolio of stocks whose performance mimics the performance of the stocks included in the stock index). [Reg. § 1.1092(d)-2.]

□ [*T. D.* 8590, 3-17-95.]

[The next page is 53,401.]

CAPITAL GAINS AND LOSSES

Treatment of Capital Gains

See p. 20,601 for regulations not amended to reflect law changes

[Reg. §1.1201-1]

§1.1201-1. Alternative tax.—
(a) *Corporations.*—(1) *In general.*—(i) If for any taxable year a corporation has net capital gain (net section 1201 gain for taxable years beginning before January 1, 1977) (as defined in section 1222 (11)), section 1201(a) imposes an alternative in lieu of the tax imposed by sections 11 and 511, but only if such alternative tax is less than the tax imposed by sections 11 and 511. The alternative tax is not in lieu of the personal holding company tax imposed by section 541 or of any other tax not specifically set forth in section 1201(a).

(ii) In the case of an insurance company, the alternative tax imposed by section 1201(a) is also in lieu of the tax imposed by sections 821(a) or (c) and 831(a), except that for taxable years beginning before January 1, 1963, the reference to section 821(a) or (c) is to be read as reference to section 821(a)(1) or (b). For taxable years beginning after December 31, 1954, and before January 1, 1958, the alternative tax imposed by section 1201(a) shall also be in lieu of the tax imposed by section 802(a), as amended by the Life Insurance Company Tax Act for 1955 (70 Stat. 38), if such alternative tax is less than the tax imposed by such section. See section 802(e), as added by the Life Insurance Company Tax Act for 1955 (70 Stat. 39). However, for taxable years beginning after December 31, 1958, and before January 1, 1962, section 802(a)(2), as amended by the Life Insurance Company Income Tax Act of 1959 (73 Stat. 115), imposes a separate tax equal to 25 percent of the amount by which the net long-term capital gain of any life insurance company (as defined in section 801(a) and paragraph (b) of §1.801-3) exceeds its net short-term capital loss. See paragraph (f) of §1.802-3. For alternative tax for life insurance companies in the case of taxable years beginning after December 31, 1961, see section 802(a)(2) and the regulations thereunder.

(iii) See section 56 and the regulations thereunder for provisions relating to the minimum tax for tax preferences.

(2) *Alternative tax.*—The alternative tax is the sum of—

(i) A partial tax computed at the rates provided in sections 11, 511, 821(a) or (c), and 831(a), on the taxable income of the taxpayer reduced by the amount of the net capital gain (net section 1201 gain for taxable years beginning before January 1, 1977), and

(ii) An amount equal to the tax determined under subparagraph (3) of this paragraph.

For taxable years beginning after December 31, 1954, and before January 1, 1958, the partial tax under subdivision (i) of this subparagraph shall also be computed at the rates provided in section 802(a). For taxable years beginning before January 1, 1963, the reference in such subdivision to section 821(a) or (c) is to be read as a reference to section 821(a) or (b).

(3) *Tax on capital gains.*—For purposes of subparagraph (2)(ii) of this paragraph, the tax shall be—

(i) In the case of a taxable year beginning after December 31, 1974, a tax of 30 percent of the net section 1201 gain (net capital gain for taxable years beginning before December 31, 1976),

(ii) In the case of a taxable year beginning after December 31, 1969, and before January 1, 1975—

(a) A tax of 25 percent of the lesser of the amount of the subsection (d) gain (as defined in section 1201(d) and paragraph (f) of this section) or the amount of the net section 1201 gain (net capital gain for taxable years beginning before December 31, 1976), plus

(b) A tax of 30 percent (28 percent in the case of a taxable year beginning after December 31, 1969, and before January 1, 1971) of the excess, if any, of the net section 1201 gain (net capital gain for taxable years beginning before December 31, 1976) over the subsection (d) gain,

(iii) In the case of a taxable year beginning after January 1, 1970, and after March 31, 1954, a tax of 25 percent of the net section 1201 gain (net capital gain for taxable years beginning before December 31, 1976), or

(iv) In the case of a taxable year beginning before April 1, 1954, a tax of 26 percent of the net section 1201 gain (net capital gain for taxable years beginning before December 31, 1976).

(4) *Determination of special deductions.*—In the computation of the partial tax described in subparagraph (2)(i) of this paragraph the special deductions provided for in sections 243, 244, 245, 247, 922, and 941 shall not be recomputed as the result of the reduction of taxable income by the net capital gain (net section 1201 gain for taxable years beginning before January 1, 1977).

(b) *Other taxpayers.*—(1) *In general.*—If for any taxable year a taxpayer (other than a corporation) has net capital gain (net section 1201 gain for taxable years beginning before January 1, 1977) (as defined in section 1222(11)), section 1201(b) imposes an alternative tax in lieu of the tax imposed by sections 1 and 511, but only if such alternative tax is less than the tax imposed by sections 1 and 511. The alternative tax is not in lieu of any other tax not specifically set forth in section 1201(b). See section 56 and the regulations thereunder for provisions relating to the minimum tax for tax preferences.

(2) *Alternative tax.*—The alternative tax is the sum of—

(i) A partial tax computed at the rates provided by sections 1 and 511 on the taxable income reduced by an amount equal to 50 percent of the net capital gain (net section 1201 gain for taxable years beginning before January 1, 1977), and

(ii) In the case of a taxable year beginning after December 31, 1969—

(a) A tax of 25 percent of the lesser of the amount of the subsection (d) gain (as defined in section 1201(d) and paragraph (f) of this section) or the amount of the net capital gain (net section 1201 gain for taxable years beginning before January 1, 1977), plus

(b) A tax computed as provided in section 1201(c) and paragraph (e) of this section on the excess, if any, of the net capital gain (net section 1201 gain for taxable years beginning before January 1, 1977) over the subsection (d) gain, or

(iii) In the case of a taxable year beginning before January 1, 1970, a tax of 25 percent of the net section 1201 gain (net capital gain for taxable years beginning before December 31, 1976).

(3) *Cross references.*—See §1.1-2(a) for rule relating to the computation of the limitation on tax in cases where the alternative tax is imposed. See §1.34-2(a) for rule relating to the computation of the dividend received credit under section 34 (for dividends received on or before December 31, 1964), and §1.35-1(a) for rule relating to the computation of credit for partially tax-exempt interest under section 35 in cases where the alternative tax is imposed.

(c) *Tax-exempt trusts and organizations.*—In applying section 1201 in the case of tax-exempt trusts or organizations subject to the tax imposed by section 511, the only amount which is taken into account as capital gain or loss is that which is taken into account in computing unrelated business taxable income under section 512. Under section 512, the only amount taken into account as capital gain or loss is that resulting from the application of section 631(a), relating to the election to treat the cutting of timber as a sale or exchange.

(d) *Joint returns.*—In the case of a joint return, the excess of any net long-term capital gain over any net short-term capital loss is to be determined by combining the long-term capital gains and losses and the short-term capital gains and losses of the spouses.

(e) *Computation of tax on capital gain in excess of subsection (d) gain.*—(1) *In general.*—The tax computed for purposes of section 1201(b)(3) and paragraph (b)(2)(ii)(b) of this section shall be the amount by which a tax determined under section 1 or 511 on an amount equal to the taxable income (but not less than 50 percent of the net capital gain (net section 1201 gain for taxable years beginning before January 1, 1977) for the taxable year exceeds a tax determined under section 1 or 511 on an amount equal to the sum of (i) the amount subject to tax under section 1201(b)(1) and paragraph (b)(2)(i) of this section for such year plus (ii) an amount equal to 50 percent of the subsection (d) gain for such year.

(2) *Limitation.*—Notwithstanding subparagraph (1) of this paragraph, the tax computed for purposes of section 1201(b)(3) and paragraph (b)(2)(ii) (b) of this section shall not exceed an amount equal to the following percentage of the excess of the net capital gain (net section 1201 gain for taxable years beginning before January 1, 1977) over the subsection (d) gain for the taxable year:

(i) $29\frac{1}{2}$ percent, in the case of a taxable year beginning after December 31, 1969, and before January 1, 1971, or

(ii) $32\frac{1}{2}$ percent, in the case of a taxable year beginning after December 31, 1970, and before January 1, 1972.

(f) *Definition of subsection (d) gain.*—(1) *In general.*—For purposes of section 1201 and this section, the term "subsection (d) gain" means the sum of the long-term capital gains for the taxable year arising—

(i) In the case of amounts received or accrued, as the case may be, before January 1, 1975 (other than any gain from a transaction described in section 631 or 1235), from—

(a) Sales or other dispositions on or before October 9, 1969, including sales or other dispositions the income from which is returned as provided in section 453(a)(1) or (b)(1), or

(b) Sales or other dispositions after October 9, 1969, pursuant to binding contracts entered into on or before that date, including sales or other dispositions the income from which is returned as provided in section 453(a)(1) or (b)(1),

(ii) From liquidating distributions made by a corporation which are made (a) before October 10, 1970, and (b) pursuant to a plan of complete liquidation adopted on or before October 9, 1969, or

(iii) In the case of a taxpayer (other than a corporation), from any other source not described in subdivision (i) or (ii) of this subparagraph, but the amount taken into account from such other sources shall be limited to the amount, if any, by which $50,000 ($25,000 in the case of a married individual filing a separate return) exceeds the sum of the gains to which subdivisions (i) and (ii) of this subparagraph apply.

(2) *Special rules.*—For purposes of subparagraph (1) of this paragraph—

(i) A binding contract entered into on or before October 9, 1969, means a contract, whether written or unwritten, which on or before that date was legally enforceable against the taxpayer under applicable law. If on or before October 9, 1969, a taxpayer grants an irrevocable option or irrevocable contractual right to another party to buy certain property and such other party exercises that option or right after October 9, 1969, the sale of such property is a sale pursuant to a binding contract entered into on or before October 9, 1969. The application of this subdivision may be illustrated by the following example:

Example. During 1964, A, B, and C formed a closely-held corporation, and A was appointed as president of the organization. On July 1, 1964, A received for consideration 100 shares of common stock in the corporation subject to the agreement that, if A should retire from the management of the corporation or die, A or his estate would first offer his shares of stock to the corporation for purchase and that, if the corporation did not buy the stock within 60 days, the stock could be sold to any party other than the corporation. On September 1, 1970, A retired from the management of the corporation and offered his shares to the corporation for purchase. Pursuant to the agreement, the corporation purchased A's stock on September 30, 1970. A's sale of such stock was pursuant to a binding contract entered into on or before October 9, 1969.

(ii) A contract which pursuant to subdivision (i) of this subparagraph constitutes a binding contract entered into on or before October 9, 1969, does not cease to qualify as such a contract by reason of the fact that after October 9, 1969, there is a modification of the terms of the contract, such as a change in the time of performance, or in the amount of the debt or in the terms and mode of payment, or in the rate of interest, or there is a change in the form or nature of the obligation or the character of the security, so long as the taxpayer is at all times on and after October 9, 1969, legally bound by such contract. The application of this subdivision may be illustrated by the following examples:

Example (1). On August 1, 1969, A sold certain capital assets to B on the installment plan and elected to return the gain therefrom under section 453, the agreement providing for payments over a period of 2 years. At the time of the sale these assets had been held by A for more than 6 months. On July 31, 1970, A and B agreed to a modification of the terms of payment under the sales agreement, the only change in the contract being that the installment payments due after July 31, 1970, would be paid over a 3-year period. For purposes of this paragraph the payments received by A after July 31, 1970, are considered amounts received from the sale on August 1, 1969. (See section 483 for rules with respect to interest on deferred payments.)

Example (2). On April 1, 1969, A sold certain capital assets to B on the installment plan and elected to return the gain therefrom under section 453, the agreement providing for payments over a period of 3 years. At the time of the sale these assets had been held by A for more than 6 months. On March 31, 1970, C assumed B's obligation to pay the balance of the installments which were due after that date. For purposes of this paragraph any installment payments received by A after March 31, 1970, from C are considered amounts received from a sale made on or before October 9, 1969.

Example (3). On May 1, 1969, A offers to sell certain capital assets to B if B accepts the offer within one year, unless it is previously withdrawn by A. B accepts the offer on November 1, 1969, and the transaction is consummated shortly thereafter. For purposes of this paragraph, any payment received by A pursuant to the sale is not considered an amount received from a sale made on or before October 9, 1969, or from a sale pursuant to a binding contract entered into on or before that date.

(iii) An amount which is considered under section 402(a)(2) or 403(a)(2) as gain of the taxpayer from the sale or exchange of a capital asset held for more than 6 months shall be treated as gain subject to the provisions of section 1201(d)(1) and subdivision (i) of such subparagraph, but only if on or before October 9, 1969, (*a*) the employee with respect to whom such amount is distributed or paid died or was otherwise separated from the service and (*b*) the terms of the plan required, or the employee elected, that the total distributions or amounts payable be paid to the taxpayer within one taxable year.

(iv) Gain described in section 1201(d)(1) or (2) with respect to a partnership, estate, or trust, which is required to be included in the gross income of a partner in such partnership, or of a beneficiary of such estate or trust, shall be treated as such gain with respect to such partner or beneficiary. Thus, for example, if during 1974 a partnership which uses the calendar year as its taxable year receives amounts which give rise to section 1201(d)(1) gain, a partner who uses the fiscal year ending June 30 as his taxable year shall treat his distributive share of such gain as subsection (d) gain for his taxable year ending June 30, 1975, even though such share is distributed to him after December 31, 1974. See § 1.706-1.

(v) An individual shall be considered married for purposes of subdivision (iii) of such subparagraph if for the taxable year he may elect with his spouse to make a joint return under section 6013(a).

(vi) In applying such subparagraph for purposes of section 21(a)(1) long-term capital gains arising from amounts received before January 1, 1970, shall be taken into account if such amounts are received during the taxable year.

(g) *Illustrations.*—The application of this section may be illustrated by the following examples in which the assumption is made that section 56 (relating to minimum tax for tax preferences) does not apply:

Example (1). A, a single individual, has for the calendar year 1954 taxable income (exclusive of capital gains and losses) of $99,400. He realizes in 1954 a gain of $50,000 on the sale of a capital asset held for 19 months and sustains a loss of $20,000 on the sale of a capital asset held for five months. He has no other capital gains or losses. Since the alternative tax is less than the tax otherwise computed under section 1, the tax payable is the alternative tax, that is $74,298. The tax is computed as follows:

Tax Under Section 1

Taxable income exclusive of capital gains and losses		$99,400
Net long-term capital gain (100 percent of $50,000)	$50,000	
Net short-term capital loss (100 percent of $20,000)	20,000	
Excess of net long-term capital gain over the net short-term capital loss		30,000
		$129,400
Deduction of 50 percent of excess of net long-term capital gain over the net short-term capital loss (section 1202)		15,000
Taxable income		$114,400
Tax under section 1		$80,136

Alternative Tax Under Section 1201(b)

Taxable income	$114,400
Less 50 percent of excess of net long-term capital gain over net short-term capital loss (section 1201(b)(1))	15,000
Taxable income exclusive of capital gains and losses	$99,400
Partial tax (tax on $99,400)	$66,798
Plus 25 percent of $30,000	7,500
Alternative tax under section 1201(b)	$74,298

Example (2). A husband and wife, who file a joint return for the calendar year 1970, have taxable income (exclusive of capital gains and losses) of $100,000. In 1970 they realize $200,000 of net long-term capital gain in excess of net short-term capital loss, including long-term capital gains of $100,000 arising from sales consummated in 1968 the income from which is returned on the installment method under section 453, and long-term capital gains of $50,000 arising in respect of distributions from X corporation made before October 10, 1970, which were pursuant to a plan of complete liquidation adopted on October 9, 1969. Since the alternative tax under section 1201(b) is less than the tax otherwise computed under section 1, the tax payable for 1970 is the alternative tax, that is, $97,430 plus the tax surcharge under section 51. The tax (without regard to the tax surcharge) is computed as follows:

Tax Under Section 1

Taxable income exclusive of capital gains and losses	$100,000
Net section 1201 gain (net capital gain for taxable years beginning before December 31, 1976) (excess of net long-term capital gain over the net short-term capital loss)	200,000
Total	$300,000
Deduction of 50 percent of net section 1201 gain (section 1202)	100,000
Taxable income	$200,000
Tax under sec. 1	$110,980

Alternative Tax Under Section 1201(b)

(1) Net section 1201 gain (net capital gain for taxable years beginning before December 31, 1976)	$200,000
(2) Subsection (d) gain:	
Sec. 1201(d)(1)	$100,000
Sec. 1201(d)(2)	50,000
Total subsection (d) gain	$150,000

(3) Net section 1201 gain (net capital gain for taxable years beginning before December 31, 1976) in excess of subsection (d) gain ($200,000 less $150,000) ... $50,000

(4) Tax under sec. 1201(b)(1):

(i) Taxable income	$200,000
(ii) Less: 50% of item (1)	100,000
(iii) Amount subject to tax under sec. 1201(b)(1)	$100,000

Partial tax (computed under sec. 1) ... $45,180

(5) Tax under sec. 1201(b)(2):

(25% of item (1) or of item (2), whichever is lesser [25% of $150,000]) 37,500

(6) Tax under sec. 1201(b)(3) on item (3):

Tax under sec. 1 on taxable income ($200,000)	$110,980
Less: Tax under sec. 1 on sum of item (4)(iii) ($100,000) plus 50% of item (2) ($75,000) (Total $175,000)	93,780
Tax under sec. 1201(c)(1)	$17,200

Limitation under sec. 1201(c)(2)(A) (29$1/2$% of item (3)) ... $14,750 ... 14,750

(7) Alternative tax under sec. 1201(b) ... $97,430

Example (3). A husband and wife, who file a joint return for the calendar year 1971, have taxable income (exclusive of capital gains and losses) of $80,000. In 1971 they realize long-term capital gain of $30,000 arising from a sale consummated on July 1, 1969, the income from which is returned on the installment method under section 453. From securities transactions in 1971 they have long-term capital gains of $60,000 and a short-term capital loss of $10,000. Since the alternative tax under section 1201(b) is less than the tax otherwise computed under section 1, the tax payable is the alternative tax, that is, $55,140. The tax is computed as follows:

Tax Under Section 1

Taxable income exclusive of capital gains and losses		$80,000
Net long-term capital gains (100% of $90,000)	$90,000	
Net short-term capital loss (100% of $10,000)	10,000	
Net section 1201 gain (net capital gain for taxable years beginning before December 31, 1976)		80,000
Total		$160,000
Deduction of 50% of net section 1201 gain (net capital gain for taxable years beginning before December 31, 1976) (sec. 1202)		40,000
Taxable income		$120,000
Tax under sec. 1		$57,580

Alternative Tax Under Section 1201(b)

(1) Net section 1201 gain (net capital gain for taxable years beginning before December 31, 1976) ... $80,000

(2) Subsection (d) gain:

Sec. 1201(d)(1)	$30,000
Sec. 1201(d)(2)	
Sec. 1201(d)(3) ($50,000 less $30,000)	20,000
Total subsection (d) gain	$50,000

(3) Net section 1201 gain (net capital gain for taxable years beginning before December 31, 1976) in excess of subsection (d) gain ($80,000 less $50,000) ... $30,000

(4) Tax under sec. 1201(b)(1):

(i) Taxable income	$120,000
(ii) Less: 50% of item (1)	40,000
(iii) Amount subject to tax under sec. 1201(b)(1)	$80,000

Partial tax (computed under sec. 1) ... $33,340

(5) Tax under sec. 1201(b)(2):

(25% of item (1) or of item (2), whichever is lesser [25% of $50,000]) ... 12,500

(6) Tax under sec. 1201(b)(3) on item (3):

Tax under sec. 1 on taxable income ($120,000)	$57,580	
Less: Tax under sec. 1 on sum of item (4)(iii) ($80,000) plus 50% of item (2) ($25,000) (Total $105,000)	48,280	
Tax under sec. 1201(c)(1)	$9,300	
Limitation under sec. 1201(c)(2)(B) (32½% of item (3))	$9,750	$9,300

(7) Alternative tax under sec. 1201(b) ... $55,140

Example (4). A husband and wife, who file a joint return for the calendar year 1973, have taxable income (exclusive of capital gains and losses) of $250,000. In 1973 they realize long-term capital gains (not described in section 1201(d)(1) or (2)) of $140,000 and a short-term capital loss of $50,000. Since the alternative tax under section 1201(b) is less than the tax otherwise computed under section 1, the tax payable is the alternative tax, that is, $172,480. The tax is computed as follows:

Tax Under Section 1

Taxable income exclusive of capital gains and losses		$250,000
Net long-term capital gains (100% of $140,000)	$140,000	
Net short-term capital loss (100% of $50,000)	50,000	
Net section 1201 gain (net capital gain for taxable years beginning before December 31, 1976)		90,000
Total		$340,000
Deduction of 50% of net section 1201 gain (sec. 1202)		45,000
Taxable income		$295,000
Tax under sec. 1		$177,480

Alternative Tax Under Section 1201(b)

(1) Net section 1201 gain (net capital gain for taxable years beginning before December 31, 1976) ... $90,000

(2) Subsection (d) gain:

Sec. 1201(d)(1)		
Sec. 1201(d)(2)		
Sec. 1201(d)(3) ($50,000)		
Total subsection (d) gain		$50,000

(3) Net section 1201 gain (net capital gain for taxable years beginning before December 31, 1976) in excess of subsection (d) gain ($90,000 less $50,000) ... $40,000

(4) Tax under sec. 1201(b)(1):

(i) Taxable income	$295,000	
(ii) Less: 50% of item (1)	45,000	
(iii) Amount subject to tax under sec. 1201(b)(1)	$250,000	
Partial tax (computed under sec. 1)		$145,980

(5) Tax under sec. 1201(b)(2):

(25% of item (1) or of item (2), whichever is lesser [25% of $50,000]) ... 12,500

(6) Tax under sec. 1201(b)(3) on item (3):

Tax under sec. 1 on taxable income ($295,000)	$177,480	
Less: Tax under sec. 1 on sum of item (4)(iii) ($250,000) plus 50% of item (2) ($25,000) (Total $275,000)	163,480	14,000

(7) Alternative tax under sec. 1201(b) ... $172,480

[Reg. § 1.1201-1.]

☐ [*T.D. 6243, 7-23-57. Amended by T.D. 6610, 8-30-62; T.D. 6681, 10-16-63; T.D. 6777, 12-15-64; T.D. 7337, 12-26-74 and T.D. 7728, 10-31-80.*]

[Reg. §1.1202-0]

§1.1202-0. Table of contents.—This section lists the major captions that appear in the regulations under §1.1202-2.

(c) Transfers by shareholders in connection with the performance of services not treated as purchases.

(d) Exceptions for termination of services, death, disability or mental incompetency, or divorce.

(1) Termination of services.

(2) Death.

(3) Disability or mental incompetency.

(4) Divorce.

(e) Effective date.

[Reg. § 1.1202-0.]

☐ [T.D. 8749, 12-30-97.]

[Reg. § 1.1202-1]

§ 1.1202-1. Deduction for capital gains.— (a) In computing gross income, adjusted gross income, taxable income, capital gain net income (net capital gain for taxable years beginning before January 1, 1977) and net capital loss, 100 percent of any gain or loss (computed under section 1001, recognized under section 1002, and taken into account without regard to subchapter P (section 1201 and following), chapter 1 of the Code), upon the sale or exchange of a capital asset shall be taken into account regardless of the period for which the capital asset has been held. Nevertheless, the net short-term capital gain or loss and the net long-term capital gain or loss must be separately computed. In computing the adjusted gross income or the taxable income of a taxpayer other than a corporation, if for any taxable year the net long-term capital gain exceeds the net short-term capital loss, 50 percent

of the amount of the excess is allowable as a deduction from gross income under section 1202.

(b) For the purpose of computing the deduction allowable under section 1202 in the case of an estate or trust, any long-term or short-term capital gains which, under section 652 and 662, are includible in the gross income of its income beneficiaries as gains derived from the sale or exchange of capital assets must be excluded in determining whether, for the taxable year of the estate or trust, its net long-term capital gain exceeds its net short-term capital loss. To determine the extent to which such gains are includible in the gross income of a beneficiary, see the regulations under sections 652 and 662. For example, during 1954 a trust realized a gain of $1,000 upon the sale of stock held for 10 months. Under the terms of the trust instrument all of such gain must be distributed during the taxable year to A, the sole income beneficiary. Assuming that under section 652 or 662 A must include all of such gain in his gross income, the trust is not entitled to any deduction with respect to such gain under section 1202. Assuming A had no other capital gains or losses for 1954, he would be entitled to a deduction of $500 under section 1202. For purposes of this section, an income beneficiary shall be any beneficiary to whom an amount is required to be distributed, or is paid or credited, which is includible in his gross income.

(c) The provisions of this section may be illustrated by the following example:

Example. A, an individual, had the following transactions in 1954:

Long-term capital gain	$6,000	
Long-term capital loss	4,000	
Net long-term capital gain		$2,000
Short-term capital loss	1,800	
Short-term capital gain	300	
Net short-term capital loss		1,500
Excess of net long-term capital gain over net short-term capital loss		
		$500

Since the net long-term capital gain exceeds the net short-term capital loss by $500, 50 percent of the excess, or $250, is allowable as a deduction under section 1202. [Reg. § 1.1202-1.]

☐ [T.D. 6243, 7-23-57. Amended by T.D. 7728, 10-31-80.]

[Reg. § 1.1202-2]

§ 1.1202-2. Qualified small business stock; effect of redemptions.—(a) *Redemptions from taxpayer or related person.—*(1) *In general.—*Stock acquired by a taxpayer is not qualified small business stock if, in one or more purchases during the 4-year period beginning on the date 2 years before the issuance of the stock, the issuing corporation purchases (directly or indirectly) more than a de minimis amount of its stock from the taxpayer or from a person related (within the meaning of section 267(b) or 707(b)) to the taxpayer.

(2) *De minimis amount.—*For purposes of this paragraph (a), stock acquired from the taxpayer or a related person exceeds a de minimis amount only if the aggregate amount paid for the stock exceeds $10,000 and more than 2 percent of the stock held by the taxpayer and related persons is acquired. The following rules apply for purposes of determining whether the 2-percent limit is exceeded. The percentage of stock acquired in any single purchase is determined by dividing the stock's value (as of the time of purchase) by the value (as of the time of purchase) of all stock held (directly or indirectly) by the taxpayer and related persons immediately before the purchase. The percentage of stock acquired in multiple purchases is the sum of the percentages determined for each separate purchase.

(b) *Significant redemptions.—*(1) *In general.—* Stock is not qualified small business stock if, in one or more purchases during the 2-year period beginning on the date 1 year before the issuance of the stock, the issuing corporation purchases more than a de minimis amount of its stock and the purchased stock has an aggregate value (as of the time of the respective purchases) exceeding 5 percent of the aggregate value of all of the issuing corporation's stock as of the beginning of such 2-year period.

(2) *De minimis amount.*—For purposes of this paragraph (b), stock exceeds a de minimis amount only if the aggregate amount paid for the stock exceeds $10,000 and more than 2 percent of all outstanding stock is purchased. The following rules apply for purposes of determining whether the 2-percent limit is exceeded. The percentage of the stock acquired in any single purchase is determined by dividing the stock's value (as of the time of purchase) by the value (as of the time of purchase) of all stock outstanding immediately before the purchase. The percentage of stock acquired in multiple purchases is the sum of the percentages determined for each separate purchase.

(c) *Transfers by shareholders in connection with the performance of services not treated as purchases.*—A transfer of stock by a shareholder to an employee or independent contractor (or to a beneficiary of an employee or independent contractor) is not treated as a purchase of the stock by the issuing corporation for purposes of this section even if the stock is treated as having first been transferred to the corporation under § 1.836(d)(1) (relating to transfers by shareholders to employees or independent contractors).

(d) *Exceptions for termination of services, death, disability or mental incompetency, or divorce.*—A stock purchase is disregarded if the stock is acquired in the following circumstances:

(1) *Termination of services.*—(i) *Employees and directors.*—The stock was acquired by the seller in connection with the performance of services as an employee or director and the stock is purchased from the seller incident to the seller's retirement or other bona fide termination of such services;

(ii) *Independent contractors.*—[Reserved];

(2) *Death.*—Prior to a decedent's death, the stock (or an option to acquire the stock) was held by the decedent or the decedent's spouse (or by both), by the decedent and joint tenant, or by a trust revocable by the decedent or the decedent's spouse (or by both), and—

(i) The stock is purchased from the decedent's estate, beneficiary (whether by bequest or lifetime gift), heir, surviving joint tenant, or surviving spouse, or from a trust established by the decedent or decedent's spouse; and

(ii) The stock is purchased within 3 years and 9 months from the date of the decedent's death;

(3) *Disability or mental incompetency.*—The stock is purchased incident to the disability or mental incompetency of the selling shareholder; or

(4) *Divorce.*—The stock is purchased incident to the divorce (within the meaning of section 1041(c)) of the selling shareholder.

(e) *Effective date.*—This section applies to stock issued after August 10, 1993. [Reg. § 1.1202-2.]

□ [T.D. 8749, 12-30-97.]

Treatment of Capital Losses

[Reg. § 1.1211-1]

§ 1.1211-1. Limitation on capital losses.—(a) *Corporations.*—(1) *General rule.*—In the case of a corporation, there shall be allowed as a deduction an amount equal to the sum of—

(i) Losses sustained during the taxable year from sales or exchanges of capital assets, plus

(ii) The aggregate of all losses sustained in other taxable years which are treated as a short-term capital loss in such taxable year pursuant to section 1212(a)(1),

but only to the extent of gains from such sales or exchanges of capital assets in such taxable year.

(2) *Banks.*—See section 582(c) for modification of the limitation under section 1211(a) in the case of a bank, as defined in section 581.

(b) *Taxpayers other than corporations.*—(1) *General rule.*—In the case of a taxpayer other than a corporation, there shall be allowed as a deduction an amount equal to the sum of—

(i) Losses sustained during the taxable year from sales or exchanges of capital assets, plus

(ii) The aggregate of all losses sustained in other taxable years which are treated either as a short-term capital loss or as a long-term capital loss in such taxable year pursuant to section 1212(b),

but only to the extent of gains from sales or exchanges of capital assets in such taxable year, plus (if such losses exceed such gains) the additional allowance or transitional additional allowance deductible under section 1211(b) from ordinary income for such taxable year. The additional allowance deductible under section 1211(b) shall be determined by application of subparagraph (2) of this paragraph, and the transitional additional allowance by application of subparagraph (3) of this paragraph.

(2) *Additional allowance.*—Except as otherwise provided by subparagraph (3) of this paragraph, the additional allowance deductible under section 1211(b) for taxable years beginning after December 31, 1969, shall be the least of—

(i) The taxable income for the taxable year reduced, but not below zero, by the zero bracket amount (in the case of taxable years beginning before January 1, 1977, the taxable income for the taxable year);

(ii) $3,000 ($2,000 for taxable years beginning in 1977; $1,000 for taxable years beginning before January 1, 1977); or

(iii) The sum of the excess of the net short-term capital loss over the net long-term capital gain, plus one-half of the excess of the net long-term capital loss over the net short-term capital gain.

(3) *Transitional additional allowance.*—(i) *In general.*—If, pursuant to the provisions of § 1.1212-1(b) and subdivision (iii) of this subparagraph, there is carried to the taxable year from a taxable year beginning before January 1, 1970, a long-term capital loss, and if for the taxable year there is an excess of net long-term capital loss over net short-term capital gain, then, in lieu of the additional allowance provided by subparagraph (2) of this paragraph, the transitional additional allowance deductible under section 1211(b) shall be the least of—

(a) The taxable income for the taxable year reduced, but not below zero, by the zero bracket amount (in the case of taxable years beginning before January 1, 1977, the taxable income for the taxable year);

(b) $3,000 ($2,000 for taxable years beginning in 1977; $1,000 for taxable years beginning before January 1, 1977); or

(c) The sum of the excess of the net short-term capital loss over the net long-term capital gain; that portion of the excess of the net long-term capital loss over the net short-term capital gain computed as provided in subdivision (ii) of this subparagraph; plus one-half of the remaining portion of the excess of the net long-term capital loss over the net short-term capital gain.

(ii) *Computation of specially treated portion of excess long-term capital loss over net short-term capital gain.*—In determining the transitional additional allowance deductible as provided by this subparagraph, there shall be applied thereto in full on a dollar-for-dollar basis the excess of net long-term capital loss over net short-term capital gain (computed with regard to capital losses carried to the taxable year) to the extent that the long-term capital losses carried to the taxable year from taxable years beginning before January 1, 1970, as provided by § 1.1212-1(b) and

subdivision (iii) of this subparagraph, exceed the sum of (a) the portion of the capital gain net income (net capital gain for taxable years beginning before January 1, 1977) actually realized in the taxable year (*i.e.,* computed without regard to capital losses carried to the taxable year) which consists of net long-term capital gain actually realized in the taxable year, plus (b) the amount by which the portion of the capital gain net income (net capital gain for taxable years beginning before January 1, 1977) actually realized in the taxable year (*i.e.,* computed without regard to capital losses carried to the taxable year) which consists of net short-term capital gain actually realized in the taxable year exceeds the total of short-term capital losses carried to the taxable year from taxable years beginning before January 1, 1970, as provided by § 1.1212-1(b) and subdivision (iv) of this subparagraph. The amount by which the net long-term capital losses carried to the taxable year from taxable years beginning before January 1, 1970, exceeds the sum of (a) plus (b) shall constitute the "transitional net long-term capital loss component" for the taxable year for the purpose of this subparagraph.

(iii) *Carryover of certain long-term capital losses not utilized in computation of transitional additional allowance.*—If for a taxable year beginning after December 31, 1969, the transitional net long-term capital loss component determined as provided in subdivision (ii) of this subparagraph exceeds the amount of such component applied to the transitional additional allowance for the taxable year as provided by subdivision (i) of this subparagraph and subparagraph (4)(ii) of this paragraph, then such excess shall for the purposes of this subparagraph be carried to the succeeding taxable year as long-term capital losses from taxable years beginning before January 1, 1970, for utilization in the computation of the transitional additional allowance in the succeeding taxable year as provided in subdivisions (i) and (ii) of this subparagraph. In no event, however, shall the amount of such component carried to the following taxable year as otherwise provided by this subdivision exceed the total of net long-term capital losses actually carried to such succeeding taxable year pursuant to section 1212(b) and § 1.1212-1(b).

(iv) *Carryover of certain short-term capital losses not utilized in computation of additional allowance or transitional additional allowance.*—If for a taxable year beginning after December 31, 1969, the total short-term capital losses carried to such year from taxable years beginning before January 1, 1970, as provided by § 1.1212-1(b) and this subdivision exceed the sum of—

(a) The portion of the capital gain net income (net capital gain for taxable years beginning before January 1, 1977) actually realized in the taxable year (*i.e.,* computed without regard to capital losses carried to the taxable year) which consists of net short-term capital gain actually realized in the taxable year, plus

(b) The amount by which the portion of the capital gain net income (net capital gain for taxable years beginning before January 1, 1977) actually realized in the taxable year (i.e., computed without regard to capital losses carried to the taxable year) which consists of net long-term capital gain actually realized in the taxable year exceeds the total long-term capital losses carried to the taxable year from taxable years beginning before January 1, 1970, as provided in § 1.1212-1(b) and subdivision (iii) of this subparagraph, then such excess shall constitute the "transitional net short-term capital loss component" for the taxable year, and to the extent such component also exceeds the net short-term capital loss applied to the additional allowance (as provided in subparagraphs (2) and (4)(i) of this paragraph) or the transitional additional allowance (as provided by subdivision (i) of this subparagraph and subparagraph (4)(i) of this paragraph) for the taxable year shall be carried to the succeeding taxable year as short-term capital losses from taxable years beginning before January 1, 1970, for utilization in such succeeding taxable year in the computation of the additional allowance (as provided by subparagraph (2) of this paragraph) or the transitional additional allowance (as provided by subdivision (i) and (ii) of this subparagraph). In no event, however, shall the amount of such component so carried to the following taxable year as otherwise provided by this subdivision exceed the total of net short- term capital losses actually carried to such succeeding taxable year pursuant to section 1212(b) and § 1.1212-1(b).

(v) *Scope of rules.*—The rules provided by this subparagraph are for the purpose of computing the amount of the transitional additional allowance deductible for the taxable year pursuant to the provisions of section 1212(b)(3) and this subparagraph. More specifically, their operation permits the limited use of a long-term capital loss carried to the taxable year from a taxable year beginning before December 31, 1969, in full on a dollar-for-dollar basis in computing the transitional additional allowance deductible for the taxable year. These rules have no application to, or effect upon, a determination of the character or amount of capital gain net income (net capital gains for taxable years beginning before January 1, 1977) reportable in the taxable year. See paragraph (b)(1) of this section and § 1.1212-1 for the determination of the amount and character of capital gains and losses reportable in the taxable year. Further, except to the extent that their application may affect the amount of the transitional additional allowance deductible for the taxable year and thus the amount to be treated as short-term capital loss for carryover purposes under section 1212(b) and § 1.1212-1(b)(2), these rules have no effect upon a determination of the character or amount

of capital losses carried to or from the taxable year pursuant to section 1212(b) and § 1.1212-1(b).

(4) *Order of application of capital losses to additional allowance or transitional additional allowance.*—In applying the excess of the net short-term capital loss over the net long-term capital gain and the excess of the net long-term capital loss over the net short-term capital gain to the additional allowance or transitional additional allowance deductible under section 1211(b) and this paragraph, such excesses shall, subject to the limitations of subparagraph (2) or (3) of this paragraph, be used in the following order:

(i) First, there shall be applied to the additional allowance or transitional additional allowance the excess, if any, of the net short-term capital loss over the net long-term capital gain.

(ii) Second, if such transitional additional allowance exceeds the amount so applied thereto as provided in subdivision (i) of this subparagraph, there shall next be applied thereto as provided in subparagraph (3) of this paragraph the excess, if any, of the net long-term capital loss over the net short-term capital gain to the extent of the transitional net long-term capital loss component for the taxable year computed as provided by subdivision (ii) of subparagraph (3) of this paragraph.

(iii) Third, if such additional allowance or transitional additional allowance exceeds the sum of the amounts so applied thereto as provided in subdivisions (i) and (ii) of this subparagraph, there shall be applied thereto one-half of the balance, if any, of the excess net long-term capital loss not applied pursuant to the provisions of subdivision (ii) of this subparagraph.

(5) *Taxable years beginning prior to January 1, 1970.*—For any taxable year beginning prior to January 1, 1970, subparagraphs (2) and (3) of this paragraph shall not apply and losses from sales or exchanges of capital assets shall be allowed as a deduction only to the extent of gains from such sales or exchanges, plus (if such losses exceed such gains) the taxable income of the taxpayer or $1,000, whichever is smaller.

(6) *Special rules.*—(i) For purposes of section 1211(b) and this paragraph, taxable income is to be computed without regard to gains or losses from sales or exchanges of capital assets and without regard to the deductions provided in section 151 (relating to personal exemptions) or any deduction in lieu thereof. For example, the deductions available to estates and trusts under section 642(b) are in lieu of the deductions allowed under section 151, and, in the case of estates and trusts, are to be added back to taxable income for the purposes of section 1211(b) and this paragraph.

(ii) For taxable years beginning before January 1, 1976, in case the tax is computed under section 3 and the regulations thereunder

Reg. §1.1211-1(b)(3)(iv)(b)

(relating to optional tax tables for individuals), the term "taxable income" as used in section 1211(b) and this paragraph shall be read as "adjusted gross income."

(iii) In the case of a joint return, the limitation under section 1211(b) and this paragraph, relating to the allowance of losses from sales or exchanges of capital assets, is to be computed and the net capital loss determined with respect to the combined taxable income and the combined capital gains and losses of the spouses.

(7) *Married taxpayers filing separate returns.*—(i) *In general.*—In the case of a husband or a wife who files a separate return for a taxable year beginning after December 31, 1969, the $3,000, $2,000, and $1,000 amounts specified in subparagraphs (2)(ii) and (3)(i)(*b*) of this paragraph shall instead be $1,500, $1,000, and $500, respectively.

(ii) *Special rule.*—If, pursuant to the provisions of § 1.1212-1(b) and subparagraph (3)(iii) or (iv) of this paragraph, there is carried to the

taxable year from a taxable year beginning before January 1, 1970, a short-term capital loss or a long-term capital loss, the $1,500, $1,000, and $500 amounts specified in subdivision (i) of this subparagraph shall instead be maximum amounts of $3,000, $2,000, and $1,000, respectively, equal to $1,500, $1,000, and $500, respectively, plus the total of the transitional net long-term capital loss component for the taxable year computed as provided by subparagraph (3)(ii) of this paragraph and the transitional net short-term capital loss component for the taxable year computed as provided by subparagraph (3)(iv) of this paragraph.

(8) *Examples.*—The provisions of section 1211(b) may be illustrated by the following examples:

Example (1). A, an unmarried individual with one exemption allowable as a deduction under section 151, has the following transactions in 1970:

Taxable income exclusive of capital gains and losses		$4,400
Deduction provided by section 151		625
Taxable income for purposes of section 1211(b)		$5,025
Long-term capital gain	$1,200	
Long-term capital loss	(5,300)	
Net long-term capital loss	($4,100)	
Losses to the extent of gains	($1,200)	
Additional allowance deductible under section 1211(b)		$1,000

The net long-term capital loss of $4,100 is deductible in 1970 only to the extent of an additional allowance of $1,000 which is smaller than the taxable income of $5,025. Under section 1211(b) and subparagraph (2) of this paragraph, $2,000 of excess net long-term capital loss was required to produce the $1,000 additional allowance. Therefore, a net long-term capital loss of $2,100 ($4,100 minus $2,000) is carried over under section 1212(b) to the succeeding taxable year. If A had the same taxable income for purposes of section 1211(b) (after reduction by the

zero bracket amount) and the same transactions in 1977, the additional allowance would be $2,000, and a net long-term capital loss of $100 would be carried over. For a taxable year beginning in 1978 or thereafter, these facts would give rise to a $2,050 additional allowance and no carryover.

Example (2). B, an unmarried individual with one exemption allowable as a deduction under section 151, has the following transactions in 1970:

Taxable income exclusive of capital gains and losses		$90
Deduction provided by section 151		625
Taxable income for purposes of section 1211(b)		$715
Long-term capital gain	$1,200	
Long-term capital loss	(5,200)	
Net long-term capital loss	($4,000)	
Losses to the extent of gains	($1,200)	
Additional allowance deductible under section 1211(b)		$715

The net long-term capital loss of $4,000 is deductible in 1970 only to the extent of an additional allowance of $715, since the $715 of taxable income for purposes of section 1211(b) is smaller than $1,000. Under section 1211(b) and subparagraph (2) of this paragraph, $1,430 of net long-term capital loss was required to produce the $715 additional allowance. Therefore a net long-term capital loss of $2,570 ($4,000 minus $1,430) is carried over under section 1212(b) to the succeeding taxable year. For illustration of

the result if the net capital loss for the taxable year is smaller than both $1,000 and taxable income for the purposes of section 1211(b), see examples (3) and (4) of this subparagraph. For carryover of a net capital loss, see § 1.1212-1. Assuming the same taxable income for purposes of section 1211(b) (after reduction by the zero bracket amount) and the same transactions for taxable years beginning in 1977 or thereafter, the same result would be reached.

Example (3). A, an unmarried individual with one exemption allowable as a deduction under section 151, has the following transactions in 1971:

Taxable income exclusive of capital gains and losses		$13,300
Deduction provided by section 151		675
Taxable income for purposes of section 1211(b)		$13,975
Long-term capital gain	$400	
Long-term capital loss	(600)	
Net long-term capital loss	($200)	
Short-term capital gain	$900	
Short-term capital loss	(1,400)	
Net short-term capital loss	($500)	
Losses to extent of gains	($1,300)	
Additional allowance deductible under section 1211(b)		$600

The $600 additional allowance deductible under section 1211(b) is the least of: (i) taxable income of $13,975, (ii) $1,000, or (iii) the sum of the excess of the net short-term capital loss of $500 over the net long-term capital gain, plus one-half of the excess of the net long-term capital loss of $200 over the net short-term capital gain. The $600 additional allowance, therefore, consists of the net short-term capital loss of $500, plus $100 (one-half of the net long-term capital loss of $200), the total of which is smaller than both $1,000 and taxable income for purposes of section 1211(b). No amount of net capital loss remains to be carried over under section 1212(b) to the succeeding taxable year since the entire

amount of the net short-term capital loss of $500 plus the entire amount of the net long-term capital loss of $200 required to produce $100 of the deduction was absorbed by the additional allowance deductible under section 1211(b) for 1971. Assuming the same taxable income for purposes of section 1211(b) (after reduction by the zero bracket amount) and the same transactions for taxable years beginning in 1977 or thereafter, the result would remain unchanged.

Example (4). A, a married individual filing a separate return with one exemption allowable as a deduction under section 151, has the following transactions in 1971:

Taxable income exclusive of capital gains and losses		$12,000
Deduction provided by section 151		675
Taxable income for purposes of section 1211(b)		$12,675
Long-term capital loss	($800)	
Long-term capital gain	300	
Net long-term capital loss	($500)	
Short-term capital loss	($500)	
Short-term capital gain	600	
Net short-term capital gain	$100	
Losses to the extent of gains		($900)
Additional allowance deductible under section 1211(b)		$200

The excess net long-term capital loss of $400 (net long-term capital loss of $500 minus net short-term capital gain of $100) is deductible in 1971 only to the extent of an additional allowance of $200 (one-half of $400) which is smaller than both $500 (married taxpayer filing a separate return for a taxable year beginning after December 31, 1969) and taxable income for purposes of section 1211(b). Since there is no net short-term capital loss in excess of net long-term capital gains for the taxable year, the $200 additional allowance deductible under section 1211(b) consists entirely of excess net long-term capital loss.

No amount of net capital loss remains to be carried over under section 1212(b) to the succeeding taxable year. Assuming the same taxable income for purposes of section 1211(b) (after reduction by the zero bracket amount) and the same transactions for taxable years beginning in 1977 or thereafter, the result would remain unchanged.

Example (5). A, an unmarried individual with one exemption allowable as a deduction under section 151, has the following transactions in 1970:

Taxable income exclusive of capital gains and losses		$13,300
Deduction provided by section 151		625
Taxable income for purposes of section 1211(b)		$13,925
Long-term capital loss	($6,000)	
Long-term capital gain	$2,000	
Net long-term capital loss	($4,000)	

Short-term capital gain	$3,000
Short-term capital loss carried to 1970 from 1969 under section 1212(b)(1)	($3,000)
Net short-term capital loss	—0—
Losses to the extent of gains	($5,000)
Additional allowance deductible under section 12(b)	$1,000

The $1,000 additional allowance deductible under section 1211(b) is the least of (i) taxable income of $13,925, (ii) $1,000, or (iii) the sum of the net short-term capital loss ($0) plus one-half the net long-term capital loss of $4,000. The $1,000 additional allowance, therefore, consists of net long-term capital loss. Since $2,000 of the net long-term capital loss of $4,000 was required to produce the $1,000 additional allowance, the $2,000 balance of the net long-term capital loss is carried over under section 1212(b) to 1971. As-

suming the same taxable income for purposes of section 1211(b) (after reduction by the zero bracket amount) and the same transactions for taxable years beginning in 1977 or thereafter, the additional allowance would be $2,000, and there would be no carryover.

Example (6). A, an unmarried individual with one exemption allowable as a deduction under section 151, has the following transactions in 1970:

Taxable income exclusive of capital gains and losses		$13,300
Deduction provided by section 151		625
Taxable income for purposes of section 1211(b)		$13,925
Long-term capital gain	$5,000	
Long-term capital loss	($7,000)	
Long-term capital loss carried to 1970 from 1969 under section 1212(b)(1)	($500)	
Net long-term capital loss	($2,500)	
Short-term capital gain	$1,100	
Short-term capital loss	(1,400)	
Net short-term capital loss	($300)	
Losses to extent of gains	($6,100)	
Transitional additional allowance deductible under section 1211(b)	$1,000	

Because a component of the net long-term capital loss for 1970 is a $500 long-term capital loss carried to 1970 from 1969, the transitional additional allowance deductible under section 1211(b) and subparagraph (3) of this paragraph is the least of (i) taxable income of $13,925, (ii) $1,000, or (iii) the sum of the net short-term capital loss of $300, plus the net long-term capital loss for 1970 to the extent of the $500 long-term capital loss carried to 1970 from 1969 and one-half of the $2,000 balance of the net long-term capital loss. The entire $500 long-term capital loss carried to 1970 from 1969 is applicable in full to the transitional additional allowance because there was no net capital gain (capital gain net income for taxable years beginning after December 31, 1976) actually realized in 1970. The $1,000 transitional additional allowance, therefore, consists of the net short-term capital loss of

$300, the $500 long-term capital loss carried to 1970 from 1969, plus one-half of enough of the balance of the 1970 net long-term capital loss ($400) to make up the $200 balance of the $1,000 transitional additional allowance. A long-term capital loss of $1,600 ($2,500 minus $900), all of which is attributable to 1970, is carried over under section 1212(b) to 1971. Assuming the same taxable income for purposes of section 1211(b) (after reduction by the zero bracket amount) and the same transactions for taxable years beginning in 1977 or thereafter, the transitional additional allowance would be $1,800. No amount would remain to be carried over to the succeeding taxable year.

Example (7). A, an unmarried individual with one exemption allowable as a deduction under section 151, has the following transactions in 1970:

Taxable income exclusive of capital gains and losses		$13,300
Deduction provided by section 151		625
Taxable income for purposes of section 1211(b)		$13,925
Long-term capital loss	($2,000)	
Long-term capital loss carried to 1970 from 1969 under section 1212(b)(1)	(500)	
Net long-term capital loss	($2,500)	
Short-term capital gain	$2,600	
Short-term capital loss carried to 1970 from 1969 under section 1211(b)(1)	($3,000)	
Net short-term capital loss	($400)	

Losses to the extent of gains	($2,600)
Transitional additional allowance deductible under section 1211(b)	$1,000

Because a component of the net long-term capital loss for 1970 is a $500 long-term capital loss carried to 1970 from 1969, the transitional additional allowance deductible under section 1211(b) and subparagraph (3) of this paragraph is the least of (i) taxable income of $13,925, (ii) $1,000, or (iii) the sum of the net short-term capital loss of $400, plus the net long-term capital loss for 1970 to the extent of the $500 long-term capital loss carried to 1970 from 1969, and one-half of the $2,000 balance of the net long-term capital loss. The entire $500 long-term capital loss carried to 1970 from 1969 is applicable in full to the transitional additional allowance because the net capital gain (capital gain net income for taxable years beginning after December 31, 1976) for the taxable year (computed without regard to capital losses carried to the taxable year) consisted entirely of net short-term capital gain not in excess of the short-term capital loss carried to 1970 from 1969. The $1,000 transitional additional allowance, therefore, consists of the net short-term capital loss of $400, the $500 long-term capital loss carried to 1970 from 1969, plus one-half of enough of the balance of the 1970 net long-term capital loss ($200) to make up the $100 balance of the $1,000 transitional additional allowance. A long-term capital loss of $1,800 ($2,500 minus $700), all of which is attributable to 1970, is carried over under section 1212(b) to 1971. Assuming the same taxable income for purposes of section 1211(b) (after reduction by the zero bracket amount) and the same transactions for taxable years beginning in 1977 or thereafter, the transitional additional allowance would be $1,900. No amount would remain to be carried over to the succeeding taxable year.

Example (8). Assume the facts in Example (7) but assume that the individual with one exemp-

tion allowable as a deduction under section 151 is married and files a separate return for 1970. The maximum transitional additional allowance to which the individual would be entitled for 1970 pursuant to subparagraph (7)(ii) of this paragraph would be the sum of $500 plus (i) $2,400 of the short-term capital loss of $3,000 carried to 1970 from 1969 (the amount by which such carryover exceeds the $600 net capital gain (capital gain net income for taxable years beginning after December 31, 1976) actually realized in 1970, all of which is net short-term capital gain) and (ii) the $500 long-term capital loss carried to 1970 from 1969. However, since this sum ($3,400) exceeds $1,000, the maximum transitional additional allowance to which the individual is entitled for 1970 is limited to $1,000. If for 1971, the same married individual had taxable income of $13,925 for purposes of section 1211(b) and no capital transactions, and filed a separate return, the additional allowance deductible under section 1211(b) for 1971 would be limited to $500 by reason of subdivision (i) of subparagraph (7) of this paragraph, since, as illustrated in Example (7), no part of the capital loss carried over to 1971 under section 1212(b) is attributable to 1969. Assuming the same taxable income for purposes of section 1211(b) (after reduction by the zero bracket amount) and the same transactions as in example (7) for a married individual filing a separate return for a taxable year beginning in 1977 or thereafter, the transitional additional allowance would be $1,900. No amount would remain to be carried over to the succeeding taxable year.

Example (9). B, an unmarried individual with one exemption allowable as a deduction under section 151, has the following transactions in 1971:

Taxable income exclusive of capital gains and losses		$10,000
Deductions provided by section 151		675
Taxable income for purposes of section 1211(b)		$10,675
Long-term capital gain	$2,500	
Long-term capital loss treated under § 1.1211-1(b)(3)(iii) as carried over from 1969	(5,000)	
Net long-term capital loss		($2,500)
Short-term capital gain	$2,700	
Short-term capital loss carried to 1971 from 1970 under section 1212(b)(1)	(1,000)	
Short-term capital loss treated under § 1.1211-1(b)(3)(iv) as carried over from 1969	(2,000)	
Net short-term capital loss		($300)
Losses to extent of gain		($5,200)
Transitional additional allowance deductible under section 1211(b)		$1,000

Because a component of the net long-term capital loss for 1971 is a long-term capital loss treated

under subparagraph (3)(iii) of this paragraph as carried over from 1969, the rules for computation of the transitional additional allowance under subparagraph (3)(i) and (ii) of this paragraph apply. The "transitional net long-term capital loss component" for 1971 under subparagraph (3)(ii) of this paragraph is $1,800, that is, the amount by which the $5,000 long-term loss treated as carried over from 1969 to 1971 exceeds (a) the net long-term capital gain of $2,500 actually realized in 1971 plus (b) the $700 excess of the $2,700 net short-term capital gain actually realized in 1971 over the $2,000 short-term capital loss treated as carried over to 1971 from 1969. The transitional additional allowance for 1971 consists of the $300 net short-term capital loss plus $700 of the net long-term capital loss attributable to 1969. A net long-term capital loss of $1,800 ($2,500 minus $700) is carried over to 1972 under section 1212(b). Only $1,100 of the $1,800 will be treated in 1972 as carried over from 1969 since under subparagraph (3)(iii) of this paragraph the "transitional net long-term capital loss component" of $1,800 is reduced by the amount ($700) applied to the transitional additional allowance for 1971. Assuming the same taxable income for purposes of section 1211(b) (after reduction by the zero bracket amount) and the same transactions for a taxable year beginning in 1977, the transitional additional allowance would be $2,000. A net long-term capital loss of $800 would remain to be carried over. Of this amount $100 would be treated as carried over from 1969. Assuming the original facts for a taxable year beginning in 1978, the transitional additional allowance would be $2,450. No amount would remain to be carried over to the succeeding taxable year. [Reg. § 1.1211-1.]

☐ [T.D. 6243, 7-23-57. Amended by T.D. 7301, 1-3-74, T.D. 7597, 3-6-79 and T.D. 7728, 10-31-80.]

[Reg. §1.1212-1]

§1.1212-1. Capital loss carryovers and carrybacks.—(a) *Corporations; other taxpayers for taxable years beginning before January 1, 1964.*— (1) *Regular net capital loss sustained for taxable years beginning before January 1, 1970.*—(i) A corporation sustaining a net capital loss for any taxable year beginning before January 1, 1970, and a taxpayer other than a corporation sustaining a net capital loss for any taxable year beginning before January 1, 1964, shall carry over such net loss to each of the five succeeding taxable years and treat it in each of such five succeeding taxable years as a short-term capital loss to the extent not allowed as a deduction against any net capital gains (capital gain net income for taxable years beginning after December 31, 1976) of any taxable years intervening between the taxable year in which the net capital loss was sustained and the taxable year to which carried. The carryover is thus applied in each succeeding taxable year to offset any net capital gain (capital gain net income for taxable years beginning after December 31, 1976) in such succeeding taxable year. The amount of the capital loss carryover may not be included in computing a new net capital loss of a taxable year which can be carried over to the next five succeeding taxable years. For purposes of this subparagraph, a net capital gain (capital gain net income for taxable years beginning after December 31, 1976) shall be computed without regard to capital loss carryovers or carrybacks. In the case of nonresident alien individuals, see section 871 for special rules on capital loss carryovers. For the rules applicable to the portion of a net capital loss of a corporation which is attributable to a foreign expropriation capital loss sustained in taxable years beginning after December 31, 1958, see subparagraph (2) of this paragraph. For the rules applicable to a taxpayer other than a corporation in the treatment of that amount of a net capital loss which may be carried over under section 1212 and this subparagraph as a short-term capital loss to the first taxable year beginning after December 31, 1963, see paragraph (b) of this section.

(ii) The practical operation of the provisions of this subparagraph may be illustrated by the following example:

Example. (a) For the taxable years 1952 to 1956, inclusive, an individual with one exemption allowable under section 151 (or corresponding provision of prior law) is assumed to have a net short-term capital loss, net short-term capital gain, net long-term capital loss, net long-term capital gain, and taxable income (net income for 1952 and 1953) as follows:

	1952	1953	1954	1955	1956
Carryover from prior years:					
From 1952		($50,000)	($29,500)	($29,500)	
From 1954				(19,500)	($13,000)
Net short-term loss (computed without regard to the carryovers)	($30,000)	(5,000)	(10,000)		
Net short-term gain (computed without regard to the carryovers)				40,000	
Net long-term loss	(20,500)		(10,000)	(5,000)	
Net long-term gain		(25,000)			15,000
Net income or taxable income, computed without regard to capital gains and losses, and, after 1953, without regard to the deduction provided by section 151	500	500	500	1,000	500

	1952	1953	1954	1955	1956
Net capital gain (capital gain net income for taxable years beginning after December 31, 1976) (computed without regard to the carryovers) ..		20,500		36,000	
Net capital loss	(50,000)		(19,500)		
Deduction allowable under section 1202					1,000
Taxable income (after deductions allowable under sections 151 and 1202)					900

(b) *Net capital loss of 1952.* The net capital loss is $50,000. This figure is the excess of the losses from sales or exchanges of capital assets over the sum of (1) gains (in this case, none) from sales or exchanges of capital assets, and (2) net income (computed without regard to capital gains and losses) of $500. This amount may be carried forward in full as a short-term loss to 1953. However, in 1953 there was a net capital gain (capital gain net income for taxable years beginning after December 31, 1976) of $20,500, as defined by section 117(a)(10)(B) of the Internal Revenue Code of 1939, and limited by section 117(e)(1) of the 1939 Code, against which this net capital loss of $50,000 is allowed in part. The remaining portion—$29,500—may be carried forward to 1954 and 1955 since there was no net capital gain (capital gain net income for taxable years beginning after December 31, 1976) in 1954. In 1955 this $29,500 is allowed in full against net capital gain (capital gain net income for taxable years beginning after December 31, 1976) of $36,000, as defined by paragraph (d) of §1.1222-1 and limited by subdivision (i) of this subparagraph.

(c) *Net capital loss of 1954.* The net capital loss is $19,500. This figure is the excess of the losses from sales or exchanges of capital assets over the sum of (1) gains (in this case, none) from sales or exchanges of capital assets and (2) taxable income (computed without regard to capital gains and losses and the deductions provided in section 151) of $500. This amount may be carried forward in full as a short-term loss to 1955. The net capital gain (capital gain net income for taxable years beginning after December 31, 1976) in 1955, before deduction of any carryovers, is $36,000. (See sections 1222(9)(B) and 1212 of the Internal Revenue Code of 1954, as it existed prior to the enactment of the Revenue Act of 1964.) The $29,500 balance of the 1952 loss is first applied against the $36,000, leaving a balance of $6,500. Against this amount the $19,500 loss arising in 1954 is applied, leaving a loss of $13,000, which may be carried forward to 1956. Since this amount is treated as a short-term capital loss in 1956 under subdivision (i) of this subparagraph, the excess of the net long-term capital gain over the net short-term capital loss is $2,000 ($15,000 minus $13,000). Half of this excess is allowable as a deduction under section 1202. Thus, after also deducting the exemption allowed as a deduction under section 151 ($600), the taxpayer has a taxable income of $900 ($2,500 minus $1,600) for 1956.

(2) *Corporations sustaining foreign expropriation capital losses for taxable years ending after December 31, 1958.*—(i) *In general.*—A corporation sustaining a net capital loss for any taxable year ending after December 31, 1958, any portion of which is attributable to a foreign expropriation capital loss, shall carry over such portion of the loss to each of the ten succeeding taxable years and treat it in each of such succeeding taxable years as a short-term capital loss to the extent and consistent with the manner provided in subparagraph (1) of this paragraph. For such purposes, the portion of any net capital loss for any taxable year which is attributable to a foreign expropriation capital loss is the amount, not in excess of the net capital loss for such year, of the foreign expropriation capital loss for such year. The portion of a net capital loss for any taxable year which is attributable to a foreign expropriation capital loss shall be treated as a separate net capital loss for that year and shall be applied, after first applying the remaining portion of such net capital loss, to offset any capital gain net income (net capital gain(s) for taxable years beginning before January 1, 1977) in a succeeding taxable year. In applying net capital losses of two or more taxable years to offset the capital gain net income (net capital gain(s) for taxable years beginning before January 1, 1977) of a subsequent taxable year, such net capital losses shall be offset against such capital gain net income (net capital gain(s) for taxable years beginning before January 1, 1977) in the order of the taxable years in which the losses were sustained, beginning with the loss for the earliest preceding taxable year, even though one or more of such net capital losses are attributable in whole or in part to a foreign expropriation capital loss.

(ii) *Foreign expropriation capital loss defined.*—For purposes of this subparagraph the term "foreign expropriation capital loss" means, for any taxable year, the sum of the losses taken into account in computing the net capital loss for such year which are—

(a) Losses sustained directly by reason of the expropriation, intervention, seizure, or similar taking of property by the government of any foreign country, any political subdivision thereof, or any agency or instrumentality of the foregoing, or

(b) Losses (treated under section 165(g)(1) as losses from the sale or exchange of capital assets) from securities which become worthless by reason of the expropriation, intervention, seizure, or similar taking of property by the government of any foreign country, any political subdivision thereof, or any agency or instrumentality of the foregoing.

(iii) *Illustrations.*—The application of this subparagraph may be illustrated by the following examples:

Example 1. X, a domestic corporation which uses the calendar year as the taxable year, owns as a capital asset 75 percent of the outstanding stock of Y, a foreign corporation operating in a foreign country. In 1961, the foreign country seizes all of the assets of Y, rendering X's stock in Y worthless and thus causing X to sustain a $40,000 foreign expropriation capital loss for such year. In 1961, X has $30,000 of other losses from the sale or exchange of capital assets and $50,000 of gains from the sale or exchange of capital assets. X's net capital loss for 1961 is $20,000 ($70,000 – $50,000). Since the foreign expropriation capital loss exceeds this amount, the entire $20,000 is a foreign expropriation capital loss for 1961.

Example 2. Z, a domestic corporation which uses the calendar year as the taxable year, has a net capital loss of $50,000 for 1961, $30,000 of which is attributable to a foreign expropriation capital loss. Pursuant to the provisions of this paragraph, $30,000 of such net capital loss shall be carried over as a short-term capital loss to each of the 10 taxable years succeeding 1961, and the remaining $20,000 of the net capital loss shall be carried over as a short-term capital loss to each of the 5 taxable years succeeding 1961. Z has a $35,000 net capital gain (capital gain net income for taxable years beginning after December 31, 1976) (determined without regard to any capital loss carryover) for 1962. In offsetting the $50,000 capital loss carryover from 1961 against the $35,000 net capital gain (capital gain net income for taxable years beginning after December 31, 1976) for 1962, the $30,000 portion of such carryover which is attributable to the foreign expropriation capital loss for 1961 is applied against the 1962 net capital gain (capital gain net income for taxable years beginning after December 31, 1976) after applying the $20,000 remaining portion of the carryover. Thus, there is a capital loss carryover of $15,000 to 1963, all of which is attributable to the foreign expropriation capital loss for 1961. Z has a net capital loss for 1963 of $10,000, no portion of which is attributable to a foreign expropriation capital loss. For 1964, Z has a net capital gain (capital gain net income for taxable years beginning after December 31, 1976) of $22,000 (determined without regard to the capital loss carryovers from 1961 and 1963). In offsetting the capital loss carryovers from 1961 and 1963 against Z's $22,000 net capital gain for 1964, the $15,000 carryover from 1961 is applied against the 1964 net capital gain (capital gain net income for taxable years beginning after December 31, 1976) before the $10,000 capi-

tal loss carryover from 1963 is applied against such gain. Thus, $3,000 of the 1963 net capital loss remains to be carried over to 1965.

(3) *Regular net capital loss sustained by a corporation for taxable years beginning after December 31, 1969.*—(i) *General rule.*—A corporation sustaining a net capital loss for any taxable year beginning after December 31, 1969 (hereinafter in this paragraph referred to as the "loss year"), shall—

(*a*) Carry back such net capital loss to each of the three taxable years preceding the loss year, but only to the extent that such net capital loss is not attributable to a foreign expropriation capital loss and the carryback of such net capital loss does not increase or produce a net operating loss (as defined in section 172(c)) for the taxable year to which it is carried back; and

(*b*) Carry over such net capital loss to each of the five taxable years succeeding the loss year,

and, subject to subdivision (ii) of this subparagraph, treat such net capital loss in each of such three preceding and five succeeding taxable years as a short-term capital loss.

(ii) *Amount treated as a short-term capital loss in each year.*—The entire amount of the net capital loss for any loss year shall be carried to the earliest of the taxable years to which such net capital loss may be carried, and the portion of such net capital loss which shall be carried to each of the other taxable years to which such net capital loss may be carried shall be the excess, if any, of such net capital loss over the total of the capital gain net income (net capital gain(s) for taxable years beginning before January 1, 1977) (computed without regard to the capital loss carryback from the loss year or any taxable year thereafter) for each of the prior taxable years to which such net capital loss may be carried.

(iii) *Special rules.*—(*a*) In the case of a net capital loss which is not a foreign expropriation capital loss and which cannot be carried back in full to a preceding taxable year by reason of section 1212(a)(1)(A)(ii) and subdivision (i)(*a*) of this subparagraph because such loss would produce or increase a net operating loss in such preceding taxable year, the capital gain net income (net capital gain(s) for taxable years beginning before January 1, 1977) for such preceding taxable year shall in no case be treated as greater than the amount of such net capital loss which can be carried back to such preceding taxable year upon the application of section 1212(a)(1)(A)(ii) and subdivision (i)(*a*) of this subparagraph.

(*b*) For the rules applicable to the portion of a net capital loss of a corporation which is attributable to a foreign expropriation capital loss sustained in a taxable year beginning after December 31, 1958, see section 1212(a)(2) and subparagraph (2) of this paragraph.

Reg. §1.1212-1(a)(3)(iii)(b)

(c) Section 1212(a)(1)(A) and subdivision (i)(a) of this subparagraph shall not apply to (and no carryback shall be allowed with respect to) the net capital loss of a corporation for any taxable year for which such corporation is an electing small business corporation under subchapter S. See § 1.1372-1.

(d) A net capital loss of a corporation for a year for which it is not an electing small business corporation under subchapter S shall not be carried back under section 1212(a)(1)(A) and subdivision (i)(a) of this subparagraph to a taxable year for which such corporation is an electing small business corporation. See section 1212(a)(3).

(e) A net capital loss of a corporation shall not be carried back under section 1212(a)(1)(A) and subdivision (i)(a) of this subparagraph to a taxable year for which the corporation was a foreign personal holding company, a regulated investment company, or a real estate investment trust, or for which an election made by the corporation under section 1247 is applicable. See section 1212(a)(4).

(f) A taxable year to which a net capital loss of a corporation cannot, by reason of (d) or (e) of this subdivision, be carried back under section 1212(a)(1)(A) and subdivision (i)(a) of this subparagraph shall nevertheless be treated as one of the 3 taxable years preceding the loss year for purposes of section 1212(a)(1)(A) and such subdivision (i)(a); but any capital gain net income (net capital gain for taxable years beginning before January 1, 1977) for such taxable year to which such net capital loss cannot be carried back shall be disregarded for purposes of subdivision (ii) of this subparagraph.

(g) A regulated investment company (as defined in section 851) sustaining a net capital loss shall carry over that loss to each of the 8 taxable years succeeding the loss year. However, the 8-year period prescribed in the preceding sentence shall be reduced (but not to less than 5 years) by the sum of (1) the number of taxable years to which the net capital loss must be carried back pursuant to subdivision (i)(a) of this subparagraph (as limited by subdivision (iii)(e) of this subparagraph) and (2) the number of taxable years, of the 8 taxable years succeeding the loss year, that the corporation failed to qualify as a regulated investment company as defined in section 851. This subdivision shall not extend the carryover period prescribed in subdivision (i)(b) of this subparagraph to a year in which a corporation is not a regulated investment company as defined in section 851.

(iv) The application of this subparagraph may be illustrated by the following examples, in each of which it is assumed that the corporation is not, and never has been, a corporation described in subdivision (iii)(c) or (d) of this subparagraph, that the corporation files its tax returns on a calendar year basis, and that no capital loss sustained is a foreign expropriation capital loss:

Example (1). A corporation has a net capital loss for 1970 which section 1212(a)(1)(A) permits to be carried back. The entire net capital loss for 1970 may be carried back to 1967, but only to the extent that a net operating loss for 1967 would not be produced or increased. The amount of the carryback to 1968 is the excess of the net capital loss for 1970 over the net capital gain (capital gain net income for taxable years beginning after December 31, 1976) for 1967, computed without regard to a capital loss carryback from 1970 or any taxable year thereafter. The amount of the carryback to 1969 is the excess of the net capital loss for 1970 over the sum of the net capital gains (capital gain net income for taxable years beginning after December 31, 1976) for 1967 and 1968, computed without regard to a capital loss carryback from 1970 or any taxable year thereafter. The amount of the carryover to 1971 is the excess of the net capital loss for 1970 over the sum of the net capital gains (capital gain net income for taxable years beginning after December 31, 1976) for 1967, 1968 and 1969, computed without regard to a capital loss carryback from 1970 or any taxable year thereafter. Similarly, the amount of the carryover to 1972, 1973, 1974 and 1975, respectively, is the excess of the net capital loss for 1970 over the sum of the net capital gains (capital gain net income for taxable years beginning after December 31, 1976) for taxable years prior to 1972, 1973, 1974, or 1975, as the case may be, to which the net capital loss for 1970 may be carried, computed without regard to a capital loss carryback from 1970 or any year thereafter.

Example (2). For the taxable years 1967 to 1975, inclusive, a corporation is assumed to have net capital loss, net capital gain, and taxable income (computed without regard to capital gains and losses) as follows [reproduced on page 53,752]:

The net capital loss of 1969, under the rules of subparagraph (1) of this paragraph, may not be carried back. Thus, the net capital loss for 1970 is carried back and partially absorbed by the net capital gain (capital gain net income for taxable years beginning after December 31, 1976) for 1967, and a portion of the net capital losses of both 1970 and 1971 are carried back to 1968. The net capital loss for 1969 is the oldest that may be carried to 1973, and thus, it is the first carried over and absorbed by the net capital gain (capital gain net income for taxable years beginning after December 31, 1976) for 1973. The net capital loss for 1972 (which is not carried back because of the net capital losses in the three years preceding 1972) may be carried over to 1973.

Example (3). For the taxable years 1967 to 1970, inclusive, a corporation which was organized on January 1, 1967, realized operating income and net capital gains (capital gain net income for taxable years beginning after December 31, 1976) and sustained operating losses and net capital losses as follows:

	Operating Income or Loss (Exclusive of Capital Gain or Loss)	Capital Gain or Loss
1967	$20,000	$24,000
1968	$20,000	—0—
1969	$20,000	—0—
1970	($25,000)	($20,000)

The net capital loss of $20,000 for 1970 is carried back to 1967 and applied against the $24,000 net capital gain (capital gain net income for taxable years beginning after December 31, 1976) realized in that year, reducing such net capital gain (capital gain net income for taxable years beginning after December 31, 1976) to $4,000. The net operating loss of $25,000 for 1970 is then carried back to 1967 and applied first to eliminate the $20,000 of operating income for that year and then to eliminate the net capital gain (capital gain net income for taxable years beginning after December 31, 1976) for that year of $4,000 (as reduced by the 1970 capital loss carryback).

Example (4). Assume the same facts as in Example (3) but substitute the following figures:

	Operating Income or Loss (Exclusive of Capital Gain or Loss)	Capital Gain or Loss
1967	($20,000)	$24,000
1968	$20,000	—0—
1969	$20,000	—0—
1970	($25,000)	($20,000)

The net capital loss of $20,000 for 1970 is carried back to 1967 and applied against the $24,000 net capital gain (capital gain net income for taxable years beginning after December 31, 1976) realized in that year only to the extent of $4,000, the maximum amount to which the 1970 capital loss carryback can be applied without producing a net operating loss for 1967. The unused $16,000 balance of the 1970 net long-term capital loss can be carried forward to 1971 and subsequent taxable years to the extent provided in subdivision (i)(b) of this subparagraph.

Example (5). Assume the same facts as in Example (3) but substitute the following figures:

	Operating Income or Loss (Exclusive of Capital Gain or Loss)	Capital Gain or Loss
1967	—0—	—0—
1968	($20,000)	—0—
1969	—0—	$24,000
1970	$20,000	($24,000)

The net capital loss of $24,000 for 1970 is carried back to 1969 and applied against the $24,000 net capital gain (capital gain net income for taxable years beginning after December 31, 1976) realized in that year to the extent of $24,000. The application of the capital loss carryback is not limited as it was in Example (4) because such carryback neither increases nor produces a net operating loss, as such, for 1969. The $20,000 net operating loss for 1968 is then carried forward to 1970 to eliminate the $20,000 of operating income for that year.

	1967	1968	1969	1970	1971	1972	1973	1974	1975
Taxable income (computed without regard to capital gains or losses)	$25,000	$25,000	$25,000	$25,000	$25,000	$25,000	$25,000	$25,000	$25,000
Net capital loss	......	......	($1,000)	($29,500)	($16,000)	($500)	......	......	......
Net capital gain (capital gain net income for taxable years beginning after December 31, 1976) (computed without regard to carrybacks or carryovers)	$14,000	$16,000	......	......	......	......	$8,000	$7,500	$6,500
Carryback or carryover:									
From 1969:	($14,000)	($15,500)	......	......	......	......	($1,000)	......	......
From 1970:	($500)	($500)	......	......	......	......	......	......	......
From 1971:	......	......	......	......	......	......	($7,000)	($7,500)	($1,000)
From 1972:									($500)

Reg. §1.1212-1(a)(3)(iv)

Example (6). Assume the same facts as in Example (3) but substitute the following figures:

	Operating Income or Loss (Exclusive of Capital Gain or Loss)	Capital Gain or Loss
1967	—0—	—0—
1968	—0—	—0—
1969	($20,000)	($24,000)
1970	$20,000	$20,000

The net capital loss of $24,000 for 1969 is carried forward to 1970 and applied against the $20,000 net capital gain realized in that year. The unused $4,000 balance of the 1969 net capital loss can be carried forward to 1971 and subsequent taxable years to the extent provided in subdivision (i)(*b*) of this subparagraph.

(b) *Taxpayers other than corporations for taxable years beginning after December 31, 1963.*—(1) *In general.*—If a taxpayer other than a corporation sustains a net capital loss for any taxable year beginning after December 31, 1963, the portion thereof which is a short-term capital loss carryover shall be carried over to the succeeding taxable year and treated as a short-term capital loss sustained in such succeeding taxable year, and the portion thereof which constitutes a long-term capital loss carryover shall be carried over to the succeeding taxable year and treated as a long-term capital loss sustained in such succeeding taxable year. The carryovers are included in the succeeding taxable year in the determination of the amount of the short-term capital loss, the net short-term capital gain or loss, the long-term capital loss, and the net long-term capital gain or loss in such year, the net capital loss in such year, and the capital loss carryovers from such year. For purposes of this subparagraph—

(i) A short-term capital loss carryover is the excess of the net short-term capital loss for the taxable year over the net long-term capital gain for such year, and

(ii) A long-term capital loss carryover is the excess of the net long-term capital loss for the taxable year over the net short-term capital gain for such year.

(2) *Special rules for determining a net short-term capital gain or loss for purposes of carryovers.*— (i) *Taxable years beginning after December 31, 1963, and before January 1, 1970.*—In determining a net short-term capital gain or loss of a taxable year beginning after December 31, 1963, and before January 1, 1970, for purposes of computing a short-term or long-term capital loss carryover to the succeeding taxable year, an amount equal to the additional allowance deductible under section 1211(b) for the taxable year (determined as provided in section 1211(b), as in effect for taxable years beginning before January 1, 1970) and § 1.1211-1(b)(5)) is treated as a short-term capital gain occurring in such year.

(ii) *Taxable years beginning after December 31, 1969.*—In determining a net short-term capi-

tal gain or loss of a taxable year beginning after December 31, 1969—

(a) For purposes of computing a short-term capital loss carryover to the succeeding taxable year, an amount equal to the additional allowance for the taxable year (determined as provided in section 1211(b) and § 1.1211-1(b)(2)) is treated as a short-term capital gain occurring in such year, and

(b) For purposes of computing a long-term capital loss carryover to the succeeding taxable year, an amount equal to the sum of the additional allowance for the taxable year (determined as provided in section 1211(b) and § 1.1211-1(b)(2)), plus the excess of such additional allowance over the net short-term capital loss (determined without regard to section 1212(b)(2) for such year) is treated as a short-term capital gain in such year.

The rules provided in this subdivision are for the purpose of taking into account the additional allowance deductible for the current taxable year under section 1211(b) and § 1.1211-1(b)(2) in determining the amount and character of capital loss carryovers from the current taxable year to the succeeding taxable year. Their practical application to a determination of the amount and character of capital loss carryovers from the current taxable year to the succeeding taxable year involves identification of the net long-term and net short-term capital loss components of the additional allowance deductible in the current taxable year as provided by § 1.1211-1(b)(2)(iii). To the extent that the additional allowance is composed of net short-term capital losses, such losses are treated as a short-term capital gain in the current taxable year in determining the capital loss carryovers to the succeeding year. To the extent that the additional allowance is composed of net long-term capital losses applied pursuant to the provisions of § 1.1211-1(b)(2)(iii), an amount equal to twice the amount of such component of the additional allowance is treated as a short-term capital gain in the current taxable year. See paragraph (4) of this section for transitional rules if any part of the additional allowance is composed of net long-term capital losses carried to the current taxable year from a taxable year beginning before January 1, 1970.

(3) *Transitional rule for net capital losses sustained in a taxable year beginning before January 1, 1964.*—A taxpayer other than a corporation sustaining a net capital loss for any taxable year beginning before January 1, 1964, shall treat as a short-term capital loss in the first taxable year beginning after December 31, 1963, any amount which would be treated as a short-term capital loss in such year under subchapter P of chapter 1 of the Code as in effect immediately before the enactment of the Revenue Act of 1964.

(4) *Transitional rule for net long-term capital losses sustained in a taxable year beginning before January 1, 1970.*—In the case of a net long-term

capital loss sustained by a taxpayer other than a corporation in a taxable year beginning prior to January 1, 1970 (referred to in this section as a "pre-1970 taxable year") which is carried over and treated as a long-term capital loss in the first taxable year beginning after December 31, 1969 (referred to in this section as a "post-1969 taxable year"), the transitional additional allowance deductible under section 1211(b) for the taxable year shall be determined by application of section 1211(b) as in effect for pre-1970 taxable years and §1.1211-1(b)(3), and the amount of such long-term capital loss carried over and treated as a long-term capital loss in the succeeding taxable year shall be determined by application of section 1212(b)(1) as in effect for pre-1970 taxable years and subparagraph (2)(i) of this paragraph (instead of under sections 1211(b) and 1212(b)(1) as in effect for post-1969 taxable years and §1.1211-1(b)(2) and subparagraph (2)(ii) of this paragraph, respectively) but only to the extent that such pre-1970 long-term capital loss constitutes a "transitional net long-term capital loss component" (determined as provided in §1.1211-1(b)(3)(ii)) in the taxable year to which such pre-1970 long-term capital loss is carried. Thus, for purposes of paragraph (2) of this section, to the extent that a component of the transitional additional allowance deductible for a post-1969 taxable year under section 1211(b) and §1.1211-1(b)(3)(i) is a transitional net long-term capital loss component carried over to such post-1969 taxable year, such component shall be treated as a short-term capital gain in determining the amount and character of capital loss carryovers from such post-1969 taxable year to the succeeding taxable year. Such component shall be so treated as a short-term capital gain in full on a dollar-for-dollar basis and shall not be doubled for this purpose as is provided by subdivision (ii) of paragraph (2) of this section in the case of a component of the additional allowance made up of net long-term capital losses applied pursuant to the provisions of §1.1211-1(b)(2)(iii). The transitional rule provided in this paragraph does not apply to a determination of the character of capital losses (as long-term or short-term) actually deductible for the current taxable year under section 1211(b) and §1.1211-1(b).

(5) *Examples.*—The application of this paragraph can be illustrated by the following examples:

Example (1). For the taxable year 1971, an unmarried individual has taxable income for purposes of section 1211(b) of $8,000, a long-term capital loss of $2,000, and no other capital gains or losses. $1,000 (one-half) of the net long-term capital loss is deductible in 1971 as the additional allowance deductible under section 1211(b). No amount of capital loss remains to be carried over to the succeeding taxable year.

Example (2). For the taxable year 1972, the same unmarried individual has taxable income

for purposes of section 1211(b) of $8,000, a long-term capital loss of $3,000 and no other capital gains or losses. $1500 (one-half of the excess net capital loss) is deductible in 1972, but limited to the $1,000 maximum additional allowance deductible under section 1211(b). By application of section 1212(b)(1), he will carry over to 1973 a long-term capital loss of $1,000 determined as follows:

Net long-term capital loss		($3,000)
Additional allowance deductible under section 1211(b)	$1,000	
Excess of additional allowance over net short-term capital loss (determined without regard to section 1212(b)(2)(B)(i))	$1,000	
Total amount treated as short-term capital gain under 1212(b)(2)(B) for purposes of determining carryover		$2,000
Long-term capital loss carryover to 1973		($1,000)

If, in 1973, he had taxable income for purposes of section 1211(b) of $8,000, but no capital gains or losses, $500 (one-half) of the net long-term capital loss carryover from 1972 would be deductible in 1973 as the additional allowance deductible under section 1211(b). No amount of capital loss would be carried over to 1974.

Example (3). For the taxable year 1971, an unmarried individual has taxable income for purposes of section 1211(b) of $9,000, a $500 short-term capital gain, a $700 short-term capital loss, a $1,000 long-term capital gain and a $1,700 long-term capital loss. He will offset $1,500 of capital losses against capital gains. The excess net capital loss of $900 is deductible in 1971 to the extent of a $550 additional allowance deductible under 1211(b) which is smaller than both $1,000 and taxable income for purposes of section 1211(b), determined as follows:

Losses allowed to the extent of gains	($1,500)
Amount allowed under section 1211(b)(1)(C)	
(i) excess of net short-term capital loss over net long-term capital gain	($200)
(ii) one-half of the excess of net long-term capital loss over net short-term capital gain	(350)
Additional allowance deductible under section 1211(b)	$550

The total amount treated as short-term capital gain under section 1212(b)(2)(B) for purposes of determining any carryover to the succeeding taxable year exceeds $900. No amount of net capital loss remains to be carried over to the succeeding taxable year.

Example (4). If in example (3) above, the long-term capital loss had been $2,800, the taxpayer would carry over $200 of long-term capital loss to 1972, determined as follows:

Losses allowed to extent of gains .... ($1,500)
Amount allowed under section 1211(b)(1)(B)
  and (C):
  (i) excess of net short-term capital loss over
      net long-term capital gain .... (200)
  (ii) one-half the excess of net long-term
      capital loss over net short-term capital
      gain .... (900)
as limited by 1211(b)(1)(B) to an additional allowance of $1,000.

Carryover under section 1212(b)(1):
Net long-term capital loss for 1971 ..... ($1,800)
Additional allowance under section
  1211(b)(1)(B) $1,000
Excess of additional allowance deductible
  under section 1211(b) over net short-
  term capital loss determined without
  regard to section 1212(b)(2)(B)(i) ($1,000
  less $200) .... $ 800
                                    _____
Total amount treated as short-term capital
  gain under section 1212(b)(2)(B) for
  purposes of determining carryover ... $1,800
Short-term capital gain for 1971 500
                                    _____
  Total short-term capital gain $2,300
Short-term capital loss for 1971 ...... ($ 700)
                                    _____
  Net short-term capital gain $1,600

Long-term capital loss carryover ($1,800 less
  $1,600) .... $ 200
                                    ========

Example (5). For 1969, an unmarried individual has taxable income for purposes of section
1211(b) of $8,000, a long-term capital loss of
$3,000, and no other capital gains or losses. He is
allowed to deduct in 1969 $1,000 as the addi-
tional allowance deductible under section
1211(b) (as in effect for pre-1970 taxable years)
and to carry over to 1970, a long-term capital loss
of $2,000 under section 1212(b) (as in effect for
pre-1970 taxable years).

If, in 1970, the same unmarried individual
with taxable income for purposes of section
1211(b) of $8,000, has no capital gains or losses,
he would deduct $1,000 of his pre-1970 capital
loss carryover as the transitional additional allowance deductible under section 1211(b) (as in
effect for pre-1970 taxable years) and carry over under
section 1212(b)(1) (as in effect for pre-1970 taxable years) to 1971 the remaining $1,000 as a
pre-1970 long-term capital loss.

If, in 1970, the same individual instead has a
long-term capital gain of $2,500, and a long-term
capital loss of $1,500, he would net these two
items with the $2,000 carried to 1970 as a long-
term capital loss. Thus, he would have a net
long-term capital loss for 1970 of $1,000 which is
deductible in 1970 as the transitional additional
allowance deductible under section 1211(b). He
would have no amount to carry over under section 1212(b)(1) to 1971.

If, in 1970, the same individual instead has a
long-term capital loss of $1,200, and a long-term
capital gain of $200, resulting in a net long-term
capital loss of $3,000 when netted with the $2,000
carried to 1970 as a long-term capital loss, he

would deduct $1,000 in respect of his pre-1970
long-term capital loss carryover as the transitional additional allowance deductible under
section 1211(b) (as in effect for pre-1970 taxable
years) and carry over under section 1212(b)(1)
(as in effect for pre-1970 taxable years) to 1971
the remaining $1,000 of the pre-1970 component
of his long-term capital loss carryover, and the
$1,000 net long-term capital loss actually sus-
tained in 1970 as the second component of his
long-term capital loss carryover.

Example (6). For 1970 a married individual
filing a separate return has taxable income of
$8,000, a long-term capital loss of $3,500 and a
short-term capital gain of $3,000. He also has a
pre-1970 short-term capital loss of $2,000 which
is carried to 1970. The $3,000 short-term capital
gain realized in 1970 would first be reduced by
the $2,000 short-term capital loss carryover, and
then the remaining $1,000 balance of the short-
term capital gain would be offset against the
$3,500 long-term capital loss, producing a net
long-term capital loss of $2,500, no part of which
is a net long-term capital loss carried over from
1969. However, under the special rule in
§ 1.1211-1(b)(7)(ii) in 1970, the taxpayer would
deduct as the additional allowance deductible
under section 1211(b), the $500 limitation in
§ 1.1211-1(b)(2)(ii) in the case of a married taxpayer filing a separate return in a taxable year
ending after December 31, 1969, plus the "transitional net short-term capital loss component" of
$2,000 computed under § 1.1211-1(b)(3)(iv), but
limited to a total deduction of $1,000. The $1,000
additional allowance deductible under section
1211(b) would absorb $2,000 of the $2,500 net
long-term capital loss, and he would carry the
unused $500 balance of such loss to 1971 for use
in that year.

Example (7). For 1970, an unmarried individual filing a separate return has taxable income
for purposes of section 1211(b) of $8,000, and a
long-term capital loss of $2,000. He also has a
pre-1970 long-term capital loss of $2,500 which is
carried to 1970. In 1970, the taxpayer would
deduct as the transitional additional allowance
deductible under section 1211(b) $1,000, absorb-
ing $1,000 of the pre-1970 long-term capital loss
of $2,500. He would carry to 1971 the unused
$1,500 balance of his pre-1970 long-term capital
loss plus the 1970 long-term capital loss of
$2,000, or a total of $3,500, for use in 1971.

For 1971, the same taxpayer filing a separate
return with taxable income for purposes of section 1211(b) of $8,000, has a $3,600 long-term
capital gain and a $2,200 long-term capital loss.
When these gains and losses are combined with
the long-term capital loss carryover from 1970 of
$3,500, a net long-term capital loss of $2,100 results. He would deduct $1,000 as the transitional
additional allowance deductible under section
1211(b). The $1,000 additional allowance would
absorb $100 of the unused pre-1970 long-term
capital loss carryover of $1,500 plus $1,800 of the

unused post-1969 long-term capital loss carry-over of $2,100 (the amount of the 1971 net long-term capital loss necessary to make up the re-maining $900 balance of the additional allow-ance). Although a component of the 1971 net long-term capital loss is the unused pre-1970 long-term capital loss carryover of $1,500, only $100 of this carryover is available for use in full on a dollar-for-dollar basis in computing the transitional additional allowance for 1971 since it only exceeds by that amount the $1,400 net capi-tal gain (capital gain net income for taxable years beginning after December 31, 1976) actually real-ized in 1971 all of which is net long-term capital gain (long-term capital gain of $3,600 reduced by long-term capital loss of $2,200). See § 1.1211-1(b)(3)(ii). The taxpayer would carry over to 1972 as a long-term capital loss the re-maining $200 of the 1971 long-term capital loss.

Example (8). For 1970, an unmarried individ-ual has taxable income for purposes of section 1211(b) of $8,000 and a short-term capital loss of $700. He also has a pre-1970 long-term capital loss carryover of $1,200. He would deduct $1,000 as the transitional additional allowance deducti-ble under section 1211(b). The $1,000 transitional additional allowance would be composed of the 1970 short-term capital loss of $700 and $300 of the pre-1970 long-term capital loss carryover. He would carry over to 1971 the unused $900 bal-ance of his $1,200 pre-1970 long-term capital loss carryover for use in 1971.

(c) *Husband and wife.*—(1) The following rules shall be applied in computing net capital loss carryovers by husband and wife:

(i) If a husband and wife making a joint return for any taxable year made separate re-turns for the preceding year, any capital loss carryovers of each spouse from such preceding taxable year may be carried forward to the taxa-ble year in accordance with paragraph (a) or (b) of this section.

(ii) If a joint return was made for the pre-ceding taxable year, any capital loss carryover from such preceding taxable year may be carried forward to the taxable year in accordance with paragraph (a) or (b) of this section.

(iii) If a husband and wife make separate returns for the first taxable year beginning after December 31, 1963, or any prior taxable year, and they made a joint return for the preceding taxable year, any capital loss carryover from such preceding taxable year shall be allocated to the spouses on the basis of their individual net capital loss which gave rise to such capital loss carryover. The capital loss carryover so allocated to each spouse may be carried forward by such spouse to the taxable year in accordance with paragraph (a) or (b) of this section.

(iv) If a husband and wife making sepa-rate returns for any taxable year following the first taxable year beginning after December 31, 1963, made a joint return for the preceding taxa-ble year, any long-term or short-term capital loss carryovers shall be allocated to the spouses on the basis of their individual net long-term and net short-term capital losses for the preceding taxable year which gave rise to such capital loss carryovers, and the portions of the long-term or short-term capital loss carryovers so allocated to each spouse may be carried forward by such spouse to the taxable year in accordance with paragraph (b) of this section.

(v) If separate returns are made both for the taxable year and the preceding taxable year, any capital loss carryover of each spouse may be carried forward by such spouse in accordance with paragraph (a) or (b) of this section.

(2) The provisions of subparagraph (1)(i), (iii), and (iv) of this paragraph may be illustrated by the following examples:

Example (1). If H and W, husband and wife, make a joint return for 1955, having made sepa-rate returns for 1954 in which H had a net capital loss of $3,000 and W had a net capital loss of $2,000, in their joint return for 1955 they would have a short-term capital loss of $5,000 (the sum of their separate capital loss carryovers from 1954), allowable in accordance with paragraph (a) of this section. If, on the other hand, they make separate returns in 1955 following a joint return in 1954 in which their net capital loss was $5,000 allocable $3,000 to H and $2,000 to W, the carryover of H as a short-term capital loss for the purpose of his 1955 separate return would be $3,000 and that of W for her separate return would be $2,000, each allowable in accordance with paragraph (a) of this section.

Example (2). H and W, husband and wife, make separate returns for 1966 following a joint return for 1965. The capital gains and losses in-curred by H and W in 1965, including those carried over by them to 1965, were as follows:

	H	W
Long-term capital gains	$8,000	$9,000
Long-term capital losses	(15,000)	(6,000)
Short-term capital gains	10,000	4,000
Short-term capital losses	(19,000)	(5,000)

Thus, in 1965 H and W had a net capital loss of $14,000 on their joint return. Of this amount, $4,000 was a long-term capital loss carryover, and $10,000 was a short-term capital loss carry-over, determined in accordance with paragraph (b) of this section. H's net long-term capital loss was $7,000 for 1965. This amount was offset on the joint return by W's net long-term capital gain of $3,000. Thus, H may carry over to his separate return for 1966, a long-term capital loss carry-over of $4,000. H and W may carry over to their separate returns for 1966, as short-term capital loss carryovers, the amounts of their respective net short-term losses from 1965, $9,000 and $1,000. [Reg. § 1.1212-1.]

☐ [*T.D. 6243, 7-23-57. Amended by T.D. 6828, 6-16-65, T.D. 6867, 12-6-65, T.D. 7301, 1-3-74, T.D. 7659, 12-14-79 and T.D. 7728, 10-31-80.*]

General Rules for Determining Capital Gains and Losses

[Reg. § 1.1221-1]

§ 1.1221-1. **Meaning of terms.**—(a) The term "capital assets" includes all classes of property not specifically excluded by section 1221. In determining whether property is a "capital asset", the period for which held is immaterial.

(b) Property used in the trade or business of a taxpayer of a character which is subject to the allowance for depreciation provided in section 167 and real property used in the trade or business of a taxpayer is excluded from the term "capital assets". Gains and losses from the sale or exchange of such property are not treated as gains and losses from the sale or exchange of capital assets, except to the extent provided in section 1231. See § 1.1231-1. Property held for the production of income, but not used in a trade or business of the taxpayer, is not excluded from the term "capital assets" even though depreciation may have been allowed with respect to such property under section 23(1) of the Internal Revenue Code of 1939 before its amendment by section 121(c) of the Revenue Act of 1942 (56 Stat. 819). However, gain or loss upon the sale or exchange of land held by a taxpayer primarily for sale to customers in the ordinary course of his business, as in the case of a dealer in real estate, is not subject to the provisions of subchapter P (section 1201 and following), chapter 1 of the Code.

(c)(1) A copyright, a literary, musical, or artistic composition, and similar property are excluded from the term "capital assets" if held by a taxpayer whose personal efforts created such property, or if held by a taxpayer in whose hands the basis of such property is determined, for purposes of determining gain from a sale or exchange, in whole or in part by reference to the basis of such property in the hands of a taxpayer whose personal efforts created such property. For purposes of this subparagraph, the phrase "similar property" includes, for example, such property as a theatrical production, a radio program, a newspaper cartoon strip, or any other property eligible for copyright protection (whether under statute or common law), but does not include a patent or an invention, or a design which may be protected only under the patent law and not under the copyright law.

(2) In the case of sales and other dispositions occurring after July 25, 1969, a letter, a memorandum, or similar property is excluded from the term "capital asset" if held by (i) a taxpayer whose personal efforts created such property, (ii) a taxpayer for whom such property was prepared or produced, or (iii) a taxpayer in whose hands the basis of such property is determined, for purposes of determining gain from a sale or exchange, in whole or in part by reference to the basis of such property in the hands of a taxpayer described in subdivision (i) or (ii) of this subparagraph. In the case of a collection of letters, memorandums, or similar property held by a person who is a taxpayer described in subdivision (i), (ii), or (iii) of this subparagraph as to some of such letters, memorandums, or similar property but not as to others, this subparagraph shall apply only to those letters, memorandums, or similar property as to which such person is a taxpayer described in such subdivision. For purposes of this subparagraph, the phrase "similar property" includes, for example, such property as a draft of a speech, a manuscript, a research paper, an oral recording of any type, a transcript of an oral recording, a transcript of an oral interview or of dictation, a personal or business diary, a log or journal, a corporate archive, including a corporate charter, office correspondence, a financial record, a drawing, a photograph, or a dispatch. A letter, memorandum, or property similar to a letter or memorandum, addressed to a taxpayer shall be considered as prepared or produced for him. This subparagraph does not apply to property, such as a corporate archive, office correspondence, or a financial record, sold or disposed of as part of a going business if such property has no significant value separate and apart from its relation to and use in such business; it also does not apply to any property to which subparagraph (1) of this paragraph applies (i.e., property to which section 1221(3) applied before its amendment by section 514(a) of the Tax Reform Act of 1969 (83 Stat. 643).

(3) For purposes of this paragraph, in general property is created in whole or in part by the personal efforts of a taxpayer if such taxpayer performs literary, theatrical, musical, artistic, or other creative or productive work which affirmatively contributes to the creation of the property, or if such taxpayer directs and guides others in the performance of such work. A taxpayer, such as corporate executive, who merely has administrative control of writers, actors, artists, or personnel and who does not substantially engage in the direction and guidance of such persons in the performance of their work, does not create property by his personal efforts. However, for purposes of subparagraph (2) of this paragraph, a letter or memorandum, or property similar to a letter or memorandum, which is prepared by personnel who are under the administrative control of a taxpayer, such as a corporate executive, shall be deemed to have been prepared or produced for him whether or not such letter, memorandum, or similar property is reviewed by him.

(4) For the application of section 1231 to the sale or exchange of property to which this paragraph applies, see § 1.1231-1. For the application of section 170 to the charitable contribution of property to which this paragraph applies, see section 170(e) and the regulations thereunder.

(d) Section 1221(4) excludes from the definition of "capital asset" accounts or notes receivable acquired in the ordinary course of trade or business for services rendered or from the sale of stock in trade or inventory or property held for sale to customers in the ordinary course of trade or business. Thus, if a taxpayer acquires a note receivable for services rendered, reports the fair market value of the note as income, and later sells the note for less than the amount previously reported, the loss is an ordinary loss. On the other hand, if the taxpayer later sells the note for more than the amount originally reported, the excess is treated as ordinary income.

(e) Obligations of the United States or any of its possessions, or of a State or Territory, or any political subdivision thereof, or of the District of Columbia, issued on or after March 1, 1941, on a discount basis and payable without interest at a fixed maturity date not exceeding one year from the date of issue, are excluded from the term "capital assets." An obligation may be issued on a discount basis even though the price paid exceeds the face amount. Thus, although the Second Liberty Bond Act (31 U.S.C. 754) provides that United States Treasury bills shall be issued on a discount basis, the issuing price paid for a particular bill may, by reason of competitive bidding, actually exceed the face amount of the bill. Since the obligations of the type described in this paragraph are excluded from the term "capital assets", gains or losses from the sale or exchange of such obligations are not subject to the limitations provided in such subchapter P. It is, therefore, not necessary for a taxpayer (other than a life insurance company taxable under part I (section 801 and following), subchapter L, chapter 1 of the Code, as amended by the Life Insurance Company Tax Act of 1955 (70 Stat. 36), and, in the case of taxable years beginning before January 1, 1955, subject to taxation only on interest, dividends, and rents) to segregate the original discount accrued and the gain or loss realized upon the sale or other disposition of any such obligation. See section 454(b) with respect to the original discount accrued. The provisions of this paragraph may be illustrated by the following examples:

Example (1). A (not a life insurance company) buys a $100,000, 90-day Treasury bill upon issuance for $99,998. As of the close of the forty-fifth day of the life of such bill, he sells it to B (not a life insurance company) for $99,999.50. The entire net gain to A of $1.50 may be taken into account as a single item of income, without allocating $1 to interest and $0.50 to gain. If B holds the bill until maturity his net gain of $0.50 may similarly be taken into account as a single item of income, without allocating $1 to interest and $0.50 to loss.

Example (2). The facts in this example are the same as in example (1) except that the selling price to B is $99,998.50. The net gain to A of $0.50 may be taken into account without allocating $1

to interest and $0.50 to loss, and, similarly, if B holds the bill until maturity his entire net gain of $1.50 may be taken into account as a single item of income without allocating $1 to interest and $0.50 to gain. [Reg. § 1.1221-1.]

☐ [*T.D. 6243, 7-23-57. Amended by T.D. 7369, 7-15-75.*]

[Reg. § 1.1221-2]

§ 1.1221-2. Hedging transactions.— (a) *Treatment of hedging transactions.*—(1) *In general.*—This section governs the treatment of hedging transactions under section 1221(a)(7). Except as provided in paragraph (g)(2) of this section, the term capital asset does not include property that is part of a hedging transaction (as defined in paragraph (b) of this section).

(2) *Short sales and options.*—This section also governs the character of gain or loss from a short sale or option that is part of a hedging transaction. Except as provided in paragraph (g)(2) of this section, gain or loss on a short sale or option that is part of a hedging transaction (as defined in paragraph (b) of this section) is ordinary income or loss.

(3) *Exclusivity.*—If a transaction is not a hedging transaction as defined in paragraph (b) of this section, gain or loss from the transaction is not made ordinary on the grounds that property involved in the transaction is a surrogate for a noncapital asset, that the transaction serves as insurance against a business risk, that the transaction serves a hedging function, or that the transaction serves a similar function or purpose.

(4) *Coordination with section 988.*—This section does not apply to determine the character of gain or loss realized on a section 988 transaction as defined in section 988(c)(1) or realized with respect to any qualified fund as defined in section 988(c)(1)(E)(iii).

(b) *Hedging transaction defined.*—Section 1221(b)(2)(A) provides that a hedging transaction is any transaction that a taxpayer enters into in the normal course of the taxpayer's trade or business primarily—

(1) To manage risk of price changes or currency fluctuations with respect to ordinary property (as defined in paragraph (c)(2) of this section) that is held or to be held by the taxpayer;

(2) To manage risk of interest rate or price changes or currency fluctuations with respect to borrowings made or to be made, or ordinary obligations incurred or to be incurred, by the taxpayer; or

(3) To manage such other risks as the Secretary may prescribe in regulations (see paragraph (d)(6) of this section).

(c) *General rules.*—(1) *Normal course.*—Solely for purposes of paragraph (b) of this section, if a transaction is entered into in furtherance of a taxpayer's trade or business, the transaction is entered into in the normal course of the taxpayer's trade or business. This rule includes managing risks relating to the expansion of an existing business or the acquisition of a new trade or business.

(2) *Ordinary property and obligations.*—Property is ordinary property to a taxpayer only if a sale or exchange of the property by the taxpayer could not produce capital gain or loss under any circumstances. Thus, for example, property used in a trade or business within the meaning of section 1231(b) (determined without regard to the holding period specified in that section) is not ordinary property. An obligation is an ordinary obligation if performance or termination of the obligation by the taxpayer could not produce capital gain or loss. For purposes of this paragraph (c)(2), the term termination has the same meaning as it does in section 1234A.

(3) *Hedging an aggregate risk.*—The term hedging transaction includes a transaction that manages an aggregate risk of interest rate changes, price changes, and/or currency fluctuations only if all of the risk, or all but a de minimis amount of the risk, is with respect to ordinary property, ordinary obligations, or borrowings.

(4) *Managing risk.*—(i) *In general.*—Whether a transaction manages a taxpayer's risk is determined based on all of the facts and circumstances surrounding the taxpayer's business and the transaction. Whether a transaction manages a taxpayer's risk may be determined on a business unit by business unit basis (for example by treating particular groups of activities, including the assets and liabilities attributable to those activities, as separate business units), provided that the business unit is within a single entity or consolidated return group that adopts the single-entity approach. A taxpayer's hedging strategies and policies as reflected in the taxpayer's minutes or other records are evidence of whether particular transactions were entered into primarily to manage the taxpayer's risk.

(ii) *Limitation of risk management transactions to those specifically described.*—Except as otherwise determined by published guidance or by private letter ruling, a transaction that is not treated as a hedging transaction under paragraph (d) does not manage risk. Moreover, a transaction undertaken for speculative purposes will not be treated as a hedging transaction.

(d) *Transactions that manage risk.*—(1) *Risk reduction transactions.*—(i) *In general.*—A transaction that is entered into to reduce a taxpayer's risk, manages a taxpayer's risk.

(ii) *Micro and macro hedges.*—(A) *In general.*—A taxpayer generally has risk of a particular type only if it is at risk when all of its operations are considered. Nonetheless, a hedge of a particular asset or liability generally will be respected as reducing risk if it reduces the risk attributable to the asset or liability and if it is reasonably expected to reduce the overall risk of the taxpayer's operations. If a taxpayer hedges particular assets or liabilities, or groups of assets or liabilities, and the hedges are undertaken as part of a program that, as a whole, is reasonably expected to reduce the overall risk of the taxpayer's operations, the taxpayer generally does not have to demonstrate that each hedge that was entered into pursuant to the program reduces its overall risk.

(B) *Example.*—The following example illustrates the rules stated in paragraph (d)(1)(ii)(A) of this section:

Example. Corporation X manages its business operations by treating particular groups of activities, including the assets and liabilities attributable to those assets, as separate business units. A separate set of books and records is maintained with respect to the activities, assets and liabilities of separate business unit *y*. As part of a risk management program that Corporation X reasonably expects to reduce the overall risks of its business operations, Corporation X enters into hedges to reduce the risks of separate business unit *y*. Corporation X may demonstrate that the hedges reduce risk by taking into account only the activities, assets and liabilities of business unit *y*.

(iii) *Written options.*—A written option may reduce risk. For example, in appropriate circumstances, a written call option with respect to assets held by a taxpayer or a written put option with respect to assets to be acquired by a taxpayer may be a hedging transaction. See also paragraph (d)(3) of this section.

(iv) *Fixed-to-floating price hedges.*—Under the principles of paragraph (d)(1)(ii)(A) of this section, a transaction that economically converts a price from a fixed price to a floating price may reduce risk. For example, a taxpayer with a fixed cost for its inventory may be at risk if the price at which the inventory can be sold varies with a particular factor. Thus, for such a taxpayer a transaction that converts its fixed price to a floating price may be a hedging transaction.

(2) *Interest rate conversions.*—A transaction that economically converts an interest rate from a fixed rate to a floating rate or that converts an interest rate from a floating rate to a fixed rate manages risk.

(3) *Transactions that counteract hedging transactions.*—If a transaction is entered into primarily to offset all or any part of the risk management effected by one or more hedging transactions, the transaction is a hedging transaction. For example, if a written option is used to reduce or

eliminate the risk reduction obtained from another position such as a purchased option, then it may be a hedging transaction.

(4) *Recycling.*—A taxpayer may enter into a hedging transaction by using a position that was a hedge of one asset or liability as a hedge of another asset or liability (recycling).

(5) *Transactions not entered into primarily to manage risk.*—(i) *Rule.*—Except as otherwise determined in published guidance or private letter ruling, the purchase or sale of a debt instrument, an equity security, or an annuity contract is not a hedging transaction even if the transaction limits or reduces the taxpayer's risk with respect to ordinary property, borrowings, or ordinary obligations. In addition, the Commissioner may determine in published guidance that other transactions are not hedging transactions.

(ii) *Examples.*—The following examples illustrate the rule stated in paragraph (d)(5)(i) of this section:

Example 1. Taxpayer borrows money and agrees to pay a floating rate of interest. Taxpayer purchases debt instruments that bear a comparable floating rate. Although taxpayer's interest rate risk from the floating rate borrowing may be reduced by the purchase of the debt instruments, the acquisition of the debt instruments is not a hedging transaction, because the transaction is not entered into primarily to manage the taxpayer's risk.

Example 2. Taxpayer undertakes obligations to pay compensation in the future. The amount of the future compensation payments is adjusted as if amounts were invested in a specified mutual fund and were increased or decreased by the earnings, gains and losses that would result from such an investment. Taxpayer invests funds in the shares of the mutual fund. Although the investment in shares of the mutual fund reduces the taxpayer's risk of fluctuation in the amount of its obligation to employees, the investment was not made primarily to manage the taxpayer's risk. Accordingly, the transaction is not a hedging transaction.

Example 3. Taxpayer provides a nonqualified retirement plan for employees that is structured like a defined contribution plan. Based on a schedule that takes into account an employee's monthly salary and years of service with the taxpayer, the taxpayer makes monthly credits to an account for each employee. Each employee may designate that the account will be treated as if it were used to pay premiums on a variable annuity contract issued by the M insurance company with a value that reflects a specified investment option. M offers a number of investment options for its variable annuity contracts. Taxpayer invests funds in M company variable annuity contracts that parallel the investment options selected by the employees. The invest-

ment is not made primarily to manage the taxpayer's risk and is not a hedging transaction.

(6) *Hedges of other risks.*—The Commissioner may, by published guidance, determine that hedging transactions include transactions entered into to manage risks other than interest rate or price changes, or currency fluctuations.

(7) *Miscellaneous provision.*—(i) *Extent of risk management.*—A taxpayer may hedge all or any portion of its risk for all or any part of the period during which it is exposed to the risk.

(ii) *Number of transactions.*—The fact that a taxpayer frequently enters into and terminates positions (even if done on a daily or more frequent basis) is not relevant to whether these transactions are hedging transactions. Thus, for example, a taxpayer hedging the risk associated with an asset or liability may frequently establish and terminate positions that hedge that risk, depending on the extent the taxpayer wishes to be hedged. Similarly, if a taxpayer maintains its level of risk exposure by entering into and terminating a large number of transactions in a single day, its transactions may nonetheless qualify as hedging transactions.

(e) *Hedging by members of a consolidated group.*—(1) *General rule: single-entity approach.*—For purposes of this section, the risk of one member of a consolidated group is treated as the risk of the other members as if all of the members of the group were divisions of a single corporation. For example, if any member of a consolidated group hedges the risk of another member of the group by entering into a transaction with a third party, that transaction may potentially qualify as a hedging transaction. Conversely, intercompany transactions are not hedging transactions because, when considered as transactions between divisions of a single corporation, they do not manage the risk of that single corporation.

(2) *Separate-entity election.*—In lieu of the single-entity approach specified in paragraph (e)(1) of this section, a consolidated group may elect separate-entity treatment of its hedging transactions. If a group makes this separate-entity election, the following rules apply:

(i) *Risk of one member not risk of other members.*—Notwithstanding paragraph (e)(1) of this section, the risk of one member is not treated as the risk of other members.

(ii) *Intercompany transactions.*—An intercompany transaction is a hedging transaction (an intercompany hedging transaction) with respect to a member of a consolidated group if and only if it meets the following requirements—

(A) The position of the member in the intercompany transaction would qualify as a hedging transaction with respect to the member (taking into account paragraph (e)(2)(i) of this section) if the member had entered into the transaction with an unrelated party; and

(B) The position of the other member (the marking member) in the transaction is marked to market under the marking member's method of accounting.

(iii) *Treatment of intercompany hedging transactions.*—An intercompany hedging transaction (that is, a transaction that meets the requirements of paragraphs (e)(2)(ii)(A) and (B) of this section) is subject to the following rules—

(A) The character and timing rules of § 1.1502-13 do not apply to the income, deduction, gain, or loss from the intercompany hedging transaction; and

(B) Except as provided in paragraph (g)(3) of this section, the character of the marking member's gain or loss from the transaction is ordinary.

(iv) *Making and revoking the election.*—Unless the Commissioner otherwise prescribes, the election described in paragraph (e)(2) of this section must be made in a separate statement that provides, "[INSERT NAME AND EMPLOYER IDENTIFICATION NUMBER OF COMMON PARENT]HEREBY ELECTS THE APPLICATION OF § 1.1221-2(e)(2) (THE SEPARATE-ENTITY APPROACH)." The statement must also indicate the date as of which the election is to be effective. The election must be filed by including the statement on or with the consolidated group's income tax return for the taxable year that includes the first date for which the election is to apply. The election applies to all transactions entered into on or after the date so indicated. The election may only be revoked with the consent of the Commissioner.

(3) *Definitions.*—For definitions of consolidated group, divisions of a single corporation, group, intercompany transactions, and member, see section 1502 and the regulations thereunder.

(4) *Examples.*—*General Facts.* In these examples, O and H are members of the same consolidated group. O's business operations give rise to interest rate risk "A," which O wishes to hedge.

O enters into an intercompany transaction with H that transfers the risk to H. O's position in the intercompany transaction is "B," and H's position in the transaction is "C." H enters into position "D" with a third party to reduce the interest rate risk it has with respect to its position C. D would be a hedging transaction with respect to risk A if O's risk A were H's risk. The following examples illustrate this paragraph (e):

Example 1. Single-entity treatment—(i) *General rule.* Under paragraph (e)(1) of this section, O's risk A is treated as H's risk, and therefore D is a hedging transaction with respect to risk A. Thus, the character of D is determined under the rules of this section, and the income, deduction, gain, or loss from D must be accounted for under a method of accounting that satisfies § 1.446-4. The intercompany transaction B-C is not a hedging transaction and is taken into account under § 1.1502-13.

(ii) *Identification.* D must be identified as a hedging transaction under paragraph (f)(1) of this section, and A must be identified as the hedged item under paragraph (f)(2) of this section. Under paragraph (f)(5) of this section, the identification of A as the hedged item can be accomplished by identifying the positions in the intercompany transaction as hedges or hedged items, as appropriate. Thus, substantially contemporaneous with entering into D, H may identify C as the hedged item and O may identify B as a hedge and A as the hedged item.

Example 2. Separate-entity election; counterparty that does not mark to market. In addition to the *General Facts* stated above, assume that the group makes a separate-entity election under paragraph (e)(2) of this section. If H does not mark C to market under its method of accounting, then B is not a hedging transaction, and the B-C intercompany transaction is taken into account under the rules of section 1502. D is not a hedging transaction with respect to A, but D may be a hedging transaction with respect to C if C is ordinary property or an ordinary obligation and if the other requirements of paragraph (b) of this section are met. If D is not part of a hedging transaction, then D may be part of a straddle for purposes of section 1092.

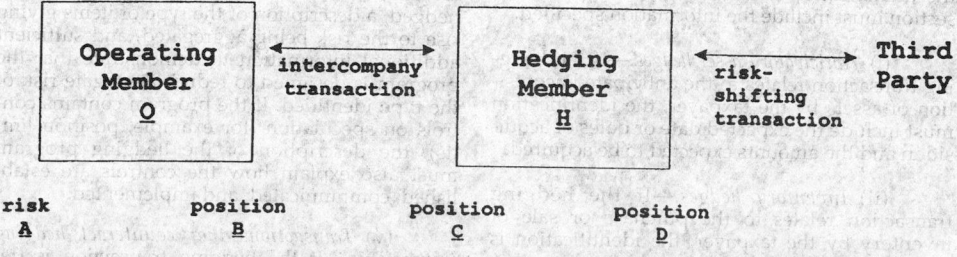

| Operating Member **O** | ◄── intercompany transaction ──► | Hedging Member **H** | ◄── risk-shifting transaction ──► | Third Party |

| risk **A** | position **B** | position **C** | position **D** |

Example 3. Separate-entity election; counterparty that marks to market. The facts are the same as in *Example 2* above, except that H marks

C to market under its method of accounting. Also assume that B would be a hedging transaction with respect to risk A if O had entered into that transaction with an unrelated party. Thus, for *O*, the *B-C* transaction is an intercompany hedging transaction with respect to *O*'s risk *A*, the character and timing rules of §1.1502-13 do not apply to the *B-C* transaction, and *H*'s income, deduction, gain, or loss from *C* is ordinary. However, other attributes of the items from the *B-C* transaction are determined under §1.1502-13. *D* is a hedging transaction with respect to *C* if it meets the requirements of paragraph (b) of this section.

(f) *Identification and recordkeeping.*—(1) *Same-day identification of hedging transactions.*—Under section 1221(a)(7), a taxpayer that enters into a hedging transaction (including recycling an existing hedging transaction) must clearly identify it as a hedging transaction before the close of the day on which the taxpayer acquired, originated, or entered into the transaction (or recycled the existing hedging transaction).

(2) *Substantially contemporaneous identification of hedged item.*—(i) *Content of the identification.*—A taxpayer that enters into a hedging transaction must identify the item, items, or aggregate risk being hedged. Identification of an item being hedged generally involves identifying a transaction that creates risk, and the type of risk that the transaction creates. For example, if a taxpayer is hedging the price risk with respect to its June purchases of corn inventory, the transaction being hedged is the June purchase of corn and the risk is price movements in the market where the taxpayer buys its corn. For additional rules concerning the content of this identification, see paragraph (f)(3) of this section.

(ii) *Timing of the identification.*—The identification required by this paragraph (f)(2) must be made substantially contemporaneously with entering into the hedging transaction. An identification is not substantially contemporaneous if it is made more than 35 days after entering into the hedging transaction.

(3) *Identification requirements for certain hedging transactions.*—In the case of the hedging transactions described in this paragraph (f)(3), the identification under paragraph (f)(2) of this section must include the information specified.

(i) *Anticipatory asset hedges.*—If the hedging transaction relates to the anticipated acquisition of assets by the taxpayer, the identification must include the expected date or dates of acquisition and the amounts expected to be acquired.

(ii) *Inventory hedges.*—If the hedging transaction relates to the purchase or sale of inventory by the taxpayer, the identification is made by specifying the type or class of inventory to which the transaction relates. If the hedging transaction relates to specific purchases or sales, the identification must also include the expected dates of the purchases or sales and the amounts to be purchased or sold.

(iii) *Hedges of debt of the taxpayer.*—(A) *Existing debt.*—If the hedging transaction relates to accruals or payments under an issue of existing debt of the taxpayer, the identification must specify the issue and, if the hedge is for less than the full issue price or the full term of the debt, the amount of the issue price and the term covered by the hedge.

(B) *Debt to be issued.*—If the hedging transaction relates to the expected issuance of debt by the taxpayer or to accruals or payments under debt that is expected to be issued by the taxpayer, the identification must specify the following information: the expected date of issuance of the debt; the expected maturity or maturities; the total expected issue price; and the expected interest provisions. If the hedge is for less than the entire expected issue price of the debt or the full expected term of the debt, the identification must also include the amount or the term being hedged. The identification may indicate a range of dates, terms, and amounts, rather than specific dates, terms, or amounts. For example, a taxpayer might identify a transaction as hedging the yield on an anticipated issuance of fixed rate debt during the second half of its fiscal year, with the anticipated amount of the debt between $75 million and $125 million, and an anticipated term of approximately 20 to 30 years.

(iv) *Hedges of aggregate risk.*—(A) *Required identification.*—If a transaction hedges aggregate risk as described in paragraph (c)(3) of this section, the identification under paragraph (f)(2) of this section must include a description of the risk being hedged and of the hedging program under which the hedging transaction was entered. This requirement may be met by placing in the taxpayer's records a description of the hedging program and by establishing a system under which individual transactions can be identified as being entered into pursuant to the program.

(B) *Description of hedging program.*—A description of a hedging program must include an identification of the type of risk being hedged, a description of the type of items giving rise to the risk being aggregated, and sufficient additional information to demonstrate that the program is designed to reduce aggregate risk of the type identified. If the program contains controls on speculation (for example, position limits), the description of the hedging program must also explain how the controls are established, communicated, and implemented.

(v) *Transactions that counteract hedging transactions.*—If the hedging transaction is described in paragraph (d)(3) of this section, the description of the hedging transaction must include an identification of the risk management transaction that is being offset and the original underlying hedged item.

(4) *Manner of identification and records to be retained.*—(i) *Inclusion of identification in tax records.*—The identification required by this paragraph (f) must be made on, and retained as part of, the taxpayer's books and records.

(ii) *Presence of identification must be unambiguous.*—The presence of an identification for purposes of this paragraph (f) must be unambiguous. The identification of a hedging transaction for financial accounting or regulatory purposes does not satisfy this requirement unless the taxpayer's books and records indicate that the identification is also being made for tax purposes. The taxpayer may indicate that individual hedging transactions, or a class or classes of hedging transactions, that are identified for financial accounting or regulatory purposes are also being identified as hedging transactions for purposes of this section.

(iii) *Manner of identification.*—The taxpayer may separately and explicitly make each identification, or, so long as paragraph (f)(4)(ii) of this section is satisfied, the taxpayer may establish a system pursuant to which the identification is indicated by the type of transaction or by the manner in which the transaction is consummated or recorded. An identification under this system is made at the later of the time that the system is established or the time that the transaction satisfies the terms of the system by being entered, or by being consummated or recorded, in the designated fashion.

(iv) *Principles of paragraph (f)(4)(iii) of this section illustrated.*—Paragraphs (f)(4)(iv)(A) through (C) of this section illustrate the principles of paragraph (f)(4)(iii) of this section and assume that the other requirements of this paragraph (f) are satisfied.

(A) A taxpayer can make an identification by designating a hedging transaction for (or placing it in) an account that has been identified as containing only hedges of a specified item (or of specified items or specified aggregate risk).

(B) A taxpayer can make an identification by including and retaining in its books and records a statement that designates all future transactions in a specified derivative product as hedges of a specified item, items, or aggregate risk.

(C) A taxpayer can make an identification by designating a certain mark, a certain form, or a certain legend as meaning that a transaction is a hedge of a specified item (or of specified items or a specified aggregate risk). Identification can be made by placing the designated mark on a record of the transaction (for example, trading ticket, purchase order, or trade confirmation) or by using the designated form or a record that contains the designated legend.

(5) *Identification of hedges involving members of the same consolidated group.*—(i) *General rule: single-entity approach.*—A member of a consolidated group must satisfy the requirements of this paragraph (f) as if all of the members of the group were divisions of a single corporation. Thus, the member entering into the hedging transaction with a third party must identify the hedging transaction under paragraph (f)(1) of this section. Under paragraph (f)(2) of this section, that member must also identify the item, items, or aggregate risk that is being hedged, even if the item, items, or aggregate risk relates primarily or entirely to other members of the group. If the members of a group use intercompany transactions to transfer risk within the group, the requirements of paragraph (f)(2) of this section may be met by identifying the intercompany transactions, and the risks hedged by the intercompany transactions, as hedges or hedged items, as appropriate. Because identification of the intercompany transaction as a hedge serves solely to identify the hedged item, the identification is timely if made within the period required by paragraph (f)(2) of this section. For example, if a member transfers risk in an intercompany transaction, it may identify under the rules of this paragraph (f) both its position in that transaction and the item, items, or aggregate risk being hedged. The member that hedges the risk outside the group may identify under the rules of this paragraph (f) both its position with the third party and its position in the intercompany transaction. Paragraph (e)(4) *Example 1* of this section illustrates this identification.

(ii) *Rule for consolidated groups making the separate-entity election.*—If a consolidated group makes the separate-entity election under paragraph (e)(2) of this section, each member of the group must satisfy the requirements of this paragraph (f) as though it were not a member of a consolidated group.

(6) *Consistency with section 1256(e)(2).*—Any identification for purposes of section 1256(e)(2) is also an identification for purposes of paragraph (f)(1) of this section.

(g) *Effect of identification and non-identification.*—(1) *Transactions identified.*—(i) *In general.*—If a taxpayer identifies a transaction as a hedging transaction for purposes of paragraph (f)(1) of this section, the identification is binding with respect to gain, whether or not all of the requirements of paragraph (f) of this section are satisfied. Thus, gain from that transaction is ordinary income. If the transaction is not in fact a hedging transaction described in paragraph (b) of this section, however, paragraphs (a)(1) and (2) of this section do not apply and the character of loss is determined without reference to whether the transaction is a surrogate for a noncapital asset, serves as insurance against a business risk, serves a hedging function, or serves a similar function or purpose. Thus, the taxpayer's identification of the transaction as a hedging transaction does not itself make loss from the transaction ordinary.

(ii) *Inadvertent identification.*—Notwithstanding paragraph (g)(1)(i) of this section, if the taxpayer identifies a transaction as a hedging transaction for purposes of paragraph (f) of this section, the character of the gain is determined as if the transaction had not been identified as a hedging transaction if—

(A) The transaction is not a hedging transaction (as defined in paragraph (b) of this section);

(B) The identification of the transaction as a hedging transaction was due to inadvertent error; and

(C) All of the taxpayer's transactions in all open years are being treated on either original or, if necessary, amended returns in a manner consistent with the principles of this section.

(2) *Transactions not identified.*—(i) *In general.*—Except as provided in paragraphs (g)(2)(ii) and (iii) of this section, the absence of an identification that satisfies the requirements of paragraph (f)(1) of this section is binding and establishes that a transaction is not a hedging transaction. Thus, subject to the exceptions, the rules of paragraphs (a)(1) and (2) of this section do not apply, and the character of gain or loss is determined without reference to whether the transaction is a surrogate for a noncapital asset, serves as insurance against a business risk, serves a hedging function, or serves a similar function or purpose.

(ii) *Inadvertent error.*—If a taxpayer does not make an identification that satisfies the requirements of paragraph (f) of this section, the taxpayer may treat gain or loss from the transaction as ordinary income or loss under paragraph (a)(1) or (2) of this section if—

(A) The transaction is a hedging transaction (as defined in paragraph (b) of this section);

(B) The failure to identify the transaction was due to inadvertent error; and

(C) All of the taxpayer's hedging transactions in all open years are being treated on either original or, if necessary, amended returns as provided in paragraphs (a)(1) and (2) of this section.

(iii) *Anti-abuse rule.*—If a taxpayer does not make an identification that satisfies all the requirements of paragraph (f) of this section but the taxpayer has no reasonable grounds for treating the transaction as other than a hedging transaction, then gain from the transaction is ordinary. The reasonableness of the taxpayer's failure to identify a transaction is determined by taking into consideration not only the requirements of paragraph (b) of this section but also the taxpayer's treatment of the transaction for financial accounting or other purposes and the taxpayer's identification of similar transactions as hedging transactions.

(3) *Transactions by members of a consolidated group.*—(i) *Single-entity approach.*—If a consolidated group is under the general rule of paragraph (e)(1) of this section (the single-entity approach), the rules of this paragraph (g) apply only to transactions that are not intercompany transactions.

(ii) *Separate-entity election.*—If a consolidated group has made the election under paragraph (e)(2) of this section, then, in addition to the rules of paragraphs (g)(1) and (2) of this section, the following rules apply:

(A) If an intercompany transaction is identified as a hedging transaction but does not meet the requirements of paragraphs (e)(2)(ii) (A) and (B) of this section, then, notwithstanding any contrary provision in §1.1502-13, each party to the transaction is subject to the rules of paragraph (g)(1) of this section with respect to the transaction as though it had incorrectly identified its position in the transaction as a hedging transaction.

(B) If a transaction meets the requirements of paragraphs (e)(2)(ii) (A) and (B) of this section but the transaction is not identified as a hedging transaction, each party to the transaction is subject to the rules of paragraph (g)(2) of this section. (Because the transaction is an intercompany hedging transaction, the character and timing rules of §1.1502-13 do not apply. See paragraph (e)(2)(iii) (A) of this section.)

(h) *Effective date.*—The rules of this section apply to transactions entered into on or after March 20, 2002.

(i) [Reserved]. For further guidance, see §1.1221-2T(i). [Temporary Reg. §1.1221-2T was removed by T.D. 9329.]

(j) *Effective/applicability date.*—Paragraph (e)(2)(iv) of this section applies to any original consolidated Federal income tax return due (without extensions) after June 14, 2007. For original consolidated Federal income tax returns due (without extensions) after May 30, 2006, and on or before June 14, 2007, see §1.1221-2T as contained in 26 CFR part 1 in effect on April 1, 2007. For original consolidated Federal income tax returns due (without extensions) on or before May 30, 2006, see §1.1221-2 as contained in 26 CFR part 1 in effect on April 1, 2006. [Reg. §1.1221-2.]

☐ [T.D. 8555, 7-13-94. *Amended by T.D. 8653,* 1-5-96; *T.D. 8985, 3-15-2002; T.D. 9264, 5-26-2006 and T.D. 9329, 6-13-2007.*]

[Reg. §1.1221-3]

§1.1221-3. Time and manner for electing capital asset treatment for certain self-created musical works.—(a) *Description.*—Section

1221(b)(3) allows an electing taxpayer to treat the sale or exchange of a musical composition or a copyright in a musical work created by the taxpayer's personal efforts (or having a basis determined by reference to the basis of such property in the hands of a taxpayer whose personal efforts created such property) as the sale or exchange of a capital asset. As a consequence, gain or loss from the sale or exchange is treated as capital gain or loss.

(b) *Time and manner for making the election.*— An election described in this section is made separately for each musical composition (or copyright in a musical work) sold or exchanged during the taxable year. An election must be made on or before the due date (including extensions) of the income tax return for the taxable year of the sale or exchange. The election is made on Schedule D, "Capital Gains and Losses," of the appropriate income tax form (for example, Form 1040, "U.S. Individual Income Tax Return;" Form 1065, "U.S. Return of Partnership Income;" Form 1120, "U.S. Corporation Income Tax Return") by treating the sale or exchange as the sale or exchange of a capital asset, in accordance with the form and its instructions.

(c) *Revocability of election.*—The election described in this section is revocable with the consent of the Commissioner. To seek consent to revoke the election, a taxpayer must submit a request for a letter ruling under the applicable administrative procedures. Alternatively, an automatic extension of 6 months from the due date of the taxpayer's income tax return (excluding extensions) is granted to revoke the election, provided the taxpayer timely filed the taxpayer's income tax return and, within this 6-month extension period, the taxpayer files an amended income tax return that treats the sale or exchange as the sale or exchange of property that is not a capital asset.

(d) *Effective/applicability date.*—This section applies to elections under section 1221(b)(3) in taxable years beginning after May 17, 2006. [Reg. § 1.1221-3.]

☐ [*T.D.* 9514, 2-4-2011.]

[Reg. § 1.1222-1]

§ 1.1222-1. Other terms relating to capital gains and losses.—(a) The phrase "short-term" applies to the category of gains and losses arising from the sale or exchange of capital assets held for 1 year (6 months for taxable years beginning before 1977; 9 months for taxable years beginning in 1977) or less; the phrase "long-term" to the category of gains and losses arising from the sale or exchange of capital assets held for more than 1 year (6 months for taxable years beginning before 1977; 9 months for taxable years beginning in 1977). The fact that some part of a loss from the sale or exchange of a capital

asset may be finally disallowed because of the operation of section 1211 does not mean that such loss is not "taken into account in computing taxable income" within the meaning of that phrase as used in sections 1222(2) and 1222(4).

(b)(1) In the definition of "net short-term capital gain", as provided in section 1222(5), the amounts brought forward to the taxable year under section 1212 (other than section 1212 (b)(1)(B)) are short-term capital losses for such taxable year.

(2) In the definition of "net long-term capital gain", as provided in section 1222(7), the amounts brought forward to the taxable year under section 1212(b)(1)(B) are long-term capital losses for such taxable year.

(c) Gains and losses from the sale or exchange of capital assets held for not more than 1 year (6 months for taxable years beginning before 1977; 9 months for taxable years beginning in 1977) (described as short-term capital gains and short-term capital losses) shall be segregated from gains and losses arising from the sale or exchange of such assets held for more than 1 year (6 months for taxable years beginning before 1977; 9 months for taxable years beginning in 1977) (described as long-term capital gains and long-term capital losses).

(d)(1) The term "capital gain net income" (net capital gain for taxable years beginning before January 1, 1977) means the excess of the gains from sales or exchanges of capital assets over the losses from sales or exchanges of capital assets, which losses include any amounts carried to the taxable year pursuant to section 1212(a) or section 1212(b).

(2) Notwithstanding subparagraph (1) of this paragraph, in the case of a taxpayer other than a corporation for taxable years beginning before January 1, 1964, the term "net capital gain" means the excess of (i) the sum of the gains from sales or exchanges of capital assets, plus the taxable income (computed without regard to gains and losses from sales or exchanges of capital assets and without regard to the deductions provided by section 151, relating to personal exemptions, or any deductions in lieu thereof) of the taxpayer or $1,000, whichever is smaller, over (ii) the losses from sales or exchanges of capital assets, which losses include amounts carried to the taxable year by such taxpayer under paragraph (a)(1) of § 1.1212-1. Thus, in the case of estates and trusts for taxable years beginning before January 1, 1964, taxable income for the purposes of this paragraph shall be computed without regard to gains and losses from sales or exchanges of capital assets and without regard to the deductions allowed by section 642(b) to estates and trusts in lieu of personal exemptions. The term "net capital gain" is not applicable in the case of a taxpayer other than a corporation for taxable years beginning after December 31, 1963, and before January 1, 1970. In the case of a taxpayer whose tax liability is computed under

section 3 for taxable years beginning before January 1, 1964, the term "taxable income", for purposes of this paragraph, shall be read as "adjusted gross income".

(e) The term "net capital loss" means the excess of the losses from sales or exchanges of capital assets over the sum allowed under section 1211. However, in the case of a corporation, amounts which are short-term capital losses under § 1.1212-1(a) are excluded in determining such "net capital loss".

(f) See section 165(g) and section 166(e), under which losses from worthless stocks, bonds, and other securities (if they constitute capital assets) are required to be treated as losses under subchapter P (section 1201 and following), chapter 1 of the Code, from the sale or exchange of capital assets, even though such securities are not actually sold or exchanged. See also section 1231 and § 1.1231-1 for the determination of whether or not gains and losses from the involuntary conversion of capital assets and from the sale, exchange, or involuntary conversion of certain property used in the trade or business shall be treated as gains and losses from the sale or exchange of capital assets. See also section 1236 and § 1.1236-1 for the determination of whether or not gains from the sale or exchange of securities by a dealer in securities shall be treated as capital gains, or whether losses from such sales or exchanges shall be treated as ordinary losses.

(g) In the case of nonresident alien individuals not engaged in trade or business within the United States, see section 871 and the regulations thereunder for the determination of the net amount of capital gains subject to tax.

(h) The term "net capital gain" ("net section 1201 gain" for taxable years beginning before January 1, 1977) means the excess of the net long-term capital gain for the taxable year over the net short-term capital loss for such year. [Reg. § 1.1222-1.]

☐ [*T.D. 6243, 7-23-57. Amended by T.D. 6828, 6-16-65; T.D. 6867, 12-6-65; T.D. 7301, 1-3-74; T.D. 7337, 12-26-74 and T.D. 7728, 10-31-80.*]

[Reg. § 1.1223-1]

§ 1.1223-1. Determination of period for which capital assets are held.—(a) The holding period of property received in an exchange by a taxpayer includes the period for which the property which he exchanged was held by him, if the property received has the same basis in whole or in part for determining gain or loss in the hands of the taxpayer as the property exchanged. However, this rule shall apply, in the case of exchanges after March 1, 1954, only if the property exchanged was at the time of the exchange a capital asset in the hands of the taxpayer or property used in his trade or business as defined in section 1231(b). For the purposes of this paragraph the term "exchange" includes the following transactions: (1) An involuntary conversion

described in section 1033, and (2) a distribution to which section 355 (or so much of section 356 as relates to section 355) applies. Thus, if property acquired as the result of a compulsory or involuntary conversion of other property of the taxpayer has under section 1033(c) the same basis in whole or in part in the hands of the taxpayer as the property so converted, its acquisition is treated as an exchange and the holding period of the newly acquired property shall include the period during which the converted property was held by the taxpayer. Thus, also, where stock of a controlled corporation is received by a taxpayer pursuant to a distribution to which section 355 (or so much of section 356 as relates to section 355) applies, the distribution is treated as an exchange and the period for which the taxpayer has held the stock of the controlled corporation shall include the period for which he held the stock of the distributing corporation with respect to which such distribution was made.

(b) The holding period of property in the hands of a taxpayer shall include the period during which the property was held by any other person, if such property has the same basis in whole or in part in the hands of the taxpayer for determining gain or loss from a sale or exchange as it would have in the hands of such other person. For example, the period for which property acquired by gift after December 31, 1920, was held by the donor must be included in determining the period for which the property was held by the taxpayer if, under the provisions of section 1015, such property has, for the purpose of determining gain or loss from the sale or exchange, the same basis in the hands of the taxpayer as it would have in the hands of the donor.

(c) In determining the period for which the taxpayer has held stock or securities received upon a distribution where no gain was recognized to the distributee under section 1081(c) (or under section 112(g) of the Revenue Act of 1928 (45 Stat. 818) or the Revenue Act of 1932 (47 Stat. 197)), there shall be included the period for which he held the stock or securities in the distributing corporation before the receipt of the stock or securities on such distribution.

(d) If the acquisition of stock or securities resulted in the nondeductibility (under section 1091, relating to wash sales) of the loss from the sale or other disposition of substantially identical stock or securities, the holding period of the newly acquired securities shall include the period for which the taxpayer held the securities with respect to which the loss was not allowable.

(e) The period for which the taxpayer has held stock, or stock subscription rights, received on a distribution shall be determined as though the stock dividend, or stock right, as the case may be, were the stock in respect of which the dividend was issued if the basis for determining gain or loss upon the sale or other disposition of such stock dividend or stock right is determined under section 307. If the basis of stock received by a taxpayer pursuant to a spin-off is determined under so much of section 1052(c) as refers to section 113(a)(23) of the Internal Revenue Code of 1939, and such stock is sold or otherwise disposed of in a taxable year which is subject to the Internal Revenue Code of 1954, the period for which the taxpayer has held the stock received in such spin-off shall include the period for which he held the stock of the distributing corporation with respect to which such distribution was made.

(f) The period for which the taxpayer has held stock or securities issued to him by a corporation pursuant to the exercise by him of rights to acquire such stock or securities from the corporation will, in every case and whether or not the receipt of taxable gain was recognized in connection with the distribution of the rights, begin with and include the day upon which the rights to acquire such stock or securities were exercised. A taxpayer will be deemed to have exercised rights received from a corporation to acquire stock or securities therein where there is an expression of assent to the terms of such rights made by the taxpayer in the manner requested or authorized by the corporation.

(g) The period for which the taxpayer has held a residence, the acquisition of which resulted under the provisions of section 1034 in the nonrecognition of any part of the gain realized on the sale or exchange of another residence, shall include the period for which such other residence had been held as of the date of such sale or exchange. See §1.1034-1. For purposes of this paragraph, the term "sale or exchange" includes an involuntary conversion occurring after December 31, 1950, and before January 1, 1954.

(h) If a taxpayer accepts delivery of a commodity in satisfaction of a commodity futures contracts, the holding period of the commodity shall include the period for which the taxpayer held the commodity futures contract, if such futures contract was a capital asset in his hands.

(i) If shares of stock in a corporation are sold from lots purchased at different dates or at different prices and the identity of the lots cannot be determined, the rules prescribed by the regulations under section 1012 for determining the cost or other basis of such stocks so sold or transferred shall also apply for the purpose of determining the holding period of such stock.

(j) In the case of a person acquiring property, or to whom property passed, from a decedent (within the meaning of section 1014(b)) dying after December 31, 1970, such person shall be considered to have held the property for more than 6 months if the property—

(1) Has a basis in the hands of such person which is determined in whole or in part under section 1014, and

(2) Is sold or otherwise disposed of by such person within 6 months after the decedent's death.

The provisions of this paragraph apply to sales of such property included in the decedent's gross estate for the purposes of the estate tax by the executor or administrator of the estate and to sales of such property by other persons who have acquired property from the decedent. The provisions of this paragraph may also be applicable to cases involving joint tenancies, community property, and properties transferred in contemplation of death. Thus, if a surviving joint tenant, who acquired property by right of survivorship, sells or otherwise disposes of such property within 1 year (6 months for taxable years beginning before 1977; 9 months for taxable years beginning in 1977) after the date of the decedent's death, and the basis of the property in his hands is determined in whole or in part under section 1014, the property shall be considered to have been held by the surviving joint tenant for more than 1 year (6 months for taxable years beginning before 1977; 9 months for taxable years beginning in 1977). Similarly, a surviving spouse's share of community property shall be considered to have been held by her for more than 1 year (6 months for taxable years beginning before 1977; 9 months for taxable years beginning in 1977) if it is sold or otherwise disposed of within 1 year (6 months for taxable years beginning before 1977; 9 months for taxable years beginning in 1977) after the date of the decedent's death, regardless of when the property was actually acquired by the marital community. For the purposes of this paragraph, it is immaterial that the sale or other disposition produces gain or loss. If property is considered to have been held for more than 1 year (6 months for taxable years beginning before 1977; 9 months for taxable years beginning in 1977) by reason of this paragraph, it also is considered to have been held for that period for purposes of section 1231 (if that section is otherwise applicable).

(k) Any reference in section 1223 or this section to another provision of the Internal Revenue Code of 1954 is, where applicable, to be deemed a reference to the corresponding provision of the Internal Revenue Code of 1939, or prior internal revenue laws. The provisions of prior internal revenue laws here intended are the sections referred to in the sections of the 1939 Code which correspond to the sections of the Internal Revenue Code of 1954 referred to in section 1223. Thus, the sections corresponding to section 1081(c) are section 371(c) of the Revenue Act of 1938 (52 Stat. 553) and section 371(c) of the Internal Revenue Code of 1939. The sections corresponding to section 1091 are section 118 of each of the following: The Revenue Acts of 1928 (45 Stat. 826), 1932 (47 Stat. 208), 1934 (48 Stat. 715), 1936 (49 Stat. 1692), and 1938 (52 Stat. 503), and

Reg. §1.1223-1(k)

the Internal Revenue Code of 1939. [Reg. § 1.1223-1.]

☐ [*T.D.* 6243, 7-23-57. *Amended by T.D.* 7238, 12-28-72 *and T.D.* 7728, 10-31-80.]

[Reg. § 1.1223-3]

§1.1223-3. Rules relating to the holding periods of partnership interests.—(a) *In general.*—A partner shall not have a divided holding period in an interest in a partnership unless—

(1) The partner acquired portions of an interest at different times; or

(2) The partner acquired portions of the partnership interest in exchange for property transferred at the same time but resulting in different holding periods (e.g., section 1223).

(b) *Accounting for holding periods of an interest in a partnership.*—(1) *General rule.*—The portion of a partnership interest to which a holding period relates shall be determined by reference to a fraction, the numerator of which is the fair market value of the portion of the partnership interest received in the transaction to which the holding period relates, and the denominator of which is the fair market value of the entire partnership interest (determined immediately after the transaction).

(2) *Special rule.*—For purposes of applying paragraph (b)(1) of this section to determine the holding period of a partnership interest (or portion thereof) that is sold or exchanged (or with respect to which gain or loss is recognized upon a distribution under section 731), if a partner makes one or more contributions of cash to the partnership and receives one or more distributions of cash from the partnership during the one-year period ending on the date of the sale or exchange (or distribution with respect to which gain or loss is recognized under section 731), the partner may reduce the cash contributions made during the year by cash distributions received on a last-in-first-out basis, treating all cash distributions as if they were received immediately before the sale or exchange (or at the time of the distribution with respect to which gain or loss is recognized under section 731).

(3) *Deemed contributions and distributions.*—For purposes of paragraphs (b)(1) and (2) of this section, deemed contributions of cash under section 752(a) and deemed distributions of cash under section 752(b) shall be disregarded to the same extent that such amounts are disregarded under § 1.704-1(b)(2)(iv)(c).

(4) *Adjustment with respect to contributed section 751 assets.*—For purposes of applying paragraph (b)(1) of this section to determine the holding period of a partnership interest (or portion thereof) that is sold or exchanged, if a partner receives a portion of the partnership interest in exchange for property described in section 751(c) or (d) (section 751 assets) within the one-

year period ending on the date of the sale or exchange of all or a portion of the partner's interest in the partnership, and the partner recognizes ordinary income or loss on account of such a section 751 asset in a fully taxable transaction (either as a result of the sale of all or part of the partner's interest in the partnership or the sale by the partnership of the section 751 asset), the contribution of the section 751 asset during the one-year period shall be disregarded. However, if, in the absence of this paragraph, a partner would not be treated as having held any portion of the interest for more than one year (e.g., because the partner's only contributions to the partnership are contributions of section 751 assets or section 751 assets and cash within the prior one-year period), this adjustment is not available.

(5) *Exception.*—The Commissioner may prescribe by guidance published in the Internal Revenue Bulletin (see § 601.601(d)(2) of this chapter) a rule disregarding certain cash contributions (including contributions of a de minimis amount of cash) in applying paragraph (b)(1) of this section to determine the holding period of a partnership interest (or portion thereof) that is sold or exchanged.

(c) *Sale or exchange of all or a portion of an interest in a partnership.*—(1) *Sale or exchange of entire interest in a partnership.*—If a partner sells or exchanges the partner's entire interest in a partnership, any capital gain or loss recognized shall be divided between long-term and short-term capital gain or loss in the same proportions as the holding period of the interest in the partnership is divided between the portion of the interest held for more than one year and the portion of the interest held for one year or less.

(2) *Sale or exchange of a portion of an interest in a partnership.*—(i) *Certain publicly traded partnerships.*—A selling partner in a publicly traded partnership (as defined under section 7704(b)) may use the actual holding period of the portion of a partnership interest transferred if—

(A) The ownership interest is divided into identifiable units with ascertainable holding periods;

(B) The selling partner can identify the portion of the partnership interest transferred; and

(C) The selling partner elects to use the identification method for all sales or exchanges of interests in the partnership after September 21, 2000. The selling partner makes the election referred to in this paragraph (c)(2)(i)(C) by using the actual holding period of the portion of the partner's interest in the partnership first transferred after September 21, 2000 in reporting the transaction for federal income tax purposes.

(ii) *Other partnerships.*—If a partner has a divided holding period in a partnership interest, and paragraph (c)(2)(i) of this section does not apply, then the holding period of the transferred interest shall be divided between long-term and short-term capital gain or loss in the same proportions as the long-term and short-term capital gain or loss that the transferor partner would realize if the entire interest in the partnership were transferred in a fully taxable transaction immediately before the actual transfer.

(d) *Distributions.*—(1) *In general.*—Except as provided in paragraph (b)(2) of this section, a partner's holding period in a partnership interest is not affected by distributions from the partnership.

(2) *Character of capital gain or loss recognized as a result of a distribution from a partnership.*—If a partner is required to recognize capital gain or loss as a result of a distribution from a partnership, then the capital gain or loss recognized shall be divided between long-term and short-term capital gain or loss in the same proportions as the long-term and short-term capital gain or loss that the distributee partner would realize if such partner's entire interest in the partnership were transferred in a fully taxable transaction immediately before the distribution.

(e) *Section 751(c) assets.*—For purposes of this section, properties and potential gain treated as unrealized receivables under section 751(c) shall be treated as separate assets that are not capital assets as defined in section 1221 or property described in section 1231.

(f) *Examples.*—The provisions of this section are illustrated by the following examples:

Example 1. Division of holding period—contribution of money and a capital asset. (i) A contributes $5,000 of cash and a nondepreciable capital asset A has held for two years to a partnership (*PRS*) for a 50 percent interest in *PRS*. A's basis in the capital asset is $5,000, and the fair market value of the asset is $10,000. After the exchange, A's basis in A's interest in *PRS* is $10,000, and the fair market value of the interest is $15,000. A received one-third of the interest in *PRS* for a cash payment of $5,000 ($5,000/$15,000). Therefore, A's holding period in one-third of the interest received (attributable to the contribution of money to the partnership) begins on the day after the contribution. A received two-thirds of the interest in *PRS* in exchange for the capital asset ($10,000/$15,000). Accordingly, pursuant to section 1223(1), A has a two-year holding period in two-thirds of the interest received in *PRS*.

(ii) Six months later, when A's basis in *PRS* is $12,000 (due to a $2,000 allocation of partnership income to A), A sells the interest in *PRS* for $17,000. Assuming *PRS* holds no inventory or unrealized receivables (as defined under section 751(c)) and no collectibles or section 1250 property, A will realize $5,000 of capital gain. As determined above, one-third of A's interest in

PRS has a holding period of one year or less, and two-thirds of A's interest in *PRS* has a holding period equal to two years and six months. Therefore, one-third of the capital gain will be short-term capital gain, and two-thirds of the capital gain will be long-term capital gain.

Example 2. Division of holding period—contribution of section 751 asset and a capital asset. A contributes inventory with a basis of $2,000 and a fair market value of $6,000 and a capital asset which A has held for more than one year with a basis of $4,000 and a fair market value of $6,000, and B contributes cash of $12,000 to form a partnership (*AB*). As a result of the contribution, one-half of A's interest in *AB* is treated as having been held for more than one year under section 1223(1). Six months later, A transfers one-half of A's interest in *AB* to C for $6,000, realizing a gain of $3,000. If *AB* were to sell all of its section 751 property in a fully taxable transaction immediately before A's transfer of the partnership interest, A would be allocated $4,000 of ordinary income on account of the inventory. Accordingly, A will recognize $2,000 of ordinary income and $1,000 of capital gain ($3,000 − $2,000) on account of the transfer to C. Because A recognizes ordinary income on account of the inventory that was contributed to *AB* within the one year period ending on the date of the sale, the inventory will be disregarded in determining the holding period of A's interest in *AB*. All of the capital gain will be long-term.

Example 3. Netting of cash contributions and distributions. (i) On January 1, 2000, A holds a 50 percent interest in the capital and profits of a partnership (*PS*). The value of A's *PS* interest is $900, and A's holding period in the entire interest is long-term. On January 2, 2000, when the value of A's *PS* interest is still $900, A contributes $100 to *PS*. On June 1, 2000, A receives a distribution of $40 cash from the partnership. On September 1, 2000, when the value of A's interest in *PS* is $1,350, A contributes an additional $230 cash to *PS*, and on October 1, 2000, A receives another $40 cash distribution from *PS*. A sells A's entire partnership interest on November 1, 2000, for $1,600. A's adjusted basis in the *PS* interest at the time of the sale is $1,000.

(ii) For purposes of netting cash contributions and distributions in determining the holding period of A's interest in *PS*, A is treated as having received a distribution of $80 on November 1, 2000. Applying that distribution on a last-in-first-out basis to reduce prior contributions during the year, the contribution made on September 1, 2000, is reduced to $150 ($230 − $80). The holding period then is determined as follows: Immediately after the contribution of $100 on January 2, 2000, A's holding period in A's *PS* interest is 90 percent long-term ($900 ÷ ($900 + $100)) and 10 percent short-term ($100 ÷ ($900 + $100)). The contribution of $150 on September 1, 2000, causes 10 percent of A's partnership interest ($150 ÷ ($1,350 + $150)) to have a short-term

Reg. §1.1223-3(f)

holding period. Accordingly, immediately after the contribution on September 1, 2000, A's holding period in A's PS interest is 81 percent long-term (.90 × .90) and 19 percent short-term ((.10 × .90) + .10). Accordingly, $486 ($600 × .81) of the gain from A's sale of the PS interest is long-term capital gain, and $114 ($600 × .19) is short-term capital gain.

Example 4. Division of holding period when capital account is increased by contribution. A, B, C, and D are equal partners in a partnership (PRS), and the fair market value of a 25 percent interest in PRS is $100. A, B, C, and D each contribute an additional $100 to partnership capital, thereby increasing the fair market value of each partner's interest to $200. As a result of the contribution, each partner has a new holding period in the portion of the partner's interest in PRS that is attributable to the contribution. That portion

equals 50 percent ($100 ÷ $200) of each partners interest in PRS.

Example 5. Sale or exchange of a portion of an interest in a partnership. (i) A, B, and C form an equal partnership (PRS). In connection with the formation, A contributes $5,000 in cash and a capital asset (capital asset 1) with a fair market value of $5,000 and a basis of $2,000; B contributes $7,000 in cash and a capital asset (capital asset 2) with a fair market value of $3,000 and a basis of $3,000; and C contributes $10,000 in cash. At the time of the contribution, A had held the contributed property for two years. Six months later, when A's basis in PRS is $7,000, A transfers one-half of A's interest in PRS to T for $7,000 at a time when PRS's balance sheet (reflecting a cash receipts and disbursements method of accounting) is as follows:

	ASSETS	
	Adjusted Basis	Market Value
Cash	$22,000	$22,000
Unrealized Receivables	0	6,000
Capital Asset 1	2,000	5,000
Capital Asset 2	3,000	9,000
Capital Assets	5,000	14,000
Total	$27,000	$42,000

(ii) Although at the time of the transfer A has not held A's interest in PRS for more than one year, 50 percent of the fair market value of A's interest in PRS was received in exchange for a capital asset with a long-term holding period. Therefore, 50 percent of A's interest in PRS has a long-term holding period.

(iii) If PRS were to sell all of its section 751 property in a fully taxable transaction immediately before A's transfer of the partnership interest, A would be allocated $2,000 of ordinary income. One-half of that amount ($1,000) is attributable to the portion of A's interest in PRS transferred to T. Accordingly, A will recognize $1,000 ordinary income and $2,500 ($3,500 − $1,000) of capital gain on account of the transfer to T of one-half of A's interest in PRS. Fifty percent ($1,250) of that gain is long-term capital gain and 50 percent ($1,250) is short-term capital gain.

Example 6. Sale of units of interests in a partnership. A publicly traded partnership (PRS) has ownership interests that are segregated into identifiable units of interest. A owns 10 limited partnership units in PRS for which A paid $10,000 on January 1, 1999. On August 1, 2000, A purchases five additional units for $10,000. At the time of purchase, the fair market value of each unit has increased to $2,000. A's holding period for one-third ($10,000/$30,000) of the interest in PRS begins on the day after the purchase of the five additional units. Less than one year later, A sells five units of ownership in PRS for $11,000. At the time, A's basis in the 15 units PRS is $20,000, and A's capital gain on the sale of 5 units is $4,333 (amount realized of $11,000 − one-third of the adjusted basis or

$6,667). For purposes of determining the holding period, A can designate the specific units of PRS sold. If A properly identifies the five units sold as five of the ten units for which A has a long-term holding period and elects to use the identification method for all subsequent sales or exchanges of interests in the partnership by using the actual holding period in reporting the transaction on A's federal income tax return, the capital gain realized will be long-term capital gain.

Example 7. Disproportionate distribution. In 1997, A and B each contribute cash of $50,000 to form and become equal partners in a partnership (PRS). More than one year later, A receives a distribution worth $22,000 from PRS, which reduces A's interest in PRS to 36 percent. After the distribution, B owns 64 percent of PRS. The holding periods of A and B in their interests in PRS are not affected by the distribution.

Example 8. Gain or loss as a result of a distribution—(i) On January 1, 1996, A contributes property with a basis of $10 and a fair market value of $10,000 in exchange for an interest in a partnership (ABC). On September 30, 2000, when A's interest in ABC is worth $12,000 (and the basis of A's partnership interest is still $10), A contributes $12,000 cash in exchange for an additional interest in ABC. A is allocated a loss equal to $10,000 by ABC for the taxable year ending December 31, 2000, thereby reducing the basis of A's partnership interest to $2,010. On February 1, 2001, ABC makes a cash distribution to A of $10,000. ABC holds no inventory or unrealized receivables. (Assume that A is allocated no gain or loss for the taxable year ending December 31, 2001, so that the basis of A's partnership interest does not increase or decrease as a result of such allocations.)

(ii) The netting rule contained in paragraph (b)(2) of this section provides that, in determining the holding period of *A*'s interest in *ABC*, the cash contribution made on September 30, 2000, must be reduced by the distribution made on February 1, 2001. Accordingly, for purposes of determining the holding period of *A*'s interest in *ABC*, *A* is treated as having made a cash contribution of $2,000 ($12,000 – $10,000) to *ABC* on September 30, 2000. *A*'s holding period in one-seventh of *A*'s interest in *ABC* ($2,000 cash contributed over the $14,000 value of the entire interest (determined as if only $2,000 were contributed rather than $12,000)) begins on the day after the cash contribution. *A* recognizes $7,990 of capital gain as a result of the distribution. See section 731(a)(1). One-seventh of the capital gain recognized as a result of the distribution is short-term capital gain, and six-sevenths of the capital gain is long-term capital gain. After the distribution, *A*'s basis in the interest in *PRS* is $0, and the holding period for the interest in *PRS* continues to be divided in the same proportions as before the distribution.

(g) *Effective date.*—This section applies to transfers of partnership interests and distributions of property from a partnership that occur on or after September 21, 2000. [Reg. § 1.1223-3.]

☐ [*T.D.* 8902, 9-20-2000.]

Special Rules for Determining Capital Gains and Losses

[Reg. § 1.1231-1]

§ 1.1231-1. **Gains and losses from the sale or exchange of certain property used in the trade or business.**—(a) *In general.*—Section 1231 provides that, subject to the provisions of paragraph (e) of this section, a taxpayer's gains and losses from the disposition (including involuntary conversion) of assets described in that section as "property used in the trade or business" and from the involuntary conversion of capital assets held for more than 1 year (6 months for taxable years beginning before 1977; 9 months for taxable years beginning in 1977) shall be treated as long-term capital gains and losses if the total gains exceed the total losses. If the total gains do not exceed the total losses, all such gains and losses are treated as ordinary gains and losses. Therefore, if the taxpayer has no gains subject to section 1231, a recognized loss from the condemnation (or from a sale or exchange under threat of condemnation) of even a capital asset held for more than 1 year (6 months for taxable years beginning before 1977; 9 months for taxable years beginning in 1977) is an ordinary loss. Capital assets subject to section 1231 treatment include only capital assets involuntarily converted. The noncapital assets subject to section 1231 treatment are (1) depreciable business property and business real property held for more than 1 year (6 months for taxable years beginning before 1977; 9 months for taxable years beginning in 1977), other than stock in trade and certain copyrights and artistic property and, in the case of sales and other dispositions occurring after July 25, 1969, other than a letter, memorandum, or property similar to a letter or memorandum; (2) timber, coal, and iron ore which do not otherwise meet the requirements of section 1231 but with respect to which section 631 applies; and (3) certain livestock and unharvested crops. See paragraph (c) of this section.

(b) *Treatment of gains and losses.*—For the purpose of applying section 1231, a taxpayer must aggregate his recognized gains and losses from—

(1) The sale, exchange, or involuntary conversion of property used in the trade or business (as defined in section 1231(b)), and

(2) The involuntary conversion (but not sale or exchange) of capital assets held for more than 1 year (6 months for taxable years beginning before 1977; 9 months for taxable years beginning in 1977).

If the gains to which section 1231 applies exceed the losses to which the section applies, the gains and losses are treated as long-term capital gains and losses and are subject to the provisions of parts I and II (section 1201 and following), subchapter P, chapter 1, of the Code, relating to capital gains and losses. If the gains to which section 1231 applies do not exceed the losses to which the section applies, the gains and losses are treated as ordinary gains and losses. Therefore, in the latter case, a loss from the involuntary conversion of a capital asset held for more than 1 year (6 months for taxable years beginning before 1977; 9 months for taxable years beginning in 1977) is treated as an ordinary loss and is not subject to the limitation on capital losses in section 1211. The phrase "involuntary conversion" is defined in paragraph (e) of this section.

(c) *Transactions to which section applies.*—Section 1231 applies to recognized gains and losses from the following:

(1) The sale, exchange, or involuntary conversion of property held for more than 1 year (6 months for taxable years beginning before 1977; 9 months for taxable years beginning in 1977) and used in the taxpayer's trade or business, which is either real property or is of a character subject to the allowance for depreciation under section 167 (even though fully depreciated), and which is not—

(i) Property of a kind which would properly be includible in the inventory of the taxpayer if on hand at the close of the taxable year, or property held by the taxpayer primarily for sale to customers in the ordinary course of business;

(ii) A copyright, a literary, musical, or artistic composition, or similar property, or (in the case of sales and other dispositions occurring after July 25, 1969) a letter, memorandum, or property similar to a letter or memorandum, held by a taxpayer described in section 1221(3); or

(iii) Livestock held for draft, breeding, dairy, or sporting purposes, except to the extent included under subparagraph (4) of this paragraph, or poultry.

(2) The involuntary conversion of capital assets held for more than 1 year (6 months for taxable years beginning before 1977; 9 months for taxable years beginning in 1977).

(3) The cutting or disposal of timber, or the disposal of coal or iron ore, to the extent considered arising from a sale or exchange by reason of the provisions of section 631 and the regulations thereunder.

(4) The sale, exchange, or involuntary conversion of livestock if the requirements of § 1.1231-2 are met.

(5) The sale, exchange, or involuntary conversion of unharvested crops on land which is (i) used in the taxpayer's trade or business and held for more than 1 year (6 months for taxable years beginning before 1977; 9 months for taxable years beginning in 1977), and (ii) sold or exchanged at the same time and to the same person. See paragraph (f) of this section. For purposes of section 1231, the phrase "property used in the trade or business" means property described in this paragraph (other than property described in subparagraph (2) of this paragraph). Notwithstanding any of the provisions of this paragraph, section 1231(a) does not apply to gains and losses under the circumstances described in paragraph (e)(2) or (3) of this section.

(d) *Extent to which gains and losses are taken into account.*—All gains and losses to which section 1231 applies must be taken into account in determining whether and to what extent the gains exceed the losses. For the purpose of this computation, the provisions of section 1211 limiting the deduction of capital losses do not apply, and no losses are excluded by that section. With that exception, gains are included in the computations under section 1231 only to the extent that they are taken into account in computing gross income, and losses are included only to the extent that they are taken into account in computing taxable income. The following are examples of gains and losses not included in the computations under section 1231:

(1) Losses of a personal nature which are not deductible by reason of section 165(c) or (d), such as losses from the sale of property held for personal use;

(2) Losses which are not deductible under section 267 (relating to losses with respect to transactions between related taxpayers) or section 1091 (relating to losses from wash sales);

(3) Gain on the sale of property (to which section 1231 applies) reported for any taxable year on the installment method under section 453, except to the extent the gain is to be reported under section 453 for the taxable year; and

(4) Gains and losses which are not recognized under section 1002, such as those to which sections 1031 through 1036, relating to common nontaxable exchanges, apply.

(e) *Involuntary conversion.*—(1) *General rule.*—For purposes of section 1231, the terms "compulsory or involuntary conversion" and "involuntary conversion" of property mean the conversion of property into money or other property as a result of complete or partial destruction, theft or seizure, or an exercise of the power of requisition or condemnation, or the threat of imminence thereof. Losses upon the complete or partial destruction, theft, seizure, requisition, or condemnation of property are treated as losses upon an involuntary conversion whether or not there is a conversion of the property into other property or money and whether or not the property is uninsured, partially insured, or totally insured. For example, if a capital asset held for more than 1 year (6 months for taxable years beginning before 1977; 9 months for taxable years beginning in 1977), with an adjusted basis of $400, but not held for the production of income, is stolen, and the loss which is sustained in the taxable year 1956 is not compensated for by insurance or otherwise, section 1231 applies to the $400 loss. For certain exceptions to this subparagraph, see subparagraphs (2) and (3) of this paragraph.

(2) *Certain uninsured losses.*—Notwithstanding the provisions of subparagraph (1) of this paragraph, losses sustained during a taxable year beginning after December 31, 1957, and before January 1, 1970, with respect to both property used in the trade or business and any capital asset held for more than 6 months and held for the production of income, which losses arise from fire, storm, shipwreck, or other casualty, or from theft, and which are not compensated for by insurance in any amount, are not losses to which section 1231(a) applies. Such losses shall not be taken into account in applying the provisions of this section.

(3) *Exclusion of gains and losses from certain involuntary conversions.*—Notwithstanding the provisions of subparagraph (1) of this paragraph, if for any taxable year beginning after December 31, 1969, the recognized losses from the involuntary conversion as a result of fire, storm, shipwreck, or other casualty, or from theft, of any property used in the trade or busi-

ness or of any capital asset held for more than 1 year (6 months for taxable years beginning before 1977; 9 months for taxable years beginning in 1977) exceed the recognized gains from the involuntary conversion of any such property as a result of fire, storm, shipwreck, or other casualty, or from theft, such gains and losses are not gains and losses to which section 1231 applies and shall not be taken into account in applying the provisions of this section. The net loss, in effect, will be treated as an ordinary loss. This subparagraph shall apply whether such property is uninsured, partially insured, or totally insured and, in the case of a capital asset held for more than 1 year (6 months for taxable years beginning before 1977; 9 months for taxable years beginning in 1977), whether the property is property used in the trade or business, property held for the production of income, or a personal asset.

(f) *Unharvested crops.*—Section 1231 does not apply to a sale, exchange or involuntary conversion of an unharvested crop if the taxpayer retains any right or option to reacquire the land the crop is on, directly or indirectly (other than a right customarily incident to a mortgage or other security transaction). The length of time for which the crop, as distinguished from the land, is held is immaterial. A leasehold or estate for years is not "land" for the purpose of section 1231.

(g) *Examples.*—The provisions of this section may be illustrated by the following examples:

Example (1). A, an individual, makes his income tax return on the calendar year basis. A's recognized gains and losses for 1957 of the kind described in section 1231 are as follows:

	Gains	Losses
1. Gain on sale of machinery, used in the business and subject to an allowance for depreciation, held for more than 6 months	$4,000	
2. Gain reported in 1957 (under sec. 453) on installment sale in 1956 of factory premises used in the business (including building and land, each held for more than 6 months)	6,000	
3. Gain reported in 1957 (under sec. 453) on installment sale in 1957 of land held for more than 6 months, used in the business as a storage lot for trucks	2,000	
4. Gain on proceeds from requisition by Government of boat, held for more than 6 months, used in the business and subject to an allowance for depreciation	500	
5. Loss upon the destruction by fire of warehouse, held for more than 6 months and used in the business (excess of adjusted basis of warehouse over compensation by insurance, etc.)		$3,000
6. Loss upon theft of unregistered bearer bonds, held for more than 6 months		5,000
7. Loss in storm of pleasure yacht, purchased in 1950 for $1,800 and having a fair market value of $1,000 at the time of the storm		1,000
8. Total gains	$12,500	
9. Total losses		$9,000
10. Excess of gains over losses	$3,500	

Since the aggregate of the recognized gains ($12,500) exceeds the aggregate of the recognized losses ($9,000), such gains and losses are treated under section 1231 as gains and losses from the sale or exchange of capital assets held for more than six months. For any taxable year ending after December 31, 1957, and before January 1, 1970, the $5,000 loss upon theft of bonds (item 6) would not be taken into account under section 1231. See paragraph (e)(2) of this section.

Example (2). If in example (1), A also had a loss of $4,000 from the sale under threat of condemnation of a capital asset acquired for profit and held for more than six months, then the gains ($12,500) would not exceed the losses ($9,000 plus $4,000 or $13,000). Neither the loss on that sale nor any of the other items set forth in example (1) would then be treated as gains and losses from the sale or exchange of capital assets, but all of such items would be treated as ordinary

gains and losses. Likewise, if A had no other gain or loss, the $4,000 loss would be treated as an ordinary loss.

Example (3). A's yacht, used for pleasure and acquired for that use in 1945 at a cost of $25,000, was requisitioned by the Government in 1957 for $15,000. A sustained no loss deductible under section 165(c) and since no loss with respect to the requisition is recognizable, the loss will not be included in the computations under section 1231.

Example (4). A, an individual, makes his income tax return on a calendar year basis. During 1970 trees on A's residential property which were planted in 1950 after the purchase of such property were destroyed by fire. The loss, which was in the amount of $2,000 after applying section 165(c)(3), was not compensated for by insurance or otherwise. During the same year A also recognized a $1,500 gain from insurance proceeds compensating him for the theft sustained in 1970 of a diamond brooch purchased in 1960 for personal use. A has no other gains or losses for 1970 from the involuntary conversion of property. Since the recognized losses exceed the recognized gains from the involuntary conversion for 1970 as a result of fire, storm, shipwreck, or other casualty, or from theft, of any property used in the trade or business or of any capital asset held for more than 6 months, neither the gain nor loss is included in making the computations under section 1231.

Example (5). The facts are the same as in example (4), except that A also recognized a gain of $1,000 from insurance proceeds compensating him for the total destruction by fire of a truck, held for more than 6 months, used in A's business and subject to an allowance for depreciation. A has no other gains or losses for 1970 from the involuntary conversion of property. Since the recognized losses ($2,000) do not exceed the recognized gains ($2,500) from the involuntary conversion for 1970 as a result of fire, storm, shipwreck, or other casualty, or from theft, of any property used in the trade or business or of any capital asset held for more than 6 months, such gains and losses are included in making the computations under section 1231. Thus, if A has no other gains or losses for 1970 to which section 1231 applies, the gains and losses from these involuntary conversions are treated under section 1231 as gains and losses from the sale or exchange of capital assets held for more than 6 months.

Example (6). The facts are the same as in example (5) except that A also has the following recognized gains and losses for 1970 to which section 1231 applies:

	Gains	Losses
Gain on sale of machinery, used in the business and subject to an allowance for depreciation, held for more than 6 months	$4,000	
Gain reported in 1970 (under sec. 453) on installment sale in 1969 of factory premises used in the business (including building and land, each held for more than 6 months)	6,000	
Gain reported in 1970 (under sec. 453) on installment sale in 1970 of land held for more than 6 months, used in the business as a storage lot for trucks	2,000	
Loss upon the sale in 1970 of warehouse, used in the business and subject to an allowance for depreciation, held for more than 6 months		$5,000
Total gains	12,000	
Total losses		5,000

Since the aggregate of the recognized gains ($14,500) exceeds the aggregate of the recognized losses ($7,000), such gains and losses are treated under section 1231 as gains and losses from the sale or exchange of capital assets held for more than 6 months.

Example (7). B, an individual, makes his income tax return on the calendar year basis. During 1970 furniture used in his business and held for more than 6 months was destroyed by fire. The recognized loss, after compensation by insurance, was $2,000. During the same year B recognized a $1,000 gain upon the sale of a parcel of real estate used in his business and held for more than 6 months, and a $6,000 loss upon the sale of stock held for more than 6 months. B has no other gains or losses for 1970 from the involuntary conversion, or the sale or exchange of, property. The $6,000 loss upon the sale of stock is not a loss to which section 1231 applies since the stock is not property used in the trade or business, as defined in section 1231(b). The $2,000 loss upon the destruction of the furniture is not a loss to which section 1231 applies since the recognized losses ($2,000) exceed the recognized gains ($0) from the involuntary conversion for 1970 as a result of fire, storm, shipwreck, or other casualty, or from theft, of any property used in the trade or business or of any capital asset held for more than 6 months. Accordingly, the $1,000 gain upon the sale of real estate is considered to be gain from the sale or exchange of a capital asset held for more than 6 months since the gains ($1,000) to which section 1231 applies exceed the losses ($0) to which such section applies.

Example (8). The facts are the same as in example (7) except that B also recognized a gain of $4,000 from insurance proceeds compensating him for the total destruction by fire of a freighter, held for more than 6 months, used in B's business and subject to an allowance for depreciation. Since the recognized losses ($2,000) do not exceed the recognized gains ($4,000) from the involuntary conversion for 1970 as a result of fire, storm, shipwreck, or other casualty, or from theft, of any property used in the trade or business or of any capital asset held for more than 6 months, such gains and losses are included in making the computations under section 1231. Since the aggregate of the recognized gains to which section 1231 applies ($5,000) exceeds the aggregate of the recognized losses to which such section applies ($2,000), such gains and losses are treated under section 1231 as gains and losses from the sale or exchange of capital assets held for more than 6 months. The $6,000 loss upon the sale of stock is not taken into account in making such computation since it is not a loss to which section 1231 applies. [Reg. § 1.1231-1.]

☐ [*T.D. 6253, 9-25-57. Amended by T.D. 6394, 7-1-59; T.D. 6841, 7-26-65; T.D. 7141, 9-21-71; T.D. 7369, 7-15-75; T.D. 7728, 10-31-80 and T.D. 7829, 8-31-82.*]

[Reg. § 1.1231-2]

§ 1.1231-2. Livestock held for draft, breeding, dairy, or sporting purposes.—(a)(1) In the case of cattle, horses, or other livestock acquired by the taxpayer after December 31, 1969, section 1231 applies to the sale, exchange, or involuntary conversion of such cattle, horses, or other livestock, regardless of age, held by the taxpayer for draft, breeding, dairy, or sporting purposes, and held by him—

(i) For 24 months or more from the date of acquisition in the case of cattle or horses, or

(ii) For 12 months or more from the date of acquisition in the case of such other livestock.

(2) In the case of livestock (including cattle or horses) acquired by the taxpayer on or before December 31, 1969, section 1231 applies to the sale, exchange, or involuntary conversion of such livestock, regardless of age, held by the taxpayer for draft, breeding, or dairy purposes, and held by him for 12 months or more from the date of acquisition.

(3) For the purposes of section 1231, the term "livestock" is given a broad, rather than a narrow, interpretation and includes cattle, hogs, horses, mules, donkeys, sheep, goats, fur-bearing animals, and other mammals. However, it does not include poultry, chickens, turkeys, pigeons, geese, other birds, fish, frogs, reptiles, etc.

(b)(1) Whether or not livestock is held by the taxpayer for draft, breeding, dairy, or sporting purposes depends upon all of the facts and circumstances in each case. The purpose for which the animal is held is ordinarily shown by the taxpayer's actual use of the animal. However, a draft, breeding, dairy, or sporting purpose may be present if an animal is disposed of within a reasonable time after its intended use for such purpose is prevented or made undesirable by reason of accident, disease, drought, unfitness of the animal for such purpose, or a similar factual circumstance. Under certain circumstances, an animal held for ultimate sale to customers in the ordinary course of the taxpayer's trade or business may be considered as held for draft, breeding, dairy, or sporting purposes. However, an animal is not held by the taxpayer for draft, breeding, dairy, or sporting purposes merely because it is suitable for such purposes or merely because it is held by the taxpayer for sale to other persons for use by them for such purposes. Furthermore, an animal held by the taxpayer for

other purposes is not considered as held for draft, breeding, dairy, or sporting purposes merely because of a negligible use of the animal for such purposes or merely because of the use of the animal for such purposes as an ordinary or necessary incident to the other purposes for which the animal is held. See paragraph (c) of this section for the rules to be used in determining when horses are held for racing purposes and, therefore, are considered as held for sporting purposes.

(2) The application of this paragraph is illustrated by the following examples:

Example (1). An animal intended by the taxpayer for use by him for breeding purposes is discovered to be sterile or unfit for the breeding purposes for which it was held, and is disposed of within a reasonable time thereafter. This animal is considered as held for breeding purposes.

Example (2). The taxpayer retires from the breeding or dairy business and sells his entire herd, including young animals which would have been used by him for breeding or dairy purposes if he had remained in business. These young animals are considered as held for breeding or dairy purposes. The same would be true with respect to young animals which would have been used by the taxpayer for breeding or dairy purposes but which are sold by him in reduction of his breeding or dairy herd, because of, for example, drought.

Example (3). A taxpayer in the business of raising hogs for slaughter customarily breeds sows to obtain a single litter to be raised by him for sale, and sells these brood sows after obtaining the litter. Even though these brood sows are held for ultimate sale to customers in the ordinary course of the taxpayer's trade or business, they are considered as held for breeding purposes.

Example (4). A taxpayer in the business of raising horses for sale to others for use by them as draft horses uses them for draft purposes on his own farm in order to train them. This use is an ordinary or necessary incident to the purpose of selling the animals, and, accordingly, these horses are not considered as held for draft purposes.

Example (5). The taxpayer is in the business of raising registered cattle for sale to others for use by them as breeding cattle. It is the business practice of this particular taxpayer to breed the offspring of his herd which he is holding for sale to others prior to sale in order to establish their fitness for sale as registered breeding cattle. In such case, the taxpayer's breeding of such offspring is an ordinary and necessary incident to his holding them for the purpose of selling them as bred heifers or proven bulls and does not demonstrate that the taxpayer is holding them for breeding purposes. However, those cattle held by the taxpayer as additions or replacements to his own breeding herd to produce calves are considered to be held for breeding purposes, even though they may not actually have produced calves.

Example (6). A taxpayer, engaged in the business of buying cattle and fattening them for slaughter, purchased cows with calf. The calves were born while the cows were held by the taxpayer. These cows are not considered as held for breeding purposes.

(c)(1) For purposes of paragraph (b) of this section, a horse held for racing purposes shall be considered as held for sporting purposes. Whether a horse is held for racing purposes shall be determined in accordance with the following rules:

(i) A horse which has actually been raced at a public race track shall, except in rare and unusual circumstances, be considered as held for racing purposes.

(ii) A horse which has not been raced at a public track shall be considered as held for racing purposes if it has been trained to race and other facts and circumstances in the particular case also indicate that the horse was held for this purpose. For example, assume that the taxpayer maintains a written training record on all horses he keeps in training status, which shows that a particular horse does not meet objective standards (including, but not limited to, such considerations as failure to achieve predetermined standards of performance during training, or the existence of a physical or other defect) established by the taxpayer for determining the fitness and quality of horses to be retained in his racing stable. Under such circumstances, if the taxpayer disposes of the horse within a reasonable time after he determined that it did not meet his objective standards for retention, the horse shall be considered as held for racing purposes.

(iii) A horse which has neither been raced at a public track nor trained for racing shall not, except in rare and unusual circumstances, be considered as held for racing purposes.

(2) This paragraph may be illustrated by the following examples:

Example (1). The taxpayer breeds, raises, and trains horses for the purpose of racing. Every year he culls some horses from his racing stable. In 1971, the taxpayer decided that in order to prevent his racing stable from getting too large to be effectively operated he must cull six horses from it. All six of the horses culled by the taxpayer had been raced at public tracks in 1970. Under subparagraph (1)(i) of this paragraph, all these horses are considered as held for racing purposes.

Example (2). Assume the same facts as in example (1). Assume further that the taxpayer decided to cull four more horses from his racing stable in 1971. All these horses had been trained to race but had not been raced at public tracks. The taxpayer culled these four horses because the training log which the taxpayer maintains on all the horses he trains showed these horses to be

unfit to remain in his racing stable. Horse A was culled because it developed shin splints during training. Horses B and C were culled because of poor temperament. B bolted every time a rider tried to mount it, and C became extremely nervous when it was placed in the starting gate. Horse D was culled because it did not qualify for retention under one of the objective standards the taxpayer had established for determining which horses to retain since it was unable to run a specified distance in a minimum time. These four horses were disposed of within a reasonable time after the taxpayer determined that they were unfit to remain in his stable. Under subparagraph (1)(ii) of this paragraph, all these horses are considered as held for racing purposes. [Reg. § 1.1231-2.]

☐ [*T.D. 6253, 9-25-57. Amended by T.D. 7141, 9-21-71.*]

[Reg. § 1.1232-1]

§ 1.1232-1. Bonds and other evidences of indebtedness; scope of section.—(a) *In general.*— Section 1232 applies to any bond, debenture, note, or certificate or other evidence of indebtedness (referred to in this section and § § 1.1232-2 through 1.1232-4 as an obligation) (1) which is a capital asset in the hands of the taxpayer, and (2) which is issued by any corporation, or by any government or political subdivision thereof. In general, section 1232(a)(1) provides that the retirement of an obligation, other than certain obligations issued before January 1, 1955, is considered to be an exchange and, therefore, is usually subject to capital gain or loss treatment. In general, section 1232(a)(2)(B) provides that in the case of a gain realized on the sale or exchange of certain obligations issued at a discount after December 31, 1954, which are either corporate bonds issued on or before May 27, 1969, or government bonds, the amount of gain equal to such discount or, under certain circumstances, the amount of gain equal to a specified portion of such discount, constitutes ordinary income. In the case of certain corporate obligations issued after May 27, 1969, in general, section 1232(a)(3) provides for the inclusion as interest in gross income of a ratable portion of original issue discount for each taxable year over the life of the obligation, section 1232(a)(3)(E) provides for an increase in basis equal to the original issue discount included in gross income, and section 1232(a)(2)(A) provides that any gain realized on such an obligation held more than 1 year (6 months for taxable years beginning before 1977; 9 months for taxable years beginning in 1977) shall be considered gain from the sale or exchange of a capital asset held more than 1 year (6 months for taxable years beginning before 1977; 9 months for taxable years beginning in 1977). For the requirements for reporting original issue discount on certain obligations issued after May 27, 1969, see section 6049(a) and the regulations thereunder. Section 1232(c) treats as ordinary income a portion of any gain realized upon the disposition of (i) coupon obligations which were acquired after August 16, 1954, and before January 1, 1958, without all coupons maturing more than 12 months after purchase attached, and (ii) coupon obligations which were acquired after December 31, 1957, without all coupons maturing after the date of purchase attached.

(b) *Requirement that obligations be capital assets.*—In order for section 1232 to be applicable, an obligation must be a capital asset in the hands of the taxpayer. See section 1221 and the regulations thereunder. Obligations held by a dealer in securities (except as provided in section 1236) or obligations arising from the sale of inventory or personal services by the holder are not capital assets. However, obligations held by a financial institution, as defined in section 582(c) (relating to treatment of losses and gains on bonds of certain financial institutions) for investment and not primarily for sale to customers in the ordinary course of the financial institution's trade or business, are capital assets. Thus, with respect to obligations held as capital assets by such a financial institution which are corporate obligations to which section 1232(a)(3) applies, there is ratable inclusion of original issue discount as interest in gross income under paragraph (a) of § 1.1232-3A, and gain on a sale or exchange (including retirement) may be subject to ordinary income treatment under section 582(c) and paragraph (a)(1) of § 1.1232-3.

(c) *Face-amount certificates.*—(1) *In general.*—For purposes of section 1232, this section and §§ 1.1232-2 through 1.1232-4, the term "other evidence of indebtedness" includes "face amount certificates" as defined in section 2(a)(15) and (4) of the Investment Company Act of 1940 (15 U.S.C. 80a-2 and 80a-4).

(2) *Amounts received in taxable years beginning prior to January 1, 1964.*—Amounts received in taxable years beginning prior to January 1, 1964 under face-amount certificates which were issued after December 31, 1954, are subject to the limitation on tax under section 72(e)(3). See paragraph (g) of § 1.72-11 (relating to limit on tax attributable to receipt of a lump sum received as an annuity payment). However, section 72(e)(3) does not apply to any such amounts received in taxable years beginning after December 31, 1963.

(3) *Certificates issued after December 31, 1975.*—In the case of a face-amount certificate issued after December 31, 1975 (other than such a certificate issued pursuant to a written commitment which was binding on such date and at all times thereafter), the provisions of section 1232(a)(3) (relating to the ratable inclusion of original issue discount in gross income) shall apply. See § 1.1232-3A(f). For treatment of any increase in basis under section 1232(a)(3)(A) as consideration paid for purposes of computing

the investment in the contract under section 72, see § 1.72-6(c)(4).

(d) *Certain deposits in financial institutions.*—For purposes of section 1232, this section and §§ 1.1232-2 through 1.1232-4, the term "other evidence of indebtedness" includes certificates of deposit, time deposits, bonus plans, and other deposit arrangements with banks, domestic building and loan associations, and similar financial institutions. For application of section 1232 to such deposits, see paragraph (e) of § 1.1232-3A. However, section 1232, this section, and §§ 1.1232-2 through 1.1232-4 shall not apply to such deposits made prior to January 1, 1971. For treatment of renewable certificates of deposit, see paragraph (e)(4) of § 1.1232-3A. [Reg. § 1.1232-1.]

☐ [T.D. 6253, 9-25-57. *Amended by* T.D. 6468, 6-6-60, T.D. 7154, 12-27-71, T.D. 7311, 3-29-74, T.D. 7336, 12-19-74; T.D. 7365, 6-30-75 *and* T.D. 7728, 10-31-80.]

[Reg. § 1.1232-2]

§ 1.1232-2. Retirement.—Section 1232(a)(1) provides that any amount received by the holder upon the retirement of an obligation shall be considered as an amount received in exchange therefor. However, section 1232(a)(1) does not apply in the case of an obligation issued before January 1, 1955, which was not issued with interest coupons or in registered form on March 1, 1954. For treatment of gain on an obligation held by certain financial institutions, see section 582(c) and paragraph (a)(1)(iii) of § 1.1232-3. [Reg. § 1.1232-2.]

☐ [T.D. 6253, 9-25-57. *Amended by* T.D. 7154, 12-27-71.]

[Reg. § 1.1232-3]

§ 1.1232-3. Gain upon sale or exchange of obligations issued at a discount.—(a) *General rule; sale or exchange.*—(1) *Obligations issued by a corporation after May 27, 1969.*—(i) *General rule.*—Under section 1232(a)(2)(A), in the case of gain realized upon the sale or exchange of an obligation issued at a discount by a corporation after May 27, 1969 (other than an obligation subject to the transitional rule of subparagraph (4) of this paragraph), and held by the taxpayer for more than 1 year (6 months for taxable years beginning before 1977; 9 months for taxable years beginning in 1977)—

(a) If at the time of original issue there was no intention to call the obligation before maturity, such gain shall be considered as long-term capital gain, or

(b) If at the time of original issue there was an intention to call the obligation before maturity, such gain shall be considered ordinary income to the extent it does not exceed the excess of—

(1) An amount equal to the entire "original issue discount", over

(2) An amount equal to the entire "original issue discount" multiplied by a fraction the numerator of which is the sum of the number of complete months and any fractional part of a month elapsed since the date of original issue and the denominator of which is the number of complete months and any fractional part of a month from the date of original issue to the stated maturity date.

The balance, if any, of the gain shall be considered as long-term capital gain. The amount described in (2) of this subdivision (*b*) in effect reduces the amount of original issue discount to be treated as ordinary income under this subdivision (*b*) by the amounts previously includible (regardless of whether included) by all holders (computed, however, as to any holder without regard to any purchase allowance under paragraph (a)(2)(ii) of §1.1232-3A and without regard to whether any holder purchased at a premium as defined in paragraph (d)(2) of §1.1232-3).

(ii) *Cross references.*—For definition of the terms "original issue discount" and "intention to call before maturity", see paragraph (b)(1) and (4) respectively of this section. For definition of the term "date of original issue", see paragraph (b)(3) of this section. For computation of the number of complete months and any fractional portion of a month, see paragraph (a)(3) of §1.1232-3A.

(iii) *Effect of section 582(c).*—Gain shall not be considered to be long-term capital gain under subdivision (i) of this subparagraph if section 582(c) (relating to treatment of losses and gains on bonds of certain financial institutions) applies.

(2) *Examples.*—The provisions of subparagraph (1) of this paragraph may be illustrated by the following examples:

Example (1). On January 1, 1970, A, a calendar-year taxpayer, purchases at original issue for cash of $7,600, M Corporation's 10-year, 5 percent bond which has a stated redemption price at maturity of $10,000. On January 1, 1972, A sells the bond to B, for $9,040. A has previously included $480 of the original issue discount in his gross income (see example (1) of paragraph (d) of §1.1232-3A) and increased his basis in the bond by that amount to $8,080 (see paragraph (c) of §1.1232-3A). Thus, if at the time of original issue there was no intention to call the bond before maturity, A's gain of $960 (amount realized, $9,040, less adjusted basis, $8,080) is considered long-term capital gain.

Example (2). (i) Assume the same facts as in example (1), except that at the time of original issue there was an intention to call the bond before maturity. The amount of the entire gain includible by A as ordinary income under sub-

paragraph (1)(ii) of this paragraph is determined as follows:

(1)	Entire original issue discount (stated redemption price at maturity, $10,000, minus issue price, $7,600)	$2,400
(2)	Less: Line (1), $2,400, multiplied by months elapsed since date of original issue, 24, divided by months from such date to stated maturity date, 120	$480
(3)	Maximum amount includible by A as ordinary income	$1,920

Since the amount in line (3) is greater than A's gain, $960, A's entire gain is includible as ordinary income.

(ii) On January 1, 1979, B, a calendar-year taxpayer, sells the bond to C for $10,150. Assume that B has included $120 of original issue discount in his gross income for each taxable year he held the bond (see example (2) of paragraph (d) of §1.1232-3A) and therefore increased his basis by $840 (*i.e.*, $120 each year × 7 years) to $9,880. B's gain is therefore $270 (amount realized, $10,150, less basis, $9,880). The amount of such gain includible by B as ordinary income under subparagraph (1)(ii) of this paragraph is determined as follows:

(1)	Entire original issue discount (as determined in part (i) of this example) .	$2,400
(2)	Less: Line (1), $2,400, multiplied by months elapsed since date of original issue, 108, divided by months from such date to stated maturity date, 120	$2,160
(3)	Maximum amount includible by B as ordinary income	$240

Since the amount in line (3) is less than B's gain, $270, only $240 of B's gain is includible as ordinary income. The remaining portion of B's gain, $30, is considered long-term capital gain.

(3) *Obligations issued by a corporation on or before May 27, 1969, and government obligations.*—Under section 1232(a)(2)(B), if gain is realized on the sale or exchange after December 31, 1957, of an obligation held by the taxpayer more than 6 months, and if the obligation either was issued at a discount after December 31, 1954, and on or before May 27, 1969, by a corporation or was issued at a discount after December 31, 1954, by or on behalf of the United States or a foreign country, or a political subdivision of either, then such gain shall be considered ordinary income to the extent it does not exceed—

(i) An amount equal to the entire "original issue discount," or

(ii) If at the time of original issue there was no intention to call the obligation before maturity, a portion of the "original issue discount" determined in accordance with paragraph (c) of this section,

and the balance, if any, of the gain shall be considered as long-term capital gain. For the definition of the terms "original issue discount" and "intention to call before maturity," see paragraph (b)(1) and (4) respectively of this section. See section 1037(b) and paragraph (b) of §1.1037-1 for special rules which are applicable in applying section 1232(a)(2)(B) and this subparagraph to gain realized on the disposition or redemption of obligations of the United States which were received from the United States in an exchange upon which gain or loss is not recognized because of section 1037(a) (or so much of section 1031(b) or (c) as relates to section 1037(a)).

(4) *Transitional rule.*—Subparagraph (3) of this paragraph (in lieu of subparagraph (1) thereof) shall apply to an obligation issued by a corporation pursuant to a written commitment which was binding on May 27, 1969, and at all times thereafter.

(5) *Obligations issued after December 31, 1954, and sold or exchanged before January 1, 1958.*—Gain realized upon the sale or exchange before January 1, 1958, of an obligation issued at a discount after December 31, 1954, and held by the taxpayer for more than 6 months, shall be considered ordinary income to the extent it equals a specified portion of the "original issue discount," and the balance, if any, of the gain shall be considered as long-term capital gain. The term "original issue discount" is defined in paragraph (b)(1) of this section. The computation of the amount of gain which constitutes ordinary income is illustrated in paragraph (c) of this section.

(6) *Obligations issued before January 1, 1955.*—Whether gain representing original issue discount realized upon the sale or exchange of obligations issued at a discount before January 1, 1955, is capital gain or ordinary income shall be determined without reference to section 1232.

(b) *Definitions.*—(1) *Original issue discount.*—(i) *In general.*—For purposes of section 1232, the term "original issue discount" means the difference between the issue price and the stated redemption price at maturity. The stated redemption price is determined without regard to optional call dates.

(ii) *De minimis rule.*—If the original issue discount is less than one-fourth of 1 percent of the stated redemption price at maturity multiplied by the number of full years from the date of original issue to maturity, then the discount shall be considered to be zero. For example, a 10-year bond with a stated redemption price at maturity of $100 issued at $98 would be regarded as having an original issue discount of zero. Thus, any gain realized by the holder would be a long-term capital gain if the bond was a capital asset in the hands of the holder and held by him for more than 1 year (6 months for taxable years beginning before 1977; 9 months for taxable years beginning in 1977). However, if the bond were issued at $97.50 or less, the original issue discount would not be considered zero.

(iii) *Stated redemption price at maturity.*—(a) *Definition.*—Except as otherwise provided in this subdivision (iii), the term "stated redemption price at maturity" means the amount fixed by the last modification of the purchase agreement, including dividends, interest, and any other amounts, however designated, payable at that time. If any amount based on a fixed rate of simple or compound interest is actually payable or will be treated as constructively received under section 451 and the regulations thereunder either—

(1) At fixed periodic intervals of one year or less during the entire term of an obligation, or

(2) Except as provided in subdivision (e) of this paragraph (b)(1)(iii), at maturity in the case of an obligation with a term of one year or less,

any such amount payable at maturity shall not be included in determining the stated redemption price at maturity. For purposes of subdivision (a)(2) of this paragraph (b)(1)(iii), the term of an obligation shall include any renewal period with respect to which, under the terms of the obligation, the holder may either take action or refrain from taking action which would prevent the actual or constructive receipt of any interest on such obligation until the expiration of any such renewal period. To illustrate this paragraph (b)(1)(iii), assume that a note which promises to pay $1,000 at the end of three years provides for additional amounts labeled as interest to be paid at the rate of $50 at the end of the first year, $50 at the end of the second year, and $120 at the end of the third year. The stated redemption price at maturity will be $1,070 since only $50 of the $120 payable at the end of the third year is based on a fixed rate of simple or compound interest. If, however, the $120 were payable at the end of the second year, so that only $50 in addition to principal would be payable at the end of the third year, then under the rule for serial obligations contained in subparagraph (2)(iv)(c) of this paragraph, the $1,000 note is treated as consisting of two series. The first series is treated as maturing at the end of the second year at a stated redemption price of $70. The second series is treated as maturing at the end of the third year at a stated redemption price of $1,000. For the calculation of issue price and the allocation of original issue discount with respect to each such series, see example (3) of subparagraph (2)(iv)(f) of this paragraph.

(b) *Special rules.*—In the case of face-amount certificates, the redemption price at maturity is the price as modified through changes such as extensions of the purchase agreement and includes any dividends which are payable at maturity. In the case of an obligation issued as part of an investment unit consisting of such

Reg. §1.1232-3(b)(1)(iii)(b)

obligation and an option (which is not excluded by (c) of this subdivision (iii)), security, or other property, the term "stated redemption price at maturity" means the amount payable on maturity in respect of the obligation, and does not include any amount payable in respect of the option, security, or other property under a repurchase agreement or option to buy or sell the option, security, or other property. For application of this subdivision to certain deposits in financial institutions, see paragraph (e) of § 1.1232-3A.

(c) *Excluded option.*—An option is excluded by this subdivision (c) if it is an option to which paragraph (a) of § 1.61-15 applies or if it is an option, referred to in paragraph (a) of § 1.83-7, granted in connection with performance of services to which section 421 does not apply.

(d) *Obligation issued in installments.*—If an obligation is issued by a corporation under terms whereby the holder makes installment payments, then the stated redemption price for each installment payment shall be computed in a manner consistent with the rules contained in subparagraph (2)(iv) of this paragraph for computing the issue price for each series of a serial obligation. For application of this subdivision (d) to certain open account deposit arrangements, see examples (1) and (2) of paragraph (e)(5)(ii) of § 1.1232-3A.

(e) *Application of definition.*—Subdivision (a)(2) of this paragraph (b)(1)(iii) shall not apply—

(1) For taxable years beginning before September 19, 1979, if for the issuer's last taxable year beginning before September 19, 1978, the rules of § 1.163-4 were properly applied by the issuer, or

(2) In the case of an obligation with a term of six months or less held by a nonresident alien individual or foreign corporation, but only for purposes of the application of sections 871 and 881.

(iv) *Carryover of original issue discount.*—If in pursuance of a plan of reorganization an obligation is received in an exchange for another obligation, and if gain or loss is not recognized in whole or in part on such exchange of obligations by reason, for example, of section 354 or 356, then the obligation received shall be considered to have the same original issue discount as the obligation surrendered reduced by the amount of gain (if any) recognized as ordinary income upon such exchange of obligations, and by the amount of original issue discount with respect to the obligation surrendered which was included as interest income under the ratable inclusion rules of section 1232(a)(3) and § 1.1232-3A. If inclusion as interest of the ratable monthly portion of original issue discount is required under section 1232(a)(3) with respect to

the obligation received, see paragraph (a)(2)(iii) of § 1.1232-3A for computation of the ratable monthly portion of original issue discount. For special rules in connection with certain exchanges of U.S. obligations, see section 1037.

(2) *Issue price defined.*—(i) *In general.*—The term "issue price" in the case of obligations registered with the Securities and Exchange Commission means the initial offering price to the public at which price a substantial amount of such obligations were sold. For this purpose, the term "the public" does not include bond houses and brokers, or similar persons or organizations acting in the capacity of underwriters or wholesalers. Ordinarily, the issue price will be the first price at which the obligations were sold to the public, and the issue price will not change if, due to market developments, part of the issue must be sold at a different price. When obligations are privately placed, the issue price of each obligation is the price paid by the first buyer of the particular obligation, irrespective of the issue price of the remainder of the issue. In the case of an obligation issued by a foreign obligor, the issue price shall be increased by the amount, if any, of interest equalization tax paid under section 4911 (and not credited, refunded, or reimbursed) on the acquisition of the obligation by the first buyer. In the case of an obligation which is convertible into stock or another obligation, the issue price includes any amount paid in respect of the conversion privilege. However, in the case of an obligation issued as part of an investment unit (as defined in subdivision (ii) (a) of this subparagraph), the issue price of the obligation includes only that portion of the initial offering price or price paid by the first buyer properly allocable to the obligation under the rules prescribed in subdivision (ii) of this subparagraph. The terms "initial offering price" and "price paid by the first buyer" include the aggregate payments made by the purchaser under the purchase agreement, including modifications thereof. Thus, all amounts paid by the purchaser under the purchase agreement or a modification of it are included in the issue price (but in the case of an obligation issued as part of an investment unit, only to the extent allocable to such obligation under subdivision (ii) of this subparagraph), such as amounts paid upon face-amount certificates or installment trust certificates in which the purchaser contracts to make a series of payments which will be returnable to the holder with an increment at a later date.

(ii) *Investment units consisting of obligations and property.*—(a) *In general.*—An investment unit, within the meaning of this subdivision (ii) and for purposes of section 1232, consists of an obligation and an option, security, or other property. For purposes of this subparagraph, the initial offering price of an investment unit shall be allocated to the individual elements of the unit on the basis of their respective fair market values. However, if the fair market value of the option, security, or other property is not readily ascertainable (within the meaning of paragraph (c) of §1.421-6), then the portion of the initial offering price or price paid by the first buyer of the unit which is allocable to the obligation issued as part of such unit shall be ascertained as of the time of acquisition of such unit by reference to the assumed price at which such obligation would have been issued had it been issued apart from such unit. The assumed price of the obligation shall be ascertained by comparison to the yields at which obligations of a similar character which are not issued as part of an investment unit are sold in arm's length transactions, and by adjusting the price of the obligation in question to this yield. This adjustment may be made by subtracting from the face amount of the obligation the total present value of the interest foregone by the purchaser as a result of purchasing the obligation at a lower yield as part of an investment unit. In most cases, assumed price may also be determined in a similar manner through the use of standard bond tables. Any reasonable method may be used in selecting the obligation for comparative purposes. Obligations of the same grade and classification shall be used to the extent possible, and proper regard shall be given, with respect to both the obligation in question and the comparative obligation, to the solvency of the issuer, the nature of the issuer's trade or business, the presence and nature of security for the obligation, the geographic area in which the loan is made, and all other factors relevant to the circumstances. An obligation which is convertible into stock or another obligation must not be used as a comparative obligation (except where the investment unit contains an obligation convertible into stock or another obligation), since such an obligation would not reflect the yield attributable solely to the obligation element of the investment unit.

(b) Agreement as to assumed price.—In the case of an investment unit which is privately placed, the assumed price at which the obligation would have been issued had it been issued apart from such unit may be agreed to by the issuer and the original purchaser of the investment unit in writing on or before the date of purchase. Alternatively, an agreement between the issuer and original purchaser may specify the rate of interest which would have been paid on the obligation if the transaction were one not involving the issuance of options, and an assumed issue price may be determined (in the manner described in (a) of this subdivision) from such agreed assumed rate of interest. An assumed price based upon such an agreement between the parties will generally be presumed to be the issue price of the obligation with respect to the issuer, original purchaser and all subsequent holders: *Provided,* That the agreement was made in arm's-length negotiations between parties having adverse interests: *And provided further,* That such price does not, under the rules stated in (a) of this subdivision, appear to be clearly erroneous. An assumed issue price agreed to by the parties as provided herein will not be considered clearly erroneous if it is not less than the face value adjusted (in the manner described in (a) of this subdivision) to a yield which is one percentage point greater than the actual rate of interest payable on the obligation. Similarly, if the agreement between the parties specifies an agreed assumed rate of interest (in lieu of an agreed assumed issue price) and such agreed rate is not more than 1 percentage point greater than the actual rate payable on the obligation, an adjusted issue price based upon such agreed assumed rate of interest will not be considered clearly erroneous.

(c) Cross references.—For rules relating to the deductibility by the issuing corporation of bond discount resulting from an allocation under the rule stated in (a) of this subdivision, see §§1.163-3 and 1.163-4. For rules relating to the basis of obligations and options, securities, or other property acquired in investment units, see §1.1012-1(d). For rules relating to certain reporting requirements with respect to options acquired in connection with evidences of indebtedness and for the tax treatment of such options, see §1.61-15, and section 1234 and the regulations thereunder. With respect to the tax consequences to the issuing corporation upon the exercise of options issued in connection with evidences of indebtedness to which this section applies, see section 1032 and the regulations thereunder.

(d) Examples.—The application of the principles set forth in this subdivision (ii) may be illustrated by the following examples in each of which it is assumed that there was no intention to call the note before maturity:

Example (1). M Corporation is a small manufacturer of electronic components located in the southwestern United States. On January 1, 1969, in consideration for the payment of $41,500, M issues to X its unsecured note for $40,000 together with warrants to purchase 3,000 shares of M stock at $10 per share at any time during the term of the note. The note is payable in 4 years and provides for interest at the rate of 5 percent per year, payable semiannually. The fair market values of the note and the warrants are not readily ascertainable. Assume that companies in the same industry as M Corporation, and similarly situated both financially and geographically, are generally able to borrow money on their unsecured notes at an annual interest rate of 6 percent. Using a present value table, the calculation of the issue price of a 5 percent, 4 year, $40,000 note, discounted to yield 6 percent compounded semiannually is made as follows:

Reg. §1.1232-3(b)(2)(ii)(d)

Semiannual interest period	(2) Amount payable at 5%	(3) Factor for present value discounted at 3% per period	(2) × (3) Present value of payment
1	$1,000	0.9709	$970.90
2	1,000	.9426	942.60
3	1,000	.9151	915.10
4	1,000	.8885	888.50
5	1,000	.8626	862.60
6	1,000	.8375	837.50
7	1,000	.8131	813.10
8	1,000	.7894	789.40
8	40,000	.7894	31,576.00

Total present value of note discounted
at 6%, compounded semiannually $38,595.70

The same result may be reached through the use of a standard bond table or by the following present value calculation:

Present value of annuity of $1,000 payable over 8 periods at 3 percent per period = 1000 ×
7.0197 = ... $7,019.70
Add: Present value of principal (as calculated above) 31,576.00

Total $38,595.70

Accordingly, the assumed price at which M's note would have been issued had it been issued without stock purchase warrants, *i.e.*, that portion of the $41,500 price paid by X which is allocable to M's note, is $38,596 (rounded). Since the price payable on redemption of M's note at maturity is $40,000, the original issue discount on M's note is $1,404 ($40,000 minus $38,596). Under the rules stated in § 1.163-3, M is entitled to a deduction, to be prorated or amortized over the life of the note, equal to this original issue discount on the note. The excess of the price for the unit over the portion of such price allocable to the note, $2,904 ($41,500 minus $38,596), is allocable to and is the basis of the stock purchase warrants acquired by X in connection with M's note. Upon the exercise of X's warrants, M will be allowed no deduction and will have no income. Upon maturity of the note X will receive $40,000 from M, of which $1,404, the amount of the original issue discount, will be taxable as ordinary income. If X were to transfer the note at its face amount to A 2 years after the issue date,

X would realize, under section 1232(a)(2)(B), ordinary income of $702 (one-half of $1,404).

Example (2). (1) On January 1, 1969, N Corporation negotiates with Y, a small business investment company, for a loan in the amount of $51,500 in consideration of which N Corporation issues to Y its unsecured 5-year note for $50,000, together with warrants to purchase 2,000 shares of N stock at $5 per share at any time during the term of the note. The note provides for interest of 6 percent, payable semiannually. The fair market values of the note and warrants are not readily ascertainable. The loan agreement between Y and N contains a provision, agreed to in arms-length bargaining between the parties, that a rate of 7 percent payable semiannually would have been applied to the loan if warrants were not issued as part of the consideration for the loan. The issue price of the note is $47,921 (rounded), determined with the use of a standard bond table, or computed in the manner illustrated in Example (1) or in the following alternative manner:

(1) Interest period	(2) Interest rate differential	(3) Principal	(4) Interest foregone for period (½%)	(5) Factor for present value discounted at 3½% per period	(4) × (5) Present value of interest foregone
1	1% (7% − 6%)	$50,000	250	0.9662	$241.55
2	1%	50,000	250	.9335	233.38
3	1%	50,000	250	.9019	225.48
4	1%	50,000	250	.8714	217.85
5	1%	50,000	250	.8420	210.50
6	1%	50,000	250	.8135	203.38
7	1%	50,000	250	.7860	196.50
8	1%	50,000	250	.7594	189.85
9	1%	50,000	250	.7337	183.43
10	1%	50,000	250	.7089	177.23

Total present value of interest foregone $2,079.15

Principal $50,000.00
Less: Total present value of interest foregone 2,079.00

Issue price $47,921.00

The calculation of present value of interest foregone may also be made as follows:

Present value of annuity of $250 discounted for 10 periods at $3\frac{1}{2}$ percent per period = $250 × 8.3166 = $2,079.15.

The total present value of interest foregone, $2,079, is also the original issue discount attributable to the note ($50,000 − $47,921). Under (b) of this subdivision, since the agreed assumed rate of interest of 7 percent is not more than 1 percentage point greater than the actual rate payable on the note, determination of the issue price of the note (and original issue discount) based upon such assumed rate will be presumed to be correct and will not be considered clearly erroneous, provided that both N and Y adhere to such determination. Under the rules in § 1.163-3, N is entitled to a deduction, to be prorated or amortized over the life of the note, equal to the original issue discount on the note. The excess of the price paid for the unit over the portion of such price allocable to the note, $3,579 ($51,500 minus $47,921) is allocable to and is the basis of the stock purchase warrants acquired by Y in connection with N's note. Upon the exercise or sale of the warrants by Y, N will be allowed no deduction and will have no income. Upon maturity of the note Y will receive $50,000 from N, of which $2,079, the amount of the original issue discount, will be taxable as ordinary income. If Y were to transfer the note at its face value to B $2\frac{1}{2}$ years after the issue date, Y would realize, under section 1232(a)(2)(B), ordinary income of $1,039.50 (one-half of $2,079).

(2) Assume that instead of the parties agreeing on as assumed interest rate at which the obligation would have been issued without the warrants, the parties agreed that the obligation at the actual 6 percent rate would have been issued without the warrants at a discounted price of $48,000. In this situation the agreed assumed issue price is presumed to be correct since it is not less than the face value adjusted (in the manner illustrated in part (1) of this example) to a yield which is one percentage point greater than the actual rate of interest payable on the obligation ($47,921).

Example (3). O Corporation is a small advertising company located in the northeastern United States. Z is a tax-exempt organization. In consideration for the payment of $60,000, O issues to Z, in a transaction not within the scope of section 503(c), its unsecured 5-year note for $60,000, together with warrants to purchase 6,000 shares of O stock at $10 per share at any time during the term of the note. The note is subject to quarterly amortization at the rate of $3,000 per quarter, and provides for interest on the outstanding unpaid balance at an annual rate of 6 percent payable quarterly ($1\frac{1}{2}$ percent per quarter). The fair market values of the notes and warrants are not readily ascertainable. The loan agreement between O and Z contains a recital that if the $60,000 note had been issued without the warrants only $45,000 would have been paid for it. An examination of relevant facts indicates that companies in the same industry as O Corporation, and similarly situated both financially and geographically, are able to borrow money on their unsecured notes at an annual interest cost of $8\frac{1}{2}$ percent payable quarterly ($2\frac{1}{8}$ percent per quarter). By reference to a present value table, it is found that the present value of O's note discounted to yield $8\frac{1}{2}$ percent compounded quarterly is $56,608 (rounded). The computation is as follows:

(1) Quarterly interest period	(2) Principal payable	(3) Interest payable ($1\frac{1}{2}$%)	(4) Total amount payable (2) + (3)	(5) Factor for present value discounted at $2\frac{1}{8}$% per quarter	(6) Present value of total payment (4) × (5)
1	$3,000	$900	$3,900	0.9792	$3,818.88
2	3,000	855	3,855	.9588	3,696.17
3	3,000	810	3,810	.9389	3,577.21
4	3,000	765	3,765	.9193	3,461.16
5	3,000	720	3,720	.9002	3,348.74
6	3,000	675	3,675	.8815	3,239.51
7	3,000	630	3,630	.8631	3,133.05
8	3,000	585	3,585	.8452	3,030.04
9	3,000	540	3,540	.8276	2,929.70
10	3,000	495	3,495	.8104	2,832.35
11	3,000	450	3,450	.7935	2,737.58
12	3,000	405	3,405	.7770	2,645.69
13	3,000	360	3,360	.7608	2,556.29
14	3,000	315	3,315	.7450	2,469.68
15	3,000	270	3,270	.7295	2,385.47
16	3,000	225	3,225	.7143	2,303.62
17	3,000	180	3,180	.6994	2,224.09
18	3,000	135	3,135	.6849	2,147.16
19	3,000	90	3,090	.6706	2,072.15
20	3,000	45	3,045	.6567	1,999.65
					$56,608.19

Reg. §1.1232-3(b)(2)(ii)(d)

This amount ($56,609) is the assumed price at which the note would have been issued had it been issued without stock purchase warrants. The assumed price of $45,000 agreed to by the parties is not presumed to be correct since it is less than the face value adjusted to a yield which is one percentage point greater than the actual rate of interest payable on the obligation. The parties did not have adverse interests in agreeing upon an assumed price (since an excessively large amount of original issue discount would benefit O, the borrower, without adversely affecting Z, an exempt organization which would pay no tax on original issue discount income), and the price agreed to appears to be clearly erroneous when compared to the $56,608 assumed issue price determined under the principles of (a) of this subdivision. Since the maturity value of O's note is $60,000, the original issue discount on O's note is $3,392 ($60,000 minus $56,608). Under the rules in § 1.163-3, O is entitled to a deduction, to be prorated or amortized over the life of the note, equal to this original issue discount on the note. The excess of the price paid for the unit over the portion of such price allocable to the note, $3,392 ($60,000 minus $56,608), is allocable to and is the basis of the stock purchase warrants acquired by Z in connection with O's note. Upon the exercise or sale of the warrants by Z, O will be allowed no deduction and will have no income.

(iii) *Issuance for property after May 27, 1969.—(a) In general.—*Except as provided in (b) of this subdivision, if an obligation or an investment unit is issued for property other than money, the issue price of such obligation shall be the stated redemption price at maturity and, therefore, no original issue discount is created as a result of the exchange. However, in such case, there may be an amount treated as interest under section 483. In the case of certain exchanges of obligations of the United States for other such obligations, see section 1037 for the determination of the amount of original issue discount on the obligation acquired in the exchange. For carryover of original issue discount in the case of certain exchanges of obligations, see subparagraph (1)(iv) of this paragraph.

(b) *Exceptions for original issue discount.*—If an obligation or investment unit is issued for property in an exchange which is not pursuant to a plan of reorganization referred to in (d) of this subdivision, and if—

(1) The obligation, investment unit, or an element of the investment unit is part of an issue a portion of which is traded on an established securities market, or

(2) The property for which such obligation or investment unit is issued is stock or securities which are traded on an established securities market,

then the issue price of the obligation or investment unit shall be the fair market value of the property for which such obligation or investment unit is issued, as determined under (c) of this subdivision. Such issue price shall control for purposes of determining the amount realized by the person exchanging the property for the obligation or unit issued and the basis of the property acquired by the holder and the issuer. An obligation which is not traded on an established securities market and which is not part of an issue or investment unit a portion of which is so traded shall not be treated as property described in (1) of this subdivision (b) even though the obligation is convertible into property so traded. For purposes of this subdivision (b), an obligation, investment unit, or element of an investment unit shall be treated as traded on an established securities market if it is so traded on or within ten "trading" days after the date it is issued. "Trading" days shall mean those days on which an established securities market is open. For purposes of this subdivision (iii), the term "established securities market" shall have the same meaning as in paragraph (d)(4) of § 1.453-3 (relating to limitations on installment method for purchaser evidences of indebtedness payable on demand or readily tradable).

(c) *Determination of fair market value in cases to which (b) of this subdivision applies.*—In general, for purposes of (b) of this subdivision, the fair market value of property for which an obligation or investment unit is issued shall be deemed to be the same as the fair market value of such obligation or investment unit, determined by reference to the fair market value of that portion of the issue, of which such obligation or unit is a part, which is traded on an established securities market. The fair market value of such obligation or unit shall be determined as of the first date after the date of issue (within the meaning of section 1232(b)(3)) that such obligation or unit is traded on an established securities market. If, however, the obligation or investment unit is not part of an issue a portion of which is traded on an established securities market, but the property for which the obligation or investment unit is issued is stock or securities which are traded on an established securities market, the fair market value of such property shall be the fair market value of such stock or securities on the date such obligation or unit is issued for such property. The fair market value of property for purposes of this subdivision (c) shall be determined as provided in § 20.2031-2 of this chapter (Estate Tax Regulations) but without applying the blockage and other special rules contained in paragraph (e) thereof.

(d) *Not in reorganization.*—An exchange which is not pursuant to a reorganization referred to in this subdivision (d) is an exchange in which the obligation or investment unit is not issued pursuant to a plan of reorganization within the meaning of section 368(a)(1) or pursuant to an insolvency reorganization within the meaning of section 371, 373, or 374. Thus, for example, no original issue discount is created on an obligation issued in a recapitalization within the meaning of section 368(a)(1)(E). Similarly, no original issue discount is created on an obligation issued in an exchange, pursuant to a plan of reorganization, to which section 361 applies regardless of the income tax consequences to any person who pursuant to such plan is the ultimate recipient of the obligation. The application of section 351 shall not preclude the creation of original issue discount. For carryover of original issue discount in the case of an exchange of obligations pursuant to a plan of reorganization, see subparagraph (1)(iv) of this paragraph.

(e) *Effective date.*—Determinations with respect to obligations issued on or before May 27, 1969, or pursuant to a written commitment which was binding on that date and at all times thereafter, shall be made without regard to this subdivision (iii).

(iv) *Serial obligations.*—(a) *In general.*—If an issue of obligations which matures serially is issued by a corporation, and if on the basis of the facts and circumstances in such case an independent issue price for each particular maturity can be established, then the obligations with each particular maturity shall be considered a separate series, and the obligations of each such series shall be treated as a separate issue with a separate issue price, maturity date, and stated redemption price at maturity. The ratable monthly portion of original issue discount attributable to each obligation within a particular series shall be determined and ratably included as interest in gross income under the rules of § 1.1232-3A.

(b) *Issue price not independently established.*—If a separate issue price cannot be established with respect to each series of an issue of obligations which matures serially, the issue price for each obligation of each series shall be its stated redemption price at maturity minus the amount of original issue discount allocated thereto in accordance with (d) of this subdivision. The amount of original issue discount so allocated shall be ratably included as interest in gross income under rules of § 1.1232-3A.

(c) *Single obligation rule.*—If a single corporate obligation provides for payments (other than payments which would not be included in the stated redemption price at maturity under subparagraph (1)(iii) of this paragraph) in two or more installments, the provisions of (b) of this subdivision shall be applied by treating such obligation as an issue of obligations consisting of more than one series each of which matures on the due date of each such installment payment.

(d) *Allocation of discount.*—For purposes of (b) and (c) of this subdivision, the original issue discount with respect to each series of an issue shall be the total original issue discount for the issue multiplied by a fraction—

(1) The numerator of which is the product of (i) the stated redemption price of such series and (ii) the number of complete years (and any fraction thereof) constituting the period for such series from the date of original issue (as defined in paragraph (b)(3) of this section) to its stated maturity date, and

(2) The denominator of which is the sum of the products determined in (1) of this subdivision (d) with respect to each such series.

If a series consists of more than one obligation, the original issue discount allocated to such series shall be apportioned to such obligations in proportion to the stated redemption price of each. Computations under this subdivision (d) may be made using periods other than years, such as, for example, months or periods of 3 months.

(e) *Effective date.*—The provisions of this subdivision (iv) shall apply with respect to corporate obligations issued after [insert date on which notice of proposed rule making is published in Federal Register]. However, no inference shall be drawn from the preceding sentence with respect to serial obligations issued prior to such date.

(f) *Examples.*—The provisions of this subdivision (iv) may be illustrated by the following examples:

Example (1). On January 1, 1972, P Corporation issued a note with a total face value of $100,000 to B for cash of $94,000. The terms of the note provide that $50,000 is payable on December 31, 1973, and the other $50,000 on December 31, 1975. Each payment is treated as the stated redemption price of a series, and the total original issue discount with respect to the note, $6,000, is allocated to each such series as follows:

Year of maturity	1973	1975	Total
(1) Stated redemption price	$50,000	$50,000	
(2) Multiply by years outstanding	2	4	
(3) Product of bond years	$100,000	$200,000	
(4) Sum of products			$300,000
(5) Fractional portion of discount	$100,000	$200,000	
	$300,000	$300,000	

(6) Multiply line (5) by discount for entire issue	6,000	6,000
(7) Discount for each series	$2,000	$4,000
(8) Issue price (line (1), minus line (7)) . . .	$48,000	$46,000

Example (2). Assume the same facts as in example (1) except that a separate note is issued for each payment. The result is the same as in example (1).

Example (3). On January 1, 1971, Y Bank, a corporation, issues a note to C for $1,000 cash. The terms of the note provide that $50 will be paid at the end of the first year, $120 at the end of the second year, and $1,050 at the end of the third year. Under (c) of this subdivision (iv), the $1,000 note is treated as consisting of two series, the first of which matures at the end of the second year, and the second of which matures at the end of the third year. The issue price and the allocation of original issue discount with respect to each series is computed as follows:

Year of maturity	1973	1975	Total
(1) Stated redemption price	$70	$1,000	
(2) Multiply by years outstanding	2	3	
(3) Product of bond years	$140	$3,000	
(4) Sum of products			$3,140
(5) Fractional portion of discount	140	3,000	
	$3,140	$3,140	
(6) Multiply line (5) by discount for entire issue	70	70	
(7) Discount for each series	$ 3.12	$66.88	
(8) Issue price (line (1) minus line (7)) . . .	$66.88	$933.12	

(3) *Date of original issue.*—In the case of issues of obligations which are registered with the Securities and Exchange Commission, the term "date of original issue" means the date on which the issue was first sold to the public at the issue price. In the case of issues which are privately placed, the term "date of original issue" means the date on which each obligation was sold to the original purchaser.

(4) *Intention to call before maturity.*—(i) *Meaning of term.*—For purposes of section 1232, the term "intention to call the bond or other evidence of indebtedness before maturity" means an understanding between (a) the issuing corporation (such corporation is hereinafter referred to as the "issuer"), and (b) the original purchaser of such obligation (or, in the case of obligations constituting part of an issue, any of the original purchasers of such obligations) that the issuer will redeem the obligation before maturity. For purposes of this subparagraph, the term "original purchaser" does not include persons or organizations acting in the capacity of underwriters or dealers, who purchased the obligation for resale in the ordinary course of their trade or business. It is not necessary that the issuer's intention to call the obligation before maturity be communicated directly to the original purchaser by the issuer. The understanding to call before maturity need not be unconditional; it may, for example, be dependent upon the financial condition of the issuer on the proposed early call date.

(ii) *Proof of intent.*—(a) *In general.*—Ordinarily the existence or non-existence of an understanding at the time of original issue that the obligation will be redeemed before maturity shall be determined by an examination of all of the circumstances under which the obligation was issued and held. The fact that the obligation is issued with provisions on its face giving the issuer the privilege of redeeming the obligation before maturity is not determinative of an intention to call before maturity; likewise, the absence of such provision is not determinative of the absence of an intention to call before maturity. However, such provision, or the absence of such provision, is one of the circumstances to be given consideration along with other factors in determining whether an understanding existed. If the obligation was part of an issue registered with the Securities and Exchange Commission and was sold to the public (whether or not sold directly to the public by the obligor) without representation to the public that the obligor intends to call the obligation before maturity, there shall be a presumption that no intention to call the obligation before maturity was in existence at the time of original issue. The existence of a provision on the face of an obligation giving the issuer the privilege of redeeming the obligation before maturity shall not in and of itself overcome the presumption set forth in the preceding sentence.

(b) *Circumstances indicating absence of understanding.*—Examples of circumstances which would be evidence that there was no understanding at the time of original issue to redeem the obligation before maturity are—

(1) The issue price and term of the obligation appear to be reasonable, taking into account the interest rate, if any, on the obligation, for a corporation in the financial condition of the issuer at the time of issue.

(2) The original purchaser and the issuer are not related within the meaning of section 267(b) and have not engaged in transactions with each other (other than concerning the obligation).

Reg. §1.1232-3(b)(3)

(3) The original purchaser is not related within the meaning of section 267(b) to any of the officers or directors of the issuer, and he has not engaged in transactions with such officers or directors (other than concerning the obligation).

(4) The officers and directors of the issuer at the time of issue of the obligation are different from those in control at the time the obligation is called or the taxpayer disposes of it.

(c) *Gain treated as ordinary income in certain cases; computation.*—The amount of gain treated as ordinary income under paragraph (a)(3)(ii) or (5) of this section is computed by multiplying the original issue discount by a fraction, the numerator of which is the number of full months the obligation was held by the holder and the denominator of which is the number of full months from the date of original issue to the date specified as the redemption date at maturity. (See paragraph (b)(3) of this section for definition of "date of original issue".) The period that the obligation was held by the taxpayer shall include any period that it was held by another person if, under chapter 1 of the Code, for the purpose of determining gain or loss from a sale or exchange, the obligation has the same basis, in whole or in part, in the hands of the taxpayer as it would have in the hands of such other person. This computation is illustrated by the following examples:

Example (1). An individual purchases a 10-year, 3 percent coupon bond for $900 on original issue on February 1, 1955, and sells it on February 20, 1960 for $940. The redemption price is $1,000. At the time of original issue, there was no intention to call the bond before maturity. The bond has been held by the taxpayer for 60 full months. (The additional days amounting to less than a full month are not taken into account.) The number of complete months from date of issue to date of maturity is 120 (10 years). The fraction 60/120 multiplied by the discount of $100 is equal to $50, which represents the proportionate part of the original issue discount attributable to the period of ownership by the taxpayer. Accordingly, any part of the gain up to $50 will be treated as ordinary income. Therefore, in this case the entire gain of $40 is treated as ordinary income.

Example (2). Assume the same facts in the preceding example, except that the selling price of the bond is $970. In this case $50 of the gain of $70 is treated as ordinary income and the balance of $20 is treated as long-term capital gain.

Example (3). Assume the same facts as in example (1), except that the selling price of the bond is $800. In this case, the individual has a long-term capital loss of $100.

Example (4). Assume the same facts as in example (1), except that the bond is purchased by the second holder February 1, 1960, for $800. The second holder keeps it to the maturity date (February 1, 1965) when it is redeemed for $1,000. Since that holder has held the bond for 60 full months, he will, upon redemption, have $50 in ordinary income and $150 in long-term capital gain.

(d) *Exceptions to the general rule.*—(1) *In general.*—Section 1232(a)(2)(C) provides that section 1232(a)(2) does not apply (i) to obligations the interest on which is excluded from gross income under section 103 (relating to certain government obligations), or (ii) to any holder who purchases an obligation at a premium.

(2) *Premium.*—For purposes of section 1232, this section, and § 1.1232-3A, "premium" means a purchase price which exceeds the stated redemption price of an obligation at its maturity. For purposes of the preceding sentence, if an obligation is acquired as part of an investment unit consisting of an option, security, or other property and an obligation, the purchase price of the obligation is that portion of the price paid or payable for the unit which is allocable to the obligation. The price paid for the unit shall be allocated to the individual elements of the unit on the basis of their respective fair market values. However, if the fair market value of the option, security, or other property is not readily ascertainable (within the meaning of paragraph (c) of § 1.421-6), then the price paid for the unit shall be allocated in accordance with the rules under paragraph (b)(2)(ii) of this section for allocating the initial offering price of an investment unit to its elements. If, under chapter 1 of the Code, the basis of an obligation in the hands of the holder is the same, in whole or in part, for the purposes of determining gain or loss from a sale or exchange, as the basis of the obligation in the hands of another person who purchased the obligation at a premium, then the holder shall be considered to have purchased the obligation at a premium. Thus, the donee of an obligation purchased at a premium by the donor will be considered a holder who purchased the obligation at a premium.

(e) *Amounts previously includible in income.*—Nothing in section 1232(a)(2) shall require the inclusion of any amount previously includible in gross income. Thus, if an amount was previously includible in a taxpayer's income on account of obligations issued at a discount and redeemable for fixed amounts increasing at stated intervals, or, under section 818(b) (relating to accrual of discount on bonds and other evidences of indebtedness held by life insurance companies), such amount is not again includible in the taxpayer's gross income under section 1232(a)(2). For example, amounts includible in gross income by a cash receipts and disbursements method taxpayer who has made an election under section 454(a) or (c) (relating to accounting rules for certain obligations issued at a discount to which section 1232(a)(3) does not apply) are not includible in gross income under section 1232(a)(2). In the case of a gain which would include, under section 1232(a)(2), an amount considered to be ordinary income and a further amount considered long-term capital gain, any amount to which this paragraph applies is first used to offset the amount considered ordinary income. For example, on January 1, 1955, A purchases a ten-year bond which is redeemable for fixed amounts increasing at stated intervals. At the time of original issue, there was no intention to call the bond before maturity. The purchase price of the bond is $75, which is also the issue price. The stated redemption price at maturity of the bond is $100. A elects to treat the annual increase in the redemption price of the bond as income pursuant to section 454(a). On January 1, 1960, A sells the bond for $90. The total stated increase in the redemption price of the bond which A has reported annually as income for the taxable year 1955 through 1959 is $7. The portion of the original issue discount of $25 attributable to this period is $12.50, computed as follows:

$$\frac{60 \text{ (months bond is held by A)}}{120 \text{ (months from date of original issue to redemption date)}} \times \$25 \text{ (original issue discount)}$$

However, $7, which represents the annual stated increase taken into income, is credited against the amount of $12.50, leaving $5.50 of the gain from the sale to be treated as ordinary income.

(f) *Record keeping requirements.*—In the case of any obligation held by a taxpayer which was issued at an original issue discount after December 31, 1954, the taxpayer shall keep a record of the issue price and issue date upon or with each such obligation (if known to or reasonably ascertainable by him). If the obligation held by the taxpayer is an obligation of the United States received from the United States in an exchange upon which gain or loss is not recognized because of section 1037(a) (or so much of section 1031(b) or (c) as relates to section 1037(a)), the taxpayer shall keep sufficient records to determine the issue price of such obligation for purposes of applying section 1037(b) and paragraphs (a) and (b) of § 1.1037-1 upon the disposition or redemption of such obligation. The issuer (or in the case of obligations first sold to the public through an underwriter or wholesaler, the underwriter or wholesaler) shall mark the issue price and issue date upon every obligation which is issued at an original issue discount after September 26, 1957, but only if the period between the date of original issue (as defined in paragraph (b)(3) of this section) and the stated maturity date is more than 6 months. [Reg. § 1.1232-3.]

☐ [*T.D. 6253, 9-25-57. Amended by T.D. 6468, 6-6-60, T.D. 6935, 11-16-67, T.D. 6984, 12-23-68, T.D. 7154, 12-27-71, T.D. 7213, 10-7-72, T.D. 7663, 12-21-79 and T.D. 7728, 10-31-80.*]

[Reg. § 1.1232-3A]

§ 1.1232-3A. Inclusion as interest of original issue discount on certain obligations issued after May 27, 1969.—(a) *Ratable inclusion as interest.*—(1) *General rule.*—Under section 1232(a)(3), the holder of any obligation issued by a corporation after May 27, 1969 (other than an obligation issued by or on behalf of the United States or a foreign country, or a political subdivision of either) shall include as interest in his gross income an amount equal to the ratable monthly portion of original issue discount multiplied by the sum of the number of complete months and any fractional part of a month such holder held the obligation during the taxable year. For increase in basis for amounts included as interest in gross income pursuant to this paragraph, see paragraph (c) of this section. For requirements for reporting original issue discount, see section 6049(a) and the regulations thereunder.

(2) *Ratable monthly portion of original issue discount.*—(i) *General rule.*—Except when subdivision (ii) of this subparagraph applies, the term "ratable monthly portion of original issue discount" means an amount equal to the original issue discount divided by the sum of the number of complete months (plus any fractional part of a month) beginning on the date of original issue and ending the day before the stated maturity date of such obligation.

(ii) *Reduction for purchase allowance.*—With respect to an obligation which has been acquired by purchase (within the meaning of subparagraph (4) of this paragraph), the term "ratable monthly portion of original issue discount" means the lesser of the amount determined under subdivision (i) of this subparagraph or an amount equal to—

(a) the excess (if any) of the stated redemption price of the obligation at maturity over its cost to the purchaser divided by

(b) The sum of the number of complete months (plus any fractional part of a month) beginning on the date of such purchase and ending the day before the stated maturity date of such obligation.

The amount of the ratable monthly portion within the meaning of this subdivision reflects a purchase allowance provided under section 1232(a)(3)(B) where a purchase is made at a price in excess of the sum of the issue price plus the portion of original issue discount previously includible (regardless of whether included) in the gross income of all previous holders (computed, however, as to such previous holders without regard to any purchase allowance under this

Rules for Determining Capital Gains and Losses
See p. 20,601 for regulations not amended to reflect law changes
53,457

subdivision and without regard to whether any previous holder purchased at a premium).

(iii) *Ratable monthly portion upon carryover to new obligation.*—In any case in which there is a carryover of original issue discount under paragraph (b)(1)(iv) of § 1.1232-3 from an obligation exchanged to an obligation received in such exchange, the ratable monthly portion of original issue discount in respect of the obligation received shall be computed by dividing the amount of original issue discount carried over by the sum of the number of complete months (plus any fractional part of a month) beginning on the date of the exchange and ending the day before the stated maturity date of the obligation received.

(iv) *Cross references.*—For definitions of the terms "original issue discount" and "date of original issue", see subparagraphs (1) and (3), respectively, of § 1.1232-3(b). For definition of the term "premium," see paragraph (d)(2) of § 1.1232-3.

(3) *Determination of number of complete months.*—(i) *In general.*—For purposes of this section—

(a) A complete month and a fractional part of a month commence with the date of original issue and the corresponding day of each succeeding calendar month (or the last day of a calendar month in which there is no corresponding day),

(b) If an obligation is acquired on any day other than the date a complete month commences, the ratable monthly portion of original issue discount for the complete month in which the acquisition occurs shall be allocated between the transferor and the transferee in accordance with the number of days in such complete month each held the obligation,

(c) In determining the allocation under (b) of this subdivision, any holder may treat each month as having 30 days,

(d) The transferee, and not the transferor, shall be deemed to hold the obligation during the entire day on the date of acquisition, and

(e) The obligor will be treated as the transferee on the date of redemption.

(ii) *Example.*—The provisions of this subparagraph may be illustrated by the following example:

Example. On February 22, 1970, A acquires an obligation of X Corporation for which February 1, 1970, is the date of original issue. B acquires the obligation on June 16, 1970. A does not choose to treat each month as having 30 days. Thus, A held the obligation for 3³/₄ months during 1970, *i.e.*, ¹/₄ of February (⁷/₂₈ days), March, April, May, ¹/₂ of June (15/30 days). The ratable monthly portion of original issue discount for the obligation is multiplied by 3³/₄

months to determine the amount included in A's gross income for 1970 pursuant to this paragraph.

(4) *Purchase.*—For purposes of this section, the term "purchase" means any acquisition (including an acquisition upon original issue) of an obligation to which this section applies, but only if the basis of such obligation is not determined in whole or in part by reference to the adjusted basis of such obligation in the hands of the person from whom it was acquired or under section 1014(a) (relating to property acquired from a decedent).

(b) *Exceptions.*—(1) *Binding commitment.*—Section 1232(a)(3) shall not apply to any obligation issued pursuant to a written commitment which was binding on May 27, 1969, and at all times thereafter.

(2) *Exception for one-year obligations.*—Section 1232(a)(3) shall not apply to any obligation in respect of which the period between the date of original issue (as defined in paragraph (b)(3) of § 1.1232-3) and the stated maturity date is one year or less. In such case, gain on the sale or exchange of such obligation shall be included in gross income as interest to the extent the gain does not exceed an amount equal to the ratable monthly portion of original issue discount multiplied by the sum of the number of complete months and any fractional part of a month such taxpayer held such obligation.

(3) *Purchase at a premium.*—Section 1232(a)(3) shall not apply to any holder who purchased the obligation at a premium (within the meaning of paragraph (d)(2) of § 1.1232-3).

(4) *Life insurance companies.*—Section 1232(a)(3) shall not apply to any holder which is a life insurance company to which section 818(b) applies. However, ratable inclusion of original issue discount as interest under section 1232(a)(3) is required by an insurance company which is subject to the tax imposed by section 821 or 831.

(c) *Basis adjustment.*—The basis of an obligation in the hands of the holder thereof shall be increased by any amount of original issue discount with respect thereto included as interest in his gross income pursuant to paragraph (a) of this section. See section 1232(a)(3)(E). However, the basis of an obligation shall not be increased by any amount that was includible as interest in gross income under paragraph (a) of this section, but was not actually included by the holder in his gross income.

(d) *Examples.*—The provisions of paragraphs (a) through (c) of this section may be illustrated by the following examples:

Example (1). On January 1, 1970, A, a calendar-year taxpayer, purchases at original issue, for cash of $7,600, M Corporation's 10-year, 5-percent bond which has a stated redemption price of $10,000. The ratable monthly portion of original issue discount, as determined under section 1232(a)(3) and this section, to be included as interest in A's gross income for each month he holds such bond is $20, computed as follows:

Original issue discount (stated redemption price, $10,000, minus issue price, $7,600)	$2,400	
Divide by: Number of months from date of original issue to stated maturity date	120	months
Ratable monthly portion	$20	

Assume that A holds the bond for all of 1970 and 1971 and includes as interest in his gross income for each such year an amount equal to the ratable monthly portion, $20, multiplied by the number of months he held the bond each such year, 12 months, or $240. Accordingly, on January 1, 1972, A's basis in the bond will have increased under paragraph (c) of this section by the amount so included, $480 (*i.e.*, $240 × 2), from his cost, $7,600, to $8,080. For results if A sells the bond on that date, see examples (1) and (2) paragraph (a)(2) of § 1.1232-3.

Example (2). Assume the same facts as in example (1). Assume further that on January 1, 1972, A sells the bond to B, a calendar-year taxpayer for $9,040.

Since B purchased the bond, he determines under paragraph (a)(2)(ii) of this section the amount of the ratable monthly portion he must include as interest in his gross income in order to reflect the amount of his purchase allowance (if any). B determines that his ratable monthly portion is $10, computed as follows:

(1) Stated redemption price at maturity	$10,000	
(2) Minus: B's cost	9,040	
(3) Excess	$960	
(4) Divide by: Number of months from date of purchase to stated maturity date	96	months
(5) Tentative ratable monthly portion	$10	
(6) Ratable monthly portion as computed in example (1)	20	

Since line (5) is lower than line (6), B's ratable monthly portion is $10. Accordingly, if B holds the bond for all of 1972, he must include $120 (*i.e.*, ratable monthly portion, $10, × 12 months) as interest in his gross income.

Example (3). (1) Assume the same facts as in example (1). Assume further that on January 1, 1975, A sells the bond to B for $10,150. Under the exception of paragraph (b)(3) of this section, B is not required to include any amount in respect of original issue discount as interest in his gross income since he has purchased the bond at a premium.

(2) On January 1, 1979, B sells the bond to C, a calendar-year taxpayer, for $9,940. Since C is now the holder of the bond (and no exception applies to him), he must include as interest in his gross income the ratable monthly portion of original issue determined under section 1232(a)(3) and this section. Since C purchased the bond he determines under paragraph (a)(2)(ii) of this section the amount of the ratable monthly portion he must include as interest in his gross income in order to reflect the amount of his purchase allowance (if any). C determines that his ratable monthly portion is $5, computed as follows:

(1) Stated redemption price at maturity	$10,000	
(2) Minus: C's cost	9,940	
(3) Excess	$ 60	
(4) Divide by: Number of months from date of purchase to stated maturity date	12	months
(5) Tentative ratable monthly portion	$ 5	
(6) Ratable monthly portion as computed in example (1)	20	

Since line (5) is lower than line (6), C's ratable monthly portion is $5. Accordingly, if C holds the bond for all of 1979, he must include $60 (*i.e.*, ratable monthly portion, $5, × 12 months) as interest in his gross income. Upon maturity of the bond on January 1, 1980, C will receive $10,000 from M, which under paragraph (c) of this section will equal his adjusted basis (the sum of his cost, $9,940, plus original issue discount included as interest in his gross income, $60).

Example (4). On January 1, 1968, D, a calendar year taxpayer, purchases at original issue, for cash of $8,000, P Corporation's 20-year, 6 percent bond which has a stated redemption price of $10,000 and which will mature on January 1, 1988. The original issue discount with respect to such bond is $2,000. However, the ratable inclusion rules of section 1232(a)(3) do not apply to D, since the bond was issued by P before May 28, 1969. On January 1, 1973, pursuant to a plan of reorganization as defined in section 368(a)(1)(E), and in which no gain or loss is recognized by D under section 354, D's 20-year bond is exchanged for a 10-year, 6 percent bond which also has a stated redemption price of $10,000 but will mature on January 1, 1983. Under paragraph (b)(1)(iv) of § 1.1232-3, the $2,000 of original issue discount is carried over to the new 10-year bond received in such exchange. Since the new bond is an obligation issued after May 27, 1969, D is required to begin ratable inclusion of the $2,000 of discount as interest in his gross income for 1973. The ratable monthly portion of original issue discount, as determined under section 1232(a)(3) to be included as interest in gross income is computed as follows:

Reg. § 1.1232-3A(d)

Amount of original issue discount
carried over $2,000
Divide by: Number of complete
months beginning on January
1,1973, and ending on December
31, 1982   120   months
Ratable monthly portion . . . . . . $ 16.67

(e) *Application of section 1232 to certain deposits in financial institutions and similar arrangements.*— (1) *In general.*—Under paragraph (d) of §1.1232-1, the term "other evidence of indebtedness" includes certificates of deposit, time deposits, bonus plans, and other deposit arrangements with banks, domestic building and loan associations, and similar financial institutions.

(2) *Adjustments where obligation redeemed before maturity.*—(i) *In general.*—If an obligation described in subparagraph (1) of this paragraph is redeemed for a price less than the stated redemption price at maturity from a taxpayer who acquired the obligation upon original issue, such taxpayer shall be allowed as a deduction, in computing adjusted gross income, the amount of the original issue discount he included in gross income but did not receive (as determined under subdivision (ii) of this subparagraph). The taxpayer's basis of such obligation (determined after any increase in basis for the taxable year under section 1232(a)(3)(E) by the amount of original issue discount included in the holder's gross income under section 1232(a)(3)) shall be decreased by the amount of such adjustment.

(ii) *Computation.*—The amount of the adjustment under subdivision (i) of this subparagraph shall be an amount equal to the excess (if any) of (a) the ratable monthly portion of the original issue discount included in the holder's gross income under section 1232(a)(3) for the period he held the obligation, over (b) the excess (if any) of the amount received upon the redemption over the issue price. Under paragraph (b)(1)(iii)(a) of §1.1232-3, if any amount based on a fixed rate of simple or compound interest is actually payable or will be treated as constructively received under section 451 and the regulations thereunder at fixed periodic intervals of one year or less during the term of the obligation, any such amount payable upon redemption shall not be included in determining the amount received upon such redemption.

(iii) *Partial redemption.*—(a) In the case of an obligation (other than a single obligation having serial maturity dates), if a portion of the obligation is redeemed prior to the stated maturity date of the entire obligation, the provisions of this subdivision shall be applied and not the provisions of subdivision (ii) of this subparagraph. In such case, the adjusted basis of the unredeemed portion of the obligation on the date of the partial redemption shall be an amount equal to the adjusted basis of the entire obligation on that date minus the amount paid upon the redemption.

(b) If the adjusted basis of the unredeemed portion (as computed under (a) of this subdivision) is equal to or in excess of the amount to be received for the unredeemed portion at maturity, no gain or loss shall be recognized at the time of the partial redemption but the holder shall be allowed a deduction, in computing adjusted gross income for the taxable year during which such partial redemption occurs, equal to the amount of such excess (if any), and no further original issue discount will be includible in the holder's gross income under section 1232(a)(3) over the remaining term of the unredeemed portion. In such case, the holder shall decrease his basis in the unredeemed portion (as computed under (a) of this subdivision) by the amount of such adjustment.

(c) If the adjusted basis of the unredeemed portion (as computed under (a) of this subdivision) is less than the redemption price of the unredeemed portion at maturity, a new computation shall be made under paragraph (a) of this section (without regard to the exception for one-year obligations in paragraph (b)(2) of this section) of the ratable monthly portion of original issue discount to be included as interest in the gross income of the holder over the remaining term of the unredeemed portion. For purposes of such computation, the adjusted basis of the unredeemed portion shall be treated as the issue price, the date of the partial redemption shall be treated as the issue date, and the amount to be paid for the unredeemed portion at maturity shall be treated as the stated redemption price.

(3) *Examples.*—The application of section 1232 to obligations to which this paragraph applies may be illustrated by the following examples:

Example (1). A is a cash method taxpayer who uses the calendar year as his taxable year. On January 1, 1971, he purchases a certificate of deposit from X bank, a corporation, for $10,000. The certificate of deposit is not redeemable until December 31, 1975, except in an emergency as defined in, and subject to the qualifications provided by, Regulation Q of the Board of Governors of the Federal Reserve. See 12 C.F.R. §217.4(d). The stated redemption price at maturity is $13,382.26. The terms of the certificate do not expressly refer to any amount as interest. A's certificate of deposit is an obligation to which section 1232 and this paragraph apply. A shall include the ratable portion of original issue discount in gross income for 1971 as determined under section 1232(a)(3). Thus, if A holds the certificate of deposit for the full calendar year 1971, the amount to be included in A's gross income for 1971 is $676.45, that is, 12/60 months, multiplied by the excess of the stated redemption price ($13,382.26) over the issue price ($10,000).

Example (2). Assume the same facts as in example (1), except that the certificate of deposit provides for payment upon redemption at December 31, 1975, of an amount equal to "$10,000, plus 6 percent compound interest from January 1, 1971, to December 31, 1975." Thus, the total amount payable upon redemption in both example (1) and this example is $13,382.26. The certificate of deposit is an obligation to which section 1232 and this paragraph apply and, since the substance of the deposit arrangement is identical to that contained in example (1), A must include the same amount in gross income.

Example (3). Assume the same facts as in example (1), except that the certificate provides for the payment of interest in the amount of $200 on December 31 of each year and $2,000 plus $10,000 (the original amount) payable upon redemption at December 31, 1975. Thus, if A holds the certificate of deposit for the full calendar year 1971, A must include in his gross income for 1971 the $200 interest payable on December 31, 1971, and $400 of original issue discount, that is 12/60 months multiplied by the excess of the stated redemption price ($12,000) over the issue price ($10,000).

Example (4). B is a cash method taxpayer who uses the calendar year as his taxable year. On January 1, 1971, B purchases a 4-year savings certificate from the Y Building and Loan Corporation for $4,000, redeemable on December 31, 1974, for $5,000. On December 31, 1973, Y redeems the certificate for $4,660. Under section 1232(a)(3), B included $250 of original issue discount in his gross income for 1971, $250 for 1972, and includes $250 in his gross income for 1973 for a total of $750. Since the excess of (i) the amount received upon the redemption, $4,660, over (ii) the issue price, $4,000, or $660, is lower than the total amount of original issue discount ($750) included in B's gross income for the period he held the certificate by $90, the $90 will be treated under subparagraph (2) of this paragraph as a deduction in computing adjusted gross income, and accordingly, will decrease the basis of his certificate by such amount. B has no gain or loss upon the redemption, as determined in accordance with the following computation:

Adjusted basis 1/1/73	$4,500
Increase under section1232(a)(3)(E)	250
Subtotal	$4,750
Decrease under subparagraph (b)(2) of this paragraph	90
Basis upon redemption	$4,660
Amount realized upon redemption	4,660
Gain or loss	$0

Example (5). On January 1, 1971, C, a cash method taxpayer who uses the calendar year as his taxable year, opens a savings account in Z bank with a $10,000 deposit. Under the terms of

the account, interest is made available semi-annually at 6 percent annual interest, compounded semi-annually. Since all of the interest on C's account in Z Bank is made available semi-annually, the stated redemption price at maturity under paragraph (b)(1)(iii)(a) of §1.1232-3 equals the issue price, and, therefore, no original issue discount is reportable by C under section 1232(a)(3). However, C must include the sum of $300 (*i.e.*, 1/2 × 6% × $10,000) plus $309 (*i.e.*, 1/2 × 6% × $10,300), or $609, of interest made available during 1971 in his gross income for 1971.

Example (6). (i) D is a cash method taxpayer who uses the calendar year as his taxable year. On January 1, 1971, D purchases a $10,000 deferred income certificate from M Bank. Under the terms of the certificate, interest accrues at 6 percent per annum, compounded quarterly. The period of the account is 10 years. In addition, the holder is permitted to withdraw the entire amount of the purchase price at any time (but not interest prior to the expiration of the 10 year term), and upon such a withdrawal of the purchase price, no further interest accrues. If the certificate is held to maturity, the issue price plus accrued interest will aggregate $18,140.18.

(ii) In respect of the certificate, the original issue discount is $8,140.18, determined by subtracting the issue price of the certificate ($10,000) from the stated redemption price at maturity ($18,140.18). Thus, under section 1232(a)(3) the ratable monthly portion of original issue discount is $67,835 (*i.e.*, 1/120 months, multiplied by $8,140.18). Under section 1232(a)(3), D includes $814.02 (*i.e.*, 12 months, multiplied by $67,835) in his gross income for each calendar year the certificate remains outstanding and under section 1232(a)(3)(E) increases his basis by that amount. Thus, on December 31, 1975, D's basis for the certificate is $14,070.10 (*i.e.*, issue price, $10,000, increased by product of $814.02 × 5 years).

(iii) On December 31, 1975, D withdraws the $10,000. Under the terms of the certificate $3,468.55 cannot be withdrawn until December 31, 1980. Under the provisions of subparagraph (2)(iii) of this paragraph, the $10,000 partial redemption shall be treated as follows:

(1) Adjusted basis of obligation at time of partialredemption	$14,070.10
(2) Amount paid upon redemption	$10,000.00
(3) Adjusted basis of unredeemed portion (line (1) less line (2))	$4,070.10
(4) Amount to be paid for unredeemed portion at maturity(December 31, 1980) . .	$3,468.55
(5) Adjustment in computing adjusted gross income (excess ofline (3) over line (4)) . . .	$601.55

Since the adjusted basis of the unredeemed portion exceeds the amount to be received for the unredeemed portion at maturity, D is allowed a deduction, in computing adjusted gross income, of $601.25 in 1975 and no further original issue discount is includible as interest in his gross income. In addition, D will decrease his basis in the unredeemed portion by $601.25, the amount of such adjustment, from $4,070.10 to $3,468.55.

Example (7). E is a cash method taxpayer who uses the calendar year as his taxable year. On January 1, 1971, E purchases a $10,000 "Bonus Savings Certificate" from N Building and Loan Corporation. Under the terms of the certificate, interest is payable at 5 percent per annum, compounded quarterly, and the period of the account is 3 years. In addition, the certificate provides that if the holder makes no withdrawals of principal or interest during the term of the certificate, a bonus payment equal to 5 percent of the purchase price of the certificate will be paid to the holder of the certificate at maturity. Thus, the amount of the bonus payment is $500 (*i.e.*, 5 percent multiplied by $10,000). Since the 5 percent annual interest is payable quarterly, the amount of such interest is not included in determining the stated redemption price at maturity under paragraph (b)(1)(iii) of §1.1232-3. However, since the bonus payment is only payable at maturity, the amount of such bonus is included as part of the stated redemption price at maturity. Thus, the stated redemption price at maturity equals $10,500 (purchase price, $10,000, plus bonus payment, $500). Accordingly, the original issue discount attributable to such certificate equals $500 (stated redemption price at maturity $10,500, minus issue price, $10,000). Therefore, E must include as interest $166.67 (*i.e.*, 12/36 months multiplied by the original issue discount, $500) in his gross income for each taxable year he holds the certificate.

(4) *Renewable certificates of deposit.*—(i) *In general.*—The renewal of a certificate of deposit shall be treated as a purchase of the certificate on the date the renewal period begins regardless of any requirement pursuant to the terms of the certificate that the holder give notice of an intention to renew or not to renew. Thus, for example, in the case of a certificate of deposit for which a renewal period begins after December 31, 1970, such renewal shall be treated as a purchase after such date whether or not the initial period began before such date.

(ii) *Computation.*—For purposes of computing the amount of original issue discount to be ratably included as interest in gross income under section 1232(a)(3) in respect of a renewable certificate of deposit for the initial period or any renewal period, the following rules apply:

(a) The issue price on the date any renewal period begins is considered to be in the case of a certificate of deposit initially purchased—

(1) After December 31, 1970, the adjusted basis of the certificate on the date such period begins,

(2) Before January 1, 1971, the amount the adjusted basis would have been on the date such period begins had the holder included all amounts of original issue discount as

interest in gross income that would have been includible if section 1232(a)(3) had applied to the certificate from the date of original purchase.

Thus, if under the terms of the certificate, no amount is forfeited upon a failure to renew, then the issue price on the date any renewal period begins is considered to be the amount which would have been received by the holder on such date had it not been renewed.

(b) The date of original issue for any renewal period shall be considered to be the date it begins.

(c) The date of maturity for the initial period or any renewal period shall be considered to be the date it ends.

(d) The stated redemption price at maturity for the initial period or any renewal period shall be considered to be the maximum amount which would be received at the end of any such period, without regard to any reduction resulting from withdrawal prior to maturity or failure to renew at any renewal date.

(iii) *Application of one-year rule.*—For purposes of paragraph (b)(2) of this section (relating to nonapplication of section 1232(a)(3) to any obligation having a term of one year or less), the period between the date of original issue (as defined in paragraph (b)(3) of §1.1232-3) of a renewable certificate of deposit and its stated maturity date shall include all renewal periods with respect to which, under the terms of the certificate, the holder may either take action or refrain from taking action which would prevent the actual or constructive receipt of any interest on such certificate until the expiration of any such renewal period whether or not the original date of issue is prior to January 1, 1971.

(iv) *Example.*—The provisions of this subparagraph may be illustrated by the following example:

Example. (a) On May 1, 1969, A purchases a 2-year renewable certificate of deposit from M bank, a corporation, for $10,000. Interest will be compounded semiannually at 6 percent on May 1 and November 1. The terms of the certificate provide that such certificate will be automatically renewed on the anniversary date every 2 years if the holder does not notify M of an intention not to renew prior to 60 days before the particular anniversary date. Thus, on May 1, 1971, and May 1, 1973, the certificate may be redeemed for $11,255.09 and $12,667.60, respectively. However, in no event shall the initial period and the renewal periods exceed 10 years. A does not notify M of an intention not to renew by March 1, 1971, and the certificate is automatically renewed for an additional 2-year period on May 1, 1971.

(b) Under subdivision (i) of this subparagraph, the May 1, 1971, renewal shall be treated as the purchase of a certificate of deposit on that date, *i.e.*, after December 31, 1970. Under subdivision (ii) of this subparagraph, the issue price is considered to be $11,255.09 and the date of maturity is considered to be May 1, 1973. Since the stated redemption price at maturity is $12,667.60, A must include $58.85 as interest in gross income for each month he holds the certificate during the renewal period beginning May 1, 1971, computed as follows:

Original issue discount (stated redemption price, $12,667.60, minus issue price, $11,255.09)	$1,412.51
Divide by: Number of months from renewal to maturity date	24 months
Ratable monthly portion	$58.85

(5) *Time deposit open account arrangements.*— (i) *In general.*—The term "time deposit open account arrangement" means an arrangement with a fixed maturity date where deposits may be made from time to time and ordinarily no interest will be paid or constructively received until such fixed maturity date. All deposits pursuant to such an arrangement constitute parts of a single obligation. The amount of original issue discount to be ratably included as interest in the gross income of the depositor for any taxable year shall be the sum of the amounts separately computed for each deposit. For this purpose, the issue price for a deposit is the amount thereof and the stated redemption price at maturity is computed under paragraph (b)(1)(iii)(d) of § 1.1232-3.

(ii) *Obligations redeemed before maturity.*— In the event of a partial redemption of a time deposit open account before maturity, the following rules, in addition to subparagraph (2) of this paragraph, shall apply:

(a) If, pursuant to the terms of the withdrawal, the amount received by the depositor is determined with reference to the principal amount of a specific deposit and interest earned from the date of such deposit, then such terms shall control for the purpose of determining which deposit was withdrawn.

(b) If (a) of this subdivision (ii) does not apply, then the withdrawal shall be deemed to be of specific deposits together with interest earned from the date of such deposits, on a first-in, first-out basis.

(iii) *Examples.*—The provisions of this subparagraph may be illustrated by the following examples:

Example (1). (i) F is a cash method taxpayer who uses the calendar year as his taxable year. On December 1, 1970, F enters into a 5-year deposit open account arrangement with M Savings and Loan Corporation. The terms of the arrangement provide that F will deposit $100 each month for a period of 5 years, and that interest will be compounded semiannually (on June 1 and December 1) at 6 percent, but will be paid only at maturity. Thus, assuming F makes deposits of $100 on the first of each month beginning with December 1, 1970, the account will have a stated redemption price of $6,998.20 at maturity on December 1, 1975. Since, however, section 1232 applies only to deposits made after December 31, 1970 (see paragraph (d) of § 1.1232-1), the $34.39 of compound interest to be earned on the first deposit of $100 over the term of the arrangement will not be subject to the ratable inclusion rules of section 1232(a)(3). F must include such $34.39 of interest in his gross income on December 1, 1975, the date it is paid.

(ii) For 1971, F must include $44.19 of original issue discount as interest in gross income, to be computed as follows:

(1) Date of $100 deposit	(2) Months to Maturity	(3) Redemption price at maturity	(4) Original issue discount (Col.3– $100)	(5) Ratable monthly portion (Col.4÷ Col. 2)	(6) Months on deposit in 1971	(7) 1971 original issue discount (Col.5 × Col. 6)
1/1/71	59	$133.73	$33.73	$0.5717	12	$6.86
2/1/71	58	133.07	33.07	0.5702	11	6.27
3/1/71	57	132.42	32.42	0.5688	10	5.69
4/1/71	56	131.77	31.77	0.5673	9	5.11
5/1/71	55	131.12	31.12	0.5658	8	4.53
6/1/71	54	130.48	30.48	0.5644	7	3.95
7/1/71	53	129.84	29.84	0.5630	6	3.38
8/1/71	52	129.20	29.20	0.5615	5	2.81
9/1/71	51	128.56	28.56	0.5600	4	2.24
10/1/71	50	127.93	27.93	0.5586	3	1.68
11/1/71	49	127.30	27.30	0.5571	2	1.11
12/1/71	48	126.68	26.68	0.5558	1	0.56

Total original issue discount to be included as interest in F's gross income for 1971 . . . . $44.19

Example (2). (i) G is a cash method taxpayer who uses the calendar year as his taxable year. On February 1, 1971, G enters into a 4-year deposit open account arrangement with T Bank, a corporation. The terms of the deposit arrangement provide that G may deposit any amount from time to time in multiples of $50 for a period of 4 years. The terms also provide that G may not redeem any amount until February 1, 1975, except in an emergency as defined in, and subject to the qualifications provided by, Regulation Q of the Board of Governors of the Federal Reserve System. See 12 CFR § 217.4(d). Interest will be compounded semiannually (on February 1 and August 1) at 6 percent, providing there is no redemption prior to February 1, 1975. However, if there is a redemption prior to such date, inter-est will be compounded semiannually at $5\frac{1}{2}$ percent.

(ii) The schedule of deposits made by G pursuant to the arrangement, and computation of ratable monthly portion for each deposit, are set forth in the table below:

(1) Date of deposit	(2) Months to maturity	(3) Amount of deposit	(4) Redemption price at maturity	(5) Original issue discount (Col. 4 – Col. 3)	(6) Ratable monthly portion (Col. 5 ÷ Col. 2)
2/1/71	48	$100	$126.68	$26.68	$0.5558
6/1/71	44	200	248.42	48.42	1.1005
12/1/71	38	500	602.95	102.95	2.7092
2/1/72	36	800	955.24	155.24	4.3122
3/1/72	35	800	950.56	150.56	4.3017
7/1/72	31	600	699.00	99.00	3.1935
8/1/72	30	250	289.82	39.82	1.3273

(iii) With respect to amounts on deposit pursuant to the arrangement, the amounts of original issue discount G must include as inter-est in his gross income for 1971 and 1972 are computed in the table below:

(1) Date of deposit	(2) Ratable monthly portion	(3) Months on deposit in 1971	(4) 1971 original issue discount (Col. 2 × Col.3)	(5) Months on deposit in 1972	(6) 1972 original issue discount (Col. 2 × Col.5)
2/1/71	$0.5558	11	$6.11	12	$6.67
6/1/71	1.1005	7	7.70	12	13.21
12/1/71	2.7092	1	2.71	12	32.51
2/1/72	4.3122			11	47.43
3/1/72	4.3017			10	43.02
7/1/72	3.1935			6	19.16
8/1/72	1.3273			5	6.64
			$16.52		$168.64

Total original issue discount includible as interest in gross income for taxable year . . . .

(6) *Certain contingent interest arrangements.*—(i) *In general.*—If under the terms of a deposit arrangement—

(a) The holder cannot receive payment of any interest or constructively receive any interest prior to a fixed maturity date,

(b) Interest is earned at a guaranteed minimum rate of compound interest,

(c) Additional contingent interest may be earned for any year at a rate not to exceed one percentage point above such guaranteed minimum rate, and

(d) Any additional contingent interest is credited at least annually to the depositor's account then any contingent interest credited to the depositor shall be treated as creating a separate obligation subject to the rules of subdivision (ii) of this subparagraph.

(ii) *Computation.*—For purposes of computing the original issue discount to be included as interest in the depositor's gross income under section 1232(a)(3) with respect to such separate obligation—

(a) The issue price shall be zero,

(b) The date of original issue shall be the date on which the contingent interest is credited to the depositor's account and begins to earn interest,

(c) The date of maturity shall be the fixed maturity date of the deposit, and

(d) The stated redemption price at maturity is the sum of the amount of such contingent interest plus interest to be earned thereon at the guaranteed minimum rate of compound interest between such dates of original issue and maturity.

(7) *Contingent interest arrangements other than those described in subparagraph (6).*—(i) *In general.*—If under the terms of a deposit arrangement, contingent interest may be earned and credited to a depositor's account, but is neither actually or constructively received before a fixed maturity date nor treated under subparagraph (6)(i) of this paragraph as creating a separate obligation, then the redemption price shall include the amount which would be credited to such account assuming the issuer, during the term of such account, credits contingent interest at the greater of the rate—

(a) Last credited on a similar account, or

(b) Equal to the average rate credited for the preceding five calendar years on a similar account.

(ii) *Adjustments for additional interest.*—The rate taken into account under this subpara-

Reg. §1.1232-3A(e)(7)(ii)

graph in computing the redemption price shall be treated as the guaranteed minimum rate for purposes of applying subparagraph (6) of this paragraph in the event the rate at which contingent interest is actually credited to the depositor's account exceeds such rate previously taken into account. If for any period the actual rate at which contingent interest is credited to the account exceeds by more than one percentage point the rate for the previous period taken into account under this subparagraph in computing the redemption price, a new computation shall be made to determine the ratable monthly portion of original issue discount to be included as interest in the gross income of the depositor over the remaining term of the account. For purposes of such computation, the date that interest is first so credited to the account shall be treated as the issue date, the adjusted basis of the account on such date shall be the issue price, and the redemption price shall equal the amount actually on deposit in the account on such date plus the amount which would be credited to such account assuming the issuer, during the remaining term of such account, continues to credit contingent interest at the new rate.

(iii) *Adjustment for reduced interest.*—If for any period the actual rate of interest at which contingent interest is credited to the depositor's account is less than the rate for the previous period taken into account under this subparagraph in computing the redemption price, the difference between the amount of interest which would have been credited to the account at the rate for such previous period and the amount actually credited shall be allowed as a deduction against the amount of original issue discount with respect to such account required to be included in the gross income of the depositor. If an account is redeemed for a price less than the adjusted basis of the account, the depositor shall be allowed as a deduction, in computing adjusted gross income, the amount of the original issue discount he included in gross income but did not receive.

(f) *Application of section 1232(a)(3) to face-amount certificates.*—(1) *In general.*—Under paragraph (c)(3) of § 1.1232-1, the provisions of section 1232 (a)(3) and this section apply in the case of a face-amount certificate issued after December 31, 1975 (other than such a certificate issued pursuant to a written commitment which was binding on such date and at all times thereafter).

(2) *Relationship with paragraph (e) of this section.*—Determinations with regard to the inclusion as interest of original issue discount on, and certain adjustments with respect to, face-amount certificates to which this section applies shall be made in a manner consistent with the rules of paragraph (e) of this section (relating to the application of section 1232 to certain deposits in financial institutions and similar arrangements).

Thus, for example, if a face-amount certificate is redeemed before maturity, the holder shall be allowed a deduction in computing adjusted gross income computed in a manner consistent with the rules of paragraph (e)(2) of this section. For a further example, if under the terms of a face-amount certificate, the issuer may grant additional credits to be paid at a fixed maturity date, computations with respect to such additional credits shall be made in a manner consistent with the rules of paragraph (e)(6) and (7) of this section (as applicable) relating to contingent interest arrangements. [Reg. § 1.1232-3A.]

☐ [*T.D. 7154, 12-27-71. Amended by T.D. 7213, 10-13-72, T.D. 7311, 3-29-74, T.D. 7336, 12-19-74 and T.D. 7365, 6-30-75.*]

[Reg. § 1.1233-1]

§ 1.1233-1. Gains and losses from short sales.—(a) *General.*—(1) For income tax purposes a short sale is not deemed to be consummated until delivery of property to close the short sale. Whether the recognized gain or loss from a short sale is capital gain or loss or ordinary gain or loss depends upon whether the property so delivered constitutes a capital asset in the hands of the taxpayer.

(2) Thus, if a dealer in securities makes a short sale of X Corporation stock, ordinary gain or loss results on closing of the short sale if the stock used to close the short sale was stock which he held primarily for sale to customers in the ordinary course of his trade or business. If the stock used to close the short sale was a capital asset in his hands, or if the taxpayer in this example was not a dealer, a capital gain or loss would result.

(3) Generally, the period for which a taxpayer holds property delivered to close a short sale determines whether long-term or short-term capital gain or loss results.

(4) Thus, if a taxpayer makes a short sale of shares of stock and covers the short sale by purchasing and delivering shares which he held for not more than 1 year (6 months for taxable years beginning before 1977; 9 months for taxable years beginning in 1977), the recognized gain or loss would be considered short-term capital gain or loss. If the short sale is made through a broker and the broker borrows property to make a delivery, the short sale is not deemed to be consummated until the obligation of the seller created by the short sale is finally discharged by delivery of property to the broker to replace the property borrowed by the broker.

(5) For rules for determining the date of sale for purposes of applying under section 1091 the 61-day period applicable to a short sale of stock or securities at a loss, see paragraph (g) of § 1.1091-1.

(b) *Hedging transactions.*—Under section 1233(g), the provisions of section 1233 and this section shall not apply to any bona fide hedging transaction in commodity futures entered into by flour millers, producers of cloth, operators of grain elevators, etc., for the purpose of their business. Gain or loss from a short sale of commodity futures which does not qualify as a hedging transaction shall be considered gain or loss from the sale or exchange of a capital asset if the commodity future used to close the short sale constitutes a capital asset in the hands of the taxpayer as explained in paragraph (a) of this section.

(c) *Special short sales.*—(1) *General.*—Section 1233 provides rules as to the tax consequences of a short sale of property if gain or loss from the short sale is considered as gain or loss from the sale or exchange of a capital asset under section 1233(a) and paragraph (a) of this section and if, at the time of the short sale or on or before the date of the closing of the short sale, the taxpayer holds property substantially identical to that sold short. The term "property" is defined for purposes of such rules to include only stocks and securities (including stocks and securities dealt with on a "when issued" basis) and commodity futures, which are capital assets in the hands of the taxpayer. Certain restrictions on the application of the section to commodity futures are provided in section 1233(e) and paragraph (d)(2) of this section. Section 1233(f) contains special provisions governing the operation of rule (2) in subparagraph (2) of this paragraph in the case of a purchase and short sale of stocks or securities in a transaction qualifying as an arbitrage operation. See paragraph (f) of this section for detailed rules relating to arbitrage operations in stocks and securities.

(2) *Treatment of special short sales.*—The first two rules, which are set forth in section 1233(b), are applicable whenever property substantially identical to that sold short has been held by the taxpayer on the date of the short sale for not more than 1 year (6 months for taxable years beginning before 1977; 9 months for taxable years beginning in 1977) (determined without regard to rule (2), contained in this subparagraph, relating to the holding period) or is acquired by him after the short sale and on or before the date of the closing thereof. These rules are:

Rule (1). Any gain upon the closing of such short sale shall be considered as a gain upon the sale or exchange of a capital asset held for not more than 1 year (6 months for taxable years beginning before 1977; 9 months for taxable years beginning in 1977) (notwithstanding the period of time any property used to close such short sale has been held); and

Rule (2). The holding period of such substantially identical property shall be considered to begin (notwithstanding the provisions of section 1223) on the date of the closing of such short sale or on the date of a sale, gift, or other disposi-

tion of such property, whichever date occurs first.

(3) *Options to sell.*—For the purpose of rule (1) and rule (2) in paragraph (2) of this paragraph, the acquisition of an option to sell property at a fixed price shall be considered a short sale, and the exercise or failure to exercise such option shall be considered as a closing of such short sale, except that any option to sell property at a fixed price acquired on or after August 17, 1954 (the day after enactment of the Internal Revenue Code of 1954), shall not be considered a short sale and the exercise or failure to exercise such option shall not be considered as the closing of a short sale provided that the option and property identified as intended to be used in its exercise are acquired on the same date. This exception shall not apply, if the option is exercised, unless it is exercised by the sale of the property so identified. In the case of any option not exercised which falls within this exception, the cost of such option shall be added to the basis of the property with which such option is identified. If the option itself does not specifically identify the property intended to be used in exercising the option, then the identification of such property shall be made by appropriate entries in the taxpayer's records within 15 days after the date such property is acquired or before November 17, 1956, whichever expiration date later occurs.

(4) *Treatment of losses.*—The third rule, which is set forth in section 1233(d), is applicable whenever property substantially identical to that sold short has been held by the taxpayer on the date of the short sale for more than 1 year (6 months for taxable years beginning before 1977; 9 months for taxable years beginning in 1977). This rule is:

Rule (3). Any loss upon the closing of such short sale shall be considered as a loss upon the sale or exchange of a capital asset held for more than 1 year (6 months for taxable years beginning before 1977; 9 months for taxable years beginning in 1977), notwithstanding the period of time any property used to close such short sale has been held. For the purpose of this rule, the acquisition of an option to sell property at a fixed price is not considered a short sale, and the exercise or failure to exercise such option is not considered as a closing of a short sale.

(5) *Application of rules.*—Rules (1) and (3) contained in subparagraphs (2) and (4) of this paragraph do not apply to the gain or loss attributable to so much of the property sold short as exceeds in quantity the substantially identical property referred to in sections 1233(b) and (d), respectively. Except as otherwise provided in section 1233(f), rule (2) in subparagraph (2) of this paragraph applies to the substantially identical property referred to in section 1233(b) in the order of the dates of the acquisition of such

property, but only to so much of such property as does not exceed the quantity sold short. If property substantially identical to that sold short has been held by the taxpayer on the date of the short sale for not more than 1 year (6 months for taxable years beginning before 1977; 9 months for taxable years beginning in 1977), or is acquired by him after the short sale and on or before the date of the closing thereof, and if property substantially identical to that sold short has been held by the taxpayer on the date of the short sale for more than 1 year (6 months for taxable years beginning before 1977; 9 months for taxable years beginning in 1977), all three rules are applicable.

(6) *Examples.*—The following examples illustrate the application of these rules to short sales of stock in the case of a taxpayer who makes his return on the basis of the calendar year:

Example (1). A buys 100 shares of X stock at $10 per share on February 1, 1955, sells short 100 shares of X stock at $16 per share on July 1, 1955, and closes the short sale on August 2, 1955, by delivering the 100 shares of X stock purchased on February 1, 1955, to the lender of the stock used to effect the short sale. Since 100 shares of X stock had been held by A on the date of the short sale for not more than 6 months, the gain of $600 realized upon the closing of the short sale is, by application of rule (1) in subparagraph (2) of this paragraph, a short-term capital gain.

Example (2). A buys 100 shares of X stock at $10 per share on February 1, 1955, sells short 100 shares of X stock at $16 per share on July 1, 1955, closes the short sale on August 1, 1955, with 100 shares of X stock purchased on that date at $18 per share, and on August 2, 1955, sells at $18 per share the 100 shares of X stock purchased on February 1, 1955. The $200 loss sustained upon the closing of the short sale is a short-term capital loss to which section 1233(d) has no application. By application of rule (2) in subparagraph (2) of this paragraph, however, the holding period of the 100 shares of X stock purchased on February 1, 1955, and sold on August 2, 1955 is considered to begin on August 1, 1955, the date of the closing of the short sale. The $800 gain realized upon the sale of such stock is, therefore, a short-term capital gain.

Example (3). A buys 100 shares of X stock at $10 per share on February 1, 1955, sells short 100 shares of X stock at $16 per share on September 1, 1955, sells on October 1, 1955, at $18 per share the 100 shares of X stock purchased on February 1, 1955, and closes the short sale on October 1, 1955, with 100 shares of X stock purchased on that date at $18 per share. The $800 gain realized upon the sale of the 100 shares of X stock purchased on February 1, 1955, is a long-term capital gain to which section 1233(b) has no application. Since A had held 100 shares of X stock on the date of the short sale for more than

6 months, the $200 loss sustained upon the closing of the short sale is, by application of rule (3) in subparagraph (4) of this paragraph, a long-term capital loss. If, instead of purchasing 100 shares of X stock on October 1, 1955, A closed the short sale with the 100 shares of stock purchased on February 1, 1955, the $600 gain realized on the closing of the short sale would be a long-term capital gain to which section 1233(b) has no application.

Example (4). A sells short 100 shares of X stock at $16 per share on February 1, 1955. He buys 250 shares of X stock on March 1, 1955, at $10 per share and holds the latter stock until September 2, 1955 (more than 6 months), at which time, 100 shares of the 250 shares of X stock are delivered to close the short sale made on February 1, 1955. Since substantially identical property was acquired by A after the short sale and before it was closed, the $600 gain realized on the closing of the short sale is, by application of rule (1) in subparagraph (2) of this paragraph, a short-term capital gain. The holding period of the remaining 150 shares of X stock is not affected by section 1233 since this amount of the substantially identical property exceeds the quantity of the property sold short.

Example (5). A buys 100 shares of X stock at $10 per share on February 1, 1955, buys an additional 100 shares of X stock at $20 per share on July 1, 1955, sells short 100 shares of X stock at $30 per share on September 1, 1955, and closes the short sale on February 1, 1956, by delivering the 100 shares of X stock purchased on February 1, 1955, to the lender of the stock used to effect the short sale. Since 100 shares of X stock had been held by A on the date of the short sale for not more than 6 months, the gain of $2,000 realized upon the closing of the short sale is, by application of rule (1) in subparagraph (2) of this paragraph a short-term capital gain and the holding period of the 100 shares of X stock purchased on July 1, 1955, is considered, by application of rule (2) in subparagraph (2) of this paragraph to begin on February 1, 1956, the date of the closing of the short sale. If, however, the 100 shares of X stock purchased on July 1, 1955, had been used by A to close the short sale, then, since 100 shares of X stock had been held by A on the date of the short sale for not more than 6 months, the gain of $1,000 realized upon the closing of the short sale would be, by application of rule (1) in subparagraph (2) of this paragraph, a short-term capital gain, but the holding period of the 100 shares of X stock purchased on February 1, 1955, would not be affected by section 1233. If, on the other hand, A purchased an additional 100 shares of X stock at $40 per share on February 1, 1956, and used such shares to close the short sale at that time, then, since 100 shares of X stock had been held by A on the date of the short sale for more than 6 months, the loss of $1,000 sustained upon the closing of the short sale would be, by application of rule (3) in subparagraph (4) of this paragraph, a long-term capital loss, and since 100 shares of X stock had been held by A on the date of the short sale for not more than 6 months, the holding period of the 100 shares of X stock purchased on July 1, 1955, would be considered by application of rule (2) in subparagraph (2) of this paragraph, to begin on February 1, 1956, but the holding period of the 100 shares of X stock purchased on February 1, 1955, would not be affected by section 1233.

Example (6). A buys 100 shares of X preferred stock at $10 per share on February 1, 1955. On July 1, 1955, he enters into a contract to sell 100 shares of XY common stock at $16 per share when, as, and if issued pursuant to a particular proposed plan of reorganization. On August 2, 1955, he receives 100 shares of XY common stock in exchange for the 100 shares of X perferred stock purchased on February 1, 1955, and delivers such common shares in performance of his July 1, 1955, contract. Assume that the exchange of the X preferred stock for the XY common stock is a tax-free exchange pursuant to section 354(a)(1), and that on the basis of all of the facts and circumstances existing on July 1, 1955, the "when issued" XY common stock is substantially identical to the X preferred stock. Since 100 shares of substantially identical property had been held by A for not more than 6 months on the date of entering into the July 1, 1955, contract of sale, the gain of $600 realized upon the closing of the contract of sale is, by application of rule (1) in subparagraph (2) of this paragraph, a short-term capital gain.

(d) *Other rules for the application of section 1233.*—(1) *Substantially identical property.*—The term "substantially identical property" is to be applied according to the facts and circumstances in each case. In general, as applied to stocks or securities, the term has the same meaning as the term "substantially identical stock or securities" used in section 1091, relating to wash sales of stocks or securities. For certain restrictions on the term as applied to commodity futures see subparagraph (2) of this paragraph. Ordinarily, stocks or securities of one corporation are not considered substantially identical to stocks or securities of another corporation. In certain situations they may be substantially identical; for example, in the case of a reorganization the facts and circumstances may be such that the stocks and securities of predecessor and successor corporations are substantially identical property. Similarly, bonds or preferred stock of a corporation are not ordinarily considered substantially identical to the common stock of the same corporation. However, in certain situations, as, for example, where the preferred stock or bonds are convertible into common stock of the same corporation, the relative values, price changes, and other circumstances may be such as to make such bonds or preferred stock and the common stock substantially identical property. Similarly, depending on the facts and circumstances, the term may apply to the stocks and securities to be received in a corporate reorganization or recapitalization, traded in on a when issued basis, as compared with the stocks or securities to be exchanged in such reorganization or recapitalization.

(2) *Commodity futures.*—(i) As provided in section 1233(e)(2)(B), in the case of futures transactions in any commodity on or subject to the rules of a board of trade or commodity exchange, a commodity future requiring delivery in one calendar month shall not be considered as property substantially identical to another commodity future requiring delivery in a different calendar month. For example, commodity futures in May wheat and July wheat are not considered, for the purpose of section 1233, substantially identical property.

Similarly, futures in different commodities which are not generally through custom of the trade used as hedges for each other (such as corn and wheat, for example) are not considered substantially identical property. If commodity futures are otherwise substantially identical property, the mere fact that they were procured through different brokers will not remove them from the scope of the term "substantially identical property". Commodity futures procured on different markets may come within the term "substantially identical property" depending upon the facts and circumstances in the case, with the historical similarity in the price movements in the two markets as the primary factor to be considered.

(ii) Section 1233(e)(3), relating to so-called "arbitrage" transactions in commodity futures, provides that where a taxpayer enters into two commodity futures transactions on the same day, one requiring delivery by him in one market and the other requiring delivery to him of the same (or substantially identical) commodity in the same calendar month in a different market, and the taxpayer subsequently closes both such transactions on the same day, section 1233 shall have no application to so much of the commodity involved in either such transaction as does not exceed in quantity the commodity involved in the other. Section 1233(f), relating to arbitrage operations in stocks or securities, has no application to arbitrage transactions in commodity futures.

(iii) The following example indicates the application of section 1233 to a commodity futures transaction:

Example. A who makes his return on the basis of the calendar year, on February 1, 1955, enters into a contract through broker X to purchase 10,000 bushels of December wheat on the Chicago market at $2 per bushel. On July 1, 1955, he enters into a contract through broker Y to sell 10,000 bushels of December wheat on the Chicago market at $2.25 per bushel. On August 2, 1955, he closes both transactions at $2.50 per bushel. The $2,500 loss sustained on the closing of the short sale is a short-term capital loss to which section 1233(d) has no application. By application of rule (2) in paragraph (c)(2) of this section, however, the holding period of the futures contract entered into on February 1, 1955, is considered to begin on August 2, 1955, the date of the closing of the short sale. The $5,000 gain realized upon the closing of such contract is, therefore, a short-term capital gain.

(3) *Husband and wife.*—Section 1233(e)(2)(C) provides that, in the case of a short sale of property by an individual, the term "taxpayer" in the application of subsections (b), (d), and (e) shall be read as "taxpayer or his spouse". Thus, if the spouse of a taxpayer holds or acquires property substantially identical to that sold short by the taxpayer, and other conditions of subsections (b), (d), and (e) are met, then the rules set forth therein are applicable to the same extent as if the taxpayer held or acquired the substantially identical property. For this purpose, an individual who is legally separated from the taxpayer under a decree of divorce or of separate maintenance shall not be considered as the spouse of the taxpayer.

(e) *Special rule for short sales by dealers in securities under certain circumstances.*—In the case of a short sale of stock (as defined in subparagraph (3) of this paragraph) after December 31, 1957, by a dealer in securities, section 1233(e)(4)(A) provides that the holding period of substantially identical stock which he has held as an investment for not more than 1 year (6 months for taxable years beginning before 1977; 9 months for taxable years beginning in 1977) shall be determined in accordance with section 1233(b)(2) unless such short sale is closed within 20 days of the date on which it was made. See rule (2) in paragraph (c)(2) of this section for the purpose of determining the holding period of such substantially identical stock. In addition, section 1233(e)(4)(B) provides that for the purpose of the special rule of section 1233(e)(4)(A), the acquisition of an option to sell property at a fixed price shall be considered a short sale, and the exercise or failure to exercise such option shall be considered a closing of such short sale. For purposes of this paragraph—

(1) Whether or not a taxpayer is a "dealer in securities" shall be determined in accordance with the meaning of the term for purposes of section 1236;

(2) Whether or not stock is "substantially identical" with other property shall be determined in accordance with the provisions of paragraph (d)(1) of this section; and

(3) The term "stock" means—

(i) Any share or certificate of stock,

(ii) Any bond or other evidence of indebtedness which is convertible into a share or certificate of stock, and

(iii) Any evidence of an interest in, or right to subscribe to or purchase, any of the items described in subdivision (i) or (ii) of this subparagraph.

(f) *Arbitrage operations in stocks and securities and holding periods.*—(1) *General rule.*—(i) In the case of a short sale entered into as part of an arbitrage operation, rule (2) of paragraph (c)(2) of this section shall apply first to substantially identical property acquired for arbitrage operations and held by the taxpayer at the close of business on the day of the short sale. The holding period of substantially identical property not acquired for arbitrage operations shall be affected only to the extent that the amount of property sold short exceeds the amount of substantially identical property acquired for arbitrage operations and held by the taxpayer at the close of business on the day of the short sale.

(ii) If the substantially identical property acquired for arbitrage operations is disposed of without closing the short sale so that a net short position in assets acquired for arbitrage operations is created, a short sale in the amount of such net short position will be deemed to have been made on the day such net short position is created. Rule (2) of paragraph (c)(2) of this section will then apply to substantially identical property not acquired for arbitrage operations to the same extent as if the taxpayer, on the day such net short position is created, sold short an amount equal to the amount of the net short position in a transaction not entered into as part of an arbitrage operation.

(iii) The following examples illustrate the application of rule (2) of paragraph (c)(2) of this section to arbitrage operations:

Example (1). On August 13, 1957, A buys 100 bonds of X Corporation for purposes other than arbitrage operations. The bonds are convertible at the option of the bondholders into common stock of X Corporation on the basis of one bond for one share of stock. On November 1, 1957, A sells short 100 shares of common stock of X Corporation in a transaction identified and intended to be part of an arbitrage operation and on the same day buys another 100 bonds of X Corporation in a transaction identified and intended to be part of the same arbitrage operation. The bonds acquired on both August 13, 1957, and November 1, 1957, are, on the basis of all the facts and circumstances, substantially identical to the common stock of X Corporation. On December 1, 1957, A closes the short sale with 100 shares of common stock of X Corporation acquired on that day. The holding period of the bonds acquired on November 1, by application of rule (2) of paragraph (c)(2) of this section, will be deemed to begin on December 1 and the holding period of the bonds acquired on August 13 will be unaffected. If, instead of purchasing the 100 shares of common stock of X Corporation on December 1, 1957, A had converted the bonds acquired on November 1 into common stock and, on December 1, 1957, used the stock so acquired to close the short sale, rule (2) of paragraph (c)(2) of this section would similarly have no effect on the holding period of the bonds acquired on August 13.

Example (2). Assume the same facts as in example (1), except that A, on December 1, sells the bonds acquired on November 1 (or converts such bonds into common stock and sells the stock), but does not close the short sale. The sale of the bonds (or stock) creates a net short position in assets acquired for arbitrage operations which is deemed to be a short sale made on December 1. Accordingly, the holding period of the bonds acquired on August 13 will, by application of rule (2) of paragraph (c)(2) of this section, begin on the date such short sale is closed or on the date of sale, gift, or other disposition of such bonds, whichever date occurs first.

(2) *Right to receive or acquire property.*— (i) For purposes of section 1233(f)(1) and (2) and subparagraph (1) of this paragraph, a taxpayer will be deemed to hold substantially identical property acquired for arbitrage operations at the close of any business day if, by virtue of the ownership of other property acquired for arbitrage operations (whether or not substantially identical) or because of any contract entered into by the taxpayer in an arbitrage operation, he then has the right to receive or acquire such substantially identical property.

(ii) The application of section 1233(f)(3) and subdivision (i) of this subparagraph may be illustrated by the following example:

Example. A acquires on August 13, 1957, 100 shares of common stock of X Corporation for purposes other than arbitrage operations. On November 1, A sells short, in a transaction identified and intended to be part of an arbitrage operation, 100 shares of X common stock. On the same day, in a transaction also identified and intended to be part of the same arbitrage operation, A contracts to purchase 100 shares of preferred stock of X. The preferred stock of X may be converted into common stock of X on the basis of one share of preferred stock for one share of common stock. The preferred stock is not actually delivered to A until November 3. Since A has contracted before the close of business on the date of the short sale, as part of an arbitrage operation, to purchase property by virtue of which he has the right to receive or acquire substantially identical property to that sold short, he will be deemed, for purposes of section 1233(f)(1) and (2), to hold such substantially identical property at the close of business on the date of the short sale. For purposes of this subparagraph, it is immaterial whether, on the basis of all the facts and circumstances, the preferred stock of X is substantially identical to the common stock of X. The short sale on November 1 does not affect the holding period of the 100

shares of X Corporation common stock purchased on August 13, 1957. Because of the operation of rule (2) of paragraph (c)(2) of this section, the holding period of the preferred stock acquired as the result of A's contract to purchase it as part of an arbitrage operation (or the common stock which A acquires by conversion of such preferred stock into common stock) will not begin until the short sale entered into in the arbitrage operation is closed.

(3) *Definition of arbitrage operations.*—For the purpose of section 1233(f), arbitrage operations are transactions involving the purchase and sale of property entered into for the purpose of profiting from a current difference between the price of the property purchased and the price of the property sold. Assets acquired for arbitrage operations include only stocks and securities and rights to acquire stocks and securities. The property purchased may be either identical to the property sold or, if not so identical, such that its acquisition will entitle the taxpayer to acquire property which is so identical. Thus, the purchase of bonds or preferred stock convertible, at the holder's option, into common stock and the short sale of the common stock which may be acquired therefor, or the purchase of stock rights and the short sale of the stock to be acquired on the exercise of such rights, may qualify as arbitrage operations. A transaction will qualify as an arbitrage operation under section 1233(f) only if the taxpayer properly identifies the transaction as an arbitrage operation on his records as soon as he is able to do so. Such identification must ordinarily be entered in the taxpayer's records on the day of the transaction. Property acquired in a transaction properly identified as part of an arbitrage operation is the only property which will be deemed acquired for an arbitrage operation. The provisions of section 1233(f) and this paragraph shall continue to apply to property acquired in a transaction properly identified as an arbitrage operation although, because of subsequent events, e.g., a change in the value of bonds so acquired or of stock into which such bonds may be converted, the taxpayer sells such property outright rather than using it to complete the arbitrage operation.

(4) *Effective date of section 1233(f).*—Section 1233(f), relating to arbitrage operations involving short sales of property, is effective only with respect to taxable years ending after August 12, 1955, and only with respect to short sales made after such date. [Reg. § 1.1233-1.]

☐ [*T.D.* 6207, *10-17-56. Amended by T.D.* 6494, *9-29-60; T.D.* 6926, *8-8-67 and T.D.* 7728, *10-31-80.*]

[Reg. § 1.1233-2]

§ 1.1233-2. Hedging transactions.—The character of gain or loss on a short sale that is (or is identified as being) part of a hedging transaction is determined under the rules of § 1.1221-2. [Reg. § 1.1233-2.]

☐ [*T.D.* 8555, 7-13-94.]

[Reg. § 1.1234-1]

§ 1.1234-1. Options to buy or sell.—(a) *Sale or exchange.*—(1) *Capital assets.*—Gain or loss from the sale or exchange of an option (or privilege) to buy or sell property which is (or if acquired would be) a capital asset in the hands of the taxpayer holding the option is considered as gain or loss from the sale or exchange of a capital asset (unless, under the provisions of subparagraph (2) of this paragraph, the gain or loss is subject to the provisions of section 1231). The period for which the taxpayer has held the option determines whether the capital gain or loss is short-term or long-term.

(2) *Section 1231 transactions.*—Gain or loss from the sale or exchange of an option to buy or sell property is considered a gain or loss subject to the provisions of section 1231 if, had the sale or exchange been of the property subject to the option, held by the taxpayer for the length of time he held the option, the sale or exchange would have been subject to the provisions of section 1231.

(3) *Other property.*—Gain or loss from the sale or exchange of an option to buy or sell property which is not (or if acquired would not be) a capital asset in the hands of the taxpayer holding the option is considered ordinary income or loss (unless under the provisions of subparagraph (2) of this paragraph, the gain or loss is subject to the provisions of section 1231).

(b) *Failure to exercise option.*—If the holder of an option to buy or sell property incurs a loss on failure to exercise the option, the option is deemed to have been sold or exchanged on the date that it expired. Any such loss to the holder of an option is treated under the general rule provided in paragraph (a) of this section. In general, any gain to the grantor of an option arising from the failure of the holder to exercise it, and any gain or loss realized by the grantor of an option as a result of a closing transaction, such as repurchasing the option from the holder, is considered ordinary income or loss. However, for the treatment of gain or loss from a closing transaction with respect to or gain on the lapse of an option granted in stock, securities, commodities, or commodity futures, see section 1234(b) and § 1.1234-3. For special rules for grantors of straddles applicable to certain options granted on or before September 1, 1976, see § 1.1234-2.

(c) *Certain options to sell property at a fixed price.*—Section 1234 does not apply to a loss on the failure to exercise an option to sell property at a fixed price which is acquired on the same day on which the property identified as intended to be used in exercising the option is acquired.

Such a loss is not recognized, but the cost of the option is added to the basis of the property with which it is identified. See section 1233(c) and the regulations thereunder.

(d) *Dealers in options to buy or sell.*—Any gain or loss realized by a dealer in options from the sale or exchange of an option to buy or sell property is considered ordinary income or loss under paragraph (a)(3) of this section. A dealer in options to buy or sell property is considered a dealer in the property subject to the option.

(e) *Other exceptions.*—Section 1234 does not apply to gain resulting from the sale or exchange of an option:

(1) To the extent that the gain is in the nature of compensation (see sections 61 and 421, and the regulations thereunder, relating to employee stock options);

(2) If the option is treated as section 306 stock (see section 306 and the regulations thereunder, relating to dispositions of certain stock); or

(3) To the extent that the gain is a distribution of earnings or profits taxable as a dividend (see section 301 and the regulations thereunder, relating to distributions of property).

(4) Acquired by the taxpayer before March 1, 1954, if in the hands of the taxpayer such option is a capital asset (whether or not the property to which the option relates is, or would be if acquired by the taxpayer, a capital asset in the hands of the taxpayer).

(f) *Limitations on effect of section.*—Losses to which section 1234 applies are subject to the limitations on losses under sections 165(c) and 1211 when applicable. Section 1234 does not permit the deduction of any loss which is disallowed under any other provision of law. In addition, section 1234 does not apply to an option to lease property, but does apply to an option to buy or sell a lease. Thus, an option to obtain all the right, title, and interest of a lessee in leased property is subject to the provisions of section 1234, but an option to obtain a sublease from the lessee is not. Furthermore, if section 1234 applies to an option to buy or sell a lease, it is the character the lease itself, if acquired, would have in the hands of the taxpayer, and not the character of the property leased, which determines the treatment of gain or loss experienced by the taxpayer with respect to such an option.

(g) *Examples.*—The rules set forth in this section may be illustrated by the following examples:

Example (1). A taxpayer is considering buying a new house for his residence and acquires an option to buy a certain house at a fixed price. Although the property goes up in value, the taxpayer decides he does not want the house for his residence and sells the option for more than he paid for it. The gain which taxpayer realized is a capital gain since the property, if acquired, would have been a capital asset in his hands.

Example (2). Assume the same facts as in example (1), except that the property goes down in value, and the taxpayer decides not to purchase the house. He sells the option at a loss. While this is a capital loss under section 1234, it is not a deductible loss because of the provisions of section 165(c).

Example (3). A dealer in industrial property acquires an option to buy an industrial site and fails to exercise the option. The loss is an ordinary loss since he would have held the property for sale to customers in the ordinary course of his trade or business if he had acquired it. [Reg. §1.1234-1.]

☐ [*T.D. 6253, 9-25-57. Amended by T.D. 6394, 7-1-59; T.D. 7152, 12-22-71 and T.D. 7652, 10-29-79.*]

[Reg. §1.1234-2]

§1.1234-2. Special rules for grantors of straddles applicable to certain options granted on or before September 1, 1976.—(a) *In general.*—Section 1234(c)(1) provides a special rule applicable in the case of gain on the lapse of an option granted by the taxpayer as part of a straddle. In such a case, the gain shall be deemed to be gain from the sale or exchange of a capital asset held for not more than 1 year (6 months for taxable years beginning before 1977; 9 months for taxable years beginning in 1977) on the day that the option expired. Thus, such gain shall be treated as a short-term capital gain, as defined in section 1222(1). Section 1234(c)(1) does not apply to any person who holds securities (including options to acquire or sell securities) for sale to customers in the ordinary course of his trade or business.

(b) *Definitions.*—The following definitions apply for purposes of section 1234(c) and this section.

(1) *Straddle.*—The term "straddle" means a simultaneously granted combination of an option to buy (i.e., a "call") and an option to sell (i.e., a "put") the same quantity of a security at the same price during the same period of time.

(2) *Security.*—The term "security" has the meaning assigned to such term by section 1236(c) and the regulations thereunder. Thus, for example, the term "security" does not include commodity futures.

(3) *Grantor.*—The term "grantor" means the writer or issuer of the option contracts making up the straddle.

(4) *Multiple option.*—The term "multiple option" means a simultaneously granted combination of an option to buy plus an option to sell plus one or more additional options to buy or sell a security.

(c) *Special rules in the case of a multiple option.*—(1) If, in the case of a multiple option, the number of the options to sell and the number of the options to buy are the same and if the terms of all of the options are identical (as to the quantity of the security, price, and period of time), then each of the options contained in the multiple option shall be deemed to be a component of a straddle for purposes of section 1234(c)(1) and paragraph (a) of this section.

(2) If, in the case of a multiple option, the number of the options to sell and the number of the options to buy are not the same or if the terms of all of the options are not identical (as to the quantity of the security, price, and period of time), then section 1234(c)(1) applies to gain on the lapse of an option granted as part of the multiple option only if—

(i) The grantor of the multiple option identified the two options which comprise each straddle contained in the multiple option in the manner prescribed in subparagraph (3) of this paragraph; or

(ii) It is clear from the facts and circumstances that the lapsed option was part of a straddle. See example (6) of paragraph (f) of this section. A multiple option to which this subdivision applies may not be regarded as consisting of a number of straddles which exceeds the lesser of the options to sell or the options to buy as the case may be. For example, if a multiple option of five puts and four calls is granted it may not be regarded as consisting of more than four straddles, although the particular facts and circumstances could dictate that the option consist of less than four straddles.

(3) The identification required under subparagraph (2)(i) of this paragraph shall be made by the grantor indicating in his records, to the extent feasible, the individual serial number of, or other characteristic symbol imprinted upon, each of the two individual options which comprise the straddle, or by adopting any other method of identification satisfactory to the Commissioner. Such identification must be made before the expiration of the fifteenth day after the day on which the multiple option is granted. The preceding sentence shall apply only with respect to multiple options granted after [the 30th day following the date of publication in the *Federal Register* of the Treasury decision]. In computing the 15-day period prescribed by this paragraph, the first day of such period is the day following the day on which the multiple option is granted.

(d) *Allocation of premium.*—The allocation of a premium received for a straddle or a multiple option between or among the component options thereof shall be made on the basis of the relative market value of such component options at the time of their issuance or on any other reasonable and consistently applied basis which is acceptable to the Commissioner.

(e) *Effective date.*—(1) *In general.*—This section, relating to special rules for grantors of straddles, shall apply only with respect to straddle transactions entered into after January 25, 1965, and before September 2, 1976.

(2) *Special rule.*—For a special rule with respect to the identification of a straddle granted as part of a multiple option, see paragraph (c).

(f) *Illustrations.*—The application of section 1234(c) and this section may be illustrated by the following examples:

Example (1). On February 1, 1971, taxpayer A, who files his income tax returns on a calendar year basis, issues a straddle for 100 shares of X Corporation stock and receives a premium of $1,000. The options comprising the straddle were to expire on August 10, 1971. A has allocated $450 (45 percent of $1,000) of the premium to the put and $550 (55 percent of $1,000) to the call. On March 1, 1971, B, the holder of the put, exercises his option. C, the holder of the call, fails to exercise his option prior to its expiration. As a result of C's failure to exercise his option, A realizes a short-term capital gain of $550 (that part of the premium allocated to the call) on August 10, 1971.

Example (2). Assume the same facts as in example (1), except that C exercises his call on March 1, 1971, and B fails to exercise his put prior to its expiration. As a result of B's failure to exercise his option, A realizes a short-term capital gain of $450 (that part of the premium allocated to the put) on August 10, 1971.

Example (3). Assume the same facts as in example (1), except that both B and C fail to exercise their respective options. As a result of the failure of B and C to exercise their options, A realizes short-term capital gains of $1,000 (the premium for granting the straddle) on August 10, 1971.

Example (4). On March 1, 1971, taxpayer D issues a multiple option containing five puts and five calls. Each put and each call is for the same number of shares of Y Corporation stock, at the same price, and for the same period of time. Thus, each of the puts and calls is deemed to be a component part of a straddle. The puts and calls comprising the multiple option were to expire on September 10, 1971. All of the puts are exercised, and all of the calls lapse. As a result of the lapse of the calls, D realizes a short-term capital gain on September 10, 1971, in the amount of that part of the premium for the multiple option which is allocable to all of the calls.

Example (5). Assume the same facts as in example (4) except that one of the puts and two of the calls lapse and the remaining puts and calls are exercised. As a result, on September 10, 1971, D realizes a short-term capital gain in the amount of that part of the premium for the multiple option which is allocable to both of the lapsed calls and the lapsed put.

Example (6). On March 1, 1971, taxpayer E issues a multiple option containing five puts and four calls. Each put and call is for the same number of shares of Y Corporation stock at the same price and for the same period of time. E does not identify the puts and calls as parts of straddles in the manner prescribed in paragraph (c)(3) of this section. However, because the terms of all of the puts and all of the calls are identical four of the puts and four of the calls are deemed to be a component part of a straddle. The puts and calls comprising the multiple option were to expire on September 10, 1971. Four of the puts are exercised and the four calls and one of the puts lapse. As a result, on September 10, 1971, E realizes short-term capital gain in the amount of that part of the premium for the multiple option which is allocable to the four lapsed calls and realizes ordinary income in the amount of that part of such premium which is allocable to the lapsed put. If E had identified four of the puts and four of the calls as constituting parts of straddles in the manner prescribed in paragraph (c)(3) of this section and the put that lapsed constituted part of a straddle, then the gain on the lapse of the put would also be short-term capital gain.

Example (7). Assume the same facts as in example (6) except that two of the puts are for Y Corporation stock at a price which is greater than that of the other puts and the other calls and that two of the calls expire on October 10, 1971. Additionally, assume that the put which lapses is at the lower price. The two puts offering the Y Corporation stock at the greater price and the two calls with the later expiration date cannot be deemed to be component parts of a straddle. Thus, only two of the puts and two of the calls are deemed to be a component part of a straddle. As a result, E realizes income as follows:

(i) On September 10, 1971, short-term capital gain in the amount of that part of the premium for the multiple option which is allocable to the two lapsed calls with the expiration date of September 10, 1971, and ordinary income in the amount of that part of such premium which is allocable to the lapsed put. If E had identified two of the puts at the lower price and the two calls with the expiration date of September 10, 1971, as constituting parts of straddles in the manner prescribed in paragraph (c)(3) of this section and if the put that lapsed was one of those identified as constituting a part of a straddle, then the gain on the lapse of that put would also be short-term capital gain.

(ii) On October 10, 1971, ordinary income in the amount of that part of the premium for the multiple option which is allocable to the lapsed calls with an expiration date of October 10, 1971. [Reg. § 1.1234-2.]

☐ [*T.D. 7152, 12-22-71. Amended by T.D. 7210, 10-2-72; T.D. 7652, 10-29-79 and T.D. 7728, 10-31-80.*]

[Reg. § 1.1234-3]

§ 1.1234-3. Special rules for the treatment of grantors of certain options granted after September 1, 1976.—(a) *In general.*—In the case of the grantor of an option (including an option granted as part of a straddle or multiple option), gain or loss from any closing transaction with respect to, and gain on the lapse of, an option in property shall be treated as a gain or loss from the sale or exchange of a capital asset held not more than 1 year (6 months for taxable years beginning before 1977; 9 months for taxable years beginning in 1977).

(b) *Definitions.*—The following definitions apply for purposes of this section.

(1) The term "closing transaction" means any termination of a grantor's obligation under an option to buy property (a "call") or an option to sell property (a "put") other than through the exercise or lapse of the option. For example, the grantor of a call may effectively terminate his obligation under the option by either (i) repurchasing the option from the holder or (ii) purchasing from an options exchange a call with terms identical to the original option granted and designating the purchase as a closing transaction. A put or call purchased to make a closing transaction is identical as to striking price and expiration date. Such put or call need not match the granted option in time of creation, date of acquisition, cost of the entire option or units therein, or number of units subject to the option. If such put or call terminates only part of a grantor's obligation under the granted option, a closing transaction is made as to that part.

(2) The term "property" means stocks and securities (including stocks and securities dealt with on a "when issued" basis), commodities, and commodity futures.

(3) The term "grantor" means the writer or issuer of an option.

(4) The term "straddle" means a simultaneously granted combination of an option to buy and an option to sell the same quantity of property at the same price during the same period of time.

(5) The term "multiple option" means a simultaneously granted combination of an option to buy plus an option to sell plus one or more additional options to buy or sell property.

(c) *Nonapplicability to broker-dealers.*—The provisions of this section do not apply to any option granted in the ordinary course of the taxpayer's trade or business of granting options. However, the provisions of this section do apply to—

(1) Gain from any closing transaction with respect to an option and gain on lapse of an option if gain on the sale or exchange of the option would be considered capital gain by a dealer in securities under section 1236(a) and the regulations thereunder, and

(2) Loss from any closing transaction with respect to an option if loss on the sale or exchange of the option would not be considered ordinary loss by a dealer in securities under section 1236(b) and the regulations thereunder.

The preceding sentence shall be applied with respect to dealers in "property" (as defined in paragraph (b)(2) of this section) and without regard to the limitation of the applicability of section 1236 to dealers in securities.

(d) *Nonapplicability to compensatory options.*—Section 1234 does not apply to options to purchase stock or other property which are issued as compensation for services, as described in sections 61, 83, and 421 and the regulations thereunder.

(e) *Premium allocation for simultaneously granted options.*—The allocation of a premium received for a straddle or multiple option between or among the component options thereof shall be made on the basis of the relative market value of the component options at the time of their issuance or on any other reasonable and consistently applied basis which is acceptable to the Commissioner.

(f) *Effective date.*—This section, relating to special rules for the treatment of grantors of certain options, shall apply to options granted after September 1, 1976. [Reg. § 1.1234-3.]

☐ [*T.D.* 7652, 10-29-79.]

[Reg. § 1.1234-4]

§ 1.1234-4. Hedging transactions.—The character of gain or loss on an acquired or a written option that is (or is identified as being) part of a hedging transaction is determined under the rules of § 1.1221-2. [Reg. § 1.1234-4.]

☐ [*T.D.* 8555, 7-13-94.]

[Reg. § 1.1235-1]

§ 1.1235-1. Sale or exchange of patents.—(a) *General rule.*—Section 1235 provides that a transfer (other than by gift, inheritance, or devise) of all substantial rights to a patent, or of an undivided interest in all such rights to a patent, by a holder to a person other than a related person constitutes the sale or exchange of a capital asset held for more than 1 year (6 months for taxable years beginning before 1977; 9 months for taxable years beginning in 1977), whether or not payments therefor are—

(1) Payable periodically over a period generally coterminous with the transferee's use of the patent, or

(2) Contingent on the productivity, use, or disposition of the property transferred.

(b) *Scope of section 1235.*—If a transfer is not one described in paragraph (a) of this section, section 1235 shall be disregarded in determining whether or not such transfer is the sale or exchange of a capital asset. For example, a transfer by a person other than a holder or a transfer by a holder to a related person is not governed by section 1235. The tax consequences of such transfers shall be determined under other provisions of the internal revenue laws.

(c) *Special rules.*—(1) *Payments for infringement.*—If section 1235 applies to the transfer of all substantial rights to a patent (or an undivided interest therein), amounts received in settlement of, or as the award of damages in, a suit for compensatory damages for infringement of the patent shall be considered payments attributable to a transfer to which section 1235 applies to the extent that such amounts relate to the interest transferred. For taxable years beginning before January 1, 1964, see section 1304, as in effect before such date, and § 1.1304a-1 for treatment of compensatory damages for patent infringement.

(2) *Payments to an employee.*—Payments received by an employee as compensation for services rendered as an employee under an employment contract requiring the employee to transfer to the employer the rights to any invention by such employee are not attributable to a transfer to which section 1235 applies. However, whether payments received by an employee from his employer (under an employment contract or otherwise) are attributable to the transfer by the employee of all substantial rights to a patent (or an undivided interest therein) or are compensation for services rendered the employer by the employee is a question of fact. In determining which is the case, consideration shall be given not only to all the facts and circumstances of the employment relationship but also to whether the amount of such payments depends upon the production, sale, or use by, or the value to, the employer of the patent rights transferred by the employee. If it is determined that payments are attributable to the transfer of patent rights, and all other requirements under section 1235 are met, such payments shall be treated as proceeds derived from the sale of a patent.

(3) *Successive transfers.*—The applicability of section 1235 to transfers of undivided interest in patents, or to successive transfers of such rights, shall be determined separately with respect to each transfer. For example, X, who is a holder, and Y, who is not a holder, transfer their respective two-thirds and one-third undivided interests in a patent to Z. Assume the transfer by X qualifies under section 1235 and that X in a later transfer acquires all the rights with respect to Y's interest, including the rights to payments from Z. One-third of all the payments thereafter received by X from Z are not attributable to a transfer to which section 1235 applies.

(d) *Payor's treatment of payments in a transfer under section 1235.*—Payments made by the transferee of patent rights pursuant to a transfer

satisfying the requirements of section 1235 are payments of the purchase price for the patent rights and are not the payment of royalties.

(e) *Effective date.*—Amounts received or accrued, and payments made or accrued, during any taxable year beginning after December 31, 1953 and ending after August 16, 1954, pursuant to a transfer satisfying the requirements of section 1235, whether such transfer occurred in a taxable year to which the Internal Revenue Code of 1954 applies, or in a year prior thereto, are subject to the provisions of section 1235.

(f) *Nonresident aliens.*—For the special rule relating to nonresident aliens who have gains arising from a transfer to which section 1235 applies, see section 871 and the regulations thereunder. For withholding of tax from income of nonresident aliens, see section 1441 and the regulations thereunder [Reg. § 1.1235-1.]

☐ [*T.D. 6263, 11-5-57. Amended by T.D. 6885, 6-1-66 and T.D. 7728, 10-31-80.*]

[Reg. § 1.1235-2]

§ 1.1235-2. **Definition of terms.**—For the purposes of section 1235 and § 1.1235-1—

(a) *Patent.*—The term "patent" means a patent granted under the provisions of title 35 of the United States Code, or any foreign patent granting rights generally similar to those under a United States patent. It is not necessary that the patent or patent application for the invention be in existence if the requirements of section 1235 are otherwise met.

(b) *All substantial rights to a patent.*—(1) The term "all substantial rights to a patent" means all rights (whether or not then held by the grantor) which are of value at the time the rights to the patent (or an undivided interest therein) are transferred. The term "all substantial rights to a patent" does not include a grant of rights to a patent—

(i) Which is limited geographically within the country of issuance;

(ii) Which is limited in duration by the terms of the agreement to a period less than the remaining life of the patent;

(iii) Which grants rights to the grantee, in fields of use within trades or industries, which are less than all the rights covered by the patent, which exist and have value at the time of the grant; or

(iv) Which grants to the grantee less than all the claims or inventions covered by the patent which exist and have value at the time of the grant.

The circumstances of the whole transaction, rather than the particular terminology used in the instrument of transfer, shall be considered in determining whether or not all substantial rights to a patent are transferred in a transaction.

(2) Rights which are not considered substantial for purposes of section 1235 may be retained by the holder. Examples of such rights are:

(i) The retention by the transferor of legal title for the purpose of securing performance or payment by the transferee in a transaction involving transfer of an exclusive license to manufacture, use, and sell for the life of the patent;

(ii) The retention by the transferor of rights in the property which are not inconsistent with the passage of ownership, such as the retention of a security interest (such as a vendor's lien), or a reservation in the nature of a condition subsequent (such as a provision for forfeiture on account of nonperformance).

(3) Examples of rights which may or may not be substantial, depending upon the circumstances of the whole transaction in which rights to a patent are transferred, are:

(i) The retention by the transferor of an absolute right to prohibit sublicensing or subassignment by the transferee;

(ii) The failure to convey to the transferee the right to use or to sell the patent property.

(4) The retention of a right to terminate the transfer at will is the retention of a substantial right for the purposes of section 1235.

(c) *Undivided interest.*—A person owns an "undivided interest" in all substantial rights to a patent when he owns the same fractional share of each and every substantial right to the patent. It does not include, for example, a right to the income from a patent, or a license limited geographically, or a license which covers some, but not all, of the valuable claims or uses covered by the patent. A transfer limited in duration by the terms of the instrument to a period less than the remaining life of the patent is not a transfer of an undivided interest in all substantial rights to a patent.

(d) *Holder.*—(1) The term "holder" means any individual—

(i) Whose efforts created the patent property and who would qualify as the "original and first" inventor, or joint inventor, within the meaning of title 35 of the United States Code, or

(ii) Who has acquired his interest in the patent property in exchange for a consideration paid to the inventor in money or money's worth prior to the actual reduction of the invention to practice (see paragraph (e) of this section), provided that such individual was neither the employer of the inventor nor related to him (see paragraph (f) of this section). The requirement that such individual is neither the employer of the inventor nor related to him must be satisfied at the time when the substantive rights as to the interest to be acquired are determined, and at the time when the consideration in money or money's worth to be paid is definitely fixed. For example, if prior to the actual reduction to prac-

tice of an invention an individual who is neither the employer of the inventor nor related to him agrees to pay the inventor a sum of money definitely fixed as to amount in return for an undivided one-half interest in rights to a patent and at a later date, when such individual has become the employer of the inventor, he pays the definitely fixed sum of money pursuant to the earlier agreement, such individual will not be denied the status of a holder because of such employment relationship.

(2) Although a partnership cannot be a holder, each member of a partnership who is an individual may qualify as a holder as to his share of a patent owned by the partnership. For example, if an inventor who is a member of a partnership composed solely of individuals uses partnership property in the development of his invention with the understanding that the patent when issued will become partnership property, each of the inventor's partners during this period would qualify as a holder. If, in this example, the partnership were not composed solely of individuals, nevertheless, each of the individual partners' distributive shares of income attributable to the transfer of all substantial rights to the patent or an undivided interest therein, would be considered proceeds from the sale or exchange of a capital asset held for more than 1 year (6 months for taxable years beginning before 1977; 9 months for taxable years beginning in 1977).

(3) An individual may qualify as a holder whether or not he is in the business of making inventions or in the business of buying and selling patents.

(e) *Actual reduction to practice.*—For the purposes of determining whether an individual is a holder under paragraph (d) of this section, the term "actual reduction to practice" has the same meaning as it does under section 102(g) of title 35 of the United States Code. Generally, an invention is reduced to actual practice when it has been tested and operated successfully under operating conditions. This may occur either before or after application for a patent but cannot occur later than the earliest time that commercial exploitation of the invention occurs.

(f) *Related person.*—(1) The term "related person" means one whose relationship to another person at the time of the transfer is described in section 267(b), except that the term does not include a brother or sister, whether of the whole or the half blood. Thus, if a holder transfers all his substantial rights to a patent to his brother or sister, or both, such transfer is not to a related person.

(2) If, prior to September 3, 1958, a holder transferred all his substantial rights to a patent to a corporation in which he owned more than 50 percent in value of the outstanding stock, he is considered as having transferred such rights to a related person for the purpose of section 1235.

On the other hand, if a holder, prior to September 3, 1958, transferred all his substantial rights to a patent to a corporation in which he owned 50 percent or less in value of the outstanding stock and his brother owned the remaining stock, he is not considered as having transferred such rights to a related person since the brother relationship is to be disregarded for purposes of section 1235.

(3) If, subsequent to September 2, 1958, a holder transfers all his substantial rights to a patent to a corporation in which he owns 25 percent or more in value of the outstanding stock, he is considered as transferring such rights to a related person for the purpose of section 1235. On the other hand if a holder, subsequent to September 2, 1958, transfers all his substantial rights to a patent to a corporation in which he owns less than 25 percent in value of the outstanding stock and his brother owns the remaining stock, he is not considered as transferring such rights to a related person since the brother relationship is to be disregarded for purposes of section 1235.

(4) If a relationship described in section 267(b) exists independently of family status, the brother-sister exception, described in subparagraphs (1), (2), and (3) of this paragraph, does not apply. Thus, if a holder transfers all his substantial rights to a patent to the fiduciary of a trust of which the holder is the grantor, the holder and the fiduciary are related persons for purposes of section 1235(d). (See section 267(b)(4).) The transfer, therefore, would not qualify under section 1235(a). This result obtains whether or not the fiduciary is the brother or sister of the holder since the disqualifying relationship exists because of the grantor-fiduciary status and not because of family status. [Reg. §1.1235-2.]

☐ [T.D. 6263, 11-5-57. *Amended by T.D. 6394,* 7-1-59, *T.D. 6852,* 10-5-65 *and T.D. 7728,* 10-31-80.]

[Reg. §1.1236-1]

§1.1236-1. Dealers in securities.—(a) *Capital gains.*—Section 1236(a) provides that gain realized by a dealer in securities from the sale or exchange of a security (as defined in paragraph (c) of this section) shall not be considered as gain from the sale or exchange of a capital asset unless—

(1) The security is, before the expiration of the thirtieth day after the date of its acquisition, clearly identified in the dealer's records as a security held for investment, or if acquired before October 20, 1951, was so identified before November 20, 1951; and

(2) The security is not held by the dealer primarily for sale to customers in the ordinary course of his trade or business at any time after the identification referred to in subparagraph (1) of this paragraph has been made. Unless both of

these requirements are met, the gain is considered as gain from the sale of assets held by the dealer primarily for sale to customers in the course of his business.

(b) *Ordinary losses.*—Section 1236(b) provides that a loss sustained by a dealer in securities from the sale or exchange of a security shall not be considered a loss from the sale or exchange of property which is not a capital asset if at any time after November 19, 1951, the security has been clearly identified in the dealer's records as a security held for investment. Once a security has been identified after November 19, 1951, as being held by the dealer for investment, it shall retain that character for purposes of determining loss on its ultimate disposition, even though at the time of its disposition the dealer holds it primarily for sale to his customers in the ordinary course of business. However, section 1236 has no application to the extent that section 582(c) applies to losses of banks.

(c) *Definitions.*—(1) *Security.*—For the purposes of this section, the term "security" means any share of stock in any corporation, any certificate of stock or interest in any corporation, any note, bond, debenture, or other evidence of indebtedness, or any evidence of any interest in, or right to subscribe to or purchase, any of the foregoing.

(2) *Dealer in securities.*—For definition of a "dealer in securities," see the regulations under section 471.

(d) *Identification of security in dealer's records.*—(1) A security is clearly identified in the dealer's records as a security held for investment when there is an accounting separation of the security from other securities, as by making appropriate entries in the dealer's books of account to distinguish the security from inventories and to designate it as an investment and by (i) indicating with such entries, to the extent feasible, the individual serial number of, or other characteristic symbol imprinted upon, the individual security, or (ii) adopting any other method of identification satisfactory to the Commissioner.

(2) In computing the 30-day period prescribed by section 1236(a), the first day of the period is the day following the date of acquisition. Thus, in the case of a security acquired on March 18, 1957, the 30-day period expires at midnight on April 17, 1957. [Reg. §1.1236-1.]

☐ [T.D. 6253, 9-25-57. *Amended by T.D. 6726,* 4-28-64.]

[Reg. §1.1237-1]

§1.1237-1. Real property subdivided for sale.—(a) *General rule.*—(1) *Introductory.*—This section provides a special rule for determining whether the taxpayer holds real property primarily for sale to customers in the ordinary course of his business under section 1221(1). This rule is to permit taxpayers qualifying under it to sell real estate from a single tract held for investment without the income being treated as ordinary income merely because of subdividing the tract or of active efforts to sell it. The rule is not applicable to dealers in real estate or to corporations, except a corporation making such sales in a taxable year beginning after December 31, 1954, if such corporation qualifies under the provisions of paragraph (c)(5)(iv) of this section.

(2) *When subdividing and selling activities are to be disregarded.*—When its conditions are met, section 1237 provides that if there is no other substantial evidence that a taxpayer holds real estate primarily for sale to customers in the ordinary course of his business, he shall not be considered a real estate dealer holding it primarily for sale merely because he has (i) subdivided the tract into lots (or parcels) and (ii) engaged in advertising, promotion, selling activities or the use of sales agents in connection with the sale of lots in such subdivision. Such subdividing and selling activities shall be disregarded in determining the purpose for which the taxpayer held real property sold from a subdivision whenever it is the only substantial evidence indicating that the taxpayer has ever held the real property sold primarily for sale to customers in the ordinary course of his business.

(3) *When subdividing and selling activities are to be taken into account.*—When other substantial evidence tends to show that the taxpayer held real property for sale to customers in the ordinary course of his business, his activities in connection with the subdivision and sale of the property sold shall be taken into account in determining the purpose for which the taxpayer held both the subdivided property and any other real property. For example, such other evidence may consist of the taxpayer's selling activities in connection with other property in prior years during which he was engaged in subdividing or selling activities with respect to the subdivided tract, his intention in prior years (or at the time of acquiring the property subdivided) to hold the tract primarily for sale in his business, his subdivision of other tracts in the same year, his holding other real property for sale to customers in the same year, or his construction of a permanent real estate office which he could use in selling other real property. On the other hand, if the only evidence of the taxpayer's purpose in holding real property consisted of not more than one of the following, in the year in question, such fact would not be considered substantial other evidence:

(i) Holding a real estate dealer's license;

(ii) Selling other real property which was clearly investment property;

(iii) Acting as a salesman for a real estate dealer, but without any financial interest in the business; or

(iv) Mere ownership of other vacant real property without engaging in any selling activity whatsoever with respect to it.

If more than one of the above exists, the circumstances may or may not constitute substantial evidence that the taxpayer held real property for sale in his business, depending upon the particular facts in each case.

(4) *Section 1237 not exclusive.*—(i) The rule in section 1237 is not exclusive in its application. Section 1237 has no application in determining whether or not real property is held by a taxpayer primarily for sale in his business if any requirement under the section is not met. Also, even though the conditions of section 1237 are met, the rules of section 1237 are not applicable if without regard to section 1237 the real property sold would not have been considered real property held primarily for sale to customers in the ordinary course of his business. Thus, the district director may at all times conclude from convincing evidence that the taxpayer held the real property solely as an investment. Furthermore, whether or not the conditions of section 1237 are met, the section has no application to losses realized upon the sale of realty from subdivided property.

(ii) If, owing solely to the application of section 1237, the real property sold is deemed not to have been held primarily for sale in the ordinary course of business, any gain realized upon such sale shall be treated as ordinary income to the extent provided in section 1237(b)(1) and (2) and paragraph (e) of this section. Any additional gain realized upon the sale shall be treated as gain arising from the sale of a capital asset or, if the circumstances so indicate, as gain arising from the sale of real property used in the trade or business as defined in section 1231(b)(1). For the relationship between sections 1237 and 1231, see paragraph (f) of this section.

(5) *Principal conditions of qualification.*—Before section 1237 applies, the taxpayer must meet three basic conditions, more fully explained later: He cannot have held any part of the tract at any time previously for sale in the ordinary course of his business, nor in the year of sale held any other real estate for sale to customers; he cannot make substantial improvements on the tract which increase the value of the lot sold substantially; and he must have owned the property 5 years, unless he inherited it. However, the taxpayer may make certain improvements if they are necessary to make the property marketable if he elects neither to add their cost to the basis of the property, or of any other property, nor to deduct the cost as an expense, and he has held the property at least 10 years. If the requirements of section 1237 are met, gain (but not more than 5 percent of the selling price of each lot) shall be treated as ordinary income in and after the year in which the sixth lot or parcel is sold.

(b) *Disqualification arising from holding real property primarily for sale.*—(1) *General rule.*—Section 1237 does not apply to any transaction if the taxpayer either—

(i) Held the lot sold (or the tract of which it was a part) primarily for sale in the ordinary course of his business in a prior year, or

(ii) Holds other real property primarily for sale in the ordinary course of his business in the same year in which such lot is sold.

Where either of these elements is present, section 1237 shall be disregarded in determining the proper treatment of any gain arising from such sale.

(2) *Method of applying general rule.*—For purposes of this paragraph, in determining whether the lot sold was held primarily for sale in the ordinary course of business in a prior year, the principles of section 1237 shall be applied, whether or not section 1237 was effective for such prior year, if the sale of the lot occurs after December 31, 1953, or, in the case of a corporation meeting the requirements of paragraph (c)(5)(iv) of this section, if the sale of the lot occurs in a taxable year beginning after December 31, 1954. Whether, on the other hand, the taxpayer holds other real property for sale in the ordinary course of his business in the same year such lot was sold shall be determined without regard to the application of section 1237 to such other real property.

(3) *Attribution rules with respect to the holding of property.*—The taxpayer is considered as holding property which he owns individually, jointly, or as a member of a partnership. He is not generally considered as holding property owned by members of his family, an estate or trust, or a corporation. See, however, paragraph (c)(5)(iv)(c) of this section for an exception to this rule. The purpose for which a prior owner held the lot or tract, or his activities, are immaterial except to the extent they indicate the purpose for which the taxpayer has held the lot or tract. See paragraph (d) of this section for rules relating to the determination of the period for which the property is held. The principles of this subparagraph may be illustrated by the following example:

Example. A dealer in real property held a tract of land for sale to customers in the ordinary course of his business for 5 years. He then made a gift of it to his son. As a result of the operation of section 1223(2) the son will have held the property for the period of time required by section 1237. However, he will not qualify for the benefits of section 1237 because, there being no evidence to the contrary, the circumstances involved establish that the son holds the property for sale to customers, as did his father.

(c) *Disqualification arising from substantial improvements.*—(1) *General rule.*—Section 1237 will not apply if the taxpayer or certain others make improvements on the tract which are substantial and which substantially increase the value of the lot sold. Certain improvements are not substantial within the meaning of section 1237(a)(2) if they are necessary to make the lot marketable at the prevailing local price and meet the other conditions of section 1237(b)(3). See subparagraph (5) of this paragraph.

(2) *Improvements made or deemed to be made by the taxpayer.*—Certain improvements made by the taxpayer or made under a contract of sale between the taxpayer and the buyer make section 1237 inapplicable.

(i) For the purposes of section 1237(a)(2) the taxpayer is deemed to have made any improvements on the tract while he held it which are made by:

(a) The taxpayer's whole or half brothers and sisters, spouse, ancestors, and lineal descendants.

(b) A corporation controlled by the taxpayer. A corporation is controlled by the taxpayer if he controls, as the result of direct ownership, constructive ownership, or otherwise, more than 50 percent of the corporation's voting stock.

(c) A partnership of which the taxpayer was a member at the time the improvements were made.

(d) A lessee if the improvement takes the place of a payment of rental income. See section 109 and the regulations thereunder.

(e) A Federal, State, or local government, or political subdivision thereof, if the improvement results in an increase in the taxpayer's basis for the property, as it would, for example, from a special tax assessment for paving streets.

(ii) The principles of subdivision (i) of this subparagraph may be illustrated by the following example:

Example. A held a tract of land for 3 years during which he made substantial improvements thereon which substantially enhanced the value of every lot on the tract. A then made a gift of the tract to his son. The son made no further improvements on the tract, but held it for 3 years and then sold several lots therefrom. The son is not entitled to the benefits of section 1237 since under section 1237(a)(2) he is deemed to have made the substantial improvements made by his father, and under section 1223(2) he is treated as having held the property for the period during which his father held it. Thus, the disqualifying improvements are deemed to have been made by the son while the tract was held by him. See paragraph (d) of this section for rules relating to the determination of the period for which the property is held.

(iii) The taxpayer is also charged with making any improvements made pursuant to a contract of sale entered into between the taxpayer and the buyer. Therefore, the buyer, as well as the taxpayer, may make improvements which prevent the application of section 1237.

(a) If a contract of sale obligates either the taxpayer or the buyer to make a substantial improvement which would substantially increase the value of the lot, the taxpayer may not claim the application of section 1237 unless the obligation to improve the lot ceases (for any reason other than that the improvement has been made) before or within the period, prescribed by section 6511, within which the taxpayer may file a claim for credit or refund of an overpayment of his tax on the gain from the sale of the lot. The following example illustrates this rule:

Example. In 1956, A sells several lots from a tract he has subdivided for sale. Section 1237 would apply to the sales of these lots except that in the contract of sale A agreed to install sewers, hard surface roads, and other utilities which would increase the value of the lots substantially. If in 1957, instead of requiring the improvements, the buyer releases A from this obligation, A may then claim the application of section 1237 to the sale of lots in 1956 in computing his income tax for 1956, since the period of limitations in which A may file a claim for credit or refund of an overpayment of his 1956 income tax has not expired.

(b) An improvement is made pursuant to a contract if the contract imposes an obligation on either party to make the improvement, but not if the contract merely places restrictions on the improvements, if any, either party may make. The following example illustrates this rule:

Example. B sells several lots from a tract which he has subdivided. Each contract of sale prohibits the purchaser from building any structure on his lot except a personal residence costing $15,000 or more. Even if the purchasers build such residences, that does not preclude B from applying section 1237 to the sales of such lots, since the contracts did not obligate the purchasers to make any improvements.

(iv) Improvements made by a bona fide lessee (other than as rent) or by others not described in section 1237(a)(2) do not preclude the use of section 1237.

(3) *When improvements substantially enhance the value of the lot sold.*—Before a substantial improvement will preclude the use of section 1237, it must substantially enhance the value of the lot sold.

(i) The increase in value to be considered is only the increase attributable to the improvement or improvements. Other changes in the market price of the lot, not arising from improvements made by the taxpayer, shall be disregarded. The difference between the value of the lot, including improvements, when the improvement has been completed and an appraisal of its value if unimproved at that time, will disclose the value added by the improvements.

(ii) Whether improvements have substantially increased the value of a lot depends upon the circumstances in each case. If improvements increase the value of a lot by 10 percent or less, such increase will not be considered as substantial, but if the value of the lot is increased by more than 10 percent, then all relevant factors must be considered to determine whether, under such circumstances, the increase is substantial.

(iii) Improvements may increase the value of some lots in a tract without equally affecting other lots in the same tract. Only the lots whose value was substantially increased are ineligible for application of the rule established by section 1237.

(4) *When an improvement is substantial.*—To prevent the application of section 1237, the improvement itself must be substantial in character. Among the improvements considered substantial are shopping centers, other commercial or residential buildings, and the installation of hard surface roads or utilities such as sewers, water, gas, or electric lines. On the other hand a temporary structure used as a field office, surveying, filling, draining, leveling and clearing operations, and the construction of minimum all-weather access roads, including gravel roads where required by the climate, are not substantial improvements.

(5) *Special rules relating to substantial improvements.*—Under certain conditions a taxpayer, including a corporation to which subdivision (iv) of this subparagraph applies, may obtain the benefits of section 1237 whether or not substantial improvements have been made. In addition, an individual taxpayer may, under certain circumstances, elect to have substantial improvements treated as necessary and not substantial.

(i) *When an improvement is not considered substantial.*—An improvement will not be considered substantial if all of the following conditions are met:

(a) The taxpayer has held the property for 10 years. The full 10-year period must elapse, whether or not the taxpayer inherited the property. Although the taxpayer must hold the property 10 years, he need not hold it for 10 years after subdividing it. See paragraph (d) of this section for rules relating to the determination of the period for which the property is held.

(b) The improvement consists of the building or installation of water, sewer, or drainage facilities (either surface, sub-surface, or both) or roads, including hard surface roads, curbs, and gutters.

(c) The district director with whom the taxpayer must file his return is satisfied that, without such improvement, the lot sold would not have brought the prevailing local price for similar building sites.

(d) The taxpayer elects, as provided in subdivision (iii) of this subparagraph, not to adjust the basis of the lot sold or any other property held by him for any part of the cost of such improvement attributable to such lot and not to deduct any part of such cost as an expense.

(ii) *Meaning of "similar building site"*.—A "similar building site" is any real property in the immediate vicinity whose size, terrain, and other characteristics are comparable to the taxpayer's property. For the purpose of determining whether a tract is marketable at the prevailing local price for similar building sites, the taxpayer shall furnish the district director with sufficient evidence to enable him to compare (a) the value of the taxpayer's property in an unimproved state with (b) the amount for which similar building sites, improved by the installation of water, sewer, or drainage facilities or roads, have recently been sold, reduced by the present cost of such improvements. Such comparison may be made and expressed in terms of dollars per square foot, dollars per acre, or dollars per front foot, or in any other suitable terms depending upon the practice generally followed by real estate dealers in the taxpayer's locality. The taxpayer shall also furnish evidence, where possible, of the best bona fide offer received for the tract or a lot thereof just before making the improvement, to assist the district director in determining the value of the tract or lot if it had been sold in its unimproved state. The operation of this subdivision and subdivision (i) of this subparagraph may be illustrated by the following examples:

Example (1). A has been offered $500 per acre for a tract without roads, water, or sewer facilities which he has owned for 15 years. The adjacent tract has been subdivided and improved with water facilities and hard surface roads, and has sold for $4,000 per acre. The estimated cost of roads and water facilities on the adjacent tract is $2,500 per acre. The prevailing local price for similar building sites in the vicinity would be $1,500 per acre (i.e., $4,000 less $2,500). If A installed roads and water facilities at a cost of $2,500 per acre, his tract would sell for approximately $4,000 per acre. Under section 1237 (b)(3) the installation of roads and water facilities does not constitute a substantial improvement if A elects to disregard the cost of such improvements ($2,500 per acre) in computing his cost or other basis for the lots sold from the tract, and in computing his basis for any other property owned by him.

Example (2). Assume the same facts as in example (1) of this subdivision, except that A can obtain $1,600 per acre for his property without improvements. The installation of any substantial improvements would not constitute a necessary improvement under section 1237(b)(3), since the prevailing local price could have been obtained without any improvement.

Example (3). Assume the same facts as in Example (1) of this subdivision, except that the adjacent tract has also been improved with sewer facilities, the present cost of which is $1,200 per acre. The installation of the substantial improvements would not constitute a necessary improvement under section 1237(b)(3) on A's part, since the prevailing local price ($4,000 less the sum of $1,200 plus $2,500, or $300) could have been obtained by A without any improvement.

(iii) *Manner of making election*.—The election required by section 1237(b)(3)(C) shall be made as follows:

(a) The taxpayer shall submit:

(1) A plat showing the subdivision and all improvements attributable to him.

(2) A list of all improvements to the tract, showing:

(i) The cost of such improvements.

(ii) Which of the improvements, without regard to the election, he considers "substantial" and which he considers not "substantial."

(iii) Those improvements which are substantial to which the election is to apply, with a fair allocation of their cost to each lot they affect, and the amount by which they have increased the values of such lots.

(iv) The date on which each lot was acquired and its basis for determining gain or loss, exclusive of the cost of any improvements listed in subdivision (iii) of this subdivision.

(3) A statement that he will neither deduct as an expense nor add to the basis of any lot sold, or of any other property, any portion of the cost of any substantial improvement which substantially increased the value of any lot in the tract and which either he listed pursuant to subdivision (2)(iii) of this subdivision or which the district director deems substantial.

(b) The election and the information required under subdivision (a) of this subdivision shall be submitted to the district director—

(1) With the taxpayer's income tax return for the taxable year in which the lots subject to the election were sold, or

(2) In the case of a return filed prior to August 14, 1957, either with a timely claim for refund, where the benefits of section 1237 have not been claimed on such return, or, independently, before November 13, 1957, where such benefits have been claimed, or

(3) If there is an obligation to make disqualifying improvements outstanding when the taxpayer files his return, with a formal claim for refund at the time of the release of the obligation, if it is then still possible to file a timely claim.

(c) Once made, the election as to the necessary improvement costs attributable to any lot sold shall be irrevocable and binding on the taxpayer unless the district director assesses an

Rules for Determining Capital Gains and Losses
53,481
See p. 20,601 for regulations not amended to reflect law changes

income tax as to such lot as if it were held for sale in the ordinary course of taxpayer's business. Under such circumstances, in computing gain, the cost or other basis shall be computed without regard to section 1237.

(iv) *Exceptions with respect to "necessary" improvements and certain corporations.*—For taxable years beginning after December 31, 1954, individual taxpayers and certain corporations may obtain the benefits of section 1237 without complying with the provisions of subdivisions (i)(c) and (d), (ii), and (iii) of this subparagraph if the requirements of section 1237 are otherwise met and if—

(a) The property in question was acquired by the taxpayer through the foreclosure of a lien thereon,

(b) The lien foreclosed secured the payment of an indebtedness to the taxpayer or (in the case of a corporation) secured the payment of an indebtedness to a creditor who has transferred the foreclosure bid to the taxpayer in exchange for all of the stock of the corporation and other consideration, and

(c) In the case of a corporate taxpayer, no shareholder of the corporation holds real property for sale to customers in the ordinary course of his trade or business or holds a controlling interest in another corporation which actually so holds real property, or which, but for the application of this subdivision, would be considered to so hold real property. Thus, in the case of such property, it is not necessary for the taxpayer to satisfy the district director that the property would not have brought the prevailing local price without improvements or to elect not to add the cost of the improvements to his basis. In addition, if 80 percent or more of the real property owned by a taxpayer is property to which this subdivision applies, the requirements of (a) and (b) of this subdivision need not be met with respect to property adjacent to such property which is also owned by the taxpayer.

(d) *Holding period required.*—(1) *General rules.*—To apply section 1237, the taxpayer must either have inherited the lot sold or have held it for 5 years. Generally, the provisions of section 1223 are applicable in determining the period for which the taxpayer has held the property. The provisions of this subparagraph may be illustrated by the following examples:

Example (1). A held a tract of land for 3 years under circumstances otherwise qualifying for section 1237 treatment. He made a gift of the tract to B at a time when the fair market value of the tract exceeded A's basis for the tract. B held the tract for 2 more years under similar circumstances. B then sold 4 lots from the tract. B is entitled to the benefits of section 1237 since under section 1223(2) he held the lots for 5 years and all the other requirements of section 1237 are met.

Example (2). C purchased all the stock in a corporation in 1955. The corporation purchased an unimproved tract of land in 1957. In 1961 the corporation was liquidated under section 333 and C acquired the tract of land. For purposes of section 1237, C's holding period commenced on the date the corporation actually acquired the land in 1957 and not on the date C purchased the stock.

(2) *Rules relating to property acquired upon death.*—If the taxpayer inherited the property there is no 5-year holding period required under section 1237. However, any holding period required by any other provision of the Code, such as section 1222, is nevertheless applicable. For purposes of section 1237, neither the survivor's one-half of community property, nor property acquired by survivorship in a joint tenancy, is property acquired by devise or inheritance. The holding period for the surviving joint tenant begins on the date the property was originally acquired.

(e) *Tax consequences if section 1237 applies.*—(1) *Introductory.*—Where there is no substantial evidence other than subdivision and related selling activities that real property is held for sale in the ordinary course of taxpayer's business and section 1237 applies, section 1237(b)(1) provides a special rule for computing taxable gain. For the relationship between sections 1237 and 1231, see paragraph (f) of this section.

(2) *Characterization of gain and its relation to selling expenses.*—(i) When the taxpayer has sold less than 6 lots or parcels from the same tract up to the end of his taxable year, the entire gain will be capital gain. (Where the land is used in a trade or business, see paragraph (f) of this section.) In computing the number of lots or parcels sold, two or more contiguous lots sold to a single buyer in a single sale will be counted as only one parcel. The following example illustrates this rule:

Example. A meets all the conditions of section 1237 in subdividing and selling a single tract. In 1956 he sells 4 lots to B, C, D, and E. In the same year F buys 3 adjacent lots. Since A has sold only 5 lots or parcels from the tract, any gain A realizes on the sales will be capital gain.

(ii) If the taxpayer has sold the sixth lot or parcel from the same tract within the taxable year, then the amount, if any, by which 5 percent of the selling price of each lot exceeds the expenses incurred in connection with its sale or exchange, shall, to the extent it represents gain, be ordinary income. Any part of the gain not treated as ordinary income will be treated as capital gain. (Where the land is used in a trade or business, see paragraph (f) of this section.) Five percent of the selling price of each lot sold from the tract in the taxable year the sixth lot is sold and thereafter is, to the extent it represents gain, considered ordinary income. However, all ex-

53,482
      Rules for Determining Capital Gains and Losses
See p. 20,601 for regulations not amended to reflect law changes

penses of sale of the lot are to be deducted first from the 5 percent of the gain which would otherwise be considered ordinary income, and any remainder of such expenses shall reduce the gain upon the sale or exchange which would otherwise be considered capital gain. Such expenses cannot be deducted as ordinary business expenses from other income. The 5-percent rule applies to all lots sold from the tract in the year the sixth lot or parcel is sold. Thus, if the taxpayer sells the first 6 lots of a single tract in one year, 5 percent of the selling price of each lot sold shall be treated as ordinary income and reduced by the selling expenses. On the other hand, if the taxpayer sells the first 3 lots of a single tract in 1955, and the next 3 lots in 1956, only the gain realized from the sales made in 1956 shall be so treated. For the effect of a 5-year interval between sales, see paragraph (g)(2) of this section. The operation of this subdivision may be illustrated by the following examples:

Example (1). Assume the selling price of the sixth lot of a tract is $10,000, the basis of the lot in the hands of the taxpayer is $5,000, and the expenses of sale are $750. The amount of gain realized by the taxpayer is $4,250, of which the amount of ordinary income attributable to the sale is zero, computed as follows:

Selling price		$10,000
Basis		5,000
Excess over basis		5,000
5 percent of selling price	$500	
Expenses of sale	750	
Amount of gain realized treated as ordinary income		0
Excess over basis		5,000
5 percent of selling price	500	
Excess of expenses over 5 percent of selling price	250	750
Amount of gain realized from sale of property not held for sale in ordinary course of business		$4,250

Example (2). Assume the same facts as in Example (1), except that the expenses of sale of such sixth lot are $300. The amount of gain realized by the taxpayer is $4,700, of which the amount of ordinary income attributable to the sale is $200, computed as follows:

Selling price		$10,000
Basis		5,000
Excess over basis		5,000
5 percent of selling price	$500	
Expenses of sale	300	
Amount of gain realized treated as ordinary income		$200
Excess over basis		5,000
5 percent of selling price	$500	
Excess of expenses over 5 percent of selling price	0	500
Amount of gain realized from sale of property not held for sale in ordinary course of business		$4,500

(iii) In the case of an exchange, the term "selling price" shall mean the fair market value of property received plus any sum of money received in exchange for the lot. See section 1031 for those exchanges in which no gain is recognized. For the purpose of subsections (b) and (c) of section 1237 and paragraphs (e) and (g) of this section, an exchange shall be treated as a sale or exchange whether or not gain or loss is recognized with respect to such exchange.

(f) *Relationship of section 1237 and section 1231.*—Application of section 1237 to a sale of real property may, in some cases, result in the property being treated as real property used in the trade or business, as described in section 1231(b)(1). Thus, assuming section 1237 is otherwise applicable, if the lot sold would be considered property described in section 1231(b)(1) except for the fact that the taxpayer subdivided the tract of which it was a part, then evidence of such subdivision and connected sales activities shall be disregarded and the lot sold shall be considered real property used in the trade or business. Under such circumstances, any gain or loss realized from the sale shall be treated as gain or loss arising from the sale of real property used in the trade or business.

(g) *Definition of "tract".*—(1) *Aggregation of properties.*—For the purposes of section 1237, the term "tract" means either (i) a single piece of real property or (ii) two or more pieces of real property if they were contiguous at any time while held by the taxpayer, or would have been contiguous but for the interposition of a road, street, railroad, stream, or similar property. Properties are contiguous if their boundaries meet at one or more points. The single piece or contiguous properties need not have been conveyed by a single deed. The taxpayer may have assembled them over a period of time and may hold them separately, jointly, or as a partner, or in any combination of such forms of ownership.

Reg. §1.1237-1(e)(2)(iii)

(2) *When a subdivision will be considered a new tract.*—If the taxpayer sells or exchanges no lots from the tract for a period of 5 years after the sale or exchange of at least 1 lot in the tract, then the remainder of the tract shall be deemed a new tract for the purpose of counting the number of lots sold from the same tract under section 1237(b)(1). The pieces in the new tract need not be contiguous. The 5-year period is measured between the dates of the sales or exchanges.

(h) *Effective date.*—This section shall apply only to gain realized on sales made after December 31, 1953, or, in the case of a person meeting the requirements of paragraph (c)(5)(iv) of this section, if the sale of the lot occurs in a taxable year beginning after December 31, 1954. Pursuant to section 7851 (a)(1)(C), the regulations prescribed in this section (other than subdivision (iv) of paragraph (c)(5)) shall also apply to taxable years beginning before January 1, 1954, and ending after December 31, 1953, and to taxable years beginning after December 31, 1953, and ending before August 17, 1954, although such years are subject to the Internal Revenue Code of 1939. Irrespective of whether the taxable year involved is subject to the Internal Revenue Code of 1939 or the Internal Revenue Code of 1954, sales or exchanges made before January 1, 1954, shall be taken into account to determine whether: (1) No sales or exchanges have been made for 5 years, under section 1237(c), and (2) more than 5 lots or parcels have been sold or exchanged from the same tract, under Section 1237(b)(1). Thus, if the taxpayer sold 5 lots from a single tract in 1950, and another lot is sold in 1954, the lot sold in 1954 constitutes the "sixth lot" sold from the original tract. On the other hand, if the first 5 lots were sold in 1948, the sale made in 1954 shall be deemed to have been made from a new tract. [Reg. § 1.1237-1.]

☐ [*T.D.* 6247, 8-13-57.]

[Reg. §1.1238-1]

§1.1238-1. Amortization in excess of depreciation.—(a) *In general.*—Section 1238 provides that if a taxpayer is entitled to a deduction for amortization of an emergency facility under section 168, and if the facility is later sold or exchanged, any gain realized shall be considered as ordinary income to the extent the amortization deduction exceeds normal depreciation. Thus, under section 1238 gain from a sale or exchange of property shall be considered as ordinary income to the extent that its adjusted basis is less than its adjusted basis would be if it were determined without regard to section 168. If an entire facility is certified under section 168(e), the taxpayer may use allowances for depreciation based on any rate and method which would have been proper if the basis of the facility were not subject to amortization under section 168, in determining what the adjusted basis of the facility would be if it were determined without regard to sec-

tion 168. If only a portion of a facility is certified under section 168(e), allowances for depreciation based on the rate and method properly used with respect to the uncertified part of the facility are used in determining what the adjusted basis of the facility would be if it were determined without regard to section 168. The principles of this paragraph may be illustrated by the following examples:

Example (1). On December 31, 1954, a taxpayer making his income tax returns on a calendar year basis acquires at a cost of $20,000 an emergency facility (used in his business) 50 percent of the adjusted basis of which has been certified under section 168(e). The facility would normally have a useful life of 20 years and a salvage value of $2,000 allocable equally between the certified and uncertified portions. Under section 168 the taxpayer elects to begin the 60-month amortization period on January 1, 1955. He takes amortization deductions with respect to the certified portion in the amount of $4,000 for the years 1955 and 1956 (24 months). On December 31, 1956, he sells the facility for a price of $19,000 which is allocable equally between the certified and uncertified portions. The adjusted basis of the certified portion on that date is $6,000 ($10,000 cost, less $4,000 amortization). With respect to the uncertified portion, the straight line method of depreciation is used and a deduction for depreciation in the amount of $450 is claimed and allowed for the year 1955. The adjusted basis of the uncertified portion on January 1, 1956, is $9,550 ($10,000 cost, less $450 depreciation). The depreciation allowance for the uncertified portion for the year 1956 would be limited to $50, the amount by which the adjusted basis of such portion at the beginning of the year exceeded its aliquot portion of the sales price. Thus, on December 31, 1956, the adjusted basis of the uncertified portion would be $9,500. Without regard to section 168, and using the rate and method the taxpayer properly applied to the uncertified portion of the facility, the adjusted basis of the certified portion on December 31, 1956, would be $9,500, computed in the same manner as the adjusted basis of the uncertified portion. The difference between the facility's actual adjusted basis ($15,500) and its adjusted basis determined without regard to section 168 ($19,000), is $3,500. Accordingly, the entire $3,500 gain on the sale of the facility ($19,000 sale price, less $15,500 adjusted basis) is treated as ordinary income.

Example (2). Assume that the entire facility in example (1) had been certified under section 168(e) and that, therefore, the adjusted basis of the facility on December 31, 1956, is $12,000. Assume further that the taxpayer adopts straight line depreciation as a proper method of depreciation for determining the adjusted basis of the facility without regard to section 168. Thus, the adjusted basis, without regard to section 168, would be $19,000. This amount is $7,000 more than the $12,000 adjusted basis under section

168. Hence, the entire $7,000 gain on the sale of the facility ($19,000 sale price less $12,000 adjusted basis) is treated as ordinary income.

(b) *Substituted basis.*—If a taxpayer acquires other property in an exchange for an emergency facility with respect to which amortization deductions have been allowed or allowable, and if the basis in his hands of the other property is determined by reference to the basis of the emergency facility, then the basis of the other property is determined with regard to section 168, and therefore the provisions of section 1238 apply with respect to gain realized on a subsequent sale or exchange of the other property. The provisions of section 1238 also apply to gain realized on the sale or exchange of an emergency facility (or other property acquired, as described in the preceding sentence, in exchange for an emergency facility) by a taxpayer in whose hands the basis of the facility (or other property) is determined by reference to its basis in the hands of another person to whom deductions were allowable or allowed with respect to the facility under section 168. [Reg. §1.1238-1.]

☐ [*T.D.* 6253, 9-25-57. *Amended by T.D.* 6825, 6-1-65.]

[Reg. §1.1239-1]

§1.1239-1. Gain from sale or exchange of depreciable property between certain related taxpayers after October 4, 1976.—(a) *In general.*—In the case of a sale or exchange of property, directly or indirectly, between related persons after October 4, 1976 (other than a sale or exchange made under a binding contract entered into on or before that date), any gain recognized by the transferor shall be treated as ordinary income if such property is, in the hands of the transferee, subject to the allowance for depreciation provided in section 167. This rule also applies to property which would be subject to the allowance for depreciation provided in section 167 except that the purchaser has elected a different form of deduction, such as those allowed under sections 169, 188, and 191.

(b) *Related persons.*—For purposes of paragraph (a), the term "related persons" means—

(1) A husband and wife,

(2) An individual and a corporation 80 percent or more in value of the outstanding stock of which is owned, directly or indirectly, by or for such individual, or

(3) Two or more corporations 80 percent or more in value of the outstanding stock of each of which is owned, directly or indirectly, by or for the same individual.

(c) *Rules of construction.*—(1) *Husband and wife.*—For purposes of paragraph (b)(1), if on the date of the sale or exchange a taxpayer is legally separated from his spouse under an interlocutory decree of divorce, the taxpayer and his spouse shall not be treated as husband and wife, provided the sale or exchange is made pursuant to the decree and the decree subsequently becomes final. Thus, if pursuant to an interlocutory decree of divorce, an individual transfers depreciable property to his spouse and, because of this section, the gain recognized on the transfer of the property is treated as ordinary income, the individual may, if the interlocutory decree becomes final after his tax return has been filed, file a claim for a refund.

(2) *Sales between commonly controlled corporations.*—In general, in the case of a sale or exchange of depreciable property between related corporations (within the meaning of paragraph (b)(3) of this section), gain which is treated as ordinary income by reason of this section shall be taxable to the transferor corporation rather than to a controlling shareholder. However, such gain shall be treated as ordinary income taxable to a controlling shareholder rather than the transferor corporation if the transferor corporation is used by a controlling shareholder as a mere conduit to make a sale to another controlled corporation, or the entity of the corporate transferor is otherwise properly disregarded for tax purposes. Sales between two or more corporations that are related within the meaning of paragraph (b)(3) of this section may also be subject to the rules of section 482 (relating to allocation of income between or among organizations, trades, or businesses which are commonly owned or controlled), and to rules requiring constructive dividend treatment to the controlling shareholder in appropriate circumstances.

(3) *Relationship determination for transfers made after January 6, 1983—taxpayer and an 80-percent owned entity.*—For purposes of paragraph (b)(2) of this section with respect to transfers made after January 6, 1983—

(i) If the transferor is an entity, the transferee and such entity are related if the entity is an 80-percent owned entity with respect to such transferee either immediately before or immediately after the sale or exchange of depreciable property, and

(ii) If the transferor is not an entity, the transferee and such transferor are related if the transferee is an 80-percent owned entity with respect to such transferor immediately after the sale or exchange of depreciable property.

(4) *Relationship determination for transfers made after January 6, 1983—two 80-percent owned entities.*—For purposes of paragraph (b)(3) of this section, with respect to transfers made after January 6, 1983, two entities are related if the same shareholder both owns 80 percent or more in value of the stock of the transferor before the sale or exchange of depreciable property and owns 80 percent or more in value of the stock of the transferee immediately after the sale or exchange of depreciable property.

(5) *Ownership of stock.*—For purposes of determining the ownership of stock under this section, the constructive ownership rules of section 318 shall be applied, except that section 318(a)(2)(C) (relating to attribution of stock ownership from a corporation) and section 318(a)(3)(C) (relating to attribution of stock ownership to a corporation) shall be applied without regard to the 50-percent limitation contained therein. The application of the constructive ownership rules of section 318 to section 1239 is illustrated by the following examples:

Example (1). A, an individual, owns 79 percent of the stock (by value) of Corporation X, and a trust for A's children owns the remaining 21 percent of the stock. A's children are deemed to own the stock owned for their benefit by the trust in proportion to their actuarial interests in the trust (section 318(a)(2)(B)). A, in turn, constructively owns the stock so deemed to be owned by his children (section 318(a)(1)(A)(ii)). Thus, A is treated as owning all the stock of Corporation X, and any gain A recognizes from the sale of depreciable property to Corporation X is treated under section 1239 as ordinary income.

Example (2). Y Corporation owns 100% in value of the stock of Z Corporation. Y Corporation sells depreciable property at a gain to Z Corporation. P and his daughter, D, own 80 percent in value of the Y Corporation stock. Under the constructive ownership rules of section 318, as applied to section 1239, P and D are each considered to own the stock in Z Corporation owned by Y Corporation. Also, P and D are each considered to own the stock in Y Corporation owned by the other. As a result, both P and D constructively own 80 percent or more in value of the stock of both Y and Z Corporations. Thus, the sale between Y and Z is governed by section 1239 and produces ordinary income to Y. [Reg. §1.1239-1.]

☐ *[T.D. 7569, 11-2-78. Amended by T.D. 8106, 11-25-86.]*

[Reg. §1.1239-2]

§1.1239-2. Gain from sale or exchange of depreciable property between certain related taxpayers on or before October 4, 1976.—Section 1239 provides in general that any gain from the sale or exchange of depreciable property between a husband and wife or between an individual and a controlled corporation on or before October 4, 1976 (and in the case of a sale or exchange occurring after that date if made under a binding contract entered into on or before that date), shall be treated as ordinary income. Thus, any gain recognized to the transferor from a sale or exchange after May 3, 1951, and on or before October 4, 1976 (or thereafter if pursuant to a binding contract entered into on or before that date), directly or indirectly, between a husband and wife or between an individual and a controlled corporation, of property which, in the hands of the transferee, is property of a character

subject to an allowance for depreciation provided in section 167 (including such property on which a deduction for amortization is allowable under sections 168 and 169) shall be considered as gain from the sale or exchange of property which is neither a capital asset nor property described in section 1231. For the purpose of section 1239, a corporation is controlled when more than 80 percent in value of all outstanding stock of the corporation is beneficially owned by the taxpayer, his spouse, and his minor children and minor grandchildren. For the purpose of this section, the terms "children" and "grandchildren" include legally adopted children and their children. The provisions of section 1239(a)(2) are applicable whether property is transferred from a corporation to a shareholder or from a shareholder to a corporation. [Reg. §1.1239-2.]

☐ *[T.D. 6253, 9-25-57. Redesignated and amended by T.D. 7569, 11-2-78.]*

[Reg. §1.1241-1]

§1.1241-1. Cancellation of lease or distributor's agreement.—(a) *In general.*—Section 1241 provides that proceeds received by lessees or distributors from the cancellation of leases or of certain distributorship agreements are considered as amounts received in exchange therefor. Section 1241 applies to leases of both real and personal property. Distributorship agreements to which section 1241 applies are described in paragraph (c) of this section. Section 1241 has no application in determining whether or not a cancellation not qualifying under that section is a sale or exchange. Further, section 1241 has no application in determining whether or not a lease or a distributorship agreement is a capital asset, even though its cancellation qualifies as an exchange under section 1241.

(b) *Definition of "cancellation".*—The term "cancellation" of a lease or a distributor's agreement, as used in section 1241, means a termination of all the contractual rights of a lessee or distributor with respect to particular premises or a particular distributorship, other than by the expiration of the lease or agreement in accordance with its terms. A payment made in good faith for a partial cancellation of a lease or a distributorship agreement is recognized as an amount received for cancellation under section 1241 if the cancellation relates to a severable economic unit, such as a portion of the premises covered by a lease, a reduction in the unexpired term of a lease or distributorship agreement, or a distributorship in one of several areas or of one of several products. Payments made for other modifications of leases or distributorship agreements, however, are not recognized as amounts received for cancellation under section 1241.

(c) *Amounts received upon cancellation of a distributorship agreement.*—Section 1241 applies to distributorship agreements only if they are for marketing or marketing and servicing of goods. It does not apply to agreements for selling intangible property or for rendering personal services as, for example, agreements establishing insurance agencies or agencies for the brokerage of securities. Further, it applies to a distributorship agreement only if the distributor has made a substantial investment of capital in the distributorship. The substantial capital investment must be reflected in physical assets such as inventories of tangible goods, equipment, machinery, storage facilities, or similar property. An investment is not considered substantial for purposes of section 1241 unless it consists of a significant fraction or more of the facilities for storing, transporting, processing, or otherwise dealing with the goods distributed, or consists of a substantial inventory of such goods. The investment required in the maintenance of an office merely for clerical operations is not considered substantial for purposes of this section. Furthermore, section 1241 shall not apply unless a substantial amount of the capital or assets needed for carrying on the operations of a distributorship are acquired by the distributor and actually used in carrying on the distributorship at some time before the cancellation of the distributorship agreement. It is immaterial for the purposes of section 1241 whether the distributor acquired the assets used in performing the functions of the distributorship before or after beginning his operations under the distributorship agreement. It is also immaterial whether the distributor is a retailer, wholesaler, jobber, or other type of distributor. The application of this paragraph may be illustrated by the following examples:

Example (1). Taxpayer is a distributor of various food products. He leases a warehouse including cold storage facilities and owns a number of motor trucks. In 1955 he obtains the exclusive rights to market certain frozen food products in his State. The marketing is accomplished by using the warehouse and trucks acquired before he entered into the agreement and entails no additional capital. Payments received upon the cancellation of the agreement are treated under section 1241 as though received upon the sale or exchange of the agreement.

Example (2). Assume that the taxpayer in example (1) entered into an exclusive distributorship agreement with the producer under which the taxpayer merely solicits orders through his staff of salesmen, the goods being shipped direct to the purchasers. Payments received upon the cancellation of the agreement would not be treated under section 1241 as though received upon the sale or exchange of the agreement.

Example (3). Taxpayer is an exclusive distributor for M city of certain frozen food products which he distributes to frozen-food freezer and locker customers. The terms of his distributorship do not make it necessary for him to have any substantial investment in inventory. Taxpayer rents a loading platform for a nominal amount, but has no warehouse space. Orders for goods from customers are consolidated by the taxpayer and forwarded to the producer from time to time. Upon receipt of these goods, taxpayer allocates them to the individual orders of customers and delivers them immediately by truck. Although it would require a fleet of fifteen or twenty trucks to carry out this operation, the distributor uses only one truck of his own and hires cartage companies to deliver the bulk of the merchandise to the customers. Payments received upon the cancellation of the distributorship agreement in such a case would not be considered received upon the sale or exchange of the agreement under section 1241 since the taxpayer does not have facilities for the physical handling of more than a small fraction of the goods involved in carrying on the distributorship and, therefore, does not have a substantial capital investment in the distributorship. On the other hand, if the taxpayer had acquired and used a substantial number of the trucks necessary for the deliveries to his customers, payments received upon the cancellation of the agreement would be considered received in exchange therefor under section 1241. [Reg. § 1.1241-1.]

☐ [*T.D.* 6253, 9-25-57.]

[Reg. § 1.1242-1]

§ 1.1242-1. Losses on small business investment company stock.—(a) *In general.*—Any taxpayer who sustains a loss for a taxable year beginning after September 2, 1958, as a result of the worthlessness, or from the sale or exchange, of the stock of a small business investment company (whether or not such stock was originally issued to such taxpayer) shall treat such loss as a loss from the sale or exchange of property which is not a capital asset, if at the time of such loss—

(1) The company which issued the stock is licensed to operate as a small business investment company pursuant to regulations promulgated by the Small Business Administration (13 CFR Part 107), and

(2) Such loss would, but for the provisions of section 1242, be a loss from the sale or exchange of a capital asset.

(b) *Treatment of losses for purposes of section 172.*—For the purposes of section 172 (relating to the net operating loss deduction), any amount of loss treated by reason of section 1242 as a loss from the sale or exchange of property which is not a capital asset shall be treated as attributable to the trade or business of the taxpayer. Accordingly, the limitation of section 172(d)(4) on the allowance of nonbusiness deductions in computing a net operating loss shall not apply to any loss with respect to the stock of a small business investment company as described in paragraph (a) of this section. See section 172(d) and § 1.172-3.

(c) *Statement to be filed with return.*—A taxpayer claiming a deduction for a loss on the stock of a small business investment company shall file with his income tax return a statement containing: the name and address of the small business investment company which issued the stock, the number of shares, basis, and selling price of the stock with respect to which the loss is claimed, the respective dates of purchase and sale of such stock, or the reason for its worthlessness and approximate date thereof. For the rules applicable in determining the worthlessness of securities, see section 165 and the regulations thereunder. [Reg. § 1.1242-1.]

☐ [*T.D.* 6449, 1-27-60.]

[Reg. § 1.1243-1]

§ 1.1243-1. Loss of small business investment company.—(a) *In general.*—(1) *Taxable years beginning after July 11, 1969.*—For taxable years beginning after July 11, 1969, a small business investment company to which section 582(c) applies, and which sustains a loss as a result of the worthlessness, or on the sale or exchange, of the stock of a small business concern (as defined in section 103(5) of the Small Business Investment Act of 1958, as amended (15 U.S.C. 662(5)) and in 13 CFR 107.3), shall treat such loss as a loss from the sale or exchange of property which is not a capital asset if—

(i) The stock was issued pursuant to the conversion privilege of the convertible debentures acquired in accordance with the provisions of section 304 of the Small Business Investment Act of 1958 (15 U.S.C. 684) and the regulations thereunder,

(ii) Such loss would, but for the provisions of section 1243, be a loss from the sale or exchange of a capital asset, and

(iii) At the time of the loss, the company is licensed to operate as a small business investment company pursuant to regulations promulgated by the Small Business Administration (13 CFR Part 107).

If section 582(c) does not apply for the taxable year, see subparagraph (2) of this paragraph.

(2) *Taxable years beginning before July 11, 1974.*—For taxable years beginning after September 2, 1958, but before July 11, 1974, a small business investment company to which section 582(c) does not apply, and which sustains a loss as a result of the worthlessness, or on the sale or exchange, of the securities of a small business concern (as defined in section 103(5) of the Small Business Investment Act of 1958, as amended (15 U.S.C. 662(5)) and in 13 CFR 107.3), shall treat such loss as a loss from the sale or exchange of property which is not a capital asset if—

(i) The securities are either the convertible debentures, or the stock issued pursuant to the conversion privilege thereof, acquired in accordance with the provisions of section 304 of the Small Business Investment Act of 1958 (15 U.S.C. 684) and the regulations thereunder,

(ii) Such loss would, but for the provisions of this subparagraph, be a loss from the sale or exchange of a capital asset, and

(iii) At the time of the loss, the company is licensed to operate as a small business investment company pursuant to regulations promulgated by the Small Business Administration (13 CFR Part 107).

If section 582(c) applies for the taxable year, see subparagraph (1) of this paragraph.

(b) *Material to be filed with return.*—A small business investment company which claims a deduction for a loss on the convertible debentures (pursuant to paragraph (a)(2) of this section) or stock (pursuant to paragraph (a)(1) or (a)(2) of this section) of a small business concern shall submit with its income tax return a statement that it is a Federal licensee under the Small Business Investment Act of 1958 (15 U.S.C. ch. 14B). The statement shall also set forth: the name and address of the small business concern with respect to whose securities the loss was sustained, the number of shares of stock or the number and denomination of debentures with respect to which the loss is claimed, the basis and selling price thereof, and the respective dates of purchase and sale of the securities, or the reason for their worthlessness and the approximate date thereof. For the rules applicable in determining the worthlessness of securities, see section 165 and the regulations thereunder. [Reg. § 1.1243-1.]

☐ [*T.D.* 6449, 1-27-60. *Amended by T.D.* 7171, 3-16-72.]

[Reg. § 1.1244(a)-1]

§ 1.1244(a)-1. Loss on small business stock treated as ordinary loss.—(a) *In general.*—Subject to certain conditions and limitations, section 1244 provides that a loss on the sale or exchange (including a transaction treated as a sale or exchange, such as worthlessness) of "section 1244 stock" which would otherwise be treated as loss from the sale or exchange of a capital asset shall be treated as a loss from the sale or exchange of an asset which is not a capital asset (referred to in this section and §§ 1.1244(b)-1 to 1.1244(e)-1, inclusive, as an "ordinary loss"). Such a loss shall be allowed as a deduction from gross income in arriving at adjusted gross income. The requirements that must be satisfied in order that stock may be considered section 1244 stock are described in §§ 1.1244(c)-1 and 1.1244(c)-2. These requirements relate to the stock itself and the corporation issuing such stock. In addition, the taxpayer who claims an ordinary loss deduction pursuant to section 1244 must satisfy the requirements of paragraph (b) of this section.

(b) *Taxpayers entitled to ordinary loss.*—The allowance of an ordinary loss deduction for a loss on section 1244 stock is permitted only to the following two classes of taxpayers:

(1) An individual sustaining the loss to whom the stock was issued by a small business corporation, or

(2) An individual who is a partner in a partnership at the time the partnership acquired the stock in an issuance from a small business corporation and whose distributive share of partnership items reflects the loss sustained by the partnership. The ordinary loss deduction is limited to the lesser of the partner's distributive share at the time of the issuance of the stock or the partner's distributive share at the time the loss is sustained. In order to claim a deduction under section 1244 the individual, or the partnership, sustaining the loss must have continuously held the stock from the date of issuance. A corporation, trust, or estate is not entitled to ordinary loss treatment under section 1244 regardless of how the stock was acquired. An individual who acquires stock from a shareholder by purchase, gift, devise, or in any other manner is not entitled to an ordinary loss under section 1244 with respect to this stock. Thus, ordinary loss treatment is not available to a partner to whom the stock is distributed by the partnership. Stock acquired through an investment banking firm, or other person, participating in the sale of an issue may qualify for ordinary loss treatment only if the stock is not first issued to the firm or person. Thus, for example, if the firm acts as a selling agent for the issuing corporation the stock may qualify. On the other hand, stock purchased by an investment firm and subsequently resold does not qualify as section 1244 stock in the hands of the person acquiring the stock from the firm.

(c) *Examples.*—The provisions of paragraph (b) of this section may be illustrated by the following examples:

Example (1). A and B, both individuals, and C, a trust, are equal partners in a partnership to which a small business corporation issues section 1244 stock. The partnership sells the stock at a loss. A's and B's distributive share of the loss may be treated as an ordinary loss pursuant to section 1244, but C's distributive share of the loss may not be so treated.

Example (2). The facts are the same as in example (1) except that the section 1244 stock is distributed by the partnership to partner A and he subsequently sells the stock at a loss. Section 1244 is not applicable to the loss since A did not acquire the stock by issuance from the small business corporation. [Reg. § 1.1244(a)-1.]

☐ [*T.D.* 6495, 10-7-60. *Amended by T.D.* 7779, 6-1-81.]

[Reg. § 1.1244(b)-1]

§ 1.1244(b)-1. **Annual limitation.**—(a) *In general.*—Subsection (b) of section 1244 imposes a limitation on the aggregate amount of loss that for any taxable year may be treated as an ordinary loss by a taxpayer by reason of that section. In the case of a partnership, the limitation is determined separately as to each partner. Any amount of loss in excess of the applicable limitation is treated as loss from the sale or exchange of a capital asset.

(b) *Amount of loss.*—(1) *Taxable years beginning after December 31, 1978.*—For any taxable year beginning after December 31, 1978, the maximum amount that may be treated as an ordinary loss under section 1244 is—

(i) $50,000, or

(ii) $100,000, if a husband and wife file a joint return under section 6013.

These limitations on the maximum amount of ordinary loss apply whether the loss or losses are sustained on pre-November 1978 stock (as defined in § 1.1244(c)-1(a)(1)), post-November 1978 stock (as defined in § 1.1244(c)-1(a)(2)), or on any combination of pre-November 1978 stock and post-November 1978 stock. The limitation referred to in (ii) applies to a joint return whether the loss or losses are sustained by one or both spouses.

(2) *Taxable years ending before November 6, 1978.*—For any taxable year ending before November 6, 1978, the maximum amount that may be treated as an ordinary loss under section 1244 is—

(i) $25,000 or

(ii) $50,000, if a husband and wife file a joint return under section 6013.

The limitation referred to in (ii) applies to a joint return whether the loss or losses are sustained by one or both spouses.

(3) *Taxable years including November 6, 1978.*—For a taxable year including November 6, 1978, the maximum amount that may be treated as ordinary loss under section 1244 is the sum of—

(i) The amount calculated by applying the limitations described in subparagraph (1) of this paragraph (b) to the amount of loss, if any, sustained during the taxable year on post-November 1978 stock, plus

(ii) The amount calculated by applying the limitations described in subparagraph (2) of this paragraph (b) to the amount of loss, if any, sustained during the taxable year on pre-November 1978 stock,

to the extent this sum does not exceed $50,000, or, if a husband and wife file a joint return under section 6013 for the taxable year, $100,000.

(4) *Examples.*—The provisions of this section may be illustrated by the following examples:

Example (1). A, a married taxpayer who files a joint return for the taxable year ending December 31, 1977, sustains a $50,000 loss qualifying under section 1244 on pre-November 1978 stock in Corporation X and an equal amount of loss qualifying under section 1244 on pre-November 1978 stock in Corporation Y. A is limited to $50,000 of ordinary loss under paragraph (b)(2)(ii). The remaining $50,000 of loss is treated as loss from the sale or exchange of a capital asset.

Example (2). For the taxable year ending December 31, 1979, B, a married taxpayer who files a joint return, sustains a $90,000 loss on post-November 1978 stock in Corporation X. In the same taxable year, C, B's spouse, sustains a $25,000 loss on post-November 1978 stock in Corporation Y. Both losses qualify under section 1244. B and C's ordinary loss is limited to $100,000 under paragraph (b)(1)(ii). The remaining $15,000 of loss is treated as loss from the sale or exchange of a capital asset.

Example (3). D, a married taxpayer who files a joint return and reports income on a fiscal year basis for the taxable year ending November 30, 1978, sustains a $60,000 loss qualifying under section 1244 on pre-November 1978 stock and a $40,000 loss qualifying under section 1244 on post-November 1978 stock. D's ordinary loss on pre-November 1978 stock is limited to $50,000 under subparagraph (3)(ii) of this paragraph (b). D's $40,000 loss on post-November 1978 stock is within the limit of subparagraph (3)(i) of this paragraph (b). The total of these losses, $90,000, is the aggregate amount deductible by D as ordinary loss under section 1244. The remaining $10,000 of loss is treated as loss from the sale or exchange of a capital asset.

Example (4). E, a married taxpayer who files a joint return for the taxable year ending December 31, 1980, sustains a $75,000 loss qualifying under section 1244 on pre-November 1978 stock and a $10,000 loss qualifying under section 1244 on post-November 1978 stock. E may deduct the total of these losses, $85,000, as ordinary loss under paragraph (b)(1)(ii).

Example (5). Assume the same facts as in the preceding example, except that the losses are sustained in the taxable year beginning January 1, 1978, and ending December 31, 1978. E is limited to $60,000 of ordinary loss ($50,000 on pre-November 1978 stock plus $10,000 on post-November 1978 stock) under paragraph (b)(3). The remaining $25,000 of loss is treated as loss from the sale or exchange of a capital asset.

Example (6). F, a married taxpayer who files a joint return for the taxable year beginning January 1, 1978, and ending December 31, 1978, sustains a $75,000 loss qualifying under section 1244 on pre-November 1978 stock and a $125,000 loss qualifying under section 1244 on post-November 1978 stock. F's loss on pre-November 1978 stock is limited to $50,000 of ordinary loss under subparagraph (3)(ii) of this paragraph (b). F's loss on post-November 1978 stock is limited to $100,000 of ordinary loss under subparagraph (3)(i) of this paragraph (b). The total of these losses, $150,000, is limited to $100,000 of ordinary loss under paragraph (b)(3). F's aggregate

amount of ordinary loss under section 1244 is $100,000. The remaining $100,000 of loss is treated as loss from the sale or exchange of a capital asset. [Reg. § 1.1244(b)-1.]

☐ [*T.D. 6495, 10-7-60. Amended by T.D. 7779, 6-1-81.*]

[Reg. § 1.1244(c)-1]

§ 1.1244(c)-1. Section 1244 stock defined.— (a) *In general.*—For purposes of § § 1.1244(a)-1 to 1.1244(e)-1, inclusive—

(1) The term "pre-November 1978 stock" means stock issued after June 30, 1958, and on or before November 6, 1978.

(2) The term "post-November 1978 stock" means stock issued after November 6, 1978.

In order that stock may qualify as section 1244 stock, the requirements described in paragraphs (b) through (e) of this section must be satisfied. In addition, the requirements of paragraph (f) of this section must be satisfied in the case of pre-November 1978 stock. Whether these requirements have been met is determined at the time the stock is issued, except for the requirement in paragraph (e) of this section. Whether the requirement in paragraph (e) of this section, relating to gross receipts of the corporation, has been satisfied is determined at the time a loss is sustained. Therefore, at the time of issuance it cannot be said with certainty that stock will qualify for the benefits of section 1244.

(b) *Common stock.*—Only common stock, either voting or nonvoting, in a domestic corporation may qualify as section 1244 stock. For purposes of section 1244, neither securities of the corporation convertible into common stock nor common stock convertible into other securities of the corporation are treated as common stock. An increase in the basis of outstanding stock as a result of a contribution to capital is not treated as an issuance of stock under section 1244. For definition of domestic corporation, see section 7701(a)(4) and the regulations under that section.

(c) *Small business corporation.*—At the time the stock is issued (or, in the case of pre-November 1978 stock, at the time of adoption of the plan described in paragraph (f)(1) of this section) the corporation must be a "small business corporation". See § 1.1244(c)-2 for the definition of a small business corporation.

(d) *Issued for money or other property.*—(1) The stock must be issued to the taxpayer for money or other property transferred by the taxpayer to the corporation. However, stock issued in exchange for stock or securities, including stock or securities of the issuing corporation, cannot qualify as section 1244 stock, except as provided in § 1.1244(d)-3, relating to certain cases where stock is issued in exchange for section 1244 stock. Stock issued for services rendered or to be rendered to, or for the benefit of, the issuing corporation does not qualify as section 1244 stock. Stock issued in consideration for cancellation of indebtedness of the corporation shall be considered issued in exchange for money or other property unless such indebtedness is evidenced by a security, or arises out of the performance of personal services.

(2) The following examples illustrate situations where stock fails to qualify as section 1244 stock as a result of the rules in subparagraph (1) of this paragraph:

Example (1). A taxpayer owns stock of Corporation X issued to him prior to July 1, 1958. Under a plan adopted in 1977, he exchanges his stock for a new issuance of stock of Corporation X. The stock received by the taxpayer in the exchange may not qualify as section 1244 stock even if the corporation has adopted a valid plan and is a small business corporation.

Example (2). A taxpayer owns stock in Corporation X. Corporation X merges into Corporation Y. In exchange for his stock, Corporation Y issues shares of its stock to the taxpayer. The stock in Corporation Y does not qualify as section 1244 stock even if the stock exchanged by the taxpayer did qualify.

Example (3). Corporation X transfers part of its business assets to Corporation Y, a new corporation, and all of the stock of Corporation Y is issued directly to the shareholders of Corporation X. Since the Corporation Y stock was not issued to the shareholders for a transfer by them of money or other property, none of the Corporation Y stock in the hands of the shareholders can qualify.

(e) *Gross receipts.*—(1)(i)(a) Except as provided in subparagraph (2) of this paragraph, stock will not qualify under section 1244 if 50 percent or more of the gross receipts of the corporation, for the period consisting of the five most recent taxable years of the corporation ending before the date the loss on such stock is sustained by the shareholders is derived from royalties, rents, dividends, interest, annuities, and sales or exchanges of stock or securities. If the corporation has not been in existence for five taxable years ending before such date, the percentage test referred to in the preceding sentence applies to the period of the taxable years ending before such date during which the corporation has been in existence; and if the loss is sustained during the first taxable year of the corporation such test applies to the period beginning with the first day of such taxable year and ending on the day before the loss is sustained. The test under this paragraph shall be made on the basis of total gross receipts, except that gross receipts from the sales or exchanges of stock or securities shall be taken into account only to the extent of gains therefrom. The term "gross receipts" as used in section 1244(c)(1)(C) is not synonymous with "gross income". Gross receipts means the total amount received or accrued under the method of

accounting used by the corporation in computing its taxable income. Thus, the total amount of receipts is not reduced by returns and allowances, cost, or deductions. For example, gross receipts will include the total amount received or accrued during the corporation's taxable year from the sale or exchange (including a sale or exchange to which section 337 applies) of any kind of property, from investments, and for services rendered by the corporation. However, gross receipts does not include amounts received in nontaxable sales or exchanges (other than those to which section 337 applies), except to the extent that gain is recognized by the corporation, nor does that term include amounts received as a loan, as repayment of a loan, as a contribution to capital, or on the issuance by the corporation of its own stock.

(b) The meaning of the term "gross receipts" as used in section 1244(c)(1)(C) may be further illustrated by the following examples:

Example (1). A corporation on the accrual method sells property (other than stock or securities) and receives payment partly in money and partly in the form of a note payable at a future time. The amount of the money and the face amount of the note would be considered gross receipts in the taxable year of the sale and would not be reduced by the adjusted basis of the property, the costs of sale, or any other amount.

Example (2). A corporation has a long-term contract as defined in paragraph (a) of §1.451-3 with respect to which it reports income according to the percentage-of-completion method as described in paragraph (b)(1) of §1.451-3. The portion of the gross contract price which corresponds to the percentage of the entire contract which has been completed during the taxable year shall be included in gross receipts for such year.

Example (3). A corporation which regularly sells personal property on the installment plan elects to report its taxable income from the sale of property (other than stock or securities) on the installment method in accordance with section 453. The installment payments actually received in a given taxable year of the corporation shall be included in gross receipts for such year.

(ii) The term "royalties" as used in subdivision (i) of this subparagraph means all royalties, including mineral, oil, and gas royalties (whether or not the aggregate amount of such royalties constitutes 50 percent or more of the gross income of the corporation for the taxable year), and amounts received for the privilege of using patents, copyrights, secret processes and formulas, good will, trademarks, trade brands, franchises, and other like property. The term "royalties" does not include amounts received upon the disposal of timber, coal, or domestic iron ore with a retained economic interest to which the special rules of section 631(b) and (c) apply or amounts received from the transfer of patent rights to which section 1235 applies. For the definition of "mineral, oil, or gas royalties," see paragraph (b)(11)(ii) and (iii) of § 1.543-1. For purposes of this subdivision, the gross amount of royalties shall not be reduced by any part of the cost of the rights under which they are received or by any amount allowable as a deduction in computing taxable income.

(iii) The term "rents" as used in subdivision (i) of this subparagraph means amounts received for the use of, or right to use, property (whether real or personal) of the corporation, whether or not such amounts constitute 50 percent or more of the gross income of the corporation for the taxable year. The term "rents" does not include payments for the use or occupancy of rooms or other space where significant services are also rendered to the occupant, such as for the use or occupancy of rooms or other quarters in hotels, boarding houses, or apartment houses furnishing hotel services, or in tourist homes, motor courts, or motels. Generally, services are considered rendered to the occupant if they are primarily for his convenience and are other than those usually or customarily rendered in connection with the rental of rooms or other space for occupancy only. The supplying of maid service, for example, constitutes such services; whereas the furnishing of heat and light, the cleaning of public entrances, exits, stairways, and lobbies, the collection of trash, etc., are not considered as services rendered to the occupant. Payments for the use or occupancy of entire private residences or living quarters in duplex or multiple housing units, of offices in an office building, etc., are generally "rents" under section 1244(c)(1)(C). Payments for the parking of automobiles ordinarily do not constitute rents. Payments for the warehousing of goods or for the use of personal property do no constitute rents if significant services are rendered in connection with such payments.

(iv) The term "dividends" as used in subdivision (i) of this subparagraph includes dividends as defined in section 316, amounts required to be included in gross income under section 551 (relating to foreign personal holding company income taxed to United States shareholders), and consent dividends determined as provided in section 565.

(v) The term "interest" as used in subdivision (i) of this subparagraph means any amounts received for the use of money (including tax-exempt interest).

(vi) The term "annuities" as used in subdivision (i) of this subparagraph means the entire amount received as an annuity under an annuity, endowment, or life insurance contract, regardless of whether only part of such amount would be includible in gross income under section 72.

(vii) For purposes of subdivision (i) of this subparagraph, gross receipts from the sales or exchanges of stock or securities are taken into account only to the extent of gains therefrom. Thus, the gross receipts from the sale of a particular share of stock will be the excess of the amount realized over the adjusted basis of such share. If the adjusted basis should equal or exceed the amount realized on the sale or exchange of a certain share of stock, bond, etc., there would be no gross receipts resulting from the sale of such security. Losses on sales or exchanges of stock or securities do not offset gains on the sales or exchanges of other stock or securities for purposes of computing gross receipts from such sales or exchanges. Gross receipts from the sale or exchange of stocks and securities include gains received from such sales or exchanges by a corporation even though such corporation is a regular dealer in stocks and securities. For the meaning of the term "stocks or securities," see paragraph (b)(5)(i) of § 1.543-1.

(2) The requirement of subparagraph (1) of this paragraph need not be satisfied if for the applicable period the aggregate amount of deductions allowed to the corporation exceeds the aggregate amount of its gross income. But for this purpose the deductions allowed by section 172, relating to the net operating loss deduction, and by sections 242, 243, 244, and 245, relating to certain special deductions for corporations, shall not be taken into account. Notwithstanding the provisions of this subparagraph and of subparagraph (1) of this paragraph, pursuant to the specific delegation of authority granted in section 1244(e) to prescribe such regulations as may be necessary to carry out the purposes of section 1244, ordinary loss treatment will not be available with respect to stock of a corporation which is not largely an operating company within the five most recent taxable years (or such lesser period as the corporation is in existence) ending before the date of the loss. Thus, for example, assume that a person who is not a dealer in real estate forms a corporation which issues stock to him which meets all the formal requirements of section 1244 stock. The corporation then acquires a piece of unimproved real estate which it holds as an investment. The property declines in value and the stockholder sells his stock at a loss. The loss does not qualify for ordinary loss treatment under section 1244 but must be treated as a capital loss.

(3) In applying subparagraphs (1) and (2) of this paragraph to a successor corporation in a reorganization described in section 368(a)(1)(F), such corporation shall be treated as the same corporation as its predecessor. See paragraph (d)(2) of § 1.1244(d)-3.

(f) *Special rules applicable to pre-November 1978 stock.*—(1)(i) Pre-November 1978 common stock must have been issued under a written plan adopted by the corporation after June 30, 1958, and on or before November 6, 1978, to offer only this stock during a period specified in the plan ending not later than 2 years after the date the plan is adopted. The 2-year requirement referred to in the preceding sentence is met if the period specified in the plan is based upon the date when, under the rules or regulations of a Government agency relating to the issuance of the stock, the stock may lawfully be sold, and it is clear that this period will end, and in fact does end, within 2 years after the plan is adopted. The plan must specifically state, in terms of dollars, the maximum amount to be received by the corporation in consideration for the stock to be issued under the plan. See § 1.1244(c)-2 for the limitation on the amount that may be received by the corporation under the plan.

(ii) To qualify, the pre-November 1978 stock must be issued during the period of the offer, which period must end not later than two years after the date the plan is adopted. Pre-November 1978 stock which is subscribed for during the period of the plan but not issued during this period cannot qualify as section 1244 stock. Pre-November 1978 stock issued on the exercise of a stock right, stock warrant, or stock option (which right, warrant, or option was not outstanding at the time the plan was adopted) will be treated as issued under a plan only if the right, warrant, or option is applicable solely to unissued stock offered under the plan and is exercised during the period of the plan.

(iii) Pre-November 1978 stock subscribed for prior to the adoption of the plan, including stock subscribed for prior to the date the corporation comes into existence, may be considered issued under a plan adopted by the corporation if the stock is not in fact issued prior to the adoption of the plan.

(iv) Pre-November 1978 stock issued for a payment which, alone or together with prior payments, exceeds the maximum amount that may be received under the plan, is not considered issued under the plan, and none of the stock can qualify as section 1244 stock. See § 1.1244(c)-2(b) for a different rule with respect to post-November 1978 stock.

(2) Pre-November 1978 stock does not qualify as section 1244 stock if at the time of the adoption of the plan under which it is issued there remains unissued any portion of a prior offering of stock. Thus, if any portion of an outstanding offering of common or preferred stock is unissued at the time of the adoption of the plan, stock issued under the plan will not qualify as section 1244 stock. An offer is outstanding unless and until it is withdrawn by affirmative action before the plan is adopted. Stock rights, stock warrants, stock options, or securities convertible into stock, that are outstanding at the time the plan is adopted, are considered prior offerings. The authorization in the corporate charter to issue stock different from stock offered under the plan or in excess of stock offered under the plan is not of itself a prior offering.

(3)(i) Even though the plan satisfies the requirements of subparagraph (1) of this paragraph (f), if another offering of pre-November 1978 stock is made by the corporation subsequent to, or simultaneous with, the adoption of the plan, pre-November 1978 stock issued under the plan after the other offering does not qualify as section 1244 stock. The issuance of stock options, stock rights, or stock warrants, at any time during the period of the plan, that are exercisable on stock other than stock offered under the plan, is considered a subsequent offering. Similarly, the issuance of pre-November 1978 stock other than that offered under the plan is considered a subsequent offering. Because stock issued upon exercise of a conversion privilege is stock issued for a security, and stock issued under a stock option granted in whole or in part for services is not issued for money or other property, the issuance of securities with a conversion privilege and the issuance of such a stock option are subsequent offerings, because the conversion privilege and the stock option are exercisable with respect to stock other than that which may properly be offered under the plan. Pre-November 1978 stock issued under the plan before a subsequent offering is not disqualified because of the subsequent offering. The rule of the subparagraph, together with the rule of subparagraph (2) of this paragraph (f), relating to offers prior to the adoption of the plan, limits pre-November 1978 section 1244 stock to stock issued by the corporation during a period when any stock issued by it must have been issued under the plan.

(ii) Any modification of a plan that changes the offering to include preferred stock, or that increases the amount of pre-November 1978 stock that may be issued under the plan to such an extent that the requirements of paragraph (c) of this section would not have been satisfied if determined with reference to this amount as of the date the plan was initially adopted, or that extends the period of time during which stock may be issued under the plan to more than 2 years from the date the plan was initially adopted, is considered a subsequent offering, and no stock issued after this offering may qualify. However, a corporation may withdraw a plan and adopt a new plan to issue stock. To determine whether stock issued under this new plan may qualify, this paragraph (f) must be applied with respect to the new plan as of the date of its adoption. For example, amounts received for stock under the prior plan must be taken into account in determining whether the statutory requirements relating to definition of small business corporation are satisfied. In applying the requirements of paragraph (c) of this section, reference should be made to equity capital as of the date the new plan is adopted. The same principles apply if the period of the initial plan expires and the corporation adopts a new plan. [Reg. § 1.1244(c)-1.]

□ [T.D. 6495, 10-7-60 *and* T.D. 6508, 12-1-60. *Amended by* T.D. 6637, 2-25-63, T.D. 6841, 7-26-65 *and* T.D. 7779, 6-1-81.]

[Reg. §1.1244(c)-2]

§1.1244(c)-2. Small business corporation defined.—(a) *In general.*—A corporation is treated as a small business corporation if it is a domestic corporation that satisfies the requirements described in paragraph (b) or (c) of this section. The requirements of paragraph (b) of this section apply if a loss is sustained on post-November 1978 stock. The requirements of paragraph (c) of this section apply if a loss is sustained on pre-November 1978 stock. If losses are sustained on both pre-November 1978 stock and post-November 1978 stock in the same taxable year, the requirements of paragraph (b) of this section are applied to the corporation at the time of the issuance of the stock (as required by paragraph (b) in the case of a loss on post-November 1978 stock) in order to determine whether the loss on post-November 1978 stock qualifies as a section 1244 loss, and the requirements of paragraph (c) of this section are applied to the corporation at the time of the adoption of the plan (as required by paragraph (c) in the case of a loss on pre-November 1978 stock) in order to determine whether the loss on pre-November 1978 stock qualifies as a section 1244 loss. For definition of domestic corporation, see section 7701(a)(4) and the regulations under that section.

(b) *Post-November 1978 stock.*—(1) *Amount received by corporation for stock.*—Capital receipts of a small business corporation may not exceed $1,000,000. For purposes of this paragraph the term "capital receipts" means the aggregate dollar amount received by the corporation for its stock, as a contribution to capital, and as paid-in surplus. If the $1,000,000 limitation is exceeded, the rules of subparagraph (2) of this paragraph (b) apply. In making these determinations, (i) property is taken into account at its adjusted basis to the corporation (for determining gain) as of the date received by the corporation, and (ii) this aggregate amount is reduced by the amount of any liability to which the property was subject and by the amount of any liability assumed by the corporation at the time the property was received. Capital receipts are not reduced by distributions to shareholders, even though the distributions may be capital distributions.

(2) *Requirement of designation in event $1,000,000 limitation exceeded.*—(i) If capital receipts exceed $1,000,000, the corporation shall designate as section 1244 stock certain shares of post-November 1978 common stock issued for money or other property in the transitional year. For purposes of this paragraph, the term "transitional year" means the first taxable year in which capital receipts exceed $1,000,000 and in which the corporation issues stock. This designation shall be made in accordance with the rules of

subdivision (iii) of this paragraph (b)(2). The amount received for designated stock shall not exceed $1,000,000, less amounts received—

(A) In exchange for stock in years prior to the transitional year;

(B) As contributions to capital in years prior to the transitional year; and

(C) As paid-in surplus in years prior to the transitional year.

(ii) Post-November 1978 common stock issued for money or other property before the transitional year qualifies as section 1244 stock without affirmative designation by the corporation. Post-November 1978 common stock issued after the transitional year does not qualify as section 1244 stock.

(iii) The corporation shall make the designation required by subdivision (i) of this paragraph (b)(2) not later than the 15th day of the third month following the close of the transitional year. However, in the case of post-November 1978 common stock issued on or before June 2, 1981 the corporation shall make the required designation by August 3, 1981 or by the 15th day of the 3rd month following the close of the transitional year, whichever is later. The designation shall be made by entering the numbers of the qualifying share certificates on the corporation's records. If the shares do not bear serial numbers or other identifying numbers or letters, or are not represented by share certificates, the corporation shall make an alternative designation in writing at the time of issuance, or, in the case of post-November 1978 common stock issued on or before June 2, 1981 by August 3, 1981. This alternative designation may be made in any manner sufficient to identify the shares qualifying for section 1244 treatment. If the corporation fails to make a designation by share certificate number or an alternative written designation as described, the rules of subparagraph (3) of this paragraph (b) apply.

(3) *Allocation of section 1244 benefit in event corporation fails to designate qualifying shares.*—If a corporation issues post-November 1978 stock in the transitional year and fails to designate certain shares of post-November 1978 common stock as section 1244 stock in accordance with the rules of subparagraph (2) of this paragraph (b), the following rules apply:

(i) Section 1244 treatment is extended to losses sustained on post-November 1978 common stock issued for money or other property in taxable years before the transitional year and is withheld from losses sustained on post-November 1978 stock issued in taxable years after the transitional year.

(ii) Post-1958 capital received before the transitional year is subtracted from $1,000,000.

(iii) Subject to the annual limitation described in §1.1244(b)-1, an ordinary loss on post-November 1978 common stock issued for money or other property in the transitional year is allowed in an amount which bears the same ratio to the total loss sustained by the individual as—

(A) The amount described in § 1.1244(c)-2(b)(3)(ii) bears to

(B) The total amount of money and other property received by the corporation in exchange for stock, as a contribution to capital, and as paid-in surplus in the transitional year.

(4) *Examples.*—The provisions of this paragraph (b) may be illustrated by the following examples:

Example (1). On December 1, 1978, Corporation W, a newly-formed corporation, issues 10,000 shares of common stock at $125 a share for an amount (determined under subparagraph (1) of this paragraph (b)) of money and other property totaling $1,250,000. The board of directors specifies that 8,000 shares are section 1244 stock and records the certificate numbers of the qualifying shares in its minutes. Because Corporation W issued post-November 1978 common stock in exchange for money and other property exceeding $1,000,000, but has designated shares of stock as section 1244 stock and the designated shares were issued in exchange for money and other property not exceeding $1,000,000 (8,000 shares × $125 price per share = $1,000,000), the 8,000 designated shares qualify as section 1244 stock.

Example (2). Corporation X comes into existence on June 1, 1979. On June 10, 1979, Corporation X issues 2,500 shares of common stock at $250 per share to shareholder A and 2,500 shares of common stock at $250 per share to shareholder B. By written agreement dated September 1, 1981, shareholder A and shareholder B determine that 1,500 of shareholder A's shares and all of shareholder B's shares will be treated as section 1244 stock. Although shareholder A's 1,500 shares and shareholder B's 2,500 shares were issued for money and other property not exceeding $1,000,000 (4,000 shares × $250 price per share = $1,000,000), these 4,000 shares do not qualify as section 1244 stock under the rules of subparagraph (2) of this paragraph (b) for three reasons: The agreement of September 1, 1979, (i) did not identify which 1,500 of shareholder A's 2,500 shares were intended to qualify for section 1244 treatment, (ii) was made by the shareholders and not by Corporation X, and (iii) was made later than the 15th day of the third month following the close of the transitional year. However,

certain of the shares issued by Corporation X may qualify as section 1244 stock under the rules of subparagraph (3) of this paragraph (b). See example (4).

Example (3). On December 1, 1980, Corporation Y issues common stock to shareholder A in exchange for $500,000 in cash. On August 1, 1981, Corporation Y issues common stock to shareholder B in exchange for property having an adjusted basis to Corporation Y of $500,000. On December 1, 1981, B transfers a tract of land having a basis in B's hands of $250,000 to Corporation Y as a contribution to capital. Under section 362(a)(2) of the Code, Corporation Y takes a basis of $250,000 in the tract of land. Corporation Y is a calendar year corporation. On February 15, 1982, it designates all of shareholder B's stock as section 1244 stock by entering the numbers of the qualifying certificates on the corporation's records. The designation made by Corporation Y is effective because it identifies which shares of its stock qualify for section 1244 treatment, was made in writing before the 15th day of the 3rd month following the close of the transitional year (1981), and because of the amount received for designated stock does not exceed $1,000,000, less amounts received (i) in exchange for stock in years prior to the transitional year; (ii) as contributions to capital in years prior to the transitional year; and (iii) as paid-in surplus in years prior to the transitional year. Nevertheless, in the event of B's sale of his stock at a loss, the increase in basis attributable to his December, 1981, contribution to capital will be treated as allocable to stock that is not section 1244 stock under § 1.1244(d)-2.

Example (4). Corporation Z, a newly-formed corporation, issues 10,000 shares of common stock at $200 per share on July 1, 1979. In exchange for its stock Corporation Z receives property (other than stock or securities) having a basis to the corporation of $400,000, and $1,600,000 in cash, for a total of $2,000,000. Corporation Z fails to designate any of the issued shares as section 1244 stock. Shareholder C purchases 2,500 shares of the 10,000 shares of Corporation Z stock for $500,000 on July 1, 1979. Subsequently, shareholder C sells the 2,500 shares for $400,000. Shareholder C may treat $50,000 of the $100,000 loss as an ordinary loss under section 1244. The amount of that loss is computed under the rule of subparagraph (3) of this paragraph (b) as follows:

$$\frac{X \text{ (C's section 1244 loss)}}{\$100,000 \text{ (C's total loss)}} = \frac{\$1,000,000 \; (\$1,000,000 - 0 = \$1,000,000)}{\$2,000,000 \; (\text{total amount received by Corporation Z})}$$

$$X = \$50,000$$

The remaining $50,000 is not treated as an ordinary loss under section 1244.

Example (5). (i) Corporation V, a newly-formed corporation, issues common stock to shareholder A and shareholder B on June 15,

1980, in exchange for $800,000 in cash ($400,000 from A and $400,000 from B). On September 15, 1981, the corporation issues common stock to shareholder C in exchange for $600,000 in cash. On January 1, 1982, common stock is issued to shareholder D in exchange for $100,000 in cash. Corporation V fails to designate any of the issued share as section 1244 stock. A, B, C, and D subsequently sell their Corporation Y stock at a loss.

(ii) Subject to the annual limitation discussed in § 1.1244(b)-1, A and B may treat their entire loss as an ordinary loss under section 1244. D may not treat any part of his loss as an ordinary loss under section 1244. Subject to the annual limitation, one-third of the loss sustained by shareholder C is treated as an ordinary loss under section 1244. These results are calculated under the rules of subparagraph (3) of this paragraph (b) as follows: First, section 1244 treatment is extended to post-November 1978 stock issued to A and B in 1980, a taxable year before the transitional year (1981); section 1244 treatment is withheld from the stock issued to D in 1982, a taxable year after the transitional year. Second, $800,000 the amount of post-1958 capital received in taxable years before the transitional year, is subtracted from $1,000,000 to leave $200,000. Third, subject to the annual limitation, an ordinary loss is allowed to C in an amount which bears the same ratio to his total loss as the amount calculated in the preceding sentence ($200,000) bears to the total amount received by the corporation in the transitional year in exchange for stock, as a contribution to capital, or as paid-in surplus ($600,000).

Example (6). Corporation V comes into existence on July 1, 1982. On that date it issues 10 shares of voting common stock to shareholder A in exchange for $500,000 and 5 shares of voting common stock to shareholder B in exchange for $250,000, designating the shares issued to both A and B as section 1244 stock. On September 15, 1982, Corporation V receives a contribution to capital from shareholders A and B having a basis in their hands of $225,000. On February 1, 1983, Corporation V issues one share of stock to shareholder C in exchange for $50,000. Corporation V may designate one-half of the share issued to shareholder C as section 1244 stock under § 1.1244(c)-2(b)(2). In 1982 the corporation received $750,000 for stock ($500,000 from A and $250,000 from B) and $225,000 as a capital contribution, totaling $975,000 in capital receipts. The receipt of $50,000 from shareholder C in exchange for stock in 1983 causes capital receipts to exceed $1,000,000 and 1983 thus becomes Corporation V's transitional year. Corporation V may receive only $25,000 for designated stock in 1983 under the rule set forth in § 1.1244(c)-2(b)(2)(i), which states that the amount received for designated stock shall not exceed $1,000,000, less amounts received (i) in exchange for stock in years prior to the transitional year ($750,000 from A and B), (ii) as contributions to capital in years prior to the transitional year ($225,000), and (iii) as paid-in surplus in years prior to the transitional year ($0). Thus, one-half of C's share (representing the receipt of $25,000) may be designated as section 1244 stock by Corporation V. In the event of the sale of A's stock or B's stock at a loss, the increase in basis attributable to their contribution to capital will be treated as allocable to stock that is not section 1244 stock under § 1.1244(d)-2.

(c) *Pre-November 1978 stock.*—(1) *Amount received by corporation for stock.*—At the time of the adoption of the plan, the sum of the aggregate dollar amount to be paid for pre-November 1978 stock that may be offered under the plan plus the aggregate amount of money and other property that has been received by the corporation after June 30, 1958, and on or before November 6, 1978, for its stock, as a contribution to capital by its shareholders, and as paid-in surplus must not exceed $500,000. In making these determinations (i) property is taken into account at its adjusted basis to the corporation (for determining gain) as of the date received by the corporation, and (ii) this aggregate amount is reduced by the amount of any liability to which the property was subject and by the amount of any liability assumed by the corporation at the time the property was received. For purposes of the $500,000 test, the total amount of money and other property received for stock, as a contribution to capital, and as paid-in surplus is not reduced by distributions to shareholders, even though the distributions may be capital distributions. Thus, once the total amount of money and other property received after June 30, 1958, reaches $500,000, the corporation is precluded from subsequently issuing pre-November 1978 stock. For a different rule that applies to post-November 1978 stock, see § 1.1244(c)-2(b).

(2) *Equity capital.*—The sum of the aggregate dollar amount to be paid for pre-November 1978 stock that may be offered under the plan plus the equity capital of the corporation (determined on the date of the adoption of the plan may not exceed $1,000,000. For this purpose, equity capital is the sum of the corporation's money and other property (in an amount equal to its adjusted basis for determining gain) less the amount of the corporation's indebtedness to persons other than its shareholders.

(3) *Examples.*—The provisions of this paragraph (c) may be illustrated by the following examples:

Example (1). Corporation W comes into existence on December 1, 1958. On that date the corporation may adopt a plan to issue common stock for an amount (determined under subparagraph (1) of this paragraph (c)) not in excess of $500,000 during a period ending not later than November 30, 1960. Such corporation will qualify as a small business corporation as of the date that the plan is adopted. However, if the corporation adopts a plan to issue stock for an amount in excess of $500,000 it is not a small business corporation at the time the plan is adopted and no stock issued under the plan may qualify as section 1244 stock. If the cost of organizing Corporation W amounted to $1,000 and constituted paid-in surplus or a contribution to capital, such amount must be taken into account in determining the amount that may be received under the plan, with the result that only $499,000 may be so received.

Example (2). On December 1, 1958, Corporation X, a newly formed corporation, adopts a plan to issue common stock for an amount (determined under subparagraph (1) of this paragraph (c)) not in excess of $500,000 during a period ending not later than November 30, 1960. By January 1, 1960, the corporation has, pursuant to the plan, issued at par, stock having an aggregate par value of $400,000, $200,000 of which was issued for $200,000 cash, and $200,000 of which was issued for property (other than stock or securities) having a basis to the corporation of $100,000 and a fair market value of $200,000. The corporation may, prior to November 30, 1960, issue stock for an amount not in excess of $200,000 cash or property having a basis to it not in excess of $200,000. Stock issued for any payment which, alone or together with any payments received after January 1, 1960, exceeds such $200,000 amount would not qualify as section 1244 stock because it would not be issued pursuant to the plan.

Example (3). Assume that on December 1, 1958, Corporation Y, a newly formed corporation, adopts a plan to issue common stock for an amount (determined under subparagraph (1) of this paragraph (c)) not in excess of $500,000 during a period ending not later than November 30, 1960. By January 1960 the corporation has received $400,000 cash for stock issued pursuant to the plan, but due to business successes the equity capital of the corporation exceeds $1,000,000. Since the equity capital test is made as of the date that the plan is adopted, the corporation may still, prior to November 30, 1960, issue section 1244 stock pursuant to the plan until the full amount specified in the plan has been received.

Example (4). Subsequent to June 30, 1958, Corporation Z receives a total of $600,000 cash on the issuance of its stock. In 1960 Corporation Z redeems shares of its stock for the total amount of $300,000 and the redemptions reduce Corporation Z's capital to substantially less than $500,000. Notwithstanding the redemptions, pre-November 1978 stock subsequently issued by Corporation Z will not qualify as section 1244 stock because the $500,000 limitation has been previously exceeded. [Reg. § 1.1244(c)-2.]

☐ [*T.D.* 6495, 10-7-60. *Amended by T.D.* 7779, 6-1-81 *and T.D.* 7837, 9-28-82.]

[Reg. § 1.1244(d)-1]

§ 1.1244(d)-1. Contributions of property having basis in excess of value.—(a) *In general.*—

(1) Section 1244(d)(1)(A) provides a special rule which limits the amount of loss on section 1244 stock that may be treated as an ordinary loss. This rule applies only when section 1244 stock is issued by a corporation in exchange for property that, immediately before the exchange, has an adjusted basis (for determining loss) in excess of its fair market value. If section 1244 stock is issued in exchange for such property and the basis of such stock in the hands of the taxpayer is determined by reference to the basis of such property, then for purposes of section 1244, the basis of such stock shall be reduced by an amount equal to the excess, at the time of the exchange, of the adjusted basis of the property over its fair market value.

(2) The provisions of section 1244(d)(1)(A) do not affect the basis of stock for purposes other than section 1244. Such provisions are to be used only in determining the portion of the total loss sustained that may be treated as an ordinary loss pursuant to section 1244.

(b) *Transfer of more than one item.*—If a taxpayer exchanges several items of property for stock in a single transaction so that the basis of the property transferred is allocated evenly among the shares of stock received, the computation under this section should be made by reference to the aggregate fair market value and the aggregate basis of the property transferred.

(c) *Examples.*—The provisions of this section may be illustrated by the following examples:

Example (1). B transfers property with an adjusted basis of $1,000 and a fair market value of $250 to a corporation for 10 shares of section 1244 stock in an exchange that qualifies under section 351. The basis of B's stock is $1,000 ($100 per share), but, solely for purposes of section 1244, the total basis of the stock must be reduced by $750, the excess of the adjusted basis of the property exchanged over its fair market value. Thus, the basis of such stock for purposes of section 1244 is $250 and the basis of each share for such purposes is $25. If B sells his 10 shares for $250, he will recognize a loss of $750, all of which must be treated as a capital loss. If he sells the 10 shares for $200, then $50 of his total loss of $800 will be treated as an ordinary loss under section 1244, assuming the various requirements of such section are satisfied, and the remaining $750 will be a capital loss.

Example (2). B owns property with a basis of $20,000. The fair market value of the property unencumbered is $15,000 but the property is subject to a $2,000 mortgage. B transfers the encumbered property to a corporation for 100 shares of section 1244 stock in an exchange that qualifies under section 351. The basis of the shares, determined in accordance with section 358, is $18,000 or $180 per share, but solely for purposes of section 1244 the basis is $13,000 ($130 per share), which is its basis for purposes other than section 1244, reduced by $5,000, the excess of the adjusted basis, immediately before the exchange, of the property transferred over its fair market value.

Example (3). C transfers business assets to a corporation for 100 shares of section 1244 stock in an exchange that qualifies under section 351. The assets transferred are as follows:

	Basis	Fair Market Value
Cash	$10,000	$10,000
Inventory	15,000	30,000
Depreciable property	50,000	20,000
Land	25,000	10,000
	$100,000	$70,000

The basis for the shares received by C is $100,000, which is applied $1,000 to each share. However, the basis of the shares for purposes of section 1244 is $70,000 ($700 per share), the basis for general purposes reduced by $30,000, the excess of the aggregate adjusted basis of the property transferred over the aggregate fair market value of such property. [Reg. § 1.1244(d)-1.]

☐ [*T.D.* 6495, 10-7-60.]

[Reg. § 1.1244(d)-2]

§ 1.1244(d)-2. Increases in basis of section 1244 stock.—(a) *In general.*—If subsequent to the time of its issuance there is for any reason, including the operation of section 1376(a), an increase in the basis of section 1244 stock, such increase shall be treated as allocable to stock which is not section 1244 stock. Therefore, a loss on stock, the basis of which has been increased subsequent to its issuance, must be apportioned between the part that qualifies as section 1244 stock and the part that does not so qualify. Only the loss apportioned to the part that so qualifies may be treated as an ordinary loss pursuant to section 1244. The amount of loss apportioned to the part that qualifies is the amount which bears the same ratio to the total loss as the basis of the stock which is treated as allocated to section 1244 stock bears to the total basis of the stock.

(b) *Example.*—The provisions of paragraph (a) of this section may be illustrated by the following example:

Example. For $10,000 a corporation issues 100 shares of section 1244 stock to X. X later contributes $2,000 to the capital of the corporation and this increases the total basis of his 100 shares to $12,000. Subsequently, he sells the 100 shares for $9,000. Of the $3,000 loss, $2,500 is allocated to the portion of the stock that qualifies as section 1244 stock

$$(\frac{\$10,000}{\$12,000} \text{ of } \$3,000)$$

and the remaining $500 is allocated to the portion of the stock that does not so qualify. Therefore, to the extent of $2,500, the loss may be treated as an ordinary loss assuming the various requirements of section 1244 stock are satisfied.

However, the remaining $500 loss must be treated as a capital loss. [Reg. § 1.1244(d)-2.]

☐ [*T.D.* 6495, 10-7-60.]

[Reg. § 1.1244(d)-3]

§ 1.1244(d)-3. Stock dividend, recapitalization, changes in name, etc..—(a) *In general.*— Section 1244(c)(1) provides that stock may not qualify for the benefits of section 1244 unless it is issued to the taxpayer for money or other property not including stock or securities. However, section 1244(d)(2) authorizes exceptions to this rule. The exceptions may apply in three situations: (1) The receipt of a stock dividend; (2) the exchange of stock for stock pursuant to a reorganization described in section 368(a)(1)(E); and (3) the exchange of stock for stock pursuant to a reorganization described in section 368(a)(1)(F).

(b) *Stock dividends.*—(1) If common stock is received by an individual or partnership in a nontaxable distribution under section 305(a) made solely with respect to stock owned by such individual or partnership which meets the requirements of section 1244 stock determinable at the time of the distribution, then the common stock so received will also be treated as meeting such requirements. For purposes of this paragraph and paragraphs (c) and (d) of this section, the requirements of section 1244 stock determinable at the time of the distribution or exchange are all of the requirements of section 1244(c)(1) other than the one described in subparagraph (C) thereof, relating to the gross receipts test.

(2) If, however, such stock dividend is received by such individual or partnership partly with respect to stock meeting the requirements of section 1244 stock determinable at the time of the distribution, and partly with respect to stock not meeting such requirements, then only part of the stock received as a stock dividend will be treated as meeting such requirements. Assuming all the shares with respect to which the dividend is received have equal rights to dividends, such part is the number of shares which bears the same ratio to the total number of shares received as the number of shares owned immediately before the stock dividend which meets such qualifications bears to the total number of shares with respect to which the stock dividend is received. In determining the basis of shares received in the stock dividend and of the shares held before the stock dividend, section 307 shall apply as if two separate nontaxable stock dividends were made, one with respect to the shares that meet the requirements and the other with respect to shares that do not meet the requirements.

(3) The provisions of subparagraphs (1) and (2) of this paragraph may be illustrated by the following examples:

Example (1). Corporation X issues 100 shares of its common stock to B for $1,000. Subsequently, in a nontaxable stock dividend B receives 5 more shares of common stock of Corporation X. If the 100 shares meet all the requirements of section 1244 stock determinable at the time of the distribution of the stock dividend, the 5 additional shares shall also be treated as meeting such requirements.

Example (2). In 1959, Corporation Y issues 100 shares of its common stock to C for $1,000 and these shares meet the requirements of section 1244 stock determinable at the time of the issuance. In 1960, C purchases an additional 200 shares of such stock from another shareholder for $3,000; however, these shares do not meet the requirements of section 1244 stock because they were not originally issued to C by the corporation. In 1961, C receives 15 shares of Corporation Y common stock as a stock dividend. Of the shares received, 5 shares, the number received with respect to the 100 shares of stock which met the requirements of section 1244 at the time of the distribution, i.e.,

$$\frac{100}{300} \times 15,$$

shall also be treated as meeting such requirements. The remaining 10 shares do not meet such requirements as they are not received with respect to section 1244 stock. The basis of such 5 shares is determined by applying section 307 as if the 5 shares were received as a separate stock dividend made solely with respect to shares that meet the requirements of section 1244 stock at the time of the distribution. Thus, the basis of the 5 shares is $47.61

$$(\frac{5}{105} \text{ of } \$1,000).$$

(c) *Recapitalizations.*—(1) If, pursuant to a recapitalization described in section 368(a)(1)(E), common stock of a corporation is received by an individual or partnership in exchange for stock of such corporation meeting the requirements of section 1244 stock determinable at the time of the exchange, such common stock shall be treated as meeting such requirements.

(2) If common stock is received pursuant to such a recapitalization partly in exchange for stock meeting the requirements of section 1244 stock determinable at the time of the exchange and partly in exchange for stock not meeting such requirements, then only part of such common stock will be treated as meeting such requirements. Such part is the number of shares which bears the same ratio to the total number of shares of common stock so received as the basis of the shares transferred which meet such requirements bears to the basis of all the shares transferred for such common stock. The basis allocable, pursuant to section 358, to the common stock which is treated as meeting such requirements is limited to the basis of stock that meets such requirements transferred in the exchange.

(3) The provisions of subparagraphs (1) and (2) of this paragraph may be illustrated by the following examples:

Example (1). A owns 500 shares of voting common stock of Corporation X. Corporation X revises its capital structure to provide for two classes of common stock: Class A voting and Class B nonvoting. In a recapitalization described in subparagraph (E) of section 368(a)(1), A exchanges his 500 shares for 750 shares of Class B nonvoting stock. If the 500 shares meet all the requirements of section 1244 stock determinable at the time of the exchange, the 750 shares received in the exchange are treated as meeting such requirements.

Example (2). B owns 500 shares of common stock of Corporation X with a basis of $5,000, and 100 shares of preferred stock of that corporation with a basis of $2,500. Pursuant to a recapitalization described in section 368(a)(1)(E), B exchanges all of his shares for 900 shares of common stock of Corporation X. The 500 common shares meet the requirements of section 1244 stock determinable at the time of the exchange, but the 100 preferred shares do not meet such requirements since only common stock may qualify. Of the 900 common shares received, 600 shares

$$(\frac{\$5,000}{\$7,500} \times 900 \text{ shares })$$

are treated as meeting the requirements of section 1244 at the time of the exchange, because they are deemed to be received in exchange for the 500 common shares which met such requirements. The remaining 300 shares do not meet such requirements as they are not deemed to be received in exchange for section 1244 stock. The basis of the 600 shares is $5,000, the basis of the relinquished shares meeting the requirements of section 1244.

(d) *Change of name, etc..*—(1) If, pursuant to a reorganization described in section 368(a)(1)(F), common stock of a successor corporation is received by an individual or partnership in exchange for stock of the predecessor corporation meeting the requirements of section 1244 stock determinable at the time of the exchange, such common stock shall be treated as meeting such requirements. If common stock is received pursuant to such a reorganization partly in exchange for stock meeting the requirements of section 1244 stock determinable at the time of the exchange and partly in exchange for stock not meeting such requirements, the principles of paragraph (c)(2) of this section apply in determining the number of shares received which are treated as meeting the requirements of section 1244 stock and the basis of those shares.

(2) For purposes of paragraphs (1)(C) and (3)(A) of section 1244(c), a successor corporation in a reorganization described in section

368(a)(1)(F) shall be treated as the same corporation as its predecessor. [Reg. § 1.1244(d)-3.]

☐ [*T.D. 6495, 10-7-60. Amended by T.D. 7779, 6-1-81.*]

[Reg. § 1.1244(d)-4]

§ 1.1244(d)-4. Net operating loss deduction.—
(a) *General rule.*—For purposes of section 172, relating to the net operating loss deduction, any amount of loss that is treated as an ordinary loss under section 1244 (taking into account the annual dollar limitation of that section) shall be treated as attributable to the trade or business of the taxpayer. Therefore, this loss is allowable in determining the taxpayer's net operating loss for a taxable year and is not subject to the application of section 172(d)(4), relating to nonbusiness deductions. A taxpayer may deduct the maximum of ordinary loss permitted under section 1244(b) even though all or a portion of the taxpayer's net operating loss carryback or carryover for the taxable year was, when incurred, a loss on section 1244 stock.

(b) *Example.*—The provisions of this section may be illustrated by the following example:

Example. A, a single individual, computes a net operating loss of $15,000 for 1980 in accordance with the rules of § 1.172-3, relating to net operating loss in case of a taxpayer other than a corporation. Included within A's computation of this net operating loss is a deduction arising under section 1244 for a loss on a small business stock. A had no taxable income in 1977, 1978, or 1979. Assume that A can carry over the entire $15,000 loss under the rules of section 172. In 1981 A has gross income of $75,000 and again sustains a loss on section 1244 stock. The amount of A's 1981 loss on section 1244 stock is $50,000. A may deduct the full $50,000 as an ordinary loss under section 1244 and the full $15,000 as a net operating loss carryover in 1981. [Reg. § 1.1244(d)-4.]

☐ [*T.D. 6495, 10-7-60. Amended by T.D. 7779, 6-1-81.*]

[Reg. § 1.1244(e)-1]

§ 1.1244(e)-1. Records to be kept.—(a) *By the corporation.*—(1) *Mandatory records.*—A plan to issue pre-November 1978 stock must appear upon the records of the corporation. Any designation of post-November 1978 stock under § 1.1244(c)-2(b)(2) also must appear upon the records of the corporation.

(2) *Discretionary records.*—In order to substantiate an ordinary loss deduction claimed by its shareholders, the corporation should maintain records showing the following:

(i) The persons to whom stock was issued, the date of issuance to these persons, and a description of the amount and type of consideration received from each;

(ii) If the consideration received is property, the basis in the hands of the shareholder and the fair market value of the property when received by the corporation;

(iii) The amount of money and the basis in the hands of the corporation of other property received for its stock, as a contribution to capital, and as paid-in surplus;

(iv) Financial statements of the corporation, such as its income tax returns, that identify the source of the gross receipt of the corporation for the period consisting of the five most recent taxable years of the corporation, or, if the corporation has not been in existence for 5 taxable years, for the period of the corporation's existence;

(v) Information relating to any tax-free stock dividend made with respect to section 1244 stock and any reorganization in which stock is transferred by the corporation in exchange for section 1244 stock; and

(vi) With respect to pre-November 1978 stock:

(A) Which certificates represent stock issued under the plan;

(B) The amount of money and the basis in the hands of the corporation of other property received after June 30, 1958, and before the adoption of the plan, for its stock, as a contribution to capital, and as paid-in surplus; and

(C) The equity capital of the corporation on the date of adoption of the plan.

(b) *By the taxpayer.*—A person who claims an ordinary loss with respect to stock under section 1244 must have records sufficient to establish that the taxpayer is entitled to the loss and satisfies the requirements of section 1244. See also section 6001, requiring records to be maintained. [Reg. § 1.1244(e)-1.]

☐ [*T.D. 6495, 10-7-60. Amended by T.D. 7779, 6-1-81 and T.D. 8594, 4-27-95.*]

[Reg. § 1.1245-1]

§ 1.1245-1. General rule for treatment of gain from dispositions of certain depreciable property.—(a) *General.*—(1) In general, section 1245(a)(1) provides that, upon a disposition of an item of section 1245 property, the amount by which the lower of (i) the "recomputed basis" of the property, or (ii) the amount realized on a sale, exchange, or involuntary conversion (or the fair market value of the property on any other disposition), exceeds the adjusted basis of the property shall be treated as gain from the sale or exchange of property which is neither a capital asset nor property described in section 1231 (that is, shall be recognized as ordinary income). The amount of such gain shall be determined separately for each item of section 1245 property. In general, the term "recomputed basis" means the adjusted basis of property plus all adjustments reflected in such adjusted basis on account of depreciation allowed or allowable for all periods after December 31, 1961. See section 1245(a)(2) and §1.1245-2. Generally, the ordinary income treatment applies even though in the absence of section 1245 no gain would be recognized under the Code. For example, if a corporation distributes section 1245 property as a dividend, gain may be recognized as ordinary income to the corporation even though, in the absence of section 1245, section 311(a) would preclude any recognition of gain to the corporation. For the definition of "section 1245 property," see section 1245(a)(3) and §1.1245-3. For exceptions and limitations to the application of section 1245(a)(1), see section 1245(b) and §1.1245-4.

(2) Section 1245(a)(1) applies to dispositions of section 1245 property in taxable years beginning after December 31, 1962, except that—

(i) In respect of section 1245 property which is an elevator or escalator, section 1245(a)(1) applies to dispositions after December 31, 1963, and

(ii) In respect of section 1245 property which is livestock (described in subparagraph (4) of §1.1245-3(a)), section 1245(a)(1) applies to dispositions made in taxable years beginning after December 31, 1969, and

(iii) [reserved].

(3) For purposes of this section and §§1.1245-2 through 1.1245-6, the term "disposition" includes a sale in a sale-and-leaseback transaction and a transfer upon the foreclosure of a security interest, but such term does not include a mere transfer of title to a creditor upon creation of a security interest or to a debtor upon termination of a security interest. Thus, for example, a disposition occurs upon a sale of property pursuant to a conditional sales contract even though the seller retains legal title to the property for purposes of security but a disposition does not occur when the seller ulitmately gives up his security interest following payment by the purchaser.

(4) For purposes of applying section 1245, the facts and circumstances of each disposition shall be considered in determining what is the appropriate item of section 1245 property. A taxpayer may treat any number of units of section 1245 property in any particular depreciation account (as defined in §1.167(a)-7) as one time of section 1245 property as long as it is reasonably clear, from the best estimates obtainable on the basis of all the facts and circumstances, that the amount of gain to which section 1245(a)(1) applies is not less than the total of the gain under section 1245(a)(1) which would be computed separately for each unit. Thus, for example, if 50 units of section 1245 property X, 25 units of section 1245 property Y, and other property are accounted for in one depreciation account, and if each such unit is sold at a gain in one transaction in which the total gain realized on the sale exceeds the sum of the adjustments reflected in the adjusted basis (as defined in paragraph (a)(2) of

§1.1245-2) of each such unit on account of depreciation allowed or allowable for periods after December 31, 1961, all 75 units may be treated as one item of section 1245 property. If, however, 5 such units of section 1245 property Y were sold at a loss, then only 70 of such units (50 of X plus the 20 of Y sold at a gain) may be treated as one item of section 1245 property.

(5) In case of a sale, exchange, or involuntary conversion of section 1245 and nonsection 1245 property in one transaction, the total amount realized upon the disposition shall be allocated between the section 1245 property and the nonsection 1245 property in proportion to their respective fair market values. In general, if a buyer and seller have adverse interests as to the allocation of the amount realized between the section 1245 property and the nonsection 1245 property, any arm's length agreement between the buyer and the seller will establish the allocation. In the absence of such an agreement, the allocation shall be made by taking into account the appropriate facts and circumstances. Some of the facts and circumstances which shall be taken into account to the extent appropriate include, but are not limited to, a comparison between the section 1245 property and all the property disposed of in such transaction of (i) the original cost and reproduction cost of construction, erection, or production, (ii) the remaining economic useful life, (iii) state of obsolescence, and (iv) anticipated expenditures to maintain, renovate, or to modernize.

(b) *Sale, exchange, or involuntary conversion.*— (1) In the case of a sale, exchange, or involuntary conversion of section 1245 property, the gain to which section 1245(a)(1) applies is the amount by which (i) the lower of the amount realized upon the disposition of the property or the recomputed basis of the property, exceeds (ii) the adjusted basis of the property.

(2) The provisions of this paragraph may be illustrated by the following examples:

Example (1). On January 1, 1964, Brown purchases section 1245 property for use in his manufacturing business. The property has a basis for depreciation of $3,300. After taking depreciation deductions of $1,300 (the amount allowable), Brown realizes after selling expenses the amount of $2,900 upon sale of the property on January 1, 1969. Brown's gain is $900 ($2,900 amount realized minus $2,000 adjusted basis). Since the amount realized upon disposition of the property ($2,900) is lower than its recomputed basis ($3,300, i.e., $2,000 adjusted basis plus $1,300 in depreciation deductions), the entire gain is treated as ordinary income under section 1245(a)(1) and not as gain from the sale or exchange of property described in section 1231.

Example (2). Assume the same facts as in example (1) except that Brown exchanges the section 1245 property for land which has a fair market value of $3,700, thereby realizing a gain of $1,700 ($3,700 amount realized minus $2,000 adjusted basis). Since the recomputed basis of the property ($3,300) is lower than the amount realized upon its disposition ($3,700), the excess of recomputed basis over adjusted basis, or $1,300, is treated as ordinary income under section 1245(a)(1). The remaining $400 of the gain may be treated as gain from the sale or exchange of property described in section 1231.

(c) *Other dispositions.*—(1) In the case of a disposition of section 1245 property other than by way of a sale, exchange, or involuntary conversion, the gain to which section 1245(a)(1) applies is the amount by which (i) the lower of the fair market value of the property on the date of disposition or the recomputed basis of the property, exceeds (ii) the adjusted basis of the property. If property is transferred by a corporation to a shareholder for an amount less than its fair market value in a sale or exchange, for purposes of applying section 1245 such transfer shall be treated as a disposition other than by way of a sale, exchange, or involuntary conversion.

(2) The provisions of this paragraph may be illustrated by the following examples:

Example (1). X Corporation distributes section 1245 property to its shareholders as a dividend. The property has an adjusted basis of $2,000 to the corporation, a recomputed basis of $3,300, and a fair market value of $3,100. Since the fair market value of the property ($3,100) is lower than its recomputed basis ($3,300), the excess of fair market value over adjusted basis, or $1,100, is treated under section 1245(a)(1) as ordinary income to the corporation even though, in the absence of section 1245, section 311(a) would preclude recognition of gain to the corporation.

Example (2). Assume the same facts as in example (1) except that X Corporation distributes the section 1245 property to its shareholders in complete liquidation of the corporation. Assume further that section 1245(b)(3) does not apply and that the fair market value of the property is $3,800 at the time of the distribution. Since the recomputed basis of the property ($3,300) is lower than its fair market value ($3,800), the excess of recomputed basis over adjusted basis, or $1,300, is treated under section 1245(a)(1) as ordinary income to the corporation even though, in the absence of section 1245, section 336 would preclude recognition of gain to the corporation.

(d) *Losses.*—Section 1245(a)(1) does not apply to losses. Thus, section 1245(a)(1) does not apply if a loss is realized upon a sale, exchange, or involuntary conversion of property, all of which is considered section 1245 property, nor does the section apply to a disposition of such property other than by way of sale, exchange, or involuntary conversion if at the time of the disposition the fair market value of such property is not greater than its adjusted basis.

(e) *Treatment of partnership and partners.*—(1) The manner of determining the amount of gain recognized under section 1245(a)(1) to a partnership may be illustrated by the following example:

Example. A partnership sells for $63 section 1245 property which has an adjusted basis to the partnership of $30 and a recomputed basis to the partnership of $60. The partnership recognizes under section 1245(a)(1) gain of $30, i.e., the lower of the amount realized ($63) or recomputed basis ($60), minus adjusted basis ($30). This result would not be changed if one or more partners had, in respect of the property, a special basis adjustment described in section 743(b) or had taken depreciation deductions in respect of such special basis adjustment.

(2)(i) Unless paragraph (e)(3) of this section applies, a partner's distributive share of gain recognized under section 1245(a)(1) by the partnership is equal to the lesser of the partner's share of total gain from the disposition of the property (gain limitation) or the partner's share of depreciation or amortization with respect to the property (as determined under paragraph (e)(2)(ii) of this section). Any gain recognized under section 1245(a)(1) by the partnership that is not allocated under the first sentence of this paragraph (e)(2)(i) (excess depreciation recapture) is allocated among the partners whose shares of total gain from the disposition of the property exceed their shares of depreciation or amortization with respect to the property. Excess depreciation recapture is allocated among those partners in proportion to their relative shares of the total gain (including gain recognized under section 1245(a)(1)) from the disposition of the property that is allocated to the partners who are not subject to the gain limitation. See *Example 2* of paragraph (e)(2)(iii) of this section.

(ii)(A) Subject to the adjustments described in paragraphs (e)(2)(ii)(B) and (e)(2)(ii)(C) of this section, a partner's share of depreciation or amortization with respect to property equals the total amount of allowed or allowable depreciation or amortization previously allocated to that partner with respect to the property.

(B) If a partner transfers a partnership interest, a share of depreciation or amortization must be allocated to the transferee partner as it would have been allocated to the transferor partner. If the partner transfers a portion of the partnership interest, a share of depreciation or amortization proportionate to the interest transferred must be allocated to the transferee partner.

(C)(1) A partner's share of depreciation or amortization with respect to property contributed by the partner includes the amount of depreciation or amortization allowed or allowable to the partner for the period before the property is contributed.

(2) A partner's share of depreciation or amortization with respect to property contributed by a partner is adjusted to account for any curative allocations. (See §1.704-3(c) for a description of the traditional method with curative allocations.) The contributing partner's share of depreciation or amortization with respect to the contributed property is decreased (but not below zero) by the amount of any curative allocation of ordinary income to the contributing partner with respect to that property and by the amount of any curative allocation of deduction or loss (other than capital loss) to the noncontributing partners with respect to that property. A noncontributing partner's share of depreciation or amortization with respect to the contributed property is increased by the noncontributing partner's share of any curative allocation of ordinary income to the contributing partner with respect to that property and by the amount of any curative allocation of deduction or loss (other than capital loss) to the noncontributing partner with respect to that property. The partners' shares of depreciation or amortization with respect to property from which curative allocations of depreciation or amortization are taken is determined without regard to those curative allocations. See *Example* 3(iii) of paragraph (e)(2)(iii) of this section.

(3) A partner's share of depreciation or amortization with respect to property contributed by a partner is adjusted to account for any remedial allocations. (See §1.704-3(d) for a description of the remedial allocation method.) The contributing partner's share of depreciation or amortization with respect to the contributed property is decreased (but not below zero) by the amount of any remedial allocation of income to the contributing partner with respect to that property. A noncontributing partner's share of depreciation or amortization with respect to the contributed property is increased by the amount of any remedial allocation of depreciation or amortization to the noncontributing partner with respect to that property. See *Example* 3(iv) of paragraph (e)(2)(iii) of this section.

(4) If, under paragraphs (e)(2)(ii)(C)(2) and (e)(2)(ii)(C)(3) of this section, the partners' shares of depreciation or amortization with respect to a contributed property exceed the adjustments reflected in the adjusted basis of the property under §1.1245-2(a) at the partnership level, then the partnership's gain recognized under section 1245(a)(1) with respect to that property is allocated among the partners in proportion to their relative shares of depreciation or amortization (subject to any gain limitation that might apply).

(5) This paragraph (e)(2)(ii)(C) also applies in determining a partner's share of depreciation or amortization with respect to property for which differences between book value and adjusted tax basis are created when a partnership revalues partnership property pursuant to §1.704-1(b)(2)(iv)(f).

(iii) Examples.—The application of this paragraph (e)(2) may be illustrated by the following examples:

Example 1. Recapture allocations. (i) *Facts.* A and B each contribute $5,000 cash to form AB, a general partnership. The partnership agreement provides that depreciation deductions will be allocated 90 percent to A and 10 percent to B, and, on the sale of depreciable property, A will first be allocated gain to the extent necessary to equalize A's and B's capital accounts. Any remaining gain will be allocated 50 percent to A and 50 percent to B. In its first year of operations, AB purchases depreciable equipment for $5,000. AB depreciates the equipment over its 5-year recovery period and elects to use the straight-line method. In its first year of operations, AB's operating income equals its expenses (other than depreciation). (To simplify this example, AB's depreciation deductions are determined without regard to any first-year depreciation conventions.)

(ii) *Year 1.* In its first year of operations, AB has $1,000 of depreciation from the partnership equipment. In accordance with the partnership agreement, AB allocates 90 percent ($900) of the depreciation to A and 10 percent ($100) of the depreciation to B. At the end of the year, AB sells the equipment for $5,200, recognizing $1,200 of gain ($5,200 amount realized less $4,000 adjusted tax basis). In accordance with the partnership agreement, the first $800 of gain is allocated to A to equalize the partners' capital accounts, and the remaining $400 of gain is allocated $200 to A and $200 to B.

(iii) *Recapture allocations.* $1,000 of the gain from the sale of the equipment is treated as section 1245(a)(1) gain. Under paragraph (e)(2)(i) of this section, each partner's share of the section 1245(a)(1) gain is equal to the lesser of the partner's share of total gain recognized on the sale of the equipment or the partner's share of total depreciation with respect to the equipment. Thus, A's share of the section 1245(a)(1) gain is $900 (the lesser of A's share of the total gain ($1,000) and A's share of depreciation ($900)). B's share of the section 1245(a)(1) gain is $100 (the lesser of B's share of the total gain ($200) and B's share of depreciation ($100)). Accordingly, $900 of the $1,000 of total gain allocated to A is treated as ordinary income and $100 of the $200 of total gain allocated to B is treated as ordinary income.

Example 2. Recapture allocation subject to gain limitation. (i) *Facts.* A, B, and C form general partnership ABC. The partnership agreement provides that depreciation deductions will be allocated equally among the partners, but that gain from the sale of depreciable property will be allocated 75 percent to A and 25 percent to B. ABC purchases depreciable personal property for $300 and subsequently allocates $100 of depreciation deductions each to A, B, and C, reducing the adjusted tax basis of the property to $0. ABC then sells the property for $440. ABC allocates $330 of the gain to A (75 percent of $440) and allocates $110 of the gain to B (25 percent of $440). No gain is allocated to C.

(ii) *Application of gain limitation.* Each partner's share of depreciation with respect to the property is $100. C's share of the total gain from the disposition of the property, however, is $0. As a result, under the gain limitation provision in paragraph (e)(2)(i) of this section, C's share of section 1245(a)(1) gain is limited to $0.

(iii) *Excess depreciation recapture.* Under paragraph (e)(2)(i) of this section, the $100 of section 1245(a)(1) gain that cannot be allocated to C under the gain limitation provision (excess depreciation recapture) is allocated to A and B (the partners not subject to the gain limitation at the time of the allocation) in proportion to their relative shares of total gain from the disposition of the property. A's relative share of the total gain allocated to A and B is 75 percent ($330 of $440 total gain). B's relative share of the total gain allocated to A and B is 25 percent ($110 of $440 total gain). However, under the gain limitation provision of paragraph (e)(2)(i) of this section, B cannot be allocated 25 percent of the excess depreciation recapture ($25) because that would result in a total allocation of $125 of depreciation recapture to B (a $100 allocation equal to B's share of depreciation plus a $25 allocation of excess depreciation recapture), which is in excess of B's share of the total gain from the disposition of the property ($110). Therefore, only $10 of excess depreciation recapture is allocated to B and the remaining $90 of excess depreciation recapture is allocated to A. A is not subject to the gain limitation because A's share of the total gain ($330) still exceeds A's share of section 1245(a)(1) gain ($190). Accordingly, all $110 of the total gain allocated to B is treated as ordinary income ($100 share of depreciation allocated to B plus $10 of excess depreciation recapture) and $190 of the total gain allocated to A is treated as ordinary income ($100 share of depreciation allocated to A plus $90 of excess depreciation recapture).

Example 3. Determination of partners' shares of depreciation with respect to contributed property. (i) *Facts.* C and D form partnership CD as equal partners. C contributes depreciable personal property C1 with an adjusted tax basis of $800 and a fair market value of $2,800. Prior to the contribution, C claimed $200 of depreciation from C1. At the time of the contribution, C1 is depreciable under the straight-line method and has four years remaining on its 5-year recovery period. D contributes $2,800 cash, which CD uses to purchase depreciable personal property D1, which is depreciable over seven years under the straight-line method. (To simplify the exam-

ple, all depreciation is determined without regard to any first-year depreciation conventions.)

(ii) *Traditional method.* C1 generates $700 of book depreciation ($1/4$ of $2,800 book value) and $200 of tax depreciation ($1/4$ of $800 adjusted tax basis) each year. C and D will each be allocated $350 of book depreciation from C1 in year 1. Under the traditional method of making section 704(c) allocations, D will be allocated the entire $200 of tax depreciation from C1 in year 1. D1 generates $400 of book and tax depreciation each year ($1/7$ of $2,800 book value and adjusted tax basis). C and D will each be allocated $200 of book and tax depreciation from D1 in year 1. As a result, after the first year of partnership operations, C's share of depreciation with respect to C1 is $200 (the depreciation taken by C prior to contribution) and D's share of depreciation with respect to C1 is $200 (the amount of tax depreciation allocated to D). C and D each have a $200 share of depreciation with respect to D1. At the end of four years, C's share of depreciation with respect to C1 will be $200 (the depreciation taken by C prior to contribution) and D's share of depreciation with respect to C1 will be $800 (four years of $200 depreciation per year). At the end of four years, C and D will each have an $800 share of depreciation with respect to D1 (four years of $200 depreciation per year).

(iii) *Effect of curative allocations.* (A) *Year 1.* If the partnership elects to make curative allocations under § 1.704-3(c) using depreciation from D1, the results will be the same as under the traditional method, except that $150 of the $200 of tax depreciation from D1 that would be allocated to C under the traditional method will be allocated to D as additional depreciation with respect to C1. As a result, after the first year of partnership operations, C's share of depreciation with respect to C1 will be reduced to $50 (the total depreciation taken by C prior to contribution ($200) decreased by the amount of the curative allocation to D ($150)). D's share of depreciation with respect to C1 will be $350 (the depreciation allocated to D under the traditional method ($200) increased by the amount of the curative allocation to D ($150)). C and D will each have a $200 share of depreciation with respect to D1.

(B) *Year 4.* At the end of four years, C's share of depreciation with respect to C1 will be reduced to $0 (the total depreciation taken by C prior to contribution ($200) decreased, but not below zero, by the amount of the curative allocations to D ($600)), and D's share of depreciation with respect to C1 will be $1,400 (the total depreciation allocated to D under the traditional method ($800) increased by the amount of the curative allocations to D ($600)). However, CD's section 1245(a)(1) gain with respect to C1 will not be more than $1,000 (CD's tax depreciation ($800) plus C's tax depreciation prior to contribution ($200)). Under paragraph (e)(2)(ii)(C)(4) of this section, because the partners' shares of

Reg. § 1.1245-1(e)(2)(iii)

depreciation with respect to C1 exceed the adjustments reflected in the property's adjusted basis, CD's section 1245(a)(1) gain will be allocated in proportion to the partners' relative shares of depreciation with respect to C1. Because C's share of depreciation with respect to C1 is $0, and D's share of depreciation with respect to C1 is $1,400, all of CD's $1,000 of section 1245(a)(1) gain will be allocated to D. At the end of four years, C and D will each have an $800 share of depreciation with respect to D1 (four years of $200 depreciation per year).

(iv) *Effect of remedial allocations.* (A) *Year 1.* If the partnership elects to make remedial allocations under §1.704-3(d), there will be $600 of book depreciation from C1 in year 1. (Under the remedial allocation method, the amount by which C1's book basis ($2,800) exceeds its tax basis ($800) is depreciated over a 5-year life, rather than a 4-year life.) C and D will each be allocated one-half ($300) of the total book depreciation. As under the traditional method, D will be allocated all $200 of tax depreciation from C1. Because the ceiling rule would cause a disparity of $100 between D's book and tax allocations of depreciation, D will also receive a $100 remedial allocation of depreciation with respect to C1, and C will receive a $100 remedial allocation of income with respect to C1. As a result, after the first year of partnership operations, D's share of depreciation with respect to C1 is $300 (the depreciation allocated to D under the traditional method ($200) increased by the amount of the remedial allocation ($100)). C's share of depreciation with respect to C1 is $100 (the total depreciation taken by C prior to contribution ($200) decreased by the amount of the remedial allocation of income ($100)). C and D will each have a $200 share of depreciation with respect to D1.

(B) *Year 5.* At the end of five years, C's share of depreciation with respect to C1 will be $0 (the total depreciation taken by C prior to contribution ($200) decreased, but not below zero, by the total amount of the remedial allocations of income to C ($600)). D's share of depreciation with respect to C1 will be $1,400 (the total depreciation allocated to D under the traditional method ($800) increased by the total amount of the remedial allocations of depreciation to D ($600)). However, CD's section 1245(a)(1) gain with respect to C1 will not be more than $1,000 (CD's tax depreciation ($800) plus C's tax depreciation prior to contribution ($200)). Under paragraph (e)(2)(ii)(C)(4) of this section, because the partners' shares of depreciation with respect to C1 exceed the adjustments reflected in the property's adjusted basis, CD's section 1245(a)(1) gain will be allocated in proportion to the partners' relative shares of depreciation with respect to C1. Because C's share of depreciation with respect to C1 is $0, and D's share of depreciation with respect to C1 is $1,400, all of CD's $1,000 of section 1245(a)(1) gain will be allocated to D. At the end of five years, C and D will each have a

$1,000 share of depreciation with respect to D1 (five years of $200 depreciation per year).

(iv) *Effective date.*—This paragraph (e)(2) is effective for properties acquired by a partnership on or after August 20, 1997. However, partnerships may rely on this paragraph (e)(2) for properties acquired before August 20, 1997, and disposed of on or after August 20, 1997.

(3)(i) If (a) a partner had a special basis adjustment under section 743(b) in respect of section 1245 property, or (b) on the date he acquired his partnership interest by way of a sale or exchange (or upon death of another partner) the partnership owned section 1245 property and an election under section 754 (relating to optional adjustment to basis of partnership property) was in effect with respect to the partnership, then the amount of gain recognized under section 1245(a)(1) by him upon a disposition by the partnership of such property shall be determined under this subparagraph.

(ii) There shall be allocated to such partner, in the same proportion as the partnership's total gain is allocated to him as his distributive share under section 704, a portion of (a) the common partnership adjusted basis for the property, and (b) the amount realized by the partnership upon the disposition, or, if nothing is realized, the fair market value of the property. There shall also be allocated to him, in the same proportion as the partnership's gain recognized under section 1245(a)(1) is allocated under subparagraph (2) of this paragraph as his distributive share of such gain, a portion of "the adjustments reflected in the adjusted basis" (as defined in paragraph (a)(2) of §1.1245-2) of such property. If on the date he acquired his partnership interest by way of a sale or exchange the partnership owned such property and an election under section 754 was in effect, then for purposes of the preceding sentence the amount of the adjustments reflected in the adjusted basis of such property on such date shall be deemed to be zero. For special rules relating to the amount of adjustments reflected in the adjusted basis of property after partnership transactions, see paragraph (c)(6) of §1.1245-2.

(iii) The partner's adjusted basis in respect of the property shall be deemed to be (a) the portion of the partnership's adjusted basis for the property allocated to the partner under subdivision (ii) of this subparagraph, (b) increased by the amount of any special basis adjustment described in section 743(b)(1) (or decreased by the amount of any special basis adjustment described in section 743(b)(2)) which the partner may have in respect of the property on the date the partnership disposed of the property.

(iv) The partner's recomputed basis in respect of the property shall be deemed to be (a) the sum of the partner's adjusted basis for the property, as determined in subdivision (iii) of this subparagraph, plus the amount of "the adjustments reflected in the adjusted basis" (as defined in paragraph (a)(2) of § 1.1245-2) for the property allocated to the partner under subdivision (ii) of this subparagraph, (b) increased by the amount by which any special basis adjustment described in section 743(b)(1) (or decreased by the amount by which any special basis adjustment described in section 743(b)(2)) in respect of the property was reduced, but only to the extent such amount was applied to adjust the amount of the deductions allowed or allowable to the partner for depreciation or amortization of section 1245 property attributable to periods referred to in paragraph (a)(2) of § 1.1245-2. The terms "allowed or allowable," "depreciation or amortization," and "attributable to periods" shall have the meanings assigned to those terms in paragraph (a) of § 1.1245-2.

(4) The application of subparagraph (3) of this paragraph may be illustrated by the following example:

Example. A, B, and C each hold a one-third interest in calendar year partnership ABC. On December 31, 1962, the firm holds section 1245 property which has an adjusted basis of $30,000 and a recomputed basis of $33,000. Depreciation deductions in respect of the property for 1962 were $3,000. On January 1, 1963, when D purchases C's partnership interest, the election under section 754 is in effect and a $5,000 special basis adjustment is made in respect of D to his one-third share of the common partnership adjusted basis for the property. For 1963 and 1964 the partnership deducts $6,000 as depreciation in respect of the property, thereby reducing its adjusted basis to $24,000, and D deducts $2,800, *i.e.*, his distributive share of partnership depreciation ($2,000) plus depreciation in respect of his special basis adjustment ($800). On March 15, 1965, the partnership sells the property for $48,000. Since the partnership's recomputed basis for the property ($33,000, i.e., $24,000 adjusted basis plus $9,000 in depreciation deductions) is lower than the amount realized upon the sale ($48,000), the excess of recomputed basis over adjusted basis, or $9,000, is treated as partnership gain under section 1245(a)(1). D's distributive share of such gain is $3,000 (⅓ of $9,000). However, the amount of gain recognized by D under section 1245(a)(1) is only $2,800, determined as follows:

(1) Adjusted basis:

D's portion of partnership adjusted basis (⅓ of $24,000)	$8,000	
D's special basis adjustment as of December 31, 1964 ($5,000 minus $800)	4,200	
D's adjusted basis		$12,200
(2) Recomputed basis:		
D's adjusted basis	$12,200	
D's portion of partnership depreciation for 1963 and 1964, *i.e.*, for periods after he acquired his partnership interest (⅓ of $6,000) .	2,000	
Depreciation for 1963 and 1964 in respect of D's special basis adjustment	800	
D's recomputed basis		$15,000
(3) D's portion of amount realized by partnership (⅓ of $48,000)		$16,000
(4) Gain recognized to D under section 1245(a)(1), *i.e.*, the lower of (2) or (3), minus (1)		$2,800

[Reg. § 1.1245-1.]

☐ [*T.D. 6832, 7-6-65. Amended by T.D. 7084, 1-7-71; T.D. 7141, 9-21-71 and T.D. 8730, 8-19-97.*]

[Reg. § 1.1245-2]

§ 1.1245-2. Definition of recomputed basis.—(a) *General rule.*—(1) *Recomputed basis defined.*—The term "recomputed basis" means, with respect to any property, an amount equal to the sum of—

(i) The adjusted basis of the property, as defined in section 1011, plus

(ii) The amount of the adjustments reflected in the adjusted basis.

(2) *Definition of adjustments reflected in adjusted basis.*—The term "adjustments reflected in the adjusted basis" means—

(i) with respect to any property other than property described in subdivision (ii), (iii), or (iv) of this subparagraph, the amount of the adjustments attributable to periods after December 31, 1961,

(ii) with respect to an elevator or escalator, the amount of the adjustments attributable to periods after June 30, 1963,

(iii) with respect to livestock (described in subparagraph (4) of § 1.1245-3(a)), the amount of the adjustments attributable to periods after December 31, 1969, or

(iv) [reserved]

which are reflected in the adjusted basis of such property on account of deductions allowed or allowable for depreciation or amortization (within the meaning of subparagraph (3) of this paragraph). For cases where the taxpayer can establish that the amount allowed for any period was less than the amount allowable, see subparagraph (7) of this paragraph. For determination of adjusted basis of property in a multiple asset account, see paragraph (c)(3) of § 1.167(a)-8.

(3) *Meaning of "depreciation or amortization".*—(i) For purposes of subparagraph (2) of

this paragraph, the term "depreciation or amortization" includes allowances (and amounts treated as allowances) for depreciation (or amortization in lieu thereof), and deductions for amortization of emergency facilities under section 168. Thus, for example, such term includes a reasonable allowance for exhaustion, wear and tear (including a reasonable allowance for obsolescence) under section 167, an expense allowance (additional first-year depreciation allowance for property placed in service before January 1, 1981) under section 179, an expenditure treated as an amount allowed under section 167 by reason of the application of section 182(d)(2)(B) (relating to expenditures by farmers for clearing land), and a deduction for depreciation of improvements under section 611 (relating to depletion). For further examples, the term "depreciation or amortization" includes periodic deductions referred to in §1.162-11 in respect of a specified sum paid for the acquisition of a leasehold and in respect of the cost to a lessee of improvements on property of which he is the lessee. However, such term does not include deductions for the periodic payment of rent.

(ii) The provisions of this subparagraph may be illustrated by the following example:

Example. On January 1, 1966, Smith purchases for $1,000, and places in service, an item of property described in section 1245(a)(3)(A). Smith deducts an additional first-year allowance for depreciation under section 179 of $200. Accordingly, the basis of the property for purposes of depreciation is $800 on January 1, 1966. Between that date and January 1, 1974, Smith deducts $640 in depreciation (the amount allowable) with respect to the property, thereby reducing its adjusted basis to $160. Since this adjusted basis reflects deductions for depreciation and amortization (within the meaning of this subparagraph) amounting to $840 ($200 plus $640), the recomputed basis of the property is $1,000 ($160 plus $840).

(4) *Adjustments of other taxpayers or in respect of other property.*—(i) For purposes of subpara-

graph (2) of this paragraph, the adjustments reflected in adjusted basis on account of depreciation or amortization which must be taken into account in determining recomputed basis are not limited to those adjustments on account of depreciation or amortization with respect to the property disposed of, nor are such adjustments limited to those on account of depreciation or amortization allowed or allowable to the taxpayer disposing of such property. Except as provided in subparagraph (7) of this paragraph, all such adjustments are taken into account, whether the deductions were allowed or allowable in respect of the same or other property and whether to the taxpayer or to any other person. For manner of determining the amount of adjustments reflected in the adjusted basis of property immediately after certain dispositions, see paragraph (c) of this section.

(ii) The provisions of this subparagraph may be illustrated by the following example:

Example. On January 1, 1966, Jones purchases machine X for use in his trade or business. The machine, which is section 1245 property, has a basis for depreciation of $10,000. After taking depreciation deductions of $2,000 (the amount allowable), Jones transfers the machine to his son as a gift on January 1, 1968. Since the exception for gifts in section 1245(b)(1) applies, Jones does not recognize gain under section 1245(a)(1). The son's adjusted basis for the machine is $8,000. On January 1, 1969, after taking a depreciation deduction of $1,000 (the amount allowable), the son exchanges machine X for machine Y in a like kind exchange described in section 1031. Since the exception for like kind exchanges in section 1245(b)(4) applies, the son does not recognize gain under section 1245(a)(1). The son's adjusted basis for machine Y is $7,000. In 1969, the son takes a depreciation deduction of $1,000 (the amount allowable) in respect of machine Y. The son sells machine Y on June 30, 1970. No depreciation was allowed or allowable for 1970, the year of the sale. The recomputed basis of machine Y on June 30, 1970, is determined in the following manner:

Adjusted basis	$6,000
Adjustments reflected in the adjusted basis:	
Depreciation deducted by Jones for 1966 and 1967 on machine X	$2,000
Depreciation deducted by son for 1968 on machine X	$1,000
Depreciation deducted by son for 1969 on machine Y	$1,000
Total adjustments reflected in the adjusted basis	$4,000
Recomputed basis	$10,000

(5) *Adjustments reflected in adjusted basis of property described in section 1245(a)(3)(B).*—For purposes of subparagraph (2) of this paragraph, the adjustments reflected in the adjusted basis of property described in section 1245(a)(3)(B), on account of depreciation or amortization which must be taken into account in determining recomputed basis, may include deductions attributable to periods during which the property is not used as an integral part of an activity, or does

not constitute a facility, specified in section 1245(a)(3)(B)(i) or (ii). Thus, for example, if depreciation deductions taken with respect to such property after December 31, 1961, amount to $10,000 (the amount allowable), of which $6,000 is attributable to periods during which the property is used as an integral part of a specified activity or constitutes a specified facility, then the entire $10,000 of depreciation deductions are adjustments reflected in the adjusted basis for purposes of determining recomputed basis. Moreover, if the property was never so used but was acquired in a transaction to which section 1245(b)(4) (relating to like kind exchanges and involuntaray conversions) applies, and if by reason of the application of paragraph (d)(3) of § 1.1245-4 the property is considered as section 1245 property described in section 1245(a)(3)(B), then the entire $10,000 of depreciation deductions would also be adjustments reflected in the adjusted basis for purposes of determining recomputed basis.

(6) *Allocation of adjustments attributable to periods after certain dates.*—(i) For purposes of determining recomputed basis, the amount of adjustments reflected in the adjusted basis of property other than property described in subparagraph (2)(ii), (iii), or (iv) of this paragraph are limited to adjustments attributable to periods after December 31, 1961. Accordingly, if depreciation deducted with respect to such property of a calendar year taxpayer is $1,000 a year (the amount allowable) for each of 10 years beginning with 1956, only the depreciation deducted in 1962 and succeeding years shall be treated as reflected in the adjusted basis for purposes of determining recomputed basis. With respect to a taxable year beginning in 1961 and ending in 1962, the deduction for depreciation or amortization shall be ascertained by applying the principles stated in paragraph (c)(3) of § 1.167(a)-8 (relating to determination of adjusted basis of retired asset). The amount of the deduction, determined in such manner, shall be allocated on a daily basis in order to determine the portion thereof which is attributable to a period after December 31, 1961. Thus, for example, if a taxpayer, whose fiscal year ends on May 31, 1962, acquires section 1245 property on November 12, 1961, and the deduction for depreciation attributable to the property for such fiscal year is ascertained (under the principles of paragraph (c)(3) of § 1.167(a)-8) to be $400, then the portion thereof attributable to a period after December 31, 1961, is $302 (151/200 of $400). If, however, the property were acquired by such taxpayer after December 31, 1961, the entire deduction for depreciation attributable to the property for such fiscal year would be allocable to a period after December 31, 1961. For treatment of certain normal retirements described in paragraph (e)(2) of § 1.167(a)-8, see paragraph (c) of § 1.1245-6. For principles of determining the amount of adjustments for depreciation or amortization reflected in the adjusted basis of property upon an abnormal retirement of property in a multiple asset account, see paragraph (c)(3) of § 1.167(a)-8.

(ii) For purposes of determining recomputed basis, the amount of adjustments reflected in the adjusted basis of an elevator or escalator are limited to adjustments attributable to periods after June 30, 1963.

(iii) For purposes of determining recomputed basis, the amount of adjustments reflected in the adjusted basis of livestock (described in subparagraph (2)(iii) of this paragraph) are limited to adjustments attributable to periods after December 31, 1969.

(7) *Depreciation or amortization allowed or allowable.*—For purposes of determining recomputed basis, generally all adjustments (for periods after Dec. 31, 1961, or, in the case of property described in subparagraph (2)(ii), (iii), or (iv) of this paragraph, for periods after the applicable date, 1969, as the case may be) attributable to allowed or allowable depreciation or amortization must be taken into account. See section 1016(a)(2) and the regulations thereunder for the meaning of "allowed" and "allowable". However, if a taxpayer can establish by adequate records or other sufficient evidence that the amount allowed for depreciation or amortization for any period was less than the amount allowable for such period, the amount to be taken into account for such period shall be the amount allowed. No adjustment is to be made on account of the tax imposed by section 56 (relating to the minimum tax for tax preferences). See paragraph (b) of this section (relating to records to be kept and information to be filed). For example, assume that in the year 1967 it becomes necessary to determine the recomputed basis of property, the $500 adjusted basis of which reflects adjustments of $1,000 with respect to depreciation deductions allowable for periods after December 31, 1961. If the taxpayer can establish by adequate records or other sufficient evidence that he had been allowed deductions amounting to $800 for the period, then in determining recomputed basis the amount added to adjusted basis with respect to the $1,000 adjustments to basis for the period will be only $800.

(8) *Exempt organizations.*—In respect of property disposed of by an organization which is or was exempt from income taxes (within the meaning of section 501(a)), adjustments reflected in the adjusted basis (within the meaning of subparagraph (2) of this paragraph) shall include only depreciation or amortization allowed or allowable (i) in computing unrelated business taxable income (as defined in section 512(a)), or (ii) in computing taxable income of the organization (or a predecessor organization) for a period during which it was not exempt or, by reason of the application of section 502, 503, or 504, was denied its exemption.

(b) *Records to be kept.*—In any case in which it is necessary to determine recomputed basis of an item of section 1245 property, the taxpayer shall have available permanent records of all the facts necessary to determine with reasonable accuracy the amount of such recomputed basis, including the following—

(1) The date, and the manner in which, the property was acquired,

(2) The taxpayer's basis on the date the property was acquired and the manner in which the basis was determined,

(3) The amount and the date of all adjustments to the basis of the property allowed or allowable to the taxpayer for depreciation or amortization and the amount and date of any other adjustments by the taxpayer to the basis of the property,

(4) In the case of section 1245 property which has an adjusted basis reflecting adjustments for depreciation or amortization taken by the taxpayer with respect to other property, or by another taxpayer with respect to the same or other property, the information described in subparagraphs (1), (2), and (3) of this paragraph with respect to such other property or such other taxpayer.

(c) *Adjustments reflected in adjusted basis immediately after certain acquisitions.*—(1) *Zero.*—(i) If on the date a person acquires property his basis for the property is determined solely by reference to its cost (within the meaning of section 1012), then on such date the amount of the adjustments reflected in his adjusted basis for the property is zero.

(ii) If on the date a person acquires property his basis for the property is determined solely by reason of the application of section 301(d) (relating to basis of property received in corporate distribution) or section 334(a) (relating to basis of property received in a liquidation in which gain or loss is recognized), then on such date the amount of the adjustments reflected in his adjusted basis for the property is zero.

(iii) If on the date a person acquires property his basis for the property is determined solely under the rules of section 334(b)(2) or (c) (relating to basis of property received in certain corporate liquidations), then on such date the amount of the adjustments reflected in his adjusted basis for the property is zero.

(iv) If as of the date a person acquires property from a decedent such person's basis is determined, by reason of the application of section 1014(a), solely by reference to the fair market value of the property on the date of the decedent's death or on the applicable date provided in section 2032 (relating to alternate valuation date), then on such date the amount of the adjustments reflected in his adjusted basis for the property is zero.

(2) *Gifts and certain tax-free transactions.*—(i) If property is disposed of in a transaction described in subdivision (ii) of this subparagraph, then the amount of the adjustments reflected in the adjusted basis of the property in the hands of a transferee immediately after the disposition shall be an amount equal to—

(a) The amount of the adjustments reflected in the adjusted basis of the property in the hands of the transferor immediately before the disposition, minus

(b) The amount of any gain taken into account under section 1245(a)(1) by the transferor upon the disposition.

(ii) The transactions referred to in subdivision (i) of this subparagraph are—

(a) A disposition which is in part a sale or exchange and in part a gift (see paragraph (a)(3) or § 1.1245-4),

(b) A disposition (other than a disposition to which section 1245(b)(6)(A) applies) which is described in section 1245(b)(3) (relating to certain tax-free transactions), or

(c) An exchange described in paragraph (e)(2) of § 1.1245-4 (relating to transfers described in section 1081(d)(1)(A)).

(iii) The provisions of this subparagraph may be illustrated by the following example:

Example. Jones transfers section 1245 property to a corporation in exchange for stock of the corporation and $1,000 cash in a transaction which qualifies under section 351 (relating to transfer to a corporation controlled by a transferor). Before the exchange the amount of the adjustments reflected in the adjusted basis of the property is $3,000. Upon the exchange $1,000 gain is recognized under section 1245(a)(1). Immediately after the exchange, the amount of the adjustments reflected in the adjusted basis of the property in the hands of the corporation is $2,000 (that is, $3,000 minus $1,000).

(3) *Certain transfers at death.*—(i) If property is acquired in transfer at death to which section 1245(b)(2) applies, the amount of the adjustments reflected in the adjusted basis of property in the hands of the transferee immediately after the transfer shall be the amount (if any) of depreciation or amortization deductions allowed the transferee before the decedent's death, to the extent that the basis of the property (determined under section 1014(a)) is required to be reduced under the second sentence of section 1014(b)(9) (relating to adjustments to basis where property is acquired from a decedent prior to his death).

(ii) The provisions of this subparagraph may be illustrated by the following example:

Example. H purchases section 1245 property in 1965 which he immediately conveys to himself and W, his wife, as tenants by the entirety. Under local law each spouse is entitled to one-half the income from the property. H and W file joint income tax returns for calendar years 1965, 1966, and 1967. Over the 3 years, depreciation deductions amounting to $4,000 (the amount allowable) are allowed in respect of the property of which one-half thereof, or $2,000, is allocable to W. On January 1, 1968, H dies and the entire value of the property at the date of death is included in H's gross estate. Since W's basis for the property (determined under section 1014(a)) is reduced (under the second sentence of section 1014(b)(9)) by the $2,000 depreciation deductions allowed W before H's death, the adjustments reflected in the adjusted basis of the property in the hands of W immediately after H's death amount to $2,000.

(4) *Property received in a like kind exchange, involuntary conversion, or F.C.C. transaction.*— (i) If property is acquired in a transaction described in subdivision (ii) of this subparagraph, then immediately after the acquisition (and before applying subparagraph (5) of this paragraph, if applicable) the amount of the adjustments reflected in the adjusted basis of the property acquired shall be an amount equal to—

(a) The amount of the adjustments reflected in the adjusted basis of the property disposed of immediately before the disposition, minus

(b) The sum of (1) the amount of any gain recognized under section 1245(a)(1) upon the disposition, plus (2) the amount of gain (if any) referred to in subparagraph (5)(ii) of this paragraph.

(ii) The transactions referred to in subdivision (i) of this subparagraph are—

(a) A disposition which is a like kind exchange or an involuntary conversion to which section 1245(b)(4) applies, or

(b) A disposition to which the provisions of section 1071 and paragraph (e)(1) of § 1.1245-4 apply.

(iii) The provisions of subdivisions (i) and (ii) of this subparagraph may be illustrated by the following examples:

Example (1). Smith exchanges machine A for machine B and $1,000 cash in a like kind exchange. Gain of $1,000 is recognized under section 1245 (a)(1). If before the exchange the amount of the adjustments reflected in the adjusted basis of machine A was $5,000, the amount of adjustments reflected in the adjusted basis of machine B after the exchange is $4,000 (that is, $5,000 minus $1,000).

Example (2). Assume the same facts as in example (1) except that machine A is destroyed by fire, that $5,000 in insurance proceeds are received of which $4,000 is used to purchase machine B, and that Smith properly elects under section 1033(a)(3)(A) to limit recognition of gain. The result is the same as in example (1), that is, the amount of adjustments reflected in the adjusted basis of machine B is $4,000 ($5,000 minus $1,000).

(iv) If more than one item of section 1245 property is acquired in a transaction referred to in subdivision (i) of this subparagraph, the total amount of the adjustments reflected in the adjusted bases of the items acquired shall be allocated to such items in proportion to their respective adjusted bases.

(5) *Property after a reduction in basis pursuant to election under section 1071 or application of section 1082(a)(2).*—If the basis of section 1245 prop-

erty is reduced pursuant to an election under section 1071 (relating to gain from sale or exchange to effectuate policies of F.C.C.), or the application of section 1082(a)(2) (relating to sale or exchange in obedience to order of S.E.C.), then immediately after the basis reduction the amount of the adjustments reflected in the adjusted basis of the property shall be the sum of—

(i) The amount of the adjustments reflected in the adjusted basis of the property immediately before the basis reduction (but after applying subparagraph (4) of this paragraph, if applicable), plus

(ii) The amount of gain which was not recognized under section 1245(a)(1) by reason of the reduction in the basis of the property. See paragraph (e)(1) of § 1.1245-4.

(6) *Partnership property after certain transactions.*—(i) For the amount of adjustments reflected in the adjusted basis of property immediately after certain distributions of the property by a partnership to a partner, see section 1245(b)(6)(B).

(ii) If under paragraph (b)(3) of § 1.751-1 (relating to certain distributions of partnership property other than section 751 property treated as sales or exchanges) a partnership is treated as purchasing section 1245 property (or a portion thereof) from a distributee who relinquishes his interest in such property (or portion), then on the date of such purchase the amount of adjustments reflected in the adjusted basis of such purchased property (or portion) shall be zero.

(iii) See paragraph (e)(3)(ii) of § 1.1245-1 for the amount of adjustments reflected in the adjusted basis of partnership property in respect of a partner who acquired his partnership interest in certain transactions when an election under section 754 (relating to optional adjustments to basis of partnership property) was in effect. [Reg. § 1.1245-2.]

☐ [*T.D. 6832, 7-6-65. Amended by T.D. 7084, 1-7-71; T.D. 7141, 9-21-71; T.D. 7564, 9-11-78; and T.D. 8121, 1-5-87.*]

[Reg. § 1.1245-3]

§ 1.1245-3. Definition of section 1245 property.—(a) *In general.*—(1) The term "section 1245 property" means any property (other than livestock excluded by the effective date limitation in subparagraph (4) of this paragraph) which is or has been property of a character subject to the allowance for depreciation provided in section 167 and which is either—

(i) Personal property (within the meaning of paragraph (b) of this section),

(ii) Property described in section 1245(a)(3)(B) (see paragraph (c) of this section), or

(iii) An elevator or an escalator within the meaning of subparagraph (C) of section 48(a)(1) (relating to the definition of "section 38 property" for purposes of the investment credit), but without regard to the limitations in such subparagraph (C).

(2) If property is section 1245 property under a subdivision of subparagraph (1) of this paragraph, a leasehold of such property is also section 1245 property under such subdivision. Thus, for example, if A owns personal property which is section 1245 property under subparagraph (1)(i) of this paragraph, and if A leases the personal property to B, B's leasehold is also section 1245 property under such provision. For a further example, if C owns and leases to D for a single lump-sum payment of $100,000 property consisting of land and a fully equipped factory building thereon, and if 40 percent of the fair market value of such property is properly allocable to section 1245 property, then 40 percent of D's leasehold is also section 1245 property. A leasehold of land is not section 1245 property.

(3) Even though property may not be of a character subject to the allowance for depreciation in the hands of the taxpayer, such property may nevertheless be section 1245 property if the taxpayer's basis for the property is determined by reference to its basis in the hands of a prior owner of the property and such property was of a character subject to the allowance for depreciation in the hands of such prior owner, or if the taxpayer's basis for the property is determined by reference to the basis of other property which in the hands of the taxpayer was property of a character subject to the allowance for depreciation. Thus, for example, if a father uses an automobile in his trade or business during a period after December 31, 1961, and then gives the automobile to his son as a gift for the son's personal use, the automobile is section 1245 property in the hands of the son.

(4) Section 1245 property includes livestock, but only with respect to taxable years beginning after December 31, 1969. For purposes of section 1245, the term "livestock" includes horses, cattle, hogs, sheep, goats, and mink and other furbearing animals, irrespective of the use to which they are put or the purpose for which they are held.

(b) *Personal property defined.*—The term "personal property" means—

(1) Tangible personal property (as defined in paragraph (c) of § 1.48-1, relating to the definition of "section 38 property" for purposes of the investment credit), and

(2) Intangible personal property.

(c) *Property described in section 1245(a)(3)(B).*—(1) The term "property described in section 1245(a)(3)(B)" means tangible property of the requisite depreciable character other than personal property (and other than a building and its structural components), but only if there are adjustments reflected in the adjusted basis of the property (within the meaning of paragraph (a)(2) of § 1.1245-2) for a period during which such property (or other property)—

(i) Was used as an integral part of manufacturing, production, or extraction, or as an integral part of furnishing transportation, communications, electrical energy, gas, water, or sewage disposal services by a person engaged in a trade or business of furnishing any such service, or

(ii) Constituted a research or storage facility used in connection with any of the foregoing activities.

Thus, even though during the period immediately preceding its disposition the property is not used as an integral part of an activity specified in subdivision (i) of this subparagraph and does not constitute a facility specified in subdivision (ii) of this subparagraph, such property is nevertheless property described in section 1245(a)(3)(B) if, for example, there are adjustments reflected in the adjusted basis of the property for a period during which the property was used as an integral part of manufacturing by the taxpayer or another taxpayer, or for a period during which other property (which was involuntarily converted into, or exchanged in a like kind exchange for, the property) was so used by the taxpayer or another taxpayer. For rules applicable to involuntary conversions and like kind exchanges, see paragraph (d)(3) of § 1.1245-4.

(2) The language used in subparagraph (1)(i) and (ii) of this paragraph shall have the same meaning as when used in paragraph (a) of § 1.48-1, and the terms "building" and "structural components" shall have the meanings assigned to those terms in paragraph (e) of § 1.48-1. [Reg. § 1.1245-3.]

☐ [*T.D. 6832, 7-6-65. Amended by T.D. 7141, 9-21-71.*]

[Reg. § 1.1245-4]

§ 1.1245-4. Exceptions and limitations.—(a) *Exception for gifts.*—(1) *General rule.*—Section 1245(b)(1) provides that no gain shall be recognized under section 1245(a)(1) upon a disposition by gift. For purposes of this paragraph, the term "gift" means, except to the extent that subparagraph (3) of this paragraph applies, a transfer of property which, in the hands of the transferee, has a basis determined under the provisions of section 1015(a) or (d) (relating to basis of property acquired by gifts). For reduction in amount of charitable contribution in case of a gift of section 1245 property, see section 170(e) and the regulations thereunder.

(2) *Examples.*—The provisions of subparagraph (1) of this paragraph may be illustrated by the following examples:

Example (1). A places section 1245 property in trust to pay the income from the property to B for his life, and after B's death to distribute the property to C. If the basis of the property to the fiduciary and to C is determined under the uniform basis rules prescribed in paragraph (b) of § 1.1015-1, and under paragraph (c) of § 1.1015-1 the time the fiduciary and C acquire their interests in the property is the time the donor relinquished dominion over the property, then section 1245(a)(1) does not apply to the transfer by A to the trust or to the distribution to C.

Example (2). Assume the same facts as in example (1), except that the fiduciary sells the section 1245 property and reinvests the proceeds in other section 1245 property which is distributed to C upon B's death. Assume further that under paragraph (f) of § 1.1015-1 C's basis for the distributed property is the cost or other basis to the fiduciary. Section 1245(a)(1) applies to the sale but not to the distribution.

(3) *Disposition in part a sale or exchange and in part a gift.*—Where a disposition of property is in part a sale or exchange and in part a gift, the gain to which section 1245(a)(1) applies is the amount by which (i) the lower of the amount realized upon the disposition of the property or the recomputed basis of the property, exceeds (ii) the adjusted basis of the property. For determination of the recomputed basis of the property in the hands of the transferee, see paragraph (c)(2) of § 1.1245-2.

(4) *Example.*—The provisions of subparagraph (3) of this paragraph may be illustrated by the following example:

Example. (i) Smith transfers section 1245 property, which he has held in excess of 1 year (6 months for taxable years beginning before 1977; 9 months for taxable years beginning in 1977), to his son for $60,000. Immediately before the transfer the property in the hands of Smith has an adjusted basis of $30,000, a fair market value of $90,000, and a recomputed basis of $110,000. Since the amount realized upon disposition of the property ($60,000) is lower than its recomputed basis ($110,000), the excess of the amount realized over adjusted basis, or $30,000, is treated as ordinary income under section 1245(a)(1) and not as gain from the sale or exchange of property described in section 1231. Smith has made a gift of $30,000 ($90,000 fair market value minus $60,000 amount realized) to which section 1245(a)(1) does not apply.

(ii) Immediately before the transfer, the amount of adjustments reflected in the adjusted basis of the property was $80,000. Under paragraph (c)(2) of § 1.1245-2, $50,000 of adjustments are reflected in the adjusted basis of the property immediately after the transfer, that is, $80,000 of such adjustments immediately before the transfer, minus $30,000 gain taken into account under section 1245(a)(1) upon the transfer. Thus, the recomputed basis of the property in the hands of the son is $110,000.

(b) *Exception for transfers at death.*—(1) *General rule.*—Section 1245(b)(2) provides that, except as provided in section 691 (relating to income in respect of a decedent), no gain shall be recognized under section 1245(a)(1) upon a transfer at death. For purposes of this paragraph, the term "transfer at death" means a transfer of property which, in the hands of the transferee, has a basis determined under the provisions of section 1014(a) (relating to basis of property acquired from a decedent) because of the death of the transferor. For recomputed basis of property acquired in a transfer at death, see paragraph (c)(1)(iv) of § 1.1245-2.

(2) *Examples.*—The provisions of this paragraph may be illustrated by the following examples:

Example (1). Smith owns section 1245 property which, upon Smith's death, is inherited by his son. Since the property is described in section 1014(b)(1), its basis in the hands of the son is determined under the provisions of section 1014(a). Therefore, section 1245(a)(1) does not apply to the transfer at Smith's death.

Example (2). H purchases section 1245 property which he conveys to himself and W, his wife, as tenants by the entirety. Upon H's death in 1970 the property (including W's share) is included in his gross estate. Since the entire property is described in section 1014(b)(1) and (9), its basis in the hands of W is determined under the provisions of section 1014(a). Therefore, section 1245(a)(1) does not apply to the transfer at H's death. For determination of the recomputed basis of the property in the hands of W, see paragraph (c)(3) of § 1.1245-2.

Example (3). Green's will provides for the bequest of section 1245 property to trustees to pay the income from the property to his wife for her lifetime, and upon her death to distribute the property to his son. If under paragraph (a)(2) of § 1.1014-4 the son's unadjusted basis for the property is its fair market value at the time the decedent died, section 1245(a)(1) does not apply to the distribution of the property to the son.

Example (4). The trustee of a trust created by will transfers section 1245 property to a beneficiary in satisfaction of a specific bequest of $10,000. If under the principles of paragraph (a)(3) of § 1.1014-4 the trust realizes a taxable gain upon the transfer, section 1245(a)(1) applies to the transfer.

(c) *Limitation for certain tax-free transactions.*—(1) *Limitation on amount of gain.*—Section 1245(b)(3) provides that upon a transfer of property described in subparagraph (2) of this paragraph, the amount of gain taken into account by the transferor under section 1245(a)(1) shall not exceed the amount of gain recognized to the transferor on the transfer (determined without regard to section 1245). For purposes of this subparagraph, in case of a transfer of both section 1245 property and non-section 1245 property in one transaction, the amount realized from the disposition of the section 1245 property (as determined under paragraph (a)(5) of § 1.1245-1) shall be deemed to consist of that portion of the fair market value of each property acquired which bears the same ratio to the fair market value of such acquired property as the amount realized from the disposition of the section 1245 property bears to the total amount realized. The preceding sentence shall be applied solely for purposes of computing the portion of the total gain (determined without regard to section 1245) which shall be recognized as ordinary income under section 1245(a)(1). For determination of the recomputed basis of the section 1245 property in the hands of the transferee, see paragraph (c)(2) of §1.1245-2. Section 1245(b)(3) does not apply to a disposition of property to an organization (other than a cooperative described in section 521) which is exempt from the tax imposed by chapter 1 of the Code.

(2) *Transfers covered.*—The transfers referred to in subparagraph (1) of this paragraph are transfers of property which the basis of the property in the hands of the transferee is determined by reference to its basis in the hands of the transferor by reason of the application of any of the following provisions:

(i) Section 332 (relating to distributions in complete liquidation of an 80-percent-or-more controlled subsidiary corporation). See subparagraph (3) of this paragraph.

(ii) Section 351 (relating to transfer to a corporation controlled by transferor).

(iii) Section 361 (relating to exchanges pursuant to certain corporate reorganizations).

(iv) Section 371(a) (relating to exchanges pursuant to certain receivership and bankruptcy proceedings).

(v) Section 374(a) (relating to exchanges pursuant to certain railroad reorganizations).

(vi) Section 721 (relating to transfers to a partnership in exchange for a partnership interest).

(vii) Section 731 (relating to distributions by a partnership to a partner). For special carry-over basis rule, see section 1245(b)(6)(A) and paragraph (f)(1) of this section.

(3) *Complete liquidation of subsidiary.*—In the case of a distribution in complete liquidation of an 80-percent-or-more controlled subsidiary to which section 332 applies, the limitation provided in section 1245(b)(3) is confined to instances in which the basis of the property in the hands of the transferee is determined, under section 334(b)(1), by reference to its basis in the hands of the transferor. Thus, for example, the limitation of section 1245(b)(3) may apply in respect of a liquidating distribution of section 1245 property by an 80-percent-or-more controlled corporation to the parent corporation, but does not apply in respect of a liquidating distribution of section 1245 property to a minority shareholder. Section 1245(b)(3) does not apply to a liquidating distribution of property by an 80-percent-or-more controlled subsidiary to its parent

if the parent's basis for the property is determined, under section 334(b)(2), by reference to its basis for the stock of the subsidiary.

(4) *Examples.*—The provisions of this paragraph may be illustrated by the following examples:

Example (1). Section 1245 property, which is owned by Smith, has a fair market value of $10,000, a recomputed basis of $8,000, and an adjusted basis of $4,000. Smith transfers the property to a corporation in exchange for stock in the corporation worth $9,000 plus $1,000 in cash in a transaction qualifying under section 351. Without regard to section 1245, Smith would recognize $1,000 gain under section 351(b), and the corporation's basis for the property would be determined under section 362(a) by reference to its basis in the hands of Smith. Since the recomputed basis of the property disposed of ($8,000) is lower than the amount realized ($10,000), the excess of recomputed basis over adjusted basis ($4,000), or $4,000, would be treated as ordinary income under section 1245(a)(1) if the provisions of section 1245(b)(3) did not apply. However, section 1245(b)(3) limits the gain taken into account by Smith under section 1245(a)(1) to $1,000. If, instead, Smith transferred the property to the corporation solely in exchange for stock of the corporation worth $10,000, then, because of the application of section 1245(b)(3), Smith would not take any gain into account under section 1245(a)(1). If, however, Smith transferred the property to the corporation for stock worth $5,000 and $5,000 cash, only $4,000 of the $5,000 gain under section 351(b) would be treated as ordinary income under section 1245(a)(1).

Example (2). Assume the same facts as in example (1) except that Smith contributes the property to a new partnership in which he has a one-half interest. Since, without regard to section 1245, no gain would be recognized to Smith under section 721, and by reason of the application of section 721 the partnership's basis for the property would be determined under section 723 by reference to its basis in the hands of Smith, the application of section 1245(b)(3) results in no gain being taken into account by Smith under section 1245(a)(1).

Example (3). Assume the same facts as in example (2) except that the property is subject to a $9,000 mortgage. Since under section 752(b) (relating to decrease in partner's liabilities) Smith is treated as receiving a distribution in money of $4,500 (one-half) of liability assumed by partnership), and since the basis of Smith's partnership interest is $4,000 (the adjusted basis of the contributed property), the $4,500 distribution results in his realizing $500 gain under section 731(a) (relating to distributions by a partnership), determined without regard to section 1245. Accordingly, the application of section 1245(b)(3) limits the gain taken into account by Smith under section 1245(a)(1) to $500.

(d) *Limitation for like kind exchanges and involuntary conversions.*—(1) *General rule.*—Section 1245(b)(4) provides that if property is disposed of and gain (determined without regard to section 1245) is not recognized in whole or in part under section 1031 (relating to like kind exchanges) or section 1033 (relating to involuntary conversions), then the amount of gain taken into account by the transferor under section 1245(a)(1) shall not exceed the sum of—

(i) The amount of gain recognized on such disposition (determined without regard to section 1245), plus

(ii) The fair market value of property acquired which is not section 1245 property and which is not taken into account under subdivision (i) of this subparagraph (that is, the fair market value of non-section 1245 property acquired which is qualifying property under section 1031 or 1033, as the case may be).

(2) *Examples.*—The provisions of subparagraph (1) of this paragraph may be illustrated by the following examples:

Example (1). Smith exchanges machine A for machine B in a like kind exchange as to which no gain is recognized under section 1031(a). Both machines are section 1245 property. No gain is recognized under section 1245(a)(1) because of the limitation contained in section 1245(b)(4). The result would be the same if machine A were involuntarily converted into machine B in a transaction as to which no gain is recognized under section 1033(a)(1).

Example (2). Jones owns property A, which is section 1245 property, with an adjusted basis of $100,000 and a recomputed basis of $116,000. The property is destroyed by fire and Jones receives $117,000 of insurance proceeds. Thus, the amount of gain under section 1245(a)(1), determined without regard to section 1245(b)(4), would be $16,000. He uses $105,000 of the proceeds to purchase section 1245 property similar or related in service or use to property A, and $9,000 of the proceeds to purchase stock in the acquisition of control of a corporation owning property similar or related in service or use to property A. Both acquisitions qualify under section 1033(a)(3)(A). Jones properly elects under section 1033(a)(3)(A) and the regulations thereunder to limit recognition of gain to the amount by which the amount realized from the conversion exceeds the cost of the stock and other property acquired to replace the converted property. Since $3,000 of the gain is recognized (without regard to section 1245) under section 1033(a)(3) (that is, $117,000 minus $114,000), and since the stock purchased for $9,000 is not section 1245 property and was not taken into account in determining the gain under section 1033, section 1245(b)(4) limits the amount of the gain taken into account under section 1245(a)(1) to $12,000 (that is, $3,000 plus $9,000). If, instead

of purchasing $9,000 in stock, Jones purchases $9,000 worth of property which is section 1245 property similar or related in use to the destroyed property, section 1245(b)(4) would limit the amount of gain taken into account under section 1245(a)(1) to $3,000.

(3) *Certain tangible property.*—If—

(i) A person disposes of section 1245 property in a transaction to which section 1245(b)(4) applies,

(ii) Adjustments are reflected in the adjusted basis (within the meaning of paragraph (a)(2) of §1.1245-2) of such property which are attributable to the use of such property (or other property) as an integral part of an activity, or as a facility, specified in section 1245(a)(3)(B)(i) or (ii), and

(iii) Property is acquired in the transaction which would be considered as section 1245 property described in section 1245(a)(3)(B) if such person used the acquired property as an integral part of such an activity, or as such a facility,

then (regardless of the use of the acquired property) the acquired property shall be considered as section 1245 property described in section 1245(a)(3)(B). For definition of property described in section 1245(a)(3)(B), see paragraph (c) of §1.1245-3. Thus, for example, if a person's section 1245 property (which is personal property) is involuntarily converted into property A which would qualify as section 1245 property only if it were devoted to a specified use, and if the person had so devoted the section 1245 property disposed of, then the acquired property is considered as section 1245 property described in section 1245(a)(3)(B) and therefore its fair market value is not taken into account under subparagraph (1)(ii) of this paragraph. For recomputed basis of property A, see paragraph (a)(5) of §1.1245-2. Moreover, if property A is not devoted to a specified use and is subsequently involuntarily converted into property B which would qualify as section 1245 property only if it were so devoted, then property B is also considered as section 1245 property described in section 1245(a)(3)(B).

(4) *Application to disposition of section 1245 property and non-section 1245 property in one transaction.*—For purposes of this paragraph, if both section 1245 property and non-section 1245 property are acquired as the result of one disposition in which both section 1245 property and non-section 1245 property are disposed of, then except as provided in subparagraph (7) of this paragraph—

(i) The total amount realized upon the disposition shall be allocated (in a manner consistent with the principles of paragraph (a)(5) of §1.1245-1) between the section 1245 property and the non-section 1245 property disposed of in proportion to their respective fair market values.

Reg. §1.1245-4(d)(4)(i)

(ii) The amount realized upon the disposition of the section 1245 property shall be deemed to consist of so much of the fair market value of the section 1245 property acquired as is not in excess of the amount realized from the section 1245 property disposed of, and the remaining portion (if any) of the amount realized upon the disposition of the section 1245 property shall be deemed to consist of so much of the fair market value of the non-section 1245 property acquired as is not in excess of the amount of such remaining portion, and

(iii) The amount realized upon the disposition of the non-section 1245 property shall be deemed to consist of so much of the fair market value of all the property acquired which was not taken into account in subdivision (ii) of this subparagraph.

(5) *Example.*—The provisions of subparagraph (4) of this paragraph may be illustrated by the following example:

Example. (i) Smith owns section 1245 property A with a fair market value of $30,000, and non-section 1245 property X with a fair market value of $20,000. Properties A and X are destroyed by fire and Smith receives insurance proceeds of $40,000. He uses all the proceeds, plus additional cash of $10,000, to purchase in a single transaction properties B and Y which qualify under section 1033(a)(3)(A), and he properly elects under section 1033(a)(3)(A) and the regulations thereunder to limit recognition of gain to the excess of the amount realized from the conversion over the costs of the qualifying properties acquired. Thus no gain would be recognized (without regard to section 1245) under section 1033(a)(3)(A). Property B is section 1245 property with a fair market value of $15,000, and property Y is nonsection 1245 property with a fair market value of $35,000.

(ii) The amount realized upon the disposition of A and X ($40,000) is allocated between A and X in proportion to their respective fair market values. Thus, the amount considered realized in respect of A is $24,000 (that is, 30/50 of $40,000). (The amount considered realized in respect of X is $16,000 (that is, 20/50 of $40,000).)

(iii) The $24,000 realized upon the disposition of A is deemed to consist of the fair market value of B ($15,000) and $9,000 of the fair market value of Y. (The $16,000 realized upon the disposition of X is deemed to consist of $16,000 of the fair market value of Y. Also, $10,000 of the fair market value of Y is attributable to the additional cash of $10,000.)

(iv) Assume that A has an adjusted basis of $5,000, and a recomputed basis of $40,000. Since the amount considered realized upon the disposition of A ($24,000) is lower than its recomputed basis ($40,000), the amount of gain which would be recognized under section 1245(a)(1), determined without regard to section 1245(b)(4), is $19,000, that is, the amount realized ($24,000),

minus the adjusted basis ($5,000). Since no gain is recognized (without regard to section 1245) under section 1033(a)(3), and since $9,000 of the property acquired in exchange for section 1245 property A is nonsection 1245 property Y, section 1245(b)(4) limits the amount of gain taken into account under section 1245(a)(1) to $9,000.

(6) *Cross references.*—For the manner of determining the recomputed basis of property acquired in a transaction to which section 1245(b)(4) applies, see paragraph (c)(4) of § 1.1245-2. For the manner of determining the basis of such property, see paragraph (a) of § 1.1245-5.

(7) *Coordination with section 1250.*—For purposes of this paragraph, if section 1245 property and section 1250 property are disposed of in one transaction in which the property acquired includes section 1250 property, the allocation rules of paragraph (d)(6) of § 1.1250-3 shall apply.

(e) *Limitation for section 1071 and 1081 transactions.*—(1) *Section 1071 and 1081(b) transactions.*—If property is disposed of and gain (determined without regard to section 1245) is not recognized in whole or in part because of the application of section 1071 (relating to gain from sale or exchange to effectuate policies of F.C.C.) or section 1081(b) (relating to gain from sale or exchange in obedience to order of S.E.C.), then the amount of gain taken into account by the transferor under section 1245(a)(1) shall not exceed the sum of—

(i) The amount of gain recognized on such disposition (determined without regard to section 1245),

(ii) In the case of a transaction to which section 1071 applies, the fair market value of property acquired which is not section 1245 property and which is not taken into account under subdivision (i) of this subparagraph, plus

(iii) The amount by which the basis of property, other than section 1245 property, is reduced (pursuant to an election under section 1071 or pursuant to the application of section 1082(a)(2)), and which is not taken into account under subdivision (i) or (ii) of this subparagraph.

(2) *Section 1081(d)(1)(A) transaction.*—No gain shall be recognized under section 1245(a)(1) upon an exchange of property as to which gain would not be recognized (without regard to section 1245) because of the application of section 1081(d)(1)(A) (relating to transfers within system group). For recomputed basis of property acquired in a transaction referred to in this subparagraph, see paragraph (c)(2) of § 1.1245-2.

(3) *Examples.*—The provisions of this paragraph may be illustrated by the following examples:

Example (1). Corporation X elects under section 1071 to treat a sale of section 1245 property for $100,000 as an involuntary conversion subject to the provisions of section 1033, but does not elect to reduce the basis of depreciable property pursuant to an election under section 1071. The corporation uses $35,000 of the proceeds to purchase section 1245 property and $40,000 to purchase other property. Both properties qualify as replacement property under section 1033. Assuming that the amount of gain under section 1245(a)(1) (determined without regard to this paragraph) would be $70,000, and that $25,000 of gain would be recognized (without regard to section 1245) upon the application of section 1071, the amount of gain taken into account under section 1245(a)(1) is $65,000 ($25,000 plus $40,000).

Example (2). (i) Assume the same facts as in example (1) except that the corporation elects under section 1071 to reduce its basis for property of a character subject to the allowance for depreciation under section 167 by the amount of gain which would be recognized without regard to the application of section 1245, that is, by $25,000. Assume further that under section 1071 the corporation may reduce the basis of depreciable property consisting of property A, which is section 1245 property with an adjusted basis of $30,000, and property B, which is property other than section 1245 property with an adjusted basis of $20,000. Under paragraph (a)(2) of §1.1071-3, the $25,000 of unrecognized gain is applied to reduce the basis of property A by $15,000 (30,000/50,000 of $25,000) and the basis of property B by $10,000 (20,000/50,000 of $25,000).

(ii) The amount of gain which would be recognized (determined without regard to section 1245) under section 1071 is zero, i.e., the amount determined in example (1) ($25,000), minus the amount of the reduction in basis of depreciable property pursuant to the election ($25,000). The amount of gain taken into account under section 1245(a)(1) is $50,000, i.e., the sum of *(a)* the gain which would be recognized without regard to section 1245 (zero), *(b)* the cost of property acquired which is not section 1245 property ($40,000), plus, *(c)* the amount by which the basis of property B is reduced ($10,000). For method of increasing basis of property B, see paragraph (b)(2) of §1.1245-5, and for recomputed basis of property A, see paragraph (c)(5) of §1.1245-2.

(f) *Limitation for property distributed by a partnership.*—(1) *In general.*—For purposes of section 1245(b)(3) (relating to certain tax-free transactions), the basis of section 1245 property distributed by a partnership to a partner shall be deemed to be determined by reference to the adjusted basis of such property to the partnership.

(2) *Adjustments reflected in the adjusted basis.*—If section 1245 property is distributed by a partnership to a partner, then, for purposes of determining the recomputed basis of the property in the hands of the distributee, the amount of the adjustments reflected in the adjusted basis of the property immediately after the distribution shall be an amount equal to—

(i) The potential section 1245 income (as defined in paragraph (c)(4) of §1.751-1) of the partnership in respect of the property immediately before the distribution, reduced by

(ii) The portion of such potential section 1245 income which is recognized as ordinary income to the partnership under paragraph (b)(2)(ii) of §1.751-1.

(3) *Examples.*—The provisions of this paragraph may be illustrated by the following examples:

Example (1). (i) A machine, which is section 1245 property owned by partnership ABC, has an adjusted basis of $9,000, a recomputed basis of $18,000, and a fair market value of $15,000. Since the fair market value of the machine is lower than its recomputed basis, the potential section 1245 income in respect of the machine is the excess of fair market value over adjusted basis, or $6,000. The partnership distributes the machine to C in a complete liquidation of his partnership interest to which section 736(a) does not apply. C, who had originally contributed the machine to the partnership, has a basis for his partnership interest of $10,000. Since section 751(b)(2)(A) provides that section 751(b)(1) does not apply to a distribution of property to the partner who contributed the property, no gain would be recognized to the partnership under section 731(b) (without regard to the application of section 1245). By reason of the application of section 731, C's basis for the property would, under section 732(b), be equal to his basis for his interest in the partnership, or $10,000.

(ii) Since section 731 applies to the distribution, and since subparagraph (1) of this paragraph provides that, for purposes of section 1245(b)(3), C's basis for the property is deemed to be determined by reference to the adjusted basis of the property to the partnership, the gain taken into account under section 1245(a)(1) by the partnership is limited by section 1245(b)(3) so as not to exceed the amount of gain which would be recognized to the partnership if section 1245 did not apply. Accordingly, the partnership does not recognize any gain under section 1245(a)(1) upon the distribution.

(iii) Immediately after the distribution, the amount of the adjustments reflected in the adjusted basis of the property is equal to $6,000 (that is, the potential section 1245 income of the partnership in respect of the property before the distribution, $6,000, minus the gain recognized by the partnership under section 751(b), zero). Accordingly, C's recomputed basis for the property is $16,000 (that is, adjusted basis, $10,000, plus adjustments reflected in the adjusted basis, $6,000).

Example (2). Assume the same facts as in example (1) except that the machine had been purchased by the partnership. Assume further that upon the distribution, the partnership recognizes $4,000 gain as ordinary income under section 751(b). Under section 1245(b)(3), gain to be taken into account under section 1245(a)(1) by the partnership is limited to $4,000. Immediately after the distribution, the amount of adjustments reflected in the adjusted basis of the property is $2,000 (that is, potential section 1245 income of the partnership, $6,000, minus gain recognized to the partnership under section 751(b), $4,000). Thus, if the adjusted basis of the machine in the hands of C were $11,333 (see, for example, the computation in paragraph (d)(2) of example (6) of paragraph (g) of §1.751-1), the recomputed basis of the machine would be $13,333 ($11,333 plus $2,000).

(g) [Reserved]

(h) *Timber property subject to amortization under section 194.*—(1) *In general.*—For purposes of section 1245(a)(2), in determining the recomputed basis of property with respect to which a deduction under section 194 was allowed for any taxable year, a taxpayer shall not take into account amortization deductions claimed under section 194 to the extent such deductions are attributable to the amortizable basis (within the meaning of section 194(c)(2)) of the taxpayer acquired before the tenth taxable year preceding the taxable year in which gain with respect to the property is recognized.

(2) *Example.*—The principles of paragraph (h)(1) of this section are illustrated by the following example:

Example. Assume A owns qualified timber property (as defined in section 194(c)(1)) with a basis of $30,000. In 1981, A incurs $12,000 of qualifying reforestation expenditures and elects to amortize the maximum $10,000 of such expenses under section 194. The $10,000 of deductions are taken during the 8-year period from 1981 to 1988. If A sells the property in 1990 for $60,000 a gain of $28,000 ($60,000 – adjusted basis of $32,000) is recognized on the sale. Since the sale took place within 10 years of the taxable year in which the reforestation expenditures were made, $10,000 of the gain is treated as ordinary income, and the remaining $18,000 of gain would be capital gain, if it otherwise qualifies for capital gain treatment. In order to avoid ordinary income treatment of the gain attributable to the reforestation expenditures incurred in 1981, A would have to wait until 1992 to dispose of the property. [Reg. §1.1245-4.]

☐ [*T.D. 6832, 7-6-65. Amended by T.D. 7084, 1-7-71, T.D. 7207, 10-3-72; T.D. 7728, 10-31-80 and T.D. 7927, 12-15-83.*]

[Reg. §1.1245-5]

§1.1245-5. Adjustments to basis.—In order to reflect gain recognized under section 1245(a)(1),

the following adjustments to the basis of property shall be made:

(a) *Property acquired in like kind exchange or involuntary conversion.*—(1) If property is acquired in a transaction to which section 1245(b)(4) applies, its basis shall be determined under the rules of section 1031(d) or 1033(c).

(2) The provisions of this paragraph may be illustrated by the following example:

Example. Jones exchanges property A, which is section 1245 property with an adjusted basis of $10,000, for property B, which has a fair market value of $9,000, and property C, which has a fair market value of $3,500, in a like kind exchange as to which no gain would be recognized under section 1031(a). Upon the exchange $2,500 gain is recognized under section 1245(a)(1), since property C is not section 1245 property. See section 1245(b)(4). Under the rules of section 1031(d), the basis of the properties received in the exchange is $12,500 (i.e., the basis of property transferred, $10,000, plus the amount of gain recognized, $2,500), of which the amount allocated to property C is $3,500 (the fair market value thereof), and the residue, $9,000, is allocated to property B.

(b) *Section 1071 and 1081 transactions.*—(1) If property is acquired in a transaction to which section 1071 and paragraph (e)(1) of §1.1245-4 (relating to limitation for section 1071 transactions, etc.) apply, its basis shall be determined in accordance with the principles of paragraph (a) of this section.

(2) If the basis of property, other than section 1245 property, is reduced pursuant to either an election under section 1071 or the application of section 1082(a)(2), then the basis of the property shall be increased to the extent of the gain recognized under section 1245(a)(1) by reason of the application of paragraph (e)(1)(iii) of §1.1245-4. [Reg. §1.1245-5.]

☐ [*T.D. 6832, 7-6-65.*]

[Reg. §1.1245-6]

§1.1245-6. Relation of section 1245 to other sections.—(a) *General.*—The provisions of section 1245 apply notwithstanding any other provision of subtitle A of the Code. Thus, unless an exception or limitation under section 1245 (b) applies, gain under section 1245(a)(1) is recognized notwithstanding any contrary nonrecognition provision or income characterizing provision. For example, since section 1245 overrides section 1231 (relating to property used in the trade or business), the gain recognized under section 1245(a)(1) upon a disposition will be treated as ordinary income and only the remaining gain, if any, from the disposition may be considered as gain from the sale or exchange of a capital asset if section 1231 is applicable. See example (2) of paragraph (b)(2) of §1.1245-1. For effect of section 1245 on basis provisions of the Code, see § 1.1245-5.

(b) *Nonrecognition sections overridden.*—The nonrecognition provisions of subtitle A of the Code which section 1245 overrides include, but are not limited to, sections 267(d), 311(a), 336, 337, 501(a), 512(b)(5), and 1039. See section 1245(b) for the extent to which section 1245(a)(1) overrides sections 332, 351, 361, 371(a), 374(a), 721, 731, 1031, 1033, 1071, and 1081(b)(1) and (d)(1)(A). For limitation on amount of adjustments reflected in adjusted basis of property disposed of by an organization exempt from income taxes (within the meaning of section 501(a)), see paragraph (a)(8) of § 1.1245-2.

(c) *Normal retirement of asset in multiple asset account.*—Section 1245(a)(1) does not require recognition of gain upon normal retirements of section 1245 property in a multiple asset account as long as the taxpayer's method of accounting, as described in paragraph (e)(2) of § 1.167(a)-8 (relating to accounting treatment of asset retirements), does not require recognition of such gain.

(d) *Installment method.*—(1) Gain from a disposition to which section 1245(a)(1) applies may be reported under the installment method if such method is otherwise available under section 453 of the Code. In such case, the income (other than interest) on each installment payment shall be deemed to consist of gain to which section 1245(a)(1) applies until all such gain has been reported, and the remaining portion (if any) of such income shall be deemed to consist of gain to which section 1245(a)(1) does not apply. For treatment of amounts as interest on certain deferred payments, see section 483.

(2) The provisions of this paragraph may be illustrated by the following example:

Example. Jones contracts to sell an item of section 1245 property for $10,000 to be paid in 10 equal payments of $1,000 each, plus a sufficient amount of interest so that section 483 does not apply. He properly elects under section 453 to report under the installment method gain of $2,000 to which section 1245(a)(1) applies and gain of $1,000 to which section 1231 applies. Accordingly, $300 of each of the first 6 installment payments and $200 of the seventh installment payment is ordinary income under section 1245(a)(1), and $100 of the seventh installment payment and $300 of each of the last 3 installment payments is gain under section 1231.

(e) *Exempt income.*—The fact that section 1245 provides for recognition of gain as ordinary income does not change into taxable income any income which is exempt under section 115 (relating to income of states, etc.), 892 (relating to income of foreign governments), or 894 (relating to income exempt under treaties).

(f) *Treatment of gain not recognized under section 1245.*—Section 1245 does not prevent gain which is not recognized under section 1245 from being considered as gain under another provision of the Code, such as, for example, section 311(c) (relating to liability in excess of basis), section 341(f) (relating to collapsible corporations), section 357(c) (relating to liabilities in excess of basis), section 1238 (relating to amortization in excess of depreciation), or section 1239 (relating to gain from sale of depreciable property between certain related persons). Thus, for example, if section 1245 property, which has an adjusted basis of $1,000 and a recomputed basis of $1,500, is sold for $1,750 in a transaction to which section 1239 applies, $500 of the gain would be recognized under section 1245(a)(1) and the remaining $250 of the gain would be treated as ordinary income under section 1239. [Reg. § 1.1245-6.]

□ [*T.D.* 6832, 7-6-65. *Amended by T.D.* 7084, 1-7-71 *and T.D.* 7400, 2-3-76.]

[Reg. § 1.1247-1]

§ 1.1247-1. Election by foreign investment companies to distribute income currently.—(a) *Election by foreign investment company.*—(1) *In general.*—If a registered foreign investment company (as defined in paragraph (b) of this section) elects, on or before December 31, 1962, with respect to each of its taxable years beginning after December 31, 1962, to comply with the requirements of subparagraph (2) of this paragraph, then section 1246 (relating to gain on foreign investment company stock) shall not apply with respect to a qualified shareholder (as defined in paragraph (b) of § 1.1247-3) of such company who disposes of his stock during any taxable year of the company to which such election applies. See section 1247(a)(1).

(2) *Requirements.*—A registered foreign investment company which makes an election under section 1247(a) shall, with respect to each of its taxable years beginning after December 31, 1962, comply with the following requirements:

(i) Under section 1247(a)(1)(A), the company shall distribute to its shareholders, during the taxable year, 90 percent or more of what its taxable income would be for such taxable year if it were a domestic corporation. To the extent elected by the company under section 1247(a)(2)(B), a distribution of taxable income made not later than 2 months and 15 days after the close of the taxable year shall be treated as distributed during such taxable year. For rules relating to computation of taxable income for a taxable year and distributions of such taxable income, see § 1.1247-2.

(ii) Under section 1247(a)(1)(B), the company shall designate to each shareholder the amount of his pro rata share of the excess of the net long-term capital gain over the net short-term capital loss for the taxable year and the amount thereof which is being distributed. For the manner of designating and the computation of such amounts, see § 1.1247-3.

(iii) Under section 1247(a)(1)(C), the company shall provide the information and maintain the records required by § 1.1247-5.

(b) *Definition of registered foreign investment company.*—The term "registered foreign investment company" means a foreign corporation which is registered within the time specified in this paragraph under the Investment Company Act of 1940, as amended (15 U.S.C. 80a-1 to 80b-2), either as a management company or as a unit investment trust. Under such Act, a company is deemed registered upon receipt by the Securities and Exchange Commission of Form N-8A entitled "Notification of Registration Filed Pursuant to section 8(a) of the Investment Company Act of 1940". See section 8(a) of such Act (15 U.S.C. 80a-8(a)) and 17 CFR 274.10. A company which computes its income on the basis of a calendar year must have registered on or before December 31, 1962, and a company which computes its income on the basis of a fiscal year must have registered on or before the last day of its fiscal year beginning in 1962 and ending in 1963.

(c) *Time and manner of making election.*—(1) *In general.*—The election provided by paragraph (a) of this section must have been made on or before December 31, 1962, by means of a letter addressed to the Director of International Operations, Internal Revenue Service, Washington 25, D.C., which clearly stated that the company elects to comply with the provisions of section 1247. The letter must have been signed by an officer of the foreign investment company who was a resident of the United States and who was duly authorized to act on behalf of the company.

(2) *Information furnished.*—The following information must have been submitted in connection with the election:

(i) The name, address, and employer identification number, if any, and the taxable year of the company;

(ii) The principal place of business of the company;

(iii) The date and the country under whose laws the company was incorporated;

(iv) The date of filing with the Securities and Exchange Commission, and the file number, of Form N-8A;

(v) The names and addresses of all of the company's directors and officers and of any custodian or agent of the company located in the United States; and

(vi) The name and address of the person (or persons) in the United States having custody of the books of account, records, and other documents of the company, and the location of such books, records, and other documents if different from such address.

(3) *Time information furnished.*—(i) If a foreign investment company was registered with the Securities and Exchange Commission on the date of election, all the information required by subparagraph (2) of this paragraph must have been submitted with the election.

(ii) If a foreign investment company made its election before it was so registered, the information required by subparagraph (2)(i), (ii), and (iii) of this paragraph must have been submitted with the election and the information required by subparagraph (2)(iv), (v), and (vi) of this paragraph must have been submitted within 60 days following receipt by the Securities and Exchange Commission of Form N-8A.

(d) *Termination of election.*—(1) *General.*—Section 1247(b) provides that the election of a foreign investment company under section 1247(a) shall permanently terminate as of the close of the taxable year preceding its first taxable year in which any of the following occurs:

(i) The company fails to comply with the provisions of section 1247(a)(1)(A), (B), or (C), unless it is shown that such failure is due to reasonable cause and not due to willful neglect;

(ii) The company is a foreign personal holding company as defined in section 552; or

(iii) The company ceases to be a registered foreign investment company which is described in paragraph (b) of this section. A company ceases to be a registered company, for example, as of the time the Securities and Exchange Commission revokes its order permitting registration of the company.

(2) *Reasonable cause.*—Whether a failure by a foreign investment company to comply with the provisions of section 1247(a)(1)(A), (B), or (C) is due to reasonable cause and not due to willful neglect depends on whether the company exercised ordinary business care and prudence. For example, if in determining its taxable income under section 1247(a) the company relied in good faith upon estimates and opinions of independent certified public accountants or other experts which are also used for purposes of its financial statements filed with the Securities and Exchange Commission under the Investment Company Act of 1940, such reliance would constitute reasonable cause for purposes of this paragraph. In such a case, the company's election under section 1247(a) for the taxable year would not be terminated nor would the company be required to make an additional distribution for such taxable year in order to comply with the provisions of section 1247(a)(1)(A). [Reg. § 1.1247-1.]

☐ [*T.D.* 6798, 2-3-65.]

[Reg. § 1.1247-2]

§ 1.1247-2. Computation and distribution of taxable income.—(a) *In general.*—Taxable income of a foreign investment company means taxable income as defined in section 63(a), computed without regard to subchapter N, chapter 1 of the Code, and in accordance with the following rules:

(1) There shall be excluded the excess, if any, of the company's net long-term capital gain over the net short-term capital loss. See § 1.1247-3 for the manner of computing such excess.

(2) The deduction provided in section 172 (relating to net operating losses) shall not be allowed.

(3) Except for the deduction provided in section 248 (relating to organizational expenditures), the special deductions provided for corporations in part VIII (sections 241 and following), subchapter B, chapter 1 of the Code shall not be allowed.

(4) In computing the amount of the deduction allowed under section 164 there shall be included taxes paid or accrued during the taxable year which are imposed by the United States or by the country under the laws of which the company is created or organized. See, however, § 1.1247-4.

(b) *Election to distribute taxable income after close of taxable year.*—A company may elect under section 1247(a)(2)(B), in respect of taxable income for a taxable year, to treat a distribution made not later than 2 months and 15 days after the close of such taxable year as a distribution made during such taxable year of such taxable income. The company shall make the election by attaching to the information return required by paragraph (c)(1) of § 1.1247-5 for such taxable year a statement setting forth the amount of each distribution (or portion thereof) to which the election applies and the date of each such distribution. The election shall be irrevocable after the expiration of the time for filing such information return. The distribution (or portion thereof) to which the election applies shall be considered as paid out of the earnings and profits of the taxable year for which such election is made, and not out of the earnings and profits of the taxable year in which the distribution is actually made. A distribution to which this paragraph applies shall be includible in the gross income of a shareholder of the foreign investment company for his taxable year in which received or accrued. [Reg. § 1.1247-2.]

☐ [*T.D.* 6798, 2-3-65.]

[Reg. § 1.1247-3]

§ 1.1247-3. Treatment of capital gains.—(a) *Treatment by the company.*—(1) *In general.*—If an election to distribute income currently pursuant to section 1247(a) is in effect for a taxable year of a foreign investment company, the company shall designate (in the manner described in subparagraph (3) of this paragraph) to each shareholder his pro rata amount of the excess of the net long-term capital gain over the net short-term capital loss for the company's taxable year, and the portion thereof which is being distributed to each such shareholder. See section 1247(a)(1)(B). Except as provided in subparagraph (2) of this paragraph, the company shall compute such excess (hereinafter referred to as "excess capital gains") as if such company were a domestic corporation, but without regard to subchapter N, chapter 1 of the Code. See paragraph (d) of § 1.1247-1 for rules relating to termination of election under section 1247(a) for failure to properly compute or to properly designate excess capital gains. A company may make an irrevocable election (by notifying its shareholders as provided in subparagraph (3) of this paragraph) to distribute, on or before the 45th day following the close of its taxable year, all or a portion of the excess capital gains and have any such distribution treated as if made during such taxable year.

(2) *Rules for computing capital gains and losses.*—Generally, the adjusted basis of property held by a foreign investment company shall be its cost adjusted in accordance with the applicable provisions of the Code. However, in respect of property held by a foreign investment company on the first day of the first taxable year for which the election under section 1247(a) applies, the amounts shown on such day in the permanent books of account, records, and other documents of the company shall, at the option of the company, be accepted as the adjusted basis of such property, if on such day such books, records, and other documents were being maintained in the manner prescribed by regulations under section 30 of the Investment Company Act of 1940 (15 U.S.C. 80a-30). In computing capital gains and losses of a foreign investment company under section 1247, the provisions of section 1212 (relating to allowance of capital loss carryover) shall not apply to any capital loss incurred in or with respect to taxable years before the first taxable year for which the election under section 1247(a) applies. See section 1247(a)(2)(C).

(3) *Notice to shareholders.*—The company shall designate by written notice, mailed on or before the 45th day following the close of its taxable year—

(i) To each person who is a shareholder at the close of such taxable year, his pro rata amount of the portion of the excess capital gains for such year which was not distributed, and

(ii) To each person who received a distribution of excess capital gains with respect to such taxable year, the amount and the date of each such distribution.

Each notice shall show the name and address of the foreign investment company and the taxable year of the company for which the designation is made.

(b) *Treatment of capital gains by qualified shareholder.*—(1) *Definition of qualified shareholder.*—(i) The term "qualified shareholder" means any shareholder of a registered foreign investment company who is a United States person (as defined in section 7701(a)(30)), other than a shareholder described in subdivision (ii) of this subparagraph.

(ii) A United States person shall not be treated as a qualified shareholder for a taxable year if in his return for such taxable year (or for any prior taxable year) he did not include, in computing his long-term capital gains, his pro rata amount of the undistributed portion of the excess capital gains which the company designated for its taxable year ending within or with such taxable year of the shareholder. Thus, for example, if a shareholder fails to include as long-term capital gain in his return for his taxable year ending December 31, 1966, the amount designated by the company as his pro rata amount of undistributed excess capital gains for the company's taxable year ending June 30, 1966, he would not be a qualified shareholder for his taxable year ending December 31, 1966, or for any subsequent taxable year. However, if the shareholder can show that his failure to include his pro rata amount of the undistributed portion of the excess capital gains in his return was due to reasonable cause and not due to willful neglect, he will continue to be a qualified shareholder. Such shareholder shall, for the year with respect to which such failure occurred, include in his taxable income his previously omitted pro rata amount of the undistributed portion of excess capital gains.

(2) *Treatment of excess capital gains.*—A qualified shareholder of a foreign investment company, for any taxable year of the company for which the election under section 1247(a) is in effect, shall include in his return in computing his long-term capital gains—

(i) For his taxable year in which received, his pro rata amount of the distributed portion of the excess capital gains for such taxable year of the company, and

(ii) For his taxable year in which or with which the taxable year of the company ends, his pro rata amount of the undistributed portion of the excess capital gains for such taxable year of the company.

(3) *Sales at end of company's taxable year.*—For purposes of determining whether the purchaser or seller of a share of foreign investment company stock is the shareholder at the close of such company's taxable year who is required to include an amount of undistributed excess capital gains in gross income, the amount of the undistributed excess capital gains shall be treated in the same manner as a cash dividend payable to shareholders of record at the close of the company's taxable year. Thus, if a cash dividend paid to shareholders of record as of the close of the foreign investment company's taxable year would be considered income to the purchaser, then the purchaser is also considered to be the shareholder of such company at the close of its taxable year for purposes of including an amount of undistributed excess capital gains in gross income. For rules for determining whether a dividend is income to the purchaser or seller of a share of stock, see paragraph (c) of §1.61-9.

(4) *Partners and partnerships.*—If the shareholder required to include an amount of undistributed excess capital gains in gross income under section 1247(d)(2) and subparagraph (2)(ii) of this paragraph is a partnership, such amount shall be taken into account by the partnership for the taxable year of the partnership in which occurs the last day of the taxable year of the foreign investment company in respect of which the undistributed portion of the excess capital gains were designated. The amount so includible by the partnership shall be taken into account by the partners as distributive shares of the partnership gains and losses from sales or exchanges of capital assets held for more than 1 year (6 months for taxable years beginning before 1977; 9 months for taxable years beginning in 1977) pursuant to section 702(a)(2) and paragraph (a)(2) of §1.702-1. The partners shall increase the basis of their partnership interests under section 705(a)(1) by their distributive shares of such gains.

(5) *Effect on earnings and profits of corporate shareholder.*—If a shareholder required to include an amount of undistributed excess capital gains in gross income under section 1247(d)(2) and subparagraph (2)(ii) of this paragraph is a corporation, such corporation, in computing its earnings and profits for the taxable year for which such amount is so includible, shall treat such amount as if it had actually been received in that year.

(6) *Example.*—The application of this paragraph may be illustrated by the following example:

Example. Smith owns one share of stock in a foreign investment company which he purchased in 1964. In respect of the company's taxable year ending June 30, 1966, during which the election under section 1247(a) was in effect, Smith receives from the company on July 15, 1966, a distribution in the amount of $8. He also receives a notice stating that for such taxable year $9 was being designated as his pro rata amount of the excess capital gains, $8 of which was distributed on July 15, 1966, and $1 of which was being designated as the undistributed portion. In order for Smith to be a qualified shareholder for his taxable year ending December 31, 1966, he must include in computing his long-term capital gains in his return for 1966, his pro rata amount of the undistributed portion of the excess capital gains, that is, $1. Smith must also

Reg. §1.1247-3(b)

include in such return his pro rata amount of the distributed portion of excess capital gains, that is, $8. If, however, Smith does not include in income his pro rata amount of the undistributed portion of excess capital gains, he is not a qualified shareholder for 1966 (or for any subsequent year). In such a case, the $8 is not treated under the provisions of section 1247(d)(1) as a distribution of long-term capital gains for such year but as a corporate distribution taxable as ordinary income to the extent provided in subchapter C, chapter 1 of the Code.

(c) *Adjustments relating to undistributed capital gains.*—(1) *Adjustments in earnings and profits of the company.*—If a foreign investment company, to which the election under section 1247(a) applies, designates an amount as the undistributed portion of excess capital gains for its taxable year, the earnings and profits of the company (within the meaning of subchapter C, chapter 1 of the Code) shall be reduced, and its capital account shall be increased, by such amount.

(2) *Increase in basis of qualified shareholder's stock.*—A qualified shareholder, who computes his long-term capital gains for a taxable year by including (in respect of each share of stock which he owns in a foreign investment company) the pro rata amount of the undistributed portion of the excess capital gains which was designated by the company for its taxable year ending with or within such taxable year of the shareholder, shall, as of the day following the close of such taxable year of the company, increase the adjusted basis of each share by such pro rata amount.

(d) *Loss on sale or exchange of certain stock held 1 year or less.*—(1) *In general.*—If—

(i) A qualified shareholder of a foreign investment company to which the election under section 1247(a) applies treats any amount designated under section 1247(a)(1)(B) with respect to a share of stock as long-term capital gain, and

(ii) Such share is held by the taxpayer for 1 year (6 months for taxable years beginning before 1977; 9 months for taxable years beginning in 1977) or less,

then any loss on the sale or exchange of such share shall, to the extent of the amount described in subdivision (i) of this subparagraph, be treated under section 1247(i) as loss from the sale or exchange of a capital asset held for more than 1 year (6 months for taxable years beginning before 1977; 9 months for taxable years beginning in 1977).

(2) *Example.*—The application of this paragraph may be illustrated by the following example:

Example. On October 1, 1966, B, a calendar year taxpayer, purchases for $100 a share of stock in a foreign investment company to which the election under section 1247(a) applies. On January 20, 1967, the company, in a notice to B, designates for its taxable year ending December 31, 1966, $8 per share as excess capital gains of which $6 was distributed on December 1, 1966, and $2 was designated as undistributed. B includes the $8 in computing his long-term capital gains in his return for 1966 and, under paragraph (c)(2) of this section, B's basis for the share is increased to $102 as of January 1, 1967. On February 1, 1967, B sells the share for $93, incurring a $9 loss of which $8 is treated as a long-term capital loss under section 1247(i) and $1 is treated as a short-term capital loss. [Reg. § 1.1247-3.]

☐ [T.D. 6798, 2-3-65. *Amended by T.D. 7728*, 10-31-80.]

[Reg. § 1.1247-4]

§ 1.1247-4. Election by foreign investment company with respect to foreign tax credit.— (a) *In general.*—(1) *Election.*—If an election to distribute income currently pursuant to section 1247(a) is in effect for a taxable year of a foreign investment company, and if at the close of such taxable year more than 50 percent of the value of the total assets of the company consists of stock or securities in foreign corporations, then the company may elect for such taxable year, in the manner provided in paragraph (d) of this section, the application of section 1247(f) in respect of foreign taxes referred to in subparagraph (2) of this paragraph which are paid during such taxable year. For purposes of this section, the term "value" shall have the same meaning as assigned to such term in section 851(c)(4) (relating to definition of regulated investment company). For definition of foreign corporation, see section 7701(a).

(2) *Taxes affected.*—The election under section 1247(f) for a taxable year applies with respect to income, war profits, and excess profits taxes described in section 901(b)(1) which are paid by the company to foreign countries and possessions of the United States. A tax paid by a foreign investment company does not include a tax which is paid by the shareholders of the company. Whether a tax is paid by the company, and whether a tax is an income, war profits, or excess profits tax described in section 901(b)(1), shall be determined under the principles of chapter 1 of the Code without regard to the law of any foreign country and without regard to any income tax convention, including any income tax convention to which the United States is a party. Section 1247(f) does not apply with respect to foreign taxes which would be deemed to have been paid by the company under section 902 if the company were a domestic corporation. For purposes of this paragraph, taxes paid to the United States are not considered foreign taxes.

(b) *Effect of election.*—(1) *Effect on company.*—If a valid election under section 1247(f) is made for a taxable year of a foreign investment company, then, for purposes of determining under section 1247(a)(1)(A) whether the company has distributed to its shareholders with respect to such taxable year 90 percent or more of what the company's taxable income would be for such year if the company were a domestic corporation, the following rules shall apply:

(i) The company shall compute such taxable income without any deduction for the foreign taxes referred to in paragraph (a)(2) of this section which were paid or accrued during the taxable year.

(ii) If the amount of taxable income (computed without regard to subdivision (i) of this subparagraph) is more than zero, the company shall treat the foreign taxes referred to in paragraph (a)(2) of this section which were paid during such taxable year of the company as distributed to its shareholders to the extent of the amount which bears the same ratio to the amount of such foreign taxes as (a) the amount actually distributed (or treated as distributed pursuant to an election under section 1247(a)(2)(B)) during such taxable year from such taxable income (determined without regard to subdivision (i) of this subparagraph), bears to (b) the amount of such taxable income (also determined without regard to such subdivision (i)). Thus, for example, if for a taxable year a foreign investment company has taxable income of $1,000 (determined after deducting foreign taxes paid of $100), and if $600 of such taxable income is distributed during the taxable year and $350 of such taxable income is distributed not later than 2 months and 15 days after the close of the taxable year, then $950 is treated as distributed for purposes of satisfying the 90-percent distribution requirement of section 1247(a)(1)(A), and the amount of foreign taxes treated as distributed under this subdivision is $95 (that is, $100 multiplied by $950/$1,000).

(iii) If the amount of taxable income (computed without regard to subdivision (i) of this subparagraph) is zero, then all foreign taxes referred to in paragraph (a)(2) of this section which were paid during the taxable year shall be treated as distributed by the company on the last day of such taxable year. Thus, for example, if for a taxable year a foreign investment company has taxable income of $500 (computed without deducting $800 of foreign taxes paid during such year), the amount of taxable income computed without regard to subdivision (i) of this paragraph is zero, and the $800 of foreign taxes is treated as distributed under this subdivision on the last day of the company's taxable year.

(2) *Effect on qualified shareholders.*—The following rules apply to a qualified shareholder of a foreign investment company which makes a valid election under section 1247(f) for a taxable year:

(i) The qualified shareholder shall include in his gross income (in addition to taxable dividends actually received) his proportionate share of the foreign taxes referred to in paragraph (a)(2) of this section which were paid during such taxable year of the company, and shall treat such proportionate share as paid by him for purposes of the deduction under section 164(a) and the foreign tax credit under section 901. See, however, paragraph (c)(1) of this section for a limitation on the amount a shareholder may treat as his proportionate share of foreign taxes.

(ii) In respect of any distribution made (or treated as made under section 1247(a)(2)(B)) during the taxable year of the company and which is received by a qualified shareholder, the term "proportionate share of foreign taxes" means, for purposes of this section, an amount which bears the same ratio to (a) the amount of the foreign taxes referred to in paragraph (a)(2) of this section which were paid during such taxable year of the company, as (b) the amount of such distribution to the shareholder out of the company's taxable income for such taxable year (determined without regard to subparagraph (1)(i) of this paragraph), bears to (c) the amount of such taxable income (also determined without regard to such subparagraph (1)(i)).

(iii) In respect of any distribution of foreign taxes treated as made under subparagraph (1)(iii) of this paragraph on the last day of the taxable year of the company, the term "proportionate share of foreign taxes" means, for purposes of this section, an amount which bears the same ratio to (a) the amount of foreign taxes referred to in paragraph (a)(2) of this section which were paid during such taxable year of the company, as (b) the fair market value of all shares of stock of the company held by such qualified shareholder on the last day of such taxable year, bears to (c) the fair market value of all such shares outstanding on such last day.

(iv) For purposes of the foreign tax credit, the qualified shareholder shall treat his proportionate share of foreign taxes as having been paid by him to the country in which the foreign investment company is created or organized.

(v) For purposes of the foreign tax credit, the qualified shareholder shall treat as gross income from sources within the country in which the foreign investment company is created or organized the sum of (a) his proportionate share of foreign taxes, (b) any dividend paid to him by such foreign investment company, and (c) his pro rata amount of distributed and undistributed portions of excess capital gains referred to in paragraph (a) of § 1.1247-3.

(vi)(a) In respect of a distribution made (or treated as made under section 1247(a)(2)(B)) during a taxable year of the company, a qualified shareholder shall consider his proportionate share of foreign taxes as having been received, and as having been paid, by him during his taxable year in which the distribution is includible in his gross income.

(b) In respect of an amount of foreign taxes treated as distributed under subparagraph (1)(iii) of this paragraph on the last day of a taxable year of the company, the qualified shareholder shall consider his proportionate share of foreign taxes as having been received, and as having been paid, by him during his taxable year in which such last day falls.

(vii) If the qualified shareholder is a corporation, it shall not be deemed under section 902 to have paid any taxes paid by the foreign investment company to which the election under section 1247(f) applied.

(3) *Effect on nonqualified shareholders.*—A shareholder who is not a qualified shareholder

Dividend income, minus operating expenses	$675,000
Foreign income taxes paid:	

Withheld by country A	$25,000	
Withheld by country B	50,000	
Income tax of country C	90,000	
Total foreign income tax paid		165,000
Taxable income for purposes of section 1247(a)(1)(A), determined without regard to section 1247(f)		$510,000

X Corporation distributes to its shareholders the amount of $459,000 (i.e., 90 percent of $510,000).

(ii) Assume that X Corporation validly elects the application of section 1274(f). Accordingly, X Corporation determines that its taxable income for purposes of section 1247(a)(1)(A) without any deduction for foreign income taxes paid or accrued is $675,000 ($510,000, plus $165,000).

(iii) Assume that X Corporation intends to distribute the least amount which would satisfy the requirements of section 1247(a)(1)(A), as modified by the election under section 1247(f). Thus, the total amount X distributes is $607,500, which consists of the sum of (a) $459,000 actually distributed, that is, 90 percent of $510,000 of taxable income (determined after the deduction for foreign taxes), plus (b) foreign taxes paid of $148,500 which are treated as distributed, that is, 90 percent of $165,000 of foreign taxes paid by X Corporation.

Example (2). Assume the same facts as in example (1) except that X Corporation distributes the entire $510,000 in the following manner: On December 15, 1964, X Corporation distributes $170,000 as a dividend of $1.70 per share. On February 25, 1965, X Corporation distributes the remaining $340,000 as a dividend of $3.40 per share pursuant to an election under section 1247(a)(2)(B) to treat such distribution as if made in 1964. Assume that Brown, a qualified shareholder, uses the calendar year as his taxable year. The amount of $0.55 per share (that is, $165,000, multiplied by $1.70/$510,000) must be treated by Brown as foreign taxes paid by him in 1964 to country C and the amount of $1.10 per share (that is, $165,000 multiplied by $3.40/$510,000) must be similarly treated by

shall not include his proportionate share of foreign taxes in gross income, and shall not be entitled to treat such proportionate share as having been paid by him to a foreign country for purposes of the deduction under section 164(a) or, except to the extent that section 902 is applicable, for purposes of the foreign tax credit under section 901.

(4) *Example.*—The application of paragraph (a) of this section and this paragraph may be illustrated by the following examples:

Example (1). (i) X Corporation, a foreign investment company incorporated in country C with 100,000 shares of stock outstanding, uses the calendar year as its taxable year. For 1964, X Corporation has the following income and pays the following foreign taxes:

Brown in 1965. The amount of $2.25 per share ($1.70 of dividends actually received plus $0.55 representing foreign taxes paid) must be reported by Brown as income considered received in 1964 from country C, and the amount of $4.50 per share ($3.40 of dividends actually received plus $1.10 representing foreign taxes paid) must be so reported by Brown in 1965.

Example (3). A foreign investment company organized under the laws of country C receives a dividend of $1,000 from X Corporation, which is also organized under the laws of country C. Under the laws of country C, the foreign investment company would, if it so elects, be considered as having paid income tax in the amount of $150 which X Corporation paid to country C with respect to the earnings from which the dividend was paid. If the foreign investment company were a domestic corporation, however, it would not be considered for purposes of section 901(b)(1) as having paid the tax actually paid by X Corporation. Accordingly, the election under section 1247(f) does not apply in respect of the $150. The result would be the same if X Corporation was organized under the laws of any other foreign country to which it paid taxes and if the laws of country C permitted the foreign investment company to be considered as the payor of such taxes.

(c) *Notice to shareholders.*—(1) *In general.*—If, in the manner provided in paragraph (d) of this section, a foreign investment company makes an election with respect to the foreign tax credit under section 1247(f), the company shall furnish to each shareholder a written notice mailed not later than 45 days after the close of the taxable

Reg. §1.1247-4(c)(1)

year of the company for which the election is made, designating the shareholder's proportionate share of the foreign taxes referred to in paragraph (a)(2) of this section which were paid by the company during such taxable year. This notice may be combined with the written notice to shareholders described in paragraph (a)(3) of § 1.1247-3 relating to excess capital gains.

(2) *Application to shareholder.*—For purposes of paragraph (b)(2) of this section, the amount which a shareholder may treat as his proportionate share of foreign taxes paid by the company shall not exceed the amounts so designated by the company in such written notice. If, however, an amount designated by the company in a notice exceeds the shareholder's proper proportionate share of such foreign taxes, the shareholder is limited to the amount correctly determined.

(d) *Manner of making election.*—(1) *In general.*—The election of a foreign investment company to have section 1247(f) apply for a taxable year shall be made by filing as part of its information return required by paragraph (c)(1) of § 1.1247-5 a Form 1118 modified so that it becomes a statement in support of the election made by the company under section 1247(f).

(2) *Irrevocability of election.*—An election under section 1247(f) for a taxable year of a foreign investment company shall be made with respect to all foreign taxes referred to in paragraph (a)(2) of this section which were paid during such taxable year, and must be made not later than the time prescribed for filing the information return under paragraph (c)(1) of § 1.1247-5. Such election, if made, shall be irrevocable with respect to the distributions, and the foreign taxes with respect thereto, to which the election applies. [Reg. § 1.1247-4.]

☐ [*T.D.* 6798, 2-3-65.]

[Reg. § 1.1247-5]

§ 1.1247-5. Information and record keeping requirements.—(a) *General.*—In order to carry out the purposes of section 1247, a foreign investment company shall keep the records and comply with the information requirements prescribed by this section for each taxable year of the company for which the election under section 1247(a) is in effect. See section 1247(a)(1)(C).

(b) *Record keeping requirements.*—The company shall maintain and preserve such permanent books of account, records, and other documents as are sufficient to establish in accordance with the provisions of § 1.1247-2 what its taxable income would be if it were a domestic corporation. Generally, if the books and records of the company are maintained in the manner prescribed by regulations under section 30 of the Investment Company Act of 1940 (15 U.S.C. 80a-30), the requirements of the preceding sentence shall be considered satisfied. Such books, records, and

other documents shall be available for inspection in the United States by authorized internal revenue officers or employees, and shall be maintained so long as the contents thereof may be material in the administration of section 1247.

(c) *Information returns.*—The company shall file, for each taxable year during which the election under section 1247(a) is in effect, on or before the 15th day of the third month following the close of its taxable year or on or before May 1, 1965, whichever is later, with the Director of International Operations, Internal Revenue Service, Washington, D.C. 20225—

(1) Form 1120, modified so as to be an annual information return, establishing the amount of its taxable income referred to in paragraph (b) of this section, and

(2) Form 2438, modified so as to be an annual information return, establishing the amount of the company's excess capital gains (referred to in paragraph (a)(1) of § 1.1247-3) for the taxable year, the distributed portion thereof, and the amount of the undistributed portion thereof. [Reg. § 1.1247-5.]

☐ [*T.D.* 6798, 2-3-65.]

[Reg. § 1.1248-1]

§ 1.1248-1. Treatment of gain from certain sales or exchanges of stock in certain foreign corporations.—(a) *In general.*—(1) If a United States person (as defined in section 7701(a)(30)) recognizes gain on a sale or exchange after December 31, 1962, of stock in a foreign corporation, and if in respect of such person the conditions of subparagraph (2) of this paragraph are satisfied, then the gain shall be included in the gross income of such person as a dividend to the extent of the earnings and profits of such corporation attributable to such stock under § 1.1248-2 or 1.1248-3, whichever is applicable, which were accumulated in taxable years of such foreign corporation beginning after December 31, 1962, during the period or periods such stock was held (or was considered as held by reason of the application of section 1223, taking into account § 1.1248-8) by such person while such corporation was a controlled foreign corporation. See section 1248(a). See § 1.1248-8 for additional rules regarding the attribution of earnings and profits to the stock of a foreign corporation following certain nonrecognition transactions. For computation of earnings and profits attributable to such stock if there are any "lower tier" corporations, see paragraph (a)(3) and (4) of § 1.1248-2 or paragraph (a) of § 1.1248-3, whichever is applicable. In general, the amount of gain to be included in a person's gross income as a dividend under section 1248(a) shall be determined separately for each share of stock sold or exchanged. However, such determination may be made in respect of a block of stock if earnings and profits attributable to the block are computed under § 1.1248-2 or 1.1248-3. See paragraph (b) of §1.1248-2 and paragraph (a)(5) of §1.1248-3. For the limitation on the tax attributable to an amount included in an individual's gross income as a dividend under section 1248(a), see section 1248(b) and §1.1248-4. For the treatment, under certain circumstances, of the sale or exchange of stock in a domestic corporation as the sale or exchange of stock held by the domestic corporation in a foreign corporation, see section 1248(e) and §1.1248-6. For the nonapplication of section 1248 in certain circumstances, see section 1248(f) and paragraph (e) of this section. For the requirement that the person establish the amount of earnings and profits attributable to the stock sold or exchanged and, for purposes of section 1248(b), the amount of certain taxes, see section 1248(g) and §1.1248-7.

(2) In respect of a United States person who sells or exchanges stock in a foreign corporation, the conditions referred to in subparagraph (1) of this paragraph are satisfied only if (i) such person owned, within the meaning of section 958(a), or was considered as owning by applying the rules of ownership of section 958(b), 10 percent or more of the total combined voting power of all classes of stock entitled to vote of such foreign corporation at any time during the 5-year period ending on the date of the sale or exchange, and (ii) at such time such foreign corporation was a controlled foreign corporation (as defined in section 957).

(3) For purposes of subparagraph (2) of this paragraph, (i) a foreign corporation shall not be considered to be a controlled foreign corporation at any time before the first day of its first taxable year beginning after December 31, 1962, and (ii) the percentage of the total combined voting power of stock of a foreign corporation owned (or considered as owned) by a United States person shall be determined in accordance with the principles of section 951(b) and the regulations thereunder.

(4) For purposes of paragraph (a)(1) of this section, if a foreign partnership sells or exchanges stock of a corporation, the partners in such foreign partnership shall be treated as selling or exchanging their proportionate share of the stock of such corporation. Stock which is considered to have been sold or exchanged by a partner by reason of the application of this paragraph (a)(4) shall for purposes of applying such sentence be treated as actually sold or exchanged by such partner.

(5) The application of this paragraph may be illustrated by the following examples:

Example (1). Corporation F is a foreign corporation which has outstanding 100 shares of one class of stock. F was a controlled foreign corporation for the period beginning on January 1, 1963, and ending on June 30, 1965, but was not a controlled foreign corporation at any time thereafter. On December 31, 1965, Brown, a United States person who has owned 15 shares of F stock since 1962, sells 7 of his 15 shares and recognizes gain with respect to each share sold. Since Brown owned stock representing at least 10 percent of the total combined voting power of F at a time during the 5-year period ending on December 31, 1965, while F was a controlled foreign corporation, the conditions of subparagraph (2) of this paragraph are satisfied. Therefore, section 1248(a) applies to the gain recognized by Brown to the extent of the earnings and profits attributable under §1.1248-3 to such shares.

Example (2). Assume the same facts as in example (1). Assume further that on February 1, 1970, Brown sells the remainder of his shares in F Corporation and recognizes gain with respect to each share sold. Even though Brown did not own stock representing at least 10 percent of the total combined voting power of F on February 1, 1970, nevertheless, in respect of each of the 8 shares of F stock which he sold on such date, the conditions of subparagraph (2) of this paragraph are satisfied since Brown owned stock representing at least 10 percent of such voting power at a time during the 5-year period ending on February 1, 1970, while F was a controlled foreign corporation. Therefore, section 1248(a) applies to the gain recognized by Brown to the extent of the earnings and profits attributable under §1.1248-3 to such shares. If, however, Brown had sold the remainder of his shares in F on July 1, 1970, since the last date on which Brown owned stock representing at least 10 percent of the total combined voting power of F while F was a controlled foreign corporation was June 30, 1965, a date which is not within the 5-year period ending July 1, 1970, the conditions of subparagraph (2) of this paragraph would not be satisfied and section 1248(a) would not apply.

Example (3). Corporation G, a foreign corporation created in 1950, has outstanding 100 shares of one class of stock and uses the calendar year as its taxable year. Corporation X, a United States person, owns 60 shares of G stock and has owned such stock since G was created. Corporation Y, a United States person, owned 15 shares of the G stock from 1950 until December 1, 1962, on which date it sold 10 of such shares. On December 31, 1963, Y sells its remaining 5 shares of the G stock and recognizes gain on the sale. Since G is not considered to be a controlled foreign corporation at any time before January 1, 1963, and since Y did not own stock representing at least 10 percent of the total combined voting power of G at any time on or after such date, the conditions of subparagraph (2) of this paragraph are not satisfied and section 1248(a) does not apply.

Example (4). (i) *Facts.* X, a domestic corporation, and Y, a foreign corporation that is not a controlled foreign corporation, are partners in foreign partnership Z. X has a 60% interest in Z, and Y has a 40% interest in Z. All parties are calendar year taxpayers. On January 1, year 1, Z forms foreign corporation H, a controlled foreign corporation that conducts a business in Country C. Z and H's functional currency is the United States dollar. In years 1 and 2, H did not earn subpart F income as defined in section 952(a). On December 31, year 2, Z sells all of the H stock for $600 when Z's adjusted basis in the stock is $100. Therefore, Z recognizes a gain of $500 on the sale, of which $300 is allocable to X as a 60% partner. At the time of the sale, H had $300 of earnings and profits, $180 of which (that is, 60% of $300) is attributable to X's 60% share of the H stock.

(ii) *Result.* Pursuant to section 1248(a) and paragraphs (a)(1) and (4) of this section, X and Y are treated as selling 60% and 40%, respectively, of the H stock. X includes in its gross income as a dividend $180 of the gain recognized on the sale. Because Y is a foreign corporation that is not a CFC, neither section 1248 nor section 964 applies to the sale of Y's 40% share of the H stock.

(iii) *Alternative facts.* If, instead, X owned its 60% interest in Z through another foreign partnership, the result would be the same.

(b) [Reserved]. For further guidance, see § 1.1248-1T(b).

(c) *Gain recognized.*—Section 1248(a) applies to a sale or exchange of stock in a foreign corporation only if gain is recognized in whole or in part upon such sale or exchange. Thus, for example, if a United States person exchanges stock in a foreign corporation, and if under section 332, 351, 354, 355, or 361 no gain is recognized as a result of a determination by the Commissioner under section 367 that the exchange is not in pursuance of a plan having as one of its principal purposes the avoidance of Federal income taxes, then no amount is includible in the gross income of such person as a dividend under section 1248(a).

(d) *Credit for foreign taxes.*—(1) If a domestic corporation includes an amount in its gross income as a dividend under section 1248(a) upon a sale or exchange of stock in a foreign corporation (referred to as a "first tier" corporation), and if on the date of the sale or exchange the domestic corporation owns directly at least 10 percent of the voting stock of the first tier corporation—

(i) The foreign tax credit provisions of sections 901 through 908 shall apply in the same manner and subject to the same conditions and limitations as if the first tier corporation on such date distributed to the domestic corporation as a dividend that portion of the amount included in gross income under section 1248(a) which does not exceed the earnings and profits of the first tier corporation attributable to the stock under § 1.1248-2 or § 1.1248-3, as the case may be, and

(ii) If on such date such first tier corporation owns directly 50 percent or more of the voting stock of a "lower tier" corporation described in paragraph (a)(3) of § 1.1248-2 or paragraph (a)(3) of § 1.1248-3, as the case may be (referred to as a "second tier" corporation), then

the foreign tax credit provisions of sections 901 through 905 shall apply in the same manner and subject to the same conditions and limitations as if on such date (*a*) the domestic corporation owned directly that percentage of the stock in the second tier corporation which such domestic corporation is considered to own by reason of the application of section 958(a)(2), and (*b*) the second tier corporation had distributed to the domestic corporation as a dividend that portion of the amount included in gross income under section 1248(a) which does not exceed the earnings and profits of the second tier corporation attributable to such stock under § 1.1248-2 or § 1.1248-3, as the case may be.

(2) A credit shall not be allowed under subparagraph (1) of this paragraph in respect of taxes which are not actually paid or accrued. For the inclusion as a dividend in the gross income of a domestic corporation of an amount equal to the taxes deemed paid by such corporation under section 902(a)(1), see section 78.

(3) If subparagraph (1)(ii) of this paragraph applies, and if the amount included in gross income under section 1248(a) upon the sale or exchange of the stock in a first tier corporation described in subparagraph (1)(ii) of this paragraph is less than the sum of the earnings and profits of the first tier corporation attributable to such stock under § 1.1248-2 or § 1.1248-3, as the case may be, plus the earnings and profits of the second tier corporation attributable to such stock under § 1.1248-2 or 1.1248-3, as the case may be, then the amount considered distributed to the domestic corporation as a dividend shall be determined by multiplying the amount included in gross income under section 1248(a) by—

(i) For purposes of applying subparagraph (1)(i) of this paragraph, the percentage that (*a*) the earnings and profits of the first tier corporation attributable to such stock under § 1.1248-2 or § 1.1248-3, as the case may be, bears to (*b*) the sum of the earnings and profits of the first tier corporation attributable to such stock under § 1.1248-2 or § 1.1248-3, as the case may be, plus the earnings and profits of the second tier corporation attributable to such stock under § 1.1248-2 or § 1.1248-3, as the case may be, and

(ii) For purposes of applying subparagraph (1)(ii) of this paragraph, the percentage that (*a*) the earnings and profits of the second tier corporation attributable to such stock under § 1.1248-2 or 1.1248-3, as the case may be, bears to (*b*) the sum referred to in subdivision (i)(*b*) of this subparagraph.

(4) The provisions of this paragraph may be illustrated by the following examples:

Example (1). On June 30, 1964, domestic corporation D owns 10 percent of the voting stock of controlled foreign corporation X. On such date, D sells a share of X stock and includes $200 of the gain on the sale in its gross income as a dividend under section 1248(a). X does not own any stock of a lower tier corporation referred to in paragraph (a)(3) of §1.1248-3. D uses the calendar year as its taxable year and instead of deducting foreign taxes under section 164, D chooses the benefits of the foreign tax credit provisions for 1964. If D had included $200 in its gross income as a dividend with respect to a distribution from X on June 30, 1964, the amount of the foreign income taxes paid by X which D would be deemed to have paid under section 902(a) in respect of such distribution would be $60. Thus, in respect of the $200 included in D's gross income as a dividend under section 1248(a), and subject to the applicable limitations and conditions of sections 901 through 905, D is entitled under this paragraph to a foreign tax credit of $60 for 1964.

Example (2). On June 30, 1965, domestic corporation D owns all of the voting stock of foreign corporation Y, and Y (the first tier corporation) owns all of the voting stock of foreign corporation Z (a second tier corporation). On such date, D sells a block of Y stock and includes $400 of the gain on the sale in its gross income as a dividend under section 1248(a). The earnings and profits attributable under §1.1248-3 to the block are $600 from Y and $1,800 from Z. D uses the calendar year as its taxable year and instead of deducting foreign taxes under section 164, D chooses the benefits of the foreign tax credit provisions for 1965. For purposes of applying the foreign tax credit provisions, Y is considered under subparagraph (3) of this paragraph to have distributed to D a dividend of $100 ($400 × 600/2400) and Z is considered to have so distributed to D a dividend of $300 ($400 × 1800/2400). If D had included $100 in its gross income as a dividend with respect to a distribution from Y on June 30, 1965, the amount of foreign income taxes paid by Y which D would be deemed to have paid under section 902(a) in respect of such distribution is $80. If D had owned the stock in Z directly, and if D had included $300 in its gross income as a dividend with respect to a distribution from Z, the amount of foreign income taxes paid by Z which D would be deemed to have paid under section 902(a) in respect of such distribution is $120. Thus, in respect of the $400 included in D's gross income as a dividend under section 1248(a), and subject to the applicable limitations and conditions of sections 901 through 905, D is entitled under this paragraph to a foreign tax credit of $200 ($80 plus $120) for 1965.

(e) *Exceptions.*—Under section 1248(f), this section and §§1.1248-2 through 1.1248-7 shall not apply to—

(1) Distributions to which section 303 (relating to distributions in redemption of stock to pay death taxes) applies;

(2) Gain realized on exchanges to which section 356 (relating to receipt of additional consideration in certain reorganizations) applies; or

(3) Any amount to the extent that such amount is, under any other provision of the Code, treated as (i) a dividend, (ii) gain from the sale of an asset which is not a capital asset, or (iii) gain from the sale of an asset held for not more than 1 year (6 months for taxable years beginning before 1977; 9 months for taxable years beginning in 1977).

(f) *Installment method.*—(1) Gain from a sale or exchange to which section 1248 applies may be reported under the installment method if such method is otherwise available under section 453 of the Code. In such case, the income (other than interest) in each installment payment shall be deemed to consist of gain which is included in gross income under section 1248 as a dividend until all such gain has been reported, and the remaining portion (if any) of such income shall be deemed to consist of gain to which section 1248 does not apply. For treatment of amounts as interest on certain deferred payments, see section 483.

(2) The application of this paragraph may be illustrated by the following example:

Example. Jones contracts to sell stock in a controlled foreign corporation for $5,000 to be paid in 10 equal payments of $500 each, plus a sufficient amount of interest so that section 483 does not apply. He properly elects under section 453 to report under the installment method gain of $1,000 which is includible in gross income under section 1248 as a dividend and gain of $500 which is a long-term capital gain. Accordingly, $150 of each of the first 6 installment payments and $100 of the seventh installment payment are included in gross income under section 1248 as a dividend, and $50 of the seventh installment payment and $150 of each of the last 3 installment payments are long-term capital gain.

(g) *Effective/applicability date.*—(1) The third sentence in paragraph (a)(1), paragraph (a)(4), and paragraph (a)(5), *Example* 4, of this section apply to income inclusions that occur on or after July 30, 2007. A taxpayer may elect to apply paragraph (a)(4) of this section to income inclusions in open taxable years provided that it consistently applies paragraph (a)(4) of this section for income inclusions in the first year for which the election is applicable and in all subsequent years.

(2) [Reserved]. For further guidance, see §1.1248-1T(g)(2).

(h) [Reserved]. For further guidance, see §1.1248-1T(h). [Reg. §1.1248-1.]

□ [*T.D. 6779, 12-21-64. Amended by T.D. 7728, 10-31-80; T.D. 7961, 6-20-84; T.D. 9345, 7-27-2007 and T.D. 9444, 2-10-2009.*]

[Reg. §1.1248-1T]

§1.1248-1T. Treatment of gain from certain sales or exchanges of stock in certain foreign

corporations (temporary).—(a) [Reserved]. For further guidance, see § 1.1248-1(a).

(b) *Sale or exchange.*—For purposes of section 1248(a), the term *sale or exchange* includes the receipt of a distribution which is treated as in exchange for stock under section 302(a) (relating to distributions in redemption of stock), section 331(a)(1) (relating to distributions in complete liquidation of a corporation), or section 331(a)(2) (relating to distributions in partial liquidation of a corporation). For purposes of section 1248(a), gain recognized by a shareholder under section 301(c)(3) in connection with a distribution of property by a corporation with respect to its stock shall be treated as gain from the sale or exchange of stock of such corporation.

(c) through (f) [Reserved]. For further guidance, see § 1.1248-1(c) through (f).

(g) *Effective/applicability dates.*—(1) [Reserved]. For further guidance, see § 1.1248-1(g)(1).

(2) Paragraph (b) of this section applies to distributions that occur on or after February 10, 2009.

(h) *Expiration date.* This section expires on or before February 10, 2012. [Temporary Reg. § 1.1248-1T.]

☐ [*T.D.* 9444, 2-10-2009.]

[Reg. § 1.1248-2]

§1.1248-2. Earnings and profits attributable to a block of stock in simple cases.—(a) *General.*—(1) *Manner of computation.*—For purposes of paragraph (a)(1) of § 1.1248-1, if a United States person sells or exchanges a block of stock (as defined in paragraph (b) of this section) in a foreign corporation, and if the conditions of paragraph (c) of this section are satisfied in respect of the block, then the earnings and profits attributable to the block which were accumulated in taxable years of the corporation beginning after December 31, 1962, during the period such block was held (or was considered to be held by reason of the application of section 1223, taking into account § 1.1248-8) by such person while such corporation was a controlled foreign corporation, shall be computed in accordance with the steps set forth in subparagraphs (2), (3), and (4) of this paragraph.

(2) *Step 1.*—(i) For each taxable year of the corporation beginning after December 31, 1962, the earnings and profits accumulated for each such taxable year by the corporation shall be computed in the manner prescribed in paragraph (d) of this section, and (ii) for the period the person held (or is considered to have held by reason of the application of section 1223, taking into account § 1.1248-8) the block, the amount of earnings and profits attributable to the block shall be computed in the manner prescribed in paragraph (e) of this section.

(3) *Step 2.*—If the conditions of paragraph (c)(5)(ii) of this section must be satisfied in respect of stock in a "lower tier" foreign corporation which such person owns within the meaning of section 958(a)(2), then (i) the earnings and profits accumulated for each such taxable year by such lower tier corporation shall be computed in the manner prescribed in paragraph (d) of this section, and (ii) for the period the person held (or is considered to have held by reason of the application of section 1223, taking into account § 1.1248-8) the block, the amount of earnings and profits of the lower tier corporation attributable to the block shall be computed in the manner prescribed in paragraph (e) of this section applied as if such person owned directly the percentage of such stock in such lower tier corporation which such person owns within the meaning of section 958(a)(2).

(4) *Step 3.*—The amount of earnings and profits attributable to the block shall be the sum of the amounts computed under steps 1 and 2.

(b) *Block of stock.*—For purposes of this section, the term "block of stock" means a group of shares sold or exchanged in one transaction, but only if—

(1) The amount realized, basis, and holding period are identical for each such share, and

(2) In case, during the period the person held (or is considered to have held by reason of the application of section 1223) such shares, any amount was included under section 951 in the gross income of the person (or another person) in respect of the shares, the excess under paragraph (e)(3)(ii) of this section (computed as if each share were a block) is identical for each such share.

(c) *Conditions to application.*—This section shall apply only if the following conditions are satisfied:

(1) (i) On each day of the period during which the block of stock was held (or is considered as held by reason of the application of section 1223) by the person during taxable years of the corporation beginning after December 31, 1962, the corporation is a controlled foreign corporation, and (ii) on no such day is the corporation a foreign personal holding company (as defined in section 552) or a foreign investment company (as defined in section 1246(b)).

(2) The corporation had only one class of stock, and the same number of shares of such stock were outstanding, on each day of each taxable year of the corporation beginning after December 31, 1962, any day of which falls within the period referred to in subparagraph (1) of this paragraph.

(3) For each taxable year referred to in subparagraph (2) of this paragraph, the corporation is not a less developed country corporation (as defined in section 902(d)).

(4) For each taxable year referred to in subparagraph (2) of this paragraph, the corporation does not make any distributions out of its earnings and profits other than distributions which, under section 316 (as modified by section 959), are considered to be out of earnings and profits accumulated in taxable years beginning after December 31, 1962, during the period such person held (or is considered to have held by reason of the application of section 1223, taking into account § 1.1248–8) the block while such corporation was a controlled foreign corporation.

(5)(i) If (a) on the date of the sale or exchange such person, by reason of his ownership of such block, owns within the meaning of section 958(a)(2) stock in another foreign corporation (referred to as a "lower tier" corporation), and (b) the conditions of paragraph (a)(2) of § 1.1248-1 would be satisfied by such person in respect of such stock in the lower tier corporation if such person were deemed to have sold or exchanged such stock in the lower tier corporation on the date he actually sold or exchanged such block in the first tier corporation, then the conditions of subdivision (ii) of this subparagraph must be satisfied.

(ii) In respect of stock in such lower tier corporation, (a) the conditions set forth in subparagraphs (1) through (4) of this paragraph (applied as if such person owned directly such stock in such lower tier corporation) must be met and (b) such person must own within the meaning of section 958(a)(2) the same percentage of the shares of such stock on each day which falls within the period referred to in subparagraph (1) of this paragraph.

(d) *Earnings and profits accumulated for a taxable year.*—(1) *General.*—For purposes of this section, the earnings and profits accumulated for a taxable year of a foreign corporation shall be the earnings and profits for such year computed in accordance with the rules prescribed in § 1.964-1 (relating to determination of earnings and profits for a taxable year of a controlled foreign corporation) and reduced by any distributions therefrom. If the stock in the corporation is sold or exchanged before any action is taken by or on behalf of the corporation under paragraph (c) of § 1.964-1, the computation of earnings and profits under § 1.964-1 for purposes of this section shall be made as if no elections had been made and no accounting method had been adopted.

(2) *Special rules.*—(i) The earnings and profits of the corporation accumulated—

(a) For any taxable year beginning before January 1, 1967 (computed without any reduction for distributions), shall not include the excess of any item includible in gross income of the foreign corporation under section 882(b) as gross income derived from sources within the United States, and

(b) For any taxable year beginning after December 31, 1966 (computed without any reduction for distributions), shall not include the excess of any item includible in gross income of the foreign corporation under section 882(b)(2) as income effectively connected for that year with the conduct by such corporation of a trade or business in the United States, whether derived from sources within or from sources without the United States,

over any deductions allocable to such item under section 882(c). However, if the sale or exchange of stock in the foreign corporation by the United States person occurs before January 1, 1967, the provisions of (a) of this subdivision apply with respect to such sale or exchange even though the taxable year begins after December 31, 1966. See section 1248(d)(4). Any item which is required to be excluded from gross income, or which is taxed at a reduced rate, under an applicable treaty obligation of the United States shall not be excluded under this subdivision from earnings and profits accumulated for a taxable year (computed without any reduction for distributions).

(ii) If a foreign corporation adopts a plan of complete liquidation in a taxable year of the corporation beginning after December 31, 1962, and if because of the application of section 337(a) gain or loss would not be recognized by the corporation from the sale or exchange of property if the corporation were a domestic corporation, then the earnings and profits of the corporation accumulated for the taxable year (computed without any reduction for distributions) shall be determined without regard to the amount of such gain or loss. See section 1248(d)(2). For the nonapplication of section 337(a) to a liquidation by a collapsible corporation (as defined in section 341) and to certain other liquidations, see section 337(c).

(e) *Earnings and profits attributable to block.*— (1) *General.*—Except as provided in subparagraph (3) of this paragraph, the earnings and profits attributable to a block of stock of a controlled foreign corporation for the period a United States person held (or is considered to have held by reason of the application of section 1223, taking into account § 1.1248–8) the block are an amount equal to—

(i) The sum of the earnings and profits accumulated for each taxable year of the corporation beginning after December 31, 1962 (computed under paragraph (d) of this section) during such period, multiplied by

(ii) The percentage that (a) the number of shares in the block, bears to (b) the total number of shares of the corporation outstanding during such period.

(2) *Special rule.*—For purposes of computing the sum referred to in subparagraph (1)(i) of this paragraph, in case the block was held (or is considered as held by reason of the application of section 1223, taking into account § 1.1248–8) during a taxable year beginning after December

Reg. § 1.1248-2(e)(2)

31, 1962, but not on each day of such taxable year, there shall be included in such sum only that portion which bears the same ratio to (i) the total earnings and profits for such taxable year computed under paragraph (d) of this section), as (ii) the number of days during such taxable year the block was held (or is considered as so held), bears to (iii) the total number of days in such taxable year.

(3) *Amounts included in gross income under section 951.*—(i) If, during the period the person held (or is considered to have held by reason of the application of section 1223, taking into account § 1.1248–8) the block, any amount was included under section 951 in the gross income of such person (or of another person whose holding of the stock sold or exchanged is, by reason of the application of section 1223, attributed to such person) in respect of the block, then the earnings and profits attributable to the block for such period shall be an amount equal to (*a*) the earnings and profits attributable to the block which would have been computed under subparagraph (1) of this paragraph if this subparagraph did not apply, reduced by (*b*) the excess computed under subdivision (ii) of this subparagraph. See section 1248(d)(1).

(ii) The excess computed under this subdivision is the excess (if any) of (*a*) amounts included under section 951 in the gross income of such person (or such other person) in respect of the block during such period, over (*b*) the portion of such amounts which, in any taxable

year of such person (or such other person), resulted in an exclusion from the gross income of such person (or such other person) under section 959(a)(1) (relating to exclusion from gross income of distributions of previously taxed earnings and profits).

(iii) This subparagraph shall apply notwithstanding an election under section 962 by such person to be subject to tax at corporate rates.

(4) *Example.*—The application of this paragraph may be illustrated by the following examples:

Example (1). On May 26, 1965, Green, a United States person, purchases at its fair market value a block of 25 of the 100 outstanding shares of the only class of stock of controlled foreign corporation F. He sells the block on January 1, 1968. In respect of the block, Green did not include any amount in his gross income under section 951. F uses the calendar year as its taxable year and does not own stock in any lower tier corporation referred to in paragraph (c)(5)(i) of this section. All of the conditions of paragraph (c) of this section are satisfied in respect of the block. The earnings and profits accumulated by F (computed under paragraph (d) of this section) are $10,000 for 1965, $13,000 for 1966, and $11,000 for 1967. The earnings and profits of F attributable to the block are $7,500, determined as follows:

Sum of earnings and profits accumulated by F during period block was held:

For 1965 (219/365 × $10,000)	$6,000
For 1966	13,000
For 1967	11,000
Sum	$30,000
Multiplied by:	
Number of shares in block (25), divided by total number of shares outstanding (100)	25%
Earnings and profits attributable to block	$7,500

Example (2). Assume the same facts as in example (1) except that in respect of the block Green includes in his gross income under section 951 the total amount of $2,800 for 1965 and 1966, and because of such inclusion the amount of $2,300 which was distributed to Green by F on January 15, 1967, is excluded from his gross income under section 959(a)(1). Accordingly, the earnings and profits of F attributable to the block are $7,000, determined as follows:

Earnings and profits attributable to the block, as computed in example (1)	$7,500
Minus:	
Excess of amount included in Green's gross income under section 951 ($2,800), over portion thereof which resulted in an exclusion under section 959(a)(1) ($2,300)	$500
Earnings and profits attributable to block	$7,000

Example (3). Assume the same facts as in example (1) except that on each day beginning on January 1, 1966 (the date controlled foreign corporation G was organized) through January 1, 1968, F owns 80 of the 100 outstanding shares of the only class of G stock. Since, by reason of his ownership of 25 shares of F stock, Green owns within the meaning of section 958(a)(2) the equivalent of 20 shares of G stock (25/100 of 80 shares), G is a lower tier corporation referred to in paragraph (c)(5)(i)(*a*) of this section. If Green

had sold the 20 shares of G stock on January 1, 1968, the date he actually sold the block of F stock, the conditions of paragraph (a)(2) of § 1.1248–1 would be satisfied in respect of the G stock, and, accordingly, the conditions of paragraph (c)(5)(ii) of this section must be satisfied. Assume further that such conditions are satisfied, that G uses the calendar year as its taxable year, and that the earnings and profits accumulated by G (computed under paragraph (d) of this section) are $19,000 for 1966 and $21,000 for

1967. The earnings and profits of F and of G attributable to the block are $15,500, determined as follows:

Sum of earnings and profits accumulated by G for period Green owned G stock within the meaning of section 958(a)(2) ($19,000 plus $21,000)	$40,000
Multiplied by: Number of G shares deemed owned within the meaning of section 958(a)(2) by Green (20), divided by total number of G shares outstanding (100)	20%
Earnings and profits of G attributable to block	$8,000
Earnings and profits of F attributable to block, as determined in example (1)	7,500
Total earnings and profits attributable to block	$15,500

[Reg. § 1.1248-2.]

☐ [*T.D. 6779, 12-21-64. Amended by T.D. 7293, 11-27-73 and T.D. 9345, 7-27-2007.*]

[Reg. §1.1248-3]

§1.1248-3. Earnings and profits attributable to stock in complex cases.—(a) *General.*—(1) *Manner of computation.*—For purposes of paragraph (a)(1) of §1.1248-1, if a United States person sells or exchanges stock in a foreign corporation, and if the provisions of §1.1248-2 do not apply, then the earnings and profits attributable to the stock which were accumulated in taxable years of the corporation beginning after December 31, 1962, during the period or periods such stock was held (or was considered to be held by reason of the application of section 1223, taking into account §1.1248-8) by such person while such corporation was a controlled foreign corporation, shall be computed in accordance with the steps set forth in subparagraphs (2), (3), and (4) of this paragraph.

(2) *Step 1.*—For each taxable year of the corporation beginning after December 31, 1962, (i) the earnings and profits accumulated for such taxable year by the corporation shall be computed in the manner prescribed in paragraph (b) of this section, (ii) the person's "tentative ratable share" of such earnings and profits shall be computed in the manner prescribed in paragraph (c) or (d) (whichever is applicable) of this section, and (iii) the person's "ratable share" of such earnings and profits shall be computed by adjusting the tentative ratable share in the manner prescribed in paragraph (e) of this section.

(3) *Step 2.*—If the provisions of paragraph (f) of this section (relating to earnings and profits of "lower tier" foreign corporations) apply, the amount of the person's ratable share of the earnings and profits accumulated by each "lower tier" corporation attributable to any such taxable year (i) shall be computed in the manner prescribed by paragraph (f) of this section,, and (ii) shall be added to such person's ratable share for such taxable year determined in step 1.

(4) *Step 3.*—The amount of earnings and profits attributable to the share shall be the sum of the ratable shares computed for each such taxable year in the manner prescribed in steps 1 and 2.

(5) *Share or block.*—In general, the computation under this paragraph shall be made separately for each share of stock sold or exchanged, except that if a group of shares constitute a block of stock the computation may be made in respect of the block. For purposes of this section, the term "block of stock" means a group of shares sold or exchanged in one transaction, but only if (i) the amount realized, basis, and holding period are identical for each such share, and (ii) the adjustments (if any) under paragraphs (e) and (f)(5) of this section of the tentative ratable shares would be identical for each such share if such adjustments were computed separately for each such share.

(6) *Deficit in earnings and profits.*—For purposes of this section and §§1.1248-4 through 1.1248-7, in respect of a taxable year, the term "earnings and profits accumulated" for a taxable year (but only if computed under paragraph (b) of this section) includes a deficit in earnings and profits accumulated for such taxable year. Similarly, a tentative ratable share, or a ratable share, may be a deficit.

(7) *Examples.*—The application of the provisions of this paragraph may be illustrated by the following examples:

Example (1). On December 31, 1967, Brown sells 10 shares of stock in foreign corporation X, which uses the calendar year as its taxable year. The 10 shares constitute a block of stock under subparagraph (5) of this paragraph. Under step 1, Brown's ratable shares of the earnings and profits of X attributable to the block are as follows:

Taxable year of X	Ratable shares
1963	$100
1964	150
1965	−50 (deficit)
1966	50
1967	100
Sum	$350

The amount of the earnings and profits attributable to such block under step 3 is $350.

Example (2). Assume the same facts as in example (1), except that in respect of X there are "lower tier" corporations Y and Z to which the provisions of paragraph (f) of this section apply. Brown's ratable shares of the earnings and profits of X, Y, and Z attributable to the block under steps 1 and 2 for each taxable year of X are as follows:

Taxable year of X	X	Ratable shares Y	Z	Total
1963	$100	$40	$20	$160
1964	150	40	–60	130
1965	–50	30	50	30
1966	50	50	30	130
1967	100	–40	40	100
Sum	$350	$120	$80	$550

The amount of the earnings and profits attributable to such block under step 3 is $550.

(b) *Earnings and profits accumulated for a taxable year.*—(1) *General.*—For purposes of this section, the earnings and profits accumulated for a taxable year of a foreign corporation shall be the earnings and profits for such year, computed in accordance with the rules prescribed in § 1.964-1 (relating to determination of earnings and profits for a taxable year of a controlled foreign corporation), except that (i) the special rules of subparagraph (2) of this paragraph shall apply, and (ii) adjustments shall be made under subparagraph (3) of this paragraph for distributions made by the corporation during such taxable year. If the stock in the corporation is sold or exchanged before any action is taken by or on behalf of the corporation under paragraph (c) of § 1.964-1, the computation of earnings and profits under § 1.964-1 for purposes of this section shall be made as if no elections had been made and no accounting method had been adopted. The amount of earnings and profits accumulated for a taxable year of a foreign corporation, as computed under this paragraph, is not necessarily the same amount as the earnings and profits of the taxable year computed under section 316(a)(2) or paragraph (d) of § 1.1248-2. Thus, for example, if a distribution with respect to stock is in excess of the amount of earnings and profits of the taxable year computed under section 316(a)(2), such excess is treated under section 316(a)(1) or paragraph (d) of § 1.1248-2 as made out of any earnings and profits accumulated in prior taxable years, whereas the amount of such excess may create, or increase, a deficit in the earnings and profits accumulated for the taxable year as computed under this paragraph. See subparagraph (3) of this paragraph.

(2) *Special rules.*—(i) The earnings and profits of the corporation accumulated—

(a) For any taxable year beginning before January 1, 1967, shall not include the excess of any item includible in gross income of the foreign corporation under section 882(b) as gross income derived from sources within the United States, and

(b) For any taxable year beginning after December 31, 1966, shall not include the excess of any item includible in gross income of the foreign corporation under section 882(b)(2) as income effectively connected for that year with the conduct by such corporation of a trade or business in the United States, whether derived

from sources within or from sources without the United States,

over any deductions allocable to such item under section 882(c). However, if the sale or exchange of stock in the foreign corporation by the U.S. person occurs before January 1, 1967, the provisions of (a) of this subdivision apply with respect to such sale or exchange even though the taxable year begins after December 31, 1966. See section 1248(d)(4). Any item which is required to be excluded from gross income, or which is taxed at a reduced rate, under an applicable treaty obligation of the United States shall not be excluded under this subdivision from earnings and profits accumulated for a taxable year.

(ii) If a foreign corporation adopts a plan of complete liquidation in a taxable year of the corporation beginning after December 31, 1962, and if because of the application of section 337(a) gain or loss would not be recognized by the corporation from the sale or exchange of property if the corporation were a domestic corporation, then the earnings and profits of the corporation accumulated for the taxable year shall be determined without regard to the amount of such gain or loss. See section 1248(d)(2). For the nonapplication of section 337(a) to a liquidation by a collapsible corporation (as defined in section 341) and to certain other liquidations, see section 337(c).

(3) *Adjustment for distributions.*—(i) The earnings and profits of a foreign corporation accumulated for a taxable year (computed without regard to this subparagraph) shall be reduced (if necessary below zero so as to create a deficit), or a deficit in such earnings and profits shall be increased, by the amount of the distributions (other than in redemption of stock under section 302(a) or 303) made by the corporation in respect of its stock during such taxable year (a) out of such earnings and profits, or (b) out of earnings and profits accumulated for prior taxable years beginning after December 31, 1962 (computed under this paragraph). Except for purposes of applying this subparagraph, the application of the preceding sentence shall not affect the amount of earnings and profits accumulated for any such prior taxable year.

(ii) The application of this subparagraph may be illustrated by the following examples:

Example (1). X Corporation, which uses the calendar year as its taxable year, was organized on January 1, 1965, and was a controlled foreign corporation on each day of 1965. The amount of X's earnings and profits accumulated for 1965 (computed under this paragraph without regard to the adjustment for distributions under this subparagraph) is $400,000, of which $100,000 is distributed by X as dividends during 1965. The amount of X's earnings and profits accumulated for 1965 (computed under this paragraph) is $300,000 (that is, $400,000 minus $100,000). The result would be the same even if X was not a controlled foreign corporation on each day of 1965.

Example (2). Assume the same facts as in example (1). Assume further that the amount of X's earnings and profits accumulated for 1966 (computed under this paragraph without regard to the adjustment for distributions under this subparagraph) is $150,000, and that X distributes the amount of $260,000 as dividends during 1966. Since $150,000 of the distribution is from earnings and profits accumulated for 1966 (computed without regard to the adjustment for distributions under this subparagraph), and since $110,000 is from earnings and profits accumulated for 1965, the earnings and profits of X accumulated for 1966 are a deficit of $110,000 (that is, $150,000 minus $260,000). However, the earnings and profits accumulated for 1965 are still $300,000 for purposes of computing in the manner prescribed in paragraph (c) of this section a person's tentative ratable share.

(c) *Tentative ratable share if earnings and profits accumulated for a taxable year not less than zero.*— (1) *General rule.*—For purposes of paragraph (a)(2)(ii) of this section, in respect of a share (or block) of stock in a foreign corporation, if the amount of the earnings and profits accumulated for a taxable year of the corporation (computed under paragraph (b) of this section), beginning after December 31, 1962, is not less than zero, then the person's tentative ratable share for such taxable year shall be equal to—

(i) *(a)* Such amount (if the computation is made in respect of a block, multiplied by the number of shares in the block), divided by *(b)* the number of shares in the corporation outstanding, or deemed under subparagraph (2) of this paragraph to be outstanding, on each day of such taxable year, multiplied by

(ii) The percentage that *(a)* the number of days in such taxable year of the corporation during the period the person held (or was considered to have held by reason of the application of section 1223, taking into account § 1.1248–8) the share (or block) while the corporation was a controlled foreign corporation, bears to *(b)* the total number of days in such taxable year.

(2) *Shares deemed outstanding for a taxable year.*—For purposes of this section and § § 1.1248-4 through 1.1248-7, if the number of shares of stock in a foreign corporation outstanding on each day of a taxable year of the corporation is not constant, then the number of such shares deemed outstanding on each such day shall be the sum of the fractional amounts in respect of each share outstanding on any day of the taxable year. The fractional amount in respect of a share shall be determined by dividing (i) the number of days in the taxable year during which such share was outstanding (excluding the day the share became outstanding, but including the day the share ceased to be outstand-

ing), by (ii) the total number of days in such taxable year.

(3) *Examples.*—The application of subparagraphs (1) and (2) of this paragraph may be illustrated by the following examples:

Example (1). On each day of 1964, S owns a block consisting of 30 of the 100 shares of the only class of stock outstanding in F Corporation, and on each such day F is a controlled foreign corporation. F uses the calendar year as its taxable year and F's earnings and profits accumulated for 1964 (computed under paragraph (b) of this section) are $10,000. S's tentative ratable share with respect to the block is $3,000, computed as follows:

Earnings and profits accumulated for taxable year	$10,000
Multiplied by:	
Number of shares in block (30), divided by number of shares outstanding (100)	30%
Multiplied by:	
Number of days in 1964 S held block while F was a controlled foreign corporation (365), divided by number of days in 1964 (365) .	100%
Tentative ratable share for block	$3,000

Example (2). On December 31, 1964, X Corporation, a controlled foreign corporation which uses the calendar year as its taxable year, had 100 shares of one class of stock outstanding, 15 of which were owned by T. T's 15 shares were redeemed by X on March 14, 1965. On December 31, 1965, in addition to the remaining 85 shares, 10 new shares of stock (which were issued on May 26, 1965) were outstanding. Thus, during 1965, 15 shares were outstanding for 73 days, 10 for 219 days, and 85 for 365 days. The earnings and profits (computed under paragraph (b) of this section) accumulated for X's taxable year ending on December 31, 1965, are $18,800. T's tentative ratable share with respect to one share of stock is $40, computed as follows:

Earnings and profits accumulated for taxable year		$18,800
Divided by:		
Number of shares deemed outstanding on each day of 1965:		
15 for 73 days (15 × 73/365)	3	
10 for 219 days (10 × 219/365)	6	
85 for 365 days (85 × 365/365)	85	
Total number of shares deemed outstanding each day of 1965 ...		94
Earnings and profits accumulated per share		$200
Multiplied by:		
Number of days in 1965 T held his share while X was a controlled foreign corporation (73), divided by number of days in 1965 (365)		20%
T's tentative ratable share per share of stock		$40

Reg. § 1.1248-3(c)(3)

Example (3). Assume the same facts as in example (2) except that X was not a controlled foreign corporation after January 31, 1965. T's tentative ratable share with respect to one share of stock for 1965 is $17, computed as follows:

Earnings and profits accumulated per share, determined in example (2)	$200
Multiplied by: Number of days in 1965 T held X stock while X was a controlled foreign corporation (31), divided by number of days in 1965 (365) . . .	8.5%
Tentative ratable share	$17

(4) *More than one class of stock.*—If a foreign corporation for a taxable year has more than one class of stock outstanding, then before applying subparagraphs (1) and (2) of this paragraph the earnings and profits accumulated for the taxable year of the corporation (computed under paragraph (b) of this section) shall be allocated to each class of stock in accordance with the principles of paragraph (e)(2) and (3) of § 1.951-1, applied as if the corporation were a controlled foreign corporation on each day of such taxable year.

(d) *Tentative ratable share if deficit in earnings and profits accumulated for taxable year.*—(1) *General rule.*—For purposes of paragraph (a)(2)(ii) of this section, in respect of a share (or block) of stock in a foreign corporation, if there is a deficit in the earnings and profits accumulated for a taxable year of the corporation (computed under paragraph (b) of this section) beginning after December 31, 1962, the person's tentative ratable share for such taxable year shall be an amount equal to the sum of the partial tentative ratable shares computed under subparagraphs (2) and (3) of this paragraph.

(2) *Operating deficit.*—The partial tentative ratable share under this subparagraph is computed in 2 steps. First, compute (under paragraph (b) of this section without regard to the adjustment for distributions under subparagraph (3) thereof) the deficit (if any) in earnings and profits accumulated for such taxable year. Second, compute the partial tentative ratable share in the same manner as the tentative ratable share for such taxable year would be computed under paragraph (c) of this section if such deficit were the amount referred to in paragraph (c)(1)(i)(*a*) of this section.

(3) *Deficit from distributions.*—The partial tentative ratable share under this subparagraph is computed in 2 steps. First, compute and treat as a deficit only that portion of the adjustment for distributions under paragraph (b)(3) of this section for such taxable year which is attributable under subparagraph (4) of this paragraph to distributions out of earnings and profits accumulated during prior taxable years of the corporation beginning after December 31, 1962, during the period or periods the corporation was a controlled foreign corporation and the share (or block) of stock was owned by a United States shareholder (as defined in section 951(b) and the regulations thereunder). Second, compute the partial tentative ratable share for such taxable year in the same manner as the tentative ratable share for such taxable year would be computed under paragraph (c) of this section if (i) such deficit were the amount referred to in paragraph (c)(1)(i)(*a*) of this section, and (ii) the corporation were a controlled foreign corporation on each day of such taxable year.

(4) *Order of distributions.*—For purposes of applying subparagraph (3) of this paragraph only, the adjustment for distributions under paragraph (b)(3) of this section for a taxable year of a foreign corporation shall be treated as attributable first to distributions of earnings and profits for the taxable year (computed under paragraph (b) of this section without regard to such adjustment) to the extent thereof, and then to distributions out of the most recent of earnings and profits accumulated during prior taxable years beginning after December 31, 1962 (computed under paragraph (b) of this section). If the foreign corporation was a controlled foreign corporation during a prior taxable year for a period or periods which was only part of such prior taxable year, then for purposes of the preceding sentence (i) such taxable year shall be divided into periods the corporation was or was not a controlled foreign corporation, (ii) distributions of the earnings and profits accumulated during such prior taxable year shall be considered made from the most recent period first, and (iii) the earnings and profits accumulated during such prior taxable year shall be allocated to a period during such year in the same proportion as the number of days in the period bears to the number of days in such year. Except for purposes of applying subparagraph (3) of this paragraph, the application of this subparagraph shall not affect the amount of earnings and profits accumulated for any such prior taxable year (computed under paragraph (b) of this section).

(5) *Examples.*—The application of this paragraph may be illustrated by the following examples:

Example (1). On each day of 1965 X Corporation, which uses the calendar year as its taxable year, was a controlled foreign corporation having 100 shares of one class of stock outstanding, a block of 25 of which were owned by T, who acquired them in 1962 and sold them in 1967. The deficit in X's earnings and profits accumulated for 1965 (computed under paragraph (b) of this section without regard to the adjustment for distributions under subparagraph (3) thereof) is $100,000, and thus in respect of the block T's partial tentative ratable share computed under subparagraph (2) of this paragraph is a deficit of $25,000 (that is, $100,000 × 25/100). During 1965 X does not make any distributions in respect of its stock, and thus in respect of the block T's partial tentative ratable share computed under subparagraph (3) of this paragraph is zero. Accordingly, T's tentative ratable share in respect of the block of X stock for 1965 is a deficit of $25,000. If, however, X was a controlled foreign corporation for only 292 days during 1965, T's tentative ratable share in respect of the block for 1965 would be a deficit of $20,000 (that is, $25,000 × 292/365).

Example (2). (i) Assume the same facts as in example (1) except that at no time during 1965 is X a controlled foreign corporation and that during 1965 X distributes $80,000 with respect to its stock. Assume further that X was a controlled foreign corporation on each day of 1964, but only for the first 146 days of 1963, and that X's earnings and profits accumulated for prior taxable years computed under paragraph (b) of this section are $70,000 for 1964 and $20,000 for 1963.

(ii) Since X was not a controlled foreign corporation on any day of 1965, in respect of the block T's partial tentative ratable share computed under subparagraph (2) of this paragraph is zero.

(iii) The partial tentative ratable share under subparagraph (3) of this paragraph is computed in the following manner: For 1965 the adjustment for distributions under paragraph (b)(3) of this section is $80,000. Under subparagraph (4) of this paragraph $70,000 of such adjustment is attributable to the distribution of all of the earnings and profits accumulated during 1964, on every day of which X was a controlled foreign corporation, and $10,000 of the adjustment is attributable to the distribution of $10,000 of the earnings and profits accumulated for 1963. The portion of the earnings and profits accumulated by X in 1963 attributable to the first 146 days in 1963 during which X was a controlled foreign corporation is $8,000 (that is, $20,000 × 146/365), and the portion attributable to the period in 1963 during which X was not a controlled foreign corporation is $12,000 (that is, $20,000 × 219/365). Under subparagraph (4)(ii) of this paragraph, the distribution in 1965 of $10,000 of earnings and profits accumulated during 1963 is attributable to the more recent period in 1963, that is, the period X was not a controlled foreign corporation. Accordingly, the portion of the adjustment for distributions under paragraph (b)(3) of this section attributable to earnings and profits accumulated during periods X was a controlled foreign corporation is $70,000, and in respect of the block T's partial tentative ratable share under subparagraph (3) of this paragraph is a deficit of $17,500 (that is, $70,000 × 25/100).

(iv) T's tentative ratable share in respect of the block of X stock for 1965 is a deficit of $17,500 (that is, the sum of the partial tentative ratable share for the block computed under subparagraph (2) of this paragraph, zero, plus the partial tentative ratable share for the block computed under subparagraph (3) of this paragraph, a deficit of $17,500).

(v) Assume that X had 100 shares of one class of stock outstanding on each day of 1964 and 1963. Notwithstanding the distributions in 1965 of earnings and profits accumulated during 1964 and 1963 (computed under paragraph (b) of this section), nevertheless, in respect of the block T's tentative ratable share for 1964 is $17,500 (that is, earnings and profits accumulated during 1964 so computed of $70,000, multiplied by 25 shares/100 shares) and in respect of the block T's tentative ratable share for 1963 is $2,000 (that is, earnings and profits accumulated during 1963 so computed of $20,000, multiplied by 25 shares/100 shares, and multiplied by the percentage that the number of days in 1963 on which X was a controlled foreign corporation bears to the total number of days in 1963, 146/365).

Example (3). Assume the same facts as in example (2) except that X was a controlled foreign corporation on each day of 1965. The tentative ratable share with respect to the block of stock for 1965 is a deficit of $42,500, that is, the sum of the partial tentative ratable share under subparagraph (2) of this paragraph (as determined in example (1)), a deficit of $25,000, plus the partial tentative ratable share under subparagraph (3) of this paragraph (as determined in example (2)), a deficit of $17,500.

(6) *More than one class of stock.*—If a foreign corporation for a taxable year has more than one class of stock outstanding, then before applying subparagraph (1) of this paragraph the earnings and profits accumulated for the taxable year of the corporation (computed under paragraph (b) of this section) shall be allocated to each class of stock in accordance with the principles of paragraph (e)(2) and (3) of §1.951-1, applied as if the corporation were a controlled foreign corporation on each day of such taxable year.

(e) *Ratable share of earnings and profits accumulated for a taxable year.*—(1) *In general.*—For purposes of paragraph (a)(2)(iii) of this section, in respect of a share (or block) of stock in a foreign corporation, the person's ratable share of the earnings and profits accumulated for a taxable year beginning after December 31, 1962, shall be an amount equal to the tentative ratable share computed under paragraph (c) or (d) (as the case may be) of this section, adjusted in the manner prescribed in subparagraphs (2) through (6) of this paragraph.

(2) *Amounts included in gross income under section 951.*—(i) In respect of a share (or block) of stock in a foreign corporation, a person's tentative ratable share for a taxable year of the corporation (computed under paragraph (c) of this section) shall be reduced (but not below zero) by the excess of *(a)* the amount, if any, included (in respect of such corporation for such taxable year) under section 951 in the gross income of such person or (during the period such share, or

block, was considered to be held by such person by reason of the application of section 1223, taking into account § 1.1248–8) in the gross income of any other person who held such share (or block), over *(b)* the portion of such amount which, in any taxable year of such person or such other person, resulted in an exclusion from the gross income of such person or such other person of an amount under section 959(a)(1) (relating to exclusion from gross income of distributions of previously taxed earnings and profits). See section 1248(d)(1). This subdivision shall apply notwithstanding an election under section 962 by such person to be subject to tax at corporate rates.

(ii) The application of this subparagraph may be illustrated by the following example:

Example. On December 31, 1975, Brown sells one share of stock in X Corporation, a controlled foreign corporation which has never been a less developed country corporation (as defined in section 902(d)). Both Brown and X use the calendar year as the taxable year. In respect of his share, Brown's tentative ratable share for 1971 (computed under paragraph (c) of this section) is $35. In respect of his share, Brown included $4 in his gross income for 1971 under section 951, and the amount of $3, which was distributed to him by X on January 15, 1972, is excluded from Brown's gross income under section 959(a)(1). In respect of the stock, Brown's ratable share for 1971 is $34, determined as follows:

Tentative ratable share	$35
Minus:	
Excess of amount of tentative ratable share included in Brown's gross income under section 951 ($4), over portion thereof which resulted in exclusion under section 959(a)(1)($3)	1
Ratable share	$34

(3) *Amounts included in gross income under section 551.*—In respect of a share (or block) of stock in a foreign corporation, a person's tentative ratable share for a taxable year of the corporation (computed under paragraph (c) of this section) shall be reduced (but not below zero) by the amount, if any, included (in respect of such corporation for such taxable year) under section 551 in the gross income of such person or (during the period such share, or block, was considered to be held by such person by reason of the application of section 1223, taking into account § 1.1248–8) in the gross income of any other person who held such share (or block).

(4) *Less developed country corporations.*—(i) If the foreign corporation was a less developed country corporation as defined in section 902(d) for a taxable year of the corporation, and if the person who sold or exchanged a share (or block) of stock in such corporation satisfies the require-

ments of paragraph (a) of § 1.1248–5 in respect of such stock, then his ratable share for such taxable year shall be zero. See section 1248(d)(3).

(ii) The application of this subparagraph may be illustrated by the following example:

Example. Assume the same facts as in the example in subparagraph (2)(ii) of this paragraph except that X was a less developed country corporation for 1971. Assume further that Brown satisfies the requirements of paragraph (a) of § 1.1248–5. Brown's ratable share in respect of the stock for 1971 is zero.

(5) *Qualified shareholder of foreign investment company.*—In respect of a share (or block) of stock in a foreign corporation which was a foreign investment company described in section 1246(b)(1), if the election under section 1247(a) to distribute income currently was in effect for a taxable year of the company, and if the person who sold or exchanged the stock (or another person who actually owned the stock during such taxable year and whose holding of the stock is attributed by reason of the application of section 1223, taking into account § 1.1248–8, to the person who sold or exchanged the stock) was a qualified shareholder (as defined in section 1247(c)) for his taxable year in which or with which such taxable year of the company ends, then the ratable share in respect of the share (or block) for such taxable year of the company shall be zero. See section 1248(d)(5). In case gain is recognized under section 1246 in respect of a share (or block), see section 1248(f)(3)(B).

(6) *Adjustment for certain distributions.*—If (i) the person who sold or exchanged the share or block (or another person who actually owned the share or block and whose holding of the share or block is attributed by reason of the application of section 1223, taking into account § 1.1248–8 to such person) received a distribution during a taxable year of the corporation, and (ii) such distribution was not included in the gross income of such person (or such other person) by reason of the application of section 959(a)(1) to amounts which were included under section 951(a)(1) in the gross income of a United States shareholder whose holding of the share or block is not attributed by reason of the application of section 1223, taking into account § 1.1248–8 to such person (or such other person), then the amount of such distribution shall be added to such person's tentative ratable share for such taxable year. Thus, for example, such tentative ratable share may be increased, or a deficit reduced, by the amount of such distribution.

(f) *Earnings and profits of subsidiaries of foreign corporations.*—(1) *Application of paragraph.*—(i) In respect of a person who sells or exchanges stock in a foreign corporation (referred to as a "first tier" corporation), the provisions of this paragraph shall apply if the following 3 conditions exist:

(a) The conditions of paragraph (a)(2) of § 1.1248-1 are satisfied by the person in respect of such stock;

(b) By reason of his ownership of such stock, on the date of such sale or exchange such person owned, within the meaning of section 958(a)(2), stock in another foreign corporation (referred to as a "lower tier" corporation); and

(c) The conditions of paragraph (a)(2) of § 1.1248-1 would be satisfied by such person in respect of such stock in the lower tier corporation if such person were deemed to have sold or exchanged such stock in the lower tier corporation on the date he actually sold or exchanged such stock in the first tier corporation.

(ii) If the provisions of this paragraph apply, *(a)* the person's tentative ratable share (or shares) of the earnings and profits accumulated by the lower tier corporation attributable to a taxable year of the first tier corporation shall be computed under subparagraph (2) or (4) of this paragraph, whichever is applicable, and *(b)* such person's ratable share (or shares) for the lower tier corporation attributable to a taxable year of the first tier corporation shall be computed under subparagraph (5) of this paragraph. For the manner of taking into account the ratable share for a lower tier corporation, see paragraph (a)(3) of this section.

(iii) The application of this subparagraph may be illustrated by the following example:

Example. On each day of 1964 and 1965 corporations X and Y are controlled foreign corporations, and each has outstanding 100 shares of one class of stock. On January 15, 1965, T, a United States person, owns one share of stock in X and X directly owns 20 shares of stock in Y. Thus, T owns, within the meaning of section 958(a)(2), stock in Y. On that date, T sells his share in X and satisfies the conditions of paragraph (a)(2) of § 1.1248-1 in respect of his stock in X. Assuming that the conditions of paragraph (a)(2) of § 1.1248-1 would be satisfied by T in respect of the stock he indirectly owns in Y if, on January 15, 1965, he were deemed to have sold such stock in Y, the provisions of this paragraph apply.

(2) *Tentative ratable share (of lower tier corporation attributable to a taxable year of first tier corporation) not less than zero.*—If the provisions of this paragraph apply to a sale or exchange by a United States person of a share (or block) of stock in a first tier corporation, and if the amount of earnings and profits accumulated (computed under paragraph (b) of this section) for a taxable year (beginning after December 31, 1962) of the lower tier corporation is not less than zero, then in respect of the share (or block) such person's tentative ratable share of the earnings and profits accumulated for such taxable year of the lower tier corporation attributable to any taxable year (beginning after December 31, 1962) of such first tier corporation shall be an amount equal to—

(i) *(a)* Such amount of earnings and profits accumulated for such taxable year of the lower tier corporation (if the computation is made in respect of a block in the first tier corporation, multiplied by the number of shares in the block), divided by *(b)* the number of shares in the first tier corporation outstanding, or deemed under paragraph (c)(2) of this section to be outstanding, on each day of such taxable year of the first tier corporation, multiplied by

(ii) The percentage that *(a)* the number of days during the period or periods in such taxable year of the first tier corporation on which such person held (or was considered to have held by reason of the application of section 1223, taking into account § 1.1248-8) the share (or block) in the first tier corporation while the first tier corporation owned (within the meaning of section 958(a)) stock of such lower tier corporation at times while such lower tier corporation was a controlled foreign corporation, bears to *(b)* the total number of days in such taxable year of the first tier corporation, multiplied by

(iii) The percentage that *(a)* the average number of shares in the lower tier corporation which were owned within the meaning of section 958(a) by the first tier corporation during such period or periods (referred to in subdivision (ii)*(a)* of this subparagraph), bears to *(b)* the total number of such shares outstanding, or deemed under the principles of paragraph (c)(2) of this section to be outstanding, during such period or periods, multiplied by

(iv) The percentage that *(a)* the number of days in such taxable year of the lower tier corporation which fall within the taxable year of the first tier corporation, bears to *(b)* the total number of days in such taxable year of the lower tier corporation.

(3) *Examples.*—The application of subparagraph (2) of this paragraph may be illustrated by the following examples:

Example (1). In a year subsequent to 1969, Brown, a United States person, sells 5 of his shares of stock in X Corporation in a transaction as to which the provisions of this paragraph apply. Brown had purchased the 5 shares prior to 1969. On each day of 1969 X Corporation actually had 100 shares of one class of stock outstanding. On each such day X Corporation directly owned all of the shares of stock in Y Corporation, and Y Corporation directly owned all of the shares of stock in Z Corporation. Z Corporation on each such day was a controlled foreign corporation. Both X and Z use the calendar year as the taxable year. Z's earnings and profits accumulated for 1969 (computed under paragraph (b) of this section) are $2,000. Brown's tentative ratable share of the earnings and profits accumulated by Z attributable to the 1969 calendar year of X is $20 per share, computed as follows:

(i) Z's earnings and profits for 1969 ($2,000), divided by the number of shares in X deemed outstanding each day of 1969 (100) $20

Multiplied by:

(ii) Since on each day of 1969 Brown (by reason of owning directly his shares in X) owned, within the meaning of section 958(a)(2), stock in Z while Z was a controlled foreign corporation, the percentage determined under subparagraph (2)(ii) of this paragraph equals 100%

Multiplied by:

(iii) Since on each day of 1969 X owned 100 percent of the stock of Y while Y owned 100 percent of the stock in Z, the percentage determined under subparagraph (2)(iii) equals 100%

Multiplied by:

(iv) Since X and Z each use the same taxable year, the percentage determined under subparagraph (2)(iv) of this paragraph equals 100%

Total $20

Example (2). Assume the same facts as in example (1), except that Brown sold his stock in X on October 19, 1969. Brown's tentative ratable share of the earnings and profits accumulated by Z attributable to the 1969 calendar year of X is $16 per share, computed as follows:

(i) The amount determined in subdivision (i) of example (1) $20

Multiplied by:

(ii) The number of days in the period during 1969 Brown (by reason of owning directly his stock in X) owned, within the meaning of section 958(a)(2), his stock in Z while Z was a controlled foreign corporation (292), divided by the number of days in 1969 (365), equals 80%

Multiplied by:

(iii) The percentage determined in subdivision (iii) of example (1) 100%

Multiplied by:

(iv) The percentage determined in subdivision (iv) of example (1) 100%

Total $16

Example (3). Assume the same facts as in examples (1) and (2), except that on each day during 1969 Y owned (within the meaning of section 958(a)(2)) 81 of the 100 shares of Z's outstanding stock. Brown's tentative ratable share of the earnings and profits accumulated by Z attributable to the 1969 calendar year of X is $12.96 per share, computed as follows:

(i) The amount determined in subdivision (i) of example (1) $20

Multiplied by:

(ii) The percentage determined in subdivision (ii) of example (2) 80%

Multiplied by:

(iii) The average number of shares in Z which were owned (within the meaning of section 958(a)) by X during the applicable period (81), divided by the total number of shares in Z during such period (100) 81%

Multiplied by:

(iv) The percentage determined in subdivision (iv) of example (1) 100%

Total $12.96

The result would be the same if X owned (within the meaning of section 958(a)(2)) 81 percent of the stock in Y while Y so owned 100 percent of the stock in X, or if X so owned 90 percent of the stock in Y while Y so owned 90 percent of the stock in Z.

Example (4). Assume the same facts as in example (3), except that Z Corporation uses a fiscal year ending June 30 as its taxable year. Assume further that Z's earnings and profits accumulated for its fiscal year ending June 30, 1969, and for its fiscal year ending June 30, 1970, are $3,000 and $2,000, respectively. Brown's tentative ratable share of the earnings and profits accumulated by Z attributable to the 1969 calendar year of X is $16.17 per share, computed as follows:

	In respect of Z's taxable year ending	
	June 30, 1969	June 30, 1970
(i) Z's earnings and profits, divided by the number of shares in X deemed outstanding on each day of 1969:		
$3,000/100	$30	
$2,000/100		$20
Multiplied by:		
(ii) The percentage determined in subdivision (ii) of example (2)	80%	80%
Multiplied by:		
(iii) The percentage determined in subdivision (iii) of example (3)	81%	81%

Reg. §1.1248-3(f)(3)

Multiplied by:

(iv) Number of days in Z's taxable year which fall within 1969, divided by total number of days in Z's taxable year:

181/365	49.6%	
184/365		50.4%
Totals	$9.64	$6.53

(v) Sum of tentative ratable shares of Z attributable to X's 1969 calendar year:

For Z's taxable year ending

June 30, 1969	$9.64
June 30, 1970	6.53
Sum	$16.17

(4) *Deficit in tentative ratable share of lower tier corporation attributable to a taxable year of first tier corporation.*—(i) If there is a deficit in the earnings and profits accumulated for a taxable year of a lower tier corporation beginning after December 31, 1962 (computed under paragraph (b) of this section), the person's tentative ratable share for such taxable year of such lower tier corporation attributable to a taxable year of a first tier corporation shall not be computed under subparagraph (2) of this paragraph but shall be an amount equal to the sum of the partial tentative ratable shares computed under subdivisions (ii) and (iii) of this subparagraph.

(ii) The partial tentative ratable share under this subdivision is computed in 2 steps. First, compute (under paragraph (b) of this section without regard to the adjustments for distributions under subparagraph (3) thereof) the deficit (if any) in earnings and profits accumulated for such taxable year of such lower tier corporation. Second, compute the partial tentative ratable share in the same manner as such tentative ratable share would be computed under subparagraph (2) of this paragraph if such deficit were the amount referred to in subparagraph (2)(i)(a) of this paragraph.

(iii) The partial tentative ratable share under this subdivision is computed in 2 steps. First, compute and treat as a deficit the portion of the adjustment for distributions under paragraph (b)(3) of this section for such taxable year which is attributable under paragraph (d)(4) of this section to distributions of earnings and profits accumulated during prior taxable years of the lower tier corporation beginning after December 31, 1962, during the period or periods such lower tier corporation was a controlled foreign corporation and the percentage of the stock of such lower tier corporation (which the person owns within the meaning of section 958(a)(2)) was owned within the meaning of section 958(a) by a United States shareholder (as defined in section 951(b) and the regulations thereunder). Second, compute the partial tentative ratable share in the same manner as such tentative ratable share would be computed under subparagraph (2) of this paragraph if (a) such deficit were the amount referred to in subparagraph (2)(i)(a) of this paragraph, and (b) such lower tier corporation were a controlled foreign corporation on each day of such taxable year.

(5) *Ratable share of lower tier corporation attributable to a first tier corporation.*—(i) If the provisions of this paragraph apply in respect of a share of stock in a first tier corporation, a person's ratable share of the earnings and profits accumulated by the lower tier corporation attributable to a taxable year of the first tier corporation shall be an amount equal to the tentative ratable share computed under subparagraph (2) or (4) of this paragraph, adjusted in the manner prescribed in this subparagraph.

(ii) If the first tier corporation and the lower tier corporation use the same taxable year, then in respect of a share (or block) of stock in the first tier corporation the person's tentative ratable share of the accumulated earnings and profits of the lower tier corporation attributable to the taxable year of the first tier corporation (computed under subparagraph (2) of this paragraph) shall be reduced (but not below zero) by the excess of (a) the amount, if any, included (in respect of such lower tier corporation for its taxable year) under section 951 in the gross income of such person or (during the period such stock was considered to be held by such person by reason of the application of section 1223, taking into account §1.1248–8) in the gross income of any other person who held such stock, over (b) the portion of such amount which, in any taxable year of such person or such other person, resulted in an exclusion from the gross income of such person or such other person of an amount under section 959(a)(1). For an illustration of the principles in the preceding sentence, see the example in paragraph (e)(2)(ii) of this section.

(iii) If the first tier corporation and the lower tier corporation do not use the same taxable year, and if there be an excess computed under subdivision (ii) of this subparagraph in respect of a taxable year of the lower tier corporation (were the taxable years of such corporations the same), then such person's tentative ratable share of the accumulated earnings and profits for a taxable year of the lower tier corporation attributable to such taxable year of the first tier corporation shall be reduced (but not below zero) by an amount which bears the same ratio to (a) such excess, as (b) the number of days in the taxable year of the lower tier corporation which fall within the taxable year of the first tier corporation, bears to (c) the total number of days in the taxable year of the first tier corporation.

Reg. §1.1248-3(f)(5)(iii)

(iv) If the first tier corporation and the lower tier corporation use the same taxable year, then in respect of a share (or block) of stock in the first tier corporation the person's tentative ratable share of the accumulated earnings and profits of the lower tier corporation attributable to the taxable year of the first tier corporation (computed under subparagraph (2) of this paragraph) shall be reduced (but not below zero) by the amount, if any, included (in respect of such corporation for such taxable year) under section 551, by reason of the application of section 555(b), in the gross income of such person or (during the period such share (or block) was considered to be held by such person by reason of the application of section 1223, taking into account §1.1248–8) in the gross income of any other person who held such share (or block).

(v) If the first tier corporation and the lower tier corporation do not use the same taxable year, and if there would be a reduction in the person's tentative ratable share of the accumulated earnings and profits of the lower tier corporation attributable to the taxable year of the first tier corporation by an amount computed under subdivision (iv) of this subparagraph in respect of a taxable year of the lower tier corporation (were the taxable years of such corporations the same), then such person's tentative ratable share of the accumulated earnings and profits for a taxable year of the lower tier corporation attributable to such taxable year of the first tier corporation shall be reduced by an amount which bears the same ratio to (a) such amount, as (b) the number of days in the taxable year of the lower tier corporation which fall within the taxable year of the first tier corporation, bears to (c) the total number of days in the taxable year of the first tier corporation.

(vi) If the lower tier corporation was a less developed country corporation as defined in section 902(d) for a taxable year of the corporation, see paragraph (g) of this section.

(g) *Lower tier corporation a less developed country corporation.*—(1) *General.*—If the lower tier corporation was a less developed country corporation as defined in section 902(d) for a taxable year of such corporation, and if the person who sold or exchanged a share (or block) of stock in the first tier corporation satisfies on the date of such sale or exchange—

(i) The requirements of paragraph (a)(1) of §1.1248-5 with respect to such stock, and

(ii) The requirements of paragraph (d)(1) of §1.1248-5 with respect to any stock of the lower tier corporation which such person, by reason of his direct ownership of such stock in the first tier corporation, owned within the meaning of section 958(a)(2),

then such person's ratable share (or a deficit in such ratable share) for such taxable year of the lower tier corporation attributable to a taxable year of the first tier corporation (determined without regard to this paragraph) shall be reduced by an amount computed by multiplying such ratable share (so determined without regard to this paragraph) by the percentage computed under either subparagraph (2) or (4) of this paragraph, whichever is applicable.

(2) *Percentage for second tier corporation.*—For purposes of subparagraph (1) of this paragraph, if stock of a lower tier corporation (hereinafter referred to as a "second tier" corporation) is owned directly by the first tier corporation on the date of the sale or exchange referred to in such subparagraph (1), the percentage under this subparagraph shall be computed by dividing (i) the number of shares of stock of the second tier corporation which the first tier corporation has owned directly for an uninterrupted 10-year period ending on such date, by (ii) the total number of shares of the stock of such second tier corporation owned directly by such first tier corporation on such date.

(3) *Examples.*—The provisions of subparagraph (2) of this paragraph may be illustrated by the following examples:

Example (1). On January 1, 1966, Smith, a United States person, recognizes gain upon the sale of one share of the only class of stock of F Corporation, which he has owned continuously since 1955. He includes a portion of the gain in his gross income as a dividend under section 1248(a). On January 1, 1966, F owns directly 60 shares of the 100 outstanding shares of the only class of stock of G Corporation, which F acquired in 1955 and owned continuously until such sale. F uses a taxable year ending June 30, and G uses the calendar year as the taxable year. For 1964, G was a less developed country corporation, and on each day of 1964 G was a controlled foreign corporation. Smith's ratable share for G's taxable year ending December 31, 1964, attributable to F's taxable year ending June 30, 1965 (determined without regard to this paragraph) is $6.00. Since the percentage computed under subparagraph (2) of this paragraph is 100 percent (60 shares divided by 60 shares), Smith's ratable share for G's taxable year ending December 31, 1964, attributable to F's taxable year ending June 30, 1965 (after the application of subparagraph (2) of this paragraph) is zero (that is, $6.00 reduced by 100 percent of $6.00).

Example (2). Assume the same facts as in example (1) except that of the 60 shares of G Corporation which F Corporation owned on January 1, 1966, 20 shares were acquired in 1961. The percentage computed under subparagraph (2) of this paragraph is 66²/₃ percent (40 shares divided by 60 shares). Accordingly, Smith's ratable share for G's taxable year ending December 31, 1964, attributable to F's taxable year ending June 30, 1965 (after the application of subparagraph (2) of this paragraph) is $2.00 (that is, $6.00 reduced by 66²/₃ percent of $6.00).

(4) *Percentage for lower tier corporations other than second tier corporation.*—For purposes of subparagraph (1) of this paragraph, if stock of a lower tier corporation (other than a second tier corporation) is owned within the meaning of section 958(a)(2) by the first tier corporation on the date of the sale or exchange referred to in such subparagraph (1), the percentage under this subparagraph shall be computed in the following manner:

(i) First, determine the percentage for the second tier corporation in accordance with subparagraph (2) of this paragraph.

(ii) Second, determine a partial percentage for each other lower tier corporation in the same manner as the percentage for the second tier corporation is determined. Thus, for example, the partial percentage for a third tier corporation is determined by dividing (*a*) the number of shares of stock of the third tier corporation which the second tier corporation has owned directly for an uninterrupted 10-year period ending on the date of the sale or exchange referred to in subparagraph (1) of this paragraph, by (*b*) the total number of shares of stock of such third tier corporation owned directly by such second tier corporation on such date.

(1)	(2)	(3)	(4)
	Shares directly owned by preceding tier—		Col. (2) divided by Col. (3) (percent)
Corporation	For uninterrupted 10-year period ending 1/1/67	On 1/1/67	
X	40	60	66²/₃
Y	30	40	75
Z	20	30	66²/₃

For 1964, the percentage referred to in subparagraph (4) of this paragraph for Z is 33¹/₃ percent (66²/₃% × 75% × 66²/₃%).

(6) *Special rule.*—For purposes of applying the provisions of this paragraph, a lower tier corporation may be treated as a second tier corporation with respect to any of its stock which is owned directly by a first tier corporation whereas such lower tier corporation may be treated as a lower tier corporation other than a second tier corporation with respect to other stock in such lower tier corporation which is owned (within the meaning of section 958(a)(2)) by such first tier corporation. Thus, for example, if corporations X, Y, and Z are foreign corporations, X is a first tier corporation owning directly 100 percent of the stock of Y and 40 percent of the stock of Z, and in addition Y owns directly 60 percent of the stock of Z, then the 40 percent of the Z stock (which X owns directly) is considered to be stock in a second tier corporation and the 60 percent of the Z stock (which Y owns directly and which X is considered to own within the meaning of section 958(a)(2)) is considered to be stock in a third tier corporation. [Reg. § 1.1248-3.]

(iii) Third, the percentage for a third tier corporation is the percentage for the second tier corporation multiplied by the partial percentage for the third tier corporation. The percentage for a fourth tier corporation is the percentage for the third tier corporation (as determined in the preceding sentence) multiplied by the partial percentage for the fourth tier corporation. In a similar manner, the percentage for any other lower tier corporation may be determined.

(5) *Example.*—The application of subparagraph (4) of this paragraph may be illustrated by the following example:

Example. On January 1, 1967, Brown, a United States person recognizes gain upon the sale of one share of the only class of stock of W Corporation, which he has owned continuously since 1955. He includes a portion of the gain in his gross income as a dividend under section 1248(a). W is the first tier corporation of a chain of foreign corporations W, X, Y, and Z. W and Z each use the calendar year as the taxable year. For 1964, Z was a less developed country corporation and on each day of 1964 Z was a controlled foreign corporation. Additional facts are set forth in the table below:

☐ [T.D. 6779, 12-21-64. *Amended by T.D. 7293,* 11-27-73; *T.D. 7545, 5-5-78 and T.D. 9345,* 7-27-2007.]

[Reg. § 1.1248-4]

§1.1248-4. Limitation on tax applicable to individuals.—(a) *General rule.*—(1) *Limitation on tax.*—Under section 1248(b), if during a taxable year an individual sells or exchanges stock in a foreign corporation, then in respect of the stock the increase in the individual's income tax liability for such taxable year which is attributable (under paragraph (b) of this section) to the amount included in his gross income as a dividend under section 1248(a) shall not be greater than an amount equal to the sum of—

(i) The excess, computed under paragraph (c) of this section in respect of the stock, of the United States taxes which would have been paid by the corporation over the taxes (including United States taxes) actually paid by the corporation, plus

(ii) An amount equal to the increase in the individual's income tax liability which would be attributable to the inclusion in his gross income for such taxable year, as long-term capital gain, of an amount equal to the excess of (*a*) the amount included in the individual's gross income as a dividend under section 1248(a) in respect of such stock, over *(b)* the excess referred to in subdivision (i) of this subparagraph.

(2) *Share or block.*—In general, the limitation on tax attributable (under paragraph (b) of this section) to the amount included in an individual's gross income as a dividend under section 1248(a) shall be determined separately for each share of stock sold or exchanged. However, such determination may be made in respect of a block of stock if earnings and profits attributable to the block are computed under §1.1248-2 or 1.1248-3. See paragraph (b) of §1.1248-2 and paragraph (a)(5) of §1.1248-3.

(3) *Application of limitation.*—The provisions of subparagraph (1) of this paragraph shall not apply unless the individual establishes—

(i) In the manner prescribed in §1.1248-7, the amount of the earnings and profits of the corporation attributable under paragraph (a)(1) of §1.1248-2 or under paragraph (a)(1) of §1.1248-3, whichever is applicable, to the stock, and

(ii) The amount equal to the sum described in subparagraph (1) of this paragraph,

computed in accordance with the provisions of this section.

(4) *Example.*—The provisions of this paragraph may be illustrated by the following example:

Example. On December 31, 1966, Smith, a United States person, sells a share of stock of X Corporation which he has owned continuously since December 31, 1965, and includes $100 of the gain on the sale in his gross income as a dividend under section 1248(a). Both X and Smith use the calendar year as the taxable year. The increase in Smith's income tax liability for 1966 which is attributable (under paragraph (b) of this section) to the inclusion of the $100 in his gross income as a dividend is $70. X was a controlled foreign corporation on each day of 1966. The excess, computed under paragraph (c) of this section in respect of the share, of the United States taxes which X would have paid over the taxes (including United States taxes) actually paid by X is $49. Under section 1248(b), the limitation on the tax attributable to the $100 included by Smith in his gross income as a dividend under section 1248(a) is $61.75, computed as follows:

(i) Excess, computed under paragraph (c) of this section, of United States taxes which X Corporation would have paid in 1966 over the taxes actually paid by X in 1966	$49.00
(ii) The amount determined under subparagraph (1)(ii) of this paragraph:	
The amount Smith included in his gross income as a dividend under section 1248(a)	$100.00
Less the excess referred to in subdivision (i) of this example	$49.00
Difference	$51.00
Increase in Smith's tax liability attributable to including $51 in his gross income as long-term capital gain (25 percent of $51)	$12.75
(iii) Limitation on tax	$61.75

(b) *Tax attributable to amount treated as dividend.*—(1) *General.*—For purposes of paragraph (a)(1) of this section, in respect of a share (or block) of stock in a foreign corporation sold or exchanged by an individual during a taxable year, the tax attributable to the amount included in his gross income as a dividend under section 1248(a) shall be the amount which bears the same ratio to (i) the excess of *(a)* his income tax liability for the taxable year determined without regard to section 1248(b) over *(b)* such tax liability determined as if the portion of the total gain recognized during the taxable year which is treated as a dividend under section 1248(a) had not been recognized, as (ii) the amount included as a dividend under section 1248(a) in respect of the share (or block), bears to (iii) the total

amount included as a dividend under section 1248(a) in the individual's gross income for such taxable year.

(2) *Examples.*—The application of this paragraph may be illustrated by the following examples:

Example (1). (i) During 1963, Brown, an unmarried United States person, sells a block of stock in a controlled foreign corporation. On the sale, he recognizes $22,000 gain, of which $18,000 is treated as a dividend under section 1248(a) and $4,000 as long-term capital gain. Brown computes his income tax liability for his taxable year ending December 31, 1963, under section 1201 (relating to alternative tax) in accordance with the additional facts assumed in the following table:

	Computation of income tax liability without regard to section 1248(b)	Computation of income tax liability as if the gain treated as a dividend under section 1248(a) had not been recognized
Income from salary	$300,000	$300,000
Long-term capital gain resulting from sale of stock, less deduction for capital gains under section 1202 ($4,000 less $2,000)	2,000	2,000
Amount treated as a dividend under section 1248(a)	$18,000	0
Adjusted gross income	$320,000	$302,000
Charitable contribution of $100,000 to church (limited under section 170(b) to 30 percent of adjusted gross income)	(96,000)	(90,600)
Other itemized deductions and personal exemption	(7,700)	(7,700)
Taxable income	$216,300	$203,700
Less 50 percent of $4,000	2,000	2,000
Amount subject to partial tax under section 1201(b)(1)	$214,300	$201,700
Partial tax	$169,833	$158,367
25 percent of $4,000	1,000	1,000
Tax liability	$170,833	$159,367

(ii) The tax attributable to the $18,000 treated as a dividend under section 1248(a) is $11,466 ($170,833 minus $159,367).

Example (2). Assume the same facts as in example (1) except that the $18,000 treated as a dividend under section 1248(a) is attributable to the sale of a block of stock in X Corporation and a block of stock in Y Corporation. Assume further that $10,000 of the gain on the block of X stock was treated as a dividend and that $8,000 of the gain on the block of Y stock was treated as a dividend. Thus, the tax attributable to the amount treated as a dividend in respect of the block of X stock is $6,370 ($10,000/$18,000 of $11,466) and the amount in respect of the block of Y stock is $5,096 ($8,000/$18,000 of $11,466). The result would be the same if both blocks of stock were blocks of stock in the same corporation.

(c) *Excess (of United States taxes which would have been paid over taxes actually paid) attributable to a share.*—(1) *General.*—For purposes of paragraph (a)(1)(i) of this section—

(i) The term "taxes" means income, war profits, or excess profits taxes, and

(ii) The excess (and the portion of such excess attributable to an individual's share or block of stock in a foreign corporation) of the United States taxes which would have been paid by the corporation over the taxes (including United States taxes) actually paid by the corporation, for the period or periods the stock was held (or was considered to be held by reason of the application of section 1223) by the individual in taxable years of the corporation beginning after December 31, 1962, while the corporation was a controlled foreign corporation, shall be computed in accordance with the steps set forth in subparagraphs (2), (3), and (4) of this paragraph.

(2) *Step 1.*—For each taxable year of the corporation beginning after December 31, 1962, in

respect of the individual's share (or block) of such stock (i) the taxable income of the corporation shall be computed in the manner prescribed in paragraph (d) of this section, and (ii) the excess (and the portion of such excess attributable to the stock) of the United States taxes which would have been paid by the corporation on such taxable income over the taxes (including United States taxes) actually paid by the corporation shall be computed in the manner prescribed in paragraph (e) of this section.

(3) *Step 2.*—If during such taxable year the corporation is a first tier corporation to which paragraph (f) of this section applies, (i) the excess (and the portion of such excess attributable to the individual's share, or block, of stock in the first tier corporation) of the United States taxes which would have been paid by any lower tier corporation over the taxes (including United States taxes) actually paid by such lower tier corporation shall be computed under paragraph (f) of this section, and (ii) such portion shall be added to the portion of the excess attributable to the individual's share (or block) of such stock as determined in step 1 for such taxable year.

(4) *Step 3.*—The excess, in respect of the individual's share (or block), of the United States taxes which would have been paid by the corporation over the taxes actually paid by the corporation shall be the sum of the portions computed for each such taxable year in the manner prescribed in steps 1 and 2.

(d) *Taxable income.*—For purposes of paragraph (c)(2)(i) of this section, taxable income shall be computed in respect of an individual's share (or block) in accordance with the following rules:

(1) *Application of principles of § 1.952-2.*—Except as otherwise provided in this paragraph, the principles of paragraphs (a)(1), (b)(1), and (c) of

§1.952-2 (other than subparagraphs (2)(iii)(b), (2)(v), (5)(i), and (6) of such paragraph (c)) shall apply.

(2) *Effect of elections.*—In respect of a taxable year of a foreign corporation, no effect shall be given to an election or an adoption of accounting method unless for such taxable year effect is given to such election or adoption of accounting method under paragraph (d)(1) of §1.1248-2 or paragraph (b)(1) of §1.1248-3, whichever is applicable.

(3) The deductions for certain dividends received provided in sections 243, 244, and 245 shall not be allowed.

(4) *Deduction for taxes.*—In computing the amount of the deduction allowed under section 164, there shall be excluded income, war profits, or excess profits taxes paid or accrued which are imposed by the authority of any foreign country or possession of the United States.

(5) *Capital loss carryover.*—In determining the amount of a net capital loss to be carried forward under section 1212 to the taxable year—

(i) No net capital loss shall be carried forward from a taxable year beginning before January 1, 1963.

(ii) The portion of a net capital loss or a capital gain net income (net capital gain for taxable years beginning before January 1, 1977) for a taxable year beginning after December 31, 1962, which shall be taken into account shall be the amount of such loss or gain (as the case may be), multiplied by the percentage which (a) the number of days in such taxable year during which the individual held (or was considered to have held by reason of the application of section 1223) the share (or block) of stock sold or exchanged while the corporation was a controlled foreign corporation, bears to (b) the total number of days in such taxable year.

(iii) The application of this subparagraph may be illustrated by the following examples:

Example (1). Corporation X is a foreign corporation which was created on January 1, 1963, and which uses the calendar year as its taxable year. X was a controlled foreign corporation on each day of the period March 15, 1963, through December 31, 1965, but was not a controlled foreign corporation on any day during the period January 1, 1963, through March 14, 1963. On December 31, 1965, Smith, a United States person, sells a share of X stock which he has owned continuously since January 1, 1963. A portion of the gain recognized on the sale is includible in Smith's gross income as a dividend under section 1248(a). X had a net capital loss (determined without regard to subchapter N, chapter 1 of the Code) of $200 for 1963. Since, however, X was a controlled foreign corporation for only 292 days in 1963, for purposes of determining the net capital loss carryover to 1964 the portion of the net capital loss of $200 for 1963

which Smith takes into account under subdivision (ii) of this subparagraph is $160 (292/365 of $200), and, accordingly, the amount of the net capital loss carryover to 1964 is $160.

Example (2). Assume the same facts as in example (1), except that X was not a controlled foreign corporation on any day of the period May 26, 1964, through June 30, 1965. Assume further that X had a net capital gain (capital gain net income for taxable years beginning after December 31, 1976) (determined without regard to subchapter N, chapter 1, of the Code) of $160 for 1964. In computing X's taxable income for 1964 under this paragraph, Smith applies the net capital loss carryover of $160 from 1963 to reduce the net capital gain (capital gain net income for taxable years beginning after December 31, 1976) of $160 for 1964 to zero. Since, however, X was a controlled foreign corporation for only 146 days in 1964, for purposes of computing the portion of the 1963 capital loss of $160 which is a net capital loss carryover to 1965, the portion of the 1964 capital gain which Smith takes into account under subdivision (ii) of this subparagraph is $63.83 (146/366 of $160). Thus, the net capital loss carryover to 1965 is $96.17 ($160 minus $63.83).

(6) *Net operating loss deduction.*—(i) The individual shall reduce the taxable income (computed under subparagraphs (1) through (5) of this paragraph) of the corporation for the taxable year by the amount of the net operating loss deduction of the corporation computed under section 172, as modified in the manner prescribed in this subparagraph.

(ii) The rules of subparagraphs (1) through (5) of this paragraph shall apply for purposes of determining the excess referred to in section 172(c) and the taxable income referred to in section 172(b)(2).

(iii) A net operating loss shall not be carried forward from, or carried back to, a taxable year beginning before January 1, 1963.

(iv) The portion of a net operating loss incurred, or of taxable income earned, in a taxable year beginning after December 31, 1962, which shall be taken into account under section 172(b)(2) shall be the amount of such loss or income (as the case may be), multiplied by the percentage which (a) the number of days in such taxable year during which the individual held (or was considered to have held by reason of the application of section 1223) the share (or block) of stock sold or exchanged while the corporation was a controlled foreign corporation, bears to (b) the total number of days in such taxable year.

(v) For illustrations of the principles of this subparagraph, see the examples relating to net capital loss carryovers in subparagraph (5)(iii) of this paragraph.

(7) *Adjustment for amount previously included in gross income of United States shareholders.*—In respect of the individual's share (or block) of

stock sold or exchanged, the taxable income of the corporation for the taxable year (determined without regard to this subparagraph and subparagraph (8) of this paragraph) shall be reduced (but not below zero) by an amount equal to the sum of the amounts included under section 951 in the gross income of United States shareholders (as defined in section 951(b)) of the corporation for the taxable year.

(8) *Adjustment for distributions.*—In respect of the individual's share (or block) of stock sold or exchanged, the taxable income of the corporation for the taxable year (determined without regard to this subparagraph) shall be reduced (but not below zero) by the amount of the distributions (other than in redemption of stock under section 302(a) or 303) made by the corporation out of earnings and profits of such taxable year (within the meaning of section 316(a)(2)). For purposes of the preceding sentence, distributions shall be taken into account only to the extent not excluded from the gross income of the United States shareholders of the corporation under section 959.

(e) *Excess attributable to a share (or block) of stock.*—(1) *Excess of United States taxes which would have been paid over taxes actually paid.*—For purposes of paragraph (c)(2)(ii) of this section, in respect of a taxable year of a foreign corporation, the portion of the excess under this subparagraph which is attributable to an individual's share (or block) of such stock shall be an amount equal to—

(i) The excess (if any) of (a) the United States taxes which would have been paid by the corporation on its taxable income (computed under paragraph (d) of this section) for the taxa-

ble year had it been taxed as a domestic corporation under chapter 1 of the Code (but without regard to subchapters F, G, H, L, M, N, S, and T thereof) for such taxable year, over (b) the income, war profits, or excess profits taxes actually paid by the corporation during such taxable year (including such taxes paid to the United States),

(ii) Multiplied by the percentage that (a) the number of days in such taxable year of the corporation during the period or periods the share (or block) was held (or was considered as held by reason of the application of section 1223) by the individual while the corporation was a controlled foreign corporation, bears to (b) the total number of days in such taxable year,

(iii) If the computation is made in respect of a block, multiplied by the number of shares in the block, and

(iv) Divided by the number of shares in the corporation outstanding, or deemed under paragraph (c)(2) of § 1.1248-3 to be outstanding, on each day of such taxable year.

(2) *Example.*—The provisions of this paragraph may be illustrated by the following example:

Example. (i) Jones, a United States person, owns on each day of 1963 10 shares of the 100 shares of the only class of outstanding stock of X Corporation. He sells one of such shares on December 31, 1963. X Corporation is a controlled foreign corporation on each day of 1963 and Jones and X each use the calendar year as the taxable year. For 1963, the excess of the United States taxes which would have been paid by X had it been taxable as a domestic corporation over the taxes (including United States taxes) actually paid by X is $23,500, computed as follows:

Amount subject to partial tax under section 1201 (a)(1), as computed by Jones:

Taxable income			$300,000
Less excess of net long-term capital gain over net short-term capital loss			100,000
Amount subject to partial tax			$200,000
Excess determined under subparagraph (1)(i) of this paragraph:			
30 percent × $25,000		$7,500	
52 percent × $175,000		91,000	
Partial tax			$98,500
25 percent × $100,000			25,000
United States taxes X would have paid (alternative tax computed under section 1201(a))			$123,500
Less income taxes X actually paid to: United States	$10,000		
foreign countries	90,000		
Total			$100,000
Excess			$23,500
Multiplied by:			
Percentage determined under subparagraph (1)(ii) of this paragraph:			
Since on each day of 1963, Jones held the share of X stock while X was a controlled foreign corporation, the percentage equals			100 %
Total			$23,500

(ii) The portion of the excess determined in subdivision (i) of this example which is attributable to the share held by Jones is $235, that is, the

amount of such excess ($23,500), divided by the number of shares of X deemed to be outstanding on each day of 1963 (100).

Reg. §1.1248-4(e)(2)

(3) *More than one class of stock.*—If a foreign corporation for a taxable year has more than one class of stock outstanding, then before applying subparagraph (1) of this paragraph the excess (if any) which would be determined under subparagraph (1)(i) of this paragraph shall be allocated to each class of stock in accordance with the principles of paragraph (e)(2) and (3) and § 1.951-1, applied as if the corporation were a controlled foreign corporation on each day of such taxable year.

(f) *Subsidiaries of foreign corporations.*—(1) *Excess for lower tier corporation attributable to taxable year of first tier corporation.*—For purposes of paragraph (c)(3) of this section, if the provisions of paragraph (a)(3) of § 1.1248-2 or paragraph (f) of § 1.1248-3 apply in the case of the sale or exchange by an individual of a share (or block) of stock in a first tier corporation, then in respect of a taxable year of a lower tier corporation (beginning after December 31, 1962) which includes at least one day which falls within a taxable year of the first tier corporation (beginning after December 31, 1962), the portion of the excess under this subparagraph attributable to the share shall be an amount equal to—

(i) The excess (if any) of (*a*) the United States taxes which would have been paid by the lower tier corporation on its taxable income (computed under paragraph (g) of this section) for such taxable year of the lower tier corporation had it been taxed as a domestic corporation under chapter 1 of the Code (but without regard to subchapters F, G, H, L, M, N, and T thereof) for such taxable year of the lower tier corporation, over (*b*) the income, war profits, or excess profits taxes actually paid by the lower tier corporation during such taxable year (including such taxes paid to the United States),

(ii) Multiplied by each of the percentages described under paragraph (f)(2)(ii), (iii), and (iv) of § 1.1248-3 in respect of such taxable year of the first tier corporation,

(iii) If the computation is made in respect of a block of stock, multiplied by the number of shares in the block, and

(iv) Divided by the number of shares in the first tier corporation outstanding, or deemed under paragraph (c)(2) of § 1.1248-3 to be outstanding, on each day of such taxable year of the first tier corporation.

(2) *More than one class of stock.*—If a foreign corporation for a taxable year has more than one class of stock outstanding, then before applying subparagraph (1) of this paragraph the principles of paragraph (e)(3) of this section shall apply.

(g) *Taxable income of lower tier corporations.*—(1) *General.*—For purposes of paragraph (f)(1)(i) of this section, in respect of the individual's share (or block) the taxable income of a lower

tier corporation shall be computed in the manner provided in paragraph (d) of this section, except as provided in this paragraph.

(2) *Capital loss carryover.*—For purposes of subparagraph (1) of this paragraph, the provisions of paragraph (d)(5)(ii) of this section shall not apply. In determining the amount of a net capital loss to be carried forward under section 1212 to the taxable year of a lower tier corporation, the portion of a net capital loss or a capital gain net income (net capital gain for taxable years beginning before January 1, 1977) for a taxable year of the lower tier corporation beginning after December 31, 1962, which shall be taken into account shall be the amount of such loss or gain (as the case may be), multiplied by the percentage which (i) the number of days in such taxable year during the period or periods the individual held (or was considered to have held by reason of the application of section 1223) the share (or block) of stock in the first tier corporation sold or exchanged while the first tier corporation owned (within the meaning of section 958(a)) stock in the lower tier corporation while the lower tier corporation was a controlled foreign corporation, bears to (ii) the total number of days in such taxable year.

(3) *Net operating loss deduction.*—For purposes of subparagraph (1) of this paragraph, the provisions of paragraph (d)(6)(iv) of this section shall not apply. In determining the amount of the net operating loss deduction for a taxable year of a lower tier corporation, the portion of a net operating loss incurred, or of taxable income earned, in a taxable year of the lower tier corporation beginning after December 31, 1962, which shall be taken into account under section 172(b)(2) shall be the amount of such loss or income (as the case may be) multiplied by the percentage described in subparagraph (2) of this paragraph for such taxable year. [Reg. § 1.1248-4.]

☐ [T.D. 6779, 12-21-64. *Amended by T.D.* 7545, 5-5-78 *and T.D.* 7728, 10-31-80.]

[Reg. § 1.1248-5]

§ 1.1248-5. Stock ownership requirements for less developed country corporations.—(a) *General rule.*—(1) *Requirements.*—For purposes of paragraph (e)(4) of § 1.1248-3, a United States person shall be considered as satisfying the requirements of this paragraph with respect to a share (or block) of stock of a foreign corporation if on the date he sells or exchanges such share (or block)—

(i) The 10-year stock ownership requirement of paragraph (b) of this section is met with respect to such share (or block), and

(ii) In the case of a United States person which is a domestic corporation, the requirement of paragraph (c) of this section, if applicable, is met.

(2) *Ownership of stock.*—For purposes of this section—

(i) The rules for determining ownership of stock prescribed by section 958(a) and (b) shall apply.

(ii) Stock owned by a United States person who is an individual, estate, or trust which was acquired by reason of the death of the predecessor in interest of such United States person shall be considered as owned by such United States person during the period such stock was owned by such predecessor in interest, and during the period such stock was owned by any other predecessor in interest if between such United States person and such other predecessor in interest there was no transfer other than by reason of the death of an individual.

(b) *10-year stock ownership requirement.*— (1) *General.*—A United States person meets the 10-year stock ownership requirement with respect to a share (or block) of stock in a foreign corporation which he sells or exchanges only if the share (or block) was owned (under the rules of paragraph (a)(2) of this section) by such person for a continuous period of at least 10 years ending on the date of the sale or exchange. See the first sentence of section 1248(d)(3). Thus, for example, if Jones, a United States person, sells a share of stock in a foreign corporation on January 1, 1965, the 10-year stock ownership requirement is met with respect to the share only if the share was owned (under the rules of paragraph (a)(2) of this section) by Jones continuously from January 1, 1955, to January 1, 1965. If a foreign corporation has not been in existence for at least 10 years on the date of the sale or exchange of the share, the 10-year stock ownership requirement cannot be met.

(2) *Special rule.*—For purposes of this paragraph, a United States person shall be considered to have owned stock during the period he was considered to have held the stock by reason of the application of section 1223.

(c) *Disqualification of domestic corporation as a result of changes in ownership of its stock.*—(1) *General.*—(i) For purposes of paragraph (a)(1)(ii) of this section, the requirement of this paragraph must be met only if, on at least one day during the 10-year period ending on the date of the sale or exchange by a domestic corporation of a share of stock in a foreign corporation, one or more noncorporate United States shareholders (as defined in subdivision (iii) of this subparagraph) own more than 50 percent of the total combined voting power of all classes of stock entitled to vote of the domestic corporation.

(ii) The requirement of this paragraph is that if one or more persons are noncorporate United States shareholders on the first such day (referred to in subdivision (i) of this subparagraph), such person or persons continue after such first day, at all times during the remainder of such 10-year period, to own in the aggregate more than 50 percent of the total combined voting power of all classes of stock entitled to vote of the domestic corporation. For purposes of determining whether a domestic corporation meets the requirement of this paragraph, the stock owned by a United States person who is a noncorporate United States shareholder of a domestic corporation on such first day shall not be counted at any time after he ceases during such ten-year period to be a noncorporate United States shareholder of such corporation.

(iii) For purposes of this paragraph, the term "noncorporate United States shareholder" means, with respect to a domestic corporation, a United States person who is an individual, estate, or trust and who owns 10 percent or more of the total combined voting power of all classes of stock of such domestic corporation.

(iv) For purposes of this paragraph, the percentage of the total combined voting power of stock of a foreign corporation owned by a United States person shall be determined in accordance with the principles of section 951(b) and the regulations thereunder.

(2) *Examples.*—The application of this paragraph may be illustrated by the following examples:

Example (1). During the entire period beginning December 31, 1954, and ending December 31, 1964, domestic corporation N owns all the stock of controlled foreign corporation X, a less developed country corporation. On December 31, 1964, N recognizes gain upon the sale of all its X stock. A, B, and C, who are unrelated individuals, were the only United States persons owning, or considered as owning, 10 percent or more of the total combined voting power of all classes of stock entitled to vote of N at any time during the 10-year period December 31, 1954, through December 31, 1964. The percentages of the total combined voting power in N, which A, B, and C owned during such 10-year period, are as follows:

Owner	Dec. 31, 1954- Apr. 1, 1957 Percent	Apr. 2, 1957- Oct. 1, 1959 Percent	Oct. 2, 1959- Dec. 31, 1964 Percent
A	20	20	20
B	9	30	30
C	30	15	9

Domestic corporation N does not meet the requirement of this paragraph with respect to the stock of controlled foreign corporation X for the following reasons:

(i) April 2, 1957, is the first day (during the 10-year period ending on December 31, 1964, the date N sells the X stock) on which noncorporate United States shareholders of N own more than

50 percent of the total combined voting power in N, and thus the requirement of this paragraph must be met. See subparagraph (1)(i) of this paragraph. Although A, B, and C did own, in the aggregate, more than 50 percent of such voting power before April 2, 1957, the voting power owned by B is not counted because B was not a noncorporate United States shareholder of N before such date.

(ii) Although C is a noncorporate United States shareholder on April 2, 1957, C ceases to own 10 percent or more of the total combined voting power in N on October 2, 1959. Thus, after October 1, 1959, the N stock which C owns is not counted for purposes of determining whether the more-than-50-percent stock ownership test is met. See subparagraph (1)(ii) of this paragraph. Accordingly, after October 1, 1959, the requirement of this paragraph is not met.

Example (2). Assume the same facts as in example (1), except that B's wife owns directly 5 percent of the total combined voting power in N from December 31, 1954, to December 31, 1964. On the basis of the assumed facts, N meets the requirement of this paragraph with respect to the stock of controlled foreign corporation X for the following reasons:

(i) December 31, 1954, is the first day (of the 10-year period ending on the date N sells the X stock) on which noncorporate United States shareholders of N own more than 50 percent of the total combined voting power in N. B is a noncorporate United States shareholder on such date because he owns, and is considered as owning, 14 percent of the total combined voting power in N (9 percent directly, and, under section 958(b), 5 percent constructively). Thus, on December 31, 1954, noncorporate United States shareholders A, B, and C own, in the aggregate, more than 50 percent of the total combined voting power in N.

(ii) A, B, and C, the noncorporate United States shareholders of N on December 31, 1954, own, and are considered as owning, more than 50 percent of the total voting power of N from December 31, 1954, to October 1, 1959. Since beginning on October 2, 1959, A owns 20 percent and B owns, and is considered as owning, 35 percent of the total combined voting power in N, A and B own, and are considered as owning, more than 50 percent of the total combined voting power in N from October 2, 1959, to December 31, 1964. Therefore, the requirement of this paragraph is met.

(d) *Application of section to lower tier corporation.*—(1) *General.*—For purposes of paragraph (g)(1)(ii) of §1.1248-3, a United States person satisfies the requirements of this subparagraph in respect of stock of a lower tier corporation which such person, by reason of his direct ownership of the share (or block) of the first tier corporation sold or exchanged, owned within the meaning of section 958(a)(2) on the date he

sold or exchanged such share (or block), if on such date—

(i) The 10-year stock ownership requirement of paragraph (b) of this section is met by such person with respect to any stock in the lower tier corporation which such person so owned, and

(ii) In the case of a United States person which is a domestic corporation, the requirement of paragraph (c) of this section, if applicable, is met.

(2) *Special rule.*—For purposes of this paragraph, in applying paragraphs (b) and (c) of this section, the sale or exchange of a share (or block) of stock in a first tier corporation by a United States person shall be deemed to be the sale or exchange of any stock in a lower tier corporation which the person, by reason of his direct ownership of such share (or block) of the first tier corporation, owned within the meaning of section 958(a)(2) on the date he actually sold or exchanged such share (or block) in the first tier corporation. [Reg. §1.1248-5.]

☐ [*T.D.* 6779, 12-21-64.]

[Reg. §1.1248-6]

§1.1248-6. Sale or exchange of stock in certain domestic corporations.—(a) *General rule.*—If a United States person recognizes gain upon the sale or exchange of a share (or block) of stock of a domestic corporation which was formed or availed of principally for the holding, directly or indirectly, of stock of one or more foreign corporations, and if the conditions of paragraph (a)(2) of §1.1248-1 would be met by such person in respect of the share (or block) if the domestic corporation were a foreign corporation, then section 1248 shall apply in respect of such gain in accordance with the rules provided in paragraph (b) of this section.

(b) *Application.*—(1) The gain referred to in paragraph (a) of this section shall be included in the gross income of the United States person as a dividend under section 1248(a) to the extent of the earnings and profits attributable under §1.1248-2 or §1.1248-3, whichever is applicable, to the share (or block), computed, however, in accordance with the following rules:

(i) The domestic corporation shall be treated as if it were a first tier foreign corporation;

(ii) If, after the application of subdivision (i) of this subparagraph, the provisions of paragraph (a)(3) of §1.1248-2 or paragraph (f) of §1.1248-3 (as the case may be) would apply in respect of a foreign corporation the stock of which is owned (within the meaning of section 958(a)) by the domestic corporation treated as the first tier corporation, such foreign corporation shall be considered a lower tier corporation;

(iii) Except to the extent provided in subdivision (iv) of this subparagraph, the earnings and profits of the domestic corporation treated as the first tier corporation accumulated for a taxable year, as computed under paragraph (d) of § 1.1248-2 or paragraph (b) of § 1.1248-3 (as the case may be), shall be considered to be zero; and

(iv) If, during a taxable year, a domestic corporation treated as the first tier corporation realizes gain upon the sale or exchange of stock in a foreign corporation, and solely by reason of the application of section 337 (relating to certain liquidations) the gain was not recognized, then the earnings and profits of such domestic corporation accumulated for the taxable year as computed under paragraph (d) of § 1.1248-2 or paragraph (b) of § 1.1248-3 (as the case may be), shall be considered to be an amount equal to the portion of such gain realized during the taxable year which, if section 337 had not applied, would have been treated as a dividend under section 1248(a).

(2) If the person selling or exchanging the stock in the domestic corporation is an individual, the limitation on tax attributable to the amount included in his gross income as a dividend under subparagraph (1) of this paragraph shall be determined, in accordance with the principles of paragraph (f) of § 1.1248-4, by treating the domestic corporation as a first tier corporation.

(3)(i) If the earnings and profits of the foreign corporation or corporations (or of the domestic corporation treated as a first tier corporation) to be taken into account under subparagraph (1) of this paragraph are not established in the manner provided in paragraph (a)(1) of § 1.1248-7, all of the gain from the sale or exchange of the share (or block) of the domestic corporation shall be treated as a dividend.

(ii) To the extent that the person does not establish, in the manner provided in paragraph (c) of § 1.1248-7, the foreign taxes paid by such foreign corporation or corporations to be taken into account for purposes of computing the limitation on tax attributable to a share, such foreign taxes shall not be taken into account for purposes of such computation.

(c) *Corporation formed or availed of principally for holding stock of foreign corporations.*—Whether or not a domestic corporation is formed or availed of principally for the holding, directly or indirectly, of stock of one or more foreign corporations shall be determined on the basis of all the facts and circumstances of each particular case. [Reg. § 1.1248-6.]

☐ [T.D. 6779, 12-21-64.]

[Reg. § 1.1248-7]

§ 1.1248-7. Taxpayer to establish earnings and profits and foreign taxes.—(a) *In general.*—(1) *Earnings and profits.*—If a taxpayer sells or exchanges stock in a foreign corporation which was a controlled foreign corporation and the Commissioner determines that the taxpayer has not established the amount of the earnings and profits of the corporation attributable to the stock under § 1.1248-2 or § 1.1248-3, whichever is applicable, all the gain from such sale or exchange shall be treated as a dividend under section 1248(a). See section 1248(g). A taxpayer shall be considered to have established such amount if—

(i) He attaches to his income tax return, filed on or before the last day prescribed by law (including extensions thereof) for his taxable year in which he sold or exchanged the stock, the schedule prescribed by paragraph (b) of this section or, if such last day is before April 1, 1965, he files such schedule before such date with the district director with whom such return was filed, and

(ii) He establishes in the manner prescribed by paragraph (d) of this section the correctness of each amount shown on such schedule.

(2) Notwithstanding an omission of information from, or an error with respect to an amount shown on, the schedule referred to in subparagraph (1)(i) of this paragraph, a taxpayer shall be considered to have complied with such subparagraph (1)(i) if—

(i) He establishes that such omission or error was inadvertent, or due to reasonable cause and not due to willful neglect, and that he has substantially complied with the requirements of this section, and

(ii) The taxpayer corrects such omission or error at the time when he complies with paragraph (d) of this section.

(3) For the requirement to establish the amount of foreign taxes to be taken into account for purposes of section 1248(b), see paragraph (c) of this section.

(b) *Schedule attached to return.*—(1) The taxpayer shall attach to his income tax return for his taxable year in which he sold or exchanged the stock, a schedule showing his name, address, and identifying number. Except to the extent provided in paragraph (e) of this section, the schedule shall also show the amount of the earnings and profits attributable under paragraph (a) of § 1.1248-2 or paragraph (a) of § 1.1248-3 (as the case may be) to the stock, and, in order to support the computation of such amount, any additional information required by subparagraphs (2), (3), (4), and (5) of this paragraph.

(2) The schedule shall also show for the first tier corporation, and for each lower tier corporation as to which information is required under subparagraph (4) of this paragraph, (i) the name of the corporation, (ii) the country under whose laws the corporation is created or organized, and (iii) the last day of the taxable year which the corporation regularly uses in computing its income.

(3) If the amount of earnings and profits attributable to a block of stock sold or exchanged

are computed under § 1.1248-2, the schedule shall also show—

(i) For each taxable year of the corporation, beginning after December 31, 1962, during the period the taxpayer held (or was considered to have held by reason of the application of section 1223, taking into account § 1.1248–8) the block, (*a*) the earnings and profits accumulated for each such taxable year computed under paragraph (d) of § 1.1248-2, and (*b*) the sum thereof computed under paragraph (e)(1)(i) and (2) of § 1.1248-2,

(ii) The number of shares in the block and the total number of shares of the corporation outstanding during such period,

(iii) If during the period the person held (or is considered to have held by reason of the application of section 1223, taking into account § 1.1248–8) the block any amount was included under section 951 in the gross income of such person (or another person) in respect of the block, the computation of the excess referred to in paragraph (e)(3)(ii) of § 1.1248-2, and

(iv) If the amount of earnings and profits of a lower tier corporation attributable to the block are computed under paragraph (a)(3) of § 1.1248-2, (*a*) the number of shares in the lower tier corporation which the taxpayer owns within the meaning of section 958(a)(2), (*b*) the total number of shares of such lower tier corporation outstanding during such period, and (*c*) in respect of such lower tier corporation, the information prescribed in subdivisions (i) and (iii) of this subparagraph.

(4) If the amount of earnings and profits attributable to a share (or block) sold or exchanged are computed under § 1.1248-3, the schedule shall also show for each taxable year of the corporation beginning after December 31, 1962, any day of which falls in a period or periods the taxpayer held (or was considered to have held by reason of the application of section 1223, taking into account § 1.1248–8) the stock while the corporation was a controlled foreign corporation—

(i) The number of days in such period or periods, but only if such number is less than the total number of days in such taxable year,

(ii) The earnings and profits accumulated for the taxable year computed under paragraph (b) of § 1.1248-3,

(iii) The number of shares in the corporation outstanding, or deemed under paragraph (c)(2) of § 1.1248-3 to be outstanding, on each day of the taxable year,

(iv) The taxpayer's tentative ratable share computed under paragraph (c) or (d) (as the case may be) of § 1.1248-3,

(v) The amount of, and a short description of each adjustment to, the tentative ratable share under paragraph (e) of § 1.1248-3, and

(vi) The amount of the ratable share referred to in paragraph (e)(1) of § 1.1248-3.

(5) In respect of a taxable year referred to in subparagraph (4) of this paragraph of a first tier corporation, if the taxpayer is required to compute under paragraph (f)(5) of § 1.1248-3 his ratable share of the earnings and profits for a taxable year of the lower tier corporation attributable to such taxable year of such first tier corporation, then for such taxable year of the lower tier corporation the schedule shall show—

(i) The earnings and profits accumulated for the taxable year of the lower tier corporation, computed under paragraph (b) of § 1.1248-3,

(ii) Each percentage described in paragraph (f)(2)(ii), (iii), and (iv) of § 1.1248-3,

(iii) The amount of the taxpayer's tentative ratable share computed under paragraph (f)(2) or (4) (as the case may be) of § 1.1248-3,

(iv) The amount of, and a short description of each adjustment to, the tentative ratable share under paragraph (f)(5) of § 1.1248-3, and

(v) The amount of the ratable share referred to in paragraph (f)(5)(i) of § 1.1248-3.

(c) *Foreign taxes.*—(1) If the taxpayer fails to establish any portion of the amount of any foreign taxes which he is required to establish by subparagraph (2) of this paragraph, then such portion shall not be taken into account under section 1248(b)(1)(B).

(2) The taxpayer shall establish in respect of the stock he sells or exchanges the amount of the foreign taxes described in section 1248(b)(1)(B) paid by the first tier corporation for each taxable year of such corporation for which the information is required under paragraph (b)(3) or (4) of this section, and the amount of such taxes paid by each lower tier corporation for each taxable year (as to which information is required under paragraph (b)(3)(iv) or (5) of this section) of each such lower tier corporation. A taxpayer shall be considered to have established the amount of such foreign taxes if—

(i) He attaches to the schedule described in paragraph (b) of this section a supplementary schedule which, except to the extent provided in paragraph (e) of this section, sets forth the amount of such foreign taxes for each taxable year (of the first tier corporation and of each such lower tier corporation) as to which such amount must be established under this subparagraph, and

(ii) He establishes in the manner prescribed by paragraph (d)(2) of this section the correctness of each amount shown on such supplementary schedule.

(d) *Establishing amounts on schedules.*—(1) A taxpayer shall be considered to have established, in respect of the stock he sold or exchanged, the correctness of an amount shown on a schedule described in paragraph (b) of this section only if he produces or provides within 180 days after demand by the district director (or within such longer period to which such director consents)—

(i) The books of original entry, or similar systematic accounting records maintained by any person or persons on a current basis as supplements to such books, which establish to the satisfaction of the district director the correctness of each such amount, and

(ii) In respect of any such books or records which are not in the English language, either an accurate English translation of any such records as are demanded, or the services of a qualified interpreter satisfactory to such director.

(2) A shareholder shall be considered to have established in respect of such stock the correctness of an amount shown on a supplementary schedule described in paragraph (c) of this section only if he produces or provides within 180 days after demand by the district director (or within such longer period to which such director consents)—

(i) Evidence described in paragraph (a)(2) of § 1.905-2 of such amount, or

(ii) Secondary evidence of such amount, in the same manner and to the same extent as would be permissible under paragraph (b) of § 1.905-2 in the case of a taxpayer who claimed the benefits of the foreign tax credit in respect of such amount

(e) *Insufficient information at time return is filed.*—If stock in a foreign corporation, which was a controlled foreign corporation, is sold or exchanged by a taxpayer during a taxable year of the corporation (or of a lower tier corporation) which ends after the last day of the taxpayer's taxable year in which the sale or exchange occurs, and if—

(1) For the taxpayer's taxable year, the last day referred to in paragraph (a)(1) of this section for filing his income tax return with a schedule prescribed in paragraph (b) of this section, and, if applicable, with a supplemental schedule prescribed in paragraph (c) of this section, or

(2) The last day referred to in paragraph (a)(1) of this section (that is, April 1, 1965) for filing any such schedule or schedules with the district director with whom such return was filed,

is not later than 90 days after the close of such taxable year of any such corporation, then such return with such schedule or schedules may be filed, or any such schedule or schedules may be filed, on the basis of estimates of amounts or percentages (for any such taxable year of any such corporation) required to be shown on any such schedule or schedules. If any such estimate differs from the actual amount or percentage, the taxpayer shall, within 90 days after the close of any such taxable year of any such corporation, file (or attach to a claim for refund or amended return filed) at the office of the district director with whom he filed the return a new schedule or schedules showing the actual amounts or percentages. [Reg. § 1.1248-7.]

□ [*T.D.* 6779, 12-21-64. *Amended by T.D.* 9345, 7-27-2007.]

[Reg. § 1.1248-8]

§ 1.1248-8. Earnings and profits attributable to stock following certain non-recognition transactions.—(a) *Scope.*—This section sets forth rules for the attribution of earnings and profits for purposes of section 1248 and § 1.1248-1(a)(1) and to supplement the rules in §§ 1.1248-2 and 1.1248-3 with respect to—

(1) *Stock that an exchanging shareholder receives, or an acquiring corporation receives, in restructuring transactions.*—Except as otherwise provided in this paragraph (a), stock of a foreign corporation that an exchanging shareholder receives, or an acquiring corporation receives, pursuant to a restructuring transaction (as defined in paragraph (b)(1)(vii) of this section) in which the holding period of such stock is determined by application of section 1223(1) or 1223(2), whichever is appropriate. This section shall not apply to an exchange otherwise described in this paragraph (a)(1) if, as a result of the exchange, the exchanging shareholder is required to include in income as a deemed dividend the section 1248 amount pursuant to § 1.367(b)-4(b). See paragraphs (b)(2) and (3) of this section;

(2) *Nonexchanging shareholders.*—Stock of a foreign corporation that participates in a restructuring transaction that is held by a non-exchanging shareholder (as defined in paragraph (b)(1)(vi) of this section) in the restructuring transaction. See paragraph (b)(4) of this section;

(3) *Application of section 381.*—Stock of a foreign corporation that receives assets in a transfer to which section 361(a) applies in connection with a reorganization described in section 368(a)(1)(A), (C), (D), (F), or (G), or in a distribution to which section 332 applies, and to which section 381(c)(2)(A) and § 1.381(c)(2)-1(a) apply. See paragraph (b)(6) of this section; or

(4) *Section 332 liquidations.*—Stock of a foreign corporation that receives the assets and liabilities of a foreign corporation in a complete liquidation described in section 332 if the foreign distributee is a foreign corporate shareholder (as defined in paragraph (b)(1)(v) of this section) of the liquidating corporation. See paragraph (c) of this section.

(b) *Earnings and profits attributable to stock following a restructuring transaction.*—(1) *Definitions.*—The following definitions apply for purposes of this section:

(i) *Acquired corporation* is a corporation whose stock or assets are acquired in exchange for stock in (or stock in and other property of) either the acquiring corporation or a foreign corporation that controls, within the meaning of

Reg. § 1.1248-8(b)(1)(i)

section 368(c), the acquiring corporation in a restructuring transaction.

(ii) *Acquiring corporation* is a corporation that acquires the stock or assets of an acquired corporation in a restructuring transaction.

(iii) *Controlled foreign corporation* is a corporation described in either section 953(c)(1)(B) or section 957.

(iv) *Exchanging shareholder* is a person that exchanges—

(A) In a restructuring transaction qualifying as a nonrecognition transaction within the meaning of section 7701(a)(45) and described in section 354, 356, or 361(a), stock in an acquired corporation for stock in either a foreign acquiring corporation or a foreign corporation that is in control, within the meaning of section 368(c), of an acquiring corporation (whether domestic or foreign); or

(B) In a restructuring transaction qualifying as a nonrecognition transaction within the meaning of section 7701(a)(45) and described in section 351, property (including stock) for stock in a foreign acquiring corporation.

(v) *Foreign corporate shareholder* is a foreign corporation that—

(A) Owns stock of another foreign corporation; and

(B) Has a section 1248 shareholder that is also a section 1248 shareholder of the other foreign corporation.

(vi) *Non-exchanging shareholder* is, at the time the acquiring corporation participates in a restructuring transaction, either a section 1248 shareholder or a foreign corporate shareholder of the acquiring corporation that is not an exchanging shareholder with respect to that corporation.

(vii) *Restructuring transaction* is a transaction qualifying as a nonrecognition transaction within the meaning of section 7701(a)(45) and described in section 351, 354, 356, or 361.

(viii) *Section 1248 shareholder* is any United States person that satisfies the ownership requirements of section 1248(a)(2) and §1.1248-1(a)(2) with respect to a foreign corporation.

(2) *Earnings and profits attributable to stock that an exchanging shareholder receives in a restructuring transaction.*—Where, in a restructuring transaction, an exchanging shareholder receives stock in a foreign corporation, the holding period of which is determined under section 1223(1), and the exchanging shareholder is either a section 1248 shareholder or a foreign corporate shareholder with respect to that foreign corporation immediately after the restructuring transaction, the earnings and profits attributable to the stock the exchanging shareholder receives shall be determined pursuant to the rules in paragraphs (b)(2)(i), (ii), and (iii) of this section.

(i) *Exchanging shareholder exchanges property that is not stock of a foreign acquired corporation with respect to which the exchanging shareholder is a section 1248 shareholder or a foreign corporate shareholder.*—Where the exchanging shareholder exchanges in a restructuring transaction property that is not stock of a foreign acquired corporation with respect to which the exchanging shareholder is a section 1248 shareholder or a foreign corporate shareholder immediately before such transaction, the earnings and profits attributable to the stock that the exchanging shareholder receives in the restructuring transaction shall be determined in accordance with §1.1248-2 or §1.1248-3, whichever is applicable, without regard to any portion of the section 1223(1) holding period in that stock that is prior to the restructuring transaction. See paragraph (b)(7) *Example 1* of this section.

(ii) *Exchanging shareholder exchanges stock of a foreign corporation with respect to which the exchanging shareholder is either a section 1248 shareholder or a foreign corporate shareholder.*—Except as provided in paragraph (b)(2)(iii) of this section, where the exchanging shareholder exchanges in a restructuring transaction stock of a foreign acquired corporation with respect to which the exchanging shareholder is either a section 1248 shareholder or a foreign corporate shareholder immediately before such restructuring transaction, the earnings and profits attributable to the stock that the exchanging shareholder receives in the restructuring transaction shall be the sum of the earnings and profits attributable to—

(A) The stock of the foreign acquired corporation exchanged (determined in accordance with §1.1248-2 or §1.1248-3, whichever is applicable, and this section, if applicable) that was accumulated before the restructuring transaction; and

(B) The stock of the foreign corporation that the exchanging shareholder receives in the restructuring transaction (determined in accordance with §1.1248-2 or §1.1248-3, whichever is applicable, and this section, if applicable), without regard to any portion of the section 1223(1) holding period in that stock that is prior to the restructuring transaction. See paragraph (b)(7) *Example 2*, *Example 4*, and *Example 6* of this section.

(iii) *Exchanging shareholder receives stock in a foreign corporation that controls a domestic acquiring corporation.*—Where the acquiring corporation is a domestic corporation and the exchanging shareholder receives in a restructuring transaction stock in a foreign corporation that controls (within the meaning of section 368(c)) the domestic acquiring corporation, the earnings and profits attributable to the stock that the exchanging shareholder receives in the restructuring transaction shall consist solely of the amount of earnings and profits attributable to such stock (determined in accordance with §1.1248-2 or §1.1248-3, whichever is applicable, and this section, if applicable) without regard to any portion of the section 1223(1) holding period in that stock that is prior to the restructuring transaction. See paragraph (b)(7) *Example 5* of this section.

(3) *Earnings and profits attributable to stock in a foreign corporation certain acquiring corporations receive in a restructuring transaction.*—Where an acquiring corporation receives, in a restructuring transaction, stock in a foreign acquired corporation, the holding period of which is determined under section 1223(2), and the acquiring corporation is either a section 1248 shareholder or a foreign corporate shareholder with respect to that foreign acquired corporation immediately after the restructuring transaction, the earnings and profits attributable to the foreign acquired corporation stock that the acquiring corporation receives shall be determined pursuant to the rules in paragraphs (b)(3)(i) and (ii) of this section.

(i) *Stock of a foreign corporation with respect to which the exchanging shareholder is neither a section 1248 shareholder nor a foreign corporate shareholder.*—The earnings and profits attributable to the stock of the foreign acquired corporation that the acquiring corporation receives in a restructuring transaction where the exchanging shareholder is neither a section 1248 shareholder nor a foreign corporate shareholder with respect to that foreign acquired corporation immediately before the restructuring transaction shall be determined in accordance with § 1.1248-2 or § 1.1248-3, whichever is applicable, without regard to any portion of the section 1223(2) holding period in that stock that is prior to the restructuring transaction.

(ii) *Stock of a foreign corporation with respect to which the exchanging shareholder is either a section 1248 shareholder or a foreign corporate shareholder.*—The earnings and profits attributable to the stock of a foreign acquired corporation that the acquiring corporation receives in the restructuring transaction where the exchanging shareholder is either a section 1248 shareholder or a foreign corporate shareholder with respect to that foreign corporation immediately before the restructuring transaction shall be determined in accordance with § 1.1248-2 or § 1.1248-3, whichever is applicable, with regard to the portion of the section 1223(2) holding period of the stock that the exchanging shareholder took into account for purposes of attributing earnings and profits to that stock (determined in accordance with this section). See paragraph (b)(7) *Example 3, Example 5,* and *Example 7* of this section.

(4) *Earnings and profits attributable to stock held by a non-exchanging shareholder in a foreign acquiring corporation.*—(i) Except to the extent paragraph (b)(4)(ii) of this section applies, the earnings and profits attributable to stock of a foreign acquiring corporation held by a non-exchanging shareholder immediately prior to a restructuring transaction continue to be attributed to such stock, and the earnings and profits of the acquired corporation accumulated prior to the restructuring transaction attributable to the stock of an acquired corporation are not attributed to the non-exchanging shareholder's stock in the foreign acquiring corporation. See § 1.1248-2 or § 1.1248-3 (whichever is applicable) and, as applicable, paragraph (b)(6) of this section; see also paragraph (b)(7) *Example 2* and *Example 4* of this section.

(ii) Where a non-exchanging shareholder holds stock in a foreign corporation that is also an exchanging shareholder and a foreign acquiring corporation in the same restructuring transaction—

(A) The earnings and profits attributable to such stock shall be the sum of the earnings and profits attributable to the stock of such foreign corporation immediately before the restructuring transaction (including amounts attributed under section 1248(c)(2)) and the earnings and profits attributable to the stock of the foreign acquiring corporation accumulated after the restructuring transaction (including amounts attributed under section 1248(c)(2)); and

(B) Paragraph (b)(6) of this section applies. See paragraph (b)(7) *Example 8* of this section.

(iii) Where the acquiring corporation is a foreign corporate shareholder with respect to stock of a foreign acquired corporation, paragraph (b)(3) of this section shall not apply for purposes of determining the earnings and profits attributable to stock in the foreign acquiring corporation owned by a non-exchanging shareholder thereof (see section 1248(c)(2)). See paragraph (b)(7) *Example 6* of this section.

(5) *Reduction in earnings and profits attributable to stock to prevent multiple inclusions with respect to the same earnings and profits.*—To the extent consistent with the principles of section 1248, adjustments to earnings and profits attributable to stock shall be made such that section 1223(1) and (2) and this section are applied in a manner that results in earnings and profits being taken into account only once. Thus, for example, when a controlled foreign corporation sells or exchanges all or part of the stock of another foreign corporation to which earnings and profits are attributable pursuant to this paragraph (b) or paragraph (c) of this section, proportionate reductions shall be made to the earnings and profits attributed to the stock of the selling foreign corporate shareholder owned by a section 1248 shareholder. See paragraph (b)(7) *Example 7* of this section.

(6) *Special rule regarding section 381.*—Solely for purposes of determining the earnings and profits (or deficit in earnings and profits) attributable to stock pursuant to this paragraph (b), the earnings and profits of a corporation shall not include earnings and profits that are treated as

received or incurred under section 381(c)(2)(A) and § 1.381(c)(2)-1(a). See paragraph (b)(7) *Example 4* of this section.

(7) *Examples.*—The application of this paragraph (b) is illustrated by the following examples. Unless otherwise indicated, in the following examples assume that—

(i) There is no immediate gain recognition pursuant to section 367(a)(1) and the regulations under that section (either through operation of the rules or because the appropriate parties have entered into a gain recognition agreement under § § 1.367(a)-3(b) and 1.367(a)-8);

(ii) There is no income inclusion required pursuant to section 367(b) and the regulations under that section, and all reporting requirements in those regulations are complied with;

(iii) References to earnings and profits are to earnings and profits that would be includible in income as a dividend under section 1248 and the regulations under that section if stock to which the earnings and profits are attributable were sold or exchanged by its shareholder;

(iv) Each corporation has only a single class of stock outstanding and uses the calendar year as its taxable year; and

(v) Each transaction is unrelated to all other transactions.

Example 1. A section 351 exchange of property other than stock in a foreign corporation with respect to which the exchanging shareholder is either a section 1248 shareholder or a foreign corporate shareholder. (i) *Facts.* DC1, a domestic corporation, has owned all the stock of CFC, a foreign corporation, since CFC's formation on January 1, year 3. On December 31, year 5, DC2, a domestic corporation unrelated to DC1, contributes property it has held since January 1, year 1, to CFC in exchange for voting stock of CFC in a restructuring transaction that is an exchange under section 351. The property that DC2 contributes is not stock in a foreign corporation with respect to which DC2 was either a section 1248 shareholder or a foreign corporate shareholder. DC2 receives 80% of the voting stock of CFC in the restructuring transaction and its holding period in that CFC stock, determined pursuant to section 1223(1), began on January 1, year 1. CFC has $100 of accumulated earnings and profits on December 31, year 5. On December 31, year 7, when the accumulated earnings and profits of CFC are $200, DC2, a section 1248 shareholder with respect to CFC, sells its CFC stock.

(ii) *Result.* Under paragraph (b)(2)(i) of this section, the earnings and profits attributable to the CFC stock sold by DC2 are $80. This amount consists of none of the $100 of earnings and profits accumulated by CFC before the restructuring transaction, and 80% of the $100 of earnings and profits of CFC accumulated after the restructuring transaction.

Example 2. A section 351 exchange of controlled foreign corporation stock by a United States person for stock in a controlled foreign corporation in a restructuring transaction. (i) *Facts.* The facts are the same as in *Example 1* except as follows. The property that DC2 contributes is 100% of the stock in CFC2, a foreign corporation. DC2 has owned all the stock of CFC2 since CFC2's formation on January 1, year 2, and CFC2 has $200 of earnings and profits as of December 31, year 5. CFC2 does not accumulate any additional earnings and profits from December 31, year 5, to December 31, year 7. On December 31, year 7, when the accumulated earnings and profits of CFC are $200, DC2, a section 1248 shareholder with respect to CFC, sells its CFC stock. Also on that date, DC1 sells its CFC stock.

(ii) *Result.* (A) *DC2 sale.* Pursuant to paragraph (b)(2)(ii) of this section, the earnings and profits attributable to the CFC stock sold by DC2 are $280. This amount consists of all of the $200 of earnings and profits of CFC2 accumulated before the restructuring transaction (see also section 1248(c)(2)), none of the $100 of earnings and profits accumulated by CFC before the restructuring transaction, and 80% of the $100 of earnings and profits of CFC accumulated after the restructuring transaction.

(B) *DC1 sale.* Pursuant to paragraph (b)(4) of this section, the earnings and profits attributable to the CFC stock sold by DC1, a non-exchanging shareholder in the restructuring transaction, are $120. This amount consists of all of the $100 of earnings and profits of CFC accumulated before the restructuring transaction, none of the $200 of earnings and profits of CFC2 accumulated before the restructuring transaction, and 20% of the $100 of earnings and profits of CFC accumulated after the restructuring transaction.

Example 3. A section 351 exchange of controlled foreign corporation stock by a United States person for stock in a domestic corporation in a restructuring transaction. (i) *Facts.* DC1, a domestic corporation, has owned all of the stock of CFC, a foreign corporation, since CFC's formation on January 1, year 1. DC1 has also owned all the stock of DC2, a domestic corporation, since DC2's formation on January 1, year 1. On December 31, year 2, DC1 contributes the stock of CFC to DC2 in exchange for stock in DC2 in a restructuring transaction that is an exchange described in section 351. On December 31, year 2, CFC has $100 of accumulated earnings and profits. DC2 has a basis in the CFC stock determined under section 362, and is considered to have held the CFC stock since January 1, year 1, pursuant to section 1223(2). On December 31, year 4, when the accumulated earnings and profits of CFC are still $100, DC2 sells its CFC stock.

(ii) *Result.* Under paragraph (b)(3)(ii) of this section, $100 of accumulated earnings and profits of CFC is attributable to the stock of CFC sold by DC2, even though DC2 did not hold the stock of CFC during the time CFC accumulated the earnings and profits.

Example 4. Acquisition of a controlled foreign corporation by a controlled foreign corporation in a reorganization described in section 368(a)(1)(C) (or section 368(a)(1)(B)). (i) *Facts.* DC1, a domestic corporation, has owned all the stock of CFC1, a foreign corporation, since its formation on January 1, year 1. DC2, a domestic corporation unrelated to DC1, has owned all of the stock of CFC2, a foreign corporation, since its formation on January 1, year 2. On December 31, year 3, pursuant to a restructuring transaction that is a reorganization described in section 368(a)(1)(C), CFC1 transfers all of its assets to CFC2 in exchange for 25% of the voting stock of CFC2. CFC1 distributes the CFC2 stock to DC1 and the CFC1 stock is cancelled. DC1's holding period in the CFC2 stock, determined under section 1223(1), begins on January 1, year 1. On December 31, year 3, CFC1 has $100 of accumulated earnings and profits and CFC2 has $200 of accumulated earnings and profits. CFC2 succeeds to the $100 of CFC1 accumulated earnings and profits in the reorganization under section 381. From January 1, year 4 to December 31, year 5, CFC2 incurred a deficit in earnings and profits in the amount of ($200). On December 31, year 5, both DC1 and DC2 sell their stock in CFC2.

(ii) *Result.* (A) *DC1.* Pursuant to paragraph (b)(2)(ii) of this section, $50 of earnings and profits is attributable to the CFC2 stock sold by DC1. This amount consists of $100 of CFC1's earnings and profits accumulated before the restructuring transaction, reduced by 25% of CFC2's ($200) post-restructuring transaction deficit in earnings and profits. None of the $200 of CFC2's earnings and profits accumulated by CFC2 prior to the reorganization is attributed to the CFC2 stock sold by DC1. Also, none of the earnings and profits CFC2 succeeded to under section 381 is attributed to the CFC2 stock sold by DC1, pursuant to paragraph (b)(6) of this section.

(B) *DC2.* Pursuant to paragraph (b)(4) of this section, there is $50 of accumulated earnings and profits attributable to the CFC2 stock sold by DC2. This amount consists of all of the $200 of CFC2's earnings and profits accumulated by CFC2 prior to the reorganization, reduced by 75% of CFC2's deficit in earnings and profits in the amount of ($200) incurred after the restructuring transaction. None of the $100 of CFC1 accumulated earnings and profits succeeded to under section 381 is attributable to the CFC2 stock sold by DC2, pursuant to paragraph (b)(6) of this section.

(C) *Section 368(a)(1)(B) reorganization.* If, instead of DC1 acquiring its 25% interest in CFC2 pursuant to a reorganization described in section 368(a)(1)(C), DC1 had transferred the stock of CFC1 to CFC2 in exchange for 25% of the voting stock of CFC2 in a reorganization described in section 368(a)(1)(B), the results would be the same as described in paragraphs (ii) (A) and (B) of this *Example 4.*

Example 5. Acquisition of the stock of a foreign corporation that controls a domestic acquiring corporation in a triangular reorganization described in section 368(a)(1)(C). (i) *Facts.* DC1, a domestic corporation, has owned all the stock of CFC1, a foreign corporation, since its formation on January 1, year 1. CFC1 has owned all the stock of CFC2, a foreign corporation, since its formation on January 1, year 1. FC, a foreign corporation that is not a controlled foreign corporation, has owned all of the stock of DC2, a domestic corporation, since its formation on January 1, year 2. On December 31, year 3, pursuant to a restructuring transaction that was a triangular reorganization described in section 368(a)(1)(C), CFC1 transfers all of its assets, including the CFC2 stock, to DC2 in exchange for 60% of the voting stock of FC. CFC1 transfers the voting stock of FC to DC1 and the CFC1 stock is cancelled. Pursuant to section 1223(1), DC1 is considered to have held the stock of FC since January 1, year 1. Under section 1223(2), DC2 is considered to have held the stock of CFC2 since January 1, year 1. On December 31, year 3, CFC1 has $100 of earnings and profits, CFC2 has $300 of earnings and profits, and FC has $200 of earnings and profits. DC1 includes the $100 all earnings and profits amount attributable to its CFC1 stock in income as a deemed dividend under §1.367(b)-3 upon the exchange of CFC1 stock for FC stock. Pursuant to the lower-tier earnings exclusion of §1.367(b)-2(d)(3)(ii), that amount does not include the $300 of earnings and profits of CFC2. From January 1, year 4, until December 31, year 5, FC (now a controlled foreign corporation) accumulates an additional $50 of earnings and profits. From January 1, year 4 until December 31, year 5, CFC2 accumulates an additional $100 of earnings and profits. On December 31, year 5, DC1 sells its stock in FC and DC2 sells its stock in CFC2.

(ii) *Result.* (A) *DC1.* Pursuant to paragraph (b)(2)(iii) of this section, there is $30 of earnings and profits attributable to the stock of FC sold by DC1. This amount consists of 60% of the $50 of earnings and profits accumulated by FC after the restructuring transaction, and none of the earnings and profits accumulated by CFC1, CFC2, or FC before the restructuring transaction.

(B) *DC2.* Pursuant to paragraph (b)(3)(ii) of this section, there is $400 of earnings and profits attributable to the stock of CFC2 sold by DC2. This amount consists of all of the earnings and profits accumulated by CFC2 during DC2's section 1223(2) holding period.

Example 6. Acquisition of the stock of a foreign corporation that controls a foreign acquiring corporation in a reorganization described in section 368(a)(1)(C). (i) *Facts.* DC1, a domestic corporation, has owned all the stock of CFC1, a foreign corporation, since its formation on January 1, year 1. CFC1 has owned all the stock of CFC2, a foreign corporation, since its formation on January 1, year 1. FC, a foreign corporation that is not a controlled foreign corporation, has owned all of the stock of FC2, a foreign corporation, since its formation on January 1, year 2. On December 31, year 3, pursuant to a restructuring transaction that was a triangular reorganization described in section 368(a)(1)(C), CFC1 transfers all of its assets, including the CFC2 stock, to FC2 in exchange for 60% of the voting stock of FC. CFC1 transfers the voting stock of FC to DC1 and the CFC1 stock is cancelled. Pursuant to section 1223(1), DC1 is considered to have held the stock of FC since January 1, year 1. Under section 1223(2), FC2 is considered to have held the stock of CFC2 since January 1, year 1. On December 31, year 3, CFC1 has $100 of earnings and profits, CFC2 has $300 of earnings and profits, FC has $200 of earnings and profits, and FC2 has no earnings and profits. From January 1, year 4, until December 31, year 5, FC (now a controlled foreign corporation) accumulates an additional $50 of earnings and profits. From January 1, year 4 until December 31, year 5, CFC2 accumulates an additional $100 of earnings and profits. FC2, a controlled foreign corporation after the restructuring transaction, accumulates $100 of earnings and profits from January 1, year 4, until December 31, year 5. On December 31, year 5, DC1 sells its stock in FC.

(ii) *Result.* Pursuant to paragraphs (b)(2)(ii) and (b)(4)(iii) of this section, there is $550 of earnings and profits attributable to the stock of FC sold by DC1. This amount consists of all $400 of the CFC1 and CFC2 earnings and profits accumulated before the restructuring transaction (see also section 1248(c)(2)), and 60% of the $250 of the earnings and profits accumulated by FC, FC2, and CFC2 after the restructuring transaction.

Example 7. Acquisition of controlled foreign corporation stock by a controlled foreign corporation in a reorganization described in section 368(a)(1)(B), followed by a sale of the acquired stock by the acquiring controlled foreign corporation. (i) *Facts.* DC1, a domestic corporation, has owned all of the outstanding stock of CFC1, a foreign corporation, since its formation on January 1, year 1. CFC1 has owned all of the outstanding stock of CFC3, a foreign corporation, since its formation on January 1, year 1. DC2, a domestic corporation unrelated to DC1, has owned all of the outstanding stock of CFC2, a foreign corporation, since its formation on January 1, year 2. On December 31, year 3, pursuant to a restructuring transaction that is a reorganization described in section 368(a)(1)(B), CFC1 transfers all of the stock of CFC3 to CFC2 in exchange for 40% of CFC2's stock. On December 31, year 3, CFC2 and CFC3 have, respectively, $40 and $20 of earnings and profits. On December 31, year 5, when the accumulated earnings and profits of CFC3 are $50 ($20 of earnings and profits as of December 31, year 3, plus $30 of earnings and profits generated from January 1, year 4, through December

31, year 5), CFC2 sells the stock of CFC3 in a transaction to which section 964(e) applies.

(ii) *Result.* (A) *CFC2.* Pursuant to paragraph (b)(3)(ii) of this section, there is $50 of earnings and profits attributable to the CFC3 stock sold by CFC2. This amount consists of the accumulated earnings and profits attributable to CFC2's entire section 1223(2) holding period in the CFC3 stock.

(B) *CFC1, DC2, and DC1.* Under paragraph (b)(5) of this section, the earnings and profits attributable to the CFC2 stock held by CFC1 and DC2, and the earnings and profits attributable to the CFC1 stock held by DC1, will be reduced (regardless of whether CFC2 recognizes gain on its sale of CFC3 stock).

(1) *CFC1.* The earnings and profits attributable to the CFC2 stock held by CFC1 will be reduced by $32, or the amount of earnings and profits as of December 31, year 5, that would have been attributable to the CFC2 stock held by CFC1 pursuant to paragraph (b)(2)(ii) of this section. This amount consists of all of the $20 of earnings and profits accumulated by CFC3 before the restructuring transaction and 40% of the $30 of earnings and profits accumulated by CFC3 after the restructuring transaction (.40 × $30 = $12).

(2) *DC1.* The earnings and profits attributable to the CFC1 stock held by DC1 will also be reduced by $32, or the amount of earnings and profits that would have been attributable to the CFC1 stock held by DC1 as of December 31, year 5.

(3) *DC2.* The earnings and profits attributable to the CFC2 stock held by DC2 will be reduced by $18, or the amount of earnings and profits that would have been attributable to the CFC2 stock held by DC2 as of December 31, year 5, under paragraph (b)(4) of this section. This amount consists of 60% of the $30 (.60 × $30 = $18) of earnings and profits accumulated by CFC3 after the restructuring transaction.

(C) *Partial sale by CFC2.* If, instead of selling 100% of the CFC3 stock, on December 31, year 5, CFC2 sells only 50% of its CFC3 stock, paragraph (b)(5) of this section requires CFC1 to reduce the earnings and profits of CFC3 attributable to its CFC2 stock to $16. Similarly, DC1 would be required to reduce the earnings and profits of CFC3 attributable to its CFC1 stock by $16. Paragraph (b)(5) of this section also requires DC2 to reduce the CFC3 earnings and profits attributable to its CFC2 stock by $9. These reductions occur without regard to whether CFC2 recognizes gain on its sale of CFC3 stock.

Example 8. Acquisition of the assets of a lower-tier controlled foreign corporation by an upper-tier controlled foreign corporation in a restructuring transaction described in section 368(a)(1)(C). (i) *Facts.* DC, a domestic corporation, has owned all the stock of CFC1, a controlled foreign corporation, since its formation on January 1, year 1. CFC1 is a holding company that has owned 79%

of the stock of CFC2, a controlled foreign corporation, since its formation on January 1, year 1. The other 21% of CFC2 stock is owned by X, an unrelated party. On December 31, year 1, CFC2 has $200 of earnings and profits. On December 31, year 1, CFC1 has no accumulated earnings and profits. On December 31, year 1, pursuant to a restructuring transaction described in section 368(a)(1)(C), CFC2 transfers all its properties to CFC1. In exchange, CFC1 assumes the liabilities of CFC2 and transfers to CFC2 voting stock representing 21% of the stock of CFC1. CFC2 distributes the voting stock to X and liquidates. The liabilities assumed do not exceed 20% of the value of the properties of CFC2. From January 1, year 2, to December 31, year 3, CFC1 accumulates $100 of earnings and profits. On December 31, year 3, DC sells its CFC1 stock.

(ii) *Result.* Pursuant to paragraph (b)(4)(ii) of this section, there is $237 of earnings and profits attributable to DC's CFC1 stock. This amount consists of 79% of CFC2's $200 of earnings and profits accumulated before the restructuring transaction (see section 1248(c)(2)), and 79% of CFC1's $100 of earnings and profits accumulated after the restructuring transaction. Pursuant to paragraph (b)(6) of this section, none of CFC2's $200 of earnings and profits to which CFC1 succeeded under section 381 would be attributable to DC's CFC1 stock.

(c) *Earnings and profits attributable to stock of a foreign distributee corporation that is a foreign corporate shareholder with respect to a foreign liquidating corporation.*—(1) *General rule.*—If a foreign corporation (liquidating corporation) makes a distribution of property in complete liquidation under section 332 to a foreign corporation (distributee), and immediately before the liquidation the distributee was a foreign corporate shareholder with respect to the liquidating foreign corporation, the amount of earnings and profits attributable to the distributee stock upon its subsequent sale or exchange will be determined under this paragraph (c)(1). The earnings and profits attributable will be the sum of the earnings and profits attributable to the stock of the distributee immediately before the liquidation (including amounts attributed under section 1248(c)(2)) and the earnings and profits attributable to the stock of the distributee accumulated after the liquidation (including amounts attributed under section 1248(c)(2)).

(2) *Special rule regarding section 381.*—Solely for purposes of determining the earnings and profits (or deficit in earnings and profits) attributable to stock under this paragraph (c), the attributed earnings and profits of a corporation shall not include earnings and profits that are treated as received or incurred pursuant to section 381(c)(2)(A) and § 1.381(c)(2)-1(a).

(3) *Example.*—(i) *Facts.*—DC, a domestic corporation, has owned all of the stock of CFC1,

a foreign corporation, since its formation on January 1, year 1. CFC1 is an operating company that has owned all of the stock of CFC2, a foreign corporation, since its formation on January 1, year 1. On December 31, year 2, CFC1 has $200 of accumulated earnings and profits and CFC2 has a ($200) deficit in earnings and profits. On December 31, year 2, CFC2 distributes all of its assets and liabilities to CFC1 in a liquidation to which section 332 applies. From January 1, year 3, until December 31, year 4, CFC1 accumulates no additional earnings and profits. On December 31, year 4, DC sells its stock in CFC1.

(ii) *Result.*—Pursuant to paragraph (c)(1) of this section, there are no earnings and profits attributable to DC's CFC1 stock. This amount consists of the sum of the earnings and profits attributable to the CFC1 stock immediately before the liquidation (100% of the $200 accumulated earnings and profits of CFC1 and 100% of CFC2's ($200) deficit in earnings and profits) and the amount of earnings and profits accumulated after the section 332 liquidation (see also section 1248(c)(2)).

(d) *Effective/applicability date.*—This section applies to income inclusions that occur on or after July 30, 2007. [Reg. § 1.1248–8.]

☐ [*T.D. 9345, 7-27-2007.*]

[Reg. § 1.1249-1]

§ 1.1249-1. Gain from certain sales or exchanges of patents, etc., to foreign corporations.—(a) *General rule.*—Section 1249 provides that if gain is recognized from the sale or exchange after December 31, 1962, of a patent, an invention, model, or design (whether or not patented), a copyright, a secret formula or process, or any other similar property right (not including property such as goodwill, a trademark, or a trade brand) to any foreign corporation by any United States person (as defined in section 7701(a)(30)) which controls such foreign corporation, and if such gain would (but for the provisions of section 1249) be gain from the sale or exchange of a capital asset or of property described in section 1231, then such gain shall be considered as gain from the sale or exchange of property which is neither a capital asset nor property described in section 1231. Section 1249 applies only to gain recognized in taxable years beginning after December 31, 1962.

(b) *Control.*—For purposes of paragraph (a) of this section, the term "control" means, with respect to any foreign corporation, the ownership, directly or indirectly, of stock possessing more than 50 percent of the total combined voting power of all classes of stock entitled to vote. For purposes of the preceding sentence, the rules for determining ownership of stock provided by section 958(a) and (b), and the principles for determining percentage of total combined voting power owned by United States shareholders provided by paragraphs (b) and (c) of § 1.957-1, shall apply. [Reg. § 1.1249-1.]

☐ [*T.D.* 6765, 11-2-64.]

[Reg. § 1.1250-1]

§ 1.1250-1. Gain from dispositions of certain depreciable realty.—(a) *Dispositions after December 31, 1969.*—(1) *Ordinary income.*—(i) In general, section 1250(a)(1) provides that, upon a disposition of an item of section 1250 property after December 31, 1969, the applicable percentage of the lower of—

(a) The additional depreciation (as defined in § 1.1250-2) attributable to periods after December 31, 1969 in respect of the property, or

(b) The excess of the amount realized on a sale, exchange, or involuntary conversion (or the fair market value of the property on any other disposition) over the adjusted basis of the property,

shall be treated as gain from the sale or exchange of property which is neither a capital asset nor property described in section 1231 (that is, shall be recognized as ordinary income). The amount of such gain shall be determined separately for each item (see subparagraph (2)(ii) of this paragraph) of section 1250 property. If the amount determined under (b) of this subdivision exceeds the amount determined under (a) of this subdivision, then such excess shall be treated as provided in subdivision (ii) of this subparagraph. For relation of section 1250 to other provisions, see paragraph (c) of this section.

(ii) If the amount determined under subdivision (i)(b) of this subparagraph exceeds the amount determined under subdivision (i)(a) of this subparagraph, then the applicable percentage of the lower of—

(a) The additional depreciation attributable to periods before January 1, 1970, or

(b) Such excess,

shall also be recognized as ordinary income.

(iii) If gain would be recognized upon a disposition of an item of section 1250 property under subdivisions (i) and (ii) of this subparagraph, and if section 1250(d) applies, then the gain recognized shall be considered as recognized first under subdivision (i) of this subparagraph. (See example (3)(i) of paragraph (c)(4) of § 1.1250-3.)

(2) *Meaning of terms.*—(i) For purposes of section 1250, the term "disposition" shall have the same meaning as in paragraph (a)(3) of § 1.1245-1. "Section 1250 property" is, in general, depreciable real property other than section 1245 property. See paragraph (e) of this section. See paragraph (d)(1) of this section for meaning of the term "applicable percentage." If, however, the property is considered to have 2 or more elements with separate periods (for example, because units thereof are placed in service on different dates, improvements are made to the

property, or because of the application of paragraph (h) of § 1.1250-3), see the special rules of § 1.1250-5.

(ii) For purposes of applying section 1250, the facts and circumstances of each disposition shall be considered in determining what is the appropriate item of section 1250 property. In general, a building is an item of section 1250 property, but in an appropriate case more than one building may be treated as a single item. For example, if two or more buildings or structures on a single tract or parcel (or contiguous tracts or parcels) of land are operated as an integrated unit (as evidenced by their actual operation, management, financing, and accounting), they may be treated as a single item of section 1250 property. For the manner of determining whether an expenditure shall be treated as an addition to capital account of an item of section 1250 property or as a separate item of section 1250 property, see paragraph (d)(2)(iii) of § 1.1250-5.

(3) *Sale, exchange, or involuntary conversion after December 31, 1969.*—(i) In the case of a disposition of section 1250 property by sale, exchange, or involuntary conversion after December 31, 1969, the gain to which section 1250(a)(1) applies is the applicable percentage for the property (determined under paragraph (d)(1) of this section) multiplied by the lower of (a) the additional depreciation in respect of the property attributable to periods after December 31, 1969, or (b) the excess (referred to as "gain realized") of the amount realized over the adjusted basis of the property.

(ii) In addition to gain recognized under section 1250(a)(1) and subdivision (i) of this subparagraph, gain may also be recognized under section 1250(a)(2) and this subdivision if the gain realized exceeds the additional depreciation attributable to periods after December 31, 1969. In such a case, the amount of gain recognized under section 1250(a)(2) and this subdivision is the applicable percentage for the property (determined under paragraph (d)(2) of this section) multiplied by the lower of (a) the additional depreciation attributable to periods before January 1, 1970, or (b) the excess (referred to as "remaining gain") of the gain realized over the additional depreciation attributable to periods after December 31, 1969.

(iii) The provisions of this subparagraph may be illustrated by the following examples:

Example (1). Section 1250 property which has an adjusted basis of $500,000 is sold for $650,000 after December 31, 1969, and thus the gain realized is $150,000. At the time of the sale the additional depreciation in respect of the property attributable to periods after December 31, 1969, is $190,000 and the applicable percentage is 100 percent (paragraph (d)(1)(i)(e) of this section). Since the gain realized ($150,000), is lower than the additional depreciation

($190,000), the amount of gain recognized as ordinary income under section 1250(a)(1) is $150,000 (that is, 100 percent of $150,000). No gain is recognized under section 1250(a)(2).

Example (2). Section 1250 property which has an adjusted basis of $440,000 is sold for $500,000 on December 31, 1974, and thus the gain realized is $60,000. The property was acquired on March 31, 1966. At the time of the sale, the additional depreciation attributable to periods after December 31, 1969, is $20,000, and the additional depreciation attributable to periods before January 1, 1970, is $60,000. The property qualified as residential rental property for each taxable year ending after December 31, 1969, and the applicable percentage is 95 percent (paragraph (d)(1)(i)(c) of this section). The applicable percentage under paragraph (d)(2) of this section is 15 percent. Since the additional depreciation attributable to periods after December 31, 1969 ($20,000), is lower than the gain realized ($60,000), the amount of gain recognized as ordinary income under section 1250(a)(1) is $19,000 (that is, 95 percent of $20,000). In addition, gain is recognized under section 1250(a)(2) since there is remaining gain of $40,000 (that is, the gain realized ($60,000) minus the additional depreciation attributable to periods after December 31, 1969 ($20,000)). Since the remaining gain of $40,000 is lower than the additional depreciation attributable to periods before January 1, 1970 ($60,000), the amount of gain recognized as ordinary income under section 1250(a)(2) is $6,000 (that is, 15 percent of $40,000). The remaining $35,000 (that is, gain realized $60,000, minus gain recognized under section 1250(a), $25,000) of the gain may be treated as gain from the sale or exchange of property described in section 1231.

(4) *Other dispositions after December 31, 1969.*—(i) In the case of a disposition of section 1250 property after December 31, 1969, other than by way of sale, exchange, or involuntary conversion, the gain to which section 1250(a)(1) applies is the applicable percentage for the property (determined under paragraph (d)(1) of this section) multiplied by the lower of (a) the additional depreciation in respect of the property attributable to periods after December 31, 1969, or (b) the excess (referred to as "potential gain") of the fair market value of the property over its adjusted basis. In addition, if the potential gain exceeds the additional depreciation attributable to periods after December 31, 1969, then the gain to which section 1250(a)(2) applies is the applicable percentage for the property (determined under paragraph (d)(2) of this section) multiplied by the lower of (c) the additional depreciation attributable to periods before January 1, 1970, or (d) the excess (referred to as "remaining potential gain") of the potential gain over the additional depreciation attributable to periods after December 31, 1969. If property is transferred by a corporation to a shareholder for an amount less than its fair market value in a sale or exchange, for purposes of applying section 1250 such transfer shall be treated as a disposition other than by way of a sale, exchange, or involuntary conversion.

(ii) The provisions of this subparagraph may be illustrated by the following examples:

Example (1). Section 1250 property having an adjusted basis of $500,000 and a fair market value of $550,000 is distributed by a corporation to a stockholder in complete liquidation of the corporation after December 31, 1969, and thus the potential gain is $50,000. At the time of the liquidation, the additional depreciation for the property attributable to periods after December 31, 1969, is $80,000 and the applicable percentage is 100 percent (paragraph (d)(1)(i)(e) of this section). Since the potential gain of $50,000 is lower than the additional depreciation attributable to periods after December 31, 1969 ($80,000), the amount of gain recognized as ordinary income under section 1250(a)(1) is $50,000 (that is, 100 percent of $50,000) even though in the absence of section 1250, section 336 would preclude recognition of gain to the corporation.

Example (2). The facts are the same as in example (1) except that the fair market value of the property is $650,000, and thus the potential gain is $150,000. Since the additional depreciation attributable to periods after December 31, 1969 ($80,000), is lower than the potential gain of $150,000, the amount of gain recognized as ordinary income under section (a)(1) is $80,000 (that is, 100 percent of $80,000). In addition, section 1250 (a)(2) applies since there is remaining potential gain of $70,000, that is, potential gain ($150,000) minus additional depreciation attributable to periods after December 31, 1969 ($80,000). The additional depreciation attributable to periods before January 1, 1970, is $90,000 and the applicable percentage under paragraph (d)(2) of this section is 50 percent. Since the remaining potential gain of $70,000 is lower than the additional depreciation attributable to periods before January 1, 1970 ($90,000), the amount of gain recognized as ordinary income under section 1250(a)(2) is $35,000 (that is, 50 percent of $70,000). Thus under section 1250(a), $115,000 (that is, $80,000 under section 1250(a)(1), plus $35,000 under section 1250(a)(2)) is recognized as ordinary income, even though in the absence of section 1250, section 336 would preclude recognition of gain to the corporation.

(5) *Instances of nonapplication.*—(i) Section 1250(a)(1) does not apply to losses. Thus, section 1250(a)(1) does not apply if a loss is realized upon a sale, exchange, or involuntary conversion of property, all of which is considered section 1250 property, nor does the section apply to a disposition of such property other than by way of sale, exchange, or involuntary conversion if at the time of the disposition the fair market value of such property is not greater than its adjusted basis.

(ii) In general, in the case of section 1250 property with a holding period under section 1223 of more than one year, section 1250(a)(1) does not apply if for periods after December 31, 1969, there are no "depreciation adjustments in excess of straight line" (as computed under section 1250(b) and paragraph (b) of § 1.1250-2).

(6) *Allocation rules.*—(i) In the case of the sale, exchange, or involuntary conversion of section 1250 property and nonsection 1250 property in one transaction after December 31, 1969, the total amount realized upon the disposition shall be allocated between the section 1250 property and the other property in proportion to their respective fair market values. Such allocation shall be made in accordance with the principles set forth in paragraph (a)(5) of § 1.1245-1 (relating to allocation between section 1245 property and nonsection 1245 property).

(ii) If an item of section 1250 property has two (or more) applicable percentages because one subdivision of paragraph (d)(1)(i) of this section applies to one portion of the taxpayer's holding period (determined under § 1.1250-4) and another subdivision of such paragraph applies with respect to another such portion, then the gain realized on a sale, exchange, or involuntary conversion, or the potential gain in the case of any other disposition, shall be allocated to each such portion of the taxpayer's holding period after December 31, 1969, in the same proportion as the additional depreciation with respect to such item for such portion bears to the additional depreciation with respect to such item for the entire holding period after December 31, 1969.

(b) *Dispositions before January 1, 1970.*—(1) *Ordinary income.*—In general, section 1250(a)(2) provides that, upon a disposition of an item of section 1250 property after December 31, 1963, and before January 1, 1970, the applicable percentage of the lower of—

(i) The additional depreciation (as defined in § 1.1250-2) attributable to periods before January 1, 1970 in respect of the property, or

(ii) The excess of the amount realized on a sale, exchange, or involuntary conversion (or the fair market value of the property on any other disposition) over the adjusted basis of the property,

shall be treated as gain from the sale or exchange of property which is neither a capital asset nor property described in section 1231 (that is, shall be recognized as ordinary income). The amount of such gain shall be determined separately for each item (see subparagraph (2)(ii) of this paragraph) of section 1250 property. For relation of section 1250 to other provisions, see paragraph (c) of this section.

(2) *Meaning of terms.*—(i) For purposes of section 1250, the term "disposition" shall have the same meaning as in paragraph (a)(3) of

§ 1.1245-1. "Section 1250 property" is, in general, depreciable real property other than section 1245 property. See paragraph (e) of this section. For purposes of this paragraph, the term "applicable percentage" means 100 percent minus 1 percentage point for each full month the property was held after the date on which the property was held 20 full months. See paragraph (d)(2) of this section. If, however, the property is considered to have two or more elements with separate holding periods (for example, because units thereof are placed in service on different dates, or improvements are made to the property), see the special rules of § 1.1250-5.

(ii) For purposes of applying section 1250, the facts and circumstances of each disposition shall be considered in determining what is the appropriate item of section 1250 property. In general, a building is an item of section 1250 property, but in an appropriate case more than one building may be treated as a single item. For manner of determining whether an expenditure shall be treated as an addition to the capital account of an item of section 1250 property or as a separate item of section 1250 property, see paragraph (d)(2)(iii) of § 1.1250-5.

(3) *Sale, exchange, or involuntary conversion before January 1, 1970.*—(i) In the case of a disposition of section 1250 property by a sale, exchange, or involuntary conversion before January 1, 1970, the gain to which section 1250(a)(2) applies is the applicable percentage for the property multiplied by the lower of (a) the additional depreciation in respect of the property or (b) the excess (referred to as "gain realized") of the amount realized over the adjusted basis of the property.

(ii) The provisions of this subparagraph may be illustrated by the following example:

Example. Section 1250 property, which has an adjusted basis of $200,000, is sold for $290,000 before January 1, 1970. At the time of the sale the additional depreciation in respect of the property is $130,000 and the applicable percentage is 60 percent. Since the gain realized ($90,000, that is, amount realized, $290,000, minus adjusted basis, $200,000) is lower than the additional depreciation ($130,000), the amount of gain recognized as ordinary income under section 1250(a)(2) is $54,000 (that is, 60 percent of $90,000). The remaining $36,000 ($90,000 minus $54,000) of the gain may be treated as gain from the sale or exchange of property described in section 1231.

(4) *Other dispositions before January 1, 1970.*— (i) In the case of a disposition of section 1250 property before January 1, 1970, other than by way of a sale, exchange, or involuntary conversion, the gain to which section 1250(a)(2) applies is the applicable percentage for the property multiplied by the lower of (a) the additional depreciation in respect of the property, or (b) the excess (referred to as "potential gain") of the fair market value of the property on the date of

disposition over its adjusted basis. If property is transferred by a corporation to a shareholder for an amount less than its fair market value in a sale or exchange, for purposes of applying section 1250 such transfer shall be treated as a disposition other than by way of a sale, exchange, or involuntary conversion.

(ii) The provisions of this subparagraph may be illustrated by the following example:

Example. Assume the same facts as in the example in subparagraph (3)(ii) of this paragraph except that the property is distributed by a corporation to a stockholder before January 1, 1970, in complete liquidation of the corporation, and that at the time of the distribution the fair market value of the property is $370,000. Since the additional depreciation ($130,000) is lower than the potential gain of $170,000 (that is, fair market value, $370,000, minus adjusted basis, $200,000), the amount of gain recognized as ordinary income under section 1250(a)(2) is $78,000 (that is, 60 percent of $130,000) even though, in the absence of section 1250, section 336 would preclude recognition of gain to the corporation.

(5) *Instances of nonapplication.*—(i) Section 1250(a)(2) does not apply to losses. Thus, section 1250(a)(2) does not apply if a loss is realized upon a sale, exchange, or involuntary conversion of property, all of which is considered section 1250 property, nor does the section apply to a disposition of such property other than by way of sale, exchange, or involuntary conversion if at the time of the disposition the fair market value of such property is not greater than its adjusted basis.

(ii) In general, in the case of section 1250 property with a holding period under section 1223 of more than one year, section 1250(a)(2) does not apply if for periods after December 31, 1963, there are no "depreciation adjustments in excess of straight line" (as computed under section 1250(b) and paragraph (b) of § 1.1250-2).

(iii) In a case in which section 1250 property (including each element thereof, if any) has a holding period under § 1.1250-4 (or paragraph (a)(2)(ii) of § 1.1250-5) of at least 10 years, section 1250(a)(2) does not apply. If within the 10-year period preceding the date the property is disposed of, an element is added to the property by reason, for example, of an addition to capital account, see § 1.1250-5.

(6) *Allocation rule.*—In the case of a sale, exchange, or involuntary conversion of section 1250 property and nonsection 1250 property in one transaction before January 1, 1970, the total amount realized upon the disposition shall be allocated between the section 1250 property and the other property in proportion to their respective fair market values. Such allocation shall be made in accordance with the principles set forth in paragraph (a)(5) of § 1.1245-1 (relating to allocation between section 1245 property and nonsection 1245 property).

(c) *Relation of section 1250 to other provisions.*—(1) *General.*—The provisions of section 1250 apply notwithstanding any other provision of subtitle A of the Code. See section 1250(i). Thus, unless an exception or limitation under section 1250(d) and § 1.1250-3 applies, gain under section 1250(a) is recognized notwithstanding any contrary nonrecognition provision or income characterizing provision. For example, since section 1250 overrides section 1231 (relating to property used in the trade or business), the gain recognized under section 1250(a) upon a disposition will be treated as ordinary income and only the remaining gain, if any, from the disposition may be considered as gain from the sale or exchange of a capital asset if section 1231 is applicable. See the example in paragraph (b)(3)(ii) of this section.

(2) *Nonrecognition sections overridden.*—The nonrecognition provisions of subtitle A of the Code which section 1250 overrides include, but are not limited to, sections 267(d), 311(a), 336, 337, 501(a), and 512(b)(5). See section 1250(d) for the extent to which section 1250(a) overrides sections 332, 351, 361, 371(a), 374(a), 721, 731, 1031, 1033, 1039, 1071, and 1081(b)(1) and (d)(1)(A). For amount of additional depreciation in respect of property disposed of by an organization exempt from income taxes (within the meaning of section 501 (a)), see paragraph (d)(6) of § 1.1250-2.

(3) *Exempt income.*—The fact that section 1250 provides for recognition of gain as ordinary income does not change into taxable income any income which is exempt under section 115 (relating to income of States, etc.), 892 (relating to income of foreign governments), or 894 (relating to income exempt under treaties).

(4) *Treatment of gain not recognized under section 1250.*—Section 1250 does not prevent gain which is not recognized under section 1250 from being considered as gain under another provision of the Code, such as, for example, section 1239 (relating to gain from sale of depreciable property between certain related persons). Thus, for example, if section 1250 property which has an adjusted basis of $10,000 is sold for $17,500 in a transaction to which section 1239 applies, and if $5,000 of the gain would be recognized under section 1250(a), then the remaining $2,500 of the gain would be treated as ordinary income under section 1239.

(5) *Normal retirement of asset in multiple asset account.*—Section 1250 (a) does not require recognition of gain upon normal retirements of section 1250 property in a multiple asset account as long as the taxpayer's method of accounting, as described in paragraph (e)(2) of § 1.167(a)-8 (relating to accounting treatment of asset retirements), does not require recognition of such gain.

Reg. § 1.1250-1(c)(5)

(6) *Installment method.*—Gain from a disposition to which section 1250(a) applies may be reported under the installment method if such method is otherwise available under section 453 of the Code. In such case, the income (other than interest) on each installment payment shall be deemed to consist of gain to which section 1250(a) applies until all such gain has been reported, and the remaining portion (if any) of such income shall be deemed to consist of other gain. For treatment of amounts as interest on certain deferred payments, see section 483.

(d) *Applicable percentage.*—(1) *Definition for purposes of section 1250(a)(1).*—(i) For purposes of section 1250(a)(1), the term "applicable percentage" means—

(a) In the case of property disposed of pursuant to a written contract which was, on July 24, 1969, and at all times thereafter binding on the owner of the property, 100 percent minus 1 percentage point for each full month the property was held after the date on which the property was held 20 full months;

(b) In the case of property constructed, reconstructed, or acquired by the taxpayer before January 1, 1975, with respect to which a mortgage is insured under section 221(d)(3) or 236 of the National Housing Act, or housing is financed or assisted by direct loan or tax abatement under similar provisions of State or local laws, and with respect to which the owner is subject to the restrictions described in section 1039(b)(1)(B) (relating to approved dispositions of certain Government-assisted housing projects), 100 percent minus one percentage point for each full month of the taxpayer's holding period for the property (determined under § 1.1250-4) during which the property qualified under this sentence, beginning after the date on which the property so qualified for 20 full months.

(c) In the case of residential rental property (as defined in section 167(j)(2)(B)) other than that covered by (a) and (b) of this subdivision, 100 percent minus 1 percentage point for each full month of the taxpayer's holding period for the property (determined under § 1.1250-4) included within a taxable year for which the property qualified as residential rental property, beginning after the date on which the property so qualified for 100 full months.

(d) In the case of property with respect to which a deduction was allowed under section 167(k) (relating to depreciation of expenditures to rehabilitate low-income rental housing), 100 percent minus 1 percentage point for each full month of the taxpayer's holding period (determined under § 1.1250-4) beginning 100 full months after the date on which the property was placed in service.

(e) In the case of all other property, 100 percent.

The provisions of (a), (b), and (c) of this subdivision shall not apply with respect to additional depreciation described in section 1250(b)(4). If the taxpayer's holding period under § 1.1250-4 includes a period before January 1, 1970, such period shall be taken into account in applying each provision of this subdivision.

(ii) A single item of property may have two (or more) applicable percentages under the provisions of subdivision (i) of this subparagraph. For example, if the provision of subdivision (i) which applies to an item of section 1250 property (or to an element of such property if the property is treated as consisting of more than one element under § 1.1250-5) in the taxable year in which the item (or element) is disposed of did not apply to the item (or element) in a prior taxable year which is included within the taxpayer's holding period under § 1.1250-4 and which ends after December 31, 1969, then each provision of subdivision (i) of this subparagraph shall apply only for the period during which the property qualified under such provision.

(iii) If the taxpayer makes rehabilitation expenditures and elects to compute depreciation under section 167(k) with respect to the property attributable to the rehabilitation expenditures, such property will generally constitute a separate improvement under paragraph (c) of § 1.1250-5 and therefore will constitute an element of section 1250 property. For computation of applicable percentage and gain recognized under section 1250(a) in such a case, see paragraph (a) of § 1.1250-5.

(iv) The principles of this subparagraph may be illustrated by the following examples:

Example (1). Section 1250 property is sold on December 31, 1970, pursuant to a written contract which was binding on the owner of the property on July 24, 1969, and at all times thereafter. The property was acquired on July 31, 1968. The applicable percentage for the property under subdivision (i)(a) of this subparagraph is 91 percent, since the property was held for 29 full months.

Example (2). Section 1250 property is sold on June 30, 1978. The property was acquired by a calendar year taxpayer on June 30, 1966. Subdivision (i)(e) of this subparagraph applies to the property in 1977 and 1978. However, subdivision (i)(c) of this subparagraph applied to the property for the taxable years of 1970 through 1976. Thus, the property has two applicable percentages under this subparagraph. The period before January 1, 1970 (42 full months), and the period from 1970 through 1976 (84 full months) are both taken into account in determining the applicable percentage under subdivision (i)(c) of this subparagraph. Thus, the applicable percentage is 74 percent (that is, 100 percent minus the excess of the holding period taken into account (126 full months) over 100 full months). The applicable percentage for the years 1977 and 1978 is 100 percent under subdivision (i)(e) of this subparagraph.

Example (3). Section 1250 property is sold on December 31, 1968. The property was acquired by a calendar year taxpayer on December 31, 1969. The taxpayer made rehabilitation expenditures in 1973 and properly elected to compute depreciation under section 167(k) on the property attributable to the expenditures for the 60-month period beginning on January 1, 1974, the date such property was placed in service. Subdivision (i)(c) applies to the property (other than the property with respect to which a deduction was allowed under section 167(k)) for the taxable years of 1970 through 1978 (108 full months) and the applicable percentage for such property is 92 percent. The applicable percentage for the property with respect to which a deduction under section 167(k) was allowed is 100 percent under subdivision (i)(d) of this subparagraph, since the holding period for purposes of such subdivision begins on the date such property is placed in service.

Example (4). Section 1250 property is sold by a calendar year taxpayer on March 31, 1974. The property was transferred to the taxpayer by gift on December 31, 1970, and under section 1250(e)(2), the taxpayer's holding period for the property for purposes of computing the applicable percentage includes the transferor's holding period of 80 full months. Subdivision (i)(c) of this subparagraph applies to the property in the years 1970 through 1974. The applicable percentage under subdivision (i)(c) of this subparagraph is 81 percent, since the period before January 1, 1970 (68 full months), and that portion of the period after December 31, 1969, during which such subdivision applied (51 full months) are taken into account.

(2) *Definition for purposes of section 1250(a)(2).*—For purposes of section 1250(a)(2), the term "applicable percentage" means—

(i) In case of property with a holding period of 20 full months or less, 100 percent;

(ii) In case of property with a holding period of more than 20 full months but less than 10 years, 100 percent minus 1 percentage point for each full month the property is held after the date on which the property is held 20 full months; and

(iii) In case of property with a holding period of at least 10 years, zero.

(3) *Holding period.*—For purposes of this paragraph, the holding period of property shall be determined under the rules of §1.1250-4, and not under the rules of section 1223, notwithstanding that the property was acquired on or before December 31, 1963. In the case of a disposition of section 1250 property which consists of 2 or more elements (within the meaning of paragraph (c) of §1.1250-5), the holding period for each element shall be determined under the rules of paragraph (a)(2)(ii) of §1.1250-5.

(4) *Full month.*—For purposes of this paragraph, the term "full month" (or "full months") means the period beginning on a date in 1 month and terminating on the date before the corresponding date in the next succeeding month (or in another succeeding month), or, if a particular succeeding month does not have such a corresponding date, terminating on the last day of such particular succeeding month.

(5) *Examples.*—The provisions of this paragraph may be illustrated by the following examples:

Example (1). Property is purchased on January 17, 1959. Under paragraph (b)(1) of §1.1250-4, its holding period begins on January 18, 1959, and thus at any time during the period beginning on October 17, 1960, and ending on November 16, 1960, the property is considered held 21 full months and has an applicable percentage under section 1250(a)(2) of 99 percent. On and after January 17, 1969, the property has a holding period of at least 120 full months (10 years) and, therefore, the applicable percentage under section 1250(a)(2) for the property is zero. Accordingly, no gain would be recognized under section 1250(a)(2) upon disposition of the property. If, however, the property consists of two or more elements, see the special rules of §1.1250-5.

Example (2). Property is purchased on January 31, 1968. Under paragraph (b)(1) of §1.1250-4 its holding period begins on February 1, 1968, and thus at any time during the period beginning on February 29, 1968, and ending on March 30, 1968, the property is considered held 1 full month. At any time during the period beginning on March 31, 1970, and ending on April 29, 1970, the property is considered held 26 full months. At any time during the period beginning on April 30, 1970, and ending on May 30, 1970, the property is considered held 27 full months.

(e) *Section 1250 property.*—(1) *Definition.*—The term "section 1250 property" means any real property (other than section 1245 property, as defined in section 1245(a)(3) and §1.1245-3) which is or has been property of a character subject to the allowance for depreciation provided in section 167. See section 1250(c).

(2) *Character of property.*—For purposes of subparagraph (1) of this paragraph, the term "is or has been property of a character subject to the allowance for depreciation provided in section 167" shall have the same meaning as when used in paragraph (a)(1) and (3) of §1.1245-3. Thus, if a father uses a house in his trade or business during a period after December 31, 1963, and then gives the house to his son as a gift for the son's personal use, the house is section 1250 property in the hands of the son. For exception to the application of section 1250(a) upon disposition of a principal residence, see section 1250(d)(7).

Reg. §1.1250-1(e)(2)

(3) *Real property.*—(i) For purposes of subparagraph (1) of this paragraph, the term "real property" means any property which is not personal property within the meaning of paragraph (b) of §1.1245-3. The term section 1250 property includes three types of depreciable real property. The first type is intangible real property. For purposes of this paragraph, a leasehold of land or of section 1250 property is intangible real property, and accordingly such a leasehold is section 1250 property. However, a fee simple interest in land is not depreciable, and therefore is not section 1250 property. The second type is a building or its structural components within the meaning of paragraph (c) of §1.1245-3. The third type is all other tangible real property except (*a*) "property described in section 1245(a)(3)(B)" as defined in paragraph (c)(1) of §1.1245-3 (relating to property used as an integral part of a specified activity or as a specified facility), and (*b*) property described in section 1245(a)(3)(D). An elevator or escalator (within the meaning of section 1245(a)(3)(C)) is not section 1250 property.

(ii) The provisions of this subparagraph may be illustrated by the following example:

Example. A owns and leases to B for a single lump-sum payment of $100,000 property consisting of land and a fully equipped factory building thereon. If 30 percent of the fair market value of such property is properly allocable to the land, 25 percent to section 1250 property (the building and its structural components), and 45 percent to section 1245 property (the equipment), then 55 percent of B's leasehold is section 1250 property.

(4) *Coordination with definition of section 1245 property.*—(i) Property may lose its character as section 1250 property and become section 1245 property. Thus, for example, if section 1250 property of the third type described in subparagraph (3)(i)(*a*) of this paragraph is converted to use as an integral part of manufacturing, the property would lose its character as section 1250 property and would become section 1245 property. However, once property in the hands of a taxpayer is section 1245 property, it can never become section 1250 property in the hands of such taxpayer. See also paragraph (a)(4) and (5) of §1.1245-2.

(ii) [Reserved]

(f) *Treatment of partnerships and partners.*—If a partnership disposes of section 1250 property, the amount of gain recognized under section 1250(a) by the partnership and by a partner shall be determined in a manner consistent with the principles provided in paragraph (e) of §1.1245-1. Thus, for example, a partner's distributive share of gain recognized by the partnership under section 1250(a) shall be determined in the same manner as his distributive share of gain recognized by the partnership under section 1245(a)(1) is determined, and, if required, additional depreciation in respect of section 1250 property shall be allocated to the partner in the same manner as the adjustments reflected in the adjusted basis of section 1245 property are allocated to the partner. For a further example, if on the date a partner acquires his partnership interest by way of a sale or exchange the partnership owns section 1250 property and an election under section 754 (relating to optional adjustment to basis of partnership property) is in effect with respect to the partnership, then such partner's additional depreciation in respect of such property on such date is deemed to be zero. For limitation on the amount of gain recognized under section 1250(a) in respect of a partnership and for the amount of additional depreciation in respect of partnership property after certain transactions, see paragraph (f) of §1.1250-3. For treatment of section 1250 property as an unrealized receivable, see section 751(c).

(g) *Examples.*—The principles of this section may be illustrated by the following examples:

Example (1). Section 1250 property which has an adjusted basis of $350,000 is sold for $630,000 on December 31, 1984. The property was acquired by a calendar year taxpayer on December 31, 1969. For the taxable years from 1970 through 1980, the property qualified as residential rental property and the applicable percentage for those years is 68 percent (paragraph (d)(1)(i)(*c*) of this section). For taxable years from 1981 through 1984, the property did not qualify as residential rental property and the applicable percentage for those years is 100 percent (paragraph (d)(1)(i)(*e*) of this section). The additional depreciation for the years from 1970 through 1980 is $120,000. The additional depreciation for the years from 1981 through 1984 is $20,000. The gain realized is $280,000 (that is, amount realized, $630,000, minus adjusted basis $350,000). The gain recognized as ordinary income under section 1250(a)(1) is computed in two steps. First, since the additional depreciation attributable to the years 1970 through 1980 ($120,000) is lower than the gain realized attributable to such years determined under paragraph (a)(6) of this section ($240,000, that is, gain realized, $280,000 multiplied by 12/14), the gain recognized as ordinary income under section 1250(a)(1) in the first step is $81,600, that is, 68 percent of $120,000. Second, since the additional depreciation attributable to the years 1981 through 1984 ($20,000) is lower than the gain realized attributable to those years ($40,000, that is, gain realized, $280,000, multiplied by 12/14), the gain recognized as ordinary income under section 1250(a)(1) for the years from 1981 through 1984 is $20,000 (that is, 100 percent of $20,000). The total gain recognized under section 1250(a)(1) is $101,600 (that is, $81,600 plus $20,000).

Example (2). Section 1250 property which has an adjusted basis of $400,000 is sold for $472,000 on December 31, 1978. The property was acquired on December 31, 1966. The additional depreciation attributable to periods before January 1, 1970, is $40,000 and the applicable percentage under paragraph (d)(2) of this section is zero percent. The property qualifies as residential rental property for the years 1970 through 1976, but fails to qualify for 1977 and 1978. Under paragraph (d)(1) of this section, the applicable percentage for the years 1970 through 1976 is 80 percent (paragraph (d)(1)(i)(c) of this section), and the applicable percentage for the years 1977 and 1978 is 100 percent (paragraph (d)(1)(i)(e) of this section). The additional depreciation attributable to the years 1970 through 1976 is $50,000, and the additional depreciation attributable to the years 1977 and 1978 is $10,000. The gain recognized as ordinary income under section 1250(a)(1) is computed in two steps. First, since the additional depreciation attributable to the years 1970 through 1976 ($50,000) is lower than the gain realized attributable to such years ($60,000, that is, $72,000 multiplied by $5/6$), the gain recognized under section 1250(a)(1) in the first step is $40,000 (that is, 80 percent of $50,000). Second, since the additional depreciation attributable to 1977 and 1978 ($10,000) is lower than the gain realized attributable to 1977 and 1978 ($10,000) is lower than the gain realized attributable to such years ($12,000, that is, $72,000 multiplied by $1/6$), the gain realized under section 1250(a)(1) in the second step is $10,000 (that is, 100 percent of $10,000). In addition, section 1250(a)(2) applies. However, since the applicable percentage is zero percent, none of the gain is recognized as ordinary income under section 1250(a)(2). Thus, the remaining $22,000 (that is, gain realized, $72,000, minus gain recognized under section 1250(a), $50,000) of the gain may be treated as gain from the sale or exchange of property described in section 1231.

Example (3). The facts are the same as in example (2) except that the property is disposed of on December 31, 1980. The property qualifies as residential rental property for the years 1979 and 1980. Thus, the applicable percentage for years 1970 through 1976, 1979, and 1980 is 56 percent (paragraph (d)(1)(i)(c) of this section). The applicable percentage for the years 1977 and 1978 is 100 percent (paragraph (d)(1)(i)(e) of this section). The additional depreciation for the years 1979 and 1980 is $8,000. The gain recognized under section 1250(a)(1) is computed in two steps. First, since the additional depreciation attributable to the years 1970 through 1976, 1979, and 1980 ($58,000) is lower than the gain realized attributable to such years ($61,412, that is, $72,000 multiplied by $58,000/$68,000), the gain recognized under section 1250(a)(1) in the first step is $32,480 (that is, 56 percent of $58,000). Second, since the additional depreciation attributable to 1977 and 1978 ($10,000) is lower than the gain realized attributable to such years ($10,588, that is, $72,000 multiplied by $10,000/$68,000) the gain recognized under section 1250(a)(1) in the second step is $10,000 (that is, 100 percent of $10,000). In addition section 1250(a)(2) applies.

However, since the applicable percentage is zero percent, none of the gain is recognized as ordinary income under section 1250(a)(2). Thus, the remaining $29,520 (that is, gain realized, $72,000, minus gain recognized under section 1250(a), $42,480) of the gain may be treated as gain from the sale or exchange of property described in section 1231. [Reg. § 1.1250-1.]

□ *[T.D. 7084, 1-7-71. Amended by T.D. 7193, 6-29-72.]*

[Reg. § 1.1250-2]

§ 1.1250-2. Additional depreciation defined.—(a) *In general.*—(1) *Definition for purposes of section 1250(b)(1).*—Except as otherwise provided in paragraph (e) of this section, for purposes of section 1250(b)(1), the term "additional depreciation" means—

(i) In case of property which at the time of disposition has a holding period under section 1223 of not more than 1 year, the "depreciation adjustments" (as defined in paragraph (d) of this section) in respect of such property for periods after December 31, 1963, and

(ii) In the case of property which at the time of disposition has a holding period under section 1223 of more than 1 year, the depreciation adjustments in excess of straight line for periods after December 31, 1963, computed under paragraph (b)(1) of this section.

(2) *Definition for purposes of section 1250(b)(4).*—Except as otherwise provided in paragraph (e) of this section, for purposes of section 1250(b)(4), the term "additional depreciation" means—

(i) In the case of property with respect to which a deduction under section 167(k) (relating to depreciation of expenditures to rehabilitate low-income rental housing) was allowed, which at the time of disposition has a holding period under section 1223 of not more than 1 year from the time the rehabilitation expenditures were incurred, the "depreciation adjustments" (as defined in paragraph (d) of this section) in respect of the property, and

(ii) In the case of property with respect to which a deduction under section 167(k) (relating to depreciation of expenditures to rehabilitate low-income rental housing) was allowed, which at the time of disposition has a holding period under section 1223 of more than 1 year from the time the rehabilitation expenditures were incurred, the depreciation adjustments in excess of straight line for the property, computed under paragraph (b)(2) of this section.

For purposes of this subparagraph, all rehabilitation expenditures which are incurred in connection with the rehabilitation of an element of section 1250 property shall be considered incurred on the date the last such expenditure is considered incurred under the accrual method of accounting, regardless of the method of accounting used by the taxpayer with regard to other items of income and expense. If the property consists of two or more elements (for example, if the property is placed in service at different times), then each element shall be treated as if it were a separate property and the expenditures attributable to each such element shall be considered incurred on the date the last such expenditure is considered incurred.

(3) *Allocation to certain periods.*—With respect to a taxable year beginning in 1963 and ending in 1964, or beginning in 1969 and ending in 1970, the amount of depreciation adjustments or of depreciation adjustments in excess of straight line (as the case may be) shall be ascertained by applying the principles of paragraph (c)(3) of §1.167(a)-8 (relating to determination of adjusted basis of retired asset), and the amount determined in such manner shall be allocated on a daily basis in order to determine the portion thereof which is attributable to a period after December 31, 1963, or after December 31, 1969, as the case may be.

(b) *Computation of depreciation adjustments in excess of straight line.*—(1) *General rule.*—For purposes of paragraph (a)(1) of this section, depreciation adjustments in excess of straight line shall be, in the case of any property, the excess of (i) the sum of the "depreciation adjustments" (as defined in paragraph (d) of this section) in respect of the property attributable to periods after December 31, 1963, over (ii) the sum such adjustments would have been for such periods if such adjustments had been determined for the entire period the property was held under the straight line method of depreciation (or, if applicable, under the lease-renewal-period provision in paragraph (c) of this section). Depreciation in excess of straight line may arise, for example, if the declining balance method, the sum of the years-digits method, or the units of production method is used, or for another example, if the cost of a leasehold improvement or of a leasehold is depreciated over a period which does not take into account certain renewal periods referred to in paragraph (c) of this section. For computations of depreciation adjustments in excess of straight line (or a deficit therein) both on an annual basis and on the basis of the entire period the property was held, see subparagraph (6) of this paragraph.

(2) *Depreciation under section 167(k).*—For purposes of paragraph (a)(2) of this section, depreciation adjustments in excess of straight line shall be, in the case of any property with respect to which a deduction was allowed under section 167(k) (relating to depreciation of expenditures to rehabilitate low-income rental housing), the excess of (i) the sum of the "depreciation adjustments" (as defined in paragraph (d) of this section) allowed in respect of the property, over (ii) the sum such adjustments would have been if

such adjustments had been determined for the entire period the property was held under the straight line method of depreciation permitted by section 167(b)(1).

(3) *General rule for computing useful life and salvage value.*—For purposes of computing under subparagraph (1)(ii) of this paragraph the sum the depreciation adjustments would have been under the straight line method, if a useful life (or salvage value) was used in determining the amount allowed as a depreciation adjustment for any taxable year, such life (or value) shall be used in determining the amount such depreciation adjustment would have been for such taxable year under the straight line method. If, however, for any taxable year a method of depreciation was used as to which a useful life was not taken into account such as, for example, the units of production method, or as to which salvage value was not taken into account in determining the annual allowances, such as, for example, the declining balance method or the amortization of a leasehold improvement over the term of a lease, then, for the purpose of determining the amount such depreciation adjustment would have been under the straight line method for such taxable year—

(i) There shall be used the useful life (or salvage value) which would have been proper if depreciation had actually been determined under the straight line method throughout the period the property was held, and

(ii) Such useful life (or such salvage value) shall be determined by taking into account for each taxable year the same facts and circumstances as would have been taken into account if the taxpayer had used such method throughout the period the property was held.

(4) *Special rule for computing useful life and salvage value (section 167(k)).*—For purposes of computing under subparagraph (2)(ii) of this paragraph the sum the depreciation adjustments would have been under the straight line method, the useful life and salvage value permitted under section 167(k) shall not apply, the useful life of the property shall be determined under paragraph (b) of §1.167(a)-1 (or, if applicable, under the lease-renewal-period provision of paragraph (c) of this section), and the salvage value of the property shall be determined under paragraph (c) of §1.167(a)-1. Such useful life or salvage value shall be determined by taking into account for each taxable year the same facts and circumstances as would have been taken into account if the taxpayer had used the straight line method permitted under section 167(b)(1) throughout the period the property was held.

(5) *Property held before January 1, 1964.*—In the case of property held before January 1, 1964—

(i) For purposes of computing under subparagraph (1)(ii) of this paragraph the sum the depreciation adjustments would have been under the straight line method, the adjusted basis of the property on such date shall be allowed or allowable before such date had been determined under the straight line method computed in accordance with subparagraph (3) of this paragraph, and

(ii) The depreciation adjustments in excess of straight line in respect of the property computed under subparagraph (1) of this paragraph, but without regard to this subdivision, shall be reduced by the amount of depreciation adjustments less than straight line for periods before January 1, 1964, that is, by the excess (if any) of the sum the depreciation adjustments would have been for periods before January 1, 1964, under the straight line method, over the sum of the depreciation adjustments attributable to periods before such date.

(6) *Determination of additional depreciation in certain cases.*—If an item of section 1250 property is subject to two (or more) applicable percentages, a separate computation of additional depreciation shall be made for the portion of the taxpayer's holding period subject to each such percentage. That is, a separate computation shall be made to determine the excess of (i) the depreciation adjustments (as defined in paragraph (d) of this section) for each such portion of the taxpayer's holding period after December 31, 1963, over (ii) the amount such adjustments would have been for each such portion if such adjustments were determined under the straight line method of depreciation (or, if applicable, under the lease-renewal-period provision in paragraph (c) of this section). Thus, for example, in the case of an item of section 1250 property acquired on January 1, 1968, and disposed of on January 1, 1973, if the applicable percentage for the period before January 1, 1970, were determined under paragraph (d)(2) of § 1.1250-1 and the applicable percentage for the period after December 31,

1969, were determined under paragraph (d)(1)(i)(e) of § 1.1250-1, the additional depreciation would be computed separately for the period before January 1, 1970, and for the period after December 31, 1969. If the additional depreciation attributable to any such portion of the taxpayer's holding period is a deficit (that is, if the depreciation adjustments for that portion are less than the amount such adjustments would have been for that portion if depreciation adjustments were determined for the entire period the property was held under the straight line method of depreciation, or, if applicable, under the lease-renewal-period provision in paragraph (c) of this section), then such deficit will be applied to reduce the additional depreciation for the other portion (or portions) of the taxpayer's holding period. (See examples (4) and (5) of subparagraph (7) of this paragraph.)

(7) *Examples.*—The provisions of this paragraph may be illustrated by the following examples:

Example (1). A calendar year taxpayer sells section 1250 property on January 1, 1968, which he purchased for $10,000 on January 1, 1963. For the period of 1963 through 1967 he computed depreciation deductions in respect of the property under the declining balance method using a rate of 200 percent of the straight line rate and a proper useful life of 10 years. Under such method salvage value is not taken into account in computing annual allowances. For purposes of applying subparagraph (3) of this paragraph, if the taxpayer had used the straight line method for such period, he would have used a salvage value of $1,000, and the depreciation under the straight line method would have been $900 each year, that is, one-tenth of $10,000 minus $1,000. As of January 1, 1968, the additional depreciation for the property is $1,123, as computed in the table below:

Year	Actual depreciation	Straight line	Additional depreciation (deficit)
1963	$2,000	$900	. . .
1964	1,600	900	$700
1965	1,280	900	380
1966	1,024	900	124
1967	819	900	(81)
Sum for periods after Dec. 31, 1963	$4,723	$3,600	$1,123

Example (2). Assume the same facts as in example (1) except that the taxpayer sells the section 1250 property on January 1, 1970. Assume further that as of January 1, 1968, the taxpayer elects under section 167(e)(1) to change to the straight line method. On that date the adjusted basis of the property is $3,277 ($10,000 minus $6,723). He redetermines the remaining useful life of the property to be 8 years and its salvage value to be $77, and thus takes depreciation deductions for 1968 and 1969 of $400 (the amount allowable) for each such year, that is,

one-eighth of $3,200 (that is, $3,277 minus $77). For purposes of applying subparagraph (3) of this paragraph, if he had used the straight line method throughout the period he held the property, the adjusted basis of the property on January 1, 1968, would have been $5,500 ($10,000 minus $4,500), and the depreciation which would have resulted under such method for 1968 and 1969 would have been $678 for each such year, that is, one-eighth of $5,423 ($5,500 minus $77). As of January 1, 1970, the additional depreciation for the property is $567, as computed in the table below:

Years	Depreciation	Straight line	Additional depreciation (deficit)
1964 through 1967	$4,723	$3,600	$1,123
1968	400	678	(278)
1969	400	678	(278)
Sum for periods after Dec. 31, 1963	$5,523	$4,956	$567

Example (3). On January 1, 1978, a calendar year taxpayer sells section 1250 property. The property, which is attributable to rehabilitation expenditures of $50,000 incurred in 1970, was placed in service on January 1, 1971. The taxpayer elected to compute depreciation for the period of 1971 through 1975 under section 167(k). Under such section salvage value is not taken into account in computing annual allowances, and the useful life of the property is deemed to be 5 years. For purposes of applying subparagraph (4) of this paragraph, if the taxpayer had used the straight line method permitted under section 167(b)(1) for such period, he would have used a salvage value of $5,000 and a useful life of 15 years. Depreciation under the straight line method would thus have been $3,000 each year, 1/15 of $45,000 (that is, $50,000 minus $5,000). As of January 1, 1978, the additional depreciation for the property is $29,000, as computed in the table below:

Year	Actual depreciation	Straight line	Additional depreciation (deficit)
1971	$10,000	$3,000	$7,000
1972	10,000	3,000	7,000
1973	10,000	3,000	7,000
1974	10,000	3,000	7,000
1975	10,000	3,000	7,000
1976		3,000	(3,000)
1977		3,000	(3,000)
Total	$50,000	$21,000	$29,000

Example (4). Section 1250 property which has an adjusted basis of $108,000 is sold for $146,000 on December 31, 1972, and thus the gain realized is $38,000. The property was acquired on December 31, 1963. The applicable percentage for the period before January 1, 1970, is 12 percent (paragraph (d)(2) of §1.1250-1) and the applicable percentage for the period after December 31, 1969, is 100 percent (paragraph (d)(1)(i)(e) of §1.1250-1). The additional depreciation must be computed separately for the period before January 1, 1970, and for the period after December 31, 1969. Assume that the additional depreciation for the period before January 1, 1970, is $32,000 and that there is a deficit in additional depreciation of $2,000 for the period after December 31, 1969. Accordingly, the additional depreciation for the period before January 1, 1970 ($32,000) is reduced to $30,000 by the $2,000 deficit in additional depreciation for the period after December 31, 1969. Although section 1250(a)(1) applies to the property, none of the gain is recognized as ordinary income under that section since there is a deficit in additional depreciation for the period after December 31, 1969. Gain is recognized under section 1250(a)(2) since there is remaining gain of $38,000 (that is, gain realized, $38,000, minus the additional depreciation attributable to periods after December 31, 1969, zero). Since the additional depreciation attributable to the period before January 1, 1970 ($30,000), is lower than the gain realized ($38,000), the amount of gain recognized under section 1250(a)(2) is $3,600 (that is, 12 percent of $30,000).

Example (5). Section 1250 property which has an adjusted basis of $207,000 is sold for $267,000 on February 24, 1988, and thus the gain realized is $60,000. The property was acquired on April 30, 1970. The applicable percentage for the period from April 30, 1970, through December 31, 1981, is 60 percent (paragraph (d)(1)(i)(c) of §1.1250-1) and the applicable percentage for the period from January 1, 1982, through February 24, 1988, is 100 percent (paragraph (d)(1)(i)(e) of §1.1250-1). The additional depreciation must be computed separately for the period before January 1, 1982, and for the period after December 31, 1981. Assume that the additional depreciation for the period before January 1, 1982, is $43,000 and that there is a deficit in additional depreciation of $6,000 for the period after December 31, 1981. Accordingly, the addition depreciation for the period before January 1, 1982 ($43,000), is reduced to $37,000 by the $6,000 deficit for the period after December 31, 1981. There is no gain recognized under section 1250(a)(1) for the period after December 31, 1981, since there is a deficit in additional depreciation for that period. The gain recognized under section 1250(a)(1) for the period before January 1, 1982, is $22,200, that is, the lower of the gain realized attributable to that period ($60,000) or the additional depreciation attributable to that period ($37,000), or $37,000, multiplied by 60 percent, the applicable percentage.

Reg. §1.1250-2(b)(7)

(c) *Property held by lessee.*—(1) *Amount depreciation would have been.*—For purposes of paragraph (b) of this section, in case of a leasehold which is section 1250 property, in determining the amount the depreciation adjustments would have been under the straight line method in respect of any building or other improvement (which is section 1250 property) erected or made on the leased property, or in respect of any cost of acquiring the lease, the lease period shall be treated as including all renewal periods. See section 1250(b)(2). For determination of the extent to which a leasehold is section 1250 property, see paragraph (e)(3) of § 1.1250-1.

(2) *Renewal period.*—(i) For purposes of this paragraph, the term "renewal period" means any period for which the lease may be renewed, extended, or continued pursuant to an option or options exercisable by the lessee (whether or not specifically provided for in the lease) except that the inclusion of one or more renewal periods shall not extend the period taken into account by more than two-thirds of the period on the basis of which the depreciation adjustments were allowed.

(ii) In respect of the cost of any building erected (or other improvement made) on the leased property by the lessee, or in respect of the portion of the cost of acquiring a leasehold which is attributable to an existing building (or other improvement) on the leasehold at the time the lessee acquires the leasehold, the inclusion of one or more renewal periods shall not extend the period taken into account to a period which exceeds the useful life remaining, at the time the leasehold is disposed of, of such building (or such other improvement). Determinations under this subdivision shall be made without regard to the proper period under section 167 or 178 for depreciating or amortizing a leasehold acquisition cost or improvement.

(iii) The provisions of this subparagraph may be illustrated by the following example:

Example. Assume that a leasehold improvement with a useful life of 30 years is properly amortized on the basis of a 10-year initial lease term. The lease is renewable for an additional 9 years. The period taken into account is $16^2/3$ years, that is, 10 years plus $2/3$ of 10 years. If, however, the leasehold improvement were disposed of at the end of 12 years, and if its remaining useful life were only 3 years, then the period taken into account would be 15 years.

(d) *Depreciation adjustments.*—(1) *General.*—For purposes of this section, the term "depreciation adjustments" means, in respect of any property, all adjustments reflected in the adjusted basis of such property on account of deductions described in subparagraph (2) of this paragraph allowed or allowable (whether in respect of the same or other property) to the taxpayer or to any other person. For cases where the taxpayer can establish that the amount allowed for any period

was less than the amount allowable, see subparagraph (4) of this paragraph. For determination of adjusted basis of property in a multiple asset account, see paragraph (c)(3) of § 1.167(a)-8. The term "depreciation adjustments" as used in this section does not have the same meaning as the term "adjustments reflected in the adjusted basis" as defined in paragraph (a)(2) of § 1.1245-2.

(2) *Deductions.*—The deductions described in this subparagraph are allowances (and amounts treated as allowances) for depreciation or amortization (other than amortization under section 168, 169 (as enacted by section 704(a), Tax Reform Act of 1969 (83 Stat. 667)), or 185). Thus, for example, such deductions include a reasonable allowance for exhaustion, wear, and tear (including a reasonable allowance for obsolescence) under section 167, the periodic deductions referred to in § 1.162-11 in respect of a specified sum paid for the acquisition of a leasehold and in respect of the cost to a lessee of improvements on property of which he is the lessee. However, such deductions do not include deductions for the periodic payment of rent.

(3) *Depreciation of other taxpayers or in respect of other property.*—(i) The depreciation adjustments (reflected in the adjusted basis) referred to in subparagraph (1) of this paragraph (*a*) are not limited to adjustments with respect to the property disposed of, nor to those allowed or allowable to the taxpayer disposing of such property, and (*b*) except as provided in subparagraph (4) of this paragraph, are taken into account, whether allowed or allowable in respect of the same or other property and whether to the taxpayer or to any other person. For manner of determining the amount of additional depreciation after certain dispositions, see paragraph (e) of this section.

(ii) The provisions of this subparagraph may be illustrated by the following example:

Example. On January 1, 1966, a calendar year taxpayer purchases for $100,000 a building for use in his trade or business. He takes depreciation deductions of $20,000 (the amount allowable), of which $3,000 is additional depreciation, and transfers the building to his son as a gift on January 1, 1968. Since the exception for gifts in section 1250(d)(1) applies, the taxpayer does not recognize gain under section 1250(a)(2). In the son's adjusted basis of $80,000 for the building there is reflected $3,000 of additional depreciation. On January 1, 1969, after taking a depreciation deduction of $10,000 (the amount allowable), of which $1,000 is additional depreciation, the son sells the building. At the time of the sale the additional depreciation is $4,000 ($3,000 allowed the father plus $1,000 allowed the son).

(4) *Depreciation allowed or allowable.*—(i) For purposes of subparagraph (1) of this paragraph, generally all deductions (described in subpara-

graph (2) of this paragraph) allowed or allowable shall be taken into account. See section 1016(a)(2) and the regulations thereunder for the meaning of "allowed" and "allowable." However, if a taxpayer can establish by adequate records or other sufficient evidence that the amount allowed for any period was less than the amount allowable for such period, the amount to be taken into account for such period shall be the amount allowed. The preceding sentence shall not apply for purposes of computing under paragraph (b)(1)(ii) of this section the amount such deductions would have been under the straight line method.

(ii) The provisions of subdivision (i) of this subparagraph may be illustrated by the following example:

Example. In the year 1969 it becomes necessary to determine the additional depreciation in respect of section 1250 property, the adjusted basis of which reflects a depreciation adjustment of $1,000 with respect to depreciation deductions allowable for the calendar year 1965 under the sum of the years-digits method. Under paragraph (b)(1)(ii) of this section, the depreciation which would have resulted under the straight line method for 1965 is $800. If the taxpayer can establish by adequate records or other sufficient evidence that he did not take, and was not allowed, any deduction for depreciation in respect of the property in 1965, then, for purposes of computing the depreciation adjustments in excess of straight line in respect of the property, the amount to be taken into account for 1965 as allowed or allowable is zero, and the amount to be taken into account in computing deductions which would have resulted under the straight line method in 1965 is $800. Thus, in effect, there is a deficit in additional depreciation for 1965 of $800.

(5) *Retired or demolished property.*—Depreciation adjustments referred to in subparagraph (1) of this paragraph generally do not include adjustments in respect of retired or demolished portions of an item of section 1250 property. If a retired or demolished portion is replaced in a disposition described in section 1250(d)(4)(A) (relating to like kind exchanges and involuntary conversions), see paragraph (d)(7) of § 1.1250-3.

(6) *Exempt organization.*—In respect of property disposed of by an organization which is or was exempt from income taxes (within the meaning of section 501(a)), the depreciation adjustments (reflected in the adjusted basis) referred to in subparagraph (1) of this paragraph shall include only adjustments allowed or allowable (i) in computing unrelated business taxable income (as defined in section 512(a)), or (ii) in computing taxable income of the organization for a period during which it was not exempt or, by reason of the application of section 502, 503, or 504, was denied its exemption.

(e) *Additional depreciation immediately after certain acquisitions.*—(1) *Zero.*—If on the date a person acquires property his basis for the property is determined solely (i) by reference to its cost (within the meaning of sec. 1012), (ii) by reason of the application of section 301(d) (relating to basis of property received in corporate distribution) or section 334(a) (relating to basis of property received in a liquidation in which gain or loss is recognized), or (iii) under the rules of section 334(b)(2) or (c) (relating to basis of property received in certain corporate liquidations), then on such date the additional depreciation for the property is zero.

(2) *Transactions referred to in section 1250(d).*—In the case of property acquired in a disposition described in section 1250(d) (relating to exceptions and limitations to application of section 1250), additional depreciation shall be computed in accordance with the rules prescribed in § 1.1250-3.

(f) *Records to be kept and information to be filed.*—(1) *Records to be kept.*—In any case in which it is necessary to determine the additional depreciation of an item of section 1250 property, the taxpayer shall have available permanent records of all the facts necessary to determine with reasonable accuracy the amount of such additional depreciation, including the following—

(i) The date, and the manner in which, the property was acquired,

(ii) The taxpayer's basis on the date the property was acquired and the manner in which the basis was determined,

(iii) The amount and date of all adjustments to the basis of the property allowed or allowable to the taxpayer for depreciation adjustments referred to in paragraph (d)(1) of this section and the amount and date of any other adjustments by the taxpayer to the basis of the property, and

(iv) In the case of section 1250 property which has an adjusted basis reflecting depreciation adjustments referred to in paragraph (d)(1) of this section taken by the taxpayer with respect to other property, or by another taxpayer with respect to the same or other property, the information described in subdivisions (i), (ii), and (iii) of this subparagraph with respect to such other property or such other taxpayer.

(2) *Information to be filed.*—If a taxpayer acquires in a transaction (other than a like kind exchange or involuntary conversion described in section 1250(d)(4)) section 1250 property which has a basis reflecting depreciation adjustments referred to in paragraph (d)(1) of this section allowed or allowable to another taxpayer, then the taxpayer shall file with its income tax return or information return for the taxable year in which the property is acquired a statement showing all information described in subpara-

Reg. § 1.1250-2(d)(4)(ii)

graph (1) of this paragraph. See section 6012 (relating to person required to make returns of income) and part III of subchapter A of chapter 61 of the Code (relating to information returns). [Reg. § 1.1250-2.]

☐ [*T.D. 7084, 1-7-71. Amended by T.D. 7193, 6-29-72.*]

[Reg. § 1.1250-3]

§ 1.1250-3. Exceptions and limitations.— (a) *Exception for gifts.*—(1) *General rule.*—Section 1250(d)(1) provides that no gain shall be recognized under section 1250(a) upon a disposition by gift. For purposes of this paragraph, the term "gift" shall have the same meaning as in paragraph (a) of § 1.1245-4. For reduction in amount of charitable contribution in case of a gift of section 1250 property, see section 170(e) and paragraph (c)(3) of § 1.170-1.

(2) *Disposition in part a sale or exchange and in part a gift.*—Where a disposition of property is in part a sale or exchange and in part a gift, the disposition shall be subject to the provisions of § 1.1250-1 and the gain to which section 1250(a) applies, shall be computed under that section.

(3) *Treatment of property in hands of transferee.*—If property is disposed of in a transaction which is a gift—

(i) The additional depreciation for the property in the hands of the transferee immediately after the disposition shall be an amount equal to (*a*) the amount of the additional depreciation for the property in the hands of the transferor immediately before the disposition, minus (*b*) the amount of any gain (in case the disposition is in part a sale or exchange and in part a gift) which would have been taken into account under section 1250(a) by the transferor upon the disposition if the applicable percentage had been 100 percent,

(ii) For purposes of computing the applicable percentage, the holding period under section 1250(e)(2) of property received as a gift in the hands of the transferee includes the transferor's holding period,

(iii) In case of a disposition which is in part a sale or exchange and in part a gift, if the adjusted basis of the property in the hands of the transferee exceeds its adjusted basis immediately before the transfer, the excess is an addition to capital account under paragraph (d)(2)(ii) of § 1.1250-5 (relating to property with two or more elements), and

(iv) If the property disposed of consists of two or more elements within the meaning of paragraph (c) of § 1.1250-5, see paragraph (e)(1) of § 1.1250-5 for the amount of additional depreciation and holding period for each element in the hands of the transferee.

(4) *Examples.*—The provisions of this paragraph may be illustrated by the following examples:

Example (1). (i) On May 15, 1967, Smith transfers section 1250 property to his son for $45,000. In the hands of Smith the property had an adjusted basis of $40,000 and a fair market value of $70,000. Thus, the gain realized is $5,000 (amount realized, $45,000, minus adjusted basis, $40,000), and Smith has made a gift of $25,000 (fair market value, $70,000, minus amount realized, $45,000).

(ii) Smith's holding period for the property is 80 full months and, thus, the applicable percentage under section 1250(a)(2) is 40 percent. The additional depreciation for the property is $10,000. Since the gain realized ($5,000) is lower than the additional depreciation ($10,000), Smith recognized as ordinary income under section 1250(a)(2) gain of $2,000 (that is, applicable percentage, 40 percent, multiplied by gain realized, $5,000) and the $3,000 remaining portion of the gain realized may be treated as gain from the sale of property described in section 1231.

(iii) On the date the son receives the property, the additional depreciation for the property in his hands is $5,000, that is, the additional depreciation for the property in the hands of the father immediately before the transfer ($10,000), minus the gain which would have been recognized under section 1250(a)(2) upon the transfer if the applicable percentage had been 100 percent ($5,000); for purposes of computing applicable percentage his holding period is his father's holding period of 80 full months; and under § 1.1015-4 his unadjusted basis for the property is $45,000, that is, the amount he paid ($45,000) plus the excess (zero) of his father's adjusted basis over such amount.

(iv) The son sells the property for $80,000 on March 15, 1968, 10 full months after he received it from his father. Thus, his holding period is 90 full months (his father's holding period of 80 full months plus the 10 full months the son actually owned the property) and the applicable percentage under section 1250(a)(2) is 30 percent. Assume that no depreciation was allowed or allowable to the son. Thus, the son's adjusted basis and additional depreciation for the property on the date of the sale is the same as on the date he received it. Accordingly, the gain realized is $35,000 (selling price of $80,000, minus adjusted basis of $45,000). Since the additional depreciation ($5,000) is lower than the gain realized ($35,000), the son recognizes as ordinary income under section 1250(a)(2) gain of $1,500, that is, applicable percentage (30 percent) multiplied by additional depreciation ($5,000).

Example (2). Assume the same facts as in example (1), except that the son sells the property on June 15, 1969, 25 full months after he received it from his father. Thus, his holding period is 105 full months (his father's holding period of 80 full months plus the 25 full months the son actually owned the property) and the applicable percentage under section 1250(a)(2) is 15 percent. Assume further that on the date of the sale the adjusted basis of the property is $39,000, and that for the period the son actually owned the property there is a deficit in additional depreciation of $2,000. Accordingly, the gain realized is $41,000 (selling price of $80,000, minus adjusted basis of $39,000), and the additional depreciation for the property is $3,000 (that is, the additional depreciation for the property in the hands of the son on the date he received it, as determined in example (1), $5,000, minus the amount of the deficit in additional depreciation for the period the son actually owned the property, $2,000). Since the additional depreciation ($3,000) is lower than the gain realized ($41,000), the son recognizes as ordinary income under section 1250(a)(2) gain of $450, that is, applicable percentage (15 percent) multiplied by additional depreciation ($3,000).

(b) *Exception for transfers at death.*—(1) *General rule.*—Section 1250(d)(2) provides that, except as provided in section 691 (relating to income in respect of a decedent), no gain shall be recognized under section 1250(a) upon a transfer at death. For purposes of this paragraph, the term "transfer at death" shall have the same meaning as in paragraph (b) of § 1.1245-4.

(2) *Treatment of transferee.*—(i) If as of the date a person acquires property from a decedent such person's basis is determined, by reason of the application of section 1014(a), solely by reference to the fair market value of the property on the date of the decedent's death or on the applicable date provided in section 2032 (relating to alternate valuation date), then (*a*) on the date of death the additional depreciation for the property is zero, and (*b*) for purposes of computing applicable percentage the holding period of the property under section 1250(e)(1)(A) is deemed to begin on the day after the date of death.

(ii) If property is acquired in a transfer at death to which section 1250(d)(2) applies, the amount of the additional depreciation for the property in the hands of the transferee immediately after the transfer shall be the amount (if any) of the additional depreciation in respect of the property allowed the transferee before the decedent's death, but only to the extent that the basis of the property (determined under section 1014(a)) is required to be reduced under the second sentence of section 1014(b)(9) (relating to adjustments to basis where property is acquired from a decedent prior to his death) by depreciation adjustments referred to in paragraph (d)(1) of § 1.1250-2 which give rise to such additional depreciation. For treatment of such property as having a special element with additional depreciation so computed, see paragraph (c)(5)(i) of § 1.1250-5 (relating to property with two or more elements). For purposes of determining applicable percentage, such special element shall have a

holding period which includes the transferee's holding period for such property for the period before the decedent's death.

(3) *Examples.*—The provisions of this paragraph may be illustrated by the following examples:

Example (1). On March 6, 1966, Smith dies owning an item of section 1250 property. On March 7, 1968, the executor distributes the property to Smith's son pursuant to a specific bequest of the property in Smith's will. Under section 1014(a)(2) and paragraph (a)(2) of § 1.1014-4, the unadjusted basis of the property in the hands of the son is its fair market value on March 6, 1966 (the date Smith died), and the son is considered to have acquired the property on such date. Under section 1250(e)(1)(A), the son's holding period for the property begins on March 7, 1966 (the day after the day he is considered to have acquired the property). Thus, on March 7, 1968 (the date the property was distributed to the son), the holding period for the property is 24 full months, and the applicable percentage under section 1250 (a)(2) is 96 percent. On such date, the additional depreciation for the property includes any additional depreciation in respect of the property for the period the property was possessed by the estate.

Example (2). H purchases section 1250 property in 1965 which he immediately conveys to himself and W, his wife, as tenants by the entirety. Under local law each spouse is entitled to one-half the income from the property. H and W file joint income tax returns for calendar years 1965, 1966, and 1967. Over the 3 years, depreciation allowed in respect of the property was $4,000 (the amount allowable) of which $500 is additional depreciation. One-half of these amounts are allocable to W. Thus, depreciation deductions of $2,000, of which $250 is additional depreciation, are allowable to W. On January 1, 1968, H dies and the entire value of the property at the date of death is included in H's gross estate. Since W's basis for the property (determined under section 1014(a)) is reduced (under the second sentence of section 1014(b)(9)) by the $2,000 depreciation deductions allowed W before H's death of which $250 is additional depreciation, the additional depreciation for the property in the hands of W immediately after H's death is $250.

(c) *Limitations for certain tax-free transactions.*—(1) *General.*—Section 1250(d)(3) provides that upon a transfer of property described in subparagraph (2) of this paragraph, the amount of gain taken into account by the transferor under section 1250(a) shall not exceed the amount of gain recognized to the transferor on the transfer (determined without regard to section 1250). For purposes of this subparagraph, in case of a transfer of both section 1250 property and nonsection 1250 property in one transaction, the amount realized from the disposition of the section 1250 property shall be deemed to consist of that portion of the fair market value of each property acquired which bears the same ratio to the fair market value of such acquired property as the amount realized from the disposition of the section 1250 property bears to the total amount realized. The preceding sentence shall be applied solely for purposes of computing the portion of the total gain (determined without regard to section 1250) which shall be recognized as ordinary income under section 1250(a). Section 1250(d)(3) does not apply to a disposition of property to an organization (other than a cooperative described in section 521) which is exempt from the tax imposed by chapter 1 of the Code.

(2) *Transfers covered.*—The transfers described in this subparagraph are transfers of property in which the basis of the property in the hands of the transferee is determined by reference to its basis in the hands of the transferor by reason of the application of any of the following provisions:

(i) Section 332 (relating to distributions in complete liquidation of an 80 percent or more controlled subsidiary corporation). For application of section 1250(d)(3) to such a complete liquidation, the principles of paragraph (c)(3) of § 1.1245-4 shall apply.

(ii) Section 351 (relating to transfer to a corporation controlled by transferor).

(iii) Section 361 (relating to exchanges pursuant to certain corporate reorganizations).

(iv) Section 371(a) (relating to exchanges pursuant to certain receivership and bankruptcy proceedings).

(v) Section 374(a) (relating to exchanges pursuant to certain railroad reorganizations).

(vi) Section 721 (relating to transfers to a partnership in exchange for a partnership interest).

(vii) Section 731 (relating to distributions by a partnership to a partner). For special carryover basis rule, see section 1250(d)(6)(A) and paragraph (f)(1) of this section.

(3) *Treatment of property in hands of transferee.*—In the case of a transfer described in subparagraph (2) (other than subdivision (vii) thereof) of this paragraph—

(i) The additional depreciation for the property in the hands of the transferee immediately after the disposition shall be an amount equal to (*a*) the amount of the additional depreciation for the property in the hands of the transferor immediately before the disposition, minus (*b*) the amount of additional depreciation necessary to produce an amount equal to the gain taken into account under section 1250(a) by the transferor upon the disposition (taking into account the applicable percentage for the property),

(ii) For purposes of computing applicable percentage, the holding period under section

1250(e)(2) of the property in the hands of the transferee includes the transferor's holding period,

(iii) If the adjusted basis of the property in the hands of the transferee exceeds its adjusted basis immediately before the transfer, the excess is an addition to capital account under paragraph (d)(2)(ii) of § 1.1250-5 (relating to property with 2 or more elements), and

(iv) If the property disposed of consists of 2 or more elements within the meaning of paragraph (c) of § 1.1250-5, see paragraph (e)(1) of § 1.1250-5 for the amount of additional depreciation and the holding period for each element in the hands of the transferee.

(4) *Examples.*—The provisions of this paragraph may be illustrated by the following examples:

Example (1). (i) Green transfers section 1250 property on March 1, 1968 to a corporation, which is not exempt from taxation, in exchange for cash of $9,000 and stock in the corporation worth $91,000, in a transaction qualifying under section 351. Thus the amount realized is $100,000 ($9,000 plus $91,000). The property has an applicable percentage under section 1250(a)(2) of 60 percent, an adjusted basis of $40,000, and additional depreciation of $20,000. The gain realized is $60,000, that is, amount realized ($100,000) minus adjusted basis ($40,000). Since the additional depreciation ($20,000) is lower than the gain realized ($60,000), the amount of gain which would be treated as ordinary income under section 1250(a)(2) would be $12,000 (60 percent of $20,000) if the limitation provided in section 1250(d)(3) did not apply. Since under section 351(b) gain in the amount of $9,000 would be recognized to the transferor without regard to section 1250, the limitation provided in section 1250(d)(3) limits the gain taken into account by the transferor under section 1250(a)(2) to $9,000.

(ii) The amount of additional depreciation for the property in the hands of the transferee immediately after the transfer is $5,000, that is, the amount of additional depreciation before the transfer ($20,000) minus the amount of additional depreciation necessary to produce an amount equal to the gain recognized under section 1250(a)(2) upon the transfer ($15,000, that is, $9,000 gain recognized divided by 60 percent, the applicable percentage). (If the property is subsequently disposed of, and for the period after the initial transfer there is additional depreciation in respect of the property, then at the time of the subsequent disposition the additional depreciation will exceed $5,000. If, however, for the period after the initial transfer there was a deficit in additional depreciation, then at the time of the subsequent disposition the additional depreciation would be less than $5,000.)

Example (2). (i) Assume the same facts as in example (1) except that the additional depreciation is $10,000. Since additional depreciation

($10,000) is lower than the gain realized ($60,000), the amount of gain which would be treated as ordinary income under section 1250(a)(2) would be $6,000 (60 percent of $10,000) if the limitation provided in section 1250(d)(3) did not apply. Since under section 351(b) gain in the amount of $9,000 would be recognized to the transferor without regard to section 1250, the limitation under section 1250(d)(3) does not prevent treatment of the entire $6,000 as ordinary income under section 1250(a)(2). The $3,000 remaining portion of the $9,000 gain may be treated as gain from the sale of property described in section 1231.

(ii) Immediately after the transfer, the amount of additional depreciation is zero, that is, the amount of additional depreciation before the transfer ($10,000) minus the amount of additional depreciation necessary to produce an amount equal to the gain taken into account under section 1250(a)(2) upon the transfer ($10,000), that is, $6,000 divided by 60 percent.

Example (3). (i) Miller transfers section 1250 property after December 31, 1969, to a corporation, which is not exempt from taxation, in exchange for cash of $9,000 and stock in the corporation worth $31,000, in a transaction qualifying under section 351. Thus, the amount realized is $40,000 ($9,000 plus $31,000). The property has an applicable percentage under paragraph (d)(1)(i)(*e*) of this section of 100 percent and an applicable percentage under paragraph (d)(2) of this section of 50 percent. The adjusted basis of the property on the date of the transfer is $24,000, and the gain realized is $16,000 (that is, amount realized, $40,000, minus adjusted basis, $24,000). The additional depreciation attributable to periods after December 31, 1969, is $8,000 and the additional depreciation attributable to periods before January 1, 1970, is $12,000. Since the additional depreciation attributable to periods after December 31, 1969 ($8,000), is lower than the gain realized ($16,000), the amount of gain which would be recognized as ordinary income under section 1250(a)(1) would be $8,000 (100 percent of $8,000) if the limitation provided in section 1250(d)(3) did not apply. In addition, gain is recognized under section 1250(a)(2) since there is a remaining potential gain of $8,000 (that is, gain realized, $16,000, minus additional depreciation attributable to periods after December 31, 1969 ($8,000)). Since the remaining potential gain ($8,000) is lower than the additional depreciation attributable to periods before January 1, 1970 ($12,000), the amount of gain which would be recognized under section 1250(a)(2) would be $4,000 (50 percent of $8,000) if the limitation in section 1250(d)(3) did not apply. Since under section 351(b) gain in the amount of $9,000 would be recognized to the transferor without regard to section 1250, the limitation in section 1250(d)(3) limits the gain taken into account by the transferor under sec-

tion 1250(a) to $9,000. Since the section 1250(a)(1) gain is considered as recognized first under paragraph (a)(1)(iii) of § 1.1250-1, of the $9,000 of gain recognized, $8,000 is recognized under section 1250(a)(1) and $1,000 is recognized under section 1250(a)(2).

(ii) The amount of additional depreciation for the property in the hands of the transferee immediately after the transfer is $10,000, the amount of additional depreciation immediately before the transfer ($20,000), minus the sum of (*a*) the amount of additional depreciation necessary to produce an amount equal to the gain recognized under section 1250(a)(1) upon the transfer, $8,000 (that is, gain recognized under section 1250(a)(1), $8,000, divided by 100 percent, the applicable percentage under section 1250(a)(1)), plus (*b*) the amount of additional depreciation necessary to produce an amount equal to the gain recognized under section 1250(a)(2) upon the transfer, $2,000 (that is, gain recognized under section 1250(a)(2), $1,000, divided by 50 percent, the applicable percentage under section 1250(a)(2)). Of this amount, zero (that is, $8,000 minus $8,000) is attributable to periods after December 31, 1969, and $10,000 ($12,000 minus $2,000) is attributable to periods before January 1, 1970.

(d) *Limitation for like kind exchanges and involuntary conversions.*—(1) *Limitation on gain.*—(i) Under section 1250(d)(4)(A), if property is disposed of and gain (determined without regard to section 1250) is not recognized in whole or in part under section 1031 (relating to like kind exchanges) or section 1033 (relating to involuntary conversions), then the amount of gain taken into account by the transferor under section 1250(a) shall not exceed the greater of the two limitations set forth in subdivisions (ii) and (iii) of this subparagraph. Immediately after the transfer the basis of the acquired property shall be determined under subparagraph (2), (3), or (4) (whichever is applicable) of this paragraph, and its additional depreciation shall be computed under subparagraph (5) of this paragraph. The holding period of the acquired property for purposes of computing applicable percentage, which is determined under section 1250(e)(1), does not include the holding period of the property disposed of. In the case of a disposition of section 1250 property and other property in one transaction, see subparagraph (6) of this paragraph. In case of a disposition described in section 1250(d)(4)(A) of a portion of this item of property, see subparagraph (7) of this paragraph.

(ii) For purposes of this subparagraph, the first limitation is the sum of—

(*a*) The amount of gain recognized on the disposition under section 1031 or 1033 (determined without regard to section 1250), plus

(*b*) An amount equal to the cost of any stock purchased in a corporation which (without regard to section 1250) would result in nonrecognition of gain under section 1033(a)(3)(A).

(iii) For purposes of this subparagraph, the second limitation is the excess (if any) of—

(a) The amount of gain which would (without regard to section 1250(d)(4)) be taken into account under section 1250(a), over

(b) The fair market value (or cost in the case of a transaction described in section 1033(a)(3)) of the section 1250 property acquired in the transaction.

(iv) The provisions of this subparagraph may be illustrated by the following example:

Example. A taxpayer receives $96,000 of insurance proceeds upon the destruction of section 1250 property by fire. If section 1250(d)(4)(A) did not apply to the disposition, $16,000 of gain would be recognized under section 1250(a). In acquisitions qualifying under

section 1033(a)(3)(A), he uses $90,000 of the proceeds to purchase property similar or related in service or use to the property destroyed, of which $42,000 is for one item of section 1250 property and $48,000 is for one piece of land, and $5,000 of the proceeds to purchase stock in the acquisition of control of a corporation owning property similar or related in service or use to the property destroyed. The taxpayer properly elects under section 1033(a)(3)(A) and the regulations thereunder to limit recognition of gain (determined without regard to section 1250) to $1,000, that is, the excess of the amount realized from the conversion ($96,000) over the cost of the property acquired in acquisitions qualifying under section 1033(a)(3)(A) ($95,000, that is, $90,000 plus $5,000). The amount of gain recognized under section 1250(a) is $6,000, determined in the following manner:

The first limitation:

(a) Amount of gain recognized under section 1033(a)(3), determined without regard to section 1250(a)	$1,000
(b) Fair market value of stock in a corporation which qualifies under section 1033(a)(3)(A)	5,000
(c) Sum of (a) plus (b)	$6,000

The second limitation:

(d) Amount of gain which would be recognized under section 1250(a) if section 1250(d)(4) did not apply	$16,000
(e) Cost of section 1250 property acquired in transaction	42,000
(f) Excess of (d) over (e)	$0

Since the first limitation ($6,000) exceeds the second limitation (zero), the amount of gain recognized under section 1250(a) is $6,000. The balance ($10,000) of the gain realized ($16,000) is not recognized.

(2) *Basis of property purchased upon involuntary conversion into money.*—(i) If section 1250 property is purchased in a compulsory or involuntary conversion to which section 1033(a)(3) applies, and if by reason of the application of section 1250(d)(4)(A) all or part of the gain computed under section 1250(a) is not taken into account, then the basis of the section 1250 property and other purchased property shall be determined under the rules prescribed in this subparagraph. See section 1250(d)(4)(D).

(ii) The total basis of all purchased property, the acquisition of which results in the nonrecognition of any part of the gain realized upon the transaction, shall be (a) its cost, reduced by (b) the portion of the total gain realized which was not recognized. To the extent that section 1250(d)(4)(A)(i) prevents the purchase of stock from resulting in nonrecognition of gain, the basis of purchased stock is its cost.

(iii) If purchased property consists of both section 1250 property and other property, the total basis computed under subdivision (ii) of this subparagraph shall be allocated between the section 1250 property (treated as a class) and the other property (treated as a class) in propor-

tion to their respective costs, except that for purposes of this subdivision (but not subdivision (iv) of this subparagraph) the cost of the section 1250 property shall be deemed to be the excess of (a) its actual cost, over (b) the gain not taken into account under section 1250(a) by reason of the application of section 1250(d)(4)(A).

(iv) If the property acquired consists of more than one item of section 1250 property (or of more than one item of other property), the total basis of the section 1250 property (or of the other property), as computed under subdivisions (ii) and (iii) of this subparagraph, shall be allocated to each item of section 1250 property (or other property) in proportion to their respective actual costs.

(v) The provisions of this subparagraph may be illustrated by the following examples:

Example (1). Assume the same facts as in the example in subparagraph (1)(iv) of this paragraph. Assume further that the portion of the gain realized which was not recognized under section 1033(a)(3) or 1250(a) upon the transaction is $60,000, of which the gain computed under section 1250(a) which is not taken into account by reason of the application of section 1250(d)(4)(A) is $10,000, that is, the excess of the gain which would have been recognized under section 1250(a) if section 1250(d)(4)(A) did not apply ($16,000) over the gain recognized under section 1250(a) ($6,000). In such example $95,000 of proceeds were used to purchase property in

Reg. §1.1250-3(d)(2)(v)

acquisitions qualifying under section 1033(a)(3)(A) of which $42,000 was for section 1250 property, $48,000 for land, and $5,000 for stock in a corporation. The basis of each acquired property is determined in the following manner:

(a) Under subdivision (ii) of this subparagraph, the total basis of the acquired properties (other than the stock) is $30,000, that is, their cost ($90,000, of which $42,000 is for section 1250 property and $48,000 is for land), reduced by the portion of the total gain realized which was not recognized ($60,000).

(b) Under subdivision (iii) of this subparagraph, such total basis is allocated between the section 1250 property and the land in proportion to their respective costs, and for this purpose the cost of the section 1250 property is considered to be $32,000, that is, its actual cost ($42,000) minus the gain not recognized under section 1250(a) by reason of the application of section 1250(d)(4)(A) ($10,000). Thus, the basis of the section 1250 property is $12,000 (32/80 of $30,000), and the basis of the land is $18,000 (48/80 of $30,000).

(c) The basis of the purchased stock is its cost of $5,000. See last sentence of subdivision (ii) of this subparagraph.

Example (2). Assume the same facts as in example (1) except that the section 1250 property purchased for $42,000 consists of 2 items of such property ($10,500 for C, and $31,500 for D), and that the land purchased for $48,000 consists of 2 pieces of land ($12,000 for X, and $36,000 for Y). Under subdivision (iv) of this subparagraph, the total basis for each class of property is allocated between the individual properties of such class in proportion to their respective actual costs. Thus, the total basis of $12,000, as determined in example (1), for the section 1250 property is allocated as follows:

To C: $12,000 × ($10,500/$42,000)	$3,000
To D: $12,000 × ($31,500/$42,000)	9,000
Total	$12,000

The total basis of $18,000, as determined in example (1), for the land is allocated as follows:

To X: $18,000 × ($12,000/$48,000)	$4,500
To Y: $18,000 × ($36,000/$48,000)	13,500
Total	$18,000

(3) *Basis of property acquired upon involuntary conversion into similar property.*—If property is involuntarily converted into property similar or related in service or use in a transaction to which section 1033(a)(1) applies, and if by reason of the application of section 1250(d)(4)(A) all or part of the gain computed under section 1250(a) is not taken into account, then—

(i) The total basis of the acquired property shall be determined under the first sentence of section 1033(c), and

(ii) If more than one item of property is acquired, such total basis shall be allocated to the individual items of property acquired in accordance with the principles prescribed in subpara-

graph (2)(iii) and (iv) of this paragraph, except that an amount equivalent to the fair market value of each item of property on the date acquired shall be treated as its actual cost.

(4) *Basis of property acquired in like kind exchange.*—If section 1250 property is transferred in an exchange described in section 1031(a) or (b), and if by reason of the application of section 1250(d)(4)(A) all or part of the gain computed under section 1250(a) is not taken into account, then—

(i) The total basis of the property (including nonsection 1250 property) acquired of the type permitted to be received under section 1031 without recognition of gain or loss shall be determined under section 1031(d), and

(ii) If more than one item of property of such type was received, such total basis shall be allocated to the individual items of property of such type in accordance with the principles prescribed in subparagraph (2)(iii) and (iv) of this paragraph, except that an amount equivalent to the fair market value of each such item of property on the date received shall be treated as its actual cost.

(5) *Additional depreciation for property acquired in like kind exchange or involuntary conversion.*—(i) If property is disposed of in a transaction described in section 1031 or 1033, and if by reason of the application of section 1250(d)(4)(A) all or part of the gain computed under section 1250(a) is not taken into account, then the additional depreciation for the acquired property immediately after the transaction (as computed under section 1250(d)(4)(E)) shall be an amount equal to the amount of gain computed under section 1250(a) which was not taken into account by reason of the application of section 1250(d)(4)(A).

(ii) In case more than one item of section 1250 property is acquired in the transaction, the additional depreciation computed under subdivision (i) of this subparagraph shall be allocated to each such item of section 1250 property in proportion to their respective adjusted bases.

(iii) The provisions of this subparagraph may be illustrated by the following examples:

Example (1). (a) On January 15, 1969, section 1250 property X is condemned and proceeds of $100,000 are received. On such date, X's adjusted basis is $25,000, the additional depreciation is $10,000, and the applicable percentage under section 1250(a)(2) is 70 percent. Since the additional depreciation ($10,000) is less than the gain realized ($75,000, that is, $100,000 minus $25,000) the amount of gain computed under section 1250(a)(2) (without regard to section 1250(d)(4)(A)) is $7,000, that is, 70 percent of $10,000.

(b) On March 1, 1969, all the proceeds are used to purchase section 1250 property Y in a transaction qualifying under section

1033(a)(3)(A) for nonrecognition of gain. Accordingly, the gain not recognized by reason of the application of section 1033(a)(3)(A) is $75,000, of which $7,000 is gain computed under section 1250(a)(2) which is not taken into account by reason of the application of section 1250(d)(4)(A). See subparagraph (1) of this paragraph.

(c) Immediately after the transaction, Y's basis is $25,000, that is, its cost ($100,000) minus the total gain realized which was not recognized ($75,000), and the additional depreciation (as computed under section 1250(d)(4)(E)) is $7,000, that is, the amount of gain not taken into account under section 1250(a)(2) by reason of the application of section 1250(d)(4)(A).

(d) On December 15, 1969, before any depreciation deductions were allowed or allowable in respect of Y, Y is sold for $90,000. Under section 1250(e)(1), the holding period of Y is 9 months, and thus, under section 1250(a)(2), the applicable percentage is 100 percent. Since the additional depreciation ($7,000) is less than the gain realized ($65,000, that is, $90,000 minus $25,000), the amount of gain recognized under section 1250(a)(2) as ordinary income is $7,000, that is, 100 percent of $7,000.

Example (2). Assume the same facts as in example (1), except that property Y was purchased on June 15, 1962, and that 90 full months thereafter, or December 15, 1969, it is sold for $35,000. Thus the applicable percentage under section 1250(a)(2) is 30 percent. Assume further that at the time of such sale Y's adjusted basis is $5,000 and additional depreciation in respect of Y for periods after it was acquired is $2,500. Thus, the additional depreciation at the time of the sale is $9,500, that is, the sum of the additional depreciation in respect of Y attributable to X as computed under section 1250(d)(4)(E) in (c) of example (1) ($7,000), plus the additional depreciation attributable to periods after Y was acquired ($2,500). Since the additional depreciation ($9,500) is less than the gain realized ($30,000, that is, $35,000 minus $5,000), the gain recognized under section 1250(a)(2) as ordinary income is $2,850, that is, 30 percent of $9,500.

(6) *Single disposition of section 1250 property and property of different class.*—(i) For purposes of this subparagraph—

(a) Section 1250 property, section 1245 property (as defined in section 1245(a)(3)), and other property shall each be treated as a separate class of property, and

(b) The term "qualifying property" means property which may be acquired without recognition of gain under the applicable provision of section 1031 or 1033 (applied without regard to section 1250 or 1245) upon the disposition of property.

(ii) If upon a sale of section 1250 property gain would be recognized under section 1250(a), and if such section 1250 property together with property of a different class or classes are disposed of in one transaction in which gain is not recognized in whole or in part under section 1031 or 1033 (without regard to sections 1245 and 1250), then—

(a) The total amount realized shall be allocated between the different classes of property disposed of in proportion to their respective fair market values,

(b) The amount realized upon the disposition of property of a class shall be deemed to consist of so much of the fair market value of qualifying property of the same class acquired as is not in excess of the amount realized from the property of such class disposed of,

(c) The remaining portion (if any) of the amount realized upon the disposition of property of such class shall be deemed to consist of so much of the fair market value of any other property acquired as is not in excess of such remaining portion, and

(d) For purposes of applying (c) of this subdivision, the fair market value of acquired property shall be taken into account only once and in such manner as the taxpayer determines.

(iii) The amounts determined under this subparagraph in respect of property shall apply for all purposes of the Code.

(iv) The application of this subparagraph may be illustrated by the following example:

Example. (a) Green owns property consisting of land and a fully equipped factory building thereon. The property is condemned and proceeds of $100,000 are received. If the property were sold for $100,000, gain of $40,000 would be recognized of which $10,000 would be recognized as ordinary income under section 1250(a). Proceeds of $95,000 are used to purchase property similar or related in service or use to the condemned property and under section 1033(a)(3)(A) (without regard to sections 1245 and 1250) recognition of gain is limited to $5,000. The fair market values by classes of the property disposed of, and of the property acquired, are summarized in the table below:

	Disposed of	Fair market value of property Acquired
Section 1245 property	$35,000	$55,000
Section 1250 property	45,000	28,000
Land	20,000	12,000
Cash		5,000
	$100,000	$100,000

Reg. §1.1250-3(d)(6)(iv)

(b) The allocations under subdivision (ii) of this subparagraph are summarized in the table below:

Property disposed of	Property acquired			Cash remaining
	Sec. 1245 property	Sec. 1250 property	Land	
$35,000 of sec. 1245 property	$35,000	...	...	...
$45,000 of sec. 1250 property	[1]17,000	$28,000	...	...
$20,000 of land	[1]3,000	...	$12,000	[1]$5,000
Total	$55,000	$28,000	$12,000	$5,000

[1] Determined by taxpayer pursuant to subdivision (ii)(d) of this subparagraph

(c) Upon the disposition of the section 1245 property, only section 1245 property is acquired, and thus gain (if any) would not be recognized under section 1245(a)(1). See section 1245(b)(4). Upon the disposition of the section 1250 property gain under section 1250(a) would not be recognized by reason of the application of section 1250(d)(4)(A). See subparagraph (1) of this paragraph. If the gain realized on the disposition of the land is not less than $5,000, then under section 1033(a)(3)(A) the gain recognized would be $5,000, that is, an amount equal to the portion of the proceeds from the disposition of the land ($5,000) not invested in qualifying property.

(7) *Disposition of portion of property.*—A disposition described in section 1250(d)(4)(A) of a portion of an item of property gives rise to an addition to capital account described in the last sentence of paragraph (d)(2)(i) of § 1.1250-5 (relating to property with 2 or more elements). If the addition to capital account is a separate improvement within the meaning of paragraph (d) of § 1.1250-5, and thus an element, then immediately after the addition is made the amount of additional depreciation for such separate improvement shall be computed under subparagraph (5) of this paragraph by treating such portion and such addition as separate properties. If the addition is not a separate improvement, then immediately after the addition is made such property is considered under paragraph (c)(5)(ii) of § 1.1250-5 as having a special element with the same amount of additional depreciation so computed. For purposes of computing applicable percentage, the holding period of the separate improvement or special element (as the case may be), which is determined under section 1250(c)(1), does not include the holding period of the property disposed of.

(e) *Sections 1071 and 1081 transactions.*—(1) *General.*—This paragraph prescribes regulations under section 1250(d)(5) which apply in the case of a disposition of section 1250 property in a transaction in which gain (determined without regard to section 1250) is not recognized in whole or in part by reason of the application of section 1071 (relating to gain from sale or exchange to effectuate policies of FCC) or section 1081 (relating to gain from sale or exchange in obedience to order of SEC).

(2) *Involuntary conversion treatment under section 1071.*—If section 1250 property is disposed of and gain (determined without regard to section 1250) is not recognized in whole or in part solely by reason of an election under the first sentence of section 1071(a) to treat the transaction as an involuntary conversion, the consequences of the transaction shall be determined under the principles of paragraph (d) of this section.

(3) *Basis reduction under section 1071 or 1082(a)(2).*—(i) If section 1250 property is disposed of and gain (determined without regard to section 1250) is not recognized in whole or in part by reason of a reduction in basis of property pursuant to an election under section 1071(a) or the application of section 1082(a)(2), then the amount of gain taken into account by the transferor under section 1250(a) shall not exceed the sum of—

(a) The amount of gain recognized on such disposition (determined without regard to section 1250), plus

(b) In case involuntary conversion treatment was also elected under section 1071(a), an amount equal to the cost of any stock purchased in a corporation which (without regard to section 1250) would result in nonrecognition of gain under section 1033(a)(3), as modified by section 1071(a), plus

(c) The portion of the gain computed under section 1250 (a) (without regard to this paragraph) which is neither taken into account under (a) or (b) of this subdivision nor applied under subdivision (ii) of this subparagraph to reduce the basis of section 1250 property.

(ii)(a) The amount of gain computed under section 1250(a) (without regard to this paragraph) which is not taken into account under subdivision (i)(a) or (b) of this subparagraph shall be applied to the amount by which the basis of the section 1250 property was reduced under section 1071(a) or 1082(a)(2), as the case may be, before other gain (which is not gain computed under section 1250(a)) is so applied.

(b) If the basis of more than one item of section 1250 property was so reduced, the gain

Reg. § 1.1250-3(d)(7)

applied under (*a*) of this subdivision to all such section 1250 properties shall be applied to such items in proportion to the amounts of their respective basis reductions.

   (*c*) Any gain not applied under (*a*) of this subdivision shall be applied to the amount by which the basis of the non-section 1250 property was reduced.

   (iii) If gain computed under section 1250 is applied under subdivision (ii) of this subparagraph to reduce the basis of section 1250 property, the amount so applied shall be treated as additional depreciation in respect of such section 1250 property. For treatment of such section 1250 property as having a special element with additional depreciation consisting of such amount, see paragraph (c)(5)(i) of § 1.1250-5. For purposes of computing applicable percentage, such special element shall have a holding period beginning on the day after the date as of which the property's basis was so reduced.

   (4) *Section 1081(d)(1)(A) transaction.*—No gain shall be recognized under section 1250(a) upon an exchange of property as to which gain is not recognized (without regard to section 1250) because of the application of section 1081(d)(1)(A) (relating to transfers within system group). For treatment of property in the hands of a transferee, the principles of paragraph (c)(3) of this section shall apply.

   (f) *Property distributed by a partnership to a partner.*—(1) *General.*—For purposes of section 1250(d)(3) and (e)(2), the basis of section 1250 property distributed by a partnership to a partner shall be determined by reference to the adjusted basis of such property to the partnership. Thus, if section 731 applies to a distribution of section 1250 property by a partnership to a partner, then even though the partner's basis is not determined for other purposes by reference to the partnership's basis, (i) the amount of gain taken into account by the partnership under section 1250(a) is limited by section 1250(d)(3) to the amount of gain recognized to the partnership upon the distribution (determined without regard to section 1250), and (ii) the holding period of the property in the hands of the partner shall, under section 1250(e)(2), include the holding period of the property in the hands of the partnership. For nonapplication of section 1250(d)(3) to a disposition to an organization (other than a cooperative described in section 521) which is exempt from the tax imposed by chapter 1 of the Code, see paragraph (c)(1) of this section.

   (2) *Treatment of property distributed by partnership.*—(i) If section 1250 property is distributed by a partnership to a partner in a distribution in which no part of the partnership's "potential section 1250 income" in respect of the property was recognized as ordinary income to the partnership under paragraph (b)(2)(ii) of § 1.751-1, the additional depreciation for the

property in the hands of the distributee attributable to periods before the distribution shall be an amount equal to the total potential section 1250 income of the partnership in respect of the property immediately before the distribution, recomputed as if the applicable percentage for the property had been 100 percent. Under paragraph (c)(4) of § 1.751-1, the potential section 1250 income is, in effect, the gain to which section 1250(a) would have applied if the property had been sold by the partnership immediately before the distribution at its fair market value at such time.

   (ii) If upon the distribution any potential section 1250 income in respect of the property was recognized to the partnership under paragraph (b)(2)(ii) of § 1.751-1, then after the distribution the additional depreciation shall be an amount equal to (*a*) the total potential section 1250 income in respect of the property, as recomputed in subdivision (i) of this subparagraph, minus (*b*) the amount of potential section 1250 income which would have been recognized to the partnership under paragraph (b)(2)(ii) of § 1.751-1 if the applicable percentage for the property had been 100 percent.

   (iii) If the partner's basis for the property immediately after the transaction exceeds the partnership's adjusted basis for the property immediately before the transaction, the excess may be an addition to capital account under paragraph (d)(2)(ii) of § 1.1250-5 (relating to property with two or more elements).

   (3) *Examples.*—The provisions of subparagraphs (1) and (2) of this paragraph may be illustrated by the following examples:

   Example (1). (i) A partnership distributes a building to Smith on January 1, 1969, in a complete liquidation of his partnership interest to which section 736(a) does not apply. On the date of the distribution, the partnership's holding period for the property is 40 full months and, accordingly, the applicable percentage under section 1250(a)(2) is 80 percent. On such date, the partnership's additional depreciation for the building ($6,250) is lower than the excess ($40,000) of its fair market value of ($140,000) over adjusted basis ($100,000). Thus, under paragraph (c)(4) of § 1.751-1, the partnership's potential section 1250 income in respect of the building is $5,000 (80 percent of $6,250). Assume that section 751(b) does not apply to the distribution. Accordingly, no gain would be recognized to the partnership under section 731(b) (without regard to the application of section 1250). Smith's basis for his partnership interest was $150,000, and under section 732(b) Smith's basis for the building is equal to his basis for his partnership interest. Thus, Smith's basis for the building is not determined by reference to the partnership's basis for the building. Nevertheless, under subparagraph (1) of this paragraph, no gain is recognized to the partnership under section 1250(a)(2) and Smith's holding period for the property includes the partnership's holding period.

(ii) Six full months after Smith receives the building in the distribution, or July 1, 1969, he sells it for $153,000. Assume that no depreciation was allowed or allowable to Smith for the building, and that the special rules under § 1.1250-5 for property with two or more elements do not apply. Since Smith's holding period for the building includes its holding period in the hands of the partnership, his holding period is 46 full months (40 full months for the partnership plus 6 full months for Smith) and the applicable percentage under section 1250(a)(2) is 74 percent.

(iii) Since no potential section 1250 income was recognized to the partnership under paragraph (b)(2)(ii) of § 1.751-1, the additional depreciation for the building attributable to periods before the distribution is determined under the provisions of subparagraph (2)(i) of this paragraph. Under such provisions, the potential section 1250 income to the partnership which was actually $5,000 (that is, 80 percent of $6,250), is recomputed as if the applicable percentage were 100 percent, and thus such additional depreciation is $6,250 (that is, 100 percent of $6,250). Since no depreciation was allowed or allowable for the building in Smith's hands, the additional depreciation for the building attributable to Smith's total holding period (46 full months) is $6,250. Since the gain realized ($3,000, that is, amount realized, $153,000, minus adjusted basis, $150,000) is lower than the additional depreciation ($6,250), the gain recognized to Smith under section 1250(a)(2) is $2,220 (that is, 74 percent of $3,000).

Example (2). Assume the facts as in example (1) except that as a result of the distribution the partnership recognizes under paragraph (b)(2)(ii) of § 1.751-1 potential section 1250 income of $1,000 (that is, 80 percent of $1,250). The additional depreciation attributable to periods before the distribution, as determined under the provisions of subparagraph (2)(ii) of this paragraph, is $5,000, that is, (*a*) the total potential section 1250 income in respect of the property, recomputed, in example (1) as if the applicable percentage were 100 percent ($6,250), minus (*b*) the amount of potential section 1250 income which would have been recognized to the partnership under paragraph (b)(2)(ii) of § 1.751-1 if the applicable percentage for the property had been 100 percent of ($1,250, that is, 100 percent of $1,250).

(4) *Treatment of partnership property after certain transactions.*—If under paragraph (b)(3) of § 1.751-1 (relating to certain distributions of partnership property other than section 751 property treated as sales or exchanges) a partnership is treated as purchasing section 1250 property (or a portion thereof) from a distributee who relinquishes his interest in such property (or portion),

then after the date of such purchase the following rules shall apply:

(i) If only a portion of the property is treated as purchased, there shall be excluded from the additional depreciation for the remaining portion any additional depreciation in respect of the purchased portion for periods before such purchase.

(ii) In respect of the purchased property (or portion), (*a*) as of the date of purchase the amount of additional depreciation shall be zero, and (*b*) for purposes of computing applicable percentage the holding period shall begin on the day after the date of such purchase.

(5) *Cross reference.*—See paragraph (f) of § 1.1250-1 for the amount of additional depreciation for partnership property in respect of a partner who acquired his partnership interest in certain transactions when an election under section 754 (relating to optional adjustments to basis of partnership property) was in effect.

(g) *Disposition of principal residence.*—(1) *In general.*—(i) Section 1250(d)(7)(A) provides that section 1250(a) shall not apply to a disposition of property by a taxpayer to the extent the property is used by the taxpayer as his principal residence (within the meaning of section 1034(a) and the regulations thereunder, relating to a sale or exchange of residence). Thus, for example, if a doctor sells a house, of which one portion was used as his principal residence within the meaning of section 1034(a) and the other portion was properly subject to the allowance for depreciation as property used in his trade or business, then, by reason of the application of section 1250(d)(7)(A), section 1250(a) does not apply in respect of the disposition of the portion used as his principal residence. The provisions of this subparagraph shall apply regardless of whether section 1034 applies. Thus, for example, if section 1034 did not apply to the sale because the doctor did not invest in a new principal residence within the period specified in section 1034, nevertheless section 1250(a) would not apply to the disposition of the portion used as a principal residence.

(ii) Section 1250(d)(7)(B) provides that section 1250(a) shall not apply to a disposition of section 1250 property by a taxpayer who, in respect of the property, satisfies the age and ownership requirements of section 121 (relating to exclusion from gross income of gain on sale or exchange of residence of individual who has attained age 65), but only to the extent the taxpayer satisfies the use requirements of section 121 in respect of such property. Thus, if a taxpayer has attained the age of 65 before the date on which he disposes of section 1250 property, and if during the 8-year period ending on the date of the disposition the property has been owned and used by the taxpayer solely as his principal residence for periods aggregating 5 years or more, then section 1250(a) does not apply in respect to the disposition. This result would not be changed even if the taxpayer does not or cannot make the election provided for in section 121 and even if section 121 applies to only a portion of the gain because the adjusted sales price exceeds the $20,000 limitation in section 121(b)(1). If, however, only a portion of the property has been used as his principal residence for such periods aggregating 5 years or more, then, by reason of the application of section 1250(d)(7)(B), section 1250(a) is inapplicable only to the portion so used. For special rules for determining whether the age, ownership, and use requirements of section 121 are treated as satisfied, and for the manner of applying such requirements, see section 121(d) and the regulations thereunder.

(2) *Concurrent operation of section 1250(d)(7) with other provisions.*—Upon the disposition of a principal residence, gain computed under section 1250(a) may not be recognized in whole or in part by reason of the application of both the provisions of section 1250(d)(7) and the provisions of one of the other exceptions or limitations enumerated in section 1250(d). Thus, for example, if an entire house is transferred as a gift, and if section 1250(d)(7) applies to only a portion of the house, then section 1250(d)(1) excepts the disposition of the entire house from the application of section 1250(a).

(3) *Special rule.*—If by reason of section 1250(d)(7) a disposition is partially excepted from the application of section 1250(a), and if no other paragraph of section 1250(d) excepts the disposition entirely from such application, then the gain to which section 1250(a) applies shall be an amount which bears the same ratio to (i) the gain computed under section 1250(a) (without regard to section 1250(d)(7)), as (ii) the fair market value of the portion of the property to which the exception in section 1250(d)(7) does not apply, bears to (iii) the total fair market value of the property. Thus, for example, if under paragraph (a)(2) of this section gain of $300 would be recognized as ordinary income under section 1250(a) (without regard to section 1250(d)(7)) upon a combined sale and gift of section 1250 property, and if the property has a fair market value of $25,000 of which $10,000 is properly allocable to a portion not used as a principal residence, then the amount of gain recognized as ordinary income under section 1250(a) would be $120 (10/25 of $300).

(4) *Treatment of property in hands of transferee.*—If property is disposed of in a transaction to which section 1250(d)(7) applies, and if its basis in the hands of the transferee is determined by reference to its basis in the hands of the transferor by reason of the application of section 1250(d)(1) (relating to gifts) or section 1250(d)(3) (relating to certain tax-free transactions), then the treatment of the property in the hands of the

transferee shall be determined under paragraph (a)(3) or (c)(3) (whichever is applicable) of this section.

(5) *Treatment of property acquired in like kind exchange or involuntary conversion.*—If property is disposed of in a transaction to which section 1250(d)(7) (relating to principal residence) and section 1250(d)(4) (relating to like kind exchanges and involuntary conversions) apply, then—

(i) The basis of the property acquired shall be determined under the applicable provisions of paragraph (d)(2), (3), or (4) of this section applied as if all gain computed under section 1250(a) (except any gain not recognized solely by reason of the application of section 1250(d)(7)) were not taken into account by reason of section 1250(d)(4)(A),

(ii) The additional depreciation for the property acquired shall be determined in the manner prescribed in paragraph (d)(5) of this section, so applied, and

(iii) For purposes of computing the applicable percentage, the holding period of the acquired property shall be determined under section 1250(e)(1).

(6) *Treatment of property acquired in section 1034 transaction.*—If a principal residence is disposed of in a transaction to which section 1250(d)(7) applies, and if by reason of the application of section 1034 (relating to sale or exchange of residence) the basis of property acquired in the transaction is determined by reference to the basis in the hands of the taxpayer of the property disposed of, then—

(i) The additional depreciation for the acquired property immediately after the transaction shall be an amount equal to (*a*) the amount of the additional depreciation for the property disposed of, minus (*b*) the amount of any gain which would have been taken into account under section 1250(a) by the transferor upon the disposition if the applicable percentage for the property had been 100 percent,

(ii) For purposes of computing the applicable percentage, the holding period of the acquired property includes the holding period of the disposed of property (see section 1250(e)(3)),

(iii) If the adjusted basis of the acquired property exceeds the adjusted basis immediately before the transfer of the property disposed of, the excess is an addition to capital account under paragraph (d)(2)(ii) of §1.1250-5 (relating to property with more than one element), and

(iv) If the property disposed of consisted of 2 or more elements within the meaning of paragraph (c) of §1.1250-5, see paragraph (e)(3) of §1.1250-5 for the amount of additional depreciation and the holding period for each element in the hands of the transferee.

(h) *Limitation for disposition of qualified low-income housing.*—(1) *Limitation on gain.*—(i) Under section 1250(d)(8)(A), if section 1250 property is disposed of and gain (determined without regard to section 1250) is not recognized in whole or in part under section 1039 (relating to certain sales of low income housing projects), then the amount of gain recognized by the transferor under section 1250(a) shall not exceed the greater of—

(a) The amount of gain recognized under section 1039 (determined without regard to section 1250), or

(b) The excess, if any, of the amount of gain which would, but for section 1250(d)(8)(A), be taken into account under section 1250(a), over the cost of the section 1250 property acquired in the transaction.

For purposes of this paragraph the term "qualified housing project", "approved disposition", "reinvestment period", and "net amount realized" shall have the same meaning as in section 1039 and § 1.1039-1.

(ii) The principles of this subparagraph may be illustrated by the following examples:

Example (1). (i) Taxpayer A owns a qualified housing project and makes an approved disposition of the project on January 1, 1971. The net amount realized upon the disposition is $550,000, of which $475,000 is attributable to section 1250 property. The adjusted basis of the section 1250 property is $250,000 and the gain realized on the disposition of section 1250 property is $225,000. The additional depreciation for the property is $100,000, the applicable percentage is 48 percent, and if section 1250(d)(8)(A) did not apply to the disposition, $48,000 of gain would be recognized under section 1250(a). Within the reinvestment period, A purchases a replacement qualified housing project at a cost of $525,000, of which $425,000 is attributable to section 1250 property. A properly elects under section 1039(a) and the regulations thereunder to limit the recognition of gain (determined without regard to section 1250) to $25,000, that is, the excess of the net amount realized ($550,000) over the cost of the replacement housing project ($525,000).

(ii) The amount of gain recognized under section 1250(a) is limited to $25,000, that is, the greater of (a) the amount of gain recognized without regard to section 1250(a) ($25,000), or (b) the excess of (1) the amount of gain which would be taken into account under section 1250(a) if section 1250(d)(8)(A) did not apply ($225,000) over (2) the cost of the replacement section 1250 property ($425,000), or zero.

Example (2). The facts are the same as in example (1) except that only $180,000 of the cost of the replacement housing project is attributable to section 1250 property. Thus, the gain recognized under section 1250(a) is limited to $45,000, the greater of (a) the excess of (1) the amount of gain which would be taken into account under section 1250(a) if section 1250(d)(8)(A) did not apply ($225,000), over (2) the cost of the replace-

ment section 1250 property ($180,000), or (b) the amount of gain recognized without regard to section 1250 ($25,000).

(2) *Replacement project consisting of more than one element.*—(i) If (a) section 1250 property is disposed of, (b) any portion of the gain which would have been recognized under section 1250(a) is not recognized by reason of section 1250(d)(8)(A), and (c) the cost of the replacement section 1250 property constructed, reconstructed, or acquired during the reinvestment period exceeds the net amount realized attributable to the section 1250 property disposed of, then the section 1250 property shall consist of two elements. For purposes of this paragraph, the "reinvestment element" is that portion of the section 1250 property constructed, reconstructed, or acquired during the reinvestment period the cost of which does not exceed the net amount realized attributable to the section 1250 property disposed of, reduced by any gain recognized with respect to such property. The "additional cost element" is that portion of the section 1250 property constructed, reconstructed, or acquired during the reinvestment period whose cost exceeds the net amount realized attributable to the section 1250 property disposed of.

(ii) The principles of this subparagraph may be illustrated by the following example:

Example. (1)(i) Taxpayer B disposes of a qualified housing project consisting of section 1250 property with an adjusted basis of $500,000 and land with a basis of $100,000. The amount realized on the disposition is $750,000 of which $650,000 is attributable to the section 1250 property. B constructs a replacement housing project at a cost of $1,000,000 of which $850,000 is attributable to section 1250 property. B elects in accordance with the provisions of section 1039(a) and the regulations thereunder not to recognize the $150,000 gain realized.

(ii) Under section 1250(d)(8)(A) no gain is recognized under section 1250(a). The replacement section 1250 property consists of the two elements. The reinvestment element has a cost of $650,000, *i.e.,* that portion of the replacement section 1250 property the cost of which does not exceed the amount realized attributable to the section 1250 property disposed of ($650,000), reduced by any gain recognized with respect to such property (zero). The additional cost element has a cost of $200,000, that is, the excess of the cost of the replacement section 1250 property ($850,000) over the amount realized attributable to the section 1250 property disposed of ($650,000).

(3) *Basis of property acquired.*—(i) If section 1250 property is disposed of and gain (determined without regard to section 1250) is not recognized in whole or in part under section 1039 (relating to certain sales of low-income housing projects), then the basis of the section 1250 property and other property acquired in the

transaction shall be determined in accordance with the rules of this subparagraph. Generally, the basis of the property acquired in a transaction to which section 1039(a) applies is its cost reduced by the amount of any gain not recognized attributable to the property disposed of (see section 1039(d)). In a case where the replacement section 1250 property constructed, reconstructed, or acquired within the reinvestment period is treated as consisting of more than one element under section 1250(d)(8)(E), the aggregate basis of the property determined under section 1039(d) shall be allocated as follows: first, to the reinvestment element of the section 1250 property, in an amount equal to the amount determined under section 1250(d)(8)(E)(i) reduced by the amount of any gain not recognized attributable to the section 1250 property disposed of; second, to the other replacement property (other than section 1250 property) in an amount equal to the amount of its cost reduced (but not below zero) by any remaining amount of gain not recognized; and finally, to the additional cost element of the section 1250 property, in an amount equal to the amount determined under section 1250(d)(8)(E)(ii) reduced by any amount of gain not recognized which has not taken into account in determining the basis of the reinvestment element and the other replacement property that is not section 1250 property. See paragraph (h)(2) of this section for definition of the terms "reinvestment element" and "additional cost element".

(ii) The principles of this subparagraph may be illustrated by the following examples:

Example (1). The facts are the same as in example (1) of subparagraph (1)(ii) of this paragraph. The basis of the replacement section 1250 property is $225,000, the amount of the reinvestment element ($425,000) minus the gain not recognized attributable to the section 1250 property disposed of ($200,000).

Example (2). Taxpayer C disposes of a qualified housing project on January 1, 1971. The adjusted basis for the project is $3,800,000, of which $3,000,000 is attributable to section 1250 property and $800,000 is attributable to land. The amount realized on the disposition is $5,000,000, of which $4,000,000 is attributable to the section 1250 property and $1,000,000 is attributable to the land. The gain realized upon the disposition is $1,200,000, that is, amount realized ($5,000,000) minus adjusted basis ($3,800,000), of which $1,000,000 is attributable to the section 1250 property disposed of. Within the reinvestment period, C purchases another qualified housing project at a cost of $5,500,000, of which $4,000,000 is attributable to section 1250 property and $1,500,000 is attributable to other property. C makes an election under section 1039(a) and the regulations thereunder and none of the $1,200,000 gain realized on the disposition is recognized (determined without regard to section 1250). Under section 1250(d)(8)(A), none of the

gain realized is recognized under section 1250(a). The basis of the replacement section 1250 property is $3,000,000, that is, the amount of the reinvestment element ($4,000,000) less the amount of gain not recognized attributable to section 1250 property disposed of ($1,000,000). The basis of the other property acquired is $1,300,000, that is, its cost ($1,500,000) reduced by the remaining gain not recognized ($200,000).

Example (3). The facts are the same as in example (2) except that the cost of the replacement section 1250 property is $4,500,000 and the cost of the other property is $1,000,000. Thus, the replacement section 1250 property consists of two elements under section 1250(d)(8)(E). The reinvestment element (section 1250(d)(8)(E)(i)) has a basis of $3,000,000, that is, $4,000,000 (that portion of the section 1250 property acquired the cost of which does not exceed the net amount realized attributable to the section 1250 property disposed of), reduced by $1,000,000 (the gain not recognized attributable to the section 1250 property disposed of). The basis of the other property is $800,000, that is, its cost ($1,000,000) reduced by the remaining gain not recognized ($200,000). The additional cost element (section 1250(d)(8)(E)(ii)) has a basis of $500,000, that is, the portion of the section 1250 property acquired the cost of which exceeds the net amount realized attributable to the section 1250 property disposed of. This amount ($500,000) is not reduced by any amount of gain not recognized because all of the gain not recognized has already been taken into account in determining the basis of the reinvestment element and the other replacement property that is not section 1250 property.

(4) *Additional depreciation for property acquired.*—(i) If a qualified housing project is disposed of in a transaction to which section 1039(a) applies, the additional depreciation for the replacement property immediately after the transaction shall be an amount equal to (*a*) the amount of additional depreciation for the property disposed of, minus (*b*) the amount of additional depreciation necessary to produce the amount of gain recognized under section 1250(a). Thus, if no gain is recognized upon a disposition of a qualified housing project, the additional depreciation for the property acquired will be the same as for the property disposed of. On the other hand, if upon disposition of a project, gain of $40,000 was recognized under section 1250(a), and if the additional depreciation for the project and the applicable percentage were $100,000 and 80 percent, respectively, the additional depreciation for the replacement housing project would be $50,000, that is, $100,000 minus $50,000, the amount of additional depreciation necessary to produce $40,000 of recognized gain where the applicable percentage is 80 percent.

(ii) If the property acquired in the transaction consists of more than one element of section 1250 property by reason of section 1250(d)(8)(E), the additional depreciation under subdivision (i) of this subparagraph shall be allocated solely to the reinvestment element.

(5) *Additional limitation.*—If, in a transaction to which section 1039(a) applies, gain is recognized by the taxpayer, the amount of gain recognized which is attributable to section 1250 property disposed of is, under section 1250(d)(8)(F)(i), limited to an amount equal to the net amount realized attributable to the section 1250 property disposed of reduced by the greater of (i) the adjusted basis of the section 1250 property disposed of or (ii) the cost of the section 1250 property acquired. The limitation of section 1250(d)(8)(F)(i) may be illustrated by the following example:

Example. Taxpayer D owns property constituting a qualified housing project under section 1039(b)(1). In an approved disposition, the project is sold for $225,000. The net amount realized on the disposition is $225,000 of which $175,000 is attributable to the section 1250 property disposed of. The adjusted basis of such property is $150,000 and thus the gain realized upon the disposition of the section 1250 property is $25,000. Assume that the total gain realized upon disposition of the project is $45,000. Within the reinvestment period, D purchases another qualified housing project at a cost of $200,000, of which $160,000 is attributable to section 1250 property. D elects, in accordance with section 1039(a) and the regulations thereunder, to limit the recognition of gain to $25,000, that is, the net amount realized ($225,000), minus the cost of the replacement housing project ($200,000). Under this subparagraph, $15,000 of the $25,000 gain recognized is attributable to the section 1250 property disposed of, that is, the net amount realized attributable to the section 1250 property disposed of ($175,000), reduced by $160,000, the greater of the adjusted basis of the section 1250 property disposed of ($150,000) or the cost of the section 1250 property acquired ($160,000).

(6) *Allocation rule.*—(i) If, in a transaction to which paragraph (h)(1) of this section applies, the section 1250 property disposed of is treated as consisting of more than one element by reason of the application of section 1250(d)(8)(E) with respect to a prior transaction, then the amount of gain recognized, the net amount realized, and the additional depreciation with respect to each such element shall be allocated to the elements of the replacement section 1250 property in accordance with the provisions of this subparagraph.

(ii) The portion of the net amount realized upon such a disposition which shall be allocated to each element of the section 1250 property disposed of is that amount which bears the same ratio to the net amount realized attributable to all the section 1250 property disposed of in the transaction as the additional depreciation

for that element bears to the total additional depreciation for all elements disposed of. If any gain is recognized upon disposition of the section 1250 property, such gain shall be allocated to each element in the same proportion as the gain realized for that element bears to the gain realized for all elements disposed of. The additional depreciation for each reinvestment element of the replacement section 1250 property shall be the same as for the corresponding element of the property disposed of, decreased by the amount of additional depreciation necessary to produce the amount of gain recognized for such element. The additional depreciation for any additional cost element shall be zero.

(iii) The principles of this subparagraph may be illustrated by the following example:

Example. Taxpayer E disposes of a qualified housing project in an approved disposition. The net amount realized is $1,090,000 of which $900,000 is attributable to section 1250 property. The section 1250 property consists of (1) a reinvestment element with an adjusted basis of $300,000, additional depreciation of $100,000, and an applicable percentage of 50 percent, and (2) an additional cost element with an adjusted basis of $200,000, additional depreciation of $50,000, and an applicable percentage of 80 percent. Gain of $400,000 is realized on the disposition of the section 1250 property, that is, amount realized ($900,000) minus adjusted basis ($500,000). Within the reinvestment period, E purchases another qualified housing project at a cost of $1,000,000 of which $840,000 is attributable to section 1250 property. E elects, in accordance with section 1039 and the regulations thereunder, to limit recognition of gain (determined without regard to section 1250) to $90,000, that is, the excess of the net amount realized ($1,090,000) over the cost of the replacement project ($1,000,000). Under section 1250(d)(8)(A), the amount of gain recognized under section 1250(a) is limited to $90,000 (see subparagraph (1) of this paragraph). Under section 1250(d)(8)(F)(ii) and this subparagraph, $600,000 of the $900,000 net amount realized attributable to the section 1250 property is allocated to the reinvestment element, that is, additional depreciation for the element ($100,000) over total additional depreciation ($150,000) times the net amount realized ($900,000). The remaining $300,000 is allocated to the additional cost element. Thus, the gain realized attributable to the reinvestment element is $300,000, that is, net amount realized ($600,000) minus adjusted basis ($300,000). The gain realized attributable to the additional cost element is $100,000, that is, net amount realized ($300,000) minus adjusted basis ($200,000). Under subparagraph (5) of this paragraph, the gain recognized attributable to the section 1250 property is limited to $60,000, that is, the net amount realized attributable to the section 1250 property disposed of ($900,000) minus the greater of the adjusted basis of such property

($500,000) or the cost of the section 1250 property acquired in the transaction ($840,000). Under section 1250(d)(8)(F)(ii) and this subparagraph, $45,000, of the $60,000 gain recognized is attributable to the reinvestment element, that is, $60,000 multiplied by a fraction whose numerator is the gain realized attributable to the reinvestment element ($300,000) and whose denominator is the total gain realized attributable to all the section 1250 property ($400,000). The remaining $15,000 of the gain recognized is attributable to the additional cost element. The new property acquired has no additional cost element. The reinvestment element of the new property acquired consists of 2 subelements corresponding to the reinvestment element and additional cost element of the property disposed of. The subelement corresponding to the reinvestment element has additional depreciation of $10,000, that is, its additional depreciation immediately before the disposition ($100,000), minus $90,000, the amount of additional depreciation necessary to produce $45,000 of section 1250(a) gain where the applicable percentage is 50 percent. The subelement corresponding to the additional cost element has additional depreciation of $31,250, that is, its additional depreciation immediately before the disposition ($50,000), minus $18,750, the amount of additional depreciation necessary to produce $15,000 of section 1250(a) gain where the applicable percentage is 80 percent. [Reg. § 1.1250-3.]

☐ [T.D. 7084, 1-7-71. Amended by T.D. 7193, 6-29-72 and T.D. 7400, 2-3-76.]

[Reg. § 1.1250-4]

§ 1.1250-4. Holding period.—(a) *General.*—In general, for purposes only of determining the applicable percentage (as defined in sec. 1250(1)(C) and (2)(B)) of section 1250 property, the holding period of the property shall be determined under the rules of section 1250(e) and this section and not under the rules of section 1223. If the property is treated as consisting of two or more elements (within the meaning of paragraph (c)(1) of § 1.1250-5), see paragraph (a)(2)(ii) of § 1.1250-5 for application of this section to determination of holding period of each element. Section 1250(e) does not affect the determination of the amount of additional depreciation in respect of section 1250 property.

(b) *Beginning of holding period.*—(1) For the purpose of determining the applicable percentage, in the case of property acquired by the taxpayer (other than by means of a transaction referred to in paragraph (c) or (d) of this section), the holding period of the property shall begin on the day after the date of its acquisition. See section 1250(e)(1)(A). Thus, for example, if a taxpayer purchases section 1250 property on January 1, 1965, the holding period of the property begins on January 2, 1965. If he sells the property on October 1, 1966, the holding period

on the day of the sale is 21 full months, and, accordingly, the applicable percentage is 99 percent. This result would not be changed even if the property initially had been used solely as the taxpayer's residence for a portion of the 21-month period. If, however, the property were sold on September 30, 1966, the holding period would be only 20 full months.

(2) For the purpose of determining the applicable percentage in the case of property constructed, reconstructed, or erected by the taxpayer, the holding period of the property shall begin on the first day of the month during which the property is placed in service. See section 1250(e)(1)(B). Thus, for example, if a taxpayer constructs section 1250 property and places it in service on January 15, 1965, its holding period begins on January 1, 1965. If the taxpayer sells the property on December 31, 1966, its holding period on the day of sale is 24 full months, and, accordingly, the applicable percentage is 96 percent. For purposes of this subparagraph, property is placed in service on the date on which it is first used, whether in a trade or business, in the production of income, or in a personal activity. Thus, for example, a residence constructed by a taxpayer for his personal use is placed in service on the date it is occupied as a residence. For purposes of determining the date property is placed in service, it is immaterial when the period begins for depreciation with respect to the property under any depreciation practice under which depreciation begins in any month other than the month in which the property is placed in service. If one or more units of a single property are placed in service on different dates before the completion of the property, see paragraph (c)(3) of § 1.1250-5 (relating to treatment of each such unit as an element).

(c) *Property with transferred basis.*—Under section 1250(e)(2), if the basis of property acquired in a transaction described in this subparagraph is determined by reference to its basis in the hands of the transferor, then the holding period of the property in the hands of the transferee shall include the holding period of the property in the hands of the transferor. The transactions described in this subparagraph are:

(1) A gift described in section 1250(d)(1).

(2) Certain transfers at death to the extent provided in paragraph (b)(2)(ii) of § 1.1250-3.

(3) Certain tax-free transactions to which section 1250(d)(3) applies. For application of section 1250(d)(3) and (e)(2) to a distribution by a partnership to a partner, see paragraph (f)(1) of § 1.1250-3.

(4) A transfer described in paragraph (e)(4) of § 1.1250-3 (relating to transaction under section 1081(d)(1)(A)).

(d) *Principal residence acquired in certain transactions.*—The holding period of a principal residence acquired in a transaction to which section 1034 and paragraph (g)(6) of § 1.1250-3 apply includes the holding period of the principal residence disposed of in such transaction. See section 1250(e)(3). The holding period of a principal residence acquired does not include the period beginning on the day after the date of the disposition and ending on the date of the acquisition.

(e) *Application of transferred basis and principal residence rules.*—The determination of holding period under this section shall be made without regard to whether a transaction occurred prior to the effective date of section 1250 and without regard to whether there was any gain upon the transaction. Thus, for example, under paragraph (c) of this section a donee's holding period for property includes his donor's holding period notwithstanding that the gift occurred on or before December 31, 1963, or that there was no additional depreciation in respect of the property at the time of the gift.

(f) *Qualified low-income housing project acquired in certain transactions.*—The holding period of a "reinvestment element" (and of subelements thereof) of section 1250 property (as defined in paragraph (h)(2) of §1.1250-3) acquired in a transaction to which sections 1039(a) and 1250(d)(8)(A) apply includes the holding period of the corresponding element of the section 1250 property disposed of. See section 1250(e)(4). The holding period of the "additional cost element" (as defined in paragraph (h)(2) of §1.1250-3) begins on the date the replacement project is acquired. The holding period of a "reinvestment element" of section 1250 property does not include the period beginning on the day after the date of the disposition and ending (1) on the date of the acquisition of the replacement housing project, or (2) on the date the replacement housing project constructed or reconstructed by the taxpayer is placed in service.

(g) *Cross reference.*—If the adjusted basis of the property in the hands of the transferee immediately after a transaction to which paragraph (c) or (d) of this section applies exceeds its adjusted basis in the hands of the transferor immediately before the transaction, the excess is an addition to capital account under paragraph (d)(2)(ii) of §1.1250-5 (relating to property with two or more elements). [Reg. §1.1250-4.]

☐ [*T.D. 7084, 1-7-71. Amended by T.D. 7400, 2-3-76.*]

[Reg. §1.1250-5]

§1.1250-5. Property with two or more elements.—(a) *Dispositions before January 1, 1970.*—(1) *Amount treated as ordinary income.*—If section 1250 property consisting of two or more elements (described in paragraph (c) of this section) is disposed of before January 1, 1970, the amount of gain taken into account under section 1250(a)(2) shall be the sum, determined in three steps under subparagraphs (2), (3), and (4) of this

paragraph, of the amounts of gain for each element.

(2) *Step 1.*—The first step is to make the following computations:

(i) In respect of the property as a whole, compute the additional depreciation (as defined in section 1250(b)), and the gain realized. For purposes of this paragraph, in the case of a transaction other than a sale, exchange or involuntary conversion, the gain realized shall be considered to be the excess of the fair market value of the property over its adjusted basis.

(ii) In respect of each element as if it were a separate property, compute the additional depreciation for the element, and the applicable percentage (as defined in section 1250(a)(2)) for the element. For additional depreciation in respect of an element of property acquired in certain transactions, see paragraph (e) of this section. For purposes of determining additional depreciation, the holding period of an element shall be determined under section 1223, applied by treating the element as a separate property. However, for the purpose of determining applicable percentage, the holding period for an element shall, except to the extent provided in paragraphs (c)(5), (e), and (f) of this section, be determined in accordance with the rules prescribed in §1.1250-4.

(3) *Step 2.*—The second step is to determine the amount of gain for each element in the following manner:

(i) If the amount of additional depreciation in respect of the property as a whole is equal to the sum of the additional depreciation in respect of each element having additional depreciation, and if such amount is not more than the gain realized, then the amount of gain to be taken into account for an element is the product of the additional depreciation for the element, multiplied by the applicable percentage for the element.

(ii) If subdivision (i) of this subparagraph does not apply, the amount of gain to be taken into account for an element is the product of—

(*a*) The additional depreciation for the element, multiplied by

(*b*) The applicable percentage for the element, and multiplied by

(*c*) A ratio, computed by dividing (1) the lower of the additional depreciation in respect of the property as a whole or the gain realized, by (2) the sum of the additional depreciation in respect of each element having additional depreciation.

(4) *Step 3.*—The third step is to compute the sum of the amounts of gain for each element, as determined in step 2.

(5) *Examples.*—The provisions of this subparagraph may be illustrated by the following examples:

Example (1). Gain of $35,000 is realized upon a sale, before January 1, 1970, of section 1250 property which consists of four elements (W, X, Y, and Z). Since on the date of the sale the amount of additional depreciation in respect of the property as a whole ($24,000) is equal to the sum of the additional depreciation in respect of each element having additional depreciation and

Element	Additional depreciation	
W	$12,000	×
X	6,000	×
Y	0	×
Z	6,000	×
Totals	$24,000	

is less than the gain realized, the additional depreciation for each element is determined under subparagraph (3)(i) of this paragraph. The amount of gain taken into account under section 1250(a)(2) is $7,500, as determined in the following table in accordance with the additional facts assumed.

Applicable percentage		Gain for element
0	=	$ 0
50	=	3,000
63	=	0
75	=	4,500
		$7,500

Example (2). Assume the same facts as in example (1), except that in respect of the property as a whole the additional depreciation is $20,000 because with respect to element Y additional depreciation allowed was $4,000 less than straight line. Accordingly, the sum of the additional depreciation for each element having additional depreciation is $24,000, that is, $4,000 greater than the additional depreciation in respect of the property as a whole. Thus, the additional depreciation for each element is

Element	Additional depreciation		Applicable percentage
W	$12,000	×	0
X	6,000	×	50
Y	0	×	63
Z	6,000	×	75
Totals	$24,000		

determined under subparagraph (3)(ii) of this paragraph. The ratio referred to in subparagraph (3)(ii)(*c*) of this paragraph is twenty twenty-fourths, that is, the lower of additional depreciation in respect of the property as a whole ($20,000) or the gain realized ($35,000), divided by the sum of the additional depreciation in respect of each element having additional depreciation ($24,000). The amount of gain taken into account under section 1250(a)(2) is $6,250, as determined in the following table:

	Ratio		Gain for element
×	20:24	=	$0
×	20:24	=	2,500
×	20:24	=	0
×	20:24	=	3,750
			$6,250

(b) Dispositions after December 31, 1969.— (1) *Amount treated as ordinary income.*—If section 1250 property consisting of two or more elements (described in paragraph (c) of this section) is disposed of after December 31, 1969, the amount of gain taken into account under section 1250(a) shall be the sum, determined in 5 steps under subparagraphs (2), (3), (4), (5), and (6) of this paragraph, of the amount of gain for each element. Steps 3 and 4 are used only if the gain realized exceeds the additional depreciation attributable to periods after December 31, 1969, in respect of the property as a whole.

(2) *Step 1.*—The first step is to make the following computations:

(i) In respect of the property as a whole, compute the additional depreciation (as defined in section 1250(b)) attributable to periods after December 31, 1969, and the gain realized. For purposes of this paragraph, in the case of a transaction other than a sale, exchange, or involuntary conversion, the gain realized shall be considered to be the excess of the fair market value of the property over its adjusted basis.

(ii) In respect of each element as if it were a separate property, compute the additional depreciation for the element attributable to periods after December 31, 1969, and the applicable percentage (as defined in section 1250(a)(1)) for the

element. For additional depreciation in respect of an element of property acquired in certain transactions, see paragraph (e) of this section. For purposes of determining additional depreciation, the holding period of an element shall be determined under section 1223, applied by treating the element as a separate property. However, for the purpose of determining applicable percentage, the holding period for an element shall, except to the extent provided in paragraphs (c)(5), (e), and (f) of this section, be determined in accordance with the rules prescribed in §1.1250-4.

(3) *Step 2.*—The second step is to determine the amount of gain recognized for each element under section 1250(a)(1) in the following manner:

(i) If the amount of additional depreciation in respect of the property as a whole attributable to periods after December 31, 1969, is equal to the sum of the additional depreciation in respect of each element having such additional depreciation, and if such amount is not more than the gain realized, then the amount of gain to be taken into account for an element under section 1250(a)(1) is the product of the additional depreciation attributable to periods after December 31, 1969, for the element multiplied by the applicable percentage for the element determined under section 1250(a)(1).

Reg. §1.1250-5(b)(3)(i)

(ii) If subdivision (i) of this subparagraph does not apply, the amount of gain to be taken into account under section 1250(a)(1) for an element is the product of—

(a) The additional depreciation attributable to periods after December 31, 1969, for the element multiplied by

(b) The applicable percentage for the element determined under section 1250(a)(1) for the element, and multiplied by

(c) A ratio, computed by dividing (1) the lower of the additional depreciation in respect of the property as a whole which is attributable to periods after December 31, 1969, or the gain realized, by (2) the sum of the additional depreciation attributable to periods after December 31, 1969, in respect of each element having such additional depreciation.

(4) *Step (3).*—If the gain realized exceeds the additional depreciation in respect of the property as a whole attributable to periods after December 31, 1969,

(i) Compute the additional depreciation attributable to periods before January 1, 1970, and the remaining gain (or remaining potential gain in the case of a transaction other than a sale, exchange, or involuntary conversion), in respect of the property as a whole.

(ii) Compute the additional depreciation attributable to periods before January 1, 1970, and the applicable percentage determined under section 1250(a)(2) in respect of each element as if it were a separate property. For additional depreciation in respect of an element of property acquired in certain transactions, see paragraph (e) of this section. For purposes of determining additional depreciation, the holding period of an element shall be determined under section 1223, applied by treating the element as a separate property. However, for the purpose of determining applicable percentage, the holding period of an element shall, except to the extent provided in paragraphs (c)(5), (e), and (f) of this section, be determined in accordance with the rules prescribed in § 1.1250-4.

(5) *Step (4).*—The fourth step is to compute the gain recognized under section 1250(a)(2) for each element (if computation was required under step (3)) in the following manner:

(i) If the amount of additional depreciation in respect of the property as a whole attributable to periods before January 1, 1970, is equal

to the sum of the additional depreciation in respect of each element having such additional depreciation, and if such amount is not more than the remaining gain (or remaining potential gain), then the amount of gain to be taken into account for an element under section 1250(a)(2) is the product of the additional depreciation attributable to periods before January 1, 1970, for the element, multiplied by the applicable percentage determined under section 1250(a)(2) for the element.

(ii) If subdivision (i) of this subparagraph does not apply, the amount of gain to be taken into account for an element under section 1250(a)(2) is the product of—

(a) The additional depreciation attributable to periods before January 1, 1970, for the element, multiplied by

(b) The applicable percentage for the element determined under section 1250(a)(2), and multiplied by

(c) A ratio, computed by dividing (1) the lower of the additional depreciation in respect of the property as a whole which is attributable to periods before January 1, 1970, or the remaining gain (or remaining potential gain), by (2) the sum of the additional depreciation attributable to periods before January 1, 1970, in respect of each element having additional depreciation.

(6) *Step (5).*—The fifth step is to compute the sum of the amount of gain for each element, as determined in steps (2) and (4).

(7) *Examples.*—The provisions of this subparagraph may be illustrated by the following examples:

Example (1). Gain of $60,000 is realized upon a sale, after December 31, 1969, of section 1250 property which was constructed by the taxpayer after such date. The property consists of 4 elements (W, X, Y, and Z). Since on the date of sale the amount of additional depreciation attributable to periods after December 31, 1969, in respect of the property as a whole ($32,000), is equal to the sum of the additional depreciation in respect of each element having such additional depreciation and is less than the gain realized, the gain recognized for each element is determined under subparagraph (3)(i) of this paragraph. The amount of gain taken into account under section 1250(a)(1) is $28,500, as determined in the following table in accordance with the additional facts assumed:

Element	Additional depreciation after 12/31/69		Applicable percentage (1250(a)(1))		Gain for element
W	$14,000	×	80	=	$11,200
X	6,000	×	90	=	5,400
Y	2,000	×	95	=	1,900
Z	10,000	×	100	=	10,000
Total	$32,000				$28,500

Example (2). Assume the same facts as in example (1), except that the property was acquired by the taxpayer before January 1, 1970. Since the gain realized ($60,000) exceeds the additional depreciation attributable to periods after December 31, 1969 ($32,000), section 1250(a)(2) applies to the remaining gain of $28,000. Since the additional depreciation in respect of the property as a whole attributable to periods before January 1, 1970 ($21,000), is equal to the sum of the additional depreciation in respect of

Element	Additional depreciation before 1/1/70	
W	$ 8,000	×
X	6,000	×
Y	2,000	×
Z	5,000	×
Total	$21,000	

each element having such additional depreciation and is less than the remaining gain ($28,000), the amount of gain recognized for each element under section 1250(a)(2) is determined under subparagraph (5)(i) of this paragraph. The amount of gain taken into account under section 1250(a)(1) is $28,500 the same as in example (1). The amount of gain taken into account under section 1250(a)(2) is $3,900, as determined in the following table in accordance with the additional facts assumed:

Applicable percentage (1250(a)(2))		Gain for element (1250(a)(2))
0	=	$ 0
10	=	600
15	=	300
60	=	3,000
		$3,900

Example (3). (i) The facts are the same as in example (2) except that element Y has a deficit in additional depreciation attributable to periods after December 31, 1969, of $6,000 and thus the additional depreciation attributable to periods after December 31, 1969, in respect of the property as a whole is $24,000. The sum of the additional depreciation for each element having additional depreciation is $30,000, or $6,000 more than the additional depreciation in respect of the property as a whole. Thus, the gain recognized for each element under section 1250(a)(1)

is determined under subparagraph (3)(ii) of this paragraph. The ratio referred to in subparagraph (3)(ii)(c) of this paragraph is 24/30, that is, the lower of the additional depreciation in respect of the property as a whole attributable to periods after December 31, 1969 ($24,000), or the gain realized ($60,000), divided by the sum of the additional depreciation in respect of each element having such additional depreciation ($30,000). The amount of gain taken into account under section 1250(a)(1) is $21,280, as determined in the following table:

Element	Additional depreciation after 12/31/69		Applicable percentage (1250(a)(1))		Ratio		Gain for element
W	$14,000	×	80	×	24/30	=	$ 8,960
X	6,000	×	90	×	24/30	=	4,320
Y	(6,000)	×	95	×	24/30	=	0
Z	10,000	×	100	×	24/30	=	8,000
Total	$24,000						$21,280

(ii) In addition, gain is recognized under section 1250(a)(2) since there is a remaining potential gain of $36,000, that is, gain realized ($60,000) minus the additional depreciation attributable to periods after December 31, 1969 ($24,000). The gain recognized in respect of each element and the gain recognized under section 1250(a)(2) ($3,900) are the same as in example (2), since the additional depreciation attributable to periods before January 1, 1970 ($21,000) is less than the remaining gain ($36,000).

(c) *Element.*—(1) *General.*—For purposes of this section, in the case of section 1250 property there shall be treated as separate elements the separate improvements, units, remaining property, special elements, and low-income housing elements which are respectively referred to in paragraphs (c)(2), (3), (4), (5) and (6) of this section.

(2) *Separate improvements.*—There shall be treated as an element each "separate improvement" (as defined in paragraph (d)(1) of this section) to the property.

(3) *Units.*—If before completion of section 1250 property one or more units thereof are placed in service, each such unit of the section 1250 property shall be treated as an element.

(4) *Remaining property.*—The remaining property which is not taken into account under subparagraph (2) or (3) of this paragraph shall be treated as an element.

(5) *Special elements.*—(i) If the basis of section 1250 property is reduced in the manner described in paragraph (b)(2)(ii) of §1.1250-3 (relating to property acquired from a decedent prior to his death) or in paragraph (e)(3)(iii) of §1.1250-3 (relating to basis reduction under section 1071 or 1082(a)(2)), then such property shall be considered as having a special element with additional depreciation equal to the amount of additional depreciation included in the depreciation adjustments (referred to in paragraph (d)(1) of §1.1250-2) to which the basis reduction is attributable. For purposes of computing applicable percentage, the holding period of a special element under this subdivision shall be deter-

Reg. §1.1250-5(c)(5)(i)

mined under paragraph (b)(2)(ii) or (e)(3)(iii) (whichever is applicable) of § 1.1250-3.

(ii) If a disposition described in section 1250(d)(4)(A) (relating to like kind exchanges and involuntary conversions) of a portion of an item of property gives rise to an addition to capital account (described in the last sentence of paragraph (d)(2)(i) of this section) which is not a separate improvement, then such property shall be considered as having a special element with additional depreciation and, for purposes of computing applicable percentage, a holding period determined under paragraph (d)(7) of § 1.1250-3.

(6) *Low-income housing elements.*—If, in an approved disposition of a qualified housing project, a replacement qualified housing project is treated as consisting of more than one element of section 1250 property by reason of section 1250(d)(8)(E) (see paragraph (h)(2) of § 1.1250-3), the elements determined under such section shall be treated as elements for purposes of this section. For definition of the terms "qualified housing project" and "approved disposition,"

Stage	Kind of element
1	unit . . . .
2	unit . . . .
3	remaining property . . . .

Example (2). Assume the same facts as in example (1) except that on January 1, 1969, two new floors, which were added after the apartment house was completed, are placed in service and that on July 1, 1972, the taxpayer disposes of the building. Assume further that the two new floors are one separate improvement (within the meaning of paragraph (d) of this section). On the date disposed of, the property consists of four elements, that is, the three elements described in example (1) and the separate improvement.

(d) *Separate improvement.*—(1) *Definition.*—For purposes of this section, with respect to any section 1250 property, the term "separate improvement" means an "addition to capital account" described in subparagraph (2) of this paragraph which qualifies as an "improvement" under the one-year test prescribed in subparagraph (3) of this paragraph and which satisfies the 36-month test prescribed in subparagraph (4) of this paragraph.

(2) *Addition to capital account.*—(i) In the case of any section 1250 property, an addition to capital account described in this subparagraph is any addition to capital account in respect of such property after its initial acquisition or completion by the taxpayer or by any person who held the property during a period included in the taxpayer's holding period (see § 1.1250-4) for the property. An addition to the capital account of section 1250 property may arise, for example, if there is an expenditure for section 1250 property which is an improvement, replacement, addition, or alteration to such property (regardless of

see section 1039(b) and the regulations thereunder.

(7) *Examples.*—The provisions of this paragraph may be illustrated by the following examples:

Example (1). A taxpayer constructs an apartment house which he places in service in three stages. The total cost is $1 million of which $350,000 is allocable to the first stage, $500,000 to the second stage, and $150,000 to the third stage. The first stage, which is placed in service on January 1, 1965, consists of 300 apartments and certain facilities including a central heating system and a common lobby. The second stage, which is placed in service on July 15, 1965, consists of 550 apartments and certain facilities including the motor for a central air-conditioning system. The third stage, which is placed in service on January 19, 1966, consists of the residue of the apartment house. On December 31, 1968, the taxpayer disposes of the apartment house. On such date, the apartment house has three elements which are described in the table below:

Cost	Full months in holding period	Applicable percentage
$350,000	48	72
500,000	42	78
150,000	36	84

whether the cost thereof is capitalized or charged against the depreciation reserve). In such a case, the "addition to capital account" is the gross addition, unreduced by amounts attributable to replaced property, to the net capital account and not the net addition to such account. Thus, if a roof has an adjusted basis of $20,000, and is replaced by constructing a new roof at a cost of $50,000, the gross addition of $50,000 is an addition to capital account. (The adjusted basis of the old roof is no longer included in the capital account for the property.) For purposes of this section, the status of an addition to capital account is not affected by whether or not it is treated as a separate property for purposes of determining depreciation adjustments. In case of an addition to the capital account of property arising after December 31, 1963, upon a disposition referred to in section 1250(d)(4) (relating to like kind exchanges and involuntary conversions) of a portion of an item of such property, the amount of such addition (and its basis for all purposes of the Code) shall be the basis thereof determined under paragraph (d)(2), (3), or (4) (whichever is applicable) of § 1.1250-3, applied by treating such portion and such addition as separate properties.

(ii) An addition to capital account may be attributable to an excess of the adjusted basis of section 1250 property in the hands of a transferee immediately after a transaction referred to in section 1250(e)(2) (relating to holding period of property with transferred basis) over its adjusted basis in the hands of the transferor immediately before the transaction. Thus, for example, such excess may arise from a gift which is in part a sale or exchange (see paragraph (a)(2) of § 1.1250-3), from an increase in basis due to gift tax paid (see section 1015(d)), from a transfer referred to in paragraph (c)(2) of § 1.1250-3 (relating to certain tax-free transactions) in which gain is partially recognized, or from a distribution by a partnership to a partner in which no gain is recognized by reason of the application of section 731. Similarly, an addition to capital account may be attributable to an excess of the adjusted basis of a principal residence acquired in a transaction referred to in section 1250(e)(3) over the adjusted basis of the principal residence disposed of, as well as to any increase in the adjusted basis of section 1250 property of a partnership by reason of an optional basis adjustment under section 734(b) or 743(b).

(iii) Whether or not an expenditure shall be treated as an addition to capital account described in this subparagraph, as distinguished from a separate item of property, may depend on how the property or properties are disposed of. Thus, for example, if a taxpayer, who owns a motel consisting of 10 buildings with common heating and plumbing systems, adds to the motel three new buildings which are connected to the common systems, and if the taxpayer sells the motel to one person in one transaction, then for purposes of this subparagraph the cost of the three new buildings shall be treated as an addition to the capital account of the motel and, if the 1-year and 36-month tests of subparagraphs (3) and (4) of this paragraph are satisfied, the motel consists of at least two elements. If, however, the 10-building group and the three-building group were individually sold in separate transactions to two different people each of whom would operate his group as a separate business, the motel would consist of two items of property.

(3) *One-year test for improvement.*—(i) An addition to capital account of section 1250 property for any taxable year (including a short taxable year and the entire taxable year in which the disposition occurs) shall be treated as an improvement only if the sum of all additions to the capital account of such property for such taxable year exceeds the greater of—

(a) $2,000, or

(b) One percent of the unadjusted basis of the property, determined as of the beginning (1) of such taxable year, or (2) of the holding period (within the meaning of § 1.1250-4) of the property, whichever is the later.

(ii) For purposes of this section, the term "unadjusted basis" means the adjusted basis of the property, determined without regard to the adjustments provided in section 1016(a)(2) and (3) (relating to adjustments for depreciation, amortization, and depletion). For purposes of this paragraph, as of any particular date the unadjusted basis of section 1250 property (a) includes the cost of any addition to capital account

for the property which arises prior to such date (regardless of whether such addition qualified under this subparagraph as an improvement), and (b) does not include the cost of a component retired before such date.

(iii) In respect of a particular disposition of section 1250 property by a person—

(a) There shall not be taken into account under the 1-year test for improvements in this subparagraph any addition to capital account which arises by reason of (or after) such disposition or which arises before the beginning of the holding period under § 1.1250-4 of such person for the property, and

(b) Such test shall be made in respect of each taxable year of such person (and of any prior transferor) any day of which is included under § 1.1250-4 in such person's holding period for the property, except that (1) such test shall be made for a taxable year of such person only if such person actually owned the property on at least 1 day of such taxable year, and (2) such test shall be made for a taxable year of such prior transferor only if such prior transferor actually owned the property on at least 1 day of such taxable year.

(iv) The provisions of this subpararaph may be illustrated by the following examples:

Example (1). The unadjusted basis of section 1250 property as of the beginning of January 1, 1960, is $300,000. During the taxable year ending on December 31, 1960, the only additions to the capital account for the property are addition A on January 1, 1960, costing $1,000, and addition B on July 1, 1960, costing $600. Since the sum of the amounts added to capital account for such taxable year is less than $2,000, A and B are not treated as improvements. This result would not be changed if addition C, costing $600, were added on December 15, 1960, since although the sum of the additions ($1,000 plus $600 plus $600, or $2,200) exceeds $2,000, such sum is less than 1 percent of the unadjusted basis of the property as of the beginning of 1960 ($3,000, that is, 1 percent of $300,000). If however, C cost $1,500, then A, B, and C would each be considered an improvement since the sum of the amounts added to capital account ($3,100) would exceed $3,000.

Example (2). Green and his son both use the calendar year as the taxable year. On February 1, 1965, Green makes addition A to a piece of section 1250 property. On June 15, 1965, Green transfers such property to his son as a gift which is in part a sale (see paragraph (a) of § 1.1250-3). Addition B arises by reason of the transfer. On August 1, 1965, the son makes addition C to the property. For purposes of determining the amount of gain recognized under section 1250(a) to Green upon the transfer, the determination of whether addition A is an improvement is made without taking into account additions B and C. For purposes of determining the amount of gain recognized under section 1250(a) upon a subse-

Reg. §1.1250-5(d)(3)(iv)

quent disposition of the property by the son, additions B and C would be taken into account in the determination of whether A is an improvement, and A would be taken into account in the determination of whether B and C are improvements.

Example (3). Assume the same facts as in example (2). Assume further that on September 15, 1965, the son transfers the property to a corporation in exchange for cash and stock in the corporation in a transaction qualifying under section 351 (see paragraph (c) of § 1.1250-3), and that the corporation uses a fiscal year ending November 30. For purposes of determining the amount of gain recognized under section 1250(a) upon a subsequent disposition by the corporation, the one-year test under subdivision (i) of this subparagraph is made for the entire taxable year of Green and of the son ending on December 31, 1965, and in respect of the corporation's taxable year ending November 30, 1965. Accordingly, if on December 7, 1965, addition D is made by the corporation, then, upon a subsequent disposition by the corporation, D is taken into account for purposes of the determination in respect of the entire taxable year of Green and of the son ending on December 31, 1965, and for the corporation's taxable year ending November 30, 1966, but not for purposes of the corporation's taxable year ending November 30, 1965. If D were made on January 3, 1966, D would still be taken into account for purposes of the determination in respect of the corporation's taxable year ending November 30, 1966. However, since neither Green nor his son actually owned the property on any day of the taxable year ending December 31, 1966, no determination is made in respect of such taxable year of Green or of the son.

(4) 36-month test for separate improvement.— (i) If, during the 36-month period ending on the last day of any taxable year (including a short taxable year and the entire taxable year in which the disposition occurs), the sum of the amounts treated under subparagraph (3) of this paragraph as improvements for such period exceeds the greatest of—

(a) 25 percent of the adjusted basis of the property,

(b) 10 percent of the unadjusted basis (determined under subparagraph (3)(ii) of this paragraph) of the property, or

(c) $5,000,

then each such improvement during such period shall be treated as a separate improvement, and thus as an element. For purposes of (a) and (b) of this subdivision, the adjusted basis (or unadjusted basis) of section 1250 property shall be determined as of the beginning of the 36-month period, or as of the beginning of the holding period of the property (within the meaning of § 1.1250-4), whichever is the later.

(ii) In respect of a particular disposition of section 1250 property by a person—

(a) There shall not be taken into account under the 36-month test for separate improvements in this subparagraph any amount treated under subparagraph (3) of this paragraph as an improvement which arises by reason of (or after) the disposition or which arises before the beginning of the holding period under § 1.1250-4 of such person for the property, and

(b) Such test shall be made in respect of each 36-month period ending on the last day of each taxable year of such person (and of any prior transferor) if at least 1 day of such period is included under § 1.1250-4 in such person's holding period for the property, except that (1) such test shall be made for a 36-month period ending on the last day of a taxable year of such person only if such person actually owned the property on at least 1 day of such period, and (2) such test shall be made for a 36-month period ending on the last day of a taxable year of such prior transferor only if such prior transferor actually owned the property on at least 1 day of such period.

(iii) For illustration of the principles of subdivision (ii) of this subparagraph, see examples (2) and (3) in subparagraph (3)(iv) of this paragraph.

(5) Example.—The application of this paragraph may be illustrated by the following example:

Example. (i) On December 31, 1967, X, a calendar year taxpayer, purchases an item of section 1250 property at a cost of $100,000. In the table below, the adjusted basis and unadjusted basis of the property are shown for the beginning of January 1 of each taxable year and it is assumed that each addition to capital was added on January 1 of the year shown.

Year	Adjusted basis	Unadjusted basis	1 percent of unadjusted basis		Addition
1969	$94,000	$100,000	$1,000	A	$10,000
1970	97,030	110,000	1,100	B	4,000
1971	94,041	114,000	1,140	C	6,000
1972	92,799	120,000	1,200		. . .
1973	86,158	120,000	1,200	D	18,000

(ii) Since each addition to capital account for the property exceeds the greater of $2,000 or one percent of unadjusted basis, determined as of the beginning of the taxable year in which made, each addition to capital account qualifies as an improvement under subparagraph (2) of this paragraph.

(iii) Since the beginning of the holding period of the property under § 1.1250-4 (Jan. 1, 1968) is later than the beginning of the 36-month period ending on December 31, 1969, the determination as to whether there are any separate improvements on the property as of December 31, 1969, is made by examining the adjusted basis (or unadjusted basis) of the property as of the beginning of January 1, 1968. As of December 31, 1969, there were no separate improvements on the property since the only amount treated as an improvement for the period beginning on January 1, 1968, and ending on December 31, 1969, is addition A (costing $10,000), which is less than $25,000, that is, 25 percent of the adjusted basis ($100,000) of the property as of the beginning of January 1, 1968.

(iv) As of December 31, 1970, there were no separate improvements on the property since the sum of the amounts treated as improvements for the 36-month period ending on December 31, 1970, is $14,000 (that is, $10,000 for A, plus $4,000 for B), and this sum is less than $25,000, that is, 25 percent of the adjusted basis ($100,000) of the property as of the beginning of January 1, 1968.

(v) As of December 31, 1971, there were no separate improvements on the property since the sum of the amounts treated as improvements for the 36-month period ending on December 31, 1971, is $20,000 (that is, $10,000 for A, plus $4,000 for B, plus $6,000 for C), and this sum is less than $23,500, that is, 25 percent of the adjusted basis ($94,000) of the property as of the beginning of January 1, 1969.

(vi) As of December 31, 1972, there were no separate improvements on the property since the sum of the amounts treated as improvements for the 36-month period ending on December 31, 1972, is $10,000 (that is, $4,000 for B plus $6,000 for C), and this sum is less than $24,258 that is, 25 percent of the adjusted basis ($97,030) of the property as of the beginning of January 1, 1970.

(vii) As of December 31, 1973, C and D are separate improvements (notwithstanding that as of December 31, 1971 and 1972, C was not a separate improvement) since the sum of the amounts added for the 36-month period ending December 31, 1973, is $24,000 (that is, $6,000 for C plus $18,000 for D), and this sum exceeds the greatest of—

(*a*) $23,510, that is, 25 percent of the adjusted basis ($94,041) of the section 1250 property as of the beginning of January 1, 1971,

(*b*) $11,400, that is, 10 percent of the unadjusted basis ($114,000) of the property as of the beginning of such first day, or

(*c*) $5,000.

(e) *Additional depreciation and holding period of property acquired in certain transactions.*—(1) *Transferred basis.*—If property consisting of two or more elements is disposed of, and if the holding period of the property in the hands of the transferee for purposes of computing applicable percentage includes the holding period of the transferor by reason of the application of paragraph (c) (other than subparagraph (2) thereof) of § 1.1250-4, then the additional depreciation for each element of the property in the hands of the transferee immediately after the transfer shall be computed in the manner set forth in this subparagraph. First, any element having a deficit in additional depreciation in the hands of the transferor immediately before such transfer shall be considered to have the same deficit in the hands of the transferee. Second, elements having additional depreciation in the hands of the transferor immediately before the transfer shall be considered to have additional depreciation in the hands of the transferee. The sum of the transferee's additional depreciation for all elements of the property having additional depreciation in the hands of the transferor shall be an amount equal to the additional depreciation in respect of the property as a whole immediately after the transfer increased by the sum of the deficits in additional depreciation for all elements having such deficits. In case there is more than one element having additional depreciation, the additional depreciation for any such element in the hands of the transferee shall be computed by multiplying (i) the amount computed under the preceding sentence by (ii) the additional depreciation for such element in the hands of the transferor divided by the sum of the additional depreciation for all such elements having additional depreciation in the hands of the transferor. For purposes of computing applicable percentage, the holding period for an element of such property in the hands of the transferee shall include the holding period of such element in the hands of the transferor.

(2) *Example.*—The provisions of subparagraph (1) of this paragraph may be illustrated by the following example:

Example. Section 1250 property has additional depreciation of $16,000 of which $12,000 is additional depreciation for element X and $4,000 for element Y. The property is transferred to a corporation in exchange for cash of $6,000 and for stock in the corporation. Assume that recognition of gain under section 1250(a) is limited to $6,000 (the amount of cash received) by reason of the application of section 351(b) (relating to transfer to corporation controlled by transferor) and section 1250(d)(3) (relating to limitation on application of section 1250 in certain tax-free transactions). Under paragraph (c)(3)(i) of § 1.1250-3, the additional depreciation for the property in the hands of the corporation immediately after the transfer is $10,000, that is, the additional depreciation for the property in the hands of the transferor immediately before the transfer ($16,000) minus the gain under section 1250 (a) recognized upon the transfer ($6,000). Under subparagraph (1) of this paragraph, in the hands of the corporation immediately after the transfer element X has additional depreciation of $7,500 ($^{12}/_{16}$ of $10,000) and element Y has additional depreciation of $2,500 ($^4/_{16}$ of $10,000). Under paragraph (d)(2)(ii) of this section there is an addition of $6,000 to the capital account for the property.

(3) *Principal residence.*—If a principal residence consisting of two or more elements is disposed of, and if for purposes of computing applicable percentage the holding period of the principal residence acquired includes the holding period of the principal residence disposed of by reason of the application of paragraph (d) of §1.1250-4, then the additional depreciation (or a deficit in additional depreciation) for an element of the principal residence acquired immediately after the transaction shall be determined in a manner consistent with the principles of subparagraph (1) of this paragraph. For purposes of computing applicable percentage, the holding period for an element of the principal residence acquired includes the holding period of such element of the principal residence disposed of, but not the period beginning on the day after the date of the disposition and ending on the date of the acquisition.

(4) [Reserved]

(f) *Holding period for small separate improvements.*—(1) *General.*—This paragraph prescribes a special holding period solely for the purpose of computing the applicable percentage of a separate improvement (as defined in paragraph (d) of this section) which is treated as an element. See paragraph (a)(2)(ii) of this section for determination of holding period under section 1223 for purposes of computing additional depreciation. In respect of section 1250 property, if the amount of a separate improvement does not exceed the greater of—

(i) $2,000, or

(ii) One percent of the unadjusted basis (within the meaning of paragraph (d)(3)(ii) of this section) of such property, determined as of the beginning of the taxable year in which such separate improvement was made,

then such separate improvement shall be treated for purposes of computing applicable percentage as placed in service on the first day, of a calendar month, which is the closest such first day to the middle of the taxable year. See the last sentence of section 1250(f)(4)(B). If two such first days are equally close to the middle of the taxable year, the earliest of such days is the applicable day.

(2) *Example.*—The application of this paragraph may be illustrated by the following example:

Example. (i) The unadjusted basis of section 1250 property as of the beginning of January 1, 1960, is $100,000. During the taxable year ending on December 31, 1960, the only additions to the capital account for the property are addition A

on March 10, 1960, costing $1,200 and addition B on September 16, 1960, costing $1,400. Since the sum of the additions ($2,600) exceeds the greater of $2,000 and one percent of unadjusted basis ($1,000, that is, one percent of $100,000), each addition is an improvement under the 1-year test of paragraph (d)(3) of this section. Assume that the 36-month test of paragraph (d)(4) of this section is satisfied and, therefore, each addition is a separate improvement treated as an element.

(ii) Since each element is less than $2,000, the provisions of this paragraph apply. Since there are 366 days in 1960, the middle of the year is at the end of 183 days, or July 1. Thus, that first day of a calendar month in 1960, which is the closest first day (of a calendar month) to the middle of the taxable year, is July 1, 1960. Accordingly, for purposes of computing applicable percentage, elements A and B are each treated as placed in service on July 1, 1960. [Reg. §1.1250-5.]

☐ [*T.D. 7084, 1-7-71. Amended by T.D. 7193, 6-29-72 and T.D. 7400, 2-3-76.*]

[Reg. §1.1252-1]

§1.1252-1. General rule for treatment of gain from disposition of farm land.—(a) *Ordinary income.*—(1) *General rule.*—(i) Except as otherwise provided in this section and §1.1252-2, if farm land is disposed of during a taxable year beginning after December 31, 1969, then under section 1252(a)(1) there shall be treated as gain from the sale or exchange of property which is neither a capital asset nor property described in section 1231 (that is, shall be recognized as ordinary income) the lower of—

(a) The applicable percentage of the amount computed in subdivision (ii) of this subparagraph, or

(b) The amount computed in subdivision (iii) of this subparagraph.

(ii) The amount computed in this subdivision is an amount equal to—

(a) The aggregate of the deductions allowed, in any taxable year any day of which falls within the period the taxpayer held (or is considered to have held) the farm land, under sections 175 (relating to soil and water conservation expenditures) and 182 (relating to expenditures by farmers for clearing land) for expenditures paid or incurred after December 31, 1969, with respect to the farm land disposed of, minus

(b) The amount of gain recognized as ordinary income under section 1251(c)(1) (relating to gain from disposition of property used in farming where farm losses offset nonfarm income) upon such disposition of such land.

(iii) The amount computed in this subdivision is an amount equal to—

(a) The gain realized, that is, the excess of the amount realized (in the case of a sale, exchange, or involuntary conversion) or the fair market value of the farm land (in the case of any other disposition), over the adjusted basis of the farm land, minus

(b) The amount of gain recognized as ordinary income under section 1251(c)(1) upon such disposition of such land.

(iv) If a deduction under section 175 is allowed in respect of the farm land disposed of for a taxable year every day of which falls within the period after the taxpayer held (or is considered to have held) the farm land, and if the deduction is attributable to expenditures paid or incurred after December 31, 1969, with respect to such land during the period the taxpayer held (or is considered to have held) the land, then the amount of such deduction shall be applied to increase the amount computed (without regard to this subdivision) under subdivision (ii)(a) of this subparagraph.

(2) *Application of section.*—Any gain treated as ordinary income under section 1252(a)(1) shall

If the farm land is disposed of—	The applicable percentage is—
Within 5 years after the date it was acquired	100 percent
Within the sixth year after it was acquired	80 percent
Within the seventh year after it was acquired	60 percent
Within the eighth year after it was acquired	40 percent
Within the ninth year after it was acquired	20 percent
Within the tenth year after it was acquired and thereafter	0 percent

(4) *Portion of parcel.*—The amount of gain to be recognized as ordinary income under section 1252(a) (1) shall be determined separately for each parcel of farm land in a manner consistent with the principles of subparagraphs (4) and (5) of § 1.1245-1(a) (relating to gain from disposition of certain depreciable property). If (i) only a portion of a parcel of farm land is disposed of in a transaction, or if two or more portions of a single parcel are disposed of in one transaction, and (ii) the aggregate of the deductions allowed under sections 175 and 182 with respect to any such portion cannot be established to the satisfaction of the Commissioner or his delegate, then the aggregate of the deductions in respect of the entire parcel shall be allocated to each portion in proportion to the fair market value of each at the time of the disposition.

(b) *Instances of non-application.*—(1) *In general.*—Section 1252 does not apply if a taxpayer disposes of farm land for which the holding period is in excess of 9 years or with respect to which no deductions have been allowed under sections 175 and 182.

(2) *Losses.*—Section 1252(a)(1) does not apply to losses. Thus, section 1252(a)(1) does not apply if a loss is realized upon a sale, exchange, or involuntary conversion of property, all of which is farm land, nor does the section apply to a disposition of such property other than by way of sale, exchange, or involuntary conversion if at the time of the disposition the fair market value of such property is not greater than its adjusted basis.

(c) *Treatment of partnerships and partners.*— [Reserved.]

be recognized as ordinary income notwithstanding any other provision of subtitle A of the Code. For special rules with respect to the application of section 1252, see § 1.1252-2. For the relation of section 1252 to other provisions see paragraph (d) of this section.

(3) *Meaning of terms.*—For purpose of section 1252—

(i) The term "farm land" means any land with respect to which deductions have been allowed under section 175 or 182. See section 1252(a)(2).

(ii) The period for which farm land shall be considered to be held shall be determined under section 1223.

(iii) The term "disposition" shall have the same meaning as in paragraph (a)(3) of § 1.1245-1.

(iv) The applicable percentage shall be determined as follows:

(d) *Relation of section 1252 to other provisions.*—(1) *General.*—The provisions of section 1252 apply notwithstanding any other provision of subtitle A of the Code. Thus, unless an exception or limitation under § 1.1252-2 applies, gain under section 1252 (a)(1) is recognized notwithstanding any contrary nonrecognition provision or income characterizing provision. For example, since section 1252 overrides section 1231 (relating to property used in the trade or business), the gain recognized under section 1252(a)(1) upon a disposition of farm land will be treated as ordinary income and only the remaining gain, if any, from the disposition may be considered as gain from the sale or exchange of a capital asset if section 1231 is applicable. See example (1) of paragraph (e) of this section.

(2) *Nonrecognition sections overridden.*—The nonrecognition of gain provisions of subtitle A of the Code which section 1252 overrides include, but are not limited to, sections 267(d), 311(a), 336, 337, and 512(b)(5). See § 1.1252-2 for the extent to which section 1252(a)(1) overrides sections 332, 351, 361, 371(a), 374(a), 721, 731, 1031, and 1033.

(3) *Installment method.*—Gain from a disposition to which section 1252 (a)(1) applies may be reported under the installment method if such method is otherwise available under section 453 of the Code. In such case, the income (other than interest) on each installment payment shall (a) first be deemed to consist of gain to which section 1251(c)(1) applies (if applicable) until all such gain has been reported, (b) the next portion (if any) of such income shall be deemed to consist of gain to which section 1252(a)(1) applies until all such gain has been reported, and (c)

finally the remaining portion (if any) of such income shall be deemed to consist of gain to which neither section 1251(c)(1) nor 1252(a)(1) applies. For treatment of amounts as interest on certain deferred payments, see section 483.

(4) *Exempt income.*—With regard to exempt income, the principles of paragraph (e) of § 1.1245-6 shall be applicable.

(5) *Treatment of gain not recognized under section 1252(a)(1).*—For treatment of gain not recognized under this section, the principles of paragraph (f) of § 1.1245-6 shall be applicable.

(e) *Examples.*—The provisions of this section may be illustrated by the following examples:

Example (1). Individual A uses the calendar year as his taxable year. On April 10, 1975 he sells for $75,000 a parcel of farm land which he had acquired on January 5, 1970, with an adjusted basis of $52,500 for a realized gain of $22,500. The aggregate of the deductions allowed under sections 175 and 182 with respect to such land is $18,000 and all of such amount was al-

lowed for 1970. Under the stated facts, none of the $22,500 gain realized is recognized as ordinary income under section 1251(c)(1) as there is no potential gain (as defined in section 1251(e)(5)) with respect to the farm land. Since no gain is recognized as ordinary income under section 1251(c)(1), and since the applicable percentage, 80 percent, of the aggregate of the deductions allowed under sections 175 and 182, $18,000, or $14,400, is lower than the gain realized, $22,500, the amount of gain recognized as ordinary income under section 1252(a)(1) is $14,400. The remaining $8,100 of the gain may be treated as gain from the sale or exchange of property described in section 1231.

Example (2). Assume the same facts as in example (2) of paragraph (b)(6) of § 1.1251-1. Assume further that the aggregate of the amount of section 175 and 182 deductions allowable to the M corporation is equal to the amount allowed. Under paragraph (a)(1) of this section, $5,000 is recognized as ordinary income under section 1252(a)(1) upon the disposition of the land as a dividend, computed as follows:

(1) Aggregate of deductions allowed under sections 175 and 182	$18,000
(2) Minus: Gain recognized as ordinary income under section 1251(c)(1)	13,000
(3) Difference	$ 5,000
(4) Multiply: Applicable percentage for property disposed of within the fifth year after it was acquired	100%
(5) Amount in paragraph (a)(1)(i)(*a*) of this section	$ 5,000
(6) Gain realized (fair market value $67,500, less adjusted basis, $45,000)	$22,500
(7) Minus: Amount in line (2)	13,000
(8) Amount in paragraph (a)(1)(i)(*b*) of this section	$ 9,500
(9) Lower of line (5) or line (8)	$ 5,000

The "gain realized", $22,500, minus the sum of the gain recognized as ordinary income under section 1251(c)(1), $13,000, and under section 1252(a)(1), $5,000, equals $4,500. Assuming section 311(d) (relating to certain distributions of appreciated property to redeem stock) does not apply, under section 311(a) the corporation does not recognize gain on account of the $4,500.

Example (3). Assume the same facts as in example (2) of this paragraph, except that M contracted to sell the land for $67,500 which would be paid in 10 equal payments of $6,750 each, plus a sufficient amount of interest so that section 483

does not apply. Assume further that the remaining gain of $4,500 is treated as gain from the sale or exchange of property described in section 1231. M properly elects under section 453 to report under the installment method gain of $13,000 to which section 1251(c)(1) applies, gain of $5,000 to which section 1252(a)(1) applies, and gain of $4,500 to which section 1231 applies. Since the total gain realized on the sale was $22,500, the gross profit realized on each installment payment is $2,250, *i.e.*, $6,750 × ($22,500/$67,500). Accordingly, the treatment of the income to be reported on each installment payment is as follows:

Payment No.	1251	Applicable sections 1252	1231
(1)	$2,250	. . .	. . .
(2)	2,250	. . .	. . .
(3)	2,250	. . .	. . .
(4)	2,250	. . .	. . .
(5)	2,250	. . .	. . .
(6)	1,750	$ 500	. . .
(7)	. . .	2,250	. . .
(8)	. . .	2,250	. . .
(9)	. . .	. . .	$2,250
(10)	. . .	. . .	2,250
Totals	$13,000	$5,000	$4,500

□ [T.D. 7418, 5-6-76.]

Reg. § 1.1252-1(d)(4)

[Reg. §1.1252-2]

§1.1252-2. Special rules.—(a) *Exception for gifts.*—(1) *General rule.*—In general, no gain shall be recognized under section 1252(a)(1) upon a disposition of farm land by gift. For purposes of section 1252 and this paragraph, the term "gift" shall have the same meaning as in paragraph (a) of §1.125-4 and, with respect to the application of this paragraph, principles illustrated by the examples of paragraph (a)(2) of §1.1245-4 shall apply. For reduction in amount of charitable contribution in case of a gift of farm land, see section 170(e) and §1.170A-4.

(2) *Disposition in part a sale or exchange and in part a gift.*—Where a disposition of farm land is in part a sale or exchange and in part a gift, the amount of gain which shall be recognized as ordinary income under section 1252(a)(1) shall be computed under paragraph (a)(1) of §1.1252-1, applied by treating the gain realized (for purposes of paragraph (a)(1)(iii)(a) of §1.1252-1) as the excess of the amount realized over the adjusted basis of the farm land.

(3) *Treatment of farm land in hands of transferee.*—See paragraph (f) of this section for treatment of the transferee in the case of a disposition to which this paragraph applies.

(4) *Examples.*—The provisions of this paragraph may be illustrated by the following examples:

(1) Aggregate of deductions allowed under sections 175 and 182	$24,000
(2) Minus: Gain recognized as ordinary income under section 1251(c)(1)	3,000
(3) Difference	$21,000
(4) Multiply: Applicable percentage for land disposed of within si xth year after it was acquired	80%
(5) Amount in paragraph (a)(1)(i)(a) of §1.1252-1	$16,800
(6) Gain realized (see subdivision (i) of this example)	$10,000
(7) Minus: Amount in line (2)	3,000
(8) Amount in paragraph (a)(1)(i)(b) of §1.1252-1, applied in accordance with subparagraph (2) of this paragraph	$7,000
(9) Lower of line (5) or line (8)	$7,000

Thus, the entire gain realized on the transfer, $10,000, is recognized as ordinary income since that amount is equal to the sum of the gain recognized as ordinary income under section 1251(c)(1), $3,000, and under section 1252(a)(1), $7,000. For treatment of the farm land in the hands of B, see example (2) of paragraph (f)(3) of this section.

(b) *Exceptions for transfers at death.*—(1) *In general.*—Except as provided in section 691 (relating to income in respect of a decedent), no gain shall be recognized under section 1252(a)(1) upon a transfer at death. For purposes of section 1252 and this paragraph, the term "transfer at death" shall have the same meaning as in paragraph (b) of §1.1245-4 and, with respect to the application of this paragraph, principles illustrated by the examples of paragraph (b)(2) of §1.1245-4 shall apply.

Example (1). On March 2, 1976, A, a calendar year taxpayer, makes a gift to B of a parcel of land having an adjusted basis of $40,000, a fair market value of $65,000, and a holding period of 6 years (A, having purchased the land on January 15, 1971). On the date of such gift, the aggregate of the deductions allowed to A under sections 175 and 182 with respect to the land is $24,000 with $21,000 of such amount attributable to 1971. Upon making the gift, A recognizes no gain under section 1251(c)(1) or section 1252(a)(1). See paragraph (a)(1) of §1.1251-4 and subparagraph (1) of this paragraph. For treatment of the farm land in the hands of B, see example (1) of paragraph (f)(3) of this section. For effect of the gift on the excess deductions accounts of A and of B, see paragraph (e)(2) of §1.1251-2.

Example (2). (i) Assume the same facts as in example (1), except that A transfers the land to B for $50,000. Thus, the gain realized is $10,000 (amount realized, $50,000, minus adjusted basis, $40,000), and A has made a gift of $15,000 (fair market value, $65,000, minus amount realized, $50,000).

(ii) Upon the transfer of the land to B, A recognizes $3,000 of gain under section 1251(c)(1). See example (2) of paragraph (a)(4) of §1.1251-4. Thus, A recognizes $7,000 as ordinary income under section 1252(a)(1), computed under subparagraph (2) of this paragraph as follows:

(2) *Treatment of farm land in hands of transferee.*—If as of the date a person acquires farm land from a decedent such person's basis is determined, by reason of the application of section 1014(a), solely by reference to the fair market value of the property on the date of the decedent's death or on the applicable date provided in section 2032 (relating to alternative valuation date), then on such date the aggregate of the section 175 and 182 deductions allowed with respect to the farm land in the hands of such transferee is zero.

(c) *Limitation for certain tax-free transactions.*—(1) *Limitation on amount of gain.*—Upon a transfer of farm land described in subparagraph (2) of this paragraph, the amount of gain recognized as ordinary income under section 1252(a)(1) shall not exceed an amount equal to the excess (if any) of (i) the amount of gain recognized to the transferor on the transfer (determined without regard to section 1252) over (ii) the amount (if any) of gain recognized as ordinary income under section 1251(c)(1). For purposes of this subparagraph, the principles of paragraph (c)(1) of § 1.1245-4 shall apply. Thus, in the case of a transfer of farm land and property other than farm land in one transaction, the amount realized from the disposition of the farm land (as determined in a manner consistent with the principles of paragraph (a)(5) of § 1.1245-1) shall be deemed to consist of that portion of the fair market value of each property acquired which bears the same ratio to the fair market value of such acquired property as the amount realized from the disposition of the farm land bears to the total amount realized. The preceding sentence shall be applied solely for purposes of computing the portion of the total gain (determined without regard to section 1252) which is eligible to be recognized as ordinary income under section 1252(a)(1). The provisions of this paragraph do not apply to a disposition of property to an organization (other than a cooperative described in section 521) which is exempt from the tax imposed by chapter 1 of the Code.

(2) *Transfers covered.*—The transfers referred to in subparagraph (1) of this paragraph are transfers of farm land in which the basis of such property in the hands of the transferee is determined by reference to its basis in the hands of the transferor by reason of the application of any of the following provisions:

(i) Section 332 (relating to distributions in complete liquidation of an 80-percent-or-more controlled subsidiary corporation). For application of subparagraph (1) of this paragraph to such a complete liquidation, the principles of paragraph (c)(3) of § 1.1245-4 shall apply. Thus, for example, the provisions of subparagraph (1) of this paragraph do not apply to a liquidating distribution of farm land by an 80-percent-or-more controlled subsidiary to its parent if the parent's basis for the property is determined, under section 334(b)(2), by reference to its basis for the stock of the subsidiary.

(ii) Section 351 (relating to transfer to a corporation controlled by transferor).

(iii) Section 361 (relating to exchanges pursuant to certain corporate reorganizations).

(iv) Section 371(a) (relating to exchanges pursuant to certain receivership and bankruptcy proceedings).

(v) Section 374(a) (relating to exchanges pursuant to certain railroad reorganizations).

(vi) Section 721 (relating to transfers to a partnership in exchange for a partnership interest). See paragraph (e) of this section.

(vii) Section 731 (relating to distributions by a partnership to a partner). For special carryover of basis rule, see paragraph (e) of this section.

(3) *Treatment of farm land in the hands of transferee.*—See paragraph (f) of this section for treatment of the transferee in the case of a disposition to which this paragraph applies.

(4) *Examples.*—The provisions of this paragraph may be illustrated by the following examples:

Example (1). On January 4, 1975, A, an individual calendar year taxpayer, owns a parcel of farm land, which he acquired on March 25, 1970, having an adjusted basis of $15,000 and a fair market value of $40,000. On that date he transfers the parcel to corporation M in exchange for stock in the corporation worth $40,000 in a transaction qualifying under section 351. On the date of such transfer, the aggregate of the deductions allowed under section 175 and 182 with respect to the land is $18,000. Without regard to section 1252, A would recognize no gain under section 351 upon the transfer and M's basis for the land would be determined under section 362(a) by reference to its basis in the hands of A. Thus, as a result of the disposition, no gain is recognized as ordinary income under section 1251(c)(1) or section 1252(a)(1) by A since the amount of gain recognized under such sections is limited to the amount of gain which is recognized under section 351 (determined without regard to sections 1251 and 1252). See paragraph (c)(1) of § 1.1251-4 and subparagraph (1) of this paragraph. For treatment of the farm land in the hands of B, see paragraph (f)(1) of this section. For effect of the transfer on the excess deductions account of A and of B, see paragraph (e)(1) of § 1.1251-2.

Example (2). Assume the same facts in example (1), except that A transferred the land to M for stock in the corporation worth $32,000 and $8,000 cash. The gain realized is $25,000 (amount realized, $40,000, minus adjusted basis, $15,000). Without regard to section 1252, A would recognize $8,000 of gain under section 351(b). Assume further that no gain is recognized as ordinary income under section 1251(c)(1). Therefore, since the applicable percentage, 100 percent, of the aggregate of the deductions allowed under sections 175 and 182, $18,000, is lower than the gain realized, $25,000, the amount of gain to be recognized as ordinary income under section 1252(a)(1) would be $18,000 if the provisions of subparagraph (1) of this paragraph do not apply. Since under section 351(b) gain in the amount of $8,000 would be recognized to the transferor without regard to section 1252, the limitation provided in subparagraph (1) of this paragraph limits the gain taken into account by A under section 1252(a)(1) to $8,000.

Example (3). Assume the same facts as in example (2), except that $5,000 of gain is recognized as ordinary income under section 1251(c)(1). The amount of gain recognized as ordinary income under section 1252(a)(1) is $3,000 computed as follows:

(1) Amount of gain under section 1252(a)(1) (determined without regard to subparagraph (1) of this paragraph):

(a) Aggregate of deductions allowed under sections 175 and 182	$18,000
(b) Minus: Gain recognized as ordinary income under section 1251(c)(1) . . .	5,000
(c) Difference	$13,000
(d) Multiply: Applicable percentage for property disposed of within the fifth year after it was acquired	100 %
(e) Amount in paragraph (a)(1)(i)(*a*) of § 1.1252-1	$13,000
(f) Gain realized (amount realized, $40,000, less adjusted basis, $15,000) . . .	$25,000
(g) Minus: Amount in line (b)	5,000
(h) Amount in paragraph (a)(1)(i)(*b*) of § 1.1252-1	$20,000
(i) Lower of line (e) or (h)	$13,000

(2) Limitation in subparagraph (1) of this paragraph:

(a) Gain recognized (determined without regard to section 1252)	$8,000
(b) Minus: Gain recognized as ordinary income under section 1251(c)(1) . . .	5,000
(c) Difference	$3,000

(3) Lower of line (1)(i) or line (2)(c)	$3,000

Thus, the entire gain recognized under section 351(b) (determined without regard to sections 1251 and 1252), $8,000, is recognized as ordinary income since that amount is equal to the sum of the gain recognized as ordinary income under section 1251(c)(1), $5,000, and under section 1252(a)(1), $3,000.

(d) *Limitation for like kind exchanges and involuntary conversions.*—(1) *General rule.*—If farm land is disposed of and gain (determined without regard to section 1252) is not recognized in whole or in part under section 1031 (relating to like kind exchanges) or section 1033 (relating to involuntary conversions), then the amount of gain recognized as ordinary income by the transferor under section 1252(a)(1) shall not exceed the sum of—

(i) The excess (if any) of (*a*) the amount of gain recognized on such disposition (determined without regard to section 1252) over (ii) the

amount (if any) of gain recognized as ordinary income under section 1251(c)(1), plus

(ii) The fair market value of property acquired which is not farm land and which is not taken into account under subdivision (i) of this subparagraph (that is, the fair market value of property other than farm land acquired which is qualifying property under section 1031 or 1033, as the case may be).

(2) *Examples.*—The provisions of subparagraph (1) of this paragraph may be illustrated by the following examples:

Example (1). (i) Assume the same facts as in example (2)(ii) of paragraph (d)(3) of § 1.1251-4. Assume further that the aggregate of the amount of sections 175 and 182 deductions allowable is equal to the amount allowed. Under paragraph (a)(1) of § 1.1252-1, $18,000 would be recognized as ordinary income under section 1252(a)(1) (determined without regard to subparagraph (1) of this paragraph), computed as follows:

(1) Aggregate of deductions allowed under sections 175 and 182	$18,000
(2) Minus: Gain recognized as ordinary income under section 1251(c)(1)	$0
(3) Difference	$18,000
(4) Multiply: Applicable percentage for property disposed of within the fifth year after it was acquired	100 %
(5) Amount in paragraph (a)(1)(i)(*a*) of § 1.1252-1	$18,000
(6) Gain realized (amount realized, $67,500, less adjusted basis, $48,000)	$19,500
(7) Minus: Amount in line (2)	0
(8) Amount in paragraph (a)(1)(i)(*b*) of § 1.1252-1	$19,500
(9) Lower of line (5) or line (8)	$18,000

(ii) Although no gain was recognized under section 1251(c)(1) and the stock purchased by A for $67,500 is farm recapture property for purposes of section 1251, it is not farm land for purposes of section 1252. Nevertheless, although no gain would be recognized under sections 1033(a)(3) and 1251(c)(1) (determined without regard to section 1252), the limitation under subparagraph (1) of this paragraph is $67,500 (that is, the fair market value of property other than farm land acquired which is qualifying property

under section 1033). Since the amount of gain which would be recognized as ordinary income under section 1252(a)(1) (determined without regard to subparagraph (1) of this paragraph), $18,000 (as computed in subdivision (i) of this example), is lower than the amount of such limitation, $67,500, accordingly, only $18,000 is recognized as ordinary income under section 1252(a)(1). For determination of basis of the stock acquired, see subparagraph (5) of this paragraph.

Example (2). (i) Assume the same facts as in example (1) of this subparagraph, except that the cost of the stock was $62,500 (its fair market value). Thus, the amount of gain recognized on the disposition under section 1033(a)(3) (determined without regard to sections 1251 and 1252) is $5,000, that is, $67,500 minus $62,500. Assume

further that $5,000 (the amount of gain recognized under section 1033(a)(3) (so determined)) was recognized as ordinary income under section 1251(c)(1). The amount of gain recognized as ordinary income under section 1252(a)(1) is $13,000, computed as follows:

(1) Amount of gain under section 1252(a)(1) (determined without regard to subparagraph (1) of this paragraph):	
(a) Aggregate of deductions allowed under sections 175 and 182	$18,000
(b) Minus: Gain recognized as ordinary income under section 1251(c)(1)	5,000
(c) Difference	$13,000
(d) Multiply: Applicable percentage for property disposed of within the fifth year after it was acquired	100 %
(e) Amount in paragraph (a)(1)(i)(*a*) of § 1.1252-1	$13,000
(f) Gain realized (amount realized, $67,500, less adjusted basis, $48,000)	$19,500
(g) Minus: Amount in line (b)	5,000
(h) Amount in paragraph (a)(1)(i)(*b*) of § 1.1252-1	$14,500
(i) Lower of line (e) or (h)	$13,000
(2) Limitation in subparagraph (1) of this paragraph:	
(a) Gain recognized (determined without regard to section 1252)	$5,000
(b) Minus: Gain recognized as ordinary income under section 1251(c)(1)	5,000
(c) Difference	$0
(d) Plus: The fair market value of property other than farm land acquired which is qualifying property under section 1033	62,500
(e) Sum of lines (c) and (d)	$62,500
(3) Lower of line (1)(i) or line (2)(e)	$13,000

(3) *Application to single disposition of farm land and property of different class.*—(i) If upon a sale of farm land gain would be recognized under section 1252(a)(1), and if such land together with property of a different class or classes is disposed of in one transaction in which gain is not recognized in whole or in part under section 1031 or 1033 (without regard to section 1252(a)(1)), then rules consistent with the principles of paragraph (d)(6) of § 1.1250-3 (relating to gain from disposition of certain depreciable realty) shall apply for purposes of allocating the amount realized to each of the classes of property disposed of and for purposes of determining what property the amount realized for each class consists of.

(ii) For purposes of this subparagraph, the classes of property other than farm recapture property (as defined in section 1251(e) and paragraph (a)(1) of § 1.1251-3) are (*a*) section 1245 property, (*b*) section 1250 property, and (*c*) other property.

(iii) For purposes of this subparagraph, the classes of farm recapture property are (*a*) land, (*b*) section 1245 property, and (*c*) other property.

(4) *Treatment of farm land received in like kind exchange or involunary conversion.*—The aggregate of the deductions allowed under sections 175 and 182 in respect of land acquired in a transaction described in subparagraph (1) of this para-

graph shall include the aggregate of the deductions allowed under sections 175 and 182 in respect of the land transferred or converted (as the case may be) in such transaction minus the amount of gain taken into account under sections 1251(c) and 1252(a) with respect to the land transferred or converted. Upon a subsequent disposition of such land, the holding period shall include the holding period with respect to the land transferred or converted.

(5) *Basis adjustment.*—In order to reflect gain recognized under section 1252(a)(1) if property is acquired in a transaction to which subparagraph (1) of this paragraph applies, its basis shall be determined under the rules of section 1031(d) or 1033(c).

(e) *Partnerships.*—[Reserved]

(f) *Treatment of farm land received by a transferee in a disposition by gift and certain tax-free transactions.*—(1) *General rule.*—If farm land is disposed of in a transaction which is either a gift to which paragraph (a)(1) of this section applies, or a completely tax-free transfer to which paragraph (c)(1) of this section applies, then for purposes of section 1252—

(i) The aggregate of the deductions allowed under section 175 and 182 in respect of the land in the hands of the transferee immediately after the disposition shall be an amount equal to the amount of such aggregate in the hands of the transferor immediately before the disposition, and

(ii) For purposes of applying section 1252 upon a subsequent disposition by the transferee (including a computation of the applicable percentage), the holding period of the transferee shall include the holding period of the transferor.

(2) *Certain partially tax-free transfers.*—If farm land is disposed of in a transaction which either is in part a sale or exchange and in part a gift to which paragraph (a)(2) of this section applies, or is partially tax-free transfer to which paragraph (c)(1) of this section applies, then for purposes of section 1252 the amount determined under subparagraph (1)(i) of this paragraph shall be reduced by the amount of gain taken into account under sections 1251(c) and 1252(a) by the transferor upon the disposition. Upon a subsequent disposition by the transferee, the holding period for purposes of computing the amount under section 1252(a)(1)(A), with respect to the 175 and 182 deductions taken by the transferor, shall include the holding period of the transferor. With respect to the 175 and 182 deductions taken by the transferee, the holding period shall not include the holding period of the transferor.

(3) *Examples.*—The provisions of subparagraphs (1) and (2) of this paragraph may be illustrated by the following examples:

Example (1). Assume the same facts as in example (1) of paragraph (a)(4) of this section. Therefore, on the date B receives the farm land in the gift transaction, under subparagraph (1) of this paragraph the aggregate of the deductions allowed under sections 175 and 182 in respect of the farm land in the hands of B is the amount in the hands of A, $24,000, and for purposes of applying section 1252 upon a subsequent disposition by B (including a computation of the applicable percentage) the holding period of B includes the holding period of A.

Example (2). Assume the same facts as in example (2) of paragraph (a)(4) of this section. Under subparagraph (2) of this paragraph, the aggregate of the sections 175 and 182 deductions which pass over to B for purposes of section 1252 is $14,000 ($24,000 deductions allowable under sections 175 and 182 minus $3,000 gain recognized under section 1251(c) in accordance with example (2) of paragraph (a)(4) of § 1.1251-4, minus $7,000 gain recognized under section 1252(a) in accordance with example (2) of paragraph

(a)(4) of this section), B's holding period includes the holding period of A (*i.e.,* the period back to January 15, 1971) with respect to A's deductions.

(g) *Disposition of farm land not specifically covered.*—If farm land is disposed of in a transaction not specifically covered under § 1.1252-1 and this section, then the principles of section 1245 shall apply. [Reg. § 1.1252-2.]

☐ [*T.D.* 7418, 5-6-76.]

[Reg. § 1.1254-0]

§ 1.1254-0. Table of contents for section 1254 recapture rules.—This section lists the major captions contained in § § 1.1254-1 through 1.1254-6.

§1.1254-3. *Section 1254 costs immediately after certain acquisitions.*

(a) Transactions in which basis is determined by reference to cost or fair market value of property transferred.

(1) Basis determined under section 1012.

(2) Basis determined under section 301(d), 334(a), or 358(a)(2).

(3) Basis determined solely under former section 334(b)(2) or former section 334(c).

(4) Basis determined by reason of the application of section 1014(a).

(b) Gifts and certain tax-free transactions.

(1) General rule.

(2) Transactions covered.

(c) Certain transfers at death.

(d) Property received in a like kind exchange or involuntary conversion.

(1) General rule.

(2) Allocation of section 1254 costs among multiple natural resource recapture property acquired.

(e) Property transferred in cases to which section 1071 or 1081(b) applies.

§1.1254-4. *Special rules for S corporations and their shareholders.*

(a) In general.

(b) Determination of gain treated as ordinary income under section 1254 upon a disposition of natural resource recapture property by an S corporation.

(1) General rule.

(2) Examples.

(c) Character of gain recognized by a shareholder upon a sale or exchange of S corporation stock.

(1) General rule.

(2) Exceptions.

(3) Examples.

(d) Section 1254 costs of a shareholder.

(e) Section 1254 costs of an acquiring shareholder after certain acquisitions.

(1) Basis determined under section 1012.

(2) Basis determined under section 1014(a).

(3) Basis determined under section 1014(b)(9).

(4) Gifts and section 1041 transfers.

(f) Special rules for a corporation that was formerly an S corporation or formerly a C corporation.

(1) Section 1254 costs of an S corporation that was formerly a C corporation.

(2) Examples.

(3) Section 1254 costs of a C corporation that was formerly an S corporation.

(g) Determination of a shareholder's section 1254 costs upon certain stock transactions

(1) Issuance of stock.

(2) Natural resource recapture property acquired in exchange for stock.

(3) Treatment of nonvested stock.

(4) Exception.

(5) Aggregate of S corporation shareholders' section 1254 costs with respect to natural resource recapture property held by the S corporation

(6) Examples.

§1.1254-5. *Special rules for partnerships and their partners.*

(a) In general.

(b) Determination of gain treated as ordinary income under section 1254 upon the disposition of natural resource recapture property by a partnership.

(1) General rule.

(2) Exception to partner level recapture in the case of abusive allocations.

(3) Examples.

(c) Section 1254 costs of a partner.

(1) General rule.

(2) Section 1254 costs of a transferee partner after certain acquisitions.

(d) Property distributed to a partner.

(1) In general.

(2) Aggregate of partners' section 1254 costs with respect to natural resource recapture property held by a partnership.

§1.1254-6. *Effective date of regulations.*
[Reg. §1.1254-0.]

☐ [*T.D.* 8586, 1-9-95. *Amended by T.D.* 8684, 10-9-96.]

[Reg. §1.1254-1]

§1.1254-1. Treatment of gain from disposition of natural resource recapture property.—
(a) *In general.*—Upon any disposition of section 1254 property or any disposition after December 31, 1975 of oil, gas, or geothermal property, gain is treated as ordinary income in an amount equal to the lesser of the amount of the section 1254 costs (as defined in paragraph (b)(1) of this section) with respect to the property, or the amount, if any, by which the amount realized on the sale, exchange, or involuntary conversion, or the fair market value of the property on any other disposition, exceeds the adjusted basis of the property. However, any amount treated as ordinary income under the preceding sentence is not included in the taxpayer's *gross income from the property* for purposes of section 613. Generally, the lesser of the amounts described in this paragraph (a) is treated as ordinary income even though, in the absence of section 1254(a), no gain would be recognized upon the disposition under any other provision of the Internal Revenue Code. For the definition of the term *section 1254 costs*, see paragraph (b)(1) of this section. For the definition of the terms *section 1254 property, oil,*

gas, or geothermal property, and natural resource recapture property, see paragraph (b)(2) of this section. For rules relating to the disposition of natural resource recapture property, see paragraphs (b)(3), (c), and (d) of this section. For exceptions and limitations to the application of section 1254(a), see § 1.1254-2.

(b) Definitions.—(1) Section 1254 costs.—(i) Property placed in service after December 31, 1986.—With respect to any property placed in service by the taxpayer after December 31, 1986, the term section 1254 costs means—

(A) The aggregate amount of expenditures that have been deducted by the taxpayer or any person under section 263, 616, or 617 with respect to such property and that, but for the deduction, would have been included in the adjusted basis of the property or in the adjusted basis of certain depreciable property associated with the property; and

(B) The deductions for depletion under section 611 that reduced the adjusted basis of the property.

(ii) Property placed in service before January 1, 1987.—With respect to any property placed in service by the taxpayer before January 1, 1987, the term section 1254 costs means—

(A) The aggregate amount of costs paid or incurred after December 31, 1975, with respect to such property, that have been deducted as intangible drilling and development costs under section 263(c) by the taxpayer or any other person (except that section 1254 costs do not include costs incurred with respect to geothermal wells commenced before October 1, 1978) and that, but for the deduction, would be reflected in the adjusted basis of the property or in the adjusted basis of certain depreciable property associated with the property; reduced by

(B) The amount (if any) by which the deduction for depletion allowed under section 611 that was computed either under section 612 or sections 613 and 613A, with respect to the property, would have been increased if the costs (paid or incurred after December 31, 1975) had been charged to capital account rather than deducted.

(iii) Deductions under section 59 and section 291.—Amounts capitalized pursuant to an election under section 59(e) or pursuant to section 291(b) are treated as section 1254 costs in the year in which an amortization deduction is claimed under section 59(e)(1) or section 291(b)(2).

(iv) Suspended deductions.—If a deduction of a section 1254 cost has been suspended as of the date of disposition of section 1254 property, the deduction is not treated as a section 1254 cost if it is included in basis for determining gain or loss on the disposition. On the other hand, if the deduction will eventually be claimed, it is a sec-

tion 1254 cost as of the date of disposition. For example, a deduction suspended pursuant to the 65 percent of taxable income limitation of section 613A(d)(1) may either be included in basis upon disposition of the property or may be deducted in a year after the year of disposition. See § 1.613A-4(a)(1). If it is included in the basis then it is not a section 1254 cost, but if it is deductible in a later year it is a section 1254 cost as of the date of the disposition.

(v) Previously recaptured amounts.—If an amount has been previously treated as ordinary income pursuant to section 1254, it is not a section 1254 cost.

(vi) Nonproductive wells.—The aggregate amount of section 1254 costs paid or incurred on any property includes the amount of intangible drilling and development costs incurred on nonproductive wells, but only to the extent that the taxpayer recognizes income on the foreclosure of a nonrecourse debt the proceeds from which were used to finance the section 1254 costs with respect to the property. For this purpose, the term nonproductive well means a well that does not produce oil or gas in commercial quantities, including a well that is drilled for the purpose of ascertaining the existence, location, or extent of an oil or gas reservoir (e.g., a delineation well). The term nonproductive well does not include an injection well (other than an injection well drilled as part of a project that does not result in production in commercial quantities).

(vii) Calculation of amount described in paragraph (b)(1)(ii)(B) of this section (hypothetical depletion offset).—(A) In general.—In calculating the amount described in paragraph (b)(1)(ii)(B) of this section, the taxpayer shall apply the following rules. The taxpayer may use the 65-percent-of-taxable-income limitation of section 613A(d)(1). If the taxpayer uses that limitation, the taxpayer is not required to recalculate the effect of such limitation with respect to any property not disposed of. That is, the taxpayer may assume that the hypothetical capitalization of intangible drilling and development costs with respect to any property disposed of does not affect the allowable depletion with respect to property retained by the taxpayer. Any intangible drilling and development costs that, if they had not been treated as expenses under section 263(c), would have properly been capitalized under § 1.612-4(b)(2) (relating to items recoverable through depreciation under section 167 or cost recovery under section 168) are treated as costs described in § 1.612-4(b)(1) (relating to items recoverable through depletion). The increase in depletion attributable to the capitalization of intangible drilling and development costs is computed by subtracting the amount of cost or percentage depletion actually claimed from the amount of cost or percentage depletion that would have been allowable if intangible drilling and development costs had been capitalized. If the remainder is zero or less than zero, the entire amount of intangible drilling and development costs attributable to the property is recapturable.

(B) *Example.*—The following example illustrates the principles of paragraph (b)(1)(vii)(A).

Example. Hypothetical depletion offset. In 1976, A purchased undeveloped property for $10,000. During 1977, A incurred $200,000 of productive well intangible drilling and development costs with respect to the property. A deducted the intangible drilling and development costs as expenses under section 263(c). Estimated reserves of 150,000 barrels of recoverable oil were discovered in 1977 and production began in 1978. In 1978, A produced and sold 30,000 barrels of oil at $8 per barrel, resulting in $240,000 of gross income. A had no other oil or gas production in 1978. A claimed a percentage depletion deduction of $52,800 (i.e., 22% of $240,000 gross income from the property). If A had capitalized the intangible drilling and development costs, assume that $200,000 of the costs would have been allocated to the depletable property and none to depreciable property. A's cost depletion deduction if the intangible drilling and development costs had been capitalized would have been $42,000 (i.e., (($200,000 intangible drilling and development costs + $10,000 acquisition costs) x 30,000 barrels of production) / 150,000 barrels of estimated recoverable reserves). Since this amount is less than A's depletion deduction of $52,800 (percentage depletion), no reduction is made to the amount of intangible drilling and development costs ($200,000). On January 1, 1979, A sold the oil property to B for $360,000 and calculated section 1254 recapture without reference to the 65-percent-of-taxable-income limitation. A's gain on the sale is the entire $360,000, because A's basis in the property at the beginning of 1979 is zero (i.e., $10,000 cost less $52,800 depletion deduction for 1978). Since the section 1254 costs ($200,000) are less than A's gain on the sale, $200,000 is treated as ordinary income under section 1254(a). The remaining amount of A's gain ($160,000) is not subject to section 1254(a).

(2) *Natural resource recapture property.*—(i) *In general.*—The term *natural resource recapture property* means section 1254 property or oil, gas, or geothermal property as those terms are defined in this section.

(ii) *Section 1254 property.*—The term *section 1254 property* means any property (within the meaning of section 614) that is placed in service by the taxpayer after December 31, 1986, if any expenditures described in paragraph (b)(1)(i)(A) of this section (relating to costs under section 263, 616, or 617) are properly chargeable to such property, or if the adjusted basis of such

property includes adjustments for deductions for depletion under section 611.

(iii) *Oil, gas, or geothermal property.*—The term *oil, gas, or geothermal property* means any property (within the meaning of section 614) that was placed in service by the taxpayer before January 1, 1987, if any expenditures described in paragraph (b)(1)(ii)(A) of this section are properly chargeable to such property.

(iv) *Property to which section 1254 costs are properly chargeable.*—(A) An expenditure is properly chargeable to property if—

(1) The property is an operating mineral interest with respect to which the expenditure has been deducted;

(2) The property is a nonoperating mineral interest (e.g., a net profits interest or an overriding royalty interest) burdening an operating mineral interest if the nonoperating mineral interest is carved out of an operating mineral interest described in paragraph (b)(2)(iv)(A)(1) of this section;

(3) The property is a nonoperating mineral interest retained by a lessor or sublessor if such lessor or sublessor held, prior to the lease or sublease, an operating mineral interest described in paragraph (b)(2)(iv)(A)(1) of this section; or

(4) The property is an operating or a nonoperating mineral interest held by a taxpayer if a party related to the taxpayer (within the meaning of section 267(b) or section 707(b)) held an operating mineral interest (described in paragraph (b)(2)(iv)(A)(1) of this section) in the same tract or parcel of land that terminated (in whole or in part) without being disposed of (e.g., a working interest which terminated after a specified period of time or a given amount of production), but only if there exists between the related parties an arrangement or plan to avoid recapture under section 1254. In such a case, the taxpayer's section 1254 costs with respect to the property include those of the related party.

(B) *Example.*—The following example illustrates the provisions of paragraph (2)(iv)(A)(4) of this section:

Example. Arrangement or plan to avoid recapture. C, an individual, owns 100% of the stock of both X Co. and Y Co. On January 1, 1998, X Co. enters into a standard oil and gas lease. X Co. immediately assigns to Y Co. 1% of the working interest for one year, and 99% of the working interest thereafter. In 1998, X Co. and Y Co. expend $300 in intangible drilling and development costs developing the tract, of which $297 are deducted by X Co. under section 263(c). On January 1, 1999, Y Co. sells its 99% share of the working interest to an unrelated person. Based on all the facts and circumstances, the arrangement between X Co. and Y Co. is part of a plan or arrangement to avoid recapture under section 1254. Therefore, Y Co. must include in its section

1254 costs the $297 of intangible drilling and development costs deducted by X Co.

(v) *Property the basis of which includes adjustments for depletion deductions.*—The adjusted basis of property includes adjustments for depletion under section 611 if—

(A) The basis of the property has been reduced by reason of depletion deductions; or

(B) The property has been carved out of or is a portion of property the basis of which has been reduced by reason of depletion deductions.

(vi) *Property held by a transferee.*—Property held by a transferee is natural resource recapture property if the property was natural resource recapture property in the hands of the transferor and the transferee's basis in the property is determined with reference to the transferor's basis in the property (e.g., a gift) or is determined under section 732.

(vii) *Property held by a transferor.*—Property held by a transferor of natural resource recapture property is natural resource recapture property if the transferor's basis in the property received is determined with reference to the transferor's basis in the property transferred by the transferor (e.g., a like kind exchange). For purposes of this paragraph (b)(2), property described in this paragraph (b)(2)(vii) is treated as placed in service at the time the property transferred by the transferor was placed in service by the transferor.

(3) *Disposition.*—(i) *General rule.*—The term *disposition* has the same meaning as in section 1245, relating to gain from dispositions of certain depreciable property.

(ii) *Exceptions.*—The term *disposition* does not include—

(A) Any transaction that is merely a financing device, such as a mortgage or a production payment that is treated as a loan under section 636 and the regulations thereunder;

(B) Any abandonment (except that an abandonment is a disposition to the extent the taxpayer recognizes income on the foreclosure of a nonrecourse debt);

(C) Any creation of a lease or sublease of natural resource recapture property;

(D) Any termination or election of the status of an S corporation;

(E) Any unitization or pooling arrangement;

(F) Any expiration or reversion of an operating mineral interest that expires or reverts by its own terms, in whole or in part; or

(G) Any conversion of an overriding royalty interest that, at the option of the grantor or successor in interest, converts to an operating mineral interest after a certain amount of production.

(iii) *Special rule for carrying arrangements.*—In a carrying arrangement, liability for section 1254 costs attributable to the entire operating mineral interest held by the carrying party prior to reversion or conversion remains attributable to the reduced operating mineral interest retained by the carrying party after a portion of the operating mineral interest has reverted to the carried party or after the conversion of an overriding royalty interest that, at the option of the grantor or successor in interest, converts to an operating mineral interest after a certain amount of production.

(c) *Disposition of a portion of natural resource recapture property.*—(1) *Disposition of a portion (other than an undivided interest) of natural resource recapture property.*—(i) *Natural resource recapture property subject to the general rules of §1.1254-1.*—For purposes of section 1254(a)(1) and paragraph (a) of this section, except as provided in paragraphs (c)(1)(ii) and (3) of this section, in the case of the disposition of a portion (that is not an undivided interest) of natural resource recapture property, the entire amount of the section 1254 costs with respect to the natural resource recapture property is treated as allocable to that portion of the property to the extent of the amount of gain to which section 1254(a)(1) applies. If the amount of the gain to which section 1254(a)(1) applies is less than the amount of the section 1254 costs with respect to the natural resource recapture property, the balance of the section 1254 costs remaining after allocation to the portion of the property that was disposed of remains subject to recapture by the taxpayer under section 1254(a)(1) upon disposition of the remaining portion of the property. For example, assume that A owns an 80-acre tract of land with respect to which A has deducted intangible drilling and development costs under section 263(c). If A sells the north 40 acres, the entire amount of the section 1254 costs with respect to the 80-acre tract is treated as allocable to the 40-acre portion sold (to the extent of the amount of gain to which section 1254(a)(1) applies).

(ii) *Natural resource recapture property subject to the exceptions and limitations of §1.1254-2.*—For purposes of section 1254(a)(1) and paragraph (a) of this section, except as provided in paragraph (b)(3) of this section, in the case of the disposition of a portion (that is not an undivided interest) of natural resource recapture property to which section 1254(a)(1) does not apply by reason of the application of §1.1254-2 (certain nonrecognition transactions), the following rule for allocation of costs applies. An amount of the section 1254 costs that bears the same ratio to the entire amount of such costs with respect to the entire natural resource recapture property as the value of the property transferred bears to the value of the entire natural resource recapture property is treated as allocable to the portion of the natural resource recapture property transferred. The balance of the section 1254 costs remaining after allocation to that portion of the transferred property remains subject to recapture by the taxpayer under section 1254(a)(1) upon disposition of the remaining portion of the property. For example, assume that A owns an 80-acre tract of land with respect to which A has deducted intangible drilling and development costs under section 263(c). If A gives away the north 40 acres, and if 60 percent of the value of the 80-acre tract were attributable to the north 40 acres given away, 60 percent of the section 1254 costs with respect to the 80-acre tract is allocable to the north 40 acres given away.

(2) *Disposition of an undivided interest.*— (i) *Natural resource recapture property subject to the general rules of §1.1254-1.*—For purposes of section 1254(a)(1), except as provided in paragraphs (b)(2)(ii) and (b)(3) of this section, in the case of the disposition of an undivided interest in natural resource recapture property (or a portion thereof), a proportionate part of the section 1254 costs with respect to the natural resource recapture property is treated as allocable to the transferred undivided interest to the extent of the amount of gain to which section 1254(a)(1) applies. For example, assume that A owns an 80-acre tract of land with respect to which A has deducted intangible drilling and development costs under section 263(c). If A sells an undivided 40 percent interest in the 80-acre tract, 40 percent of the section 1254 costs with respect to the 80-acre tract is allocable to the transferred 40 percent interest in the 80-acre tract. However, if the amount of gain recognized on the sale of the 40 percent undivided interest were equal to only 35 percent of the amount of section 1254 costs attributable to the 80-acre tract, only 35 percent of the section 1254 costs would be treated as attributable to the undivided 40 percent interest. See paragraph (c)(3) of this section for an alternative allocation rule.

(ii) *Natural resource recapture property subject to the exceptions and limitations of §1.1254-2.*— For purposes of section 1254(a)(1) and paragraph (a) of this section, except as provided in paragraph (b)(3) of this section, in the case of a disposition of an undivided interest in natural resource recapture property (or a portion thereof) to which section 1254(a)(1) does not apply by reason of §1.1254-2, a proportionate part of the section 1254 costs with respect to the natural resource recapture property is treated as allocable to the transferred undivided interest. See paragraph (c)(3) of this section for an alternative allocation rule.

(3) *Alternative allocation rule.*—(i) *In general.*—The rules for the allocation of costs set forth in section 1254(a)(2) and paragraphs (c)(1) and (2) of this section do not apply with respect to section 1254 costs that the taxpayer establishes to the satisfaction of the Commissioner do not

relate to the transferred property. Except as provided in paragraphs (c)(3)(ii) and (iii) of this section, a taxpayer may satisfy this requirement only by receiving a private letter ruling from the Internal Revenue Service that the section 1254 costs do not relate to the transferred property.

(ii) *Portion of property.*—Upon the transfer of a portion of a natural resource recapture property (other than an undivided interest) with respect to which section 1254 costs have been incurred, a taxpayer may treat section 1254 costs as not relating to the transferred portion if the transferred portion does not include any part of any deposit with respect to which the costs were incurred.

(iii) *Undivided interest.*—Upon the transfer of an undivided interest in a natural resource recapture property with respect to which section 1254 costs have been incurred, a taxpayer may treat costs as not relating to the transferred interest if the undivided interest is an undivided interest in a portion of the natural resource recapture property, and the portion would be eligible for the alternative allocation rule under paragraph (c)(3)(ii) of this section.

(iv) *Substantiation.*—If a taxpayer treats section 1254 costs incurred with respect to a natural resource recapture property as not relating to a transferred interest in a portion of the property, the taxpayer must indicate on his or her tax return that the costs do not relate to the transferred portion and maintain the records and supporting evidence that substantiate this position.

(d) *Installment method.*—Gain from a disposition to which section 1254(a)(1) applies is reported on the installment method if that method otherwise applies under section 453 or 453A of the Internal Revenue Code and the regulations thereunder. The portion of each installment payment as reported that represents income (other than interest) is treated as gain to which section 1254(a)(1) applies until all of the gain (to which section 1254(a)(1) applies) has been reported, and the remaining portion (if any) of the income is then treated as gain to which section 1254(a)(1) does not apply. For treatment of amounts as interest on certain deferred payments, see sections 483, 1274, and the regulations thereunder. [Reg. §1.1254-1.]

☐ [T.D. 8586, 1-9-95.]

[Reg. §1.1254-2]

§1.1254-2. Exceptions and limitations.— (a) *Exception for gifts and section 1041 transfers.*— (1) *General rule.*—No gain is recognized under section 1254(a)(1) upon a disposition of natural resource recapture property by a gift or by a transfer in which no gain or loss is recognized pursuant to section 1041 (relating to transfers between spouses). For purposes of this paragraph (a), the term *gift* means, except to the extent that paragraph (a)(2) of this section applies, a transfer of natural resource recapture property that, in the hands of the transferee, has a basis determined under the provisions of sections 1015(a) or (d) (relating to basis of property acquired by gift). For rules concerning the potential reduction in the amount of the charitable contribution in the case of natural resource recapture property, see section 170(e) and § 1.170A-4. See § 1.1254-3(b)(1) for determination of potential recapture of section 1254 costs on property acquired by gift. See § 1.1254-1(c)(1)(ii) and (c)(2)(ii) for apportionment of section 1254 costs on a gift of a portion of natural resource recapture property.

(2) *Part gift transactions.*—If a disposition of natural resource recapture property is in part a sale or exchange and in part a gift, the gain that is treated as ordinary income pursuant to section 1254(a)(1) is the lower of the section 1254 costs with respect to the property or the excess of the amount realized upon the disposition of the property over the adjusted basis of the property. In the case of a transfer subject to section 1011(b) (relating to bargain sales to charitable organizations), the adjusted basis for purposes of the preceding sentence is the adjusted basis for determining gain or loss under section 1011(b).

(b) *Exception for transfers at death.*—Except as provided in section 691 (relating to income in respect of a decedent), no gain is recognized under section 1254(a)(1) upon a transfer at death. For purposes of this paragraph, the term *transfer at death* means a transfer of natural resource recapture property that, in the hands of the transferee, has a basis determined under the provisions of section 1014(a) (relating to basis of property acquired from a decedent) because of the death of the transferor. See § 1.1254-3(a)(4) and (c) for the determination of potential recapture of section 1254 costs on property acquired in a transfer at death.

(c) *Limitation for certain tax-free transactions.*—(1) *General rule.*—Upon a transfer of property described in paragraph (c)(3) of this section, the amount of gain treated as ordinary income by the transferor under section 1254(a)(1) may not exceed the amount of gain recognized to the transferor on the transfer (determined without regard to section 1254). In the case of a transfer of both natural resource recapture property and property that is not natural resource recapture property in one transaction, the amount realized from the disposition of the natural resource recapture property is deemed to be equal to the amount that bears the same ratio to the total amount realized as the fair market value of the natural resource recapture property bears to the aggregate fair market value of all the property transferred. The preceding sentence is applied solely for purposes of computing the portion of

the total gain (determined without regard to section 1254) that may be recognized as ordinary income under section 1254(a)(1).

(2) *Special rule for dispositions to certain tax exempt organizations.*—Paragraph (c)(1) of this section does not apply to a disposition of natural resource recapture property to an organization (other than a cooperative described in section 521) that is exempt from the tax imposed by chapter I of the Internal Revenue Code. The preceding sentence does not apply to a disposition of natural resource recapture property to an organization described in section 511(a)(2) or (b)(2) (relating to imposition of tax on unrelated business income of charitable, etc., organizations) if, immediately after the disposition, the organization uses the property in an unrelated trade or business as defined in section 513. If any property with respect to which gain is not recognized by reason of the exception of this paragraph (c)(2) ceases to be used in an unrelated trade or business of the organization acquiring the property, that organization is, for purposes of section 1254, treated as having disposed of the property on the date of the cessation.

(3) *Transfers described.*—The transfers referred to in paragraph (c)(1) of this section are transfers of natural resource recapture property in which the basis of the natural resource recapture property in the hands of the transferee is determined by reference to its basis in the hands of the transferor by reason of the application of any of the following provisions:

(i) Section 332 (relating to certain liquidations of subsidiaries). See paragraph (c)(4) of this section.

(ii) Section 351 (relating to transfer to a corporation controlled by transferor).

(iii) Section 361 (relating to exchanges pursuant to certain corporate reorganizations).

(iv) Section 721 (relating to transfers to a partnership in exchange for a partnership interest).

(v) Section 731 (relating to distributions by a partnership to a partner). For purposes of this paragraph, the basis of natural resource recapture property distributed by a partnership to a partner is deemed to be determined by reference to the adjusted basis of such property to the partnership.

(4) *Special rules for section 332 transfers.*—In the case of a distribution in complete liquidation of a subsidiary to which section 332 applies, the limitation provided in this paragraph (c) is confined to instances in which the basis of the natural resource recapture property in the hands of the transferee is determined, under section 334(b)(1), by reference to its basis in the hands of the transferor. Thus, for example, the limitation may apply in respect of a liquidating distribution of natural resource recapture property by a subsidiary corporation to the parent corporation,

but does not apply in respect of a liquidating distribution of natural resource recapture property to a minority shareholder. This paragraph (c) does not apply to a liquidating distribution of natural resource recapture property by a subsidiary to its parent if the parent's basis for the property is determined under section 334(b)(2) (as in effect before enactment of the Tax Reform Act of 1986), by reference to its basis for the stock of the subsidiary. This paragraph (c) does not apply to a liquidating distribution under section 332 of natural resource recapture property by a subsidiary to its parent if gain is recognized and there is a corresponding increase in the parent's basis in the property (e.g., certain distributions to a tax-exempt or foreign corporation).

(d) *Limitation for like kind exchanges and involuntary conversions.*—(1) *General rule.*—If natural resource recapture property is disposed of and gain (determined without regard to section 1254) is not recognized in whole or in part under section 1031 (relating to like kind exchanges) or section 1033 (relating to involuntary conversions), the amount of gain taken into account by the transferor under section 1254(a)(1) may not exceed the sum of—

(i) The amount of gain recognized on the disposition (determined without regard to section 1254); plus

(ii) The fair market value of property acquired that is not natural resource recapture property (determined without regard to §1.1254-1(b)(2)(vii)) and is not taken into account under paragraph (d)(1)(i) of this section (that is, qualifying property under section 1031 or 1033 that is not natural resource recapture property).

(2) *Disposition and acquisition of both natural resource recapture property and other property.*—For purposes of this paragraph (d), if both natural resource recapture property and property that is not natural resource recapture property are acquired as the result of one disposition in which both natural resource recapture property and property that is not natural resource recapture property are disposed of—

(i) The total amount realized upon the disposition is allocated between the natural resource recapture property and the property that is not natural resource recapture property disposed of in proportion to their respective fair market values;

(ii) The amount realized upon the disposition of the natural resource recapture property is deemed to consist of so much of the fair market value of the natural resource recapture property acquired as is not in excess of the amount realized from the natural resource recapture property disposed of, and the remaining portion (if any) of the amount realized upon the disposition of such property is deemed to consist of so much of the fair market value of the property

that is not natural resource recapture property acquired as is not in excess of the remaining portion; and

(iii) The amount realized upon the disposition of the property that is not natural resource recapture property is deemed to consist of so much of the fair market value of all the property acquired which was not taken into account under paragraph (d)(2)(ii) of this section. Except as provided in section 1060 and the regulations thereunder, if a buyer and seller have adverse interests as to such allocation of the amount realized, any arm's-length agreement between the buyer and seller is used to establish the allocation. In the absence of such an agreement, the allocation is made by taking into account the appropriate facts and circumstances. [Reg. §1.1254-2.]

☐ [*T.D. 8586, 1-9-95. Amended by T.D. 8684,* 10-9-96.]

[Reg. §1.1254-3]

§1.1254-3. Section 1254 costs immediately after certain acquisitions.—(a) *Transactions in which basis is determined by reference to cost or fair market value of property transferred.*—(1) *Basis determined under section 1012.*—If, on the date a person acquires natural resource recapture property, the person's basis for the property is determined solely by reference to its cost (within the meaning of section 1012), the amount of section 1254 costs with respect to the natural resource recapture property in the person's hands is zero on the acquisition date.

(2) *Basis determined under section 301(d), 334(a), or 358(a)(2).*—If, on the date a person acquires natural resource recapture property, the person's basis for the property is determined solely by reason of the application of section 301(d) (relating to basis of property received in a corporate distribution), section 334(a) (relating to basis of property received in a liquidation in which gain or loss is recognized), or section 358(a)(2) (relating to basis of other property received in certain exchanges), the amount of the section 1254 costs with respect to the natural resource recapture property in the person's hands is zero on the acquisition date.

(3) *Basis determined solely under former section 334(b)(2) or former section 334(c).*—If, on the date a person acquires natural resource recapture property, the person's basis for the property is determined solely under the provisions of section 334(b)(2) (prior to amendment of that section by the Tax Equity and Fiscal Responsibility Act of 1982) or (c) (prior to repeal of that section by the Tax Reform Act of 1986) (relating to basis of property received in certain corporate liquidations), the amount of section 1254 costs with respect to the natural resource recapture property in the person's hands is zero on the acquisition date.

(4) *Basis determined by reason of the application of section 1014(a).*—If, on the date a person acquires natural resource recapture property from a decedent, the person's basis is determined, by reason of the application of section 1014(a), solely by reference to the fair market value of the property on the date of the decedent's death or on the applicable date provided in section 2032 (relating to alternate valuation date), the amount of section 1254 costs with respect to the natural resource recapture property in the person's hands is zero on the acquisition date. See paragraph (c) of this section for the treatment of certain transfers at death.

(b) *Gifts and certain tax-free transactions.*— (1) *General rule.*—If natural resource recapture property is transferred in a transaction described in paragraph (b)(2) of this section, the amount of section 1254 costs with respect to the natural resource recapture property in the hands of the transferee immediately after the disposition is an amount equal to—

(i) The amount of section 1254 costs with respect to the natural resource recapture property in the hands of the transferor immediately before the disposition (and in the case of an S corporation or partnership transferor, the section 1254 costs of the shareholders or partners with respect to the natural resource recapture property); minus

(ii) The amount of any gain taken into account as ordinary income under section 1254(a)(1) by the transferor upon the disposition (and in the case of an S corporation or partnership transferor, any such gain taken into account as ordinary income by the shareholders or partners).

(2) *Transactions covered.*—The transactions to which paragraph (b)(1) of this section apply are—

(i) A disposition that is a gift or in part a sale or exchange and in part a gift;

(ii) A transaction described in section 1041(a); or

(iii) A disposition described in § 1.1254-2(c)(3) (relating to certain tax-free transactions).

(c) *Certain transfers at death.*—If natural resource recapture property is acquired in a transfer at death, the amount of section 1254 costs with respect to the natural resource recapture property in the hands of the transferee immediately after the transfer includes the amount, if any, of the section 1254 costs deducted by the transferee before the decedent's death, to the extent that the basis of the natural resource recapture property (determined under section 1014(a)) is required to be reduced under the second sentence of section 1014(b)(9) (relating to adjustments to basis where the property is acquired from a decedent prior to death).

(d) *Property received in a like kind exchange or involuntary conversion.*—(1) *General rule.*—If natural resource recapture property is disposed of in a like kind exchange under section 1031 or involuntary conversion under section 1033, then immediately after the disposition the amount of section 1254 costs with respect to any natural resource recapture property acquired for the property transferred is an amount equal to—

(i) The amount of section 1254 costs with respect to the natural resource recapture property disposed of (including the section 1254 costs of the shareholders of an S corporation or of the partners of a partnership with respect to the natural resource recapture property); minus

(ii) The amount of any gain taken into account as ordinary income under section 1254(a)(1) by the transferor upon the disposition (and in the case of an S corporation or partnership transferor, any such gain taken into account as ordinary income by the shareholders or partners).

(2) *Allocation of section 1254 costs among multiple natural resource recapture properties acquired.*—If more than one parcel of natural resource recapture property is acquired at the same time from the same person in a transaction referred to in paragraph (d)(1) of this section, the total amount of section 1254 costs with respect to the parcels is allocated to the parcels in proportion to their respective adjusted bases.

(e) *Property transferred in cases to which section 1071 or 1081(b) applies.*—Rules similar to the rules of section 1245(b)(5) shall apply under section 1254. [Reg. § 1.1254-3.]

□ [*T.D. 8586, 1-9-95. Amended by T.D. 8684, 10-9-96.*]

[Reg. § 1.1254-4]

§ 1.1254-4. Special rules for S corporations and their shareholders.—(a) *In general.*—This section provides rules for applying the provisions of section 1254 to S corporations and their shareholders upon the disposition by an S corporation (and a corporation that was formerly an S corporation) of natural resource recapture property and upon the disposition by a shareholder of stock of an S corporation that holds natural resource recapture property.

(b) *Determination of gain treated as ordinary income under section 1254 upon a disposition of natural resource recapture property by an S corporation.*— (1) *General rule.*—Upon a disposition of natural resource recapture property by an S corporation, the amount of gain treated as ordinary income under section 1254 is determined at the shareholder level. Each shareholder must recognize as ordinary income under section 1254 the lesser of—

(i) The shareholder's section 1254 costs with respect to the property disposed of; or

(ii) The shareholder's share of the amount, if any, by which the amount realized on the sale, exchange, or involuntary conversion, or the fair market value of the property upon any other disposition (including a distribution), exceeds the adjusted basis of the property.

(2) *Examples.*—The following examples illustrate the provisions of paragraph (b)(1) of this section:

Example 1. Disposition of natural resource recapture property other than oil and gas property. A and B are equal shareholders in X, an S corporation. On January 1, 1997, X acquires for $90,000 an undeveloped mineral property, its sole property. During 1997, X expends and deducts $100,000 in developing the property. On January 15, 1998, X sells the property for $250,000 when X's basis in the property is $90,000. Thus, X recognizes gain of $160,000 on the sale. A and B's share of the $160,000 gain recognized is $80,000 each. Each shareholder has $50,000 of section 1254 costs with respect to the property. Under these circumstances, A and B each are required to recognize $50,000 of the $80,000 of gain on the sale of the property as ordinary income under section 1254.

Example 2. Disposition of oil and gas property the adjusted basis of which is allocated to the shareholders under section 613A(c)(11). C and D are equal shareholders in Y, an S corporation. On January 1, 1997, Y acquires for $150,000 an undeveloped oil and gas property, its sole property. During 1997, Y expends in developing the property $40,000 in intangible drilling costs which it elects to expense under section 263(c). On January 15, 1998, Y sells the property for $200,000. C and D's share of the $200,000 amount realized on the sale is $100,000 each. C and D each have a basis of $75,000 in the property and $20,000 of section 1254 costs with respect to the property. Under these circumstances, C and D each are required to recognize $20,000 of the $25,000 gain on the sale of the property as ordinary income under section 1254.

(c) *Character of gain recognized by a shareholder upon a sale or exchange of S corporation stock.*—(1) *General rule.*—Except as provided in paragraph (c)(2) of this section, if an S corporation shareholder recognizes gain upon a sale or exchange of stock in the S corporation (determined without regard to section 1254), the gain is treated as ordinary income under section 1254 to the extent of the shareholder's section 1254 costs (with respect to the shares sold or exchanged).

(2) *Exceptions.*—(i) *Gain not attributable to section 1254 costs.*—(A) *General rule.*—Paragraph (c)(1) of this section does not apply to any portion of the gain recognized on the sale or exchange of the stock that the taxpayer establishes is not attributable to section 1254 costs. The portion of the gain recognized that is not attributable to section 1254 costs is that portion of the gain recognized that exceeds the amount of ordinary income that the shareholder would have recognized under section 1254 (with respect to the shares sold or exchanged) if, immediately prior to the sale or exchange of the stock, the corporation had sold at fair market value all of the corporation's property the disposition of which would result in the recognition by the shareholder of ordinary income under section 1254.

(B) *Substantiation.*—To establish that a portion of the gain recognized is not attributable to a shareholder's section 1254 costs so as to qualify for the exception contained in paragraph (c)(2)(i)(A) of this section, the shareholder must attach to the shareholder's tax return a statement detailing the shareholder's share of the fair market value and basis, and the shareholder's section 1254 costs, for each of the S corporation's natural resource recapture properties held immediately before the sale or exchange of stock.

(ii) *Transactions entered into as part of a plan to avoid recognition of ordinary income under section 1254.*—In the case of a contribution of property prior to a sale or exchange of stock pursuant to a plan a principal purpose of which is to avoid recognition of ordinary income under section 1254, paragraph (c)(1) of this section does not apply. Instead, the amount recognized as ordinary income under section 1254 is the amount of ordinary income the selling or exchanging shareholder would have recognized under section 1254 (with respect to the shares sold or exchanged) had the S corporation sold its natural resource recapture property the disposition of which would have resulted in the recognition of ordinary income under section 1254. The amount recognized as ordinary income under the preceding sentence reduces the amount realized on the sale or exchange of the stock. This reduced amount realized is used in determining any gain or loss on the sale or exchange.

(3) *Examples.*—The following examples illustrate the provisions of this paragraph (c):

Example 1. Application of general rule upon a sale of S corporation stock. C and D are equal shareholders in Y, an S corporation. As of January 1, 1997, Y holds two mining properties: Blackacre, with an adjusted basis of $5,000 and a fair market value of $35,000, and Whiteacre, with an adjusted basis of $20,000 and a fair market value of $15,000. Y also holds securities with a basis of $5,000 and a fair market value of $10,000. On January 1, 1997, D sells 50 percent of D's Y stock to E for $15,000. As of the date of the sale, D's adjusted basis in the Y stock sold is $7,500, and D has $18,000 of section 1254 costs with respect to Blackacre and $12,000 of section 1254 costs with respect to Whiteacre. Under this paragraph (c), the gain recognized by D upon the sale of Y stock is treated as ordinary income to the extent of D's section 1254 costs with respect to the stock sold, unless D establishes that a portion of such excess is not attributable to D's section 1254 costs. However, because D would recognize $7,500 in ordinary income under section 1254 with respect to the stock sold if Y sold Blackacre (the only asset the disposition of which would result in ordinary income to D under section 1254), the $7,500 of gain recognized by D upon the sale of D's Y stock is attributable to D's section 1254 costs. Therefore, upon the sale of stock to E, D recognizes $7,500 of ordinary income under this paragraph (c).

Example 2. Sale of S corporation stock where gain is not entirely attributable to section 1254 costs. Assume the same facts as in *Example 1*, except that Blackacre has a fair market value of $25,000, and the securities have a fair market value of $20,000. Immediately prior to the sale of stock to E, if Y had sold Blackacre (its only asset the disposition of which would result in the recognition of ordinary income to D under section 1254), D would recognize $5,000 in ordinary income with respect to the stock sold under section 1254. D attaches a statement to D's tax return for 1997 detailing D's share of the fair market values and bases, and D's section 1254 costs with respect to Blackacre and Whiteacre. Therefore, upon the sale of stock to E, of the $7,500 gain recognized by D, $5,000 is ordinary income under this paragraph (c).

Example 3. Contribution of property prior to sale of S corporation stock as part of a plan to avoid recognition of ordinary income under section 1254. H owns all of the stock of Z, an S corporation. As of January 1, 1997, H has $3,000 of section 1254 costs with respect to property P, which is natural resource recapture property and Z's only asset. Property P has an adjusted basis of $5,000 and a fair market value of $8,000. H has a basis of $5,000 in Z stock, which has a fair market value of $8,000. On January 1, 1997, H contributes securities to Z which have a basis of $7,000 and a fair market value of $4,000. On April 15, 1997, H sells all of the Z stock to J for $12,000. On that date, H's adjusted basis in the Z stock is also $12,000. Based on all the facts and circumstances, the sale of stock is part of a plan (along with the contribution by H of the securities to Z) that has a principal purpose to avoid recognition of ordinary income under section 1254. Consequently, under paragraph (c)(2)(ii) of this section, H must recognize $3,000 as ordinary income under section 1254, the amount of ordinary income that H would recognize as ordinary income under section 1254 if property P were sold at fair market value. In addition, H reduces the amount realized on the sale of the stock ($12,000) by $3,000. As a result, H also recognizes a $3,000 capital loss on the sale of the stock ($9,000 amount realized less $12,000 adjusted basis).

(d) *Section 1254 costs of a shareholder.*—An S corporation shareholder's section 1254 costs with respect to any natural resource recapture property held by the corporation include all of the shareholder's section 1254 costs with respect to the property in the hands of the S corporation. See §1.1254-1(b)(1) for the definition of section 1254 costs.

(e) *Section 1254 costs of an acquiring shareholder after certain acquisitions.*—(1) *Basis determined under section 1012.*—If stock in an S corporation that holds natural resource recapture property is acquired and the acquiring shareholder's basis for the stock is determined solely by reference to its cost (within the meaning of section 1012), the amount of section 1254 costs with respect to the property held by the corporation in the acquiring shareholder's hands is zero on the acquisition date.

(2) *Basis determined under section 1014(a).*—If stock in an S corporation that holds natural resource recapture property is acquired from a decedent and the acquiring shareholder's basis is determined, by reason of the application of section 1014(a), solely by reference to the fair market value of the stock on the date of the decedent's death or on the applicable date provided in section 2032 (relating to alternate valuation date), the amount of section 1254 costs with respect to the property held by the corporation in the acquiring shareholder's hands is zero on the acquisition date.

(3) *Basis determined under section 1014(b)(9).*—If stock in an S corporation that holds natural resource recapture property is acquired before the death of the decedent, the amount of section 1254 costs with respect to the property held by the corporation in the acquiring shareholder's hands includes the amount, if any, of the section 1254 costs deducted by the acquiring shareholder before the decedent's death, to the extent that the basis of the stock (determined under section 1014(a)) is required to be reduced under section 1014(b)(9) (relating to adjustments to basis when the property is acquired before the death of the decedent).

(4) *Gifts and section 1041 transfers.*—If stock is acquired in a transfer that is a gift, in a transfer that is a part sale or exchange and part gift, or in a transfer that is described in section 1041(a), the amount of section 1254 costs with respect to the property held by the corporation in the acquiring shareholder's hands immediately after the transfer is an amount equal to—

(i) The amount of section 1254 costs with respect to the property held by the corporation in the hands of the transferor immediately before the transfer; minus

(ii) The amount of any gain recognized as ordinary income under section 1254 by the transferor upon the transfer.

(f) *Special rules for a corporation that was formerly an S corporation or formerly a C corporation.*—(1) *Section 1254 costs of an S corporation that was formerly a C corporation.*—In the case of a C

Reg. §1.1254-4(f)(1)

corporation that holds natural resource recapture property and that elects to be an S corporation, each shareholder's section 1254 costs as of the beginning of the corporation's first taxable year as an S corporation include a pro rata share of the section 1254 costs of the corporation as of the close of the last taxable year that the corporation was a C corporation.

(2) *Examples.*—The following examples illustrate the application of the provisions of paragraph (f)(1) of this section:

Example 1. Sale of natural resource recapture property held by an S corporation that was formerly a C corporation—(i) Y is a C corporation that elects to be an S corporation effective January 1, 1997. On that date, Y owns Oil Well, which is natural resource recapture property and a capital asset. Y has section 1254 costs of $20,000 as of the close of the last taxable year that it was a C corporation. On January 1, 1997, Oil Well has a value of $200,000 and a basis of $100,000. Thus, under section 1374, Y's net unrealized built-in gain is $100,000. Also on that date, Y's basis in Oil Well is allocated to A, Y's sole shareholder, under section 613A(c)(11) and the section 1254 costs are allocated to A under paragraph (f)(1) of this section. In addition, A has a basis in A's Y stock of $100,000.

(ii) On November 1, 1997, Y sells Oil Well for $250,000. During 1997, Y has taxable income greater than $100,000, and no other transactions or items treated as recognized built-in gain or loss. Under section 1374, Y has net recognized built-in gain of $100,000. Assuming a tax rate of 35 percent on capital gain, Y has a tax of $35,000 under section 1374. The tax of $35,000 is treated as a capital loss under section 1366(f)(2). A has a realized gain on the sale of $150,000 ($250,000 minus $100,000) of which $20,000 is recognized as ordinary income under section 1254, and $130,000 is recognized as capital gain. Consequently, A recognizes ordinary income of $20,000 and net capital gain of $95,000 ($130,000 minus $35,000) on the sale.

Example 2. Sale of stock followed by sale of natural resource recapture property held by an S corporation that was formerly a C corporation—(i) Assume the same facts as in *Example 1*(i). On November 1, 1997, A sells all of A's Y stock to P for $250,000. A has a realized gain on the sale of $150,000 ($250,000 minus $100,000) of which $20,000 is recognized as ordinary income under section 1254, and $130,000 is recognized as capital gain.

(ii) On November 2, 1997, Y sells Oil Well for $250,000. During 1997, Y has taxable income greater than $100,000, and no other transactions or items treated as recognized built-in gain or loss. Under section 1374, Y has net recognized built-in gain of $100,000. Assuming a tax rate of 35 percent on capital gain, Y has a tax of $35,000 under section 1374. The tax of $35,000 is treated as a capital loss under section 1366(f)(2). P has a

realized gain on the sale of $150,000 ($250,000 minus $100,000), which is recognized as capital gain. Consequently, P recognizes net capital gain of $115,000 ($150,000 minus $35,000) on the sale.

(3) *Section 1254 costs of a C corporation that was formerly an S corporation.*—In the case of an S corporation that becomes a C corporation, the C corporation's section 1254 costs with respect to any natural resource recapture property held by the corporation as of the beginning of the corporation's first taxable year as a C corporation include the sum of its shareholders' section 1254 costs with respect to the property as of the close of the last taxable year that the corporation was an S corporation. In the case of an S termination year as defined in section 1362(e)(4), the shareholders' section 1254 costs are determined as of the close of the S short year as defined in section 1362(e)(1)(A). See paragraph (g)(5) of this section for rules on determining the aggregate amount of the shareholders' section 1254 costs.

(g) *Determination of a shareholder's section 1254 costs upon certain stock transactions.*—(1) *Issuance of stock.*—Upon an issuance of stock (whether such stock is newly-issued or had been held as treasury stock) by an S corporation in a reorganization described in section 368 or otherwise—

(i) Each recipient of shares must be allocated a pro rata share (determined solely with respect to the shares issued in the transaction) of the aggregate of the S corporation shareholders' section 1254 costs with respect to natural resource recapture property held by the S corporation immediately before the issuance (as determined pursuant to paragraph (g)(5) of this section); and

(ii) Each pre-existing shareholder must reduce his or her section 1254 costs with respect to natural resource recapture property held by the S corporation immediately before the issuance by an amount equal to the pre-existing shareholder's section 1254 costs immediately before the issuance multiplied by the percentage of stock of the corporation issued in the transaction.

(2) *Natural resource recapture property acquired in exchange for stock.*—If natural resource recapture property is transferred to an S corporation in exchange for stock of the S corporation (for example, in a section 351 transaction, or in a reorganization described in section 368), the S corporation must allocate to its shareholders a pro rata share of the S corporation's section 1254 costs with respect to the property immediately after the transaction (as determined under §1.1254-3(b)(1)).

(3) *Treatment of nonvested stock.*—Stock issued in connection with the performance of services that is substantially nonvested (within the meaning of §1.83-3(b)) is treated as issued for purposes of this section at the first time it is

treated as outstanding stock of the S corporation for purposes of section 1361.

(4) *Exception.*—Paragraph (g)(1) of this section does not apply to stock issued in exchange for stock of the same S corporation (as for example, in a recapitalization described in section 368(a)(1)(E)).

(5) *Aggregate of S corporation shareholders' section 1254 costs with respect to natural resource recapture property held by the S corporation.*—(i) *In general.*—The aggregate of S corporation shareholders' section 1254 costs is equal to the sum of each shareholder's section 1254 costs. The S corporation must determine each shareholder's section 1254 costs under either paragraph (g)(5)(ii) (written data) or paragraph (g)(5)(iii) (assumptions) of this section. The S corporation may determine the section 1254 costs of some shareholders under paragraph (g)(5)(ii) of this section and of others under paragraph (g)(5)(iii) of this section.

(ii) *Written data.*—An S corporation may determine a shareholder's section 1254 costs by using written data provided by a shareholder showing the shareholder's section 1254 costs with respect to natural resource recapture property held by the S corporation unless the S corporation knows or has reason to know that the written data is inaccurate. If an S corporation does not receive written data upon which it may rely, the S corporation must use the assumptions provided in paragraph (g)(5)(iii) of this section in determining a shareholder's section 1254 costs.

(iii) *Assumptions.*—An S corporation that does not use written data pursuant to paragraph (g)(5)(ii) of this section to determine a shareholder's section 1254 costs must use the following assumptions to determine the shareholder's section 1254 costs—

(A) The shareholder deducted his or her share of the amount of deductions under sections 263(c), 616, and 617 in the first year in which the shareholder could claim a deduction for such amounts, unless in the case of expenditures under sections 263(c) or 616 the S corporation elected to capitalize such amounts;

(B) The shareholder was not subject to the following limitations with respect to the shareholder's depletion allowance under section 611, except to the extent a limitation applied at the corporate level: the taxable income limitation of section 613(a); the depletable quantity limitations of section 613A(c); or the limitations of sections 613A(d)(2), (3), and (4) (exclusion of retailers and refiners).

(6) *Examples.*—The following examples illustrate the provisions of this paragraph (g):

Example 1. Transfer of natural resource recapture property to an S corporation in a section 351 transaction. As of January 1, 1997, A owns all the stock (20 shares) in X, an S corporation. X holds property that is not natural resource recapture property that has a fair market value of $2,000 and an adjusted basis of $2,000. On January 1, 1997, B transfers natural resource recapture property, Property P, to X in exchange for 80 shares of X stock in a transaction that qualifies under section 351. Property P has a fair market value of $8,000 and an adjusted basis of $5,000. Pursuant to section 351, B does not recognize gain on the transaction. Immediately prior to the transaction, B's section 1254 costs with respect to Property P equaled $6,000. Under § 1.1254-2(c)(1), B does not recognize any gain under section 1254 on the section 351 transaction and, under § 1.1254-3(b)(1), X's section 1254 costs with respect to Property P immediately after the contribution equal $6,000. Under paragraph (g)(2) of this section, each shareholder is allocated a pro rata share of X's section 1254 costs. The pro rata share of X's section 1254 costs that is allocated to A equals $1,200 (20 percent interest in X multiplied by X's $6,000 of section 1254 costs). The pro rata share of X's section 1254 costs that is allocated to B equals $4,800 (80 percent interest in X multiplied by X's $6,000 of section 1254 costs).

Example 2. Contribution of money in exchange for stock of an S corporation holding natural resource recapture property. As of January 1, 1997, A and B each own 50 percent of the stock (50 shares each) in X, an S corporation. X holds natural resource recapture property, Property P, which has a fair market value of $20,000 and an adjusted basis of $14,000. A's and B's section 1254 costs with respect to Property P are $4,000 and $1,500, respectively. On January 1, 1997, C contributes $20,000 to X in exchange for 100 shares of X's stock. Under paragraph (g)(1)(i) of this section, X must allocate to C a pro rata share of its shareholders' section 1254 costs. Using the assumptions set forth in paragraph (g)(5)(iii) of this section, X determines that A's section 1254 costs with respect to natural resource recapture property held by X equal $4,500. Using written data provided by B, X determines that B's section 1254 costs with respect to Property P equal $1,500. Thus, the aggregate of X's shareholders' section 1254 costs equals $6,000. C's pro rata share of the $6,000 of section 1254 costs equals $3,000 (C's 50 percent interest in X multiplied by $6,000). Under paragraph (g)(1)(ii) of this section, A's section 1254 costs are reduced by $2,000 (A's actual section 1254 costs ($4,000) multiplied by 50 percent). B's section 1254 costs are reduced by $750 (B's actual section 1254 costs ($1,500) multiplied by 50 percent).

Example 3. Merger involving an S corporation that holds natural resource recapture property. X, an S corporation with one shareholder, A, holds as its sole asset natural resource recapture property that has a fair market value of $120,000 and an adjusted basis of $40,000. A has section 1254 costs with respect to the property of $60,000. For valid business reasons, X merges into Y, an S corporation with one shareholder, B, in a reorganization described in section 368(a)(1)(A). Y holds property that is not natural resource recapture property that has a fair market value of $120,000 and basis of $120,000. Under paragraph (c) of this section, A does not recognize ordinary income under section 1254 upon the exchange of stock in the merger because A did not otherwise recognize gain on the merger. Under paragraph (g)(2) of this section, Y must allocate to A and B a pro rata share of its $60,000 of section 1254 costs. Thus, A and B are each allocated $30,000 of section 1254 costs (50 percent interest in X, each, multiplied by $60,000). [Reg. § 1.1254-4.]

□ [T.D. 8586, 1-9-95. Amended by T.D. 8684, 10-9-96.]

[Reg. § 1.1254-5]

§ 1.1254-5. Special rules for partnerships and their partners.—(a) In general.—This section provides rules for applying the provisions of section 1254 to partnerships and their partners upon the disposition of natural resource recapture property by the partnership and certain distributions of property by a partnership. See section 751 and the regulations thereunder for rules concerning the treatment of gain upon the transfer of a partnership interest.

(b) Determination of gain treated as ordinary income under section 1254 upon the disposition of natural resource recapture property by a partnership.—(1) General rule.—Upon a disposition of natural resource recapture property by a partnership, the amount treated as ordinary income under section 1254 is determined at the partner level. Each partner must recognize as ordinary income under section 1254 the lesser of—

(i) The partner's section 1254 costs with respect to the property disposed of; or

(ii) The partner's share of the amount, if any, by which the amount realized upon the sale, exchange, or involuntary conversion, or the fair market value of the property upon any other disposition, exceeds the adjusted basis of the property.

(2) Exception to partner level recapture in the case of abusive allocations.—Paragraph (b)(1) of this section does not apply in determining the amount treated as ordinary income under section 1254 upon a disposition of section 1254 property by a partnership if the partnership has allocated the amount realized or gain recognized from the disposition with a principal purpose of avoiding the recognition of ordinary income under section 1254. In such case, the amount of gain on the disposition recaptured as ordinary income under section 1254 is determined at the partnership level.

(3) Examples.—The provisions of paragraphs (a) and (b) of this section are illustrated by the following examples which assume

that capital accounts are maintained in accordance with section 704(b) and the regulations thereunder:

Example 1. Partner level recapture—In general. A, B, and C, have equal interests in capital in Partnership ABC that was formed on January 1, 1985. The partnership acquired an undeveloped domestic oil property on January 1, 1985, for $120,000. The partnership allocated the property's basis to each partner in proportion to the partner's interest in partnership capital, so each partner was allocated $40,000 of basis. In 1985, the partnership incurred $60,000 of productive well intangible drilling and development costs with respect to the property. The partnership elected to deduct the intangible drilling and development costs as expenses under section 263(c). Each partner deducted $20,000 of the intangible drilling and development costs. Assume that depletion allowable under section 613A(c)(7)(D) for each partner for 1985 was $10,000. On January 1, 1986, the partnership sold the oil property to an unrelated third party for $210,000. Each partner's allocable share of the amount realized is $70,000. Each partner's basis in the oil property at the end of 1985 is $30,000 ($40,000 cost – $10,000 depletion deductions claimed). Each partner has a gain of $40,000 on the sale of the oil property ($70,000 amount realized – $30,000 adjusted basis in the oil property). Assume that each partner's depletion allowance would not have been increased if the intangible drilling and development costs had been capitalized. Each partner's section 1254 costs with respect to the property are $20,000. Thus, A, B, and C each must treat $20,000 of gain recognized as ordinary income under section 1254(a).

Example 2. Special allocation of intangible drilling and development costs. K and L form a partnership on January 1, 1997, to acquire and develop a geothermal property as defined under section 613(e)(2). The partnership agreement provides that all intangible drilling and development costs will be allocated to partner K, and that all other items of income, gain, or loss will be allocated equally between the two partners. Assume these allocations have substantial economic effect under section 704(b) and the regulations thereunder. The partnership acquires a lease covering undeveloped acreage located in the United States for $50,000. In 1997, the partnership incurs $50,000 of intangible drilling and development costs that are allocated to partner K. The partnership also has $30,000 of depletion deductions, which are allocated equally between K and L. On January 1, 1998, the partnership sells the geothermal property to an unrelated third party for $160,000 and recognizes a gain of $140,000 ($160,000 amount realized less $20,000 adjusted basis ($50,000 unadjusted basis less $30,000 depletion deductions)). This gain is allocated equally between K and L. Because K's section 1254 costs are $65,000 and L's section 1254 costs are $15,000, K recognizes $65,000 as ordinary income under section 1254(a) and L recognizes $15,000 as ordinary income under section 1254(a). The remaining $5,000 of gain allocated to K and $55,000 of gain allocated to L is characterized without regard to section 1254.

Example 3. Section 59(e) election to capitalize intangible drilling and development costs. Partnership DK has 50 equal partners. On January 1, 1995, the partnership purchases an undeveloped oil and gas property for $100,000. The partnership allocates the property's basis equally among the partners, so each partner is allocated $2,000 of basis. In January 1995, the partnership incurs $240,000 of intangible drilling and development costs with respect to the property. The partnership elects to deduct the intangible drilling and development costs as expenses under section 263(c). Each partner is allocated $4,800 of intangible drilling and development costs. One of the partners, H, elects under section 59(e) to capitalize his $4,800 share of intangible drilling and development costs. Therefore, H is permitted to amortize his $4,800 share of intangible drilling and development costs over 60 months. H takes a $960 amortization deduction in 1995. Each of the remaining 49 partners deducts his $4,800 share of intangible drilling and development costs in 1995. Assume that depletion allowable for each partner under section 613A(c)(7)(D) for 1995 is $1,000. On December 31, 1995, the partnership sells the property for $300,000. Each partner is allocated $6,000 of amount realized. Each partner that deducted the intangible drilling and development costs has a basis in the oil property at the end of 1995 of $1,000 ($2,000 cost − $1,000 depletion deductions claimed). Each of these partners has a gain of $5,000 on the sale of the oil property ($6,000 amount realized − $1,000 adjusted basis in the property). The section 1254 costs of each partner that deducted intangible drilling and development costs are $5,800 ($4,800 intangible drilling and development costs deducted + $1,000 depletion deductions claimed). Because each partner's section 1254 costs ($5,800) exceed each partner's share of amount realized less each partner's adjusted basis ($5,000), each partner must treat his $5,000 gain recognized on the sale of the oil property as ordinary income under section 1254(a). Because H elected under section 59(e) to capitalize the $4,800 of intangible drilling and development costs and amortized only $960 of the costs in 1995, the $3,840 of unamortized intangible drilling and development costs are included in H's basis in the oil property. Therefore, at the end of 1995 H's basis in the oil property is $4,840 (($2,000 cost + $4,800 capitalized intangible drilling and development costs) − ($960 intangible drilling and development costs amortized + $1,000 depletion deduction claimed)). H's gain on the sale of the oil property is $1,160 ($6,000 amount realized − $4,840 adjusted basis). H's section 1254 costs are $1,960 ($960 intangible drilling and development costs amortized + $1,000 depletion deductions

claimed). Because H's section 1254 costs ($1,960) exceed H's share of amount realized less H's adjusted basis ($1,160), H must treat the $1,160 of gain recognized as ordinary income under section 1254(a).

(c) *Section 1254 costs of a partner.*—(1) *General rule.*—A partner's section 1254 costs with respect to property held by a partnership include all of the partner's section 1254 costs with respect to the property in the hands of the partnership. In the case of property contributed to a partnership in a transaction described in section 721, a partner's section 1254 costs include all of the partner's section 1254 costs with respect to the property prior to contribution. Section 1.1254-1(b)(1)(iv), which provides rules concerning the treatment of suspended deductions, applies to amounts not deductible pursuant to section 704(d).

(2) *Section 1254 costs of a transferee partner after certain acquisitions.*—(i) *Basis determined under section 1012.*—If a person acquires an interest in a partnership that holds natural resource recapture property (transferee partner) and the transferee partner's basis for the interest is determined by reference to its cost (within the meaning of section 1012), the amount of the transferee partner's section 1254 costs with respect to the property held by the partnership is zero on the acquisition date.

(ii) *Basis determined by reason of the application of section 1014(a).*—If a transferee partner acquires an interest in a partnership that holds natural resource recapture property from a decedent and the transferee partner's basis is determined, by reason of the application of section 1014(a), solely by reference to the fair market value of the partnership interest on the date of the decedent's death or on the applicable date provided in section 2032 (relating to alternate valuation date), the amount of the transferee partner's section 1254 costs with respect to property held by the partnership is zero on the acquisition date.

(iii) *Basis determined by reason of the application of section 1014(b)(9).*—If an interest in a partnership that holds natural resource recapture property is acquired before the death of the decedent, the amount of the transferee partner's section 1254 costs with respect to property held by the partnership shall include the amount, if any, of the section 1254 costs deducted by the transferee partner before the decedent's death, to the extent that the basis of the partner's interest (determined under section 1014(a)) is required to be reduced under section 1014(b)(9) (relating to adjustments to basis when the property is acquired before the death of the decedent).

(iv) *Gifts and section 1041 transfers.*—If an interest in a partnership is transferred in a transfer that is a gift, a part sale or exchange and part gift, or a transfer that is described in section 1041(a), the amount of the transferee partner's section 1254 costs with respect to property held by the partnership immediately after the transfer is an amount equal to—

(A) The amount of the transferor partner's section 1254 costs with respect to the property immediately before the transfer; minus

(B) The amount of any gain recognized as ordinary income under section 1254 by the transferor partner upon the transfer.

(d) *Property distributed to a partner.*—(1) *In general.*—The section 1254 costs for any natural resource recapture property received by a partner in a distribution with respect to part or all of an interest in a partnership include—

(i) The aggregate of the partners' section 1254 costs with respect to the natural resource recapture property immediately prior to the distribution; reduced by

(ii) The amount of any gain taken into account as ordinary income under section 751 by the partnership or the partners (as constituted after the distribution) on the distribution of the natural resource recapture property.

(2) *Aggregate of partners' section 1254 costs with respect to natural resource recapture property held by a partnership.*—(i) *In general.*—The aggregate of partners' section 1254 costs is equal to the sum of each partner's section 1254 costs. The partnership must determine each partner's section 1254 costs under either paragraph (d)(2)(i)(A) (written data) or paragraph (d)(2)(i)(B) (assumptions) of this section. The partnership may determine the section 1254 costs of some of the partners under paragraph (d)(2)(i)(A) of this section and of others under paragraph (d)(2)(i)(B) of this section.

(A) *Written data.*—A partnership may determine a partner's section 1254 costs by using written data provided by a partner showing the partner's section 1254 costs with respect to natural resource recapture property held by the partnership unless the partnership knows or has reason to know that the written data is inaccurate. If a partnership does not receive written data upon which it may rely, the partnership must use the assumptions provided in paragraph (d)(2)(i)(B) of this section in determining a partner's section 1254 costs.

(B) *Assumptions.*—A partnership that does not use written data pursuant to paragraph (d)(2)(i)(A) of this section to determine a partner's section 1254 costs must use the following assumptions to determine the partner's section 1254 costs:

(1) The partner deducted his or her share of deductions under section 263(c), 616, or 617 for the first year in which the partner could claim a deduction for such amounts, unless in the case of expenditures under section 263(c) or

616, the partnership elected to capitalize such amounts;

(2) The partner was not subject to the following limitations with respect to the partner's depletion allowance under section 611, except to the extent a limitation applied at the partnership level: the taxable income limitation of section 613(a); the depletable quantity limitations of section 613A(c); or the limitations of section 613A(d)(2), (3), and (4) (exclusion of retailers and refiners). [Reg. § 1.1254-5.]

☐ [*T.D.* 8586, 1-9-95.]

[Reg. § 1.1254-6]

§ 1.1254-6. Effective date of regulations.—Sections 1.1254-1 through 1.1254-3 and § 1.1254-5 are effective with respect to any disposition of natural resource recapture property occurring after March 13, 1995. The rule in § 1.1254-1(b)(2)(iv)(A)(2), relating to a nonoperating mineral interest carved out of an operating mineral interest with respect to which an expenditure has been deducted, is effective with respect to any disposition occurring after March 13, 1995, of property (within the meaning of section 614) that is placed in service by the taxpayer after December 31, 1986. Section 1.1254-4 applies to dispositions of natural resource recapture property by an S corporation (and a corporation that was formerly an S corporation) and dispositions of S corporation stock occurring on or after October 10, 1996. Sections 1.1254-2(d)(1)(ii) and 1.1254-3(b)(1)(i) and (ii) and (d)(1)(i) are effective for dispositions of property occurring on or after October 10, 1996. [Reg. § 1.1254-6.]

☐ [*T.D.* 8586, 1-9-95. *Amended by T.D.* 8684, 10-9-96.]

[Reg. § 16A.1255-1]

§ 16A.1255-1. General rule for treatment of gain from disposition of section 126 property (Temporary).—(a) *Ordinary income.*—(1) *General rule.*—Except as otherwise provided in this section and § 16A.1255-2, if section 126 property is disposed of after September 30, 1979, then under section 1255(a)(1) there shall be recognized as ordinary income the lesser of—

(i) The "excludable portion" under section 126, or

(ii)(A) The excess of the amount realized (in the case of a sale, exchange, or involuntary conversion), or the fair market value of the section 126 property (in the case of any other disposition), over the adjusted basis of the property, less

(B) The amount recognized as ordinary income under the other provisions of chapter 1, subchapter P, part IV of the Code.

(2) *Application of section.*—Any gain treated as ordinary income under section 1255(a)(1) shall

be recognized as ordinary income notwithstanding any other provision of subtitle A of the Code except that section 1255 does not apply to the extent the gain is recognized as ordinary income under the other provisions of subchapter P, part IV of the Code. For special rules with respect to the application of section 1255, see § 16A.1255-2. For the relation of section 1255 to other provisions, see paragraph (c) of this section.

(3) *Meaning of terms.*—For purposes of section 1255 and these regulations—

(i) The term "section 126 property" means any property acquired, improved, or otherwise modified as a result of a payment listed in section 126(a) which has been certified by the Secretary of Agriculture as primarily for the purpose of conservation;

(ii) The term "excludable portion" is defined in § 16A.126-1(b)(5);

(iii) The term "disposition" has the same meaning as in § 1.1245-1(a)(3);

(iv) The term "date of receipt of the section 126 payment" means the last date the government made a payment for the improvements.

(4) *Applicable percentage.*—If section 126 property is disposed of less than 10 years after the date of receipt of the last payment which has been certified by the Secretary of Agriculture as primarily for the purpose of conservation, the "applicable percentage" is 100 percent; if section 126 property is disposed of more than 10 years after that date, the applicable percentage is 100 percent reduced (but not below zero) by 10 percent for each year or part thereof in excess of 10 years such property was held after the date of the section 126 payment.

(5) *Portion of parcel.*—The amount of gain to be recognized as ordinary income under section 1255(a)(1) shall be determined separately for each parcel of section 126 property in a manner consistent with the principles of § 1.1245-1(a)(4) and (5) relating to gain from disposition of certain depreciable property. If (i) only a portion of a parcel of section 126 property is disposed of in a transaction, or if two or more portions of a single parcel are disposed of in one transaction, and (ii) the aggregate of "excludable portions" with respect to any such portion cannot be established to the satisfaction of the Commissioner, then the aggregate of the "excludable portions" in respect of the entire parcel shall be allocated to each portion in proportion to the fair market value of each at the time of the disposition.

(b) *Instances of nonapplication.*—(1) *In general.*—Section 1255 does not apply if a taxpayer disposes of section 126 property more than 20 years after receipt of the last section 126 payment with respect to the property.

(2) *Losses.*—Section 1255(a)(1) does not apply to losses. Thus, section 1255(a)(1) does not

apply if a loss is realized upon a sale, exchange, or involuntary conversion of property, all of which is section 126 property, nor does the section apply to a disposition of the property other than by way of sale, exchange, or involuntary conversion if at the time of the disposition the fair market value of the property is not greater than its adjusted basis.

(c) *Relation of section 1255 to other provisions.*— (1) *General.*—The provisions of section 1255 apply notwithstanding any other provisions of subtitle A of the Code except that they do not apply to the extent gain is recognized as ordinary income under the other provisions of subchapter P, part IV of the Code. Thus, unless an exception or limitation under § 16A.1255-2 applies, gain under section 1255(a)(1) is recognized notwithstanding any contrary nonrecognition provision or income characterizing provision. For example, since section 1255 overrides section 1231 (relating to property used in the trade or business), the gain recognized under section 1255 upon a disposition of section 126 property will be treated as ordinary income and only the remaining gain, if any, from the disposition may be considered as gain from the sale or exchange of property to which section 1231 applies. See example (1) of paragraph (d) of this section.

(2) *Nonrecognition sections overridden.*—The nonrecognition of gain provisions of subtitle A of the Code which section 1255 overrides include, but are not limited to, sections 267(d), 311(a), 336, 337, and 512(b)(5). See § 16A.1255-2 for the extent to which section 1255(a)(1) overrides sections 332, 351, 361, 371(a), 374(a), 721, 731, 1031, and 1033.

(3) *Installment method.*—Gain from a disposition to which section 1255(a)(1) applies may be reported under the installment method if such method is otherwise available under section 453 of the Code. In such a case, the portion of the installment payment that is gain is treated as follows: first as ordinary gain under other sections of chapter I, subchapter P, part IV of the Code until all that gain has been reported; next as ordinary gain to which section 1255 applies until all that gain is reported; and finally as gain under other sections of chapter I, subchapter D, part IV of the Code. For treatment of amounts as interest on certain deferred payments, see section 483.

(4) *Exempt income.*—With regard to exempt income, the principles of § 1.1245-6(e) shall be applicable.

(5) *Treatment of gain not recognized under section 1255(a)(1).*—For treatment of gain not recognized under this section, the principles of § 1.1245-6(f) shall be applicable.

(d) *Example.*—The provisions of this section may be illustrated by the following example:

Reg. § 16A.1255-1(d)

Example (1). Individual A uses the calendar year as his taxable year. On April 10, 1995, A sells for $75,000 section 126 property with an adjusted basis of $52,500 for a realized gain of $22,500. The excludable portion under section 126 was $18,000. A received the section 126 payment on January 5, 1990. No gain is recognized as ordinary gain under sections 1231 through 1254. Because the applicable percentage, 100 percent, of the aggregate of the section 126 improvements ($18,000), $18,000, is lower than the gain realized, $22,500, the amount of gain recognized as ordinary income under section 1255(a)(1) is $18,000. The remaining $4,500 of the gain may be treated as gain from the sale or exchange of property described in section 1231. [Temporary Reg. § 16A.1255-1.]

☐ *[T.D. 7778, 5-18-81.]*

[Reg. § 16A.1255-2]

§ 16A.1255-2. Special rules (Temporary).—
(a) *Exception for gifts.*—(1) *General rule.*—In general, no gain shall be recognized under section 1255(a)(1) upon a disposition of section 126 property by gift. For purposes of section 1255 and this paragraph, the term "gift" shall have the same meaning as in § 1.1245-4(a) and, with respect to the application of this paragraph, principles illustrated by the examples of § 1.1245-4(a)(2) shall apply.

(2) *Disposition in part a sale or exchange and in part a gift.*—Where a disposition of section 126 property is in part a sale or exchange and in part a gift, the amount of gain which shall be recognized as ordinary income under section 1255(a)(1) shall be computed under

§ 16A.1255-1(a)(1), applied by treating the gain realized (for purposes of § 16A.1255-1(a)(1)(ii)), as the excess of the amount realized over the adjusted basis of the section 126 property.

(3) *Treatment of section 126 property in hands of transferee.*—See paragraph (d) of this section for treatment of the transferee in the case of a disposition to which this paragraph applies.

(4) *Examples.*—The provisions of this paragraph may be illustrated by the following examples:

Example (1). On March 2, 1986, A makes a gift to B of a parcel of land having an adjusted basis of $40,000 and fair market value of $65,000. On the date of that gift, the aggregate of excludable portions under section 126 was $24,000. The section 126 payments were all received on January 15, 1981. Upon making the gift, A recognizes no gain under section 1255(a)(1). See paragraph (a)(1) of this section. For treatment of the property in the hands of B, see example (1) of paragraph (d)(3) of this section.

Example (2). (i) Assume the same facts as in example (1), except that A transfers the land to B for $50,000. Assume further that no gain is recognized as ordinary income under any other provision of chapter I, subchapter P, part IV of the Code. Thus, the gain realized is $10,000 (amount realized, $50,000, minus adjusted basis, $40,000), and A has made a gift of $15,000 (fair market value, $65,000, minus amount realized, $50,000).

(ii) Upon the transfer of the land to B, A recognizes $10,000 as ordinary income under section 1255(a)(1), computed under paragraph (a)(2) of this section as follows:

(1) Aggregate of excludable portions under section 126	$24,000
(2) Multiply: Applicable percentage for land disposed if within sixth year after section 126 payments were received	100 %
(3) Amount in § 16A.1255-1(a)(1)(i)	$24,000
(4) Gain realized (see (i) of this example)	$10,000
(5) Amount in § 16A.1255-1(a)(1)(ii) applied in accordance with paragraph (a)(2) of this section	$10,000
(6) Lower of line (3) or line (5)	$10,000

Thus, the entire gain realized on the transfer, $10,000, is recognized as ordinary income. For treatment of the farm land in the hands of B, see example (2) of paragraph (d)(3) of this section.

(b) *Exception for transfer at death.*—(1) *In general.*—Except as provided in section 691 (relating to income in respect of a decedent), no gain shall be recognized under section 1255(a)(1) upon a transfer at death. For purposes of section 1255 and this paragraph, the term "transfer at death" shall have the same meaning as in § 1.1245-4(b) and, with respect to the application of this paragraph, principles illustrated by the examples of § 1.1245-4(b)(2) shall apply.

(2) *Treatment of section 126 property in hands of transferee.*—If, as of the date a person acquires section 126 property from a decedent, the person's basis is determined by reason of the application of section 1014(a), solely by reference to the fair market value of the property on the date of the decedent's death, or on the applicable date provided in section 2032 (relating to alternative valuation date), then on that date the aggregate of excludable portions under section 126 in the hands of such transferee is zero.

(c) *Limitation for certain tax-free transactions.*—(1) *Limitation on amount of gain.*—Upon a transfer of section 126 property described in paragraph (c)(2) of this section, the amount of gain recognized as ordinary income under section 1255(a)(1) shall not exceed an amount equal to the excess (if any) or (i) the amount of gain recognized to the transferor on the transfer (determined without regard to section 1255) over (ii) the amount (if any) of gain recognized as ordinary income under the other provisions of chapter I, subchapter P, part IV of the Code. For purposes of paragraph (c)(1) of this section, the principles of § 1.1245-4(c)(1) shall apply. Thus, in the case of a transfer of section 126 property and other property in one transaction, the amount realized from the disposition of the section 126 property (as determined in a manner consistent with the principles of § 1.1245-1(a)(5)) shall consist of that portion of the fair market value of each property acquired which bears the same ratio to the fair market value of the acquired property as the amount realized from the disposition of the section 126 property bears to the total amount realized. The preceding sentence shall be applied solely for purposes of computing the portion of the total gain (determined without regard to section 1255) which is eligible to be recognized as ordinary income under section 1255(a)(1). The provisions of this paragraph do not apply to a disposition of property to an organization (other than a cooperative described in section 521) which is exempt from the tax imposed by chapter 1 of the Code.

(2) *Transfers covered.*—The transfers referred to in paragraph (c)(1) of this section are transfers of section 126 property in which the basis of the property in the hands of the transferee is determined by reference to its basis in the hands of the transferor by reason of the application of any of the following provisions:

(i) Section 332 (relating to distributions in complete liquidation of an 80-percent-or-more controlled subsidiary corporation). For application of paragraph (c)(1) of this section to such a complete liquidation, the principles of § 1.1245-4(c)(3) shall apply. Thus, for example, the provisions of paragraph (c)(1) of this section do not apply to a liquidating distribution of section 126 property by an 80-percent-or-more controlled subsidiary to its parent if the parent's basis for the property is determined, under section 334(b)(2), by reference to its basis for the stock of the subsidiary.

(ii) Section 351 (relating to transfer to a corporation controlled by the transferor).

(iii) Section 361 (relating to exchanges pursuant to certain corporate reorganizations).

(iv) Section 371(a) (relating to exchanges pursuant to certain receivership and bankruptcy proceedings).

(v) Section 374(a) (relating to exchanges pursuant to certain railroad reorganizations).

(vi) Section 721 (relating to transfers to a partnership in exchange for a partnership interest). See paragraph (e) of this section.

(vii) Section 731 (relating to distributions by a partnership to a partner). For special carryover of basis rule, see paragraph (e) of this section.

(viii) Section 1031 (relating to like kind exchanges).

(ix) Section 1034 (relating to rollover of gain on the sale of a principal residence).

(3) *Treatment of section 126 property in the hands of transferee.*—See paragraph (d) of this section for treatment of the transferee in the case of a disposition to which this paragraph applies.

(4) *Examples.*—The provisions of this paragraph may be illustrated by the following examples:

Example (1). On January 4, 1986, A holds a parcel of property that is section 126 property having an adjusted basis of $15,000 and a fair market value of $40,000. On that date he transfers the parcel to corporation M in exchange for stock in the corporation worth $40,000 in a transaction qualifying under section 351. On the date of the transfer, the aggregate of excludable portions under section 126 with respect to the transferred property is $18,000 and all of such amount was received on March 25, 1981. With regard to section 1255, A would recognize no gain under section 351 upon the transfer and M's basis for the land would be determined under section 362(a) by reference to its basis in the hands of A. Thus, as a result of the disposition, no gain is recognized as ordinary income under section 1255 by A since the amount of gain recognized under that section is limited to the amount of gain which is recognized under section 351 (determined without regard to section 1255). See paragraph (c)(1) of this section. For treatment of the section 126 property in the hands of B, see paragraph (d)(1) of this section.

Example (2). Assume the same facts in example (1), except that A transferred the property to M for stock in the corporation worth $32,000 and $8,000 cash. The gain realized is $25,000 (amount realized, $40,000, minus adjusted basis, $15,000). Without regard to section 1255, A would recognize $8,000 of gain under section 351(b). Assume further that no gain is recognized as ordinary income under the other provisions of chapter 1, subchapter P, part IV of the Code. Therefore, since the applicable percentage, 100 percent of the aggregate excludable portions under section 126, $18,000, is lower than the gain realized, $25,000, the amount of gain to be recognized as ordinary income under section 1255(a)(1) would be $18,000 if the provisions of paragraph (c)(1) of this section do not apply. Since under section 351(b) gain in the amount of $8,000 would be recognized to the transferor without regard to section 1255, the limitation provided in paragraph (c)(1) of this section limits the gain taken into account by A under section 1255(a)(1) to $8,000.

Example (3). Assume the same facts as in example (2), except that $5,000 of gain is recognized as ordinary income under section 1251(c)(1). The amount of gain recognized as ordinary income under section 1255(a)(1) is $3,000 computed as follows:

(1) Amount of gain under section 1255(a)(1) (determined without regard to paragraph (c)(1) of this section):	
(a) Aggregate of excludable portions under section 126	$18,000
(b) Multiply: Applicable percentage for property disposed of within the fifth year after section 126 payments were received	100 %
(c) Amount in § 16A.1255-1(a)(1)(i)	$18,000
(d) Gain realized (amount realized $40,000 less adjusted basis, $15,000)	$25,000
(e) Lower of line (c) or line (d)	$18,000
(2) Limitation in paragraph (c)(1) of this section:	
(a) Gain recognized (determined without regard to section 1255)	$8,000
(b) Minus: Gain recognized as ordinary income under section 1251(c)(1)	$5,000
(c) Difference	$3,000
(3) Lower of line (1)(e) or line (2)(c)	$3,000

Thus, the entire gain recognized under section 351(b) (determined without regard to sections 1251 and 1255), $8,000, is recognized as ordinary income since that amount is equal to the sum of the gain recognized as ordinary income under section 1251(c)(1), $5,000, and under section 1255(a)(1), $3,000.

(d) *Treatment of section 126 property received by a transferee in a disposition by gift and certain tax-free transactions.*—(1) *General rule.*—If section 126 property is disposed of in a transaction which is either a gift to which paragraph (a)(1) of this section applies, or a completely tax-free transfer to which paragraph (c)(1) of this section applies, then for purposes of section 1255—

(i) The aggregate of the excludable portions under section 126 in respect of the land in the hands of the transferee immediately after the disposition shall be an amount equal to the amount of such aggregate in the hands of the transferor immediately before the disposition, and

(ii) For purposes of applying section 1255 upon a subsequent disposition by the transferee (including a computation of the applicable percentage), the dates of receipt of section 126 payments shall not be affected by the dispositions.

(2) *Certain partially tax-free transfers.*—If section 126 property is disposed of in a transaction which either is in part a sale or exchange and in part a gift to which paragraph (a)(2) of this section applies, or is a partially tax-free transfer to which paragraph (c)(1) of this section applies, then for purposes of section 1255 the amount determined under paragraph (d)(1) of this section shall be reduced by the amount of gain taken into account under section 1255 by the transferor upon the disposition. Upon a subsequent disposition by the transferee, the dates of receipt of section 126 payments remain the same in the hands of the transferee as they were in the hands of the transferor. With respect to the 175 and 182 deductions taken by the transferee, the holding period shall not include the holding period of the transferor.

(3) *Examples.*—The provisions of this paragraph may be illustrated by the following examples:

Example (1). Assume the same facts as in example (1) of paragraph (a)(4) of this section. Therefore, on the date B receives the land in the gift transaction, under paragraph (d)(1) of this section the aggregate of excludable portions under section 126 in respect of the land in the hands of B is the amount in the hands of A, $24,000, and for purposes of applying section 1255 upon a subsequent disposition by B (including a computation of the applicable percentage) the date the section 126 payments were received is the same as it was when the property was in A's hands (January 15, 1981).

Example (2). Assume the same facts as in example (2) of paragraph (a)(4) of this section. Under paragraph (d)(2) of this section, the aggregate of excludable portions under section 126 which pass over to B for purposes of section 1255 is $14,000 ($24,000 excluded under section 126 minus $10,000 gain recognized under section 1255(d)(1) in accordance with example (2) of paragraph (a)(4) of this section). The date the section 126 payments were received is the same as when the property was in B's hands (January 15, 1981).

(e) *Disposition of section 126 property not specifically covered.*—If section 126 property is disposed of in a transaction not specifically covered under § 16A.1255-1, and this section, then the principles of section 1245 shall apply. [Temporary Reg. § 16A.1255-2.]

☐ [T.D. 7778, 5-18-81.]

Reg. § 16A.1255-2(d)

[Reg. §1.1256(e)-1]

§1.1256(e)-1. Identification of hedging transactions.—(a) *Identification and recordkeeping requirements.*—Under section 1256(e)(2), a taxpayer that enters into a hedging transaction must identify the transaction as a hedging transaction before the close of the day on which the taxpayer enters into the transaction.

(b) *Requirements for identification.*—The identification of a hedging transaction for purposes of section 1256(e)(2) must satisfy the requirements of §1.1221-2(f)(1). Solely for purposes of section 1256(f)(1), however, an identification that does not satisfy all of the requirements of §1.1221-2(f)(1) is nevertheless treated as an identification under section 1256(e)(2).

(c) *Consistency with §1.1221-2.*—Any identification for purposes of §1.1221-2(f)(1) is also an identification for purposes of this section. If a taxpayer satisfies the requirements of §1.1221-2(g)(1)(ii), the transaction is treated as if it were not identified as a hedging transaction for purposes of section 1256(e)(2).

(d) *Effective date.*—The rules of this section apply to transactions entered into on or after March 20, 2002. [Reg. §1.1256(e)-1.]

☐ [*T.D. 8555, 7-13-94. Amended by T.D. 8985, 3-15-2002 (corrected 5-10-2002).*]

[Reg. §1.1258-1]

§1.1258-1. Netting rule for certain conversion transactions.—(a) *Purpose.*—The purpose of this section is to provide taxpayers with a method to net certain gains and losses from positions of the same conversion transaction before determining the amount of gain treated as ordinary income under section 1258(a).

(b) *Netting of gain and loss for identified transactions.*—(1) In general. If a taxpayer disposes of or terminates all the positions of an identified netting transaction (as defined in paragraph (b)(2) of this section) within a 14-day period in a single taxable year, all gains and losses on those positions taken into account for federal tax purposes within that period (other than built-in losses as defined in paragraph (c) of this section) are netted solely for purposes of determining the amount of gain treated as ordinary income under section 1258(a). For purposes of the preceding sentence, a taxpayer is treated as disposing of any position that is treated as sold under any provision of the Code or regulations thereunder (for example, under section 1256(a)(1)).

(2) *Identified netting transaction.*—For purposes of this section, an identified netting transaction is a conversion transaction (as defined in section 1258(c)) that the taxpayer identifies as an identified netting transaction on its books and records. Identification of each position of the conversion transaction must be made before the close of the day on which the position becomes part of the conversion transaction. No particular form of identification is necessary, but all the positions of a single conversion transaction must be identified as part of the same transaction and must be distinguished from all other positions.

(c) *Definition of built-in loss.*—For purposes of this section, built-in loss means—

(1) Built-in loss as defined in section 1258(d)(3)(B); and

(2) If a taxpayer realizes gain or loss on any one position of a conversion transaction (for example, under section 1256), as of the date that gain or loss is realized, any unrecognized loss in any other position of the conversion transaction that is not disposed of, terminated, or treated as sold under any provision of the Code or regulations thereunder within 14 days of and within the same taxable year as the realization event.

(d) *Examples.*—These examples illustrate this section:

Example 1. Identified netting transaction with simultaneous actual dispositions. (i) On December 1, 1995, A purchases 1,000 shares of XYZ stock for $100,000 and enters into a forward contract to sell 1,000 shares of XYZ stock on November 30, 1997, for $110,000. The XYZ stock is actively traded as defined in §1.1092(d)-1(a) and is a capital asset in A's hands. A maintains books and records on which, on December 1, 1995, it identifies the two positions as all the positions of a single conversion transaction. A owns no other XYZ stock. On December 1, 1996, when the applicable imputed income amount for the transaction is $7,000, A sells the 1,000 shares of XYZ stock for $95,000. On the same day, A terminates its forward contract with its counterparty, receiving $10,200. No dividends were received on the stock during the time it was part of the conversion transaction.

(ii) The XYZ stock and forward contract are positions of a conversion transaction. Under section 1258(c)(1), substantially all of A's expected return from the overall transaction is attributable to the time value of the net investment in the transaction. Under section 1258(c)(2)(B), the transaction is an applicable straddle as defined in section 1258(d)(1).

(iii) A disposed of or terminated all the positions of the conversion transaction within 14 days and within the same taxable year as required by paragraph (b)(1) of this section. The transaction is an identified netting transaction because it meets the identification requirement of paragraph (b)(2) of this section. Solely for purposes of section 1258(a), the $5,000 loss realized ($100,000 basis less $95,000 amount realized) on the disposition of the XYZ stock is netted against the $10,200 gain recognized on the disposition of the forward contract. Thus, the net gain from the conversion transaction for purposes of section 1258(a) is $5,200 ($10,200 gain less $5,000 loss). Only the $5,200 net gain is recharacterized as ordinary income under section 1258(a) even though the applicable imputed income amount is $7,000. For federal tax purposes other than section 1258(a), *A* has recognized a $10,200 gain on the disposition of the forward contract ($5,200 of which is treated as ordinary income) and realized a separate $5,000 loss on the sale of the *XYZ* stock.

Example 2. Identified netting transaction with built-in loss. (i) The facts are the same as in *Example 1*, except that *A* had purchased the *XYZ* stock for $104,000 on May 15, 1995. The *XYZ* stock had a fair market value of $100,000 on December 1, 1995, the date it became part of a conversion transaction.

(ii) The results are the same as in *Example 1*, except that *A* has built-in loss (in addition to the $5,000 loss that arose economically during the period of the conversion transaction), as defined in section 1258(d)(3)(B), of $4,000 on the *XYZ* stock. That $4,000 built-in loss is not netted against the $10,200 gain on the forward contract for purposes of section 1258(a). Thus, the net gain from the conversion transaction for purposes of section 1258(a) is $5,200, the same as in *Example 1*. The $4,000 built-in loss is recognized and has a character determined without regard to section 1258.

(e) *Effective date and transition rule.*—(1) *In general.*—These regulations are effective for conversion transactions that are outstanding on or after December 21, 1995.

(2) *Transition rule for identification requirements.*—In the case of a conversion transaction entered into before February 20, 1996, paragraph (b)(2) of this section is treated as satisfied if the identification is made before the close of business on February 20, 1996. [Reg. §1.1258-1.]

□ [*T.D.* 8649, 12-20-95.]

Special Rules for Bonds and Other Debt Instruments

[Reg. §1.1271-0]

§1.1271-0. Original issue discount; effective date; table of contents.—(a) *Effective date.*—Except as otherwise provided, §§1.1271-1 through 1.1275-5 apply to debt instruments issued on or after April 4, 1994. Taxpayers, however, may rely on these sections (as contained in 26 CFR part 1 revised April 1, 1996) for debt instruments issued after December 21, 1992, and before April 4, 1994.

(b) *Table of contents.*—This section lists captioned paragraphs contained in §§1.1271-1 through 1.1275-7T.

§1.1272-3. *Election by a holder to treat all interest on a debt instrument as OID.*

(a) Election.

(b) Scope of election.

(1) In general.

(2) Exceptions, limitations, and special rules.

(c) Mechanics of the constant yield method.

(1) In general.

(2) Special rules to determine adjusted basis.

(d) Time and manner of making the election.

(e) Revocation of election.

(f) Effective date.

§1.1273-1. *Definition of OID.*

(a) In general.

(b) Stated redemption price at maturity.

(c) Qualified stated interest.

(1) Definition.

(2) Debt instruments subject to contingencies.

(3) Variable rate debt instrument.

(4) Stated interest in excess of qualified stated interest.

(5) Short-term obligations.

(d) *De minimis* OID.

(1) In general.

(2) *De minimis* amount.

(3) Installment obligations.

(4) Special rule for interest holidays, teaser rates, and other interest shortfalls.

(5) Treatment of *de minimis* OID by holders.

(e) Definitions.

(1) Installment obligation.

(2) Self-amortizing installment obligation.

(3) Weighted average maturity.

(f) Examples.

§1.1273-2. *Determination of issue price and issue date.*

(a) Debt instruments issued for money.

(1) Issue price.

(2) Issue date.

(b) Publicly traded debt instruments issued for property.

(1) Issue price.

(2) Issue date.

(c) Debt instruments issued for publicly traded property.

(1) Issue price.

(2) Issue date.

(d) Other debt instruments.

(1) Issue price.

(2) Issue date.

(e) Special rule for certain sales to bond houses, brokers, or similar persons.

(f) Traded on an established market (publicly traded).

(1) In general.

(2) Exchange listed property.

(3) Market traded property.

(4) Property appearing on a quotation medium.

(5) Readily quotable debt instruments.

(6) Effect of certain temporary restrictions on trading.

(7) Convertible debt instruments.

(g) Treatment of certain cash payments incident to lending transactions.

(1) Applicability.

(2) Payments from borrower to lender.

(3) Payments from lender to borrower.

(4) Payments between lender and third party.

(5) Examples.

(h) Investment units.

(1) In general.

(2) Consistent allocation by holders and issuer.

(i) [Reserved]

(j) Convertible debt instruments.

(k) Below-market loans subject to section 7872(b).

(l) [Reserved]

(m) Treatment of amounts representing pre-issuance accrued interest.

(1) Applicability.

(2) Exclusion of pre-issuance accrued interest from issue price.

(3) Example.

§1.1274-1. *Debt instruments to which section 1274 applies.*

(a) In general.

(b) Exceptions.

(1) Debt instrument with adequate stated interest and no OID.

(2) Exceptions under sections 1274(c)(1)(B), 1274(c)(3), 1274A(c), and 1275(b)(1).

(3) Other exceptions to section 1274.

(c) Examples.

§1.1274-2. *Issue price of debt instruments to which section 1274 applies.*

(a) In general.

(b) Issue price.

(1) Debt instruments that provide for adequate stated interest; stated principal amount.

(2) Debt instruments that do not provide for adequate stated interest; imputed principal amount.

(3) Debt instruments issued in a potentially abusive situation; fair market value.

Reg. §1.1271-0

(c) Determination of whether a debt instrument provides for adequate stated interest.

(1) In general.

(2) Determination of present value.

(d) Treatment of certain options.

(e) Mandatory sinking funds.

(f) Treatment of variable rate debt instruments.

(1) Stated interest at a qualified floating rate.

(2) Stated interest at a single objective rate.

(g) Treatment of contingent payment debt instruments.

(h) Examples.

(i) [Reserved]

(j) Special rules for tax-exempt obligations.

(1) Certain variable rate debt instruments.

(2) Contingent payment debt instruments.

(3) Effective date.

§1.1274-3. Potentially abusive situations defined.

(a) In general.

(b) Operating rules.

(1) Debt instrument exchanged for nonrecourse financing.

(2) Nonrecourse debt with substantial down payment.

(3) Clearly excessive interest.

(c) Other situations to be specified by Commissioner.

(d) Consistency rule.

§1.1274-4. Test rate.

(a) Determination of test rate of interest.

(1) In general.

(2) Test rate for certain debt instruments.

(b) Applicable Federal rate.

(c) Special rules to determine the term of a debt instrument for purposes of determining the applicable Federal rate.

(1) Installment obligations.

(2) Certain variable rate debt instruments.

(3) Counting of either the issue date or the maturity date.

(4) Certain debt instruments that provide for principal payments uncertain as to time.

(d) Foreign currency loans.

(e) Examples.

§1.1274-5. Assumptions.

(a) In general.

(b) Modifications of debt instruments.

(1) In general.

(2) Election to treat buyer as modifying the debt instrument.

(c) Wraparound indebtedness.

(d) Consideration attributable to assumed debt.

§1.1274A-1. Special rules for certain transactions where stated principal amount does not exceed $2,800,000.

(a) In general.

(b) Rules for both qualified and cash method debt instruments.

(1) Sale-leaseback transactions.

(2) Debt instruments calling for contingent payments.

(3) Aggregation of transactions.

(4) Inflation adjustment of dollar amounts.

(c) Rules for cash method debt instruments.

(1) Time and manner of making cash method election.

(2) Successors of electing parties.

(3) Modified debt instrument.

(4) Debt incurred or continued to purchase or carry a cash method debt instrument.

§1.1275-1. Definitions.

(a) Applicability.

(b) Adjusted issue price.

(1) In general.

(2) Adjusted issue price for subsequent holders.

(c) OID.

(d) Debt instrument.

(e) Tax-exempt obligations.

(f) Issue.

(1) Debt instruments issued on or after March 13, 2001.

(2) Debt instruments issued before March 13, 2001.

(3) Transition rule.

(4) Cross-references for reopening and aggregation rules.

(g) Debt instruments issued by a natural person.

(h) Publicly offered debt instrument.

(i) [Reserved]

(j) Life annuity exception under section 1275(a)(1)(B)(i).

(1) Purpose.

(2) General rule.

(3) Availability of a cash surrender option.

(4) Availability of a loan secured by the contract.

(5) Minimum payout provision.

(6) Maximum payout provision.

(7) Decreasing payout provision.

(8) Effective dates.

(k) Exception under section 1275(a)(1)(B)(ii) for annuities issued by an insurance company subject to tax under subchapter L of the Internal Revenue Code.

(1) Rule.

(2) Examples.

(3) Effective date.

§ 1.1275-2. Special rules relating to debt instruments.

(a) Payment ordering rule.

(1) In general.

(2) Exceptions.

(b) Debt instruments distributed by corporations with respect to stock.

(1) Treatment of distribution.

(2) Issue date.

(c) Aggregation of debt instruments.

(1) General rule.

(2) Exception if separate issue price established.

(3) Special rule for debt instruments that provide for the issuance of additional debt instruments.

(4) Examples.

(d) Special rules for Treasury securities.

(1) Issue price and issue date.

(2) Reopenings of Treasury securities.

(e) Disclosure of certain information to holders.

(f) Treatment of pro rata prepayments.

(1) Treatment as retirement of separate debt instrument.

(2) Definition of pro rata prepayment.

(g) Anti-abuse rule.

(1) In general.

(2) Unreasonable result.

(3) Examples.

(4) Effective date.

(h) Remote and incidental contingencies.

(1) In general.

(2) Remote contingencies.

(3) Incidental contingencies.

(4) Aggregation rule.

(5) Consistency rule.

(6) Subsequent adjustments.

(7) Effective date.

(i) [Reserved]

(j) Treatment of certain modifications.

(k) Reopenings.

(1) In general.

(2) Definitions.

(3) Qualified reopening.

(4) Issuer's treatment of a qualified reopening.

(5) Effective date.

§ 1.1275-3. OID information reporting requirements.

(a) In general.

(b) Information required to be set forth on face of debt instruments that are not publicly offered.

(1) In general.

(2) Time for legending.

(3) Legend must survive reissuance upon transfer.

(4) Exceptions.

(c) Information required to be reported to Secretary upon issuance of publicly offered debt instruments.

(1) In general.

(2) Time for filing information return.

(3) Exceptions.

(d) Application to foreign issuers and U.S. issuers of foreign-targeted debt instruments.

(e) Penalties.

(f) Effective date.

§ 1.1275-4. Contingent payment debt instruments.

(a) Applicability.

(1) In general.

(2) Exceptions.

(3) Insolvency and default.

(4) Convertible debt instruments.

(5) Remote and incidental contingencies.

(b) Noncontingent bond method.

(1) Applicability.

(2) In general.

(3) Description of method.

(4) Comparable yield and projected payment schedule.

(5) Qualified stated interest.

(6) Adjustments.

(7) Adjusted issue price, adjusted basis, and retirement.

(8) Character on sale, exchange, or retirement.

(9) Operating rules.

(c) Method for debt instruments not subject to the noncontingent bond method.

(1) Applicability.

(2) Separation into components.

(3) Treatment of noncontingent payments.

(4) Treatment of contingent payments.

(5) Basis different from adjusted issue price.

(6) Treatment of a holder on sale, exchange, or retirement.

(7) Examples.

(d) Rules for tax-exempt obligations.

(1) In general.

(2) Certain tax-exempt obligations with interest-based or revenue-based payments

(3) All other tax-exempt obligations.

(4) Basis different from adjusted issue price.

Reg. §1.1271-0

(e) Amounts treated as interest under this section.

(f) Effective date.

§1.1275-5. Variable rate debt instruments.

(a) Applicability.

(1) In general.

(2) Principal payments.

(3) Stated interest.

(4) Current value.

(5) No contingent principal payments.

(6) Special rule for debt instruments issued for nonpublicly traded property.

(b) Qualified floating rate.

(1) In general.

(2) Certain rates based on a qualified floating rate.

(3) Restrictions on the stated rate of interest.

(c) Objective rate.

(1) Definition.

(2) Other objective rates to be specified by Commissioner.

(3) Qualified inverse floating rate.

(4) Significant front-loading or back-loading of interest.

(5) Tax-exempt obligations.

(d) Examples.

(e) Qualified stated interest and OID with respect to a variable rate debt instrument.

(1) In general.

(2) Variable rate debt instrument that provides for annual payments of interest at a single variable rate.

(3) All other variable rate debt instruments except for those that provide for a fixed rate.

(4) Variable rate debt instrument that provides for a single fixed rate.

(f) Special rule for certain reset bonds.

§1.1275-6. Integration of qualifying debt instruments.

(a) In general.

(b) Definitions.

(1) Qualifying debt instrument.

(2) Section 1.1275-6 hedge.

(3) Financial instrument.

(4) Synthetic debt instrument.

(c) Integrated transaction.

(1) Integration by taxpayer.

(2) Integration by Commissioner.

(d) Special rules for legging into and legging out of an integrated transaction.

(1) Legging into.

(2) Legging out.

(e) Identification requirements.

(f) Taxation of integrated transactions.

(1) General rule.

(2) Issue date.

(3) Term.

(4) Issue price.

(5) Adjusted issue price.

(6) Qualified stated interest.

(7) Stated redemption price at maturity.

(8) Source of interest income and allocation of expense.

(9) Effectively connected income.

(10) Not a short-term obligation.

(11) Special rules in the event of integration by the Commissioner.

(12) Retention of separate transaction rules for certain purposes.

(13) Coordination with consolidated return rules.

(g) Predecessors and successors.

(h) Examples.

(i) [Reserved]

(j) Effective date.

§1.1275-7. Inflation-indexed debt instruments.

(a) Overview.

(b) Applicability.

(1) In general.

(2) Exceptions.

(c) Definitions.

(1) Inflation-indexed debt instrument.

(2) Reference index.

(3) Qualified inflation index.

(4) Inflation-adjusted principal amount.

(5) Minimum guarantee payment.

(d) Coupon bond method.

(1) In general.

(2) Applicability.

(3) Qualified stated interest.

(4) Inflation adjustments.

(5) Example.

(e) Discount bond method.

(1) In general.

(2) No qualified stated interest.

(3) OID.

(4) Example.

(f) Special rules.

(1) Deflation adjustments.

(2) Adjusted basis.

(3) Subsequent holders.

(4) Minimum guarantee.

(5) Temporary unavailability of a qualified inflation index.

(g) Reopenings.

(h) Effective date.

[Reg. §1.1271-0.]

☐ [*T.D. 8517*, 1-27-94. *Amended by T.D. 8674*, 6-11-96; *T.D. 8709*, 12-31-96; *T.D. 8754*, 1-7-98; *T.D. 8838*, 9-3-99; *T.D. 8840*, 11-3-99; *T.D. 8934*, 1-11-2001 *and T.D. 8993*, 5-6-2002.]

[Reg. § 1.1271-1]

§ 1.1271-1. Special rules applicable to amounts received on retirement, sale, or exchange of debt instruments.—(a) *Intention to call before maturity.*—(1) *In general.*—For purposes of section 1271(a)(2), all or a portion of gain realized on a sale or exchange of a debt instrument to which section 1271 applies is treated as interest income if there was an intention to call the debt instrument before maturity. An intention to call a debt instrument before maturity means a written or oral agreement or understanding not provided for in the debt instrument between the issuer and the original holder of the debt instrument that the issuer will redeem the debt instrument before maturity. In the case of debt instruments that are part of an issue, the agreement or understanding must be between the issuer and the original holders of a substantial amount of the debt instruments in the issue. An intention to call before maturity can exist even if the intention is conditional (e.g., the issuer's decision to call depends on the financial condition of the issuer on the potential call date) or is not legally binding. For purposes of this section, original holder means the first holder (other than an underwriter or dealer that purchased the debt instrument for resale in the ordinary course of its trade or business).

(2) *Exceptions.*—In addition to the exceptions provided in sections 1271(a)(2)(B) and 1271(b), section 1271(a)(2) does not apply to—

(i) A debt instrument that is publicly offered (as defined in § 1.1275-1(h));

(ii) A debt instrument to which section 1272(a)(6) applies (relating to certain interests in or mortgages held by a REMIC, and certain other debt instruments with payments subject to acceleration); or

(iii) A debt instrument sold pursuant to a private placement memorandum that is distributed to more than ten offerees and that is subject to the sanctions of section 12(2) of the Securities Act of 1933 (15 U.S.C 77l) or the prohibitions of section 10(b) of the Securities Exchange Act of 1934 (15 U.S.C. 78j).

(b) *Short-term obligations.*—(1) *In general.*—Under sections 1271(a)(3) and (a)(4), all or a portion of the gain realized on the sale or exchange of a short-term government or nongovernment obligation is treated as interest income. Sections 1271(a)(3) and (a)(4), however, do not apply to any short-term obligation subject to section 1281. See § 1.1272-1(f) for rules to determine if an obligation is a short-term obligation.

(2) *Method of making elections.*—Elections to accrue on a constant yield basis under sections 1271(a)(3)(E) and (a)(4)(D) are made on an obligation-by-obligation basis by reporting the transaction on the basis of daily compounding on the taxpayer's timely filed Federal income tax return

for the year of the sale or exchange. These elections are irrevocable.

(3) *Counting conventions.*—In computing the ratable share of acquisition discount under section 1271(a)(3) or OID under section 1271(a)(4), any reasonable counting convention may be used (e.g., 30 days per month/360 days per year). [Reg. § 1.1271-1.]

☐ [*T.D. 8517, 1-27-94.*]

[Reg. § 1.1272-1]

§ 1.1272-1. Current inclusion of OID in income.—(a) *Overview.*—(1) *In general.*—Under section 1272(a)(1), a holder of a debt instrument includes accrued OID in gross income (as interest), regardless of the holder's regular method of accounting. A holder includes qualified stated interest (as defined in § 1.1273-1(c)) in income under the holder's regular method of accounting. See §§ 1.446-2 and 1.451-1.

(2) *Debt instruments not subject to OID inclusion rules.*—Sections 1272(a)(2) and 1272(c) list exceptions to the general inclusion rule of section 1272(a)(1). For purposes of section 1272(a)(2)(E) (relating to certain loans between natural persons), a loan does not include a stripped bond or stripped coupon within the meaning of section 1286(e), and the rule in section 1272(a)(2)(E)(iii), which treats a husband and wife as 1 person, does not apply to loans made between a husband and wife.

(b) *Accrual of OID.*—(1) *Constant yield method.*—Except as provided in paragraphs (b)(2) and (b)(3) of this section, the amount of OID includible in the income of a holder of a debt instrument for any taxable year is determined using the constant yield method as described under this paragraph (b)(1).

(i) *Step one: Determine the debt instrument's yield to maturity.*—The yield to maturity or yield of a debt instrument is the discount rate that, when used in computing the present value of all principal and interest payments to be made under the debt instrument, produces an amount equal to the issue price of the debt instrument. The yield must be constant over the term of the debt instrument and, when expressed as a percentage, must be calculated to at least two decimal places. See paragraph (c) of this section for rules relating to the yield of certain debt instruments subject to contingencies.

(ii) *Step two: Determine the accrual periods.*—An accrual period is an interval of time over which the accrual of OID is measured. Accrual periods may be of any length and may vary in length over the term of the debt instrument, provided that each accrual period is no longer than 1 year and each scheduled payment of principal or interest occurs either on the final day of an accrual period or on the first day of an accrual period. In general, the computation of OID is simplest if accrual periods correspond to the intervals between payment dates provided by the terms of the debt instrument. In computing the length of accrual periods, any reasonable counting convention may be used (e.g., 30 days per month/360 days per year).

(iii) *Step three: Determine the OID allocable to each accrual period.*—Except as provided in paragraph (b)(4) of this section, the OID allocable to an accrual period equals the product of the adjusted issue price of the debt instrument (as defined in § 1.1275-1(b)) at the beginning of the accrual period and the yield of the debt instrument, less the amount of any qualified stated interest allocable to the accrual period. In performing this calculation, the yield must be stated appropriately taking into account the length of the particular accrual period. *Example 1* in paragraph (j) of this section provides a formula for converting a yield based upon an accrual period of one length to an equivalent yield based upon an accrual period of a different length.

(iv) *Step four: Determine the daily portions of OID.*—The daily portions of OID are determined by allocating to each day in an accrual period the ratable portion of the OID allocable to the accrual period. The holder of the debt instrument includes in income the daily portions of OID for each day during the taxable year on which the holder held the debt instrument.

(2) *Exceptions.*—Paragraph (b)(1) of this section does not apply to—

(i) A debt instrument to which section 1272(a)(6) applies (certain interests in or mortgages held by a REMIC, and certain other debt instruments with payments subject to acceleration);

(ii) A debt instrument that provides for contingent payments, other than a debt instrument described in paragraph (c) or (d) of this section or except as provided in § 1.1275-4; or

(iii) A variable rate debt instrument to which § 1.1275-5 applies, except as provided in § 1.1275-5.

(3) *Modifications.*—The amount of OID includible in income by a holder under paragraph (b)(1) of this section is adjusted if—

(i) The holder purchased the debt instrument at a premium or an acquisition premium (within the meaning of § 1.1272-2); or

(ii) The holder made an election for the debt instrument under § 1.1272-3 to treat all interest as OID.

(4) *Special rules for determining the OID allocable to an accrual period.*—The following rules apply to determine the OID allocable to an accrual period under paragraph (b)(1)(iii) of this section.

(i) *Unpaid qualified stated interest allocable to an accrual period.*—In determining the OID allocable to an accrual period, if an interval between payments of qualified stated interest contains more than 1 accrual period—

(A) The amount of qualified stated interest payable at the end of the interval (including any qualified stated interest that is payable on the first day of the accrual period immediately following the interval) is allocated on a pro rata basis to each accrual period in the interval; and

(B) The adjusted issue price at the beginning of each accrual period in the interval must be increased by the amount of any qualified stated interest that has accrued prior to the first day of the accrual period but that is not payable until the end of the interval. See *Example 2* of paragraph (j) of this section for an example illustrating the rules in this paragraph (b)(4)(i).

(ii) *Final accrual period.*—The OID allocable to the final accrual period is the difference between the amount payable at maturity (other than a payment of qualified stated interest) and the adjusted issue price at the beginning of the final accrual period.

(iii) *Initial short accrual period.*—If all accrual periods are of equal length, except for either an initial shorter accrual period or an initial and a final shorter accrual period, the amount of OID allocable to the initial accrual period may be computed using any reasonable method. See *Example 3* in paragraph (j) of this section.

(iv) *Payment on first day of an accrual period.*—The adjusted issue price at the beginning of an accrual period is reduced by the amount of any payment (other than a payment of qualified stated interest) that is made on the first day of the accrual period.

(c) *Yield and maturity of certain debt instruments subject to contingencies.*—(1) *Applicability.*—This paragraph (c) provides rules to determine the yield and maturity of certain debt instruments that provide for an alternative payment schedule (or schedules) applicable upon the occurrence of a contingency (or contingencies). This paragraph (c) applies, however, only if the timing and amounts of the payments that comprise each payment schedule are known as of the issue date and the debt instrument is subject to paragraph (c)(2), (3), or (5) of this section. A debt instrument does not provide for an alternative payment schedule merely because there is a possibility of impairment of a payment (or payments) by insolvency, default, or similar circumstances. See § 1.1275-4 for the treatment of a debt instrument that provides for a contingency that is not described in this paragraph (c). See § 1.1273-1(c) to determine whether stated interest on a debt instrument subject to this paragraph (c) is qualified stated interest.

(2) *Payment schedule that is significantly more likely than not to occur.*—If, based on all the facts and circumstances as of the issue date, a single payment schedule for a debt instrument, including the stated payment schedule, is significantly more likely than not to occur, the yield and maturity of the debt instrument are computed based on this payment schedule.

(3) *Mandatory sinking fund provision.*—Notwithstanding paragraph (c)(2) of this section, if a debt instrument is subject to a mandatory sinking fund provision, the provision is ignored for purposes of computing the yield and maturity of the debt instrument if the use and terms of the provision meet reasonable commercial standards. For purposes of the preceding sentence, a mandatory sinking fund provision is a provision that meets the following requirements:

(i) The provision requires the issuer to redeem a certain amount of debt instruments in an issue prior to maturity.

(ii) The debt instruments actually redeemed are chosen by lot or purchased by the issuer either in the open market or pursuant to an offer made to all holders (with any proration determined by lot).

(iii) On the issue date, the specific debt instruments that will be redeemed on any date prior to maturity cannot be identified.

(4) *Consistency rule.*—[Reserved]

(5) *Treatment of certain options.*—Notwithstanding paragraphs (c)(2) and (3) of this section, the rules of this paragraph (c)(5) determine the yield and maturity of a debt instrument that provides the holder or issuer with an unconditional option or options, exercisable on one or more dates during the term of the debt instrument, that, if exercised, require payments to be made on the debt instrument under an alternative payment schedule or schedules (e.g., an option to extend or an option to call a debt instrument at a fixed premium). Under this paragraph (c)(5), an issuer is deemed to exercise or not exercise an option or combination of options in a manner that minimizes the yield on the debt instrument, and a holder is deemed to exercise or not exercise an option or combination of options in a manner that maximizes the yield on the debt instrument. If both the issuer and the holder have options, the rules of this paragraph (c)(5) are applied to the options in the order that they may be exercised. See paragraph (j) *Example 5* through *Example 8* of this section.

(6) *Subsequent adjustments.*—If a contingency described in this paragraph (c) (including the exercise of an option described in paragraph (c)(5) of this section) actually occurs or does not occur, contrary to the assumption made pursuant to this paragraph (c) (a change in circumstances), then, solely for purposes of sections 1272 and 1273, the debt instrument is treated as

retired and then reissued on the date of the change in circumstances for an amount equal to its adjusted issue price on that date. See paragraph (j) *Example 5* and *Example 7* of this section. If, however, the change in circumstances results in a substantially contemporaneous pro-rata prepayment as defined in § 1.1275-2(f)(2), the pro-rata prepayment is treated as a payment in retirement of a portion of the debt instrument, which may result in gain or loss to the holder. See paragraph (j) *Example 6* and *Example 8* of this section.

(7) *Effective date.*—This paragraph (c) applies to debt instruments issued on or after August 13, 1996.

(d) *Certain debt instruments that provide for a fixed yield.*—If a debt instrument provides for one or more contingent payments but all possible payment schedules under the terms of the instrument result in the same fixed yield, the yield of the debt instrument is the fixed yield. For example, the yield of a debt instrument with principal payments that are fixed in total amount but that are uncertain as to time (such as a demand loan) is the stated interest rate if the issue price of the instrument is equal to the stated principal amount and interest is paid or compounded at a fixed rate over the entire term of the instrument. This paragraph (d) applies to debt instruments issued on or after August 13, 1996.

(e) *Convertible debt instruments.*—For purposes of section 1272, an option is ignored if it is an option to convert a debt instrument into the stock of the issuer, into the stock or debt of a related party (within the meaning of section 267(b) or 707(b)(1)), or into cash or other property in an amount equal to the approximate value of such stock or debt.

(f) *Special rules to determine whether a debt instrument is a short-term obligation.*—(1) *Counting of either the issue date or maturity date.*—For purposes of determining whether a debt instrument is a short-term obligation (i.e., a debt instrument with a fixed maturity date that is not more than 1 year from the date of issue), the term of the debt instrument includes either the issue date or the maturity date, but not both dates.

(2) *Coordination with paragraph (c) of this section for certain sections of the Internal Revenue Code.*—Notwithstanding paragraph (c) of this section, solely for purposes of determining whether a debt instrument is a short-term obligation under sections 871(g)(1)(B)(i), 881, 1271(a)(3), 1271(a)(4), 1272(a)(2)(C), and 1283(a)(1), the maturity date of a debt instrument is the last possible date that the instrument could be outstanding under the terms of the instrument. For purposes of the preceding sentence, the last possible date that the debt instrument could be outstanding is determined without re-

gard to §1.1275-2(h) (relating to payments subject to remote or incidental contingencies).

(g) *Basis adjustment.*—The basis of a debt instrument in the hands of the holder is increased by the amount of OID included in the holder's gross income and decreased by the amount of any payment from the issuer to the holder under the debt instrument other than a payment of qualified stated interest. See, however, §1.1275-2(f) for rules regarding basis adjustments on a pro rata prepayment.

(h) *Debt instruments denominated in a currency other than the U.S. dollar.*—Section 1272 and this section apply to a debt instrument that provides for all payments denominated in, or determined by reference to, the functional currency of the taxpayer or qualified business unit of the taxpayer (even if that currency is other than the U.S. dollar). See §1.988-2(b) to determine interest income or expense for debt instruments that provide for payments denominated in, or determined by reference to, a nonfunctional currency.

(i) [Reserved]

(j) *Examples.*—The following examples illustrate the rules of this section. Each example assumes that all taxpayers use the calendar year as the taxable year. In addition, each example assumes a 30-day month, 360-day year, and that

$$r = c \{ (1 + i/b)^{b/c} - 1 \}$$

In which:

i	=	The yield based on compounding b times per year expressed as a decimal
r	=	The equivalent yield based on compounding c times per year expressed as a decimal
b	=	The number of compounding periods in a year on which i is based (for example, 12, if i is based on monthly compounding)
c	=	The number of compounding periods in a year on which r is based

(iv) *Determination of OID allocable to each accrual period.* Assume that A decides to compute OID on the debt instrument using semiannual accrual periods. Under paragraph (b)(1)(iii) of this section, the OID allocable to the first semiannual accrual period is $27,022.56: the product of the issue price ($675,564.17) and the yield properly adjusted for the length of the accrual period (8 percent/2), less qualified stated interest allocable to the accrual period ($0). The daily portion of OID for the first semiannual period is $150.13 ($27,022.56/180).

(v) *Determination of OID if monthly accrual periods are used.* Alternatively, assume that A decides to compute OID on the debt instrument using monthly accrual periods. Using the above formula, the yield on the debt instrument reflecting monthly compounding is 7.87 percent, compounded monthly $(12 \{ (1 + .08/2)^{2/12} - 1 \})$. Under paragraph (b)(1)(iii) of this section, the OID allocable to the first monthly accrual period is $4,430.48: the product of the issue price ($675,564.17) and the yield properly adjusted for

the initial accrual period begins on the issue date and the final accrual period ends on the day before the stated maturity date. Although, for purposes of simplicity, the yield as stated is rounded to two decimal places, the computations do not reflect any such rounding convention.

Example 1. Accrual of OID on zero coupon debt instrument; choice of accrual periods—(i) *Facts.* On July 1, 1994, A purchases at original issue, for $675,564.17, a debt instrument that matures on July 1, 1999, and provides for a single payment of $1,000,000 at maturity.

(ii) *Determination of yield.* Under paragraph (b)(1)(i) of this section, the yield of the debt instrument is 8 percent, compounded semiannually.

(iii) *Determination of accrual period.* Under paragraph (b)(1)(ii) of this section, accrual periods may be of any length, provided that each accrual period is no longer than 1 year and each scheduled payment of principal or interest occurs either on the first or final day of an accrual period. The yield to maturity to be used in computing OID accruals in any accrual period, however, must reflect the length of the accrual period chosen. A yield based on compounding b times per year is equivalent to a yield based on compounding c times per year as indicated by the following formula:

the length of the accrual period (7.87 percent/12), less qualified stated interest allocable to the accrual period ($0). The daily portion of OID for the first monthly accrual period is $147.68 ($4,430.48/30).

Example 2. Accrual of OID on debt instrument with qualified stated interest—(i) *Facts.* On September 1, 1994, A purchases at original issue, for $90,000, B corporation's debt instrument that matures on September 1, 2004, and has a stated principal amount of $100,000, payable on that date. The debt instrument provides for semiannual payments of interest of $3,000, payable on September 1 and March 1 of each year, beginning on March 1, 1995.

(ii) *Determination of yield.* The debt instrument is a 10-year debt instrument with an issue price of $90,000 and a stated redemption price at maturity of $100,000. The semiannual payments of $3,000 are qualified stated interest payments. Under paragraph (b)(1)(i) of this section, the yield is 7.44 percent, compounded semiannually.

Reg. §1.1272-1(g)

(iii) *Accrual of OID if semiannual accrual periods are used.* Assume that A decides to compute OID on the debt instrument using semiannual accrual periods. Under paragraph (b)(1)(iii) of this section, the OID allocable to the first semiannual accrual period equals the product of the issue price ($90,000) and the yield properly adjusted for the length of the accrual period (7.44 percent/2), less qualified stated interest allocable to the accrual period ($3,000). Therefore, the amount of OID for the first semiannual accrual period is $345.78 ($3,345.78 – $3,000).

(iv) *Adjustment for accrued but unpaid qualified stated interest if monthly accrual periods are used.* Assume, alternatively, that A decides to compute OID on the debt instrument using monthly accrual periods. The yield, compounded monthly, is 7.32 percent. Under paragraph (b)(1)(iii) of this section, the OID allocable to the first monthly accrual period is the product of the issue price ($90,000) and the yield properly adjusted for the length of the accrual period (7.32 percent/12), less qualified stated interest allocable to the accrual period. Under paragraph (b)(4)(i)(A) of this section, the qualified stated interest allocable to the first monthly accrual period is the pro rata amount of qualified stated interest allocable to the interval between payment dates ($3,000 × $1/6$, or $500). Therefore, the amount of OID for the first monthly accrual period is $49.18 ($549.18 – $500). Under paragraph (b)(4)(i)(B) of this section, the adjusted

issue price of the debt instrument for purposes of determining the amount of OID for the second monthly accrual period is $90,549.18 ($90,000 + $49.18 + $500). Although the adjusted issue price of the debt instrument for this purpose includes the amount of qualified stated interest allocable to the first monthly accrual period, A includes the qualified stated interest in income based on A's regular method of accounting (e.g., an accrual method or the cash receipts and disbursements method).

Example 3. Accrual of OID for debt instrument with initial short accrual period—(i) *Facts.* On May 1, 1994, G purchases, at original issue, for $80,000, H corporation's debt instrument maturing on July 1, 2004. The debt instrument provides for a single payment at maturity of $250,000. G computes its OID using 6-month accrual periods ending on January 1 and July 1 of each year and an initial short 2-month accrual period from May 1, 1994, through June 30, 1994.

(ii) *Determination of yield.* The yield on the debt instrument is 11.53 percent, compounded semiannually.

(iii) *Determination of OID allocable to initial short accrual period.* Under paragraph (b)(4)(iii) of this section, G may use any reasonable method to compute OID for the initial short accrual period. One reasonable method is to calculate the amount of OID pursuant to the following formula:

$$OID_{short} = IP \times (i/k) \times f$$

In which:

OID_{short}	=	The amount of OID allocable to the initial short accrual period
IP	=	The issue price of the debt instrument
i	=	The yield to maturity expressed as a decimal
k	=	The number of accrual periods in a year
f	=	A fraction whose numerator is the number of days in the initial short accrual period, and whose denominator is the number of days in a full accrual period

(iv) *Amount of OID for the initial short accrual period.* Under this method, the amount of OID for the initial short accrual period is $1,537 ($80,000 × (11.53 percent/2) × (60/180)).

(v) *Alternative method.* Another reasonable method is to calculate the amount of OID for the initial short accrual period using the yield based on bi-monthly compounding, computed pursuant to the formula set forth in *Example 1* of paragraph (j) of this section. Under this method, the amount of OID for the initial short accrual period is $1,508.38 ($80,000 × (11.31 percent/6)).

Example 4. Impermissible accrual of OID using a method other than constant yield method—(i) *Facts.* On July 1, 1994, B purchases at original issue, for $100,000, C corporation's debt instrument that matures on July 1, 1999, and has a stated principal amount of $100,000. The debt instrument provides for a single payment at maturity of $148,024.43. The yield of the debt instrument is 8 percent, compounded semiannually.

(ii) *Determination of yield.* Assume that C uses 6 monthly accrual periods to compute its OID for 1994. The yield must reflect monthly compounding (as determined using the formula described in *Example 1* of paragraph (j) of this section). As a result, the monthly yield of the debt instrument is 7.87 percent, divided by 12. C may not compute its monthly yield for the last 6 months in 1994 by dividing 8 percent by 12.

Example 5. Debt instrument subject to put option—(i) *Facts.* On January 1, 1995, G purchases at original issue, for $70,000, H corporation's debt instrument maturing on January 1, 2010, with a stated principal amount of $100,000, payable at maturity. The debt instrument provides for semiannual payments of interest of $4,000, payable on January 1 and July 1 of each year, beginning on July 1, 1995. The debt instrument gives G an unconditional right to put the bond back to H, exercisable on January 1, 2005, in return for $85,000 (exclusive of the $4,000 of stated interest payable on that date).

(ii) *Determination of yield and maturity.* Yield determined without regard to the put option is 12.47 percent compounded semiannually. Yield determined by assuming that the put option is exercised (i.e., by using January 1, 2005, as the maturity date and $85,000 as the stated principal amount payable on that date) is 12.56 percent, compounded semiannually. Thus, under paragraph (c)(5) of this section, it is assumed that G will exercise the put option, because exercise of the option would increase the yield of the debt instrument. Thus, for purposes of calculating OID, the debt instrument is assumed to be a 10-year debt instrument with an issue price of $70,000, a stated redemption price at maturity of $85,000, and a yield of 12.56 percent, compounded semiannually.

(iii) *Consequences if put option is, in fact, not exercised.* If the put option is in fact, not exercised, then, under paragraph (c)(6) of this section, the debt instrument is treated, solely for purposes of sections 1272 and 1273, as if it were reissued on January 1, 2005, for an amount equal to its adjusted issue price on that date, $85,000. The new debt instrument matures on January 1, 2010, with a stated principal amount of $100,000 payable on that date and provides for semiannual payments of interest of $4,000. The yield of the new debt instrument is 12.08 percent, compounded semiannually.

Example 6. Debt instrument subject to partial call option—(i) *Facts.* On January 1, 1995, H purchases at original issue, for $95,000, J corporation's debt instrument that matures on January 1, 2000, and has a stated principal amount of $100,000, payable on that date. The debt instrument provides for semiannual payments of interest of $4,000, payable on January 1 and July 1 of each year, beginning on July 1, 1995. On January 1, 1998, J has an unconditional right to call 50 percent of the principal amount of the debt instrument for $55,000 (exclusive of the $4,000 of stated interest payable on that date). If the call is exercised, the semiannual payments of interest made after the call date will be reduced to $2,000.

(ii) *Determination of yield and maturity.* Yield determined without regard to the call option is 9.27 percent, compounded semiannually. Yield determined by assuming J exercises its call option is 10.75 percent, compounded semiannually. Thus, under paragraph (c)(5) of this section, it is assumed that J will not exercise the call option because exercise of the option would increase the yield of the debt instrument. Thus, for purposes of calculating OID, the debt instrument is assumed to be a 5-year debt instrument with a single principal payment at maturity of $100,000, and a yield of 9.27 percent, compounded semiannually.

(iii) *Consequences if the call option is, in fact, exercised.* If the call option is, in fact, exercised, then under paragraph (c)(6) of this section, the debt instrument is treated as if the issuer made a pro rata prepayment of $55,000 that is subject to § 1.1275-2(f). Consequently, under § 1.1275-2(f)(1), the instrument is treated as consisting of two debt instruments, one that is retired on the call date and one that remains outstanding after the call date. The adjusted issue price, adjusted basis in the hands of the holder, and accrued OID of the original debt instrument is allocated between the two instruments based on the portion of the original instrument treated as retired. Since each payment remaining to be made after the call date is reduced by one-half, one-half of the adjusted issue price, adjusted basis, and accrued OID is allocated to the debt instrument that is treated as retired. The adjusted issue price of the original debt instrument immediately prior to the call date is $97,725.12, which equals the issue price of the original debt instrument ($95,000) increased by the OID previously includible in gross income ($2,725.12). One-half of this adjusted issue price is allocated to the debt instrument treated as retired, and the other half is allocated to the debt instrument that is treated as remaining outstanding. Thus, the debt instrument treated as remaining outstanding has an adjusted issue price immediately after the call date of $97,725.12/2, or $48,862.56. The yield of this debt instrument continues to be 9.27 percent, compounded semiannually. In addition, the portion of H's adjusted basis allocated to the debt instrument treated as retired is $97,725.12/2 or $48,862.56. Accordingly, under section 1271, H realizes a gain on the deemed retirement equal to $6,137.44 ($55,000 − $48,862.56).

Example 7. Debt instrument issued at par that provides for payment of interest in kind—(i) *Facts.* On January 1, 1995, A purchases at original issue, for $100,000, X corporation's debt instrument maturing on January 1, 2000, at a stated principal amount of $100,000, payable on that date. The debt instrument provides for annual payments of interest of $6,000 on January 1 of each year, beginning on January 1, 1996. The debt instrument gives X the unconditional right to issue, in lieu of the first interest payment, a second debt instrument (PIK instrument) maturing on January 1, 2000, with a stated principal amount of $6,000. The PIK instrument, if issued, would provide for annual payments of interest of $360 on January 1 of each year, beginning on January 1, 1997.

(ii) *Aggregation of PIK instrument with original debt instrument.* Under § 1.1275-2(c)(3), the issuance of the PIK instrument is not considered a payment made on the original debt instrument, and the PIK instrument is aggregated with the original debt instrument. The issue date of the PIK instrument is the same as the original debt instrument.

(iii) *Determination of yield and maturity.* The right to issue the PIK instrument is treated as an option to defer the initial interest payment until maturity. Yield determined without regard to the option is 6 percent, compounded annually. Yield determined by assuming X exercises the option is 6 percent, compounded annually. Thus, under paragraph (c)(5) of this section, it is assumed that X will not exercise the option by issuing the PIK instrument because exercise of the option would not decrease the yield of the debt instrument. For purposes of calculating OID, the debt instrument is assumed to be a 5-year debt instrument with a single principal payment at maturity of $100,000 and ten semiannual interest payments of $6,000, beginning on January 1, 1996. As a result, the yield is 6 percent, compounded annually.

(iv) *Determination of OID.* Under the payment schedule that would result if the option was exercised, none of the interest on the debt instrument would be qualified stated interest. Accordingly, under § 1.1273-1(c)(2), no payments on the debt instrument are qualified stated interest payments. Thus, $6,000 of OID accrues during the first annual accrual period. If the PIK instrument is not issued, $6,000 of OID accrues during each annual accrual period.

(v) *Consequences if the PIK instrument is issued.* Under paragraph (c)(6) of this section, if X issues the PIK instrument on January 1, 1996, the issuance of the PIK instrument is not a payment on the debt instrument. Solely for purposes of sections 1272 and 1273, the debt instrument is deemed reissued on January 1, 1996, for an issue price of $106,000. The recomputed yield is 6 percent, compounded annually. The OID for the first annual accrual period after the deemed reissuance is $6,360. The adjusted issue price of the debt instrument at the beginning of the next annual accrual period is $106,000 ($106,000 + $6,360 – $6,360). The OID for each of the four remaining annual accrual periods is $6,360.

Example 8. Debt instrument issued at a discount that provides for payment of interest in kind—(i) *Facts.* On January 1, 1995, T purchases at original issue, for $75,500, U corporation's debt instrument maturing on January 1, 2000, at a stated principal amount of $100,000, payable on that date. The debt instrument provides for annual payments of interest of $4,000 on January 1 of each year, beginning on January 1, 1996. The debt instrument gives U the unconditional right to issue, in lieu of the first interest payment, a second debt instrument (PIK instrument) maturing on January 1, 2000, with a stated principal amount of $4,000. The PIK instrument, if issued, would provide for annual payments of interest of $160 on January 1 of each year, beginning on January 1, 1997.

(ii) *Aggregation of PIK instrument with original debt instrument.* Under § 1.1275-2(c)(3), the issuance of the PIK instrument is not considered a payment made on the original debt instrument, and the PIK instrument is aggregated with the original debt instrument. The issue date of the PIK instrument is the same as the original debt instrument.

(iii) *Determination of yield and maturity.* The right to issue the PIK instrument is treated as an option to defer the initial interest payment until maturity. Yield determined without regard to the option is 10.55 percent, compounded annually. Yield determined by assuming U exercises the option is 10.32 percent, compounded annually. Thus, under paragraph (c)(5) of this section, it is assumed that U will exercise the option by issuing the PIK instrument because exercise of the option would decrease the yield of the debt instrument. For purposes of calculating OID, the debt instrument is assumed to be a 5-year debt instrument with a single principal payment at maturity of $104,000 and four annual interest payments of $4,160, beginning on January 1, 1997. As a result, the yield is 10.32 percent, compounded annually.

(iv) *Consequences if the PIK instrument is not issued.* Assume that T chooses to compute OID accruals on the basis of an annual accrual period. On January 1, 1996, the adjusted issue price of the debt instrument, and T's adjusted basis in the instrument, is $83,295.15. Under paragraph (c)(6) of this section, if U actually makes the $4,000 interest payment on January 1, 1996, the debt instrument is treated as if U made a pro rata prepayment (within the meaning of § 1.1275-2(f)(2)) of $4,000, which reduces the amount of each payment remaining on the instrument by a factor of $^4/_{104}$, or $^1/_{26}$. Thus, under § 1.1275-2(f)(1) and section 1271, T realizes a gain of $796.34 ($4,000 – ($83,295.15/26)). The adjusted issue price of the debt instrument and T's adjusted basis immediately after the payment is $80,091.49 ($83,295.15 × 25/26) and the yield continues to be 10.32 percent, compounded annually.

Example 9. Debt instrument with stepped interest rate—(i) *Facts.* On July 1, 1994, G purchases at original issue, for $85,000, H corporation's debt instrument maturing on July 1, 2004. The debt instrument has a stated principal amount of $100,000, payable on the maturity date and provides for semiannual interest payments on January 1 and July 1 of each year, beginning on January 1, 1995. The amount of each payment is $2,000 for the first 5 years and $5,000 for the final 5 years.

(ii) *Determination of OID.* Assume that G computes its OID using 6-month accrual periods ending on January 1 and July 1 of each year. The yield of the debt instrument, determined under paragraph (b)(1)(i) of this section, is 8.65 percent, compounded semiannually. Interest is unconditionally payable at a fixed rate of at least 4 percent, compounded semiannually, for the entire term of the debt instrument. Consequently, under § 1.1273-1(c)(1), the semiannual payments are qualified stated interest payments to the extent of $2,000. The amount of OID for the first 6-month accrual period is $1,674.34 (the issue price of the debt instrument ($85,000) times the yield of the debt instrument for that accrual period (.0865/2) less the amount of any qualified stated interest allocable to that accrual period ($2,000).

Example 10. Debt instrument payable on demand that provides for interest at a constant rate—(i) *Facts.* On January 1, 1995, V purchases at original issue, for $100,000, W corporation's debt instrument. The debt instrument calls for interest to accrue at a rate of 9 percent, compounded annually. The debt instrument is redeemable at any time at the option of V for an amount equal to $100,000, plus accrued interest. V uses annual accrual periods to accrue OID on the debt instrument.

(ii) *Amount of OID.* Pursuant to paragraph (d) of this section, the yield of the debt instrument is 9 percent, compounded annually. If the debt instrument is not redeemed during 1995, the amount of OID allocable to the year is $9,000. [Reg. § 1.1272-1.]

□ [*T.D.* 8517, 1-27-94. *Amended by T.D.* 8674, 6-11-96.]

[Reg. § 1.1272-2]

§ 1.1272-2. Treatment of debt instruments purchased at a premium.—(a) *In general.*— Under section 1272(c)(1), if a holder purchases a debt instrument at a premium, the holder does not include any OID in gross income. Under section 1272(a)(7), if a holder purchases a debt instrument at an acquisition premium, the holder reduces the amount of OID includible in gross income by the fraction determined under paragraph (b)(4) of this section.

(b) *Definitions and special rules.*— (1) *Purchase.*—For purposes of section 1272 and this section, purchase means any acquisition of a debt instrument, including the acquisition of a newly issued debt instrument in a debt-for-debt exchange or the acquisition of a debt instrument from a donor.

(2) *Premium.*—A debt instrument is purchased at a premium if its adjusted basis, immediately after its purchase by the holder (including a purchase at original issue), exceeds the sum of all amounts payable on the instrument after the purchase date other than payments of qualified stated interest (as defined in § 1.1273-1(c)).

(3) *Acquisition premium.*—A debt instrument is purchased at an acquisition premium if its adjusted basis, immediately after its purchase (including a purchase at original issue), is—

(i) Less than or equal to the sum of all amounts payable on the instrument after the purchase date other than payments of qualified stated interest (as defined in § 1.1273-1(c)); and

(ii) Greater than the instrument's adjusted issue price (as defined in § 1.1275-1(b)).

(4) *Acquisition premium fraction.*—In applying section 1272(a)(7), the cost of a debt instru-

ment is its adjusted basis immediately after its acquisition by the purchaser. Thus, the numerator of the fraction determined under section 1272(a)(7)(B) is the excess of the adjusted basis of the debt instrument immediately after its acquisition by the purchaser over the adjusted issue price of the debt instrument. The denominator of the fraction determined under section 1272(a)(7)(B) is the excess of the sum of all amounts payable on the debt instrument after the purchase date, other than payments of qualified stated interest, over the instrument's adjusted issue price.

(5) *Election to accrue discount on a constant yield basis.*—Rather than applying the acquisition premium fraction, a holder of a debt instrument purchased at an acquisition premium may elect under § 1.1272-3 to compute OID accruals by treating the purchase as a purchase at original issuance and applying the mechanics of the constant yield method.

(6) *Special rules for determining basis.*— (i) *Debt instruments acquired in exchange for other property.*—For purposes of section 1272(a)(7), section 1272(c)(1), and this section, if a debt instrument is acquired in an exchange for other property (other than in a reorganization defined in section 368) and the basis of the debt instrument is determined, in whole or in part, by reference to the basis of the other property, the basis of the debt instrument may not exceed its fair market value immediately after the exchange. For example, if a debt instrument is distributed by a partnership to a partner in a liquidating distribution and the partner's basis in the debt instrument would otherwise be determined under section 732, the partner's basis in the debt instrument may not exceed its fair market value for purposes of this section.

(ii) *Acquisition by gift.*—For purposes of this section, a donee's adjusted basis in a debt instrument is the donee's basis for determining gain under section 1015(a).

(c) *Examples.*—The following examples illustrate the rules of this section.

Example 1. Debt instrument purchased at an acquisition premium—(i) *Facts.* On July 1, 1994, A purchased at original issue, for $500, a debt instrument issued by Corporation X. The debt instrument matures on July 1, 1999, and calls for a single payment at maturity of $1,000. Under section 1273(a), the debt instrument has a stated redemption price at maturity of $1,000 and, thus, OID of $500. On July 1, 1996, when the debt instrument's adjusted issue price is $659.75, A sells the debt instrument to B for $750 in cash.

(ii) *Acquisition premium fraction.* Because the cost to B of the debt instrument is less than the amount payable on the debt instrument after the purchase date, but is greater than the debt instrument's adjusted issue price, B has paid an acquisition premium for the debt instrument. Accordingly, the daily portion of OID for any day that B holds the debt instrument is reduced by a fraction, the numerator of which is $90.25 (the excess of the cost of the debt instrument over its adjusted issue price) and the denominator of which is $340.25 (the excess of the sum of all payments after the purchase date over its adjusted issue price).

Example 2. Debt-for-debt exchange where holder is considered to purchase new debt instrument at a premium—(i) *Facts.* On January 1, 1995, H purchases at original issue, for $1,000, a debt instrument issued by Corporation X. On July 1, 1997, when H's adjusted basis in the debt instrument is $1,000, Corporation X issues a new debt instrument with a stated redemption price at maturity of $750 to H in exchange for the old debt instrument. Assume that the issue price of the new debt instrument is $600. Thus, under section 1273(a), the debt instrument has OID of $150. The exchange qualifies as a recapitalization under section 368(a)(1)(E), with the consequence that, under sections 354 and 358, H recognizes no loss on the exchange and has an adjusted basis in the new debt instrument of $1,000.

(ii) *Application of section 1272(c)(1).* Under paragraphs (b)(1) and (b)(2) of this section, H purchases the new debt instrument at a premium of $250. Accordingly, under section 1272(c)(1), H is not required to include OID in income with respect to the new debt instrument.

Example 3. Debt-for-debt exchange where holder is considered to purchase new debt instrument at an acquisition premium—(i) *Facts.* The facts are the same as in *Example 2* of paragraph (c) of this section, except that H purchases the old debt instrument from another holder on July 1, 1995, and on July 1, 1997, H's adjusted basis in the old debt instrument is $700. Under section 1273(a), the new debt instrument is issued with OID of $150.

(ii) *Application of section 1272(a)(7).* Under paragraphs (b)(1) and (b)(3) of this section, H purchases the new debt instrument at an acquisition premium of $100. Accordingly, the daily portion of OID that is includible in H's income is reduced by the fraction determined under section 1272(a)(7).

Example 4. Treatment of acquisition premium for debt instrument acquired by gift—(i) *Facts.* On July 1, 1994, D receives as a gift a debt instrument with a stated redemption price at maturity of $1,000 and an adjusted issue price of $800. On that date, the fair market value of the debt instrument is $900 and the donor's adjusted basis in the debt instrument is $950.

(ii) *Application of section 1272(a)(7).* Under paragraphs (b)(1), (b)(3), and (b)(6)(ii) of this section, D is considered to have purchased the debt instrument at an acquisition premium of $150. Accordingly, the daily portion of OID that is includible in D's income is reduced by the

fraction determined under section 1272(a)(7). [Reg. § 1.1272-2.]

□ [*T.D. 8517, 1-27-94.*]

[Reg. § 1.1272-3]

§ 1.1272-3. Election by a holder to treat all interest on a debt instrument as OID.—(a) *Election.*—A holder of a debt instrument may elect to include in gross income all interest that accrues on the instrument by using the constant yield method described in paragraph (c) of his section. For purposes of this election, interest includes stated interest, acquisition discount, OID, de minimis OID, market discount, de minimis market discount, and unstated interest, as adjusted by any amortizable bond premium or acquisition premium.

(b) *Scope of election.*—(1) *In general.*—Except as provided in paragraph (b)(2) of this section, a holder may make the election for any debt instrument.

(2) *Exceptions, limitations, and special rules.*—(i) *Debt instrument with amortizable bond premium (as determined under section 171).*—(A) A holder may make the election for a debt instrument with amortizable bond premium only if the instrument qualifies as a bond under section 171(d).

(B) If a holder makes the election under this section for a debt instrument with amortizable bond premium, the holder is deemed to have made the election under section 171(c)(2) for the taxable year in which the instrument was acquired. If the holder has previously made the election under section 171(c)(2), the requirements of that election with respect to any debt instrument are satisfied by electing to amortize the bond premium under the rules provided by this section.

(ii) *Debt instrument with market discount.*—(A) A holder may make the election under this section for a debt instrument with market discount only if the holder is eligible to make an election under section 1278(b).

(B) If a holder makes the election under this section for a debt instrument with market discount, the holder is deemed to have made both the election under section 1276(b)(2) for that instrument and the election under section 1278(b) for the taxable year in which the instrument was acquired. If the holder has previously made the election under section 1278(b), the requirements of that election with respect to any debt instrument are satisfied by electing to include the market discount in income in accordance with the rules provided by this section.

(iii) *Tax-exempt debt instrument.*—A holder may not make the election for a tax-exempt obligation as defined in section 1275(a)(3).

(c) *Mechanics of the constant yield method.*—(1) *In general.*—For purposes of this section, the amount of interest that accrues during an accrual period is determined under rules similar to those under section 1272 (the constant yield method). In applying the constant yield method, however, a debt instrument subject to the election is treated as if—

    (i) The instrument is issued for the holder's adjusted basis immediately after its acquisition by the holder;

    (ii) The instrument is issued on the holder's acquisition date; and

    (iii) None of the interest payments provided for in the instrument are qualified stated interest payments.

    (2) *Special rules to determine adjusted basis.*—For purposes of paragraph (c)(1)(i) of this section—

    (i) If the debt instrument is acquired in an exchange for other property (other than in a reorganization defined in section 368) and the basis of the debt instrument is determined, in whole or in part, by reference to the basis of the other property, the, adjusted basis of the debt instrument may not exceed its fair market value immediately after the exchange; and

    (ii) If the debt instrument was acquired with amortizable bond premium (as determined under section 171), the adjusted basis of the debt instrument is reduced by an amount equal to the value attributable to any conversion feature.

(d) *Time and manner of making the election.*—The election must be made for the taxable year in which the holder acquires the debt instrument. A holder makes the election by attaching to the holder's timely filed Federal income tax return a statement that the holder is making an election under this section and that identifies the debt instruments subject to the election. A holder may make the election for a class or group of debt instruments by attaching a statement describing the type or types of debt instruments being designated for the election.

(e) *Revocation of election.*—The election may not be revoked unless approved by the Commissioner.

(f) *Effective date.*—This section applies to debt instruments acquired on or after April 4, 1994. [Reg. § 1.1272-3.]

☐ [T.D. 8517, 1-27-94.]

[Reg. § 1.1273-1]

§ 1.1273-1. Definition of OID.—(a) *In general.*—Section 1273(a)(1) defines OID as the excess of a debt instrument's stated redemption price at maturity over its issue price. Section 1.1273-2 defines issue price, and paragraph (b) of this section defines stated redemption price at maturity. Paragraph (d) of this section provides

rules for de minimis amounts of OID. Although the total amount of OID for a debt instrument may be indeterminate, § 1.1272-1(d) provides a rule to determine OID accruals on certain debt instruments that provide for a fixed yield. See *Example 10* in § 1.1272-1(j).

(b) *Stated redemption price at maturity.*—A debt instrument's stated redemption price at maturity is the sum of all payments provided by the debt instrument other than qualified stated interest payments. If the payment schedule of a debt instrument is determined under § 1.1272-1(c) (relating to certain debt instruments subject to contingencies), that payment schedule is used to determine the instrument's stated redemption price at maturity.

(c) *Qualified stated interest.*—(1) *Definition.*—(i) *In general.*—Qualified stated interest is stated interest that is unconditionally payable in cash or in property (other than debt instruments of the issuer), or that will be constructively received under section 451, at least annually at a single fixed rate (within the meaning of paragraph (c)(1)(iii) of this section).

    (ii) *Unconditionally payable.*—Interest is unconditionally payable only if reasonable legal remedies exist to compel timely payment or the debt instrument otherwise provides terms and conditions that make the likelihood of late payment (other than a late payment that occurs within a reasonable grace period) or nonpayment a remote contingency (within the meaning of § 1.1275-2(h)). For purposes of the preceding sentence, remedies or other terms and conditions are not taken into account if the lending transaction does not reflect arm's length dealing and the holder does not intend to enforce the remedies or other terms and conditions. For purposes of determining whether interest is unconditionally payable, the possibility of nonpayment due to default, insolvency, or similar circumstances, or due to the exercise of a conversion option described in § 1.1272-1(e) is ignored. This paragraph (c)(1)(ii) applies to debt instruments issued on or after August 13, 1996.

    (iii) *Single fixed rate.*—(A) *In general.*—Interest is payable at a single fixed rate only if the rate appropriately takes into account the length of the interval between payments. Thus, if the interval between payments varies during the term of the debt instrument, the value of the fixed rate on which a payment is based generally must be adjusted to reflect a compounding assumption that is consistent with the length of the interval preceding the payment. See *Example 1* in paragraph (f) of this section.

    (B) *Special rule for certain first and final payment intervals.*—Notwithstanding paragraph (c)(1)(iii)(A) of this section, if a debt instrument provides for payment intervals that are equal in length throughout the term of the instrument, except that the first or final payment interval differs in length from the other payment intervals, the first or final interest payment is considered to be made at a fixed rate if the value of the rate on which the payment is based is adjusted in any reasonable manner to take into account the length of the interval. See *Example 2* of paragraph (f) of this section. The rule in this paragraph (c)(1)(iii)(B) also applies if the lengths of both the first and final payment intervals differ from the length of the other payment intervals.

(2) *Debt instruments subject to contingencies.*—The determination of whether a debt instrument described in § 1.1272-1(c) (a debt instrument providing for an alternative payment schedule (or schedules) upon the occurrence of one or more contingencies) provides for qualified stated interest is made by analyzing each alternative payment schedule (including the stated payment schedule) as if it were the debt instrument's sole payment schedule. Under this analysis, the debt instrument provides for qualified stated interest to the extent of the lowest fixed rate at which qualified stated interest would be payable under any payment schedule. See *Example 4* of paragraph (f) of this section.

(3) *Variable rate debt instrument.*—In the case of a variable rate debt instrument, qualified stated interest is determined under § 1.1275-5(e).

(4) *Stated interest in excess of qualified stated interest.*—To the extent that stated interest payable under a debt instrument exceeds qualified stated interest, the excess is included in the debt instrument's stated redemption price at maturity.

(5) *Short-term obligations.*—In the case of a debt instrument with a term that is not more than 1 year from the date of issue, no payments of interest are treated as qualified stated interest payments.

(d) *De minimis OID.*—(1) *In general.*—If the amount of OID with respect to a debt instrument is less than the de minimis amount, the amount of OID is treated as zero, and all stated interest (including stated interest that would otherwise be characterized as OID) is treated as qualified stated interest.

(2) *De minimis amount.*—The de minimis amount is an amount equal to 0.0025 multiplied by the product of the stated redemption price at maturity and the number of complete years to maturity from the issue date.

(3) *Installment obligations.*—In the case of an installment obligation (as defined in paragraph (e)(1) of this section), paragraph (d)(2) of this section is applied by substituting for the number of complete years to maturity the weighted average maturity (as defined in paragraph (e)(3) of this section). Alternatively, in the case of a debt

instrument that provides for payments of principal no more rapidly than self-amortizing installment obligation (as defined in paragraph (e)(2) of this section), the de minimis amount defined in paragraph (d)(2) of this section may be calculated by substituting 0.00167 for 0.0025.

(4) *Special rule for interest holidays, teaser rates, and other interest shortfalls.*—(i) *In general.*—This paragraph (d)(4) provides a special rule to determine whether a debt instrument with a teaser rate (or rates), an interest holiday, or any other interest shortfall has de minimis OID. This rule applies if—

(A) The amount of OID on the debt instrument is more than the de minimis amount as otherwise determined under paragraph (d) of this section; and

(B) All stated interest provided for in the debt instrument would be qualified stated interest under paragraph (c) of this section except that for 1 or more accrual periods the interest rate is below the rate applicable for the remainder of the instrument's term (e.g., if as a result of an interest holiday, none of the stated interest is qualified stated interest).

(ii) *Redetermination of OID for purposes of the de minimis test.*—For purposes of determining whether a debt instrument described in paragraph (d)(4)(i) of this section has de minimis OID, the instrument's stated redemption price at maturity is treated as equal to the instrument's issue price plus the greater of the amount of foregone interest or the excess (if any) of the instrument's stated principal amount over its issue price. The amount of foregone interest is the amount of additional stated interest that would be required to be payable on the debt instrument during the period of the teaser rate, holiday, or shortfall so that all stated interest would be qualified stated interest under paragraph (c) of this section. See *Example 5* and *Example 6* of paragraph (f) of this section. In addition, for purposes of computing the de minimis amount of OID the weighted average maturity of the debt instrument is determined by treating all stated interest payments as qualified stated interest payments.

(5) *Treatment of de minimis OID by holders.*—(i) *Allocation of de minimis OID to principal payments.*—The holder of a debt instrument includes any de minimis OID (other than de minimis OID treated as qualified stated interest under paragraph (d)(1) of this section, such as de minimis OID attributable to a teaser rate or interest holiday) in income as stated principal payments are made. The amount includible in income with respect to each principal payment equals the product of the total amount of de minimis OID on the debt instrument and a fraction, the numerator of which is the amount of the principal payment made, and the denominator of which is the stated principal amount of the instrument.

Reg. § 1.1273-1(d)(5)(i)

(ii) *Character of de minimis OID.*—(A) *De minimis OID treated as gain recognized on retirement.*—Any amount of de minimis OID includible in income under this paragraph (d)(5) is treated as gain recognized on retirement of the debt instrument. See section 1271 to determine whether a retirement is treated as an exchange of the debt instrument.

(B) *Treatment of de minimis OID on sale or exchange.*—Any gain attributable to de minimis OID that is recognized on the sale or exchange of a debt instrument is capital gain if the debt instrument is a capital asset in the hands of the seller.

(iii) *Treatment of subsequent holders.*—If a subsequent holder purchases a debt instrument issued with de minimis OID at a premium (as defined in § 1.1272-2(b)(2)), the subsequent holder does not include the de minimis OID in income. Otherwise, a subsequent holder includes any discount in income under the market discount rules (sections 1276 through 1278) rather than under the rules of this paragraph (d)(5).

(iv) *Cross-reference.*—See § 1.1272-3 for an election by a holder to treat de minimis OID as OID.

(e) *Definitions.*—(1) *Installment obligation.*—An installment obligation is a debt instrument that provides for the payment of any amount other than qualified stated interest before maturity.

(2) *Self-amortizing installment obligation.*—A self-amortizing installment obligation is an obligation that provides for equal payments composed of principal and qualified stated interest that are unconditionally payable at least annually during the entire term of the debt instrument with no additional payment required at maturity.

(3) *Weighted average maturity.*—The weighted average maturity of a debt instrument is the sum of the following amounts determined for each payment under the instrument (other than a payment of qualified stated interest)—

(i) The number of complete years from the issue date until the payment is made, multiplied by

(ii) A fraction, the numerator of which is the amount of the payment and the denominator of which is the debt instrument's stated redemption price at maturity.

(f) *Examples.*—The following examples illustrate the rules of this section.

Example 1. Qualified stated interest—(i) *Facts.* On January 1, 1995, A purchases at original issue for $100,000, a debt instrument that matures on January 1, 1999, and has a stated principal amount of $100,000, payable at maturity. The debt instrument provides for interest payments of $8,000 on January 1, 1996, and January 1, 1997, and quarterly interest payments of $1,942.65, beginning on April 1, 1997.

(ii) *Amount of qualified stated interest.* The annual payments of $8,000 and the quarterly payments of $1,942.65 are payable at a single fixed rate because 8 percent, compounded annually, is equivalent to 7.77 percent, compounded quarterly. Consequently, all stated interest payments under the debt instrument are qualified stated interest payments.

Example 2. Qualified stated interest with short initial payment interval. On October 1, 1994, A purchases at original issue, for $100,000, a debt instrument that matures on January 1, 1998, and has a stated principal amount of $100,000, payable at maturity. The debt instrument provides for an interest payment of $2,000 on January 1, 1995, and interest payments of $8,000 on January 1, 1996, January 1, 1997, and January 1, 1998. Under paragraph (c)(1)(iii)(B) of this section, all stated interest payments on the debt instrument are computed at a single fixed rate and are qualified stated interest payments.

Example 3. Stated interest in excess of qualified stated interest—(i) *Facts.* On January 1, 1995, B purchases at original issue, for $100,000, C corporation's 5-year debt instrument. The debt instrument provides for a principal payment of $100,000, payable at maturity, and calls for annual interest payments of $10,000 for the first 3 years and annual interest payments of $10,600 for the last 2 years.

(ii) *Payments in excess of qualified stated interest.* All of the first three interest payments and $10,000 of each of the last two interest payments are qualified stated interest payments within the meaning of paragraph (c)(1) of this section. Under paragraph (c)(4) of this section, the remaining $600 of each of the last two interest payments is included in the stated redemption price at maturity, so that the stated redemption price at maturity is $101,200. Pursuant to paragraph (e)(3) of this section, the weighted average maturity of the debt instrument is 4.994 years [(4 years × $600/$101,200) + (5 years × $100,600/$101,200)]. The de minimis amount, or one-fourth of 1 percent of the stated redemption price at maturity multiplied by the weighted average maturity, is $1,263.50. Because the actual amount of discount, $1,200, is less than the de minimis amount, the instrument is treated as having no OID, and, under paragraph (d)(1) of this section, all of the interest payments are treated as qualified stated interest payments.

Example 4. Qualified stated interest on a debt instrument that is subject to an option—(i) *Facts.* On January 1, 1997, A issues, for $100,000, a 10-year debt instrument that provides for a $100,000 principal payment at maturity and for annual interest payments of $10,000. Under the terms of the debt instrument, A has the option, exercisable on January 1, 2002, to lower the annual interest payments to $8,000. In addition, the debt instrument gives the holder an unconditional right to put the debt instrument back to A, exercisable on January 1, 2002, in return for $100,000.

(ii) *Amount of qualified stated interest.* Under paragraph (c)(2) of this section, the debt instrument provides for qualified stated interest to the extent of the lowest fixed rate at which qualified stated interest would be payable under any payment schedule. If the payment schedule determined by assuming that the issuer's option will be exercised and the put option will not be exercised were treated as the debt instrument's sole payment schedule, only $8,000 of each annual interest payment would be qualified stated interest. Under any other payment schedule, the debt instrument would provide for annual qualified stated interest payments of $10,000. Accordingly, only $8,000 of each annual interest payment is qualified stated interest. Any excess of each annual interest payment over $8,000 is included in the debt instrument's stated redemption price at maturity.

Example 5. De minimis OID; interest holiday—(i) *Facts.* On January 1, 1995, C purchases at original issue, for $97,561, a debt instrument that matures on January 1, 2007, and has a stated principal amount of $100,000, payable at maturity. The debt instrument provides for an initial interest holiday of 1 quarter and quarterly interest payments of $2,500 thereafter (beginning on July 1, 1995). The issue price of the debt instrument is $97,561. C chooses to accrue OID based on quarterly accrual periods.

(ii) *De minimis amount of OID.* But for the interest holiday, all stated interest on the debt instrument would be qualified stated interest. Under paragraph (d)(4) of this section, for purposes of determining whether the debt instrument has de minimis OID, the stated, redemption price at maturity of the instrument is $100,061 ($97,561 (issue price) plus $2,500, (the greater of the amount of foregone interest ($2,500) and the amount equal to the excess of the instrument's stated principal amount over its issue price ($2,439)). Thus, the debt instrument is treated as having OID of $2,500 ($100,061 minus $97,561). Because this amount is less than the de minimis amount of $3,001.83 (0.0025 multiplied by $100,061 multiplied by 12 complete years to maturity), the debt instrument is treated as having no OID, and all stated interest is treated as qualified stated interest.

Example 6. De minimis OID; teaser rate—(i) *Facts.* The facts are the same as in *Example 5* of this paragraph (f) except that C uses an initial semiannual accrual period rather than an initial quarterly accrual period.

(ii) *De minimis amount of OID.* The debt instrument provides for an initial teaser rate because the interest rate for the semiannual accrual period is less than the interest rate applicable to the subsequent quarterly accrual periods. But for the initial teaser rate, all stated interest on the debt instrument would be qualified stated interest. Under paragraph (d)(4) of this section, for pur-

poses of determining whether the debt instrument has de minimis OID, the stated redemption price at maturity of the instrument is $100,123.50 ($97,561 (issue price) plus $2,562.50 (the greater of the amount of foregone interest ($2,562.50) and the amount equal to the excess of the instrument's stated principal amount over its issue price ($2,439)). Thus, the debt instrument is treated as having OID of $2,562.50 ($100,123.50 minus $97,561). Because this amount is less than the de minimis amount of $3,003.71 (0.0025 multiplied by $100,123.50 multiplied by 12 complete years to maturity), the debt instrument is treated as having no OID, and all stated interest is treated as qualified stated interest. [Reg. §1.1273-1.]

☐ [*T.D.* 8517, 1-27-94. *Amended by T.D.* 8674, 6-11-96.]

[Reg. §1.1273-2]

§1.1273-2. Determination of issue price and issue date.—(a) *Debt instruments issued for money.*—(1) *Issue price.*—If a substantial amount of the debt instruments in an issue is issued for money, the issue price of each debt instrument in the issue is the first price at which a substantial amount of the debt instruments is sold for money. Thus, if an issue consists of a single debt instrument that is issued for money, the issue price of the debt instrument is the amount paid for the instrument. For example, in the case of a debt instrument evidencing a loan to a natural person, the issue price of the instrument is the amount loaned. See §1.1275-2(d) for rules regarding Treasury securities. For purposes of this paragraph (a), money includes functional currency and, in certain circumstances, nonfunctional currency. See §1.988-2(b)(2) for circumstances when nonfunctional currency is treated as money rather than as property.

(2) *Issue date.*—The issue date of an issue described in paragraph (a)(1) of this section is the first settlement date or closing date, whichever is applicable, on which a substantial amount of the debt instruments in the issue is sold for money.

(b) *Publicly traded debt instruments issued for property.*—(1) *Issue price.*—If a substantial amount of the debt instruments in an issue is traded on an established market (within the meaning of paragraph (f) of this section) and the issue is not described in paragraph (a)(1) of this section, the issue price of each debt instrument in the issue is the fair market value of the debt instrument, determined as of the issue date (as defined in paragraph (b)(2) of this section).

(2) *Issue date.*—The issue date of an issue described in paragraph (b)(1) of this section is the first date on which a substantial amount of the traded debt instruments in the issue is issued.

(c) *Debt instruments issued for publicly traded property.*—(1) *Issue price.*—If a substantial amount of the debt instrument in an issue is issued for property that is traded on an established market (within the meaning of paragraph (f) of this section) and the issue is not described in paragraph (a)(1) or (b)(1) of this section, the issue price of each debt instrument in the issue is the fair market value of the property, determined as of the issue date (as defined in paragraph (c)(2) of this section). For purposes of the preceding sentence, property means a debt instrument, stock, security, contract, commodity, or nonfunctional currency. But see § 1.988-2(b)(2) for circumstances when nonfunctional currency is treated as money rather than as property.

(2) *Issue date.*—The issue date of an issue described in paragraph (c)(1) of this section is the first date on which a substantial amount of the debt instruments in the issue is issued for traded property.

(d) *Other debt instruments.*—(1) *Issue price.*—If an issue of debt instruments is not described in paragraph (a)(1), (b)(1), or (c)(1) of this section, the issue price of each debt instrument in the issue is determined as if the debt instrument were a separate issue. If the issue price of a debt instrument that is treated as a separate issue under the preceding sentence is not determined under paragraph (a)(1), (b)(1), or (c)(1) of this section, and if section 1274 applies to the debt instrument, the issue price of the instrument is determined under section 1274. Otherwise, the issue price of the debt instrument is its stated redemption price at maturity under section 1273(b)(4). See section 1274(c) and § 1.1274-1 to determine if section 1274 applies to a debt instrument.

(2) *Issue date.*—The issue date of an issue described in paragraph (d)(1) of this section is the date on which the debt instrument is issued for money or in a sale or exchange.

(e) *Special rule for certain sales to bond houses, brokers, or similar persons.*—For purposes of determining the issue price and issue date of a debt instrument under this section, sales to bond houses, brokers, or similar persons or organizations acting in the capacity of underwriters, placement agents, or wholesalers are ignored.

(f) *Traded on an established market (publicly traded).*—(1) *In general.*—Property (including a debt instrument described in paragraph (b)(1) of this section) is traded on an established market for purposes of this section if, at any time during the 60-day period ending 30 days after the issue date, the property is described in paragraph (f)(2), (f)(3), (f)(4), or (f)(5) of this section.

(2) *Exchange listed property.*—Property is described in this paragraph (f)(2) if it is listed on—

(i) A national securities exchange registered under section 6 of the Securities Exchange Act of 1934 (15 U.S.C. 78f);

(ii) An interdealer quotation system sponsored by a national securities association registered under section 15A of the Securities Exchange Act of 1934 (15 U.S.C. 78o-3); or

(iii) The International Stock Exchange of the United Kingdom and the Republic of Ireland, Limited, the Frankfurt Stock Exchange, the Tokyo Stock Exchange, or any other foreign exchange or board of trade that is designated by the Commissioner in the Internal Revenue Bulletin (see § 601.601(d)(2)(ii) of this chapter).

(3) *Market traded property.*—Property is described in this paragraph (f)(3) if it is property of a kind that is traded either on a board of trade designated as a contract market by the Commodities Futures Trading Commission or on an interbank market.

(4) *Property appearing on a quotation medium.*—Property is described in this paragraph (f)(4) if it appears on a system of general circulation (including a computer listing disseminated to subscribing brokers, dealers, or traders) that provides a reasonable basis to determine fair market value by disseminating either recent price quotations (including rates, yields, or other pricing information) of one or more identified brokers, dealers, or traders or actual prices (including rates, yields, or other pricing information) of recent sales transactions (a quotation medium). A quotation medium does not include a directory or listing of brokers, dealers, or traders for specific securities, such as yellow sheets, that provides neither price quotations nor actual prices of recent sales transactions.

(5) *Readily quotable debt instruments.*—(i) *In general.*—A debt instrument is described in this paragraph (f)(5) if price quotations are readily available from dealers, brokers, or traders.

(ii) *Safe harbors.*—A debt instrument is not considered to be described in paragraph (f)(5)(i) of this section if—

(A) No other outstanding debt instrument of the issuer (or of any person who gurantees the debt instrument) is described in paragraph (f)(2), (f)(3), or (f)(4) of this section (other traded debt);

(B) The original stated principal amount of the issue that includes the debt instrument does not exceed $25 million;

(C) The conditions and covenants relating to the issuer's performance with respect to the debt instrument are materially less restrictive than the conditions and covenants included in all of the issuer's other traded debt (e.g., the debt instrument is subject to an economically significant subordination provision whereas the issuer's other traded debt is senior); or

Reg. § 1.1273-2(c)

(D) The maturity date of the debt instrument is more than 3 years after the latest maturity date of the issuer's other traded debt.

(6) *Effect of certain temporary restrictions on trading.*—If there is any temporary restriction on trading a purpose of which is to avoid the characterization of the property as one that is traded on an established market for Federal income tax purposes, then the property is treated as traded on an established market. For purposes of the preceding sentence, a temporary restriction on trading need not be imposed by the issuer.

(7) *Convertible debt instruments.*—A debt instrument is not treated as traded on an established market solely because the debt instrument is convertible into property that is so traded.

(g) *Treatment of certain cash payments incident to lending transactions.*—(1) *Applicability.*—The provisions of this paragraph (g) apply to cash payments made incident to private lending transactions (including seller financing).

(2) *Payments from borrower to lender.*—(i) *Money lending transaction.*—In a lending transaction to which section 1273(b)(2) applies, a payment from the borrower to the lender (other than a payment for property or for services provided by the lender, such as commitment fees or loan processing costs) reduces the issue price of the debt instrument evidencing the loan. However, solely for purposes of determining the tax consequences to the borrower, the issue price is not reduced if the payment is deductible under section 461(g)(2).

(ii) *Section 1274 transaction.*—In a lending transaction to which section 1274 applies, a payment from the buyer-borrower to the seller-lender that is designated as interest or points reduces the stated principal amount of the debt instrument evidencing the loan, but is included in the purchase price of the property. If the payment is deductible under section 461(g)(2), however, the issuer price of the debt instrument (as otherwise determined under section 1274 and the rule in the preceding sentence) is increased by the amount of the payment to compute the buyer-borrower's interest deductions under section 163.

(3) *Payments from lender to borrower.*—A payment from the lender to the borrower in a lending transaction is treated as an amount loaned.

(4) *Payments between lender and third party.*—If, as part of a lending transaction, a party other than the borrower (the third party) makes a payment to the lender, that payment is treated in appropriate circumstances as made from the third party to the borrower followed by a payment in the same amount from the borrower to the lender and governed by the provisions of paragraph (g)(2) of this section. If, as part of a lending transaction, the lender makes a payment to a third party, that payment is treated in appropriate circumstances as an additional amount loaned to the borrower and then paid by the borrower to the third party. The character of the deemed payment between the borrower and the third party depends on the substance of the transaction.

(5) *Examples.*—The following examples illustrate the rules of this paragraph (g).

Example 1. Payments from borrower to lender in a cash transaction—(i) *Facts.* A lends $100,000 to B for a term of 10 years. At the time the loan is made, B pays $4,000 in points to A. Assume that the points are not deductible by B under section 461(g)(2) and that the stated redemption price at maturity of the debt instrument is $100,000.

(ii) *Payment results in OID.* Under paragraph (g)(2)(i) of this section, the issue price of B's debt instrument evidencing the loan is $96,000. Because the amount of OID on the debt instrument ($4,000) is more than a de minimis amount of OID, A accounts for the OID under § 1.1272-1. B accounts for the OID under § 1.163-7.

Example 2. Payments from borrower to lender in a section 1274 transaction—(i) *Facts.* A sells property to B for $1,000,000 in a transaction that is not a potentially abusive situation (within the meaning of § 1.1274-3). In consideration for the property, B gives A $300,000 and issues a 5-year debt instrument that has a stated principal amount of $700,000, payable at maturity, and that calls for semiannual payments of interest at a rate of 8.5 percent. In addition to the cash downpayment, B pays A $14,000 designated as points on the loan. Assume that the points are not deductible under section 461(g)(2).

(ii) *Issue price.* Under paragraph (g)(2)(ii) of this section, the stated principal amount of B's debt instrument is $686,000 ($700,000 minus $14,000). Assuming a test rate of 9 percent, compounded semiannually, the imputed principal amount of B's debt instrument under § 1.1274-2(c)(1) is $686,153. Under § 1.1274-2(b)(1), the issue price of B's debt instrument is the stated principal amount of $686,000. Because the amount of OID on the debt instrument ($700,000 − $686,000, or $14,000) is more than a de minimis amount of OID, A accounts for the OID under § 1.1272-1 and B accounts for the OID under § 1.163-7. B's basis in the property purchased is $1,000,000 ($686,000 debt instrument plus $314,000 cash payments).

Example 3. Payments between lender and third party (seller-paid points)—(i) *Facts.* A sells real property to B for $500,000 in a transaction that is not a potentially abusive situation (within the meaning of § 1.1274-3). B makes a cash down payment of $100,000 and borrows $400,000 of the purchase price from a lender, L, repayable in annual installments over a term of 15 years calling for interest at a rate of 9 percent, compounded annually. As part of the transaction, A makes a payment of $8,000 to L to facilitate the loan to B.

(ii) *Payment results in a de minimis amount of OID.* Under the provisions of paragraphs (g)(2)(i) and (g)(4) of this section, B is treated as having made an $8,000 payment directly to L and a payment of only $492,000 to A for the property. Thus, B's basis in the property is $492,000. The payment to L reduces the issue price of B's debt instrument to $392,000, resulting in $8,000 of OID ($400,000 − $392,000). Because the amount of OID is de minimis under §1.1273-1(d), L accounts for the de minimis OID under §1.1273-1(d)(5). But see §1.1272-3 (election to treat de minimis OID as OID). B accounts for the de minimis OID under §1.163-7.

(h) *Investment units.*—(1) *In general.*—Under section 1273(c)(2), an investment unit is treated as if the investment unit were a debt instrument. The issue price of the investment unit is determined under paragraph (a)(1), (b)(1), or (c)(1) of this section, if applicable. The issue price of the investment unit is then allocated between the debt instrument and the property right (or rights) that comprise the unit based on their relative fair market values. If paragraphs (a)(1), (b)(1), and (c)(1) of this section are not applicable, however, the issue price of the debt instrument that is part of the investment unit is determined under section 1273(b)(4) or 1274, whichever is applicable.

(2) *Consistent allocation by holders and issuer.*—The issuer's allocation of the issue price of the investment unit is binding on all holders of the investment unit. However, the issuer's determination is not binding on a holder that explicitly discloses that its allocation is different from the issuer's allocation. Unless otherwise provided by the Commissioner, the disclosure must be made on a statement attached to the holder's timely filed Federal income tax return for the taxable year that includes the acquisition date of the investment unit. See §1.1275-2(e) for rules relating to the issuer's obligation to disclose certain information to holders.

(i) [Reserved]

(j) *Convertible debt instruments.*—The issue price of a debt instrument includes any amount paid for an option to convert the instrument into stock (or another debt instrument) of either the issuer or a related party (within the meaning of section 267(b) or 707(b)(1)) or into cash or other property in an amount equal to the approximate value of such stock (or debt instrument).

(k) *Below-market loans subject to section 7872(b).*—The issue price of a below-market loan subject to section 7872(b) (a term loan other than a gift loan) is the issue price determined under this section, reduced by the excess amount determined under section 7872(b)(1).

(l) [Reserved]

(m) *Treatment of amounts representing pre-issuance accrued interest.*—(1) *Applicability.*—Paragraph (m)(2) of this section provides an alternative to the general rule of this section for determining the issue price of a debt instrument if—

(i) A portion of the initial purchase price of the instrument is allocable to interest that has accrued prior to the issue date (pre-issuance accrued interest); and

(ii) The instrument provides for a payment of stated interest on the first payment date within 1 year of the issue date that equals or exceeds the amount of the pre-issuance accrued interest.

(2) *Exclusiion of pre-issuance accrued interest from issue price.*—If a debt instrument meets the requirements of paragraph (m)(1) of this section, the instrument's issue price may be computed by subtracting from the issue price (as otherwise computed under this section) the amount of pre-issuance accrued interest. If the issue price of the debt instrument is computed in this manner, a portion of the stated interest payable on the first payment date must be treated as a return of the excluded pre-issuance accrued interest, rather than as an amount payable on the instrument.

(3) *Example.*—The following example illustrates the rule of paragraph (m) of this section.

Example. (i) *Facts.* On January 15, 1995, A purchases at original issue, for $1,005, B corporation's debt instrument. The debt instrument provides for a payment of principal of $1,000 on January 1, 2005, and provides for semiannual interest payments of $60 on January 1 and July 1 of each year, beginning on July 1, 1995.

(ii) *Determination of pre-issuance accrued interest.* Under paragraphs (m)(1) and (m)(2) of this section, $5 of the $1,005 initial purchase price of the debt instrument is allocable to pre-issuance accrued interest. Accordingly, the debt instrument's issue price may be computed by subtracting the amount of pre-issuance accrued interest ($5) from the issue price otherwise computed under this section ($1,005), resulting in an issue price of $1,000. If the issue price is computed in this manner, $5 of the $60 payment made on July 1, 1995, must be treated as a repayment by B of the pre-issuance accrued interest. [Reg. §1.1273-2.]

☐ [*T.D.* 8517, 1-27-94.]

[Reg. §1.1274-1]

§1.1274-1. Debt instruments to which section 1274 applies.—(a) *In general.*—Subject to the exceptions and limitations in paragraph (b) of this section, section 1274 and this section apply to any debt instrument issued in consideration for the sale or exchange of property. For purposes of section 1274, property includes debt instruments and investment units, but does not include money, services, or the right to use property. For the treatment of certain obligations given in exchange for services or the use of property, see sections 404 and 467. For purposes of this paragraph (a), money includes functional currency and, in certain circumstances, nonfunctional currency. See § 1.988-2(b)(2) for circumstances when nonfunctional currency is treated as money rather than as property.

(b) *Exceptions.*—(1) *Debt instrument with adequate stated interest and no OID.*—Section 1274 does not apply to a debt instrument if—

(i) All interest payable on the instrument is qualified stated interest;

(ii) The stated rate of interest is at least equal to the test rate of interest (as defined in § 1.1274-4);

(iii) The debt instrument is not issued in a potentially abusive situation (as defined in § 1.1274-3); and

(iv) No payment from the buyer-borrower to the seller-lender designated as points or interest is made at the time of issuance of the debt instrument.

(2) *Exceptions under sections 1274(c)(1)(B), 1274(c)(3), 1274A(c), and 1275(b)(1).*—(i) *In general.*—Sections 1274(c)(1)(B), 1274(c)(3), 1274A(c), and 1275(b)(1) describe certain transactions to which section 1274 does not apply. This paragraph (b)(2) provides certain rules to be used in applying those exceptions.

(ii) *Special rules for certain exceptions under section 1274(c)(3).*—(A) *Determination of sales price for certain sales of farms.*—For purposes of section 1274(c)(3)(A), the determination as to whether the sales price cannot exceed $1,000,000 is made without regard to any other exception to, or limitation on, the applicability of section 1274 (e.g., without regard to the special rules regarding sales of principal residences and land transfers between related persons). In addition, the sales price is determined without regard to section 1274 and without regard to any stated interest. The sales price includes the amount of any liability included in the amount realized from the sale or exchange. See § 1.1001-2.

(B) *Sales involving total payments of $250,000 or less.*—Under section 1274(c)(3)(C), the determination of the amount of payments due under all debt instruments and the amount of other consideration to be received is made as of the date of the sale or exchange or, if earlier, the contract date. If the precise amount due under any debt instrument or the precise amount of any other consideration to be received cannot be determined as of that date, section 1274(c)(3)(C) applies only if it can be determined that the maximum of the aggregate amount of payments due under the debt instruments and other consideration to be received cannot exceed $250,000. For purposes of section 1274(c)(3)(C), if a liability is assumed or property is taken subject to a liability, the aggregate amount of payments due includes the outstanding principal balance or adjusted issue price (in the case of an obligation originally issued at a discount) of the obligation.

(C) *Coordination with section 1273 and § 1.1273-2.*—In accordance with section 1274(c)(3)(D), section 1274 and this section do not apply if the issue price of a debt instrument issued in consideration for the sale or exchange of property is determined under paragraph (a)(1), (b)(1), or (c)(1) of § 1.1273-2.

(3) *Other exceptions to section 1274.*—(i) *Holders of certain below-market instruments.*—Section 1274 does not apply to any holder of a debt instrument that is issued in consideration for the sale or exchange of personal use property (within the meaning of section 1275(b)(3)) in the hands of the issuer and that evidences a below-market loan described in section 7872(c)(1).

(ii) *Transactions involving certain demand loans.*—Section 1274 does not apply to any debt instrument that evidences a demand loan that is a below-market loan described in section 7872(c)(1).

(iii) *Certain transfers subject to section 1041.*—Section 1274 does not apply to any debt instrument issued in consideration for a transfer of property subject to section 1041 (relating to transfers of property between spouses or incident to divorce).

(c) *Examples.*—The following examples illustrate the rules of this section.

Example 1. Single stated rate paid semiannually. A debt instrument issued in consideration for the sale of nonpublicly traded property in a transaction that is not a potentially abusive situation calls for the payment of a principal amount of $1,000,000 at the end of a 10-year term and 20 semiannual interest payments of $60,000. Assume that the test rate of interest is 12 percent, compounded semiannually. The debt instrument is not subject to section 1274 because it provides for interest equal to the test rate and all interest payable on the instrument is qualified stated interest.

Example 2. Sale of farm for debt instrument with contingent interest—(i) *Facts.* On July 1, 1995, A, an individual, sells to B land used as a farm within the meaning of section 6420(c)(2). As partial consideration for the sale, B issues a debt instrument calling for a single $500,000 payment due in 10 years unless profits from the land in each of the 10 years preceding maturity of the debt instrument exceed a specified amount, in which case B is to make a payment of $1,200,000. The debt instrument does not provide for interest.

(ii) *Total payments may exceed $1,000,000.* Even though the total payments ultimately payable under the contract may be less than $1,000,000, at the time of the sale or exchange it cannot be determined that the sales price cannot exceed $1,000,000. Thus, the sale of the land used as a farm is not an excepted transaction described in section 1274(c)(3)(A).

Example 3. Sale between related parties subject to section 483(e)—(i) *Facts.* On July 1, 1995, A, an individual, sells land (not used as a farm within the meaning of section 6420(c)(2)) to A's child B for $650,000. In consideration for the sale, B issues a 10-year debt instrument to A that calls for a payment of $650,000. No other consideration is given. The debt instrument does not provide for interest.

(ii) *Treatment of debt instrument.* For purposes of section 483(e), the $650,000 debt instrument is treated as two separate debt instruments: a $500,000 debt instrument and a $150,000 debt instrument. The $500,000 debt instrument is subject to section 483(e), and accordingly is covered by the exception from section 1274 described in section 1274(c)(3)(F). Because the amount of the payments due as consideration for the sale exceeds $250,000, however, the $150,000 debt instrument is subject to section 1274.

[Reg. § 1.1274-1.]

☐ [*T.D.* 8517, 1-27-94.]

[Reg. § 1.1274-2]

§ 1.1274-2. Issue price of debt instruments to which section 1274 applies.—(a) *In general.*—If section 1274 applies to a debt instrument, section 1274 and this section determine the issue price of the debt instrument. For rules relating to the determination of the amount and timing of OID to be included in income, see section 1272 and the regulations thereunder.

(b) *Issue price.*—(1) *Debt instruments that provide for adequate stated interest; stated principal amount.*—The issue price of a debt instrument that provides for adequate stated interest is the stated principal amount of the debt instrument. For purposes of section 1274, the stated principal amount of a debt instrument is the aggregate amount of all payments due under the debt instrument, excluding any amount of stated interest. Under § 1.1273-2(g)(2)(ii), however, the stated principal amount of a debt instrument is reduced by any payment from the buyer-borrower to the seller-lender that is designated as interest or points. See *Example 2* of § 1.1273-2(g)(5).

(2) *Debt instruments that do not provide for adequate stated interest; imputed principal amount.*—The issue price of a debt instrument that does not provide for adequate stated interest is the imputed principal amount of the debt instrument.

(3) *Debt instruments issued in a potentially abusive situation; fair market value.*—Notwithstanding paragraphs (b)(1) and (b)(2) of this section, in the case of a debt instrument issued in a potentially abusive situation (as defined in § 1.1274-3), the issue price of the debt instrument is the fair market value of the property received in exchange for the debt instrument, reduced by the fair market value of any consideration other than the debt instrument issued in consideration for the sale or exchange.

(c) *Determination of whether a debt instrument provides for adequate stated interest.*—(1) *In general.*—A debt instrument provides for adequate stated interest if its stated principal amount is less than or equal to its imputed principal amount. Imputed principal amount means the sum of the present values, as of the issue date, of all payments, including payments of stated interest, due under the debt instrument (determined by using a discount rate equal to the test rate of interest as determined under § 1.1274-4). If a debt instrument has a single fixed rate of interest that is paid or compounded at least annually, and that rate is equal to or greater than the test rate, the debt instrument has adequate stated interest.

(2) *Determination of present value.*—The present value of a payment is determined by discounting the payment from the date it becomes due to the date of the sale or exchange at the test rate of interest. To determine present value, a compounding period must be selected, and the test rate must be based on the same compounding period.

(d) *Treatment of certain options.*—This paragraph (d) provides rules for determining the issue price of a debt instrument to which section 1274 applies (other than a debt instrument issued in a potentially abusive situation) that is subject to one or more options described in both paragraphs (c)(1) and (c)(5) of § 1.1272-1. Under this paragraph (d), an issuer will be deemed to exercise or not exercise an option or combination of options in a manner that minimizes the instrument's imputed principal amount, and a holder will be deemed to exercise or not exercise an option or combination of options in a manner that maximizes the instrument's imputed principal amount. If both the issuer and the holder have options, the rules of this paragraph (d) are applied to the options in the order that they may be exercised. Thus, the deemed exercise of one option may eliminate other options that are later in time. See § 1.1272-1(c)(5) to determine the debt instrument's yield and maturity for purposes of determining the accrual of OID with respect to the instrument.

(e) *Mandatory sinking funds.*—In determining the issue price of a debt instrument to which section 1274 applies (other than a debt instrument issued in a potentially abusive situation) and that is subject to a mandatory sinking fund provision described in § 1.1272-1(c)(3), the mandatory sinking fund provision is ignored.

(f) *Treatment of variable rate debt instruments.*— (1) *Stated interest at a qualified floating rate.*—(i) *In general.*—For purposes of paragraph (c) of this section, the imputed principal amount of a variable rate debt instrument (within the meaning of § 1.1275-5(a)) that provides for stated interest at a qualified floating rate (or rates) is determined by assuming that the instrument provides for a fixed rate of interest for each accrual period to which a qualified floating rate applies. For purposes of the preceding sentence, the assumed fixed rate in each accrual period is the greater of—

(A) The value of the applicable qualified floating rate as of the first date on which there is a binding written contract that substantially sets forth the terms under which the sale or exchange is ultimately consummated; or

(B) The value of the applicable qualified floating rate as of the date on which the sale or exchange occurs.

(ii) *Interest rate restrictions.*—Notwithstanding paragraph (f)(1)(i) of this section, if, as a result of interest rate restrictions (such as an interest rate cap), the expected yield of the debt instrument taking the restrictions into account is significantly less than the expected yield of the debt instrument without regard to the restrictions, the interest payments on the debt instrument (other than any fixed interest payments) are treated as contingent payments. Reasonably symmetric interest rate caps and floors, or reasonably symmetric governors, that are fixed throughout the term of the debt instrument do not result in the debt instrument being subject to this rule.

(2) *Stated interest at a single objective rate.*— For purposes of paragraph (c) of this section, the imputed principal amount of a variable rate debt instrument (within the meaning of § 1.1275-5(a)) that provides for stated interest at a single objective rate is determined by treating the interest payments as contingent payments.

(g) *Treatment of contingent payment debt instruments.*—Notwithstanding paragraph (b) of this section, if a debt instrument subject to section 1274 provides for one or more contingent payments, the issue price of the debt instrument is the lesser of the instrument's noncontingent principal payments and the sum of the present values of the noncontingent payments (as determined under paragraph (c) of this section). However, if the debt instrument is issued in a potentially abusive situation, the issue price of the debt instrument is the fair market value of the noncontingent payments. For additional rules relating to a debt instrument that provides

for one or more contingent payments, see § 1.1275-4. This paragraph (g) applies to debt instruments issued on or after August 13, 1996.

(h) *Examples.*—The following examples illustrate the rules of this section. Each example assumes a 30-day month, 360-day year. In addition, each example assumes that the debt instrument is not a qualified debt instrument (as defined in section 1274A(b)) and is not issued in a potentially abusive situation.

Example 1. Debt instrument without a fixed rate over its entire term—(i) *Facts.* On January 1, 1995, A sells nonpublicly traded property to B for a stated purchase price of $3,500,000. In consideration for the sale, B makes a down payment of $500,000 and issues a 10-year debt instrument with a stated principal amount of $3,000,000, payable at maturity. The debt instrument calls for no interest in the first 2 years and interest at a rate of 15 percent payable annually over the remaining 8 years of the debt instrument. The first interest payment of $450,000 is due on December 31, 1997, and the last interest payment is due on December 31, 2004, together with the $3,000,000 payment of principal. Assume that the test rate of interest applicable to the debt instrument is 10.5 percent, compounded annually.

(ii) *Applicability of section 1274.* Because the debt instrument does not provide for any interest during the first 2 years, none of the interest on the debt instrument is qualified stated interest. Therefore, the issue price of the debt instrument is determined under section 1274. See § 1.1274-1(b)(1). If the debt instrument has adequate stated interest, the issue price of the instrument is its stated principal amount. Otherwise, the issue price of the debt instrument is its imputed principal amount. The debt instrument has adequate stated interest only if the stated principal amount is less than or equal to the imputed principal amount.

(iii) *Determination of imputed principal amount.* To compute the imputed principal amount of the debt instrument, all payments due under the debt instrument are discounted back to the issue date at 10.5 percent, compounded annually, as follows:

(A) The present value of the $3,000,000 principal payment payable on December 31, 2004, is $1,105,346.59, determined as follows:

$$\$1{,}105{,}346.59 = \frac{\$3{,}000{,}000}{(1 + .105/1)^{10}}$$

(B) The present value of the eight interest payments of $450,000 as of January 1, 1997, is $2,357,634.55, determined as follows:

$$\$2{,}357{,}634.55 = \$450{,}000 \times \frac{1 - (1 + .105/1)^{-8}}{(.105/1)}$$

Reg. §1.1274-2(h)

(C) The present value of this interim amount as of January 1, 1995, is $1,930,865.09, determined as follows:

$$1,930,865.09 = \frac{\$2,357,634.55}{(1 + .105/.1)^2}$$

(iv) *Determination of issue price.* The debt instrument's imputed principal amount (that is, the present value of all payments due under the debt instrument) is $3,036,211.68 ($1,105,346.59 + $1,930,865.09). Because the stated principal amount ($3,000,000) is less than the imputed principal amount, the debt instrument provides for adequate stated interest. Therefore, the issue price of the debt instrument is its stated principal amount ($3,000,000).

Example 2. Debt instrument subject to issuer call option—(i) *Facts.* On January 1, 1995, in partial consideration for the sale of nonpublicly traded property, H corporation issues to G a 10-year debt instrument, maturing on January 1, 2005, with a stated principal amount of $10,000,000, payable on that date. The debt instrument provides for annual payments of interest of 8 percent for the first 5 years and 14 percent for the final 5 years, payable on January 1 of each year, beginning on January 1, 1996. In addition, the debt instrument provides H with the unconditional option to call (prepay) the debt instrument at the end of 5 years for its stated principal amount of $10,000,000. Assume that the Federal mid-term and long-term rates applicable to the sale based on annual compounding are 9 percent and 10 percent, respectively.

(ii) *Option presumed exercised.* Assuming exercise of the call option, the imputed principal amount as determined under paragraph (d) of this section is $9,611,034.87 (the present value of all of the payments due within a 5-year term discounted at a test rate of 9 percent, compounded annually). Assuming nonexercise of the call option, the imputed principal amount is $10,183,354.78 (the present value of all of the payments due within a 10-year term discounted at a test rate of 10 percent, compounded annually). For purposes of determining the imputed principal amount, the option is presumed exercised because the imputed principal amount, assuming exercise of the option, is less than the imputed principal amount, assuming the option is not exercised. Because the option is presumed exercised, the debt instrument fails to provide for adequate stated interest because the imputed principal amount ($9,611,034.87) is less than the stated principal amount ($10,000,000). Thus, the issue price of the debt instrument is $9,611,034.87.

Example 3. Variable rate debt instrument with a single rate over its entire term—(i) *Facts.* On January 1, 1995, A sells B nonpublicly traded property. In partial consideration for the sale, B issues a debt instrument in the principal amount of $1,000,000, payable in 5 years. The debt instrument calls for interest payable monthly at a rate

of 1 percentage point above the average prime lending rate of a major bank for the month preceding the month of the interest payment. Assume that the test rate of interest applicable to the debt instrument is 10.5 percent, compounded monthly. Assume also that 1 percentage point above the prime lending rate of the designated bank on the date of the sale is 12.5 percent, compounded monthly, which is greater than 1 percentage point above the prime lending rate of the designated bank on the first date on which there is a binding written contract that substantially sets forth the terms under which the sale is consummated.

(ii) *Debt instrument has adequate stated interest.* The debt instrument is a variable rate debt instrument (within the meaning of § 1.1275-5) that provides for stated interest at a qualified floating rate. Under paragraph (f)(1)(i) of this section, the debt instrument is treated as if it provided for a fixed rate of interest equal to 12.5 percent, compounded monthly. Because the test rate of interest is 10.5 percent, compounded monthly, the debt instrument provides for adequate stated interest.

Example 4. Debt instrument with a capped variable rate. On July 1, 1995, A sells nonpublicly traded property to B in return for a debt instrument with a stated principal amount of $10,000,000, payable on July 1, 2005. Interest is payble on July 1 of each year, beginning on July 1, 1996, at the Federal short-term rate for June of the same year. The debt instrument provides, however, that the interest rate cannot rise above 8.5 percent, compounded annually. Assume that, as of the date the test rate of interest for the debt instrument is determined, the Federal short-term rate is 8 percent, compounded annually. Assume further that, as a result of the interest rate cap of 8.5 percent, compounded annually, the expected yield of the debt instrument is significantly less than the expected yield of the debt instrument if it did not include the interest rate cap. Under paragraph (f)(1)(ii) of this section, the variable payments are treated as contingent payments for purposes of this section.

(i) [Reserved]

(j) *Special rules for tax-exempt obligations.*— (1) *Certain variable rate debt instruments.*—Notwithstanding paragraph (b) of this section, if a tax-exempt obligation (as defined in section 1275(a)(3)) is a variable rate debt instrument (within the meaning of § 1.1275-5) that pays interest at an objective rate and is subject to section 1274, the issue price of the obligation is the greater of the obligation's fair market value and its stated principal amount.

(2) *Contingent payment debt instruments.*— Notwithstanding paragraphs (b) and (g) of this section, if a tax-exempt obligation (as defined in section 1275(a)(3)) is subject to section 1274 and § 1.1275-4, the issue price of the obligation is the fair market value of the obligation. However, in

the case of a tax-exempt obligation that is subject to § 1.1275-4(d)(2) (an obligation that provides for interest-based or revenue-based payments), the issue price of the obligation is the greater of the obligation's fair market value and its stated principal amount.

(3) *Effective date.*—This paragraph (j) applies to debt instruments issued on or after August 13, 1996. [Reg. § 1.1274-2.]

☐ [*T.D. 8517, 1-27-94. Amended by T.D. 8674, 6-11-96.*]

[Reg. § 1.1274-3]

§ 1.1274-3. Potentially abusive situations defined.—(a) *In general.*—For purposes of section 1274, a potentially abusive situation means—

(1) A tax shelter (as defined in section 6662(d)(2)(C)(ii)); or

(2) Any other situation involving—

(i) A recent sales transaction;

(ii) Nonrecourse financing;

(iii) Financing with a term in excess of the useful life of the property; or

(iv) A debt instrument with clearly excessive interest.

(b) *Operating rules.*—(1) *Debt instrument exchanged for nonrecourse financing.*—Nonrecourse financing does not include an exchange of a nonrecourse debt instrument for an outstanding recourse or nonrecourse debt instrument.

(2) *Nonrecourse debt with substantial down payment.*—Nonrecourse financing does not include a sale or exchange of a real property interest financed by a nonrecourse debt instrument if, in addition to the nonrecourse debt instrument, the purchaser makes a down payment in money that equals or exceeds 20 percent of the total stated purchase price of the real property interest. For purposes of the preceding sentence, a real property interest means any interest, other than an interest solely as a creditor, in real property.

(3) *Clearly excessive interest.*—Interest on a debt instrument is clearly excessive if the interest, in light of the terms of the debt instrument and the creditworthiness of the borrower, is clearly greater than the arm's length amount of interest that would have been charged in a cash lending transaction between the same two parties.

(c) *Other situations to be specified by Commissioner.*—The Commissioner may designate in the Internal Revenue Bulletin situations that, although described in paragraph (a)(2) of this section, will not be treated as potentially abusive because they do not have the effect of significantly misstating basis or amount realized (see § 601.601(d)(2)(ii) of this chapter).

(d) *Consistency rule.*—The issuer's determination that the debt instrument is or is not issued in a potentially abusive situation is binding on all holders of the debt instrument. However, the issuer's determination is not binding on a holder who explicitly discloses a position that is inconsistent with the issuer's determination. Unless otherwise prescribed by the Commissioner, the disclosure must be made on a statement attached to the holder's timely filed Federal income tax return for the taxable year that includes the acquisition date of the debt instrument. See § 1.1275-2(e) for rules relating to the issuer's obligation to disclose certain information to holders. [Reg. § 1.1274-3.]

☐ [*T.D. 8517, 1-27-94.*]

[Reg. § 1.1274-4]

§ 1.1274-4. Test rate.—(a) *Determination of test rate of interest.*—(1) *In general.*—(i) *Test rate is the 3-month rate.*—Except as provided in paragraph (a)(2) of this section, the test rate of interest for a debt instrument issued in consideration for the sale or exchange of property is the 3-month rate.

(ii) *The 3-month rate.*—Except as provided in paragraph (a)(1)(iii) of this section, the 3-month rate is the lower of—

(A) The lowest applicable Federal rate (based on the appropriate compounding period) in effect during the 3-month period ending with the first month in which there is a binding written contract that substantially sets forth the terms under which the sale or exchange is ultimately consummated; or

(B) The lowest applicable Federal rate (based on the appropriate compounding period) in effect during the 3-month period ending with the month in which the sale or exchange occurs.

(iii) *Special rule if there is no binding written contract.*—If there is no binding written contract that substantially sets forth the terms under which the sale or exchange is ultimately consummated, the 3-month rate is the lowest applicable Federal rate (based on the appropriate compounding period) in effect during the 3-month period ending with the month in which the sale or exchange occurs.

(2) *Test rate for certain debt instruments.*—(i) *Sale-leaseback transactions.*—Under section 1274(e) (relating to certain sale-leaseback transactions), the test rate is 110 percent of the 3-month rate determined under paragraph (a)(1) of this section. For purposes of section 1274(e)(3), related party means a person related to the transferor within the meaning of section 267(b) or 707(b)(1).

(ii) *Qualified debt instrument.*—Under section 1274A(a), the test rate for a qualified debt instrument is no greater than 9 percent, compounded semiannually, or an equivalent rate based on an appropriate compounding period.

(iii) *Alternative test rate for short-term obligations.*—(A) *Requirements.*—This paragraph (a)(2)(iii)(A) provides an alternative test rate under section 1274(d)(1)(D) for a debt instrument with a maturity of 1 year or less. This alternative test rate applies, however, only if the debt instrument provides for adequate stated interest using the alternative test rate, the issuer provides on the face of the debt instrument that the instrument qualifies as having adequate stated interest under section 1274(d)(1)(D), and the issuer and holder treat or agree to treat the instrument as having adequate stated interest.

(B) *Alternative test rate.*—For purposes of paragraph (a)(2)(iii)(A), the alternative test rate is the market yield on U.S. Treasury bills with the same maturity date as the debt instrument. If the same maturity date is not available, the market yield on U.S. Treasury bills that mature in the same week or month as the debt instrument is used. The alternative test rate is determined as of the date on which there is a binding written contract that substantially sets forth the terms under which the sale or exchange is ultimately consummated or as of the date of the sale or exchange, whichever date results in a lower rate. If there is no binding written contract, however, the alternative test rate is determined as of the date of the sale or exchange.

(b) *Applicable Federal rate.*—Except as otherwise provided in this section, the applicable Federal rate for a debt instrument is based on the term of the instrument (i.e., short-term, mid-term, or long-term). See section 1274(d)(1). The Internal Revenue Service publishes the applicable Federal rates for each month in the Internal Revenue Bulletin (see §601.601(d)(2)(ii) of this chapter). The applicable Federal rates are based on the yield to maturity of outstanding marketable obligations of the United States of similar maturities during the one month period ending on the 14th day of the month preceding the month for which the rates are applicable.

(c) *Special rules to determine the term of a debt instrument for purposes of determining the applicable Federal rate.*—(1) *Installment obligation.*—If a debt instrument is an installment obligation (as defined in §1.1273-1(e)(1)), the term of the instrument is the instrument's weighted average maturity (as defined in §1.1273-1(e)(3)).

(2) *Certain variable rate debt instruments.*— (i) *In general.*—Except as otherwise provided in paragraph (c)(2)(ii) of this section, if a variable rate debt instrument (as defined in §1.1275-5(a)) provides for stated interest at a qualified floating rate (or rates), the term of the instrument is determined by reference to the longest interval between interest adjustment dates, or, if the variable rate debt instrument provides for a fixed rate, the interval between the issue date and the last day on which the fixed rate applies, if this interval is longer.

(ii) *Restrictions on adjustments.*—If, due to significant restrictions on variations in a qualified floating rate or the use of certain formulae pursuant to §1.1275-5(b)(2) (e.g., 15 percent of 1-year LIBOR, plus 800 basis points), the rate in substance resembles a fixed rate, the applicable Federal rate is determined by reference to the term of the debt instrument.

(3) *Counting of either the issue date or the maturity date.*—The term of a debt instrument includes either the issue date or the maturity date, but not both dates.

(4) *Certain debt instruments that provide for principal payments uncertain as to time.*—If a debt instrument provides for principal payments that are fixed in total amount but uncertain as to time, the term of the instrument is determined by reference to the latest possible date on which a principal payment can be made or, in the case of an installment obligation, by reference to the longest weighted average maturity under any possible payment schedule.

(d) *Foreign currency loans.*—If all of the payments of a debt instrument are denominated in, or determined by reference to, a currency other than the U.S. dollar, the applicable Federal rate for the debt instrument is a foreign currency rate of interest that is analogous to the applicable Federal rate described in this section. For this purpose, an analogous rate of interest is a rate based on yields (with the appropriate compounding period) of the highest grade of outstanding marketable obligations denominated in such currency (excluding any obligations that benefit from special tax exemptions or preferential tax rates not available to debt instruments generally) with due consideration given to the maturities of the obligations.

(e) *Examples.*—The following examples illustrate the rules of this section.

Example 1. Variable rate debt instrument that limits the amount of increase and decrease in the rate— (i) *Facts.* On July 1, 1996, A sells nonpublicly traded property to B in return for a 5-year debt instrument that provides for interest to be paid on July 1 of each year, beginning on July 1, 1997, based on the prime rate of a local bank on that date. However, the interest rate cannot increase or decrease from one year to the next by more than .25 percentage points (25 basis points).

(ii) *Significant restriction.* The debt instrument is a variable rate debt instrument (as defined in §1.1275-5) that provides for stated interest at a qualified floating rate. Assume that based on all the facts and circumstances, the restriction is a significant restriction on the variations in the rate of interest. Under paragraph (c)(2)(ii) of this section, the applicable Federal rate is determined by reference to the term of the debt instrument, and the applicable Federal rate is the Federal midterm rate.

Example 2. Installment obligation—(i) *Facts.* On January 1, 1996, A sells nonpublicly traded property to B in exchange for a debt instrument that calls for a payment of $500,000 on January 1, 2001, and a payment of $1,000,000 on January 1, 2006. The debt instrument does not provide for any stated interest.

(ii) *Determination of term.* The debt instrument is an installment obligation. Under paragraph (c)(1) of this section, the term of the debt instrument is its weighted average maturity (as defined in § 1.1273-1(e)(3)). The debt instrument's weighted average maturity is 8.33 years, which is the sum of (A) the ratio of the first payment to total payments (500,000/1,500,000), multiplied by the number of complete years from the issue date until the payment is due (5 years), and (b) the ratio of the second payment to total payments (1,000,000/1,500,000), multiplied by the number of complete years from the issue date until the second payment is due (10 years).

(iii) *Applicable Federal rate.* Based on the calculation in paragraph (ii) of this example, the term of the debt instrument is treated as 8.33 years. Consequently, the applicable Federal rate is the Federal mid-term rate.

[Reg. § 1.1274-4.]

☐ [*T.D.* 8517, 1-27-94.]

[Reg. § 1.1274-5]

§ 1.1274-5. Assumptions.—(a) *In general.*— Section 1274 does not apply to a debt instrument if the debt instrument is assumed, or property is taken subject to the debt instrument, in connection with a sale or exchange of property, unless the terms of the debt instrument, as part of the sale or exchange, are modified in a manner that would constitute an exchange under section 1001.

(b) *Modifications of debt instruments.*—(1) *In general.*—Except as provided in paragraph (b)(2) of this section, if a debt instrument is assumed, or property is taken subject to a debt instrument, in connection with a sale or exchange of property, the terms of the debt instrument are modified as part of the sale or exchange, and the modification triggers an exchange under section 1001, the modification is treated as a separate transaction taking place immediately before the sale or exchange and is attributed to the seller of the property. For purposes of this paragraph (b), a debt instrument is not considered to be modified as part of the sale or exchange unless the seller knew or had reason to know about the modification.

(2) *Election to treat buyer as modifying the debt instrument.*—(i) *In general.*—Rather than having the rules in paragraph (b)(1) of this section apply, the seller and buyer may jointly elect to treat the transaction as one in which the buyer first assumed the original (unmodified) debt instrument and then subsequently modified the debt

instrument. For this purpose, the modification is treated as a separate transaction taking place immediately after the sale or exchange.

(ii) *Time and manner of making the election.*—The buyer and seller make the election under paragraph (b)(2)(i) of this section by jointly signing a statement that includes the names, addresses, and taxpayer identification numbers of the seller and buyer, and a clear indication that the election is being made under paragraph (b)(2)(i) of this section. Both the buyer and the seller must sign this statement not later than the earlier of the last day (including extensions) for filing the Federal income tax return of the buyer or seller for the taxable year in which the sale or exchange of the property occurs. The buyer and seller should attach this signed statement (or a copy thereof) to their timely filed Federal income tax returns.

(c) *Wraparound indebtedness.*—For purposes of paragraph (a) of this section, the issuance of wraparound indebtedness is not considered an assumption.

(d) *Consideration attributable to assumed debt.*— If as part of the consideration for the sale or exchange of property, the buyer assumes, or takes the property subject to, an indebtedness that was issued with OID (including a debt instrument issued in a prior sale or exchange to which section 1274 applied), the portion of the buyer's basis in the property and the seller's amount realized attributable to the debt instrument equals the adjusted issue price of the debt instrument as of the date of the sale or exchange. [Reg. § 1.1274-5.]

☐ [*T.D.* 8517, 1-27-94.]

[Reg. § 1.1274A-1]

§ 1.1274A-1. Special rules for certain transactions where stated principal amount does not exceed $2,800,000.—(a) *In general.*—Section 1274A allows the use of a lower test rate for purposes of sections 483 and 1274 in the case of a qualified debt instrument (as defined in section 1274A(b)) and, if elected by the borrower and the lender, the use of the cash receipts and disbursements method of accounting for interest on a cash method debt instrument (as defined in section 1274A(c)(2)). This section provides special rules for qualified debt instruments and cash method debt instruments.

(b) *Rules for both qualified and cash method debt instruments.*—(1) *Sale-leaseback transactions.*—A debt instrument issued in a sale-leaseback transaction (within the meaning of section 1274(e)) cannot be either a qualified debt instrument or a cash method debt instrument.

(2) *Debt instruments calling for contingent payments.*—A debt instrument that provides for contingent payments cannot be a qualified debt

Reg. § 1.1274A-1(b)(2)

instrument unless it can be determined at the time of the sale or exchange that the maximum stated principal amount due under the debt instrument cannot exceed the amount specified in section 1274A(b). Similarly, a debt instrument that provides for contingent payments cannot be a cash method debt instrument unless it can be determined at the time of the sale or exchange that the maximum stated principal amount due under the debt instrument cannot exceed the amount specified in section 1274A(c)(2)(A).

(3) *Aggregation of transactions.*—(i) *General rule.*—The aggregation rules of section 1274A(d)(1) are applied using a facts and circumstances test.

(ii) *Examples.*—The following examples illustrate the application of section 1274A(d)(1) and paragraph (b)(3)(i) of this section.

Example 1. Aggregation of two sales to a single person. In two transactions evidenced by separate sales agreements, A sells undivided half interests in Blackacre to B. The sales are pursuant to a plan for the sale of a 100 percent interest in Blackacre to B. These sales or exchanges are part of a series of related transactions and, thus, are treated as a single sale for purposes of section 1274A.

Example 2. Aggregation of two purchases by unrelated individuals. Pursuant to a plan, unrelated individuals X and Y purchase undivided half interests in Blackacre from A and subsequently contribute these interests to a partnership in exchange for equal interests in the partnership. These purchases are treated as part of the same transaction and, thus, are treated as a single sale for purposes of section 1274A.

Example 3. Aggregation of sales made pursuant to a tender offer. Fifteen unrelated individuals own all of the stock of X Corporation. Y Corporation makes a tender offer to these 15 shareholders. The terms offered to each shareholder are identical. Shareholders holding a majority of the shares of X Corporation elect to tender their shares pursuant to Y Corporation's offer. These sales are part of the same transaction and, thus, are treated as a single sale for purposes of section 1274A.

Example 4. No aggregation for separate sales of similar property to unrelated persons. Pursuant to a newspaper advertisement, X Corporation offers for sale similar condominiums in a single building. The prices of the units vary due to a variety of factors, but the financing terms offered by X Corporation to all buyers are identical. The units are purchased by unrelated buyers who decided whether to purchase units in the building at the price and on the terms offered by X Corporation, without regard to the actions of other buyers. Because each buyer acts individually, the sales are not part of the same transaction or a series of related transactions and, thus, are treated as separate sales.

(4) *Inflation adjustment of dollar amounts.*—Under section 1274A(d)(2), the dollar amounts specified in sections 1274A(b) and 1274A(c)(2)(A) are adjusted for inflation. The dollar amounts, adjusted for inflation, are published in the Internal Revenue Bulletin (see § 601.601(d)(2)(ii) of this chapter).

(c) *Rules for cash method debt instruments.*—(1) *Time and manner of making cash method election.*—The borrower and lender make the election described in section 1274A(c)(2)(D) by jointly signing a statement that includes the names, addresses, and taxpayer identification numbers of the borrower and lender, a clear indication that an election is being made under section 1274A(c)(2), and a declaration that debt instrument with respect to which the election is being made fulfills the requirements of a cash method debt instrument. Both the borrower and the lender must sign this statement not later than the earlier of the last day (including extensions) for filing the Federal income tax return of the borrower or lender for the taxable year in which the debt instrument is issued. The borrower and lender should attach this signed statement (or a copy thereof) to their timely filed Federal income tax returns.

(2) *Successors of electing parties.*—Except as othewise provided in this paragraph (c)(2), the cash method election under section 1274A(c) applies to any successor of the electing lender or borrower. Thus, for any period after the transfer of a cash method debt instrument, the successor takes into account the interest (including unstated interest) on the instrument under the cash receipts and disbursements method of accounting. Nevertheless, if the lender (or any successor thereof) transfers the cash method debt instrument to a taxpayer who uses an accrual method of accounting, section 1272 rather than section 1274A(c) applies to the successor of the lender with respect to the debt instrument for any period after the date of the transfer. The borrower (or any successor thereof), however, remains on the cash receipts and disbursements method of accounting with respect to the cash method debt instrument.

(3) *Modified debt instrument.*—In the case of a debt instrument issued in a debt-for-debt exchange that qualifies as an exchange under section 1001, the debt instrument is eligible for the election to be a cash method debt instrument if the other prerequisites to making the election in section 1274A(c) are met. However, if a principal purpose of the modification is to defer interest income or deductions through the use of the election, then the debt instrument is not eligible for the election.

(4) *Debt incurred or continued to purchase or carry a cash method debt instrument.*—If a debt instrument is incurred or continued to purchase or carry a cash method debt instrument, rules

similar to those under section 1277 apply to determine the timing of the interest deductions for the debt instrument. For purposes of the preceding sentence, rules similar to those under section 265(a)(2) apply to determine whether a debt instrument is incurred or continued to purchase or carry a cash method debt instrument. [Reg. § 1.1274A-1.]

☐ [T.D. 8517, 1-27-94.]

[Reg. § 1.1275-1]

§ 1.1275-1. Definitions.—(a) *Applicability.*— The definitions contained in this section apply for purposes of sections 163(e) and 1271 through 1275 and the regulations therunder.

(b) *Adjusted issue price.*—(1) *In general.*—The adjusted issue price of a debt instrument at the beginning of the first accrual period is the issue price. Thereafter, the adjusted issue price of the debt instrument is the issue price of the debt instrument—

(i) Increased by the amount of OID previously includible in the gross income of any holder (determined without regard to section 1272(a)(7) and section 1272(c)(1)); and

(ii) Decreased by the amount of any payment previously made on the debt instrument other than a payment of qualified stated interest. See § 1.1275-2(f) for rules regarding adjustments to adjusted issue price on a pro rata prepayment.

(2) *Bond issuance premium.*—If a debt instrument is issued with bond issuance premium (as defined in § 1.163-13(c)), for purposes of determining the issuer's adjusted issue price, the adjusted issue price determined under paragraph (b)(1) of this section is also decreased by the amount of bond issuance premium previously allocable under § 1.163-13(d)(3).

(3) *Adjusted issue price for subsequent holders.*—for purposes of calculating OID accruals, acquisition premium, or market discount, a holder (other than a purchaser at original issuance) determines adjusted issue price in any manner consistent with the regulations under sections 1271 through 1275.

(c) *OID.*—OID means original issue discount (as defined in section 1273(a) and § 1.1273-1).

(d) *Debt instrument.*—Except as provided in section 1275(a)(1)(B) (relating to certain annuity contracts; see paragraph (j) of this section), debt instrument means any instrument or contractual arrangement that constitutes indebtedness under general principles of Federal income tax law (including, for example, a certificate of deposit or a loan). Nothing in the regulations under sections 163(e), 483, and 1271 through 1275, however, shall influence whether an instrument constitutes indebtedness for Federal income tax purposes.

(e) *Tax-exempt obligations.*—For purposes of section 1275(a)(3)(B), exempt from tax means exempt from Federal income tax.

(f) *Issue.*—(1) *Debt instruments issued on or after March 13, 2001.*—Except as provided in paragraph (f)(3) of this section, two or more debt instruments are part of the same issue if the debt instruments—

(i) Have the same credit and payment terms;

(ii) Are issued either pursuant to a common plan or as part of a single transaction or a series of related transactions;

(iii) Are issued within a period of thirteen days beginning with the date on which the first debt instrument that would be part of the issue is issued to a person other than a bond house, broker, or similar person or organization acting in the capacity of an underwriter, placement agent, or wholesaler; and

(iv) Are issued on or after March 13, 2001.

(2) *Debt instruments issued before March 13, 2001.*—Except as provided in paragraph (f)(3) of this section, two or more debt instruments are part of the same issue if the debt instruments—

(i) Have the same credit and payment terms;

(ii) Are sold reasonably close in time either pursuant to a common plan or as part of a single transaction or a series of related transactions; and

(iii) Are issued on or after April 4, 1994, and before March 13, 2001.

(3) *Transition rule.*—If the issue date of any of the debt instruments that would be part of the same issue (determined as if each debt instrument were part of a separate issue) is on or after March 13, 2001, then the definition of the term *issue* in paragraph (f)(1) of this section applies rather than the definition in paragraph (f)(2) of this section to determine if the debt instruments are part of the same issue.

(4) *Cross-references for reopening and aggregation rules.*—See § 1.1275-2(d) and (k) for rules that treat debt instruments issued in certain reopenings as part of an issue of original (outstanding) debt instruments. See § 1.1275-2(c) for rules that treat two or more debt instruments as a single debt instrument.

(g) *Debt instruments issued by a natural person.*—If an entity is a primary obligor under a debt instrument, the debt instrument is considered to be issued by the entity and not by a natural person even if a natural person is a co-maker and is jointly liable for the debt instrument's repayment. A debt instrument issued by a partnership is considered to be issued by the partnership as an entity even if the partnership is composed entirely of natural persons.

Reg. § 1.1275-1(g)

(h) *Publicly offered debt instrument.*—A debt instrument is publicly offered if it is part of an issue of debt instruments the initial offering of which—

(1) Is registered with the Securities and Exchange Commission; or

(2) Would be required to be registered under the Securities Act of 1933 (15 U.S.C. 77a et seq.) but for an exemption from registration—

(i) Under section 3 of the Securities Act of 1933 (relating to exempted securities);

(ii) Under any law (other than the Securities Act of 1933) because of the identity of the issuer or the nature of the security; or

(iii) Because the issue is intended for distribution to persons who are not United States persons.

(i) [Reserved]

(j) *Life annuity exception under section 1275(a)(1)(B)(i).*—(1) *Purpose.*—Section 1275(a)(1)(B)(i) excepts an annuity contract from the definition of *debt instrument* if section 72 applies to the contract and the contract depends (in whole or in substantial part) on the life expectancy of one or more individuals. This paragraph (j) provides rules to ensure that an annuity contract qualifies for the exception in section 1275(a)(1)(B)(i) only in cases where the life contingency under the contract is real and significant.

(2) *General rule.*—(i) *Rule.*—For purposes of section 1275(a)(1)(B)(i), an annuity contract depends (in whole or in substantial part) on the life expectancy of one or more individuals only if—

(A) The contract provides for periodic distributions made not less frequently than annually for the life (or joint lives) of an individual (or a reasonable number of individuals); and

(B) The contract does not contain any terms or provisions that can significantly reduce the probability that total distributions under the contract will increase commensurately with the longevity of the annuitant (or annuitants).

(ii) *Terminology.*—For purposes of this paragraph (j):

(A) *Contract.*—The term *contract* includes all written or unwritten understandings among the parties as well as any person or persons acting in concert with one or more of the parties.

(B) *Annuitant.*—The term *annuitant* refers to the individual (or reasonable number of individuals) referred to in paragraph (j)(2)(i)(A) of this section.

(C) *Terminating death.*—The phrase *terminating death* refers to the annuitant death that can terminate periodic distributions under the contract. (See paragraph (j)(2)(i)(A) of this section.) For example, if a contract provides for periodic distributions until the later of the death of the last-surviving annuitant or the end of a term certain, the terminating death is the death of the last-surviving annuitant.

(iii) *Coordination with specific rules.*—Paragraphs (j)(3) through (7) of this section describe certain terms and conditions that can significantly reduce the probability that total distributions under the contract will increase commensurately with the longevity of the annuitant (or annuitants). If a term or provision is not specifically described in paragraphs (j)(3) through (7) of this section, the annuity contract must be tested under the general rule of paragraph (j)(2)(i) of this section to determine whether it depends (in whole or in substantial part) on the life expectancy of one or more individuals.

(3) *Availability of a cash surrender option.*—(i) *Impact on life contingency.*—The availability of a cash surrender option can significantly reduce the probability that total distributions under the contract will increase commensurately with the longevity of the annuitant (or annuitants). Thus, the availability of any cash surrender option causes the contract to fail to be described in section 1275(a)(1)(B)(i). A cash surrender option is available if there is reason to believe that the issuer (or a person acting in concert with the issuer) will be willing to terminate or purchase all or a part of the annuity contract by making one or more payments of cash or property (other than an annuity contract described in this paragraph (j)).

(ii) *Examples.*—The following examples illustrate the rules of this paragraph (j)(3):

Example 1. (i) *Facts.* On March 1, 1998, X issues a contract to A for cash. The contract provides that, effective on any date chosen by A (the annuity starting date), X will begin equal monthly distributions for A's life. The amount of each monthly distribution will be no less than an amount based on the contract's account value as of the annuity starting date, A's age on that date, and permanent purchase rate guarantees contained in the contract. The contract also provides that, at any time before the annuity starting date, A may surrender the contract to X for the account value less a surrender charge equal to a declining percentage of the account value. For this purpose, the initial account value is equal to the cash invested. Thereafter, the account value increases annually by at least a minimum guaranteed rate.

(ii) *Analysis.* The ability to obtain the account value less the surrender charge, if any, is a cash surrender option. This ability can significantly reduce the probability that total distributions under the contract will increase commensurately with A's longevity. Thus, the contract fails to be described in section 1275(a)(1)(B)(i).

Example 2. (i) *Facts.* On March 1, 1998, X issues a contract to B for cash. The contract provides that beginning on March 1, 1999, X will distribute to B a fixed amount of cash each month for B's life. Based on X's advertisements, marketing literature, or illustrations or on oral representations by X's sales personnel, there is reason to believe that an affiliate of X stands ready to purchase B's contract for its commuted value.

(ii) *Analysis.* Because there is reason to believe that an affiliate of X stands ready to purchase B's contract for its commuted value, a cash surrender option is available within the meaning of paragraph (j)(3)(i) of this section. This availability can significantly reduce the probability that total distributions under the contract will increase commensurately with B's longevity. Thus, the contract fails to be described in section 1275(a)(1)(B)(i).

(4) *Availability of a loan secured by the contract.*—(i) *Impact on life contingency.*—The availability of a loan secured by the contract can significantly reduce the probability that total distributions under the contract will increase commensurately with the longevity of the annuitant (or annuitants). Thus, the availability of any such loan causes the contract to fail to be described in section 1275(a)(1)(B)(i). A loan secured by the contract is available if there is reason to believe that the issuer (or a person acting in concert with the issuer) will be willing to make a loan that is directly or indirectly secured by the annuity contract.

(ii) *Example.*—The following example illustrates the rules of this paragraph (j)(4):

Example. (i) *Facts.* On March 1, 1998, X issues a contract to C for $100,000. The contract provides that, effective on any date chosen by C (the annuity starting date), X will begin equal monthly distributions for C's life. The amount of each monthly distribution will be no less than an amount based on the contract's account value as of the annuity starting date, C's age on that date, and permanent purchase rate guarantees contained in the contract. From marketing literature circulated by Y, there is reason to believe that, at any time before the annuity starting date, C may pledge the contract to borrow up to $75,000 from Y. Y is acting in concert with X.

(ii) *Analysis.* Because there is reason to believe that Y, a person acting in concert with X, is willing to lend money against C's contract, a loan secured by the contract is available within the meaning of paragraph (j)(4)(i) of this section. This availability can significantly reduce the probability that total distributions under the contract will increase commensurately with C's longevity. Thus, the contract fails to be described in section 1275(a)(1)(B)(i).

(5) *Minimum payout provision.*—(i) *Impact on life contingency.*—The existence of a minimum payout provision can significantly reduce the probability that total distributions under the contract will increase commensurately with the longevity of the annuitant (or annuitants). Thus, the existence of any minimum payout provision causes the contract to fail to be described in section 1275(a)(1)(B)(i).

(ii) *Definition of minimum payout provision.*—A minimum payout provision is a contractual provision (for example, an agreement to make distributions over a term certain) that provides for one or more distributions made—

(A) After the terminating death under the contract; or

(B) By reason of the death of any individual (including distributions triggered by or increased by terminal or chronic illness, as defined in section 101(g)(1)(A) and (B)).

(iii) *Exceptions for certain minimum payouts.*—(A) *Recovery of consideration paid for the contract.*—Notwithstanding paragraphs (j)(2)(i)(A) and (j)(5)(i) of this section, a contract does not fail to be described in section 1275(a)(1)(B)(i) merely because it provides that, after the terminating death, there will be one or more distributions that, in the aggregate, do not exceed the consideration paid for the contract less total distributions previously made under the contract.

(B) *Payout for one-half of life expectancy.*—Notwithstanding paragraphs (j)(2)(i)(A) and (j)(5)(i) of this section, a contract does not fail to be described in section 1275(a)(1)(B)(i) merely because it provides that, if the terminating death occurs after the annuity starting date, distributions under the contract will continue to be made after the terminating death until a date that is no later than the halfway date. This exception does not apply unless the amounts distributed in each contract year will not exceed the amounts that would have been distributed in that year if the terminating death had not occurred until the expected date of the terminating death, determined under paragraph (j)(5)(iii)(C) of this section.

(C) *Definition of halfway date.*—For purposes of this paragraph (j)(5)(iii), the halfway date is the date halfway between the annuity starting date and the expected date of the terminating death, determined as of the annuity starting date, with respect to all then-surviving annuitants. The expected date of the terminating death must be determined by reference to the applicable mortality table prescribed under section 417(e)(3)(A)(ii)(I).

(iv) *Examples.*—The following examples illustrate the rules of this paragraph (j)(5):

Example 1. (i) *Facts.* On March 1, 1998, X issues a contract to D for cash. The contract provides that, effective on any date D chooses (the annuity starting date), X will begin equal monthly distributions for the greater of D's life or 10 years, regardless of D's age as of the annuity starting date. The amount of each monthly distribution will be no less than an amount based on the contract's account value as of the annuity starting date, D's age on that date, and permanent purchase rate guarantees contained in the contract.

(ii) *Analysis.* A minimum payout provision exists because, if D dies within 10 years of the annuity starting date, one or more distributions will be made after D's death. The minimum payout provision does not qualify for the exception in paragraph (j)(5)(iii)(B) of this section because D may defer the annuity starting date until his remaining life expectancy is less than 20 years. If, on the annuity starting date, D's life expectancy is less than 20 years, the minimum payout period (10 years) will last beyond the halfway date. The minimum payout provision, therefore, can significantly reduce the probability that total distributions under the contract will increase commensurately with D's longevity. Thus, the contract fails to be described in section 1275(a)(1)(B)(i).

Example 2. (i) *Facts.* The facts are the same as in *Example 1* of this paragraph (j)(5)(iv) except that the monthly distributions will last for the greater of D's life or a term certain. D may choose the length of the term certain subject to the restriction that, on the annuity starting date, the term certain must not exceed one-half of D's life expectancy as of the annuity starting date. The contract also does not provide for any adjustment in the amount of distributions by reason of the death of D or any other individual, except for a refund of D's aggregate premium payments less the sum of all prior distributions under the contract.

(ii) *Analysis.* The minimum payout provision qualifies for the exception in paragraph (j)(5)(iii)(B) of this section because distributions under the minimum payout provision will not continue past the halfway date and the contract does not provide for any adjustments in the amount of distributions by reason of the death of D or any other individual, other than a guaranteed death benefit described in paragraph (j)(5)(iii)(A) of this section. Accordingly, the existence of this minimum payout provision does not prevent the contract from being described in section 1275(a)(1)(B)(i).

(6) *Maximum payout provision.*—(i) *Impact on life contingency.*—The existence of a maximum payout provision can significantly reduce the probability that total distributions under the contract will increase commensurately with the longevity of the annuitant (or annuitants). Thus, the existence of any maximum payout provision causes the contract to fail to be described in section 1275(a)(1)(B)(i).

(ii) *Definition of maximum payout provision.*—A maximum payout provision is a contractual provision that provides that no distributions under the contract may be made after some date (the termination date), even if the terminating death has not yet occurred.

(iii) *Exception.*—Notwithstanding paragraphs (j)(2)(i)(A) and (j)(6)(i) of this section, an annuity contract does not fail to be described in section 1275(a)(1)(B)(i) merely because the contract contains a maximum payout provision, provided that the period of time from the annuity starting date to the termination date is at least twice as long as the period of time from the annuity starting date to the expected date of the terminating death, determined as of the annuity starting date, with respect to all then-surviving annuitants. The expected date of the terminating death must be determined by reference to the applicable mortality table prescribed under section 417(e)(3)(A)(ii)(I).

(iv) *Example.*—The following example illustrates the rules of this paragraph (j)(6):

Example. (i) *Facts.* On March 1, 1998, X issues a contract to E for cash. The contract provides that beginning on April 1, 1998, X will distribute to E a fixed amount of cash each month for E's life but that no distributions will be made after April 1, 2018. On April 1, 1998, E's life expectancy is 9 years.

(ii) *Analysis.* A maximum payout provision exists because if E survives beyond April 1, 2018, E will receive no further distributions under the contract. The period of time from the annuity starting date (April 1, 1998) to the termination date (April 1, 2018) is 20 years. Because this 20-year period is more than twice as long as E's life expectancy on April 1, 1998, the maximum payout provision qualifies for the exception in paragraph (j)(6)(iii) of this section. Accordingly, the existence of this maximum payout provision does not prevent the contract from being described in section 1275(a)(1)(B)(i).

(7) *Decreasing payout provision.*—(i) *General rule.*—If the amount of distributions during any contract year (other than the last year during which distributions are made) may be less than the amount of distributions during the preceding year, this possibility can significantly reduce the probability that total distributions under the contract will increase commensurately with the longevity of the annuitant (or annuitants). Thus, the existence of this possibility causes the contract to fail to be described in section 1275(a)(1)(B)(i).

(ii) *Exception for certain variable distributions.*—Notwithstanding paragraph (j)(7)(i) of this section, if an annuity contract provides that the amount of each distribution must increase and decrease in accordance with investment experience, cost of living indices, or similar fluctuating criteria, then the possibility that the amount of a distribution may decrease for this reason does not significantly reduce the probability that the distributions under the contract will increase commensurately with the longevity of the annuitant (or annuitants).

(iii) *Examples.*—The following examples illustrate the rules of this paragraph (j)(7):

Example 1. (i) *Facts.* On March 1, 1998, X issues a contract to F for $100,000. The contract provides that beginning on March 1, 1999, X will make distributions to F each year until F's death. Prior to March 1, 2009, distributions are to be made at a rate of $12,000 per year. Beginning on March 1, 2009, distributions are to be made at a rate of $3,000 per year.

(ii) *Analysis.* If F is alive in 2009, the amount distributed in 2009 ($3,000) will be less than the amount distributed in 2008 ($12,000). The exception in paragraph (j)(7)(ii) of this section does not apply. The decrease in the amount of any distributions made on or after March 1, 2009, can significantly reduce the probability that total distributions under the contract will increase commensurately with F's longevity. Thus, the contract fails to be described in section 1275(a)(1)(B)(i).

Example 2. (i) *Facts.* On March 1, 1998, X issues a contract to G for cash. The contract provides that, effective on any date G chooses (the annuity starting date), X will begin monthly distributions to G for G's life. Prior to the annuity starting date, the account value of the contract reflects the investment return, including changes in the market value, of an identifiable pool of assets. When G chooses the annuity starting date, G must also choose whether the distributions are to be fixed or variable. If fixed, the amount of each monthly distribution will remain constant at an amount that is no less than an amount based on the contract's account value as of the annuity starting date, G's age on that date, and permanent purchase rate guarantees contained in the contract. If variable, the monthly distributions will fluctuate to reflect the investment return, including changes in the market value, of the pool of assets. The monthly distributions under the contract will not otherwise decline from year to year.

(ii) *Analysis.* Because the only possible year-to-year declines in annuity distributions are described in paragraph (j)(7)(ii) of this section, the possibility that the amount of distributions may decline from the previous year does not reduce the probability that total distributions under the contract will increase commensurately with G's longevity. Thus, the potential fluctuation in the annuity distributions does not cause the contract to fail to be described in section 1275(a)(1)(B)(i).

(8) *Effective dates.*—(i) *In general.*—Except as provided in paragraph (j)(8)(ii) and (iii) of this section, this paragraph (j) is applicable for interest accruals on or after February 9, 1998 on annuity contracts held on or after February 9, 1998.

(ii) *Grandfathered contracts.*—This paragraph (j) does not apply to an annuity contract that was purchased before April 7, 1995. For purposes of this paragraph (j)(8), if any additional investment in such a contract is made on or after April 7, 1995, and the additional investment is not required to be made under a binding contractual obligation that was entered into before April 7, 1995, then the additional investment is treated as the purchase of a contract after April 7, 1995.

(iii) *Contracts consistent with the provisions of FI-33-94, published at 1995-1 C.B. 920. See § 601.601(d)(2)(ii)(b) of this chapter.*—This paragraph (j) does not apply to a contract purchased on or after April 7, 1995, and before February 9, 1998, if all payments under the contract are periodic payments that are made at least annually for the life (or lives) of one or more individuals, do not increase at any time during the term of the contract, and are part of a series of distributions that begins within one year of the date of the initial investment in the contract. An annuity contract that is otherwise described in the preceding sentence does not fail to be described therein merely because it also provides for a payment (or payments) made by reason of the death of one or more individuals.

(k) *Exception under section 1275(a)(1)(B)(ii) for annuities issued by an insurance company subject to tax under subchapter L of the Internal Revenue Code.*—(1) *Rule.*—For purposes of section 1275(a)(1)(B)(ii), an annuity contract issued by a foreign insurance company is considered as issued by an insurance company subject to tax under subchapter L if the insurance company is subject to tax under subchapter L with respect to income earned on the annuity contract.

(2) *Examples.*—The following examples illustrate the rule of paragraph (k)(1) of this section. Each example assumes that the annuity contract is a contract to which section 72 applies and was issued in a transaction where there is no consideration other than cash or another qualifying annuity contract, pursuant to the exercise of an election under an insurance contract by a beneficiary thereof on the death of the insured party, or in a transaction involving a qualified pension or employee benefit plan. The examples are as follows:

Example 1. Company X is an insurance company that is organized, licensed and doing business in Country Y. Company X does not have a U.S. trade or business and is not, under section 842, subject to U.S. income tax under subchapter L with respect to income earned on annuity contracts. A, a U.S. taxpayer, purchases an annuity contract from Company X in Country Y. The annuity contract is not excepted from the definition of a debt instrument by section 1275(a)(1)(B)(ii).

Example 2. The facts are the same as in *Example 1*, except that Company X has a U.S. trade or business. A purchased the annuity from Company X's U.S. trade or business. Under section 842(a), Company X is subject to tax under subchapter L with respect to income earned on the annuity contract. Under these facts, the annuity contract is excepted from the definition of a debt instrument by section 1275(a)(1)(B)(ii).

Example 3. The facts are the same as in *Example 2*, except that there is a tax treaty between Country Y and the United States. Company X is a resident of Country Y for purposes of the U.S.-Country Y tax treaty. Company X's activities in the U.S. do not constitute a permanent establishment under the U.S.-Country Y tax treaty. Because Company X does not have a U.S. permanent establishment, Company X is not subject to tax under subchapter L with respect to income earned on the annuity contract. Thus, the annuity contract is not excepted from the definition of a debt instrument by section 1275(a)(1)(B)(ii).

Example 4. The facts are the same as in *Example 1*, except that Company X is a foreign insurance corporation controlled by a U.S. shareholder. Company X does not make an election under section 953(d) to be treated as a domestic corporation. The controlling U.S. shareholder is required under sections 953 and 954 to include income earned on the annuity contract in its taxable income under subpart F. However, Company X is not subject to tax under subchapter L with respect to income earned on the annuity contract. Thus, the annuity contract is not excepted from the definition of a debt instrument by section 1275(a)(1)(B)(ii).

Example 5. The facts are the same as in *Example 4*, except that Company X properly elects under section 953(d) to be treated as a domestic corporation. By reason of its election, Company X is subject to tax under subchapter L with respect to income earned on the annuity contract. Thus, the annuity contract is excepted from the definition of a debt instrument by section 1275(a)(1)(B)(ii).

(3) *Effective date.*—This paragraph (k) is applicable for interest accruals on or after June 6, 2002. This paragraph (k) does not apply to an annuity contract that was purchased before January 12, 2001. For purposes of this paragraph (k), if any additional investment in a contract purchased before January 12, 2001, is made on or after January 12, 2001, and the additional investment is not required to be made under a binding written contractual obligation that was entered into before that date, then the additional investment is treated as the purchase of a contract after January 12, 2001. [Reg. §1.1275-1.]

☐ [T.D. 8517, 1-27-94. *Amended by T.D. 8746, 12-30-97; T.D. 8754, 1-7-98; T.D. 8934, 1-11-2001 and T.D. 8993, 5-6-2002.*]

[Reg. §1.1275-2]

§1.1275-2. Special rules relating to debt instruments.—(a) *Payment ordering rule.*—(1) *In general.*—Except as provided in paragraph (a)(2) of this section, each payment under a debt instrument is treated first as a payment of OID to the extent of the OID that has accrued as of the date the payment is due and has not been allocated to prior payments, and second as a payment of principal. Thus, no portion of any payment is treated as prepaid interest.

(2) *Exceptions.*—The rule in paragraph (a)(1) of this section does not apply to—

(i) A payment of qualified stated interest;

(ii) A payment of points deductible under section 461(g)(2), in the case of the issuer;

(iii) A pro rata prepayment described in paragraph (f)(2) of this section; or

(iv) A payment of additional interest or a similar charge provided with respect to amounts that are not paid when due.

(b) *Debt instruments distributed by corporations with respect to stock.*—(1) *Treatment of distribution.*—For purposes of determining the issue price of a debt instrument distributed by a corporation with respect to its stock, the instrument is treated as issued by the corporation for property. See section 1275(a)(4). Thus, under section 1273(b)(3), the issue price of a distributed debt instrument that is traded on an established market is its fair market value. The issue price of a distributed debt instrument that is not traded on an established market is determined under section 1274 or section 1273(b)(4).

(2) *Issue date.*—The issue date of a debt instrument distributed by a corporation with respect to its stock is the date of the distribution.

(c) *Aggregation of debt instruments.*—(1) *General rule.*—Except as provided in paragraph (c)(2) of this section, debt instruments issued in connection with the same transaction or related transactions (determined based on all the facts and circumstances) are treated as a single debt instrument for purposes of sections 1271 through 1275 and the regulations thereunder. This rule ordinarily applies only to debt instruments of a single issuer that are issued to a single holder. The Commissioner may, however, aggregate debt instruments that are issued by more than one issuer or that are issued to more than one holder if the debt instruments are issued in an arrangement that is designed to avoid the aggregation rule (e.g., debt instruments issued by or to related parties or debt instruments originally issued to different holders with the understanding that the debt instruments will be transferred to a single holder).

(2) *Exception if separate issue price established.*—Paragraph (c)(1) of this section does not apply to a debt instrument if—

(i) The debt instrument is part of an issue a substantial portion of which is traded on an established market within the meaning of § 1.1273-2(f); or

(ii) The debt instrument is part of an issue a substantial portion of which is issued for money (or for property traded on an established market within the meaning of § 1.1273-2(f)) to parties who are not related to the issuer or holder and who do not purchase other debt instruments of the same issuer in connection with the same transaction or related transactions.

(3) *Special rule for debt instruments that provide for the issuance of additional debt instruments.*—If, under the terms of a debt instrument (the original debt instrument), the holder may receive one or more additional debt instruments of the issuer, the additional debt instrument or instruments are aggregated with the original debt instrument. Thus, the payments made pursuant to an additional debt instrument are treated as made on the original debt instrument, and the distribution by the issuer of the additional debt instrument is not considered to be a payment made on the original debt instrument. This paragraph (c)(3) applies regardless of whether the right to receive an additional debt instrument is fixed as of the issue date or is contingent upon subsequent events. See § 1.1272-1(c) for the treatment of certain rights to issue additional debt instruments in lieu of cash payments.

(4) *Examples.*—The following examples illustrate the rules set forth in paragraphs (c)(1) and (c)(2) of this section.

Example 1. Exception for debt instruments issued separately to other purchasers. On January 1, 1995, Corporation M issues two series of bonds, Series A and Series B. The two series are sold for cash and have different terms. Although some holders purchase bonds from both series, a substantial portion of the bonds is issued to different holders. H purchases bonds from both series. Under the exception in paragraph (c)(2)(ii) of this section, the Series A and Series B bonds purchased by H are not aggregated.

Example 2. Tiered REMICs. Z forms a dual tier real estate mortgage investment conduit (REMIC). In the dual tier structure, Z forms REMIC A to acquire a pool of real estate mortgages and to issue a residual interest and several classes of regular interests. Contemporaneously, Z forms REMIC B to acquire as qualified mortgages all of the regular interests in REMIC A. REMIC B issues several classes of regular interests and a residual interest, and Z sells all of those interests to unrelated parties in a public offering. Under the general rule set out in paragraph (c)(1) of this section, all of the regular interests issued by REMIC A and held by REMIC B are treated as a single debt instrument for purposes of sections 1271 through 1275.

(d) *Special rules for Treasury securities.*—(1) *Issue price and issue date.*—The issue price of an issue of Treasury securities is the average price of the securities sold. The issue date of an issue of Treasury securities is the first settlement date on which a substantial amount of the securities in the issue is sold. For an issue of Treasury securities sold from November 1, 1998, to March 13, 2001, the issue price of the issue is the price of the securities sold at auction.

(2) *Reopenings of Treasury securities.*—(i) *Treatment of additional Treasury securities.*—Notwithstanding § 1.1275-1(f), additional Treasury securities issued in a qualified reopening are part of the same issue as the original Treasury securities. As a result, the additional Treasury securities have the same issue price, issue date, and (with respect to holders) the same adjusted issue price as the original Treasury securities. This paragraph (d)(2) applies to qualified reopenings that occur on or after March 25, 1992.

(ii) *Definitions.*—(A) *Additional Treasury securities.*—Additional Treasury securities are Treasury securities with terms that are in all respects identical to the terms of the original Treasury securities.

(B) *Original Treasury securities.*—Original Treasury securities are securities comprising any issue of outstanding Treasury securities.

(C) *Qualified reopening—reopenings on or after March 13, 2001.*—For a reopening of Treasury securities that occurs on or after March 13, 2001, a qualified reopening is a reopening that occurs not more than one year after the original Treasury securities were first issued to the public or, under paragraph (k)(3)(iii) of this section, a reopening in which the additional Treasury securities are issued with no more than a de minimis amount of OID.

(D) *Qualified reopening—reopenings before March 13, 2001.*—For a reopening of Treasury securities that occurs before March 13, 2001, a qualified reopening is a reopening that occurs not more than one year after the original Treasury securities were first issued to the public. However, for a reopening of Treasury securities (other than Treasury Inflation-Indexed Securities) that occurred prior to November 5, 1999, a qualified reopening is a reopening of Treasury securities that satisfied the preceding sentence and that was intended to alleviate an acute, protracted shortage of the original Treasury securities.

(e) *Disclosure of certain information to holders.*—Certain provisions of the regulations under section 163(e) and sections 1271 through 1275 provide that the issuer's determination of an item controls the holder's treatment of the item. In such a case, the issuer must provide the relevant information to the holder in a reasonable manner. For example, the issuer may provide the name or title and either the address or telephone number of a representative of the issuer who will make available to holders upon request the information required for holders to comply with these provisions of the regulations.

(f) *Treatment of pro rata prepayments.*—(1) *Treatment as retirement of separate debt instrument.*—A pro rata prepayment is treated as a payment in retirement of a portion of a debt instrument, which may result in a gain or loss to the holder. Generally, the gain or loss is calculated by assuming that the original debt instrument consists of two instruments, one that is retired and one that remains outstanding. The adjusted issue price, holder's adjusted basis, and accrued but unpaid OID of the original debt instrument, determined immediately before the pro rata prepayment, are allocated between these two instruments based on the portion of the instrument that is treated as retired by the pro rata prepayment.

(2) *Definition of pro rata prepayment.*—For purposes of paragraph (f)(1) of this section, a pro rata prepayment is a payment on a debt instrument made prior to maturity that—

(i) Is not made pursuant to the instrument's payment schedule (including a payment schedule determined under §1.1272-1(c)); and

(ii) Results in a substantially pro rata reduction of each payment remaining to be paid on the instrument.

(g) *Anti-abuse rule.*—(1) *In general.*—If a principal purpose in structuring a debt instrument or engaging in a transaction is to achieve a result that is unreasonable in light of the purposes of section 163(e), sections 1271 through 1275, or any related section of the Code, the Commissioner can apply or depart from the regulations under the applicable sections as necessary or appropriate to achieve a reasonable result. For example, if this paragraph (g) applies to a debt instrument that provides for a contingent payment, the Commissioner can treat the contingency as if it were a separate position. See also §1.988-2(b)(18) for debt instruments with payments denominated in (or determined by reference to) a currency other than the taxpayer's functional currency.

(2) *Unreasonable result.*—Whether a result is unreasonable is determined based on all the facts and circumstances. In making this determination, a significant fact is whether the treatment of the debt instrument is expected to have a substantial effect on the issuer's or a holder's U.S. tax liability. In the case of a contingent payment debt instrument, another significant fact is whether the result is obtainable without the application of §1.1275-4 and any related provisions (e.g., if the debt instrument and the contingency were entered into separately). A result will not be considered unreasonable, however, in the absence of an expected substantial effect on the present value of a taxpayer's tax liability.

(3) *Examples.*—The following examples illustrate the provisions of this paragraph (g):

Example 1. A issues a current-pay, increasing-rate note that provides for an early call option. Although the option is deemed exercised on the call date under §1.1272-1(c)(5), the option is not expected to be exercised by A. In addition, a principal purpose of including the option in the terms of the note is to limit the amount of interest income includible by the holder in the period prior to the call date by virtue of the option rules in §1.1272-1(c)(5). Moreover, the application of the option rules is expected to substantially reduce the present value of the holder's tax liability. Based on these facts, the application of §1.1272-1(c)(5) produces an unreasonable result. Therefore, under this paragraph (g), the Commissioner can apply the regulations (in whole or in part) to the note without regard to §1.1272-1(c)(5).

Example 2. C, a foreign corporation not subject to U.S. taxation, issues to a U.S. holder a debt instrument that provides for a contingent payment. The debt instrument is issued for cash and is subject to the noncontingent bond method in §1.1275-4(b). Six months after issuance, C and the holder modify the debt instrument so that there is a deemed reissuance of the instrument under section 1001. The new debt instrument is subject to the rules of §1.1275-4(c) rather than §1.1275-4(b). The application of §1.1275-4(c) is expected to substantially reduce the present value of the holder's tax liability as compared to the application of §1.1275-4(b). In addition, a principal purpose of the modification is to substantially reduce the present value of the holder's tax liability through the application of §1.1275-4(c). Based on these facts, the application of §1.1275-4(c) produces an unreasonable result. Therefore, under this paragraph (g), the Commissioner can apply the noncontingent bond method to the modified debt instrument.

Example 3. D issues a convertible debt instrument rather than an economically equivalent investment unit consisting of a debt instrument and a warrant. The convertible debt instrument is issued at par and provides for annual payments of interest. D issues the convertible debt instrument rather than the investment unit so that the debt instrument would not have OID. See §1.1273-2(j). In general, this is a reasonable result in light of the purposes of the applicable statutes. Therefore, the Commissioner generally will not use the authority under this paragraph (g) to depart from the application of §1.1273-2(j) in this case.

(4) *Effective date.*—This paragraph (g) applies to debt instruments issued on or after August 13, 1996.

Reg. §1.1275-2(f)(1)

(h) Remote and incidental contingencies.—*(1) In general.*—This paragraph (h) applies to a debt instrument if one or more payments on the instrument are subject to either a remote or incidental contingency. Whether a contingency is remote or incidental is determined as of the issue date of the debt instrument, including any date there is a deemed reissuance of the debt instrument under paragraph (h)(6)(ii) or (j) of this section or § 1.1272-1(c)(6). Except as otherwise provided, the treatment of the contingency under this paragraph (h) applies for all purposes of sections 163(e) (other than sections 163(e)(5)) and 1271 through 1275 and the regulations thereunder. For purposes of this paragraph (h), the possibility of impairment of a payment by insolvency, default, or similar circumstances is not a contingency.

(2) Remote contingencies.—A contingency is remote if there is a remote likelihood either that the contingency will occur or that the contingency will not occur. If there is a remote likelihood that the contingency will occur, it is assumed that the contingency will not occur. If there is a remote likelihood that the contingency will not occur, it is assumed that the contingency will occur.

(3) Incidental contingencies.—*(i) Contingency relating to amount.*—A contingency relating to the amount of a payment is incidental if, under all reasonably expected market conditions, the potential amount of the payment is insignificant relative to the total expected amount of the remaining payments on the debt instrument. If a payment on a debt instrument is subject to an incidental contingency described in this paragraph (h)(3)(i), the payment is ignored until the payment is made. However, see paragraph (h)(6)(i)(B) of this section for the treatment of the debt instrument if a change in circumstances occurs prior to the date the payment is made.

(ii) Contingency relating to time.—A contingency relating to the timing of a payment is incidental if, under all reasonably expected market conditions, the potential difference in the timing of the payment (from the earliest date to the latest date) is insignificant. If a payment on a debt instrument is subject to an incidental contingency described in this paragraph (h)(3)(ii), the payment is treated as made on the earliest date that the payment could be made pursuant to the contingency. If the payment is not made on this date, a taxpayer makes appropriate adjustments to take into account the delay in payment. However, see paragraph (h)(6)(i)(C) of this section for the treatment of the debt instrument if the delay is not insignificant.

(4) Aggregation rule.—For purposes of paragraph (h)(2) of this section, if a debt instrument provides for multiple contingencies each of which has a remote likelihood of occurring but, when all of the contingencies are considered together, there is a greater than remote likelihood that at least one of the contingencies will occur, none of the contingencies is treated as a remote contingency. For purposes of paragraph (h)(3)(i) of this section, if a debt instrument provides for multiple contingencies each of which is incidental but the potential total amount of all of the payments subject to the contingencies is not, under reasonably expected market conditions, insignificant relative to the total expected amount of the remaining payments on the debt instrument, none of the contingencies is treated as incidental.

(5) Consistency rule.—For purposes of paragraphs (h)(2) and (3) of this section, the issuer's determination that a contingency is either remote or incidental is binding on all holders. However, the issuer's determination is not binding on a holder that explicitly discloses that its determination is different from the issuer's determination. Unless otherwise prescribed by the Commissioner, the disclosure must be made on a statement attached to the holder's timely filed federal income tax return for the taxable year that includes the acquisition date of the debt instrument. See § 1.1275-2(e) for rules relating to the issuer's obligation to disclose certain information to holders.

(6) Subsequent adjustments.—*(i) Applicability.*—This paragraph (h)(6) applies to a debt instrument when there is a change in circumstances. For purposes of the preceding sentence, there is a change in circumstances if—

(A) A remote contingency actually occurs or does not occur, contrary to the assumption made in paragraph (h)(2) of this section;

(B) A payment subject to an incidental contingency described in paragraph (h)(3)(i) of this section becomes fixed in an amount that is not insignificant relative to the total expected amount of the remaining payments on the debt instrument; or

(C) A payment subject to an incidental contingency described in paragraph (h)(3)(ii) of this section becomes fixed such that the difference between the assumed payment date and the due date of the payment is not insignificant.

(ii) In general.—If a change in circumstances occurs, solely for purposes of sections 1272 and 1273, the debt instrument is treated as retired and then reissued on the date of the change in circumstances for an amount equal to the instrument's adjusted issue price on that date.

(iii) Contingent payment debt instruments.—Notwithstanding paragraph (h)(6)(ii) of this section, in the case of a contingent payment debt instrument subject to § 1.1275-4, if a change in circumstances occurs, no retirement or reissuance is treated as occurring, but any payment that is fixed as a result of the change in circum-

stances is governed by the rules in § 1.1275-4 that apply when the amount of a contingent payment becomes fixed.

(7) *Effective date.*—This paragraph (h) applies to debt. instruments issued on or after August 13, 1996.

(i) [Reserved]

(j) *Treatment of certain modifications.*—If the terms of a debt instrument are modified to defer one or more payments, and the modification does not cause an exchange under section 1001, then, solely for purposes of sections 1272 and 1273, the debt instrument is treated as retired and then reissued on the date of the modification for an amount equal to the instrument's adjusted issue price on that date. This paragraph (j) applies to debt instruments issued on or after August 13, 1996.

(k) *Reopenings.*—(1) *In general.*—Notwithstanding § 1.1275-1(f), additional debt instruments issued in a qualified reopening are part of the same issue as the original debt instruments. As a result, the additional debt instruments have the same issue date, the same issue price, and (with respect to holders) the same adjusted issue price as the original debt instruments.

(2) *Definitions.*—(i) *Original debt instruments.*—Original debt instruments are debt instruments comprising any single issue of outstanding debt instruments. For purposes of determining whether a particular reopening is a qualified reopening, debt instruments issued in prior qualified reopenings are treated as original debt instruments and debt instruments issued in the particular reopening are not so treated.

(ii) *Additional debt instruments.*—Additional debt instruments are debt instruments that, without the application of this paragraph (k)—

(A) Are part of a single issue of debt instruments;

(B) Are not part of the same issue as the original debt instruments; and

(C) Have terms that are in all respects identical to the terms of the original debt instruments as of the reopening date.

(iii) *Reopening date.*—The reopening date is the issue date of the additional debt instruments (determined without the application of this paragraph (k)).

(iv) *Announcement date.*—The announcement date is the later of seven days before the date on which the price of the additional debt instruments is established or the date on which the issuer's intent to reopen a security is publicly announced through one or more media, including an announcement reported on the standard electronic news services used by security broker-

dealers (for example, Reuters, Telerate, or Bloomberg).

(3) *Qualified reopening.*—(i) *Definition.*—A qualified reopening is a reopening of original debt instruments that is described in paragraph (k)(3)(ii) or (iii) of this section. In addition, see paragraph (d)(2) of this section to determine if a reopening of Treasury securities is a qualified reopening.

(ii) *Reopening within six months.*—A reopening is described in this paragraph (k)(3)(ii) if—

(A) The original debt instruments are publicly traded (within the meaning of § 1.1273-2(f));

(B) The reopening date of the additional debt instruments is not more than six months after the issue date of the original debt instruments; and

(C) On the date on which the price of the additional debt instruments is established (or, if earlier, the announcement date), the yield of the original debt instruments (based on their fair market value) is not more than 110 percent of the yield of the original debt instruments on their issue date (or, if the original debt instruments were issued with no more than a de minimis amount of OID, the coupon rate).

(iii) *Reopening with de minimis OID.*—A reopening (including a reopening of Treasury securities) is described in this paragraph (k)(3)(iii) if—

(A) The original debt instruments are publicly traded (within the meaning of § 1.1273-2(f)); and

(B) The additional debt instruments are issued with no more than a de minimis amount of OID (determined without the application of this paragraph (k)).

(iv) *Exceptions.*—This paragraph (k)(3) does not apply to a reopening of tax-exempt obligations (as defined in section 1275(a)(3)) or contingent payment debt instruments (within the meaning of § 1.1275-4).

(4) *Issuer's treatment of a qualified reopening.*—See § 1.163-7(e) for the issuer's treatment of the debt instruments that are part of a qualified reopening.

(5) *Effective date.*—This paragraph (k) applies to debt instruments that are part of a reopening where the reopening date is on or after March 13, 2001. [Reg. § 1.1275-2.]

☐ [*T.D. 8517, 1-27-94. Amended by T.D. 8674, 6-11-96; T.D. 8840, 11-3-99; T.D. 8934, 1-11-2001 and T.D. 9157, 8-27-2004.*]

[Reg. § 1.1275-3]

§ 1.1275-3. OID information reporting requirements.—(a) *In general.*—This section provides legending and information reporting requirements intended to facilitate the reporting of OID.

(b) *Information required to be set forth on face of debt instruments that are not publicly offered.*— (1) *In general.*—Except as provided in paragraph (b)(4) or paragraph (d) of this section, this paragraph (b) applies to any debt instrument that is not publicly offered (within the meaning of § 1.1275-1(h)), is issued in physical form, and has OID. The issuer of any such debt instrument must legend the instrument by stating on the face of the instrument that the debt instrument was issued with OID. In addition, the issuer must either—

(i) Set forth on the face of the debt instrument the issue price, the amount of OID, the issue date, the yield to maturity, and, in the case of a debt instrument subject to the rules of § 1.1275-4(b), the comparable yield and projected payment schedule; or

(ii) Provide the name or title and either the address or telephone number of a representative of the issuer who will, beginning no later than 10 days after the issue date, promptly make available to holders upon request the information described in paragraph (b)(1)(i) of this section.

(2) *Time for legending.*—An issuer may satisfy the requirements of this paragraph (b) by legending the debt instrument when it is first issued in physical form. Legending is not required, however, before the first holder of the debt instrument disposes of the instrument.

(3) *Legend must survive reissuance upon transfer.*—Any new security that is issued (for example, upon registration of transfer of ownership) must contain any required legend.

(4) *Exceptions.*—Paragraph (b)(1) of this section does not apply to debt instruments described in section 1272(a)(2) (relating to debt instruments not subject to the periodic OID inclusion rules), debt instruments issued by natural persons (as defined in § 1.6049-4(f)(2)), REMIC regular interests or other debt instruments subject to section 1272(a)(6), or stripped bonds and coupons within the meaning of section 1286.

(c) *Information required to be reported to Secretary upon issuance of publicly offered debt instruments.*— (1) *In general.*—Except as provided in paragraph (c)(3) or paragraph (d) of this section, the information reporting requirements of this paragraph (c) apply to any debt instrument that is publicly offered and has original issue discount. The issuer of any such debt instrument must make an information return on the form prescribed by the Commissioner (Form 8281, as of September 2, 1992). The prescribed form must be filed with the Internal Revenue Service in the manner specified on the form. The taxpayer must use the prescribed form even if other information returns are filed using other methods (e.g., electronic media), unless the Commissioner announces otherwise in a revenue procedure.

(2) *Time for filing information return.*—The prescribed form must be filed for each issue of publicly offered debt instruments within 30 days after the issue date of the issue.

(3) *Exceptions.*—The rules of paragraph (c)(1) of this section do not apply to debt instruments described in section 1272(a)(2), debt instruments issued by natural persons (as defined in § 1.6049-4(f)(2)), certificates of deposit, REMIC regular interests or other debt instruments subject to section 1272(a)(6), or (unless otherwise required by the Commissioner pursuant to a revenue ruling or revenue procedure) stripped bonds and coupons (within the meaning of section 1286).

(d) *Application to foreign issuers and U.S. issuers of foreign-targeted debt instruments.*—A foreign or domestic issuer is subject to the rules of this section with respect to an issue of debt instruments unless the issue is not offered for sale or resale in the United States in connection with its original issuance.

(e) *Penalties.*—See section 6706 for rules relating to the penalty imposed for failure to meet the information reporting requirements imposed by this section.

(f) *Effective date.*—Paragraphs (c), (d), and (e) of this section are effective for an issue of debt instruments issued after September 2, 1992. [Reg. § 1.1275-3.]

☐ [*T.D.* 8431, 9-2-92. *Amended by T.D.* 8517, 1-27-94 *and T.D.* 8674, 6-11-96.]

[Reg. § 1.1275-4]

§ 1.1275-4. Contingent payment debt instruments.—(a) *Applicability.*—(1) *In general.*—Except as provided in paragraph (a)(2) of this section, this section applies to any debt instrument that provides for one or more contingent payments. In general, paragraph (b) of this section applies to a contingent payment debt instrument that is issued for money or publicly traded property and paragraph (c) of this section applies to a contingent payment debt instrument that is issued for nonpublicly traded property. Paragraph (d) of this section provides special rules for tax-exempt obligations. See § 1.1275-6 for a taxpayer's treatment of a contingent payment debt instrument and a hedge.

(2) *Exceptions.*—This section does not apply to—

(i) A debt instrument that has an issue price determined under section 1273(b)(4) (e.g., a debt instrument subject to section 483);

(ii) A variable rate debt instrument (as defined in § 1.1275-5);

(iii) A debt instrument subject to § 1.1272-1(c) (a debt instrument that provides for certain contingencies) or § 1.1272-1(d) (a debt instrument that provides for a fixed yield);

(iv) A debt instrument subject to section 988 (except as provided in § 1.988-6);

(v) A debt instrument to which section 1272(a)(6) applies (certain interests in or mortgages held by a REMIC, and certain other debt instruments with payments subject to acceleration);

(vi) A debt instrument (other than a tax-exempt obligation) described in section 1272(a)(2) (e.g., U.S. savings bonds, certain loans between natural persons, and short-term taxable obligations);

(vii) An inflation-indexed debt instrument (as defined in § 1.1275-7); or

(viii) A debt instrument issued pursuant to a plan or arrangement if—

(A) The plan or arrangement is created by a state statute;

(B) A primary objective of the plan or arrangement is to enable the participants to pay for the costs of post-secondary education for themselves or their designated beneficiaries; and

(C) Contingent payments on the debt instrument are related to such objective.

(3) *Insolvency and default.*—A payment is not contingent merely because of the possibility of impairment by insolvency, default, or similar circumstances.

(4) *Convertible debt instruments.*—A debt instrument does not provide for contingent payments merely because it provides for an option to convert the debt instrument into the stock of the issuer, into the stock or debt of a related party (within the meaning of section 267(b) or 707(b)(1)), or into cash or other property in an amount equal to the approximate value of such stock or debt.

(5) *Remote and incidental contingencies.*—A payment is not a contingent payment merely because of a contingency that, as of the issue date, is either remote or incidental. See § 1.1275-2(h) for the treatment of remote and incidental contingencies.

(b) *Noncontingent bond method.*—(1) *Applicability.*—The noncontingent bond method described in this paragraph (b) applies to a contingent payment debt instrument that has an issue price determined under § 1.1273-2 (e.g., a contingent payment debt instrument that is issued for money or publicly traded property).

(2) *In general.*—Under the noncontingent bond method, interest on a debt instrument must be taken into account whether or not the amount of any payment is fixed or determinable in the

taxable year. The amount of interest that is taken into account for each accrual period is determined by constructing a projected payment schedule for the debt instrument and applying rules similar to those for accruing OID on a noncontingent debt instrument. If the actual amount of a contingent payment is not equal to the projected amount, appropriate adjustments are made to reflect the difference.

(3) *Description of method.*—The following steps describe how to compute the amount of income, deductions, gain, and loss under the noncontingent bond method:

(i) *Step one: Determine the comparable yield.*—Determine the comparable yield for the debt instrument under the rules of paragraph (b)(4) of this section. The comparable yield is determined as of the debt instrument's issue date.

(ii) *Step two: Determine the projected payment schedule.*—Determine the projected payment schedule for the debt instrument under the rules of paragraph (b)(4) of this section. The projected payment schedule is determined as of the issue date and remains fixed throughout the term of the debt instrument (except under paragraph (b)(9)(ii) of this section, which applies to a payment that is fixed more than 6 months before it is due).

(iii) *Step three: Determine the daily portions of interest.*—Determine the daily portions of interest on the debt instrument for a taxable year as follows. The amount of interest that accrues in each accrual period is the product of the comparable yield of the debt instrument (properly adjusted for the length of the accrual period) and the debt instrument's adjusted issue price at the beginning of the accrual period. See paragraph (b)(7)(ii) of this section to determine the adjusted issue price of the debt instrument. The daily portions of interest are determined by allocating to each day in the accrual period the ratable portion of the interest that accrues in the accrual period. Except as modified by paragraph (b)(3)(iv) of this section, the daily portions of interest are includible in income by a holder for each day in the holder's taxable year on which the holder held the debt instrument and are deductible by the issuer for each day during the issuer's taxable year on which the issuer was primarily liable on the debt instrument.

(iv) *Step four: Adjust the amount of income or deductions for differences between projected and actual contingent payments.*—Make appropriate adjustments to the amount of income or deductions attributable to the debt instrument in a taxable year for any differences between projected and actual contingent payments. See paragraph (b)(6) of this section to determine the amount of an adjustment and the treatment of the adjustment.

(4) Comparable yield and projected payment schedule.—This paragraph (b)(4) provides rules for determining the comparable yield and projected payment schedule for a debt instrument. The comparable yield and projected payment schedule must be supported by contemporaneous documentation showing that both are reasonable, are based on reliable, complete, and accurate data, and are made in good faith.

(i) Comparable yield.—*(A) In general.*—Except as provided in paragraph (b)(4)(i)(B) of this section, the comparable yield for a debt instrument is the yield at which the issuer would issue a fixed rate debt instrument with terms and conditions similar to those of the contingent payment debt instrument (the comparable fixed rate debt instrument), including the level of subordination, term, timing of payments, and general market conditions. For example, if a §1.1275-6 hedge (or the substantial equivalent) is available, the comparable yield is the yield on the synthetic fixed rate debt instrument that would result if the issuer entered into the §1.1275-6 hedge. If a §1.1275-6 hedge (or the substantial equivalent) is not available, but similar fixed rate debt instruments of the issuer trade at a price that reflects a spread above a benchmark rate, the comparable yield is the sum of the value of the benchmark rate on the issue date and the spread. In determining the comparable yield, no adjustments are made for the riskiness of the contingencies or the liquidity of the debt instrument. The comparable yield must be a reasonable yield for the issuer and must not be less than the applicable Federal rate (based on the overall maturity of the debt instrument).

(B) Presumption for certain debt instruments.—This paragraph (b)(4)(i)(B) applies to a debt instrument if the instrument provides for one or more contingent payments not based on market information and the instrument is part of an issue that is marketed or sold in substantial part to persons for whom the inclusion of interest under this paragraph (b) is not expected to have a substantial effect on their U.S. tax liability. If this paragraph (b)(4)(i)(B) applies to a debt instrument, the instrument's comparable yield is presumed to be the applicable Federal rate (based on the overall maturity of the debt instrument). A taxpayer may overcome this presumption only with clear and convincing evidence that the comparable yield for the debt instrument should be a specific yield (determined using the principles in paragraph (b)(4)(i)(A) of this section) that is higher than the applicable Federal rate. The presumption may not be overcome with appraisals or other valuations of non-publicly traded property. Evidence used to overcome the presumption must be specific to the issuer and must not be based on comparable issuers or general market conditions.

(ii) Projected payment schedule.—The projected payment schedule for a debt instrument includes each noncontingent payment and an amount for each contingent payment determined as follows:

(A) Market-based payments.—If a contingent payment is based on market information (a market-based payment), the amount of the projected payment is the forward price of the contingent payment. The forward price of a contingent payment is the amount one party would agree, as of the issue date, to pay an unrelated party for the right to the contingent payment on the settlement date (e.g., the date the contingent payment is made). For example, if the right to a contingent payment is substantially similar to an exchange-traded option, the forward price is the spot price of the option (the option premium) compounded at the applicable Federal rate from the issue date to the date the contingent payment is due.

(B) Other payments.—If a contingent payment is not based on market information (a non-market-based payment), the amount of the projected payment is the expected value of the contingent payment as of the issue date.

(C) Adjustments to the projected payment schedule.—The projected payment schedule must produce the comparable yield. If the projected payment schedule does not produce the comparable yield, the schedule must be adjusted consistent with the principles of this paragraph (b)(4) to produce the comparable yield. For example, the adjusted amounts of non-market-based payments must reasonably reflect the relative expected values of the payments and must not be set to accelerate or defer income or deductions. If the debt instrument contains both market-based and non-market-based payments, adjustments are generally made first to the non-market-based payments because more objective information is available for the market-based payments.

(iii) Market information.—For purposes of this paragraph (b), market information is any information on which an objective rate can be based under §1.1275-5(c)(1) or (2).

(iv) Issuer/holder consistency.—The issuer's projected payment schedule is used to determine the holder's interest accruals and adjustments. The issuer must provide the projected payment schedule to the holder in a manner consistent with the issuer disclosure rules of §1.1275-2(e). If the issuer does not create a projected payment schedule for a debt instrument or the issuer's projected payment schedule is unreasonable, the holder of the debt instrument must determine the comparable yield and projected payment schedule for the debt instrument under the rules of this paragraph (b)(4). A holder that determines its own projected payment schedule must

explicitly disclose this fact and the reason why the holder set its own schedule (e.g., why the issuer's projected payment schedule is unreasonable). Unless otherwise prescribed by the Commissioner, the disclosure must be made on a statement attached to the holder's timely filed federal income tax return for the taxable year that includes the acquisition date of the debt instrument.

(v) *Issuer's determination respected.*— (A) *In general.*—If the issuer maintains the contemporaneous documentation required by this paragraph (b)(4), the issuer's determination of the comparable yield and projected payment schedule will be respected unless either is unreasonable.

(B) *Unreasonable determination.*—For purposes of paragraph (b)(4)(v)(A) of this section, a comparable yield or projected payment schedule generally will be considered unreasonable if it is set with a purpose to overstate, understate, accelerate, or defer interest accruals on the debt instrument. In a determination of whether a comparable yield or projected payment schedule is unreasonable, consideration will be given to whether the treatment of the debt instrument under this section is expected to have a substantial effect on the issuer's or holder's U.S. tax liability. For example, if a taxable issuer markets a debt instrument to a holder not subject to U.S. taxation, the comparable yield will be given close scrutiny and will not be respected unless contemporaneous documentation shows that the yield is not too high.

(C) *Exception.*—Paragraph (b)(4)(v)(A) of this section does not apply to a debt instrument subject to paragraph (b)(4)(i)(B) of this section (concerning a yield presumption for certain debt instruments that provide for non-market-based payments).

(vi) *Examples.*—The following examples illustrate the provisions of this paragraph (b)(4). In each example, assume that the instrument described is a debt instrument for federal income tax purposes. No inference is intended, however, as to whether the instrument is a debt instrument for federal income tax purposes.

Example 1. Market-based payment—(i) *Facts.* On December 31, 1996, X corporation issues for $1,000,000 a debt instrument that matures on December 31, 2006. The debt instrument provides for annual payments of interest, beginning in 1997, at the rate of 6 percent and for a payment at maturity equal to $1,000,000 plus the excess, if any, of the price of 10,000 shares of publicly traded stock in an unrelated corporation on the maturity date over $350,000, or less the excess, if any, of $350,000 over the price of 10,000 shares of the stock on the maturity date. On the issue date, the forward price to purchase 10,000 shares of the stock on December 31, 2006, is $350,000.

(ii) *Comparable yield.* Under paragraph (b)(4)(i) of this section, the debt instrument's comparable yield is the yield on the synthetic debt instrument that would result if X corporation entered into a § 1.1275-6 hedge. A § 1.1275-6 hedge in this case is a forward contract to purchase 10,000 shares of the stock on December 31, 2006. If X corporation entered into this hedge, the resulting synthetic debt instrument would yield 6 percent, compounded annually. Thus, the comparable yield on the debt instrument is 6 percent, compounded annually.

(iii) *Projected payment schedule.* Under paragraph (b)(4)(ii) of this section, the projected payment schedule for the debt instrument consists of 10 annual payments of $60,000 and a projected amount for the contingent payment at maturity. Because the right to the contingent payment is based on market information, the projected amount of the contingent payment is the forward price of the payment. The right to the contingent payment is substantially similar to a right to a payment of $1,000,000 combined with a cash-settled forward contract for the purchase of 10,000 shares of the stock for $350,000 on December 31, 2006. Because the forward price to purchase 10,000 shares of the stock on December 31, 2006, is $350,000, the amount to be received or paid under the forward contract is projected to be zero. As a result, the projected amount of the contingent payment at maturity is $1,000,000, consisting of the $1,000,000 base amount and no additional amount to be received or paid under the forward contract.

(A) Assume, alternatively, that on the issue date the forward price to purchase 10,000 shares of the stock on December 31, 2006, is $370,000. If X corporation entered into a § 1.1275-6 hedge (a forward contract to purchase the shares for $370,000), the resulting synthetic debt instrument would yield 6.15 percent, compounded annually. Thus, the comparable yield on the debt instrument is 6.15 percent, compounded annually. The projected payment schedule for the debt instrument consists of 10 annual payments of $60,000 and a projected amount for the contingent payment at maturity. The projected amount of the contingent payment is $1,020,000, consisting of the $1,000,000 base amount plus the excess $20,000 of the forward price of the stock over the purchase price of the stock under the forward contract.

(B) Assume, alternatively, that on the issue date the forward price to purchase 10,000 shares of the stock on December 31, 2006, is $330,000. If X corporation entered into a § 1.1275-6 hedge, the resulting synthetic debt instrument would yield 5.85 percent, compounded annually. Thus, the comparable yield on the debt instrument is 5.85 percent, compounded annually. The projected payment schedule for the debt instrument consists of 10 annual payments of $60,000 and a projected amount for the contingent payment at maturity. The projected amount of the contingent payment is $980,000, consisting of the $1,000,000 base amount minus the excess $20,000 of the purchase price of the stock under the forward contract over the forward price of the stock.

Example 2. Non-market-based payments—(i) *Facts.* On December 31, 1996, Y issues to Z for $1,000,000 a debt instrument that matures on December 31, 2000. The debt instrument has a stated principal amount of $1,000,000, payable at maturity, and provides for payments on December 31 of each year, beginning in 1997, of $20,000 plus 1 percent of Y's gross receipts, if any, for the year. On the issue date, Y has outstanding fixed rate debt instruments with maturities of 2 to 10 years that trade at a price that reflects an average of 100 basis points over Treasury bonds. These debt instruments have terms and conditions similar to those of the debt instrument. Assume that on December 31, 1996, 4-year Treasury bonds have a yield of 6.5 percent, compounded annually, and that no § 1.1275-6 hedge is available for the debt instrument. In addition, assume that the interest inclusions attributable to the debt instru-

Date	
12/31/1997	. . . .
12/31/1998	. . . .
12/31/1999	. . . .
12/31/2000	. . . .

(5) *Qualified stated interest.*—No amounts payable on a debt instrument to which this paragraph (b) applies are qualified stated interest within the meaning of § 1.1273-1(c).

(6) *Adjustments.*—This paragraph (b)(6) provides rules for the treatment of positive and negative adjustments under the noncontingent bond method. A taxpayer takes into account only those adjustments that occur during a taxable year while the debt instrument is held by the taxpayer or while the taxpayer is primarily liable on the debt instrument.

(i) *Determination of positive and negative adjustments.*—If the amount of a contingent payment is more than the projected amount of the contingent payment, the difference is a positive adjustment on the date of the payment. If the amount of a contingent payment is less than the projected amount of the contingent payment, the difference is a negative adjustment on the date of the payment (or on the scheduled date of the payment if the amount of the payment is zero).

(ii) *Treatment of net positive adjustments.*— The amount, if any, by which total positive adjustments on a debt instrument in a taxable year exceed the total negative adjustments on the debt instrument in the taxable year is a net positive adjustment. A net positive adjustment is treated as additional interest for the taxable year.

(iii) *Treatment of net negative adjustments.*— The amount, if any, by which total negative adjustments on a debt instrument in a taxable year

ment are expected to have a substantial effect on Z's U.S. tax liability.

(ii) *Comparable yield.* The comparable yield for the debt instrument is equal to the value of the benchmark rate (i.e., the yield on 4-year Treasury bonds) on the issue date plus the spread. Thus, the debt instrument's comparable yield is 7.5 percent, compounded annually.

(iii) *Projected payment schedule.* Y anticipates that it will have no gross receipts in 1997, but that it will have gross receipts in later years, and those gross receipts will grow each year for the next three years. Based on its business projections, Y believes that it is not unreasonable to expect that its gross receipts in 1999 and each year thereafter will grow by between 6 percent and 13 percent over the prior year. Thus, Y must take these expectations into account in establishing a projected payment schedule for the debt instrument that results in a yield of 7.5 percent, compounded annually. Accordingly, Y could reasonably set the following projected payment schedule for the debt instrument:

Noncontingent payment	Contingent payment
$20,000	$0
20,000	70,000
20,000	75,600
1,020,000	83,850

exceed the total positive adjustments on the debt instrument in the taxable year is a net negative adjustment. A taxpayer's net negative adjustment on a debt instrument for a taxable year is treated as follows:

(A) *Reduction of interest accruals.*—A net negative adjustment first reduces interest for the taxable year that the taxpayer would otherwise account for on the debt instrument under paragraph (b)(3)(iii) of this section.

(B) *Ordinary income or loss.*—If the net negative adjustment exceeds the interest for the taxable year that the taxpayer would otherwise account for on the debt instrument under paragraph (b)(3)(iii) of this section, the excess is treated as ordinary loss by a holder and ordinary income by an issuer. However, the amount treated as ordinary loss by a holder is limited to the amount by which the holder's total interest inclusions on the debt instrument exceed the total amount of the holder's net negative adjustments treated as ordinary loss on the debt instrument in prior taxable years. The amount treated as ordinary income by an issuer is limited to the amount by which the issuer's total interest deductions on the debt instrument exceed the total amount of the issuer's net negative adjustments treated as ordinary income on the debt instrument in prior taxable years.

(C) *Carryforward.*—If the net negative adjustment exceeds the sum of the amounts treated by the taxpayer as a reduction of interest and as ordinary income or loss (as the case may

Reg. § 1.1275-4(b)(6)(iii)(C)

be) on the debt instrument for the taxable year, the excess is a negative adjustment carryforward for the taxable year. In general, a taxpayer treats a negative adjustment carryforward for a taxable year as a negative adjustment on the debt instrument on the first day of the succeeding taxable year. However, if a holder of a debt instrument has a negative adjustment carryforward on the debt instrument in a taxable year in which the debt instrument is sold, exchanged, or retired, the negative adjustment carryforward reduces the holder's amount realized on the sale, exchange, or retirement. If an issuer of a debt instrument has a negative adjustment carryforward on the debt instrument for a taxable year in which the debt instrument is retired, the issuer takes the negative adjustment carryforward into account as ordinary income.

(D) *Treatment under section 67.*—A net negative adjustment is not subject to section 67 (the 2-percent floor on miscellaneous itemized deductions).

(iv) *Cross-references.*—If a holder has a basis in a debt instrument that is different from the debt instrument's adjusted issue price, the holder may have additional positive or negative adjustments under paragraph (b)(9)(i) of this section. If the amount of a contingent payment is fixed more than 6 months before the date it is due, the amount and timing of the adjustment are determined under paragraph (b)(9)(ii) of this section.

(7) *Adjusted issue price, adjusted basis, and retirement.*—(i) *In general.*—If a debt instrument is subject to the noncontingent bond method, this paragraph (b)(7) provides rules to determine the adjusted issue price of the debt instrument, the holder's basis in the debt instrument, and the treatment of any scheduled or unscheduled retirements. In general, because any difference between the actual amount of a contingent payment and the projected amount of the payment is taken into account as an adjustment to income or deduction, the projected payments are treated as the actual payments for purposes of making adjustments to issue price and basis and determining the amount, of any contingent payment made on a scheduled retirement.

(ii) *Definition of adjusted issue price.*—The adjusted issue price of a debt instrument is equal to the debt instrument's issue price, increased by the interest previously accrued on the debt instrument under paragraph (b)(3)(iii) of this section (determined without regard to any adjustments taken into account under paragraph (b)(3)(iv) of this section), and decreased by the amount of any noncontingent payment and the projected amount of any contingent payment previously made on the debt instrument. See paragraph (b)(9)(ii) of this section for special rules that apply when a contingent payment is fixed more than 6 months before it is due.

(iii) *Adjustments to basis.*—A holder's basis in a debt instrument is increased by the interest previously accrued by the holder on the debt instrument under paragraph (b)(3)(iii) of this section (determined without regard to any adjustments taken into account under paragraph (b)(3)(iv) of this section), and decreased by the amount of any noncontingent payment and the projected amount of any contingent payment previously made on the debt instrument to the holder. See paragraph (b)(9)(i) of this section for special rules that apply when basis is different from adjusted issue price and paragraph (b)(9)(ii) of this section for special rules that apply when a contingent payment is fixed more than 6 months before it is due.

(iv) *Scheduled retirements.*—For purposes of determining the amount realized by a holder and the repurchase price paid by the issuer on the scheduled retirement of a debt instrument, a holder is treated as receiving, and the issuer is treated as paying, the projected amount of any contingent payment due at maturity. If the amount paid or received is different from the projected amount, see paragraph (b)(6) of this section for the treatment of the difference by the taxpayer. Under paragraph (b)(6)(iii)(C) of this section, the amount realized by a holder on the retirement of a debt instrument is reduced by any negative adjustment carryforward determined in the taxable year of the retirement.

(v) *Unscheduled retirements.*—An unscheduled retirement of debt instrument (or the receipt of a pro-rata prepayment that is treated as a retirement of a portion of a debt instrument under § 1.1275-2(f)) is treated as a repurchase of the debt instrument (or a pro-rata portion of the debt instrument) by the issuer from the holder for the amount paid by the issuer to the holder.

(vi) *Examples.*—The following examples illustrate the following provisions of paragraphs (b)(6) and (7) of this section. In each example, assume that the instrument described is a debt instrument for federal income tax purposes. No inference is intended, however, as to whether the instrument is a debt instrument for federal income tax purposes.

Example 1. Treatment of positive and negative adjustments—(i) *Facts.* On December 31, 1996, Z, a calendar year taxpayer, purchases a debt instrument subject to this paragraph (b) at original issue for $1,000. The debt instrument's comparable yield is 10 percent, compounded annually, and the projected payment schedule provides for payments of $500 on December 31, 1997 (consisting of a noncontingent payment of $375 and a projected amount of $125) and $660 on December 31, 1998 (consisting of a noncontingent payment of $600 and a projected amount of $60). The debt instrument is a capital asset in the hands of Z.

Reg. § 1.1275-4(b)(6)(iii)(D)

(ii) *Adjustment in 1997.* Based on the projected payment schedule, Z's total daily portions of interest on the debt instrument are $100 for 1997 (issue price of $1,000 × 10 percent). Assume that the payment actually made on December 31, 1997, is $375, rather than the projected $500. Under paragraph (b)(6)(i) of this section, Z has a negative adjustment of $125 on December 31, 1997, attributable to the difference between the amount of the actual payment and the amount of the projected payment. Because Z has no positive adjustments for 1997, Z has a net negative adjustment of $125 on the debt instrument for 1997. This net negative adjustment reduces to zero the $100 total daily portions of interest Z would otherwise include in income in 1997. Accordingly, Z has no interest income on the debt instrument for 1997. Because Z had no interest inclusions on the debt instrument for prior taxable years, the remaining $25 of the net negative adjustment is a negative adjustment carryforward for 1997 that results in a negative adjustment of $25 on January 1, 1998.

(iii) *Adjustment to issue price and basis.* Z's total daily portions of interest on the debt instrument are $100 for 1997. The adjusted issue price of the debt instrument and Z's adjusted basis in the debt instrument are increased by this amount, despite the fact that Z does not include this amount in income because of the net negative adjustment for 1997. In addition, the adjusted issue price of the debt instrument and Z's adjusted basis in the debt instrument are decreased on December 31, 1997, by the projected amount of the payment on that date ($500). Thus, on January 1, 1998, Z's adjusted basis in the debt instrument and the adjusted issue price of the debt instrument are $600.

(iv) *Adjustments in 1998.* Based on the projected payment schedule, Z's total daily portions of interest are $60 for 1998 (adjusted issue price of $600 × 10 percent). Assume that the payment actually made on December 31, 1998, is $700, rather than the projected $660. Under paragraph (b)(6)(i) of this section, Z has a positive adjustment of $40 on December 31, 1998, attributable to the difference between the amount of the actual payment and the amount of the projected payment. Because Z also has a negative adjustment of $25 on January 1, 1998, Z has a net positive adjustment of $15 on the debt instrument for 1998 (the excess of the $40 positive adjustment over the $25 negative adjustment). As a result, Z has $75 of interest income on the debt instrument for 1998 (the $15 net positive adjustment plus the $60 total daily portions of interest that are taken into account by Z in that year).

(v) *Retirement.* Based on the projected payment schedule, Z's adjusted basis in the debt instrument immediately before the payment at maturity is $660 ($600 plus $60 total daily portions of interest for 1998). Even though Z receives $700 at maturity, for purposes of

determining the amount realized by Z on retirement of the debt instrument, Z is treated as receiving the projected amount of the contingent payment on December 31, 1998. Therefore, Z is treated as receiving $660 on December 31, 1998. Because Z's adjusted basis in the debt instrument immediately before its retirement is $660, Z recognizes no gain or loss on the retirement.

Example 2. Negative adjustment carryforward for year of sale—(i) *Facts.* Assume the same facts as in *Example 1* of this paragraph (b)(7)(vi), except that Z sells the debt instrument on January 1, 1998, for $630.

(ii) *Gain on sale.* On the date the debt instrument is sold, Z's adjusted basis in the debt instrument is $600. Because Z has a negative adjustment of $25 on the debt instrument on January 1, 1998, and has no positive adjustments on the debt instrument in 1998, Z has a net negative adjustment for 1998 of $25. Because Z has not included in income any interest on the debt instrument, the entire $25 net negative adjustment is a negative adjustment carryforward for the taxable year of the sale. Under paragraph (b)(6)(iii)(C) of this section, the $25 negative adjustment carryforward reduces the amount realized by Z on the sale of the debt instrument from $630 to $605. Thus, Z has a gain on the sale of $5 ($605-$600). Under paragraph (b)(8)(i) of this section, the gain is treated as interest income.

Example 3. Negative adjustment carryforward for year of retirement—(i) *Facts.* Assume the same facts as in *Example 1* of this paragraph (b)(7)(vi), except that the payment actually made on December 31, 1998, is $615, rather than the projected $660.

(ii) *Adjustments in 1998.* Under paragraph (b)(6)(i) of this section, Z has a negative adjustment of $45 on December 31, 1998, attributable to the difference between the amount of the actual payment and the amount of the projected payment. In addition, Z has a negative adjustment of $25 on January 1, 1998. See *Example 1* (ii) of this paragraph (b)(7)(vi). Because Z has no positive adjustments in 1998, Z has a net negative adjustment of $70 for 1998. This net negative adjustment reduces to zero the $60 total daily portions of interest Z would otherwise include in income for 1998. Therefore, Z has no interest income on the debt instrument for 1998. Because Z had no interest inclusions on the debt instrument for 1997, the remaining $10 of the net negative adjustment is a negative adjustment carryforward for 1998 that reduces the amount realized by Z on retirement of the debt instrument.

(iii) *Loss on retirement.* Immediately before the payment at maturity, Z's adjusted basis in the debt instrument is $660. Under paragraph (b)(7)(iv) of this section, Z is treated as receiving the projected amount of the contingent payment, or $660, as the payment at maturity. Under paragraph (b)(6)(iii)(C) of this section, however, this amount is reduced by any negative adjustment carryforward determined for the taxable year of retirement to calculate the amount Z realizes on retirement of the debt instrument. Thus, Z has a loss of $10 on the retirement of the debt instrument, equal to the amount by which Z's adjusted basis in the debt instrument ($660) exceeds the amount Z realizes on the retirement of the debt instrument ($660 minus the $10 negative adjustment carryforward). Under paragraph (b)(8)(ii) of this section, the loss is a capital loss.

(8) *Character on sale, exchange, or retirement.*—(i) *Gain.*—Any gain recognized by a holder on the sale, exchange, or retirement of a debt instrument subject to this paragraph (b) is interest income.

(ii) *Loss.*—Any loss recognized by a holder on the sale, exchange, or retirement of a debt instrument subject to this paragraph (b) is ordinary loss to the extent that the holder's total interest inclusions on the debt instrument exceed the total net negative adjustments on the debt instrument the holder took into account as ordinary loss. Any additional *loss is* treated as *loss* from the sale, exchange, or retirement of the debt instrument. However, any loss that would otherwise be ordinary under this paragraph (b)(8)(ii) and that is attributable to the holder's basis that could not be amortized under section 171(b)(4) is loss from the sale, exchange, or retirement of the debt instrument.

(iii) *Special rule if there are no remaining contingent payments on the debt instrument.*—(A) *In general.*—Notwithstanding paragraphs (b)(8)(i) and (ii) of this section, if, at the time of the sale, exchange, or retirement of the debt instrument, there are no remaining contingent payments due on the debt instrument under the projected payment schedule, any gain or loss recognized by the holder is gain or loss from the sale, exchange, or retirement of the debt instrument. See paragraph (b)(9)(ii) of this section to determine whether there are no remaining contingent payments on a debt instrument that provides for fixed but deferred contingent payments.

(B) *Exception for certain positive adjustments.*—Notwithstanding paragraph (b)(8)(iii)(A) of this section, if a positive adjustment on a debt instrument is spread under paragraph (b)(9)(ii)(F) or (G) of this section, any gain recognized by the holder on the sale, exchange, or retirement of the instrument is treated as interest income to the extent of the positive adjustment that has not yet been accrued and included in income by the holder.

(iv) *Examples.*—The following examples illustrate the provisions of this paragraph (b)(8). In each example, assume that the instrument described is a debt instrument for federal income tax purposes. No inference is intended, however,

as to whether the instrument is a debt instrument for federal income tax purposes.

Example 1. Gain on sale—(i) *Facts.* On January 1, 1998, D, a calendar year taxpayer, sells a debt instrument that is subject to paragraph (b) of this section for $1,350. The projected payment schedule for the debt instrument provides for contingent payments after January 1, 1998. On January 1, 1998, D has an adjusted basis in the debt instrument of $1,200. In addition, D has a negative adjustment carryforward of $50 for 1997 that, under paragraph (b)(6)(iii)(C) of this section, results in a negative adjustment of $50 on January 1, 1998. D has no positive adjustments on the debt instrument on January 1, 1998.

(ii) *Character of gain.* Under paragraph (b)(6) of this section, the $50 negative adjustment on January 1, 1998, results in a negative adjustment carryforward for 1998, the taxable year of the sale of the debt instrument. Under paragraph (b)(6)(iii)(C) of this section, the negative adjustment carryforward reduces the amount realized by D on the sale of the debt instrument from $1,350 to $1,300. As a result, D realizes a $100 gain on the sale of the debt instrument, equal to the $1,300 amount realized minus D's $1,200 adjusted basis in the debt instrument. Under paragraph (b)(8)(i) of this section, the gain is interest income to D.

Example 2. Loss on sale—(i) *Facts.* On December 31, 1996, E, a calendar year taxpayer, purchases a debt instrument at original issue for $1,000. The debt instrument is a capital asset in the hands of E. The debt instrument provides for a single payment on December 31, 1998 (the maturity date of the instrument), of $1,000 plus an amount based on the increase, if any, in the price of a specified commodity over the term of the instrument. The comparable yield for the debt instrument is 9.54 percent, compounded annually, and the projected payment schedule provides for a payment of $1,200 on December 31, 1998. Based on the projected payment schedule, the total daily portions of interest are $95 for 1997 and $105 for 1998.

(ii) *Ordinary loss.* Assume that E sells the debt instrument for $1,050 on December 31, 1997. On that date, E has an adjusted basis in the debt instrument of $1,095 ($1,000 original basis, plus total daily portions of $95 for 1997). Therefore, E realizes a $45 loss on the sale of the debt instrument ($1,050 - $1,095). The loss is ordinary to the extent E's total interest inclusions on the debt instrument ($95) exceed the total net negative adjustments on the instrument that E took into account as an ordinary loss. Because E has not had any net negative adjustments on the debt instrument, the $45 loss is an ordinary loss.

(iii) *Capital loss.* Alternatively, assume that E sells the debt instrument for $990 on December 31, 1997. E realizes a $105 loss on the sale of the debt instrument ($990 - $1,095). The loss is ordinary to the extent E's total interest inclusions on the debt instrument ($95) exceed the total net negative adjustments on the instrument that E took into account as an ordinary loss. Because E has not had any net negative adjustments on the debt instrument, $95 of the $105 loss is an ordinary loss. The remaining $10 of the $105 loss is a capital loss.

(9) *Operating rules.*—The rules of this paragraph (b)(9) apply to a debt instrument subject to the noncontingent bond method notwithstanding any other rule of this paragraph (b).

(i) *Basis different from adjusted issue price.*— This paragraph (b)(9)(i) provides rules for a holder whose basis in a debt instrument is different from the adjusted issue price of the debt instrument (e.g., a subsequent holder that purchases the debt instrument for more or less than the instrument's adjusted issue price).

(A) *General rule.*—The holder accrues interest under paragraph (b)(3)(iii) of this section and makes adjustments under paragraph (b)(3)(iv) of this section based on the projected payment schedule determined as of the issue date of the debt instrument. However, upon acquiring the debt instrument, the holder must reasonably allocate any difference between the adjusted issue price and the basis to daily portions of interest or projected payments over the remaining term of the debt instrument. Allocations are taken into account under paragraphs (b)(9)(i)(B) and (C) of this section.

(B) *Basis greater than adjusted issue price.*—If the holder's basis in the debt instrument exceeds the debt instrument's adjusted issue price, the amount of the difference allocated to a daily portion of interest or to a projected payment is treated as a negative adjustment on the date the daily portion accrues or the payment is made. On the date of the adjustment, the holder's adjusted basis in the debt instrument is reduced by the amount the holder treats as a negative adjustment under this paragraph (b)(9)(i)(B). See paragraph (b)(9)(ii)(E) of this section for a special rule that applies when a contingent payment is fixed more than 6 months before it is due.

(C) *Basis less than adjusted issue price.*— If the holder's basis in the debt instrument is less than the debt instrument's adjusted issue price, the amount of the difference allocated to a daily portion of interest or to a projected payment is treated as a positive adjustment on the date the daily portion accrues or the payment is made. On the date of the adjustment, the holder's adjusted basis in the debt instrument is increased by the amount the holder treats as a positive adjustment under this paragraph (b)(9)(i)(C). See paragraph (b)(9)(ii)(E) of this section for a special rule that applies when a contingent payment is fixed more than 6 months before it is due.

(D) *Premium and discount rules do not apply.*—The rules for accruing premium and discount in sections 171, 1272(a)(7), 1276, and 1281 do not apply. Other rules of those sections, such as section 171(b)(4), continue to apply to the extent relevant.

(E) *Safe harbor for exchange listed debt instruments.*—If the debt instrument is exchange listed property (within the meaning of § 1.1273-2(f)(2), it is reasonable for the holder to allocate any difference between the holder's basis and the adjusted issue price of the debt instrument pro-rata to daily portions of interest (as determined under paragraph (b)(3)(iii) of this section) over the remaining term of the debt instrument. A pro-rata allocation is not reasonable, however, to the extent the holder's yield on the debt instrument, determined after taking into account the amounts allocated under this paragraph (b)(9)(i)(E), is less than the applicable Federal rate for the instrument. For purposes of the preceding sentence, the applicable Federal rate for the debt instrument is determined as if the purchase date were the issue date and the remaining term of the instrument were the term of the instrument.

(F) *Examples.*—The following examples illustrate the provisions of this paragraph (b)(9)(i). In each example, assume that the instrument described is a debt instrument for federal income tax purposes. No inference is intended, however, as to whether the instrument is a debt instrument for federal income tax purposes. In addition, assume that each instrument is not exchange listed property.

Example 1. Basis greater than adjusted issue price—(i) *Facts.* On July 1, 1998, Z purchases for $1,405 a debt instrument that matures on December 31, 1999, and promises to pay on the maturity date $1,000 plus the increase, if any, in the price of a specified amount of a commodity from the issue date to the maturity date. The debt instrument was originally issued on December 31, 1996, for an issue price of $1,000. The comparable yield for the debt instrument is 10.25 percent, compounded semiannually, and the projected payment schedule for the debt instrument (determined as of the issue date) provides for a single payment at maturity of $1,350. At the time of the purchase, the debt instrument has an adjusted issue price of $1,162, assuming semiannual accrual periods ending on December 31 and June 30 of each year. The increase in the value of the debt instrument over its adjusted issue price is due to an increase in the expected amount of the contingent payment and not to a decrease in market interest rates. The debt instrument is a capital asset in the hands of Z. Z is a calendar year taxpayer.

(ii) *Allocation of the difference between basis and adjusted issue price.* Z's basis in the debt instrument on July 1, 1998, is $1,405. Under paragraph (b)(9)(i)(A) of this section, Z allocates the

$243 difference between basis ($1,405) and adjusted issue price ($1,162) to the contingent payment at maturity. Z's allocation of the difference between basis and adjusted issue price is reasonable because the increase in the value of the debt instrument over its adjusted issue price is due to an increase in the expected amount of the contingent payment.

(iii) *Treatment of debt instrument for 1998.* Based on the projected payment schedule, $60 of interest accrues on the debt instrument from July 1, 1998 to December 31, 1998 (the product of the debt instrument's adjusted issue price on July 1, 1998 ($1,162) and the comparable yield properly adjusted for the length of the accrual period (10.25 percent/2)). Z has no net negative or positive adjustments for 1998. Thus, Z includes in income $60 of total daily portions of interest for 1998. On December 31, 1998, Z's adjusted basis in the debt instrument is $1,465 ($1,405 original basis, plus total daily portions of $60 for 1998).

(iv) *Effect of allocation to contingent payment at maturity.* Assume that the payment actually made on December 31, 1999, is $1,400, rather than the projected $1,350. Thus, under paragraph (b)(6)(i) of this section, Z has a positive adjustment of $50 on December 31, 1999. In addition, under paragraph (b)(9)(i)(B) of this section, Z has a negative adjustment of $243 on December 31, 1999, which is attributable to the difference between Z's basis in the debt instrument on July 1, 1998, and the instrument's adjusted issue price on that date. As a result, Z has a net negative adjustment of $193 for 1999. This net negative adjustment reduces to zero the $128 total daily portions of interest Z would otherwise include in income in 1999. Accordingly, Z has no interest income on the debt instrument for 1999. Because Z had $60 of interest inclusions for 1998, $60 of the remaining $65 net negative adjustment is treated by Z as an ordinary loss for 1999. The remaining $5 of the net negative adjustment is a negative adjustment carryforward for 1999 that reduces the amount realized by Z on the retirement of the debt instrument from $1,350 to $1,345.

(v) *Loss at maturity.* On December 31, 1999, Z's basis in the debt instrument is $1,350 ($1,405 original basis, plus total daily portions of $60 for 1998 and $128 for 1999, minus the negative adjustment of $243). As a result, Z realizes a loss of $5 on the retirement of the debt instrument (the difference between the amount realized on the retirement ($1,345) and Z's adjusted basis in the debt instrument ($1,350)). Under paragraph (b)(8)(ii) of this section, the $5 loss is treated as loss from the retirement of the debt instrument. Consequently, Z realizes a total loss of $65 on the debt instrument for 1999 (a $60 ordinary loss and a $5 capital loss).

Example 2. Basis less than adjusted issue price—(i) *Facts.* On January 1, 1999, Y purchases for $910 a debt instrument that pays 7 percent interest semiannually on June 30 and December 31 of each year, and that promises to pay on December 31, 2001, $1,000 plus or minus $10 times the positive or negative difference, if any, between a specified amount and the value of an index on December 31, 2001. However, the payment on December 31, 2001, may not be less than $650. The debt instrument was originally issued on December 31, 1996, for an issue price of $1,000. The comparable yield for the debt instrument is 9.80 percent, compounded semiannually, and the projected payment schedule for the debt instrument (determined as of the issue date) provides for semiannual payments of $35 and a contingent payment at maturity of $1,175. On January 1, 1999, the debt instrument has an adjusted issue price of $1,060, assuming semiannual accrual periods ending on December 31 and June 30 of each year. Y is a calendar year taxpayer.

(ii) *Allocation of the difference between basis and adjusted issue price.* Y's basis in the debt instrument on January 1, 1999, is $910. Under paragraph (b)(9)(i)(A) of this section, Y must allocate the $150 difference between basis ($910) and adjusted issue price ($1,060) to daily portions of interest or to projected payments. These amounts will be positive adjustments taken into account at the time the daily portions accrue or the payments are made.

(A) Assume that, because of a decrease in the relevant index, the expected value of the payment at maturity has declined by about 9 percent. Based on forward prices on January 1, 1999, Y determines that approximately $105 of the difference between basis and adjusted issue price is allocable to the contingent payment. Y allocates the remaining $45 to daily portions of interest on a pro-rata basis (i.e., the amount allocated to an accrual period equals the product of $45 and a fraction, the numerator of which is the total daily portions for the accrual period and the denominator of which is the total daily portions remaining on the debt instrument on January 1, 1999). This allocation is reasonable.

(B) Assume alternatively that, based on yields of comparable debt instruments and its purchase price for the debt instrument, Y determines that an appropriate yield for the debt instrument is 13 percent, compounded semiannually. Based on this determination, Y allocates $55.75 of the difference between basis and adjusted issue price to daily portions of interest as follows: $15.19 to the daily portions of interest for the taxable year ending December 31, 1999; $18.40 to the daily portions of interest for the taxable year ending December 31, 2000; and $22.16 to the daily portions of interest for the taxable year ending December 31, 2001. Y allocates the remaining $94.25 to the contingent payment at maturity. This allocation is reasonable.

(ii) *Fixed but deferred contingent payments.*—This paragraph (b)(9)(ii) provides rules that apply when the amount of a contingent payment becomes fixed before the payment is due. For purposes of paragraph (b) of this section, if a contingent payment becomes fixed within the 6-month period ending on the due date of the payment, the payment is treated as a contingent payment even after the payment is fixed. If a contingent payment becomes fixed more than 6 months before the payment is due, the following rules apply to the debt instrument.

(A) *Determining adjustments.*—The amount of the adjustment attributable to the contingent payment is equal to the difference between the present value of the amount that is fixed and the present value of the projected amount of the contingent payment. The present value of each amount is determined by discounting the amount from the date the payment is due to the date the payment becomes fixed, using a discount rate equal to the comparable yield on the debt instrument. The adjustment is treated as a positive or negative adjustment, as appropriate, on the date the contingent payment becomes fixed. See paragraph (b)(9)(ii)(G) of this section to determine the timing of the adjustment if all remaining contingent payments on the debt instrument become fixed substantially contemporaneously.

(B) *Payment schedule.*—The contingent payment is no longer treated as a contingent payment after the date the amount of the payment becomes fixed. On the date the contingent payment becomes fixed, the projected payment schedule for the debt instrument is modified prospectively to reflect the fixed amount of the payment. Therefore, no adjustment is made under paragraph (b)(3)(iv) of this section when the contingent payment is actually made.

(C) *Accrual period.*—Notwithstanding the determination under § 1.1272-1(b)(1)(ii) of accrual periods for the debt instrument, an accrual period ends on the day the contingent payment becomes fixed, and a new accrual period begins on the day after the day the contingent payment becomes fixed.

(D) *Adjustments to basis and adjusted issue price.*—The amount of any positive adjustment on a debt instrument determined under paragraph (b)(9)(ii)(A) of this section increases the adjusted issue price of the instrument and the holder's adjusted basis in the instrument. Similarly, the amount of any negative adjustment on a debt instrument determined under paragraph (b)(9)(ii)(A) of this section decreases the adjusted issue price of the instrument and the holder's adjusted basis in the instrument.

(E) *Basis different from adjusted issue price.*—If a holder's basis in a debt instrument exceeds the debt instrument's adjusted issue price, the amount allocated to a projected payment under paragraph (b)(9)(i) of this section is treated as a negative adjustment on the date the

payment becomes fixed. If a holder's basis in a debt instrument is less than the debt instrument's adjusted issue price, the amount allocated to a projected payment under paragraph (b)(9)(i) of this section is treated as a positive adjustment on the date the payment becomes fixed.

(F) *Special rule for certain contingent interest payments.*—Notwithstanding paragraph (b)(9)(ii)(A) of this section, this paragraph (b)(9)(ii)(F) applies to contingent stated interest payments that are adjusted to compensate for contingencies regarding the reasonableness of the debt instrument's stated rate of interest. For example, this paragraph (b)(9)(ii)(F) applies to a debt instrument that provides for an increase in the stated rate of interest if the credit quality of the issuer or liquidity of the debt instrument deteriorates. Contingent stated interest payments of this type are recognized over the period to which they relate in a reasonable manner.

(G) *Special rule when all contingent payments become fixed.*—Notwithstanding paragraph (b)(9)(ii)(A) of this section, if all the remaining contingent payments on a debt instrument become fixed substantially contemporaneously, any positive or negative adjustments on the instrument are taken into account in a reasonable manner over the period to which they relate. For purposes of the preceding sentence, a payment is treated as a fixed payment if all remaining contingencies with respect to the payment are remote or incidental (within the meaning of § 1.1275-2(h)).

(H) *Example.*—The following example illustrates the provisions of this paragraph (b)(9)(ii). In this example, assume that the instrument described is a debt instrument for federal income tax purposes. No inference is intended, however, as to whether the instrument is a debt instrument for federal income tax purposes.

Example. Fixed but deferred payments—(i) *Facts.* On December 31, 1996, B, a calendar year taxpayer, purchases a debt instrument at original issue for $1,000. The debt instrument matures on December 31, 2002, and provides for a payment of $1,000 at maturity. In addition, on December 31, 1999, and December 31, 2002, the debt instrument provides for payments equal to the excess of the average daily value of an index for the 6-month period ending on September 30 of the preceding year over a specified amount. The debt instrument's comparable yield is 10 percent, compounded annually, and the instrument's projected payment schedule consists of a payment of $250 on December 31, 1999, and a payment of $1,439 on December 31, 2002. B uses annual accrual periods.

(ii) *Interest accrual for 1997.* Based on the projected payment schedule, B includes a total of $100 of daily portions of interest in income in 1997. B's adjusted basis in the debt instrument

Reg. § 1.1275-4(b)(9)(ii)(H)

and the debt instrument's adjusted issue price on December 31, 1997, is $1,100.

(iii) *Interest accrual for 1998*—(A) *Adjustment*. Based on the projected payment schedule, B would include $110 of total daily portions of interest in income in 1998. However, assume that on September 30, 1998, the payment due on December 31, 1999, fixes at $300, rather than the projected $250. Thus, on September 30, 1998, B has an adjustment equal to the difference between the present value of the $300 fixed amount and the present value of the $250 projected amount of the contingent payment. The present values of the two payments are determined by discounting each payment from the date the payment is due (December 31, 1999) to the date the payment becomes fixed (September 30, 1998), using a discount rate equal to 10 percent, compounded annually. The present value of the fixed payment is $266.30 and the present value of the projected amount of the contingent payment is $221.91. Thus, on September 30, 1998, B has a positive adjustment of $44.39 ($266.30 - $221.91).

(B) *Effect of adjustment*. Under paragraph (b)(9)(ii)(C) of this section, B's accrual period ends on September 30, 1998. The daily portions of interest on the debt instrument for the period from January 1, 1998 to September 30, 1998 total $81.51. The adjusted issue price of the debt instrument and B's adjusted basis in the debt instrument are thus increased over this period by $125.90 (the sum of the daily portions of interest of $81.51 and the positive adjustment of $44.39 made at the end of the period) to $1,225.90. For purposes of all future accrual periods, including the new accrual period from October 1, 1998, to December 31, 1998, the debt instrument's projected payment schedule is modified to reflect a fixed payment of $300 on December 31, 1999. Based on the new adjusted issue price of the debt instrument and the new projected payment schedule, the yield on the debt instrument does not change.

(C) *Interest accrual for 1998*. Based on the modified projected payment schedule, $29.56 of interest accrues during the accrual period that ends on December 31, 1998. Because B has no other adjustments during 1998, the $44.39 positive adjustment on September 30, 1998, results in a net positive adjustment for 1998, which is additional interest for that year. Thus, B includes $155.46 ($81.51 + $29.56 + $44.39) of interest in income in 1998. B's adjusted basis in the debt instrument and the debt instrument's adjusted issue price on December 31, 1998, is $1,255.46 ($1,225.90 from the end of the prior accrual period plus $29.56 total daily portions for the current accrual period).

(iii) *Timing contingencies*.—This paragraph (b)(9)(iii) provides rules for debt instruments that have payments that are contingent as to time.

(A) *Treatment of certain options*.—If a taxpayer has an unconditional option to put or call the debt instrument, to exchange the debt instrument for other property, or to extend the maturity date of the debt instrument, the projected payment schedule is determined by using the principles of § 1.1272-1(c)(5).

(B) *Other timing contingencies.*— [Reserved]

(iv) *Cross-border transactions.*—(A) *Allocation of deductions*.—For purposes of § 1.861-8, the holder of a debt instrument shall treat any deduction or loss treated as an ordinary loss under paragraph (b)(6)(iii)(B) or (b)(8)(ii) of this section as a deduction that is definitely related to the class of gross income to which income from such debt instrument belongs. Accordingly, if a U.S. person holds a debt instrument issued by a related controlled foreign corporation and, pursuant to section 904(d)(3) and the regulations thereunder, any interest accrued by such U.S. person with respect to such debt instrument would be treated as foreign source general limitation income, any deductions relating to a net negative adjustment will reduce the U.S. person's foreign source general limitation income. The holder shall apply the general rules relating to allocation and apportionment of deductions to any other deduction or loss realized by the holder with respect to the debt instrument.

(B) *Investments in United States real property*.—Notwithstanding paragraph (b)(8)(i) of this section, gain on the sale, exchange, or retirement of a debt instrument that is a United States real property interest is treated as gain for purposes of sections 897, 1445, and 6039C.

(v) *Coordination with subchapter M and related provisions*.—For purposes of sections 852(c)(2) and 4982 and § 1.852-11, any positive adjustment, negative adjustment, income, or loss on a debt instrument that occurs after October 31 of a taxable year is treated in the same manner as foreign currency gain or loss that is attributable to a section 988 transaction.

(vi) *Coordination with section 1092*.—A holder treats a negative adjustment and an issuer treats a positive adjustment as a loss with respect to a position in a straddle if the debt instrument is a position in a straddle and the contingency (or any portion of the contingency) to which the adjustment relates would be part of the straddle if entered into as a separate position.

(c) *Method for debt instruments not subject to the noncontingent bond method*.—(1) *Applicability*.—This paragraph (c) applies to a contingent payment debt instrument (other than a tax-exempt obligation) that has an issue price determined under § 1.1274-2. For example, this paragraph (c) generally applies to a contingent payment debt instrument that is issued for nonpublicly traded property.

(2) *Separation into components.*—If paragraph (c) of this section applies to a debt instrument (the overall debt instrument), the noncontingent payments are subject to the rules in paragraph (c)(3) of this section, and the contingent payments are accounted for separately under the rules in paragraph (c)(4) of this section.

(3) *Treatment of noncontingent payments.*— The noncontingent payments are treated as a separate debt instrument. The issue price of the separate debt instrument is the issue price of the overall debt instrument, determined under § 1.1274-2(g). No interest payments on the separate debt instrument are qualified stated interest payments (within the meaning of § 1.1273-1(c)) and the de minimis rules of section 1273(a)(3) and § 1.1273-1(d) do not apply to the separate debt instrument.

(4) *Treatment of contingent payments.*—(i) *In general.*—Except as provided in paragraph (c)(4)(iii) of this section, the portion of a contingent payment treated as interest under paragraph (c)(4)(ii) of this section is includible in gross income by the holder and deductible from gross income by the issuer in their respective taxable years in which the payment is made.

(ii) *Characterization of contingent payments as principal and interest.*—(A) *General rule.*—A contingent payment is treated as a payment of principal in an amount equal to the present value of the payment, determined by discounting the payment at the test rate from the date the payment is made to the issue date. The amount of the payment in excess of the amount treated as principal under the preceding sentence is treated as a payment of interest.

(B) *Test rate.*—The test rate used for purposes of paragraph (c)(4)(ii)(A) of this section is the rate that would be the test rate for the overall debt instrument under § 1.1274-4 if the term of the overall debt instrument began on the issue date of the overall debt instrument and ended on the date the contingent payment is made. However, in the case of a contingent payment that consists of a payment of stated principal accompanied by a payment of stated interest at a rate that exceeds the test rate determined under the preceding sentence, the test rate is the stated interest rate.

(iii) *Certain delayed contingent payments.*— (A) *General rule.*—Notwithstanding paragraph (c)(4)(ii) of this section, if a contingent payment becomes fixed more than 6 months before the payment is due, the issuer and holder are treated as if the issuer had issued a separate debt instrument on the date the payment becomes fixed, maturing on the date the payment is due. This separate debt instrument is treated as a debt

instrument to which section 1274 applies. The stated principal amount of this separate debt instrument is the amount of the payment that becomes fixed. An amount equal to the issue price of this debt instrument is characterized as interest or principal under the rules of paragraph (c)(4)(ii) of this section and accounted for as if this amount had been paid by the issuer to the holder on the date that the amount of the payment becomes fixed. To determine the issue price of the separate debt instrument, the payment is discounted at the test rate from the maturity date of the separate debt instrument to the date that the amount of the payment becomes fixed.

(B) *Test rate.*—The test rate used for purposes of paragraph (c)(4)(iii)(A) of this section is determined in the same manner as the test rate under paragraph (c)(4)(ii)(B) of this section is determined except that the date the contingent payment is due is used rather than the date the contingent payment is made.

(5) *Basis different from adjusted issue price.*— This paragraph (c)(5) provides rules for a holder whose basis in a debt instrument is different from the instrument's adjusted issue price (e.g., a subsequent holder). This paragraph (c)(5), however, does not apply if the holder is reporting income under the installment method of section 453.

(i) *Allocation of basis.*—The holder must allocate basis to the noncontingent component (i.e., the right to the noncontingent payments) and to any separate debt instruments described in paragraph (c)(4)(iii) of this section in an amount up to the total of the adjusted issue price of the noncontingent component and the adjusted issue prices of the separate debt instruments. The holder must allocate the remaining basis, if any, to the contingent component (i.e., the right to the contingent payments).

(ii) *Noncontingent component.*—Any difference between the holder's basis in the noncontingent component and the adjusted issue price of the noncontingent component, and any difference between the holder's basis in a separate debt instrument and the adjusted issue price of the separate debt instrument, is taken into account under the rules for market discount, premium, and acquisition premium that apply to a noncontingent debt instrument.

(iii) *Contingent component.*—Amounts received by the holder that are treated as principal payments under paragraph (c)(4)(ii) of this section reduce the holder's basis in the contingent component. If the holder's basis in the contingent component is reduced to zero, any additional principal payments on the contingent component are treated as gain from the sale or exchange of the debt instrument. Any basis remaining on the contingent component on the date the final contingent payment is made in-

Reg. § 1.1275-4(c)(5)(iii)

creases the holder's adjusted basis in the noncontingent component (or, if there are no remaining noncontingent payments, is treated as loss from the sale or exchange of the debt instrument).

(6) *Treatment of a holder on sale, exchange, or retirement.*—This paragraph (c)(6) provides rules for the treatment of a holder on the sale, exchange, or retirement of a debt instrument subject to this paragraph (c). Under this paragraph (c)(6), the holder must allocate the amount received from the sale, exchange, or retirement of a debt instrument first to the noncontingent component and to any separate debt instruments described in paragraph (c)(4)(ii) of this section in an amount up to the total of the adjusted issue price of the noncontingent component and the adjusted issue prices of the separate debt instruments. The holder must allocate the remaining amount received, if any, to the contingent component.

(i) *Amount allocated to the noncontingent component.*—The amount allocated to the noncontingent component and any separate debt instruments is treated as an amount realized from the sale, exchange, or retirement of the noncontingent component or separate debt instrument.

(ii) *Amount allocated to the contingent component.*—The amount allocated to the contingent component is treated as a contingent payment that is made on the date of the sale, exchange, or retirement and is characterized as interest and principal under the rules of paragraph (c)(4)(ii) of this section.

(7) *Examples.*—The following examples illustrate the provisions of this paragraph (c). In each example, assume that the instrument described is a debt instrument for federal income tax purposes. No inference is intended, however, as to whether the instrument is a debt instrument for federal income tax purposes.

Example 1. Contingent interest Payments—(i) *Facts.* A owns Blackacre, unencumbered depreciable real estate. On January 1, 1997, A sells Blackacre to B. As consideration for the sale, B makes a downpayment of $1,000,000 and issues to A a debt instrument that matures on December 31, 2001. The debt instrument provides for a payment of principal at maturity of $5,000,000 and a contingent payment of interest on December 31 of each year equal to a fixed percentage of the gross rents B receives from Blackacre in that year. Assume that the debt instrument is not issued in a potentially abusive situation. Assume also that on January 1, 1997, the short-term applicable Federal rate is 5 percent, compounded annually, and the mid-term applicable Federal rate is 6 percent, compounded annually.

(ii) *Determination of issue price.* Under §1.1274-2(g), the issue price of the debt instrument is $3,736,291, which is the present value, as of the issue date, of the $5,000,000 noncontingent

payment due at maturity, calculated using a discount rate equal to the mid-term applicable Federal rate. Under §1.1012-1(g)(1), B's basis in Blackacre on January 1, 1997, is $4,736,291 ($1,000,000 down payment plus the $3,736,291 issue price of the debt instrument).

(iii) *Noncontingent payment treated as separate debt instrument.* Under paragraph (c)(3) of this section, the right to the noncontingent payment of principal at maturity is treated as a separate debt instrument. The issue price of this separate debt instrument is $3,736,291 (the issue price of the overall debt instrument). The separate debt instrument has a stated redemption price at maturity of $5,000,000 and, therefore, OID of $1,263,709.

(iv) *Treatment of contingent payments.* Assume that the amount of contingent interest that is fixed and paid on December 31, 1997, is $200,000. Under paragraph (c)(4)(ii) of this section, this payment is treated as consisting of a payment of principal of $190,476, which is the present value of the payment, determined by discounting the payment at the test rate of 5 percent, compounded annually, from the date the payment is made to the issue date. The remainder of the $200,000 payment ($9,524) is treated as interest. The additional amount treated as principal gives B additional basis in Blackacre on December 31, 1997. The portion of the payment treated as interest is includible in gross income by A and deductible by B in their respective taxable years in which December 31, 1997 occurs. The remaining contingent payments on the debt instrument are accounted for similarly, using a test rate of 5 percent, compounded annually, for the contingent payments due on December 31, 1998, and December 31, 1999, and a test rate of 6 percent, compounded annually, for the contingent payments due on December 31, 2000, and December 31, 2001.

Example 2. Fixed but deferred payment—(i) *Facts.* The facts are the same as in paragraph (c)(7) *Example 1* of this section, except that the contingent payment of interest that is fixed on December 31, 1997, is not payable until December 31, 2001, the maturity date.

(ii) *Treatment of deferred contingent payment.* Assume that the amount of the payment that becomes fixed on December 31, 1997, is $200,000. Because this amount is not payable until December 31, 2001, under paragraph (c)(4)(iii) of this section, a separate debt instrument to which section 1274 applies is treated as issued by B on December 31, 1997 (the date the payment is fixed). The maturity date of this separate debt instrument is December 31, 2001 (the date on which the payment is due). The stated principal amount of this separate debt instrument is $200,000, the amount of the payment that becomes fixed. The imputed principal amount of the separate debt instrument is $158,419, which is the present value, as of December 31, 1997, of the $200,000 payment, computed using a discount rate equal to the test rate of the overall debt instrument (6 percent, compounded annually). An amount equal to the issue price of the separate debt instrument is treated as an amount paid on December 31, 1997, and characterized as interest and principal under the rules of paragraph (c)(4)(ii) of this section. The amount of the deemed payment characterized as principal is equal to $150,875, which is the present value, as of January 1, 1997 (the issue date of the overall debt instrument), of the deemed payment, computed using a discount rate of 5 percent, compounded annually. The amount of the deemed payment characterized as interest is $7,544 ($158,419 – $150,875), which is includible in gross income by A and deductible by B in their respective taxable years in which December 31, 1997 occurs.

(d) *Rules for tax-exempt obligations.*—(1) *In general.*—Except as modified by this paragraph (d), the noncontingent bond method described in paragraph (b) of this section applies to a tax-exempt obligation (as defined in section 1275(a)(3)) to which this section applies. Paragraph (d)(2) of this section applies to certain tax-exempt obligations that provide for interest-based payments or revenue-based payments and paragraph (d)(3) of this section applies to all other obligations. Paragraph (d)(4) of this section provides rules for a holder whose basis in a tax-exempt obligation is different from the adjusted issue price of the obligation.

(2) *Certain tax-exempt obligations with interest-based or revenue-based payments.*—(i) *Applicability.*—This paragraph (d)(2) applies to a tax-exempt obligation that provides for interest-based payments or revenue-based payments.

(ii) *Interest-based payments.*—A tax-exempt obligation provides for interest-based payments if the obligation would otherwise qualify as a variable rate debt instrument under § 1.1275-5 except that—

(A) The obligation provides for more than one fixed rate;

(B) The obligation provides for one or more caps, floors, or governors (or similar restrictions) that are fixed as of the issue date;

(C) The interest on the obligation is not compounded or paid at least annually; or

(D) The obligation provides for interest at one or more rates equal to the product of a qualified floating rate and a fixed multiple greater than zero and less than .65, or at one or more rates equal to the product of a qualified floating rate and a fixed multiple greater than zero and less than .65, increased or decreased by a fixed rate.

(iii) *Revenue-based payments.*—A tax-exempt obligation provides for revenue-based payments if the obligation—

(A) Is issued to refinance (including a series of refinancings) an obligation (in a series of refinancings, the original obligation), the proceeds of which were used to finance a project or enterprise; and

(B) Would otherwise qualify as a variable rate debt instrument under § 1.1275-5 except that it provides for stated interest payments at least annually based on a single fixed percentage of the revenue, value, change in value, or other similar measure of the performance of the refinanced project or enterprise.

(iv) *Modifications to the noncontingent bond method.*—If a tax-exempt obligation is subject to this paragraph (d)(2), the following modifications to the noncontingent bond method described in paragraph (b) of this section apply to the obligation.

(A) *Daily portions and net positive adjustments.*—The daily portions of interest determined under paragraph (b)(3)(iii) of this section and any net positive adjustment on the obligation are interest for purposes of section 103.

(B) *Net negative adjustments.*—A net negative adjustment for a taxable year reduces the amount of tax-exempt interest the holder would otherwise account for on the obligation for the taxable year under paragraph (b)(3)(iii) of this section. If the net negative adjustment exceeds this amount, the excess is a nondeductible, noncapitalizable loss. If a regulated investment company (RIC) within the meaning of section 851 has a net negative adjustment in a taxable year that would be a nondeductible, noncapitalizable loss under the prior sentence, the RIC must use this loss to reduce its tax-exempt interest income on other tax-exempt obligations held during the taxable year.

(C) *Gains.*—Any gain recognized on the sale, exchange, or retirement of the obligation is gain from the sale or exchange of the obligation.

(D) *Losses.*—Any loss recognized on the sale, exchange, or retirement of the obligation is treated the same as a net negative adjustment under paragraph (d)(2)(iv)(B) of this section.

(E) *Special rule for losses and net negative adjustments.*—Notwithstanding paragraphs (d)(2)(iv)(B) and (D) of this section, on the sale, exchange, or retirement of the obligation, the holder may claim a loss from the sale or exchange of the obligation to the extent the holder has not received in cash or property the sum of its original investment in the obligation and any amounts included in income under paragraph (d)(4)(ii) of this section.

(3) *All other tax-exempt obligations.*—(i) *Applicability.*—This paragraph (d)(3) applies to a tax-exempt obligation that is not subject to paragraph (d)(2) of this section.

(ii) *Modifications to the noncontingent bond method.*—If a tax-exempt obligation is subject to this paragraph (d)(3), the following modifications to the noncontingent bond method described in paragraph (b) of this section apply to the obligation.

(A) *Modification to projected payment schedule.*—The comparable yield for the obligation is the greater of the obligation's yield, determined without regard to the contingent payments, and the tax-exempt applicable Federal rate that applies to the obligation. The Internal Revenue Service publishes the tax-exempt applicable Federal rate for each month in the Internal Revenue Bulletin (see §601.601(d)(2)(ii) of this chapter).

(B) *Daily portions.*—The daily portions of interest determined under paragraph (b)(3)(iii) of this section are interest for purposes of section 103.

(C) *Adjustments.*—A net positive adjustment on the obligation is treated as gain to the holder from the sale or exchange of the obligation in the taxable year of the adjustment. A net negative adjustment on the obligation is treated as a loss to the holder from the sale or exchange of the obligation in the taxable year of the adjustment.

(D) *Gains and losses.*—Any gain or loss recognized on the sale, exchange, or retirement of the obligation is gain or loss from the sale or exchange of the obligation.

(4) *Basis different from adjusted issue price.*—This paragraph (d)(4) provides rules for a holder whose basis in a tax-exempt obligation is different from the adjusted issue price of the obligation. The rules of paragraph (b)(9)(i) of this section do not apply to tax-exempt obligations.

(i) *Basis greater than adjusted issue price.*—If the holder's basis in the obligation exceeds the obligation's adjusted issue price, the holder, upon acquiring the obligation, must allocate this difference to daily portions of interest on a yield to maturity basis over the remaining term of the obligation. The amount allocated to a daily portion of interest is not deductible by the holder. However, the holder's basis in the obligation is reduced by the amount allocated to a daily portion of interest on the date the daily portion accrues.

(ii) *Basis less than adjusted issue price.*—If the holder's basis in the obligation is less than the obligation's adjusted issue price, the holder, upon acquiring the obligation, must allocate this difference to daily portions of interest on a yield to maturity basis over the remaining term of the obligation. The amount allocated to a daily portion of interest is includible in income by the holder as ordinary income on the date the daily portion accrues. The holder's adjusted basis in the obligation is increased by the amount includible in income by the holder under this paragraph (d)(4)(ii) on the date the daily portion accrues.

(iii) *Premium and discount rules do not apply.*—The rules for accruing premium and discount in sections 171, 1276, and 1288 do not apply. Other rules of those sections continue to apply to the extent relevant.

(e) *Amounts treated as interest under this section.*—Amounts treated as interest under this section are treated as OID for all purposes of the Internal Revenue Code.

(f) *Effective date.*—This section applies to debt instruments issued on or after August 13, 1996. [Reg. §1.1275-4.]

☐ [*T.D. 8674, 6-11-96. Amended by T.D. 8709, 12-31-96; T.D. 8838, 9-3-99 and T.D. 9157, 8-27-2004.*]

[Reg. §1.1275-5]

§1.1275-5. Variable rate debt instruments.—(a) *Applicability.*—(1) *In general.*—This section provides rules for variable rate debt instruments. Except as provided in paragraph (a)(6) of this section, a variable rate debt instrument is a debt instrument that meets the conditions described in paragraphs (a)(2), (3), (4), and (5) of this section. If a debt instrument that provides for a variable rate of interest does not qualify as a variable rate debt instrument, the debt instrument is a contingent payment debt instrument. See §1.1275-4 for the treatment of a contingent payment debt instrument. See §1.1275-6 for a taxpayer's treatment of a variable rate debt instrument and a hedge.

(2) *Principal payments.*—The issue price of the debt instrument must not exceed the total noncontingent principal payments by more than an amount equal to the lesser of—

(i) .015 multiplied by the product of the total noncontingent principal payments and the number of complete years to maturity from the issue date (or, in the case of an installment obligation, the weighted average maturity as defined in §1.1273-1(e)(3)); or

(ii) 15 percent of the total noncontingent principal payments.

(3) *Stated interest.*—(i) *General rule.*—The debt instrument must not provide for any stated interest other than stated interest (compounded or paid at least annually) at—

(A) One or more qualified floating rates;

(B) a single fixed rate and one or more qualified floating rates;

(C) A single objective rate; or

(D) A single fixed rate and a single objective rate that is a qualified inverse floating rate.

(ii) *Certain debt instruments bearing interest at a fixed rate for an initial period.*—If interest on a debt instrument is stated at a fixed rate for an initial period of 1 year or less followed by a variable rate that is either a qualified floating rate or an objective rate for a subsequent period, and the value of the variable rate on the issue date is intended to approximate the fixed rate, the fixed rate and the variable rate together constitute a single qualified floating rate or objective rate. A fixed rate and a variable rate will be conclusively presumed to meet the requirements of the preceding sentence if the value of the variable rate on the issue date does not differ from the value of the fixed rate by more than .25 percentage points (25 basis points).

(4) *Current value.*—The debt instrument must provide that a qualified floating rate or objective rate in effect at any time during the term of the instrument is set at a current value of that rate. A current value is the value of the rate on any day that is no earlier than 3 months prior to the first day on which that value is in effect and no later than 1 year following that first day.

(5) *No contingent principal payments.*—Except as provided in paragraph (a)(2) of this section, the debt instrument must not provide for any principal payments that are contingent (within the meaning of §1.1275-4(a)).

(6) *Special rule for debt instruments issued for nonpublicly traded property.*—A debt instrument (other than a tax-exempt obligation) that would otherwise qualify as a variable rate debt instrument under this section is not a variable rate debt instrument if section 1274 applies to the instrument and any stated interest payments on the instrument are treated as contingent payments under §1.1274-2. This paragraph (a)(6) applies to debt instruments issued on or after August 13, 1996.

(b) *Qualified floating rate.*—(1) *In general.*—A variable rate is a qualified floating rate if variations in the value of the rate can reasonably be expected to measure contemporaneous variations in the cost of newly borrowed funds in the currency in which the debt instrument is denominated. The rate may measure contemporaneous variations in borrowing costs for the issuer of the debt instrument or for issuers in general. Except as provided in paragraph (b)(2) of this section, a multiple of a qualified floating rate is not a qualified floating rate. If a debt instrument provides for two or more qualified floating rates that can reasonably be expected to have approximately the same values throughout the term of the instrument, the qualified floating rates together constitute a single qualified floating rate. Two or more qualified floating rates will be conclusively presumed to meet the requirements of the preceding sentence if the values of all rates on the issue date are within .25 percentage points (25 basis points) of each other.

(2) *Certain rates based on a qualified floating rate.*—For a debt instrument issued on or after August 13, 1996, a variable rate is a qualified floating rate if it is equal to either—

(i) The product of a qualified floating rate described in paragraph (b)(1) of this section and a fixed multiple that is greater than .65 but not more than 1.35; or

(ii) The product of a qualified floating rate described in paragraph (b)(1) of this section and a fixed multiple that is greater than .65 but not more than 1.35, increased or decreased by a fixed rate.

(3) *Restrictions on the stated rate of interest.*—A variable rate is not a qualified floating rate if it is subject to a restriction or restrictions on the maximum stated interest rate (cap), a restriction or restrictions on the minimum stated interest rate (floor), a restriction or restrictions on the amount of increase or decrease in the stated interest rate (governor), or other similar restrictions. Notwithstanding the preceding sentence, the following restrictions will not cause a variable rate to fail to be a qualified floating rate—

(i) A cap, floor, or governor that is fixed throughout the term of the debt instrument;

(ii) A cap or similar restriction that is not reasonably expected as of the issue date to cause the yield on the debt instrument to be significantly less than the expected yield determined without the cap;

(iii) A floor or similar restriction that is not reasonably expected as of the issue date to cause the yield on the debt instrument to be significantly more than the expected yield determined without the floor; or

(iv) A governor or similar restriction that is not reasonably expected as of the issue date to cause the yield on the debt instrument to be significantly more or significantly less than the expected yield determined without the governor.

(c) *Objective rate.*—(1) *Definition.*—(i) *In general.*—For debt instruments issued on or after August 13, 1996, an objective rate is a rate (other than a qualified floating rate) that is determined using a single fixed formula and that is based on objective financial or economic information. For example, an objective rate generally includes a rate that is based on one or more qualified floating rates or on the yield of actively traded personal property (within the meaning of section 1092(d)(1)).

(ii) *Exception.*—For purposes of paragraph (c)(1)(i) of this section, an objective rate does not include a rate based on information that is within the control of the issuer (or a related party within the meaning of section 267(b) or 707(b)(1)) or that is unique to the circumstances of the issuer (or a related party within the meaning of section 267(b) or 707(b)(1)), such as dividends, profits, or the value of the issuer's stock.

However, a rate does not fail to be an objective rate merely because it is based on the credit quality of the issuer.

(2) *Other objective rates to be specified by Commissioner.*—The Commissioner may designate in the Internal Revenue Bulletin variable rates other than those described in paragraph (c)(1) of this section that will be treated as objective rates (see § 601.601(d)(2)(ii) of this chapter).

(3) *Qualified inverse floating rate.*—An objective rate described in paragraph (c)(1) of this section is a qualified inverse floating rate if—

(i) The rate is equal to a fixed rate minus a qualified floating rate; and

(ii) The variations in the rate can reasonably be expected to inversely reflect contemporaneous variations in the qualified floating rate (disregarding any restrictions on the rate that are described in paragraphs (b)(3)(i), (b)(3)(ii), (b)(3)(iii), and (b)(3)(iv) of this section).

(4) *Significant front-loading or back-loading of interest.*—Notwithstanding paragraph (c)(1) of this section, a variable rate of interest on a debt instrument is not an objective rate if it is reasonably expected that the average value of the rate during the first half of the instrument's term will be either significantly less than or significantly greater than average value of the rate during the final half of the instrument's term.

(5) *Tax-exempt obligations.*—Notwithstanding paragraph (c)(1) of this section, in the case of a tax-exempt obligation (within the meaning of section 1275(a)(3)), a variable rate is an objective rate only if it is a qualified inverse floating rate or a qualified inflation rate. A rate is a qualified inflation rate if the rate measures contemporaneous changes in inflation based on a general inflation index.

(d) *Examples.*—The following examples illustrate the rules of paragraphs (b) and (c) of this section. For purposes of these examples, assume that the debt instrument is not a tax-exempt obligation. In addition, unless otherwise provided, assume that the rate is not reasonably expected to result in a significant front-loading or back-loading of interest and that the rate is not based on objective financial or economic information that is within the control of the issuer (or a related party) or that is unique to the circumstances of the issuer (or a related party).

Example 1. Rate based on LIBOR. X issues a debt instrument that provides for annual payments of interest at a rate equal to the value of the 1-year London Interbank Offered Rate (LIBOR) at the end of each year. Variations in the value of 1-year LIBOR over the term of the debt instrument can reasonably be expected to measure contemporaneous variations in the cost of newly borrowed funds over that term. Accordingly, the rate is a qualified floating rate.

Example 2. Rate increased by a fixed amount. X issues a debt instrument that provides for annual payments of interest at a rate equal to 200 basis points (2 percent) plus the current value, at the end of each year, of the average yield on 1-year Treasury securities as published in Federal Reserve bulletins. Variations in the value of this interest rate can reasonably be expected to measure contemporaneous variations in the cost of newly borrowed funds. Accordingly, the rate is a qualified floating rate.

Example 3. Rate based on commercial paper rate. X issues a debt instrument that provides for a rate of interest that is periodically adjusted to equal the current interest rate of Bank's commercial paper. Variations in the value of this interest rate can reasonably be expected to measure contemporaneous variations in the cost of newly-borrowed funds. Accordingly, the rate is a qualified floating rate.

Example 4. Rate based on changes in the value of a commodity index. On January 1, 1997, X issues a debt instrument that provides for annual interest payments at the end of each year at a rate equal to the percentage increase, if any, in the value of an index for the year immediately preceding the payment. The index is based on the prices of several actively traded commodities. Variations in the value of this interest rate cannot reasonably be expected to measure contemporaneous variations in the cost of newly borrowed funds. Accordingly, the rate is not a qualified floating rate. However, because the rate is based on objective financial information using a single fixed formula, the rate is an objective rate.

Example 5. Rate based on a percentage of S&P 500 Index. On January 1, 1997, X issues a debt instrument that provides for annual interest payments at the end of each year based on a fixed percentage of the value of the S&P 500 Index. Variations in the value of this interest rate cannot reasonably be expected to measure contemporaneous variations in the cost of newly borrowed funds and, therefore, the rate is not a qualified floating rate. Although the rate is described in paragraph (c)(1)(i) of this section, the rate is not an objective rate because, based on historical data, it is reasonably expected that the average value of the rate during the first half of the instrument's term will be significantly less than the average value of the rate during the final half of the instrument's term.

Example 6. Rate based on issuer's profits. On January 1, 1997, Z issues a debt instrument that provides for annual interest payments equal to 1 percent of Z's gross profits earned during the year immediately preceding the payment. Variations in the value of this interest rate cannot reasonably be expected to measure contemporaneous variations in the cost of newly borrowed funds. Accordingly, the rate is not a qualified floating rate. In addition, because the rate is based on information that is unique to the is-

Reg. § 1.1275-5(c)(2)

suer's circumstances, the rate is not an objective rate.

Example 7. Rate based on a multiple of an interest index. On January 1, 1997, Z issues a debt instrument with annual interest payments at a rate equal to two times the value of 1-year LIBOR as of the payment date. Because the rate is a multiple greater than 1.35 times a qualified floating rate, the rate is not a qualified floating rate. However, because the rate is based on objective financial information using a single fixed formula, the rate is an objective rate.

Example 8. Variable rate based on the cost of borrowed funds in a foreign currency. On January 1, 1997, Y issues a 5-year dollar denominated debt instrument that provides for annual interest payments at a rate equal to the value of 1-year French franc LIBOR as of the payment date. Variations in the value of French franc LIBOR do not measure contemporaneous changes in the cost of newly borrowed funds in dollars. As a result, the rate is not a qualified floating rate for an instrument denominated in dollars. However, because the rate is based on objective financial information using a single fixed formula, the rate is an objective rate.

Example 9. Qualified inverse floating rate. On January 1, 1997, X issues a debt instrument that provides for annual interest payments at the end of each year at a rate equal to 12 percent minus the value of 1-year LIBOR as of the payment date. On the issue date, the value of 1-year LIBOR is 6 percent. Because the rate can reasonably be expected to inversely reflect contemporaneous variations in 1-year LIBOR, it is a qualified inverse floating rate. However, if the value of 1-year LIBOR on the issue date were 11 percent rather than 6 percent, the rate would not be a qualified inverse floating rate because the rate could not reasonably be expected to inversely reflect contemporaneous variations in 1-year LIBOR.

Example 10. Rate based on an inflation index. On January 1, 1997, X issues a debt instrument that provides for annual interest payments at the end of each year at a rate equal to 400 basis points (4 percent) plus the annual percentage change in a general inflation index (e.g., the Consumer Price Index, U.S. City Average, All Items, for all Urban Consumers, seasonally unadjusted). The rate, however, may not be less than zero. Variations in the value of this interest rate cannot reasonably be expected to measure contemporaneous variations in the cost of newly borrowed funds. Accordingly, the rate is not a qualified floating rate. However, because the rate is based on objective economic information using a single fixed formula, the rate is an objective rate.

(e) *Qualified stated interest and OID with respect to a variable rate debt instrument.*—(1) *In general.*— This paragraph (e) provides rules to determine the amount and accrual of OID and qualified stated interest on a variable rate debt instrument.

In general, the rules convert the debt instrument into a fixed rate debt instrument and then apply the general OID rules to the debt instrument. The issue price of a variable rate debt instrument, however, is not determined under this paragraph (e). See §§ 1.1273-2 and 1.1274-2 to determine the issue price of a variable rate debt instrument.

(2) *Variable rate debt instrument that provides for annual payments of interest at a single variable rate.*—If a variable rate debt instrument provides for stated interest at a single qualified floating rate or objective rate and the interest is unconditionally payable in cash or in property (other than debt instruments of the issuer), or will be constructively received under section 451, at least annually, the following rules apply to the instrument:

(i) All stated interest with respect to the debt instrument is qualified stated interest.

(ii) The amount of qualified stated interest and the amount of OID, if any, that accrues during an accrual period is determined under the rules applicable to fixed rate debt instruments by assuming that the variable rate is a fixed rate equal to—

(A) In the case of a qualified floating rate or qualified inverse floating rate, the value, as of the issue date, of the qualified floating rate or qualified inverse floating rate; or

(B) In the case of an objective rate (other than a qualified inverse floating rate), a fixed rate that reflects the yield that is reasonably expected for the debt instrument.

(iii) The qualified stated interest allocable to an accrual period is increased (or decreased) if the interest actually paid during an accrual period exceeds (or is less than) the interest assumed to be paid during the accrual period under paragraph (e)(2)(ii) of this section.

(3) *All other variable rate debt instruments except for those that provide for a fixed rate.*—If a variable rate debt instrument is not described in paragraph (e)(2) of this section and does not provide for interest payable at a fixed rate (other than an initial fixed rate described in paragraph (a)(3)(ii) of this section), the amount of interest and OID accruals for the instrument are determined under this paragraph (e)(3).

(i) *Step one: Determine the fixed rate substitute for each variable rate provided under the debt instrument.*—(A) *Qualified floating rate.*—The fixed rate substitute for each qualified floating rate provided for in the debt instrument is the value of each rate as of the issue date. If, however, a variable rate debt instrument provides for two or more qualified floating rates with different intervals between interest adjustment dates, the fixed rate substitutes for the rates must be based on intervals that are equal in length. For example, if a 4-year debt instrument provides for 24 monthly interest payments based on the value of the 30-day commercial paper rate on each payment date followed by 8 quarterly interest payments based on the value of quarterly LIBOR on each payment date, the fixed rate substitutes may be based on the values as of the issue date, of the 90-day commercial paper rate and quarterly LIBOR. Alternatively, the fixed rate substitutes may be based on the values, as of the issue date, of the 30-day commercial paper rate and monthly LIBOR.

(B) *Qualified inverse floating rate.*—The fixed rate substitute for a qualified inverse floating rate is the value of the qualified inverse floating rate as of the issue date.

(C) *Objective rate.*—The fixed rate substitute for an objective rate (other than a qualified inverse floating rate) is a fixed rate that reflects the yield that is reasonably expected for the debt instrument.

(ii) *Step two: Construct the equivalent fixed rate debt instrument.*—The equivalent fixed rate debt instrument has terms that are identical to those provided under the variable rate debt instrument, except that the equivalent fixed rate debt instrument provides for the fixed rate substitutes (determined in paragraph (e)(3)(i) of this section) in lieu of the qualified floating rates or objective rate provided under the variable rate debt instrument.

(iii) *Step three: Determine the amount of qualified stated interest and OID with respect to the equivalent fixed rate debt instrument.*—The amount of qualified stated interest and OID, if any, are determined for the equivalent fixed rate debt instrument under the rules applicable to fixed rate debt instruments and are taken into account as if the holder held the equivalent fixed rate debt instrument.

(iv) *Step four: Make appropriate adjustments for actual variable rates.*—Qualified stated interest or OID allocable to an accrual period must be increased (or decreased) if the interest actually accrued or paid during an accrual period exceeds (or is less than) the interest assumed to be accrued or paid during the accrual period under the equivalent fixed rate debt instrument. This increase or decrease is an adjustment to qualified stated interest for the accrual period if the equivalent fixed rate debt instrument (as determined under paragraph (e)(3)(ii) of this section) provides for qualified stated interest and the increase or decrease is reflected in the amount actually paid during the accrual period. Otherwise, this increase or decrease is an adjustment to OID for the accrual period.

(v) *Examples.*—The following examples illustrate the rules in paragraphs (e)(2) and (3) of this section.

Example 1. Equivalent fixed rate debt instrument—(i) *Facts.* X purchases at original issue a 6-year variable rate debt instrument that provides for semiannual payments of interest. For the first 3 years, the rate of interest is the value of 6-month LIBOR on the payment date. For the final 3 years, the rate is the value of the 6-month T-bill rate on the payment date. On the issue date, the value of 6-month LIBOR is 3 percent, compounded semiannually, and the 6-month T-bill rate is 2 percent, compounded semiannually.

(ii) *Determination of equivalent fixed rate debt instrument.* Under paragraph (e)(3)(i) of this section, the fixed rate substitute for 6-month LIBOR is 3 percent, compounded semiannually, and the fixed rate substitute for the 6-month T-bill rate is 2 percent, compounded semiannually. Under paragraph (e)(3)(ii) of this section, the equivalent fixed rate debt instrument is a 6-year debt instrument that provides for semiannual payments of interest at 3 percent, compounded semiannually, for the first 3 years followed by 2 percent, compounded semiannually, for the final 3 years.

Example 2. Equivalent fixed rate debt instrument with de minimis OID—(i) *Facts.* Y purchases at original issue, for $100,000, a 4-year variable rate debt instrument that has a stated principal amount of $100,000, payable at maturity. The debt instrument provides for monthly payments of interest at the end of each month. For the first year, the interest rate is the monthly commercial paper rate and for the last 3 years, the interest rate is the monthly commercial paper rate plus 100 basis points. On the issue date, the monthly commercial paper rate is 3 percent, compounded monthly.

(ii) *Equivalent fixed rate debt instrument.* Under paragraph (e)(3)(ii) of this section, the equivalent fixed rate debt instrument for the variable rate debt instrument is a 4-year debt instrument that has an issue price and stated principal amount of $100,000. The equivalent fixed rate debt instrument provides for monthly payments of interest at 3 percent, compounded monthly, for the first year ($250 per month) and monthly payments of interest at 4 percent, compounded monthly, for the last 3 years ($333.33 per month).

(iii) *De minimis OID.* Under §1.1273-1(a), because a portion (100 basis points) of each interest payment in the final 3 years is not a qualified stated interest payment, the equivalent fixed rate debt instrument has OID of $2,999.88 ($102,999.88 − $100,000) However, under §1.1273-1(d)(4) (the *de minimis* rule relating to teaser rates and interest holidays), the stated redemption price at maturity of the equivalent fixed rate debt instrument is $100,999.96 ($100,000 (issue price) plus $999.96 (the greater of the amount of foregone interest ($999.96) and the amount equal to the excess of the instrument's stated principal amount over its issue price ($0)). Thus, the equivalent fixed rate debt instrument is treated as having OID of $999.96 ($100,999.96 − $100,000). Because this amount is less than the *de minimis* amount of $1,010 (0.0025 multiplied by $100,999.96 multiplied by 4 complete years to maturity), the equivalent fixed rate debt instrument has *de minimis* OID. Therefore, the variable rate debt instrument has zero OID and all stated interest payments are qualified stated interest payments.

Example 3. Adjustment to qualified stated interest for actual payment of interest—(i) *Facts.* On January 1, 1995, Z purchases at original issue, for $90,000, a variable rate debt instrument that matures on January 1, 1997, and has a stated principal amount of $100,000, payable at maturity. The debt instrument provides for annual payments of interest on January 1 of each year, beginning on January 1, 1996. The amount of interest payable is the value of annual LIBOR on the payment date. The value of annual LIBOR on January 1, 1995, and January 1, 1996, is 5 percent, compounded annually. The value of annual LIBOR on January 1, 1997, is 7 percent, compounded annually.

(ii) *Accrual of OID and qualified stated interest.* Under paragraph (e)(2) of this section, the variable rate debt instrument is treated as a 2-year debt instrument that has an issue price of $90,000, a stated principal amount of $100,000, and interest payments of $5,000 at the end of each year. The debt instrument has $10,000 of OID and the annual interest payments of $5,000 are qualified stated interest payments. Under § 1.1272-1, the debt instrument has a yield of 10.82 percent, compounded annually. The amount of OID allocable to the first annual accrual period (assuming Z uses annual accrual periods) is $4,743.25 (($90,000 × .1082) – $5,000), and the amount of OID allocable to the second annual accrual period is $5,256.75 ($100,000 – $94,743.25). Under paragraph (e)(2)(iii) of this section, the $2,000 difference between the $7,000 interest payment actually made at maturity and the $5,000 interest payment assumed to be made at maturity under the equivalent fixed rate debt instrument is treated as additional qualified stated interest for the period.

(4) *Variable rate debt instrument that provides for a single fixed rate.*—(i) *General rule.*—If a variable rate debt instrument provides for stated interest either at one or more qualified floating rates or at a qualified inverse floating rate and in addition provides for stated interest at a single fixed rate (other than an initial fixed rate described in paragraph (a)(3)(ii) of this section), the amount of interest and OID are determined using the method of paragraph (e)(3) of this section, as modified by this paragraph (e)(4). For purposes of paragraphs (e)(3)(i) through (e)(3)(iii) of this section, the variable rate debt instrument is treated as if it provided for a qualified floating rate (or a qualified inverse floating rate, if the debt instrument provides for a qualified inverse floating rate), rather than the fixed rate. The qualified floating rate (or qualified in-

verse floating rate) replacing the fixed rate must be such that the fair market value of the variable rate debt instrument as of the issue date would be approximately the same as the fair market value of an otherwise identical debt instrument that provides for the qualified floating rate (or qualified inverse floating rate) rather than the fixed rate.

(ii) *Example.*—The following example illustrates the rule in paragraph (e)(4)(i) of this section.

Example. Variable rate debt instrument that provides for a single fixed rate—(i) *Facts.* On January 1, 1995, X purchases at original issue, for $100,000, a variable rate debt instument that matures on January 1, 2001, and that has a stated principal amount of $100,000. The debt instrument provides for payments of interest on January 1 of each year, beginning on January 1, 1996. For the first 4 years, the interest rate is 4 percent, compounded annually, and for the last 2 years the interest rate is the value of 1-year LIBOR, as of the payment date, plus 200 basis points. On January 1, 1995, the value of 1-year LIBOR is 2 percent, compounded annually. In addition, assume that on January 1, 1995, the variable, rate debt instrument has approximately the same fair market value as an otherwise identical debt instrument that provides for an interest rate equal to the value of 1-year LIBOR, as of the payment date, for the first 4 years.

(ii) *Equivalent fixed rate debt instrument.* Under paragraph (e)(4)(i) of this section, for purposes of paragraphs (e)(3)(i) through (e)(3)(iii) of this section, the variable rate debt instrument is treated as if it provided for an interest rate equal to the value of 1-year LIBOR, as of the payment date, for the first 4 years. Under paragraph (e)(3)(ii) of this section, the equivalent fixed rate debt instrument for the variable rate debt instrument is a 6-year debt instrument that has an issue price and stated principal amount of $100,000. The equivalent fixed rate debt instrument provides for interest payments of $2,000 for the first 4 years and $4,000 for the last 2 years.

(iii) *Accrual of OID and qualified stated interest.* Under § 1.1273-1, the equivalent fixed rate debt instrument has OID of $4,000 because a portion (200 basis points) of each interest payment in the last 2 years is not a qualified stated interest payment. The $4,000 of OID is allocable over the 6-year term of the debt instrument under § 1.1272-1. Under paragraph (e)(3)(iv) of this section, the difference between the $4,000 payment made in the first 4 years and the $2,000 payment assumed to be made on the equivalent fixed rate debt instrument in those years is an adjustment to qualified stated interest. In addition, any difference between the amount actually paid in each of the last 2 years and the $4,000 payment assumed to be made on the equivalent fixed rate debt instrument is an adjustment to qualified stated interest.

(f) Special rule for certain reset bonds.—Notwithstanding paragraph (e) of this section, this paragraph (f) provides a special rule for a variable rate debt instrument that provides for stated interest at a fixed rate for an initial interval, and provides that on the date immediately following the end of the initial interval (the effective date) the stated interest rate will be a rate determined under a procedure (such as an auction procedure) so that the fair market value of the instrument on the effective date will be a fixed amount (the reset value). Solely for purposes of calculating the accrual of OID, the variable rate debt instrument is treated as—

(1) Maturing on the date immediately preceding the effective date for an amount equal to the reset value; and

(2) Reissued on the effective date for an amount equal to the reset value. [Reg. §1.1275-5.]

☐ [*T.D. 8517, 1-27-94. Amended by T.D. 8674, 6-11-96.*]

[Reg. §1.1275-6]

§1.1275-6. Integration of qualifying debt instruments.—(a) *In general.*—This section generally provides for the integration of a qualifying debt instrument with a hedge or combination of hedges if the combined cash flows of the components are substantially equivalent to the cash flows on a fixed or variable rate debt instrument. The integrated transaction is generally subject to the rules of this section rather than the rules to which each component of the transaction would be subject on a separate basis. The purpose of this section is to permit a more appropriate determination of the character and timing of income, deductions, gains, or losses than would be permitted by separate treatment of the components. The rules of this section affect only the taxpayer who holds (or issues) the qualifying debt instrument and enters into the hedge.

(b) *Definitions.*—(1) *Qualifying debt instrument.*—A qualifying debt instrument is any debt instrument (including an integrated transaction as defined in paragraph (c) of this section) other than—

(i) A tax-exempt obligation as defined in section 1275(a)(3);

(ii) A debt instrument to which section 1272(a)(6) applies (certain interests in or mortgages held by a REMIC, and certain other debt instruments with payments subject to acceleration); or

(iii) A debt instrument that is subject to §1.483-4 or §1.1275-4(c) (certain contingent payment debt instruments issued for nonpublicly traded property).

(2) *Section 1.1275-6 hedge.*—(i) *In general.*—A §1.1275-6 hedge is any financial instrument (as defined in paragraph (b)(3) of this section) if the combined cash flows of the financial instrument and the qualifying debt instrument permit the calculation of a yield to maturity (under the principles of section 1272), or the right to the combined cash flows would qualify under §1.1275-5 as a variable rate debt instrument that pays interest at a qualified floating rate or rates (except for the requirement that the interest payments be stated as interest). A financial instrument is not a §1.1275-6 hedge, however, if the resulting synthetic debt instrument does not have the same term as the remaining term of the qualifying debt instrument. A financial instrument that hedges currency risk is not a §1.1275-6 hedge.

(ii) *Limitations.*—(A) A debt instrument issued by a taxpayer and a debt instrument held by the taxpayer cannot be part of the same integrated transaction.

(B) A debt instrument can be a §1.1275-6 hedge only if it is issued substantially contemporaneously with, and has the same maturity (including rights to accelerate or delay payments) as, the qualifying debt instrument.

(3) *Financial instrument.*—For purposes of this section, a financial instrument is a spot, forward, or futures contract, an option, a notional principal contract, a debt instrument, or a similar instrument, or combination or series of financial instruments. Stock is not a financial instrument for purposes of this section.

(4) *Synthetic debt instrument.*—The synthetic debt instrument is the hypothetical debt instrument with the same cash flows as the combined cash flows of the qualifying debt instrument and the §1.1275-6 hedge.

(c) *Integrated transaction.*—(1) *Integration by taxpayer.*—Except as otherwise provided in this section, a qualifying debt instrument and a §1.1275-6 hedge are an integrated transaction if all of the following requirements are satisfied:

(i) The taxpayer satisfies the identification requirements of paragraph (e) of this section on or before the date the taxpayer enters into the §1.1275-6 hedge.

(ii) None of the parties to the §1.1275-6 hedge are related within the meaning of section 267(b) or 707(b)(1), or, if the parties are related, the party providing the hedge uses, for federal income tax purposes, a mark-to-market method of accounting for the hedge and all similar or related transactions.

(iii) Both the qualifying debt instrument and the §1.1275-6 hedge are entered into by the same individual, partnership, trust, estate, or corporation (regardless of whether the corporation is a member of an affiliated group of corporations that files a consolidated return).

(iv) If the taxpayer is a foreign person engaged in a U.S. trade or business and the taxpayer issues or acquires a qualifying debt instrument, or enters into a §1.1275-6 hedge, through the trade or business, all items of income and expense associated with the qualifying debt instrument and the §1.1275-6 hedge (other than interest expense that is subject to §1.882-5) would have been effectively connected with the U.S. trade or business throughout the term of the qualifying debt instrument had this section not applied.

(v) Neither the qualifying debt instrument, nor any other debt instrument that is part of the same issue as the qualifying debt instrument, nor the §1.1275-6 hedge was, with respect to the taxpayer, part of an integrated transaction that was terminated or otherwise legged out of within the 30 days immediately preceding the date that would be the issue date of the synthetic debt instrument.

(vi) The qualifying debt instrument is issued or acquired by the taxpayer on or before the date of the first payment on the §1.1275-6 hedge, whether made or received by the taxpayer (including a payment made to purchase the hedge). If the qualifying debt instrument is issued or acquired by the taxpayer after, but substantially contemporaneously with, the date of the first payment on the §1.1275-6 hedge, the qualifying debt instrument is treated, solely for purposes of this paragraph (c)(1)(vi), as meeting the requirements of the preceding sentence.

(vii) Neither the §1.1275-6 hedge nor the qualifying debt instrument was, with respect to the taxpayer, part of a straddle (as defined in section 1092(c)) prior to the issue date of the synthetic debt instrument.

(2) *Integration by Commissioner.*—The Commissioner may treat a qualifying debt instrument and a financial instrument (whether entered into by the taxpayer or by a related party) as an integrated transaction if the combined cash flows on the qualifying debt instrument and financial instrument are substantially the same as the combined cash flows required for the financial instrument to be a §1.1275-6 hedge. The Commissioner, however, may not integrate a transaction unless the qualifying debt instrument either is subject to §1.1275-4 or is subject to §1.1275-5 and pays interest at an objective rate. The circumstances under which the Commissioner may require integration include, but are not limited to, the following:

(i) A taxpayer fails to identify a qualifying debt instrument and the §1.1275-6 hedge under paragraph (e) of this section.

(ii) A taxpayer issues or acquires a qualifying debt instrument and a related party (within the meaning of section 267(b) or 707(b)(1)) enters into the §1.1275-6 hedge.

(iii) A taxpayer issues or acquires a qualifying debt instrument and enters into the §1.1275-6 hedge with a related party (within the meaning of section 267(b) or 707(b)(1)).

(iv) The taxpayer legs out of an integrated transaction and within 30 days enters into a new §1.1275-6 hedge with respect to the same qualifying debt instrument or another debt instrument that is part of the same issue.

(d) *Special rules for legging into and legging out of an integrated transaction.*—(1) *Legging into.*—(i) *Definition.*—Legging into an integrated transaction under this section means that a §1.1275-6 hedge is entered into after the date the qualifying debt instrument is issued or acquired by the taxpayer, and the requirements of paragraph (c)(1) of this section are satisfied on the date the §1.1275-6 hedge is entered into (the leg-in date).

(ii) *Treatment.*—If a taxpayer legs into an integrated transaction, the taxpayer treats the qualifying debt instrument under the applicable rules for taking interest and OID into account up to the leg-in date, except that the day before the leg-in date is treated as the end of an accrual period. As of the leg-in date, the qualifying debt instrument is subject to the rules of paragraph (f) of this section.

(iii) *Anti-abuse rule.*—If a taxpayer legs into an integrated transaction with a principal purpose of deferring or accelerating income or deductions on the qualifying debt instrument, the Commissioner may—

(A) Treat the qualifying debt instrument as sold for its fair market value on the leg-in date; or

(B) Refuse to allow the taxpayer to integrate the qualifying debt instrument and the §1.1275-6 hedge.

(2) *Legging out.*—(i) *Definition.*—(A) *Legging out if the taxpayer has integrated.*—If a taxpayer has integrated a qualifying debt instrument and a §1.1275-6 hedge under paragraph (c)(1) of this section, legging out means that, prior to the maturity of the synthetic debt instrument, the §1.1275-6 hedge ceases to meet the requirements for a §1.1275-6 hedge, the taxpayer fails to meet any requirement of paragraph (c)(1) of this section, or the taxpayer disposes of or otherwise terminates all or a part of the qualifying debt instrument or §1.1275-6 hedge. If the taxpayer fails to meet the requirements of paragraph (c)(1) of this section but meets the requirements of paragraph (c)(2) of this section, the Commissioner may treat the taxpayer as not legging out.

(B) *Legging out if the Commissioner has integrated.*—If the Commissioner has integrated a qualifying debt instrument and a financial instrument under paragraph (c)(2) of this section, legging out means that, prior to the maturity of the synthetic debt instrument, the requirements for Commissioner integration under paragraph (c)(2) of this section are not met or the taxpayer fails to meet the requirements for taxpayer integration under paragraph (c)(1) of this section and the Commissioner agrees to allow the taxpayer to be treated as legging out.

Reg. §1.1275-6(d)(2)(i)(B)

(C) *Exception for certain nonrecognition transactions.*—If, in a single nonrecognition transaction, a taxpayer disposes of, or ceases to be primarily liable on, the qualifying debt instrument and the §1.1275-6 hedge, the taxpayer is not treated as legging out. Instead, the integrated transaction is treated under the rules governing the nonrecognition transaction. For example, if a holder of an integrated transaction is acquired in a reorganization under section 368(a)(1)(A), the holder is treated as disposing of the synthetic debt instrument in the reorganization rather than legging out. If the successor holder is not eligible for integrated treatment, the successor is treated as legging out.

(ii) *Operating rules.*—If a taxpayer legs out (or is treated as legging out) of an integrated transaction, the following rules apply:

(A) The transaction is treated as an integrated transaction during the time the requirements of paragraph (c)(1) or (2) of this section, as appropriate, are satisfied.

(B) Immediately before the taxpayer legs out, the taxpayer is treated as selling or otherwise terminating the synthetic debt instrument for its fair market value and, except as provided in paragraph (d)(2)(ii)(D) of this section, any income, deduction, gain, or loss is realized and recognized at that time.

(C) If, immediately after the taxpayer legs out, the taxpayer holds or remains primarily liable on the qualifying debt instrument, adjustments are made to reflect any difference between the fair market value of the qualifying debt instrument and the adjusted issue price of the qualifying debt instrument. If, immediately after the taxpayer legs out, the taxpayer is a party to a §1.1275-6 hedge, the §1.1275-6 hedge is treated as entered into at its fair market value.

(D) If a taxpayer legs out of an integrated transaction by disposing of or otherwise terminating a §1.1275-6 hedge within 30 days of legging into the integrated transaction, then any loss or deduction determined under paragraph (d)(2)(ii)(B) of this section is not allowed. Appropriate adjustments are made to the qualifying debt instrument for any disallowed loss. The adjustments are taken into account on a yield to maturity basis over the remaining term of the qualifying debt instrument.

(E) If a holder of a debt instrument subject to §1.1275-4 legs into an integrated transaction with respect to the instrument and subsequently legs out of the integrated transaction, any gain recognized under paragraph (d)(2)(ii)(B) or (C) of this section is treated as interest income to the extent determined under the principles of §1.1275-4(b)(8)(iii)(B) (rules for determining the character of gain on the sale of a debt instrument all of the payments on which have been fixed). If the synthetic debt instrument would qualify as a variable rate debt instrument,

the equivalent fixed rate debt instrument determined under §1.1275-5(e) is used for this purpose.

(e) *Identification requirements.*—For each integrated transaction, a taxpayer must enter and retain as part of its books and records the following information—

(1) The date the qualifying debt instrument was issued or acquired (or is expected to be issued or acquired) by the taxpayer and the date the §1.1275-6 hedge was entered into by the taxpayer;

(2) A description of the qualifying debt instrument and the §1.1275-6 hedge; and

(3) A summary of the cash flows and accruals resulting from treating the qualifying debt instrument and the §1.1275-6 hedge as an integrated transaction (i.e., the cash flows and accruals on the synthetic debt instrument).

(f) *Taxation of integrated transactions.*—(1) *General rule.*—An integrated transaction is generally treated as a single transaction by the taxpayer during the period that the transaction qualifies as an integrated transaction. Except as provided in paragraph (f)(12) of this section, while a qualifying debt instrument and a §1.1275-6 hedge are part of an integrated transaction, neither the qualifying debt instrument nor the §1.1275-6 hedge is subject to the rules that would apply on a separate basis to the debt instrument and the §1.1275-6 hedge, including section 1092 or §1.446-4. The rules that would govern the treatment of the synthetic debt instrument generally govern the treatment of the integrated transaction. For example, the integrated transaction may be subject to section 263(g) or, if the synthetic debt instrument would be part of a straddle, section 1092. Generally, the synthetic debt instrument is subject to sections 163(e) and 1271 through 1275, with terms as set forth in paragraphs (f)(2) through (13) of this section.

(2) *Issue date.*—The issue date of the synthetic debt instrument is the first date on which the taxpayer entered into all of the components of the synthetic debt instrument.

(3) *Term.*—The term of the synthetic debt instrument is the period beginning on the issue date of the synthetic debt instrument and ending on the maturity date of the qualifying debt instrument.

(4) *Issue price.*—The issue price of the synthetic debt instrument is the adjusted issue price of the qualifying debt instrument on the issue date of the synthetic debt instrument. If, as a result of entering into the §1.1275-6 hedge, the taxpayer pays or receives one or more payments that are substantially contemporaneous with the issue date of the synthetic debt instrument, the payments reduce or increase the issue price as appropriate.

(5) *Adjusted issue price.*—In general, the adjusted issue price of the synthetic debt instrument is determined under the principles of § 1.1275-1(b).

(6) *Qualified stated interest.*—No amounts payable on the synthetic debt instrument are qualified stated interest within the meaning of § 1.1273-1(c).

(7) *Stated redemption price at maturity.*— (i) *Synthetic debt instruments that are borrowings.*—In general, if the synthetic debt instrument is a borrowing, the instrument's stated redemption price at maturity is the sum of all amounts paid or to be paid on the qualifying debt instrument and the § 1.1275-6 hedge, reduced by any amounts received or to be received on the § 1.1275-6 hedge.

(ii) *Synthetic debt instruments that are held by the taxpayer.*—In general, if the synthetic debt instrument is held by the taxpayer, the instrument's stated redemption price at maturity is the sum of all amounts received or to be received by the taxpayer on the qualifying debt instrument and the § 1.1275-6 hedge, reduced by any amounts paid or to be paid by the taxpayer on the § 1.1275-6 hedge.

(iii) *Certain amounts ignored.*—For purposes of this paragraph (f)(7), if an amount paid or received on the § 1.1275-6 hedge is taken into account under paragraph (f)(4) of this section to determine the issue price of the synthetic debt instrument, the amount is not taken into account to determine the synthetic debt instrument's stated redemption price at maturity.

(8) *Source of interest income and allocation of expense.*—The source of interest income from the synthetic debt instrument is determined by reference to the source of income of the qualifying debt instrument under sections 861(a)(1) and 862(a)(1). For purposes of section 904, the character of interest from the synthetic debt instrument is determined by reference to the character of the interest income from the qualifying debt instrument. Interest expense is allocated and apportioned under regulations under section 861 or under § 1.882-5.

(9) *Effectively connected income.*—If the requirements of paragraph (c)(1)(iv) of this section are satisfied, any interest income resulting from the synthetic debt instrument entered into by the foreign person is treated as effectively connected with a U.S. trade or business, and any interest expense resulting from the synthetic debt instrument entered into by the foreign person is allocated and apportioned under § 1.882-5.

(10) *Not a short-term obligation.*—For purposes of section 1272(a)(2)(C), a synthetic debt instrument is not treated as a short-term obligation.

(11) *Special rules in the event of integration by the Commissioner.*—If the Commissioner requires integration, appropriate adjustments are made to the treatment of the synthetic debt instrument, and, if necessary, the qualifying debt instrument and financial instrument. For example, the Commissioner may treat a financial instrument that is not a § 1.1275-6 hedge as a § 1.1275-6 hedge when applying the rules of this section. The issue date of the synthetic debt instrument is the date determined appropriate by the Commissioner to require integration.

(12) *Retention of separate transaction rules for certain purposes.*—This paragraph (f)(12) provides for the retention of separate transaction rules for certain purposes. In addition, by publication in the Internal Revenue Bulletin (see § 601.601(d)(2)(ii) of this chapter), the Commissioner may require use of separate transaction rules for any aspect of an integrated transaction.

(i) *Foreign persons that enter into integrated transactions giving rise to U.S. source income not effectively connected with a U.S. trade or business.*— If a foreign person enters into an integrated transaction that gives rise to U.S. source interest income (determined under the source rules for the synthetic debt instrument) not effectively connected with a U.S. trade or business of the foreign person, paragraph (f) of this section does not apply for purposes of sections 871(a), 881, 1441, 1442, and 6049. These sections of the Internal Revenue Code are applied to the qualifying debt instrument and the § 1.1275-6 hedge on a separate basis.

(ii) *Relationship between taxpayer and other persons.*—Because the rules of this section affect only the taxpayer that enters into an integrated transaction (i.e., either the issuer or a particular holder of a qualifying debt instrument), any provisions of the Internal Revenue Code or regulations that govern the relationship between the taxpayer and any other person are applied on a separate basis. For example, taxpayers must comply with any reporting or disclosure requirements on any qualifying debt instrument as if it were not part of an integrated transaction. Thus, if required under § 1.1275-4(b)(4), an issuer of a contingent payment debt instrument subject to integrated treatment must provide the projected payment schedule to holders. Similarly, if a U.S. corporation enters into an integrated transaction that includes a notional principal contract, the source of any payment received by the counterparty on the notional principal contract is determined under § 1.863-7 as if the contract were not part of an integrated transaction, and, if received by a foreign person who is not engaged in a U.S. trade or business, the payment is non-U.S. source income that is not subject to U.S. withholding tax.

(13) *Coordination with consolidated return rules.*—If a taxpayer enters into a § 1.1275-6

hedge with a member of the same consolidated group (the counterparty) and the § 1.1275-6 hedge is part of an integrated transaction for the taxpayer, the § 1.1275-6 hedge is not treated as an intercompany transaction for purposes of § 1.1502-13. If the taxpayer legs out of integrated treatment, the taxpayer and the counterparty are each treated as disposing of its position in the § 1.1275-6 hedge under the principles of paragraph (d)(2) of this section. If the § 1.1275-6 hedge remains in existence after the leg-out date, the § 1.1275-6 hedge is treated under the rules that would otherwise apply to the transaction (including § 1.1502-13 if the transaction is between members).

(g) *Predecessors and successors.*—For purposes of this section, any reference to a taxpayer, holder, issuer, or person includes, where appropriate, a reference to a predecessor or successor. For purposes of the preceding sentence, a predecessor is a transferor of an asset or liability (including an integrated transaction) to a transferee (the successor) in a nonrecognition transaction. Appropriate adjustments, if necessary, are made in the application of this section to predecessors and successors.

(h) *Examples.*—The following examples illustrate the provisions of this section. In each example, assume that the qualifying debt instrument is a debt instrument for federal income tax purposes. No inference is intended, however, as to whether the debt instrument is a debt instrument for federal income tax purposes.

Example 1. Issuer hedge—(i) *Facts.* On January 1, 1997, V, a domestic corporation, issues a 5-year debt instrument for $1,000. The debt instrument provides for annual payments of interest at a rate equal to the value of 1-year LIBOR and a principal payment of $1,000 at maturity. On the same day, V enters into a 5-year interest rate swap agreement with an unrelated party. Under the swap, V pays 6 percent and receives 1-year LIBOR on a notional principal amount of $1,000. The payments on the swap are fixed and made on the same days as the payments on the debt instrument. On January 1, 1997, V identifies the debt instrument and the swap as an integrated transaction in accordance with the requirements of paragraph (e) of this section.

(ii) *Eligibility for integration.* The debt instrument is a qualifying debt instrument. The swap is a § 1.1275-6 hedge because it is a financial instrument and a yield to maturity on the combined cash flows of the swap and the debt instrument can be calculated. V has met the identification requirements, and the other requirements of paragraph (c)(1) of this section are satisfied. Therefore, the transaction is an integrated transaction under this section.

(iii) *Treatment of the synthetic debt instrument.* The synthetic debt instrument is a 5-year debt instrument that has an issue price of $1,000 and provides for annual interest payments of $60 and a principal payment of $1,000 at maturity. Under paragraph (f)(6) of this section, no amounts payable on the synthetic debt instrument are qualified stated interest. Thus, under paragraph (f)(7)(i) of this section, the synthetic debt instrument has a stated redemption price at maturity of $1,300 (the sum of all amounts to be paid on the qualifying debt instrument and the swap, reduced by amounts to be received on the swap). The synthetic debt instrument, therefore, has $300 of OID.

Example 2. Issuer hedge with an option—(i) *Facts.* On December 31, 1996, W, a domestic corporation, issues for $1,000 a debt instrument that matures on December 31, 1999. The debt instrument has a stated principal amount of $1,000 payable at maturity. The debt instrument also provides for a payment at maturity equal to $10 times the increase, if any, in the value of a nationally known composite index of stocks from December 31, 1996, to the maturity date. On December 31, 1996, W purchases from an unrelated party an option that pays $10 times the increase, if any, in the stock index from December 31, 1996, to December 31, 1999. W pays $250 for the option. On December 31, 1996, W identifies the debt instrument and option as an integrated transaction in accordance with the requirements of paragraph (e) of this section.

(ii) *Eligibility for integration.* The debt instrument is a qualifying debt instrument. The option is a § 1.1275-6 hedge because it is a financial instrument and a yield to maturity on the combined cash flows of the option and the debt instrument can be calculated. W has met the identification requirements, and the other requirements of paragraph (c)(1) of this section are satisfied. Therefore, the transaction is an integrated transaction under this section.

(iii) *Treatment of the synthetic debt instrument.* Under paragraph (f)(4) of this section, the issue price of the synthetic debt instrument is equal to the issue price of the debt instrument ($1,000) reduced by the payment for the option ($250). As a result, the synthetic debt instrument is a 3-year debt instrument with an issue price of $750. Under paragraph (f)(7) of this section, the synthetic debt instrument has a stated redemption price at maturity of $1,000 (the $250 payment for the option is not taken into account). The synthetic debt instrument, therefore, has $250 of OID.

Example 3. Hedge with prepaid swap—(i) *Facts.* On January 1, 1997, H purchases for £ 1,000 a 5-year debt instrument that provides for semiannual payments based on 6-month pound LIBOR and a payment of the £1,000 principal at maturity. On the same day, H enters into a swap with an unrelated third party under which H receives semiannual payments, in pounds, of 10 percent, compounded semiannually, and makes semiannual payments, in pounds, of 6-month pound LIBOR on a notional principal amount of £ 1,000. Payments on the swap are fixed and made on the same dates as the payments on the debt instrument. H also makes a £162 prepayment on the swap. On January 1, 1997, H identifies the swap and the debt instrument as an integrated transaction in accordance with the requirements of paragraph (e) of this section.

(ii) *Eligibility for integration.* The debt instrument is a qualifying debt instrument. The swap is a § 1.1275-6 hedge because it is a financial instrument and a yield to maturity on the combined cash flows of the swap and the debt instrument can be calculated. Although the debt instrument is denominated in pounds, the swap hedges only interest rate risk, not currency risk. Therefore, the transaction is an integrated transaction under this section. See § 1.988-5(a) for the treatment of a debt instrument and a swap if the swap hedges currency risk.

(iii) *Treatment of the synthetic debt instrument.* Under paragraph (f)(4) of this section, the issue price of the synthetic debt instrument is equal to the issue price of the debt instrument (£1,000) increased by the prepayment on the swap (£162). As a result, the synthetic debt instrument is a 5-year debt instrument that has an issue price of £1,162 and provides for semiannual interest payments of £50 and a principal payment of £1,000 at maturity. Under paragraph (f)(6) of this section, no amounts payable on the synthetic debt instrument are qualified stated interest. Thus, under paragraph (f)(7)(ii) of this section, the synthetic debt instrument's stated redemption price at maturity is £1,500 (the sum of all amounts to be received on the qualifying debt instrument and the § 1.1275-6 hedge, reduced by all amounts to be paid on the § 1.1275-6 hedge other than the £162 prepayment for the swap). The synthetic debt instrument, therefore, has £338 of OID.

Example 4. Legging into an integrated transaction by a holder—(i) *Facts.* On December 31, 1996, X corporation purchases for $1,000,000 a debt instrument that matures on December 31, 2006. The debt instrument provides for annual payments of interest at the rate of 6 percent and for a payment at maturity equal to $1,000,000, increased by the excess, if any, of the price of 1,000 units of a commodity on December 31, 2006, over $350,000, and decreased by the excess, if any, of $350,000 over the price of 1,000 units of the commodity on that date. The projected amount of the payment at maturity determined under § 1.1275-4(b)(4) is $1,020,000. On December 31, 1999, X enters into a cash-settled forward contract with an unrelated party to sell 1,000 units of the commodity on December 31, 2006, for $450,000. On December 31, 1999, X also identifies the debt instrument and the forward contract as an integrated transaction in accordance with the requirements of paragraph (e) of this section.

(ii) *Eligibility for integration.* X meets the requirements for integration as of December 31, 1999. Therefore, X legged into an integrated transaction on that date. Prior to that date, X treats the debt instrument under the applicable rules of § 1.1275-4.

(iii) *Treatment of the synthetic debt instrument.* As of December 31, 1999, the debt instrument and the forward contract are treated as an integrated transaction. The issue price of the synthetic debt instrument is equal to the adjusted issue price of the qualifying debt instrument on the leg-in date, $1,004,804 (assuming one year accrual periods). The term of the synthetic debt instrument is from December 31, 1999, to December 31, 2006. The synthetic debt instrument provides for annual interest payments of $60,000 and a principal payment at maturity of $1,100,000 ($1,000,000 + $450,000 − $350,000). Under paragraph (f)(6) of this section, no amounts payable on the synthetic debt instrument are qualified stated interest. Thus, under paragraph (f)(7)(ii) of this section, the synthetic debt instrument's stated redemption price at maturity is $1,520,000 (the sum of all amounts to be received by X on the qualifying debt instrument and the § 1.1275-6 hedge, reduced by all amounts to be paid by X on the § 1.1275-6 hedge). The synthetic debt instrument, therefore, has $515,196 of OID.

Example 5. Abusive leg-in—(i) *Facts.* On January 1, 1997, Y corporation purchases for $1,000,000 a debt instrument that matures on December 31, 2001. The debt instrument provides for annual payments of interest at the rate of 6 percent, a payment on December 31, 1999, of the increase, if any, in the price of a commodity from January 1, 1997, to December 31, 1999, and a payment at maturity of $1,000,000 and the increase, if any, in the price of the commodity from December 31, 1999 to maturity. Because the debt instrument is a contingent payment debt instrument subject to § 1.1275-4, Y accrues interest based on the projected payment schedule.

(ii) *Leg-in.* By late 1999, the price of the commodity has substantially increased, and Y expects a positive adjustment on December 31, 1999. In late 1999, Y enters into an agreement to exchange the two commodity based payments on the debt instrument for two payments on the same dates of $100,000 each. Y identifies the transaction as an integrated transaction in accordance with the requirements of paragraph (e) of this section. Y disposes of the hedge in early 2000.

(iii) *Treatment.* The legging into an integrated transaction has the effect of deferring the positive adjustment from 1999 to 2000. Because Y legged into the integrated transaction with a principal purpose to defer the positive adjustment, the Commissioner may treat the debt instrument as sold for its fair market value on the leg-in date or refuse to allow integration.

Example 6. Integration of offsetting debt instruments—(i) *Facts.* On January 1, 1997, Z issues two 10-year debt instruments. The first, Issue 1, has an issue price of $1,000, pays interest annually at 6 percent, and, at maturity, pays $1,000, increased by $1 times the increase, if any, in the value of the S&P 100 Index over the term of the instrument and reduced by $1 times the decrease, if any, in the value of the S&P 100 Index over the term of the instrument. However, the amount paid at maturity may not be less than $500 or more than $1,500. The second, Issue 2, has an issue price of $1,000, pays interest annually at 8 percent, and, at maturity, pays $1,000, reduced by $1 times the increase, if any, in the value of the S&P 100 Index over the term of the instrument and increased by $1 times the decrease, if any, in the value of the S&P 100 Index over the term of the instrument. The amount paid at maturity may not be less than $500 or more than $1,500. On January 1, 1997, Z identifies Issue 1 as the qualifying debt instrument, Issue 2 as a §1.1275-6 hedge, and otherwise meets the identification requirements of paragraph (e) of this section.

(ii) *Eligibility for integration.* Both Issue 1 and Issue 2 are qualifying debt instruments. Z has met the identification requirements by identifying Issue 1 as the qualifying debt instrument and Issue 2 as the §1.1275-6 hedge. The other requirements of paragraph (c)(1) of this section are satisfied. Therefore, the transaction is an integrated transaction under this section.

(iii) *Treatment of the synthetic debt instrument.* The synthetic debt instrument has an issue price of $2,000, provides for a payment at maturity of $2,000, and, in addition, provides for annual payments of $140. Under paragraph (f)(6) of this section, no amounts payable on the synthetic debt instrument are qualified stated interest. Thus, under paragraph (f)(7)(i) of this section, the synthetic debt instrument's stated redemption price at maturity is $3,400 (the sum of all amounts to be paid on the qualifying debt instrument and the §1.1275-6 hedge, reduced by amounts to be received on the §1.1275-6 hedge other than the $1,000 payment received on the issue date). The synthetic debt instrument, therefore, has $1,400 of OID.

Example 7. Integrated transaction entered into by a foreign person—(i) *Facts.* X, a foreign person, enters into an integrated transaction by purchasing a qualifying debt instrument that pays U.S. source interest and entering into a notional principal contract with a U.S. corporation. Neither the income from the qualifying debt instrument nor the income from the notional principal contract is effectively connected with a U.S. trade or business. The notional principal contract is a §1.1275-6 hedge.

(ii) *Treatment of integrated transaction.* Under paragraph (f)(8) of this section, X will receive U.S. source income from the integrated transaction. However, under paragraph (f)(12)(i) of this section, the qualifying debt instrument and the notional principal contract are treated as if they are not part of an integrated transaction for purposes of determining whether tax is due and must be withheld on income. Accordingly, because the §1.1275-6 hedge would produce for-

eign source income under §1.863-7 to X if it were not part of an integrated transaction, any income on the §1.1275-6 hedge generally will not be subject to tax under sections 871(a) and 881, and the U.S. corporation that is the counterparty will not be required to withhold tax on payments under the §1.1275-6 hedge under sections 1441 and 1442.

(i) [Reserved]

(j) *Effective date.*—This section applies to a qualifying debt instrument issued on or after August 13, 1996. This section also applies to a qualifying debt instrument acquired by the taxpayer on or after August 13, 1996, if—

(1) The qualifying debt instrument is a fixed rate debt instrument or a variable rate debt instrument; or

(2) The qualifying debt instrument and the §1.1275-6 hedge are acquired by the taxpayer substantially contemporaneously. [Reg. §1.1275-6.]

☐ [T.D. 8674, 6-11-96.]

[Reg. §1.1275-7]

§1.1275-7. **Inflation-indexed debt instruments.**—(a) *Overview.*—This section provides rules for the federal income tax treatment of an inflation-indexed debt instrument. If a debt instrument is an inflation-indexed debt instrument, one of two methods will apply to the instrument: the coupon bond method (as described in paragraph (d) of this section) or the discount bond method (as described in paragraph (e) of this section). Both methods determine the amount of OID that is taken into account each year by a holder or an issuer of an inflation-indexed debt instrument.

(b) *Applicability.*—(1) *In general.*—Except as provided in paragraph (b)(2) of this section, this section applies to an inflation-indexed debt instrument as defined in paragraph (c)(1) of this section. For example, this section applies to Treasury Inflation-Indexed Securities.

(2) *Exceptions.*—This section does not apply to an inflation-indexed debt instrument that is also—

(i) A debt instrument (other than a tax-exempt obligation) described in section 1272(a)(2) (for example, U.S. savings bonds, certain loans between natural persons, and short-term taxable obligations); or

(ii) A debt instrument subject to section 529 (certain debt instruments issued by qualified state tuition programs).

(c) *Definitions.*—The following definitions apply for purposes of this section:

(1) *Inflation-indexed debt instrument.*—An inflation-indexed debt instrument is a debt instrument that satisfies the following conditions:

(i) *Issued for cash.*—The debt instrument is issued for U.S. dollars and all payments on the instrument are denominated in U.S. dollars.

(ii) *Indexed for inflation and deflation.*—Except for a minimum guarantee payment (as defined in paragraph (c)(5) of this section), each payment on the debt instrument is indexed for inflation and deflation. A payment is indexed for inflation and deflation if the amount of the payment is equal to—

    (A) The amount that would be payable if there were no inflation or deflation over the term of the debt instrument, multiplied by

    (B) A ratio, the numerator of which is the value of the reference index for the date of the payment and the denominator of which is the value of the reference index for the issue date.

(iii) *No other contingencies.*—No payment on the debt instrument is subject to a contingency other than the inflation contingency or the contingencies described in this paragraph (c)(1)(iii). A debt instrument may provide for—

    (A) A minimum guarantee payment as defined in paragraph (c)(5) of this section; or

    (B) Payments under one or more alternate payment schedules if the payments under each payment schedule are indexed for inflation and deflation and a payment schedule for the debt instrument can be determined under §1.1272-1(c). (For purposes of this section, the rules of §1.1272-1(c) are applied to the debt instrument by assuming that no inflation or deflation will occur over the term of the instrument.)

(2) *Reference index.*—The reference index is an index used to measure inflation and deflation over the term of a debt instrument. To qualify as a reference index, an index must satisfy the following conditions:

(i) The value of the index is reset once a month to a current value of a single qualified inflation index (as defined in paragraph (c)(3) of this section). For this purpose, a value of a qualified inflation index is current if the value has been updated and published within the preceding six month period.

(ii) The reset occurs on the same day of each month (the reset date).

(iii) The value of the index for any date between reset dates is determined through straight-line interpolation.

(3) *Qualified inflation index.*—A qualified inflation index is a general price or wage index that is updated and published at least monthly by an agency of the United States Government (for example, the non-seasonally adjusted U.S. City Average All Items Consumer Price Index for All Urban Consumers (CPI-U), which is published by the Bureau of Labor Statistics of the Department of Labor).

(4) *Inflation-adjusted principal amount.*—For any date, the inflation-adjusted principal amount of an inflation-indexed debt instrument is an amount equal to—

(i) The outstanding principal amount of the debt instrument (determined as if there were no inflation or deflation over the term of the instrument), multiplied by

(ii) A ratio, the numerator of which is the value of the reference index for the date and the denominator of which is the value of the reference index for the issue date.

(5) *Minimum guarantee payment.*—In general, a minimum guarantee payment is an additional payment made at maturity on a debt instrument if the total amount of inflation-adjusted principal paid on the instrument is less than the instrument's stated principal amount. The amount of the additional payment must be no more than the excess, if any, of the debt instrument's stated principal amount over the total amount of inflation-adjusted principal paid on the instrument. An additional payment is not a minimum guarantee payment unless the qualified inflation index used to determine the reference index is either the CPI-U or an index designated for this purpose by the Commissioner in the Federal Register or the Internal Revenue Bulletin (see §601.601(d)(2)(ii) of this chapter). See paragraph (f)(4) of this section for the treatment of a minimum guarantee payment.

(d) *Coupon bond method.*—(1) *In general.*—This paragraph (d) describes the method (coupon bond method) to be used to account for qualified stated interest and inflation adjustments (OID) on an inflation-indexed debt instrument described in paragraph (d)(2) of this section.

(2) *Applicability.*—The coupon bond method applies to an inflation-indexed debt instrument that satisfies the following conditions:

(i) *Issued at par.*—The debt instrument is issued at par. A debt instrument is issued at par if the difference between its issue price and principal amount for the issue date is less than the de minimis amount. For this purpose, the de minimis amount is determined using the principles of §1.1273-1(d).

(ii) *All stated interest is qualified stated interest.*—All stated interest on the debt instrument is qualified stated interest. For purposes of this paragraph (d), stated interest is qualified stated interest if the interest is unconditionally payable in cash, or is constructively received under section 451, at least annually at a single fixed rate. Stated interest is payable at a single fixed rate if the amount of each interest payment is determined by multiplying the inflation adjusted principal amount for the payment date by the single fixed rate.

Reg. §1.1275-7(d)(2)(ii)

(3) *Qualified stated interest.*—Under the coupon bond method, qualified stated interest is taken into account under the taxpayer's regular method of accounting. The amount of accrued but unpaid qualified stated interest as of any date is determined by using the principles of §1.446-3(e)(2)(ii) (relating to notional principal contracts). For example, if the interval between interest payment dates spans two taxable years, a taxpayer using an accrual method of accounting determines the amount of accrued qualified stated interest for the first taxable year by reference to the inflation-adjusted principal amount at the end of the first taxable year.

(4) *Inflation adjustments.*—(i) *Current accrual.*—Under the coupon bond method, an inflation adjustment is taken into account for each taxable year in which the debt instrument is outstanding.

(ii) *Amount of inflation adjustment.*—For any relevant period (such as the taxable year or the portion of the taxable year during which a taxpayer holds an inflation-indexed debt instrument), the amount of the inflation adjustment is equal to—

(A) The sum of the inflation-adjusted principal amount at the end of the period and the principal payments made during the period, minus

(B) The inflation-adjusted principal amount at the beginning of the period.

(iii) *Positive inflation adjustments.*—A positive inflation adjustment is OID.

(iv) *Negative inflation adjustments.*—A negative inflation adjustment is a deflation adjustment that is taken into account under the rules of paragraph (f)(1) of this section.

(5) *Example.*—The following example illustrates the coupon bond method:

Example. (i) *Facts.* On October 15, 1997, X purchases at original issue, for $100,000, a debt instrument that is indexed for inflation and deflation. The debt instrument matures on October 15, 1999, has a stated principal amount of $100,000, and has a stated interest rate of 5 percent, compounded semiannually. The debt instrument provides that the principal amount is indexed to the CPI-U. Interest is payable on April 15 and October 15 of each year. The amount of each interest payment is determined by multiplying the inflation-adjusted principal amount for each interest payment date by the stated interest rate, adjusted for the length of the accrual period. The debt instrument provides for a single payment of the inflation-adjusted principal amount at maturity. In addition, the debt instrument provides for an additional payment at maturity equal to the excess, if any, of $100,000 over the inflation-adjusted principal amount at maturity. X uses the cash receipts and disbursements method of accounting and the calendar year as its taxable year.

(ii) *Indexing methodology.* The debt instrument provides that the inflation-adjusted principal amount for any day is determined by multiplying the principal amount of the instrument for the issue date by a ratio, the numerator of which is the value of the reference index for the day the inflation-adjusted principal amount is to be determined and the denominator of which is the value of the reference index for the issue date. The value of the reference index for the first day of a month is the value of the CPI-U for the third preceding month. The value of the reference index for any day other than the first day of a month is determined based on a straight-line interpolation between the value of the reference index for the first day of the month and the value of the reference index for the first day of the next month.

(iii) *Inflation-indexed debt instrument subject to the coupon bond method.* Under paragraph (c)(1) of this section, the debt instrument is an inflation-indexed debt instrument. Because there is no difference between the debt instrument's issue price ($100,000) and its principal amount for the issue date ($100,000) and because all stated interest is qualified stated interest, the coupon bond method applies to the instrument.

(iv) *Reference index values.* Assume the following table lists the relevant reference index values for 1997 through 1999:

Date	Reference index value
October 15, 1997	100
January 1, 1998	101
April 15, 1998	103
October 15, 1998	105
January 1, 1999	99

(v) *Treatment of X in 1997.* X does not receive any payments of interest on the debt instrument in 1997. Therefore, X has no qualified stated interest income for 1997. X, however, must take into account the inflation adjustment for 1997. The inflation-adjusted principal amount for January 1, 1998, is $101,000 ($100,000 × 101/100). Therefore, the inflation adjustment for 1997 is $1,000, the inflation-adjusted principal amount for January 1, 1998 ($101,000) minus the principal amount for the issue date ($100,000). X includes the $1,000 inflation adjustment in income as OID in 1997.

(vi) *Treatment of X in 1998.* In 1998, X receives two payments of interest: On April 15, 1998, X receives a payment of $2,575 ($100,000 × 103/100 × .05/2), and on October 15, 1998, X receives a payment of $2,625 ($100,000 × 105/100 × .05/2). Therefore, X's qualified stated interest income for 1998 is $5,200 ($2,575 + $2,625). X also must take into account the inflation adjustment for 1998. The inflation-adjusted principal amount for January 1, 1999, is $99,000 ($100,000 × 99/100). Therefore, the inflation adjustment for 1998 is negative $2,000, the inflation-adjusted principal amount for January 1, 1999 ($99,000) minus the inflation-adjusted principal amount for January 1, 1998 ($101,000). Because the amount of the inflation adjustment is negative, it is a deflation adjustment. Under paragraph (f)(1)(i) of this section, X uses this $2,000 deflation adjustment to reduce the interest otherwise includible in income by X with respect to the debt instrument in 1998. Therefore, X includes $3,200 in income for 1998, the qualified stated interest income for 1998 ($5,200) minus the deflation adjustment ($2,000).

(e) *Discount bond method.*—(1) *In general.*— This paragraph (e) describes the method (discount bond method) to be used to account for OID on an inflation-indexed debt instrument that does not qualify for the coupon bond method.

(2) *No qualified stated interest.*—Under the discount bond method, no interest on an inflation-indexed debt instrument is qualified stated interest.

(3) *OID.*—Under the discount bond method, the amount of OID that accrues on an inflation-indexed debt instrument is determined as follows:

(i) *Step one: Determine the debt instrument's yield to maturity.*—The yield of the debt instrument is determined under the rules of § 1.1272-1(b)(1)(i). In calculating the yield under those rules for purposes of this paragraph (e)(3)(i), the payment schedule of the debt instrument is determined as if there were no inflation or deflation over the term of the instrument.

(ii) *Step two: Determine the accrual periods.*—The accrual periods are determined under the rules of § 1.1272-1(b)(1)(ii). However, no accrual period can be longer than 1 month.

(iii) *Step three: Determine the percentage change in the reference index during the accrual period.*—The percentage change in the reference index during the accrual period is equal to—

(A) The ratio of the value of the reference index at the end of the period to the value of the reference index at the beginning of period,

(B) Minus one.

(iv) *Step four: Determine the OID allocable to each accrual period.*—The OID allocable to an accrual period (n) is determined by using the following formula:

$$OID_{(n)} = AIP_{(n)} \times [r + \inf_{(n)} + (r \times \inf_{(n)})]$$ in which,

r = yield of the debt instrument as determined under paragraph (e)(3)(i) of this section (adjusted for the length of the accrual period);

$\inf_{(n)}$ = percentage change in the value of the reference index for period (n) as determined under paragraph (e)(3)(iii) of this section; and

$AIP_{(n)}$ = adjusted issue price at the beginning of period (n).

(v) *Step five: Determine the daily portions of OID.*—The daily portions of OID are determined and taken into account under the rules of § 1.1272-1(b)(1)(iv). If the daily portions determined under this paragraph (e)(3)(v) are negative amounts, however, these amounts (deflation adjustments) are taken into account under the rules for deflation adjustments described in paragraph (f)(1) of this section.

(4) *Example.*—The following example illustrates the discount bond method:

Example. (i) *Facts.* On November 15, 1997, X purchases at original issue, for $91,403, a zero-coupon debt instrument that is indexed for inflation and deflation. The principal amount of the debt instrument for the issue date is $100,000. The debt instrument provides for a single payment on November 15, 2000. The amount of the payment will be determined by multiplying $100,000 by a fraction, the numerator of which is the CPI-U for September 2000, and the denominator of which is the CPI-U for September 1997. The debt instrument also provides that in no event will the payment on November 15, 2000, be less than $100,000. X uses the cash receipts and disbursements method of accounting and the calendar year as its taxable year.

(ii) *Inflation-indexed debt instrument.* Under paragraph (c)(1) of this section, the instrument is an inflation-indexed debt instrument. The debt instrument's principal amount for the issue date ($100,000) exceeds its issue price ($91,403) by $8,597, which is more than the de minimis amount for the debt instrument ($750). Therefore, the coupon bond method does not apply to the debt instrument. As a result, the discount bond method applies to the debt instrument.

(iii) *Yield and accrual period.* Assume X chooses monthly accrual periods ending on the 15th day of each month. The yield of the debt instrument is determined as if there were no inflation or deflation over the term of the instrument. Therefore, based on the issue price of $91,403 and an assumed payment at maturity of $100,000, the yield of the debt instrument is 3 percent, compounded monthly.

(iv) *Percentage change in reference index.* Assume that the CPI-U for September 1997 is 160; for October 1997 is 161.2; and for November 1997 is 161.7. The value of the reference index for November 15, 1997, is 160, the value of the CPI-U for September 1997. Similarly, the value of the reference index for December 15, 1997, is 161.2, and for January 15, 1998, is 161.7. The percentage change in the reference index from November 15, 1997, to December 15, 1997, ($\inf_1$) is 0.0075 (161.2/160 − 1); the percentage change in the reference index from December 15, 1997, to January 15, 1998, ($\inf_2$) is 0.0031 (161.7/161.2 − 1).

(v) *Treatment of X in 1997.* For the accrual period ending on December 15, 1997, r is .0025

(.03/12), inf_1 is .0075, and the product of r and inf_1 is .00001875. Under paragraph (e)(3) of this section, the amount of OID allocable to the accrual period ending on December 15, 1997, is $916. This amount is determined by multiplying the issue price of the debt instrument ($91,403) by .01001875 (the sum of r, inf_1, and the product of r and inf_1). The adjusted issue price of the debt instrument on December 15, 1997, is $92,319 ($91,403 + $916). For the accrual period ending on January 15, 1998, r is .0025 (.03/12), inf_2 is .0031, and the product of r and inf_2 is .00000775. Under paragraph (e)(3) of this section, the amount of OID allocable to the accrual period ending on January 15, 1998, is $518. This amount is determined by multiplying the adjusted issue price of the debt instrument ($92,319) by .00560775 (the sum of r, inf_2, and the product of r and inf_2). Because the accrual period ending on January 15, 1998, spans two taxable years, only $259 of this amount ($518/30 days × 15 days) is allocable to 1997. Therefore, X includes $1,175 of OID in income for 1997 ($916 + $259).

(f) *Special rules.*—The following rules apply to an inflation-indexed debt instrument:

(1) *Deflation adjustments.*—(i) *Holder.*—A deflation adjustment reduces the amount of interest otherwise includible in income by a holder with respect to the debt instrument for the taxable year. For purposes of this paragraph (f)(1)(i), interest includes OID, qualified stated interest, and market discount. If the amount of the deflation adjustment exceeds the interest otherwise includible in income by the holder with respect to the debt instrument for the taxable year, the excess is treated as an ordinary loss by the holder for the taxable year. However, the amount treated as an ordinary loss is limited to the amount by which the holder's total interest inclusions on the debt instrument in prior taxable years exceed the total amount treated by the holder as an ordinary loss on the debt instrument in prior taxable years. If the deflation adjustment exceeds the interest otherwise includible in income by the holder with respect to the debt instrument for the taxable year and the amount treated as an ordinary loss for the taxable year, this excess is carried forward to reduce the amount of interest otherwise includible in income by the holder with respect to the debt instrument for subsequent taxable years.

(ii) *Issuer.*—A deflation adjustment reduces the interest otherwise deductible by the issuer with respect to the debt instrument for the taxable year. For purposes of this paragraph (f)(1)(ii), interest includes OID and qualified stated interest. If the amount of the deflation adjustment exceeds the interest otherwise deductible by the issuer with respect to the debt instrument for the taxable year, the excess is treated as ordinary income by the issuer for the taxable year. However, the amount treated as ordinary income is limited to the amount by which the issuer's total interest deductions on the debt instrument in prior taxable years exceed the total amount treated by the issuer as ordinary income on the debt instrument in prior taxable years. If the deflation adjustment exceeds the interest otherwise deductible by the issuer with respect to the debt instrument for the taxable year and the amount treated as ordinary income for the taxable year, this excess is carried forward to reduce the interest otherwise deductible by the issuer with respect to the debt instrument for subsequent taxable years. If there is any excess remaining upon the retirement of the debt instrument, the issuer takes the excess amount into account as ordinary income.

(2) *Adjusted basis.*—A holder's adjusted basis in an inflation-indexed debt instrument is determined under § 1.1272-1(g). However, a holder's adjusted basis in the debt instrument is decreased by the amount of any deflation adjustment the holder takes into account to reduce the amount of interest otherwise includible in income or treats as an ordinary loss with respect to the instrument during the taxable year. The decrease occurs when the deflation adjustment is taken into account under paragraph (f)(1) of this section.

(3) *Subsequent holders.*—A holder determines the amount of acquisition premium or market discount on an inflation-indexed debt instrument by reference to the adjusted issue price of the instrument on the date the holder acquires the instrument. A holder determines the amount of bond premium on an inflation-indexed debt instrument by assuming that the amount payable at maturity on the instrument is equal to the instrument's inflation-adjusted principal amount for the day the holder acquires the instrument. Any premium or market discount is taken into account over the remaining term of the debt instrument as if there were no further inflation or deflation. See section 171 for additional rules relating to the amortization of bond premium and sections 1276 through 1278 for additional rules relating to market discount.

(4) *Minimum guarantee.*—Under both the coupon bond method and the discount bond method, a minimum guarantee payment is ignored until the payment is made. If there is a minimum guarantee payment, the payment is treated as interest on the date it is paid.

(5) *Temporary unavailability of a qualified inflation index.*—Notwithstanding any other rule of this section, an inflation-indexed debt instrument may provide for a substitute value of the qualified inflation index if and when the publication of the value of the qualified inflation index is temporarily delayed. The substitute value may be determined by the issuer under any reasonable method. For example, if the CPI-U is not reported for a particular month, the debt instru-

ment may provide that a substitute value may be determined by increasing the last reported value by the average monthly percentage increase in the qualified inflation index over the preceding twelve months. The use of a substitute value does not result in a reissuance of the debt instrument.

(g) *Reopenings.*—For rules concerning a reopening of Treasury Inflation-Indexed Securities, see paragraphs (d)(2) and (k)(3)(iii) of § 1.1275-2.

(h) *Effective date.*—This section applies to an inflation-indexed debt instrument issued on or after January 6, 1997. [Reg. § 1.1275-7.]

☐ [*T.D. 8709, 12-31-96. Redesignated by T.D. 8838, 9-3-99. Amended by T.D. 8840, 11-3-99 and T.D. 8934, 1-11-2001.*]

[Reg. § 1.1286-1]

§ 1.1286-1. Tax treatment of certain stripped bonds and stripped coupons.—(a) *De minimis OID.*—If the original issue discount determined under section 1286(a) with respect to the purchase of a stripped bond or stripped coupon is less than the amount computed under subparagraphs (A) and (B) of section 1273(a)(3) and the regulations thereunder, then the amount of original issue discount with respect to that purchase (other than any tax-exempt portion thereof, determined under section 1286(d)(2)) shall be considered to be zero. For purposes of this computation, the number of complete years to maturity is measured from the date the stripped bond or stripped coupon is purchased.

(b) *Treatment of certain stripped bonds as market discount bonds.*—(1) *In general.*—By publication in the Internal Revenue Bulletin (see § 601.601(d)(2)(ii)(b) of the Statement of Procedural Rules), the Internal Revenue Service may (subject to the limitation of paragraph (b)(2) of this section) provide that certain mortgage loans that are stripped bonds are to be treated as market discount bonds under section 1278. Thus, any purchaser of such a bond is to account for any discount on the bond as market discount rather than original issue discount.

(2) *Limitation.*—This treatment may be provided for a stripped bond only if, immediately after the most recent disposition referred to in section 1286(b)—

(i) The amount of original issue discount with respect to the stripped bond is determined under paragraph (a) of this section (concerning *de minimis* OID); or

(ii) The annual stated rate of interest payable on the stripped bond is no more than 100 basis points lower than the annual stated rate of interest payable on the original bond from which it and any other stripped bond or bonds and any stripped coupon or coupons were stripped.

(c) *Effective date.*—This section is effective on and after August 8, 1991. [Reg. § 1.1286-1.]

☐ [*T.D. 8463, 12-28-92.*]

[Reg. § 1.1286-2]

§ 1.1286-2. Stripped inflation-indexed debt instruments.—*Stripped inflation-indexed debt instruments.* If a Treasury Inflation-Indexed Security is stripped under the Department of the Treasury's Separate Trading of Registered Interest and Principal of Securities (STRIPS) program, the holders of the principal and coupon components must use the discount bond method (as described in § 1.1275-7(e)) to account for the original issue discount on the components. [Reg. § 1.1286-2.]

☐ [*T.D. 8709, 12-31-96. Redesignated and amended by T.D. 8838, 9-3-99.*]

[Reg. § 1.1287-1]

§ 1.1287-1. Denial of capital gains treatment for gains on registration-required obligations not in registered form.—(a) *In general.*—Except as provided in paragraph (c) of this section, any gain on the sale or other disposition of a registration-required obligation held after December 31, 1982, that is not in registered form shall be treated as ordinary income unless the issuance of the obligation was subject to tax under section 4701. The term "registration-required obligation" has the meaning given to that term in section 163(f)(2), except that clause (iv) of subparagraph (A) thereof shall not apply. Therefore, although an obligation that is not in registered form is described in § 1.163-5(c)(1), the holder of such an obligation shall be required to treat the gain on the sale or other disposition of such obligation as ordinary income. The term "holder" means the person that would be denied a loss deduction under section 165(j)(1) or denied capital gain treatment under section 1287(a).

(b) *Registered form.*—(1) *Obligations issued after September 21, 1984.*—With respect to any obligation originally issued after September 21, 1984, the term "registered form" has the meaning given that term in section 103(j)(3) and the regulations thereunder. Therefore, an obligation that would otherwise be in registered form is not considered to be in registered form if it can be transferred at that time or at any time until its maturity by any means not described in § 5f.103-1(c). An obligation that, as of a particular time, is not considered to be in registered form because it can be transferred by any means not described in § 5f.103-1(c) is considered to be in registered form at all times during the period beginning with a later time and ending with the maturity of the obligation in which the obligation can be transferred only by a means described in § 5f.103-1(c).

(2) *Obligations issued after December 31, 1982 and on or before September 21, 1984.*—With respect

to any obligation originally issued after December 31, 1982 and on or before September 21, 1984 or an obligation originally issued after September 21, 1984 pursuant to the exercise of a warrant or the conversion of a convertible obligation, which warrant or obligation (including conversion privilege) was issued after December 31, 1982 and on or before September 21, 1984 that obligation will be considered to be in registered form if it satisfied § 5f.163-1 or the proposed regulations provided in § 1.163-5(c) and published in the Federal Register on September 2, 1983 (48 FR 39953).

(c) *Registration-required obligations not in registered form which are not subject to section 1287(c).—*

Notwithstanding the fact that an obligation is a registration-required obligation that is not in registered form, the holder will not be subject to section 1287(a) if the holder meets the conditions of § 1.165-12(c).

(d) *Effective date.—*These regulations apply generally to obligations issued after January 20, 1987. However, a taxpayer may choose to apply the rules of § 1.1287-1 with respect to an obligation issued after December 31, 1982 and on or before January 20, 1987, which obligation is held after January 20, 1987. [Reg. § 1.1287-1.]

☐ [T.D. 8110, 12-16-86.]

Passive Foreign Investment Companies

[Reg. § 1.1291-0]

§ 1.1291-0. Treatment of shareholders of certain passive foreign investment companies; table of contents.—This section contains a listing of the headings for §§ 1.1291-1, 1.1291-9, and 1.1291-10.

§ 1.1291-1. Taxation of U.S. persons that are shareholders of section 1291 funds.
  (a) through (b) [Reserved].
  (c) Coordination with other PFIC rules.
    (1) and (2) [Reserved].
    (3) Coordination with section 1296: distributions and dispositions.
    (4) Coordination with mark to market rules under chapter 1 of the Internal Revenue Code other than section 1296.
      (i) In general.
      (ii) Coordination rule.
  (d) [Reserved].
  (e) Exempt organization as shareholder.
    (1) In general.
    (2) Effective date.
  (f) through (i) [Reserved].
  (j) Effective date.

§ 1.1291-9. Deemed dividend election.
  (a) Deemed dividend election.
    (1) In general.
    (2) Post-1986 earnings and profits defined.
      (i) In general.
      (ii) Pro rata share of post-1986 earnings and profits attributable to shareholder's stock.
        (A) In general.
        (B) Reduction for previously taxed amounts.
  (b) Who may make the election.
  (c) Time for making the election.
  (d) Manner of making the election.
    (1) In general.
    (2) Attachment to Form 8621

  (e) Qualification date.
    (1) In general.
    (2) Elections made after March 31, 1995, and before January 27, 1997.
      (i) In general.
      (ii) Exception.
    (3) Examples.
  (f) Adjustment to basis.
  (g) Treatment of holding period.
  (i) Election inapplicable to shareholder of former PFIC.
    (1) [Reserved].
    (2) Former PFIC.
  (j) Definitions.
    (1) Passive foreign investment company (PFIC).
    (2) Types of PFICs.
      (i) Qualified electing fund (QEF).
      (ii) Pedigreed QEF.
      (iii) Unpedigreed QEF.
      (iv) Former PFIC.
    (3) Shareholder.
  (k) Effective date.

§ 1.1291-10. Deemed sale election.
  (a) Deemed sale election.
  (b) Who may make the election.
  (c) Time for making the election.
  (d) Manner of making the election.
  (e) Qualification date.
    (1) In general.
    (2) Elections made after March 31, 1995, and before January 27, 1997.
      (i) In general.
      (ii) Exception.
  (f) Adjustments to basis.
    (1) In general.
    (2) Adjustment to basis for section 1293 inclusion with respect to deemed sale election made after March 31, 1995, and before January 27, 1997.
  (g) Treatment of holding period.

(h) Election inapplicable to shareholder of former PFIC.

(i) Effective date.

[Reg. § 1.1291-0.]

☐ [*T.D. 8701, 12-26-96. Amended by T.D. 8750, 12-31-97 and T.D. 9123, 4-30-2004.*]

[Reg. § 1.1291-0T]

§ 1.1291-0T. [Reserved].

☐ [*T.D. 8178, 2-26-88. Amended by T.D. 8404, 3-31-92; T.D. 8701, 12-26-96 and T.D. 8750, 12-31-97.*]

[Reg. § 1.1291-1]

§ 1.1291-1. Taxation of U.S. persons that are shareholders of section 1291 funds.—(a) and (b) [Reserved].

(c) *Coordination with other PFIC rules.*

(1) and (2) [Reserved].

(3) *Coordination with section 1296: distributions and dispositions.*—If PFIC stock is marked to market under section 1296 for any taxable year, then, except as provided in § 1.1296-1(i), section 1291 and the regulations thereunder shall not apply to any distribution with respect to section 1296 stock (as defined in § 1.1296-1(a)(2)), or to any disposition of such stock, for such taxable year.

(4) *Coordination with mark to market rules under chapter 1 of the Internal Revenue Code other than section 1296.*—(i) *In general.*—If PFIC stock is marked to market for any taxable year under section 475 or any other provision of chapter 1 of the Internal Revenue Code, other than section 1296, regardless of whether the application of such provision is mandatory or results from an election by the taxpayer or another person, then, except as provided in paragraph (c)(4)(ii) of this section, section 1291 and the regulations thereunder shall not apply to any distribution with respect to such PFIC stock or to any disposition of such PFIC stock for such taxable year. See §§ 1.1295-1(i)(3) and 1.1296-1(h)(3)(i) for rules regarding the automatic termination of an existing election under section 1295 or section 1296 when a taxpayer marks to market PFIC stock under section 475 or any other provision of chapter 1 of the Internal Revenue Code.

(ii) *Coordination rule.*—(A) Notwithstanding any provision in this section to the contrary, the rule of paragraph (c)(4)(ii)(B) of this section shall apply to the first taxable year in which a United States person marks to market its PFIC stock under a provision of chapter 1 of the Internal Revenue Code, other than section 1296, if such foreign corporation was a PFIC for any taxable year, prior to such first taxable year, during the United States person's holding period (as defined in section 1291(a)(3)(A) and § 1.1296-1(f)) in such stock, and for which such

corporation was not treated as a QEF with respect to such United States person.

(B) For the first taxable year of a United States person that marks to market its PFIC stock under any provision of chapter 1 of the Internal Revenue Code, other than section 1296, such United States person shall, in lieu of the rules under which the United States person marks to market, apply the rules of § 1.1296-1(i)(2) and (3) as if the United States person had made an election under section 1296 for such first taxable year.

(d) [Reserved].

(e) *Exempt organization as shareholder.*—(1) *In general.*—If the shareholder of a PFIC is an organization exempt from tax under this chapter, section 1291 and these regulations apply to such shareholder only if a dividend from the PFIC would be taxable to the organization under subchapter F.

(2) *Effective date.*—Paragraph (e)(1) of this section is applicable on and after April 1, 1992.

(f) through (i) [Reserved].

(j) *Effective dates.*—This section applies for taxable years beginning on or after May 3, 2004, except as otherwise provided in paragraph (e)(2) of this section. [Reg. § 1.1291-1.]

☐ [*T.D. 8750, 12-31-97. Redesignated by T.D. 8870, 2-4-2000. Amended by T.D. 9123, 4-30-2004.*]

[Reg. § 1.1291-9]

§ 1.1291-9. Deemed dividend election.—(a) *Deemed dividend election.*—(1) *In general.*—This section provides rules for making the election under section 1291(d)(2)(B) (deemed dividend election). Under that section, a shareholder (as defined in paragraph (j)(3) of this section) of a PFIC that is an unpedigreed QEF may elect to include in income as a dividend the shareholder's pro rata share of the post-1986 earnings and profits of the PFIC attributable to the stock held on the qualification date (as defined in paragraph (e) of this section), provided the PFIC is a controlled foreign corporation (CFC) within the meaning of section 957(a) for the taxable year for which the shareholder elects under section 1295 to treat the PFIC as a QEF (section 1295 election). If the shareholder makes the deemed dividend election, the PFIC will become a pedigreed QEF with respect to the shareholder. The deemed dividend is taxed under section 1291 as an excess distribution received on the qualification date. The excess distribution determined under this paragraph (a) is allocated under section 1291(a)(1)(A) only to those days in the shareholder's holding period during which the foreign corporation qualified as a PFIC. For purposes of the preceding sentence, the holding period of the PFIC stock with respect to which the election is made ends on the day before the qualification date. For the definitions of PFIC,

QEF, unpedigreed QEF, and pedigreed QEF, see paragraph (j)(1) and (2) of this section.

(2) *Post-1986 earnings and profits defined.—* (i) *In general.*—For purposes of this section, the term post-1986 earnings and profits means the undistributed earnings and profits, within the meaning of section 902(c)(1), as of the day before the qualification date, that were accumulated and not distributed in taxable years of the PFIC beginning after 1986 and during which it was a PFIC, but without regard to whether the earnings relate to a period during which the PFIC was a CFC.

(ii) *Pro rata share of post-1986 earnings and profits attributable to shareholder's stock.*—(A) *In general.*—A shareholder's pro rata share of the post-1986 earnings and profits of the PFIC attributable to the stock held by the shareholder on the qualification date is the amount of post-1986 earnings and profits of the PFIC accumulated during any portion of the shareholder's holding period ending at the close of the day before the qualification date and attributable, under the principles of section 1248 and the regulations under that section, to the PFIC stock held on the qualification date.

(B) *Reduction for previously taxed amounts.*—A shareholder's pro rata share of the post-1986 earnings and profits of the PFIC does not include any amount that the shareholder demonstrates to the satisfaction of the Commissioner (in the manner provided in paragraph (d)(2) of this section) was, pursuant to another provision of the law, previously included in the income of the shareholder, or of another U.S. person if the shareholder's holding period of the PFIC stock includes the period during which the stock was held by that other U.S. person.

(b) *Who may make the election.*—A shareholder of an unpedigreed QEF that is a CFC for the taxable year of the PFIC for which the shareholder makes the section 1295 election may make the deemed dividend election provided the shareholder held stock of that PFIC on the qualification date. A shareholder is treated as holding stock of the PFIC on the qualification date if its holding period with respect to that stock under section 1223 includes the qualification date. A shareholder may make the deemed dividend election without regard to whether the shareholder is a United States shareholder within the meaning of section 951(b). A deemed dividend election may be made by a shareholder whose pro rata share of the post-1986 earnings and profits of the PFIC attributable to the PFIC stock held on the qualification date is zero.

(c) *Time for making the election.*—The shareholder makes the deemed dividend election in the shareholder's return for the taxable year that includes the qualification date. If the shareholder and the PFIC have the same taxable year, the shareholder makes the deemed dividend election in either the original return for the taxable year for which the shareholder makes the section 1295 election, or in an amended return for that year. If the shareholder and the PFIC have different taxable years, the deemed dividend election must be made in an amended return for the taxable year that includes the qualification date. If the deemed dividend election is made in an amended return, the amended return must be filed by a date that is within three years of the due date, as extended under section 6081, of the original return for the taxable year that includes the qualification date.

(d) *Manner of making the election.*—(1) *In general.*—A shareholder makes the deemed dividend election by filing Form 8621 and the attachment to Form 8621 described in paragraph (d)(2) of this section with the return for the taxable year of the shareholder that includes the qualification date, reporting the deemed dividend as an excess distribution pursuant to section 1291(a)(1), and paying the tax and interest due on the excess distribution. A shareholder that makes the deemed dividend election after the due date of the return (determined without regard to extensions) for the taxable year that includes the qualification date must pay additional interest, pursuant to section 6601, on the amount of the underpayment of tax for that year.

(2) *Attachment to Form 8621.*—The shareholder must attach a schedule to Form 8621 that demonstrates the calculation of the shareholder's pro rata share of the post-1986 earnings and profits of the PFIC that is treated as distributed to the shareholder on the qualification date pursuant to this section. If the shareholder is claiming an exclusion from its pro rata share of the post-1986 earnings and profits for an amount previously included in its income or the income of another U.S. person, the shareholder must include the following information:

(i) The name, address, and taxpayer identification number of each U.S. person that previously included an amount in income, the amount previously included in income by each such U.S. person, the provision of the law pursuant to which the amount was previously included in income, and the taxable year or years of inclusion of each amount; and

(ii) A description of the transaction pursuant to which the shareholder acquired, directly or indirectly, the stock of the PFIC from another U.S. person, and the provisions of law pursuant to which the shareholder's holding period includes the period the other U.S. person held the CFC stock.

(e) *Qualification date.*—(1) *In general.*—Except as otherwise provided in this paragraph (e), the qualification date is the first day of the PFIC's first taxable year as a QEF (first QEF year).

(2) *Elections made after March 31, 1995, and before January 27, 1997.*—(i) *In general.*—The qualification date for deemed dividend elections made after March 31, 1995, and before January 27, 1997, is the first day of the shareholder's election year. The shareholder's election year is the taxable year of the shareholder for which it made the section 1295 election.

(ii) *Exception.*—A shareholder who made the deemed dividend election after May 1, 1992, and before January 27, 1997, may elect to change its qualification date to the first day of the first QEF year, provided the periods of limitations on assessment for the taxable year that includes that date and for the shareholder's election year have not expired. A shareholder changes the qualification date by filing amended returns, with revised Forms 8621 and the attachments described in paragraph (d)(2) of this section, for the shareholder's election year and the shareholder's taxable year that includes the first day of the first QEF year, and making all appropriate adjustments and payments.

(3) *Examples.*—The rules of this paragraph (e) are illustrated by the following examples:

Example 1—(i) *Eligibility to make deemed dividend election.* A is a U.S. person who files its income tax return on a calendar year basis. On January 2, 1994, A purchased one percent of the stock of M, a PFIC with a taxable year ending November 30. M was both a CFC and a PFIC, but not a QEF, for all of its taxable years. On December 3, 1996, M made a distribution to its shareholders. A received $100, all of which A reported in its 1996 return as an excess distribution as provided in section 1291(a)(1). A decides to make the section 1295 election in A's 1997 taxable year to treat M as a QEF effective for M's taxable year beginning December 1, 1996. Because A did not make the section 1295 election in 1994, the first year in its holding period of M stock that M qualified as a PFIC, M would be an unpedigreed QEF and A would be subject to both sections 1291 and 1293. A, however, may elect under section 1291(d)(2) to purge the years M was not a QEF from A's holding period. If A makes the section 1291(d)(2) election, the December 3 distribution will not be taxable under section 1291(a). Because M is a CFC, even though A is not a U.S. shareholder within the meaning of section 951(b), A may make the deemed dividend election under section 1291(d)(2)(B).

(ii) *Making the election.* Under paragraph (e)(1) of this section, the qualification date, and therefore the date of the deemed dividend, is December 1, 1996. Accordingly, to make the deemed dividend election, A must file an amended return for 1996, and include the deemed dividend in income in that year. As a result, M will be a pedigreed QEF as of December 1, 1996, and the December 3, 1996, distribution will not be taxable as an excess distribution. Therefore, in its amended return, A may report

the December 3, 1996, distribution consistent with section 1293 and the general rules applicable to corporate distributions.

Example 2. X, a U.S. person, owned a five percent interest in the stock of FC, a PFIC with a taxable year ending June 30. X never made the section 1295 election with respect to FC. X transferred her interest in FC to her granddaughter, Y, a U.S. person, on February 14, 1996. The transfer qualified as a gift for federal income tax purposes, and no gain was recognized on the transfer (see Regulation Project INTL-656-87, published in 1992-1 C.B. 1124; see § 601.601(d)(2)(ii)(*b*) of this chapter). As provided in section 1223(2), Y's holding period includes the period that X held the FC stock. Y decides to make the section 1295 election in her 1996 return to treat FC as a QEF for its taxable year beginning July 1, 1995. However, because Y's holding period includes the period that X held the FC stock, and FC was a PFIC but not a QEF during that period, FC will be an unpedigreed QEF with respect to Y unless Y makes a section 1291(d)(2) election. Although Y did not actually own the stock of FC on the qualification date (July 1, 1995), Y's holding period includes that date. Therefore, provided FC is a CFC for its taxable year beginning July 1, 1995, Y may make a section 1291(d)(2)(B) election to treat FC as a pedigreed QEF.

(f) *Adjustment to basis.*—A shareholder that makes the deemed dividend election increases its adjusted basis of the stock of the PFIC owned directly by the shareholder by the amount of the deemed dividend. If the shareholder makes the deemed dividend election with respect to a PFIC of which it is an indirect shareholder, the shareholder's adjusted basis of the stock or other property owned directly by the shareholder, through which ownership of the PFIC is attributed to the shareholder, is increased by the amount of the deemed dividend. In addition, solely for purposes of determining the subsequent treatment under the Code and regulations of a shareholder of the stock of the PFIC, the adjusted basis of the direct owner of the stock of the PFIC is increased by the amount of the deemed dividend.

(g) *Treatment of holding period.*—For purposes of applying sections 1291 through 1297 to the shareholder after the deemed dividend, the shareholder's holding period of the stock of the PFIC begins on the qualification date. For other purposes of the Code and regulations, this holding period rule does not apply.

(h) *Coordination with section 959(e).*—For purposes of section 959(e), the entire deemed dividend is treated as included in gross income under section 1248(a).

(i) *Election inapplicable to shareholder of a former PFIC or of a section 1297(e) PFIC.*—A shareholder may not make the section 1295 and deemed dividend elections if the foreign corporation is a former PFIC (as defined in paragraph (j)(2)(iv) of this section) or a section 1297(e) PFIC (as defined in paragraph (j)(2)(v) of this section) with respect to the shareholder. For the rules regarding the election by a shareholder of a former PFIC, see § 1.1298-3. For the rules regarding the election by a shareholder of a section 1297(e) PFIC, see § 1.1297-3.

(j) *Definitions.*—(1) *Passive foreign investment company (PFIC).*—A passive foreign investment company (PFIC) is a foreign corporation that satisfies either the income test of section 1296(a)(1) or the asset test of section 1296(a)(2). A corporation will not be treated as a PFIC with respect to a shareholder for those days included in the shareholder's holding period when the shareholder, or a person whose holding period of the stock is included in the shareholder's holding period, was not a United States person within the meaning of section 7701(a)(30).

(2) *Types of PFICs.*—(i) *Qualified electing fund (QEF).*—A PFIC is a qualified electing fund (QEF) with respect to a shareholder that has elected, under section 1295, to be taxed currently on its share of the PFIC's earnings and profits pursuant to section 1293.

(ii) *Pedigreed QEF.*—A PFIC is a pedigreed QEF with respect to a shareholder if the PFIC has been a QEF with respect to the shareholder for all taxable years during which the corporation was a PFIC that are included wholly or partly in the shareholder's holding period of the PFIC stock.

(iii) *Unpedigreed QEF.*—A PFIC is an unpedigreed QEF for a taxable year if—

(A) An election under section 1295 is in effect for that year;

(B) The PFIC has been a QEF with respect to the shareholder for at least one, but not all, of the taxable years during which the corporation was a PFIC that are included wholly or partly in the shareholder's holding period of the PFIC stock; and

(C) The shareholder has not made an election under section 1291(d)(2) and this section or § 1.1291-10 with respect to the PFIC to purge the nonQEF years from the shareholder's holding period.

(iv) *Former PFIC.*—A foreign corporation is a former PFIC with respect to a shareholder if the corporation satisfies neither the income test of section 1297(a)(1) nor the asset test of section 1297(a)(2), but its stock, held by that shareholder, is treated as stock of a PFIC, pursuant to section 1298(b)(1), because the corporation was a PFIC that was not a QEF at some time during the shareholder's holding period of the stock.

(v) *Section 1297(e) PFIC.*—A foreign corporation is a section 1297(e) PFIC with respect to

a shareholder (as defined in paragraph (j)(3) of this section) if—

(A) The foreign corporation qualifies as a PFIC under section 1297(a) on the first day on which the qualified portion of the shareholder's holding period in the foreign corporation begins, as determined under section 1297(e)(2); and

(B) The stock of the foreign corporation held by the shareholder is treated as stock of a PFIC, pursuant to section 1298(b)(1), because, at any time during the shareholder's holding period of the stock, other than the qualified portion, the corporation was a PFIC that was not a QEF.

(3) *Shareholder.*—A shareholder is a U.S. person that is a direct or indirect shareholder as defined in Regulation Project INTL-656-87 published in 1992-1 C.B. 1124; see § 601.601(d)(2)(ii)(*b*) of this chapter.

(k) *Effective/applicability date.*—(1) The rules of this section, except for paragraph (j)(2)(v) of this section, are applicable as of April 1, 1995.

(2) The rules of paragraph (j)(2)(v) of this section are applicable as of December 8, 2005. [Reg. § 1.1291-9.]

☐ [*T.D.* 8701, 12-26-96. *Amended by T.D.* 8750, 12-31-97; *T.D.* 9231, 12-7-2005 *and T.D.* 9360, 9-26-2007.]

[Reg. § 1.1291-10]

§ 1.1291-10. Deemed sale election.— (a) *Deemed sale election.*—This section provides rules for making the election under section 1291(d)(2)(A) (deemed sale election). Under that section, a shareholder (as defined in § 1.1291-9(j)(3)) of a PFIC that is an unpedigreed QEF may elect to recognize gain with respect to the stock of the unpedigreed QEF held on the qualification date (as defined in paragraph (e) of this section). If the shareholder makes the deemed sale election, the PFIC will become a pedigreed QEF with respect to the shareholder. A shareholder that makes the deemed sale election is treated as having sold, for its fair market value, the stock of the PFIC that the shareholder held on the qualification date. The gain recognized on the deemed sale is taxed under section 1291 as an excess distribution received on the qualification date. In the case of an election made by an indirect shareholder, the amount of gain to be recognized and taxed as an excess distribution is the amount of gain that the direct owner of the stock of the PFIC would have realized on an actual sale or other disposition of the stock of the PFIC indirectly owned by the shareholder. Any loss realized on the deemed sale is not recognized. For the definitions of PFIC, QEF, unpedigreed QEF, and pedigreed QEF, see § 1.1291-9(j)(1) and (2).

(b) *Who may make the election.*—A shareholder of an unpedigreed QEF may make the deemed sale election provided the shareholder held stock of that PFIC on the qualification date. A shareholder is treated as holding stock of the PFIC on the qualification date if its holding period with respect to that stock under section 1223 includes the qualification date. A deemed sale election may be made by a shareholder that would realize a loss on the deemed sale.

(c) *Time for making the election.*—The shareholder makes the deemed sale election in the shareholder's return for the taxable year that includes the qualification date. If the shareholder and the PFIC have the same taxable year, the shareholder makes the deemed sale election in either the original return for the taxable year for which the shareholder makes the section 1295 election, or in an amended return for that year. If the shareholder and the PFIC have different taxable years, the deemed sale election must be made in an amended return for the taxable year that includes the qualification date. If the deemed sale election is made in an amended return, the amended return must be filed by a date that is within three years of the due date, as extended under section 6081, of the original return for the taxable year that includes the qualification date.

(d) *Manner of making the election.*—A shareholder makes the deemed sale election by filing Form 8621 with the return for the taxable year of the shareholder that includes the qualification date, reporting the gain as an excess distribution pursuant to section 1291(a), and paying the tax and interest due on the excess distribution. A shareholder that makes the deemed sale election after the due date of the return (determined without regard to extensions) for the taxable year that includes the qualification date must pay additional interest, pursuant to section 6601, on the amount of the underpayment of tax for that year. A shareholder that realizes a loss on the deemed sale reports the loss on Form 8621, but does not recognize the loss.

(e) *Qualification date.*—(1) *In general.*—Except as otherwise provided in this paragraph (e), the qualification date is the first day of the PFIC's first taxable year as a QEF (first QEF year).

(2) *Elections made after March 31, 1995, and before January 27, 1997.*—(i) *In general.*—The qualification date for deemed sale elections made after March 31, 1995, and before January 27, 1997, is the first day of the shareholder's election year. The shareholder's election year is the taxable year of the shareholder for which it made the section 1295 election.

(ii) *Exception.*—A shareholder who made the deemed sale election after May 1, 1992, and before January 27, 1997, may elect to change its qualification date to the first day of the first QEF year, provided the periods of limitations on assessment for the taxable year that includes that

date and for the shareholder's election year have not expired. A shareholder changes the qualification date by filing amended returns, with revised Forms 8621, for the shareholder's election year and the shareholder's taxable year that includes the first day of the first QEF year, and making all appropriate adjustments and payments.

(f) *Adjustments to basis.*—(1) *In general.*—A shareholder that makes the deemed sale election increases its adjusted basis of the PFIC stock owned directly by the amount of gain recognized on the deemed sale. If the shareholder makes the deemed sale election with respect to a PFIC of which it is an indirect shareholder, the shareholder's adjusted basis of the stock or other property owned directly by the shareholder, through which ownership of the PFIC is attributed to the shareholder, is increased by the amount of gain recognized by the shareholder. In addition, solely for purposes of determining the subsequent treatment under the Code and regulations of a shareholder of the stock of the PFIC, the adjusted basis of the direct owner of the stock of the PFIC is increased by the amount of gain recognized on the deemed sale. A shareholder shall not adjust the basis of any stock with respect to which the shareholder realized a loss on the deemed sale.

(2) *Adjustment of basis for section 1293 inclusion with respect to deemed sale election made after March 31, 1995, and before January 27, 1997.*—For purposes of determining the amount of gain recognized with respect to a deemed sale election made after March 31, 1995, and before January 27, 1997, by a shareholder that treats the first day of the shareholder's election year as the qualification date, the adjusted basis of the stock deemed sold includes the shareholder's section 1293(a) inclusion attributable to the period beginning with the first day of the PFIC's first QEF year and ending on the day before the qualification date.

(g) *Treatment of holding period.*—For purposes of applying sections 1291 through 1297 to the shareholder after the deemed sale, the shareholder's holding period of the stock of the PFIC begins on the qualification date, without regard to whether the shareholder recognized gain on the deemed sale. For other purposes of the Code and regulations, this holding period rule does not apply.

(h) *Election inapplicable to shareholder of former PFIC.*—A shareholder may not make the section 1295 and deemed sale elections if the foreign corporation is a former PFIC (as defined in § 1.1291-9(j)(2)(iv)) with respect to the shareholder. For the rules regarding the election by a shareholder of a former PFIC, see 1.1297-3T.

(i) *Effective date.*—The rules of this section are applicable as of April 1, 1995. [Reg. § 1.1291-10.]

☐ [T.D. 8701, 12-26-96.]

[Reg. § 1.1293-0]

§ 1.1293-0. Table of contents.—This section contains a listing of the headings for § 1.1293-1.

☐ [*T.D. 8750, 12-31-97. Amended by T.D. 8870, 2-4-2000 (corrected 3-27-2000).*]

[Reg. § 1.1293-1]

§ 1.1293-1. Current taxation of income from qualified electing funds.—(a) *In general.*—[Reserved].

(1) *Other rules.*—[Reserved].

(2) *Net capital gain defined.*—(i) *In general.*—This paragraph (a)(2) defines the term net capital gain for purposes of sections 1293 and 1295 and the regulations under those sections. The QEF, as defined in § 1.1291-9(j)(2)(i), in determining its net capital gain for a taxable year, may either—

(A) Calculate and report the amount of each category of long-term capital gain provided in section 1(h) that was recognized by the PFIC in the taxable year;

(B) Calculate and report the amount of net capital gain recognized by the PFIC in the taxable year, stating that that amount is subject to the highest capital gain rate of tax applicable to the shareholder; or

(C) Calculate its earnings and profits for the taxable year and report the entire amount as ordinary earnings.

(ii) *Effective date.*—Paragraph (a)(2)(i) of this section is applicable to sales by QEFs during their taxable years ending on or after May 7, 1997.

(b) *Other rules.*—[Reserved].

(c) *Application of rules of inclusion with respect to stock held by a pass through entity.*—(1) *In general.*—If a domestic pass through entity makes a section 1295 election, as provided in paragraph (d)(2) of this section, with respect to the PFIC shares that it owns, directly or indirectly, the domestic pass through entity takes into account its pro rata share of the ordinary earnings and net capital gain attributable to the QEF shares held by the pass through entity. A U.S. person that indirectly owns QEF shares through the domestic pass through entity accounts for its pro rata shares of ordinary earnings and net capital gain attributable to the QEF shares according to the general rules applicable to inclusions of income from the domestic pass through entity. For the definition of pass through entity, see § 1.1295-1(j).

(2) *QEF stock transferred to a pass through entity.*—(i) *Pass through entity makes a section 1295 election.*—If a shareholder transfers stock subject to a section 1295 election to a domestic pass through entity of which it is an interest holder and the pass through entity makes a section 1295 election with respect to that stock, as provided in § 1.1295-1(d)(2), the shareholder takes into account its pro rata shares of the ordinary earnings and net capital gain attributable to the QEF shares under the rules applicable to inclusions of income from the pass through entity.

(ii) *Pass through entity does not make a section 1295 election.*—If the pass through entity does not make a section 1295 election with respect to the PFIC, the shares of which were transferred to the pass through entity subject to the 1295 election of the shareholder, the shareholder continues to be subject, in its capacity as an indirect shareholder, to the income inclusion rules of section 1293 and reporting rules required of shareholders of QEFs. Proper adjustments to reflect an inclusion in income under section 1293 by the indirect shareholder must be made, under the principles of § 1.1291-9(f), to the basis of the indirect shareholder's interest in the pass through entity.

(3) *Effective date.*—Paragraph (c) of this section is applicable to taxable years of shareholders beginning after December 31, 1997. [Reg. § 1.1293-1.]

☐ [*T.D. 8750, 12-31-97. Redesignated and amended by T.D. 8870, 2-4-2000.*]

[Reg. § 1.1294-0]

§ 1.1294-0. Table of contents.—This section contains a listing of the headings for § 1.1294-1T.

(3) Undistributed earnings.

   (i) In general.

   (ii) Effect of loan, pledge or guarantee.

(c) Time for making the election.

   (1) In general.

   (2) Exception.

(d) Manner of making the election.

   (1) In general.

   (2) Information to be included in the election.

(e) Termination of the extension.

(f) Undistributed PFIC earnings tax liability.

(g) Authority to require a bond.

(h) Annual reporting requirement.

[Reg. § 1.1294-0.]

☐ [*T.D.* 8750, 12-31-97.]

[Reg. § 1.1294-1T]

§ 1.1294-1T. Election to extend the time for payment of tax on undistributed earnings of a qualified electing fund (Temporary).— (a) *Purpose and scope.*—This section provides rules for making the annual election under section 1294. Under that section, a U.S. person that is a shareholder in a qualified electing fund (QEF) may elect to extend the time for payment of its tax liability which is attributable to its share of the undistributed earnings of the QEF. In general, a QEF is a passive foreign investment company (PFIC), as defined in section 1296, that makes the election under section 1295. Under section 1293, a U.S. person that owns, or is treated as owning, stock of a QEF at any time during the taxable year of the QEF shall include in gross income, as ordinary income, its pro rata share of the ordinary earnings of the QEF for the taxable year and, as long-term capital gain, its pro rata share of the net capital gain of the QEF for the taxable year. The shareholder's share of the earnings shall be included in the shareholder's taxable year in which or with which the taxable year of the QEF ends.

(b) *Election to extend time for payment.*—(1) *In general.*—A U.S. person that is a shareholder of a QEF on the last day of the QEF's taxable year may elect under section 1294 to extend the time for payment of that portion of its tax liability which is attributable to the inclusion in income pursuant to section 1293 of the shareholder's share of the QEF's undistributed earnings. The election under section 1294 may be made only with respect to undistributed earnings, and interest is imposed under section 6601 on the amount of the tax liability which is subject to the extension. This interest must be paid on the termination of the election.

(2) *Exception.*—An election under this § 1.1294-1T cannot be made for a taxable year of the shareholder if any portion of the QEF's earnings is includible in the gross income of the shareholder for such year under either section 551 (relating to foreign personal holding companies) or section 951 (relating to controlled foreign corporations).

(3) *Undistributed earnings.*—(i) *In general.*— For purposes of this § 1.1294-1T the term "undistributed earnings" means the excess, if any, of the amount includible in gross income by reason of section 1293(a) for the shareholder's taxable year (the includible amount) over the sum of (A) the amount of any distribution to the shareholder during the QEF's taxable year and (B) the portion of the includible amount that is attributable to stock in the QEF that the shareholder transferred or otherwise disposed of before the end of the QEF's year. For purposes of this paragraph, a distribution will be treated as made from the most recently accumulated earnings and profits.

(ii) *Effect of a loan, pledge or guarantee.*—A loan, pledge, or guarantee described in § 1.1294-1T(e)(2) or (4) will be treated as a distribution of earnings for purposes of paragraph (b)(3)(i)(A). If earnings are treated as distributed in a taxable year by reason of a loan, pledge or guarantee described in § 1.1294-1T(e)(2) or (4), but the amount of the deemed distribution resulting therefrom was less than the amount of the actual loan by the QEF (or the amount of the loan secured by the pledge or guarantee), earnings derived by the QEF in a subsequent taxable year will be treated as distributed in such subsequent year to the shareholder for purposes of paragraph (b)(3)(i)(A) by virtue of such loan, but only to the extent of the difference between the outstanding principal balance on the loan in such subsequent year and the prior years' deemed distributions resulting from the loan. For this purpose, the outstanding principal balance on a loan in a taxable year shall be treated as equal to the greatest amount of the outstanding balance at any time during such year.

Example (1). (i) *Facts.* FC is a PFIC that made the election under section 1295 to be a QEF for its taxable year beginning January 1, 1987. S owned 500 shares, or 50 percent, of FC throughout the first six months of 1987, but on June 30, 1987 sold 10 percent, or 50 shares, of the FC stock that it held. FC had $100,000x$ of ordinary earnings but no net capital gain in 1987. No part of FC's earnings is includible in S's income under either section 551 or 951. FC made no distributions to its shareholders in 1987. S's pro rata share of income is determined by attributing FC's income ratably to each day in FC's year. Accordingly, FC's daily earnings are $274x$ ($100,000x/365). S's share of the earnings of FC is $47,484x$, determined as follows.

FC's daily earnings	×	number of days percentage held by	×	percentage ownership in FC.

Accordingly, S's pro rata share of FC's earnings for the first six months of FC's year deemed earned while S held 50 percent of FC's stock is $24,797x ($274x × 181 days × 50%). S's pro rata share of FC's earnings for the remainder of FC's year deemed earned while S held 45 percent of FC's stock is $22,687x ($274x × 184 days × 45%). Therefore, S's total share of FC's earnings to be included in income under section 1293 is $47,484x ($24,797x + $22,687x).

(ii) *Election.* S intends to make the election under section 1294 to defer the payment of its tax liability that is attributable to the undistributed earnings of FC. The amount of current year undistributed earnings as defined in § 1.1294-1T(b)(3) with respect to which S can make the election is the excess of S's inclusion in gross income under section 1293(a) for the taxable year over the sum of (1) the cash and other property distributed to S during FC's tax year out of earnings included in income pursuant to section 1293(a), and (2) the earnings attributable to stock disposed of during FC's tax year. Because S sold 10 percent, or 50 shares, of the FC stock that it held during the first six months of the year, 10 percent of its share of the earnings for that part of the year, which is $2,480x ($24,797x × 10%), is attributable to the shares sold. S therefore cannot make the election under section 1294 to extend the time for payment of its tax liability on that amount. Accordingly, S can make the election under section 1294 with respect to its tax on $45,004x ($47,484x less $2,480x), which is its pro rata share of FC's earnings, reduced by the earnings attributable to the stock disposed of during the year.

Example (2). (i) *Facts.* The facts are the same as in Example (1) with the following exceptions. S did not sell any FC stock during 1987. Therefore, because S held 50 percent of the FC stock throughout 1987, S's pro rata share of FC's ordinary earnings was $50,000x, no part of which was includible in S's income under either section 551 or 951. There were no actual distributions of earnings to S in 1988. On December 31, 1987, S pledged the FC stock as security for a bank loan of $75,000x. The pledge is treated as a disposition of the FC stock and therefore a distribution of S's share of the undistributed earnings of FC up to the amount of the loan principal. S's entire share of the undistributed earnings of FC are deemed distributed as a result of the pledge of the FC stock. S therefore cannot make the election under section 1294 to extend the time for payment of its tax liability on its share of FC's earnings for 1987.

(ii) *Deemed distribution.* In 1988, FC has ordinary earnings of $100,000x but no net capital gain. S's pro rata share of FC's 1988 ordinary earnings was $50,000x. S's loan remained outstanding throughout 1988; the highest loan balance during 1988 was $74,000x. Of S's share of the ordinary earnings of FC of $50,000x, $24,000x is deemed distributed to S. This is the amount by which the highest loan balance for the year

($74,000x) exceeds the portion of the undistributed earnings of FC deemed distributed to S in 1987 by reason of the pledge ($50,000x). S may make the election under section 1294 to extend the time for payment of its tax liability on $26,000x, which is the amount by which S's includible amount for 1988 exceeds the amount deemed distributed to S during 1988.

(c) *Time for making the election.*—(1) *In general.*—An election under this § 1.1294-1T may be made for any taxable year in which a shareholder reports income pursuant to section 1293. Except as provided in paragraph (c)(2), the election shall be made by the due date, as extended, of the tax return for the shareholder's taxable year for which the election is made.

(2) *Exception.*—An election under this section may be made within 60 days of receipt of notification from the QEF of the shareholder's pro rata share of the ordinary earnings and net capital gain if notification is received after the time for filing the election provided in paragraph (c)(1) (and requires the filing of an amended return to report income pursuant to section 1293). If the notification reports an increase in the shareholder's pro rata share of the earnings previously reported to the shareholder by the QEF, the shareholder may make the election under this paragraph (c)(2) only with respect to the amount of such increase.

(d) *Manner of making the election.*—(1) *In general.*—A shareholder shall make the election by (i) attaching to its return for the year of the election Form 8621 or a statement containing the information and representations required by this section and (ii) filing a copy of Form 8621 or the statement with the Internal Revenue Service Center, P.O. Box 21086, Philadelphia, Pennsylvania 19114.

(2) *Information to be included in the election statement.*—If a statement is used in lieu of Form 8621, the statement should be identified, in a heading, as an election under section 1294 of the Code. The statement must include the following information and representations:

(i) The name, address, and taxpayer identification number of the electing shareholder and the taxable year of the shareholder for which the election is being made;

(ii) The name, address and taxpayer identification number of the QEF if provided to the shareholder;

(iii) A statement that the shareholder is making the election under section 1294 of the Code;

(iv) A schedule containing the following information:

(A) the ordinary earnings and net capital gain for the current year included in the shareholder's income under section 1293;

(B) the amount of cash and other property distributed by the QEF during its taxable year with respect to stock held directly or indirectly by the shareholder during that year, identifying the amount of such distributions that is paid out of current earnings and profits and the amount paid out of each prior year's earnings and profits; and

(C) the undistributed PFIC earnings tax liability (as defined in paragraph (f) of this section) for the taxable year, payment of which is being deferred by reason of the election under section 1294;

(v) The number of shares of stock held in the QEF during the QEF's taxable year which gave rise to the section 1293 inclusion and the number of such shares transferred, deemed transferred or otherwise disposed of by the electing shareholder before the end of the QEF's taxable year, and the date of transfer; and

(vi) The representations of the electing shareholder that—

(A) No part of the QEF's earnings for the taxable year is includible in the electing shareholder's gross income under either section 551 or 951 of the Code;

(B) The election is made only with respect to the shareholder's pro rata share of the undistributed earnings of the QEF; and

(C) The electing shareholder, upon termination of the election to extend the date for payment, shall pay the undistributed PFIC earnings tax liability attributable to those earnings to which the termination applies as well as interest on such tax liability pursuant to section 6601. Payment of this tax and interest must be made by the due date (determined without extensions) of the tax return for the taxable year in which termination occurs.

(e) *Termination of the extension.*—The election to extend the date for payment of tax will be terminated in whole or in part upon the occurrence of any of the following events:

(1) The QEF's distribution of earnings to which the section 1294 extensic pay tax is attributable; the extension will terminate only with respect to the tax attributable to the earnings that were distributed.

(2) The electing shareholder's transfer of stock in the QEF (or use thereof as security for a loan) with respect to which an election under this § 1.1294-1T was made. The election will be terminated with respect to the undistributed earnings attributable to the shares of the stock transferred. In the case of a pledge of the stock, the election will be terminated with respect to

undistributed earnings equal to the amount of the loan for which the stock is pledged.

(3) Revocation of the QEF's election as a QEF or cessation of the QEF's status as a PFIC. A revocation of the QEF election or cessation of PFIC status will result in the complete termination of the extension.

(4) A loan of property by the QEF directly or indirectly to the electing shareholder or related person, or a pledge or guarantee by the QEF with respect to a loan made by another party to the electing shareholder or related person. The election will be terminated with respect to undistributed earnings in an amount equal to the amount of the loan, pledge, or guarantee.

(5) A determination by the District Director pursuant to section 1294(c)(3) that collection of the tax is in jeopardy. The amount of undistributed earnings with respect to which the extension is terminated under this paragraph (d)(5) will be left to the discretion of the District Director.

(f) *Undistributed PFIC earnings tax liability.*— The electing shareholder's tax liability attributable to the ordinary earnings and net capital gain included in gross income under section 1293 shall be the excess of the tax imposed under chapter 1 of the Code for the taxable year over the tax that would be imposed for the taxable year without regard to the inclusion in income under section 1293 of the undistributed earnings as defined in paragraph (b)(3) of this section.

Example. The facts are the same as in § 1.1294-1T(b)(3), *Example (1),* with the following exceptions. S, a domestic corporation, did not dispose of any FC stock in 1987. Therefore, because S held 50 percent of the FC stock throughout 1987, S's pro rata share of FC's ordinary earnings was $50,000x. In addition to $50,000x of ordinary earnings from FC, S had $12,500x of domestic source income and $6,000x of expenses (other than interest expense) not definitely related to any gross income. These expenses are apportioned, pursuant to § 1.861-8(c)(2), on a pro rata basis between the domestic and foreign source income—$1,200x of expenses, or one-fifth, to domestic source income, and $4,800x of expenses, or four-fifths, to the section 1293 inclusion. FC paid foreign taxes of $25,000x in 1987. Accordingly, S is entitled to claim as an indirect foreign tax credit pursuant to section 1293(f) a proportionate amount of the foreign taxes paid by FC, which is $12,500x ($25,000x × $50,000x/ $100,000x). S is taxed in the U.S. at the rate of 34 percent. The amount for payment is determined as follows:

1987 Tax Liability (with section 1293 inclusion)

Source	U.S.	Foreign
Income	12,500 x	0
Section 1293	0	50,000 x
Expenses	−1,200 x	−4,800 x
Taxable income	11,300 x	45,200 x

Reg. § 1.1294-1T(f)

Total taxable income	56,500 x
U.S. income tax rate	×34 %
Pre-credit U.S. tax	19,210 x
Foreign tax credit	−12,500 x
1987 Tax Liability	6,710 x

1987 Tax Liability (without section 1293 inclusion)

Source	U.S.	Foreign
Income	12,500 x	0
Expenses	−6,000 x	
Taxable income	6,500 x	
U.S. tax rate	×34 %	
U.S. tax	2,210 x	
Foreign tax credit	0	
Hypothetical 1987 Tax Liability	2,210 x	

The amount of tax, payment of which S may defer pursuant to section 1294, is $4,500x ($6,710x less $2,210x).

(g) *Authority to require a bond.*—Pursuant to the authority granted in section 6165 and in the manner provided therein, and subject to notification, the District Director may require the electing shareholder to furnish a bond to secure payment of the tax, the time for payment of which is extended under this section. If the electing shareholder does not furnish the bond within 60 days after receiving a request from the District Director, the election will be revoked.

(h) *Annual reporting requirement.*—The electing shareholder must attach Form 8621 or a statement to its income tax return for each year during which an election under this section is outstanding. The statement must contain the following information: (1) the total amount of undistributed earnings as of the end of the taxable year to which the outstanding elections apply; (2) the total amount of the undistributed PFIC earnings tax liability and accrued interest charge as of the end of the year; (3) the total amount of distributions received during the taxable year; and (4) a description of the occurrence of any other termination event described in paragraph (e) of this section that occurred during the taxable year. The electing shareholder also shall file by the due date, as extended, for its return a copy of Form 8621 or the statement with the Philadelphia Service Center, P.O. Box 21086, Philadelphia, Pennsylvania 19114. [Temporary Reg. § 1.1294-1T.]

☐ [T.D. 8178, 2-26-88.]

[Reg. § 1.1295-0]

§ 1.1295-0. Table of contents.—This section contains a listing of the headings for § § 1.1295-1 and 1.1295-3.

§ 1.1295-1. Qualified electing funds.

(a) In general. [Reserved].

(b) Application of section 1295 election. [Reserved].

(1) Election personal to shareholder. [Reserved].

(2) Election applicable to specific corporation only.

(i) In general. [Reserved].

(ii) Stock of QEF received in a nonrecognition transfer. [Reserved].

(iii) Exception for options.

(3) Application of general rules to stock held by a pass through entity.

(i) Stock subject to a section 1295 election transferred to a pass through entity.

(ii) Limitation on application of pass through entity's section 1295 election.

(iii) Effect of partnership termination on section 1295 election.

(iv) Characterization of stock held through a pass through entity.

(4) Application of general rules to a taxpayer filing a joint return under section 6013.

(c) Effect of section 1295 election.

(1) In general.

(2) Years to which section 1295 election applies.

(i) In general.

(ii) Effect of PFIC status on election.

(iii) Effect on election of complete termination of a shareholder's interest in the PFIC.

(iv) Effect on section 1295 election of transfer of stock to a domestic pass through entity.

(v) Examples.

(d) Who may make a section 1295 election.

(1) General rule.

(2) Application of general rule to pass through entities.

(i) Partnerships.

(A) Domestic partnership.

(B) Foreign partnership.

(ii) S corporation.

(iii) Trust or estate.

(ii) Elimination of prejudice to the interests of the United States government.

(4) Procedural requirements.

(i) Filing instructions.

(ii) Affidavit from shareholder.

(iii) Affidavits from other persons.

(iv) Other information.

(v) Notification of Internal Revenue Service.

(vi) Who requests special consent under this paragraph (f) and who enters into a closing agreement.

(g) Time for and manner of making a retroactive election.

(1) Time for making a retroactive election.

(i) In general.

(ii) Transition rule.

(iii) Ownership not required at time retroactive election is made.

(2) Manner of making a retroactive election.

(3) Who makes the retroactive election.

(4) Other elections.

(i) Section 1291(d)(2) election.

(ii) Section 1294 election.

(h) Effective date.

[Reg. § 1.1295-0.]

☐ [*T.D. 8750, 12-31-97. Amended by T.D. 8870, 2-4-2000 and T.D. 9123, 4-30-2004.*]

[Reg. § 1.1295-1]

§1.1295-1. Qualified electing funds.—(a) *In general.*—[Reserved].

(b) *Application of section 1295 election.*— [Reserved].

(1) *Election personal to shareholder.*— [Reserved].

(2) *Election applicable to specific corporation only.*—(i) *In general.*—[Reserved].

(ii) *Stock of QEF received in a nonrecognition transfer.*—[Reserved].

(iii) *Exception for options.*—A shareholder's section 1295 election does not apply to any option to buy stock of the PFIC.

(3) *Application of general rules to stock held by a pass through entity.*—(i) *Stock subject to a section 1295 election transferred to a pass through entity.*— A shareholder's section 1295 election will not apply to a domestic pass through entity to which the shareholder transfers stock subject to a section 1295 election, or to any other U.S. person that is an interest holder or beneficiary of the domestic pass through entity. However, as provided in paragraph (c)(2)(iv) of this section (relating to a transfer to a domestic pass through entity of stock subject to a section 1295 election),

a shareholder that transfers stock subject to a section 1295 election to a pass through entity will continue to be subject to the section 1295 election with respect to the stock indirectly owned through the pass through entity and any other stock of that PFIC owned by the shareholder.

(ii) *Limitation on application of pass through entity's section 1295 election.*—Except as provided in paragraph (c)(2)(iv) of this section, a section 1295 election made by a domestic pass through entity does not apply to other stock of the PFIC held directly or indirectly by the interest holder or beneficiary.

(iii) *Effect of partnership termination on section 1295 election.*—Termination of a section 1295 election made by a domestic partnership by reason of the termination of the partnership under section 708(b) will not terminate the section 1295 election with respect to partners of the terminated partnership that are partners of the new partnership. Except as otherwise provided, the stock of the PFIC of which the new partners are indirect shareholders will be treated as stock of a QEF only if the new domestic partnership makes a section 1295 election with respect to that stock.

(iv) *Characterization of stock held through a pass through entity.*—Stock of a PFIC held through a pass through entity will be treated as stock of a pedigreed QEF with respect to an interest holder or beneficiary only if—

(A) In the case of PFIC stock acquired (other than in a transaction in which gain is not recognized pursuant to regulations under section 1291(f) with respect to that stock) and held by a domestic pass through entity, the pass through entity makes the section 1295 election and the PFIC has been a QEF with respect to the pass through entity for all taxable years that are included wholly or partly in the pass through entity's holding period of the PFIC stock and during which the foreign corporation was a PFIC within the meaning of § 1.1291-9(j)(1); or

(B) In the case of PFIC stock transferred by an interest holder or beneficiary to a pass through entity in a transaction in which gain is not fully recognized (including pursuant to regulations under section 1291(f)), the pass through entity makes the section 1295 election with respect to the PFIC stock transferred for the taxable year in which the transfer was made. The PFIC stock transferred will be treated as stock of a pedigreed QEF by the pass through entity, however, only if that stock was treated as stock of a pedigreed QEF with respect to the interest holder or beneficiary at the time of the transfer, and the PFIC has been a QEF with respect to the pass through entity for all taxable years of the PFIC that are included wholly or partly in the pass through entity's holding period of the PFIC stock during which the foreign corporation was a PFIC within the meaning of § 1.1291-9(j).

(v) *Characterization of stock distributed by a partnership.*—In the case of PFIC stock distributed by a partnership to a partner in a transaction in which gain is not fully recognized, the PFIC stock will be treated as stock of a pedigreed QEF by the partners only if that stock was treated as stock of a pedigreed QEF with respect to the partnership for all taxable years of the PFIC that are included wholly or partly in the partnership's holding period of the PFIC stock during which the foreign corporation was a PFIC within the meaning of § 1.1291-9(j), and the partner has a section 1295 election in effect with respect to the distributed PFIC stock for the partner's taxable year in which the distribution was made. If the partner does not have a section 1295 election in effect, the stock shall be treated as stock in a section 1291 fund. See paragraph (k) of this section for special applicability date of paragraph (b)(3)(v) of this section.

(4) *Application of general rules to a taxpayer filing a joint return under section 6013.*—A section 1295 election made by a taxpayer in a joint return, within the meaning of section 6013, will be treated as also made by the spouse that joins in the filing of that return. See paragraph (k) of this section for special applicability date of paragraph (b)(4) of this section.

(c) *Effect of section 1295 election.*—(1) *In general.*—Except as otherwise provided in this paragraph (c), the effect of a shareholder's section 1295 election is to treat the foreign corporation as a QEF with respect to the shareholder for each taxable year of the foreign corporation ending with or within a taxable year of the shareholder for which the election is effective. A section 1295 election is effective for the shareholder's election year and all subsequent taxable years of the shareholder unless invalidated, terminated or revoked as provided in paragraph (i) of this section. The terms shareholder and shareholder's election year are defined in paragraph (j) of this section.

(2) *Years to which section 1295 election applies.*—(i) *In general.*—Except as otherwise provided in this paragraph (c), a foreign corporation with respect to which a section 1295 election is made will be treated as a QEF for its taxable year ending with or within the shareholder's election year and all subsequent taxable years of the foreign corporation that are included wholly or partly in the shareholder's holding period (or periods) of stock of the foreign corporation.

(ii) *Effect of PFIC status on election.*—A foreign corporation will not be treated as a QEF for any taxable year of the foreign corporation that the foreign corporation is not a PFIC under section 1297(a) and is not treated as a PFIC under section 1298(b)(1). Therefore, a shareholder shall not be required to include pursuant to section 1293 the shareholder's pro rata share of ordinary earnings and net capital gain for such year and

shall not be required to satisfy the section 1295 annual reporting requirement of paragraph (f)(2) of this section for such year. Cessation of a foreign corporation's status as a PFIC will not, however, terminate a section 1295 election. Thus, if the foreign corporation is a PFIC in any taxable year after a year in which it is not treated as a PFIC, the shareholder's original election under section 1295 continues to apply and the shareholder must take into account its pro rata share of ordinary earnings and net capital gain for such year and comply with the section 1295 annual reporting requirement.

(iii) *Effect on election of complete termination of a shareholder's interest in the PFIC.*—Complete termination of a shareholder's direct and indirect interest in stock of a foreign corporation will not terminate a shareholder's section 1295 election with respect to the foreign corporation. Therefore, if a shareholder reacquires a direct or indirect interest in any stock of the foreign corporation, that stock is considered to be stock for which an election under section 1295 has been made and the shareholder is subject to the income inclusion and reporting rules required of a shareholder of a QEF.

(iv) *Effect on section 1295 election of transfer of stock to a domestic pass through entity.*—The transfer of a shareholder's direct or indirect interest in stock of a foreign corporation to a domestic pass through entity (as defined in paragraph (j) of this section) will not terminate the shareholder's section 1295 election with respect to the foreign corporation, whether or not the pass through entity makes a section 1295 election. For the rules concerning the application of section 1293 to stock transferred to a domestic pass through entity, see § 1.1293-1(c).

(v) *Examples.*—The following examples illustrate the rules of this paragraph (c)(2).

Example 1. In 1998, C, a U.S. person, purchased stock of FC, a foreign corporation that is a PFIC. Both FC and C are calendar year taxpayers. C made a timely section 1295 election to treat FC as a QEF in C's 1998 return, and FC was therefore a pedigreed QEF. C included its shares of FC's 1998 ordinary earnings and net capital gain in C's 1998 income and did not make a section 1294 election to defer the time for payment of tax on that income. In 1999, 2000, and 2001, FC did not satisfy either the income or asset test of section 1296(a), and therefore was neither a PFIC nor a QEF. C therefore did not have to include its pro rata shares of the ordinary earnings and net capital gain of FC pursuant to section 1293, or satisfy the section 1295 annual reporting requirements for any of those years. FC qualified as a PFIC again in 2002. Because C had made a section 1295 election in 1998, and the election had not been invalidated, terminated, or revoked, within the meaning of paragraph (i) of this section, C's section 1295 election remains in effect for 2002. C therefore is subject in 2002 to the income inclusion and reporting rules required of shareholders of QEFs.

Example 2. The facts are the same as in Example (1) except that FC did not lose PFIC status in any year and C sold all the FC stock in 1999 and repurchased stock of FC in 2002. Because C had made a section 1295 election in 1998 with respect to stock of FC, and the election had not been invalidated, terminated, or revoked, within the meaning of paragraph (i) of this section, C's section 1295 election remained in effect and therefore applies to the stock of FC purchased by C in 2002. C therefore is subject in 2002 to the income inclusion and reporting rules required of shareholders of QEFs.

Example 3. The facts are the same as in Example (2) except that C is a partner in domestic partnership P and C transferred its FC stock to P in 1999. Because C had made a section 1295 election in 1998 with respect to stock of FC, and the election had not been invalidated, terminated, or revoked, within the meaning of paragraph (i) of this section, C's section 1295 election remains in effect with respect to its indirect interest in the stock of FC. If P does not make the section 1295 election with respect to the FC stock, C will continue to be subject, in C's capacity as an indirect shareholder of FC, to the income inclusion and reporting rules required of shareholders of QEFs in 1999 and subsequent years for that portion of the FC stock C is treated as owning indirectly through the partnership. If P makes the section 1295 election, C will take into account its pro rata shares of the ordinary earnings and net capital gain of the FC under the rules applicable to inclusions of income from P.

(d) *Who may make a section 1295 election.*— (1) *General rule.*—Except as otherwise provided in this paragraph (d), any U.S. person that is a shareholder (as defined in paragraph (j) of this section) of a PFIC, including a shareholder that holds stock of a PFIC in bearer form, may make a section 1295 election with respect to that PFIC. The shareholder need not own directly or indirectly any stock of the PFIC at the time the shareholder makes the section 1295 election provided the shareholder is a shareholder of the PFIC during the taxable year of the PFIC that ends with or within the taxable year of the shareholder for which the section 1295 election is made. Except in the case of a shareholder that is an exempt organization that may not make a section 1295 election, as provided in paragraph (d)(6) of this section, in a chain of ownership only the first U.S. person that is a shareholder of the PFIC may make the section 1295 election.

(2) *Application of general rule to pass through entities.*—(i) *Partnerships.*—(A) *Domestic partnership.*—A domestic partnership that holds an interest in stock of a PFIC makes the section 1295 election with respect to that PFIC. The partnership election applies only to the stock of the

PFIC held directly or indirectly by the partnership and not to any other stock held directly or indirectly by any partner. As provided in § 1.1293-1(c)(1), shareholders owning stock of a QEF by reason of an interest in the partnership take into account the section 1293 inclusions with respect to the QEF shares owned by the partnership under the rules applicable to inclusions of income from the partnership.

(B) *Foreign partnership.*—A U.S. person that holds an interest in a foreign partnership that, in turn, holds an interest in stock of a PFIC makes the section 1295 election with respect to that PFIC. A partner's election applies to the stock of the PFIC owned directly or indirectly by the foreign partnership and to any other stock of the PFIC owned by that partner. A section 1295 election by a partner applies only to that partner.

(ii) *S corporation.*—An S corporation that holds an interest in stock of a PFIC makes the section 1295 election with respect to that PFIC. The S corporation election applies only to the stock of the PFIC held directly or indirectly by the S corporation and not to any other stock held directly or indirectly by any S corporation shareholder. As provided in § 1.1293-1(c)(1), shareholders owning stock of a QEF by reason of an interest in the S corporation take into account the section 1293 inclusions with respect to the QEF shares under the rules applicable to inclusions of income from the S corporation.

(iii) *Trust or estate.*—(A) *Domestic trust or estate.*—(1) *Nongrantor trust or estate.*—A domestic nongrantor trust or a domestic estate that holds an interest in stock of a PFIC makes the section 1295 election with respect to that PFIC. The trust or estate's election applies only to the stock of the PFIC held directly or indirectly by the trust or estate and not to any other stock held directly or indirectly by any beneficiary. As provided in § 1.1293-1(c)(1), shareholders owning stock of a QEF by reason of an interest in a domestic trust or estate take into account the section 1293 inclusions with respect to the QEF shares under the rules applicable to inclusions of income from the trust or estate.

(2) *Grantor trust.*—A U.S. person that is treated under sections 671 through 678 as the owner of the portion of a domestic trust that owns an interest in stock of a PFIC makes the section 1295 election with respect to that PFIC. If that person ceases to be treated as the owner of the portion of the trust that owns an interest in the PFIC stock and is a beneficiary of the trust, that person's section 1295 election will continue to apply to the PFIC stock indirectly owned by that person under the rules of paragraph (c)(2)(iv) of this section as if the person had transferred its interest in the PFIC stock to the trust. However, the stock will be treated as stock of a PFIC that is not a QEF with respect to other beneficiaries of the trust, unless the trust makes

the section 1295 election as provided in paragraph (d)(2)(iii)(A)(1) of this section.

(B) *Foreign trust or estate.*—(1) *Nongrantor trust or estate.*—A U.S. person that is a beneficiary of a foreign nongrantor trust or estate that holds an interest in stock of a PFIC makes the section 1295 election with respect to that PFIC. A beneficiary's section 1295 election applies to all the PFIC stock owned directly and indirectly by the trust or estate and to the other PFIC stock owned directly or indirectly by the beneficiary. A section 1295 election by a beneficiary applies only to that beneficiary.

(2) *Grantor trust.*—A U.S. person that is treated under sections 671 through 679 as the owner of the portion of a foreign trust that owns an interest in stock of a PFIC stock makes the section 1295 election with respect to that PFIC. If that person ceases to be treated as the owner of the portion of the trust that owns an interest in the PFIC stock and is a beneficiary of the trust, that person's section 1295 election will continue to apply to the PFIC stock indirectly owned by that person under the rules of paragraph (c)(2)(iv) of this section. However, as provided in paragraph (d)(2)(iii)(B)(1) of this section, any other shareholder that is a beneficiary of the trust and that wishes to treat the PFIC as a QEF must make the section 1295 election.

(iv) *Indirect ownership of the pass through entity or the PFIC.*—The rules of this paragraph (d)(2) apply whether or not the shareholder holds its interest in the pass through entity directly or indirectly and whether or not the pass through entity holds its interest in the PFIC directly or indirectly.

(3) *Indirect ownership of a PFIC through other PFICs.*—(i) *In general.*—An election under section 1295 shall apply only to the foreign corporation for which an election is made. Therefore, if a shareholder makes an election under section 1295 to treat a PFIC as a QEF, that election applies only to stock in that foreign corporation and not to the stock in any other corporation which the shareholder is treated as owning by virtue of its ownership of stock in the QEF.

(ii) *Example.*—The following example illustrates the rules of paragraph (d)(3)(i) of this section:

Example. In 1988, T, a U.S. person, purchased stock of FC, a foreign corporation that is a PFIC. FC also owns the stock of SC, a foreign corporation that is a PFIC. T makes an election under section 1295 to treat FC as a QEF. T's section 1295 election applies only to the stock T owns in FC, and does not apply to the stock T indirectly owns in SC.

(4) *Member of consolidated return group as shareholder.*—Pursuant to § 1.1502-77(a), the common parent of an affiliated group of corporations that join in filing a consolidated income tax return makes a section 1295 election for all members of the affiliated group. An election by a common parent will be effective for all members of the affiliated group with respect to interests in PFIC stock held at the time the election is made or at any time thereafter. A separate election must be made by the common parent for each PFIC of which a member of the affiliated group is a shareholder.

(5) *Option holder.*—A holder of an option to acquire stock of a PFIC may not make a section 1295 election that will apply to the option or to the stock subject to the option.

(6) *Exempt organization.*—A tax-exempt organization that is not taxable under section 1291, pursuant to § 1.1291-1(e), with respect to a PFIC may not make a section 1295 election with respect to that PFIC. In addition, such an exempt organization will not be subject to any section 1295 election made by a domestic pass through entity.

(e) *Time for making a section 1295 election.*—(1) *In general.*—Except as provided in § 1.1295-3, a shareholder making the section 1295 election must make the election on or before the due date, as extended under section 6081 (election due date), for filing the shareholder's income tax return for the first taxable year to which the election will apply. The section 1295 election must be made in the original return for that year, or in an amended return, provided the amended return is filed on or before the election due date.

(2) *Examples.*—The following examples illustrate the rules of paragraph (e)(1) of this section:

Example 1. In 1998, C, a domestic corporation, purchased stock of FC, a foreign corporation that is a PFIC. Both C and FC are calendar year taxpayers. C wishes to make the section 1295 election for its taxable year ended December 31, 1998. The section 1295 election must be made on or before March 15, 1999, the due date of C's 1998 income tax return as provided by section 6072(b). On March 14, 1999, C files a request for a three-month extension of time to file its 1998 income tax return under section 6081(b). C's time to file its 1998 income tax return and to make the section 1295 election is thereby extended to June 15, 1999.

Example 2. The facts are the same as in *Example 1* except that on May 1, 1999, C filed its 1998 income tax return and failed to include the section 1295 election. C may file an amended income tax return for 1998 to make the section 1295 election provided the amended return is filed on or before the extended due date of June 15, 1999.

(f) *Manner of making a section 1295 election and the annual election requirements of the shareholder.*—(1) *Manner of making the election.*—A shareholder must make a section 1295 election by—

(i) Completing Form 8621 in the manner required by that form and this section for making the section 1295 election;

(ii) Attaching Form 8621 to its federal income tax return filed by the election due date for the shareholder's election year; and

(iii) Receiving and reflecting in Form 8621 the information provided in the PFIC Annual Information Statement described in paragraph (g)(1) of this section, the Annual Intermediary Statement described in paragraph (g)(3) of this section, or the applicable combined statement described in paragraph (g)(4) of this section, for the taxable year of the PFIC ending with or within the taxable year for which Form 8621 is being filed. If the PFIC Annual Information Statement contains a statement described in paragraph (g)(1)(ii)(C) of this section, the shareholder must attach a statement to Form 8621 that indicates that the shareholder rather than the PFIC calculated the PFIC's ordinary earnings and net capital gain.

(2) *Annual election requirements.*—(i) *In general.*—A shareholder that makes a section 1295 election with respect to a PFIC held directly or indirectly, for each taxable year to which the section 1295 election applies, must—

(A) Complete Form 8621 in the manner required by that form and this section;

(B) Attach Form 8621 to its federal income tax return filed by the due date of the return, as extended; and

(C) Receive and reflect in Form 8621 the PFIC Annual Information Statement described in paragraph (g)(1) of this section, the Annual Intermediary Statement described in paragraph (g)(3) of this section, or the applicable combined statement described in paragraph (g)(4) of this section, for the taxable year of the PFIC ending with or within the taxable year for which Form 8621 is being filed. If the PFIC Annual Information Statement contains a statement described in paragraph (g)(1)(ii)(C) of this section, the shareholder must attach a statement to its Form 8621 that the shareholder rather than the PFIC provided the calculations of the PFIC's ordinary earnings and net capital gain.

(ii) *Retention of documents.*—For all taxable years subject to the section 1295 election, the shareholder must retain copies of all Forms 8621, with their attachments, and PFIC Annual Information Statements or Annual Intermediary Statements. Failure to produce those documents at the request of the Commissioner in connection with an examination may result in invalidation or termination of the shareholder's section 1295 election.

(3) *Effective date.*—See paragraph (k) of this section for special applicability date of paragraph (f) of this section.

(g) *Annual election requirements of the PFIC or intermediary.*—(1) *PFIC Annual Information Statement.*—For each year of the PFIC ending in a taxable year of a shareholder to which the shareholder's section 1295 election applies, the PFIC must provide the shareholder with a PFIC Annual Information Statement. The PFIC Annual Information Statement is a statement of the PFIC, signed by the PFIC or an authorized representative of the PFIC, that contains the following information and representations—

(i) The first and last days of the taxable year of the PFIC to which the PFIC Annual Information Statement applies;

(ii) Either—

(A) The shareholder's pro rata shares of the ordinary earnings and net capital gain (as defined in § 1.1293-1(a)(2)) of the PFIC for the taxable year indicated in paragraph (g)(1)(i) of this section; or

(B) Sufficient information to enable the shareholder to calculate its pro rata shares of the PFIC's ordinary earnings and net capital gain, for that taxable year; or

(C) A statement that the foreign corporation has permitted the shareholder to examine the books of account, records, and other documents of the foreign corporation for the shareholder to calculate the amounts of the PFIC's ordinary earnings and the net capital gain according to federal income tax accounting principles and to calculate the shareholder's pro rata shares of the PFIC's ordinary earnings and net capital gain;

(iii) The amount of cash and the fair market value of other property distributed or deemed distributed to the shareholder during the taxable year of the PFIC to which the PFIC Annual Information Statement pertains; and

(iv) Either—

(A) A statement that the PFIC will permit the shareholder to inspect and copy the PFIC's permanent books of account, records, and such other documents as may be maintained by the PFIC to establish that the PFIC's ordinary earnings and net capital gain are computed in accordance with U.S. income tax principles, and to verify these amounts and the shareholder's pro rata shares thereof; or

(B) In lieu of the statement required in paragraph (g)(1)(iv)(A) of this section, a description of the alternative documentation requirements approved by the Commissioner, with a copy of the private letter ruling and the closing agreement entered into by the Commissioner and the PFIC pursuant to paragraph (g)(2) of this section.

(2) *Alternative documentation.*—In rare and unusual circumstances, the Commissioner will consider alternative documentation requirements necessary to verify the ordinary earnings and net capital gain of a PFIC other than the documentation requirements described in para-

graph (g)(1)(iv)(A) of this section. Alternative documentation requirements will be allowed only pursuant to a private letter ruling and a closing agreement entered into by the Commissioner and the PFIC describing an alternative method of verifying the PFIC's ordinary earnings and net capital gain. If the PFIC has not obtained a private letter ruling from the Commissioner approving an alternative method of verifying the PFIC's ordinary earnings and net capital gain by the time a shareholder is required to make a section 1295 election, the shareholder may not use an alternative method for that taxable year.

(3) *Annual Intermediary Statement.*—In the case of a U.S. person that is an indirect shareholder of a PFIC that is owned through an intermediary, as defined in paragraph (j) of this section, an Annual Intermediary Statement issued by an intermediary containing the information described in paragraph (g)(1) of this section and reporting the indirect shareholder's pro rata share of the ordinary earnings and net capital gain of the QEF as described in paragraph (g)(1)(ii)(A) of this section, may be provided to the indirect shareholder in lieu of the PFIC Annual Information Statement if the following conditions are satisfied—

(i) The intermediary receives a copy of the PFIC Annual Information Statement or the intermediary receives an annual intermediary statement from another intermediary which contains a statement that the other intermediary has received a copy of the PFIC Annual Information Statement and represents that the conditions of paragraphs (g)(3)(ii) and (g)(3)(iii) of this section are met;

(ii) The representations and information contained in the Annual Intermediary Statement reflect the representations and information contained in the PFIC Annual Information Statement; and

(iii) The PFIC Annual Information Statement issued to the intermediary contains either the representation set forth in paragraph (g)(1)(iv)(A) of this section, or, if alternative documentation requirements were approved by the Commissioner pursuant to paragraph (g)(2) of this section, a copy of the private letter ruling and closing agreement between the Commissioner and the PFIC, agreeing to an alternative method of verifying PFIC ordinary earnings and net capital gain as described in paragraph (g)(2) of this section;

(4) *Combined statements.*—(i) *PFIC Annual Information Statement.*—A PFIC that owns directly or indirectly any stock of one or more PFICs with respect to which a shareholder may make the section 1295 election may prepare a PFIC Annual Information Statement that combines with its own information and representations the information and representations of all the PFICs. The PFIC may use any format for a

combined PFIC Annual Information Statement provided the required information and representations are separately stated and identified with the respective corporations.

(ii) *Annual Intermediary Statement.*—An intermediary described in paragraph (g)(3) of this section that owns directly or indirectly stock of one or more PFICs with respect to which an indirect shareholder may make the section 1295 election may prepare an Annual Intermediary Statement that combines with its own information and representations the information and representations with respect to all the PFICs. The intermediary may use any format for a combined Annual Intermediary Statement provided the required information and representations are separately stated and identified with the intermediary and the respective corporations.

(5) *Effective date.*—See paragraph (k) of this section for special applicability date of paragraph (g) of this section.

(h) *Transition rules.*—Taxpayers may rely on Notice 88-125 (1988-2 C.B. 535) (see §601.601(d)(2) of this chapter), for rules on making and maintaining elections for shareholder election years (as defined in paragraph (j) of this section) beginning after December 31, 1986, and before January 1, 1998. Elections made under Notice 88-125 must be maintained as provided in §1.1295-1 for taxable years beginning after December 31, 1997. A section 1295 election made prior to February 2, 1998, that was intended to be effective for the taxable year of the PFIC that began during the shareholder's election year will be effective for that taxable year of the foreign corporation provided that it is clear from all the facts and circumstances that the shareholder intended the election to be effective for that taxable year of the foreign corporation.

(i) *Invalidation, termination, or revocation of section 1295 election.*—(1) *Invalidation or termination of election at the discretion of the Commissioner.*—(i) *In general.*—The Commissioner, in its discretion, may invalidate or terminate a section 1295 election applicable to a shareholder if the shareholder, the PFIC, or any intermediary fails to satisfy the requirements for making a section 1295 election or the annual election requirements of this section to which the shareholder, PFIC, or intermediary is subject, including the requirement to provide, on request, copies of the books and records of the PFIC or other documentation substantiating the ordinary earnings and net capital gain of the PFIC.

(ii) *Deferral of section 1293 inclusion.*—The Commissioner may invalidate any pass through entity section 1295 election with respect to an interest holder or beneficiary if the section 1293 inclusion with respect to that interest holder or beneficiary is not included in the gross income of either the pass through entity, an intermediate pass through entity, or the interest holder or beneficiary within two years of the end of the PFIC's taxable year due to nonconforming taxable years of the interest holder and the pass through entity or any intermediate pass through entity.

(iii) *When effective.*—Termination of a shareholder's section 1295 election will be effective for the taxable year of the PFIC determined by the Commissioner in the Commissioner's discretion. An invalidation of a shareholder's section 1295 election will be effective for the first taxable year to which the section 1295 election applied, and the shareholder whose election is invalidated will be treated as if the section 1295 election was never made.

(2) *Shareholder revocation.*—(i) *In general.*—In the Commissioner's discretion, upon a finding of a substantial change in circumstances, the Commissioner may consent to a shareholder's request to revoke a section 1295 election. Request for revocation must be made by the shareholder that made the election and at the time and in the manner provided in paragraph (i)(2)(ii) of this section.

(ii) *Time for and manner of requesting consent to revoke.*—(A) *Time.*—The shareholder must request consent to revoke the section 1295 election no later than 12 calendar months after the discovery of the substantial change of circumstances that forms the basis for the shareholder's request to revoke the section 1295 election.

(B) *Manner of making request.*—A shareholder requests consent to revoke a section 1295 election by filing a ruling request with the Office of the Associate Chief Counsel (International). The ruling request must satisfy the requirements, including payment of the user fee, for filing ruling requests with that office.

(iii) *When effective.*—Unless otherwise determined by the Commissioner, revocation of a section 1295 election will be effective for the first taxable year of the PFIC beginning after the date the Commissioner consents to the revocation.

(3) *Automatic termination.*—If a United States person, or the United States shareholder on behalf of a controlled foreign corporation, makes an election pursuant to section 1296 and the regulations thereunder with respect to PFIC stock for which a QEF election is in effect, or marks to market such stock under another provision of chapter 1 of the Internal Revenue Code, the QEF election is automatically terminated with respect to such stock that is marked to market under section 1296 or another provision of chapter 1 of the Internal Revenue Code. Such termination shall be effective on the last day of the shareholder's taxable year preceding the first taxable year for which the section 1296 election is in effect or such stock is marked to market under

another provision of chapter 1 of the Internal Revenue Code.

Example. Corp Y, a domestic corporation, owns directly 100 shares of marketable stock in foreign corporation FX, a PFIC. Corp Y also owns a 50 percent interest in FP, a foreign partnership that owns 200 shares of FX stock. Accordingly, under section 1298(a)(3) and §1.1296-1(e)(1), Corp Y is treated as indirectly owning 100 shares of FX stock. Corp Y also owns 100 percent of the stock of FZ, a foreign corporation that is not a PFIC. FZ owns 100 shares of FX stock, and therefore under section 1298(a)(2)(A), Corp Y is treated as owning the 100 shares of FX stock owned by FZ. For taxable year 2005, Corp Y has a QEF election in effect with respect to all 300 shares of FX stock that it owns directly or indirectly. See generally §1.1295-1(c)(1). For taxable year 2006, Corp Y makes a timely election pursuant to section 1296 and the regulations thereunder. For purposes of section 1296, Corp Y is treated as owning stock held indirectly through a partnership, but not through a foreign corporation. Section 1296(g); §1.1296-1(e)(1). Accordingly, Corp Y's section 1296 election covers the 100 shares it owns directly and the 100 shares it owns indirectly through FP, but not the 100 shares owned by FZ. With respect to the first 200 shares, Corp Y's QEF election is automatically terminated effective December 31, 2005. With respect to the 100 shares Corp Y owns through foreign FZ, Corp Y's QEF election remains in effect unless invalidated, terminated, or revoked pursuant to this paragraph (i).

(4) *Effect of invalidation, termination, or revocation.*—An invalidation, termination, or revocation of a section 1295 election—

(i) Terminates all section 1294 elections, as provided in §1.1294-1T(e), and the undistributed PFIC earnings tax liability and interest thereon are due by the due date, without regard to extensions, for the return for the last taxable year of the shareholder to which the section 1295 election applies;

(ii) In the Commissioner's discretion, results in a deemed sale of the QEF stock on the last day of the PFIC's last taxable year as a QEF, in which gain, but not loss, will be recognized and with respect to which appropriate basis and holding period adjustments will be made; and

(iii) Subjects the shareholder to any other terms and conditions that the Commissioner determines are necessary to ensure the shareholder's compliance with sections 1291 through 1298 or any other provisions of the Code.

(5) *Effect after invalidation, termination, or revocation.*—(i) *In general.*—Without the Commissioner's consent, a shareholder whose section 1295 election was invalidated, terminated, or revoked under this paragraph (i) may not make the section 1295 election with respect to the PFIC before the sixth taxable year in which the invali-

dation, termination, or revocation became effective.

(ii) *Special rule.*—Notwithstanding paragraph (i)(5)(i) of this section, a shareholder whose section 1295 election was terminated pursuant to paragraph (i)(3) of this section, and either whose section 1296 election has subsequently been terminated because its PFIC stock ceased to be marketable or who no longer marks to market such stock under another provision of chapter 1 of the Internal Revenue Code, may make a section 1295 election with respect to its PFIC stock before the sixth taxable year in which its prior section 1295 election was terminated.

(j) *Definitions.*—For purposes of this section—

Intermediary is a nominee or shareholder of record that holds stock on behalf of the shareholder or on behalf of another person in a chain of ownership between the shareholder and the PFIC, and any direct or indirect beneficial owner of PFIC stock (including a beneficial owner that is a pass through entity) in the chain of ownership between the shareholder and the PFIC.

Pass through entity is a partnership, S corporation, trust, or estate.

Shareholder has the same meaning as the term shareholder in § 1.1291-9(j)(3), except that for purposes of this section, a partnership and an S corporation also are treated as shareholders. Furthermore, unless otherwise provided, an interest holder of a pass through entity, which is treated as a shareholder of a PFIC, also will be treated as a shareholder of the PFIC.

Shareholder's election year is the taxable year of the shareholder for which it made the section 1295 election.

(k) *Effective dates.*—Except as otherwise provided, paragraphs (b)(2)(iii), (b)(3), (b)(4), and (c) through (j) of this section are applicable to taxable years of shareholders beginning after December 31, 1997. However, taxpayers may apply the rules under paragraphs (b)(4), (f) and (g) of this section to a taxable year beginning before January 1, 1998, provided the statute of limitations on the assessment of tax has not expired as of April 27, 1998, and, in the case of paragraph (b)(4) of this section, the taxpayers who filed the joint return have consistently applied the rules of that section to all taxable years following the year the election was made. Paragraph (b)(3)(v) of this section is applicable as of February 7, 2000, however, a taxpayer may apply the rules to a taxable year prior to the applicable date provided the statute of limitations on the assessment of tax for that taxable year has not expired. Paragraphs (i)(3) and (i)(5)(ii) of this section are applicable for taxable years beginning on or after May 3, 2004. [Reg. § 1.1295-1.]

☐ [*T.D. 8750, 12-31-97. Redesignated and amended by T.D. 8870, 2-4-2000. Amended by T.D. 9123, 4-30-2004.*]

[Reg. § 1.1295-3]

§ 1.1295-3. Retroactive elections.—(a) *In general.*—This section prescribes the exclusive rules under which a shareholder, as defined in § 1.1295-1(j), may make a section 1295 election for a taxable year after the election due date, as defined in § 1.1295-1(e) (retroactive election). Therefore, a shareholder may not seek such relief under any other provision of the law, including § 301.9100 of this chapter. Paragraph (b) of this section describes the general rules for a shareholder to preserve the ability to make a retroactive election. These rules require that the shareholder possess reasonable belief as of the election due date that the foreign corporation was not a PFIC for its taxable year that ended in the shareholder's taxable year to which the election due date pertains, and that the shareholder file a Protective Statement to preserve its ability to make a retroactive election. Paragraph (c) of this section establishes the terms, conditions and other requirements with respect to a Protective Statement required to be filed under the general rules. Paragraph (d) of this section sets forth factors that establish a shareholder's reasonable belief that a foreign corporation was not a PFIC. Paragraph (e) of this section prescribes special rules for certain shareholders that are deemed to satisfy the reasonable belief requirement and therefore are not required to file a Protective Statement. Paragraph (f) of this section describes the limited circumstances under which the Commissioner may permit a shareholder that lacked the requisite reasonable belief or failed to satisfy the requirements of paragraph (b) or (e) of this section to make a retroactive election. Paragraph (g) of this section provides the time for and manner of making a retroactive election. Paragraph (h) of this section provides the effective date of this section.

(b) *General rule.*—Except as provided in paragraphs (e) and (f) of this section, a shareholder may make a retroactive election for a taxable year of the shareholder (retroactive election year) only if the shareholder—

(1) Reasonably believed, within the meaning of paragraph (d) of this section, that as of the election due date, as defined in § 1.1295-1(e), the foreign corporation was not a PFIC for its taxable year that ended during the retroactive election year;

(2) Filed a Protective Statement with respect to the foreign corporation, applicable to the retroactive election year, in which the shareholder described the basis for its reasonable belief and extended, in the manner provided in paragraph (c)(4) of this section, the periods of limitations on the assessment of taxes determined under sections 1291 through 1298 with respect to the foreign corporation (PFIC related taxes) for all taxable years of the shareholder to which the Protective Statement applies; and

(3) Complied with the other terms and conditions of the Protective Statement.

(c) *Protective Statement.*—(1) *In general.*—A Protective Statement is a statement executed under penalties of perjury by the shareholder, or a person authorized to sign a federal income tax return on behalf of the shareholder, that preserves the shareholder's ability to make a retroactive election. To file a Protective Statement that applies to a taxable year of the shareholder, the shareholder must reasonably believe as of the election due date that the foreign corporation was not a PFIC for the foreign corporation's taxable year that ended during the retroactive election year. The Protective Statement must contain—

(i) The shareholder's reasonable belief statement, as described in paragraph (c)(2) of this section;

(ii) The shareholder's agreement extending the periods of limitations on the assessment of PFIC related taxes for all taxable years to which the Protective Statement applies, as provided in paragraph (c)(4) of this section; and

(iii) The following information and representations—

(A) The shareholder's name, address, taxpayer identification number, and the shareholder's first taxable year to which the Protective Statement applies;

(B) The foreign corporation's name, address, and taxpayer identification number, if any; and

(C) The highest percentage of shares of each class of stock of the foreign corporation held directly or indirectly by the shareholder during the shareholder's first taxable year to which the Protective Statement applies.

(2) *Reasonable belief statement.*—The Protective Statement must contain a reasonable belief statement, as described in paragraph (c)(1) of this section. The reasonable belief statement is a description of the shareholder's basis for its reasonable belief that the foreign corporation was not a PFIC for its taxable year that ended with or within the shareholder's first taxable year to which the Protective Statement applies. If the Protective Statement applies to a taxable year or years described in paragraph (c)(5)(ii) of this section, the reasonable belief statement must describe the shareholder's basis for its reasonable belief that the foreign corporation was not a PFIC for the foreign corporation's taxable year or years that ended in such taxable year or years of the shareholder. The reasonable belief statement must discuss the application of the income and asset tests to the foreign corporation and the factors, including those stated in paragraph (d) of this section, that affect the results of those tests.

(3) *Who executes and files the Protective Statement.*—The person that executes and files the Protective Statement is the person that makes the section 1295 election, as provided in §1.1295-1(d).

(4) *Waiver of the periods of limitations.*— (i) *Time for and manner of extending periods of limitations.*—(A) *In general.*—A shareholder that files the Protective Statement with the Commissioner must extend the periods of limitations on the assessment of all PFIC related taxes for all of the shareholder's taxable years to which the Protective Statement applies, as provided in this paragraph (c)(4). The shareholder is required to execute the waiver on such form as the Commissioner may prescribe for purposes of this paragraph (c)(4). Until that form is published, the shareholder must execute a statement in which the shareholder agrees to extend the periods of limitations on the assessment of all PFIC related taxes for all the shareholder's taxable years to which the Protective Statement applies, as provided in this paragraph (c)(4), and agrees to the restrictions in paragraph (c)(4)(ii)(A) of this section. The shareholder or a person authorized to sign the shareholder's federal income tax return must sign the form or statement. A properly executed form or statement authorized by this paragraph (c)(4) will be deemed consented to and signed by a Service Center Director or the Assistant Commissioner (International) for purposes of §301.6501(c)-1(d) of this chapter.

(B) *Application of general rule to domestic partnerships.*—(1) *In general.*—A domestic partnership that holds an interest in stock of a PFIC satisfies the waiver requirement of paragraph (c)(4) of this section pursuant to the rules of this paragraph (c)(4)(i)(B)(1). The partnership must file one or more waivers obtained or arranged under this paragraph (c)(4)(i)(B) as part of the Protective Statement, as provided in paragraph (c)(1) of this section. The partnership must either—

(i) Obtain from each partner the partner's waiver of the periods of limitations;

(ii) Obtain from each partner a duly executed power of attorney under §601.501 of this chapter authorizing the partnership to extend that partner's periods of limitations, and execute a waiver on behalf of the partners; or

(iii) In the case of a domestic partnership governed by the unified audit and litigation procedures of sections 6221 through 6233 (TEFRA partnership), arrange for the tax matters partner (or any other person authorized to enter into an agreement to extend the periods of limitations), as provided in section 6229(b), to execute a waiver on behalf of all the partners.

(2) *Special rules.*—(i) *Addition of partner to non-TEFRA partnership.*—In the case of any individual who becomes a partner in a domestic partnership other than a TEFRA partnership (non-TEFRA partnership) in a taxable year subsequent to the year in which the partnership

filed a Protective Statement, the partner and the partnership must comply with the rules applicable to non-TEFRA partnerships, as provided in paragraph (c)(4)(i)(B)(1) of this section, by the due date, as extended, for the federal income tax return of the partnership for the taxable year during which the individual became a partner. Failure to so comply will render the Protective Statement invalid with respect to the partnership and partners.

(ii) *Change in status from non-TEFRA partnership to TEFRA partnership.*—If a partnership is a non-TEFRA partnership in one taxable year but becomes a TEFRA partnership in a subsequent taxable year, the partnership must file one or more waivers obtained or arranged under this paragraph (c)(4)(i)(B)(2)(ii), as part of the Protective Statement, as provided in paragraph (c)(1) of this section. The partnership must either obtain from any new partner the partner's waiver described in this paragraph (c)(4); obtain from the new partner a duly executed power of attorney under §601.501 of this chapter authorizing the partnership to extend the partner's periods of limitations, and execute a waiver on behalf of the new partner; or arrange for the tax matters partner (or any other person authorized to enter into an agreement to extend the periods of limitations) to execute a waiver on behalf of all the partners. In each case, the partnership must attach any new waiver of a partner's periods of limitations, and a copy of the Protective Statement to its federal income tax return for that taxable year.

(C) *Application of general rule to domestic nongrantor trusts and domestic estates.*—A domestic nongrantor trust or a domestic estate that holds an interest in stock of a PFIC satisfies the waiver requirement of this paragraph (c)(4) at the entity level. For this purpose, such entity must comply with rules similar to those applicable to non-TEFRA partnerships, as provided in paragraph (c)(4)(i)(B)(1) of this section.

(D) *Application of general rule to S corporations.*—An S corporation that holds an interest in stock of a PFIC satisfies the waiver requirement of this paragraph (c)(4) at the S corporation level. For this purpose, the S corporation must comply with rules similar to those applicable to non-TEFRA partnerships, as provided in paragraph (c)(4)(i)(B)(1) of this section. However, in the case of an S corporation that was governed by the unified audit corporate proceedings of sections 6241 through 6245 for any taxable year to which a Protective Statement applies (former TEFRA S corporation), the tax matters person (or any other person authorized to enter into such an agreement), as was provided in sections 6241 through 6245, may execute a waiver described in this paragraph (c)(4) that applies to such taxable year; for any other taxable year, the former TEFRA S corporation must comply with rules

similar to those applicable to non-TEFRA partnerships.

(E) *Effect on waiver of complete termination of a pass through entity or pass through entity's business.*—The complete termination of a pass through entity described in paragraphs (c)(4)(i)(B) through (D) of this section, or a pass through entity's trade or business, will not terminate a waiver that applies to a partner, shareholder, or beneficiary.

(F) *Application of general rule to foreign partnerships, foreign trusts, domestic or foreign grantor trusts, and foreign estates.*—A U.S. person that is a partner or beneficiary of a foreign partnership, foreign trust, or foreign estate that holds an interest in stock of a PFIC satisfies the waiver requirement of this paragraph (c)(4) at the partner or beneficiary level. A U.S. person that is treated under sections 671 through 679 as the owner of the portion of a domestic or foreign trust that owns an interest in PFIC stock also satisfies the waiver requirement at the owner level. A waiver by a partner or beneficiary applies only to that partner or beneficiary, and is not affected by a complete termination of the entity or the entity's trade or business.

(ii) *Terms of waiver.*—(A) *Scope of waiver.*—The waiver of the periods of limitations is limited to the assessment of PFIC related taxes. If the period of limitations for a taxable year affected by a retroactive election has expired with respect to the assessment of other non-PFIC related taxes, no adjustments, other than consequential changes, may be made by the Internal Revenue Service or by the shareholder to any other items of income, deduction, or credit for that year. If the period of limitations for refunds or credits for a taxable year affected by a retroactive election is open only by virtue of the assessment period extension and section 6511(c), no refund or credit is allowable on grounds other than adjustments to PFIC related taxes and consequential changes.

(B) *Period of waiver.*—The extension of the periods of limitations on the assessment of PFIC related taxes will be effective for all of the shareholder's taxable years to which the Protective Statement applies. In addition, the waiver, to the extent it applies to the period of limitations for a particular year, will terminate with respect to that year no sooner than three years from the date on which the shareholder files an amended return, as provided in paragraph (g) of this section, for that year. For the suspension of the running of the period of limitations for the collection of taxes for which a shareholder has elected under section 1294 to extend the time for payment, as provided in paragraph (g)(3)(ii) of this section, see sections 6503(i) and 6229(h).

(5) *Time of and manner for filing a Protective Statement.*—(i) *In general.*—Except as provided

in paragraph (c)(5)(ii) of this section, a Protective Statement must be attached to the shareholder's federal income tax return for the shareholder's first taxable year to which the Protective Statement will apply. The shareholder must file its return and the copy of the Protective Statement by the due date, as extended under section 6081, for the return.

(ii) *Special rule for taxable years ended before January 2, 1998.*—A shareholder may file a Protective Statement that applies to the shareholder's taxable year or years that ended before January 2, 1998, provided the period of limitations on the assessment of taxes for any such year has not expired (open year). The shareholder must file the Protective Statement applicable to such open year or years, as provided in paragraph (c)(5)(i) of this section, by the due date, as extended, for the shareholder's return for the first taxable year ending after January 2, 1998.

(6) *Applicability of the Protective Statement.*—(i) *In general.*—Except as otherwise provided in this paragraph (c)(6), a Protective Statement applies to the shareholder's first taxable year for which the Protective Statement was filed and to each subsequent taxable year. The Protective Statement will not apply to any taxable year of the shareholder during which the shareholder does not own any stock of the foreign corporation or to any taxable year thereafter. Accordingly, if the shareholder has not made a retroactive election with respect to the previously owned stock by the time the shareholder reacquires stock of the foreign corporation, the shareholder must file another Protective Statement to preserve its right to make a retroactive election with respect to the later acquired stock. For the rule that provides that a section 1295 election made with respect to a foreign corporation applies to stock of that corporation acquired after a lapse in ownership, see § 1.1295-1(c)(2)(iii).

(ii) *Invalidity of the Protective Statement.*—A shareholder will be treated as if it never filed a Protective Statement if—

(A) The shareholder failed to make a retroactive election by the date prescribed for making the retroactive election in paragraph (g)(1) of this section; or

(B) The waiver of the periods of limitations terminates (by reason of a court decision or other determination) with respect to any taxable year before the expiration of three years from the date of filing of an amended return for that year pursuant to paragraph (g) of this section.

(7) *Retention of Protective Statement and information demonstrating reasonable belief.*—A shareholder that files a Protective Statement must retain a copy of the Protective Statement and its attachments and must, for each taxable year of the shareholder to which the Protective Statement applies, retain information sufficient to demonstrate the shareholder's reasonable belief that the foreign corporation was not a PFIC for the taxable year of the foreign corporation ending during each such taxable year of the shareholder.

(d) *Reasonable belief.*—(1) *In general.*—A foreign corporation is a PFIC for a taxable year if the foreign corporation satisfies either the income or asset test of section 1297(a). To determine whether a shareholder had reasonable belief that the foreign corporation is not a PFIC under section 1297(a), the shareholder must consider all relevant facts and circumstances. Reasonable belief may be based on a variety of factors, including reasonable asset valuations as well as reasonable interpretations of the applicable provisions of the Code, regulations, and administrative guidance regarding the direct or indirect ownership of the income or assets of the foreign corporation, the proper character of that income or those assets, and similar issues. Reasonable belief may be based on reasonable predictions regarding income to be earned and assets to be owned in subsequent years where qualification of the foreign corporation as a PFIC for the current taxable year will depend on the qualification of the corporation as a PFIC in a subsequent year. Reasonable belief may be based on an analysis of generally available financial information of the foreign corporation. To determine whether a shareholder had reasonable belief that the foreign corporation was not a PFIC, the Commissioner may consider the size of the shareholder's interest in the foreign corporation.

(2) *Knowledge of law required.*—Reasonable belief must be based on a good faith effort to apply the Code, regulations, and related administrative guidance. Any person's failure to know or apply these provisions will not form the basis of reasonable belief.

(e) *Special rules for qualified shareholders.*—(1) *In general.*—A shareholder that is a qualified shareholder, as defined in paragraph (e)(2) of this section, for a taxable year of the shareholder is not required to satisfy the reasonable belief requirement of paragraph (b)(1) of this section or file a Protective Statement to preserve its ability to make a retroactive election with respect to such taxable year. Accordingly, a qualified shareholder may make a retroactive election for any open taxable year in the shareholder's holding period. The retroactive election will be treated as made in the earliest taxable year of the shareholder during which the foreign corporation qualified as a PFIC (including a taxable year ending prior January 2, 1998) and the shareholder will be treated as a shareholder of a pedigreed QEF, as defined in § 1.1291-9(j)(2)(ii), provided the shareholder—

(i) Has been a qualified shareholder with respect to the foreign corporation for all taxable years of the shareholder included in the shareholder's holding period during which the foreign corporation was a PFIC, or in the case of taxable years ending before January 2, 1998, the shareholder satisfies the criteria of a qualified shareholder, for all such years; or

(ii) Has been a qualified shareholder, or in the case of taxable years ending before January 2, 1998, satisfies the criteria of a qualified shareholder, for all taxable years in its holding period before it filed a Protective Statement, which Protective Statement is applicable to all subsequent years, beginning with the first taxable year in which the shareholder is not a qualified shareholder.

(2) *Qualified shareholder.*—A shareholder will be treated as a qualified shareholder for a taxable year if the shareholder did not file a Protective Statement applicable to an earlier taxable year included in the shareholder's holding period of the stock of the foreign corporation currently held and—

(i) At all times during the taxable year the shareholder owned, within the meaning of section 958, directly, indirectly, or constructively, less than two percent of the vote and value of each class of stock of the foreign corporation; and

(ii) With respect to the taxable year of the foreign corporation ending within the shareholder's taxable year, the foreign corporation or U.S. counsel for the foreign corporation indicated in a public filing, disclosure statement or other notice provided to U.S. persons that are shareholders of the foreign corporation (corporate filing) that the foreign corporation—

(A) Reasonably believes that it is not or should not constitute a PFIC for the corporation's taxable year; or

(B) Is unable to conclude that it is not or should not be a PFIC (due to certain asset valuation or interpretation issues, or because PFIC status will depend on the income or assets of the foreign corporation in the corporation's subsequent taxable years) but reasonably believes that, more likely than not, it ultimately will not be a PFIC.

(3) *Exceptions.*—Notwithstanding paragraph (e)(2)(ii) of this section, a shareholder will not be treated as a qualified shareholder for a taxable year of the shareholder if the shareholder knew or had reason to know that a corporate filing regarding the foreign corporation's PFIC status was inaccurate, or knew that the foreign corporation was a PFIC for the taxable year of the foreign corporation ending with or within such taxable year of the shareholder. For purposes of this paragraph, a shareholder will be treated as knowing that a foreign corporation was a PFIC if the principal activity of the foreign corporation, directly or indirectly, is owning or

trading a diversified portfolio of stock, securities, or other financial contracts.

(f) *Special consent.*—(1) *In general.*—A shareholder that has not satisfied the requirements of paragraph (b) or (e) of this section may request the consent of the Commissioner to make a retroactive election for a taxable year of the shareholder provided the shareholder satisfies the requirements set forth in this paragraph (f). The Commissioner will grant relief under this paragraph (f) only if—

(i) The shareholder reasonably relied on a qualified tax professional, within the meaning of paragraph (f)(2) of this section;

(ii) Granting consent will not prejudice the interests of the United States government, as provided in paragraph (f)(3) of this section;

(iii) The shareholder requests consent under paragraph (f) of this section before a representative of the Internal Revenue Service raises upon audit the PFIC status of the corporation for any taxable year of the shareholder; and

(iv) The shareholder satisfies the procedural requirements set forth in paragraph (f)(4) of this section.

(2) *Reasonable reliance on a qualified tax professional.*—(i) *In general.*—Except as provided in paragraph (f)(2)(ii) of this section, a shareholder is deemed to have reasonably relied on a qualified tax professional only if the shareholder reasonably relied on a qualified tax professional (including a tax professional employed by the shareholder) who failed to identify the foreign corporation as a PFIC or failed to advise the shareholder of the consequences of making, or failing to make, the section 1295 election. A shareholder will not be considered to have reasonably relied on a qualified tax professional if the shareholder knew, or reasonably should have known, that the foreign corporation was a PFIC and of the availability of a section 1295 election, or knew or reasonably should have known that the qualified tax professional—

(A) Was not competent to render tax advice with respect to the ownership of shares of a foreign corporation; or

(B) Did not have access to all relevant facts and circumstances.

(ii) *Shareholder deemed to have not reasonably relied on a qualified tax professional.*—For purposes of this paragraph (f)(2), a shareholder is deemed to have not reasonably relied on a qualified tax professional if the shareholder was informed by the qualified tax professional that the foreign corporation was a PFIC and of the availability of the section 1295 election and related tax consequences, but either chose not to make the section 1295 election or was unable to make a valid section 1295 election.

(3) *Prejudice to the interests of the United States government.*—(i) *General rule.*—Except as

otherwise provided in paragraph (f)(3)(ii) of this section, the Commissioner will not grant consent under paragraph (f) of this section if doing so would prejudice the interests of the United States government. The interests of the United States government are prejudiced if granting relief would result in the shareholder having a lower tax liability, taking into account applicable interest charges, in the aggregate for all years affected by the retroactive election (other than by a de minimis amount) than the shareholder would have had if the shareholder had made the section 1295 election by the election due date. The time value of money is taken into account for purposes of this computation.

(ii) *Elimination of prejudice to the interests of the United States government.*—Notwithstanding the general rule of paragraph (f)(3)(i) of this section, if granting relief would prejudice the interests of the United States government, the Commissioner may, in the Commissioner's sole discretion, grant consent to make the election provided the shareholder enters into a closing agreement with the Commissioner that requires the shareholder to pay an amount sufficient to eliminate any prejudice to the United States government as a consequence of the shareholder's inability to file amended returns for closed taxable years.

(4) *Procedural requirements.*—(i) *Filing instructions.*—A shareholder requests consent under paragraph (f) of this section to make a retroactive election by filing with the Office of the Associate Chief Counsel (International) a ruling request that includes the affidavits required by this paragraph (f)(4). The ruling request must satisfy the requirements, including payment of the user fee, for ruling requests filed with that office.

(ii) *Affidavit from shareholder.*—The shareholder, or a person authorized to sign a federal income tax return on behalf of the shareholder, must submit a detailed affidavit describing the events that led to the failure to make a section 1295 election by the election due date, and to the discovery thereof. The shareholder's affidavit must describe the engagement and responsibilities of the qualified tax professional as well as the extent to which the shareholder relied on the tax professional. The shareholder must sign the affidavit under penalties of perjury. An individual who signs for an entity must have personal knowledge of the facts and circumstances at issue.

(iii) *Affidavits from other persons.*—The shareholder must submit detailed affidavits from individuals having knowledge or information about the events that led to the failure to make a section 1295 election by the election due date, and to the discovery thereof. These individuals must include the qualified tax professional upon whose advice the shareholder relied, as well as

any individual (including an employee of the shareholder) who made a substantial contribution to the return's preparation, and any accountant or attorney, knowledgeable in tax matters, who advised the shareholder with regard to its ownership of the stock of the foreign corporation. Each affidavit must describe the individual's engagement and responsibilities as well as the advice concerning the tax treatment of the foreign corporation that the individual provided to the shareholder. Each affidavit also must include the individual's name, address, and taxpayer identification number, and must be signed by the individual under penalties of perjury.

(iv) *Other information.*—In connection with a request for consent under this paragraph (f), a shareholder must provide any additional information requested by the Commissioner.

(v) *Notification of Internal Revenue Service.*—The shareholder must notify the branch of the Associate Chief Counsel (International) considering the request for relief under this paragraph (f) if, while the shareholder's request for consent is pending, the Internal Revenue Service begins an examination of the shareholder's return for the retroactive election year or for any subsequent taxable year during which the shareholder holds stock of the foreign corporation.

(vi) *Who requests special consent under this paragraph (f) and who enters into a closing agreement.*—The person that requests consent under this paragraph (f) is the person that makes the section 1295 election, as provided in §1.1295-1(d). If a shareholder is required to enter into a closing agreement with the Commissioner, as described in paragraph (f)(3)(ii) of this section, rules similar to those under paragraphs (c)(4)(i)(B) through (E) of this section apply for purposes of determining the person that enters into the closing agreement.

(g) *Time for and manner of making a retroactive election.*—(1) *Time for making a retroactive election.*—(i) *In general.*—Except as otherwise provided in paragraph (g)(1)(ii) of this section, a shareholder must make a retroactive election, in the manner provided in paragraph (g)(2) of this section, on or before the due date, as extended, for the shareholder's return—

(A) In the case of a shareholder that makes a retroactive election pursuant to paragraph (b) or (e) of this section, for the taxable year in which the shareholder determines or reasonably should have determined that the foreign corporation was a PFIC; or

(B) In the case of a shareholder that obtains the consent of the Commissioner pursuant to paragraph (f) of this section, for the taxable year in which such consent is granted.

(ii) *Transition rule.*—A shareholder that files a Protective Statement for a taxable year described in paragraph (c)(5)(ii) of this section may make a retroactive election by the due date, as extended, for the return for the first taxable year ended after January 2, 1998, even if the shareholder determined or should have determined that the foreign corporation was a PFIC for a year described in paragraph (c)(5)(ii) of this section at any time on or before January 2, 1998.

(iii) *Ownership not required at time retroactive election is made.*—The shareholder need not own shares of the foreign corporation at the time the shareholder makes a retroactive election with respect to the foreign corporation.

(2) *Manner of making a retroactive election.*—A shareholder that has satisfied the requirements of paragraph (b) or (e) of this section, or a shareholder that has been granted consent under paragraph (f) of this section, must make a retroactive election in the manner provided in Form 8621 for making a section 1295 election, and must attach Form 8621 to an amended return for the later of the retroactive election year or the earliest open taxable year of the shareholder. The shareholder also must file an amended return for each of its subsequent taxable years affected by the retroactive election. In each amended return the shareholder must redetermine its income tax liability for that year to take into account the assessment of PFIC related taxes. If the period of limitations for the assessment of taxes for a taxable year affected by the retroactive election has expired except to the extent the waiver of limitations, described in paragraph (c)(4) of this section, has extended such period, no adjustments, other than consequential changes, may be made to any other items of income, deduction, or credit in that year. In addition, the shareholder must pay all taxes and interest owing by reason of the PFIC and QEF status of the foreign corporation in those years (except to the extent a section 1294 election extends the time to pay the taxes and interest). A shareholder that filed a Protective Statement must attach to Form 8621 filed with each amended return a representation that the shareholder, until the taxable year in which it determined or reasonably should have determined that the foreign corporation was a PFIC, reasonably believed, within the meaning of paragraph (d) of this section, that the foreign corporation was not a PFIC in the taxable year for which the amended return is filed, and in all other taxable years to which the Protective Statement applies. A shareholder that entered into a closing agreement must comply with the terms of that agreement, as provided in paragraph (f)(3)(ii) of this section, to eliminate any prejudice to the United States government's interests, as described in paragraph (f)(3) of this section.

(3) *Who makes the retroactive election.*—The person that makes the retroactive election is the person that makes the section 1295 election, as provided in § 1.1295-1(d). A partner, shareholder, or beneficiary for which a pass through entity, as described in paragraphs (c)(4)(i)(B) through (D) of this section, filed a Protective Statement may make a retroactive election, if the pass through entity completely terminates its business or otherwise ceases to exist.

(4) *Other elections.*—(i) *Section 1291(d)(2) election.*—If the foreign corporation for which the shareholder makes a retroactive election will be treated as an unpedigreed QEF, as defined in § 1.1291-9(j)(2)(iii), with respect to the shareholder, the shareholder may make an election under section 1291(d)(2) to purge its holding period of the years or parts of years before the effective date of the retroactive election. If the qualification date, within the meaning of § 1.1291-9(e) or 1.1291-10(e), falls in a taxable year for which the period of limitations has expired, the shareholder may treat the first day of the retroactive election year as the qualification date. The shareholder may make a section 1291(d)(2) election at the time that it makes the retroactive election, but no later than two years after the date that the amended return in which the retroactive election is made is filed. For the requirements for making a section 1291(d)(2) election, see §§ 1.1291-9 and 1.1291-10.

(ii) *Section 1294 election.*—A shareholder may make an election under section 1294 to extend the time for payment of tax on the shareholder's pro rata shares of the ordinary earnings and net capital gain of the foreign corporation reported in the shareholder's amended return, and section 6621 interest attributable to such tax, but only to the extent the tax and interest are attributable to earnings that have not been distributed to the shareholder. The shareholder must make a section 1294 election for a taxable year at the time that it files its amended return for that year, as provided in paragraph (g)(1) of this section. For the requirements for making a section 1294 election, see § 1.1294-1T.

(h) *Effective date.*—The rules of this section are effective as of January 2, 1998. [Reg. § 1.1295-3.]

☐ *[T.D. 8750, 12-31-97. Redesignated and amended by T.D. 8870, 2-4-2000.]*

[Reg. § 1.1296-1]

§ 1.1296-1. Mark to market election for marketable stock.—(a) *Definitions.*—(1) *Eligible RIC.*—An *eligible RIC* is a regulated investment company that offers for sale, or has outstanding, any stock of which it is the issuer and which is redeemable at net asset value, or that publishes net asset valuations at least annually.

(2) *Section 1296 stock.*—The term *section 1296 stock* means marketable stock in a passive foreign investment company (PFIC), including any PFIC stock owned directly or indirectly by an eligible RIC, for which there is a valid section 1296 elec-

tion. Section 1296 stock does not include stock of a foreign corporation that previously had been a PFIC, and for which a section 1296 election remains in effect.

(3) *Unreversed inclusions.*—(i) *General rule.*— The term *unreversed inclusions* means with respect to any section 1296 stock, the excess, if any, of—

(A) The amount of mark to market gain included in gross income of the United States person under paragraph (c)(1) of this section with respect to such stock for prior taxable years; over

(B) The amount allowed as a deduction to the United States person under paragraph (c)(3) of this section with respect to such stock for prior taxable years.

(ii) *Section 1291 adjustment.*—The amount referred to in paragraph (a)(3)(i)(A) of this section shall include any amount subject to section 1291 under the coordination rule of paragraph (i)(2)(ii) of this section.

(iii) *Example.*—An example of the computation of unreversed inclusions is as follows:

Example. A, a United States person, acquired stock in Corp X, a foreign corporation, on January 1, 2005 for $150. At such time and at all times thereafter, Corp X was a PFIC and A's stock in Corp X was marketable. For taxable years 2005 and 2006, Corp X was a nonqualified fund subject to taxation under section 1291. A made a timely section 1296 election with respect to the X stock, effective for taxable year 2007. The fair market value of the X stock was $200 as of December 31, 2006, and $240 as of December 31, 2007. Additionally, Corp X made no distribution with respect to its stock for the taxable years at issue. In 2007, pursuant to paragraph (i)(2)(ii) of this section, A must include the $90 gain in the X stock in accordance with the rules of section 1291 for purposes of determining the deferred tax amount and any applicable interest. Nonetheless, for purposes of determining the amount of the unreversed inclusions pursuant to paragraph (a)(3)(ii) of this section, A will include the $90 of gain that was taxed under section 1291 and not the interest thereon.

(iv) *Special rule for regulated investment companies.*—In the case of a regulated investment company which had elected to mark to market the PFIC stock held by such company as of the last day of the taxable year preceding such company's first taxable year for which such company makes a section 1296 election, the amount referred to in paragraph (a)(3)(i)(A) of this section shall include amounts previously included in gross income by the company pursuant to such mark to market election with respect to such stock for prior taxable years. For further guidance, see Notice 92-53 (1992-2 C.B. 384) (see also 601.601(d)(2) of this chapter).

(b) *Application of section 1296 election.*—(1) *In general.*—Any United States person and any controlled foreign corporation (CFC) that owns directly, or is treated as owning under this section, marketable stock, as defined in §1.1296-2, in a PFIC may make an election to mark to market such stock in accordance with the provisions of section 1296 and this section.

(2) *Election applicable to specific United States person.*—A section 1296 election applies only to the United States person (or CFC that is treated as a U.S. person under paragraph (g)(2) of this section) that makes the election. Accordingly, a United States person's section 1296 election will not apply to a transferee of section 1296 stock.

(3) *Election applicable to specific corporation only.*—A section 1296 election is made with respect to a single foreign corporation, and thus a separate section 1296 election must be made for each foreign corporation that otherwise meets the requirements of this section. A United States persons section 1296 election with respect to stock in a foreign corporation applies to all marketable stock of the corporation that the person owns directly, or is treated as owning under paragraph (e) of this section, at the time of the election or that is subsequently acquired.

(c) *Effect of election.*—(1) *Recognition of gain.*— If the fair market value of section 1296 stock on the last day of the United States person's taxable year exceeds its adjusted basis, the United States person shall include in gross income for its taxable year the excess of the fair market value of such stock over its adjusted basis (mark to market gain).

(2) *Character of gain.*—Mark to market gain, and any gain on the sale or other disposition of section 1296 stock, shall be treated as ordinary income.

(3) *Recognition of loss.*—If the adjusted basis of section 1296 stock exceeds its fair market value on the last day of the United States persons taxable year, such person shall be allowed a deduction for such taxable year equal to the lesser of the amount of such excess or the unreversed inclusions with respect to such stock (mark to market loss).

(4) *Character of loss.*—(i) *Losses not in excess of unreversed inclusions.*—Any mark to market loss allowed as a deduction under paragraph (c)(3) of this section, and any loss on the sale or other disposition of section 1296 stock, to the extent that such loss does not exceed the unreversed inclusions attributable to such stock, shall be treated as an ordinary loss, deductible in computing adjusted gross income.

(ii) *Losses in excess of unreversed inclusions.*—Any loss recognized on the sale or other disposition of section 1296 stock in excess of any prior unreversed inclusions will be subject to the rules generally applicable to losses provided elsewhere in the Internal Revenue Code and the regulations thereunder.

(5) *Application of election to separate lots of stock.*—In the case in which a United States person purchased or acquired shares of stock in a PFIC at different prices, the rules of this section shall be applied in a manner consistent with the rules of § 1.1012-1.

(6) *Source rules.*—The source of any amount included in gross income under paragraph (c)(1) of this section, or the allocation and apportionment of any amount allowed as a deduction under paragraph (c)(3) of this section, shall be determined in the same manner as if such amounts were gain or loss (as the case may be) from the sale of stock in the PFIC.

(7) *Examples.*—The following examples illustrate this paragraph (c):

Example 1. Treatment of gain as ordinary income. A, a United States individual, purchases stock in FX, a foreign corporation that is not a PFIC, in 1990 for $1,000. On January 1, 2005, when the fair market value of the FX stock is $1,100, FX becomes a PFIC. A makes a timely section 1296 election for taxable year 2005. On December 31, 2005, the fair market value of the FX stock is $1,200. For taxable year 2005, A includes $200 of mark to market gain (the excess of the fair market value of FX stock ($1,200) over A's adjusted basis ($1,000)) in gross income as ordinary income and pursuant to paragraph (d)(1) of this section increases his basis in the FX stock by that amount.

Example 2. Treatment of gain as capital gain. The facts are the same as in *Example 1*. For taxable year 2006, FX does not satisfy either the asset test or the income test of section 1297(a). A does not revoke the section 1296 election it made with respect to the FX stock. On December 1, 2006, A sells the FX stock when the fair market value of the stock is $1,500. For taxable year 2006, A includes $300 of gain (the excess of the fair market value of FX stock ($1,500) over A's adjusted basis ($1,200)) in gross income as long-term capital gain because at the time of sale of the FX stock by A, FX did not qualify as a PFIC, and, therefore, the FX stock was not section 1296 stock at the time of the disposition. Further, A's holding period for non-PFIC purposes was more than one year.

Example 3. Treatment of losses as ordinary where they do not exceed unreversed inclusions. The facts are the same as in *Example 1*. On December 1, 2006, A sells the stock in FX for $1,100. At that time, A's unreversed inclusions (the amount A included in income as mark to market gain) with respect to the stock in FX are $200. Accordingly, for taxable year 2006, A recognizes a loss on the sale of the FX stock of $100, (the fair market value of the FX stock ($1,100) minus A's adjusted basis ($1,200) in the stock) that is treated as an ordinary loss because the loss does not exceed the unreversed inclusions attributable to the stock of FX.

Example 4. Treatment of losses as long-term capital losses. The facts are the same as in *Example 3*, except that FX does not satisfy either the asset test or the income test of section 1297(a) for taxable year 2006. For taxable year 2006, A's $100 loss from the sale of the FX stock is treated as long-term capital loss because at the time of the sale of the FX stock by A FX did not qualify as a PFIC, and, therefore, the FX stock was not section 1296 stock at the time of the disposition. Further, A's holding period in the FX stock for non-PFIC purposes was more than one year.

Example 5. Long-term capital loss treatment of losses in excess of unreversed inclusions. The facts are the same as in *Example 3*, except that A sells his FX stock for $900. At the time of A's sale of the FX stock on December 1, 2006, A's unreversed inclusions with respect to the FX stock are $200. Accordingly, the $300 loss recognized by A on the disposition is treated as an ordinary loss to the extent of his unreversed inclusions ($200). The amount of the loss in excess of A's unreversed inclusions ($100) will be treated as a long-term capital loss because A's holding period in the FC stock for non-PFIC purposes was more than one year.

Example 6. Application of section 1296 election to separate lots of stock. On January 1, 2005, Corp A, a domestic corporation, purchased 100 shares (first lot) of stock in FX, a PFIC, for $500 ($5 per share). On June 1, 2005, Corp A purchased 100 shares (second lot) of FX stock for $1,000 ($10 per share). Corp A made a timely section 1296 election with respect to its FX stock for taxable year 2005. On December 31, 2005, the fair market value of FX stock was $8 per share. For taxable year 2005, Corp A includes $300 of gain in gross income as ordinary income under paragraph (c)(1) of this section with respect to the first lot, and adjusts its basis in that lot to $800 pursuant to paragraph (d)(1) of this section. With respect to the second lot, Corp A is not permitted to recognize a loss under paragraph (c)(3) of this section for taxable year 2005. Although Corp A's adjusted basis in that stock exceeds its fair market value by $200, Corp A has no unreversed inclusions with respect to that particular lot of stock. On July 1, 2006, Corp A sells 100 shares of FX stock for $900. Assuming that Corp A adequately identifies (in accordance with the rules of § 1.1012-1(c)) the shares of FX stock sold as being from the second lot, Corp A recognizes $100 of long term capital loss pursuant to paragraph (c)(4)(ii) of this section.

(d) *Adjustment to basis.*—(1) *Stock held directly.*—The adjusted basis of the section 1296 stock shall be increased by the amount included in the gross income of the United States person under paragraph (c)(1) of this section with respect to such stock, and decreased by the amount allowed as a deduction to the United States person under paragraph (c)(3) of this section with respect to such stock.

(2) *Stock owned through certain foreign entities.*—(i) In the case of section 1296 stock that a United States person is treated as owning through certain foreign entities pursuant to paragraph (e) of this section, the basis adjustments under paragraph (d)(1) of this section shall apply to such stock in the hands of the foreign entity actually holding such stock, but only for purposes of determining the subsequent treatment under chapter 1 of the Internal Revenue Code of the United States person with respect to such stock. Such increase or decrease in the adjusted basis of the section 1296 stock shall constitute an adjustment to the basis of partnership property only with respect to the partner making the section 1296 election. Corresponding adjustments shall be made to the adjusted basis of the United States person's interest in the foreign entity and in any intermediary entity described in paragraph (e) of this section through which the United States person holds the PFIC stock.

(ii) *Example.*—The following example illustrates this paragraph (d)(2):

Example. FP is a foreign partnership. Corp A, a domestic corporation, owns a 20 percent interest in FP. Corp B, a domestic corporation, owns a 30 percent interest in FP. Corp C, a foreign corporation, with no direct or indirect shareholders that are U.S. persons, owns a 50% interest in FP. Corp A, Corp B, and FP all use a calendar year for their taxable year. In 2005, FP purchases stock in FX, a foreign corporation and a PFIC, for $1,000. Corp A makes a timely section 1296 election for taxable year 2005. On December 31, 2005, the fair market value of the PFIC stock is $1,100. Corp A includes $20 of ordinary income in taxable year 2005 under paragraphs (c)(1) and (2) of this section. Corp A increases its basis in its FP partnership interest by $20. FP increases its basis in the FX stock to $1,020 solely for purposes of determining the subsequent treatment of Corp A, under chapter 1 of the Internal Revenue Code, with respect to such stock. In 2006, FP sells the FX stock for $1,200. For purposes of determining the amount of gain of Corp A, FP will be treated as having $180 in gain of which $20 is allocated to Corp A. Corp A's $20 of gain will be treated as ordinary income under paragraph (c)(2) of this section. For purposes of determining the amount of gain attributable to Corp B, FP will be treated as having $200 gain, $60 of which will be allocated to Corp B.

(3) *Stock owned indirectly by an eligible RIC.*—Paragraph (d)(2) of this section shall also apply to an eligible RIC which is an indirect shareholder under §1.1296-2(f) of stock in a PFIC and has a valid section 1296 election in effect with respect to the PFIC stock.

(4) *Stock acquired from a decedent.*—In the case of stock of a PFIC which is acquired by bequest, devise, or inheritance (or by the decedent's estate) and with respect to which a section 1296 election was in effect as of the date of the decedent's death, notwithstanding section 1014, the basis of such stock in the hands of the person so acquiring it shall be the adjusted basis of such stock in the hands of the decedent immediately before his death (or, if lesser, the basis which would have been determined under section 1014 without regard to this paragraph).

(5) *Transition rule for individuals becoming subject to United States income taxation.*—(i) *In general.*—If any individual becomes a United States person in a taxable year beginning after December 31, 1997, solely for purposes of this section, the adjusted basis, before adjustments under this paragraph (d), of any section 1296 stock owned by such individual on the first day of such taxable year shall be treated as being the greater of its fair market value or its adjusted basis on such first day.

(ii) An example of the transition rule for individuals becoming subject to United States income taxation is as follows:

Example. A, a nonresident alien individual, purchases marketable stock in FX, a PFIC, for $50 in 1995. On January 1, 2005, A becomes a United States person and makes a timely section 1296 election with respect to the stock in accordance with paragraph (h) of this section. The fair market value of the FX stock on January 1, 2005, is $100. The fair market value of the FX stock on December 31, 2005, is $110. Under paragraph (d)(5)(i) of this section, A computes the amount of mark to market gain or loss for the FX stock in 2005 by reference to an adjusted basis of $100, and therefore A includes $10 in gross income as mark to market gain under paragraph (c)(1) of this section. Additionally, under paragraph (d)(1) of this section, A's adjusted basis in the FX stock for purposes of this section is increased to $110 (and to $60 for all other tax purposes). A sells the FX stock in 2006 for $120. For purposes of applying section 1001, A must use its original basis of $50, with any adjustments under paragraph (d)(1) of this section, $10 in this case, and therefore A recognizes $60 of gain. Under paragraph (c)(2) of this section (which is applied using an adjusted basis of $110), $10 of such gain is treated as ordinary income. The remaining $50 of gain from the sale of the FX stock is long term capital gain because A held such stock for more than one year.

(e) *Stock owned through certain foreign entities.*—(1) *In general.*—Except as provided in paragraph (e)(2) of this section, the following rules shall apply in determining stock ownership for purposes of this section. PFIC stock owned, directly or indirectly, by or for a foreign partnership, foreign trust (other than a foreign trust described in sections 671 through 679), or foreign estate shall be considered as being owned proportionately by its partners or beneficiaries. PFIC stock owned, directly or indirectly, by or for a foreign trust described in sections 671 through 679 shall be considered as being owned proportionately by its grantors or other persons treated as owners under sections 671 through 679 of any portion of the trust that includes the stock. The determination of a person's proportionate interest in a foreign partnership, foreign trust or foreign estate will be made on the basis of all the facts and circumstances. Stock considered owned by reason of this paragraph shall, for purposes of applying the rules of this section, be treated as actually owned by such person.

(2) *Stock owned indirectly by eligible RICs.*— The rules for attributing ownership of stock contained in §1.1296-2(f) will apply to determine the indirect ownership of PFIC stock by an eligible RIC.

(f) *Holding period.*—Solely for purposes of sections 1291 through 1298, if section 1296 applied to stock with respect to the taxpayer for any prior taxable year, the taxpayer's holding period in such stock shall be treated as beginning on the first day of the first taxable year beginning after the last taxable year for which section 1296 so applied.

(g) *Special rules.*—(1) *Certain dispositions of stock.*—To the extent a United States person is treated as actually owning stock in a PFIC under paragraph (e) of this section, any disposition which results in the United States person being treated as no longer owning such stock, and any disposition by the person owning such stock, shall be treated as a disposition by the United States person of the stock in the PFIC.

(2) *Treatment of CFC as a United States person.*—In the case of a CFC that owns, or is treated as owning under paragraph (e) of this section, section 1296 stock:

(i) Other than with respect to the sourcing rules in paragraph (c)(6) of this section, this section shall apply to the CFC in the same manner as if such corporation were a United States person. The CFC will be treated as a foreign person for purposes of applying the source rules of paragraph (c)(6).

(ii) For purposes of subpart F of part III of subchapter N of the Internal Revenue Code—

(A) Amounts included in the CFC's gross income under paragraph (c)(1) or (i)(2)(ii) of this section shall be treated as foreign personal holding company income under section 954(c)(1)(A); and

(B) Amounts allowed as a deduction under paragraph (c)(3) of this section shall be treated as a deduction allocable to foreign personal holding company income for purposes of computing net foreign base company income under §1.954-1(c).

(iii) A United States shareholder, as defined in section 951(b), of the CFC shall not be subject to section 1291 with respect to any stock of the PFIC for the period during which the section 1296 election is in effect for that stock, and the holding period rule of paragraph (f) of this section shall apply to such United States shareholder.

(iv) The rules of this paragraph (g)(2) shall not apply to a United States person that is a shareholder of the PFIC for purposes of section 1291, but is not a United States shareholder under section 951(b) with respect to the CFC making a section 1296 election.

(3) *Timing of inclusions for stock owned through certain foreign entities.*—In the case of section 1296 stock that a United States person is treated as owning through certain foreign entities pursuant to paragraph (e) of this section, the mark to market gain or mark to market loss is determined in accordance with paragraphs (c) and (i)(2)(ii) of this section as of the last day of the taxable year of the foreign partnership, foreign trust or foreign estate and then included in the taxable year of such United States person that includes the last day of the taxable year of the entity.

(h) *Elections.*—(1) *Timing and manner for making a section 1296 election.*—(i) *United States persons.*—A United States person that owns marketable stock in a PFIC, or is treated as owning marketable stock under paragraph (e) of this section, on the last day of the taxable year of such person, and that wants to make a section 1296 election, must make a section 1296 election for such taxable year on or before the due date (including extensions) of the United States person's income tax return for that year. The section 1296 election must be made on the Form 8621, "Return by a Shareholder of a Passive Foreign Investment Company or Qualified Electing Fund", included with the original tax return of the United States person for that year, or on an amended return, provided that the amended return is filed on or before the election due date.

(ii) *Controlled foreign corporations.*—A section 1296 election by a CFC shall be made by its controlling United States shareholders, as defined in §1.964-1(c)(5), and shall be included with the Form 5471, "Information Return of U.S. Persons With Respect To Certain Foreign Corporations", for that CFC by the due date (including extensions) of the original income tax returns of the controlling United States shareholders for that year. A section 1296 election by a CFC shall be binding on all United States shareholders of the CFC.

(iii) *Retroactive elections for PFIC stock held in prior years.*—A late section 1296 election may be permitted only in accordance with §301.9100 of this chapter.

(2) *Effect of section 1296 election.*—(i) A section 1296 election will apply to the taxable year for which such election is made and remain in effect for each succeeding taxable year unless such election is revoked or terminated pursuant to paragraph (h)(3) of this section.

(ii) *Cessation of a foreign corporation as a PFIC.*—A United States person will not include mark to market gain or loss pursuant to paragraph (c) of this section with respect to any stock of a foreign corporation for any taxable year that such foreign corporation is not a PFIC under section 1297 or treated as a PFIC under section 1298(b)(1) (taking into account the holding period rule of paragraph (f) of this section). Cessation of a foreign corporation's status as a PFIC will not, however, terminate a section 1296 election. Thus, if a foreign corporation is a PFIC in a taxable year after a year in which it is not treated as a PFIC, the United States person's original election (unless revoked or terminated in accordance with paragraph (h)(3) of this section) continues to apply and the shareholder must include any mark to market gain or loss in such year.

(3) *Revocation or termination of election.*— (i) *In general.*—A United States person's section 1296 election is terminated if the section 1296 stock ceases to be marketable; if the United States person elects, or is required, to mark to market the section 1296 stock under another provision of chapter 1 of the Internal Revenue Code; or if the Commissioner, in the Commissioner's discretion, consents to the United States person's request to revoke its section 1296 election upon a finding of a substantial change in circumstances. A substantial change in circumstances for this purpose may include a foreign corporation ceasing to be a PFIC.

(ii) *Timing of termination or revocation.*— Where a section 1296 election is terminated automatically (e.g., the stock ceases to be marketable), section 1296 will cease to apply beginning with the taxable year in which such termination occurs. Where a section 1296 election is revoked with the consent of the Commissioner, section 1296 will cease to apply beginning with the first taxable year of the United States person after the revocation is granted unless otherwise provided by the Commissioner.

(4) *Examples.*—The operation of the rules of this paragraph (h) is illustrated by the following examples:

Example 1. A, a United States person, owns stock in FX, a PFIC. A makes a QEF election in 1996 with respect to the FX stock. For taxable year 2005, A makes a timely section 1296 election with respect to its stock, and thus its QEF election is automatically terminated pursuant to § 1.1295-1(i)(3). In 2006, A's stock in FX ceases to be marketable, and therefore its section 1296

election is automatically terminated under paragraph (h)(3) of this section. Beginning with taxable year 2006, A is subject to the rules of section 1291 with respect to its FX stock unless it makes a new QEF election. See § 1.1295-1(i)(5).

Example 2. The facts are the same as in *Example 1*, except that A's stock in FX becomes marketable again in 2007. A may make a new section 1296 election with respect to the FX stock for its taxable year 2007, or thereafter. A will be subject to the coordination rules under paragraph (i) of this section unless it made a new QEF election in 2006.

(i) *Coordination rules for first year of election.*— (1) *In general.*—Notwithstanding any provision in this section to the contrary, the rules of this paragraph (i) shall apply to the first taxable year in which a section 1296 election is effective with respect to marketable stock of a PFIC if such foreign corporation was a PFIC for any taxable year, prior to such first taxable year, during the United States person's holding period (as defined in paragraph (f) of this section) in such stock, and for which such corporation was not treated as a QEF with respect to such United States person.

(2) *Shareholders other than regulated investment companies.*—For the first taxable year of a United States person (other than a regulated investment company) for which a section 1296 election is in effect with respect to the stock of a PFIC, such United States person shall, in lieu of the rules of paragraphs (c) and (d) of this section—

(i) Apply the rules of section 1291 to any distributions with respect to, or disposition of, section 1296 stock;

(ii) Apply section 1291 to the amount of the excess, if any, of the fair market value of such section 1296 stock on the last day of the United States person's taxable year over its adjusted basis, as if such amount were gain recognized from the disposition of stock on the last day of the taxpayer's taxable year; and

(iii) Increase its adjusted basis in the section 1296 stock by the amount of excess, if any, subject to section 1291 under paragraph (i)(2)(ii) of this section.

(3) *Shareholders that are regulated investment companies.*—For the first taxable year of a regulated investment company for which a section 1296 election is in effect with respect to the stock of a PFIC, such regulated investment company shall increase its tax under section 852 by the amount of interest that would have been imposed under section 1291(c)(3) for such taxable year if such regulated investment company were subject to the rules of paragraph (i)(2) of this section, and not this paragraph (i)(3). No deduction or increase in basis shall be allowed for the increase in tax imposed under this paragraph (i)(3).

(4) The operation of the rules of this paragraph (i) is illustrated by the following examples:

Example (1). A, a United States person and a calendar year taxpayer, owns marketable stock in FX, a PFIC that it acquired on January 1, 1992. At all times, A's FX stock was a nonqualified fund subject to taxation under section 1291. A made a timely section 1296 election effective for taxable year 2005. At the close of taxable year 2005, the fair market value of A's FX stock exceeded its adjusted basis by $10. Pursuant to paragraph (i)(2)(ii) of this section, A must treat the $10 gain under section 1291 as if the FX stock were disposed of on December 31, 2005. Further, A increases its adjusted basis in the FX stock by the $10 in accordance with paragraph (i)(2)(iii) of this section.

Example (2). Assume the same facts as in *Example (1)*, except that A is a RIC that had not made an election prior to 2005 to mark to market the PFIC stock. In taxable year 2005, A includes $10 of ordinary income under paragraph (c)(1) of this section, and such amount is not subject to section 1291. A also increases its tax imposed under section 852 by the amount of interest that would have been determined under section 1291(c)(3), and no deduction is permitted for such amount. Finally, under paragraph (d)(1) of this section, A increases its adjusted basis in the FX stock by $10.

(j) *Effective date.*—The provisions in this section are applicable for taxable years beginning on or after May 3, 2004. [Reg. § 1.1296-1.]

☐ [*T.D. 9123*, 4-30-2004.]

[Reg. § 1.1296-2]

§ 1.1296-2. Definition of marketable stock.— (a) *General rule.*—For purposes of section 1296, the term *marketable stock* means—

(1) Passive foreign investment company (PFIC) stock that is regularly traded, as defined in paragraph (b) of this section, on a qualified exchange or other market, as defined in paragraph (c) of this section;

(2) Stock in certain PFICs, as described in paragraph (d) of this section; and

(3) Options on stock that is described in paragraph (a)(1) or (2) of this section, to the extent provided in paragraph (e) of this section.

(b) *Regularly traded.*—(1) *General rule.*—For purposes of paragraph (a)(1) of this section, a class of stock that is traded on one or more qualified exchanges or other markets, as defined in paragraph (c) of this section, is regularly traded on such exchanges or markets for any calendar year during which such class of stock is traded, other than in de minimis quantities, on at least 15 days during each calendar quarter.

(2) *Special rule for year of initial public offering.*—For the calendar year in which a corporation initiates a public offering of a class of stock for trading on one or more qualified exchanges or other markets, as defined in paragraph (c) of this section, such class of stock meets the requirements of paragraph (b)(1) of this section for such year if the stock is regularly traded on such exchanges or markets, other than in de minimis quantities, on 1/6 of the days remaining in the quarter in which the offering occurs, and on at least 15 days during each remaining quarter of the taxpayer's calendar year. In cases where a corporation initiates a public offering of a class of stock in the fourth quarter of the calendar year, such class of stock meets the requirements of paragraph (b)(1) of this section in the calendar year of the offering if the stock is regularly traded on such exchanges or markets, other than in de minimis quantities, on the greater of 1/6 of the days remaining in the quarter in which offering occurs, or 5 days.

(3) *Anti-abuse rule.*—Trades that have as one of their principal purposes the meeting of the trading requirements of paragraph (b)(1) or (2) of this section shall be disregarded. Further, a class of stock shall not be treated as meeting the trading requirement of paragraph (b)(1) or (2) of this section if there is a pattern of trades conducted to meet the requirement of paragraph (b)(1) or (2) of this section. Similarly, paragraph (b)(2) of this section shall not apply to a public offering of stock that has as one of its principal purposes to avail itself of the reduced trading requirements under the special rule for the calendar year of an initial public offering. For purposes of applying the immediately preceding sentence, consideration will be given to whether the trading requirements of paragraph (b)(1) of this section are satisfied in the subsequent calendar year.

(c) *Qualified exchange or other market.*—(1) *General rule.*—For purposes of paragraph (a)(1) of this section, the term *qualified exchange or other market* means, for any calendar year—

(i) A national securities exchange that is registered with the Securities and Exchange Commission or the national market system established pursuant to section 11A of the Securities Exchange Act of 1934 (15 U.S.C. 78f); or

(ii) A foreign securities exchange that is regulated or supervised by a governmental authority of the country in which the market is located and which has the following characteristics—

(A) The exchange has trading volume, listing, financial disclosure, surveillance, and other requirements designed to prevent fraudulent and manipulative acts and practices, to remove impediments to and perfect the mechanism of a free and open, fair and orderly, market, and to protect investors; and the laws of the country in which the exchange is located and the rules of the exchange ensure that such requirements are actually enforced; and

(B) The rules of the exchange effectively promote active trading of listed stocks.

(2) *Exchange with multiple tiers.*—If an exchange in a foreign country has more than one tier or market level on which stock may be separately listed or traded, each such tier shall be treated as a separate exchange.

(d) *Stock in certain PFICs.*—(1) *General rule.*—Except as provided in paragraph (d)(2) of this section, a foreign corporation is a corporation described in section 1296(e)(1)(B), and paragraph (a)(2) of this section, if the foreign corporation offers for sale or has outstanding stock of which it is the issuer and which is redeemable at its net asset value and if the foreign corporation satisfies the following conditions with respect to the class of shares held by the electing taxpayer—

(i) At all times during the calendar year, the foreign corporation has more than one hundred shareholders with respect to the class, other than shareholders who are related under section 267(b);

(ii) At all times during the calendar year, the class of shares of the foreign corporation is readily available for purchase by the general public at its net asset value and the foreign corporation does not require a minimum initial investment of greater than $10,000 (U.S.);

(iii) At all times during the calendar year, quotations for the class of shares of the foreign corporation are determined and published no less frequently than on a weekly basis in a widely-available permanent medium not controlled by the issuer of the shares, such as a newspaper of general circulation or a trade publication;

(iv) No less frequently than annually, independent auditors prepare financial statements of the foreign corporation that include balance sheets (statements of assets, liabilities, and net assets) and statements of income and expenses, and those statements are made available to the public;

(v) The foreign corporation is supervised or regulated as an investment company by a foreign government or an agency or instrumentality thereof that has broad inspection and enforcement authority and effective oversight over investment companies;

(vi) At all times during the calendar year, the foreign corporation has no senior securities authorized or outstanding, including any debt other than in de minimis amounts;

(vii) Ninety percent or more of the gross income of the foreign corporation for its taxable year is passive income, as defined in section 1297(a)(1) and the regulations thereunder; and

(viii) The average percentage of assets held by the foreign corporation during its taxable year which produce passive income or which are held for the production of passive income, as defined in section 1297(a)(2) and the regulations thereunder, is at least 90 percent.

(2) *Anti-abuse rule.*—If a foreign corporation undertakes any actions that have as one of their principal purposes the manipulation of the net asset value of a class of its shares, for the calendar year in which the manipulation occurs, the shares are not marketable stock for purposes of paragraph (d)(1) of this section.

(e) [Reserved]

(f) *Special rules for regulated investment companies (RICs).*—(1) *General rule.*—In the case of any RIC that is offering for sale, or has outstanding, any stock of which it is the issuer and which is redeemable at net asset value, if the RIC owns directly or indirectly, as defined in section 1298(a), stock in any passive foreign investment company, that stock will be treated as marketable stock owned by that RIC for purposes of section 1296. Except as provided in paragraph (f)(2) of this section, in the case of any other RIC that publishes net asset valuations at least annually, if the RIC owns directly or indirectly, as defined in section 1298(a), stock in any passive foreign investment company, that stock will be treated as marketable stock owned by that RIC for purposes of section 1296.

(2) [Reserved]

(g) *Effective date.*—This section applies to shareholders whose taxable year ends on or after January 25, 2000 for stock in a foreign corporation whose taxable year ends with or within the shareholder's taxable year. In addition, shareholders may elect to apply these regulations to any taxable year beginning after December 31, 1997, for stock in a foreign corporation whose taxable year ends with or within the shareholder's taxable year. [Reg. §1.1296-2.]

☐ [*T.D.* 8867, 1-25-2000. *Redesignated and amended by T.D.* 9123, 4-30-2004.]

[Reg. §1.1297-0]

§1.1297-0. Table of contents.—This section contains a listing of the headings for §1.1297-3.

§1.1297-3 Deemed sale or deemed dividend election by a U.S. person that is a shareholder of a section 1297(e) PFIC.

(a) In general

(b) Application of deemed sale election rules.

(1) Eligibility to make the deemed sale election.

(2) Effect of the deemed sale election.

(3) Time for making the deemed sale election.

(4) Manner of making the deemed sale election.

(5) Adjustments to basis.

(6) Treatment of holding period.

(c) Application of deemed dividend election rules.

   (1) Eligibility to make the deemed dividend election.

   (2) Effect of the deemed dividend election.

   (3) Post-1986 earnings and profits defined.

   (4) Time for making the deemed dividend election.

   (5) Manner of making the deemed dividend election.

   (6) Adjustments to basis.

   (7) Treatment of holding period.

   (8) Coordination with section 959(e).

(d) CFC qualification date.

(e) Late purging elections requiring special consent.

   (1) In general.

   (2) Prejudice to the interests of the U.S. government.

   (3) Procedural requirements.

   (4) Time and manner of making late election.

   (5) Multiple late elections.

(f) Effective/applicability date.
[Reg. § 1.1297-0.]

☐ [*T.D. 8750, 12-31-97. Amended by T.D. 9231, 12-7-2005 and T.D. 9360, 9-26-2007.*]

[Reg. § 1.1297-3]

§1.1297-3. Deemed sale or deemed dividend election by a U.S. person that is a shareholder of a section 1297(e) PFIC.—(a) *In general.*—A shareholder (as defined in §1.1291-9(j)(3)) of a foreign corporation that is a section 1297(e) passive foreign investment company (PFIC) (as defined in §1.1291-9(j)(2)(v)) with respect to such shareholder, shall be treated for tax purposes as holding stock in a PFIC and therefore continues to be subject to taxation under section 1291 unless the shareholder makes a purging election under section 1298(b)(1). A purging election under section 1298(b)(1) is made under rules similar to the rules of section 1291(d)(2). Section 1291(d)(2) allows a shareholder to purge the continuing PFIC taint by either making a deemed sale election or a deemed dividend election.

(b) *Application of deemed sale election rules.*—(1) *Eligibility to make the deemed sale election.*—A shareholder of a foreign corporation that is a section 1297(e) PFIC with respect to such shareholder may make a deemed sale election under section 1298(b)(1) by applying the rules of this paragraph (b).

   (2) *Effect of the deemed sale election.*—A shareholder making the deemed sale election with respect to a section 1297(e) PFIC shall be treated as having sold all of its stock in the section 1297(e) PFIC for its fair market value on the controlled foreign corporation (CFC) qualification date, as defined in paragraph (d) of this section. A deemed sale under this section is treated as a disposition subject to taxation under section 1291. Thus, the gain from the deemed sale is taxed as an excess distribution received on the CFC qualification date. In the case of an election made by an indirect shareholder, the amount of gain to be recognized and taxed as an excess distribution is the amount of gain that the direct owner of the stock of the PFIC would have realized on an actual sale or disposition of the stock of the PFIC indirectly owned by the shareholder. Any loss realized on the deemed sale is not recognized. After the deemed sale election, the shareholder's stock with respect to which the election was made under this paragraph (b) shall not be treated as stock in a PFIC and the shareholder shall not be subject to taxation under section 1291 with respect to such stock unless the qualified portion of the shareholder's holding period ends, as determined under section 1297(e)(2), and the foreign corporation thereafter qualifies as a PFIC under section 1297(a).

   (3) *Time for making the deemed sale election.*—Except as provided in paragraph (e) of this section, a shareholder shall make the deemed sale election under this paragraph (b) and section 1298(b)(1) in the shareholder's original or amended return for the taxable year that includes the CFC qualification date (election year). If the deemed sale election is made in an amended return, the return must be filed by a date that is within three years of the due date, as extended under section 6081, of the original return for the election year.

   (4) *Manner of making the deemed sale election.*—A shareholder makes the deemed sale election under this paragraph (b) by filing Form 8621, "Return by a Shareholder of a Passive Foreign Investment Company or Qualified Electing Fund", with the return of the shareholder for the election year, reporting the gain as an excess distribution pursuant to section 1291(a) as if such sale occurred under section 1291(d)(2), and paying the tax and interest due on the excess distribution. A shareholder that makes the deemed sale election after the due date of the return (determined without regard to extensions) for the election year must pay additional interest, pursuant to section 6601, on the amount of underpayment of tax for that year. An electing shareholder that realizes a loss on Form 8621, but shall not recognize the loss.

   (5) *Adjustments to basis.*—A shareholder that makes the deemed sale election increases its adjusted basis of the PFIC stock owned directly by the amount of gain recognized on the deemed sale. If the shareholder makes the deemed sale election with respect to a PFIC of which it is an indirect shareholder, the shareholder's adjusted basis of the stock or other property owned directly by the shareholder, through which ownership of the PFIC is attributed to the shareholder, is increased by the amount of gain recognized by

Reg. § 1.1297-3(b)(5)

the shareholder. In addition, solely for purposes of determining the subsequent treatment under the Internal Revenue Code (Code) and regulations of a shareholder of the stock of the PFIC, the adjusted basis of the direct owner of the stock of the PFIC is increased by the amount of gain recognized on the deemed sale. A shareholder shall not adjust the basis of any stock with respect to which the shareholder realized a loss on the deemed sale, which loss is not recognized under paragraph (b)(2) of this section.

(6) *Treatment of holding period.*—If a shareholder of a foreign corporation has made a deemed sale election, then, for purposes of applying sections 1291 through 1298 to such shareholder after the deemed sale, the shareholder's holding period in the stock of the foreign corporation begins on the CFC qualification date, without regard to whether the shareholder recognized gain on the deemed sale. For other purposes of the Code and regulations, this holding period rule does not apply.

(c) *Application of deemed dividend election rules.*—(1) *Eligibility to make the deemed dividend election.*—A shareholder of a foreign corporation that is a section 1297(e) PFIC with respect to such shareholder may make the deemed dividend election under the rules of this paragraph (c). A deemed dividend election may be made by a shareholder whose pro rata share of the post-1986 earnings and profits of the PFIC attributable to the PFIC stock held on the CFC qualification date is zero.

(2) *Effect of the deemed dividend election.*—A shareholder making the deemed dividend election with respect to a section 1297(e) PFIC shall include in income as a dividend its pro rata share of the post-1986 earnings and profits of the PFIC attributable to all of the stock it held, directly or indirectly on the CFC qualification date, as defined in paragraph (d) of this section. The deemed dividend is taxed under section 1291 as an excess distribution received on the CFC qualification date. The excess distribution determined under this paragraph (c) is allocated under section 1291(a)(1)(A) only to each day of the shareholder's holding period of the stock during which the foreign corporation qualified as a PFIC. For purposes of the preceding sentence, the shareholder's holding period of the PFIC stock ends on the day before the CFC qualification date. After the deemed dividend election, the shareholder's stock with respect to which the election was made under this paragraph (c) shall not be treated as stock in a PFIC and the shareholder shall not be subject to taxation under section 1291 with respect to such stock unless the qualified portion of the shareholder's holding period ends, as determined under section 1297(e)(2), and the foreign corporation thereafter qualifies as a PFIC under section 1297(a).

(3) *Post-1986 earnings and profits defined.*—(i) *In general.*—(A) *General rule.*—For purposes of this section, the term post-1986 earnings and profits means the post-1986 undistributed earnings, within the meaning of section 902(c)(1) (determined without regard to section 902(c)(3)), as of the day before the CFC qualification date, that were accumulated and not distributed in taxable years of the PFIC beginning after 1986 and during which it was a PFIC, without regard to whether the earnings related to a period during which the PFIC was a CFC.

(B) *Special rule.*—If the CFC qualification date is a day that is after the first day of the taxable year, the term post-1986 earnings and profits means the post-1986 undistributed earnings, within the meaning of section 902(c)(1) (determined without regard to section 902(c)(3)), as of the close of the taxable year that includes the CFC qualification date. For purposes of this computation, only earnings and profits accumulated in taxable years during which the foreign corporation was a PFIC shall be taken into account, but without regard to whether the earnings related to a period during which the PFIC was a CFC.

(ii) *Pro rata share of post-1986 earnings and profits attributable to shareholder's stock.*—(A) *In general.*—A shareholder's pro rata share of the post-1986 earnings and profits of the PFIC attributable to the stock held by the shareholder on the CFC qualification date is the amount of post-1986 earnings and profits of the PFIC accumulated during any portion of the shareholder's holding period ending at the close of the day before the CFC qualification date and attributable, under the principles of section 1248 and the regulations under that section, to the PFIC stock held on the CFC qualification date.

(B) *Reduction for previously taxed amounts.*—A shareholder's pro rata share of the post-1986 earnings and profits of the PFIC does not include any amount that the shareholder demonstrates to the satisfaction of the Commissioner (in the manner provided in paragraph (c)(5)(ii) of this section) was, pursuant to another provision of the law, previously included in the income of the shareholder, or of another U.S. person if the shareholder's holding period of the PFIC stock includes the period during which the stock was held by that other U.S. person.

(4) *Time for making the deemed dividend election.*—Except as provided in paragraph (e) of this section, the shareholder shall make the deemed dividend election under this paragraph (c) and section 1298(b)(1) in the shareholder's original or amended return for the taxable year that includes the CFC qualification date (election year). If the deemed dividend election is made in an amended return, the return must be filed by a date that is within three years of the due date, as

extended under section 6081, of the original return for the election year.

(5) *Manner of making the deemed dividend election.*—(i) *In general.*—A shareholder makes the deemed dividend election by filing Form 8621 and the attachment to Form 8621 described in paragraph (c)(5)(ii) of this section with the return of the shareholder for the election year, reporting the deemed dividend as an excess distribution pursuant to section 1291(a)(1), and paying the tax and interest due on the excess distribution. A shareholder that makes the deemed dividend election after the due date of the return (determined without regard to extensions) for the election year must pay additional interest, pursuant to section 6601, on the amount of underpayment of tax for that year.

(ii) *Attachment to Form 8621.*—The shareholder must attach a schedule to Form 8621 that demonstrates the calculation of the shareholder's pro rata share of the post-1986 earnings and profits of the PFIC that is treated as distributed to the shareholder on the CFC qualification date, pursuant to this paragraph (c). If the shareholder is claiming an exclusion from its pro rata share of the post-1986 earnings and profits for an amount previously included in its income or the income of another U.S. person, the shareholder must include the following information:

(A) The name, address and taxpayer identification number of each U.S. person that previously included an amount in income, the amount previously included in income by each such U.S. person, the provision of law, pursuant to which the amount was previously included in income, and the taxable year or years of inclusion of each amount.

(B) A description of the transaction pursuant to which the shareholder acquired, directly or indirectly, the stock of the PFIC from another U.S. person, and the provision of law pursuant to which the shareholder's holding period includes the period the other U.S. person held the CFC stock.

(6) *Adjustments to basis.*—A shareholder that makes the deemed dividend election increases its adjusted basis of the stock of the PFIC owned directly by the shareholder by the amount of the deemed dividend. If the shareholder makes the deemed dividend election with respect to a PFIC of which it is an indirect shareholder, the shareholder's adjusted basis of the stock or other property owned directly by the shareholder, through which ownership of the PFIC is attributed to the shareholder, is increased by the amount of the deemed dividend. In addition, solely for purposes of determining the subsequent treatment under the Code and regulations of a shareholder of the stock of the PFIC, the adjusted basis of the direct owner of the stock of the PFIC is increased by the amount of the deemed dividend.

(7) *Treatment of holding period.*—If the shareholder of a foreign corporation has made a deemed dividend election, then, for purposes of applying sections 1291 through 1298 to such shareholder after the deemed dividend, the shareholder's holding period of the stock of the foreign corporation begins on the CFC qualification date. For other purposes of the Code and regulations, this holding period rule does not apply.

(8) *Coordination with section 959(e).*—For purposes of section 959(e), the entire deemed dividend is treated as having been included in gross income under section 1248(a).

(d) *CFC qualification date.*—For purposes of this section, the CFC qualification date is the first day on which the qualified portion of the shareholder's holding period in the section 1297(e) PFIC begins, as determined under section 1297(e).

(e) *Late purging elections requiring special consent.*—(1) *In general.*—This section prescribes the exclusive rules under which a shareholder of a section 1297(e) PFIC may make a section 1298(b)(1) election after the time prescribed in paragraph (b)(3) or (c)(4) of this section for making a deemed sale or a deemed dividend election has elapsed (late purging election). Therefore, a shareholder may not seek such relief under any other provisions of the law, including § 301.9100-3 of this chapter. A shareholder may request the consent of the Commissioner to make a late deemed sale or deemed dividend election for the taxable year of the shareholder that includes the CFC qualification date provided the shareholder satisfies the requirements set forth in this paragraph (e). The Commissioner may, in his discretion, grant relief under this paragraph (e) only if--

(i) In a case where the shareholder is requesting consent under this paragraph (e) after December 31, 2005, the shareholder requests such consent before a representative of the Internal Revenue Service (IRS) raises upon audit the PFIC status of the foreign corporation for any taxable year of the shareholder;

(ii) The shareholder has agreed in a closing agreement with the Commissioner, described in paragraph (e)(3) of this section, to eliminate any prejudice to the interests of the U.S. government, as determined under paragraph (e)(2) of this section, as a consequence of the shareholder's inability to file amended returns for its taxable year in which the CFC qualification date falls or an earlier closed taxable year in which the shareholder has taken a position that is inconsistent with the treatment of the foreign corporation as a PFIC; and

(iii) The shareholder satisfies the procedural requirements set forth in paragraph (e)(3) of this section.

(2) *Prejudice to the interests of the U.S. government.*—The interests of the U.S. government are prejudiced if granting relief would result in the shareholder having a lower tax liability (other than by a de minimis amount), taking into account applicable interest charges, for the taxable year that includes the CFC qualification date (or a prior taxable year in which the taxpayer took a position on a return that was inconsistent with the treatment of the foreign corporation as a PFIC) than the shareholder would have had if the shareholder had properly made the section 1298(b)(1) election in the time prescribed in paragraph (b)(2) or (c)(3) of this section (or had not taken a position in a return for an earlier year that was inconsistent with the status of the foreign corporation as a PFIC). The time value of money is taken into account for purposes of this computation.

(3) *Procedural requirements.*—(i) *In general.*—The amount due with respect to a late purging election is determined in the same manner as if the purging election had been timely filed. However, the shareholder is also liable for interest on the amount due, pursuant to section 6601, determined for the period beginning on the due date (without extensions) for the taxpayer's income tax return for the year in which the CFC qualification date falls and ending on the date the late purging election is filed with the IRS.

(ii) *Filing instructions.*—A late purging election is made by filing a completed Form 8621-A, "Return by a Shareholder Making Certain Late Elections to End Treatment as a Passive Foreign Investment Company."

(4) *Time and manner of making late election.*—(i) *Time for making a late purging election.*—A shareholder may make a late purging election in the manner provided in paragraph (e)(4)(ii) of this section at any time. The date the election is filed with the IRS will determine the amount of interest due under paragraph (e)(3) of this section.

(ii) *Manner of making a late purging election.*—A shareholder makes a late purging election by completing Form 8621-A in the manner required by that form and this section and filing that form with the Internal Revenue Service, DP 8621-A, Ogden, UT 84201.

(5) *Multiple late elections.*—(i) *General rule.*—A shareholder of a foreign corporation may make multiple late purging elections under the rules of this paragraph (e) or §1.1298-3(e) to the same extent such multiple purging elections could have been made if those purging elections had been filed within the time prescribed under paragraph (b)(3) or (c)(4) of this section or §1.1298-3(b)(3) or (c)(4).

(ii) *Example.*—The rule of this paragraph (e)(5) is illustrated by the following example:

Example. (i) In 1991, X, a U.S person, acquired a five percent interest in the stock of FC, a controlled foreign corporation, as defined in section 957(a). In years 1991, 1992, 1995, 1996 and 1997, FC satisfied either the income test or the asset test of section 1297(a). X did not make a QEF election with regard to FC. In years 1993 and 1994, FC did not satisfy either the income or the asset test of section 1297(a). In 1998, X acquired additional stock in FC such that X was a U.S. shareholder (as defined in section 951(b)) of FC.

(ii) Because FC qualified as a PFIC in 1991, FC will be treated as a PFIC with respect to all of the stock held by X, under the "once a PFIC always a PFIC" rule of section 1298(b)(1), unless X makes an election to purge the PFIC taint. Because X ceased to satisfy either the income or asset test in 1993, X could have made an election under §1.1298-3 to purge the PFIC taint of FC for that year if X had filed such an election within the time prescribed under §1.1298-3(b)(3) or (c)(4). If X had done so, the stock X held in FC would not be treated as stock in a PFIC for the years 1993 and 1994. Because X became a U.S. shareholder of FC in 1998, X then could have made a deemed sale or deemed dividend election under this section to purge the PFIC taint of FC for the years 1995 through 1997 if X had filed within the time prescribed under paragraph (b)(3) or (c)(4) of this section. Accordingly, X may make a late purging election to purge the PFIC taint of FC for the years 1991 and 1992 under the rules of §1.1298-3(e) and may also make a late purging election to purge the PFIC taint of FC for the years 1995 through 1997 under the rules of this paragraph (e).

(f) *Effective/applicability date.*—The rules of this section are applicable as of December 8, 2005. [Reg. §1.1297-3.]

☐ [*T.D.* 9360, 9-26-2007 (*corrected* 10-17-2007).]

[Reg. §1.1298-0]

§1.1298-0. Table of contents.—This section contains a listing of the paragraph headings for §1.1298-3.

§1.1298-3 Deemed sale or deemed dividend election by a U.S. person that is a shareholder of a former PFIC.

(a) In general.

(b) Application of deemed sale election rules.

(1) Eligibility to make the deemed sale election.

(2) Effect of the deemed sale election.

(3) Time for making the deemed sale election.

(4) Manner of making the deemed sale election.

(5) Adjustments to basis.

(6) Treatment of holding period.

(c) Application of deemed dividend election rules.

   (1) Eligibility to make the deemed dividend election.

   (2) Effect of the deemed dividend election.

   (3) Post-1986 earnings and profits defined.

   (4) Time for making the deemed dividend election.

   (5) Manner of making the deemed dividend election.

   (6) Adjustments to basis.

   (7) Treatment of holding period.

   (8) Coordination with section 959(e).

(d) Termination date.

(e) Late purging elections requiring special consent.

   (1) In general.

   (2) Prejudice to the interests of the U.S. government.

   (3) Procedural requirements.

   (4) Time and manner of making late election.

   (5) Multiple late elections.

(f) Effective/applicability date.

[Reg. § 1.1298-0.]

□ [*T.D.* 9231, 12-7-2005. *Amended by T.D.* 9360, 9-26-2007.]

[Reg. § 1.1298-3]

§ 1.1298-3. Deemed sale or deemed dividend election by a U.S. person that is a shareholder of a former PFIC.—(a) *In general.*—A shareholder (as defined in § 1.1291-9(j)(3)) of a foreign corporation that is a former PFIC, (as defined in § 1.1291-9(j)(2)(iv)) with respect to such shareholder, shall be treated for tax purposes as holding stock in a PFIC and therefore continues to be subject to taxation under section 1291 unless the shareholder makes a purging election under section 1298(b)(1). A purging election under section 1298(b)(1) is made under rules similar to the rules of section 1291(d)(2). Section 1291(d)(2) allows a shareholder to purge the continuing PFIC taint by making either a deemed sale election or a deemed dividend election.

(b) *Application of deemed sale election rules.*—(1) *Eligibility to make the deemed sale election.*—A shareholder of a foreign corporation that is a former PFIC with respect to such shareholder may make a deemed sale election under section 1298(b)(1) by applying the rules of this paragraph (b).

(2) *Effect of deemed sale election.*—A shareholder making the deemed sale election with respect to a former PFIC shall be treated as having sold all its stock in the former PFIC for its fair market value on the termination date, as defined in paragraph (d) of this section. A deemed sale is treated as a disposition subject to taxation under section 1291. Thus, gain from the deemed sale is taxed under section 1291 as an excess distribution received on the termination date. In the case of an election made by an indirect shareholder, the amount of gain to be recognized and taxed as an excess distribution is the amount of gain that the direct owner of the stock of the PFIC would have realized on an actual sale or disposition of the stock of the PFIC indirectly owned by the shareholder. Any loss realized on the deemed sale is not recognized. After the deemed sale election, the shareholder's stock with respect to which the election was made under this paragraph (b) shall not be treated as stock in a PFIC and the shareholder shall not be subject to taxation under section 1291 with respect to such stock unless the foreign corporation thereafter qualifies as a PFIC under section 1297(a).

(3) *Time for making the deemed sale election.*—Except as provided in paragraph (e) of this section, the shareholder shall make the deemed sale election under this paragraph (b) and section 1298(b)(1) in the shareholder's original or amended return for the taxable year that includes the termination date (election year). If the deemed sale election is made in an amended return, the return must be filed by a date that is within three years of the due date, as extended under section 6081, of the original return for the election year.

(4) *Manner of making the deemed sale election.*—A shareholder makes the deemed sale election under this paragraph (b) by filing Form 8621 ("Return by a Shareholder of a Passive Foreign Investment Company or Qualified Electing Fund") with the return of the shareholder for the election year, reporting the gain as an excess distribution pursuant to section 1291(a) as if such deemed sale occurred under section 1291(d)(2), and paying the tax and interest due on the excess distribution. A shareholder that makes the deemed sale election after the due date of the return (determined without regard to extensions) for the election year must pay additional interest, pursuant to section 6601, on the amount of underpayment of tax for that year. An electing shareholder that realizes a loss shall report the loss on Form 8621, but shall not recognize the loss.

(5) *Adjustments to basis.*—A shareholder that makes the deemed sale election increases its adjusted basis of the PFIC stock owned directly by the amount of gain recognized on the deemed sale. If the shareholder makes the deemed sale election with respect to a PFIC of which it is an indirect shareholder, the shareholder's adjusted basis of the stock or other property owned directly by the shareholder, through which ownership of the PFIC is attributed to the shareholder, is increased by the amount of gain recognized by the shareholder. In addition, solely for purposes of determining the subsequent treatment under the Code and regulations of a shareholder of the stock of the PFIC, the adjusted basis of the direct

owner of the stock of the PFIC is increased by the amount of gain recognized on the deemed sale. A shareholder shall not adjust the basis of any stock with respect to which the shareholder realized a loss on the deemed sale, but which loss is not recognized under paragraph (b)(2) of this section.

(6) *Treatment of holding period.*—If a shareholder of a foreign corporation has made a deemed sale election, then, for purposes of applying sections 1291 through 1298 to such shareholder after the deemed sale, the shareholder's holding period in the stock of the foreign corporation begins on the day following the termination, without regard to whether the shareholder recognized gain on the deemed sale. For other purposes of the Code and regulations, this holding period rule does not apply.

(c) *Application of deemed dividend election rules.*—(1) *Eligibility to make the deemed dividend election.*—A shareholder of a foreign corporation that is a former PFIC with respect to such shareholder may make the deemed dividend election under the rules of this paragraph (c) provided the foreign corporation was a controlled foreign corporation (as defined in section 957(a) (CFC)) during its last taxable year as a PFIC. A shareholder may make the deemed dividend election without regard to whether the shareholder is a United States shareholder within the meaning of section 951(b). A deemed dividend election may be made by a shareholder whose pro rata share of the post-1986 earnings and profits of the PFIC attributable to the PFIC stock held on the termination date is zero.

(2) *Effect of the deemed dividend election.*—A shareholder making the deemed dividend election with respect to a former PFIC shall include in income as a dividend its pro rata share of the post-1986 earnings and profits of the PFIC attributable to all of the stock it held, directly or indirectly on the termination date, as defined in paragraph (d) of this section. The deemed dividend is taxed under section 1291 as an excess distribution received on the termination date. The excess distribution determined under this paragraph (c) is allocated under section 1291(a)(1)(A) only to each day of the shareholder's holding period of the stock during which the foreign corporation qualified as a PFIC. For purposes of the preceding sentence, the shareholder's holding period of the PFIC stock ends on the termination date. After the deemed dividend election, the shareholder's stock with respect to which the election was made under this paragraph (c) shall not be treated as stock in a PFIC and the shareholder shall not be subject to taxation under section 1291 with respect to such stock unless the foreign corporation thereafter qualifies as a PFIC under section 1297(a).

(3) *Post-1986 earnings and profits defined.*—(i) *In general.*—For purposes of this section, the term *post-1986 earnings and profits* means the post-1986 undistributed earnings, within the meaning of section 902(c)(1) (determined without regard to section 902(c)(3)), as of the close of the taxable year that includes the termination date. For purposes of this computation, only earnings and profits accumulated in taxable years during which the foreign corporation was a PFIC shall be taken into account, without regard to whether the earnings relate to a period during which the PFIC was a CFC.

(ii) *Pro rata share of post-1986 earnings and profits attributable to shareholder's stock.*—(A) *In general.*—A shareholder's pro rata share of the post-1986 earnings and profits of the PFIC attributable to the stock held by the shareholder on the termination date is the amount of post-1986 earnings and profits of the PFIC accumulated during any portion of the shareholder's holding period ending at the close of the termination date and attributable, under the principles of section 1248 and the regulations under that section, to the PFIC stock held on the termination date.

(B) *Reduction for previously taxed amounts.*—A shareholder's pro rata share of the post-1986 earnings and profits of the PFIC does not include any amount that the shareholder demonstrates to the satisfaction of the Commissioner (in the manner provided in paragraph (c)(5)(ii) of this section) was, pursuant to another provision of the law, previously included in the income of the shareholder, or of another U.S. person if the shareholder's holding period of the PFIC stock includes the period during which the stock was held by that other U.S. person.

(4) *Time for making the deemed dividend election.*—Except as provided in paragraph (e) of this section, the shareholder shall make the deemed dividend election under this paragraph (c) and section 1298(b)(1) in the shareholder's original or amended return for the taxable year that includes the termination date (election year). If the deemed dividend election is made in an amended return, the return must be filed by a date that is within three years of the due date, as extended under section 6081, of the original return for the election year.

(5) *Manner of making the deemed dividend election.*—(i) *In general.*—A shareholder makes the deemed dividend election by filing Form 8621 and the attachment to Form 8621 described in paragraph (c)(5)(ii) of this section with the return of the shareholder for the election year, reporting the deemed dividend as an excess distribution pursuant to section 1291(a)(1), and paying the tax and interest due on the excess distribution. A shareholder that makes the deemed dividend election after the due date of the return (determined without regard to extensions) for the elec-

tion year must pay additional interest, pursuant to section 6601, on the amount of underpayment of tax for that year.

(ii) *Attachment to Form 8621.*—The shareholder must attach a schedule to Form 8621 that demonstrates the calculation of the shareholder's pro rata share of the post-1986 earnings and profits of the PFIC that is treated as distributed to the shareholder on the termination date pursuant to this paragraph (c). If the shareholder is claiming an exclusion from its pro rata share of the post-1986 earnings and profits for an amount previously included in its income or the income of another U.S. person, the shareholder must include the following information:

(A) The name, address, and taxpayer identification number of each U.S. person that previously included an amount in income, the amount previously included in income by each such U.S. person, the provision of law pursuant to which the amount was previously included in income, and the taxable year or years of inclusion of each amount.

(B) A description of the transaction pursuant to which the shareholder acquired, directly or indirectly, the stock of the PFIC from another U.S. person, and the provision of law pursuant to which the shareholder's holding period includes the period the other U.S. person held the CFC stock.

(6) *Adjustments to basis.*—A shareholder that makes the deemed dividend election increases its adjusted basis of the stock of the PFIC owned directly by the shareholder by the amount of the deemed dividend. If the shareholder makes the deemed dividend election with respect to a PFIC of which it is an indirect shareholder, the shareholder's adjusted basis of the stock or other property owned directly by the shareholder, through which ownership of the PFIC is attributed to the shareholder, is increased by the amount of the deemed dividend. In addition, solely for purposes of determining the subsequent treatment under the Code and regulations of a shareholder of the stock of the PFIC, the adjusted basis of the direct owner of the stock of the PFIC is increased by the amount of the deemed dividend.

(7) *Treatment of holding period.*—If the shareholder of a foreign corporation has made a deemed dividend election, then, for purposes of applying sections 1291 through 1298 to such shareholder after the deemed dividend, the shareholder's holding period of the stock of the foreign corporation begins on the day following the termination date. For other purposes of the Code and regulations, this holding period rule does not apply.

(8) *Coordination with section 959(e).*—For purposes of section 959(e), the entire deemed

dividend is treated as having been included in gross income under section 1248(a).

(d) *Termination date.*—For purposes of this section, the termination date is the last day of the last taxable year of the foreign corporation during which it qualified as a PFIC under section 1297(a).

(e) *Late purging elections requiring special consent.*—(1) *In general.*—This section prescribes the exclusive rules under which a shareholder of a former PFIC may make a section 1298(b)(1) election after the time prescribed in paragraph (b)(3) or (c)(4) of this section for making a deemed sale or a deemed dividend election has elapsed (late purging election). Therefore, a shareholder may not seek such relief under any other provisions of the law, including § 301.9100-3 of this chapter. A shareholder may request the consent of the Commissioner to make a late purging election for the taxable year of the shareholder that includes the termination date provided the shareholder satisfies the requirements set forth in this paragraph (e). The Commissioner may, in his discretion, grant relief under this paragraph (e) only if—

(i) In a case where the shareholder is requesting consent under this paragraph (e) after December 31, 2005, the shareholder requests such consent before a representative of the Internal Revenue Service raises upon audit the PFIC status of the foreign corporation for any taxable year of the shareholder;

(ii) The shareholder has agreed in a closing agreement with the Commissioner, described in paragraph (e)(3) of this section, to eliminate any prejudice to the interests of the U.S. government, as determined under paragraph (e)(2) of this section, as a consequence of the shareholder's inability to file amended returns for its taxable year in which the termination date falls or an earlier closed taxable year in which the shareholder has taken a position that is inconsistent with the treatment of the foreign corporation as a PFIC; and

(iii) The shareholder satisfies the procedural requirements set forth in paragraph (e)(3) of this section.

(2) *Prejudice to the interests of the U.S. government.*—The interests of the U.S. government are prejudiced if granting relief would result in the shareholder having a lower tax liability (other than by a de minimis amount), taking into account applicable interest charges, for the taxable year that includes the termination date (or a prior taxable year in which the taxpayer took a position on a return that was inconsistent with the treatment of the foreign corporation as a PFIC) than the shareholder would have had if the shareholder had properly made the section 1298(b)(1) election in the time prescribed in paragraph (b)(2) or (c)(3) of this section (or had not taken a position in a return for an earlier year

that was inconsistent with the status of the foreign corporation as a PFIC). The time value of money is taken into account for purposes of this computation.

(3) *Procedural requirements.*—(i) *In general.*—The amount due with respect to a late purging election is determined in the same manner as if the purging election had been timely filed. However, the shareholder is also liable for interest on the amount due, pursuant to section 6601, determined for the period beginning on the due date (without extensions) for the taxpayer's income tax return for the year in which the termination date falls and ending on the date the late purging election is filed with the IRS.

(ii) *Filing instructions.*—A late purging election is made by filing a completed Form 8621-A, "Return by a Shareholder Making Certain Late Elections to End Treatment as a Passive Foreign Investment Company."

(4) *Time and manner of making late election.*—(i) *Time for making a late purging election.*—A shareholder may make a late purging election in the manner provided in paragraph (e)(4)(ii) of this section at any time. The date the election is filed with the IRS will determine the amount of interest due under paragraph (e)(3) of this section.

(ii) *Manner of making a late purging election.*—A shareholder makes a late purging election by completing Form 8621-A in the manner required by that form and this section and filing that form with the Internal Revenue Service, DP 8621-A, Ogden, UT 84201.

(5) *Multiple late elections.*—For rules regarding the circumstances under which a shareholder of a foreign corporation may make multiple late purging elections under this paragraph (e) or § 1.1297-3(e), see § 1.1297-3(e)(5).

(f) *Effective/applicability date.*—The rules of this section are applicable as of December 8, 2005 [Reg. § 1.1298-3.]

☐ [*T.D. 9231, 12-7-2005. Amended by T.D. 9360, 9-26-2007.*]

READJUSTMENT OF TAX BETWEEN YEARS AND SPECIAL LIMITATIONS

Income Averaging

[Reg. § 1.1301-1]

§ 1.1301-1. **Averaging of farm and fishing income.**—(a) *Overview.*—An individual engaged in a farming or fishing business may make a farm income averaging election to compute current year (election year) income tax liability under section 1 by averaging, over the prior three-year period (base years), all or a portion of the individual's current year electible farm income as defined in paragraph (e) of this section. Electible farm income includes income from both farming and fishing businesses. An individual who makes a farm income averaging election—

(1) Designates all or a portion of the individual's electible farm income for the election year as elected farm income; and

(2) Determines the election year section 1 tax by calculating the sum of—

(i) The section 1 tax that would be imposed for the election year if taxable income for the year were reduced by elected farm income; plus

(ii) The amount by which the section 1 tax would be increased if taxable income for each base year were increased by one-third of elected farm income.

(b) *Individual engaged in a farming or fishing business.*—(1) *In general.*—(i) *Farming or fishing business.*—"Farming business" has the same meaning as provided in section 263A(e)(4) and the regulations under that section. *Fishing business* means the conduct of commercial fishing as defined in section 3 of the Magnuson-Stevens Fishery Conservation and Management Act (16 U.S.C. 1802(4)). Accordingly, a fishing business is fishing in which the fish harvested are intended to or do enter commerce through sale, barter, or trade. *Fishing* means the catching, taking, or harvesting of fish; the attempted catching, taking, or harvesting of fish; any activities that reasonably can be expected to result in the catching, taking, or harvesting of fish; or any operations at sea in support of or in preparation for the catching, taking, or harvesting of fish. Fishing does not include any scientific research activity conducted by a scientific research vessel. *Fish* means finfish, mollusks, crustaceans, and all other forms of marine animal and plant life, other than marine mammals and birds. *Catching, taking, or harvesting* includes activities that result in the killing of fish or the bringing of live fish on board a vessel.

(ii) *Exxon Valdez settlement payments.*—For purposes of this section, a qualified taxpayer who receives qualified settlement income in any taxable year is treated as engaged in a fishing business, and the income is treated as income attributable to a fishing business, for that taxable year. A *qualified taxpayer* is an individual plaintiff in the civil action *In re Exxon Valdez*, No. 89-095-CV (HRH) (Consolidated) (D. Alaska). *Qualified taxpayer* also means any individual who is a beneficiary of the estate of such a plaintiff, was the spouse or immediate relative of that plaintiff, and acquired the right to receive the settlement income from that plaintiff. *Qualified settlement income* means any interest and punitive damage awards that are received in connection with the civil action *In re Exxon Valdez* (whether as lump-sum or periodic payments, whether pre- or post-judgment, and whether related to a settlement or to a judgment) and that are otherwise includible in income.

(iii) *Form of business.*—An individual engaged in a farming or fishing business includes a sole proprietor of a farming or fishing business, a partner in a partnership engaged in a farming or fishing business, and a shareholder of an S corporation engaged in a farming or fishing business. Except as provided in paragraph (e)(1)(i) of this section, services performed as an employee are disregarded in determining whether an individual is engaged in a farming or fishing business for purposes of section 1301 of the Internal Revenue Code.

(iv) *Base years.*—An individual is not required to have been engaged in a farming or fishing business in any of the base years in order to make a farm income averaging election.

(2) *Certain landlords.*—A landlord is engaged in a farming business for purposes of section 1301 with respect to rental income that is based on a share of production from a tenant's farming business and, with respect to amounts received on or after January 1, 2003, is determined under a written agreement entered into before the tenant begins significant activities on the land. A landlord is not engaged in a farming business for purposes of section 1301 with respect to either fixed rent or, with respect to amounts received on or after January 1, 2003, rental income based on a share of a tenant's production determined under an unwritten agreement or a written agreement entered into after the tenant begins significant activities on the land. Whether the landlord materially participates in the tenant's farming business is irrelevant for purposes of section 1301.

(3) *Lessors of vessels used in fishing.*—A lessor of a vessel is engaged in a fishing business for purposes of section 1301 with respect to payments that are received under the lease and are based on a share of the catch from the lessee's use of the vessel in a fishing business (or a share of the proceeds from the sale of the catch) if this manner of payment is determined under a written lease agreement entered into before the lessee begins any significant fishing activities resulting in the catch. A lessor of a vessel is not engaged in a fishing business for purposes of section 1301 with respect to fixed lease payments or with respect to lease payments based on a share of the lessee's catch (or a share of the proceeds from the sale of the catch) if the share is

determined under either an unwritten agreement or a written agreement entered into after the lessee begins significant fishing activities resulting in the catch.

(c) *Making, changing, or revoking an election.*—(1) *In general.*—A farm income averaging election is made by filing Schedule J, "Income Averaging for Farmers and Fishermen," with an individual's Federal income tax return for the election year (including a late or amended return if the period of limitation on filing a claim for credit or refund has not expired).

(2) *Changing or revoking an election.*—An individual may change the amount of the elected farm income in a previous election or revoke a previous election if the period of limitations on filing a claim for credit or refund has not expired for the election year.

(d) *Guidelines for calculation of section 1 tax.*—(1) *Actual taxable income not affected.*—Under paragraph (a)(2) of this section, a determination of the section 1 tax for the election year involves a computation of the section 1 tax that would be imposed if taxable income for the election year were reduced by elected farm income and taxable income for each of the base years were increased by one-third of elected farm income. The reduction and increases required for purposes of this computation do not affect the actual taxable income for either the election year or the base years. Thus, for each of those years, the actual taxable income is taxable income determined without regard to any hypothetical reduction or increase required for purposes of the computation under paragraph (a)(2) of this section. The following illustrates this principle:

(i) Any reduction or increase in taxable income required for purposes of the computation under paragraph (a)(2) of this section is disregarded in determining the taxable year in which a net operating loss carryover or net capital loss carryover is applied.

(ii) The net section 1231 gain or loss and the character of any section 1231 items for the election year is determined without regard to any reduction in taxable income required for purposes of the computation under paragraph (a)(2) of this section.

(iii) The section 68 overall limitation on itemized deductions for the election year is determined without regard to any reduction in taxable income required for purposes of the computation under paragraph (a)(2) of this section. Similarly, the section 68 limitation for a base year is not recomputed to take into account any allocation of elected farm income to the base year for such purposes.

(iv) If a base year had a partially used capital loss, the remaining capital loss may not be applied to reduce the elected farm income allocated to the year for purposes of the computation under paragraph (a)(2) of this section.

Reg. §1.1301-1(d)(1)(iv)

(v) If a base year had a partially used credit, the remaining credit may not be applied to reduce the section 1 tax attributable to the elected farm income allocated to the year for purposes of the computation under paragraph (a)(2) of this section.

(2) *Computation in base years.*—(i) *In general.*—As provided in paragraph (a)(2)(ii) of this section, the election year section 1 tax includes the amounts by which the section 1 tax for each base year would be increased if taxable income for the year were increased by one-third of elected farm income. For this purpose, all allowable deductions (including the full amount of any net operating loss carryover) are taken into account in determining the taxable income for the base year even if the deductions exceed gross income and the result is negative. If the result is negative, however, any amount that may provide a benefit in another taxable year is added back in determining base year taxable income. Amounts that may provide a benefit in another year include—

(A) The net operating loss (as defined in section 172(c)) for the base year;

(B) The net operating loss for any other year to the extent carried forward from the base year under section 172(b)(2); and

(C) The capital loss deduction allowed for the base year under section 1211(b)(1) or (2) to the extent such deduction does not reduce the capital loss carryover from the base year because it exceeds adjusted taxable income (as defined in section 1212(b)(2)(B)).

(ii) *Example.*—The rules of this paragraph (d)(2)are illustrated by the following example:

Example. In 2001, F and F's spouse on their joint return elect to average $24,000 of income attributable to a farming business. One-third of the elected farm income, $8,000, is added to the 1999 base year income. In 1999, F and F's spouse reported adjusted gross income of $7,300 and claimed a standard deduction of $7,200 and a deduction for personal exemptions of $8,250. Therefore, their 1999 base year taxable income is – $8,150 [$7,300 – ($7,200 + $8,250)]. After adding the elected farm income to the negative taxable income, their 1999 base year taxable income would be zero [$8,000 + (–$8,150) = – $150]. If F and F's spouse elected to income average in 2002, and made the adjustments described in paragraph (d)(3) of this section to account for the 2001 election, their 1999 base year taxable income for the 2002 election would be – $150.

(3) *Effect on subsequent elections.*—(i) *In general.*—The reduction and increases in taxable income assumed in computing the election year section 1 tax (within the meaning of paragraph (a)(2) of this section) for an election year are treated as having actually occurred for purposes of computing the election year section 1 tax for any subsequent election year. Thus, if a base year for a farm income averaging election is also an election year for another farm income averaging election, the increase in the section 1 tax for that base year is determined after reducing taxable income by the elected farm income from the earlier election year. Similarly, if a base year for a farm income averaging election is also a base year for another farm income averaging election, the increase in the section 1 tax for that base year is determined after increasing taxable income by elected farm income allocated to the year from the earlier election year.

(ii) *Example.*—The rules of this paragraph (d)(3) are illustrated by the following example:

Example. (i) T is a fisherman who uses the calendar taxable year. In each of the years 2007, 2008, and 2009, T's taxable income is $20,000, none of which is electible farm income. In 2010, T has taxable income of $30,000 (prior to any farm income averaging election), $10,000 of which is electible farm income. T makes a farm income averaging election with respect to $9,000 of the electible farm income for 2010. Under paragraph (a)(2)(ii) of this section, $3,000 of elected farm income is allocated to each of the base years 2007, 2008, and 2009. Under paragraph (a)(2) of this section, T's 2010 tax liability is the sum of the following amounts:

(A) The section 1 tax on $21,000, which is T's taxable income of $30,000, minus elected farm income of $9,000.

(B) For each of the base years 2007, 2008, and 2009, the amount by which the section 1 tax would be increased if one-third of elected farm income were allocated to each year. The amount for each year is the section 1 tax on $23,000 (T's taxable income of $20,000, plus $3,000, which is one-third of elected farm income for the 2010 election year), minus the section 1 tax on $20,000.

(ii) In 2011, T has taxable income of $50,000, $12,000 of which is electible farm income. T makes a farm income averaging election with respect to all $12,000 of the electible farm income for 2011. Under paragraph (a)(2)(ii) of this section, $4,000 of elected farm income is allocated to each of the base years 2008, 2009, and 2010. Under paragraph (a)(2) of this section, T's 2011 tax liability is the sum of the following amounts:

(A) The section 1 tax on $38,000, which is T's taxable income of $50,000, minus elected farm income of $12,000.

(B) For each of the base years 2008 and 2009, the amount by which section 1 tax would be increased if, after adjustments for previous farm income averaging elections pursuant to paragraph (d)(3)(i) of this section, one-third of 2011 elected farm income were allocated to each year. The amount for each year is the section 1 tax on $27,000 (T's taxable income of $20,000 increased by $3,000 for T's 2010 farm income averaging election and further increased by $4,000, which is one-third of elected farm income for the 2011 election year), minus the section 1 tax on $23,000 (T's taxable income of $20,000 increased by $3,000 for T's 2010 farm income averaging election).

(C) For base year 2010, the amount by which section 1 tax would be increased if, after adjustments for previous farm income averaging elections pursuant to paragraph (d)(3)(i) of this section, one-third of elected farm income were allocated to that year. This amount is the section 1 tax on $25,000 (T's 2010 taxable income of $30,000 reduced by $9,000 for T's 2010 farm income averaging election and increased by $4,000, which is one-third of elected farm income for the 2011 election year), minus the section 1 tax on $21,000 (T's taxable income of $30,000 reduced by $9,000 for T's 2010 farm income averaging election).

(4) *Deposits into Merchant Marine Capital Construction Fund.*—(i) *Reductions to taxable income and electible farm income.*—Under section 7518(c)(1)(A), certain deposits to a Merchant Marine Capital Construction Fund (CCF) reduce taxable income for purposes of the Internal Revenue Code (the CCF reduction). The amount of the CCF reduction is limited under section 7518(a)(1)(A) to the taxpayer's taxable income (determined without regard to the reduction) attributable to specified maritime operations including operations in fisheries of the United States. The CCF reduction is taken into account in determining the taxable income used in computations under this section. In addition, except to the extent the amount described in section 7518(a)(1)(A) is not attributable to the individual's fishing business, the CCF reduction is treated in computing electible farm income as an item of deduction attributable to the individual's fishing business.

(ii) *Example.*—The rules of this paragraph (d)(4) are illustrated by the following example:

Example. (i) T is a fisherman who uses the calendar taxable year. In each of the years 2007, 2008, and 2009, T's taxable income (before taking any CCF reduction into account) is $20,000. For taxable year 2008, all of T's income is described in section 7518(a)(1)(A)section 7518(a)(1)(A) and is attributable to T's fishing business. T makes a $5,000 deposit into a CCF for taxable year 2008. In 2010, T has total taxable income of $30,000 (before taking any CCF reduction into account). T's electible farm income for 2010 (before taking the CCF reduction into account) is $10,000, all of which is described in section 7518(a)(1)(A) and is attributable to T's fishing business. For taxable year 2010, T makes a $4,000 deposit into a CCF.

(ii) The amount of the 2010 CCF deposit reduces taxable income. Accordingly, T's taxable income for 2010 is $26,000 ($30,000 - $4,000). In addition, the entire amount of the CCF reduction is treated as an item of deduction attributable to T's fishing business. Accordingly, T's electible farm income for 2010 is $6,000 ($10,000 - $4,000).

Similarly, the amount of the 2008 CCF deposit reduces T's taxable income for 2008. Accordingly, T's taxable income for 2008 is $15,000 ($20,000 - $5,000).

(iii) T makes an income averaging election with respect to all $6,000 of the electible farm income for 2010. Under paragraph (a)(2)(ii) of this section, $2,000 of elected farm income is allocated to each of the base years 2007, 2008, and 2009. Under paragraph (a)(2) of this section, T's 2010 tax liability is the sum of the following amounts:

(A) The section 1 tax on $20,000, which is T's taxable income of $26,000 ($30,000 reduced by the $4,000 CCF deposit), minus elected farm income of $6,000.

(B) For each of the base years 2007, 2008, and 2009, the amount by which section 1 tax would be increased if one-third of elected farm income were allocated to each year. The amount for base years 2007 and 2009 is the section 1 tax on $22,000, (T's taxable income of $20,000, plus $2,000, which is one-third of elected farm income for the election year), minus the section 1 tax on $20,000. The amount for base year 2008 is the section 1 tax on $17,000, which is T's taxable income of $15,000 ($20,000 reduced by the $5,000 CCF deposit), plus $2,000 (one-third of elected farm income for the election year), minus the section 1 tax on $15,000.

(e) *Electible farm income.*—(1) *Identification of items attributable to a farming or fishing business.*—(i) *In general.*—Farm and fishing income includes items of income, deduction, gain, and loss attributable to an individual's farming or fishing business. Farm and fishing losses include, to the extent attributable to a farming or fishing business, any net operating loss carryover or carryback or net capital loss carryover to an election year. Income, gain, or loss from the sale of development rights, grazing rights, and other similar rights is not treated as attributable to a farming business. In general, farm and fishing income does not include compensation received as an employee. However, a shareholder of an S corporation engaged in a farming or fishing business may treat compensation received from the corporation as farm or fishing income if the compensation is paid by the corporation in the conduct of the farming or fishing business. If a crewmember on a vessel engaged in commercial fishing (within the meaning of section 3 of the Magnuson-Stevens Fishery Conservation and Management Act, 16 U.S.C. 1802(4)) is compensated by a share of the boat's catch of fish or a share of the proceeds from the sale of the catch, the crewmember is treated for purposes of section 1301 as engaged in a fishing business and the compensation is treated for such purposes as income from a fishing business.

(ii) *Gain or loss on sale or other disposition of property.*—(A) *In general.*—Gain or loss from the sale or other disposition of property that was

Reg. § 1.1301-1(e)(1)(ii)(A)

regularly used in the individual's farming or fishing business for a substantial period of time is treated as attributable to a farming or fishing business. For this purpose, the term *property* does not include land, but does include structures affixed to land. Property that has always been used solely in the farming or fishing business by the individual is deemed to meet both the regularly used and substantial period tests. Whether property not used solely in the farming or fishing business was regularly used in the farming or fishing business for a substantial period of time depends on all of the facts and circumstances.

(B) *Cessation of a farming or fishing business.*—If gain or loss described in paragraph (e)(1)(ii)(A) of this section is realized after cessation of a farming or fishing business, the gain or loss is treated as attributable to a farming or fishing business only if the property is sold within a reasonable time after cessation of the farming or fishing business. A sale or other disposition within one year of cessation of the farming or fishing business is presumed to be within a reasonable time. Whether a sale or other disposition that occurs more than one year after cessation of the farming or fishing business is within a reasonable time depends on all of the facts and circumstances.

(2) *Determination of amount that may be elected farm income.*—(i) *Electible farm income.*—(A) The maximum amount of income that an individual may elect to average (electible farm income) is the sum of any farm and fishing income and gains, minus any farm and fishing deductions or losses (including loss carryovers and carrybacks) that are allowed as a deduction in computing the individual's taxable income.

(B) Individuals conducting both a farming business and a fishing business must calculate electible farm income by combining income, gains, deductions, and losses derived from the farming business and the fishing business.

(C) Except as otherwise provided in paragraph (d)(4) of this section, the amount of any CCF reduction is treated as a deduction from income attributable to a fishing business in calculating electible farm income.

(D) Electible farm income may not exceed taxable income, and electible farm income from net capital gain attributable to a farming or fishing business may not exceed total net capital gain. Subject to these limitations, an individual who has both ordinary income and net capital gain from a farming or fishing business may elect to average any combination of the ordinary income and net capital gain.

(ii) *Examples.*—The rules of this paragraph (e)(2) are illustrated by the following examples:

Example 1. A has ordinary income from a farming business of $200,000 and deductible ex-

penses from a farming business of $50,000. A's taxable income is $150,000 ($200,000 - $50,000). Under paragraph (e)(2)(i) of this section, A's electible farm income is $150,000, all of which is ordinary income.

Example 2. B has capital gain of $20,000 that is not from a farming or fishing business, capital loss from a farming business of $30,000, and ordinary income from a farming business of $100,000. Under section 1211(b), B's allowable capital loss is limited to $23,000. B's taxable income is $97,000 (($20,000 - $23,000) + $100,000). B has a capital loss carryover from a farming business of $7,000 ($30,000 total loss - $23,000 allowable loss). Under paragraph (e)(2)(i) of this section, B's electible farm income is $77,000 ($100,000 ordinary income from a farming business, minus $23,000 capital loss from a farming business), all of which is ordinary income.

Example 3. C has ordinary income from a fishing business of $200,000 and ordinary loss from a farming business of $60,000. C's taxable income is $140,000 ($200,000 - $60,000). Under paragraph (e)(2)(i)(B) of this section, C must deduct the farm loss from the fishing income in determining C's electible farm income. Therefore, C's electible farm income is $140,000 ($200,000 - $60,000), all of which is ordinary income.

Example 4. D has ordinary income from a farming business of $200,000 and ordinary loss of $50,000 that is not from a farming or fishing business. D's taxable income is $150,000 ($200,000 - $50,000). Under paragraph (e)(2)(i)(D) of this section, electible farm income may not exceed taxable income. Therefore, D's electible farm income is $150,000, all of which is ordinary income.

Example 5. E has capital gain from a farming business of $50,000, capital loss of $40,000 that is not from a farming or fishing business, and ordinary income from a farming business of $60,000. E's taxable income is $70,000 (($50,000 - $40,000) + $60,000). Under paragraph (e)(2)(i)(D) of this section, electible farm income may not exceed taxable income, and electible farm income from net capital gain attributable to a farming or fishing business may not exceed total net capital gain. Therefore, E's electible farm income is $70,000 of which $10,000 is capital gain and $60,000 is ordinary income.

(f) *Miscellaneous rules.*—(1) *Short taxable year.*—(i) *In general.*—If a base year or an election year is a short taxable year, the rules of section 443 and the regulations thereunder apply for purposes of calculating the section 1 tax.

(ii) *Base year is a short taxable year.*—If a base year is a short taxable year, elected farm income is allocated to such year for purposes of paragraph (a)(2) of this section after the taxable income for such year has been annualized.

(iii) *Election year is a short taxable year.*—In applying paragraph (a)(2) of this section for purposes of determining tax computed on the annual basis (within the meaning of section 443(b)(1)) for an election year that is a short taxable year—

(A) The taxable income and the electible farm income for the year are annualized; and

(B) The taxpayer may designate all or any part of the annualized electible farm income as elected farm income.

(2) *Changes in filing status.*—An individual is not prohibited from making a farm income averaging election solely because the individual's filing status is not the same in an election year and the base years. For example, an individual who is married and files a joint return in the election year, who filed as single in one or more of the base years, may elect to average farm or fishing income, by using the single filing status to compute the increase in section 1 taxes for the base years in which the individual filed as single.

(3) *Employment tax.*—A farm income averaging election has no effect in determining the amount of wages for purposes of the Federal Insurance Contributions Act (FICA), the Federal Unemployment Tax Act (FUTA), and the Collection of Income Tax at Source on Wages (Federal income tax withholding), or the amount of net earnings from self-employment for purposes of the Self-Employment Contributions Act (SECA).

(4) *Alternative minimum tax.*—A farm income averaging election is disregarded in computing the tentative minimum tax and the regular tax under section 55 for the election year or any base year. The election is taken into account, however, in determining the regular tax liability under section 53(c) for the election year.

(5) *Unearned income of minor child.*—In an election year, if a minor child's investment income is taxable under section 1(g) and a parent makes a farm income averaging election, the tax rate used for purposes of applying section 1(g) is the rate determined after application of the election. In a base year, however, the tax on a minor child's investment income is not affected by a farm income averaging election.

(g) *Effective/applicability date.*—This section applies for taxable years beginning after December 15, 2010. See the provisions of §§ 1.1301–1 and 1.1301–1T as in effect on December 14, 2010 for rules that apply for taxable years beginning on or before December 15, 2010. In addition, a taxpayer may apply paragraph (b)(1)(ii) of this section in taxable years beginning after December 31, 2003. [Reg. § 1.1301–1.]

☐ [*T.D.* 8972, 1-7-2002 (*corrected* 2-4-2002). *Amended by T.D.* 9417, 7-21-2008 and *T.D.* 9509, 12-14-2010.]

[Reg. § 5c.1305-1T]

§ 5c.1305-1T. Special income averaging rules for taxpayers otherwise required to compute tax in accordance with § 5c.1256-3 (Temporary).—(a) *In general.*—If an eligible individual (as defined in section 1303 and the regulations thereunder) is described in the first sentence of § 5c.1256-3(a), chooses the benefits of income averaging and otherwise complies with the special rules under section 1304 and the regulations thereunder, and has averagable income (as defined in section 1302 and the regulations thereunder) in excess of $3,000, then the individual shall compute the tax under section 1301 as provided in this section. The computation under this section shall be in lieu of the computation under § 5c.1256-3.

(b) *Computation of tax.*—The individual shall compute the tax under section 1301 as follows:

Step (1). Compute tax under section 1301 and the regulations thereunder on all taxable income, including gains or losses on regulated futures contracts subject to section 1256(a) and the regulations thereunder, using rates applicable to the taxpayer for the taxable year which includes June 23, 1981.

Step (2). Compute tax under section 1301 and the regulations thereunder on all taxable income, including gains or losses on regulated futures contracts subject to section 1256(a) and the regulations thereunder, using rates applicable to the taxpayer for taxable years beginning in 1982.

Step (3). Compute the percentage of adjusted gross income attributable to all sources except regulated futures contracts subject to section 1256(a) and the regulations thereunder.

Step (4). Compute the percentage of adjusted gross income attributable to regulated futures contracts subject to section 1256(a) and the regulations thereunder. Both the percentage in Step (3) and the percentage in Step (4) are to be rounded to the nearest percent. The sum of both percentages must equal 100 percent.

Step (5). Multiply the result of Step (1) with the result of Step (3).

Step (6). Multiply the result of Step (2) with the result of Step (4).

Step (7). Add the result of Step (5) and the result of Step (6). This is the tax for the individual under section 1301 for the taxable year which includes June 23, 1981.

(c) *Option to defer tax.*—If an individual computes the tax under section 1301 as provided in paragraph (a) of this section, the individual may also opt to pay part or all of the deferrable tax under income averaging (as defined in paragraph (d) of this section) for the taxable year which includes June 23, 1981, in 2 or more, but not more than 5, equal installments in accordance with this section. Such individual may not opt to pay part or all of the deferrable tax in installments under § 5c.1256-3. An individual opting to defer payment must attach a statement to Form 6781 indicating the computation of deferrable tax under income averaging, the number of installments in which the individual opts to pay the deferrable tax under income averaging, and the amount of each such payment.

(d) *Deferrable tax under income averaging.*—The deferrable tax under income averaging is the excess of—

(1) The tax for the taxable year which includes June 23, 1981, computed pursuant to paragraph (b) of this section, over

(2) The tax for the taxable year which includes June 23, 1981, computed pursuant to paragraph (b) of this section, except that pretransitional year gain or loss (as described in §5c.1256-2(g)) is omitted for purposes of recomputing the percentage in Step (4). As computed under this subparagraph (2), the sum of the percentage in Step (3) and Step (4) will not equal 100 percent.

(e) *Rules of application.*—The provisions of §5c.1256-3(c), (f), (g), (h), (i), and (j) shall apply in computing the tax and in determining the deferrable tax under income averaging under this section.

(f) *Examples.*—The application of this section may be illustrated by the following examples:

Example (1). Individual A is a single, calendar year taxpayer with no dependents.

A reported the following amounts for the following years on line 34 of Form 1040:

1977 —	$ 80,000
1978 —	$90,000
1979 —	$100,000
1980 —	$110,000

A reports the following amounts for the following lines on Form 1040 for 1981:

line 7 —	$120,000
line 12 —	$600,000
line 32b —	$ 19,000
line 33 —	$ 1,000

The amount on line 12 is computed as follows: $937,500 of gain is attributable to regulated futures contracts subject to section 1256(a). Of that total, 40 percent is short term capital gain ($375,000) and 60 percent is long term capital gain ($562,500). Of the long term capital gain, 40 percent is taxable ($225,000). Therefore, A reports $600,000 on line 12 ($375,000 + $225,000).

The result of Step (1) is $464,013.41. The result of Step (2) is $337,051.52. The result of Step (3) is 17 percent. The result of Step (4) is 83 percent. The result of Step (5) is $78,882.28. The result of Step (6) is $279,752.76. The result of Step (7) is $358,635.04. This is A's tax for 1981 under section 1301.

Example (2). The facts are the same as in Example (1), except that $703,125 of the $937,500 gain attributable to regulated futures contracts is pretransitional year gain or loss (as described in §5c.1256-2(g)). A's tax for 1981 under section 1301 is $358,635.04. A may opt to pay in installments a maximum of $221,004.68 of the tax due in 1981. If A opts to defer the maximum amount and pay in 5 equal installments, A must pay for 1981 a tax of $181,831.30. Each of the 4 succeeding installments is $44,200.94 plus interest computed in accordance with §5c.1256-3(g)(3). [Temporary Reg. §5c.1305-1.]

☐ [*T.D.* 7826, 8-27-82.]

Mitigation of Effect of Limitations—Other Provisions

[Reg. §1.1311(a)-1]

§1.1311(a)-1. Introduction.—(a) Part II (section 1311 and following) subchapter Q, chapter 1 of the Code, provides certain rules for the correction of the effect of an erroneous treatment of an item in a taxable year which is closed by the statute of limitations or otherwise, in cases where, in connection with the ascertainment of the tax for another taxable year, it has been determined that there was an erroneous treatment of such item in the closed year.

(b) In most situations falling within this part the correction of the effect of the error on a closed year can be made only if either the Commissioner or the taxpayer has taken a position in another taxable year which is inconsistent with the erroneous treatment of the item in the closed year. If a refund or credit would result from the correction of the error in the closed year, then the Commissioner must be the one maintaining the inconsistent position. For example, if the taxpayer erroneously included an item of income on his return for an earlier year which is now closed and the Commissioner successfully requires it to be included in a later year, then the correction of the effect of the erroneous inclusion of that item in the closed year may be made since the Commissioner has maintained a position inconsistent with the treatment of such item in such closed year. On the other hand, if an additional assessment would result from the correction of the error in the closed year, then the taxpayer must be the one maintaining the inconsistent position. For example, if the taxpayer deducted an item in an earlier year which is now closed and he successfully contends that the item should be deducted in a later year, then the correction of the effect of the erroneous deduction of that item in the closed year may be made since the taxpayer has taken a position inconsistent with the treatment of such item in such earlier year.

(c) There are two special circumstances which fall within this part but which do not require that an inconsistent position be maintained. One of these circumstances relates to the inclusion of an item of income in the correct year and the other relates to the allowance of a deduction in the correct year. In the first situation, if the Commissioner takes the position by a deficiency notice or before the Tax Court that an item of income should be included in the gross income of a taxpayer for a particular year and it is ultimately determined that such item was not so includible, then such item can be included in the income of the proper year if that year was not closed at the time the Commissioner took his position. In the second situation, if the taxpayer claims that a deduction should be allowed for a particular year and it is ultimately determined that the deduction was not allowable in that year, then the taxpayer may take the deduction in the proper year if that year was not closed at the time the taxpayer first claimed a deduction. [Reg. § 1.1311(a)-1.]

☐ [T.D. 6162, 2-8-56.]

[Reg. § 1.1311(a)-2]

§ 1.1311(a)-2. Purpose and scope of section 1311.—(a) Section 1311 provides for the correction of the effect of certain errors under circumstances specified in section 1312 when one or more provisions of law, such as the statute of limitations, would otherwise prevent such correction. Section 1311 may be applied to correct the effect of certain errors if, on the date of a determination (as defined in section 1313(a) and the regulations thereunder), correction is prevented by the operation of any provision of law other than sections 1311 through 1315 and section 7122 (relating to compromises) and the corresponding provisions of prior revenue laws. Examples of provisions preventing such corrections are sections 6501, 6511, 6532, and 6901(c), (d) and (e), relating to periods of limitations; sections 6212(c) and 6512 relating to the effect of petition to the Tax Court of the United States on further deficiency letters and on credits or refunds; section 7121 relating to closing agreements; and sections 6401 and 6514 relating to payments, refunds, or credits after the period of limitations has expired. Section 1311 may also be applied to correct the effect of an error if, on the date of the determination, correction of the error is prevented by the operation of any rule of law, such as res judicata or estoppel.

(b) The determination (including a determination under section 1313(a)(4)) may be with respect to any of the taxes imposed by subtitle A of the Internal Revenue Code of 1954, by chapter 1 and subchapters A, B, D, and E of chapter 2 of the Internal Revenue Code of 1939, or by the corresponding provisions of any prior revenue act, or by more than one of such provisions. Section 1311 may be applied to correct the effect of the error only as to the tax or taxes with respect to which the error was made which correspond to the tax or taxes with respect to which the determination relates. Thus, if the determination relates to a tax imposed by chapter 1 of the

Internal Revenue Code of 1954, the adjustment may be only with respect to the tax imposed by such chapter or by the corresponding provisions of prior law.

(c) Section 1311 is not applicable if, on the date of the determination, correction of the effect of the error is permissible without recourse to said section.

(d) If the tax liability for the year with respect to which the error was made has been compromised under section 7122 or the corresponding provisions of prior revenue laws, no adjustment may be made under section 1311 with respect to said year.

(e) No adjustment may be made under section 1311 for any taxable year beginning prior to January 1, 1932. See section 1314(d).

(f) Section 1311 applies only to a determination (as defined in section 1313(a) and §§ 1.1313(a)-1 to 1.1313(a)-4, inclusive) made after November 14, 1954. Section 3801 of the Internal Revenue Code of 1939 and the regulations thereunder apply to determinations, as defined therein, made on or before November 14, 1954. See section 1315. [Reg. § 1.1311(a)-2.]

☐ [T.D. 6162, 2-8-56.]

[Reg. § 1.1311(b)-1]

§ 1.1311(b)-1. Maintenance of an inconsistent position.—(a) In general.—Under the circumstances stated in § 1.1312-1, § 1.1312-2, paragraph (a) of § 1.1312-3, § 1.1312-5, § 1.1312-6, and § 1.1312-7, the maintenance of an inconsistent position is a condition necessary for adjustment. The requirement in such circumstances is that a position maintained with respect to the taxable year of the determination and which is adopted in the determination be inconsistent with the erroneous inclusion, exclusion, omission, allowance, disallowance, recognition, or nonrecognition, as the case may be, with respect to the taxable year of the error. That is, a position successfully maintained with respect to the taxable year of the determination must be inconsistent with the treatment accorded an item which was the subject of an error in the computation of the tax for the closed taxable year. Adjustments under the circumstances stated in paragraph (b) of § 1.1312-3 and in § 1.1312-4 are made without regard to the maintenance of an inconsistent position.

(b) Adjustments resulting in refund or credit.—(1) An adjustment under any of the circumstances stated in § 1.1312-1, § 1.1312-5, § 1.1312-6, or § 1.1312-7 which would result in the allowance of a refund or credit is authorized only if (i) the Commissioner, in connection with a determination, has maintained a position which is inconsistent with the erroneous inclusion, omission, disallowance, recognition, or nonrecognition, as the case may be, in the year of the error, and (ii) such inconsistent position is adopted in the determination.

Example. A taxpayer who keeps his books on the cash method erroneously included as income on his return for 1954 an item of accrued interest. After the period of limitations on refunds for 1954 had expired, the district director, on behalf of the Commissioner, proposed an adjustment for the year 1955 on the ground that the item of interest was received in 1955 and, therefore, was properly includible in gross income for that year. The taxpayer and the district director entered into an agreement which meets all of the requirements of § 1.1313(a)-4 and which determines that the interest item was includible in gross income for 1955. The Commissioner has maintained a position inconsistent with the inclusion of the interest item for 1954. As the determination (the agreement pursuant to § 1.1313(a)-4) adopted such inconsistent position, an adjustment is authorized for the year 1954.

(2) An adjustment under circumstances stated in § 1.1312-1, § 1.1312-5, § 1.1312-6, or § 1.1312-7 which would result in the allowance of a refund or credit is not authorized if the taxpayer with respect to whom the determination is made, and not the Commissioner, has maintained such inconsistent position.

Example. In the example in subparagraph (1) of this paragraph, assume that the Commissioner asserted a deficiency for 1955 based upon other items for that year but, in computing the net income upon which such deficiency was based, did not include the item of interest. The taxpayer appealed to the Tax Court and in his petition asserted that the interest item should be included in gross income for 1955. The Tax Court in 1960 included the item of interest in its redetermination of tax for the year 1955. In such case no adjustment would be authorized for 1954 as the taxpayer, and not the Commissioner, maintained a position inconsistent with the erroneous inclusion of the item of interest in the gross income of the taxpayer for that year.

(c) *Adjustments resulting in additional assessments.*—(1) An adjustment under any of the circumstances stated in § 1.1312-2, paragraph (a) of § 1.1312-3, § 1.1312-5, § 1.1312-6, or § 1.1312-7, which would result in an additional assessment is authorized only if (i) the taxpayer with respect to whom the determination is made has, in connection therewith, maintained a position which is inconsistent with the erroneous exclusion, omission, allowance, recognition, or nonrecognition, as the case may be, in the year of the error, and (ii) such inconsistent position is adopted in the determination.

Example. A taxpayer in his return for 1950 claimed and was allowed a deduction for a loss arising from a casualty. After the taxpayer had filed his return for 1951 and after the period of limitations upon the assessment of a deficiency for 1950 had expired, it was discovered that the loss actually occurred in 1951. The taxpayer, therefore, filed a claim for refund for the year

1951 based upon the allowance of a deduction for the loss in that year, and the claim was allowed by the Commissioner in 1955. The taxpayer thus has maintained a position inconsistent with the allowance of the deduction for 1950 by filing a claim for refund for 1951 based upon the same deduction. As the determination (the allowance of the claim for refund) adopts such inconsistent position, an adjustment is authorized for the year 1950.

(2) An adjustment under the circumstances stated in § 1.1312-2, paragraph (a) of § 1.1312-3, § 1.1312-5, § 1.1312-6, or § 1.1312-7 which would result in an additional assessment is not authorized if the Commissioner, and not the taxpayer, has maintained such inconsistent position.

Example. In the example in subparagraph (1) of this paragraph, assume that the taxpayer did not file a claim for refund for 1951 but the Commissioner issued a notice of deficiency for 1951 based upon other items. The taxpayer filed a petition with the Tax Court of the United States and the Commissioner in his answer voluntarily proposed the allowance for 1951 of a deduction for the loss previously allowed for 1950. The Tax Court took the deduction into account in its redetermination in 1955 of the tax for the year 1951. In such case no adjustment would be authorized for the year 1950 as the Commissioner, and not the taxpayer, has maintained a position inconsistent with the allowance of a deduction for the loss in that year. [Reg. § 1.1311(b)-1.]

☐ [*T.D.* 6162, 2-8-56. *Amended by T.D.* 6617, 11-6-62.]

[Reg. § 1.1311(b)-2]

§ 1.1311(b)-2. **Correction not barred at time of erroneous action.**—(a) An adjustment under the circumstances stated in paragraph (b) of § 1.1312-3 (relating to the double exclusion of an item of gross income) which would result in an additional assessment, is authorized only if assessment of a deficiency against the taxpayer or related taxpayer for the taxable year in which the item is includible was not barred by any law or rule of law at the time the Commissioner first maintained, in a notice of deficiency sent pursuant to section 6212 (or section 272(a) of the Internal Revenue Code of 1939) or before the Tax Court of the United States, that the item described in paragraph (b) of § 1.1312-3 should be included in the gross income of the taxpayer in the taxable year to which the determination relates.

(b) An adjustment under the circumstances stated in § 1.1312-4 (relating to the double disallowance of a deduction or credit), which would result in the allowance of a credit or refund, is authorized only if a credit or refund to the taxpayer or related taxpayer, attributable to such adjustment, was not barred by any law or rule of law when the taxpayer first maintained in writing before the Commissioner or the Tax Court that he was entitled to such deduction or credit for the taxable year to which the determination relates. The taxpayer will be considered to have first maintained in writing before the Commissioner or the Tax Court that he was entitled to such deduction or credit when he first formally asserts his right to such deduction or credit as, for example, in a return, in a claim for refund, or in a petition (or an amended petition) before the Tax Court.

(c) Under the circumstances of adjustment with respect to which the conditions stated in this section are applicable, the conditions stated in § 1.1311(b)-1 (maintenance of an inconsistent position) are not required. See paragraph (b) of § 1.1312-3 and § 1.1312-4 for examples of the application of this section. [Reg. § 1.1311(b)-2.]

[*T.D.* 6162, 2-8-56.]

[Reg. § 1.1311(b)-3]

§ 1.1311(b)-3. Existence of relationship in case of adjustment by way of deficiency assessment.—(a) Except for cases described in paragraph (b) of § 1.1312-3, no adjustment by way of a deficiency assessment shall be made, with respect to a related taxpayer, unless the relationship existed both at some time during the taxable year with respect to which the error was made and at the time the taxpayer with respect to whom the determination is made first maintained the inconsistent position with respect to the taxable year to which the determination relates. In the case of an adjustment by way of a deficiency assessment under the circumstance described in paragraph (b) of § 1.1312-3 (where the maintenance of an inconsistent position is not required), the relationship need exist only at some time during the taxable year in which the error was made.

(b) If the inconsistent position is maintained in a return, claim for refund, or petition (or amended petition) to the Tax Court of the United States for the taxable year in respect to which the determination is made, the requisite relationship must exist on the date of filing such document. If the inconsistent position is maintained in more than one of such documents, the requisite date is the date of filing of the document in which it was first maintained. If the inconsistent position was not thus maintained, then the relationship must exist on the date of the determination as, for example, where at the instance of the taxpayer a deduction is allowed, the right to which was not asserted in a return, claim for refund, or petition to the Tax Court, and a determination is effected by means of a closing agreement or an agreement under section 1313(a)(4). [Reg. § 1.1311(b)-3.]

[*T.D.* 6162, 2-8-56.]

[Reg. § 1.1312-1]

§ 1.1312-1. Double inclusion of an item of gross income.—(a) Paragraph (1) of section 1312

applies if the determination requires the inclusion in a taxpayer's gross income of an item which was erroneously included in the gross income of the same taxpayer for another taxable year or of a related taxpayer for the same or another taxable year.

(b) The application of paragraph (a) of this section may be illustrated by the following examples:

Example (1). A taxpayer who keeps his books on the cash method erroneously included in income on his return for 1947 an item of accrued rent. In 1952, after the period of limitation on refunds for 1947 had expired, the Commissioner discovered that the taxpayer received this rent in 1948 and asserted a deficiency for the year 1948 which is sustained by the Tax Court of the United States in 1955. An adjustment in favor of the taxpayer is authorized with respect to the year 1947. If the taxpayer had returned the rent for both 1947 and 1948 and by a determination was denied a refund claim for 1948 on account of the rent item, a similar adjustment is authorized.

Example (2). A husband assigned to his wife salary to be earned by him in the year 1952. The wife included such salary in her separate return for that year and the husband omitted it. The Commissioner asserted a deficiency against the wife for 1952 with respect to a different item; she contested that deficiency, and the Tax Court entered an order in her case which became final in 1955. The wife would therefore be barred by section 6512(a) from claiming a refund for 1952. Thereafter, the Commissioner asserted a deficiency against the husband on account of the omission of such salary from his return for 1952. In 1955 the husband and the Commissioner enter into a closing agreement for the year 1952 in which the salary is taxed to the husband. An adjustment is authorized with respect to the wife's tax for 1952. [Reg. § 1.1312-1.]

[*T.D.* 6162, 2-8-56.]

[Reg. § 1.1312-2]

§ 1.1312-2. Double allowance of a deduction or credit.—(a) Paragraph (2) of section 1312 applies if the determination allows the taxpayer a deduction or credit which was erroneously allowed the same taxpayer for another taxable year or a related taxpayer for the same or another taxable year.

(b) The application of paragraph (a) of this section may be illustrated by the following examples:

Example (1). A taxpayer in his return for 1950 claimed and was allowed a deduction for destruction of timber by a forest fire. Subsequently, it was discovered that the forest fire occurred in 1951 rather than 1950. After the expiration of the period of limitations for the assessment of a deficiency for 1950, the taxpayer filed a claim for refund for 1951 based upon a deduction for the fire loss in that year. The Commissioner in 1955 allows the claim for refund. An adjustment is authorized with respect to the year 1950.

Example (2). The beneficiary of a testamentary trust in his return for 1949 claimed, and was allowed, a deduction for depreciation of the trust property. The Commissioner asserted a deficiency against the beneficiary for 1949 with respect to a different item and a final decision of the Tax Court of the United States was rendered in 1951, so that the Commissioner was thereafter barred by section 272(f) of the Internal Revenue Code of 1939 from asserting a further deficiency against the beneficiary for 1949. The trustee thereafter filed a timely refund claim contending that, under the terms of the will, the trust, and not the beneficiary, was entitled to the allowance for depreciation. The court in 1955 sustains the refund claim. An adjustment is authorized with respect to the beneficiary's tax for 1949. [Reg. § 1.1312-2.]

☐ [*T.D.* 6162, 2-8-56.]

[Reg. § 1.1312-3]

§ 1.1312-3. Double exclusion of an item of gross income.—(a) *Items included in income or with respect to which a tax was paid.*—(1) Paragraph (3)(A) of section 1312 applies if the determination requires the exclusion, from a taxpayer's gross income, of an item included in a return filed by the taxpayer, or with respect to which tax was paid, and which was erroneously excluded or omitted from the gross income of the same taxpayer for another taxable year or of a related taxpayer for the same or another taxable year.

(2) The application of subparagraph (1) of this paragraph may be illustrated by the following examples:

Example (1). (i) A taxpayer received payments in 1951 under a contract for the performance of services and included the payments in his return for that year. After the expiration of the period of limitations for the assessment of a deficiency for 1950, the Commissioner issued a notice of deficiency to the taxpayer for the year 1951 based upon adjustments to other items, and the taxpayer filed a petition with the Tax Court of the United States and maintained in the proceeding before the Tax Court that he kept his books on the accrual basis and that the payments received in 1951 were on income that had accrued and was properly taxable in 1950. A final decision of the Tax Court was rendered in 1955 excluding the payments from 1951 income. An adjustment in favor of the Commissioner is authorized with respect to the year 1950, whether or not a tax had been paid on the income reported in the 1951 return.

(ii) Assume the same facts as in (i), except that the taxpayer had not included the payments in any return and had not paid a tax thereon. No adjustment would be authorized under section 1312(3)(A) with respect to the year 1950. If the taxpayer, however, had paid a deficiency asserted for 1951 based upon the inclusion of the payments in 1951 income and thereafter successfully sued for refund thereof, an adjustment would be authorized with respect to the year 1950. (See paragraph (b) of this section for circumstances under which correction is authorized with respect to items not included in income and on which a tax was not paid.)

Example (2). A father and son conducted a partnership business, each being entitled to one-half of the net profits. The father included the entire net income of the partnership in his return for 1948, and the son included no portion of this income in his return for that year. Shortly before the expiration of the period of limitations with respect to deficiency assessments and refund claims for both father and son for 1948, the father filed a claim for refund of that portion of his 1948 tax attributable to the half of the partnership income which should have been included in the son's return. The court sustains the claim for refund in 1955. An adjustment is authorized with respect to the son's tax for 1948.

(b) *Items not included in income and with respect to which the tax was not paid.*—(1) Paragraph (3)(B) of section 1312 applies if the determination requires the exclusion from gross income of an item not included in a return filed by the taxpayer and with respect to which a tax was not paid, but which is includible in the gross income of the same taxpayer for another taxable year, or in the gross income of a related taxpayer for the same or another taxable year. This is one of the two circumstances in which the maintenance of an inconsistent position is not a requirement for an adjustment, but the requirements in paragraph (a) of § 1.1311(b)-2 must be fulfilled (correction not barred at time of erroneous action).

(2) The application of subparagraph (1) of this paragraph may be illustrated by the following examples:

Example (1). The taxpayer, A, who computes his income by use of the accrual method of accounting, performed in 1949 services for which he received payments in 1949 and 1950. He did not include in his return for either 1949 or 1950 the payments which he received in 1950, and he paid no tax with respect to such payments. In 1952 the Commissioner sent a notice of deficiency to A with respect to the year 1949, contending that A should have included all of such payments in his return for that year. A contested the deficiency on the basis that in 1949 he had no accruable right to the payments which he received in 1950. In 1955 (after the expiration of the period of limitations for assessing deficiencies with respect to 1950), the Tax Court sustains A's position. The Commissioner may assess a deficiency for 1950, since a deficiency assessment for that year was not barred when he sent the notice of deficiency with respect to 1949.

Example (2). B and C were partners in 1950, each being entitled to one-half of the profits of the partnership business. During 1950, B received an item of income which he treated as partnership income so that his return for that year reflected only 50 percent of such item. C, however, included no part of such item in any return and paid no tax with respect thereto. In 1952, the Commissioner sent to C a notice of deficiency with respect to 1950, contending that his return for that year should have reflected 50 percent of such item. C contested the deficiency on the basis that such item was not partnership income. In 1955, after the expiration of the period of limitations for assessing deficiencies with respect to 1950, the Tax Court sustained C's position. The Commissioner may assess a deficiency against B with respect to 1950 requiring him to include the entire amount of such item in his income since assessment of the deficiency was not barred when the Commissioner sent the notice of deficiency with respect to such item to C. [Reg. § 1.1312-3.]

☐ [*T.D.* 6162, 2-8-56.]

[Reg. § 1.1312-4]

§ 1.1312-4. Double disallowance of a deduction or credit.—(a) Paragraph (4) of section 1312 applies if the determination disallows a deduction or credit which should have been, but was not, allowed to the same taxpayer for another taxable year or to a related taxpayer for the same or another taxable year. This is one of the two circumstances in which the maintenance of an inconsistent position is not a requirement for an adjustment but the requirements in paragraph (b) of § 1.1311(b)-2 must be fulfilled (correction not barred at time of erroneous action).

(b) The application of paragraph (a) of this section may be illustrated by the following examples:

Example (1). The taxpayer, A, who computes his income by use of the accrual method of accounting, deducted in his return for the taxable year 1951 an item of expense which he paid in such year. At the time A filed his return for 1951, the statute of limitations for 1950 had not expired. Subsequently, the Commissioner asserted a deficiency for 1951 based on the position that the liability for such expense should have been accrued for the taxable year 1950. In 1955, after the period of limitations on refunds for 1950 had expired, there was a determination by the Tax Court disallowing such deduction for the taxable year 1951. A is entitled to an adjustment for the taxable year 1950. However, if such liability should have been accrued for the taxable year 1946 instead of 1950, A would not be entitled to an adjustment, if a credit or refund with respect to 1946 was already barred when he deducted such expense for the taxable year 1951.

Example (2). The taxpayer, B, in his return for 1951 claimed a deduction for a charitable contri-

bution. The Commissioner asserted a deficiency for such year contending that 50 percent of the deduction should be disallowed, since the contribution was made from community property 50 percent of which was attributable to B's spouse. The deficiency is sustained by the Tax Court in 1956, subsequent to the period of limitations within which B's spouse could claim a refund with respect to 1951. An adjustment is permitted to B's spouse, a related taxpayer, since a refund attributable to a deduction by her of such contribution was not barred when B claimed the deduction. [Reg. § 1.1312-4.]

☐ [*T.D.* 6162, 2-8-56.]

[Reg. § 1.1312-5]

§ 1.1312-5. Correlative deductions and inclusions for trusts or estates and legatees, beneficiaries, or heirs.—(a) Paragraph (5) of section 1312 applies to distributions by a trust or an estate to the beneficiaries, heirs, or legatees. If the determination relates to the amount of the deduction allowed by sections 651 and 661 or the inclusion in taxable income of the beneficiary required by sections 652 and 662 (including amounts falling within subpart D, of subchapter J, chapter 1 of the Code, relating to treatment of excess distributions by trusts), or if the determination relates to the additional deduction (or inclusion) specified in section 162(b) and (c) of the Internal Revenue Code of 1939 (or the corresponding provisions of a prior revenue act), with respect to amounts paid, credited, or required to be distributed to the beneficiaries, heirs, and legatees, and such determination requires:

(1) The allowance to the estate or trust of the deduction when such amounts have been erroneously omitted or excluded from the income of the beneficiaries, heirs, or legatees; or

(2) The inclusion of such amounts in the income of the beneficiaries, heirs, or legatees when the deduction has been erroneously disallowed to or omitted by the estate or trust; or

(3) The disallowance to an estate or trust of the deduction when such amounts have been erroneously included in the income of the beneficiaries, heirs, or legatees; or

(4) The exclusion of such amounts from the income of the beneficiaries, heirs, or legatees when the deduction has been erroneously allowed to the estate or trust.

(b) The application of paragraph (a)(1) of this section may be illustrated by the following example:

Example. For the taxable year 1954, a trustee, directed by the trust instrument to accumulate the trust income, made no distribution to the beneficiary and returned the entire income as taxable to the trust. Accordingly the beneficiary did not include the trust income in his return for the year 1954. In 1957, a State court holds invalid the clause directing accumulation and determines that the income is required to be currently distributed. It also rules that certain extraordinary dividends which the trustee in good faith allocated to corpus in 1954 were properly allocable to income. In 1958, the trustee, relying upon the court decision, files a claim for refund of the tax paid on behalf of the trust for the year 1954 and thereafter files a suit in the District Court. The claim is sustained by the court (except as to the tax on the extraordinary dividends) in 1959 after the expiration of the period of limitations upon deficiency assessments against the beneficiary for the year 1954. An adjustment is authorized with respect to the beneficiary's tax for the year 1954. The treatment of the distribution to the beneficiary of the extraordinary dividends shall be determined under subpart D of subchapter J.

(c) The application of paragraph (a)(2) of this section may be illustrated by the following example:

Example. Assume the same facts as in the example in paragraph (b) of this section, except that, instead of the trustee's filing a refund claim, the Commissioner, relying upon the decision of the State court, asserts a deficiency against the beneficiary for 1954. The deficiency is sustained by final decision of the Tax Court of the United States in 1959, after the expiration of the period for filing claim for refund on behalf of the trust for 1954. An adjustment is authorized with respect to the trust for the year 1954.

(d) The application of paragraph (a)(3) of this section may be illustrated by the following example:

Example. A trustee claimed in the trust return for 1954 for amounts paid to the beneficiary a deduction to the extent of distributable net income. This amount was included by the beneficiary in gross income in his return for 1954. In computing distributable net income the trustee had included short and long-term capital gains. In 1958, the Commissioner asserts a deficiency against the trust on the ground that the capital gains were not includible in distributable net income, and that, therefore, the gains were taxable to the trust, not the beneficiary. The deficiency is sustained by a final decision of the Tax Court in 1960, after the expiration of the period for filing claims for refund by the beneficiary for 1954. An adjustment is authorized with respect to the beneficiary's tax for the year 1954, based on the exclusion from 1954 gross income of the capital gains previously considered distributed by the trust under section 662.

(e) The application of paragraph (a)(4) of this section may be illustrated by the following example:

Example. Assume the same facts as in the example in paragraph (d) of this section, except that, instead of the Commissioner's asserting a deficiency, the beneficiary filed a refund claim for 1954 on the same ground. The claim is sustained by the court in 1960 after the expiration of

the period of limitations upon deficiency assessments against the trust for 1954. An adjustment is authorized with respect to the trust for the year 1954. [Reg. § 1.1312-5.]

☐ [*T.D.* 6162, 2-8-56.]

[Reg. § 1.1312-6]

§ 1.1312-6. Correlative deductions and credits for certain related corporations.—(a) Paragraph (6) of section 1312 applies if the determination allows or disallows a deduction (including a credit) to a corporation, and if a correlative deduction or credit has been erroneously allowed, omitted, or disallowed in respect of a related taxpayer described in section 1313(c)(7).

(b) The application of paragraph (a) of this section may be illustrated by the following examples:

Example (1). X Corporation is a wholly-owned subsidiary of Y Corporation. In 1955, X Corporation paid $5,000 to Y Corporation and claimed an interest deduction for this amount in its return for 1955. Y Corporation included this amount in its gross income for 1955. In 1958, the Commissioner asserted a deficiency against X Corporation for 1955, contending that the deduction for interest paid should be disallowed on the ground that the payment was in reality the payment of a dividend to Y Corporation. X Corporation contested the deficiency, and ultimately in June 1959, a final decision of the Tax Court sustained the Commissioner. Since the amount of the payment is a dividend, Y Corporation should have been allowed for 1955 the corporate dividends-received deduction under section 243 with respect to such payment. However, the Tax Court's decision sustaining the deficiency against X Corporation occurred after the expiration of the period for filing claim for refund by Y Corporation for 1955. An adjustment is authorized with respect to Y Corporation for 1955.

Example (2). Assume the same facts as in example (1) except that, instead of the Commissioner asserting a deficiency against X Corporation for 1955, Y Corporation filed a claim for refund in 1958, alleging that the payment received in 1955 from X Corporation was in reality a dividend to which the corporate dividends-received deduction (section 243) applies. The Commissioner denied the claim, and ultimately in June 1959, the district court, in a final decision, sustained Y Corporation. Since the amount of the payment is a dividend, X Corporation should not have been allowed an interest deduction for the amount paid to Y Corporation. However, the district court's decision sustaining the claim for refund occurred after the expiration of the period of limitations for assessing a deficiency against X Corporation for the year 1955. An adjustment is authorized with respect to X Corporation's tax for 1955. [Reg. § 1.1312-6.]

☐ [*T.D.* 6617, 11-6-62.]

[Reg. §1.1312-7]

§1.1312-7. **Basis of property after erroneous treatment of a prior transaction.**—(a) Paragraph (7) of section 1312 applies if the determination establishes the basis of property, and there occurred one of the following types of errors in respect of a prior transaction upon which such basis depends, or in respect of a prior transaction which was erroneously treated as affecting such basis:

(1) An erroneous inclusion in, or omission from, gross income, or

(2) An erroneous recognition or nonrecognition of gain or loss, or

(3) An erroneous deduction of an item properly chargeable to capital account or an erroneous charge to capital account of an item properly deductible.

(b) For this section to apply, the taxpayer with respect to whom the erroneous treatment occurred must be—

(1) The taxpayer with respect to whom the determination is made, or

(2) A taxpayer who acquired title to the property in the erroneously treated transaction and from whom, mediately or immediately, the taxpayer with respect to whom the determination is made derived title in such a manner that he will have a basis ascertained by reference to the basis in the hands of the taxpayer who acquired title to the property in the erroneously treated transaction, or

(3) A taxpayer who had title to the property at the time of the erroneously treated transaction and from whom, mediately or immediately, the taxpayer with respect to whom the determination is made derived title, if the basis of the property in the hands of the taxpayer with respect to whom the determination is made is determined under section 1015(a) (relating to the basis of property acquired by gift).

No adjustment is authorized with respect to the transferor of the property in a transaction upon which the basis of the property depends, when the determination is with respect to the original transferee or a subsequent transferee of such original transferee.

(c) The application of this section may be illustrated by the following examples:

Example (1). In 1949 taxpayer A transferred property which had cost him $5,000 to the X Corporation in exchange for an original issue of shares of its stock having a fair market value of $10,000. In his return for 1949 taxpayer A treated the exchange as one in which the gain or loss was not recognizable:

(i) In 1955 the X Corporation maintains that the gain should have been recognized in the exchange in 1949 and therefore the property it received had a $10,000 basis for depreciation. Its position is adopted in a closing agreement. No adjustment is authorized with respect to the tax of the X Corporation for 1949, as none of the

three types of errors specified in paragraph (a) of this section occurred with respect to the X Corporation in the treatment of the exchange in 1949. Moreover, no adjustment is authorized with respect to taxpayer A, as he is not within any of the three classes of taxpayers described in paragraph (b) of this section.

(ii) In 1953 taxpayer A sells the stock which he received in 1949 and maintains that, as gain should have been recognized in the exchange in 1949 the basis for computing the profit on the sale is $10,000. His position is confirmed in a closing agreement executed in 1955. An adjustment is authorized with respect to his tax for the year 1949 as the basis for computing the gain on the sale depends upon the transaction in 1949, and in respect of that transaction there was an erroneous nonrecognition of gain to taxpayer A, the taxpayer with respect to whom the determination is made.

Example (2). In 1950 taxpayer A was the owner of 10 shares of the common stock of the Z Corporation which had a basis of $1,500. In that year he received as a dividend thereon 10 shares of the preferred stock of the same corporation having a fair market value of $1,000. On his books, entries were made reducing the basis of the common stock by allocating $500 of the basis to the preferred stock, and on his return for 1950 he did not include the dividend in gross income.

(i) In 1951 taxpayer A made a gift of the preferred stock of the Z Corporation to taxpayer B, an unrelated individual. Taxpayer B sold the stock in 1953 and on his return for that year he reported the sale and claimed a basis of $1,000, contending that the dividend of preferred stock was taxable to A in 1950 at its fair market value of $1,000. The basis of $1,000 is confirmed by a closing agreement executed in 1955. An adjustment is authorized with respect to taxpayer A's tax for 1950, as the closing agreement determines basis of property, and in a prior transaction upon which such basis depends there was an erroneous omission from gross income of taxpayer A, a taxpayer who acquired title to the property in the erroneously treated transaction and from whom, immediately, the taxpayer with respect to whom the determination is made derived title.

(ii) Assuming the same facts as in (i) except that the common stock instead of the preferred stock was the subject of the gift, and the basis claimed by taxpayer B and confirmed in the closing agreement was $1,500. An adjustment is authorized with respect to taxpayer A's tax for 1950, as the closing agreement determines the basis of property, and in a prior transaction which was erroneously treated as affecting such basis there was an erroneous omission from gross income of taxpayer A, a taxpayer who had title to the property at the time of the erroneously treated transaction, and from whom, immediately, taxpayer B, with respect to whom the determination is made, derived title. The basis of the property in taxpayer B's hands with respect to whom the determination is made is determined under section 1015(a) (relating to the basis of property acquired by gift).

Example (3). In 1950 taxpayer A sold property acquired at a cost of $5,000 to taxpayer B for $10,000. In his return for 1950 taxpayer A failed to include the profit on such sale. In 1953 taxpayer B sold the property for $12,000, and in his return for 1953 reported a gain of $2,000 upon the sale which is confirmed by a closing agreement executed in 1955. No adjustment is authorized with respect to the tax of taxpayer A for 1950, as he does not come within any of the three classes of taxpayers described in paragraph (b) of this section.

Example (4). In 1950 a taxpayer who owned 100 shares of stock in Corporation Y received $1,000 from the corporation which amount the taxpayer reported on his return for 1950 as a taxable dividend. In 1952 Corporation Y was completely liquidated and the taxpayer received in that year liquidating distributions totalling $8,000. In his return for 1952 the taxpayer reported the receipt of the $8,000 and computed his gain or loss upon the liquidation by using as a basis the amount which he paid for the stock. The Commissioner maintained that the distribution in 1950 was a distribution out of capital and that in computing the taxpayer's gain or loss upon the liquidation in 1952, the basis of the stock should be reduced by the $1,000. This position is adopted in a closing agreement executed in 1955 with respect to the year 1952. An adjustment is authorized with respect to the year 1950 as the basis for computing gain or loss in 1952 depends upon the transaction in 1950, and in respect of the 1950 transaction (upon which the basis of the property depends) there was an erroneous inclusion in gross income of the taxpayer with respect to whom the determination is made.

Example (5). In 1946 a taxpayer received 100 shares of stock of the X Corporation having a fair market value of $5,000, in exchange for shares of stock in the Y Corporation which he had acquired at a cost of $12,000. In his return for 1946 the taxpayer treated the exchange as one in which gain or loss was not recognizable. The taxpayer sold 50 shares of the X Corporation stock in 1947 and in his return for that year treated such shares as having a $6,000 basis. In 1952, the taxpayer sold the remaining 50 shares of stock of the X Corporation for $7,500 and reported $1,500 gain in his return for 1952. After the expiration of the period of limitations on deficiency assessments and on refund claims for 1946 and 1947, the Commissioner asserted a deficiency for 1952 on the ground that the loss realized on the exchange in 1946 was erroneously treated as nonrecognizable, and the basis for computing gain upon the sale in 1952 was $2,500, resulting in a gain of $5,000. The deficiency is sustained by the Tax Court in 1955. An adjustment is authorized with respect to the year 1946 as to the entire $7,000 loss realized on the exchange, as the Court's decision determines the basis of property, and in a prior transaction upon which such basis depends there was an erroneous nonrecognition of loss to the taxpayer with respect to whom the determination was made. No adjustment is authorized with respect to the year 1947 as the basis for computing gain upon the sale of the 50 shares in 1952 does not depend upon the transaction in 1947 but upon the transaction in 1946. [Reg. § 1.1312-7.]

☐ [*T.D.* 6162, 2-8-56. *Amended by T.D. 6617,* 11-6-62.]

[Reg. § 1.1312-8]

§ 1.1312-8. Law applicable in determination of error.—The question whether there was an erroneous inclusion, exclusion, omission, allowance, disallowance, recognition, or nonrecognition is determined under the provisions of the internal revenue laws applicable with respect to the year as to which the inclusion, exclusion, omission, allowance, disallowance, recognition, or nonrecognition, as the case may be, was made. The fact that the inclusion, exclusion, omission, allowance, disallowance, recognition, or nonrecognition, as the case may be, was in pursuance of an interpretation, either judicial or administrative, accorded such provisions of the internal revenue laws at the time of such action is not necessarily determinative of this question. For example, if a later judicial decision authoritatively alters such interpretation so that such action was contrary to such provisions of the internal revenue laws as later interpreted, the inclusion, exclusion, omission, allowance, disallowance, recognition, or nonrecognition, as the case may be, is erroneous within the meaning of section 1312. [Reg. § 1.1312-8.]

☐ [*T.D.* 6162, 2-8-56. *Amended by T.D. 6617,* 11-6-62.]

[Reg. § 1.1313(a)-1]

§ 1.1313(a)-1. Decision by Tax Court or other court as a determination.—(a) A determination may take the form of a decision by the Tax Court of the United States or a judgment, decree, or other order by any court of competent jurisdiction, which has become final.

(b) The date upon which a decision by the Tax Court becomes final is prescribed in section 7481.

(c) The date upon which a judgment of any other court becomes final must be determined upon the basis of the facts in the particular case. Ordinarily, a judgment of a United States district court becomes final upon the expiration of the time allowed for taking an appeal, if no such appeal is duly taken within such time; and a judgment of the United States Court of Claims becomes final upon the expiration of the time allowed for filing a petition for certiorari if no such petition is duly filed within such time. [Reg. § 1.1313(a)-1.]

☐ [*T.D.* 6162, 2-8-56.]

[Reg. § 1.1313(a)-2]

§ 1.1313(a)-2. Closing agreement as a determination.—A determination may take the form of a closing agreement authorized by section 7121. Such an agreement may relate to the total tax liability of the taxpayer for a particular taxable year or years or to one or more separate items affecting such liability. A closing agreement becomes final for the purpose of this section on the date of its approval by the Commissioner. [Reg. § 1.1313(a)-2.]

☐ [*T.D. 6162, 2-8-56.*]

[Reg. § 1.1313(a)-3]

§ 1.1313(a)-3. Final disposition of claim for refund as a determination.—(a) *In general.*—A determination may take the form of a final disposition of a claim for refund. Such disposition may result in a determination with respect to two classes of items, i.e., items included by the taxpayer in a claim for refund and items applied by the Commissioner to offset the alleged overpayment. The time at which a disposition in respect of a particular item becomes final may depend not only upon what action is taken with respect to that item but also upon whether the claim for refund is allowed or disallowed.

(b) *Items with respect to which the taxpayer's claim is allowed.*—(1) The disposition with respect to an item as to which the taxpayer's contention in the claim for refund is sustained becomes final on the date of allowance of the refund or credit if—

(i) The taxpayer's claim for refund is unqualifiedly allowed; or

(ii) The taxpayer's contention with respect to an item is sustained and with respect to other items is denied, so that the net result is an allowance of refund or credit; or

(iii) The taxpayer's contention with respect to an item is sustained, but the Commissioner applies other items to offset the amount of the alleged overpayment and the items so applied do not completely offset such amount but merely reduce it so that the net result is an allowance of refund or credit.

(2) If the taxpayer's contention in the claim for refund with respect to an item is sustained but the Commissioner applies other items to offset the amount of the alleged overpayment so that the net result is a disallowance of the claim for refund, the date of mailing, by registered mail, of the notice of disallowance (see section 6532) is the date of the final disposition as to the item with respect to which the taxpayer's contention is sustained.

(c) *Items with respect to which the taxpayer's claim is disallowed.*—The disposition with respect to an item as to which the taxpayer's contention in the claim for refund is denied becomes final upon the expiration of the time allowed by section 6532 for instituting suit on the claim for refund, unless the suit is instituted prior to the expiration of such period, if—

(1) The taxpayer's claim for refund is unqualifiedly disallowed; or

(2) The taxpayer's contention with respect to an item is denied and with respect to other items is sustained so that the net result is an allowance of refund or credit; or

(3) The taxpayer's contention with respect to an item is sustained in part and denied in part. For example, assume that the taxpayer claimed a deductible loss of $10,000 and a consequent overpayment of $2,500 and the Commissioner concedes that a deductible loss was sustained, but only in the amount of $5,000. The disposition of the claim for refund with respect to the allowance of the $5,000 and the disallowance of the remaining $5,000 becomes final upon the expiration of the time for instituting suit on the claim for refund unless suit is instituted prior to the expiration of such period.

(d) *Items applied by the Commissioner in reduction of the refund or credit.*—If the Commissioner applies an item in reduction of the overpayment alleged in the claim for refund, and the net result is an allowance of refund or credit, the disposition with respect to the item so applied by the Commissioner becomes final upon the expiration of the time allowed by section 6532 for instituting suit on the claim for refund, unless suit is instituted prior to the expiration of such period. If such application of the item results in the assertion of a deficiency, such action does not constitute a final disposition of a claim for refund within the meaning of § 1.1313(a)-3, but subsequent action taken with respect to such deficiency may result in a determination under §§ 1.1313(a)-1, 1.1313(a)-2, or 1.1313(a)-4.

(e) *Elimination of waiting period.*—The necessity of waiting for the expiration of the 2-year period of limitations provided in section 6532 may be avoided in such cases as are described in paragraph (c) or (d) of this section by the use of a closing agreement (see § 1.1313(a)-2) or agreement under § 1.1313(a)-4 to effect a determination. [Reg. § 1.1313(a)-3.]

☐ [*T.D. 6162, 2-8-56.*]

[Reg. § 1.1313(a)-4]

§ 1.1313(a)-4. Agreement pursuant to section 1313(a)(4) as a determination.—(a) *In general.*—(1) A determination may take the form of an agreement made pursuant to this section. This section is intended to provide an expeditious method for obtaining an adjustment under section 1311 and for offsetting deficiencies and refunds whenever possible. The provisions of part II (section 1311 and following), subchapter Q, chapter 1 of the Code, must be strictly complied with in any such agreement.

(2) An agreement made pursuant to this section will not, in itself, establish the tax liability for the open taxable year to which it relates, but it will state the amount of the tax, as then determined, for such open year. The tax may be the amount of tax shown on the return as filed by the taxpayer, but if any changes in the amount have been made, or if any are being made by documents executed concurrently with the execution of said agreement, such changes must be taken into account. For example, an agreement pursuant to this section may be executed concurrently with the execution of a waiver of restrictions on assessment and collection of a deficiency or acceptance of an overassessment with respect to the open taxable year, or concurrently with the execution and filing of a stipulation in a proceeding before the Tax Court of the United States, where an item which is to be the subject of an adjustment under section 1311 is disposed of by the stipulation and is not left for determination by the court.

(b) *Contents of agreement.*—An agreement made pursuant to this section shall be so designated in the heading of the agreement, and it shall contain the following:

(1) A statement of the amount of the tax determined for the open taxable year to which the agreement relates, and if said liability is established or altered by a document executed concurrently with the execution of the agreement, a reference to said document.

(2) A concise statement of the material facts with respect to the item that was the subject of the error in the closed taxable year or years, and a statement of the manner in which such item was treated in computing the tax liability set forth pursuant to subparagraph (1) of this paragraph.

(3) A statement as to the amount of the adjustment ascertained pursuant to §1.1314(a)-1 for the taxable year with respect to which the error was made and, where applicable, a statement as to the amount of the adjustment or adjustments ascertained pursuant to §1.1314(a)-2 with respect to any other taxable year or years; and

(4) A waiver of restrictions on assessment and collection of any deficiencies set forth pursuant to subparagraph 3 of this paragraph.

(c) *Execution and effect of agreement.*—An agreement made pursuant to this section shall be signed by the taxpayer with respect to whom the determination is made, or on the taxpayer's behalf by an agent or attorney acting pursuant to a power of attorney on file with the Internal Revenue Service. If an adjustment is to be made in a case of a related taxpayer, the agreement shall be signed also by the related taxpayer, or on the related taxpayer's behalf by an agent or attorney acting pursuant to a power of attorney on file

with the Internal Revenue Service. It may be signed on behalf of the Commissioner by the district director, or such other person as is authorized by the Commissioner. When duly executed, such agreement will constitute the authority for an allowance of any refund or credit agreed to therein, and for the immediate assessment of any deficiency agreed to therein for the taxable year with respect to which the error was made, or any closed taxable year or years affected, or treated as affected, by a net operating loss deduction or capital loss carryover determined with reference to the taxable year with respect to which the error was made.

(d) *Finality of determination.*—A determination made by an agreement pursuant to this section becomes final when the tax liability for the open taxable year to which the determination relates becomes final. During the period, if any, that a deficiency may be assessed or a refund or credit allowed with respect to such year, either the taxpayer or the Commissioner may properly pursue any of the procedures provided by law to secure a further modification of the tax liability for such year. For example, if the taxpayer subsequently files a claim for refund, or if the Commissioner subsequently issues a notice of deficiency with respect to such year, either may adopt a position with respect to the item that was the subject of the adjustment that is at variance with the manner in which said item was treated in the agreement. Any assessment, refund, or credit that is subsequently made with respect to the tax liability for such open taxable year, to the extent that it is based upon a revision in the treatment of the item that was the subject of the adjustment, shall constitute an alteration or revocation of the determination for the purpose of a redetermination of the adjustment pursuant to paragraph (d) of §1.1314 (b)-1. [Reg. §1.1313(a)-4.]

☐ [T.D. 6162, 2-8-56.]

[Reg. §1.1313(c)-1]

§1.1313(c)-1. **Related taxpayer.**—An adjustment in the case of the taxpayer with respect to whom the error was made may be authorized under section 1311 although the determination is made with respect to a different taxpayer, provided that such taxpayers stand in one of the relationships specified in section 1313(c). The concept of "related taxpayer" has application to all of the circumstances of adjustment specified in §1.1312-1 through §1.1312-5 if the related taxpayer is one described in section 1313(c); it has application to the circumstances of adjustment specified in §1.1312-6 only if the related taxpayer is one described in section 1313(c)(7); it does not apply in the circumstances specified in §1.1312-7. If such relationship exists, it is not essential that the error involve a transaction made possible only by reason of the existence of the relationship. For example, if the error with respect to which an adjustment is sought under section 1311 grew out of an assignment of rents between taxpayer A and taxpayer B, who are partners, and the determination is with respect to taxpayer A, an adjustment with respect to taxpayer B may be permissible despite the fact that the assignment had nothing to do with the business of the partnership. The relationship need not exist throughout the entire taxable year with respect to which the error was made, but only at some time during that taxable year. For example, if a taxpayer on February 15 assigns to his fiancee the net rents of a building which the taxpayer owns, and the two are married before the end of a taxable year, an adjustment may be permissible if the determination relates to such rents despite the fact that they were not husband and wife at the time of the assignment. See § 1.1311(b)-3 for the requirement in certain cases that the relationship exist at the time an inconsistent postion is first maintained. [Reg. § 1.1313(c)-1.]

☐ [*T.D. 6162*, 2-8-56. *Amended by T.D. 6617*, 11-6-62.]

[Reg. § 1.1314(a)-1]

§ 1.1314(a)-1. Ascertainment of amount of adjustment in year of error.—(a) In computing the amount of the adjustment under sections 1311 to 1315, inclusive, there must first be ascertained the amount of the tax previously determined for the taxpayer as to whom the error was made for the taxable year with respect to which the error was made. The tax previously determined for any taxable year may be the amount of tax shown on the taxpayer's return, but if any changes in that amount have been made, they must be taken into account. In such cases, the tax previously determined will be the sum of the amount shown as the tax by the taxpayer upon his return and the amounts previously assessed (or collected without assessment) as deficiencies, reduced by the amount of any rebates made. The amount shown as the tax by the taxpayer upon his return and the amount of any rebates or deficiencies shall be determined in accordance with the provisions of section 6211 and the regulations thereunder.

(b)(1) The tax previously determined may consist of tax for any taxable year beginning after December 31, 1931, imposed by subtitle A of the Internal Revenue Code of 1954, by chapter 1 and subchapters A, B, D, and E of chapter 2 of the Internal Revenue Code of 1939, or by the corresponding provisions of prior internal revenue laws, or by any one or more of such provisions.

(2) After the tax previously determined has been ascertained, a recomputation must then be made under the laws applicable to said taxable year to ascertain the increase or decrease in tax, if any, resulting from the correction of the error.

The difference between the tax previously determined and the tax as recomputed after correction of the error will be the amount of the adjustment.

(c) No change shall be made in the treatment given any item upon which the tax previously determined was based other than in the correction of the item or items with respect to which the error was made. However, due regard shall be given to the effect that such correction may have on the computation of gross income, taxable income, and other matters under chapter 1 of the Code. If the treatment of any item upon which the tax previously determined was based, or if the application of any provisions of the internal revenue laws with respect to such tax, depends upon the amount of income (e.g., charitable contributions, foreign tax credit, dividends received credit, medical expenses, and percentage depletion), readjustment in these particulars will be necessary as part of the recomputation in conformity with the change in the amount of the income which results from the correct treatment of the item or items in respect of which the error was made.

(d) Any interest or additions to the tax collected as a result of the error shall be taken into account in determining the amount of the adjustment.

(e) The application of this section may be illustrated by the following example:

Example. (1) For the taxable year 1949 a taxpayer with no dependents, who kept his books on the cash receipts and disbursements method, filed a joint return with his wife disclosing adjusted gross income of $42,000, deductions amounting to $12,000, and a net income of $30,000. Included among other items in the gross income were salary in the amount of $15,000 and rents accrued but not yet received in the amount of $5,000. During the taxable year he donated $10,000 to the American Red Cross and in his return claimed a deduction of $6,300 on account thereof, representing the maximum deduction allowable under the 15-percent limitation imposed by section 23(o) of the Internal Revenue Code of 1939 as applicable to the year 1949. In computing his net income he omitted interest income amounting to $6,000 and neglected to take a deduction for interest paid in the amount of $4,500. The return disclosed a tax liability of $7,788, which was assessed and paid. After the expiration of the period of limitations upon the assessment of a deficiency or the allowance of a refund for 1949, the Commissioner included the item of rental income amounting to $5,000 in the taxpayer's gross income for the year 1950 and asserted a deficiency for that year. As a result of a final decision of the Tax Court of the United States in 1955 sustaining the deficiency for 1950, an adjustment is authorized for the year 1949.

(2) The amount of the adjustment is computed as follows:

Reg. § 1.1314(a)-1(e)

Tax previously determined for 1949	$7,788
Net income for 1949 upon which tax previously determined was based	$30,000
Less: Rents erroneously included	5,000
Balance	$25,000
Adjustment for contributions (add 15 percent of $5,000)	750
Net income as adjusted	$25,750
Tax as recomputed	$6,152
Tax previously determined	7,788
Difference	$1,636
Amount of adjustment to be refunded or credited	1,636

(3) In accordance with the provisions of paragraph (c) of this section, the recomputation to determine the amount of the adjustment does not take into consideration the item of $6,000 representing interest received, which was omitted from gross income, or the item of $4,500 representing interest paid, for which no deduction was allowed. [Reg. § 1.1314(a)-1.]

☐ [T.D. 6162, 2-8-56.]

[Reg. § 1.1314(a)-2]

§ 1.1314(a)-2. Adjustment to other barred taxable years.—(a) An adjustment is authorized under section 1311 with respect to a taxable year or years other than the year of the error, but only if all of the following requirements are met:

(1) The tax liability for such other year or years must be affected, or must have been treated as affected, by a net operating loss deduction (as defined in section 172) or by a capital loss carryback or carryover (as defined in section 1212).

(2) The net operating loss deduction or capital loss carryback or carryover must be determined with reference to the taxable year with respect to which the error was made.

(3) On the date of the determination, the adjustment with respect to such other year or years must be prevented by some law or rule of law, other than sections 1311 through 1315 and section 7122 and the corresponding provisions of prior revenue laws.

(b) The amount of the adjustment for such other year or years shall be computed in a manner similar to that provided in § 1.1314(a)-1. The tax previously determined for such other year or years shall be ascertained. A recomputation must then be made to ascertain the increase or decrease in tax, if any, resulting solely from the correction of the net operating loss deduction or capital loss carryback or carryover. The difference between the tax previously determined and the tax as recomputed is the amount of the adjustment. In the recomputation, no consideration shall be given to items other than the following: (1) the items upon which the tax previously determined for such other year or years was based, and (2) the net operating loss deduction or capital loss carryback or carryover as corrected. In determining the correct net operating loss deduction or capital loss carryback or carryover, no changes shall be made in taxable income (net income in the case of taxable years subject to the provisions of the Internal Revenue Code of 1939 or prior revenue laws), net operating loss or capital loss, for any barred taxable year, except as provided in section 1314. Section 172 and the corresponding provisions of prior revenue laws, and the regulations promulgated thereunder, prescribe the methods of computing the net operating loss deduction. Section 1212 and the corresponding provisions of prior revenue laws, and the regulations promulgated thereunder, prescribe the methods of computing the capital loss carryback or carryover.

(c) A net operating loss deduction or a capital loss carryback or carryover determined with reference to the year of the error may affect, or may have been treated as affecting, a taxable year with respect to which an adjustment is not prevented by the operation of any law or rule of law. In such case, the appropriate adjustment shall be made with respect to such open taxable year. However, the redetermination of the tax for such open taxable year is not made pursuant to part II (section 1311 and following), subchapter Q, chapter 1 of the Code, and the adjustment for such open year and the method of computation are not limited by the provisions of said sections.

(d) The application of this section may be illustrated by the following example:

Example. The taxpayer is a corporation which makes its income tax returns on a calendar year basis. Its net income in 1949, computed without any net operating loss deduction was $10,000, but because of a net operating loss deduction in excess of that amount resulting from a carryback of a net operating loss claimed for 1950, it paid no income tax for 1949. On its return for 1950 it showed an excess of deductions over gross income of $14,000, and it paid no income tax for 1950. For the year 1951 its net income, computed without any net operating loss deduction, was $15,000, and a net operating loss deduction of $13,000 was allowed ($4,000 of which was attributable to the carryover from 1950 and $9,000 of which was attributable to the carryback of a net operating loss of $9,000 sustained in 1952). In 1957 the assessment of deficiencies or the allowance of refunds for all of said years are barred by the statute of limitations.

(i) A Tax Court decision entered in 1957 with respect to the taxable year 1953 constituted a determination under which an adjustment is authorized to the taxable year 1950, the year with respect to which the error was made. This adjustment increases income for said year by $15,000, so that instead of a net operating loss of $14,000, its corrected net income is $1,000 for 1950, and the tax computed on that income will be assessed as a deficiency for 1950. An adjustment is authorized under this section with respect to each of the years 1949 and 1951, as the tax liability for each year was treated as affected by a net operating loss deduction which was determined by a computation in which reference was made to the year 1950. In the recomputation of the tax for 1949, the net operating loss carryback from 1950 will be eliminated, and in the recomputation of the tax for 1951 the net operating loss carryover from 1950 will be eliminated; for each of the years 1949 and 1951 there will be an adjustment which will be treated as a deficiency for said year.

(ii) Assuming the same facts except that the correction with respect to the year 1950 increases the net operating loss for said year from $14,000 to $20,000. As a result of this correction, there will be no change in the tax due for 1949 and 1950. However, the net operating loss deduction for 1951 is recomputed to be $19,000, the aggregate of the $10,000 carryover from 1950 and the $9,000 carryback from 1952 (the carryover from 1950 is the excess of the $20,000 net operating loss for 1950 over the $10,000 net income for 1949, such 1949 income being determined without any net operating loss deduction). As a result of the correction of the net operating loss deduction for 1951, the tax recomputation will show no tax due for said year, and the adjustment for 1951 will result in a refund or credit of the tax previously paid. Moreover, computations resulting from this adjustment will disclose a net operating loss carryover from 1952 to 1953 of $4,000, that is, the excess of the $9,000 net operating loss for 1952 over the $5,000 net income for 1951 (such net income for 1951 being computed as the $15,000 reduced by the carryover of $10,000 from 1950, the carryback from 1952 not being taken into account). A further adjustment is authorized under section 1311 with respect to any subsequent barred year in which the tax liability is affected by a carryover of the net operating loss from 1952, inasmuch as such carryover from 1952 has been determined by a computation in which reference was made to 1950, the taxable year of the error. [Reg. § 1.1314(a)-2.]

☐ [T.D. 6162, 2-8-56. *Amended by T.D. 7301,* 1-3-74.]

[Reg. § 1.1314(b)-1]

§ 1.1314(b)-1. Method of adjustment.—(a) If the amount of the adjustment ascertained pursuant to § 1.1314(a)-1 or § 1.1314(a)-2 represents an increase in tax, it is to be treated as if it were a deficiency determined by the Commissioner with respect to the taxpayer as to whom the error was made and for the taxable year or years with respect to which such adjustment was made. The amount of such adjustment is thus to be assessed and collected under the law and regulations applicable to the assessment and collection of deficiencies, subject, however, to the limitations imposed by § 1.1314(c)-1. Notice of deficiency, unless waived, must be issued with respect to such amount or amounts, and the taxpayer may contest the deficiency before the Tax Court of the United States or, if he chooses, may pay the deficiency and later file claim for refund. If the amount of the adjustment ascertained pursuant to § 1.1314(a)-1 or § 1.1314(a)-2 represents a decrease in tax, it is to be treated as if it were an overpayment claimed by the taxpayer with respect to whom the error was made for the taxable year or years with respect to which such adjustment was made. Such amount may be recovered under the law and regulations applicable to overpayments of tax, subject however, to the limitations imposed by § 1.1314(c)-1. The taxpayer must file a claim for refund thereof, unless the overpayment is refunded without such claim, and if the claim is denied or not acted upon by the Commissioner within the prescribed time, the taxpayer may then file suit for refund.

(b) For the purpose of the adjustments authorized by section 1311, the period of limitations upon the making of an assessment or upon refund or credit, as the case may be, for the taxable year of an adjustment shall be considered as if, on the date of the determination, one year remained before the expiration of such period. The Commissioner thus has one year from the date of the determination within which to mail a notice of deficiency in respect of the amount of the adjustment where such adjustment is treated as if it were a deficiency. The issuance of such notice of deficiency, in accordance with the law and regulations applicable to the assessment of deficiencies will suspend the running of the 1-year period of limitations provided in section 1314(b). In accordance with the applicable law and regulations governing the collection of deficiencies, the period of limitation for collection of the amount of the adjustment will commence to run from the date of assessment of such amount. (See section 6502 and corresponding provisions of prior revenue laws.) Similarly, the taxpayer has a period of one year from the date of the determination within which to file a claim for refund in respect of the amount of the adjustment where such adjustment is treated as if it were an overpayment. Where the amount of the adjustment is treated as if it were a deficiency and the taxpayer chooses to pay such deficiency and contest it by way of a claim for refund, the period of limitation upon filing a claim for refund will commence to run from the date of such payment. See section 6511 and corresponding provisions of prior revenue laws.

(c) The amount of an adjustment treated as if it were a deficiency or an overpayment, as the case may be, will bear interest and be subject to additions to the tax to the extent provided by the internal revenue laws applicable to deficiencies and overpayments for the taxable year with respect to which the adjustment is made. In the case of an adjustment resulting from an increase or decrease in a net operating loss or net capital loss which is carried back to the year of adjustment, interest shall not be collected or paid for any period prior to the close of the taxable year in which the net operating loss or net capital loss arises.

(d) If, as a result of a determination provided for in § 1.1313(a)-4, an adjustment has been made by the assessment and collection of a deficiency or the refund or credit of an overpayment, and subsequently such determination is altered or revoked, the amount of the adjustment ascertained under § 1.1314(a)-1 and § 1.1314(a)-2 shall be redetermined on the basis of such alteration or revocation, and any overpayment or deficiency resulting from such redetermination shall be refunded or credited, or assessed and collected, as the case may be, as an adjustment under section 1311. For the circumstances under which such an agreement can be altered or revoked, see paragraph (d) of § 1.1313(a)-4. [Reg. § 1.1314(b)-1.]

☐ [*T.D. 6162, 2-8-56. Amended by T.D. 7301, 1-3-74.*]

[Reg. § 1.1314(c)-1]

§ 1.1314(c)-1. Adjustment unaffected by other items.—(a) The amount of any adjustment ascertained under § 1.1314(a)-1 or § 1.1314(a)-2 shall not be diminished by any credit or set-off based upon any item other than the one that was the subject of the adjustment.

(b) The application of this section may be illustrated by the following examples:

Example (1). In the example set forth in paragraph (e) of § 1.1314(a)-1, if, after the amount of the adjustment had been ascertained, the taxpayer filed a refund claim for the amount thereof, the Commissioner could not diminish the amount of that claim by offsetting against it the amount of tax which should have been paid with respect to the $6,000 interest item omitted from gross income for the year 1949; nor could the court, if suit were brought on such claim for refund, offset against the amount of the adjustment the amount of tax which should have been paid with respect to such interest. Similarly, the amount of the refund could not be increased by any amount attributable to the taxpayer's failure to deduct the $4,500 interest paid in the year 1949.

Example (2). Assume that a taxpayer included in his gross income for the year 1953 an item which should have been included in his gross income for the year 1952. After the expiration of the period of limitations upon the assessment of a deficiency or the allowance of a refund for 1952, the taxpayer filed a claim for refund for the year 1953 on the ground that such item was not properly includible in gross income for that year. The claim for refund was allowed by the Commissioner and as a result of such determination an adjustment was authorized under section 1311 with respect to the tax for 1952. If, in such case, the Commissioner issued a notice of deficiency for the amount of the adjustment and the taxpayer contested the deficiency before the Tax Court of the United States, the taxpayer could not in such proceeding claim an offset based upon his failure to take an allowable deduction for the year 1952; nor could the Tax Court in its decision offset against the amount of the adjustment any overpayment for the year 1952 resulting from the failure to take such deduction.

(c) If the Commissioner has refunded the amount of an adjustment under section 1311, the amount so refunded may not subsequently be recovered by the Commissioner in any suit for erroneous refund based upon any item other than the one that was the subject of the adjustment.

Example. In the example set forth in paragraph (e) of § 1.1314(a)-1, if the Commissioner had refunded the amount of the adjustment, no part of the amount so refunded could subsequently be recovered by the Commissioner by a suit for erroneous refund based on the ground that there was no overpayment for 1949, as the taxpayer had failed to include in gross income the $6,000 item of interest received in that year.

(d) If the Commissioner has assessed and collected the amount of an adjustment under section 1311, no part thereof may be recovered by the taxpayer in any suit for refund based upon any item other than the one that was the subject of the adjustment.

Example. In example (2) of paragraph (b) of this section, if the taxpayer had paid the amount of the adjustment, he could not subsequently recover any part of such payment in a suit for refund based upon the failure to take an allowable deduction for the year 1952.

(e) If the amount of the adjustment is considered an overpayment, it may be credited, under applicable law and regulations, together with any interest allowed thereon, against any liability in respect of an internal revenue tax on the part of the person who made such overpayment. Likewise, if the amount of the adjustment is considered as a deficiency, any overpayment by the taxpayer of any internal revenue tax may be credited against the amount of such adjustment in accordance with the applicable law and regulations thereunder. (See section 6402 and the corresponding provisions of prior revenue laws.) Accordingly, it may be possible in one transaction between the Commissioner and the taxpayer to settle the taxpayer's tax liability for the year with respect to which the determination is made and to make the adjustment under section 1311 for the year with respect to which the error was made or for a year which is affected, or treated as affected, by a net operating loss deduction or a capital loss carryover from the year of the error. [Reg. § 1.1314(c)-1.]

☐ [*T.D.* 6162, 2-8-56.]

Claim of Right

[Reg. § 1.1341-1]

§ 1.1341-1. Restoration of amounts received or accrued under claim of right.—(a) *In general.*—(1) If, during the taxable year, the taxpayer is entitled under other provisions of chapter 1 of the Internal Revenue Code of 1954 to a deduction of more than $3,000 because of the restoration to another of an item which was included in the taxpayer's gross income for a prior taxable year (or years) under a claim of right, the tax imposed by chapter 1 of the Internal Revenue Code of 1954 for the taxable year shall be the tax provided in paragraph (b) of this section.

(2) For the purpose of this section "income included under a claim of right" means an item included in gross income because it appeared from all the facts available in the year of inclusion that the taxpayer had an unrestricted right to such item, and "restoration to another" means a restoration resulting because it was established after the close of such prior taxable year (or years) that the taxpayer did not have an unrestricted right to such item (or portion thereof).

(3) For purposes of determining whether the amount of a deduction described in section 1341(a)(2) exceeds $3,000 for the taxable year, there shall be taken into account the aggregate of all such deductions with respect to each item of income (described in section 1341(a)(1)) of the same class.

(b) *Determination of tax.*—(1) Under the circumstances described in paragraph (a) of this section, the tax imposed by chapter 1 of the Internal Revenue Code of 1954 for the taxable year shall be the lesser of—

(i) The tax for the taxable year computed under section 1341 (a)(4), that is, with the deduction taken into account, or

(ii) The tax for the taxable year computed under section 1341 (a)(5), that is, without taking such deduction into account, minus the decrease in tax (net of any increase in tax imposed by section 56, relating to the minimum tax for tax preferences) (under chapter 1 of the Internal Revenue Code of 1954, under chapter 1 (other than subchapter E) and subchapter E of chapter 2 of the Internal Revenue Code of 1939, or under the corresponding provisions of prior revenue laws) for the prior taxable year (or years) which would result solely from the exclusion from the gross income of all or that portion of the income included under a claim of right to which the deduction is attributable. For the purpose of this subdivision, the amount of the decrease in tax is not limited to the amount of the tax for the taxable year. See paragraph (i) of this section where the decrease in tax for the prior taxable year (or years) exceeds the tax for the taxable year.

(iii) For purposes of computing, under section 1341(a)(4) and subdivision (i) of this subparagraph, the tax for a taxable year beginning after December 31, 1961, if the deduction of the amount of the restoration results in a net operating loss for the taxable year of restoration, such net operating loss shall, pursuant to section 1341(b)(4)(A), be carried back to the same extent and in the same manner as is provided under section 172 (relating to the net operating loss deduction) and the regulations thereunder. If the aggregate decrease in tax for the taxable year (or years) to which such net operating loss is carried back is greater than the excess of—

(*a*) The amount of decrease in tax for a prior taxable year (or years) computed under section 1341(a)(5)(B), over

(*b*) The tax for the taxable year computed under section 1341(a)(5)(A),

the tax imposed for the taxable year under chapter 1 shall be the tax determined under section 1341(a)(4) and subdivision (i) of this subparagraph. If the tax imposed for the taxable year is determined under section 1341(a)(4) and subdivision (i) of this subparagraph, the decrease in tax for the taxable year (or years) to which the net operating loss is carried back shall be an overpayment of tax for the taxable year (or years) to which the net operating loss is carried back and shall be refunded or credited as an overpayment for such taxable year (or years). See section 6511(d)(2), relating to special period of limitation with respect to net operating loss carrybacks.

(2) Except as otherwise provided in section 1341(b)(4)(B) and paragraph (d)(1)(ii) and (4)(ii) of this section, if the taxpayer computes his tax for the taxable year under the provisions of section 1341(a)(5) and subparagraph (1)(ii) of this paragraph, the amount of the restoration shall not be taken into account in computing taxable income or loss for the taxable year, including the computation of any net operating loss carryback or carryover or any capital loss carryover. However, the amount of such restoration shall be taken into account in adjusting earnings and profits for the current taxable year.

(3) If the tax determined under subparagraph (1)(i) of this paragraph is the same as the tax determined under subparagraph (1)(ii) of

this paragraph, the tax imposed for the taxable year under chapter 1 shall be the tax determined under subparagraph (1)(i) of this paragraph, and section 1341 and this section shall not otherwise apply.

(4) After it has been determined whether the tax imposed for a taxable year of restoration beginning after December 31, 1961, shall be computed under the provisions of section 1341(a)(4) or under the provisions of section 1341(a)(5), the net operating loss, if any, which remains after the application of section 1341(b)(4)(A) or the net operating loss or capital loss, if any, which remains after the application of section 1341(b)(4)(B) shall be taken into account in accordance with the following rules—

(i) If it is determined that section 1341(a)(4) and subparagraph (1)(i) of this paragraph apply, then that portion, if any, of the net operating loss for the taxable year which remains after the application of section 1341(b)(4)(A) and subparagraph (1)(iii) of this paragraph shall be taken into account under section 172 for taxable years subsequent to the taxable year of restoration to the same extent and in the same manner as a net operating loss sustained in such taxable year of restoration. Thus, if the net operating loss for the taxable year of restoration (computed with the deduction referred to in section 1341(a)(4)) exceeds the taxable income (computed with the modifications prescribed in section 172) for the taxable year (or years) to which it is carried back, such excess shall be available as a carryover to taxable years subsequent to the taxable year of restoration.

(ii) If it is determined that section 1341(a)(5) and subparagraph (1)(ii) of this paragraph apply, then that portion, if any, of a net operating loss or capital loss which remains after the application of section 1341(b)(4)(B) and paragraph (d)(4) of this section shall be taken into account under section 172 or section 1212, as the case may be, for taxable years subsequent to the taxable year of restoration to the same extent and in the same manner as a net operating loss or capital loss sustained in the prior taxable year (or years). For example, if the net operating loss for the prior taxable year (computed with the exclusion referred to in section 1341(a)(5)(B)) exceeds the taxable income (computed with the modifications prescribed in section 172) for prior taxable years to which such net operating loss is carried back or carried over (including for this purpose the taxable year of restoration), such excess shall be available as a carryover to taxable years subsequent to the taxable year of restoration in accordance with the rules prescribed in section 172 which are applicable to such prior taxable year (or years).

(c) *Application to deductions which are capital in nature.*—Section 1341 and this section shall also apply to a deduction which is capital in nature otherwise allowable in the taxable year. If the deduction otherwise allowable is capital in nature, the determination of whether the taxpayer is entitled to the benefits of section 1341 and this section shall be made without regard to the net capital loss limitation imposed by section 1211. For example, if a taxpayer restores $4,000 in the taxable year and such amount is a long-term capital loss, the taxpayer will, nevertheless, be considered to have met the $3,000 deduction requirement for purposes of applying this section, although the full amount of the loss might not be allowable as a deduction for the taxable year. However, if the tax for the taxable year is computed with the deduction taken into account, the deduction allowable will be subject to the limitation on capital losses provided in section 1211, and the capital loss carryover provided in section 1212.

(d) *Determination of decrease in tax for prior taxable years.*—(1) *Prior taxable years.*—(i) Except as otherwise provided in subsection (ii) of this subparagraph, the prior taxable year (or years) referred to in paragraph (b) of this section is the year (or years) in which the item to which the deduction is attributable was included in gross income under a claim of right and, in addition, any other prior taxable year (or years) the tax for which will be affected by the exclusion from gross income in such prior taxable year (or years) of such income.

(ii) For purposes of applying section 1341(b)(4)(B) in computing the amount of the decrease referred to in paragraph (b)(1)(ii) of this section for any taxable year beginning after December 31, 1961, the term "prior taxable year (or years)" includes the taxable year of restoration. Under section 1341(b)(4)(B), for taxable years of restoration beginning after December 31, 1961, in any case where the exclusion referred to in section 1341(a)(5)(B) and paragraph (b)(1)(ii) of this section results in a net operating loss or capital loss for the prior taxable year (or years), such loss shall, for purposes of computing the decrease in tax for the prior taxable year (or years) under such section 1341(a)(5)(B) and such paragraph (b)(1)(ii) of this section, be carried back and carried over to the same extent and in the same manner as is provided under section 172 (relating to the net operating loss deduction) or section 1212 (relating to capital loss carryover), except that no carryover beyond the taxable year shall be taken into account. See subparagraph (4) of this paragraph for rules relating to the computation of the amount of decrease in tax.

(2) *Amount of exclusion from gross income in prior taxable years.*—(i) The amount to be excluded from gross income for the prior taxable year (or years) in determining the decrease in tax under section 1341(a)(5)(B) and paragraph (b)(1)(ii) of this section shall be the amount restored in the taxable year, but shall not exceed the amount included in gross income in the prior taxable year (or years) under the claim of right to

which the deduction for the restoration is attributable, and shall be adjusted as provided in subdivision (ii) of this subparagraph.

(ii) If the amount included in gross income for the prior taxable year (or years) under the claim of right in question was reduced in such year (or years) by a deduction allowed under section 1202 (or section 117(b) of the Internal Revenue Code of 1939 or corresponding provisions of prior revenue laws), then the amount determined under subdivision (i) of this subparagraph to be excluded from gross income for such year (or years) shall be reduced in the same proportion that the amount included in gross income under a claim of right was reduced.

(iii) The determination of the amount of the exclusion from gross income of the prior taxable year shall be made without regard to the capital loss limitation contained in section 1211 applicable in computing taxable income for the current taxable year. The amount of the exclusion from gross income in a prior taxable year (or years) shall not exceed the amount which would, but for the application of section 1211, be allowable as a deduction in the taxable year of restoration.

(iv) The rule provided in subdivision (iii) of this subparagraph may be illustrated as follows:

Example. For the taxable year 1952, and individual taxpayer had long-term capital gains of $50,000 and long-term capital losses of $10,000, a net long-term gain of $40,000. He also had other income of $5,000. In 1956, taxpayer restored the $50,000 of long-term gain. He had no capital gains or losses in 1956 but had other income of $5,000. If his tax liability for 1956, the taxable year of restoration, is computed by taking the deduction into account, the taxpayer would be entitled to a deduction under section 1211 of only $1,000 on account of the capital loss. However, if the taxpayer computes his tax under section 1341(a)(5) and paragraph (b)(1)(ii) of this

section, it is necessary to determine the decrease in tax for 1952. In such a determination, $50,000 is to be excluded from gross income for that year, resulting in a net capital loss for that year of $10,000, and a capital loss deduction of $1,000 under section 117(d) of the Internal Revenue Code of 1939 (corresponding to section 1211 of the Internal Revenue Code of 1954) with carryover privileges. The difference between the tax previously determined and the tax as recomputed after such exclusion for the years affected will be the amount of the decrease.

(3) *Determination of amount of deduction attributable to prior taxable years.*—(i) If the deduction otherwise allowable for the taxable year relates to income included in gross income under a claim of right in more than one prior taxable year and the amount attributable to each such prior taxable year cannot be readily identified, then the portion attributable to each such prior taxable year shall be that proportion of the deduction otherwise allowable for the taxable year which the amount of the income included under the claim of right in question for the prior taxable year bears to the total of all such income included under the claim of right for all such prior taxable years.

(ii) The rule provided in subdivision (i) of this subparagraph may be illustrated as follows:

Example. Under a claim of right, A included in his gross income over a period of three taxable years an aggregate of $9,000 for services to a certain employer, in amounts as follows: $2,000 for taxable year 1952, $4,000 for taxable year 1953, and $3,000 for taxable year 1954. In 1955 it is established that A must restore $6,750 of these amounts to his employer, and that A is entitled to a deduction of this amount in the taxable year 1955. The amount of the deduction attributable to each of the prior taxable years cannot be identified. Accordingly, the amount of the deduction attributable to each prior taxable year is:

$$1952—\$6,750 \times \frac{\$2,000}{\$9,000} = \$1,500$$

$$1953—\$6,750 \times \frac{\$4,000}{\$9,000} = \$3,000$$

$$1954—\$6,750 \times \frac{\$3,000}{\$9,000} = \$2,250$$

(4) *Computation of amount of decrease in tax.*—(i) In computing the amount of decrease in tax for a prior taxable year (or years) resulting from the exclusion from gross income of the income included under a claim of right, there must first be ascertained the amount of tax previously determined for the taxpayer for such prior taxable year (or years). The tax previously determined shall be the sum of the amounts shown by the taxpayer on his return or returns, plus any amounts which have been previously assessed (or collected without assessment) as deficiencies

or which appropriately should be assessed or collected, reduced by the amount of any refunds or credits which have previously been made or which appropriately should be made. For taxable years beginning after December 31, 1961, if the provisions of section 1341(b)(4)(B) are applicable, the tax previously determined shall include the tax for the taxable year of restoration computed without taking the deduction for the amount of the restoration into account. After the tax previously determined has been ascertained, a recomputation must then be made to determine the decrease in tax, if any, resulting from the exclusion from gross income of all or that portion of the income included under a claim of right to which the deduction otherwise allowable in the taxable year is attributable.

(ii) No item other than the exclusion of the income previously included under a claim of right shall be considered in computing the amount of decrease in tax if reconsideration of such other item is prevented by the operation of any provision of the internal revenue laws or any other rule of law. However, if the amounts of other items in the return are dependent upon the amount of adjusted gross income, taxable income, or net income (such as charitable contributions, foreign tax credit, deductions for depletion, and net operating loss), appropriate adjustment shall be made as part of the computation of the decrease in tax. For the purpose of determining the decrease in tax for the prior taxable year (or years) which would result from the exclusion from gross income of the item included under a claim of right, the exclusion of such item shall be given effect not only in the prior taxable year in which it was included in gross income but in all other prior taxable years (including the taxable year of restoration if such

year begins after December 31, 1961, and section 1341(b)(4)(B) applies, see subparagraph (1)(ii) of this paragraph) affected by the inclusion of the item (for example, prior taxable years affected by a net operating loss carryback or carryover or capital loss carryover).

(iii) The rules provided in this subparagraph may be illustrated as follows:

Example (1). For the taxable year 1954, a corporation had taxable income of $35,000, on which it paid a tax of $12,700. Included in gross income for the year was $20,000 received under a claim of rights as royalties. In 1957, the corporation is required to return $10,000 of the royalties. It otherwise has taxable income in 1957 of $5,000, so that without the application of section 1341 it has a net operating loss of $5,000 in that year. Facts also come to light in 1957 which entitle the corporation to an additional deduction of $5,000 for 1954. When a computation is made under paragraph (b)(1)(i) of this section, the corporation has no tax for the taxable year 1957. When a computation is made under paragraph (b)(1)(ii) of this section, the tax for 1957, without taking the restoration into account, is $1,500, based on a taxable income of $5,000. The decrease in tax for 1954 is computed as follows:

Tax shown on return for 1954		$12,700
Taxable income for 1954 upon which tax shown on return was based		$35,000
Less: Additional deduction (on account of which credit or refund could be made)		5,000
Total		$30,000
Tax on $30,000 (adjusted taxable income for 1954)		10,100
Tax on $30,000 (adjusted taxable income for 1954)		$10,100
Taxable income for 1954, as adjusted	$30,000	
Less exclusion of amount restored	10,000	
Taxable income for 1954 by applying paragraph (b)(1)(ii) of this section	$20,000	
Tax on $20,000		$6,000
Decrease in tax for 1954 by applying paragraph (b)(1)(ii) of this section		$4,100
Tax for 1957 without taking the restoration into account		1,500
Amount by which decrease exceeds the tax for 1957 computed without taking restoration into account		$2,600

(The $2,600 is treated as having been paid on the last day prescribed by law for the payment of the tax for 1957 and is available as a refund. In addition the taxpayer has made an overpayment of $2,600 ($12,700 less $10,100) for 1954 because of the additional deduction of $5,000.)

Example (2). Assume the same facts as in example (1) except that, instead of the corporation being entitled to an additional deduction of $5,000 for 1954, it is determined that the corporation failed to include an item of $5,000 in gross income for that year. The decrease in tax for 1954 is computed as follows:

Tax shown on return for 1954		$12,700
Taxable income for 1954 upon which tax shown on return was based		$35,000
Plus: Additional income (on account of which deficiency assessment could be made)		5,000
Total		$40,000
Tax on $40,000 (adjusted taxable income for 1954)		$15,300
Tax on $40,000 (adjusted taxable income for 1954)		$15,300
Taxable income for 1954 as adjusted	$40,000	
Less: Exclusion of amount restored	10,000	
Taxable income for 1954 by applying paragraph (b)(1)(ii) of this section	30,000	

Tax on $30,000	10,100
Decrease in tax for 1954 by applying paragraph (b)(1)(ii) of this section	$ 5,200
Tax for 1957 without taking the restoration into account	1,500
Amount by which decrease exceeds the tax for 1957 computed without taking the restoration into account	$ 3,700

(The $3,700 is treated as having been paid on the last day prescribed by law for the payment of the tax for 1957 and is available as a refund. In addition the taxpayer has a deficiency of $2,600 ($15,300 less $12,700) for 1954 because of the additional income of $5,000.)

Example (3). For the taxable year 1954, a corporation had taxable income of $25,000, on which it paid a tax of $7,500. Included in gross income for the year was $10,000 received under a claim of right as commissions. In 1956, the corporation is required to return $5,000 of the commissions. The corporation has a net operating loss of $10,000 for 1956, excluding the deduction for the $5,000 restored. When a computation is made under either paragraph (b)(1)(i) or paragraph (b)(1)(ii) of this section, the corporation has no tax for the taxable year 1956. The decrease in tax for 1954 is computed as follows:

Tax shown on return for 1954		$7,500
Taxable income for 1954 upon which tax shown on return was based		$25,000
Less: Additional deduction (on account of net operating loss carryback from 1956)		10,000
Net income as adjusted		$15,000
Tax on $15,000 (adjusted taxable income for 1954)		4,500
Tax on $15,000 (adjusted taxable income for 1954)		$4,500
Taxable income for 1954, as adjusted	$15,000	
Less: Exclusion of amount restored	5,000	
Taxable income for 1954 by applying paragraph (b)(1)(ii) of this section	10,000	
Tax on $10,000		3,000
Decrease in tax for 1954 by applying paragraph (b)(1)(ii) of this section		$1,500
Tax for 1956 without taking the restoration into account		None
Amount by which decrease exceeds the tax for 1956 computed without taking the restoration into account		$1,500

(The $1,500 is treated as having been paid on the last day prescribed by law for the payment of the tax for 1956 and is available as a refund. In addition, the taxpayer has an overpayment of $3,000 ($7,500 less $4,500) for 1954 because of the net operating loss deduction of $10,000.)

Example (4). For the taxable year 1946 a married man with no dependents, who kept his books on the cash receipts and disbursements basis, filed a return (claiming two exemptions) disclosing adjusted gross income of $42,000, deductions amounting to $12,000, and a net income of $30,000. Gross income included among other items salary in the amount of $15,000 and rental income in the amount of $5,000. During the taxable year he donated $10,000 to the American Red Cross and in his return claimed a deduction of $6,300 on account thereof, representing the maximum deduction allowable under the 15-percent limitation imposed by section 23(o) of the Internal Revenue Code of 1939 for the year 1946. In computing his net income he omitted interest income amounting to $6,000 and neglected to take a deduction for interest paid in the amount of $4,500. The return disclosed a tax liability of $11,970, which was assessed and paid. In 1955, after the expiration of the period of limitations upon the assessment of a deficiency or the allowance of a refund for 1946, the taxpayer had to restore the $5,000 included in his gross income in 1946 as rental income. The amount of the decrease in tax for 1946 is $2,467.62, computed as follows:

Tax previously determined for 1946	$11,970.00
Net income for 1946 upon which tax previously determined was based	$30,000.00
Less: Rents included under claim of right	$ 5,000.00
Balance	25,000.00
Adjustment for contributions (add 15 percent of $5,000)	750.00
Net income as adjusted	25,750.00
Tax on $25,750	9,502.38
Amount of decrease in tax for 1946:	
Tax previously determined	$11,970.00
Tax as recomputed	9,502.38
Decrease in tax	$ 2,467.62

The recomputation to determine the amount of the decrease in tax for 1946 does not take into consideration the barred item of $6,000 representing interest received, which was omitted from gross income, or the barred item of $4,500 representing interest paid for which no deduction was allowed. See subdivision (ii) of this subparagraph.

Example (5). (a) Facts. For the taxable year 1959, a corporation reporting income on the calendar year basis had taxable income of $20,000 on which it paid a tax of $6,000. Included in gross income for such year was $100,000 received under a claim of right as royalties. For each of its taxable years 1956, 1957, 1958, 1960, 1961, and 1962, the corporation had taxable income of $10,000 on which it paid tax of $3,000 for each year. In 1963, the corporation returns the entire amount of $100,000 of the royalties. In such taxable year the corporation has taxable income of $25,000 (without taking the deduction of $100,000 into account), and has a net operating loss of $75,000 (taking the deduction of $100,000 into account). In determining whether section 1341(a)(4) or section 1341(a)(5) applies, the corporation will compute the lesser amount of tax referred to in section 1341(a) by applying the rules provided in section 1341(b)(4).

(b) Tax under section 1341(a)(4) and (b)(4)(A). The net operating loss of $75,000 for 1963 (taking into account the deduction of $100,000) is carried back to the three taxable years (1960, 1961, and 1962) in the manner provided under section 172. For purposes of this example it is assumed that no modifications under section 172 are necessary. Since the aggregate taxable income for such three taxable years

is only $30,000 the entire taxable income for such years is eliminated by the carryback, and the corporation would be entitled to a refund of the tax for such years in the aggregate amount of $9,000. (In addition, the remaining $45,000 of the net operating loss for 1963 would be available as a carryover to taxable years after the taxable year (1963) to the extent and in the manner provided by section 172.)

(c) Tax under section 1341(a)(5) and (b)(4)(B). The tax for the taxable year (1963) on $25,000 of taxable income (computed without the deduction of $100,000) is $7,500. The exclusion of $100,000 from gross income for the taxable year 1959 (the year in which the item was included) results in a net operating loss of $80,000 for such year ($20,000 taxable income minus the $100,000 exclusion, no adjustments under section 172 being necessary), thus decreasing the tax for such year by the entire amount of $6,000 paid. The resulting net operating loss of $80,000 for 1959 is available as a carryback to 1956, 1957, and 1958, and as a carryover to 1960, 1961, 1962, and 1963. For purposes of this example it is assumed that no modifications under section 172 are necessary. Since the aggregate taxable income for such taxable years is $85,000, all except $5,000 of the 1963 taxable income is eliminated by such carryback and carryover. The tax on such remaining $5,000 of taxable income for 1963 is $1,500, thus decreasing the tax determined for such year by $6,000 ($7,500 minus $1,500). Under section 1341(a)(5) and (b)(4)(B), the decrease in tax for the prior taxable years exceeds the tax for the taxable year of restoration computed without the deduction of the amount of the restoration by $22,500, computed as follows:

Tax for taxable year 1963 (on taxable income of $25,000 without the deduction)			$7,500
Decrease in tax for prior taxable years:			
Due to exclusion (1959)		$6,000	
Due to net operating loss carryback:			
1956	$3,000		
1957	3,000		
1958	3,000	$9,000	
Due to net operating loss carryover:			
1961	3,000		
1962	3,000		
1963	6,000	15,000	30,000
Excess of the decrease in tax for the prior taxable years over the tax for taxable year 1963 ($30,000 less $7,500 tax for the taxable year).			$22,500

(d) Application of section 1341(a)(4) or section 1341(a)(5). Since the computation under section 1341(a)(4) and (b)(4)(A) results in an available refund of only $9,000 tax for the taxable years to which the net operating loss for 1963 is carried back, and since the computation under section 1341(a)(5) and (b)(4)(B) results in an overpayment of $22,500, it is determined that section 1341(a)(5) applies. Accordingly, the $22,500 is treated as having been paid on the last day prescribed by law for the payment of tax for 1963 and is available as a refund.

(e) Method of accounting.—The provisions of section 1341 and this section shall be applicable in the case of a taxpayer on the cash receipts and disbursements method of accounting only to the taxable year in which the item of income included in a prior year (or years) under a claim of right is actually repaid. However, in the case of a taxpayer on the cash receipts and disbursements method of accounting who constructively received an item of income under a claim of right and included such item of income in gross income in a prior year (or years), the provisions of section 1341 and this section shall be applicable

Reg. §1.1341-1(e)

to the taxable year in which the taxpayer is required to relinquish his right to receive such item of income. Such provisions shall be applicable in the case of other taxpayers only to the taxable year which is the proper taxable year (under the method of accounting used by the taxpayer in computing taxable income) for taking into account the deduction resulting from the restoration of the item of income included in a prior year (or years) under a claim of right. For example, if the taxpayer is on an accrual method of accounting, the provisions of this section shall apply to the year in which the obligation properly accrues for the repayment of the item included under a claim of right.

(f) *Inventory items, stock in trade, and property held primarily for sale in the ordinary course of trade or business.*—(1) Except for amounts specified in subparagraphs (2) and (3) of this paragraph, the provisions of section 1341 and this section do not apply to deductions attributable to items which were included in gross income by reason of the sale or other disposition of stock in trade of the taxpayer (or other property of a kind which would properly have been included in the inventory of the taxpayer if on hand at the close of the prior taxable year) or property held by the taxpayer primarily for sale to customers in the ordinary course of the taxpayer's trade or business. This section is, therefore, not applicable to sales returns and allowances and similar items.

(2)(i) In the case of taxable years beginning after December 31, 1957, the provisions of section 1341 and this section apply to deductions which arise out of refunds or repayments with respect to rates made by a regulated public utility, as defined in section 7701(a)(33) without regard to the limitation contained in the last two sentences thereof (for taxable years beginning before January 1, 1964, as defined in 1503(c)(1) or (3) and paragraph (g) of § 1.1502-2A (as contained in the 26 C.F.R. edition revised as of April 1, 1996)), if such refunds or repayments are required to be made by the Government, political subdivision, agency, or instrumentality referred to in such section, or are required to be made by an order of a court, or are made in settlement of litigation or under threat or imminence of litigation. Thus, deductions attributable to refunds of charges for the sale of natural gas under rates approved temporarily by a proper governmental authority are, in the case of taxable years beginning after December 31, 1957, eligible for the benefits of section 1341 and this section, if such refunds are required by the governmental authority, or by an order of a court, or are made in settlement of litigation or under threat or imminence of litigation.

(ii) In the case of taxable years beginning before January 1, 1958, the provisions of section 1341 and this section apply to deductions which arise out of refunds or repayments (whether or not with respect to rates) made by a regulated public utility, as defined in section 7701(a)(33)

without regard to the limitation contained in the last two sentences thereof (for taxable years beginning before January 1, 1964, as defined in section 1503(c)(1) or (3) and paragraph (g) of § 1.1502-2A), if such refunds or repayments are required to be made by the Government, political subdivision, agency, or instrumentality referred to in such section. Thus, in the case of taxable years beginning before January 1, 1958, deductions attributable to refunds or repayments may be eligible for the benefits of section 1341 and this section, even though such refunds or repayments are not with respect to rates. On the other hand, in the case of such taxable years, section 1341 and this section do not apply to any deduction which arises out of a refund or repayment (whether or not with respect to rates) which is required to be made by an order of a court, or which is made in settlement of litigation or under threat or imminence of litigation.

(3) The provisions of section 1341 and this section apply to a deduction which arises out of a payment or repayment made pursuant to a price redetermination provision in a subcontract—

(i) If such subcontract was entered into before January 1, 1958, between persons other than those bearing a relationship set forth in section 267(b);

(ii) If such subcontract is subject to statutory renegotiation; and

(iii) If section 1481 (relating to mitigation of effect of renegotiation of Government contracts) does not apply to such payment or repayment solely because such payment or repayment is not paid or repaid to the United States or any agency thereof.

Thus, a taxpayer who enters into a subcontract to furnish items to a prime contractor with the United States may, pursuant to a price redetermination provision in the subcontract, be required to refund an amount to the prime contractor or to another subcontractor. Since the refund would be made directly to the prime contractor or to another subcontractor, and not directly to the United States, the taxpayer would be unable to avail himself of the benefits of section 1481. However, the provisions of section 1341 and this section will apply in such a case, if the conditions set forth in subdivisions (i), (ii), and (iii) of this subparagraph are met. For provisions relating to the mitigation of the effect of a redetermination of price with respect to subcontracts entered into after December 31, 1957, when repayment is made to a party other than the United States or any agency thereof, see section 1482.

(g) *Bad debts.*—The provisions of section 1341 and this section do not apply to deductions attributable to bad debts.

(h) *Legal fees and other expenses.*—Section 1341 and this section do not apply to legal fees or other expenses incurred by a taxpayer in contesting the restoration of an item previously included in income. This rule may be illustrated by the following example:

Example. A sold his personal residence to B in a prior taxable year and realized a capital gain on the sale. C claimed that under an agreement with A he was entitled to a 5-percent share of the purchase price since he brought the parties together and was instrumental in closing the sale. A rejected C's demand and included the entire amount of the capital gain in gross income for the year of sale. C instituted action and in the taxable year judgment is rendered against A who pays C the amount involved. In addition, A pays legal fees in the taxable year which were incurred in the defense of the action. Section 1341 applies to the payment of the 5-percent share of the purchase price to C. However, the payment of the legal fees, whether or not otherwise deductible, does not constitute an item restored for purposes of section 1341 (a) and paragraph (a) of this section.

(i) *Refunds.*—If the decrease in tax for the prior taxable year (or years) determined under section 1341(a)(5)(B) and paragraph (b)(1)(ii) of this section exceeds the tax imposed by chapter 1 of the Code for the taxable year computed without the deduction, and for taxable years beginning after December 31, 1961, if such excess is greater than the decrease in tax for the taxable year (or years) to which the net operating loss described in section 1341(b)(4)(A) and paragraph (b)(1)(iii) of this section is carried back, such excess shall be considered to be a payment of tax for the taxable year of restoration. Such payment is deemed to have been made on the last day prescribed by law for the payment of tax for the taxable year and shall be refunded or credited in the same manner as if it were an overpayment of tax for such taxable year. However, no interest shall be allowed or paid if such an excess results from the application of section 1341(a)(5)(B) in the case of a deduction described in paragraph (f)(3) of this section (relating to payments or repayments pursuant to price redetermination). If the tax for the taxable year of restoration is computed under section 1341(a)(4) and results in a decrease in tax for the taxable year (or years) to which a net operating loss described in section 1341(b)(4)(A) is carried back, see paragraph (b)(1)(iii) of this section. [Reg. § 1.1341-1.]

□ [*T.D.* 6242, 7-19-57. *Amended by T.D.* 6617, 11-6-62; *T.D.* 6747, 7-20-64; *T.D.* 7244, 12-29-72; *T.D.* 7564, 9-11-78 *and T.D.* 8677, 6-26-96.]

S Corporations and Their Shareholders

[Reg. § 1.1361-0]

§ 1.1361-0. Table of contents.—This section lists captions contained in §§ 1.1361-1, 1.1361-2, 1.1361-3, 1.1361-4, 1.1361-5, and 1.1361-6.

[Reg. § 1.1361-0.]

☐ [*T.D. 8104, 9-25-86. Amended by T.D. 8419, 5-28-92; T.D. 8600, 7-20-95; T.D. 8869, 1-20-2000; T.D. 8994, 5-13-2002 and T.D. 9422, 8-13-2008.*]

[Reg. § 1.1361-1]

§ 1.1361-1. S corporation defined.—(a) *In general.*—For purposes of this title, with respect to any taxable year

(1) The term *S corporation* means a small business corporation (as defined in paragraph (b) of this section) for which an election under section 1362(a) is in effect for that taxable year.

(2) The term *C corporation* means a corporation that is not an S corporation for that taxable year.

(b) *Small business corporation defined.*—(1) *In general.*—For purposes of subchapter S, chapter 1 of the Code and the regulations thereunder, the term *small business corporation* means a domestic corporation that is not an ineligible corporation (as defined in section 1361(b)(2)) and that does not have—

(i) More than the number of shareholders provided in section 1361(b)(1)(A);

(ii) As a shareholder, a person (other than an estate, a trust described in section 1361(c)(2), or, for taxable years beginning after December 31, 1997, an organization described in section 1361(c)(6)) who is not an individual;

(iii) A nonresident alien as a shareholder; or

(iv) More than one class of stock.

(2) *Estate in bankruptcy.*—The term *estate*, for purposes of this paragraph, includes the estate of an individual in a case under title 11 of the United States Code.

(3) *Treatment of restricted stock.*—For purposes of subchapter S, stock that is issued in connection with the performance of services (within the meaning of §1.83-3(f)) and that is substantially nonvested (within the meaning of §1.83-3(b)) is not treated as outstanding stock of the corporation, and the holder of that stock is not treated as a shareholder solely by reason of holding the stock, unless the holder makes an election with respect to the stock under section 83(b). In the event of such an election, the stock is treated as outstanding stock of the corporation, and the holder of the stock is treated as a shareholder for purposes of subchapter S. See paragraphs (l)(1) and (3) of this section for rules for determining whether substantially nonvested stock with respect to which an election under section 83(b) has been made is treated as a second class of stock.

(4) *Treatment of deferred compensation plans.*—For purposes of subchapter S, an instrument, obligation, or arrangement is not outstanding stock if it—

(i) Does not convey the right to vote;

(ii) Is an unfunded and unsecured promise to pay money or property in the future;

(iii) Is issued to an individual who is an employee in connection with the performance of services for the corporation or to an individual who is an independent contractor in connection with the performance of services for the corporation (and is not excessive by reference to the services performed); and

(iv) Is issued pursuant to a plan with respect to which the employee or independent contractor is not taxed currently on income.

A deferred compensation plan that has a current payment feature (*e.g.*, payment of dividend equivalent amounts that are taxed currently as compensation) is not for that reason excluded from this paragraph (b)(4).

(5) *Treatment of straight debt.*—For purposes of subchapter S, an instrument or obligation that satisfies the definition of straight debt in paragraph (l)(5) of this section is not treated as outstanding stock.

(6) *Effective date provision.*—Section 1.1361-1(b) generally applies to taxable years of a corporation beginning on or after May 28, 1992. However, a corporation and its shareholders may apply this §1.1361-1(b) to prior taxable years. In addition, substantially nonvested stock issued on or before May 28, 1992, that has been treated as outstanding by the corporation is treated as outstanding for purposes of subchapter S, and the fact that it is substantially

nonvested and no section 83(b) election has been made with respect to it will not cause the stock to be treated as a second class of stock.

(c) *Domestic corporation.*—For purposes of paragraph (b) of this section, the term *domestic corporation* means a domestic corporation as defined in §301.7701-5 of this chapter, and the term *corporation* includes an entity that is classified as an association taxable as a corporation under §301.7701-2 of this chapter.

(d) *Ineligible corporation.*—(1) *General rule.*—Except as otherwise provided in this paragraph (d), the term *ineligible corporation* means a corporation that is—

(i) For taxable years beginning on or after January 1, 1997, a financial institution that uses the reserve method of accounting for bad debts described in section 585 (for taxable years beginning prior to January 1, 1997, a financial institution to which section 585 applies (or would apply but for section 585(c)) or to which section 593 applies);

(ii) An insurance company subject to tax under subchapter

(iii) A corporation to which an election under section 936 applies; or

(iv) A DISC or former DISC.

(2) *Exceptions.*—See the special rules and exceptions provided in sections 6(c)(2), (3) and (4) of Pub. L. 97-354 that are applicable for certain casualty insurance companies and qualified oil corporations.

(e) *Number of shareholders.*—(1) *General rule.*—A corporation does not qualify as a small business corporation if it has more than the number of shareholders provided in section 1361(b)(1)(A). Ordinarily, the person who would have to include in gross income dividends distributed with respect to the stock of the corporation (if the corporation were a C corporation) is considered to be the shareholder of the corporation. For example, if stock (owned other than by a husband and wife or members of a family described in section 1361(c)(1)) is owned by tenants in common or joint tenants, each tenant in common or joint tenant is generally considered to be a shareholder of the corporation. (For special rules relating to stock owned by husband and wife or members of a family, see paragraphs (e)(2) and (3) of this section, respectively; for special rules relating to restricted stock, see paragraphs (b)(3) and (6) of this section.) The person for whom stock of a corporation is held by a nominee, guardian, custodian, or an agent is considered to be the shareholder of the corporation for purposes of this paragraph (e) and paragraphs (f) and (g) of this section. For example, a partnership may be a nominee of S corporation stock for a person who qualifies as a shareholder of an S corporation. However, if the partnership is the beneficial owner of the stock, then the partnership is the shareholder, and the corporation does not qualify as a small business corporation. In addition, in the case of stock held for a minor under a uniform transfers to minors act or similar statute, the minor and not the custodian is the shareholder. Except as otherwise provided in paragraphs (h) and (j) of this section, and for purposes of this paragraph (e) and paragraphs (f) and (g) of this section, if stock is held by a decedent's estate or a trust described in section 1361(c)(2)(A)(ii) or (iii), the estate or trust (and not the beneficiaries of the estate or trust) is considered to be the shareholder; however, if stock is held by a subpart E trust (which includes a voting trust) or an electing QSST described in section 1361(d)(1), the deemed owner of the trust is considered to be the shareholder. If stock is held by an ESBT described in section 1361(c)(2)(A)(v), each potential current beneficiary of the trust shall be treated as a shareholder, except that the trust shall be treated as the shareholder during any period in which there is no potential current beneficiary of the trust. If stock is held by a trust described in section 1361(c)(2)(A)(vi), the individual for whose benefit the trust was created shall be treated as the shareholder. See paragraph (h) of this section for special rules relating to trusts.

(2) *Special rules relating to stock owned by husband and wife.*—For purposes of paragraph (e)(1) of this section, stock owned by a husband and wife (or by either or both of their estates) is treated as if owned by one shareholder, regardless of the form in which they own the stock. For example, if husband and wife are owners of a subpart E trust, they will be treated as one individual. Both husband and wife must be U.S. citizens or residents, and a decedent spouse's estate must not be a foreign estate as defined in section 7701(a)(31). The treatment described in this paragraph (e)(2) will cease upon dissolution of the marriage for any reason other than death.

(3) *Special rules relating to stock owned by members of a family.*—(i) *In general.*—For purposes of paragraph (e)(1) of this section, stock owned by members of a family is treated as owned by one shareholder. Members of a family include a common ancestor, any lineal descendant of the common ancestor (without any generational limit), and any spouse (or former spouse) of the common ancestor or of any lineal descendants of the common ancestor. An individual shall not be considered to be a common ancestor if, on the applicable date, the individual is more than six generations removed from the youngest generation of shareholders who would be members of the family determined by deeming that individual as the common ancestor. For purposes of this six-generation test, a spouse (or former spouse) is treated as being of the same generation as the individual to whom the spouse is or was married. This test is applied on the

latest of the date the election under section 1362(a) is made for the corporation, the earliest date that a member of the family (determined by deeming that individual as the common ancestor) holds stock in the corporation, or October 22, 2004. For this purpose, the date the election under section 1362(a) is made for the corporation is the effective date of the election, not the date it is signed or received by any person. The test is only applied as of the applicable date, and lineal descendants (and spouses) more than six generations removed from the common ancestor will be treated as members of the family even if they acquire stock in the corporation after that date. The members of a family are treated as one shareholder under this paragraph (e)(3) solely for purposes of section 1361(b)(1)(A), and not for any other purpose, whether under section 1361 or any other provision. Specifically, each member of the family who owns or is deemed to own stock must meet the requirements of sections 1361(b)(1)(B) and (C) (regarding permissible shareholders) and section 1362(a)(2) (regarding shareholder consents to an S corporation election). Although a person may be a member of more than one family under this paragraph (e)(3), each family (not all of whose members are also members of the other family) will be treated as one shareholder. For purposes of this paragraph (e)(3), any legally adopted child of an individual, any child who is lawfully placed with an individual for legal adoption by that individual, and any eligible foster child of an individual (within the meaning of section 152(f)(1)(C)), shall be treated as a child of such individual by blood.

(ii) *Certain entities treated as members of a family.*—For purposes of this paragraph (e)(3), the estate or trust (described in section 1361(c)(2)(A)(ii) or (iii)) of a deceased member of the family will be considered to be a member of the family during the period in which the estate or such trust (if the trust is described in section 1361(c)(2)(A)(ii) or (iii)), holds stock in the S corporation. The members of the family also will include—

(A) In the case of an ESBT, each potential current beneficiary who is a member of the family;

(B) In the case of a QSST, the income beneficiary who makes the QSST election, if that income beneficiary is a member of the family;

(C) In the case of a trust created primarily to exercise the voting power of stock transferred to it, each beneficiary who is a member of the family;

(D) The individual for whose benefit a trust described in section 1361(c)(2)(A)(vi) was created, if that individual is a member of the family;

(E) The deemed owner of a trust described in section 1361(c)(2)(A)(i) if that deemed owner is a member of the family; and

Reg. §1.1361-1(e)(3)(ii)(E)

(F) The owner of an entity disregarded as an entity separate from its owner under §301.7701-3 of this chapter, if that owner is a member of the family.

(f) *Shareholder must be an individual or estate.*— Except as otherwise provided in paragraph (e)(1) of this section (relating to nominees), paragraph (h) of this section (relating to certain trusts), and, for taxable years beginning after December 31, 1997, section 1361(c)(6) (relating to certain exempt organizations), a corporation in which any shareholder is a corporation, partnership, or trust does not qualify as a small business corporation.

(g) *Nonresident alien shareholder.*—(1) *General rule.*—(i) A corporation having a shareholder who is a nonresident alien as defined in section 7701(b)(1)(B) does not qualify as a small business corporation. If a U.S. shareholder's spouse is a nonresident alien who has a current ownership interest (as opposed, for example, to a survivorship interest) in the stock of the corporation by reason of any applicable law, such as a state community property law or a foreign country's law, the corporation does not qualify as a small business corporation from the time the nonresident alien spouse acquires the interest in the stock. If a corporation's S election is inadvertently terminated as a result of a nonresident alien spouse being considered a shareholder, the corporation may request relief under section 1362(f).

(ii) The following examples illustrate this paragraph (g)(1)(i):

Example 1. In 1990, W, a U.S. citizen, married H, a citizen of a foreign country. At all times H is a nonresident alien under section 7701(b)(1)(B). Under the foreign country's law, all property acquired by a husband and wife during the existence of the marriage is community property and owned jointly by the husband and wife. In 1996 while residing in the foreign country, W formed X, a U.S. corporation, and X simultaneously filed an election to be an S corporation. X issued all of its outstanding stock in W's name. Under the foreign country's law, X's stock became the community property of and jointly owned by H and W. Thus, X does not meet the definition of a small business corporation and therefore could not file a valid S election because H, a nonresident alien, has a current interest in the stock.

Example 2. Assume the same facts as *Example 1*, except that in 1991, W and H filed a section 6013(g) election allowing them to file a joint U.S. tax return and causing H to be treated as a U.S. resident for purposes of chapters 1, 5, and 24 of the Internal Revenue Code. The section 6013(g) election applies to the taxable year for which made and to all subsequent taxable years until terminated. Because H is treated as a U.S. resident under section 6013(g), X does meet the definition of a small business corporation. Thus,

the election filed by X to be an S corporation is valid.

(2) *Special rule for dual residents.*—[Reserved]

(h) *Special rules relating to trusts.*—(1) *General rule.*—In general, a trust is not a permitted small business corporation shareholder. However, except as provided in paragraph (h)(2) of this section, the following trusts are permitted shareholders:

(i) *Qualified subpart E trust.*—A trust all of which is treated (under subpart E, part I, subchapter J, chapter 1) as owned by an individual (whether or not the grantor) who is a citizen or resident of the United States (a qualified subpart E trust). This requirement applies only during the period that the trust holds S corporation stock.

(ii) *Subpart E trust ceasing to be a qualified subpart E trust after the death of deemed owner.*—A trust that was a qualified subpart E trust immediately before the death of the deemed owner and that continues in existence after the death of the deemed owner, but only for the 2-year period beginning on the day of the deemed owner's death. A trust is considered to continue in existence if the trust continues to hold the stock pursuant to the terms of the will or the trust agreement, or if the trust continues to hold the stock during a period reasonably necessary to wind up the affairs of the trust. See §1.641(b)-3 for rules concerning the termination of trusts for federal income tax purposes.

(iii) *Electing qualified subchapter S trusts.*— A qualified subchapter S trust (QSST) that has a section 1361(d)(2) election in effect (an electing QSST). See paragraph (j) of this section for rules concerning QSSTs including the manner for making the section 1361(d)(2) election.

(iv) *Testamentary trusts.*—A trust (other than a qualified subpart E trust, an electing QSST, or an electing small business trust) to which S corporation stock is—

(A) Transferred pursuant to the terms of a will, but only for the 2-year period beginning on the day the stock is transferred to the trust except as otherwise provided in paragraph (h)(3)(i)(D) of this section; or

(B) Transferred pursuant to the terms of an electing trust as defined in §1.645-1(b)(2) during the election period as defined in §1.645-1(b)(6), or deemed to be distributed at the close of the last day of the election period pursuant to §1.645-1(h)(1), but in each case only for the 2-year period beginning on the day the stock is transferred or deemed distributed to the trust except as otherwise provided in paragraph (h)(3)(i)(D) of this section.

(v) *Qualified voting trusts.*—A trust created primarily to exercise the voting power of S corporation stock transferred to it. To qualify as a voting trust for purposes of this section (a qualified voting trust), the beneficial owners must be treated as the owners of their respective portions of the trust under subpart E and the trust must have been created pursuant to a written trust agreement entered into by the shareholders, that—

(A) Delegates to one or more trustees the right to vote;

(B) Requires all distributions with respect to the stock of the corporation held by the trust to be paid to, or on behalf of, the beneficial owners of that stock;

(C) Requires title and possession of that stock to be delivered to those beneficial owners upon termination of the trust; and

(D) Terminates, under its terms or by state law, on or before a specific date or event.

(vi) *Electing small business trusts.*—An electing small business trust (ESBT) under section 1361(e). See paragraph (m) of this section for rules concerning ESBTs including the manner of making the election to be an ESBT under section 1361(e)(3).

(vii) *Individual retirement accounts.*—In the case of a corporation which is a bank (as defined in section 581) or a depository institution holding company (as defined in section 3(w)(1) of the Federal Deposit Insurance Act (12 U.S.C. 1813(w)(1)), a trust which constitutes an individual retirement account under section 408(a), including one designated as a Roth IRA under section 408A, but only to the extent of the stock held by such trust in such bank or company as of October 22, 2004. Individual retirement accounts (including Roth IRAs) are not otherwise eligible S corporation shareholders.

(2) *Foreign trust.*—For purposes of paragraph (h)(1) of this section, in any case where stock is held by a foreign trust as defined in section 7701(a)(31), the trust is considered to be the shareholder and is an ineligible shareholder. Thus, even if a foreign trust qualifies as a subpart E trust (e.g., a qualified voting trust), any corporation in which the trust holds stock does not qualify as a small business corporation.

(3) *Determination of shareholders.*—(i) *General rule.*—For purposes of paragraph (b) of this section (qualification as a small business corporation), and, except as provided in paragraph (h)(3)(ii) of this section, for purposes of sections 1366 (relating to the pass-through of items of income, loss, deduction, or credit), 1367 (relating to adjustments to basis of shareholder's stock), and 1368 (relating to distributions), the shareholder of S corporation stock held by a trust that is a permitted shareholder under paragraph (h)(1) of this section is determined as follows:

(A) If stock is held by a qualified subpart E trust, the deemed owner of the trust is treated as the shareholder.

(B) If stock is held by a trust defined in paragraph (h)(1)(ii) of this section, the estate of the deemed owner is generally treated as the shareholder as of the day of the deemed owner's death. However, if stock is held by such a trust in a community property state, the decedent's estate is the shareholder only of the portion of the trust included in the decedent's gross estate (and the surviving spouse continues to be the shareholder of the portion of the trust owned by that spouse under the applicable state's community property law). The estate ordinarily will cease to be treated as the shareholder upon the earlier of the transfer of the stock by the trust or the expiration of the 2-year period beginning on the day of the deemed owner's death. If the trust qualifies and becomes an electing QSST, the beneficiary and not the estate is treated as the shareholder as of the effective date of the QSST election, and the rules provided in paragraph (j)(7) of this section apply. If the trust qualifies and becomes an ESBT, the shareholders are determined under paragraphs (h)(3)(i)(F) and (h)(3)(ii) of this section as of the effective date of the ESBT election, and the rules provided in paragraph (m) of this section apply.

(C) If stock is held by an electing QSST, see paragraph (j)(7) of this section for the rules on who is treated as the shareholder.

(D) If stock is transferred or deemed distributed to a testamentary trust described in paragraph (h)(1)(iv) of this section (other than a qualified subpart E trust, an electing QSST, or an ESBT), the estate of the testator is treated as the shareholder until the earlier of the transfer of that stock by the trust or the expiration of the 2-year period beginning on the day that the stock is transferred or deemed distributed to the trust. If the trust qualifies and becomes an electing QSST, the beneficiary and not the estate is treated as the shareholder as of the effective date of the QSST election, and the rules provided in paragraph (j)(7) of this section apply. If the trust qualifies and becomes an ESBT, the shareholders are determined under paragraphs (h)(3)(i)(F) and (h)(3)(ii) of this section as of the effective date of the ESBT election, and the rules provided in paragraph (m) of this section apply.

(E) If stock is held by a qualified voting trust, each beneficial owner of the stock, as determined under subpart E, is treated as a shareholder with respect to the owner's proportionate share of the stock held by the trust.

(F) If S corporation stock is held by an ESBT, each potential current beneficiary is treated as a shareholder. However, if for any period there is no potential current beneficiary of the ESBT, the ESBT is treated as the shareholder during such period. See paragraph (m)(4) of this section for the definition of potential current beneficiary.

Reg. §1.1361-1(h)(3)(i)(F)

(G) If stock in an S corporation bank or depository institution holding company is held by an individual retirement account (including a Roth IRA) described in paragraph (h)(1)(vii) of this section, the individual for whose benefit the trust was created shall be treated as the shareholder.

(ii) *Exceptions.*—See § 1.641(c)-1 for the rules for the taxation of an ESBT. Solely for purposes of section 1366, 1367, and 1368 the shareholder of S corporation stock held by a trust is determined as follows—

(A) If stock is held by a trust as defined in paragraph (h)(1)(ii) of this section (other than an electing QSST or an ESBT), the trust is treated as the shareholder. If the trust continues to own the stock after the expiration of the 2-year period, the corporation's S election will terminate unless the trust is otherwise a permitted shareholder.

(B) If stock is transferred or deemed distributed to a testamentary trust described in paragraph (h)(1)(iv) of this section (other than a qualified subpart E trust, an electing QSST, or an ESBT), the trust is treated as the shareholder. If the trust continues to own the stock after the expiration of the 2-year period, the corporation's S election will terminate unless the trust otherwise qualifies as a permitted shareholder.

(i) [Reserved]

(j) *Qualified subchapter S trust.*—(1) *Definition.*—A qualified subchapter S trust (QSST) is a trust (whether intervivos or testamentary), other than a foreign trust described in section 7701(a)(31), that satisfies the following requirements:

(i) All of the income (within the meaning of § 1.643(b)-1) of the trust is distributed (or is required to be distributed) currently to one individual who is a citizen or resident of the United States. For purposes of the preceding sentence, unless otherwise provided under local law (including pertinent provisions of the governing instrument that are effective under local law), income of the trust includes distributions to the trust from the S corporation for the taxable year in question, but does not include the trust's pro rata share of the S corporation's items of income, loss, deduction, or credit determined under section 1366. See § § 1.651(a)-2(a) and 1.663(b)-1(a) for rules relating to the determination of whether all of the income of a trust is distributed (or is required to be distributed) currently. If under the terms of the trust income is not required to be distributed currently, the trustee may elect under section 663(b) to consider a distribution made in the first 65 days of a taxable year as made on the last day of the preceding taxable year. See section 663(b) and § 1.663(b)-2 for rules on the time and manner for making the election. The income distribution requirement must be satisfied for the taxable year of the trust or for that part of the

trust's taxable year during which it holds S corporation stock.

(ii) The terms of the trust must require that—

(A) During the life of the current income beneficiary, there will be only one income beneficiary of the trust;

(B) Any corpus distributed during the life of the current income beneficiary may be distributed only to that income beneficiary;

(C) The current income beneficiary's income interest in the trust will terminate on the earlier of that income beneficiary's death or the termination of the trust; and

(D) Upon termination of the trust during the life of the current income beneficiary, the trust will distribute all of its assets to that income beneficiary.

(iii) The terms of the trust must satisfy the requirements of paragraph (j)(1)(ii) of this section from the date the QSST election is made or from the effective date of the QSST election, whichever is earlier, throughout the entire period that the current income beneficiary and any successor income beneficiary is the income beneficiary of the trust. If the terms of the trust do not preclude the possibility that any of the requirements stated in paragraph (j)(1)(ii) of this section will not be met, the trust will not qualify as a QSST. For example, if the terms of the trust are silent with respect to corpus distributions, and distributions of corpus to a person other than the current income beneficiary are permitted under local law during the life of the current income beneficiary, then the terms of the trust do not preclude the possibility that corpus may be distributed to a person other than the current income beneficiary and, therefore, the trust is not a QSST.

(2) *Special rules.*—(i) If a husband and wife are income beneficiaries of the same trust, the husband and wife file a joint return, and each is a U.S. citizen or resident, the husband and wife are treated as one beneficiary for purposes of paragraph (j) of this section. If a husband and wife are treated by the preceding sentence as one beneficiary, any action required by this section to be taken by an income beneficiary requires joinder of both of them. For example, each spouse must sign the QSST election, continue to be a U.S. citizen or resident, and continue to file joint returns for the entire period that the QSST election is in effect.

(ii)(A) *Terms of the trust and applicable local law.*—The determination of whether the terms of a trust meet all of the requirements under paragraph (j)(1)(ii) of this section depends upon the terms of the trust instrument and the applicable local law. For example, a trust whose governing instrument provides that A is the sole income beneficiary of the trust is, nevertheless, considered to have two income beneficiaries if, under the applicable local law, A and B are considered to be the income beneficiaries of the trust.

(B) *Legal obligation to support.*—If under local law a distribution to the income beneficiary is in satisfaction of the grantor's legal obligation of support to that income beneficiary, the trust will not qualify as a QSST as of the date of distribution because, under section 677(b), if income is distributed, the grantor will be treated as the owner of the ordinary income portion of the trust or, if trust corpus is distributed, the grantor will be treated as a beneficiary under section 662. See § 1.677(b)-1 for rules on the treatment of trusts for support and § 1.662(a)-4 for rules concerning amounts used in discharge of a legal obligation.

(C) *Example.*—The following example illustrates the rules of paragraph (j)(2)(ii)(B) of this section:

Example. F creates a trust for the benefit of F's minor child, G. Under the terms of the trust, all income is payable to G until the trust terminates on the earlier of G's attaining age 35 or G's death. Upon the termination of the trust, all corpus must be distributed to G or G's estate. The trust includes all of the provisions prescribed by section 1361(d)(3)(A) and paragraph (j)(1)(ii) of this section, but does not preclude the trustee from making income distributions to G that will be in satisfaction of F's legal obligation to support G. Under the applicable local law, distributions of trust income to G will satisfy F's legal obligation to support G. If the trustee distributes income to G in satisfaction of F's legal obligation to support G, the trust will not qualify as a QSST because F will be treated as the owner of the ordinary income portion of the trust. Further, the trust will not be a qualified subpart E trust because the trust will be subject to tax on the income allocable to corpus.

(iii) If, under the terms of the trust, a person (including the income beneficiary) has a special power to appoint, during the life of the income beneficiary, trust income or corpus to any person other than the current income beneficiary, the trust will not qualify as a QSST. However, if the power of appointment results in the grantor being treated as the owner of the entire trust under the rules of subpart E, the trust may be a permitted shareholder under section 1361(c)(2)(A)(i) and paragraph (h)(1)(i) of this section.

(iv) If the terms of a trust or local law do not preclude the current income beneficiary from transferring the beneficiary's interest in the trust or do not preclude a person other than the current income beneficiary named in the trust instrument from being treated as a beneficiary of the trust under § 1.643(c)-1, the trust will still qualify as a QSST. However, if the income beneficiary transfers or assigns the income interest or a portion of the income interest to another, the trust may no longer qualify as a QSST, depending on the facts and circumstances, because any transferee of the current income beneficiary's income interest and any person treated as a beneficiary under § 1.643(c)-1 will be treated as a current income beneficiary for purposes of paragraph (j)(1)(ii) of this section and the trust may no longer meet the QSST requirements.

(v) If the terms of the trust do not preclude a person other than the current income beneficiary named in the trust instrument from being awarded an interest in the trust by the order of a court, the trust will qualify as a QSST assuming the trust meets the requirements of paragraphs (j)(1)(i) and (ii) of this section. However, if as a result of such court order, the trust no longer meets the QSST requirements, the trust no longer qualifies as a QSST and the corporation's S election will terminate.

(vi) A trust may qualify as a QSST even though a person other than the current income beneficiary is treated under subpart E as the owner of a part or all of that portion of a trust which does not consist of the S corporation stock, provided the entire trust meets the QSST requirements stated in paragraphs (j)(1)(i) and (ii) of this section.

(3) *Separate and independent shares of a trust.*—For purposes of sections 1361(c) and (d), a substantially separate and independent share of a trust, within the meaning of section 663(c) and the regulations thereunder, is treated as a separate trust. For a separate share which holds S corporation stock to qualify as a QSST, the terms of the trust applicable to that separate share must meet the QSST requirements stated in paragraphs (j)(1)(i) and (ii) of this section.

(4) *Qualified terminable interest property trust.*—If property, including S corporation stock, or stock of a corporation that intends to make an S election, is transferred to a trust and an election is made to treat all or a portion of the transferred property as qualified terminable interest property (QTIP) under section 2056(b)(7), the income beneficiary may make the QSST election if the trust meets the requirements set out in paragraphs (j)(1)(i) and (ii) of this section. However, if property is transferred to a QTIP trust under section 2523(f), the income beneficiary may not make a QSST election even if the trust meets the requirements set forth in paragraph (j)(1)(ii) of this section because the grantor would be treated as the owner of the income portion of the trust under section 677. In addition, if property is transferred to a QTIP trust under section 2523(f), the trust does not qualify as a permitted shareholder under section 1361(c)(2)(A)(i) and paragraph (h)(1)(i) of this section (a qualified subpart E trust), unless under the terms of the QTIP trust, the grantor is treated as the owner of the entire trust under sections 671 to 677. If the grantor ceases to be the income beneficiary's spouse, the trust may qualify as a QSST if it

otherwise satisfies the requirements under paragraphs (j)(1)(i) and (ii) of this section.

(5) *Ceasing to meet the QSST requirements.*—If a QSST for which an election under section 1361(d)(2) has been made (as described in paragraph (j) (6) of this section) ceases to meet any of the requirements specified in paragraph (j)(1)(ii) of this section, the provisions of this paragraph (j) will cease to apply as of the first day on which that requirement ceases to be met. If such a trust ceases to meet the income distribution requirement specified in paragraph (j)(1)(i) of this section, but continues to meet all of the requirements in paragraph (j)(1)(ii) of this section, the provisions of this paragraph (j) will cease to apply as of the first day of the first taxable year beginning after the first taxable year for which the trust ceased to meet the income distribution requirement of paragraph (j)(1)(i) of this section. If a corporation's S election is inadvertently terminated as a result of a trust ceasing to meet the QSST requirements, the corporation may request relief under section 1362(f).

(6) *Qualified subchapter S trust election.*— (i) *In general.*—This paragraph (j)(6) applies to the election provided in section 1361(d)(2) (the QSST election) to treat a QSST (as defined in paragraph (j)(1) of this section) as a trust described in section 1361(c)(2)(A)(i), and thus a permitted shareholder. This election must be made separately with respect to each corporation whose stock is held by the trust. The QSST election does not itself constitute an election as to the status of the corporation; the corporation must make the election provided by section 1362(a) to be an S corporation. Until the effective date of a corporation's S election, the beneficiary is not treated as the owner of the stock of the corporation for purposes of section 678. Any action required by this paragraph (j) to be taken by a person who is under a legal disability by reason of age may be taken by that person's guardian or other legal representative, or if there be none, by that person's natural or adoptive parent.

(ii) *Filing the QSST election.*—The current income beneficiary of the trust must make the election by signing and filing with the service center with which the corporation files its income tax return the applicable form or a statement that—

(A) Contains the name, address, and taxpayer identification number of the current income beneficiary, the trust, and the corporation;

(B) Identifies the election as an election made under section 1361(d)(2);

(C) Specifies the date on which the election is to become effective (not earlier than 15 days and two months before the date on which the election is filed);

(D) Specifies the date (or dates) on which the stock of the corporation was transferred to the trust; and

(E) Provides all information and representations necessary to show that:

(1) Under the terms of the trust and applicable local law—

(i) During the life of the current income beneficiary, there will be only one income beneficiary of the trust (if husband and wife are beneficiaries, that they will file joint returns and that both are U.S. residents or citizens);

(ii) Any corpus distributed during the life of the current income beneficiary may be distributed only to that beneficiary;

(iii) The current beneficiary's income interest in the trust will terminate on the earlier of the beneficiary's death or upon termination of the trust; and

(iv) Upon the termination of the trust during the life of such income beneficiary, the trust will distribute all its assets to such beneficiary.

(2) The trust is required to distribute all of its income currently, or that the trustee will distribute all of its income currently if not so required by the terms of the trust.

(3) No distribution of income or corpus by the trust will be in satisfaction of the grantor's legal obligation to support or maintain the income beneficiary.

(iii) *When to file the QSST election.*—(A) If S corporation stock is transferred to a trust, the QSST election must be made within the 16-day-and-2-month period beginning on the day that the stock is transferred to the trust. If a C corporation has made an election under section 1362(a) to be an S corporation (S election) and, before that corporation's S election is in effect, stock of that corporation is transferred to a trust, the QSST election must be made within the 16-day-and-2-month period beginning on the day that the stock is transferred to the trust.

(B) If a trust holds C corporation stock and that C corporation makes an S election effective for the first day of the taxable year in which the S election is made, the QSST election must be made within the 16-day-and-2-month period beginning on the day that the S election is effective. If a trust holds C corporation stock and that C corporation makes an S election effective for the first day of the taxable year following the taxable year in which the S election is made, the QSST election must be made within the 16-day-and-2-month period beginning on the day that the S election is made. If a trust holds C corporation stock and that corporation makes an S election intending the S election to be effective for the first day of the taxable year in which the S election is made but, under § 1.1362-6(a)(2), such S election is subsequently treated as effective for the first day of the taxable year following the taxable year in which the S election is made, the fact that the QSST election states that the effective date of the QSST election is the first day of the taxable year in which the S election is made will not cause the QSST election to be ineffective for the first year in which the corporation's S election is effective.

(C) If a trust ceases to be a qualified subpart E trust, satisfies the requirements of a QSST, and intends to become a QSST, the QSST election must be filed within the 16-day-and-2-month period beginning on the date on which the trust ceases to be a qualified subpart E trust. If the estate of the deemed owner of the trust is treated as the shareholder under paragraph (h)(3)(i) of this section, the QSST election may be filed at any time, but no later than the end of the 16-day-and-2-month period beginning on the date on which the estate of the deemed owner ceases to be treated as a shareholder.

(D) If a testamentary trust is a permitted shareholder under paragraph (h)(1)(iv) of this section, satisfies the requirements of a QSST, and intends to become a QSST, the QSST election may be filed at any time, but no later than the end of the 16-day-and-2-month period beginning on the day after the end of the 2-year period.

(E) If a corporation's S election terminates because of a late QSST election, the corporation may request inadvertent termination relief under section 1362(f). See § 1.1362-4 for rules concerning inadvertent terminations.

(iv) *Protective QSST election when a person is an owner under subpart E.*—If the grantor of a trust is treated as the owner under subpart E of all of the trust, or of a portion of the trust which consists of S corporation stock, and the current income beneficiary is not the grantor, the current income beneficiary may not make the QSST election, even if the trust meets the QSST requirements stated in paragraph (j)(1)(ii) of this section. See paragraph (j)(6)(iii)(C) of this section as to when the QSST election may be made. See also paragraph (j) (2) (vi) of this section. However, if the current income beneficiary (or beneficiaries who are husband and wife, if both spouses are U.S. citizens or residents and file a joint return) of a trust is treated under subpart E as owning all or a portion of the trust consisting of S corporation stock, the current income beneficiary (or beneficiaries who are husband and wife, if both spouses are U.S. citizens or residents and file a joint return) may make the QSST election. See *Example 8* of paragraph (k) (l) of this section.

(7) *Treatment as shareholder.*—(i) The income beneficiary who makes the QSST election and is treated (for purposes of section 678(a)) as the owner of that portion of the trust that consists of S corporation stock is treated as the shareholder for purposes of sections 1361(b)(1), 1366, 1367, and 1368.

(ii) If, upon the death of an income beneficiary, the trust continues in existence, continues to hold S corporation stock but no longer satisfies the QSST requirements, is not a qualified

subpart E trust, and does not qualify as an ESBT, then, solely for purposes of section 1361(b)(1), as of the date of the income beneficiary's death, the estate of that income beneficiary is treated as the shareholder of the S corporation with respect to which the income beneficiary made the QSST election. The estate ordinarily will cease to be treated as the shareholder for purposes of section 1361(b)(1) upon the earlier of the transfer of that stock by the trust or the expiration of the 2-year period beginning on the day of the income beneficiary's death. During the period that the estate is treated as the shareholder for purposes of section 1361(b)(1), the trust is treated as the shareholder for purposes of sections 1366, 1367, and 1368. If, after the 2-year period, the trust continues to hold S corporation stock and does not otherwise qualify as a permitted shareholder, the corporation's S election terminates. If the termination is inadvertent, the corporation may request relief under section 1362(f).

(8) *Coordination with grantor trust rules.*—If a valid QSST election is made, the income beneficiary is treated as the owner, for purposes of section 678(a), of that portion of the trust that consists of the stock of the S corporation for which the QSST election was made. However, solely for purposes of applying the preceding sentence to a QSST, an income beneficiary who is a deemed section 678 owner only by reason of section 1361(d)(1) will not be treated as the owner of the S corporation stock in determining and attributing the federal income tax consequences of a disposition of the stock by the QSST. For example, if the disposition is a sale, the QSST election terminates as to the stock sold and any gain or loss recognized on the sale will be that of the trust, not the income beneficiary. Similarly, if a QSST distributes its S corporation stock to the income beneficiary, the QSST election terminates as to the distributed stock and the consequences of the distribution are determined by reference to the status of the trust apart from the income beneficiary's terminating ownership status under sections 678 and 1361(d)(1). The portions of the trust other than the portion consisting of S corporation stock are subject to subparts A through D of subchapter J of chapter 1, except as otherwise required by subpart E of the Internal Revenue Code. However, solely for purposes of applying sections 465 and 469 to the income beneficiary, a disposition of S corporation stock by a QSST shall be treated as a disposition by the income beneficiary.

(9) *Successive income beneficiary.*—(i) If the income beneficiary of a QSST who made a QSST election dies, each successive income beneficiary of that trust is treated as consenting to the election unless a successive income beneficiary affirmatively refuses to consent to the election. For this purpose, the term *successive income beneficiary* includes a beneficiary of a trust whose interest is a separate share within the meaning of

section 663(c), but does not include any beneficiary of a trust that is created upon the death of the income beneficiary of the QSST and which is a new trust under local law.

(ii) The application of this paragraph (j)(9) is illustrated by the following examples:

Example 1. Shares of stock in Corporation X, an S corporation, are held by Trust A, a QSST for which a QSST election was made. B is the sole income beneficiary of Trust A. On B's death, under the terms of Trust A, J and K become the current income beneficiaries of Trust A. J and K each hold a separate and independent share of Trust A within the meaning of section 663(c). J and K are successive income beneficiaries of Trust A, and they are treated as consenting to B's QSST election.

Example 2. Assume the same facts as in *Example 1,* except that on B's death, under the terms of Trust A and local law, Trust A terminates and the principal is to be divided equally and held in newly created Trust B and Trust C. The sole income beneficiaries of Trust B and Trust C are J and K, respectively. Because Trust A terminated, J and K are not successive income beneficiaries of Trust A. J and K must make QSST elections for their respective trusts to qualify as QSSTs, if they qualify. The result is the same whether or not the trustee of Trusts B and C is the same as the trustee of trust A.

(10) *Affirmative refusal to consent.*— (i) *Required statement.*—A successive income beneficiary of a QSST must make an affirmative refusal to consent by signing and filing with the service center where the corporation files its income tax return a statement that—

(A) Contains the name, address, and taxpayer identification number of the successive income beneficiary, the trust, and the corporation for which the election was made;

(B) Identifies the refusal as an affirmative refusal to consent under section 1361(d)(2); and

(C) Sets forth the date on which the successive income beneficiary became the income beneficiary.

(ii) *Filing date and effectiveness.*—The affirmative refusal to consent must be filed within 15 days and 2 months after the date on which the successive income beneficiary becomes the income beneficiary. The affirmative refusal to consent will be effective as of the date on which the successive income beneficiary becomes the current income beneficiary.

(11) *Revocation of QSST election.*—A QSST election may be revoked only with the consent of the Commissioner. The Commissioner will not grant a revocation when one of its purposes is the avoidance of federal income taxes or when the taxable year is closed. The application for consent to revoke the election must be submitted

to the Internal Revenue Service in the form of a letter ruling request under the appropriate revenue procedure. The application must be signed by the current income beneficiary and must—

(i) Contain the name, address, and taxpayer identification number of the current income beneficiary, the trust, and the corporation with respect to which the QSST election was made;

(ii) Identify the election being revoked as an election made under section 1361(d)(2); and

(iii) Explain why the current income beneficiary seeks to revoke the QSST election and indicate that the beneficiary understands the consequences of the revocation.

(12) *Converting a QSST to an ESBT.*—For a trust that seeks to convert from a QSST to an ESBT, the consent of the Commissioner is hereby granted to revoke the QSST election as of the effective date of the ESBT election, if all the following requirements are met:

(i) The trust meets all of the requirements to be an ESBT under paragraph (m)(1) of this section except for the requirement under paragraph (m)(1)(iv)(A) of this section that the trust not have a QSST election in effect.

(ii) The trustee and the current income beneficiary of the trust sign the ESBT election. The ESBT election must be filed with the service center where the S corporation files its income tax return. This ESBT election must state at the top of the document "ATTENTION ENTITY CONTROL—CONVERSION OF A QSST TO AN ESBT PURSUANT TO SECTION 1.1361-1(j)" and include all information otherwise required for an ESBT election under paragraph (m)(2) of this section. A separate election must be made with respect to the stock of each S corporation held by the trust.

(iii) The trust has not converted from an ESBT to a QSST within the 36-month period preceding the effective date of the new ESBT election.

(iv) The date on which the ESBT election is to be effective cannot be more than 15 days and two months prior to the date on which the election is filed and cannot be more than 12 months after the date on which the election is filed. If an election specifies an effective date more than 15 days and two months prior to the date on which the election is filed, it will be effective on the day that is 15 days and two months prior to the date on which it is filed. If an election specifies an effective date more than 12 months after the date on which the election is filed, it will be effective on the day that is 12 months after the date it is filed.

(k)(1) *Examples.*—The provisions of paragraphs (h) and (j) of this section are illustrated by the following examples in which it is assumed that all noncorporate persons are citizens or residents of the United States:

Example 1. (i) *Terms of the trust.* In 1996, A and A's spouse, B, created an intervivos trust and each funded the trust with separately owned stock of an S corporation. Under the terms of the trust, A and B designated themselves as the income beneficiaries and each, individually, retained the power to amend or revoke the trust with respect to the trust assets attributable to their respective trust contributions. Upon A's death, the trust is to be divided into two separate parts; one part attributable to the assets A contributed to the trust and one part attributable to B's contributions. Before the trust is divided, and during the administration of A's estate, all trust income is payable to B. The part of the trust attributable to B's contributions is to continue in trust under the terms of which B is designated as the sole income beneficiary and retains the power to amend or revoke the trust. The part attributable to A's contributions is to be divided into two separate trusts both of which have B as the sole income beneficiary for life. One trust, the *Credit Shelter Trust,* is to be funded with an amount that can pass free of estate tax by reason of A's available estate tax unified credit. The terms of the Credit Shelter Trust meet the requirements of section 1361(d)(3) as a QSST. The balance of the property passes to a Marital Trust, the terms of which satisfy the requirements of section 1361(d)(3) as a QSST and section 2056(b)(7) as QTIP. The appropriate fiduciary under § 20.2056(b)-7(b)(3) is directed to make an election under section 2056(b)(7).

(ii) *Results after deemed owner's death.* On February 3, 1997, A dies and the portion of the trust assets attributable to A's contributions including the S stock contributed by A, is includible in A's gross estate under sections 2036 and 2038. During the administration of A's estate, the trust holds the S corporation stock. Under section 1361(c)(2)(B)(ii), A's estate is treated as the shareholder of the S corporation stock that was included in A's gross estate for purposes of section 1361(b)(1); however, for purposes of sections 1366, 1367, and 1368, the trust is treated as the shareholder. B's part of the trust continues to be a qualified subpart E trust of which B is the owner under sections 676 and 677. B, therefore, continues to be treated as the shareholder of the S corporation stock in that portion of the trust. On May 13, 1997, during the continuing administration of A's estate, the trust is divided into separate trusts in accordance with the terms of the trust instrument. The S corporation stock that was included in A's gross estate is distributed to the Marital Trust and to the Credit Shelter Trust. A's estate will cease to be treated as the shareholder of the S corporation under section 1361(c)(2)(B)(ii) on May 13, 1997 (the date on which the S corporation stock was transferred to the trusts). B, as the income beneficiary of the Marital Trust and the Credit Shelter Trust, must make the QSST election for each trust by July 28, 1997 (the end of the 16-day-and-2-month period

beginning on the date the estate ceases to be treated as a shareholder) to have the trusts become permitted shareholders of the S corporation.

Example 2. (i) *Qualified subpart E trust as shareholder.* In 1997, A, an individual established a trust and transferred to the trust A's shares of stock of Corporation M, an S corporation. A has the power to revoke the entire trust. The terms of the trust require that all income be paid to B and otherwise meet the requirements of a QSST under section 1361(d)(3). The trust will continue in existence after A's death. The trust is a qualified subpart E trust described in section 1361(c)(2)(A)(i) during A's life, and A (not the trust) is treated as the shareholder for purposes of sections 1361(b)(1), 1366, 1367, and 1368.

(ii) *Trust ceasing to be a qualified subpart E trust on deemed owner's death.* Assume the same facts as paragraph (i) of this *Example 2,* except that A dies without having exercised A's power to revoke. Upon A's death, the trust ceases to be a qualified subpart E trust described in section 1361(c)(2)(A)(i). A's estate (and not the trust) is treated as the shareholder for purposes of section 1361(b)(1). A's estate will cease to be treated as the shareholder for purposes of section 1361(b)(1) upon the earlier of the transfer of the Corporation M stock by the trust (other than to A's estate), the expiration of the 2-year period beginning on the day of A's death, or the effective date of a QSST or ESBT election if the trust qualifies as a QSST or ESBT. However, until that time, because the trust continues in existence after A's death and will receive any distributions with respect to the stock it holds, the trust is treated as the shareholder for purposes of sections 1366, 1367, and 1368. If no QSST or ESBT election is made effective upon the expiration of the 2-year period, the corporation ceases to be an S corporation, but the trust continues as the shareholder of a C corporation.

(iii) *Trust continuing to be a qualified subpart E trust on deemed owner's death.* Assume the same facts as paragraph (ii) of this *Example 2,* except that the terms of the trust also provide that if A does not exercise the power to revoke before A's death, B will have the sole power to withdraw all trust property at any time after A's death. The trust continues to qualify as a qualified subpart E trust after A's death because, upon A's death, B is deemed to be the owner of the entire trust under section 678. Because the trust does not cease to be a qualified subpart E trust upon A's death, B (and not A's estate) is treated as the shareholder for purposes of sections 1361(b)(1), 1366, 1367, and 1368. Since the trust qualifies as a QSST, B may make a protective QSST election under paragraph (j) (6) (iv) of this section.

Example 3. (i) *2-year rule under section 1361(c)(2)(A)(ii) and (iii).* F owns stock of Corporation P, an S corporation. In addition, F is the deemed owner of a qualified subpart E trust that holds stock in Corporation O, an S corporation. F dies on July 1, 2003. The trust continues in existence after F's death but is no longer a qualified subpart E trust. On August 1, 2003, F's shares of stock in Corporation P are transferred to the trust pursuant to the terms of F's will. Because the stock of Corporation P was not held by the trust when F died, section 1361(c)(2)(A)(ii) does not apply with respect to that stock. Under section 1361(c)(2)(A)(iii), the last day on which the trust could be treated as a permitted shareholder of Corporation P is July 31, 2005 (that is, the last day of the 2-year period that begins on the date of the transfer from the estate to the trust). With respect to the shares of stock in Corporation O held by the trust at the time of F's death, section 1361(c)(2)(A)(ii) applies and the last day on which the trust could be treated as a permitted shareholder of Corporation O is June 30, 2005 (that is, the last day of the 2-year period that begins on the date of F's death).

(ii) *Section 645 electing trust and successor trust.* Assume the same facts as in paragraph (i) of this *Example 3*, except that F's trust is a qualified revocable trust for which a valid section 645 election is made on October 1, 2003 (electing trust). Because under section 645 the electing trust is treated and taxed for purposes of subtitle A of the Code as part of F's estate, the trust may continue to hold the O stock pursuant to § 1361(b)(1)(B), without causing the termination of Corporation O's S election, for the duration of the section 645 election period. However, on January 1, 2004, during the election period, the shares of stock in Corporation O are transferred pursuant to the terms of the electing trust to a successor trust. Because the successor trust satisfies the definition of a testamentary trust under paragraph (h)(1)(iv) of this section, the successor trust is a permitted shareholder until the earlier of the expiration of the 2-year period beginning on January 1, 2004, or the effective date of a QSST or ESBT election for the successor trust.

Example 4. (i) *QSST when terms do not require current distribution of income.* Corporation Q, a calender year corporation, makes an election to be an S corporation effective for calendar year 1996. On July 1, 1996, G, a shareholder of Corporation Q, transfers G's shares of Corporation Q stock to a trust with H as its current income beneficiary. The terms of the trust otherwise satisfy the QSST requirements, but authorize the trustee in its discretion to accumulate or distribute the trust income. However, the trust, which uses the calendar year as its taxable year, initially satisfies the income distribution requirement because the trustee is currently distributing all of the income. On August 1, 1996, H makes a QSST election with respect to Corporation Q that is effective as of July 1, 1996. Accordingly, as of July 1, 1996, the trust is a QSST and H is treated as the shareholder for purposes of sections 1361(b)(1), 1366, 1367, and 1368.

(ii) *QSST when trust income is not distributed currently.* Assume the same facts as in paragraph

(i) of this *Example 4,* except that, for the taxable year ending on December 31, 1997, the trustee accumulates some trust income. The trust ceases to be a QSST on January 1, 1998, because the trust failed to distribute all of its income for the taxable year ending December 31, 1997. Thus, Corporation Q ceases to be an S corporation as of January 1, 1998, because the trust is not a permitted shareholder.

(iii) *QSST when a person other than the current income beneficiary may receive trust corpus.* Assume the same facts as in paragraph (i) of this *Example 4,* except that the events occur in 2003 and H dies on November 1, 2003, and the trust does not qualify as an ESBT. Under the terms of the trust, after H's death, L is the income beneficiary of the trust and the trustee is authorized to distribute trust corpus to L as well as to J. The trust ceases to be a QSST as of November 1, 2003, because corpus distributions may be made to someone other than L, the current (successive) income beneficiary. Under section 1361(c)(2)(B)(ii), H's estate (and not the trust) is considered to be the shareholder for purposes of section 1361(b)(1) for the 2-year period beginning on November 1, 2003. However, because the trust continues in existence after H's death and will receive any distributions from the corporation, the trust (and not H's estate) is treated as the shareholder for purposes of sections 1366, 1367, and 1368, during that 2-year period. After the 2-year period, the S election terminates and the trust continues as a shareholder of a C corporation. If the termination is inadvertent, Corporation Q may request relief under section 1362(f). However, the S election would not terminate if the trustee distributed all Corporation Q shares to L, J, or both on or before October 31, 2005, (the last day of the 2-year period) assuming that neither L nor J becomes the 76th shareholder of Corporation Q as a result of the distribution.

Example 5. QSST when current income beneficiary assigns the income interest to a person not named in the trust. On January 1, 1996, stock of Corporation R, a calendar year S corporation, is transferred to a trust that satisfies all of the requirements to be a QSST. Neither the terms of the trust nor local law preclude the current income beneficiary, K, from assigning K's income interest in the trust. K files a timely QSST election that is effective January 1, 1996. On July 1, 1996, K assigns the income interest in the trust to N. Under applicable state law, the trustee is bound as a result of the assignment to distribute the trust income to N. Thus, the QSST will cease to qualify as a QSST under section 1361(d)(3)(A)(iii) because N's interest will terminate on K's death (rather than on N's death). Accordingly, as of the date of the assignment, the trust ceases to be a QSST and Corporation R ceases to be an S corporation.

Example 6. QSST when terms fail to provide for distribution of trust assets upon termination during life of current income beneficiary. A contributes S corporation stock to a trust the terms of which provide for one income beneficiary, annual distributions of income, discretionary invasion of corpus only for the benefit of the income beneficiary, and termination of the trust only upon the death of the current income beneficiary. Since the trust can terminate only upon the death of the income beneficiary, the governing instrument fails to provide for any distribution of trust assets during the income beneficiary's life. The governing instrument's silence on this point does not disqualify the trust under section 1361(d)(3)(A)(ii) or (iv).

Example 7. QSST when settlor of trust retains a reversion in the trust. On January 10, 1996, M transfers to a trust shares of stock in corporation X, an S corporation. D, who is 13 years old and not a lineal descendant of M, is the sole income beneficiary of the trust. On termination of the trust, the principal (including the X shares) is to revert to M. The trust instrument provides that the trust will terminate upon the earlier of D's death or D's 21st birthday. The terms of the trust satisfy all of the requirements to be a QSST except those of section 1361(d)(3)(A)(ii) (that corpus may be distributed during the current income beneficiary's life only to that beneficiary) and (iv) (that, upon termination of the trust during the life of the current income beneficiary, the corpus, must be distributed to that beneficiary). On February 10, 1996, M makes a gift of M's reversionary interest to D. Until M assigns M's reversion in the trust to D, M is deemed to own the entire trust under section 673(a) and the trust is a qualified subpart E trust. For purposes of section 1361(b)(1), 1366, 1367, and 1368, M is the shareholder of X. The trust ceases to be a qualified subpart E trust on February 10, 1996. Assuming that, by virtue of the assignment to D of M's reversionary interest, D (upon his 21st birthday) or D's estate (in the case of D's death before reaching age 21) is entitled under local law to receive the trust principal, the trust will be deemed as of February 10, 1996, to have satisfied the conditions of section 1361(d)(3)(A)(ii) and (iv) even though the terms of the trust do not explicitly so provide. D must make a QSST election by no later than April 25, 1996 (the end of the 16-day-and-2-month period that begins on February 10, 1996, the date on which the X stock is deemed transferred to the trust by M). See example (5) of § 1.1001-2(c) of the regulations.

Example 8. QSST when the income beneficiary has the power to withdraw corpus. On January 1, 1996, F transfers stock of an S corporation to an irrevocable trust whose income beneficiary is F's son, C. Under the terms of the trust, C is given the noncumulative power to withdraw from the corpus of the trust the greater of $5,000 or 5 percent of the value of the corpus on a yearly basis. The terms of the trust meet the QSST requirements. Assuming the trust distributions are not in satisfaction of F's legal obligation to support C, the trust qualifies as a QSST. C (or if

C is a minor, C's legal representative) must make the QSST election no later than March 16, 1996 (the end of the 16-day-and-2-month period that begins on the date the stock is transferred to the trust).

Example 9. (i) *Filing the QSST election.* On January 1, 1996, stock of Corporation T, a calendar year C corporation, is transferred to a trust that satisfies all of the requirements to be a QSST. On January 31, 1996, Corporation T files an election to be an S corporation that is to be effective for its taxable year beginning on January 1, 1996. In order for the S election to be effective for the 1996 taxable year, the QSST election must be effective January 1, 1996, and must be filed within the period beginning on January 1, 1996, and ending March 16, 1996 (the 16-day-and-2-month period beginning on the first day of the first taxable year for which the election to be an S corporation is intended to be effective).

(ii) *QSST election when the S election is filed late.* Assume the same facts as in paragraph (i) of this *Example 9,* except that Corporation T's election to be an S corporation is filed on April 1, 1996 (after the 15th day of the 3rd month of the first taxable year for which it is to be effective but before the end of that taxable year). Because the election to be an S corporation is not timely filed for the 1996 taxable year, under section 1362(b)(3), the S election is treated as made for the taxable year beginning on January 1, 1997. The QSST election must be filed within the 16-day-and-2-month period beginning on April 1, 1996, the date the S election was made, and ending on June 16, 1996.

Example 10. (i) *Transfers to QTIP trust.* On June 1, 1996, A transferred S corporation stock to a trust for the benefit of A's spouse B, the terms of which satisfy the requirements of section 2523(f)(2) as qualified terminable interest property. Under the terms of the trust, B is the sole income beneficiary for life. In addition, corpus may be distributed to B, at the trustee's discretion, during B's lifetime. However, under section 677(a), A is treated as the owner of the trust. Accordingly, the trust is a permitted shareholder of the S corporation under section 1361(c)(2)(A)(i), and A is treated as the shareholder for purposes of sections 1361(b)(1), 1366, 1367, and 1368.

(ii) *Transfers to QTIP trust where husband and wife divorce.* Assume the same facts as in paragraph (i) of this *Example 10,* except that A and B divorce on May 2, 1997. Under section 682, A ceases to be treated as the owner of the trust under section 677(a) because A and B are no longer husband and wife. Under section 682, after the divorce, B is the income beneficiary of the trust and corpus of the trust may only be distributed to B. Accordingly, assuming the trust otherwise meets the requirements of section 1361(d)(3), B must make the QSST election within 2 months and 15 days after the date of the divorce.

(iii) *Transfers to QTIP trust where no corpus distribution is permitted.* Assume the same facts as in paragraph (i) of this *Example 10,* except that the terms of the trust do not permit corpus to be distributed to B and require its retention by the trust for distribution to A and B's surviving children after the death of B. Under section 677, A is treated as the owner of the ordinary income portion of the trust, but the trust will be subject to tax on gross income allocable to corpus. Accordingly, the trust does not qualify as an eligible shareholder of the S corporation because it is neither a qualified subpart E trust nor a QSST.

(2) *Effective date.*—(i) *In general.*—Paragraph (a) of this section, and paragraphs (c) through (k) of this section (as contained in the 26 CFR edition revised April 1, 2003) apply to taxable years of a corporation beginning after July 21, 1995. For taxable years beginning on or before July 21, 1995, to which paragraph (a) of this section and paragraphs (c) through (k) of this section (as contained in the 26 CFR edition revised April 1, 2003) do not apply, see § 18.1361-1 of this chapter (as contained in the 26 CFR edition revised April 1, 1995). However, paragraphs (h)(1)(vi), (h)(3)(i)(F), (h)(3)(ii), and (i)(12) of this section (as contained in the 26 CFR edition revised April 1, 2003) are applicable for taxable years beginning on and after May 14, 2002. Otherwise, paragraphs (b)(1)(ii), (f), (h)(1)(ii), (h)(1)(iv), (h)(3)(i)(B), (h)(3)(i)(D), (h)(3)(ii)(A), (h)(3)(ii)(B), (j)(6)(iii)(C), (j)(6)(iii)(D), (j)(7)(ii), and (k)(1) *Example 2*(ii) fourth and last sentences, *Example 3,* and *Example 4*(iii) of this section apply on and after July 17, 2003. Paragraphs (b)(1)(i), (e)(1), (e)(3), (h)(1)(vii), (h)(3)(i)(G), and the fifth sentence of paragraph (j)(8) are effective on August 14, 2008.

(ii) *Transition rules.*—Taxpayers may apply paragraph (h)(1)(iv)(B) of this section on and after December 24, 2002, and before July 17, 2003, to treat a trust as a testamentary trust, but not during any period for which a QSST or ESBT election was in effect for the trust. In addition, the Internal Revenue Service will not challenge the treatment of a trust described in paragraph (h)(1)(iv)(B) of this section as a permitted shareholder of an S corporation for periods after August 5, 1997, and before the earlier of July 17, 2003, or the effective date of any QSST or ESBT election for that trust.

(iii) *Exception.*—If a QSST has sold or otherwise disposed of all or a portion of its S corporation stock in a tax year that is open for the QSST and the income beneficiary but on or before July 21, 1995, the QSST and the income beneficiary may both treat the transaction as if the beneficiary was the owner of the stock sold or disposed of, and thus recognize any gain or loss, or as if the QSST was the owner of the stock sold or disposed of as described in paragraph (j)(8) of this section. This exception applies only if the QSST and the income beneficiary take consistent reporting positions. The QSST and the income beneficiary must disclose by a statement on their respective returns (or amended returns), that they are taking consistent reporting positions.

(l) *Classes of stock.*—(1) *General rule.*—A corporation that has more than one class of stock does not qualify as a small business corporation. Except as provided in paragraph (l)(4) of this section (relating to instruments, obligations, or arrangements treated as a second class of stock), a corporation is treated as having only one class of stock if all outstanding shares of stock of the corporation confer identical rights to distribution and liquidation proceeds. Differences in voting rights among shares of stock of a corporation are disregarded in determining whether a corporation has more than one class of stock. Thus, if all shares of stock of an S corporation have identical rights to distribution and liquidation proceeds, the corporation may have voting and nonvoting common stock, a class of stock that may vote only on certain issues, irrevocable proxy agreements, or groups of shares that differ with respect to rights to elect members of the board of directors.

(2) *Determination of whether stock confers identical rights to distribution and liquidation proceeds.*—(i) *In general.*—The determination of whether all outstanding shares of stock confer identical rights to distribution and liquidation proceeds is made based on the corporate charter, articles of incorporation, bylaws, applicable state law, and binding agreements relating to distribution and liquidation proceeds (collectively, the governing provisions). A commercial contractual agreement, such as a lease, employment agreement, or loan agreement, is not a binding agreement relating to distribution and liquidation proceeds and thus is not a governing provision unless a principal purpose of the agreement is to circumvent the one class of stock requirement of section 1361(b)(1)(D) and this paragraph (l). Although a corporation is not treated as having more than one class of stock so long as the governing provisions provide for identical distribution and liquidation rights, any distributions (including actual, constructive, or deemed distributions) that differ in timing or amount are to be given appropriate tax effect in accordance with the facts and circumstances.

(ii) *State law requirements for payment and withholding of income tax.*—State laws may require a corporation to pay or withhold state income taxes on behalf of some or all of the corporation's shareholders. Such laws are disregarded in determining whether all outstanding shares of stock of the corporation confer identical rights to distribution and liquidation proceeds, within the meaning of paragraph (l)(1) of this section, provided that, when the constructive distributions resulting from the payment or withholding of taxes by the corporation are taken into account, the outstanding shares confer identical rights to distribution and liquidation proceeds. A difference in timing between the constructive distributions and the actual distributions to the other shareholders does not cause the corporation to be treated as having more than one class of stock.

(iii) *Buy-sell and redemption agreements.*— (A) *In general.*—Buy-sell agreements among shareholders, agreements restricting the transferability of stock, and redemption agreements are disregarded in determining whether a corporation's outstanding shares of stock confer identical distribution and liquidation rights unless—

(1) A principal purpose of the agreement is to circumvent the one class of stock requirement of section 1361(b)(1)(D) and this paragraph (1), and

(2) The agreement establishes a purchase price that, at the time the agreement is entered into, is significantly in excess of or below the fair market value of the stock.

Agreements that provide for the purchase or redemption of stock at book value or at a price between fair market value and book value are not considered to establish a price that is significantly in excess of or below the fair market value of the stock and, thus, are disregarded in determining whether the outstanding shares of stock confer identical rights. For purposes of this paragraph (l)(2)(iii)(A), a good faith determination of fair market value will be respected unless it can be shown that the value was substantially in error and the determination of the value was not performed with reasonable diligence. Although an agreement may be disregarded in determining whether shares of stock confer identical distribution and liquidation rights, payments pursuant to the agreement may have income or transfer tax consequences.

(B) *Exception for certain agreements.*— Bona fide agreements to redeem or purchase stock at the time of death, divorce, disability, or termination of employment are disregarded in determining whether a corporation's shares of stock confer identical rights. In addition, if stock that is substantially nonvested (within the meaning of § 1.83-3(b)) is treated as outstanding under these regulations, the forfeiture provisions that cause the stock to be substantially nonvested are disregarded. Furthermore, the Commissioner may provide by Revenue Ruling or other published guidance that other types of bona fide agreements to redeem or purchase stock are disregarded.

(C) *Safe harbors for determinations of book value.*—A determination of book value will be respected if—

(1) The book value is determined in accordance with Generally Accepted Accounting

Principles (including permitted optional adjustments); or

(2) The book value is used for any substantial nontax purpose.

(iv) *Distributions that take into account varying interests in stock during a taxable year.*—A governing provision does not, within the meaning of paragraph (l)(2)(i) of this section, alter the rights to liquidation and distribution proceeds conferred by an S corporation's stock merely because the governing provision provides that, as a result of a change in stock ownership, distributions in a taxable year are to be made on the basis of the shareholders' varying interests in the S corporation's income in the current or immediately preceding taxable year. If distributions pursuant to the provision are not made within a reasonable time after the close of the taxable year in which the varying interests occur, the distributions may be recharacterized depending on the facts and circumstances, but will not result in a second class of stock.

(v) *Special rule for section 338(h)(10) elections.*—If the shareholders of an S corporation sell their stock in a transaction for which an election is made under section 338(h)(10) and § 1.338(h)(10)-1, the receipt of varying amounts per share by the shareholders will not cause the S corporation to have more than one class of stock, provided that the varying amounts are determined in arm's length negotiations with the purchaser.

(vi) *Examples.*—The application of paragraph (l)(2) of this section may be illustrated by the following examples. In each of the examples, the S corporation requirements of section 1361 are satisfied except as otherwise stated, the corporation has in effect an S election under section 1362, and the corporation has only the shareholders described.

Example 1. Determination of whether stock confers identical rights to distribution and liquidation proceeds. (i) The law of State A requires that permission be obtained from the State Commissioner of Corporations before stock may be issued by a corporation. The Commissioner grants permission to S, a corporation, to issue its stock subject to the restriction that any person who is issued stock in exchange for property, and not cash, must waive all rights to receive distributions until the shareholders who contributed cash for stock have received distributions in the amount of their cash contributions.

(ii) The condition imposed by the Commissioner pursuant to state law alters the rights to distribution and liquidation proceeds conferred by the outstanding stock of S so that those rights are not identical. Accordingly, under paragraph (l)(2)(i) of this section, S is treated as having more than one class of stock and does not qualify as a small business corporation.

Reg. §1.1361-1(l)(2)(vi)

Example 2. Distributions that differ in timing. (i) S, a corporation, has two equal shareholders, A and B. Under S's bylaws, A and B are entitled to equal distributions. S distributes $50,000 to A in the current year, but does not distribute $50,000 to B until one year later. The circumstances indicate that the difference in timing did not occur by reason of a binding agreement relating to distribution or liquidation proceeds.

(ii) Under paragraph (l)(2)(i) of this section, the difference in timing of the distributions to A and B does not cause S to be treated as having more than one class of stock. However, section 7872 or other recharacterization principles may apply to determine the appropriate tax consequences.

Example 3. Treatment of excessive compensation. (i) S, a corporation, has two equal shareholders, C and D, who are each employed by S and have binding employment agreements with S. The compensation paid by S to C under C's employment agreement is reasonable. The compensation paid by S to D under D's employment agreement, however, is found to be excessive. The facts and circumstances do not reflect that a principal purpose of D's employment agreement is to circumvent the one class of stock requirement of section 1361(b)(1)(D) and this paragraph (l).

(ii) Under paragraph (l)(2)(i) of this section, the employment agreements are not governing provisions. Accordingly, S is not treated as having more than one class of stock by reason of the employment agreements, even though S is not allowed a deduction for the excessive compensation paid to D.

Example 4. Agreement to pay fringe benefits. (i) S, a corporation, is required under binding agreements to pay accident and health insurance premiums on behalf of certain of its employees who are also shareholders. Different premium amounts are paid by S for each employee-shareholder. The facts and circumstances do not reflect that a principal purpose of the agreements is to circumvent the one class of stock requirement of section 1361(b)(1)(D) and this paragraph (l).

(ii) Under paragraph (l)(2)(i) of this section, the agreements are not governing provisions. Accordingly, S is not treated as having more than one class of stock by reason of the agreements. In addition, S is not treated as having more than one class of stock by reason of the payment of fringe benefits.

Example 5. Below-market corporation-shareholder loan. (i) E is a shareholder of S, a corporation. S makes a below-market loan to E that is a corporation-shareholder loan to which section 7872 applies. Under section 7872, E is deemed to receive a distribution with respect to S stock by reason of the loan. The facts and circumstances do not reflect that a principal purpose of the loan is to circumvent the one class of stock require-

ment of section 1361(b)(1)(D) and this paragraph (l).

(ii) Under paragraph (l)(2)(i) of this section, the loan agreement is not a governing provision. Accordingly, S is not treated as having more than one class of stock by reason of the below-market loan to E.

Example 6. Agreement to adjust distributions for state tax burdens. (i) S, a corporation, executes a binding agreement with its shareholders to modify its normal distribution policy by making upward adjustments of its distributions to those shareholders who bear heavier state tax burdens. The adjustments are based on a formula that will give the shareholders equal after-tax distributions.

(ii) The binding agreement relates to distribution or liquidation proceeds. The agreement is thus a governing provision that alters the rights conferred by the outstanding stock of S to distribution proceeds so that those rights are not identical. Therefore, under paragraph (l)(2)(i) of this section, S is treated as having more than one class of stock.

Example 7. State law requirements for payment and withholding of income tax. (i) The law of State X requires corporations to pay state income taxes on behalf of nonresident shareholders. The law of State X does not require corporations to pay state income taxes on behalf of resident shareholders. S is incorporated in State X. S's resident shareholders have the right (for example, under the law of State X or pursuant to S's bylaws or a binding agreement) to distributions that take into account the payments S makes on behalf of its nonresident shareholders.

(ii) The payment by S of state income taxes on behalf of its nonresident shareholders are generally treated as constructive distributions to those shareholders. Because S's resident shareholders have the right to equal distributions, taking into account the constructive distributions to the nonresident shareholders, S's shares confer identical rights to distribution proceeds. Accordingly, under paragraph (l)(2)(ii) of this section, the state law requiring S to pay state income taxes on behalf of its nonresident shareholders is disregarded in determining whether S has more than one class of stock.

(iii) The same result would follow if the payments of state income taxes on behalf of nonresident shareholders are instead treated as advances to those shareholders and the governing provisions require the advances to be repaid or offset by reductions in distributions to those shareholders.

Example 8. Redemption agreements. (i) F, G, and H are shareholders of S, a corporation. F is also an employee of S. By agreement, S is to redeem F's shares on the termination of F's employment.

(ii) On these facts, under paragraph (l)(2)(iii)(B) of this section, the agreement is disregarded in determining whether all outstanding shares of S's stock confer identical rights to distribution and liquidation proceeds.

Example 9. Analysis of redemption agreements. (i) J, K, and L are shareholders of S, a corporation. L is also an employee of S. L's shares were not issued to L in connection with the performance of services. By agreement, S is to redeem L's shares for an amount significantly below their fair market value on the termination of L's employment or if S's sales fall below certain levels.

(ii) Under paragraph (l)(2)(iii)(B) of this section, the portion of the agreement providing for redemption of L's stock on termination of employment is disregarded. Under paragraph (l)(2)(iii)(A), the portion of the agreement providing for redemption of L's stock if S's sales fall below certain levels is disregarded unless a principal purpose of that portion of the agreement is to circumvent the one class of stock requirement of section 1361(b)(1)(D) and this paragraph (l).

(3) *Stock taken into account.*—Except as provided in paragraphs (b)(3), (4), and (5) of this section (relating to restricted stock, deferred compensation plans, and straight debt), in determining whether all outstanding shares of stock confer identical rights to distribution and liquidation proceeds, all outstanding shares of stock of a corporation are taken into account. For example, substantially nonvested stock with respect to which an election under section 83(b) has been made is taken into account in determining whether a corporation has a second class of stock, and such stock is not treated as a second class of stock if the stock confers rights to distribution and liquidation proceeds that are identical, within the meaning of paragraph (l)(1) of this section, to the rights conferred by the other outstanding shares of stock.

(4) *Other instruments, obligations, or arrangements treated as a second class of stock.*—(i) *In general.*—Instruments, obligations, or arrangements are not treated as a second class of stock for purposes of this paragraph (l) unless they are described in paragraphs (l)(4)(ii) or (iii) of this section. However, in no event are instruments, obligations, or arrangements described in paragraph (b)(4) of this section (relating to deferred compensation plans), paragraphs (l)(4)(iii)(B) and (C) of this section (relating to the exceptions and safe harbor for options), paragraph (l)(4)(ii)(B) of this section (relating to the safe harbors for certain short-term unwritten advances and proportionally-held debt), or paragraph (l)(5) of this section (relating to the safe harbor for straight debt), treated as a second class of stock for purposes of this paragraph (l).

(ii) *Instruments, obligations, or arrangements treated as equity under general principles.*—(A) *In general.*—Except as provided in paragraph (l)(4)(i) of this section, any instrument, obligation, or arrangement issued by a corpora-

tion (other than outstanding shares of stock described in paragraph (l)(3) of this section), regardless of whether designated as debt, is treated as a second class of stock of the corporation—

(1) If the instrument, obligation, or arrangement constitutes equity or otherwise results in the holder being treated as the owner of stock under general principles of Federal tax law; and

(2) A principal purpose of issuing or entering into the instrument, obligation, or arrangement is to circumvent the rights to distribution or liquidation proceeds conferred by the outstanding shares of stock or to circumvent the limitation on eligible shareholders contained in paragraph (b)(1) of this section.

(B) *Safe harbor for certain short-term unwritten advances and proportionately held obligations.*—(1) *Short-term unwritten advances.*—Unwritten advances from a shareholder that do not exceed $10,000 in the aggregate at any time during the taxable year of the corporation, are treated as debt by the parties, and are expected to be repaid within a reasonable time are not treated as a second class of stock for that taxable year, even if the advances are considered equity under general principles of Federal tax law. The failure of an unwritten advance to meet this safe harbor will not result in a second class of stock unless the advance is considered equity under paragraph (l)(4)(ii)(A)(1) of this section and a principal purpose of the advance is to circumvent the rights of the outstanding shares of stock or the limitation on eligible shareholders under paragraph (l)(4)(ii)(A)(2) of this section.

(2) *Proportionately-held obligations.*—Obligations of the same class that are considered equity under general principles of Federal tax law, but are owned solely by the owners of, and in the same proportion as, the outstanding stock of the corporation, are not treated as a second class of stock. Furthermore, an obligation or obligations owned by the sole shareholder of a corporation are always held proportionately to the corporation's outstanding stock. The obligations that are considered equity that do not meet this safe harbor will not result in a second class of stock unless a principal purpose of the obligations is to circumvent the rights of the outstanding shares of stock or the limitation on eligible shareholders under paragraph (l)(4)(ii)(A)(2) of this section.

(iii) *Certain call options, warrants or similar instruments.*—(A) *In general.*—Except as otherwise provided in this paragraph (l)(4)(iii), a call option, warrant, or similar instrument (collectively, call option) issued by a corporation is treated as a second class of stock of the corporation if, taking into account all the facts and circumstances, the call option is substantially certain to be exercised (by the holder or a potential transferee) and has a strike price substantially below the fair market value of the underlying stock on the date that the call option is issued, transferred by a person who is an eligible shareholder under paragraph (b)(1) of this section to a person who is not an eligible shareholder under paragraph (b)(1) of this section, or materially modified. For purposes of this paragraph (l)(4)(iii), if an option is issued in connection with a loan and the time period in which the option can be exercised is extended in connection with (and consistent with) a modification of the terms of the loan, the extension of the time period in which the option may be exercised is not considered a material modification. In addition, a call option does not have a strike price substantially below fair market value if the price at the time of exercise cannot, pursuant to the terms of the instrument, be substantially below the fair market value of the underlying stock at the time of exercise.

(B) *Certain exceptions.*—*(1)* A call option is not treated as a second class of stock for purposes of this paragraph (l) if it is issued to a person that is actively and regularly engaged in the business of lending and issued in connection with a commercially reasonable loan to the corporation. This paragraph (l)(4)(iii)(B)(*1*) continues to apply if the call option is transferred with the loan (or if a portion of the call option is transferred with a corresponding portion of the loan). However, if the call option is transferred without a corresponding portion of the loan, this paragraph (l)(4)(iii)(B)(*1*) ceases to apply. Upon that transfer, the call option is tested under paragraph (l)(4)(iii)(A) (notwithstanding anything in that paragraph to the contrary) if, but for this paragraph, the call option would have been treated as a second class of stock on the date it was issued.

(*2*) A call option that is issued to an individual who is either an employee or an independent contractor in connection with the performance of services for the corporation or a related corporation (and that is not excessive by reference to the services performed) is not treated as a second class of stock for purposes of this paragraph (l) if—

(*i*) The call option is nontransferable within the meaning of § 1.83-3(d); and

(*ii*) The call option does not have a readily ascertainable fair market value as defined in § 1.83-7(b) at the time the option is issued.

If the call option becomes transferable, this paragraph (l)(4)(iii)(B)(2) ceases to apply. Solely for purposes of this paragraph (l)(4)(iii)(B)(2), a corporation is related to the issuing corporation if more than 50 percent of the total voting power and total value of its stock is owned by the issuing corporation.

(*3*) The Commissioner may provide other exceptions by Revenue Ruling or other published guidance.

(C) *Safe harbor for certain options.*—A call option is not treated as a second class of stock if, on the date the call option is issued, transferred by a person who is an eligible shareholder under paragraph (b)(1) of this section to a person who is not an eligible shareholder under paragraph (b)(1) of this section, or materially modified, the strike price of the call option is at least 90 percent of the fair market value of the underlying stock on that date. For purposes of this paragraph (l)(4)(iii)(C), a good faith determination of fair market value by the corporation will be respected unless it can be shown that the value was substantially in error and the determination of the value was not performed with reasonable diligence to obtain a fair value. Failure of an option to meet this safe harbor will not necessarily result in the option being treated as a second class of stock.

(iv) *Convertible debt.*—A convertible debt instrument is considered a second class of stock if—

(A) It would be treated as a second class of stock under paragraph (l)(4)(ii) of this section (relating to instruments, obligations, or arrangements treated as equity under general principles); or

(B) It embodies rights equivalent to those of a call option that would be treated as a second class of stock under paragraph (l)(4)(iii) of this section (relating to certain call options, warrants, and similar instruments).

(v) *Examples.*—The application of this paragraph (l)(4) may be illustrated by the following examples. In each of the examples, the S corporation requirements of section 1361 are satisfied except as otherwise stated, the corporation has in effect an S election under section 1362, and the corporation has only the shareholders described.

Example 1. Transfer of call option by eligible shareholder to ineligible shareholder. (i) S, a corporation, has 10 shareholders. S issues call options to A, B, and C, individuals who are U.S. residents. A, B, and C are not shareholders, employees, or independent contractors of S. The options have a strike price of $40 and are issued on a date when the fair market value of S stock is also $40. A year later, P, a partnership, purchases A's option. On the date of transfer, the fair market value of S stock is $80.

(ii) On the date the call option is issued, its strike price is not substantially below the fair market value of the S stock. Under paragraph (l)(4)(iii)(A) of this section, whether a call option is a second class of stock must be redetermined if the call option is transferred by a person who is an eligible shareholder under paragraph (b)(1) of this section to a person who is not an eligible shareholder under paragraph (b)(1) of this section. In this case, A is an eligible shareholder of S under paragraph (b)(1) of this section, but P is not. Accordingly, the option is retested on the date it is transferred to D.

(iii) Because on the date the call option is transferred to P its strike price is 50% of the fair market value, the strike price is substantially below the fair market value of the S stock. Accordingly, the call option is treated as a second class of stock as of the date it is transferred to P if, at that time, it is determined that the option is substantially certain to be exercised. The determination of whether the option is substantially certain to be exercised is made on the basis of all the facts and circumstances.

Example 2. Call option issued in connection with the performance of services. (i) E is a bona fide employee of S, a corporation. S issues to E a call option in connection with E's performance of services. At the time the call option is issued, it is not transferable and does not have a readily ascertainable fair market value. However, the call option becomes transferable before it is exercised by E.

(ii) While the option is not transferable, under paragraph (l)(4)(iii)(B)(2) of this section, it is not treated as a second class of stock, regardless of its strike price. When the option becomes transferable, that paragraph ceases to apply, and the general rule of paragraph (l)(4)(iii)(A) of this section applies. Accordingly, if the option is materially modified or is transferred to a person who is not an eligible shareholder under paragraph (b)(1) of this section, and on the date of such modification or transfer, the option is substantially certain to be exercised and has a strike price substantially below the fair market value of the underlying stock, the option is treated as a second class of stock.

(iii) If E left S's employment before the option became transferable, the exception provided by paragraph (l)(4)(iii)(B)(2) would continue to apply until the option became transferable.

(5) *Straight debt safe harbor.*—(i) *In general.*—Notwithstanding paragraph (l)(4) of this section, straight debt is not treated as a second class of stock. For purposes of section 1361(c)(5) and this section, the term straight debt means a written unconditional obligation, regardless of whether embodied in a formal note, to pay a sum certain on demand, or on a specified due date, which—

(A) Does not provide for an interest rate or payment dates that are contingent on profits, the borrower's discretion, the payment of dividends with respect to common stock, or similar factors;

(B) Is not convertible (directly or indirectly) into stock or any other equity interest of the S corporation; and

(C) Is held by an individual (other than a nonresident alien), an estate, or a trust described in section 1361(c)(2).

(ii) *Subordination.*—The fact that an obligation is subordinated to other debt of the corporation does not prevent the obligation from qualifying as straight debt.

(iii) *Modification or transfer.*—An obligation that originally qualifies as straight debt ceases to so qualify if the obligation—

(A) Is materially modified so that it no longer satisfies the definition of straight debt; or

(B) Is transferred to a third party who is not an eligible shareholder under paragraph (b)(1) of this section.

(iv) *Treatment of straight debt for other purposes.*—An obligation of an S corporation that satisfies the definition of straight debt in paragraph (l)(5)(i) of this section is not treated as a second class of stock even if it is considered equity under general principles of Federal tax law. Such an obligation is generally treated as debt and when so treated is subject to the applicable rules governing indebtedness for other purposes of the Code. Accordingly, interest paid or accrued with respect to a straight debt obligation is generally treated as interest by the corporation and the recipient and does not constitute a distribution to which section 1368 applies. However, if a straight debt obligation bears a rate of interest that is unreasonably high, an appropriate portion of the interest may be recharacterized and treated as a payment that is not interest. Such a recharacterization does not result in a second class of stock.

(v) *Treatment of C corporation debt upon conversion to S status.*—If a C corporation has outstanding an obligation that satisfies the definition of straight debt in paragraph (l)(5)(i) of this section, but that is considered equity under general principles of Federal tax law, the obligation is not treated as a second class of stock for purposes of this section if the C corporation converts to S status. In addition, the conversion from C corporation status to S corporation status is not treated as an exchange of debt for stock with respect to such an instrument.

(6) *Inadvertent terminations.*—See section 1362(f) and the regulations thereunder for rules relating to inadvertent terminations in cases where the one class of stock requirement has been inadvertently breached.

(7) *Effective date.*—Section 1.1361-1(l) generally applies to taxable years of a corporation beginning on or after May 28, 1992. However, §1.1361-1(l) does not apply to: an instrument, obligation, or arrangement issued or entered into before May 28, 1992, and not materially modified after that date; a buy-sell agreement, redemption agreement, or agreement restricting transferabil-

ity entered into before May 28, 1992, and not materially modified after that date; or a call option or similar instrument issued before May 28, 1992, and not materially modified after that date. In addition, a corporation and its shareholders may apply this §1.1361-1(l) to prior taxable years.

(m) *Electing small business trust (ESBT).*— (1) *Definition.*—(i) *General rule.*—An electing small business trust (ESBT) means any trust if it meets the following requirements: the trust does not have as a beneficiary any person other than an individual, an estate, an organization described in section 170(c)(2) through (5), or an organization described in section 170(c)(1) that holds a contingent interest in such trust and is not a potential current beneficiary; no interest in the trust has been acquired by purchase; and the trustee of the trust makes a timely ESBT election for the trust.

(ii) *Qualified beneficiaries.*—(A) *In general.*—For purposes of this section, a beneficiary includes a person who has a present, remainder, or reversionary interest in the trust.

(B) *Distributee trusts.*—A distributee trust is the beneficiary of the ESBT only if the distributee trust is an organization described in section 170(c)(2) or (3). In all other situations, any person who has a beneficial interest in a distributee trust is a beneficiary of the ESBT. A distributee trust is a trust that receives or may receive a distribution from an ESBT, whether the rights to receive the distribution are fixed or contingent, or immediate or deferred.

(C) *Powers of appointment.*—A person in whose favor a power of appointment could be exercised is not a beneficiary of an ESBT until the holder of the power of appointment actually exercises the power in favor of such person.

(D) *Nonresident aliens.*—A nonresident alien as defined in section 7701(b)(1)(B) is an eligible beneficiary of an ESBT. However, see paragraph (m)(4)(i) and (m)(5)(iii) of this section if the nonresident alien is a potential current beneficiary of the ESBT (which would result in an ineligible shareholder and termination of the S corporation election).

(iii) *Interests acquired by purchase.*—A trust does not qualify as an ESBT if any interest in the trust has been acquired by purchase. Generally, if a person acquires an interest in the trust and thereby becomes a beneficiary of the trust as defined in paragraph (m)(1)(ii)(A), and any portion of the basis in the acquired interest in the trust is determined under section 1012, such interest has been acquired by purchase. This includes a net gift of a beneficial interest in the trust, in which the person acquiring the benefi-

cial interest pays the gift tax. The trust itself may acquire S corporation stock or other property by purchase or in a part-gift, part-sale transaction.

(iv) *Ineligible trusts.*—An ESBT does not include—

(A) Any qualified subchapter S trust (as defined in section 1361(d)(3)) if an election under section 1361(d)(2) applies with respect to any corporation the stock of which is held by the trust;

(B) Any trust exempt from tax or not subject to tax under subtitle A; or

(C) Any charitable remainder annuity trust or charitable remainder unitrust (as defined in section 664(d)).

(2) *ESBT election.*—(i) *In general.*—The trustee of the trust must make the ESBT election by signing and filing, with the service center where the S corporation files its income tax return, a statement that meets the requirements of paragraph (m)(2)(ii) of this section. If there is more than one trustee, the trustee or trustees with authority to legally bind the trust must sign the election statement. If any one of several trustees can legally bind the trust, only one trustee needs to sign the election statement. Generally, only one ESBT election is made for the trust, regardless of the number of S corporations whose stock is held by the ESBT. However, if the ESBT holds stock in multiple S corporations that file in different service centers, the ESBT election must be filed with all the relevant service centers where the corporations file their income tax returns. This requirement applies only at the time of the initial ESBT election; if the ESBT later acquires stock in an S corporation which files its income tax return at a different service center, a new ESBT election is not required.

(ii) *Election statement.*—The election statement must include—

(A) The name, address, and taxpayer identification number of the trust, the potential current beneficiaries, and the S corporations in which the trust currently holds stock. If the trust includes a power described in paragraph (m)(4)(vi)(B) of this section, then the election statement must include a statement that such a power is included in the instrument, but does not need to include the name, address, or taxpayer identification number of any particular charity or any other information regarding the power.

(B) An identification of the election as an ESBT election made under section 1361(e)(3);

(C) The first date on which the trust owned stock in each S corporation;

(D) The date on which the election is to become effective (not earlier than 15 days and two months before the date on which the election is filed); and

(E) *Representations signed by the trustee stating that—*

(1) The trust meets the definitional requirements of section 1361(e)(1); and

(2) All potential current beneficiaries of the trust meet the shareholder requirements of section 1361(b)(1).

(iii) *Due date for ESBT election.*—The ESBT election must be filed within the time requirements prescribed in paragraph (j)(6)(iii) of this section for filing a qualified subchapter S trust (QSST) election.

(iv) *Election by a trust described in section 1361(c)(2)(A)(ii) or (iii).*—A trust that is a qualified S corporation shareholder under section 1361(c)(2)(A)(ii) or (iii) may elect ESBT treatment at any time during the 2-year period described in those sections or the 16-day-and-2-month period beginning on the date after the end of the 2-year period. If the trust makes an ineffective ESBT election, the trust will continue nevertheless to qualify as an eligible S corporation shareholder for the remainder of the period described in section 1361(c)(2)(A)(ii) or (iii).

(v) *No protective election.*—A trust cannot make a conditional ESBT election that would be effective only in the event the trust fails to meet the requirements for an eligible trust described in section 1361(c)(2)(A)(i) through (iv). If a trust attempts to make such a conditional ESBT election and it fails to qualify as an eligible S corporation shareholder under section 1361(c)(2)(A)(i) through (iv), the S corporation election will be ineffective or will terminate because the corporation will have an ineligible shareholder. Relief may be available under section 1362(f) for an inadvertent ineffective S corporation election or an inadvertent S corporation election termination. In addition, a trust that qualifies as an ESBT may make an ESBT election notwithstanding that the trust is a wholly-owned grantor trust.

(3) *Effect of ESBT election.*—(i) *General rule.*—If a trust makes a valid ESBT election, the trust will be treated as an ESBT for purposes of chapter 1 of the Internal Revenue Code as of the effective date of the ESBT election.

(ii) *Employer Identification Number.*—An ESBT has only one employer identification number (EIN). If an existing trust makes an ESBT election, the trust continues to use the EIN it currently uses.

(iii) *Taxable year.*—If an ESBT election is effective on a day other than the first day of the trust's taxable year, the ESBT election does not cause the trust's taxable year to close. The termination of the ESBT election (including a termination caused by a conversion of the ESBT to a QSST) other than on the last day of the trust's taxable year also does not cause the trust's taxable year to close. In either case, the trust files one tax return for the taxable year.

(iv) *Allocation of S corporation items.*—If, during the taxable year of an S corporation, a trust is an ESBT for part of the year and an eligible shareholder under section 1361(c)(2)(A)(i) through (iv) for the rest of the year, the S corporation items are allocated between the two types of trusts under section 1377(a). See § 1.1377-1(a)(2)(iii).

(v) *Estimated taxes.*—If an ESBT election is effective on a day other than the first day of the trust's taxable year, the trust is considered one trust for purposes of estimated taxes under section 6654.

(4) *Potential current beneficiaries.*—(i) *In general.*—For purposes of determining whether a corporation is a small business corporation within the meaning of section 1361(b)(1), each potential current beneficiary of an ESBT generally is treated as a shareholder of the corporation. Subject to the provisions of this paragraph (m)(4), a potential current beneficiary generally is, with respect to any period, any person who at any time during such period is entitled to, or in the discretion of any person may receive, a distribution from the principal or income of the trust. A person is treated as a shareholder of the S corporation at any moment in time when that person is entitled to, or in the discretion of any person may, receive a distribution of principal or income of the trust. No person is treated as a potential current beneficiary solely because that person holds any future interest in the trust.

(ii) *Grantor trusts.*—If all or a portion of an ESBT is treated as owned by a person under subpart E, part I, subchapter J, chapter 1 of the Internal Revenue Code, such owner is a potential current beneficiary in addition to persons described in paragraph (m)(4)(i) of this section.

(iii) *Special rule for dispositions of stock.*—Notwithstanding the provisions of paragraph (m)(4)(i) of this section, if a trust disposes of all of the stock which it holds in an S corporation, then, with respect to that corporation, any person who first met the definition of a potential current beneficiary during the 1-year period ending on the date of such disposition is not a potential current beneficiary and thus is not a shareholder of that corporation.

(iv) *Distributee trusts.*—(A) *In general.*—This paragraph (m)(4)(iv) contains the rules for determining who are the potential current beneficiaries of an ESBT if a distributee trust becomes entitled to, or at the discretion of any person, may receive a distribution from principal or income of an ESBT. A distributee trust does not include a trust that is not currently in existence. For this purpose, a trust is not currently in existence if the trust has no assets and no items of income, loss, deduction, or credit. Thus, if a trust instrument provides for a trust to be funded at

Reg. § 1.1361-1(m)(4)(iv)(A)

some future time, the future trust is not currently a distributee trust.

(B) If the distributee trust is not a trust described in section 1361(c)(2)(A), then the distributee trust is the potential current beneficiary of the ESBT and the corporation's S corporation election terminates.

(C) If the distributee trust is a trust described in section 1361(c)(2)(A), the persons who would be its potential current beneficiaries (as defined in paragraphs (m)(4)(i) and (ii) of this section) if the distributee trust were an ESBT are treated as the potential current beneficiaries of the ESBT. Notwithstanding the preceding sentence, however, if the distributee trust is a trust described in section 1361(c)(2)(A)(ii) or (iii), the estate described in section 1361(c)(2)(B)(ii) or (iii) is treated as the potential current beneficiary of the ESBT for the 2-year period during which such trust would be permitted as a shareholder.

(D) For the purposes of paragraph (m)(4)(iv)(C) of this section, a trust will be deemed to be described in section 1361(c)(2)(A) if such trust would qualify for a QSST election under section 1361(d) or an ESBT election under section 1361(e) if it owned S corporation stock.

(v) *Contingent distributions.*—A person who is entitled to receive a distribution only after a specified time or upon the occurrence of a specified event (such as the death of the holder of a power of appointment) is not a potential current beneficiary until such time or the occurrence of such event.

(vi) *Currently exercisable powers of appointment and other powers.*—(A) *Powers of appointment.*—A person to whom a distribution may be made during any period pursuant to a power of appointment (as described for transfer tax purposes in section 2041 and §20.2041-1(b) of this chapter and section 2514 and §25.2514-1(b) of this chapter) is not a potential current beneficiary unless the power is exercised in favor of that person during the period. It is immaterial for purposes of this paragraph (m)(4)(vi)(A) whether such power of appointment is a "general power of appointment" for transfer tax purposes as described in §§20.2041-1(c) and 25.2514-1(c) of this chapter. The mere existence of one or more powers of appointment during the lifetime of a power holder that would permit current distributions from the trust to be made to more than the number of persons described in section 1361(b)(1)(A) or to a person described in section 1361(b)(1)(B) or (C) will not cause the S corporation election to terminate unless one or more of such powers are exercised, collectively, in favor of an excessive number of persons or in favor of a person who is ineligible to be an S corporation shareholder. For purposes of this paragraph (m)(4)(vi)(A), a "power of appointment" includes a power, regardless of by whom held, to add a beneficiary or class of beneficiaries to the class of potential current beneficiaries, but

generally does not include a power held by a fiduciary who is not also a beneficiary of the trust to spray or sprinkle trust distributions among beneficiaries. Nothing in this paragraph (m)(4)(vi)(A) alters the definition of "power of appointment" for purposes of any provision of the Internal Revenue Code or the regulations.

(B) *Powers to distribute to certain organizations not pursuant to powers of appointment.*—If a trustee or other fiduciary has a power (that does not constitute a power of appointment for transfer tax purposes as described in §§20.2041-1(b) and 25.2514-1(b) of this chapter) to make distributions from the trust to one or more members of a class of organizations described in section 1361(c)(6), such organizations will be counted collectively as only one potential current beneficiary for purposes of this paragraph (m), except that each organization receiving a distribution also will be counted as a potential current beneficiary. This paragraph (m)(4)(vi)(B) shall not apply to a power to currently distribute to one or more particular charitable organizations described in section 1361(c)(6). Each of such organizations is a potential current beneficiary of the trust.

(vii) *Number of shareholders.*—Each potential current beneficiary of the ESBT, as defined in paragraphs (m)(4)(i) through (vi) of this section, is counted as a shareholder of any S corporation whose stock is owned by the ESBT. During any period in which the ESBT has no potential current beneficiaries, the ESBT is counted as the shareholder. A person is counted as only one shareholder of an S corporation even though that person may be treated as a shareholder of the S corporation by direct ownership and through one or more eligible trusts described in section 1361(c)(2)(A). Thus, for example, if a person owns stock in an S corporation and is a potential current beneficiary of an ESBT that owns stock in the same S corporation, that person is counted as one shareholder of the S corporation. Similarly, if a husband owns stock in an S corporation and his wife is a potential current beneficiary of an ESBT that owns stock in the same S corporation, the husband and wife will be counted as one shareholder of the S corporation.

(viii) *Miscellaneous.*—Payments made by an ESBT to a third party on behalf of a beneficiary are considered to be payments made directly to the beneficiary. The right of a beneficiary to assign the beneficiary's interest to a third party does not result in the third party being a potential current beneficiary until that interest is actually assigned.

(5) *ESBT terminations.*—(i) *Ceasing to meet ESBT requirements.*—A trust ceases to be an ESBT on the first day the trust fails to meet the definition of an ESBT under section 1361(e). The last day the trust is treated as an ESBT is the day

before the date on which the trust fails to meet the definition of an ESBT.

(ii) *Disposition of S stock.*—In general, a trust ceases to be an ESBT on the first day following the day the trust disposes of all S corporation stock. However, if the trust is using the installment method to report income from the sale or disposition of its stock in an S corporation, the trust ceases to be an ESBT on the day following the earlier of the day the last installment payment is received by the trust or the day the trust disposes of the installment obligation.

(iii) *Potential current beneficiaries that are ineligible shareholders.*—If a potential current beneficiary of an ESBT is not an eligible shareholder of a small business corporation within the meaning of section 1361(b)(1), the S corporation election terminates. For example, the S corporation election will terminate if a nonresident alien becomes a potential current beneficiary of an ESBT. Such a potential current beneficiary is treated as an ineligible shareholder beginning on the day such person becomes a potential current beneficiary, and the S corporation election terminates on that date. However, see the special rule of paragraph (m)(4)(iii) of this section. If the S corporation election terminates, relief may be available under section 1362(f).

(6) *Revocation of ESBT election.*—An ESBT election may be revoked only with the consent of the Commissioner. The application for consent to revoke the election must be submitted to the Internal Revenue Service in the form of a letter ruling request under the appropriate revenue procedure.

(7) *Converting an ESBT to a QSST.*—For a trust that seeks to convert from an ESBT to a QSST, the consent of the Commissioner is hereby granted to revoke the ESBT election as of the effective date of the QSST election, if all the following requirements are met:

(i) The trust meets all of the requirements to be a QSST under section 1361(d).

(ii) The trustee and the current income beneficiary of the trust sign the QSST election. The QSST election must be filed with the service center where the S corporation files its income tax return. This QSST election must state at the top of the document "ATTENTION ENTITY CONTROL—CONVERSION OF AN ESBT TO A QSST PURSUANT TO SECTION 1.1361-1(m)" and include all information otherwise required for a QSST election under § 1.1361-1(j)(6). A separate QSST election must be made with respect to the stock of each S corporation held by the trust.

(iii) The trust has not converted from a QSST to an ESBT within the 36-month period preceding the effective date of the new QSST election.

(iv) The date on which the QSST election is to be effective cannot be more than 15 days and two months prior to the date on which the election is filed and cannot be more than 12 months after the date on which the election is filed. If an election specifies an effective date more than 15 days and two months prior to the date on which the election is filed, it will be effective on the day that is 15 days and two months prior to the date on which it is filed. If an election specifies an effective date more than 12 months after the date on which the election is filed, it will be effective on the day that is 12 months after the date it is filed.

(8) *Examples.*—The provisions of this paragraph (m) are illustrated by the following examples in which it is assumed, unless otherwise specified, that all noncorporate persons are citizens or residents of the United States:

Example 1. (i) *ESBT election with section 663(c) separate shares.* On January 1, 2003, *M* contributes S corporation stock to Trust for the benefit of *M's* three children *A, B,* and *C.* Pursuant to section 663(c), each of Trust's separate shares for *A, B,* and *C* will be treated as separate trusts for purposes of determining the amount of distributable net income (DNI) in the application of sections 661 and 662. On January 15, 2003, the trustee of Trust files a valid ESBT election for Trust effective January 1, 2003. Trust will be treated as a single ESBT and will have a single S portion taxable under section 641(c).

(ii) *ESBT acquires stock of an additional S corporation.* On February 15, 2003, Trust acquires stock of an additional S corporation. Because Trust is already an ESBT, Trust does not need to make an additional ESBT election.

(iii) *Section 663(c) shares of ESBT convert to separate QSSTs.* Effective January 1, 2004, *A, B, C,* and Trust's trustee elect to convert each separate share of Trust into a separate QSST pursuant to paragraph (m)(7) of this section. For each separate share, they file a separate election for each S corporation whose stock is held by Trust. Each separate share will be treated as a separate QSST.

Example 2. (i) *Invalid potential current beneficiary.* Effective January 1, 2005, Trust makes a valid ESBT election. On January 1, 2006, *A,* a nonresident alien, becomes a potential current beneficiary of Trust. Trust does not dispose of all of its S corporation stock within one year after January 1, 2006. As of January 1, 2006, *A* is the potential current beneficiary of Trust and therefore is treated as a shareholder of the S corporation. Because *A* is not an eligible shareholder of an S corporation under section 1361(b)(1), the S corporation election of any corporation in which Trust holds stock terminates effective January 1, 2006. Relief may be available under section 1362(f).

(ii) *Invalid potential current beneficiary and disposition of S stock.* Assume the same facts as in *Example 2* (i) except that within one year after

Reg. § 1.1361-1(m)(8)

January 1, 2006, trustee of Trust disposes of all Trust's S corporation stock. *A* is not considered a potential current beneficiary of Trust and therefore is not treated as a shareholder of any S corporation in which Trust previously held stock.

Example 3. Subpart E trust. M transfers stock in *X*, an S corporation, and other assets to Trust for the benefit of *B* and *B*'s siblings. *M* retains no powers or interest in Trust. Under section 678(a), *B* is treated as the owner of a portion of the *X* stock. No beneficiary has acquired any portion of his or her interest in Trust by purchase, and Trust is not an ineligible trust under paragraph (m)(1)(iv) of this section. Trust is eligible to make an ESBT election.

Example 4. Subpart E trust continuing after grantor's death. On January 1, 2003, M transfers stock in *X*, an S corporation, and other assets to Trust. Under the terms of Trust, the trustee of Trust has complete discretion to distribute the income or principal to *M* during *M*'s lifetime and to *M*'s children upon *M*'s death. During *M*'s life, *M* is treated as the owner of Trust under section 677. The trustee of Trust makes a valid election to treat Trust as an ESBT effective January 1, 2003. On March 28, 2004, *M* dies. Under applicable local law, Trust does not terminate on *M*'s death. Trust continues to be an ESBT after *M*'s death, and no additional ESBT election needs to be filed for Trust after *M*'s death.

Example 5. Potential current beneficiaries and distributee trust holding S corporation stock. Trust-1 has a valid ESBT election in effect. The trustee of Trust-1 has the power to make distributions to *A* directly or to any trust created for the benefit of *A*. On January 1, 2003, M creates Trust-2 for the benefit of *A*. Also on January 1, 2003, the trustee of Trust-1 distributes some S corporation stock to Trust-2. *A*, as the current income beneficiary of Trust-2, makes a timely and effective election to treat Trust-2 as a QSST. Because Trust-2 is a valid S corporation shareholder, the distribution to Trust-2 does not terminate the ESBT election of Trust-1. Trust-2 itself will not be counted toward the shareholder limit of section 1361(b)(1)(A). Additionally, because *A* is already counted as an S corporation shareholder because of *A*'s status as a potential current income beneficiary of Trust-1, *A* is not counted again by reason of *A*'s status as the deemed owner of Trust-2.

Example 6. Potential current beneficiaries and distributee trust not holding S corporation stock. (i) *Distributee trust that would itself qualify as an ESBT.* Trust-1 holds stock in *X*, an S corporation, and has a valid ESBT election in effect. Under the terms of Trust-1, the trustee has discretion to make distributions to *A*, *B*, and Trust-2, a trust for the benefit of *C*, *D*, and *E*. Trust-2 would qualify to be an ESBT, but it owns no S corporation stock and has made no ESBT election. Under paragraph (m)(4)(iv) of this section, Trust-2's potential current beneficiaries are treated as the

potential current beneficiaries of Trust-1 and are counted as shareholders for purposes of section 1361(b)(1). Thus, *A*, *B*, *C*, *D*, and *E* are potential current beneficiaries of Trust-1 and are counted as shareholders for purposes of section 1361(b)(1). Trust-2 itself will not be counted as a shareholder of Trust-1 for purposes of section 1361(b)(1).

(ii) *Distributee trust that would not qualify as an ESBT or a QSST.* Assume the same facts as in paragraph (i) of this *Example 6* except that *D* is a nonresident alien. Trust-2 would not be eligible to make an ESBT or QSST election if it owned S corporation stock and therefore Trust-2 is a potential current beneficiary of Trust-1. Since Trust-2 is not an eligible shareholder, *X*'s S corporation election terminates.

(iii) *Distributee trust that is a section 1361(c)(2)(A)(ii) trust.* Assume the same facts as in paragraph (i) of this *Example 6* except that Trust-2 is a trust treated as owned by *A* under section 676 because *A* has the power to revoke Trust-2 at any time prior to *A*'s death. On January 1, 2003, *A* dies. Because Trust-2 is a trust described in section 1361(c)(2)(A)(ii) during the 2-year period beginning on the day of *A*'s death, under paragraph (m)(4)(iv)(C) of this section, Trust-2's only potential current beneficiary is the person listed in section 1361(c)(2)(B)(ii), *A*'s estate. Thus, *B* and *A*'s estate are potential current beneficiaries of Trust-1 and are counted as shareholders for purposes of section 1361(b)(1).

Example 7. Potential current beneficiaries and powers of appointment. M creates Trust from which *A* has a right to all net income and funds it with S corporation stock. *A* also has a currently exercisable power to appoint income or principal to anyone except *A*, *A*'s creditors, *A*'s estate, and the creditors of *A*'s estate. The potential current beneficiaries of Trust for any period will be *A* and each person who receives a distribution from Trust pursuant to *A*'s exercise of *A*'s power of appointment during that period.

Example 8. Power to distribute to an unlimited class of charitable organizations not pursuant to a power of appointment. M creates Trust from which *A* has a right to all net income and funds it with S corporation stock. In addition, the trustee of Trust, who is not *A* or a descendant of *M*, has the power to make discretionary distributions of principal to the living descendants of *M* and to any organizations described in section 1361(c)(6). The potential current beneficiaries of Trust for any period will be *A*, each then-living descendant of *M*, and each exempt organization described in section 1361(c)(6) that receives a distribution during that period. In addition, the class of exempt organizations will be counted as one potential current beneficiary.

Example 9. Power to distribute to a class of named charitable organizations not pursuant to a power of appointment. M creates Trust from which *A* has a right to all net income and funds it with S corporation stock. In addition, the trustee of

Trust, who is not A or a descendant of M, has the power to make discretionary distributions of principal to the living descendants of M and to X, Y, and Z, each of which is an organization described in section 1361(c)(6). The potential current beneficiaries of Trust for any period will be A, X, Y, Z, and each living descendant of M.

(9) *Effective date.*—This paragraph (m) is applicable for taxable years of ESBTs beginning on and after May 14, 2002. Paragraphs (m)(2)(ii)(A), (m)(4)(iii) and (vi), and (m)(8), *Example 2, Example 5, Example 7, Example 8,* and *Example 9* of this section are effective on August 14, 2008. [Reg. § 1.1361-1.]

☐ [*T.D.* 8419, 5-28-92. *Amended by T.D.* 8600, 7-20-95; *T.D.* 8869, 1-20-2000; *T.D.* 8940, 2-12-2001; *T.D.* 8994, 5-13-2002; *T.D.* 9078, 7-16-2003 *and T.D.* 9422, 8-13-2008.]

[Reg. § 1.1361-2]

§ 1.1361-2. Definitions relating to S corporation subsidiaries.—(a) *In general.*—The term *qualified subchapter S subsidiary* (QSub) means any domestic corporation that is not an ineligible corporation (as defined in section 1361(b)(2) and the regulations thereunder), if—

(1) 100 percent of the stock of such corporation is held by an S corporation; and

(2) The S corporation properly elects to treat the subsidiary as a QSub under § 1.1361-3.

(b) *Stock treated as held by S corporation.*—For purposes of satisfying the 100 percent stock ownership requirement in section 1361(b)(3)(B)(i) and paragraph (a)(1) of this section—

(1) Stock of a corporation is treated as held by an S corporation if the S corporation is the owner of that stock for Federal income tax purposes; and

(2) Any outstanding instruments, obligations, or arrangements of the corporation which would not be considered stock for purposes of section 1361(b)(1)(D) if the corporation were an S corporation are not treated as outstanding stock of the QSub.

(c) *Straight debt safe harbor.*—Section 1.1361-1(1)(5)(iv) and (v) apply to an obligation of a corporation for which a QSub election is made if that obligation would satisfy the definition of straight debt in § 1.1361-1(1)(5) if issued by the S corporation.

(d) *Examples.*—The following examples illustrate the application of this section:

Example 1. X, an S corporation, owns 100 percent of Y, a corporation for which a valid QSub election is in effect for the taxable year. Y owns 100 percent of Z, a corporation otherwise eligible for QSub status. X may elect to treat Z as a QSub under section 1361(b)(3)(B)(ii).

Example 2. Assume the same facts as in *Example 1,* except that Y is a business entity that is disregarded as an entity separate from its owner under § 301.7701-2(c)(2) of this chapter. X may elect to treat Z as a QSub.

Example 3. Assume the same facts as in *Example 1,* except that Y owns 50 percent of Z, and X owns the other 50 percent. X may elect to treat Z as a QSub.

Example 4. Assume the same facts as in *Example 1,* except that Y is a C corporation. Although Y is a domestic corporation that is otherwise eligible to be a QSub, no QSub election has been made for Y. Thus, X is not treated as holding the stock of Z. Consequently, X may not elect to treat Z as a QSub.

Example 5. Individuals A and B own 100 percent of the stock of corporation X, an S corporation, and, except for C's interest (described below), X owns 100 percent of corporation Y, a C corporation. Individual C holds an instrument issued by Y that is considered to be equity under general principles of tax law but would satisfy the definition of straight debt under § 1.1361-1(1)(5) if Y were an S corporation. In determining whether X owns 100 percent of Y for purposes of making the QSub election, the instrument held by C is not considered outstanding stock. In addition, under § 1.1361-1(1)(5)(v), the QSub election is not treated as an exchange of debt for stock with respect to such instrument, and § 1.1361-1(1)(5)(iv) applies to determine the tax treatment of payments on the instrument while Y's QSub election is in effect.

[Reg. § 1.1361-2.]

☐ [*T.D.* 8869, 1-20-2000.]

[Reg. § 1.1361-3]

§ 1.1361-3. QSub election.—(a) *Time and manner of making election.*—(1) *In general.*—The corporation for which the QSub election is made must meet all the requirements of section 1361(b)(3)(B) at the time the election is made and for all periods for which the election is to be effective.

(2) *Manner of making election.*—Except as provided in section 1361(b)(3)(D) and § 1.1361-5(c) (five-year prohibition on reelection), an S corporation may elect to treat an eligible subsidiary as a QSub by filing a completed form to be prescribed by the IRS. The election form must be signed by a person authorized to sign the S corporation's return required to be filed under section 6037. Unless the election form provides otherwise, the election must be submitted to the service center where the subsidiary filed its most recent tax return (if applicable), and, if an S corporation forms a subsidiary and makes a valid QSub election (effective upon the date of the subsidiary's formation) for the subsidiary, the election should be submitted to the service center where the S corporation filed its most recent return.

(3) *Time of making election.*—A QSub election may be made by the S corporation parent at any time during the taxable year.

(4) *Effective date of election.*—A QSub election will be effective on the date specified on the election form or on the date the election form is filed if no date is specified. The effective date specified on the form cannot be more than two months and 15 days prior to the date of filing and cannot be more than 12 months after the date of filing. For this purpose, the definition of the term *month* found in § 1.1362-6(a)(2)(ii)(C) applies. If an election form specifies an effective date more than two months and 15 days prior to the date on which the election form is filed, it will be effective two months and 15 days prior to the date it is filed. If an election form specifies an effective date more than 12 months after the date on which the election is filed, it will be effective 12 months after the date it is filed.

(5) *Example.*—The following example illustrates the application of paragraph (a)(4) of this section:

Example. X has been a calendar year S corporation engaged in a trade or business for several years. X acquires the stock of Y, a calendar year C corporation, on April 1, 2002. On August 10, 2002, X makes an election to treat Y as a QSub. Unless otherwise specified on the election form, the election will be effective as of August 10, 2002. If specified on the election form, the election may be effective on some other date that is not more than two months and 15 days prior to August 10, 2002, and not more than 12 months after August 10, 2002.

(6) *Extension of time for making a QSub election.*—An extension of time to make a QSub election may be available under the procedures applicable under § § 301.9100-1 and 301.9100-3 of this chapter.

(b) *Revocation of QSub election.*—(1) *Manner of revoking QSub election.*—An S corporation may revoke a QSub election under section 1361 by filing a statement with the service center where the S corporation's most recent tax return was properly filed. The revocation statement must include the names, addresses, and taxpayer identification numbers of both the parent S corporation and the QSub, if any. The statement must be signed by a person authorized to sign the S corporation's return required to be filed under section 6037.

(2) *Effective date of revocation.*—The revocation of a QSub election is effective on the date specified on the revocation statement or on the date the revocation statement is filed if no date is specified. The effective date specified on the revocation statement cannot be more than two months and 15 days prior to the date on which the revocation statement is filed and cannot be more than 12 months after the date on which the

revocation statement is filed. If a revocation statement specifies an effective date more than two months and 15 days prior to the date on which the statement is filed, it will be effective two months and 15 days prior to the date it is filed. If a revocation statement specifies an effective date more than 12 months after the date on which the statement is filed, it will be effective 12 months after the date it is filed.

(3) *Revocation after termination.*—A revocation may not be made after the occurrence of an event that renders the subsidiary ineligible for QSub status under section 1361(b)(3)(B).

(4) *Revocation before QSub election effective.*—For purposes of Section 1361(b)(3)(D) and § 1.1361-5(c) (five-year prohibition on re-election), a revocation effective on the first day the QSub election was to be effective will not be treated as a termination of a QSub election. [Reg. § 1.1361-3.]

☐ [*T.D.* 8869, 1-20-2000.]

[Reg. § 1.1361-4]

§ 1.1361-4. Effect of QSub election.—(a) *Separate existence ignored.*—(1) *In general.*—Except as otherwise provided in paragraphs (a)(3), (a)(6), (a)(7), (a)(8), and (a)(9) of this section, for Federal tax purposes—

(i) A corporation that is a QSub shall not be treated as a separate corporation; and

(ii) All assets, liabilities, and items of income, deduction, and credit of a QSub shall be treated as assets, liabilities, and items of income, deduction, and credit of the S corporation.

(2) *Liquidation of subsidiary.*—(i) *In general.*—If an S corporation makes a valid QSub election with respect to a subsidiary, the subsidiary is deemed to have liquidated into the S corporation. Except as provided in paragraph (a)(5) of this section, the tax treatment of the liquidation or of a larger transaction that includes the liquidation will be determined under the Internal Revenue Code and general principles of tax law, including the step transaction doctrine. Thus, for example, if an S corporation forms a subsidiary and makes a valid QSub election (effective upon the date of the subsidiary's formation) for the subsidiary, the transfer of assets to the subsidiary and the deemed liquidation are disregarded, and the corporation will be deemed to be a QSub from its inception.

(ii) *Examples.*—The following examples illustrate the application of this paragraph (a)(2)(i) of this section:

Example 1. Corporation X acquires all of the outstanding stock of solvent corporation Y from an unrelated individual for cash and short-term notes. Thereafter, as part of the same plan, X immediately makes an S election and a QSub election for Y. Because X acquired all of the stock of Y in a qualified stock purchase within the meaning of section 338(d)(3), the liquidation described in paragraph (a)(2) of this section is respected as an independent step separate from the stock acquisition, and the tax consequences of the liquidation are determined under sections 332 and 337.

Example 2. Corporation X, pursuant to a plan, acquires all of the outstanding stock of corporation Y from the shareholders of Y solely in exchange for 10 percent of the voting stock of X. Prior to the transaction, Y and its shareholders are unrelated to X. Thereafter, as part of the same plan, X immediately makes an S election and a QSub election for Y. The transaction is a reorganization described in section 368(a)(1)(C), assuming the other conditions for reorganization treatment (e.g., continuity of business enterprise) are satisfied.

Example 3. After the expiration of the transition period provided in paragraph (a)(5)(i) of this section, individual A, pursuant to a plan, contributes all of the outstanding stock of Y to his wholly owned S corporation, X, and immediately causes X to make a QSub election for Y. The transaction is a reorganization under section 368(a)(1)(D), assuming the other conditions for reorganization treatment (e.g., continuity of business enterprise) are satisfied. If the sum of the amount of liabilities of Y treated as assumed by X exceeds the total of the adjusted basis of the property of Y, then section 357(c) applies and such excess is considered as gain from the sale or exchange of a capital asset or of property which is not a capital asset, as the case may be.

(iii) *Adoption of plan of liquidation.*—For purposes of satisfying the requirement of adoption of a plan of liquidation under section 332, unless a formal plan of liquidation that contemplates the QSub election is adopted on an earlier date, the making of the QSub election is considered to be the adoption of a plan of liquidation immediately before the deemed liquidation described in paragraph (a)(2)(i) of this section.

(iv) *Example.*—The following example illustrates the application of paragraph (a)(2)(iii) of this section:

Example. Corporation X owns 75 percent of a solvent corporation Y, and individual A owns the remaining 25 percent of Y. As part of a plan to make a QSub election for Y, X causes Y to redeem A's 25 percent interest on June 1 for cash and makes a QSub election for Y effective on June 3. The making of the QSub election is considered to be the adoption of a plan of liquidation immediately before the deemed liquidation. The deemed liquidation satisfies the requirements of section 332.

(v) *Stock ownership requirements of section 332.*—The deemed exercise of an option under §1.1504-4 and any instruments, obligations, or arrangements that are not considered stock under §1.1361-2(b)(2) are disregarded in determining if the stock ownership requirements of section 332(b) are met with respect to the deemed liquidation provided in paragraph (a)(2)(i) of this section.

(3) *Treatment of banks.*—(i) *In general.*—If an S corporation is a bank, or if an S corporation makes a valid QSub election for a subsidiary that is a bank, any special rules applicable to banks under the Internal Revenue Code continue to apply separately to the bank parent or bank subsidiary as if the deemed liquidation of any QSub under paragraph (a)(2) of this section had not occurred (except as other published guidance may apply section 265(b) and section 291(a)(3) and (e)(1)(B) not only to the bank parent or bank subsidiary but also to any QSub deemed to have liquidated under paragraph (a)(2) of this section). For any QSub that is a bank, however, all assets, liabilities, and items of income, deduction, and credit of the QSub, as determined in accordance with the special bank rules, are treated as assets, liabilities, and items of income, deduction, and credit of the S corporation. For purposes of this paragraph (a)(3)(i), the term *bank* has the same meaning as in section 581.

(ii) *Examples.*—The following examples illustrate the application of this paragraph (a)(3):

Example 1. X, an S corporation, is a bank as defined in section 581. X owns 100 percent of Y and Z, corporations for which valid QSub elections are in effect. Y is a bank as defined in section 581, and Z is not a financial institution. Pursuant to paragraph (a)(3)(i) of this section, any special rules applicable to banks under the Internal Revenue Code continue to apply separately to X and Y and do not apply to Z. Thus, for example, section 265(b), which provides special rules for interest expense deductions of banks, applies separately to X and Y. That is, X and Y each must make a separate determination under section 265(b) of interest expense allocable to tax-exempt interest, and no deduction is allowed for that interest expense. Section 265(b) does not apply to Z except as published guidance may provide otherwise.

Example 2. X, an S corporation, is a bank holding company and thus is not a bank as defined in section 581. X owns 100 percent of Y, a corporation for which a valid QSub election is in effect. Y is a bank as defined in section 581. Pursuant to paragraph (a)(3)(i) of this section, any special rules applicable to banks under the Internal Revenue Code continue to apply to Y and do not apply to X. However, all of Y's assets, liabilities, and items of income, deduction, and credit, as determined in accordance with the special bank rules, are treated as those of X. Thus, for example, section 582(c), which provides special rules for sales and exchanges of debt by banks, applies only to sales and exchanges by Y. However, any gain or loss on such a transaction by Y that is considered ordinary income or ordinary loss pursuant to section 582(c) is treated as ordinary income or ordinary loss of X.

(iii) *Effective date.*—This paragraph (a)(3) applies to taxable years beginning after December 31, 1996.

(4) *Treatment of stock of QSub.*—Except for purposes of section 1361(b)(3)(B)(i) and §1.1361-2(a)(1), the stock of a QSub shall be disregarded for all Federal tax purposes.

(5) *Transitional relief.*—(i) *General rule.*—If an S corporation and another corporation (the related corporation) are persons specified in section 267(b) prior to an acquisition by the S corporation of some or all of the stock of the related corporation followed by a QSub election for the related corporation, the step transaction doctrine will not apply to determine the tax consequences of the acquisition. This paragraph (a)(5) shall apply to QSub elections effective before January 1, 2001.

(ii) *Examples.*—The following examples illustrate the application of this paragraph (a)(5):

Example 1. Individual A owns 100 percent of the stock of X, an S corporation. X owns 79 percent of the stock of Y, a solvent corporation, and A owns the remaining 21 percent. On May 4, 1998, A contributes its Y stock to X in exchange for X stock. X makes a QSub election with respect to Y effective immediately following the transfer. The liquidation described in paragraph (a)(2) of this section is respected as an independent step separate from the stock acquisition, and the tax consequences of the liquidation are determined under sections 332 and 337. The contribution by A of the Y stock qualifies under section 351, and no gain or loss is recognized by A, X, or Y.

Example 2. Individual A owns 100 percent of the stock of two solvent S corporations, X and Y. On May 4, 1998, A contributes the stock of Y to X. X makes a QSub election with respect to Y immediately following the transfer. The liquidation described in paragraph (a)(2) of this section is respected as an independent step separate from the stock acquisition, and the tax consequences of the liquidation are determined under sections 332 and 337. The contribution by A of the Y stock to X qualifies under section 351, and no gain or loss is recognized by A, X, or Y. Y is not treated as a C corporation for any period solely because of the transfer of its stock to X, an ineligible shareholder. Compare *Example 3* of §1.1361-4(a)(2)(ii).

(6) *Treatment of certain QSubs.*—(i) *In general.*—A QSub, even though it is generally not treated as a corporation separate from the S corporation, is treated as a separate corporation for purposes of:

(A) Federal tax liabilities of the QSub with respect to any taxable period for which the QSub was treated as a separate corporation.

(B) Federal tax liabilities of any other entity for which the QSub is liable.

(C) Refunds or credits of Federal tax.

(ii) *Examples.*—The following examples illustrate the application of paragraph (a)(6)(i) of this section:

Example 1. X has owned all of the outstanding stock of Y, a domestic corporation that reports its taxes on a calendar year basis, since 2001. X and Y do not report their taxes on a consolidated basis. For 2003, X makes a timely S election and simultaneously makes a QSub election for Y. In 2004, the Internal Revenue Service (IRS) seeks to extend the period of limitations on assessment for Y's 2001 taxable year. Because Y was treated as a separate corporation for its 2001 taxable year, Y is the proper party to sign the consent to extend the period of limitations.

Example 2. The facts are the same as in *Example 1*, except that in 2004, the IRS determines that Y miscalculated and underreported its income tax liability for 2001. Because Y was treated as a separate corporation for its 2001 taxable year, the deficiency for Y's 2001 taxable year may be assessed against Y and, in the event that Y fails to pay the liability after notice and demand, a general tax lien will arise against all of Y's property and rights to property.

Example 3. X is a QSub of Y. In 2001, Z, a domestic corporation that reports its taxes on a calendar year basis, merges into X in a state law merger. Z was not a member of a consolidated group at any time during its taxable year ending in December 2000. Under the applicable state law, X is the successor to Z and is liable for all of Z's debts. In 2003, the IRS seeks to extend the period of limitations on assessment for Z's 2000 taxable year. Because X is the successor to Z and is liable for Z's 2000 taxes that remain unpaid, X is the proper party to execute the consent to extend the period of limitations on assessment.

(iii) *Effective date.*—This paragraph (a)(6) applies on or after April 1, 2004.

(7) *Treatment of QSubs for purposes of employment taxes.*—(i) *In general.*—A QSub is treated as a separate corporation for purposes of Subtitle C—Employment Taxes and Collection of Income Tax (Chapters 21, 22, 23, 23A, 24, and 25 of the Internal Revenue Code).

(ii) *Effective/applicability date.*—This paragraph (a)(7) applies with respect to wages paid on or after January 1, 2009.

(8) *Treatment of QSubs for purposes of certain excise taxes.*—(i) *In general.*—A QSub is treated as a separate corporation for purposes of—

(A) Federal tax liabilities imposed by Chapters 31, 32 (other than section 4181), 33, 34, 35, 36 (other than section 4461), and 38 of the Internal Revenue Code, or any floor stocks tax imposed on articles subject to any of these taxes;

(B) Collection of tax imposed by Chapter 33 of the Internal Revenue Code;

(C) Registration under sections 4101, 4222, and 4412; and

(D) Claims of a credit (other than a credit under section 34), refund, or payment related to a tax described in paragraph (a)(8)(i)(A) of this section or under section 6426 or 6427.

(ii) *Effective/applicability date.*—This paragraph (a)(8) applies to liabilities imposed and actions first required or permitted in periods beginning on or after January 1, 2008.

(9) *Information returns.*—(i) *In general.*—Except to the extent provided by the Secretary or Commissioner in guidance (including forms or instructions), paragraph (a)(1) of this section shall not apply to part III of subchapter A of chapter 61, relating to information returns.

(ii) *Effective/applicability date.*—This paragraph (a)(9) is effective on August 14, 2008.

(b) *Timing of the liquidation.*—(1) *In general.*—Except as otherwise provided in paragraph (b)(3) or (4) of this section, the liquidation described in paragraph (a)(2) of this section occurs at the close of the day before the Qsub election is effective. Thus, for example, if a C corporation elects to be treated as an S corporation and makes a QSub election (effective the same date as the S election) with respect to a subsidiary, the liquidation occurs immediately before the S election becomes effective, while the S electing parent is still a C corporation.

(2) *Application to elections in tiered situations.*—When QSub elections for a tiered group of subsidiaries are effective on the same date, the S corporation may specify the order of the liquidations. If no order is specified, the liquidations that are deemed to occur as a result of the QSub elections will be treated as occurring first for the lowest tier entity and proceed successively upward until all of the liquidations under paragraph (a)(2) of this section have occurred. For example, S, an S corporation, owns 100 percent of C, the common parent of an affiliated group of corporations that includes X and Y. C owns all of the stock of X and X owns all of the stock of Y. S elects under §1.1361-3 to treat C, X and Y as QSubs effective on the same date. If no order is specified for the elections, the following liquidations are deemed to occur as a result of the elections, with each successive liquidation occurring on the same day immediately after the preceding liquidation: Y is treated as liquidating into X, then X is treated as liquidating into C, and finally C is treated as liquidating into S.

(3) *Acquisitions.*—(i) *In general.*—If an S corporation does not own 100 percent of the stock of the subsidiary on the day before the QSub election is effective, the liquidation described in paragraph (a)(2) of this section occurs immediately

after the time at which the S corporation first owns 100 percent of the stock.

(ii) *Special rules for acquired S corporations.*—Except as provided in paragraph (b)(4) of this section, if a corporation (Y) for which an election under section 1362(a) was in effect is acquired, and a QSub election is made effective on the day Y is acquired, Y is deemed to liquidate into the S corporation at the beginning of the day the termination of its S election is effective. As a result, if corporation X acquires Y, an S corporation, and makes an S election for itself and a QSub election for Y effective on the day of acquisition, Y liquidates into X at the beginning of the day when X's S election is effective, and there is no period between the termination of Y's S election and the deemed liquidation of Y during which Y is a C corporation. Y's taxable year ends for all Federal income tax purposes at the close of the preceding day. Furthermore, if Y owns Z, a corporation for which a QSub election was in effect prior to the acquisition of Y by X, and X makes QSub elections for Y and Z, effective on the day of acquisition, the transfer of assets to Z and the deemed liquidation of Z are disregarded. See §§1.1361-4(a)(2) and 1.1361-5(b)(1)(i).

(4) *Coordination with section 338 election.*—An S corporation that makes a qualified stock purchase of a target may make an election under section 338 with respect to the acquisition if it meets the requirements for the election, and may make a QSub election with respect to the target. If an S corporation makes an election under section 338 with respect to a subsidiary acquired in a qualified stock purchase, a QSub election made with respect to that subsidiary is not effective before the day after the acquisition date (within the meaning of section 338(h)(2)). If the QSub election is effective on the day after the acquisition date, the liquidation under paragraph (a)(2) of this section occurs immediately after the deemed asset purchase by the new target corporation under section 338. If an S corporation makes an election under section 338 (without a section 338(h)(10) election) with respect to a target, the target must file a final return as a C corporation reflecting the deemed sale. See §1.338-10(a). If the target was an S corporation on the day before the acquisition date, the final return as a C corporation must reflect the activities of the target for the acquisition date, including the deemed sale. See §1.338-10(a)(3).

(c) *Carryover of disallowed losses and deductions.*—If an S corporation (S1) acquires the stock of another S corporation (S2), and S1 makes a QSub election with respect to S2 effective on the day of the acquisition, see §1.1366-2(c)(1) for provisions relating to the carryover of losses and deductions with respect to a former shareholder of S2 that may be available to that shareholder as a shareholder of S1.

(d) *Examples.*—The following examples illustrate the application of this section:

Example 1. X, an S corporation, owns 100 percent of the stock of Y, a C corporation. On June 2, 2002, X makes a valid QSub election for Y, effective June 2, 2002. Assume that, under general principles of tax law, including the step transaction doctrine, X's acquisition of the Y stock and the subsequent QSub election would not be treated as related. The liquidation described in paragraph (a)(2) of this section occurs at the close of the day on June 1, 2002, the day before the QSub election is effective, and the plan of liquidation is considered adopted on that date. Y's taxable year and separate existence for Federal tax purposes end at the close of June 1, 2002.

Example 2. X, a C corporation, owns 100 percent of the stock of Y, another C corporation. On December 31, 2002, X makes an election under section 1362 to be treated as an S corporation and a valid QSub election for Y, both effective January 1, 2003. Assume that, under general principles of tax law, including the step transaction doctrine, X's acquisition of the Y stock and the subsequent QSub election would not be treated as related. The liquidation described in paragraph (a)(2) of this section occurs at the close of December 31, 2002, the day before the QSub election is effective. The QSub election for Y is effective on the same day that X's S election is effective, and the deemed liquidation is treated as occurring before the S election is effective, when X is still a C corporation. Y's taxable year ends at the close of December 31, 2002. See § 1.381(b)-1.

Example 3. On June 1, 2002, X, an S corporation, acquires 100 percent of the stock of Y, an existing S corporation, for cash in a transaction meeting the requirements of a qualified stock purchase (QSP) under section 338. X immediately makes a QSub election for Y effective June 2, 2002, and also makes a joint election under section 338(h)(10) with the shareholder of Y. Under section 338(a) and § 1.338(h)(10)-1(d)(3), Y is treated as having sold all of its assets at the close of the acquisition date, June 1, 2002. Y is treated as a new corporation which purchased all of those assets as of the beginning of June 2, 2002, the day after the acquisition date. Section 338(a)(2). The QSub election is effective on June 2, 2002, and the liquidation under paragraph (a)(2) of this section occurs immediately after the deemed asset purchase by the new corporation.

Example 4. X, an S corporation, owns 100 percent of Y, a corporation for which a QSub election is in effect. On May 12, 2002, a date on which the QSub election is in effect, X issues Y a $10,000 note under state law that matures in ten years with a market rate of interest. Y is not treated as a separate corporation, and X's issuance of the note to Y on May 12, 2002, is disregarded for Federal tax purposes.

Example 5. X, an S corporation, owns 100 percent of the stock of Y, a C corporation. At a time

when Y is indebted to X in an amount that exceeds the fair market value of Y's assets, X makes a QSub election effective on the date it is filed with respect to Y. The liquidation described in paragraph (a)(2) of this section does not qualify under sections 332 and 337 and, thus, Y recognizes gain or loss on the assets distributed, subject to the limitations of section 267.

[Reg. § 1.1361-4.]

□ [*T.D. 8869, 1-20-2000 (corrected 3-27-2000). Amended by T.D. 8940, 2-12-2001; T.D. 9183, 2-24-2005; T.D. 9356, 8-15-2007 and T.D. 9422, 8-13-2008.*]

[Reg. §1.1361-5]

§1.1361-5. Termination of QSub election.—(a) *In general.*—(1) *Effective date.*—The termination of a QSub election is effective—

(i) On the effective date contained in the revocation statement if a QSub election is revoked under §91.1361-3(b);

(ii) At the close of the last day of the parent's last taxable year as an S corporation if the parent's S election terminates under §1.1362-2; or

(iii) At the close of the day on which an event (other than an event described in paragraph (a)(1)(ii) of this section) occurs that renders the subsidiary ineligible for QSub status under section 1361(b)(3)(B).

(2) *Information to be provided upon termination of QSub election by failure to qualify as a Qsub.*—If a QSub election terminates because an event renders the subsidiary ineligible for QSub status, the S corporation must attach to its return for the taxable year in which the termination occurs a notification that a QSub election has terminated, the date of the termination, and the names, addresses, and employer identification numbers of both the parent corporation and the QSub.

(3) *QSub joins a consolidated group.*—If a QSub election terminates because the S corporation becomes a member of a consolidated group (and no election under section 338(g) is made) the principles of § 1.1502-76(b)(1)(ii)(A)(2) (relating to a special rule for S corporations that join a consolidated group) apply to any QSub of the S corporation that also becomes a member of the consolidated group at the same time as the S corporation. See *Example 4* of paragraph (a)(4) of this section.

(4) *Examples.*—The following examples illustrate the application of this paragraph (a):

Example 1. Termination because parent's S election terminates. X, an S corporation, owns 100 percent of Y. A QSub election is in effect with respect to Y for 2001. Effective on January 1, 2002, X revokes its S election. Because X is no longer an S corporation, Y no longer qualifies as a QSub at the close of December 31, 2001.

Example 2. Termination due to transfer of QSub stock. X, an S corporation, owns 100 percent of. Y. A QSub-election is in effect with respect to Y. On December 10, 2002, X sells one share of Y stock to A, an individual. Because X no longer owns 100 percent of the stock of Y, Y no longer qualifies as a QSub. Accordingly, the QSub election made with respect to Y terminates at the close of December 10, 2002.

Example 3. No termination on stock transfer between QSub and parent. X, an S corporation, owns 100 percent of the stock of Y, and Y owns 100 percent of the stock of Z. QSub elections are in effect with respect to both Y and Z. Y transfers all of its Z stock to X. Because X is treated as owning the stock of Z both before and after the transfer of stock solely for purposes of determining whether the requirements of section 1361(b)(3)(B)(i) and §1.1361-2(a)(1) have been satisfied, the transfer of Z stock does not terminate Z's QSub election. Because the stock of Z is disregarded for all other Federal tax purposes, no gain is recognized under section 311.

Example 4. Termination due to acquisition of S parent by a consolidated group. X, an S corporation, owns 100 percent of Y, a corporation for which a QSub election is in effect. Z, the common parent of a consolidated group of corporations, acquires 80 percent of the stock of X on June 1, 2002. Z does not make an election under section 338(g) with respect to the purchase of X stock. X's S election terminates as of the close of the preceding day, May 31, 2002. Y's QSub election also terminates at the close of May 31, 2002. Under §1.1502-76(b)(1)(ii)(A)(2) and paragraph (a)(3) of this section, X and Y become members of Z's consolidated group of corporations as of the beginning of the day June 1, 2002.

Example 5. Termination due to acquisition of QSub by a consolidated group. The facts are the same as in *Example 4*, except that Z acquires 80 percent of the stock of Y (instead of X) on June 1, 2002. In this case, Y's QSub election terminates as of the close of June 1, 2002, and, under §1.1502-76(b)(1)(ii)(A)(1), Y becomes a member of the consolidated group at that time.

(b) *Effect of termination of QSub election.*— (1) *Formation of new corporation.*—(i) *In general.*— If a QSub election terminates under paragraph (a) of this section, the former QSub is treated as a new corporation acquiring all of its assets (and assuming all of its liabilities) immediately before the termination from the S corporation parent in exchange for stock of the new corporation. The tax treatment of this transaction or of a larger transaction that includes this transaction will be determined under the Internal Revenue Code and general principles of tax law, including the step transaction doctrine. For purposes of determining the application of section 351 with respect to this transaction, instruments, obligations, or other arrangements that are not treated as stock of the QSub under §1.1361-2(b)

are disregarded in determining control for purposes of section 368(c) even if they are equity under general principles of tax law.

(ii) *Termination for tiered QSubs.*—If QSub elections terminate for tiered QSubs on the same day, the formation of any higher tier subsidiary precedes the formation of its lower tier subsidiary. See *Example 6* in paragraph (b)(3) of this section.

(2) *Carryover of disallowed losses and deductions.*—If a QSub terminates because the S corporation distributes the QSub stock to some or all of the S corporation's shareholders in a transaction to which section 368(a)(1)(D) applies by reason of section 355 (or so much of section 356 as relates to section 355), see §1.1366-2(c)(2) for provisions relating to the carryover of disallowed losses and deductions that may be available.

(3) *Examples.*—The following examples illustrate the application of this paragraph (b):

Example 1. X, an S corporation, owns 100 percent of the stock of Y, a corporation for which a QSub election is in effect. X sells 21 percent of the Y stock to Z, an unrelated corporation, for cash, thereby terminating the QSub election. Y is treated as a new corporation acquiring all of its assets (and assuming all of its liabilities) in exchange for Y stock immediately before the termination from the S corporation. The deemed exchange by X of assets for Y stock does not qualify under section 351 because X is not in control of Y within the meaning of section 368(c) immediately after the transfer as a result of the sale of stock to Z. Therefore, X must recognize gain, if any, on the assets transferred to Y in exchange for its stock. X's losses, if any, on the assets transferred are subject to the limitations of section 267.

Example 2. (i) X, an S corporation, owns 100 percent of the stock of Y, a corporation for which a QSub election is in effect. As part of a plan to sell a portion of Y, X causes Y to merge into T, a limited liability company wholly owned by X that is disregarded as an entity separate from its owner for Federal tax purposes. X then sells 21 percent of T to Z, an unrelated corporation, for cash. Following the sale, no entity classification election is made under §301.7701-3(c) of this chapter to treat the limited liability company as an association for Federal tax purposes.

(ii) The merger of Y into T causes a termination of Y's QSub election. The new corporation (Newco) that is formed as a result of the termination is immediately merged into T, an entity that is disregarded for Federal tax purposes. Because, at the end of the series of transactions, the assets continue to be held by X for Federal tax purposes, under step transaction principles, the formation of Newco and the transfer of assets pursuant to the merger of Newco into T are disregarded. The sale of 21 percent of T is treated as a sale of a 21 percent undivided interest in each of T's assets. Immediately thereafter, X and Z are treated as contributing their respective interests in those assets to a partnership in exchange for ownership interests in the partnership.

(iii) Under section 1001, X recognizes gain or loss from the deemed sale of the 21 percent interest in each asset of the limited liability company to Z. Under section 721(a), no gain or loss is recognized by X and Z as a result of the deemed contribution of their respective interests in the assets to the partnership in exchange for ownership interests in the partnership.

Example 3. Assume the same facts as in *Example 1*, except that, instead of purchasing Y stock, Z contributes to Y an operating asset in exchange for 21 percent of the Y stock. Y is treated as a new corporation acquiring all of its assets (and assuming all of its liabilities) in exchange for Y stock immediately before the termination. Because X and Z are co-transferors that control the transferee immediately after the transfer, the transaction qualifies under section 351.

Example 4. X, an S corporation, owns 100 percent of the stock of Y, a corporation for which a QSub election is in effect. X distributes all of the Y stock pro rata to its shareholders, and the distribution terminates the QSub election. The transaction can qualify as a distribution to which sections 368(a)(1)(D) and 355 apply if the transaction otherwise satisfies the requirements of those sections.

Example 5. X, an S corporation, owns 100 percent of the stock of Y, a corporation for which a QSub election is in effect. X subsequently revokes the QSub election. Y is treated as a new corporation acquiring all of its assets (and assuming all of its liabilities) immediately before the revocation from its S corporation parent in a deemed exchange for Y stock. On a subsequent date, X sells 21 percent of the stock of Y to Z, an unrelated corporation, for cash. Assume that under general principles of tax law including the step transaction doctrine, the sale is not taken into account in determining whether X is in control of Y immediately after the deemed exchange of assets for stock. The deemed exchange by X of assets for Y stock and the deemed assumption by Y of its liabilities qualify under section 351 because, for purposes of that section, X is in control of Y within the meaning of section 368(c) immediately after the transfer.

Example 6. (i) X, an S corporation, owns 100 percent of the stock of Y, and Y owns 100 percent of the stock of Z. Y and Z are corporations for which QSub elections are in effect. X subsequently revokes the QSub elections and the effective date specified on each revocation statement is June 26, 2002, a date that is less than 12 months after the date on which the revocation statements are filed.

(ii) Immediately before the QSub elections terminate, Y is treated as a new corporation ac-

quiring all of its assets (and assuming all of its liabilities) directly from X in exchange for the stock of Y. Z is treated as a new corporation acquiring all of its assets (and assuming all of its liabilities) directly from Y in exchange for the stock of Z.

Example 7. (i) The facts are the same as in *Example 6*, except that, prior to June 26, 2002 (the effective date of the revocations), Y distributes the Z stock to X under state law.

(ii) Immediately before the QSub elections terminate, Y is treated as a new corporation acquiring all of its assets (and assuming all of its liabilities) directly from X in exchange for the stock of Y. Z is also treated as a new corporation acquiring all of its assets (and assuming all of its liabilities) directly from X in exchange for the stock of Z.

Example 8. Merger of parent into QSub. X, an S corporation, owns 100 percent of the stock of Y, a corporation for which a QSub election is in effect. X merges into Y under state law, causing the QSub election for Y to terminate, and Y survives the merger. The formation of the new corporation, Y, and the merger of X into Y can qualify as a reorganization described in section 368(a)(1)(F) if the transaction otherwise satisfies the requirements of that section.

Example 9. Transfer of 100 percent of QSub. X, an S corporation, owns 100 percent of the stock of Y, a corporation for which a QSub election is in effect. Z, an unrelated C corporation, acquires 100 percent of the stock of Y. The deemed formation of Y by X (as a consequence of the termination of Y's QSub election) is disregarded for Federal income tax purposes. The transaction is treated as a transfer of the assets of Y to Z, followed by Z's transfer of these assets to the capital of Y in exchange for Y stock. Furthermore, if Z is an S corporation and makes a QSub election for Y effective as of the acquisition, Z's transfer of the assets of Y in exchange for Y stock, followed by the immediate liquidation of Y as a consequence of the QSub election are disregarded for Federal income tax purposes.

(c) *Election after QSub termination.*—(1) *In general.*—Absent the Commissioner's consent, and except as provided in paragraph (c)(2) of this section, a corporation whose QSub election has terminated under paragraph (a) of this section (or a successor corporation as defined in § 1.1362-5(b)) may not make an S election under section 1362 or have a QSub election under section 1361(b)(3)(B)(ii) made with respect to it for five taxable years (as described in section 1361(b)(3)(D)). The Commissioner may permit an S election by the corporation or a new QSub election with respect to the corporation before the five-year period expires. The corporation requesting consent to make the election has the burden of establishing that, under the relevant facts and circumstances, the Commissioner should consent to a new election.

(2) *Exception.*—In the case of S and QSub elections effective after December 31, 1996, if a corporation,'s QSub election terminates, the corporation may, without requesting the Commissioner's consent, make an S election or have a QSub election made with respect to it before the expiration of the five-year period described in section 1361(b)(3)(D) and paragraph (c)(1) of this section, provided that—

(i) Immediately following the termination, the corporation (or its successor corporation) is otherwise eligible to make an S election or have a QSub election made for it; and

(ii) The relevant election is made effective immediately following the termination of the QSub election.

(3) *Examples.*—The following examples illustrate the application of this paragraph (c):

Example 1. Termination upon distribution of QSub stock to shareholders of parent. X, an S corporation, owns Y, a QSub. X distributes all of its Y stock to X's shareholders. The distribution terminates the QSub election because Y no longer satisfies the requirements of a QSub. Assuming Y is otherwise eligible to be treated as an S corporation, Y's shareholders may elect to treat Y as an S corporation effective on the date of the stock distribution without requesting the Commissioner's consent.

Example 2. Sale of 100 percent of QSub stock. X, an S corporation, owns Y, a QSub. X sells 100 percent of the stock of Y to Z, an unrelated S corporation. Z may elect to treat Y as a QSub effective on the date of purchase without requesting the Commissioner's consent. [Reg. § 1.1361-5.]

☐ [*T.D.* 8869, 1-20-2000 (*corrected* 10-23-2002).]

[Reg. § 1.1361-6]

§ 1.1361-6. Effective date.—Except as provided in §§ 1.1361-4(a)(3)(iii), 1.1361-4(a)(5)(i), 1.1361-4(a)(6)(iii), 1.1361-4(a)(7)(ii), 1.1361-4(a)(8)(ii), 1.1361-4(a)(9), and 1.1361-5(c)(2), the provisions of §§ 1.1361-2 through 1.1361-5 apply to taxable years beginning on or after January 20, 2000; however, taxpayers may elect to apply the regulations in whole, but not in part (aside from those sections with special dates of applicability), for taxable years beginning on or after January 1, 2000, provided all affected taxpayers apply the regulations in a consistent manner. To make this election, the corporation and all affected taxpayers must file a return or an amended return that is consistent with these rules for the taxable year for which the election is made. For purposes of this section, affected taxpayers means all taxpayers whose returns are affected by the election to apply the regulations. [Reg. § 1.1361-6.]

☐ [*T.D.* 8869, 1-20-2000. *Amended by T.D.* 9356, 8-15-2007 *and T.D.* 9422, 8-13-2008.]

[Reg. § 18.0]

§ 18.0. Effective date of temporary regulations under the Subchapter S Revision Act of 1982.—The temporary regulations provided under §§ 18.1377-1, 18.1379-1, and 18.1379-2 are effective with respect to taxable years beginning after 1982, and the temporary regulations provided under § 18.1378-1 are effective with respect to elections made after October 19, 1982. [Temporary Reg. § 18.0.]

☐ [*T.D.* 7872, 1-21-83. *Amended by T.D.* 7976, 9-5-84 *and by T.D.* 8600, 7-20-95.]

[Reg. § 1.1362-0]

§ 1.1362-0. Table of contents.—This section lists the captions that appear in the regulations under section 1362.

(A) Royalties.

(1) In general.

(2) Royalties derived in the ordinary course of a trade or business.

(3) Copyright, mineral, oil and gas, and active business computer software royalties.

(B) Rents.

(1) In general.

(2) Rents derived in the active trade or business of renting property.

(3) Produced film rents.

(4) Income from leasing self-produced tangible property.

(C) Dividends.

(D) Interest.

(1) In general.

(2) Interest on obligations acquired in the ordinary course of a trade or business.

(E) Annuities.

(F) Gross receipts from the sale of stock or securities.

(G) Identified income.

(iii) Special rules.

(A) Options or commodities dealers.

(B) Treatment of certain lending, financing and other businesses.

(1) In general.

(2) Directly derived.

(C) Payment to a patron of a cooperative.

(6) Examples.

§ 1.1362-3. Treatment of S termination year.

(a) In general.

(b) Allocations other than pro rata.

(1) Elections under section 1362(e)(3).

(2) Purchase of stock treated as an asset purchase.

(3) 50 percent change in ownership during S termination year.

(c) Special rules.

(1) S corporation that is a partner in a partnership.

(2) Tax for the C short year.

(3) Each short year treated as taxable year.

(4) Year for carryover purposes.

(5) Due date for S short year return.

(6) Year in which income from S short year is includible.

(d) Examples.

§ 1.1362-4. Inadvertent terminations and inadvertently invalid elections.

(a) In general.

(b) Inadvertent termination.

(c) Corporation's request for determination of an inadvertent termination.

(d) Adjustments.

(e) Corporation and shareholder consents.

(f) Status of corporation.

(g) Effective/applicability date.

§ 1.1362-5. Election after termination.

(a) In general.

(b) Successor corporation.

(c) Automatic consent after certain terminations.

§ 1.1362-6. Elections and consents.

(a) Time and manner of making elections.

(1) In general.

(2) Election to be an S corporation.

(i) Manner of making election.

(ii) Time of making election.

(A) In general.

(B) Elections made during the first $2^1/2$ months treated as made for the following taxable year.

(C) Definition of month and beginning of the taxable year.

(iii) Examples.

(3) Revocation of S election.

(i) Manner of revoking election.

(ii) Time of revoking election.

(iii) Examples.

(4) Rescission of a revocation.

(i) Manner of rescinding a revocation.

(ii) Time of rescinding a revocation.

(5) Election not to apply pro rata allocation.

(b) Shareholders' consents.

(1) Manner of consents in general.

(2) Persons required to consent.

(i) Community interest in stock.

(ii) Minor.

(iii) Estate.

(iv) Trust.

(3) Special rules for consent of shareholder to election to be an S corporation.

(i) In general.

(ii) Examples.

(iii) Extension of time for filing consents to an election.

(A) In general.

(B) Required consents.

§ 1.1362-7. Effective date.

(a) In general.

(b) Special effective date for passive investment income provisions.

§ 1.1362-8. Dividends received from affiliated subsidiaries.

(a) In general.

(b) Determination of active or passive earnings and profits.

(1) In general.

(2) Lower tier subsidiaries.

(3) De minimis exception.

(4) Special rules for earnings and profits accumulated by a C corporation prior to 80 percent acquisition.

(5) Gross receipts safe harbor.

(c) Allocating distributions to active or passive earnings and profits.

(1) Distributions from current earnings and profits.

(2) Distributions from accumulated earnings and profits.

(3) Adjustments to active earnings and profits.

(4) Special rules for consolidated groups.

(d) Examples.

(e) Effective date.

[Reg. § 1.1362-0.]

☐ [*T.D. 8449, 11-24-92. Amended by T.D. 8869, 1-20-2000 and T.D. 9422, 8-13-2008.*]

[Reg. § 1.1362-1]

§ 1.1362-1. Election to be an S corporation.— (a) *In general.*—Except as provided in § 1.1362-5, a small business corporation as defined in section 1361 may elect to be an S corporation under section 1362(a). An election may be made only with the consent of all of the shareholders of the corporation at the time of the election. See § 1.1362-6(a) for rules concerning the time and manner of making this election.

(b) *Years for which election is effective.*—An election under section 1362(a) is effective for the entire taxable year of the corporation for which it is made and for all succeeding taxable years of the corporation, until the election is terminated. [Reg. § 1.1362-1.]

☐ [*T.D. 8449, 11-24-92.*]

[Reg. § 1.1362-2]

§ 1.1362-2. Termination of election.— (a) *Termination by revocation.*—(1) *In general.*—An election made under section 1362(a) is terminated if the corporation revokes the election for any taxable year of the corporation for which the election is effective, including the first taxable year. A revocation may be made only with the consent of shareholders who, at the time the revocation is made, hold more than one-half of the number of issued and outstanding shares of stock (including non-voting stock) of the corporation. See § 1.1362-6(a) for rules concerning the time and manner of revoking an election made under section 1362(a).

(2) *When effective.*—(i) *In general.*—Except as provided in paragraph (a)(2)(ii) of this section, a revocation made during the taxable year and before the 16th day of the third month of the taxable year is effective on the first day of the taxable year and a revocation made after the 15th day of the third month of the taxable year is effective for the following taxable year. If a corporation makes an election to be an S corpora-

tion that is to be effective beginning with the next taxable year and revokes its election on or before the first day of the next taxable year, the corporation is deemed to have revoked its election on the first day of the next taxable year.

(ii) *Revocations specifying a prospective revocation date.*—If a corporation specifies a date for revocation and the date is expressed in terms of a stated day, month, and year that is on or after the date the revocation is filed, the revocation is effective on and after the date so specified.

(3) *Effect on taxable year of corporation.*—In the case of a corporation that revokes its election to be an S corporation effective on the first day of the first taxable year for which its election is to be effective, any statement made with the election regarding a change in the corporation's taxable year has no effect.

(4) *Rescission of a revocation.*—A corporation may rescind a revocation made under paragraph (a)(2) of this section at any time before the revocation becomes effective. A rescission may be made only with the consent of each person who consented to the revocation and by each person who became a shareholder of the corporation within the period beginning on the first day after the date the revocation was made and ending on the date on which the rescission is made. See § 1.1362-6(a) for rules concerning the time and manner of rescinding a revocation.

(b) *Termination by reason of corporation ceasing to be a small business corporation.*—(1) *In general.*—If a corporation ceases to be a small business corporation, as defined in section 1361(b), at any time on or after the first day of the first taxable year for which its election under section 1362(a) is effective, the election terminates. In the event of a termination under this paragraph (b)(1), the corporation should attach to its return for the taxable year in which the termination occurs a notification that a termination has occurred and the date of the termination.

(2) *When effective.*—If an election terminates because of a specific event that causes the corporation to fail to meet the definition of a small business corporation, the termination is effective as of the date on which the event occurs. If a corporation makes an election to be an S corporation that is effective beginning with the following taxable year and is not a small business corporation on the first day of that following taxable year, the election is treated as having terminated on that first day. If a corporation is a small business corporation on the first day of the taxable year for which its election is effective, its election does not terminate even if the corporation was not a small business corporation during all or part of the period beginning after the date the election was made and ending before the first day of the taxable year for which the election is effective.

Reg. § 1.1362-2(b)(2)

(3) *Effect on taxable year of corporation.*—In the case of a corporation that fails to meet the definition of a small business corporation on the first day of the first taxable year for which its election to be an S corporation is to be effective, any statement made with the election regarding a change in the corporation's taxable year has no effect.

(c) *Termination by reason of excess passive investment income.*—(1) *In general.*—A corporation's election under section 1362(a) terminates if the corporation has subchapter C earnings and profits at the close of each of three consecutive taxable years and, for each of those taxable years, has passive investment income in excess of 25 percent of gross receipts. See section 1375 for the tax imposed on excess passive investment income.

(2) *When effective.*—A termination under this paragraph (c) is effective on the first day of the first taxable year beginning after the third consecutive year in which the S corporation had excess passive investment income.

(3) *Subchapter C earnings and profits.*—For purposes of this paragraph (c), *subchapter C earnings and profits* of a corporation are the earnings and profits of any corporation, including the S corporation or an acquired or predecessor corporation, for any period with respect to which an election under section 1362(a) (or under section 1372 of prior law) was not in effect. The subchapter C earnings and profits of an S corporation are modified as required by section 1371(c).

(4) *Gross receipts.*—(i) *In general.*—For purposes of this paragraph (c), *gross receipts* generally means the total amount received or accrued under the method of accounting used by the corporation in computing its taxable income and is not reduced by returns and allowances, cost of goods sold, or deductions.

(ii) *Special rules for sales of capital assets, stock and securities.*—(A) *Sales of capital assets.*—For purposes of this paragraph (c), gross receipts from the sales or exchanges of capital assets (as defined in section 1221), other than stock and securities, are taken into account only to the extent of capital gain net income (as defined in section 1222).

(B) *Sales of stock or securities.*—(1) *In general.*—For purposes of this paragraph (c), gross receipts from the sales or exchanges of stock or securities are taken into account only to the extent of gains therefrom. In addition, for purposes of computing gross receipts from sales or exchanges of stock or securities, losses do not offset gains.

(2) *Treatment of certain liquidations.*—Gross receipts from the sales or exchanges of stock or securities do not include amounts described in section 1362(d)(3)(D)(iv), relating to

the treatment of certain liquidations. For purposes of section 1362(d)(3)(D)(iv), stock of the liquidating corporation owned by an S corporation shareholder is not treated as owned by the S corporation.

(3) *Definition of stock or securities.*—For purposes of this paragraph (c), *stock or securities* includes shares or certificates of stock, stock rights or warrants, or an interest in any corporation (including any joint stock company, insurance company, association, or other organization classified as a corporation under section 7701); an interest as a limited partner in a partnership; certificates of interest or participation in any profit-sharing agreement, or in any oil, gas, or other mineral property, or lease; collateral trust certificates; voting trust certificates; bonds; debentures; certificates of indebtedness; notes; car trust certificates; bills of exchange; or obligations issued by or on behalf of a State, Territory, or political subdivision thereof.

(4) *General partner interests.*—(i) *In general.*—Except as provided in paragraph (c)(4)(ii)(B)(4)(ii) of this section, if an S corporation disposes of a general partner interest, the gain on the disposition is treated as gain from the sale of stock or securities to the extent of the amount the S corporation would have received as a distributive share of gain from the sale of stock or securities held by the partnership if all of the stock and securities held by the partnership had been sold by the partnership at fair market value at the time the S corporation disposes of the general partner interest. In applying this rule, the S corporation's distributive share of gain from the sale of stock or securities held by the partnership is not reduced to reflect any loss that would be recognized from the sale of stock or securities held by the partnership. In the case of tiered partnerships, the rules of this section apply by looking through each tier.

(ii) *Exception.*—An S corporation that disposes of a general partner interest may treat the disposition, for purposes of this paragraph (c), in the same manner as the disposition of an interest as a limited partner.

(iii) *Other exclusions from gross receipts.*—For purposes of this paragraph (c), gross receipts do not include—

(A) Amounts received in nontaxable sales or exchanges except to the extent that gain is recognized by the corporation on the sale or exchange; or

(B) Amounts received as a loan, as a repayment of a loan, as a contribution to capital, or on the issuance by the corporation of its own stock.

(5) *Passive investment income.*—(i) *In general.*—In general, *passive investment income* means gross receipts (as defined in paragraph (c)(4) of this section) derived from royalties, rents, divi-

dends, interest, annuities, and gains from the sales or exchanges of stock or securities.

(ii) *Definitions.*—For purposes of this paragraph (c)(5), the following definitions apply:

(A) *Royalties.*—*(1) In general.*—*Royalties* means all royalties, including mineral, oil, and gas royalties, and amounts received for the privilege of using patents, copyrights, secret processes and formulas, good will, trademarks, tradebrands, franchises, and other like property. The gross amount of royalties is not reduced by any part of the cost of the rights under which the royalties are received or by any amount allowable as a deduction in computing taxable income.

(2) *Royalties derived in the ordinary course of a trade or business.*—*Royalties* does not include royalties derived in the ordinary course of a trade or business of franchising or licensing property. Royalties received by a corporation are derived in the ordinary course of a trade or business of franchising or licensing property only if, based on all the facts and circumstances, the corporation—

(i) Created the property; or

(ii) Performed significant services or incurred substantial costs with respect to the development or marketing of the property.

(3) *Copyright, mineral, oil and gas, and active business computer software royalties.*—*Royalties* does not include copyright royalties, nor mineral, oil and gas royalties if the income from those royalties would not be treated as personal holding company income under sections 543(a)(3) and (a)(4) if the corporation were a C corporation; amounts received upon disposal of timber, coal, or domestic iron ore with respect to which the special rules of sections 631(b) and (c) apply; and active business computer software royalties as defined under section 543(d) (without regard to paragraph (d)(5) of section 543).

(B) *Rents.*—*(1) In general.*—*Rents* means amounts received for the use of, or right to use, property (whether real or personal) of the corporation.

(2) *Rents derived in the active trade or business of renting property.*—*Rents* does not include rents derived in the active trade or business of renting property. Rents received by a corporation are derived in an active trade or business of renting property only if, based on all the facts and circumstances, the corporation provides significant services or incurs substantial costs in the rental business. Generally, significant services are not rendered and substantial costs are not incurred in connection with net leases. Whether significant services are performed or substantial costs are incurred in the rental business is determined based upon all the facts and circumstances including, but not limited to, the number of persons employed to provide the ser-vices and the types and amounts of costs and expenses incurred (other than depreciation).

(3) *Produced film rents.*—*Rents* does not include produced film rents as defined under section 543(a)(5).

(4) *Income from leasing self-produced tangible property.*—*Rents* does not include compensation, however designated, for the use of, or right to use, any real or tangible personal property developed, manufactured, or produced by the taxpayer, if during the taxable year the taxpayer is engaged in substantial development, manufacturing, or production of real or tangible personal property of the same type.

(C) *Dividends.*—*Dividends* includes dividends as defined in section 316, amounts to be included in gross income under section 551 (relating to foreign personal holding company income taxed to U.S. shareholders), and consent dividends as provided in section 565. See paragraphs (c)(5)(iii)(B) and (C) of this section for special rules for the treatment of certain dividends and certain payments to a patron of a cooperative. See § 1.1362-8 for special rules regarding the treatment of dividends received by an S corporation from a C corporation in which the S corporation holds stock meeting the requirements of section 1504(a)(2).

(D) *Interest.*—*(1) In general.*—*Interest* means any amount received for the use of money (including tax-exempt interest and amounts treated as interest under section 483, 1272, 1274, or 7872). See paragraph (c)(5)(iii)(B) of this section for a special rule for the treatment of interest derived in certain businesses.

(2) *Interest on obligations acquired in the ordinary course of a trade or business.*—*Interest* does not include interest on any obligation acquired from the sale of property described in section 1221(1) or the performance of services in the ordinary course of a trade or business of selling the property or performing the services.

(E) *Annuities.*—*Annuities* means the entire amount received as an annuity under an annuity, endowment, or life insurance contract, if any part of the amount would be includible in gross income under section 72.

(F) *Gross receipts from the sale of stock or securities.*—Gross receipts from the sales or exchanges of stock or securities, as described in paragraph (c)(4)(ii)(B) of this section, are passive investment income to the extent of gains therefrom. See paragraph (c)(5)(iii)(B) of this section for a special rule for the treatment of gains derived in certain businesses.

(G) *Identified income.*—Passive investment income does not include income identified by the Commissioner by regulations, revenue ruling, or revenue procedure as income derived

Reg. § 1.1362-2(c)(5)(ii)(G)

in the ordinary course of a trade or business for purposes of this section.

(iii) *Special rules.*—For purposes of this paragraph (c)(5), the following special rules apply:

(A) *Options or commodities dealers.*—In the case of an options dealer or commodities dealer, *passive investment income* does not include any gain or loss (in the normal course of the taxpayer's activity of dealing in or trading section 1256 contracts) from any section 1256 contract or property related to the contract. *Options dealer, commodities dealer*, and *section 1256 contract* have the same meaning as in section 1362(d)(3)(E)(ii).

(B) *Treatment of certain lending, financing and other businesses.*—*(1) In general.*—*Passive investment income* does not include gross receipts that are directly derived in the ordinary course of a trade or business of—

(i) Lending or financing;

(ii) Dealing in property;

(iii) Purchasing or discounting accounts receivable, notes, or installment obligations; or

(iv) Servicing mortgages.

(2) *Directly derived.*—For purposes of this paragraph (c)(5)(iii)(B), gross receipts directly derived in the ordinary course of business includes gain (as well as interest income) with respect to loans originated in a lending business, or interest income (as well as gain) from debt obligations of a dealer in such obligations. However, interest earned from the investment of idle funds in short-term securities does not constitute gross receipts directly derived in the ordinary course of business. Similarly, a dealer's income or gain from an item of property is not directly derived in the ordinary course of its trade or business if the dealer held the property for investment at any time before the income or gain is recognized.

(C) *Payment to a patron of a cooperative.*—*Passive investment income* does not include amounts included in the gross income of a patron of a cooperative (within the meaning of section 1381(a), without regard to paragraph (2)(A) or (C) of section 1381(a)) by reason of any payment or allocation to the patron based on patronage occurring in the case of a trade or business of the patron.

(6) *Examples.*—The principles of paragraphs (c)(4) and (c)(5) of this section are illustrated by the following examples. Unless otherwise provided in an example, *S* is an S corporation with subchapter C earnings and profits, and *S*'s gross receipts from operations are gross receipts not derived from royalties, rents, dividends, interest, annuities, or gains from the sales or exchanges of stock or securities. *S* is a calendar year taxpayer

and its first taxable year as an S corporation is 1993.

Example 1. Sales of capital assets, stock and securities. (i) *S* uses an accrual method of accounting and sells:

(1) a depreciable asset, held for more than 6 months, which is used in the corporation's business;

(2) a capital asset (other than stock or securities) for a gain;

(3) a capital asset (other than stock or securities) for a loss; and

(4) securities.

S receives payment for each asset partly in money and partly in the form of a note payable at a future time, and elects not to report the sales on the installment method.

(ii) The amount of money and the face amount (or issue price if different) of the note received for the business asset are considered gross receipts in the taxable year of sale and are not reduced by the adjusted basis of the property, costs of sale, or any other amount. With respect to the sales of the capital assets, gross receipts include the cash down payment and face amount (or issue price if different) of any notes, but only to the extent of *S*'s capital gain net income. In the case of the sale of the securities, gross receipts include the cash down payment and face amount (or issue price if different) of the notes, but only to the extent of gain on the sale. In determining gross receipts from sales of securities, losses are not netted against gains.

Example 2. Long-term contract reported on percentage-of-completion method. *S* has a long-term contract as defined in § 1.460-1(b)(1) with respect to which it reports income according to the percentage-of-completion method as described in § 1.460-4(b). The portion of the gross contract price which corresponds to the percentage of the entire contract which has been completed during the taxable year is included in *S*'s gross receipts for the year.

Example 3. Income reported on installment sale method. For its 1993 taxable year, *S* sells personal property on the installment plan and elects to report its taxable income from the sale of the property (other than property qualifying as a capital asset or stock or securities) on the installment method in accordance with section 453. The installment payment actually received in a given taxable year of *S* is included in gross receipts for the year.

Example 4. Partnership interests. In 1993, *S* and two of its shareholders contribute cash to form a general partnership, *PRS*. *S* receives a 50 percent interest in the capital and profits of *PRS*. *S* formed *PRS* to indirectly invest in marketable stocks and securities. The only assets of *PRS* are the stock and securities, and certain real and tangible personal property. In 1994, *S* needs cash in its business and sells its partnership interest at a gain rather than having *PRS* sell the marketable stock or securities that have appreciated. Under paragraph (c)(4)(ii)(B)(4) of this section, the gain on S's disposition of its interest in PRS is treated as gain from the sale or exchange of stock or securities to the extent of the amount the distributive share of gain S would have received from the sale of stock or securities held by PRS if PRS has sold all of its stock or securities at fair market value at the time S disposed of its interest in PRS.

Example 5. Royalties derived in ordinary course of trade or business. (i) In 1993, S has gross receipts of $75,000. Of this amount, $5,000 is from royalty payments with respect to Trademark A, $8,000 is from royalty payments with respect to Trademark B, and $62,000 is gross receipts from operations. S created Trademark A, but S did not create Trademark B or perform significant services or incur substantial costs with respect to the development or marketing of Trademark B.

(ii) Because S created Trademark A, the royalty payments with respect to Trademark A are derived in the ordinary course of S's business and are not included within the definition of *royalties* for purposes of determining S's passive

$110,000	Gross receipts from operations and from gain on the sale of stock in the ordinary course of a trade or business
10,000	Gross dividend receipts
25,000	Gain on sale of P stock (Loss on O stock not taken into account)
$145,000	Total gross receipts

(iii) S's passive investment income is determined as follows:

$10,000	Gross dividend receipts
25,000	Gain on sale of P stock (Loss on O stock not taken into account)
$35,000	Total passive investment income

(iv) S's passive investment income percentage for its first year as an S corporation is 24.1% ($35,000/$145,000). This does not exceed 25 percent of S's gross receipts and consequently the three-year period described in section 1362(d)(3) does not begin to run.

Example 7. Interest on accounts receivable; netting of gain on sale of real property investments. (i) In 1993, S receives $6,000 of interest on accounts receivable arising from S's sales of inventory property. S also receives dividends with respect

$90,000	Gross receipts from operations
6,000	Gross interest receipts
1,500	Gross dividend receipts
2,000	Net gain on sale of real property investments
$99,500	Total gross receipts

(iii) Under paragraph (c)(5)(ii)(D) of this section, S's gross interest receipts are not passive investment income. In addition, gain on the sale of real property ($2,000) is not passive investment income. S's passive investment income includes only the $1,500 of gross dividend receipts. Accordingly, S's passive investment income percentage for its first year as an S corporation is 1.51% ($1,500/$99,500). This does not exceed 25 percent of S's gross receipts and consequently

investment income. However, the royalty payments with respect to Trademark B are included within the definition of *royalties* for purposes of determining S's passive investment income. See paragraph (c)(5)(ii)(A) of this section. S's passive investment income for the year is $8,000, and S's passive investment income percentage for the taxable year is 10.67% ($8,000/$75,000). This does not exceed 25 percent of S's gross receipts and consequently the three-year period described in section 1362(d)(3) does not begin to run.

Example 6. Dividends; gain on sale of stock derived in the ordinary course of trade or business. (i) In 1993, S receives dividends of $10,000 on stock of corporations P and O, recognizes a gain of $25,000 on sale of the P stock, and recognizes a loss of $12,000 on sale of the O stock. S held the P and O stock for investment, rather than for sale in the ordinary course of a trade or business. S has gross receipts from operations and from gain on the sale of stock in the ordinary course of its trade or business of $110,000.

(ii) S's gross receipts are calculated as follows:

to stock held for investment of $1,500. In addition, S sells two parcels of real property (Property J and Property K) that S had purchased and held for investment. S sells Property J, in which S has a basis of $5,000, for $10,000 (a gain of $5,000). S sells Property K, in which S has a basis of $12,000, for $9,000 (a loss of $3,000). S has gross receipts from operations of $90,000.

(ii) S's gross receipts are calculated as follows:

the three-year period described in section 1362(d)(3) does not begin to run.

Example 8. Interest received in the ordinary course of a lending business. (i) In 1993, S has gross receipts of $100,000 from loans and investments made in the ordinary course of S's mortgage banking business. This includes, for example, mortgage servicing fees, interest earned on mortgages prior to sale of the mortgages, and gain on sale of mortgages. In addition, S receives, from the investment of idle funds in short-term securities, $15,000 of gross interest income and $5,000 of gain.

(ii) *S's* gross receipts are calculated as follows:

$100,000	Gross receipts from operations
15,000	Gross interest receipts
5,000	Gain on sale of securities
$120,000	Total gross receipts

(iii) *S's* passive investment income is determined as follows:

$15,000	Gross interest receipts
5,000	Gain on sale of securities
$20,000	Total passive investment income

(iv) *S's* passive investment income percentage for its first year as an S corporation is 16.67% ($20,000/$120,000). This does not exceed 25 percent of *S's* gross receipts and consequently the three-year period described in section 1362(d)(3) does not begin to run. [Reg. §1.1362-2.]

☐ [*T.D. 8449, 11-24-92. Amended by T.D. 8869, 1-20-2000 and T.D. 8995, 5-14-2002.*]

[Reg. §1.1362-3]

§1.1362-3. Treatment of S termination year.—(a) *In general.*—If an S election terminates under section 1362(d) on a date other than the first day of a taxable year of the corporation, the corporation's taxable year in which the termination occurs is an S termination year. The portion of the S termination year ending at the close of the day prior to the termination is treated as a short taxable year for which the corporation is an S corporation (the *S short year*). The portion of the S termination year beginning on the day the termination is effective is treated as a short taxable year for which the corporation is a C corporation (the *C short year*). Except as provided in paragraphs (b) and (c)(1) of this section, the corporation allocates income or loss for the entire year on a pro rata basis as described in section 1362(e)(2). To the extent that income or loss is not allocated on a pro rata basis under this section, items of income, gain, loss, deduction, and credit are assigned to each short taxable year on the basis of the corporation's normal method of accounting as determined under section 446. See, however, §1.1502-76(b)(1)(ii)(A)(2) for special rules for an S election that terminates under section 1362(d) immediately before the S corporation becomes a member of a consolidated group (within the meaning of §1.1502-1(h)). See §1.460-4(k)(3)(iv)(D) for rules relating to the computation of the S corporation's income or loss from a contract accounted for under a long-term contract method of accounting in the S termination year.

(b) *Allocations other than pro rata.*—(1) *Elections under section 1362(e)(3).*—The pro rata allocation rules of section 1362(e)(2) do not apply if the corporation elects to allocate its S termination year income on the basis of its normal tax accounting method. This election may be made

only with the consent of each person who is a shareholder in the corporation at any time during the S short year and of each person who is a shareholder in the corporation on the first day of the C short year. See §1.1362-6(a) for rules concerning the time and manner of making this election.

(2) *Purchase of stock treated as an asset purchase.*—The pro rata allocation rules of section 1362(e)(2) do not apply with respect to any item resulting from the application of section 338.

(3) *50 percent change in ownership during S termination year.*—The pro rata allocation rules of section 1362(e)(2) do not apply if at any time during the S termination year, as a result of sales or exchanges of stock in the corporation during that year, there is a change in ownership of 50 percent or more of the issued and outstanding shares of stock of the corporation. If stock has already been sold or exchanged during the S termination year, subsequent sales or exchanges of that stock are not taken into account for purposes of this paragraph (b)(3).

(c) *Special rules.*—(1) *S corporation that is a partner in a partnership.*—For purposes of section 706(c) only, the termination of the election of an S corporation that is a partner in a partnership during any portion of the S short year under §1.1362-2(a) or (b), is treated as a sale or exchange of the corporation's entire interest in the partnership on the last day of the S short year, if—

(i) The pro rata allocation rules do not apply to the corporation; and

(ii) Any taxable year of the partnership ends with or within the C short year.

(2) *Tax for the C short year.*—The taxable income for the C short year is determined on an annualized basis as described in section 1362(e)(5).

(3) *Each short year treated as taxable year.*—Except as otherwise provided in paragraph (c)(4) of this section, the S and C short years are treated as two separate years for purposes of all provisions of the Internal Revenue Code.

(4) *Year for carryover purposes.*—The S and C short years are treated as one year for purposes of determining the number of taxable years to which any item may be carried back or forward by the corporation.

(5) *Due date for S short year return.*—The date by which the return for the S short year must be filed is the same as the date by which the return for the C short year must be filed (including extensions).

(6) *Year in which income from S short year is includible.*—A shareholder must include in taxable income the shareholder's pro rata share of the items described in section 1366(a) for the S

short year for the taxable year with or within which the S termination year ends.

(d) *Examples.*—The provisions of this section are illustrated by the following examples:

Example 1. S termination year not created. (i) On January 1, 1993, the first day of its taxable year, a subchapter C corporation had three eligible shareholders. During 1993, the corporation properly elected to be treated as an S corporation effective January 1, 1994, the first day of the succeeding taxable year. Subsequently, a transfer of some of the stock in the corporation was made to an ineligible shareholder. The ineligible shareholder still holds the stock on January 1, 1994.

(ii) The corporation fails to meet the definition of a small business corporation on January 1, 1994, and its election is treated as having terminated on that date. See § 1.1362-2(b)(2) for the termination rules. Because the corporation ceases to be a small business corporation on the first day of a taxable year, an S termination year is not created. In addition, if the corporation in the future meets the definition of a small business corporation and desires to elect to be treated as an S corporation, the corporation is automatically granted consent to reelect before the expiration of the 5-year waiting period. See § 1.1362-5 for special rules concerning automatic consent to reelect.

Example 2. More than 50 percent change in ownership during S short year. A, an individual, owns all 100 outstanding shares of stock of S, a calendar year S corporation. On January 31, 1993, A sells 60 shares of S stock to B, an individual. On June 1, 1993, A sells 5 shares of S stock to PRS, a partnership. S ceases to be a small business corporation on June 1, 1993, and pursuant to section 1362(d)(2), its election terminates on that date. Because there was a more than 50 percent change in ownership of the issued and outstanding shares of S stock, S must assign the items of income, loss, deduction, or credit for the S termination year to the two short taxable years on the basis of S's normal method of accounting under the rules of paragraph (b)(3) of this section.

Example 3. More than 50 percent change in ownership during C short year. A, an individual, owns all 100 outstanding shares of stock of S, a calendar year S corporation. On June 1, 1993, A sells 5 shares of S stock to PRS, a partnership. S ceases to be a small business corporation on that date and pursuant to section 1362(d)(3), its election terminates on that date. On July 1, 1993, A sells 60 shares of S stock to B, an individual. Since there was a more than 50 percent change in ownership of the issued and outstanding shares of S stock during the S termination year, S must assign the items of income, loss, deduction, or credit for the S termination year to the two short taxable years on the basis of S's normal method of accounting under the rules of paragraph (b)(3) of this section.

Example 4. Stock acquired other than by sale or exchange. C and D are shareholders in S, a calendar year S corporation. Each owns 50 percent of the issued and outstanding shares of the corporation on December 31, 1993. On March 1, 1994, C makes a gift of his entire shareholder interest to T, a trust not permitted as a shareholder under section 1361(c)(2). S ceases to be a small business corporation on March 1, 1994, and pursuant to section 1362(d)(2), its S corporation election terminates effective on that date. As a result of the gift, T owns 50 percent of S's issued and outstanding stock. However, because T acquired the stock by gift from C rather than by sale or exchange, there has not been a more than 50 percent change in ownership by sale or exchange of S that would cause the rules of paragraph (b)(3) of this section to apply. [Reg. § 1.1362-3.]

☐ [*T.D. 8449, 11-24-92. Amended by T.D. 8842, 11-9-99 and T.D. 9137, 7-15-2004.*]

[Reg. § 1.1362-4]

§ 1.1362-4. Inadvertent terminations and inadvertently invalid elections.—(a) *In general.*— A corporation is treated as continuing to be an S corporation or a QSub (or, an invalid election to be either an S corporation or a QSub is treated as valid) during the period specified by the Commissioner if—

(1) The corporation made a valid election under section 1362(a) or section 1361(b)(3) and the election terminated or the corporation made an election under section 1362(a) or section 1361(b)(3) that was invalid;

(2) The Commissioner determines that the termination or invalidity was inadvertent;

(3) Within a reasonable period of time after discovery of the terminating event or invalid election, steps were taken so that the corporation for which the election was made or the termination occurred is a small business corporation or a QSub, as the case may be, or to acquire the required shareholder consents; and

(4) The corporation and shareholders agree to adjustments that the Commissioner may require for the period.

(b) *Inadvertent termination or inadvertently invalid election.*—For purposes of paragraph (a) of this section, the determination of whether a termination or invalid election was inadvertent is made by the Commissioner. The corporation has the burden of establishing that under the relevant facts and circumstances the Commissioner should determine that the termination or invalid election was inadvertent. The fact that the terminating event or invalidity of the election was not reasonably within the control of the corporation and, in the case of a termination, was not part of a plan to terminate the election, or the fact that the terminating event or circumstance took place without the knowledge of the corporation, notwithstanding its due diligence to safeguard itself against such an event or circumstance, tends to establish that the termination or invalidity of the election was inadvertent.

(c) *Corporation's request for determination of an inadvertent termination or invalid election.*—A corporation that believes that the termination or invalidity of its election was inadvertent may request a determination from the Commissioner that the termination or invalidity of its election was inadvertent. The request is made in the form of a ruling request and should set forth all relevant facts pertaining to the event or circumstance including, but not limited to, the facts described in paragraph (b) of this section, the date of the corporation's election (or intended election) under section 1362(a) or 1361(b)(3), a detailed explanation of the event or circumstance causing the termination or invalidity, when and how the event or circumstance was discovered, and the steps taken under paragraph (a)(3) of this section.

(d) *Adjustments.*—The Commissioner may require any adjustments that are appropriate. In general, the adjustments required should be consistent with the treatment of the corporation as an S corporation or QSub during the period specified by the Commissioner. In the case of stock held by an ineligible shareholder that causes an inadvertent termination or invalid election for an S corporation under section 1362(f), the Commissioner may require the ineligible shareholder to be treated as a shareholder of the S corporation during the period the ineligible shareholder actually held stock in the corporation. Moreover, the Commissioner may require protective adjustments that prevent the loss of any revenue due to the holding of stock by an ineligible shareholder (for example, a nonresident alien).

(e) *Corporation and shareholder consents.*—The corporation and all persons who were shareholders of the corporation at any time during the period specified by the Commissioner must consent to any adjustments that the Commissioner may require. Each consent should be in the form of a statement agreeing to make the adjustments. The statement must be signed by the shareholder (in the case of shareholder consent) or a person authorized to sign the return required by section 6037 (in the case of corporate consent). See §1.1362-6(b)(2) for persons required to sign consents. A shareholder's consent statement should include the name, address, and taxpayer identification numbers of the corporation and shareholder, the number of shares of stock owned by the shareholder, and the dates on which the shareholder owned any stock. The corporate consent statement should include the name, address, and taxpayer identification numbers of the corporation and each shareholder.

(f) *Status of corporation.*—The status of the corporation after the terminating event or invalid election and before the determination of inadvertence is determined by the Commissioner. Inadvertent termination or inadvertent invalid election relief may be granted retroactively for all years for which the terminating event or circumstance giving rise to invalidity is effective, in which case the corporation is treated as if its election was valid or had not terminated. Alternatively, relief may be granted only for the period in which the corporation became eligible for subchapter S or QSub treatment, in which case the corporation is treated as a C corporation or, in the case of a QSub with an inadvertently terminated or invalid election, as a separate C corporation, during the period for which the corporation was not eligible for its intended status.

(g) *Effective/applicability date.*—Paragraphs (a), (b), (c), (d), and (f) of this section are effective on August 14, 2008. [Reg. §1.1362-4.]

☐ [*T.D.* 8449, 11-24-92. *Amended by T.D. 9422,* 8-13-2008.]

[Reg. §1.1362-5]

§1.1362-5. Election after termination.—(a) *In general.*—Absent the Commissioner's consent, an S corporation whose election has terminated (or a successor corporation) may not make a new election under section 1362(a) for five taxable years as described in section 1362(g). However, the Commissioner may permit the corporation to make a new election before the 5-year period expires. The corporation has the burden of establishing that under the relevant facts and circumstances, the Commissioner should consent to a new election. The fact that more than 50 percent of the stock in the corporation is owned by persons who did not own any stock in the corporation on the date of the termination tends to establish that consent should be granted. In the absence of this fact, consent ordinarily is denied unless the corporation shows that the event causing termination was not reasonably within the control of the corporation or shareholders having a substantial interest in the corporation and was not part of a plan on the part of the corporation or of such shareholders to terminate the election.

(b) *Successor corporation.*—A corporation is a *successor corporation* to a corporation whose election under section 1362 has been terminated if—

(1) 50 percent or more of the stock of the corporation (the new corporation) is owned, directly or indirectly, by the same persons who, on the date of the termination, owned 50 percent or more of the stock of the corporation whose election terminated (the old corporation); and

(2) Either the new corporation acquires a substantial portion of the assets of the old corporation, or a substantial portion of the assets of the new corporation were assets of the old corporation.

(c) *Automatic consent after certain terminations.*—A corporation may, without requesting the Commissioner's consent, make a new election under section 1362(a) before the 5-year period described in section 1362(g) expires if the termination occurred because the corporation—

(1) Revoked its election effective on the first day of the first taxable year for which its election was to be effective (see § 1.1362-2(a)(2)); or

(2) Failed to meet the definition of a small business corporation on the first day of the first taxable year for which its election was to be effective (see § 1.1362-2(b)(2)). [Reg. § 1.1362-5.]

☐ [T.D. 8449, 11-24-92.]

[Reg. § 1.1362-6]

§ 1.1362-6. Elections and consents.—(a) *Time and manner of making elections.*—(1) *In general.*— An election statement made under this section must identify the election being made, set forth the name, address, and taxpayer identification number of the corporation, and be signed by a person authorized to sign the return required to be filed under section 6037.

(2) *Election to be an S corporation.*— (i) *Manner of making election.*—A small business corporation makes an election under section 1362(a) to be an S corporation by filing a completed Form 2553. The election form must be filed with the service center designated in the instructions applicable to Form 2553. The election is not valid unless all shareholders of the corporation at the time of the election consent to the election in the manner provided in paragraph (b) of this section. However, once a valid election is made, new shareholders need not consent to that election.

(ii) *Time of making election.*—(A) *In general.*—The election described in paragraph (a)(2)(i) of this section may be made by a small business corporation at any time during the taxable year that immediately precedes the taxable year for which the election is to be effective, or during the taxable year for which the election is to be effective provided that the election is made before the 16th day of the third month of the year. If a corporation makes an election for a taxable year, and the election meets all the requirements of this section but is made during the period beginning after the 15th day of the third month of the taxable year, the election is treated as being made for the following taxable year provided that the corporation meets all the requirements of section 1361(b) at the time the election is made. For taxable years of 2½ months or less, an election made before the 16th day of the third month after the first day of the taxable year is treated as made during that year.

(B) *Elections made during the first 2½ months treated as made for the following taxable year.*—A timely election made by a small business corporation during the taxable year for which it is intended to be effective is nonetheless treated as made for the following taxable year if—

(1) The corporation is not a small business corporation during the entire portion of the taxable year which occurs before the date the election is made; or

(2) Any person who held stock in the corporation at any time during the portion of the taxable year which occurs before the time the election is made, and who does not hold stock at the time the election is made, does not consent to the election.

(C) *Definition of month and beginning of the taxable year.*—*Month* means a period commencing on the same numerical day of any calendar month as the day of the calendar month on which the taxable year began and ending with the close of the day preceding the numerically corresponding day of the succeeding calendar month or, if there is no corresponding day, with the close of the last day of the succeeding calendar month. In addition, the taxable year of a new corporation begins on the date that the corporation has shareholders, acquires assets, or begins doing business, whichever is the first to occur. The existence of incorporators does not necessarily begin the taxable year of a new corporation.

(iii) *Examples.*—The provisions of this section are illustrated by the following examples:

Example 1. Effective election; no prior taxable year. A calendar year small business corporation begins its first taxable year on January 7, 1993. To be an S corporation beginning with its first taxable year, the corporation must make the election set forth in this section during the period that begins January 7, 1993, and ends before March 22, 1993. Because the corporation had no taxable year immediately preceding the taxable year for which the election is to be effective, an election made earlier than January 7, 1993, will not be valid.

Example 2. Effective election; taxable year less than 2½ months. A calendar year small business corporation begins its first taxable year on November 8, 1993. To be an S corporation beginning with its first taxable year, the corporation must make the election set forth in this section during the period that begins November 8, 1993, and ends before January 23, 1994.

Example 3. Election effective for the following taxable year; ineligible shareholder. On January 1, 1993, two individuals and a partnership own all of the stock of a calendar year subchapter C corporation. On January 31, 1993, the partnership dissolved and distributed its shares in the corporation to its five partners, all individuals. On February 28, 1993, the seven shareholders of the corporation consented to the corporation's election of subchapter S status. The corporation files a properly completed Form 2553 on March

2, 1993. The corporation is not eligible to be a subchapter S corporation for the 1993 taxable year because during the period of the taxable year prior to the election it had an ineligible shareholder. However, under paragraph (a)(2)(ii)(B) of this section, the election is treated as made for the corporation's 1994 taxable year.

(3) *Revocation of S election.*—(i) *Manner of revoking election.*—To revoke an election, the corporation files a statement that the corporation revokes the election made under section 1362(a). The statement must be filed with the service center where the election was properly filed. The revocation statement must include the number of shares of stock (including non-voting stock) issued and outstanding at the time the revocation is made. A revocation may be made only with the consent of shareholders who, at the time the revocation is made, hold more than one-half of the number of issued and outstanding shares of stock (including non-voting stock) of the corporation. Each shareholder who consents to the revocation must consent in the manner required under paragraph (b) of this section. In addition, each consent should indicate the number of issued and outstanding shares of stock (including non-voting stock) held by each shareholder at the time of the revocation.

(ii) *Time of revoking election.*—For rules concerning when a revocation is effective, see § 1.1362-2(a)(2).

(iii) *Examples.*—The principles of this paragraph (a)(3) are illustrated by the following examples:

Example 1. Revocation; consent of shareholders owning more than one-half of issued and outstanding shares. A calendar year S corporation has issued and outstanding 40,000 shares of class A voting common stock and 20,000 shares of class B non-voting common stock. The corporation wishes to revoke its election of subchapter S status. Shareholders owning 11,000 shares of class A stock sign revocation consents. Shareholders owning 20,000 shares of class B stock sign revocation consents. The corporation has obtained the required shareholder consent to revoke its subchapter S election because shareholders owning more than one-half of the total number of issued and outstanding shares of stock of the corporation consented to the revocation.

Example 2. Effective prospective revocation. In June 1993, a calendar year S corporation determines that it will revoke its subchapter S election effective August 1, 1993. To do so it must file its revocation statement with consents attached on or before August 1, 1993, and the statement must indicate that the revocation is intended to be effective August 1, 1993.

(4) *Rescission of a revocation.*—(i) *Manner of rescinding a revocation.*—To rescind a revocation,

the corporation files a statement that the corporation rescinds the revocation made under section 1362(d)(1). The statement must be filed with the service center where the revocation was properly filed. A rescission may be made only with the consent (in the manner required under paragraph (b)(1) of this section) of each person who consented to the revocation and of each person who became a shareholder of the corporation within the period beginning on the first day after the date the revocation was made and ending on the date on which the rescission is made.

(ii) *Time of rescinding a revocation.*—If the rescission statement is filed before the revocation becomes effective and is filed with proper service center, the rescission is effective on the date it is so filed.

(5) *Election not to apply pro rata allocation.*— To elect not to apply the pro rata allocation rules to an S termination year, a corporation files a statement that it elects under section 1362(e)(3) not to apply the rules provided in section 1362(e)(2). In addition to meeting the requirements of paragraph (a)(1) of this section, the statement must set forth the cause of the termination and the date thereof. The statement must be filed with the corporation's return for the C short year. This election may be made only with the consent of all persons who are shareholders of the corporation at any time during the S short year and all persons who are shareholders of the corporation on the first day of the C short year (in the manner required under paragraph (b)(1) of this section).

(b) *Shareholders' consents.*—(1) *Manner of consents in general.*—A shareholder's consent required under paragraph (a) of this section must be in the form of a written statement that sets forth the name, address, and taxpayer identification number of the shareholder, the number of shares of stock owned by the shareholder, the date (or dates) on which the stock was acquired, the date on which the shareholder's taxable year ends, the name of the S corporation, the corporation's taxpayer identification number, and the election to which the shareholder consents. The statement must be signed by the shareholder under penalties of perjury. Except as provided in paragraph (b)(3)(iii) of this section, the election of the corporation is not valid if any required consent is not filed in accordance with the rules contained in this paragraph (b). The consent statement should be attached to the corporation's election statement.

(2) *Persons required to consent.*—The following rules apply in determining persons required to consent:

(i) *Community interest in stock.*—When stock of the corporation is owned by husband and wife as community property (or the income from the stock is community property), or is owned by tenants in common, joint tenants, or tenants by the entirety, each person having a community interest in the stock or income therefrom and each tenant in common, joint tenant and tenant by the entirety must consent to the election.

(ii) *Minor.*—The consent of a minor must be made by the minor or by the legal representative of the minor (or by a natural or an adoptive parent of the minor if no legal representative has been appointed).

(iii) *Estate.*—The consent of an estate must be made by an executor or administrator thereof, or by any other fiduciary appointed by testamentary instrument or appointed by the court having jurisdiction over the administration of the estate.

(iv) *Trusts.*—In the case of a trust described in section 1361(c)(2)(A) (including a trust treated under section 1361(d)(1)(A) as a trust described in section 1361(c)(2)(A)(i) and excepting an electing small business trust described in section 1361(c)(2)(A)(v) (ESBT)), only the person treated as the shareholder for purposes of section 1361(b)(1) must consent to the election. When stock of the corporation is held by a trust, both husband and wife must consent to any election if the husband and wife have a community interest in the trust property. See paragraph (b)(2)(i) of this section for rules concerning community interests in S corporation stock. In the case of an ESBT, the trustee and the owner of any portion of the trust that consists of the stock in one or more S corporations under subpart E, part I, subchapter J, chapter 1 of the Internal Revenue Code must consent to the S corporation election. If there is more than one trustee, the trustee or trustees with authority to legally bind the trust must consent to the S corporation election.

(3) *Special rules for consent of shareholder to election to be an S corporation.*—(i) *In general.*—The consent of a shareholder to an election by a small business corporation under section 1362(a) may be made on Form 2553 or on a separate statement in the manner described in paragraph (b)(1) of this section. In addition, the separate statement must set forth the name, address, and taxpayer identification number of the corporation. A shareholder's consent is binding and may not be withdrawn after a valid election is made by the corporation. Each person who is a shareholder (including any person who is treated as a shareholder under section 1361(c)(2)(B)) at the time the election is made) must consent to the election. If the election is made before the 16th day of the third month of the taxable year and is intended to be effective for that year, each person who was a shareholder (including any person who was treated as a shareholder under section 1361(c)(2)(B)) at any time during the portion of that year which occurs before the time the

election is made, and who is not a shareholder at the time the election is made, must also consent to the election. If the election is to be effective for the following taxable year, no consent need be filed by any shareholder who is not a shareholder on the date of the election. Any person who is considered to be a shareholder under applicable state law solely by virtue of his or her status as an incorporator is not treated as a shareholder for purposes of this paragraph (b)(3)(i).

(ii) *Examples.*—The principles of this section are illustrated by the following examples:

Example 1. Effective election; shareholder consents. On January 1, 1993, the first day of its taxable year, a subchapter C corporation had 15 shareholders. On January 30, 1993, two of the C corporation's shareholders, A and B, both individuals, sold their shares in the corporation to P, Q, and R, all individuals. On March 1, 1993, the corporation filed its election to be an S corporation for the 1993 taxable year. The election will be effective (assuming the other requirements of section 1361(b) are met) provided that all of the shareholders as of March 1, 1993, as well as former shareholders A and B, consent to the election.

Example 2. Consent of new shareholder unnecessary. On January 1, 1993, three individuals own all of the stock of a calendar year subchapter C corporation. On April 15, 1993, the corporation, in accordance with paragraph (a)(2) of this section, files a properly completed Form 2553. The corporation anticipates that the election will be effective beginning January 1, 1994, the first day of the succeeding taxable year. On October 1, 1993, the three shareholders collectively sell 75% of their shares in the corporation to another individual. On January 1, 1994, the corporation's shareholders are the three original individuals and the new shareholder. Because the election was valid and binding when made, it is not necessary for the new shareholder to consent to the election. The corporation's subchapter S election is effective on January 1, 1994 (assuming the other requirements of section 1361(b) are met).

(iii) *Extension of time for filing consents to an election.*—(A) *In general.*—An election that is timely filed for any taxable year and that would be valid except for the failure of any shareholder to file a timely consent is not invalid if consents are filed as required under paragraph (b)(3)(iii)(B) of this section and it is shown to the satisfaction of the district director or director of the service center with which the corporation files its income tax return that—

(1) There was reasonable cause for the failure to file the consent;

(2) The request for the extension of time to file a consent is made within a reasonable time under the circumstances; and

Reg. § 1.1362-6(b)(3)(iii)(A)(2)

(3) The interests of the Government will not be jeopardized by treating the election as valid.

(B) Required consents.—Consents must be filed within the extended period of time as may be granted by the Internal Revenue Service, by all persons who—

(1) Were shareholders of the corporation at any time during the period beginning as of the date of the invalid election and ending on the date on which an extension of time is granted in accordance with this paragraph (b)(3)(iii); and

(2) Have not previously consented to the election. [Reg. § 1.1362-6.]

☐ [*T.D.* 8449, 11-24-92. *Amended by T.D.* 8994, 5-13-2002.]

[Reg. § 1.1362-7]

§ 1.1362-7. Effective dates.—*(a) In general.*— The provisions of §§ 1.1362-1 through 1.1362-6 apply to taxable years of corporations beginning after December 31, 1992. For taxable years to which these regulations do not apply, corporations and shareholders subject to the provisions of section 1362 must take reasonable return positions taking into consideration the statute; its legislative history; the provisions of §§ 18.1362-1 through 18.1362-5 (see 26 CFR part 18 as contained in the CFR edition revised as of April 1, 1992). In addition, following these regulations is a reasonable return position. See Notice 92-56, 1992-49 I.R.B. (see § 601.601(d)(2)(ii)(*b*) of this chapter), for additional guidance regarding reasonable return positions for years to which §§ 1.1362-1 through 1.1362-6 do not apply. Section 1.1362-6(b)(2)(iv) is applicable for taxable years beginning on and after May 14, 2002.

(b) Special effective date for passive investment income provisions.—For taxable years of an S corporation and all affected shareholders that are not closed, the S corporation and all affected shareholders may elect to apply the provisions of § 1.1362-2(c)(5). To make the election, the corporation and all affected shareholders must file a return or an amended return that is consistent with these rules for the taxable year for which the election is made and each subsequent taxable year. For purposes of this section, *affected shareholders* means all shareholders who received distributive shares of S corporation items in the taxable year for which the election is made and all shareholders of the S corporation for all subsequent taxable years. However, the Commissioner may, in appropriate circumstances, permit taxpayers to make this election even if all affected shareholders cannot file consistent returns. [Reg. § 1.1362-7.]

☐ [*T.D.* 8449, 11-24-92. *Amended by T.D.* 8994, 5-13-2002.]

[Reg. § 1.1362-8]

§ 1.1362-8. Dividends received from affiliated subsidiaries.—*(a) In general.*—For purposes of section 1362(d)(3), if an S corporation holds stock in a C corporation meeting the requirements of section 1504(a)(2), the term *passive investment income* does not include dividends from the C corporation to the extent those dividends are attributable to the earnings and profits of the C corporation derived from the active conduct of a trade or business (active earnings and profits). For purposes of applying section 1362(d)(3), earnings and profits of a C corporation are active earnings and profits to the extent that the earnings and profits are derived from activities that would not produce passive investment income (as defined in section 1362(d)(3)) if the C corporation were an S corporation.

(b) Determination of active or passive earnings and profits.—*(1) In general.*—An S corporation may use any reasonable method to determine the amount of dividends that are not treated as passive investment income under section 1362(d)(3)(E). Paragraph (b)(5) of this section describes a method of determining the amount of dividends that are not treated as passive investment income under section 1362(d)(3)(E) that is deemed to be reasonable under all circumstances.

(2) Lower tier subsidiaries.—If a C corporation subsidiary (upper tier corporation) holds stock in another C corporation (lower tier subsidiary) meeting the requirements of section 1504(a)(2), the upper tier corporation's gross receipts attributable to a dividend from the lower tier subsidiary are considered to be derived from the active conduct of a trade or business to the extent the lower tier subsidiary's earnings and profits are attributable to the active conduct of a trade or business by the subsidiary under paragraph (b)(1), (3), (4), or (5) of this section. For purposes of this section, distributions by the lower tier subsidiary will be considered attributable to active earnings and profits according to the rule in paragraph (c) of this section. This paragraph (b)(2) does not apply to any member of a consolidated group (as defined in § 1.1502-1(h)).

(3) De minimis exception.—If less than 10 percent of a C corporation's earnings and profits for a taxable year are derived from activities that would produce passive investment income if the C corporation were an S corporation, all earnings and profits produced by the corporation during that taxable year are considered active earnings and profits.

(4) Special rules for earnings and profits accumulated by a C corporation prior to 80 percent acquisition.—A C corporation may treat all earnings and profits accumulated by the corporation in all taxable years ending before the S corporation

held stock meeting the requirements of section 1504(a)(2) as active earnings and profits in the same proportion as the C corporation's active earnings and profits for the three taxable years ending prior to the time when the S corporation acquired 80 percent of the C corporation bears to the C corporation's total earnings and profits for those three taxable years.

(5) *Gross receipts safe harbor.*—A corporation may treat its earnings and profits for a year as active earnings and profits in the same proportion as the corporation's gross receipts (as defined in § 1.1362-2(c)(4)) derived from activities that would not produce passive investment income (if the C corporation were an S corporation), including those that do not produce passive investment income under paragraphs (b)(2) through (b)(4) of this section, bear to the corporation's total gross receipts for the year in which the earnings and profits are produced.

(c) *Allocating distributions to active or passive earnings and profits.*—(1) *Distributions from current earnings and profits.*—Dividends distributed by a C corporation from current earnings and profits are attributable to active earnings and profits in the same proportion as current active earnings and profits bear to total current earnings and profits of the C corporation.

(2) *Distributions from accumulated earnings and profits.*—Dividends distributed by a C corporation out of accumulated earnings and profits for a taxable year are attributable to active earnings and profits in the same proportion as accumulated active earnings and profits for that taxable year bear to total accumulated earnings and profits for that taxable year immediately prior to the distribution.

(3) *Adjustments to active earnings and profits.*—For purposes of applying paragraph (c)(1) or (2) of this section to a distribution, the active earnings and profits of a corporation shall be reduced by the amount of any prior distribution properly treated as attributable to active earnings and profits from the same taxable year.

(4) *Special rules for consolidated groups.*—For purposes of applying section 1362(d)(3) and this section to dividends received by an S corporation from the common parent of a consolidated group (as defined in § 1.1502-1(h)), the following rules apply—

(i) The current earnings and profits, accumulated earnings and profits, and active earnings and profits of the common parent shall be determined under the principles of § 1.1502-33 (relating to earnings and profits of any member of a consolidated group owning stock of another member); and

(ii) The gross receipts of the common parent shall be the sum of the gross receipts of each member of the consolidated group (including the common parent), adjusted to eliminate gross receipts from intercompany transactions (as defined in § 1.1502-13(b)(1)(i)).

(d) *Examples.*—The following examples illustrate the principles of this section:

Example 1. (i) X, an S corporation, owns 85 percent of the one class of stock of Y. On December 31, 2002, Y declares a dividend of $100 ($85 to X), which is equal to Y's current earnings and profits. In 2002, Y has total gross receipts of $1,000, $200 of which would be passive investment income if Y were an S corporation.

(ii) One-fifth ($200/$1,000) of Y's gross receipts for 2002 is attributable to activities that would produce passive investment income. Accordingly, one-fifth of the $100 of earnings and profits is passive, and $17 ($\frac{1}{5}$ of $85) of the dividend from Y to X is passive investment income.

Example 2. (i) The facts are the same as in *Example 1*, except that Y owns 90 percent of the stock of Z. Y and Z do not join in the filing of a consolidated return. In 2002, Z has gross receipts of $15,000, $12,000 of which are derived from activities that would produce passive investment income. On December 31, 2002, Z declares a dividend of $1,000 ($900 to Y) from current earnings and profits.

(ii) Four-fifths ($12,000/$15,000) of the dividend from Z to Y are attributable to passive earnings and profits. Accordingly, $720 ($\frac{4}{5}$ of $900) of the dividend from Z to Y is considered gross receipts from an activity that would produce passive investment income. The $900 dividend to Y gives Y a total of $1,900 ($1,000 + $900) in gross receipts, $920 ($200 + $720) of which is attributable to passive investment income-producing activities. Under these facts, $41 ($920/$1,900 of $85) of Y's distribution to X is passive investment income to X.

(e) *Effective date.*—This section applies to dividends received in taxable years beginning on or after January 20, 2000; however, taxpayers may elect to apply the regulations in whole, but not in part, for taxable years beginning on or after January 1, 2000, provided all affected taxpayers apply the regulations in a consistent manner. To make this election, the corporation and all affected taxpayers must file a return or an amended return that is consistent with these rules for the taxable year for which the election is made. For purposes of this section, affected taxpayers means all taxpayers whose returns are affected by the election to apply the regulations. [Reg. § 1.1362-8.]

☐ [*T.D.* 8869, 1-20-2000 (*corrected* 3-27-2000).]

[Reg. § 1.1363-1]

§ 1.1363-1. Effect of election on corporation.—(a) *Exemption of corporation from income tax.*—(1) *In general.*—Except as provided in this paragraph (a), a small business corporation that makes a valid election under section 1362(a) is exempt from the taxes imposed by chapter 1 of the Internal Revenue Code with respect to taxable years of the corporation for which the election is in effect.

(2) *Corporate level taxes.*—An S corporation is not exempt from the tax imposed by section 1374 (relating to the tax imposed on certain built-in gains), or section 1375 (relating to the tax on excess passive investment income). See also section 1363(d) (relating to the recapture of LIFO benefits) for the rules regarding the payment by an S corporation of LIFO recapture amounts.

(b) *Computation of corporate taxable income.*—The taxable income of an S corporation is computed as described in section 1363(b).

(c) *Elections of the S corporation.*—(1) *In general.*—Any elections (other than those described in paragraph (c)(2) of this section) affecting the computation of items derived from an S corporation are made by the corporation. For example, elections of methods of accounting, of computing depreciation, of treating soil and water conservation expenditures, and the option to deduct as expenses intangible drilling and development costs, are made by the corporation and not by the shareholders separately. All corporate elections are applicable to all shareholders.

(2) *Exceptions.*—(i) Each shareholder's pro rata share of expenses described in section 617 paid or accrued by the S corporation is treated according to the shareholder's method of treating those expenses, notwithstanding the treatment of the expenses by the corporation.

(ii) Each shareholder may elect to amortize that shareholder's pro rata share of any qualified expenditure described in section 59(e) paid or accrued by the S corporation.

(iii) Each shareholder's pro rata share of taxes described in section 901 paid or accrued by the S corporation to foreign countries or possessions of the United States (according to its method of treating those taxes) is treated according to the shareholder's method of treating those taxes, and each shareholder may elect to use the total amount either as a credit against tax or as a deduction from income.

(d) *Effective date.*—This section applies to taxable years of corporations beginning after December 31, 1992. For taxable years to which this section does not apply, corporations and shareholders subject to the provisions of section 1363 must take reasonable return positions taking into consideration the statute, its legislative history and these regulations. See Notice 92-56, 1992-49 I.R.B. (see § 601.601(d)(2)(ii)(*b*) of this chapter), for additional guidance regarding reasonable return positions for taxable years to which this section does not apply. [Reg. § 1.1363-1.]

☐ [*T.D.* 8449, 11-24-92.]

[Reg. § 1.1363-2]

§ 1.1363-2. Recapture of LIFO benefits.—(a) *In general.*—A C corporation must include the LIFO recapture amount (as defined in section 1363(d)(3)) in its gross income—

(1) In its last taxable year as a C corporation if the corporation inventoried assets under the LIFO method for its last taxable year before its S corporation election becomes effective; or

(2) In the year of transfer by the C corporation to an S corporation of the LIFO inventory assets if paragraph (a)(1) of this section does not apply and the C corporation—

(i) Inventoried assets under the LIFO method during the taxable year of the transfer of those LIFO inventory assets; and

(ii) Transferred the LIFO inventory assets to the S corporation in a nonrecognition transaction (within the meaning of section 7701(a)(45)) in which the transferred assets constitute transferred basis property (within the meaning of section 7701(a)(43)).

(b) *LIFO inventory held indirectly through partnership.*—A C corporation must include the lookthrough LIFO recapture amount (as defined in paragraph (c)(4) of this section) in its gross income—

(1) In its last taxable year as a C corporation if, on the last day of the corporation's last taxable year before its S corporation election becomes effective, the corporation held a lookthrough partnership interest (as defined in paragraph (c)(3) of this section); or

(2) In the year of transfer by the C corporation to an S corporation of a lookthrough partnership interest if the corporation transferred its lookthrough partnership interest to the S corporation in a nonrecognition transaction (within the meaning of section 7701(a)(45)) in which the transferred interest constitutes transferred basis property (within the meaning of section 7701(a)(43)).

(c) *Definitions and special rules.*—(1) *Recapture date.*—In the case of a transaction described in paragraph (a)(1) or (b)(1) of this section, the recapture date is the day before the effective date of the S corporation election. In the case of a transaction described in paragraph (a)(2) or (b)(2) of this section, the recapture date is the date of the transfer of the partnership interest to the S corporation.

(2) *Determination of LIFO recapture amount.*—The LIFO recapture amount shall be determined as of the end of the recapture date for transactions described in paragraph (a)(1) of this section, and as of the moment before the transfer occurs for transactions described in paragraph (a)(2) of this section.

(3) *Lookthrough partnership interest.*—A partnership interest is a lookthrough partnership in-

terest if the partnership owns (directly or indirectly through one or more partnerships) assets accounted for under the last-in, first-out (LIFO) method (LIFO inventory).

(4) *Lookthrough LIFO recapture amount.*— (i) *In general.*—For purposes of this section, a corporation's lookthrough LIFO recapture amount is the amount of income that would be allocated to the corporation, taking into account section 704(c) and §1.704-3, if the partnership sold all of its LIFO inventory for the inventory's FIFO value. For this purpose, the FIFO value of inventory is the inventory amount of the inventory assets under the first-in, first-out method of accounting authorized by section 471, determined in accordance with section 1363(d)(4)(C).

(ii) *Determination of lookthrough LIFO recapture amount.*—Except as provided in paragraph (c)(4)(iii) of this section, the lookthrough LIFO recapture amount shall be determined as of the end of the recapture date for transactions described in paragraph (b)(1) of this section, and as of the moment before the transfer occurs for transactions described in paragraph (b)(2) of this section.

(iii) *Alternative rule.*—If the partnership is not otherwise required to determine the inventory amount of the inventory using the LIFO method (the LIFO value) on the recapture date, the partnership may determine the lookthrough LIFO recapture amount as though the FIFO and LIFO values of the inventory on the recapture date equaled the FIFO and LIFO values of the opening inventory for the partnership's taxable year that includes the recapture date. For this purpose, the opening inventory includes inventory contributed by a partner to the partnership on or before the recapture date and excludes inventory distributed by the partnership to a partner on or before the recapture date. A partnership that applies the alternative method of this paragraph (c)(4)(iii) to calculate the lookthrough LIFO recapture amount must take into account any adjustments to the partnership's basis in its LIFO inventory that result from transactions occurring after the start of the partnership's taxable year and before the end of the recapture date. For example, the lookthrough LIFO recapture amount must be adjusted to take into account any adjustments to the basis of LIFO inventory during that period under sections 734(b), 737(c), or 751(b).

(d) *Payment of tax.*—Any increase in tax caused by including the LIFO recapture amount or the lookthrough LIFO recapture amount in the gross income of the C corporation is payable in four equal installments. The C corporation must pay the first installment of this payment by the due date of its return, determined without regard to extensions, for the last taxable year it operated as a C corporation if paragraph (a)(1) or (b)(1) of this section applies, or for the taxable

year of the transfer if paragraph (a)(2) or (b)(2) of this section applies. The three succeeding installments must be paid—

(1) For a transaction described in paragraph (a)(1) or (b)(1) of this section, by the corporation that made the election under section 1362(a) to be an S corporation, on or before the due date for the corporation's returns (determined without regard to extensions) for the succeeding three taxable years; and

(2) For a transaction described in paragraph (a)(2) or (b)(2) of this section, by the transferee S corporation on or before the due date for the transferee corporation's returns (determined without regard to extensions) for the succeeding three taxable years.

(e) *Basis adjustments.*—(1) *General rule.*—Appropriate adjustments to the basis of inventory are to be made to reflect any amount included in income under paragraph (a) of this section.

(2) *LIFO inventory owned through a partnership.*—(i) *Basis of corporation's partnership interest.*—Appropriate adjustments to the basis of the corporation's lookthrough partnership interest are to be made to reflect any amount included in income under paragraph (b) of this section.

(ii) *Basis of partnership assets.*—A partnership directly holding LIFO inventory that is taken into account under paragraph (b) of this section may elect to adjust the basis of that LIFO inventory. In addition, a partnership that holds, through another partnership, LIFO inventory that is taken into account under paragraph (b) of this section may elect to adjust the basis of that partnership interest. Any adjustment under this paragraph (e)(2) to the basis of inventory held by the partnership is equal to the amount of LIFO recapture attributable to the inventory. Likewise, any adjustment under this paragraph (e)(2) to the basis of a lookthrough partnership interest held by the partnership is equal to the amount of LIFO recapture attributable to the interest. A basis adjustment under this paragraph (e)(2) is treated in the same manner and has the same effect as an adjustment to the basis of partnership property under section 743(b). See §1.743-1(j).

(3) *Election.*—A partnership elects to adjust the basis of its inventory and any lookthrough partnership interest that it owns by attaching a statement to its original or amended income tax return for the first taxable year ending on or after the date of the S corporation election or transfer described in paragraph (b) of this section. This statement shall state that the partnership is electing under this paragraph (e)(3) and must include the names, addresses, and taxpayer identification numbers of any corporate partner liable for tax under paragraph (d) of this section and of the partnership, as well as the amount of the adjustment and the portion of the adjustment that is

attributable to each pool of inventory or look-through partnership interest that is held by the partnership.

(f) *Examples.*—The following examples illustrate the rules of this section:

Example 1. (i) G is a C corporation with a taxable year ending on June 30. GH is a partnership with a calendar year taxable year. G has a 20 percent interest in GH. The remaining 80 percent interest is owned by an individual. On April 25, 2005, G contributed inventory that is LIFO inventory to GH, increasing G's interest in the partnership to 50 percent. GH holds no other LIFO inventory, and there are no other adjustments to the partnership's basis in its LIFO inventory between January 1, 2005 and the end of the recapture date. G elects to be an S corporation effective July 1, 2005. The recapture date is June 30, 2005 under paragraph (c)(1) of this section. GH elects to use the LIFO method for the inventory and determines that the FIFO and LIFO values of the opening inventory for GH's 2005 taxable year, including the inventory contributed by G, are $200 and $120, respectively.

(ii) Under paragraph (c)(4)(iii) of this section, GH is not required to determine the FIFO and LIFO values of the inventory on the recapture date. Instead, GH may determine the lookthrough LIFO recapture amount as though the FIFO and LIFO values of the inventory on the recapture date equaled the FIFO and LIFO values of the opening inventory for the partnership's taxable year (2005) that includes the recapture date. For this purpose, under paragraph (c)(4) of this section, the opening inventory includes the inventory contributed by G. The amount by which the FIFO value ($200) exceeds the LIFO value ($120) in GH's opening inventory is $80. Thus, if GH sold all of its LIFO inventory for $200, it would recognize $80 of income. G's lookthrough LIFO recapture amount is $80, the amount of income that would be allocated to G, taking into account section 704(c) and § 1.704-3, if GH sold all of its LIFO inventory for the FIFO value. Under paragraph (b)(1) of this section, G must include $80 in income in its taxable year ending on June 30, 2005. Under paragraph (e)(2) of this section, G must increase its basis in its interest in GH by $80. Under paragraphs (e)(2) and (3) of this section, and in accordance with section 743(b) principles, GH may elect to increase the basis (with respect to G only) of its LIFO inventory by $80.

Example 2. (i) J is a C corporation with a calendar year taxable year. JK is a partnership with a calendar year taxable year. J has a 30 percent interest in the partnership. JK owns LIFO inventory that is not section 704(c) property. J elects to be an S corporation effective January 1, 2005. The recapture date is December 31, 2004 under paragraph (c)(1) of this section. JK determines that the FIFO and LIFO values of the inventory on

December 31, 2004 are $240 and $140, respectively.

(ii) The amount by which the FIFO value ($240) exceeds the LIFO value ($140) on the recapture date is $100. Thus, if JK sold all of its LIFO inventory for $240, it would recognize $100 of income. J's lookthrough LIFO recapture amount is $30, the amount of income that would be allocated to J if JK sold all of its LIFO inventory for the FIFO value (30 percent of $100). Under paragraph (b)(1) of this section, J must include $30 in income in its taxable year ending on December 31, 2004. Under paragraph (e)(2) of this section, J must increase its basis in its interest in JK by $30. Under paragraphs (e)(2) and (3) of this section, and in accordance with section 743(b) principles, JK may elect to increase the basis (with respect to J only) of its inventory by $30.

(g) *Effective dates.*—(1) The provisions of paragraph (a)(1) of this section apply to S elections made after December 17, 1987. For an exception, see section 10227(b)(2) of the Revenue Act of 1987.

(2) The provisions of paragraph (a)(2) of this section apply to transfers made after August 18, 1993.

(3) The provisions of paragraphs (b), (c), (d), (e)(2), (e)(3), and (f) of this section apply to S elections and transfers made on or after August 13, 2004. The rules that apply to S elections and transfers made before August 13, 2004, are contained in § 1.1363-2 as in effect prior to August 13, 2004 (see 26 CFR part 1 revised as of April 1, 2005). [Reg. § 1.1363-2.]

☐ [*T.D.* 8567, 10-6-94. *Amended by T.D.* 9210, 7-11-2005.]

[Reg. § 1.1366-0]

§ 1.1366-0. Table of contents.—The following table of contents is provided to facilitate the use of § § 1.1366-1 through 1.1366-5:

(c) Gross income of a shareholder.

(1) In general.

(2) Gross income for substantial omission of items.

(d) Shareholders holding stock subject to community property laws.

(e) Net operating loss deduction of shareholder of S corporation.

(f) Cross-reference.

§ 1.1366-2. *Limitations on deduction of passthrough items of an S corporation to its shareholders.*

(a) In general.

(1) Limitation on losses and deductions.

(2) Carryover of disallowance.

(3) Basis limitation amount.

(i) Stock portion.

(ii) Indebtedness portion.

(4) Limitation on losses and deductions allocated to each item.

(5) Nontransferability of losses and deductions.

(i) In general.

(ii) Exceptions for transfers of stock under section 1041(a).

(iii) Examples.

(6) Basis of stock acquired by gift.

(b) Special rules for carryover of disallowed losses and deductions to post-termination transition period described in section 1377(b).

(1) In general.

(2) Limitation on losses and deductions.

(3) Limitation on losses and deductions allocated to each item.

(4) Adjustment to the basis of stock.

(c) Carryover of disallowed losses and deductions in the case of liquidations, reorganizations, and divisions.

(1) Liquidations and reorganizations.

(2) Corporate separations to which section 368(a)(1)(D) applies.

§ 1.1366-3. *Treatment of family groups.*

(a) In general.

(b) Examples.

§ 1.1366-4. *Special rules limiting the passthrough of certain items of an S corporation to its shareholders.*

(a) Passthrough inapplicable to section 34 credit.

(b) Reduction in passthrough for tax imposed on built-in gains.

(c) Reduction in passthrough for tax imposed on excess net passive income.

§ 1.1366-5. *Effective date.*
[Reg. § 1.1366-0.]

☐ [*T.D. 8852, 12-21-99. Amended by T.D. 9422, 8-13-2008.*]

[Reg. § 1.1366-1]

§ 1.1366-1. Shareholder's share of items of an S corporation.—(a) *Determination of shareholder's tax liability.*—(1) *In general.*—An S corporation must report, and a shareholder is required to take into account in the shareholder's return, the shareholder's pro rata share, whether or not distributed, of the S corporation's items of income, loss, deduction, or credit described in paragraphs (a)(2), (3), and (4) of this section. A shareholder's pro rata share is determined in accordance with the provisions of section 1377(a) and the regulations thereunder. The shareholder takes these items into account in determining the shareholder's taxable income and tax liability for the shareholder's taxable year with or within which the taxable year of the corporation ends. If the shareholder dies (or if the shareholder is an estate or trust and the estate or trust terminates) before the end of the taxable year of the corporation, the shareholder's pro rata share of these items is taken into account on the shareholder's final return. For the limitation on allowance of a shareholder's pro rata share of S corporation losses or deductions, see section 1366(d) and § 1.1366-2.

(2) *Separately stated items of income, loss, deduction, or credit.*—Each shareholder must take into account separately the shareholder's pro rata share of any item of income (including tax-exempt income), loss, deduction, or credit of the S corporation that if separately taken into account by any shareholder could affect the shareholder's tax liability for that taxable year differently than if the shareholder did not take the item into account separately. The separately stated items of the S corporation include, but are not limited to, the following items—

(i) The corporation's combined net amount of gains and losses from sales or exchanges of capital assets grouped by applicable holding periods, by applicable rate of tax under section 1(h), and by any other classification that may be relevant in determining the shareholder's tax liability;

(ii) The corporation's combined net amount of gains and losses from sales or exchanges of property described in section 1231 (relating to property used in the trade or business and involuntary conversions), grouped by applicable holding periods, by applicable rate of tax under section 1(h), and by any other classification that may be relevant in determining the shareholder's tax liability;

(iii) Charitable contributions, grouped by the percentage limitations of section 170(b), paid by the corporation within the taxable year of the corporation;

(iv) The taxes described in section 901 that have been paid (or accrued) by the corporation to foreign countries or to possessions of the United States;

(v) Each of the corporation's separate items involved in the determination of credits against tax allowable under part IV of subchapter A (section 21 and following) of the Internal Revenue Code, except for any credit allowed under section 34 (relating to certain uses of gasoline and special fuels);

(vi) Each of the corporation's separate items of gains and losses from wagering transactions (section 165(d)); soil and water conservation expenditures (section 175); deduction under an election to expense certain depreciable business expenses (section 179); medical, dental, etc., expenses (section 213); the additional itemized deductions for individuals provided in part VII of subchapter B (section 212 and following) of the Internal Revenue Code; and any other itemized deductions for which the limitations on itemized deductions under sections 67 or 68 applies;

(vii) Any of the corporation's items of portfolio income or loss, and expenses related thereto, as defined in the regulations under section 469;

(viii) The corporation's tax-exempt income. For purposes of subchapter S, tax-exempt income is income that is permanently excludible from gross income in all circumstances in which the applicable provision of the Internal Revenue Code applies. For example, income that is excludible from gross income under section 101 (certain death benefits) or section 103 (interest on state and local bonds) is tax-exempt income, while income that is excludible from gross income under section 108 (income from discharge of indebtedness) or section 109 (improvements by lessee on lessor's property) is not tax-exempt income;

(ix) The corporation's adjustments described in sections 56 and 58, and items of tax preference described in section 57; and

(x) Any item identified in guidance (including forms and instructions) issued by the Commissioner as an item required to be separately stated under this paragraph (a)(2).

(3) *Nonseparately computed income or loss.*—Each shareholder must take into account separately the shareholder's pro rata share of the nonseparately computed income or loss of the S corporation. For this purpose, nonseparately computed income or loss means the corporation's gross income less the deductions allowed to the corporation under chapter 1 of the Internal Revenue Code, determined by excluding any item requiring separate computation under paragraph (a)(2) of this section.

(4) *Separate activities requirement.*—An S corporation must report, and each shareholder must take into account in the shareholder's return, the shareholder's pro rata share of an S corporation's items of income, loss, deduction, or credit described in paragraphs (a)(2) and (3) of this section for each of the corporation's activities as

defined in section 469 and the regulations thereunder.

(5) *Aggregation of deductions or exclusions for purposes of limitations.*—(i) *In general.*—A shareholder aggregates the shareholder's separate deductions or exclusions with the shareholder's pro rata share of the S corporation's separately stated deductions or exclusions in determining the amount of any deduction or exclusion allowable to the shareholder under subtitle A of the Internal Revenue Code as to which a limitation is imposed.

(ii) *Example.*—The provisions of paragraph (a)(5)(i) of this section are illustrated by the following example:

Example. In 1999, Corporation M, a calendar year S corporation, purchases and places in service section 179 property costing $10,000. Corporation M elects to expense the entire cost of the property. Shareholder A owns 50 percent of the stock of Corporation M. Shareholder A's pro rata share of this item after Corporation M applies the section 179(b) limitations is $5,000. Because the aggregate amount of Shareholder A's pro rata share and separately acquired section 179 expense may not exceed $19,000 (the aggregate maximum cost that may be taken into account under section 179(a) for the applicable taxable year), Shareholder A may elect to expense up to $14,000 of separately acquired section 179 property that is purchased and placed in service in 1999, subject to the limitations of section 179(b).

(b) *Character of items constituting pro rata share.*—(1) *In general.*—Except as provided in paragraph (b)(2) or (3) of this section, the character of any item of income, loss, deduction, or credit described in section 1366(a)(1)(A) or (B) and paragraph (a) of this section is determined for the S corporation and retains that character in the hands of the shareholder. For example, if an S corporation has capital gain on the sale or exchange of a capital asset, a shareholder's pro rata share of that gain will also be characterized as a capital gain regardless of whether the shareholder is otherwise a dealer in that type of property. Similarly, if an S corporation engages in an activity that is not for profit (as defined in section 183), a shareholder's pro rata share of the S corporation's deductions will be characterized as not for profit. Also, if an S corporation makes a charitable contribution to an organization qualifying under section 170(b)(1)(A), a shareholder's pro rata share of the S corporation's charitable contribution will be characterized as made to an organization qualifying under section 170(b)(1)(A).

(2) *Exception for contribution of noncapital gain property.*—If an S corporation is formed or availed of by any shareholder or group of shareholders for a principal purpose of selling or exchanging contributed property that in the hands

of the shareholder or shareholders would not have produced capital gain if sold or exchanged by the shareholder or shareholders, then the gain on the sale or exchange of the property recognized by the corporation is not treated as a capital gain.

(3) *Exception for contribution of capital loss property.*—If an S corporation is formed or availed of by any shareholder or group of shareholders for a principal purpose of selling or exchanging contributed property that in the hands of the shareholder or shareholders would have produced capital loss if sold or exchanged by the shareholder or shareholders, then the loss on the sale or exchange of the property recognized by the corporation is treated as a capital loss to the extent that, immediately before the contribution, the adjusted basis of the property in the hands of the shareholder or shareholders exceeded the fair market value of the property.

(c) *Gross income of a shareholder.*—(1) *In general.*—Where it is necessary to determine the amount or character of the gross income of a shareholder, the shareholder's gross income includes the shareholder's pro rata share of the gross income of the S corporation. The shareholder's pro rata share of the gross income of the S corporation is the amount of gross income of the corporation used in deriving the shareholder's pro rata share of S corporation taxable income or loss (including items described in section 1366(a)(1)(A) or (B) and paragraph (a) of this section). For example, a shareholder is required to include the shareholder's pro rata share of S corporation gross income in computing the shareholder's gross income for the purposes of determining the necessity of filing a return (section 6012(a)) and the shareholder's gross income derived from farming (sections 175 and 6654(i)).

(2) *Gross income for substantial omission of items.*—(i) *In general.*—For purposes of determining the applicability of the 6-year period of limitation on assessment and collection provided in section 6501(e) (relating to omission of more than 25 percent of gross income), a shareholder's gross income includes the shareholder's pro rata share of S corporation gross income (as described in section 6501(e)(1)(A)(i)). In this respect, the amount of S corporation gross income used in deriving the shareholder's pro rata share of any item of S corporation income, loss, deduction, or credit (as included or disclosed in the shareholder's return) is considered as an amount of gross income stated in the shareholder's return for purposes of section 6501(e).

(ii) *Example.*—The following example illustrates the provisions of paragraph (c)(2)(i) of this section:

Example. Shareholder A, an individual, owns 25 percent of the stock of Corporation N, an S corporation that has $10,000 gross income

and $2,000 taxable income. A reports only $300 as A's pro rata share of N's taxable income. A should have reported $500 as A's pro rata share of taxable income, derived from A's pro rata share, $2,500, of N's gross income. Because A's return included only $300 without a disclosure meeting the requirements of section 6501(e)(1)(A)(ii) describing the difference of $200, A is regarded as having reported on the return only $1,500 ($300/$500 of $2,500) as gross income from N.

(d) *Shareholders holding stock subject to community property laws.*—If a shareholder holds S corporation stock that is community property, then the shareholder's pro rata share of any item or items listed in paragraphs (a)(2), (3), and (4) of this section with respect to that stock is reported by the husband and wife in accordance with community property rules.

(e) *Net operating loss deduction of shareholder of S corporation.*—For purposes of determining a net operating loss deduction under section 172, a shareholder of an S corporation must take into account the shareholder's pro rata share of items of income, loss, deduction, or credit of the corporation. See section 1366(b) and paragraph (b) of this section for rules on determining the character of the items. In determining under section 172(d)(4) the nonbusiness deductions allowable to a shareholder of an S corporation (arising from both corporation sources and any other sources), the shareholder separately takes into account the shareholder's pro rata share of the deductions of the corporation that are not attributable to a trade or business and combines this amount with the shareholder's nonbusiness deductions from any other sources. The shareholder also separately takes into account the shareholder's pro rata share of the gross income of the corporation not derived from a trade or business and combines this amount with the shareholder's nonbusiness income from all other sources. See section 172 and the regulations thereunder.

(f) *Cross-reference.*—For rules relating to the consistent tax treatment of subchapter S items, see section 6037(c). [Reg. § 1.1366-1.]

☐ [*T.D.* 8852, 12-21-99.]

[Reg. § 1.1366-2]

§ 1.1366-2. Limitations on deduction of pass-through items of an S corporation to its shareholders.—(a) *In general.*—(1) *Limitation on losses and deductions.*—The aggregate amount of losses and deductions taken into account by a shareholder under § 1.1366-1(a)(2), (3), and (4) for any taxable year of an S corporation cannot exceed the sum of—

(i) The adjusted basis of the shareholder's stock in the corporation (as determined under paragraph (a)(3)(i) of this section); and

(ii) The adjusted basis of any indebtedness of the corporation to the shareholder (as determined under paragraph (a)(3)(ii) of this section).

(2) *Carryover of disallowance.*—A shareholder's aggregate amount of losses and deductions for a taxable year in excess of the sum of the adjusted basis of the shareholder's stock in an S corporation and of any indebtedness of the S corporation to the shareholder is not allowed for the taxable year. However, any disallowed loss or deduction retains its character and is treated as incurred by the corporation in the corporation's first succeeding taxable year, and subsequent taxable years, with respect to the shareholder. For rules on determining the adjusted bases of stock of an S corporation and indebtedness of the corporation to the shareholder, see paragraphs (a)(3)(i) and (ii) of this section.

(3) *Basis limitation amount.*—(i) *Stock portion.*—A shareholder generally determines the adjusted basis of stock for purposes of paragraphs (a)(1)(i) and (2) of this section (limiting losses and deductions) by taking into account only increases in basis under section 1367(a)(1) for the taxable year and decreases in basis under section 1367(a)(2)(A), (D) and (E) (relating to distributions, noncapital, nondeductible expenses, and certain oil and gas depletion deductions) for the taxable year. In so determining this loss limitation amount, the shareholder disregards decreases in basis under section 1367(a)(2)(B) and (C) (for losses and deductions, including losses and deductions previously disallowed) for the taxable year., However, if the shareholder has in effect for the taxable year an election under § 1.1367-1(g) to decrease basis by items of loss and deduction prior to decreasing basis by noncapital, nondeductible expenses and certain oil and gas depletion deductions, the shareholder also disregards decreases in basis under section 1367(a)(2)(D) and (E). This basis limitation amount for stock is determined at the time prescribed under § 1.1367-1(d)(1) for adjustments to the basis of stock.

(ii) *Indebtedness portion.*—A shareholder determines the shareholder's adjusted basis in indebtedness of the corporation for purposes of paragraphs (a)(1)(ii) and (2) of this section (limiting losses and deductions) without regard to any adjustment under section 1367(b)(2)(A) for the taxable year. This basis limitation amount for indebtedness is determined at the time prescribed under § 1.1367-2(d)(1) for adjustments to the basis of indebtedness.

(4) *Limitation on losses and deductions allocated to each item.*—If a shareholder's pro rata share of the aggregate amount of losses and deductions specified in § 1.1366-1(a)(2), (3), and (4) exceeds the sum of the adjusted basis of the

shareholder's stock in the corporation (determined in accordance with paragraph (a)(3)(i) of this section) and the adjusted basis of any indebtedness of the corporation to the shareholder (determined in accordance with paragraph (a)(3)(ii) of this section), then the limitation on losses and deductions under section 1366(d)(1) must be allocated among the shareholder's pro rata share of each loss or deduction. The amount of the limitation allocated to any loss or deduction is an amount that bears the same ratio to the amount of the limitation as the loss or deduction bears to the total of the losses and deductions. For this purpose, the total of losses and deductions for the taxable year is the sum of the shareholder's pro rata share of losses and deductions for the taxable year, and the losses and deductions disallowed and carried forward from prior years pursuant to section 1366(d)(2).

(5) *Nontransferability of losses and deductions.*—(i) *In general.*—Except as provided in paragraph (a)(5)(ii) of this section, any loss or deduction disallowed under paragraph (a)(1) of this section is personal to the shareholder and cannot in any manner be transferred to another person. If a shareholder transfers some but not all of the shareholder's stock in the corporation, the amount of any disallowed loss or deduction under this section is not reduced and the transferee does not acquire any portion of the disallowed loss or deduction. If a shareholder transfers all of the shareholder's stock in the corporation, any disallowed loss or deduction is permanently disallowed.

(ii) *Exceptions for transfers of stock under section 1041(a).*—If a shareholder transfers stock of an S corporation after December 31, 2004, in a transfer described in section 1041(a), any loss or deduction with respect to the transferred stock that is disallowed to the transferring shareholder under paragraph (a)(1) of this section shall be treated as incurred by the corporation in the following taxable year with respect to the transferee spouse or former spouse. The amount of any loss or deduction with respect to the stock transferred shall be determined by prorating any losses or deductions disallowed under paragraph (a)(1) of this section for the year of the transfer between the transferor and the spouse or former spouse based on the stock ownership at the beginning of the following taxable year. If a transferor claims a deduction for losses in the taxable year of transfer, then under paragraph (a)(4) of this section, if the transferor's pro rata share of the losses and deductions in the year of transfer exceeds the transferor's basis in stock and the indebtedness of the corporation to the transferor, then the limitation must be allocated among the transferor spouse's pro rata share of each loss or deduction, including disallowed losses and deductions carried over from the prior year.

Reg. § 1.1366-2(a)(1)(ii)

(iii) *Examples.*—The following examples illustrates the provisions of paragraph (a)(5)(ii) of this section:

Example 1. A owns all 100 shares in X, a calendar year S corporation. For X's taxable year ending December 31, 2006, A has zero basis in the shares and X does not have any indebtedness to A. For the 2006 taxable year, X had $100 in losses that A cannot use because of the basis limitation in section 1366(d)(1) and that are treated as incurred by the corporation with respect to A in the following taxable year. Halfway through the 2007 taxable year, A transfers 50 shares to B, A's former spouse in a transfer to which section 1041(a) applies. In the 2007 taxable year, X has $80 in losses. On A's 2007 individual income tax return, A may use the entire $100 carryover loss from 2006, as well as A's share of the $80 2007 loss determined under section 1377(a) ($60), assuming A acquires sufficient basis in the X stock. On B's 2007 individual income tax return, B may use B's share of the $80 2007 loss determined under section 1377(a) ($20), assuming B has sufficient basis in the X stock. If any disallowed 2006 loss is disallowed to A under section 1366(d)(1) in 2007, that loss is prorated between A and B based on their stock ownership at the beginning of 2008. On B's 2008 individual income tax return, B may use that loss, assuming B acquires sufficient basis in the X stock. If neither A nor B acquires any basis during the 2007 taxable year, then as of the beginning of 2008, the corporation will be treated as incurring $50 of loss with respect to A and $50 of loss with respect to B for the $100 of disallowed 2006 loss, and the corporation will be treated as incurring $60 of loss with respect to A and $20 with respect to B for the $80 of disallowed 2007 loss.

Example 2. Assume the same facts as *Example 1*, except that during the 2007 taxable year, A acquires $10 of basis in A's shares in X. For the 2007 taxable year, A may claim a $10 loss deduction, which represents $6.25 of the disallowed 2006 loss of $100 and $3.75 of A's 2007 loss of $60. The disallowed 2006 loss is reduced to $93.75. As of the beginning of 2008, the corporation will be treated as incurring half of the remaining $93.75 of loss with respect to A and half of that loss with respect to B for the remaining $93.75 of disallowed 2006 loss, and if B does not acquire any basis during 2007, the corporation will be treated as incurring $56.25 of loss with respect to A and $20 with respect to B for the remaining disallowed 2007 loss.

(6) *Basis of stock acquired by gift.*—For purposes of section 1366(d)(1)(A) and paragraphs (a)(1)(i) and (2) of this section, the basis of stock in a corporation acquired by gift is the basis of the stock that is used for purposes of determining loss under section 1015(a).

(b) *Special rules for carryover of disallowed losses and deductions to post-termination transition period*

described in section 1377(b).—(1) *In general.*—If, for the last taxable year of a corporation for which it was an S corporation, a loss or deduction was disallowed to a shareholder by reason of the limitation in paragraph (a) of this section, the loss or deduction is treated under section 1366(d)(3) as incurred by that shareholder on the last day of any post-termination transition period (within the meaning of section 1377(b)).

(2) *Limitation on losses and deductions.*—The aggregate amount of losses and deductions taken into account by a shareholder under paragraph (b)(1) of this section cannot exceed the adjusted basis of the shareholder's stock in the corporation determined at the close of the last day of the post-termination transition period. For this purpose, the adjusted basis of a shareholder's stock in the corporation is determined at the close of the last day of the post-termination transition period without regard to any reduction required under paragraph (b)(4) of this section. If a shareholder disposes of a share of stock prior to the close of the last day of the post-termination transition period, the adjusted basis of that share is its basis as of the close of the day of disposition. Any losses and deductions in excess of a shareholder's adjusted stock basis are permanently disallowed. For purposes of section 1366(d)(3)(B) and this paragraph (b)(2), the basis of stock in a corporation acquired by gift is the basis of the stock that is used for purposes of determining loss under section 1015(a).

(3) *Limitation on losses and deductions allocated to each item.*—If the aggregate amount of losses and deductions treated as incurred by the shareholder under paragraph (b)(1) of this section exceeds the adjusted basis of the shareholder's stock determined under paragraph (b)(2) of this section, the limitation on losses and deductions under section 1366(d)(3)(B) must be allocated among each loss or deduction. The amount of the limitation allocated to each loss or deduction is an amount that bears the same ratio to the amount of the limitation as the amount of each loss or deduction bears to the total of all the losses and deductions.

(4) *Adjustment to the basis of stock.*—The shareholder's basis in the stock of the corporation is reduced by the amount allowed as a deduction by reason of this paragraph (b). For rules regarding adjustments to the basis of a shareholder's stock in an S corporation, see §1.1367-1.

(c) *Carryover of disallowed losses and deductions in the case of liquidations, reorganizations, and divisions.*—(1) *Liquidations and reorganizations.*—If a corporation acquires the assets of an S corporation in a transaction to which section 381(a) applies, any loss or deduction disallowed under paragraph (a) of this section with respect to a shareholder of the distributor or transferor S corporation is available to that shareholder as a

Reg. §1.1366-2(c)(1)

shareholder of the acquiring corporation. Thus, where the acquiring corporation is an S corporation, a loss or deduction of a shareholder of the distributor or transferor S corporation disallowed prior to or during the taxable year of the transaction is treated as incurred by the acquiring S corporation with respect to that shareholder if the shareholder is a shareholder of the acquiring S corporation after the transaction. Where the acquiring corporation is a C corporation, a post-termination transition period arises the day after the last day that an S corporation was in existence and the rules provided in paragraph (b) of this section apply with respect to any shareholder of the acquired S corporation that is also a shareholder of the acquiring C corporation after the transaction. See the special rules under section 1377 for the availability of the post-termination transition period if the acquiring corporation is a C corporation.

(2) *Corporate separations to which section 368(a)(1)(D) applies.*—If an S corporation transfers a portion of its assets constituting an active trade or business to another corporation in a transaction to which section 368(a)(1)(D) applies, and immediately thereafter the stock and securities of the controlled corporation are distributed in a distribution or exchange to which section 355 (or so much of section 356 as relates to section 355) applies, any loss or deduction disallowed under paragraph (a) of this section with respect to a shareholder of the distributing S corporation immediately before the transaction is allocated between the distributing corporation and the controlled corporation with respect to the shareholder. Such allocation shall be made according to any reasonable method, including a method based on the relative fair market value of the shareholder's stock in the distributing and controlled corporations immediately after the distribution, a method based on the relative adjusted basis of the assets in the distributing and controlled corporations immediately after the distribution, or, in the case of losses and deductions clearly attributable to either the distributing or controlled corporation, any method that allocates such losses and deductions accordingly. [Reg. § 1.1366-2.]

☐ *[T.D. 8247, 4-4-89. Amended by T.D. 8852, 12-21-99 and T.D. 9422, 8-13-2008.]*

[Reg. § 1.1366-3]

§ 1.1366-3. Treatment of family groups.—
(a) *In general.*—Under section 1366(e), if an individual, who is a member of the family of one or more shareholders of an S corporation, renders services for, or furnishes capital to, the corporation without receiving reasonable compensation, the Commissioner shall prescribe adjustments to those items taken into account by the individual and the shareholders as may be necessary to reflect the value of the services rendered or capital furnished. For these purposes, in determining

the reasonable value for services rendered, or capital furnished, to the corporation, consideration will be given to all the facts and circumstances, including the amount that ordinarily would be paid in order to obtain comparable services or capital from a person (other than a member of the family) who is not a shareholder in the corporation. In addition, for purposes of section 1366(e), if a member of the family of one or more shareholders of the S corporation holds an interest in a passthrough entity (e.g., a partnership, S corporation, trust, or estate), that performs services for, or furnishes capital to, the S corporation without receiving reasonable compensation, the Commissioner shall prescribe adjustments to the passthrough entity and the corporation as may be necessary to reflect the value of the services rendered or capital furnished. For purposes of section 1366(e), the term *family* of any shareholder includes only the shareholder's spouse, ancestors, lineal descendants, and any trust for the primary benefit of any of these persons.

(b) *Examples.*—The provisions of this section may be illustrated by the following examples:

Example 1. The stock of an S corporation is owned 50 percent by F and 50 percent by T, the minor son of F. For the taxable year, the corporation has items of taxable income equal to $70,000. Compensation of $10,000 is paid by the corporation to F for services rendered during the taxable year, and no compensation is paid to T, who rendered no services. Based on all the relevant facts and circumstances, reasonable compensation for the services rendered by F would be $30,000. In the discretion of the Internal Revenue Service, up to an additional $20,000 of the $70,000 of the corporation's taxable income, for tax purposes, may be allocated to F as compensation for services rendered. If the Internal Revenue Service allocates $20,000 of the corporation's taxable income to F as compensation for services, taxable income of the corporation would be reduced by $20,000 to $50,000, of which F and T each would be allocated $25,000. F would have $30,000 of total compensation paid by the corporation for services rendered.

Example 2. The stock of an S corporation is owned by A and B. For the taxable year, the corporation has paid compensation to a partnership that rendered services to the corporation during the taxable year. The spouse of A is a partner in that partnership. Consequently, if based on all the relevant facts and circumstances the partnership did not receive reasonable compensation for the services rendered to the corporation, the Internal Revenue Service, in its discretion, may make adjustments to those items taken into account by the partnership and the corporation as may be necessary to reflect the value of the services rendered.

[Reg. § 1.1366-3.]

☐ *[T.D. 8852, 12-21-99.]*

[Reg. § 1.1366-4]

§ 1.1366-4. Special rules limiting the pass-through of certain items of an S corporation to its shareholders.—(a) *Passthrough inapplicable to section 34 credit.*—Section 1.1366-1(a) does not apply to any credit allowable under section 34 (relating to certain uses of gasoline and special fuels).

(b) *Reduction in passthrough for tax imposed on built-in gains.*—For purposes of § 1.1366-1(a), if for any taxable year of the S corporation a tax is imposed on the corporation under section 1374, the amount of the tax imposed is treated as a loss sustained by the S corporation during the taxable year. The character of the deemed loss is determined by allocating the loss proportionately among the net recognized built-in gains giving rise to the tax and attributing the character of each net recognized built-in gain to the allocable portion of the loss.

(c) *Reduction in passthrough for tax imposed on excess net passive income.*—For purposes of § 1.1366-1(a), if for any taxable year of the S corporation a tax is imposed on the corporation under section 1375, each item of passive investment income shall be reduced by an amount that bears the same ratio to the amount of the tax as the net amount of the item bears to the total net passive investment income for that taxable year. [Reg. § 1.1366-4.]

☐ [*T.D.* 8852, 12-21-99 (*corrected* 3-8-2000).]

[Reg. § 1.1366-5]

§ 1.1366-5. Effective date.—Sections 1.1366-1 through 1.1366-4 apply to taxable years of an S corporation beginning on or after August 18, 1998. Sections 1.1366-2(a)(5)(i), (ii) and (iii) are effective on August 14, 2008. [Reg. § 1.1366-5.]

☐ [*T.D.* 8852, 12-21-99. *Amended by T.D.* 9422, 8-13-2008.]

[Reg. § 1.1367-0]

§ 1.1367-0. Table of contents.—The following table of contents is provided to facilitate the use of §§ 1.1367-1 through 1.1367-3.

[Reg. § 1.1367-0.]

☐ [*T.D.* 8508, 12-30-93. *Amended by T.D.* 8852, 12-21-99.]

[Reg. § 1.1367-1]

§ 1.1367-1. Adjustments to basis of shareholder's stock in an S corporation.—(a) *In general.*—(1) *Adjustments under section 1367.*—This section provides rules relating to adjustments required by section 1367 to the basis of a shareholder's stock in an S corporation. Paragraph (b) of this section provides rules concerning increases in the basis of a shareholder's stock, and paragraph (c) of this section provides rules concerning decreases in the basis of a shareholder's stock.

(2) *Applicability of other Internal Revenue Code provisions.*—In addition to the adjustments required by section 1367 and this section, the basis of stock is determined or adjusted under other applicable provisions of the Internal Revenue Code.

(b) *Increase in basis of stock.*—(1) *In general.*— Except as provided in § 1.1367-2(c) (relating to restoration of basis of indebtedness to the shareholder), the basis of a shareholder's stock in an S corporation is increased by the sum of the items described in section 1367(a)(1). The increase in basis described in section 1367(a)(1)(C) for the excess of the deduction for depletion over the basis of the property subject to depletion does not include the depletion deduction attributable to oil or gas property. See section 613(A)(c)(11).

(2) *Amount of increase in basis of individual shares.*—The basis of a shareholder's share of stock is increased by an amount equal to the shareholder's pro rata portion of the items described in section 1367(a)(1) that is attributable to that share, determined on a per share, per day basis in accordance with section 1377(a).

(c) *Decrease in basis of stock.*—(1) *In general.*— The basis of a shareholder's stock in an S corporation is decreased (but not below zero) by the sum of the items described in section 1367(a)(2).

(2) *Noncapital, nondeductible expenses.*—For purposes of section 1367(a)(2)(D), expenses of the corporation not deductible in computing its taxable income and not properly chargeable to a capital account (*noncapital, nondeductible expenses*) are only those items for which no loss or deduction is allowable and do not include items the deduction for which is deferred to a later taxable year. Examples of noncapital, nondeductible expenses include (but are not limited to) the following: illegal bribes, kickbacks, and other payments not deductible under section 162(c); fines and penalties not deductible under section 162(f); expenses and interest relating to tax-exempt income under section 265; losses for which the deduction is disallowed under section 267(a)(1); the portion of meals and entertainment expenses disallowed under section 274; and the two-thirds portion of treble damages paid for violating antitrust laws not deductible under section 162.

(3) *Amount of decrease in basis of individual shares.*—The basis of a shareholder's share of stock is decreased by an amount equal to the shareholder's pro rata portion of the pass-through items and distributions described in section 1367(a)(2) attributable to that share, determined on a per share, per day basis in accordance with section 1377(a). If the amount attributable to a share exceeds its basis, the excess is applied to reduce (but not below zero) the remaining bases of all other shares of stock in the corporation owned by the shareholder in proportion to the remaining basis of each of those shares.

(d) *Time at which adjustments to basis of stock are effective.*—(1) *In general.*—The adjustments described in section 1367(a) to the basis of a share-holder's stock are determined as of the close of the corporation's taxable year, and the adjustments generally are effective as of that date. However, if a shareholder disposes of stock during the corporation's taxable year, the adjustments with respect to that stock are effective immediately prior to the disposition.

(2) *Adjustment for nontaxable item.*—An adjustment for a nontaxable item is determined for the taxable year in which the item would have been includible or deductible under the corporation's method of accounting for federal income tax purposes if the item had been subject to federal income taxation.

(3) *Effect of election under section 1377(a)(2) or § 1.1368-1(g)(2).*—If an election under section 1377(a)(2) (to terminate the year in the case of the termination of a shareholder's interest) or under § 1.1368-1(g)(2) (to terminate the year in the case of a qualifying disposition) is made with respect to the taxable year of a corporation, this paragraph (d) applies as if the taxable year consisted of separate taxable years, the first of which ends at the close of the day on which either the shareholder's interest is terminated or a qualifying disposition occurs, whichever the case may be.

(e) *Ordering rules for taxable years beginning before January 1, 1997.*—For any taxable year of a corporation beginning before January 1, 1997, except as provided in paragraph (g) of this section, the adjustments required by section 1367(a) are made in the following order—

(1) Any increase in basis attributable to the income items described in section 1367(a)(1)(A) and (B) and the excess of the deductions for depletion described in section 1367(a)(1)(C);

(2) Any decrease in basis attributable to noncapital, nondeductible expenses described in section 1367(a)(2)(D) and the oil and gas depletion deduction described in section 1367(a)(2)(E);

(3) Any decrease in basis attributable to items of loss or deduction described in section 1367(a)(2)(B) and (C); and

(4) Any decrease in basis attributable to a distribution by the corporation described in section 1367(a)(2)(A).

(f) *Ordering rules for taxable years beginning on or after August 18, 1998.*—For any taxable year of a corporation beginning on or after August 18, 1998, except as provided in paragraph (g) of this section, the adjustments required by section 1367(a) are made in the following order—

(1) Any increase in basis attributable to the income items described in section 1367(a)(1)(A) and (B), and the excess of the deductions for depletion described in section 1367(a)(1)(C);

(2) Any decrease in basis attributable to a distribution by the corporation described in section 1367(a)(2)(A);

(3) Any decrease in basis attributable to noncapital, nondeductible expenses described in section 1367(a)(2)(D), and the oil and gas depletion deduction described in section 1367(a)(2)(E); and

(4) Any decrease in basis attributable to items of loss or deduction described in section 1367(a)(2)(B) and (C).

(g) *Elective ordering rule.*—A shareholder may elect to decrease basis under paragraph (e)(3) or (f)(4) of this section, whichever applies, prior to decreasing basis under paragraph (e)(2) or (f)(3) of this section, whichever applies. If a shareholder makes this election, any amount described in paragraph (e)(2) or (f)(3) of this section, whichever applies, that is in excess of the shareholder's basis in stock and indebtedness is treated, solely for purposes of this section, as an amount described in paragraph (e)(2) or (f)(3) of this section, whichever applies, in the succeeding taxable year. A shareholder makes the election under this paragraph by attaching a statement to the shareholder's timely filed original or amended return that states that the shareholder agrees to the carryover rule of the preceding sentence. Once a shareholder makes an election under this paragraph with respect to an S corporation, the shareholder must continue to use the rules of this paragraph for that S corporation in future taxable years unless the shareholder receives the permission of the Commissioner.

(h) *Examples.*—The following examples illustrate the principles of §1.1367-1. In each example, the corporation is a calendar year S corporation:

Example 1. Adjustments to basis of stock for taxable years beginning before January 1, 1997. (i) On December 31, 1994, A owns a block of 50 shares of stock with an adjusted basis per share of $6 in Corporation S. On December 31, 1994, A purchases for $400 an additional block of 50 shares of stock with an adjusted basis of $8 per share. Thus, A holds 100 shares of stock for each day of the 1995 taxable year. For S's 1995 taxable year, A's pro rata share of the amount of the items described in section 1367(a)(1)(A) (relating to increases in basis of stock) is $300, and A's pro rata share of the amount of the items described in section 1367(a)(2)(B) and (D) (relating to decreases in basis of stock) is $500. S makes a distribution to A in the amount of $100 during 1995.

(ii) Pursuant to the ordering rules of paragraph (e) of this section, A increases the basis of each share of stock by $3 ($300 ÷ 100 shares) and decreases the basis of each share of stock by $5 ($500 ÷ 100 shares). Then A reduces the basis of each share by $1 ($100 ÷ 100 shares) for the distribution. Thus, on January 1, 1996, A has a

basis of $3 per share in his original block of 50 shares ($6 + $3 − $5 − $1) and a basis of $5 per share in the second block of 50 shares ($8 + $3 − $5 − $1).

Example 2. Adjustments to basis of stock for taxable years beginning on or after August 18, 1998. (i) On December 31, 2001, A owns a block of 50 shares of stock with an adjusted basis per share of $6 in Corporation S. On December 31, 2001, A purchases for $400 an additional block of 50 shares of stock with an adjusted basis of $8 per share. Thus, A holds 100 shares of stock for each day of the 2002 taxable year. For S's 2002 taxable year, A's pro rata share of the amount of items described in section 1367(a)(1)(A) (relating to increases in basis of stock) is $300, A's pro rata share of the amount of the items described in section 1367(a)(2)(B) (relating to decreases in basis of stock attributable to items of loss and deduction) is $300, and A's pro rata share of the amount of the items described in section 1367(a)(2)(D) (relating to decreases in basis of stock attributable to noncapital, nondeductible expenses) is $200. S makes a distribution to A in the amount of $100 during 2002.

(ii) Pursuant to the ordering rules of paragraph (f) of this section, A first increases the basis of each share of stock by $3 ($300/100 shares) and then decreases the basis of each share by $1 ($100/100 shares) for the distribution. A next decreases the basis of each share by $2 ($200/100 shares) for the noncapital, nondeductible expenses and then decreases the basis of each share by $3 ($300/100 shares) for the items of loss. Thus, on January 1, 2003, A has a basis of $3 per share in the original block of 50 shares ($6 + $3 − $1 − $2 − $3) and a basis of $5 per share in the second block of 100 shares ($8 + $3 − $1 − $2 − $3).

Example 3. Adjustments attributable to basis of individual shares of stock. (i) On December 31, 1993, B owns one share of S corporation's 10 outstanding shares of stock. The basis of B's share is $30. On July 2, 1994, B purchases from another shareholder two shares for $25 each. During 1994, S corporation has no income or deductions but incurs a loss of $365. Under section 1377(a)(1)(A) and paragraph (c)(3) of this section, the amount of the loss assigned to each day of S's taxable year is $1.00 ($365/365 days). For each day, $.10 is allocated to each outstanding share ($1.00 amount of loss assigned to each day/10 shares).

(ii) B owned one share for 365 days and, therefore, reduces the basis of that share by the amount of loss attributable to it, *i.e.*, $36.50 ($.10 × 365 days). B owned two shares for 182 days and, therefore, reduces the basis of each of those shares by the amount of the loss attributable to each, *i.e.*, $18.20 ($.10 × 182 days).

(iii) The bases of the shares are decreased as follows:

Share	Original Basis	Decrease	Adjusted Basis	Excess Basis Reduction
No. 1	$30.00	$36.50	$0	$6.50
No. 2	25.00	18.20	6.80	0
No. 3	25.00	18.20	6.80	0
Total remaining basis			13.60	

(iv) Because the decrease in basis attributable to share No. 1 exceeds the basis of share No. 1 by $6.50 ($36.50 – $30.00), the excess is applied to reduce the bases of shares No. 2 and No. 3 in proportion to their remaining bases. Therefore, the bases of share No. 2 and share No. 3 are each decreased by an additional $3.25 ($6.50 × $6.80/$13.60). After this decrease, Share No. 1 has a basis of zero, Share No. 2 has a basis of $3.55, and Share No. 3 has a basis of $3.55.

Example 4. Effects of section 1377(a)(2) election and distribution on basis of stock for taxable years beginning before January 1, 1997. (i) On January 1, 1994, individuals B and C each own 50 of the 100 shares of issued and outstanding stock of Corporation S. B's adjusted basis in each share of stock is $120, and C's is $80. On June 30, 1994, S distributes $6,000 to B and $6,000 to C. On June 30, 1994, B sells all of her S stock for $10,000 to D. S elects under section 1377(a)(2) to treat its 1994 taxable year as consisting of two taxable years, the first of which ends at the close of June 30, the date on which B terminates her interest in S.

(ii) For the period January 1, 1994, through June 30, 1994, S has nonseparately computed income of $6,000 and a separately stated deduction item of $4,000. Therefore, on June 30, 1994, B and C, pursuant to the ordering rules of paragraph (e) of this section, increase the basis of each share by $60 ($6,000/100 shares) and decrease the basis of each share by $40 ($4,000/100 shares). Then B and C reduce the basis of each share by $120 ($12,000/100 shares) for the distribution.

(iii) The basis of B's stock is reduced from $120 to $20 per share ($120 + $60 – $40 – $120). The basis of C's stock is reduced from $80 to $0 per share ($80 + $60 – $40 – $120). See section 1368 and §1.1368-1(c) and (d) for rules relating to the tax treatment of the distributions.

(iv) Pursuant to paragraph (d)(3) of this section, the net reduction in the basis of B's shares of the S stock required by section 1367 and this section is effective immediately prior to B's sale of her stock. Thus, B's basis for determining gain or loss on the sale of the S stock is $20 per share, and B has a gain on the sale of $180 ($200 – $20) per share.

Example 5. Effects of section 1377(a)(2) election and distribution on basis of stock for taxable years beginning on or after August 18, 1998. (i) The facts are the same as in *Example 4*, except that all of the events occur in 2001 rather than in 1994 and except as follows: On June 30, 2001, B sells 25 shares of her stock for $5,000 to D and 25 shares back to Corporation S for $5,000. Under section 1377(a)(2)(B) and §1.1377-1(b)(2), B, C, and D are affected shareholders because B has transferred shares to Corporations S and D. Pursuant to section 1377(a)(2)(A) and §1.1377-1(b)(1), B, C, and D, the affected shareholders, and Corporation S agree to treat the taxable year 2001 as if it consisted of two separate taxable years for all affected shareholders for the purposes set forth in §1.1377-1(b)(3)(i).

(ii) On June 30, 2001, B and C, pursuant to the ordering rules of paragraph (f)(1) of this section, increase the basis of each share by $60 ($6,000/100 shares) for the nonseparately computed income. Then B and C reduce the basis of each share by $120 ($12,000/100 shares) for the distribution. Finally, B and C decrease the basis of each share by $40 ($4,000/100 shares) for the separately stated deduction item.

(iii) The basis of the stock of B is reduced from $120 to $20 per share ($120 + $60 – $120 – $40). Prior to accounting for the separately stated deduction item, the basis of the stock of C is reduced from $80 to $20 ($80 + $60 – $120). Finally, because the period from January 1 through June 30, 2001 is treated under §1.1377-1(b)(3)(i) as a separate taxable year for purposes of making adjustments to the basis of stock, under section 1366(d) and §1.1366-2(a)(2), C may deduct only $20 per share of the remaining $40 of the separately stated deduction item, and the basis of the stock of C is reduced from $20 per share to $0 per share. Under section 1366 and §1.1366-2(a)(2), C's remaining separately stated deduction item of $20 per share is treated as having been incurred in the first succeeding taxable year of Corporation S, which, for this purpose, begins on July 1, 2001.

(i) [Reserved]

(j) *Adjustments for items of income in respect of a decedent.*—The basis determined under section 1014 of any stock in an S corporation is reduced by the portion of the value of the stock that is attributable to items constituting income in respect of a decedent. For the determination of items realized by an S corporation constituting income in respect of a decedent, see sections 1367(b)(4)(A) and 691 and applicable regulations thereunder. For the determination of the allowance of a deduction for the amount of estate tax attributable to income in respect of a decedent, see section 691(c) and applicable regulations thereunder. [Reg. §1.1367-1.]

☐ [T.D. 8508, 12-30-93. *Amended by T.D. 8852, 12-21-99 (corrected 3-8-2000).*]

[Reg. §1.1367-2]

§1.1367-2. **Adjustments to basis of indebtedness to shareholder.**—(a) *In general.*—(1) *Adjustments under section 1367.*—This section provides rules relating to adjustments required by subchapter S to the basis of indebtedness (including open account debt as described in paragraph (a)(2) of this section) of an S corporation to a shareholder. The basis of indebtedness of the S corporation to a shareholder is reduced as provided in paragraph (b) of this section and restored as provided in paragraph (c) of this section in accordance with the timing rules in paragraph (d) of this section.

(2) *Open account debt.*—(i) *General rule.*—The term *open account debt* means shareholder advances not evidenced by separate written instruments and repayments on the advances, the aggregate outstanding principal of which does not exceed $25,000 of indebtedness of the S corporation to the shareholder at the close of the S corporation's taxable year. Advances and repayments on open account debt are treated as a single indebtedness.

(ii) *Exception.*—If the shareholder advances not evidenced by a separate written instrument, net of repayments, exceeds an aggregate outstanding principal amount of $25,000 at the close of the S corporation's taxable year, for any subsequent taxable year the aggregate principal amount of that indebtedness is treated in the same manner as indebtedness evidenced by a separate written instrument for purposes of this section. For any subsequent taxable year, that indebtedness is not open account debt and is subject to all basis adjustment rules applicable to basis of indebtedness of an S corporation to a shareholder in this section.

(b) *Reduction in basis of indebtedness.*—(1) *General rule.*—If, after making the adjustments required by section 1367(a)(1) for any taxable year of the S corporation, the amounts specified in section 1367(a)(2)(B), (C), (D), and (E) (relating to losses, deductions, noncapital, nondeductible expenses, and certain oil and gas depletion deductions) exceed the basis of a shareholder's stock in the corporation, the excess is applied to reduce (but not below zero) the basis of any indebtedness of the S corporation to the shareholder held by the shareholder at the close of the corporation's taxable year. Any such indebtedness that has been satisfied by the corporation, or disposed of or forgiven by the shareholder, during the taxable year, is not held by the shareholder at the close of that year and is not subject to basis reduction.

(2) *Termination of shareholder's interest in corporation during taxable year.*—If a shareholder terminates his or her interest in the corporation during the taxable year, the rules of this paragraph (b) are applied with respect to any indebtedness of the S corporation held by the shareholder immediately prior to the termination of the shareholder's interest in the corporation.

(3) *Multiple indebtedness.*—If a shareholder holds more than one indebtedness at the close of the corporation's taxable year or, if applicable,

immediately prior to the termination of the shareholder's interest in the corporation, the reduction in basis is applied to each indebtedness in the same proportion that the basis of each indebtedness bears to the aggregate bases of the indebtedness to the shareholder.

(c) *Restoration of basis.*—(1) *General rule.*—If, for any taxable year of an S corporation beginning after December 31, 1982, there has been a reduction in the basis of an indebtedness of the S corporation to a shareholder under section 1367(b)(2)(A), any *net increase* in any subsequent taxable year of the corporation is applied to restore that reduction. For purposes of this section, *net increase* with respect to a shareholder means the amount by which the shareholder's pro rata share of the items described in section 1367(a)(1) (relating to income items and excess deduction for depletion) exceed the items described in section 1367(a)(2) (relating to losses, deductions, noncapital, nondeductible expenses, certain oil and gas depletion deductions, and certain distributions) for the taxable year. These restoration rules apply only to indebtedness held by a shareholder as of the beginning of the taxable year in which the net increase arises. The reduction in basis of indebtedness must be restored before any net increase is applied to restore the basis of a shareholder's stock in an S corporation. In no event may the shareholder's basis of indebtedness be restored above the adjusted basis of the indebtedness under section 1016(a), excluding any adjustments under section 1016(a)(17) for prior taxable years, determined as of the beginning of the taxable year in which the net increase arises.

(2) *Multiple indebtedness.*—If a shareholder holds more than one indebtedness (including any open account debt and any debt treated as a single indebtedness under paragraph (a)(2)(ii) of this section) as of the beginning of an S corporation's taxable year, any net increase is applied first to restore the reduction of basis in any indebtedness repaid (in whole or in part) in that taxable year to the extent necessary to offset any gain that would otherwise be realized on the repayment. Any remaining net increase is applied to restore each outstanding indebtedness (including any open account debt and any debt treated as a single indebtedness under paragraph (a)(2)(ii) of this section) in proportion to the amount that the basis of each outstanding indebtedness has been reduced under section 1367(b)(2)(A) and paragraph (b) of this section and not restored under section 1367(b)(2)(B) and this paragraph (c).

(d) *Time at which adjustments to basis of indebtedness are effective.*—(1) *In general.*—The amounts of the adjustments to basis of indebtedness (including open account debt) provided in section 1367(b)(2) and this section are determined as of the close of the S corporation's taxable year, and the adjustments are generally effective as of the

Reg. § 1.1367-2(d)(1)

close of the S corporation's taxable year. However, if the shareholder is not a shareholder in the S corporation at that time, these adjustments are effective immediately before the shareholder terminates his or her interest in the S corporation. Except as provided in paragraph (d)(2) of this section, if a debt is disposed of or repaid in whole or in part before the close of the taxable year, the basis of that indebtedness is restored under paragraph (c) of this section, effective immediately before the disposition or the first repayment on the debt during the taxable year. To the extent any indebtedness of the S corporation to the shareholder is disposed of or repaid (in whole or in part) during the taxable year and the shareholder's basis in that indebtedness has been reduced under paragraph (b) of this section and is not restored completely under paragraph (c) of this section, the disposition or repayment is a recognition event effective immediately before the indebtedness is disposed of or repaid (in whole or in part).

(2) *Open account debt.*—(i) *In general.*—All advances and repayments on open account debt (as described in paragraph (a)(2)(i) of this section) during the S corporation's taxable year are netted at the close of the S corporation's taxable year to determine the amount of any net advance or net repayment. The net advance or net repayment is combined with the outstanding aggregate principal balance of the existing open account debt and that amount is carried forward to the beginning of the subsequent taxable year as the outstanding aggregate principal amount of the open account debt (unless the aggregate principal amount meets the exception defined in paragraph (a)(2)(ii) of this section at the close of the taxable year). However, if the shareholder in the S corporation is not a shareholder of the S corporation at the close of the S corporation's taxable year, such advances and repayments on open account debt are netted, and the basis of that indebtedness is restored under paragraph (c) of this section, effective immediately before the shareholder terminates his or her interest in the S corporation. If any open account debt is disposed of before or upon the close of the taxable year, the disposition is effective at the close of the S corporation's taxable year, and all advances and repayments are netted immediately prior to the disposition and the basis of that indebtedness is restored under paragraph (c) of this section, effective at the close of the S corporation's taxable year.

(ii) *Exception.*—Shareholder indebtedness that is open account debt at the beginning of the taxable year but meets the exception defined in paragraph (a)(2)(ii) of this section at the close of the taxable year, adjustments to the basis of the indebtedness for that taxable year follow the provisions for open account debt. The resulting aggregate principal amount of indebtedness is treated as the principal amount of a debt evidenced by a separate written instrument for any

subsequent taxable year, and is no longer subject to the open account debt provisions of this section.

(3) *Effect of election under section 1377(a)(2) or §1.1368-1(g)(2)*.—If an election is made under section 1377(a)(2) (to terminate the year in the case of the termination of a shareholder's interest) or under §1.1368-1(g)(2) (to terminate the year in the case of a qualifying disposition), this paragraph (d) applies as if the taxable year consisted of separate taxable years, the first of which ends at the close of the day on which the shareholder either terminates his or her interest in the corporation or disposes of a substantial amount of stock, whichever the case may be.

(e) *Examples.*—The following examples illustrate the principles of §1.1367-2. In each example, the corporation is a calendar year S corporation. The lending transactions described in the examples do not result in foregone interest (within the meaning of section 7872(e)(2)), original issue discount (within the meaning of section 1273), or total unstated interest (within the meaning of section 483(b)).

Example 1. Reduction in basis of indebtedness. (i) A has been the sole shareholder in Corporation S since 1992. In 1993, A loans S $1,000 (Debt No. 1), which is evidenced by a ten-year promissory note in the face amount of $1,000. In 1996, A loans S $5,000 (Debt No. 2), which is evidenced by a demand promissory note. On December 31, 1996, the basis of A's stock is zero; the basis of Debt No. 1 has been reduced under paragraph (b) of this section to $0; and the basis of Debt No. 2 has been reduced to $1,000. On January 1, 1997, A loans S $4,000 (Debt No. 3), which is evidenced by a demand promissory note. For S's 1997 taxable year, the sum of the amounts specified in section 1367(a)(1) (in this case, nonseparately computed income and the excess deduction for depletion) is $6,000, and the sum of the amounts specified in section 1367(a)(2)(B), (D) and (E) (in this case, items of separately stated deductions and losses, noncapital, nondeductible expenses, and certain oil and gas depletion deductions—there is no nonseparately computed loss) is $10,000. Corporation S makes no payments to A on any of the loans during 1997.

(ii) The $4,000 excess of loss and deduction items is applied to reduce the basis of each indebtedness in proportion to the basis of that indebtedness over the aggregate bases of the indebtedness to the shareholder (determined immediately before any adjustment under section 1367(b)(2)(A) and paragraph (b) of this section is effective for the taxable year). Thus, the basis of Debt No. 2 is reduced in an amount equal to $800 ($4,000 (excess) × $1,000 (basis of Debt No. 2)/$5,000 (total basis of all debt)). Similarly, the basis in Debt No. 3 is reduced in an amount equal to $3,200 ($4,000 × $4,000/$5,000). Accordingly, on December 31, 1997, A's basis in his stock is zero and his bases in the three debts are as follows:

Debt	1/1/96 Basis	12/31/96 Reduction	1/1/97 Basis	12/31/97 Reduction	1/1/98 Basis
No. 1	$1,000	$1,000	$0	$0	$0
No. 2	5,000	4,000	1,000	800	200
No. 3			4,000	3,200	800

Example 2. Restoration of basis of indebtedness. (i) The facts are the same as in *Example 1.* On July 1, 1998, S completely repays Debt No. 3, and, for S's 1998 taxable year, the net increase (within the meaning of paragraph (c) of this section) with respect to A equals $4,500.

(ii) The net increase is applied first to restore the bases in the debts held on January 1, 1998, before any of the net increase is applied to increase A's basis in his shares of S stock. The net increase is applied to restore first the reduction of basis in indebtedness repaid in 1998. Any remaining net increase is applied to restore the bases of the outstanding debts in proportion to the amount that each of these outstanding debts have been reduced previously under paragraph (b) of this section and have not been restored. As

Original Basis	Amount Reduced
$1,000	$1,000
5,000	4,800

Example 3. Full restoration of basis in indebtedness when debt is repaid in part during the taxable year. (i) C has been a shareholder in Corporation S since 1992. In 1997, C loans S $1,000. S issues its note to C in the amount of $1,000, of which $950 is payable on March 1, 1998, and $50 is payable on March 1, 1999. On December 31, 1997, C's basis in all her shares of S stock is zero and her basis in the note has been reduced under paragraph (b) of this section to $900. For 1998, the net increase (within the meaning of paragraph (c) of this section) with respect to C is $300.

(ii) Because C's basis of indebtedness was reduced in a prior taxable year under § 1.1367-2(b), the net increase for 1998 is applied to restore this reduction. The restored basis cannot exceed the adjusted basis of the debt as of the beginning of the first day of 1998, excluding prior adjustments under section 1367, or $1,000. Therefore, $100 of the $300 net increase is applied to restore the basis of the debt from $900 to $1,000 effective immediately before the repayment on March 1, 1998. The remaining net increase of $200 increases C's basis in her stock.

Example 4. Determination of net increase—distribution in excess of increase in basis. (i) D has been the sole shareholder in Corporation S since 1990. On January 1, 1996, D loans S $10,000 in return for a note from S in the amount of $10,000 of which $5,000 is payable on each of January 1, 2000, and January 1, 2001. On December 31, 1997, the basis of D's shares of S stock is zero, and his basis in the note has been reduced under paragraph (b) of this section to $8,000. During 1998, the sum of the items under section 1367(a)(1) (relating to increases in basis of stock)

of December 31, 1998, the total reduction in A's debts held on January 1, 1998 equals $9,000. Thus, the basis of Debt No. 3 is restored by $3,200 (the amount of the previous reduction) to $4,000. A's basis in Debt No. 3 is treated as restored immediately before that debt is repaid. Accordingly, A does not realize any gain on the repayment. The remaining net increase of $1,300 ($4,500 − $3,200) is applied to restore the bases of Debt No. 1 and Debt No. 2. As of December 31, 1998, the total reduction in these outstanding debts is $5,800 ($9,000 − $3,200). The basis of Debt No. 1 is restored in an amount equal to $224 ($1,300 × $1,000/$5,800). Similarly, the basis in Debt No. 2 is restored in an amount equal to $1,076 ($1,300 × $4,800/$5,800). On December 31, 1998, A's basis in his S stock is zero and his bases in the two remaining debts are as follows:

1/1/98 Basis	Amount Restored	12/31/98 Basis
$0	$224	$224
200	1,076	1,276

with respect to D equals $10,000 (in this case, nonseparately computed income), and the sum of the items under section 1367(a)(2)(B), (C), (D), and (E) (relating to decreases in basis of stock) with respect to D equals $0. During 1998, S also makes distributions to D totaling $11,000. This distribution is an item that reduces basis of stock under section 1367(a)(2)(A) and must be taken into account for purposes of determining whether there is a net increase for the taxable year. Thus, for 1998, there is no net increase with respect to D because the amount of the items provided in section 1367(a)(1) do not exceed the amount of the items provided in section 1367(a)(2).

(ii) Because there is no net increase with respect to D for 1998, none of the 1997 reduction in D's basis in the indebtedness is restored. The $10,000 increase in basis under section 1367(a)(1) is applied to increase D's basis in his S stock. Under section 1367(a)(2)(A), the $11,000 distribution with respect to D's stock reduces D's basis in his shares of S stock to $0. See section 1368 and § 1.1368-1(c) and (d) for the tax treatment of the $1,000 distribution in excess of D's basis.

Example 5. Distributions less than increase in basis. (i) The facts are the same as in *Example 4,* except that in 1998 S makes distributions to D totaling $8,000. On these facts, for 1998, there is a net increase with respect to D of $2,000 (the amount by which the items provided in section 1367(a)(1) exceed the amount of the items provided in section 1367(a)(2)).

(ii) Because there is a net increase of $2,000 with respect to D for 1998, $2,000 of the $10,000 increase in basis under section 1367(a)(1) is first

Reg. § 1.1367-2(e)

applied to restore D's basis in the indebtedness to $10,000 ($8,000 + $2,000). Accordingly, on December 31, 1998, D has a basis in his shares of S stock of $0 ($0 + $8,000 (increase in basis remaining after restoring basis in indebtedness) − $8,000 (distribution)) and a basis in the note of $10,000.

Example 6. The $25,000 aggregate principal amount applies to each shareholder. (i) A and B have been the two shareholders in Corporation S since 2000. As of the end of the 2008 taxable year, the bases of A's and B's stock are both zero. On June 1, 2009, A advances S $16,000, which is not evidenced by a written instrument. On August 1, 2009, B advances S $22,000, which is not evidenced by a written instrument. Both the $16,000 advance and the $22,000 advance are open account debt and remain outstanding at those amounts during 2009. There is no net increase under paragraph (c) of this section in year 2009.

(ii) At the close of the 2009 taxable year, A's open account debt does not exceed $25,000. A therefore carries forward to the beginning of the 2010 taxable year the $16,000 as open account debt.

(iii) At the close of the 2009 taxable year, B's open account debt does not exceed $25,000. B therefore carries forward to the beginning of the 2010 taxable year the $22,000 as open account debt.

Example 7. Treatment of open account debt. (i) The facts are the same as in *Example 6*, in addition to which, on December 31, 2009, A's basis in the open account debt is reduced under paragraph (b) of this section to $8,000. On April 1, 2010, S repays A $4,000 of the open account indebtedness. On September 1, 2010, A advances S an additional $1,000, which is not evidenced by a written instrument. There is no net increase under paragraph (c) of this section in year 2010.

(ii) The $4,000 April repayment S makes to A and A's $1,000 September advance are netted to result in a net repayment of $3,000 for the taxable year on A's $16,000 open account debt carried forward from 2009. Because there is no net increase in 2010, no basis of indebtedness is restored for the 2010 taxable year, and A realizes $1,500 of income on the $3,000 net repayment at the close of the 2010 taxable year.

(iii) At close of the 2010 taxable year, A's open account debt does not exceed $25,000. The net repayment of $3,000 for the taxable year on A's $16,000 open account debt carried forward from 2009, leaves A with an open account debt of $13,000 to carry forward as open account debt to the beginning of the 2011 taxable year.

Example 8. Treatment of shareholder indebtedness not evidenced by a written instrument which exceeds $25,000. (i) The facts are the same as in *Example 7*, in addition to which, on February 1, 2011, S repays $5,000 of the open account debt and on March 1, 2011, A advances S $20,000, which is not evidenced by a written instrument.

(ii) At the close of the 2010 taxable year, A has an open account debt of $13,000 to carry forward

as open account debt to the beginning of the 2011 taxable year.

(iii) The 2011 advances and repayments are netted to result in a net advance of $15,000 on A's $13,000 open account debt carried forward from 2010, increasing A's open account debt to $28,000 as of the close of the 2011 taxable year. Because A's open account debt exceeds $25,000, for any subsequent taxable year the $28,000 indebtedness will be treated in the same manner as indebtedness evidenced by a separate written instrument for the purposes of this section. Because there is no net increase in 2011, no basis of indebtedness is restored for the 2011 taxable year. [Reg. § 1.1367-2.]

☐ [T.D. 8508, 12-30-93. *Amended by* T.D. 9428, 10-17-2008 (*corrected* 11-13-2008).]

[Reg. § 1.1367-3]

§ 1.1367-3. Effective/Applicability date.—Section 1.1367-2(a), (c)(2), (d)(2), and (e) *Example 6, Example 7,* and *Example 8* apply to any shareholder advances to the S corporation made on or after October 20, 2008, and repayments on those advances by the S corporation. The rules that apply with respect to shareholder advances to the S corporation made before October 20, 2008, are contained in § 1.1367-3 in effect prior to October 20, 2008. (See 26 CFR part 1 revised as of April 1, 2007.) Shareholders have the option to apply these rules to shareholder advances to the S corporation made before October 20, 2008, and repayments on those advances by the S corporation. [Reg. § 1.1367-3.]

☐ [T.D. 8508, 12-30-93. *Amended by* T.D. 8852, 12-21-99 *and* T.D. 9428, 10-17-2008.]

[Reg. § 1.1368-0]

§ 1.1368-0. Table of contents.—The following table of contents is provided to facilitate the use of §§ 1.1368-1 through 1.1368-4.

(iii) Corporation with subchapter C and subchapter S earnings and profits.

(3) Election to make a deemed dividend.

(4) Election to forego previously taxed income.

(5) Time and manner of making elections.

(i) For earnings and profits.

(ii) For previously taxed income and deemed dividends.

(iii) Corporate statement regarding elections.

(iv) Irrevocable elections.

(g) Special rule.

(1) Election to terminate year under §1.1368-1(g)(2).

(2) Election in case of a qualifying disposition

(i) In general.

(ii) Effect of the election.

(iii) Time and manner of making election.

(iv) Coordination with election under section 1377(a)(2).

§1.1368-2. *Accumulated adjustments account (AAA).*

(a) Accumulated adjustments account.

(1) In general.

(2) Increases to the AAA.

(3) Decreases to the AAA.

(i) In general.

(ii) Extent of allowable reduction.

(iii) Decrease to the AAA for distributions.

(4) Ordering rules for the AAA for taxable years beginning before January 1, 1997.

(5) Ordering rules for the AAA for taxable years beginning on or after August 18, 1998.

(b) Distributions in excess of the AAA.

(1) In general.

(2) Amount of the AAA allocated to each distribution.

(c) Distribution of money and loss property.

(1) In general.

(2) Allocating the AAA to loss property.

(d) Adjustment in the case of redemptions, liquidations, reorganizations, and divisions.

(1) Redemptions.

(i) General rule.

(ii) Special rule for years in which a corporation makes both ordinary and redemption distributions.

(iii) Adjustments to earnings and profits.

(2) Liquidations and reorganizations.

(3) Corporate separations to which section 368(a)(1)(D) applies.

(e) Election to terminate year under section 1377(a)(2) or §1.1368-1(g)(2).

§1.1368-3. *Examples.*

§1.1368-4. *Effective date and transition rule.* [Reg. §1.1368-0.]

☐ [T.D. 8508, 12-30-93. *Amended by* T.D. 8696, 12-20-96; T.D. 8852, 12-21-99 *and* T.D. 8869, 1-20-2000.]

[Reg. §1.1368-1]

§1.1368-1. Distributions by S corporations.— (a) *In general.*—This section provides rules for distributions made by an S corporation with respect to its stock which, but for section 1368(a) and this section, would be subject to section 301(c) and other rules of the Internal Revenue Code that characterize a distribution as a dividend.

(b) *Date distribution made.*—For purposes of section 1368, a distribution is taken into account on the date the corporation makes the distribution, regardless of when the distribution is treated as received by the shareholder.

(c) *S corporation with no earnings and profits.*—A distribution made by an S corporation that has no accumulated earnings and profits as of the end of the taxable year of the S corporation in which the distribution is made is treated in the manner provided in section 1368(b).

(d) *S corporation with earnings and profits.*— (1) *General treatment of distribution.*—Except as provided in paragraph (d)(2) of this section, a distribution made with respect to its stock by an S corporation that has accumulated earnings and profits as of the end of the taxable year of the S corporation in which the distribution is made is treated in the manner provided in section 1368(c). See section 316 and §1.316-2 for provisions relating to the allocation of earnings and profits among distributions.

(2) *Previously taxed income.*—This paragraph (d)(2) applies to distributions by a corporation that has both accumulated earnings and profits and previously taxed income (within the meaning of section 1375(d)(2), as in effect prior to its amendment by the Subchapter S Revision Act of 1982, and the regulations thereunder) with respect to one or more shareholders. In the case of such a distribution, that portion remaining after the application of section 1368(c)(1) (relating to distributions from the accumulated adjustments account (AAA) as defined in §1.1368-2(a)) is treated in the manner provided in section 1368(b) (relating to S corporations without earnings and profits) to the extent that portion is a distribution of money and does not exceed the shareholder's net share immediately before the distribution of the corporation's previously taxed income. The AAA and the earnings and profits of the corporation are not decreased by that portion of the distribution. Any distribution remaining after the application of this paragraph

Reg. §1.1368-1(d)(2)

(d)(2) is treated in the manner provided in section 1368(c)(2) and (3).

(e) *Certain adjustments taken into account.*— (1) *Taxable years beginning before January 1, 1997.*—For any taxable year of the corporation beginning before January 1, 1997, paragraphs (c) and (d) of this section are applied only after taking into account—

(i) The adjustments to the basis of the shares of a shareholder's stock described in section 1367 (without regard to section 1367(a)(2)(A) (relating to decreases attributable to distributions not includible in income)) for the S corporation's taxable year; and

(ii) The adjustments to the AAA required by section 1368(e)(1)(A) (but without regard to the adjustments for distributions under §1.1368-2(a)(3)(iii)) for the S corporation's taxable year.

(2) *Taxable years beginning on or after August 18, 1998.*—For any taxable year of the corporation beginning on or after August 18, 1998, paragraphs (c) and (d) of this section are applied only after taking into account—

(i) The adjustments to the basis of the shares of a shareholder's stock described in section 1367(a)(1) (relating to increases in basis of stock) for the S corporation's taxable year; and

(ii) The adjustments to the AAA required by section 1368(e)(1)(A) (but without regard to the adjustments for distributions under §1.1368-2(a)(3)(iii)) for the S corporation's taxable year. Any net negative adjustment (as defined in section 1368(e)(1)(C)(ii)) for the taxable year shall not be taken into account.

(f) *Elections relating to source of distributions.*— (1) *In general.*—An S corporation may modify the application of paragraphs (c) and (d) of this section by electing (pursuant to paragraph (f)(5) of this section)—

(i) To distribute earnings and profits first as described in paragraph (f)(2) of this section;

(ii) To make a deemed dividend as described in paragraph (f)(3) of this section; or

(iii) To forego previously taxed income as described in paragraph (f)(4) of this section.

(2) *Election to distribute earnings and profits first.*—(i) *In general.*—An S corporation with accumulated earnings and profits may elect under this paragraph (f)(2) for any taxable year to distribute earnings and profits first as provided in section 1368(e)(3). Except as provided in paragraph (f)(2)(ii) of this section, distributions made by an S corporation making this election are treated as made first from earnings and profits under section 1368(c)(2) and second from the AAA under section 1368(c)(1). Any remaining portion of the distribution is treated in the manner provided in section 1368(b). This election is effective for all distributions made during the year for which the election is made.

(ii) *Previously taxed income.*—If a corporation to which paragraph (d)(2) of this section (relating to corporations with previously taxed income) applies makes the election provided in this paragraph (f)(2) for the taxable year, and does not make the election to forego previously taxed income under paragraph (f)(4) of this section, distributions by the S corporation during the taxable year are treated as made first, from previously taxed income under paragraph (d)(2) of this section; second, from earnings and profits under section 1368(c)(2); and third, from the AAA under section 1368(c)(1). Any portion of a distribution remaining after the previously taxed income, earnings and profits, and the AAA are exhausted is treated in the manner provided in section 1368(b).

(iii) *Corporation with subchapter C and subchapter S earnings and profits.*—If an S corporation that makes the election provided in this paragraph (f)(2) has both subchapter C earnings and profits (as defined in section 1362(d)(3)(B)) and subchapter S earnings and profits in a taxable year of the corporation in which the distribution is made, the distribution is treated as made first from subchapter C earnings and profits, and second from subchapter S earnings and profits. *Subchapter S earnings and profits* are earnings and profits accumulated in a taxable year beginning before January 1, 1983 (or in the case of a qualified casualty insurance electing small business corporation or a qualified oil corporation, earnings and profits accumulated in any taxable year), for which an election under subchapter S of chapter 1 of the Internal Revenue Code was in effect.

(3) *Election to make a deemed dividend.*—An S corporation may elect under this paragraph (f)(3) to distribute all or part of its subchapter C earnings and profits through a deemed dividend. If an S corporation makes the election provided in this paragraph (f)(3), the S corporation will be considered to have made the election provided in paragraph (f)(2) of this section (relating to the election to distribute earnings and profits first). The amount of the deemed dividend may not exceed the subchapter C earnings and profits of the corporation on the last day of the taxable year, reduced by any actual distributions of subchapter C earnings and profits made during the taxable year. The amount of the deemed dividend is considered, for all purposes of the Internal Revenue Code, as if it were distributed in money to the shareholders in proportion to their stock ownership, received by the shareholders, and immediately contributed by the shareholders to the corporation, all on the last day of the corporation's taxable year.

(4) *Election to forego previously taxed income.*—An S corporation may elect to forego distributions of previously taxed income. If such an election is made, paragraph (d)(2) of this section

(relating to corporations with previously taxed income) does not apply to any distribution made during the taxable year. Thus, distributions by a corporation that makes the election to forego previously taxed income for a taxable year under this paragraph (f)(4) and does not make the election to distribute earnings and profits first under paragraph (f)(2) of this section are treated in the manner provided in section 1368(c) (relating to distributions by corporations with earnings and profits). Distributions by a corporation that makes both the election to distribute earnings and profits first under paragraph (f)(2) of this section and the election to forego previously taxed income under this paragraph (f)(4), are treated in the manner provided in paragraph (f)(2)(i) of this section.

(5) *Time and manner of making elections.*— (i) *For earnings and profits.*—If an election is made under paragraph (f)(2) of this section to distribute earnings and profits first, see section 1368(e)(3) regarding the consent required by shareholders.

(ii) *For previously taxed income and deemed dividends.*—If an election is made to forego previously taxed income under paragraph (f)(4) of this section or to make a deemed dividend under paragraph (f)(3) of this section, consent by each "affected shareholder," as defined in section 1368(e)(3)(B), is required.

(iii) *Corporate statement regarding elections.*—A corporation makes an election for a taxable year under §1.1368-1(f) by attaching a statement to a timely filed (including extensions) original or amended return required to be filed under section 6037 for that taxable year. In the statement, the corporation must identify the election it is making under §1.1368-1(f) and must state that each shareholder consents to the election. In the case of elections for taxable years beginning before January 1, 2003, an officer of the corporation must sign under penalties of perjury the statement on behalf of the corporation. In the case of elections for taxable years beginning after December 31, 2002, the statement described in this paragraph (f)(5)(iii) shall be verified by signing the return. A statement of election to make a deemed dividend under §1.1368-1(f) must include the amount of the deemed dividend that is distributed to each shareholder.

(iv) *Irrevocable elections.*—The elections under this paragraph (f) are irrevocable and are effective only for the taxable year for which they are made. In applying the preceding sentence to elections under this paragraph (f), an election to terminate the taxable year under section 1377(a)(2) or §1.1368-1(g)(2) is disregarded.

(g) *Special rule.*—(1) *Election to terminate year under §1.1368-1(g)(2).*—If an election is made under paragraph (g)(2) of this section to termi-

nate the year when there is a qualifying disposition, this section applies as if the taxable year consisted of separate taxable years, the first of which ends at the close of the day on which there is a qualifying disposition of stock.

(2) *Election in case of a qualifying disposition.*—(i) *In general.*—In the case of a qualifying disposition, a corporation may elect under this paragraph (g)(2)(i) to treat the year as if it consisted of separate taxable years, the first of which ends at the close of the day on which the qualifying disposition occurs. A *qualifying disposition* is—

(A) A disposition by a shareholder of 20 percent or more of the outstanding stock of the corporation in one or more transactions during any thirty-day period during the corporation's taxable year;

(B) A redemption treated as an exchange under section 302(a) or section 303(a) of 20 percent or more of the outstanding stock of the corporation from a shareholder in one or more transactions during any thirty-day period during the corporation's taxable year; or

(C) An issuance of an amount of stock equal to or greater than 25 percent of the previously outstanding stock to one or more new shareholders during any thirty-day period during the corporation's taxable year.

(ii) *Effect of the election.*—A corporation making an election under paragraph (g)(2)(i) of this section must treat the taxable year as separate taxable years for purposes of allocating items of income and loss; making adjustments to the AAA, earnings and profits, and basis; and determining the tax effect of distributions under section 1368(b) and (c). An election made under paragraph (g)(2)(i) of this section may be made upon the occurrence of any qualifying disposition. Dispositions of stock that are taken into account as part of a qualifying disposition are not taken into account in determining whether a subsequent qualifying disposition has been made.

(iii) *Time and manner of making election.*—A corporation makes an election under §1.1368-1(g)(2)(i) for a taxable year by attaching a statement to a timely filed (including extensions) original or amended return required to be filed under section 6037 for a taxable year (without regard to the election under §1.1368-1(g)(2)(i)). In the statement, the corporation must state that it is electing for the taxable year under §1.1368-1(g)(2)(i) to treat the taxable year as if it consisted of separate taxable years. The corporation also must set forth facts in the statement relating to the qualifying disposition (e.g., sale, gift, stock issuance, or redemption), and state that each shareholder who held stock in the corporation during the taxable year (without regard to the election under §1.1368-1(g)(2)(i)) consents to this election. For purposes of this election, a shareholder of the corporation for the taxable year is a shareholder as described in section 1362(a)(2). A single election statement may be filed for all elections made under §1.1368-1(g)(2)(i) for the taxable year. An election made under §1.1368-1(g)(2)(i) is irrevocable. In the case of elections for taxable years beginning before January 1, 2003, the statement through which a corporation makes an election under §1.1368-1(g)(2)(i) must be signed by an officer of the corporation under penalties of perjury. In the case of elections for taxable years beginning after December 31, 2002, the statement described in the preceding sentence shall be verified by signing the return.

(iv) *Coordination with election under section 1377(a)(2).*—If the event resulting in a qualifying disposition also results in a termination of a shareholder's entire interest as described in §1.1377-1(b)(4), the election under this paragraph (g)(2) cannot be made. Rather, the election under section 1377(a)(2) and §1.1377-1(b) may be made. See §1.1377-1(b) (concerning the election under section 1377(a)(2)). [Reg. §1.1368-1.]

☐ [T.D. 8508, 12-30-93. *Amended by T.D.* 8696, 12-20-96; *T.D.* 8852, 12-21-99; *T.D.* 9100, 12-18-2003 *and T.D.* 9300, 12-7-2006.]

[Reg. §1.1368-2]

§1.1368-2. Accumulated adjustments account (AAA).—(a) *Accumulated adjustments account.*—(1) *In general.*—The accumulated adjustments account is an account of the S corporation and is not apportioned among shareholders. The AAA is relevant for all taxable years beginning on or after January 1, 1983, for which the corporation is an S corporation. On the first day of the first year for which the corporation is an S corporation, the balance of the AAA is zero. The AAA is increased in the manner provided in paragraph (a)(2) of this section and is decreased in the manner provided in paragraph (a)(3) of this section. For the adjustments to the AAA in the case of redemptions, liquidations, reorganizations, and corporate separations, see paragraph (d) of this section.

(2) *Increases to the AAA.*—The AAA is increased for the taxable year of the corporation by the sum of the following items with respect to the corporation for the taxable year:

(i) The items of income described in section 1366(a)(1)(A) other than income that is exempt from tax;

(ii) Any nonseparately computed income determined under section 1366(a)(1)(B); and

(iii) The excess of the deductions for depletion over the basis of property subject to depletion unless the property is an oil or gas property the basis of which has been allocated to shareholders under section 613A(c)(11).

(3) *Decreases to the AAA.*—(i) *In general.*—The AAA is decreased for the taxable year of the corporation by the sum of the following items with respect to the corporation for the taxable year—

(A) The items of loss or deduction described in section 1366(a)(1)(A);

(B) Any nonseparately computed loss determined under section 1366(a)(1)(B);

(C) Any expense of the corporation not deductible in computing its taxable income and not properly chargeable to a capital account, other than—

(1) Federal taxes attributable to any taxable year in which the corporation was a C corporation; and

(2) Expenses related to income that is exempt from tax; and

(D) The sum of the shareholders' deductions for depletion for any oil or gas property held by the corporation described in section 1367(a)(2)(E).

(ii) *Extent of allowable reduction.*—The AAA may be decreased under paragraph (a)(3)(i) of this section below zero. The AAA is decreased by noncapital, nondeductible expenses under paragraph (a)(3)(i)(C) of this section even though a portion of the noncapital, nondeductible expenses is not taken into account by a shareholder under §1.1367-1(g) (relating to the elective ordering rule). The AAA is also decreased by the entire amount of any loss or deduction even though a portion of the loss or deduction is not taken into account by a shareholder under section 1366(d)(1) or is otherwise not currently deductible under the Internal Revenue Code. However, in any subsequent taxable year in which the loss, deduction, or noncapital, nondeductible expense is treated as incurred by the corporation with respect to the shareholder under section 1366(d)(2) or §1.1367-1(g) (or in which the loss or deduction is otherwise allowed to the shareholder), no further adjustment is made to the AAA.

(iii) *Decrease to the AAA for distributions.*—The AAA is decreased (but not below zero) by any portion of a distribution to which section 1368(b) or (c)(1) applies.

(4) *Ordering rules for the AAA for taxable years beginning before January 1, 1997.*—For any taxable year beginning before January 1, 1997, the adjustments to the AAA are made in the following order—

(i) The AAA is increased under paragraph (a)(2) of this section before it is decreased under paragraph (a)(3) of this section for the taxable year;

(ii) The AAA is decreased under paragraph (a)(3)(i) of this section before it is decreased under paragraph (a)(3) (iii) of this section;

(iii) The AAA is decreased (but not below zero) by any portion of an ordinary distribution to which section 1368(b) or (c)(1) applies; and

(iv) The AAA is adjusted (whether negative or positive) for redemption distributions under paragraph (d)(1) of this section.

(5) *Ordering rules for the AAA for taxable years beginning on or after August 18, 1998.*—For any taxable year of the S corporation beginning on or after August 18, 1998, the adjustments to the AAA are made in the following order—

(i) The AAA is increased under paragraph (a)(2) of this section before it is decreased under paragraph (a)(3)(i) of this section for the taxable year;

(ii) The AAA is decreased under paragraph (a)(3)(i) of this section (without taking into account any net negative adjustment (as defined in section 1368(e)(1)(C)(ii)) before it is decreased under paragraph (a)(3)(iii) of this section;

(iii) The AAA is decreased (but not below zero) by any portion of an ordinary distribution to which section 1368(b) or (c)(1) applies;

(iv) The AAA is decreased by any net negative adjustment (as defined in section 1368(e)(1)(C)(ii)); and

(v) The AAA is adjusted (whether negative or positive) for redemption distributions under paragraph (d)(1) of this section.

(b) *Distributions in excess of the AAA.*—(1) *In general.*—A portion of the AAA (determined under paragraph (b)(2) of this section) is allocated to each of the distributions made for the taxable year if—

(i) An S corporation makes more than one distribution of property with respect to its stock during the taxable year of the corporation (including an S short year as defined under section 1362(e)(1)(A));

(ii) The AAA has a positive balance at the close of the year; and

(iii) The sum of the distributions made during the corporation's taxable year exceeds the balance of the AAA at the close of the year.

(2) *Amount of the AAA allocated to each distribution.*—The amount of the AAA allocated to each distribution is determined by multiplying the balance of the AAA at the close of the current taxable year by a fraction, the numerator of which is the amount of the distribution and the denominator of which is the amount of all distributions made during the taxable year. For purposes of this paragraph (b)(2), the term *all distributions made during the taxable year* does not include any distribution treated as from earnings and profits or previously taxed income pursuant to an election made under section 1368(e)(3) and §1.1368-1(f)(2). See paragraph (d)(1) of this section for rules relating to the adjustments to the AAA for redemptions and distributions in the year of a redemption.

(c) *Distribution of money and loss property.*—(1) *In general.*—The amount of the AAA allocated to a distribution under this section must be further allocated (under paragraph (c)(2) of this section) if the distribution—

(i) Consists of property the adjusted basis of which exceeds its fair market value on the date of the distribution and money;

(ii) Is a distribution to which §1.1368-1(d)(1) applies; and

(iii) Exceeds the amount of the corporation's AAA properly allocable to that distribution.

(2) *Allocating the AAA to loss property.*—The amount of the AAA allocated to the property other than money is equal to the amount of the AAA allocated to the distribution multiplied by a fraction, the numerator of which is the fair market value of the property other than money on the date of distribution and the denominator of which is the amount of the distribution. The amount of the AAA allocated to the money is equal to the amount of the AAA allocated to the distribution reduced by the amount of the AAA allocated to the property other than money.

(d) *Adjustment in the case of redemptions, liquidations, reorganizations, and divisions.*—(1) *Redemptions.*—(i) *General Rule.*—In the case of a redemption distribution by an S corporation that is treated as an exchange under section 302(a) or section 303(a) (a *redemption distribution*), the AAA of the corporation is adjusted in an amount equal to the ratable share of the corporation's AAA (whether negative or positive) attributable to the redeemed stock as of the date of the redemption.

(ii) *Special rule for years in which a corporation makes both ordinary and redemption distributions.*—In any year in which a corporation makes one or more distributions to which section 1368(a) applies (*ordinary distributions*) and makes one or more redemption distributions, the AAA of the corporation is adjusted first for any ordinary distributions and then for any redemption distributions.

(iii) *Adjustments to earnings and profits.*—Earnings and profits are adjusted under section 312 independently of any adjustments made to the AAA.

(2) *Liquidations and reorganizations.*—An S corporation acquiring the assets of another S corporation in a transaction to which section 381(a) applies will succeed to and merge its AAA (whether positive or negative) with the AAA (whether positive or negative) of the distributor or transferor S corporation as of the close of the date of distribution or transfer. Thus, the AAA of the acquiring corporation after the transaction is the sum of the AAAs of the corporations prior to the transaction.

(3) *Corporate separations to which section 368(a)(1)(D) applies.*—If an S corporation with accumulated earnings and profits transfers a part of its assets constituting an active trade or business to another corporation in a transaction to which section 368(a)(1)(D) applies, and immediately thereafter the stock and securities of the controlled corporation are distributed in a distribution or exchange to which section 355 (or so much of section 356 as relates to section 355) applies, the AAA of the distributing corporation immediately before the transaction is allocated between the distributing corporation and the controlled corporation in a manner similar to the manner in which the earnings and profits of the distributing corporation are allocated under section 312(h). See § 1.312-10(a).

(e) *Election to terminate year under section 1377(a)(2) or § 1.1368-1(g)(2).*—If an election is made under section 1377(a)(2) (to terminate the year in the case of termination of a shareholder's interest) or § 1.1368-1(g)(2) (to terminate the year in the case of a qualifying disposition), this section applies as if the taxable year consisted of separate taxable years, the first of which ends at the close of the day on which the shareholder terminated his or her interest in the corporation or makes a substantial disposition of stock, whichever the case may be. [Reg. § 1.1368-2.]

☐ [*T.D. 8508, 12-30-93. Amended by T.D. 8852, 12-21-99 and T.D. 8869, 1-20-2000.*]

[Reg. § 1.1368-3]

§ 1.1368-3. Examples.—The principles of §§ 1.1368-1 and 1.1368-2 are illustrated by the examples below. In each example Corporation S is a calendar year corporation:

Example 1. Distributions by S corporations without C corporation earnings and profits for taxable years beginning before January 1, 1997. (i) Corporation S, an S corporation, has no earnings and profits as of January 1, 1996, the first day of its 1996 taxable year. S's sole shareholder, A, holds 10 shares of S stock with a basis of $1 per share as of that date. On March 1, 1996, S makes a distribution of $38 to A. For S's 1996 taxable year, A's pro rata share of the amount of the items described in section 1367(a)(1) (relating to increases in basis of stock) is $50 and A's pro rata share of the amount of the items described in section 1367(a)(2)(B) through (D) (relating to decreases in basis of stock for items other than distributions) is $26.

(ii) Under section 1368(d)(1) and § 1.1368-1(e)(1), the adjustments to the bases of A's stock in S described in section 1367 are made before the distribution rules of section 1368 are applied. Thus, A's basis per share in the stock is $3.40 ($1 + [($50 – $26) / 10 shares]) before taking into account the distribution. Under section 1367(a)(2)(A), the basis of A's stock is decreased by distributions to A that are not includible in A's income. Under § 1.1367-1(c)(3),

the amount of the distribution that is attributable to each share of A's stock is $3.80 ($38 distribution / 10 shares). However, A only has a basis of $3.40 in each share, and basis may not be reduced below zero. Therefore, the basis of each share of his stock is reduced by $3.40 to zero, and the remaining $4.00 of the distribution ([$3.80 – $3.40] × 10 shares) is treated as gain from the sale or exchange of property. As of January 1, 1997, A has a basis of $0 in his shares of S stock.

Example 2. Distributions by S corporations without earnings and profits for taxable years beginning on or after August 18, 1998. (i) Corporation S, an S corporation, has no earnings and profits as of January 1, 2001, the first day of its 2001 taxable year. S's sole shareholder, A, holds 10 shares of S stock with a basis of $1 per share as of that date. On March 1, 2001, S makes a distribution of $38 to A. The balance in Corporation S's AAA is $100. For S's 2001 taxable year, A's pro rata share of the amount of the items described in section 1367(a)(1) (relating to increases in basis of stock) is $50. A's pro rata share of the amount of the items described in sections 1367(a)(2)(B) through (D) (relating to decreases in basis of stock for items other than distributions) is $26, $20 of which is attributable to items described in section 1367(a)(2)(B) and (C) and $6 of which is attributable to items described in section 1367(a)(2)(D) (relating to decreases in basis attributable to noncapital, nondeductible expenses).

(ii) Under section 1368(d)(1) and § 1.1368-1(e)(1) and (2), the adjustments to the basis of A's stock in S described in sections 1367(a)(1) are made before the distribution rules of section 1368 are applied. Thus, A's basis per share in the stock is $6.00 ($1 + [$50/10]) before taking into account the distribution. Under section 1367(a)(2)(A), the basis of A's stock is decreased by distributions to A that are not includible in A's income. Under § 1.1367-1(c)(3), the amount of the distribution that is attributable to each share of A's stock is $3.80 ($38 distribution/10 shares). Thus, A's basis per share in the stock is $2.20 ($6.00 – $3.80), after taking into account the distribution. Under section 1367(a)(2)(D), the basis of each share of A's stock in S after taking into account the distribution, $2.20, is decreased by $.60 ($6 noncapital, nondeductible expenses/10). Thus, A's basis per share after taking into account the nondeductible, noncapital expenses is $1.60. Under section 1367(a)(2)(B) and (C), A's basis per share is further decreased by $2 ($20 items described in section 1367(a)(2)(B) and (C) /10 shares). However, basis may not be reduced below zero. Therefore, the basis of each share of A's stock is reduced to zero. As of January 1, 2002, A has a basis of $0 in his shares of S stock. Pursuant to section 1366(d)(2), the $.40 of loss in excess of A's basis in each of his shares of S stock is treated as incurred by the corporation in the succeeding taxable year with respect to A.

Example 3. Distributions by S corporations with C corporation earnings and profits for taxable years beginning before January 1, 1997. (i) Corporation S properly elects to be an S corporation beginning January 1, 1997, and as of that date has accumulated earnings and profits of $30. B, an individual and sole shareholder of Corporation S, has 10 shares of S stock with a basis of $12 per share. In addition, B lends $30 to S evidenced by a demand note.

(ii) During 1997, S has a nonseparately computed loss of $150. S makes no distributions to B during 1997. Under section 1366(d)(1), B is allowed a loss equal to $150, the amount equal to the sum of B's bases in his shares of stock and his basis in the debt. Under section 1367, the loss reduces B's adjusted basis in his stock and debt to $0. Under § 1.1368-2(a)(3), S's AAA as of December 31, 1997, has a deficit of $150 as a result of S's loss for the year.

(iii) For 1998, S has $220 of separately stated income and distributes $110 to B. The balance in the AAA (negative $150 from 1997) is increased by $220 for S's income for the year and decreased to $0 for the portion of the distribution that is treated as being from the AAA ($70). Under § 1.1367-2(c), B's net increase is $150, determined by reducing the $220 of income by the $70 of the distribution not includible in income by B. Thus, B's basis in the debt is fully restored to $30, and B's basis in S stock (before accounting for the distribution) is increased from zero to $19 per share ([$220 − $30 applied to the debt]/10). Thirty dollars of the distribution is considered a dividend to the extent of S's $30 of earnings and profits, and the remaining $10 of the distribution reduces B's basis in the S stock. Thus, B's basis in the S stock as of December 31, 1998, is $11 per share ($19 − [$70 AAA distribution/10] − [10 distribution treated as a reduction in basis/10]). The balance in the AAA is $0, S's earnings and profits are $0, and B's basis in the loan is $30.

Example 4. Distributions by S corporations with earnings and profits and no net negative adjustment for taxable years beginning on or after August 18, 1998. (i) Corporation S, an S corporation, has accumulated earnings and profits of $1,000 and a balance in the AAA of $2,000 on January 1, 2001. S's sole shareholder B holds 100 shares of stock with a basis of $20 per share as of January 1, 2001. On April 1, 2001, S makes a distribution of $1,500 to B. B's pro rata share of the income earned by S during 2001 is $2,000 and B's pro rata share of S's losses is $1,500. For the taxable year ending December 31, 2001, S does not have a net negative adjustment as defined in section 1368(e)(1)(C). S does not make the election under section 1368(e)(3) and § 1.1368-1(f)(2) to distribute its earnings and profits before its AAA.

(ii) The AAA is increased from $2,000 to $4,000 for the $2,000 of income earned during the 2001 taxable year. The AAA is decreased from $4,000 to $2,500 for the $1,500 of losses. The AAA is decreased from $2,500 to $1,000 for the portion of

the distribution ($1,500) to B that does not exceed the AAA.

(iii) As of December 31, 2001, B's basis in his stock is $10 ($20 + $20 ($2,000 income/100 shares) − $15 ($1,500 distribution/100 shares) − $15 ($1,500 loss/100 shares)).

Example 5. Distributions by S corporations with earnings and profits and net negative adjustment for taxable years beginning on or after August 18, 1998. (i) Corporation S, an S corporation, has accumulated earnings and profits of $1,000 and a balance in the AAA of $2,000 on January 1, 2001. S's sole shareholder B holds 100 shares of stock with a basis of $20 per share as of January 1, 2001. On April 1, 2001, S makes a distribution of $2,000 to B. B's pro rata share of the income earned by S during 2001 is $2,000 and B's pro rata share of S's losses is $3,500. For the taxable year ending December 31, 2001, S has a net negative adjustment as defined in section 1368(e)(1)(C). S does not make the election under section 1368(e)(3) and § 1.1368-1(f)(2) to distribute its earnings and profits before its AAA.

(ii) The AAA is increased from $2,000 to $4,000 for the $2,000 of income earned during the 2001 taxable year. Because under section 1368(e)(1)(C)(ii) and § 1.1368-2(a)(ii), the net negative adjustment is not taken into account, the AAA is decreased from $4,000 to $2,000 for the portion of the losses ($2,000) that does not exceed the income earned during the 2001 taxable year. The AAA is reduced from $2,000 to zero for the portion of the distribution to B ($2,000) that does not exceed the AAA. The AAA is decreased from zero to a negative $1,500 for the portion of the $3,500 of loss that exceeds the $2,000 of income earned during the 2001 taxable year.

(iii) Under § 1.1367-1(c)(1), the basis of a shareholder's share in an S corporation stock may not be reduced below zero. Accordingly, as of December 31, 2001, B's basis per share in his stock is zero ($20 + $20 income − $20 distribution −$35 loss). Pursuant to section 1366(d)(2), the $15 of loss in excess of B's basis in each of his shares of S stock is treated as incurred by the corporation in the succeeding taxable year with respect to B.

Example 6. Election in case of disposition of substantial amount of stock. (i) Corporation S, an S corporation, has earnings and profits of $3,000 and a balance in the AAA of $1,000 on January 1, 1997. C, an individual and the sole shareholder of Corporation S, has 100 shares of S stock with a basis of $10 per share. On July 3, 1997, C sells 50 shares of his S stock to D, an individual, for $250. For 1997, S has taxable income of $1,000, of which $500 was earned on or before July 3, 1997, and $500 earned after July 3, 1997. During its 1997 taxable year, S distributes $1,000 to C on February 1 and $1,000 to each of C and D on August 1. S does not make the election under section 1368(e)(3) and § 1.1368-1(f)(2) to distribute its earnings and profits before its AAA. S makes the election under § 1.1368-1(g)(2) to treat its taxable year as if it consisted of separate taxable years, the first of which ends at the close of July 3, 1997, the date of the qualifying disposition.

(ii) Under section § 1.1368-1(g)(2), for the period ending on July 3, 1997, S's AAA is $500 ($1,000 (AAA as of January 1, 1997) + $500 (income earned from January 1, 1997 through July 3, 1997) – $1,000 (distribution made on February 1, 1997)). C's bases in his shares of stock is decreased to $5 per share ($10 (original basis) + $5 (increase per share for income) – $10 (decrease per share for distribution)).

(iii) The AAA is adjusted at the end of the taxable year for the period July 4 through December 31, 1997. It is increased from $500 (AAA as of the close of July 3, 1997) to $1,000 for the income earned during this period and is decreased by $1,000, the portion of the distribution ($2,000 in total) made to C and D on August 1 that does not exceed the AAA. The $1,000 portion of the distribution that remains after the AAA is reduced to zero is attributable to earnings and profits. Therefore C and D each have a dividend of $500, which does not affect their basis or S's AAA. The earnings and profits account is reduced from $3,000 to $2,000.

(iv) As of December 31, 1997, C and D have bases in their shares of stock of zero ($5 (basis as of July 4) + $5 ($500 income/100 shares) – $10 ($1,000 distribution/100 shares)). C and D each will report $500 as dividend income, which does not affect their basis or S's AAA.

Example 7. Election to distribute earnings and profits first. (i) Corporation S has been a calendar year C corporation since 1975. For 1982, S elects for the first time to be taxed under subchapter S, and during 1982 has $60 of earnings and profits. As of December 31, 1995, S has an AAA of $10 and earnings and profits of $160, consisting of $100 of subchapter C earnings and profits and $60 of subchapter S earnings and profits. For 1996, S has $200 of taxable income and the AAA is increased to $210 (before taking distributions into account). During 1996, S distributes $240 to its shareholders. With its 1996 tax return, S properly elects under section 1368(e)(3) and § 1.1368-1(f)(2) to distribute its earnings and profits before its AAA.

(ii) Because S elected to distribute its earnings and profits before its AAA, the first $100 of the distribution is characterized as a distribution from subchapter C earnings and profits; the next $60 of the distribution is characterized as a distribution from subchapter S earnings and profits. Because $160 of the distribution is from earnings and profits, the shareholders of S have a $160 dividend. The remaining $80 of the distribution is a distribution from S's AAA and is treated by the shareholders as a return of capital or gain from the sale or exchange of property, as appropriate, under § 1.1368-1(d)(1). S's AAA, as of December 31, 1996, equals $130 ($210 – $80).

Example 8. Distributions in excess of the AAA. (i) On January 1, 1995, Corporation S has $40 of earnings and profits and a balance in the AAA of $100. S has two shareholders, E and F, each of whom own 50 shares of S's stock. For 1995, S has taxable income of $50, which increases the AAA to $150 as of December 31, 1995 (before taking into account distributions made during 1995). On February 1, 1995, S distributes $60 to each shareholder. On September 1, 1995, S distributes $30 to each shareholder. S does not make the election under section 1368(e)(3) and § 1.1368-1(f)(2) to distribute its earnings and profits before its AAA.

(ii) The sum of the distributions exceed S's AAA. Therefore, under § 1.1368-2(b), a portion of S's $150 balance in the AAA as of December 31, 1995, is allocated to each of the February 1 and September 1 distributions based on the respective sizes of the distributions. Accordingly, S must allocate $100 ($150 (AAA) × ($120 (February 1 distribution) / $180 (the sum of the distributions))) of the AAA to the February 1 distribution, and $50 ($150 × ($60 / $180)) to the September 1 distribution. The portions of the distributions to which the AAA is allocated are treated by the shareholder as a return of capital or gain from the sale or exchange of property, as appropriate. The remainder of the two distributions is treated as a dividend to the extent that it does not exceed S's earnings and profits. E and F must each report $10 of dividend income for the February 1 distribution. For the September 1 distribution, E and F must each report $5 of dividend income.

Example 9. Ordinary and redemption distributions in the same taxable year. (i) On January 1, 1995, Corporation S, an S corporation, has $20 of earnings and profits and a balance in the AAA of $10. S has two shareholders, G and H, each of whom owns 50 shares of S's stock. For 1995, S has taxable income of $16, which increases the AAA to $26 as of December 31, 1995 (before taking into account distributions made during 1995). On February 1, 1995, S distributes $10 to each shareholder. On December 31, 1995, S redeems for $13 all of shareholder G's stock in a redemption that is treated as a sale or exchange under section 302(a).

(ii) The sum of the ordinary distributions does not exceed S's AAA. Therefore, S must reduce the $26 balance in the AAA by $20 for the February 1 ordinary distribution. The portions of the distribution by which the AAA is reduced are treated by the shareholders as a return of capital or gain from the sale or exchange of property. S must adjust the remaining AAA, $6, in an amount equal to the ratable share of the remaining AAA attributable to the redeemed stock, or $3 (50% × $6).

(iii) S also must adjust the earnings and profits of $20 in an amount equal to the ratable share of the earnings and profits attributable to the redeemed stock. Therefore, S adjusts the earnings and profits by $10 (50% × $20), the ratable share

of the earnings and profits attributable to the redeemed stock.
[Reg. § 1.1368-3.]

☐ [*T.D.* 8508, 12-30-93. *Amended by T.D.* 8852, 12-21-99.]

[Reg. § 1.1368-4]

§ 1.1368-4. Effective date and transition rule.—Except for § § 1.1368-1(e)(2), 1.1368-2(a)(5), and 1.1368-3 *Example 2, Example 4*, and *Example 5*, § § 1.1368-1, 1.1368-2, and 1.1368-3 apply to taxable years of the corporation beginning on or after January 1, 1994. Section 1.1368-1(e)(2), § 1.1368-2(a)(5), and § 1.1368-3 *Example 2, Example 4*, and *Example 5* apply only to taxable years of the corporation beginning on or after August 18, 1998. For taxable years beginning before January 1, 1994, and taxable years beginning on or after January 1, 1997, and before August 18, 1998, the treatment of distributions by an S corporation to its shareholders must be determined in a reasonable manner, taking into account the statute and legislative history. Except with regard to the deemed dividend rule under § 1.1368-1(f)(3), § 1.1368-1(e)(2), § 1.1368-2(a)(5), and § 1.1368-3 *Example 2, Example 4*, and *Example 5*, return positions consistent with § § 1.1368-1, 1.1368-2, and 1.1368-3 are reasonable for taxable years beginning before January 1, 1994. Return positions consistent with § § 1.1368-1(e)(2), 1.1368-2(a)(5), and 1.1368-3 *Example 2, Example 4*, and *Example 5* are reasonable for taxable years beginning on or after January 1, 1997, and before August 18, 1998. [Reg. § 1.1368-4].

☐ [*T.D.* 8508, 12-30-93. *Amended by T.D.* 8852, 12-21-99.]

[Reg. § 18.1371-1]

§ 18.1371-1. Election to treat distributions as dividends during certain post-termination transition periods (Temporary).—A corporation may make an election under section 1371(e) (as amended by section 721(o) of the Act) to treat all distributions of money made during the post-termination transition period described in section 1377(b)(1)(A) as coming out of the corporation's earnings and profits (after earnings and profits have been eliminated, the distributions are applied against and reduce the adjusted basis of the stock). The election may be made only with the consent of each shareholder to whom the corporation makes a distribution (whether or not it is a cash distribution) during such post-termination transition period. Any such election shall be made by the corporation by attaching to its income tax return for the C year in which such post-termination transition period ends a statement which clearly indicates that the corporation elects to have section 1371(e)(1) not apply to all distributions made during such post-termination transition period. The election shall not be effective unless such statement is signed by a person authorized to sign the return required to be filed under section 6012 and by each share-

holder required to consent to the election. [Temporary Reg. § 18.1371-1.]

☐ [*T.D.* 7976, 9-5-84.]

[Reg. § 1.1374-0]

§ 1.1374-0. Table of contents.—This section lists the major paragraph headings for § § 1.1374-1 through 1.1374-10.

Reg. § 1.1374-0

(4) RBIG and RBIL limitations.

  (i) Sale of partnership interest.

  (ii) Amounts of limitations.

(5) Small interest exception.

  (i) In general.

  (ii) Contributed assets.

  (iii) Anti-abuse rule.

(6) Section 704(c) gain or loss.

(7) Disposition of distributed partnership asset.

(8) Examples.

§ 1.1374-5. *Loss carryforwards.*

  (a) In general.

  (b) Example.

§ 1.1374-6. *Credits and credit carryforwards.*

  (a) In general.

  (b) Limitations.

  (c) Examples.

§ 1.1374-7. *Inventory.*

  (a) Valuation.

  (b) Identity of dispositions.

§ 1.1374-8. *Section 1374(d)(8) transactions.*

  (a) In general.

  (b) Effective date of section 1374(d)(8).

  (c) Separate determination of tax.

  (d) Taxable income limitation.

  (e) Examples.

§ 1.1374-9. *Anti-stuffing rule.*

§ 1.1374-10. *Effective date and additional rules.*

  (a) In general.

  (b) Additional rules.

    (1) Certain transfers to partnerships.

    (2) Certain inventory dispositions.

    (3) Certain contributions of built-in loss assets.

    (4) Certain installment sales.

      (i) In general.

      (ii) Examples.

  (c) Revocation and re-election of S corporation status.

    (1) In general.

    (2) Example.

[Reg. § 1.1374-0.]

☐ [*T.D.* 8579, 12-23-94. *Amended by T.D.* 9236, 12-20-2005.]

[Reg. § 1.1374-1]

§ 1.1374-1. General rules and definitions.— (a) *Computation of tax.*—The tax imposed on the income of an S corporation by section 1374(a) for any taxable year during the recognition period is computed as follows—

(1) Step One: Determine the net recognized built-in gain of the corporation for the taxable year under section 1374(d)(2) and § 1.1374-2;

(2) Step Two: Reduce the net recognized built-in gain (but not below zero) by any net operating loss and capital loss carryforward allowed under section 1374(b)(2) and § 1.1374-5;

(3) Step Three: Compute a tentative tax by applying the rate of tax determined under section 1374(b)(1) for the taxable year to the amount determined under paragraph (a)(2) of this section;

(4) Step Four: Compute the final tax by reducing the tentative tax (but not below zero) by any credit allowed under section 1374(b)(3) and § 1.1374-6.

(b) *Anti-trafficking rules.*—If section 382, 383, or 384 would have applied to limit the use of a corporation's recognized built-in loss or section 1374 attributes at the beginning of the first day of the recognition period if the corporation had remained a C corporation, these sections apply to limit their use in determining the S corporation's pre-limitation amount, taxable income limitation, net unrealized built-in gain limitation, deductions against net recognized built-in gain, and credits against the section 1374 tax.

(c) *Section 1374 attributes.*—Section 1374 attributes are the loss carryforwards allowed under section 1374(b)(2) as a deduction against net recognized built-in gain and the credit and credit carryforwards allowed under section 1374(b)(3) as a credit against the section 1374 tax.

(d) *Recognition period.*—The recognition period is the 10-year (120-month) period beginning on the first day the corporation is an S corporation or the day an S corporation acquires assets in a section 1374(d)(8) transaction. For example, if the first day of the recognition period is July 14, 1996, the last day of the recognition period is July 13, 2006. If the recognition period for certain assets ends during an S corporation's taxable year (for example, because the corporation was on a fiscal year as a C corporation and changed to a calendar year as an S corporation or because an S corporation acquired assets in a section 1374(d)(8) transaction during a taxable year), the S corporation must determine its pre-limitation amount (as defined in § 1.1374-2(a)(1)) for the year as if the corporation's books were closed at the end of the recognition period.

(e) *Predecessor corporation.*—For purposes of section 1374(c)(1), if the basis of an asset of the S corporation is determined (in whole or in part) by reference to the basis of the asset (or any other property) in the hands of another corporation, the other corporation is a predecessor corporation of the S corporation. [Reg. § 1.1374-1.]

☐ [*T.D.* 8579, 12-23-94.]

[Reg. §1.1374-1A]

§1.1374-1A. Tax imposed on certain capital gains.—(a) *General rule.*—Except as otherwise provided in paragraph (c) of this section, if for a taxable year beginning after 1982 of an S corporation—

(1) The net capital gain of such corporation exceeds $25,000, and

(2) The net capital gain of such corporation exceeds 50 percent of its taxable income (as defined in paragraph (d) of this section) for such year, and

(3) The taxable income of such corporation (as defined in paragraph (d) of this section) for such year exceeds $25,000,

section 1374 imposes a tax (computed under paragraph (b) of this section) on the income of such corporation. The tax is imposed on the S corporation and not on the shareholders.

(b) *Amount of tax.*—The amount of tax shall be the lower of—

(1) An amount equal to the tax, determined as provided in section 1201(a)(2), on the amount by which the net capital gain of the corporation for the taxable year exceeds $25,000, or

(2) An amount equal to the tax which would be imposed by section 11 on the taxable income of the corporation (as defined in paragraph (d) of this section) for the taxable year were it not an S corporation.

No credit shall be allowable under Part IV of Subchapter A of Chapter 1 of the Internal Revenue Code of 1954 (other than under section 34) against the tax imposed by section 1374(a) and this section. See section 1375(c)(2) and §1.1375-1(c)(2) for a special rule that reduces the amount of the net capital gain of the corporation for purposes of this paragraph (b) in cases where a net capital gain is taxed as excess net passive income under section 1375. See section 1374(c)(3) and paragraph (c)(1)(ii) of this section for a special rule that limits the amount of tax on property with a substituted basis in certain cases.

(c) *Exceptions to taxation.*—(1) *New corporations and corporations with election in effect for 3 immediately preceding years.*—(i) *In general.*—If an S corporation would be subject to the tax imposed by section 1374 for a taxable year pursuant to paragraph (a) of this section, the corporation shall, nevertheless, not be subject to such tax for such year, if:

(A) The election under section 1362(a) which is in effect with respect to such corporation for such year has been in effect for the corporation's three immediately preceding taxable years, or

(B) An election under section 1362(a) has been in effect with respect to such corporation for each of its taxable years for which it has been in existence, unless there is a net capital gain for the taxable year which is attributable to property with a substituted basis within the meaning of paragraph (c)(1)(iii) of this section.

(ii) *Amount of tax on net capital gain attributable to property with a substituted basis.*—If for a taxable year of an S corporation either paragraph (c)(1)(i)(A) or (B) of this section is satisfied, but the S corporation has a net capital gain for such taxable year which is attributable to property with a substituted basis (within the meaning of paragraph (c)(1)(iii) of this section), then paragraph (a) of this section shall apply for the taxable year, but the amount of tax determined under paragraph (b) of this section shall not exceed a tax, determined as provided in section 1201(a), on the net capital gain attributable to property with a substituted basis.

(iii) *Property with substituted basis.*—For purposes of this section, the term "property with a substituted basis" means:

(A) Property acquired by a corporation ("the acquiring corporation") during the period beginning 36 months before the first day of the acquiring corporation's taxable year and ending on the last day of such year;

(B) The basis of such property in the hands of the acquiring corporation is determined in whole or in part by reference to the basis of any property in the hands of another corporation; and

(C) Such other corporation was not an S corporation throughout the period beginning the later of:

(1) 36 months before the first day of the acquiring corporation's taxable year, or

(2) The time such other corporation came into existence, and ending on the date such other corporation transferred the property, the basis of which is used to determine, in whole or in part, the basis of the property in the hands of the acquiring corporation. An S corporation and any predecessor corporation shall not be treated as one corporation for purposes of this paragraph (c)(1).

(vi) *Existence of a corporation.*—For purposes of this section, a corporation shall not be considered to be in existence for any month which precedes the first month in which such corporation has shareholders or acquires assets or begins business, whichever is first to occur.

(v) *References to prior law included.*—For purposes of this paragraph (c), the term "S corporation" shall include an electing small business corporation under prior subchapter S law, and the term "election under section 1362(a)" shall include an election under section 1372 of prior subchapter S law.

(vi) *Examples.*—The provisions of this paragraph may be illustrated by the following examples:

Reg. §1.1374-1A(c)(1)(vi)

Example (1). M Corporation was organized and began business in 1977. M subsequently made an election under section 1362(a) which was effective for its 1984 taxable year. If such election does not terminate under section 1362 for its taxable years 1984, 1985, and 1986, M is not subject to the tax imposed by section 1374 for its taxable year 1987, or for any subsequent year for which such election remains in effect, unless it has, for any such year, an excess of net long-term capital gain over net short-term capital loss attributable to property with a substituted basis. If there is such an excess for any such year, and the requirements of paragraph (a) of this section are met, M will be subject to the tax for such year. If there is no such excess for any year after 1986, M will not be subject to the tax for any such year even though the requirements of paragraph (a) of this section are met.

Example (2). N corporation was organized in 1983, and was an S corporation for its first taxable year. N is not subject to the tax imposed by section 1374 for 1983, or for any subsequent year for which its original election under section 1362(a) has not terminated under section 1362(d), unless, for any such year, it has an excess of net long-term capital gain over net short-term capital loss attributable to property with a substituted basis and the requirements of paragraph (a) of this section are met.

(2) *Treatment of certain gains of options and commodities dealers.*—(i) *Exclusion of certain capital gains.*—For purposes of this section, the net capital gain of any options dealer or commodities dealer shall be determined by not taking into account any gain or loss (in the normal course of the taxpayer's activity of dealing in or trading section 1256 contracts) from any section 1256 contract or property related to such a contract.

(ii) *Definitions.*—For purposes of this paragraph (c)(2)—

(A) *Options dealer.*—The term "options dealer" has the meaning given to such term by section 1256(g)(8).

(B) *Commodities dealer.*—The term "commodities dealer" means a person who is actively engaged in trading section 1256 contracts and is registered with a domestic board of trade which is designated as a contract market by the Commodities Futures Trading Commission.

(C) *Section 1256 contracts.*—The term "section 1256 contracts" has the meaning given to such term by section 1256(b).

(iii) *Effective dates.*—(A) *In general.*—Except as otherwise provided in this paragraph (c)(2)(iii), this paragraph (c)(2) shall apply to positions established after July 18, 1984, in taxable years ending after such date.

(B) *Special rule for options on regulated futures contracts.*—In the case of any option with respect to a regulated futures contract (within the meaning of section 1256), this paragraph (c)(2) shall apply to positions established after October 31, 1983, in taxable years ending after such date.

(C) *Elections with respect to property held on or before July 18, 1984.*—See §§ 1.1256(h)-1T and 1.1256(h)-2T for rules concerning an election to have this paragraph (c)(2) apply to certain property held on or before July 18, 1984.

(d) *Determination of taxable income.*—(1) *General rule.*—For purposes of this section, taxable income of the corporation shall be determined under section 63(a) as if the corporation were a C corporation rather than an S corporation, except that the following deductions shall not apply in the computation—

(i) The deduction allowed by section 172 (relating to net operating loss deduction), and

(ii) The deductions allowed by Part VIII of Subchapter B (other than the deduction allowed by section 248, relating to organization expenditures).

For any taxable year in which a tax under this section is imposed on an S corporation, the S corporation shall attach a Form 1120 completed in accordance with this paragraph (d) and the instructions to Form 1120S to its tax return filed for such taxable year.

(2) *Special rule for net capital gains taxed as excess net passive income under section 1375.*—See section 1375(c)(2) and § 1.1375-1(c)(2) for a special rule that reduces the taxable income of the corporation for purposes of section 1374(b)(2) and § 1.1374-1(b)(2) in cases where a net capital gain is taxed as excess net passive income under section 1375.

(e) *Reduction in pass-thru for tax imposed on capital gain.*—See section 1366(f)(2) for a special rule reducing the S corporation's long-term capital gains and the corporation's gain from sales or exchanges of property described in section 1231 for purposes of section 1366(a) by an amount of tax imposed under section 1374 and this section.

(f) *Examples.*—The following examples illustrate the principles of this section and assume that a tax will not be imposed under section 1375:

Example (1). Corporation M is an S corporation for its taxable year beginning January 1, 1983. For 1983, M has an excess of net long-term capital gain over net short-term capital loss in the amount of $30,000. However, its taxable income for the year is only $20,000 as a result of other deductions in excess of other income. Thus, although the excess of the net long-term capital gain over the net short-term capital loss exceeds $25,000 and also exceeds 50 percent of taxable income, M is not subject to the tax imposed by

Reg. § 1.1374-1A(c)(2)

section 1374 for 1983 because its taxable income does not exceed $25,000.

Example (2). Corporation N is an S corporation for its 1983 taxable year. For 1983, N has an excess of net long-term capital gain over net short-term capital loss in the amount of $30,000, and taxable income of $65,000. Thus, although N's net capital gain ($30,000) exceeds $25,000, it does not exceed 50 percent of the corporation's taxable income for the year (50 percent of $65,000, or $32,500), and therefore N is not subject to the tax imposed by section 1374 for such year.

Example (3). Assume that Corporation O, an S corporation, is subject to the tax imposed by section 1374 for its taxable year 1983. For 1983, O has an excess of net long-term capital gain over net short-term capital loss in the amount of $73,000, and taxable income within the meaning of section 1374, which includes capital gains and losses, of $100,000. The amount of tax computed under paragraph (b)(1) of this section is 28 percent of $48,000 ($73,000 − $25,000), or $13,440. Since this is lower than the amount computed under paragraph (b)(2) of this section, which is $25,750 ($3,750 + $4,500 + $7,500 + $10,000), $13,440 is the amount of tax imposed by section 1374.

Example (4). Assume that in example (3) the taxable income of O for 1983 is $35,000. This results from an excess of deductions over income with respect to items which were not included in determining the excess of the net long-term capital gain over the net short-term capital loss. In such case, the amount of tax, computed under paragraph (b)(2) of this section, is $5,550. Since this is lower than the amount computed under paragraph (b)(1) of this section, $5,550 is the amount of tax imposed by section 1374.

Example (5). Corporation P, an S corporation, for its taxable year 1983 has an excess of net long-term capital gain over net short-term capital loss in the amount of $65,000 and has taxable income of $80,000. P's election under section 1362 has been in effect for its three immediately preceding taxable years, but P, nevertheless, is subject to the tax imposed by section 1374 for 1983 since it has an excess of net long-term capital gain over net short-term capital loss (in the amount of $20,000) attributable to property with a substituted basis. The tax computed under paragraph (b)(1) of this section, $11,200 (28 percent of $40,000 ($65,000 − $25,000)), is less than the tax computed under paragraph (b)(2) of this section, $17,750. However, under the limitation provided in paragraph (c) of this section which is applicable in this factual situation, the tax imposed by section 1374 for 1983 may not exceed $5,600 (28 percent of $20,000, the excess of net long-term capital gain over net short-term capital loss attributable to property with substituted basis). [Reg. § 1.1374-1A.]

☐ [*T.D.* 8104, 9-25-86. *Amended by T.D.* 8419, 5-28-92. *Redesignated by T.D.* 8579, 12-23-94.]

[Reg. §1.1374-2]

§1.1374-2. Net recognized built-in gain.— (a) *In general.*—An S corporation's net recognized built-in gain for any taxable year is the least of—

(1) Its taxable income determined by using all rules applying to C corporations and considering only its recognized built-in gain, recognized built-in loss, and recognized built-in gain carryover (pre-limitation amount);

(2) Its taxable income determined by using all rules applying to C corporations as modified by section 1375(b)(1)(B) (taxable income limitation); and

(3) The amount by which its net unrealized built-in gain exceeds its net recognized built-in gain for all prior taxable years (net unrealized built-in gain limitation).

(b) *Allocation rule.*—If an S corporation's pre-limitation amount for any taxable year exceeds its net recognized built-in gain for that year, the S corporation's net recognized built-in gain consists of a ratable portion of each item of income, gain, loss, and deduction included in the pre-limitation amount.

(c) *Recognized built-in gain carryover.*—If an S corporation's net recognized built-in gain for any taxable year is equal to its taxable income limitation, the amount by which its pre-limitation amount exceeds its taxable income limitation is a recognized built-in gain carryover included in its pre-limitation amount for the succeeding taxable year. The recognized built-in gain carryover consists of that portion of each item of income, gain, loss, and deduction not included in the S corporation's net recognized built-in gain for the year the carryover arose, as determined under paragraph (b) of this section.

(d) *Accounting methods.*—In determining its taxable income for pre-limitation amount and taxable income limitation purposes, a corporation must use the accounting method(s) it uses for tax purposes as an S corporation.

(e) *Example.*—The rules of this section are illustrated by the following example.

Example. Net recognized built-in gain. X is a calendar year C corporation that elects to become an S corporation on January 1, 1996. X has a net unrealized built-in gain of $50,000 and no net operating loss or capital loss carryforwards. In 1996, X has a pre-limitation amount of $20,000, consisting of ordinary income of $15,000 and capital gain of $5,000, a taxable income limitation of $9,600, and a net unrealized built-in gain limitation of $50,000. Therefore, X's net recognized built-in gain for 1996 is $9,600, because that is the least of the three amounts described in paragraph (a) of this section. Under paragraph (b) of this section, X's net recognized built-in gain consists of recognized built-in ordinary income of $7,200 [$15,000 × ($9,600/$20,000) = $7,200] and recognized built-in capital gain of $2,400 [$5,000 × ($9,600/$20,000) = $2,400]. Under paragraph (c) of this section, X has a recognized built-in gain carryover to 1997 of $10,400 ($20,000 − $9,600 = $10,400), consisting of $7,800 ($15,000 − $7,200 = $7,800) of recognized built-in ordinary income and $2,600 ($5,000 − $2,400 = $2,600) of recognized built-in capital gain.

[Reg. § 1.1374-2.]

☐ [T.D. 8579, 12-23-94.]

[Reg. § 1.1374-3]

§ 1.1374-3. Net unrealized built-in gain.— (a) *In general.*—An S corporation's net unrealized built-in gain is the total of the following—

(1) The amount that would be the amount realized if, at the beginning of the first day of the recognition period, the corporation had remained a C corporation and had sold all its assets at fair market value to an unrelated party that assumed all its liabilities; decreased by

(2) Any liability of the corporation that would be included in the amount realized on the sale referred to in paragraph (a)(1) of this section, but only if the corporation would be allowed a deduction on payment of the liability; decreased by

(3) The aggregate adjusted bases of the corporation's assets at the time of the sale referred to in paragraph (a)(1) of this section; increased or decreased by

(4) The corporation's section 481 adjustments that would be taken into account on the sale referred to in paragraph (a)(1) of this section; and increased by

(5) Any recognized built-in loss that would not be allowed as a deduction under section 382, 383, or 384 on the sale referred to in paragraph (a)(1) of this section.

(b) *Adjustment to net unrealized built-in gain.*— (1) *In general.*—If section 1374(d)(8) applies to an S corporation's acquisition of assets, some or all of the stock of the corporation from which such assets were acquired was taken into account in the computation of the net unrealized built-in gain for a pool of assets of the S corporation, and some or all of such stock is redeemed or canceled in such transaction, then, subject to the limitations of paragraph (b)(2) of this section, such net unrealized built-in gain is adjusted to eliminate any effect that any built-in gain or built-in loss in the redeemed or canceled stock (other than stock with respect to which a loss under section 165 is claimed) had on the initial computation of net unrealized built-in gain for that pool of assets. For purposes of this paragraph, stock described in section 1374(d)(6) shall be treated as taken into account in the computation of the net unrealized built-in gain for a pool of assets of the S corporation.

(2) *Limitations on adjustment.*—(i) *Recognized built-in gain or loss.*—Net unrealized built-in gain

for a pool of assets of the S corporation is only adjusted under paragraph (b)(1) of this section to reflect built-in gain or built-in loss in the redeemed or canceled stock that has not resulted in recognized built-in gain or recognized built-in loss during the recognition period.

(ii) *Anti-duplication rule.*—Paragraph (b)(1) of this section shall not be applied to duplicate an adjustment to the net unrealized built-in gain for a pool of assets made pursuant to paragraph (b)(1) of this section.

(3) *Effect of adjustment.*—Any adjustment to the net unrealized built-in gain made pursuant to this paragraph (b) only affects computations of the amount subject to tax under section 1374 for taxable years that end on or after the date of the acquisition to which section 1374(d)(8) applies.

(4) *Pool of assets.*—For purposes of this section, a pool of assets means—

(i) The assets held by the corporation on the first day it became an S corporation, if the corporation was previously a C corporation; or

(ii) The assets the S corporation acquired from a C corporation in a section 1374(d)(8) transaction.

(c) *Examples.*—The following examples illustrate the rules of this section:

Example 1. Computation of net unrealized built-in gain. (i)(A) X, a calendar year C corporation using the cash method, elects to become an S corporation on January 1, 1996. On December 31, 1995, X has assets and liabilities as follows:

Assets	FMV	Basis
Factory	$500,000	$900,000
Accounts Receivable	300,000	0
Goodwill	250,000	0
Total	1,050,000	900,000

Liabilities	Amount	
Mortgage	$200,000	
Accounts Payable	100,000	
Total	300,000	

(B) Further, X must include a total of $60,000 in taxable income in 1996, 1997, and 1998 under section 481(a).

(ii) If, on December 31, 1995, X sold all its assets to a third party that assumed all its liabilities, X's amount realized would be $1,050,000 ($750,000 cash received + $300,000 liabilities assumed = $1,050,000). Thus, X's net unrealized built-in gain is determined as follows:

Amount realized	$1,050,000
Deduction allowed (A/P)	(100,000)
Basis of X's assets	(900,000)
Section 481 adjustments	60,000
Net unrealized built-in gain	110,000

Example 2. Adjustment to net unrealized built-in gain for built-in gain in eliminated C corporation stock. (i) X, a calendar year C corporation, elects to become an S corporation effective January 1, 2005. On that date, X's assets (the first pool of assets) have a net unrealized built-in gain of $15,000. Among the assets in the first pool of assets is all of the outstanding stock of Y, a C corporation, with a fair market value of $33,000 and an adjusted basis of $18,000. On March 1, 2009, X sells an asset that it owned on January 1, 2005, and as a result has $10,000 of recognized built-in gain. X has had no other recognized built-in gain or built-in loss. X's taxable income limitation for 2009 is $50,000. Effective June 1, 2009, X elects under section 1361 to treat Y as a qualified subchapter S subsidiary (QSub). The election is treated as a transfer of Y's assets to X in a liquidation to which sections 332 and 337(a) apply.

(ii) Under paragraph (b) of this section, the net unrealized built in-gain of the first pool of assets is adjusted to account for the elimination of the Y stock in the liquidation. The net unrealized built-in gain of the first pool of assets, therefore, is decreased by $15,000, the amount by which the fair market value of the Y stock exceeded its adjusted basis as of January 1, 2005. Accordingly, for taxable years ending after June 1, 2009, the net unrealized built-in gain of the first pool of assets is $0.

(iii) Under § 1.1374-2(a), X's net recognized built-in gain for any taxable year equals the least of X's pre-limitation amount, taxable income limitation, and net unrealized built-in gain limitation. In 2009, X's pre-limitation amount is $10,000, X's taxable income limitation is $50,000, and X's net unrealized built-in gain limitation is $0. Because the net unrealized built-in gain of the first pool of assets has been adjusted to $0, despite the $10,000 of recognized built-in gain in 2009, X has $0 net recognized built-in gain for the taxable year ending on December 31, 2009.

Example 3. Adjustment to net unrealized built-in gain for built-in loss in eliminated C corporation stock. (i) X, a calendar year C corporation, elects to become an S corporation effective January 1, 2005. On that date, X's assets (the first pool of assets) have a net unrealized built-in gain of negative $5,000. Among the assets in the first pool of assets is 10 percent of the outstanding stock of Y, a C corporation, with a fair market value of $18,000 and an adjusted basis of $33,000. On March 1, 2009, X sells an asset that it owned on January 1, 2005, resulting in $8,000 of recognized built-in gain. X has had no other recognized built-in gains or built-in losses. X's taxable income limitation for 2009 is $50,000. On June 1, 2009, Y transfers its assets to X in a reorganization under section 368(a)(1)(C).

(ii) Under paragraph (b) of this section, the net unrealized built in-gain of the first pool of assets is adjusted to account for the elimination of the Y stock in the reorganization. The net unrealized built-in gain of the first pool of assets, therefore, is increased by $15,000, the amount by which the adjusted basis of the Y stock exceeded its fair market value as of January 1, 2005. Accordingly, for taxable years ending after June 1, 2009, the net unrealized built-in gain of the first pool of assets is $10,000.

(iii) Under § 1.1374-2(a), X's net recognized built-in gain for any taxable year equals the least of X's pre-limitation amount, taxable income limitation, and net unrealized built-in gain limitation. In 2009, X's pre-limitation amount is $8,000 and X's taxable income limitation is $50,000. The net unrealized built-in gain of the first pool of assets has been adjusted to $10,000, so X's net unrealized built-in gain limitation is $10,000. X, therefore, has $8,000 net recognized built-in gain for the taxable year ending on December 31, 2009. X's net unrealized built-in gain limitation for 2010 is $2,000.

Example 4. Adjustment to net unrealized built-in gain in case of prior gain recognition. (i) X, a calendar year C corporation, elects to become an S corporation effective January 1, 2005. On that date, X's assets (the first pool of assets) have a net unrealized built-in gain of $30,000. Among the assets in the first pool of assets is all of the outstanding stock of Y, a C corporation, with a fair market value of $45,000 and an adjusted basis of $10,000. Y has no current or accumulated earnings and profits. On April 1, 2007, Y distributes $18,000 to X, $8,000 of which is treated as gain to X from the sale or exchange of property under section 301(c)(3). That $8,000 is recognized built-in gain to X under section 1374(d)(3), and results in $8,000 of net recognized built-in gain to X for 2007. X's net unrealized built-in gain limitation for 2008 is $22,000. On June 1, 2009, Y transfers its assets to X in a liquidation to which sections 332 and 337(a) apply.

(ii) Under paragraph (b) of this section, the net unrealized built in-gain of the first pool of assets is adjusted to account for the elimination of the Y stock in the liquidation. The net unrealized built-in gain of that pool of assets, however, can only be adjusted to reflect the amount of built-in gain that was inherent in the Y stock on January 1, 2005 that has not resulted in recognized built-in gain during the recognition period. In this case, therefore, the net unrealized built-in gain of the first pool of assets cannot be reduced by more than $27,000 ($35,000, the amount by which the fair market value of the Y stock exceeded its adjusted basis as of January 1, 2005, minus $8,000, the recognized built-in gain with respect to the stock during the recognition period). Accordingly, for taxable years ending after June 1, 2009, the net unrealized built-in gain of the first pool of assets is $3,000. The net unrealized built-in gain limitation for 2009 is $0.

[Reg. § 1.1374-3.]

□ [*T.D.* 8579, 12-23-94. *Amended by T.D.* 9180, 2-22-2005.]

[Reg. §1.1374-4]

§1.1374-4. Recognized built-in gain or loss.—(a) *Sales and exchanges.*—(1) *In general.*— Section 1374(d)(3) or 1374(d)(4) applies to any gain or loss recognized during the recognition period in a transaction treated as a sale or exchange for federal income tax purposes.

(2) *Oil and gas property.*—For purposes of paragraph (a)(1) of this section, an S corporation's adjusted basis in oil and gas property equals the sum of the shareholders' adjusted bases in the property as determined in section 613A(c)(11)(B).

(3) *Examples.*—The rules of this paragraph (a) are illustrated by the following examples.

Example 1. Production and sale of oil. X is a C corporation that purchased a working interest in an oil and gas property for $100,000 on July 1, 1993. X elects to become an S corporation effective January 1, 1996. On that date, the working interest has a fair market value of $250,000 and an adjusted basis of $50,000, but no oil has as yet been extracted. In 1996, X begins production of the working interest, sells oil that it has produced to a refinery for $75,000, and includes that amount in gross income. Under paragraph (a)(1) of this section, the $75,000 is not recognized built-in gain because as of the beginning of the recognition period X held only a working interest in the oil and gas property (since the oil had not yet been extracted from the ground), and not the oil itself.

Example 2. Sale of oil and gas property. Y is a C corporation that elects to become an S corporation effective January 1, 1996. Y has two shareholders, A and B. A and B each own 50 percent of Y's stock. In addition, Y owns a royalty interest in an oil and gas property with a fair market value of $300,000 and an adjusted basis of $200,000. Under section 613A(c)(11)(B), Y's $200,000 adjusted basis in the royalty interest is allocated $100,000 to A and $100,000 to B. During 1996, A and B take depletion deductions with respect to the royalty interest of $10,000 and $15,000, respectively. As of January 1, 1997, A and B have a basis in the royalty interest of $90,000 and $85,000, respectively. On January 1, 1997, Y sells the royalty interest for $250,000. Under paragraph (a)(1) of this section, Y has gain recognized and recognized built-in gain of $75,000 ($250,000 − ($90,000 + $85,000) = $75,000) on the sale.

(b) *Accrual method rule.*—(1) *Income items.*— Except as otherwise provided in this section, any item of income properly taken into account during the recognition period is recognized built-in gain if the item would have been properly included in gross income before the beginning of the recognition period by an accrual method taxpayer (disregarding any method of accounting for which an election by the taxpayer must be made unless the taxpayer actually used the method when it was a C corporation).

(2) *Deduction items.*—Except as otherwise provided in this section, any item of deduction properly taken into account during the recognition period is recognized built-in loss if the item would have been properly allowed as a deduction against gross income before the beginning of the recognition period to an accrual method taxpayer (disregarding any method of accounting for which an election by the taxpayer must be made unless the taxpayer actually used the method when it was a C corporation). In determining whether an item would have been properly allowed as a deduction against gross income by an accrual method taxpayer for purposes of this paragraph, section 461(h)(2)(C) and §1.461-4(g) (relating to liabilities for tort, worker's compensation, breach of contract, violation of law, rebates, refunds, awards, prizes, jackpots, insurance contracts, warranty contracts, service contracts, taxes, and other liabilities) do not apply.

(3) *Examples.*—The rules of this paragraph (b) are illustrated by the following examples.

Example 1. Accounts receivable. X is a C corporation using the cash method that elects to become an S corporation effective January 1, 1996. On January 1, 1996, X has $50,000 of accounts receivable for services rendered before that date. On that date, the accounts receivable have a fair market value of $40,000 and an adjusted basis of $0. In 1996, X collects $50,000 on the accounts receivable and includes that amount in gross income. Under paragraph (b)(1) of this section, the $50,000 included in gross income in 1996 is recognized built-in gain because it would have been included in gross income before the beginning of the recognition period if X had been an accrual method taxpayer. However, if X instead disposes of the accounts receivable for $45,000 on July 1, 1996, in a transaction treated as a sale or exchange for federal income tax purposes, X would have recognized built-in gain of $40,000 on the disposition.

Example 2. Contingent liability. Y is a C corporation using the cash method that elects to become an S corporation effective January 1, 1996. In 1995, a lawsuit was filed against Y claiming $1,000,000 in damages. In 1996, Y loses the lawsuit, pays a $500,000 judgment, and properly claims a deduction for that amount. Under paragraph (b)(2) of this section, the $500,000 deduction allowed in 1996 is not recognized built-in loss because it would not have been allowed as a deduction against gross income before the beginning of the recognition period if Y had been an accrual method taxpayer (even disregarding section 461(h)(2)(C) and §1.461-4(g)).

Example 3. Deferred payment liabilities. X is a C corporation using the cash method that elects to become an S corporation on January 1, 1996. In 1995, X lost a lawsuit and became obligated to pay $150,000 in damages. Under section

461(h)(2)(C), this amount is not allowed as a deduction until X makes payment. In 1996, X makes payment and properly claims a deduction for the amount of the payment. Under paragraph (b)(2) of this section, the $150,000 deduction allowed in 1996 is recognized built-in loss because it would have been allowed as a deduction against gross income before the beginning of the recognition period if X had been an accrual method taxpayer (disregarding section 461(h)(2)(C) and §1.461-4(g)).

Example 4. Deferred prepayment income. Y is a C corporation using an accrual method that elects to become an S corporation effective January 1, 1996. In 1995, Y received $2,500 for services to be rendered in 1996, and properly elected to include the $2,500 in gross income in 1996 under Rev. Proc. 71-21, 1971-2 C.B. 549 (see §601.601(d)(2)(ii)(*b*) of this chapter). Under paragraph (b)(1) of this section, the $2,500 included in gross income in 1996 is not recognized built-in gain because it would not have been included in gross income before the beginning of the recognition period by an accrual method taxpayer using the method that Y actually used before the beginning of the recognition period.

Example 5. Change in method. X is a C corporation using an accrual method that elects to become an S corporation effective January 1, 1996. In 1995, X received $5,000 for services to be rendered in 1996, and properly included the $5,000 in gross income. In 1996, X properly elects to include the $5,000 in gross income in 1996 under Rev. Proc. 71-21, 1971-2 C.B. 549 (see §601.601(d)(2)(ii)(*b*) of this chapter). As a result of the change in method of accounting, X has a $5,000 negative section 481(a) adjustment. Under paragraph (b)(1) of this section, the $5,000 included in gross income in 1996 is recognized built-in gain because it would have been included in gross income before the beginning of the recognition period by an accrual method taxpayer using the method that X actually used before the beginning of the recognition period. In addition, the $5,000 negative section 481(a) adjustment is recognized built-in loss because it relates to an item (the $5,000 X received for services in 1995) attributable to periods before the beginning of the recognition period under the principles for determining recognized built-in gain or loss in this section. See paragraph (d) of this section for rules regarding section 481(a) adjustments.

(c) *Section 267(a)(2) and 404(a)(5) deductions.*— (1) *Section 267(a)(2).*—Notwithstanding paragraph (b)(2) of this section, any amount properly deducted in the recognition period under section 267(a)(2), relating to payments to related parties, is recognized built-in loss to the extent—

(i) All events have occurred that establish the fact of the liability to pay the amount, and the exact amount of the liability can be determined, as of the beginning of the recognition period; and

(ii) The amount is paid—

(A) In the first two and one-half months of the recognition period; or

(B) To a related party owning, under the attribution rules of section 267, less than 5 percent, by voting power and value, of the corporation's stock, both as of the beginning of the recognition period and when the amount is paid.

(2) *Section 404(a)(5).*—Notwithstanding paragraph (b)(2) of this section, any amount properly deducted in the recognition period under section 404(a)(5), relating to payments for deferred compensation, is recognized built-in loss to the extent—

(i) All events have occurred that establish the fact of the liability to pay the amount, and the exact amount of the liability can be determined, as of the beginning of the recognition period; and

(ii) The amount is not paid to a related party to which section 267(a)(2) applies.

(3) *Examples.*—The rules of this paragraph (c) are illustrated by the following examples.

Example 1. Fixed annuity. X is a C corporation that elects to become an S corporation effective January 1, 1996. On December 31, 1995, A is age 60, has provided services to X as an employee for 20 years, and is a vested participant in X's unfunded nonqualified retirement plan. Under the plan, A receives $1,000 per month upon retirement until death. The plan provides no additional benefits. A retires on December 31, 1997, after working for X for 22 years. A at no time is a shareholder of X. X's deductions under section 404(a)(5) in the recognition period on paying A the $1,000 per month are recognized built-in loss because all events have occurred that establish the fact of the liability to pay the amount, and the exact amount of the liability can be determined, as of the beginning of the recognition period.

Example 2. Increase in annuity for working beyond 20 years. The facts are the same as *Example 1,* except that under the plan A receives $1,000 per month, plus $100 per month for each year A works for X beyond 20 years, upon retirement until death. X's deductions on paying A the $1,000 per month are recognized built-in loss. However, X's deductions on paying A the $200 per month for the two years A worked for X beyond 20 years are not recognized built-in loss because all events have not occurred that establish the fact of the liability to pay the amount, and the exact amount of the liability cannot be determined, as of the beginning of the recognition period.

Example 3. Cost of living adjustment. The facts are the same as *Example 1,* except that under the plan A receives $1,000 per month, plus annual cost of living adjustments, upon retirement until death. X's deductions under section 404(a)(5) on paying A the $1,000 per month are recognized built-in loss. However, X's deductions under section 404(a)(5) on paying A the annual cost of living adjustment are not recognized built-in loss because all events have not occurred that establish the fact of the liability to pay the amount, and the exact amount of the liability cannot be determined, as of the beginning of the recognition period.

(d) *Section 481(a) adjustments.*—(1) *In general.*—Any section 481(a) adjustment taken into account in the recognition period is recognized built-in gain or loss to the extent the adjustment relates to items attributable to periods before the beginning of the recognition period under the principles for determining recognized built-in gain or loss in this section. The principles for determining recognized built-in gain or loss in this section include, for example, the accrual method rule under paragraph (b) of this section.

(2) *Examples.*—The rules of this paragraph (d) are illustrated by the following examples.

Example 1. Omitted item attributable to pre-recognition period. X is a C corporation that elects to become an S corporation effective January 1, 1996. X improperly capitalizes repair costs and recovers the costs through depreciation of the related assets. In 1999, X properly changes to deducting repair costs as they are incurred. Under section 481(a), the basis of the related assets are reduced by an amount equal to the excess of the repair costs incurred before the year of change over the repair costs recovered through depreciation before the year of change. In addition, X has a negative section 481(a) adjustment equal to the basis reduction. Under paragraph (d)(1) of this section, the portion of X's negative section 481(a) adjustment relating to the repair costs incurred before the recognition period is recognized built-in loss because those repair costs are items attributable to periods before the beginning of the recognition period under the principles for determining recognized built-in gain or loss in this section.

Example 2. Duplicated item attributable to pre-recognition period. Y is a C corporation that elects to become an S corporation effective January 1, 1996. Y improperly uses an accrual method without regard to the economic performance rules of section 461(h) to account for worker's compensation claims. As a result, Y takes deductions when claims are filed. In 1999, Y properly changes to an accrual method with regard to the economic performance rules under section 461(h)(2)(C) for worker's compensation claims. As a result, Y takes deductions when claims are paid. The positive section 481(a) adjustment resulting from the change is equal to the amount of claims filed, but unpaid, before the year of change. Under paragraph (b)(2) of this section, the deduction allowed in the recognition period for claims filed, but unpaid, before the recognition period is recognized built-in loss because a deduction was allowed for those claims before the recognition period under an accrual method without regard to section 461(h)(2)(C). Under paragraph (d)(1) of this section, the portion of Y's positive section 481(a) adjustment relating to claims filed, but unpaid, before the recognition period is recognized built-in gain because those claims are items attributable to periods before the beginning of the recognition period under the principles for determining recognized built-in gain or loss in this section.

(e) *Section 995(b)(2) deemed distributions.*—Any item of income properly taken into account during the recognition period under section 995(b)(2) is recognized built-in gain if the item results from a DISC termination or disqualification occurring before the beginning of the recognition period.

(f) *Discharge of indebtedness and bad debts.*—Any item of income or deduction properly taken into account during the first year of the recognition period as discharge of indebtedness income under section 61(a)(12) or as a bad debt deduction under section 166 is recognized built-in gain or loss if the item arises from a debt owed by or to an S corporation at the beginning of the recognition period.

(g) *Completion of contract.*—Any item of income properly taken into account during the recognition period under the completed contract method (as described in §1.460-4(d)) where the corporation began performance of the contract before the beginning of the recognition period is recognized built-in gain if the item would have been included in gross income before the beginning of the recognition period under the percentage of completion method (as described in §1.460-4(b)). Any similar item of deduction is recognized built-in loss if the item would have been allowed as a deduction against gross income before the beginning of the recognition period under the percentage of completion method.

(h) *Installment method.*—(1) *In general.*—If a corporation sells an asset before or during the recognition period and reports the income from the sale using the installment method under section 453 during or after the recognition period, that income is subject to tax under section 1374.

(2) *Limitation on amount subject to tax.*—For purposes of paragraph (h)(1) of this section, the taxable income limitation under §1.1374-2(a)(2) is equal to the amount by which the S corporation's net recognized built-in gain would have been increased from the year of the sale to the earlier of the year the income is reported under

the installment method or the last year of the recognition period, assuming all income from the sale had been reported in the year of the sale and all provisions of section 1374 applied. For purposes of the preceding sentence, if the corporation sells the asset before the recognition period, the income from the sale that is not reported before the recognition period is treated as having been reported in the first year of the recognition period.

(3) *Rollover rule.*—If the limitation in paragraph (h)(2) of this section applies, the excess of the amount reported under the installment method over the amount subject to tax under the limitation is treated as if it were reported in the succeeding taxable year(s), but only for succeeding taxable year(s) in the recognition period. The amount reported in the succeeding taxable year(s) under the preceding sentence is reduced to the extent that the amount not subject to tax under the limitation in paragraph (h)(2) of this section was not subject to tax because the S corporation had an excess of recognized built-in loss over recognized built-in gain in the taxable year of the sale and succeeding taxable year(s) in the recognition period.

(4) *Use of losses and section 1374 attributes.*— If income is reported under the installment method by an S corporation for a taxable year after the recognition period and the income is subject to tax under paragraph (h)(1) of this section, the S corporation's section 1374 attributes may be used to the extent their use is allowed under all applicable provisions of the Code in determining the section 1374 tax. However, the S corporation's loss recognized for a taxable year after the recognition period that would have been recognized built-in loss if it had been recognized in the recognition period may not be used in determining the section 1374 tax.

(5) *Examples.*—The rules of this paragraph (h) are illustrated by the following examples.

Example 1. Rollover rule. X is a C corporation that elects to become an S corporation effective January 1, 1996. On that date, X sells Blackacre with a basis of $0 and a value of $100,000 in exchange for a $100,000 note bearing a market rate of interest payable on January 1, 2001. X does not make the election under section 453(d) and, therefore, reports the $100,000 gain using the installment method under section 453. In the year 2001, X has income of $100,000 on collecting the note, unexpired C year attributes of $0, recognized built-in loss of $0, current losses of $100,000, and taxable income of $0. If X had reported the $100,000 gain in 1996, X's net recognized built-in gain from 1996 through 2001 would have been $75,000 greater than otherwise. Under paragraph (h) of this section, X has $75,000 net recognized built-in gain subject to tax under section 1374. X also must treat the $25,000 excess of the amount reported, $100,000, over the

amount subject to tax, $75,000, as income reported under the installment method in the succeeding taxable year(s) in the recognition period, except to the extent X establishes that the $25,000 was not subject to tax under section 1374 in the year 2001 because X had an excess of recognized built-in loss over recognized built-in gain in the taxable year of the sale and succeeding taxable year(s) in the recognition period.

Example 2. Use of losses. Y is a C corporation that elects to become an S corporation effective January 1, 1996. On that date, Y sells Whiteacre with a basis of $0 and a value of $250,000 in exchange for a $250,000 note bearing a market rate of interest payable on January 1, 2006. Y does not make the election under section 453(d) and, therefore, reports the $250,000 gain using the installment method under section 453. In the year 2006, Y has income of $250,000 on collecting the note, unexpired C year attributes of $0, loss of $100,000 that would have been recognized built-in loss if it had been recognized in the recognition period, current losses of $150,000, and taxable income of $0. If Y had reported the $250,000 gain in 1996, X's net recognized built-in gain from 1996 through 2005 (that is, during the recognition period) would have been $225,000 greater than otherwise. Under paragraph (h) of this section, X has $225,000 net recognized built-in gain subject to tax under section 1374.

Example 3. Use of section 1374 attribute. Z is a C corporation that elects to become an S corporation effective January 1, 1996. On that date, Z sells Greenacre with a basis of $0 and a value of $500,000 in exchange for a $500,000 note bearing a market rate of interest payable on January 1, 2011. Z does not make the election under section 453(d) and, therefore, reports the $500,000 gain using the installment method under section 453. In the year 2011, Z has income of $500,000 on collecting the note, loss of $0 that would have been recognized built-in loss if it had been recognized in the recognition period, current losses of $0, taxable income of $500,000, and a minimum tax credit of $60,000 arising in 1995. None of Z's minimum tax credit is limited under sections 53(c) or 383. If Z had reported the $500,000 gain in 1996, Z's net recognized built-in gain from 1996 through 2005 (that is, during the recognition period) would have been $350,000 greater than otherwise. Under paragraph (h) of this section, Z has $350,000 net recognized built-in gain subject to tax under section 1374, a tentative section 1374 tax of $122,500 ($350,000 × .35 = $122,500), and a section 1374 tax after using its minimum tax credit arising in 1995 of $62,250 ($122,500 − $60,000 = $62,250).

(i) *Partnership interests.*—(1) *In general.*—If an S corporation owns a partnership interest at the beginning of the recognition period or transfers property to a partnership in a transaction to which section 1374(d)(6) applies during the recognition period, the S corporation determines the effect on net recognized built-in gain from its distributive share of partnership items as follows—

(i) Step One: Apply the rules of section 1374(d) to the S corporation's distributive share of partnership items of income, gain, loss, or deduction included in income or allowed as a deduction under the rules of subchapter K to determine the extent to which it would have been treated as recognized built-in gain or loss if the partnership items had originated in and been taken into account directly by the S corporation (partnership 1374 items);

(ii) Step Two: Determine the S corporation's net recognized built-in gain without partnership 1374 items;

(iii) Step Three: Determine the S corporation's net recognized built-in gain with partnership 1374 items; and

(iv) Step Four: If the amount computed under Step Three (paragraph (i)(1)(iii) of this section) exceeds the amount computed under Step Two (paragraph (i)(1)(ii) of this section), the excess (as limited by paragraph (i)(2)(i) of this section) is the S corporation's partnership RBIG, and the S corporation's net recognized built-in gain is the sum of the amount computed under Step Two (paragraph (i)(1)(ii) of this section) plus the partnership RBIG. If the amount computed under Step Two (paragraph (i)(1)(ii) of this section) exceeds the amount computed under Step Three (paragraph (i)(1)(iii) of this section), the excess (as limited by paragraph (i)(2)(ii) of this section) is the S corporation's partnership RBIL, and the S corporation's net recognized built-in gain is the remainder of the amount computed under Step Two (paragraph (i)(1)(ii) of this section) after subtracting the partnership RBIL.

(2) *Limitations.*—(i) *Partnership RBIG.*—An S corporation's partnership RBIG for any taxable year may not exceed the excess (if any) of the S corporation's RBIG limitation over its partnership RBIG for prior taxable years. The preceding sentence does not apply if a corporation forms or avails of a partnership with a principal purpose of avoiding the tax imposed under section 1374.

(ii) *Partnership RBIL.*—An S corporation's partnership RBIL for any taxable year may not exceed the excess (if any) of the S corporation's RBIL limitation over its partnership RBIL for prior taxable years.

(3) *Disposition of partnership interest.*—If an S corporation disposes of its partnership interest, the amount that may be treated as recognized built-in gain may not exceed the excess (if any) of the S corporation's RBIG limitation over its partnership RBIG during the recognition period. Similarly, the amount that may be treated as recognized built-in loss may not exceed the excess (if any) of the S corporation's RBIL limitation over its partnership RBIL during the recognition period.

(4) *RBIG and RBIL limitations.*—(i) *Sale of partnership interest.*—An S corporation's RBIG or RBIL limitation is the total of the following—

(A) The amount that would be the amount realized if, at the beginning of the first day of the recognition period, the corporation had remained a C corporation and had sold its partnership interest (and any assets the corporation contributed to the partnership during the recognition period) at fair market value to an unrelated party; decreased by

(B) The corporation's adjusted basis in the partnership interest (and any assets the corporation contributed to the partnership during the recognition period) at the time of the sale referred to in paragraph (i)(4)(i)(A) of this section; and increased or decreased by

(C) The corporation's allocable share of the partnership's section 481(a) adjustments at the time of the sale referred to in paragraph (i)(4)(i)(A) of this section.

(ii) *Amounts of limitations.*—If the result in paragraph (i)(4)(i) of this section is a positive amount, the S corporation has a RBIG limitation equal to that amount and a RBIL limitation of $0, but if the result in paragraph (i)(4)(i) of this section is a negative amount, the S corporation has a RBIL limitation equal to that amount and a RBIG limitation of $0.

(5) *Small interest exception.*—(i) *In general.*—Paragraph (i)(1) of this section does not apply to a taxable year in the recognition period if the S corporation's partnership interest represents less than 10 percent of the partnership's capital and profits at all times during the taxable year and prior taxable years in the recognition period, and the fair market value of the S corporation's partnership interest as of the beginning of the recognition period is less than $100,000.

(ii) *Contributed assets.*—For purposes of paragraph (i)(5)(i) of this section, if the S corporation contributes any assets to the partnership during the recognition period and the S corporation held the assets as of the beginning of the recognition period, the fair market value of the S corporation's partnership interest as of the beginning of the recognition period is determined as if the assets were contributed to the partnership before the beginning of the recognition period (using the fair market value of each contributed asset as of the beginning of the recognition period). The contribution does not affect whether paragraph (i)(5)(i) of this section applies for taxable years in the recognition period before the taxable year in which the contribution was made.

(iii) *Anti-abuse rule.*—Paragraph (i)(5)(i) of this section does not apply if a corporation forms or avails of a partnership with a principal purpose of avoiding the tax imposed under section 1374.

(6) *Section 704(c) gain or loss.*—Solely for purposes of section 1374, an S corporation's section 704(c) gain or loss amount with respect to any asset is not reduced during the recognition period, except for amounts treated as recognized built-in gain or loss with respect to that asset under this paragraph.

(7) *Disposition of distributed partnership asset.*—If on the first day of the recognition period an S corporation holds an interest in a partnership that holds an asset and during the recognition period the partnership distributes the asset to the S corporation that thereafter disposes of the asset, the asset is treated as having been held by the S corporation on the first day of the recognition period and as having the fair market value and adjusted basis in the hands of the S corporation that it had in the hands of the partnership on that day.

(8) *Examples.*—The rules of this paragraph (i) are illustrated by the following examples.

Example 1. Pre-conversion partnership interest. X is a C corporation that elects to become an S corporation on January 1, 1996. On that date, X owns a 50 percent interest in partnership P and P owns (among other assets) Blackacre with a basis of $25,000 and a value of $45,000. In 1996, P buys Whiteacre for $50,000. In 1999, P sells Blackacre for $55,000 and recognizes a gain of $30,000 of which $15,000 is included in X's distributive share. P also sells Whiteacre in 1999 for $42,000 and recognizes a loss of $8,000 of which $4,000 is included in X's distributive share. Under this paragraph and section 1374(d)(3), X's $15,000 gain is presumed to be recognized built-in gain and thus treated as a partnership 1374 item, but this presumption is rebutted if X establishes that P's gain would have been only $20,000 ($45,000 − $25,000 = $20,000) if Blackacre had been sold on the first day of the recognition period. In such a case, only X's distributive share of the $20,000 built-in gain, $10,000, would be treated as a partnership 1374 item. Under this paragraph and section 1374(d)(4), X's $4,000 loss is not treated as a partnership 1374 item because P did not hold Whiteacre on the first day of the recognition period.

Example 2. Post-conversion contribution. Y is a C corporation that elects to become an S corporation on January 1, 1996. On that date, Y owns (among other assets) Blackacre with a basis of $100,000 and a value of $200,000. On January 1, 1998, when Blackacre has a basis of $100,000 and a value of $200,000, Y contributes Blackacre to partnership P for a 50 percent interest in P. On January 1, 2000, P sells Blackacre for $300,000 and recognizes a gain of $200,000 on the sale ($300,000 − $100,000 = $200,000). P is allocated $100,000 of the gain under section 704(c), and another $50,000 of the gain for its fifty percent share of the remainder, for a total of $150,000. Under this paragraph and section 1374(d)(3), if Y establishes that P's gain would have been only $100,000 ($200,000 − $100,000 = $100,000) if Blackacre had been sold on the first day of the recognition period, Y would treat only $100,000 as a partnership 1374 item.

Example 3. RBIG limitation of $100,000 or $50,000. X is a C corporation that elects to become an S corporation on January 1, 1996. On that date, X owns a 50 percent interest in partnership P with a RBIG limitation of $100,000 and a RBIL limitation of $0. P owns (among other assets) Blackacre with a basis of $50,000 and a value of $200,000. In 1996, P sells Blackacre for $200,000 and recognizes a gain of $150,000 of which $75,000 is included in X's distributive share and treated as a partnership 1374 item. X's net recognized built-in gain for 1996 computed without partnership 1374 items is $35,000 and with partnership 1374 items is $110,000. Thus, X has a partnership RBIG of $75,000 except as limited under paragraph (i)(2)(i) of this section. Because X's RBIG limitation is $100,000, X's partnership RBIG of $75,000 is not limited and X's net recognized built-in gain for the year is $110,000 ($35,000 + $75,000 = $110,000). However, if X had a RBIG limitation of $50,000 instead of $100,000, X's partnership RBIG would be limited to $50,000 under paragraph (i)(2)(i) of this section and X's net recognized built-in gain would be $85,000 ($35,000 + $50,000 = $85,000).

Example 4. RBIL limitation of $60,000 or $40,000. Y is a C corporation that elects to become an S corporation on January 1, 1996. On that date, Y owns a 50 percent interest in partnership P with a RBIG limitation of $0 and a RBIL limitation of $60,000. P owns (among other assets) Blackacre with a basis of $225,000 and a value of $125,000. In 1996, P sells Blackacre for $125,000 and recognizes a loss of $100,000 of which $50,000 is included in Y's distributive share and treated as a partnership 1374 item. Y's net recognized built-in gain for 1996 computed without partnership 1374 items is $75,000 and with partnership 1374 items is $25,000. Thus, Y has a partnership RBIL of $50,000 for the year except as limited under paragraph (i)(2)(ii) of this section. Because Y's RBIL limitation is $60,000, Y's partnership RBIL for the year is not limited and Y's net recognized built-in gain for the year is $25,000 ($75,000 − $50,000 = $25,000). However, if Y had a RBIL limitation of $40,000 instead of $60,000, Y's partnership RBIL would be limited to $40,000 under paragraph (i)(2)(ii) of this section and Y's net recognized built-in gain for the year would be $35,000 ($75,000 − $40,000 = $35,000).

Example 5. RBIG limitation of $0. (i) X is a C corporation that elects to become an S corporation on January 1, 1996. X owns a 50 percent interest in partnership P with a RBIG limitation of $0 and a RBIL limitation of $25,000.

(a) In 1996, P's partnership 1374 items are—

(1) Ordinary income of $25,000; and

(2) Capital gain of $75,000.

(b) X itself has—

(1) Recognized built-in ordinary income of $40,000; and

(2) Recognized built-in capital loss of $90,000.

(ii) X's net recognized built-in gain for 1996 computed without partnership 1374 items is $40,000 and with partnership 1374 items is $65,000 ($40,000 + $25,000 = $65,000). Thus, X's partnership RBIG is $25,000 for the year except as limited under paragraph (i)(2)(i) of this section. Because X's RBIG limitation is $0, X's partnership RBIG of $25,000 is limited to $0 and X's net recognized built-in gain for the year is $40,000.

Example 6. RBIL limitation of $0. (i) Y is a C corporation that elects to become an S corporation on January 1, 1996. Y owns a 50 percent interest in partnership P with a RBIG limitation of $60,000 and a RBIL limitation of $0.

(a) In 1996, P's partnership 1374 items are—

(1) Ordinary income of $25,000; and

(2) Capital loss of $90,000.

(b) Y itself has—

(1) recognized built-in ordinary income of $40,000; and

(2) recognized built-in capital gain of $75,000.

(ii) Y's net recognized built-in gain for 1996 computed without partnership 1374 items is $115,000 ($40,000 + $75,000 = $115,000) and with partnership 1374 items is $65,000 ($40,000 + $25,000 = $65,000). Thus, Y's partnership RBIL is $50,000 for the year except as limited under paragraph (i)(2)(ii) of this section. Because Y's RBIL limitation is $0, Y's partnership RBIL of $50,000 is limited to $0 and Y's net recognized built-in gain is $115,000.

Example 7. Disposition of partnership interest. X is a C corporation that elects to become an S corporation on January 1, 1996. On that date, X owns a 50 percent interest in partnership P with a RBIG limitation of $200,000 and a RBIL limitation of $0. P owns (among other assets) Blackacre with a basis of $20,000 and a value of $140,000. In 1996, P sells Blackacre for $140,000 and recognizes a gain of $120,000 of which $60,000 is included in X's distributive share and treated as a partnership 1374 item. X's net recognized built-in gain for 1996 computed without partnership 1374 items is $95,000 and with partnership 1374 items is $155,000. Thus, X has a partnership RBIG of $60,000. In 1999, X sells its entire interest in P for $350,000 and recognizes a gain of $250,000. Under paragraph (i)(3) of this section, X's recognized built-in gain on the sale is limited by its RBIG limitation to $140,000 ($200,000 – $60,000 = $140,000).

Example 8. Section 704(c) case. Y is a C corporation that elects to become an S corporation on January 1, 1996. On that date, Y contributes Asset 1, 5-year property with a value of $40,000 and a basis of $0, and an unrelated party contributes $40,000 in cash, each for a 50 percent interest in

partnership P. The partnership adopts the traditional method under § 1.704-3(b). If P sold Asset 1 for $40,000 immediately after it was contributed by Y, P's $40,000 gain would be allocated to Y under section 704(c). Instead, Asset 1 is sold by P in 1999 for $36,000 and P recognizes gain of $36,000 ($36,000 – $0 = $36,000) on the sale. However, because book depreciation of $8,000 per year has been taken on Asset 1 in 1996, 1997, and 1998, Y is allocated only $16,000 of P's $36,000 gain ($40,000 – (3 × $8,000) = ($16,000 – $0) = $16,000) under section 704(c). The remaining $20,000 of P's $36,000 gain ($36,000 – $16,000 = $20,000) is allocated 50 percent to each partner under section 704(b). Thus, a total of $26,000 ($16,000 + $10,000 = $26,000) of P's $36,000 gain is allocated to Y. However, under paragraph (i)(6) of this section, Y treats $36,000 as a partnership 1374 item on P's sale of Asset 1.

Example 9. Disposition of distributed partnership asset. X is a C corporation that elects to become an S corporation on January 1, 1996. On that date, X owns a fifty percent interest in partnership P and P owns (among other assets) Blackacre with a basis of $20,000 and a value of $40,000. On January 1, 1998, P distributes Blackacre to X, when Blackacre has a basis of $20,000 and a value of $50,000. Under section 732(a)(1), X has a transferred basis of $20,000 in Blackacre. On January 1, 1999, X sells Blackacre for $60,000 and recognizes a gain of $40,000. Under paragraph (i)(7) of this section and section 1374(d)(3), X has recognized built-in gain from the sale of $20,000, the amount of built-in gain in Blackacre on the first day of the recognition period. [Reg. § 1.1374-4.]

☐ [*T.D.* 8579, 12-23-94. *Amended by T.D.* 8995, 5-14-2002.]

[Reg. § 1.1374-5]

§ 1.1374-5. Loss carryforwards.—(a) *In general.*—The loss carryforwards allowed as deductions against net recognized built-in gain under section 1374(b)(2) are allowed only to the extent their use is allowed under the rules applying to C corporations. Any other loss carryforwards, such as charitable contribution carryforwards under section 170(d)(2), are not allowed as deductions against net recognized built-in gain.

(b) *Example.*—The rules of this section are illustrated by the following example.

Example. Section 382 limitation. X is a C corporation that has an ownership change under section 382(g)(1) on January 1, 1994. On that date, X has a fair market value of $500,000, NOL carryforwards of $400,000, and a net unrealized built-in gain under section 382(h)(3)(A) of $0. Assume X's section 382 limitation under section 382(b)(1) is $40,000. X elects to become an S corporation on January 1, 1998. On that date, X has NOL carryforwards of $240,000 (having used $160,000 of its pre-change net operating losses in its 4 preceding taxable years) and a section 1374 net unrealized built-in gain of $250,000. In 1998, X has net recognized built-in gain of $100,000. X may use $40,000 of its NOL carryforwards as a deduction against its $100,000 net recognized built-in gain, because X's section 382 limitation is $40,000. [Reg. § 1.1374-5.]

[T.D. 8579, 12-23-94.]

[Reg. § 1.1374-6]

§ 1.1374-6. Credits and credit carryforwards.—(a) *In general.*—The credits and credit carryforwards allowed as credits against the section 1374 tax under section 1374(b)(3) are allowed only to the extent their use is allowed under the rules applying to C corporations. Any other credits or credit carryforwards, such as foreign tax credits under section 901, are not allowed as credits against the section 1374 tax.

(b) *Limitations.*—The amount of business credit carryforwards and minimum tax credit allowed against the section 1374 tax are subject to the limitations described in section 38(c) and section 53(c), respectively, as modified by this paragraph. The tentative tax determined under paragraph (a)(3) of § 1.1374-1 is treated as the regular tax liability described in sections 38(c)(1) and 53(c)(1), and as the net income tax and net regular tax liability described in section 38(c)(1). The tentative minimum tax described in section 55(b) is determined using the rate of tax applicable to corporations and without regard to any alternative minimum tax foreign tax credit described in that section and by treating the net recognized built-in gain determined under § 1.1374-2, modified to take into account the adjustments of sections 56 and 58 applicable to corporations and the preferences of section 57, as the alternative minimum taxable income described in section 55(b)(2).

(c) *Examples.*—The rules of this section are illustrated by the following examples.

Example 1. Business credit carryforward. X is a C corporation that elects to become an S corporation effective January 1, 1996. On that date, X has a $500,000 business credit carryforward from a C year and Asset #1 with a fair market value of $400,000, a basis for regular tax purposes of $95,000, and a basis for alternative minimum tax purposes of $150,000. In 1996, X has net recognized built-in gain of $305,000 from selling Asset #1 for $400,000. Thus, X's tentative tax under paragraph (a)(3) of § 1.1374-1 and regular tax liability under paragraph (b) of this section is $106,750 ($400,000 − $95,000 = $305,000 × .35 = $106,750, assuming a 35 percent tax rate). Also, X's tentative minimum tax determined under paragraph (b) of this section is $47,000 [$400,000 − $150,000 = $250,000 − $15,000 ($40,000 corporate exemption amount − $25,000 phase-out = $15,000) = $235,000 × .20 = $47,000, assuming a 20 percent tax rate]. Thus, the business credit limitation under section 38(c) is $59,750 [$106,750

− $47,000 (the greater of $47,000 or $20,438 (.25 × $81,750 ($106,750 − $25,000 = $81,750))) = $59,750]. As a result, X's section 1374 tax is $47,000 ($106,750 − $59,750 = $47,000) for 1996 and X has $440,250 ($500,000 − $59,750 = $440,250) of business credit carryforwards for succeeding taxable years.

Example 2. Minimum tax credit. Y is a C corporation that elects to become an S corporation effective January 1, 1996. On that date, Asset #1 has a fair market value of $5,000,000, a basis for regular tax purposes of $4,000,000, and a basis for alternative minimum tax purposes of $4,750,000. Y also has a minimum tax credit of $310,000 from 1995. Y has no other assets, no net operating or capital loss carryforwards, and no business credit carryforwards. In 1996, Y's only transaction is the sale of Asset #1 for $5,000,000. Therefore, Y has net recognized built-in gain in 1996 of $1,000,000 ($5,000,000 − $4,000,000 = $1,000,000) and a tentative tax under paragraph (a)(3) of § 1.1374-1 of $350,000 ($1,000,000 × .35 = $350,000, assuming a 35 percent tax rate). Also, Y's tentative minimum tax determined under paragraph (b) of this section is $47,000 [$5,000,000 − $4,750,000 = $250,000 − $15,000 ($40,000 corporate exemption amount − $25,000 phase-out = $15,000) = $235,000 × .20 = $47,000, assuming a 20 percent tax rate]. Thus, Y may use its minimum tax credit in the amount of $303,000 ($350,000 − $47,000 = $303,000) to offset its section 1374 tentative tax. As a result, Y's section 1374 tax is $47,000 ($350,000 − $303,000 = $47,000) in 1996 and Y has a minimum tax credit attributable to years for which Y was a C corporation of $7,000 ($310,000 − $303,000 = $7,000). [Reg. § 1.1374-6.]

[T.D. 8579, 12-23-94.]

[Reg. § 1.1374-7]

§ 1.1374-7. Inventory.—(a) *Valuation.*—The fair market value of the inventory of an S corporation on the first day of the recognition period equals the amount that a willing buyer would pay a willing seller for the inventory in a purchase of all the S corporation's assets by a buyer that expects to continue to operate the S corporation's business. For purposes of the preceding sentence, the buyer and seller are presumed not to be under any compulsion to buy or sell and to have reasonable knowledge of all relevant facts.

(b) *Identity of dispositions.*—The inventory method used by an S corporation for tax purposes must be used to identify whether the inventory it disposes of during the recognition period is inventory it held on the first day of that period. Thus, a corporation using the LIFO method does not dispose of inventory it held on the first day of the recognition period unless the carrying value of its inventory for a taxable year during that period is less than the carrying value of its inventory on the first day of the recognition period (determined using the LIFO method as described in section 472). However, if a corporation changes its method of accounting for inventory (for example, from the FIFO method to the LIFO method or from the LIFO method to the FIFO method) with a principal purpose of avoiding the tax imposed under section 1374, it must use its former method to identify its dispositions of inventory. [Reg. § 1.1374-7.]

☐ [T.D. 8579, 12-23-94.]

[Reg. § 1.1374-8]

§ 1.1374-8. Section 1374(d)(8) transactions.—
(a) *In general.*—If any S corporation acquires any asset in a transaction in which the S corporation's basis in the asset is determined (in whole or in part) by reference to a C corporation's basis in the assets (or any other property) (a section 1374(d)(8) transaction), section 1374 applies to the net recognized built-in gain attributable to the assets acquired in any section 1374(d)(8) transaction.

(b) *Effective date of section 1374(d)(8).*—Section 1374(d)(8) applies to any section 1374(d)(8) transaction, as defined in paragraph (a)(1) of this section, that occurs on or after December 27, 1994, without regard to the date of the corporation's election to be an S corporation under section 1362.

(c) *Separate determination of tax.*—For purposes of the tax imposed under section 1374(d)(8), a separate determination of tax is made with respect to the assets the S corporation acquires in one section 1374(d)(8) transaction from the assets the S corporation acquires in another section 1374(d)(8) transaction and from the assets the corporation held when it became an S corporation. Thus, an S corporation's section 1374 attributes when it became an S corporation may only be used to reduce the section 1374 tax imposed on dispositions of assets the S corporation held at that time. Similarly, an S corporation's section 1374 attributes acquired in a section 1374(d)(8) transaction may only be used to reduce a section 1374 tax imposed on dispositions of assets the S corporation acquired in the same transaction. If an S corporation makes QSub elections under section 1361(b)(3) for a tiered group of subsidiaries effective on the same day, see § 1.1361-4(b)(2).

(d) *Taxable income limitation.*—For purposes of paragraph (a) of this section, an S corporation's taxable income limitation under § 1.1374-2(a)(2) for any taxable year is allocated between or among each of the S corporation's separate determinations of net recognized built-in gain for that year (determined without regard to the taxable income limitation) based on the ratio of each of those determinations to the sum of all of those determinations.

(e) *Examples.*—The rules of this section are illustrated by the following examples.

Example 1. Separate determination of tax. (i) X is a C corporation that elected to become an S corporation effective January 1, 1986 (before section 1374 was amended in the Tax Reform Act of 1986). X has a net operating loss carryforward of $20,000 arising in 1985 when X was a C corporation. On January 1, 1996, Y (an unrelated C corporation) merges into X in a transaction to which section 368(a)(1)(A) applies. Y has no loss carryforwards, credits, or credit carryforwards. The assets X acquired from Y are subject to tax under section 1374 and have a net unrealized built-in gain of $150,000.

(ii) In 1996, X has a pre-limitation amount of $50,000 on dispositions of assets acquired from Y and a taxable income limitation of $100,000 (because only one group of assets is subject to section 1374, there is no allocation of the taxable income limitation). As a result, X has a net recognized built-in gain on those assets of $50,000. X's $20,000 net operating loss carryforward may not be used as a deduction against its $50,000 net recognized built-in gain on the assets X acquired from Y. Therefore, X has a section 1374 tax of $17,500 ($50,000 × .35 = $17,500, assuming a 35 percent tax rate) for its 1996 taxable year.

Example 2. Allocation of taxable income limitation. (i) Y is a C corporation that elects to become an S corporation effective January 1, 1996. The assets Y holds when it becomes an S corporation have a net unrealized built-in gain of $5,000. Y has no loss carryforwards, credits, or credit carryforwards. On January 1, 1997, Z (an unrelated C corporation) merges into Y in a transaction to which section 368(a)(1)(A) applies. Z has no loss carryforwards, credits, or credit carryforwards. The assets Y acquired from Z are subject to tax under section 1374 and have a net unrealized built-in gain of $80,000.

(ii) In 1997, Y has a pre-limitation amount on the assets it held when it became an S corporation of $15,000, a pre-limitation amount on the assets Y acquired from Z of $15,000, and a taxable income limitation of $10,000. However, because the assets Y held on becoming an S corporation have a net unrealized built-in gain of $5,000, its net recognized built-in gain on those assets is limited to $5,000 before taking into account the taxable income limitation. Y's taxable income limitation of $10,000 is allocated between the assets Y held on becoming an S corporation and the assets Y acquired from Z for purposes of determining the net recognized built-in gain from each pool of assets. Thus, Y's net recognized built-in gain on the assets Y held on becoming an S corporation is $2,500 [$10,000 × ($5,000/$20,000) = $2,500]. Y's net recognized built-in gain on the assets Y acquired from Z is $7,500 [$10,000 × ($15,000/$20,000) = $7,500]. Therefore, Y has a section 1374 tax of $3,500 [($2,500 + $7,500) × .35 = $3,500, assuming a 35 percent tax rate] for its 1997 taxable year.

[Reg. § 1.1374-8.]

☐ [*T.D.* 8579, 12-23-94. *Amended by T.D.* 8869, 1-20-2000; *T.D.* 9170, 12-21-2004 *and T.D.* 9236, 12-20-2005.]

[Reg. §1.1374-9]

§1.1374-9. Anti-stuffing rule.—If a corporation acquires an asset before or during the recognition period with a principal purpose of avoiding the tax imposed under section 1374, the asset and any loss, deduction, loss carryforward, credit, or credit carryforward attributable to the asset is disregarded in determining the S corporation's pre-limitation amount, taxable income limitation, net unrealized built-in gain limitation, deductions against net recognized built-in gain, and credits against the section 1374 tax. [Reg. §1.1374-9.]

☐ [*T.D.* 8579, 12-23-94.]

[Reg. §1.1374-10]

§1.1374-10. Effective date and additional rules.—(a) *In general.*—Sections 1.1374-1 through 1.1374-9, other than §1.1374-3(b) and (c) *Examples* 2 through 4, apply for taxable years ending on or after December 27, 1994, but only in cases where the S corporation's return for the taxable year is filed pursuant to an S election or a section 1374(d)(8) transaction occurring on or after December 27, 1994. Section 1.1374-3(b) and (c) *Examples* 2 through 4 apply to section 1374(d)(8) transactions that occur in taxable years beginning after February 23, 2005. In addition, an S corporation may apply §1.1374-3(b) and (c) *Examples* 2 through 4 to section 1374(d)(8) transactions that occur in taxable years beginning on or before February 23, 2005, if the S corporation (and any predecessors or successors) and all affected shareholders file original or amended returns that are consistent with these provisions for taxable years of the S corporation during the recognition period of the pool of assets the net unrealized built-in gain of which would be adjusted pursuant to those provisions that are not closed as of the first date after February 23, 2005 that the S corporation files an original or amended return. For purposes of this section, affected shareholders means all shareholders who received contributive shares of S corporation items in such taxable years. However, the Commissioner may, in appropriate circumstances, permit taxpayers to apply these provisions even if all affected shareholders cannot file consistent returns. In addition, for this purpose, a predecessor of an S corporation is a corporation that transfers its assets to the S corporation in a transaction to which section 381 applies. A successor of an S corporation is a corporation to which the S corporation transfers its assets in a transaction to which section 381 applies.

(b) *Additional rules.*—This paragraph (b) provides rules applicable to certain S corporations,

assets, or transactions to which §§1.1374-1 through 1.1374-9 do not apply.

(1) *Certain transfers to partnerships.*—If a corporation transfers an asset to a partnership in a transaction to which section 721(a) applies and the transfer is made in contemplation of an S election or during the recognition period, section 1374 applies on a disposition of the asset by the partnership as if the S corporation had disposed of the asset itself. This paragraph (b)(1) applies as of the effective date of section 1374, unless the recognition period with respect to the contributed asset is pursuant to an S election or a section 1374(d)(8) transaction occurring on or after December 27, 1994.

(2) *Certain inventory dispositions.*—For purposes of section 1374(d)(2)(A), the inventory method used by the taxpayer for tax purposes (FIFO, LIFO, etc.) must be used to identify whether goods disposed of following conversion to S corporation status were held by the corporation at the time of conversion. Thus, for example, a corporation using the LIFO inventory method will not be subject to the built-in gain tax with respect to sales of inventory except to the extent that a LIFO layer existing prior to the beginning of the first taxable year as an S corporation is invaded after the beginning of that year. This paragraph (b)(2) applies as of the effective date of section 1374, unless the recognition period with respect to the inventory is pursuant to an S election or a section 1374(d)(8) transaction occurring on or after December 27, 1994.

(3) *Certain contributions of built-in loss assets.*—If a built-in loss asset (that is, an asset with an adjusted tax basis in excess of its fair market value) is contributed to a corporation within 2 years before the earlier of the beginning of its first taxable year as an S corporation, or the filing of its S election, the loss inherent in the asset will not reduce net unrealized built-in gain, as defined in section 1374(d)(1), unless the taxpayer demonstrates a clear and substantial relationship between the contributed property and the conduct of the corporation's current or future business enterprises. This paragraph (b)(3) applies as of the effective date of section 1374, unless the recognition period with respect to the contributed asset is pursuant to an S election or a section 1374(d)(8) transaction occurring on or after December 27, 1994.

(4) *Certain installment sales.*—(i) *In general.*—If a taxpayer sells an asset either prior to or during the recognition period and recognizes income either during or after the recognition period from the sale under the installment method, the income will, when recognized, be taxed under section 1374 to the extent it would have been so taxed in prior taxable years if the selling corporation had made the election under section 453(d) not to report the income under the installment method. For purposes of determin-

ing the extent to which the income would have been subject to tax if the section 453(d) election had not been made, the taxable income limitation of section 1374(d)(2)(A)(ii) and the built-in gain carryover rule of section 1374(d)(2)(B) will be taken into account. This paragraph (b)(4) applies for installment sales occurring on or after March 26, 1990, and before December 27, 1994.

(ii) *Examples.*—The rules of this paragraph (b)(4) are illustrated by the following examples.

Example 1. In year 1 of the recognition period under section 1374, a corporation realizes a gain of $100,000 on the sale of an asset with built-in gain. The corporation is to receive full payment for the asset in year 11. Because the corporation does not make an election under section 453(d), all $100,000 of the gain from the sale is reported under the installment method in year 11. If the corporation had made an election under section 453(d) with respect to the sale, the gain would have been recognized in year 1 and, taking into account the corporation's income and gains from other sources, application of the taxable income limitation of section 1374(d)(2)(A)(ii) and the built-in gain carryover rule of section 1374(d)(2)(B) would have resulted in $40,000 of the gain being subject to tax during the recognition period under section 1374. Therefore, $40,000 of the gain recognized in year 11 is subject to tax under section 1374.

Example 2. In year 1 of the recognition period under section 1374, a corporation realizes a gain of $100,000 on the sale of an asset with built-in gain. The corporation is to receive full payment for the asset in year 6. Because the corporation does not make an election under section 453(d), all $100,000 of the gain from the sale is reported under the installment method in year 6. If the corporation had made an election under section 453(d) with respect to the sale, the gain would have been recognized in year 1 and, taking into account the corporation's income and gains from other sources, application of the taxable income limitation of section 1374(d)(2)(A)(ii) and the built-in gain carryover rule of section 1374(d)(2)(B) would have resulted in all of the gain being subjected to tax under section 1374 in years 1 through 5. Therefore, notwithstanding that the taxable income limitation of section 1374(d)(2)(A)(ii) might otherwise limit the taxation of the gain recognized in year 6, the entire $100,000 of gain will be subject to tax under section 1374 when it is recognized in year 6.

(c) *Termination and re-election of S corporation status.*—(1) *In general.*—For purposes of section 633(d)(8) of the Tax Reform Act of 1986, as amended, any reference to an election to be an S corporation under section 1362 shall be treated as a reference to the corporation's most recent election to be an S corporation under section 1362. This paragraph (c) applies for taxable years beginning after December 22, 2004, without re-

gard to the date of the corporation's most recent election to be an S corporation under section 1362.

(2) *Example.*—The following example illustrates the rules of this paragraph (c):

Example. (i) Effective January 1, 1988, X, a C corporation that is a qualified corporation under section 633(d) of the Tax Reform Act of 1986, as amended, elects to be an S corporation under section 1362. Effective January 1, 1990, X revokes its S status and becomes a C corporation. On January 1, 2004, X again elects to be an S corporation under section 1362. X disposes of assets in 2006, 2007, and 2008, recognizing gain.

(ii) X is not eligible for treatment under the transition rule of section 633(d)(8) of the Tax Reform Act of 1986, as amended, with respect to these assets. Accordingly, X is subject to section 1374, as amended by the Tax Reform Act of 1986 and the Technical and Miscellaneous Revenue Act of 1988, and the 10-year recognition period begins on January 1, 2004.

(iii) To the extent the gain that X recognizes on the asset sales in 2006, 2007, and 2008 reflects built-in gain inherent in such assets in X's hands on January 1, 2004, such gain is subject to tax under section 1374 as amended by the Tax Reform Act of 1986 and the Technical and Miscellaneous Revenue Act of 1988.

[Reg. §1.1374-10.]

☐ [T.D. 8579, 12-23-94. *Amended by* T.D. 9170, 12-21-2004; T.D. 9180, 2-22-2005 *and* T.D. 9236, 12-20-2005.]

[Reg. §1.1375-1]

§1.1375-1. Tax imposed when passive investment income of corporation having subchapter C earnings and profits exceeds 25 percent of gross receipts.—(a) *General rule.*—For taxable years beginning after 1981, section 1375(a) imposes a tax on the income of certain S corporations that have passive investment income. In the case of a taxable year beginning during 1982, an electing small business corporation may elect to have the rules under this section not apply. See the regulations under section 1362 for rules on the election. For purposes of this section, the term "S corporation" shall include an electing small business corporation under prior law. This tax shall apply to an S corporation for a taxable year if the S corporation has—

(1) Subchapter C earnings and profits at the close of such taxable year, and

(2) Gross receipts more than 25 percent of which are passive investment income.

If the S corporation has no subchapter C earnings and profits at the close of the taxable year (because, for example, such earnings and profits were distributed in accordance with section 1368), the tax shall not be imposed even though the S corporation has passive investment income for the taxable year. If the tax is imposed, the tax shall be computed by multiplying the excess net passive income (as defined in paragraph (b) of this section) by the highest rate of tax specified in section 11(b).

(b) *Definitions.*—(1) *Excess net passive income.*—(i) *In general.*—The term "excess net passive income" is defined in section 1375(b)(1), and can be expressed by the following formula:

$$\text{ENPI} = \text{NPI} \times \frac{\text{PII} - (.25 \times \text{GR})}{\text{PII}}$$

Where:
ENPI = excess net passive income
NPI = net passive income
PII = passive investment income
GR = total gross receipts

(ii) *Limitation.*—The amount of the excess net passive income for any taxable year shall not exceed the corporation's taxable income for the taxable year (determined in accordance with section 1374(d) and § 1.1374-1(d)).

(2) *Net passive income.*—The term "net passive income" means—

(i) Passive investment income, reduced by

(ii) The deductions allowable under chapter 1 of the Internal Revenue Code of 1954 which are directly connected (within the meaning of (b)(3) of this section) with the production of such income (other than deductions allowable under section 172 and part VIII of subchapter B).

(3) *Directly connected.*—(i) *In general.*—For purposes of paragraph (b)(2)(ii) of this section to be directly connected with the production of income, an item of deduction must have proximate and primary relationship to the income. Expenses, depreciation, and similar items attributable solely to such income qualify for deduction.

(ii) *Allocation of deduction.*—If an item of deduction is attributable (within the meaning of paragraph (b)(3)(i) of this section) in part to passive investment income and in part to income other than passive investment income, the deduction shall be allocated between the two types of items on a reasonable basis. The portion of any deduction so allocated to passive investment income shall be treated as proximately and primarily related to such income.

(4) *Other definitions.*—The terms "subchapter C earnings and profits," "passive investment income," and "gross receipts" shall have the same meaning given these terms in section 1362(d)(3) and the regulations thereunder.

(c) *Special rules.*—(1) *Disallowance of credits.*—No credit is allowed under part IV of subchapter A of chapter 1 of the Code (other than section 34)

against the tax imposed by section 1375(a) and this section.

(2) *Coordination with section 1374.*—If any gain—

(i) Is taken into account in determining passive income for purposes of this section, and

(ii) Is taken into account under section 1374, the amount of such gain taken into account under section 1374(b) and § 1.1374-1(b)(1) and (2) in determining the amount of tax shall be reduced by the portion of the excess net passive income for the taxable year which is attributable (on a pro rata basis) to such gain. For purposes of the preceding sentence, the portion of excess net passive income for the taxable year which is attributable to such capital gain is equal to the amount determined by multiplying the excess net passive income by the following fraction:

$$\frac{\text{NCG} = \text{E}}{\text{NPI}}$$

Where:
NCG = net capital gain
NPI = net passive income
E = Expense attributable to net capital gain

(d) *Waiver of tax in certain cases.*—(1) *In general.*—If an S corporation establishes to the satisfaction of the Commissioner that—

(i) It determined in good faith that it had no subchapter C earnings and profits at the close of the taxable year, and

(ii) During a reasonable period of time after it was determined that it did have subchapter C earnings and profits at the close of such taxable year such earnings and profits were distributed,

the Commissioner may waive the tax imposed by section 1375 for such taxable year. The S corporation has the burden of establishing that under the relevant facts and circumstances the Commissioner should waive the tax. For example, if an S corporation establishes that in good faith and using due diligence it determined that it had no subchapter C earnings and profits at the close of a taxable year, but it was later determined on audit that it did have subchapter C earnings and profits at the close of such taxable year, and if the corporation establishes that it distributed such earnings and profits within a reasonable time after the audit, it may be appropriate for the Commissioner to waive the tax on passive income for such taxable year.

(2) *Corporation's request for a waiver.*—A request for waiver of the tax imposed by section 1375 shall be made in writing to the district director request and shall contain all relevant facts to establish that the requirements of paragraph (d)(1) of this section are met. Such request shall contain a description of how and on what date the S corporation in good faith and using

due diligence determined that it had no subchapter C earnings and profits at the close of the taxable year, a description of how and on what date it was determined that the S corporation had subchapter C earnings and profits at the close of the year and a description (including dates) of any steps taken to distribute such earnings and profits. If the earnings and profits have not yet been distributed, the request shall contain a timetable for distribution and an explanation of why such timetable is reasonable. On the date the waiver is to become effective, all subchapter C earnings and profits must have been distributed.

(e) *Reduction in pass-thru for tax imposed on excess net passive income.*—See section 1366(f)(3) for a special rule reducing each item of the corporation's passive investment income for purposes of section 1366(a) if a tax is imposed on the corporation under section 1375.

(f) *Examples.*—The following examples illustrate the principles of this section:

Example (1). Assume Corporation M, an S corporation, has for its taxable year total gross receipts of $200,000, passive investment income of $100,000, $60,000 of which is interest income, and expenses directly connected with the production of such interest income in the amount of $10,000. Assume also that at the end of the taxable year Corporation M has subchapter C earnings and profits. Since more than 25 percent of Corporation M's total gross receipts are passive investment income, and since Corporation M has subchapter C earnings and profits at the end of the taxable year, Corporation M will be subject to the tax imposed by section 1375. The amount of excess net passive investment income is $45,000 ($90,000 × ($50,000/$100,000)). Assume that the other $40,000 of passive investment income is attributable to net capital gain and that there are no expenses directly connected with such gain. Under these facts, $20,000 of the excess net passive income is attributable to the net capital gain ($45,000 × ($40,000/$90,000)). Accordingly, the amount of gain taken into account under section 1374(b)(1) and the taxable income of Corporation M under section 1374(b)(2) shall be reduced by $20,000.

Example (2). Assume an S corporation with subchapter C earnings and profits has tax-exempt income of $400, its only passive income, gross receipts of $1,000 and taxable income of $250 and there are no expenses associated with the tax-exempt income. The corporation's excess net passive income for the taxable year would total $150 (400 × ((400 − 250)/400)). This amount is subject to the tax imposed by section 1375, notwithstanding that such amount is otherwise tax-exempt income. [Reg. § 1.1375-1.]

☐ [*T.D.* 8104, 9-25-86. *Amended by T.D.* 8419, 5-28-92.]

[Reg. § 1.1377-0.]

☐ [*T.D.* 8696, 12-20-96. *Amended by T.D.* 8994, 5-13-2002.]

[Reg. §1.1377-1]

§1.1377-1. Pro rata share.—(a) *Computation of pro rata shares.*—(1) *In general.*—For purposes of subchapter S of chapter 1 of the Internal Revenue Code and this section, each shareholder's pro rata share of any S corporation item described in section 1366(a) for any taxable year is the sum of the amounts determined with respect to the shareholder by assigning an equal portion of the item to each day of the S corporation's taxable year, and then dividing that portion pro rata among the shares outstanding on that day. See paragraph (b) of this section for rules pertaining to the computation of each shareholder's pro rata share when an election is made under section 1377(a)(2) to treat the taxable year of an S corporation as if it consisted of two taxable years in the case of a termination of a shareholder's entire interest in the corporation. See § 1.460-4(k)(3)(iv)(D) for rules relating to the computation of the shareholders' pro rata share of S corporation's income or loss from a contract accounted for under a long-term contract method of accounting.

(2) *Special rules.*—(i) *Days on which stock has not been issued.*—Solely for purposes of determining a shareholder's pro rata share of an item for a taxable year under section 1377(a) and this section, the beneficial owners of the corporation are treated as the shareholders of the corporation for any day on which the corporation has not issued any stock.

(ii) *Determining shareholder for day of stock disposition.*—A shareholder who disposes of stock in an S corporation is treated as the shareholder for the day of the disposition. A shareholder who dies is treated as the shareholder for the day of the shareholder's death.

(iii) *Shareholder trust conversions.*—If, during the taxable year of an S corporation, a trust that is an eligible shareholder of the S corporation converts from a trust described in section 1361(c)(2)(A)(i), (ii), (iii), or (v) for the first part of the year to a trust described in a different subpart of section 1361(c)(2)(A)(i), (ii), or (v) for the remainder of the year, the trust's share of the S corporation items is allocated between the two types of trusts. The first day that a qualified subchapter S trust (QSST) or an electing small business trust (ESBT) is treated as an S corporation shareholder is the effective date of the QSST or ESBT election. Upon the conversion, the trust is not treated as terminating its entire interest in the S corporation for purposes of paragraph (b) of this section, unless the trust was a trust described in section 1361(c)(2)(A)(ii) or (iii) before the conversion.

(b) *Election to terminate year.*—(1) *In general.*—If a shareholder's entire interest in an S corporation is terminated during the S corporation's taxable year and the corporation and all affected shareholders agree, the S corporation may elect under section 1377(a)(2) and this paragraph (b) (terminating election) to apply paragraph (a) of this section to the affected shareholders as if the corporation's taxable year consisted of two separate taxable years, the first of which ends at the close of the day on which the shareholder's entire interest in the S corporation is terminated. If the event resulting in the termination of the shareholder's entire interest also constitutes a qualifying disposition as described in

§ 1.1368-1(g)(2)(i), the election under § 1.1368-1(g)(2) cannot be made. An S corporation may not make a terminating election if the cessation of a shareholder's interest occurs in a transaction that results in a termination under section 1362(d)(2) of the corporation's election to be an S corporation. (See section 1362(e)(3) for an election to have items assigned to each short taxable year under normal tax accounting rules in the case of a termination of a corporation's election to be an S corporation.) A terminating election is irrevocable and is effective only for the terminating event for which it is made.

(2) *Affected shareholders.*—For purposes of the terminating election under section 1377(a)(2) and paragraph (b) of this section, the term *affected shareholders* means the shareholder whose interest is terminated and all shareholders to whom such shareholder has transferred shares during the taxable year. If such shareholder has transferred shares to the corporation, the term *affected shareholders* includes all persons who are shareholders during the taxable year.

(3) *Effect of the terminating election.*—(i) *In general.*—An S corporation that makes a terminating election for a taxable year must treat the taxable year as separate taxable years for all affected shareholders for purposes of allocating items of income (including tax-exempt income), loss, deduction, and credit; making adjustments to the accumulated adjustments account, earnings and profits, and basis; and determining the tax effect of a distribution. An S corporation that makes a terminating election must assign items of income (including tax-exempt income), loss, deduction, and credit to each deemed separate taxable year using its normal method of accounting as determined under section 446(a).

(ii) *Due date of S corporation return.*—A terminating election does not affect the due date of the S corporation's return required to be filed under section 6037(a) for a taxable year (determined without regard to a terminating election).

(iii) *Taxable year of inclusion by shareholder.*—A terminating election does not affect the taxable year in which an affected shareholder must take into account the affected shareholder's pro rata share of the S corporation's items of income, loss, deduction, and credit.

(iv) *S corporation that is a partner in a partnership.*—A terminating election by an S corporation that is a partner in a partnership is treated as a sale or exchange of the corporation's entire interest in the partnership for purposes of section 706(c) (relating to closing the partnership taxable year), if the taxable year of the partnership ends after the shareholder's interest is terminated and within the taxable year of the S corporation (determined without regard to any terminating election) for which the terminating election is made.

(4) *Determination of whether an S shareholder's entire interest has terminated.*—For purposes of the terminating election under section 1377(a)(2) and paragraph (b) of this section, a shareholder's entire interest in an S corporation is terminated on the occurrence of any event through which a shareholder's entire stock ownership in the S corporation ceases, including a sale, exchange, or other disposition of all of the stock held by the shareholder; a gift under section 102(a) of all the shareholder's stock; a spousal transfer under section 1041(a) of all the shareholder's stock; a redemption, as defined in section 317(b), of all the shareholder's stock, regardless of the tax treatment of the redemption under section 302; and the death of the shareholder. A shareholder's entire interest in an S corporation is not terminated if the shareholder retains ownership of any stock (including an interest treated as stock under § 1.1361-1(1)) that would result in the shareholder continuing to be considered a shareholder of the corporation for purposes of section 1362(a)(2). Thus, in determining whether a shareholder's entire interest in an S corporation has been terminated, any interest held by the shareholder as a creditor, employee, director, or in any other non-shareholder capacity is disregarded.

(5) *Time and manner of making a terminating election.*—(i) *In general.*—An S corporation makes a terminating election by attaching a statement to its timely filed original or amended return required to be filed under section 6037(a) (that is, a Form 1120S) for the taxable year during which a shareholder's entire interest is terminated. A single election statement may be filed by the S corporation for all terminating elections for the taxable year. The election statement must include—

(A) A declaration by the S corporation that it is electing under section 1377(a)(2) and this paragraph to treat the taxable year as if it consisted of two separate taxable years;

(B) Information setting forth when and how the shareholder's entire interest was terminated (for example, a sale or gift);

(C) The signature on behalf of the S corporation of an authorized officer of the corporation under penalties of perjury, except that for taxable years beginning after December 31, 2002, the election statement described in § 1.1377-1(b)(5)(i) of this section shall be verified, and the requirement of this paragraph (b)(5)(i)(C) is satisfied, by the signature on the Form 1120S filed by the S corporation.

(D) A statement by the corporation that the corporation and each affected shareholder consent to the S corporation making the terminating election.

(ii) *Affected shareholders required to consent.*—For purposes of paragraph (b)(5)(i)(D) of this section, a shareholder of the S corporation for the taxable year is a shareholder as described in section 1362(a)(2). For example, the person who under § 1.1362-6(b)(2) must consent to a corporation's S election in certain special cases is the person who must consent to the terminating election. In addition, an executor or administrator of the estate of a deceased affected shareholder may consent to the terminating election on behalf of the deceased affected shareholder.

(iii) *More than one terminating election.*—A shareholder whose entire interest in an S corporation is terminated in an event for which a terminating election was made is not required to consent to a terminating election made with respect to a subsequent termination within the same taxable year unless the shareholder is an affected shareholder with respect to the subsequent termination.

(c) *Examples.*—The following examples illustrate the provisions of this section:

Example 1. Shareholder's pro rata share in the case of a partial disposition of stock. (i) On January 6, 1997, X incorporates as a calendar year corporation, issues 100 shares of common stock to each of A and B, and files an election to be an S corporation for its 1997 taxable year. On July 24, 1997, B sells 50 shares of X stock to C. Thus, in 1997, A owned 50 percent of the outstanding shares of X on each day of X's 1997 taxable year, B owned 50 percent on each day from January 6, 1997, to July 24, 1997 (200 days), and 25 percent from July 25, 1997, to December 31, 1997 (160 days), and C owned 25 percent from July 25, 1997, to December 31, 1997 (160 days).

(ii) Because B's entire interest in X is not terminated when B sells 50 shares to C on July 24, 1997, X cannot make a terminating election under section 1377(a)(2) and paragraph (b) of this section for B's sale of 50 shares to C. Although B's sale of 50 shares to C is a qualifying disposition under § 1.1368-1(g)(2)(i), X does not make an election to terminate its taxable year under § 1.1368-1(g)(2). During its 1997 taxable year, X has nonseparately computed income of $720,000.

(iii) For each day in X's 1997 taxable year, A's daily pro rata share of X's nonseparately computed income is $1,000 ($720,000/360 days × 50%). Thus, A's pro rata share of X's nonseparately computed income for 1997 is $360,000 ($1,000 × 360 days). B's daily pro rata share of X's nonseparately computed income is $1,000 ($720,000/360 × 50%) for the first 200 days of X's 1997 taxable year, and $500 ($720,000/360 × 25%) for the following 160 days in 1997. Thus, B's pro rata share of X's nonseparately computed income for 1997 is $280,000 (($1,000 × 200 days) + ($500 × 160 days)). C's daily pro rata share of X's nonseparately computed income is $500 ($720,000/360 × 25%) for 160 days in 1997. Thus, C's pro rata share of X's nonseparately computed income for 1997 is $80,000 ($500 × 160 days).

Example 2. Shareholder's pro rata share when an S corporation makes a terminating election under section 1377(a)(2). (i) On January 6, 1997, X incorporates as a calendar year corporation, issues 100 shares of common stock to each of A and B, and files an election to be an S corporation for its 1997 taxable year. On July 24, 1997, B sells B's entire 100 shares of X stock to C. With the consent of B and C, X makes an election under section 1377(a)(2) and paragraph (b) of this section for the termination of B's entire interest arising from B's sale of 100 shares to C. As a result of the election, the pro rata shares of B and C are determined as if X's taxable year consisted of two separate taxable years, the first of which ends on July 24, 1997, the date B's entire interest in X terminates. Because A is not an affected shareholder as defined by section 1377(a)(2)(B) and paragraph (b)(2) of this section, the treatment as separate taxable years does not apply to A.

(ii) During its 1997 taxable year, X has nonseparately computed income of $720,000. Under X's normal method of accounting, $200,000 of the $720,000 of nonseparately computed income is allocable to the period of January 6, 1997, through July 24, 1997 (the first deemed taxable year), and the remaining $520,000 is allocable to the period of July 25, 1997, through December 31, 1997 (the second deemed taxable year).

(iii) B's pro rata share of the $200,000 of nonseparately computed income for the first deemed taxable year is determined by assigning the $200,000 of nonseparately computed income to each day of the first deemed taxable year ($200,000/200 days = $1,000 per day). Because B held 50% of X's authorized and issued shares on each day of the first deemed taxable year, B's daily pro rata share for each day of the first deemed taxable year is $500 ($1,000 per day × 50%). Thus, B's pro rata share of the $200,000 of nonseparately computed income for the first deemed taxable year is $100,000 ($500 per day x 200 days). B must report this amount for B's taxable year with or within which X's full taxable year ends (December 31, 1997).

(iv) C's pro rata share of the $520,000 of nonseparately computed income for the second deemed taxable year is determined by assigning the $520,000 of nonseparately computed income to each day of the second deemed taxable year ($520,000/160 days = $3,250 per day). Because C held 50% of X's authorized and issued shares on each day of the second deemed taxable year, C's daily pro rata shares for each day of the second deemed taxable year is $1,625 ($3,250 per day × 50%). Therefore, C's pro rata share of the $520,000 of nonseparately computed income is $260,000 ($1,625 per day × 160 days). C must report this amount for C's taxable year with or within which X's full taxable year ends (December 31, 1997).

Example 3. Effect of conversion of a qualified subchapter S trust (QSST) to an electing small business trust (ESBT). (i) On January 1, 2003, Trust receives stock of S corporation. Trust's current income beneficiary makes a timely QSST election under section 1361(d)(2), effective January 1, 2003. Subsequently, the trustee and current income beneficiary of Trust elect, pursuant to § 1.1361-1(j)(12), to terminate the QSST election and convert to an ESBT, effective July 1, 2004. The taxable year of S corporation is the calendar year. In 2004, Trust's pro rata share of S corporation's nonseparately computed income is $100,000.

(ii) For purposes of computing the income allocable to the QSST and to the ESBT, Trust is treated as a QSST through June 30, 2004, and Trust is treated as an ESBT beginning July 1, 2004. Pursuant to section 1377(a)(1), the pro rata share of S corporation income allocated to the QSST is $49,727 ($100,000 × 182 days/366 days), and the pro rata share of S corporation income allocated to the ESBT is $50,273 ($100,000 × 184 days/366 days).

[Reg. § 1.1377-1.]

☐ [*T.D.* 8696, 12-20-96. *Amended by T.D.* 8994, 5-13-2002; *T.D.* 9100, 12-18-2003; *T.D.* 9137, 7-15-2004 *and T.D.* 9300, 12-7-2006.]

[Reg. § 1.1377-2]

§ 1.1377-2. Post-termination transition period.—(a) *In general.*—For purposes of subchapter S of chapter 1 of the Internal Revenue Code (Code) and this section, the term *post-termination transition period* means—

(1) The period beginning on the day after the last day of the corporation's last taxable year as an S corporation and ending on the later of—

(i) The day which is 1 year after such last day; or

(ii) The due date for filing the return for the last taxable year as an S corporation (including extensions);

(2) The 120-day period beginning on the date of any determination pursuant to an audit of the taxpayer which follows the termination of the corporation's election and which adjusts a subchapter S item of income, loss, or deduction of the corporation arising during the S period (as defined in section 1368(e)(2)); and

(3) The 120-day period beginning on the date of a determination that the corporation's election under section 1362(a) had terminated for a previous taxable year.

(b) *Special rules for post-termination transition period.*—Pursuant to section 1377(b)(1) and paragraph (a)(1) of this section, a post-termination transition period arises the day after the last day that an S corporation was in existence if a C corporation acquires the assets of the S corporation in a transaction to which section 381(a)(2) applies. However, if an S corporation acquires the assets of another S corporation in a transaction to which section 381(a)(2) applies, a post-

Reg. § 1.1377-2(b)

termination transition period does not arise. (See §1.1368-2(d)(2) for the treatment of the acquisition of the assets of an S corporation by another S corporation in a transaction to which section 381(a)(2) applies.) The special treatment under section 1371(e)(1) of distributions of money by a corporation with respect to its stock during the post-termination transition period is available only to those shareholders who were shareholders in the S corporation at the time of the termination.

(c) *Determination defined.*—For purposes of section 1377(b)(1) and paragraph (a) of this section, the term *determination* means—

(1) A determination as defined in section 1313(a);

(2) A written agreement between the corporation and the Commissioner (including a statement acknowledging that the corporation's election to be an S corporation terminated under section 1362(d)) that the corporation failed to qualify as an S corporation;

(3) For a corporation subject to the audit and assessment provisions of subchapter C of chapter 63 of subtitle A of the Code, the expiration of the period specified in section 6226 for filing a petition for readjustment of a final S corporation administrative adjustment finding that the corporation failed to qualify as an S corporation, provided that no petition was timely filed before the expiration of the period; and

(4) For a corporation not subject to the audit and assessment provisions of subchapter C of chapter 63 of subtitle A of the Code, the expiration of the period for filing a petition under section 6213 for the shareholder's taxable year for which the Commissioner has made a finding that the corporation failed to qualify as an S corporation, provided that no petition was timely filed before the expiration of the period.

(d) *Date a determination becomes effective.*—(1) *Determination under section 1313(a).*—A determination under paragraph (c)(1) of this section becomes effective on the date prescribed in section 1313 and the regulations thereunder.

(2) *Written agreement.*—A determination under paragraph (c)(2) of this section becomes effective when it is signed by the district director having jurisdiction over the corporation (or by another Service official to whom authority to sign the agreement is delegated) and by an officer of the corporation authorized to sign on its behalf. Neither the request for a written agreement nor the terms of the written agreement suspend the running of any statute of limitations.

(3) *Implied agreement.*—A determination under paragraph (c)(3) or (4) of this section becomes effective on the day after the date of expiration of the period specified under section 6226 or 6213, respectively. [Reg. §1.1377-2.]

☐ [*T.D.* 8696, 12-20-96.]

[Reg. §1.1377-3]

§1.1377-3. **Effective dates.**—Section 1.1377-1 and 1.1377-2 apply to taxable years of an S corporation beginning after December 31, 1996, except that §1.1377-1(a)(2)(iii), and (c) *Example 3* are applicable for taxable years beginning on and after May 14, 2002. [Reg. §1.1377-3.]

☐ [*T.D.* 8696, 12-20-96. *Amended by T.D.* 8994, 5-13-2002.]

[Reg. §1.1378-1]

§1.1378-1. **Taxable year of S corporation.**—(a) *In general.*—The taxable year of an S corporation must be a permitted year. A permitted year is the required taxable year (i.e., a taxable year ending on December 31), a taxable year elected under section 444, a 52-53-week taxable year ending with reference to the required taxable year or a taxable year elected under section 444, or any other taxable year for which the corporation establishes a business purpose to the satisfaction of the Commissioner under section 442.

(b) *Adoption of taxable year.*—An electing S corporation may adopt, in accordance with §1.441-1(c), its required taxable year, a taxable year elected under section 444, or a 52-53-week taxable year ending with reference to its required taxable year or a taxable year elected under section 444 without the approval of the Commissioner. See §1.441-1. An electing S corporation that wants to adopt any other taxable year, must establish a business purpose and obtain the approval of the Commissioner under section 442.

(c) *Change in taxable year.*—(1) *Approval required.*—An S corporation or electing S corporation that wants to change its taxable year must obtain the approval of the Commissioner under section 442 or make an election under section 444. However, an S corporation or electing S corporation may obtain automatic approval for certain changes, including a change to its required taxable year, pursuant to administrative procedures published by the Commissioner.

(2) *Short period tax return.*—An S corporation or electing S corporation that changes its taxable year must make its return for a short period in accordance with section 443, but must not annualize the corporation's taxable income.

(d) *Retention of taxable year.*—In certain cases, an S corporation or electing S corporation will be required to change its taxable year unless it obtains the approval of the Commissioner under section 442, or makes an election under section 444, to retain its current taxable year. For example, a corporation using a June 30 fiscal year that elects to be an S corporation and, as a result, is required to use the calendar year must obtain the approval of the Commissioner to retain its current fiscal year.

(e) *Procedures for obtaining approval or making a section 444 election.*—(1) *In general.*—See §1.442-1(b) for procedures to obtain the approval of the Commissioner (automatically or otherwise) to adopt, change, or retain a taxable year. See §§1.444-1T and 1.444-2T for qualifications, and 1.444-3T for procedures, for making an election under section 444.

(2) *Special rules for electing S corporations.*—An electing S corporation that wants to adopt, change to, or retain a taxable year other than its required taxable year must request approval of the Commissioner on Form 2553, "Election by a Small Business Corporation," when the election to be an S corporation is filed pursuant to section 1362(b) and §1.1362-6. See §1.1362-6(a)(2)(i) for the manner of making an election to be an S corporation. If such corporation receives permission to adopt, change to, or retain a taxable year other than its required taxable year, the election to be an S corporation will be effective. Denial of the request renders the election ineffective unless the corporation agrees that, in the event the request to adopt, change to, or retain a taxable year other than its required taxable year is denied, it will adopt, change to, or retain its required taxable year or, if applicable, make an election under section 444.

(f) *Effective date.*—The rules of this section are applicable for taxable years ending on or after May 17, 2002. [Reg. §1.1378-1.]

☐ [*T.D.* 8996, 5-16-2002.]

[Reg. §18.1379-1]

§18.1379-1. Transitional rules on enactment (Temporary).—(a) *Prior elections.*—Any election that was made under section 1372(a) (as in effect before the enactment of the Subchapter S Revision Act of 1982), and that is still in effect as of the first day of a taxable year beginning in 1983, shall be treated as being an election made under section 1362(a). In addition, any election that was made under section 1371(g)(2) (as in effect before the enactment of that Act), and that is still in effect as of the first day of a taxable year beginning in 1983, shall be treated as being an election made under section 1362(d)(2) [1361(d)(2)].

(b) *Prior terminations.*—For purposes of section 1362(g), any termination under section 1372(e) (as in effect before the enactment of the Subchapter S Revision Act of 1982) shall not be taken into account.

(c) *Time and manner of making an election under section 6(c)(3)(B) of the Subchapter S Revision Act of 1982.*—In the case of a qualified oil corporation (as defined in section 6(c)(3)(B) of the Subchapter S Revision Act of 1982), the corporation may elect under that section of the Act to have the amendments made by the Act not apply and to have subchapter S (as in effect on July 1, 1982), chapter 1 of the Internal Revenue Code of 1954 apply. The election shall be made by the corporation by filing a statement that—

(1) Contains the name, address, and taxpayer identification number of the corporation and of each shareholder,

(2) Identifies the election as an election under section 6(c)(3)(B) of the Subchapter S Revision Act of 1982, and

(3) Provides all information necessary in the judgment of the district director to show that the corporation meets the requirements (other than the requirement of making this election) of a qualified oil corporation.

The statement shall be signed by any person authorized to sign the return required to be filed under section 6037 and by each person who is or was a shareholder in the corporation at any time during the taxable year beginning in 1983 and shall be filed with the return for that taxable year. [Temporary Reg. §18.1379-1.]

☐ [*T.D.* 7872, 1-21-83.]

[Reg. §18.1379-2]

§18.1379-2. Special rules for all elections, consents, and refusals (Temporary).—(a) *Additional information required.*—If later regulations issued under the section of the Code or of the Subchapter S Revision Act of 1982 under which the election, consent, or refusal was made require the furnishing of information in addition to that which was furnished with the statement of election, consent, or refusal as provided by Part 18 of this Title, and if an office of the Internal Revenue Service requests the taxpayer to provide the additional information, the taxpayer shall furnish the additional information in a statement filed with that office of the Internal Revenue Service within 60 days after the date on which the request is made. This statement shall also—

(1) Contain the name, address, and taxpayer identification number of each party identified in connection with the election, consent, or refusal,

(2) Identify the election, consent, or refusal by reference to the section of the Code or Act under which the election, consent, or refusal was made, and

(3) Specify the scope of the election, consent, or refusal.

If the additional information is not provided within 60 days after the date on which the request is made, the election, consent, or refusal may, at the discretion of the Commissioner, be held invalid.

(b) *State law incorporator.*—For purposes of any election, consent, or refusal provided in Part

18 of this Title, any person who is considered to be a shareholder for state law purposes solely by virtue of his or her status as an incorporator shall not be treated as a shareholder. [Temporary Reg. §18.1379-2.]

☐ [*T.D.* 7872, 1-21-83.]

COOPERATIVES AND THEIR PATRONS

Cooperatives

[Reg. §1.1381-1]

§1.1381-1. Organizations to which part applies.—(a) *In general.*—Except as provided in paragraph (b) of this section, part I, subchapter T, chapter 1 of the Code, applies to any corporation operating on a cooperative basis and allocating amounts to patrons on the basis of the business done with or for such patrons.

(b) *Exceptions.*—Part I of such subchapter T does not apply to—

(1) Any organization which is exempt from income taxes under chapter 1 of the Code (other than an exempt farmers' cooperative described in section 521);

(2) Any organization which is subject to the provisions of part II (section 591 and following), subchapter H, chapter 1 of the Code (relating to mutual savings banks, etc.);

(3) Any organization which is subject to the provisions of subchapter L (section 801 and following), chapter 1 of the Code (relating to insurance companies); or

(4) Any organization which is engaged in generating, transmitting, or otherwise furnishing electric energy, or which provides telephone service, to persons in rural areas. The terms "rural areas" and "telephone service" shall have the meaning assigned to them in section 5 of the Rural Electrification Act of 1936, as amended (7 U.S.C. 924). [Reg. §1.1381-1.]

☐ [*T.D.* 6643, 4-1-63.]

[Reg. §1.1381-2]

§1.1381-2. Tax on certain farmers' cooperatives.—(a) *In general.*—(1) For taxable years beginning after December 31, 1962, farmers', fruit growers', or like associations, organized and operated in compliance with the requirements of section 521 and §1.521-1, shall be subject to the taxes imposed by section 11 or section 1201. Although such associations are subject to both normal tax and surtax, as in the case of corporations generally, certain special deductions are provided for them in section 1382(c) and §1.1382-3. For the purpose of any law which refers to organizations exempt from income taxes such an association shall, however, be considered as an organization exempt under section 501. Thus, the provisions of section 243, providing a credit for dividends received from a domestic corporation subject to taxation, are not applicable to dividends received from a cooperative association organized and operated in compliance with the requirements of section 521 and §1.521-1. The provisions of section 1501, relating to consolidated returns, are likewise not applicable.

(2) Rules governing the manner in which amounts paid as patronage dividends are allowable as deductions in computing the taxable income of such an association are set forth in section 1382(b) and §1.1382-2. For the tax treatment, as to patrons, of amounts received during the taxable year as patronage dividends, see section 1385 and the regulations thereunder.

(b) *Cross references.*—For tax treatment of exempt cooperative associations for taxable years beginning before January 1, 1963, or for taxable years beginning after December 31, 1962, with respect to payments attributable to patronage occurring during taxable years beginning before January 1, 1963, see section 522 and the regulations thereunder. For requirements of annual returns by such associations, see sections 6012 and 6072(d) and paragraph (f) of §1.6012-2. [Reg. §1.1381-2.]

☐ [*T.D.* 6643, 4-1-63.]

[Reg. §1.1382-1]

§1.1382-1. Taxable income of cooperatives; gross income.—(a) *Introduction.*—Section 1382(b) provides that the amount of certain patronage dividends (and amounts paid in redemption of nonqualified written notices of allocation) shall not be taken into account by a cooperative organization in determining its taxable income. Such section also provides that, for purposes of the Internal Revenue Code, an amount not taken into account is to be treated in the same manner as an item of gross income and as a deduction therefrom. Therefore, such an amount is treated as a deduction for purposes of applying the Internal Revenue Code and the regulations thereunder and, for simplicity, is referred to as a deduction in the regulations under such Code. However, this should not be regarded as a determination of the character of the amount for other purposes.

(b) *Computation of gross income.*—Any cooperative organization to which part I, subchapter T, chapter 1 of the Code, applies shall not, for any purpose under the Code, exclude from its gross income (as a reduction in gross receipts, an increase in cost of goods sold, or otherwise) the amount of any allocation or distribution to a patron out of the net earnings of such organization with respect to patronage occurring during a taxable year beginning after December 31, 1962. See, however, section 1382(b) and §1.1382-2 for deductions for certain amounts paid to patrons out of net earnings. [Reg. §1.1382-1.]

☐ [*T.D.* 6643, 4-1-63.]

[Reg. §1.1382-2]

§1.1382-2. Taxable income of cooperatives; treatment of patronage dividends.—(a) *In general.*—(1) In determining the taxable income of any cooperative organization to which part I, subchapter T, chapter 1 of the Code, applies, there shall be allowed as deductions from gross income, in addition to the other deductions allowable under chapter 1 of the Code, the deductions with respect to patronage dividends provided in section 1382(b) and paragraphs (b) and (c) of this section.

(2) For the definition of terms used in this section see section 1388 and §1.1388-1; to determine the payment period for a taxable year, see section 1382(d) and §1.1382-4.

(b) *Deduction for patronage dividends.*—(1) *In general.*—In the case of a taxable year beginning after December 31, 1962, there is allowed as a deduction from the gross income of any cooperative organization to which part I of subchapter T applies, amounts paid to patrons during the payment period for the taxable year as patronage dividends with respect to patronage occurring during such taxable year, but only to the extent that such amounts are paid in money, qualified written notices of allocation, or other property (other than nonqualified written notices of allocation). See section 1382(e) and (f) and §§1.1382-5 and 1.1382-6 for special rules relating to the time when patronage is deemed to occur where products are marketed under a pooling arrangement or where earnings are includible in the gross income of the cooperative organization for a taxable year after the year in which the patronage occurred. For purposes of this paragraph, a written notice of allocation is considered paid when it is issued to the patron. A patronage dividend shall be treated as paid in money during the payment period for the taxable year to the extent it is paid by a qualified check which is issued during the payment period for such taxable year and endorsed and cashed on or before the ninetieth day after the close of such payment period. In determining the amount paid which is allowable as a deduction under this paragraph, property (other than written notices of allocation) shall be taken into account at its fair market value when paid, and a qualified written notice of allocation shall be taken into account at its stated dollar amount.

(2) *Special rule for certain taxable years.*—No deduction is allowed under this section for amounts paid during taxable years beginning before January 1, 1963, or for amounts paid during taxable years beginning after December 31, 1962, with respect to patronage occurring during taxable years beginning before January 1, 1963. With respect to such amounts, the Internal Revenue Code of 1954 (including section 522 and the regulations thereunder) shall be applicable without regard to subchapter T.

(c) *Deduction for amounts paid in redemption of certain nonqualified written notices of allocation.*—In the case of a taxable year beginning after December 31, 1962, there is allowed as a deduction from the gross income of a cooperative organization to which part I of subchapter T applies, amounts paid by such organization during the payment period for such taxable year in redemption of a nonqualified written notice of allocation which was previously paid as a patronage dividend during the payment period for the taxable year during which the patronage occurred, but only to the extent such amounts (1) are paid in money or other property (other than written notices of allocation) and (2) do not exceed the stated dollar amount of such written notice of allocation. No deduction shall be allowed under this paragraph, however, for amounts paid in redemption of nonqualified written notices of allocation which were paid with respect to patronage occurring during a taxable year beginning before January 1, 1963. For purposes of this paragraph, if an amount is paid within the payment period for two or more taxable years, it will be allowable as a deduction only for the earliest of such taxable years. Thus, if a cooperative which reports its income on a calendar year basis pays an amount in redemption of a nonqualified written notice of allocation on January 15, 1966, it will be allowed a deduction for such amount only for its 1965 taxable year. In determining the amount paid which is allowable as a deduction under this paragraph, property (other than written notices of allocation) shall be taken into account at its fair market value when paid. Amounts paid in redemption of a nonqualified written notice of allocation in excess of its stated dollar amount shall be treated under the applicable provisions of the Code. For example, if such excess is in the nature of interest, its deductibility will be governed by section 163 and the regulations thereunder. [Reg. §1.1382-2.]

☐ [*T.D.* 6643, 4-1-63.]

[Reg. §1.1382-3]

§1.1382-3. Taxable income of cooperatives; special deductions for exempt farmers' cooperatives.—(a) *In general.*—(1) Section 1382(c) provides that in determining the taxable income of a farmers', fruit growers', or like association, described in section 1381(a)(1) and organized and operated in compliance with the requirements of section 521 and §1.521-1, there shall be allowed as deductions from the gross income of such organization, in addition to the other deductions allowable under chapter 1 of the Code (including the deductions allowed by section 1382(b)) the special deductions provided in section 1382(c) and paragraphs (b), (c), and (d) of this section.

(2) For the definition of terms used in this section, see section 1388 and § 1.1388-1; to determine the payment period for a taxable year, see section 1382(d) and § 1.1382-4.

(b) *Deduction for dividends paid on capital stock.*—In the case of a taxable year beginning after December 31, 1962, there is allowed as a deduction from the gross income of a cooperative association operated in compliance with the requirements of section 521 and § 1.521-1, amounts paid as dividends during the taxable year on the capital stock of such cooperative association. For the purpose of the preceding sentence, the term "capital stock" includes common stock (whether voting or nonvoting), preferred stock, or any other form of capital represented by capital retain certificates, revolving fund certificates, letters of advice, or other evidence of a proprietary interest in a cooperative association. Such deduction is applicable only to the taxable year in which the dividends are actually or constructively paid to the holder of capital stock or other proprietary interest of the cooperative association. If a dividend is paid by check and the check bearing a date within the taxable year is deposited in the mail, in a cover properly stamped and addressed to the shareholder at his last known address, at such time that in the ordinary handling of the mails the check would be received by such holder within the taxable year, a presumption arises that the dividend was paid to such holder in such year. The determination of whether a dividend has been paid to such holder by the corporation during its taxable year is in no way dependent upon the method of accounting regularly employed by the corporation in keeping its books. For further rules as to the determination of the right to a deduction for dividends paid, under certain specific circumstances, see section 561 and the regulations thereunder.

(c) *Deduction for amounts allocated from income not derived from patronage.*—(1) *In general.*—In the case of a taxable year beginning after December 31, 1962, there is allowed as a deduction from the gross income of a cooperative association operated in compliance with the requirements of section 521 and § 1.521-1, amounts paid to patrons, during the payment period for the taxable year, on a patronage basis with respect to its income derived during such taxable year either from business done with or for the United States or any of its agencies or from sources other than patronage, but only to the extent such amounts are paid in money, qualified written notices of allocation, or other property (other than nonqualified written notices of allocation). For purposes of this subparagraph a written notice of allocation is considered paid when it is issued to

the patron. An amount shall be treated as paid in money during the payment period for the taxable year to the extent it is paid by a qualified check which is issued during the payment period for such taxable year and endorsed and cashed on or before the ninetieth day after the close of such payment period. In determining the amount paid which is allowable as a deduction under this paragraph, property (other than written notices of allocation) shall be taken into account at its fair market value when paid, and a qualified written notice of allocation shall be taken into account at its stated dollar amount.

(2) *Definition.*—As used in this paragraph, the term "income derived from sources other than patronage" means incidental income derived from sources not directly related to the marketing, purchasing, or service activities of the cooperative association. For example, income derived from the lease of premises, from investment in securities, or from the sale or exchange of capital assets, constitutes income derived from sources other than patronage.

(3) *Basis of distribution.*—In order that the deduction for amounts paid with respect to income derived from business done with or for the United States or any of its agencies or from sources other than patronage may be applicable, it is necessary that the amount sought to be deducted be paid on a patronage basis in proportion, insofar as is practicable, to the amount of business done by or for patrons during the period to which such income is attributable. For example, if capital gains are realized from the sale or exchange of capital assets acquired and disposed of during the taxable year, income realized from such gains must be paid to patrons of such year in proportion to the amount of business done by such patrons during the taxable year. Similarly, if capital gains are realized by the association from the sale or exchange of capital assets held for a period extending into more than one taxable year income realized from such gains must be paid, insofar as is practicable, to the persons who were patrons during the taxable years in which the asset was owned by the association in proportion to the amount of business done by such patrons during such taxable years.

(4) *Special rules for certain taxable years.*—No deduction is allowable under this paragraph for amounts paid during taxable years beginning before January 1, 1963, or for amounts paid during taxable years beginning after December 31, 1962, with respect to income derived during taxable years beginning before January 1, 1963. With respect to such amounts, the Internal Revenue Code of 1954 (including section 522 and the regulations thereunder) shall be applicable without regard to subchapter T.

(d) *Deduction for amounts paid in redemption of certain nonqualified written notices of allocation.*—In the case of a taxable year beginning after December 31, 1962, there is allowed as a deduction from the gross income of a cooperative association operated in compliance with the requirements of section 521 and § 1.521-1, amounts paid by such association during the payment period for such taxable year in redemption of certain nonqualified written notices of allocation, but only to the extent such amounts (1) are paid in money or other property (other than written notices of allocation) and (2) do not exceed the stated dollar amount of such nonqualified written notices of allocation. The nonqualified written notices of allocation referred to in the preceding sentence are those which were previously paid to patrons on a patronage basis with respect to earnings derived either from business done with or for the United States or any of its agencies or from sources other than patronage, provided that such nonqualified written notices of allocation were paid during the payment period for the taxable year during which such earnings were derived. No deduction shall be allowed under this paragraph, however, for amounts paid in redemption of nonqualified written notices of allocation which were paid with respect to earnings derived during a taxable year beginning before January 1, 1963. For purposes of this paragraph, if an amount is paid within the payment period for two or more taxable years, it will be allowable as a deduction only for the earliest of such taxable years. In determining the amount paid which is allowable as a deduction under this paragraph, property (other than written notices of allocation) shall be taken into account at its fair market value when paid. Amounts paid in redemption of a nonqualified written notice of allocation in excess of its stated dollar amount shall be treated under the applicable provisions of the Code. [Reg. § 1.1382-3.]

☐ [*T.D.* 6643, 4-1-63.]

[Reg. § 1.1382-4]

§ 1.1382-4. Taxable income of cooperatives; payment period for each taxable year.—The payment period for a taxable year is the period beginning with the first day of such taxable year and ending with the fifteenth day of the ninth month following the close of such year. [Reg. § 1.1382-4.]

☐ [*T.D.* 6643, 4-1-63.]

[Reg. § 1.1382-5]

§ 1.1382-5. Taxable income of cooperatives; products marketed under pooling arrangements.—For purposes of section 1382(b) and § 1.1382-2, in the case of a pooling arrangement for the marketing of products the patronage under such pool shall be treated as occurring during the taxable year in which the pool closes. The determination of when a pool is closed will be made on the basis of the facts and circumstances in each case, but generally the practices and operations of the cooperative organization

shall control. This section may be illustrated by the following example:

Example. Farmer A delivers to the X Cooperative 100 bushels of wheat on August 15, 1963, at which time he receives a "per bushel" advance. (Both farmer A and the X Cooperative file returns on a calendar year basis.) On October 15, 1963 farmer A receives an additional "per bushel" payment. The pool sells some of its wheat in 1963 and the remainder in January of 1964. The pool is closed on February 15, 1964. For purposes of section 1382(b), A's patronage is considered as occurring in 1964. [Reg. § 1.1382-5.]

☐ [*T.D.* 6643, 4-1-63.]

[Reg. § 1.1382-6]

§ 1.1382-6. Taxable income of cooperatives; treatment of earnings received after patronage occurred.—If earnings derived from business done with or for patrons are includible in the gross income of the cooperative organization for a taxable year after the taxable year during which the patronage occurred, then, for purposes of determining whether the cooperative is allowed a deduction under section 1382(b) and § 1.1382-2, the patronage to which these earnings relate shall be considered to have occurred during the taxable year for which such earnings are includible in the cooperative's gross income. Thus, if the cooperative organization pays these earnings out as patronage dividends during the payment period for the taxable year for which the earnings are includible in its gross income, it will be allowed a deduction for such payments under section 1382(b)(1) and paragraph (b) of § 1.1382-2, to the extent they are paid in money, qualified written notices of allocation, or other property (other than written notices of allocation). [Reg. § 1.1382-6.]

☐ [*T.D.* 6643, 4-1-63.]

[Reg. § 1.1382-7]

§ 1.1382-7. Special rules applicable to cooperative associations exempt from tax before January 1, 1952.—(a) *Basis of property.*—The adjustments to the cost or other basis provided in sections 1011 and 1016 and the regulations thereunder, are applicable for the entire period since the acquisition of the property. Thus, proper adjustment to basis must be made under section 1016 for depreciation, obsolescence, amortization, and depletion for all taxable years beginning prior to January 1, 1952, although the cooperative association was exempt from tax under section 521 or corresponding provisions of prior law for such years. However, no adjustment for percentage or discovery depletion is to be made for any year during which the association was exempt from tax. If a cooperative association has made a proper election in accordance with section 1020 and the regulations prescribed thereunder with respect to a taxable year beginning before 1952 in which the association was not exempt from tax, the adjustment to basis for depreciation for such years shall be limited in accordance with the provisions of section 1016(a)(2).

(b) *Amortization of bond premium.*—In the case of tax exempt and partially taxable bonds purchased at a premium and subject to amortization under section 171, proper adjustment to basis must be made to reflect amortization with respect to such premium from the date of acquisition of the bond. (For principles governing the method of computation, see the example in paragraph (b) of §1.1016-9, relating to mutual savings banks, building and loan associations, and cooperative banks.) The basis of a fully taxable bond purchased at a premium shall be adjusted from the date of the election to amortize such premium in accordance with the provisions of section 171 except that no adjustment shall be allowable for such portion of the premium attributable to the period prior to the election.

(c) *Amortization of mortgage premium.*—In the case of a mortgage acquired at a premium where the principal of such mortgage is payable in installments, adjustments to the basis for the premium must be made for all taxable years (whether or not the association was exempt from tax under section 521 during such years) in which installment payments are received. Such adjustments may be made on an individual mortgage basis or on a composite basis by reference to the average period of payments of the mortgage loans of such association. For the purpose of this adjustment, the term "premium" includes the excess of the acquisition value of the mortgage over its maturity value. The acquisition value of the mortgage is the cost including buying commissions, attorneys' fees, or brokerage fees, but such value does not include amounts paid for accrued interest. [Reg. §1.1382-7.]

☐ [*T.D. 6643, 4-1-63.*]

[Reg. §1.1383-1]

§1.1383-1. Computation of tax where cooperative redeems nonqualified written notices of allocation.—(a) *General rule.*—(1) If, during the taxable year, a cooperative organization is entitled to a deduction under section 1382(b)(2) or (c)(2)(B) for amounts paid in redemption of nonqualified written notices of allocation, the tax imposed for the taxable year by chapter 1 of the Code shall be the lesser of—

(i) The tax for the taxable year computed under section 1383(a)(1), that is, with such deduction taken into account, or

(ii) The tax for the taxable year computed under section 1383(a)(2), that is, without taking such deduction into account, minus the decrease in tax (under chapter 1 of the Code) for any prior taxable year (or years) which would result solely

from treating all such nonqualified written notices of allocation redeemed during the taxable year as qualified written notices of allocation when paid. For the purpose of this subdivision, the amount of the decrease in tax is not limited to the amount of the tax for the taxable year. See paragraph (c) of this section for rules relating to a refund of tax where the decrease in tax for the prior taxable year (or years) exceeds the tax for the taxable year.

(2) If the cooperative organization computes its tax for the taxable year under the provisions of section 1383(a)(2) and subparagraph (1)(ii) of this paragraph, then no deduction under section 1382(b)(2) or (c)(2)(B) shall be taken into account in computing taxable income or loss for the taxable year, including the computation of any net operating loss carryback or carryover. However, the amount of the deduction shall be taken into account in adjusting earnings and profits for the taxable year.

(3) If the tax determined under subparagraph (1)(i) of this paragraph is the same as the tax determined under subparagraph (1)(ii) of this paragraph, the tax imposed for the taxable year under chapter 1 of the Code shall be the tax determined under subparagraph (1)(i) of this paragraph, and section 1383 and this section shall not otherwise apply. The tax imposed for the taxable year shall be the tax determined under subparagraph (1)(ii) of this paragraph in any case when a credit or refund would be allowable for the taxable year under section 1383(b)(1).

(b) *Determination of decrease in tax for prior taxable years.*—(1) *Prior taxable years.*—The prior taxable year (or years) referred to in paragraph (a) of this section is the year (or years) within the payment period for which the nonqualified written notices of allocation were paid and, in addition, any other prior taxable year (or years) which is affected by the adjustment to income by reason of treating such nonqualified written notices of allocation as qualified written notices of allocation when paid.

(2) *Adjustment to income in prior taxable years.*—The deduction for the prior taxable year (or years) in determining the decrease in tax under section 1383(a)(2)(B) and paragraph (a)(1)(ii) of this section shall be the amount paid in redemption of the nonqualified written notices of allocation which, without regard to section 1383, is allowable as a deduction under section 1382(b)(2) or (c)(2)(B) for the current taxable year.

(3) *Computation of decrease in tax for prior taxable years.*—In computing the amount of decrease in tax for a prior taxable year (or years) resulting under this section, there must first be ascertained the amount of tax previously determined for the taxpayer for such prior taxable year (or years). The tax previously determined

shall be the sum of the amounts shown as such tax by the taxpayer on his return or returns, plus any amounts which have been previously assessed (or collected without assessment) as deficiencies, reduced by the amount of any rebates which have previously been made. The amount shown as the tax by the taxpayer on his return and the amount of any rebates or deficiencies shall be determined in accordance with the provisions of section 6211 and the regulations thereunder. After the tax previously determined has been ascertained, a recomputation must then be made to determine the decrease in tax, if any, resulting under this section. In determining the decrease in tax for the prior taxable year (or years), appropriate adjustment shall be made to any item which is dependent upon the amount of gross income or taxable income (such as charitable contributions, net operating losses, the foreign tax credit, and the dividends received credit).

(c) *Refunds.*—If the decrease in tax for the prior taxable year (or years) determined under section 1383(a)(2)(B) and paragraph (a)(1)(ii) of this section exceeds the tax imposed by chapter 1 of the Code for the taxable year computed without the deduction under section 1382(b) or (c)(2)(B), the excess shall be considered to be a payment of tax for the taxable year of the deduction. Such payment is deemed to have been made on the last day prescribed by law for the payment of tax for the taxable year and shall be refunded or credited in the same manner as if it were an overpayment of tax for such taxable year. See section 6151 and the regulations thereunder, for rules relating to time and place for paying tax shown on returns.

(d) *Example.*—The application of section 1383 may be illustrated by the following example:

Example. The X Cooperative (which reports its income on a calendar year basis) pays patronage

dividends of $100,000 in nonqualified written notices of allocation on February 1, 1964, with respect to patronage occurring in 1963. Since the patronage dividends of $100,000 were paid in nonqualified written notices of allocation the X Cooperative is not allowed a deduction for that amount for 1963. On December 1, 1966, the X Cooperative redeems these nonqualified written notices of allocation for $50,000. Under section 1382(b)(2), a deduction of $50,000 is allowable in computing its taxable income for 1966. However, the X Cooperative has a loss for 1966 determined without regard to this deduction. The X Cooperative, therefore, makes the computation under the alternative method provided in section 1383(a)(2). Under this alternative method, it will claim a credit or refund (as an overpayment of tax for 1966) of the decrease in tax for 1963 and for such other years prior to 1966 as are affected which results from recomputing its tax for 1963 (and such other years affected) as if patronage dividends of $50,000 had been paid on February 1, 1964, in qualified written notices of allocation. In addition, under this alternative the X Cooperative cannot use the $50,000 as a deduction for 1966 so as to increase its net operating loss for such year for purposes of computing a net operating loss carryback or carryover. If the X Cooperative also redeems on December 1, 1966, nonqualified written notices of allocation which were paid as patronage dividends on February 1, 1965, with respect to patronage occurring in 1964, it will claim a credit or refund (as an overpayment of tax for 1966) of the decrease in tax for 1964 and for such other years prior to 1966 as are affected. It shall not, however, apply one method for computing the tax with respect to the redemptions in 1966 of the nonqualified written notices of allocation paid in 1964 and the other method with respect to the redemption in 1966 of the nonqualified written notices of allocation paid in 1965. [Reg. § 1.1383-1.]

☐ [T.D. 6643, 4-1-63.]

Tax Treatment of Patronage Dividends, Etc.

[Reg. § 1.1385-1]

§ 1.1385-1. Amounts includible in patron's gross income.—(a) *General rules.*—Section 1385(a) requires every person to include in gross income the following amounts received by him during the taxable year, to the extent paid by the organization in money, a qualified written notice of allocation, or other property (other than a nonqualified written notice of allocation):

(1) The amount of any patronage dividend received from an organization subject to the provisions of part I, subchapter T, chapter 1 of the Code, unless such amount is excludable from gross income under the provisions of section 1385(b) and paragraph (c) of this section, and

(2) The amount of any distribution received from a farmers', fruit growers', or like associa-

tion, organized and operated in compliance with the requirements of section 521 and § 1.521-1, which is paid on a patronage basis with respect to earnings derived by such association either from business done with or for the United States or any of its agencies or from sources other than patronage.

The amounts described in subparagraphs (1) and (2) of this paragraph are includible in gross income for the taxable year in which they are received even though the cooperative organization was allowed a deduction for such amounts for its preceding taxable year because they were paid during the payment period for such preceding taxable year. Similarly, such amounts are includible in gross income even though the cooperative organization is not permitted any deduction for such amounts under the provisions

Reg. § 1.1385-1(a)(2)

of section 1382 because such amounts were not paid within the time prescribed by such section.

(b) *Treatment of certain nonqualified notices of allocation.*—(1) Except as provided in paragraph (c) of this section, any gain on the redemption, sale, or other disposition of a nonqualified written notice of allocation described in subparagraph (2) of this paragraph shall, to the extent that the stated dollar amount of such written notice of allocation exceeds its basis, be considered as gain from the sale or exchange of property which is not a capital asset, whether such gain is realized by the patron who received the nonqualified written notice of allocation initially or by any subsequent holder. Any amount realized on the redemption, sale, or other disposition of such a nonqualified written notice of allocation in excess of its stated dollar amount will be treated under the applicable provisions of the Code. For example, amounts received in redemption of a nonqualified written notice of allocation which are in excess of the stated dollar amount of such written notice of allocation and which, in effect, constitute interest shall be treated by the recipient as interest.

(2) The nonqualified written notices of allocation to which subparagraph (1) of this paragraph applies are the following:

(i) A nonqualified written notice of allocation which was paid as a patronage dividend (within the meaning of section 1388(a) and paragraph (a) of § 1.1388-1), by a cooperative organization subject to the provisions of part I of subchapter T, and

(ii) A nonqualified written notice of allocation which was paid by a farmers', fruit growers', or like association, organized and operated in compliance with the requirements of section 521 and § 1.521-1, to patrons on a patronage basis with respect to earnings derived either from business done with or for the United States or any of its agencies or from sources other than patronage.

(3) The basis of any nonqualified written notice of allocation described in subparagraph (2) of this paragraph, in the hands of the patron to whom such written notice of allocation was initially paid shall be zero, and the basis of such a written notice of allocation which was acquired from a decedent shall be its basis in the hands of the decedent.

(4) The application of this paragraph may be illustrated by the following example:

Example. A, a farmer, receives a patronage dividend from the X Cooperative, in the form of a nonqualified written notice of allocation, which is attributable to the sale of his crop to that cooperative organization. The stated dollar amount of the nonqualified written notice of allocation is $100. The basis of the written notice of allocation in the hands of A is zero and he must report any amount up to $100 received by him on its redemption, sale, or other disposition,

as ordinary income. If A gives the written notice of allocation to his son B, B takes A's (the donor's) basis which is zero, and any gain up to $100 which B later realizes on its redemption, sale, or other disposition is ordinary income. Similarly, if A dies before realizing any gain on the nonqualified written notice of allocation, B, his legatee, has a zero basis for such written notice of allocation and any gain up to $100 which he then realizes on its redemption, sale, or other disposition is also ordinary income. Such gain is income in respect of a decedent within the meaning of section 691(a) and § 1.691(a)-1.

(c) *Treatment of patronage dividends received with respect to certain property.*—(1) *Exclusions from gross income.*—Except as provided in subparagraph (2) of this paragraph, gross income shall not include—

(i) Any amount of a patronage dividend described in paragraph (a)(1) of this section which is received with respect to the purchase of supplies, equipment, or services, which were not used in the trade or business and the cost of which was not deductible under section 212, or which is received with respect to the marketing or purchasing of a capital asset (as defined in section 1221) or property used in the trade or business of a character which is subject to the allowance for depreciation provided in section 167; and

(ii) Any amount (to the extent treated as ordinary income under paragraph (b) of this section) received on the redemption, sale, or other disposition of a nonqualified written notice of allocation which was received as a patronage dividend with respect to the purchase of supplies, equipment, or services, which were not used in the trade or business and the cost of which was not deductible under section 212, or which was received as a patronage dividend with respect to the marketing or purchasing of a capital asset (as defined in section 1221) or property used in the trade or business of a character which is subject to the allowance for depreciation provided in section 167.

(2) *Special rules.*—(i) If an amount described in subparagraph (1) of this paragraph relates to the purchase of a capital asset (as defined in section 1221), or property used in the trade or business of a character which is subject to the allowance for depreciation provided in section 167, and the person receiving such amount owned such asset or property at any time during the taxable year in which such amount is received, then such amount shall be taken into account as an adjustment to the basis of such property or asset as of the first day of the taxable year in which such amount is received. To the extent that such amount exceeds the adjusted basis of such property it shall be taken into account as ordinary income.

(ii) If an amount described in subparagraph (1) of this paragraph relates to the marketing or purchasing of a capital asset (as defined in section 1221), or property used in the trade or business of a character which is subject to the allowance for depreciation provided in section 167, and the person receiving such amount did not own the asset or property at any time during the taxable year in which such amount is received, then such amount shall be included in gross income as ordinary income except that—

(a) If such amount relates to a capital asset (as defined in section 1221) which was held by the recipient for more than 1 year (6 months for taxable years beginning before 1977; 9 months for taxable years beginning in 1977) and with respect to which a loss was or would have been deductible under section 165, such amount shall be taken into account as gain from the sale or exchange of a capital asset held for more than 1 year (6 months for taxable years beginning before 1977; 9 months for taxable years beginning in 1977);

(b) If such amount relates to a capital asset (as defined in section 1221) with respect to which a loss was not or would not have been deductible under section 165, such amount shall not be taken into account.

(iii) If an amount described in subparagraph (1) of this paragraph relates to the marketing of a capital asset (as defined in section 1221) or property used in the trade or business of a character which is subject to the allowance for depreciation provided in section 167, and such amount is received by the patron in the same taxable year during which he marketed the asset to which it relates, such amount shall be treated as an additional amount received on the sale or other disposition of such asset.

(iv) If a person receiving a patronage dividend or an amount on the redemption, sale, or other disposition of a nonqualified written notice of allocation which was received as a patronage dividend is unable to determine the item to which it relates, he shall include such patronage dividend or such amount in gross income as ordinary income in the manner and to the extent provided in paragraph (a) or (b) of this section, whichever is applicable.

(3) The application of this paragraph may be illustrated by the following examples:

Example (1). On July 1, 1964, P, a patron of a cooperative association, purchases an implement for use in his farming business from such association for $2,900. The implement has an estimated useful life of three years and has an estimated salvage value of $200 which P chooses to take into account in the computation of depreciation. P files his income tax returns on a calendar year basis. For 1964 P claims depreciation of $450 with respect to the implement pursuant to his use of the straight-line method at the rate of $900 per year. On July 1, 1965, the cooperative association pays a patronage dividend to P of $300 in cash with respect to his purchase of the farm implement. P will adjust the basis of the implement and will compute his depreciation deduction for 1965 (and subsequent taxable years) as follows:

Cost of farm implement, July 1, 1964		$2,900
Less:		
Salvage value	$200	
Depreciation for 1964 (6 mos.)	450	
Adjustment as of Jan. 1, 1965 for cash patronage dividend	300	950
Basis for depreciation for the remaining 2½ years of estimated life		1,950
Depreciation deduction for 1965 ($1,950 divided by the 2½ years of remaining life)		780

Example (2). Assume the same facts as in example (1), except that on July 1, 1965, the cooperative association paid a patronage dividend to P with respect to his purchase of the implement in the form of a nonqualified written notice of allocation having a stated dollar amount of $300. Since such written notice of allocation was not qualified, no amount of the patronage dividend was taken into account by P as an adjustment to the basis of the implement, or in computing his depreciation deduction, for the year 1965. In 1968, P receives $300 cash from the association in full redemption of the written notice of allocation. Prior to 1968, he had recovered through depreciation $2,700 of the cost of the implement, leaving an adjusted basis of $200 (the salvage value). For the year 1968, the redemption proceeds of $300 are applied against the adjusted basis of $200, reducing the basis of the implement to zero, and the balance of the redemption proceeds, $100, is includible as ordinary income in P's gross income for the calendar year 1968. If the patronage dividend paid to P on July 1, 1965, had been in the form of $60 cash (20 percent of $300) and a qualified written notice of allocation with a stated dollar amount of $240, then the tax treatment of such patronage dividend would be that illustrated in example (1).

Example (3). Assume the same facts as in example (2), except that the nonqualified written notice of allocation is redeemed in cash on July 1, 1966. The full $300 received on redemption will reduce the adjusted basis of the implement as of January 1, 1966, and the depreciation allowances for 1966 and 1967 are computed as follows:

Cost of farm implement, July 1, 1964		$2,900
Less:		
Salvage value	$200	
Depreciation for 1964 (6 mos.)	450	

Depreciation for 1965	900
Adjustment as of Jan. 1, 1966 for proceeds of the redemption . . .	300
	1,850
Basis for depreciation on Jan. 1, 1966	1,050

If P uses the implement in his business until fully depreciated, he would be entitled to the following depreciation allowances with respect to such implement:

For 1966	$700
For 1967	350
	$1,050
Balance to be depreciated	0

Example (4). Assume the same facts as in example (3), except that P sells the implement in 1965. The entire $300 received in 1966 in redemption of the nonqualified written notice of allocation is includible as ordinary income in P's gross income for the year 1966.

(d) *Determination of amount received.*—In determining the amount received for purposes of this section—

(1) Property (other than written notices of allocation) shall be taken into account at its fair market value when received;

(2) A qualified written notice of allocation shall be taken into account at its stated dollar amount; and

(3) The amount of a qualified check shall be considered an amount received in money during the taxable year in which such check is received if the check is endorsed and cashed on or before the ninetieth day after the close of the payment period for the taxable year of the cooperative organization in which the patronage to which such amount relates occurred.

(e) *Effective date.*—This section shall not apply to any distribution or allocation received from a cooperative organization, or to any gain or loss on the redemption, sale, or other disposition of any allocation received from such an organization, if such distribution or allocation was received with respect to patronage occurring in a taxable year of the organization beginning before January 1, 1963. See § 1.61-5 for the tax treatment by patrons of such distributions or allocations. [Reg. § 1.1385-1.]

☐ [*T.D.* 6643, 4-1-63. *Amended by T.D.* 7728, 10-31-80.]

Definitions; Special Rules

[Reg. § 1.1388-1]

§ 1.1388-1. Definitions and special rules.— (a) *Patronage dividend.*—(1) *In general.*—The term "patronage dividend" means an amount paid to a patron by a cooperative organization subject to the provisions of Part I, subchapter T, chapter 1 of the Code, which is paid—

(i) On the basis of quantity or value of business done with or for such patron,

(ii) Under a valid enforceable written obligation of such organization to the patron to pay such amount, which obligation existed before the cooperative organization received the amount so paid, and

(iii) Which is determined by reference to the net earnings of the cooperative organization from business done with or for its patrons.

For the purpose of subdivision (ii) of this subparagraph, amounts paid by a cooperative organization are paid under a valid enforceable written obligation if such payments are required by State law or are paid pursuant to provisions of the bylaws, articles of incorporation, or other written contract, whereby the organization is obligated to make such payment. The term "net earnings", for purposes of subdivision (iii) of this subparagraph includes the excess of amounts retained (or assessed) by the organization to cover expenses or other items over the amount of such expenses or other items. For purposes of such subdivision (iii), net earnings shall not be reduced by any taxes imposed by subtitle A of the Code, but shall be reduced by dividends paid on capital stock or other proprietary capital interests.

(2) *Exceptions.*—The term "patronage dividend" does not include the following:

(i) An amount paid to a patron by a cooperative organization to the extent that such amount is paid out of earnings not derived from business done with or for patrons.

(ii) An amount paid to a patron by a cooperative organization to the extent that such amount is paid out of earnings from business done with or for other patrons to whom no amounts are paid, or to whom smaller amounts are paid, with respect to substantially identical transactions. Thus, if a cooperative organization does not pay any patronage dividends to nonmembers, any portion of the amounts paid to members which is out of net earnings from patronage with nonmembers, and which would have been paid to the nonmembers if all patrons were treated alike, is not a patronage dividend.

(iii) An amount paid to a patron by a cooperative organization to the extent that such amount is paid in redemption of capital stock, or in redemption or satisfaction of certificates of indebtedness, revolving fund certificates, retain certificates, letters of advice, or other similar documents, even if such documents were originally paid as patronage dividends.

(iv) An amount paid to a patron by a cooperative organization to the extent that such amount is fixed without reference to the net earnings of the cooperative organization from business done with or for its patrons.

(3) *Examples.*—The application of subparagraphs (1) and (2) of this paragraph may be illustrated by the following examples:

Example (1). (i) Cooperative A, a marketing association operating on a pooling basis, receives the products of patron W on January 5, 1964. On the same day cooperative A advances to W 45 cents per unit for the products so delivered and allocates to him a "retain certificate" having a face value calculated at the rate of 5 cents per unit. During the operation of the pool, and before substantially all the products in the pool are disposed of, cooperative A advances to W an additional 40 cents per unit, the amount being determined by reference to the market price of the products sold and the anticipated price of the unsold products. At the close of the pool on November 10, 1964, cooperative A determines the excess of its receipts over the sum of its expenses and its previous advances to patrons, and allocates to W an additional 3 cents per unit and shares of the capital stock of A having an aggregate stated dollar amount calculated at the rate of 2 cents per unit. Under the provisions of section 1382(e), W's patronage is deemed to occur in 1964, the year in which the pool is closed.

(ii) The patronage dividend paid to W during 1964 amounts to 5 cents per unit, consisting of the aggregate of the following per-unit allocations: The amount of the cash distribution (3 cents), and the stated dollar amount of the capital stock of A (2 cents), which are fixed with reference to the net earnings of A. The amount of the two distributions in cash (85 cents) and the face amount of the "retain certificate" (5 cents), which are fixed without reference to the net earnings of A, do not constitute patronage dividends.

Example (2). Cooperative B, a marketing association operating on a pooling basis, receives the products of patron X on March 5, 1964. On the same day cooperative B pays to X $1.00 per unit for such products, this amount being determined by reference to the market price of the product when received, and issues to him a participation certificate having no face value but which entitles X on the close of the pool to the proceeds derived from the sale of his products less the previous payment of $1.00 and the expenses and other charges attributable to such products. On March 5, 1967, cooperative B, having sold the products in the pool, having deducted the previous payments for such products, and having determined the expenses and other charges of the pool pays to X, in cash, 10 cents per unit pursuant to the participation certificate. Under the provisions of section 1382(e), X's patronage is deemed to occur in 1967, the year in which the pool is closed. The payment made to X during 1967, amounting to 10 cents per unit, is a patronage dividend. Neither the payment to X in 1964 of $1.00 nor the issuance to him of the participation certificate in that year constitutes a patronage dividend.

Example (3). Cooperative C, a purchasing association, obtains supplies for patron Y on May 1, 1964, and receives in return therefor $100. On February 1, 1965, cooperative C, having determined the excess of its receipts over its costs and expenses, pays to Y a cash distribution of $1.00 and a revolving fund certificate with a stated dollar amount of $1.00. The amount of patronage dividend paid to Y in 1965 is $2.00, the aggregate of the cash distribution ($1.00) and the stated dollar amount of the revolving fund certificate ($1.00).

Example (4). Cooperative D, a service association, sells the products of members on a fee basis. It receives the products of patron Z under an agreement not to pool his products with those of other members, to sell his products, and to deliver to him the proceeds of the sale. Patron Z makes payments to cooperative D during 1964 aggregating $75 for service rendered him by cooperative D during that year. On May 15, 1965, cooperative D, having determined the excess of its receipts over its costs and expenses, pays to Z a cash distribution of $2.00. Such amount is a patronage dividend paid by cooperative D during 1965.

(b) *Written notice of allocation.*—The term "written notice of allocation" means any capital stock, revolving fund certificate, retain certificate, certificate of indebtedness, letter of advice, or other written notice, which discloses to the patron the stated dollar amount allocated to him on the books of the cooperative organization, and the portion thereof, if any, which constitutes a patronage dividend. Thus, a mere credit to the account of a patron on the books of the organization without disclosure to the patron, is not a written notice of allocation. A written notice of allocation may disclose to the patron the amount of the allocation which constitutes a patronage dividend either as a dollar amount or as a percentage of the stated dollar amount of the written notice of allocation.

(c) *Qualified written notice of allocation.*—(1) *In general.*—The term "qualified written notice of allocation" means a written notice of allocation—

(i) Which meets the requirements of subparagraph (2) or (3) of this paragraph, and

(ii) Which is paid as part of a patronage dividend, or as part of a payment by a cooperative association organized and operated in compliance with the provisions of section 521 and

§ 1.521-1 to patrons on a patronage basis with respect to earnings derived from business done with or for the United States or any of its agencies or from sources other than patronage, that also includes a payment in money or by qualified check equal to at least 20 percent of such patronage dividend or such payment.

In determining, for purposes of subdivision (ii) of this subparagraph, whether 20 percent of a patronage dividend or a payment with respect to nonpatronage earnings is paid in money or by qualified check, any portion of such dividend or payment which is paid in nonqualified written notices of allocation may be disregarded. Thus, if a cooperative pays a patronage dividend of $100 in the form of a nonqualified written notice of allocation with a stated dollar amount of $50, a written notice of allocation with a stated dollar amount of $40, and money in the amount of $10, the written notice of allocation with a stated dollar amount of $40 will constitute a qualified written notice of allocation if it meets the requirements of subparagraph (2) or (3) of this paragraph. A "payment in money", as that term is used in subdivision (ii) of this subparagraph, includes a payment by a check drawn on a bank but does not include a credit against amounts owed by the patron to the cooperative organization, a credit against the purchase price of a share of stock or of a membership in such organization, nor does it include a payment by means of a document redeemable by such organization for money.

(2) *Written notice of allocation redeemable in cash.*—The term "qualified written notice of allocation" includes a written notice of allocation which meets the requirement of subparagraph (1)(ii) of this paragraph and which may be redeemed in cash at its stated dollar amount at any time within a period beginning on the date such written notice of allocation is paid and ending not earlier than 90 days from such date, but only if the distributee receives written notice of the right of redemption at the time he receives such written notice of allocation. The written notice of the right of redemption referred to in the preceding sentence shall be given separately to each patron. Thus, a written notice of the right of redemption which is published in a newspaper or posted at the cooperative's place of business would not be sufficient to qualify a written notice of allocation which is otherwise described in this subparagraph.

(3) *Consent of patron.*—The term "qualified written notice of allocation" also includes a written notice of allocation which meets the requirement of subparagraph (1)(ii) of this paragraph and which the distributee has consented, in a manner provided in this subparagraph, to take into account at its stated dollar amount as provided in section 1385 and § 1.1385-1.

(i) *Consent in writing.*—A distributee may consent to take the stated dollar amount of written notices of allocation into account under section 1385 by signing and furnishing a written consent to the cooperative organization. No special form is required for the written consent so long as the document on which it is made clearly discloses the terms of the consent. Thus, the written consent may be made on a signed invoice, sales slip, delivery ticket, marketing agreement, or other document, on which appears the appropriate consent. Unless the written consent specifically provides to the contrary, it shall be effective with respect to all patronage occurring during the taxable year of the cooperative organization in which such consent is received by such organization and, unless revoked under section 1388(c)(3)(B), for all subsequent taxable years. Section 1388(c)(3)(B)(i) provides that a written consent may be revoked by the patron at any time. Thus, any written consent which is, by its terms, irrevocable is not a consent that would qualify a written notice of allocation. A revocation, to be effective, must be in writing, signed by the patron, and furnished to the cooperative organization. Such a revocation shall be effective only with respect to patronage occurring after the close of the taxable year of the cooperative organization during which the revocation is filed with it. In the case of a pooling arrangement described in section 1382(e) and § 1.1382-5, a written consent which is made at any time before the close of the taxable year of the cooperative organization during which the pool closes shall be effective with respect to all patronage under that pool. In addition, any subsequent revocation of such consent by the patron will not be effective for that pool or any other pool with respect to which he has been a patron before such revocation.

(ii) *Consent by membership.*—(a) A distributee may consent to take the stated dollar amount of written notices of allocation into account under section 1385 by obtaining or retaining membership in the cooperative organization after such organization has adopted a valid bylaw providing that membership in such cooperative organization constitutes such consent, but such consent shall take effect only after the distributee has received a written notification of the adoption of the bylaw provision and a copy of such bylaw. The bylaw must have been adopted by the cooperative organization after October 16, 1962, and must contain a clear statement that membership in the cooperative organization constitutes the prescribed consent. The written notification from the cooperative organization must inform the patron that this bylaw has been adopted and of its significance. The notification and copy of the bylaw shall be given separately to each member (or prospective member); thus, a written notice and copy of the bylaw which are published in a newspaper or posted at the cooperative's place of business are not sufficient to qualify a written notice of allocation under this subdivision. A member (or prospective member) is presumed to have received the notification and copy of the bylaw if they were sent to his last known address by ordinary mail. A prospective member must receive the notification and copy of the bylaw before he becomes a member of the organization in order to have his membership in the organization constitute consent. A consent made in the manner described in this subdivision shall be effective only with respect to patronage occurring after the patron has received a copy of the bylaw and the prerequisite notice and while he is a member of the organization. Thus, any such consent shall not be effective with respect to any patronage occurring after the patron ceases to be a member of the cooperative organization or after the bylaw provision is repealed by such organization. In the case of a pooling arrangement described in section 1382(e) and § 1.1382-5, a consent made under this subdivision will be effective only with respect to the patron's actual patronage occurring after he receives the notification and copy of the bylaw and while he is a member of the cooperative organization. Thus such a consent shall not be effective with respect to any patronage under a pool after the patron ceases to be a member of the cooperative organization or after the bylaw provision is repealed by the organization.

(b) The following is an example of a bylaw provision which would meet the requirements prescribed in (a) of this subdivision.

Example. Each person who hereafter applies for and is accepted to membership in this cooperative and each member of this cooperative on the effective date of this bylaw who continues as a member after such date shall, by such act alone, consent that the amount of any distributions with respect to his patronage occurring after . . . ., which are made in written notices of allocation (as defined in 26 U.S.C. 1388) and which are received by him from the cooperative, will be taken into account by him at their stated dollar amounts in the manner provided in 26 U.S.C. 1385(a) in the taxable year in which such written notices of allocation are received by him.

(c) For purposes of this subdivision the term "member" means a person who is entitled to participate in the management of the cooperative organization.

(iii) *Consent by qualified check.*—(a) A distributee may consent to take the stated dollar amount of a written notice of allocation into account under section 1385 by endorsing and cashing a qualified check which is paid as a part of the same patronage dividend or payment described in subparagraph (1)(ii) of this paragraph of which the written notice of allocation is also a part. In order to constitute an effective consent under this subdivision, however, the qualified check must be endorsed and cashed by the payee on or before the ninetieth day after the close of the payment period for the taxable year of the cooperative organization with respect to which the patronage dividend or payment is paid (or on or before such earlier day as may be prescribed by the cooperative organization). The endorsing and cashing of a qualified check shall be considered a consent only with respect to written notices of allocation which are part of the same patronage dividend or payment as the qualified check and for which a consent under subdivision (i) or (ii) of this subparagraph is not in effect. A qualified check is presumed to be endorsed and cashed within the 90-day period if the earliest bank endorsement which appears thereon bears a date no later than 3 days after the end of such 90-day period (excluding Saturdays, Sundays, and legal holidays).

(b) The term "qualified check" means a check, or other instrument redeemable in money, which is paid as a part of a patronage dividend or payment described in subparagraph (1)(ii) of this paragraph, on which there is clearly imprinted a statement that the endorsement and cashing of the check or other instrument constitutes the consent of the payee to take into account, as provided in the Federal income tax laws, the stated dollar amount of any written notices of allocation which are paid as a part of the patronage dividend or payment of which such check or other instrument is also a part. A qualified check need not be in the form of an ordinary check which is payable through the banking system. It may, for example, be in the form of an instrument which is redeemable in money by the cooperative organization. The term "qualified check" does not include a check or other instrument paid as part of a patronage dividend or payment with respect to which a consent under subdivision (i) or (ii) of this subparagraph is in effect. In addition, the term "qualified check" does not include a check or other instrument which is paid as part of a patronage dividend or payment, if such patronage dividend or payment does not also include a written notice of allocation (other than a written notice of allocation that may be redeemed in cash at its stated dollar amount which meets the requirements of section 1388(c)(1)(A) and subparagraph (2) of this paragraph). Thus, a check which is paid as part of a patronage dividend is not a qualified check (even though it has the required statement imprinted on it) if the remaining portion of such patronage dividend is paid in cash or if the only written notices of allocation included in the payment are qualified under section 1388(c)(1)(A) and subparagraph (2) of this paragraph (relating to certain written notices of allocation which are redeemable by the patron within a period of at least 90 days).

(c) The provisions of this subdivision may be illustrated by the following example:

Reg. § 1.1388-1(c)(3)(iii)(c)

Example. (1) The A Cooperative is a cooperative organization filing its income tax returns on a calendar year basis. None of its patrons have consented in the manner prescribed in section 1388(c)(2)(A) or (B). On August 1, 1964, the A Cooperative pays patronage dividends to its patrons with respect to their 1963 patronage, and the payment to each such patron is partly by a qualified check and partly in the form of a written notice of allocation which is not redeemable for cash. Each patron who endorses and cashes his qualified check on or before December 14, 1964 (the ninetieth day following the close of the 1963 payment period) shall be considered to have consented with respect to the accompanying written notice of allocation and the amount of such check is treated as a patronage dividend paid in money on August 1, 1964.

(2) As to any patron who has not endorsed and cashed his qualified check by December 14, 1964, there is no consent and both the written notice of allocation and the qualified check constitute nonqualified written notices of allocation within the meaning of section 1388(d) and paragraph (d) of this section. If such a patron then cashes his check on January 2, 1965, he shall treat the amount received as an amount received on January 2, 1965, in redemption of a nonqualified written notice of allocation. Likewise, the cooperative shall treat the amount of the check as an amount paid on January 2, 1965, in redemption of a nonqualified written notice of allocation.

(d) *Nonqualified written notice of allocation.*— The term "nonqualified written notice of allocation" means a written notice of allocation which is not a qualified written notice of allocation described in section 1388(c) and paragraph (c) of this section, or a qualified check which is not cashed on or before the ninetieth day after the close of the payment period for the taxable year of the cooperative organization for which the payment of which it is a part is paid.

(e) *Patron.*—The term "patron" includes any person with whom or for whom the cooperative association does business on a cooperative basis, whether a member or a non-member of the cooperative association, and whether an individual, a trust, estate, partnership, company, corporation, or cooperative association. [Reg. § 1.1388-1.]

☐ [*T.D.* 6643, 4-1-63.]

EMPOWERMENT ZONES, ENTERPRISE COMMUNITIES, AND RURAL DEVELOPMENT INVESTMENT AREAS

[Reg. § 1.1394-0]

§ 1.1394-0. Table of contents.—This section lists the major paragraph headings contained in § 1.1394-1.

(q) Effective dates.

(1) In general.

(2) Elective retroactive application in whole.

[Reg. § 1.1394-0.]

☐ [T.D. 8673, 5-30-96.]

[Reg. § 1.1394-1]

§ 1.1394-1. Enterprise zone facility bonds.— (a) *Scope.*—This section contains rules relating to tax-exempt bonds under section 1394 (enterprise zone facility bonds) to provide enterprise zone facilities in both empowerment zones and enterprise communities (zones). See sections 1394, 1397B, and 1397C for other rules and definitions.

(b) *Period of compliance.*—(1) *In general.*—Except as provided in paragraphs (b)(2) and (c) of this section, the requirements under sections 1394(a) and (b) applicable to enterprise zone facility bonds must be complied with throughout the greater of the following—

(i) The remainder of the period during which the zone designation is in effect under section 1391 (zone designation period); and

(ii) The period that ends on the weighted average maturity date of the enterprise zone facility bonds.

(2) *Compliance after an issue is retired.*—Except as provided in paragraph (c)(3) of this section, the requirements applicable to enterprise zone facility bonds do not apply to an issue after the date on which no enterprise zone facility bonds of the issue are outstanding.

(3) *Deemed compliance.*—(i) *General rule.*— An issue is deemed to comply with the requirements of sections 1394(a) and (b) if—

(A) The issuer and the principal user in good faith attempt to meet the requirements of sections 1394(a) and (b) throughout the period of compliance required under this section; and

(B) Any failure to meet these requirements is corrected within a one-year period after the failure is first discovered.

(ii) *Exception.*—The provisions of paragraph (b)(3)(i) of this section do not apply to the requirements of section 1397B(d)(5)(A) (relating to certain prohibited business activities).

(iii) *Good faith.*—In order to satisfy the good faith requirement of paragraph (b)(3)(i)(A) of this section, the principal user must at least annually demonstrate to the issuer the principal user's monitoring of compliance with the requirements of sections 1394(a) and (b).

(c) *Special rules for requirements of sections 1397B and 1397C.*—(1) *Start of compliance period.*—Except as provided in paragraph (c)(2) of this section, the requirements of sections 1397B (relating to qualification as an enterprise zone business) and 1397C (relating to satisfaction of

the rules for qualified zone property) do not apply prior to the *initial testing date* (as defined in paragraph (c)(4) of this section) if—

(i) The issuer and the principal user reasonably expect on the issue date of the enterprise zone facility bonds that those requirements will be met by the principal user on or before the initial testing date; and

(ii) The issuer and the principal user exercise due diligence to meet those requirements prior to the initial testing date.

(2) *Compliance period for certain prohibited activities.*—The requirements of section 1397B(d)(5)(A) (relating to certain prohibited business activities) must be complied with throughout the term of the enterprise zone facility bonds.

(3) *Minimum compliance period.*—The requirements of sections 1397B(b) or (c) and 1397C must be satisfied for a continuous period of at least three years after the initial testing date, notwithstanding that—

(i) The period of compliance required under paragraph (b)(1) of this section expires before the end of the three-year period; or

(ii) The enterprise zone facility bonds are retired before the end of the three-year period.

(4) *Initial testing date.*—(i) *In general.*—Except as otherwise provided in paragraph (c)(4)(ii) of this section, the initial testing date is the date that is 18 months after the later of the issue date of the enterprise zone facility bonds or the date on which the financed property is placed in service; provided, however, it is not later than—

(A) Three years after the issue date; or

(B) Five years after the issue date, if the issue finances a construction project for which both the issuer and a licensed architect or engineer certify on or before the issue date of the enterprise zone facility bonds that more than three years after the issue date is necessary to complete construction of the project.

(ii) *Alternative initial testing date.*—If the issuer identifies as the initial testing date a date after the issue date of the enterprise zone facility bonds and prior to the initial testing date that would have been determined under paragraph (c)(4)(i) of this section, that earlier date is treated as the initial testing date.

(d) *Testing on an average basis.*—Compliance with each of the requirements of section 1397B(b) or (c) is tested each taxable year. Compliance with any of the requirements may be tested on an average basis, taking into account up to four immediately preceding taxable years plus the current taxable year. The earliest taxable year that may be taken into account for purposes of the preceding sentence is the taxable year that includes the initial testing date. A taxable year is disregarded if the part of the taxable year that falls in a required compliance period does not exceed 90 days.

(e) *Resident employee requirements.*—(1) *Determination of employee status.*—For purposes of the requirement of section 1397B(b)(6) or (c)(5) that at least 35 percent of the employees are residents of the zone, the issuer and the principal user may rely on a certification, signed under penalties of perjury by the employee, provided—

(i) The certification provides to the principal user the address of the employee's principal residence;

(ii) The employee is required by the certification to notify the principal user of a change of the employee's principal residence; and

(iii) Neither the issuer nor the principal user has actual knowledge that the principal residence set forth in the certification is not the employee's principal residence.

(2) *Employee treated as zone resident.*—If an issue fails to comply with the requirement of section 1397B(b)(6) or (c)(5) because an employee who initially resided in the zone moves out of the zone, that employee is treated as still residing in the zone if—

(i) That employee was a bona fide resident of the zone at the time of the certification described in paragraph (e)(1) of this section;

(ii) That employee continues to perform services for the principal user in an enterprise zone business and substantially all of those services are performed in the zone; and

(iii) A resident of the zone meeting the requirements of section 1397B(b)(5) or (c)(4) is hired by the principal user for the next available comparable (or lesser) position.

(3) *Resident employee percentage.*—For purposes of meeting the requirement of section 1397B(b)(6) or (c)(5) that at least 35 percent of the employees of an enterprise zone business are residents of a zone, paragraphs (e)(3)(i) and (ii) of this section apply.

(i) The term *employee* includes a self-employed individual within the meaning of section 401(c)(1).

(ii) The resident employee percentage is determined on any reasonable basis consistently applied throughout the period of compliance required under this section. The per-employee fraction (as defined in paragraph (e)(3)(ii)(A) of this section) or the employee actual work hour fraction (as defined in paragraph (e)(3)(ii)(B) of this section) are both reasonable methods.

(A) The term *per-employee fraction* means the fraction, the numerator of which is, during the taxable year, the number of employees who work at least 15 hours a week for the principal user, who reside in the zone, and who are employed for at least 90 days, and the denominator of which is, during the same taxable year, the aggregate number of all employees who work at least 15 hours a week for the principal user and who are employed for at least 90 days.

(B) The term *employee actual work hour fraction* means the fraction, the numerator of which is the aggregate total actual hours of work for the principal user of employees who reside in the zone during a taxable year, and the denominator of which is the aggregate total actual hours of work for the principal user of all employees during the same taxable year.

(f) *Application to pooled financing bond and loan recycling programs.*—In the case of a pooled financing bond program described in paragraph (g)(2) of this section or a loan recycling program described in paragraph (m)(2)(ii) of this section, the requirements of paragraphs (b) through (e) of this section apply on a loan-by-loan basis. See also paragraphs (g)(2) (relating to limitation on amount of bonds), (m)(2) (relating to maturity limitations), (m)(3) (relating to volume cap), and (m)(4) (relating to remedial actions) of this section.

(g) *Limitation on amount of bonds.*—(1) *Determination of outstanding amount.*—Whether an issue satisfies the requirements of section 1394(c) (relating to the $3 million and $20 million aggregate limitations on the amount of outstanding enterprise zone facility bonds) is determined as of the issue date of that issue, based on the issue price of that issue and the adjusted issue price of outstanding enterprise zone facility bonds. Amounts of outstanding enterprise zone facility bonds allocable to any entity are determined under rules contained in section 144(a)(10)(C) and the underlying regulations. Thus, the definition of *principal user* for purposes of section 1394(c) is different from the definition of *principal user* for purposes of paragraph (j) of this section.

(2) *Pooled financing bond programs.*—(i) *In general.*—The limitations of section 1394(c) for an issue for a pooled financing bond program are determined with regard to the amount of the actual loans to enterprise zone businesses rather than the amount lent to *intermediary lenders* as defined in paragraph (g)(2)(ii) of this section. This paragraph (g)(2) applies only to the extent the proceeds of those enterprise zone facility bonds are loaned to one or more enterprise zone businesses within 42 months of the issue date of the enterprise zone facility bonds or are used to redeem enterprise zone facility bonds of the issue within that 42-month period.

(ii) *Pooled financing bond program defined.*—For purposes of this section, a *pooled financing bond program* is a program in which the issuer of enterprise zone facility bonds, in order to provide loans to enterprise zone businesses, lends the proceeds of the enterprise zone facility bonds to a bank or similar intermediary (intermediary lender) which must then relend the proceeds to two or more enterprise zone businesses.

(h) *Original use requirement for purposes of qualified zone property.*—In general, for purposes of section 1397C(a)(1)(B), the term *original use* means the first use to which the property is put within the zone. For purposes of section 1394, if property is vacant for at least a one-year period including the date of zone designation, use prior to that period is disregarded for purposes of determining original use. For this purpose, de minimis incidental uses of property, such as renting the side of a building for a billboard, are disregarded.

(i) *Land.*—The determination of whether land is functionally related and subordinate to qualified zone property is made in a manner consistent with the rules for exempt facilities under section 142.

(j) *Principal user.*—(1) *In general.*—Except as provided in paragraph (j)(2) of this section, the term *principal user* means the owner of financed property.

(2) *Rental of real property.*—(i) *A lessee as the principal user.*—If an owner of real property financed with enterprise zone facility bonds is not an enterprise zone business within the meaning of section 1397B, but the rental of the property is a qualified business within the meaning of section 1397B(d)(2), the term *principal user* for purposes of sections 1394(b) and (e) means the lessee or lessees.

(ii) *Allocation of enterprise zone facility bonds.*—If a lessee is the principal user of real property under paragraph (j)(2)(i) of this section, then proceeds of enterprise zone facility bonds may be allocated to expenditures for real property only to the extent of the property allocable to the lessee's leased space, including expenditures for common areas.

(3) *Pooled financing bond program.*—An intermediary lender in a pooled financing bond program described in paragraph (g)(2) of this section is not treated as the principal user.

(k) *Treatment as separately incorporated business.*—For purposes of section 1394(b)(3)(B), a trade or business may be treated as separately incorporated if allocations of income and activities attributable to the business conducted within the zone are made using a reasonable allocation method and if that trade or business has evidence of those allocations sufficient to establish compliance with the requirements of paragraphs (b) through (f) of this section. Whether an allocation method is reasonable will depend upon the facts and circumstances. An allocation method will not be considered to be reasonable unless the allocation method is applied consistently by the trade or business and is consistent with the purposes of section 1394.

(l) *Substantially all.*—For purposes of sections 1397B and 1397C(a), the term *substantially all* means 85 percent.

(m) *Application of sections 142 and 146 through 150.*—(1) *In general.*—Except as provided in this paragraph (m), enterprise zone facility bonds are treated as exempt facility bonds that are described in section 142(a), and all regulations generally applicable to exempt facility bonds apply to enterprise zone facility bonds. For this purpose, enterprise zone businesses are treated as meeting the public use requirement. Sections 147(c)(1)(A) (relating to limitations on financing the acquisition of land), 147(d) (relating to financing the acquisition of existing property), and 142(b)(2) (relating to limitations on financing office space) do not apply to enterprise zone facility bonds. See also paragraph (n)(4) of this section.

(2) *Maturity limitation.*—(i) *Requirements.*—An issue of enterprise zone facility bonds, the proceeds of which are to be used as part of a loan recycling program, satisfies the requirements of section 147(b) if—

(A) Each loan satisfies the requirements of section 147(b) (determined by treating each separate loan as a separate issue); and

(B) The term of the issue does not exceed 30 years.

(ii) *Loan recycling program defined.*—A *loan recycling program* is a program in which—

(A) The issuer reasonably expects as of the issue date of the enterprise zone facility bonds that loan repayments from principal users will be used to make additional loans during the zone designation period;

(B) Repayments of principal on loans (including prepayments) received during the zone designation period are used within six months of the date of receipt either to make new loans to enterprise zone businesses or to redeem enterprise zone facility bonds that are part of the issue; and

(C) Repayments of principal on loans (including prepayments) received after the zone designation period are used to redeem enterprise zone facility bonds that are part of the issue within six months of the date of receipt.

(3) *Volume cap.*—For purposes of applying section 146(f)(5)(A) (relating to elective carryforward of unused volume limitation), issuing enterprise zone facility bonds is a carryforward purpose.

(4) *Remedial actions.*—In the case of a pooled financing bond program described in paragraph (g)(2) of this section or a loan recycling program described in paragraph (m)(2)(ii) of this section, if a loan fails to meet the requirements of paragraphs (b) through (f) of this section, within six months of noncompliance (after taking into

account the deemed compliance provisions of paragraph (b)(3) of this section, if applicable), an amount equal to the outstanding loan principal must be prepaid and the issuer must—

(i) Reloan the amount of the prepayment; or

(ii) Use the prepayment to redeem an amount of outstanding enterprise zone facility bonds equal to the outstanding principal amount of the loan that no longer meets those requirements.

(n) *Continuing compliance and change of use penalties.*—(1) *In general.*—The penalty provisions of section 1394(e) apply throughout the period of compliance required under paragraph (b) (1) of this section.

(2) *Coordination with deemed compliance provisions.*—Section 1394(e)(2) does not apply during any period during which the issue is deemed to comply with the requirements of section 1394 under the deemed compliance provisions of paragraph (b)(3) of this section.

(3) *Application to pooled financing bond and loan recycling programs.*—In the case of a pooled financing bond program described in paragraph (g)(2) of this section or a loan recycling program described in paragraph (m)(2)(ii) of this section, section 1394(e) applies on a loan-by-loan basis.

(4) *Section 150(b)(4) inapplicable.*—Section 150(b)(4) does not apply to enterprise zone facility bonds.

(o) *Refunding bonds.*—(1) *In general.*—An issue of bonds issued after the zone designation period to refund enterprise zone facility bonds (other than in an advance refunding) are treated as enterprise zone facility bonds if the refunding issue and the prior issue, if treated as a single combined issue, would meet all of the requirements for enterprise zone facility bonds, except the requirements in section 1394(c). For example, the compliance period described in paragraph(b)(1) of this section is calculated taking into account any extension of the weighted average maturity of the refunding issue compared to the remaining weighted average maturity of the prior issue. The proceeds of the refunding issue are allocated to the same expenditures and purpose investments as the prior issue.

(2) *Maturity limitation.*—The maturity limitation of section 147(b) is applied to a refunding issue by taking into account the issuer's reasonable expectations about the economic life of the financed property as of the issue date of the prior issue and the actual weighted average maturity of the combined refunding issue and prior issue.

(p) *Examples.*—The following examples illustrate paragraphs (a) through (o) of this section:

Example 1. Averaging of enterprise zone business requirements. City C issues enterprise zone facility bonds, the proceeds of which are loaned by C to Corporation B to finance the acquisition of equipment for its existing business located in a zone. On the issue date of the enterprise zone facility bonds, B meets all of the requirements of section 1397B(b), except that only 25% of B's employees reside in the zone. C and B reasonably expect on the issue date to meet all requirements of section 1397B(b) by the date that 18 months after the equipment is placed in service (the initial testing date). In each of the first, second, and third taxable years after the initial testing date, 35% 40% and 45%, respectively, of B's employees are zone residents. In the fourth year after the testing date, only 25% of B's employees are zone residents. B continues to meet the 35% resident employee requirement, because the average of zone resident employees for those four taxable years is approximately 36%. The percentage of zone residents employed by B before the initial testing date is not included in determining whether B continues to comply with the 35% resident employee requirement.

Example 2. Measurement of resident employee percentage. Authority D issues enterprise zone facility bonds, the proceeds of which are loaned to Sole Proprietor F to establish an accounting business in a zone. In the first year after the initial testing date, the staff working for F includes F, who works 40 hours per week and does not live in the zone, one employee who resides in the zone and works 40 hours per week, one employee who does not reside in the zone and works 20 hours per week, and one employee who does not reside in the zone and works 10 hours per week. F meets the 35% resident employee test by calculating the percentage on the basis of employee actual work hours as described in paragraph (e)(3)(ii)(B) of this section. If F uses the per-employee basis as described in paragraph (e)(3)(ii)(A) of this section to determine if the resident employee test is met, the percentage of employees who are zone residents on a per-employee basis is only 33% because F must exclude from the numerator and the denominator the employee who works only 10 hours per week. If F calculates the resident employee test as a percentage of employee actual work hours as described in paragraph (e)(3)(ii)(B) of this section in the first year, F must calculate the resident employee test as a percentage of employee actual work hours each year.

Example 3. Active conduct of business within the zone. State G issues enterprise zone facility bonds and loans the proceeds to Corporation H to finance the acquisition of equipment for H's mail order clothing business, which is located in a zone. H purchases the supplies for its clothing business from suppliers located both within and outside of the zone and expects that orders will be received both from customers who will reside or work within the zone and from others outside the zone. All orders are received and filled at, and are shipped from, H's clothing business located in the zone. H meets the requirement that at least 80% of its gross income is derived from the active conduct of business within the zone.

Example 4. Enterprise zone business definition. City J issues enterprise zone facility bonds, the proceeds of which are loaned to Partnership K to finance the acquisition of equipment for its printing operation located in the zone. All orders are taken and completed, and all billing and accounting activities are performed, at the print shop located in the zone. K, on occasion, uses its equipment (including its trucks) and employees to deliver large print jobs to customers who reside outside -of the zone. So long as K is able to establish that its trucks are used in the zone at least 85% of the time and its employees perform at least 85% of services for K in the zone, K meets the requirements of sections 1397B(b)(3) and (5).

Example 5. Treatment as a separately incorporated business. The facts are the same as in *Example 4* except that six years after the issue date of the enterprise zone facility bonds, K determines to expand its operations to a second location outside of the boundaries of the zone. Although the expansion would result in the failure of K to meet the tests of 1397B(b), K, using a reasonable allocation method, allocates income and activities to its operations within the zone and has evidence of these allocations sufficient to establish compliance with the requirements of paragraphs (b) through (f) of this section. The bonds will not fail to be enterprise zone facility bonds merely because of the expansion.

Example 6. Treatment of pooled financing bond programs. Authority L issues bonds in the aggregate principal amount of $5,000,000 and loans the proceeds to Bank M pursuant to a loans-to-lenders program. M does not meet the definition of enterprise zone business contained in section 1397B. Prior to the issue date of the bonds, L held a public hearing regarding issuance of the bonds for the loans-to-lenders program, describing the projects of identified borrowers to be financed initially with $4,000,000 of the proceeds of the bonds. The applicable elected representative of L approved issuance of the bonds subsequent to the public hearing. The loan agreement between L and N provides that the other proceeds of the bonds will be held by M and loaned to borrowers that qualify as enterprise zone businesses, following a public hearing and approval by the applicable elected representative of L of each loan by M to an enterprise zone business. None of the loans will be in principal amounts in excess of $3,000,000. The loans by M will otherwise meet the requirements of section 1394. The bonds will be enterprise zone facility bonds.

Example 7. Original use requirement for purposes of qualified zone property. City N issues enterprise zone facility bonds, the proceeds of which are loaned to Corporation P to finance the acquisition of equipment. P uses the proceeds after the zone designation date to purchase used equipment located outside of the zone and places the equipment in service at its location in the zone. Substantially all of the use of the equipment is in the zone and is in the active conduct of a qualified business by P. The equipment is treated as qualified enterprise zone property under section 1397C because P makes the first use of the property within the zone after the zone designation date.

Example 8. Principal user. State R issues enterprise zone facility bonds and loans the proceeds to Partnership S to finance the construction of a small shopping center to be located in a zone. S is in the business of commercial real estate. S is not an enterprise zone business, but has secured one anchor lessee, Corporation T, for the shopping center. T would qualify as an enterprise zone business. S will derive 60% of its gross rental income of the shopping center from T. S does not anticipate that the remaining rental income will come from enterprise zone businesses. T will occupy 60% of the total rentable space in the shopping center. S can use enterprise zone facility bond proceeds to finance the portion of the costs of the shopping center allocable to T (60%) because T is treated as the principal user of the enterprise zone facility bond proceeds.

Example 9. Remedial actions. State W issues pooled financing enterprise zone facility bonds, the proceeds of which will be loaned to several enterprise zone businesses in the two enterprise communities and one empowerment zone in W. Proceeds of the pooled financing bonds are loaned to Corporation X, an enterprise zone business, for a term of 10 years. Six years after the date of the loan, X expands its operations beyond the empowerment zone and is no longer able to meet the requirements of section 1394. X does not reasonably expect to be able to cure the noncompliance. The loan documents provide that X must prepay its loan in the event of noncompliance. W does not expect to be able to reloan the prepayment by X within six months of noncompliance. X's noncompliance will not affect the qualification of the pooled financing bonds as enterprise zone facility bonds if W uses the proceeds from the loan prepayment to redeem outstanding enterprise zone facility bonds within six months of noncompliance in an amount comparable to the outstanding amount of the loan immediately prior to prepayment. X will be denied an interest expense deduction for the interest accruing from the first day of the taxable year in which the noncompliance began.

(q) *Effective dates.*—(1) *In general.*—Except as otherwise provided in this section, the provisions of this section apply to all issues issued after July 30, 1996, and subject to section 1394.

(2) *Elective retroactive application in whole.*— An issuer may apply the provisions of this section in whole, but not in part, to any issue that is

outstanding on July 30, 1996, and is subject to section 1394. [Reg. § 1.1394-1.]

☐ [T.D. 8673, 5-30-96.]

[Reg. § 1.1396-1]

§ 1.1396-1. Qualified zone employees.—
(a) *In general.*—A qualified zone employee of an employer is an employee who satisfies the location-of-services requirement and the abode requirement with respect to the same empowerment zone and is not otherwise excluded by section 1396(d).

(1) *Location-of-services requirement.*—The location-of-services requirement is satisfied if substantially all of the services performed by the employee for the employer are performed in the empowerment zone in a trade or business of the employer.

(2) *Abode requirement.*—The abode requirement is satisfied if the employee's principal place of abode while performing those services is in the empowerment zone.

(b) *Period for applying location-of-services requirement.*—In applying the location-of-services requirement, an employer may use either the pay period method described in paragraph (b)(1) of this section or the calendar year method described in paragraph (b)(2) of this section. For each taxable year of an employer, the employer must either use the pay period method with respect to all of its employees or use the calendar year method with respect to all of its employees. The employer may change the method applied to all of its employees from one taxable year to the next.

(1) *Pay period method.*—(i) *Relevant period.*—Under the pay period method, the relevant period for applying the location-of-services requirement is each pay period in which an employee provides services to the employer during the calendar year with respect to which the credit is being claimed (i.e., the calendar year that ends with or within the relevant taxable year). If an employer has one pay period for certain employees and a different pay period for other employees (*e.g.*, a weekly pay period for hourly wage employees and a bi-weekly pay period for salaried employees), the pay period actually applicable to a particular employee is the relevant pay period for that employee under this method.

(ii) *Application of method.*—Under this method, an employee does not satisfy the location-of-services requirement during a pay period unless substantially all of the services performed by the employee for the employer during that pay period are performed within the empowerment zone in a trade or business of the employer.

(2) *Calendar year method.*—(i) *Relevant Period.*—Under the calendar year method, the relevant period for an employee is the entire calendar year with respect to which the credit is being claimed. However, for any employee who is employed by the employer for less than the entire calendar year, the relevant period is the portion of that calendar year during which the employee is employed by the employer.

(ii) *Application of method.*—Under this method, an employee does not satisfy the location-of-services requirement during any part of a calendar year unless substantially all of the services performed by the employee for the employer during that calendar year (or, if the employee is employed by the employer for less than the entire calendar year, the portion of that calendar year during which the employee is employed by the employer) are performed within the empowerment zone in a trade or business of the employer.

(3) *Examples.*—This paragraph (b) may be illustrated by the following examples. In each example, the following assumptions apply. The employees satisfy the abode requirement at all relevant times and all services performed by the employees for their employer are performed in a trade or business of the employer. The employees are not precluded from being qualified zone employees by section 1396(d)(2) (certain employees ineligible). No portion of the employees' wages is precluded from being qualified zone wages by section 1396(c)(2) (only first $15,000 of wages taken into account) or section 1396(c)(3) (coordination with targeted jobs credit and work opportunity credit). The examples are as follows:

Example 1. (i) Employer X has a weekly pay period for all its employees. Employee A works for X throughout 1997. During each of the first 20 weekly pay periods in 1997, substantially all of A's work for X is performed within the empowerment zone in which A resides. A also works in the zone at various times during the rest of the year, but there is no other pay period in which substantially all of A's work for X is performed within the empowerment zone. Employer X uses the pay period method.

(ii) For each of the first 20 pay periods of 1997, A is a qualified zone employee, all of A's wages from X are qualified zone wages, and X may claim the empowerment zone employment credit with respect to those wages. X cannot claim the credit with respect to any of A's wages for the rest of 1997.

Example 2. (i) Employer Y has a weekly pay period for its factory workers and a bi-weekly pay period for its office workers. Employee B works for Y in various factories and Employee C works for Y in various offices. Employer Y uses the pay period method.

(ii) Y must use B's weekly pay periods to determine the periods (if any) in which B is a qualified zone employee. Y may claim the empowerment zone employment credit with respect to B's wages only for the weekly pay periods for which B is a qualified zone employee, because those are B's only wages that are qualified zone wages. Y must use C's bi-weekly pay periods to determine the periods (if any) in which C is a qualified zone employee. Y may claim the credit with respect to C's wages only for the bi-weekly pay periods for which C is a qualified zone employee, because those are C's only wages that are qualified zone wages.

Example 3. (i) Employees D and E work for Employer Z throughout 1997. Although some of D's work for Z in 1997 is performed outside the empowerment zone in which D resides, substantially all of it is performed within that empowerment zone. E's work for Z is performed within the empowerment zone in which E resides for several weeks of 1997 but outside the zone for the rest of the year so that, viewed on an annual basis, E's work is not substantially all performed within the empowerment zone. Employer Z uses the calendar year method.

(ii) D is a qualified zone employee for the entire year, all of D's 1997 wages from Z are qualified zone wages, and Z may claim the empowerment zone employment credit with respect to all of those wages, including the portion attributable to work outside the zone. Under the calendar year method, E is not a qualified zone employee for any part of 1997, none of E's 1997 wages are qualified zone wages, and Z cannot claim any empowerment zone employment credit with respect to E's wages for 1997. Z cannot use the calendar year method for D and the pay period method for E because Z must use the same method for all employees. For 1998, however, Z can switch to the pay period method for E if Z also switches to the pay period method for D and all of Z's other employees.

(c) *Effective date.*—This section applies with respect to wages paid or incurred on or after December 21, 1994. [Reg. § 1.1396-1.]

☐ [*T.D.* 8747, 12-29-97.]

[Reg. § 1.1397E-1]

§ 1.1397E-1. Qualified zone academy bonds.—(a) *In general.*—(1) *Overview.*—In general, a qualified zone academy bond (QZAB or QZABs) is a taxable bond issued by a state or local government the proceeds of which are used to improve certain eligible public schools. An eligible taxpayer that holds a QZAB generally is allowed annual Federal income tax credits in lieu of periodic interest payments. These credits compensate the eligible taxpayer for lending money to the issuer and function as payments of interest on the bond. Accordingly, this section generally treats the allowance of a credit as if it were a payment of interest on the bond. This section also provides other rules for QZABs, including rules governing the credit rate, the private business contribution requirement, the maximum

term, use and expenditure of proceeds, remedial actions, eligible issuers, arbitrage investment restrictions, and information reporting.

(2) *Certain definitions.*—(i) *In general.*—For purposes of this section, except as otherwise provided in this section, the following definitions apply: the definitions set forth in this section; the definitions used for general tax-exempt bond purposes in § 1.150-1; and the definitions used for purposes of the arbitrage investment restrictions on tax-exempt bonds in § 1.148-1(b).

(ii) *Applicable definition of proceeds.*—(A) *Use and expenditure provisions.*—Except as provided in paragraphs (a)(2)(ii)(B) and (a)(2)(ii)(C) of this section, for purposes of all applicable requirements regarding use and expenditure of proceeds of QZABs under section 1397E and this section, "proceeds" means "sale proceeds," as defined in § 1.148-1(b), plus "investment proceeds," as defined in § 1.148-1(b).

(B) *Private business contribution requirement.*—For purposes of the private business contribution requirement of section 1397E(d)(2), "proceeds" means "sale proceeds," as defined in § 1.148-1(b).

(C) *Arbitrage investment restrictions.*—For purposes of the scope of application of the arbitrage investment restrictions under section 1397E(g) and paragraph (i) of this section, "proceeds" generally means gross proceeds, as defined in § 1.148-1(b). In addition, in applying the arbitrage investment restrictions under paragraph (i) of this section and under section 148, the various applicable definitions of the various types of proceeds of tax-exempt bonds under § 1.148-1(b) shall apply.

(b) *Credit rate.*—The Secretary shall determine monthly (or more often as deemed necessary by the Secretary) the credit rate the Secretary estimates will generally permit the issuance of a qualified zone academy bond without discount and without interest cost to the issuer. The manner for ascertaining the credit rate for a qualified zone academy bond as determined by the Secretary shall be set forth in procedures, notices, forms, or instructions prescribed by the Commissioner.

(c) *Private business contribution requirement.*—(1) *Reasonable discount rate.*—To determine the present value (as of the issue date) of qualified contributions from private entities under section 1397E(d)(2), the issuer must use a reasonable discount rate. The credit rate determined under paragraph (b) of this section is a reasonable discount rate.

(2) *Definition of private entities.*—For purposes of section 1397E(d)(2)(A), the term *private entities* includes any person (as defined in section 7701(a)) other than the United States, a State or local government, or any agency or instrumen-

tality thereof or related party with respect thereto. To determine whether a person is related to the United States or a State or local government under this paragraph (c)(2), rules similar to those for determining whether a person is a related party under § 1.150-1(b) shall apply (treating the United States as a governmental unit for purposes of § 1.150-1(b)).

(3) *Qualified contribution.*—For purposes of section 1397E(d)(2)(A), the term *qualified contribution* means any contribution (of a type and quality acceptable to the eligible local education agency) of any property or service described in section 1397E(d)(2)(B)(i), (ii), (iii), (iv) or (v). In addition, cash received with respect to a qualified zone academy from a private entity (other than cash received indirectly from a person that is not a private entity as part of a plan to avoid the requirements of section 1397E) constitutes a qualified contribution if it is to be used to purchase any property or service described in section 1397E(d)(2)(B)(i), (ii), (iii), (iv) or (v). Services of employees of the eligible local education agency do not constitute qualified contributions.

(d) *Maximum term.*—The maximum term for a QZAB is determined under section 1397E(d)(3) by using a discount rate equal to 110 percent of the long-term adjusted applicable Federal rate (AFR), compounded semi-annually, for the month in which the bond is sold. The Internal Revenue Service publishes this figure each month in a revenue ruling that is published in the Internal Revenue Bulletin. See § 601.601(d)(2)(ii)(b) of this chapter. A bond is sold on the sale date, as defined in § 1.150-1(c)(6), which is the first day on which there is a binding contract in writing for the sale or exchange of the bond.

(e) *Tax credit.*—(1) *Eligible taxpayer.*—An eligible taxpayer (within the meaning of section 1397E(d)(6)) that holds a qualified zone academy bond on a credit allowance date is allowed a tax credit against the federal income tax imposed on the taxpayer for the taxable year that includes the credit allowance date. The amount of the credit is equal to the product of the credit rate and the outstanding principal amount of the bond on the credit allowance date. The credit is subject to a limitation based on the eligible taxpayer's income tax liability. See section 1397E(c).

(2) *Ineligible taxpayer.*—A taxpayer that is not an eligible taxpayer is not allowed a credit.

(f) *Treatment of the allowance of the credit as a payment of interest.*—(1) *General rule.*—The holder of a qualified zone academy bond must treat the bond as if it pays qualified stated interest (within the meaning of § 1.1273-1(c)) on each credit allowance date. The amount of the deemed payment of interest on each credit allowance date is equal to the product of the credit rate and the outstanding principal amount of the

bond on that date. Thus, for example, if the holder uses an accrual method of accounting, the holder must accrue as interest income the amount of the credit over the one-year accrual period that ends on the credit allowance date.

(2) *Adjustment if the holder cannot use the credit to offset a tax liability.*—If a holder holds a qualified zone academy bond on the credit allowance date but cannot use all or a portion of the credit to reduce its income tax liability (for example, because the holder is not an eligible taxpayer or because the limitation in section 1397E(c) applies), the holder is allowed a deduction for the taxable year that includes the credit allowance date (or, at the option of the holder, the next succeeding taxable year). The amount of the deduction is equal to the amount of the unused credit deemed paid on the credit allowance date.

(g) *Not a tax-exempt obligation.*—A qualified zone academy bond is not an obligation the interest on which is excluded from gross income under section 103(a).

(h) *Use of proceeds.*—(1) *In general.*—Section 1397E(d)(1) provides that a bond issued as part of an issue is a QZAB only if, among other requirements, at least 95 percent of the proceeds of the issue are to be used for a qualified purpose with respect to a qualified zone academy established by an eligible local education agency (as defined in section 1397E(d)(4)(B)), and the issue meets the requirements of section 1397E(f) and (g). Section 1397E(d)(5) defines *qualified purpose*, with respect to any qualified zone academy, as rehabilitating or repairing the public school facility in which such academy is established, providing equipment for use at such academy, developing course materials for education to be provided at such academy, and training teachers and other school personnel in such academy. Section 1397E(d)(4)(A) defines *qualified zone academy* as any public school (or academic program within a public school) that is established by and operated under the supervision of an eligible local education agency to provide education or training below the postsecondary level and that meets the requirements of section 1397E(d)(4)(A)(i), (ii), (iii) and (iv).

(2) *Use of proceeds requirements.*—An issue meets the requirements of sections 1397E (d)(1)(A) and (f) only if—

(i) The issuer reasonably expects, as of the issue date of the issue, that—

(A) At least 95 percent of the proceeds from the sale of the issue are to be spent for qualified purposes with respect to qualified zone academies within the 5-year period beginning on the issue date of the QZAB;

(B) A binding commitment with a third party to spend at least 10 percent of the proceeds from the sale of the issue will be incurred within the 6-month period beginning on the issue date of the QZAB;

(C) At least 95 percent of the proceeds from the sale of the issue will be spent for qualified purposes with respect to a qualified zone academy with due diligence (with due diligence measured by the reasonableness standard under § 1.148-1(b)); and

(D) At least 95 percent of the proceeds of the issue will be used for qualified purposes with respect to a qualified zone academy for the entire term of the issue (without regard to any redemption provision); and

(ii) Except as otherwise provided in paragraph (h)(8) of this section, at least 95 percent of the proceeds of the issue are actually used for qualified purposes with respect to a qualified academy for the entire term of the issue (without regard to any redemption provision).

(3) *Extension of 5-year period.*—The Commissioner may extend the period described in paragraph (h)(2)(i)(A) of this section if the issuer, prior to the end of such period, submits a private ruling request, and establishes to the satisfaction of the Commissioner that—

(i) The failure to satisfy the 5-year spending requirement is due to reasonable cause; and

(ii) The expenditure of at least 95 percent of the proceeds from the sale of the issue for a qualified purpose with respect to a qualified zone academy will continue to proceed with due diligence.

(4) *Unspent proceeds.*—For purposes of paragraphs (h)(2)(i)(D) and (h)(2)(ii) of this section, during the period described in paragraph (h)(2)(i)(A) of this section, including any extension under paragraph (h)(3) of this section, unspent proceeds are treated as used for a qualified purpose with respect to a qualified zone academy if the issuer reasonably expects to proceed with due diligence to spend those proceeds for a qualified purpose with respect to a qualified zone academy during that period.

(5) *Proceeds spent for rehabilitation, repair or equipment.*—(i) *In general.*—Under section 1397E(d)(5)(A) the term *qualified purpose* with respect to any qualified zone academy includes rehabilitating or repairing the public school facility in which such academy is established. For this purpose, in determining whether proceeds are spent for rehabilitation, rules similar to those under section 47(c) (other than sections 47(c)(1)(B) and 47(c)(2)(B)(iv))shall apply. Under section 1397E(d)(5)(B) the term *qualified purpose* also includes providing equipment for use at such academy. If proceeds of an issue are spent for a purpose described in section 1397E(d)(5)(A) or (B) with respect to a qualified zone academy, then those proceeds are treated as used for a qualified purpose with respect to the academy during any period after such expenditure that—

(A) The property financed with those proceeds is used for the purposes of the academy; and

(B) The academy maintains its status as a qualified zone academy under section 1397E(d)(4).

(ii) *Retirement from service.*—The retirement from service of financed property due to normal wear or obsolescence does not cause the property to fail to be used for a qualified purpose with respect to a qualified zone academy.

(6) *Proceeds spent to develop course materials or train teachers.*—Section 1397E(d)(5)(C) and (D) provides that the term *qualified purpose* with respect to any qualified zone academy includes developing course materials for education to be provided at such academy, and training teachers and other school personnel in such academy. If proceeds of an issue are spent for a purpose described in section 1397E(d)(5)(C) or (D) with respect to a qualified zone academy, then those proceeds are treated as used for a qualified purpose with respect to the academy during any period after such expenditure.

(7) *Special rule for determining status as qualified zone academy.*—Section 1397E(d)(4)(A)(iv) provides that a public school (or academic program within a public school) is a qualified zone academy only if, among other requirements, the public school is located in an empowerment zone or enterprise community (as defined in section 1393), or there is a reasonable expectation (as of the issue date of the issue) that at least 35 percent of the students attending the school or participating in the program (as the case may be) will be eligible for free or reduced-cost lunches under the school lunch program established under the Richard B. Russell National School Lunch Act. For purposes of determining whether an issue complies with section 1397E(d)(4)(A)(iv)—

(i) A public school is treated as located in an empowerment zone or enterprise community for the entire term of the issue if the public school is located in an empowerment zone or enterprise community on the issue date of the issue; and

(ii) The determination of whether there is a reasonable expectation (as of the issue date of the issue) that at least 35 percent of the students attending the school or participating in the program (as the case may be) will be eligible for free or reduced-cost lunches under the school lunch program established under the Richard B. Russell National School Lunch Act is based on expectations regarding the one-year period following the issue date.

(8) *Remedial actions.*—(i) *General rule.*—If less than 95 percent of the proceeds of an issue are properly used (as determined under paragraph (h)(8)(ii)(D) of this section), the issue will

be treated as meeting the requirements of section 1397E(d)(1)(A) if the issue met the requirements of paragraph (h)(2)(i) of this section and a remedial action is taken under paragraph (h)(8)(ii) or (iii) of this section.

(ii) *Redemption or defeasance.*—(A) *In general.*—A remedial action is taken under this paragraph (h)(8)(ii) if the requirements of paragraphs (h)(8)(ii)(B) and (C) of this section are met.

(B) *Retirement of nonqualified bonds.*—(1) *In general.*—The requirements of this paragraph (h)(8)(ii)(B) are met if—

(i) All of the nonqualified bonds of the issue (as determined under § 1.142-2(e)) are redeemed within 90 days after the date on which the failure to properly use proceeds occurs; or

(ii) To the extent proceeds of the issue that have been actually spent for a qualified purpose with respect to a qualified zone academy, if any nonqualified bonds of the issue are not redeemed within 90 days after the date on which the failure to properly use such proceeds occurs (the unredeemed nonqualified bonds), a defeasance escrow is established for the unredeemed nonqualified bonds within 90 days after the date on which the failure to properly use proceeds occurs.

(2) *Special rule for dispositions for cash.*—If the failure to properly use proceeds occurs because of a disposition of financed property described in section 1397E(d)(5)(A) or (B) and the consideration for the disposition is exclusively cash, the requirements of this paragraph (h)(8)(ii)(B) are met if all of the disposition proceeds (as defined in paragraph (h)(8)(iv) of this section) are used within 90 days after the date of the disposition to redeem, or establish a defeasance escrow for, the nonqualified bonds (as determined under § 1.142-2(e)).

(3) *Definition of defeasance escrow.*—For purposes of this section, a defeasance escrow is an irrevocable escrow established to retire nonqualified bonds on the earliest call date after the date on which the failure to properly use proceeds occurs in an amount that is sufficient to retire nonqualified bonds on that call date. At least 90 percent of the weighted average amount in a defeasance escrow must be invested in investments (as defined in § 1.148-1(b)), except that no amount in a defeasance escrow may be invested in any investment the obligor (or any person that is a related party with respect to the obligor within the meaning of § 1.150-1(b)) of which is a user of proceeds of the bonds. All purchases or sales of an investment in a defeasance escrow must be made at the fair market value of the investment within the meaning of § 1.148-5(d)(6).

(C) *Additional rules.*—(1) *Limitation on source of funding.*—Proceeds of an issue of QZABs (other than unspent proceeds of the issue

for which the failure to properly use proceeds occurs) must not be used to redeem or defease nonqualified bonds under paragraph (h)(8)(ii)(B) of this section.

(2) *Rebate requirement.*—The issuer must pay to the United States, at the same time and in the same manner as rebate amounts are required to be paid under § 1.148-3 (or at such other time or in such other manner as the Commissioner may prescribe), any investment earnings on amounts in a defeasance escrow established under paragraph (h)(8)(ii)(B) of this section that are in excess of the yield on the issue of QZABs with respect to which the defeasance escrow was established. For this purpose, the first computation period begins on the date on which the defeasance escrow is established.

(3) *Notice of defeasance.*—The issuer must provide written notice to the Commissioner, at the place designated in § 1.150-5(a), of the establishment of the defeasance escrow within 90 days of the date the defeasance escrow is established.

(D) *When a failure to properly use proceeds occurs.*—(1) *Unspent proceeds.*—For unspent proceeds, a failure to properly use proceeds occurs on the earliest of—

(i) The first date on which the public school (or academic program within the public school) fails to constitute a qualified zone academy;

(ii) The first date on which the issuer fails to have a reasonable expectation to proceed with due diligence to spend at least 95 percent of the proceeds of the issue for a qualified purpose with respect to a qualified zone academy; or

(iii) The last day of the period described in paragraph (h)(2)(i)(A) of this section, including any extension, if less than 95 percent of the proceeds of the issue are actually spent for a qualified purpose with respect to a qualified zone academy.

(2) *Proceeds spent for rehabilitation, repair or equipment.*—For proceeds that have been spent for a purpose described in section 1397E(d)(5)(A) or (B) with respect to a qualified zone academy, a failure to properly use proceeds occurs on the earlier of—

(i) The first date on which the public school (or academic program within the public school) fails to constitute a qualified zone academy; and

(ii) The first date on which an action is taken that causes the issuer to fail actually to use at least 95 percent of the proceeds of the issue for a qualified purpose with respect to a qualified zone academy.

(3) *Proceeds spent for course materials or training.*—If proceeds have been spent for a

purpose described in section 1397E(d)(5)(C) or (D) with respect to a qualified zone academy, no event subsequent to such expenditure shall constitute a failure to properly use such proceeds.

(iii) *Alternative use of disposition proceeds.*— A remedial action is taken under this paragraph (h)(8)(iii) if all of the requirements of paragraphs (h)(8)(iii)(A) through (D) of this section are met—

(A) The failure to properly use proceeds (as determined under paragraph (h)(8)(ii)(D) of this section) is a disposition of financed property described in section 1397E(d)(5)(A) or (B) and the consideration for the disposition is exclusively cash;

(B) The issuer reasonably expects as of the date of the disposition that—

(1) All of the disposition proceeds will be spent within the two-year period beginning with the date of the disposition for a qualified purpose with respect to a qualified zone academy; or

(2) To the extent not expected to be so spent, the disposition proceeds will be used within 90 days after the date of the disposition to redeem or defease bonds in a manner that meets the requirements of paragraph (h)(8)(ii) of this section;

(C) The disposition proceeds are treated as proceeds for purposes of section 1397E; and

(D) If all of the disposition proceeds are not actually used in the manner described in paragraph (h)(8)(iii)(B) of this section, the remainder of such amounts are used within 90 days after the end of the period described in paragraph (h)(8)(iii)(B)(1) of this section for a remedial action that meets the requirements of paragraph (h)(8)(ii) of this section.

(iv) *Definition of disposition proceeds and allocation among multiple funding sources.*—For purposes of this paragraph (h)(8), *disposition proceeds* means disposition proceeds, as defined in §1.141-12(c)(1), plus amounts derived from investing disposition proceeds. If property has been financed with an issue of QZABs and one or more other funding sources, any disposition proceeds from that property are allocated to the issue under the principles of §1.141-12(c)(3).

(9) *Payment of principal, interest or redemption price.*—(i) *In general.*—Except as provided in paragraphs (h)(9)(ii) and (h)(9)(iii) of this section, the use of proceeds of a bond to pay principal, interest, or redemption price of the bond or another bond is not a qualified purpose within the meaning of section 1397E(d)(5).

(ii) *Exception for certain eligible reimbursements of interim refinancings.*—The use of proceeds of a bond (the refinancing bond) to pay principal, interest, or redemption price of another bond (the prior bond) is a qualified purpose within the meaning of section 1397E(d)(5) to the extent that—

(A) The prior bond was not a QZAB (and, in the case of a series of refinancings, no earlier bond in the series was a QZAB);

(B) The proceeds of the prior bond (or the original bond in the case of a series of refinancings, as applicable) were spent for a qualified purpose under section 1397E(d)(5) with respect to a qualified zone academy (the original expenditure); and

(C) The issuer makes a valid reimbursement allocation to allocate the proceeds of the refinancing bond to the payment of the original expenditure (the reimbursement allocation), which allocation satisfies the requirements for reimbursements under paragraph (h)(10) of this section. For purposes of applying the rules for reimbursement, a refinancing bond which otherwise meets the requirements of this paragraph (h)(9)(ii) is eligible for reimbursement and is not treated as a disqualified refunding under §1.150-2(g).

(iii) *Reissuance of a QZAB.*—For purposes of determining whether the establishing of a defeasance escrow under paragraph (h)(8)(ii)(B)(1)(ii) of this section results in an exchange under §1.1001-1(a), the QZAB is treated as a tax-exempt bond under §1.1001-3(e)(5)(ii)(B)(1).

(10) *Reimbursement.*—An expenditure for a qualified purpose may be reimbursed with proceeds of a QZAB. For this purpose, rules similar to those on reimbursement of expenditures in §1.142-4(b) and §1.150-2 shall apply. In applying these reimbursement rules, expenditures eligible for reimbursement under §1.150-2(d)(3) shall be deemed to mean any expenditure for a qualified purpose under section 1397E(d)(5).

(i) *Arbitrage investment restrictions.*—(1) *In general.*—Under section 1397E(g) and this paragraph (i), and except as otherwise provided in this paragraph (i), the arbitrage investment restrictions and rebate requirements under section 148 and §§1.148-1 through 1.148-11, inclusive, and the exceptions to those restrictions, apply broadly to gross proceeds of QZABs issued under section 1397E to the same extent and in the same manner as they apply to gross proceeds of taxexempt state or local governmental bonds. For this purpose, references in those sections to tax-exempt bonds generally shall be deemed to refer to QZABs and, to the extent that any particular arbitrage restriction depends on whether bonds are private activity bonds under section 141, the determination of whether QZABs are private activity bonds shall be based on the general definition of private activity bonds under section 141. In applying section 148 and the regulations under that section to QZABs, the modifications set forth in paragraphs (i)(2) through (i)(6) of this section shall apply.

Reg. §1.1397E-1(i)(1)

(2) *5-year temporary period exception to arbitrage yield restriction.*—If an issue of QZABs meets the requirements of section 1397E(f)(1) and paragraph (h)(2)(i) of this section, then the proceeds of the issue of QZABs are treated as qualifying for a 5-year temporary period exception to arbitrage yield restriction under §1.148-2(e)(2) beginning on the issue date of the issue.

(3) *Disregard QZAB credit in QZAB yield for arbitrage purposes.*—In determining the yield on an issue of QZABs for arbitrage purposes under §1.148-4, the QZAB credit allowed under section 1397E(a) is disregarded.

(4) *Non-AMT tax-exempt bond investment exception inapplicable.*—The exception to arbitrage yield restriction for investments of gross proceeds of tax-exempt bonds in specified tax-exempt bond investments not subject to section 148(b)(3)(B) (relating to an exception to the definition of "investment property" for specified tax-exempt bonds) and §1.148-2(d)(2)(v) (relating to a corresponding exception to arbitrage yield limitations) is inapplicable.

(5) *Application of small issuer exception to the arbitrage rebate requirement.*—Except as otherwise provided in paragraph (i)(6) of this section, for purposes of the small issuer exception to the arbitrage rebate requirement under section 148(f)(4)(D) and §1.148-8, QZABs that are actually issued or reasonably expected to be issued by the QZAB issuer (and applicable entities aggregated under section 148(f)(4)(D)) within a calendar year are taken into account in measuring the applicable size limitation.

(6) *Certain defeasance escrow earnings.*—With respect to a defeasance escrow established in a remedial action for an issue of QZABs that meets the special rebate requirement under paragraph (h)(8)(ii)(C)(2) of this section, the QZAB issuer is treated as ineligible for the small issuer exception to arbitrage rebate under section 148(f)(4)(D) and paragraph (i)(5) of this section and compliance with that special rebate requirement is treated as satisfying applicable arbitrage investment restrictions under section 148 for that defeasance escrow.

(j) *Information reporting requirement.*—Under section 1397E(h) and this paragraph (j), issuers of QZABs are required to submit information reporting returns to the IRS similar to the information reporting returns required to be submitted to the IRS under section 149(e) for tax-exempt state or local governmental bonds at the same time and in the same manner as those reports are required to be submitted to the IRS on such forms as shall be prescribed by the Commissioner for such purpose.

(k) *State or local government.*—(1) *In general.*—For purposes of section 1397E(d)(1)(B), the term *State or local government* means a State or political subdivision as defined for purposes of section 103(c).

(2) *On behalf of issuer.*—A qualified zone academy bond may be issued on behalf of a State or local government under rules similar to those for determining whether a bond issued on behalf of a State or political subdivision constitutes an obligation of that State or political subdivision for purposes of section 103.

(l) *Cross-references.*—See section 171 and the regulations thereunder for rules relating to amortizable bond premium. See §1.61-7(d) for the seller's treatment of a bond sold between interest payment dates (credit allowance dates) and §1.61-7(c) for the buyer's treatment of a bond purchased between interest payment dates (credit allowance dates).

(m) *Effective/applicability dates.*—(1) *In general.*—Except as otherwise provided in this paragraph (m), this section applies to bonds issued under section 1397E that are sold on or after September 14, 2007.

(2) *Special effective dates.*—(i) *Effective dates for paragraphs (h)(2), (h)(3), (h)(4), (i), and (j) of this section in general.*—Paragraphs (h)(2), (h)(3), (h)(4), (i), and (j) of this section apply to bonds issued under section 1397E pursuant to allocations of the national qualified zone academy bond volume cap authority for calendar years after 2005 and sold on or after September 14, 2007.

(ii) *Permissive retroactive application.*—(A) *In general.*—Except as otherwise provided in this paragraph (m), issuers and taxpayers may apply this section in whole, but not in part, to bonds issued under section 1397E that are sold before September 14, 2007.

(B) *Special rule for certain provisions.*—For purposes of the permissive retroactive application rule in paragraph (m)(2)(ii)(A) of this section, paragraphs (h)(2), (h)(3), (h)(4), (i), and (j) of this section need not be applied to any bonds issued under section 1397E to which those provisions do not otherwise apply under the general effective date provisions for those provisions in paragraph (m)(2)(i) of this section.

(C) *Definition of proceeds.*—Issuers and taxpayers may apply paragraph (h) of this section, without regard to the definition of proceeds in paragraph (a)(2)(ii) of this section, to bonds issued under section 1397E that are sold before September 14, 2007.

(D) *Bonds issued before July 1, 1999.*—Paragraphs (b) and (h)(10) of this section may not be applied to bonds issued under section 1397E that are issued before July 1, 1999.

(3) *Scope of reliance for bonds issued under sections 54A and 54E.*—Except to the extent inconsistent with the successor statutory provisions for QZABs in sections 54A and 54E or applicable public administrative or regulatory guidance under those provisions and except as otherwise provided in this paragraph (m)(3), issuers and taxpayers may apply these regulations to QZABs issued under sections 54A and 54E that are sold after October 3, 2008. In the case of QZABs that are issued under sections 54A and 54E for which the issuer makes an irrevocable election under section 6431(f) to receive payments with respect to credits under section 6431, issuers and taxpayers may not apply the remedial action provisions under paragraph (h)(8) of this section. [Reg. § 1.1397E-1.]

☐ [*T.D.* 8903, 9-25-2000. *Amended by T.D.* 9339, 7-13-2007 *and T.D.* 9495, 7-29-2010 (*corrected* 8-24-2010).]

TITLE 11 CASES

[Reg. § 1.1398-1]

§ 1.1398-1. Treatment of passive activity losses and passive activity credits in individuals' title 11 cases.—(a) *Scope.*—This section applies to cases under chapter 7 or chapter 11 of title 11 of the United States Code, but only if the debtor is an individual.

(b) *Definitions and rules of general application.*— For purposes of this section—

(1) *Passive activity* and *former passive activity* have the meanings given in section 469(c) and (f)(3);

(2) The unused passive activity loss (determined as of the first day of a taxable year) is the passive activity loss (as defined in section 469(d)(1)) that is disallowed under section 469 for the previous taxable year; and

(3) The unused passive activity credit (determined as of the first day of a taxable year) is the passive activity credit (as defined in section 469(d)(2)) that is disallowed under section 469 for the previous taxable year.

(c) *Estate succeeds to losses and credits upon commencement of case.*—The bankruptcy estate (estate) succeeds to and takes into account, beginning with its first taxable year, the debtor's unused passive activity loss and unused passive activity credit (determined as of the first day of the debtor's taxable year in which the case commences).

(d) *Transfers from estate to debtor.*—(1) *Transfer not treated as taxable event.*—If, before the termination of the estate, the estate transfers an interest in a passive activity or former passive activity to the debtor (other than by sale or exchange), the transfer is not treated as a disposition for purposes of any provision of the Internal Revenue Code assigning tax consequences to a disposition. The transfers to which this rule applies include transfers from the estate to the debtor of property that is exempt under section 522 of title 11 of the United States Code and abandonments of estate property to the debtor under section 554(a) of such title.

(2) *Treatment of passive activity loss and credit.*—If, before the termination of the estate, the estate transfers an interest in a passive activity or former passive activity to the debtor (other than by sale or exchange)—

(i) The estate must allocate to the transferred interest, in accordance with § 1.469-1(f)(4), part or all of the estate's unused passive activity loss and unused passive activity credit (determined as of the first day of the estate's taxable year in which the transfer occurs); and

(ii) The debtor succeeds to and takes into account, beginning with the debtor's taxable year in which the transfer occurs, the unused passive activity loss and unused passive activity credit (or part thereof) allocated to the transferred interest.

(e) *Debtor succeeds to loss and credit of the estate upon its termination.*—Upon termination of the estate, the debtor succeeds to and takes into account, beginning with the debtor's taxable year in which the termination occurs, the passive activity loss and passive activity credit disallowed under section 469 for the estate's last taxable year.

(f) *Effective date.*—(1) *Cases commencing on or after November 9, 1992.*—This section applies to cases commencing on or after November 9, 1992.

(2) *Cases commencing before November 9, 1992.*—(i) *Election required.*—This section applies to a case commencing before November 9, 1992, and terminating on or after that date if the debtor and the estate jointly elect its application in the manner prescribed in paragraph (f)(2)(v) of this section (the election). The caption "ELECTION PURSUANT TO § 1.1398-1" must be placed prominently on the first page of each of the debtor's returns that is affected by the election (other than returns for taxable years that begin after the termination of the estate) and on the first page of each of the estate's returns that is affected by the election. In the case of returns that are amended under paragraph (f)(2)(iii) of this section, this requirement is satisfied by placing the caption on the amended return.

(ii) *Scope of election.*—This election applies to the passive and former passive activities and unused passive activity losses and passive activity credits of the taxpayers making the election.

(iii) *Amendment of previously filed returns.*—The debtor and the estate making the election must amend all returns (except to the extent they are for a year that is a closed year within the meaning of paragraph (f)(2)(iv)(D) of this section) they filed before the date of the election to the extent necessary to provide that no claim of a deduction or credit is inconsistent with the succession under this section to unused losses and credits. The Commissioner may revoke or limit the effect of the election if either the debtor or the estate fails to satisfy the requirement of this paragraph (f)(2)(iii).

(iv) *Rules relating to closed years.*—(A) *Estate succeeds to debtor's passive activity loss and credit as of the commencement date.*—If, by reason of an election under this paragraph (f), this section applies to a case that was commenced in a closed year, the estate, nevertheless, succeeds to and takes into account the unused passive activity loss and unused passive activity credit of the debtor (determined as of the first day of the debtor's taxable year in which the case commenced).

(B) *No reduction of unused passive activity loss and credit for passive activity loss and credit not claimed for a closed year.*—In determining a taxpayer's carryover of a passive activity loss or credit to its taxable year following a closed year, a deduction or credit that the taxpayer failed to claim in the closed year, if attributable to an unused passive activity loss or credit to which the taxpayer succeeded under this section, is treated as a deduction or credit that was disallowed under section 469.

(C) *Passive activity loss and credit to which taxpayer succeeds reflects deductions of prior holder in a closed year.*—A loss or credit to which a taxpayer would otherwise succeed under this section is reduced to the extent the loss or credit was allowed to its prior holder for a closed year.

(D) *Closed year.*—For purposes of this paragraph (f)(2)(iv), a taxable year is closed to the extent the assessment of a deficiency or refund of an overpayment is prevented, on the date of the election and at all times thereafter, by any law or rule of law.

(v) *Manner of making election.*—(A) *Chapter 7 cases.*—In a case under chapter 7 of title 11 of the United States Code, the election is made by obtaining the written consent of the bankruptcy trustee and filing a copy of the written consent with the returns (or amended returns) of the debtor and the estate for their first taxable years ending after November 9, 1992.

(B) *Chapter 11 cases.*—In a case under chapter 11 of title 11 of the United States Code, the election is made by incorporating the election into a bankruptcy plan that is confirmed by the bankruptcy court or into an order of such court and filing the pertinent portion of the plan or order with the returns (or amended returns) of the debtor and the estate for their first taxable years ending after November 9, 1992.

(vi) *Election is binding and irrevocable.*—Except as provided in paragraph (f)(2)(iii) of this section, the election, once made, is binding on both the debtor and the estate and is irrevocable. [Reg. § 1.1398-1.]

☐ [*T.D. 8537, 5-12-94.*]

[Reg. § 1.1398-2]

§ 1.1398-2. Treatment of section 465 losses in individuals' title 11 cases.—(a) *Scope.*—This section applies to cases under chapter 7 or chapter 11 of title 11 of the United States Code, but only if the debtor is an individual.

(b) *Definition and rules of general application.*—For purposes of this section—

(1) *Section 465 activity* means an activity to which section 465 applies; and

(2) For each section 465 activity, the unused section 465 loss from the activity (determined as of the first day of a taxable year) is the loss (as defined in section 465(d)) that is not allowed under section 465(a)(1) for the previous taxable year.

(c) *Estate succeeds to losses upon commencement of case.*—The bankruptcy estate (the estate) succeeds to and takes into account, beginning with its first taxable year, the debtor's unused section 465 losses (determined as of the first day of the debtor's taxable year in which the case commences).

(d) *Transfers from estate to debtor.*—(1) *Transfer not treated as taxable event.*—If, before the termination of the estate, the estate transfers an interest in a section 465 activity to the debtor (other than by sale or exchange), the transfer is not treated as a disposition for purposes of any provision of the Internal Revenue Code assigning tax consequences to a disposition. The transfers to which this rule applies include transfers from the estate to the debtor of property that is exempt under section 522 of title 11 of the United States Code and abandonments of estate property to the debtor under section 554(a) of such title.

(2) *Treatment of section 465 losses.*—If, before the termination of the estate, the estate transfers an interest in a section 465 activity to the debtor (other than by sale or exchange) the debtor succeeds to and takes into account, beginning with the debtor's taxable year in which the transfer occurs, the transferred interest's share of the estate's unused section 465 loss from the activity (determined as of the first day of the estate's taxable year in which the transfer occurs). For this purpose, the transferred interest's share of such loss is the amount, if any, by which such

loss would be reduced if the transfer had occurred as of the close of the preceding taxable year of the estate and been treated as a disposition on which gain or loss is recognized.

(e) *Debtor succeeds to losses of the estate upon its termination.*—Upon termination of the estate, the debtor succeeds to and takes into account, beginning with the debtor's taxable year in which the termination occurs, the losses not allowed under section 465 for the estate's last taxable year.

(f) *Effective date.*—(1) *Cases commencing on or after November 9, 1992.*—This section applies to cases commencing on or after November 9, 1992.

(2) *Cases commencing before November 9, 1992.*—(i) *Election required.*—This section applies to a case commencing before November 9, 1992, and terminating on or after that date if the debtor and the estate jointly elect its application in the manner prescribed in paragraph (f)(2)(v) of this section (the election). The caption "ELECTION PURSUANT TO § 1.1398-2" must be placed prominently on the first page of each of the debtor's returns that is affected by the election (other than returns for taxable years that begin after the termination of the estate) and on the first page of each of the estate's returns that is affected by the election. In the case of returns that are amended under paragraph (f)(2)(iii) of this section, this requirement is satisfied by placing the caption on the amended return.

(ii) *Scope of election.*—This election applies to the section 465 activities and unused losses from section 465 activities of the taxpayers making the election.

(iii) *Amendment of previously filed returns.*—The debtor and the estate making the election must amend all returns (except to the extent they are for a year that is a closed year within the meaning of paragraph (f)(2)(iv)(D) of this section) they filed before the date of the election to the extent necessary to provide that no claim of a deduction is inconsistent with the succession under this section to unused losses from section 465 activities. The Commissioner may revoke or limit the effect of the election if either the debtor or the estate fails to satisfy the requirement of this paragraph (f)(2)(iii).

(iv) *Rules relating to closed years.*—(A) *Estate succeeds to debtor's section 465 loss as of the commencement date.*—If, by reason of an election under this paragraph (f), this section applies to a case that was commenced in a closed year, the estate, nevertheless, succeeds to and takes into account the section 465 losses of the debtor (determined as of the first day of the debtor's taxable year in which the case commenced).

(B) *No reduction of unused section 465 loss for loss not claimed for a closed year.*—In determining a taxpayer's carryover of an unused section 465 loss to its taxable year following a closed year, a deduction that the taxpayer failed to claim in the closed year, if attributable to an unused section 465 loss to which the taxpayer succeeds under this section, is treated as a deduction that was not allowed under section 465.

(C) *Loss to which taxpayer succeeds reflects deductions of prior holder in a closed year.*—A loss to which a taxpayer would otherwise succeed under this section is reduced to the extent the loss was allowed to its prior holder for a closed year.

(D) *Closed year.*—For purposes of this paragraph (f)(2)(iv), a taxable year is closed to the extent the assessment of a deficiency or refund of an overpayment is prevented, on the date of the election and at all times thereafter, by any law or rule of law.

(v) *Manner of making election.*—(A) *Chapter 7 cases.*—In a case under chapter 7 of title 11 of the United States Code, the election is made by obtaining the written consent of the bankruptcy trustee and filing a copy of the written consent with the returns (or amended returns) of the debtor and the estate for their first taxable years ending after November 9, 1992.

(B) *Chapter 11 cases.*—In a case under chapter 11 of title 11 of the United States Code, the election is made by incorporating the election into a bankruptcy plan that is confirmed by the bankruptcy court or into an order of such court and filing the pertinent portion of the plan or order with the returns (or amended returns) of the debtor and the estate for their first taxable years ending after November 9, 1992.

(vi) *Election is binding and irrevocable.*—Except as provided in paragraph (f)(2)(iii) of this section, the election, once made, is binding on both the debtor and the estate and is irrevocable. [Reg. § 1.1398-2.]

☐ [*T.D.* 8537, 5-12-94.]

[Reg. § 1.1398-3]

§ 1.1398-3. Treatment of section 121 exclusion in individuals' title 11 cases.—(a) *Scope.*—This section applies to cases under chapter 7 or chapter 11 of title 11 of the United States Code, but only if the debtor is an individual.

(b) *Definition and rules of general application.*—For purposes of this section, section 121 exclusion means the exclusion of gain from the sale or exchange of a debtor's principal residence available under section 121.

(c) *Estate succeeds to exclusion upon commencement of case.*—The bankruptcy estate succeeds to and takes into account the section 121 exclusion with respect to the property transferred into the estate.

Reg. § 1.1398-3(c)

(d) *Effective date.*—This section is applicable for sales or exchanges on or after December 24, 2002. [Reg. § 1.1398-3.]

☐ [*T.D.* 9030, 12-23-2002.]

SHORT-TERM REGIONAL BENEFITS

See p. 20,601 for regulations not amended to reflect law changes

[Reg. § 1.1400L(b)-1]

§ 1.1400L(b)-1. Additional first year depreciation deduction for qualified New York Liberty Zone property.—(a) *Scope.*—This section provides the rules for determining the 30-percent additional first year depreciation deduction allowable under section 1400L(b) for qualified New York Liberty Zone property.

(b) *Definitions.*—For purposes of section 1400L(b) and this section, the definitions of the terms in § 1.168(k)-1(a)(2) apply and the following definitions also apply:

(1) *Building* and *structural components* have the same meanings as those terms are defined in § 1.48-1(e).

(2) *New York Liberty Zone* is the area located on or south of Canal Street, East Broadway (east of its intersection with Canal Street), or Grand Street (east of its intersection with East Broadway) in the Borough of Manhattan in the City of New York, New York.

(3) *Nonresidential real property* and *residential rental property* have the same meanings as those terms are defined in section 168(e)(2).

(4) *Real property* is a building or its structural components, or other tangible real property.

(c) *Qualified New York Liberty Zone property.*—(1) *In general.*—Qualified New York Liberty Zone property is depreciable property that meets all the following requirements in the first taxable year in which the property is subject to depreciation by the taxpayer whether or not depreciation deductions for the property are allowable—

(i) The requirements in § 1.1400L(b)-1(c)(2) (description of property);

(ii) The requirements in § 1.1400L(b)-1(c)(3) (substantial use);

(iii) The requirements in § 1.1400L(b)-1(c)(4) (original use);

(iv) The requirements in § 1.1400L(b)-1(c)(5) (acquisition of property by purchase); and

(v) The requirements in § 1.1400L(b)-1(c)(6) (placed-in-service date).

(2) *Description of qualified New York Liberty Zone property.*—(i) *In general.*—Depreciable property will meet the requirements of this paragraph (c)(2) if the property is—

(A) Described in § 1.168(k)-1(b)(2)(i); or

(B) Nonresidential real property or residential rental property depreciated under section

168, but only to the extent it rehabilitates real property damaged, or replaces real property destroyed or condemned, as a result of the terrorist attacks of September 11, 2001. Property is treated as replacing destroyed or condemned property if, as part of an integrated plan, the property replaces real property that is included in a continuous area that includes real property destroyed or condemned. For purposes of this section, real property is considered as destroyed or condemned only if an entire building or structure was destroyed or condemned as a result of the terrorist attacks of September 11, 2001. Otherwise, the real property is considered damaged real property. For example, if certain structural components (for example, walls, floors, and plumbing fixtures) of a building are damaged or destroyed as a result of the terrorist attacks of September 11, 2001, but the building is not destroyed or condemned, then only costs related to replacing the damaged or destroyed structural components qualify under this paragraph (c)(2)(i)(B).

(ii) *Property not eligible for additional first year depreciation deduction.*—Depreciable property will not meet the requirements of this paragraph (c)(2) if—

(A) Section 168(k) or § 1.168(k)-1 applies to the property;

(B) The property is described in section 168(f);

(C) The property is required to be depreciated under the alternative depreciation system of section 168(g) pursuant to section 168(g)(1)(A) through (D) or other provisions of the Internal Revenue Code (for example, property described in section 263A(e)(2)(A) if the taxpayer (or any related person) has made an election under section 263A(d)(3), or property described in section 280F(b)(1));

(D) The property is included in any class of property for which the taxpayer elects not to deduct the additional first year depreciation under paragraph (e) of this section; or

(E) The property is qualified New York Liberty Zone leasehold improvement property as described in section 1400L(c)(2).

(3) *Substantial use.*—Depreciable property will meet the requirements of this paragraph (c)(3) if substantially all of the use of the property is in the New York Liberty Zone and is in the active conduct of a trade or business by the taxpayer in New York Liberty Zone. For pur-

poses of this paragraph (c)(3), "substantially all" means 80 percent or more.

(4) *Original use.*—Depreciable property will meet the requirements of this paragraph (c)(4) if the original use of the property commences with the taxpayer in the New York Liberty Zone after September 10, 2001. The original use rules in § 1.168(k)-1(b)(3) apply for purposes of this paragraph (c)(4). In addition, used property will satisfy the original use requirement in this paragraph (c)(4) so long as the property has not been previously used within the New York Liberty Zone.

(5) *Acquisition of property by purchase.*—(i) *In general.*—Depreciable property will meet the requirements of this paragraph (c)(5) if the property is acquired by the taxpayer by purchase (as defined in section 179(d) and § 1.179-4(c)) after September 10, 2001, but only if no written binding contract for the acquisition of the property was in effect before September 11, 2001. For purposes of this paragraph (c)(5), the rules in § 1.168(k)-1(b)(4)(ii) (binding contract), the rules in § 1.168(k)-1(b)(4)(iii) (self-constructed property), and the rules in § 1.168(k)-1(b)(4)(iv) (disqualified transactions) apply. For purposes of the preceding sentence, the rules in § 1.168(k)-1(b)(4)(iii) shall be applied without regard to 'and before January 1, 2005.'

(ii) *Exception for certain transactions.*—For purposes of this section, the new partnership of a transaction described in § 1.168(k)-1(f)(1)(ii) (technical termination of a partnership) or the transferee of a transaction described in § 1.168(k)-1(f)(1)(iii) (section 168(i)(7) transactions) is deemed to acquire the depreciable property by purchase.

(6) *Placed-in-service date.*—Depreciable property will meet the requirements of this paragraph (c)(6) if the property is placed in service by the taxpayer on or before December 31, 2006. However, nonresidential real property and residential rental property described in paragraph (c)(2)(i)(B) of this section must be placed in service by the taxpayer on or before December 31, 2009. The rules in § 1.168(k)-1(b)(5)(ii) (relating to sale-leaseback and syndication transactions), the rules in § 1.168(k)-1(b)(5)(iii) (relating to a technical termination of a partnership under section 708(b)(1)(B)), and the rules in § 1.168(k)-1(b)(5)(iv) (relating to section 168(i)(7) transactions) apply for purposes of this paragraph (c)(6).

(d) *Computation of depreciation deduction for qualified New York Liberty Zone property.*—The computation of the allowable additional first year depreciation deduction and the otherwise allowable depreciation deduction for qualified New York Liberty Zone property is made in accordance with the rules for qualified property in § 1.168(k)-1(d)(1)(i) and (2).

(e) *Election not to deduct additional first year depreciation.*—(1) *In general.*—A taxpayer may make an election not to deduct the 30-percent additional first year depreciation for any class of property that is qualified New York Liberty Zone property placed in service during the taxable year. If a taxpayer makes an election under this paragraph (e), the election applies to all qualified New York Liberty Zone property that is in the same class of property and placed in service in the same taxable year, and no additional first year depreciation deduction is allowable for the class of property.

(2) *Definition of class of property.*—For purposes of this paragraph (e), the term class of property means—

(i) Except for the property described in paragraphs (e)(2)(ii), (iv), and (v) of this section, each class of property described in section 168(e) (for example, 5-year property);

(ii) Water utility property as defined in section 168(e)(5) and depreciated under section 168;

(iii) Computer software as defined in, and depreciated under, section 167(f)(1) and the regulations thereunder;

(iv) Nonresidential real property as defined in paragraph (b)(3) of this section and as described in paragraph (c)(2)(B) of this section; or

(v) Residential rental property as defined in paragraph (b)(3) of this section and as described in paragraph (c)(2)(B) of this section.

(3) *Time and manner for making election.*—(i) *Time for making election.*—Except as provided in paragraph (e)(4) of this section, the election specified in paragraph (e)(1) of this section must be made by the due date (including extensions) of the federal tax return for the taxable year in which the qualified New York Liberty Zone property is placed in service by the taxpayer.

(ii) *Manner of making election.*—Except as provided in paragraph (e)(4) of this section, the election specified in paragraph (e)(1) of this section must be made in the manner prescribed on Form 4562, "Depreciation and Amortization," and its instructions. The election is made separately by each person owning qualified New York Liberty Zone property (for example, for each member of a consolidated group by the common parent of the group, by the partnership, or by the S corporation). If Form 4562 is revised or renumbered, any reference in this section to that form shall be treated as a reference to the revised or renumbered form.

(4) *Special rules for 2000 or 2001 returns.*—For the election specified in paragraph (e)(1) of this section for qualified New York Liberty Zone property placed in service by the taxpayer during the taxable year that included September 11, 2001, the taxpayer should refer to the guidance

Reg. § 1.1400L(b)-1(e)(4)

provided by the Internal Revenue Service for the time and manner of making this election on the 2000 or 2001 federal tax return for the taxable year that included September 11, 2001 (for further guidance, see sections 3.03(3) and 4 of Rev. Proc. 2002-33 (2002-1 C.B. 963), Rev. Proc. 2003-50 (2003-29 I.R.B. 119), and § 601.601(d)(2)(ii)(b) of this chapter).

(5) *Failure to make election.*—If a taxpayer does not make the election specified in paragraph (e)(1) of this section within the time and in the manner prescribed in paragraph (e)(3) or (e)(4) of this section, the amount of depreciation allowable for that property under section 167(f)(1) or under section 168, as applicable, must be determined for the placed-in-service year and for all subsequent taxable years by taking into account the additional first year depreciation deduction. Thus, the election specified in paragraph (e)(1) of this section shall not be made by the taxpayer in any other manner (for example, the election cannot be made through a request under section 446(e) to change the taxpayer's method of accounting).

(6) *Alternative minimum tax.*—If a taxpayer makes an election under this paragraph (e) for a class of property, the depreciation adjustments under section 56 and the regulations under section 56 apply to the property to which the election applies for purposes of computing the taxpayer's alternative minimum taxable income.

(7) *Revocation of election.*—(i) *In general.*— Except as provided in paragraph (e)(7)(ii) of this section, an election under this paragraph (e), once made, may be revoked only with the written consent of the Commissioner of Internal Revenue. To seek the Commissioner's consent, the taxpayer must submit a request for a letter ruling.

(ii) *Automatic 6-month extension.*—If a taxpayer made an election under this paragraph (e) for a class of property, an automatic extension of 6 months from the due date of the taxpayer's Federal tax return (excluding extensions) for the placed-in-service year of the class of property is granted to revoke that election, provided the taxpayer timely filed the taxpayer's Federal tax return for the placed-in-service year of the class of property and, within this 6-month extension period, the taxpayer (and all taxpayers whose tax liability would be affected by the election) files an amended Federal tax return for the placed-in-service year of the class of property in a manner that is consistent with the revocation of the election.

(f) *Special rules.*—(1) *Property placed in service and disposed of in the same taxable year.*—Rules similar to those provided in § 1.168(k)-1(f)(1) apply for purposes of this paragraph (f)(1).

(2) *Redetermination of basis.*—If the unadjusted depreciable basis (as defined in § 1.168(k)-1(a)(2)(iii)) of qualified New York Liberty Zone property is redetermined (for example, due to contingent purchase price or discharge of indebtedness) on or before December 31, 2006 (or on or before December 31, 2009, for nonresidential real property and residential rental property described in paragraph (c)(2)(i)(B) of this section), the additional first year depreciation deduction allowable for the qualified New York Liberty Zone property is redetermined in accordance with the rules provided in § 1.168(k)-1(f)(2).

(3) *Section 1245 and 1250 depreciation recapture.*—The rules provided in § 1.168(k)-1(f)(3) apply for purposes of this paragraph (f)(3).

(4) *Coordination with section 169.*—Rules similar to those provided in § 1.168(k)-1(f)(4) apply for purposes of this paragraph (f)(4).

(5) *Like-kind exchanges and involuntary conversions.*—This paragraph (f)(5) applies to acquired MACRS property (as defined in § 1.168(k)-1(f)(5)(ii)(A)) or acquired computer software (as defined in § 1.168(k)-1(f)(5)(ii)(C)) that is eligible for the additional first year depreciation deduction under section 1400L(b) at the time of replacement provided the time of replacement is after September 10, 2001, and on or before December 31, 2006, or in the case of acquired MACRS property or acquired computer software that is qualified New York Liberty Zone property described in paragraph (c)(2)(i)(B) of this section, the time of replacement is after September 10, 2001, and on or before December 31, 2009. The rules and definitions similar to those provided in § 1.168(k)-1(f)(5) apply for purposes of this paragraph (f)(5).

(6) *Change in use.*—Rules similar to those provided in § 1.168(k)-1(f)(6) apply for purposes of this paragraph (f)(6).

(7) *Earnings and profits.*—The rule provided in § 1.168(k)-1(f)(7) applies for purposes of this paragraph (f)(7).

(8) *Section 754 election.*—Rules similar to those provided in § 1.168(k)-1(f)(9) apply for purposes of this paragraph (f)(8).

(9) *Coordination with section 47.*—Rules similar to those provided in § 1.168(k)-1(f)(10) apply for purposes of this paragraph (f)(9).

(10) *Coordination with section 514(a)(3).*— Rules similar to those provided in § 1.168(k)-1(f)(11) apply for purposes of this paragraph (f)(10).

(g) *Effective date.*—(1) *In general.*—Except as provided in paragraphs (g)(2), (3), and (5) of this section, this section applies to qualified New

York Liberty Zone property acquired by a taxpayer after September 10, 2001.

(2) *Technical termination of a partnership or section 168(i)(7) transactions.*—If qualified New York Liberty Zone property is transferred in a technical termination of a partnership under section 708(b)(1)(B) or in a transaction described in section 168(i)(7) for a taxable year ending on or before September 8, 2003, and the additional first year depreciation deduction allowable for the property was not determined in accordance with paragraph (f)(1) of this section, the Internal Revenue Service will allow any reasonable method of determining the additional first year depreciation deduction allowable for the property in the year of the transaction that is consistently applied to the property by all parties to the transaction.

(3) *Like-kind exchanges and involuntary conversions.*—If a taxpayer did not claim on a federal tax return for a taxable year ending on or before September 8, 2003, the additional first year depreciation deduction for the remaining carryover basis of qualified New York Liberty Zone property acquired in a transaction described in section 1031(a), (b), or (c), or in a transaction to which section 1033 applies and the taxpayer did not make an election not to deduct the additional first year depreciation deduction for the class of property applicable to the remaining carryover basis, the Internal Revenue Service will treat the taxpayer's method of not claiming the additional first year depreciation deduction for the remaining carryover basis as a permissible method of accounting and will treat the amount of the additional first year depreciation deduction allowable for the remaining carryover basis as being equal to zero, provided the taxpayer does not claim the additional first year depreciation deduction for the remaining carryover basis in accordance with paragraph (g)(4)(ii) of this section.

(4) *Change in method of accounting.*—(i) *Special rules for 2000 or 2001 returns.*—If a taxpayer did not claim on the federal tax return for the taxable year that included September 11, 2001, any additional first year depreciation deduction for a class of property that is qualified New York Liberty Zone property and did not make an election not to deduct the additional first year depreciation deduction for that class of property, the taxpayer should refer to the guidance provided by the Internal Revenue Service for the time and manner of claiming the additional first year depreciation deduction for the class of property (for further guidance, see section 4 of Rev. Proc. 2002-33 (2002-1 C.B. 963), Rev. Proc. 2003-50 (2003-29 I.R.B. 119), and § 601.601(d)(2)(ii)(b) of this chapter).

(ii) *Like-kind exchanges and involuntary conversions.*—If a taxpayer did not claim on a federal tax return for any taxable year ending on or before September 8, 2003, the additional first

year depreciation deduction allowable for the remaining carryover basis of qualified New York Liberty Zone property acquired in a transaction described in section 1031(a), (b), or (c), or in a transaction to which section 1033 applies and the taxpayer did not make an election not to deduct the additional first year depreciation deduction for the class of property applicable to the remaining carryover basis, the taxpayer may claim the additional first year depreciation deduction allowable for the remaining carryover basis in accordance with paragraph (f)(5) of this section either—

(A) By filing an amended return (or a qualified amended return, if applicable (for further guidance, see Rev. Proc. 94-69 (1994-2 C.B. 804) and § 601.601(d)(2)(ii)(b) of this chapter)) on or before December 31, 2003, for the year of replacement and any affected subsequent taxable year; or,

(B) By following the applicable administrative procedures issued under § 1.446-1(e)(3)(ii) for obtaining the Commissioner's automatic consent to a change in method of accounting (for further guidance, see Rev. Proc. 2002-9 (2002-1 C.B. 327) and § 601.601(d)(2)(ii)(b) of this chapter).

(iii) *Revisions made in paragraphs (b)(4) and (c)(2)(ii) of this section.*—If a taxpayer did not claim on a Federal tax return for a taxable year ending on or after September 11, 2001, and on or before September 1, 2006, any additional first year depreciation deduction for qualified New York Liberty Zone property because of the application of § 1.1400L(b)-1T(b)(4) or because the taxpayer made an election under § 1.168(k)-1T(e)(1) for a class of property that included such qualified New York Liberty Zone property, the taxpayer may claim the additional first year depreciation deduction for such qualified New York Liberty Zone property under this section in accordance with the applicable administrative procedures issued under § 1.446-1(e)(3)(ii) for obtaining the Commissioner's consent to a change in method of accounting. Section 481(a) applies to a request to claim the additional first year depreciation deduction for such qualified New York Liberty Zone property under this paragraph (g)(4)(iii).

(5) *Revision to paragraphs (b)(4) and (b)(6).*—The addition of "(or, in the case of multiple units of property subject to the same lease, within three months after the date the final unit is placed in service, so long as the period between the time the first unit is placed in service and the time the last unit is placed in service does not exceed 12 months)" to § 1.168(k)-1(b)(3)(iii)(B) and § 1.168(k)-1(b)(5)(ii)(B) applies to property sold after June 4, 2004, for purposes of paragraphs (b)(4) and (b)(6) of this section.

(6) *Rehabilitation credit.*—If a taxpayer did not claim on a Federal tax return for a taxable

Reg. § 1.1400L(b)-1(g)(6)

year ending on or before September 1, 2006, the rehabilitation credit provided by section 47(a) with respect to the portion of the basis of a qualified rehabilitated building that is attributable to qualified rehabilitation expenditures and the qualified rehabilitation expenditures are qualified New York Liberty Zone property, and the taxpayer did not make the election specified in paragraph (e)(1) of this section for the class of property that includes the qualified rehabilitation expenditures, the taxpayer may claim the rehabilitation credit for the remaining rehabilitated basis (as defined in § 1.168(k)-1(f)(10)(i)(B)) of the qualified rehabilitated building that is attributable to the qualified rehabilitation expenditures (assuming all the requirements of section

47 are met) in accordance with paragraph (f)(9) of this section by filing an amended Federal tax return for the taxable year for which the rehabilitation credit is to be claimed. The amended Federal tax return must include the adjustment to the tax liability for the rehabilitation credit and any collateral adjustments to taxable income or to the tax liability (for example, the amount of depreciation allowed or allowable in that taxable year for the qualified rehabilitated building). Such adjustments must also be made on amended Federal tax returns for any affected succeeding taxable years. [Reg. § 1.1400L(b)-1.]

☐ [*T.D. 9091, 9-5-2003 (corrected 11-7-2003). Redesignated and amended by T.D. 9283, 8-28-2006.*]

[The next page is 56,501.]

Tax on Self-Employment Income

See p. 20,601 for regulations not amended to reflect law changes

[Reg. §1.1401-1]

§1.1401-1. Tax on self-employment income.—(a) There is imposed, in addition to other taxes, a tax upon the self-employment income of every individual at the rates prescribed in section 1401(a) (old-age, survivors, and disability insurance) and (b) (hospital insurance). (See subparagraphs (1) and (2) of paragraph (b) of this section.) This tax shall be levied, assessed, and collected as part of the income tax imposed by subtitle A of the Code and, except as otherwise expressly provided, will be included with the tax imposed by section 1 or 3 in computing any deficiency or overpayment and in computing the interest and additions to any deficiency, overpayment, or tax. Since the tax on self-employment income is part of the income tax, it is subject to the jurisdiction of the Tax Court of the United States to the same extent and in the same manner as the other taxes under subtitle A of the Code. Furthermore, with respect to taxable years beginning after December 31, 1966, this tax must be taken into account in computing any estimate of the taxes required to be declared under section 6015.

(b) The rates of tax on self-employment income are as follows:

(1) For old-age, survivors, and disability insurance:

Taxable Year	Percent
Beginning before January 1, 1957	3
Beginning after December 31, 1956 and before January 1, 1959	3.375
Beginning after December 31, 1958 and before January 1, 1960	3.75
Beginning after December 31, 1959 and before January 1, 1962	4.5
Beginning after December 31, 1961 and before January 1, 1963	4.7
Beginning after December 31, 1962 and before January 1, 1966	5.4
Beginning after December 31, 1965 and before January 1, 1967	5.8
Beginning after December 31, 1966 and before January 1, 1968	5.9
Beginning after December 31, 1967 and before January 1, 1969	5.8
Beginning after December 31, 1968 and before January 1, 1971	6.3
Beginning after December 31, 1970 and before January 1, 1973	6.9
Beginning after December 31, 1972	7.0

(2) For hospital insurance:

Taxable Year	Percent
Beginning after December 31, 1965 and before January 1, 1967	0.35
Beginning after December 31, 1966 and before January 1, 1968	.50
Beginning after December 31, 1967 and before January 1, 1973	.60
Beginning after December 31, 1972 and before January 1, 1974	1.00
Beginning after December 31, 1973 and before January 1, 1978	.90
Beginning after December 31, 1977 and before January 1, 1981	1.10
Beginning after December 31, 1980 and before January 1, 1986	1.35
Beginning after December 31, 1985	1.50

(c) In general, self-employment income consists of the net earnings derived by an individual (other than a nonresident alien) from a trade or business carried on by him as sole proprietor or by a partnership of which he is a member, including the net earnings of certain employees as set forth in §1.1402(c)-3, and of crew leaders, as defined in section 3121(o) (see such section and the regulations thereunder in Part 31 of this chapter (Employment Tax Regulations)). See, however, the exclusions, exceptions, and limitations set forth in §§1.1402(a)-1 through 1.1402(h)-1. [Reg. §1.1401-1.]

☐ [T.D. 6196, 8-13-56. *Amended by T.D.* 6691, 12-2-63, *T.D.* 6993, 1-17-69 *and T.D.* 7333, 12-19-74.]

[Reg. §1.1402(a)-1]

§1.1402(a)-1. Definition of net earnings from self-employment.—(a) Subject to the special rules set forth in §§1.1402(a)-3 to 1.1402(a)-17, inclusive, and to the exclusions set forth in §§1.1402(c)-2 to 1.1402(c)-7, inclusive, the term "net earnings from self-employment" means—

(1) The gross income derived by an individual from any trade or business carried on by such individual, less the deductions allowed by chapter 1 of the Code which are attributable to such trade or business, plus

(2) His distributive share (whether or not distributed), as determined under section 704, of the income (or minus the loss), described in section 702(a)(9) and as computed under section 703, from any trade or business carried on by any partnership of which he is a member.

(b) Gross income derived by an individual from a trade or business includes payments received by him from a partnership of which he is a member for services rendered to the partnership or for the use of capital by the partnership, to the extent the payments are determined without regard to the income of the partnership. However, such payments received from a partnership not engaged in a trade or business within the meaning of section 1402(c) and §1.1402(c)-1 do not constitute gross income derived by an individual from a trade or business. See section 707(c) and the regulations thereunder, relating to guaranteed payments to a member of a partnership for services or the use of capital. See also section 706(a) and the regulations thereunder, relating to the taxable year of the partner in which such guaranteed payments are to be included in computing taxable income.

(c) Gross income derived by an individual from a trade or business includes gross income received (in the case of an individual reporting income on the cash receipts and disbursements method) or accrued (in the case of an individual reporting income on the accrual method) in the taxable year from a trade or business even though such income may be attributable in whole or in part to services rendered or other acts performed in a prior taxable year as to which the individual was not subject to the tax on self-employment income. [Reg. § 1.1402(a)-1.]

☐ [*T.D. 6196, 8-13-56. Amended by T.D. 6691, 12-2-63, and T.D. 7333, 12-19-74.*]

[Reg. § 1.1402(a)-2]

§ 1.1402(a)-2. Computation of net earnings from self-employment.—(a) *General rule.*—In general, the gross income and deductions of an individual attributable to a trade or business (including a trade or business conducted by an employee referred to in paragraphs (b), (c), (d), or (e) of § 1.1402(c)-3), for the purpose of ascertaining his net earnings from self-employment, are to be determined by reference to the provisions of law and regulations applicable with respect to the taxes imposed by sections 1 and 3. Thus, if an individual uses the accrual method of accounting in computing taxable income from a trade or business for the purpose of the tax imposed by section 1 or 3, he must use the same method in determining net earnings from self-employment. Likewise, if a taxpayer engaged in a trade or business of selling property on the installment plan elects, under the provisions of section 453, to use the installment method in computing income for purposes of the tax under section 1 or 3, he must use the same method in determining net earnings from self-employment. Income which is excludable from gross income under any provision of subtitle A of the Internal Revenue Code is not taken into account in determining net earnings from self-employment except as otherwise provided in § 1.1402(a)-9, relating to certain residents of Puerto Rico, in § 1.1402(a)-11, relating to ministers or members of religious orders, and in § 1.1402(a)-12, relating to the term "possession of the United States" as used for purposes of the tax on self-employment income. Thus, in the case of a citizen of the United States conducting, in a foreign country, a trade or business in which both personal services and capital are material income-producing factors, any part of the income therefrom which is excluded from gross income as earned income under the provisions of section 911 and the regulations thereunder is not taken into account in determining net earnings from self-employment.

(b) *Trade or business carried on.*—The trade or business must be carried on by the individual, either personally or through agents or employees. Accordingly, income derived from a trade or business carried on by an estate or trust is not included in determining the net earnings from self-employment of the individual beneficiaries of such estate or trust.

(c) *Aggregate net earnings.*—Where an individual is engaged in more than one trade or business within the meaning of section 1402(c) and § 1.1402(c)-1, his net earnings from self-employment consist of the aggregate of the net income and losses (computed subject to the special rules provided in § § 1.1402(a)-1 to 1.1402(a)-17, inclusive) of all such trades or businesses carried on by him. Thus, a loss sustained in one trade or business carried on by an individual will operate to offset the income derived by him from another trade or business.

(d) *Partnerships.*—The net earnings from self-employment of an individual include, in addition to the earnings from a trade or business carried on by him, his distributive share of the income or loss, described in section 702(a)(9), from any trade or business carried on by each partnership of which he is a member. An individual's distributive share of such income or loss of a partnership shall be determined as provided in section 704, subject to the special rules set forth in section 1402(a) and in § § 1.1402(a)-1 to 1.1402(a)-17, inclusive, and to the exclusions provided in section 1402(c) and § § 1.1402(c)-2 to 1.1402(c)-7, inclusive. For provisions relating to the computation of the taxable income of a partnership, see section 703.

(e) *Different taxable years.*—If the taxable year of a partner differs from that of the partnership, the partner shall include, in computing net earnings from self-employment, his distributive share of the income or loss, described in section 702(a)(9), of the partnership for its taxable year ending with or within the taxable year of the partner. For the special rule in case of the termination of a partner's taxable year as result of death, see § § 1.1402(f) and 1.1402(f)-1.

(f) *Meaning of partnerships.*—For the purpose of determining net earnings from self-employment, a partnership is one which is recognized as such for income tax purposes. For income tax purposes, the term "partnership" includes not only a partnership as known at common law, but, also, a syndicate, group, pool, joint venture, or other unincorporated organization which carries on any trade or business, financial operation, or venture, and which is not, within the meaning of the Code, a trust, estate, or a corporation. An organization described in the preceding sentence shall be treated as a partnership for purposes of the tax on self-employment income even though such organization has elected, pursuant to section 1361 and the regulations thereunder, to be taxed as a domestic corporation.

(g) *Nature of partnership interest.*—The net earnings from self-employment of a partner include his distributive share of the income or loss, described in section 702(a)(9), of the partnership of which he is a member, irrespective of the nature of his membership. Thus, in determining his net earnings from self-employment, a limited or inactive partner includes his distributive share of such partnership income or loss. In the case of a partner who is a member of a partnership with respect to which an election has been made pursuant to section 1361 and the regulations thereunder to be taxed as a domestic corporation, net earnings from self-employment include his distributive share of the income or loss, described in section 702(a)(9), from the trade or business carried on by the partnership computed without regard to the fact that the partnership has elected to be taxed as a domestic corporation.

(h) *Proprietorship taxed as domestic corporation.*—A proprietor of an unincorporated business enterprise with respect to which an election has been made pursuant to section 1361 and the regulations thereunder to be taxed as a domestic corporation shall compute his net earnings from self-employment without regard to the fact that such election has been made. [Reg. § 1.1402(a)-2.]

☐ *[T.D. 6691, 12-2-63. Amended by T.D. 7333, 12-19-74.]*

[Reg. § 1.1402(a)-3]

§ 1.1402(a)-3. Special rules for computing net earnings from self-employment.—For the purpose of computing net earnings from self-employment, the gross income derived by an individual from a trade or business carried on by him, the allowable deductions attributable to such trade or business, and the individual's distributive share of the income or loss, described in section 702(a)(9), from any trade or business carried on by a partnership of which he is a member shall be computed in accordance with the special rules set forth in §§ 1.1402(a)-4 to 1.1402(a)-17, inclusive. [Reg. § 1.1402(a)-3.]

☐ *[T.D. 6691, 12-2-63. Amended by T.D. 7710, 7-28-80.]*

[Reg. § 1.1402(a)-4]

§ 1.1402(a)-4. Rentals from real estate.—(a) *In general.*—Rentals from real estate and from personal property leased with the real estate (including such rentals paid in crop shares) and the deductions attributable thereto, unless such rentals are received by an individual in the course of a trade or business as a real-estate dealer, are excluded. Whether or not an individual is engaged in the trade or business of a real-estate dealer is determined by the application of the principles followed in respect of the taxes im-

posed by sections 1 and 3. In general, an individual who is engaged in the business of selling real estate to customers with a view to the gains and profits that may be derived from such sales is a real-estate dealer. On the other hand, an individual who merely holds real estate for investment or speculation and receives rentals therefrom is not considered a real-estate dealer. Where a real-estate dealer holds real estate for investment or speculation in addition to real estate held for sale to customers in the ordinary course of his trade or business as a real-estate dealer, only the rentals from the real estate held for sale to customers in the ordinary course of his trade or business as a real-estate dealer, and the deductions attributable thereto, are included in determining net earnings from self-employment; the rentals from the real estate held for investment or speculation, and the deductions attributable thereto, are excluded. Rentals paid in crop shares include income derived by an owner or lessee of land under an agreement entered into with another person pursuant to which such other person undertakes to produce a crop or livestock on such land and pursuant to which (1) the crop or livestock, or the proceeds thereof, are to be divided between such owner or lessee and such other person, and (2) the share of the owner or lessee depends on the amount of the crop or livestock produced. See, however, paragraph (b) of this section.

(b) *Special rule for "includible farm rental income".*—(1) *In general.*—Notwithstanding the rules set forth in paragraph (a) of this section, there shall be included in determining net earnings from self-employment for taxable years ending after 1955 any income derived by an owner or tenant of land, if the following requirements are met with respect to such income:

(i) The income is derived under an arrangement between the owner or tenant of land and another person which provides that such other person shall produce agricultural or horticultural commodities on such land, and that there shall be material participation by the owner or tenant in the production or the management of the production of such agricultural or horticultural commodities; and

(ii) There is material participation by the owner or tenant with respect to any such agricultural or horticultural commodity.

Income so derived shall be referred to in this section as "includible farm rental income".

(2) *Requirement that income be derived under an arrangement.*—In order for rental income received by an owner or tenant of land to be treated as includible farm rental income, such income must be derived pursuant to a sharefarming or other rental arrangement which contemplates material participation by the owner or tenant in the production or management of production of agricultural or horticultural commodities.

(3) *Nature of arrangement.*—(i) The arrangement between the owner or tenant and the person referred to in subparagraph (1) of this paragraph may be either oral or written. The arrangement must impose upon such other person the obligation to produce one or more agricultural or horticultural commodities (including livestock, bees, poultry, and fur-bearing animals and wildlife) on the land of the owner or tenant. In addition, it must be within the contemplation of the parties that the owner or tenant will participate in the production or the management of the production of the agricultural or horticultural commodities required to be produced by the other person under such arrangement to an extent which is material with respect either to the production or to the management of production of such commodities or is material with respect to the production and management of production when the total required participation in connection with both is considered.

(ii) The term "production", wherever used in this paragraph, refers to the physical work performed and the expenses incurred in producing a commodity. It includes such activities as the actual work of planting, cultivating, and harvesting crops, and the furnishing of machinery, implements, seed, and livestock. An arrangement will be treated as contemplating that the owner or tenant will materially participate in the "production" of the commodities required to be produced by the other person under the arrangement if under the arrangement it is understood that the owner or tenant is to engage to a material degree in the physical work related to the production of such commodities. The mere undertaking to furnish machinery, implements, and livestock and to incur expenses is not, in and of itself, sufficient. Such factors may be significant, however, in cases where the degree of physical work intended of the owner or tenant is not material. For example, if under the arrangement it is understood that the owner or tenant is to engage periodically in physical work to a degree which is not material in and of itself and, in addition, to furnish a substantial portion of the machinery, implements, and livestock to be used in the production of the commodities or to furnish or advance funds or assume financial responsibility for a substantial part of the expense involved in the production of the commodities, the arrangement will be treated as contemplating material participation of the owner or tenant in the production of such commodities.

(iii) The term "management of the production", wherever used in this paragraph, refers to services performed in making managerial decisions relating to the production, such as when to plant, cultivate, dust, spray, or harvest the crop, and includes advising and consulting, making inspections, and making decisions as to matters such as rotation of crops, the type of crops to be grown, the type of livestock to be raised, and the type of machinery and implements to be furnished. An arrangement will be treated as contemplating that the owner or tenant is to participate materially in the "management of the production" of the commodities required to be produced by the other person under the arrangement if the owner or tenant is to engage to a material degree in the management decisions related to the production of such commodities. The services which are considered of particular importance in making such management decisions are those services performed in making inspections of the production activities and in advising and consulting with such person as to the production of the commodities. Thus, if under the arrangement it is understood that the owner or tenant is to advise or consult periodically with the other person as to the production of the commodities required to be produced by such person under the arrangement and to inspect periodically the production activities on the land, a strong inference will be drawn that the arrangement contemplates participation by the owner or tenant in the management of the production of such commodities. The mere undertaking to select the crops or livestock to be produced or the type of machinery and implements to be furnished or to make decisions as to the rotation of crops generally is not, in and of itself, sufficient. Such factors may be significant, however, in making the over-all determination of whether the arrangement contemplates that the owner or tenant is to materially participate in the management of the production of the commodities. Thus, if in addition to the understanding that the owner or tenant is to advise or consult periodically with the other person as to the production of the commodities and inspect periodically the production activities on the land, it is also understood that the owner is to select the type of crops and livestock to be produced and the type of machinery and implements to be furnished and to make decisions as to the rotation of crops, the arrangement will be treated as contemplating material participation of the owner or tenant in the management of production of such commodities.

(4) *Actual participation.*—In order for the rental income received by the owner or tenant of land to be treated as includible farm rental income, not only must it be derived pursuant to the arrangement described in subparagraph (1) of this paragraph, but also the owner or tenant must actually participate to a material degree in the production or in the management of the production of any of the commodities required to be produced under the arrangement, or he must actually participate in both the production and the management of the production to an extent that his participation in the one when combined with his participation in the other will be considered participation to a material degree. If the owner or tenant shows that he periodically advises or consults with the other person, who

under the arrangement produces the agricultural or horticultural commodities, as to the production of any of these commodities and also shows that he periodically inspects the production activities on the land, he will have presented strong evidence of the existence of the degree of participation contemplated by section 1402(a)(1). If, in addition to the foregoing, the owner or tenant shows that he furnishes a substantial portion of the machinery, implements, and livestock used in the production of the commodities or that he furnishes or advances funds, or assumes financial responsibility, for a substantial part of the expense involved in the production of the commodities, he will have established the existence of the degree of participation contemplated by section 1402(a)(1) and this paragraph.

(5) *Employees or agents.*—An agreement entered into by an employee or agent of an owner or tenant and another person is considered to be an arrangement entered into by the owner or tenant for purposes of satisfying the requirement set forth in paragraph (b)(2) that the income must be derived under an arrangement between the owner or tenant and another person. For purposes of determining whether the arrangement satisfies the requirement set forth in paragraph (b)(3) that the parties contemplate that the owner or tenant will materially participate in the production or management of production of a commodity, services which will be performed by an employee or agent of the owner or tenant are not considered to be services which the arrangement contemplates will be performed by the owner or tenant. Services actually performed by such employee or agent are not considered services performed by the owner or tenant in determining the extent to which the owner or tenant has participated in the production or management of production of a commodity. For taxable years beginning before January 1, 1974, contemplated or actual services of an agent or an employee of the owner or tenant are deemed to be contemplated or actual services of the owner or tenant under paragraphs (b)(3) and (b)(4) of this section.

(6) *Examples.*—Application of the rules prescribed in this paragraph may be illustrated by the following examples:

Example (1). After the death of her husband, Mrs. A rents her farm, together with its machinery and equipment, to B for one-half of the proceeds from the commodities produced on such farm by B. It is agreed that B will live in the tenant house on the farm and be responsible for the over-all operation of the farm, such as planting, cultivating, and harvesting the field crops, caring for the orchard and harvesting the fruit and caring for the livestock and poultry. It also is agreed that Mrs. A will continue to live in the farm residence and help B operate the farm. Under the agreement it is contemplated that Mrs. A will regularly operate and clean the

cream separator and feed the poultry flock and collect the eggs. When possible she will assist B in such work as spraying the fruit trees, penning livestock, culling the poultry, and controlling weeds. She will also assist in preparing the meals when B engages seasonal workers. The agreement between Mrs. A and B clearly provides that she will materially participate in the over-all production operations to be conducted on her farm by B. In actual practice, Mrs. A performs such regular and intermittent services. The regularly performed services are material to the production of an agricultural commodity, and the intermittent services performed are material to the production operations to which they relate. The furnishing of a substantial portion of the farm machinery and equipment also adds support to a conclusion that Mrs. A has materially participated. Accordingly, the rental income Mrs. A receives from her farm should be included in net earnings from self-employment.

Example (2). D agrees to produce a crop on C's cotton farm under an arrangement providing that C and D will each receive one-half of the proceeds from such production. C agrees to furnish all the necessary equipment, and it is understood that he is to advise D when to plant the cotton and when it needs to be chopped, plowed, sprayed, and picked. It is also understood that during the growing season C is to inspect the crop every few days to determine whether D is properly taking care of the crop. Under the arrangement, D is required to furnish all labor needed to grow and harvest the crop. C, in fact, renders such advice, makes such inspections, and furnishes such equipment. C's contemplated participation in management decisions is considered material with respect to the management of the cotton production operation. C's actual participation pursuant to the arrangement is also considered to be material with respect to the management of the production of cotton. Accordingly, the income C receives from his cotton farm is to be included in computing his net earnings from self-employment.

Example (3). E owns a grain farm and turns its operation over to his son, F. By the oral rental arrangement between E and F, the latter agrees to produce crops of grain on the farm, and E agrees that he will be available for consultation and advice and will inspect and help to harvest the crops. E furnishes most of the equipment, including a tractor, a combine, plows, wagons, drills, and harrows; he continues to live on the farm and does some of the work such as repairing barns and farm machinery, going to town for supplies, cutting weeds, etc.; he regularly inspects the crops during the growing season; and he helps F to harvest the crops. Although the final decisions are made by F, he frequently consults with his father regarding the production of the crops. An evaluation of all of E's actual activities indicates that they are sufficiently substantial and regular to support a conclusion that he is

Reg. § 1.1402(a)-4(b)(6)

materially participating in the crop production operations and the management thereof. If it can be shown that the degree of E's actual participation was contemplated by the arrangement, E's income from the grain farm will be included in computing net earnings from self-employment.

Example (4). G owns a fully-equipped farm which he rents to H under an arrangement which contemplates that G shall materially participate in the management of the production of crops raised on the farm pursuant to the arrangement. G lives in town about 5 miles from the farm. About twice a month he visits the farm and looks over the buildings and equipment. G may occasionally, in an emergency, discuss with H some phase of a crop production activity. In effect, H has complete charge of the management of farming operations regardless of the understanding between him and G. Although G pays one-half of the cost of the seed and fertilizer and is charged for the cost of materials purchased by H to make all necessary repairs, G's activities do not constitute material participation in the crop production activities. Accordingly, G's income from the crops is not included in computing net earnings from self-employment.

Example (5). I owned a farm several miles from the town in which he lived. He rented the farm to J under an arrangement which contemplated I's material participation in the management of production of wheat. I furnished one-half of the seed and fertilizer and all the farm equipment and livestock. He employed K to perform all the services in advising, consulting, and inspecting contemplated by the arrangement. I is not materially participating in the management of production of wheat by J. The work done by I's employee, K, is not attributable to I in determining the extent of I's participation. I's rental income from the arrangement is, therefore, not to be included in computing his net earnings from self-employment. For taxable years beginning before January 1, 1974, however, I's rental income would be includible in those earnings.

Example (6). L, a calendar-year taxpayer, appointed M as his agent to rent his fully equipped farm for 1974. M entered into a rental arrangement with N under which M was to direct the planting of crops, inspect them weekly during the growing season, and consult with N on any problems that might arise in connection with irrigation, etc., while N furnished all the labor needed to grow and harvest the crops. M did in fact fulfill its responsibilities under the arrangement. Although the arrangement entered into by M and N is considered to have been made by L, M's services are not attributable to L, and L's furnishing of a fully equipped farm is insufficient by itself to constitute material participation in the production of the crops. Accordingly, L's rental income from the arrangement is not included in his net earnings from self-employment for that year. For taxable years beginning before

January 1, 1974, however, L's rental income would be includible in those earnings.

(c) *Rentals from living quarters.*—(1) *No services rendered for occupants.*—Payments for the use or occupancy of entire private residences or living quarters in duplex or multiple-housing units are generally rentals from real estate. Except in the case of real-estate dealers, such payments are excluded in determining net earnings from self-employment even though such payments are in part attributable to personal property furnished under the lease.

(2) *Services rendered for occupants.*—Payments for the use or occupancy of rooms or other space where services are also rendered to the occupant, such as for the use or occupancy of rooms or other quarters in hotels, boarding houses, or apartment houses furnishing hotel services, or in tourist camps or tourist homes, or payments for the use or occupancy of space in parking lots, warehouses, or storage garages, do not constitute rentals from real estate; consequently, such payments are included in determining net earnings from self-employment. Generally, services are considered rendered to the occupant if they are primarily for his convenience and are other than those usually or customarily rendered in connection with the rental of rooms or other space for occupancy only. The supplying of maid service, for example, constitutes such service; whereas the furnishing of heat and light, the cleaning of public entrances, exits, stairways and lobbies, the collection of trash, and so forth, are not considered as services rendered to the occupant.

(3) *Example.*—The application of this paragraph may be illustrated by the following example:

Example. A, an individual, owns a building containing four apartments. During the taxable year, he receives $1,400 from apartments numbered 1 and 2, which are rented without services rendered to the occupants, and $3,600 from apartments numbered 3 and 4, which are rented with services rendered to the occupants. His fixed expenses for the four apartments aggregate $1,200 during the taxable year. In addition, he has $500 of expenses attributable to the services rendered to the occupants of apartments 3 and 4. In determining his net earnings from self-employment, A includes the $3,600 received from apartments 3 and 4, and the expenses of $1,100 ($500 plus one-half of $1,200) attributable thereto. The rentals and expenses attributable to apartments 1 and 2 are excluded. Therefore, A has $2,500 of net earnings from self-employment for the taxable year from the building.

(d) *Treatment of business income which includes rentals from real estate.*—Except in the case of a real-estate dealer, where an individual or a partnership is engaged in a trade or business the income of which is classifiable in part as rentals from real estate, only that portion of such income which is not classifiable as rentals from real estate, and the expenses attributable to such portion, are included in determining net earnings from self-employment. [Reg. § 1.1402(a)-4.]

☐ [T.D. 6691, 12-2-63. *Amended by T.D. 7710, 7-28-80.*]

[Reg. § 1.1402(a)-5]

§ 1.1402(a)-5. Dividends and interest.— (a) All dividends on shares of stock are excluded unless they are received by an individual in the course of his trade or business as a dealer in stocks or securities.

(b) Interest on any bond, debenture, note, or certificate, or other evidence of indebtedness, issued with interest coupons or in registered form by any corporation (including one issued by a government or political subdivision thereof) is excluded unless such interest is received in the course of a trade or business as a dealer in stocks or securities. However, interest with respect to which a credit against tax is allowable as provided in section 35, that is, interest on certain obligations of the United States and its instrumentalities, is not included in net earnings from self-employment even though received in the course of a trade or business as a dealer in stocks or securities. Only interest on bonds, debentures, notes, or certificates, or other evidence of indebtedness, issued with interest coupons or in registered form by a corporation, is excluded in the case of all persons other than dealers in stocks or securities; other interest received in the course of any trade or business (such as interest received by a pawnbroker on his loans or interest received by a merchant on his accounts or notes receivable) is not excluded.

(c) Dividends and interest of the character excludable under paragraphs (a) and (b) of this section received by an individual on stocks or securities held for speculation or investment are excluded whether or not the individual is a dealer in stocks or securities.

(d) A dealer in stocks or securities is a merchant of stocks or securities with an established place of business, regularly engaged in the business of purchasing stocks or securities and reselling them to customers; that is, he is one who as a merchant buys stocks or securities and sells them to customers with a view to the gains and profits that may be derived therefrom. Persons who buy and sell or hold stocks or securities for investment or speculation, irrespective of whether such buying or selling constitutes the carrying on of a trade or business, are not dealers in stocks or securities. [Reg. § 1.1402(a)-5.]

☐ [T.D. 6691, 12-2-63.]

[Reg. § 1.1402(a)-6]

§ 1.1402(a)-6. Gain or loss from disposition of property.— (a) There is excluded any gain or loss: (1) Which is considered as gain or loss from the sale or exchange of a capital asset; (2) from the cutting of timber or the disposal of timber, coal, or iron ore, even though held primarily for sale to customers, if section 631 is applicable to such gain or loss; and (3) from the sale, exchange, involuntary conversion, or other disposition of property if such property is neither (i) stock in trade or other property of a kind which would properly be includible in inventory if on hand at the close of the taxable year, nor (ii) property held primarily for sale to customers in the ordinary course of a trade or business. For the purpose of the special rule in subparagraph (3) of this paragraph, it is immaterial whether a gain or loss is treated as a capital gain or loss or as an ordinary gain or loss for purposes other than determining net earnings from self-employment. For instance, where the character of a loss is governed by the provisions of section 1231, such loss is excluded in determining net earnings from self-employment even though such loss is treated under section 1231 as an ordinary loss. For the purposes of this special rule, the term "involuntary conversion" means a compulsory or involuntary conversion of property into other property or money as a result of its destruction in whole or in part, theft or seizure, or an exercise of the power of requisition or condemnation or the threat or imminence thereof; and the term "other disposition" includes the destruction or loss, in whole or in part, of property by fire, storm, shipwreck, or other casualty, or by theft, even though there is no conversion of such property into other property or money.

(b) The application of this section may be illustrated by the following example:

Example. During the taxable year 1954, A, who owns a grocery store, realized a net profit of $1,500 from the sale of groceries and a gain of $350 from the sale of a refrigerator case. During the same year, he sustained a loss of $2,000 as a result of damage by fire to the store building. In computing taxable income, all of these items are taken into account. In determining net earnings from self-employment, however, only the $1,500 of profit derived from the sale of groceries is included. The $350 gain and the $2,000 loss are excluded. [Reg. § 1.1402(a)-6.]

☐ [T.D. 6691, 12-2-63. *Amended by T.D. 6841, 7-26-65.*]

[Reg. § 1.1402(a)-7]

§ 1.1402(a)-7. Net operating loss deduction.— The deduction provided by section 172, relating to net operating losses sustained in years other than the taxable year, is excluded. [Reg. § 1.1402(a)-7.]

☐ [T.D. 6691, 12-2-63.]

[Reg. § 1.1402(a)-8]

§ 1.1402(a)-8. Community income.—(a) *In case of an individual.—*If any of the income derived by an individual from a trade or business (other than a trade or business carried on by a partnership) is community income under community property laws applicable to such income, all of the gross income, and the deductions attributable to such income, shall be treated as the gross income and deductions of the husband unless the wife exercises substantially all of the management and control of such trade or business, in which case all of such gross income and deductions shall be treated as the gross income and deductions of the wife. For the purpose of this special rule, the term "management and control" means management and control in fact, not the management and control imputed to the husband under the community property laws. For example, a wife who operates a beauty parlor without any appreciable collaboration on the part of her husband will be considered as having substantially all of the management and control of such business despite the provision of any community property law vesting in the husband the right of management and control of community property; and the income and deductions attributable to the operation of such beauty parlor will be considered the income and deductions of the wife.

(b) *In case of a partnership.*—Even though a portion of a partner's distributive share of the income or loss, described in section 702(a)(9), from a trade or business carried on by a partnership is community income or loss under the community property laws applicable to such share, all of such distributive share shall be included in computing the net earnings from self-employment of such partner; no part of such share shall be taken into account in computing the net earnings from self-employment of the spouse of such partner. In any case in which both spouses are members of the same partnership, the distributive share of the income or loss of each spouse is included in computing the net earnings from self-employment of that spouse. [Reg. § 1.1402(a)-8.]

☐ [*T.D.* 6691, 12-2-63.]

[Reg. § 1.1402(a)-9]

§ 1.1402(a)-9. **Puerto Rico.**—(a) *Residents.*—A resident of Puerto Rico, whether or not a bona fide resident thereof during the entire taxable year, and whether or not an alien, a citizen of the United States, or a citizen of Puerto Rico, shall compute his net earnings from self-employment in the same manner as would a citizen of the United States residing in the United States. See paragraph (d) of § 1.1402(b)-1 for regulations relating to nonresident aliens. For the purposes of the tax on self-employment income, the gross income of such a resident of Puerto Rico also includes income from Puerto Rican sources. Thus, under this special rule, income from Puerto Rican sources will be included in determining net earnings from self-employment of a resident of Puerto Rico engaged in the active conduct of a trade or business in Puerto Rico despite the fact that, under section 933, such income may not be taken into account for purposes of the tax under section 1 or 3.

(b) *Nonresidents.*—A citizen of Puerto Rico who is also a citizen of the United States and who is not a resident of Puerto Rico will compute his net earnings from self-employment in the same manner and subject to the same provisions of law and regulations as other citizens of the United States. [Reg. § 1.1402(a)-9.]

☐ [*T.D.* 6691, 12-2-63.]

[Reg. § 1.1402(a)-10]

§ 1.1402(a)-10. **Personal exemption deduction.**—The deduction provided by section 151, relating to personal exemptions, is excluded. [Reg. § 1.1402(a)-10.]

☐ [*T.D.* 6691, 12-2-63.]

[Reg. § 1.1402(a)-11]

§ 1.1402(a)-11. **Ministers and members of religious orders.**—(a) *In general.*—For each taxable year ending after 1954 in which a minister or member of a religious order is engaged in a trade or business, within the meaning of section 1402(c) and § 1.1402(c)-5, with respect to service performed in the exercise of his ministry or in the exercise of duties required by such order, net earnings from self-employment from such trade or business include the gross income derived during the taxable year from any such service, less the deductions attributable to such gross income. For each taxable year ending on or after December 31, 1957, such minister or member of a religious order shall compute his net earnings from self-employment derived from the performance of such service without regard to the exclusions from gross income provided by section 107 (relating to rental value of parsonages) and section 119 (relating to meals and lodging furnished for the convenience of the employer). Thus, a minister who is subject to self-employment tax with respect to his services as a minister will include in the computation of his net earnings from self-employment for a taxable year ending on or after December 31, 1957, the rental value of a home furnished to him as remuneration for services performed in the exercise of his ministry or the rental allowance paid to him as remuneration for such services irrespective of whether such rental value or rental allowance is excluded from gross income by section 107. Similarly, the value of any meals or lodging furnished to a minister or to a member of a religious order in connection with service performed in the exercise of his ministry or as a member of such order will be included in the computation of his net earnings from self-employment for a taxable year ending on or after December 31, 1957, notwithstanding the exclusion of such value from gross income by section 119.

(b) *In employ of American employer.*—If a minister or member of a religious order engaged in a trade or business described in section 1402(c) and § 1.1402(c)-5 is a citizen of the United States and performs service, in his capacity as a minister or member of a religious order, as an employee of an American employer, as defined in section 3121(h) and the regulations thereunder in Part 31 of this chapter (Employment Tax Regulations), his net earnings from self-employment derived from such service shall be computed as provided in paragraph (a) of this section but without regard to the exclusions from gross income provided in section 911, relating to earned income from sources without the United States, and section 931, relating to income from sources within certain possessions of the United States. Thus, even though all the income of the minister or member for service of the character to which this paragraph is applicable was derived from sources without the United States, or from sources within certain possessions of the United States, and therefore may be excluded from gross income, such income is included in computing net earnings from self-employment.

(c) *Minister in a foreign country whose congregation is composed predominantly of citizens of the United States.*—(1) *Taxable years ending after 1956.*—For any taxable year ending after 1956, a minister of a church, who is engaged in a trade or business within the meaning of section 1402(c) and § 1.1402(c)-5, is a citizen of the United States, is performing service in the exercise of his ministry in a foreign country, and has a congregation composed predominantly of United States citizens, shall compute his net earnings from self-employment derived from his services as a minister for such taxable year without regard to the exclusion from gross income provided in section 911, relating to earned income from sources without the United States. For taxable years ending on or after December 31, 1957, such minister shall also disregard sections 107 and 119 in the computation of his net earnings from self-employment. (See paragraph (a) of this section.) For purposes of section 1402(a)(8) and this paragraph a "congregation composed predominantly of citizens of the United States" means a congregation the majority of which throughout the greater portion of its minister's taxable year were United States citizens.

(2) *Election for taxable years ending after 1954 and before 1957.*—(i) A minister described in subparagraph (1) of this paragraph who, for a taxable year ending after 1954 and before 1957, had income from service described in such subparagraph which would have been included in computing net earnings from self-employment if such income had been derived in a taxable year ending after 1956 by an individual who had filed a waiver certificate under section 1402(e), may elect to have section 1402(a)(8) and subparagraph (1) of this paragraph apply to his income

from such service for his taxable years ending after 1954 and before 1957. If such minister filed a waiver certificate prior to August 1, 1956, in accordance with § 1.1402(e)(1)-1, or he files such a waiver certificate on or before the due date of his return (including any extensions thereof) for his last taxable year ending before 1957, he must make such election on or before the due date of his return (including any extensions thereof) for such taxable year or before April 16, 1957, whichever is the later. If the waiver certificate is not so filed, the minister must make his election on or before the due date of the return (including any extensions thereof) for his first taxable year ending after 1956. Notwithstanding the expiration of the period prescribed by section 1402(e)(2) for filing such waiver, the minister may file a waiver certificate at the time he makes the election. In no event shall an election be valid unless the minister files prior to or at the time of the election a waiver certificate in accordance with § 1.1402(e)(1)-1.

(ii) The election shall be made by filing with the district director of internal revenue with whom the waiver certificate, Form 2031, is filed a written statement indicating that, by reason of the Social Security Amendments of 1956, the minister desires to have the Federal old-age, survivors, and disability insurance system established by title II of the Social Security Act extended to his services performed in a foreign country as a minister of a congregation composed predominantly of United States citizens beginning with the first taxable year ending after 1954 and prior to 1957 for which he had income from such services. The statement shall be dated and signed by the minister and shall clearly state that it is an election for retroactive self-employment tax coverage under the Self-Employment Contributions Act of 1954. In addition, the statement shall include the following information:

(a) The name and address of the minister.

(b) His social security account number, if he has one.

(c) That he is a duly ordained, commissioned, or licensed minister of a church.

(d) That he is a citizen of the United States.

(e) That he is performing services in the exercise of his ministry in a foreign country.

(f) That his congregation is composed predominantly of citizens of the United States.

(g) (1) That he has filed a waiver certificate and, if so, where and under what circumstances the certificate was filed and the taxable year for which it is effective; or (2) That he is filing a waiver certificate with his election for retroactive coverage and, if so, the taxable year for which it is effective.

(h) That he has or has not filed income tax returns for his taxable years ending after 1954 and before 1957. If he has filed such returns, he

Reg. § 1.1402(a)-11(c)(2)(ii)(h)

shall state the years for which they were filed and indicate the district director of internal revenue with whom they were filed.

(iii) Notwithstanding section 1402(e)(3), a waiver certificate filed pursuant to §1.1402(e)(1)-1 by a minister making an election under this paragraph shall be effective (regardless of when such certificate is filed) for such minister's first taxable year ending after 1954 in which he had income from service described in subparagraph (1) of this paragraph or for the taxable year of the minister prescribed by section 1402(e)(3), if such taxable year is earlier, and for all succeeding taxable years.

(iv) No interest or penalty shall be assessed or collected for failure to file a return within the time prescribed by law if such failure arises solely by reason of an election made by a minister pursuant to this paragraph or for any underpayment of self-employment income tax arising solely by reason of such election, for the period ending with the date such minister makes an election pursuant to this paragraph.

(d) *Treatment of certain remuneration paid in 1955 and 1956 as wages.*—For treatment of remuneration paid to an individual for service described in section 3121(b)(8)(A) which was erroneously treated by the organization employing him as employment within the meaning of chapter 21 of the Internal Revenue Code, see §1.1402(e)(4)-1. [Reg. §1.1402(a)-11.]

☐ [*T.D. 6691, 12-2-63. Amended by T.D. 9194, 4-6-2005.*]

[Reg. §1.1402(a)-12]

§1.1402(a)-12. Continental shelf and certain possessions of the United States.—(a) *Certain possessions.*—For purposes of the tax on self-employment income, the exclusion from gross income provided by section 931 (relating to bona fide residents of certain possessions of the United States) will not apply. Net earnings from self-employment are subject to the tax on self-employment income even if such amounts are excluded from gross income under section 931.

(b) *Continental shelf.*—For the definition of the term "United States" and for other geographical definitions relating to the continental shelf, see section 638 and §1.638-1.

(c) *Effective/applicability date.*—This section applies to taxable years ending after April 9, 2008. [Reg. §1.1402(a)-12.]

☐ [*T.D. 6691, 12-2-63. Amended by T.D. 7277, 5-14-73; T.D. 9194, 4-6-2005 and T.D. 9391, 4-4-2008.*]

[Reg. §1.1402(a)-13]

§1.1402(a)-13. Income from agricultural activity.—(a) *Agricultural trade or business.*—(1) An agricultural trade or business is one in which, if the trade or business were carried on

exclusively by employees, the major portion of the services would constitute agricultural labor as defined in section 3121(g) and the regulations thereunder in Part 31 of this chapter (Employment Tax Regulations). In case the services are in part agricultural and in part nonagricultural, the time devoted to the performance of each type of service is the test to be used to determine whether the major portion of the services would constitute agricultural labor. If more than half of the time spent in performing all the services is spent in performing services which would constitute agricultural labor under section 3121(g), the trade or business is agricultural. If only half, or less, of the time spent in performing all the services is spent in performing services which would constitute agricultural labor under section 3121(g), the trade or business is not agricultural. In every case the time spent in performing the services will be computed by adding the time spent in the trade or business during the taxable year by every individual (including the individual carrying on such trade or business and the members of his family) in performing such services. The operation of this special rule is not affected by section 3121(c), relating to the included-excluded rule for determining employment.

(2) The rules prescribed in subparagraph (1) of this paragraph have no application where the nonagricultural services are performed in connection with an enterprise which constitutes a trade or business separate and distinct from the trade or business conducted as an agricultural enterprise. Thus, the operation of a roadside automobile service station on farm premises constitutes a trade or business separate and distinct from the agricultural enterprise, and the gross income derived from such service station, less the deductions attributable thereto, is to be taken into account in determining net earnings from self-employment.

(b) *Farm operator's income for taxable years ending before 1955.*—Income derived in a taxable year ending before 1955 from any agricultural trade or business (see paragraph (a) of this section), and all deductions attributable to such income, are excluded in computing net earnings from self-employment.

(c) *Farm operator's income for taxable years ending after 1954.*—Income derived in a taxable year ending after 1954 from an agricultural trade or business (see paragraph (a) of this section) is includible in computing net earnings from self-employment. Income derived from an agricultural trade or business includes income derived by an individual under an agreement entered into by such individual with another person pursuant to which such individual undertakes to produce agricultural or horticultural commodities (including livestock, bees, poultry, and fur-bearing animals and wildlife) on land owned or leased by such other person and pursuant to which the agricultural or horticultural commodities produced by such individual, or the proceeds therefrom, are to be divided between such individual and such other person, and the amount of such individual's share depends on the amount of the agricultural or horticultural commodities produced. However, except as provided in paragraph (d) of this section, relating to arrangements involving material participation, the income derived under such an agreement by the owner or lessee of the land is not includible in computing net earnings from self-employment. See § 1.1402(a)-4. For options relating to the computation of net earnings from self-employment, see §§ 1.1402(a)-14 and 1.1402(a)-15.

(d) *Includible farm rental income for taxable years ending after 1955.*—For taxable years ending after 1955, income derived from an agricultural trade or business (see paragraph (a) of this section) includes also income derived by the owner or tenant of land under an arrangement between such owner or tenant and another person, if such arrangement provides that such other person shall produce agricultural or horticultural commodities (including livestock, bees, poultry, and fur-bearing animals and wildlife) on such land, and that there shall be material participation by the owner or tenant in the production or the management of the production of such agricultural or horticultural commodities, and if there is material participation by the owner or tenant with respect to any such agricultural or horticultural commodity. See paragraph (b) of § 1.1402(a)-4. For options relating to the computation of net earnings from self-employment, see §§ 1.1402(a)-14 and 1.1402(a)-15.

(e) *Income from service performed after 1956 as a crew leader.*—Income derived by a crew leader (see section 3121(o) and the regulations thereunder in Part 31 of this chapter (Employment Tax Regulations)) from service performed after 1956 in furnishing individuals to perform agricultural labor for another person and from service performed after 1956 in agricultural labor as a member of the crew is considered to be income derived from a trade or business for purposes of § 1.1402(c)-1. Whether such trade or business is an agricultural trade or business shall be determined by applying the rules set forth in this section. [Reg. § 1.1402(a)-13.]

☐ [*T.D. 6691, 12-2-63.*]

[Reg. § 1.1402(a)-14]

§ 1.1402(a)-14. Options available to farmers in computing net earnings from self-employment for taxable years ending after 1954 and before December 31, 1956.—[This regulation is now obsolete.—CCH.]

[Reg. § 1.1402(a)-15]

§ 1.1402(a)-15. Options available to farmers in computing net earnings from self-employment for taxable years ending on or after December 31, 1956.—(a) *Computation of net earnings.*—In the case of any trade or business which is carried on by an individual or by a partnership and in which, if such trade or business were carried on exclusively by employees, the major portion of the services would constitute agricultural labor as defined in section 3121(g) (see paragraph (a) of § 1.1402(a)-13), net earnings from self-employment may, for a taxable year ending on or after December 31, 1956, at the option of the taxpayer, be computed as follows:

(1) *In case of an individual.*—(i) *Gross income of less than specified amount.*—If the gross income, computed as provided in paragraph (b) of this section, from such trade or business is $2,400 or less ($1,800 or less for a taxable year ending on or after December 31, 1956, and beginning before January 1, 1966), the taxpayer may, at his option, treat as net earnings from self-employment from such trade or business an amount equal to 66⅔ percent of such gross income. If the taxpayer so elects, the amount equal to 66⅔ percent of such gross income shall be used in computing his self-employment income in lieu of his actual net earnings from such trade or business, if any.

(ii) *Gross income in excess of specified amount.*—If the gross income, computed as provided in paragraph (b) of this section, from such trade or business is more than $2,400 ($1,800 for a taxable year ending on or after December 31, 1956, and beginning before January 1, 1966), and the net earnings from self-employment from such trade or business (computed without regard to this section) are less than $1,600 ($1,200 for a taxable year ending on or after December 31, 1956, and beginning before January 1, 1966), the taxpayer may, at his option, treat $1,600 ($1,200 for a taxable year ending on or after December 31, 1956, and beginning before January 1, 1966) as net earnings from self-employment. If the taxpayer so elects, $1,600 ($1,200 for a taxable year ending on or after December 31, 1956, and beginning before January 1, 1966) shall be used in computing his self-employment income in lieu of his actual net earnings from such trade or business, if any. However, if the taxpayer's actual net earnings from such trade or business, as computed in accordance with the applicable provisions of §§ 1.1402(a)-1 to 1.1402(a)-13, inclusive, are $1,600 or more ($1,200 or more for a taxable year ending on or after December 31, 1956, and beginning before January 1, 1966) such actual net earnings shall be used in computing his self-employment income.

(2) *In case of a member of a partnership.*—(i) *Distributive share of gross income of less than specified amount.*—If a taxpayer's distributive share of the gross income of a partnership (as such gross income is computed under the provisions of paragraph (b) of this section) derived

from such trade or business (after such gross income has been reduced by the sum of all payments to which section 707(c) applies) is $2,400 or less ($1,800 or less for a taxable year ending on or after December 31, 1956, and beginning before January 1, 1966), the taxpayer may, at his option, treat as his distributive share of income described in section 702(a)(9) derived from such trade or business an amount equal to 66²/₃ percent of his distributive share of such gross income (after such gross income has been reduced by the sum of all payments to which section 707(c) applies). If the taxpayer so elects, the amount equal to 66²/₃ percent of his distributive share of such gross income shall be used by him in the computation of his net earnings from self-employment in lieu of the actual amount of his distributive share of income described in section 702(a)(9) from such trade or business, if any.

(ii) *Distributive share of gross income in excess of specified amount.*—If a taxpayer's distributive share of the gross income of a partnership (as such gross income is computed under the provisions of paragraph (b) of this section) derived from such trade or business (after such gross income has been reduced by the sum of all payments to which section 707(c) applies) is more than $2,400 ($1,800 for a taxable year ending on or after December 31, 1956, and beginning before January 1, 1966) and the actual amount of his distributive share (whether or not distributed) of income described in section 702(a)(9) derived from such trade or business (computed without regard to this section) is less than $1,600 ($1,200 for a taxable year ending on or after December 31, 1956, and beginning before January 1, 1966), the taxpayer may, at his option, treat $1,600 ($1,200 for a taxable year ending on or after December 31, 1956, and beginning before January 1, 1966) as his distributive share of income described in section 702(a)(9) derived from such trade or business. If the taxpayer so elects, $1,600 ($1,200 for a taxable year ending on or after December 31, 1956, and beginning before January 1, 1966) shall be used by him in the computation of his net earnings from self-employment in lieu of the actual amount of his distributive share of income described in section 702(a)(9) from such trade or business, if any. However, if the actual amount of the taxpayer's distributive share of income described in section 702(a)(9) from such trade or business, as computed in accordance with the applicable provisions of §§ 1.1402(a)-1 to 1.1402(a)-13, inclusive, is $1,600 or more ($1,200 or more for a taxable year ending on or after December 31, 1956, and beginning before January 1, 1966), such actual amount of the taxpayer's distributive share shall be used in computing his net earnings from self-employment.

(iii) *Cross reference.*—For a special rule in the case of certain deceased partners, see paragraph (c) of § 1.1402(f)-1.

(b) *Computation of gross income.*—For purposes of this section gross income has the following meanings:

(1) In the case of any such trade or business in which the income is computed under a cash receipts and disbursements method, the gross receipts from such trade or business reduced by the cost or other basis of property which was purchased and sold in carrying on such trade or business (see paragraphs (a) and (c), other than paragraph (a)(5), of § 1.61-4), adjusted (after such reduction) in accordance with the applicable provisions of §§ 1.1402(a)-3 to 1.1402(a)-13, inclusive.

(2) In the case of any such trade or business in which the income is computed under an accrual method (see paragraphs (b) and (c), other than paragraph (b)(5), of § 1.61-4), the gross income from such trade or business, adjusted in accordance with the applicable provisions of §§ 1.1402(a)-3 to 1.1402(a)-13, inclusive.

(c) *Two or more agricultural activities.*—If an individual (including a member of a partnership) derives gross income (as defined in paragraph (b) of this section) from more than one agricultural trade or business, such gross income (including his distributive share of the gross income of any partnership derived from any such trade or business) shall be deemed to have been derived from one trade or business. Thus, such an individual shall aggregate his gross income derived from each agricultural trade or business carried on by him (which includes, under paragraph (b) of § 1.1402(a)-1, any guaranteed payment, within the meaning of section 707(c), received by him from a farm partnership of which he is a member) and his distributive share of partnership gross income (after such gross income has been reduced by any guaranteed payment within the meaning of section 707(c)) derived from each farm partnership of which he is a member. Such gross income is the amount to be considered for purposes of the optional method provided in this section for computing net earnings from self-employment. If the aggregate gross income of an individual includes income derived from an agricultural trade or business carried on by him and a distributive share of partnership income derived from an agricultural trade or business carried on by a partnership of which he is a member, such aggregate gross income shall be treated as income derived from a single trade or business carried on by him, and such individual shall apply the optional method applicable to individuals set forth in paragraph (a)(1) of this section for purposes of computing his net earnings from self-employment.

(d) *Examples.*—The application of this section may be illustrated by the following examples:

Example (1). F is engaged in the business of farming and computes his income under the cash receipts and disbursements method. He files his income tax returns on the basis of the calendar year. During the year 1966, F's gross income from the business of farming (computed in accordance with paragraph (b)(1) of this section) is $2,325. His actual net earnings from self-employment derived from such business are $1,250. As his net earnings from self-employment, F may report $1,250 or, by the optional computation method, he may report $1,550 (66 2/3 percent of $2,325).

Example (2). G is engaged in the business of farming and computes his income under the accrual method. His income tax returns are filed on the calendar year basis. For the year 1966, G's gross income from the operation of his farm (computed in accordance with paragraph (b)(2) of this section) is $2,800. He has actual net earnings from self-employment derived from such farm in the amount of $1,250. As his net earnings from self-employment derived from his farm, G may report his actual net earnings of $1,250, or by the optional method he may report $1,600. If G's actual net earnings from self-employment from his farming activities for 1966 were in an amount of $1,600 or more, he would be required to report such amount in computing his self-employment income.

Example (3). M, who files his income tax returns on a calendar year basis, is one of the three partners of the XYZ Company, a partnership, engaged in the business of farming. The taxable year of the partnership is the calendar year, and its income is computed under the cash receipts and disbursements method. For M's services in connection with the planting, cultivating, and harvesting of the crops during the year 1966 the partnership agrees to pay him $500, the full amount of which is determined without regard to the income of the partnership and constitutes a guaranteed payment within the meaning of section 707(c). This guaranteed payment to M is the only such payment made during such year. The gross income derived from the business for the year 1966 computed in accordance with paragraph (b)(1) of this section and after being reduced by the guaranteed payment of $500 made to M, is $3,000. One-third of the $3,000 ($1,000), is M's distributive share of such gross income. Under paragraph (c) of this section, the guaranteed payment ($500) received by M and his distributive share of the partnership gross income ($1,000) are deemed to have been derived from one trade or business, and such amounts must be aggregated for purposes of the optional method of computing net earnings from self-employment. Since M's combined gross income from his two agricultural businesses ($1,000 and $500) is not more than $2,400 and since such income is deemed to be derived from one trade or business, M's net earnings from self-employment derived from such farming business may, at his option, be deemed to be $1,000 (66 2/3 percent of $1,500).

Example (4). A is one of the two partners of the AB partnership which is engaged in the business of farming. The taxable year of the partnership is the calendar year and its income is computed under the accrual method. A files his income tax returns on the calendar year basis. The partnership agreement provides for an equal sharing in the profits and losses of the partnership by the two partners. A is an experienced farmer and for his services as manager of the partnership's farm activities during the year 1966 he receives $6,000 which amount constitutes a guaranteed payment within the meaning of section 707(c). The gross income of the partnership derived from such business for the year 1966, computed in accordance with paragraph (b)(2) of this section and after being reduced by the guaranteed payment made to A, is $9,600. A's distributive share of such gross income is $4,800 and his distributive share of income described in section 702(a)(9) derived from the partnership's business is $1,900. Under paragraph (c) of this section, the guaranteed payment received by A and his distributive share of the partnership gross income are deemed to have been derived from one trade or business, and such amounts must be aggregated for purposes of the optional method of computing his net earnings from self-employment. Since the aggregate of A's guaranteed payment ($6,000) and his distributive share of partnership gross income ($4,800) is more than $2,400 and since the aggregate of A's guaranteed payment ($6,000) and his distributive share ($1,900) of partnership income described in section 702(a)(9) is not less than $1,600, the optional method of computing net earnings from self-employment is not available to A.

Example (5). F is a member of the EFG partnership which is engaged in the business of farming. F files his income tax returns on the calendar year basis. The taxable year of the partnership is the calendar year, and its income is computed under a cash receipts and disbursements method. Under the partnership agreement the partners are to share equally the profits or losses of the business. The gross income derived from the partnership business for the year 1966, computed in accordance with paragraph (b)(1) of this section is $7,500. F's share of such gross income is $2,500. Due to drought and an epidemic among the livestock, the partnership sustains a net loss of $7,800 for the year 1966 of which loss F's share is $2,600. Since F's distributive share of gross income derived from such business is in excess of $2,400 and since F does not receive income described in section 702(a)(9) of $1,600 or more from such business, he may, at his option, be deemed to have received $1,600 as his distributive share of income described in section 702(a)(9) from such business. [Reg. § 1.1402(a)-15.]

□ [T.D. 6691, 12-2-63. Amended by T.D. 6993, 1-17-69.]

Reg. § 1.1402(a)-15(d)

[Reg. § 1.1402(a)-16]

§ 1.1402(a)-16. Exercise of option.—A taxpayer shall, for each taxable year with respect to which he is eligible to use the optional method described in § 1.1402(a)-14 or § 1.1402(a)-15, make a determination as to whether his net earnings from self-employment are to be computed in accordance with such method. If the taxpayer elects the optional method for a taxable year, he shall signify such election by computing net earnings from self-employment under the optional method as set forth in Schedule F (Form 1040) of the income tax return filed by the taxpayer for such taxable year. If the optional method is not elected at the time of the filing of the return for a taxable year with respect to which the taxpayer is eligible to elect such optional method, such method may be elected on an amended return (or on such other form as may be prescribed for such use) filed within the period prescribed by section 6501 and the regulations thereunder for the assessment of the tax for such taxable year. If the optional method is elected on a return for a taxable year, the taxpayer may revoke such election by filing an amended return (or such other form as may be prescribed for such use) for the taxable year within the period prescribed by section 6501 and the regulations thereunder for the assessment of the tax for such taxable year. If the taxpayer is deceased or unable to make an election, the person designated in section 6012(b) and the regulations thereunder may, within the period prescribed in this section elect the optional method for any taxable year with respect to which the taxpayer is eligible to use the optional method and revoke an election previously made by or for the taxpayer. [Reg. § 1.1402(a)-16.]

☐ [T.D. 6691, 12-2-63.]

[Reg. § 1.1402(a)-17]

§ 1.1402(a)-17. Retirement payments to retired partners.—(a) *In general.*—There shall be excluded, in computing net earnings from self-employment for taxable years ending on or after December 31, 1967, certain payments made on a periodic basis by a partnership, pursuant to a written plan of the partnership, to a retired partner on account of his retirement. The exclusion applies only if the payments are made pursuant to a plan which meets the requirements prescribed in paragraph (b) of this section, and, in addition, the conditions set forth in paragraph (c) of this section are met.

(b) *Retirement plan of partnership.*—(1) To meet the requirements of section 1402(a)(10), the written plan of the partnership must set forth the terms and conditions of the program or system established by the partnership for the purpose of making payments to retired partners on account of their retirement. To qualify as payments on account of retirement, the payments must consti-

tute bona fide retirement income. Thus, payments of benefits not customarily included in a pension or retirement plan such as layoff benefits are not payments on account of retirement. Eligibility for retirement generally is established on the basis of age, physical condition, or a combination of age or physical condition and years of service. Generally, retirement benefits are measured by, and based on, such factors as years of service and compensation received. In determining whether the plan of the partnership provides for payments on account of retirement, factors, formulas, etc., reflected in public, and in broad based private, pension or retirement plans in prescribing eligibility requirements and in computing benefits may be taken into account.

(2) The plan of the partnership must provide for payments on account of retirement—

(i) To partners generally or to a class or classes of partners,

(ii) On a periodic basis, and

(iii) Which continue at least until the partner's death.

For purposes of subdivision (i) of this subparagraph, a class of partners may, in an appropriate case, contain only one member. Payments are made on a periodic basis if made at regularly recurring intervals (usually monthly) not exceeding one year.

(c) *Conditions relating to exclusion.*—(1) *In general.*—A payment made pursuant to a written plan of a partnership which meets the requirements of paragraph (b) of this section shall be excluded, in computing net earnings from self-employment, only if—

(i) The retired partner to whom the payment is made rendered no service with respect to any trade or business carried on by the partnership (or its successors) during the taxable year of the partnership (or its successors), which ends within or with the taxable year of the retired partner and in which the payment was received by him;

(ii) No obligation (whether certain in amount or contingent on a subsequent event) exists (as of the close of the partnership's taxable year referred to in subdivision (i) of this subparagraph) from the other partners to the retired partner except with respect to retirement payments under the plan or rights such as benefits payable on account of sickness, accident, hospitalization, medical expenses, or death; and

(iii) The retired partner's share (if any) of the capital of the partnership has been paid to him in full before the close of the partnership's taxable year referred to in subdivision (i) of this subparagraph.

By application of the conditions set forth in this subparagraph, either all payments on account of retirement received by a retired partner during the taxable year of the partnership ending within or with his taxable year are excluded or none of the payments are excluded. Subdivision (ii) of this subparagraph has application only to obligations from other partners in their capacity as partners as distinguished from an obligation which arose and exists from a transaction unrelated to the partnership or to a trade or business carried on by the partnership. The effect of the conditions set forth in subdivisions (ii) and (iii) of this subparagraph is that the exclusion may apply with respect to payments received by a retired partner during the taxable year of the partnership ending within or with his taxable year only if at the close of the partnership's taxable year the retired partner had no financial interest in the partnership except for the right to retirement payments.

(2) *Examples.*—The application of subparagraph (1) of this paragraph may be illustrated by the following examples. Each example assumes that the partnership plan pursuant to which the payments are made meets the requirements of paragraph (b) of this section.

Example (1). A, who files his income tax returns on a calendar year basis, is a partner in the ABC partnership. The taxable year of the partnership is the period July 1 to June 30, inclusive. A retired from the partnership on January 1, 1973, and receives monthly payments on account of his retirement. As of June 30, 1973, no obligation existed from the other partners to A (except with respect to retirement payments under the plan) and A's share of the capital of the partnership had been paid to him in full. The monthly retirement payments received by A from the partnership in his taxable year ending on December 31, 1973, are not excluded from net earnings from self-employment since A rendered service to the partnership during a portion of the partnership's taxable year (July 1, 1972, through June 30, 1973) which ends within A's taxable year ending on December 31, 1973.

Example (2). D, a partner in the DEF partnership, retired from the partnership as of the close of December 31, 1972. The taxable year of both D and the partnership is the calendar year. During the partnership's taxable year ending December 31, 1973, D rendered no service with respect to any trade or business carried on by the partnership. On or before December 31, 1973, all obligations (other than with respect to retirement payments under the plan) from the other partners to D have been liquidated, and D's share of the capital of the partnership has been paid to him. Retirement payments received by D pursuant to the partnership's plan in his taxable year ending December 31, 1973, are excluded in determining his net earnings from self-employment (if any) for that taxable year.

Example (3). Assume the same facts as in example (2) except that as of the close of December 31, 1973, D has a right to a fixed percentage of any amounts collected by the partnership after that date which are attributable to services rendered by him prior to his retirement for clients of

the partnership. The monthly payments received by D in his taxable year ending December 31, 1973, are not excluded from net earnings from self-employment since as of the close of the partnership's taxable year which ends with D's taxable year, an obligation (other than an obligation with respect to retirement payments) exists from the other partners to D. [Reg. §1.1402(a)-17.]

☐ [*T.D.* 7333, 12-19-74.]

[Reg. §1.1402(a)-18]

§1.1402(a)-18. Split-dollar life insurance arrangements.—See §§1.61-22 and 1.7872-15 for rules relating to the treatment of split-dollar life insurance arrangements.

☐ [*T.D.* 9092, 9-11-2003.]

[Reg. §1.1402(b)-1]

§1.1402(b)-1. Self-employment income.—(a) *In general.*—Except for the exclusions in paragraphs (b) and (c) of this section and the exception in paragraph (d) of this section, the term "self-employment income" means the net earnings from self-employment derived by an individual during a taxable year.

(b) *Maximum self-employment income.*—(1) *General rule.*—Subject to the special rules described in subparagraph (2) of this paragraph, the maximum self-employment income of an individual for a taxable year (whether a period of 12 months or less) is—

(i) For any taxable year beginning in a calendar year after 1974, an amount equal to the contribution and benefit base (as determined under section 230 of the Social Security Act) which is effective for such calendar year; and

(ii) For any taxable year—

Ending before 1955	$3,600
Ending after 1954 and before 1959	4,200
Ending after 1958 and before 1966	4,800
Ending after 1965 and before 1968	6,600
Ending after 1967 and beginning before 1972	7,800
Beginning after 1971 and before 1973	9,000
Beginning after 1972 and before 1974	10,800
Beginning after 1973 and before 1975	13,200

(2) *Special rules.*—(i) If an individual is paid wages as defined in subparagraph (3) of this paragraph in a taxable year, the maximum self-employment income for such taxable year is computed as provided in subdivision (ii) or (iii) of this subparagraph.

(ii) If an individual is paid wages as defined in subparagraph (3)(i) or (ii) of this paragraph in a taxable year, the maximum self-employment income of such individual for such taxable year is the excess of the amounts indicated in subparagraph (1) of this paragraph over the amount of the wages, as defined in subparagraph (3)(i) and (ii) of this paragraph, paid to him during the taxable year. For example, if for his taxable year beginning in 1974, an individual has $15,000 of net earnings from self-employment and during such taxable year is paid $1,000 of wages as defined in section 3121(a) (see subparagraph (3)(i) of this paragraph), he has $12,200 ($13,200 – $1,000) of self-employment income for the taxable year.

(iii) For taxable years ending on or after December 31, 1968, wages, as defined in subparagraph (3)(iii) of this paragraph, are taken into account in determining the maximum self-employment income of an individual for purposes of the tax imposed under section 1401(b) (hospital insurance), but not for purposes of the tax imposed under section 1401(a) (old-age, survivors, and disability insurance). If an individual is paid wages as defined in subparagraph (3)(iii) of this paragraph in a taxable year, his maximum self-employment income for such taxable year for purposes of the tax imposed under section 1401(a) is computed under subparagraph (1) of this paragraph or subdivision (ii) of this subparagraph (whichever is applicable), and his maximum self-employment income for such taxable year for purposes of the tax imposed under section 1401(b) is the excess of his section 1401(a) maximum self-employment income over the amount of wages, as defined in subparagraph (3)(iii) of this paragraph, paid to him during the taxable year. For purposes of this subdivision, wages as defined in subparagraph (3)(iii) of this paragraph are deemed paid to an individual in the period with respect to which the payment is made, that is, the period in which the compensation was earned or deemed earned within the meaning of section 3231(e). For an explanation of the term "compensation" and for provisions relating to when compensation is earned, see the regulations under section 3231(e) in Part 31 of this chapter (Employment Tax Regulations). The application of the rules set forth in this subdivision may be illustrated by the following example:

Example. M, a calendar-year taxpayer, has $15,000 of net earnings from self-employment for 1974 and during the taxable year is paid $1,000 of wages as defined in section 3121(a) (see subparagraph (3)(i) of this paragraph) and $1,600 of compensation subject to tax under section 3201 (see subparagraph (3)(iii) of this paragraph). Of the $1,600 of taxable compensation, $1,200 represents compensation for services rendered in 1974 and the balance ($400) represents compensation which pursuant to the provisions of section 3231(e) is earned or deemed earned in 1973. M's maximum self-employment income for 1974 for purposes of the tax imposed under section 1401(a), computed as provided in subdivision (ii) of this subparagraph, is $12,200 ($13,200 – $1,000), and for purposes of the tax imposed under section 1401(b) is $11,000 ($12,200 – $1,200). However, M may recompute his maximum self-employment income for 1973 for pur-

poses of the tax imposed under section 1401(b) by taking into account the $400 of compensation which is deemed paid in 1973.

(3) *Meaning of term "wages".*—For the purpose of the computation described in subparagraph (2) of this paragraph, the term "wages" includes:

(i) Wages as defined in section 3121(a);

(ii) Such remuneration paid to an employee for services covered by—

(a) An agreement entered into pursuant to section 218 of the Social Security Act (42 U.S.C. 418), which section provides for extension of the Federal old-age, survivors and disability insurance system to State and local government employees under voluntary agreements between the States and the Secretary of Health, Education, and Welfare (Federal Security Administrator before April 11, 1953), or

(b) An agreement entered into pursuant to the provisions of section 3121(1), relating to coverage of citizens of the United States who are employees of foreign subsidiaries of domestic corporations,

as would be wages under section 3121(a) if such services constituted employment under section 3121(b). For an explanation of the term "wages", see the regulations under section 3121(a) in Part 31 of this chapter (Employment Tax Regulations); and

(iii) Compensation, as defined in section 3231(e), which is subject to the employee tax imposed by section 3201 or the employee representative tax imposed by section 3211.

(c) *Minimum net earnings from self-employment.*—Self-employment income does not include the net earnings from self-employment of an individual when the amount of such earnings for the taxable year is less than $400. Thus, an individual having only $300 of net earnings from self-employment for the taxable year would not have any self-employment income. However, an individual having net earnings from self-employment of $400 or more for the taxable year may, by application of paragraph (b)(2) of this section, have less than $400 of self-employment income for purposes of the tax imposed under section 1401(a) and the tax imposed under section 1401(b) or may have self-employment income of $400 or more for purposes of the tax imposed under section 1401(a) and of less than $400 for purposes of the tax imposed under section 1401(b). This could occur in a case in which the amount of the individual's net earnings from self-employment is $400 or more for a taxable year and the amount of such net earnings from self-employment plus the amount of wages, as defined in paragraph (b)(3) of this section, paid to him during the taxable year exceed the maximum self-employment income, as set forth in paragraph (b)(1) of this section, for the taxable year. However, the result occurs only if such maximum self-employment income exceeds the amount of such wages. The application of this paragraph may be illustrated by the following example:

Example. For 1974 M, a calendar-year taxpayer, has net earnings from self-employment of $2,000 and wages (as defined in paragraph (b)(3)(i) and (ii) of this section) of $12,500. Since M's net earnings from self-employment plus his wages exceed the maximum self-employment income for 1974 ($13,200), his self-employment income for 1974 is $700 ($13,200 − $12,500). If M also had wages, as defined in paragraph (b)(3)(iii) of this section, of $200, his self-employment income would be $700 for purposes of the tax imposed under section 1401(a) and $500 ($13,200 − $12,700 ($12,500 + $200)) for purposes of the tax imposed under section 1401(b).

For provisions relating to when wages as defined in paragraph (b)(3)(iii) of this section are treated as paid, see paragraph (b)(2)(iii) of this section.

(d) *Nonresident aliens.*—A nonresident alien individual never has self-employment income. While a nonresident alien individual who derives income from a trade or business carried on within the United States, Puerto Rico, the Virgin Islands, Guam, or American Samoa (whether by agents or employees, or by a partnership of which he is a member) may be subject to the applicable income tax provisions on such income, such nonresident alien individual will not be subject to the tax on self-employment income, since any net earnings which he may have from self-employment do not constitute self-employment income. For the purpose of the tax on self-employment income, an individual who is not a citizen of the United States but who is a resident of the Commonwealth of Puerto Rico, the Virgin Islands, or, for taxable years beginning after 1960, of Guam or American Samoa is not considered to be a nonresident alien individual. [Reg. § 1.1402(b)-1.]

☐ *[T.D. 6196, 8-13-56. Amended by T.D. 6691, 12-2-63, T.D. 6993, 1-17-69 and T.D. 7333, 12-19-74.]*

[Reg. § 1.1402(c)-1]

§ 1.1402(c)-1. **Trade or business.**—In order for an individual to have net earnings from self-employment, he must carry on a trade or business, either as an individual or as a member of a partnership. Except for the exclusions discussed in § § 1.1402(c)-2 to 1.1402(c)-7, inclusive, the term "trade or business", for the purpose of the tax on self-employment income, shall have the same meaning as when used in section 162. An individual engaged in one of the excluded activities specified in such sections of the regulations may also be engaged in carrying on activities which constitute a trade or business for purposes of the tax on self-employment income. Whether or not he is also engaged in carrying on a trade or business will be dependent upon all of the facts and circumstances in the particular case. An individual who is a crew leader, as defined in section 3121(o) (see such section and the regulations thereunder in Part 31 of this chapter (Employment Tax Regulations)), is considered to be engaged in carrying on a trade or business with respect to services performed by him after 1956 in furnishing individuals to perform agricultural labor for another person or services performed by him after 1956 as a member of the crew. [Reg. § 1.1402(c)-1.]

☐ *[T.D. 6196, 8-13-56. Amended by T.D. 6691, 12-2-63 and T.D. 6978, 10-29-68.]*

[Reg. § 1.1402(c)-2]

§ 1.1402(c)-2. **Public office.**—(a) *In general.*—(1) *General rule.*—Except as otherwise provided in subparagraph (2) of this paragraph, the performance of the functions of a public office does not constitute a trade or business.

(2) *Fee basis public officials.*—(i) *In general.*—If an individual receives fees after 1967 for the performance of the functions of a public office of a State or a political subdivision thereof for which he is compensated solely on a fee basis, and if the service performed in such office is eligible for (but is not made the subject of) an agreement between the State and the Secretary of Health, Education, and Welfare pursuant to section 218 of the Social Security Act to extend social security coverage thereto, the service for which such fees are received constitutes a trade or business within the meaning of section 1402(c) and § 1.1402(c)-1. If an individual performs service for a State or a political subdivision thereof in any period in more than one position, each position is treated separately for purposes of the preceding sentence. See also paragraph (f) of § 1.1402(c)-3 relating to the performance of service by an individual as an employee of a State or a political subdivision thereof in a position compensated solely on a fee basis.

(ii) *Election with respect to fees received in 1968.*—(A) Any individual who in 1968 receives fees for service performed by him with respect to the functions of a public office of a State or a political subdivision thereof in any period in which the functions are performed in a position compensated solely on a fee basis may elect, if the performance of the service for which such fees are received constitutes a trade or business pursuant to the provisions of subdivision (i) of this subparagraph, to have such performance of service treated as excluded from the term "trade or business" for the purpose of the tax on self-employment income, pursuant to the provisions of section 122(c)(2) of the Social Security Amendments of 1967 (as quoted in § 1.1402(c)). Such election shall not be limited to service to which the fees received in 1968 are attributable but must also be applicable to service (if any) in subsequent years which, except for the election,

Reg. § 1.1402(c)-2(a)(2)(ii)(A)

would constitute a trade or business pursuant to the provisions of subdivision (i) of this subparagraph. An election made pursuant to the provisions of this subparagraph is irrevocable.

(B) The election referred to in subdivision (ii)(A) of this subparagraph shall be made by filing a certificate of election of exemption (Form 4415) on or before the due date of the income tax return (see section 6072), including any extension thereof (see section 6081), for the taxable year of the individual making the election which begins in 1968. The certificate of election of exemption shall be filed with an internal revenue office in accordance with the instructions on the certificate.

(b) *Meaning of public office.*—The term "public office" includes any elective or appointive office of the United States or any possession thereof, of the District of Columbia, of a State or its political subdivisions, or of a wholly-owned instrumentality of any one or more of the foregoing. For example, the President, the Vice President, a governor, a mayor, the Secretary of State, a member of Congress, a State representative, a county commissioner, a judge, a justice of the peace, a county or city attorney, a marshal, a sheriff, a constable, a registrar of deeds, or a notary public performs the functions of a public office. (However, the service of a notary public could not be made the subject of a section 218 agreement under the Social Security Act because notaries are not "employees" within the meaning of that section. Accordingly, such service does not constitute a trade or business.) [Reg. § 1.1402(c)-2.]

☐ [*T.D. 6691, 12-2-63. Amended by T.D. 7333, 12-19-74 and T.D. 7372, 7-23-75.*]

[Reg. § 1.1402(c)-3]

§ 1.1402(c)-3. Employees.—(a) *General rule.*—Generally, the performance of service by an individual as an employee, as defined in the Federal Insurance Contributions Act (chapter 21 of the Internal Revenue Code) does not constitute a trade or business within the meaning of section 1402(c) and § 1.1402(c)-1. However, in six cases set forth in paragraphs (b) to (g), inclusive, of this section, the performance of service by an individual is considered to constitute a trade or business within the meaning of section 1402(c) and § 1.1402(c)-1. (As to when an individual is an employee, see section 3121(d) and (o) and section 3506 and the regulations under those sections in part 31 of this chapter (Employment Tax Regulations).)

(b) *Newspaper vendors.*—Service performed by an individual who has attained the age of 18 constitutes a trade or business for purposes of the tax on self-employment income within the meaning of section 1402(c) and § 1.1402(c)-1 if performed in, and at the time of, the sale of newspapers or magazines to ultimate consumers, under an arrangement under which the newspapers or magazines are to be sold by him at a fixed price, his compensation being based on the retention of the excess of such price over the amount at which the newspapers or magazines are charged to him, whether or not he is guaranteed a minimum amount of compensation for such service, or is entitled to be credited with the unsold newspapers or magazines turned back.

(c) *Sharecroppers.*—Service performed by an individual under an arrangement with the owner or tenant of land pursuant to which—

(1) Such individual undertakes to produce agricultural or horticultural commodities (including livestock, bees, poultry, and furbearing animals and wildlife) on such land,

(2) The agricultural or horticultural commodities produced by such individual, or the proceeds therefrom, are to be divided between such individual and such owner or tenant, and

(3) The amount of such individual's share depends on the amount of the agricultural or horticultural commodities produced,

constitutes a trade or business within the meaning of section 1402(c) and § 1.1402(c)-1.

(d) *Employees of foreign government, instrumentality wholly owned by foreign government, or international organization.*—Service performed in the United States, as defined in section 3121(e)(2) (see such section and the regulations thereunder in Part 31 of this chapter (Employment Tax Regulations)), by an individual who is a citizen of the United States constitutes a trade or business within the meaning of section 1402(c) and § 1.1402(c)-1 if such service is excepted from employment, for purposes of the Federal Insurance Contributions Act (chapter 21 of the Code), by—

(1) Section 3121(b)(11), relating to service in the employ of a foreign government (for regulations under section 3121(b)(11), see § 31.3121(b)(11)-1 of this chapter);

(2) Section 3121(b)(12), relating to service in the employ of an instrumentality wholly owned by a foreign government (for regulations under section 3121(b)(12), see § 31.3121(b)(12)-1 of this chapter); or

(3) Section 3121(b)(15), relating to service in the employ of an international organization (for regulations under section 3121(b)(15), see § 31.3121(b)(15)-1 of this chapter).

This paragraph is applicable to service performed in any taxable year ending on or after December 31, 1960, except that it does not apply to service performed before 1961 in Guam or American Samoa.

(e) *Ministers and members of religious orders.*—(1) *Taxable years ending before 1968.*—Service described in section 1402(c)(4) performed by an individual during taxable years ending before 1968 for which a certificate filed pursuant to section 1402(e) is in effect constitutes a trade or business within the meaning of section 1402(c) and § 1.1402(c)-1. See also § 1.1402(c)-5.

(2) *Taxable years ending after 1967.*—Service described in section 1402(c)(4) performed by an individual during taxable years ending after 1967 constitutes a trade or business within the meaning of section 1402(c) and § 1.1402(c)-1 unless an exemption under section 1402(e) (see § § 1.1402(e)-1A through 1.1402(e)-4A) is efffective with respect to such individual for the taxable year during which the service is performed. See also § 1.1402(c)-5.

(f) *State and local government employees compensated on fee basis.*—(1) *In general.*—(i) Section 1402(c)(2)(E) and this paragraph are applicable only with respect to fees received by an individual after 1967 for services performed by him as an employee of a State or a political subdivision thereof in a position compensated solely on a fee basis. If an individual performs service for a State or a political subdivision thereof in more than one position, each position is treated separately for purposes of determining whether the service performed in such position is performed by an employee and whether compensation for service performed in the position is solely on a fee basis.

(ii) If an individual receives fees after 1967 for service performed by him as an employee of a State or a political subdivision thereof in a position compensated solely on a fee basis, the service for which such fees are received constitutes a trade or business within the meaning of section 1402(c) and § 1.1402(c)-1 except that if service performed in such position is covered under an agreement entered into by the State and the Secretary of Health, Education, and Welfare pursuant to section 218 of the Social Security Act at the time a fee is received, the service to which such fee relates does not constitute a trade or business. See also paragraph (a) of § 1.1402(c)-2, relating, in part, to the performance of the functions of a public office of a State or a political subdivision thereof by an individual.

(2) *Election with respect to fees received in 1968.*—(i) Any individual who in 1968 receives fees for service as an employee of a State or a political subdivision thereof in a position compensated solely on a fee basis may elect, if the performance of the service for which such fees are received constitutes a trade or business pursuant to the provisions of subparagraph (1) of this paragraph, to have such performance of service treated as excluded from the term "trade or business" for the purpose of the tax on self-employment income, pursuant to the provisions of section 122(c)(2) of the Social Security Amendments of 1967 (as quoted in § 1.1402(c)). Such election shall not be limited to service to which the fees received in 1968 are attributable but must also be applicable to service (if any) in subsequent years which, except for the election,

would constitute a trade or business pursuant to the provisions of subparagraph (1) of this paragraph. An election made pursuant to the provisions of this subparagraph is irrevocable.

(ii) The election referred to in subdivision (i) of this subparagraph shall be made by filing a certificate of election of exemption (Form 4415) on or before the due date of the income tax return (see section 6072), including any extension thereof (see section 6081), for the taxable year of the individual making the election which begins in 1968. The certificate of election of exemption shall be filed with an internal revenue office in accordance with the instructions on the certificate.

(g) *Individuals engaged in fishing.*—For taxable years ending after December 31, 1954, service performed by an individual on a boat engaged in catching fish or other forms of aquatic animal life (hereinafter "fish") constitutes a trade or business within the meaning of section 1402(c) and § 1.1402(c)-1 if the service is excepted from the definition of employment by section 3121(b)(20) and § 31.3121(b)(20)-1(a). However, the preceding sentence does not apply to services performed after December 31, 1954, and before October 4, 1976, on a boat engaged in catching fish if the owner or operator of the boat treated the individual as an employee in the manner described in § 31.3121(b)(20)-1(b). [Reg. § 1.1402(c)-3.]

☐ [*T.D. 6691, 12-2-63. Amended by T.D. 6978, 10-29-68, T.D. 7333, 12-19-74, T.D. 7691, 4-8-80 and T.D. 7716, 8-26-80.*]

[Reg. § 1.1402(c)-4]

§ 1.1402(c)-4. Individuals under Railroad Retirement System.—The performance of service by an individual as an employee or employee representative as defined in section 3231(b) and (c), respectively (see § § 31.3231(b)-1 and 31.3231(c)-1 of Part 31 of this chapter (Employment Tax Regulations)), that is, an individual covered under the railroad retirement system, does not constitute a trade or business. [Reg. § 1.1402(c)-4.]

☐ [*T.D. 6691, 12-2-63.*]

[Reg. § 1.1402(c)-5]

§ 1.1402(c)-5. Ministers and members of religious orders.—(a) *In general.*—(1) *Taxable years ending before 1968.*—For taxable years ending before 1955, a duly ordained, commissioned, or licensed minister of a church or a member of a religious order is not engaged in carrying on a trade or business with respect to service performed by him in the exercise of his ministry or in the exercise of duties required by such order. However, for taxable years ending after 1954 and before 1968, any individual who is a duly ordained, commissioned, or licensed minister of a church or a member of a religious order (other than a member of a religious order who has taken a vow of poverty as a member of such order) may elect, as provided in § 1.1402(e)(1)-1, to have the Federal old-age, survivors, and disability insurance system established by title II of the Social Security Act extended to service performed by him in his capacity as such a minister or member. If such a minister or a member of a religious order makes an election pursuant to § 1.1402(e)(1)-1 he is, with respect to service performed by him in such capacity, engaged in carrying on a trade or business for each taxable year to which the election is effective. An election by a minister or member of a religious order has no application to service performed by such minister or member which is not in the exercise of his ministry or in the exercise of duties required by such order.

(2) *Taxable years ending after 1967.*—For any taxable year ending after 1967, a duly ordained, commissioned, or licensed minister of a church or a member of a religious order (other than a member of a religious order who has taken a vow of poverty as a member of such order) is engaged in carrying on a trade or business with respect to service performed by him in the exercise of his ministry or in the exercise of duties required by such order unless an exemption under section 1402(e) (see § § 1.1402(e)-1A through 1.1402(e)-4A) is effective with respect to such individual for the taxable year during which the service is performed. An exemption which is effective with respect to a minister or a member of a religious order has no application to service performed by such minister or member which is not in the exercise of his ministry or in the exercise of duties required by such order.

(b) *Service by a minister in the exercise of his ministry.*—(1)(i) A certificate of election filed by a duly ordained, commissioned, or licensed minister of a church under the provisions of § 1.1402(e)(1)-1 has application only to service performed by him in the exercise of his ministry.

(ii) An exemption under section 1402(e) (see § § 1.1402(e)-1A through 1.1402(e)-4A) which is effective with respect to a duly ordained, commissioned, or licensed minister of a church has application only to service performed by him in the exercise of his ministry.

(2) Except as provided in paragraph (c)(3) of this section, service performed by a minister in the exercise of his ministry includes the ministration of sacerdotal functions and the conduct of religious worship, and the control, conduct, and maintenance of religious organizations (including the religious boards, societies, and other integral agencies of such organizations), under the authority of a religious body constituting a church or church denomination. The following rules are applicable in determining whether services performed by a minister are performed in the exercise of his ministry:

(i) Whether service performed by a minister constitutes the conduct of religious worship or the ministration of sacerdotal functions depends on the tenets and practices of the particular religious body constituting his church or church denomination.

(ii) Service performed by a minister in the control, conduct, and maintenance of a religious organization relates to directing, managing, or promoting the activities of such organization. Any religious organization is deemed to be under the authority of a religious body constituting a church or church denomination if it is organized and dedicated to carrying out the tenets and principles of a faith in accordance with either the requirements or sanctions governing the creation of institutions of the faith. The term "religious organization" has the same meaning and application as is given to the term for income tax purposes.

(iii) If a minister is performing service in the conduct of religious worship or the ministration of sacerdotal functions, such service is in the exercise of his ministry whether or not it is performed for a religious organization. The application of this rule may be illustrated by the following example:

Example. M, a duly ordained minister, is engaged to perform service as chaplain at N University. M devotes his entire time to performing his duties as chaplain which include the conduct of religious worship, offering spiritual counsel to the university students, and teaching a class in religion. M is performing service in the exercise of his ministry.

(iv) If a minister is performing service for an organization which is operated as an integral agency of a religious organization under the authority of a religious body constituting a church or church denomination, all service performed by the minister in the conduct of religious worship, in the ministration of sacerdotal functions, or in the control, conduct, and maintenance of such organization (see subparagraph (2)(ii) of this paragraph) is in the exercise of his ministry. The application of this rule may be illustrated by the following example:

Example. M, a duly ordained minister, is engaged by the N Religious Board to serve as director of one of its departments. He performs no other service. The N Religious Board is an integral agency of O, a religious organization operating under the authority of a religious body constituting a church denomination. M is performing service in the exercise of his ministry.

(v) If a minister, pursuant to an assignment or designation by a religious body constituting his church, performs service for an organization which is neither a religious organization nor operated as an integral agency of a religious organization, all service performed by him, even though such service may not involve the conduct of religious worship or the ministration of sacerdotal functions, is in the exercise of his ministry. The application of this rule may be illustrated by the following example:

    Example. M, a duly ordained minister, is assigned by X, the religious body constituting his church, to perform advisory service to Y Company in connection with the publication of a book dealing with the history of M's church denomination. Y is neither a religious organization nor operated as an integral agency of a religious organization. M performs no other service for X or Y. M is performing service in the exercise of his ministry.

    (c) *Service by a minister not in the exercise of his ministry.*—(1)(i) A certificate filed by a duly ordained, commissioned, or licensed minister of a church under the provisions of § 1.1402(e)(1)-1 has no application to service performed by him which is not in the exercise of his ministry.

    (ii) An exemption under section 1402(e) (see § § 1.1402(e)-1A through 1.1402(e)-4A) which is effective with respect to a duly ordained, commissioned, or licensed minister of a church has no application to service performed by him which is not in the exercise of his ministry.

    (2) If a minister is performing service for an organization which is neither a religious organization nor operated as an integral agency of a religious organization and the service is not performed pursuant to an assignment or designation by his ecclesiastical superiors, then only the service performed by him in the conduct of religious worship or the ministration of sacerdotal functions is in the exercise of his ministry. See, however, subparagraph (3) of this paragraph. The application of the rule in this subparagraph may be illustrated by the following example:

    Example. M, a duly ordained minister, is engaged by N University to teach history and mathematics. He performs no other service for N although from time to time he performs marriages and conducts funerals for relatives and friends. N University is neither a religious organization nor operated as an integral agency of a religious organization. M is not performing the service for N pursuant to an assignment or designation by his ecclesiastical superiors. The service performed by M for N University is not in the exercise of his ministry. However, service performed by M in performing marriages and conducting funerals is in the exercise of his ministry.

    (3) Service performed by a duly ordained, commissioned, or licensed minister of a church as an employee of the United States, or a State, Territory, or possession of the United States, or the District of Columbia, or a foreign government, or a political subdivision of any of the foregoing, is not considered to be in the exercise of his ministry for purposes of the tax on self-employment income, even though such service may involve the ministration of sacerdotal functions or the conduct of religious worship. Thus, for example, service performed by an individual

as a chaplain in the Armed Forces of the United States is considered to be performed by a commissioned officer in his capacity as such, and not by a minister in the exercise of his ministry. Similarly, service performed by an employee of a State as a chaplain in a State prison is considered to be performed by a civil servant of the State and not by a minister in the exercise of his ministry.

    (d) *Service in the exercise of duties required by a religious order.*—(1) *Certificate of election.*—A certificate of election filed by a member of a religious order (other than a member of a religious order who has taken a vow of poverty as a member of such order) under the provisions of § 1.1402(e)(1)-1 has application to all duties required of him by such order.

    (2) *Exemption.*—An exemption under section 1402(e) (see § § 1.1402(e)-1A through 1.1402(e)-4A) which is effective with respect to a member of a religious order (other than a member of a religious order who has taken a vow of poverty as a member of such order) has application only to the duties required of him by such order.

    (3) *Service.*—For purposes of subparagraphs (1) and (2) of this paragraph, the nature or extent of the duties required of the member by the order is immaterial so long as it is a service which he is directed or required to perform by his ecclesiastical superiors. [Reg. § 1.1402(c)-5.]

    ☐ *[T.D. 6691, 12-2-63. Amended by T.D. 6978, 10-29-68.]*

[Reg. § 1.1402(c)-6]

    § 1.1402(c)-6. Members of certain professions.—(a) *Periods of exclusion.*—(1) *Taxable years ending before 1955.*—For taxable years ending before 1955, an individual is not engaged in carrying on a trade or business with respect to the performance of service in the exercise of his profession as a physician, lawyer, dentist, osteopath, veterinarian, chiropractor, naturopath, optometrist, Christian Science practitioner, architect, certified public accountant, accountant registered or licensed as an accountant under State or municipal law, full-time practicing public accountant, funeral director, or professional engineer.

    (2) *Taxable years ending in 1955.*—Except as provided in paragraph (b) of this section, for a taxable year ending in 1955 an individual is not engaged in carrying on a trade or business with respect to the performance of service in the exercise of his profession as a physician, lawyer, dentist, osteopath, veterinarian, chiropractor, naturopath, optometrist, or Christian Science practitioner.

    (3) *Taxable years ending after 1955.*—(i) *Doctors of medicine.*—For taxable years ending after 1955 and before December 31, 1965, an

individual is not engaged in carrying on a trade or business with respect to the performance of service in the exercise of his profession as a doctor of medicine. For taxable years ending after December 30, 1965, an individual is engaged in carrying on a trade or business with respect to the performance of service in the exercise of his profession as a doctor of medicine.

(ii) *Christian Science practitioners.*—Except as provided in paragraph (b)(1), of this section, for taxable years ending after 1955 and before 1968, an individual is not engaged in carrying on a trade or business with respect to the performance of service in the exercise of his profession as a Christian Science practitioner. For provisions relating to the performance of service in taxable years ending after 1967 by an individual in the exercise of his profession as a Christian Science practitioner, see paragraph (b)(2) of this section.

(b) *Christian Science practitioner.*—(1) *Certain taxable years ending before 1968; election.*—For taxable years ending after 1954 and before 1968, a Christian Science practitioner may elect, as provided in § 1.1402(e)(1)-1, to have the Federal old-age, survivors, and disability insurance system established by title II of the Social Security Act extended to service performed by him in the exercise of his profession as a Christian Science practitioner. If an election is made pursuant to § 1.1402(e)(1)-1, the Christian Science practitioner is, with respect to the performance of service in the exercise of such profession, engaged in carrying on a trade or business for each taxable year for which the election is effective. An election by a Christian Science practitioner has no application to service performed by him which is not in the exercise of his profession as a Christian Science practitioner.

(2) *Taxable years ending after 1967; exemption.*—For a taxable year ending after 1967, a Christian Science practitioner is, with respect to the performance of service in the exercise of his profession as a Christian Science practitioner, engaged in carrying on a trade or business unless an exemption under section 1402(e) (see §§ 1.1402(e)-1A through 1.1402(e)-4A) if effective with respect to him for the taxable year during which the service is performed. An exemption which is effective with respect to a Christian Science practitioner has no application to service performed by him which is not in the exercise of his profession as a Christian Science practitioner.

(c) *Meaning of terms.*—The designations in this section are to be given their commonly accepted meanings. For taxable years ending after 1955, an individual who is a doctor of osteopathy, and who is not a doctor of medicine within the commonly accepted meaning of that term, is deemed, for purposes of this section, not to be engaged in carrying on a trade or business in the exercise of the profession of doctor of medicine.

(d) *Legal requirements.*—The exclusions specified in paragraph (a) of this section apply only if the individuals meet the legal requirements, if any, for practicing their professions in the place where they perform the service.

(e) *Partnerships.*—In the case of a partnership engaged in the practice of any of the designated excluded professions, the partnership shall not be considered as carrying on a trade or business for the purpose of the tax on self-employment income, and none of the distributive shares of the income or loss, described in section 702(a)(9), of such partnership shall be included in computing net earnings from self-employment of any member of the partnership. On the other hand, where a partnership is engaged in a trade or business not within any of the designated excluded professions, each partner must include his distributive share of the income or loss, described in section 702(a)(9), of such partnership in computing his net earnings from self-employment, irrespective of whether such partner is engaged in the practice of one or more of such professions and contributes his professional services to the partnership. [Reg. § 1.1402(c)-6.]

☐ [*T.D.* 6691, 12-2-63. *Amended by T.D.* 6978, 10-29-68.]

[Reg. § 1.1402(c)-7]

§ 1.1402(c)-7. Members of religious groups opposed to insurance.—The performance of service by an individual—

(a) Who is a member of a recognized religious sect or division thereof, and

(b) Who is an adherent of established tenets or teachings of such sect or division by reason of which he is conscientiously opposed to acceptance of the benefits of any private or public insurance which makes payments in the event of death, disability, old age, or retirement or makes payments toward the cost of, or provides services for, medical care (including the benefits of any insurance system established by the Social Security Act),

during any taxable year for which he is granted a tax exemption, pursuant to section 1402(h), does not constitute a trade or business within the meaning of section 1402(c) and § 1.1402(c)-1. See also §§ 1.1402(h) and 1.1402(h)-1. [Reg. § 1.1402(c)-7.]

☐ [*T.D.* 6993, 1-17-69.]

[Reg. § 1.1402(d)-1]

§ 1.1402(d)-1. Employee and wages.—For the purpose of the tax on self-employment income, the term "employee" and the term "wages" shall have the same meaning as when used in the Federal Insurance Contributions Act. For an explanation of these terms, see Subpart B of Part 31 of this chapter (Employment Tax Regulations). [Reg. § 1.1402(d)-1.]

☐ [*T.D.* 6196, 8-13-56. *Amended by T.D.* 6691, 12-2-63.]

[Reg. §1.1402(e)-1A]

§1.1402(e)-1A. Application of regulations under section 1402(e).—The regulations in §§1.1402(e)-2A through 1.1402(e)-4A relate to section 1402(e) as amended by section 115(b)(2) of the Social Security Amendments of 1967 (81 Stat. 839) and apply to taxable years ending after 1967. Section 1.1402(e)-5A reflects changes made by section 1704(a) of the Tax Reform Act of 1986 (100 Stat. 2085, 2779) and applies to applications for exemption under section 1402(e) filed after December 31, 1986. For regulations under section 1402(e) (as in effect prior to amendment by the Social Security Amendments of 1967) applicable to taxable years ending before 1968, see §§1.1402(e)(1)-1 through 1.1402(e)(6)-1. [Reg. §1.1402(e)-1A.]

☐ [*T.D. 6978, 10-29-68. Amended by T.D. 8221, 8-30-88.*]

[Reg. §1.1402(e)-2A]

§1.1402(e)-2A. Ministers, members of religious orders and Christian Science practitioners; application for exemption from self-employment tax.—(a) *In general.*—(1) Subject to the limitations set forth in subparagraphs (2) and (3) of this paragraph, any individual who is (i) a duly ordained, commissioned, or licensed minister of a church or a member of a religious order (other than a member of a religious order who has taken a vow of poverty as a member of such order) or (ii) a Christian Science practitioner may request an exemption from the tax on self-employment income (see §§1.1401 and 1.1401-1) with respect to services performed by him in his capacity as a minister or member, or as a Christian Science practitioner, as the case may be. Such a request shall be made by filing an application for exemption on Form 4361 in the manner provided in paragraph (b) of this section and within the time specified in §1.1402(e)-3A. For provisions relating to the taxable year or years for which an exemption from the tax on self-employment income with respect to service performed by a minister or member or a Christian Science practitioner in his capacity as such is effective, see §1.1402(e)-4A. For additional provisions applicable to services performed by individuals referred to in this subparagraph, see paragraph (e) of §1.1402(c)-3 and §1.1402(c)-5 relating to ministers and members of religious orders, and paragraphs (a)(3)(ii) and (b) of §1.1402(c)-6 relating to Christian Science practitioners.

(2) The application for exemption shall contain, or there shall be filed with such application, a statement to the effect that the individual making application for exemption is conscientiously opposed to, or because of religious principles is opposed to, the acceptance (with respect to services performed by him in his capacity as a minister, member, or Christian Science practitioner) of any public insurance which makes payments in the event of death, disability, old age, or retirement or makes payments toward the cost of, or provides services for, medical care (including the benefits of any insurance system established by the Social Security Act). Thus, ministers, members of religious orders, and Christian Science practitioners requesting exemption from social security coverage must meet either of two alternative tests: (1) A religious principles test which refers to the institutional principles and discipline of the particular religious denomination to which he belongs, or (2) a conscientious opposition test which refers to the opposition because of religious considerations of individual ministers, members of religious orders, and Christian Science practitioners (rather than opposition based upon the general conscience of any such individual or individuals). The term "public insurance," as used in section 1402(e) and this paragraph, refers to governmental, as distinguished from private, insurance and does not include insurance carried with a commercial insurance carrier. To be eligible to file an application for exemption on Form 4361, a minister, member, or Christian Science practitioners need not be opposed to the acceptance of all public insurance making payments of this specified type; he must, however, be opposed on religious grounds to the acceptance of any such payment which, in whole or in part, is based on, or measured by earnings from, services performed by him in his capacity as a minister or member (see §1.1402(c)-5) or in his capacity as a Christian Science practitioner (see paragraph (b)(2) of §1.1402(c)-6). For example, a minister performing service in the exercise of his ministry may be eligible to file an application for exemption on Form 4361 even though he is not opposed to the acceptance of benefits under the Social Security Act with respect to service performed by him which is not in the exercise of his ministry.

(3) An exemption from the tax imposed on self-employment income with respect to service performed by a minister, member, or Christian Science practitioner in his capacity as such may not be granted to a minister, member, or practitioner who (in accordance with the provisions of section 1402(e) as in effect prior to amendment by section 115(b)(2) of the Social Security Amendments of 1967 (81 Stat. 839)) filed a valid waiver certificate on Form 2031 electing to have the Federal old-age, survivors, and disability insurance system established by title II of the Social Security Act extended to service performed by him in the exercise of his ministry or in the exercise of duties required by the order of which he is a member, or in the exercise of his profession as a Christian Science practitioner. For provisions relating to waiver certificates on Form 2031, see §§1.1402(e)(1)-1 through 1.1402(e)(6)-1.

(b) *Application for exemption.*—An application for exemption on Form 4361 shall be filed in triplicate with the internal revenue officer or the internal revenue office, as the case may be, designated in the instructions relating to the application for exemption. The application for exemption must be filed within the time prescribed in § 1.1402(e)-3A. If the last original Federal income tax return of an individual to whom paragraph (a) of this section applies which was filed before the expiration of such time limitation for filing an application for exemption shows no liability for tax on self-employment income, such return will be treated as an application for exemption, provided that before February 28, 1975 such individual also files a properly executed Form 4361.

(c) *Approval of application for exemption.*—The filing of an application for exemption on Form 4361 by a minister, a member of a religious order, or a Christian Science practitioner does not constitute an exemption from the tax on self-employment income with respect to services performed by him in his capacity as a minister, member, or practitioner. The exemption is granted only if the application is approved by an appropriate internal revenue officer. See § 1.1402(e)-4A relating to the period for which an exemption is effective. [Reg. § 1.1402(e)-2A.]

☐ [T.D. 7333, 12-19-74.]

[Reg. § 1.1402(e)-3A]

§ 1.1402(e)-3A. Time limitation for filing application for exemption.—(a) *General rule.*—(1) Any individual referred to in paragraph (a) of § 1.1402(e)-2A who desires an exemption from the tax on self-employment income with respect to service performed by him in his capacity as a minister or member of a religious order or as a Christian Science practitioner must file the application for exemption (Form 4361) prescribed by § 1.1402(e)-2A on or before whichever of the following dates is later:

　　(i) The due date of the income tax return (see section 6072), including any extension thereof (see section 6081), for his second taxable year ending after 1967, or

　　(ii) The due date of the income tax return, including any extension thereof, for his second taxable year beginning after 1953 for which he has net earnings from self-employment of $400 or more, any part of which—

　　　　(a) In the case of a duly ordained, commissioned, or licensed minister of a church, consists of remuneration for service performed in the exercise of his ministry, or

　　　　(b) In the case of a member of a religious order who has not taken a vow of poverty as a member of such order, consists of remuneration for service performed in the exercise of duties required by such order, or

　　　　(c) In the case of a Christian Science practitioner, consists of remuneration for service performed in the exercise of his profession as a Christian Science practitioner.

See paragraph (c) of this section for provisions relating to the computation of net earnings from self-employment.

(2) If a minister, a member of a religious order, or a Christian Science practitioner derives gross income in a taxable year both from service performed in such capacity and from the conduct of another trade or business, and the deductions allowed by chapter 1 of the Internal Revenue Code which are attributable to the gross income derived from service performed in such capacity equal or exceed the gross income derived from service performed in such capacity, no part of the net earnings from self-employment (computed as prescribed in paragraph (c) of this section) for the taxable year shall be considered as derived from service performed in such capacity.

(3) The application of the rules set forth in subparagraphs (1) and (2) of this paragraph may be illustrated by the following examples:

Example (1). M, who makes his income tax returns on a calendar year basis, was ordained as a minister in January 1960. During each of two or more taxable years ending before 1968 M has net earnings from self-employment in excess of $400, some part of which is from service performed in the exercise of his ministry. M has not filed an effective waiver certificate on Form 2031 (see paragraph (a)(3) of § 1.1402(e)-2A). If M desires an exemption from the tax on self-employment income with respect to service performed in the exercise of his ministry, he must file an application for exemption on or before the due date of his income tax return for 1969 (his second taxable year ending after 1967), or any extension thereof.

Example (2). M, who makes his income tax returns on a calendar year basis, was ordained as a minister in January 1966. M has net earnings of $350 for the taxable year 1966 and has net earnings in excess of $400 for each of his taxable years 1967 and 1968 (some part or all of which is derived from service performed in the exercise of his ministry). M has not filed an effective waiver certificate on Form 2031 (see paragraph (a)(3) of § 1.1402(e)-2A). If M desires an exemption from the tax on self-employment income with respect to service performed in the exercise of his ministry, he must file an application for exemption on or before the due date of his income tax return for 1969 (his second taxable year ending after 1967), or any extension thereof.

Example (3). Assume the same facts as in example (2) except that M has net earnings in excess of $400 for each of his taxable years 1967 and 1969 (but less than $400 in 1968). The application for exemption must be filed on or before the due date of his income tax return for 1969, or any extension thereof.

Example (4). M was ordained as a minister in May 1973. During each of the taxable years 1973 and 1975, M, who makes his income tax returns on a calendar year basis, derives net earnings in excess of $400 from his activities as a minister. M has net earnings of $350 for the taxable year 1974, $200 of which is derived from service performed by him in the exercise of his ministry. If M desires an exemption from the tax on self-employment income with respect to service performed in the exercise of his ministry, he must file an application for exemption on or before the due date of his income tax return for 1975, or any extension thereof.

Example (5). M, who was ordained a minister in January 1973, is employed as a toolmaker by the XYZ Corporation for the taxable years 1973 and 1974 and also engages in activities as a minister on weekends. M makes his income tax returns on the basis of a calendar year. During each of the taxable years 1973 and 1974 M receives wages of $14,000 from the XYZ Corporation and derives net earnings of $400 from his activities as a minister. If M desires an exemption from the tax on self-employment income with respect to service performed in the exercise of his ministry, he must file an application for exemption on or before the due date of his income tax return for 1974, or any extension thereof. It should be noted that although by reason of section 1402(b)(1)(G) and (H) no part of the $400 represents "self-employment income," nevertheless the entire $400 constitutes "net earnings from self-employment" for purposes of fulfilling the requirements of section 1402(e)(2).

Example (6). M, who files his income tax returns on a calendar year basis, was ordained as a minister in March 1973. During 1973 he receives $410 for service performed in the exercise of his ministry. In addition to his ministerial services, M is engaged during the year 1973 in a mercantile venture from which he derives net earnings from self-employment in the amount of $4,000. The expenses incurred by him in connection with his ministerial services during 1973 and which are allowable deductions under chapter 1 of the Internal Revenue Code amount to $410. During 1974 and 1975, M has net earnings from self-employment in amounts of $4,600 and $4,800, respectively, and some part of each of these amounts is from the exercise of his ministry. The deductions allowed in each of the years 1974 and 1975 by chapter 1 which are attributable to the gross income derived by M from the exercise of his ministry in each of such years, respectively, do not equal or exceed such gross income in such year. If M desires an exemption from the tax on self-employment income with respect to service performed in the exercise of his ministry, he must file an application for exemption on or before the due date of his income tax return for 1975, or an extension thereof.

(b) *Effect of death.*—The right of an individual to file an application for exemption shall cease upon his death. Thus, the surviving spouse, administrator, or executor of a decedent shall not be permitted to file an application for exemption for such decedent.

(c) *Computation of net earnings.*—(1) *Taxable years ending before 1968.*—For purposes of this section net earnings from self-employment for taxable years ending before 1968 shall be determined without regard to the fact that, without an election under section 1402(e) (as in effect prior to amendment by section 115(b)(2) of the Social Security Amendments of 1967, see § 1.1402(e)-1A), the performance of services by a duly ordained, commissioned, or licensed minister of a church in the exercise of his ministry, or by a member of a religious order in the exercise of duties required by such order, or the performance of service by an individual in the exercise of his profession as a Christian Science practitioner, does not constitute a trade or business for purposes of the tax on self-employment income.

(2) *Taxable years ending after 1967.*—For purposes of this section and § 1.1402(e)-4A net earnings from self-employment for taxable years ending after 1967 shall be determined without regard to section 1402(c)(4) and (5). See § 1.1402(c)-3(e)(2) and § 1.1402(c)-5 relating to ministers and members of religious orders, and paragraphs (a)(3)(ii) and (b) of § 1.1402(c)-6 relating to Christian Science practitioners. [Reg. § 1.1402(e)-3A.]

☐ [*T.D.* 7333, 12-19-74.]

[Reg. § 1.1402(e)-4A]

§ 1.1402(e)-4A. Period for which exemption is effective.—(a) *In general.*—If an application for exemption on Form 4361—

(1) Is filed by a minister, a member of a religious order, or a Christian Science practitioner eligible to file such an application (see particularly paragraph (a)(2) and (3) of § 1.1402(e)-2A), and

(2) Is approved (see paragraph (c) of § 1.1402(e)-2A),

the exemption from the tax on self-employment income shall be effective for the first taxable year ending after 1967 for which such minister, member, or practitioner has net earnings from self-employment of $400 or more any part of which was derived from the performance of service in his capacity as a minister, member, or practitioner, and for all succeeding taxable years. See, however, paragraphs (b)(1)(ii) and (d)(2) of § 1.1402(c)-5 relating to ministers and members of religious orders and paragraph (b)(2) of § 1.1402(c)-6 relating to Christian Science practitioners.

(b) *Exemption irrevocable.*—An exemption granted to a minister, a member of a religious order, or a Christian Science practitioner pursuant to the provisions of section 1402(e) is irrevocable. [Reg. § 1.1402(e)-4A.]

☐ [T.D. 7333, 12-19-74.]

[Reg. § 1.1402(e)-5A]

§1.1402(e)-5A. Applications for exemption from self-employment taxes filed after December 31, 1986, by ministers, certain members of religious orders, and Christian Science practitioners.—(a) *In general.*—(1) Except as provided in paragraph (a)(2) of this section, this section applies to any individual who is a duly ordained, commissioned, or licensed minister of a church, member of a religious order (other than a member of a religious order who has taken a vow of poverty as a member of such order), or a Christian Science practitioner who files an application after December 31, 1986, for exemption from the tax on self-employment income (see section 1401 and § 1.1401-1) with respect to services performed by him or her in his or her capacity as a minister, member, or practitioner pursuant to §§ 1.1402(e)-2A through 1.1402(e)-4A. This section does not apply to applications for exemption under section 1402(e) that are filed before January 1, 1987.

(2) *Application of this section to Christian Science practitioners.*—Paragraph (b) of this section does not apply to Christian Science practitioners. Thus, Christian Science practitioners filing applications for exemption from self-employment taxes under section 1402(e) should follow the procedures set forth in §§ 1.1402(e)-2A through 1.1402(e)-4A, and are not required to include the statement described in paragraph (b)(1)(ii) of this section. However, see paragraph (c) of this section for verification procedures with respect to applications for exemption from self-employment taxes filed after December 31, 1986, by Christian Science practitioners.

(b) *Church or order must be informed.*—(1) *In general.*—Any individual, other than a Christian Science practitioner, who files an application for exemption from the tax on self-employment income under section 1402(e) after December 31, 1986:

(i) Shall file such application in accordance with the procedures set forth in §§ 1.1402(e)-2A through 1.1402(e)-4A, and

(ii) Shall include with such application a statement to the effect that the individual making application for exemption has informed the ordaining, commissioning, or licensing body of the church or order that he or she is opposed to the acceptance (for services performed as a minister or member of a religious order not under a vow of poverty) of any public insurance that makes payments in the event of death, disability, old age, or retirement, or that makes payments toward the cost of, or provides services for, medical care (including the benefits of any insurance system established by the Social Security Act).

(2) *Statement to be filed with Form.*—If the form provided by the Service for applying for exemption under 1402(e) does not contain the statement set forth in paragraph (b)(1)(ii) of this section, any individual required to include this statement with his or her application under this paragraph (b) shall file such statement with the individual's application at the time and place prescribed for filing such application under §§ 1.1402(e)-2A and 1.1402(e)-3A. The statement shall contain the information set forth in paragraph (b)(1)(ii) of this section and shall be signed by such individual under penalties of perjury.

(c) *Verification of Application.*—(1) *In general.*—The Service will approve an application for an exemption filed by an individual to whom this section applies only after verifying that the individual applying for the exemption is aware of the grounds on which the individual may receive an exemption under section 1402(e) (see § 1.1402(e)-2A) and that the individual seeks exemption on such grounds in accordance with the procedures set forth in paragraph (c)(2) of this section.

(2) *Verification procedure.*—Upon receipt of an application for exemption from self-employment taxes under section 1402(e) and this section, the Service will mail to the applicant a statement that describes the grounds on which an individual may receive an exemption under section 1402(e). The individual filing the application shall certify that he or she has read the statement and that he or she seeks exemption from self-employment taxes on the grounds listed in the statement. The certification shall be made by signing a copy of the statement under penalties of perjury and mailing the signed copy to the Service Center from which the statement was issued not later than 90 days after the date on which the statement was mailed to the individual. If the signed copy of the statement is not mailed to the Service Center within 90 days of the date on which the statement was mailed to the individual, that individual's exemption will not be effective until the date that the signed copy of the statement is received at the Service Center. [Reg. § 1.1402(e)-5A.]

☐ [T.D. 8821, 8-30-88.]

[Reg. § 1.1402(f)-1]

§1.1402(f)-1. Computation of partner's net earnings from self-employment for taxable years ending as result of his death.—(a) *Taxable years ending after August 28, 1958.*—(1) *In general.*—The rules for the computation of a partner's net earnings from self-employment are set forth in paragraphs (d) to (g), inclusive, of § 1.1402(a)-2. In addition to the net earnings from self-employment computed under such rules for the last taxable year of a deceased partner, if a partner's taxable year ends after August 28, 1958, solely because of death, and on a day other than the last day of the partnership's taxable year, the deceased partner's net earnings from self-employment for such year shall also include so much of the deceased partner's distributive share of partnership ordinary income or loss (see subparagraph (3) of this paragraph) for the taxable year of the partnership in which his death occurs as is attributable to an interest in the partnership prior to the month following the month of his death.

(2) *Computation.*—(i) The deceased partner's distributive share of partnership ordinary income or loss for the partnership taxable year in which he died shall be determined by applying the rules contained in paragraphs (d) to (g), inclusive, of § 1.1402(a)-2, except that paragraph (e) shall not apply.

(ii) The portion of such distributive share to be included under this section in the deceased partner's net earnings from self-employment for his last taxable year shall be determined by treating the ordinary income or loss constituting such distributive share as having been realized or sustained ratably over the period of the partnership taxable year during which the deceased partner had an interest in the partnership and during which his estate, or any other person succeeding by reason of his death to rights with respect to his partnership interest, held such interest in the partnership or held a right with respect to such interest. The amount to be included under this section in the deceased partner's net earnings from self-employment for his last taxable year will, therefore, be determined by multiplying the deceased partner's distributive share of partnership ordinary income or loss for the partnership taxable year in which he died, as determined under subdivision (i) of this subparagraph, by a fraction, the denominator of which is the number of calendar months in the partnership taxable year over which the ordinary income or loss constituting the deceased partner's distributive share of partnership income or loss for such year is treated as having been realized or sustained under the preceding sentence and the numerator of which is the number of calendar months in such partnership taxable year that precede the month following the month of his death.

(3) *Definition of "deceased partner's distributive share."*.—For the purpose of this section, the term "deceased partner's distributive share" includes the distributive share of his estate or of any other person succeeding, by reason of his death, to rights with respect to his partnership interest. It does not include any share attributable to a partnership interest which was not held by the deceased partner at the time of his death. Thus, if a deceased partner's estate should acquire an interest in a partnership additional to the interest to which it succeeded upon the death of the deceased partner, the amount of the distributive share attributable to such additional interest acquired by the estate would not be in-

cluded in computing the "deceased partner's distributive share" of the partnership's ordinary income or loss for the partnership taxable year.

(4) *Examples.*—The application of this paragraph may be illustrated by the following examples:

Example (1). B, an individual who files his income tax returns on the calendar year basis, is a member of the ABC partnership, the taxable year of which ends on June 30. B dies on October 17, 1958, and his estate succeeds to his partnership interest and continues as a partner in its own right under local law until June 30, 1959. B's distributive share of the partnership's ordinary income, as determined under paragraphs (d) to (g), inclusive, of § 1.1402(a)-2, for the taxable year of the partnership ended June 30, 1958 is $2,400. His distributive share, including the share of his estate, of such partnership's ordinary income, as determined under paragraphs (d) to (g), inclusive, of § 1.1402(a)-2 (with the exception of paragraph (e)), for the taxable year of the partnership ended June 30, 1959 is $4,500. The portion of such $4,500 attributable to an interest in the partnership prior to the month following the month in which he died is $4,500 × $4/12$ (4 being the number of months in the partnership taxable year in which B died which precede the month following the month of his death and 12 being the number of months in such partnership taxable year in which B and his estate had an interest in the partnership) or $1,500. The amount to be included in the deceased partner's net earnings from self-employment for his last taxable year in $3,900 ($2,400 plus $1,500).

Example (2). If in the preceding example B's estate is entitled to only $1,000, the amount of B's distributive share of partnership ordinary income for the period July 1, 1958 through October 17, 1958, such $1,000 is considered to have been realized ratably over the period preceding B's death and will be included in B's net earnings from self-employment for his last taxable year.

Example (3). X, who reports his income on a calendar year basis, is a member of a partnership which also reports its income on a calendar year basis. X dies on June 30, 1959, and his estate succeeds to his partnership interest and continues as a partner in its own right under local law. On September 15, 1959, X's estate sells the partnership interest to which it succeeded on the death of X. X's distributive share of partnership income for 1959 is $5,500. $600 of such amount is X's share of the gain from the sale of a capital asset which occurs on May 1, 1959, and $400 of such amount is the estate's share of the gain from the sale of a capital asset which occurs on July 15, 1959. The remainder of such amount is income from services rendered. X's distributive share of partnership ordinary income for 1959, as determined under paragraphs (d) to (g), inclusive, of § 1.1402(a)-2 (with the exception of paragraph (e)), is $4,500 ($5,500 minus $1,000). The portion of such share attributable to an interest in the partnership prior to the month following the month of his death is $4,500 × 6/8.5 (6 being the number of months in the partnership taxable year in which X died as precede the month following the month of his death and 8.5 being the number of months in such partnership taxable year in which X and his estate had an interest in the partnership) or $3,176.47.

(b) *Options available to farmers.*—(1) *Special rule.*—In determining whether the optional method available to a member of a farm partnership in computing his net earnings from self-employment may be applied, and in applying such method, it is necessary to determine the partner's distributive share of partnership gross income and the partner's distributive share of income described in section 702(a)(9). See section 1402(a) and §1.1402(a)-15. If section 1402(f) and this section apply, or may be made applicable under section 403(b)(2) of the Social Security Amendments of 1958 and paragraph (c) of this section, for the last taxable year of a deceased partner, such partner's distributive share of income described in section 702(a)(9) for his last taxable year shall be determined by including therein any amount which is included under section 1402(f) and this section in his net earnings from self-employment for such taxable year. Such a partner's distributive share of partnership gross income for his last taxable year shall be determined by including therein so much of the deceased partner's distributive share (see paragraph (a)(3) of this section) of partnership gross income, as defined in section 1402(a) and paragraph (b) of §1.1402(a)-15, for the partnership taxable year in which he died as is attributable to an interest in the partnership prior to the month following the month of his death. Such allocation shall be made in the same manner as is prescribed in paragraph (a)(2) of this section for determining the portion of a deceased partner's distributive share of partnership ordinary income or loss to be included under section 1402(f) and this section in his net earnings from self-employment for his last taxable year.

(2) *Examples.*—The principles set forth in this paragraph may be illustrated by the following examples:

Example (1). X, an individual who files his income tax returns on a calendar year basis, is a member of the XYZ farm partnership, the taxable year of which ends on March 31. X dies on May 31, 1967, and his estate succeeds to his partnership interest and continues as a partner in its own right under local law until March 31, 1968. X's distributive share of the partnership's ordinary income, determined under paragraphs (d) to (g), inclusive, of §1.1402(a)-2, for the taxable year of the partnership ended March 31, 1967, is $1,600. His distributive share, including the share of his estate, of such partnership's ordinary loss as determined under paragraphs (d) to

(g), inclusive, of §1.1402(a)-2 (with the exception of paragraph (e)), for the taxable year of the partnership ended March 31, 1968, is $1,200. The portion of such $1,200 attributable to an interest in the partnership prior to the month following the month in which he died is $1,200 × 2/12 (2 being the number of months in the partnership taxable year in which X died which precede the month following the month of his death and 12 being the number of months in such partnership taxable year in which X and his estate had an interest in the partnership) or $200. X is also a member of the ABX farm partnership, the taxable year of which ends on May 31. His distributive share of the partnership loss described in section 702(a)(9) for the partnership taxable year ending May 31, 1967, is $300. Section 1402(f) and this section do not apply with respect to such $300 since X's last taxable year ends, as a result of his death, with the taxable year of the ABX partnership. Under this paragraph the $200 loss must be included in determining X's distributive share of XYZ partnership income described in section 702(a)(9) for the purpose of applying the optional method available to farmers for computing net earnings from self-employment. Further, the resulting $1,400 of income must be aggregated, pursuant to paragraph (c) of §1.1402(a)-15, with the $300 loss, X's distributive share of ABX partnership loss described in section 702(a)(9), for purposes of applying such option. The representative of X's estate may exercise the option described in paragraph (a)(2)(ii) of §1.1402(a)-15, provided the portion of X's distributive share of XYZ partnership gross income for the taxable year ended March 31, 1968, attributable to an interest in the partnership prior to the month following the month in which he died (the allocation being made in the manner prescribed for allocating his $1,200 distributive share of XYZ partnership loss for such year), when aggregated with his distributive share of XYZ partnership gross income for the partnership taxable year ended March 31, 1967, and with his distributive share of ABX partnership gross income for the partnership taxable year ended May 31, 1967, results in X having more than $2,400 of gross income from the trade or business of farming. If such aggregate amount of gross income is not more than $2,400, the option described in paragraph (a)(2)(i) of §1.1402(a)-15, is available.

Example (2). A, a sole proprietor engaged in the business of farming, files his income tax returns on a calendar year basis. A is also a member of a partnership engaged in an agricultural activity. The partnership files its returns on the basis of a fiscal year ending March 31. A dies June 29, 1967. A's gross income from farming as a sole proprietor for the 6-month period comprising his taxable year which ends because of death is $1,600 and his actual net earnings from self-employment based thereon are $400. As of March 31, 1967, A's distributive share of the gross income of the farm partnership is $2,200 and his distributive share of income described in section 702(a)(9) based thereon is $1,000. The amount of A's distributive share of the partnership's ordinary income for its taxable year ended March 31, 1968, which may be included in his net earnings from self-employment under section 1402(f) and paragraph (a) of this section is $300. The amount of the deceased partner's distributive share of partnership gross income attributable to an interest in the partnership prior to the month following the month of his death as is determined, pursuant to subparagraph (1) of this paragraph, under paragraph (a) of this section is $2,000. An aggregation of the above figures produces a gross income from farming of $5,800 and actual net earnings from self-employment of $1,700. Under these circumstances none of the options provided by section 1402(a) may be used. If the actual net earnings from self-employment had been less than $1,600, the option described in paragraph (a)(2)(ii) of §1.1402(a)-15 would have been available.

(c) *Taxable years ending after 1955 and on or before August 28, 1958.*—(1) *Requirement of election.*—If a partner's taxable year ended, as a result of his death, after 1955 and on or before August 28, 1958, the rules set forth in paragraph (a) of this section may be made applicable in computing the deceased partner's net earnings from self-employment for his last taxable year provided that—

(i) Before January 1, 1960, there is filed, by the person designated in section 6012(b)(1) and paragraph (b)(1) of §1.6012-3, a return (or amended return) of the tax imposed by chapter 2 for the taxable year ending as a result of death, and

(ii) Such return, if filed solely for the purpose of reporting net earnings from self-employment resulting from the enactment of section 1402(f), is accompanied by the amount of tax attributable to such net earnings.

(2) *Administrative rule of special application.*—Notwithstanding the provisions of sections 6601, 6651, and 6653 (see such sections and the regulations thereunder) no interest or penalty shall be assessed or collected on the amount of any self-employment tax due solely by reason of the operation of section 1402(f) in the case of an individual who died after 1955 and before August 29, 1958. [Reg. §1.1402(f)-1.]

☐ [*T.D.* 6691, 12-2-63. *Amended by T.D.* 6993, 1-17-69.]

[Reg. §1.1402(g)-1]

§1.1402(g)-1. **Treatment of certain remuneration erroneously reported as net earnings from self-employment.**—(a) *General rule.*—If an amount is erroneously paid as self-employment tax, for any taxable year ending after 1954 and before 1962, with respect to remuneration for service (other than service described in section 3121(b)(8)(A)) performed in the employ of an organization described in section 501(c)(3) and exempt from income tax under section 501(a), and if such remuneration is reported as self-employment income on a return filed on or before the due date prescribed for filing such return (including any extension thereof), the individual who paid such amount (or a fiduciary acting for such individual or his estate, or his survivor (within the meaning of section 205(c)(1)(C) of the Social Security Act)), may request that such remuneration be deemed to constitute net earnings from self-employment. If such request is filed during the period September 14, 1960, to April 16, 1962, inclusive, and on or after the date on which the organization which paid such remuneration to such individual for services performed in its employ has filed, pursuant to section 3121(k), a certificate waiving exemption from taxes under the Federal Insurance Contributions Act, and if no credit or refund of any portion of the amount erroneously paid for such taxable year as self-employment tax (other than a credit or refund which would be allowable if such tax were applicable with respect to such remuneration) has been obtained before the date on which such request is filed or, if obtained, the amount credited or refunded (including any interest under section 6611) is repaid on or before such date, then, for purposes of the Self-Employment Contributions Act of 1954 and the Federal Insurance Contributions Act, any amount of such remuneration which is paid to such individual before the calendar quarter in which such request is filed (or before the succeeding quarter if such certificate first becomes effective with respect to services performed by such individual in such succeeding quarter) and with respect to which no tax (other than an amount erroneously paid as tax) has been paid under the Federal Insurance Contributions Act, shall be deemed to constitute net earnings from self-employment and not remuneration for employment. If the certificate filed by such organization pursuant to section 3121(k) is not effective with respect to services performed by such individual on or before the first day of the calendar quarter in which the request is filed, then, for purposes of section 3121(b)(8)(B)(ii) and (iii), such individual shall be deemed to have become an employee of such organization (or to have become a member of a group, described in section 3121(k)(1)(E), of employees of such organization) on the first day of the succeeding quarter.

(b) *Request for validation.*—(1) No particular form is prescribed for making a request under paragraph (a) of this section. The request should be in writing, should be signed and dated by the person making the request, and should indicate clearly that it is a request that, pursuant to section 1402(g) of the Code, remuneration for service described in section 3121(b)(8) (other than service described in section 3121(b)(8)(A)) erroneously reported as self-employment income for one or more specified years be deemed to constitute net earnings from self-employment and not renumeration for employment. In addition, the following information shall be shown in connection with the request:

(i) The name, address, and social security account number of the individual with respect to whose remuneration the request is made.

(ii) The taxable year or years (ending after 1954 and before 1962) to which the request relates.

(iii) A statement that the remuneration was erroneously reported as self-employment income on the individual's return for each year specified and that the return was filed on or before its due date (including any extension thereof).

(iv) Location of the office of the district director with whom each return was filed.

(v) A statement that no portion of the amount erroneously paid by the individual as self-employment tax with respect to the remuneration has been credited or refunded (other than a credit or refund which would have been allowable if the tax had been applicable with respect to the remuneration); or, if a credit or refund of any portion of such amount has been obtained, a statement identifying the credit or refund and showing how and when the amount credited or refunded, together with any interest received in connection therewith, was repaid.

(vi) The name and address of the organization which paid the remuneration to the individual.

(vii) The date on which the organization filed a waiver certificate on Form SS-15, and the location of the office of the district director with whom it was filed.

(viii) The date on which the certificate became effective with respect to services performed by the individual.

(ix) If the request is made by a person other than the individual to whom the remuneration was paid, the name and address of that person and evidence which shows the authority of such person to make the request.

(2) The request should be filed with the district director of internal revenue with whom the latest of the returns specified in the request pursuant to subparagraph (1)(iii) of this paragraph was filed.

(c) *Cross references.*—For regulations relating to section 3121(b)(8) and (k), see §§ 31.3121(b)(8)-2 and 31.3121(k)-1 of Subpart B of Part 31 of this chapter (Employment Tax Regulations). For regulations relating to exemption from income tax of an organization described in section 501(c)(3), see § 1.501(c)(3)-1. [Reg. § 1.1402(g)-1.]

☐ [T.D. 6691, 12-2-63.]

[Reg. § 1.1402(h)-1]

§ 1.1402(h)-1. Members of certain religious groups opposed to insurance.—(a) *In general.*— An individual—

(1) Who is a member of a recognized religious sect or division thereof and

(2) Who is an adherent of established tenets or teachings of such sect or division and by reason thereof is conscientiously opposed to acceptance of the benefits of any private or public insurance which makes payments in the event of death, disability, old age, or retirement or makes payments toward the cost of, or provides services for, medical care (including the benefits of any insurance system established by the Social Security Act), may file an application for exemption from the tax under section 1401. The form of insurance to which section 1402(h) and this section refer does not include liability insurance of a kind that provides only for the protection of other persons, or property of other persons, who may be injured or damaged by or on property belonging to, or by an action of, an individual who otherwise meets the requirements of this section. An application for exemption under section 1402(h) and this section shall be made in the manner provided in paragraph (b) of this section and within the time specified in paragraph (c) of this section. For provisions relating to the filing of an application for exemption by a fiduciary or survivor, see paragraph (d) of this section.

(b) *Application for exemption.*—The application for exemption shall be filed on Form 4029 in duplicate with the internal revenue official or office designated on the form. The filing of a return by a member of a religious group opposed to insurance showing no self-employment income or self-employment tax shall not be construed as an application for exemption referred to in paragraph (a) of this section.

(c) *Time limitation for filing application for exemption.*—(1) *Taxable years ending before December 31, 1967.*—A member of a religious group opposed to insurance within the meaning of paragraph (a) of this section—

(i) Who has self-employment income (determined without regard to subsections (c)(6) and (h) of section 1402 and this section) for one or more taxable years ending before December 31, 1967, and

(ii) Who desires to be exempt from the payment of the self-employment tax under section 1401,

must file the application for exemption on or before December 31, 1968.

(2) *Taxable year ending on or after December 31, 1967.*—(i) *General rule.*—Except as provided in subdivision (ii) of this subparagraph, a member of a religious group opposed to insurance within the meaning of paragraph (a) of this section—

(a) Who has no self-employment income (determined without regard to subsections (c)(6) and (h) of section 1402 and this section) for any taxable year ending before December 31, 1967, and

(b) Who desires to be exempt from the payment of the self-employment tax under section 1401 for any taxable year ending on or after December 31, 1967,

must file the application for exemption on or before the due date of the income tax return (see section 6072), including any extension thereof (see section 6081), for the first taxable year ending on or after December 31, 1967, for which he has self-employment income (determined without regard to subsections (c)(6) and (h) of section 1402 and this section).

(ii) *Exception to general rule.*—If an individual to whom subdivision (i) of this subparagraph applies—

(a) Is notified in writing by a district director of internal revenue or the Director of International Operations that he has not filed the application for exemption on or before the date specified in such subdivision (i), and

(b) Files the application for exemption on or before the last day of the third calendar month following the calendar month in which he is so notified,

such application shall be considered a timely filed application for exemption.

(d) *Application by fiduciary or survivor.*—If an individual who was a member of a religious group opposed to insurance dies before the expiration of the time prescribed in section 1402(h)(2) and paragraph (c) of this section during which an application could have been filed by him, an application for exemption with respect to such deceased individual may be filed by a fiduciary acting for such individual's estate or by such individual's survivor within the meaning of section 205(c)(1)(C) of the Social Security Act. An application for exemption with respect to a deceased individual executed by a fiduciary or survivor may be approved only if it could have been approved if the individual were not deceased and had filed the application on the date the application was filed by the fiduciary or executor.

(e) *Approval of application for exemption.*—(1) *In general.*—The filing of an application for exemption on Form 4029 by a member of a religious group opposed to insurance does not constitute an exemption from the payment of the tax on self-employment income. An individual who files such an application is exempt from the payment of the tax only if the application is approved by the official with whom the application is required to be filed (see paragraph (b) of this section).

(2) *Conditions relating to approval or disapproval of application.*—An application for exemption on Form 4029 will not be approved unless the Secretary of Health, Education, and Welfare finds with respect to the religious sect or division thereof of which the individual filing the application is a member—

(i) That the sect or division thereof has the established tenets or teachings by reason of which the individual applicant is conscientiously opposed to the benefits of insurance of the type referred to in section 1402(h) (see paragraph (a) of this section),

(ii) That it is the practice, and has been for a period of time which the Secretary of Health, Education, and Welfare deems to be substantial, for members of such sect or division thereof to make provisions for their dependent members which, in the judgment of such Secretary, is reasonable in view of the general level of living of the members of the sect or division thereof; and

(iii) That the sect or division thereof has been in existence continuously since December 31, 1950.

In addition, an application for exemption on Form 4029 will not be approved if any benefit or other payment under title II or title XVIII of the Social Security Act became payable (or, but for section 203, relating to reduction of insurance benefits, or 222(b), relating to reduction of insurance benefits on account of refusal to accept rehabilitation services, of the Social Security Act would have been payable) at or before the time of the filing of the application for exemption. Any determination required to be made pursuant to the preceding sentence will be made by the Secretary of Health, Education, and Welfare.

(f) *Period for which exemption is effective.*—(1) *General rule.*—An application for exemption shall be in effect (if approved as provided in paragraph (e) of this section) for all taxable years beginning after December 31, 1950 except as otherwise provided in subparagraph (2) of this paragraph.

(2) *Exceptions.*—An application for exemption referred to in subparagraph (1) of this paragraph shall not be effective for any taxable year which—

(i) Begins (a) before the taxable year in which the individual filing the application first met the requirements of subparagraphs (1) and (2) of paragraph (a) of this section, or (b) before the time as of which the Secretary of Health, Education, and Welfare finds that the sect or division thereof of which the individual is a member met the requirements of subparagraphs (C) and (D) of section 1402(h)(1) (see subdivisions (i) and (ii) of paragraph (e)(2) of this section), or

(ii) Ends (a) after the time at which the individual filing the application ceases to meet

Reg. §1.1402(h)-1(f)(2)(ii)

the requirements of subparagraphs (1) and (2) of paragraph (a) of this section, or (b) after the time as of which the Secretary of Health, Education, and Welfare finds that the sect or division thereof of which the individual is a member ceases to meet the requirements of subparagraphs (C) and (D) of section 1402(h)(1) (see subdivisions (i) and (ii) of paragraph (e)(2) of this section).

(g) *Refund or credit.*—An application for exemption on Form 4029 filed on or before December 31, 1968 (if approved as provided in paragraph (e) of this section), shall constitute a claim for refund or credit of any tax on self-employment income under section 1401 (or under section 480 of the Internal Revenue Code of 1939) paid or incurred in respect of any taxable year beginning after December 31, 1950, and ending before December 31, 1967, for which an exemption is granted. Refund or credit of any tax referred to in the preceding sentence may be made, pursuant to the provisions of section 501(c) of the Social Security Amendments of 1967 (81 Stat. 933), notwithstanding that the refund or credit would otherwise be prevented by operation of any law or rule of law. No interest shall be allowed or paid in respect of any refund or credit made or allowed in connection with a claim for refund or credit made on Form 4029. [Reg. § 1.1402(h)-1.]

☐ [*T.D.* 6993, 1-17-69.]

[Reg. § 1.1403-1]

§ 1.1403-1. Cross references.—For provisions relating to the requirement for filing returns with respect to net earnings from self-employment, see § 1.6017-1. For provisions relating to declarations of estimated tax on self-employment income, see § § 1.6015(a)-1 to 1.6015(j)-1, inclusive. For other administrative provisions relating to the tax on self-employment income, see the applicable sections of the regulations in this part (§ 1.6001-1 et seq.) and the applicable sections of the regulations in Part 301 of this chapter (Regulations on Procedure and Administration). [Reg. § 1.1403-1.]

☐ [*T.D.* 6196, 8-13-56. *Amended by T.D.* 7427, 8-9-76.]

Withholding of Tax on Nonresident Aliens and Foreign Corporations

NONRESIDENT ALIENS AND FOREIGN CORPORATIONS

See p. 20,601 for regulations not amended to reflect law changes

[Reg. § 1.1441-0]

§ 1.1441-0. Outline of regulation provisions for section 1441.—This section lists captions contained in § § 1.1441-1 through 1.1441-9.

§ 1.1441-1. Requirement for the deduction and withholding of tax on payments to foreign persons.

(a) Purpose and scope.

(b) General rules of withholding.

(1) Requirement to withhold on payments to foreign persons.

(2) Determination of payee and payee's status.

(i) In general.

(ii) Payments to a U.S. agent of a foreign person.

(iii) Payments to wholly-owned entities.

(A) Foreign-owned domestic entity.

(B) Foreign entity.

(iv) Payments to a U.S. branch of certain foreign banks or foreign insurance companies

(A) U.S. branch treated as a U.S. person in certain cases.

(B) Consequences to the withholding agent.

(C) Consequences to the U.S. branch.

(D) Definition of payment to a U.S. branch.

(E) Payments to other U.S. branches.

(v) Payments to a foreign intermediary.

(A) Payments treated as made to persons for whom the intermediary collects the payment.

(B) Payments treated as made to foreign intermediary.

(vi) Other payees.

(vii) Rules for reliably associating a payment with a withholding certificate or other appropriate documentation.

(A) Generally.

(B) Special rules applicable to a withholding certificate from a nonqualified intermediary or flow-through entity.

(C) Special rules applicable to a withholding certificate provided by a qualified intermediary that does not assume primary withholding responsibility.

(D) Special rules applicable to a withholding certificate provided by a qualified intermediary that assumes primary withholding responsibility under chapter 3 of the Internal Revenue Code.

(E) Special rules applicable to a withholding certificate provided by a qualified intermediary that assumes primary Form 1099 reporting and backup withholding responsibility but not primary withholding under chapter 3.

(F) Special rules applicable to a withholding certificate provided by a qualified intermediary that assumes primary withholding responsibility under chapter 3 and primary Form 1099 reporting and backup withholding responsibility and a withholding certificate provided by a withholding foreign partnership.

(3) Presumptions regarding payee's status in the absence of documentation.

(i) General rules.

(ii) Presumptions of classification as individual, corporation, partnership, etc.

(A) In general.

(B) No documentation provided.

(C) Documentary evidence furnished for offshore account.

(iii) Presumption of U.S. or foreign status.

(A) Payments to exempt recipients.

(B) Scholarships and grants.

(C) Pensions, annuities, etc.

(D) Certain payments to offshore accounts.

(iv) Grace period.

(v) Special rules applicable to payments to foreign intermediaries.

(A) Reliance on claim of status as foreign intermediary.

(B) Beneficial owner documentation or allocation information is lacking or unreliable.

(C) Information regarding allocation of payment is lacking or unreliable.

(D) Certification that the foreign intermediary has furnished documentation for all of the persons to whom the intermediary certificate relates is lacking or unreliable.

(vi) U.S. branches.

(vii) Joint payees.

(A) In general.

(B) Special rule for offshore accounts.

(viii) Rebuttal of presumptions.

(ix) Effect of reliance on presumptions and of actual knowledge or reason to know otherwise.

(A) General rule.

(B) Actual knowledge or reason to know that amount of withholding is greater than is required under the presumptions or that reporting of the payment is required.

(x) Examples.

(4) List of exemptions from, or reduced rates of, withholding under chapter 3 of the Code.

(5) Establishing foreign status under applicable provisions of chapter 61 of the Code.

(6) Rules of withholding for payments by a foreign intermediary or certain U.S. branches.

(i) In general.

(ii) Example.

(7) Liability for failure to obtain documentation timely or to act in accordance with applicable presumptions.

(i) General rule.

(ii) Proof that tax liability has been satisfied.

(iii) Liability for interest and penalties.

(iv) Special effective date.

(v) Examples.

(8) Adjustments, refunds, or credits of overwithheld amounts.

(9) Payments to joint owners.

(c) Definitions.

(1) Withholding.

(2) Foreign and U.S. person.

(3) Individual.

(i) Alien individual.

(ii) Nonresident alien individual.

(4) Certain foreign corporations.

(5) Financial institution and foreign financial institution.

(6) Beneficial owner.

(i) General rule.

(ii) Special rules.

(A) General rule.

(B) Foreign partnerships.

(C) Foreign simple trusts and foreign grantor trusts.

(D) Other foreign trusts and foreign estates.

(7) Withholding agent.

(8) Person

(9) Source of income.

(10) Chapter 3 of the Code.

(11) Reduced rate.

(12) Payee.

(13) Intermediary.

(14) Nonqualified intermediary.

(15) Qualified intermediary.

(16) Withholding certificate.

(17) Documentary evidence; other appropriate documentation.

(18) Documentation.

(19) Payor.

(20) Exempt recipient.

(21) Non-exempt recipient.

(22) Reportable amounts.

(23) Flow-through entity.

(24) Foreign simple trust.

(25) Foreign complex trust.

(26) Foreign grantor trust.

(27) Partnership.

(28) Nonwithholding foreign partnership.

(29) Withholding foreign partnership.

(d) Beneficial owner's or payee's claim of U.S. status.

(1) In general.

(2) Payments for which a Form W-9 is otherwise required.

Reg. §1.1441-0

(3) Payments for which a Form W-9 is not otherwise required.

(4) When a payment to an intermediary or flow-through entity may be treated as made to a U.S. payee.

(e) Beneficial owner's claim of foreign status.

(1) Withholding agent's reliance.

(i) In general.

(ii) Payments that a withholding agent may treat as made to a foreign person that is a beneficial owner.

(A) General rule.

(B) Additional requirements.

(2) Beneficial owner withholding certificate.

(i) In general.

(ii) Requirements for validity of certificate.

(3) Intermediary, flow-through, or U.S. branch withholding certificate.

(i) In general.

(ii) Intermediary withholding certificate from a qualified intermediary.

(iii) Intermediary withholding certificate from a nonqualified intermediary.

(iv) Withholding statement provided by nonqualified Intermediary.

(A) In general.

(B) General requirements.

(C) Content of withholding statement.

(D) Alternative procedures.

(E) Notice procedures.

(v) Withholding certificate from certain U.S. branches.

(vi) Reportable amounts.

(4) Applicable rules.

(i) Who may sign the certificate.

(ii) Period of validity.

(A) Three-year period.

(B) Indefinite validity period.

(C) Withholding certificate for effectively connected income.

(D) Change in circumstances.

(iii) Retention of withholding certificate.

(iv) Electronic transmission of information.

(A) In general.

(B) Requirements.

(C) Special requirements for transmission of Forms W-8 by an intermediary. [Reserved]

(v) Electronic confirmation of taxpayer identifying number on withholding certificate.

(vi) Acceptable substitute form.

(vii) Requirement of taxpayer identifying number.

(viii) Reliance rules.

(A) Classification.

(B) Status of payee as an intermediary or as a person acting for its own account.

(ix) Certificates to be furnished for each account unless exception applies.

(A) Coordinated account information system in effect.

(B) Family of mutual funds.

(C) Special rule for brokers.

(5) Qualified intermediaries.

(i) General rule.

(ii) Definition of qualified intermediary.

(iii) Withholding agreement.

(A) In general.

(B) Terms of the withholding agreement.

(iv) Assignment of primary withholding responsibility.

(v) Withholding statement.

(A) General rule.

(B) Content of withholding statement.

(C) Withholding rate pools.

(f) Effective date.

(1) In general.

(2) Transition rules.

(i) Special rules for existing documentation.

(ii) Lack of documentation for past years.

§ 1.1441-2. *Amounts subject to withholding*.

(a) In general.

(b) Fixed or determinable annual or periodical income.

(1) In general.

(i) Definition.

(ii) Manner of payment.

(iii) Determinability of amount.

(2) Exceptions.

(3) Original issue discount.

(i) Amount subject to tax.

(ii) Amounts subject to withholding.

(4) Securities lending transactions and equivalent transactions.

(5) REMIC residual interests.

(c) Other income subject to withholding.

(d) Exceptions to withholding where no money or property is paid or lack of knowledge.

(1) General rule.

(2) Cancellation of debt.

(3) Satisfaction of liability following underwithholding by withholding agent.

(4) Withholding exemption inapplicable.

(e) Payment.

(1) General rule.

(2) Income allocated under section 482.

(3) Blocked income.

(4) Special rules for dividends.

(5) Certain interest accrued by a foreign corporation.

(6) Payments other than in U.S. dollars.

(f) Effective/applicability date.

§1.1441-3. *Determination of amounts to be withheld.*

(a) Withholding on gross amount.

(b) Withholding on payments on certain obligations.

(1) Withholding at time of payment of interest.

(2) No withholding between interest payment dates.

(i) In general.

(ii) Anti-abuse rule.

(c) Corporate distributions.

(1) General rule.

(2) Exception to withholding on distributions.

(i) In general.

(ii) Reasonable estimate of accumulated and current earnings and profits on the date of payment.

(A) General rule.

(B) Procedures in case of underwithholding.

(C) Reliance by intermediary on reasonable estimate.

(D) Example.

(3) Special rules in the case of distributions from a regulated investment company.

(i) General rule

(ii) Reliance by intermediary on reasonable estimate.

(4) Coordination with withholding under section 1445.

(i) In general.

(A) Withholding under section 1441.

(B) Withholding under both sections 1441 and 1445.

(C) Coordination with REIT withholding.

(ii) Intermediary reliance rule.

(d) Withholding on payments that include an undetermined amount of income.

(1) In general.

(2) Withholding on certain gains.

(e) Payments other than in U.S. dollars.

(1) In general.

(2) Payments in foreign currency.

(f) Tax liability of beneficial owner satisfied by withholding agent.

(1) General rule.

(2) Example.

(g) Conduit financing arrangements

(h) Effective date.

§1.1441-4. *Exemptions from withholding for certain effectively connected income and other amounts.*

(a) Certain income connected with a U.S. trade or business.

(1) In general.

(2) Withholding agent's reliance on a claim of effectively connected income.

(i) In general.

(ii) Special rules for U.S. branches of foreign persons.

(A) U.S. branches of certain foreign banks or foreign insurance companies.

(B) Other U.S. branches.

(3) Income on notional principal contracts.

(i) General rule.

(ii) Exception for certain payments.

(b) Compensation for personal services of an individual.

(1) Exemption from withholding.

(2) Manner of obtaining withholding exemption under tax treaty.

(i) In general.

(ii) Withholding certificate claiming withholding exemption.

(iii) Review by withholding agent.

(iv) Acceptance by withholding agent.

(v) Copies of Form 8233.

(3) Withholding agreements.

(4) Final payments exemption.

(i) General rule.

(ii) Final payment of compensation for personal services.

(iii) Manner of applying for final payment exemption.

(iv) Letter to withholding agent.

(5) Requirement of return.

(6) Personal exemption.

(i) In general.

(ii) Multiple exemptions.

(iii) Special rule where both certain scholarship and compensation income are received.

(c) Special rules for scholarship and fellowship income.

(1) In general.

(2) Alternate withholding election.

(d) Annuities received under qualified plans.

(e) Per diem of certain alien trainees.

(f) Failure to receive withholding certificates timely or to act in accordance with applicable presumptions.

(g) Effective date.

(1) General rule.

(2) Transition rules.

§1.1441-5. Withholding on payments to partnerships, trusts, and estates.

(a) In general.

(b) Rules applicable to U.S. partnerships, trusts, and estates.

(1) Payments to U.S. partnerships, trusts, and estates.

(2) Withholding by U.S. payees.

(i) U.S. partnerships.

(A) In general.

(B) Effectively connected income of partners.

(ii) U.S. simple trusts.

(iii) U.S. complex trusts and U.S. estates.

(iv) U.S. grantor trusts

(v) Subsequent distribution

(c) Foreign partnerships.

(1) Determination of payee.

(i) Payments treated as made to partners.

(ii) Payments treated as made to the partnership.

(iii) Rules for reliably associating a payment with documentation.

(iv) Examples.

(2) Withholding foreign partnerships.

(i) Reliance on claim of withholding foreign partnership status.

(ii) Withholding agreement.

(iii) Withholding responsibility.

(iv) Withholding certificate from a withholding foreign partnership.

(3) Nonwithholding foreign partnerships.

(i) Reliance on claim of foreign partnership status.

(ii) Reliance on claim of reduced withholding by a partnership for its partners.

(iii) Withholding certificate from a nonwithholding foreign partnership.

(iv) Withholding statement provided by nonwithholding foreign partnership.

(v) Withholding and reporting by a foreign partnership.

(d) Presumption rules.

(1) In general.

(2) Determination of partnership's status as domestic or foreign in the absence of documentation.

(3) Determination of partners' status in the absence of certain documentation.

(4) Determination by a withholding foreign partnership of the status of its partners.

(e) Foreign trusts and estates.

(1) In general.

(2) Payments to foreign complex trusts and estates.

(3) Payees of payments to foreign simple trusts and foreign grantor trusts.

(i) Payments for which beneficiaries and owners are payees.

(ii) Payments for which trust is payee.

(4) Reliance on claim of foreign complex trust or foreign estate status.

(5) Foreign simple trust and foreign grantor trust.

(i) Reliance on claim of foreign simple trust or foreign grantor trust status.

(ii) Reliance on claim of reduced withholding by a foreign simple trust or foreign grantor trust for its beneficiaries or owners.

(iii) Withholding certificate from foreign simple trust or foreign grantor trust.

(iv) Withholding statement provided by a foreign simple trust or foreign grantor trust.

(v) Withholding foreign trusts.

(6) Presumption rules

(i) In general

(ii) Determination of status as U.S. or foreign trust or estate in the absence of documentation.

(iii) Determination of beneficiary or owner's status in the absence of certain documentation.

(f) Failure to receive withholding certificate timely or to act in accordance with applicable presumptions.

(g) Effective date.

(1) General rule.

(2) Transition rules.

§1.1441-6. Claim of reduced withholding under an income tax treaty.

(a) In general.

(b) Reliance on claim of reduced withholding under an income tax treaty.

(1) In general.

(2) Payment to fiscally transparent entity.

(i) In general.

(ii) Certification by qualified intermediary.

(iii) Dual treatment.

(iv) Examples.

(3) Certified TIN

(4) Claim of benefits under an income tax treaty by a U.S. person.

(c) Exemption from requirement to furnish a taxpayer identifying number and special documentary evidence rules for certain income.

(1) In general.

(2) Income to which special rules apply.

(3) Certificate of residence.

(4) Documentary evidence establishing residence in the treaty country.

(i) Individuals.

(ii) Persons other than individuals.

(5) Statements regarding entitlement to treaty benefits.

(i) Statement regarding conditions under a limitation on benefits provision.

(ii) Statement regarding whether the taxpayer derives the income.

(d) Joint owners.

(e) Competent authority.

(f) Failure to receive withholding certificate timely.

(g) Special taxpayer identifying number rule for certain foreign individuals claiming treaty benefits.

(1) General rule.

(2) Special rule.

(3) Requirement that an ITIN be requested during the first business day following payment.

(4) Definition of unexpected payment.

(5) Examples.

(h) Effective dates.

(1) General rule.

(2) Transition rules.

§ 1.1441-7. General provisions relating to withholding agents.

(a) Withholding agent defined.

(1) In general.

(2) Examples.

(b) Standards of knowledge.

(1) In general.

(2) Reason to know.

(3) Financial institutions—limits on reason to know.

(4) Rules applicable to withholding certificates.

(i) In general.

(ii) Examples.

(5) Withholding certificate—establishment of foreign status.

(6) Withholding certificate—claim of reduced rate of withholding under treaty.

(7) Documentary evidence.

(8) Documentary evidence—establishment of foreign status.

(9) Documentary evidence—claim of reduced rate of withholding under treaty.

(10) Limits on reason to know—indirect account holders.

(11) Additional guidance.

(c) Authorized agent.

(1) In general.

(2) Authorized foreign agent.

(3) Notification.

(4) Liability of U.S. withholding agent.

(5) Filing of returns.

(d) United States obligations.

(e) Assumed obligations.

(f) Conduit financing arrangements.

(g) Effective date.

§ 1.1441-8. Exemption from withholding for payments to foreign governments, international organizations, foreign central banks of issue, and the Bank for International Settlements.

(a) Foreign governments.

(b) Reliance on claim of exemption by foreign government.

(c) Income of a foreign central bank of issue or the Bank for International Settlements.

(1) Certain interest income.

(2) Bankers' acceptances.

(d) Exemption for payments to international organizations.

(e) Failure to receive withholding certificate timely and other applicable procedures.

(f) Effective date.

(1) In general.

(2) Transition rules.

§ 1.1441-9. Exemption from withholding on exempt income of a foreign tax-exempt organization, including foreign private foundations.

(a) Exemption from withholding for exempt income.

(b) Reliance on foreign organization's claim of exemption from withholding.

(1) General rule.

(2) Withholding certificate.

(3) Presumptions in the absence of documentation.

(4) Reason to know.

(c) Failure to receive withholding certificate timely and other applicable procedures.

(d) Effective date.

(1) In general.

(2) Transition rules.

[Reg. § 1.1441-0.]

☐ [T.D. 8734, 10-6-97 (T.D. 8804 delayed the effective date of T.D. 8734 from January 1, 1999, to January 1, 2000; T.D. 8856 further delayed the effective date of T.D. 8734 until January 1, 2001). *Amended by T.D. 8881, 5-15-2000; T.D. 9023,* 11-21-2002; *T.D. 9272, 7-31-2006 and T.D. 9415,* 7-11-2008.]

[Reg. § 1.1441-1]

§ 1.1441-1. Requirement for the deduction and withholding of tax on payments to foreign persons.—(a) *Purpose and scope.*—This section, §§ 1.1441-2 through 1.1441-9, and 1.1443-1 provide rules for withholding under sections 1441, 1442, and 1443 when a payment is made to a foreign person. This section provides definitions of terms used in chapter 3 of the Internal Revenue Code (Code) and regulations thereunder. It prescribes procedures to determine whether an amount must be withheld under chapter 3 of the Code and documentation that a withholding agent may rely upon to determine the status of a payee or a beneficial owner as a U.S. person or as a foreign person and other relevant characteristics of the payee that may affect a withholding agent's obligation to withhold under chapter 3 of the Code and the regulations thereunder. Special procedures regarding payments to foreign persons that act as intermediaries are also provided. Section 1.1441-2 defines the income subject to withholding under section 1441, 1442, and 1443 and the regulations under these sections. Section 1.1441-3 provides rules regarding the amount subject to withholding. Section 1.1441-4 provides exemptions from withholding for, among other things, certain income effectively connected with the conduct of a trade or business in the United States, including certain compensation for the personal services of an individual. Section 1.1441-5 provides rules for withholding on payments made to flow-through entities and other similar arrangements. Section 1.1441-6 provides rules for claiming a reduced rate of withholding under an income tax treaty. Section 1.1441-7 defines the term *withholding agent* and provides due diligence rules governing a withholding agent's obligation to withhold. Section 1.1441-8 provides rules for relying on claims of exemption from withholding for payments to a foreign government, an international organization, a foreign central bank of issue, or the Bank for International Settlements. Sections 1.1441-9 and 1.1443-1 provide rules for relying on claims of exemption from withholding for payments to foreign tax exempt organizations and foreign private foundations.

(b) *General rules of withholding.*—(1) *Requirement to withhold on payments to foreign persons.*—A withholding agent must withhold 30-percent of any payment of an amount subject to withholding made to a payee that is a foreign person unless it can reliably associate the payment with documentation upon which it can rely to treat the payment as made to a payee that is a U.S. person or as made to a beneficial owner that is a foreign person entitled to a reduced rate of withholding. However, a withholding agent making a payment to a foreign person need not withhold where the foreign person assumes responsibility for withholding on the payment under chapter 3 of the Code and the regulations thereunder as a qualified intermediary (see paragraph (e)(5) of this section), as a U.S. branch of a foreign person (see paragraph (b)(2)(iv) of this section), as a withholding foreign partnership (see § 1.1441-5(c)(2)(i)), or as an authorized foreign agent (see § 1.1441-7(c)(1)). This section (dealing with general rules of withholding and claims of foreign or U.S. status by a payee or a beneficial owner), and § § 1.1441-4, 1.1441-5, 1.1441-6, 1.1441-8, 1.1441-9, and 1.1443-1 provide rules for determining whether documentation is required as a condition for reducing the rate of withholding on a payment to a foreign beneficial owner or to a U.S. payee and if so, the nature of the documentation upon which a withholding agent may rely in order to reduce such rate. Paragraph (b)(2) of this section prescribes the rules for determining who the payee is, the extent to which a payment is treated as made to a foreign payee, and reliable association of a payment with documentation. Paragraph (b)(3) of this section describes the applicable presumptions for determining the payee's status as U.S. or foreign and the payee's other characteristics (i.e., as an owner or intermediary, as an individual, partnership, corporation, etc.). Paragraph (b)(4) of this section lists the types of payments for which the 30-percent withholding rate may be reduced. Because the treatment of a payee as a U.S. or a foreign person also has consequences for purposes of making an information return under the provisions of chapter 61 of the Code and for withholding under other provisions of the Code, such as sections 3402, 3405 or 3406, paragraph (b)(5) of this section lists applicable provisions outside chapter 3 of the Code that require certain payees to establish their foreign status (e.g., in order to be exempt from information reporting). Paragraph (b)(6) of this section describes the withholding obligations of a foreign person making a payment that it has received in its capacity as an intermediary. Paragraph (b)(7) of this section describes the liability of a withholding agent that fails to withhold at the required 30-percent rate in the absence of documentation. Paragraph (b)(8) of this section deals with adjustments and refunds in the case of overwithholding. Paragraph (b)(9) of this section deals with determining the status of the payee when the payment is jointly owned. See paragraph (c)(6) of this section for a definition of beneficial owner. See § 1.1441-7(a) for a definition of withholding agent. See § 1.1441-2(a) for the determination of an amount subject to withholding. See § 1.1441-2(e) for the definition of a payment and when it is considered made. Except as otherwise provided, the provisions of this section apply only for purposes of determining a withholding agent's obligation to withhold under chapter 3 of the Code and the regulations thereunder.

(2) *Determination of payee and payee's status.*—(i) *In general.*—Except as otherwise provided in this paragraph (b)(2) and § 1.1441-5(c)(1) and (e)(3), a payee is the person to whom a payment is made, regardless of whether such person is the beneficial owner of the amount (as defined in paragraph (c)(6) of this section). A foreign payee is a payee who is a foreign person. A U.S. payee is a payee who is a U.S. person. Generally, the determination by a withholding agent of the U.S. or foreign status of a payee and of its other relevant characteristics (e.g., as a beneficial owner or intermediary, or as an individual, corporation, or flow-through entity) is made on the basis of a withholding certificate that is a Form W-8 or a Form 8233 (indicating foreign status of the payee or beneficial owner) or a Form W-9 (indicating U.S. status of the payee). The provisions of this paragraph (b)(2), paragraph (b)(3) of this section, and § 1.1441-5(c), (d), and (e) dealing with determinations of payee and applicable presumptions in the absence of documentation, apply only to payments of amounts subject to withholding

under chapter 3 of the Code (within the meaning of § 1.1441-2(a)). Similar payee and presumption provisions are set forth under § 1.6049-5(d) for payments of amounts that are not subject to withholding under chapter 3 of the Code (or the regulations thereunder) but that may be reportable under provisions of chapter 61 of the Code (and the regulations thereunder). See paragraph (d) of this section for documentation upon which the withholding agent may rely in order to treat the payee or beneficial owner as a U.S. person. See paragraph (e) of this section for documentation upon which the withholding agent may rely in order to treat the payee or beneficial owner as a foreign person. For applicable presumptions of status in the absence of documentation, see paragraph (b)(3) of this section and § 1.1441-5(d). For definitions of a foreign person and U.S. person, see paragraph (c)(2) of this section.

(ii) *Payments to a U.S. agent of a foreign person.*—A withholding agent making a payment to a U.S. person (other than to a U.S. branch that is treated as a U.S. person pursuant to paragraph (b)(2)(iv) of this section) and who has actual knowledge that the U.S. person receives the payment as an agent of a foreign person must treat the payment as made to the foreign person. However, the withholding agent may treat the payment as made to the U.S. person if the U.S. person is a financial institution and the withholding agent has no reason to believe that the financial institution will not comply with its obligation to withhold. See paragraph (c)(5) of this section for the definition of a financial institution.

(iii) *Payments to wholly-owned entities.*— (A) *Foreign-owned domestic entity.*—A payment to a wholly-owned domestic entity that is disregarded for federal tax purposes under § 301.7701-2(c)(2) of this chapter as an entity separate from its owner and whose single owner is a foreign person shall be treated as a payment to the owner of the entity, subject to the provisions of paragraph (b)(2)(iv) of this section. For purposes of this paragraph (b)(2)(iii)(A), a domestic entity means a person that would be treated as a U.S. person if it had an election in effect under § 301.7701-3(c)(1)(i) of this chapter to be treated as a corporation. For example, a limited liability company, A, organized under the laws of the State of Delaware, opens an account at a U.S. bank. Upon opening of the account, the bank requests A to furnish a Form W-9 as required under section 6049(a) and the regulations under that section. A does not have an election in effect under § 301.7701-3(c)(1)(i) of this chapter and, therefore, is not treated as an organization taxable as a corporation, including for purposes of the exempt recipient provisions in § 1.6049-4(c)(1). If A has a single owner and the owner is a foreign person (as defined in paragraph (c)(2) of this section), then A may not furnish a Form W-9 because it may not represent

that it is a U.S. person for purposes of the provisions of chapters 3 and 61 of the Code, and section 3406. Therefore, A must furnish a Form W-8 with the name, address, and taxpayer identifying number (TIN) (if required) of the foreign person who is the single owner in the same manner as if the account were opened directly by the foreign single owner. See § § 1.894-1T(d) and 1.1441-6(b)(2) for special rules where the entity's owner is claiming a reduced rate of withholding under an income tax treaty.

(B) *Foreign entity.*—A payment to a wholly-owned foreign entity that is disregarded under § 301.7701-2(c)(2) of this chapter as an entity separate from its owner shall be treated as a payment to the single owner of the entity, subject to the provisions of paragraph (b)(2)(iv) of this section if the foreign entity has a U.S. branch in the United States. For purposes of this paragraph (b)(2)(iii)(B), a foreign entity means a person that would be treated as a foreign person if it had an election in effect under § 301.7701-3(c)(1)(i) of this chapter to be treated as a corporation. See § § 1.894-1T(d) and 1.1441-6(b)(2) for special rules where the foreign entity or its owner is claiming a reduced rate of withholding under an income tax treaty. Thus, for example, if the foreign entity's single owner is a U.S. person, the payment shall be treated as a payment to a U.S. person. Therefore, based on the saving clause in U.S. income tax treaties, such an entity may not claim benefits under an income tax treaty even if the entity is organized in a country with which the United States has an income tax treaty in effect and treats the entity as a non-fiscally transparent entity. See § 1.894-1T(d)(6), *Example 10.* Unless it has actual knowledge or reason to know that the foreign entity to whom the payment is made is disregarded under § 301.7701-2(c)(2) of this chapter, a withholding agent may treat a foreign entity as an entity separate from its owner unless it can reliably associate the payment with a withholding certificate from the entity's owner.

(iv) *Payments to a U.S. branch of certain foreign banks or foreign insurance companies.*— (A) *U.S. branch treated as a U.S. person in certain cases.*—A payment to a U.S. branch of a foreign person is a payment to a foreign person. However, a U.S. branch described in this paragraph (b)(2)(iv)(A) and a withholding agent (including another U.S. branch described in this paragraph (b)(2)(iv)(A)) may agree to treat the branch as a U.S. person for purposes of withholding on specified payments to the U.S. branch. Notwithstanding the preceding sentence, a withholding agent making a payment to a U.S. branch treated as a U.S. person under this paragraph (b)(2)(iv)(A) shall not treat the branch as a U.S. person for purposes of reporting the payment made to the branch. Therefore, a payment to such U.S. branch shall be reported on Form 1042-S under § 1.1461-1(c). Further, a U.S. branch that is

Reg. § 1.1441-1(b)(2)(iv)(A)

treated as a U.S. person under this paragraph (b)(2)(iv)(A) shall not be treated as a U.S. person for purposes of the withholding certificate it may provide to a withholding agent. Therefore, the U.S. branch must furnish a U.S. branch withholding certificate on Form W-8 as provided in paragraph (e)(3)(v) of this section and not a Form W-9. An agreement to treat a U.S. branch as a U.S. person must be evidenced by a U.S. branch withholding certificate described in paragraph (e)(3)(v) of this section furnished by the U.S. branch to the withholding agent. A U.S. branch described in this paragraph (b)(2)(iv)(A) is any U.S. branch of a foreign bank subject to regulatory supervision by the Federal Reserve Board or a U.S. branch of a foreign insurance company required to file an annual statement on a form approved by the National Association of Insurance Commissioners with the Insurance Department of a State, a Territory, or the District of Columbia. In addition, a financial institution organized in a possession of the United States will be treated as a U.S. branch for purposes of this paragraph (b)(2)(iv)(A). The Internal Revenue Service (IRS) may approve a list of U.S. branches that may qualify for treatment as a U.S. person under this paragraph (b)(2)(iv)(A) (see §601.601(d)(2) of this chapter). See §1.6049-5(c)(5)(vi) for the treatment of U.S. branches as U.S. payors if they make a payment that is subject to reporting under chapter 61 of the Internal Revenue Code. Also see §1.6049-5(d)(1)(ii) for the treatment of U.S. branches as foreign payees under chapter 61 of the Internal Revenue Code.

(B) *Consequences to the withholding agent.*—Any person that is otherwise a withholding agent regarding a payment to a U.S. branch described in paragraph (b)(2)(iv)(A) of this section shall treat the payment in one of the following ways—

(1) As a payment to a U.S. person, in which case the withholding agent is not responsible for withholding on such payment to the extent it can reliably associate the payment with a withholding certificate described in paragraph (e)(3)(v) of this section that has been furnished by the U.S. branch under its agreement with the withholding agent to be treated as U.S. person;

(2) As a payment directly to the persons whose names are on withholding certificates or other appropriate documentation forwarded by the U.S. branch to the withholding agent when no agreement is in effect to treat the U.S. branch as a U.S. person for such payment, to the extent the withholding agent can reliably associate the payment with such certificates or documentation; or

(3) As a payment to a foreign person of income that is effectively connected with the conduct of a trade or business in the United States if the withholding agent cannot reliably associate the payment with a withholding certificate from the U.S. branch or any other certificate or other appropriate documentation from another person. See §1.1441-4(a)(2)(ii).

(C) *Consequences to the U.S. branch.*— A U.S. branch that is treated as a U.S. person under paragraph (b)(2)(iv)(A) of this section shall be treated as a separate person solely for purposes of section 1441(a) and all other provisions of chapter 3 of the Internal Revenue Code and the regulations thereunder (other than for purposes of reporting the payment to the U.S. branch under §1.1461-1(c) or for purposes of the documentation such a branch must furnish under paragraph (e)(3)(v) of this section) for any payment that it receives as such. Thus, the U.S. branch shall be responsible for withholding on the payment in accordance with the provisions under chapter 3 of the Internal Revenue Code and the regulations thereunder and other applicable withholding provisions of the Internal Revenue Code. For this purpose, it shall obtain and retain documentation from payees or beneficial owners of the payments that it receives as a U.S. person in the same manner as if it were a separate entity. For example, if a U.S. branch receives a payment on behalf of its home office and the home office is a qualified intermediary, the U.S. branch must obtain a qualified intermediary withholding certificate described in paragraph (e)(3)(ii) of this section from its home office. In addition, a U.S. branch that has not provided documentation to the withholding agent for a payment that is, in fact, not effectively connected income is a withholding agent with respect to that payment. See paragraph (b)(6) of this section and §1.1441-4(a)(2)(ii).

(D) *Definition of payment to a U.S. branch.*—A payment is treated as a payment to a U.S. branch of a foreign bank or foreign insurance company if the payment is credited to an account maintained in the United States in the name of a U.S. branch of the foreign person, or the payment is made to an address in the United States where the U.S. branch is located and the name of the U.S. branch appears on documents (in written or electronic form) associated with the payment (e.g., the check mailed or a letter addressed to the branch).

(E) *Payments to other U.S. branches.*— Similar withholding procedures may apply to payments to U.S. branches that are not described in paragraph (b)(2)(iv)(A) of this section to the extent permitted by the district director or the Assistant Commissioner (International). Any such branch must establish that its situation is analogous to that of a U.S. branch described in paragraph (b)(2)(iv)(A) of this section regarding its registration with, and regulation by, a U.S. governmental institution, the type and amounts of assets it is required to, or actually maintains in the United States, and the personnel who carry out the activities of the branch in the United

States. In the alternative, the branch must establish that the withholding and reporting requirements under chapter 3 of the Code and the regulations thereunder impose an undue administrative burden and that the collection of the tax imposed by section 871(a) or 881(a) on the foreign person (or its members in the case of a foreign partnership) will not be jeopardized by the exemption from withholding. Generally, an undue administrative burden will be found to exist in a case where the person entitled to the income, such as a foreign insurance company, receives from the withholding agent income on securities issued by a single corporation, some of which is, and some of which is not, effectively connected with conduct of a trade or business within the United States and the criteria for determining the effective connection are unduly difficult to apply because of the circumstances under which such securities are held. No exemption from withholding shall be granted under this paragraph (b)(2)(iv)(E) unless the person entitled to the income complies with such other requirements as may be imposed by the district director or the Assistant Commissioner (International) and unless the district director or the Assistant Commissioner (International) is satisfied that the collection of the tax on the income involved will not be jeopardized by the exemption from withholding. The IRS may prescribe such procedures as are necessary to make these determinations (see § 601.601(d)(2) of this chapter).

(v) *Payments to a foreign intermediary.*— (A) *Payments treated as made to persons for whom the intermediary collects the payment.*—Except as otherwise provided in paragraph (b)(2)(v)(B) of this section, the payee of a payment to a person that the withholding agent may treat as a foreign intermediary in accordance with the provisions of paragraph (b)(3)(ii)(C) or (b)(3)(v)(A) of this section is the person or persons for whom the intermediary collects the payment. Thus, for example, the payee of a payment that the withholding agent can reliably associate with a withholding certificate from a qualified intermediary (defined in paragraph (e)(5)(ii) of this section) that does not assume primary withholding responsibility or a payment to a nonqualified intermediary are the persons for whom the qualified intermediary or nonqualified intermediary acts and not to the intermediary itself. See paragraph (b)(3)(v) of this section for presumptions that apply if the payment cannot be reliably associated with valid documentation. For similar rules for payments to flow-through entities, see § 1.1441-5(c)(1) and (e)(3).

(B) *Payments treated as made to foreign intermediary.*—The payee of a payment to a person that the withholding agent may treat as a qualified intermediary is the qualified intermediary to the extent that the qualified intermediary assumes primary withholding responsibility

under paragraph (e)(5)(iv) of this section for the payment. For example if a qualified intermediary assumes primary withholding responsibility under chapter 3 of the Internal Revenue Code but does not assume primary reporting or withholding responsibility under chapter 61 or section 3406 of the Internal Revenue Code and therefore provides Forms W-9 for U.S. non-exempt recipients, the qualified intermediary is the payee except to the extent the payment is reliably associated with a Form W-9 from a U.S. non-exempt recipient.

(vi) *Other payees.*—A payment to a person described in § 1.6049-4(c)(1)(ii) that the withholding agent would treat as a payment to a foreign person without obtaining documentation for purposes of information reporting under section 6049 (if the payment were interest) is treated as a payment to a foreign payee for purposes of chapter 3 of the Code and the regulations thereunder (or to a foreign beneficial owner to the extent provided in paragraph (e)(1)(ii)(A)(6) or (7) of this section). Further, payments that the withholding agent can reliably associate with documentary evidence described in § 1.6049-5(c)(1) relating to the payee is treated as a payment to a foreign payee. A payment that the withholding agent may treat as a payment to an authorized foreign agent (as defined in § 1.1441-7(c)(2)) is treated as a payment to the agent and not to the persons for whom the agent collects the payment. See § 1.1441-5(b)(1) and (c)(1) for payee determinations for payments to partnerships. See § 1.1441-5(e) for payee determinations for payments to foreign trusts or foreign estates.

(vii) *Rules for reliably associating a payment with a withholding certificate or other appropriate documentation.*—(A) *Generally.*—The presumption rules of paragraph (b)(3) of this section and §§ 1.1441-5(d) and (e)(6) and 1.6049-5(d) apply to any payment, or portion of a payment, that a withholding agent cannot reliably associate with valid documentation. Generally, a withholding agent can reliably associate a payment with valid documentation if, prior to the payment, it holds valid documentation (either directly or through an agent), it can reliably determine how much of the payment relates to the valid documentation, and it has no actual knowledge or reason to know that any of the information, certifications, or statements in, or associated with, the documentation are incorrect. Special rules apply for payments made to intermediaries, flow-through entities, and certain U.S. branches. See paragraph (b)(2)(vii)(B) through (F) of this section. The documentation referred to in this paragraph (b)(2)(vii) is documentation described in paragraphs (c)(16) and (17) of this section upon which a withholding agent may rely to treat the payment as a payment made to a payee or beneficial owner, and to ascertain the characteristics of the payee or beneficial owner that are relevant to withholding or reporting under chapter 3 of the Internal Revenue Code and the regulations thereunder. For purposes of this paragraph (b)(2)(vii), documentation also includes the agreement that the withholding agent has in effect with an authorized foreign agent in accordance with §1.1441-7(c)(2)(i). A withholding agent that is not required to obtain documentation with respect to a payment is considered to lack documentation for purposes of this paragraph (b)(2)(vii). For example, a withholding agent paying U.S. source interest to a person that is an exempt recipient, as defined in §1.6049-4(c)(1)(ii), is not required to obtain documentation from that person in order to determine whether an amount paid to that person is reportable under an applicable information reporting provision under chapter 61 of the Internal Revenue Code. The withholding agent must, however, treat the payment as made to an undocumented person for purposes of chapter 3 of the Internal Revenue Code. Therefore, the presumption rules of paragraph (b)(3)(iii) of this section apply to determine whether the person is presumed to be a U.S. person (in which case, no withholding is required under this section), or whether the person is presumed to be a foreign person (in which case 30-percent withholding is required under this section). See paragraph (b)(3)(v) of this section for special reliance rules in the case of a payment to a foreign intermediary and §1.1441-5(d) and (e)(6) for special reliance rules in the case of a payment to a flow-through entity.

(B) *Special rules applicable to a withholding certificate from a nonqualified intermediary or flow-through entity.*—(1) In the case of a payment made to a nonqualified intermediary, a flow-through entity (as defined in paragraph (c)(23) of this section), and a U.S. branch described in paragraph (b)(2)(iv) of this section (other than a branch that is treated as a U.S. person), a withholding agent can reliably associate the payment with valid documentation only to the extent that, prior to the payment, the withholding agent can allocate the payment to a valid nonqualified intermediary, flow-through, or U.S. branch withholding certificate; the withholding agent can reliably determine how much of the payment relates to valid documentation provided by a payee as determined under paragraph (c)(12) of this section (i.e., a person that is not itself an intermediary, flow-through entity, or U.S. branch); and the withholding agent has sufficient information to report the payment on Form 1042-S or Form 1099, if reporting is required. See paragraph (e)(3)(iii) of this section for the requirements of a nonqualified intermediary withholding certificate, paragraph (e)(3)(v) of this section for the requirements of a U.S. branch certificate, and §§1.1441-5(c)(3)(iii) and (e)(5)(iii) for the requirements of a flow-through withholding certificate. Thus, a payment cannot be reliably associated with valid documentation

provided by a payee to the extent such documentation is lacking or unreliable, or to the extent that information required to allocate and report all or a portion of the payment to each payee is lacking or unreliable. If a withholding certificate attached to an intermediary, U.S. branch, or flow-through withholding certificate is another intermediary, U.S. branch, or flow-through withholding certificate, the rules of this paragraph (b)(2)(vii)(B) apply by treating the share of the payment allocable to the other intermediary, U.S. branch, or flow-through entity as if the payment were made directly to such other entity. See paragraph (e)(3)(iv)(D) of this section for rules permitting information allocating a payment to documentation to be received after the payment is made.

(2) The rules of paragraph (b)(2)(vii)(B)(1) of this section are illustrated by the following examples:

Example 1. WH, a withholding agent, makes a payment of U.S. source interest to NQI, an intermediary that is a nonqualified intermediary. NQI provides a valid intermediary withholding certificate under paragraph (e)(3)(iii) of this section. NQI does not, however, provide valid documentation from the persons on whose behalf it receives the interest payment, and, therefore, the interest payment cannot be reliably associated with valid documentation provided by a payee. WH must apply the presumption rules of paragraph (b)(3)(v) of this section to the payment.

Example 2. The facts are the same as in *Example 1*, except that NQI does attach valid beneficial owner withholding certificates (as defined in paragraph (e)(2)(i) of this section) from A, B, C, and D establishing their status as foreign persons. NQI does not, however, provide WH with any information allocating the payment among A, B, C, and D and, therefore, WH cannot determine the portion of the payment that relates to each beneficial owner withholding certificate. The interest payment cannot be reliably associated with valid documentation from a payee and WH must apply the presumption rules of paragraph (b)(3)(v) of this section to the payment. See, however, paragraph (e)(3)(iv)(D) of this section providing special rules permitting allocation information to be received after a payment is made.

Example 3. The facts are the same as in *Example 2*, except that NQI does provide allocation information associated with its intermediary withholding certificate indicating that 25 percent of the interest payment is allocable to A and 25 percent to B. NQI does not provide any allocation information regarding the remaining 50 percent of the payment. WH may treat 25 percent of the payment as made to A and 25 percent as made to B. The remaining 50 percent of the payment cannot be reliably associated with valid documentation from a payee, however, since NQI did not provide information allocating the payment. Thus, the remaining 50 percent of the payment is subject to the presumption rules of paragraph (b)(3)(v) of this section.

Example 4. WH makes a payment of U.S. source interest to NQI1, an intermediary that is not a qualified intermediary. NQI1 provides WH with a valid nonqualified intermediary withholding certificate as well a valid beneficial owner withholding certificates from A and B and a valid nonqualified intermediary withholding certificate from NQI2. NQI2 has provided valid beneficial owner documentation from C sufficient to establish C's status as a foreign person. Based on information provided by NQI1, WH can allocate 20 percent of the interest payment to A, and 20 percent to B. Based on information that NQI2 provided NQI1 and that NQI1 provides to WH, WH can allocate 60 percent of the payment to NQI 2, but can only allocate one half of that payment (30 percent) to C. Therefore, WH cannot reliably associate 30 percent of the payment made to NQI2 with valid documentation and must apply the presumption rules of paragraph (b)(3)(v) of this section to that portion of the payment.

(C) *Special rules applicable to a withholding certificate provided by a qualified intermediary that does not assume primary withholding responsibility.*—(1) If a payment is made to a qualified intermediary that does not assume primary withholding responsibility under chapter 3 of the Internal Revenue Code or primary Form 1099 reporting and backup withholding responsibility under chapter 61 and section 3406 of the Internal Revenue Code for the payment, a withholding agent can reliably associate the payment with valid documentation only to the extent that, prior to the payment, the withholding agent has received a valid qualified intermediary withholding certificate and the withholding agent can reliably determine the portion of the payment that relates to a withholding rate pool, as defined in paragraph (e)(5)(v)(C) of this section. In the case of a withholding rate pool attributable to a U.S. non-exempt recipient, a payment cannot be reliably associated with valid documentation unless, prior to the payment, the qualified intermediary has provided the U.S. person's Form W-9 (or, in the absence of the form, the name, address, and TIN, if available, of the U.S. person) and sufficient information for the withholding agent to report the payment on Form 1099. See paragraph (e)(5)(v)(C)(2) of this section for special rules regarding allocation of payments among U.S. non-exempt recipients.

(2) The rules of this paragraph (b)(2)(vii)(C) are illustrated by the following examples:

Example 1. WH, a withholding agent, makes a payment of U.S. source dividends to QI. QI provides WH with a valid qualified intermediary withholding certificate on which it indicates that it does not assume primary withholding responsibility under chapter 3 of the Internal Revenue Code or primary Form 1099 reporting and backup withholding responsibility under chapter 61 and section 3406 of the Internal Revenue Code. QI does not provide any information allocating the dividend to withholding rate pools. WH cannot reliably associate the payment with valid payee documentation and therefore must apply the presumption rules of paragraph (b)(3)(v) of this section.

Example 2. WH makes a payment of U.S. source dividends to QI. QI has 5 customers: A, B, C, D, and E. QI has obtained documentation from A and B establishing their entitlement to a 15 percent rate of tax on U.S. source dividends under an income tax treaty. C is a U.S. person that is an exempt recipient as defined in paragraph (c)(20) of this section. D and E are U.S. non-exempt recipients who have provided Forms W-9 to QI. A, B, C, D, and E are each entitled to 20 percent of the dividend payment. QI provides WH with a valid qualified intermediary withholding certificate as described in paragraph (e)(2)(ii) of this section with which it associates the Forms W-9 from D and E. QI associates the following allocation information with its qualified intermediary withholding certificate: 40 percent of the payment is allocable to the 15 percent withholding rate pool, and 20 percent is allocable to each of D and E. QI does not provide any allocation information regarding the remaining 20 percent of the payment. WH cannot reliably associate 20 percent of the payment with valid documentation and, therefore, must apply the presumption rules of paragraph (b)(3)(v) of this section to that portion of the payment. The 20 percent of the payment allocable to the 15 percent withholding rate pool, and the portion of the payments allocable to D and E are payments that can be reliably associated with documentation.

(D) *Special rules applicable to a withholding certificate provided by a qualified intermediary that assumes primary withholding responsibility under chapter 3 of the Internal Revenue Code.*—(1) In the case of a payment made to a qualified intermediary that assumes primary withholding responsibility under chapter 3 of the Internal Revenue Code with respect to that payment (but does not assume primary Form 1099 reporting and backup withholding responsibility under chapter 61 and section 3406 of the Internal Revenue Code), a withholding agent can reliably associate the payment with valid documentation only to the extent that, prior to the payment, the withholding agent has received a valid qualified intermediary withholding certificate and the withholding agent can reliably determine the portion of the payment that relates to the withholding rate pool for which the qualified intermediary assumes primary withholding responsibility under chapter 3 of the Internal Revenue Code and the portion of the payment attributable to withholding rate pools for each U.S. non-exempt recipient for whom the qualified intermediary has provided a Form W-9 (or, in absence of the form, the name, address, and TIN, if available, of the U.S. non-exempt recipient). See paragraph (e)(5)(v)(C)(2) of this section for alternative allocation procedures for payments made to U.S. persons that are not exempt recipients.

(2) *Examples.*—The following examples illustrate the rules of paragraph (b)(2)(vii)(D)(1) of this section:

Example 1. WH makes a payment of U.S. source interest to QI, a qualified intermediary. QI provides WH with a withholding certificate that indicates that QI will assume primary withholding responsibility under chapter 3 of the Internal Revenue Code with respect to the payment. In addition, QI attaches a Form W-9 from A, a U.S. nonexempt recipient, as defined in paragraph (c)(21) of this section, and provides the name, address, and TIN of B, a U.S. person that is also a non-exempt recipient but who has not provided a Form W-9. QI associates a withholding statement with its qualified intermediary withholding certificate indicating that 10 percent of the payment is attributable to A, and 10 percent to B, and that QI will assume primary withholding responsibility with respect to the remaining 80 percent of the payment. WH can reliably associate the entire payment with valid documentation. Although under the presumption rule of paragraph (b)(3)(v) of this section, an undocumented person receiving U.S. source interest is generally presumed to be a foreign person, WH has actual knowledge that B is a U.S. non-exempt recipient and therefore must report the payment on Form 1099 and backup withhold on the interest payment under section 3406.

Example 2. The facts are the same as in *Example 1*, except that no Forms W-9 or other information have been provided for the 20 percent of the payment that is allocable to A and B. Thus, QI has accepted withholding responsibility for 80 percent of the payment, but has provided no information for the remaining 20 percent. In this case, 20 percent of the payment cannot be reliably associated with valid documentation, and WH must apply the presumption rule of paragraph (b)(3)(v) of this section.

(E) *Special rules applicable to a withholding certificate provided by a qualified intermediary that assumes primary Form 1099 reporting and backup withholding responsibility but not primary withholding under chapter 3.*—(1) If a payment is made to a qualified intermediary that assumes primary Form 1099 reporting and backup withholding responsibility for the payment (but does not assume primary withholding responsibility under chapter 3 of the Internal Revenue Code), a withholding agent can reliably associate the payment with valid documentation only to the extent that, prior to the payment, the withholding

agent has received a valid qualified intermediary withholding certificate and the withholding agent can reliably determine the portion of the payment that relates to a withholding rate pool or pools provided as part of the qualified intermediary's withholding statement and the portion of the payment for which the qualified intermediary assumes primary Form 1099 reporting and backup withholding responsibility.

(2) The following example illustrates the rules of paragraph (b)(2)((vii)(D)(1) of this section:

Example. WH makes a payment of U.S. source dividends to QI, a qualified intermediary. QI has provided WH with a valid qualified intermediary withholding certificate. QI states on its withholding statement accompanying the certificate that it assumes primary Form 1099 reporting and backup withholding responsibility but does not assume primary withholding responsibility under chapter 3 of the Internal Revenue Code. QI represents that 15 percent of the dividend is subject to a 30 percent rate of withholding, 75 percent of the dividend is subject to a 15 percent rate of withholding, and that QI assumed primary Form 1099 reporting and backup withholding for the remaining 10 percent of the payment. The entire payment can be reliably associated with valid documentation.

(F) *Special rules applicable to a withholding certificate provided by a qualified intermediary that assumes primary withholding responsibility under chapter 3 and primary Form 1099 reporting and backup withholding responsibility and a withholding certificate provided by a withholding foreign partnership.*—If a payment is made to a qualified intermediary that assumes both primary withholding responsibility under chapter 3 of the Internal Revenue Code and primary Form 1099 reporting and backup withholding responsibility under chapter 61 and section 3406 of the Internal Revenue Code for the payment, a withholding agent can reliably associate a payment with valid documentation provided that it receives a valid qualified intermediary withholding certificate as described in paragraph (e)(3)(ii) of this section. In the case of a payment made to a withholding foreign partnership, the withholding agent can reliably associate the payment with valid documentation to the extent it can associate the payment with a valid withholding certificate described in § 1.1441-5(c)(2)(iv).

(3) *Presumptions regarding payee's status in the absence of documentation.*—(i) *General rules.*—A withholding agent that cannot, prior to the payment, reliably associate (within the meaning of paragraph (b)(2)(vii) of this section) a payment of an amount subject to withholding (as described in § 1.1441-2(a)) with valid documentation may rely on the presumptions of this paragraph (b)(3) to determine the status of the payee as a U.S. or a foreign person and the payee's other relevant characteristics (e.g., as an owner

or intermediary, as an individual, trust, partnership, or corporation). The determination of withholding and reporting requirements applicable to payments to a person presumed to be a foreign person is governed only by the provisions of chapter 3 of the Code and the regulations thereunder. For the determination of withholding and reporting requirements applicable to payments to a person presumed to be a U.S. person, see chapter 61 of the Code, sections 3402, 3405, or 3406, and the regulations under these provisions. A presumption that a payee is a foreign payee is not a presumption that the payee is a foreign beneficial owner. Therefore, the provisions of this paragraph (b)(3) have no effect for purposes of reducing the withholding rate if associating the payment with documentation of foreign beneficial ownership is required as a condition for such rate reduction. See paragraph (b)(3)(ix) of this section for consequences to a withholding agent that fails to withhold in accordance with the presumptions set forth in this paragraph (b)(3) or if the withholding agent has actual knowledge or reason to know of facts that are contrary to the presumptions set forth in this paragraph (b)(3). See paragraph (b)(2)(vii) of this section for rules regarding the extent which a withholding agent can reliably associate a payment with documentation.

(ii) *Presumptions of classification as individual, corporation, partnership, etc.*.—(A) *In general.*—A withholding agent that cannot reliably associate a payment with a valid withholding certificate or that has received valid documentary evidence under §§ 1.1441-1(e)(1)(ii)(2) and 1.6049-5(c)(1) or (4) but cannot determine a payee's classification from the documentary evidence must apply the rules of this paragraph (b)(3)(ii) to determine the payee's classification as an individual, trust, estate, corporation, or partnership. The fact that a payee is presumed to have a certain status under the provisions of this paragraph (b)(3)(ii) does not mean that it is excused from furnishing documentation if documentation is otherwise required to obtain a reduced rate of withholding under this section. For example, if, for purposes of this paragraph (b)(3)(ii), a payee is presumed to be a tax-exempt organization based on § 1.6049-4(c)(1)(ii)(B), the withholding agent cannot rely on this presumption to reduce the rate of withholding on payments to such person (if such person is also presumed to be a foreign person under paragraph (b)(3)(iii)(A) of this section) because a reduction in the rate of withholding for payments to a foreign tax-exempt organization generally requires that a valid Form W-8 described in § 1.1441-9(b)(2) be furnished to the withholding agent.

(B) *No documentation provided.*—If the withholding agent cannot reliably associate a payment with a valid withholding certificate or valid documentary evidence, it must presume that the payee is an individual, a trust, or an estate, if the payee appears to be such person (e.g., based on the payee's name or other indications). In the absence of reliable indications that the payee is an individual, trust, or an estate, the withholding agent must presume that the payee is a corporation or one of the persons enumerated under § 1.6049-4(c)(1)(ii)(B) through (Q) if it can be so treated under § 1.6049-4(c)(1)(ii)(A)(*1*) or any one of the paragraphs under § 1.6049-4(c)(1)(ii)(B) through (Q) without the need to furnish documentation. If the withholding agent cannot treat a payee as a person described in § 1.6049-4(c)(1)(ii)(A)(*1*) through (Q), then the payee shall be presumed to be a partnership. If such a partnership is presumed to be foreign, it is not the beneficial owner of the income paid to it. See paragraph (c)(6) of this section. If such a partnership is presumed to be domestic, it is a U.S. non-exempt recipient for purposes of chapter 61 of the Internal Revenue Code.

(C) *Documentary evidence furnished for offshore account.*—If the withholding agent receives valid documentary evidence, as described in § 1.6049-5(c)(1) or (4), with respect to an offshore account from an entity but the documentary evidence does not establish the entity's classification as a corporation, trust, estate, or partnership, the withholding agent may presume (in the absence of actual knowledge otherwise) that the entity is the type of person enumerated under § 1.6049-4(c)(1)(ii)(B) through (Q) if it can be so treated under any one of those paragraphs without the need to furnish documentation. If the withholding agent cannot treat a payee as a person described in § 1.6049-4(c)(1)(ii)(B) through (Q), then the payee shall be presumed to be a corporation unless the withholding agent knows, or has reason to know, that the entity is not classified as a corporation for U.S. tax purposes. If a payee is, or is presumed to be, a corporation under this paragraph (b)(3)(ii)(C) and a foreign person under paragraph (b)(3)(iii) of this section, a withholding agent shall not treat the payee as the beneficial owner of income if the withholding agent knows, or has reason to know, that the payee is not the beneficial owner of the income. For this purpose, a withholding agent shall have reason to know that the payee is not a beneficial owner if the documentary evidence indicates that the payee is a bank, broker, intermediary, custodian, or other agent, or is treated under § 1.6049-4(c)(1)(ii)(B) through (Q) as such a person. A withholding agent may, however, treat such a person as a beneficial owner if the foreign person provides a statement, in writing and signed by a person with authority to sign the statement, that is attached to the documentary evidence stating it is the beneficial owner of the income.

Reg. §1.1441-1(b)(3)(ii)(C)

(iii) *Presumption of U.S. or foreign status.*— A payment that the withholding agent cannot reliably associate with documentation is presumed to be made to a U.S. person, except as otherwise provided in this paragraph (b)(3)(iii), in paragraphs (b)(3)(iv) and (v) of this section, or in § 1.1441-5(d) or (e).

(A) *Payments to exempt recipients.*—If a withholding agent cannot reliably associate a payment with documentation from the payee and the payee is an exempt recipient (as determined under the provisions of § 1.6049-4(c)(1)(ii) in the case of interest, or under similar provisions under chapter 61 of the Code applicable to the type of payment involved, but not including a payee that the withholding agent may treat as a foreign intermediary in accordance with paragraph (b)(3)(v) of this section), the payee is presumed to be a foreign person and not a U.S. person—

(1) If the withholding agent has actual knowledge of the payee's employer identification number and that number begins with the two digits "98";

(2) If the withholding agent's communications with the payee are mailed to an address in a foreign country;

(3) If the name of the payee indicates that the entity is the type of entity that is on the per se list of foreign corporations contained in § 301.7701-2(b)(8)(i) of this chapter; or

(4) If the payment is made outside the United States (as defined in § 1.6049-5(e)).

(B) *Scholarships and grants.*—A payment representing taxable scholarship or fellowship grant income that does not represent compensation for services (but is not excluded from tax under section 117) and that a withholding agent cannot reliably associate with documentation is presumed to be made to a foreign person if the withholding agent has a record that the payee has a U.S. visa that is not an immigrant visa. See section 871(c) and § 1.1441-4(c) for applicable tax rate and withholding rules.

(C) *Pensions, annuities, etc..*—A payment from a trust described in section 401(a), an annuity plan described in section 403(a), a payment with respect to any annuity, custodial account, or retirement income account described in section 403(b), or a payment from an individual retirement account or individual retirement annuity described in section 408 that a withholding agent cannot reliably associate with documentation is presumed to be made to a U.S. person only if the withholding agent has a record of a Social Security number for the payee and relies on a mailing address described in the following sentence. A mailing address is an address used for purposes of information reporting or otherwise communicating with the payee that is an address in the United States or in a foreign country with which the United States has an income

tax treaty in effect and the treaty provides that the payee, if an individual resident in that country, would be entitled to an exemption from U.S. tax on amounts described in this paragraph (b)(3)(iii)(C). Any payment described in this paragraph (b)(3)(iii)(C) that is not presumed to be made to a U.S. person is presumed to be made to a foreign person. A withholding agent making a payment to a person presumed to be a foreign person may not reduce the 30-percent amount of withholding required on such payment unless it receives a withholding certificate described in paragraph (e)(2)(i) of this section furnished by the beneficial owner. For reduction in the 30-percent rate, see §§ 1.1441-4(e) or 1.1441-6(b).

(D) *Certain payments to offshore accounts.*—A payment is presumed made to a foreign payee if the payment is made outside the United States (as defined in § 1.6049-5(e)) to an offshore account (as defined in § 1.6049-5(c)(1)) and the withholding agent does not have actual knowledge that the payee is a U.S. person. See § 1.6049-5(d)(2) and (3) for exceptions to this rule.

(E) *Certain payments for services.*—A payment for services is presumed to be made to a foreign person if—

(1) The payee is an individual;

(2) The withholding agent does not know, or have reason to know, that the payee is a U.S. citizen or resident;

(3) The withholding agent does not know, or have reason to know, that the income is (or may be) effectively connected with the conduct of a trade or business within the United States; and

(4) All of the services for which the payment is made were performed by the payee outside of the United States.

(iv) *Grace period.*—A withholding agent may choose to apply the provisions of § 1.6049-5(d)(2)(ii) regarding a 90-day grace period for purposes of this paragraph (b)(3) (by applying the term *withholding agent* instead of the term *payor*) to amounts described in § 1.1441-6(c)(2) and to amounts covered by a Form 8233 described in § 1.1441-4(b)(2)(ii). Thus, for these amounts, a withholding agent may choose to treat an account holder as a foreign person and withhold under chapter 3 of the Internal Revenue Code (and the regulations thereunder) while awaiting documentation. For purposes of determining the rate of withholding under this section, the withholding agent must withhold at the unreduced 30-percent rate at the time that the amounts are credited to an account. However, a withholding agent who can reliably associate the payment with a withholding certificate that is otherwise valid within the meaning of the applicable provisions except for the fact that it is transmitted by facsimile may rely on that facsimile form for purposes of withholding at the claimed reduced rate. For reporting of amounts credited both before and after the grace period, see § 1.1461-1(c)(4)(i)(A). The following adjustments shall be made at the expiration of the grace period:

(A) If, at the end of the grace period, the documentation is not furnished in the manner required under this section and the account holder is presumed to be a U.S. nonexempt recipient, then backup withholding applies to amounts credited to the account after the expiration of the grace period only. Amounts credited to the account during the grace period shall be treated as owned by a foreign payee and adjustments must be made to correct any underwithholding on such amounts in the manner described in § 1.1461-2.

(B) If, at the end of the grace period, the documentation is not furnished in the manner required under this section, or if documentation is furnished that does not support the claimed rate reduction, and the account holder is presumed to be a foreign person then adjustments must be made to correct any underwithholding on amounts credited to the account during the grace period, based on the adjustment procedures described in § 1.1461-2.

(v) *Special rules applicable to payments to foreign intermediaries.*—(A) *Reliance on claim of status as foreign intermediary.*—The presumption rules of paragraph (b)(3)(v)(B) of this section apply to a payment made to an intermediary (whether the intermediary is a qualified or nonqualified intermediary) that has provided a valid withholding certificate under paragraph (e)(3)(ii) or (iii) of this section (or has provided documentary evidence described in paragraph (b)(3)(ii)(C) of this section that indicates it is a bank, broker, custodian, intermediary, or other agent) to the extent the withholding agent cannot treat the payment as being reliably associated with valid documentation under the rules of paragraph (b)(2)(vii) of this section. For this purpose, a U.S. person's foreign branch that is a qualified intermediary defined in paragraph (e)(5)(ii) of this section shall be treated as a foreign intermediary. A payee that the withholding agent may not reliably treat as a foreign intermediary under this paragraph (b)(3)(v)(A) is presumed to be a payee other than an intermediary whose classification as an individual, corporation, partnership, etc., must be determined in accordance with paragraph (b)(3)(ii) of this section to the extent relevant. In addition, such payee is presumed to be a U.S. or a foreign payee based upon the presumptions described in paragraph (b)(3)(iii) of this section. The provisions of paragraph (b)(3)(v)(B) of this section are not relevant to a withholding agent that can reliably associate a payment with a withholding certificate from a person representing to be a qualified intermediary to the extent the qualified intermediary has assumed primary withholding respon-

sibility in accordance with paragraph (e)(5)(iv) of this section.

(B) *Beneficial owner documentation or allocation information is lacking or unreliable.*—Any portion of a payment that the withholding agent may treat as made to a foreign intermediary (whether a nonqualified or a qualified intermediary) but that the withholding agent cannot treat as reliably associated with valid documentation under the rules of paragraph (b)(2)(vii) of this section is presumed made to an unknown, undocumented foreign payee. As a result, a withholding agent must deduct and withhold 30 percent from any payment of an amount subject to withholding. If a withholding certificate attached to an intermediary certificate is another intermediary withholding certificate or a flow-through withholding certificate, the rules of this paragraph (b)(3)(v)(B) (or § 1.1441-5(d)(3) or (e)(6)(iii)) apply by treating the share of the payment allocable to the other intermediary or flow-through entity as if it were made directly to the other intermediary or flow-through entity. Any payment of an amount subject to withholding that is presumed made to an undocumented foreign person must be reported on Form 1042-S. See § 1.1461-1(c). See § 1.6049-5(d) for payments that are not subject to withholding.

(vi) *U.S. branches.*—The rules of paragraph (b)(3)(v)(B) of this section shall apply to payments to a U.S. branch described in paragraph (b)(2)(iv)(A) of this section that has provided a withholding certificate as described in paragraph (e)(3)(v) of this section on which it has not agreed to be treated as a U.S. person.

(vii) *Joint payees.*—(A) *In general.*—Except as provided in paragraph (b)(3)(vii)(B) of this section, if a withholding agent makes a payment to joint payees and cannot reliably associate a payment with valid documentation from all payees, the payment is presumed made to an unidentified U.S. person. However, if one of the joint payees provides a Form W-9 furnished in accordance with the procedures described in §§ 31.3406(d)-1 through 31.3406(d)-5 of this chapter, the payment shall be treated as made to that payee. See § 31.3406(h)-2 of this chapter for rules to determine the relevant payee if more than one Form W-9 is provided. For purposes of applying this paragraph (b)(3), the grace period rules in paragraph (b)(3)(iv) of this section shall apply only if each payee meets the conditions described in paragraph (b)(3)(iv) of this section.

(B) *Special rule for offshore accounts.*—If a withholding agent makes a payment to joint payees and cannot reliably associate a payment with valid documentation from all payees, the payment is presumed made to an unknown foreign payee if the payment is made outside the United States (as defined in § 1.6049-5(e)) to an offshore account (as defined in § 1.6049-5(c)(1)).

(viii) *Rebuttal of presumptions.*—A payee or beneficial owner may rebut the presumptions described in this paragraph (b)(3) by providing reliable documentation to the withholding agent or, if applicable, to the IRS.

(ix) *Effect of reliance on presumptions and of actual knowledge or reason to know otherwise.*— (A) *General rule.*—Except as otherwise provided in paragraph (b)(3)(ix)(B) of this section, a withholding agent that withholds on a payment under section 3402, 3405 or 3406 in accordance with the presumptions set forth in this paragraph (b)(3) shall not be liable for withholding under this section even it is later established that the beneficial owner of the payment is, in fact, a foreign person. Similarly, a withholding agent that withholds on a payment under this section in accordance with the presumptions set forth in this paragraph (b)(3) shall not be liable for withholding under section 3402 or 3405 or for backup withholding under section 3406 even if it is later established that the payee or beneficial owner is, in fact, a U.S. person. A withholding agent that, instead of relying on the presumptions described in this paragraph (b)(3), relies on its own actual knowledge to withhold a lesser amount, not withhold, or not report a payment, even though reporting of the payment or withholding a greater amount would be required if the withholding agent relied on the presumptions described in this paragraph (b)(3) shall be liable for tax, interest, and penalties to the extent provided under section 1461 and the regulations under that section. See paragraph (b)(7) of this section for provisions regarding such liability if the withholding agent fails to withhold in accordance with the presumptions described in this paragraph (b)(3).

(B) *Actual knowledge or reason to know that amount of withholding is greater than is required under the presumptions or that reporting of the payment is required.*—Notwithstanding the provisions of paragraph (b)(3)(ix)(A) of this section, a withholding agent may not rely on the presumptions described in this paragraph (b)(3) to the extent it has actual knowledge or reason to know that the status or characteristics of the payee or of the beneficial owner are other than what is presumed under this paragraph (b)(3) and, if based on such knowledge or reason to know, it should withhold (under this section or another withholding provision of the Code) an amount greater than would be the case if it relied on the presumptions described in this paragraph (b)(3) or it should report (under this section or under another provision of the Code) an amount that would not otherwise be reportable if it relied on the presumptions described in this paragraph (b)(3). In such a case, the withholding agent must rely on its actual knowledge or reason to know rather than on the presumptions set forth in this paragraph (b)(3). Failure to do so and, as a result, failure to withhold the higher amount or

to report the payment, shall result in liability for tax, interest, and penalties to the extent provided under sections 1461 and 1463 and the regulations under those sections.

(x) *Examples.*—The provisions of this paragraph (b)(3) are illustrated by the following examples:

Example 1. A withholding agent, W, makes a payment of U.S. source dividends to person X, Inc. at an address outside the United States. W cannot reliably associate the payment to X with documentation. Under §§ 1.6042-3(b)(1)(vii) and 1.6049-4(c)(1)(ii)(A)(*1*), W may treat X as a corporation. Thus, under the presumptions described in paragraph (b)(3)(iii) of this section, W must presume that X is a foreign person (because the payment is made outside the United States). However, W knows that X is a U.S. person who is an exempt recipient. W may not rely on its actual knowledge to not withhold under this section. If W's knowledge is, in fact, incorrect, W would be liable for tax, interest, and, if applicable, penalties, under section 1461. W would be permitted to reduce or eliminate its liability for the tax by establishing, in accordance with paragraph (b)(7) of this section, that the tax is not due or has been satisfied. If W's actual knowledge is, in fact, correct, W may nevertheless be liable for tax, interest, or penalties under section 1461 for the amount that W should have withheld based upon the presumptions. W would be permitted to reduce or eliminate its liability for the tax by establishing, in accordance with paragraph (b)(7) of this section, that its actual knowledge was, in fact, correct and that no tax or a lesser amount of tax was due.

Example 2. A withholding agent, W, makes a payment of U.S. source dividends to Y who does not qualify as an exempt recipient under §§ 1.6042-3(b)(1)(vii) and 1.6049-4(c)(1)(ii). W cannot reliably associate the payment to Y with documentation. Under the presumptions described in paragraph (b)(3)(iii) of this section, W must presume that Y is a U.S. person who is not an exempt recipient for purposes of section 6042. However, W knows that Y is a foreign person. W may not rely on its actual knowledge to withhold under this section rather than backup withhold under section 3406. If W's knowledge is, in fact, incorrect, W would be liable for tax, interest, and, if applicable, penalties, under section 3403. If W's actual knowledge is, in fact, correct, W may nevertheless be liable for tax, interest, or penalties under section 3403 for the amount that W should have withheld based upon the presumptions. Paragraph (b)(7) of this section does not apply to provide relief from liability under section 3403.

Example 3. A withholding agent, W, makes a payment of U.S. source dividends to X, Inc. W cannot reliably associate the payment to X, Inc. with documentation. X, Inc. presents none of the indicia of foreign status described in paragraph (b)(3)(iii)(A) of this section, but W has actual knowledge that X, Inc. is a foreign corporation. W may treat X, Inc. as an exempt recipient under §1.6042-3(b)(1)(vii). Because there are no indicia of foreign status, W would, absent actual knowledge or reason to know otherwise, be permitted to treat X, Inc. as a domestic corporation in accordance with the presumptions of paragraph (b)(3)(iii) of this section. However, under paragraph (b)(3)(ix)(B) of this section, W may not rely on the presumption of U.S. status since reliance on its actual knowledge requires that it withhold an amount greater than would be the case under the presumptions.

Example 4. A withholding agent, W, is a plan administrator who makes pension payments to person X with a mailing address in a foreign country with which the United States has an income tax treaty in effect. Under that treaty, the type of pension income paid to X is taxable solely in the country of residence. The plan administrator has a record of X's U.S. social security number. W has no actual knowledge or reason to know that X is a foreign person. W may rely on the presumption of paragraph (b)(3)(iii)(C) of this section in order to treat X as a U.S. person. Therefore, any withholding and reporting requirements for the payment are governed by the provisions of section 3405 and the regulations under that section.

(4) *List of exemptions from, or reduced rates of, withholding under chapter 3 of the Code.*—A withholding agent that has determined that the payee is a foreign person for purposes of paragraph (b)(1) of this section must determine whether the payee is entitled to a reduced rate of withholding under section 1441, 1442, or 1443. This paragraph (b)(4) identifies items for which a reduction in the rate of withholding may apply and whether the rate reduction is conditioned upon documentation being furnished to the withholding agent. Documentation required under this paragraph (b)(4) is documentation that a withholding agent must be able to associate with a payment upon which it can rely to treat the payment as made to a foreign person that is the beneficial owner of the payment in accordance with paragraph (e)(1)(ii) of this section. This paragraph (b)(4) also cross-references other sections of the Code and applicable regulations in which some of these exceptions, exemptions, or reductions are further explained. See, for example, paragraph (b)(4)(viii) of this section, dealing with effectively connected income, that cross-references §1.1441-4(a); see paragraph (b)(4)(xv) of this section, dealing with exemptions from, or reductions of, withholding under an income tax treaty, that cross-references §1.1441-6. This paragraph (b)(4) is not an exclusive list of items to which a reduction of the rate of withholding may apply and, thus, does not preclude an exemption from, or reduction in, the rate of withholding that may otherwise be al-

lowed under the regulations under the provisions of chapter 3 of the Code for a particular item of income identified in this paragraph (b)(4).

(i) Portfolio interest described in section 871(h) or 881(c) and substitute interest payments described in §1.871-7(b)(2) or 1.881-2(b)(2) are exempt from withholding under section 1441(a). See §1.871-14 for regulations regarding portfolio interest and section 1441(c)(9) for exemption from withholding. Documentation establishing foreign status is required for interest on an obligation in registered form to qualify as portfolio interest. See section 871(h)(2)(B)(ii) and §1.871-14(c)(1)(ii)(C). For special documentation rules regarding foreign-targeted registered obligations described in §1.871-14(e)(2), see §1.871-14(e)(3) and (4) and, in particular, §1.871-14(e)(4)(i)(A) and (ii)(A) regarding the time when the withholding agent must receive the documentation. The documentation furnished for purposes of qualifying interest as portfolio interest serves as the basis for the withholding exemption for purposes of this section and for purposes of establishing foreign status for purposes of section 6049. See §1.6049-5(b)(8). Documentation establishing foreign status is not required for qualifying interest on an obligation in bearer form described in §1.871-14(b)(1) as portfolio interest. However, in certain cases, documentation for portfolio interest on a bearer obligation may have to be furnished in order to establish foreign status for purposes of the information reporting provisions of section 6049 and backup withholding under section 3406. See §1.6049-5(b)(7).

(ii) Bank deposit interest and similar types of deposit interest (including original issue discount) described in section 871(i)(2)(A) or 881(d) that are from sources within the United States are exempt from withholding under section 1441(a). See section 1441(c)(10). Documentation establishing foreign status is not required for purposes of this withholding exemption but may have to be furnished for purposes of the information reporting provisions of section 6049 and backup withholding under section 3406. See §1.6049-5(d)(3)(iii) for exceptions to the foreign payee and exempt recipient rules regarding this type of income. See also §1.6049-5(b)(11) for applicable documentation exemptions for certain bank deposit interest paid on obligations in bearer form.

(iii) Bank deposit interest (including original issue discount) described in section 861(a)(1)(B) is exempt from withholding under sections 1441(a) as income that is not from U.S. sources. Documentation establishing foreign status is not required for purposes of this withholding exemption but may have to be furnished for purposes of the information reporting provisions of section 6049 and backup withholding under section 3406. Reporting requirements for payments of such interest are governed by section

6049 and the regulations under that section. See §1.6049-5(b)(12) and alternative documentation rules under §1.6049-5(c)(1).

(iv) Interest or original issue discount from sources within the United States on certain short-term obligations described in section 871(g)(1)(B) or 881(a)(3) is exempt from withholding under sections 1441(a). Documentation establishing foreign status is not required for purposes of this withholding exemption but may have to be furnished for purposes of the information reporting provisions of section 6049 and backup withholding under section 3406. See §1.6049-5(b)(12) for applicable documentation for establishing foreign status and §1.6049-5(d)(3)(iii) for exceptions to the foreign payee and exempt recipient rules regarding this type of income. See also §1.6049-5(b)(10) for applicable documentation exemptions for certain obligations in bearer form.

(v) Income from sources without the United States is exempt from withholding under sections 1441(a). Documentation establishing foreign status is not required for purposes of this withholding exemption but may have to be furnished for purposes of the information reporting provisions of section 6049 or other applicable provisions of chapter 61 of the Code and backup withholding under section 3406. See, for example, §1.6049-5(b)(6) and (12) and alternative documentation rules under §1.6049-5(c). See also paragraph (b)(5) of this section for cross references to other applicable provisions of the regulations under chapter 61 of the Code.

(vi) Distributions from certain domestic corporations described in section 871(i)(2)(B) or 881(d) are exempt from withholding under section 1441(a). See section 1441(c)(10). Documentation establishing foreign status is not required for purposes of this withholding exemption but may have to be furnished for purposes of the information reporting provisions of section 6042 and backup withholding under section 3406. See §1.6042-3(b)(1)(iii) through (vi).

(vii) Dividends paid by certain foreign corporations that are treated as income from sources within the United States by reason of section 861(a)(2)(B) are exempt from withholding under section 884(e)(3) to the extent that the distributions are paid out of earnings and profits in any taxable year that the corporation was subject to branch profits tax for that year. Documentation establishing foreign status is not required for purposes of this withholding exemption but may have to be furnished for purposes of the information reporting provisions of section 6042 and backup withholding under section 3406. See §1.6042-3(b)(1)(iii) through (vii).

(viii) Certain income that is effectively connected with the conduct of a U.S. trade or business is exempt from withholding under section 1441(a). See section 1441(c)(1). Documentation establishing foreign status and status of the income as effectively connected must be furnished for purposes of this withholding exemption to the extent required under the provisions of §1.1441-4(a). Documentation furnished for this purpose also serves as documentation establishing foreign status for purposes of applicable information reporting provisions under chapter 61 of the Code and for backup withholding under section 3406. See, for example, §1.6041-4(a)(1).

(ix) Certain income with respect to compensation for personal services of an individual that are performed in the United States is exempt from withholding under section 1441(a). See section 1441(c)(4) and §1.1441-4(b). However, such income may be subject to withholding as wages under section 3402. Documentation establishing foreign status must be furnished for purposes of any withholding exemption or reduction to the extent required under §1.1441-4(b) or 31.3401(a)(6)-1(e) and (f) of this chapter. Documentation furnished for this purpose also serves as documentation establishing foreign status for purposes of information reporting under section 6041. See §1.6041-4(a)(1).

(x) Amounts described in section 871(f) that are received as annuities from certain qualified plans are exempt from withholding under section 1441(a). See section 1441(c)(7). Documentation establishing foreign status must be furnished for purposes of the withholding exemption as required under §1.1441-4(d). Documentation furnished for this purpose also serves as documentation establishing foreign status for purposes of information reporting under section 6041. See §1.6041-4(a)(1).

(xi) Payments to a foreign government (including a foreign central bank of issue) that are excludable from gross income under section 892(a) are exempt from withholding under section 1442. See §1.1441-8(b). Documentation establishing status as a foreign government is required for purposes of this withholding exemption. Payments to a foreign government are exempt from information reporting under chapter 61 of the Code (see §1.6049-4(c)(1)(ii)(F)).

(xii) Payments of certain interest income to a foreign central bank of issue or the Bank for International Settlements that are exempt from tax under section 895 are exempt from withholding under section 1442. Documentation establishing eligibility for such exemption is required to the extent provided in §1.1441-8(c)(1). Payments to a foreign central bank of issue or to the Bank for International Settlements are exempt from information reporting under chapter 61 of the Code (see §1.6049-4(c)(1)(ii)(H) and (M)).

(xiii) Amounts derived by a foreign central bank of issue from bankers' acceptances described in section 871(i)(2)(C) or 881(d) are exempt from tax and, therefore, from withholding. See section 1441(c)(10). Documentation establishing foreign status is not required for purposes of this withholding exemption if the name of the payee and other facts surrounding the payment reasonably indicate that the beneficial owner of the payment is a foreign central bank of issue as defined in §1.861-2(b)(4). See §1.1441-8(c)(2) for withholding procedures. See also §§1.6049-4(c)(1)(ii)(H) and 1.6041-3(q)(8) for a similar exemption from information reporting.

(xiv) Payments to an international organization from investments in the United States of stocks, bonds, or other domestic securities or from interest on deposits in banks in the United States of funds belonging to such international organization are exempt from tax under section 892(b) and, thus, from withholding. Documentation establishing status as an international organization is not required if the name of the payee and other facts surrounding the payment reasonably indicate that the beneficial owner of the payment is an international organization within the meaning of section 7701(a)(18). See §1.1441-8(d). Payments to an international organization are exempt from information reporting under chapter 61 of the Code (see §1.6049-4(c)(1)(ii)(G)).

(xv) Amounts may be exempt from, or subject to a reduced rate of, withholding under an income tax treaty. Documentation establishing eligibility for benefits under an income tax treaty is required for this purpose as provided under §§1.1441-6. Documentation furnished for this purpose also serves as documentation establishing foreign status for purposes of applicable information reporting provisions under chapter 61 of the Code and for backup withholding under section 3406. See, for example, §1.6041-4(a)(1).

(xvi) Amounts of scholarships and grants paid to certain exchange or training program participants that do not represent compensation for services but are not excluded from tax under section 117 are subject to a reduced rate of withholding of 14-percent under section 1441(b). Documentation establishing foreign status is required for purposes of this reduction in rate as provided under §1.1441-4(c). This income is not subject to information reporting under chapter 61 of the Code nor to backup withholding under section 3406. The compensatory portion of a scholarship or grant is reportable as wage income. See §1.6041-3(o).

(xvii) Amounts paid to a foreign organization described in section 501(c) are exempt from withholding under section 1441 to the extent that the amounts are not income includible under section 512 in computing the organization's unrelated business taxable income and are not subject to the tax imposed by section 4948(a). Documentation establishing status as a tax-exempt organization is required for purposes of this exemption to the extent provided in §1.1441-9. Amounts includible under section 512 in computing the organization's unrelated business taxable income are subject to withholding to the extent provided in section 1443(a) and

§1.1443-1(a). Gross investment income (as defined in section 4940(c)(2)) of a private foundation is subject to withholding at a 4-percent rate to the extent provided in section 1443(b) and §1.1443-1(b). Payments to a tax-exempt organization are exempt from information reporting under chapter 61 of the Code and the regulations thereunder (see §1.6049-4(c)(1)(ii)(B)(1)).

(xviii) Per diem amounts for subsistence paid by the U.S. government to a nonresident alien individual who is engaged in any program of training in the United States under the Mutual Security Act of 1954 are exempt from withholding under section 1441(a). See section 1441(c)(6). Documentation of foreign status is not required under §1.1441-4(e) for purposes of establishing eligibility for this exemption. See §1.6041-3(p).

(xix) Interest with respect to tax-free covenant bonds issued prior to 1934 is subject to special withholding procedures set forth in §1.1461-1 in effect prior to January 1, 2001 (see §1.1461-1 as contained in 26 CFR part 1, revised April 1, 1999).

(xx) Income from certain gambling winnings of a nonresident alien individual is exempt from tax under section 871(j) and from withholding under section 1441(a). See section 1441(c)(11). Documentation establishing foreign status is not required for purposes of this exemption but may have to be furnished for purposes of the information reporting provisions of section 6041 and backup withholding under section 3406. See §§1.6041-1 and 1.6041-4(a)(1).

(xxi) Any payments not otherwise mentioned in this paragraph (b)(4) shall be subject to withholding at the rate of 30-percent if it is an amount subject to withholding (as defined in §1.1441-2(a)) unless and to the extent the IRS may otherwise prescribe in published guidance (see §601.601(d)(2) of this chapter) or unless otherwise provided in regulations under chapter 3 of the Code.

(5) *Establishing foreign status under applicable provisions of chapter 61 of the Code.*—This paragraph (b)(5) identifies relevant provisions of the regulations under chapter 61 of the Code that exempt payments from information reporting, and therefore, from backup withholding under section 3406, based on the payee's status as a foreign person. Many of these exemptions require that the payee's foreign status be established in order for the exemption to apply. The regulations under applicable provisions of chapter 61 of the Code generally provide that the documentation described in this section may be relied upon for purposes of determining foreign status.

(i) Payments to a foreign person that are governed by section 6041 (dealing with certain trade or business income) are exempt from information reporting under §1.6041-4(a).

(ii) Payments to a foreign person that are governed by section 6041A (dealing with remuneration for services and certain sales) are exempt from information reporting under § 1.6041A-1(d)(3).

(iii) Payments to a foreign person that are governed by section 6042 (dealing with dividends) are exempt from information reporting under § 1.6042-3(b)(1)(iii) through (vi).

(iv) Payments to a foreign person that are governed by section 6044 (dealing with patronage dividends) are exempt from information reporting under § 1.6044-3(c)(1).

(v) Payments to a foreign person that are governed by section 6045 (dealing with broker proceeds) are exempt from information reporting under § 1.6045-1(g).

(vi) Payments to a foreign person that are governed by section 6049 (dealing with interest) to a foreign person are exempt from information reporting under § 1.6049-5(b)(6) through (15).

(vii) Payments to a foreign person that are governed by section 6050N (dealing with royalties) are exempt from information reporting under § 1.6050N-1(c).

(viii) Payments to a foreign person that are governed by section 6050P (dealing with income from cancellation of debt) are exempt from information reporting under section 6050P or the regulations under that section except to the extent provided in Notice 96-61 (1996-2 C.B. 227); see also § 601.601(b)(2) of this chapter.

(6) *Rules of withholding for payments by a foreign intermediary or certain U.S. branches.*—(i) *In general.*—A foreign intermediary described in paragraph (e)(3)(i) of this section or a U.S. branch described in paragraph (b)(2)(iv) of this section that receives an amount subject to withholding (as defined in § 1.1441-2(a)) shall be required to withhold (if another withholding agent has not withheld the full amount required) and report such payment under chapter 3 of the Internal Revenue Code and the regulations thereunder except as otherwise provided in this paragraph (b)(6). A nonqualified intermediary or U.S. branch described in paragraph (b)(2)(iv) of this section (other than a branch that is treated as a U.S. person) shall not be required to withhold or report if it has provided a valid nonqualified intermediary withholding certificate or a U.S. branch withholding certificate, it has provided all of the information required by paragraph (e)(3)(iv) of this section (withholding statement), and it does not know, and has no reason to know, that another withholding agent failed to withhold the correct amount or failed to report the payment correctly under § 1.1461-1(c). A qualified intermediary's obligations to withhold and report shall be determined in accordance with its qualified intermediary withholding agreement.

(ii) *Examples.*—The following examples illustrate the rules of paragraph (b)(6)(i) of this section:

Example 1. FB, a foreign bank, acts an intermediary for five different persons, A, B, C, D, and E, each of whom owns U.S. securities that generate U.S. source dividends. The dividends are paid by USWA, a U.S. withholding agent. FB furnished USWA with a nonqualified intermediary withholding certificate, described in paragraph (e)(3)(iii) of this section, to which it attached the withholding certificates of each of A, B, C, D, and E. The withholding certificates from A and B claim a 15 percent reduced rate of withholding under an income tax treaty. C, D, and E claim no reduced rate of withholding. FB provides a withholding statement that meets all of the requirements of paragraph (e)(3)(iv) of this section, including information allocating 20 percent of each dividend payment to each of A, B, C, D, and E. FB does not have actual knowledge or reason to know that USWA did not withhold the correct amounts or report the dividends on Forms 1042-S to each of A, B, C, D, and E. FB is not required to withhold or to report the dividends to A, B, C, D, and E.

Example 2. The facts are the same as in *Example 1*, except that FB did not provide any information for USWA to determine how much of the dividend payments were made to A, B, C, D, and E. Because USWA could not reliably associate the dividend payments with documentation under paragraph (b)(2)(vii) of this section, USWA applied the presumption rules of paragraph (b)(3)(v) of this section and withheld 30 percent from all dividend payments. In addition, USWA filed a single Form 1042-S reporting the payment to an unknown foreign payee. FB is deemed to know that USWA did not report the payment to A, B, C, D, and E because it did not provide all of the information required on a withholding statement under paragraph (e)(3)(iv) of this section (i.e., allocation information). Although FB is not required to withhold on the payment because the full 30 percent withholding was imposed by USWA, it is required to report the payments on Forms 1042-S to A, B, C, D, and E. FB's intentional failure to do so will subject it to intentional disregard penalties under sections 6721 and 6722.

(7) *Liability for failure to obtain documentation timely or to act in accordance with applicable presumptions.*—(i) *General rule.*—A withholding agent that cannot reliably associate a payment with documentation on the date of payment and that does not withhold under this section, or withholds at less than the 30-percent rate prescribed under section 1441(a) and paragraph (b)(1) of this section, is liable under section 1461 for the tax required to be withheld under chapter 3 of the Code and the regulations thereunder, without the benefit of a reduced rate unless—

(A) The withholding agent has appropriately relied on the presumptions described in paragraph (b)(3) of this section (including the grace period described in paragraph (b)(3)(iv) of this section) in order to treat the payee as a U.S.

person or, if applicable, on the presumptions described in § 1.1441-4(a)(2)(ii) or (3)(i) to treat the payment as effectively connected income; or

(B) The withholding agent can demonstrate to the satisfaction of the district director or the Assistant Commissioner (International) that the proper amount of tax, if any, was in fact paid to the IRS; or

(C) No documentation is required under section 1441 or this section in order for a reduced rate of withholding to apply.

(D) The withholding agent has complied with the provisions of § 1.1441-6(c) or (g).

(ii) *Proof that tax liability has been satisfied.*—Proof of payment of tax may be established for purposes of paragraph (b)(7)(i)(B) of this section on the basis of a Form 4669 (or such other form as the IRS may prescribe in published guidance (see § 601.601(d)(2) of this chapter)), establishing the amount of tax, if any, actually paid by or for the beneficial owner on the income. Proof that a reduced rate of withholding was, in fact, appropriate under the provisions of chapter 3 of the Code and the regulations thereunder may also be established after the date of payment by the withholding agent on the basis of a valid withholding certificate or other appropriate documentation furnished after that date. However, in the case of a withholding certificate or other appropriate documentation received after the date of payment (or after the grace period specified in paragraph (b)(3)(iv) of this section), the district director or the Assistant Commissioner (International) may require additional proof if it is determined that the delays in obtaining the withholding certificate affect its reliability.

(iii) *Liability for interest and penalties.*—For payments made after December 31, 2000, if a withholding agent fails to deduct and withhold any tax imposed under sections 1441 or 1442, and the tax against which such tax may be credited under section 1462 is paid, then the amount of tax required to be deducted and withheld shall not be collected from the withholding agent. However, the withholding agent is not relieved from liability for interest or any penalties or additions to the tax otherwise applicable in respect of the failure to deduct and withhold. See section 1463. Further, in the event that a tax liability is assessed against the beneficial owner under section 871, 881, or 882 and interest under section 6601(a) is assessed against, and collected from, the beneficial owner, the interest charge imposed on the withholding agent shall be abated to that extent so as to avoid the imposition of a double interest charge.

(iv) *Special effective date.*—See paragraph (f)(2)(ii) of this section for the special effective date applicable to this paragraph (b)(7).

(8) *Adjustments, refunds, or credits of overwithheld amounts.*—If the amount withheld under section 1441, 1442, or 1443 is greater than the tax due by the withholding agent or the taxpayer, adjustments may be made in accordance with the procedures described in § 1.1461-2(a). Alternatively, refunds or credits may be claimed in accordance with the procedures described in § 1.1464-1, relating to refunds or credits claimed by the beneficial owner, or § 1.6414-1, relating to refunds or credits claimed by the withholding agent. If an amount was withheld under section 3406 or is subsequently determined to have been paid to a foreign person, see paragraph (b)(3)(vii) of this section and § 31.6413(a)-3(a)(1) of this chapter.

(9) *Payments to joint owners.*—A payment to joint owners that requires documentation in order to reduce the rate of withholding under chapter 3 of the Code and the regulations thereunder does not qualify for such reduced rate unless the withholding agent can reliably associate the payment with documentation from each owner. Notwithstanding the preceding sentence, a payment to joint owners qualifies as a payment exempt from withholding under this section if any one of the owners provides a certificate of U.S. status on a Form W-9 in accordance with paragraph (d)(2) or (3) of this section or the withholding agent can associate the payment with an intermediary or flow-through withholding certificate upon which it can rely to treat the payment as made to a U.S. payee under paragraph (d)(4) of this section. See § 31.3406(h)-2(a)(3)(i)(B) of this chapter.

(c) *Definitions.*—(1) *Withholding.*—The term *withholding* means the deduction and withholding of tax at the applicable rate from the payment.

(2) *Foreign and U.S. person.*—The term *foreign person* means a nonresident alien individual, a foreign corporation, a foreign partnership, a foreign trust, a foreign estate, and any other person that is not a U.S. person described in the next sentence. Solely for purposes of the regulations under chapter 3 of the Internal Revenue Code, the term *foreign person* also means, with respect to a payment by a withholding agent, a foreign branch of a U.S. person that furnishes an intermediary withholding certificate described in paragraph (e)(3)(ii) of this section. Such a branch continues to be a U.S. payor for purposes of chapter 61 of the Internal Revenue Code. See § 1.6049-5(c)(4). A U.S. person is a person described in section 7701(a)(30), the U.S. government (including an agency or instrumentality thereof), a State (including an agency or instrumentality thereof), or the District of Columbia (including an agency or instrumentality thereof).

(3) *Individual.*—(i) *Alien individual.*—The term *alien individual* means an individual who is

not a citizen or a national of the United States. See § 1.1-1(c).

(ii) *Nonresident alien individual.*—The term *nonresident alien individual* means a person described in section 7701(b)(1)(B), an alien individual who is a resident of a foreign country under the residence article of an income tax treaty and § 301.7701(b)-7(a)(1) of this chapter, or an alien individual who is a resident of Puerto Rico, Guam, the Commonwealth of Northern Mariana Islands, the U.S. Virgin Islands, or American Samoa as determined under § 301.7701(b)-1(d) of this chapter. An alien individual who has made an election under section 6013(g) or (h) to be treated as a resident of the United States is nevertheless treated as a nonresident alien individual for purposes of withholding under chapter 3 of the Code and the regulations thereunder.

(4) *Certain foreign corporations.*—For purposes of this section, a corporation created or organized in Guam, the Commonwealth of Northern Mariana Islands, the U.S. Virgin Islands, and American Samoa, is not treated as a foreign corporation if the requirements of sections 881(b)(1)(A), (B), and (C) are met for such corporation. Further, a payment made to a foreign government or an international organization shall be treated as a payment made to a foreign corporation for purposes of withholding under chapter 3 of the Code and the regulations thereunder.

(5) *Financial institution and foreign financial institution.*—For purposes of the regulations under chapter 3 of the Code, the term *financial institution* means a person described in § 1.165-12(c)(1)(iv) (not including a person providing pension or other similar benefits or a regulated investment company or other mutual fund, unless otherwise indicated) and the term *foreign financial institution* means a financial institution that is a foreign person, as defined in paragraph (c)(2) of this section.

(6) *Beneficial owner.*—(i) *General rule.*—This paragraph (c)(6) defines the term *beneficial owner* for payments of income other than a payment for which a reduced rate of withholding is claimed under an income tax treaty. The term *beneficial owner* means the person who is the owner of the income for tax purposes and who beneficially owns that income. A person shall be treated as the owner of the income to the extent that it is required under U.S. tax principles to include the amount paid in gross income under section 61 (determined without regard to an exclusion or exemption from gross income under the Internal Revenue Code). Beneficial ownership of income is determined under the provisions of section 7701(l) and the regulations under that section and any other applicable general U.S. tax principles, including principles governing the determination of whether a transaction is a conduit transaction. Thus, a person receiving income in a

capacity as a nominee, agent, or custodian for another person is not the beneficial owner of the income. In the case of a scholarship, the student receiving the scholarship is the beneficial owner of that scholarship. In the case of a payment of an amount that is not income, the beneficial owner determination shall be made under this paragraph (c)(6) as if the amount were income.

(ii) *Special rules.*—(A) *General rule.*—The beneficial owners of income paid to an entity described in this paragraph (c)(6)(ii) are those persons described in paragraphs (c)(6)(ii)(B) through (D) of this section.

(B) *Foreign partnerships.*—The beneficial owners of income paid to a foreign partnership (whether a nonwithholding or a withholding foreign partnership) are the partners in the partnership, unless they themselves are not the beneficial owners of the income under this paragraph (c)(6). For example, a partnership (first tier) that is a partner in another partnership (second tier) is not the beneficial owner of income paid to the second tier partnership since the first tier partnership is not the owner of the income under U.S. tax principles. Rather, the partners of the first tier partnership are the beneficial owners (to the extent they are not themselves persons that are not beneficial owners under this paragraph (c)(6)). See § 1.1441-5(b) for applicable withholding procedures for payments to a domestic partnership. See also § 1.1441-5(c)(3)(ii) for applicable withholding procedures for payments to a foreign partnership where one of the partners (at any level in the chain of tiers) is a domestic partnership.

(C) *Foreign simple trusts and foreign grantor trusts.*—The beneficial owners of income paid to a foreign simple trust, as described in paragraph (c)(23) of this section, are the beneficiaries of the trust, unless they themselves are not the beneficial owners of the income under this paragraph (c)(6). The beneficial owners of income paid to a foreign grantor trust, as described in paragraph (c)(26) of this section, are the persons treated as the owners of the trust, unless they themselves are not the beneficial owners of the income under this paragraph (c)(6).

(D) *Other foreign trusts and foreign estates.*—The beneficial owner of income paid to a foreign complex trust as defined in paragraph (c)(25) of this section or to a foreign estate is the foreign complex trust or estate itself.

(7) *Withholding agent.*—For a definition of the term *withholding agent* and applicable rules, see § 1.1441-7.

(8) *Person.*—For purposes of the regulations under chapter 3 of the Code, the term *person* shall mean a person described in section 7701(a)(1) and the regulations under that section

and a U.S. branch to the extent treated as a U.S. person under paragraph (b)(2)(iv) of this section. For purposes of the regulations under chapter 3 of the Code, the term *person* does not include a wholly-owned entity that is disregarded for federal tax purposes under § 301.7701-2(c)(2) of this chapter as an entity separate from its owner. See paragraph (b)(2)(iii) of this section for procedures applicable to payments to such entities.

(9) *Source of income.*—The source of income is determined under the provisions of part I (section 861 and following) , subchapter N, chapter 1 of the Code and the regulations under those provisions.

(10) *Chapter 3 of the Code.*—For purposes of the regulations under sections 1441, 1442, and 1443, any reference to chapter 3 of the Code shall not include references to sections 1445 and 1446, unless the context indicates otherwise.

(11) *Reduced rate.*—For purposes of regulations under chapter 3 of the Code, and other withholding provisions of the Code, the term *reduced rate*, when used in regulations under chapter 3 of the Code, shall include an exemption from tax.

(12) *Payee.*—For purposes of chapter 3 of the Internal Revenue Code, the term *payee* of a payment is determined under paragraph (b)(2) of this section, § 1.1441-5(c)(1) (relating to partnerships), and § 1.1441-5(e)(2) and (3) (relating to trusts and estates) and includes foreign persons, U.S. exempt recipients, and U.S. non-exempt recipients. A nonqualified intermediary and a qualified intermediary (to the extent it does not assume primary withholding responsibility) are not payees if they are acting as intermediaries and not the beneficial owner of income. In addition, a flow-through entity is not a payee unless the income is (or is deemed to be) effectively connected with the conduct of a trade or business in the United States. See § 1.6049-5(d)(1) for rules to determine the payee for purposes of chapter 61 of the Internal Revenue Code. See § § 1.1441-1(b)(3), 1.1441-5(d), and (e)(6) and 1.6049-5(d)(3) for presumption rules that apply if a payee's identity cannot be determined on the basis of valid documentation.

(13) *Intermediary.*—An *intermediary* means, with respect to a payment that it receives, a person that, for that payment, acts as a custodian, broker, nominee, or otherwise as an agent for another person, regardless of whether such other person is the beneficial owner of the amount paid, a flow-through entity, or another intermediary.

(14) *Nonqualified intermediary.*—A *nonqualified intermediary* means any intermediary that is not a U.S. person and not a qualified intermediary, as defined in paragraph (e)(5)(ii) of this section, or a qualified intermediary that is not

acting in its capacity as a qualified intermediary with respect to a payment. For example, to the extent an entity that is a qualified intermediary provides another withholding agent with a foreign beneficial owner withholding certificate as defined in paragraph (e)(2)(i) of this section, the entity is not acting in its capacity as a qualified intermediary. Notwithstanding the preceding sentence, a qualified intermediary is acting as a qualified intermediary to the extent it provides another withholding agent with Forms W-9, or other information regarding U.S. non-exempt recipients pursuant to its qualified intermediary agreement with the IRS.

(15) *Qualified intermediary.*—The term *qualified intermediary* is defined in paragraph (e)(5)(ii) of this section.

(16) *Withholding certificate.*—The term *withholding certificate* means a Form W-8 described in paragraph (e)(2)(i) of this section (relating to foreign beneficial owners), paragraph (e)(3)(i) of this section (relating to foreign intermediaries), § 1.1441-5(c)(2)(iv), (c)(3)(iii), and (e)(3)(iv) (relating to flow-through entities), a Form 8233 described in § 1.1441-4(b)(2), a Form W-9 as described in paragraph (d) of this section, a statement described in § 1.871-14(c)(2)(v) (relating to portfolio interest), or any other certificates that under the Internal Revenue Code or regulations certifies or establishes the status of a payee or beneficial owner as a U.S. or a foreign person.

(17) *Documentary evidence: other appropriate documentation.*—The terms *documentary evidence* or *other appropriate documentation* refer to documents other than a withholding certificate that may be provided for payments made outside the United States to offshore accounts or any other evidence that under the Internal Revenue Code or regulations certifies or establishes the status of a payee or beneficial owner as a U.S. or foreign person. See § § 1.1441-6(b)(2), (c)(3) and (4) (relating to treaty benefits), and 1.6049-5(c)(1) and (4) (relating to chapter 61 reporting). Also see § 1.1441-4(a)(3)(ii) regarding documentary evidence for notional principal contracts.

(18) *Documentation.*—The term *documentation* refers to both withholding certificates, as defined in paragraph (c)(16) of this section, and documentary evidence or other appropriate documentation, as defined in paragraph (c)(17) of this section.

(19) *Payor.*—The term *payor* is defined in § 31.3406(a)-2 of this chapter and § 1.6049-4(a)(2) and generally includes a withholding agent, as defined in § 1.1441-7(a). The term also includes any person that makes a payment to an intermediary, flow-through entity, or U.S. branch that is not treated as a U.S. person to the extent the intermediary, flow-through, or U.S. branch provides a Form W-9 or other appropriate information relating to a payee so that the payment can

Reg. §1.1441-1(c)(19)

be reported under chapter 61 of the Internal Revenue Code and, if required, subject to backup withholding under section 3406. This latter rule does not preclude the intermediary, flow-through entity, or U.S. branch from also being a payor.

(20) *Exempt recipient.*—The term *exempt recipient* means a person that is exempt from reporting under chapter 61 of the Internal Revenue Code and backup withholding under section 3406 and that is described in §§1.6041-3(q), 1.6045-2(b)(2)(i), and 1.6049-4(c)(1)(ii), and §5f.6045-1(c)(3)(i)(B) of this chapter. Exempt recipients are not exempt from withholding under chapter 3 of the Internal Revenue Code unless they are U.S. persons or foreign persons entitled to an exemption from withholding under chapter 3.

(21) *Non-exempt recipient.*—A *non-exempt recipient* is any person that is not an exempt recipient under paragraph (c)(20) of this section.

(22) *Reportable amounts.*—*Reportable amounts* are defined in paragraph (e)(3)(vi) of this section.

(23) *Flow-through entity.*—A *flow-through entity* means any entity that is described in this paragraph (c)(23) and that may provide documentation on behalf of others to a withholding agent. The entities described in this paragraph are a foreign partnership (other than a withholding foreign partnership), a foreign simple trust (other than a withholding foreign trust) that is described in paragraph (c)(24) of this section, a foreign grantor trust (other than a withholding foreign trust) that is described in paragraph (c)(25) of this section, or, for any payments for which a reduced rate of withholding under an income tax treaty is claimed, any entity to the extent the entity is considered to be fiscally transparent under section 894 with respect to the payment by an interest holder's jurisdiction.

(24) *Foreign simple trust.*—A *foreign simple trust* is a foreign trust that is described in section 651(a).

(25) *Foreign complex trust.*—A *foreign complex trust* is a foreign trust other than a trust described in section 651(a) or sections 671 through 679.

(26) *Foreign grantor trust.*—A *foreign grantor trust* is a foreign trust but only to the extent all or a portion of the income of the trust is treated as owned by the grantor or another person under sections 671 through 679.

(27) *Partnership.*—The term *partnership* means any entity treated as a partnership under §301.7701-2 or -3 of this chapter.

(28) *Nonwithholding foreign partnership.*—A *nonwithholding foreign partnership* is a foreign partnership that is not a withholding foreign partnership, as defined in §1.1441-5(c)(2)(i).

(29) *Withholding foreign partnership.*—A withholding foreign partnership is defined in §1.1441-5(c)(2)(i).

(30) *Possessions of the United States.*—For purposes of the regulations under chapters 3 and 61 of the Internal Revenue Code, *possessions of the United States* means Guam, American Samoa, the Northern Mariana Islands, Puerto Rico, and the Virgin Islands.

(d) *Beneficial owner's or payee's claim of U.S. status.*—(1) *In general.*—Under paragraph (b)(1) of this section, a withholding agent is not required to withhold under chapter 3 of the Code on payments to a U.S. payee, to a person presumed to be a U.S. payee in accordance with the provisions of paragraph (b)(3) of this section, or to a person that the withholding agent may treat as a U.S. beneficial owner of the payment. Absent actual knowledge or reason to know otherwise, a withholding agent may rely on the provisions of this paragraph (d) in order to determine whether to treat a payee or beneficial owner as a U.S. person.

(2) *Payments for which a Form W-9 is otherwise required.*—A withholding agent may treat as a U.S. payee any person who is required to furnish a Form W-9 and who furnishes it in accordance with the procedures described in §§31.3406(d)-1 through 31.3406(d)-5 of this chapter (including the requirement that the payee furnish its taxpayer identifying number (TIN)) if the withholding agent meets all the requirements described in §31.3406(h)-3(e) of this chapter regarding reliance by a payor on a Form W-9. Providing a Form W-9 or valid substitute form shall serve as a statement that the person whose name is on the form is a U.S. person. Therefore, a foreign person, including a U.S. branch treated as a U.S. person under paragraph (b)(2)(iv) of this section, shall not provide a Form W-9. A U.S. branch of a foreign person may establish its status as a foreign person exempt from reporting under chapter 61 and backup withholding under section 3406 by providing a withholding certificate on Form W-8.

(3) *Payments for which a Form W-9 is not otherwise required.*—In the case of a payee who is not required to furnish a Form W-9 under section 3406 (e.g., a person exempt from reporting under chapter 61 of the Internal Revenue Code), the withholding agent may treat the payee as a U.S. payee if the payee provides the withholding agent with a Form W-9 or a substitute form described in §31.3406(h)-3(c)(2) of this chapter (relating to forms for exempt recipients) that contains the payee's name, address, and TIN. The form must be signed under penalties of perjury by the payee if so required by the form or by §31.3406(h)-3 of this chapter. Providing a

Form W-9 or valid substitute form shall serve as a statement that the person whose name is on the certificate is a U.S. person. A Form W-9 or valid substitute form shall not be provided by a foreign person, including any U.S. branch of a foreign person whether or not the branch is treated as a U.S. person under paragraph (b)(2)(iv) of this section. See paragraph (e)(3)(v) of this section for withholding certificates provided by U.S. branches described in paragraph (b)(2)(iv) of this section. The procedures described in § 31.3406(h)-2(a) of this chapter shall apply to payments to joint payees. A withholding agent that receives a Form W-9 to satisfy this paragraph (d)(3) must retain the form in accordance with the provisions of § 31.3406(h)-3(g) of this chapter, if applicable, or of paragraph (e)(4)(iii) of this section (relating to the retention of withholding certificates) if § 31.3406(h)-3(g) of this chapter does not apply. The rules of this paragraph (d)(3) are only intended to provide a method by which a withholding agent may determine that a payee is a U.S. person and do not otherwise impose a requirement that documentation be furnished by a person who is otherwise treated as an exempt recipient for purposes of the applicable information reporting provisions under chapter 61 of the Internal Revenue Code (e.g., § 1.6049-4(c)(1)(ii) for payments of interest).

(4) *When a payment to an intermediary or flow-through entity may be treated as made to a U.S. payee.*—A withholding agent that makes a payment to an intermediary (whether a qualified intermediary or nonqualified intermediary), a flow-through entity, or a U.S. branch described in paragraph (b)(2)(iv) of this section may treat the payment as made to a U.S. payee to the extent that, prior to the payment, the withholding agent can reliably associate the payment with a Form W-9 described in paragraph (d)(2) or (3) of this section attached to a valid intermediary, flow-through, or U.S. branch withholding certificate described in paragraph (e)(3)(i) of this section or to the extent the withholding agent can reliably associate the payment with a Form W-8 described in paragraph (e)(3)(v) of this section that evidences an agreement to treat a U.S. branch described in paragraph (b)(2)(iv) of this section as a U.S. person. In addition, a withholding agent may treat the payment as made to a U.S. payee only if it complies with the electronic confirmation procedures described in paragraph (e)(4)(v) of this section, if required, and it has not been notified by the IRS that any of the information on the withholding certificate or other documentation is incorrect or unreliable. In the case of a Form W-9 that is required to be furnished for a reportable payment that may be subject to backup withholding, the withholding agent may be notified in accordance with section 3406(a)(1)(B) and the regulations under that section. See applicable procedures under section 3406(a)(1)(B) and the regulations under that section for payors who have been notified with

regard to such a Form W-9. Withholding agents who have been notified in relation to other Forms W-9, including under section 6724(b) pursuant to section 6721, may rely on the withholding certificate or other documentation only to the extent provided under procedures as prescribed by the IRS (see § 601.601(d)(2) of this chapter).

(e) *Beneficial owner's claim of foreign status.*—(1) *Withholding agent's reliance.*—(i) *In general.*—Absent actual knowledge or reason to know otherwise, a withholding agent may treat a payment as made to a foreign beneficial owner in accordance with the provisions of paragraph (e)(1)(ii) of this section. See paragraph (e)(4)(viii) of this section for applicable reliance rules. See paragraph (b)(4) of this section for a description of payments for which a claim of foreign status is relevant for purposes of claiming a reduced rate of withholding for purposes of section 1441, 1442, or 1443. See paragraph (b)(5) of this section for a list of payments for which a claim of foreign status is relevant for other purposes, such as claiming an exemption from information reporting under chapter 61 of the Code.

(ii) *Payments that a withholding agent may treat as made to a foreign person that is a beneficial owner.*—(A) *General rule.*—The withholding agent may treat a payment as made to a foreign person that is a beneficial owner if it complies with the requirements described in paragraph (e)(1)(ii)(B) of this section and, then, only to the extent—

(1) That the withholding agent can reliably associate the payment with a beneficial owner withholding certificate described in paragraph (e)(2) of this section furnished by the person whose name is on the certificate or attached to a valid foreign intermediary, flow-through, or U.S. branch withholding certificate;

(2) That the payment is made outside the United States (within the meaning of § 1.6049-5(e)) to an offshore account (within the meaning of § 1.6049-5(c)(1)) and the withholding agent can reliably associate the payment with documentary evidence described in §§ 1.1441-6(c)(3) or (4), or 1.6049-5(c)(1) relating to the beneficial owner;

(3) That the withholding agent can reliably associate the payment with a valid qualified intermediary withholding certificate, as described in paragraph (e)(3)(ii) of this section, and the qualified intermediary has provided sufficient information for the withholding agent to allocate the payment to a withholding rate pool other than a withholding rate pool or pools established for U.S. non-exempt recipients;

(4) That the withholding agent can reliably associate the payment with a withholding certificate described in § 1.1441-5(c)(3)(iii) or (e)(5)(iii) from a flow-through entity claiming the income is effectively connected income;

(5) That the withholding agent identifies the payee as a U.S. branch described in

Reg. § 1.1441-1(e)(1)(ii)(A)(5)

paragraph (b)(2)(iv) of this section, the payment to which it treats as effectively connected income in accordance with § 1.1441-4(a)(2)(ii) or (3);

(6) That the withholding agent identifies the payee as an international organization (or any wholly-owned agency or instrumentality thereof) as defined in section 7701(a)(18) that has been designated as such by executive order (pursuant to 22 U.S.C. 288 through 288(f)); or

(7) That the withholding agent pays interest from bankers' acceptances and identifies the payee as a foreign central bank of issue (as defined in § 1.861-2(b)(4)).

(B) *Additional requirements.*—In order for a payment described in paragraph (e)(1)(ii)(A) of this section to be treated as made to a foreign beneficial owner, the withholding agent must hold the documentation (if required) prior to the payment, comply with the electronic confirmation procedures described in paragraph (e)(4)(v) of this section (if required), and must not have been notified by the IRS that any of the information on the withholding certificate or other documentation is incorrect or unreliable. If the withholding agent has been so notified, it may rely on the withholding certificate or other documentation only to the extent provided under procedures prescribed by the IRS (see § 601.601(d)(2) of this chapter). See paragraph (b)(2)(vii) of this section for rules regarding reliable association of a payment with a withholding certificate or other appropriate documentation.

(2) *Beneficial owner withholding certificate.*—(i) *In general.*—A beneficial owner withholding certificate is a statement by which the beneficial owner of the payment represents that it is a foreign person and, if applicable, claims a reduced rate of withholding under section 1441. A separate withholding certificate must be submitted to each withholding agent. If the beneficial owner receives more than one type of payment from a single withholding agent, the beneficial owner may have to submit more than one withholding certificate to the single withholding agent for the different types of payments as may be required by the applicable forms and instructions, or as the withholding agent may require (such as to facilitate the withholding agent's compliance with its obligations to determine withholding under this section or the reporting of the amounts under § 1.1461-1(b) and (c)). For example, if a beneficial owner claims that some but not all of the income it receives is effectively connected with the conduct of a trade or business in the United States, it may be required to submit two separate withholding certificates, one for income that is not effectively connected and one for income that is so connected. See § 1.1441-6(b)(2) for special rules for determining who must furnish a beneficial owner withholding certificate when a benefit is claimed under an income tax treaty. See paragraph (e)(4)(ix) of this section for reliance rules in the case of certificates

held by another person or at a different branch location of the same person.

(ii) *Requirements for validity of certificate.*—A beneficial owner withholding certificate is valid only if it is provided on a Form W-8, or a Form 8233 in the case of personal services income described in § 1.1441-4(b) or certain scholarship or grant amounts described in § 1.1441-4(c) (or a substitute form described in paragraph (e)(4)(vi) of this section, or such other form as the IRS may prescribe). A Form W-8 is valid only if its validity period has not expired, it is signed under penalties of perjury by the beneficial owner, and it contains all of the information required on the form. The required information is the beneficial owner's name, permanent residence address, and TIN (if required), the country under the laws of which the beneficial owner is created, incorporated, or governed (if a person other than an individual), the classification of the entity, and such other information as may be required by the regulations under section 1441 or by the form or accompanying instructions in addition to, or in lieu of, the information described in this paragraph (e)(2)(ii). A person's permanent residence address is an address in the country where the person claims to be a resident for purposes of that country's income tax. In the case of a certificate furnished in order to claim a reduced rate of withholding under an income tax treaty, the residence must be determined in the manner prescribed under the applicable treaty. See § 1.1441-6(b). The address of a financial institution with which the beneficial owner maintains an account, a post office box, or an address used solely for mailing purposes is not a residence address for this purpose. If the beneficial owner is an individual who does not have a tax residence in any country, the permanent residence address is the place at which the beneficial owner normally resides. If the beneficial owner is not an individual and does not have a tax residence in any country, then the permanent residence address is the place at which the person maintains its principal office. See paragraph (e)(4)(vii) of this section for circumstances in which a TIN is required on a beneficial owner withholding certificate. See paragraph (f)(2)(i) of this section for continued validity of certificates during a transition period.

(3) *Intermediary, flow-through, or U.S. branch withholding certificate.*—(i) *In general.*—An intermediary withholding certificate is a Form W-8 by which a payee represents that it is a foreign person and that it is an intermediary (whether a qualified or nonqualified intermediary) with respect to a payment and not the beneficial owner. See paragraphs (e)(3)(ii) and (iii) of this section. A flow-through withholding certificate is a Form W-8 used by a flow-through entity as defined in paragraph (c)(23) of this section. See § 1.1441-5(c)(3)(iii) (a nonwithholding foreign partnership), § 1.1441-5(e)(5)(iii) (a foreign sim-

ple trust or foreign grantor trust) or § 1.1441-6(b)(2) (foreign entity presenting claims on behalf of its interest holders for a reduced rate of withholding under an income tax treaty). A U.S. branch certificate is a Form W-8 furnished under paragraph (e)(3)(v) of this section by a U.S. branch described in paragraph (b)(2)(iv) of this section. See paragraph (e)(4)(viii) of this section for applicable reliance rules.

(ii) *Intermediary withholding certificate from a qualified intermediary.*—A qualified intermediary shall provide a qualified intermediary withholding certificate for reportable amounts received by the qualified intermediary. See paragraph (e)(3)(vi) of this section for the definition of reportable amount. A qualified intermediary-withholding certificate is valid only if it is furnished on a Form W-8, an acceptable substitute form, or such other form as the IRS may prescribe, it is signed under penalties of perjury by a person with authority to sign for the qualified intermediary, its validity has not expired, and it contains the following information, statement, and certifications—

(A) The name, permanent residence address (as described in paragraph (e)(2)(ii) of this section), qualified intermediary employer identification number (QI-EIN), and the country under the laws of which the intermediary is created, incorporated, or governed. A qualified intermediary that does not act in its capacity as a qualified intermediary must not use its QI-EIN. Rather the intermediary should provide a nonqualified intermediary withholding certificate, if it is acting as an intermediary, and should use the taxpayer identification number, if any, that it uses for all other purposes;

(B) A certification that, with respect to accounts it identifies on its withholding statement (as described in paragraph (e)(5)(v) of this section), the qualified intermediary is not acting for its own account but is acting as a qualified intermediary;

(C) A certification that the qualified intermediary has provided, or will provide, a withholding statement as required by paragraph (e)(5)(v) of this section; and

(D) Any other information, certifications, or statements as may be required by the form or accompanying instructions in addition to, or in lieu of, the information and certifications described in this paragraph (e)(3)(ii) or paragraph (e)(3)(v) of this section. See paragraph (e)(5)(v) of this section for the requirements of a withholding statement associated with the qualified intermediary withholding certificate.

(iii) *Intermediary withholding certificate from a nonqualified intermediary.*—A nonqualified intermediary shall provide a nonqualified intermediary withholding certificate for reportable amounts received by the nonqualified intermediary. See paragraph (e)(3)(vi) of this section for the definition of reportable amount. A nonqualified intermediary withholding certificate is valid only to the extent it is furnished on a Form W-8, an acceptable substitute form, or such other form as the IRS may prescribe, it is signed under penalties of perjury by a person authorized to sign for the nonqualified intermediary, it contains the information, statements, and certifications described in this paragraph (e)(3)(iii) and paragraph (e)(3)(iv) of this section, its validity has not expired, and the withholding certificates and other appropriate documentation for all persons to whom the certificate relates are associated with the certificate. Withholding certificates and other appropriate documentation consist of beneficial owner withholding certificates described in paragraph (e)(2)(i) of this section, intermediary and flow-through withholding certificates described in paragraph (e)(3)(i) of this section, withholding foreign partnership certificates described in § 1.1441-5(c)(2)(iv), documentary evidence described in §§ 1.1441-6(c)(3) or (4) and 1.6049-5(c)(1), and any other documentation or certificates applicable under other provisions of the Internal Revenue Code or regulations that certify or establish the status of the payee or beneficial owner as a U.S. or a foreign person. If a nonqualified intermediary is acting on behalf of another nonqualified intermediary or a flow-through entity, then the nonqualified intermediary must associate with its own withholding certificate the other nonqualified intermediary withholding certificate or the flow-through withholding certificate and separately identify all of the withholding certificates and other appropriate documentation that are associated with the withholding certificate of the other nonqualified intermediary or flow-through entity. Nothing in this paragraph (e)(3)(iii) shall require an intermediary to furnish original documentation. Copies of certificates or documentary evidence may be transmitted to the U.S. withholding agent, in which case the nonqualified intermediary must retain the original documentation for the same time period that the copy is required to be retained by the withholding agent under paragraph (e)(4)(iii) of this section and must provide it to the withholding agent upon request. For purposes of this paragraph (e)(3)(iii), a valid intermediary withholding certificate also includes a statement described in § 1.871-14(c)(2)(v) furnished for interest to qualify as portfolio interest for purposes of sections 871(h) and 881(c). The information and certifications required on a Form W-8 described in this paragraph (e)(3)(iii) are as follows—

(A) The name and permanent resident address (as described in paragraph (e)(2)(ii) of this section) of the nonqualified intermediary, and the country under the laws of which the nonqualified intermediary is created, incorporated, or governed;

(B) A certification that the nonqualified intermediary is not acting for its own account;

(C) If the nonqualified intermediary withholding certificate is used to transmit withholding certificates or other appropriate documentation for more than one person on whose behalf the nonqualified intermediary is acting, a withholding statement associated with the Form W-8 that provides all the information required by paragraph (e)(3)(iv) of this section; and

(D) Any other information, certifications, or statements as may be required by the form or accompanying instructions in addition to, or in lieu of, the information, certifications, and statements described in this paragraph (e)(3)(iii) or paragraph (e)(5)(iv) of this section.

(iv) *Withholding statement provided by nonqualified intermediary.*—(A) *In general.*—A nonqualified intermediary shall provide a withholding statement required by this paragraph (e)(3)(iv) to the extent the nonqualified intermediary is required to furnish, or does furnish, documentation for payees on whose behalf it receives reportable amounts (as defined in paragraph (e)(3)(vi) of this section) or to the extent it otherwise provides the documentation of such payees to a withholding agent. A nonqualified intermediary is not required to disclose information regarding persons for whom it collects reportable amounts unless it has actual knowledge that any such person is a U.S. non-exempt recipient as defined in paragraph (c)(21) of this section. Information regarding U.S. non-exempt recipients required under this paragraph (e)(3)(iv) must be provided irrespective of any requirement under foreign law that prohibits the disclosure of the identity of an account holder of a nonqualified intermediary or financial information relating to such account holder. Although a nonqualified intermediary is not required to provide documentation and other information required by this paragraph (e)(3)(iv) for persons other than U.S. non-exempt recipients, a withholding agent that does not receive documentation and such information must apply the presumption rules of paragraph (b) of this section, §§ 1.1441-5(d) and (e)(6) and 1.6049-5(d) or the withholding agent shall be liable for tax, interest, and penalties. A withholding agent must apply the presumption rules even if it is not required under chapter 61 of the Internal Revenue Code to obtain documentation to treat a payee as an exempt recipient and even though it has actual knowledge that the payee is a U.S. person. For example, if a nonqualified intermediary fails to provide a withholding agent with a Form W-9 for an account holder that is a U.S. exempt recipient, the withholding agent must presume (even if it has actual knowledge that the account holder is a U.S. exempt recipient), that the account holder is an undocumented foreign person with respect to amounts subject to withholding. See paragraph (b)(3)(v) of this section for applicable presumptions. Therefore, the withholding agent must withhold 30 percent from the payment even though if a

Form W-9 had been provided, no withholding or reporting on the payment attributable to a U.S. exempt recipient would apply. Further, a nonqualified intermediary that fails to provide the documentation and the information under this paragraph (e)(3)(iv) for another withholding agent to report the payments on Forms 1042-S and Forms 1099 is not relieved of its responsibility to file information returns. See paragraph (b)(6) of this section. Therefore, unless the nonqualified intermediary itself files such returns and provides copies to the payees, it shall be liable for penalties under sections 6721 (failure to file information returns), and 6722 (failure to furnish payee statements), including the penalties under those sections for intentional failure to file information returns. In addition, failure to provide either the documentation or the information required by this paragraph (e)(3)(iv) results in a payment not being reliably associated with valid documentation. Therefore, the beneficial owners of the payment are not entitled to reduced rates of withholding and if the full amount required to be held under the presumption rules is not withheld by the withholding agent, the nonqualified intermediary must withhold the difference between the amount withheld by the withholding agent and the amount required to be withheld. Failure to withhold shall result in the nonqualified intermediary being liable for tax under section 1461, interest, and penalties, including penalties under section 6656 (failure to deposit) and section 6672 (failure to collect and pay over tax).

(B) *General requirements.*—A withholding statement must be provided prior to the payment of a reportable amount and must contain the information specified in paragraph (e)(3)(iv)(C) of this section. The statement must be updated as often as required to keep the information in the withholding statement correct prior to each subsequent payment. The withholding statement forms an integral part of the withholding certificate provided under paragraph (e)(3)(iii) of this section, and the penalties of perjury statement provided on the withholding certificate shall apply to the withholding statement. The withholding statement may be provided in any manner the nonqualified intermediary and the withholding agent mutually agree, including electronically. If the withholding statement is provided electronically, there must be sufficient safeguards to ensure that the information received by the withholding agent is the information sent by the nonqualified intermediary and all occasions of user access that result in the submission or modification of the withholding statement information must be recorded. In addition, an electronic system must be capable of providing a hard copy of all withholding statements provided by the nonqualified intermediary. A withholding agent will be liable for tax, interest, and penalties in accordance with paragraph (b)(7) of this section to the extent it does not follow the presumption rules of paragraph (b)(3) of this section or §§1.1441-5(d) and (e)(6), and 1.6049-5(d) for any payment of a reportable amount, or portion thereof, for which it does not have a valid withholding statement prior to making a payment.

(C) *Content of withholding statement.*— The withholding statement provided by a nonqualified intermediary must contain the information required by this paragraph (e)(3)(iv)(C).

(1) The withholding statement must contain the name, address, TIN (if any) and the type of documentation (documentary evidence, Form W-9, or type of Form W-8) for every person from whom documentation has been received by the nonqualified intermediary and provided to the withholding agent and whether that person is a U.S. exempt recipient, a U.S. non-exempt recipient, or a foreign person. See paragraphs (c)(2), (20), and (21) of this section for the definitions of foreign person, U.S. exempt recipient, and U.S. non-exempt recipient. In the case of a foreign person, the statement must indicate whether the foreign person is a beneficial owner or an intermediary, flow-through entity, or U.S. branch described in paragraph (b)(2)(iv) of this section and include the type of recipient, based on recipient codes used for filing Forms 1042-S, if the foreign person is a recipient as defined in §1.1461-1 (c)(1)(ii).

(2) The withholding statement must allocate each payment, by income type, to every payee (including U.S. exempt recipients) for whom documentation has been provided. Any payment that cannot be reliably associated with valid documentation from a payee shall be treated as made to an unknown payee in accordance with the presumption rules of paragraph (b) of this section and §§1.1441-5(d) and (e)(6) and 1.6049-5(d). For this purpose, a type of income is determined by the types of income required to be reported on Forms 1042-S or 1099, as appropriate. Notwithstanding the preceding sentence, deposit interest (including original issue discount) described in section 871(i)(2)(A) or 881(d) and interest or original issue discount on short-term obligations as described in section 871(g)(1)(B) or 881(e) is only required to be allocated to the extent it is required to be reported on Form 1099 or Form 1042-S. See §1.6049-8 (regarding reporting of bank deposit interest to certain foreign persons). If a payee receives income through another nonqualified intermediary, flow-through entity, or U.S. branch described in paragraph (e)(2)(iv) of this section (other than a U.S. branch treated as a U.S. person), the withholding statement must also state, with respect to the payee, the name, address, and TIN, if known, of the other nonqualified intermediary or U.S. branch from which the payee directly receives the payment or the flow-through entity in which the payee has a direct ownership interest. If another nonqualified intermediary, flow-through entity, or U.S. branch

fails to allocate a payment, the name of the nonqualified intermediary, flow-through entity, or U.S. branch that failed to allocate the payment shall be provided with respect to such payment.

(3) If a payee is identified as a foreign person, the nonqualified intermediary must specify the rate of withholding to which the payee is subject, the payee's country of residence and, if a reduced rate of withholding is claimed, the basis for that reduced rate (e.g., treaty benefit, portfolio interest, exempt under section 501(c)(3), 892, or 895). The allocation statement must also include the taxpayer identification numbers of those foreign persons for whom such a number is required under paragraph (e)(4)(vii) of this section or §1.1441-6(b)(1) (regarding claims for treaty benefits). In the case of a claim of treaty benefits, the nonqualified intermediary's withholding statement must also state whether the limitation on benefits and section 894 statements required by §1.1441-6(c)(5) have been provided, if required, in the beneficial owner's Form W-8 or associated with such owner's documentary evidence.

(4) The withholding statement must also contain any other information the withholding agent reasonably requests in order to fulfill its obligations under chapter 3, chapter 61 of the Internal Revenue Code, and section 3406.

(D) *Alternative procedures.*—(1) *In general.*—Under the alternative procedures of this paragraph (e)(3)(iv)(D), a nonqualified intermediary may provide information allocating a payment of a reportable amount to each payee (including U.S. exempt recipients) otherwise required under paragraph (e)(3)(iv)(B)(2) of this section after a payment is made. To use the alternative procedure of this paragraph (e)(3)(iv)(D), the nonqualified intermediary must inform the withholding agent on a statement associated with its nonqualified intermediary withholding certificate that it is using the procedure under this paragraph (e)(3)(iv)(D) and the withholding agent must agree to the procedure. If the requirements of the alternative procedure are met, a withholding agent, including the nonqualified intermediary using the procedures, can treat the payment as reliably associated with documentation and, therefore, the presumption rules of paragraph (b)(3) of this section and §§1.1441-5(d) and (e)(6) and 1.6049-5(d) do not apply even though information allocating the payment to each payee has not been received prior to the payment. See paragraph (e)(3)(iv)(D)(7) of this section, however, for a nonqualified intermediary's liability for tax and penalties if the requirements of this paragraph (e)(3)(iv)(D) are not met. These alternative procedures shall not be used for payments that are allocable to U.S. non-exempt recipients. Therefore, a nonqualified intermediary is required to provide a withholding agent with information allocating payments of reportable amounts to

Reg. §1.1441-1(e)(3)(iv)(D)(1)

U.S. non-exempt recipients prior to the payment being made by the withholding agent.

(2) *Withholding rate pools.*—In place of the information required in paragraph (e)(3)(iv)(C)(2) of this section allocating payments to each payee, the nonqualified intermediary must provide a withholding agent with withholding rate pool information prior to the payment of a reportable amount. The withholding statement must contain all other information required by paragraph (e)(3)(iv)(C) of this section. Further, each payee listed in the withholding statement must be assigned to an identified withholding rate pool. To the extent a nonqualified intermediary is required to, or does provide, documentation, the alternative procedures do not relieve the nonqualified intermediary from the requirement to provide documentation prior to the payment being made. Therefore, withholding certificates or other appropriate documentation and all information required by paragraph (e)(3)(iv)(C) of this section (other than allocation information) must be provided to a withholding agent before any new payee receives a reportable amount. In addition, the withholding statement must be updated by assigning a new payee to a withholding rate pool prior to the payment of a reportable amount. A withholding rate pool is a payment of a single type of income, determined in accordance with the categories of income used to file Form 1042-S, that is subject to a single rate of withholding. A withholding rate pool may be established by any reasonable method to which the nonqualified intermediary and a withholding agent agree (e.g., by establishing a separate account for a single withholding rate pool, or by dividing a payment made to a single account into portions allocable to each withholding rate pool). The nonqualified intermediary shall determine withholding rate pools based on valid documentation or, to the extent a payment cannot be reliably associated with valid documentation, the presumption rules of paragraph (b)(3) of this section and §§ 1.1441-5(d) and (e)(6) and 1.6049-5(d).

(3) *Allocation information.*—The nonqualified intermediary must provide the withholding agent with sufficient information to allocate the income in each withholding rate pool to each payee (including U.S. exempt recipients) within the pool no later than January 31 of the year following the year of payment. Any payments that are not allocated to payees for whom documentation has been provided shall be allocated to an undocumented payee in accordance with the presumption rules of paragraph (b)(3) of this section and §§ 1.1441-5(d) and (e)(6) and 1.6049-5(d). Notwithstanding the preceding sentence, deposit interest (including original issue discount) described in section 871(i)(2)(A) or 881(d) and interest or original issue discount on short-term obligations as described in section 871(g)(1)(B) or 881(e) is not required to be allocated to a U.S. exempt recipient or a foreign payee, except as required under § 1.6049-8 (regarding reporting of deposit interest paid to certain foreign persons).

(4) *Failure to provide allocation information.*—If a nonqualified intermediary fails to provide allocation information, if required, by January 31 for any withholding rate pool, a withholding agent shall not apply the alternative procedures of this paragraph (e)(3)(iv)(D) to any payments of reportable amounts paid after January 31 in the taxable year following the calendar year for which allocation information was not given and any subsequent taxable year. Further, the alternative procedures shall be unavailable for any other withholding rate pool even though allocation information was given for that other pool. Therefore, the withholding agent must withhold on a payment of a reportable amount in accordance with the presumption rules of paragraph (b)(3) of this section, and §§ 1.1441-5(d) and (e)(6) and 1.6049-5(d), unless the nonqualified intermediary provides all of the information, including information sufficient to allocate the payment to each specific payee, required by paragraph (e)(3)(iv)(A) through (C) of this section prior to the payment. A nonqualified intermediary must allocate at least 90 percent of the income required to be allocated for each withholding rate pool or the nonqualified intermediary will be treated as having failed to provide allocation information for purposes of this paragraph (e)(3)(iv)(D). See paragraph (e)(3)(iv)(D)(7) of this section for liability for tax and penalties if a nonqualified intermediary fails to provide allocation information in whole or in part.

(5) *Cure provision.*—A nonqualified intermediary may cure any failure to provide allocation information by providing the required allocation information to the withholding agent no later than February 14 following the calendar year of payment. If the withholding agent receives the allocation information by that date, it may apply the adjustment procedures of § 1.1461-2 to any excess withholding for payments made on or after February 1 and on or before February 14. Any nonqualified intermediary that fails to cure by February 14, may request the ability to use the alternative procedures of this paragraph (e)(3)(iv)(D) by submitting a request, in writing, to the Assistant Commissioner (International). The request must state the reason that the nonqualified intermediary did not comply with the alternative procedures of this paragraph (e)(3)(iv)(D) and steps that the nonqualified intermediary has taken, or will take, to ensure that no failures occur in the future. If the Assistant Commissioner (International) determines that the alternative procedures of this paragraph (e)(3)(iv)(D) may apply, a determination to that effect will be is-

Reg. § 1.1441-1(e)(3)(iv)(D)(2)

sued by the IRS to the nonqualified intermediary.

     (6) Form 1042-S reporting in case of allocation failure.—If a nonqualified intermediary fails to provide allocation information by February 14 following the year of payment for a withholding rate pool, the withholding agent must file Forms 1042-S for payments made to each payee in that pool (other than U.S. exempt recipients) in the prior calendar year by pro rating the payment to each payee (including U.S. exempt recipients) listed in the withholding statement for that withholding rate pool. If the nonqualified intermediary fails to allocate 10 percent or less of an amount required to be allocated for a withholding rate pool, a withholding agent shall report the unallocated amount as paid to a single unknown payee in accordance with the presumption rules of paragraph (b) of this section and §§1.1441-5(d) and (e)(6) and 1.6049-5(d). The portion of the payment that can be allocated to specific recipients, as defined in §1.1461-1(c)(1)(ii), shall be reported to each recipient in accordance with the rules of §1.1461-1(c).

     (7) Liability for tax, interest, and penalties.—If a nonqualified intermediary fails to provide allocation information by February 14 following the year of payment for all or a portion of the payments made to any withholding rate pool, the withholding agent from whom the nonqualified intermediary received payments of reportable amounts shall not be liable for any tax, interest, or penalties, due solely to the errors or omissions of the nonqualified intermediary. See §1.1441-7(b)(2) through (10) for the due diligence requirements of a withholding agent. Because failure by the nonqualified intermediary to provide allocation information results in a payment not being reliably associated with valid documentation, the beneficial owners for whom the nonqualified intermediary acts are not entitled to a reduced rate of withholding. Therefore, the nonqualified intermediary, as a withholding agent, shall be liable for any tax not withheld by the withholding agent in accordance with the presumption rules, interest on the under withheld tax if the nonqualified intermediary fails to pay the tax timely, and any applicable penalties, including the penalties under sections 6656 (failure to deposit), 6721 (failure to file information returns) and 6722 (failure to file payee statements). Failure to provide allocation information for more than 10 percent of the payments made to a particular withholding rate pool will be presumed to be an intentional failure within the meaning of sections 6721(e) and 6722(c). The nonqualified intermediary may rebut the presumption.

     (8) Applicability to flow-through entities and certain U.S. branches.—See paragraph (e)(3)(v) of this section and §1.1441-5(c)(3)(iv)

and (e)(5)(iv) for the applicability of this paragraph (e)(3)(iv) to U.S. branches described in paragraph (b)(2)(iv) of this section (other than U.S. branches treated as U.S. persons) and flow-through entities.

     (E) *Notice procedures.*—The IRS may notify a withholding agent that the alternative procedures of paragraph (e)(3)(iv)(D) of this section are not applicable to a specified nonqualified intermediary, a U.S. branch described in paragraph (b)(2)(iv) of this section, or a flow-through entity. If a withholding agent receives such a notice, it must commence withholding in accordance with the presumption rules of paragraph (b)(3) of this section and §§1.1441-5(d) and (e)(6) and 1.6049-5(d) unless the nonqualified intermediary, U.S. branch, or flow-through entity complies with the procedures in paragraphs (e)(3)(iv)(A) through (C) of this section. In addition, the IRS may notify a withholding agent, in appropriate circumstances, that it must apply the presumption rules of paragraph (b)(3) of this section and §§1.1441-5(d) and (e)(6) and 1.6049-5(d) to payments made to a nonqualified intermediary, a U.S. branch, or a flow-through entity even if the nonqualified intermediary, U.S. branch or flow-through entity provides allocation information prior to the payment. A withholding agent that receives a notice under this paragraph (e)(3)(iv)(E) must commence withholding in accordance with the presumption rules within 30 days of the date of the notice. The IRS may withdraw its prohibition against using the alternative procedures of paragraph (e)(3)(iv)(D) of this section, or its requirement to follow the presumption rules, if the nonqualified intermediary, U.S. branch, or flow-through entity can demonstrate to the satisfaction of the Assistant Commissioner (International) or his delegate that it is capable of complying with the rules under chapter 3 of the Internal Revenue Code and any other conditions required by the Assistant Commissioner (International).

     (v) *Withholding certificate from certain U.S. branches.*—A U.S. branch certificate is a withholding certificate provided by a U.S. branch described in paragraph (b)(2)(iv) of this section that is not the beneficial owner of the income. The withholding certificate is provided with respect to reportable amounts and must state that such amounts are not effectively connected with the conduct of a trade or business in the United States. The withholding certificate must either transmit the appropriate documentation for the persons for whom the branch receives the payment (i.e., as an intermediary) or be provided as evidence of its agreement with the withholding agent to be treated as a U.S. person with respect to any payment associated with the certificate. A U.S. branch withholding certificate is valid only if it is furnished on a Form W-8, an acceptable substitute form, or such other form as the IRS may prescribe, it is signed under penalties of perjury by a person authorized to sign for the branch, its validity has not expired, and it contains the information, statements, and certifications described in this paragraph (e)(3)(v). If the certificate is furnished to transmit withholding certificates and other documentation, it must contain the information, certifications, and statements described in paragraphs (e)(3)(v)(A) through (C) of this section and in paragraphs (e)(3)(iii) and (iv) (alternative procedures) of this section, applying the term *U.S. branch* instead of the term *nonqualified intermediary*. If the certificate is furnished pursuant to an agreement to treat the U.S. branch as a U.S. person, the information and certifications required on the withholding certificate are limited to the following—

(A) The name of the person of which the branch is a part and the address of the branch in the United States;

(B) A certification that the payments associated with the certificate are not effectively connected with the conduct of its trade or business in the United States; and

(C) Any other information, certifications, or statements as may be required by the form or accompanying instructions in addition to, or in lieu of, the information and certification described in this paragraph (e)(3)(v).

(vi) *Reportable amounts.*—For purposes of chapter 3 of the Internal Revenue Code, a nonqualified intermediary, qualified intermediary, flow-through entity, and U.S. branch described in paragraph (b)(2)(iv) of this section (other than a U.S. branch that agrees to be treated as a U.S. person) must provide a withholding certificate and associated documentation and other information with respect to reportable amounts. For purposes of the regulations under chapter 3 of the Internal Revenue Code, the term reportable amount means an amount subject to withholding within the meaning of §1.1441-2(a), bank deposit interest (including original issue discount) and similar types of deposit interest described in section 871(i)(2)(A) or 881(d) that are from sources within the United States, and any amount of interest or original issue discount from sources within the United States on the redemption of certain short-term obligations described in section 871(g)(1)(B) or 881(e). Reportable amounts shall not include amounts received on the sale or exchange (other than a redemption) of an obligation described in section 871(g)(1)(B) or 881(e) that is effected at an office outside the United States. See §1.6045-1(g)(3) to determine whether a sale is effected at an office outside the United States. Reportable amounts also do not include payments with respect to deposits with banks and other financial institutions that remain on deposit for a period of two weeks or less, to amounts of original issue discount arising from a sale and repurchase transaction that is completed within a period of two weeks or less, or to amounts described in

§1.6049-5(b)(7), (10) or (11) (relating to certain obligations issued in bearer form). While short-term OID and bank deposit interest are not subject to withholding under chapter 3 of the Internal Revenue Code, such amounts may be subject to information reporting under section 6049 if paid to a U.S. person who is not an exempt recipient described in §1.6049-4(c)(1)(ii) and to backup withholding under section 3406 in the absence of documentation. See §1.6049-5(d)(3)(iii) for applicable procedures when such amounts are paid to a foreign intermediary.

(4) *Applicable rules.*—The provisions in this paragraph (e)(4) describe procedures applicable to withholding certificates on Form W-8 or Form 8233 (or a substitute form) or documentary evidence furnished to establish foreign status. These provisions do not apply to Forms W-9 (or their substitutes). For corresponding provisions regrading Form W-9 (or a substitute form), see section 3406 and the regulations under that section.

(i) *Who may sign the certificate.*—A withholding certificate (or other acceptable substitute) may be signed by any person authorized to sign a declaration under penalties of perjury on behalf of the person whose name is on the certificate as provided in section 6061 and the regulations under that section (relating to who may sign generally for an individual, estate, or trust, which includes certain agents who may sign returns and other documents), section 6062 and the regulations under that section (relating to who may sign corporate returns), and section 6063 and the regulations under that section (relating to who may sign partnership returns).

(ii) *Period of validity.*—(A) *Three-year period.*—A withholding certificate described in paragraph (e)(2)(i) of this section, or a certificate described in §1.871-14(c)(2)(v) (furnished to qualify interest as portfolio interest for purposes of sections 871(h) and 881(c)), shall remain valid until the earlier of the last day of the third calendar year following the year in which the withholding certificate is signed or the day that a change in circumstances occurs that makes any information on the certificate incorrect. For example, a withholding certificate signed on September 30, 2001, remains valid through December 31, 2004, unless circumstances change that make the information on the form no longer correct. Documentary evidence described in §§1.1441-6(c)(3) or (4) or 1.6049-5(c)(1) shall remain valid until the earlier of the last day of the third calendar year following the year in which the documentary evidence is provided to the withholding agent or the day that a change in circumstances occurs that makes any information on the documentary evidence incorrect.

(B) *Indefinite validity period.*—Notwithstanding paragraph (e)(4)(ii)(A) of this section, the following certificates or parts of certificates shall remain valid until the status of the person whose name is on the certificate is changed in a way relevant to the certificate or circumstances change that make the information on the certificate no longer correct:

(1) A withholding certificate described in paragraph (e)(2)(ii) of this section that is furnished with a TIN, provided that the withholding agent reports at least one payment annually to the beneficial owner under § 1.1461-1(c) or the TIN furnished on the certificate is reported to the IRS under the procedures described in § 1.1461-1(d). For example, assume a withholding agent receives a Form W-8 in 2001 from a beneficial owner with respect to an account that contains bonds, the interest on which must be reported on Form 1042-S under § 1.1461-1(c). The Form W-8 contains a valid TIN and the withholding agent reports on Forms 1042-S interest to the beneficial owner for 2001 through 2005. In 2005, the beneficial owner sells some of the bonds. For purposes of the exemption from Form 1099 reporting under § 1.6045-1(g), the withholding agent may consider the Form W-8 as valid, even though the payment of the sales proceeds is not reportable on Form 1042-S under § 1.1461-1(c) and even though the Form W-8 was provided more than three years previously.

(2) certificate described in paragraph (e)(3)(ii) of this section (a qualified intermediary withholding certificate) but not including the withholding certificates, documentary evidence, statements or other information associated with the certificate.

(3) A certificate described in paragraph (e)(3)(iii) of this section (a nonqualified intermediary certificate), but not including the withholding certificates, documentary evidence, statements or other information associated with the certificate.

(4) A certificate described in paragraph (e)(3)(v) of this section (a U.S. branch withholding certificate), but not including the withholding certificates, documentary evidence, statements or other information associated with the certificate.

(5) A certificate described in § 1.1441-5(c)(2)(iv) (dealing with a certificate from a person representing to be a withholding foreign partnership).

(6) A certificate described in § 1.1441-5(c)(3)(iii) (a withholding certificate from a nonwithholding foreign partnership) but not including the withholding certificates, documentary evidence, statements or other information required to be associated with the certificate.

(7) A certificate furnished by a person representing to be an integral part of a foreign government (within the meaning of § 1.892-2T(a)(2)) in accordance with § 1.1441-8(b), or by a person representing to be a foreign central bank of issue (within the meaning of § 1.861-2(b)(4)) or the Bank for International Settlements in accordance with § 1.1441-8(c)(1).

(8) A withholding certificate described in § 1.1441-5(e)(5)(iii) provided by a foreign simple trust or a foreign grantor trust to transmit documentation of beneficiaries or owners, but not including the withholding certificates, documentary evidence, statements or other information associated with the certificate.

(C) *Withholding certificate for effectively connected income.*—Notwithstanding paragraph (e)(4)(ii)(B)(1) of this section, the period of validity of a withholding certificate furnished to a withholding agent to claim a reduced rate of withholding for income that is effectively connected with the conduct of a trade or business within the United States shall be limited to the three-year period described in paragraph (e)(4)(ii)(A) of this section.

(D) *Change in circumstances.*—If a change in circumstances makes any information on a certificate or other documentation incorrect, then the person whose name is on the certificate or other documentation must inform the withholding agent within 30 days of the change and furnish a new certificate or new documentation. A certificate or documentation becomes invalid from the date that the withholding agent holding the certificate or documentation knows or has reason to know that circumstances affecting the correctness of the certificate or documentation have changed. However, a withholding agent may choose to apply the provisions of paragraph (b)(3)(iv) of this section regarding the 90-day grace period as of that date while awaiting a new certificate or documentation or while seeking information regarding changes, or suspected changes, in the person's circumstances. If an intermediary (including a U.S. branch described in paragraph (b)(2)(iv)(A) of this section that passes through certificates to a withholding agent) or a flow-through entity becomes aware that a certificate or other appropriate documentation it has furnished to the person from whom it collects the payment is no longer valid because of a change in the circumstances of the person who issued the certificate or furnished the other appropriate documentation, then the intermediary or flow-through entity must notify the person from whom it collects the payment of the change of circumstances. It must also obtain a new withholding certificate or new appropriate documentation to replace the existing certificate or documentation whose validity has expired due to the change in circumstances. If a beneficial owner withholding certificate is used to claim foreign status only (and not, also, residence in a particular foreign country for purposes of an income tax treaty), a change of address is a change in circumstances for purposes of this paragraph (e)(4)(ii)(D) only if it changes to an address in the United States. Further, a change of address within the same foreign country is not a change in circumstances for purposes of this paragraph (e)(4)(ii)(D). A change in the circumstances affecting the withholding information provided to the withholding agent in accordance with the provisions in paragraph (e)(3)(iv) or (5)(v) of this section or in § 1.1441-5(c)(3)(iv) shall terminate the validity of the withholding certificate with respect to the information that is no longer reliable unless the information is updated. A withholding agent may rely on a certificate without having to inquire into possible changes of circumstances that may affect the validity of the statement, unless it knows or has reason to know that circumstances have changed. A withholding agent may require a new certificate at any time prior to a payment, even though the withholding agent has no actual knowledge or reason to know that any information stated on the certificate has changed.

(iii) *Retention of withholding certificate.*—A withholding agent must retain each withholding certificate and other documentation for as long as it may be relevant to the determination of the withholding agent's tax liability under section 1461 and § 1.1461-1.

(iv) *Electronic transmission of information.*—(A) *In general.*—A withholding agent may establish a system for a beneficial owner or payee to electronically furnish a Form W-8, an acceptable substitute Form W-8, or such other form as the Internal Revenue Service may prescribe. The system must meet the requirements described in paragraph (e)(4)(iv)(B) of this section. A withholding agent may accept Forms W-8 that are furnished electronically on or after January 1, 2000, provided the requirements of paragraph (e)(4)(iv)(B) of this section are met.

(B) *Requirements.*—(1) *In general.*—The electronic system must ensure that the information received is the information sent, and must document all occasions of user access that result in the submission renewal, or modification of a Form W-8. In addition, the design and operation of the electronic system, including access procedures, must make it reasonably certain that the person accessing the system and furnishing Form W-8 is the person named in the Form.

(2) *Same information as paper Form W-8.*—The electronic transmission must provide the withholding agent or payor with exactly the same information as the paper Form W-8.

(3) *Perjury statement and signature requirements.*—The electronic transmission must contain an electronic signature by the person whose name is on the Form W-8 and the signature must be under penalties of perjury in the manner described in this paragraph (e)(4)(iv)(B)(3).

(i) *Perjury statement.*—The perjury statement must contain the language that appears on the paper Form W-8. The electronic system must inform the person whose name is on the Form W-8 that the person must make the declaration contained in the perjury statement and that the declaration is made by signing the Form W-8. The instructions and the language of the perjury statement must immediately follow the person's certifying statements and immediately precede the person's electronic signature.

(ii) *Electronic signature.*—The act of the electronic signature must be effected by the person whose name is on the electronic Form W-8. The signature must also authenticate and verify the submission. For this purpose, the terms *authenticate* and *verify* have the same meanings as they do when applied to a written signature on a paper Form W-8. An electronic signature can be in any form that satisfies the foregoing requirements. The electronic signature must be the final entry in the person's Form W-8 submission.

(4) *Requests for electronic Form W-8 data.*—Upon request by the Internal Revenue Service during an examination, the withholding agent must supply a hard copy of the electronic Form W-8 and a statement that, to the best of the withholding agent's knowledge, the electronic Form W-8 was filed by the person whose name is on the form. The hard copy of the electronic Form W-8 must provide exactly the same information as, but need not be identical to, the paper Form W-8.

(C) *Special requirements for transmission of Forms W-8 by an intermediary.*—[Reserved]

(v) *Electronic confirmation of taxpayer identifying number on withholding certificate.*—The Commissioner may prescribe procedures in a revenue procedure (see § 601.601(d)(2) of this chapter) or other appropriate guidance to require a withholding agent to confirm electronically with the IRS information concerning any TIN stated on a withholding certificate.

(vi) *Acceptable substitute form.*—A withholding agent may substitute its own form instead of an official Form W-8 or 8233 (or such other official form as the IRS may prescribe). Such a substitute for an official form will be acceptable if it contains provisions that are substantially similar to those of the official form, it contains the same certifications relevant to the transactions as are contained on the official form and these certifications are clearly set forth, and the substitute form includes a signature-under-penalties-of-perjury statement identical to the one stated on the official form. The substitute form is acceptable even if it does not contain all of the provisions contained on the official form, so long as it contains those provisions that are relevant to the transaction for which it is furnished. For example, a withholding agent that pays no income for which treaty benefits are claimed may develop a substitute form that is identical to the official form, except that it does not include information regarding claim of benefits under an income tax treaty. A withholding agent who uses a substitute form must furnish instructions relevant to the substitute form only to the extent and in the manner specified in the instructions to the official form. A withholding agent may refuse to accept a certificate from a payee or beneficial owner (including the official Form W-8 or 8233) if the certificate is not provided on the acceptable substitute form provided by the withholding agent. However, a withholding agent may refuse to accept a certificate provided by a payee or beneficial owner only if the withholding agent furnishes the payee or beneficial owner with an acceptable substitute form immediately upon receipt of an unacceptable form or within 5 business days of receipt of an unacceptable form from the payee or beneficial owner. In that case, the substitute form is acceptable only if it contains a notice that the withholding agent has refused to accept the form submitted by the payee or beneficial owner and that the payee or beneficial owner must submit the acceptable form provided by the withholding agent in order for the payee or beneficial owner to be treated as having furnished the required withholding certificate.

(vii) *Requirement of taxpayer identifying number.*—A TIN must be stated on a withholding certificate when required by this paragraph (e)(4)(vii). A TIN is required to be stated on—

(A) A withholding certificate on which a beneficial owner is claiming the benefit of a reduced rate under an income tax treaty (other than for amounts described in § 1.1441-6(c)(2);

(B) A withholding certificate on which a beneficial owner is claiming exemption from withholding because income is effectively connected with a U.S. trade or business;

(C) A withholding certificate on which a beneficial owner is claiming exemption from withholding under section 871(f) for certain annuities received under qualified plans;

(D) A withholding certificate on which a beneficial owner is claiming an exemption based solely on a foreign organization's claim of tax exempt status under section 501(c) or private foundation status (however, a TIN is not required from a foreign private foundation that is subject to the 4-percent tax under section 4948(a) on income if that income would be exempt from withholding but for section 4948(a) (e.g., portfolio interest));

(E) A withholding certificate from a person representing to be a qualified intermediary described in paragraph (e)(5)(ii) of this section;

(F) A withholding certificate from a person representing to be a withholding foreign partnership described in § 1.1441-5(c)(2)(i));

(G) A withholding certificate provided by a foreign organization that is described in section 501(c);

(H) A withholding certificate from a person representing to be a U.S. branch described in paragraph (b)(2)(iv) of this section.

(viii) *Reliance rules.*—A withholding agent may rely on the information and certifications stated on withholding certificates or other documentation without having to inquire into the truthfulness of this information or certification, unless it has actual knowledge or reason to know that the same is untrue. In the case of amounts described in § 1.1441-6(c)(2), a withholding agent described in § 1.1441-7(b)(2)(ii) has reason to know that the information or certifications on a certificate are untrue only to the extent provided in § 1.1441-7(b)(2)(ii). See § 1.1441-6(b)(1) for reliance on representations regarding eligibility for a reduced rate under an income tax treaty. Paragraphs (e)(4)(viii)(A) and (B) of this section provide examples of such reliance.

(A) *Classification.*—A withholding agent may rely on the claim of entity classification indicated on the withholding certificate that it receives from or for the beneficial owner, unless it has actual knowledge or reason to know that the classification claimed is incorrect. A withholding agent may not rely on a person's claim of classification other than as a corporation if the name of the corporation indicates that the person is a per se corporation described in § 301.7701-2(b)(8)(i) of this chapter unless the certificate contains a statement that the person is a grandfathered per se corporation described in § 301.7701-2(b)(8) of this chapter and that its grandfathered status has not been terminated. In the absence of reliable representation or information regarding the classification of the payee or beneficial owner, see § 1.1441-1(b)(3)(ii) for applicable presumptions.

(B) *Status of payee as an intermediary or as a person acting for its own account.*—A withholding agent may rely on the type of certificate furnished as indicative of the payee's status as an intermediary or as an owner, unless the withholding agent has actual knowledge or reason to know otherwise. For example, a withholding agent that receives a beneficial owner withholding certificate from a foreign financial institution may treat the institution as the beneficial owner, unless it has information in its records that would indicate otherwise or the certificate contains information that is not consistent with beneficial owner status (e.g., sub-account numbers or names). If the financial institution also acts as an intermediary, the withholding agent may request that the institution furnish two certificates, i.e., a beneficial owner certificate described in paragraph (e)(2)(i) of this section for the amounts that it receives as a beneficial owner, and an intermediary withholding certificate described in paragraph (e)(3)(i) of this section for the amounts that it receives as an intermediary. In the absence of reliable representation or information regarding the status of the payee as an owner or as an intermediary, see paragraph (b)(3)(v)(A) for applicable presumptions.

(ix) *Certificates to be furnished for each account unless exception applies.*—Unless otherwise provided in this paragraph (e)(4)(ix), a withholding agent that is a financial institution with which a customer may open an account shall obtain withholding certificates or other appropriate documentation on an account-by-account basis.

(A) *Coordinated account information system in effect.*—A withholding agent may rely on the withholding certificate or other appropriate documentation furnished by a customer for a pre-existing account under any one or more of the circumstances described in this paragraph (e)(4)(ix)(A).

(1) A withholding agent may rely on documentation furnished by a customer for another account if all such accounts are held at the same branch location.

(2) A withholding agent may rely on documentation furnished by a customer for an account held at another branch location of the same withholding agent or at a branch location of a person related to the withholding agent if the withholding agent and the related person are part of a universal account system that uses a customer identifier that can be used to retrieve systematically all other accounts of the customer. See § 31.3406(c)-1(c)(3)(ii) and (iii)(C) of this chapter for an identical procedure for purposes of backup withholding. For purposes of this paragraph (e)(4)(ix)(A), a withholding agent is related to another person if it is related within the meaning of section 267(b) or 707(b).

(3) A withholding agent may rely on documentation furnished by a customer for an account held at another branch location of the same withholding agent or at a branch location of a person related to the withholding agent if the withholding agent and the related person are part of an information system other than a universal account system and the information system is described in this paragraph (e)(4)(ix)(A)(3). The system must allow the withholding agent to easily access data regarding the nature of the documentation, the information contained in the documentation, and its validity status, and must allow the withholding agent to easily transmit data into the system regarding any facts of which it becomes aware that may affect the reliability of the documentation. The withholding agent must be able to establish how and when it has accessed the data regarding the documentation and, if applicable, how and when it has transmitted data regarding any facts of which it became aware that may affect the relia-

bility of the documentation. In addition, the withholding agent or the related party must be able to establish that any data it has transmitted to the information system has been processed and appropriate due diligence has been exercised regarding the validity of the documentation.

(4) A withholding agent may rely on documentation furnished by a beneficial owner or payee to an agent of the withholding agent. The agent may retain the documentation as part of an information system maintained for a single or multiple withholding agents provided that the system permits any withholding agent that uses the system to easily access data regarding the nature of the documentation, the information contained in the documentation, and its validity, and must allow the withholding agent to easily transmit data into the system regarding any facts of which it becomes aware that may affect the reliability of the documentation. The withholding agent must be able to establish how and when it has accessed the data regarding the documentation and, if applicable, how and when it has transmitted data regarding any facts of which it became aware that may affect the reliability of the documentation. In addition, the withholding agent must be able to establish that any data it has transmitted to the information system has been processed and appropriate due diligence has been exercised regarding the validity of the documentation.

(B) *Family of mutual funds.*—An interest in a mutual fund that has a common investment advisor or common principal underwriter with other mutual funds (within the same family of funds) may, in the discretion of the mutual fund, be represented by one single withholding certificate where shares are acquired or owned in any of the funds. See § 31.3406(h)-3(a)(2) of this chapter for an identical procedures for purposes of backup withholding.

(C) *Special rule for brokers.*—*(1) In general.*—A withholding agent may rely on the certification of a broker that the broker holds a valid beneficial owner withholding certificate described in paragraph (e)(2)(i) of this section or other appropriate documentation for that beneficial owner with respect to any readily tradable instrument, as defined in § 31.3406(h)-1(d) of this chapter, if the broker is a United States person (including a U.S. branch treated as a U.S. person under paragraph (b)(2)(iv) of this section) that is acting as the agent of a beneficial owner and the U.S. broker has been provided a valid Form W-8 or other appropriate documentation. The certification must be in writing or in electronic form and contain all of the information required of a nonqualified intermediary under paragraphs (e)(3)(iv)(B) and (C) of this section. If a U.S. broker chooses to use this paragraph (e)(4)(ix)(C), that U.S. broker will be solely responsible for applying the rules of § 1.1441-7(b) to the withholding certificates or other appropriate documentation. For purposes of this paragraph (c)(4)(ix)(C), the term broker means a person treated as a broker under §1.6045-1(a).

(2) The following example illustrates the rules of this paragraph (e)(4)(ix)(C):

Example. SCO is a U.S. securities clearing organization that provides clearing services for correspondent broker, CB, a U.S. corporation. Pursuant to a fully disclosed clearing agreement, CB fully discloses the identity of each of its customers to SCO. Part of SCO's clearing duties include the crediting of income and gross proceeds of readily tradeable instruments (as defined in §31.3406(h)-1(d)) to each customer's account. For each disclosed customer that is a foreign beneficial owner, CB provides SCO with information required under paragraphs (e)(3)(iv)(B) and (C) of this section that is necessary to apply the correct rate of withholding and to file Forms 1042-S. SCO may use the representations and beneficial owner information provided by CB to determine the proper amount of withholding and to file Forms 1042-S. CB is responsible for determining the validity of the withholding certificates or other appropriate documentation under §1.1441-1(b).

(5) *Qualified intermediaries.*—(i) *General rule.*—A qualified intermediary, as defined in paragraph (e)(5)(ii) of this section, may furnish a qualified intermediary withholding certificate to a withholding agent. The withholding certificate provides certifications on behalf of other persons for the purpose of claiming and verifying reduced rates of withholding under section 1441 or 1442 and for the purpose of reporting and withholding under other provisions of the Internal Revenue Code, such as the provisions under chapter 61 and section 3406 (and the regulations under those provisions). Furnishing such a certificate is in lieu of transmitting to a withholding agent withholding certificates or other appropriate documentation for the persons for whom the qualified intermediary receives the payment, including interest holders in a qualified intermediary that is fiscally transparent under the regulations under section 894. Although the qualified intermediary is required to obtain withholding certificates or other appropriate documentation from beneficial owners, payees, or interest holders pursuant to its agreement with the IRS, it is generally not required to attach such documentation to the intermediary withholding certificate. Notwithstanding the preceding sentence a qualified intermediary must provide a withholding agent with the Forms W-9, or disclose the names, addresses, and taxpayer identifying numbers, if known, of those U.S. non-exempt recipients for whom the qualified intermediary receives reportable amounts (within the meaning of paragraph (e)(3)(vi) of this section) to the extent required in the qualified intermediary's agreement with the IRS. A person may claim qualified intermediary status

before an agreement is executed with the IRS if it has applied for such status and the IRS authorizes such status on an interim basis under such procedures as the IRS may prescribe.

(ii) *Definition of qualified intermediary.*— With respect to a payment to a foreign person, the term *qualified intermediary* means a person that is a party to a withholding agreement with the IRS and such person is—

(A) A foreign financial institution or a foreign clearing organization (as defined in §1.163-5(c)(2)(i)(D)(8), without regard to the requirement that the organization hold obligations for members, other than a U.S. branch or U.S. office of such institution or organization;

(B) A foreign branch or office of a U.S. financial institution or a foreign branch or office of a U.S. clearing organization (as defined in §1.163-5(c)(2)(i)(D)(8), without regard to the requirement that the organization hold obligations for members);

(C) A foreign corporation for purposes of presenting claims of benefits under an income tax treaty on behalf of its shareholders; or

(D) Any other person acceptable to the IRS.

(iii) *Withholding agreement.*—(A) *In general.*—The IRS may, upon request, enter into a withholding agreement with a foreign person described in paragraph (e)(5)(ii) of this section pursuant to such procedures as the IRS may prescribe in published guidance (see §601.601(d)(2) of this chapter). Under the withholding agreement, a qualified intermediary shall generally be subject to the applicable withholding and reporting provisions applicable to withholding agents and payors under chapters 3 and 61 of the Internal Revenue Code, section 3406, the regulations under those provisions, and other withholding provisions of the Internal Revenue Code, except to the extent provided under the agreement.

(B) *Terms of the withholding agreement.*— Generally, the agreement shall specify the type of certifications and documentation upon which the qualified intermediary may rely to ascertain the classification (e.g., corporation or partnership) and status (i.e., U.S. or foreign) of beneficial owners and payees who receive payments collected by the qualified intermediary and, if necessary, entitlement to the benefits of a reduced rate under an income tax treaty. The agreement shall specify if, and to what extent, the qualified intermediary may assume primary withholding responsibility in accordance with paragraph (e)(5)(iv) of this section. It shall also specify the extent to which applicable return filing and information reporting requirements are modified so that, in appropriate cases, the qualified intermediary may report payments to the IRS on an aggregated basis, without having to disclose the identity of beneficial owners and payees. How-

Reg. §1.1441-1(e)(5)(iii)(B)

ever, the qualified intermediary may be required to provide to the IRS the name and address of those foreign customers who benefit from a reduced rate under an income tax treaty pursuant to the qualified intermediary arrangement for purposes of verifying entitlement to such benefits, particularly under an applicable limitation on benefits provision. Under the agreement, a qualified intermediary may agree to act as an acceptance agent to perform the duties described in § 301.6109-1(d)(3)(iv)(A) of this chapter. The agreement may specify the manner in which applicable procedures for adjustments for underwithholding and overwithholding, including refund procedures, apply in the context of a qualified intermediary arrangement and the extent to which applicable procedures may be modified. In particular, a withholding agreement may allow a qualified intermediary to claim refunds of overwithheld amounts. If relevant, the agreement shall specify the manner in which the qualified intermediary may deal with payments to other intermediaries and flow-through entities. In addition, the agreement shall specify the manner in which the IRS will verify compliance with the agreement. In appropriate cases, the IRS may agree to rely on audits performed by an intermediary's approved auditor. In such a case, the IRS's audit may be limited to the audit of the auditor's records (including work papers of the auditor and reports prepared by the auditor indicating the methodology employed to verify the entity's compliance with the agreement). For this purpose, the agreement shall specify the auditor or class of auditors that are approved. Generally, an auditor will not be approved if the auditor is not subject to laws, regulations, or rules that impose sanctions for failure to exercise its independence and to perform the audit competently. The agreement may include provisions for the assessment and collection of tax in the event that failure to comply with the terms of the agreement results in the failure by the withholding agent or the qualified intermediary to withhold and deposit the required amount of tax. Further, the agreement may specify the procedures by which deposits of amounts withheld are to be deposited, if different from the deposit procedures under the Internal Revenue Code and applicable regulations. To determine whether to enter a qualified intermediary withholding agreement and the terms of any particular withholding agreement, the IRS will consider appropriate factors including whether or not the foreign person agrees to assume primary withholding responsibility, the type of local know-your-customer laws and practices to which it is subject, the extent and nature of supervisory and regulatory control exercised under the laws of the foreign country over the foreign person, the volume of investments in U.S. securities (determined in dollar amounts and number of account holders), the financial condition of the foreign person, and whether the qualified intermediary is a resident of a country with which the United States has an income tax treaty.

(iv) *Assignment of primary withholding responsibility.*—Any person who meets the definition of a withholding agent under § 1.1441-7(a) (whether a U.S. person or a foreign person) is required to withhold and deposit any amount withheld under § 1.1461-1(a) and to make the returns prescribed by § 1.1461-1(b) and (c). If permitted by its qualified intermediary agreement, a qualified intermediary agreement may, however, inform a withholding agent from which it receives a payment that it will assume the primary obligation to withhold, deposit, and report amounts under chapter 3 of the Internal Revenue Code and/or under chapter 61 of the Internal Revenue Code and section 3406. If a withholding agent makes a payment of an amount subject to withholding, as defined in § 1.1441-2(a), or a reportable payment, as defined in section 3406(b), to a qualified intermediary that represents to the withholding agent that it has assumed primary withholding responsibility for the payment, the withholding agent is not required to withhold on the payment. The withholding agent is not required to determine that the qualified intermediary agreement actually permits the qualified intermediary to assume primary withholding responsibility. A qualified intermediary that assumes primary withholding responsibility under chapter 3 of the Internal Revenue Code or primary reporting and backup withholding responsibility under chapter 61 and section 3406 is not required to assume primary withholding responsibility for all accounts it has with a withholding agent but must assume primary withholding responsibility for all payments made to any one account that it has with the withholding agent. A qualified intermediary may agree with the withholding agent to assume primary withholding responsibility under chapter 3 and section 3406, only if expressly permitted to do so under its agreement with the IRS.

(v) *Withholding statement.*—(A) *In general.*—A qualified intermediary must provide each withholding agent from which it receives reportable amounts, as defined in paragraph (e)(3)(vi) of this section, as a qualified intermediary with a written statement (the withholding statement) containing the information specified in paragraph (e)(5)(v)(B) of this section. A withholding statement is not required, however, if all of the information a withholding agent needs to fulfill its withholding and reporting requirements is contained in the withholding certificate. The qualified intermediary agreement may require, in appropriate circumstances, the qualified intermediary to include information in its withholding statement relating to payments other than payments of reportable amounts. The withholding statement forms an integral part of the qualified intermediary's qualified intermediary withholding certificate and the penalties of perjury statement provided on the withholding certificate shall apply to the withholding statement as well. The withholding statement may be provided in any manner, and in any form, to which qualified intermediary and the withholding agent mutually agree, including electronically. If the withholding statement is provided electronically, there must be sufficient safeguards to ensure that the information received by the withholding agent is the information sent by qualified intermediary and must also document all occasions of user access that result in the submission or modification of withholding statement information. In addition, the electronic system must be capable of providing a hard copy of all withholding statements provided by the qualified intermediary. The withholding statement shall be updated as often as necessary for the withholding agent to meet its reporting and withholding obligations under chapters 3 and 61 of the Internal Revenue Code and section 3406. A withholding agent will be liable for tax, interest, and penalties in accordance with paragraph (b)(7) of this section to the extent it does not follow the presumption rules of paragraph (b)(3) of this section, §§ 1.1441-5(d) and (e)(6), and 1.6049-5(d) for any payment, or portion thereof, for which it does not have a valid withholding statement prior to making a payment.

     (B) *Content of withholding statement.*—The withholding statement must contain sufficient information for a withholding agent to apply the correct rate of withholding on payments from the accounts identified on the statement and to properly report such payments on Forms 1042-S and Forms 1099, as applicable. The withholding statement must—

     (1) Designate those accounts for which the qualified intermediary acts as a qualified intermediary;

     (2) Designate those accounts for which qualified intermediary assumes primary withholding responsibility under chapter 3 of the Internal Revenue Code and/or primary reporting and backup withholding responsibility under chapter 61 and section 3406; and

     (3) Provide information regarding withholding rate pools, as described in paragraph (e)(5)(v)(C) of this section.

     (C) *Withholding rate pools.*—(1) In general.—Except to the extent it has assumed both primary withholding responsibility under chapter 3 of the Internal Revenue Code and primary reporting and backup withholding responsibility under chapter 61 and section 3406 with respect to a payment, a qualified intermediary shall provide as part of its withholding statement the withholding rate pool information that is required for the withholding agent to meet its withholding and reporting obligations under chapters 3 and 61 of the Internal Revenue Code and section 3406. A withholding rate pool is a payment of a single type of income, determined

in accordance with the categories of income reported on Form 1042-S or Form 1099, as applicable, that is subject to a single rate of withholding. A withholding rate pool may be established by any reasonable method on which the qualified intermediary and a withholding agent agree (e.g., by establishing a separate account for a single withholding rate pool, or by dividing a payment made to a single account into portions allocable to each withholding rate pool). To the extent a qualified intermediary does not assume primary reporting and backup withholding responsibility under chapter 61 and section 3406, a qualified intermediary's withholding statement must establish a separate withholding rate pool for each U.S. non-exempt recipient account holder that the qualified intermediary has disclosed to the withholding agent unless the qualified intermediary uses the alternative procedures in paragraph (e)(5)(v)(C)(2) of this section. A qualified intermediary shall determine withholding rate pools based on valid documentation that it obtains under its withholding agreement with the IRS, or if a payment cannot be reliably associated with valid documentation, under the applicable presumption rules. If a qualified intermediary has an account holder that is another intermediary (whether a qualified intermediary or a nonqualified intermediary) or a flow-through entity, the qualified intermediary may combine the account holder information provided by the intermediary or flow-through entity with the qualified intermediary's direct account holder information to determine the qualified intermediary's withholding rate pools.

     (2) *Alternative procedure for U.S. non-exempt recipients.*—If permitted under its agreement with the IRS, a qualified intermediary may, by mutual agreement with a withholding agent, establish a single zero withholding rate pool that includes U.S. non-exempt recipient account holders for whom the qualified intermediary has provided Forms W-9 prior to the withholding agent paying any reportable payments, as defined in the qualified intermediary agreement, and a separate withholding rate pool (subject to 31-percent withholding) that includes only U.S. non-exempt recipient account holders for whom a qualified intermediary has not provided Forms W-9 prior to the withholding agent paying any reportable payments. If a qualified intermediary chooses the alternative procedure of this paragraph (e)(5)(v)(C)(2), the qualified intermediary must provide the information required by its qualified intermediary agreement to the withholding agent no later than January 15 of the year following the year in which the payments are paid. Failure to provide such information will result in the application of penalties to the qualified intermediary under sections 6721 and 6722, as well as any other applicable penalties, and may result in the termination of the qualified intermediary's withholding agreement with the IRS. A withholding agent shall not be liable

for tax, interest, or penalties for failure to backup withhold or report information under chapter 61 of the Internal Revenue Code due solely to the errors or omissions of the qualified intermediary. If a qualified intermediary fails to provide the allocation information required by this paragraph (e)(5)(v)(C)(2), with respect to U.S. nonexempt recipients, the withholding agent shall report the unallocated amount paid from the withholding rate pool to an unknown recipient, or otherwise in accordance with the appropriate Form 1099 and the instructions accompanying the form.

(f) *Effective date.*—(1) *In general.*—This section applies to payments made after December 31, 2000.

(2) *Transition rules.*—(i) *Special rules for existing documentation.*—For purposes of paragraphs (d)(3) and (e)(2)(i) of this section, the validity of a withholding certificate (namely, Form W-8, 8233, 1001, 4224, or 1078 , or a statement described in §1.1441-5 in effect prior to January 1, 2001 (see §1.1441-5 as contained in 26 CFR part 1, revised April 1, 1999)) that was valid on January 1, 1998 under the regulations in effect prior to January 1, 2001 (see 26 CFR parts 1 and 35a, revised April 1, 1999) and expired, or will expire, at any time during 1998, is extended until December 31, 1998. The validity of a withholding certificate that is valid on or after January 1, 1999, remains valid until its validity expires under the regulations in effect prior to January 1, 2001 (see 26 CFR parts 1 and 35a, revised April 1, 1999) but in no event will such withholding certificate remain valid after December 31, 2000. The rule in this paragraph (f)(2)(i), however, does not apply to extend the validity period of a withholding certificate that expires solely by reason of changes in the circumstances of the person whose name is on the certificate. Notwithstanding the first three sentences of this paragraph (f)(2)(i), a withholding agent may choose to not take advantage of the transition rule in this paragraph (f)(2)(i) with respect to one or more withholding certificates valid under the regulations in effect prior to January 1, 2001 (see 26 CFR parts 1 and 35a, revised April 1, 1999) and, therefore, to require withholding certificates conforming to the requirements described in this section (new withholding certificates). For purposes of this section, a new withholding certificate is deemed to satisfy the documentation requirement under the regulations in effect prior to January 1, 2001 (see 26 CFR parts 1 and 35a, revised April 1, 1999). Further, a new withholding certificate remains valid for the period specified in paragraph (e)(4)(ii) of this section, regardless of when the certificate is obtained.

(ii) *Lack of documentation for past years.*—A taxpayer may elect to apply the provisions of paragraphs (b)(7)(i)(B), (ii), and (iii) of this section, dealing with liability for failure to obtain documentation timely, to all of its open tax years, including tax years that are currently under examination by the IRS. The election is made by simply taking action under those provisions in the same manner as the taxpayer would take action for payments made after December 31, 2000. [Reg. §1.1441-1.]

☐ [*T.D. 6187, 7-5-56. Amended by T.D. 6592, 2-27-62; T.D. 6908, 12-30-66; T.D. 7157, 12-29-71; T.D. 7385, 10-28-75; T.D. 7670, 1-30-80; T.D. 8734, 10-6-97; T.D. 8804, 12-30-98; T.D. 8856, 12-29-99 (corrected 3-27-2000); T.D. 8881, 5-15-2000 (corrected 4-5-2001); T.D. 9023, 11-21-2002; T.D. 9253, 3-13-2006 and T.D. 9323, 4-11-2007.*]

[Reg. §1.1441-2]

§1.1441-2. Amounts subject to withholding.—(a) *In general.*—For purposes of the regulations under chapter 3 of the Internal Revenue Code, the term *amounts subject to withholding* means amounts from sources within the United States that constitute either fixed or determinable annual or periodical income described in paragraph (b) of this section or other amounts subject to withholding described in paragraph (c) of this section. For purposes of this paragraph (a), an amount shall be treated as being from sources within the United States if the source of the amount cannot be determined at the time of payment. See §1.1441-3(d)(1) for determining the amount to be withheld from a payment in the absence of information at the time of payment regarding the source of the amount. Amounts subject to withholding include amounts that are not fixed or determinable annual or periodical income and upon which withholding is specifically required under a provision of this section or another section of the regulations under chapter 3 of the Internal Revenue Code (such as corporate distributions upon which withholding is required under §1.1441-3(c)(1) that do not constitute dividend income). Amounts subject to withholding do not include—

(1) Amounts described in §1.1441-1(b)(4)(i) to the extent they involve interest on obligations in bearer form or on foreign-targeted registered obligations (but, in the case of a foreign-targeted registered obligation, only to the extent of those amounts paid to a registered owner that is a financial institution within the meaning of section 871(h)(5)(B) or a member of a clearing organization which member is the beneficial owner of the obligation);

(2) Amounts described in §1.1441-1(b)(4)(ii) (dealing with bank deposit interest and similar types of interest (including original issue discount) described in section 871(i)(2)(A) or 881(d));

(3) Amounts described in §1.1441-1(b)(4)(iv) (dealing with interest or original issue discount on certain short-term obligations described in section 871(g)(1)(B) or 881(e));

(4) Amounts described in §1.1441-1(b)(4)(xx) (dealing with income from certain gambling winnings exempt from tax under section 871(j));

(5) Amounts paid as part of the purchase price of an obligation sold or exchanged between interest payment dates, unless the sale or exchange is part of a plan the principal purpose of which is to avoid tax and the withholding agent has actual knowledge or reason to know of such plan;

(6) Original issue discount paid as part of the purchase price of an obligation sold or exchanged in a transaction other than a redemption of such obligation, unless the purchase is part of a plan the principal purpose of which is to avoid tax and the withholding agent has actual knowledge or reason to know of such plan; and

(7) Insurance premiums paid with respect to a contract that is subject to the section 4371 excise tax.

(b) *Fixed or determinable annual or periodical income.*—(1) *In general.*—(i) *Definition.*—For purposes of chapter 3 of the Internal Revenue Code and the regulations thereunder, fixed or determinable annual or periodical income includes all income included in gross income under section 61 (including original issue discount) except for the items specified in paragraph (b)(2) of this section. Items of income that are excluded from gross income under a provision of law without regard to the U.S. or foreign status of the owner of the income, such as interest excluded from gross income under section 103(a) or qualified scholarship income under section 117, shall not be treated as fixed or determinable annual or periodical income under chapter 3 of the Internal Revenue Code. Income excluded from gross income under section 892 (income of foreign governments) or section 115 (income of a U.S. possession) is fixed or determinable annual or periodical income since the exclusion from gross income under those sections is dependent on the foreign status of the owner of the income. See §1.306-3(h) for treating income from the disposition of section 306 stock as fixed or determinable annual or periodical income.

(ii) *Manner of payment.*—The term *fixed or determinable annual or periodical* is merely descriptive of the character of a class of income. If an item of income falls within the class of income contemplated in the statute and described in paragraph (a) of this section, it is immaterial whether payment of that item is made in a series of payments or in a single lump sum. Further, the income need not be paid annually if it is paid periodically; that is to say, from time to time, whether or not at regular intervals. The fact that a payment is not made annually or periodically does not, however, prevent it from being fixed or determinable annual or periodical income (e.g., a lump sum payment). In addition, the fact that

the length of time during which the payments are to be made may be increased or diminished in accordance with someone's will or with the happening of an event does not disqualify the payment as determinable or periodical. For this purpose, the share of the fixed or determinable annual or periodical income of an estate or trust from sources within the United States which is required to be distributed currently, or which has been paid or credited during the taxable year, to a nonresident alien beneficiary of such estate or trust constitutes fixed or determinable annual or periodical income.

(iii) *Determinability of amount.*—An item of income is fixed when it is to be paid in amounts definitely pre-determined. An item of income is determinable if the amount to be paid is not known but there is a basis of calculation by which the amount may be ascertained at a later time. For example, interest is determinable even if it is contingent in that its amount cannot be determined at the time of payment of an amount with respect to a loan because the calculation of the interest portion of the payment is contingent upon factors that are not fixed at the time of payment. For purposes of this section, an amount of income does not have to be determined at the time that the payment is made in order to be determinable. An amount of income described in paragraph (a) of this section which the withholding agent knows is part of a payment it makes but which it cannot calculate exactly at the time of payment, is nevertheless determinable if the determination of the exact amount depends upon events expected to occur at a future date. In contrast, a payment which may be income in the future based upon events that are not anticipated at the time the payment is made is not determinable. For example, loan proceeds may become income to the borrower when and to the extent the loan is canceled without repayment. While the cancellation of the debt is income to the borrower when it occurs, it is not determinable at the time the loan proceeds are disbursed to the borrower if the lack of repayment leading to the cancellation of part or all of the debt was not anticipated at the time of disbursement. The fact that the source of an item of income cannot be determined at the time that the payment is made does not render a payment not determinable. See §1.1441-3(d)(1) for determining the amount to be withheld from a payment in the absence of information at the time of payment regarding the source of the amount.

(2) *Exceptions.*—For purposes of chapter 3 of the Code and the regulations thereunder, the items of income described in this paragraph (b)(2) are not fixed or determinable annual or periodical income—

(i) Gains derived from the sale of property (including market discount and option premiums), except for gains described in paragraph (b)(3) or (c) of this section; and

(ii) Any other income that the Internal Revenue Service (IRS) may determine, in published guidance (see § 601.601(d)(2) of this chapter), is not fixed or determinable annual or periodical income.

(3) *Original issue discount.*—(i) *Amount subject to tax.*—An amount representing original issue discount is fixed or determinable annual or periodical income that is subject to tax under sections 871(a)(1)(C) and 881(a)(3) to the extent provided in those sections and this paragraph (b)(3) if not otherwise excluded under paragraph (a) of this section. An amount of original issue discount is subject to tax with respect to a foreign beneficial owner of an obligation carrying original issue discount upon a sale or exchange of the obligation or when a payment is made on such obligation. The amount taxable is the amount of original issue discount that accrued while the foreign person held the obligation up to the time that the obligation is sold or exchanged or that a payment is made on the obligation, reduced by any amount of original issue discount that was taken into account prior to that time (due to a payment made on the obligation). In the case of a payment made on the obligation, the tax due on the amount of original issue discount may not exceed the amount of the payment reduced by the tax imposed on any portion of the payment that is qualified stated interest.

(ii) *Amounts subject to withholding.*—A withholding agent must withhold on the taxable amount of original issue discount paid on the redemption of an original issue discount obligation unless an exception to withholding applies (e.g., portfolio interest or treaty exception). In addition, withholding is required on the taxable amount of original issue discount upon the sale or exchange of an original issue discount obligation, other than in a redemption, to the extent the withholding agent has actual knowledge or reason to know that the sale or exchange is part of a plan the principal purpose of which is to avoid tax. If a withholding agent cannot determine the taxable amount of original issue discount on the redemption of an original issue discount obligation (or on the sale or exchange of such an obligation if the principal purpose of the sale is to avoid tax), then it must withhold on the entire amount of original issue discount accrued from the date of issue until the date of redemption (or the date the obligation is sold or exchanged) determined on the basis of the most recently published "List of Original Issue Discount Instruments" (IRS Publication 1212, available from the IRS Forms Distribution Center) or similar list published by the IRS as if the beneficial owner of the obligation had held the obligation since its original issue.

(iii) *Exceptions to withholding.*—To the extent that this paragraph (b)(3) applies to require withholding by a person other than an issuer of an original issue discount obligation, or the issuer's agent, it shall apply only to obligations issued after December 31, 2000.

(4) *Securities lending transactions and equivalent transactions.*—See §§ 1.871-7(b)(2) and 1.881-2(b)(2) regarding the character of substitute payments as fixed and determinable annual or periodical income. Such amounts constitute income subject to withholding to the extent they are from sources within the United States, as determined under section §§ 1.861-2(a)(7) and 1.861-3(a)(6). See §§ 1.6042-3(a)(2) and 1.6049-5(a)(5) for reporting requirements applicable to substitute dividend and interest payments, respectively.

(5) *REMIC residual interests.*—Amounts subject to withholding include an excess inclusion described in § 1.860G-3(b)(2) and the portion of an amount described in § 1.860G-3(b)(1) that is an excess inclusion.

(c) *Other income subject to withholding.*—Withholding is also required on the following items of income—

(1) Gains described in sections 631(b) or (c), relating to treatment of gain on disposal of timber, coal, or domestic iron ore with a retained economic interest; and

(2) Gains subject to the 30-percent tax under section 871(a)(1)(D) or 881(a)(4), relating to contingent payments received from the sale or exchange of patents, copyrights, and similar intangible property.

(d) *Exceptions to withholding where no money or property is paid or lack of knowledge.*—(1) *General rule.*—A withholding agent who is not related to the recipient or beneficial owner has an obligation to withhold under section 1441 only to the extent that, at any time between the date that the obligation to withhold would arise (but for the provisions of this paragraph (d)) and the due date for the filing of return on Form 1042 (including extensions) for the year in which the payment occurs, it has control over, or custody of money or property owned by the recipient or beneficial owner from which to withhold an amount and has knowledge of the facts that give rise to the payment. The exemption from the obligation to withhold under this paragraph (d) shall not apply, however, to distributions with respect to stock or if the lack of control or custody of money or property from which to withhold is part of a pre-arranged plan known to the withholding agent to avoid withholding under section 1441, 1442, or 1443. For purposes of this paragraph (d), a withholding agent is related to the recipient or beneficial owner if it is related within the meaning of section 482. Any exemption from withholding pursuant to this paragraph (d) applies without a requirement that documentation be furnished to the withholding agent. However, documentation may have to be furnished for purposes of the information reporting provisions under chapter 61 of the Code and backup withholding under section 3406. The exemption from withholding under this paragraph (d) is not a determination that the amounts are not fixed or determinable annual or periodical income, nor does it constitute an exemption from reporting the amount under § 1.1461-1(b) and (c).

(2) *Cancellation of debt.*—A lender of funds who forgives any portion of the loan is deemed to have made a payment of income to the borrower under § 1.61-12 at the time the event of forgiveness occurs. However, based on the rules of paragraph (d)(1) of this section, the lender shall have no obligation to withhold on such amount to the extent that it does not have custody or control over money or property of the borrower at any time between the time that the loan is forgiven and the due date (including extensions) of the Form 1042 for the year in which the payment is deemed to occur. A payment received by the lender from the borrower in partial settlement of the debt obligation does not, for this purpose, constitute an amount of money or property belonging to the borrower from which the withholding tax liability can be satisfied.

(3) *Satisfaction of liability following underwithholding by withholding agent.*—A withholding agent who, after failing to withhold the proper amount from a payment, satisfies the underwithheld amount out of its own funds may cause the beneficial owner to realize income to the extent of such satisfaction or may be considered to have advanced funds to the beneficial owner. Such determination depends upon the contractual arrangements governing the satisfaction of such tax liability (e.g., arrangements in which the withholding agent agrees to pay the amount due under section 1441 for the beneficial owner) or applicable laws governing the transaction. If the satisfaction of the tax liability is considered to constitute an advance of funds by the withholding agent to the beneficial owner and the withholding agent fails to collect the amount from the beneficial owner, a cancellation of indebtedness may result, giving rise to income to the beneficial owner under § 1.61-12. While such income is annual or periodical fixed or determinable, the withholding agent shall have no liability to withhold on such income to the extent the conditions set forth in paragraphs (d)(1) and (2) of this section are satisfied with respect to this income. Contrast the rules of this paragraph (d)(3) with the rules in § 1.1441-3(f)(1) dealing with a situation in which the satisfaction of the beneficial owner's tax liability itself constitutes additional income to the beneficial owner. See, also, § 1.1441-3(c)(2)(ii)(B) for a special rule regarding underwithholding on corporate distributions due to underestimating an amount of earnings and profits.

(4) *Withholding exemption inapplicable.*—The exemption in § 1.1441-2(d) from the obligation to withhold shall not apply to amounts described in § 1.860G-3(b)(1) (regarding certain partnership allocations of REMIC net income with respect to a REMIC residual interest).

(e) *Payment.*—(1) *General rule.*—A payment is considered made to a person if that person realizes income whether or not such income results from an actual transfer of cash or other property. For example, realization of income from cancellation of debt results in a deemed payment. A payment is considered made when the amount would be includible in the income of the beneficial owner under the U.S. tax principles governing the cash basis method of accounting. A payment is considered made whether it is made directly to the beneficial owner or to another person for the benefit of the beneficial owner (e.g., to the agent of the beneficial owner). Thus, a payment of income is considered made to a beneficial owner if it is paid in complete or partial satisfaction of the beneficial owner's debt to a creditor. In the event of a conflict between the rules of this paragraph (e)(1) governing whether a payment has occurred and its timing and the rules of § 31.3406(a)-4 of this chapter, the rules in § 31.3406(a)-4 of this chapter shall apply to the extent that the application of section 3406 is relevant to the transaction at issue.

(2) *Income allocated under section 482.*—A payment is considered made to the extent income subject to withholding is allocated under section 482. Further, income arising as a result of a secondary adjustment made in conjunction with a reallocation of income under section 482 from a foreign person to a related U.S. person is considered paid to a foreign person unless the taxpayer to whom the income is reallocated has entered into a repatriation agreement with the IRS and the agreement eliminates the liability for withholding under this section. For purposes of determining the liability for withholding, the payment of income is deemed to have occurred on the last day of the taxable year in which the transactions that give rise to the allocation of income and the secondary adjustments, if any, took place.

(3) *Blocked income.*—Income is not considered paid if it is blocked under executive authority, such as the President's exercise of emergency power under the Trading with the Enemy Act (50 U.S.C. App. 5), or the International Emergency Economic Powers Act (50 U.S.C. 1701 et seq).. However, on the date that the blocking restrictions are removed, the income that was blocked is considered constructively received by the beneficial owner (and therefore paid for purposes of this section) and subject to withholding under § 1.1441-1. Any exemption from withholding pursuant to this paragraph (e)(3) applies without a requirement that documentation be

furnished to the withholding agent. However, documentation may have to be furnished for purposes of the information reporting provisions under chapter 61 of the Code and backup withholding under section 3406. The exemption from withholding granted by this paragraph (e)(3) is not a determination that the amounts are not fixed or determinable annual or periodical income.

(4) *Special rules for dividends.*—For purposes of sections 1441 and 6042, in the case of stock for which the record date is earlier than the payment date, dividends are considered paid on the payment date. In the case of a corporate reorganization, if a beneficial owner is required to exchange stock held in a former corporation for stock in a new corporation before dividends that are to be paid with respect to the stock in the new corporation will be paid on such stock, the dividend is considered paid on the date that the payee or beneficial owner actually exchanges the stock and receives the dividend. See §31.3406(a)-4(a)(2) of this chapter.

(5) *Certain interest accrued by a foreign corporation.*—For purposes of sections 1441 and 6049, a foreign corporation shall be treated as having made a payment of interest as of the last day of the taxable year if it has made an election under §1.884-4(c)(1) to treat accrued interest as if it were paid in that taxable year.

(6) *Payments other than in U.S. dollars.*—For purposes of section 1441, a payment includes amounts paid in a medium other than U.S. dollars. See §1.1441-3(e) for rules regarding the amount subject to withholding in the case of such payments.

(f) *Effective/applicability date.*—This section applies to payments made after December 31, 2000. Paragraphs (b)(5) and (d)(4) of this section apply to payments made after August 1, 2006. [Reg. §1.1441-2.]

☐ [*T.D.* 6187, 7-5-56. *Amended by T.D.* 6464, 5-11-60, *T.D.* 6592, 2-27-62, *T.D.* 6841, 7-26-65, *T.D.* 6873, 1-24-66, *T.D.* 6908, 12-30-66; *T.D.* 7977, 9-19-84; *T.D.* 8734, 10-6-97; *T.D.* 8804, 12-30-98; *T.D.* 8856, 12-29-99; *T.D.* 8881, 5-15-2000; *T.D.* 9272, 7-31-2006 *and T.D.* 9415, 7-11-2008 (*corrected* 8-5-2008).]

[Reg. §1.1441-3]

§1.1441-3. Determination of amounts to be withheld.—(a) *Withholding on gross amount.*—Except as otherwise provided in regulations under section 1441, the amount subject to withholding under §1.1441-1 is the gross amount of income subject to withholding that is paid to a foreign person. The gross amount of income subject to withholding may not be reduced by any deductions, except to the extent that one or more personal exemptions are allowed as provided under §1.1441-4(b)(6).

(b) *Withholding on payments on certain obligations.*—(1) *Withholding at time of payment of interest.*—When making a payment on an interest-bearing obligation, a withholding agent must withhold under §1.1441-1 upon the gross amount of stated interest payable on the interest payment date, regardless of whether the payment constitutes a return of capital or the payment of income within the meaning of section 61. To the extent an amount was withheld on an amount of capital rather than interest, see the rules for adjustments, refunds, or credits under §1.1441-1(b)(8).

(2) *No withholding between interest payment dates.*—(i) *In general.*—A withholding agent is not required to withhold under §1.1441-1 upon interest accrued on the date of a sale or exchange of a debt obligation when that sale occurs between two interest payment dates (even though the amount is treated as interest under §1.61-7(c) or (d) and is subject to tax under section 871 or 881). See §1.6045-1(c) for reporting requirements by brokers with respect to sale proceeds. See §1.61-7(c) regarding the character of payments received by the acquirer of an obligation subsequent to such acquisition (that is, as a return of capital or interest accrued after the acquisition). Any exemption from withholding pursuant to this paragraph (b)(2)(i) applies without a requirement that documentation be furnished to the withholding agent. However, documentation may have to be furnished for purposes of the information reporting provisions under section 6045 or 6049 and backup withholding under section 3406. The exemption from withholding granted by this paragraph (b)(2) is not a determination that the accrued interest is not fixed or determinable annual or periodical income under section 871 (a) or 881(a).

(ii) *Anti-abuse rule.*—The exemption in paragraph (b)(2)(i) of this section does not apply if the sale of securities is part of a plan the principal purpose of which is to avoid tax by selling and repurchasing securities and the withholding agent has actual knowledge or reason to know of such plan.

(c) *Corporate distributions.*—(1) *General rule.*—A corporation making a distribution with respect to its stock or any intermediary (described in §1.1441-1(c)(13)) making a payment of such a distribution is required to withhold under section 1441, 1442, or 1443 on the entire amount of the distribution, unless it elects to reduce the amount of withholding under the provisions of this paragraph (c). Any exceptions from withholding provided by this paragraph (c) apply without any requirement to furnish documentation to the withholding agent. However, documentation may have to be furnished for purposes of the information reporting provisions under section 6042 or 6045 and backup withholding under section 3406. See §1.1461-1(c) to determine whether amounts excepted from withholding under this section are considered amounts that are subject to reporting.

(2) *Exception to withholding on distributions.*—(i) *In general.*—An election described in paragraph (c)(1) of this section is made by actually reducing the amount of withholding at the time that the payment is made. An intermediary that makes a payment of a distribution is not required to reduce the withholding based on the distributing corporation's estimates under this paragraph (c)(2), even if the distributing corporation itself elects to reduce the withholding on payments of distributions that it itself makes to foreign persons. Conversely, an intermediary may elect to reduce the amount of withholding with respect to the payment of a distribution even if the distributing corporation does not so elect for the payments of distributions that it itself makes of distributions to foreign persons. The amounts with respect to which a distributing corporation or intermediary may elect to reduce the withholding are as follows:

(A) A distributing corporation or intermediary may elect to not withhold on a distribution to the extent it represents a nontaxable distribution payable in stock or stock rights.

(B) A distributing corporation or intermediary may elect to not withhold on a distribution to the extent it represents a distribution in part or full payment in exchange for stock.

(C) A distributing corporation or intermediary may elect to not withhold on a distribution (actual or deemed) to the extent it is not paid out of accumulated earnings and profits or current earnings and profits, based on a reasonable estimate determined under paragraph (c)(2)(ii) of this section.

(D) A regulated investment company or intermediary may elect to not withhold on a distribution representing a capital gain dividend (as defined in section 852(b)(3)(C)) or an exempt interest dividend (as defined in section 852(b)(5)(A)) based on the applicable procedures described under paragraph (c)(3) of this section.

(E) A U.S. Real Property Holding Corporation (defined in section 897(c)(2)) or a real estate investment trust (defined in section 856) or intermediary may elect to not withhold on a distribution to the extent it is subject to withholding under section 1445 and the regulations under that section. See paragraph (c)(4) of this section for applicable procedures.

(ii) *Reasonable estimate of accumulated and current earnings and profits on the date of payment.*—(A) *General rule.*—A reasonable estimate for purposes of paragraph (c)(2)(i)(C) of this section is a determination made by the distributing corporation at a time reasonably close to the date of payment of the extent to which the distribution will constitute a dividend, as defined in section 316. The determination is based upon the anticipated amount of accumulated earnings and profits and current earnings and profits for the taxable year in which the distribution is made, the distributions made prior to the distribution for which the estimate is made and all other relevant facts and circumstances. A reasonable estimate may be made based on the procedures described in § 31.3406(b)(2)-4(c)(2) of this chapter.

(B) *Procedures in case of underwithholding.*—A distributing corporation or intermediary that is a withholding agent with respect to a distribution and that determines at the end of the taxable year in which the distribution is made that it underwithheld under section 1441 on the distribution shall be liable for the amount underwithheld as a withholding agent under section 1461. However, for purposes of this section and § 1.1461-1, any amount underwithheld paid by a distributing corporation, its paying agent, or an intermediary shall not be treated as income subject to additional withholding even if that amount is treated as additional income to the shareholders unless the additional amount is income to the shareholder as a result of a contractual arrangement between the parties regarding the satisfaction of the shareholder's tax liabilities. In addition, no penalties shall be imposed for failure to withhold and deposit the tax if—

(1) The distributing corporation made a reasonable estimate as provided in paragraph (c)(2)(ii)(A) of this section; and

(2) Either—

(i) The corporation or intermediary pays over the underwithheld amount on or before the due date for filing a Form 1042 for the calendar year in which the distribution is made, pursuant to § 1.1461-2(b); or

(ii) The corporation or intermediary is not a calendar year taxpayer and it files an amended return on Form 1042X (or such other form as the Commissioner may prescribe) for the calendar year in which the distribution is made and pays the underwithheld amount and interest within 60 days after the close of the taxable year in which the distribution is made.

(C) *Reliance by intermediary on reasonable estimate.*—For purposes of determining whether the payment of a corporate distribution is a dividend, a withholding agent that is not the distributing corporation may, absent actual knowledge or reason to know otherwise, rely on representations made by the distributing corporation regarding the reasonable estimate of the anticipated accumulated and current earnings and profits made in accordance with paragraph (c)(2)(ii)(A) of this section. Failure by the withholding agent to withhold the required amount due to a failure by the distributing corporation to reasonably estimate the portion of the distribution treated as a dividend or to properly communicate the information to the withholding agent shall be imputed to the distributing corporation.

Reg. § 1.1441-3(c)(2)(ii)(C)

In such a case, the Internal Revenue Service (IRS) may collect from the distributing corporation any underwithheld amount and subject the distributing corporation to applicable interest and penalties as a withholding agent.

(D) *Example.*—The rules of this paragraph (c)(2) are illustrated by the following example:

Example. (i) *Facts.* Corporation X, a publicly traded corporation with both U.S. and foreign shareholders and a calendar year taxpayer, has an accumulated deficit in earnings and profits at the close of 2000. In 2001, Corporation X generates $1 million of current earnings and profits each month and makes an $18 million distribution, resulting in a $12 million dividend. Corporation X plans to make an additional $18 million distribution on October 1, 2002. Approximately one month before that date, Corporation X's management receives an internal report from its legal and accounting department concerning Corporation X's estimated current earnings and profits. The report states that Corporation X should generate only $5.1 million of current earnings and profits by the close of the third quarter due to costs relating to substantial organizational and product changes, but these changes will enable Corporation X to generate $1.3 million of earnings and profits monthly for the last quarter of the 2002 fiscal year. Thus, the total amount of current and earnings and profits for 2002 is estimated to be $9 million.

(ii) *Analysis.* Based on the facts in paragraph (i) of this *Example,* including the fact that earnings and profits estimate was made within a reasonable time before the distribution, Corporation X can rely on the estimate under paragraph (c)(2)(ii)(A) of this section. Therefore, Corporation X may treat $9 million of the $18 million of the October 1, 2002, distribution to foreign shareholders as a non-dividend distribution.

(3) *Special rules in the case of distributions from a regulated investment company.*—(i) *General rule.*—If the amount of any distributions designated as being subject to section 852(b)(3)(C) or (5)(A), or 871(k)(1)(C) or (2)(C), exceeds the amount that may be designated under those sections for the taxable year, then no penalties will be asserted for any resulting underwithholding if the designations were based on a reasonable estimate (made pursuant to the same procedures as are described in paragraph (c)(2)(ii)(A) of this section) and the adjustments to the amount withheld are made within the time period described in paragraph (c)(2)(ii)(B) of this section. Any adjustment to the amount of tax due and paid to the IRS by the withholding agent as a result of underwithholding shall not be treated as a distribution for purposes of section 562(c) and the regulations thereunder. Any amount of U.S. tax that a foreign shareholder is treated as having paid on the undistributed capital gain of a regulated investment company under section 852(b)(3)(D) may be claimed by the foreign shareholder as a credit or refund under § 1.1464-1.

(ii) *Reliance by intermediary on reasonable estimate.*—For purposes of determining whether a payment is a distribution designated as subject to section 852(b)(3)(C) or (5)(A), or 871(k)(1)(C) or (2)(C), a withholding agent that is not the distributing regulated investment company may, absent actual knowledge or reason to know otherwise, rely on the designations that the distributing company represents have been made in accordance with paragraph (c)(3)(i) of this section. Failure by the withholding agent to withhold the required amount due to a failure by the regulated investment company to reasonably estimate the required amounts or to properly communicate the relevant information to the withholding agent shall be imputed to the distributing company. In such a case, the IRS may collect from the distributing company any underwithheld amount and subject the company to applicable interest and penalties as a withholding agent.

(4) *Coordination with withholding under section 1445.*—(i) *In general.*—A distribution from a U.S. Real Property Holding Corporation (USRPHC) (or from a corporation that was a USRPHC at any time during the five-year period ending on the date of distribution) with respect to stock that is a U.S. real property interest under section 897(c) or from a Real Estate Investment Trust (REIT) with respect to its stock is subject to the withholding provisions under section 1441 (or section 1442 or 1443) and section 1445. A USRPHC making a distribution shall be treated as satisfying its withholding obligations under both sections if it withholds in accordance with one of the procedures described in either paragraph (c)(4)(i)(A) or (B) of this section. A USRPHC must apply the same withholding procedure to all the distributions made during the taxable year. However, the USRPHC may change the applicable withholding procedure from year to year. For rules regarding distributions by REITs, see paragraph (c)(4)(i)(C) of this section.

(A) *Withholding under section 1441.*—The USRPHC may choose to withhold on a distribution only under section 1441 (or 1442 or 1443) and not under section 1445. In such a case, the USRPHC must withhold under section 1441 (or 1442 or 1443) on the full amount of the distribution, whether or not any portion of the distribution represents a return of basis or capital gain. If a reduced tax rate under an income tax treaty applies to the distribution by the USRPHC, then the applicable rate of withholding on the distribution shall be no less than 10-percent, unless the applicable treaty specifies an applicable lower rate for distributions from a

USRPHC, in which case the lower rate may apply.

(B) *Withholding under both sections 1441 and 1445.*—As an alternative to the procedure described in paragraph (c)(4)(i)(A) of this section, a USRPHC may choose to withhold under both sections 1441 (or 1442 or 1443) and 1445 under the procedures set forth in this paragraph (c)(4)(i)(B). The USRPHC must make a reasonable estimate of the portion of the distribution that is a dividend under paragraph (c)(2)(ii)(A) of this section, and must—

(1) Withhold under section 1441 (or 1442 or 1443) on the portion of the distribution that is estimated to be a dividend under paragraph (c)(2)(ii)(A) of this section; and

(2) Withhold under section 1445(e)(3) and § 1.1445-5(e) on the remainder of the distribution or on such smaller portion based on a withholding certificate obtained in accordance with § 1.1445-5(e)(2)(iv).

(C) *Coordination with REIT withholding.*—Withholding is required under section 1441 (or 1442 or 1443) on the portion of a distribution from a REIT that is not designated as a capital gain dividend, a return of basis, or a distribution in excess of a shareholder's adjusted basis in the stock of the REIT that is treated as a capital gain under section 301(c)(3). A distribution in excess of a shareholder's adjusted basis in the stock of the REIT is, however, subject to withholding under section 1445, unless the interest in the REIT is not a U.S. real property interest (e.g., an interest in a domestically controlled REIT under section 897(h)(2)). In addition, withholding is required under section 1445 on the portion of the distribution designated by a REIT as a capital gain dividend. See § 1.1445-8.

(ii) *Intermediary reliance rule.*—A withholding agent that is not the distributing USRPHC must withhold under paragraph (c)(4)(i) of this section, but may, absent actual knowledge or reason to know otherwise, rely on representations made by the USRPHC regarding the determinations required under paragraph (c)(4)(i) of this section. Failure by the withholding agent to withhold the required amount due to a failure by the distributing USRPHC to make these determinations in a reasonable manner or to properly communicate the determinations to the withholding agent shall be imputed to the distributing USRPHC. In such a case, the IRS may collect from the distributing USRPHC any underwithheld amount and subject the distributing USRPHC to applicable interest and penalties as a withholding agent.

(d) *Withholding on payments that include an undetermined amount of income.*—(1) *In general.*—Where the withholding agent makes a payment and does not know at the time of payment the amount that is subject to withholding because the determination of the source of the income or the calculation of the amount of income subject to tax depends upon facts that are not known at the time of payment, then the withholding agent must withhold an amount under § 1.1441-1 based on the entire amount paid that is necessary to assure that the tax withheld is not less than 30 percent (or other applicable percentage) of the amount that will subsequently be determined to be from sources within the United States or to be income subject to tax. The amount so withheld shall not exceed 30 percent of the amount paid. In the alternative, the withholding agent may make a reasonable estimate of the amount from U.S. sources or of the taxable amount and set aside a corresponding portion of the amount due under the transaction and hold such portion in escrow until the amount from U.S. sources or the taxable amount can be determined, at which point withholding becomes due under § 1.1441-1. See § 1.1441-1(b)(8) regarding adjustments in the case of overwithholding. The provisions of this paragraph (d)(1) shall not apply to the extent that other provisions of the regulations under chapter 3 of the Internal Revenue Code (Code) specify the amount to be withheld, if any, when the withholding agent lacks knowledge at the time of payment (e.g., lack of reliable knowledge regarding the status of the payee or beneficial owner, addressed in § 1.1441-1(b)(3), or lack of knowledge regarding the amount of original issue discount under § 1.1441-2(b)(3)).

(2) *Withholding on certain gains.*—Absent actual knowledge or reason to know otherwise, a withholding agent may rely on a claim regarding the amount of gain described in § 1.1441-2(c) if the beneficial owner withholding certificate, or other appropriate withholding certificate, states the beneficial owner's basis in the property giving rise to the gain. In the absence of a reliable representation on a withholding certificate, the withholding agent must withhold an amount under § 1.1441-1 that is necessary to assure that the tax withheld is not less than 30 percent (or other applicable percentage) of the recognized gain. For this purpose, the recognized gain is determined without regard to any deduction allowed by the Code from the gains. The amount so withheld shall not exceed 30 percent of the amount payable by reason of the transaction giving rise to the recognized gain. See § 1.1441-1(b)(8) regarding adjustments in the case of overwithholding.

(e) *Payments other than in U.S. dollars.*—(1) *In general.*—The amount of a payment made in a medium other than U.S. dollars is measured by the fair market value of the property or services provided in lieu of U.S. dollars. The withholding agent may liquidate the property prior to payment in order to withhold the required amount of tax under section 1441 or obtain payment of the tax from an alternative source. However, the obligation to withhold under section 1441 is not deferred even if no alternative source can be located. Thus, for purposes of withholding under chapter 3 of the Code, the provisions of § 31.3406(h)-2(b)(2)(ii) of this chapter (relating to backup withholding from another source) shall not apply. If the withholding agent satisfies the tax liability related to such payments, the rules of paragraph (f) of this section apply.

(2) *Payments in foreign currency.*—If the amount subject to withholding tax is paid in a currency other than the U.S. dollar, the amount of withholding under section 1441 shall be determined by applying the applicable rate of withholding to the foreign currency amount and converting the amount withheld into U.S. dollars on the date of payment at the spot rate (as defined in § 1.988-1(d)(1)) in effect on that date. A withholding agent making regular or frequent payments in foreign currency may use a month-end spot rate or a monthly average spot rate. In addition, such as withholding agent may use the spot rate on the date the amount of tax is deposited (within the meaning of § 1.6302-2(a)), provided that such deposit is made within seven days of the date of the payment giving rise to the obligation to withhold. A spot rate convention must be used consistently for all non-dollar amounts withheld and from year to year. Such convention cannot be changed without the consent of the Commissioner. The U.S. dollar amount so determined shall be treated by the beneficial owner as the amount of tax paid on the income for purposes of determining the final U.S. tax liability and, if applicable, claiming a refund or credit of tax.

(f) *Tax liability of beneficial owner satisfied by withholding agent.*—(1) *General rule.*—In the event that the satisfaction of a tax liability of a beneficial owner by a withholding agent constitutes income to the beneficial owner and such income is of a type that is subject to withholding, the amount of the payment deemed made by the withholding agent for purposes of this paragraph (f) shall be determined under the gross-up formula provided in this paragraph (f)(1). Whether the payment of the tax by the withholding agent constitutes a satisfaction of the beneficial owner's tax liability and whether, as such, it constitutes additional income to the beneficial owner, must be determined under all the facts and circumstances surrounding the transaction, including any agreements between the parties and applicable law. The formula described in this paragraph (f)(1) is as follows:

$$\text{Payment} = \frac{\text{Gross payment without withholding}}{1 - (\text{tax rate})}$$

(2) *Example.*—The following example illustrates the provisions of this paragraph (f):

Example. College X awards a qualified scholarship within the meaning of section 117(b) to foreign student, FS, who is in the United States on an F visa. FS is a resident of a country that does not have an income tax treaty with the United States. The scholarship is $20,000 to be applied to tuition, mandatory fees and books, plus benefits in kind consisting of room and board and roundtrip air transportation. College X agrees to pay any U.S. income tax owed by FS with respect to the scholarship. The fair market value of the room and board measured by the amount College X charges non-scholarship students is $6,000. The cost of the roundtrip air transportation is $2,600. Therefore, the total fair market value of the scholarship received by FS is $28,600. However, the amount taxable is limited to the fair market value of the benefits in kind ($8,600) because the portion of the scholarship amount for tuition, fees, and books is not included in gross income under section 117. The applicable rate of withholding is 14 percent under section 1441(b). Therefore, under the gross-up formula, College X is deemed to make a payment of $10,000 ($8,600 divided by (1 – .14). The U.S. tax that must be deducted and withheld from the payment under section 1441(b) is $1,400 (.14 × $10,000). College X reports scholarship income of $30,000 and $1,400 of U.S. tax withheld on Forms 1042 and 1042-S.

(g) *Conduit financing arrangements.*—(1) *Duty to withhold.*—A financed entity or other person required to withhold tax under section 1441 with respect to a financing arrangement that is a conduit financing arrangement within the meaning of § 1.881-3(a)(2)(iv) shall be required to withhold under section 1441 as if the district director had determined, pursuant to § 1.881-3(a)(3), that all conduit entities that are parties to the conduit financing arrangement should be disregarded. The amount of tax required to be withheld shall be determined under § 1.881-3(d). The withholding agent may withhold tax at a reduced rate if the financing entity establishes that it is entitled to the benefit of a treaty that provides a reduced rate of tax on a payment of the type deemed to have been paid to the financing entity. Section 1.881-3(a)(3)(ii)(E) shall not apply for purposes of determining whether any person is required to deduct and withhold tax pursuant to this paragraph (g), or whether any party to a financing arrangement is liable for failure to withhold or entitled to a refund of tax under sections 1441 or 1461 to 1464 (except to the extent the amount withheld exceeds the tax liability determined under § 1.881-3(d)). See § 1.1441-7(f) relating to withholding tax liability of the withholding agent in conduit financing arrangements subject to § 1.881-3.

(2) *Effective date.*—This paragraph (g) is effective for payments made by financed entities on or after September 11, 1995. This paragraph shall not apply to interest payments covered by

section 127(g)(3) of the Tax Reform Act of 1984, and to interest payments with respect to other debt obligations issued prior to October 15, 1984 (whether or not such debt was issued by a Netherlands Antilles corporation).

(h) *Effective date.*—Except as otherwise provided in paragraph (g) of this section, this section applies to payments made after December 31, 2000. [Reg. § 1.1441-3.]

☐ [*T.D. 6187, 7-5-56. Amended by T.D. 6592, 2-27-62; T.D. 6636, 2-25-63; T.D. 6669, 8-26-63; T.D. 6777, 12-15-64; T.D. 6908, 12-30-66; T.D. 7378, 9-29-75; T.D. 7977, 9-19-84; T.D. 8611, 8-10-95; T.D. 8734, 10-6-97; T.D. 8804, 12-30-98; T.D. 8856, 12-29-99; T.D. 8881, 5-15-2000 and T.D. 9253, 3-13-2006.*]

[Reg. § 1.1441-4]

§ 1.1441-4. Exemptions from withholding for certain effectively connected income and other amounts.—(a) *Certain income, connected with a U.S. trade or business.*—(1) *In general.*—No withholding is required under section 1441 on income otherwise subject to withholding if the income is (or is deemed to be) effectively connected with the conduct of a trade or business within the United States and is includible in the beneficial owner's gross income for the taxable year. For purposes of this paragraph (a), an amount is not deemed to be includible in gross income if the amount is (or is deemed to be) effectively connected with the conduct of a trade or business within the United States and the beneficial owner claims an exemption from tax under an income tax treaty because the income is not attributable to a permanent establishment in the United States. To claim a reduced rate of withholding because the income is not attributable to a permanent establishment, see § 1.1441-6(b)(1). This paragraph (a) does not apply to income of a foreign corporation to which section 543(a)(7) applies for the taxable year or to compensation for personal services performed by an individual. See paragraph (b) of this section for compensation for personal services performed by an individual.

(2) *Withholding agent's reliance on a claim of effectively connected income.*—(i) *In general.*—Absent actual knowledge or reason to know otherwise, a withholding agent may rely on a claim of exemption based upon paragraph (a)(1) of this section if, prior to the payment to the foreign person, the withholding agent can reliably associate the payment with a Form W-8 upon which it can rely to treat the payment as made to a foreign beneficial owner in accordance with § 1.1441-1(e)(1)(ii). For purposes of this paragraph (a), a withholding certificate is valid only if, in addition to other applicable requirements, it includes the taxpayer identifying number of the person whose name is on the Form W-8 and represents, under penalties of perjury, that the

amounts for which the certificate is furnished are effectively connected with the conduct of a trade or business in the United States and is includable in the beneficial owner's gross income for the taxable year. In the absence of a reliable claim that the income is effectively connected with the conduct of a trade or business in the United States, the income is presumed not to be effectively connected, except as otherwise provided in paragraph (a)(2)(ii) or (3) of this section. See § 1.1441-1(e)(4)(ii)(C) for the period of validity applicable to a certificate provided under this section and § 1.1441-1(e)(4)(ii)(D) for changes in circumstances arising during the taxable year indicating that the income to which the certificate relates is not, or is no longer expected to be, effectively connected with the conduct of a trade or business within the United States. A withholding certificate shall be effective only for the item or items of income specified therein. The provisions of § 1.1441-1(b)(3)(iv) dealing with a 90-day grace period shall apply for purposes of this section.

(ii) *Special rules for U.S. branches of foreign persons.*—(A) *U.S. branches of certain foreign banks or foreign insurance companies.*—A payment to a U.S. branch described in § 1.1441-1(b)(2)(iv)(A) is presumed to be effectively connected with the conduct of a trade or business in the United States without the need to furnish a certificate, unless the U.S. branch provides a U.S. branch withholding certificate described in § 1.1441-1(e)(3)(v) that represents otherwise. If no certificate is furnished but the income is not, in fact, effectively connected income, then the branch must withhold whether the payment is collected on behalf of other persons or on behalf of another branch of the same entity. See § 1.1441-1(b)(2)(iv) and (6) for general rules applicable to payments to U.S. branches of foreign persons.

(B) *Other U.S. branches.*—See § 1.1441-1(b)(2)(iv)(E) for similar procedures for other U.S. branches to the extent provided in a determination letter from the district director or the Assistant Commissioner (International).

(3) *Income on notional principal contracts.*—(i) *General rule.*—A withholding agent that pays amounts attributable to a notional principal contract described in § 1.863-7(a) or 1.988-2(e) shall have no obligation to withhold on the amounts paid under the terms of the notional principal contract regardless of whether a withholding certificate is provided. However, a withholding agent must file returns under § 1.1461-1(b) and (c) reporting the income that it must treat as effectively connected with the conduct of a trade or business in the United States under the provisions of this paragraph (a)(3). Except as otherwise provided in paragraph (a)(3)(ii) of this section, a withholding agent must treat the income as effectively connected with the conduct

of a U.S. trade or business if the income is paid to, or to the account of, a qualified business unit of a foreign person located in the United States or, if the payment is paid to, or to the account of, a qualified business unit of a foreign person located outside the United States, the withholding agent knows, or has reason to know, the payment is effectively connected with the conduct of a trade or business within the United States. Income on a notional principal contract does not include the amount characterized as interest under the provisions of § 1.446-3(g)(4).

(ii) *Exception for certain payments.*—A payment shall not be treated as effectively connected with the conduct of a trade or business within the United States for purposes of paragraph (a)(3)(i) of this section even if no withholding certificate is furnished if the payee provides a representation in a master agreement that governs the transactions in notional principal contracts between the parties (for example an International Swaps and Derivatives Association (ISDA) Agreement, including the Schedule thereto) or in the confirmation on the particular notional principal contract transaction that the payee is a U.S. person or a non-U.S. branch of a foreign person.

(b) *Compensation for personal services of an individual.*—(1) *Exemption from withholding.*—Withholding is not required under § 1.1441-1 from salaries, wages, remuneration, or any other compensation for personal services of a nonresident alien individual if such compensation is effectively connected with the conduct of a trade or business within the United States and—

(i) Such compensation is subject to withholding under section 3402 (relating to withholding on wages) and the regulations under that section;

(ii) Such compensation would be subject to withholding under section 3402 but for the provisions of section 3401(a) (not including section 3401(a)(6)) and the regulations under that section. This paragraph (b)(1)(ii) does not apply to payments to a nonresident alien individual from any trust described in section 401(a), any annuity plan described in section 403(a), any annuity, custodial account, or retirement income account described in section 403(b), or an individual retirement account or individual retirement annuity described in section 408. Instead, these payments are subject to withholding under this section to the extent they are exempted from the definition of wages under section 3401(a)(12) or to the extent they are from an annuity, custodial account, or retirement income account described in section 403(b), or an individual retirement account or individual retirement annuity described in section 408. Thus, for example, payments to a nonresident alien individual from a trust described in section 401 (a) are subject to withholding under section 1441 and not under section 3405 or section 3406;

(iii) Such compensation is for services performed by a nonresident alien individual who is a resident of Canada or Mexico and who enters and leaves the United States at frequent intervals;

(iv) Such compensation is, or will be, exempt from the income tax imposed by chapter 1 of the Code by reason of a provision of the Internal Revenue Code or a tax treaty to which the United States is a party;

(v) Such compensation is paid after January 3, 1979 as a commission or rebate paid by a ship supplier to a nonresident alien individual, who is employed by a nonresident alien individual, foreign partnership, or foreign corporation in the operation of a ship or ships of foreign registry, for placing orders for supplies to be used in the operation of such ship or ships with the supplier. See section 162(c) and the regulations thereunder for denial of deductions for illegal bribes, kickbacks, and other payments; or

(vi) Compensation that is exempt from withholding under section 3402 by reason of section 3402(e), provided that the employee and his employer enter into an agreement under section 3402(p) to provide for the withholding of income tax upon payments of amounts described in § 31.3401(a)-3(b)(1) of this chapter. An employee who desires to enter into such an agreement should furnish his employer with Form W-4 (withholding exemption certificate) (or such other form as the Internal Revenue Service (IRS) may prescribe). See section 3402(f) and the regulations thereunder and § 31.3402(p)-1 of this chapter.

(2) *Manner of obtaining withholding exemption under tax treaty.*—(i) *In general.*—In order to obtain the exemption from withholding by reason of a tax treaty, provided by paragraph (b)(1)(iv) of this section, a nonresident alien individual must submit a withholding certificate (described in paragraph (b)(2)(ii) of this section) to each withholding agent from whom amounts are to be received. A separate withholding certificate must be filed for each taxable year of the alien individual. If the withholding agent is satisfied that an exemption from withholding is warranted (see paragraph (b)(2)(iii) of this section), the withholding certificate shall be accepted in the manner set forth in paragraph (b)(2)(iv) of this section. The exemption from withholding becomes effective for payments made at least ten days after a copy of the accepted withholding certificate is forwarded to the Assistant Commissioner (International). The withholding agent may rely on an accepted withholding certificate only if the IRS has not objected to the certificate. For purposes of this paragraph (b)(2)(i), the IRS will be considered to have not objected to the certificate if it has not notified the withholding agent within a 10-day period beginning from the date that the withholding certificate is forwarded to the IRS pursuant to paragraph (b)(2)(v) of this

section. After expiration of the 10-day period, the withholding agent may rely on the withholding certificate retroactive to the date of the first payment covered by the certificate. The fact that the IRS does not object to the withholding certificate within the 10-day period provided in this paragraph (b)(2)(i) shall not preclude the IRS from examining the withholding agent at a later date in light of facts that the withholding agent knew or had reason to know regarding the payment and eligibility for a reduced rate and that were not disclosed to the IRS as part of the 10-day review process.

(ii) *Withholding certificate claiming withholding exemption.*—The statement claiming an exemption from withholding shall be made on Form 8233 (or an acceptable substitute or such other form as the IRS may prescribe). Form 8233 shall be dated, signed by the beneficial owner under penalties of perjury, and contain the following information—

(A) The individual's name, permanent residence address, taxpayer identifying number (or a copy of a completed Form W-7 or SS-5 showing that a number has been applied for), and the U.S. visa number, if any;

(B) The individual's current immigration status and visa type;

(C) The individual's original date of entry into the United States;

(D) The country that issued the individual's passport and the number of such passport, or the individual's permanent address if a citizen of Canada or Mexico;

(E) The taxable year, for which the statement is to apply the compensation to which it relates, and the amount (or estimated amount if exact amount not known) of such compensation;

(F) A statement that the individual is not a citizen or resident of the United States;

(G) The number of personal exemptions claimed by the individual;

(H) A statement as to whether the compensation to be paid to him or her during the taxable year is or will be exempt from income tax and the reason why the compensation is exempt;

(I) If the compensation is exempt from withholding by reason of an income tax treaty to which the United States is a party, the tax treaty and provision under which the exemption from withholding is claimed and the country of which the individual is a resident;

(J) Sufficient facts to justify the claim in exemption from withholding; and

(K) Any other information as may be required by the form or accompanying instructions in addition to, or in lieu of, the information described in this paragraph (b)(2)(ii).

(iii) *Review by withholding agent.*—The exemption from withholding provided by paragraph (b)(1)(iv) of this section shall not apply unless the withholding agent accepts (in the manner provided in paragraph (b)(2)(iv) of this section) the statement on Form 8233 supplied by the nonresident alien individual. Before accepting the statement the withholding agent must examine the statement. If the withholding agent knows or has reason to know that any of the facts or assertions on Form 8233 may be false or that the eligibility of the individual's compensation for the exemption cannot be readily determined, the withholding agent may not accept the statement on Form 8233 and is required to withhold under this section. If the withholding agent accepts the statement and subsequently finds that any of the facts or assertions contained on Form 8233 may be false or that the eligibility of the individual's compensation for the exemption can no longer be readily determined, then the withholding agent shall promptly so notify the Assistant Commissioner (International) by letter, and the withholding agent is not relieved of liability to withhold on any amounts still to be paid. If the withholding agent is notified by the Assistant Commissioner (International) that the eligibility of the individual's compensation for the exemption is in doubt or that such compensation is not eligible for the exemption, the withholding agent is required to withhold under this section. The rules of this paragraph are illustrated by the following examples.

Example 1. C, a nonresident alien individual, submits Form 8233 to W, a withholding agent. The statement on Form 8233 does not include all the information required by paragraph (b)(2)(ii) of this section. Therefore, W has reason to know that he or she cannot readily determine whether C's compensation for personal services is eligible for an exemption from withholding and, therefore, W must withhold.

Example 2. D, a nonresident alien, is performing services for W, a withholding agent. W has accepted a statement on Form 8233 submitted by D, according to the provisions of this section. W receives notice from the Internal Revenue Service that the eligibility of D's compensation for a withholding exemption is in doubt. Therefore, W has reason to know that the eligibility of the compensation for a withholding exemption cannot be readily determined, as of the date W receives the notification, and W must withhold tax under section 1441 on amounts paid after receipt of the notification.

Example 3. E, a nonresident alien individual, submits Form 8233 to W, a withholding agent for whom E is to perform personal services. The statement contains all the information requested on Form 8233. E claims an exemption from withholding based on a personal exemption amount computed on the number of days E will perform personal services for W in the United States. If W does not know or have reason to know that any statement on the Form 8233 is false or that the eligibility of E's compensation for the withholding exemption cannot be readily determined, W can accept the statement on Form 8233 and exempt from withholding the appropriate amount of E's income.

(iv) *Acceptance by withholding agent.*—If after the review described in paragraph (b)(2)(iii) of this section the withholding agent is satisfied that an exemption from withholding is warranted, the withholding agent may accept the statement by making a certification, verified by a declaration that it is made under the penalties of perjury, on Form 8233. The certification shall be—

(A) That the withholding agent has examined the statement,

(B) That the withholding agent is satisfied that an exemption from withholding is warranted, and

(C) That the withholding agent does not know or have reason to know that the individual's compensation is not entitled to the exemption or that the eligibility of the individual's compensation for the exemption cannot be readily determined.

(v) *Copies of Form 8233.*—The withholding agent shall forward one copy of each Form 8233 that is accepted under paragraph (b)(2)(iv) of this section to the Assistant Commissioner (International), within five days of such acceptance. The withholding agent shall retain a copy of Form 8233.

(3) *Withholding agreements.*—Compensation for personal services of a nonresident alien individual who is engaged during the taxable year in the conduct of a trade or business within the United States may be wholly or partially exempted from the withholding required by § 1.1441-1 if an agreement is reached between the Assistant Commissioner (International) and the alien individual with respect to the amount of withholding required. Such agreement shall be available in the circumstances and in the manner set forth by the Internal Revenue Service, and shall be effective for payments covered by the agreement that are made after the agreement is executed by all parties. The alien individual must agree to timely file an income tax return for the current taxable year.

(4) *Final payment exemption.*—(i) *General rule.*—Compensation for independent personal services of a nonresident alien individual who is engaged during the taxable year in the conduct of a trade or business within the United States may be wholly or partially exempted from the withholding required by § 1.1441-1 from the final payment of compensation for independent personal services. This exemption does not apply to wages. This exemption from withholding is available only once during an alien individual's taxable year and is obtained by the alien individual presenting to the withholding agent a letter in duplicate from a district director stating the amount of compensation subject to the exemption and the amount that would otherwise be withheld from such final payment under section 1441 that shall be paid to the alien individual due to the exemption. The alien individual shall attach a copy of the letter to his or her income tax return for the taxable year for which the exemption is effective.

(ii) *Final payment of compensation for personal services.*—For purposes of this paragraph, final payment of compensation for personal services means the last payment of compensation, other than wages, for personal services rendered within the United States that the individual expects to receive from any withholding agent during the taxable year.

(iii) *Manner of applying for final payment exemption.*—In order to obtain the final payment exemption provided by paragraph (b)(4)(i) of this section, the nonresident alien individual (or his or her agent) must file the forms and provide the information required by the district director. Ordinary and necessary business expenses may be taken into account if substantiated to the satisfaction of the district director. The alien individual must submit a statement, signed by him or her and verified by a declaration that it is made under the penalties of perjury, that all the information provided is true and that to his or her knowledge no relevant information has been omitted. The information required to be submitted includes, but is not limited to—

(A) A statement by each withholding agent from whom amounts of gross income effectively connected with the conduct of a trade or business within the United States have been received by the alien individual during the taxable year, of the amount of such income paid and the amount of tax withheld, signed and verified by a declaration that it is made under penalties of perjury;

(B) A statement by the withholding agent from whom the final payment of compensation for personal services will be received, of the amount of such final payment and the amount which would be withheld under § 1.1441-1 if a final payment exemption under paragraph (b)(4)(i) of this section is not granted, signed and verified by a declaration that it is made under penalties of perjury;

(C) A statement by the individual that he or she does not intend to receive any other amounts of gross income effectively connected with the conduct of a trade or business within the United States during the current taxable year;

(D) The amount of tax which has been withheld (or paid) under any other provision of the Code or regulations with respect to any income effectively connected with the conduct of a trade or business within the United States during the current taxable year;

(E) The amount of any outstanding tax liabilities (and interest and penalties relating thereto) from the current taxable year or prior taxable periods; and

(F) The provision of any income tax treaty under which a partial or complete exemption from withholding may be claimed, the country of the individual's residence, and a statement of sufficient facts to justify an exemption pursuant to such treaty.

(iv) *Letter to withholding agent.*—If the district director is satisfied that the information provided under paragraph (b)(4)(iii) of this section is sufficient, the district director will, after coordination with the Director of the Foreign Operations District, ascertain the amount of the alien individual's tentative income tax for the taxable year with respect to gross income that is effectively connected with the conduct of a trade or business within the United States. After the tentative tax has been ascertained, the district director will provide the alien individual with a letter to the withholding agent stating the amount of the final payment of compensation for personal services that is exempt from withholding, and the amount that would otherwise be withheld under section 1441 that shall be paid to the alien individual due to the exemption. The amount of compensation for personal services exempt from withholding under this paragraph (b)(4) shall not exceed $5,000.

Example 1. On July 15, 1983, B, a nonresident alien individual, appears before a district director with the information required by paragraph (b)(4)(iii) of this section. B has received personal service income in 1983 from which $3,000 has been withheld under section 1441. On August 1, 1983, B will receive $5,000 in personal service income from W. B does not intend to receive any other income subject to U.S. tax during 1983. Taking into account B's substantiated deductible business expenses, the district director computes the tentative tax liability on B's income effectively connected with the conduct of a trade or business in the United States during 1983 (including the $5,000 payment to be made on August 1, 1983) to be $3,300. B does not owe U.S. tax for any other taxable periods. The amount of B's final payment exemption is determined as follows:

(1) The amount of total withholding is $4,500 ($3,000 previously withheld plus $1,500, 30% of the $5,000 final payment);

(2) The amount of tentative excess withholding is $1,200 (total withholding of $4,500 minus B's tentative tax liability of $3,300); and

(3) To allow B to receive $1,200 of the amount which would otherwise have been withheld from the final payment, the district director allows a withholding exemption for $4,000 of B's final payment. W must withhold $300 from the final payment.

Example 2. The facts are the same as in Example 1 except B will receive a final payment of compensation on August 1, 1983, in the amount of $10,000 and B's tentative tax liability is $3,900. The amount of B's final payment exemption is determined as follows:

(1) The amount of total withholding is $6,000 ($3,000 previously withheld plus $3,000, 30% of the $10,000 final payment);

(2) The amount of tentative excess withholding is $2,100 (total withholding of $6,000 minus B's tentative tax liability of $3,900); and

(3) To allow B to receive $2,100 of the amount which would otherwise be withheld from the final payment, $7,000 of the final payment would have to be exempt from withholding; however, as no more than $5,000 of the final payment can be exempt from withholding under this paragraph (b)(4), the district director allows a withholding exemption for $5,000 of B's final payment. B must file a claim for refund at the end of the taxable year to obtain a refund of $600. W must withhold $1,500 from the final payment.

(5) *Requirement of return.*—The tentative tax determined by the district director under paragraph (b)(4)(iv) of this section or by the Director of the Foreign Operations District under the withholding agreement procedure of paragraph (b)(3) of this section shall not constitute a final determination of the income tax liability of the nonresident alien individual, nor shall such determination constitute a tax return of the nonresident alien individual for any taxable period. An alien individual who applies for or obtains an exemption from withholding under the procedures of paragraphs (b)(2), (3), or (4) of this section is not relieved of the obligation to file a return of income under section 6012.

(6) *Personal exemption.*—(i) *In general.*—To determine the tax to be withheld at source under §1.1441-1 from remuneration paid for personal services performed within the United States by a nonresident alien individual and from scholarship and fellowship income described in paragraph (c) of this section, a withholding agent may take into account one personal exemption pursuant to sections 873(b)(3) and 151 regardless of whether the income is effectively connected. For purposes of withholding under section 1441 on remuneration for personal services, the exemption must be prorated upon a daily basis for the period during which the personal services are performed within the United States by the nonresident alien individual by dividing by 365 the number of days in the period during which the individual is present in the United States for the purpose of performing the services and multiplying the result by the amount of the personal exemption in effect for the taxable year. See §31.3402(f)(6)-1 of this chapter.

Reg. §1.1441-4(b)(6)(i)

(ii) *Multiple exemptions.*—More than one personal exemption may be claimed in the case of a resident of a contiguous country or a national of the United States under section 873(b)(3). In addition, residents of a country with which the United States has an income tax treaty in effect may be eligible to claim more than one personal exemption if the treaty so provides. Claims for more than one personal exemption shall be made on the withholding certificate furnished to the withholding agent. The exemption must be prorated on a daily basis in the same manner as described in paragraph (b)(6)(i) of this section.

(iii) *Special rule where both certain scholarship and compensation income are received.*—The fact that both non-compensatory scholarship income and compensation income (including compensatory scholarship income) are received during the taxable year does not entitle the taxpayer to claim more than one personal exemption amount (or more than the additional amounts permitted under paragraph (b)(6)(ii) of this section). Thus, if a nonresident alien student receives non-compensatory taxable scholarship income from one withholding agent and compensation income from another withholding agent, no more than the total personal exemption amount permitted under the Internal Revenue Code or under an income tax treaty may be taken into account by both withholding agents. For this purpose, the withholding agent may rely on a representation from the beneficial owner that the exemption amount claimed does not exceed the amount permissible under this section.

(c) *Special rules for scholarship and fellowship income.*—(1) *In general.*—Under section 871(c), certain amounts paid as a scholarship or fellowship for study, training, or research in the United States to a nonresident alien individual temporarily present in the United States as a nonimmigrant under section 101(a)(15)(F), (J), (M), or (Q) of the Immigration and Nationality Act are treated as income effectively connected with the conduct of a trade or business within the United States. The amounts described in the preceding sentence are those amounts that do not represent compensation for services. Such amounts (as described in the second sentence of section 1441(b)) are subject to withholding under section 1441, but at the lower rate of 14 percent. That rate may be reduced under the provisions of an income tax treaty. Claims of a reduced rate under an income tax treaty shall be made under the procedures described in § 1.1441-6(b)(1). Therefore, claims for reduction in withholding under an income tax treaty on amounts described in this paragraph (c)(1) may not be made on a Form 8233. However, if the payee is receiving both compensation for personal services (including compensatory scholarship income) and non-compensatory scholarship income described in this paragraph (c)(1) from the same withholding agent, claims for reduction of withholding on both types of income may be made on Form 8233.

(2) *Alternate withholding election.*—A withholding agent may elect to withhold on the amounts described in paragraph (c)(1) of this section at the rates applicable under section 3402, as if the income were wages. Such election shall be made by obtaining a Form W-4 (or an acceptable substitute or such other form as the IRS may prescribe) from the beneficial owner. The fact that the withholding agent asks the beneficial owner to furnish a Form W-4 for such fellowship or scholarship income or to take such income into account in preparing such Form W-4 shall serve as notice to the beneficial owner that the income is being treated as wages for purposes of withholding tax under section 1441.

(d) *Annuities received under qualified plans.*—Withholding is not required under section § 1.1441-1 in the case of any amount received as an annuity if the amount is exempt from tax under section 871(f) and the regulations under that section. The withholding agent may exempt the payment from withholding if, prior to payment, it can reliably associate the payment with documentation upon which it can rely to treat the payment as made to a beneficial owner in accordance with § 1.1441-1(e)(1)(ii). A beneficial owner withholding certificate furnished for purposes of claiming the benefits of the exemption under this paragraph (d) is valid only if, in addition to other applicable requirements, it contains a taxpayer identifying number.

(e) *Per diem of certain alien trainees.*—Withholding is not required under section 1441(a) and § 1.1441-1 on per diem amounts paid for subsistence by the United States Government (directly or by contract) to any nonresident alien individual who is engaged in any program of training in the United States under the Mutual Security Act of 1954, as amended (22 U.S.C. chapter 24). This rule shall apply even though such amounts are subject to tax under section 871. Any exemption from withholding pursuant to this paragraph (e) applies without a requirement that documentation be furnished to the withholding agent. However, documentation may have to be furnished for purposes of the information reporting provisions under section 6041 and backup withholding under section 3406. The exemption from withholding granted by this paragraph (e) is not a determination that the amounts are not fixed or determinable annual or periodical income.

(f) *Failure to receive withholding certificates timely or to act in accordance with applicable presumptions.*—See applicable procedures described in § 1.1441-1(b)(7) in the event the withholding agent does not hold an appropriate withholding certificate or other appropriate documentation at the time of payment or does not act in accordance with applicable presumptions described in paragraph (a)(2)(i), (2)(ii), or (3) of this section.

(g) *Effective date.*—(1) *General rule.*—This section applies to payments made after December 31, 2000.

(2) *Transition rules.*—The validity of a Form 4224 or 8233 that was valid on January 1, 1998, under the regulations in effect prior to January 1, 2001 (see 26 CFR part 1, revised April 1, 1999) and expired, or will expire, at any time during 1998, is extended until December 31, 1998. The validity of a Form 4224 or 8233 that is valid on or after January 1, 1999, remains valid until its validity expires under the regulations in effect prior to January 1, 2001 (see 26 CFR part 1, revised April 1, 1999) but in no event will such form remain valid after December 31, 2000. The rule in this paragraph (g)(2), however, does not apply to extend the validity period of a Form 4224 or 8223 that expires solely by reason of changes in the circumstances of the person whose name is on the certificate. Notwithstanding the first three sentences of this paragraph (g)(2), a withholding agent may choose to not take advantage of the transition rule in this paragraph (g)(2) with respect to one or more withholding certificates valid under the regulations in effect prior to January 1, 2001 (see 26 CFR part 1, revised April 1, 1999) and, therefore, to require withholding certificates conforming to the requirements described in this section (new withholding certificates). For purposes of this section, a new withholding certificate is deemed to satisfy the documentation requirement under the regulations in effect prior to January 1, 2001 (see 26 CFR part 1, revised April 1, 1999). Further, a new withholding certificate remains valid for the period specified in § 1.1441-1(e)(4)(ii), regardless of when the certificate is obtained. [Reg. § 1.1441-4.]

☐ [T.D. 6187, 7-5-56. *Amended by T.D.* 6229, 4-22-57; *T.D.* 6592, 2-27-62; *T.D.* 6908, 12-30-66; *T.D.* 6922, 6-16-67; *T.D.* 7378, 9-29-75; *T.D.* 7582, 1-2-79; *T.D.* 7777, 5-18-81; *T.D.* 7842, 11-2-82; *T.D.* 7977, 9-19-84; *T.D.* 8015, 3-25-85; *T.D.* 8288, 2-2-90; *T.D.* 8734, 10-6-97; *T.D.* 8804, 12-30-98; *T.D.* 8856, 12-29-99 *and T.D.* 8881, 5-15-2000.]

[Reg. § 1.1441-5]

§ 1.1441-5. Withholding on payments to partnerships, trusts, and estates.—(a) *In general.*—This section describes the rules that apply to payments made to partnerships, trusts, and estates. Paragraph (b) of this section prescribes the rules that apply to a withholding agent making a payment to a U.S. partnership, trust, or estate. It also prescribes the obligations of a U.S. partnership, trust, or estate that makes a payment to a foreign partner, beneficiary, or owner. Paragraph (c) of this section prescribes rules that apply to a withholding agent that makes a payment to a foreign partnership. Paragraph (d) of this section provides presumption rules that apply to payments made to foreign partnerships. Paragraph (e) of this section prescribes rules, including presumption rules, that apply to a withholding agent that makes a payment to a foreign trust or foreign estate.

(b) *Rules applicable to U.S. partnerships, trusts, and estates.*—(1) *Payments to U.S. partnerships, trusts, and estates.*—No withholding is required under section 1.1441-1(b)(1) on a payment of an amount subject to withholding (as defined in § 1.1441-2(a)) that a withholding agent may treat as made to a U.S. payee. Therefore, if a withholding agent can reliably associate (within the meaning of § 1.1441-2(b)(vii)) a Form W-9 provided in accordance with § 1.1441-1(d)(2) or (4) by a U.S. partnership, U.S. trust, or a U.S. estate the withholding agent may treat the payment as made to a U.S. payee and the payment is not subject to withholding under section 1441 even though the partnership, trust, or estate may have foreign partners, beneficiaries, or owners. A withholding agent is also not required to withhold under section 1441 on a payment it makes to an entity presumed to be a U.S. payee under paragraphs (d)(2) and (e)(6)(ii) of this section.

(2) *Withholding by U.S. payees.*—(i) *U.S. partnerships.*—(A) *In general.*—A U.S. partnership is required to withhold under § 1.1441-1 as a withholding agent on an amount subject to withholding (as defined in § 1.1441-2(a)) that is includible in the gross income of a partner that is a foreign person. Subject to paragraph (b)(2)(v) of this section, a U.S. partnership shall withhold when any distributions that include amounts subject to withholding (including guaranteed payments made by a U.S. partnership) are made. To the extent a foreign partner's distributive share of income subject to withholding has not actually been distributed to the foreign partner, the U.S. partnership must withhold on the foreign partner's distributive share of the income on the earlier of the date that the statement required under section 6031(b) is mailed or otherwise provided to the partner or the due date for furnishing the statement.

(B) *Effectively connected income of partners.*—Withholding on items of income that are effectively connected income in the hands of the partners who are foreign persons is governed by section 1446 and not by this section. In such a case, partners in a domestic partnership are not required to furnish a withholding certificate in order to claim an exemption from withholding under section 1441(c)(1) and § 1.1441-4.

(ii) *U.S. simple trusts.*—A U.S. trust that is described in section 651(a) (a U.S. simple trust) is required to withhold under chapter 3 of the Internal Revenue Code as a withholding agent on the distributable net income includible in the gross income of a foreign beneficiary to the extent the distributable net income is an amount subject to withholding (as defined in § 1.1441-2(a)). A U.S. simple trust shall withhold when a distribution is made to a foreign beneficiary. The U.S. trust may make a reasonable estimate of the portion of the distribution that constitutes distributable net income consisting of an amount subject to withholding and apply the appropriate rate of withholding to the estimated amount. If, at the end of the taxable year in which the distribution is made, the U.S. simple trust determines that it underwithheld under section 1441 or 1442, the trust shall be liable as a withholding agent for the amount under withheld under section 1461. No penalties shall be imposed for failure to withhold and deposit the tax if the U.S. simple trust's estimate was reasonable and the trust pays the underwithheld amount on or before the due date of Form 1042 under section 1461. Any payment of underwithheld amounts by the U.S. simple trust shall not be treated as income subject to additional withholding even if that amount is treated as additional income to the foreign beneficiary, unless the additional amount is income to the foreign beneficiary as a result of a contractual arrangement between the parties regarding the satisfaction of the foreign beneficiary's tax liability. To the extent a U.S. simple trust is required to, but does not, distribute such income to a foreign beneficiary, the U.S. trust must withhold on the foreign beneficiary's allocable share at the time the income is required (without extension) to be reported on Form 1042-S under § 1.1461-1(c).

(iii) *U.S. complex trusts and U.S. estates.*— A U.S. trust that is not a trust described in section 651(a) (a U.S. complex trust) is required to withhold under chapter 3 of the Internal Revenue Code as a withholding agent on the distributable net income includible in the gross income of a foreign beneficiary to the extent the distributable net income consists of an amount subject to withholding (as defined in § 1.1441-2(a)) that is, or is required to be, distributed currently. The U.S. complex trust shall withhold when a distribution is made to a foreign beneficiary. The trust may use the same procedures regarding an estimate of the amount subject to withholding as a U.S. simple trust under paragraph (b)(2)(ii) of this section. To the extent an amount subject to withholding is required to be, but is not actually distributed, the U.S. complex trust must withhold on the foreign beneficiary's allocable share at the time the income is required to be reported on Form 1042-S under § 1.1461-1(c), without extension. A U.S. estate is required to withhold under chapter 3 of the Internal Revenue Code on the distributable net income includible in the gross income of a foreign beneficiary to the extent the distributable net income consists of an amount subject to withholding (as defined in § 1.1441-2(a)) that is actually distributed. A U.S. estate may also use the reasonable estimate procedures of paragraph (b)(2)(ii) of this section.

However, those procedures apply to an estate that has a taxable year other than a calendar year only if the estate files an amended return on Form 1042 for the calendar year in which the distribution was made and pays the underwithheld tax and interest within 60 days after the close of the taxable year in which the distribution was made.

(iv) *U.S. grantor trusts.*—A U.S. trust that is described in section 671 through 679 (a U.S. grantor trust) must withhold on any income includible in the gross income of a foreign person that is treated as an owner of the grantor trust to the extent the amount includible consists of an amount that is subject to withholding (as described in § 1.1441-2(a)). The withholding must occur at the time the income is received by, or credited to, the trust.

(v) *Subsequent distribution.*—If a U.S. partnership or U.S. trust withholds on a foreign partner, beneficiary, or owner's share of an amount subject to withholding before the amount is actually distributed to the partner, beneficiary, or owner, withholding is not required when the amount is subsequently distributed.

(c) *Foreign partnerships.*—(1) *Determination of payee.*—(i) *Payments treated as made to partners.*— Except as otherwise provided in paragraph (c)(1)(ii) of this section, the payees of a payment to a person that the withholding agent may treat as a nonwithholding foreign partnership under paragraph (c)(3)(i) or (d)(2) of this section are the partners (looking through partners that are foreign intermediaries or flow-through entities) as follows—

(A) If the withholding agent can reliably associate a partner's distributive share of the payment with a valid Form W-9 provided under § 1.1441-1 (d), the partner is a U.S. payee;

(B) If the withholding agent can reliably associate a partner's distributive share of the payment with a valid Form W-8, or other appropriate documentation, provided under § 1.1441-1 (e)(1)(ii), the partner is a payee that is a foreign beneficial owner;

(C) If the withholding agent can reliably associate a partner's distributive share of the payment with a qualified intermediary withholding certificate under § 1.1441-1(e)(3)(ii), a nonqualified intermediary withholding certificate under § 1.1441-1(e)(3)(iii), or a U.S. branch certificate under § 1.1441-1(e)(3)(v), then the rules of § 1.1441-1(b)(2)(v) shall apply to determine who the payee is in the same manner as if the partner's distributive share of the payment had been paid directly to such intermediary or U.S. branch;

(D) If the withholding agent can reliably associate the partner's distributive share with a withholding foreign partnership certificate under paragraph (c)(2)(iv) of this section or a nonwithholding foreign partnership certificate under paragraph (c)(3)(iii) of this section, then the rules of this paragraph (c)(1)(i) or paragraph (c)(1)(ii) of this section shall apply to determine whether the payment is treated as made to the partners of the higher-tier partnership under this paragraph (c)(1)(i) or to the higher-tier partnership itself (under the rules of paragraph (c)(1)(ii) of this section) in the same manner as if the partner's distributive share of the payment had been paid directly to the higher-tier foreign partnership;

(E) If the withholding agent can reliably associate the partner's distributive share with a withholding certificate described in paragraph (e) of this section regarding a foreign trust or estate, then the rules of paragraph (e) of this section shall apply to determine who the payees are; and

(F) If the withholding agent cannot reliably associate the partner's distributive share with a withholding certificate or other appropriate documentation, the partners are considered to be the payees and the presumptions described in paragraph (d)(3) of this section shall apply to determine their classification and status.

(ii) *Payments treated as made to the partnership.*—A payment to a person that the withholding agent may treat as a foreign partnership is treated as a payment to the foreign partnership and not to its partners only if—

(A) The withholding agent can reliably associate the payment with a withholding certificate described in paragraph (c)(2)(iv) of this section (withholding certificate of a withholding foreign partnership);

(B) The withholding agent can reliably associate the payment with a withholding certificate described in paragraph (c)(3)(iii) of this section (nonwithholding foreign partnership) certifying that the payment is income that is effectively connected with the conduct of a trade or business in the United States; or

(C) The withholding agent can treat the income as effectively connected income under the presumption rules of § 1.1441-4(a)(2)(ii) or (3)(i).

(iii) *Rules for reliably associating a payment with documentation.*—For rules regarding the reliable association of a payment with documentation, see § 1.1441-1(b)(2)(vii). In the absence of documentation, see § § 1.1441-1(b)(3) and 1.6049-5(d) and paragraphs (d) and (e)(6) of this section for applicable presumptions.

(iv) *Examples.*—The rules of paragraphs (c)(1)(i) and (ii) of this section are illustrated by the following examples:

Example 1. FP is a nonwithholding foreign partnership organized in Country X. FP has two partners, FC, a foreign corporation, and USP, a U.S. partnership. USWH, a U.S. withholding agent, makes a payment of U.S. source interest to FP. FP has provided USWH with a valid nonwithholding foreign partnership certificate, as described in paragraph (c)(3)(iii) of this section, with which it associates a beneficial owner withholding certificate from FC and a Form W-9 from USP together with the withholding statement required by paragraph (c)(3)(iv) of this section. USWH can reliably associate the payment of interest with the withholding certificates from FC and USP. Under paragraph (c)(1)(i) of this section, the payees of the interest payment are FC and USP.

Example 2. The facts are the same as in *Example 1,* except that FP1, a nonwithholding foreign partnership, is a partner in FP rather than USP. FP1 has two partners, A and B, both foreign persons. FP provides USWH with a valid nonwithholding foreign partnership certificate, as described in paragraph (c)(3)(iii) of this section, with which it associates a beneficial owner withholding certificate from FC and a nonwithholding foreign partnership certificate from FP1. In addition, foreign beneficial owner withholding certificates from A and B are associated with the nonwithholding foreign partnership withholding certificate from FP1. FP also provides the withholding statement required by paragraph (c)(3)(iv) of this section. USWH can reliably associate the interest payment with the withholding certificates provided by FC, A, and B. Therefore, under paragraph (c)(1)(i) of this section, the payees of the interest payment are FC, A, and B.

Example 3. USWH makes a payment of U.S. source dividends to WFP, a withholding foreign partnership. WFP has two partners, FC1 and FC2, both foreign corporations. USWH can reliably associate the payment with a valid withholding foreign partnership withholding certificate from WFP. Therefore, under paragraph(c)(1)(ii)(A) of this section, WFP is the payee of the dividends.

Example 4. USWH makes a payment of U.S. source royalties to FP, a foreign partnership. USWH can reliably associate the royalties with a valid withholding certificate from FP on which FP certifies that the income is effectively connected with the conduct of a trade or business in the United States. Therefore, under paragraph (c)(1)(ii)(B) of this section, FP is the payee of the royalties.

(2) *Withholding foreign partnerships.*— (i) *Reliance on claim of withholding foreign partnership status.*—A withholding foreign partnership is a foreign partnership that has entered into an agreement with the Internal Revenue Service (IRS), as described in paragraph (c)(2)(ii) of this section, with respect to distributions and guaranteed payments it makes to its partners. A withholding agent that can reliably associate a payment with a certificate described in paragraph (c)(2)(iv) of this section may treat the person to whom it makes the payment as a withholding foreign partnership for purposes of

withholding under chapter 3 of the Internal Revenue Code, information reporting under chapter 61 of the Internal Revenue Code, backup withholding under section 3406, and withholding under other provisions of the Internal Revenue Code. Furnishing such a certificate is in lieu of transmitting to a withholding agent withholding certificates or other appropriate documentation for its partners. Although the withholding foreign partnership generally will be required to obtain withholding certificates or other appropriate documentation from its partners pursuant to its agreement with the IRS, it will generally not be required to attach such documentation to its withholding foreign partnership withholding certificate. A foreign partnership may act as a qualified intermediary under § 1.1441-1(e)(5) with respect to payments it makes to persons other than its partners. In addition, the IRS may permit a foreign partnership to act as a qualified intermediary under § 1.1441-1(e)(5)(ii)(D) with respect to its partners in appropriate circumstances.

(ii) *Withholding agreement.*—The IRS may, upon request, enter into a withholding agreement with a foreign partnership pursuant to such procedures as the IRS may prescribe in published guidance (see § 601.601(d)(2) of this chapter). Under the withholding agreement, a foreign partnership shall generally be subject to the applicable withholding and reporting provisions applicable to withholding agents and payors under chapters 3 and 61 of the Internal Revenue Code, section 3406, the regulations under those provisions, and other withholding provisions of the Internal Revenue Code, except to the extent provided under the agreement. Under the agreement, a foreign partnership may agree to act as an acceptance agent to perform the duties described in § 301.6109-1(d)(3)(iv)(A) of this chapter. The agreement may specify the manner in which applicable procedures for adjustments for underwithholding and overwithholding, including refund procedures, apply to the withholding foreign partnership and its partners and the extent to which applicable procedures may be modified. In particular, a withholding agreement may allow a withholding foreign partnership to claim refunds of overwithheld amounts on behalf of its customers. In addition, the agreement must specify the manner in which the IRS will audit the foreign partnership's books and records in order to verify the partnership's compliance with its agreement. A withholding foreign partnership must file a return on Form 1042 and information returns on Form 1042-S. The withholding foreign partnership agreement may also require a withholding foreign partnership to file a partnership return under section 6031(a) and partner statements under 6031(b).

(iii) *Withholding responsibility.*—A withholding foreign partnership must assume primary withholding responsibility under chapter 3 of the Internal Revenue Code. It is not required to provide information to the withholding agent regarding each partner's distributive share of the payment. The withholding foreign partnership will be responsible for reporting the payments under § 1.1461-1(c) and chapter 61 of the Internal Revenue Code. A withholding agent making a payment to a withholding foreign partnership is not required to withhold any amount under chapter 3 of the Internal Revenue Code on a payment to the withholding foreign partnership, unless it has actual knowledge or reason to know that the foreign partnership is not a withholding foreign partnership. The withholding foreign partnership shall withhold the payments under the same procedures and at the same time as prescribed for withholding by a U.S. partnership under paragraph (b)(2) of this section, except that, for purposes of determining the partner's status, the provisions of paragraph (d)(4) of this section shall apply.

(iv) *Withholding certificate from a withholding foreign partnership.*—The rules of § 1.1441-1(e)(4) shall apply to withholding certificates described in this paragraph (c)(2)(iv). A withholding certificate furnished by a withholding foreign partnership is valid with regard to any partner on whose behalf the certificate is furnished only if it is furnished on a Form W-8, an acceptable substitute form, or such other form as the IRS may prescribe, it is signed under penalties of perjury by a partner with authority to sign for the partnership, its validity has not expired, and it contains the information, statement, and certifications described in this paragraph (c)(2)(iv) as follows—

(A) The name, permanent residence address (as described in § 1.1441-1(e)(2)(ii)), and the employer identification number of the partnership, and the country under the laws of which the partnership is created or governed;

(B) A certification that the partnership is a withholding foreign partnership within the meaning of paragraph (c)(2)(i) of this section; and

(C) Any other information, certifications or statements as may be required by the withholding foreign partnership agreement with the IRS or the form or accompanying instructions in addition to, or in lieu of, the information, statements, and certifications described in this paragraph (c)(2)(iv).

(3) *Nonwithholding foreign partnerships.*—(i) *Reliance on claim of foreign partnership status.*—A withholding agent may treat a person as a nonwithholding foreign partnership if it receives from that person a nonwithholding foreign partnership withholding certificate as described in paragraph (c)(3)(iii) of this section. A withholding agent that does not receive a nonwithholding foreign partnership withholding certificate, or does not receive a valid withholding certificate,

from an entity it knows, or has reason to know, is a foreign partnership, must apply the presumption rules of §§ 1.1441-1(b)(3) and 1.6049-5(d) and paragraphs (d) and (e)(6) of this section. In addition, to the extent a withholding agent cannot, prior to a payment, reliably associate the payment with valid documentation from a payee that is associated with the nonwithholding foreign partnership withholding certificate or has insufficient information to report the payment on Form 1042-S or Form 1099, to the extent reporting is required, must also apply the presumption rules. See § 1.1441-1(b)(2)(vii)(A) and (B) for rules regarding reliable association. See paragraph (c)(3)(iv) of this section and § 1.1441-1(e)(3)(iv) for alternative procedures permitting allocation information to be received after a payment is made.

(ii) *Reliance on claim of reduced withholding by a partnership for its partners.*—This paragraph (c)(3)(ii) describes the manner in which a withholding agent may rely on a claim of reduced withholding when making a payment to a nonwithholding foreign partnership. To the extent that a withholding agent treats a payment to a nonwithholding foreign partnership as a payment to the nonwithholding foreign partnership's partners (whether direct or indirect) in accordance with paragraph (c)(1)(i) of this section, it may rely on a claim for reduced withholding by the partner if, prior to the payment, the withholding agent can reliably associate the payment (within the meaning of § 1.1441-1(b)(2)(vii)) with a valid withholding certificate or other appropriate documentation from the partner that establishes entitlement to a reduced rate of withholding. A withholding certificate or other appropriate documentation that establishes entitlement to a reduced rate of withholding is a beneficial owner withholding certificate described in § 1.1441-1(e)(2)(i), documentary evidence described in § 1.1441-6(c)(3) or (4) or 1.6049-5(c)(1) (for a partner claiming to be a foreign person and a beneficial owner, determined under the provisions of § 1.1441-1(c)(6)), a Form W-9 described in § 1.1441-1(d) (for a partner claiming to be a U.S. payee), or a withholding foreign partnership withholding certificate described in paragraph (c)(2)(iv) of this section. Unless a nonwithholding foreign partnership withholding certificate is provided for income claimed to be effectively connected with the conduct of a trade or business in the United States, a claim must be presented for each portion of the payment that represents an item of income includible in the distributive share of a partner as required under paragraph (c)(3)(iii)(C) of this section. When making a claim for several partners, the partnership may present a single nonwithholding foreign partnership withholding certificate to which the partners' certificates or other appropriate documentation are associated. Where the nonwithholding foreign partnership withholding certificate is provided for

income claimed to be effectively connected with the conduct of a trade or business in the United States under paragraph (c)(3)(iii)(D) of this section, the claim may be presented without having to identify any partner's distributive share of the payment.

(iii) *Withholding certificate from a nonwithholding foreign partnership.*—A nonwithholding foreign partnership shall provide a nonwithholding foreign partnership withholding certificate with respect to reportable amounts received by the nonwithholding foreign partnership. A nonwithholding foreign partnership withholding certificate is valid only to the extent it is furnished on a Form W-8 (or an acceptable substitute form or such other form as the IRS may prescribe), it is signed under penalties of perjury by a partner with authority to sign for the partnership, its validity has not expired, and it contains the information, statements, and certifications described in this paragraph (c)(3)(iii) and paragraph (c)(3)(iv) of this section, and the withholding certificates and other appropriate documentation for all the persons to whom the certificate relates are associated with the certificate. The rules of § 1.1441-1(e)(4) shall apply to withholding certificates described in this paragraph (c)(3)(iii). No withholding certificates or other appropriate documentation from persons who derive income through a partnership (whether or not U.S. exempt recipients) are required to be associated with the nonwithholding foreign partnership withholding certificate if the certificate is furnished solely for income claimed to be effectively connected with the conduct of a trade or business in the United States. Withholding certificates and other appropriate documentation that may be associated with the nonwithholding foreign partnership withholding certificate consist of beneficial owner withholding certificates under § 1.1441-1(e)(2)(i), intermediary withholding certificates under § 1.1441-1(e)(3)(i), withholding foreign partnership withholding certificates under paragraph (c)(2)(iv) of this section, nonwithholding foreign partnership withholding certificates under this paragraph (c)(3)(iii), withholding certificates from foreign trusts or estates under paragraph (e) of this section, documentary evidence described in § 1.1441-6(c)(3) or (4) or documentary evidence described in § 1.6049-5(c)(1), and any other documentation or certificates applicable under other provisions of the Internal Revenue Code or regulations that certify or establish the status of the payee or beneficial owner as a U.S. or a foreign person. Nothing in this paragraph (c)(3)(iii) shall require a nonwithholding foreign partnership to furnish original documentation. Copies of certificates or documentary evidence may be transmitted to the U.S. withholding agent, in which case the nonwithholding foreign partnership must retain the original documentation for the same time period that the copy is required to be retained by the withholding agent under §1.1441-1(e)(4)(iii) and must provide it to the withholding agent upon request. The information, statement, and certifications required on the withholding certificate are as follows—

(A) The name, permanent residence address (as described in §1.1441-1(e)(2)(ii)), and the employer identification number of the partnership, if any, and the country under the laws of which the partnership is created or governed;

(B) A certification that the person whose name is on the certificate is a foreign partnership;

(C) A withholding statement associated with the nonwithholding foreign partnership withholding certificate that provides all of the information required by paragraph (c)(3)(iv) of this section and §1.1441-1(e)(3)(iv). No withholding statement is required, however, for a nonwithholding foreign partnership withholding certificate furnished for income claimed to be effectively connected with the conduct of a trade or business in the United States;

(D) A certification that the income is effectively connected with the conduct of a trade or business in the United States, if applicable; and

(E) Any other information, certifications, or statements required by the form or accompanying instructions in addition to, or in lieu of, the information and certifications described in this paragraph (c)(3)(iii).

(iv) *Withholding statement provided by nonwithholding foreign partnership.*—The provisions of §1.1441-1(e)(3)(iv) (regarding a withholding statement) shall apply to a nonwithholding foreign partnership by substituting the term nonwithholding foreign partnership for the term nonqualified intermediary.

(v) *Withholding and reporting by a foreign partnership.*—A nonwithholding foreign partnership described in this paragraph (c)(3) that receives an amount subject to withholding (as defined in §1.1441-2(a)) shall be required to withhold and report such payment under chapter 3 of the Internal Revenue Code and the regulations thereunder except as otherwise provided in this paragraph (c)(3)(v). A nonwithholding foreign partnership shall not be required to withhold and report if it has provided a valid nonwithholding foreign partnership withholding certificate, it has provided all of the information required by paragraph (c)(3)(iv) of this section (withholding statement), and it does not know, and has no reason to know, that another withholding agent failed to withhold the correct amount or failed to report the payment correctly under §1.1461-1(c). A withholding foreign partnership's obligations to withhold and report shall be determined in accordance with its withholding foreign partnership agreement.

(d) *Presumption rules.*—(1) *In general.*—This paragraph (d) contains the applicable presumptions for a withholding agent (including a partnership) to determine the classification and status of a partnership and its partners in the absence of documentation. The provisions of §1.1441-1(b)(3)(iv) (regarding the 90-day grace period) and §1.1441-1(b)(3)(vii) through (ix) shall apply for purposes of this paragraph (d).

(2) *Determination of partnership status as U.S. or foreign in the absence of documentation.*—In the absence of a valid representation of U.S. partnership status in accordance with paragraph (b)(1) of this section or of foreign partnership status in accordance with paragraph (c)(2)(i) or (3)(i) of this section, the withholding agent shall determine the classification of the payee under the presumptions set forth in §1.1441-1(b)(3)(ii). If the withholding agent treats the payee as a partnership under §1.1441-1(b)(3)(ii), the withholding agent shall presume the partnership to be a U.S. partnership unless there are indicia of foreign status. If there are indicia of foreign status, the withholding agent may presume the partnership to be foreign. Indicia of foreign status exist only if the withholding agent has actual knowledge of the payee's employer identification number and that number begins with the two digits "98," the withholding agent's communications with the payee are mailed to an address in a foreign country, or the payment is made outside the United States (as defined in §1.6049-5(e)). For rules regarding reliable association with a withholding certificate from a domestic or a foreign partnership, see §1.1441-1(b)(2)(vii).

(3) *Determination of partners' status in the absence of certain documentation.*—If a nonwithholding foreign partnership has provided a nonwithholding foreign partnership withholding certificate under paragraph (c)(3)(iii) of this section that would be valid except that the withholding agent cannot reliably associate all or a portion of the payment with valid documentation from a partner of the partnership, then the withholding agent may apply the presumption rule of this paragraph (d)(3) with respect to all or a portion of the payment for which documentation has not been received. See §1.1441-1(b)(2)(vii)(A) and (B) for rules regarding reliable association. The presumption rule of this paragraph (d)(3) also applies to a person that is presumed to be a foreign partnership under the rule of paragraph (d)(2) of this section. Any portion of a payment that the withholding agent cannot treat as reliably associated with valid documentation from a partner may be presumed made to a foreign payee. As a result, any payment of an amount subject to withholding is subject to withholding at a rate of 30 percent. Any payment that is presumed to be made to an undocumented foreign payee must be reported on Form 1042-S. See §1.1461-1(c).

(4) *Determination by a withholding foreign partnership of the status of its partners.*—A with-

holding foreign partnership shall determine whether the partners or some other persons are the payees of the partners' distributive shares of any payment made by a withholding foreign partnership by applying the rules of § 1.1441-1(b)(2), paragraph (c)(1) of this section (in the case of a partner that is a foreign partnership), and paragraph (e)(3) of this section (in the case of a partner that is a foreign estate or a foreign trust). Further, the provisions of paragraph (d)(3) of this section shall apply to determine the status of partners and the applicable withholding rates to the extent that, at the time the foreign partnership is required to withhold on a payment, it cannot reliably associate the amount with documentation for any one or more of its partners.

(e) *Foreign trusts and estates.*—(1) *In general.*— This paragraph (e) provides rules applicable to payments of amounts subject to withholding (as defined in § 1.1441-2(a)) that a withholding agent may treat as made to any foreign trust or a foreign estate. For rules relating to payments to a U.S. trust or a U.S. estate, see paragraph (b) of this section. For the definitions of foreign simple trust, foreign complex trust, and foreign grantor trust, see § 1.1441-1(c)(24), (25), and (26).

(2) *Payments to foreign complex trusts and foreign estates.*—Under § 1.1441-1(c)(6)(ii)(D), a foreign complex trust or foreign estate is generally considered to be the beneficial owner of income paid to the foreign complex trust or foreign estate. See paragraph (e)(4) of this section for rules describing when a withholding agent may treat a payment as made to a foreign complex trust or a foreign estate.

(3) *Payees of payments to foreign simple trusts and foreign grantor trusts.*—(i) *Payments for which beneficiaries and owners are payees.*—For purposes of the regulations under chapters 3 and 61 of the Internal Revenue Code and section 3406, a foreign simple trust is not a beneficial owner or a payee of a payment. Also, a foreign grantor trust (or a portion of a trust that is a foreign grantor trust) is not considered a beneficial owner or a payee of a payment. Except as otherwise provided in paragraph (e)(3)(ii) of this section, the payees of a payment made to a person that the withholding agent may treat as a foreign simple trust or a foreign grantor trust (or a portion of a trust that is a foreign grantor trust) are determined under the rules of this paragraph (e)(3)(i). The payees shall be treated as the beneficial owners if they may be so treated under § 1.1441-1(c)(6)(ii)(C) and they provide documentation supporting their status as the beneficial owners. The payees of a payment to a foreign simple trust or foreign grantor trust are determined as follows—

(A) If the withholding agent can reliably associate a payment with a valid Form W-9 provided under § 1.1441-1(d) from a beneficiary

or owner of the foreign trust, then the beneficiary or owner is a U.S. payee;

(B) If the withholding agent can reliably associate a payment with a valid Form W-8, or other appropriate documentation, provided under § 1.1441-1(e)(1)(ii) from a beneficiary or owner of the foreign trust, then the beneficiary or owner is a payee that is a foreign beneficial owner;

(C) If the withholding agent can reliably associate a payment with a qualified intermediary withholding certificate under § 1.1441-1(e)(3)(ii), a nonqualified intermediary withholding certificate under § 1.1441-1(e)(3)(ii), or a U.S. branch withholding certificate under § 1.1441-1(e)(3)(v), then the rules of § 1.1441-1(b)(2)(v) shall apply to determine the payee in the same manner as if the payment had been paid directly to such intermediary or U.S. branch;

(D) If the withholding agent can reliably associate a payment with a withholding foreign partnership withholding certificate under paragraph (c)(2)(iv) of this section or a nonwithholding foreign partnership withholding certificate under paragraph (c)(3)(iii) of this section, then the rules of paragraph (c)(1)(i) or (ii) of this section shall apply to determine the payee;

(E) If the withholding agent can reliably associate the payment with a foreign simple trust withholding certificate or a foreign grantor trust withholding certificate (both described in paragraph (e)(5)(iii) of this section) from a second or higher-tier foreign simple trust or foreign grantor trust, then the rules of this paragraph (e)(3)(i) or paragraph (e)(3)(ii) of this section shall apply to determine whether the payment is treated as made to a beneficiary or owner of the higher-tier trust or to the trust itself in the same manner as if the payment had been made directly to the higher-tier trust; and

(F) If the withholding agent cannot reliably associate a payment with a withholding certificate or other appropriate documentation, the payees shall be determined by applying the presumptions described in paragraph (e)(6) of this section.

(ii) *Payments for which trust is payee.*—A payment to a person that the withholding agent may treat as made to a foreign trust under paragraph (e)(5)(iii) of this section is treated as a payment to the trust, and not to a beneficiary of the trust, only if—

(A) The withholding agent can reliably associate the payment with a foreign complex trust withholding certificate under paragraph (e)(4) of this section;

(B) The withholding agent can reliably associate the payment with a foreign simple trust withholding certificate under paragraph (e)(5)(iii) of this section certifying that the payment is income that is treated as effectively connected with the conduct of a trade or business in the United States; or

(C) The withholding agent can treat the income as effectively connected income under the presumption rules of § 1.1441-4(a)(3)(i).

(4) *Reliance on claim of foreign complex trust or foreign estate status.*—A withholding agent may treat a payment as made to a foreign complex trust or a foreign estate if the withholding agent can reliably associate the payment with a beneficial owner withholding certificate described in § 1.1441-1(e)(2)(i) or other documentary evidence under § 1.1441-6(c)(3) or (4) (regarding a claim for treaty benefits) or § 1.6049-5(c)(1) (regarding documentary evidence to establish foreign status for purposes of chapter 61 of the Internal Revenue Code) that establishes the foreign complex trust or foreign estate's status as a beneficial owner. See paragraph (e)(6) of this section for presumption rules if documentation is lacking.

(5) *Foreign simple trust and foreign grantor trust.*—(i) *Reliance on claim of foreign simple trust or foreign grantor trust status.*—A withholding agent may treat a person as a foreign simple trust or foreign grantor trust if it receives from that person a foreign simple trust or foreign grantor trust withholding certificate as described in paragraph (e)(5)(iii) of this section. A withholding agent must apply the presumption rules of §§ 1.1441-1(b)(3) and 1.6049-5(d) and paragraphs (d) and (e)(6) of this section to the extent it cannot, prior to the payment, reliably associate a payment (within the meaning of § 1.1441-1(b)(2)(vii)) with a valid foreign simple trust or foreign grantor trust withholding certificate, it cannot reliably determine how much of the payment relates to valid documentation provided by a payee (e.g., a person that is not itself a nonqualified intermediary, flow-through entity, or U.S. branch) associated with the foreign simple trust or foreign grantor trust withholding certificate, or it does not have sufficient information to report the payment on Form 1042-S or Form 1099, if reporting is required. See § 1.1441-1(b)(2)(vii)(A) and (B).

(ii) *Reliance on claim of reduced withholding by a foreign simple trust or foreign grantor trust for its beneficiaries or owners.*—This paragraph (e)(5)(ii) describes the manner in which a withholding agent may rely on a claim of reduced withholding when making a payment to a foreign simple trust or foreign grantor trust. To the extent that a withholding agent treats a payment to a foreign simple trust or foreign grantor trust as a payment to payees other than the trust in accordance with paragraph (e)(3)(i) of this section, it may rely on a claim for reduced withholding by a beneficiary or owner if, prior to the payment, the withholding agent can reliably associate the payment (within the meaning of § 1.1441-1(b)(2)(vii)) with a valid withholding certificate or other appropriate documentation

from a payee or beneficial owner that establishes entitlement to a reduced rate of withholding. A withholding certificate or other appropriate documentation that establishes entitlement to a reduced rate of withholding is a beneficial owner withholding certificate described in § 1.1441-1(e)(2)(i) or documentary evidence described in § 1.1441-6(c)(3) or (4) or in § 1.6049-5(c)(1) (for a beneficiary or owner claiming to be a foreign person and a beneficial owner, determined under the provisions of § 1.1441-1(c)(6)), a Form W-9 described in § 1.1441-1(d) (for a beneficiary or owner claiming to be a U.S. payee), or a withholding foreign partnership withholding certificate described in paragraph (c)(2)(iv) of this section. Unless a foreign simple trust or foreign grantor trust withholding certificate is provided for income treated as income effectively connected with the conduct of a trade or business in the United States, a claim must be presented for each payee's portion of the payment. When making a claim for several payees, the trust may present a single foreign simple trust or foreign grantor trust withholding certificate with which the payees' certificates or other appropriate documentation are associated. Where the foreign simple trust or foreign grantor trust withholding certificate is provided for income that is treated as effectively connected with the conduct of a trade or business in the United States under paragraph (e)(5)(iii)(D) of this section, the claim may be presented without having to identify any beneficiary's or grantor's distributive share of the payment.

(iii) *Withholding certificate from foreign simple trust or foreign grantor trust.*—A withholding certificate furnished by a foreign simple trust or a foreign grantor trust that is not a withholding foreign trust (within the meaning of paragraph (e)(5)(v) of this section) is valid only if it is furnished on a Form W-8, an acceptable substitute form, or such other form as the IRS may prescribe, it is signed under penalties of perjury by a trustee, its validity has not expired, it contains the information, statements, and certifications required by this paragraph (e)(5)(iii) and § 1.1441-1(e)(3)(iv), and the withholding certificates or other appropriate documentation for all of the payees (as determined under paragraph (e)(3)(i) of this section) to whom the certificate relates are associated with the foreign simple trust or foreign grantor trust withholding certificate. The rules of § 1.1441-1(e)(4) shall apply to withholding certificates described in this paragraph (e)(5)(iii). No withholding certificates or other appropriate documentation from persons who derive income through a foreign simple trust or a foreign grantor trust (whether or not U.S. exempt recipients) are required to be associated with the foreign simple trust or foreign grantor trust withholding certificate if the certificate is furnished solely for income that is treated as effectively connected with the conduct of a trade or business in the United States. Withholding certificates and other appropriate documentation (as determined under paragraph (e)(3)(i) of this section) that may be associated with a foreign simple trust or foreign grantor trust withholding certificate consist of beneficial owner withholding certificates under §1.1441-1(e)(2)(i), intermediary withholding certificates under §1.1441-1(e)(3)(i), withholding foreign partnership withholding certificates under paragraph (c)(2)(iv) of this section, nonwithholding foreign partnership withholding certificates under paragraph (c)(3)(iii) of this section, withholding certificates from foreign trusts or estates under paragraph (e)(4) or (5)(iii) of this section, documentary evidence described in §§1.1441-6(c)(3) or (4), or 1.6049-5(c)(1), and any other documentation or certificates applicable under other provisions of the Internal Revenue Code or regulations that certify or establish the status of the payee or beneficial owner as a U.S. or a foreign person. Nothing in this paragraph (e)(5)(iii) shall require a foreign simple trust or foreign grantor trust to provide original documentation. Copies of certificates or documentary evidence may be passed up to the U.S. withholding agent, in which case the foreign simple trust or foreign grantor trust must retain the original documentation for the same time period that the copy is required to be retained by the withholding agent under §1.1441-1(e)(4)(iii) and must provide it to the withholding agent upon request. The information, statement, and certifications required on a foreign simple trust or foreign grantor trust withholding certificate are as follows—

(A) The name, permanent residence address (as described in §1.1441-1(e)(2)(ii)), and the employer identification number, if required, of the trust and the country under the laws of which the trust is created;

(B) A certification that the person whose name is on the certificate is a foreign simple trust or a foreign grantor trust;

(C) A withholding statement associated with the foreign simple trust or foreign grantor trust withholding certificate that provides all of the information required by paragraph (e)(5)(iv) of this section. No withholding statement is required, however, for a foreign simple trust withholding certificate furnished for income that is treated as effectively connected with the conduct of a trade or business in the United States;

(D) A certification on a foreign simple trust withholding certificate that the income is treated as effectively connected with the conduct of a trade or business in the United States, if applicable; and

(E) Any other information, certifications, or statements required by the form or accompanying instructions in addition to, or in lieu of, the information, certifications, and statements described in this paragraph (e)(5)(iii);

(iv) *Withholding statement provided by a foreign simple trust or foreign grantor trust.*—The provisions of §1.1441-1(e)(3)(iv) (regarding a withholding statement) shall apply to a foreign simple trust or foreign grantor trust by substituting the term foreign simple trust or foreign grantor trust for the term nonqualified intermediary.

(v) *Withholding foreign trusts.*—The IRS may enter an agreement with a foreign trust to treat the trust or estate as a withholding foreign trust. Such an agreement shall generally follow the same principles as an agreement with a withholding foreign partnership under paragraph (c)(2)(ii) of this section. A withholding agent may treat a payment to a withholding foreign trust in the same manner the withholding agent would treat a payment to a withholding foreign partnership. The IRS may also enter an agreement to treat a trust as a qualified intermediary in appropriate circumstances. See §1.1441-1(e)(5)(ii)(D).

(6) *Presumption rules.*—(i) *In general.*—This paragraph (e)(6) contains the applicable presumptions for a withholding agent (including a trust or estate) to determine the classification and status of a trust or estate and its beneficiaries or owners in the absence of valid documentation. The provisions of §1.1441-1(b)(3)(iv) (regarding the 90-day grace period) and §1.1441-1(b)(3)(vii) through (ix) shall apply for purposes of this paragraph (e)(6).

(ii) *Determination of status as U.S. or foreign trust or estate in the absence of documentation.*—In the absence of valid documentation that establishes the U.S. status of a trust or estate under paragraph (b)(1) of this section and of documentation that establishes the foreign status of a trust or estate under paragraph (e)(4) or (5)(iii) of this section, the withholding agent shall determine the classification of the payee based upon the presumptions set forth in §1.1441-1(b)(3)(ii). If, based upon those presumptions, the withholding agent classifies the payee as a trust or estate, the trust or estate shall be presumed to be a U.S. trust or U.S. estate unless there are indicia of foreign status, in which case the trust or estate shall be presumed to be foreign. Indicia of foreign status exists if the withholding agent has actual knowledge of the payee's employer identification number and that number begins with the two digits "98," the withholding agent's communications with the payee are mailed to an address in a foreign country, or the payment is made outside the United States (as defined in §1.6049-5(e)). If an undocumented payee is presumed to be a foreign trust it shall be presumed to be a foreign complex trust. If a withholding agent has documentary evidence that establishes that an entity is a foreign trust, but the withholding agent cannot determine whether the foreign trust is a complex trust, a simple trust, or foreign

Reg. §1.1441-5(e)(6)(ii)

grantor trust, the withholding agent may presume that the trust is a foreign complex trust.

(iii) *Determination of beneficiary or owner's status in the absence of certain documentation.*—If a foreign simple trust or foreign grantor trust has provided a foreign simple trust or foreign grantor trust withholding certificate under paragraph (e)(5)(iii) of this section but the payment to such trust cannot be reliably associated with valid documentation from a specific beneficiary or owner of the trust, then any portion of a payment that a withholding agent cannot treat as reliably associated with valid documentation from a beneficiary or owner may be presumed made to a foreign payee. As a result, any payment of an amount subject to withholding is subject to withholding at a rate of 30 percent. Any such payment that is presumed to be made to an undocumented foreign person must be reported on Form 1042-S. See § 1.1461-1(c).

(f) *Failure to receive withholding certificate timely or to act in accordance with applicable presumptions.*—See applicable procedures described in § 1.1441-1(b)(7) in the event the withholding agent does not hold an appropriate withholding certificate or other appropriate documentation at the time of payment or fails to rely on the presumptions set forth in § 1.1441-1(b)(3) or in paragraph (d) or (e) of this section.

(g) *Effective date.*—(1) *General rule.*—This section applies to payments made after December 31, 2000.

(2) *Transition rules.*—The validity of a withholding certificate that was valid on January 1, 1998, under the regulations in effect prior to January 1, 2001 (see 26 CFR parts 1 and 35a, revised April 1, 1999) and expired, or will expire, at any time during 1998, is extended until December 31, 1998. The validity of a withholding certificate that is valid on or after January 1, 1999, remains valid until its validity expires under the regulations in effect prior to January 1, 2001 (see 26 CFR parts 1 and 35a, revised April 1, 1999) but in no event will such a withholding certificate remain valid after December 31, 2000. The rule in this paragraph (g)(2), however, does not apply to extend the validity period of a withholding certificate that expires solely by reason of changes in the circumstances of the person whose name is on the certificate. Notwithstanding the first three sentences of this paragraph (g)(2) , a withholding agent may choose to not take advantage of the transition rule in this paragraph (g)(2) with respect to one or more withholding certificates valid under the regulations in effect prior to January 1, 2001 (see 26 CFR parts 1 and 35a, revised April 1, 1999) and, therefore, to require withholding certificates conforming to the requirements described in this section (new withholding certificates). For purposes of this section, a new withholding certificate is deemed to satisfy the documentation requirement under the regulations in effect prior to January 1, 2001 (see 26 CFR parts 1 and 35a, revised April 1, 1999). Further, a new withholding certificate remains valid for the period specified in § 1.1441-1(e)(4)(ii), regardless of when the certificate is obtained. [Reg. § 1.1441-5.]

☐ [T.D. 6187, 7-5-56. Amended by T.D. 6238, 6-10-57; T.D. 6908, 12-30-66; T.D. 7277, 5-14-73; T.D. 7842, 11-2-82; T.D. 7977, 9-19-84; T.D. 8160, 9-8-87; T.D. 8411, 4-24-92; T.D. 8734, 10-6-97; T.D. 8804, 12-30-98; T.D. 8856, 12-29-99 and T.D. 8881, 5-15-2000 (corrected 4-5-2001).]

[Reg. § 1.1441-6]

§ 1.1441-6. Claim of reduced withholding under an income tax treaty.—(a) *In general.*—The rate of withholding on a payment of income subject to withholding may be reduced to the extent provided under an income tax treaty in effect between the United States and a foreign country. Most benefits under income tax treaties are to foreign persons who reside in the treaty country. In some cases, benefits are available under an income tax treaty to U.S. citizens or U.S. residents or to residents of a third country. See paragraph (b)(5) of this section for claims of benefits by U.S. persons. If the requirements of this section are met, the amount withheld from the payment may be reduced at source to account for the treaty benefit. See also § 1.1441-4(b)(2) for rules regarding claims of reduced rate of withholding under an income tax treaty in the case of compensation from personal services.

(b) *Reliance on claim of reduced withholding under an income tax treaty.*—(1) *In general.*—The withholding imposed under section 1441, 1442, or 1443 on any payment to a foreign person is eligible for reduction under the terms of an income tax treaty only to the extent that such payment is treated as derived by a resident of an applicable treaty jurisdiction, such resident is a beneficial owner, and all other requirements for benefits under the treaty are satisfied. See section 894 and the regulations thereunder to determine whether a resident of a treaty country derives the income. Absent actual knowledge or reason to know otherwise, a withholding agent may rely on a claim that a beneficial owner is entitled to a reduced rate of withholding based upon an income tax treaty if, prior to the payment, the withholding agent can reliably associate the payment with a beneficial owner withholding certificate, as described in § 1.1441-1(e)(2), that contains the information necessary to support the claim, or, in the case of a payment of income described in paragraph (c)(2) of this section made outside the United States with respect to an offshore account, documentary evidence described in paragraphs (c)(3), (4), and (5) of this section. See § 1.6049-5(e) for the definition of payments made outside the United States and § 1.6049-5(c)(1) for the definition of offshore account. For purposes of this paragraph (b)(1), a beneficial owner withholding certificate described in §1.1441-1(e)(2)(i) contains information necessary to support the claim for a treaty benefit only if it includes the beneficial owner's taxpayer identifying number (except as otherwise provided in paragraph (c)(1) of this section and §1.1441-6(g)) and the representations that the beneficial owner derives the income under section 894 and the regulations thereunder, if required, and meets the limitation on benefits provisions of the treaty, if any. The withholding certificate must also contain any other representations required by this section and any other information, certifications, or statements as may be required by the form or accompanying instructions in addition to, or in place of, the information and certifications described in this section. Absent actual knowledge or reason to know that the claims are incorrect (and subject to the standards of knowledge in §1.1441-7(b)), a withholding agent may rely on the claims made on a withholding certificate or on documentary evidence. A withholding agent may also rely on the information contained in a withholding statement provided under §§1.1441-1(e)(3)(iv) and 1.1441-5(c)(3)(iv) and (e)(5)(iv) to determine whether the appropriate statements regarding section 894 and limitation on benefits have been provided in connection with documentary evidence. The Internal Revenue Service (IRS) may apply the provisions of §1.1441-1(e)(1)(ii)(B) to notify the withholding agent that the certificate cannot be relied upon to grant benefits under an income tax treaty. See §1.1441-1(e)(4)(viii) regarding reliance on a withholding certificate by a withholding agent. The provisions of §1.1441-1(b)(3)(iv) dealing with a 90-day grace period shall apply for purposes of this section.

(2) *Payment to fiscally transparent entity.*— (i) *In general.*—If the person claiming a reduced rate of withholding under an income tax treaty is the interest holder of an entity that is considered to be fiscally transparent (as defined in the regulations under section 894) by the interest holder's jurisdiction with respect to an item of income, then, with respect to such income derived by that person through the entity, the entity shall be treated as a flow-through entity and may provide a flow-through withholding certificate with which the withholding certificate or other documentary evidence of the interest holder that supports the claim for treaty benefits is associated. For purposes of the preceding sentence, interest holders do not include any direct or indirect interest holders that are themselves treated as fiscally transparent entities with respect to that income by the interest holder's jurisdiction. See §1.1441-1(c)(23) and (e)(3)(i) for the definition of flow-through entity and flow-through withholding certificate. The entity may provide a beneficial owner withholding certificate, or beneficial owner documentation, with respect to any remaining portion of the income to the extent the

entity is receiving income and is not treated as fiscally transparent by its own jurisdiction. Further, the entity may claim a reduced rate of withholding with respect to the portion of a payment for which it is not treated as fiscally transparent if it meets all the requirements to make such a claim and, in the case of treaty benefits, it provides the documentation required by paragraph (b)(1) of this section. If dual claims, as described in paragraph (b)(2)(iii) of this section, are made, multiple withholding certificates may have to be furnished. Multiple withholding certificates may also have to be furnished if the entity receives income for which a reduction of withholding is claimed under a provision of the Internal Revenue Code (e.g., portfolio interest) and income for which a reduction of withholding is claimed under an income tax treaty.

(ii) *Certification by qualified intermediary.*— Notwithstanding paragraph (b)(2)(i) of this section, a foreign entity that is fiscally transparent, as defined in the regulations under section 894, that is also a qualified intermediary for purposes of claiming a reduced rate of withholding under an income tax treaty for its interest holders (who are deriving the income paid to the entity as residents of an applicable treaty jurisdiction) may furnish a single qualified intermediary withholding certificate, as described in §1.1441-1(e)(3)(ii), for amounts for which it claims a reduced rate of withholding under an income tax treaty on behalf of its interest holders.

(iii) *Dual treatment.*—Under paragraph (b)(2)(i) of this section, a withholding agent may make a payment to a foreign entity that is simultaneously claiming to be the beneficial owner of a portion of the income (whether or not it is also claiming a reduced rate of tax on its own behalf) and a reduced rate on behalf of persons in their capacity as interest holders in the entity with respect to the same, or a different, portion of the income. If the same portion of a payment may be reliably associated with both the entity's claim and an interest holder's claim, the withholding agent may choose to reject both claims and request new documentation and information allocating the payment among the beneficial owners of the payment or the withholding agent may choose which claim to apply. If the entity and the interest holder's claims are reliably associated with separate portions of the payment, the withholding agent may, at its option, accept such dual claims based on withholding certificates or other appropriate documentation furnished by the entity and its interest holders with respect to their respective shares of the payment even though this will result in the withholding agent treating the entity differently with respect to different portions of the same payment. Alternatively, the withholding agent may choose to apply only the claim made by the entity, provided the entity may be treated as a beneficial owner of the income. If the withholding agent does not accept claims for a reduced rate of withholding presented by any one or more of the interest holders, or by the entity, any interest holder or the entity may subsequently claim a refund or credit of any amount so withheld to the extent the interest holder's or entity's share of such withholding exceeds the amount of tax due.

(iv) *Examples*.—The following examples illustrate the rules of this paragraph (b)(2):

Example 1. (i) *Facts*. Entity E is a business organization formed under the laws of country Y. Country Y has an income tax treaty with the United States. The treaty contains a limitation on benefits provision. E receives U.S. source royalties from withholding agent W and claims a reduced rate of withholding under the U.S.-Y tax treaty on its own behalf (rather than on behalf of its interest holders). E furnishes a beneficial owner withholding certificate described in paragraph (b)(1) of this section that represents that E is a resident of country Y (within the meaning of the U.S.-Y tax treaty), is the beneficial owner of the income, derives the income under section 894 and the regulations thereunder, and is not precluded from claiming benefits by the treaty's limitation on benefits provision.

(ii) *Analysis*. Absent actual knowledge or reason to know otherwise, W may rely on the representations made by E to apply a reduced rate of withholding.

Example 2. (i) *Facts*. The facts are the same as under *Example 1*, except that one of E's interest holders, H, is an entity organized in country Z. The U.S.-Z tax treaty reduces the rate on royalties to zero whereas the rate on royalties under the U.S.-Y tax treaty applicable to E is 5 percent. H is not fiscally transparent under country Z's tax law with respect to such income. H furnishes a beneficial owner withholding certificate to E that represents that H derives, within the meaning of section 894 and the regulations thereunder, its share of the royalty income paid to E as a resident of country Z, is the beneficial owner of the royalty income, and is not precluded from claiming treaty benefits by virtue of the limitation on benefits provision in the U.S.-Z treaty. E furnishes to W a flow-through withholding certificate described in §1.1441-1(e)(3)(i) to which it attaches H's beneficial owner withholding certificate and a withholding statement for the portion of the payment that H claims as its distributive share of the royalty income. E also furnishes to W a beneficial owner withholding certificate for itself for the portion of the payment that H does not claim as its distributive share.

(ii) *Analysis*. Absent actual knowledge or reason to know otherwise, W may rely on the documentation furnished by E to treat the royalty payment to a single foreign entity (E) as derived by different residents of tax treaty countries as a result of the claims presented under different treaties. W may, at its option, grant dual treatment, that is, a reduced rate of zero percent under the U.S.-Z treaty on the portion of the royalty payment that H claims to derive as a resident of country Z and a reduced rate of 5 percent under the U.S.-Y treaty for the balance. However, under paragraph (b)(2)(iii) of this section, W may, at its option, treat E as the only relevant person deriving the royalty and grant benefits under the U.S.-Y treaty only.

Example 3. (i) *Facts*. E is a business organization formed under the laws of country X. Country X has an income tax treaty with the United States. E has two interest holders, H1, organized in country Y, and H2, organized in country Z. E receives from W, a U.S. withholding agent, U.S. source royalties and interest that is eligible for the portfolio interest exception under sections 871(h) and 881(c), provided W receives the appropriate beneficial owner statement required under section 871(h)(5). E is classified as a corporation under U.S. tax law principles. Country X, E's country of organization, treats E as an entity that is not fiscally transparent with respect to items of income under the regulations under section 894. Under the U.S.-X income tax treaty, royalties are subject to 5 percent rate of withholding. Country Y, H1's country of organization, treats E as fiscally transparent with respect to items of income under section 894 and H1 as not fiscally transparent with respect to items of income. Under the country Y-U.S. income tax treaty, royalties are exempt from U.S. tax. Country Z, H2's country of organization, treats E as not fiscally transparent under section 894 with respect to items of income. E provides W with a flow-through beneficial owner withholding certificate with which it associates a beneficial owner withholding certificate from H1. H1's withholding certificate states that H1 is a resident of country Y, derives the royalty income under section 894, meets the applicable limitations on benefits provisions of the U.S.-Y treaty, and is the beneficial owner of the income. The withholding statement attached to E's flow-through withholding certificate allocates one-half of the royalty payment to H1. E also provides W with a beneficial owner withholding certificate for the interest income and the remaining one-half of the royalty income. The withholding certificate states that E is a resident of country X, derives the royalty income under section 894, meets the limitation on benefits provisions of the U.S.-X treaty, and is the beneficial owner of the income.

(ii) *Analysis*. Absent actual knowledge or reason to know that the claims are incorrect, W may treat one-half of the royalty derived by E as subject to a 5 percent withholding rate and one-half of the royalty as derived by H1 and subject to no withholding. Further, it may treat all of the interest as being paid to E and as qualifying for the portfolio interest exception. W can, at its option, treat the entire royalty as paid to E and subject it to withholding at a 5 percent rate of withholding. In that case, H1 would be entitled to claim a refund with respect to its one-half of the royalty.

(3) *Certified TIN.*—The IRS may issue guidance requiring a foreign person claiming treaty benefits and for whom a TIN is required to establish with the IRS, at the time the TIN is requested or after the TIN is issued, that the person is a resident in a treaty country and meets other conditions (such as limitation on benefits provisions) of the treaty. See §601.601(d)(2) of this chapter.

(4) *Claim of benefits under an income tax treaty by a U.S. person.*—In certain cases, a U.S. person may claim the benefit of an income tax treaty. For example, under certain treaties, a U.S. citizen residing in the treaty country may claim a reduced rate of U.S. tax on certain amounts representing a pension or an annuity from U.S. sources. Claims of treaty benefits by a U.S. person may be made by furnishing a Form W-9 to the withholding agent or such other form as the IRS may prescribe in published guidance (see §601.601(d)(2) of this chapter).

(c) *Exemption from requirement to furnish a taxpayer identifying number and special documentary evidence rules for certain income.*—(1) *General rule.*—In the case of income described in paragraph (c)(2) of this section, a withholding agent may rely on a beneficial owner withholding certificate described in paragraph (b)(1) of this section without regard to the requirement that the withholding certificate include the beneficial owner's taxpayer identifying number. In the case of payments of income described in paragraph (c)(2) of this section made outside the United States (as defined in §1.6049-5(e)) with respect to an offshore account (as defined in §1.6049-5(c)(1)), a withholding agent may, as an alternative to a withholding certificate described in paragraph (b)(1) of this section, rely on a certificate of residence described in paragraph (c)(3) of this section or documentary evidence described in paragraph (c)(4) of this section, relating to the beneficial owner, that the withholding agent has reviewed and maintains in its records in accordance with §1.1441-1(e)(4)(iii). In the case of a payment to a person other than an individual, the certificate of residence or documentary evidence must be accompanied by the statements described in paragraphs (c)(5)(i) and (ii) of this section regarding limitation on benefits and whether the amount paid is derived by such person or by one of its interest holders. The withholding agent maintains the reviewed documents by retaining either the documents viewed or a photocopy thereof and noting in its records the date on which, and by whom, the documents were received and reviewed. This paragraph (c)(1) shall not apply to amounts that are exempt from withholding based on a claim that the in-

come is effectively connected with the conduct of a trade or business in the United States.

(2) *Income to which special rules apply.*—The income to which paragraph (c)(1) of this section applies is dividends and interest from stocks and debt obligations that are actively traded, dividends from any redeemable security issued by an investment company registered under the Investment Company Act of 1940 (15 U.S.C. 80a-1), dividends, interest, or royalties from units of beneficial interest in a unit investment trust that are (or were upon issuance) publicly offered and are registered with the Securities and Exchange Commission under the Securities Act of 1933 (15 U.S.C. 77a) and amounts paid with respect to loans of securities described in this paragraph (c)(2). For purposes of this paragraph (c)(2), a stock or debt obligation is actively traded if it is actively traded within the meaning of section 1092(d) and §1.1092(d)-1 when documentation is provided.

(3) *Certificate of residence.*—A certificate of residence referred to in paragraph (c)(1) of this section is a certification issued by an appropriate tax official of the treaty country of which the taxpayer claims to be a resident that the taxpayer has filed its most recent income tax return as a resident of that country (within the meaning of the applicable tax treaty). The certificate of residence must have been issued by such official within three years prior to its being presented to the withholding agent, or such other period as the IRS may prescribe in published guidance (see §601.601(d)(2) of this chapter). See §1.1441-1(e)(4)(ii)(A) for the period during which a withholding agent may rely on a certificate of residence. The competent authorities may agree to a different procedure for certifying residence, in which case such procedure shall govern for payments made to a person claiming to be a resident of the country with which such an agreement is in effect.

(4) *Documentary evidence establishing residence in the treaty country.*—(i) *Individuals.*—For an individual, the documentary evidence referred to in paragraph (c)(1) of this section is any documentation that includes the individuals name, address, and photograph, is an official document issued by an authorized governmental body (i.e., a government or agency thereof, or a municipality), and has been issued no more than three years prior to presentation to the withholding agent. A document older than three years may be relied upon as proof of residence only if it is accompanied by additional evidence of the person's residence in the treaty country (e.g., a bank statement, utility bills, or medical bills). Documentary evidence must be in the form of original documents or certified copies thereof.

(ii) *Persons other than individuals.*—For a person other than an individual, the documentary evidence referred to in paragraph (c)(1) of this section is any documentation that includes the name of the entity and the address of its principal office in the treaty country, and is an official document issued by an authorized governmental body (e.g., a government or agency thereof, or a municipality).

(5) *Statements regarding entitlement to treaty benefits.*—(i) *Statement regarding conditions under a limitation on benefits provision.*—In addition to the documentary evidence described in (c)(4)(ii) of this section, a taxpayer that is not an individual must provide a statement that it meets one or more of the conditions set forth in the limitation on benefits article (if any, or in a similar provision) contained in the applicable tax treaty.

(ii) *Statement regarding whether the taxpayer derives the income.*—A taxpayer that is not an individual must also provide, in addition to the documentary evidence and the statement described in paragraph (c)(5)(i) of this section, a statement that any income for which it intends to claim benefits under an applicable income tax treaty is income that will properly be treated as derived by itself as a resident of the applicable treaty jurisdiction within the meaning of section 894 and the regulations thereunder. This requirement does not apply if the taxpayer furnishes a certificate of residence that certifies that fact.

(d) *Joint owners.*—In the case of a payment to joint owners, each owner must furnish a withholding certificate or, if applicable, documentary evidence or a certificate of residence. The applicable rate of withholding on a payment of income to joint owners shall be the highest applicable rate.

(e) *Competent authority.*—The procedures described in this section may be modified to the extent the U.S. competent authority may agree with the competent authority of a country with which the United States has an income tax treaty in effect.

(f) *Failure to receive withholding certificate timely.*—See applicable procedures described in § 1.1441-1(b)(7) in the event the withholding agent does not hold an appropriate withholding certificate or other appropriate documentation at the time of payment.

(g) *Special taxpayer identifying number rule for certain foreign individuals claiming treaty benefits.*—(1) *General rule.*—Except as provided in paragraph (c) or (g)(2) of this section, for purposes of paragraph (b)(1) of this section, a withholding agent may not rely on a beneficial owner withholding certificate, described in paragraph (b)(1) of this section, that does not include the beneficial owner's taxpayer identifying number (TIN).

(2) *Special rule.*—For purposes of satisfying the TIN requirement of paragraph (b)(1) of this section, a withholding agent may rely on a bene-

ficial owner withholding certificate, described in such paragraph, without regard to the requirement that the withholding certificate include the beneficial owner's TIN, if—

(i) A withholding agent, who is also an acceptance agent, as defined in § 301.6109-1(d)(3)(iv) of this chapter (the payor), has entered into an acceptance agreement that permits the acceptance agent to request an individual taxpayer identification number (ITIN) on an expedited basis because of the circumstances of payment or unexpected nature of payments required to be made by the payor;

(ii) The payor was required to make an unexpected payment to the beneficial owner who is a foreign individual;

(iii) An ITIN for the beneficial owner cannot be received by the payor from the Internal Revenue Service (IRS) because the IRS is not issuing ITINs at the time of payment or any time prior to the time of payment when the payor has knowledge of the unexpected payment;

(iv) The unexpected payment to the beneficial owner could not be reasonably delayed to permit the payor to obtain an ITIN for the beneficial owner on an expedited basis; and

(v) The payor satisfies the provisions of paragraph (g)(3) of this section.

(3) *Requirement that an ITIN be requested during the first business day following payment.*—The payor must submit a beneficial owner payee application for an ITIN (Form W-7 "Application for IRS Individual Taxpayer Identification Number") that complies with the requirements of § 301.6109-1(d)(3)(ii) of this chapter, and also the certification described in § 301.6109-1(d)(3)(iv)(A)(4) of this chapter, to the IRS during the first business day after payment is made.

(4) *Definition of unexpected payment.*—For purposes of this section, an *unexpected payment* is a payment that, because of the nature of the payment or the circumstances in which it is made, could not reasonably have been anticipated by the payor or beneficial owner during a time when the payor or beneficial owner could obtain an ITIN from the IRS. For purposes of this paragraph (g)(4), a payor or beneficial owner will not lack the requisite knowledge of the forthcoming payment solely because the amount of the payment is not fixed.

(5) *Examples.*—The rules of this paragraph (g) are illustrated by the following examples:

Example 1. G, a citizen and resident of Country Y, a country with which the United States has an income tax treaty that exempts U.S. source gambling winnings from U.S. tax, is visiting the United States for the first time. During his visit, G visits Casino B, a casino that has entered into a special acceptance agent agreement with the IRS that permits Casino B to request an ITIN on an expedited basis. During that visit, on a Sunday,

G wins $5000 in slot machine play at Casino B and requests immediate payment from Casino B. ITINs are not available from the IRS on Sunday and would not again be available until Monday. G, who does not have an individual taxpayer identification number, furnishes a beneficial owner withholding certificate, described in § 1.1441-1(e)(2), to the Casino upon winning at the slot machine. The beneficial owner withholding certificate represents that G is a resident of Country Y (within the meaning of the U.S.—Y tax treaty) and meets all applicable requirements for claiming benefits under the U.S.—Y tax treaty. The beneficial owner withholding certificate does not, however, contain an ITIN for G. On the following Monday, Casino B faxes a completed Form W-7, including the required certification, for G, to the IRS for an expedited ITIN. Pursuant to paragraph (b) and (g)(2) of this section, absent actual knowledge or reason to know otherwise, Casino B, may rely on the documentation furnished by G at the time of payment and pay the $5000 to G without withholding U.S. tax based on the treaty exemption.

Example 2. The facts are the same as *Example 1,* except G visits Casino B on Monday. G requests payment Monday afternoon. In order to pay the winnings to G without withholding the 30 percent tax, Casino B must apply for and obtain an ITIN for G because an expedited ITIN is available from the IRS at the time of the $5000 payment to G.

Example 3. The facts are the same as *Example 1,* except G requests payment fifteen minutes before the time when the IRS begins issuing ITINs. Under these facts, it would be reasonable for Casino B to delay payment to G. Therefore, Casino B must apply for and obtain an ITIN for G if G wishes to claim an exemption from U.S. withholding tax under the U.S.—Y tax treaty at the time of payment.

Example 4. P, a citizen and resident of Country Z, is a lawyer and a well-known expert on real estate transactions. P is scheduled to attend a three-day seminar on complex real estate transactions, as a participant, at University U, a U.S. university, beginning on a Saturday and ending on the following Monday, which is a holiday. University U has entered into a special acceptance agent agreement with the IRS that permits University U to request an ITIN on an expedited basis. Country Z is a country with which the United States has an income tax treaty that exempts certain income earned from the performance of independent personal services from U.S. tax. It is P's first visit to the United States. On Saturday, prior to the start of the seminar, Professor Q, one of the lecturers at the seminar, cancels his lecture. That same day the Dean of University U offers P $5000, to replace Professor Q at the seminar, payable at the conclusion of the seminar on Monday. P agrees. P gives her lecture Sunday afternoon. ITINs are not available from the IRS on that Saturday, Sunday, or Mon-

day. After the seminar ends on Monday, P, who does not have an ITIN, requests payment for her teaching. P furnishes a beneficial owner withholding certificate, described in § 1.1441-1(e)(2), to University U that represents that P is a resident of Country Z (within the meaning of the U.S.—Z tax treaty) and meets all applicable requirements for claiming benefits under the U.S.—Z tax treaty. The beneficial owner withholding certificate does not, however, contain an ITIN for P. On Tuesday, University U faxes a completed Form W-7, including the required certification, for P, to the IRS for an expedited ITIN. Pursuant to paragraph (b) and (g)(2) of this section, absent actual knowledge or reason to know otherwise, University U may rely on the documentation furnished by P and pay $5000 to P without withholding U.S. tax based on the treaty exemption.

(h) *Effective dates.*—(1) *General rule.*—This section applies to payments made after December 31, 2000, except for paragraph (g) of this section which applies to payments made after December 31, 2001.

(2) *Transition rules.*—For purposes of this section, the validity of a Form 1001 or 8233 that was valid on January 1, 1998, under the regulations in effect prior to January 1, 2001 (see 26 CFR parts 1 and 35a, revised April 1, 1999) and expired, or will expire, at any time during 1998, is extended until December 31, 1998. The validity of a Form 1001 or 8233 that is valid on or after January 1, 1999, remains valid until its validity expires under the regulations in effect prior to January 1, 2001 (see 26 CFR parts 1 and 35a, revised April 1, 1999) but in no event will such a form remain valid after December 31, 2000. The rule in this paragraph (h)(2), however, does not apply to extend the validity period of a Form 1001 or 8233 that expires solely by reason of changes in the circumstances of the person whose name is on the certificate or in interpretation of the law under the regulations under § 1.894-1T(d). Notwithstanding the first three sentences of this paragraph (h)(2), a withholding agent may choose to not take advantage of the transition rule in this paragraph (h)(2) with respect to one or more withholding certificates valid under the regulations in effect prior to January 1, 2001 (see 26 CFR parts 1 and 35a, revised April 1, 1999) and, therefore, to require withholding certificates conforming to the requirements described in this section (new withholding certificates). For purposes of this section, a new withholding certificate is deemed to satisfy the documentation requirement under the regulations in effect prior to January 1, 2001 (see 26 CFR parts 1 and 35a, revised April 1, 1999). Further, a new withholding certificate remains valid for the period specified in § 1.1441-1(e)(4)(ii), regardless of when the certificate is obtained. [Reg. § 1.1441-6.]

Reg. § 1.1441-6(h)(2)

☐ [*T.D. 7157*, 12-29-71. *Amended by T.D. 7842*, 11-2-82; *T.D. 7977*, 9-19-84; *T.D. 8734*, 10-6-97; *T.D. 8804*, 12-30-98; *T.D. 8856*, 12-29-99 (*corrected* 3-27-2000); *T.D. 8881*, 5-15-2000; *T.D. 8977*, 1-16-2002; *T.D. 9023*, 11-21-2002 *and T.D. 9253*, 3-13-2006 (*corrected* 5-1-2006).]

[Reg. §1.1441-7]

§1.1441-7. General provisions relating to withholding agents.—(a) *Withholding agent defined.*—(1) *In general.*—For purposes of chapter 3 of the Internal Revenue Code and the regulations under such chapter, the term *withholding agent* means any person, U.S. or foreign, that has the control, receipt, custody, disposal, or payment of an item of income of a foreign person subject to withholding, including (but not limited to) a foreign intermediary described in §1.1441-1(e)(3)(i), a foreign partnership, or a U.S. branch described in §1.1441-1(b)(2)(iv)(A) or (E). See §§1.1441-1(b)(2) and (3) and 1.1441-5(c), (d), and (e), for rules to determine whether a payment is considered made to a foreign person. Any person who meets the definition of a withholding agent is required to deposit any tax withheld under §1.1461-1(a) and to make the returns prescribed by §1.1461-1(b) and (c), except as otherwise may be required by a qualified intermediary withholding agreement, a withholding foreign partnership agreement, or a withholding foreign trust agreement. When several persons qualify as withholding agents with respect to a single payment, only one tax is required to be withheld and deposited. See §1.1461-1. A person who, as a nominee described in §1.6031(c)-1T, has furnished to a partnership all of the information required to be furnished under §1.6031(c)-1T(a) shall not be treated as a withholding agent if it has notified the partnership that it is treating the provision of information to the partnership as a discharge of its obligations as a withholding agent.

(2) *Examples.*—The following examples illustrate the rules of paragraph (a)(1) of this section:

Example 1. USB is a broker organized in the United States. USB pays U.S. source dividends and interest, which are amounts subject to withholding under §1.1441-2(a), to FC, a foreign corporation that has an investment account with USB. USB is a withholding agent as defined in paragraph (a)(1) of this section.

Example 2. USB is a bank organized in the United States. FB is a bank organized in country X. X has an omnibus account with USB through which FB invests in debt and equity instruments that pay amounts subject to withholding as defined in §1.1441-2(a). FB is a nonqualified intermediary, as defined in §1.1441-1(c)(14). Both USB and FB are withholding agents as defined in paragraph (a)(1) of this section.

Example 3. The facts are the same as in *Example 2*, except that FB is a qualified intermediary.

Both USB and FB are withholding agents as defined in paragraph (a)(1) of this section.

Example 4. FB is a bank organized in country X. FB has a branch in the United States. FB's branch has customers that are foreign persons who receive amounts subject to withholding, as defined in §1.1441-2(a). FB is a withholding agent under paragraph (a)(1) of this section and is required to withhold and report payments of amounts subject to withholding in accordance with chapter 3 of the Internal Revenue Code.

Example 5. X is a foreign corporation. X pays dividends to shareholders who are foreign persons. Under section 861(a)(2)(B), a portion of the dividends are from sources within the United States and constitute amounts subject to withholding within the meaning of §1.1441-2(a). The dividends are not subject to tax under section 884(a). See 884(e)(3). X is a withholding agent under paragraph (a)(1) of this section.

(b) *Standards of knowledge.*—(1) *In general.*—A withholding agent must withhold at the full 30-percent rate under section 1441, 1442, or 1443(a) or at the full 4-percent rate under section 1443(b) if it has actual knowledge or reason to know that a claim of U.S. status or of a reduced rate of withholding under section 1441, 1442, or 1443 is unreliable or incorrect. A withholding agent shall be liable for tax, interest, and penalties to the extent provided under sections 1461 and 1463 and the regulations under those sections if it fails to withhold the correct amount despite its actual knowledge or reason to know the amount required to be withheld. For purposes of the regulations under sections 1441, 1442, and 1443, a withholding agent may rely on information or certifications contained in, or associated with, a withholding certificate or other documentation furnished by or for a beneficial owner or payee unless the withholding agent has actual knowledge or reason to know that the information or certifications are incorrect or unreliable and, if based on such knowledge or reason to know, it should withhold (under chapter 3 of the Code or another withholding provision of the Code) an amount greater than would be the case if it relied on the information or certifications, or it should report (under chapter 3 of the Code or under another provision of the Code) an amount that would not otherwise be reportable if it relied on the information or certifications. See §1.1441-1(e)(4)(viii) for applicable reliance rules. A withholding agent that has received notification by the Internal Revenue Service (IRS) that a claim of U.S. status or of a reduced rate is incorrect has actual knowledge beginning on the date that is 30 calendar days after the date the notice is received. A withholding agent that fails to act in accordance with the presumptions set forth in §§1.1441-1(b)(3), 1.1441-4(a), 1.1441-5(d) and (e), or 1.1441-9(b)(3) may also be liable for tax, interest, and penalties. See §1.1441-1(b)(3)(ix) and (7).

(2) *Reason to know.*—A withholding agent shall be considered to have reason to know if its knowledge of relevant facts or of statements contained in the withholding certificates or other documentation is such that a reasonably prudent person in the position of the withholding agent would question the claims made.

(3) *Financial institutions—limits on reason to know.*—For purposes of this paragraph (b)(3) and paragraphs (b)(4) through (b)(10) of this section, the terms *withholding certificate*, *documentary evidence*, and *documentation* are defined in § 1.1441-1(c)(16), (17) and (18). Except as otherwise provided in paragraphs (b)(4) through (b)(9) of this section, a withholding agent that is a financial institution (including a regulated investment company) that has a direct account relationship with a beneficial owner (a direct account holder) has a reason to know, with respect to amounts described in § 1.1441-6(c)(2), that documentation provided by the direct account holder is unreliable or incorrect only if one or more of the circumstances described in paragraphs (b)(4) through (b)(9) of this section exist. If a direct account holder has provided documentation that is unreliable or incorrect under the rules of paragraph (b)(4) through (b)(9) of this section, the withholding agent may require new documentation. Alternatively, the withholding agent may rely on the documentation originally provided if the rules of paragraphs (b)(4) through (b)(9) of this section permit such reliance based on additional statements and documentation. Paragraph (b)(10) of this section provides limits on reason to know for financial institutions that receive beneficial owner documentation from persons (indirect account holders) that have an account relationship with, or an ownership interest in, a direct account holder. For rules regarding reliance on Form W-9, see § 31.3406(g)-3(e)(2) of this chapter.

(4) *Rules applicable to withholding certificates.*—(i) *In general.*—A withholding agent has reason to know that a beneficial owner withholding certificate provided by a direct account holder in connection with a payment of an amount described in § 1.1441-6(c)(2) is unreliable or incorrect if the withholding certificate is incomplete with respect to any item on the certificate that is relevant to the claims made by the direct account holder, the withholding certificate contains any information that is inconsistent with the direct account holder's claim, the withholding agent has other account information that is inconsistent with the direct account holder's claim, or the withholding certificate lacks information necessary to establish entitlement to a reduced rate of withholding. For purposes of establishing a direct account holder's status as a foreign person or resident of a treaty country a withholding certificate shall be considered unreliable or inconsistent with an account holder's claims only if it is not reliable under the rules of

paragraphs (b)(5) and (6) of this section. A withholding agent that relies on an agent to review and maintain a withholding certificate is considered to know or have reason to know the facts within the knowledge of the agent.

(ii) *Examples.*—The rules of paragraph (b)(4) of this section are illustrated by the following examples:

Example 1. F, a foreign person that has a direct account relationship with USB, a bank that is a U.S. person, provides USB with a beneficial owner withholding certificate for the purpose of claiming a reduced rate of withholding on U.S. source dividends. F resides in a treaty country that has a limitation on benefits provision in its income tax treaty with the United States. The withholding certificate, however, does not contain a statement regarding limitations on benefits or deriving the income under section 894 as required by § 1.1441-6(b)(1). USB cannot rely on the withholding certificate to grant a reduced rate of withholding because it is incomplete with respect to the claim made by F.

Example 2. F, a foreign person that has a direct account relationship with USB, a broker that is a U.S. person, provides USB with a withholding certificate for the purpose of claiming the portfolio interest exception under section 881(c), which applies to foreign corporations. F indicates on its withholding certificate, however, that it is a partnership. USB may not treat F as a beneficial owner of the interest for purposes of the portfolio interest exception because F has indicated on its withholding certificate that it is a foreign partnership, and therefore under § 1.1441-1(c)(6)(ii) it is not the beneficial owner of the interest payment.

(5) *Withholding certificate—establishment of foreign status.*—A withholding agent has reason to know that a beneficial owner withholding certificate (as defined in § 1.1441-1(e)(2)) provided by a direct account holder in connection with a payment of an amount described in § 1.1441-6(c)(2) is unreliable or incorrect for purposes of establishing the account holder's status as a foreign person if the certificate is described in paragraph (b)(5)(i) or (ii) of this section.

(i) A withholding certificate is unreliable or incorrect if the withholding certificate has a permanent residence address (as defined in § 1.1441-1(e)(2)(ii)) in the United States, the withholding certificate has a mailing address in the United States, the withholding agent has a residence or mailing address as part of its account information that is an address in the United States, or the direct account holder notifies the withholding agent of a new residence or mailing address in the United States (whether or not provided on a withholding certificate). A withholding agent may, however, rely on the beneficial owner withholding certificate as establishing the account holder's foreign status if it may do so under the provisions of paragraph (b)(5)(i)(A) or (B) of this section.

(A) A withholding agent may treat a direct account holder as a foreign person if the beneficial owner withholding certificate has been provided by an individual and—

(1) The withholding agent has in its possession or obtains documentary evidence (which does not contain a U.S. address) that has been provided within the past three years, was valid at the time it was provided, the documentary evidence supports the claim of foreign status, and the direct account holder provides the withholding agent with a reasonable explanation, in writing, supporting the account holder's foreign status; or

(2) The account is maintained at an office of the withholding agent outside the United States and the withholding agent is required to report annually a payment to the direct account holder on a tax information statement that is filed with the tax authority of the country in which the office is located and that country has an income tax treaty in effect with the United States.

(B) A withholding agent may treat an account holder as a foreign person if the beneficial owner withholding certificate has been provided by an entity that the withholding agent does not know, or does not have reason to know, is a flow-through entity and—

(1) The withholding agent has in its possession, or obtains, documentation that substantiates that the entity is actually organized or created under the laws of a foreign country; or

(2) The account is maintained at an office of the withholding agent outside the United States and the withholding agent is required to report annually a payment to the direct account holder on a tax information statement that is filed with the tax authority of the country in which the office is located and that country has an income tax treaty in effect with the United States.

(ii) A beneficial owner withholding certificate is unreliable or incorrect if it is provided with respect to an offshore account (as defined in § 1.6049-5(c)(1)) and the direct account holder has standing instructions directing the withholding agent to pay amounts from its account to an address or an account maintained in the United States. The withholding agent may treat the direct account holder as a foreign person, however, if the direct account holder provides a reasonable explanation in writing that supports its foreign status.

(6) *Withholding certificate—claim of reduced rate of withholding under treaty.*—A withholding agent has reason to know that a withholding certificate (other than Form W-9) provided by a direct account holder in connection with a payment of an amount described in § 1.1441-6(c)(2) is unreliable or incorrect for purposes of establishing that the direct account holder is a resident of a country with which the United States has an income tax treaty if it is described in paragraphs (b)(6)(i) through (iii) of this section.

(i) A beneficial owner withholding certificate is unreliable or incorrect if the permanent residence address on the beneficial owner withholding certificate is not in the country whose treaty is invoked, or the direct account holder notifies the withholding agent of a new permanent residence address that is not in the treaty country. A withholding agent may, however, treat a direct account holder as entitled to a reduced rate of withholding under an income tax treaty if the direct account holder provides a reasonable explanation for the permanent residence address outside the treaty country (e.g., the address is the address of a branch of the beneficial owner located outside the treaty country in which the entity is a resident) or the withholding agent has in its possession, or obtains, documentary evidence that establishes residency in a treaty country.

(ii) A beneficial owner withholding certificate is unreliable or incorrect if the permanent residence address on the withholding certificate is in the applicable treaty country but the withholding certificate contains a mailing address outside the treaty country or the withholding agent has a mailing address as part of its account information that is outside the treaty country. A mailing address that is a P.O. Box, in-care-of address, or address at a financial institution (if the financial institution is not a beneficial owner) shall not preclude a withholding agent from treating the direct account holder as a resident of a treaty country if such address is in the treaty country. If a withholding agent has a mailing address (whether or not contained on the withholding certificate) outside the applicable treaty country, the withholding agent may nevertheless treat a direct account holder as a resident of an applicable treaty country if—

(A) The withholding agent has in its possession, or obtains, additional documentation supporting the direct account holder's claim of residence in the applicable treaty country (and the additional documentation does not contain an address outside the treaty country);

(B) The withholding agent has in its possession, or obtains, documentation that establishes that the direct account holder is an entity organized in a treaty country (or an entity managed and controlled in a treaty country, if the applicable treaty so requires);

(C) The withholding agent knows that the address outside the applicable treaty country (other than a P.O. box, or in-care-of address) is a branch of a bank or insurance company that is a resident of the applicable treaty country; or

(D) The withholding agent obtains a written statement from the direct account holder that reasonably establishes entitlement to treaty benefits.

(iii) A beneficial owner withholding certificate is unreliable or incorrect to establish entitlement to a reduced rate of withholding under an income tax treaty if the direct account holder has standing instructions for the withholding agent to pay amounts from its account to an address or an account outside the treaty country unless the direct account holder provides a reasonable explanation, in writing, establishing the direct account holder's residence in the applicable treaty country.

(7) *Documentary evidence.*—A withholding agent shall not treat documentary evidence provided by a direct account holder as valid if the documentary evidence does not reasonably establish the identity of the person presenting the documentary evidence. For example, documentary evidence is not valid if it is provided in person by a direct account holder that is a natural person and the photograph or signature on the documentary evidence, if any, does not match the appearance or signature of the person presenting the document. A withholding agent shall not rely on documentary evidence to reduce the rate of withholding that would otherwise apply under the presumption rules of §§ 1.1441-1(b)(3), 1.1441-5(d) and (e)(6), and 1.6049-5(d) if the documentary evidence contains information that is inconsistent with the direct account holder's claim of a reduced rate of withholding, the withholding agent has other account information that is inconsistent with the direct account holder's claim, or the documentary evidence lacks information necessary to establish entitlement to a reduced rate of withholding. For example, if a direct account holder provides documentary evidence to claim treaty benefits and the documentary evidence establishes the direct account holder's status as a foreign person and a resident of a treaty country, but the account holder fails to provide the treaty statements required by § 1.1441-6(c)(5), the documentary evidence does not establish the direct account holder's entitlement to a reduced rate of withholding. For purposes of establishing a direct account holder's status as a foreign person or resident of a country with which the United States has an income tax treaty with respect to income described in § 1.1441-6(c)(2), documentary evidence shall be considered unreliable or incorrect only if it is not reliable under the rules of paragraph (b)(8) and (9) of this section.

(8) *Documentary evidence—establishment of foreign status.*—A withholding agent has reason to know that documentary evidence provided in connection with a payment of an amount described in § 1.1441-6(c)(2) is unreliable or incorrect for purposes of establishing the direct account holder's status as a foreign person if the documentary evidence is described in paragraphs (b)(8)(i), (ii), (iii) or (iv) of this section.

(i) A withholding agent shall not treat documentary evidence provided by an account holder after December 31, 2000, as valid for purposes of establishing the direct account holder's foreign status if the only mailing or residence address that is available to the withholding agent is an address at a financial institution (unless the financial institution is a beneficial owner of the income), an in-care-of address, or a P.O. box. In this case, the withholding agent must obtain additional documentation that is sufficient to establish the direct account holder's status as a foreign person. A withholding agent shall not treat documentary evidence provided by an account holder before January 1, 2001, as valid for purposes of establishing a direct account holder's status as a foreign person if it has actual knowledge that the direct account holder is a U.S. person or if it has a mailing or residence address for the direct account holder in the United States. If a withholding agent has an address for the direct account holder in the United States, the withholding agent may nevertheless treat the direct account holder as a foreign person if it can so treat the direct account holder under the rules of paragraph (b)(8)(ii) of this section.

(ii) Documentary evidence is unreliable or incorrect to establish a direct account holder's status as a foreign person if the withholding agent has a mailing or residence address (whether or not on the documentation) for the direct account holder in the United States or if the direct account holder notifies the withholding agent of a new address in the United States. A withholding agent may, however, rely on documentary evidence as establishing the direct account holder's foreign status if it may do so under the provisions of paragraph (b)(8)(ii)(A) or (B) of this section.

(A) A withholding agent may treat a direct account holder that is an individual as a foreign person even if it has a mailing or residence address for the direct account holder in the United States if the withholding agent—

(1) Has in its possession or obtains additional documentary evidence (which does not contain a U.S. address) supporting the claim of foreign status and a reasonable explanation in writing supporting the account holder's foreign status;

(2) Has in its possession or obtains a valid beneficial owner withholding certificate on Form W-8 and the Form W-8 contains a permanent residence address outside the United States and a mailing address outside the United States (or if a mailing address is inside the United States the direct account holder provides a reasonable explanation in writing supporting the direct account holder's foreign status); or

(3) The account is maintained at an office of the withholding agent outside the United States and the withholding agent is required to report annually a payment to the direct

Reg. § 1.1441-7(b)(8)(ii)(A)(3)

account holder on a tax information statement that is filed with the tax authority of the country in which the office is located and that country has an income tax treaty in effect with the United States.

(B) A withholding agent may treat a direct account holder that is an entity (other than a flow-through entity) as a foreign person even if it has a mailing or residence address for the direct account holder in the United States if the withholding agent—

(1) Has in its possession, or obtains, documentation that substantiates that the entity is actually organized or created under the laws of a foreign country;

(2) Obtains a valid beneficial owner withholding certificate on Form W-8 and the Form W-8 contains a permanent residence address outside the United States and a mailing address outside the United States (or if a mailing address is inside the United States the direct account holder provides additional documentary evidence sufficient to establish the direct account holder's foreign status); or

(3) The account is maintained at an office of the withholding agent outside the United States and the withholding agent is required to report annually a payment to the direct account holder on a tax information statement that is filed with the tax authority of the country in which the office is located and that country has an income tax treaty in effect with the United States.

(iii) Documentary evidence is unreliable or incorrect if the direct account holder has standing instructions directing the withholding agent to pay amounts from its account to an address or an account maintained in the United States. The withholding agent may treat the direct account holder as a foreign person, however, if the account holder provides a reasonable explanation in writing that supports its foreign status.

(9) *Documentary evidence—claim of reduced rate of withholding under treaty.*—A withholding agent has reason to know that documentary evidence provided in connection with a payment of an amount described in § 1.1441-6(c)(2) is unreliable or incorrect for purposes of establishing that a direct account holder is a resident of a country with which the United States has an income tax treaty if it is described in paragraph (b)(9)(i) or (ii) of this section.

(i) Documentary evidence is unreliable or incorrect if the withholding agent has a mailing or residence address for the direct account holder (whether or not on the documentary evidence) that is outside the applicable treaty country, or the only address that the withholding agent has (whether in or outside of the applicable treaty country) is a P.O. box, an in-care-of address, or the address of a financial institution (if the financial institution is not the beneficial

owner). If a withholding agent has a mailing or residence address for the direct account holder outside the applicable treaty country, the withholding agent may nevertheless treat a direct account holder as a resident of an applicable treaty country if the withholding agent—

(A) Has in its possession, or obtains, additional documentary evidence supporting the direct account holder's claim of residence in the applicable treaty country (and the documentary evidence does not contain an address outside the applicable treaty country, a P.O. box, an in-care-of address, or the address of a financial institution);

(B) Has in its possession, or obtains, documentary evidence that establishes the direct account holder is an entity organized in a treaty country (or an entity managed and controlled in a treaty country, if the applicable treaty so requires); or

(C) Obtains a valid beneficial owner withholding certificate on Form W-8 that contains a permanent residence address and a mailing address in the applicable treaty country.

(ii) Documentary evidence is unreliable or incorrect if the direct account holder has standing instructions directing the withholding agent to pay amounts from its account to an address or an account maintained outside the treaty country unless the direct account holder provides a reasonable explanation, in writing, establishing the direct account holder's residence in the applicable treaty country.

(10) *Limits on reason to know—indirect account holders.*—A financial institution that receives documentation from a payee through a nonqualified intermediary, a flow-through entity, or a U.S. branch described in § 1.1441-1(b)(2)(iv) (other than a U.S. branch that is treated as a U.S. person) with respect to a payment of an amount described in § 1.1441-6(c)(2) has reason to know that the documentation is unreliable or incorrect if a reasonably prudent person in the position of a withholding agent would question the claims made. This standard requires, but is not limited to, a withholding agent's compliance with the rules of paragraphs (b)(10)(i) through (iii).

(i) The withholding agent must review the withholding statement described in § 1.1441-1(e)(3)(iv) and may not rely on information in the statement to the extent the information does not support the claims made for any payee. For this purpose, a withholding agent may not treat a payee as a foreign person if an address in the United States is provided for such payee and may not treat a person as a resident of a country with which the United States has an income tax treaty if the address for that person is outside the applicable treaty country. Notwithstanding a U.S. address or an address outside a treaty country, the withholding agent may treat a payee as a foreign person or a foreign person as a resident of a treaty country if a reasonable explanation is provided, in writing, by the non-qualified intermediary, flow-through entity, or U.S. branch supporting the payee's foreign status or the foreign person's residency in a treaty country.

(ii) The withholding agent must review each withholding certificate in accordance with the requirements of paragraphs (b)(5) and (6) of this section and verify that the information on the withholding certificate is consistent with the information on the withholding statement required under § 1.1441-1(e)(3)(iv). If there is a discrepancy between the withholding certificate and the withholding statement, the withholding agent may choose to rely on the withholding certificate, if valid, and instruct the nonqualified intermediary, flow-through entity, or U.S. branch to correct the withholding statement or apply the presumption rules of §§ 1.1441-1(b), 1.1441-5(d) and (e)(6), and 1.6049-5(d) to the payment allocable to the payee who provided the withholding certificate. A withholding agent that receives a withholding certificate before December 31,2001, is not required to review the information on withholding certificates or determine if it is consistent with the information on the withholding statement until December 31, 2001. A withholding agent may withhold and report in accordance with a withholding statement until December 31, 2001, unless it has actually performed the verification procedures required by this paragraph (b)(10)(ii) and determined that the withholding statement is inaccurate with respect to a particular payee.

(iii) The withholding agent must review the documentary evidence provided by the non-qualified intermediary, flow-through entity, or U.S. branch to determine that there is no obvious indication that the payee is a U.S. non-exempt recipient or that the documentary evidence does not establish the identity of the person who provided the documentation (e.g., the documentary evidence does not appear to be an identification document).

(11) *Additional guidance.*—The IRS may prescribe other circumstances for which a withholding certificate or documentary evidence is unreliable or incorrect in addition to the circumstances described in paragraph (b) of this section to establish an account holder's status as a foreign person or a beneficial owner entitled to a reduced rate of withholding in published guidance (see § 601.601(d)(2) of this chapter).

(c) *Authorized agent.*—(1) *In general.*—The acts of an agent of a withholding agent (including the receipt of withholding certificates, the payment of amounts of income subject to withholding, and the deposit of tax withheld) are imputed to the withholding agent on whose behalf it is acting. However, if the agent is a foreign person, a withholding agent that is a U.S. person may treat the acts of the foreign agent as its own for pur-

poses of determining whether it has complied with the provisions of this section, but only if the agent is an authorized foreign agent, as defined in paragraph (c)(2) of this section. An authorized foreign agent cannot apply the provisions of this paragraph (c) to appoint another person its authorized foreign agent with respect to the payments it receives from the withholding agent.

(2) *Authorized foreign agent.*—An agent is an authorized foreign agent only if—

(i) There is a written agreement between the withholding agent and the foreign person acting as agent;

(ii) The notification procedures described in paragraph (c)(3) of this section have been complied with;

(iii) Books and records and relevant personnel of the foreign agent are available (on a continuous basis, including after termination of the relationship) for examination by the IRS in order to evaluate the withholding agent's compliance with the provisions of chapters 3 and 61 of the Code, section 3406, and the regulations under those provisions; and

(iv) The U.S. withholding agent remains fully liable for the acts of its agent and does not assert any of the defenses that may otherwise be available, including under common law principles of agency in order to avoid tax liability under the Internal Revenue Code.

(3) *Notification.*—A withholding agent that appoints an authorized agent to act on its behalf for purposes of § 1.871-14(c)(2), the withholding provisions of chapter 3 of the Code, section 3406 or other withholding provisions of the Internal Revenue Code, or the reporting provisions of chapter 61 of the Code, is required to file notice of such appointment with the Office of the Assistant Commissioner (International). Such notice shall be filed before the first payment for which the authorized agent acts as such. Such notice shall acknowledge the withholding agent liability as provided in paragraph (c)(2)(iv) of this section.

(4) *Liability of U.S. withholding agent.*—An authorized foreign agent is subject to the same withholding and reporting obligations that apply to any withholding agent under the provisions of chapter 3 of the Code and the regulations thereunder. In particular, an authorized foreign agent does not benefit from the special procedures or exceptions that may apply to a qualified intermediary. A withholding agent acting through an authorized foreign agent is liable for any failure of the agent, such as failure to withhold an amount or make payment of tax, in the same manner and to the same extent as if the agent's failure had been the failure of the U.S. withholding agent. For this purpose, the foreign agent's actual knowledge or reason to know shall be imputed to the U.S. withholding agent. The U.S. withholding agent's liability

shall exist irrespective of the fact that the authorized foreign agent is also a withholding agent and is itself separately liable for failure to comply with the provisions of the regulations under section 1441, 1442, or 1443. However, the same tax, interest, or penalties shall not be collected more than once.

(5) *Filing of returns.*—See § 1.1461-1(b)(2)(iii) and (c)(4)(iii) regarding returns required to be made where a U.S. withholding agent acts through an authorized foreign agent.

(d) *United States obligations.*—If the United States is a withholding agent for an item of interest, including original issue discount, on obligations of the United States or of any agency or instrumentality thereof, the withholding obligation of the United States is assumed and discharged by—

(1) The Commissioner of the Public Debt, for interest paid by checks issued through the Bureau of the Public Debt;

(2) The Treasurer of the United States, for interest paid by him or her, whether by check or otherwise;

(3) Each Federal Reserve Bank, for interest paid by it, whether by check or otherwise; or

(4) Such other person as may be designated by the IRS.

(e) *Assumed obligations.*—If, in connection with the sale of a corporation's property, payment on the bonds or other obligations of the corporation is assumed by a person, then that person shall be a withholding agent to the extent amounts subject to withholding are paid to a foreign person. Thus, the person shall withhold such amounts under § 1.1441-1 as would be required to be withheld by the seller or corporation had no such sale or assumption been made.

(f) *Conduit financing arrangements.*—(1) *Liability of withholding agent.*—Subject to paragraph (f)(2) of this section, any person that is required to deduct and withhold tax under § 1.1441-3(g) is made liable for that tax by section 1461. A person that is required to deduct and withhold tax but fails to do so is liable for the payment of the tax and any applicable penalties and interest.

(2) *Exception for withholding agents that do not know of conduit financing arrangement.*—(i) *In general.*—A withholding agent will not be liable under paragraph (f)(1) of this section for failing to deduct and withhold with respect to a conduit financing arrangement unless the person knows or has reason to know that the financing arrangement is a conduit financing arrangement. This standard shall be satisfied if the withholding agent knows or has reason to know of facts sufficient to establish that the financing arrangement is a conduit financing arrangement, including facts sufficient to establish that the participation of the intermediate entity in the

financing arrangement is pursuant to a tax avoidance plan. A withholding agent that knows only of the financing transactions that comprise the financing arrangement will not be considered to know or have reason to know of facts sufficient to establish that the financing arrangement is a conduit financing arrangement.

(ii) *Examples.*—The following examples illustrate the operation of paragraph (d)(2) of this section.

Example 1. (i) DS is a U.S. subsidiary of FP, a corporation organized in Country N, a country that does not have an income tax treaty with the United States. FS is a special purpose subsidiary of FP that is incorporated in Country T, a country that has an income tax treaty with the United States that prohibits the imposition of withholding tax on payments of interest. FS is capitalized with $10,000,000 in debt from BK, a Country N bank, and $1,000,000 in capital from FS.

(ii) On May 1, 1995, C, a U.S. person, purchases an automobile from DS in return for an installment note. On July 1, 1995, DS sells a number of installment notes, including C's, to FS in exchange for $10,000,000. DS continues to service the installment notes for FS and C is not notified of the sale of its obligation and continues to make payments to DS. But for the withholding tax on payments of interest by DS to BK, DS would have borrowed directly from BK, pledging the installment notes as collateral.

(iii) The C installment note is a financing transaction, whether held by DS or by FS, and the FS note held by BK also is a financing transaction. After FS purchases the installment note, and during the time the installment note is held by FS, the transactions constitute a financing arrangement, within the meaning of § 1.881-3(a)(2)(i). BK is the financing entity, FS is the intermediate entity, and C is the financed entity. Because the participation of FS in the financing arrangement reduces the tax imposed by section 881 and because there was a tax avoidance plan, FS is a conduit entity.

(iv) Because C does not know or have reason to know of the tax avoidance plan (and by extension that the financing arrangement is a conduit financing arrangement), C is not required to withhold tax under section 1441. However, DS, who knows that FS's participation in the financing arrangement is pursuant to a tax avoidance plan and is a withholding agent for purposes of section 1441, is not relieved of its withholding responsibilities.

Example 2. Assume the same facts as in *Example 1*, except that C receives a new payment booklet on which DS is described as "agent". Although C may deduce that its installment note has been sold, without more C has no reason to know of the existence of a financing arrangement. Accordingly, C is not liable for failure to withhold, although DS still is not relieved of its withholding responsibilities.

Reg. § 1.1441-7(c)(5)

Example 3. (i) DC is a U.S. corporation that is in the process of negotiating a loan of $10,000,000 from BK1, a bank located in Country N, a country that does not have an income tax treaty with the United States. Before the loan agreement is signed, DC's tax lawyers point out that interest on the loan would not be subject to withholding tax if the loan were made by BK2, a subsidiary of BK1 that is incorporated in Country T, a country that has an income tax treaty with the United States that prohibits the imposition of withholding tax on payments of interest. BK1 makes a loan to BK2 to enable BK2 to make the loan to DC. Without the loan from BK1 to BK2, BK2 would not have been able to make the loan to DC.

(ii) The loan from BK1 to BK2 and the loan from BK2 to DC are both financing transactions and together constitute a financing arrangement within the meaning of § 1.881-3(a)(2)(i). BK1 is the financing entity, BK2 is the intermediate entity, and DC is the financed entity. Because the participation of BK2 in the financing arrangement reduces the tax imposed by section 881 and because there is a tax avoidance plan, BK2 is a conduit entity.

(iii) Because DC is a party to the tax avoidance plan (and accordingly knows of its existence), DC must withhold tax under section 1441. If DC does not withhold tax on its payment of interest, BK2, a party to the plan and a withholding agent for purposes of section 1441, must withhold tax as required by section 1441.

Example 4. (i) DC is a U.S. corporation that has a long-standing banking relationship with BK2, a U.S. subsidiary of BK1, a bank incorporated in Country N, a country that does not have an income tax treaty with the United States. DC has borrowed amounts of as much as $75,000,000 from BK2 in the past. On January 1, 1995, DC asks to borrow $50,000,000 from BK2. BK2 does not have the funds available to make a loan of that size. BK2 considers asking BK1 to enter into a loan with DC but rejects this possibility because of the additional withholding tax that would be incurred. Accordingly, BK2 borrows the necessary amount from BK1 with the intention of on-lending to DC. BK1 does not make the loan directly to DC because of the withholding tax that would apply to payments of interest from DC to BK1. DC does not negotiate with BK1 and has no reason to know that BK1 was the source of the loan.

(ii) The loan from BK2 to DC and the loan from BK1 to BK2 are both financing transactions and together constitute a financing arrangement within the meaning of § 1.881-3(a)(2)(i). BK1 is the financing entity, BK2 is the intermediate entity, and DC is the financed entity. The participation of BK2 in the financing arrangement reduces the tax imposed by section 881. Because the participation of BK2 in the financing arrangement reduces the tax imposed by section 881 and be-

cause there was a tax avoidance plan, BK2 is a conduit entity.

(iii) Because DC does not know or have reason to know of the tax avoidance plan (and by extension that the financing arrangement is a conduit financing arrangement), DC is not required to withhold tax under section 1441. However, BK2, who is also a withholding agent under section 1441 and who knows that the financing arrangement is a conduit financing arrangement, is not relieved of its withholding responsibilities.

(3) *Effective date.*—This paragraph (f) is effective for payments made by financed entities on or after September 11, 1995. This paragraph shall not apply to interest payments covered by section 127(g)(3) of the Tax Reform Act of 1984, and to interest payments with respect to other debt obligations issued prior to October 15, 1984 (whether or not such debt was issued by a Netherlands Antilles corporation).

(g) *Effective date.*—Except as otherwise provided in paragraph (f)(3) of this section, this section applies to payments made after December 31, 2000. [Reg. § 1.1441-7.]

☐ [T.D. 7977, 9-19-84. *Amended by T.D.* 8611, 8-10-95; *T.D.* 8734, 10-6-97; *T.D.* 8804, 12-30-98; *T.D.* 8856, 12-29-99 *and T.D.* 8881, 5-15-2000 (*corrected* 4-5-2001).]

[Reg. § 1.1441-8]

§ 1.1441-8. Exemption from withholding for payments to foreign governments, international organizations, foreign central banks of issue, and the Bank for International Settlements.—(a) *Foreign governments.*—Under section 892, certain specific types of income received by foreign governments are excluded from gross income and are exempt from taxation, unless derived from the conduct of a commercial activity or received from or by a controlled commercial entity. Accordingly, withholding is not required under § 1.1441-1 with regard to any item of income which is exempt from taxation under section 892.

(b) *Reliance on claim of exemption by foreign government.*—Absent actual knowledge or reason to know otherwise, the withholding agent may rely upon a claim of exemption made by the foreign government if, prior to the payment, the withholding agent can reliably associate the payment with documentation upon which it can rely to treat the payment as made to a beneficial owner in accordance with § 1.1441-1(e)(1)(ii). A Form W-8 furnished by a foreign government for purposes of claiming an exemption under this paragraph (b) is valid only if, in addition to other applicable requirements, it certifies that the income is, or will be, exempt from taxation under section 892 and the regulations under that section and whether the person whose name is on the certificate is an integral part of a foreign government (as defined in §1.892-2T(a)(2)) or a controlled entity (as defined in §1.892-2T(a)(3)).

(c) *Income of a foreign central bank of issue or the Bank for International Settlements.*—(1) *Certain interest income.*—Section 895 provides for the exclusion from gross income of certain income derived by a foreign central bank of issue, or by the Bank for International Settlements, from obligations of the United States or of any agency or instrumentality thereof or from interest on deposits with persons carrying on the banking business if the bank is the owner of the obligations or deposits and does not hold the obligations or deposits for, or use them in connection with, the conduct of a commercial banking function or other commercial activity by such bank. See §1.895-1. Absent actual knowledge or reason to know that a foreign central bank of issue, or the Bank for International Settlements, is operating outside the scope of the exclusion granted by section 895 and the regulations under that section, the withholding agent may rely on a claim of exemption if, prior to the payment, the withholding agent can reliably associate the payment with documentation upon which it can rely to treat the foreign central bank of issue or the Bank for International Settlements as the beneficial owner of the payment in accordance with §1.1441-1(e)(1)(ii). A Form W-8 furnished by a foreign central bank of issue or the Bank for International Settlements for purposes of claiming an exemption under this paragraph (c)(1) is valid only if, in addition to other applicable requirements, it certifies that the person whose name is on the certificate is a foreign central bank of issue, or the Bank for International Settlements, and that the bank does not, and will not, hold the obligations or the bank deposits covered by the Form W-8 for, or use them in connection with, the conduct of a commercial banking function or other commercial activity.

(2) *Bankers' acceptances.*—Interest derived by a foreign central bank of issue from bankers' acceptances is exempt from tax under sections 871(i)(2)(C) and 881(d) and §1.861-2(b)(4). With respect to bankers' acceptances, a withholding agent may treat a payee as a foreign central bank of issue without requiring a withholding certificate if the name of the payee and other facts surrounding the payment reasonably indicate that the payee or beneficial owner is a foreign central bank of issue, as defined in §1.861-2(b)(4).

(d) *Exemption for payments to international organizations.*—A payment to an international organization (within the meaning of section 7701(a)(18)) is exempt from withholding on any payment. A withholding agent may treat a payee as an international organization without requiring a withholding certificate if the name of the payee is one that is designated as an international organization by executive order (pursuant to 22 U.S.C. 288 through 288(f)) and other facts surrounding the transaction reasonably indicate that the international organization is the beneficial owner of the payment.

(e) *Failure to receive withholding certificate timely and other applicable procedures.*—See applicable procedures described in §1.1441-1(b)(7) in the event the withholding agent does not hold a valid withholding certificate described in paragraph (b) or (c)(1) of this section or other appropriate documentation at the time of payment. Further, the provisions of §1.1441-1(e)(4) shall apply to withholding certificates and other documents related thereto furnished under the provisions of this section.

(f) *Effective date.*—(1) *In general.*—This section applies to payments made after December 31, 2000.

(2) *Transition rules.*—For purposes of this section, the validity of a Form 8709 that was valid on January 1, 1998, under the regulations in effect prior to January 1, 2001 (see 26 CFR part 1, revised April 1, 1999) and expired, or will expire, at any time during 1998, is extended until December 31, 1998. The validity of a Form 8709 that is valid on or after January 1, 1999, remains valid until its validity expires under the regulations in effect prior to January 1, 2001 (see 26 CFR part 1, revised April 1, 1999) but in no event shall such a form remain valid after December 31, 2000. The rule in this paragraph (f)(2), however, does not apply to extend the validity period of a Form 8709 that expires solely by reason of changes in the circumstances of the person whose name is on the certificate. Notwithstanding the first three sentences of this paragraph (f)(2), a withholding agent may choose to not take advantage of the transition rule in this paragraph (f)(2) with respect to one or more withholding certificates valid under the regulations in effect prior to January 1, 2001 (see 26 CFR part 1, revised April 1, 1999) and, therefore, to require withholding certificates conforming to the requirements described in this section (new withholding certificates). For purposes of this section, a new withholding certificate is deemed to satisfy the documentation requirement under the regulations in effect prior to January 1, 2001 (see 26 CFR part 1, revised April 1, 1999). Further, a new withholding certificate remains valid for the period specified in §1.1441-1(e)(4)(ii), regardless of when the certificate is obtained. [Reg. §1.1441-8.]

☐ [T.D. 8211, 6-24-88. *Redesignated and amended by T.D. 8734, 10-6-97 and amended by T.D. 8804, 12-30-98 and T.D. 8856, 12-29-99.*]

[Reg. §1.1441-9]

§1.1441-9. Exemption from withholding on exempt income of a foreign tax-exempt organization, including foreign private foundations.—(a) *Exemption from withholding for exempt* *income.*—No withholding is required under section 1441(a) or 1442, and the regulations under those sections, on amounts paid to a foreign organization that is described in section 501(c) to the extent that the amounts are not income includible under section 512 in computing the organization's unrelated business taxable income. See, however, §1.1443-1 for withholding on payments of unrelated business income to foreign tax-exempt organizations and on payments subject to tax under section 4948. For a foreign organization to claim an exemption from withholding under section 1441(a) or 1442 based on its status as an organization described in section 501(c), it must furnish the withholding agent with a withholding certificate described in paragraph (b)(2) of this section. A foreign organization described in section 501(c) may choose to claim a reduced rate of withholding under the procedures described in other sections of the regulations under section 1441 and not under this section. In particular, if an organization chooses to claim benefits under an income tax treaty, the withholding procedures applicable to claims of such a reduced rate are governed solely by the provisions of §1.1441-6 and not of this section.

(b) *Reliance on foreign organization's claim of exemption from withholding.*—(1) *General rule.*—A withholding agent may rely on a claim of exemption under this section only if, prior to the payment, the withholding agent can reliably associate the payment with a valid withholding certificate described in paragraph (b)(2) of this section.

(2) *Withholding certificate.*—A withholding certificate under this paragraph (b)(2) is valid only if it is a Form W-8 and if, in addition to other applicable requirements, the Form W-8 includes the taxpayer identifying number of the organization whose name is on the certificate, and it certifies that the Internal Revenue Service (IRS) has issued a favorable determination letter (and the date thereof) that is currently in effect, what portion, if any, of the amounts paid constitute income includible under section 512 in computing the organization's unrelated business taxable income, and, if the organization is described in section 501(c)(3), whether it is a private foundation described in section 509. Notwithstanding the preceding sentence, if the organization cannot certify that it has been issued a favorable determination letter that is still in effect, its withholding certificate is nevertheless valid under this paragraph (b)(2) if the organization attaches to the withholding certificate an opinion that is acceptable to the withholding agent from a U.S. counsel (or any other person as the IRS may prescribe in published guidance (see §601.601(d)(2) of this chapter)) concluding that the organization is described in section 501(c). If the determination letter or opinion of counsel to which the withholding certificate refers concludes that the organization is described in section 501(c)(3), and the certificate further certifies that the organization is not a private foundation described in section 509, an affidavit of the organization setting forth sufficient facts concerning the operations and support of the organization for the Internal Revenue Service (IRS) to determine that such organization would be likely to qualify as an organization described in section 509(a)(1), (2), (3), or (4) must be attached to the withholding certificate. An organization that provides an opinion of U.S. counsel or an affidavit may provide the same opinion or affidavit to more than one withholding agent provided that the opinion is acceptable to each withholding agent who receives it in conjunction with a withholding certificate. Any such opinion of counsel or affidavit must be renewed whenever there is a change in facts or circumstances that are relevant to determine the organization's status under section 501(c) or, if relevant, that the organization is or is not a private foundation described in section 509.

(3) *Presumptions in the absence of documentation.*—Notwithstanding paragraph (b)(1) of this section, if the organization's certification with respect to whether amounts paid constitute income includible under section 512 in computing the organization's unrelated business taxable income is not reliable or is lacking but all other certifications are reliable, the withholding agent may rely on the certificate but the amounts paid are presumed to be income includible under section 512 in computing the organization's unrelated business taxable income. If the certification regarding private foundation status is not reliable, the withholding agent may rely on the certificate but the amounts paid are presumed to be paid to a foreign beneficial owner that is a private foundation.

(4) *Reason to know.*—Reliance by a withholding agent on the information and certifications stated on a withholding certificate is subject to the agent's actual knowledge or reason to know that such information or certification is incorrect as provided in §1.1441-7(b). For example, a withholding agent must cease to treat a foreign organization's claim for exemption from withholding based on the organization's tax-exempt status as valid beginning on the earlier of the date on which such agent knows that the IRS has given notice to such foreign organization that it is not an organization described in section 501(c) or the date on which the IRS gives notice to the public that such foreign organization is not an organization described in section 501(c). Similarly, a withholding agent may no longer rely on a certification that an amount is not subject to tax under section 4948 beginning on the earlier of the date on which such agent knows that the IRS has given notice to such foreign organization that it is subject to tax under section 4948 or the date on which the IRS

Reg. §1.1441-9(b)(4)

gives notice that such foreign organization is a private foundation within the meaning of section 509(a).

(c) *Failure to receive withholding certificate timely and other applicable procedures.*—See applicable procedures described in §1.1441-1(b)(7) in the event the withholding agent does not hold a valid withholding certificate or other appropriate documentation at the time of payment. Further, the provisions of §1.1441-1(e)(4) shall apply to withholding certificates and other documents related thereto furnished under the provisions of this section.

(d) *Effective date.*—(1) *In general.*—This section applies to payments made after December 31, 2000.

(2) *Transition rules.*—For purposes of this section, the validity of a Form W-8, 1001, or 4224 or a statement that was valid on January 1, 1998, under the regulations in effect prior to January 1, 2001 (see 26 CFR parts 1 and 35a, revised April 1, 1999) and expired, or will expire, at any time during 1998, is extended until December 31, 1998. The validity of a Form W-8, 1001, or 4224 or a statement that is valid on or after January 1, 1999 remains valid until its validity expires under the regulations in effect prior to January 1, 2001 (see 26 CFR parts 1 and 35a, revised April 1, 1999) but in no event shall such form or statement remain valid after December 31, 2000. The rule in this paragraph (d)(2), however, does not apply to extend the validity period of a Form W-8, 1001, or 4224 or a statement that expires solely by reason of changes in the circumstances of the person whose name is on the certificate. Notwithstanding the first three sentences of this paragraph (d)(2), a withholding agent may choose to not take advantage of the transition rule in this paragraph (d)(2) with respect to one or more withholding certificates valid under the regulations in effect prior to January 1, 2001 (see 26 CFR parts 1 and 35a, revised April 1, 1999) and, therefore, to require withholding certificates conforming to the requirements described in this section (new withholding certificates). For purposes of this section, a new withholding certificate is deemed to satisfy the documentation requirement under the regulations in effect prior to January 1, 2001 (see 26 CFR parts 1 and 35a, revised April 1, 1999). Further, a new withholding certificate remains valid for the period specified in §1.1441-1(e)(4)(ii), regardless of when the certificate is obtained. [Reg. §1.1441-9.]

☐ [*T.D. 8734, 10-6-97. Amended by T.D. 8804, 12-30-98; T.D. 8856, 12-29-99 and T.D. 8881, 5-15-2000.*]

[Reg. §1.1441-10]

§1.1441-10. Withholding agents with respect to fast-pay arrangements.—(a) *In general.*—A corporation that issues fast-pay stock in a fast-pay arrangement described in §1.7701(l)-3(b)(1) is a withholding agent with respect to payments made on the fast-pay stock and payments deemed made under the recharacterization rules of §1.7701(l)-3. Except as provided in this paragraph (a) or in paragraph (b) of this section, the withholding tax rules under section 1441 and section 1442 apply with respect to a fast-pay arrangement described in §1.7701(l)-3(c)(1)(i) in accordance with the recharacterization rules provided in §1.7701(l)-3(c). In all cases, notwithstanding paragraph (b) of this section, if at any time the withholding agent knows or has reason to know that the Commissioner has exercised the discretion under either §1.7701(l)-3(c)(1)(ii) to apply the recharacterization rules of §1.7701(l)-3(c), or §1.7701(l)-3(d) to depart from the recharacterization rules of §1.7701(l)-3(c) for a taxpayer, the withholding agent must withhold on payments made (or deemed made) to that taxpayer in accordance with the characterization of the fast-pay arrangement imposed by the Commissioner under §1.7701(l)-3.

(b) *Exception.*—If at any time the withholding agent knows or has reason to know that any taxpayer entered into a fast-pay arrangement with a principal purpose of applying the recharacterization rules of §1.7701(l)-3(c) to avoid tax under section 871(a) or section 881, then for each payment made or deemed made to such taxpayer under the arrangement, the withholding agent must withhold, under section 1441 or section 1442, the higher of—

(1) The amount of withholding that would apply to such payment determined under the form of the arrangement; or

(2) The amount of withholding that would apply to deemed payments determined under the recharacterization rules of §1.7701(l)-3(c).

(c) *Liability.*—Any person required to deduct and withhold tax under this section is made liable for that tax by section 1461, and is also liable for applicable penalties and interest for failing to comply with section 1461.

(d) *Examples.*—The following examples illustrate the rules of this section:

Example 1. REIT W issues shares of fast-pay stock to foreign individual A, a resident of Country C. United States source dividends paid to residents of C are subject to a 30 percent withholding tax. W issues all shares of benefited stock to foreign individuals who are residents of Country D. D's income tax convention with the United States reduces the United States withholding tax on dividends to 15 percent. Under §1.7701(l)-3(c), the dividends paid by W to A are deemed to be paid by W to the benefited shareholders. W has reason to know that A entered into the fast-pay arrangement with a principal purpose of using the recharacterization rules of §1.7701(l)-3(c) to reduce United States withholding tax. W must withhold at the 30 percent rate because the amount of withholding that applies to the payments determined under the form of the arrangement is higher than the amount of withholding that applies to the payments determined under § 1.7701(l)-3(c).

Example 2. The facts are the same as in *Example 1* of this paragraph (d) except that W does not know, or have reason to know, that A entered into the arrangement with a principal purpose of using the recharacterization rules of § 1.7701(l)-3(c) to reduce United States withholding tax. Further, the Commissioner has not exercised the discretion under § 1.7701(l)-3(d) to depart from the recharacterization rules of § 1.7701(l)-3(c). Accordingly, W must withhold tax at a 15 percent rate on the dividends deemed paid to the benefited shareholders.

(e) *Effective date.*—This section applies to payments made (or deemed made) on or after January 6, 1999. [Reg. § 1.1441-10.]

☐ [T.D. 8853, 1-7-2000.]

[Reg. § 1.1442-1]

§ 1.1442-1. Withholding of tax on foreign corporations.—For regulations concerning the withholding of tax at source under section 1442 in the case of foreign corporations, foreign governments, international organizations, foreign tax-exempt corporations, or foreign private foundations, see § § 1.1441-1 through 1.1441-9. [Reg. § 1.1442-1.]

☐ [T.D. 6187, 7-5-56. *Amended by T.D.* 6908, 12-30-66 *and T.D.* 8734, 10-6-97 (T.D. 8804 delayed the effective date of T.D. 8734 from January 1, 1999, to January 1, 2000; T.D. 8856 further delayed the effective date of T.D. 8734 until January 1, 2001).]

[Reg. § 1.1442-2]

§ 1.1442-2. Exemption under a tax treaty.— For regulations providing for a claim of reduced withholding tax under section 1442 by certain foreign corporations pursuant to the provisions of an income tax treaty, see § 1.1441-6. [Reg. § 1.1442-2.]

☐ [T.D. 6908, 12-30-66. *Amended by T.D.* 8734, 10-6-97 (T.D. 8804 delayed the effective date of T.D. 8734 from January 1, 1999, to January 1, 2000; T.D. 8856 further delayed the effective date of T.D. 8734 until January 1, 2001).]

[Reg. § 1.1442-3]

§ 1.1442-3. Tax exempt income of a foreign tax-exempt corporation.—For regulations providing for a claim of exemption for income exempt from tax under section 501(a) of a foreign tax-exempt corporation, see § 1.1441-9. See § 1.1443-1 for withholding rules applicable to foreign private foundations and to the unrelated business income of foreign tax-exempt organizations. [Reg. § 1.1442-3.]

☐ [T.D. 8734, 10-6-97 (T.D. 8804 delayed the effective date of T.D. 8734 from January 1, 1999, to January 1, 2000; T.D. 8856 further delayed the effective date of T.D. 8734 until January 1, 2001).]

[Reg. § 1.1443-1]

§ 1.1443-1. Foreign tax-exempt organizations.—(a) *Income includible in computing unrelated business taxable income.*—In the case of a foreign organization that is described in section 501(c), amounts paid or effectively connected taxable income allocable to the organization that are includible under section 512 and section 513 in computing the organization's unrelated business taxable income are subject to withholding under § § 1.1441-1, 1.1441-4, 1.1441-6, and 1.1446-1 through 1.1446-6, in the same manner as payments or allocations of effectively connected taxable income of the same amounts made to any foreign person that is not a tax-exempt organization. Therefore, a foreign organization receiving amounts includible under section 512 and section 513 in computing the organization's unrelated business taxable income may claim an exemption from withholding or a reduced rate of withholding with respect to that income in the same manner as a foreign person that is not a tax-exempt organization. See § 1.1441-9(b)(3) for a presumption that amounts are includible under section 512 and section 513 in computing the organization's unrelated business taxable income in the absence of reliable certification. See also § 1.1446-3(c)(3), applying this presumption in the context of section 1446.

(b) *Income subject to tax under section 4948.*— (1) *In general.*—The gross investment income (as defined in section 4940(c)(2)) of a foreign private foundation is subject to withholding under section 1443(b) at the rate of 4 percent to the extent that the income is from sources within the United States and is subject to the tax imposed by section 4948(a) and the regulations under that section. Withholding under this paragraph (b) is required irrespective of the fact that the income may be effectively connected with the conduct of a trade or business in the United States by the foreign organization. See § 1.1441-9(b)(3) for applicable presumptions that amounts are subject to tax under section 4948. The withholding imposed under this paragraph (b)(1) does not obviate a private foundation's obligation to file any return required by law with respect to such organization, such as the form that the foundation is required to file under section 6033 for the taxable year.

(2) *Reliance on a foreign organization's claim of foreign private foundation status.*—For reliance by a withholding agent on a foreign organization's claim of foreign private foundation status, see § 1.1441-9(b) and (c).

(3) *Applicable procedures.*—A withholding agent withholding the 4-percent amount pursu-

Reg. § 1.1443-1(b)(3)

ant to paragraph (b)(1) of this section shall treat such withholding as withholding under section 1441(a) or 1442(a) for all purposes, including reporting of the payment on a Form 1042 and a Form 1042-S pursuant to §1.1461-1(b) and (c). Similarly, the foreign private foundation shall treat the 4-percent withholding as withholding under section 1441(a) or 1442(a), including for purposes of claims for refunds and credits.

(4) *Claim of benefits under an income tax treaty.*—The withholding procedures applicable to claims of a reduced rate under an income tax treaty are governed solely by the provisions of §1.1441-6 and not by this section.

(c) *Effective date.*—(1) *In general.*—This section applies to payments made after December 31, 2000, except that the references in paragraph (a) of this section to effectively connected taxable income and withholding under section 1446 shall apply to partnership taxable years beginning after May 18, 2005, or such earlier time as the regulations under §§1.1446-1 through 1.1446-5 apply by reason of an election under §1.1446-7.

(2) *Transition rules.*—For purposes of this section, the validity of an affidavit or opinion of counsel described in §1.1443-1(b)(4)(i) in effect prior to January 1, 2001 (see §1.1443-1(b)(4)(i) as contained in 26 CFR part 1, revised April 1, 1999) is extended until December 31, 2000. However, a withholding agent may chose to not take advantage of the transition rule in this paragraph (c)(2) with respect to one or more withholding certificates valid under the regulations in effect prior to January 1, 2001 (see CFR part 1, revised April 1, 1999) and, therefore, to require withholding certificates conforming to the requirements described in this section (new withholding certificates). For purposes of this section, a new withholding certificate is deemed to satisfy the documentation requirement under the regulations in effect prior to January 1, 2001 (see 26 CFR part 1, revised April 1, 1999). Further, a new withholding certificate remains valid for the period specified in §1.1441-1(e)(4)(ii), regardless of when the certificate is obtained. [Reg. §1.1443-1.]

☐ [*T.D. 6187, 7-5-56. Amended by T.D. 6908, 12-30-66; T.D. 7229, 12-20-72; T.D. 7247, 12-29-72; T.D. 8734, 10-6-97; T.D. 8804, 12-30-98; T.D. 8856, 12-29-99; T.D. 9200, 5-13-2005 and T.D. 9394, 4-28-2008.*]

[Reg. §1.1445-1]

§1.1445-1. Withholding on dispositions of U.S. real property interests by foreign persons: In general.—(a) *Purpose and scope of regulations.*—These regulations set forth rules relating to the withholding requirements of section 1445. In general, section 1445(a) provides that any person who acquires a U.S. real property interest from a foreign person must withhold a tax of 10 percent from the amount realized by the trans-

feror foreign person (or a lesser amount established by agreement with the Internal Revenue Service). Section 1445(e) provides special rules requiring withholding on distributions and certain other transactions by corporations, partnerships, trusts, and estates. This §1.1445-1 provides general rules concerning the withholding requirement of section 1445(a), as well as definitions applicable under both sections 1445(a) and 1445(e). Section 1.1445-2 provides for various situations in which withholding is not required under section 1445(a). Section 1.1445-3 provides for adjustments to the amount required to be withheld by transferees under section 1445(a). Section 1.1445-4 prescribes the duties of agents in transactions subject to withholding under either section 1445(a) or 1445(e). Section 1.1445-5 provides rules concerning the withholding required under section 1445(e), while §1.1445-6 provides for adjustments to the amount required to be withheld under section 1445(e). Finally, §1.1445-7 provides rules concerning the treatment of a foreign corporation that has made an election under section 897(i) to be treated as a domestic corporation.

(b) *Duty to withhold.*—(1) *In general.*—Transferees of U.S. real property interests are required to deduct and withhold a tax equal to 10 percent of the amount realized by the transferor, if the transferor is a foreign person and the disposition takes place on or after January 1, 1985. Neither the transferee's duty to withhold nor the amount required to be withheld is affected by the amount of cash to be paid by the transferee. Amounts withheld must be reported and paid over in accordance with the requirements of paragraph (c) of this section. Failures to withhold and pay over are subject to the liabilities set forth in paragraph (e) of this section. If two or more persons are joint transferees of a U.S. real property interest, each such person is subject to the obligation to withhold. That obligation is fulfilled with respect to each such person if any one of them withholds and pays over the required amount in accordance with the rules of this section. If the amount realized (as defined in paragraph (g)(5) of this section) by the transferor is zero, then no withholding is required. For example, if a real property interest is transferred as a gift (i.e., the recipient does not assume any liabilities or furnish any other consideration to the transferor) then no withholding is required. Withholding is not required with respect to dispositions that take place before January 1, 1985, even if the first payment of consideration is made after December 31, 1984.

(2) *U.S. real property interest owned jointly by foreign and non-foreign transferors.*—The amount subject to withholding under paragraph (b)(1) of this section with respect to the transfer of a U.S. real property interest owned by one or more foreign persons (as defined in §1.897-1(k)) and one or more non-foreign persons shall be deter-

mined by allocating the amount realized from the transfer between (or among) such transferors based upon the capital contribution of each transferor with respect to the property and by aggregating the amounts allocated to any foreign person (or persons). For this purpose, a husband and wife will each be deemed to have contributed 50 percent of the aggregate capital contributed by such husband and wife. See § 1.1445-1(f)(3)(iv) with respect to the crediting of the amount withheld between or among joint foreign transferors.

(3) *Options to acquire a U.S. real property interest.*—(i) *No withholding on grant of option.*—No withholding is required under section 1445 with respect to any amount realized by the grantor on the grant of an option to acquire a U.S. real property interest.

(ii) *No withholding upon lapse of option.*— No withholding is required under section 1445 with respect to any amount realized by the grantor upon the lapse of an option to acquire a U.S. real property interest.

(iii) *Withholding required upon the sale or exchange of option.*—A transferee of an option to acquire a U.S. real property interest must deduct and withhold a tax equal to 10 percent of the amount realized by the transferor upon the disposition. This § 1.1445-1(b)(3)(iii) does not apply to require withholding upon the initial grant of an option.

(iv) *Withholding required on exercise of option.*—If the holder exercises an option to purchase a U.S. real property interest, the amount paid for the option shall be considered an amount realized by the grantor/transferor upon the transfer of the property with respect to which the option was granted, and shall thus be subject to withholding on the day that such underlying property is transferred. The preceding sentence applies regardless of whether or not the terms of the option specifically provide that the option price is applied to the purchase price.

(4) *Exceptions and modifications.*—The duty to withhold under section 1445(a) is subject to the exceptions and modifications contained in §§ 1.1445-2 and 1.1445-3. Generally, § 1.1445-2 provides rules for determining that withholding is not required because either the transferor is not a foreign person or the interest transferred is not a U.S. real property interest. In addition, § 1.1445-2 provides exceptions to the withholding requirement, including a rule that exempts from withholding any person who acquires a U.S. real property interest for use as a residence for a contract price of $300,000 or less. If withholding is required under section 1445(a), § 1.1445-3 allows the amount withheld to be modified pursuant to a withholding certificate issued by the Internal Revenue Service. If a transferee cannot withhold the full amount re-

quired because the first payment of consideration for the transfer does not involve sufficient cash (or other liquid assets convertible into cash, such as foreign currency), then a withholding certificate must be obtained pursuant to § 1.1445-3.

(c) *Reporting and paying over of withheld amounts.*—(1) *In general.*—A transferee must report and pay over any tax withheld by the 20th day after the date of the transfer. Forms 8288 and 8288-A are used for this purpose, and must be filed at the location as provided in the instructions to Forms 8288 and 8288-A. Pursuant to section 7502 and regulations thereunder, the timely mailing of Forms 8288 and 8288-A will be treated as their timely filing. Form 8288-A will be stamped by the IRS to show receipt, and a stamped copy will be mailed by the IRS to the transferor (at the address reported on the form) for the transferor's use. See §§ 1.1445-1(f) and 1.1445-3(f). Forms 8288 and 8288-A are required to include the identifying numbers of both the transferor and the transferee, as provided in paragraph (d) of this section. If any identifying number as required by such forms is not provided, the transferee must still report and pay over any tax withheld on Form 8288, although the transferor cannot obtain a credit or refund of tax on the basis of a Form 8288-A that does not include the transferor's identifying number (see paragraph (f)(2) of this section).

(2) *Pending application for withholding certificate.*—(i) *In general.*—(A) *Delayed reporting and payment with respect to application submitted by transferee.*—If an application for a withholding certificate with respect to a transfer of a U.S. real property interest is submitted to the Internal Revenue Service by the transferee on the day of or at any time prior to the transfer, the transferee must withhold 10 percent of the amount realized as required by paragraph (b) of this section. However, the amount withheld, or a lesser amount as determined by the Service, need not be reported and paid over to the Service until the 20th day following the Service's final determination with respect to the application for a withholding certificate. For this purpose, the Service's final determination occurs on the day when the withholding certificate is mailed to the transferee by the Service or when a notification denying the request for a withholding certificate is mailed to the transferee by the Service. An application is submitted to the Service on the day it is actually received by the Service at the address provided in § 1.1445-1(g)(10) or, under the rules of section 7502, on the day it is mailed to the Service at the address provided in § 1.1445-1(g)(10).

(B) *Delayed reporting and payment with respect to application submitted by transferor.*—If an application for a withholding certificate with respect to a transfer of a U.S. real property interest

Reg. § 1.1445-1(c)(2)(i)(B)

is submitted to the Internal Revenue Service by the transferor on the day of or any time prior to the transfer, such transferor must provide notice to the transferee prior to the transfer. No particular form is required but the notice must set forth the name, address, and taxpayer identification number of the transferor, a brief description of the property which is the subject of the application, and the date the application was submitted to the Service. The transferee must withhold 10 percent of the amount realized as required in paragraph (b) of this section but need not report or pay over to the Service such amount (or a lesser amount as determined by the Service) until the 20th day following the Service's final determination with respect to the application. The Service will send a copy of the withholding certificate or copy of the notification denying the request for a withholding certificate to the transferee. For this purpose, the Service's final determination will be deemed to occur on the day when the copy of the withholding certificate or the copy of the notification denying the request for a withholding certificate is mailed by the Service to the transferee (or transferees). An application is submitted to the Service on the day it is actually received by the Service at the address provided in § 1.1445-1(g)(10) or, under the rules of § 7502, on the day it is mailed to the Service at the address provided in § 1.1445-1(g)(10).

(ii) *Anti-abuse rule.*—(A) *In general.*—A transferee that in reliance upon the rules of this paragraph (c)(2) fails to report and pay over amounts withheld by the 20th day following the date of the transfer, shall be subject to the payment of interest and penalties if the relevant application for a withholding certificate (or an amendment to the application for a withholding certificate) was submitted for a principal purpose of delaying the transferee's payment to the IRS of the amount withheld. Interest and penalties shall be assessed on the amount that is ultimately paid over (or collected pursuant to the agreement) with respect to the period between the 20th day after the date of the transfer and the date on which payment is made (or collected).

(B) *Presumption.*—A principal purpose of delaying payment of the amount withheld shall be presumed if—

(1) The transferee applies for a withholding certificate pursuant to § 1.1445-3(c) based on a determination of the transferor's maximum tax liability, and

(2) Such liability is ultimately determined to be equal to 90 percent or more of the amount that was otherwise required to be withheld and paid over.

However, the presumption created by the previous sentence may be rebutted by evidence establishing that delaying payment of the amount withheld was not a principal purpose of the transaction.

(d) *Contents of Forms 8288 and 8288-A.*—(1) *Transactions subject to section 1445(a).*—Any person that is required to file Forms 8288 and 8288-A pursuant to section 1445(a) and the rules of this section must set forth thereon the following information:

(i) The name, identifying number, and home address (in the case of an individual) or office address (in the case of any entity) of the transferee(s) filing the return;

(ii) The name, identifying number, and home address (in the case of an individual) or office address (in the case of any entity) of the transferor(s);

(iii) A brief description of the U.S. real property interest transferred, including its location and the nature of any substantial improvements in the case of real property, and the class or type and amount of interests transferred in the case of interests in a corporation that constitute U.S. real property interests;

(iv) The date of the transfer;

(v) The amount realized by the transferor, as defined in paragraph (g)(5) of this section;

(vi) The amount withheld by the transferee and whether withholding is at the statutory or reduced rate; and

(vii) Such other information as the Commissioner may require.

For purposes of paragraph (d)(1)(i) and (ii), mailing addresses may be provided in addition to, but not in lieu of, home addresses or office addresses.

(2) *Transactions subject to section 1445(e).*—Any person that is required to file Forms 8288 and 8288-A pursuant to the rules of § 1.1445-5 must set forth thereon the following information:

(i) The name, identifying number, and office address of the entity or fiduciary filing the return;

(ii) The amount withheld by the entity or fiduciary;

(iii) The date of the transfer;

(iv) In the case of a transaction subject to withholding pursuant to section 1445(e)(1) and § 1.1445-5(c):

(A) A brief description of the U.S. real property interest transferred, as described in paragraph (d)(1)(iii) of this section;

(B) The name, identifying number, and home address (in the case of an individual) or office address (in the case of an entity) of each holder of an interest in the entity that is a foreign person; and

(C) Each such interest-holder's pro rata share of the amount withheld;

(v) In the case of a distribution subject to withholding pursuant to section 1445(e)(2) and § 1.1445-5(d):

(A) A brief description of the U.S. real property interest transferred, as described in paragraph (d)(1)(iii) of this section; and

Reg. § 1.1445-1(c)(2)(ii)(A)

(B) The amount of gain recognized upon the distribution by the corporation.

(vi) In the case of a distribution subject to withholding pursuant to section 1445(e)(3) and § 1.1445-5(e):

(A) A brief description of the property distributed by the corporation;

(B) The name, identifying number, and home address (in the case of an individual) or office address (in the case of an entity) of each holder of an interest in the entity that is a foreign person;

(C) The amount realized upon the distribution by each such foreign interest holder; and

(D) Each foreign interest-holder's pro rata share of the amount withheld; and

(vii) Such other information as the Commissioner may require.

(e) *Liability of transferee upon failure to withhold.*—(1) *In general.*—Every person required to deduct and withhold tax under section 1445 is made liable for that tax by section 1461. Therefore, a person that is required to deduct and withhold tax but fails to do so may be held liable for the payment of the tax and any applicable penalties and interest.

(2) *Transferor's liability not otherwise satisfied.*—(i) *Tax and penalties.*—Except as provided in paragraph (e)(3) of this section, if a transferee is required to deduct and withhold tax under section 1445 but fails to do so, then the tax shall be assessed against and collected from that transferee. Such person may also be subject to any of the civil and criminal penalties that apply. Corporate officers or other responsible persons may be subject to a civil penalty under section 6672 equal to the amount that should have been withheld and paid over.

(ii) *Interest.*—If a transferee is required to deduct and withhold tax under section 1445 but fails to do so, then such transferee shall be liable for the payment of interest pursuant to section 6601 and the regulations thereunder. Interest shall be payable with respect to the period between—

(A) The last date on which the tax imposed under section 1445 was required to be paid over by the transferee, and

(B) The date on which such tax is actually paid. Interest shall be payable with respect to the entire amount that is required to be deducted and withheld. However, if the Service issues a withholding certificate providing for withholding of a reduced amount, then, for the period after the issuance of the certificate, interest shall be payable with respect to that reduced amount.

(3) *Transferor's liability otherwise satisfied.*—(i) *Tax and penalties.*—If a transferee is required

to deduct and withhold tax under section 1445 but fails to do so, and the transferor's tax liability with respect to the transfer was satisfied (or was established to be zero) by—

(A) The transferor's filing of an income tax return (and payment of any tax due) with respect to the transfer, or

(B) The issuance of a withholding certificate by the Internal Revenue Service establishing that the transferor's maximum tax liability is zero,

then the tax required to be withheld under section 1445 shall not be collected from the transferee. Such transferee's liability for tax, and the requirement that such person file Forms 8288 and 8288-A, shall be deemed to have been satisfied as of the date on which the transferor's income tax return was filed or the withholding certificate was issued. No penalty shall be imposed on or collected from such person for failure to return or pay the tax, unless such failure was fraudulent and for the purpose of evading payment. A transferee that seeks to avoid liability for tax and penalties pursuant to the rule of paragraph (e)(3)(i) must provide sufficient information for the Service to determine whether the transferor's tax liability was satisfied (or was established to be zero).

(ii) *Interest.*—If a transferee is required to deduct and withhold tax under section 1445 but fails to do so, then such person shall be liable for the payment of interest under section 6601 and regulations thereunder. Such transferee's liability for the payment of interest shall not be excused by reason of the deemed satisfaction, pursuant to subdivision (i) of this paragraph (e)(3), of the transferee's liability under section 1445, because the deemed satisfaction of that liability is the equivalent of the late payment of a liability, on which interest must be paid. Interest shall be payable with respect to the period between—

(A) The last date on which the tax imposed under section 1445 was required to be paid over, and

(B) The date (established from information supplied to the Service by the transferee) on which any tax due is paid with respect to the transferor's relevant income tax return, or the date the withholding certificate is issued establishing that the transferor's maximum tax liability is zero.

Interest shall be payable with respect to the entire amount that is required to be deducted and withheld. However, if the Service issues a withholding certificate providing for withholding of a reduced amount, then for the period after the issuance of the certificate interest shall be payable with respect to that reduced amount.

(4) *Coordination with entity withholding rules.*—For purposes of section 1445(e) and §§ 1.1445-5, 1.1445-6, 1.1445-7, and 1.1445-8T, the rules of this paragraph (e) shall be applied by—

(i) Substituting the words "person required to withhold" for the word "transferee" each place it appears in this paragraph (e), and

(ii) Substituting the words "person subject to withholding" for the word "transferor" each place it appears in this paragraph (e).

(f) *Effect of withholding on transferor.*—(1) *In general.*—The withholding of tax under section 1445(a) does not excuse a foreign person that disposes of a U.S. real property interest from filing a U.S. tax return with respect to the income arising from the disposition. Form 1040NR, 1041, or 1120F, as appropriate, must be filed, and any tax due must be paid, by the filing deadline generally applicable to such person. (The return may be filed by such later date as is provided in an extension granted by the Internal Revenue Service.) Any tax withheld under section 1445(a) shall be credited against the amount of income tax as computed in such return.

(2) *Manner of obtaining credit or refund.*—A stamped copy of Form 8288-A will be provided to the transferor by the Service (under paragraph (c) of this section) if the Form 8288-A is complete, including the transferor's identifying number. Except as provided in paragraph (f)(3) of this section, a stamped copy of Form 8288-A must be attached to the transferor's return to establish the amount withheld that is available as a credit. If the amount withheld under section 1445(a) constitutes less than the full amount of the transferor's U.S. tax liability for that taxable year, then a payment of estimated tax may be required to be made pursuant to section 6154 or 6654 prior to the filing of the income tax return for that year. Alternatively, if the amount withheld under section 1445(a) exceeds the transferor's maximum tax liability with respect to the disposition (as determined by the IRS), then the transferor may seek an early refund of the excess pursuant to §1.1445-3T(g), or a normal refund upon filing of a tax return.

(3) *Special rules.*—(i) *Failure to receive Form 8288-A.*—If a stamped copy of Form 8288-A has not been provided to the transferor by the Service, the transferor may establish the amount of tax withheld by the transferee by attaching to its return substantial evidence (*e.g.*, closing documents) of such amount. Such a transferor must attach to its return a statement which supplies all of the information required by §1.1445-1(d), including the transferor's identifying number.

(ii) *U.S. persons subjected to withholding.*—If a transferee withholds tax under section 1445(a) with respect to a person who is not a foreign person, such person may credit the amount of any tax withheld against his income tax liability in accordance with the provisions of this §1.1445-1(f) or apply for an early refund under §1.1445-3(g).

(iii) *Refund in case of installment sale.*—A transferor that takes gain into account in accordance with the provisions of section 453 shall not be entitled to a refund of the amount withheld, unless a withholding certificate providing for such a refund is obtained from the Internal Revenue Service pursuant to the provisions of §1.1445-3.

(iv) *Joint foreign transferors.*—If two or more foreign persons jointly transfer a U.S. real property interest, each transferor shall be credited with such portion of the amount withheld as such transferors mutually agree. Such transferors must request that the transferee reflect the agreed-upon crediting of the amount withheld on the Forms 8288-A filed by the transferee. If the foreign transferors fail to request that the transferee reflect the agreed-upon crediting of the amount withheld by the 10th day after the date of transfer, the transferee must credit the amount withheld equally between (or among) the foreign transferors. In such case, the transferee is indemnified pursuant to section 1461 against any claim by a transferor objecting to the resulting division of credits. For rules regarding the amount realized allocated to joint foreign and non-foreign transferors, see §1.1445-1(b)(2).

(g) *Definitions.*—(1) *In general.*—Unless otherwise specified, the definitions of terms provided in §1.897-1 shall apply for purposes of this section and §§1.1445-2 through 1.1445-7. For purposes of section 1445 and the regulations thereunder, definitions of other relevant terms are provided in this paragraph (g). In addition, the term "residence" is defined in §1.1445-2(d)(1), the terms "transferor's agent" and "transferee's agent" are defined in §1.1445-4(f), and the term "relevant taxpayer" is defined in §1.1445-6(a)(2).

(2) *Transfer.*—The term "transfer" means any transaction that would constitute a disposition for any purpose of the Internal Revenue Code and regulations thereunder. For purposes of §§1.1445-5 and 1.1445-6, the term includes distributions to shareholders of a corporation, partners of a partnership, and beneficiaries of a trust or estate.

(3) *Transferor.*—The term "transferor" means any person, foreign or domestic, that disposes of a U.S. real property interest by sale, exchange, gift or any other transfer. The term "U.S. real property interest" is defined in §1.897-1(c).

(4) *Transferee.*—The term "transferee" means any person, foreign or domestic, that acquires a U.S. real property interest by purchase, exchange, gift, or any other transfer.

(5) *Amount realized.*—The amount realized by the transferor for the transfer of a U.S. real property interest is the sum of:

(i) The cash paid, or to be paid,

(ii) The fair market value of other property transferred, or to be transferred, and

(iii) The outstanding amount of any liability assumed by the transferee or to which the U.S. real property interest is subject immediately before and after the transfer. The term "cash paid or to be paid" does not include stated or unstated interest or original issue discount (as determined under the rules of sections 1271 through 1275).

(6) *Contract price.*—The contract price of a U.S. real property interest is the sum that is agreed to by the transferee and transferor as the total amount of consideration to be paid for the property. That amount will generally be equal to the amount realized by the transferor, as defined in paragraph (b)(5) of this section.

(7) *Fair market value.*—The fair market value of property means the price at which the property would change hands between an unrelated willing buyer and willing seller, neither being under any compulsion to buy or to sell and both having reasonable knowledge of all relevant facts.

(8) *Date of transfer.*—The date of transfer of a U.S. real property interest is the first date on which consideration is paid (or a liability assumed) by the transferee. However, for purposes of section 1445(e)(2), (3), and (4) and §1.1445-5(c)(1)(iii) and 1.1445-5(c)(3) only, the date of transfer is the date of the distribution that gives rise to the obligation to withhold. For purposes of this paragraph (g)(8), the payment of consideration does not include the payment, prior to the passage of legal or equitable title (other than pursuant to an initial contract for purchase), of earnest money, a good-faith deposit, or any similar sum that is primarily intended to bind the transferee or transferor to the entering or performance of a contract. Such a payment will not constitute a payment of consideration solely because it may ultimately be applied against the amount owed to the transferor by the transferee. Such a payment is presumed to be earnest money, a good faith deposit, or a similar sum if it is subject to forfeiture in the event of a failure to enter into a contract or a breach of contract. However, a payment that is not forfeitable may nevertheless be found to constitute earnest money, a good faith deposit, or a similar sum.

(9) *Identifying number.*—Pursuant to §1.897-1(p), an individual's identifying number is the social security number or the identification number assigned by the Internal Revenue Service (see §301.6109-1 of this chapter). The identifying number of any other person is its United States employer identification number.

(10) *Address of the Director, Philadelphia Service Center.*—Any written communication directed to the Director, Philadelphia Service Center is to be addressed as follows: P.O. Box 21086, Drop Point 8731, FIRPTA Unit, Philadelphia, PA 19114-0586.

(h) *Effective date for taxpayer identification numbers.*—The requirement in paragraphs (c)(2)(i)(B), (d)(1)(i) and (ii), (d)(2)(i), (d)(2)(iv)(B), and (d)(2)(vi)(B) of this section that taxpayer identification numbers be provided (in all cases) is applicable for dispositions of U.S. real property interests occurring after November 3, 2003. [Reg. §1.1445-1.]

☐ [*T.D.* 8113, 12-18-86. *Amended by T.D.* 8647, 12-20-95 *and T.D.* 9082, 8-4-2003.]

[Reg. §1.1445-2]

§1.1445-2. Situations in which withholding is not required under section 1445(a).—(a) *Purpose and scope of section.*—This section provides rules concerning various situations in which withholding is not required under section 1445(a). In general, a transferee has a duty to withhold under section 1445(a) only if both of the following are true:

(1) The transferor is a foreign person; and

(2) The transferee is acquiring a U.S. real property interest.

Thus, paragraphs (b) and (c) of this section provide rules under which a transferee of property can ascertain that he has no duty to withhold because one or the other of the two key elements is missing. Under paragraph (b), a transferee may determine that no withholding is required because the transferor is not a foreign person. Under paragraph (c), a transferee may determine that no withholding is required because the property acquired is not a U.S. real property interest. Finally, paragraph (d) of this section provides rules concerning exceptions to the withholding requirement.

(b) *Transferor not a foreign person.*—(1) *In general.*—No withholding is required under section 1445 if the transferor of a U.S. real property interest is not a foreign person. Therefore, paragraph (b)(2) of this section provides rules pursuant to which the transferor can provide a certification of non-foreign status to inform the transferee that withholding is not required. A transferee that obtains such a certification must retain that document for five years, as provided in paragraph (b)(3) of this section. Except to the extent provided in paragraph (b)(4) of this section, the obtaining of this certification excuses the transferee from any liability otherwise imposed by section 1445 and §1.1445-1(e). However, section 1445 and the rules of this section do not impose any obligation upon a transferee to obtain a certification from the transferor; thus, a transferee may instead rely upon other means to ascertain the non-foreign status of the transferor. If, however, the transferee relies upon other means and the transferor was, in fact, a foreign person, then the transferee is subject to the liability imposed by section 1445 and § 1.1445-1(e).

A transferee is in no event required to rely upon other means to ascertain the non-foreign status of the transferor and may demand a certification of non-foreign status. If the certification is not provided, the transferee may withhold tax under section 1445 and will be considered, for purposes of sections 1461 through 1463, to have been required to withhold such tax.

(2) *Transferor's certification of non-foreign status.*—(i) *In general.*—A transferee of a U.S. real property interest is not required to withhold under section 1445(a) if, prior to or at the time of the transfer, the transferor furnishes to the transferee a certification that—

(A) States that the transferor is not a foreign person,

(B) Sets forth the transferor's name, identifying number and home address (in the case of an individual) or office address (in the case of an entity), and

(C) Is signed under penalties of perjury.

In general, a foreign person is a nonresident alien individual, foreign corporation, foreign partnership, foreign trust, or foreign estate, but not a resident alien individual. In this regard, see § 1.897-1(k). However, a foreign corporation that has made a valid election under section 897(i) is generally not treated as a foreign person for purposes of section 1445. In this regard, see § 1.1445-7. Pursuant to § 1.897-1(p), an individual's identifying number is the individual's Social Security number and any other person's identifying number is its U.S. employer identification number. A certification pursuant to this paragraph (b) must be verified as true and signed under penalties of perjury by a responsible officer in the case of a corporation, by a general partner in the case of a partnership, and by a trustee, executor, or equivalent fiduciary in the case of a trust or estate. No particular form is needed for a certification pursuant to this paragraph (b), nor is any particular language required, so long as the document meets the requirements of this paragraph (b)(2)(i). Samples of acceptable certifications are provided in paragraph (b)(2)(iii) of this section.

(ii) *Foreign corporation that has made election under section 897(i).*—A foreign corporation that has made a valid election under section 897(i) to be treated as a domestic corporation for purposes of section 897 may provide a certification of non-foreign status pursuant to this paragraph (b)(2). However, an electing foreign corporation must attach to such certification a copy of the acknowledgment of the election provided to the corporation by the Internal Revenue Service pursuant to § 1.897-3(d)(4). An acknowledgement is valid for this purpose only if it states that the information required by § 1.897-3 has been determined to be complete.

(iii) *Disregarded entities.*—A disregarded entity may not certify that it is the transferor of a U.S. real property interest, as the disregarded entity is not the transferor for U.S. tax purposes, including sections 897 and 1445. Rather, the owner of the disregarded entity is treated as the transferor of property and must provide a certificate of non-foreign status to avoid withholding under section 1445. A disregarded entity for these purposes means an entity that is disregarded as an entity separate from its owner under § 301.7701-3 of this chapter, a qualified REIT subsidiary as defined in section 856(i), or a qualified subchapter S subsidiary under section 1361(b)(3)(B). Any domestic entity must include in its certification of non-foreign status with respect to the transfer a certification that it is not a disregarded entity. This paragraph (b)(2)(iii) and the sample certification provided in paragraph (b)(2)(iv)(B) of this section (to the extent it addresses disregarded entities) is applicable for dispositions occurring [after]September 4, 2003.

(iv) *Sample certifications.*—(A) *Individual transferor.*—"Section 1445 of the Internal Revenue Code provides that a transferee (buyer) of a U.S. real property interest must withhold tax if the transferor (seller) is a foreign person. To inform the transferee (buyer) that withholding of tax is not required upon my disposition of a U.S. real property interest, I, [*name of transferor*], hereby certify the following:

1. I am not a nonresident alien for purposes of U.S. income taxation;

2. My U.S. taxpayer identifying number (Social Security number) is _____; and

3. My home address is

_____

_____

I understand that this certification may be disclosed to the Internal Revenue Service by the transferee and that any false statement I have made here could be punished by fine, imprisonment, or both.

Under penalties of perjury I declare that I have examined this certification and to the best of my knowledge and belief it is true, correct, and complete.

[Signature and Date]"

(B) *Entity transferor.*—"Section 1445 of the Internal Revenue Code provides that a transferee of a U.S. real property interest must withhold tax if the transferor is a foreign person. For U.S. tax purposes (including section 1445), the owner of a disregarded entity (which has legal title to a U.S. real property interest under local law) will be the transferor of the property and not the disregarded entity. To inform the transferee that withholding of tax is not required upon the disposition of a U.S. real property interest by [name of transferor], the undersigned hereby certifies the following on behalf of [name of the transferor]:

1. [Name of transferor] is not a foreign corporation, foreign partnership, foreign trust, or foreign estate (as those terms are defined in the Internal Revenue Code and Income Tax Regulations);

2. [Name of transferor] is not a disregarded entity as defined in § 1.1445-2(b)(2)(iii);

3. [Name of transferor]'s U.S. employer identification number is _____; and

4. [Name of transferor]'s office address is _____.

[Name of transferor] understands that this certification may be disclosed to the Internal Revenue Service by transferee and that any false statement contained herein could be punished by fine, imprisonment, or both.

Under penalties of perjury I declare that I have examined this certification and to the best of my knowledge and belief it is true, correct, and complete, and I further declare that I have authority to sign this document on behalf of [name of transferor].

[Signature(s) and date]

[Title(s)]"

(3) *Transferee must retain certification.*—If a transferee obtains a transferor's certification pursuant to the rules of this paragraph (b), then the transferee must retain that certification until the end of the fifth taxable year following the taxable year in which the transfer takes place. The transferee must retain the certification, and make it available to the Internal Revenue Service when requested in accordance with the requirements of section 6001 and regulations thereunder.

(4) *Reliance upon certification not permitted.*— (i) *In general.*—A transferee may not rely upon a transferor's certification pursuant to this paragraph (b) under the circumstances set forth in either subdivision (ii) or (iii) of this paragraph (b)(4). In either of those circumstances, a transferee's withholding obligation shall apply as if a certification had never been obtained, and the transferee is fully liable pursuant to section 1445 and § 1445-1(e) for any failure to withhold.

(ii) *Failure to attach IRS acknowledgment of election.*—A transferee that knows that the transferor is a foreign corporation may not rely upon a certification of non-foreign status provided by the corporation on the basis of election under section 897(i), unless there is attached to the certification a copy of the acknowledgment by the Internal Revenue Service of the corporation's election, as required by paragraph (b)(2)(ii) of this section.

(iii) *Knowledge of falsity.*—A transferee is not entitled to rely upon a transferor's certification if prior to or at the time of the transfer the transferee either—

(A) Has actual knowledge that the transferor's certification is false; or

(B) Receives a notice that the certification is false from a transferor's or transferee's agent, pursuant to § 1.1445-4.

(iv) *Belated notice of false certification.*—If after the date of the transfer a transferee receives a notice that a certification is false, then that transferee is entitled to rely upon the certification only with respect to consideration that was paid prior to receipt of the notice. Such a transferee is required to withhold a full 10 percent of the amount realized from the consideration that remains to be paid to the transferor if possible. Thus, if 10 percent or more of the amount realized remains to be paid to the transferor then the transferee is required to withhold and pay over the full 10 percent. The transferee must do so by withholding and paying over the entire amount of each successive payment of consideration to the transferor until the full 10 percent of the amount realized has been withheld and paid over. Amounts so withheld must be reported and paid over by the 20th day following the date on which each such payment of consideration is made. A transferee that is subject to the rules of this paragraph (b)(4)(iv) may not obtain a withholding certificate pursuant to § 1.1445-3, but must instead withhold and pay over the amounts required by this paragraph.

(c) *Transferred property not a U.S. real property interest.*—(1) *In general.*—No withholding is required under section 1445 if the transferee acquires only property that is not a U.S. real property interest. As defined in section 897(c) and § 1.897-1(c), a U.S. real property interest includes certain interests in U.S. corporations, as well as direct interests in real property and certain associated personal property. This paragraph (c) provides rules pursuant to which a person acquiring an interest in a U.S. corporation may determine that withholding is not required because that interest is not a U.S. real property interest. To determine whether an interest in tangible property constitutes a U.S. real property interest the acquisition of which would be subject to withholding, see § 1.897-1(b) and (c).

(2) *Interests in publicly traded entities.*—No withholding is required under section 1445(a) upon the acquisition of an interest in a domestic corporation if any class of stock of the corporation is regularly traded on an established securities market. This exemption shall apply if the disposition is incident to an initial public offering of stock pursuant to a registration statement filed with the Securities and Exchange Commission. Similarly, no withholding is required under section 1445(a) upon the acquisition of an interest in a publicly traded partnership or trust. However, the rule of this paragraph (c)(2) shall not apply to the acquisition, from a single transferor (or related transferors as defined in § 1.897-1(i)) in a single transaction (or related transactions), of an interest described in

§ 1.897-1(c)(2)(iii)(B) (relating to substantial amounts of non-publicly traded interests in publicly traded corporations) or to similar interests in publicly traded partnerships or trusts. The person making an acquisition described in the preceding sentence must otherwise determine whether withholding is required, pursuant to section 1445 and the regulations thereunder. Transactions shall be deemed to be related if they are undertaken within 90 days of one another or if it can otherwise be shown that they were undertaken in pursuance of a prearranged plan.

(3) *Transferee receives statement that interest in corporation is not a U.S. real property interest.*— (i) *In general.*—No withholding is required under section 1445(a) upon the acquisition of an interest in a domestic corporation, if the transferor provides the transferee with a copy of a statement, issued by the corporation pursuant to § 1.897-2(h), certifying that the interest is not a U.S. real property interest. In general, a corporation may issue such a statement only if the corporation was not a U.S. real property holding corporation at any time during the previous five years (or the period in which the interest was held by its present holder, if shorter) or if interests in the corporation ceased to be United States real property interests under section 897(c)(1)(B). (A corporation may not provide such a statement based on its determination that the interest in question is an interest solely as a creditor.) See § 1.897-2(f) and (h). The corporation may provide such a statement directly to the transferee at the transferor's request. The transferor must request such a statement prior to the transfer, and shall, to the extent possible, specify the anticipated date of the transfer. A corporation's statement may be relied upon for purposes of this paragraph (c)(3) only if the statement is dated not more than 30 days prior to the date of the transfer. A transferee may also rely upon a corporation's statement that is voluntarily provided by the corporation in response to a request from the transferee, if that statement otherwise complies with the requirements of this paragraph (c)(3) and § 1.897-2(h).

(ii) *Reliance on statement not permitted.*—A transferee is not entitled to rely upon a statement that a corporation is not a U.S. real property holding corporation if, prior to or at the time of the transfer, the transferee either—

(A) Has actual knowledge that the statement is false, or

(B) Receives a notice that the statement is false from a transferor's or transferee's agent, pursuant to § 1.1445-4.

Such a transferee's withholding obligations shall apply as if a statement had never been given, and such a transferee may be held fully liable pursuant to § 1.1445-1(e) for any failure to withhold.

(iii) *Belated notice of false statement.*—If after the date of the transfer, a transferee receives notice that a statement provided under § 1.1445-2(c)(3)(i) (that an interest in a corporation is not a U.S. real property interest) is false, then such transferee may rely on the statement only with respect to consideration that was paid prior to the receipt of the notice. Such a transferee is required to withhold a full 10 percent of the amount realized from the consideration that remains to be paid to the transferor, if possible. Thus, if 10 percent or more of the amount realized remains to be paid to the transferor, then the transferee is required to withhold any pay over the full 10 percent. The transferee must do so by withholding and paying over the entire amount of each successive payment of consideration to the transferor, until the full 10 percent of the amount realized has been withheld and paid over. Amounts so withheld must be reported and paid over by the 20th day following the date on which each such payment of consideration is made. A transferee that is subject to the rules of this paragraph 1.1445-2(c)(3)(iii) may not obtain a withholding certificate pursuant to § 1.1445-3, but must instead withhold and pay over the amounts required by this paragraph.

(d) *Exceptions to requirement of withholding.*— (1) *Purchase of residence for $300,000 or less.*—No withholding is required under section 1445(a) if one or more individual transferees acquire a U.S. real property interest for use as a residence and the amount realized on the transaction is $300,000 or less. For purposes of this section, a U.S. real property interest is acquired for use as a residence if on the date of the transfer the transferee (or transferees) has definite plans to reside at the property for at least 50 percent of the number of days that the property is used by any person during each of the first two 12-month periods following the date of the transfer. The number of days that the property will be vacant is not taken into account in determining the number of days such property is used by any person. A transferee shall be considered to reside at a property on any day on which a member of the transferee's family, as defined in section 267(c)(4), resides at the property. No form or other document need be filed with the Internal Revenue Service to establish a transferee's entitlement to rely upon the exception provided by this paragraph (d)(1). A transferee who fails to withhold in reliance upon this exception, but who does not in fact reside at the property for the minimum number of days set forth above, shall be liable for the failure to withhold (if the transferor was a foreign person and did not pay the full U.S. tax due on any gain recognized upon the transfer). However, if the transferee establishes that the failure to reside the minimum number of days was caused by a change in circumstances that could not reasonably have been anticipated at the time of the transfer, then the transferee shall not be liable for the failure to

Reg. § 1.1445-2(c)(3)

withhold. The exception provided by paragraph (d)(1) does not apply in any case where the transferee is other than an individual even if the property is acquired for or on behalf of an individual who will use the property as a residence. However, this exception applies regardless of the organizational structure of the transferor (i.e., regardless of whether the transferor is an individual, partnership, trust, corporation, etc.).

(2) *Coordination with nonrecognition provisions.*—(i) *In general.*—A transferee shall not be required to withhold under section 1445(a) with respect to the transfer of a U.S. real property interest if—

(A) The transferor notifies the transferee, in the manner described in paragraph (d)(2)(iii) of this section, that by reason of the operation of a nonrecognition provision of the Internal Revenue Code or the provisions of any United States treaty the transferor is not required to recognize any gain or loss with respect to the transfer; and

(B) By the 20th day after the date of the transfer the transferee provides a copy of the transferor's notice to the Director, Philadelphia Service Center, at the address provided in § 1.1445-1(g)(10), together with a cover letter setting forth the name, identifying number, and home address (in the case of an individual) or office address (in the case of an entity) of the transferee providing the notice to the Service.

The rule of this paragraph (d)(2)(i) is subject to the exceptions set forth in paragraph (d)(2)(ii). For purposes of this paragraph (d)(2) a nonrecognition provision is any provision of the Internal Revenue Code for not recognizing gain or loss.

(ii) *Exceptions.*—A transferee may not rely upon the rule of paragraph (d)(2)(i) of this section, and must therefore withhold under section 1445(a) with respect to the transfer of a U.S. real property interest, if either:

(A) The transferor qualifies for nonrecognition treatment with respect to part, but not all, of the gain realized by the transferor upon the transfer; or

(B) The transferee knows or has reason to know that the transferor is not entitled to the nonrecognition treatment claimed by the transferor.
In either of the above circumstances the transferee or transferor may request a withholding certificate from the Internal Revenue Service pursuant to the rules of § 1.1445-3.

(iii) *Contents of the notice.*—No particular form is required for a transferor's notice to a transferee that the transferor is not required to recognize gain or loss with respect to a transfer. The notice must be verified as true and signed under penalties of perjury by the transferor, by a responsible officer in the case of a corporation, by a general partner in the case of a partnership, and by a trustee or equivalent fiduciary in the case of a trust or estate. The following information must be set forth in paragraphs labeled to correspond with the designation set forth as follows—

(A) A statement that the document submitted constitutes a notice of a nonrecognition transaction or a treaty provision pursuant to the requirements of § 1.1445-2(d)(2);

(B) The name, identifying number, and home address (in the case of an individual) or office address (in the case of an entity) of the transferor submitting the notice;

(C) A statement that the transferor is not required to recognize any gain or loss with respect to the transfer;

(D) A brief description of the transfer; and

(E) A brief summary of the law and facts supporting the claim that recognition of gain or loss is not required with respect to the transfer.

(iv) *No notice allowed.*—The provisions of this paragraph (d)(2) do not apply to exclusions from income under section 121, to simultaneous like-kind exchanges under section 1031 that do not qualify for nonrecognition treatment in their entirety (see paragraph (d)(2)(ii)(A) of this section), and to nonsimultaneous like-kind exchanges under section 1031 where the transferee cannot determine that the exchange has been completed and all the conditions for nonrecognition have been satisfied at the time it is otherwise required to pay the section 1445 withholding tax and file the withholding tax return (Form 8288, "U.S. Withholding Tax Return for Dispositions by Foreign Persons of U.S. Real Property Interests"). In these cases, the transferee is excused from withholding only upon the timely application for and receipt of a withholding certificate under § 1.1445-3 (see § 1.1445-3(b)(5) and (6) for specific rules applicable to transactions under sections 121 and 1031). This paragraph (d)(2)(iv) is applicable for dispositions and exchanges occurring [after] September 4, 2003.

(3) *Special procedural rules applicable to foreclosures.*—(i) *Amount to be withheld.*—(A) *Foreclosures.*—A transferee that acquires a U.S. real property interest pursuant to a repossession or foreclosure on such property under a mortgage, security agreement, deed of trust or other instrument securing a debt must withhold tax under section 1445(a) equal to 10 percent of the amount realized on such sale. Such amount must be reported and paid over to the Service under the general rules of § 1.1445-1. However, if the transferee complies with the notice requirements of § 1.1445-2(d)(3)(ii) and (iii), such transferee may report and pay over to the Service on or before the 20th day following the final determination by a court or trustee with jurisdiction over the foreclosure action, the lesser of:

(1) the amount otherwise required to be withheld under section 1445(a), or

(2) the "alternative amount" as defined in the succeeding sentence.

The alternative amount is the entire amount, if any, determined by a court or trustee with jurisdiction over the matter, that accrues to the debtor/transferor out of the amount realized from the foreclosure sale. The amount of any mortgage, lien, or other security agreement secured by the property, that is terminated, assumed by another person, or otherwise extinguished (as to the debtor/transferor) shall not be treated as an amount that accrues to the debtor/transferor for purposes of this §1.1445-2(d)(3)(i)(A). If the alternative amount is zero, no withholding is required. Any difference between the amount withheld at the time of the foreclosure sale and the amount to be reported and paid over to the Service must be transferred to the court or trustee with jurisdiction over the foreclosure action. Amounts withheld, if any, are to be reported and paid over to the Service by using Forms 8288 and 8288-A in conformity with §1.1445-1(d).

(B) *Deeds in lieu of foreclosures.*—A transferee of a U.S. real property interest pursuant to a deed in lieu of foreclosure must withhold tax equal to 10 percent of the amount realized by the debtor/transferor on the transfer. However, no withholding is required if:

(1) The transferee is the only person with a security interest in the property,

(2) No cash or other property (other than incidental fees incurred with respect to the transfer) is paid, directly or indirectly, to any person with respect to the transfer, and

(3) The notice requirements of §1.1445-2(d)(3) are satisfied.

The amount withheld, if any, must be reported and paid over to the Service not later than the 20th day following the date of transfer. In a case where withholding would otherwise be required, a withholding certificate may be requested in accordance with §1.1445-3.

(ii) *Notice to the court or trustee in a foreclosure action.*—(A) *Notice on day of purchase.*—A transferee in a foreclosure sale that chooses to use the special rules applicable to foreclosures must provide notice to the court or trustee with jurisdiction over the foreclosure action on the day the property is transferred with respect to such transferee's withholding obligation. No particular form is necessary but the notice must set forth the transferee's name, home address in the case of an individual, office address in the case of an entity, a brief description of the property, the date of the transfer, the amount realized on the sale of the foreclosed property and the amount withheld under section 1445(a).

(B) *Notice whether amount withheld or alternative amount is reported and paid over the Ser-*vice.—A purchaser/transferee in a foreclosure that chooses to use the special rules applicable to foreclosures must provide notice to the court or trustee with jurisdiction over the foreclosure action regarding whether the amount withheld or the alternative amount will be (or has been) reported and paid over to the Service. The notice should set forth all the information required by the preceding paragraph (d)(3)(ii)(A), the amount withheld or alternative amount that will be (or has been) reported and paid over to the Service, and the amount that will be (or has been) paid over to the court or trustee.

(iii) *Notice to the Service.*—(A) *General rule.*—A transferee that in reliance upon the rules of this paragraph (d)(3) withholds an alternative amount (or does not withhold because the alternative amount is zero) must, on or before the 20th day following the final determination by a court or trustee in a foreclosure action or on or before the 20th day following the date of the transfer with respect to a transfer pursuant to a deed in lieu of foreclosure, provide notice thereof to the Assistant Commissioner (International) at the address provided in §1.1445-1(g)(10). (The filing of such a notice shall not relieve a creditor of any obligation it may have to file a notice pursuant to section 6050J and the regulations thereunder.) No particular form is required but the following information must be set forth in paragraphs labelled to correspond with the numbers set forth below.

(1) A statement that the notice constitutes a notice of foreclosure action or transfer pursuant to a deed in lieu of foreclosure under §1.1445-2(d)(3).

(2) The name, identifying number, and home address (in the case of an individual) or office address (in the case of an entity) of the purchaser/transferee.

(3) The name, identifying number, and home address (in the case of an individual) or office address (in the case of an entity) of the debtor/transferor.

(4) In a foreclosure action, the date of the final determination by a court or trustee regarding the distribution of the amount realized from the foreclosure sale. In a transfer pursuant to a deed in lieu of foreclosure, the date the property is transferred to the purchaser/transferee.

(5) A brief description of the property.

(6) The amount realized from the foreclosure sale or with respect to the transfer pursuant to a deed in lieu of foreclosure.

(7) The alternative amount.

(B) *Special rule for lenders required to file Form 1099-A where the alternative amount is zero.*— A person required under section 6050J to file Form 1099-A does not have to comply with the notice requirement of §1.1445-2(d)(3)(iii)(A) if the alternative amount is zero. In such case, the filing of the Form 1099-A will be deemed to satisfy the notice requirement of § 1.1445-2(d)(3)(iii)(A).

(iv) *Requirements not applicable.*—A transferee is not required to withhold tax or provide notice pursuant to the rules of this paragraph (d)(3) if no substantive withholding liability applies to the transfer of the property by the debtor/transferor. For example, if the debtor/transferor provides the transferee with a certification of non-foreign status pursuant to paragraph (b) of this section, then no substantive withholding liability would exist with respect to the acquisition of the property from the debtor transferor. In such a case, no withholding of tax or notice to the Internal Revenue Service is required of the transferee with respect to the repossession or foreclosure.

(v) *Anti-abuse rule.*—If a U.S. real property interest is transferred in foreclosure or pursuant to a deed in lieu of foreclosure for a principal purpose of avoiding the requirements of section 1445(a), then the provisions of this paragraph (d)(3) shall not apply to the transfer and the transferee shall be fully liable for any failure to withhold with respect to the transfer. A principal purpose to avoid section 1445(a) will be presumed (subject to rebuttal on the basis of all relevant facts and circumstances) if:

(A) The transferee acquires property in which it, or a related party, has a security interest;

(B) The security interest did not arise in connection with the debtor/transferor's or a related party's or predecessor in interest's acquisition, improvement, or maintenance of the property; and

(C) The total amount of all debts secured by the property exceeds 90 percent of the fair market value of the property.

(4) *Installment payments.*—A transferee of a U.S. real property interest is not required to withhold under section 1445 when making installment payments on an obligation arising out of a disposition that took place before January 1, 1985. With respect to dispositions that take place after December 31, 1984, the transferee shall be required to satisfy its entire withholding obligation within the time specified in § 1.1445-1(c) regardless of the amount actually paid by the transferee. Thereafter, no withholding is required upon further installment payments on an obligation arising out of the transfer. A transferee that is unable to satisfy its entire withholding obligation within the time specified in § 1.1445-1(c) may request a withholding certificate pursuant to § 1.1445-3.

(5) *Acquisitions by governmental bodies.*—No withholding of tax is required under section 1445 with respect to any acquisition of property by

the United States, a state or possession of the United States, a political subdivision thereof, or the District of Columbia.

(6) [Reserved.]

(7) *Withholding certificate obtained by transferee or transferor.*—No withholding is required under section 1445(a) if the transferee is provided with a withholding certificate that so specifies. Either the transferor or the transferee may seek a withholding certificate from the Internal Revenue Service, pursuant to the provisions of § 1.1445-3.

(8) *Amount realized by transferor is zero.*—If the amount realized by the transferor on a transfer of a U.S. real property interest is zero, no withholding is required.

(e) *Effective date for taxpayer identification numbers.*—The requirement in paragraphs (d)(2)(i)(B), (d)(2)(iii)(B), and (d)(3)(iii)(A)(2) and (3) of this section that taxpayer identification numbers be provided (in all cases) is applicable for dispositions of U.S. real property interests occurring after November 3, 2003. [Reg. § 1.1445-2.]

□ [*T.D.* 8113, 12-18-86. *Amended by T.D.* 8198, 5-4-88 *and T.D.* 9082, 8-4-2003.]

[Reg. § 1.1445-3]

§ 1.1445-3. Adjustments to amount required to be withheld pursuant to withholding certificate.—(a) *In general.*—Withholding under section 1445(a) may be reduced or eliminated pursuant to a withholding certificate issued by the Internal Revenue Service in accordance with the rules of this section. A withholding certificate may be issued by the Service in cases where reduced withholding is appropriate (see paragraph (c) of this section), where the transferor is exempt from U.S. tax (see paragraph (d) of this section), or where an agreement for the payment of tax is entered into with the Service (see paragraph (e) of this section). A withholding certificate that is obtained prior to a transfer notifies the transferee that no withholding is required. A withholding certificate that is obtained after a transfer has been made may authorize a normal refund or an early refund pursuant to paragraph (g) of this section. Either a transferee or transferor may apply for a withholding certificate. The Internal Revenue Service will act upon an application for a withholding certificate not later than the 90th day after it is received. Solely for this purpose (i.e., determining the day upon which the 90-day period commences), an application is received by the Service on the date that all information necessary for the Service to make a determination is provided by the applicant. In no event, however, will a withholding certificate be issued without the transferor's identifying number. (For rules regarding whether an application for a withholding certificate has been timely submitted, see § 1.1445-1(c)(2).) The Service may deny a request for a withholding certificate where, after due notice, an applicant fails to provide information necessary for the Service to make a determination. The Service will act upon an application for an early refund not later than the 90th day after it is received. An application for an early refund must either (1) include a copy of a withholding certificate issued by the Service with respect to the transaction, or (2) be combined with an application for a withholding certificate. Where an application for an early refund is combined with an application for a withholding certificate, the Service will act upon both applications not later than the 90th day after receipt. In the case of an application for a certificate based on nonconforming security under paragraph (e)(3)(v) of this section, and in unusually complicated cases, the Service may be unable to provide a final withholding certificate by the 90th day. In such a case the Service will notify the applicant, by the 45th day after receipt of the application, that additional processing time will be necessary. The Service's notice may request additional information or explanation concerning particular aspects of the application, and will provide a target date for final action (contingent upon the applicant's timely submission of any requested information). A withholding certificate issued pursuant to the provisions of this section serves to fulfill the requirements of section 1445(b)(4) concerning qualifying statements, section 1445(c)(1) concerning the transferor's maximum tax liability, or section 1445(c)(2) concerning the Secretary's authority to prescribe reduced withholding.

(b) *Applications for withholding certificates.*— (1) *In general.*—An application for a withholding certificate must be submitted to the Director, Philadelphia Service Center, at the address provided in §1.1445-1(g)(10). An application for a withholding certificate must be signed by a responsible officer in the case of a corporation, by a general partner in the case of a partnership, by a trustee, executor, or equivalent fiduciary in the case of a trust or estate, and in the case of an individual by the individual himself. A duly authorized agent may sign the application but the application must contain a valid power of attorney authorizing the agent to sign the application on behalf of the applicant. The person signing the application must verify under penalties of perjury that all representations made in connection with the application are true, correct, and complete to his knowledge and belief. No particular form is required for an application, but the application must set forth the information described in paragraphs (b)(2), (3), and (4), and to the extent applicable, paragraph (b)(5) or (6) of this section.

(2) *Parties to the transaction.*—The application must set forth the name, address, and identifying number of the person submitting the application (specifying whether that person is the transferee or transferor), and the name, address, and identifying number of other parties to the transaction (specifying whether each such party is a transferee or transferor). The Service will deny the application if complete information, including the identifying numbers of all the parties, is not provided. Thus, for example, the applicant should determine if an identifying number exists for each party, and, if none exists for a particular party, the applicant should notify the particular party of the obligation to get an identifying number before the application can be submitted to the Service. The address provided in the case of an individual must be that individual's home address, and the address provided in the case of an entity must be that entity's office address. A mailing address may be provided in addition to, but not in lieu of, a home address or office address.

(3) *Real property interest to be transferred.*— The application must set forth information concerning the U.S. real property interest with respect to which the withholding certificate is sought, including the type of interest, the contract price, and, in the case of an interest in real property, its location and general description, or in the case of an interest in a U.S. real property holding corporation, the class or type and amount of the interest.

(4) *Basis for certificate.*—(i) *Reduced withholding.*—If a withholding certificate is sought on the basis of a claim that reduced withholding is appropriate, the application must include:

(A) A calculation of the maximum tax that may be imposed on the disposition in accordance with paragraph (c)(2) of this section. Such calculation must be accompanied by a copy of the relevant contract and depreciation schedules or other evidence that confirms the contract price and adjusted basis of the property. If no depreciation schedules are provided, the application must state the nature of the use of the property and why depreciation was not allowable. Evidence that supports any claimed adjustment to the maximum tax on the disposition must also be provided;

(B) A calculation of the transferor's unsatisfied withholding liability, or evidence supporting the claim that no such liability exists, in accordance with paragraph (c)(3) of this section; and

(C) In the case of a request for a special reduction of withholding pursuant to paragraph (c)(4) of this section, a statement of law and facts in support of the request.

(ii) *Exemption.*—If a withholding certificate is sought on the basis of the transferor's exemption from U.S. tax, the application must set forth a brief statement of the law and facts that support the claimed exemption. In this regard, see paragraph (d) of this section.

(iii) *Agreement.*—If a withholding certificate is sought on the basis of an agreement for the payment of tax, the application must include a signed copy of the agreement proposed by the applicant and a copy of the security instrument (if any) proposed by the applicant. In this regard, see paragraph (e) of this section.

(5) *Special rule for exclusions from income under section 121.*—A withholding certificate may be sought on the basis of a section 121 exclusion as a reduction in the amount of tax due under paragraph (c)(2)(v) of this section. The application must include information establishing that the transferor, who is a nonresident alien individual at the time of the sale (and is therefore subject to sections 897 and 1445) is entitled to claim the benefits of section 121. For example, a claim for reduced withholding as a result of section 121 must include information that the transferor occupied the U.S. real property interest as his or her personal residence for the required period of time.

(6) *Special rule for like-kind exchanges under Section 1031.*—A withholding certificate may be requested with respect to a like-kind exchange under section 1031 as a transaction subject to a nonrecognition provision under paragraph (c)(2)(ii) of this section. The application must include information substantiating the requirements of section 1031. The IRS may require additional information during the course of the application process to determine that the requirements of section 1031 are satisfied. In the case of a deferred like-kind exchange, the withholding agent is excused from reporting and paying the withholding tax to the IRS within 20 days after the transfer only if an application for a withholding certificate is submitted prior to or on the date of transfer. See § 1.1445-1(c)(2) for rules concerning delayed reporting and payment where an application for a withholding certificate has been submitted to the IRS prior to or on the date of transfer.

(c) *Adjustment of amount required to be withheld.*—(1) *In general.*—The Internal Revenue Service may issue a withholding certificate that excuses withholding or that permits the transferee to withhold an adjusted amount reflecting the transferor's maximum tax liability. The transferor's maximum tax liability is the sum of—

(i) The maximum amount which could be imposed as tax under section 871 or 882 upon the transferor's disposition of the subject real property interest, as determined under paragraph (c)(2) of this section, and

(ii) The transferor's unsatisfied withholding liability with respect to the subject real property interest, as determined under paragraph (c)(3) of this section.

In addition, the Internal Revenue Service may issue a withholding certificate that permits the transferee to withhold a reduced amount if the Service determines pursuant to paragraph (c)(4) of this section that reduced withholding will not jeopardize the collection of tax.

(2) *Maximum tax imposed on disposition.*— The first element of the transferor's maximum tax liability is the maximum amount which the transferor could be required to pay as tax upon the disposition of the subject real property interest. In the case of an individual transferor that amount will generally be the contract price of the property minus its adjusted basis, multiplied by the maximum individual income tax rate applicable to long-term capital gain. In the case of a corporate transferor, that amount will generally be the contract price of the property minus its adjusted basis, multiplied by the maximum corporate income tax rate applicable to long-term capital gain. However, that amount must be adjusted to take into account the following:

(i) Any reduction of tax to which the transferor is entitled under the provisions of a U.S. income tax treaty;

(ii) The effect of any nonrecognition provision that is applicable to the transaction;

(iii) Any losses realized and recognized upon the previous disposition of U.S. real property interests during the taxable year;

(iv) Any amount that is required to be treated as ordinary income; and

(v) Any other factor that may increase or reduce the tax upon the disposition.

(3) *Transferor's unsatisfied withholding liability.*—(i) *In general.*—The second element of the transferor's maximum tax liability is the transferor's unsatisfied withholding liability. That liability is the amount of any tax that the transferor was required to but did not withhold and pay over under section 1445 upon the acquisition of the subject U.S. real property interest or a predecessor interest. The transferor's unsatisfied withholding liability is included in the calculation of maximum tax liability so that such prior withholding liability can be satisfied by the transferee's withholding upon the current transfer. Alternatively, the transferor's unsatisfied withholding liability may be disregarded for purposes of calculating the maximum tax liability, if either—

(A) Such prior withholding liability is fully satisfied by a payment that is made with the application submitted pursuant to this section; or

(B) An agreement is entered into for the payment of that liability pursuant to the rules of paragraph (e) of this section. Because section 1445 only requires withholding after December 31, 1984, no transferor's unsatisfied withholding liability can exist unless the transferor acquired the subject or predecessor real property interest after that date. For purposes of this paragraph (c), a predecessor interest is one that was exchanged for the subject U.S. real property interest in a transaction in which the transferor was not required to recognize the full amount of the gain or loss realized upon the transfer.

(ii) *Evidence that no unsatisfied withholding liability exists.*—For purposes of paragraph (b)(4)(i)(B) of this section (concerning information that must be submitted with an application for a withholding certificate), evidence that the transferor has no unsatisfied withholding liability includes any one of the following documents:

(A) Evidence that the transferor acquired the subject or predecessor real property interest prior to January 1, 1985;

(B) A copy of the Form 8288 that was filed by the transferor, and proof of payment of the amount shown due thereon, with respect to the transferor's acquisition of the subject or predecessor real property interest;

(C) A copy of a withholding certificate with respect to the transferor's acquisition of the subject or predecessor real property interest, plus a copy of Form 8288 and proof of payment with respect to any withholding required under that certificate;

(D) A copy of the non-foreign certification furnished by the person from whom the subject or predecessor U.S. real property interest was acquired, executed at the time of that acquisition;

(E) Evidence that the transferor purchased the subject or predecessor real property for $300,000 or less, and a statement, signed by the transferor under penalties of perjury, that the transferor purchased the property for use as a residence within the meaning of §1.1445-2(d)(1);

(F) Evidence that the person from whom the transferor acquired the subject or predecessor U.S. real property interest fully paid any tax imposed on that transaction pursuant to section 897;

(G) A copy of a notice of nonrecognition treatment provided to the transferor pursuant to §1.1445-2(d)(2) by the person from whom the transferor acquired the subject or predecessor U.S. real property interest; and

(H) A statement, signed by the transferor under penalties of perjury, setting forth the facts and circumstances that supported the transferor's conclusion that no withholding was required under section 1445(a) with respect to the transferor's acquisition of the subject or predecessor real property interest.

(4) *Special reduction of amount required to be withheld.*—The Internal Revenue Service may, in its discretion, issue a withholding certificate that permits the transferee to withhold a reduced amount based upon a determination that reduced withholding will not jeopardize the collection of tax. A transferor that requests a withholding certificate pursuant to this paragraph (c)(4) is required pursuant to paragraph (b)(4)(i)(C) of this section to submit a statement

of law and facts in support of the request. That statement must explain why the transferor is unable to enter into an agreement for the payment of tax pursuant to paragraph (e) of this section.

(d) *Transferor's exemption from U.S. tax.*—(1) *In general.*—The Internal Revenue Service will issue a withholding certificate that excuses all withholding by a transferee if it is established that:

(i) The transferor's gain from the disposition of the subject U.S. real property interest will be exempt from U.S. tax, and

(ii) The transferor has no unsatisfied withholding liability.

For the available exemptions, see paragraph (d)(2) of this section. The transferor's unsatisfied withholding liability shall be determined in accordance with the provisions of paragraph (c)(3) of this section. A transferor that is entitled to a reduction of (rather than an exemption from) U.S. tax may obtain a withholding certificate to that effect pursuant to the provisions of paragraph (c) of this section.

(2) *Available exemptions.*—A transferor's gain from the disposition of a U.S. real property interest may be exempt from U.S. tax because either:

(i) The transferor is an integral part or controlled entity of a foreign government and the disposition of the subject property is not a commercial activity, as determined pursuant to section 892 and the regulations thereunder; or

(ii) The transferor is entitled to the benefits of an income tax treaty that provides for such an exemption (subject to the limitations imposed by section 1125(c) of Pub. L. 96-499, which, in general, overrides such benefits as of January 1, 1985).

(e) *Agreement for the payment of tax.*—(1) *In general.*—The Internal Revenue Service will issue a withholding certificate that excuses withholding or that permits a transferee to withhold a reduced amount, if either the transferee or the transferor enters into an agreement for the payment of tax pursuant to the provisions of this paragraph (e). An agreement for the payment of tax is a contract between the Service and any other person that consists of two necessary elements. Those elements are—

(i) A contract between the Service and the other person, setting forth in detail the rights and obligations of each; and

(ii) A security instrument or other form of security acceptable to the Director, Foreign Operations District.

(2) *Contents of agreement.*—(i) *In general.*—An agreement for the payment of tax must cover an amount described in subdivision (ii) or (iii) of this paragraph (e)(2). The agreement may either provide adequate security for the payment of the chosen amount in accordance with paragraph (e)(3) of this section, or provide for the payment

of that amount through a combination of security and withholding of tax by the transferee.

(ii) *Tax that would otherwise be withheld.*—An agreement for the payment of tax may cover the amount of tax that would otherwise be required to be withheld pursuant to section 1445(a). In addition to the amount computed pursuant to section 1445(a), the applicant must agree to pay interest upon that amount, at the rate established under section 6621, with respect to the period between the date on which the tax imposed by section 1445(a) would otherwise be due (*i.e.*, the 20th day after the date of transfer) and the date on which the transferor's payment of tax with respect to the disposition will be due under the agreement. The amount of interest agreed upon must be paid by the applicant regardless of whether or not the Service is required to draw upon any security provided pursuant to the agreement. The interest may be paid either with the return or by the Service drawing upon the security.

(iii) *Maximum tax liability.*—An agreement for the payment of tax may cover the transferor's maximum tax liability, determined in accordance with paragraph (c) of this section. The agreement must also provide for the payment of an additional amount equal to 25 percent of the amount determined under paragraph (c) of this section. This additional amount secures the interest and penalties that would accrue between the date of a failure to file a return and pay tax with respect to the disposition, and the date on which the Service collects upon that liability pursuant to the agreement. Such additional amount will only be collected if the Service finds it necessary to draw upon any security provided due to the transferor's failure to file a return and pay tax with respect to the relevant disposition.

(3) *Major types of security.*—(i) *In general.*—The following are the major types of security acceptable to the Service. Further details with respect to the terms and conditions of each type may be specified by Revenue Procedure.

(ii) *Bond with surety or guarantor.*—The Service may accept as security with respect to a transferor's tax liability a bond that is executed with a satisfactory surety or guarantor. Only the following persons may act as surety or guarantor for this purpose:

(A) A surety company holding a certificate of authority from the Secretary as an acceptable surety on Federal bonds, as listed in Treasury Department Circular No. 570, published annually in the Federal Register on the first working day of July;

(B) A person that is engaged within or without the United States in the conduct of a banking, financing, or similar business under the principles of § 1.864-4(c)(5) and that is subject to

U.S. or foreign local or national regulation of such business, if that person is otherwise acceptable to the Service; and

(C) A person that is engaged within or without the United States in the conduct of an insurance business that is subject to U.S. or foreign local or national regulation, if that person is otherwise acceptable to the Service.

(iii) *Bond with collateral.*—The Service may accept as security with respect to a transferor's tax liability a bond that is secured by acceptable collateral. All collateral must be deposited with a responsible financial institution acting as escrow agent or, in the Service's discretion, with the Service. Only the following types of collateral are acceptable:

(A) Bonds, notes, or other public debt obligations of the United States, in accordance with the rules of 31 CFR Part 225; and

(B) A certified cashier's, or treasurer's check, drawn on an entity acceptable to the Service that is engaged within or without the United States in the conduct of a banking, financing, or similar business under the principles of § 1.864-4(c)(5) and that is subject to U.S. or foreign local or national regulation of such business.

(iv) *Letter of credit.*—The Service may accept as security with respect to a transferor's tax liability an irrevocable letter of credit. The Service may accept a letter of credit issued by an entity acceptable to the Service that is engaged within or without the United States in the conduct of a banking, financing or similar business under the principles of § 1.884-4(c)(5) and that is subject to U.S. or foreign local or national regulation of such business. However, the Director will accept a letter of credit from an entity that is not engaged in trade or business in the United States only if such letter may be drawn on an advising bank within the United States.

(v) *Guarantees and other nonconforming security.*—(A) *Guarantee.*—The Service may in its discretion accept as security with respect to a transferor's tax liability the applicant's guarantee that it will pay such liability. The Service will in general accept such a guarantee only from a corporation, foreign or domestic, any class of stock of which is regularly traded on an established securities market on the date of the transfer.

(B) *Other forms of security.*—The Service may in unusual circumstances and at its discretion accept any form of security that it finds to be adequate. An application for a withholding certificate that proposes a form of security that does not conform with any of the preferred types set forth in paragraph (e)(3)(ii) through (iv) of this section or any relevant Revenue Procedure must include:

Reg. § 1.1445-3(e)(3)(v)(B)

(1) A detailed statement of the facts and circumstances supporting the use of the proposed form of security, and

(2) A memorandum of law concerning the validity and enforceability of the proposed form of security.

(4) *Terms of security instrument.*—Any security instrument that is furnished pursuant to this section must provide that—

(i) The amount of each deposit of estimated tax that will be required with respect to the gain realized on the subject disposition may be collected by levy upon the security as of the date following the date on which each such deposit is due (unless such deposit is timely made);

(ii) The entire amount of the liability may be collected by levy upon the security at any time during the nine months following the date on which the payment of tax with respect to the subject disposition is due, subject to release of the security upon the full payment of the tax and any interest and penalties due. If the transferor requests an extension of time to file a return with respect to the disposition, then the Director may require that the term of the security instrument be extended until the date that is nine months after the filing deadline as extended.

(f) *Amendments to application for withholding certificate.*—(1) *In general.*—An applicant for a withholding certificate may amend an otherwise complete application by submitting an amending statement to the Director, Philadelphia Service Center, at the address provided in §1.1445-1(g)(10). The amending statement shall provide the information required by §1.1445-3(f)(3) and must be signed and accompanied by a penalties of perjury statement in accordance with §1.1445-3(b)(1).

(2) *Extension of time for the Service to process requests for withholding certificates.*—(i) *In general.*—If an amending statement is submitted, the time in which the Internal Revenue Service must act upon the amended application shall be extended by 30 days.

(ii) *Substantial amendments.*—If an amending statement is submitted and the Service finds that the statement substantially amends the facts of the underlying application or substantially alters the terms of the withholding certificate as requested in the initial application, the time within which the Service must act upon the amended application shall be extended by 60 days. The applicant shall be so notified.

(iii) *Amending statement received after the requested withholding certificate has been signed by the Director, Philadelphia Service Center.*—If an amending statement is received after the withholding certificate, drafted in response to the underlying application, has been signed by the Director, Philadelphia Service Center, or his delegate and prior to the day such certificate is mailed to the applicant, the time in which the Service must act upon the amended application shall be extended by 90 days. The applicant will be so notified.

(3) *Information required to be submitted.*—No particular form is required for an amending statement but the statement must provide the following information:

(i) *Identification of applicant.*—The amending statement must set forth the name, address and identifying number of the person submitting the amending statement (specifying whether that person is the transferee or transferor).

(ii) *Date of underlying application.*—The amending statement must set forth the date of the underlying application for a withholding certificate.

(iii) *Real property interest to be (or that has been) transferred.*—The amending statement must set forth a brief description of the real property interest with respect to which the underlying application for a withholding certificate was submitted.

(iv) *Amending information.*—The amending statement must fully set forth the basis for the amendment including any modification of the facts supporting the application for a withholding certificate and any change sought in the terms of the withholding certificate.

(g) *Early refund of overwithheld amounts.*—If a transferor receives a withholding certificate pursuant to this section, and an amount greater than that specified in the certificate was withheld by the transferee, then pursuant to the rules of this paragraph (g) the transferor may apply for a refund (without interest) of the excess amount prior to the date on which the transferor's tax return is due (without extensions). (Any interest payable on refunds issued after the filing of a tax return shall be determined in accordance with the provisions of section 6611 and regulations thereunder.) An application for an early refund must be addressed to the Director, Philadelphia Service Center, at the address provided in §1.1445-1(g)(10). No particular form is required for the application, but the following information must be set forth in separate paragraphs numbered to correspond with the number given below:

(1) Name, address, and identifying number of the transferor seeking the refund;

(2) Amount required to be withheld pursuant to the withholding certificate issued by Internal Revenue Service;

(3) Amount withheld by the transferee (attach a copy of Form 8288-A stamped by IRS pursuant to §1.1445-1(c));

(4) Amount to be refunded to the transferor. An application for an early refund cannot be processed unless the required copy of Form

8288-A (or substantial evidence of the amount withheld in the case of a failure to receive Form 8288-A as provided in § 1.1445-1(f)(3)) is attached to the application. If an application for a withholding certificate based upon the transferor's maximum tax liability is submitted after the transfer takes place, then that application may be combined with an application for an early refund. The Service will act upon a claim for refund within the time limits set forth in paragraph (a) of this section.

(h) *Effective date for taxpayer identification numbers.*—The requirement in paragraphs (b)(2), (f)(3)(i), and (g)(1) of this section that taxpayer identification numbers be provided (in all cases) is applicable for dispositions of U.S. real property interests occurring after November 3, 2003. [Reg. § 1.1445-3.]

☐ [*T.D.* 8113, 12-18-86. *Amended by T.D.* 9082, 8-4-2003.]

[Reg. §1.1445-4]

§1.1445-4. Liability of agents.—(a) *Duty to provide notice of false certification or statement to transferee.*—A transferee's or transferor's agent must provide notice to the transferee if either—

(1) The transferee is furnished with a non-U.S. real property interest statement pursuant to § 1.1445-2(c)(3) and the agent knows that the statement is false; or

(2) The transferee is furnished with a nonforeign certification pursuant to § 1.1445-2(b)(2) and either (i) the agent knows that the certification is false, or (ii) the agent represents a transferor that is a foreign corporation.

An agent that represents a transferor that is a foreign corporation is not required to provide notice to the transferee if the foreign corporation provided a nonforeign certification to the transferee prior to such agent's employment and the agent does not know that the corporation did so.

(b) *Duty to provide notice of false certification or statement to entity or fiduciary.*—A transferee's or transferor's agent must provide notice to an entity or fiduciary that plans to carry out a transaction described in section 1445(e)(1), (2), (3), or (4) if either—

(1) The entity or fiduciary is furnished with a non-U.S. real property interest statement pursuant to § 1.1445-5(b)(4)(iii) and the agent knows that such statement is false; or

(2) The entity or fiduciary is furnished with a non-foreign certification pursuant to § 1.1445-5(b)(3)(ii) and either (i) the agent knows that such certification is false, or (ii) the agent represents a foreign corporation that made such a certification.

(c) *Procedural requirements.*—(1) *Notice to transferee, entity, or fiduciary.*—An agent who is required by this section to provide notice must do so in writing as soon as possible after learning of the false certification or statement, but not later than the date of the transfer (prior to the transferee's payment of consideration). If an agent first learns of a false certification or statement after the date of the transfer, notice must be given by the third day following that discovery. The notice must state that the certification or statement is false and may not be relied upon. The notice must also explain the possible consequences to the recipient of a failure to withhold. The notice need not disclose the information on which the agent's statement is based. The following is an example of an acceptable notice: "This is to notify you that you may be required to withhold tax in connection with (*describe transaction*). You have been provided with a certification of nonforeign status (or a non-U.S. real property interest statement) in connection with that transaction. I have learned that that document is false. Therefore, you may not rely upon it as a basis for failing to withhold under section 1445 of the Internal Revenue Code. Section 1445 provides that any person who acquires a U.S. real property interest from a foreign person must withhold a tax equal to 10 percent of the total purchase price. (The term 'U.S. real property interest' includes real property, stock in U.S. corporations whose assets are primarily real property, and some personal property associated with realty.) Any person who is required to withhold but fails to do so can be held liable for the tax. Thus, if you do not withhold the 10 percent tax from the total that you pay on this transaction, you could be required to pay the tax yourself, if what you are acquiring is a U.S. real property interest and the transferor is a foreign person. Tax that is withheld must be promptly paid over to the IRS using Form 8288. For further information see sections 897 and 1445 of the Internal Revenue Code and the related regulations."

(2) *Notice to be filed with IRS.*—An agent who is required by paragraph (a) or (b) of this section to provide notice to a transferee, entity, or fiduciary must furnish a copy of that notice to the Internal Revenue Service by the date on which the notice is required to be given to the transferee, entity, or fiduciary. The copy of the notice must be delivered to the Director, Philadelphia Service Center, at the address provided in § 1.1445-1(g)(10), and must be accompanied by a cover letter stating that the copy is being filed pursuant to the requirements of this § 1.1445-4(c)(2).

(d) *Effect on recipient.*—A transferee, entity, or fiduciary that receives a notice pursuant to this section prior to the date of the transfer from any agent of the transferor or transferee may not rely upon the subject certification or statement for purposes of excusing withholding pursuant to § 1.1445-2 or § 1.1445-5. Therefore, the recipient of a notice may be held liable for any failure to deduct and withhold tax under section 1445 as if such certification or statement had never been given. For special rules concerning the effect of the receipt of a notice after the date of the transfer, see §§ 1.1445-2(b)(4)(iv) and 1.1445-5(c), (d) and (e).

(e) *Failure to provide notice.*—Any agent who is required to provide notice but who fails to do so in the manner required by paragraph (a) or (b) of this section shall be held liable for the tax that the recipient of the notice would have been required to withhold under section 1445 if such notice had been given. However, an agent's liability under this paragraph (e) is limited to the amount of compensation that that agent derives from the transaction. In addition, an agent who assists in the preparation of, or fails to disclose knowledge of, a false certification or statement may be liable for civil or criminal penalties.

(f) *Definition of transferor's or transferee's agent.*—(1) *In general.*—For purposes of this section, the terms "transferor's agent" and "transferee's agent" mean any person who represents the transferor or transferee (respectively)—

(i) In any negotiation with another person (or another person's agent) relating to the transaction; or

(ii) In settling the transaction.

(2) *Transactions subject to section 1445(e).*—In the case of transactions subject to section 1445(e), the following definitions apply.

(i) The term "transferor's agent" means any person that represents or advises an entity or fiduciary with respect to the planning, arrangement, or consummation by the entity of a transaction described in section 1445(e)(1), (2), (3), or (4).

(ii) The term "transferee's agent" means any person that represents or advises the holder of an interest in an entity with respect to the planning, arrangement or consummation by the entity of a transaction described in section 1445(e)(1), (2), (3), or (4).

(3) *Exclusion of settlement officers and clerical personnel.*—For purposes of this section, a person shall not be treated as a transferor's agent or transferee's agent with respect to any transaction solely because such person performs one or more of the following activities:

(i) The receipt and disbursement of any portion of the consideration for the transaction;

(ii) The recording of any document in connection with the transaction; or

(iii) Typing, copying, and other clerical tasks;

(iv) The obtaining of title insurance reports and reports concerning the condition of the real property that is the subject of the transaction; or

(v) The transmission or delivery of documents between the parties.

(4) *Exclusion for governing body of a condominium association and the board of directors of a cooperative housing corporation.*—The members of a board, committee or other governing body of a condominium association and the board of directors and officers of a cooperative housing corporation will not be deemed agents of the transferor or transferee if such individuals function exclusively in their capacity as representatives of such association or corporation with respect to the transaction. In addition, the managing agent of a cooperative housing corporation or condominium association will not be deemed to be an agent of the transferee or transferor if such person functions exclusively in its capacity as a managing agent. If a person's activities include advising the transferee or transferor with respect to the transfer, this exclusion shall not apply. [Reg. § 1.1445-4.]

☐ [*T.D. 8113, 12-18-86. Amended by T.D. 9082, 8-4-2003.*]

[Reg. § 1.1445-5]

§ 1.1445-5. **Special rules concerning distributions and other transactions by corporations, partnerships, trusts, and estates.**—(a) *Purpose and scope.*—This section provides special rules concerning the withholding that is required under section 1445(e) upon distributions and other transactions involving domestic or foreign corporations, partnerships, trusts, and estates. Paragraph (b) of this section provides rules that apply generally to the various withholding requirements set forth in this section. Under section 1445(e)(1) and paragraph (c) of this section, a domestic partnership or the fiduciary of a domestic trust or estate is required to withhold tax upon the entity's disposition of a U.S. real property interest if any foreign persons are partners or beneficiaries of the entity. Paragraph (d) provides rules concerning the requirement of section 1445(e)(2) that a foreign corporation withhold tax upon its distribution of a U.S. real property interest to its interest-holders. Finally, under section 1445(e)(3) and paragraph (e) of this section a domestic U.S. real property holding corporation is required to withhold tax upon certain distributions to interest-holders that are foreign persons. Paragraphs (f) and (g) of this section are reserved to provide rules concerning transactions involving interests in partnerships, trusts, and estates that will be subject to withholding pursuant to section 1445(e)(4) and (5).

(b) *Rules of general application.*—(1) *Double withholding not required.*—If tax is required to be withheld with respect to a transfer of property in accordance with the rules of this section, then no additional tax is required to be withheld by the transferee of the property with respect to that transfer pursuant to the general rules of section 1445(a) and § 1.1445-1. For rules coordinating the withholding under section 1441 (or section 1442 or 1443) and under section 1445 on distributions from a corporation, see §1.1441-3(b)(4). If a transfer of a U.S. real property interest described in section 1445(e) is exempt from withholding under the rules of this section, then no withholding is required under the general rules of section 1445(a) and §1.1445-1.

(2) *Coordination with nonrecognition provisions.*—(i) *In general.*—Withholding shall not be required under the rules of this section with respect to a transfer described in section 1445(e) of a U.S. real property interest if—

    (A) By reason of the operation of a nonrecognition provision of the Internal Revenue Code or the provisions of any treaty of the United States no gain or loss is required to be recognized by the foreign person with respect to which withholding would otherwise be required; and

    (B) The entity or fiduciary that is otherwise required to withhold complies with the notice requirements of paragraph (b)(2)(ii) of this section. The entity or fiduciary must determine whether gain or loss is required to be recognized pursuant to the rules of section 897 and the applicable nonrecognition provisions of the Internal Revenue Code. An entity or fiduciary may obtain a withholding certificate from the Internal Revenue Service that confirms the applicability of a nonrecognition provision, but is not required to do so. For purposes of this paragraph (b)(2), a nonrecognition provision is any provision of the Internal Revenue Code for not recognizing gain or loss. If nonrecognition treatment is available only with respect to part of the gain realized on a transfer, the exemption from withholding provided by this paragraph (b)(2) shall not apply. In such cases a withholding certificate may be sought pursuant to the provisions of §1.1445-6.

    (ii) *Notice of nonrecognition transfer.*—An entity or fiduciary that fails to withhold tax with respect to a transfer in reliance upon the rules of this paragraph (b)(2) must by the 20th day after the date of the transfer deliver a notice thereof to the Director, Philadelphia Service Center, at the address provided in §1.1445-1(g)(10). No particular form is required for a notice of transfer, but the following information must be set forth in paragraphs labelled to correspond with the letter set forth below:

    (A) A statement that the document submitted constitutes a notice of a nonrecognition transfer pursuant to the requirements of §1.1445-5(b)(2)(ii);

    (B) The name, office address, and identifying number of the entity of fiduciary submitting the notice;

    (C) The name, identifying number, and home address (in the case of an individual) or office address (in the case of an entity) of each foreign person with respect to which withholding would otherwise be required;

    (D) A brief description of the transfer; and

    (E) A brief statement of the law and facts supporting the claim that recognition of gain or loss is not required with respect to the transfer.

(3) *Interest-holder not a foreign person.*—(i) *In general.*—Pursuant to the provisions of paragraphs (c) and (e) of this section, an entity or fiduciary is required to withhold with respect to certain transfers of property if a holder of an interest in the entity is a foreign person. For purposes of determining whether a holder of an interest is a foreign person, an entity or fiduciary may rely upon a certification of non-foreign status provided by that person in accordance with paragraph (b)(3)(ii) of this section. Except to the extent provided in paragraph (b)(3)(iii) of this section, such a certification excuses the entity or fiduciary from any liability otherwise imposed pursuant to section 1445(e) and regulations thereunder. However, no obligation is imposed upon an entity or fiduciary to obtain certifications from interest-holders; an entity or fiduciary may instead rely upon other means to ascertain the non-foreign status of an interest-holder. If the entity or fiduciary does rely upon other means but the interest-holder proves, in fact, to be a foreign person, then the entity or fiduciary is subject to any liability imposed pursuant to section 1445 and regulations thereunder. An entity or fiduciary is not required to rely upon other means to ascertain the non-foreign status of an interest-holder and may demand a certification of non-foreign status. If the certification is not provided, the entity or fiduciary may withhold tax under section 1445 and will be considered, for purposes of sections 1461 through 1463, to have been required to withhold such tax.

    (ii) *Interest-holder's certification of non-foreign status.*—(A) *In general.*—For purposes of this section, an entity or fiduciary may treat any holder of an interest in the entity as a U.S. person if that interest-holder furnishes to the entity or fiduciary a certification stating that the interest-holder is not a foreign person, in accordance with the provisions of paragraph (b)(3)(ii)(B) of this section. In general, a foreign person is a nonresident alien individual, foreign corporation, foreign partnership, foreign trust, or foreign estate, but not a resident alien individual. In this regard, see §1.897-1(k).

    (B) *Procedural rules.*—An interest-holder's certification of non-foreign status must—

    (1) State that the interest-holder is not a foreign person;

    (2) Set forth the interest-holder's name, identifying number, home address (in the case of an individual) or office address (in the case of an entity), and place of incorporation (in the case of a corporation); and

    (3) Be signed under penalties of perjury.

Reg. §1.1445-5(b)(3)(ii)(B)(3)

Pursuant to §1.897-1(p), an individual's identifying number is the individual's Social Security number and any other person's identifying number is its U.S. employer identification number. The certification must be signed by a responsible officer in the case of a corporation, by a general partner in the case of a partnership, and by a trustee, executor, or equivalent fiduciary in the case of a trust or estate. No particular form is needed for a certification pursuant to this paragraph (b)(3)(ii)(B), nor is any particular language required, so long as the document meets the requirements of this paragraph. Samples of acceptable certifications are provided in paragraph (b)(3)(ii)(D) of this section. An entity may rely upon a certification pursuant to this paragraph (b)(3)(ii)(B) for a period of two calendar years following the close of the calendar year in which the certification was given. If an interest holder becomes a foreign person within the period described in the preceding sentence, the interest holder must notify the entity prior to any further dispositions or distributions and upon receipt of such notice (or any other notification of the foreign status of the interest holder) the entity may no longer rely upon the prior certification. An entity that obtains and relies upon a certification must retain that certification with its books and records for a period of three calendar years following the close of the last calendar year in which the entity relied upon the certification.

(C) *Foreign corporation that has made an election under section 897(i).*—A foreign corporation that has made a valid election under section 897(i) to be treated as a domestic corporation for purposes of section 897 may provide a certification of non-foreign status pursuant to this paragraph (b)(3)(ii). However, an electing foreign corporation must attach to such certification a copy of the acknowledgment of the election provided to the corporation by the Internal Revenue Service pursuant to §1.897-3(d)(4).

An acknowledgment is valid for this purpose only if it states that the information required by §1.897-3 has been determined to be complete.

(D) *Sample certifications.*—(1) *Individual interest-holder.*—"Under section 1445(e) of the Internal Revenue Code, a corporation, partnership, trust or estate must withhold tax with respect to certain transfers of property if a holder of an interest in the entity is a foreign person. To inform [*name of entity*] that no withholding is required with respect to my interest in it, I, [*name of interest-holder*], hereby certify the following:

1. I am not a nonresident alien for purposes of U.S. income taxation;

2. My U.S. taxpayer identifying number (Social Security number) is ———; and

3. My home address is

I agree to inform [name of entity] promptly if I become a nonresident alien at any time during the three years immediately following the date of this notice.

I understand that this certification may be disclosed to the Internal Revenue Service by [*name of entity*] and that any false statement I have made here could be punished by fine, imprisonment, or both.

Under penalties of perjury I declare that I have examined this certification and to the best of my knowledge and belief it is true, correct, and complete.

[*Signature and date*]"

(2) *Entity interest-holder.*—"Under section 1445(e) of the Internal Revenue Code, a corporation, partnership, trust, or estate must withhold tax with respect to certain transfers of property if a holder of an interest in the entity is a foreign person. To inform [*name of entity*] that no withholding is required with respect to [*name of interest-holder*]'s interest in it, the undersigned hereby certifies the following on behalf of [*name of interest-holder*]:

1. [*Name of interest-holder*] is not a foreign corporation, foreign partnership, foreign trust, or foreign estate (as those terms are defined in the Internal Revenue Code and Income Tax Regulations);

2. [*Name of interest-holder*]'s U.S. employer identification number is _____; and

3. [*Name of interest-holder*]'s office address is

_____

and place of incorporation (if applicable) is

_____

[Name of interest holder] agrees to inform [name of entity] if it becomes a foreign person at any time during the three year period immediately following the date of this notice.

[*Name of interest-holder*] understands that this certification may be disclosed to the Internal Revenue Service by [*name of entity*] and that any false statement contained herein could be punished by fine, imprisonment, or both.

Under penalties of perjury I declare that I have examined this certification and to the best of my knowledge and belief it is true, correct, and complete, and I further declare that I have authority to sign this document on behalf of [*name of interest-holder*].

[*Signature and date*]

[*Title*]"

(iii) *Reliance upon certification not permitted.*—An entity or fiduciary may not rely upon an interest-holder's certification of non-foreign status if, prior to or at the time of the transfer with respect to which withholding would be required, the entity or fiduciary either—

(A) Has actual knowledge that the certification is false;

(B) Has received a notice that the certification is false from a transferor's or transferee's agent, pursuant to § 1.1445-4; or

(C) Has received from a corporation that it knows to be a foreign corporation a certification that does not have attached to it a copy of the IRS acknowledgment of the corporation's election under section 897(i), as required by paragraph (b)(3)(ii)(C) of this section.

Such an entity's or fiduciary's withholding obligations shall apply as if a statement had never been given, and such an entity or fiduciary may be held fully liable pursuant to § 1.1445-1(e) for any failure to withhold. For special rules concerning an entity's belated receipt of a notice concerning a false certification, see paragraphs (c)(2)(ii) and (e)(2)(iii) of this section.

(4) *Property transferred not a U.S. real property interest.*—(i) *In general.*—Pursuant to the provisions of paragraphs (c) and (d) of this section, an entity or fiduciary is required to withhold with respect to certain transfers of property, if the property transferred is a U.S. real property interest. (In addition, taxable distributions of U.S. real property interests by domestic or foreign partnerships, trusts, and estates will be subject to withholding pursuant to section 1445(e)(4) and paragraph (f) of this section after publication of a Treasury decision under sections 897(e)(2) and (g).) As defined in section 897(c) and § 1.897-1(c), a U.S. real property interest includes certain interests in U.S. corporations, as well as direct interests in real property and certain associated personal property. This paragraph (b)(4) provides rules pursuant to which an entity (or fiduciary thereof) that transfers an interest in a U.S. corporation may determine that withholding is not required because the interest transferred is not a U.S. real property interest. To determine whether an interest in tangible property constitutes a U.S. real property interest the transfer of which would be subject to withholding, see § 1.897-1(b) and (c).

(ii) *Interests in publicly traded entities.*—Withholding is not required under paragraph (c) or (d) of this section upon an entity's transfer of an interest in a domestic corporation if any class of stock of the corporation is regularly traded on an established securities market. This exemption shall apply to a disposition incident to an initial public offering of stock pursuant to a registration statement filed with the Securities and Exchange Commission. Similarly, no withholding is required under paragraph (c) or (d) of this section upon an entity's transfer of an interest in a publicly traded partnership or trust. However, the rule of this paragraph (b)(4)(ii) shall not apply to the transfer, to a single transferee (or related transferees as defined in § 1.897-1(i)) in a single

transaction (or related transactions), of an interest described in § 1.897-1(c)(2)(iii)(B) (relating to substantial amounts of non-publicly traded interests in publicly traded corporations) or of similar interests in publicly traded partnerships or trusts. The entity making a transfer described in the preceding sentence must otherwise determine whether withholding is required, pursuant to section 1445(e) and the regulations thereunder. Transactions shall be deemed to be related if they are undertaken within 90 days of one another or if if can otherwise be shown that they were undertaken in pursuance of a prearranged plan.

(iii) *Corporation's statement that interest is not a U.S. real property interest.*—(A) *In general.*—No withholding is required under paragraph (c) or (d) of this section upon an entity's transfer of an interest in a domestic corporation if, prior to the transfer, the entity or fiduciary obtains a statement, issued by the corporation pursuant to § 1.897-2(h), certifying that the interest is not a U.S. real property interest. In general, a corporation may issue such a statement only if the corporation was not a U.S. real property holding corporation at any time during the previous five years (or the period in which the interest was held by its present holder, if shorter) or if interests in the corporation ceased to be United States real property interests under section 897(c)(1)(B). (A corporation may not provide such a statement based on its determination that the interest in question is an interest solely as a creditor.) See § 1.897-2(f) and (h). A corporation's statement may be relied upon for purposes of this paragraph (b)(4)(iii) only if the statement is dated not more than 30 days prior to the date of the transfer.

(B) *Reliance on statement not permitted.*—An entity or fiduciary is not entitled to rely upon a statement that an interest in a corporation is not a U.S. real property interest if, prior to or at the time of the transfer, the entity or fiduciary either—

(1) Has actual knowledge that the statement is false, or

(2) Receives a notice that the statement is false from a transferor's or transferee's agent, pursuant to § 1.1445-4.

Such an entity's or fiduciary's withholding obligations shall apply as if a statement had never been given, and such an entity or fiduciary may be held fully liable pursuant to § 1.1445-1(e) for any failure to withhold. For special rules concerning an entity's belated receipt of a notice concerning a false statement, see paragraphs (c)(2)(iii) and (d)(2)(i) of this section.

(5) *Reporting and paying over of withheld amounts.*—(i) *In general.*—An entity or fiduciary must report and pay over to the Internal Revenue Service any tax withheld pursuant to section 1445(e) and this section by the 20th day after the

date of the transfer (as defined in §1.1445-1(g)(8)). Forms 8288 and 8288-A are used for this purpose and must be filed at the location as provided in the instructions to Forms 8288 and 8288-A. The contents of Forms 8288 and 8288-A are described in §1.1445-1(d). Pursuant to section 7502 and regulations thereunder, the timely mailing of Forms 8288 and 8288-A by U.S. mail will be treated as their timely filing. Form 8288-A will be stamped by the Internal Revenue Service to show receipt, and a stamped copy will be mailed by the Service to the interest holder if the Form 8288 is complete, including the transferor's identifying number, at the address shown on the form, for the interest-holder's use. See paragraph (b)(7) of this section.

If an application for a withholding certificate with respect to a transfer of a U.S. real property interest was submitted to the Internal Revenue Service on the day of or at any time prior to the transfer, the entity or fiduciary must withhold the amount required under section 1445(e) and the rules of this section. However, the amount withheld, or a lesser amount as determined by the Service, need not be reported and paid over to the Service until the 20th day following the Service's final determination. For this purpose, the Service's final determination occurs on the day when the withholding certificate is mailed to the applicant by the Service or when notification denying the request for a withholding certificate is mailed to the applicant by the Service. An application is submitted to the Service on the day it is actualy received by the Service at the address provided in §1.1445-1(g)(10) or, under the rules of section 7502, on the day it is mailed to the Service at the address provided in §1.1445-1(g)(10), concerning the issuance of withholding certificates see §1.1445-6.

(ii) *Anti-abuse rule.*—An entity or fiduciary that in reliance upon the rules of this paragraph (b)(5)(ii) fails to report and pay over amounts withheld by the 20th day following the date of the transfer, shall be subject to the payment of interest and penalties if the relevant application for a withholding certificate (or an amendment of the application for a withholding certificate) was submitted for a principle purpose of delaying the payment to the IRS of the amount withheld. Interest and penalties shall be assessed on the amount that is ultimately paid over with respect to the period between the 20th day after the date of the transfer and the date on which payment is made.

(6) *Liability upon failure to withhold.*—For rules regarding liability upon failure to withhold under section 1445(e) and this §1.1445-5, see §1.1445-1(e).

(7) *Effect of withholding by entity or fiduciary upon interest holder.*—The withholding of tax under section 1445(e) does not excuse a foreign person that is subject to U.S. tax by reason of the operation of section 897 from filing a U.S. tax return. Thus, Form 1040NR, 1041, or 1120F as appropriate must be filed and any tax due must be paid by the filing date otherwise applicable to such person (or any extension therof). The tax withheld with respect to the foreign person under section 1445(e) (as shown on Form 8288-A) shall be credited against the amount of income tax as computed in such return, but only if the stamped copy of Form 8288-A provided to the entity or fiduciary (under paragraph (b)(5) of this section) is attached to the return or substantial evidence of the amount of tax withheld is attached to the return in accordance with the succeeding sentence. If a stamped copy of Form 8288-A has not been provided to the interest-holder by the Service, the interest-holder may establish the amount of tax withheld by the entity or fiduciary by attaching to its return substantial evidence of such amount. Such an interest-holder must attach to its return a statement which supplies all of the information required by §1.1445-1(d)(2). If the amount withheld under section 1445(e) constitutes less than the full amount of the foreign person's U.S. tax liability for that taxable year, then a payment of estimated tax may be required to be made pursuant to section 6154 or 6654 prior to the filing of the income tax return for that year. Alternatively, if the amount withheld under section 1445(e) exceeds the foreign person's maximum tax liability with respect to the transaction (as *reflected* in a withholding certificate issued by the Internal Revenue Service pursuant to §1.1445-6), then the foreign person may seek an early refund of the excess pursuant to §1.1445-6(g). A foreign person that takes gain into account in accordance with the provisions of section 453 shall not be entitled to a refund of the amount withheld unless a withholding certificate providing for such a refund is obtained pursuant to §1.1445-6.

If an entity or fiduciary withholds tax under section 1445(e) with respect to a beneficial owner of an interest who is not a foreign person, such beneficial owner may credit the amount of any tax withheld against his income tax liability in accordance with the provisions of this §1.1445-5(b)(7) or apply for an early refund under §1.1445-6(g).

(8) *Effective dates.*—(i) *Partnership, trust, and estate dispositions of U.S. real property interests.*—The provisions of section 1445(e)(1) and paragraph (c) of this section, requiring withholding upon certain dispositions of U.S. real property interests by domestic partnerships, trusts and estates, shall apply to any disposition on or after January 1, 1985.

(ii) *Certain distributions by foreign corporations.*—The provisions of section 1445(e)(2) and paragraph (d) of this section requiring withholding upon distributions of U.S. real property interest by foreign corporations, shall apply to distributions made on or after January 1, 1985.

(iii) *Distributions by certain domestic corporations to foreign shareholders.*—The provisions of section 1445(e)(3) and paragraph (e)(1) of this section, requiring withholding upon distributions in redemption of stock under section 302(a) or liquidating distributions under Part II of subchapter C of the Internal Revenue Code by U.S. real property holding corporations to foreign shareholders, shall apply to distributions made on or after January 1, 1985. The provisions of section 1445(e)(3) and paragraph (e)(1) of this section requiring withholding on distributions under section 301 by U.S. real property holding corporations to foreign shareholders shall apply to distributions made after August 20, 1996. The provisions of paragraph (e) of this section providing for the coordination of withholding between sections 1445 and 1441 (or 1442 or 1443) for distributions under section 301 by U.S. real property holding corporations to foreign shareholders apply to distributions after December 31, 2000 (see § 1.1441-3(c)(4) and (h)).

(iv) *Taxable distributions by domestic or foreign partnerships, trusts, and estates.*—The provisions of section 1445(e)(4), requiring withholding upon certain taxable distributions by domestic or foreign partnerships, trusts, and estates, shall apply to distributions made on or after the effective date of a Treasury decision under section 897(e)(2)(B)(ii) and (g).

(v) [Removed]

(vi) *Tiered partnerships.*—No withholding is required upon the disposition of a U.S. real property interest by a partnership which is directly owned, in whole or in part, by another domestic partnership (but only to the extent that the amount realized is attributable to the partnership interest of that other partnership) until the effective date of a Treasury Decision published under section 1445(e) providing rules governing this matter.

(c) *Dispositions of U.S. real property interests by domestic partnerships, trusts, and estates.*— (1) *Withholding required.*—(i) *In general.*—If a domestic partnership, trust, or estate disposes of a U.S. real property interest and any partner, beneficiary, or owner of the entity is a foreign person, then the partnership or the trustee, executor, or equivalent fiduciary of the trust or estate must withhold tax with respect to each such foreign person in accordance with the provisions of subdivision (ii), (iii), or (iv) of this paragraph (c)(1) (as applicable). The withholding obligation imposed by this paragraph (c) applies to the fiduciary of a trust even if the grantor of the trust or another person is treated as the owner of the trust or any portion thereof for purposes of the Internal Revenue Code. Thus, the withholding obligation imposed by this paragraph (c) applies to the trustee of a land trust or similar arrangement, even if such a trustee is not ordinarily treated under the applicable provisions of local law as a true fiduciary.

(ii) *Disposition by partnership.*—A partnership must withhold a tax equal to 35 percent (or the highest rate specified in section 1445(e)(1)) of each foreign partner's distributive share of the gain realized by the partnership upon the disposition of each U.S. real property interest. Such distributive share of the gain must be determined pursuant to the principles of section 704 and the regulations thereunder. For the rules applicable to partnerships, interests in which are regularly traded on an established securities market, see § 1.1445-8.

(iii) *Disposition by trust or estate.*—(A) *In general.*—A trustee, fiduciary, executor or equivalent fiduciary (hereafter collectively referred to as the fiduciary) of a trust or estate having one or more foreign beneficiaries must withhold tax in accordance with the rules of this § 1.1445-5(c)(1)(iii). Such a fiduciary must establish a U.S. real property interest account and must enter in such account all gains and losses realized during the taxable year of the trust or estate from dispositions of U.S. real property interests. The fiduciary must withhold 35 percent (or the highest rate specified in section 1445(e)(1)) of any distribution to a foreign beneficiary that is attributable to the balance in the U.S. real property interest account on the day of the distribution. A distribution from a trust or estate to a beneficiary (domestic or foreign) shall, solely for purposes of section 1445(e)(1), be deemed to be attributable first to any balance in the U.S. real property interest account and then to other amounts. However, a distribution that occurs prior to the transfer of a U.S. real property interest in a taxable year or at any other time when the amount contained in the U.S. real property interest account is zero, is not subject to withholding under this § 1.1445-5(c)(1)(iii). The U.S. real property interest account is reduced by the amount distributed to all beneficiaries (domestic and foreign) attributable to such account during the taxable year of the trust or estate. Any ending balance of the U.S. real property interest account not distributed by the close of the taxable year of the trust or estate is cancelled and is not carried over (or carried back) to any other year. Thus, the beginning balance of such account in any taxable year of the trust or estate is always zero. For rules applicable to grantor trusts see § 1.1445-5(c)(1)(iv). For rules applicable to trusts, interests in which are regularly traded on an established securities market and real estate investment trusts, see § 1.1445-8.

(B) *Example.*—The following example illustrates the rules of paragraph (c)(1)(iii)(A) of this section.

On January 1, 1994, A establishes a domestic trust (which has as its taxable year, the calendar year) for the benefit of B, a nonresident alien, and C, a U.S. citizen. The trust is not a trust subject to sections 671 through 679. Under the terms of the trust, the trustee, T, is given discretion to distribute income and corpus of the trust to provide for the reasonable needs of B and C.

During the trust's 1994 tax year, T disposes of three parcels of vacant land located in the United States. The following chart illustrates the computation of the amount subject to withholding under section 1445 with respect to distributions made by T to B and C during 1994.

Date	Parcel sold	Gains or (loss) realized	Distributions to C	Distributions to B (before withholding)	Section 1445 withholding (35% rate)	U.S. real property interest account
1/01/94						-0-
3/01/94	Parcel 1	140,000				140,000
3/05/94			5,000	10,000	3,500	125,000
3/15/94			10,000	5,000	1,750	110,000
5/01/94	Parcel 2	300,000				410,000
5/15/94	Parcel 3	(50,000)				360,000
12/01/94			170,000	170,000	59,500	20,000
1/01/95						-0-

(iv) *Disposition by grantor trust.*—The trustee or equivalent fiduciary of a trust that is subject to the provisions of subpart E of part I of subchapter J (sections 671 through 679) must withhold a tax equal to 35 percent (or the highest rate specified in section 1445(e)(1)) of the gain realized from each disposition of a U.S. real property interest to the extent such gain is allocable to a portion of the trust treated as owned by a foreign person under subpart E of part I of subchapter J.

(2) *Withholding not required under paragraph (c).*—(i) [Removed]

(ii) *Interest-holder not a foreign person.*—(A) *In general.*—A domestic partnership, trust, or estate that disposes of a U.S. real property interest shall not be required to withhold with respect to any partner or beneficiary that it determines, pursuant to the rules of paragraph (b)(3) of this section, not to be a foreign person.

(B) *Belated notice of false certification.*—If after the date of the transfer a partnership or fiduciary learns that a partner's or beneficiary's certification of non-foreign status is false, then that partnership or fiduciary shall be required to withhold, with respect to the foreign partner or beneficiary that gave the false certification, the lesser of—

(1) The amount otherwise required to be withheld under the rules of this paragraph (c), or

(2) An amount equal to that partner's or beneficiary's remaining interests in the income or assets of the partnership, trust, or estate.

Amounts so withheld must be reported and paid over by the 60th day following the date on which the partnership or fiduciary learns that the certification is false. For rules concerning the notifications of false certifications that may be required to be given to partnerships and fiduciaries, see § 1.1445-4(b).

(iii) *Property disposed of not a U.S. real property interest.*—(A) *In general.*—No withholding is required under this paragraph (c) if a domestic partnership, trust, or estate that disposes of property determines pursuant to the rules of paragraph (b)(4) of this section that the property disposed of is not a U.S. real property interest.

(B) *Belated notice of false statement.*—If after the date of the transfer a partnership or fiduciary learns that a corporation's statement (that an interest in the corporation is not a U.S. real property interest) is false, then that partnership or fiduciary shall be required to withhold, with respect to each foreign partner or beneficiary, the lesser of—

(1) The amount otherwise required to be withheld under the rules of this paragraph (c), or

(2) An amount equal to that partner's or beneficiary's remaining interests in the income or assets of the partnership, trust, or estate.

Amounts so withheld must be reported and paid over by the 60th day following the date on which the partnership or fiduciary learns that the statement is false. For rules concerning the notifications of false statements that may be required to be given to partnerships or fiduciaries, see § 1.1445-4(b).

(iv) *Withholding certificate.*—No withholding is required under this paragraph (c) with respect to the transfer of a U.S. real property interest if the Internal Revenue Service issues a withholding certificate that so provides. For rules concerning the issuance of withholding certificates, see § 1.1445-6.

(v) *Nonrecognition transactions.*—For special rules concerning transactions entitled to nonrecognition of gain or loss, see paragraph (b)(2) of this section.

(3) *Large partnerships or trusts.*—(i) *In general.*—If a partnership or trust has more than 100

partners or beneficiaries, then the partnership or fiduciary of the trust may elect to withhold in accordance with the provisions of this § 1.1445-5(c)(3) in lieu of withholding in the manner required by § 1.1445-5(c)(1). However, the rules of this § 1.1445-5(c)(3) shall not apply to any partnership or trust interests in which are regularly traded on an established securities market except as described in § 1.1445-8(c)(1). The rules of this § 1.1445-5(c)(3) shall not apply to any real estate investment trust. *See* § 1.1445-8.

(ii) *Amount to be withheld.*—A partnership or trust electing to withhold under this § 1.1445-5(c)(3) shall withhold from each distribution to a foreign person an amount equal to 35 percent (or the highest rate specified in section 1445(e)(1)) of the amount attributable to section 1445(e)(1) transfers.

(iii) *Amounts attributable to section 1445(e)(1) transfers.*—A distribution is attributable to section 1445(e)(1) transfers to the extent of the partner's or beneficiary's proportionate share of the current balance of the entity's section 1445(e)(1) account. A distribution from a partnership or trust that has made an election under this § 1.1445-5(c)(3) shall be deemed first to be attributable to a section 1445(e)(1) transfer to the extent of the balance in the section 1445(e)(1) account. An entity's section 1445(e)(1) account shall be equal to—

(A) The total amount of net gain realized by the entity upon all transfers of U.S. real property interests carried out by the entity after the date of its election under this § 1.1445-5(c)(3); minus

(B) The total amount of all distributions by the entity to domestic and foreign distributees from such account.

(iv) *Special rules for entities that make recurring sales of growing crops and timber.*—An entity that makes an election under § 1.1445-5(c)(3) and that makes recurring sales of growing crops and timber may further elect to determine the amount subject to withholding under the rules of this § 1.1445-5(c)(3)(iv). Such an entity must withhold from each distribution to a foreign partner or beneficiary an amount equal to 10 percent of such partner's or beneficiary's proportionate share of the current balance of the entity's gross section 1445(e)(1) account. An entity's gross section 1445(e)(1) account equals—

(A) The total amount realized by the entity upon all transfers of U.S. real property interests carried out by the entity after the date of its election under this § 1.1445-5(c)(3)(iv); minus

(B) The total amount of all distributions to domestic and foreign distributees from such account.

An entity that elects to compute the amount subject to withholding under this § 1.1445-5(c)(3)(iv), shall make such election in accordance with § 1.1445-5(c)(3)(vi) and shall be subject to the provisions otherwise applicable under § 1.1445-5(c)(3).

(v) *Procedural rules.*—An election under paragraph (c)(3) may be made by filing a notice thereof with the Director, Philadelphia Service Center, at the address provided in § 1.1445-1(g)(10). The notice must be submitted by a general partner (in the case of a partnership) or the trustee or equivalent fiduciary (in the case of a trust). The notice must set forth the name, office address, and identifying number of the partnership or fiduciary making the election, and, in the case of a partnership, must include the name, office address, and identifying number of the general partner submitting the election. An election under this paragraph (c)(3) may be revoked only with the consent of the Internal Revenue Service. Consent of the Service may be requested by filing an application to revoke the election with the Director, Philadelphia Service Center, at the address stated above. This application must include all information provided to the Service with the election notice and must provide an explanation of the reasons for revoking the election. The application to revoke an election must also specify the amount remaining to be distributed in the section 1445(e)(1) account or the gross section 1445(e)(1) account. An entity that ceases to qualify under section 1.1445-5(c)(3) because such entity does not have more than 100 partners or beneficiaries may revoke its election only with the consent of the Internal Revenue Service.

(d) *Distributions of U.S. real property interests by foreign corporations.*—(1) *In general.*—A foreign corporation that distributes a U.S. real property interest must deduct and withhold a tax equal to 35 percent (or the rate specified in section 1445(e)(2)) of the amount of gain recognized by the corporation on the distribution. The amount of gain required to be recognized by the corporation must be detemined pursuant to the rules of section 897 and any other applicable section. For special rules concerning the applicability of a nonrecognition provision to a distribution, see paragraph (b)(2) of this section. The withholding liability imposed by this paragraph (d) applies to the same taxpayer that owes the related substantive income tax liability pursuant to the operation of section 897. Only one such liability will be assessed and collected from a foreign corporation, but separate penalties for failures to comply with the two requirements will be asserted.

(2) *Withholding not required.*—(i) *Property distributed not a U.S. real property interest.*—(A) *In general.*—No withholding is required under this paragraph (d) if a foreign corporation that distributes property determines pursuant to the rules of paragraph (b)(3) of this section that the property distributed is not a U.S. real property interest.

Reg. § 1.1445-5(d)(2)(i)(A)

(B) *Belated notice of false statement.*—If after the date of a distribution described in paragraph (d)(1) of this section a foreign corporation learns that another corporation's statement (that an interest in that other corporation is not a U.S. real property interest) is false, then the foreign corporation may not rely upon that statement for any purpose. Such a foreign corporation's withholding obligations under this paragraph (d) shall apply as if a statement had never been given, and such a corporation may be held fully liable pursuant to §1.1445-5(b)(5) for any failure to withhold. Amounts withheld pursuant to the rule of this paragraph (d)(2)(i)(B) must be reported and paid over by the 60th day following the date on which the foreign corporation learns that the statement is false. No penalties or interest will be assessed for failures to withhold prior to that date. For rules concerning the notifications of false statements that may be required to be given to foreign corporations, see §1.1445-4(b).

(ii) *Withholding certificate.*—No withholding is required under this paragraph (d) with respect to a foreign corporation's distribution of a U.S. real property interest if the distributing corporation obtains a withholding certificate from the Internal Revenue Service that so provides. For rules concerning the issuance of withholding certificates, see §1.1445-6.

(e) *Distributions to foreign persons by U.S. real property holding corporations.*—(1) *In general.*—A domestic corporation that distributes any property to a foreign person that holds an interest in the corporation must deduct and withhold a tax equal to 10 percent of the fair market value of the property distributed to the foreign person, if—

(i) The foreign person's interest in the corporation constitutes a U.S. real property interest under the provisions of section 897 and regulations thereunder; and

(ii) There is a distribution of property in redemption of stock treated as an exchange under section 302(a), in liquidation of the corporation pursuant to the provisions of Part II of subchapter C of the Internal Revenue Code (sections 331 through section 346), or with respect to stock under section 301 that is not made out of earnings and profits of the corporation.

(2) *Coordination rules for Section 301 distributions.*—If a domestic corporation makes a distribution of property under section 301 to a foreign person whose interest in such corporation constitutes a U.S. real property interest under the provisions of section 897 and the regulations thereunder, then see §1.1441-3(c)(4) for rules coordinating withholding obligations under sections 1445 and 1441 (or 1442 or 1443)).

(3) *Withholding not required.*—(i) *Foreign person's interest not a U.S. real property interest.*—Withholding is required under this paragraph (e) only with respect to distributions to foreign persons holding interests in the corporation that constitute U.S. real property interests. In general, a foreign person's interest in a domestic corporation constitutes a U.S. real property interest if the corporation was a U.S. real property holding corporation at any time during the shorter of (A) the period in which the foreign person held the interest or (B) the previous five years (but not earlier than June 19, 1980). See section 897(c) and §§1.897-1(c) and 1.897-2(b) and (h). However, an interest in such a corporation ceases to be a U.S. real property interest after all of the U.S. real property interests held by the corporation itself are disposed of in transactions on which gain or loss is recognized. See section 897(c)(1)(B) and §1.897-2(f)(2). Thus, if a U.S. real property holding corporation in the process of liquidation does not elect section 337 nonrecognition treatment upon its sale of all U.S. real property interests held by the corporation, and recognizes gain or loss upon such sales, interests in that corporation cease to be U.S. real property interests. Therefore, no withholding would be required with respect to that corporation's subsequent liquidating distribution to a foreign shareholder of property other than a U.S. real property interest.

(ii) *Nonrecognition transactions.*—For special rules concerning the applicability of a nonrecognition provision to a distribution described in paragraph (e)(1) of this section, see paragraph (b)(2) of this section.

(iii) *Interest-holder not a foreign person.*—(A) *In general.*—A domestic corporation shall not be required to withhold under this paragraph (e) with respect to a distribution of property to any distributee that it determines, pursuant to the rules of paragraph (b)(3) of this section, not to be a foreign person.

(B) *Belated notice of false certification.*—If after the date of a distribution described in paragraph (e)(1) of this section a domestic corporation learns that an interest-holder's certification of non-foreign status is false, then the corporation may rely upon that certification only if the person providing the false certification holds (or held) less than 10 percent of the value of the outstanding stock of the corporation. With respect to less than 10 percent interest-holders, no withholding is required under this paragraph (e) upon receipt of a belated notice of false certification. With respect to 10 percent or greater interest-holders, the corporation's withholding obligations under this paragraph (e) shall apply as if a certification had never been given, and such a corporation may be held fully liable pursuant to §1.1445-5(b)(6) for any failure to withhold as of the date specified in this §1.1445-5(e)(3)(iii)(B). Amounts withheld pursuant to the rule of this paragraph (e)(3)(iii)(B) must be reported and paid over by the 60th day following the date on which the corporation learns that the certification is false. No penalties or interest for failures to withhold will be assessed prior to that date. For rules concerning the notifications of false certifications that may be required to be given to U.S. real property holding corporations, see § 1.1445-4(b).

(iv) *Withholding certificate.*—No withholding, or reduced withholding, is required under this paragraph (e) with respect to a domestic corporation's distribution of property if the distributing corporation obtains a withholding certificate from the Internal Revenue Service that so provides. For rules concerning the issuance of withholding certificates, see § 1.1445-6.

(f) *Taxable distributions by domestic or foreign partnerships, trusts, or estates.*—[Reserved]

(g) *Dispositions of interests in partnerships, trusts, and estates.*—[Reserved]

(h) *Effective date for taxpayer identification numbers.*—The requirement in paragraphs (b)(2)(ii)(B) and (C) of this section that taxpayer identification numbers be provided (in all cases) is is applicable for dispositions of U.S. real property interests occurring after November 3, 2003. [Reg. § 1.1445-5.]

☐ [*T.D.* 8113, 12-18-86. *Amended by T.D.* 8198, 5-4-88; *T.D.* 8321, 12-6-90; *T.D.* 8647, 12-20-95; *T.D.* 8734, 10-6-97 (T.D. 8804 delayed the effective date of T.D. 8734 from January 1, 1999, to January 1, 2000; T.D. 8856 further delayed the effective date of T.D. 8734 until January 1, 2001) *and T.D.* 9082, 8-4-2003.]

[Reg. § 1.1445-6]

§ 1.1445-6. Adjustments pursuant to withholding certificate of amount required to be withheld under section 1445(e).— (a) *Withholding certificate for purposes of section 1445(e).*—(1) *In general.*—Pursuant to the provisions of § 1.1445-5(c)(2)(iv), (d)(2)(ii), and (e)(2)(iv), withholding under section 1445(e) may be reduced or eliminated pursuant to a withholding certificate issued by the Internal Revenue Service in accordance with the rules of this § 1.1445-6. A withholding certificate may be issued in cases where adjusted withholding is appropriate (e.g., because of the applicability of a nonrecognition provision—see paragraph (c) of this section), where the relevant taxpayers are exempt from U.S. tax (see paragraph (d) of this section), or where an agreement for the payment of tax is entered into with the Service (see paragraph (e) of this section). A withholding certificate that is obtained prior to a transfer allows the entity or fiduciary to withhold a reduced amount or excuses withholding entirely. A withholding certificate that is obtained after a transfer has been made may authorize a normal refund or an early refund pursuant to paragraph (g) of this section. The Internal Revenue Service will act

upon an application for a withholding certificate not later than the 90th day after it is received. (The Service may deny a request for a withholding certificate where, after due notice, an applicant fails to provide the information necessary to make a determination.) Solely for this purpose (i.e., determining the day upon which the 90 day period commences), an application is received by the Service on the date when all information necessary for the Service to make a determination is provided by the applicant. In no event, however, will a withholding certificate be issued without the transferor's identifying number. (For rules regarding whether an application has been timely submitted, see § 1.1445-5(b)(5).) The Internal Revenue Service will act upon an application for an early refund not later than the 90th day after it is received. An application for an early refund must either (i) include a copy of a withholding certificate issued by the Service with respect to the transaction, or (ii) be combined with an application for a withholding certificate. Where an application for an early refund is combined with an application for a withholding certificate, the Service will act upon both applications not later than the 90th day after receipt. Either an entity, a fiduciary, or a relevant taxpayer (as defined in paragraph (a)(2) of this section) may apply for a withholding certificate. An entity or fiduciary may apply for a withholding certificate with respect to all or less than all relevant taxpayers. For special rules concerning the issuance of a withholding certificate to a foreign corporation that has made an election under section 897(i), see § 1.1445-7(d).

(2) *Relevant taxpayer.*—For purposes of this section, the term "relevant taxpayer" means any foreign person that will bear substantive income tax liability by reason of the operation of section 897 with respect to a transaction upon which withholding is required under section 1445(e).

(b) *Applications for withholding certificates.*— (1) *In general.*—An application for a withholding certificate pursuant to this § 1.1445-6 must be submitted in the manner provided in § 1.1445-3(b). However, in lieu of the information required to be submitted pursuant to § 1.1445-3(b)(4), the applicant must provide the information required by paragraph (b)(2) of this section. In addition, the information required by paragraph (b)(3) of this section must be submitted with the application.

(2) *Basis for certificate.*—(i) *Adjusted withholding.*—If a withholding certificate is sought on the basis of a claim that adjusted withholding is appropriate, the application must include a calculation, in accordance with paragraph (c) of this section, of the maximum tax that may be imposed on each relevant taxpayer with respect to which adjusted withholding is sought. The application must also include all evidence necessary to substantiate the claimed calculation, such

Reg. § 1.1445-6(b)(2)(i)

as records of adjustments to basis or appraisals of fair market value.

(ii) *Exemption.*—If a withholding certificate is sought on the basis of a relevant taxpayer's exemption from U.S. tax, the application must set forth a brief statement of the law and facts that support the claimed exemption. See paragraph (d) of this section.

(iii) *Agreement.*—If a withholding certificate is sought on the basis of an agreement for the payment of tax, the application must include a copy of the agreement proposed by the applicant and a copy of the security instrument (if any) proposed by the applicant. In this regard, see paragraph (e) of this section.

(3) *Relevant taxpayers.*—An application for withholding certificate pursuant to this section must include all of the following information: the name, identifying number, and home address (in the case of an individual) or office address (in the case of an entity) of each relevant taxpayer with respect to which adjusted withholding is sought.

(c) *Adjustment of amount required to be withheld.*—The Internal Revenue Service may issue a withholding certificate that excuses withholding, or that permits an entity or fiduciary to withhold an adjusted amount reflecting the relevant taxpayers' maximum tax liability. A relevant taxpayer's maximum tax liability is the maximum amount which that taxpayer could be required to pay as tax by reason of the transaction upon which withholding is required. In the case of an individual taxpayer that amount will generally be the gain realized by the individual, multiplied by the maximum individual income tax rate applicable to long term capital gain. In the case of a corporate taxpayer, that amount will generally be the gain realized by the corporation, multiplied by the maximum corporate income tax rate applicable to long term capital gain. However, that amount must be adjusted to take into account the following:

(1) Any reduction of tax to which the relevant taxpayer is entitled under the provisions of a U.S. income tax treaty;

(2) The effect of any nonrecognition provision that is applicable to the transaction;

(3) Any losses previously realized and recognized by the relevant taxpayer during the taxable year by reason of the operation of section 897;

(4) Any amount realized upon the subject transfer by the relevant taxpayer that is required to be treated as ordinary income under any provision of the Code; and

(5) Any other factor that may increase or reduce the tax upon the transaction.

(d) *Relevant taxpayer's exemption from U.S. tax.*—(1) *In general.*—The Internal Revenue Ser-

vice will issue a withholding certificate that excuses withholding by an entity or fiduciary if it is established that a relevant taxpayer's income from the transaction will be exempt from U.S. tax. For the available exemptions, see paragraph (d)(2) of this section. If a relevant taxpayer is entitled to a reduction of (rather than an exemption from) U.S. tax, then the entity or fiduciary may obtain a withholding certificate to that effect pursuant to the provisions of paragraph (c) of this section.

(2) *Available exemptions.*—A relevant taxpayer's income from a transaction with respect to which withholding is required under section 1445(e) may be exempt from U.S. tax because either:

(i) The relevant taxpayer is an integral part or controlled entity of a foreign government and the subject income is exempt from U.S. tax pursuant to section 892 and the regulations thereunder; or

(ii) The relevant taxpayer is entitled to the benefits of an income tax treaty that provides for such an exemption (subject to the limitations imposed by section 1125(c) of Pub. L. 96-499, which, in general, overrides such benefits as of January 1, 1985).

(e) *Agreement for the payment of tax.*—(1) *In general.*—The Internal Revenue Service will issue a withholding certificate that excuses withholding or that permits an entity or fiduciary to withhold a reduced amount, if the entity, fiduciary, or a relevant taxpayer enters into an agreement for the payment of tax pursuant to the provisions of this paragraph (e). An agreement for the payment of tax is a contract between the Service and the entity, fiduciary, or relevant taxpayer that consists of two necessary elements. Those elements are—

(i) A contract between the Service and the other person, setting forth in detail the rights and obligations of each; and

(ii) A security instrument or other form of security acceptable to the Assistant Commissioner (International).

(2) *Contents of agreement.*—(i) *In general.*—An agreement for the payment of tax must cover an amount described in subdivision (ii) or (iii) of this paragraph (e)(2). The agreement may either provide adequate security for the payment of the chosen amount with respect to the relevant taxpayer in accordance with paragraph (e)(3) of this section, or provide for the payment of that amount through a combination of security and withholding of tax by the entity or fiduciary.

(ii) *Tax that would otherwise be withheld.*—An agreement for the payment of tax may cover the amount of tax that would otherwise be required to be withheld with respect to the relevant taxpayer pursuant to section 1445(e). In addition to the amount computed pursuant to section 1445(e), the applicant must agree to pay interest upon that amount, at the rate established under section 6621, with respect to the period between the date on which withholding tax under section 1445(e) would otherwise be due and the date on which the relevant taxpayer's payment of tax with respect to the disposition will be due. The amount of interest agreed upon must be paid by the applicant regardless of whether or not the Service is required to draw upon any security provided pursuant to the agreement. The interest may be paid either with the return or by the Service drawing upon the security.

(iii) *Maximum tax liability.*—An agreement for the payment of tax may cover the relevant taxpayer's maximum tax liability, determined in accordance with paragraph (c) of this section. The agreement must also provide for the payment of an additional amount equal to 25 percent of the amount determined under paragraph (c) of this section. This additional amount secures the interest and penalties that would accrue between the date of the relevant taxpayer's failure to file a return and pay tax with respect to the disposition, and the date on which the Service collects upon that liability pursuant to the agreement.

(iv) *Allocation of payment.*—An agreement for the payment of tax pursuant to this section must set forth an allocation of the payment provided for by the agreement among the relevant taxpayers with respect to which the withholding certificate is sought. In the case of an agreement that covers an amount described in subdivision (ii) of this paragraph (e)(2), such allocation must be based upon the amount that would otherwise be required to be withheld with respect to each relevant taxpayer. In the case of an agreement that covers an amount described in subdivision (iii) of this paragraph (e)(2), such allocation must be based upon each relevant taxpayer's maximum tax liability.

(3) *Major types of security.*—The major types of security that are acceptable to the Internal Revenue Service for purposes of this section are described in §1.1445-3(e)(3).

(4) *Terms of security instrument.*—Any security instrument that is furnished pursuant to this section must contain the terms described in §1.1445-3(e)(4).

(f) *Amendments to application for withholding certificates.*—(1) *In general.*—An applicant for a withholding certificate may amend an otherwise complete application by submitting an amending statement to the Director, Philadelphia Service Center, at the address provided in §1.1445-1(g)(10). The amending statement shall provide the information required by §1.1445-6(f)(3) and must be signed and accom-panied by a penalties of perjury statement in accordance with §1.1445-6(b).

(2) *Extension of time for the Service to process requests for withholding certificates.*—(i) *In general.*—If an amending statement is submitted, the time in which the Internal Revenue Service must act upon the amended application shall be extended by 30 days.

(ii) *Substantial amendments.*—If an amending statement is submitted and the Service finds that the statement substantially amends to the facts of the underlying application or substantially alters the terms of the withholding certificate as requested in the initial application, the time within which the Service must act upon the amended application shall be extended by 60 days. The applicant shall be so notified.

(iii) *Amending statement received after the requested withholding certificate has been signed by the Director, Philadelphia Service Center.*—If an amending statement is received after the withholding certificate, drafted in response to the underlying application, has been signed by the Director, Philadelphia Service Center, or his delegate and prior to the day such certificate is mailed to the applicant, the time in which the Service must act upon the amended application shall be extended by 90 days.

(3) *Information required to be submitted.*—No particular form is required for an amending statement but the statement must provide the following information:

(i) *Identification of applicant.*—The amending statement must set forth the name, address, and identifying number of the person submitting the amending statement.

(ii) *Date of application.*—The amending statement must set forth the date of the underlying application for a withholding certificate.

(iii) *Real property interest to be (or that has been) transferred.*—The amending statement must set forth a brief description of the real property interest with respect to which the underlying application for a withholding certificate was submitted.

(iv) *Amending information.*—The amending statement must fully set forth the basis for the amendment including any modification of the facts supporting the application for a withholding certificate and any change sought in the terms of the withholding certificate.

(g) *Early refund of overwithheld amounts.*—If the Internal Revenue Service issues a withholding certificate pursuant to this section, and an amount greater than that specified in the certificate was withheld by the entity or fiduciary, then pursuant to the rules of this paragraph (g) a relevant taxpayer may apply for an early refund of a proportionate share of the excess amount (without interest) prior to the date on which the relevant taxpayer's return is due (without extensions). An application for an early refund must be addressed to the Director, Philadelphia Service Center, at the address provided in § 1.1445-1(g)(10). No particular form is required for the application, but the following information must be set forth in separate paragraphs numbered to correspond with the numbers given below:

(1) Name, address, and identifying number of the relevant taxpayer seeking the refund;

(2) Amount required to be withheld pursuant to withholding certificate;

(3) Amount withheld by entity or fiduciary (attach a copy of Form 8388-A stamped by IRS pursuant to § 1.1445-5(b)(4) or provide substantial evidence of the amount withheld in the case of a failure to receive Form 8288-A, as provided in § 1.1445-5(b)(7));

(4) Amount to be refunded to the relevant taxpayer.

An application for an early refund cannot be processed unless the required copy of Form 8288-A or substantial evidence of the amount withheld in the case of a failure to receive Form 8288-A (as provided in § 1.1445-5(b)(7)) is attached to the application. If an application for a withholding certificate is submitted after the transfer takes place, then that application may be combined with an application for an early refund. The Service will act upon a claim for refund within the time limits set forth in § 1.1445-6(a)(1).

(h) *Effective date for taxpayer identification numbers.*—The requirement in paragraphs (b)(3), (f)(3)(i), and (g)(1) of this section that taxpayer identification numbers be provided (in all cases) is applicable for dispositions of U.S. real property interests occurring after November 3, 2003. [Reg. § 1.1445-6.]

☐ [*T.D.* 8113, 12-18-86. *Amended by T.D.* 9082, 8-4-2003.]

[Reg. § 1.1445-7]

§ 1.1445-7. Treatment of foreign corporation that has made an election under section 897(i) to be treated as a domestic corporation.—(a) *In general.*—Pursuant to section 897(i) a foreign corporation may elect to be treated as a domestic corporation for purposes of sections 897 and 6039C. A foreign corporation that has made such an election shall also be treated as a domestic corporation for purposes of the withholding required under section 1445, in accordance with the provisions of this section.

(b) *Withholding under section 1445(a).*—(1) *Dispositions by corporation.*—A foreign corporation that has made an election under section 897(i) may provide a transferee with a certification of non-foreign status in connection with the corpo-

ration's disposition of a U.S. real property interest. However, in accordance with the provisions of §§ 1.1445-2(b)(2)(ii) and 1.1445-5(b)(3)(ii)(C), such an electing foreign corporation must attach to such certification a copy of the acknowledgment of the election provided to the corporation by the Internal Revenue Service pursuant to § 1.897-3(d)(4) which states that the information required by § 1.897-3 has been determined to be complete.

(2) *Dispositions of interests in corporation.*—Dispositions of interests in electing foreign corporations shall be subject to the withholding requirements of section 1445(a) and the rules of §§ 1.1445-1 through 1.1445-4. Therefore, if a foreign person disposes of an interest in such a corporation, and that interest is a U.S. real property interest under the provisions of section 897 and regulations thereunder, then the transferee is required to withhold under section 1445(a).

(c) *Withholding under section 1445(e).*—Because a foreign corporation that has made an election under section 897(i) is treated as a domestic corporation for purposes of determining withholding obligations under section 1445, such a corporation is not subject to the requirement of section 1445(e)(2) that a foreign corporation withhold at the corporate capital gain rate from the gain recognized upon the distribution of a U.S. real property interest. Such a corporation is subject to the provisions of section 1445(e)(3). Thus, if interests in an electing corporation constitute U.S. real property interests, then the corporation is required to withhold with respect to the non-dividend distribution of any property to an interest-holder that is a foreign person. See § 1.1445-5(e). Dividend distributions (distributions that are described in section 301) shall be treated as provided in sections 897(f), 1441 and 1442. In addition, if interests in an electing foreign corporation do not constitute U.S. real property interests, then distributions by such corporation shall be treated as provided in sections 897(f) (if applicable), 1441 and 1442. Approved by the Office of Management and Budget under control number 545-0902. [Reg. § 1.1445-7.]

☐ [*T.D.* 8113, 12-18-86.]

[Reg. § 1.1445-8]

§ 1.1445-8. Special rules regarding publicly traded partnerships, publicly traded trusts and real estate investment trusts (REITS).—(a) *Entities to which this section applies.*—The rules of this section apply to—

(1) Any partnership or trust, interests in which are regularly traded on an established securities market (regardless of the number of its partners or beneficiaries), and

(2) Any REIT (regardless of the form of its organization).

For purposes of paragraph (a)(1) of this section, the rules of section 1445(e)(1) and this section shall not apply to a publicly traded partnership (as defined in section 7704) which is treated as a corporation under section 7704(a), or to those entities that are classified as "associations" and taxed as corporations. See § 301.7701-2.

(b) *Obligation to withhold.*—(1) *In general.*—An entity described in paragraph (a) of this section is not required to withhold under the provisions of § 1.1445-5(c), which states the withholding requirements of domestic partnerships, trusts and estates upon the disposition of U.S. real property interests. Except as otherwise provided in this paragraph (b), an entity described in paragraph (a) of this section shall be liable to withhold tax upon the distribution of any amount attributable to the disposition of a U.S. real property interest, with respect to each holder of an interest in the entity that is a foreign person. The amount to be withheld is described in paragraph (c) of this section.

(2) *Publicly traded partnerships.*—Publicly traded partnerships which comply with the withholding procedures under section 1446 will be deemed to have satisfied their withholding obligations under this paragraph (b).

(3) *Special rule for certain distributions to nominees.*—In the case of a person that—

(i) Is a nominee (as defined in paragraph (d) of this section),

(ii) Receives a distribution attributable to the disposition of a U.S. real property interest directly from an entity described in paragraph (a) of this section or indirectly from such entity through a nominee,

(iii) Receives the distribution for payment to any foreign person, or the account of any foreign person, and

(iv) Receives a qualified notice pursuant to paragraph (f) of this section,

then the obligation to withhold in accordance with the general rules of section 1445(e)(1) and this paragraph (b) shall be imposed solely on that person to the extent of the amount specified by the qualified notice. A person obligated to withhold by reason of this paragraph (b)(3) is referred to as a withholding agent.

(4) *Person designated to act for withholding agent.*—The rules stated in § 1.1441-7(b)(1) and (2) regarding a person designated to act for a withholding agent shall apply for purposes of this section.

(5) *Effect of withholding exemption granted under § 1.1441-4(f).*—A letter issued by a district director under the provisions of § 1.1441-4(f), which exempts a person from withholding under section 1441 or section 1442, shall also exempt that person from withholding under this paragraph (b), if—

(i) The letter identifies another person as the withholding agent for purposes of section 1441 or 1442, and

(ii) Such other person enters into a written agreement, with the district director who issued the letter, to be the withholding agent for purposes of this paragraph (b).

The exemption granted, and the corresponding withholding obligation imposed, by this paragraph (b)(5) shall apply with respect to the first distribution made after execution of the agreement described in the preceding sentence and shall continue to apply to all distributions made during the period in which the exemption granted under § 1.1441-4(f) is in effect.

(6) *Payment other than in money.*—The rule stated in § 1.1441-7(c) regarding payment other than in money shall apply for purposes of this section.

(c) *Amount to be withheld.*—(1) *Distribution from a publicly traded partnership or publicly traded trust.*—The amount to be withheld under this section with respect to a distribution by a publicly traded partnership or publicly traded trust shall be computed in the manner described in § 1.1445-5(c)(3)(ii) and (iii), subject to the rules of this section.

(2) *REITs.*—(i) *In general.*—The amount to be withheld with respect to a distribution by a REIT, under this section shall be equal to 35 percent (or the highest rate specified in section 1445(e)(1)) of the amount described in paragraph (c)(2)(ii) of this section.

(ii) *Amount subject to withholding.*—(A) *In general.*—Except as otherwise provided in paragraph (c)(2)(ii)(C) of this section, the amount subject to withholding is the amount of any distribution, determined with respect to each share or certificate of beneficial interest, designated by a REIT as a capital gain dividend, multiplied by the number of shares or certificates of beneficial interest owned by the foreign person. Solely for purposes of this paragraph, the largest amount of any distribution occurring after March 7, 1991 that could be designated as a capital gain dividend under section 857(b)(3)(C) shall be deemed to have been designated by a REIT as a capital gain dividend regardless of the amount actually designated.

(B) *Distribution attributable to net short-term capital gain from the disposition of a U.S. real property interest.*—[Reserved]

(C) *Designation of prior distribution as capital gain dividend.*—If a REIT makes an actual designation of a prior distribution, in whole or in part, as a capital gain dividend, such prior distribution shall not be subject to withholding under this section. Rather, a REIT must characterize and treat as a capital gain dividend distribution (solely for purposes of section 1445(e)(1)) each distribution, determined with respect to each share or certificate of beneficial interest, made on the day of, or any time subsequent to, such designation as a capital gain dividend until such characterized amounts equal the amount of the prior distribution designated as a capital gain dividend. The provisions of this paragraph shall not be applicable in any taxable year in which the REIT adopts a formal or informal resolution or plan of complete liquidation.

(iii) *Example.*—The following example illustrates the rules of paragraph (c)(2)(ii)(C) of this section.

In the first quarter of 1988, XYZ REIT makes a dividend distribution of $2X. In the second quarter of 1988, XYZ sells real property, recognizing a long term capital gain of $15X, and makes a dividend distribution of $5X. In the third quarter of 1988, XYZ makes a distribution of $3X. In the fourth quarter of 1988, XYZ sells real property recognizing a long term capital loss of $2X. Within 30 days after the close of the taxable year, XYZ designates a capital gain dividend for the year of $13X. It subsequently makes a fourth quarter distribution of $7X. Since XYZ has made an actual designation of prior distributions during the taxable year as capital gain dividends, withholding on those prior distributions will not be required. However, the REIT must characterize, solely for purposes of § 1445(e)(1), a total amount of $13X of dividend distributions as capital gain dividends. Therefore, the fourth quarter dividend distribution of $7X must be characterized as a capital gain dividend subject to withholding under this section. In addition, XYZ will be required to characterize an additional $6X of subsequent dividend distributions as capital gain dividends.

(d) *Definition of nominee.*—For purposes of this section, the term "nominee" means a domestic person that holds an interest in an entity described in paragraph (a) of this section on behalf of another domestic or foreign person.

(e) *Determination of non-foreign status by withholding agent.*—A withholding agent may rely on a certificate of non-foreign status pursuant to § 1.1445-2(b) or on the statements and address provided to it on Form W-9 or a form that is substantially similar to such form, to determine whether an interest holder is a domestic person. Reliance on these documents will excuse the withholding agent from liability imposed under section 1445(e)(1) in the absence of actual knowledge that the interest holder is a foreign person. A withholding agent may also employ other means to determine the status of an interest holder, but, if the agent relies on such other means and the interest holder proves, in fact, to be a foreign person, then the withholding agent is subject to any liability imposed pursuant to section 1445 and the regulations thereunder for failure to withhold.

(f) *Qualified notice.*—A qualified notice for purposes of paragraph (b)(3)(iv) of this section is a notice given by a partnership, trust or REIT regarding a distribution that is attributable to the disposition of a U.S. real property interest in accordance with the notice requirements with respect to dividends described in 17 C.F.R. 240.10b-17(b)(1) or (3) issued pursuant to the Securities Exchange Act of 1934, 15 U.S.C. §78a *et seq.* In the case of a REIT, a qualified notice is only a notice of a distribution, all or any portion of which the REIT actually designates, or characterizes in accordance with paragraph (c)(2)(ii)(C) of this section, as a capital gain dividend in accordance with 17 C.F.R. 240.10b-17(b)(1) or (3), with respect to each share or certificate of beneficial interest. A deemed designation under paragraph (c)(2)(ii)(A) of this section may not be the subject of a qualified notice under this paragraph (f). A person described in paragraph (b)(3) of this section shall be treated as receiving a qualified notice at the time such notice is published in accordance with 17 C.F.R. 240.10b-17(b)(1) or (3).

(g) *Reporting and paying over withheld amounts.*—With respect to an amount withheld under this section, a withholding agent is not required to conform to the requirements of § 1.1445-5(b)(5) but is required to report and pay over to the Internal Revenue Service any amount required to be withheld pursuant to the rules and procedures of section 1461, the regulations thereunder and § 1.6302-2. Forms 1042 and 1042S are to be used for this purpose.

(h) *Early refund procedure not available.*—The early refund procedure set forth in § 1.1445-6(g) shall not apply to amounts withheld under the rules of this section. For adjustment of over-withheld amounts, see § 1.1461-4.

(i) *Liability upon failure to withhold.*—For rules regarding liability upon failure to withhold under § 1445(e) and this section, see § 1.1445-1(e). [Reg. § 1.1445-8.]

☐ [*T.D.* 8321, 12-6-90. *Amended by T.D.* 8647, 12-20-95.]

[Reg. § 1.1445-10T]

§ 1.1445-10T. Special rule for foreign governments (Temporary).—(a) This section provides a temporary regulation that, if and when adopted as a final regulation, will add a new paragraph (d)(6) to § 1.1445-2. Paragraph (b) of this section would then appear as paragraph (d) (6) of § 1.1445-2.

(b) *Foreign government.*—(1) *As transferor.*—A foreign government is subject to U.S. taxation under section 897 on the disposition of a U.S. real property interest except to the extent specifically otherwise provided in the regulations issued under section 892. A foreign government that disposes of a U.S. real property interest that is not subject to taxation as specifically provided by the regulations under section 892 may present a notice of nonrecognition treatment pursuant to paragraph (d)(2) of this section that specifically cites the provision of such regulation, and thereby avoids withholding by the transferee of the property. A foreign government that disposes of a U.S. real property interest or the transferee of the property may obtain a withholding certificate from the Internal Revenue Service that confirms the applicability of section 892, but neither is required to do so. Rules concerning the issuance of withholding certificates are provided in § 1.1445-3.

(2) *As transferee.*—A foreign government or international organization that acquires a U.S. real property interest is fully subject to section 1445 and the regulations thereunder. Therefore, such an entity is required to withhold tax upon the acquisition of a U.S. real property interest from a foreign person.

(c) *Effective date.*—The rules of this section shall be effective for transfers, exchanges, distributions and other dispositions occurring on or after June 6, 1988. [Temporary Reg. § 1.1445-10T.]

☐ [*T.D.* 8198, 5-4-88.]

[Reg. § 1.1445-11T]

§ 1.1445-11T. Special rules requiring withholding under § 1.1445-5 (Temporary).— (a) *Purpose and scope.*—This section provides temporary regulations that, if and when adopted as a final regulation, will add certain new paragraphs within § 1.1445-5(b) and (c). The paragraphs of this section would then appear as set forth below. Paragraph (b) of this section would then appear as paragraph (b)(8)(v) of § 1.1445-5. Paragraph (c) of this section would then appear as paragraph (c)(2)(i) of § 1.1445-5. Paragraph (d) of this section would then appear as paragraph (g) of § 1.1445-5.

(b) *Disposition of interests in partnerships, trusts, and estates.*—The provisions of section 1445(e)(5), requiring withholding upon certain dispositions of interests in partnerships, trusts, and estates, that own directly or indirectly a U.S. real property interest shall apply to dispositions on or after the effective date of a later Treasury decision under section 897(g) of the Code except in the case of dispositions of interests in partnerships in which fifty percent of the value of the gross assets consist of U.S. real property interests and ninety percent or more of the value of the gross assets consist of U.S. real property interests plus any cash or cash equivalents. The provisions of section 1445(e)(5), shall apply, however, to dispositions after June 6, 1988, of interests in partnerships in which fifty percent or more of the value of the gross assets consist of U.S. real property interests, and ninety percent or more of the value of the gross assets consist of U.S. real property interests plus any cash or cash equivalents. See paragraph (d) of this section.

(c) *Transactions covered elsewhere.*—No withholding is required under this paragraph (c) with respect to the distribution of a U.S. real property interest by a partnership, trust, or estate. Such distributions shall be subject to withholding under section 1445(e)(4) and paragraph (f) of this § 1.1445-5 on the effective date of a later Treasury decision published under section 897(g) of the Code. No withholding is required at this time for distributions described in the preceding sentence. See paragraph (b)(8)(iv) of this § 1.1445-5. No withholding is required under this paragraph with respect to the disposition of an interest in a trust, estate, or partnership except in the case of a partnership in which fifty percent or more of the value of the gross assets consist of U.S. real property interests, and ninety percent or more of the value of the gross assets consist of U.S. real property interests plus any cash or cash equivalents. See paragraph (b)(8)(v) of § 1.1445-5. Withholding shall be required as provided in section 1445(e)(5) and paragraph (g) of this section with respect to the disposition after June 6, 1988, of an interest in a partnership in which fifty percent or more of the value of the gross assets consist of U.S. real property interests, and ninety percent or more of the value of the gross assets consist of U.S. real property interests plus any cash or cash equivalents.

(d) *Dispositions of interests in partnerships, trusts, and estates.*—(1) *Withholding required on disposition of certain partnership interests.*—Withholding is required under section 1445(e)(5) and this paragraph with respect to the disposition by a foreign partner of an interest in a domestic or foreign partnership in which fifty percent or more of the value of the gross assets consist of U.S. real property interests, and ninety percent or more of the value of the gross assets consist of U.S. real property interests plus any cash or cash equivalents. For purposes of this paragraph cash equivalents means any asset readily convertible into cash (whether or not denominated in U.S. dollars), including, but not limited to, bank accounts, certificates of deposit, money market accounts, commercial paper, U.S. and foreign treasury obligations and bonds, corporate obligations and bonds, precious metals or commodities, and publicly traded instruments. The taxpayer on filing an income tax return for the year of the disposition may demonstrate the extent to which the gain on the disposition of the interest is not attributable to U.S. real property interests. A taxpayer is also permitted by § 1.1445-3 to apply for a withholding certificate in instances where reduced withholding is appropriate.

(2) *Withholding not required.*—(i) *Transferee receives statement that interest in partnership is not described in paragraph (d)(1).*—No withholding is required under paragraph (d)(1) of this section upon the disposition of a partnership interest otherwise described in that paragraph if the

transferee is provided a statement, issued by the partnership and signed by a general partner under penalties of perjury no earlier than 30 days before the transfer, certifying that fifty percent or more of the value of the gross assets does not consist of U.S. real property interests, or that ninety percent or more of the value of the gross assets of the partnership does not consist of U.S. real property interests plus cash or cash equivalents.

(ii) *Reliance on statement not permitted.*—A transferee is not entitled to rely upon a statement described in paragraph (d)(2)(i) of this section if, prior to or at the time of the transfer, the transferee either—

(A) Has actual knowledge that the statement is false, or

(B) Receives a notice, pursuant to §1.1445-4.

Such a transferee's withholding obligations shall apply as if the statement had never been given, and such a transferee may be held fully liable pursuant to §1.1445-1(e) for any failure to withhold.

(iii) *Belated notice of false statement.*—If, after the date of the transfer, a transferee receives notice that a statement provided under paragraph (d)(2)(i) of this section is false, then such transferee may rely on the statement only with respect to consideration that was paid prior to the receipt of the notice. Such a transferee is required to withhold a full 10 percent of the amount realized from the consideration that remains to be paid to the transferor. Thus, if 10 percent or more of the amount realized remains to be paid to the transferor, then the transferee is required to withhold and pay over the full 10 percent. The transferee must do so by withholding and paying over the entire amount of each successive payment of consideration to the transferor, until the full 10 percent of the amount realized has been withheld and paid over. Amounts so withheld must be reported and paid over by the 20th day following the date on which each such payment of consideration is made. A transferee that is subject to the rules of this §1.1445-10T(d)(2)(iii) may not obtain a withholding certificate pursuant to §1.1445-3, but must instead withhold and pay over the amounts required by this paragraph.

(e) *Effective date.*—The rules of this section are effective for transactions after June 6, 1988. [Temporary Reg. §1.1445-11T.]

☐ [T.D. 8198, 5-4-88.]

[Reg. §1.1446-0]

§1.1446-0. **Table of contents.**—This section lists the captions contained in §§1.1446-1 through 1.1446-7.

§1.1446-1 *Withholding tax on foreign partners' share of effectively connected taxable income.*

(a) In general.

(b) Steps in determining 1446 tax obligation.

(c) Determining whether a partnership has a foreign partner.

(1) In general.

(2) Submission of Forms W-8BEN, W-8IMY, W-8ECI, W-8EXP, and W-9.

(i) In general.

(ii) Withholding certificate applicable to each type of partner.

(A) U.S. person.

(B) Nonresident alien.

(C) Foreign partnership.

(D) Disregarded entities.

(E) Domestic and foreign grantor trusts.

(F) Nominees.

(G) Foreign governments, foreign tax-exempt organizations and other foreign persons.

(H) Foreign corporations, certain foreign trusts, and foreign estates

(iii) Effect of Forms W-8BEN, W-8IMY, W-8ECI, W-8EXP, W-9, and statement.

(A) Partnership reliance on withholding certificate.

(B) Reason to know.

(C) Subsequent knowledge and impact on penalties.

(iv) Requirements for certificates to be valid.

(A) When period of validity expires.

(B) Required information for Forms W-8BEN, W-8IMY, W-8ECI, and W-8EXP.

(v) Partner must provide new withholding certificate when there is a change in circumstances.

(vi) Partnership must retain withholding certificates.

(3) Presumptions in the absence of valid Form W-8BEN, Form W-8IMY, Form W-8ECI, Form W-8EXP, Form W-9, or statement.

(4) Consequences when partnership knows or has reason to know that Form W-8BEN, Form W-8IMY, Form W-8ECI, Form W-8EXP, or Form W-9 is incorrect or unreliable and does not withhold.

(5) Acceptable substitute form.

§1.1446-2 *Determining a partnership's effectively connected taxable income allocable to foreign partners under section 704.*

(a) In general.

(b) Computation.

(1) In general.

(2) Income and gain rules.

(i) Application of the principles of section 864.

(ii) Income treated as effectively connected.

(iii) Exempt income.

(3) Deductions and losses.

(i) Oil and gas interests.

(ii) Charitable contributions.

(iii) Net operating losses and other suspended or carried losses.

(iv) Interest deductions.

(v) Limitation on capital losses.

(vi) Other deductions.

(vii) Limitations on deductions.

(4) Other rules.

(i) Exclusion of items allocated to U.S. partners.

(ii) Partnership credits.

(5) Examples.

§ 1.1446-3 *Time and manner of calculating and paying over the 1446 tax.*

(a) In general.

(1) Calculating 1446 tax.

(2) Applicable percentage.

(i) In general.

(ii) Special types of income or gain.

(b) Installment payments.

(1) In general.

(2) Calculation.

(i) General application of the principles of section 6655.

(ii) Annualization methods.

(iii) Partner's estimated tax payments.

(iv) Partner whose interest terminates during the partnership's taxable year.

(v) Exceptions and modifications to the application of the principles under section 6655.

(A) Inapplicability of special rules for large corporations.

(B) Inapplicability of special rules regarding early refunds.

(C) Period of underpayment.

(D) Other taxes.

(E) 1446 tax treated as tax under section 11.

(F) Application of section 6655(f).

(G) Application of section 6655(i).

(H) Current year tax safe harbor.

(I) Prior year tax safe harbor.

(3) 1446 tax safe harbor.

(i) In general.

(ii) Permission to change to standard annualization method.

(c) Coordination with other withholding rules.

(1) Fixed or determinable, annual or periodical income.

(2) Real property gains.

(i) Domestic partnerships.

(ii) Foreign partnerships.

(3) Coordination with section 1443.

(d) Reporting and crediting the 1446 tax.

(1) Reporting 1446 tax.

(i) Reporting of installment tax payments and notification to partners of installment tax payments.

(ii) Payment due dates.

(iii) Annual return and notification to partners.

(iv) Information provided to beneficiaries of foreign trusts and estates.

(v) Attachments required of foreign trusts and estates.

(vi) Attachments required of beneficiaries of foreign trusts and estates.

(vii) Information provided to beneficiaries of foreign trusts and estates that are partners in certain publicly traded partnerships.

(2) Crediting 1446 tax against a partner's U.S. tax liability.

(i) In general.

(ii) Substantiation for purposes of claiming the credit under section 33.

(iii) Special rules for apportioning the tax credit under section 33.

(A) Foreign trusts and estates.

(B) Use of domestic trusts to circumvent section 1446.

(iv) Refunds to withholding agent.

(v) 1446 tax treated as cash distribution to partners.

(vi) Examples.

(e) Liability of partnership for failure to withhold.

(1) In general.

(2) Proof that tax liability has been satisfied and deemed payment of 1446 tax.

(3) Liability for interest, penalties, and additions to the tax.

(i) Partnership.

(ii) Foreign partner.

(4) Examples.

(f) Effect of withholding on partner.

§ 1.1446-4 *Publicly traded partnerships.*

(a) In general.

(b) Definitions.

(1) Publicly traded partnership.

(2) Applicable percentage.

(3) Nominee.

(4) Qualified notice.

(c) Paying and reporting 1446 tax.

(d) Rules for designation of nominees to withhold tax under section 1446.

(e) Determining foreign status of partners.

(f) Distributions subject to withholding.

(1) In general.

(2) In-kind distributions.

(3) Ordering rule relating to distributions.

(4) Coordination with section 1445(e) (1).

Reg. § 1.1446-0

§1.1446-5 *Tiered partnership structures.*
  (a) In general.
  (b) Reporting requirements.
    (1) In general.
    (2) Publicly traded partnerships.
  (c) Look through rules for foreign upper-tier partnerships.
  (d) Publicly traded partnerships.
    (1) Upper-tier publicly traded partnership.
    (2) Lower-tier publicly traded partnership.
  (e) Election by a domestic upper-tier partnership to apply look through rules.
    (1) In general.
    (2) Information required for valid election statement.
    (3) Consent of lower-tier partnership.
  (f) Examples.

§1.1446-6 *Special rules to reduce a partnership's 1446 tax with respect to a foreign partner's allocable share of effectively connected taxable income.*
  (a) In general.
    (1) Purpose and scope.
    (2) Reasonable reliance on a certificate.
  (b) Foreign partners to whom this section applies.
    (1) In general.
    (2) Definitions.
      (i) U.S. income tax return.
      (ii) Timely-filed.
      (iii) Qualifying U.S. income tax return.
    (3) Special rules.
  (c) Reduction of 1446 tax with respect to a foreign partner.
    (1) General rules.
      (i) Certified deductions and losses.
        (A) Deductions and losses from the partnership.
        (B) Deductions and loss from other sources.
        (C) Limit on the consideration of a partner's net operating loss deduction.
        (D) Limitation on losses subject to certain partner level limitations.
        (E) Certification of deductions and losses to other partnerships.
        (F) Partner level use of deductions and losses certified to a partnership.
      (ii) De minimis certificate for nonresident alien individual partners.
        (A) In general.
        (B) Requirements for exception.
      (iii) Consideration of certain current year state and local taxes.
    (2) Form and time of certification.
      (i) Form of certification.
      (ii) Time of certification provided to partnership.

      (A) First certificate submitted for a partnership's taxable year.
      (B) Updated certificates and status updates.
        (1) Preceding year tax returns not yet filed.
        (2) Other circumstances requiring an updated certificate.
        (3) Form and content of updated certificate.
        (4) Partnership consideration of an updated certificate.
    (3) Notification to partnership when a partner's certificate cannot be relied upon.
    (4) Partner to receive copy of notice.
    (5) Notification to partnership when no foreign partner's certificate can be relied upon.
    (6) Partnership notification to partner regarding use of deductions and losses.
    (7) Partner's certificate valid only for partnership taxable year for which submitted.
  (d) Effect of certificate of deductions and losses on partner and partnership.
    (1) Effect on partner.
      (i) No effect on liability for income tax of foreign partner.
      (ii) No effect on partner's estimated tax obligations.
      (iii) No effect on partner's obligation to file U.S. income tax return.
    (2) Effect on partnership.
      (i) Reasonable reliance to relieve partnership from addition to tax under section 6665.
      (ii) Continuing liability for withholding tax under section 1461 and for applicable interest and penalties.
        (A) In general.
        (B) Certificate defective because of amount or character of deductions and losses.
    (3) Partnership level rules and requirements.
      (i) Filing requirement.
      (ii) Reasonable cause for failure to timely file a valid certificate and computation.
        (A) Determining reasonable cause.
        (B) Notification.
  (e) Examples.
  (f) Effective/Applicability date.
  (g) Transition rule.

§1.1446-7 *Effective/Applicability date.*
[Reg. §1.1446-0.]

  ☐ [*T.D.* 9200, 5-13-2005. *Amended by T.D. 9394,* 4-28-2008.]

[Reg. §1.1446-1]

§1.1446-1. Witholding tax on foreign partners' share of effectively connected taxable income.—(a) *In general.*—If a domestic or foreign partnership has effectively connected taxable income (ECTI) as computed under §1.1446-2 for any partnership tax year, and any portion of such taxable income is allocable under section 704 to a foreign partner, then the partnership must pay a withholding tax under section 1446 (1446 tax) at the time and in the manner prescribed in this section, and §§ 1.1446-2 through 1.1446-6.

(b) *Steps in determining 1446 tax obligation.*—In general, a partnership determines its 1446 tax as follows. The partnership determines whether it has any foreign partners in accordance with paragraph (c) of this section. If the partnership does not have any foreign partners (including any person presumed to be foreign under paragraph (c) of this section and any domestic trust treated as foreign under § 1.1446-3(d)) during its taxable year, it generally will not have a 1446 tax obligation. If the partnership has one or more foreign partners, it then determines under § 1.1446-2 whether it has ECTI any portion of which is allocable under section 704 to one or more of the foreign partners. If the partnership has ECTI allocable under section 704 to one or more of its foreign partners, the partnership computes its 1446 tax, pays over 1446 tax, and reports the amount paid in accordance with the rules in § 1.1446-3. For special rules applicable to publicly traded partnerships, see § 1.1446-4. For special rules applicable to tiered partnership structures, see § 1.1446-5. For special rules that may apply in determining the amount of 1446 tax due with respect to a partner, see § 1.1446-6.

(c) *Determining whether a partnership has a foreign partner.*—(1) *In general.*—Except as otherwise provided in this section, § 1.1446-3, and § 1.1446-5, only a partnership that has at least one foreign partner during the partnership's taxable year can have a 1446 tax liability. Generally, the term foreign partner means any partner of the partnership that is not a U.S. person within the meaning of section 7701(a)(30). Thus, a partner of the partnership is generally a foreign partner if the partner is a nonresident alien, foreign partnership (see § 1.1446-5 for rules that allow a lower-tier partnership to look through an upper-tier foreign partnership to the partners of such partnership for purposes of computing its 1446 tax), foreign corporation (which includes a foreign government pursuant to section 892(a) (3)), foreign estate or trust (see paragraph (c) (2) of this section for rules that instruct a partnership to consider the grantor or other owner of a trust under subpart E of subchapter J as the partner for purposes of computing the partnership's 1446 tax), as those terms are defined under section 7701 and the regulations thereunder, or a foreign organization described in section 501(c), or other foreign person. A person also is a foreign partner if the person is presumed to be a foreign person under paragraph (c)(3) of this section. For purposes of this section, a partner that is treated as a U.S. person for all income tax purposes (by election or otherwise, see e.g., sec-

tions 953(d) and 1504(d)) will not be a foreign partner, provided the partner has provided the partnership a valid Form W-9, "Request for Taxpayer Identification Number and Certification," or the partnership uses other means to determine that the partner is not a foreign partner (see paragraph (c)(3) of this section). A partner that is treated as a U.S. person only for certain specified purposes is considered a foreign partner for purposes of section 1446, and a partnership must pay 1446 tax on the portion of ECTI allocable to that partner. For example, a partnership must generally pay 1446 tax on ECTI allocable to a foreign corporate partner that has made an election under section 897(i).

(2) *Submission of Forms W-8BEN, W-8IMY, W-8ECI, W-8EXP, and W-9.*—(i) *In general.*—Except as otherwise provided in this paragraph (c)(2) or paragraph (c)(3) of this section, a partnership must generally determine whether a partner is a foreign partner, and the partner's tax classification (e.g., corporate or non-corporate), by obtaining a withholding certificate from the partner that is a Form W-8BEN, "Certificate of Foreign Status of Beneficial Owner for United States Tax Withholding," Form W-8IMY, "Certificate of Foreign Intermediary, Flow-Through Entity, or Certain U.S. Branches for United States Tax Withholding," Form W-8ECI, "Certificate of Foreign Person's Claim for Exemption from Withholding on Income Effectively Connected With the Conduct of a Trade or Business in the United States," Form W-8EXP, "Certificate of Foreign Government or other Foreign Organization for United States Tax Withholding," or a Form W-9, as applicable, or an acceptable substitute form permitted under paragraph (c)(5) of this section. Generally, a foreign partner that is a nonresident alien, a foreign estate or trust (other than a grantor trust described in this paragraph (c) (2)), a foreign corporation, or a foreign government should provide a valid Form W-8BEN.

(ii) *Withholding certificate applicable to each type of partner.*—A partner that submits a valid Form W-8 (e.g., Form W-8BEN) for purposes of section 1441 or 1442 will generally satisfy the documentation requirements of this section provided that the submission of such form is not inconsistent with the rules of this paragraph (c)(2) or paragraph (c)(3) of this section. The following rules shall apply for purposes of this section.

(A) *U.S. person.*—A partner that is a U.S. person (other than a grantor trust described in this paragraph (c)(2)), including a domestic partnership and domestic simple or complex trust (including an estate), shall provide a valid Form W-9.

(B) *Nonresident alien.*—A Form W-8 (e.g., Form W-8BEN) submitted by a nonresident alien for purposes of withholding under section 1441 will generally be accepted for purposes of section 1446. If no such form is submitted for purposes of section 1441, such nonresident alien shall submit Form W-8BEN for purposes of section 1446.

(C) *Foreign partnership.*—A partner that is a foreign partnership generally shall provide a valid Form W-8IMY for purposes of section 1446. See § 1.1446-5 (permitting a lower-tier partnership to look through an upper-tier foreign partnership in certain circumstances when computing 1446 tax).

(D) *Disregarded entities.*—An entity that is disregarded as an entity separate from its owner under § 301.7701-3 of this chapter (whether domestic or foreign) shall not submit a Form W-8 (e.g., Form W-8BEN) or Form W-9. Instead, the owner of such entity for Federal tax purposes shall submit appropriate documentation to comply with this section. See § § 301.7701-1 through 301.7701-3 of this chapter for determining the U.S. Federal tax classification of a partner.

(E) *Domestic and foreign grantor trusts.*— To the extent that a grantor or other person is treated as the owner of any portion of a trust under subpart E of subchapter J of the Internal Revenue Code, such trust shall provide documentation under this paragraph (c)(2) to identify the trust as a grantor trust and provide documentation on behalf of the grantor or other person treated as the owner of all or a portion of such trust as required by this paragraph (c)(2). If such trust is a foreign trust, the trust shall submit Form W-8IMY to the partnership identifying itself as a foreign grantor trust and shall provide such documentation (e.g., Forms W-8BEN, W-8IMY, W-8ECI, W-8EXP, or W-9) and information pertaining to its grantor or other owner to the partnership that permits the partnership to reliably associate (within the meaning of § 1.1441-1(b)(2)(vii)) such portion of the trust's allocable share of partnership ECTI with the grantor or other person that is the owner of such portion of the trust. If such trust is a domestic trust, the trust shall furnish the partnership a statement under penalty of perjury that the trust is, in whole or in part, a domestic grantor trust and such statement shall identify that portion of the trust that is treated as owned by a grantor or another person under subpart E of subchapter J of the Internal Revenue Code. The trust shall also provide such documentation and information (e.g., Forms W-8BEN, W-8IMY, W-8ECI, W-8EXP, or W-9) pertaining to its grantor or other owner(s) to the partnership that permits the partnership to reliably associate (within the meaning of § 1.1441-1(b)(2)(vii)) such portion of the trust's allocable share of partnership ECTI with the grantor or other person that is the owner of such portion of the trust.

(F) *Nominees.*—Where a nominee holds an interest in a partnership on behalf of another person, the beneficial owner of the partnership interest, not the nominee, shall submit a Form W-8 (e.g., Form W-8BEN) or Form W-9 to the partnership or nominee that is the withholding agent.

(G) *Foreign governments, foreign tax-exempt organizations and other foreign persons.*—A Form W-8 (e.g., Form W-8EXP) submitted by a partner that is a foreign government, foreign tax-exempt organization, or other foreign person for purposes of withholding under § § 1441 through 1443 will also operate to establish the foreign status of such partner under this section. However, except as set forth in § 1.1446-3(c)(3) (regarding certain tax-exempt organizations described in section 501(c)), the submission of Form W-8EXP will have no effect on whether there is a 1446 tax due with respect to such partner's allocable share of partnership ECTI. For example, a partnership must still pay 1446 tax with respect to a foreign government partner's allocable share of ECTI because such partner is treated as a foreign corporation under section 892(a)(3). If no Form W-8 is submitted for purposes of withholding under sections 1441 through 1443, then such government, tax-exempt organization, or person must generally submit Form W-8BEN.

(H) *Foreign corporations, certain foreign trusts, and foreign estates.*—Consistent with the rules of this paragraph (c)(2) and paragraph (c)(3) of this section, a foreign corporation, a foreign trust (other than a foreign grantor trust described in paragraph (c)(2)(ii)(E) of this section), or a foreign estate may generally submit any appropriate Form W-8 (e.g., Form W-8BEN) to the partnership to establish its foreign status for purposes of section 1446.

(iii) *Effect of Forms W-8BEN, W-8IMY, W-8ECI, W-8EXP, W-9, and statement.*— (A) *Partnership reliance on withholding certificate.*—In general, for purposes of this section, a partnership may rely on a valid Form W-8 (e.g., Form W-8BEN) or Form W-9, or statement described in this paragraph (c)(2) from a partner, beneficial owner, or grantor trust to determine whether that person, beneficial owner, or the owner of a grantor trust, is a non-foreign or foreign partner for purposes of computing 1446 tax, and if such person is a foreign partner, to determine whether or not such person is a corporation for U.S. tax purposes. The rules of paragraph (c)(3) of this section shall apply to a partnership that receives a Form W-8IMY from a foreign grantor trust or a statement described in this paragraph (c)(2) from a domestic grantor trust, but does not receive a Form W-8 (e.g., Form W-8BEN) or Form W-9 identifying such grantor or other person. Further, a partnership may not rely on a Form W-8 or Form W-9, or statement described in this paragraph (c)(2), and such form or statement is therefore not valid for any installment period or Form 8804 filing date during which the partnership has actual knowledge or has reason to know that any information on the withholding certificate or statement is incorrect or unreliable and, if based on such knowledge or reason to know, the partnership should pay 1446 tax in an amount greater than would be the case if it relied on the certificate or statement.

(B) *Reason to know.*—A partnership has reason to know that information on a withholding certificate or statement is incorrect or unreliable if its knowledge of relevant facts or statements contained on the form or other documentation is such that a reasonably prudent person in the position of the withholding agent would question the claims made. See §§ 1.1441-1(e)(4)(viii) and 1.1441-7(b)(1) and (2).

(C) *Subsequent knowledge and impact on penalties.*—If the partnership does not have actual knowledge or reason to know that a Form W-8BEN, Form W-8IMY, Form W-8ECI, Form W-8EXP, Form W-9, or statement received from a partner, beneficial owner, or grantor trust contains incorrect or unreliable information, but it subsequently determines that the certificate or statement contains incorrect or unreliable information, and, based on such knowledge the partnership should pay 1446 tax in an amount greater than would be the case if it relied on the certificate or statement, then the partnership will not be subject to penalties for its failure to pay the 1446 tax in reliance on such certificate or statement for any installment payment date prior to the date that the determination is made. See §§ 1.1446-1(c)(4) and 1.1446-3 concerning penalties for failure to pay the withholding tax when a partnership knows or has reason to know that a withholding certificate or statement is incorrect or unreliable.

(iv) *Requirements for certificates to be valid.*—Except as otherwise provided in this paragraph (c), for purposes of this section, the validity of a Form W-9 shall be determined under section 3406 and § 31.3406(h)-3(e) of this chapter which establish when such form may be reasonably relied upon. A Form W-8BEN, Form W-8IMY, Form W-8ECI, or Form W-8EXP is only valid for purposes of this section if its validity period has not expired, the partner submitting the form has signed it under penalties of perjury, and it contains all the required information.

(A) *When period of validity expires.*—For purposes of this section, a Form W-8BEN, Form W-8IMY, Form W-8ECI, or Form W-8EXP submitted by a partner shall be valid until the end of the period of validity determined for such form under § 1.1441-1(e). With respect to a foreign partnership submitting Form W-8IMY, the period of validity of such form shall be determined under § 1.1441-1(e) as if such foreign partnership

submitted the form required of a nonwithholding foreign partnership. See § 1.1441-1(e)(4)(ii).

(B) *Required information for Forms W-8BEN, W-8IMY, W-8ECI, and W-8EXP.*—Forms W-8BEN, W-8IMY, W-8ECI, and W-8EXP submitted under this section must contain the partner's name, permanent address and Taxpayer Identification Number (TIN), the country under the laws of which the partner is formed, incorporated or governed (if the person is not an individual), the classification of the partner for U.S. Federal tax purposes (e.g., partnership, corporation), and any other information required to be submitted by the forms or instructions for such form, as applicable.

(v) *Partner must provide new withholding certificate when there is a change in circumstances.*—The principles of § 1.1441-1(e)(4)(ii)(D) shall apply when a change in circumstances has occurred (including situations where the status of a U.S. person changes) that requires a partner to provide a new withholding certificate.

(vi) *Partnership must retain withholding certificates.*—A partnership or nominee who has responsibility for paying 1446 tax under this section or § 1.1446-4 must retain each withholding certificate, statement, and other information received from its direct and indirect partners for as long as it may be relevant to the determination of the withholding agent's 1446 tax liability under section 1461 and the regulations thereunder.

(3) *Presumptions in the absence of valid Form W-8BEN, Form W-8IMY, Form W-8ECI, Form W-8EXP, Form W-9, or statement.*—Except as otherwise provided in this paragraph (c)(3), a partnership that does not receive a valid Form W-8BEN, Form W-8IMY, Form W-8ECI, Form W-8EXP, Form W-9, or statement required by paragraph (c)(2) of this section from a partner, beneficial owner, or grantor trust, or a partnership that receives a withholding certificate or statement but has actual knowledge or reason to know that the information on the certificate or statement is incorrect or unreliable, must presume that the partner is a foreign person. Except as provided in § 1.1446-3(a)(2) and § 1.1446-5(c)(2), a partnership that knows that a partner is an individual shall treat the partner as a nonresident alien. Except as provided in § 1.1446-3(a)(2) and § 1.1446-5(c)(2), a partnership that knows that a partner is an entity shall treat the partner as a corporation if the entity is a corporation as defined in § 301.7701-2(b)(8) of this chapter. See § 1.1446-3(a)(2) which prohibits a partnership in certain circumstances from considering preferential tax rates in computing its 1446 tax when the presumption and rules of this paragraph (c)(3) apply. In all other cases, the partnership shall treat the partner as either a nonresident alien or a foreign corporation, whichever classification results in a higher 1446

tax being due, and shall pay the 1446 tax in accordance with this presumption. Except as provided in § 1.1446-5(c)(2), the presumption set forth in this paragraph (c)(3) that a partner is a foreign person shall not apply to the extent that the partnership relies on other means to ascertain the non-foreign status of a partner and the partnership is correct in its determination that such partner is a U.S. person. A partnership is in no event required to rely upon other means to determine the non-foreign status of a partner and may demand that a partner furnish an acceptable certificate under this section. If a certificate is not provided in such circumstances, the partnership may presume that the partner is a foreign partner, and for purposes of sections 1461 through 1463, will be considered to have been required to pay 1446 tax on such partner's allocable share of partnership ECTI.

(4) *Consequences when partnership knows or has reason to know that Form W-8BEN, Form W-8IMY, Form W-8ECI, Form W-8EXP, or Form W-9 is incorrect or unreliable and does not withhold.*—If a partnership has actual knowledge or has reason to know that a Form W-8BEN, Form W-8IMY, Form W-8ECI, Form W-8EXP, Form W-9, or statement required by paragraph (c)(2) of this section submitted by a partner, beneficial owner, or grantor trust contains incorrect or unreliable information (either because the certificate or statement when given to the partnership contained incorrect information or because there has been a change in facts that makes information on the certificate or statement incorrect), and the partnership pays less than the full amount of 1446 tax due on ECTI allocable to that partner, the partnership shall be fully liable under section 1461 and § 1.1461-3 (§ 1.1461-1 for publicly traded partnerships subject to § 1.1446-4) and § 1.1446-3, and for all applicable penalties and interest, for any failure to pay the 1446 tax for the period during which the partnership has such knowledge or reason to know that the certificate contained incorrect or unreliable information and for all subsequent installment periods. If a partner, beneficial owner, or grantor trust submits a new valid Form W-8BEN, Form W-8IMY, Form W-8ECI, Form W-8EXP, Form W-9, or statement, as applicable, the partnership may rely on that documentation when paying 1446 tax (or any installment of such tax) for any payment date that has not passed at the time such form is received.

(5) *Acceptable substitute form.*—A partnership or withholding agent responsible for paying 1446 tax (or any installment of such tax) may substitute its own form for the official version of Form W-8 (e.g., Form W-8BEN) that is recognized under this section to ascertain the identity of its partners, provided such form is consistent with § 1.1441-1(e)(4)(vi). All references under this section or § § 1.1446-2 through 1.1446-6 to a Form W-8 (e.g., Form W-8BEN, Form W-8IMY, Form W-8ECI, Form W-8EXP) shall include the acceptable substitute form recognized under this paragraph (c)(5). [Reg. § 1.1446-1.]

☐ [*T.D. 9200, 5-13-2005. Amended by T.D. 9394, 4-28-2008.*]

[Reg. § 1.1446-2]

§ 1.1446-2. Determining a partnership's effectively connected taxable income allocable to foreign partners under section 704.—(a) *In general.*—A partnership's effectively connected taxable income (ECTI) is generally the partnership's taxable income as computed under section 703, with adjustments as provided in section 1446(c) and this section, and computed with consideration of only those partnership items which are effectively connected (or treated as effectively connected) with the conduct of a trade or business in the United States. For purposes of determining the section 1446 withholding tax (1446 tax) or any installment of such tax under § 1.1446-3, partnership ECTI allocable under section 704 to foreign partners is the sum of the allocable shares of ECTI of each of the partnership's foreign partners as determined under paragraph (b) of this section. See § 1.1446-6 (special rules permitting the partnership to consider partner-level deductions and losses to reduce the partnership's 1446 tax). The calculation of partnership ECTI allocable to foreign partners as set forth in paragraph (b) of this section and the partnership's withholding tax obligation are partnership-level computations solely for purposes of determining the 1446 tax. Therefore, any deduction that is not taken into account in calculating a partner's allocable share of partnership ECTI (e.g., percentage depletion), but which is a deduction that under U.S. tax law the foreign partner is otherwise entitled to claim, can still be claimed by the foreign partner when computing its U.S. tax liability and filing its U.S. income tax return, subject to any restriction or limitation that otherwise may apply.

(b) *Computation.*—(1) *In general.*—A foreign partner's allocable share of partnership ECTI for the partnership's taxable year that is allocable under section 704 to a particular foreign partner is equal to that foreign partner's distributive share of partnership gross income and gain for the partnership's taxable year that is effectively connected and properly allocable to the partner under section 704 and the regulations thereunder, reduced by the foreign partner's distributive share of partnership deductions for the partnership taxable year that are connected with such income under section 873(a) or 882(c) and properly allocable to the partner under section 704 and the regulations thereunder, in each case, after application of the rules of this section. See § 1.1446-6 (special rules permitting the partnership to consider partner-level deductions and losses to reduce the partnership's 1446 tax). For these purposes, a foreign partner's distributive share of effectively connected gross income and gain and the deductions connected with such income shall be computed by considering allocations that are respected under the rules of section 704 and § 1.704-1(b)(1), including special allocations in the partnership agreement (as defined in § 1.704-1(b)(2)(ii) (*h*)), and adjustments to the basis of partnership property described in section 743 pursuant to an election by the partnership under section 754 (see § 1.743-1(j)). The character of effectively connected partnership items (capital versus ordinary) shall be separately considered only to the extent set forth in paragraph (b)(3)(v) of this section and, when applicable, sections 1.1446-3(a)(2) (consideration of preferential rates when computing 1446 tax) and section 1.1446-6 (special rules permitting the partnership to consider partner-level deductions and losses to reduce the partnership's 1446 tax).

(2) *Income and gain rules.*—For purposes of computing a foreign partner's allocable share of partnership ECTI under this paragraph (b), the following rules shall apply with respect to partnership income and gain.

(i) *Application of the principles of section 864.*—The determination of whether a partnership's items of gross income are effectively connected shall be made by applying the principles of section 864 and the regulations thereunder.

(ii) *Income treated as effectively connected.*— A partnership's items of gross income that are effectively connected include any income that is treated as effectively connected income, including partnership income subject to a partner's election under section 871(d) or section 882(d), any partnership income treated as effectively connected with the conduct of a U.S. trade or business pursuant to section 897, and any other items of partnership income treated as effectively connected under another provision of the Internal Revenue Code, without regard to whether those amounts are taxable to the partner. A partner that makes the election under section 871(d) or section 882(d) shall furnish to the partnership a statement that indicates that such election has been made. See § 1.871-10(d)(3). If a partnership receives a valid Form W-8ECI from a partner, the partner is deemed, for purposes of section 1446, to have effectively connected income subject to withholding under section 1446 to the extent of the items identified on the form.

(iii) *Exempt income.*—A foreign partner's allocable share of partnership ECTI does not include income or gain exempt from U.S. tax by reason of a provision of the Internal Revenue Code. A foreign partner's allocable share of partnership ECTI also does not include income or gain exempt from U.S. tax by operation of any U.S. income tax treaty or reciprocal agreement. In the case of income excluded by reason of a treaty provision, such income must be derived

by a resident of an applicable treaty jurisdiction, the resident must be the beneficial owner of the item, and all other requirements for benefits under the treaty must be satisfied. The partnership must have received from the partner a valid withholding certificate, that is, Form W-8BEN (see § 1.1446-1(c)(2)(iii) regarding when a Form W-8BEN is valid for purposes of this section), containing the information necessary to support the claim for treaty benefits required in the forms and instructions. In addition, for purposes of this section, the withholding certificate must contain the beneficial owner's taxpayer identification number.

(3) *Deductions and losses.*—For purposes of computing a foreign partner's allocable share of partnership ECTI under this paragraph (b), the following rules shall apply with respect to deductions and losses.

(i) *Oil and gas interests.*—The deduction for depletion with respect to oil and gas wells shall be allowed, but the amount of such deduction shall be determined without regard to sections 613 and 613A.

(ii) *Charitable contributions.*—The deduction for charitable contributions provided in section 170 shall not be allowed.

(iii) *Net operating losses and other suspended or carried losses.*—Except as provided in § 1.1446-6, the net operating loss deduction of any foreign partner provided in section 172 shall not be taken into account. Further, except as provided in § 1.1446-6, the partnership shall not take into account any suspended losses (e.g., losses in excess of a partner's basis in the partnership, see section 704(d)) or any capital loss carrybacks or carryovers available to a foreign partner.

(iv) *Interest deductions.*—The rules of this paragraph (b)(3)(iv) shall apply for purposes of determining the amount of interest expense that is allocable to income which is (or is treated as) effectively connected with the conduct of a trade or business for purposes of calculating a foreign partner's allocable share of partnership ECTI. In the case of a non-corporate foreign partner, the rules of § 1.861-9T(e)(7) shall apply. In the case of a corporate foreign partner, the rules of § 1.882-5 shall apply by treating the partnership as a foreign corporation and using the partner's pro-rata share of the partnership's assets and liabilities for these purposes. For these purposes, the rules governing elections under § 1.882-5(a)(7) shall be made at the partnership level.

(v) *Limitation on capital losses.*—Losses from the sale or exchange of capital assets allocable under section 704 to a partner shall be allowed only to the extent of gains from the sale or exchange of capital assets allocable under section 704 to such partner.

Reg. § 1.1446-2(b)(3)(v)

(vi) *Other deductions.*—No deduction shall be allowed for personal exemptions provided in section 151 or the additional itemized deductions for individuals provided in part VII of subchapter B of the Internal Revenue Code (section 211 and following).

(vii) *Limitations on deductions.*—Except as provided in § 1.1446-6 and this paragraph (b)(3), any limitations on losses or deductions that apply at the partner level when determining ECTI allocable to a foreign partner shall not be taken into account.

(4) *Other rules.*—(i) *Exclusion of items allocated to U.S. partners.*—Except as provided in § 1.1446-5(e), in computing partnership ECTI, the partnership shall not take into account any item of income, gain, loss, or deduction to the extent allocable to any partner that is not a foreign partner, as that term is defined in § 1.1446-1(c).

(ii) *Partnership credits.*—See § 1.1446-3(a) providing that the 1446 tax is computed without regard to a partner's distributive share of the partnership's tax credits.

(5) *Examples.*—The following examples illustrate the application of this section. In considering the examples, disregard the potential application of § 1.1446-3(b)(2)(v)(F) (relating to the de minimis exception to paying 1446 tax). The examples are as follows:

Example 1. Limitation on capital losses. PRS partnership has two equal partners, A and B. A is a nonresident alien and B is a U.S. citizen. A provides PRS with a valid Form W-8BEN, and B provides PRS with a valid Form W-9. PRS has the following annualized tax items for the relevant installment period, all of which are effectively connected with its U.S. trade or business and are allocated equally between A and B: $100 of long-term capital gain, $400 of long-term capital loss, $300 of ordinary income, and $100 of ordinary deductions. Assume that these allocations are respected under section 704(b) and the regulations thereunder. Accordingly, A's allocable share of PRS's effectively connected items includes $50 of long-term capital gain, $200 of long-term capital loss, $150 of ordinary income, and $50 of ordinary deductions. In determining A's allocable share of partnership ECTI, the amount of the long-term capital loss that may be taken into account pursuant to paragraph (b)(3)(v) of this section is limited to A's allocable share of gain from the sale or exchange of capital assets. Accordingly, A's share of partnership ECTI allocable under section 704 pursuant to § 1.1446-2 is $100 ($150 of ordinary income less $50 of ordinary deductions, plus $50 of capital gain less $50 of capital loss).

Example 2. Limitation on capital losses—special allocations. PRS partnership has two equal partners, A and B. A and B are both nonresident aliens. A and B each provide PRS with a valid Form W-8BEN. PRS has the following annualized tax items for the relevant installment period, all of which are effectively connected with its U.S. trade or business: $200 of long-term capital gain, $200 of long-term capital loss, and $400 of ordinary income. A and B have equal shares in the ordinary income, however, pursuant to the partnership agreement, capital gains and losses are subject to special allocations. The long-term capital gain is allocable to A, and the long-term capital loss is allocable to B. Assume that these allocations are respected under section 704(b) and the regulations thereunder. Pursuant to paragraph (b)(3)(v) of this section, A's allocable share of partnership ECTI under § 1.1446-2 is $400 (consisting of $200 of ordinary income and $200 of long-term capital gain), and B's allocable share of partnership ECTI is $200 (consisting of $200 of ordinary income).

Example 3. Withholding tax obligation where partner has net operating losses. PRS partnership has two equal partners, FC, a foreign corporation, and DC, a domestic corporation. FC and DC provide a valid Form W-8BEN and Form W-9, respectively, to PRS. Both FC and PRS are on a calendar taxable year. PRS is engaged in the conduct of a trade or business in the United States and for its first installment period during its taxable year has $100 of annualized ECTI that is allocable to FC. As of the beginning of the taxable year, FC had an unused effectively connected net operating loss carryover in the amount of $300. FC's net operating loss carryover is not taken into account in determining FC's allocable share of partnership ECTI under § 1.1446-2 and, absent the application of § 1.1446-6 (permitting a foreign partner to certify deductions and losses reasonably expected to be available to reduce the partner's U.S. income tax liability on the effectively connected income or gain allocable from the partnership), is not considered in computing the 1446 tax installment payment due on behalf of FC. Accordingly, PRS must pay 1446 tax with respect to the $100 of ECTI allocable to FC.

[Reg. § 1.1446-2.]

☐ [*T.D. 9200, 5-13-2005. Amended by T.D. 9394, 4-28-2008.*]

[Reg. § 1.1446-3]

§ 1.1446-3. Time and manner of calculating and paying over the 1446 tax.—(a) *In general.*—(1) *Calculating 1446 tax.*—This section provides rules for calculating, reporting, and paying over the section 1446 withholding tax (1446 tax). A partnership's 1446 tax equals the amount determined under this section and shall be paid in installments during the partnership's taxable year (see paragraph (d)(1) of this section for installment payment due dates), with any remaining tax due paid with the partnership's annual return required to be filed pursuant to paragraph (d) of this section. For these purposes, a partnership shall not take into account either a partner's liability for any other tax imposed under any other provision of the Internal Revenue Code (e.g., section 55 or 884) or a partner's distributive share of the partnership's tax credits when determining the amount of the partnership's 1446 tax.

(2) *Applicable percentage.*—(i) *In general.*—Except as provided in this paragraph (a)(2), in the case of a foreign partner that is a corporation for U.S. tax purposes, the applicable percentage is the highest rate of tax specified in section 11(b)(1) for such taxable year. Except as provided in this paragraph (a)(2) and § 1.1446-5, in the case of a foreign partner that is not a corporation for U.S. tax purposes (e.g., a partnership, individual, trust or estate), the applicable percentage is the highest rate of tax specified in section 1.

(ii) *Special types of income or gain.*—Except as otherwise provided, a partnership is permitted to consider as the applicable percentage under this paragraph (a)(2) the highest rate of tax applicable to a particular type of income or gain allocable to a partner (e.g., long-term capital gain allocable to a non-corporate partner, unrecaptured section 1250 gain, collectibles gain under section 1(h)), to the extent of a partner's allocable share of such income or gain. Consideration of the highest rate of tax applicable to a particular type of income or gain under the previous sentence shall be made without regard to the amount of such partner's income. A partnership is not permitted to consider the highest rate of tax applicable to a particular type of income or gain under this paragraph (a)(2)(ii) if the application of the preferential rate depends upon the corporate or non-corporate status of the person reporting the income or gain and, either no documentation has been provided to the partnership under § 1.1446-1 to establish the corporate or non-corporate status of the partner required to pay tax on the income or gain, or the partnership is otherwise required to compute and pay 1446 tax on such portion of the income or gain using the highest applicable percentage under section 1446(b). See e.g., § § 1.1446-1(c)(3) (presumption of foreign status in the absence of documentation) and 1.1446-5(c)(2) (requirement to pay 1446 tax at higher of rates in section 1446(b) where a lower-tier partnership cannot reliably associate income with a partner of the upper-tier partnership).

(b) *Installment payments.*—(1) *In general.*—Except as provided in § 1.1446-4 for certain publicly traded partnerships, a partnership must pay its 1446 tax by making installment payments of the 1446 tax based on the amount of partnership effectively connected taxable income (ECTI) allocable under section 704 to its foreign partners, without regard to whether the partnership makes any distributions to its partners during the partnership's taxable year. The amount of the installment payments is determined in accordance with this paragraph (b), and the tax must be paid at the times set forth in paragraph (d) of this section. Subject to paragraphs (b)(2)(v) and (b)(3)(ii) of this section, in computing its first installment of 1446 tax for a taxable year, a partnership must decide whether it will pay its 1446 tax for the entire taxable year by using the safe harbor set forth in paragraph (b)(3)(i) of this section, or by using one of several annualization methods available under paragraph (b)(2)(ii) of this section for computing partnership ECTI allocable to foreign partners. In the case of a partnership's underpayment of an installment of 1446 tax, the partnership shall be subject to an addition to the tax equal to the amount determined under section 6655, as modified by this section, as if such partnership were a corporation, as well as any other applicable interest and penalties. See § 1.1446-3(f). Section 6425 (permitting an adjustment for an overpayment of estimated tax by a corporation) shall not apply to a partnership's payment of its 1446 tax.

(2) *Calculation.*—(i) *Application of the principles of section 6655.*—(A) *In general.*—Installment payments of 1446 tax required during the partnership's taxable year are based upon partnership ECTI for the portion of the partnership taxable year to which the payments relate, and, except as set forth in this paragraph (b)(2) or paragraph (b)(3) of this section, shall be calculated using the principles of section 6655. The principles of section 6655, except as otherwise provided in § 1.6655-2, are applied to annualize the partnership's items of effectively connected income, gain, loss, and deduction to determine each foreign partner's allocable share of partnership ECTI. Each foreign partner's allocable share of partnership ECTI is then multiplied by the relevant applicable percentage for the type of income allocable to the foreign partner under paragraph (a)(2) of this section. The respective 1446 tax amounts are then added for each foreign partner to yield an annualized 1446 tax with respect to such partner. The installment of 1446 tax due with respect to a foreign partner equals the excess of the section 6655(e)(2)(B)(ii) percentage of the annualized 1446 tax for that partner (or, if applicable, the adjusted seasonal amount) for the relevant installment period, over the aggregate amount of 1446 tax installment payments previously paid with respect to that partner during the partnership's taxable year. The partnership's total 1446 tax installment payment equals the sum of the installment payments due for such period on behalf of all the partnership's foreign partners.

(B) *Calculation rules when certificates are submitted under § 1.1446-6.*—(1) To the extent applicable, in computing the 1446 tax due with respect to a foreign partner, a partnership may consider a certificate received from such partner under § 1.1446-6(c)(1)(i) or (ii) and the amount of state and local taxes permitted to be considered under §1.1446-6(c)(1)(iii). For this purpose, a partnership shall first annualize the partner's allocable share of the partnership's items of effectively connected income, gain, deduction, and loss before—

(*i*) Considering under §1.1446-6(c)(1)(i) the partner's certified deductions and losses;

(*ii*) Determining under §1.1446-6(c)(1)(ii) whether the 1446 tax otherwise due with respect to that partner is less than $1,000 (determined with regard to any certified deductions or losses); or

(*iii*) Considering under §1.1446-6 (c)(1)(iii) the amount of state and local taxes withheld and remitted on behalf of the partner.

(*2*) The amount of the limitation provided in §1.1446-6(c)(1)(i)(C) shall be based on the partner's allocable share of these annualized amounts. For any installment period in which the partnership considers a partner's certificate, the partnership must also consider the following events to the extent they occur prior to the due date for paying the 1446 tax for such installment period—

(*i*) The receipt of an updated certificate or status update from the partner under §1.1446-6(c)(2)(ii)(B) certifying an amount of deductions or losses that is less than the amount reflected on the superseded certificate (see §1.1446-6(e)(2) *Example 4*);

(*ii*) The failure to receive an updated certificate or status update from the partner that should have been provided under §1.1446-6(c)(2)(ii)(B); and

(*iii*) The receipt of a notification from the IRS under §1.1446-6(c)(3) or (c)(5) (see §1.1446-6(e)(2) *Example 5*).

(ii) *Annualization methods.*—A partnership that decides to annualize its income for the taxable year shall use one of the annualization methods set forth in section 6655(e) and the regulations thereunder, and as described in the forms and instructions for Form 8804, "Annual Return for Partnership Withholding Tax (Section 1446)," Form 8805, "Foreign Partner's Information Statement of Section 1446 Withholding Tax," and Form 8813, "Partnership Withholding Tax Payment Voucher."

(iii) *Partner's estimated tax payments.*—In computing its installment payments of 1446 tax, a partnership may not take into account a partner's estimated tax payments.

(iv) *Partner whose interest terminates during the partnership's taxable year.*—If a partner's interest in the partnership terminates prior to the end of the partnership's taxable year, the partnership shall take into account the income that is allocable to the partner for the portion of the partnership taxable year that the person was a partner.

(v) *Exceptions and modifications to the application of the principles under section 6655.*—To the extent not otherwise modified in §§1.1446-1 through 1.1446-7 or inconsistent with those rules, the principles of section 6655 apply to the calculation of the installment payments of 1446 tax made by a partnership as set forth in this paragraph (b)(2)(v).

(A) *Inapplicability of special rules for large corporations.*—The principles of section 6655(d)(2), concerning large corporations (as defined in section 6655(g)(2)), shall not apply.

(B) *Inapplicability of special rules regarding early refunds.*—The principles of section 6655(h), applicable to amounts excessively credited or refunded under section 6425, shall not apply. See paragraph (b)(1) of this section providing that section 6425 shall not apply for purposes of the 1446 tax. This paragraph (b)(2)(v)(B) shall apply to 1446 tax paid by a partnership or nominee, as well as to amounts that a partner is deemed to have paid for estimated tax purposes by reason of the partnership's or nominee's 1446 tax payments under §1.1446-3(d)(1)(i).

(C) *Period of underpayment.*—The period of the underpayment set forth in section 6655(b)(2) shall end on the earlier of the 15th day of the 4th month following the close of the partnership's taxable year (or, in the case of a partnership described in §1.6081-5(a)(1) of this chapter, the 15th day of the 6th month following the close of the partnership's taxable year), or with respect to any portion of the underpayment, the date on which such portion is paid.

(D) *Other taxes.*—Section 6655 shall be applied without regard to any references to alternative minimum taxable income and modified alternative minimum taxable income.

(E) *1446 tax treated as tax under section 11.*—The principles of section 6655(g)(1) shall be applied to treat the 1446 tax as a tax imposed by section 11, and any partnership required to pay such tax shall be treated as a corporation.

(F) *Application of section 6655(f).*—A partnership subject to section 1446 shall apply section 6655(f) after aggregating the 1446 tax due (or any installment of such tax) for all its foreign partners. See §1.1446-6(c)(1)(ii) for an exception to this rule when a nonresident alien partner certifies to the partnership that the partnership investment is the nonresident alien partner's only activity giving rise to effectively connected items.

(G) *Application of section 6655(i).*—If a partnership has a taxable year of less than 12 months, the partnership is required to pay 1446 tax (including installments of such tax) in accordance with this section §1.1446-3, if the partnership has ECTI allocable under section 704 to foreign partners. In such a case, the partnership shall adjust its installment payments of 1446 tax in a reasonable manner (e.g., the annualized amounts of ECTI estimated to be allocable to a foreign partner, and the section 6655(e)(2)(B)(ii) percentage to be applied to each installment) to account for the short-taxable year. However, if the partnership's taxable year is a period of less than 4 months, the partnership shall not be required to make installment payments of 1446 tax, but will only be required to file Forms 8804 and 8805 in accordance with this section §1.1446-3, and report and pay the appropriate 1446 tax for the short-taxable year.

(H) *Current year tax safe harbor.*—The safe harbor set forth in section 6655(d)(1)(B)(i) shall apply to a partnership subject to section 1446.

(I) *Prior year tax safe harbor.*—The safe harbor set forth in section 6655(d)(1)(B)(ii) shall not apply and instead the safe harbor set forth in paragraph (b)(3) of this section applies.

(3) *1446 tax safe harbor.*—(i) *In general.*—The addition to tax under section 6655 shall not apply to a partnership with respect to a current installment of 1446 tax if—

(A) The average of the amount of the current installment and prior installments during the taxable year is at least 25 percent of the total 1446 tax (without regard to §1.1446-6) for the prior taxable year;

(B) The prior taxable year consisted of twelve months;

(C) The partnership timely files (including extensions) an information return under section 6031 for the prior year; and

(D) The amount of ECTI for the prior taxable year is not less than 50 percent of the ECTI shown on the annual return of section 1446 withholding tax that is (or will be) timely filed for the current year.

(ii) *Permission to change to standard annualization method.*—Except as otherwise provided in this paragraph (b)(3)(ii), if a partnership decides to pay its 1446 tax for the first installment period based upon the safe harbor method set forth in paragraph (b)(3)(i), the partnership must use the safe harbor method for each installment payment made during the partnership's taxable year. Notwithstanding the previous sentence, if a partnership paying over 1446 tax during the taxable year pursuant to this paragraph (b)(3) determines during an installment period (based upon the standard option annualization method set forth in section 6655(e) and the regulations thereunder, as modified by the forms and instructions to Forms 8804, 8805, and 8813) that it will not qualify for the safe harbor in this paragraph (b)(3) because the prior year's ECTI will not meet the 50-percent threshold in paragraph (b)(3)(i)(D) of this section, then the partnership is permitted, without being subject to the addition to the tax under section 6655 (as applied through this section), to pay over its 1446 tax for the period in which such determination is made, and all subsequent installment periods during the taxable year, using the standard option annualization method. A change pursuant to this paragraph shall be disclosed in a statement attached to the Form 8804 the partnership files for the taxable year and shall include information to allow the IRS to determine whether the change was appropriate.

(c) *Coordination with other withholding rules.*—(1) *Fixed or determinable, annual or periodical income.*—Fixed or determinable, annual or periodical income subject to tax under section 871(a) or section 881 is not subject to withholding under section 1446, and such income is subject to the withholding requirements of sections 1441 and 1442 and the regulations thereunder.

(2) *Real property gains.*—(i) *Domestic partnerships.*—Except as otherwise provided in this paragraph (c)(2), a domestic partnership that is otherwise subject to the withholding requirements of sections 1445 and 1446 will be subject to the payment and reporting requirements of section 1446 only and not section 1445(e)(1) and the regulations thereunder, with respect to partnership gain from the disposition of a U.S. real property interest (as defined in section 897(c)). A partnership that has complied with the requirements of section 1446 will be deemed to satisfy the withholding requirements of section 1445 and the regulations thereunder. However, a domestic partnership that would otherwise be exempt from section 1445 withholding by operation of a nonrecognition provision must continue to comply with the requirements of §1.1445-5(b)(2). In the event that amounts are withheld under section 1445(e) at the time of the disposition of a U.S. real property interest, such amounts may be credited against the partnership's 1446 tax. A partnership that fails to comply fully with the requirements of section 1446 pursuant to this paragraph (c)(2) shall be liable for any unpaid 1446 tax and subject to any applicable addition to the tax, interest, and penalties under section 1446. See §1.1446-4(f)(4) for rules coordinating the withholding liability of publicly traded partnerships under sections 1445 and 1446.

(ii) *Foreign partnerships.*—A foreign partnership that is subject to withholding under section 1445(a) during its taxable year may credit the amount withheld under section 1445(a) against its section 1446 tax liability for that taxable year only to the extent such amount is allocable to foreign partners.

(3) *Coordination with section 1443.*—A partnership that has ECTI allocable under section 704 to a foreign organization described in section 501(c) shall be required to pay 1446 tax on such

Reg. §1.1446-3(c)(3)

ECTI only to the extent such ECTI is includible under section 512 and section 513 in computing the organization's unrelated business taxable income. The certificate procedure available under § 1.1441-9(b)(1) by which a partner may set forth the amounts it believes will and will not be includible in its computation of unrelated business taxable income under section 512 and section 513 shall also apply to a partner in a partnership subject to section 1446. Such certificate shall be made by a partner in the same manner as under § 1.1441-9(b)(2). A partnership that determines that the partner's certificate as to certain partnership items is unreliable or lacking must presume, consistent with § 1.1441-9(b)(3) (regarding amounts includible under section 512 in computing the organization's unrelated business taxable income), that such partnership items would be includible in computing the partner's UBTI.

(d) *Reporting and crediting the 1446 tax.*— (1) *Reporting 1446 tax.*—This paragraph (d) sets forth the rules for reporting and crediting the 1446 tax paid by a partnership. To the extent that 1446 tax is paid on ECTI allocable to a domestic trust (including a grantor or other person treated as an owner of a portion of such trust) or a grantor or other person treated as the owner of a portion of a foreign trust, the rules of this paragraph (d) applicable to a foreign trust or its beneficiaries shall be applied to such domestic or foreign trust and its beneficiaries or owners, as applicable, so that appropriate credit for the 1446 tax may be claimed by the trust, beneficiary, grantor, or other person.

(i) *Reporting of installment tax payments and notification to partners of installment tax payments.*—Each partnership required to make an installment payment of 1446 tax must file Form 8813, "Partnership Withholding Tax Payment Voucher (Section 1446)," in accordance with the instructions to that form. Form 8813 is generally used to transmit an installment payment of 1446 tax to the IRS with respect to partnership ECTI estimated to be allocated to foreign partners. However, see § 1.1446-6(d)(3) (relating to circumstances where a partnership must file Form 8813 when no payment is required under section 1446). Except as provided in this section, a partnership must notify each foreign partner of the 1446 tax paid on the partner's behalf when the partnership makes an installment payment of 1446 tax. The notice required to be given to a foreign partner under the previous sentence must be provided within 10 days of the installment payment due date, or, if paid later, the date such installment payment is made. A foreign partner generally may credit an installment of 1446 tax paid by the partnership on the partner's behalf against the partner's estimated tax that the partner must pay during the partner's own taxable year. See § 1.1446-5(b) (relating to tiered partnership structures). However, a foreign part-

ner may not obtain an early refund of such amounts under the estimated tax rules. See § 1.1446-3(b)(2)(v)(B). See paragraph (d)(2) of this section for the amount of 1446 tax a partner may credit against its U.S. income tax liability. No particular form is required for a partnership's notification to a foreign partner, but each notification must include the partnership's name, the partnership's Taxpayer Identification Number (TIN), the partnership's address, the partner's name, the partner's TIN, the partner's address, the annualized ECTI estimated to be allocated to the foreign partner (or prior year's safe harbor amount, if applicable), and the amount of tax paid on behalf of the partner for both the current and any prior installment periods during the partnership's taxable year. Notwithstanding any other provision of this paragraph (d), a withholding agent is not required to notify a partner of an installment of 1446 tax paid on the partner's behalf, unless requested by the partner, if—

(A) The partnership's agent responsible for providing notice pursuant to this paragraph is the same person that acts as an agent of the foreign partner for purposes of filing the partner's U.S. Federal income tax return for the partner's taxable year that includes the installment payment date; or

(B) The partnership has at least 500 foreign partners and the total 1446 tax that the partnership determines will be required to be paid for the partnership taxable year on behalf of such partner (based on paragraph (b)(2)(ii) or (3) of this section) with respect to the partner's allocable share of ECTI is less than $1,000.

(ii) *Payment due dates.*—The 1446 tax is calculated based on partnership ECTI allocable under section 704 to foreign partners during the partnership's taxable year, as determined under section 706. Installment payments of the 1446 tax generally must be made during the partnership's taxable year in which such income is derived. A partnership must pay to the Internal Revenue Service a portion of its estimated annual 1446 tax in installments on or before the 15th day of the fourth, sixth, ninth, and twelfth months of the partnership's taxable year as provided in section 6655. Any additional amount determined to be due is to be paid with the filing of the annual return of tax required under paragraph (d)(1)(iii) of this section and clearly designated as for the prior taxable year. Form 8813 should not be submitted for a payment made under the preceding sentence.

(iii) *Annual return and notification to partners.*—Every partnership (except a publicly traded partnership subject to § 1.1446-4) that has effectively connected gross income for the partnership's taxable year allocable under section 704 to one or more of its foreign partners (or is treated as having paid 1446 tax under § 1.1446-5(b)), must file Form 8804, "Annual Return for Partnership Withholding Tax (Section

1446)." Additionally, every partnership that is required to file Form 8804 also must file Form 8805, "Foreign Partner's Information Statement of Section 1446 Withholding Tax," for each of its foreign partners on whose behalf it paid 1446 tax, and furnish Form 8804 and the Forms 8805 to the Internal Revenue Service and the respective Form 8805 to each of its partners. Notwithstanding the previous sentence, a partnership that considers a foreign partner's certificate under § 1.1446-6 when computing its 1446 tax on Form 8804 is required to furnish such partner and the Internal Revenue Service a Form 8805, even if the form submitted to the partner shows no payment of 1446 tax on behalf of the partner. Forms 8804 and 8805 are separate from Form 1065, "U.S. Return of Partnership Income," and the attachments thereto, and are not to be filed as part of the partnership's Form 1065. A partnership must generally file Forms 8804 and 8805 on or before the due date for filing the partnership's Form 1065. See § 1.6031(a)-1(c) for rules concerning the due date of a partnership's Form 1065. However, with respect to partnerships described in § 1.6081-5(a)(1), Forms 8804 and 8805 are not due until the 15th day of the sixth month following the close of the partnership's taxable year.

(iv) *Information provided to beneficiaries of foreign trusts and estates.*—A foreign trust or estate that is a partner in a partnership subject to withholding under section 1446 shall be provided Form 8805 by the partnership. The foreign trust or estate must provide to each of its beneficiaries a copy of the Form 8805 furnished by the partnership. In addition, the foreign trust or estate must provide a statement for each of its beneficiaries to inform each beneficiary of the amount of the credit that may be claimed under section 33 (as determined under this section) for the 1446 tax paid by the partnership. Until an official Internal Revenue Service form is available, the statement from a foreign trust or estate that is described in this paragraph (d)(1)(iv) shall contain the following information—

(A) Name, address, and TIN of the foreign trust or estate;

(B) Name, address, and TIN of the partnership;

(C) The amount of the partnership's ECTI allocated to the foreign trust or estate for the partnership taxable year (as shown on the Form 8805 provided to the trust or estate);

(D) The amount of 1446 tax paid by the partnership on behalf of the foreign trust or estate (as shown on Form 8805 to the trust or estate);

(E) Name, address, and TIN of the beneficiary of the foreign trust or estate;

(F) The amount of the partnership's ECTI allocated to the trust or estate for purposes of section 1446 that is to be included in the beneficiary's gross income; and

(G) The amount of 1446 tax paid by the partnership on behalf of the foreign trust or estate that the beneficiary is entitled to claim on its return as a credit under section 33.

(v) *Attachments required of foreign trusts and estates.*—The statement furnished to each foreign beneficiary under this paragraph (d)(1) must also be attached to the foreign trust or estate's U.S. Federal income tax return filed for the taxable year that includes the installment periods to which the statement relates.

(vi) *Attachments required of beneficiaries of foreign trusts and estates.*—The beneficiary of the foreign trust or estate must attach the statement provided by the trust or estate pursuant to paragraph (d)(1)(iv) of this section, along with a copy of the Form 8805 furnished by the partnership to such trust or estate, to its U.S. income tax return for the year in which it claims a credit for the 1446 tax. See § 1.1446-3(d)(2)(ii) for additional rules regarding a partner or beneficial owner claiming a credit for the 1446 tax.

(vii) *Information provided to beneficiaries of foreign trusts and estates that are partners in certain publicly traded partnerships.*—A statement similar to the statement required by paragraph (d)(1)(iv) of this section shall be provided by trusts or estates that hold interests in publicly traded partnerships subject to § 1.1446-4.

(2) *Crediting 1446 tax against a partner's U.S. tax liability.*—(i) *In general.*—A partnership's payment of 1446 tax on the portion of ECTI allocable to a foreign partner generally relates to the partner's U.S. income tax liability for the partner's taxable year in which the partner is subject to U.S. tax on that income. Subject to paragraphs (d)(2)(ii) and (iii) of this section, a partner may claim as a credit under section 33 the 1446 tax paid by the partnership with respect to ECTI allocable to that partner. The partner may not claim an early refund of these amounts under the estimated tax rules. See paragraph (d)(1)(i) of this section regarding a partner's ability to credit an installment of 1446 tax paid on the partner's behalf against the partner's estimated tax payments due for the taxable year. See also § 1.1446-5(b) (relating to tiered partnership structures).

(ii) *Substantiation for purposes of claiming the credit under section 33.*—A partner may credit the amount paid under section 1446 with respect to such partner against its U.S. income tax liability only if it attaches proof of payment to its U.S. income tax return for the partner's taxable year in which the items comprising such partner's allocable share of partnership ECTI are included in the partner's income. Except as provided in the next sentence, proof of payment consists of a copy of the Form 8805 the partnership provides to the partner (or in the case of a beneficiary of a foreign trust or estate, the statement required under paragraph (d)(1)(iv) or (vii) of this section to be provided by such trust or estate and a copy of the related Form 8805 furnished to such trust or estate), but only if the name and TIN on the Form 8805 (or the statement provided by a foreign trust or estate) match the name and TIN on the partner's U.S. tax return, and such form (or statement) identifies the partner (or beneficiary) as the person entitled to the credit under section 33. In the case of a partner of a publicly traded partnership that is subject to withholding on distributions under §1.1446-4, proof of payment consists of a copy of the Form 1042-S, "Foreign Person's U.S. Source Income Subject to Withholding," provided to the partner by the partnership.

(iii) *Special rules for apportioning the tax credit under section 33.*—(A) *Foreign trusts and estates.*—Section 1446 tax paid on the portion of ECTI allocable under section 704 to a foreign trust or estate that the foreign trust or estate may claim as a credit under section 33 shall bear the same ratio to the total 1446 tax paid on behalf of the trust or estate as the total ECTI allocable to such trust or estate and not distributed (or treated as distributed) to the beneficiaries of such trust or estate, and, accordingly not deducted under section 651 or section 661 in calculating the trust or estate's taxable income, bears to the total ECTI allocable to such trust or estate. The 1446 tax that a foreign trust or estate is not entitled to claim as a credit under this paragraph (d)(2) may be claimed as a credit by the beneficiary of such trust or estate that includes the partnership ECTI allocated to the trust or estate in gross income under section 652 or section 662 (whether distributed or deemed to be distributed and with the same character as effectively connected income as in the hands of the trust or estate). In the case of a foreign trust or estate with multiple beneficiaries, each beneficiary may claim a portion of the 1446 tax that may be claimed by all beneficiaries under the previous sentence as a credit in the same proportion as the amount of ECTI included in such beneficiary's gross income bears to the total amount of ECTI included by all beneficiaries. The trust or estate must provide each beneficiary with a copy of the Form 8805 provided to it by the partnership and prepare the statement required by paragraph (d)(1)(iv) of this section.

(B) *Use of domestic trusts to circumvent section 1446.*—This paragraph (d)(2)(iii)(B) shall apply if a partnership knows or has reason to know that a foreign person holds its interest in the partnership through a domestic trust, and such domestic trust was formed or availed of with a principal purpose of avoiding the 1446 tax. The use of a domestic trust may have a principal purpose of avoiding the 1446 tax even though the tax avoidance purpose is outweighed by other purposes when taken together. In such case, a partnership is required to pay 1446 tax

under this paragraph as if the domestic trust was a foreign trust for purposes of section 1446 and the regulations thereunder. Accordingly, all applicable additions to the tax, interest, and penalties shall apply to the partnership for its failure to pay 1446 tax under this paragraph (d)(2)(iii)(B), commencing with the installment period during which the partnership knows or has reason to know that this paragraph (d)(2)(iii)(B) applies. A publicly traded partnership within the meaning of §1.1446-4 (or a nominee required to pay 1446 tax under §1.1446-4) will not be considered to know or have reason to know a domestic trust is being used to avoid the 1446 tax under this paragraph (d)(2)(iii)(B), provided the interest held in such entity by the domestic trust is publicly traded.

(iv) *Refunds to withholding agent.*—A withholding agent (i.e., the partnership) may obtain a refund of the 1446 tax paid (or deemed paid under §1.1446-5(b)) to the extent of the excess of the amount paid to the Internal Revenue Service by the partnership, over the partnership's section 1446 tax liability as determined by the sum of the total tax creditable to each partner indicated on all Forms 8805 for the taxable year. If a partnership issues Form 8805 to a partner, then the partnership may not claim a refund for any amount of tax shown on that form as paid on behalf of the partner. If a partnership incorrectly withholds upon a United States person under section 1446 of the Internal Revenue Code and issues a Form 8805 to that person, the partnership may not file for a refund of the amount incorrectly withheld. Instead, the United States person may file for a refund of that amount on its annual return. For rules concerning refunds to withholding agents who pay 1446 tax on distributions of effectively connected income or gain under §1.1446-4 (i.e., publicly traded partnerships or nominees), see §1.1464-1.

(v) *1446 tax treated as cash distribution to partners.*—Except as otherwise provided in this paragraph (d)(2)(v), a partnership's payment of 1446 tax on behalf of a foreign partner is treated under section 1446(d) and this section as a deemed distribution of money to the partner on the earliest of the day on which the partnership paid the tax, the last day of the partnership's taxable year for which the amount was paid, or the last day on which the partner owned an interest in the partnership during the taxable year for which the tax was paid. However, a deemed distribution of money under section 1446(d) resulting from a partnership's installment payment of 1446 tax on behalf of a partner is treated as an advance or drawing of money under §1.731-1(a)(1)(ii) to the extent of the partner's distributive share of income for the partnership taxable year. The rule treating a deemed distribution as an advance or drawing of money under this paragraph (d)(2)(v) applies only for purposes of determining the tax results of the

Reg. §1.1446-3(d)(2)(iii)

deemed distribution to the partner under sections 705, 731, and 733, and does not affect the date that the partnership is considered to have paid any installment of 1446 tax for purposes of section 6655 (as applied through this section) or the date a foreign partner is deemed to have paid estimated tax by reason of such installment payment. See paragraph (d)(1)(i) of this section (permitting a partner to credit 1446 tax paid on the partner's behalf against the partner's estimated tax obligation). An amount treated as an advance or drawing of money is taken into account at the end of the partnership taxable year or the last day during the partnership's taxable year on which the partner owned an interest in the partnership. Any 1446 tax paid after the close of the partnership's taxable year, including amounts paid with the filing of Form 8804, that are on account of partnership ECTI allocated to partners for the prior taxable year shall be treated under section 1446(d) and this section as a distribution from the partnership on the earlier of the last day of the partnership's prior taxable year for which the tax is paid, or the last day in such prior taxable year on which such foreign partner held an interest in the partnership.

(vi) *Examples.*—The following examples illustrate the application of this section. In considering the examples, disregard the potential application of paragraph (b)(2)(v)(F) of this section (relating to the de minimis exception to paying 1446 tax). The examples are as follows:

Example 1. Simple trust that reports entire amount of ECTI. PRS is a partnership that has two partners, FT, a foreign trust, and A, a U.S. person. FT is a simple trust under section 651. FT and A each provide PRS with a valid Form W-8BEN and Form W-9, respectively. FT has one beneficiary, NRA, a nonresident alien. PRS and FT each maintain a calendar taxable year. PRS estimated for each installment period during the partnership's taxable year that FT would be allocated $100 of ECTI for the taxable year, and that all such ECTI would be ordinary in character. Assume that the allocation of the $100 would be respected under section 704(b) and the regulations thereunder. PRS pays installments of 1446 tax based upon its estimates and timely pays a total of $35 of 1446 tax over the course of the partnership's taxable year ($100 ECTI × .35). Assume that PRS' estimates of ECTI allocable to FT during the taxable year equal the actual amount of ECTI allocable to FT for the taxable year. Assume also that FT's only income for the taxable year is the $100 of income from PRS, and that, pursuant to the terms of the trust's governing instrument and local law, the $100 of ECTI is not included in FT's fiduciary accounting income and the deemed distribution of the $35 withholding tax paid under paragraph (d)(2)(v) of this section is not included in FT's fiduciary accounting income. Accordingly, the $100 of ECTI is not income required to be distributed by FT, and FT may not claim a deduction under

section 651 for this amount. FT must report the $100 of ECTI in its gross income and may claim a credit under section 33 as determined under paragraph (d)(2)(iii) of this section of $35 for the 1446 tax paid by PRS. NRA is not required to include any of the ECTI in gross income and accordingly may not claim a credit for any amount of the $35 of 1446 tax PRS paid.

Example 2. Simple trust that distributes a portion of ECTI to the beneficiary. Assume the same facts as in *Example 1,* except that PRS distributes $60 to FT, which FT includes in its fiduciary accounting income under local law. FT will report the $100 of ECTI in its gross income and may claim a deduction for the $60 required to be distributed under section 651(a) to NRA. Pursuant to paragraph (d)(2)(iii) of this section, FT may claim a $14 credit under section 33 for the 1446 tax PRS paid ($40/$100 multiplied by $35). NRA is required to include the $60 of the ECTI in gross income under section 652 (as ECTI) and may claim a $21 credit under section 33 for the 1446 tax PRS paid ($35 less $14 or $60/$100 multiplied by $35).

Example 3. Complex trust that distributes entire ECTI to the beneficiary. Assume the same facts as in *Example 1,* except that FT is a complex trust under section 661. PRS distributes $60 to FT, which FT includes in its fiduciary accounting income. FT distributes the $60 of fiduciary accounting income to NRA and also properly distributes an additional $40 to NRA from FT's principal. FT will report the $100 of ECTI in its gross income and may deduct the $60 required to be distributed to NRA under section 661(a)(1) and may deduct the $40 distributed to NRA under section 661(a)(2). Pursuant to paragraph (d)(2)(iii) of this section, FT may not claim a credit under section 33 for any of the $35 of 1446 tax paid by PRS. NRA is required to include $100 of the ECTI in gross income under section 662 (as ECTI) and may claim a $35 credit under section 33 for the 1446 tax paid by PRS ($35 less $0).

(e) *Liability of partnership for failure to withhold.*—(1) *In general.*—Every partnership required to pay 1446 tax is made liable for that tax by section 1461. Therefore, a partnership that is required to pay 1446 tax but fails to do so, or pays less than the amount required under this section, is liable under section 1461 for the payment of the tax required to be withheld under chapter 3 of the Internal Revenue Code and the regulations thereunder unless, and to the extent, the partnership can demonstrate pursuant to paragraph (e)(2) of this section, to the satisfaction of the Commissioner or his delegate, that a foreign partner has paid the full amount of tax required to be paid by such partner to the Internal Revenue Service. See paragraph (e)(3) of this section and section 1463 regarding a partnership's liability for penalties and interest even though a foreign partner has satisfied the underlying tax liability. See also § 1.1461-3 for applicable penalties when a partnership fails to pay

1446 tax. See paragraph (b) of this section for an addition to the tax under section 6655 when there is an underpayment of 1446 tax.

(2) *Proof that tax liability has been satisfied and deemed payment of 1446 tax.*—Proof of payment of tax may be established for purposes of paragraph (e)(1) of this section consistent with §1.1445-1(e)(3). Under that standard, a partnership must provide sufficient information to the IRS to determine that the partner's tax liability was satisfied or established to be zero in accordance with the rules of this section. Under this section, a partnership's liability for 1446 tax shall be deemed to have been satisfied (deemed payment), to the extent of the 1446 tax due with respect to the ECTI allocable to a foreign partner, on the later of the date that such partner is considered to have paid all tax that is required to be shown on such partner's U.S. income tax return under section 6513(a) and (b)(2) (prescribing the date tax is considered paid for purposes of sections 6511(b)(2), (c), and 6512), or the last date for payment of the 1446 tax without extensions (the unextended due date for Form 8804). The deemed payment rule of this paragraph (e)(2) shall apply for purposes sections of 1446, 1461, and 1463, and any additions to the tax, interest, or penalties potentially applicable to such partnership under section 1446, including sections 6601, 6651, and 6655. Any deemed payment of 1446 tax under this paragraph (e)(2) shall not be treated as a deemed distribution under section 1446(d) and this section.

(3) *Liability for interest, penalties, and additions to the tax.*—(i) *Partnership.*—Notwithstanding paragraph (e)(2) of this section, a partnership that fails to pay 1446 tax is not relieved from liability under section 6655 (as applied through this section) or for interest under section 6601, when applicable. See §1.1463-1. Such liability may exist even if there is no underlying tax liability due from a foreign partner on its allocable share of partnership ECTI. The addition to the tax under section 6655 or the interest charge under section 6601 that is required by those sections shall be imposed as set forth in those sections, as modified by this section. The section 6601 interest charge shall accrue beginning on the last date prescribed for payment of the 1446 tax due under section 1461 (which is the due date, without extensions, for filing Form 8804). The section 6601 interest charge shall stop accruing on the 1446 tax liability on the date, and to the extent, that the unpaid tax liability under section 1446 is satisfied (or is deemed satisfied under this paragraph (e)). Further, a partnership's liability under section 6655 (as applied through this section) for any underpaid installment payment shall accrue beginning on the relevant installment payment date, and shall stop accruing on the earlier of the date (and to the extent) that the 1446 tax liability is actually satisfied or the date prescribed in paragraph

(b)(2)(v)(C) of this section. See paragraph (e)(4) of this section for examples illustrating that a partner's payment of estimated tax has no effect on the partnership's calculation of its addition to the tax under section 6655 and this section. See §1.1461-3 for a list of the additions to tax, interest, and penalties that may apply to a partnership that fails to comply with section 1446. See §1.1446-6(d)(2)(i) for exceptions to the application of the addition to the tax under section 6655 (as applied through this section) when a partnership reasonably relies on a foreign partner's certificate to reduce 1446 tax.

(ii) *Foreign partner.*—A foreign partner is permitted to reduce any addition to the tax under section 6654 or section 6655 by the amount of any section 6655 addition to the tax paid by the partnership with respect to the partnership's failure to pay adequate installment payments of the 1446 tax on ECTI allocable to the foreign partner.

(4) *Examples.*—The following examples illustrate the application of this section. In considering the examples, disregard the potential application of paragraph (b)(2)(v)(F) of this section (relating to the de minimis exception to paying 1446 tax). Further, in each of the examples where a partnership is deemed to have paid 1446 tax with respect to ECTI allocable to a partner, it is assumed that the partnership has presented to the IRS the appropriate information under paragraph (e)(2) of this section for the IRS to conclude that the deemed payment is appropriate. The examples are as follows:

Example 1. Foreign partnership fails to pay 1446 tax and sole foreign partner fails to pay all tax required to be shown on partner's U.S. income tax return.

(i) PRS is a foreign partnership engaged in a trade or business in the United States and has two equal partners, A, a U.S. person, and B, a nonresident alien. PRS is described in §1.6081-5(a) (PRS keeps its books and records outside the United States and Puerto Rico) and, therefore, is required to file Form 8804 by the 15th day of the 6th month following the close of its taxable year. Both partners and PRS are calendar year taxpayers. PRS has received a valid Form W-9 and W-8BEN from A and B, respectively, but has not received any other documents or certificates. B is engaged in multiple trades or businesses (including the PRS partnership) that give rise to effectively connected income. PRS will use an acceptable annualization method under this section for computing its 1446 tax.

(ii) In PRS's first year of operations (Year 1), PRS estimates for each installment period described in §1.1446-3 that B will be allocated $100 of ordinary ECTI for the taxable year. Therefore, for each installment period PRS is required to pay one fourth of the tax on the annualized ECTI allocable to B, or $8.75 (.25 × ($100 × .35)). PRS fails to make any installment payments. PRS's operations actually result in $100 of ECTI allocated to B. Therefore, PRS was required to have paid 1446 tax of $35 on or before the due date, without extensions, for filing its Form 8804 which is June 15, Year 2 (the last date prescribed for payment of the 1446 tax). PRS does not file Forms 8804 or 8805.

(iii) B pays estimated taxes and makes the following payments on the following dates: June 15, Year 1 – $20, September 15, Year 1 – $15, and January 15, Year 2 – $10. B's total estimated tax payments equal $45. B files its U.S. Federal income tax return timely on June 15, Year 2, and reports all effectively connected income required to be shown on its return. Assume that B's total correct tax liability as shown on the return is $50. B does not make a payment with its return and so B still owes $5 to the Internal Revenue Service (excluding any interest, penalties, and additions to the tax that may apply). Assume that B is not subject to an addition to the tax under section 6654.

(iv) Under the rules of paragraph (e)(2) of this section, for purposes of sections 1446, 1461, and 1463, PRS is not considered to have paid any 1446 tax because B has not paid all of B's U.S. income tax liability.

(v) Further, under the principles of section 6655 and the rules of § 1.1446-3(e), a partner's estimated tax payments will not affect the calculation of a partnership's addition to the tax. Accordingly, PRS will be liable under the principles of section 6655 and § 1.1446-3 for failing to withhold for each installment payment. The addition to the tax will accrue beginning with the due date of each installment payment on the $8.75 underpayment for each respective installment period and will continue to accrue until June 15, Year 2 (the date prescribed in paragraph (b)(2)(v)(C) of this section).

(vi) Further, beginning on June 15, Year 2 (the last date prescribed for payment of 1446 tax without extensions), PRS will be liable for interest under section 6601 with respect to the unpaid 1446 tax, $35. This interest will stop accruing on the earlier of the date that the 1446 tax is paid by PRS or is deemed paid under paragraph (e)(2) of this section by reason of B's payment of its full tax liability.

(vii) Further, beginning on June 15, Year 2 (the due date for filing Form 8804), PRS will be liable for the addition to the tax under section 6651(a)(1) for failing to file Form 8804. This addition to the tax accrues on the amount required to be shown as the 1446 tax liability on Form 8804, $35. This addition to the tax will accrue at the rate of 5 percent per month until the date that PRS files Form 8804 for Year 1, or the maximum accrual of the penalty (25 percent of the tax required to be shown on the return) under that section has been reached.

(viii) PRS may be liable for other penalties and additions to the tax for its failure to withhold or to furnish statements to its foreign part-

ner B. See § 1.1461-3 for a list of the penalties that may apply.

Example 2. Foreign partnership fails to pay 1446 tax but sole foreign partner pays all tax required to be shown on the partner's U.S. income tax return. The facts are the same as *Example 1*, except that B pays $5 with the filing of B's return and has therefore paid all tax required to be shown on B's return within the meaning of paragraph (e)(2) of this section.

(i) For purposes of sections 1446, 1461, and 1463, PRS is deemed to have paid its 1446 tax liability under paragraph (e) (2) of this section as of the later of the date that B is considered to have paid its tax under section 6513(a) and (b)(2) (June 15, Year 2) and the last date for PRS to pay its 1446 tax without extensions (also June 15, Year 2). Therefore, PRS is deemed to have paid all of its 1446 tax liability as of June 15, Year 2. PRS has no continuing liability for 1446 tax under section 1461, however, additions to the tax, interest, and penalties may apply.

(ii) For purposes of section 6655 and § 1.1446-3, under paragraph (e)(2) PRS is deemed to have paid its 1446 tax on June 15, Year 2. Even if B had fully paid its tax liability as of March 15, Year 2, the rule in paragraph (e) (2) of this section would not deem PRS to have paid its 1446 tax until June 15, Year 2. As a result, B's estimated tax payments will have no effect on PRS's calculation of its addition to the tax. The addition to the tax under 6655 and § 1.1446-3 shall begin to accrue on each installment date with respect to the underpaid installment ($8.75), and will stop accruing on June 15, Year 2, the date prescribed in paragraph (b)(2)(v)(C) of this section.

(iii) Because PRS is deemed to have paid its full 1446 tax liability as of June 15, Year 2 (the last date prescribed for payment of 1446 tax without extensions), PRS is not subject to an interest charge under section 6601, or a failure to file penalty under section 6651 (see section 6651(b)(1)).

(iv) PRS may be liable for other penalties and additions to the tax for its failure to withhold or to furnish statements to its foreign partner B. See § 1.1461-3 for a list of the penalties that may apply.

(v) If PRS had several foreign partners, PRS would conduct the same analysis as set forth above with respect to each partner. That is, under paragraph (e) of this section, PRS may be deemed to have paid 1446 tax with respect to the ECTI allocable to some but not all of its foreign partners.

Example 3. Domestic partnership fails to pay 1446 tax but sole foreign partner fully pays all tax required to be shown on partner's U.S. income tax return. The facts are the same as *Example 2*, except that PRS is a domestic partnership whose last date prescribed for paying 1446 tax without extensions (i.e., generally the unextended due date for Form 8804) is April 15, Year 2.

Reg. § 1.1446-3(e)(4)

(i) For purposes of sections 1446, 1461, and 1463, PRS is deemed to have paid its 1446 tax liability on the later of the date that B is considered to have paid tax under section 6513(a) and (b)(2) (June 15, Year 2) and the last date for paying 1446 tax without extensions (i.e., the unextended due date for Form 8804, April 15, Year 2). Accordingly, PRS is not considered to have fully paid its 1446 tax liability until June 15, Year 2. PRS has no continuing liability for 1446 tax under section 1461, however, additions to the tax, interest, and penalties may apply.

(ii) For purposes of section 6655 and §1.1446-3, PRS is subject to an underpayment addition to the tax that accrues on the same amount as in *Example 1* and *Example 2* because PRS is not deemed to have paid 1446 tax under paragraph (e)(2) of this section until June 15, Year 2. The addition to the tax will stop accruing on the date prescribed in paragraph (b)(2)(v)(C) of this section (i.e., April 15, Year 2, the due date, without extensions, for filing Form 8804).

(iii) For purposes of section 6601, as of the last date prescribed for paying 1446 tax without extensions (April 15, Year 2), PRS has not paid or been deemed to have paid any 1446 tax. Accordingly, the interest charge under section 6601 shall begin to accrue on April 15, Year 2, and shall accrue until the 1446 liability is paid or deemed to have been paid. In this case, the interest charge will accrue until June 15, Year 2, the date that PRS is deemed to have paid its 1446 tax under paragraph (e)(2) of this section.

(iv) For purposes of section 6651(a)(1), as of April 15, Year 2, PRS's amount required to be shown as tax on its Form 8804 is $35. This amount cannot be reduced under section 6651(b)(1) because PRS is not deemed to have paid 1446 tax under paragraph (e)(2) of this section until June 15, Year 2, a date falling after the last date for PRS to pay its 1446 tax, April 15, Year 2. Accordingly, the failure to file penalty will begin to accrue on April 15, Year 2 (filing due date for Form 8804), and shall stop accruing on the earlier of the date that PRS files Form 8804 or the maximum accrual of the penalty (25 percent of the amount required to be shown as tax on the return) is reached.

(v) PRS may be liable for other penalties and additions to the tax for its failure to withhold or to furnish statements to its foreign partner B. See §1.1461-3 for a list of the penalties that may apply.

(f) *Effect of withholding on partner.*—The payment of the 1446 tax by a partnership does not excuse a foreign partner to which a portion of ECTI is allocable from filing a U.S. tax or informational return, as appropriate, with respect to that income. Information concerning installment payments of 1446 tax paid during the partnership's taxable year on behalf of a foreign partner shall be provided to such foreign partner in accordance with paragraph (d) of this section and such information may be taken into account by the foreign partner when computing the partner's estimated tax liability during the taxable year. Form 1040NR, "U.S. Nonresident Alien Income Tax Return," Form 1065, "U.S. Return of Partnership Income," Form 1120F, "U.S. Income Tax Return of a Foreign Corporation," or such other return as appropriate, must be filed by the partner, and any tax due must be paid, by the filing deadline (including extensions) generally applicable to such person. Pursuant to paragraph (d) of this section, a partner may generally claim a credit under section 33 for its share of any 1446 tax paid by the partnership against the amount of income tax (or 1446 tax in the case of tiers of partnerships) as computed in such partner's return. See §1.1446-3(e)(3)(ii) for rules permitting a partner to reduce its addition to tax under section 6654 or section 6655. [Reg. §1.1446-3.]

☐ [*T.D. 9200, 5-13-2005. Amended by T.D. 9394, 4-28-2008.*]

[Reg. §1.1446-4]

§1.1446-4. Publicly traded partnerships.— (a) *In general.*—This section sets forth rules for applying the section 1446 withholding tax (1446 tax) to publicly traded partnerships. A publicly traded partnership (as defined in paragraph (b) of this section) that has effectively connected gross income, gain or loss must pay 1446 tax by withholding from distributions to a foreign partner. Publicly traded partnerships that withhold on distributions must pay over and report any 1446 tax as provided in paragraph (c) of this section, and generally are not to pay over and report the 1446 tax under the rules in §1.1446-3. The amount of the withholding tax on distributions, other than distributions excluded under paragraph (f) of this section, that are made during any partnership taxable years, equals the applicable percentage (defined in paragraph (b)(2) of this section) of such distributions. For penalties and additions to the tax for failure to comply with this section, see §§1.1461-1 and 1.1461-3.

(b) *Definitions.*—(1) *Publicly traded partnership.*—For purposes of this section, the term publicly traded partnership has the same meaning as in section 7704 (including the regulations thereunder), but does not include a publicly traded partnership treated as a corporation under that section.

(2) *Applicable percentage.*—For purposes of this section, applicable percentage shall have the meaning as set forth in §1.1446-3(a)(2), except that the partnership or nominee required to pay 1446 tax may not consider a preferential rate in computing the 1446 tax due with respect to a partner.

(3) *Nominee.*—For purposes of this section, the term nominee means a domestic person that

holds an interest in a publicly traded partnership on behalf of a foreign person.

(4) *Qualified notice.*—For purposes of this section, a qualified notice is a notice given by a publicly traded partnership regarding a distribution that is attributable to effectively connected income, gain or loss of the partnership, and in accordance with the notice requirements with respect to dividends described in 17 CFR 240.10b-17(b)(1) or (3) issued pursuant to the Securities Exchange Act of 1934 (15 U.S.C. 78a). See paragraph (d) of this section regarding when a nominee is considered to have received a qualified notice.

(c) *Paying and reporting 1446 tax.*—The withholding tax required under this section is to be paid pursuant to the rules and procedures of section 1461, §§1.1461-1, 1.1461-2, and 1.6302-2, as supplemented by the rules of this section. However, the reimbursement and set-off procedures set forth in §1.1461-2 shall not apply. A withholding agent under this section must use Form 1042,"Annual Withholding Tax Return for U.S. Source Income of Foreign Persons," and Form 1042-S,"Foreign Person's U.S. Source Income Subject to Withholding," to report withholding from distributions under this section. See §1.1461-1(b). Further, a withholding agent under this section may obtain a refund for 1446 tax paid in accordance with section 1464 and the regulations thereunder. See §1.1446-3(d)(1)(iv) and (vii) (relating to a foreign trust or estate that holds an interest in a publicly traded partnership) and §1.1446-5(d) (relating to a publicly traded partnership that is part of a tiered partnership structure) for additional guidance.

(d) *Rules for designation of nominees to withhold tax under section 1446.*—A nominee that receives a distribution from a publicly traded partnership subject to withholding under this section, and which is to be paid to (or for the account of) any foreign person, may be treated as a withholding agent under this section. A nominee is treated as a withholding agent under this section only to the extent of the amount specified in the qualified notice (as defined in paragraph (b)(4) of this section) received by the nominee. A nominee is treated as receiving a qualified notice at the time such notice is published in accordance with 17 CFR 240.10b-17(b)(1) or (3). Where a nominee is designated as a withholding agent with respect to a foreign partner of the partnership, the obligation to withhold on distributions to such foreign partner in accordance with the rules of this section shall be imposed solely on the nominee. A nominee responsible for withholding under the rules of this section shall be subject to liability under sections 1461 and 6655, as well as all applicable penalties and interest, as if such nominee was a partnership responsible for withholding under this section.

(e) *Determining foreign status of partners.*—The rules of §1.1446-1 shall apply in determining whether a partner of a publicly traded partnership is a foreign partner for purposes of the 1446 tax. A partnership or nominee obligated to withhold under this section shall be entitled to rely on any of the forms acceptable under §1.1446-1 received from persons on whose behalf it holds interests in the partnership to the same extent a partnership is entitled to rely on such forms under those rules.

(f) *Distributions subject to withholding.*—(1) *In general.*—Except as provided in this paragraph (f)(1), a publicly traded partnership must withhold at the applicable percentage with respect to any actual distribution made to a foreign partner. The amount of a distribution subject to 1446 tax includes the amount of any 1446 tax required to be withheld on the distribution. In the case of a partnership (upper-tier partnership) that receives a partnership distribution from another partnership in which it is a partner (lower-tier partnership) (i.e., a tiered structure described in §1.1446-5), any 1446 tax that was paid by the lower-tier partnership may be credited by the upper-tier partnership and shall be treated as a distribution under section 1446. For example, a foreign publicly traded partnership, UTP, owns an interest in domestic publicly traded partnership, LTP. LTP makes a distribution subject to section 1446 of $100 to UTP during its taxable year beginning January 1, 2005, and withholds 35 percent (the highest rate in section 1) ($35) of that distribution under section 1446. UTP receives a net distribution of $65 which it immediately redistributes to its partners. UTP has a liability to pay 35 percent of the total actual and deemed distribution it makes to its foreign partners as a section 1446 withholding tax. UTP may credit the $35 withheld by LTP against this liability as if it were paid by UTP. See §1.1462-1(b) and §1.1446-5(b)(1). When UTP distributes the $65 it actually receives from LTP to its partners, UTP is treated for purposes of section 1446 as if it made a distribution of $100 to its partners ($65 actual distribution and $35 deemed distribution). UTP's partners (U.S. and foreign) may claim a credit against their U.S. income tax liability for their allocable share of the $35 of 1446 tax paid on their behalf.

(2) *In-kind distributions.*—If a publicly traded partnership distributes property other than money, the partnership shall not release the property until it has funds sufficient to enable the partnership to pay over in money the required 1446 tax.

(3) *Ordering rule relating to distributions.*—Distributions from publicly traded partnerships are deemed to be paid out of the following types of income in the order indicated—

(i) Amounts attributable to income described in section 1441 or 1442 that are not effectively connected, without regard to whether such amounts are subject to withholding because of a treaty or statutory exemption;

(ii) Amounts effectively connected with a U.S. trade or business, but not subject to withholding under section 1446 (e.g., amounts exempt by treaty);

(iii) Amounts subject to withholding under section 1446; and

(iv) Amounts not listed in paragraphs (f)(3)(i) through (iii) of this section.

(4) *Coordination with section 1445(e)(1).*—Except as otherwise provided in this section, a publicly traded partnership that complies with the requirements of withholding under section 1446 and this section will be deemed to have satisfied the requirements of section 1445(e)(1) and the regulations thereunder. Notwithstanding the excluded amounts set forth in paragraph (f)(3) of this section, distributions subject to withholding at the applicable percentage shall include the following—

(i) Amounts subject to withholding under section 1445(e)(1) upon distribution pursuant to an election under § 1.1445-5(c)(3) of the regulations; and

(ii) Amounts not subject to withholding under section 1445 because the distributee is a partnership or is a foreign corporation that has made an election under section 897(i). [Reg. § 1.1446-4.]

☐ [*T.D.* 9200, 5-13-2005.]

[Reg. § 1.1446-5]

§ 1.1446-5. Tiered partnership structures.—
(a) *In general.*—The rules of this section shall apply in cases where a partnership (lower-tier partnership) that has effectively connected taxable income (ECTI), has a partner that is a partnership (upper-tier partnership). Except as provided in paragraph (e) of this section, if an upper-tier domestic partnership directly owns an interest in a lower-tier partnership, the lower-tier partnership is not required to pay the section 1446 withholding tax (1446 tax) with respect to the upper-tier partnership's allocable share of net income, regardless of whether the upper-tier domestic partnership's partners are foreign. Paragraph (b) of this section prescribes the reporting requirements for upper-tier and lower-tier partnerships subject to section 1446. Paragraph (c) of this section prescribes rules requiring a lower-tier partnership to look through an upper-tier foreign partnership to a partner of such upper-tier partnership to the extent it has sufficient documentation to determine the status of such partner and determine such partner's indirect share of the lower-tier partnership's effectively connected taxable income (ECTI). Paragraph (d) of this section prescribes rules applicable to a publicly traded partnership in a tiered partnership structure. Paragraph (e) of this section

prescribes rules permitting a domestic upper-tier partnership to elect to apply the look through rules of paragraph (c) of this section. Paragraph (f) of this section sets forth examples illustrating the rules of this section.

(b) *Reporting requirements.*—(1) *In general.*—Notwithstanding paragraph (c) of this section, to the extent that an upper-tier partnership that is a foreign partnership is a partner in a lower-tier partnership, and the lower-tier partnership has paid 1446 tax (including installment payments of such tax) with respect to ECTI allocable to the upper-tier partnership, the lower-tier partnership shall comply with §§ 1.1446-1 through 1.1446-3 and provide the upper-tier partnership notice of such payments and a copy of the statements and forms filed with respect to the upper-tier partnership's interest in the lower-tier partnership (e.g., Form 8805, "Foreign Partner's Information Statement of Section 1446 Withholding Tax"). The upper-tier partnership may treat the 1446 tax (or any installment of such tax) paid by the lower-tier partnership on its behalf as a credit against its liability to pay 1446 tax (or any installment of such tax), as if the upper-tier partnership actually paid over the amounts at the time that the amounts were paid by the lower-tier partnership. See § 1.1462-1(b) and § 1.1446-3(d). To the extent required in § 1.1446-3(d)(1)(iii), the upper-tier partnership will file Form 8804, "Annual Return for Partnership Withholding Tax (Section 1446)," and Form 8805, "Foreign Partner's Information Statement of Section 1446 Withholding Tax," for each of its foreign partners with respect to its 1446 tax obligation. To the extent the upper-tier partnership does not claim a refund of the 1446 tax it paid (or is considered to have paid), the upper-tier partnership will pass the credit for the 1446 tax paid to its partners on the Forms 8805 it issues. See § 1.1446-3(d). The rules of this paragraph (b) shall apply to an upper-tier and lower-tier partnership to the extent that an election has been made and consented to under paragraph (e) of this section.

(2) *Publicly traded partnerships.*—In the case of an upper-tier foreign partnership that is a publicly traded partnership, the rules of § 1.1446-4(c) shall apply. See also paragraph (d) of this section.

(c) *Look through rules for foreign upper-tier partnerships.*—For purposes of computing the 1446 tax obligation of a lower-tier partnership, if an upper-tier foreign partnership owns an interest in the lower-tier partnership, the upper-tier partnership's allocable share of ECTI from the lower-tier partnership shall be treated as allocable to a partner of the upper-tier partnership, to the extent of such partner's indirect share of such ECTI (as if such partner were a direct partner in the lower-tier partnership), if—

(1) The upper-tier foreign partnership furnishes the lower-tier partnership a valid Form W-8IMY, "Certificate of Foreign Intermediary, Flow Through Entity, or Certain U.S. Branches for United States Tax Withholding," indicating that it is a look-through foreign partnership for purposes of section 1446; and

(2) The lower-tier partnership can reliably associate (within the meaning of § 1.1441-1(b)(2)(vii)) effectively connected partnership items allocable to the upper-tier partnership (and indirectly to such partner) with a Form W-8 (e.g., Form W-8BEN), Form W-9, "Request for Taxpayer Identification Number and Certification," or other form acceptable under § 1.1446-1, establishing the status of such partner provided by the upper-tier partnership. The lower-tier partnership required to pay 1446 tax must be able to provide the information necessary for the IRS to determine the chain of ownership, allocation of effectively connected items at each partnership level, as well as to the ultimate beneficial owner of the effectively connected items, and whether the amount of 1446 tax paid was appropriate. This information should permit each partnership in the tiered structure and the IRS to reliably associate any effectively connected items allocable to such upper-tier partnership, as well as to the ultimate beneficial owner of the effectively connected items. The principles of § 1.1441-1(b)(2)(vii) shall apply to determine whether a lower-tier partnership can reliably associate effectively connected partnership items allocable to the upper-tier partnership with a partner of the upper-tier partnership. To the extent the lower-tier partnership receives a valid Form W-8IMY from the upper-tier partnership but cannot reliably associate a portion of the upper-tier partnership's allocable share of effectively connected partnership items with a partner of such upper-tier partnership, then the lower-tier partnership shall pay 1446 tax on such portion at the higher of the applicable percentages in section 1446(b). See § 1.1446-3(a)(2) for the treatment of any income or gain potentially subject to a preferential rate. If a lower-tier partnership has not received a valid Form W-8IMY from the upper-tier partnership, the lower-tier partnership shall withhold on the upper-tier partnership's entire allocable share of ECTI at the higher of the applicable percentages in section 1446(b). The look through regime set forth in this paragraph (c) is for purposes of computing the lower-tier partnership's 1446 tax obligation only and does not alter the persons considered to be partners in the lower-tier partnership for partnership reporting purposes (e.g., issuing Form 8805, Schedule K-1).

(d) *Publicly traded partnerships.*—(1) *Upper-tier publicly traded partnership.*—The rules set forth in paragraph (c) shall not apply to look through an upper-tier partnership whose interests are publicly traded (as defined in § 1.1446-4(b)(1)).

(2) *Lower-tier publicly traded partnership.*—The look through rules of paragraph (c) of this section shall apply, if the requirements of that paragraph are met, to a lower-tier partnership that is a publicly traded partnership within the meaning of § 1.1446-4(b)(1) only if the upper-tier partnership is not described in paragraph (d)(1) of this section. For example, a lower-tier publicly traded partnership (or nominee) shall look through an upper-tier foreign partnership (or domestic partnership to the extent an election is made and consented to under paragraph (e) of this section) when computing its 1446 tax liability, provided the upper-tier partnership is not a publicly traded partnership and the appropriate documentation needed to satisfy the standards set forth in § 1.1441-1(b)(2)(vii) and paragraph (c) of this section have been furnished.

(e) *Election by a domestic upper-tier partnership to apply look through rules.*—(1) *In general.*—Subject to the rules of this paragraph (e), a domestic partnership that is a partner in a lower-tier partnership may elect to apply the rules of this section 1.1446-5 and have the lower-tier partnership look through such upper-tier partnership to the partners of such domestic partnership for purposes of computing the lower-tier partnership's 1446 tax liability. A domestic partnership shall make this election by attaching to the Form W-9 submitted to the lower-tier partnership, a written statement and information (described in paragraph (e)(2) of this section) that identifies the upper-tier partnership as a domestic partnership and that states that such partnership is making the election under this paragraph (e). This paragraph (e)(1) shall not apply to a publicly traded partnership described in § 1.1446-4(b)(1). See paragraph (d)(1) of this section.

(2) *Information required for valid election statement.*—In addition to the requirements of paragraphs (e)(1) and (3) of this section, the election statement submitted under this paragraph (e)(2) is not valid and cannot be accepted by the lower-tier partnership pursuant to paragraph (e)(3) of this section unless the upper-tier partnership attaches valid documentation pursuant to § 1.1446-1 (e.g., Form W-8BEN) with respect to one or more of its foreign partners. The information and documentation submitted with the election must comply with the rules of this section to permit the lower-tier partnership to reliably associate (within the meaning of § 1.1441-1(b)(2)(vii)) at least a portion of the upper-tier partnership's allocable share of ECTI with one or more foreign partners of the upper-tier partnership. The election statement must identify the upper-tier partnership by name, address, and TIN, and specify the percentage interest the domestic partnership holds in the lower-tier partnership. The statement may also include such information the upper-tier partnership deems necessary to enable the lower-tier partnership to apply the provisions of this section. If

at any time the upper-tier partnership determines that the information or documentation previously provided to the lower- tier partnership is no longer correct, the upper-tier partnership shall update such information and documentation. Except as provided in paragraph (e)(3) of this section, an election that is effective under this paragraph (e) shall apply for subsequent taxable years until such upper-tier partnership revokes the election in writing. A revocation under this section shall be effective for any installment due date arising more than 15 days subsequent to the date that the lower-tier partnership receives such revocation.

(3) *Consent of lower-tier partnership.*—An election made under this paragraph (e) is not effective until the lower-tier partnership consents in writing to the upper-tier partnership that it agrees to apply the provisions of this section. A lower-tier partnership may not consent to an election submitted under this paragraph (e) for any installment date or Form 8804 filing date arising within 15 days of the lower-tier partnership's receipt of such election. The lower-tier partnership's written consent must specify the extent to which it will look through the upper-tier partnership in computing its 1446 tax (or any installment of such tax). To the extent that the lower-tier partnership does not consent to an election to apply the look through provisions of paragraph (c) of this section, the lower-tier partnership shall consider such portion of the upper-tier partnership's allocable share of ECTI as allocable to a domestic person for purposes of computing its 1446 tax obligation. A lower-tier partnership that has consented to an election under this paragraph (e) may revoke or modify its consent, in writing, at any time.

(f) *Examples.*—The following examples illustrate the provisions of this section. In considering the examples, disregard the potential application of § 1.1446-3(b)(2)(v)(F) (relating to the de minimis exception to paying 1446 tax). The examples are as follows:

Example 1. Sufficient documentation—tiered partnership structure. (i) Nonresident alien (NRA) and foreign corporation (FC) are partners in PRS, a foreign partnership, and share profits and losses in PRS 70 and 30 percent, respectively. All of PRS's partnership items are allocated based upon each partner's respective ownership interest and it is assumed that these allocations are respected under section 704(b) and the regulations thereunder. NRA and FC each furnish PRS with a valid Form W-8BEN establishing themselves as a foreign individual and foreign corporation, respectively. PRS holds a 40 percent interest in the profits, losses and capital of LTP, a lower-tier partnership. NRA holds the remaining 60 percent interest in profits, losses and capital of LTP. All of LTP's partnership items are allocated based upon each partner's respective ownership interest and it is assumed that these allocations

are respected under section 704(b) and the regulations thereunder. LTP has $100 of annualized ECTI for the relevant installment period. All of this income is ordinary income and there is no potential application of a preferential rate applicable percentage under § 1.1446-3(a)(2). Further, § 1.1446-6 does not apply. PRS has no income other than the income allocated from LTP. PRS provides LTP with a valid Form W-8IMY indicating that it is a foreign partnership and attaches the valid Form W-8BENs executed by NRA and FC, as well as a statement describing the allocation of PRS's effectively connected items among its partners. The information that PRS submits to LTP is sufficient to permit LTP to reliably associate (within the meaning of § 1.1441-1(b)(2)(vii)) PRS's allocable share of effectively connected items with NRA and FC pursuant to this section. Further, NRA provides a valid Form W-8BEN to LTP.

(ii) LTP must pay 1446 tax on the $60 allocable to its direct partner NRA using the applicable percentage for non-corporate partners (the highest rate in section 1).

(iii) With respect to the effectively connected partnership items that LTP can reliably associate with NRA through PRS (70 percent of PRS's 40 percent allocable share ($40), or $28), LTP will pay 1446 tax on NRA's allocable share of LTP's ECTI (as determined by looking through PRS) using the applicable percentage for non-corporate partners (the highest rate in section 1).

(iv) With respect to the effectively connected partnership items that LTP can reliably associate with FC through PRS (30 percent of PRS's 40 percent allocable share ($40), or $12), LTP will pay 1446 tax on FC's allocable share of LTP's ECTI (as determined by looking through PRS) using the applicable percentage for corporate partners (the highest rate in section 11).

(v) LTP's payment of the 1446 tax is treated as a distribution to NRA and PRS, its direct partners, that those partners may credit against their respective tax obligations. PRS will report its 1446 tax obligation with respect to its direct foreign partners, NRA and FC, on the Form 8804 and Forms 8805 that it files with the Internal Revenue Service pursuant to paragraph (b) of this section and will credit the amount withheld by LTP on its Form 8804. This credit will satisfy PRS's 1446 tax liability as reported on the Form 8804 it files because PRS's only income is from LTP, and LTP paid 1446 tax with respect to all of PRS's allocable share in LTP by looking through to PRS's partners NRA and FC. Further, PRS will pass along the credit for the 1446 tax withheld by LTP to its partners, NRA and FC on the Form 8805 issued to each partner. The credit passed to each partner on Form 8805 will be treated as a distribution to the respective partners under section 1446(d).

Example 2. Insufficient documentation—tiered partnership structure. (i) LTP is a domestic partnership that has two equal partners A and PRS.

A is a nonresident alien and PRS is a foreign partnership that has two equal foreign partners, C and D. Neither A nor PRS provides LTP with a valid Form W-8 or Form W-9. Neither C nor D provides PRS with a valid Form W-8 or Form W-9. Pursuant to § 1.1446-1(c)(3), LTP must presume that PRS is a foreign person subject to withholding under section 1446 at the higher of the highest rate under section 1 or section 11(b)(1). LTP has also not received any documentation with respect to A. LTP must presume that A is a foreign person, and, if LTP knows that A is an individual, compute and pay 1446 tax, subject to § 1.1446-3(a)(2), based on that knowledge.

(ii) Assume a change of facts where C provides a form W-8 (e.g., Form W-8BEN) to PRS, and PRS in turn, furnishes that form to LTP along with its Form W-8IMY, and information regarding how effectively connected items are allocated to C and D. Based upon the additional facts, LTP can reliably associate one-half of PRS's allocable share of ECTI with documentation related with C. Therefore, under paragraph (c)(2) of this section, LTP will look through PRS to C when computing its 1446 tax to the extent of C's indirect share and will not look through with respect to the remainder of PRS's allocable share (D's indirect share).

[Reg. § 1.1446-5.]

□ [*T.D. 9200, 5-13-2005. Amended by T.D. 9394, 4-28-2008.*]

[Reg. §1.1446-6]

§1.1446-6. Special rules to reduce a partnership's 1446 tax with respect to a foreign partner's allocable share of effectively connected taxable income.—(a) *In general.*—(1) *Purpose and scope.*—This section provides rules regarding when a partnership required to pay withholding tax under section 1446 (1446 tax), or an installment of 1446 tax, may consider certain partner-level deductions and losses in computing its 1446 tax obligation under § 1.1446-3, or otherwise not pay a de minimis amount of 1446 tax due with respect to a nonresident alien individual partner. A partnership determines the applicability of the rules of this section on a partner-by-partner basis for each installment period and when completing its Form 8804, "Annual Return for Partnership Withholding Tax (Section 1446)," and paying 1446 tax for the partnership taxable year. Except with respect to certain state and local taxes paid by the partnership on behalf of the partner, to apply the rules of this section with respect to a foreign partner, the partnership must receive a certificate from such partner for each partnership taxable year. Paragraph (b) of this section identifies the foreign partners to which this section applies. Paragraph (c) of this section identifies the deductions and losses that a foreign partner may certify to the partnership as well as the state and local taxes paid by the partnership on behalf of the foreign partner that

can be taken into account without a certification, and establishes an exception that permits a partnership to not pay a de minimis amount of 1446 tax with respect to a nonresident alien partner. Paragraph (c) of this section also sets forth the requirements for a valid certificate. Paragraphs (a)(2) and (d) of this section establish when a partnership may rely on and consider a foreign partner's certificate in computing its 1446 tax, and the effects of relying on such a certificate. Paragraph (d) of this section also describes the effects of a partnership relying on a certificate (including an updated certificate) and the reporting requirements of a partnership with respect to a certificate. Paragraph (e) of this section sets forth examples that illustrate the rules of this section. Paragraph (f) of this section provides the Effective/Applicability date. Paragraph (g) of this section provides a transition rule.

(2) *Reasonable reliance on a certificate.*—Subject to § 1.1446-2 and the rules of this section, a partnership receiving a certificate (including an updated certificate or status update under paragraph (c)(2)(ii)(B) of this section) of deductions and losses from a partner provided in accordance with the provisions of this section may reasonably rely on such certificate (to the extent of the certified deductions and losses or other representations set forth in the certificate) until such time that it has actual knowledge or reason to know that the certificate is defective or that the time for receiving an updated certificate or status update from the partner under paragraph (c)(2)(ii)(B) of this section has expired. For this purpose, a partnership shall be considered to have actual knowledge or reason to know that a certificate is defective upon receipt of written notification from the IRS under paragraph (c)(3) or (c)(5) of this section.

(b) *Foreign partner to whom this section applies.*—(1) *In general.*—Except as otherwise provided in paragraph (b)(3) of this section, a foreign partner to whom this section applies is a foreign partner that meets the requirements of this paragraph (b)(1).

(i) The partner has provided valid documentation to the partnership to which a certificate is submitted under this section in accordance with § 1.1446-1.

(ii) If the partner's current taxable year is the first taxable year in which the partner submits a certificate to any partnership, the partner has filed (or will file) a qualifying U.S. income tax return for each of its three taxable years ending before the end of the partnership's taxable year for which the partner is submitting a certificate (regardless of whether it was a partner in that partnership during each of these years). A qualifying U.S. income tax return for a taxable year that is prior to the first taxable year the partner submits a certificate to any partnership is a U.S. income tax return filed within the time specified in paragraph (b)(2)(iii) of this section.

(iii) If the current taxable year of the partner is not the first taxable year in which the partner submits a certificate to any partnership, the partner met the requirements in paragraph (b)(1)(ii) of this section for the first taxable year in which it submitted a certificate to any partnership and has filed (or will file) a qualifying U.S. income tax return for its first taxable year in which it submitted a certificate to any partnership and each subsequent taxable year ending before the beginning of the current taxable year (regardless of whether it was a partner in any partnership during each of those years). A qualifying U.S. income tax return for a taxable year that is prior to the taxable year the partner submits a certificate to any partnership is a U.S. income tax return filed within the time specified in paragraph (b)(2)(iii) of this section.

(iv) The partner files a qualifying U.S. income tax return (within the meaning of paragraph (b)(2)(iii) of this section) for its taxable year in which a certificate is provided to any partnership.

(2) *Definitions.*—(i) *U.S. income tax return.*— A U.S. income tax return means a Form 1040NR, "U.S. Nonresident Alien Income Tax Return," in the case of a nonresident alien individual and a Form 1120F, "U.S. Income Tax Return of a Foreign Corporation," in the case of a foreign corporation.

(ii) *Timely-filed.*—Only for purposes of this section, a U.S. income tax return shall be considered timely-filed if the return is filed on or before the due date set forth in section 6072(c), plus any extension of time to file such return granted under section 6081.

(iii) *Qualifying U.S. income tax return.*—A U.S. income tax return shall constitute a qualifying U.S. income tax return if the return reports income or gain that is effectively connected with a U.S. trade or business or deductions or losses properly allocated and apportioned to such activities and if the return is described in paragraph (b)(2)(iii)(A), (B), or (C) of this section. A protective return described in §1.874-1(b)(6) or §1.882-4(a)(3)(vi) is not a qualifying U.S. income tax return for purposes of this section.

(A) A U.S. income tax return for a partner's preceding taxable year in which it did not submit a certificate to any partnership (but not including a taxable year following the first taxable year in which the partner submitted a certificate to any partnership), with a due date as set forth in section 6072(c), not including any extensions of time to file, which falls before the beginning of the current partnership taxable year for which the certificate is provided is described in this paragraph (b)(2)(iii)(A) if the return is filed and all amounts due with respect to such return (including interest, penalties, and additions to tax, if any) are paid on or before the earlier of—

(1) The date that is one year after the due date set forth in section 6072(c) for such return, not including any extensions of time to file; or

(2) The date on which the certificate for the current partnership taxable year is submitted to the partnership.

(B) A U.S. income tax return for a partner's preceding taxable year in which it did not submit a certificate to any partnership (but not including a taxable year following the first taxable year in which the partner submitted a certificate to any partnership), with a due date as set forth in section 6072(c), not including any extensions of time to file, which falls within the current partnership taxable year for which the certificate is provided is described in this paragraph (b)(2)(iii)(B) if the return is timely-filed and all amounts due with respect to such return are timely paid.

(C) A U.S. income tax return for a taxable year in which the partner submits a certificate to any partnership and for a taxable year following the first taxable year in which the partner submits a certificate to any partnership is described in this paragraph (b)(2)(iii)(C) if the return is timely-filed and all amounts due with such return are timely paid with respect to such return.

(3) *Special rules.*—(i) In the case of a partnership (upper-tier partnership) that is a partner in another partnership (lower-tier partnership)—

(A) The rules of this section may apply to reduce or eliminate the 1446 tax (or any installment of such tax) of the lower-tier partnership with respect to a foreign partner of the upper-tier partnership only to the extent the provisions of §1.1446-5 apply to look through the upper-tier partnership to the foreign partner of such upper-tier partnership and the certificate described in paragraph (c) of this section is provided by such foreign partner to the upper-tier partnership and, in turn, provided to the lower-tier partnership with other appropriate documentation (see §1.1446-5(c) and (e));

(B) An upper-tier partnership that submits a certificate of deductions and losses or a de minimis certificate to a lower-tier partnership may not submit that certificate to another lower-tier partnership;

(C) An upper-tier partnership that relies on a certificate submitted to it by a foreign partner under this section for computing its 1446 tax due on effectively connected taxable income (ECTI) allocable to that partner (other than ECTI allocable to it from a lower-tier partnership) may not submit that certificate to any lower-tier partnership; and

(D) In addition to any other information required by this section, a lower-tier partnership must submit with a Form 8813, "Partnership Withholding Tax Payment Voucher (Section 1446)," and Form 8805, "Foreign Partner's Information Statement of Section 1446 Withholding Tax," for which it relies on a certificate from an upper-tier partnership to reduce the 1446 tax due with respect to a foreign partner of the upper-tier partnership, sufficient information so that the IRS may reliably associate the ECTI and the certificate of deductions and losses with the partner in the upper-tier partnership submitting the certificate, including the name, taxpayer identification number (TIN) and allocation of effectively connected items at each partnership tier, as well as to the ultimate upper-tier partner submitting the certificate.

(ii) This section shall not apply to a partner that is a foreign estate or its beneficiaries.

(iii) This section shall not apply to a partner that is a trust or to its beneficiaries, except to the extent that such trust is owned by a grantor or other person under subpart E of subchapter J of the Internal Revenue Code, the documentation requirements of § 1.1446-1 have been met by the grantor or other owner of such trust, and the certificate described in paragraph (c) of this section is provided by the grantor or other owner of such trust to the partnership.

(iv) This section shall not apply to a partner in a publicly-traded partnership subject to § 1.1446-4.

(c) *Reduction of 1446 tax with respect to a foreign partner.*—(1) *General rules.*—Under paragraph (c)(1)(i) of this section a foreign partner to whom this section applies may certify to a partnership for a partnership taxable year that it has certain deductions (other than charitable deductions) and losses properly allocated and apportioned to gross income that is effectively connected (or treated as effectively connected) with the conduct of the partner's trade or business in the United States, and that the partner reasonably expects those deductions and losses to be available and claimed on the partner's U.S. income tax return to be filed for that taxable year. Under paragraph (c)(1)(ii) of this section, a nonresident alien individual partner to whom this section applies may also certify to a partnership for a partnership taxable year that its only investment or activity giving rise to effectively connected items for the partnership's taxable year that ends with or within the partner's taxable year is (and will be) the partner's investment in the partnership. A certificate submitted by a foreign partner to a partnership under this section must be in accordance with the form and requirements set forth in paragraph (c)(2)(ii) of this section. Under paragraph (c)(1)(iii) of this section, a partnership may take into account certain state and local taxes withheld by the partnership on behalf of the partner.

(i) *Certified deductions and losses.*— (A) *Deductions and losses from the partnership.*— Under this paragraph (c)(1)(i)(A), a partner may certify to a partnership for a partnership taxable year deductions (other than charitable deduc-

tions) and losses properly allocated and apportioned to gross income which is effectively connected (or treated as effectively connected) with the conduct of the partner's trade or business in the United States, that are reported on a Form 1065 (Schedule K-1), "Partner's Share of Income, Credits, Deductions, etc.," issued (or to be issued) to the partner by the partnership for a prior partnership taxable year, that are (or will be) reported on a qualifying U.S. income tax return for a partner's taxable year that ends before the installment due date or the close of the partnership taxable year for which the partner is certifying such deductions and losses, and that the partner reasonably expects to be available and claimed on a qualifying U.S. income tax return for the partner's taxable year ending with or after the close of the partnership taxable year. A partner that has a loss reported on a Form 1065 (Schedule K-1) issued (or to be issued) to the partner by the partnership for a prior partnership taxable year, but that is not (and will not be) reported on a qualifying U.S. income tax return for a prior taxable year of the partner because the loss is suspended under section 704(d) may also certify such suspended loss to the partnership under this paragraph (c)(1)(i)(A).

(B) *Deductions and losses from other sources.*—Under this paragraph (c)(1)(i)(B), a foreign partner may certify to a partnership for a partnership taxable year deductions (other than charitable deductions) and losses properly allocated and apportioned to gross income that is effectively connected (or treated as effectively connected) with the conduct of the partner's trade or business in the United States and that are from sources other than the partnership to whom the certificate is submitted if the deductions and losses are (or will be) reported on a qualifying U.S. income tax return of the partner for a taxable year that ends before the installment due date or the close of the partnership taxable year for which the partner is certifying the deductions and losses and the partner reasonably expects the deductions and losses to be available and claimed on the a qualifying U.S. income tax return filed for its taxable year ending with or after the close of the partnership taxable year. Any deductions and losses certified under this paragraph (c)(1)(i)(B) that are allocated to the partner from another partnership must be reported on a Form 1065 (Schedule K-1) issued (or to be issued) to the partner by such other partnership. However, the partner may not certify any deduction or loss allocated to it from another partnership that is suspended under section 704(d).

(C) *Limit on the consideration of a partner's net operating loss deduction.*—A partnership may not consider a net operating loss deduction (as determined under section 172) certified by the partner under this paragraph (c)(1)(i) in an amount greater than the percentage limitation, if any, provided in section 56(a)(4) and (d) multiplied by the partner's allocable share of ECTI from the partnership reduced by all other certified deductions and losses whether or not taken into account by the partnership, as well as deductions considered under paragraph (c)(1)(iii) of this section.

(D) *Limitation on losses subject to certain partner level limitations.*—Pursuant to paragraph (c)(2)(i) of this section, a partner must identify any certified losses or deductions that are subject to special limitations at the partner level (for example, sections 465 and 469) and provide information to the partnership that will allow the partnership to take the special limitations into account. For example, where a partner certifies a loss to the partnership that is a passive activity loss under section 469, the partner shall identify the activities the partnership conducts that the partner expects will be passive activities. The partnership shall then ensure that these limitations are taken into account when determining the 1446 tax due with respect to the partner.

(E) *Certification of deductions and losses to other partnerships.*—Deductions and losses certified to a partnership for a taxable year of the partnership may not be certified for the taxable year of another partnership that begins or ends with or within the taxable year of the partnership to which the deductions and losses were certified.

(F) *Partner level use of deductions and losses certified to a partnership.*—Any deductions and losses certified to a partnership for a taxable year of the partner and considered by the partnership in computing its section 1446 tax due may not be considered by that partner for the same taxable year in computing the amount of its required installments under section 6654(d) or 6655(d) on income unrelated to the partnership to which the partner has submitted the certificate.

(ii) *De minimis certificate for nonresident alien individual partners.*—(A) *In general.*—Under this paragraph (c)(1)(ii), a nonresident alien individual partner to whom this section applies and that satisfies the requirements of paragraph (c)(1)(ii)(B) of this section may certify to a partnership that its only activity giving rise to effectively connected income, gain, deduction, or loss for the partnership's taxable year that ends with or within the partner's taxable year is (and will be) the partner's investment in the partnership. A partnership that receives a certificate from a nonresident alien partner under this paragraph (c)(1)(ii) and that may reasonably rely on such certificate is not required to pay 1446 tax (or any installment of such tax) with respect to such partner if the partnership estimates that the annualized (or, in the case of a partnership completing its Form 8804, the actual) 1446 tax otherwise due with respect to such partner is less

than $1,000, without taking into account any deductions or losses certified by the partner to the partnership under paragraph (c)(1)(i) of this section or any amounts under paragraph (c)(1)(iii) of this section.

(B) *Requirements for exception.*—The requirements of this paragraph (c)(1)(ii)(B) are met if the nonresident individual alien partner's only activity giving rise to effectively connected income, gain, deduction, or loss for the partnership taxable year that ends with or within the partner's taxable year is (and will be) the partner's investment in the partnership. For this purpose, if the partner has (or has reason to expect to have) income or gain described in section 864(c)(6), such income or gain shall be considered derived from a separate investment activity. A certificate submitted by a nonresident alien individual partner under this paragraph (c)(1)(ii) is valid even if such certificate does not certify deductions and losses to partnership under this section. A nonresident alien individual partner that submits a certificate to a partnership under this paragraph (c)(1)(ii) must notify the partnership in writing and revoke such certificate within 10 days of the date that the partner invests or otherwise engages in another activity that may give rise to effectively connected income, gain, deduction, or loss for the partner's taxable year. For example, while an investment in a U.S. real property interest (as defined in section 897(c)) would not give rise to an activity requiring a notification (unless an election is in effect under section 871(d)), the disposition of the U.S. real property interest would give rise to an activity requiring a notification.

(iii) *Consideration of certain current year state and local taxes.*—In addition to any deductions and losses certified by a foreign partner to a partnership under paragraph (c)(1)(i) of this section, the partnership may consider as a deduction of such partner 90-percent of any state and local income taxes withheld and remitted by the partnership on behalf of such partner with respect to the partner's allocable share of partnership ECTI. The partnership may consider the amount of state and local taxes of the foreign partner determined under this paragraph (c)(1)(iii) regardless of whether the foreign partner submits a certificate to the partnership under paragraph (c)(1)(i) or (ii) of this section.

(2) *Form and time of certification.*—(i) *Form of certification.*—A partner's certification to a partnership under paragraph (c)(1)(i) or (iii) of this section shall be made using Form 8804-C, "Certificate Of Partner-Level Items to Reduce Section 1446 Withholding" in accordance with the instructions of the form and the rules of this section.

(ii) *Time for certification provided to partnership.*—(A) *First certificate submitted for a partnership's taxable year.*—Provided the other requirements of this section are met, a partnership may only rely on the first certificate received from a foreign partner for any 1446 tax installment due or Form 8804 filing due (without regard to extensions) on or after the date on which the certificate is received. See §1.1446-3 for 1446 tax installment due dates. See also paragraph (e) of this section for examples illustrating the rules of this paragraph (c)(2).

    (B) *Updated certificates and status updates.*—(1) *Preceding year tax returns not yet filed.*—If a foreign partner's U.S. income tax return for a preceding taxable year has not been filed as of the time the partner submits to the partnership its first certificate under this paragraph (c), the certificate shall specify this fact and set forth the filing due date for such return set forth in section 6072(c), plus any extension of time to file such return granted under section 6081 and the regulations under section 6081. The partner shall also submit an updated certificate to the partnership in accordance with this paragraph (c) within 10 days of the date the partner files its U.S. income tax return for any such taxable year. In addition, prior to the partnership's final 1446 tax installment due date the partner shall provide to the partnership, under penalties of perjury, a status update regarding any U.S. income tax return for the prior taxable year that has not (or will not) be filed as of the final installment due date. The status update must identify the due date, set forth in section 6072(c), plus any extension of time to file such return granted under section 6081 and the regulations under section 6081, for any un-filed return identified in the first certificate and state whether the first certificate submitted may continue to be considered by the partnership. If the partnership does not receive an updated certificate or a status update from the partner prior to the partnership's final installment due date, the partnership shall disregard the partner's certificate when computing the 1446 tax due with respect to that partner for the final installment period and when completing its Form 8804 for the taxable year. In addition, the foreign partner shall not be permitted to submit an additional or substitute certificate for the disregarded certificate. See §1.1446-3(b)(2)(i) for computation requirements for installment payments of 1446 tax when a partnership receives, or fails to receive, an updated certificate or status update. See also paragraph (e)(2) *Examples 4 and 8* of this section. Notwithstanding this paragraph (c)(2)(ii)(B)(1), a partner that can meet the requirements of this section for a subsequent partnership taxable year may submit a certificate to the partnership under this section for such taxable year.

    (2) *Other circumstances requiring an updated certificate.*—If at any time during the partnership taxable year the partner determines that its most recent certificate furnished to the partnership for such taxable year is incorrect,

then the partner shall submit to the partnership an updated certificate in accordance with this paragraph (c) within 10 days of such determination. For example, if the partner determines that the amount or character of the certified deductions or losses is incorrect, the partner shall submit an updated certificate to the partnership. See §1.1446-3(b)(2)(i) for computation requirements for installment payments of 1446 tax when a partnership receives an updated certificate.

    (3) *Form and content of updated certificate.*—The updated certificate required by this paragraph (c)(2)(ii) must be provided using the form and instructions identified in paragraph (c)(2)(i) of this section. The updated certificate must indicate that it is an updated certificate filed in accordance with this paragraph (c)(2)(ii). The partner is not required to attach to the updated certificate a copy of the certificate that is being updated (superseded certificate).

    (4) *Partnership consideration of an updated certificate.*—A partnership may consider an updated certificate, that meets the requirements of this paragraph (c), that is received prior to an installment due date in the same partnership taxable year for which the superseded certificate was provided, or prior to the due date of its Form 8804 (without regard to extensions) to be filed for the year the superseded certificate was provided. A partnership must consider an updated certificate that meets all the requirements of this paragraph (c) if it would increase the amount of 1446 tax the partnership would pay by the next installment due date, if any, or the due date of its Form 8804. An updated certificate considered by the partnership under this paragraph (c)(2)(ii)(B)(4) supersedes all prior certificates submitted by the foreign partner for the same partnership taxable year, beginning with the installment period or Form 8804 filing date for which the partnership considers the updated certificate. See paragraph (e)(2) *Example 4* of this section.

    (3) *Notification to partnership when a partner's certificate cannot be relied upon.*—If the IRS determines, in its discretion based on all the facts and circumstances, that a foreign partner's certificate is defective (or that it lacks information sufficient to make this determination after providing written request for such information to the partnership), the IRS shall notify the partnership of such determination in writing. Upon receipt of such written notification, the partnership shall not rely on any certificate submitted by that foreign partner for the partnership taxable year to which the defective certificate relates (or any subsequent partnership taxable year), until the IRS provides written notification to the partnership revoking or modifying the original written notification. For purposes of this section, a foreign partner's certificate of deductions and losses shall be defective if—

(i) The partner is not described in paragraph (b) of this section;

(ii) Any deductions or losses set forth in such certificate are not described in paragraph (c)(1)(i) of this section;

(iii) The timing requirements under paragraph (c)(2) of this section for submitting an original certificate, an updated certificate or a status update to the partnership are not met;

(iv) The certificate does not include all of the information required by paragraph (c)(2)(i) of this section;

(v) Any representation made on the certificate is incorrect;

(vi) The actual amount of deductions and losses available to the partner is less than the amount of deductions and losses certified to the partnership for the partnership taxable year and considered by the partnership in determining its 1446 tax due; or

(vii) There is a failure to comply with any other provision of this section.

(4) *Partner to receive copy of notice.*—If the IRS notifies a partnership under paragraph (c)(3) of this section that a certificate of a foreign partner is defective, the IRS shall send a copy of such notice to the partner's address as shown on the certificate. The partnership shall also promptly furnish a copy of the IRS notice to such partner.

(5) *Notification to partnership when no foreign partner's certificate can be relied upon.*—If the IRS determines, in its discretion based on all the facts and circumstances, that there would be a substantial reduction in section 1446 tax as a result of the submission of one or more defective certificates or that a substantial portion of all certificates being submitted by partners to the partnership and by the partnership to the IRS are defective (or lack information sufficient to make this determination), then the IRS shall notify the partnership of such determination in writing. Upon receipt of such written notification, the partnership shall not rely on any certificate submitted by any partner for the partnership taxable year to which the notice relates or any subsequent partnership taxable year, until the IRS provides written notification to the partnership revoking or modifying the original notice.

(6) *Partnership notification to partner regarding use of deductions and losses.*—Unless § 1.1446-3(d)(1)(i)(A) or (B) applies (relating to waiver of notice of tax paid during the partnership taxable year), a partnership must notify each foreign partner of the amount of such partner's certified deductions and losses and state and local taxes, if any, taken into account under this paragraph (c) in determining the 1446 tax due with respect to such partner for each installment period or Form 8804 filing date, as applicable.

(7) *Partner's certificate valid only for partnership taxable year for which submitted.*—A partnership that receives a certificate from a partnership under this paragraph (c) shall consider such certificate only for the partnership taxable year for which the certificate is submitted, as set forth on the certificate.

(d) *Effect of certificate of deductions and losses on partners and partnership.*—(1) *Effect on partner.*—(i) *No effect on liability for income tax of foreign partner.*—A foreign partner that certifies deductions and losses to a partnership under this section is not relieved of liability for income tax on its allocable share of ECTI from the partnership. Further, the submission of a certificate under this section does not constitute an acceptance by the IRS of the amount or character of the deductions or losses certified therein.

(ii) *No effect on partner's estimated tax obligations.*—A foreign partner that certifies deductions and losses to a partnership under this section is not relieved of any estimated tax obligation otherwise applicable to such partner with respect to income or gain allocated to such partner from the partnership.

(iii) *No effect on partner's obligation to file U.S. income tax return.*—The submission of a certificate under paragraph (c) of this section does not relieve the foreign partner from its obligation to file a U.S. income tax return even if as a result of the partnership considering the certificate the partner would have no additional tax due with such return. See also § 1.1446-3(f).

(2) *Effect on partnership.*—(i) *Reasonable reliance to relieve partnership from addition to tax under section 6655.*—A partnership that has reasonably relied on a certificate received from a foreign partner and complied with the filing requirements of paragraph (d)(3)(i) of this section, shall not be liable for any addition to tax under section 6655 (as applied through § 1.1446-3) for any period during which the partnership reasonably relied on such certificate, even if such certificate is later determined to be defective or the partner submits an updated certificate under paragraph (c)(2) of this section that increases the 1446 tax due with respect to such partner.

(ii) *Continuing liability for withholding tax under section 1461 and for applicable interest and penalties.*—(A) *In general.*—Except as otherwise provided in this section, a partnership that has reasonably relied on a certificate received from a foreign partner and complied with the filing requirements of paragraph (d)(3)(i) of this section, is not relieved from liability for the 1446 tax (or any installment of such tax) under section 1461, any additions to the tax, interest or penalties. However, the partnership may be relieved of additions to the tax or penalties in certain circumstances. See §§ 301.6651-1(c) and 301.6724-1 of this chapter. Further, see § 1.1446-3(e) which deems a partnership to have paid 1446 tax with respect to ECTI allocable to a partner in certain circumstances. See also paragraph (e)(2) *Example 5* of this section.

(B) *Certificate defective because of amount or character of deductions and losses.*—If a certificate is determined to be defective because the actual amount of deductions and losses available to the partner is less than the amount reflected on the certificate (other than when it is determined that the partner certified the same deduction or loss to more than one partnership), or because the character of the certified deductions and losses is erroneous, the partnership shall be liable for 1446 tax under section 1461 (or any installment of such tax) with respect to such partner to the extent the partnership considered an amount of certified deductions and losses greater than the amount actually available to the partner and permitted to be used under §§ 1.1446-1 through 1.1446-5 and this section, or to the extent that the proper character of the certified deductions and losses results in a greater amount of 1446 tax due with respect to such partner. See paragraph (e)(2) *Example 6* of this section.

(3) *Partnership level rules and requirements.*— (i) *Filing requirement.*—A partnership that relies in whole or in part on a certificate received from a partner under this section in computing its 1446 tax due with respect to such partner must still file Form 8813 or Form 8804 and 8805, whichever is applicable, for the period for which the certificate is considered, even if as a result of relying on the certificate no 1446 tax (or an installment of such tax) is due with respect to such foreign partner. See generally § 1.1446-3(d)(1). Except as otherwise provided in this paragraph (d)(3)(i), the partnership must attach a copy of the foreign partner's certificate, and the computation of the 1446 tax due with respect to such partner, to both the Form 8813 and Form 8805 filed with the IRS for any installment period or year for which such certificate is considered in computing the partnership's 1446 tax. See § 1.1446-3(d)(1)(iii) requiring the partnership to furnish Form 8805 to the IRS and such foreign partner even if no 1446 tax is paid on behalf of the partner. The partnership must include in that computation the amount of state and local taxes described in paragraph (c)(1)(iii) of this section taken into account in computing the 1446 tax due with respect to that partner. The partnership must also attach a computation of the 1446 tax due with respect to a partner for whom only state and local taxes described in paragraph (c)(1)(iii) are taken into account. For an installment period other than the first installment period for which the partnership considers a foreign partner's certificate or updated certificate, the partnership may, instead of attaching any partner's certificate, attach to Form 8813 a list containing the name, TIN, the amount of

certified deductions and losses, and the amount of state and local taxes the partnership may consider under paragraph (c)(1)(iii) of this section for each foreign partner whose certificate was relied upon. For purposes of the preceding sentence, if the partnership is relying on a certificate received under paragraph (c)(1)(ii) of this section, instead of providing the amounts described in the prior sentence, it should attach a statement to Form 8813 which provides that, relying on that certificate, no 1446 tax is due with respect to that partner.

(ii) *Reasonable cause for failure to timely file a valid certificate and computation.*—This paragraph (d)(3)(ii) provides the sole source of relief for a partnership that fails to timely file a valid certificate or attach a computation of 1446 tax as required under paragraph (d)(3)(i) of this section. To permit the partnership to reasonably rely on such certificate, the partnership shall be considered to have satisfied the requirements of paragraph (d)(3)(i) of this section if the partnership demonstrates that such failure was due to reasonable cause and not willful neglect and if once the partnership becomes aware of the failure, the partnership attaches the certificate and computation, as well as a written statement setting forth the reasons for the failure to comply with the requirements of paragraph (d)(3)(i) of this section, to an amended Form 8813 or amended Forms 8804 and 8805 for the relevant period. All such submissions should be sent to the address provided in the instructions to Form 8804-C.

(A) *Determining reasonable cause.*—In determining whether the partnership has reasonable cause, the Director shall consider whether the partnership acted reasonably and in good faith considering all the facts and circumstances.

(B) *Notification.*—If the IRS has notified, as provided in paragraph (c)(3) of this section, the partnership that the certificate is defective or that no foreign partner's certificate may be relied upon, as provided in paragraph (c)(5) of this section, the partnership will be deemed not to have acted reasonably and in good faith. Otherwise, the Director shall notify the partnership in writing within 120 days of the amended filing if it is determined that the failure to comply was not due to reasonable cause, or if additional time will be needed to make such determination. If the Director fails to notify the partnership within 120 days of the amended filing, the partnership shall be considered to have demonstrated to the Director that such failure was due to reasonable cause and not willful neglect.

(e) *Examples.*—(1) The rules of this section are illustrated by the examples in paragraph (e)(2) of this section. Except as otherwise provided, in each example assume:

(i) Section 1.1446-3(b)(2)(v)(F) (relating to the de minimis exception to paying 1446 tax) does not apply;

(ii) Paragraph (c)(1)(ii) of this section (relating to a nonresident alien individual partner whose sole investment generating effectively connected income or gain is the partnership) does not apply;

(iii) All income and losses are ordinary;

(iv) For purposes of applying paragraph (c)(1)(i)(C) of this section, the percentage limitation under section 56(a)(4) and (d) is 90 percent;

(v) Any loss is not a passive activity loss within the meaning of section 469;

(vi) The partnership uses an acceptable annualization method under §1.1446-3;

(vii) NRA is a nonresident alien individual who maintains a calendar taxable year for U.S. tax purpose;

(viii) B and C are U.S. individuals who maintain a calendar taxable year; and

(ix) Any partnership maintains a calendar taxable year.

(2) The examples are as follows:

Example 1. Qualifying U.S. income tax return. (i) NRA and B form a partnership (PRS) in year 4 to conduct a trade or business in the United States. NRA and B provide PRS appropriate documentation under §1.1446-1 to establish their status for purposes of section 1446. NRA submits a certificate to PRS (using Form 8804-C) on March 20, year 4, to be considered by PRS in determining its 1446 tax due with respect to NRA for the first installment period in the year 4. The Form 8804-C states that NRA reasonably expects to have an effectively connected net operating loss of $5,000 available to offset its allocable share of ECTI from PRS in year 4. Prior to year 4, NRA had not submitted a certificate to a partnership under this section. NRA filed (or will file) its year 1 U.S. income tax return on March 11, year 3; its year 2 U.S. income tax return on February 12, year 4; its year 3 U.S. income tax return on April 13, year 4; and its year 4 U.S. income tax return on May 14, year 5. NRA paid or (will pay) all amounts due with respect to the returns (including interest, penalties, and additions to tax, if any) by the date they are filed. NRA's years 1 though 3 U.S. income tax returns report income or gain effectively connected with a U.S. trade or business or deductions or losses properly allocated and apportioned to such activities.

(ii) To be eligible to submit a certificate of deductions and losses to PRS under this section, NRA must satisfy the requirements of paragraph (b)(1) of this section. In accordance with §1.1446-1, NRA provided valid documentation to PRS to establish its status for purposes of section 1446. NRA's year 1 U.S. income tax return is a qualifying U.S. income tax return because it reported income or gain effectively connected with a U.S. trade or business or deductions or losses properly allocated and apportioned to such activities and is described under paragraph (b)(2)(iii)(A) of this section. Although

NRA filed its year 1 return after the due date of the return (determined under section 6072(c) without regard to any extension of time to file) the return was filed on March 11, year 3, which was on or before the earlier of June 15, year 3, the date one year after its section 6072(c) due date without regard to any extension of time to file, and March 20, year 4, the date on which NRA submitted the certificate to PRS. NRA's year 2 U.S. income tax return is a qualifying U.S. income tax return because it reported income or gain effectively connected with a U.S. trade or business or deductions or losses properly allocated and apportioned to such activities and is described under paragraph (b)(2)(iii)(A) of this section. Although NRA filed its year 2 return after the due date of the return (determined under section 6072(c) without regard to any extension of time to file) the return was filed on February 12, year 4, which was on or before the earlier of June 15, year 4, the date one year after its section 6072(c) due date without regard to any extension of time to file, and March 20, year 4, the date on which NRA submitted the certificate to PRS. NRA's year 3 U.S. income tax return is a qualifying U.S. income tax return because it reported income or gain effectively connected with a U.S. trade or business or deductions or losses properly allocated and apportioned to such activities and is described under paragraph (b)(2)(iii)(B) of this section. Because NRA filed its year 3 U.S. income tax return on April 13, year 4, the return will be considered timelyfiled under paragraph (b)(2)(ii) of this section, as the due date under section 6072(c) was June 15, year 4. NRA's year 4 U.S. income tax return is a qualifying U.S. income tax return because it reported income or gain effectively connected with a U.S. trade or business or deductions or losses properly allocated and apportioned to such activities and is described under paragraph (b)(2)(iii)(C) of this section. Because NRA filed its year 4 U.S. income tax return on May 14, year 5, the return will be considered timelyfiled under paragraph (b)(2)(ii) of this section. Accordingly, NRA meets the conditions of paragraph (b)(1) of this section and is eligible to provide a certificate of deductions and losses to PRS for year 4.

Example 2. Subsequent year qualifying U.S. income tax return. (i) Assume the same facts as in Example 1. Further, NRA and C form a second partnership (XYZ) in year 7 to conduct a trade or business in the United States. NRA and C provide XYZ appropriate documentation under §1.1446-1 to establish their status for purposes of section 1446. NRA did not submit a certificate under this section to any partnership for years 5 and 6. NRA submits a certificate to XYZ (using Form 8804-C) on April 10, year 7, to be considered by XYZ in determining its 1446 tax due with respect to NRA for its first installment period in year 7. The certificate states that NRA reasonably expects to have an effectively connected net operating loss of $8,000 available to offset its allocable share of ECTI from XYZ in year 7. Further, the certificate contains all of the necessary representations required under this section. NRA will file its U.S. income tax return for year 5 on March 25, year 7, (after its section 6072(c) due date and any extension of time to file that could have been granted under section 6081), its U.S. income tax return for year 6 on April 26, year 7; and its U.S. income tax return for year 7 on May 27, year 8. NRA will pay all amounts due with the returns (including interest, penalties, and additions to tax, if any) by the dates they are filed. NRA's years 5, 6, and 7 U.S. income tax returns will report income or gain that is effectively connected with a U.S. trade or business or deductions or losses properly allocated and apportioned to such activities.

(ii) To be eligible to submit a certificate of deductions and losses to XYZ under this section, NRA must satisfy the requirements of paragraph (b)(1) of this section. NRA provided valid documentation to XYZ in accordance with § 1.1446-1. As described in Example 1, NRA's year 4 U.S. income tax return is a qualifying U.S. income tax return because it will report income or gain effectively connected with a U.S. trade or business and is described under paragraph (b)(2)(iii)(C) of this section. Although NRA's year 5 U.S. income tax return reports income or gain effectively connected with a U.S. trade or business or deductions or losses properly allocated and apportioned to such activities it is not qualifying U.S. tax return under paragraph (b)(2)(iii) of this section. Because NRA submitted a certificate to PRS in year 4, to constitute a qualifying U.S. tax income return the year 5 U.S. income tax return must be timely-filed and all amounts due with such return must be timely paid. See paragraph (b)(2)(iii)(C) of this section. However, NRA will not file its U.S. income tax return for year 5 until March 25, year 7, (after its section 6072(c) due date and any extension of time to file that could have been granted under section 6081). Because the year 5 tax return is not a qualifying U.S. income tax return under paragraph (b)(2)(iii) of this section, NRA does not satisfy the requirements of paragraph (b)(1)(ii) of this section and, therefore, may not submit a certificate of deductions and losses to XYZ under this section in year 7.

Example 3. General application of the rules of this section. NRA and B form a partnership (PRS) to conduct a trade or business in the United States. NRA and B are equal partners under the partnership agreement. NRA and B provide PRS appropriate documentation under § 1.1446-1 to establish their status for purposes of section 1446. Prior to the formation of PRS, NRA had not invested in or engaged in the conduct of a U.S. trade or business. PRS incurs a $1,500 effectively connected net operating loss in years 1 and 2. The loss incurred in each is allocated equally between NRA and B. NRA has filed a qualifying U.S. income tax return (within the meaning of

paragraph (b)(2)(iii) of this section) for years 1 and 2 that report its allocable share of effective connected net operating loss allocated to it from PRS, as reported on the Form 1065 (Schedule K-1) issued to NRA for each year.

(i) In year 3, NRA may not submit a certificate to PRS under paragraph (c) because it will not have filed qualifying U.S. income tax returns for the preceding three years. In year 3, PRS has ECTI of $1,000 that is allocated equally between NRA and B. PRS satisfies its 1446 tax obligation with respect to NRA for year 3.

(ii) In year 4, PRS estimates that it will have ECTI of $4,000, which will be allocated equally between NRA and B. On or before April 15th of year 4 (the first installment due date), NRA submits a certificate to PRS under this section (using Form 8804-C) certifying that it reasonably expects to have an effectively connected net operating loss of $1,000 ($750 loss in both years 1 and 2, less $500 of income in year 3) available to offset its allocable share of ECTI from PRS in year 4. As of the date the certificate is submitted, NRA has received the Form 1065 (Schedule K-1) from PRS for year 3 but has not yet filed its U.S. income tax return for year 3.

(iii) With respect to year 4, and based upon paragraph (b)(1) of this section, NRA can include year 3 (NRA's preceding taxable year) as one of the preceding three years that it has filed or will file qualifying U.S. income tax returns (within the meaning of paragraph (b)(2)(iii) of this section). Therefore, provided PRS has, in accordance with paragraph (a)(2) of this section, no actual knowledge or reason to know the certificate is defective, PRS may reasonably rely on NRA's certificate. Accordingly, PRS may consider NRA's certificate to reduce the 1446 tax that would otherwise be required to be paid on NRA's behalf. Specifically, subject to paragraph (c)(1)(i)(C) of this section, the $1,000 of net losses that have been reported on Forms 1065 (Schedule K-1) issued to NRA that are available to reduce NRA's U.S. income tax on NRA's allocable share of effectively connected income or gain allocable from PRS may be used to reduce the $2,000 of ECTI estimated to be allocable to NRA. As a result, PRS must pay 1446 tax on only $1,100 of NRA's allocable share of partnership ECTI for the first installment period in year 5 ($2,000 − ($1,000 × .90)). PRS must pay 1446 tax of $96.25 for its first installment period with respect to the ECTI allocable to NRA ($1,100 (net ECTI after considering certified losses) x .35 (withholding tax rate) x .25 (section 6655(e)(2)(B) percentage for the first installment period)). See § 1.1446-3(b)(2). Pursuant to paragraph (d)(3) of this section, PRS must attach NRA's certificate and PRS's computation of its 1446 tax obligation with respect to NRA to its Form 8813, "Partnership Withholding Tax Payment Voucher (Section 1446)," filed for the first installment period. Under paragraph (c)(2)(ii)(B) of this section, NRA is required to provide an updated certificate on or before the 10th day after NRA files its U.S. income tax return for year 3, even if the updated certificate results in no change to the amount of deductions and losses reported on the superseded certificate.

(iv) The results are the same if NRA had not yet received a Form 1065 (Schedule K-1) from PRS for year 3. See paragraph (c)(1)(i)(A) of this section.

Example 4. Updated certificate submitted for losses. On January 1, year 8, NRA and B form a partnership (PRS) to conduct a trade or business in the United States. NRA and B are equal partners in PRS. NRA and B provide PRS appropriate documentation under §1.1446-1 to establish their status for purposes of section 1446. During years 1 through 7 NRA held an interest in another partnership (XYZ) that conducted a trade or business in the United States. NRA timely-filed (within the meaning of paragraph (b)(2) of this section) U.S. income tax returns for years 1 through 6 reporting its allocable year of ECTI (or loss) from XYZ (and timely paid all tax shown on such returns). NRA files its U.S. income tax return for year 7 on June 9, year 8 (and timely pays all tax due with such return). Therefore, NRA has filed qualifying U.S. income tax returns (within the meaning of paragraph (b)(2)(iii) of this section) for years 1 through 7. During years 1 through 7, NRA's only investment generating effectively connected items was its interest in XYZ. The XYZ partnership liquidated and ceased doing business on December 31, year 7.

(i) On or before April 15, year 8, PRS receives from NRA a valid certificate under this section using Form 8804-C in which NRA certifies that it reasonably expects to have available effectively connected net operating losses in the amount of $5,000. Among other statements made in accordance with paragraph (c) of this section, NRA represents that it has not yet filed its year 7 U.S. income tax return, but will timely file such return (and timely pay all tax due with such return). For its first installment period in year 8, PRS estimates that it will earn taxable income of $10,000 for the year which will be allocated equally to NRA and B (NRA's allocable share of PRS's ECTI is $5,000).

(ii) Provided PRS has, in accordance with paragraph (a)(2) of this section, no actual knowledge or reason to know the certificate is defective, PRS may reasonably rely on NRA's certificate when computing its 1446 tax obligation for the first installment period. PRS is limited under paragraph (c)(1)(i)(C) of this section and PRS may only consider $4,500 ($5,000 × .90) of the certified net operating loss. After consideration of the certified loss, PRS owes 1446 tax in the amount of $43.75 for the first installment period ($5,000 estimated allocable ECTI less $4,500 (certified loss as limited under paragraph (c)(1)(i)(C)) × .35 (1446 tax applicable percentage) × .25 (section 6655(e)(2)(B) percentage for the

first installment period)). See §1.1446-3(b)(2). Pursuant to paragraph (d)(3) of this section, PRS must attach a copy of NRA's certificate and the computation of 1446 tax due with respect to NRA to the Form 8813 filed with respect to NRA.

(iii) PRS's estimate of ECTI allocable to NRA for the second installment period remains unchanged from the first installment period. On June 10, year 8, NRA provides PRS an updated certificate reporting that NRA now reasonably expects to have an effectively connected net operating loss of $4,000 available to offset its allocable share of ECTI from PRS in year 4. NRA provided the updated certificate within 10 days of filing its U.S. income tax return for the year 7 taxable year, as required by paragraph (c)(2)(ii)(B) of this section. Provided the updated certificate is otherwise valid, PRS may rely on the updated certificate for the second installment period (due date June 15, year 8). Even if the updated certificate were not valid, PRS could no longer rely on the original certificate.

(iv) Under paragraph (d) of this section, PRS is not relieved from liability for the 1446 tax due with respect to NRA under section 1461 if it relies on a certificate determined to be defective, or if it receives an updated certificate reporting an amount of deductions and losses less than the amount reported on the superseded certificate. Under the principles of section 6655 (as applied through §1.1446-3), PRS is required to have paid 50-percent of the annualized 1446 tax due with respect to NRA on or before the due date of the second installment period (section 6655(e)(2)(B) percentage for the second installment period). Under paragraph (c)(2)(ii)(B) of this section, because NRA's updated certificate is valid for the second installment period, if PRS considers a certificate for that period it must consider the updated certificate. Under paragraph (c)(1)(i)(C) of this section, PRS can only consider $3,600 ($4,000 × .90) of NRA's updated effectively connected net operating loss. Assuming PRS considers NRA's updated certificate for the second installment period, PRS must have paid a total of $245 of 1446 tax with respect to the ECTI estimated to be allocable to NRA as of the second installment due date ($1,400 ($5,000 ECTI less $3,600 net operating loss deduction) × .35 (withholding tax rate) × .50 (section 6655(e)(2)(B) percentage for the second installment period)). After considering PRS's payment of 1446 tax for the first installment period, PRS is required to pay $201.25 for the second installment period ($245 less previous payment of $43.75). See §1.1446-3(b)(2). Further, if PRS considers NRA's updated certificate for the second installment period, when PRS files Form 8813 it must attach the updated certificate along with PRS's computation of 1446 tax due with respect to NRA.

(v) Under paragraph (d) of this section, PRS is not liable for the addition to the tax under section 6655 (as applied through §1.1446-3) for the first installment period because PRS reasonably relied on NRA's certificate of losses for that period.

(vi) Assume that PRS's estimate of its ECTI allocable to NRA for the third and fourth installment periods is the same as for the first and second installment periods. Assume PRS may reasonably rely on NRA's updated certificate in calculating its payment of 1446 tax for the third and fourth installment periods. The third installment of 1446 tax would be $122.50 (($5,000 − $3,600) × .35 × .75 = $367.50 − $245 (total previous payments)). The fourth installment of 1446 tax would be $122.50 (($5,000− $3,600) × .35 × 1.00 = $490 − $367.50 (total previous payments)). See § 1.1446- 3(b)(2). PRS must attach to each Form 8813 a computation of the 1446 tax due with respect to NRA that takes into account the amount of effectively connected net operating loss reported on NRA's updated certificate.

(vii) Because NRA's certified net operating loss has not changed for the third and fourth installments, in lieu of attaching NRA's certificate, PRS may attach a statement containing NRA's name, TIN, and the certified net operating loss amount. However, PRS must attach NRA's certificate and a computation of the 1446 tax due with respect to NRA that takes into account NRA's certified net operating loss to the Form 8805 filed with respect to NRA. See paragraph (d)(3) of this section.

Example 5. IRS determines in subsequent taxable year that partner's certificate is defective because partner failed to timely file a U.S. income tax return. NRA and B form a partnership (PRS) in year 1 to conduct a trade or business in the United States. NRA and B provide PRS appropriate documentation under § 1.1446-1 to establish their status for purposes of section 1446. In year 4, NRA timely submits a certificate under this section (using Form 8804-C) to be considered by PRS for its first installment period. The certificate reports that NRA reasonably expects to have an effectively connected net operating loss of $5,000 available to offset its allocable share of ECTI from PRS in year 4. Further, the certificate contains all of the necessary representations required under this section. PRS estimates for each installment period that NRA's allocable share of ECTI will be $5,000 for the taxable year. PRS's actual operating results for the year result in $5,000 of ECTI allocable to NRA.

(i) PRS reasonably relies on (within the meaning of paragraph (a)(2) of this section) NRA's certificate when computing each installment payment during year 4 and the 1446 tax due on Form 8804 and appropriately considers the limitation in paragraph (c)(1)(i)(C) of this section. As a result, PRS paid $175 of 1446 tax on behalf of NRA for the taxable year ($5,000 of ECTI less $4,500 net operating loss deduction x .35 applicable percentage). As required under paragraph (d) of this section, PRS attached the certificate to the Form 8813 for the first installment period and the Form 8805 for year 4. Be-

cause NRA did not submit an updated certificate to PRS in year 4, PRS attached to the Forms 8813 for the second, third and fourth installment periods a statement containing NRA's name, TIN, and the certified net operating loss as well as the computation of 1446 tax due with respect to NRA reflecting the amount of net operating loss considered.

(ii) In year 5, NRA timely submits to PRS a certificate under this section to be considered for the first installment period. The certificate represents that NRA reasonably expects to have an effectively connected net operating loss of $5,000 available to offset its allocable share of ECTI from PRS in year 5. For the first installment period, PRS estimates that NRA's allocable share of partnership ECTI is $5,000. PRS reasonably relies on the certificate for the first installment period and determines that it is required to make a 1446 tax installment payment of $43.75 ($5,000 allocable ECTI less $4,500 (certified net operating loss as limited under paragraph (c)(1)(i)(C) of this section) x .35 (1446 tax applicable percentage) x .25 (section 6655(e)(2)(B) percentage for the first installment period)). See § 1.1446-3(b)(2). PRS makes the installment payment with the Form 8813 filed for the first installment period, and complies with paragraph (d)(3) of this section by attaching NRA's certificate and the computation of 1446 tax due with respect to NRA to the Form 8813.

(iii) The IRS provides written notification to PRS on June 1, year 5, (pursuant to paragraph (c)(3) of this section) that the certificate received from NRA in year 4 is defective because NRA failed to file a qualifying U.S. income tax return (within the meaning of paragraph (b)(2)(iii) of this section) for one of the preceding taxable years as required under paragraph (b)(1) of this section. The notice further states that PRS is not to rely on any certificate received from NRA in year 5.

(iv) Under paragraph (d)(2)(ii) of this section, because the certificate submitted by NRA in year was determined to be defective for a reason other than the amount or character of the certified deductions and losses, under section 1461 PRS is fully liable for the 1446 tax due with respect to NRA's allocable share of ECTI year 4 without regard to the certificate. The total 1446 tax due for year 4 without regard to the certificate is $1,750 ($5,000 ECTI x .35) and PRS paid $175 of 1446 tax in year 4. Therefore, PRS owes $1,575 of 1446 tax. However, PRS may be deemed to have paid the outstanding 1446 tax due if NRA paid all of its U.S. tax due in year 4. See § 1.1446- 3(e).

(v) However, because PRS did not have actual knowledge or reason to know that the certificate NRA submitted in year 4 was defective, PRS reasonably relied on the certificate for purposes of paragraph (d)(2) of this section. Therefore, PRS is not liable for an addition to the tax with respect to its underpayment of 1446 tax under the principles of section 6655 (as applied through § 1.1446-3) for any installment period in year 4.

(vi) However, PRS is generally liable for interest under section 6601 and for the failure to pay addition to tax under section 6651(a)(2) on the $1,575 of 1446 tax due for year 4 for the period from April 15, year 5 (last date prescribed for payment of 1446 tax) to the date PRS pays the 1446 tax or is deemed to have paid the 1446 tax under § 1.1446-3(e).

(vii) With respect to the year 5, PRS reasonably relied on NRA's certificate when computing its first installment payment (due on April 15, year 5). Therefore, in accordance with paragraph (d)(2)(i) of this section, PRS will not be liable for an addition to the tax under the principles of section 6655 (as applied through § 1.1446-3) for the first installment period. However, because the IRS provided written notification to PRS on June 1, year 5, to disregard any certificate received from NRA for year 5, PRS may not rely on any certificate received from NRA certificate (or any new certificate provided by NRA) when it computes its second installment payment in year 5. PRS is not permitted to consider any certificate submitted by NRA until the IRS provides written notification to PRS revoking or modifying the original notice. PRS's second installment payment in year 5 must include the additional amount of 1446 tax it would have paid for the first installment period without regard to the certificate received from NRA.

Example 6. IRS determines in subsequent taxable year that partner's certificate is defective because partner's actual losses are less than amount certified and considered by the partnership. Assume the same facts as in *Example 5*, except that the IRS determines that NRA's certificate submitted in year 4 is defective because the actual effectively connected net operating loss available to NRA for year 4 was $1,000 rather than the $5,000 certified.

(i) Under paragraph (d)(2)(ii) of this section, PRS is not relieved from its liability for 1446 tax under section 1461 when it relies on a certificate of losses from a foreign partner that is later determined to be defective. However, when the IRS determines that a partner's certificate is defective because of the amount of the certified deductions and losses, the partnership is liable for the 1446 tax, interest, additions to tax, and penalties to the extent the amount of certified deductions and losses taken into account when computing 1446 tax (or, unless there was reasonable reliance on the certificate, any installment of such tax) is greater than the actual amount of available deductions and losses. Here, PRS considered the certified deductions and losses in the amount of $4,500. The IRS subsequently determined that NRA only had $1,000 of actual losses, only $900 of which were permitted to be considered under paragraph (c)(1)(i)(C) of this section. Accordingly, PRS is liable for the 1446 tax due

with respect to the portion of the overstated losses that it considered when computing its 1446 tax. The remaining 1446 tax due for year 4 is $1,260 ($3,600 ($4,500 less $900) of excess losses considered x .35). However, PRS may be deemed to have paid the $1,260 of 1446 tax under § 1.1446-3(e) if NRA has paid all of NRA's U.S. income tax.

(ii) If PRS had considered only $900 (or a lesser amount) of NRA's certified net operating loss when computing and paying its 1446 tax during year 4 then, under paragraph (d)(2)(iii) of this section, PRS would not be liable for 1446 tax because it did not consider a net operating loss greater than the amount actually available to NRA.

Example 7. Partner with different taxable year than partnership. PRS partnership has two equal partners, FC, a foreign corporation, and DC, a domestic corporation. PRS conducts a trade or business in the United States and generates effectively connected income. FC maintains a June 30 fiscal taxable year end, while DC and PRS maintain a calendar taxable year end. FC and DC provide a valid Form W-8BEN and Form W-9, respectively, to PRS. FC and DC are the only persons that have ever been partners in PRS. For its year 1 through year 3 taxable years, PRS issued Forms 1065 (Schedule K-1) reporting in the aggregate $100 of net loss to each partner. For its year 4 taxable year, PRS issued Forms 1065 (Schedule K-1) to its partners reporting $150 of loss to each partner. All of the losses reported on the Forms 1065 (Schedule K-1) are effectively connected to PRS's and FC's trade or business in the United States.

(i) Assume that FC submits a valid certificate under this section certifying losses to the partnership for the partnership's year 5 taxable year. Further, assume that FC's only source of effectively connected income, gain, deduction, or loss is the activity of PRS.

(ii) For PRS's first installment period in year 5, FC may only certify deductions and losses under this section in the amount of $100 (the losses as reported on the Forms 1065 (Schedule K-1) issued for PRS's year 1 through 3 taxable years). Under section 706, the taxable income of a partner shall include the income, gain, loss, deduction, or credit of the partnership for the partnership taxable year ending within or with the taxable year of the partner. PRS's year 4 calendar taxable year ends during FC's fiscal taxable year ending June 30, year 5. Therefore, under paragraph (c)(1) of this section, as of April 15, year 5 (the last date FC may submit its first certificate under paragraph (c) of this section to have it considered for PRS's first installment due date of April 15, year 5), FC's allocable share of the PRS losses for years 1 through 3 are the only losses that FC can represent have been or will be reported on an FC U.S. income tax return filed for a taxable year ending prior to such installment due date.

(iii) The result in paragraph (ii) of this *Example 7* is the same for the year 5 second installment period, the due date of which is June 15, year 5.

(iv) FC may submit an updated certificate under this section after June 30, year 5, which includes the $150 loss for year 4. PRS may consider such an updated certificate for its third installment period (due date September 15, year 5), provided the updated certificate is received by the due date for such installment in accordance with paragraph (c) of this section.

Example 8. Failure to provide status update with respect to prior year unfiled returns. FC, a foreign corporation, and DC, a domestic corporation, form a partnership (PRS) to conduct a trade or business in the United States. FC and DC provide PRS appropriate documentation under §1.1446-1 to establish their status for purposes of section 1446. FC and DC are equal partners in PRS, and all partnership items are allocated equally between FC and DC.

(i) In the current taxable year FC submits a certificate under this section using Form 8804-C prior to PRS's first installment due date. FC represents that it has filed or will file a qualifying U.S. income tax return (within the meaning of paragraph (b)(2)(iii) of this section) in each of the preceding three taxable years. FC specifies that it has not filed its U.S. income tax return for the immediately preceding taxable year. FC also represents that it will timely file its U.S. income tax return for the partnership taxable year during which the certificate is considered (and will timely pay all tax due with such return). Assume all other requirements under paragraph (c) of this section are met for FC's certificate to be valid.

(ii) Provided that PRS does not possess actual knowledge or reason to know that FC's certificate is defective under paragraph (a)(2) of this section, PRS may reasonably rely on FC's certificate for its first, second, and third installment payments.

(iii) If FC does not submit to PRS either an updated certificate or a status update as required by paragraph (c)(2)(ii)(B)(1) of this section by December 15th (PRS's final installment due date), PRS must disregard FC's certificate when computing its fourth installment payment of 1446 tax and when completing its Form 8804 for the taxable year. PRS's payment of 1446 tax for its fourth installment period must include the additional amount of 1446 tax it would have paid in the first, second and third installment periods had it not considered FC's certificate. Further, even if the status update is provided by December 15th, PRS may only rely on the certificate if the status update does not contradict the original certificate and such update indicates that the immediately preceding year's return will be timely filed. Finally, even if the status update is provided by December 15th, FC must also submit an updated certificate to the partnership in accordance with paragraph (c) of this section within 10 days of the date FC timely files its U.S. income tax return for the preceding taxable year.

Example 9. Partnership consideration of certified deductions and losses or de minimis certificate. For purposes of this example assume paragraph (c)(1)(ii) of this section may apply. On January 1, year 4, NRA and B form a partnership (PRS) to conduct a trade or business in the United States. NRA and B are equal partners in PRS and all partnership items are shared equally. NRA and B provide PRS appropriate documentation under §1.1446-1 to establish their status for purposes of section 1446. During years 1 through 3, NRA's only activity generating effectively connected items was an interest in partnership XYZ. XYZ allocated NRA a loss for all three years. NRA filed qualifying U.S. income tax returns (within the meaning of paragraph (b)(2)(iii) of this section) reporting its allocable share of losses from XYZ in years 1 through 3. The XYZ partnership dissolved on December 31, year 3.

(i) In year 4, NRA's only activity giving rise to effectively connected income, gain, deduction, or loss is its interest in PRS. NRA submits to PRS a valid certificate (using Form 8804-C) certifying under paragraph (c)(1)(i) its effectively connected net operating losses from years 1 through 3 and under (c)(1)(ii) of this section that its only activity giving rise to effectively connected income, gain, deduction, or loss for the PRS taxable year that ends with or within its taxable year is (and will be) its investment in PRS.

(ii) During year 4, PRS allocates ECTI to NRA. If the 1446 tax otherwise due on the annualized amount allocated to NRA is less than $1,000, determined without regard to any deductions and losses certified by NRA under paragraph (c)(1)(i) of this section, PRS may consider the certificate received from NRA under paragraph (c)(1)(ii) of this section and not pay 1446 tax (or any installment of such tax) with respect to NRA. Alternatively, PRS may consider the deductions and losses certified by NRA under paragraph (c)(1)(i) of this section.

(iii) Regardless of whether PRS considers NRA's certification under paragraph (c)(1)(i) or (c)(1)(ii) of this section in computing its 1446 tax due with respect to NRA, PRS must file Form 8813 for all installment periods as well as a Form 8805 for NRA with its Form 8804. If PRS considers NRA's certification under paragraph (c)(1)(i) or (c)(1)(ii) of this section, PRS must attach to each Form 8813, as well as to the Form 8805, a computation of the 1446 tax with respect to NRA that takes into account its consideration of NRA's certificate. In addition, PRS must attach NRA's certificate to the Form 8813 for the first installment period it considers the certificate, as well as to the Form 8805. For all subsequent installment periods, PRS may attach a statement containing NRA's name, and TIN. If PRS is relying on NRA's certified losses under paragraph (c)(1)(i) of this section, the statement must indicate the amount of losses and deductions NRA certified. If PRS is relying on NRA's certification under paragraph (c)(ii) of this section, the statement must indicate that it is relying on NRA meeting the requirements under paragraph (c)(1)(ii) of this section and the 1446 tax on the annualized amount allocated to NRA is less than $1,000. See paragraph (d)(3)(i) of this section.

Example 10. Application of transition rule. NRA and B form a partnership (PRS) on January 1, 2004, to conduct a trade or business in the United States. NRA and B are equal partners in PRS and all partnership items are shared equally. NRA and B provide PRS appropriate documentation under § 1.1446-1 to establish their status for purposes of section 1446. For its 2004 through 2007 tax years, PRS issued Forms 1065 (Schedule K-1) to NRA and B reporting a $1,000 net loss from its U.S. trade or business to each partner for each year (for an aggregate loss of $4,000 per partner). During the 2004 through 2007 tax years, NRA's only activity generating effectively connected items was its investment in PRS.

(i) On February 10, 2008, NRA submitted a certificate to PRS, reporting its aggregate $4,000 effectively connected loss to PRS, that met the requirements of § 1.1446-6T(c) (See 26 CFR Part 1, revised as of April 1, 2007), as in effect before January 1, 2008. The certificate stated that NRA had timely filed its U.S. income tax returns for the 2004, 2005 and 2006 tax years, and that it would timely file a U.S. income tax return for its 2007 tax year. For the first and second installments period in 2008, PRS estimates that it will earn ECTI of $10,000.

(ii) Because the certificate submitted by NRA to PRS on February 10, 2008, met the requirements of § 1.1446-6T (See 26 CFR Part 1, revised as of April 1, 2007), as in effect before January 1, 2008, PRS may consider such certificate when computing its 1446 tax due for the first and second installment period even if the certificate does not meet all the requirements of paragraph (c) of this section.

(iii) NRA timely files its U.S. income tax return for the 2007 tax year on July 24, 2008. In accordance with paragraph (c)(2)(ii)(B)(1) of this section, within 10 days of filing such return NRA prepares an updated certificate to be submitted to PRS certifying that it reasonably expects to have only $3,500 of losses available to reduce its allocable share of ECTI from PRS. Because the updated certificate will be submitted after July 28, 2008, to be valid the updated certificate must meet the requirements of paragraph (c) this section.

(f) *Effective/Applicability date.*—Except as otherwise provided in this paragraph (f), the rules of this section are applicable for partnership taxable years beginning after December 31, 2007. The rules of paragraphs (b)(3)(i)(B) through (D) shall apply to partnership taxable years beginning after July 28, 2008.

(g) *Transition rule.*—A certificate that met the requirements of § 1.1446-6T(c) (See 26 CFR Part 1, revised as of April 1, 2007), as in effect before January 1, 2008, submitted on or before July 28, 2008 by a partner that met the requirements of § 1.1446-6T(b) (See 26 CFR Part 1, revised as of April 1, 2007), as in effect before January 1, 2008, shall not be considered defective because it does not meet the requirements of this section. However, any certificate (including any updated certificates and status updates) submitted, or required to be submitted, under paragraph (c) of this section after July 28, 2008, must meet the requirements of this section. See paragraph (e)(2) *Example 10* of this section. [Reg. § 1.1446-6.]

☐ [*T.D.* 9394, 4-28-2008 (*corrected* 4-1-2009).]

[Reg. § 1.1446-7]

§ 1.1446-7. Effective/Applicability date.—Sections 1.1446-1 through 1.1446-5 shall apply to partnership taxable years beginning after May 18, 2005. However, a partnership may elect to apply all of the provisions of § § 1.1446-1 through 1.1446-5 to partnership taxable years beginning after December 31, 2004. A partnership shall make the election under this section by complying with the provisions of § § 1.1446-1 through § 1.1446-5 and attaching a statement to the Form 8804 or Form 1042 annual return, filed for the taxable year in which the regulation provisions first apply, that indicates that the partnership is making the election under this section. The revisions to § § 1.1446-3(b)(2), 1.1446-3(b)(3)(i)(A) and 1.1446-5(c)(2) contained in the final regulations published in 2008 apply to partnership taxable years beginning after December 31, 2007. See § 1.1446-6(f) and (g) for the Effective/Applicability date and Transition rule for § 1.1446-6. [Reg. § 1.1446-7.]

☐ [*T.D.* 9200, 5-13-2005. *Amended by T.D.* 9394, 4-28-2008.]

Application of Withholding Provisions

See p. 20,601 for regulations not amended to reflect law changes

[Reg. § 1.1461-1]

§ 1.1461-1. Payment and returns of tax withheld.—(a) *Payment of withheld tax.*—(1) *Deposits of tax.*—Every withholding agent who withholds tax pursuant to chapter 3 of the Internal Revenue Code (Code) and the regulations under such chapter shall deposit such amount of tax as provided in § 1.6302-2(a). If for any reason the total amount of tax required to be returned for any calendar year pursuant to paragraph (b) of this section has not been deposited pursuant to

§ 1.6302-2, the withholding agent shall pay the balance of tax due for such year at such place as the Internal Revenue Service (IRS) shall specify. The tax shall be paid when filing the return required under paragraph (b)(1) of this section for such year, unless the IRS specifies otherwise. With respect to withholding under section 1446, this section shall only apply to publicly traded partnerships. See § 1.1461-3 for penalties applicable to partnerships that fail to withhold under section 1446 on effectively connected taxable income allocable to foreign partners. The previous two sentences shall apply to partnership taxable years beginning after May 18, 2005, or such earlier time as the regulations under §§ 1.1446-1 through 1.1446-5 apply by reason of an election under § 1.1446-7.

(2) *Penalties for failure to pay tax.*—For penalties and additions to the tax for failure to timely pay the tax required to be withheld under chapter 3 of the Code, see sections 6656, 6672, and 7202 and the regulations under those sections.

(b) *Income tax return.*—(1) *General rule.*—A withholding agent shall make an income tax return on Form 1042 (or such other form as the IRS may prescribe) for income paid during the preceding calendar year that the withholding agent is required to report on an information return on Form 1042-S (or such other form as the IRS may prescribe) under paragraph (c)(1) of this section. See section 6011 and § 1.6011-1(c). The withholding agent must file the return on or before March 15 of the calendar year following the year in which the income was paid. The return must show the aggregate amount of income paid and tax withheld required to be reported on all the Forms 1042-S for the preceding calendar year by the withholding agent, in addition to such information as is required by the form and accompanying instructions. Withholding certificates or other statements or information provided to a withholding agent are not required to be attached to the return. A return must be filed under this paragraph (b)(1) even though no tax was required to be withheld during the preceding calendar year. The withholding agent must retain a copy of Form 1042 for the applicable statute of limitations on assessments and collection with respect to the amounts required to be reported on the Form 1042. See section 6501 and the regulations thereunder for the applicable statute of limitations. Adjustments to the total amount of tax withheld, as described in § 1.1461-2, shall be stated on the return as prescribed by the form and accompanying instructions.

(2) *Amended returns.*—An amended return may be filed on a Form 1042 or such other form as the IRS may prescribe. An amended return must include such information as the form or accompanying instructions shall require, including, with respect to any information that has changed from the time of the filing of the return, the information that was shown on the original return and the corrected information.

(c) *Information returns.*—(1) *Filing requirement.*—(i) *In general.*—A withholding agent (other than an individual who is not acting in the course of a trade or business with respect to a payment) must make an information return on Form 1042-S (or such other form as the IRS may prescribe) to report the amounts subject to reporting, as defined in paragraph (c)(2) of this section, that were paid during the preceding calendar year. Notwithstanding the preceding sentence, any person that withholds or is required to withhold an amount under sections 1441, 1442, 1443, or § 1.1446-4(a) (applicable to publicly traded partnerships required to pay tax under section 1446 on distributions) must file a Form 1042-S, "Foreign Person's U.S. Source Income Subject to Withholding," for the payment withheld upon whether or not that person is engaged in a trade or business and whether or not the payment is an amount subject to reporting. The reference in the previous sentence to withholding under § 1.1446-4 shall apply to partnership taxable years beginning after May 18, 2005, or such earlier time as the regulations under §§ 1.1446-1 through 1.1446-5 apply by reason of an election under § 1.1446-7. A Form 1042-S shall be prepared for each recipient of an amount subject to reporting. The Form 1042-S shall be prepared in such manner as the form and accompanying instructions prescribe. One copy of the Form 1042-S shall be filed with the IRS on or before March 15 of the calendar year following the year in which the amount subject to reporting was paid. It shall be filed with a transmittal form as provided in the instructions to the Form 1042-S and to the transmittal form. Withholding certificates, documentary evidence, or other statements or documentation provided to a withholding agent are not required to be attached to the form. Another copy of the Form 1042-S must be furnished to the recipient for whom the form is prepared (or any other person, as required under this paragraph (c) or the instructions to the form) on or before March 15 of the calendar year following the year in which the amount subject to reporting was paid. The withholding agent must retain a copy of each Form 1042-S for the statute of limitations on assessment and collection applicable to the Form 1042 to which the Form 1042-S relates.

(ii) *Recipient.*—(A) *Defined.*—For purposes of this section, the term *recipient* means—

(1) A beneficial owner as defined in § 1.1441-1(c)(6), including a foreign estate or a foreign complex trust, as defined in § 1.1441-1(c)(25);

(2) A qualified intermediary as defined in § 1.1441-1(e)(5)(ii);

(3) A withholding foreign partnership as defined in § 1.1441-5(c)(2) or a withholding foreign trust under § 1.1441-5(e)(5)(v);

(4) An authorized foreign agent as defined in § 1.1441-7(c);

(5) A U.S. branch that is treated as a U.S. person under § 1.1441-1(b)(2)(iv)(A);

(6) A nonwithholding foreign partnership or a foreign simple trust as defined in § 1.1441-1(c)(24), but only to the extent the income is (or is treated as) effectively connected with the conduct of a trade or business in the United States by such entity;

(7) A payee, as defined in § 1.1441-1(b)(2) that is presumed to be a foreign person under the presumption rules of § 1.1441-1(b)(3); 1.1441-5(d) or (e)(6), or 1.6049-5(d); and

(8) A partner receiving a distribution from a publicly traded partnership subject to withholding under section 1446 and § 1.1446-4 on distributions of effectively connected income. This paragraph (c)(1)(ii)(A)(*8*) shall apply to partnership taxable years beginning after May 18, 2005, or such earlier time as the regulations under § § 1.1446-1 through 1.1446-5 apply by reason of an election under § 1.1446-7.

(9) Any other person as required on Form 1042-S or the instructions to the form.

(B) Persons that are not recipients.—A recipient does not include—

(1) A nonqualified intermediary;

(2) A payment to a wholly-owned entity that is disregarded under § 301.7701-2(c)(2) of this chapter as an entity separate from its owner;

(3) A flow-through entity, as defined in § 1.1441-1(c)(23) (to the extent it is receiving amounts subject to reporting other than income effectively connected with the conduct of a trade or business in the United States); and

(4) A U.S. branch described in § 1.1441-1(b)(2)(iv) that is not treated as a U.S. person under that section.

(2) Amounts subject to reporting.—(i) *In general.*—Subject to the exceptions described in paragraph (c)(2)(ii) of this section, amounts subject to reporting on Form 1042-S are amounts paid to a foreign payee or partner (including persons presumed to be foreign) that are amounts subject to withholding as defined in § 1.1441-2(a) or § 1.1446-4(a) (addressing publicly traded partnerships required to pay withholding tax under section 1446 on distributions of effectively connected income). The reference in the previous sentence to withholding under § 1.1446-4 shall apply to partnership taxable years beginning after May 18, 2005, or such earlier time as the regulations under § § 1.1446-1 through 1.1446-5 apply by reason of an election under § 1.1446-7. Amounts subject to reporting include amounts subject to withholding even if no amount is deducted and withheld from the payment because of a treaty or Internal Revenue Code exception to taxation or because an amount withheld was reimbursed to the payee under the adjustment procedures of § 1.1461-2. In addition, amounts subject to reporting include any amounts paid to a foreign payee on which a withholding agent withheld an amount (either under chapter 3 of the Internal Revenue Code or section 3406) whether or not the amount is subject to withholding. Amounts subject to reporting include, but are not limited to, the following items—

(A) The entire amount of a corporate distribution (whether actual or deemed) irrespective of any estimate of the portion of the distribution that represents a taxable dividend;

(B) Interest, including the portion of a notional principal contract payment that is characterized as interest. Interest shall also be reported on Form 1042-S if it is bank deposit interest paid to nonresident alien individuals as required under § 1.6049-8;

(C) Rents;

(D) Royalties;

(E) Compensation for dependent and independent personal services performed in the United States;

(F) Annuities;

(G) Pension distributions and other deferred income;

(H) Gambling winnings that are not exempt from tax under section 871(j);

(I) Income from the cancellation of indebtedness unless the withholding agent is unrelated to the debtor and does not have knowledge of the facts that give rise to the payment (see § 1.1441-2(d));

(J) Amounts that are (or are presumed to be) effectively connected with the conduct of a trade or business in the United States (including deposit interest as defined in sections 871(i)(2)(A) and 881(d)) even if no withholding certificate is required to be furnished by the payee or beneficial owner. In the case of amounts paid on a notional principal contract described in § 1.1441-4(a)(3) that are presumed to be effectively connected with the conduct of a trade or business in the United States, the amount required to be reported is limited to the amount of cash paid from the notional principal contract;

(K) Scholarship, fellowship, or grant income and compensation for personal services that is not excludible from gross income under section 117 (whether or not the taxable scholarship, fellowship, grant income, or compensation for personal services is exempt from tax under an income tax treaty) paid to foreign students, trainees, teachers, or researchers;

(L) Amounts paid to foreign governments, international organizations, or the Bank for International Settlements, whether or not documentation must be provided; and

(M) Original issue discount paid on the redemption of an OID obligation. The amount to be reported is the amount of OID includible in the gross income of the holder of the obligation, if known, or, if not known, the total amount of original issue discount determined as if the holder held the obligation from its original issuance. A withholding agent may determine the total amount of OID by using the most recently published "List of Original Issue Discount Instruments," (Publication 1212, available from the IRS Forms Distribution Centers).

(ii) *Exceptions to reporting.*—The amounts listed in this paragraph (c)(2)(ii) are not required to be reported on Form 1042-S—

(A) Interest (including original issue discount) that is deposit interest under sections 871(i)(2)(A) and 881(d) and that is not effectively connected with the conduct of a trade or business in the United States, unless reporting is required under § 1.6049-8 (regarding payments to certain foreign residents) or is interest that is effectively connected with the conduct of a trade or business in the United States;

(B) Interest or original issue discount on certain short-term obligations, described in section 871(g)(1)(B) or 881(a)(3);

(C) Interest paid on obligations sold between interest payment dates and the portion of the purchase price of an OID obligation that is sold or exchanged in a transaction other than a redemption, unless the sale or exchange is part of a plan, the principal purpose of which is to avoid tax and the withholding agent has actual knowledge or reason to know of such plan (see § 1.1441-2(a)(5) and (6));

(D) Any item required to be reported on a Form W-2, including an item required to be shown on Form W-2 solely by reason of § 1.6041-2 (relating to return of information for payments to employees) or § 1.6052-1 (relating to information regarding payment of wages in the form of group-term life insurance);

(E) Any item required to be reported on Form 1099, and such other forms as are prescribed pursuant to the information reporting provisions of sections 6041 through 6050P and the regulations under those sections;

(F) Amounts paid on a notional principal contract described in § 1.1441-4(a)(3)(i) that are not effectively connected with the conduct of a trade or business in the United States (or not treated as effectively connected pursuant to § 1.1441-4(a)(3)(ii));

(G) Amounts required to be reported on Form 8288 (U.S. Withholding Tax Return for Dispositions by Foreign Persons of U.S. Real Property Interests) or Form 8804 (Annual Return for Partnership Withholding Tax (section 1446)). A withholding agent that must report a distribution partly on a Form 8288 or 8804 and partly on a Form 1042-S may elect to report the entire amount on a Form 8288 or 8804;

(H) Interest (including original issue discount) paid with respect to foreign-targeted registered obligations described in § 1.871-14(e)(2) to the extent the documentation requirements described in § 1.871-14(e)(3) and (4) are required to be satisfied (taking into account the provisions of § 1.871-14(e)(4)(ii), if applicable;

(I) Interest on a foreign targeted bearer obligation (see § § 1.1441-1(b)(4)(i) and 1.1441-2(a);

(J) Gain described in section 301(c)(3); and

(K) Amounts described in § 1.1441-1(b)(4)(xviii) (dealing with certain amounts paid by the U.S. government).

(3) *Required information.*—The information required to be furnished under this paragraph (c)(3) shall be based upon the information provided by or on behalf of the recipient of an amount subject to reporting (as corrected and supplemented based on the withholding agent's actual knowledge) or the presumption rules of § § 1.1441-1(b)(3), 1.1441-4(a), 1.1441-5(d) and (e); 1.1441-9(b)(3), 1.1446-1(c)(3) (as applied to publicly traded partnerships required to pay tax under section 1446 on distributions of effectively connected income) or 1.6049-5(d). The reference in the previous sentence to presumption rules applicable to withholding under section 1446 shall apply to partnership taxable years beginning after May 18, 2005, or such earlier time as the regulations under § § 1.1446-1 through 1.1446-5 apply by reason of an election under § 1.1446-7. The Form 1042-S must include the following information, if applicable—

(i) The name, address, and taxpayer identifying number of the withholding agent;

(ii) A description of each category of income paid based on the income codes provided on the form (e.g., interest, dividends, royalties, etc.) and the aggregate amount in each category expressed in U.S. dollars;

(iii) The rate of withholding applied or the basis for exempting the payment from withholding (based on exemption codes provided on the form);

(iv) The name and address of the recipient;

(v) The name and address of any nonqualified intermediary, flow-through entity, or U.S. branch as described in § 1.1441-1(b)(2)(iv) (other than a branch that is treated as a U.S. person) to which the payment was made;

(vi) The taxpayer identifying number of the recipient if required under § 1.1441-1(e)(4)(vii) or if actually known to the withholding agent making the return;

(vii) The taxpayer identifying number of a nonqualified intermediary or flow-through entity (to the extent it is not a recipient) or other flow-through entity to the extent it is known to the withholding agent;

Reg. § 1.1461-1(c)(3)(vii)

(viii) The country (based on the country codes provided on the form) of the recipient and of any nonqualified intermediary or flow-through entity the name of which appears on the form; and

(ix) Such information as the form or the instructions may require in addition to, or in lieu of, information required under this paragraph (c)(3).

(4) *Method of reporting.*—(i) *Payments by U.S. withholding agents to recipients.*—A withholding agent that is a U.S. person (other than a foreign branch of a U.S. person that is a qualified intermediary as defined in §1.1441-1(e)(5)(ii)) and that makes payments of amounts subject to reporting on Form 1042-S must file a separate Form 1042-S for each recipient who receives such amount. For purposes of this paragraph (c)(4), a U.S. person includes a U.S. branch described in §1.1441-1(e)(2)(iv)(A) or (E) that agrees to be treated as a U.S. person. Except as may otherwise be required on Form 1042-S or the instructions to the form, only payments for which the income code, exemption code, withholding rate and recipient code are the same may be reported on a single Form 1042-S. See paragraph (c)(4)(ii) of this section for reporting of payments made to a person that is not a recipient.

(A) *Payments to beneficial owners.*—If a U.S. withholding agent makes a payment directly to a beneficial owner it must complete Form 1042-S treating the beneficial owner as the recipient. Under the grace period rule of §1.1441-1(b)(3)(iv), a U.S. withholding agent may, under certain circumstances, treat a payee as a foreign person while the withholding agent awaits a valid withholding certificate. A U.S. withholding agent who relies on the grace period rule to treat a payee as a foreign person must file a Form 1042-S to report all payments on Form 1042-S during the period that person was presumed to be foreign even if that person is later determined to be a U.S. person based on appropriate documentation or is presumed to be a U.S. person after the grace period ends. In the case of joint owners, a withholding agent may provide a single Form 1042-S made out to the owner whose status the U.S. withholding agent relied upon to determine the applicable rate of withholding. If, however, any one of the owners requests its own Form 1042-S, the withholding agent must furnish a Form 1042-S to the person who requests it. If more than one Form 1042-S is issued for a single payment, the aggregate amount paid and tax withheld that is reported on all Forms 1042-S cannot exceed the total amounts paid to joint owners and the tax withheld thereon.

(B) *Payments to a qualified intermediary, a withholding foreign partnership, or a withholding foreign trust.*—A U.S. withholding agent that makes payments to a qualified intermediary (whether or not the qualified intermediary assumes primary withholding responsibility), a withholding foreign partnership, or a withholding foreign trust shall complete Forms 1042-S treating the qualified intermediary or withholding foreign partnership as the recipient. The U.S. withholding agent must complete a separate Form 1042-S for each withholding rate pool. A withholding rate pool is a payment of a single type of income (determined by the income codes on Form 1042-S) that is subject to a single rate of withholding. A qualified intermediary that does not assume primary withholding responsibility on all payments it receives provides information regarding the proportions of income subject to a particular withholding rate to the withholding agent on a withholding statement associated with a qualified intermediary withholding certificate. A qualified intermediary may provide a U.S. withholding agent with information regarding withholding rate pools for U.S. non-exempt recipients (as defined under §1.1441-1(c)(21)). Amounts paid with respect to such withholding rate pools must be reported on Form 1099 completed for each U.S. non-exempt recipient to the extent they are subject to Form 1099 reporting. These amounts must not be reported on Form 1042-S. In addition, the qualified intermediary may provide the U.S. withholding agent information regarding withholding rate pools for U.S. persons that are exempt recipients as defined under §1.1441-1(c)(20). If such information is provided, a U.S. withholding agent should not report such withholding rate pools on Form 1042-S.

(C) *Amounts paid to U.S. branches treated as U.S. persons.*—A U.S. withholding agent making a payment to a U.S. branch of a foreign person described in §1.1441-1(b)(2)(iv) shall complete Form 1042-S as follows—

(1) If the branch has provided the U.S. withholding agent with a withholding certificate that evidences its agreement with the withholding agent to be treated as a U.S. person, the U.S. withholding agent files Forms 1042-S treating the U.S. branch as the recipient;

(2) If the branch has provided the U.S. withholding agent with a withholding certificate that transmits information regarding beneficial owners, qualified intermediaries, withholding foreign partnerships, or other recipients, the U.S. withholding agent must complete a separate Form 1042-S for each recipient whose documentation is associated with the U.S. branch's withholding certificate; or

(3) If the U.S. withholding agent cannot reliably associate a payment with a valid withholding certificate from the U.S. branch, it shall treat the U.S. branch as the recipient and report the income as effectively connected with the conduct of a trade or business in the United States.

(D) Amounts paid to an authorized foreign agent.—If a U.S. withholding agent makes a payment to an authorized foreign agent, the withholding agent files Forms 1042-S treating the authorized foreign agent as the recipient, provided that the authorized foreign agent reports the payments on Forms 1042-S to each recipient to which it makes payments. If the authorized foreign agent fails to report the amounts paid on Forms 1042-S for each recipient to which the payment is made, the U.S. withholding agent remains responsible for such reporting.

(E) Dual claims.—A U.S. withholding agent may make a payment to a foreign entity that is simultaneously claiming a reduced rate of tax on its own behalf for a portion of the payment and a reduced rate on behalf of persons in their capacity as interest holders in that entity on the remaining portion. See § 1.1441-6(b)(2)(iii). If the claims are consistent and the withholding agent accepts the multiple claims, the withholding agent must file a separate Form 1042-S for those payments for which the entity is treated as the beneficial owner and Forms 1042-S for each of the interest holder in the entity for which the interest holder is treated as the recipient. For those payments for which the interest holder in an entity is treated as the recipient, the U.S. withholding agent shall prepare the Form 1042-S in the same manner as a payment made to a nonqualified intermediary or flow-through entity as set forth in paragraph (c)(4)(ii) of this section. If the claims are consistent but the withholding agent has not chosen to accept the multiple claims, or if the claims are inconsistent, the withholding agent must file a separate Form 1042-S for the person or persons it has chosen to treat as the recipients.

(ii) Payments made by U.S. withholding agents to persons that are not recipients.— (A) *Amounts paid to a nonqualified intermediary, a flow-through entity, and certain U.S. branches.*—If a U.S. withholding agent makes a payment to a nonqualified intermediary, a flow-through entity, or a U.S. branch described in § 1.1441-1(b)(2)(iv) (other than a branch that agrees to be treated as a U.S. person), it must complete a separate Form 1042-S for each recipient to the extent the withholding agent can reliably associate a payment with valid documentation (within the meaning of § 1.1441-1(b)(2)(vii)) from the recipient which is associated with the withholding certificate provided by the nonqualified intermediary, flow-through entity, or U.S. branch. If a payment is made through tiers of nonqualified intermediaries or flow-through entities, the withholding agent must nevertheless complete Form 1042-S for the recipients to the extent it can reliably associate the payment with documentation from the recipients. A withholding agent that is completing a Form 1042-S for a recipient that receives a payment through a nonqualified intermediary, a flow-through entity, or a U.S. branch must include on the Form 1042-S the name of the nonqualified intermediary or flow-through entity from which the recipient directly receives the payment. If a U.S. withholding agent cannot reliably associate the payment, or any portion of the payment, with valid documentation from a recipient either because no such documentation has been provided or because the nonqualified intermediary, flow-through entity, or U.S. branch has failed to provide sufficient allocation information so that the withholding agent can associate the payment, or any portion thereof, with valid documentation, then the withholding agent must report the payments as made to an unknown recipient in accordance with the appropriate presumption rules for that payment. Thus, if under the presumption rules the payment is presumed to be made to a foreign person, the withholding agent must generally withhold 30 percent of the payment and report the payment on Form 1042-S made out to an unknown recipient and shall also include the name of the nonqualified intermediary or flow-through entity that received the payment on behalf of the unknown recipient. If, however, the recipient is presumed to be a U.S. non-exempt recipient (as defined in § 1.1441-1(c)(21)), the withholding agent must withhold on the payment as required under section 3406 and report the payment as made to an unknown recipient on the appropriate Form 1099 as required under chapter 61 of the Internal Revenue Code.

(B) Disregarded entities.—If a U.S. withholding agent makes a payment to a disregarded entity but receives a valid withholding certificate or other documentary evidence from a foreign person that is the single owner of a disregarded entity, the withholding agent must file a Form 1042-S treating the foreign single owner as the recipient. The taxpayer identifying number on the Form 1042-S, if required, must be the foreign single owner's TIN.

(iii) Reporting by qualified intermediaries, withholding foreign partnerships, and withholding foreign trusts.—A qualified intermediary, a withholding foreign partnership, and a withholding foreign trust shall report payments on Form 1042-S as provided in their agreements with the IRS and the instructions to the form.

(iv) Reporting by a nonqualified intermediary, flow-through entity, and certain U.S. branches.—A nonqualified intermediary, flow-through entity, or U.S. branch described in § 1.1441-1(e)(2)(iv) (other than a U.S. branch that is treated as a U.S. person) is a withholding agent and must file Forms 1042-S for amounts paid to recipients in the same manner as a U.S. withholding agent. A Form 1042-S will not be required, however, if another withholding agent has reported the same amount to the same recipient for which the nonqualified intermediary,

Reg. § 1.1461-1(c)(4)(iv)

flow-through entity, or U.S. branch would be required to file a return and the entire amount that should be withheld from such payment has been withheld. A nonqualified intermediary, flow-through entity, or U.S. branch must report payments made to recipients to the extent it has failed to provide the appropriate documentation to another withholding agent together with the information required for that withholding agent to reliably associate the payment with the recipient documentation or to the extent it knows, or has reason to know, that less than the required amount has been withheld. A nonqualified intermediary or flow-through entity that is required to report a payment on Form 1042-S must follow the same rules as apply to a U.S. withholding agent under paragraph (c)(4)(i) and (ii) of this section.

(v) *Pro rata reporting for allocation failures.*—If a nonqualified intermediary, flow-through entity, or U.S. branch described in §1.1441-1(b)(2)(iv) (other than a branch treated as a U.S. person) that uses the alternative procedures of §1.1441-1(e)(3)(iv)(D) fails to provide information sufficient to allocate the amount subject to reporting paid to a withholding rate pool to the payees identified for that pool, then the withholding agent shall report the payment in accordance with the rule provided in §1.1441-1(e)(3)(iv)(D)(6).

(vi) *Other withholding agents.*—Any person that is a withholding agent not described in paragraph (c)(4)(i), (iii), or (iv) of this section (e.g., a foreign person that is not a qualified intermediary, flow-through entity, or U.S. branch) shall file Form 1042-S in the same manner as a U.S. withholding agent and in accordance with the instructions to the form.

(5) *Magnetic media reporting.*—A withholding agent that makes 250 or more Form 1042-S information returns for a taxable year must file Form 1042-S returns on magnetic media. See §301.6011-2 of this chapter for requirements applicable to a withholding agent that files Forms 1042-S with the IRS on magnetic media and publications of the IRS relating to magnetic media filing.

(d) *Report of taxpayer identifying numbers.*—When so required under procedures that the IRS may prescribe in published guidance (see §601.601(d)(2) of this chapter), a withholding agent must attach to the Form 1042 a list of all the taxpayer identifying numbers (and corresponding names) that have been furnished to the withholding agent and upon which the withholding agent has relied to grant a reduced rate of withholding and that are not otherwise required to be reported on a Form 1042-S under the provisions of this section.

(e) *Indemnification of withholding agent.*—A withholding agent is indemnified against the claims and demands of any person for the amount of any tax it deducts and withholds in accordance with the provisions of chapter 3 of the Code and the regulations under that chapter. A withholding agent that withholds based on a reasonable belief that such withholding is required under chapter 3 of the Code and the regulations under that chapter is treated for purposes of section 1461 and this paragraph (e) as having withheld tax in accordance with the provisions of chapter 3 of the Code and the regulations under that chapter. In addition, a withholding agent is indemnified against the claims and demands of any person for the amount of any payments made in accordance with the grace period provisions set forth in §1.1441-1(b)(3)(iv). This paragraph (e) does not apply to relieve a withholding agent from tax liability under chapter 3 of the Code or the regulations under that chapter.

(f) *Amounts paid not constituting gross income.*—Any amount withheld in accordance with §1.1441-3 shall be reported and paid in accordance with this section, even though the amount paid to the beneficial owner may not constitute gross income in whole or in part. For this purpose, a reference in this section and §1.1461-2 to an amount shall, where appropriate, be deemed to refer to the amount subject to withholding under §1.1441-3.

(g) *Extensions of time to file Forms 1042 and 1042-S.*—The IRS may grant an extension of time in which to file a Form 1042 or a Form 1042-S. Form 2758, Application for Extension of Time to File Certain Excise, Income, Information, and Other Returns (or such other form as the IRS may prescribe), must be used to request an extension of time for a Form 1042. Form 8809, Request for Extension of Time to File Information Returns (or such other form as the IRS may prescribe) must be used to request an extension of time for a Form 1042-S. The request must contain a statement of the reasons for requesting the extension and such other information as the forms or instructions may require. It must be mailed or delivered not later than March 15 of the year following the end of the calendar year for which the return will be filed.

(h) *Penalties.*—For penalties and additions to the tax for failure to file returns or furnish statements in accordance with this section, see sections 6651, 6662, 6663, 6721, 6722, 6723, 6724(c), 7201, 7203, and the regulations under those sections.

(i) *Effective date.*—Unless otherwise provided in this section, this section shall apply to returns required for payments made after December 31, 2000. [Reg. § 1.1461-1.]

☐ [*T.D. 6187, 7-5-56. Amended by T.D. 6213, 11-20-56; T.D. 6908, 12-30-66; T.D. 7157, 12-29-71; T.D. 7977, 9-19-84; T.D. 8734, 10-6-97; T.D. 8804,*

12-30-98; *T.D.* 8856, 12-29-99; *T.D.* 8881, 5-15-2000 (*corrected* 4-5-2001); *T.D.* 8952, 6-25-2001; *T.D.* 9200, 5-13-2005 *and T.D.* 9507, 12-2-2010.]

[Reg. §1.1461-2]

§1.1461-2. Adjustments for overwithholding or underwithholding of tax.—(a) *Adjustments of overwithheld tax.*—(1) *In general.*—Except for partnerships or nominees required to withhold under section 1446, a withholding agent that has overwithheld under chapter 3 of the Internal Revenue Code, and made a deposit of the tax as provided in §1.6302-2(a) may adjust the overwithheld amount either pursuant to the reimbursement procedure described in paragraph (a)(2) of this section or pursuant to the set-off procedure described in paragraph (a)(3) of this section. References in the previous sentence excepting from this section certain partnerships withholding under section 1446 shall apply to partnership taxable years beginning after May 18, 2005, or such earlier time as the regulations under §§1.1446-1 through 1.1446-5 apply by reason of an election under §1.1446-7. Adjustments under this paragraph (a) may only be made within the time prescribed under paragraph (a)(2) or (3) of this section. After such time, a refund of the amount overwithheld can only be claimed by the beneficial owner with the Internal Revenue Service (IRS) pursuant to the procedures described in chapter 65 of the Code. For purposes of this section, the term overwithholding means any amount actually withheld (determined before application of the adjustment procedures under this section) from an item of income pursuant to chapter 3 of the Code or the regulations thereunder in excess of the actual tax liability due, regardless of whether such overwithholding was in error or appeared correct at the time it occurred.

(2) *Reimbursement of tax.*—(i) *General rule.*— Under the reimbursement procedure, the withholding agent repays the beneficial owner or payee for the amount overwithheld. In such a case, the withholding agent may reimburse itself by reducing, by the amount of tax actually repaid to the beneficial owner or payee, the amount of any deposit of tax made by the withholding agent under §1.6302-2(a)(1)(iii) for any subsequent payment period occurring before the end of the calendar year following the calendar year of overwithholding. Any such reduction that occurs for a payment period in the calendar year following the calendar year of overwithholding shall be allowed only if—

(A) The withholding agent states, on a timely filed (not including extensions) Form 1042-S for the calendar year of overwithholding, the amount of tax withheld and the amount of any actual repayment; and

(B) The withholding agent states on a timely filed (not including extensions) Form 1042 for the calendar year of overwithholding, that the filing of the Form 1042 constitutes a claim for credit in accordance with §1.6414-1.

(ii) *Record maintenance.*—If the beneficial owner is repaid an amount of withholding tax under the provisions of this paragraph (a)(2), the withholding agent shall keep as part of its records a receipt showing the date and amount of repayment and the withholding agent must provide a copy of such receipt to the beneficial owner. For this purpose, a canceled check or an entry in a statement is sufficient provided that the check or statement contains a specific notation that it is a refund of tax overwithheld.

(3) *Set-offs.*—Under the set-off procedure, the withholding agent may repay the beneficial owner or payee by applying the amount overwithheld against any amount which otherwise would be required under chapter 3 of the Code or the regulations thereunder to be withheld from income paid by the withholding agent to such person before the earlier of the due date (without regard to extensions) for filing the Form 1042-S for the calendar year of overwithholding or the date that the Form 1042-S is actually filed with the IRS. For purposes of making a return on Form 1042 or 1042-S (or an amended form) for the calendar year of overwithholding and for purposes of making a deposit of the amount withheld, the reduced amount shall be considered the amount required to be withheld from such income under chapter 3 of the Code and the regulations thereunder.

(4) *Examples.*—The principles of this paragraph (a) are illustrated by the following examples:

Example 1. (i) N is a nonresident alien individual who is a resident of the United Kingdom. In December 2001, a domestic corporation C pays a dividend of $100 to N, at which time C withholds $30 and remits the balance of $70 to N. On February 10, 2002, prior to the time that C files its Form 1042, N furnishes a valid Form W-8 described in §1.1441-1(e)(2)(i) upon which C may rely to reduce the rate of withholding to 15 percent under the provisions of the U.S.-U.K. tax treaty. Consequently, N advises C that its tax liability is only $15 and not $30 and requests reimbursement of $15. Although C has already deposited the $30 that was withheld, as required by §1.6302-2(a)(1)(iv), C repays N in the amount of $15.

(ii) During 2001, C makes no other payments upon which tax is required to be withheld under chapter 3 of the Code; accordingly, its return on Form 1042 for such year, which is filed on March 15, 2002, shows total tax withheld of $30, an adjusted total tax withheld of $15, and $30 previously paid for such year. Pursuant to §1.6414-1(b), C claims a credit for the overpayment of $15 shown on the Form 1042 for 2001. Accordingly, it is permitted to reduce by $15 any deposit required by §1.6302-2 to be made of tax withheld during the calendar year 2002. The Form 1042-S required to be filed by C with respect to the dividend of $100 paid to N in 2001 is required to show tax withheld of $30 and tax released of $15.

Example 2. The facts are the same as in *Example 1.* In addition, during 2002, C makes payments to N upon which it is required to withhold $200 under chapter 3 of the Code, all of which is withheld in June 2002. Pursuant to §1.6302-2(a)(1)(iii), C deposits the amount of $185 on July 15, 2002 ($200 less the $15 for which credit is claimed on the Form 1042 for 2001). On March 15, 2003, C Corporation files its return on Form 1042 for calendar year 2002, which shows total tax withheld of $200, $185 previously deposited by C, and $15 allowable credit.

Example 3. The facts are the same as in *Example 1.* Under §1.6032-2(a)(1)(ii)), C is required to deposit on a quarter-monthly basis the tax withheld under chapter 3 of the Code. C withholds tax of $100 between February 8 and February 15, 2002, and deposits $75 [($100 × 90 percent) less $15]of the withheld tax within 3 banking days after February 15, 2002, and by depositing $10 [($100 − $15) less $75]within 3 banking days after March 15, 2002.

(b) *Withholding of additional tax when underwithholding occurs.*—A withholding agent may withhold from future payments (or distributions of effectively connected income under section 1446) made to a beneficial owner the tax that should have been withheld from previous payments (or distributions subject to section 1446) to such beneficial owner under chapter 3 of the Internal Revenue Code. In the alternative, the withholding agent may satisfy the tax from property that it holds in custody for the beneficial owner or property over which it has control. Such additional withholding or satisfaction of the tax owed may only be made before the date that the Form 1042 is required to be filed (not including extensions) for the calendar year in which the underwithholding occurred. See §1.6302-2 for making deposits of tax or §1.1461-1(a) for making payment of the balance due for a calendar year. See also §§1.1461-1, 1.1461-3, and 1.1446-1 through 1.1446-7 for rules relating to withholding under section 1446. References in this paragraph (b) to withholding under section 1446 shall apply to partnership taxable years beginning after May 18, 2005, or such earlier time as the regulations under §§1.1446-1 through 1.1446-5 apply by reason of an election under §1.1446-7.

(c) *Definition.*—For purposes of this section, the term *payment period* means the period for which the withholding agent is required by §1.6302-2(a)(1) to make a deposit of tax withheld under chapter 3 of the Code.

(d) *Effective date.*—Unless otherwise provided in this section, this section applies to payments made after December 31, 2000. [Reg. §1.1461-2.]

☐ [*T.D. 6187,* 7-5-56. *Amended by T.D. 6213,* 11-20-56, *T.D. 6922,* 6-16-67, *T.D. 7157,* 12-29-71, *T.D. 7284,* 8-2-73; *T.D. 7977,* 9-19-84; *T.D. 8734,* 10-6-97; *T.D. 8804,* 12-30-98; *T.D. 8856,* 12-29-99 *and T.D. 9200,* 5-13-2005.]

[Reg. §1.1461-3]

§1.1461-3. Withholding under section 1446.—For rules relating to the withholding tax liability of a partnership or nominee under section 1446, see §§1.1446-1 through 1.1446-7. For interest, penalties, and additions to the tax for failure to timely pay the tax required to be paid under section 1446, see sections 6601, 6651, 6655 (in the case of publicly traded partnerships, see section 6656), 6672, and 7202 and the regulations under those sections. For additional penalties and additions to the tax for failure to comply with the regulations under section 1446, see sections 6651, 6662, 6663, 6721, 6722, 6723, 6724(c), 7201, 7203, and the regulations under those sections. This section shall apply to partnership taxable years beginning after May 18, 2005, or such earlier time as the regulations under §§1.1446-1 through 1.1446-5 apply by reason of an election under §1.1446-7. [Reg. §1.1461-3.]

☐ [*T.D. 9200,* 5-13-2005.]

[Reg. §1.1462-1]

§1.1462-1. Withheld tax as credit to recipient of income.—(a) *Creditable tax.*—The entire amount of the income from which the tax is required to be withheld (including amounts calculated under the gross-up formula in §1.1441-3(f)(1)) shall be included in gross income in the return required to be made by the beneficial owner of the income, without deduction for the amount required to be or actually withheld, but the amount of tax actually withheld shall be allowed as a credit against the total income tax computed in the beneficial owner's return.

(b) *Amounts paid to persons who are not the beneficial owner.*—Amounts withheld at source under chapter 3 of the Internal Revenue Code on payments to (or effectively connected taxable income allocable to) a fiduciary, partnership, or intermediary are deemed to have been paid by the taxpayer ultimately liable for the tax upon such income. Thus, for example, if a beneficiary of a trust is subject to the taxes imposed by section 1, 2, 3, or 11 upon any portion of the income received from a foreign trust, the part of any amount withheld at source which is properly allocable to the income so taxed to such beneficiary shall be credited against the amount of the income tax computed upon the beneficiary's return, and any excess shall be refunded. See §1.1446-3 for examples applying this rule in the context of a partnership interest held by a foreign trust or estate. Further, if a partnership withholds an amount under chapter 3 of the Internal Revenue Code with respect to the allocable share of a partner that is a partnership (upper-tier partnership) or with respect to the allocable share of partners in an upper-tier partnership, such amount is deemed to have been withheld by the upper-tier partnership. See §1.1446-5 for rules applicable to tiered partnership structures. References in this paragraph (b) to withholding under section 1446 shall apply to partnership taxable years beginning after May 18, 2005, or such earlier time as the regulations under §§1.1446-1 through 1.1446-5 apply by reason of an election under §1.1446-7.

(c) *Effective date.*—Unless otherwise provided in this section, this section applies to payments made after December 31, 2000. [Reg. §1.1462-1.]

☐ [*T.D. 6187, 7-5-56. Amended by T.D. 7977, 9-19-84; T.D. 8734, 10-6-97; T.D. 8804, 12-30-98; T.D. 8856, 12-29-99 and T.D. 9200, 5-13-2005.*]

[Reg. §1.1463-1]

§1.1463-1. Tax paid by recipient of income.— (a) *Tax paid.*—If the tax required to be withheld under chapter 3 of the Internal Revenue Code is paid by the beneficial owner of the income or by the withholding agent, it shall not be re-collected from the other, regardless of the original liability therefor. However, this section does not relieve the person that did not withhold tax from liability for interest or any penalties or additions to tax otherwise applicable. See §1.1441-7(b) for additional applicable rules. See §1.1446-3(e) and (f) for application of the rule of this paragraph (a), and for additional rules, where the withholding tax was required to be paid under section 1446. The previous sentence shall apply to partnership taxable years beginning after May 18, 2005, or such earlier time as the regulations under §§1.1446-1 through 1.1446-5 apply by reason of an election under §1.1446-7.

(b) *Effective date.*—Unless otherwise provided in this section, this section applies to failures to withhold occurring after December 31, 2000. [Reg. §1.1463-1.]

☐ [*T.D. 6187, 7-5-56. Amended by T.D. 8734, 10-6-97; T.D. 8804, 12-30-98; T.D. 8856, 12-29-99 and T.D. 9200, 5-13-2005.*]

[Reg. §1.1464-1]

§1.1464-1. Refunds or credits.—(a) *In general.*—The refund or credit under chapter 65 of the Code of an overpayment of tax which has actually been withheld at the source under chapter 3 of the Code shall be made to the taxpayer from whose income the amount of such tax was in fact withheld. To the extent that the overpayment under chapter 3 was not in fact withheld at the source, but was paid, by the withholding agent the refund or credit under chapter 65 of the overpayment shall be made to the withhold-

ing agent. Thus, where a debtor corporation assumes liability pursuant to its tax-free covenant for the tax required to be withheld under chapter 3 upon interest and pays the tax in behalf of its bondholder, and it can be shown that the bondholder is not in fact liable for any tax, the overpayment of tax shall be credited or refunded to the withholding agent in accordance with chapter 65 since the tax was not actually deducted and withheld from the interest paid to the bondholder. In further illustration, where a withholding agent who is required by chapter 3 to withhold $300 tax from rents paid to a nonresident alien individual mistakenly withholds $320 and mistakenly pays $350 as internal revenue tax, the amount of $30 shall be credited or refunded to the withholding agent in accordance with chapter 65 and the amount of $20 shall be credited or refunded in accordance with such chapter to the person from whose income such amount has been withheld. With respect to section 1446, this section shall only apply to a publicly traded partnership described in §1.1446-4.

(b) *Tax repaid to payee.*—For purposes of this section and §1.6414-1, any amount of tax withheld under chapter 3 of the Code, which, pursuant to paragraph (a)(1) of §1.1461-2, is repaid by the withholding agent to the person from whose income such amount was erroneously withheld shall be considered as tax which, within the meaning of sections 1464 and 6414, was not actually withheld by the withholding agent.

(c) *Effective/Applicability date.*—The last sentence in paragraph (a) of this section shall apply to partnership taxable years beginning after April 29, 2008. [Reg. §1.1464-1.]

☐ [*T.D. 6187, 7-5-56. Amended by T.D. 6922, 6-16-67; T.D. 8804, 12-30-98 and T.D. 9394, 4-28-2008 (corrected 4-1-2009).*]

[Reg. §1.1491-1]

§1.1491-1. Imposition of tax.—Section 1491 imposes an excise tax upon transfers of stock or securities by a citizen or resident of the United States, or by a domestic corporation or partnership, or by a trust which is not a foreign trust, to a foreign corporation as paid-in surplus or as a contribution to capital, or to a foreign trust, or to a foreign partnership. The tax is in an amount equal to $27\frac{1}{2}$ percent of the excess of (a) the value of the stock or securities so transferred over (b) its adjusted basis, as provided in section 1011, for determining gain in the hands of the transferor. [Reg. §1.1491-1.]

☐ [*T.D. 6127, 3-17-55.*]

[Reg. §1.1492-1]

§1.1492-1. Nontaxable transfers.—(a) The tax imposed by section 1491 does not apply:

(1) If the transferee is an organization (other than an organization described in section 401(a))

exempt from income tax under the provisions of sections 501 to 504, inclusive; or

(2) If before the transfer it has been established to the satisfaction of the Commissioner that the transfer is not in pursuance of a plan having as one of its principal purposes the avoidance of Federal income taxes.

(b) Whether a transfer of stock or securities is in pursuance of a plan having as one of its principal purposes the avoidance of Federal income taxes is a question to be determined from the facts and circumstances of each particular case. In any such case where a transferor desires to establish that the transfer is not in pursuance of such a plan, a statement of the facts relating to the plan under which the transfer is to be made or was made, together with a copy of the plan if in writing, shall be forwarded to the Commissioner of Internal Revenue, Washington 25, D.C., for a ruling. This statement shall contain, or be verified by, a written declaration that it is made under the penalties of perjury. A letter notifying the transferor of the Commissioner's determination will be mailed to the transferor. [Reg. § 1.1492-1.]

☐ [T.D. 6127, 3-17-55.]

[Reg. § 1.1494-1]

§ 1.1494-1. Returns; payment and collection of tax.—(a) *Returns and payment.*—Every person making a transfer described in section 1491 shall make a return to the district director on the day on which the transfer is made and, unless the transfer is nontaxable under section 1492, pay the tax due on such transfer. This return, which shall contain, or be verified by, a written declaration that it is made under the penalties of perjury, shall be made on Form 926 and shall be filed with the district director to whom the transferor's return of income is required to be made. The return shall set forth in detail the following information:

(1) Name and address of transferor, and place of organization or creation, if a corporation, partnership, or trust.

(2) Name and address of transferee, place of organization or creation, and whether the transferee is a foreign corporation, a foreign trust, or a foreign partnership. If the transferee is a foreign trust or a foreign partnership, the name and address of the fiduciary and each beneficiary, in the case of a trust, or of each partner, in the case of a partnership, must be shown.

(3) Description and amount of stock or securities transferred, the date of transfer, and a complete statement showing all the facts relating to the transfer, accompanied by a copy of the plan under which the transfer was made.

(4) The fair market value of the stock or securities transferred as of the date of transfer, and the adjusted basis provided in section 1011 for determining gain in the hands of the transferor.

(5) Whether the transfer was made in pursuance of a plan submitted to and approved by the Commissioner as not having as one of its principal purposes the avoidance of Federal income taxes. If the plan has been so approved, a copy of the Commissioner's letter approving the plan shall accompany the return.

(6) Such other information as may be required by the return form.

(b) *Certificate.*—(1) If the transferee of the stock or securities, the transfer of which is reported in the return, is a foreign organization meeting the tests of exemption from income tax provided in part I (section 501 and following), subchapter F, chapter 1 of the Code, and the transferor on that account claims that no liability for tax is imposed by section 1491, such transferor must file with Form 926 a certificate establishing the exemption of the transferee under such part I. This certificate, which shall contain, or be verified by, a written declaration that it is made under the penalties of perjury, shall contain complete information showing the character of the transferee, the purpose for which it was organized, its actual activities, the source of its income and the disposition of such income, whether or not any of its income is credited to surplus or may inure to the benefit of any private shareholder or individual, and in general all facts relating to its operations which affect its right to exemption. To such certificate shall be attached a copy of the charter or articles of incorporation, the by-laws of the organization, and the latest financial statement showing the assets, liabilities, receipts, and disbursements of the organization.

(2) If the transferee is a foreign organization which has been held to be exempt from income tax under such part I (or corresponding provisions of prior law), a copy of the Commissioner's letter so holding shall be filed with Form 926 in lieu of the above certificate and attachments.

(c) *Assessment and collection.*—The determination, assessment, and collection of the tax and the examination of returns and claims filed pursuant to chapter 5 of the Code will be made under such procedure as may be prescribed from time to time by the Commissioner. [Reg. § 1.1494-1.]

☐ [T.D. 6127, 3-17-55.]

[Reg. § 1.1494-2]

§ 1.1494-2. Effective date.—Chapter 5 (section 1491 and following) of the Internal Revenue Code of 1954 and the regulations prescribed thereunder apply with respect to transfers occurring after December 31, 1954. (See section 7851(a)(1)(B).) Chapter 7 (section 1250 and following) of the Internal Revenue Code of 1939 and the regulations applicable thereto apply with respect to transfers occurring prior to January 1, 1955. [Reg. § 1.1494-2.]

☐ [T.D. 6127, 3-17-55.]

Consolidated Returns

RETURNS AND PAYMENT OF TAX

See p. 20,601 for regulations not amended to reflect law changes

[Reg. § 1.1502-0]

§ 1.1502-0. Effective dates.—(a) The regulations under section 1502 are applicable to taxable years beginning after December 31, 1965, except as otherwise provided therein.

(b) The provisions of §§ 1.1502-0A through 1.1502-3A, 1.1502-10A through 1.1502-19A, and 1.1502-30A through 1.1502-51A (as contained in the 26 CFR part 1 edition revised April 1, 1996) are applicable to taxable years beginning before January 1, 1966. [Reg. § 1.1502-0.]

☐ [*T.D. 6894, 9-7-66. Amended by T.D. 8677, 6-26-96.*]

[Reg. § 1.1502-1]

§ 1.1502-1. Definitions.—(a) *Group.*—The term "group" means an affiliated group of corporations as defined in section 1504. See § 1.1502-75 (d) as to when a group remains in existence. Except as the context otherwise requires, references to a group are references to a consolidated group (as defined in paragraph (h) of this section).

(b) *Member.*—The term *member* means a corporation (including the common parent) that is included in the group, or as the context may require, a corporation that is included in a subgroup.

(c) *Subsidiary.*—The term "subsidiary" means a corporation other than the common parent which is a member of such group.

(d) *Consolidated return year.*—The term "consolidated return year" means a taxable year for which a consolidated return is filed or required to be filed by such group.

(e) *Separate return year.*—The term "separate return year" means a taxable year of a corporation for which it files a separate return or for which it joins in the filing of a consolidated return by another group.

(f) *Separate return limitation year.*—(1) *In general.*—Except as provided in paragraphs (f)(2) and (3) of this section, the term *separate return limitation year* (or *SRLY*) means any separate return year of a member or of a predecessor of a member.

(2) *Exceptions.*—The term *separate return limitation year* (or *SRLY*) does not include:

(i) A separate return year of the corporation which is the common parent for the consolidated return year to which the tax attribute is to be carried (except as provided in § 1.1502-75(d)(2)(ii) and subparagraph (3) of this paragraph),

(ii) A separate return year of any corporation which was a member of the group for each day of such year, or

(iii) A separate return year of a predecessor of any member if such predecessor was a member of the group for each day of such year,

provided that an election under section 1562(a) (relating to the privilege to elect multiple surtax exemptions) was never effective (or is no longer effective as a result of a termination of such election) for such year. An election under section 1562(a) which is effective for a taxable year beginning in 1963 and ending in 1964 shall be disregarded.

(3) *Reverse acquisitions.*—In the event of an acquisition to which § 1.1502-75(d)(3) applies, all taxable years of the first corporation and of each of its subsidiaries ending on or before the date of the acquisition shall be treated as separate return limitation years, and the separate return years (if any) of the second corporation and each of its subsidiaries shall not be treated as separate return limitation years (unless they were so treated immediately before the acquisition). For example, if corporation P merges into corporation T, and the persons who were stockholders of P immediately before the merger, as a result of owning the stock of P, own more than 50 percent of the fair market value of the outstanding stock of T, then a loss incurred before the merger by T (even though it is the common parent), or by a subsidiary of T, is treated as having been incurred in a separate return limitation year. Conversely, a loss incurred before the merger by P, or by a subsidiary of P in a separate return year during all of which such subsidiary was a member of the group of which P was the common parent and for which section 1562 was not effective, is treated as having been incurred in a year which is not a separate return limitation year.

(4) *Predecessor and successors.*—The term *predecessor* means a transferor or distributor of assets to a member (the successor) in a transaction—

(i) To which section 381(a) applies; or

(ii) That occurs on or after January 1, 1997, in which the successor's basis for the assets is determined, directly or indirectly, in whole or in part, by reference to the basis of the assets of the transferor or distributor, but in the case of a transaction that occurs before June 25, 1999, only if the amount by which basis differs from value, in the aggregate, is material. For a transaction that occurs before June 25, 1999, only one member may be considered a predecessor to or a successor of one other member.

(g) *Consolidated return change of ownership.*—(1) *In general.*—A consolidated return change of ownership occurs during any taxable year (referred to in this subparagraph as the "year of change") of the corporation which is the common parent for the taxable year to which the tax attribute is to be carried, if, at the end of the year of change—

(i) Any one or more of the persons described in section 382(a) (2) own a percentage of the fair market value of the outstanding stock of such corporation which is more than 50 percentage points greater than such person or persons owned at—

(a) The beginning of such taxable year, or

(b) The beginning of the preceding taxable year, and

(ii) The increase in percentage points at the end of such year is attributable to—

(a) A purchase (within the meaning of section 382(a)(4)) by such person or persons of such stock, the stock of another corporation owning stock in such corporation, or an interest in a partnership or trust owning stock in such corporation, or

(b) A decrease in the amount of such stock outstanding or the amount of stock outstanding of another corporation owning stock in such corporation, except a decrease resulting from a redemption to pay death taxes to which section 303 applies.

For purposes of subdivision (i)(a) and (b) of this subparagraph, the beginning of the taxable years specified therein shall be the beginning of such taxable years or October 1, 1965, whichever occurs later.

(2) *Operating rules.*—For purposes of this paragraph—

(i) The term "stock" means all shares except nonvoting stock which is limited and preferred as to dividends, and

(ii) Section 318 (relating to constructive ownership of stock) shall apply in determining the ownership of stock, except that section 318(a)(2)(C) and (3)(C) shall be applied without regard to the 50-percent limitation contained therein.

(3) *Old members.*—The term "old members" of a group means—

(i) Those corporations which were members of such group immediately preceding the first day of the taxable year in which the consolidated return change of ownership occurs, or

(ii) If the group was not in existence prior to the taxable year in which the consolidated return change of ownership occurs, the corporation which is the common parent for the taxable year to which the tax attribute is to be carried.

(4) *Reverse acquisitions.*—If there has been a consolidated return change of ownership of a corporation under subparagraph (1) of this paragraph and the stock or assets of such corporation are subsequently acquired by another corporation in an acquisition to which § 1.1502-7(d)(3) applies so that the group of which the former corporation is the common parent is treated as continuing in existence, then the "old members", as defined in subparagraph (3) of this paragraph, of such group immediately before the acquisition shall continue to be treated as "old members" immediately after the acquisition. For example, assume that corporations P and S comprise group PS, and PS undergoes a consolidated return change of ownership. Subsequently, the stock of P, the common parent, is acquired by corporation T, the common parent of group TU, in an acquisition to which section 368(a)(1)(B) and § 1.1502-75(d)(3) apply. The PS group is treated as continuing in existence with T as the common parent. P and S continue to be treated as old members, as defined in subparagraph (3) of this paragraph.

(h) *Consolidated group.*—The term "consolidated group" means a group filing (or required to file) consolidated returns for the tax year.

(i) [Reserved]

(j) *Affiliated.*—Corporations are affiliated if they are members of a group with each other. [Reg. § 1.1502-1.]

☐ [*T.D.* 6894, 9-7-66. *Amended by T.D.* 7246, 12-29-72; *T.D.* 8319, 11-19-90; *T.D.* 8560, 8-12-94; *T.D.* 8677, 6-26-96 *and T.D.* 8823, 6-25-99.]

[Reg. § 1.1502-2]

§ 1.1502-2. Computation of tax liability.—The tax liability of a group for a consolidated return year shall be determined by adding together—

(a) The tax imposed by section 11 on the consolidated taxable income for such year (see § 1.1502-11 for the computation of consolidated taxable income);

(b) The tax imposed by section 541 on the consolidated undistributed personal holding company income;

(c) If paragraph (b) of this section does not apply, the aggregate of the taxes imposed by section 541 on the separate undistributed personal holding company income of the members of the group which are personal holding companies;

(d) If paragraph (b) of this section does not apply, the tax imposed by section 531 on the consolidated accumulated taxable income (see § 1.1502-43);

(e) The tax imposed by section 594(a) in lieu of the taxes imposed by section 11 or 1201 on the taxable income of a life insurance department of the common parent of a group which is a mutual savings bank;

(f) The tax imposed by section 802(a) on consolidated life insurance company taxable income;

(g) The tax imposed by section 831(a) on the consolidated insurance company taxable income of the members which are subject to such tax;

(h) The tax imposed by section 1201, instead of the taxes computed under paragraphs (a) and (g) of this section, computed by reference to the net capital gain of the group (see § 1.1502-22) (or, for consolidated return years to which § 1.1502-22 does not apply, computed by reference to the excess of the consolidated net long-term capital gain over the consolidated net short-term capital loss (see § 1.1502-41A for the determination of the consolidated net long-term capital gain and the consolidated net short-term capital loss));

(i) [Reserved]

(j) The tax imposed by section 1333 on war loss recoveries; and

by allowing as a credit against such taxes the investment credit under section 38 (see § 1.1502-3) and the foreign tax credit under section 33 (see § 1.1502-4). For purposes of this section, the surtax exemption of the group for a consolidated return year is $25,000, or if a lesser amount is allowed under section 1561, such lesser amount. See § 1.1561-2(a)(2). For increase in tax due to the application of section 47, see § 1.1502-3(f). For amount of tax surcharge, see section 51 and § 1.1502-7. [Reg. § 1.1502-2.]

□ [*T.D. 6894, 9-7-66. Amended by T.D. 7093, 3-12-71; T.D. 7937, 1-26-84; T.D. 8677, 6-26-96 and T.D. 8823, 6-25-99.*]

[Reg. § 1.1502-3]

§ 1.1502-3. Consolidated tax credits.— (a) *Determination of amount of consolidated credit.*—(1) *In general.*—The credit allowed by section 38 for a consolidated return year of a group shall be equal to the consolidated credit earned. The consolidated credit earned is equal to the aggregate of the credit earned (as determined under subparagraph (2) of this paragraph) by all members of the group for the consolidated return year.

(2) *Determination of credit earned.*—The credit earned of a member of the group is an amount equal to 7 percent of such member's qualified investment (determined under section 46(c)). For purposes of computing a member's qualified investment, the basis of property shall not include any gain or loss realized with respect to such property by another member in an inter company transaction (as defined in § 1.1502-13(b)), whether or not such gain or loss is deferred.

Thus, if section 38 property acquired in an intercompany transaction has a basis of $100 to the purchasing member, and if the selling member has a $20 gain with respect to such property, the basis of such property for purposes of computing the purchaser's qualified investment is only $80. Such $80 basis shall also be used for purposes of applying section 47 to such property. See paragraph (f) of this section.

(3) *Consolidated limitation based on amount of tax.*—(i) Notwithstanding the amount of the consolidated credit earned for the taxable year, the consolidated credit allowed by section 38 to the group for the consolidated return year is limited to—

(a) So much of the consolidated liability for tax as does not exceed $25,000, plus

(b) For taxable years ending on or before March 9, 1967, 25 percent of the consolidated liability for tax in excess of $25,000, or

(c) For taxable years ending after March 9, 1967, 50 percent of the consolidated liability for tax in excess of $25,000.

The $25,000 amount referred to in the preceding sentence shall be reduced by any part of such $25,000 amount apportioned under § 1.46-1 to component members of the controlled group (as defined in section 46(a)(5)) which do not join in the filing of the consolidated return. For further rules for computing the limitation based on amount of tax with respect to the suspension period (as defined in section 48(j)), see section 46(a)(2). The amount determined under this subparagraph is referred to in this section as the "consolidated limitation based on amount of tax."

(ii) If an organization to which section 593 applies or a cooperative organization described in section 1381(a) joins in the filing of the consolidated return, the $25,000 amount referred to in subdivision (i) of this subparagraph (reduced as provided in such subdivision) shall be apportioned equally among the members of the group filing the consolidated return. The amount so apportioned equally to any such organization shall then be decreased in accordance with the provisions of section 46(d). Finally, the sum of all such equal portions (as decreased under section 46(d)) of each member of the group shall be substituted for the $25,000 amount referred to in subdivision (i) of this subparagraph.

(4) *Consolidated liability for tax.*—For purposes of subparagraph (3) of this paragraph, the consolidated liability for tax shall be the income tax imposed for the taxable year upon the group by chapter 1 of the Code, reduced by the consolidated foreign tax credit allowable under § 1.1502-4. The tax imposed by section 56 (relating to minimum tax for tax preferences), section 531 (relating to accumulated earnings tax), section 541 (relating to personal holding company tax), and any additional tax imposed by section 1351(d)(1) (relating to recoveries of foreign ex-

propriation losses), shall not be considered tax imposed by chapter 1 of the Code. In addition, any increase in tax resulting from the application of section 47 (relating to certain dispositions, etc., of section 38 property) shall not be treated as tax imposed by chapter 1 for purposes of computing the consolidated liability for tax.

(b) *Carryback and carryover of unused credits.*—(1) *Allowance of unused credit as consolidated carryback or carryover.*—A group shall be allowed to add to the amount allowable as a credit under paragraph (a)(1) of this section for any consolidated return year an amount equal to the aggregate of the consolidated investment credit carryovers and carrybacks to such year. The consolidated investment credit carryovers and carrybacks to the taxable year shall consist of any consolidated unused credits of the group, plus any unused credits of members of the group arising in separate return years of such members, which may be carried over or back to the taxable year under the principles of section 46(b). However, such consolidated carryovers and carrybacks shall not include any consolidated unused credits apportioned to a corporation for a separate return year pursuant to paragraph (c) of § 1.1502-79 and shall be subject to the limitations contained in paragraphs (c) and (e) of this section. A consolidated unused credit for any consolidated return year is the excess of the consolidated credit earned over the consolidated limitation based on amount of tax for such year.

(2) *Absorption rules.*—For purposes of determining the amount, if any, of an unused credit (whether consolidated or separate) which can be carried to a taxable year (consolidated or separate), the amount of such unused credit which is absorbed in a prior consolidated return year under section 46(b) shall be determined by—

(i) Applying all unused credits which can be carried to such prior year in the order of the taxable years in which such unused credits arose, beginning with the taxable year which ends earliest, and

(ii) Applying all such unused credits which can be carried to such prior year from taxable years ending on the same date on a pro rata basis.

(3) *Example.*—The provisions of paragraphs (a) and (b) of this section may be illustrated by the following example:

Example. (i) Corporation P is incorporated on January 1, 1966. On that same day P incorporates corporation S, a wholly owned subsidiary. P and S file consolidated returns for calendar years 1966 and 1967. P's and S's credit earned, the consolidated credit earned, and the consolidated limitation based on amount of tax for 1966 and 1967 are as follows:

	Credit earned	Consolidated credit earned	Consolidated limitation based on amount of tax
1966:			
P	$60,000		
S	$30,000	$90,000	$100,000
1967:			
P	$40,000		
S	$25,000	$65,000	$50,000

(ii) P's and S's credit earned for 1966 are aggregated, and the group's consolidated credit earned, $90,000, is allowable in full to the group as a credit under section 38 for 1966 since such amount is less than the consolidated limitation based on amount of tax for 1966, $100,000.

(iii) Since the consolidated limitation based on amount of tax for 1967 is $50,000, only $50,000 of the $65,000 consolidated credit earned for such year is allowable to the group under section 38 as a credit for 1967. The consolidated unused credit for 1967 of $15,000 ($65,000 less $50,000) is a consolidated investment credit carryback and carryover to the years prescribed in section 46(b). In this case the consolidated unused credit is a consolidated investment credit carryback to 1966 (since P and S were not in existence in 1964 and 1965) and a consolidated investment credit carryover to 1968 and subsequent years. The portion of the consolidated unused credit for 1967 which is allowable as a credit for 1966 is $10,000. This amount shall be added to the amount allowable as a credit to the group for 1966. The balance of the consolidated unused credit for 1967 to be carried to 1968 is $5,000. These amounts are computed as follows:

Consolidated carryback to 1966		$15,000
1966 consolidated limitation based on tax	$100,000	
Less: Consolidated credit earned for 1966	$90,000	
Consolidated unused credits attributable to years preceding 1967	0	$90,000
Limit on amount of 1967 consolidated unused credit which may be added as a credit for 1966		$10,000
Balance of 1967 consolidated unused credit to be carried to 1968		$5,000

(c) *Limitation on investment credit carryovers and carrybacks from separate return limitation years applicable for consolidated return years for which the due date of the return is on or before March 13, 1998.*—(1) *General rule.*—In the case of an unused credit of a member of the group arising in a separate return limitation year (as defined in §1.1502-1(f)) of such member (and in a separate return limitation year of any predecessor of such member), the amount which may be included under paragraph (b) of this section (computed without regard to the limitation contained in paragraph (e) of this section) shall not exceed the amount determined under paragraph (c)(2) of this section.

(2) *Computation of limitation.*—The amount referred to in paragraph (c)(1) of this section with respect to a member of the group is the excess, if any, of—

(i) The limitation based on amount of tax of the group, minus such limitation recomputed by excluding the items of income, deduction, and foreign tax credit of such member; over

(ii) The sum of the investment credit earned by such member for such consolidated return year, and the unused credits attributable to such member which may be carried to such consolidated return year arising in unused credit years ending prior to the particular separate return limitation year.

(3) *Special effective date.*—This paragraph (c) applies to consolidated return years for which the due date of the income tax return (without extensions) is on or before March 13, 1998. See paragraph (d) of this section for the rule that limits the group's use of a section 38 credit carryover or carryback from a SRLY for a consolidated return year for which the due date of the income tax return (without extensions) is after March 13, 1998. See also paragraph (d)(4) of this section for an optional effective date rule (generally making the rules of this paragraph (c) inapplicable to a consolidated return year beginning after December 31, 1996, if the due date of the income tax return (without extensions) for such year is on or before March 13, 1998).

(4) *Examples.*—The provisions of this paragraph (c) may be illustrated by the following examples:

Example 1. (i) Assume the same facts as in the example contained in paragraph (b)(3) of this section, except that all the stock of corporation T, also a calendar year taxpayer, is acquired by P on January 1, 1968, and that P, S, and T file a consolidated return for 1968. In 1966, T had an unused credit of $10,000 which has not been absorbed and is available as an investment credit carryover to 1968. Such carryover is from a separate return limitation year. P's and S's credit earned for 1968 is $10,000 each, and T's credit earned is $8,000; the consolidated credit earned is therefore $28,000. The group's consolidated limitation based on amount of tax for 1968 is $50,000. Such limitation recomputed by excluding the items of income, deduction, and foreign tax credit of T is $30,000. Thus, the amount determined under paragraph (c)(2)(i) of this section is $20,000 ($50,000 minus $30,000). Accordingly, the limitation on the carryover of T's unused credit is $12,000, the excess of $20,000 over $8,000 (the sum of T's credit earned for the taxable year and any carryovers from prior unused credit years (none in this case)). Therefore T's $10,000 unused credit from 1966 may be carried over to the consolidated return year without limitation.

(ii) The group's consolidated credit earned for 1968, $28,000, is allowable in full as a credit under section 38 since such amount is less than the consolidated limitation based on amount of tax, $50,000.

(iii) The group's consolidated investment credit carryover to 1968 is $15,000, consisting of the consolidated unused credits of the group ($5,000) plus T's separate return year unused credit ($10,000). The entire $15,000 consolidated carryover shall be added to the amount allowable to the group as a credit under section 38 for 1968, since such amount is less than $22,000 (the excess of the consolidated limitation based on tax, $50,000, over the sum of the consolidated credit earned for 1968, $28,000, and unused credits arising in prior unused credit years, zero).

Example 2. Assume the same facts as in *Example 1,* except that the amount determined under paragraph (c)(2)(i) of this section is $12,000. Therefore, the limitation on the carryover of T's unused credit is $4,000. Accordingly, the consolidated investment credit carryover is only $9,000 since the amount of T's separate return year unused credit which may be added to the group's $ 5,000 consolidated unused credit is $4,000. These amounts are computed as follows:

T's carryover to 1968		$10,000
Consolidated limitation based on amount of tax minus recomputed limitation		$12,000
Less: T's credit earned for 1968	$8,000	
Unused credits attributable to T arising in unused credit years preceding 1966	0	$8,000
Limit on amount of 1966 unused credit of T which may be added to consolidated investment credit carryover		$4,000
Balance of 1966 unused credit of T to be carried to 1969 (subject to the limitation contained in paragraph (c) of this section)		$6,000

Reg. §1.1502-3(c)(4)

(d) *Limitation on tax credit carryovers and carrybacks from separate return limitation years applicable for consolidated return years for which the due date of the return is after March 13, 1998.*—(1) *General rule.*—The aggregate of a member's unused section 38 credits arising in SRLYs that are included in the consolidated section 38 credits for all consolidated return years of the group may not exceed—

(i) The aggregate for all consolidated return years of the member's contributions to the consolidated section 38(c) limitation for each consolidated return year; reduced by

(ii) The aggregate of the member's section 38 credits arising and absorbed in all consolidated return years (whether or not absorbed by the member).

(2) *Computational rules.*—(i) *Member's contribution to the consolidated section 38(c) limitation.*—If the consolidated section 38(c) limitation for a consolidated return year is determined by reference to the consolidated tentative minimum tax (see section 38(c)(1)(A)), then a member's contribution to the consolidated section 38(c) limitation for such year equals the member's share of the consolidated net income tax minus the member's share of the consolidated tentative minimum tax. If the consolidated section 38(c) limitation for a consolidated return year is determined by reference to the consolidated net regular tax liability (see section 38(c)(1)(B)), then a member's contribution to the consolidated section 38(c) limitation for such year equals the member's share of the consolidated net income tax minus 25 percent of the quantity which is equal to so much of the member's share of the consolidated net regular tax liability less its portion of the $25,000 amount specified in section 38(c)(1)(B). The group computes the member's shares by applying to the respective consolidated amounts the principles of section 1552 and the percentage method under § 1.1502-33(d)(3), assuming a 100% allocation of any decreased tax liability. The group must make proper adjustments so that taxes and credits not taken into account in computing the limitation under section 38(c) are not taken into account in computing the member's share of the consolidated net income tax, etc. (See, for example, the taxes described in section 26(b) that are disregarded in computing regular tax liability.) Also, the group may apportion all or a part of the $25,000 amount (or lesser amount if reduced by section 38(c)(3)) for any year to one or more members.

(ii) *Years included in computation.*—For purposes of computing the limitation under this paragraph (d), the consolidated return years of the group include only those years, including the year to which a credit is carried, that the member has been continuously included in the group's consolidated return, but exclude—

(A) For carryovers, any years ending after the year to which the credit is carried; and

(B) For carrybacks, any years ending after the year in which the credit arose.

(iii) *Subgroups and successors.*—The SRLY subgroup principles under § 1.1502-21(c)(2) apply for purposes of this paragraph (d). The predecessor and successor principles under § 1.1502-21(f) also apply for purposes of this paragraph (d).

(iv) *Overlap with section 383.*—The principles under § 1.1502-21(g) apply for purposes of this paragraph (d). For example, an overlap of paragraph (d) of this section and the application of section 383 with respect to a credit carryover occurs if a corporation becomes a member of a consolidated group (the SRLY event) within six months of the change date of an ownership change giving rise to a section 383 credit limitation with respect to that carryover (the section 383 event), with the result that the limitation of this paragraph (d) does not apply. See §§ 1.1502-21(g)(2)(ii)(A) and 1.383-1; see also § 1.1502-21(g)(4) (subgroup rules).

(3) *Effective date.*—(i) *In general.*—This paragraph (d) generally applies to consolidated return years for which the due date of the income tax return (without extensions) is after March 13, 1998.

(A) *Contribution years.*—Except as provided in paragraph (d)(4)(ii) of this section, a group does not take into account a consolidated taxable year for which the due date of the income tax return (without extensions) is on or before March 13, 1998, in determining a member's (or subgroup's) contributions to the consolidated section 38(c) limitation under this paragraph (d).

(B) *Special subgroup rule.*—In the event that the principles of § 1.1502-21(g)(1) do not apply to a particular credit carryover in the current group, then solely for purposes of applying paragraph (d) of this section to determine the limitation with respect to that carryover and with respect to which the SRLY register (the aggregate of the member's or subgroup's contribution to consolidated section 38(c) limitation reduced by the aggregate of the member's or subgroup's section 38 credits arising and absorbed in all consolidated return years) began in a taxable year for which the due date of the return is on or before May 25, 2000, the principles of § 1.1502-21(c)(2) shall be applied without regard to the phrase "or for a carryover that was subject to the overlap rule described in paragraph (g) of this section or §1.1502-15(g) with respect to another group (the former group)."

(ii) *Overlap rule.*—Paragraph (d)(2)(iv) of this section (relating to overlap with section 383) applies to taxable years for which the due date (without extensions) of the consolidated return is after May 25, 2000. For purposes of this section, only an ownership change to which section 383, as amended by the Tax Reform Act of 1986 (100 Stat. 2085), applies and which results in a section 383 credit limitation shall constitute a section 383 event.

(4) *Optional effective date of January 1, 1997.*— (i) For consolidated taxable years beginning on or after January 1, 1997, for which the due date of the income tax return (without extensions) is on or before March 13, 1998, in lieu of paragraphs (c) and (e)(3) of this section (relating to the general business credit), §1.1502-4(f)(3) and (g)(3) (relating to the foreign tax credit), the next to last sentence of §1.1502-9A(a)(2), §1.1502-9A(b)(1)(v) (relating to overall foreign losses), and §1.1502-55(h)(4)(iii) (relating to the alternative minimum tax credit), a consolidated group may apply the corresponding provisions as they appear in 1998-1 C.B. 655 through 661 (see §601.601(d)(2) of this chapter) (treating references in such corresponding provisions to §§1.1502-9(b)(1)(ii), (iii), and (iv) as references to §§1.1502-9A(b)(1)(ii), (iii), and (iv)). Also, in the case of a consolidated return change of ownership that occurs on or after January 1, 1997, in a taxable year for which the due date of the income tax return (without extensions) is on or before March 13, 1998, a consolidated group may choose not to apply paragraph (e) of this section and §1.1502-4(g) to taxable years ending after December 31, 1996. A consolidated group making the choices described in the two preceding sentences generally must apply all such corresponding provisions (including not applying paragraph (e) of this section and §1.1502-4(g)) for all relevant years. However, a consolidated group making the election provided in §1.1502-9A(b)(1)(vi) (electing not to apply §1.1502-9A(b)(1)(v) to years beginning before January 1, 1998) may nevertheless choose to apply all such corresponding provisions referred to in this paragraph (d)(4)(i) other than the provision corresponding to §1.1502-9A(b)(1)(v) for all relevant years.

(ii) If a consolidated group chooses to apply the corresponding provisions referred to in paragraph (d)(4)(i) of this section, the consolidated group shall not take into account a consolidated taxable year beginning before January 1, 1997, in determining a member's (or subgroup's) contributions to the consolidated section 38(c) limitation under this paragraph (d).

(5) *Example.*—The following example illustrates the provisions of this paragraph (d):

Example. (i) Individual A owns all of the stock of P and T. P is the common parent of the P group. P acquires all the stock of T at the beginning of Year 2. T carries over an unused section 38 general business credit from Year 1 of $100,000. The table in paragraph (i) of this *Example* shows the group's net consolidated income tax, consolidated tentative minimum tax, and consolidated net regular tax liabilities, and T's share of such taxes computed under the principles of section 1552 and the percentage method under §1.1502-33(d)(3), assuming a 100% allocation of any decreased tax liability, for Year 2. (The effects of the lower section 11 brackets are ignored, there are no other tax credits affecting a group amount or member's share, and $1,000s are omitted.)

Year 2

	Group	P's share of col. 1	T's share of col. 1
1. consolidated taxable income	$2,000	$1,200	$800
2. consolidated net regular tax	$700	$420	$280
3. consolidated alternative minimum taxable income	$4,000	$3,200	$800
4. consolidated tentative minimum tax	$800	$640	$160
5. consolidated net income tax	$800	$520	$280
6. greater of line 4 or 25% of (line 2 minus $25,000) *for the group*	$800		
7. consolidated §38(c) limitation (line 5 minus line 6)	$0		

(ii) T's Year 1 is a SRLY with respect to the P group. See §1.1502-1(f)(2)(ii). T did not undergo an ownership change giving rise to a section 383 credit limitation within 6 months of joining the P group. Thus, T's $100,000 general business credit arising in Year 1 is subject to a SRLY limitation in the P group. The amount of T's unused section 38 credits from Year 1 that are included in the consolidated section 38 credits for Year 2 may not exceed T's contribution to the consolidated section 38(c) limitation. For Year 2, the group determines the consolidated section 38(c) limitation by reference to consolidated tentative minimum tax for Year 2. Therefore, T's contribution to the consolidated section 38(c) limitation for Year 2 equals its share of consolidated net income tax minus its share of consolidated tentative minimum tax. T's contribution is $280,000 minus $160,000, or $120,000. However, because the group has a consolidated section 38 limitation of zero, it may not include any of T's unused

section 38 credits in the consolidated section 38 credits for Year 2.

(iii) The following table shows similar information for the group for Year 3:

Year 3

	Group	P's share of col. 1	T's share of col. 1
1. consolidated taxable income	$1,200	$1,500	$(300)
2. consolidated net regular tax	$420	$525	$(105)
3. consolidated alternative minimum taxable income	$1,500	$1,700	$(200)
4. consolidated tentative minimum tax	$300	$340	$(40)
5. consolidated net income tax	$420	$525	$(105)
6. greater of line 4 or 25% of (line 2 minus $25,000) *for the group*	$300		
7. consolidated §38(c) limitation (line 5 minus line 6)	$120		

(iv) The amount of T's unused section 38 credits from Year 1 that are included in the consolidated section 38 credits for Year 3 may not exceed T's aggregate contribution to the consolidated section 38(c) limitation for Years 2 and 3. For Year 3, the group determines the consolidated section 38(c) limitation by reference to the consolidated tentative minimum tax for Year 3. Therefore, T's contribution to the consolidated section 38(c) limitation for Year 3 equals its share of consolidated net income tax minus its share of consolidated tentative minimum tax. Applying the principles of section 1552 and §1.1502-33(d) (taking into account, for example, that T's positive earnings and profits adjustment under §1.1502-33(d) reflects its losses actually absorbed by the group), T's contribution is $(105,000) minus $(40,000), or $(65,000). T's aggregate contribution to the consolidated section 38(c) limitation for Years 2 and 3 is $120,000 + $(65,000), or $55,000. The group may include $55,000 of T's Year 1 unused section 38 credits in its consolidated section 38 tax credit in Year 3.

(e) *Limitation on investment credit carryovers where there has been a consolidated return change of ownership.*—(1) *General rule.*—If a consolidated return change of ownership (as defined in paragraph (g) of §1.1502-1) occurs during the taxable year or an earlier taxable year, the amount which may be included under paragraph (b) of this section in the consolidated investment credit carryovers to the taxable year with respect to the aggregate unused credits attributable to old members of the group (as defined in paragraph (g)(3) of §1.1502-1) arising in taxable years (consolidated or separate) ending on the same day and before the taxable year in which the consolidated return change of ownership occurred shall not exceed the amount determined under subparagraph (2) of this paragraph.

(2) *Computation of limitation.*—The amount referred to in subparagraph (1) of this paragraph

shall be the excess of the consolidated limitation based on the amount of tax for the taxable year, recomputed by including only the items of income, deduction, and foreign tax credit of the old members, over the sum of—

(i) The aggregate investment credits earned by the old members for the taxable year, and

(ii) The aggregate unused investment credits attributable to the old members which may be carried to the taxable year arising in unused credit years ending prior to the particular unused credit year or years.

(3) *Special effective date.*—This paragraph (e) applies only to a consolidated return change of ownership that occurred during a consolidated return year for which the due date of the income tax return (without extensions) is on or before March 13, 1998. See paragraph (d)(4) of this section for an optional effective date rule (generally making the rules of this paragraph (e) also inapplicable if the consolidated return change of ownership occurred on or after January 1, 1997, and during a consolidated return year for which the due date of the income tax return (without extensions) is on or before March 13, 1998).

(f) *Early dispositions, etc., of section 38 property.*—(1) *Dispositions of section 38 property during and after consolidated return year.*—If property is subject to section 47(a)(1) or (2) with respect to a member during a consolidated return year, any increase in tax shall be added to the tax liability of the group under §1.1502-2 (regardless of whether the property was placed in service in a consolidated or separate return year). Also, if property is subject to section 47(a)(1) or (2) with respect to a corporation during a taxable year for which such corporation files on a separate return basis, any increase in tax shall be added to the tax liability of such corporation (regardless of whether such property was placed in service in a consolidated or separate return year).

(2) *Exception for transfer to another member.*—
(i) Except as provided in subdivisions (ii) and
(iii) of this subparagraph, a transfer of section 38
property from one member of the group to another member of such group during a consolidated return year shall not be treated as a
disposition or cessation within the meaning of
section 47(a)(1). If such section 38 property is
disposed of, or otherwise ceases to be section 38
property or becomes public utility property with
respect to the transferee, before the close of the
estimated useful life which was taken into account in computing qualified investment, then
section 47(a)(1) or (2) shall apply to the transferee with respect to such property (determined
by taking into account the period of use, qualified investment, other dispositions, etc., of the
transferor). Any increase in tax due to the application of section 47(a)(1) or (2) shall be added to
the tax liability of such transferee (or the tax
liability of a group, if the transferee joins in the
filing of a consolidated return).

(ii) Except as provided in subdivision (iii)
of this subparagraph, if section 38 property is
disposed of during a consolidated return year by
one member of the group to another member of
such group which is an organization to which
section 593 applies or a cooperative organization
described in section 1381(a), the tax under chapter 1 of the Code for such consolidated return
year shall be increased by an amount equal to
the aggregate decrease in the credits allowed
under section 38 for all prior taxable years which
would result solely from treating such property,
for purposes of determining qualified investment, as placed in service by such organization
to which section 593 applies or such cooperative
organization described in section 1381(a), as the
case may be, but with due regard to the use of
the property before such transfer.

(iii) Section 47(a)(1) shall apply to a transfer of section 38 property by a corporation during a consolidated return year if such
corporation is liquidated in a transaction to
which section 334(b)(2) applies.

(3) *Examples.*—The provisions of this paragraph may be illustrated by the following
examples:

Example (1). P, S, and T file a consolidated
return for calendar year 1967. In such year S
places in service section 38 property having an
estimated useful life of more than 8 years. In
1968, P, S, and T file a consolidated return, and
in such year S sells such property to T. Such sale
will not cause section 47(a)(1) to apply.

Example (2). Assume the same facts as in
example (1), except that P, S, and T filed separate
returns for 1967. The sale from S to T will not
cause section 47(a)(1) to apply.

Example (3). Assume the same facts as in
example (1), except that P, S, and T continue to
file consolidated returns through 1971 and in
such year T disposes of the property to individ-

ual A. Section 47(a)(1) will apply to the group
and any increase in tax shall be added to the tax
liability of the group. For the purposes of determining the actual period of use by T, such period
shall include S's period of use.

Example (4). Assume the same facts as in
example (3), except that T files a separate return
in 1971. Again, the actual periods of use by S and
T will be combined in applying section 47. If the
disposition results in an increase in tax under
section 47(a)(1), such additional tax shall be
added to the separate tax liability of T.

Example (5). Assume the same facts as in
example (1), except that in 1969, P sells all the
stock of T to a third party. Such sale will not
cause section 47(a)(1) to apply.
[Reg. § 1.1502-3.]

☐ [*T.D. 6894, 9-7-66. Amended by T.D. 7246,*
12-29-72; T.D. 8597, 7-12-95; T.D. 8751, 1-9-98;
T.D. 8766, 3-13-98 and T.D. 8884, 5-24-2000 (cor-
rected 8-7-2000).]

[Reg. § 1.1502-4]

§ 1.1502-4. Consolidated foreign tax credit.—
(a) *In general.*—The credit under section 901 for
taxes paid or accrued to any foreign country or
possession of the United States shall be allowed
to the group only if the common parent corporation chooses to use such credit in the computation of the tax liability of the group for the
consolidated return year. If this choice is made,
no deduction may be taken on the consolidated
return for such taxes paid or accrued by any
member of the group. See section 275(a)(4).

(b) *Limitation effective under section 904(a) for*
the group.—(1) *Common parent's limitation effective*
for group.—The determination of whether the
overall limitation or the per-country limitation
applies for a consolidated return year shall be
made by reference to the limitation effective with
respect to the common parent corporation for
such year. If the limitation effective with respect
to a member for its immediately preceding separate return year differs from the limitation effective with respect to the common parent
corporation for the consolidated return year,
then such member shall, if the overall limitation
is effective with respect to the common parent,
be deemed to have made an election to use such
overall limitation, or, if the per-country limitation is effective with respect to the common parent, be deemed to have revoked its election to
use the overall limitation. Consent of the Secretary or his delegate (if otherwise required) is
hereby given to such member for such election
or revocation. Any such election or revocation
shall apply only prospectively beginning with
such consolidated return year.

(2) *Limitation effective for subsequent years.*—
The limitation effective with respect to a member
for the last year for which it joins in the filing of
a consolidated return with a group shall remain

in effect for a subsequent separate return year and may be changed by such corporation for such subsequent year only in accordance with the provisions of section 904(b) (and this paragraph if it joins in the filing of a consolidated return with another group). Any retroactive change in the limitation by the common parent corporation for such member's last consolidated return year shall change the election effective with respect to such member for such last period. Thus, if the common parent (P) elects the overall limitation with respect to calendar year 1966, such election would be effective with respect to its subsidiary S for 1966. If S leaves the group at the beginning of calendar year 1967, such election shall be effective for 1967 with respect to S (unless S revokes such election for 1967 or a subsequent year in accordance with section 904(b), or this paragraph if it joins in the filing of a consolidated return with another group). However, if P retroactively changes back to the per-country limitation with respect to 1966, such limitation would be effective with respect to S for 1966 and subsequent years (unless S elects the overall limitation for any such subsequent year).

(c) *Computation of consolidated foreign tax credit.*—The foreign tax credit for the consolidated return year shall be determined on a consolidated basis under the principles of sections 901 through 905 and section 960. For example, if the per-country limitation applies to the consolidated return year, taxes paid or accrued for such year (including those deemed paid or accrued under sections 902 and 960(a) and paragraph (e) of this section) to each foreign country or possession by the members of the group shall be aggregated. If the overall limitation applies, taxes paid or accrued for such year (including those deemed paid or accrued) to all foreign countries and possessions by members of the group shall be aggregated. If the overall limitation applies and a member of the group qualifies as a Western Hemisphere trade corporation, see section 1503(b).

(d) *Computation of limitation on credit.*—For purposes of computing the group's applicable limitation under section 904(a), the following rules shall apply:

(1) *Computation of taxable income from foreign sources.*—The numerator of the applicable limiting fraction under section 904(a) shall be an amount (not in excess of the amount determined under subparagraph (2) of this paragraph) equal to the aggregate of the separate taxable incomes of the members from sources within each foreign country or possession of the United States (if the per-country limitation is applicable), or from sources without the United States (if the overall limitation is applicable), determined under §1.1502-12, adjusted for the following items

taken into account in the computation of consolidated taxable income:

(i) The portion of the consolidated net operating loss deduction, the consolidated charitable contributions deduction, the consolidated dividends received deduction, and the consolidated section 922 deduction, attributable to such foreign source income;

(ii) Any such foreign source capital gain net income (net capital gain for taxable years beginning before January 1, 1977) (determined without regard to any net capital loss carryover or carryback);

(iii) Any such foreign source net capital loss and section 1231 net loss, reduced by the portion of the consolidated net capital loss attributable to such foreign source loss; and

(iv) The portion of any consolidated net capital loss carryover or carryback attributable to such foreign source income which is absorbed in the taxable year.

(2) *Computation of entire taxable income.*—The denominator of the applicable limiting fraction under section 904(a) (that is, the entire taxable income of the group) shall be the consolidated taxable income of the group computed in accordance with §1.1502-11.

(3) *Computation of tax against which credit is taken.*—The tax against which the limiting fraction under section 904(a) is applied shall be the consolidated tax liability of the group determined under §1.1502-2, but without regard to paragraphs (b), (c), (d), and (j) thereof, and without regard to any credit against such liability.

(e) *Carryover and carryback of unused foreign tax.*—(1) *Allowance of unused foreign tax as consolidated carryover or carryback.*—The aggregate of the consolidated unused foreign tax carryovers and carrybacks to the taxable year, to the extent absorbed for such year under the principles of section 904(d), shall be deemed to be paid or accrued to a foreign country or possession for such year. The consolidated unused foreign tax carryovers and carrybacks to the taxable year shall consist of any consolidated unused foreign tax, plus any unused foreign tax of members for separate return years of such members, which may be carried over or back to the taxable year under the principles of section 904(d) and (e). However, such consolidated carryovers and carrybacks shall not include any consolidated unused foreign taxes apportioned to a corporation for a separate return year pursuant to §1.1502-79(d) and shall be subject to the limitations contained in paragraphs (f) and (g) of this section. A consolidated unused foreign tax is the excess of the foreign taxes paid or accrued by the group (or deemed paid or accrued by the group, other than by reason of section 904(d)) over the applicable limitation for the consolidated return year.

Reg. §1.1502-4(c)

(2) *Absorption rules.*—For purposes of determining the amount, if any, of an unused foreign tax (consolidated or separate) which can be carried to a taxable year (consolidated or separate), the amount of such unused tax which is absorbed in a prior consolidated return year under section 904(d) shall be determined by—

(i) Applying all unused foreign taxes which can be carried to such prior year in the order of the taxable years in which such unused taxes arose, beginning with the taxable year which ends earliest, and

(ii) Applying all such unused taxes which can be carried to such prior year from taxable years ending on the same date on a pro rata basis.

(f) *Limitation on unused foreign tax carryover or carryback from separate return limitation years.*— (1) *General rule.*—In the case of an unused foreign tax of a member of the group arising in a separate return limitation year (as defined in paragraph (f) of § 1.1502-1) of such member, the amount which may be included under paragraph (e) of this section (computed without regard to the limitation contained in paragraph (g) of this section) shall not exceed the amount determined under subparagraph (2) of this paragraph.

(2) *Computation of limitation.*—The amount referred to in subparagraph (1) of this paragraph with respect to a member of the group is the excess, if any, of—

(i) The section 904(a) limitation of the group, minus such limitation recomputed by excluding the items of income and deduction of such member, over

(ii) The sum of (*a*) the foreign taxes paid (or deemed paid, other than be reason of section 904(d)) by such member for the consolidated return year, and (*b*) the unused foreign tax attributable to such member which may be carried to such consolidated return year arising in taxable years ending prior to the particular separate return limitation year.

(3) *Limitation on unused foreign tax credit carryover or carryback from separate return limitation years.*—Paragraphs (f)(1) and (2) of this section do not apply for consolidated return years for which the due date of the income tax return (without extensions) is after March 13, 1998. For consolidated return years for which the due date of the income tax return (without extensions) is after March 13, 1998, a group shall include an unused foreign tax of a member arising in a SRLY without regard to the contribution of the member to consolidated tax liability for the consolidated return year. See also § 1.1502-3(d)(4) for an optional effective date rule (generally making the rules of paragraphs (f)(1) and (2) of this section also inapplicable to a consolidated return year beginning on or after January 1, 1997, if the due date of the income tax return (without ex-

tensions) for such year is on or before March 13, 1998).

(g) *Limitation on unused foreign tax carryover where there has been a consolidated return change of ownership.*—(1) *General rule.*—If a consolidated return change of ownership (as defined in paragraph (g) of § 1.1502-1) occurs during the taxable year or an earlier taxable year, the amount which may be included under paragraph (e) of this section in the consolidated unused foreign tax carryovers to the taxable year with respect to the aggregate unused credits attributable to the old members of the group (as defined in paragraph (g)(3) of § 1.1502-1) arising in taxable years (consolidated or separate) ending on the same day and before the taxable year in which the consolidated return change of ownership occurred shall not exceed the amount determined under subparagraph (2) of this paragraph.

(2) *Computation of limitation.*—The amount referred to in subparagraph (1) of this paragraph shall be the excess of the section 904(a) limitation of the group for the taxable year, recomputed by including only the items of income and deduction of the old members of the group, over the sum of—

(i) The aggregate foreign taxes paid (or deemed paid, other than by reason of section 904(d)) by the old members for the taxable year, and

(ii) The aggregate unused foreign tax attributable to the old members which can be carried to the taxable year arising in taxable years ending prior to the particular unused foreign tax year or years.

(3) *Special effective date for CRCO limitation.*—Paragraphs (g)(1) and (2) of this section apply only to a consolidated return change of ownership that occurred during a consolidated return year for which the due date of the income tax return (without extensions) is on or before March 13, 1998. See also § 1.1502-3(d)(4) for an optional effective date rule (generally making the rules of paragraph (g)(1) and (2) of this section also inapplicable if the consolidated return change of ownership occurred on or after January 1, 1997, and during a consolidated return year for which the due date of the income tax return (without extensions) is on or before March 13, 1998).

(h) *Amount of credit with respect to interest income.*—If any member of the group has interest income described in section 904(f)(2) (for a year for which it filed on a consolidated or separate basis), the group's foreign tax credit with respect to such interest shall be computed separately in accordance with the principles of section 904(f) and this section.

(i) [Reserved]

(j) *Examples.*—The provisions of this section may be illustrated by the following examples:

Example (1). Domestic corporation P is incorporated on January 1, 1966. On that same day it also incorporates domestic corporations S and T, wholly owned subsidiaries. P, S, and T file consolidated returns for 1966 and 1967 on the basis of a calendar year. T engages in business solely in country A. S transacts business solely in countries A and B. P does business solely in the United States. During 1966 T sold an item of inventory to P at a profit of $2,000. Under §1.1502-13 (as contained in the 26 CFR part 1 edition revised as of April 1, 1995) such profit is deferred and none of the circumstances of restoration contained in paragraph (d), (e), or (f) of §1.1502-13 have occurred as of the close of 1966. The taxable income for 1966 from foreign and United States sources, and the foreign taxes paid on such foreign income are as follows:

| Corporation | U.S. Taxable income | Country A | | Country B | | Total Taxable income |
		Taxable income	Foreign tax paid	Taxable income	Foreign tax paid	
P	$40,000	....	....	....	....	$40,000
T	....	$20,000	$12,000	....	....	20,000
S	....	10,000	6,000	$10,000	$3,000	20,000
						$80,000

Such taxable income was computed by taking into account the rules provided in §1.1502-12. Thus, the $2,000 deferred profit is not included in T's taxable income for 1966 (but will be included for the taxable year for which one of the events specified in paragraph (d), (e), or (f) of §1.1502-13 occurs). The consolidated taxable income of the group (computed in accordance with §1.1502-11 is $80,000. The consolidated tax liability against which the credit may be taken (computed in accordance with paragraph (d)(3) of this section) is $31,900.

(i) Assuming P chooses to use the foreign taxes paid as a credit and the group is subject to the per-country limitation, the group may take as a credit against the consolidated tax liability $11,962.50 of the amount paid to country A, plus the $3,000 paid to country B. Such amounts are computed as follows: The aggregate taxes paid to country A of $18,000 is limited to $11,962.50 ($31,900 times $30,000/$80,000). The unused foreign tax with respect to country A is $6,037.50 ($18,000 less $11,962.50), and is a consolidated unused foreign tax which shall be carried to the years prescribed by section 904(d). A credit of $3,000 is available with respect to the taxes paid to country B since such amount is less than the limitation of $3,987.50 ($31,900 times $10,000/$80,000).

(ii) Assuming the overall limitation is in effect for the taxable year, the group may take $15,950 as a credit, computed as follows: The aggregate taxes paid to all foreign countries of $21,000 is limited to $15,950 ($31,900 times $40,000/$80,000). The unused foreign tax is $5,050 ($21,000 less $15,950), and is a consolidated unused foreign tax which shall be carried to the years prescribed by section 904(d).

Example (2). Assume the same facts as in example (1), except that T has a $10,000 long-term capital gain (derived from a sale to a nonmember in country A) and P has a $10,000 long-term capital loss (derived from a sale to a nonmember in the United States). Notwithstanding that the consolidated net capital gain (capital gain net income for taxable years beginning after December 31, 1976) of the group is zero, T's capital gain shall be reflected in full in the computation of taxable income from foreign sources.

Example (3). Assume the same facts as in example (1), except that the group had a consolidated section 172 deduction of $8,000 which is attributable to a net operating loss sustained by T. The $8,000 consolidated net operating loss deduction is offset against T's income from country A, thus reducing T's taxable income from country A to $12,000. [Reg. §1.1502-4.]

☐ [T.D. 6894, 9-7-66. *Amended by* T.D. 7637, 8-6-79; T.D. 7728, 10-31-80; T.D. 8597, 7-12-95; T.D. 8751, 1-9-98; T.D. 8766, 3-13-98 *and* T.D. 8884, 5-24-2000.]

[Reg. §1.1502-5]

§1.1502-5. Estimated tax.—(a) *General rule.*—(1) *Consolidated estimated tax.*—If a group files a consolidated return for two consecutive taxable years, it must make payments of estimated tax on a consolidated basis for each subsequent taxable year, until such time as separate returns are properly filed. Until such time, the group is treated as a single corporation for purposes of section 6154 (relating to payment of estimated tax by corporations). If separate returns are filed by the members for a taxable year, the amount of any estimated tax payments made with respect to a consolidated payment of estimated tax for such year shall be credited against the separate tax liabilities of the members in any manner designated by the common parent which is satisfactory to the Commissioner. The consolidated payments of estimated tax shall be deposited with the authorized financial institution with which the common parent deposits its estimated tax payments. A statement should be attached to the payment setting forth the name, address, employer identification number, and internal revenue service center of each member.

(2) *First two consolidated return years.*—For the first 2 years for which a group files a consolidated return, it may make payments of esti-

mated tax on either a consolidated or separate basis. If a consolidated return is filed for such year, the amount of any estimated tax payments made for such year by any member shall be credited against the tax liability of the group.

(3) *Effective date.*—This section applies to taxable years for which the due date (without extensions) for filing returns is after August 6, 1979. For prior taxable years see 26 CFR § 1.1502-5. (Revised as of April 1, 1978).

(b) *Addition to tax for failure to pay estimated tax under section 6655.*—(1) *Consolidated return filed.*—For the first two taxable years for which a group files a consolidated return, the group may compute the amount of the penalty (if any) under section 6655 on a consolidated basis or separate member basis, regardless of the method of payment. Thereafter, for a taxable year for which the group files a consolidated return, the group must compute the penalty on a consolidated basis.

(2) *Computation of penalty on consolidated basis.*—(i) This paragraph (b)(2) gives the rules for computing the penalty under section 6655 on a consolidated basis.

(ii) The tax and facts shown on the return for the preceding taxable year referred to in section 6655(d)(1) and (2) are, if a consolidated return was filed for that preceding year, such items shown on the consolidated return for that preceding year or, if one was not filed for that preceding year, the aggregate taxes and the facts shown on the separate returns of the common parent and any other corporation that was a member of the same affiliated group as the common parent for that preceding year.

(iii) If estimated tax was not paid on a consolidated basis, then the amount of the group's payments of estimated tax for the taxable year is the aggregate of the payments made by all members for the year.

(iv) Section 6655(d)(1) applies only if the common parent's consolidated return, or each member's separate return, for the preceding taxable year (as the case may be) was a taxable year of 12 months.

(3) *Computation of penalty on separate member basis.*—To compute any penalty under section 6655 on a separate member basis, for purposes of section 6655(b)(1), the "tax shown on the return for the taxable year" is the portion of the tax shown on the consolidated return allocable to the member under paragraph (b)(5) of this section. If the member was included in the consolidated return filed by the group for the preceding taxable year then—

(i) For purposes of section 6655(d)(1), the "tax shown on the return" for any member shall be the portion of the tax shown on the consolidated return for the preceding year allocable to

the member under paragraph (b)(5) of this section.

(ii) For purposes of section 6655(d)(2), the "facts shown on the return" shall be the facts shown on the consolidated return for the preceding year and the tax computed under that section shall be allocated under the rules of paragraph (b)(5) of this section.

(4) *Consolidated payments if separate returns filed.*—If the group does not file a consolidated return for the taxable year, but makes payments of estimated tax on a consolidated basis, for purposes of section 6655(b)(2), the "amount, if any of the installment paid" by any member is an amount apportioned to the member in a manner designated by the common parent that is satisfactory to the Commissioner. If the member was included in the consolidated return filed by the group for the preceding taxable year, the amount of a member's penalty under section 6655 is computed on the separate member basis described in paragraph (b)(3)(i) and (ii) of this section.

(5) *Rules for allocation of consolidated tax liability.*—For purposes of subparagraphs (1) and (2) of this paragraph, the tax shown on a consolidated return shall be allocated to the members of the group under the method which the group has elected pursuant to section 1552 and § 1.1502-33(d)(2).

(c) *Examples.*—The provisions of this section may be illustrated by the following examples:

Example (1). Corporations P and S-1 file a consolidated return for the first time for calendar year 1978. P and S-1 also file consolidated returns for 1979 and 1980. For 1978 and 1979, P and S-1 may make payments of estimated tax on either a separate or consolidated basis. For 1980, however, the group must pay its estimated tax on a consolidated basis. In determining whether P and S-1 come within the exception provided in section 6655(d)(1) for 1980, the "tax shown on the return" is the tax shown on the consolidated return for 1979.

Example (2). Assume the same facts as in example (1). Assume further that corporation S-2 is a member of the group during 1979, and joins in the filing of the consolidated return for such year, but ceases to be a member of the group on September 15, 1980. In determining whether the group (which no longer includes S-2) comes within the exception provided in section 6655(d)(1) for 1980, the "tax shown on the return" is the tax shown on the consolidated return for 1979.

Example (3). Assume the same facts as in example (1). Assume further that corporation S-2 becomes a member of the group on July 1, 1980, and joins in the filing of the consolidated return for 1980. In determining whether the group (which now includes S-2) comes within the exception provided in section 6655(d)(1) for 1980, the "tax shown on the return" is the tax shown on the consolidated return for 1979. Any tax of S-2 for any separate return year is not included as a part of the "tax shown on the return" for purposes of applying section 6655(d)(1).

Example (4). Corporations X and Y filed consolidated returns for the calendar years 1977 and 1978 and separate returns for 1979. In determining whether X or Y comes within the exception provided in section 6655(d)(1) for 1979, the "tax shown on the return" is the amount of tax shown on the consolidated return for 1978 allocable to X and to Y in accordance with paragraph (b)(5) of this section.

(d) *Cross reference.*—For provisions relating to quick refunds of corporate estimated tax payments, see §1.1502-78, and §1.6425-1 through §1.6425-3, of this chapter. [Reg. §1.1502-5.]

□ [*T.D. 6894, 9-7-66. Amended by T.D. 7059, 9-16-70; T.D. 7637, 8-6-79 and T.D. 8952, 6-25-2001.*]

[Reg. §1.1502-6]

§1.1502-6. Liability for tax.—(a) *Several liability of members of group.*—Except as provided in paragraph (b) of this section, the common parent corporation and each subsidiary which was a member of the group during any part of the consolidated return year shall be severally liable for the tax for such year computed in accordance with the regulations under section 1502 prescribed on or before the due date (not including extensions of time) for the filing of the consolidated return for such year.

(b) *Liability of subsidiary after withdrawal.*—If a subsidiary has ceased to be a member of the group and if such cessation resulted from a bona fide sale or exchange of its stock for fair value and occurred prior to the date upon which any deficiency is assessed, the Commissioner may, if he believes that the assessment or collection of the balance of the deficiency will not be jeopardized, make assessment and collection of such deficiency from such former subsidiary in an amount not exceeding the portion of such deficiency which the Commissioner may determine to be allocable to it. If the Commissioner makes assessment and collection of any part of a deficiency from such former subsidiary, then for purposes of any credit or refund of the amount collected from such former subsidiary the agency of the common parent under the provisions of §1.1502-77 shall not apply.

(c) *Effect of intercompany agreements.*—No agreement entered into by one or more members of the group with any other member of such group or with any other person shall in any case have the effect of reducing the liability prescribed under this section. [Reg. §1.1502-6.]

□ [*T.D. 6894, 9-7-66. Amended by T.D. 9002, 6-27-2002.*]

[Reg. §1.1502-9]

§1.1502-9. Consolidated overall foreign losses, separate limitation losses, and overall domestic losses.—[Reserved]. For further guidance, see §1.1502-9T.

□ [*T.D. 8833, 8-10-99. Amended by T.D. 9371, 12-20-2007.*]

[Reg. §1.1502-9T]

§1.1502-9T. Consolidated overall foreign losses, separate limitation losses, and overall domestic losses (temporary).—(a) *In general.*—This section provides rules for applying section 904(f) and (g) (including its definitions and nomenclature) to a group and its members. Generally, section 904(f) concerns rules relating to overall foreign losses (OFLs) and separate limitation losses (SLLs) and the consequences of such losses. Under section 904(f)(5), losses are computed separately in each category of income described in section 904(d)(1) or §1.904-4(m) (separate category). Section 904(g) concerns rules relating to overall domestic losses (ODLs) and the consequences of such losses. Paragraph (b) of this section defines terms and provides computational and accounting rules, including rules regarding recapture. Paragraph (c) of this section provides rules that apply to OFLs, SLLs, and ODLs when a member becomes or ceases to be a member of a group. Paragraph (d) of this section provides a predecessor and successor rule. Paragraph (e) of this section provides effective dates.

(b) *Consolidated application of section 904(f) and (g).*—A group applies section 904(f) and (g) for a consolidated return year in accordance with that section, subject to the following rules:

(1) *Computation of CSLI or CSLL and consolidated U.S.-source taxable income or CDL.*—The group computes its consolidated separate limitation income (CSLI) or consolidated separate limitation loss (CSLL) for each separate category under the principles of §1.1502-11 by aggregating each member's foreign-source taxable income or loss in such separate category computed under the principles of §1.1502-12, and taking into account the foreign portion of the consolidated items described in §1.1502-11(a)(2) through (8) for such separate category. The group computes its consolidated U.S.-source taxable income or consolidated domestic loss (CDL) under similar principles.

(2) *Netting CSLLs, CSLIs, and consolidated U.S.-source taxable income.*—The group applies section 904(f)(5) to determine the extent to which a CSLL for a separate category reduces CSLI for another separate category or consolidated U.S.-source taxable income.

(3) *Netting CDL and CSLI.*—The group applies section 904(g)(2) to determine the extent to which a CDL reduces CSLI.

(4) *CSLL, COFL, and CODL accounts.*—To the extent provided in section 904(f), the amount by which a CSLL for a separate category (the loss category) reduces CSLI for another separate category (the income category) shall result in the creation of (or addition to) a CSLL account for the loss category with respect to the income category. Likewise, the amount by which a CSLL for a loss category reduces consolidated U.S.-source taxable income will create (or add to) a consolidated overall foreign loss account (a COFL account). To the extent provided in section 904(g), the amount by which a CDL reduces CSLI shall result in the creation of (or addition to) a consolidated overall domestic loss (CODL) account for the income category reduced by the CDL.

(5) *Recapture of COFL, CSLL, and CODL accounts.*—In the case of a COFL account for a loss category, section 904(f)(1) and (3) recharacterizes some or all of the foreign-source income in the loss category as U.S.-source income. In the case of a CSLL account for a loss category with respect to an income category, section 904(f)(5)(C) and (F) recharacterizes some or all of the foreign-source income in the loss category as foreign-source income in the income category. In the case of a CODL account, section 904(g)(3) recharacterizes some of the U.S.-source income as foreign-source income in the separate category that was offset by the CDL. The COFL account, CSLL account, or CODL account is reduced to the extent income is recharacterized with respect to such account.

(6) *Intercompany transactions.*— (i) *Nonapplication of section 904(f) disposition rules.*—Neither section 904(f)(3) (in the case of a COFL account) nor section 904(f)(5)(F) (in the case of a CSLL account) applies at the time of a disposition that is an intercompany transaction to which § 1.1502-13 applies. Instead, section 904(f)(3) and (5)(F) applies only at such time and only to the extent that the group is required under § 1.1502-13 (without regard to section 904(f)(3) and (5)(F)) to take into account any intercompany items resulting from the disposition, based on the COFL or CSLL account existing at the end of the consolidated return year during which the group takes the intercompany items into account.

(ii) *Examples.*—Paragraph (b)(6)(i) of this section is illustrated by the following examples. The identity of the parties and the basic assumptions set forth in § 1.1502-13(c)(7)(i) apply to the examples. Except as otherwise stated, assume further that the consolidated group recognizes no foreign-source income other than as a result of the transactions described. The examples are as follows:

Example 1. (i) On June 10, year 1, S transfers nondepreciable property with a basis of $100 and a fair market value of $250 to B in a transaction to which section 351 applies. The property was predominantly used without the United States in a trade or business, within the meaning of section 904(f)(3). B continues to use the property without the United States. The group has a COFL account in the relevant loss category of $120 as of December 31, year 1.

(ii) Because the contribution from S to B is an intercompany transaction, section 904(f)(3) does not apply to result in any gain recognition in year 1. See paragraph (b)(5)(i) of this section.

(iii) On January 10, year 4, B ceases to be a member of the group. Because S did not recognize gain in year 1 under section 351, no gain is taken into account in year 4 under § 1.1502-13. Thus, no portion of the group's COFL account is recaptured in year 4. For rules requiring apportionment of a portion of the COFL account to B, see paragraph (c)(2) of this section.

Example 2. (i) The facts are the same as in paragraph (i) of *Example 1*. On January 10, year 4, B sells the property to X for $300. As of December 31, year 4, the group's COFL account is $40. (The COFL account was reduced between year 1 and year 4 due to unrelated foreign-source income taken into account by the group.)

(ii) B takes into account gain of $200 in year 4. The $40 COFL account in year 4 recharacterizes $40 of the gain as U.S. source. See section 904(f)(3).

Example 3. (i) On June 10, year 1, S sells nondepreciable property with a basis of $100 and a fair market value of $250 to B for $250 cash. The property was predominantly used without the United States in a trade or business, within the meaning of section 904(f)(3). The group has a COFL account in the relevant loss category of $120 as of December 31, year 1. B predominantly uses the property in a trade or business without the United States.

(ii) Because the sale is an intercompany transaction, section 904(f)(3) does not require the group to take into account any gain in year 1. Thus, under paragraph (b)(5)(i) of this section, the COFL account is not reduced in year 1.

(iii) On January 10, year 4, B sells the property to X for $300. As of December 31, year 4, the group's COFL account is $60. (The COFL account was reduced between year 1 and year 4 due to unrelated foreign-source income taken into account by the group.)

(iv) In year 4, S's $150 intercompany gain and B's $50 corresponding gain are taken into account to produce the same effect on consolidated taxable income as if S and B were divisions of a single corporation. See § 1.1502-13(c). All of B's $50 corresponding gain is recharacterized under section 904(f)(3). If S and B were divisions of a single corporation and the intercompany sale were a transfer between the divisions, B would succeed to S's $100 basis in the property and would have $200 of gain ($60 of which would be recharacterized under section 904(f)(3)), instead of a $50 gain. Consequently, S's $150 intercompany gain and B's $50 corre-

Reg. §1.1502-9T(b)(6)(ii)

sponding gain are taken into account, and $10 of S's gain is recharacterized under section 904(f)(3) as U.S. source income to reflect the $10 difference between B's $50 recharacterized gain and the $60 recomputed gain that would have been recharacterized.

(c) *Becoming or ceasing to be a member of a group.*—(1) *Adding separate accounts on becoming a member.*—At the time that a corporation becomes a member of a group (a new member), the group adds to the balance of its COFL, CSLL or CODL account the balance of the new member's corresponding OFL account, SLL account or ODL account. A new member's OFL account corresponds to a COFL account if the account is for the same loss category. A new member's SLL account corresponds to a CSLL account if the account is for the same loss category and with respect to the same income category. A new member's ODL account corresponds to a CODL account if the account is with respect to the same income category. If the group does not have a COFL, CSLL or CODL account corresponding to the new member's account, it creates a COFL, CSLL or CODL account with a balance equal to the balance of the member's account.

(2) *Apportionment of consolidated account to departing member.*—(i) *In general.*—A group apportions to a member that ceases to be a member (a departing member) a portion of each COFL, CSLL and CODL account as of the end of the year during which the member ceases to be a member and after the group makes the additions or reductions to such account required under paragraphs (b)(4), (b)(5) and (c)(1) of this section (other than an addition under paragraph (c)(1) of this section attributable to a member becoming a member after the departing member ceases to be a member). The group computes such portion under paragraph (c)(2)(ii) of this section, as limited by paragraph (c)(2)(iii) of this section. The departing member carries such portion to its first separate return year after it ceases to be a member. Also, the group reduces each account by such portion and carries such reduced amount to its first consolidated return year beginning after the year in which the member ceases to be a member. If two or more members cease to be members in the same year, the group computes the portion allocable to each such member (and reduces its accounts by such portion) in the order that the members cease to be members.

(ii) *Departing member's portion of group's account.*—A departing member's portion of a group's COFL, CSLL or CODL account for a loss category is computed based upon the member's share of the group's assets that generate income subject to recapture at the time that the member ceases to be a member. Under the characterization principles of §§1.861-9T(g)(3) and 1.861-12T, the group identifies the assets of the departing member and the remaining members

that generate U.S.-source income (domestic assets) and foreign-source income (foreign assets) in each separate category. The assets are characterized based upon the income that the assets are reasonably expected to generate after the member ceases to be a member. The member's portion of a group's COFL or CSLL account for a loss category is the group's COFL or CSLL account, respectively, multiplied by a fraction, the numerator of which is the value of the member's foreign assets for the loss category and the denominator of which is the value of the foreign assets of the group (including the departing member) for the loss category. The member's portion of a group's CODL account for each income category is the group's CODL account multiplied by a fraction, the numerator of which is the value of the member's domestic assets and the denominator of which is the value of the domestic assets of the group (including the departing member). The value of the domestic and foreign assets is determined under the asset valuation rules of §1.861-9T(g)(1) and (2) using either tax book value or fair market value under the method chosen by the group for purposes of interest apportionment as provided in §1.861-9T(g)(1)(ii). For purposes of this paragraph (c)(2)(ii), §1.861-9T(g)(2)(iv) (assets in intercompany transactions) shall apply, but §1.861-9T(g)(2)(iii) (adjustments for directly allocated interest) shall not apply. If the group uses the tax book value method, the member's portions of COFL, CSLL, and CODL accounts are limited by paragraph (c)(2)(iii) of this section. In addition, for purposes of this paragraph (c)(2)(ii), the tax book value of assets transferred in intercompany transactions shall be determined without regard to previously deferred gain or loss that is taken into account by the group as a result of the transaction in which the member ceases to be a member. The assets should be valued at the time the member ceases to be a member, but values on other dates may be used unless this creates substantial distortions. For example, if a member ceases to be a member in the middle of the group's consolidated return year, an average of the values of assets at the beginning and end of the year (as provided in §1.861-9T(g)(2)) may be used or, if a member ceases to be a member in the early part of the group's consolidated return year, values at the beginning of the year may be used, unless this creates substantial distortions.

(iii) *Limitation on member's portion for groups using tax book value method.*—If a group uses the tax book value method of valuing assets for purposes of paragraph (c)(2)(ii) of this section and the aggregate of a member's portions of CCFL and CSLL accounts for a loss category (with respect to one or more income categories) determined under paragraph (c)(2)(ii) of this section exceeds 150 percent of the actual fair market value of the member's foreign assets in the loss category, the member's portion of the COFL or

CSLL accounts for the loss category shall be reduced (proportionately, in the case of multiple accounts) by such excess. In addition, if the aggregate of a member's portions of CODL accounts (with respect to one or more income categories) determined under paragraph (c)(2)(ii) of this section exceeds 150 percent of the actual fair market value of the member's domestic assets, the member's portion of the CODL accounts shall be reduced (proportionately, in the case of multiple accounts) by such excess. This rule does not apply in the case of COFL or CSLL accounts if the departing member and all other members that cease to be members as part of the same transaction own all (or substantially all) the foreign assets in the loss category. In the case of CODL accounts, this rule does not apply if the departing member and all other members that cease to be members as part of the same transaction own all (or substantially all) the domestic assets.

(iv) *Determination of values of domestic and foreign assets binding on departing member.*—The group's determination of the value of the member's and the group's domestic and foreign assets for a loss category is binding on the member, unless the Commissioner concludes that the determination is not appropriate. The common parent of the group must attach a statement to the return for the taxable year that the departing member ceases to be a member of the group that sets forth the name and taxpayer identification number of the departing member, the amount of each COFL and CSLL for each loss category and each CODL that is apportioned to the departing member under this paragraph (c)(2), the method used to determine the value of the member's and the group's domestic and foreign assets in each such loss category, and the value of the member's and the group's domestic and foreign assets in each such loss category. The common parent must also furnish a copy of the statement to the departing member.

(v) *Anti-abuse rule.*—If a corporation becomes a member and ceases to be a member, and a principal purpose of the corporation becoming and ceasing to be a member is to transfer the corporation's OFL account, SLL account or ODL account to the group or to transfer the group's COFL, CSLL or CODL account to the corporation, appropriate adjustments will be made to eliminate the benefit of such a transfer of accounts. Similarly, if any member acquires assets or disposes of assets (including a transfer of assets between members of the group and the departing member) with a principal purpose of affecting the apportionment of accounts under paragraph (c)(2)(i) of this section, appropriate adjustments will be made to eliminate the benefit of such acquisition or disposition.

(vi) *Examples.*—The following examples illustrate the rules of this paragraph (c):

Example 1. (i) On November 6, year 1, S, a member of the P group, a consolidated group with a calendar consolidated return year, ceases to be a member of the group. On December 31, year 1, the P group has a $40 COFL account for the general category, a $20 CSLL account for the general category (that is, the loss category) with respect to the passive category (that is, the income category), and a $10 CODL account with respect to the passive category (that is, the income category). No member of the group has foreign-source income or loss in year 1. The group apportions its interest expense according to the tax book value method.

(ii) On November 6, year 1, the group identifies S's assets and the group's assets (including S's assets) expected to produce foreign-source general category income. Use of end-of-the-year values will not create substantial distortions in determining the relative values of S's and the group's relevant assets on November 6, year 1. The group determines that S's relevant assets have a tax book value of $2,000 and a fair market value of $2,200. Also, the group's relevant assets (including S's assets) have a tax book value of $8,000. On November 6, year 1, S has no assets expected to produce U.S. source income.

(iii) Under paragraph (c)(2)(ii) of this section, S takes a $10 COFL account for the general category ($40 × $2000/$8000) and a $5 CSLL account for the general category with respect to the passive category ($20 × $2000/$8000). S does not take any portion of the CODL account. The limitation described in paragraph (c)(2)(iii) of this section does not apply because the aggregate of the COFL and CSLL accounts for the general category that are apportioned to S ($15) is less than 150 percent of the actual fair market value of S's general category foreign assets ($2,200 × 150%).

Example 2. (i) Assume the same facts as in *Example 1,* except that the fair market value of S's general category foreign assets is $4 as of November 6, year 1.

(ii) Under paragraph (c)(2)(iii) of this section, S's COFL and CSLL accounts for the general category must be reduced by $9, which is the excess of $15 (the aggregate amount of the accounts apportioned under paragraph (c)(2)(ii) of this section) over $6 (150 percent of the $4 actual fair market value of S's general category foreign assets). S thus takes a $4 COFL account for the general category ($10 − ($9 × $10/$15)) and a $2 CSLL account for the general category with respect to the passive category ($5 − ($9 × $5/$15)).

Example 3. (i) Assume the same facts as in *Example 1,* except that S also has assets that are expected to produce U.S. source income.

(ii) On November 6, year 1, the group identifies S's assets and the group's assets (including S's assets) expected to produce U.S. source income. Use of end-of-the-year values will not create substantial distortions in deter-

Reg. §1.1502-9T(c)(2)(vi)

mining the relative values of S's and the group's relevant assets on November 6, year 1. The group determines that S's relevant assets have a tax book value of $3,000 and a fair market value of $2,500. Also, the group's relevant assets (including S's assets) have a tax book value of $6,000.

(iii) Under paragraph (c)(2)(ii) of this section, S takes a $5 CODL account ($10 × $3,000/$6,000), in addition to the COFL and CSLL accounts determined in *Example 1*. The limitation described in paragraph (c)(2)(iii) of this section does not apply because the CODL account that is apportioned to S ($5) is less than 150 percent of the actual fair market value of S's U.S. assets ($2,500 × 150%).

(d) *Predecessor and successor.*—A reference to a member includes, as the context may require, a reference to a predecessor or successor of the member. See § 1.1502-1(f).

(e) *Effective/applicability date.*—This section applies to consolidated return years beginning after December 21, 2007. Taxpayers may choose to apply the provisions of this section relating to overall domestic losses to other consolidated return years beginning after December 31, 2006, as well. For rules relating to overall foreign losses and separate limitation losses in consolidated return years beginning on or before December 21, 2007 see 26 CFR 1.1502-9 (revised as of April 1, 2007).

(f) *Expiration date.*—The applicability of this section expires on December 20, 2010. [Temporary Reg. § 1.1502-9T.]

☐ [*T.D.* 9371, 12-20-2007.]

[Reg. § 1.1502-9A]

§ 1.1502-9A. Application of overall foreign loss recapture rules to corporations filing consolidated returns due on or before August 11, 1999.—(a) *Scope.*—(1) *Effective date.*—This section applies only to consolidated return years for which the due date of the income tax return (without extensions) is on or before August 11, 1999.

(2) *In general.*—An affiliated group of corporations filing a consolidated return sustains an overall foreign loss (a consolidated overall foreign loss) in any taxable year in which its gross income from sources without the United States subject to a separate limitation (as defined in § 1.904(f)-1(c)(2)) is exceeded by the sum of the deductions properly allocated and apportioned thereto. However, for taxable years prior to 1983, affiliated groups may have determined their overall foreign losses for income subject to the passive interest limitation, DISC dividend limitation, and general limitation on a combined basis in accordance with the rules in § 1.904(f)-1(c)(1). The rules contained in §§ 1.904(f)-1 through 1.904(f)-6 are applicable to affiliated groups filing

consolidated returns. This section provides special rules for applying those sections to such groups. Paragraph (b) provides rules for additions and subtractions of a portion of overall foreign losses to and from consolidated overall foreign loss accounts. Paragraph (c) requires that separate notional overall foreign loss accounts be kept for each member of the group that contributes to a consolidated overall foreign loss account and provides for allocation of a portion of the group's overall foreign loss account to a member when the member leaves the group prior to recapture of the entire amount of the loss account. These rules are similar to the rules provided in § 1.1502-21(b)(2) (or § 1.1502-79A, as appropriate) concerning the apportionment of consolidated net operating losses to a member who leaves the group. However, the rules differ somewhat because the absorption rule of § 1.1502-21(b)(1) (or § 1.1502-79A, as appropriate) is applied year-by-year, consistently with the sequence rules of section 172(b), and recapture of overall foreign losses is based on overall foreign loss accounts that may consist of losses in more than one year. Paragraph (d) provides rules for recapture of amounts in consolidated overall foreign loss accounts. Paragraph (e) provides special rules pertaining to section 904(f)(3) dispositions between members of a group. Paragraphs (b), (c), and (e) also contain special rules that apply to overall foreign losses that arise in separate return limitation years; the principles therein also apply to overall foreign losses when there has been a consolidated return change of ownership (as defined in § 1.1502-1(g)). See § 1.1502-9T(b)(1)(v) for the rule that ends the separate return limitation year limitation for consolidated return years for which the due date of the income tax return (without extensions) is after March 13, 1998, and § 1.1502-9T(b)(1)(vi) for an election to continue the separate return limitation year limitation for consolidated return years beginning before January 1, 1998. See also § 1.1502-3(d)(4) for an optional effective date rule (generally making the rules of paragraphs (b)(1)(iii) and (iv) of this section inapplicable for a consolidated return year beginning after December 31, 1996, if the due date of the income tax return (without extensions) for such year is on or before March 13, 1998).

(b) *Consolidated overall foreign loss accounts.*—Any group that sustains an overall foreign loss (or acquires a member with a balance in an overall foreign loss account) must establish a consolidated overall foreign loss account for such loss, and amounts shall be added to and subtracted from such account as provided in §§ 1.904(f)-1 through 1.904(f)-6 and this section.

(1) *Additions to the consolidated overall foreign loss accounts.*—(i) *Consolidated overall foreign losses.*—Any consolidated overall foreign loss shall be added to the applicable consolidated

overall foreign loss account for such separate limitation, to the extent that the overall foreign loss has reduced United States source income, in accordance with the rules of §§ 1.904(f)-1 and 1.904(f)-3.

(ii) *Overall foreign losses from separate return years.*—If a corporation joins in the filing of a consolidated return in a taxable year in which such corporation has a balance in an overall foreign loss account from a prior separate return year that is not a separate return limitation year, such balance shall be added to the applicable consolidated overall foreign loss account in such year and treated as a consolidated overall foreign loss incurred in the previous year (and shall therefore be subject to recapture, in accordance with paragraph (d) of this section, beginning in the same year in which it is added to the consolidated overall foreign loss account).

(iii) *Overall foreign losses from separate return limitation years.*—If a corporation joins in the filing of a consolidated return in a taxable year in which such corporation has a balance in an overall foreign loss account from a prior separate return limitation year, such balance shall be added to the applicable consolidated overall foreign loss account in such consolidated return year to the extent of the lesser of the balance in the overall foreign loss account from the separate return limitation year or 50 percent (or such larger percentage as the taxpayer may elect) of the difference between the consolidated foreign source taxable income subject to the same separate limitation (computed in accordance with §§ 1.904(f)-2(b) and 1.1502-4(d)(1) minus such consolidated foreign source taxable income recomputed by excluding the items of income and deduction of such corporation (but not less than zero). The amount added to a consolidated overall foreign loss account in any taxable year under this paragraph (b)(1)(iii) shall be treated as a consolidated overall foreign loss in the previous year (and shall therefore be subject to recapture, in accordance with paragraph (d) of this section, beginning in the same year in which it is added to the consolidated overall foreign loss account).

(iv) *Overall foreign losses that are part of a net operating loss or net capital loss carried over from a separate return limitation year.*—Overall foreign losses that are part of a net operating loss or net capital loss carryover from a separate return limitation year of a member that is absorbed in a consolidated return year shall be treated as though they were added to an overall foreign loss account in a separate return limitation year of such member and will be subject to the limitation on recapture of SRLY losses contained in paragraph (b)(1)(iii) of this section. See paragraph (c)(2) of this section for rules regarding the addition of such losses to the applicable overall foreign loss account of such member.

(v) *Special effective date for SRLY limitation.*—Except as provided in paragraph (b)(1)(vi) of this section, paragraphs (b)(1)(iii) and (iv) of this section apply only to consolidated return years for which the due date of the income tax return (without extensions) is on or before March 13, 1998. For consolidated return years for which the due date of the income tax return (without extensions) is after March 13, 1998, the rules of paragraph (b)(1)(ii) of this section shall apply to overall foreign losses from separate return years that are separate return limitation years. For purposes of applying paragraph (b)(1)(ii) of this section in such years, the group treats a member with a balance in an overall foreign loss account from a separate return limitation year on the first day of the first consolidated return year for which the due date of the income tax return (without extensions) is after March 13, 1998, as a corporation joining the group on such first day. An overall foreign loss that is part of a net operating loss or net capital loss carryover from a separate return limitation year of a member that is absorbed in a consolidated return year for which the due date of the income tax return (without extensions) is after March 13, 1998, shall be added to the appropriate consolidated overall foreign loss account in the year that it is absorbed. For consolidated return years for which the due date of the income tax return (without extensions) is after March 13, 1998, similar principles apply to overall foreign losses when there has been a consolidated return change of ownership (regardless of when the change of ownership occurred). See also § 1.1502-3(d)(4) for an optional effective date rule (generally making this paragraph (b)(1)(v) applicable to a consolidated return year beginning after December 31, 1996, if the due date of the income tax return (without extensions) for such year is on or before March 13, 1998).

(vi) *Election to defer application of special effective date.*—A consolidated group may elect not to apply paragraph (b)(1)(v) of this section to consolidated return years beginning before January 1, 1998. To make this election, a consolidated group must write "Election Pursuant to Notice 98-40" across the top of page 1 of an original or amended tax return for each consolidated return year subject to the election. For the first consolidated return year to which the overall foreign loss provisions of paragraph (b)(1)(v) of this section apply (i.e., the first year beginning on or after January 1, 1998), such consolidated group must write "Notice 98-40 Election in Effect in Prior Years" across the top of page 1 of the consolidated tax return for that year. For purposes of applying paragraph (b)(1)(ii) of this section with respect to such year, any member with a balance in an overall foreign loss account from a separate return limitation year on the first day of such year shall be treated as joining the group on such first day.

Reg. § 1.1502-9A(b)(1)(vi)

(2) *Reductions of the consolidated overall foreign loss accounts.*—(i) *Amounts allocated to members leaving the group.*—When a member leaves the group, each applicable consolidated overall foreign loss account shall be reduced by the amount allocated from such account to such member in accordance with paragraph (c)(3)(i) of this section.

(ii) *Amounts recaptured.*—A consolidated overall foreign loss account shall be reduced by the amount of any overall foreign loss under the same separate limitation that is recaptured from consolidated income in accordance with § 1.904(f)-2.

(c) *Allocation of overall foreign losses among members of an affiliated group.*—(1) *Notional overall foreign loss accounts.*—Separate notional overall foreign loss accounts shall be established for each member of a group that contributes to a consolidated overall foreign loss account. Additions to and reductions of such notional accounts shall be made when additions or reductions are made to consolidated overall foreign loss accounts in accordance with paragraph (b) of this section and § 1.904(f)-1.

(i) *Additions to notional accounts.*—(A) *Consolidated overall foreign losses.*—When a consolidated overall foreign loss is added to a consolidated overall foreign loss account, each member shall add its pro rata share of the amount of such loss to the member's notional overall foreign loss account. A member's pro rata share of a consolidated overall foreign loss for any taxable year is determined by multiplying the consolidated loss by a fraction. The numerator of this fraction is the amount by which the member's separate gross income for the taxable year from sources without the United States subject to the applicable separate limitation is exceeded by the sum of the deductions properly allocated and apportioned thereto (including such member's share of any consolidated net operating loss deduction and consolidated net capital loss carryovers and carrybacks to the taxable year), for each member with such deductions in excess of such income. The denominator of this fraction is the sum of the numerators of this fraction for all such members of the group.

(B) *Overall foreign losses from separate return years and separate return limitation years.*—When an amount from a member's overall foreign loss account from a separate return year or separate return limitation year is added to a consolidated overall foreign loss account in accordance with paragraph (b)(1)(ii) or (iii) of this section, such amount shall also be added to that member's notional overall foreign loss account for such separate limitation.

(ii) *Reductions of notional accounts.*—When a consolidated overall foreign loss account is reduced by recapture, in accordance with para-

graph (b)(2)(ii) of this section, each member of the group shall reduce its notional overall foreign loss account for that separate limitation by its pro rata share of the amount by which the consolidated overall foreign loss account is reduced. A member's pro rata share of the amount by which a consolidated overall foreign loss account is reduced is determined by multiplying the amount recaptured by a fraction, the numerator of which is the amount in such member's notional account under such separate limitation, and the denominator of which is the amount in the consolidated overall foreign loss account under such separate limitation before reduction for the amount recaptured for that taxable year.

(2) *Overall foreign losses that are part of a net operating loss or net capital loss from a separate return limitation year.*—An overall foreign loss that is part of a net operating loss or net capital loss carryover from a separate return limitation year of a member that is absorbed in a consolidated return year shall be treated as an overall foreign loss of such member (rather than the group) and shall be added to such member's separate overall foreign loss account to the extent it reduces United States source income, in accordance with § 1.904(f)-1(d)(5). Such overall foreign losses shall be added to the appropriate consolidated overall foreign loss account in later years in accordance with paragraph (b)(1)(iii) of this section.

(3) *Allocation of a portion of overall foreign loss accounts to a member leaving the group.*—(i) *Consolidated overall foreign losses.*—When a corporation ceases to be a member of an affiliated group filing consolidated returns, a portion of the balance in each applicable consolidated overall foreign loss account shall be allocated to such corporation. The amount allocated to such corporation shall be equal to the amount, if any, in such member's notional overall foreign loss account under the same separate limitation.

(ii) *Overall foreign losses from separate return limitation years.*—When a corporation ceases to be a member of an affiliated group filing consolidated returns, it shall take with it the remaining portion of each separate overall foreign loss account for overall foreign losses from separate return limitation years (including amounts added to such accounts under paragraph (c)(2) of this section).

(d) *Recapture of consolidated overall foreign losses.*—The amount in any consolidated overall foreign loss account shall be recaptured under § § 1.904(f)-1 through 1.904(f)-6 by recharacterizing consolidated foreign source taxable income subject to the separate limitation under which the loss arose as United States source taxable income. For purposes of recapture, consolidated foreign source taxable income subject to the separate limitation under which the loss arose shall be determined in accordance with § § 1.904(f)-2 and 1.1502-4. Amounts in a member's excess loss account that are included in income under § 1.1502-19 shall be subject to recapture to the extent that they are included in consolidated foreign source taxable income subject to the separate limitation under which the loss arose.

(e) *Dispositions of property between members of the same affiliated group during a consolidated return year.*—(1) *In general.*—Except as provided in paragraph (2) with respect to overall foreign losses of a selling member from a separate return limitation year, the rules of § 1.1502-13 with respect to intercompany transactions will apply to dispositions of property to which section 904(f)(3)(A) applies.

(2) *Recapture of overall foreign loss from a separate return limitation year.*—Paragraph (1) will not apply and gain will be recognized to the extent that the selling member has a balance in its overall foreign loss account from a separate return limitation year unless the selling member adds the entire amount of its overall foreign loss account from separate return limitation years to the applicable consolidated overall foreign loss account and treats such amount as an overall foreign loss incurred in the previous year. Such loss shall be subject to recapture, in accordance with paragraph (d) of § 1.1502-9, beginning in the same year in which it is added to the consolidated overall foreign loss account.

(f) *Illustrations.*—The provisions of this section are illustrated by the following examples. All foreign source income or loss in these examples is subject to the general limitation.

Example (1). A, B, and C are the members of an affiliated group of corporations (as defined in section 1504), and all use the calendar year as their taxable year. For 1983, A, B, and C file a consolidated return. ABC has United States source income of $1,000 and foreign source losses (overall foreign loss) of $400. In accordance with paragraph (b)(1)(i) of this section, ABC adds $400 to its consolidated overall foreign loss account at the end of 1983. For 1983, the separate foreign source taxable income (or loss) of A is $400, of B is ($200), and of C is ($600). Under paragraph (c)(1) of this section, B and C must establish separate notional overall foreign loss accounts. Under paragraph (c)(1)(i)(A) of this section, the amount added to each notional account is the pro rata share of the consolidated overall foreign loss of each member contributing to such loss. The pro rata share is determined by multiplying the consolidated loss by the member's proportionate share of the total foreign source losses of all members having such losses. B's foreign source loss is $200 and C's foreign source loss is $600, totaling $800. B must add $400 × 200/800, or $100, to its notional overall foreign loss account. C must add $400 × 600/800, or $300, to its notional overall foreign loss account.

Example (2). The facts are the same as in example (1). In 1984, ABC has consolidated foreign source taxable income of $200. Under paragraph (d) of this section and § 1.904(f)-2, ABC is required to recapture $100 of the amount in its consolidated overall foreign loss account, which reduces that account by $100 under paragraph (b)(2)(ii) of this section. In accordance with paragraph (c)(1)(ii) of this section, B reduces its notional account by $100 × 100/400, or $25, and C reduces its notional account by $100 × 300/400, or $75. At the end of 1984 ABC has $300 in its consolidated overall foreign loss account, B has $75 in its notional account, and C has $225 in its notional account.

Example (3). D and E are members of an affiliated group and file separate returns using the calendar year as their taxable year for 1980. In 1980, D has an overall foreign loss of $200, which it adds to its overall foreign loss account, and E has no overall foreign losses. For 1981, D and E file a consolidated return, and DE must establish a consolidated overall foreign loss account, to which D's overall foreign loss from 1980 is added under paragraph (b)(1)(ii) of this section. D also adds the same amount $200 to its notional account under paragraph (c)(1)(i)(B) of this section. In 1981, DE has consolidated foreign source taxable income of $300. Since the amount added to the consolidated overall foreign loss account in 1981 is treated as a consolidated overall foreign loss from 1980, DE must recapture $150 in 1981 under paragraph (d) of this section and § 1.904(f)-2. DE's consolidated overall foreign loss account is reduced by $150 under paragraph (b)(2)(ii) of this section, and D's notional account is reduced by $150 under paragraph (c)(1)(ii) of this section, leaving balances of $50 in each of those accounts at the end of 1981.

Example (4). F and G are not members of an affiliated group in 1980, and G has an overall foreign loss of $200, which it adds to its overall foreign loss account. F has no overall foreign loss. On January 1, 1981, F acquires G, and FG files a consolidated return for the calendar year 1981. In 1981, F has no foreign source taxable income or loss, and G has $100 of foreign source taxable income. FG's consolidated foreign source taxable income, $100, minus such income without G's items of income and deduction, $0, is $100. Therefore 50% of that amount, $50, of G's overall foreign loss from its 1980 separate return limitation year is added to FG's consolidated overall foreign loss account under paragraph (b)(1)(iii) of this section, and the same amount is added to G's notional account under paragraph (c)(1)(i)(B) of this section. In accordance with paragraph (d) of this section and § 1.904(f)-2, FG must recapture the $50 balance in its consolidated overall foreign loss account in 1981 because the amount added from G's separate return limitation year is treated as a 1980 consolidated overall foreign loss. At the end of 1981, FG has a balance of $0 in its consolidated overall foreign loss account, G has $0 in its notional account, and G also has $150 remaining from its 1980 overall foreign loss that has not yet been added to the consolidated overall foreign loss account.

On January 1, 1982, F sells G and G leaves the affiliated group. Under paragraph (c)(3)(i) of this section, G takes with it the balance in its overall foreign loss account from 1980 (its prior separate return limitation year) that has not been added to the consolidated account. G has $150 of overall foreign loss in its overall foreign loss account. Because the amount in the consolidated overall foreign loss account is zero, no amount from that account is allocated to G.

Example (5). (i) In 1982 corporation H has United States source income of $300 and foreign source losses of $500, resulting in a net operating loss of $200 and a balance in H's overall foreign loss account at the end of 1982 of $300.

(ii) On January 1, 1983, H is acquired by J, and for the calendar year 1983 JH files a consolidated return. JH has consolidated taxable income of $700 in 1983, including a consolidated net operating loss deduction of $100. This net operating loss deduction is $100 of H's $200 net operating loss from 1982 (a separate return limitation year), which is limited by §1.1502-21A(c). For 1983, H has separate taxable income of $100, comprised

Consolidated foreign source taxable income	
Consolidated foreign source taxable income recomputed by excluding H's foreign source income and deductions	
× 50%	
Amount from H's separate return limitation year overall foreign loss account added to the consolidated overall foreign loss account	

This amount is subject to recapture beginning in the same taxable year, as it is treated as a consolidated overall foreign loss incurred in a previous year. Therefore, under paragraph (d) of this section and §1.904(f)-2, JH also recaptures this $100, reducing the consolidated overall foreign loss account to $0. H has $300 remaining in its separate overall foreign loss account at the end of 1984.

(iv) In 1985, H has separate taxable income of $400, comprised of $100 of United States source

Consolidated foreign source taxable income	
Consolidated foreign source taxable income recomputed by excluding H's foreign source income and deductions	

of $100 of United States source taxable income and zero foreign source taxable income, and J has separate taxable income of $700, comprised of $700 of United States source taxable income and zero foreign source taxable income. Under paragraph (c)(2) of this section, H adds $100 to its separate overall foreign loss account, since that amount of its net operating loss has reduced United States source income. H has $400 in its separate overall foreign loss account at the end of 1983, none of which has been added to a consolidated overall foreign loss account.

(iii) In 1984, H has separate taxable income of $400, comprised of $100 of United States source taxable income and $300 of foreign source taxable income. J has separate taxable income of $900, comprised of $700 of United States source taxable income and $200 of foreign source taxable income. JH has consolidated taxable income of $1200, which includes $100 of consolidated net operating loss deduction from H's 1982 net operating loss. Since this net operating loss deduction is allocated to foreign source income, it does not reduce United States source income and will not be added to an overall foreign loss account. Under paragraph (b)(1)(iii) of this section, $100 from H's overall foreign loss is added to the consolidated overall foreign loss account computed as follows:

	$400
	−200
	$200
	$100
	$100

taxable income and $300 of foreign source taxable income. J has separate taxable income of $300 comprised of $600 of United States source taxable income and $300 of foreign source losses. JH has consolidated taxable income of $700, all of which is United States source. Under paragraph (b)(1)(iii) of this section, an additional $150 from H's separate overall foreign loss is added to the consolidated overall foreign loss account, computed as follows:

	$0
	−(300)
	$300

× 50%
Amount from H's separate return
limitation year overall foreign
loss account added to the
consolidated overall foreign
loss account $150

$150

Thus, an additional $150 of H's separate overall foreign loss is added to the consolidated overall foreign loss account, and, under paragraph (c)(1)(i)(B) of this section, the same amount is added to J's notional account. While this amount is subject to recapture beginning in the same taxable year, JH has no consolidated foreign source taxable income in 1985, so no overall foreign loss is recaptured. H has a remaining balance of $150 in its separate return limitation year overall foreign loss account and HJ has $150 in its consolidated overall foreign loss account.

Example (6). A, B, and C are members of an affiliated group of corporations (as defined in section 1504), and all use the calendar year as their taxable year. For 1986, A, B, and C file a consolidated return. A has an overall foreign loss account which arose in a separate return limitation year. The amount in the overall foreign loss account is $2,000. A makes a disposition of all its assets to B on January 1, 1986. The gain on the transfer is $1,500, all of which would be recognized under section 904(f)(3). However, if A adds the total amount of its overall foreign loss from separate return limitation years to ABC's consolidated overall foreign loss account, no gain will be recognized on the transfer until the intercompany gain is taken into account under § 1.1502-13. In the interim, any foreign source gain of the purchasing member (or any other member of the consolidated group) may be used to recapture on a consolidated basis the amount in ABC's consolidated overall foreign loss account. [Reg. § 1.1502-9A.]

☐ [*T.D. 8153, 8-21-87. Amended by T.D. 8597, 7-12-95; T.D. 8677, 6-26-96; T.D. 8751, 1-9-98; T.D. 8766, 3-13-98; T.D. 8800, 12-28-98 and T.D. 8823, 6-25-99. Redesignated and amended by T.D. 8833, 8-10-99. Amended by T.D. 8884, 5-24-2000.*]

[Reg. § 1.1502-11]

§ 1.1502-11. Consolidated taxable income.—
(a) *In general.*—The consolidated taxable income for a consolidated return year shall be determined by taking into account—

(1) The separate taxable income of each member of the group (see § 1.1502-12 for the computation of separate taxable income);

(2) Any consolidated net operating loss deduction (see § 1.1502-21 (or 1.1502-21A, as appropriate) for the computation of the consolidated net operating loss deduction);

(3) Any consolidated capital gain net income (net capital gain for taxable years beginning before January 1, 1977) (see § 1.1502-22 (or 1.1502-22A, as appropriate) for the computation of the consolidated capital gain net income (net

capital gain for taxable years beginning before January 1, 1977));

(4) Any consolidated section 1231 net loss (see § 1.1502-23 (or 1.1502-23A, as appropriate) for the computation of the consolidated section 1231 net loss);

(5) Any consolidated charitable contributions deduction (see § 1.1502-24 for the computation of the consolidated charitable contributions deduction);

(6) Any consolidated section 922 deduction (see § 1.1502-25 for the computation of the consolidated section 922 deduction);

(7) Any consolidated dividends received deduction (see § 1.1502-26 for the computation of the consolidated dividends received deduction); and

(8) Any consolidated section 247 deduction (see § 1.1502-27 for the computation of the consolidated section 247 deduction).

(b) *Elimination of circular stock basis adjustments when there is no excluded COD income.*—(1) *In general.*—If one member (P) disposes of the stock of another member (S), this paragraph (b) limits the use of S's deductions and losses in the year of disposition and the carryback of items to prior years. The purpose of the limitation is to prevent P's income or gain from the disposition of S's stock from increasing the absorption of S's deductions and losses, because the increased absorption would reduce P's basis (or increase its excess loss account) in S's stock under § 1.1502-32 and, in turn, increase P's income or gain. See paragraph (b)(3) of this section for the application of these principles to P's deduction or loss from the disposition of S's stock, and paragraph (b)(4) of this section for the application of these principles to multiple stock dispositions. This paragraph (b) applies only when no member realizes discharge of indebtedness income that is excluded from gross income under section 108(a) (excluded COD income) during the taxable year of the disposition. See paragraph (c) of this section for rules that apply when a member realizes excluded COD income during the taxable year of the disposition. See § 1.1502-19(c) for the definition of disposition.

(2) *Limitation on deductions and losses.*—(i) *Determination of amount of limitation.*—If P disposes of one or more shares of S's stock, the extent to which S's deductions and losses for the tax year of the disposition (and its deductions and losses carried over from prior years) may offset income and gain is subject to limitation. The amount of S's deductions and losses that may offset income and gain is determined by

tentatively computing taxable income (or loss) for the year of disposition (and any prior years to which the deductions or losses may be carried) without taking into account P's income and gain from the disposition.

(ii) *Application of limitation.*—S's deductions and losses offset income and gain only to the extent of the amount determined under paragraph (b)(2)(i) of this section. To the extent S's deductions and losses in the year of disposition cannot offset income or gain because of the limitation under this paragraph (b), the items are carried to other years under the applicable provisions of the Internal Revenue Code and regulations as if they were the only items incurred by S in the year of disposition. For example, to the extent S incurs an operating loss in the year of disposition that is limited, the loss is treated as a separate net operating loss attributable to S arising in that year. The tentative computation does not affect the manner in which S's unlimited deductions and losses are absorbed or the manner in which deductions and losses of other members are absorbed. (If the amount of S's unlimited deductions and losses actually absorbed is less than the amount absorbed in the tentative computation, P's stock basis adjustments under §1.1502-32 reflect only the amounts actually absorbed.)

(iii) *Examples.*—For purposes of the examples in this paragraph (b), unless otherwise stated, P owns all of the only class of S's stock for the entire year, S owns no stock of lower-tier members, the tax year of all persons is the calendar year, all persons use the accrual method of accounting, the facts set forth the only corporate activity, all transactions are between unrelated persons, and tax liabilities are disregarded. The principles of this paragraph (b)(2) are illustrated by the following examples.

Example 1. Limitation on losses with respect to stock gain. (a) P has a $500 basis in S's stock. For Year 1, P has ordinary income of $30 (determined without taking P's gain or loss from the disposition of S's stock into account) and S has an $80 ordinary loss. P sells S's stock for $520 at the close of Year 1.

(b) To determine the amount of the limitation on S's loss under paragraph (b)(2)(i) of this section, and the effect under §1.1502-32(b) of the absorption of S's loss on P's basis in S's stock, P's gain or loss from the disposition of S's stock is not taken into account. The group is tentatively treated as having a consolidated net operating loss of $50 (P's $30 of income minus S's $80 loss). Thus, $50 of S's loss is limited under this paragraph (b).

(c) Because $30 of S's loss is absorbed in the determination of consolidated taxable in-

come under paragraph (b)(2)(ii) of this section, P's basis in S's stock is reduced under §1.1502-32(b) from $500 to $470 immediately before the disposition. Consequently, P recognizes a $50 gain from the sale of S's stock and the group has consolidated taxable income of $50 for Year 1 (P's $30 of ordinary income and $50 gain from the sale of S's stock, less the $30 of S's loss). In addition, S's limited loss of $50 is treated as a separate net operating loss attributable to S and, because S ceases to be a member, the loss is apportioned to S under §1.1502-21 (or §1.1502-79A, as appropriate) and carried to its first separate return year.

Example 2. Carrybacks and carryovers. (a) For Year 1, the P group has consolidated taxable income of $30, and a consolidated net capital loss of $100 ($50 attributable to P and $50 to S). At the beginning of Year 2, P has a $300 basis in S's stock. For Year 2, P has ordinary income of $30, and a $20 capital gain (determined without taking the $100 consolidated net capital loss carryover or P's gain or loss from the disposition of S's stock into account), and S has a $100 ordinary loss. P sells S's stock for $280 at the close of Year 2.

(b) To determine the amount of the limitation under paragraph (b)(2)(i) of this section on S's losses, and the effect of the absorption of S's losses on P's basis in S's stock under §1.1502-32(b), P's gain or loss from the disposition of S's stock is not taken into account. For Year 2, the P group is tentatively treated as having a $70 consolidated net operating loss (S's $100 ordinary loss, less P's $30 of ordinary income). The P group is also treated as having no consolidated net capital gain in Year 2, because P's $20 capital gain is reduced by $20 of the consolidated net capital loss carryover from Year 1 under section 1212(a) (the absorption of which is attributed equally to P and S). In addition, of the $70 consolidated net operating loss, $30 is carried back to Year 1 and offsets P's ordinary income in that year, and $40 is carried forward. Consequently, $40 of S's operating loss from Year 2, and $40 of the consolidated net capital loss carryover from Year 1 attributable to S, are limited under this paragraph (b).

(c) Under paragraph (b)(2)(ii) of this section, the limitation under this paragraph (b) does not affect the absorption of any deductions and losses attributable to P, $60 of S's operating loss from Year 2, and $10 of the consolidated net capital loss from Year 1 attributable to S. Consequently, P's basis in S's stock is reduced under §1.1502-32(b) by $70, from $300 to $230, and P recognizes a $50 gain from the sale of S's stock in Year 2. Thus, the P group is treated as having a $20 unlimited net operating loss that is carried back to Year 1:

Ordinary income:

P	$30
S (excluding the $40 limited loss)	(60)
Sub Total	$(30)

Consolidated net capital gain:

P ($20 + $50 from S stock – $50 from Year 1)	$20
S (–$10 from Year 1)	(10)
Sub Total	$10
Consolidated taxable income	$(20)

(d) Under paragraph (b)(2)(ii) of this section, S's $40 ordinary loss from Year 2 that is limited under this paragraph (b) is treated as a separate net operating loss arising in Year 2. Similarly, $40 of the consolidated net capital loss from Year 1 attributable to S is treated as a separate net capital loss carried over from Year 1. Because S ceases to be a member, the $40 net operating loss from Year 2 and the $40 consolidated net capital loss from Year 1 are allocated to S under §§ 1.1502-21 and 1.1502-22, respectively (or § 1.1502-79A, as appropriate) and are carried to S's first separate return year.

Example 3. Allocation of basis adjustments. (a) For Year 1, the P group has consolidated taxable income of $100. At the beginning of Year 2, P has a $40 basis in each of the 10 shares of S's stock. For Year 2, P has an $80 ordinary loss (determined without taking into account P's gain or loss from the disposition of S's stock) and S has an $80 ordinary loss. P sells 2 shares of S's stock for $85 each at the close of Year 2.

(b) Under paragraph (b)(2)(i) of this section, the amount of the limitation on S's loss is determined by tentatively treating the P group as having a $160 consolidated net operating loss for Year 2. Of this amount, $100 is carried back under section 172 and absorbed in Year 1 ($50 attributable to S and $50 attributable to P). Consequently, $30 of S's loss is limited under this paragraph (b).

(c) Under paragraph (b)(2)(ii) of this section, the limitation under this paragraph (b) does not affect the absorption of P's $80 ordinary loss or $50 of S's ordinary loss. Consequently, P's basis in each share of S's stock is reduced from $40 to $35 under § 1.1502-32(b), and P recognizes a $100 gain from the sale of the 2 shares. Thus, the P group is treated as having a $30 unlimited net operating loss:

Ordinary loss:

P	$(80)
S (excluding the $30 limited loss)	(50)
Sub Total	$(130)

Consolidated net capital gain:

P	$100
S	0
Sub Total	$100
Unlimited consolidated net operating loss	$(30)

(d) A portion of the $130 of unlimited operating losses for Year 2 is fully absorbed in that year, and a portion is carried back to Year 1. Thus, $61.50 of P's $80 loss ($100 multiplied by $80/$130) and $38.50 of S's $50 unlimited loss ($100 multiplied by $50/$130) are absorbed in Year 2. P's remaining $18.50 of loss and S's remaining $11.50 of loss are not subject to limitation and are carried back and absorbed in Year 1.

(e) Under paragraph (b)(2)(ii) of this section, S's $30 limited under this paragraph (b) is treated as a separate net operating loss.

(3) *Loss dispositions.*—(i) *General rule.*—The principles of paragraph (b)(2) of this section apply to the extent necessary to carry out the purposes of paragraph (b)(1) of this section if P recognizes a deduction or loss from the disposition of S's stock.

(ii) *Example.*—The principles of this paragraph (b)(3) are illustrated by the following example.

Example. (a) P has a $400 basis in S's stock. For Year 1, P has a capital gain of $100 (determined without taking P's gain or loss from the disposition of S's stock into account) and S has both a $60 capital loss and a $200 ordinary loss. P sells S's stock for $140 at the close of Year 1.

(b) Under paragraph (b)(3) of this section, the amount of S's ordinary and capital losses that may offset income and gain is determined by tentatively computing the group's consolidated net operating loss and consolidated net capital loss without taking into account P's loss from the disposition of S's stock. The limitation is necessary to prevent P's loss from the disposition of S's stock from affecting the absorption of S's losses and thereby the adjustments to P's basis in S's stock under § 1.1502-32(b) (which would, in turn, affect P's loss).

(c) Under the principles of paragraph (b)(2)(i) of this section, the amount of the limitation on S's loss is determined by tentatively treating the P group as having a $40 consolidated net capital gain and a $200 ordinary loss, which results in a $160 consolidated net operating loss for Year 1, all of which is attributable to S. Thus, $160 of S's ordinary loss is limited under this paragraph (b). See also §§ 1.337(d)-2, 1.1502-35, and 1.1502-36 for rules relating to basis adjustments and allowance of stock loss on dispositions of stock of a subsidiary member.

(4) *Multiple dispositions.*—(i) *Stock of a member.*—To the extent income, gain, deduction, or loss from a prior disposition of S's stock is deferred under any rule of law, the limitation under paragraph (b)(2) of this section is determined by treating the year the deferred amount is taken into account as the year of the disposition.

(ii) *Stock of different members.*—If S is a higher-tier corporation with respect to another member (T), and all of T's items of income, gain, deduction, and loss (including the absorption of T's deduction or loss) would be fully reflected in P's basis in S's stock under § 1.1502-32, the limitation under paragraph (b)(2)(i) of this section with respect to T's deductions and losses is determined without taking into account any income, gain, deduction, or loss from the disposition of the stock of S or T (or of the stock of members owned in the chain connecting S and T). However, this paragraph (b) does not otherwise limit the absorption of one member's deduction or loss with respect to the disposition of another member's stock.

(iii) *Examples.*—The principles of this paragraph (b)(4) are illustrated by the following examples.

Example 1. Chain of subsidiaries. (a) P owns all of S's stock with a $500 basis, and S owns all of T's stock with a $500 basis. For Year 1, P has ordinary income of $30, S has no income or loss, and T has an $80 ordinary loss. P sells S's stock for $520 at the close of Year 1.

(b) Under paragraph (b)(4) of this section, to determine the amount of the limitation under paragraph (b) of this section on T's loss, and the effect of the absorption of T's loss on P's basis in S's stock under § 1.1502-32(b), P's gain or loss from the disposition of S's stock is not taken into account. The group is tentatively treated as having a consolidated net operating loss of $50 (P's $30 of income minus T's $80 loss). Because only $30 of T's loss offsets income or gain, P's basis in S's stock is reduced under § 1.1502-32(b) from $500 to $470 immediately before the disposition of S's stock. Thus, P takes into account a $50 gain from the sale of S's stock.

(c) The facts are the same as in paragraph (a) of this *Example 1*, except that S has a $10 excess loss account in T's stock (rather than a $500 basis). Under paragraph (b)(4) of this section, neither P's gain or loss from the disposition of S's stock nor S's gain or loss from the disposition of T's stock (under § 1.1502-19) are taken into account for purposes of the tentative computations and the effect of any absorption under § 1.1502-32(b) on P's basis in S's stock and S's excess loss account in T's stock. The group is tentatively treated as having a consolidated net operating loss of $50 (P's $30 of income minus

T's $80 loss), and only $30 of T's loss may offset the group's income or gain. Under § 1.1502-32(b), the absorption of $30 of T's loss increases S's excess loss account in T's stock to $40 and, under § 1.1502-19, the excess loss account is taken into account. Moreover, under § 1.1502-32(b), P's basis in S's stock is increased immediately before the sale by $10 (S's $40 gain under § 1.1502-19(b) minus T's $30 loss absorbed and tiered up under § 1.1502-32(b)), from $500 to $510. Thus, P takes into account a $10 gain from the sale of S's stock, and S takes into account a $40 gain from its excess loss account in T's stock.

Example 2. Brother-sister subsidiaries. (a) P owns all of the stock of S1 and S2, each with a $50 basis. For Year 1, the group has a $100 consolidated net operating loss ($50 of which is attributable to S1, and $50 to S2) determined without taking gain or loss from the disposition of member stock into account. At the close of Year 1, P sells the stock of S1 and S2 for $100 each.

(b) Paragraph (b)(4) of this section does not limit the loss of S1 or S2 with respect to the disposition of stock of the other. Consequently, each subsidiary's loss may offset P's gain from the disposition of the stock of the other subsidiary. Because this absorption results in a $50 reduction in P's basis in the stock of each subsidiary under § 1.1502-32(b), P's aggregate gain from the stock dispositions is increased from $100 to $200, $100 of which is offset by the losses of the subsidiaries.

(5) *Effective date.*—This paragraph (b) applies to stock dispositions occurring in consolidated return years beginning on or after January 1, 1995. For prior years, see § 1.1502-11(b) as contained in the 26 CFR part 1 edition revised as of April 1, 1994.

(c) *Elimination of circular stock basis adjustments when there is excluded COD income.*—(1) *In general.*—If one member (P) disposes of the stock of another member (S) in a year during which any member realizes excluded COD income, this paragraph (c) limits the use of S's deductions and losses in the year of disposition and the carryback of items to prior years, the amount of the attributes of certain members that can be reduced in respect of excluded COD income of certain other members, and the attributes that can be used to offset an excess loss account taken into account by reason of the application of § 1.1502-19(c)(1)(iii)(B). In addition to the purpose set forth in paragraph (b)(1) of this section, the purpose of these limitations is to prevent the reduction of tax attributes in respect of excluded COD income from affecting P's income, gain, or loss on the disposition of S stock (including a disposition of S stock that results from the application of § 1.1502-19(c)(1)(iii)(B)) and, in turn, affecting the attributes available for reduction pursuant to sections 108 and 1017 and

§ 1.1502-28. See § 1.1502-19(c) for the definition of disposition.

(2) *Computation of tax liability, reduction of attributes, and computation of limits on absorption and reduction of attributes.*—If a member realizes excluded COD income in the taxable year during which P disposes of S stock, the steps used to compute tax liability, to effect the reduction of attributes, and to compute the limitations on the absorption and reduction of attributes are as follows. These steps also apply to determine whether and to what extent an excess loss account must be taken into account as a result of the application of § 1.1502-19(b)(1) and (c)(1)(iii)(B).

(i) *Limitation on deductions and losses to offset income or gain.*—First, the determination of the extent to which S's deductions and losses for the tax year of the disposition (and its deductions and losses carried over from prior years) may offset income and gain is made pursuant to paragraphs (b)(2) and (3) of this section.

(ii) *Tentative adjustment of stock basis.*—Second, § 1.1502-32 is tentatively applied to adjust the basis of the S stock to reflect the amount of S's income and gain included, and unlimited deductions and losses that are absorbed, in the tentative computation of taxable income or loss for the year of the disposition (and any prior years) that is made pursuant to paragraph (b)(2) of this section, but not to reflect the realization of excluded COD income and the reduction of attributes in respect thereof.

(iii) *Tentative computation of stock gain or loss.*—Third, in the case of a disposition of S stock that does not result from the application of § 1.1502-19(c)(1)(iii)(B), P's income, gain, or loss from the disposition of S stock is computed. For this purpose, the result of the computation pursuant to paragraph (c)(2)(ii) of this section is treated as the basis of such stock.

(iv) *Tentative computation of tax imposed.*—Fourth, the tax imposed by chapter 1 of the Internal Revenue Code for the year of disposition (and any prior years) is tentatively computed. For this purpose, in the case of a disposition of S stock that does not result from the application of § 1.1502-19(c)(1)(iii)(B), the tentative computation of tax imposed takes into account P's income, gain, or loss from the disposition of S stock computed pursuant to paragraph (c)(2)(iii) of this section. The tentative computation of tax imposed is made without regard to whether all or a portion of an excess loss account in a share of S stock is required to be taken into account pursuant to § 1.1502-19(b)(1) and (c)(1)(iii)(B).

(v) *Tentative reduction of attributes.*—Fifth, the rules of sections 108 and 1017 and § 1.1502-28 are tentatively applied to reduce the attributes

remaining after the tentative computation of tax imposed pursuant to paragraph (c)(2)(iv) of this section.

(vi) *Actual adjustment of stock basis.*—Sixth, § 1.1502-32 is applied to reflect the amount of S's income and gain included, and unlimited deductions and losses that are absorbed, in the tentative computation of tax imposed for the year of the disposition (and any prior years) made pursuant to paragraph (c)(2)(iv) of this section, and the excluded COD income applied to reduce attributes and the attributes tentatively reduced in respect of the excluded COD income pursuant to paragraph (c)(2)(v) of this section.

(vii) *Actual computation of stock gain or loss.*—Seventh, the group's actual gain or loss on the disposition of S stock (including a disposition that results from the application of § 1.1502-19(c)(1)(iii)(B)) is computed. The result of the computation pursuant to paragraph (c)(2)(vi) of this section is treated as the basis of such stock.

(viii) *Actual computation of tax imposed.*—Eighth, the tax imposed by chapter 1 of the Internal Revenue Code for the year of the disposition (and any prior years) is computed. The actual tax imposed on the group for the year of the disposition is computed by applying the limitation computed pursuant to paragraph (c)(2)(i) of this section, and by including the gain or loss recognized on the disposition of S stock computed pursuant to paragraph (c)(2)(vii) of this section. However, attributes that were tentatively used in the computation of tax imposed pursuant to paragraph (c)(2)(iv) of this section and attributes that were tentatively reduced pursuant to paragraph (c)(2)(v) of this section cannot offset any excess loss account taken into account as a result of the application of § 1.1502-19(b)(1) and (c)(1)(iii)(B).

(ix) *Actual reduction of attributes.*—Ninth, the rules of sections 108 and 1017 and § 1.1502-28 are actually applied to reduce the attributes remaining after the actual computation of tax imposed pursuant to paragraph (c)(2)(viii) of this section.

(A) *S or a lower-tier corporation realizes excluded COD income.*—If S or a lower-tier corporation of S realizes excluded COD income, the aggregate amount of excluded COD income that is applied to reduce attributes attributable to members other than S and any lower-tier corporation of S pursuant to this paragraph (c)(2)(ix) shall not exceed the aggregate amount of excluded COD income that was tentatively applied to reduce attributes attributable to members other than S and any lower-tier corporation of S pursuant to paragraph (c)(2)(v) of this section. The amount of the actual reduction of attributes attributable to S and any lower-tier corporation of S that may be reduced in respect of the excluded COD income of S or a lower-tier corporation of S shall not be so limited.

(B) *A member other than S or a lower-tier corporation realizes excluded COD income.*—If a member other than S or a lower-tier corporation of S realizes excluded COD income, the aggregate amount of excluded COD income that is applied to reduce attributes (other than credits) attributable to S and any lower-tier corporation of S pursuant to this paragraph (c)(2)(ix) shall not exceed the aggregate amount of excluded COD income that was tentatively applied to reduce attributes (other than credits) attributable to S and any lower-tier corporation of S pursuant to paragraph (c)(2)(v) of this section. The amount of the actual reduction of attributes attributable to any member other than S and any lower-tier corporation of S that may be reduced in respect of the excluded COD income of S or a lower-tier corporation of S shall not be so limited.

(3) *Special rules.*—(i) If the reduction of attributes attributable to a member is prevented as a result of a limitation described in paragraph (c)(2)(ix)(B) of this section, the excluded COD income that would have otherwise been applied to reduce such attributes is applied to reduce the remaining attributes of the same type that are available for reduction under § 1.1502-28(a)(4), on a pro rata basis, prior to reducing attributes of a different type. The reduction of such remaining attributes, however, is subject to any applicable limitation described in paragraph (c)(2)(ix)(B) of this section.

(ii) To the extent S's deductions and losses in the year of disposition (or those of a lower-tier corporation of S) cannot offset income or gain because of the limitation under paragraph (b) of this section or this paragraph (c) and are not reduced pursuant to sections 108 and 1017 and § 1.1502-28, such items are carried to other years under the applicable provisions of the Internal Revenue Code and regulations as if they were the only items incurred by S (or a lower-tier corporation of S) in the year of disposition. For example, to the extent S incurs an operating loss in the year of disposition that is limited and is not reduced pursuant to section 108 and § 1.1502-28, the loss is treated as a separate net operating loss attributable to S arising in that year.

(4) *Definition of lower-tier corporation.*—A corporation is a lower-tier corporation of S if all of its items of income, gain, deduction, and loss (including the absorption of deduction or loss and the reduction of attributes other than credits) would be fully reflected in P's basis in S's stock under § 1.1502-32.

(5) *Examples.*—For purposes of the examples in this paragraph (c), unless otherwise stated, the tax year of all persons is the calendar year, all persons use the accrual method of accounting, the facts set forth the only corporate

activity, all transactions are between unrelated persons, tax liabilities are disregarded, and no election under section 108(b)(5) is made. The principles of this paragraph (c) are illustrated by the following examples:

Example 1. Departing member realizes excluded COD income. (i) *Facts.* P owns all of S's stock with a $90 basis. For Year 1, P has ordinary income of $30, and S has an $80 ordinary loss and $100 of excluded COD income from the discharge of non-intercompany indebtedness. P sells the S stock for $20 at the close of Year 1. As of the beginning of Year 2, S has Asset A with a basis of $0 and a fair market value of $20.

(ii) *Analysis.* The steps used to compute the tax imposed on the group, to effect the reduction of attributes, and to compute the limitations on the use and reduction of attributes are as follows:

(A) *Computation of limitation on deductions and losses to offset income or gain.* To determine the amount of the limitation under paragraph (c)(2)(i) of this section on S's loss and the effect of the absorption of S's loss on P's basis in S's stock under § 1.1502-32(b), P's gain or loss from the disposition of S's stock is not taken into account. The group is tentatively treated as having a consolidated net operating loss of $50 (P's $30 of income minus S's $80 loss). Thus, $30 of S's loss is unlimited and $50 of S's loss is limited under paragraph (c)(2)(i) of this section. Under the principles of § 1.1502-21(b)(2)(iv), all of the consolidated net operating loss is attributable to S.

(B) *Tentative adjustment of stock basis.* Then, pursuant to paragraph (c)(2)(ii) of this section, § 1.1502-32 is tentatively applied to adjust the basis of S stock. For this purpose, however, adjustments attributable to the excluded COD income and the reduction of attributes in respect thereof are not taken into account. Under § 1.1502-32(b), the absorption of $30 of S's loss decreases P's basis in S's stock by $30 to $60.

(C) *Tentative computation of stock gain or loss.* Then, P's income, gain, or loss from the sale of S stock is computed pursuant to paragraph (c)(2)(iii) of this section using the basis computed in the previous step. Thus, P is treated as recognizing a $40 loss from the sale of S stock.

(D) *Tentative computation of tax imposed.* Pursuant to paragraph (c)(2)(iv) of this section, the tax imposed for the year of disposition is then tentatively computed, taking into account P's $40 loss on the sale of the S stock computed pursuant to paragraph (c)(2)(iii) of this section. The group has a $50 consolidated net operating loss for Year 1 that, under the principles of § 1.1502-21(b)(2)(iv), is wholly attributable to S and a consolidated capital loss of $40 that, under the principles of § 1.1502-21(b)(2)(iv), is wholly attributable to P.

(E) *Tentative reduction of attributes.* Next, pursuant to paragraph (c)(2)(v) of this section, the rules of sections 108 and 1017 and § 1.1502-28 are tentatively applied to reduce attributes remaining after the tentative computation of the tax imposed. Pursuant to §1.1502-28(a)(2), the tax attributes attributable to S would first be reduced to take into account its $100 of excluded COD income. Accordingly, the consolidated net operating loss for Year 1 would be reduced by $50, the portion of that consolidated net operating loss attributable to S under the principles of §1.1502-21(b)(2)(iv), to $0. Then, pursuant to §1.1502-28(a)(4), S's remaining $50 of excluded COD income would reduce the consolidated capital loss attributable to P of $40 by $40 to $0. The remaining $10 of excluded COD income would have no effect.

(F) *Actual adjustment of stock basis.* Pursuant to paragraph (c)(2)(vi) of this section, §1.1502-32 is applied to reflect the amount of S's income and gain included, and unlimited deductions and losses that are absorbed, in the tentative computation of the tax imposed for the year of the disposition and the excluded COD income tentatively applied to reduce attributes and the attributes reduced in respect of the excluded COD income pursuant to the previous step. Under §1.1502-32(b), the absorption of $30 of S's loss, the application of $90 of S's excluded COD income to reduce attributes of P and S, and the reduction of the $50 loss attributable to S in respect of the excluded COD income results in a positive adjustment of $10 to P's basis in the S stock. P's basis in the S stock, therefore, is $100.

(G) *Actual computation of stock gain or loss.* Pursuant to paragraph (c)(2)(vii) of this section, P's actual gain or loss on the sale of the S stock is computed using the basis computed in the previous step. Accordingly, P recognizes an $80 loss on the disposition of the S stock.

(H) *Actual computation of tax imposed.* Pursuant to paragraph (c)(2)(viii) of this section, the tax imposed is computed by taking into account P's $80 loss from the sale of S stock. Before the application of §1.1502-28, therefore, the group has a consolidated net operating loss of $50 that is wholly attributable to S under the principles of §1.1502-21(b)(2)(iv), and a consolidated capital loss of $80 that is wholly attributable to P under the principles of §1.1502-21(b)(2)(iv).

(I) *Actual reduction of attributes.* Pursuant to paragraph (c)(2)(ix) of this section, sections 108 and 1017 and §1.1502-28 are then actually applied to reduce attributes remaining after the actual computation of the tax imposed. Pursuant to §1.1502-28(a)(2), the tax attributes attributable to S must first be reduced to take into account its $100 of excluded COD income. Accordingly, the consolidated net operating loss for Year 1 is reduced by $50, the portion of that consolidated net operating loss attributable to S under the principles of §1.1502-21(b)(2)(iv), to $0. Then, pursuant to §1.1502-28(a)(4), S's remaining $50 of excluded COD income reduces consolidated tax attributes. In particular, without regard to the limitation imposed by paragraph (c)(2)(ix)(A) of this section, the $80 consolidated capital loss, which under the principles of

§1.1502-21(b)(2)(iv) is attributable to P, would be reduced by $50 from $80 to $30. However, the limitation imposed by paragraph (c)(2)(ix)(A) of this section prevents the reduction of the consolidated capital loss attributable to P by more than $40. Therefore, the consolidated capital loss attributable to P is reduced by only $40 in respect of S's excluded COD income. The remaining $10 of excluded COD income has no effect.

Example 2. Member other than departing member realizes excluded COD income. (i) *Facts.* P owns all of S1's and S2's stock. P's basis in S2's stock is $600. For Year 1, P has ordinary income of $30, S1 has a $100 ordinary loss and $100 of excluded COD income from the discharge of non-intercompany indebtedness, and S2 has $200 of ordinary loss. P sells the S2 stock for $600 at the close of Year 1. As of the beginning of Year 2, S1 has Asset A with a basis of $0 and a fair market value of $10.

(ii) *Analysis.* The steps used to compute the tax imposed on the group, to effect the reduction of attributes, and to compute the limitations on the use and reduction of attributes are as follows:

(A) *Computation of limitation on deductions and losses to offset income or gain.* To determine the amount of the limitation under paragraph (c)(2)(i) of this section on S2's loss and the effect of the absorption of S2's loss on P's basis in S2's stock under §1.1502-32(b), P's gain or loss from the sale of S2's stock is not taken into account. The group is tentatively treated as having a consolidated net operating loss of $270 (P's $30 of income minus S1's $100 loss and S2's $200 loss). Consequently, $20 of S2's loss from Year 1 is unlimited and $180 of S2's loss from Year 1 is limited under paragraph (c)(2)(i) of this section. Under the principles of §1.1502-21(b)(2)(iv), $90 of the consolidated net operating loss is attributable to S1 and $180 of the consolidated net operating loss is attributable to S2.

(B) *Tentative adjustment of stock basis.* Then, pursuant to paragraph (c)(2)(ii) of this section, §1.1502-32 is tentatively applied to adjust the basis of S2's stock. For this purpose, however, adjustments to the basis of S2's stock attributable to the reduction of attributes in respect of S1's excluded COD income are not taken into account. Under §1.1502-32(b), the absorption of $20 of S2's loss decreases P's basis in S2's stock by $20 to $580.

(C) *Tentative computation of stock gain or loss.* Then, P's income, gain, or loss from the disposition of S2 stock is computed pursuant to paragraph (c)(2)(iii) of this section using the basis computed in the previous step. Thus, P is treated as recognizing a $20 gain from the sale of the S2 stock.

(D) *Tentative computation of tax imposed.* Pursuant to paragraph (c)(2)(iv) of this section, the tax imposed for the year of disposition is then tentatively computed, taking into account P's $20 gain from the sale of S2 stock computed pursuant to paragraph (c)(2)(iii) of this section.

Reg. §1.1502-11(c)(5)

Although S2's limited loss cannot be used to offset P's $20 gain from the sale of S2's stock under the rules of this section, S1's loss will offset that gain. Therefore, the group is tentatively treated as having a consolidated net operating loss of $250, $70 of which is attributable to S1 and $180 of which is attributable to S2 under the principles of § 1.1502-21(b)(2)(iv).

(E) *Tentative reduction of attributes.* Next, pursuant to paragraph (c)(2)(v) of this section, the rules of sections 108 and 1017 and § 1.1502-28 are tentatively applied to reduce attributes remaining after the tentative computation of the tax imposed. Pursuant to § 1.1502-28(a)(2), the tax attributes attributable to S1 would first be reduced to take into account its $100 of excluded COD income. Accordingly, the consolidated net operating loss for Year 1 would be reduced by $70, the portion of that consolidated net operating loss attributable to S1 under the principles of § 1.1502-21(b)(2)(iv), to $0. Then, pursuant to § 1.1502-28(a)(4), S1's remaining $30 of excluded COD income would reduce the consolidated net operating loss for Year 1 attributable to S2 of $180 by $30 to $150.

(F) *Actual adjustment of stock basis.* Pursuant to paragraph (c)(2)(vi) of this section, § 1.1502-32 is applied to reflect the amount of S2's income and gain included, and unlimited deductions and losses that are absorbed, in the tentative computation of the tax imposed for the year of the disposition and the excluded COD income tentatively applied to reduce attributes and the attributes reduced in respect of the excluded COD income pursuant to the previous step. Under § 1.1502-32(b), the absorption of $20 of S2's loss to offset a portion of P's income and the application of $30 of S1's excluded COD income to reduce attributes attributable to S2 results in a negative adjustment of $50 to P's basis in the S2 stock. P's basis in the S2 stock, therefore, is $550.

(G) *Actual computation of stock gain or loss.* Pursuant to paragraph (c)(2)(vii) of this section, P's actual gain or loss on the sale of the S2 stock is computed using the basis computed in the previous step. Therefore, P recognizes a $50 gain on the disposition of the S2 stock.

(H) *Actual computation of tax imposed.* Pursuant to paragraph (c)(2)(viii) of this section, the tax imposed is computed by taking into account P's $50 gain from the disposition of the S2 stock. Before the application of § 1.1502-28, therefore, the group has a consolidated net operating loss of $220, $40 of which is attributable to S1 and $180 of which is attributable to S2 under the principles of § 1.1502-21(b)(2)(iv).

(I) *Actual reduction of attributes.* Pursuant to paragraph (c)(2)(ix) of this section, sections 108 and 1017 and § 1.1502-28 are then actually applied to reduce attributes remaining after the actual computation of the tax imposed. Pursuant to § 1.1502-28(a)(2), the tax attributes attributable to S1 must first be reduced to take into account its $100 of excluded COD income. Accordingly,

the consolidated net operating loss for Year 1 is reduced by $40, the portion of that consolidated net operating loss attributable to S1 under the principles of § 1.1502-21(b)(2)(iv), to $0. Then, pursuant to § 1.1502-28(a)(4), without regard to the limitation imposed by paragraph (c)(2)(ix)(B) of this section, S1's remaining $60 of excluded COD income would reduce S2's net operating loss of $180 to $120. However, the limitation imposed by paragraph (c)(2)(ix)(B) of this section prevents the reduction of S2's loss by more than $30. Therefore, S2's loss of $180 is reduced by $30 to $150 in respect of S1's excluded COD income. The remaining $30 of excluded COD income has no effect.

Example 3. Lower-tier corporation of departing member realizes excluded COD income. (i) *Facts.* P owns all of S1's stock, S2's stock, and S3's stock. S1 owns all of S4's stock. P's basis in S1's stock is $50 and S1's basis in S4's stock is $50. For Year 1, P has $50 of ordinary loss, S1 has $100 of ordinary loss, S2 has $150 of ordinary loss, S3 has $50 of ordinary loss, and S4 has $50 of ordinary loss and $80 of excluded COD income from the discharge of non-intercompany indebtedness. P sells the S1 stock for $100 at the close of Year 1. As of the beginning of Year 2, S4 has Asset A with a fair market value of $10. After the computation of tax imposed for Year 1 and before the application of sections 108 and 1017 and § 1.1502-28, Asset A has a basis of $0.

(ii) *Analysis.* The steps used to compute the tax imposed on the group, to effect the reduction of attributes, and to compute the limitations on the use and reduction of attributes are as follows:

(A) *Computation of limitation on deductions and losses to offset income or gain.* To determine the amount of the limitation under paragraph (c)(2)(i) of this section on S1's and S4's losses and the effect of the absorption of S1's and S4's losses on P's basis in S1's stock under § 1.1502-32(b), P's gain or loss from the sale of S1's stock is not taken into account. The group is tentatively treated as having a consolidated net operating loss of $400. Consequently, $100 of S1's loss and $50 of S4's loss is limited under paragraph (c)(2)(i) of this section.

(B) *Tentative adjustment of stock basis.* Then, pursuant to paragraph (c)(2)(ii) of this section, § 1.1502-32 is tentatively applied to adjust the basis of S1's stock. For this purpose, adjustments to the basis of S1's stock attributable to S4's realization of excluded COD income and the reduction of attributes in respect of such excluded COD income are not taken into account. There is no adjustment under § 1.1502-32 to the basis of the S1 stock. Therefore, P's basis in the S1 stock for this purpose is $50.

(C) *Tentative computation of stock gain or loss.* Then, P's income, gain, or loss from the sale of S1 stock is computed pursuant to paragraph (c)(2)(iii) of this section using the basis computed in the previous step. Thus, P is treated as recognizing a $50 gain from the sale of the S1 stock.

(D) *Tentative computation of tax imposed.* Pursuant to paragraph (c)(2)(iv) of this section, the tax imposed for the year of disposition is then tentatively computed, taking into account P's $50 gain from the sale of the S1 stock computed pursuant to paragraph (c)(2)(iii) of this section. Although S1's and S4's limited losses cannot be used to offset P's $50 gain from the sale of S1's stock under the rules of this section, $10 of P's loss, $30 of S2's loss, and $10 of S3's loss will offset that gain. Therefore, the group is tentatively treated as having a consolidated net operating loss of $350, $40 of which is attributable to P, $100 of which is attributable to S1, $120 of which is attributable to S2, $40 of which is attributable to S3, and $50 of which is attributable to S4 under the principles of § 1.1502-21(b)(2)(iv).

(E) *Tentative reduction of attributes.* Next, pursuant to paragraph (c)(2)(v) of this section, the rules of sections 108 and 1017 and § 1.1502-28 are tentatively applied to reduce attributes remaining after the tentative computation of the tax imposed. Pursuant to § 1.1502-28(a)(2), the tax attributes attributable to S4 would first be reduced to take into account its $80 of excluded COD income. Accordingly, the consolidated net operating loss for Year 1 would be reduced by $50, the portion of the consolidated net operating loss attributable to S4 under the principles of § 1.1502-21(b)(2)(iv), to $300. Then, pursuant to § 1.1502-28(a)(4), S4's remaining $30 of excluded COD income would reduce the consolidated net operating loss for Year 1 that is attributable to other members. Therefore, the consolidated net operating loss for Year 1 would be reduced by $30. Of that amount, $4 is attributable to P, $10 is attributable to S1, $12 is attributable to S2, and $4 is attributable to S3.

(F) *Actual adjustment of stock basis.* Pursuant to paragraph (c)(2)(vi) of this section, § 1.1502-32 is applied to reflect the amount of S1's and S4's income and gain included, and unlimited deductions and losses that are absorbed, in the tentative computation of tax imposed for the year of the disposition and the excluded COD income tentatively applied to reduce attributes and the attributes reduced in respect of the excluded COD income pursuant to the previous step. Under § 1.1502-32(b), the application of $80 of S4's excluded COD income to reduce attributes, and the reduction of S4's loss in the amount of $50 and S1's loss in the amount of $10 in respect of the excluded COD income results in a positive adjustment of $20 to P's basis in the S1 stock. Accordingly, P's basis in S1 stock is $70.

(G) *Actual computation of stock gain or loss.* Pursuant to paragraph (c)(2)(vii) of this section, P's actual gain or loss on the sale of the S1 stock is computed using the basis computed in the previous step. Accordingly, P recognizes a $30 gain on the disposition of the S1 stock.

(H) *Actual computation of tax imposed.* Pursuant to paragraph (c)(2)(viii) of this section, the tax imposed is computed by taking into account

P's $30 gain from the sale of S1 stock. Before the application of § 1.1502-28, therefore, the group has a consolidated net operating loss of $370, $44 of which is attributable to P, $100 of which is attributable to S1, $132 of which is attributable to S2, $44 of which is attributable to S3, and $50 of which is attributable to S4.

(I) *Actual reduction of attributes.* Pursuant to paragraph (c)(2)(ix) of this section, sections 108 and 1017 and § 1.1502-28 are then actually applied to reduce attributes remaining after the actual computation of the tax imposed. Pursuant to § 1.1502-28(a)(2), the tax attributes attributable to S4 must first be reduced to take into account its $80 of excluded COD income. Accordingly, the consolidated net operating loss for Year 1 is reduced by $50, the portion of that consolidated net operating loss attributable to S4 under the principles of § 1.1502-21(b)(2)(iv), to $320. Then, pursuant to § 1.1502-28(a)(4), without regard to the limitation imposed by paragraph (c)(2)(ix)(A) of this section, S4's remaining $30 of excluded COD income would reduce the consolidated net operating loss for Year 1 by $30 ($4.12 of the consolidated net operating loss attributable to P, $9.38 of the consolidated net operating loss attributable to S1, $12.38 of the consolidated net operating loss attributable to S2, and $4.12 of the consolidated net operating loss attributable to S3) to $290. However, the limitation imposed by paragraph (c)(2)(ix)(A) of this section prevents the reduction of the consolidated net operating loss attributable to P, S2, and S3 by more than $4, $12, and $4 respectively. The $.62 of excluded COD income that would have otherwise reduced the consolidated net operating loss attributable to P, S2, and S3 is applied to reduce the consolidated net operating loss attributable to S1. Therefore, S1 carries forward $90 of loss.

Example 4. Excess loss account taken into account. (i) *Facts.* P is the common parent of a consolidated group. On Day 1 of Year 2, P acquired all of the stock of S1. As of the beginning of Year 2, S1 had a $30 net operating loss carryover from Year 1, a separate return limitation year. A limitation under § 1.1502-21(c) applies to the use of that loss by the P group. For Years 1 and 2, the P group had no consolidated taxable income or loss. On Day 1 of Year 3, S1 acquired all of the stock of S2 for $10. In Year 3, P had ordinary income of $10, S1 had ordinary income of $25, and S2 had an ordinary loss of $50. In addition, in Year 3, S2 realized $20 of excluded COD income from the discharge of non-intercompany indebtedness. After the discharge of this indebtedness, S2 had no liabilities. As of the beginning of Year 4, S2 had Asset A with a fair market value of $10. After the computation of tax imposed for Year 3 and before the application of sections 108 and 1017 and § 1.1502-28, Asset A has a basis of $0. S2 had no taxable income (or loss) for Year 1 and Year 2.

(ii) *Analysis.* The steps used to compute the tax imposed on the group, to effect the reduction

Reg. § 1.1502-11(c)(5)

of attributes, and to compute the limitations on the use and reduction of attributes are as follows:

(A) *Computation of limitation on deductions and losses to offset income or gain, tentative basis adjustments, tentative computation of stock gain or loss.* Because it is not initially apparent that there has been a disposition of stock, paragraph (c)(2)(i) of this section does not limit the use of deductions to offset income or gain, no adjustments to the basis are required pursuant to paragraph (c)(2)(ii) of this section, and no stock gain or loss is computed pursuant to paragraph (c)(2)(iii) of this section or taken into account in the tentative computation of tax imposed pursuant to paragraph (c)(2)(iv) of this section.

(B) *Tentative computation of tax imposed.* Pursuant to paragraph (c)(2)(iv) of this section, the tax imposed for Year 3 is tentatively computed. For Year 3, the P group has a consolidated taxable loss of $15, all of which is attributable to S2 under the principles of §1.1502-21(b)(2)(iv).

(C) *Tentative reduction of attributes.* Next, pursuant to paragraph (c)(2)(v) of this section, the rules of sections 108 and 1017 and §1.1502-28 are tentatively applied to reduce attributes remaining after the tentative computation of tax imposed. Pursuant to §1.1502-28(a)(2), the tax attributes attributable to S2 would first be reduced to take into account its $20 of excluded COD income. Accordingly, the consolidated net operating loss for Year 3 is reduced by $15, the portion of that consolidated net operating loss attributable to S2 under the principles of §1.1502-21(b)(2)(iv), to $0. The remaining $5 of excluded COD income is not applied to reduce attributes as there are no remaining attributes that are subject to reduction.

(D) *Actual adjustment of stock basis.* Pursuant to paragraph (c)(2)(vi) of this section, §1.1502-32 is applied to reflect the amount of S2's income and gain included, and unlimited deductions and losses that are absorbed, in the tentative computation of tax imposed for the year of the disposition and the excluded COD income tentatively applied to reduce attributes and the attributes reduced in respect of the excluded COD income pursuant to the previous step. Under §1.1502-32, the absorption of $35 of S2's loss, the application of $15 in respect of S2's excluded COD income to reduce attributes, and the reduction of $15 in respect of the loss attributable to S2 reduced in respect of the excluded COD income results in a negative adjustment of $35 to the basis of the S2 stock. Therefore, S1 has an excess loss account of $25 in the S2 stock.

(E) *Actual computation of stock gain or loss.* Pursuant to paragraph (c)(2)(vii) of this section, S1's actual gain or loss, if any, on the S2 stock is computed. Because S2 realized $5 of excluded COD income that was not applied to reduce attributes, pursuant to §1.1502-19(b)(1) and (c)(1)(iii)(B), S1 is required to take into account $5 of its excess loss account in the S2 stock.

(F) *Actual computation of tax imposed.* Pursuant to paragraph (c)(2)(viii) of this section, the tax imposed is computed by taking into account the $5 of the excess loss account in the S2 stock required to be taken into account. See §1.1502-28(b)(6) (requiring an excess loss account that is required to be taken into account as a result of the application of §1.1502-19(c)(1)(iii)(B) to be included in the group's tax return for the year that includes the date of the debt discharge). However, pursuant to paragraph (c)(2)(viii) of this section, such amount may not be offset by any of the consolidated net operating loss attributable to S2. It may, however, subject to applicable limitations, be offset by the separate net operating loss of S1 from Year 1.

(G) *Actual reduction of attributes.* Pursuant to paragraph (c)(2)(ix) of this section, sections 108 and 1017 and §1.1502-28 are then actually applied to reduce attributes remaining after the actual computation of the tax imposed. Attributes will be actually reduced in the same way that they were tentatively reduced.

(6) *Additional rules for multiple dispositions.*—[Reserved]

(7) *Effective date.*—This paragraph (c) applies to dispositions of subsidiary stock that occur after March 22, 2005. Taxpayers may apply §1.1502-11(c) of REG-167265-03 (2004-15 IRB 730) (see §601.601(d)(2) of this chapter) in whole, but not in part, to any disposition of subsidiary stock that occurs on or before March 22, 2005, if a member of the group realized excluded COD income after August 29, 2003, in the taxable year that includes the date of the disposition of such subsidiary stock.

(d) *Disallowance of loss attributable to pre-1966 distributions.*—No loss shall be allowed upon the sale or other disposition of stock, bonds, or other obligations of a member or former member to the extent that such loss is attributable to a distribution made in an affiliated year beginning before January 1, 1966, out of earnings and profits accumulated before the distributing corporation became a member. [Reg. §1.1502-11.]

☐ [T.D. 6894, 9-7-66. *Amended by T.D. 7246,* 12-29-72; *T.D. 7728,* 10-31-80; *T.D. 8560,* 8-12-94; *T.D. 8677,* 6-26-96; *T.D. 8823,* 6-25-99; *T.D. 9048,* 3-11-2003; *T.D. 9187,* 3-2-2005 *T.D. 9192,* 3-21-2005 (*corrected* 4-15-2005); *T.D. 9254,* 3-9-2006 *and T.D. 9424,* 9-9-2008.]

[Reg. §1.1502-12]

§1.1502-12. Separate taxable income.—The separate taxable income of a member (including a case in which deductions exceed gross income) is computed in accordance with the provisions of the Code covering the determination of taxable income of separate corporations, subject to the following modifications:

(a) Transactions between members and transactions with respect to stock, bonds, or other obligations of members shall be reflected according to the provisions of § 1.1502-13;

(b) Any deduction which is disallowed under §§ 1.1502-15A or 1.1502-15 shall be taken into account as provided in those sections;

(c) The limitation on deductions provided in section 615(c) or section 617(h) shall be taken into account as provided in § 1.1502-16;

(d) The method of accounting under which such computation is made and the adjustments to be made because of any change in method of accounting shall be determined under § 1.1502-17;

(e) Inventory adjustments shall be made as provided in § 1.1502-18;

(f) Any amount included in income under § 1.1502-19 shall be taken into account;

(g) In the computation of the deduction under section 167, property shall not lose its character as new property as a result of a transfer from one member to another member during a consolidated return year if—

(1) The transfer occurs on or before January 4, 1973, or

(2) The transfer occurs after January 4, 1973, and the transfer is an intercompany transaction as defined in § 1.1502-13 or the basis of the property in the hands of the transferee is determined (in whole or in part) by reference to its basis in the hands of the transferor;

(h) No net operating loss deduction shall be taken into account;

(i) [Reserved]

(j) No capital gains or losses shall be taken into account;

(k) No gains and losses subject to section 1231 shall be taken into account;

(l) No deduction under section 170 with respect to charitable contributions shall be taken into account;

(m) No deduction under section 922 (relating to the deduction for Western Hemisphere trade corporations) shall be taken into account;

(n) No deductions under section 243(a)(1), 244(a), 245, or 247 (relating to deductions with respect to dividends received and dividends paid) shall be taken into account;

(o) Basis shall be determined under §§ 1.1502-31 and 1.1502-32, and earnings and profits shall be determined under § 1.1502-33; and

(p) The limitation on deductions provided in section 613A shall be taken into account for each member's oil and gas properties as provided in § 1.1502-44.

(q) A thrift institution's deduction under section 593(b)(2) (relating to the addition to the reserve for bad debts of a thrift institution under the percentage of taxable income method) shall be determined under § 1.1502-42.

The term "separate taxable income" shall include a case in which the determination under this section results in an excess of deductions over gross income.

(r) See §§ 1.337(d)-2, 1.1502-35, and 1.1502-36 for rules relating to basis adjustments and allowance of stock loss on dispositions or transfers of subsidiary stock. [Reg. § 1.1502-12.]

☐ [*T.D. 6894, 9-7-66. Amended by T.D. 7192, 6-29-72; T.D. 7246, 12-29-72; T.D. 7725, 9-30-80; T.D. 7876, 3-14-83; T.D. 8294, 3-9-90; T.D. 8319, 11-19-90; T.D. 8364, 9-13-91; T.D. 8597, 7-12-95; T.D. 8677, 6-26-96; T.D. 8823, 6-25-99; T.D. 9048, 3-11-2003 T.D 9187, 3-2-2005; T.D. 9254, 3-9-2006 and T.D. 9424, 9-9-2008.*]

[Reg. § 1.1502-13]

§ 1.1502-13. Intercompany transactions.— (a) *In general.*—(1) *Purpose.*—This section provides rules for taking into account items of income, gain, deduction, and loss of members from intercompany transactions. The purpose of this section is to provide rules to clearly reflect the taxable income (and tax liability) of the group as a whole by preventing intercompany transactions from creating, accelerating, avoiding, or deferring consolidated taxable income (or consolidated tax liability).

(2) *Separate entity and single entity treatment.*—Under this section, the selling member (S) and the buying member (B) are treated as separate entities for some purposes but as divisions of a single corporation for other purposes. The *amount* and *location* of S's intercompany items and B's corresponding items are determined on a separate entity basis (separate entity treatment). For example, S determines its gain or loss from a sale of property to B on a separate entity basis, and B has a cost basis in the property. The *timing*, and the *character, source,* and other *attributes* of the intercompany items and corresponding items, although initially determined on a separate entity basis, are redetermined under this section to produce the effect of transactions between divisions of a single corporation (single entity treatment). For example, if S sells land to B at a gain and B sells the land to a nonmember, S does not take its gain into account until B's sale to the nonmember.

(3) *Timing rules as a method of accounting.*— (i) *In general.*—The timing rules of this section are a method of accounting for intercompany transactions, to be applied by each member in addition to the member's other methods of accounting. See § 1.1502-17 and, with regard to consolidated return years beginning on or after November 7, 2001, § 1.446-1(c)(2)(iii). To the extent the timing rules of this section are inconsistent with a member's otherwise applicable methods of accounting, the timing rules of this section control. For example, if S sells property to B in exchange for B's note, the timing rules of

Reg. § 1.1502-13(a)(3)(i)

this section apply instead of the installment sale rules of section 453. S's or B's application of the timing rules of this section to an intercompany transaction clearly reflects income only if the effect of that transaction as a whole (including, for example, related costs and expenses) on consolidated taxable income is clearly reflected.

(ii) *Automatic consent for joining and departing members.*—(A) *Consent granted.*—Section 446(e) consent under this section to the extent a change in method of accounting is necessary solely by reason of the timing rules of this section—

(1) For each member, with respect to its intercompany transactions, in the first consolidated return year which follows a separate return year and in which the member engages in an intercompany transaction; and

(2) For each former member, with respect to its transactions with members that would otherwise be intercompany transactions if the former member were still a member, in the first separate return year in which the former member engages in such a transaction.

(B) *Cut-off basis.*—Any change in method of accounting described in paragraph (a)(3)(ii)(A) of this section is to be effected on a cut-off basis for transactions entered into on or after the first day of the year for which consent is granted under paragraph (a)(3)(ii)(A) of this section.

(4) *Application of other rules of law.*—See § 1.1502-80(a) regarding the general applicability of other rules of law and a limitation on duplicative adjustments. The rules of this section apply

in addition to other applicable law (including nonstatutory authorities). For example, this section applies in addition to sections 267(f) (additional rules for certain losses), 269 (acquisitions to evade or avoid income tax), and 482 (allocations among commonly controlled taxpayers). Thus, an item taken into account under this section can be deferred, disallowed, or eliminated under other applicable law, for example, section 1091 (losses from wash sales).

(5) *References.*—References in other sections to this section include, as appropriate, references to prior law. For effective dates and prior law see paragraph (1) of this section.

(6) *Overview.*—(i) *In general.*—The principal rules of this section that implement single entity treatment are the matching rule and the acceleration rule of paragraphs (c) and (d) of this section. Under the matching rule, S and B are generally treated as divisions of a single corporation for purposes of taking into account their items from intercompany transactions. The acceleration rule provides additional rules for taking the items into account if the effect of treating S and B as divisions cannot be achieved (for example, if S or B becomes a nonmember). Paragraph (b) of this section provides definitions. Paragraph (e) of this section provides simplifying rules for certain transactions. Paragraphs (f) and (g) of this section provide additional rules for stock and obligations of members. Paragraphs (h) and (j) of this section provide anti-avoidance rules and miscellaneous operating rules.

(ii) *Table of examples.*—Set forth below is a table of the examples contained in this section.

Matching rule. (§ 1.1502-13(c)(7)(ii))
   Example 1. Intercompany sale of land.
   Example 2. Dealer activities.
   Example 3. Intercompany section 351 transfer.
   Example 4. Depreciable property.
   Example 5. Intercompany sale followed by installment sale.
   Example 6. Intercompany sale of installment obligation.
   Example 7. Performance of services.
   Example 8. Rental of property.
   Example 9. Intercompany sale of a partnership interest.
   Example 10. Net operating losses subject to section 382 or the SRLY rules.
   Example 11. Section 475.
   Example 12. Section 1092.
   Example 13. [Reserved].
   Example 14. Source of income under section 863.
   Example 15. Section 1248.
   Example 16. Intercompany stock distribution followed by section 332 liquidation.
   Example 17. Intercompany stock sale followed by section 355 distribution.
Acceleration rule. (§ 1.1502-13(d)(3))
   Example 1. Becoming a nonmember—timing.
   Example 2. Becoming a nonmember—attributes.
   Example 3. Selling member's disposition of installment note.
   Example 4. Cancellation of debt and attribute reduction under section 108(b).
   Example 5. Section 481.

Reg. § 1.1502-13(a)(3)(ii)

(b) *Definitions.*—For purposes of this section—

(1) *Intercompany transactions.*—(i) *In general.*—An intercompany transaction is a transaction between corporations that are members of the same consolidated group immediately after the transaction. S is the member transferring property or providing services, and B is the member receiving the property or services. Intercompany transactions include—

(A) S's sale of property (or other transfer, such as an exchange or contribution) to B, whether or not gain or loss is recognized;

(B) S's performance of services for B, and B's payment or accrual of its expenditure for S's performance;

(C) S's licensing of technology, rental of property, or loan of money to B, and B's payment or accrual of its expenditure; and

(D) S's distribution to B with respect to S stock.

(ii) *Time of transaction.*—If a transaction occurs in part while S and B are members and in part while they are not members, the transaction is treated as occurring when performance by either S or B takes place, or when payment for performance would be taken into account under the rules of this section if it were an intercompany transaction, whichever is earliest. Appropriate adjustments must be made in such cases by, for example, dividing the transaction into two separate transactions reflecting the extent to which S or B has performed.

(iii) *Separate transactions.*—Except as otherwise provided in this section, each transaction is analyzed separately. For example, if S simultaneously sells two properties to B, one at a gain and the other at a loss, each property is treated as sold in a separate transaction. Thus, the gain and loss cannot be offset or netted against each other for purposes of this section. Similarly, each payment or accrual of interest on a loan is a separate transaction. In addition, an accrual of premium is treated as a separate transaction, or as an offset to interest that is not a separate transaction, to the extent required under separate entity treatment. If two members exchange property, each member is S with respect to the property it transfers and B with respect to the property it receives. If two members enter into a notional principal contract, each payment under the contract is a separate transaction and the member making the payment is B with respect to that payment and the member receiving the payment is S. See paragraph (j)(4) of this section for rules aggregating certain transactions.

(2) *Intercompany items.*—(i) *In general.*—S's income, gain, deduction, and loss from an intercompany transaction are its intercompany items. For example, S's gain from the sale of property to B is intercompany gain. An item is an intercompany item whether it is directly or indirectly from an intercompany transaction.

(ii) *Related costs or expenses.*—S's costs or expenses related to an intercompany transaction are included in determining its intercompany items. For example, if S sells inventory to B, S's direct and indirect costs properly includible under section 263A are included in determining its intercompany income. Similarly, related costs or expenses that are not capitalized under S's separate entity method of accounting are included in determining its intercompany items. For example, deductions for employee wages, in addition to other related costs, are included in determining S's intercompany items from performing services for B, and depreciation deductions are included in determining S's intercompany items from renting property to B.

(iii) *Amounts not yet recognized or incurred.*—S's intercompany items include amounts from an intercompany transaction that are not yet taken into account under its separate entity method of accounting. For example, if S is a cash method taxpayer, S's intercompany income might be taken into account under this section even if the cash is not yet received. Similarly, an amount reflected in basis (or an amount equivalent to basis) under S's separate entity method of accounting that is a substitute for income, gain, deduction or loss from an intercompany transaction is an intercompany item.

(3) *Corresponding items.*—(i) *In general.*—B's income, gain, deduction, and loss from an intercompany transaction, or from property acquired in an intercompany transaction, are its corresponding items. For example, if B pays rent to S, B's deduction for the rent is a corresponding deduction. If B buys property from S and sells it to a nonmember, B's gain or loss from the sale to the nonmember is a corresponding gain or loss; alternatively, if B recovers the cost of the property through depreciation, B's depreciation deductions are corresponding deductions. An

item is a corresponding item whether it is directly or indirectly from an intercompany transaction (or from property acquired in an intercompany transaction).

(ii) *Disallowed or eliminated amounts.*—B's corresponding items include amounts that are permanently disallowed or permanently eliminated, whether directly or indirectly. Thus, corresponding items include amounts disallowed under section 265 (expenses relating to tax-exempt income), and amounts not recognized under section 311(a) (nonrecognition of loss on distributions), section 332 (nonrecognition on liquidating distributions), or section 355(c) (certain distributions of stock of a subsidiary). On the other hand, an amount is not permanently disallowed or permanently eliminated (and therefore is not a corresponding item) to the extent it is not recognized in a transaction in which B receives a successor asset within the meaning of paragraph (j)(1) of this section. For example, B's corresponding items do not include amounts not recognized from a transaction with a nonmember to which section 1031 applies or from another transaction in which B receives exchanged basis property.

(4) *Recomputed corresponding items.*—The recomputed corresponding item is the corresponding item that B would take into account if S and B were divisions of a single corporation and the intercompany transaction were between those divisions. For example, if S sells property with a $70 basis to B for $100, and B later sells the property to a nonmember for $90, B's corresponding item is its $10 loss, and the recomputed corresponding item is $20 of gain (determined by comparing the $90 sales price with the $70 basis the property would have if S and B were divisions of a single corporation). Although neither S nor B actually takes the recomputed corresponding item into account, it is computed as if B did take it into account (based on reasonable and consistently applied assumptions, including any provision of the Internal Revenue Code or regulations that would affect its timing or attributes).

(5) *Treatment as a separate entity.*—Treatment as a separate entity means treatment without application of the rules of this section, but with the application of the other consolidated return regulations. For example, if S sells the stock of another member to B, S's gain or loss on a separate entity basis is determined with the application of § 1.1502-80(b) (non-applicability of section 304), but without redetermination under paragraph (c) or (d) of this section.

(6) *Attributes.*—The attributes of an intercompany item or corresponding item are all of the item's characteristics, except *amount, location,* and *timing,* necessary to determine the item's effect on taxable income (and tax liability). For example, attributes include character, source,

treatment as excluded from gross income or as a noncapital, nondeductible amount, and treatment as built-in gain or loss under section 382(h) or 384. In contrast, the characteristics of property, such as a member's holding period, or the fact that property is included in inventory, are not attributes of an item, but these characteristics might affect the determination of the attributes of items from the property.

(c) *Matching rule.*—For each consolidated return year, B's corresponding items and S's intercompany items are taken into account under the following rules:

(1) *Attributes and holding periods.*— (i) *Attributes.*—The separate entity attributes of S's intercompany items and B's corresponding items are redetermined to the extent necessary to produce the same effect on consolidated taxable income (and consolidated tax liability) as if S and B were divisions of a single corporation, and the intercompany transaction were a transaction between divisions. Thus, the activities of both S and B might affect the attributes of both intercompany items and corresponding items. For example, if S holds property for sale to unrelated customers in the ordinary course of its trade or business, S sells the property to B at a gain and B sells the property to an unrelated person at a further gain, S's intercompany gain and B's corresponding gain might be ordinary because of S's activities with respect to the property. Similar principles apply if S performs services, rents property, or engages in any other intercompany transaction.

(ii) *Holding periods.*—The holding period of property transferred in an intercompany transaction is the aggregate of the holding periods of S and B. However, if the basis of the property is determined by reference to the basis of other property, the property's holding period is determined by reference to the holding period of the other property. For example, if S distributes stock to B in a transaction to which section 355 applies, B's holding period in the distributed stock is determined by reference to B's holding period in the stock of S.

(2) *Timing.*—(i) *B's items.*—B takes its corresponding items into account under its accounting method, but the redetermination of the attributes of a corresponding item might affect its timing. For example, if B's sale of property acquired from S is treated as a dealer disposition because of S's activities, section 453(b) prevents any corresponding income of B from being taken into account under the installment method.

(ii) *S's items.*—S takes its intercompany item into account to reflect the difference for the year between B's corresponding item taken into account and the recomputed corresponding item.

(3) *Divisions of a single corporation.*—As divisions of a single corporation, S and B are treated as engaging in their actual transaction and owning any actual property involved in the transaction (rather than treating the transaction as not occurring). For example, S's sale of land held for investment to B for cash is not disregarded, but is treated as an exchange of land for cash between divisions (and B therefore succeeds to S's basis in the property). Similarly, S's issuance of its own stock to B in exchange for property is not disregarded, B is treated as owning the stock it receives in the exchange, and section 1032 does not apply to B on its subsequent sale of the S stock. Although treated as divisions, S and B nevertheless are treated as:

(i) Operating separate trades or businesses. See, e.g., § 1.446-1(d) (accounting methods for a taxpayer engaged in more than one business).

(ii) Having any special status that they have under the Internal Revenue Code or regulations. For example, a bank defined in section 581, a domestic building and loan association defined in section 7701(a)(19), and an insurance company to which section 801 or 831 applies are treated as divisions having separate special status. On the other hand, the fact that a member holds property for sale to customers in the ordinary course of its trade or business is not a special status.

(4) *Conflict or allocation of attributes.*—This paragraph (c)(4) provides special rules for redetermining and allocating attributes under paragraph (c)(1)(i) of this section.

(i) *Offsetting amounts.*—(A) *In general.*— To the extent B's corresponding item offsets S's intercompany item in amount, the attributes of B's corresponding item, determined based on both S's and B's activities, control the attributes of S's offsetting intercompany item. For example, if S sells depreciable property to B at a gain and B depreciates the property, the attributes of B's depreciation deduction (ordinary deduction) control the attributes of S's offsetting intercompany gain. Accordingly, S's gain is ordinary.

(B) *B controls unreasonable.*—To the extent the results under paragraph (c)(4)(i)(A) are inconsistent with treating S and B as divisions of a single corporation, the attributes of the offsetting items must be redetermined in a manner consistent with treating S and B as divisions of a single corporation. To the extent, however, that B's corresponding item on a separate entity basis is excluded from gross income, is a noncapital, nondeductible amount, or is otherwise permanently disallowed or eliminated, the attributes of B's corresponding item always control the attributes of S's offsetting intercompany item.

(ii) *Allocation.*—To the extent S's intercompany item and B's corresponding item do not offset in amount, the attributes redetermined

Reg. § 1.1502-13(c)(4)(ii)

under paragraph (c)(1)(i) of this section must be allocated to S's intercompany item and B's corresponding item by using a method that is reasonable in light of all the facts and circumstances, including the purposes of this section and any other rule affected by the attributes of S's intercompany item and B's corresponding item. A method of allocation or redetermination is unreasonable if it is not used consistently by all members of the group from year to year.

(5) *Special status.*—Notwithstanding the general rule of paragraph (c)(1)(i) of this section, to the extent an item's attributes determined under this section are permitted or not permitted to a member under the Internal Revenue Code or regulations by reason of the member's special status, the attributes required under the Internal Revenue Code or regulations apply to that member's items (but not the other member). For example, if S is a bank to which section 582(c) applies, and sells debt securities at a gain to B, a nonbank, the character of S's intercompany gain is ordinary as required under section 582(c), but the character of B's corresponding item as capital or ordinary is determined under paragraph (c)(1)(i) of this section without the application of section 582(c). For other special status issues, see, for example, sections 595(b) (foreclosure on property securing loans), 818(b) (life insurance company treatment of capital gains and losses), and 1503(c) (limitation on absorption of certain losses).

(6) *Treatment of intercompany items if corresponding items are excluded or nondeductible.*— (i) *In general.*—Under paragraph (c)(1)(i) of this section, S's intercompany item might be redetermined to be excluded from gross income or treated as a noncapital, nondeductible amount. For example, S's intercompany loss from the sale of property to B is treated as a noncapital, nondeductible amount if B distributes the property to a nonmember shareholder at no further gain or loss (because, if S and B were divisions of a single corporation, the loss would not have been recognized under section 311(a)). Paragraph (c)(6)(ii) of this section, however, provides limitations on the application of this rule to intercompany income or gain. See also §§ 1.1502-32 and 1.1502-33 (adjustments to S's stock basis and earnings and profits to reflect amounts so treated).

(ii) *Limitation on treatment of intercompany items as excluded from gross income.*—Notwithstanding the general rule of paragraph (c)(1)(i) of this section, S's intercompany income or gain is redetermined to be excluded from gross income only to the extent one of the following applies:

(A) *Disallowed amounts.*—B's corresponding item is a deduction or loss and, in the taxable year the item is taken into account under this section, it is permanently and explicitly disallowed under another provision of the Internal

Revenue Code or regulations. For example, deductions that are disallowed under section 265 are permanently and explicitly disallowed. An amount is not permanently and explicitly disallowed, for example, to the extent that—

(1) The Internal Revenue Code or regulations provide that the amount is not recognized (for example, a loss that is realized but not recognized under section 332 or section 355(c) is not permanently and explicitly disallowed, notwithstanding that it is a corresponding item within the meaning of paragraph (b)(3)(ii) of this section (certain disallowed or eliminated amounts));

(2) A related amount might be taken into account by B with respect to successor property, such as under section 280B (demolition costs recoverable as capitalized amounts);

(3) A related amount might be taken into account by another taxpayer, such as under section 267(d) (disallowed loss under section 267(a) might result in nonrecognition of gain for a related person);

(4) A related amount might be taken into account as a deduction or loss, including as a carryforward to a later year, under any provision of the Internal Revenue Code or regulations (whether or not the carryforward expires in a later year); or

(5) The amount is reflected in the computation of any credit against (or other reduction of) Federal income tax (whether allowed for the taxable year or carried forward to a later year).

(B) *Section 311.*—The corresponding item is a loss that is realized, but not recognized under section 311(a) on a distribution to a nonmember (even though the loss is not a permanently and explicitly disallowed amount within the meaning of paragraph (c)(6)(ii)(A) of this section).

(C) *Certain intercompany gains on stock.*—(1) *In general.*—Notwithstanding paragraph (c)(6)(ii)(A)(1) of this section, intercompany gain with respect to a member's stock that was created by reason of an intercompany transfer of the stock, and that would not otherwise be taken into account upon a subsequent elimination of the stock's basis but for the transfer, is redetermined to be excluded from gross income if—

(i) B or S becomes a successor (as defined in paragraph (j)(2) of this section) to the other party (either B or S), or a third member becomes a successor to both B and S;

(ii) Immediately before the intercompany gain would be taken into account, the successor member holds the member's stock with respect to which the intercompany gain was realized;

(iii) The successor member's basis in the member's stock that reflects the intercompany gain that is taken into account is eliminated without the recognition of gain or loss (and such eliminated basis is not further reflected in the basis of any successor asset);

(iv) The effects of the intercompany transaction have not previously been reflected, directly or indirectly, on the group's consolidated return; and

(v) The group has not derived, and no taxpayer will derive, any Federal income tax benefit from the intercompany transaction that gave rise to the intercompany gain or the redetermination of the intercompany gain (including any adjustment to basis in member stock under § 1.1502-32). For this purpose, the redetermination of the intercompany gain is not itself considered a Federal income tax benefit.

(2) *Effect on earnings and profits and investment adjustments.*—Any amount excluded from gross income under paragraph (c)(6)(ii)(C)(*1*) of this section shall not be taken into account as earnings and profits of any member and shall not be treated as tax-exempt income under§ 1.1502-32(b)(2)(ii).

(D) *Other amounts.*—(*1*) The Commissioner may determine that treating S's intercompany item as excluded from gross income is consistent with the purposes of this section and other applicable provisions of the Internal Revenue Code, regulations, and published guidance, if the following conditions are met, depending on whether the intercompany item is an item of income or an item of gain:

(i) In the case of an intercompany item of income, the corresponding item is permanently disallowed; or

(ii) If the intercompany item constitutes gain, the conditions described in paragraphs (c)(6)(ii)(C)(*1*)(*iv*) and (c)(6)(ii)(C)(*1*)(*v*) of this section are satisfied.

(2) A determination by the Commissioner may be obtained only through a letter ruling request.

(7) *Examples.*—(i) *In general.*—For purposes of the examples in this section, unless otherwise stated, P is the common parent of the P consolidated group, P owns all of the only class of stock of subsidiaries S and B, X is a person unrelated to any member of the P group, the taxable year of all persons is the calendar year, all persons use the accrual method of accounting, tax liabilities are disregarded, the facts set forth the only corporate activity, no member has any special status, and the transaction is not otherwise subject to recharacterization. If a member acts as both a selling member and a buying member (e.g., with respect to different aspects of a single transaction, or with respect to related transactions), the member is referred to as M, M1, or M2 (rather than as S or B).

(ii) *Matching rule.*—The matching rule of this paragraph (c) is illustrated by the following examples.

Example 1. Intercompany sale of land followed by sale to a nonmember. (a) *Facts.* S holds land for investment with a basis of $70. S has held the land for more than one year. On January 1 of Year 1, S sells the land to B for $100. B also holds the land for investment. On July 1 of Year 3, B sells the land to X for $110.

(b) *Definitions.* Under paragraph (b)(1) of this section, S's sale of the land to B is an intercompany transaction, S is the selling member, and B is the buying member. Under paragraphs (b)(2) and (3) of this section, S's $30 gain from the sale to B is its intercompany item, and B's $10 gain from the sale to X is its corresponding item.

(c) *Attributes.* Under the matching rule of paragraph (c) of this section, S's $30 intercompany gain and B's $10 corresponding gain are taken into account to produce the same effect on consolidated taxable income (and consolidated tax liability) as if S and B were divisions of a single corporation. In addition, the holding periods of S and B for the land are aggregated. Thus, the group's entire $40 of gain is long-term capital gain. Because both S's intercompany item and B's corresponding item on a separate entity basis are long-term capital gain, the attributes are not redetermined under paragraph (c)(1)(i) of this section.

(d) *Timing.* For each consolidated return year, S takes its intercompany item into account under the matching rule to reflect the difference for the year between B's corresponding item taken into account and the recomputed corresponding item. If S and B were divisions of a single corporation and the intercompany sale were a transfer between the divisions, B would succeed to S's $70 basis in the land and would have a $40 gain from the sale to X in Year 3, instead of a $10 gain. Consequently, S takes no gain into account in Years 1 and 2, and takes the entire $30 gain into account in Year 3, to reflect the $30 difference in that year between the $10 gain B takes into account and the $40 recomputed gain (the recomputed corresponding item). Under §§ 1.1502-32 and 1.1502-33, P's basis in its S stock and the earnings and profits of S and P do not reflect S's $30 gain until the gain is taken into account in Year 3. (Under paragraph (a)(3) of this section, the results would be the same if S sold the land to B in an installment sale to which section 453 would otherwise apply, because S must take its intercompany gain into account under this section.)

(e) *Intercompany loss followed by sale to a nonmember at a gain.* The facts are the same as in paragraph (a) of this *Example 1*, except that S's basis in the land is $130 (rather than $70). The attributes and timing of S's intercompany loss and B's corresponding gain are determined under the matching rule in the manner provided in paragraphs (c) and (d) of this *Example 1*. If S and B were divisions of a single corporation and the intercompany sale were a transfer between the divisions, B would succeed to S's $130 basis in the land and would have a $20 loss from the sale to X instead of a $10 gain. Thus, S takes its entire $30 loss into account in Year 3 to reflect the $30 difference between B's $10 gain taken into account and the $20 recomputed loss. (The results are the same under section 267(f).) S's $30 loss is long-term capital loss, and B's $10 gain is long-term capital gain.

(f) *Intercompany gain followed by sale to a nonmember at a loss.* The facts are the same as in paragraph (a) of this *Example* 1 except that B sells the land to X for $90 (rather than $110). The attributes and timing of S's intercompany gain and B's corresponding loss are determined under the matching rule. If S and B were divisions of a single corporation and the intercompany sale were a transfer between the divisions, B would succeed to S's $70 basis in the land and would have a $20 gain from the sale to X instead of a $10 loss. Thus, S takes its entire $30 gain into account in Year 3 to reflect the $30 difference between B's $10 loss taken into account and the $20 recomputed gain. S's $30 gain is long-term capital gain, and B's $10 loss is long-term capital loss.

(g) *Intercompany gain followed by distribution to a nonmember at a loss.* The facts are the same as in paragraph (a) of this *Example 1,* except that B distributes the land to X, a minority shareholder of B, and at the time of the distribution the land has a fair market value of $90. The attributes and timing of S's intercompany gain and B's corresponding loss are determined under the matching rule. Under section 311(a), B does not recognize its $10 loss on the distribution to X. If S and B were divisions of a single corporation and the intercompany sale were a transfer between divisions, B would succeed to S's $70 basis in the land and would have a $20 gain from the distribution to X instead of an unrecognized $10 loss. Under paragraph (b)(3)(ii) of this section, B's loss that is not recognized under section 311(a) is a corresponding item. Thus, S takes its $30 gain into account under the matching rule in Year 3 to reflect the difference between B's $10 corresponding unrecognized loss and the $20 recomputed gain. B's $10 corresponding loss offsets $10 of S's intercompany gain and, under paragraph (c)(4)(i) of this section, the attributes of B's corresponding item control the attributes of S's intercompany item. Paragraph (c)(6) of this section does not prevent the redetermination of S's intercompany item as excluded from gross income. (See paragraph (c)(6)(ii)(B) of this section). Thus, $10 of S's $30 gain is redetermined to be excluded from gross income.

(h) *Intercompany sale followed by section 1031 exchange with nonmember.* The facts are the same as in paragraph (a) of this *Example 1, except,* that, instead of selling the land to X, B exchanges the land for land owned by X in a transaction to which section 1031 applies. There is no difference in Year 3 between B's $0 corresponding item taken into account and the $0 recomputed corresponding item. Thus, none of S's intercompany gain is taken into account under the matching rule as a result of the section 1031 exchange. Instead, B's gain is preserved in the land received from X and, under the successor asset rule of paragraph (j)(1) of this section, S's intercompany gain is taken into account by reference to the replacement property. (If B takes gain into account as a result of boot received in the exchange, S's intercompany gain is taken into account under the matching rule to the extent the boot causes a difference between B's gain taken into account and the recomputed gain.)

(i) *Intercompany sale followed by section 351 transfer to nonmember.* The facts are the same as in paragraph (a) of this *Example 1,* except that, instead of selling the land to X, B transfers the land to X in a transaction to which section 351(a) applies and X remains a nonmember. There is no difference in Year 3 between B's $0 corresponding item taken into account and the $0 recomputed corresponding item. Thus, none of S's intercompany gain is taken into account under the matching rule as a result of the section 351(a) transfer. However, S's entire gain is taken into account in Year 3 under the acceleration rule of paragraph (d) of this section (because X, a nonmember, reflects B's $100 cost basis in the land under section 362).

Example 2. Dealer activities. (a) *Facts.* S holds land for investment with a basis of $70. On January 1 of Year 1, S sells the land to B for $100. B develops the land as residential real estate, and sells developed lots to customers during Year 3 for an aggregate amount of $110.

(b) *Attributes.* S and B are treated under the matching rule as divisions of a single corporation for purposes of determining the attributes of S's intercompany item and B's corresponding item. Thus, although S held the land for investment, whether the gain is treated as from the sale of property described in section 1221(1) is based on the activities of both S and B. If, based on both's S's and B's activities, the land is described in section 1221(1), both S's and B's gain are ordinary income.

Example 3. Intercompany section 351 transfer. (a) *Facts.* S holds land with a $70 basis and a $100 fair market value for sale to customers in the ordinary course of business. On January 1 of Year 1, S transfers the land to B in exchange for all of the stock of B in a transaction to which section 351 applies. S has no gain or loss under section 351(a), and its basis in the B stock is $70 under section 358. Under section 362, B's basis in the land is $70. B holds the land for investment. On July 1 of Year 3, B sells the land to X for $100. Assume that if S and B were divisions of a single corporation, B's gain from the sale would be ordinary income because of S's activities.

Reg. §1.1502-13(c)(7)(ii)

(b) *Timing and attributes.* Under paragraph (b)(1) of this section, S's transfer to B is an intercompany transaction. Under paragraph (c)(3) of this section, S is treated as transferring the land in exchange for B's stock even though, as divisions, S could not own stock of B. S has no intercompany item, but B's $30 gain from its sale of the land to X is a corresponding item because the land was acquired in an intercompany transaction. B's $30 gain is ordinary income that is taken into account under B's method of accounting.

(c) *Intercompany section 351 transfer with boot* The facts are the same as in paragraph (a) of this *Example 3, except,* that S receives $10 cash in addition to the B stock in the transfer. S recognizes $10 of gain under section 351(b), and its basis in the B stock is $70 under section 358. Under section 362, B's basis in the land is $80. S takes its $10 intercompany gain into account in Year 3 to reflect the $10 difference between B's $20 corresponding gain taken into account and the $30 recomputed gain. Both S's $10 gain and B's $20 gain are ordinary income.

(d) *Partial disposition.* The facts are the same as in paragraph (c) of this *Example 3,* except B sells a only a one-half, undivided interest in the land to X for $50. The timing and attributes are determined in the manner provided in paragraph (b) of this *Example 3,* except that S takes only $5 of its gain into account in Year 3 to reflect the $5 difference between B's $10 gain taken into account and the $15 recomputed gain.

Example 4. Depreciable property. (a) *Facts.* On January 1 of Year 1, S buys 10-year recovery property for $100 and depreciates it under the straight-line method. On January 1 of Year 3, S sells the property to B for $130. Under .section 168(i)(7), B is treated as S for purposes of section 168 to the extent B's $130 basis does not exceed S's adjusted basis at the time of the sale. B's additional basis is treated as new 10-year recovery property for which B elects the straight-line method of recovery. (To simplify the example, the half-year convention is disregarded.)

(b) *Depreciation through Year 3; intercompany gain.* S claims $10 of depreciation for each of Years 1 and 2 and has an $80 basis at the time of the sale to B. Thus, S has a $50 intercompany gain from its sale to B. For Year 3, B has $10 of depreciation with respect to $80 of its basis (the portion of its $130 basis not exceeding S's adjusted basis). In addition, B has $5 of depreciation with respect to the $50 of its additional basis that exceeds S's adjusted basis.

(c) *Timing.* S's $50 gain is taken into account to reflect the difference for each consolidated return year between B's depreciation taken into account with respect to the property and the recomputed depreciation. For Year 3, B takes $15 of depreciation into account. If the intercompany transaction were a transfer between divisions of a single corporation, B would succeed to S's adjusted basis in the property and take into ac-

count only $10 of depreciation for Year 3. Thus, S takes $5 of gain into account in Year 3. In each subsequent year that B takes into account $15 of depreciation with respect to the property, S takes into account $5 of gain.

(d) *Attributes.* Under paragraph (c)(1)(i) of this section, the attributes of S's gain and B's depreciation must be redetermined to the extent necessary to produce the same effect on consolidated taxable income as if the intercompany transaction were between divisions of a single corporation (the group must have a net depreciation deduction of $10). In each year, $5 of B's corresponding depreciation deduction offsets S's $5 intercompany gain taken into account and, under paragraph (c)(4)(i) of this section, the attributes of B's corresponding item control the attributes of S's intercompany item. Accordingly, S's intercompany gain that is taken into account as a result of B's depreciation deduction is ordinary income.

(e) *Sale of property to a nonmember.* The facts are the same as in paragraph (a) of this *Example 4,* except that B sells the property to X on January 1 of Year 5 for $110. As set forth in paragraphs (c) and (d) of this *Example 4,* B has $15 of depreciation with respect to the property in each of Years 3 and 4, causing S to take $5 of intercompany gain into account in each year as ordinary income. The $40 balance of S's intercompany gain is taken into account in Year 5 as a result of B's sale to X, to reflect the $40 difference between B's $10 gain taken into account and the $50 of recomputed gain ($110 of sale proceeds minus the $60 basis B would have if the intercompany sale were a transfer between divisions of a single corporation). Treating S and B as divisions of a single corporation, $40 of the gain is section 1245 gain and $10 is section 1231 gain. On a separate entity basis, S would have more than $10 treated as section 1231 gain, and B would have no amount treated as section 1231 gain. Under paragraph (c)(4)(ii) of this section, all $10 of the section 1231 gain is allocated to S. S's remaining $30 of gain, and all of B's $10 gain, is treated as section 1245 gain.

Example 5. Intercompany sale followed by installment sale. (a) *Facts.* S holds land for investment with a basis of $70x. On January 1 of Year 1, S sells the land to B for $100x. B also holds the land for investment. On July 1 of Year 3, B sells the land to X in exchange for X's $110x note. The note bears a market rate of interest in excess of the applicable Federal rate, and provides for principal payments of $55x in Year 4 and $55x in Year 5. The interest charge under section 453A(c) applies to X's note.

(b) *Timing and attributes.* S takes its $30x gain into account to reflect the difference in each consolidated return year between B's gain taken into account for the year and the recomputed gain. Under section 453, B takes into account $5x of gain in Year 4 and $5x of gain in Year 5. Thus, S takes into account $15x of gain in Year 4 and

$15x of gain in Year 5 to reflect the $15x difference in each of those years between B's $5x gain taken into account and the $20x recomputed gain. Both S's $30x gain and B's $10x gain are subject to the section 453A(c) interest charge beginning in Year 3.

(c) *Election out under section 453(d).* If, under the facts in paragraph (a) of this *Example 5,* the P group wishes to elect not to apply section 453 with respect to S's gain, an election under section 453(d) must be made for Year 3 with respect to B's gain. This election will cause B's $10x gain to be taken into account in Year 3. Under the matching rule, this will result in S's $30x gain being taken into account in Year 3. (An election by the P group solely with respect to S's gain has no effect because the gain from S's sale to B is taken into account under the matching rule, and therefore must reflect the difference between B's gain taken into account and the recomputed gain.)

(d) *Sale to a nonmember at a loss, but overall gain.* The facts are the same as in paragraph (a) of this *Example 5,* except that B sells the land to X in exchange for X's $90x note (rather than $110x note). If S and B were divisions of a single corporation, B would succeed to S's basis in the land, and the sale to X would be eligible for installment reporting under section 453, because it resulted in an overall gain. However, because only gains may be reported on the installment method, B's $10x corresponding loss is taken into account in, Year 3. Under paragraph (b)(4) of this section the recomputed corresponding item is $20x gain that would be taken into account under the installment method, $0 in Year 3 and $10x in each of Years 4 and 5. Thus, in Year 3 S takes $10x of gain into account to reflect the difference between B's $10x loss taken into account and the $0 recomputed gain for Year 3. Under paragraph (c)(4)(i) of this section, B's $10x corresponding loss offsets $10x of S's intercompany gain, and B's attributes control. S takes $10x of gain into account in each of Years 4 and 5 to reflect the difference in those years between B's $0 gain taken into account and the $10x recomputed gain that would be taken into account under the installment method. only the $20x of S's gain taken into account in Years 4 and 5 is subject to the interest charge under section 453A(c) beginning in Year 3. (If P elects under section 453(d) for Year 3 not to apply section 453 with respect to the gain, all of S's $30x gain will be taken into account in Year 3 to reflect the difference between B's $10x loss taken into account and the $20x recomputed gain.)

(e) *Intercompany loss, installment gain.* The facts are the same as in paragraph (a) of this *Example 5,* except that S has a $130x (rather than $70x) basis in the land. Under paragraph (c)(1)(i) of this section, the separate entity attributes of S's and B's items from the intercompany transaction must be redetermined to produce the same effect on consolidated taxable income (and tax

liability) as if the transaction had been a transfer between divisions. If S and B were divisions of a single corporation, B would succeed to S's basis in the land and the group would have $20x loss from the sale to X, installment reporting would be unavailable, and the interest charge under section 453A(c) would not apply. Accordingly, B's gain from the transaction is not eligible for installment treatment under section 453. B takes its $10x gain into account in Year 3, and S takes its $30x of loss into account in Year 3 to reflect the difference between B's $10x gain and the $20x recomputed loss.

(f) *Recapture income.* The facts are the same as in paragraph (a) of this *Example 5,* except that S bought depreciable property (rather than land) for $100x, claimed depreciation deductions, and reduced the property's basis to $70x before Year 1. (To simplify the example, B's depreciation is disregarded.) If the intercompany sale of property had been a transfer between divisions of a single corporation, $30x of the $40x gain from the sale to X would be section 1245 gain (which is ineligible for installment reporting) and $10x would be section 1231 gain (which is eligible for installment reporting). On a separate entity basis, S would have $30x of section 1245 gain and B would have $10x of section 1231 gain. Accordingly, the attributes are not redetermined under paragraph (c)(1)(i) of this section. All of B's $10x gain is eligible for installment reporting and is taken into account $5x each in Years 4 and 5 (and is subject to the interest charge under section 453A(c)). S's $30x gain is taken into account in Year 3 to reflect the difference between B's $0 gain taken into account and the $30x of recomputed gain. (If S had bought the depreciable property for $110X and its recomputed basis under section 1245 had been $110x (rather than $100x), B's $10x gain and S's $30x gain would both be recapture income ineligible for installment reporting.)

Example 6. Intercompany sale of installment obligation. (a) *Facts.* S holds land for investment with a basis of $70x. On January 1 of Year 1, S sells the land to X in exchange for X's $100x note, and S reports its gain on the installment method under section 453. X's note bears interest at a market rate of interest in excess of the applicable Federal rate, and provides for principal payments of $50x in Year 5 and $50x in Year 6. Section 453A applies to X's note. On July 1 of Year 3, S sells X's note to B for $100x, resulting in $30x gain from S's prior sale of the land to X under section 453B(a).

(b) *Timing and attributes.* S's sale of X's note to B is an intercompany transaction, and S's $30x gain is intercompany gain. S takes $15x of the gain into account in each of Years 5 and 6 to reflect the $15x difference in each year between B's $0 gain taken into account and the $15x recomputed gain. S's gain continues to be treated as its gain from the sale to X, and the deferred tax liability remains subject to the interest charge under section 453A(c).

(c) *Worthlessness.* The facts are the same as in paragraph (a) of this *Example 6,* except that X's note becomes worthless on December 1 of Year 3 and B has a $100x short-term capital loss under section 165(g) on a separate entity basis. Under paragraph (c)(1)(i) of this section, B's holding period for X's note is aggregated with S's holding period. Thus, B's loss is a long-term capital loss. S takes its $30x gain into account in Year 3 to reflect the $30x difference between B's $100x loss taken into account and the $70x recomputed loss. Under paragraph (c)(1)(i) of this section, S's gain is long-term capital gain.

(d) *Pledge.* The facts are the same as in paragraph (a) of this *Example 6, except,* that, on December 1 of Year 3, B borrows $100x from an unrelated bank and secures the indebtedness with X's note. X's note remains subject to section 453A(d) following the sale to B. Under section 453A(d), B's $100x of proceeds from the secured indebtedness is treated as an amount received on December 1 of Year 3 by B on X's note. Thus, S takes its entire $30x gain into account in Year 3.

Example 7. Performance of services. (a) *Facts.* S is a driller of water wells. B operates a ranch in a remote location, and B's taxable income from the ranch is not subject to section 447. B's ranch requires water to maintain its cattle. During Year 1, S drills an artesian well on B's ranch in exchange for $100 from B, and S incurs $80 of expenses (e.g., for employees and equipment). B capitalizes its $100 cost for the well under section 263, and takes into account $10 of cost recovery deductions in each of Years 2 through 11. Under its separate entity method of accounting, S would take its income and expenses into account in Year 1. If S and B were divisions of a single corporation, the costs incurred in drilling the well would be capitalized.

(b) *Definitions.* Under paragraph (b)(1) of this section, the service transaction is an intercompany transaction, S is the selling member, and B is the buying member. Under paragraph (b)(2)(ii) of this section, S's $100 of income and $80 of related expenses are both included in determining its intercompany income of $20.

(c) *Timing and attributes.* S's $20 of intercompany income is taken into account under the matching rule to reflect the $20 difference between B's corresponding items taken into account (based on its $100 cost basis in the well) and the recomputed corresponding items (based on the $80 basis that B would have if S and B were divisions of a single corporation and B's basis were determined by reference to S's $80 of expenses). In Year 1, S takes into account $80 of its income and the $80 of expenses. In each of Years 2 through 11, S takes $2 of its $20 intercompany income into account to reflect the annual $2 difference between B's $10 of cost recovery deductions taken into account and the $8 of recomputed cost recovery deductions. S's $100 income

and $80 expenses, and B's cost recovery deductions, are ordinary items (because S's and B's items would be ordinary on a separate entity basis, the attributes are not redetermined under paragraph (c)(1)(i) of this section). If S's offsetting $80 of income and expense would not be taken into account in the same year under its separate entity method of accounting, they nevertheless must be taken into account under this section in a manner that clearly reflects consolidated taxable income. See paragraph (a)(3)(i) of this section.

(d) *Sale of capitalized services.* The facts are the same as in paragraph (a) of this *Example 7,* except that B sells the ranch before Year 11 and recognizes gain attributable to the well. To the extent of S's income taken into account as a result of B's cost recovery deductions, as well as S's offsetting $80 of income and expense, the timing and attributes are determined in the manner provided in paragraph (c) of this *Example 7.* The attributes of the remainder of S's $20 of income and B's gain from the sale are redetermined to produce the same effect on consolidated taxable income as if S and B were divisions of a single corporation. Accordingly, S's remaining intercompany income is treated as recapture income or section 1231 gain, even though it is from S's performance of services.

Example 8. Rental of property. B operates a ranch that requires grazing land for its cattle. S owns undeveloped land adjoining B's ranch. On January 1 of Year 1, S leases grazing rights to B for Year 1. B's $100 rent expense is deductible for Year 1 under its separate entity accounting method. Under paragraph (b)(1) of this section, the rental transaction is an intercompany transaction, S is the selling member, and B is the buying member. S takes its $100 of income into account in Year 1 to reflect the $100 difference between B's rental deduction taken into account and the $0 recomputed rental deduction. S's income and B's deduction are ordinary items (because S's intercompany item and B's corresponding item would both be ordinary on a separate entity basis, the attributes are not redetermined under paragraph (c)(1)(i) of this section).

Example 9. Intercompany sale of a partnership interest. (a) *Facts.* S owns a 20% interest in the capital and profits of a general partnership. The partnership holds land for investment with a basis equal to its value, and operates depreciable assets which have value in excess of basis. S's basis in its partnership interest equals its share of the adjusted basis of the partnership's land and depreciable assets. The partnership has an election under section 754 in effect. On January 1 of Year 1, S sells its partnership interest to B at a gain. During Years 1 through 10, the partnership depreciates the operating assets, and B's depreciation deductions from the partnership reflect the increase in the basis of the depreciable assets under section 743(b).

Reg. §1.1502-13(c)(7)(ii)

(b) *Timing and attributes.* S's gain is taken into account during Years 1 though 10 to reflect the difference in each year between B's depreciation deductions from the partnership taken into account and the recomputed depreciation deductions from the partnership. Under paragraphs (c)(1)(i) and (c)(4)(i) of this section, S's gain taken into account is ordinary income. (The acceleration rule does not apply to S's gain as a result of the section 743(b) adjustment, because the adjustment is solely with respect to B and therefore no nonmember reflects any part of the intercompany transaction.)

(c) *Partnership sale of assets.* The facts are the same as in paragraph (a) of this *Example 9,* and the partnership sells some of its depreciable assets to X at a gain on December 31 of Year 4. In addition to the intercompany gain taken into account as a result of the partnership's depreciation, S takes intercompany gain into account in Year 4 to reflect the difference between B's partnership items taken into account from the sale (which reflect the basis increase under section 743(b)) and the recomputed partnership items. The attributes of S's additional gain are redetermined to produce the same effect on consolidated taxable income as if S and B were divisions of a single corporation (recapture income or section 1231 gain).

(d) *B's sale of partnership interest.* The facts are the same as in paragraph (a) of this *Example 9,* and on December 31 of Year 4, B sells its partnership interest to X at no gain or loss. In addition to the intercompany gain taken into account as a result of the partnership's depreciation, the remaining balance of S's intercompany gain is taken into account in Year 4 to reflect the difference between B's $0 taken into account from the sale of the partnership interest and the recomputed gain The character of S's remaining intercompany item and B's corresponding item are determined on a separate entity basis under section 751, and then redetermined to the extent necessary to produce the same effect as treating the intercompany transaction as occurring between divisions of a single corporation.

(e) *No section 754 election.* The facts are the same as in paragraph (d) of this *Example 9,* except that the partnership does not have a section 754 election in effect, and B recognizes a capital loss from its sale of the partnership interest to X on December 31 of Year 4. Because there is no difference between B's depreciation deductions from the partnership taken into account and the recomputed depreciation deductions, S does not take any of its gain into account during Years 1 through 4 as a result of B's partnership's items. Instead, S's entire intercompany gain is taken into account in Year 4 to reflect the difference between B's loss taken into account from the sale to X and the recomputed partnership gain or loss.

Example 10. Net operating losses subject to section 382 or the SRLY rules. (a) *Facts.* On January 1 of Year 1, P buys all of S's stock. S has net operating loss carryovers from prior years. P's acquisition results in an ownership change under section 382 with respect to S's loss carryovers, and S has a net unrealized built-in gain (within the meaning of section 382(h)(3)). S owns nondepreciable property with a $70 basis and $100 value. On July 1 of Year 3, S sells the property to B for $100, and its $30 gain is recognized built-in gain (within the meaning of section 382(h)(2)) on a separate entity basis. On December 1 of Year 5, B sells the property to X for $90.

(b) *Timing and attributes.* S's $30 gain is taken into account in Year 5 to reflect the $30 difference between B's $10 loss taken into account and the recomputed $20 gain. S and B are treated as divisions of a single corporation for purposes of applying section 382 in connection with the intercompany transaction. Under a single entity analysis, the single corporation has losses subject to limitation under section 382, and this limitation may be increased under section 382(h) if the single corporation has recognized built-in gain with respect to those losses. B's $10 corresponding loss offsets $10 of S's intercompany gain, and thus, under paragraph (c)(4)(i) of this section, $10 of S's intercompany gain is redetermined not to be recognized built-in gain. S's remaining $20 intercompany gain continues to be treated as recognized built-in gain.

(c) *B's recognized built-in gain.* The facts are the same as in paragraph (a) of this *Example 10,* except that the property declines in value after S becomes a member of the P group, S sells the property to B for its $70 basis, and B sells the property to X for $90 during Year 5. Treating S and B as divisions of a single corporation, S's sale to B does not cause the property to cease to be built-in gain property. Thus, B's $20 gain from its sale to X is recognized built-in gain that increases the section 382 limitation applicable to S's losses.

(d) *SRLY limitation.* The facts are the same as in paragraph (a) of this *Example 10,* except that P's acquisition of S is not subject to the overlap rule of § 1.1502-21(g), and S's net operating loss carryovers are subject to the separate return limitation year (SRLY) rules. See § 1.1502-21(c). The application of the SRLY rules depends on S's status as a separate corporation having losses from separate return limitation years. Under paragraph (c)(5), the attribute of S's intercompany item as it relates to S's SRLY limitation is not redetermined, because the SRLY limitation depends on S's special status. Accordingly, S's $30 intercompany gain is included in determining its SRLY limitation for Year 5.

Example 11. Section 475. (a) *Facts.* S, a dealer in securities within the meaning of section 475(c), owns a security with a basis of $70. The security is held for sale to customers and is not identified under section 475(b) as within an exception to marking to market. On July 1 of Year 1, S sells the security to B for $100. B is not a dealer and holds the security for investment. On December 31 of Year 1, the fair market value of the security is $100. On July 1 of Year 2, B sells the security to X for $110.

(b) *Attributes.* Under section 475, a dealer in securities can treat a security as within an exception to marking to market under section 475(b) only if it timely identifies the security as so described. Under the matching rule, attributes must be redetermined by treating S and B as divisions of a single corporation. As a result of S's activities, the single corporation is treated as a dealer with respect to securities, and B must continue to mark to market the security acquired from S. Thus, B's corresponding items and the recomputed corresponding items are determined by continuing to treat the security as not within an exception to marking to market. Under section 475(d)(3), it is possible for the character of S's intercompany items to differ from the character of B's corresponding items.

(c) *Timing and character.* S has a $30 gain when it disposes of the security by selling it to B. This gain is intercompany gain that is taken into account in Year 1 to reflect the $30 difference between B's $0 gain taken into account from marking the security to market under section 475 and the recomputed $30 gain that would be taken into account. The character of S's gain and B's gain are redetermined as if the security were transferred between divisions. Accordingly, S's gain is ordinary income under section 475(d)(3)(A)(i), but under section 475(d)(3)(B)(ii) B's $10 gain from its sale to X is capital gain that is taken into account in Year 2.

(d) *Nondealer to dealer.* The facts are the same as in paragraph (a) of this *Example 11*, except that S is not a dealer and holds the security for investment with a $70 basis, B is a dealer to which section 475 applies and, immediately after acquiring the security from S for $100, B holds the security for sale to customers in the ordinary course of its trade or business. Because S is not a dealer and held the security for investment, the security is treated as properly identified as held for investment under section 475(b)(1) until it is sold to B. Under section 475(b)(3), the security thereafter ceases to be described in section 475(b)(1) because B holds the security for sale to customers. The mark-to-market requirement applies only to changes in the value of the security after B's acquisition. B's mark-to-market gain taken into account and the recomputed mark-to-market gain are both determined based on changes from the $100 value of the security at the time of B's acquisition. There is no difference between B's $0 mark-to-market gain taken into account in Year 1 and the $0 recomputed mark-to-market gain. Therefore, none of S's gain is taken into account in Year 1 as a result of B's marking the security to market in Year 1. In Year 2, B has a $10 gain when it disposes of the security by selling it to X, but would have had a $40 gain if S and B were

divisions of a single corporation. Thus, S takes its $30 gain into account in Year 2 under the matching rule. Under section 475(d)(3), S's gain is capital gain even though B's subsequent gain or loss from marking to market or disposing of the security is ordinary gain or loss. If B disposes of the security at a $10 loss in Year 2, S's gain taken into account in Year 2 is still capital because on a single entity basis section 475(d)(3) would provide for $30 of capital gain and $10 of ordinary loss. Because the attributes are not redetermined under paragraph (c)(1)(i) of this section, paragraph (c)(4)(i) of this section does not apply. Furthermore, if B held the security for investment, and so identified the security under section 475(b)(1), the security would continue to be excepted from marking to market.

Example 12. Section 1092. (a) *Facts.* On July 1 of Year 1, S enters into offsetting long and short positions with respect to actively traded personal property. The positions are not section 1256 contracts, and they are the only positions taken into account for purposes of applying section 1092. On August 1 of Year 1, S sells the long position to B at an $11 loss, and there is $11 of unrealized gain in the offsetting short position. On December 1 of Year 1, B sells the long position to X at no gain or loss. On December 31 of Year 1, there is still $11 of unrealized gain in the short position. On February 1 of Year 2, S closes the short position at an $11 gain.

(b) *Timing and attributes.* If the sale from S to B were a transfer between divisions of a single corporation, the $11 loss on the sale to X would have been deferred under section 1092(a)(1)(A). Accordingly, there is no difference in Year 1 between B's corresponding item of $0 and the recomputed corresponding item of $0. S takes its $11 loss into account in Year 2 to reflect the difference between B's corresponding item of $0 taken into account in Year 2 and the recomputed loss of $11 that would have been taken into account in Year 2 under section 1092(a)(1)(B) if S and B had been divisions of a single corporation. (The results are the same under section 267(f).)

Example 13. [Reserved.]

Example 14. Source of income under section 863. (a) *Intercompany sale with no independent factory price.* S manufactures inventory in the United States, and recognizes $75 of income on sales to B in Year 1. B distributes the inventory in Country Y and recognizes $25 of income on sales to X, also in Year 1. Title passes from S to B, and from B to X, in Country Y. There is no independent factory price (as defined in regulations under section 863) for the sale from S to B. Under the matching rule, S's $75 intercompany income and B's $25 corresponding income are taken into account in Year 1. In determining the source of income, S and B are treated as divisions of a single corporation, and section 863 applies as if $100 of income were recognized from producing in the United States and selling in Country Y. Assume that applying the section 863 regulations on a single entity basis, $50 is treated as foreign source income and $50 as U.S. source income. Assume further that on a separate entity basis, S would have $37.50 of foreign source income and $37.50 of U.S. source income, and that all of B's $25 of income would be foreign source income. Thus, on a separate entity basis, S and B would have $62.50 of combined foreign source income and $37.50 of U.S. source income. Accordingly, under single entity treatment, $12.50 that would be treated as foreign source income on a separate entity basis is redetermined to be U.S. source income. Under paragraph (c)(1)(i) of this section, attributes are redetermined only to the extent of the $12.50 necessary to achieve the same effect as a single entity determination. Under paragraph (c)(4)(ii) of this section, the redetermined attribute must be allocated between S and B using a reasonable method. For example, it may be reasonable to recharacterize only S's foreign source income as U.S. source income because only S would have any U.S. source income on a separate entity basis. However, it may also be reasonable to allocate the redetermined attribute between S and B in proportion to their separate entity amounts of foreign source income (in a 3:2 ratio, so that $7.50 of S's foreign source income is redetermined to be U.S. source and $5 of B's foreign source income is redetermined to be U.S. source), provided the same method is applied to all similar transactions within the group.

(b) *Intercompany sale with independent factory price.* The facts are the same as in paragraph (a) of this *Example 14,* except that an independent factory price exists for the sale by S to B such that $70 of S's $75 of income is attributable to the production function. Assume that on a single entity basis, $70 is treated as U.S. source income (because of the existence of the independent factory price) and $30 is treated as foreign source income. Assume that on a separate entity basis, $70 of S's income would be treated as U.S. source, $5 of S's income would be treated as foreign source income, and all of B's $25 income would be treated as foreign source income. Because the results are the same on a single entity basis and a separate entity basis, the attributes are not redetermined under paragraph (c)(1)(i) of this section.

(c) *Sale of property reflecting intercompany services or intangibles.* S earns $10 of income performing services in the United States for B. B capitalizes S's fees into the basis of property that it manufactures in the United States and sells to an unrelated person in Year 1 at a $90 profit, with title passing in Country Y. Under the matching rule, S's $10 income and B's $90 income are taken into account in Year 1. In determining the source of income, S and B are treated as divisions of a single corporation, and section 863 applies as if $100 were earned from manufacturing in the United States and selling in Country Y. Assume that on a single entity basis

$50 is treated as foreign source income and $50 is treated as U.S. source income. Assume that on a separate entity basis, S would have $10 of U.S. source income, and B would have $45 of foreign source income and $45 of U.S. source income. Accordingly, under single entity treatment, $5 of income that would be treated as U.S. source income on a separate entity basis is redetermined to be foreign source income. Under paragraph (c)(1)(i) of this section, attributes are redetermined only to the extent of the $5 necessary to achieve the same effect as a single entity determination. Under paragraph (c)(4)(ii) of this section, the redetermined attribute must be allocated between S and B using a reasonable method. (If instead of performing services, S licensed an intangible to B and earned $10 that would be treated as U.S. source income on a separate entity basis, the results would be the same.)

Example 15. Section 1248. (a) *Facts.* On January 1 of Year 1, S forms FT, a wholly owned foreign subsidiary, with a $10 contribution. During Years 1 through 3, FT has earnings and profits of $40. None of the earnings and profits is taxed as subpart F income under section 951, and FT distributes no dividends to S during this period. On January 1 of Year 4, S sells its FT stock to B for $50. While B owns FT, FT has a deficit in earnings and profits of $10. On July 1 of Year 6, B sells its FT stock for $70 to X, an unrelated foreign corporation.

(b) *Timing.* S's $40 of intercompany gain is taken into account in Year 6 to reflect the difference between B's $20 of gain taken into account and the $60 recomputed gain.

(c) *Attributes.* Under the matching rule, the attributes of S's intercompany gain and B's corresponding gain are redetermined to have the same effect on consolidated taxable income (and consolidated tax liability) as if S and B were divisions of a single corporation. On a single entity basis, there is $60 of gain and the portion which is characterized as a dividend under section 1248 is determined on the basis of FT's $30 of earnings and profits at the time of the sale of FT to X (the sum of FT's $40 of earnings and profits while held by S and FT's $10 deficit in earnings and profits while held by B). Therefore, $30 of the $60 gain is treated as a dividend under section 1248. The remaining $30 is treated as capital gain. On a separate entity basis, all of S's $40 gain would be treated as a dividend under section 1248 and all of B's $20 gain would be treated as capital gain. Thus, as a result of the single entity determination, $10 that would be treated as a dividend under section 1248 on a separate entity basis is redetermined to be capital gain. Under paragraph (c)(4)(ii) of this section, this redetermined attribute must be allocated between S's intercompany item and B's corresponding item by using a reasonable method. On a separate entity basis, only S would have any amount treated as a dividend under section 1248 available for redetermination. Accordingly, $10 of S's income is redetermined to be not subject to section 1248, with the result that $30 of S's intercompany gain is treated as a dividend and the remaining $10 is treated as capital gain. All of B's corresponding gain is treated as capital gain, as it would be on a separate entity basis.

(d) *B has loss.* The facts are the same as in paragraph (a) of this *Example 15*, except that FT has no earnings and profits or deficit in earnings and profits while B owns FT, and B sells the FT stock to X for $40. On a single entity basis, there is $30 of gain, and section 1248 is applied on the basis of FT's $40 earnings and profits at the time of the sale of FT to X. Under section 1248, the amount treated as a dividend is limited to $30 (the amount of the gain). On a separate entity basis, S's entire $40 gain would be treated as a dividend under section 1248, and B's $10 loss would be a capital loss. B's $10 corresponding loss offsets $10 of S's intercompany gain and, under paragraph (c)(4)(i) of this section, the attributes of B's corresponding item control. Accordingly, $10 of S's gain must be redetermined to be capital gain. B's $10 loss remains a capital loss. (If, however, S sold FT to B at a loss and B sold FT to X at a gain, it may be unreasonable for the attributes of B's corresponding gain to control S's offsetting intercompany loss. If B's attributes were to control, for example, the group could possibly claim a larger foreign tax credit than would be available if S and B were divisions of a single corporation.)

Example 16. Intercompany stock distribution followed by section 332 liquidation. (a) *Facts.* P owns all of the stock of S, S owns all the stock of T, a member of the P group, and T owns all of the stock of T1, also a member of the P group. On January 1 of Year 1, S distributes all of the T stock to P in a distribution to which section 301 applies. At the time of this distribution, the value of the T stock is $100 and S has a $40 basis in the T stock. Under section 311(b), the distribution creates $60 of intercompany gain to S. Under section 301(d), P's basis in the T stock is $100. S will take its $60 intercompany gain into account under the matching rule. On January 1 of Year 4, in an independent transaction, S distributes all of its assets to P in a complete liquidation to which section 332 applies, and, under paragraph (j)(2) of this section, P succeeds to S's $60 gain. On January 1 of Year 7, T distributes all of its T1 stock to P in a transaction to which section 355 applies. At the time of this distribution, P has a basis in the T stock of $100, the value of the T stock (without regard to T1) is $75, and the value of the T1 stock is $25. Under section 358, P allocates $25 of its $100 basis in the T stock to the T1 stock, and, under paragraph (j)(1) of this section, the T1 stock becomes a successor asset to the T stock. On January 1 of Year 9, in an independent transaction, T distributes all of its assets

to P in a complete liquidation to which section 332 applies.

(b) *Analysis.* Under paragraphs (b)(1) and (f)(2) of this section, S's distribution in Year 1 of the T stock to P is an intercompany transaction, S is the selling member, and P is the buying member. In Year 9 when T liquidates, P has no gain or loss under section 332. Under paragraph (b)(3)(ii) of this section, P's $0 gain or loss with respect to the T stock under section 332 is a corresponding item. P takes $45 (75/100 × $60) of its intercompany gain into account under the matching rule in Year 9 to reflect the difference between P's $0 of unrecognized gain and P's $45 of recomputed unrecognized gain. (If P and S were divisions of a single corporation, P would have had a $40 basis in the T stock, and, after the Year 7 distribution of the T1 stock, would have held the T stock with a $30 basis.) However, paragraph (c)(6) of this section does not prevent the redetermination of P's intercompany gain as excluded from gross income provided P succeeds to S's intercompany item; P and S are a single entity; P's basis in the T stock that reflects the $45 intercompany gain taken into account is eliminated without the recognition of gain or loss (and this eliminated basis is not further reflected in the basis of any successor asset); the group has not derived and no taxpayer will derive any Federal income tax benefit from the basis in the T stock and will not derive any Federal income tax benefit from a redetermination of this portion of the gain; and the effects of the intercompany transaction have not previously been reflected, directly or indirectly, on the P group's consolidated return. (See paragraph (c)(6)(ii)(C) of this section.) Accordingly, under paragraph (c)(6)(ii)(C) of this section, the $45 intercompany gain that P takes into account is redetermined to be excluded from gross income. P's basis in its T1 stock continues to reflect $15 of intercompany gain.

Example 17. Intercompany stock sale followed by section 355 distribution. (a) *Facts.* The facts are the same as *Example 16*, except that T does not distribute the stock of T1, instead, in Year 7, T makes a distribution of $50 to P in a transaction to which section 301 applies. Under § 1.1502-32, P's basis in its T stock is reduced by $50 and, under paragraph (f)(2)(ii) of this section, the intercompany distribution is excluded from P's gross income. Further, in Year 9, instead of liquidating T, P distributes the T stock to its shareholders in a transaction to which section 355 applies.

(b) *Analysis.* On the distribution of the T stock in Year 9, P has $0 of unrecognized gain under section 355(c). Under paragraph (b)(3)(ii) of this section, P's $0 of unrecognized gain or loss with respect to the T stock under section 355(c) is a corresponding item. P takes its $60 intercompany gain into account under the matching rule in Year 9 to reflect the difference between P's $0 of unrecognized gain and P's $60 of recomputed gain ($50 unrecognized gain and $10 recognized gain). (If P and S were divisions of a single corporation, P would have had a $40 basis in the T stock, and, after the Year 7 distribution, would have held the T stock with a $10 excess loss account.) See paragraph (f)(7), *Example* 2 of this section. Paragraph (c)(6) of this section does not prevent the redetermination of P's intercompany gain as excluded from gross income provided P succeeds to S's intercompany item; P and S are a single entity; P's basis in the T stock that reflects the $60 intercompany gain taken into account is eliminated without the recognition of gain or loss (and this eliminated basis is not further reflected in any successor asset); the group has not derived any Federal income tax benefit from the basis in the T stock and will not derive any Federal income tax benefit from a redetermination of this portion of the gain; and the effects of the intercompany transaction have not previously been reflected, directly or indirectly, on the P group's consolidated return. (See paragraph (c)(6)(ii)(C) of this section.) The intercompany transaction with respect to the T stock resulted in an increase in the basis of the T stock, and this increase in the basis of the T stock prevented P from holding the T stock with a $10 excess loss account (as a result of the Year 7 distribution) at the time of the section 355 distribution. Accordingly, the group derived a Federal income tax benefit from the intercompany transaction to the extent of $10 and, under paragraph (c)(6)(ii)(C) of this section, only $50 of the $60 intercompany gain that P takes into account is redetermined to be excluded from gross income.

(c) *Application of section 355(e)*. If it were determined that section 355(e) applied to P's distribution of the T stock, P would recognize $0 of gain and derive a Federal income tax benefit to the extent of the full $60 increase in the basis of the T stock. Therefore, no portion of P's intercompany gain would be redetermined to be excluded from gross income under paragraph (c)(6)(ii)(C) of this section.

(iii) *Effective/applicability date.*—(A) *In general.*—Paragraphs (c)(6)(ii)(C), (c)(6)(ii)(D), and (c)(7)(ii) *Examples 16* and *17* of this section apply with respect to items taken into account on or after March 4, 2011.

(B) *Prior periods.*—For items taken into account on or after March 7, 2008, and before March 4, 2011, see § 1.1502-13T(c)(6)(ii)(C) and (f)(7), *Examples 7* and *8* as contained in 26 CFR part 1 in effect on April 1, 2009. For items taken into account before March 7, 2008, see § 1.1502-13 as contained in 26 CFR part 1 in effect on April 1, 2007.

(d) *Acceleration rule.*—S's intercompany items and B's corresponding items are taken into account under this paragraph (d) to the extent they cannot be taken into account to produce the effect of treating S and B as divisions of a single

corporation. For this purpose, the following rules apply:

(1) *S's items.*—(i) *Timing.*—S takes its intercompany items into account to the extent they cannot be taken into account to produce the effect of treating S and B as divisions of a single corporation. The items are taken into account immediately before it first becomes impossible to achieve this effect. For this purpose, the effect cannot be achieved—

(A) To the extent an intercompany item or corresponding item will not be taken into account in determining the group's consolidated taxable income (or consolidated tax liability) under the matching rule (for example, if S or B becomes a nonmember, or if S's intercompany item is no longer reflected in the difference between B's basis (or an amount equivalent to basis) in property and the basis (or equivalent amount) the property would have if S and B were divisions of a single corporation); or

(B) To the extent a nonmember reflects, directly or indirectly, any aspect of the intercompany transaction (e.g., if B's cost basis in property purchased from S is reflected by a nonmember under section 362 following a section 351 transaction).

(ii) *Attributes.*—The attributes of S's intercompany items taken into account under this paragraph (d)(1) are determined as follows:

(A) *Sale, exchange, or distribution.*—If the item is from an intercompany sale, exchange, or distribution of property, its attributes are determined under the principles of the matching rule as if B sold the property, at the time the item is taken into account under paragraph (d)(1)(i) of this section, for a cash payment equal to B's adjusted basis in the property (i.e., at no net gain or loss), to the following person:

(1) *Property leaves the group.*—If the property is owned by a nonmember immediately after S's item is taken into account, B is treated as selling the property to that nonmember. If the nonmember is related for purposes of any provision of the Internal Revenue Code or regulations to any party to the intercompany transaction (or any related transaction) or to the common parent, the nonmember is treated as related to B for purposes of that provision. For example, if the nonmember is related to P within the meaning of section 1239(b), the deemed sale is treated as being described in section 1239(a). See paragraph (j)(6) of this section, under which property is not treated as being owned by a nonmember if it is owned by the common parent after the common parent becomes the only remaining member.

(2) *Property does not leave the group.*—If the property is not owned by a nonmember immediately after S's item is taken into account, B is treated as selling the property to an affiliated corporation that is not a member of the group.

(B) *Other transactions.*—If the item is from an intercompany transaction other than a sale, exchange, or distribution of property (e.g., income from S's services capitalized by B), its attributes are determined on a separate entity basis.

(2) *B's items.*—(i) *Attributes.*—The attributes of B's corresponding items continue to be redetermined under the principles of the matching rule, with the following adjustments:

(A) If S and B continue to join with each other in the filing of consolidated returns, the attributes of B's corresponding items (and any applicable holding periods) are determined by continuing to treat S and B as divisions of a single corporation.

(B) Once S and B no longer join with each other in the filing of consolidated returns, the attributes of B's corresponding items are determined as if the S division (but not the B division) were transferred by the single corporation to an unrelated person. Thus, S's activities (and any applicable holding period) before the intercompany transaction continue to affect the attributes of the corresponding items (and any applicable holding period).

(ii) *Timing.*—If paragraph (d)(1) of this section applies to S, B nevertheless continues to take its corresponding items into account under its accounting method. However, the redetermination of the attributes of a corresponding item under this paragraph (d)(2) might affect its timing.

(3) *Examples.*—The acceleration rule of this paragraph (d) is illustrated by the following examples.

Example 1. Becoming a nonmember—timing. (a) *Facts.* S owns land with a basis of $70. On January 1 of Year 1, S sells the land to B for $100. On July 1 of Year 3, P sells 60% of S's stock to X for $60 and, as a result, S becomes a nonmember.

(b) *Matching rule.* Under the matching rule, none of S's $30 gain is taken into account in Years 1 through 3 because there is no difference between B's $0 gain or loss taken into account and the recomputed gain or loss.

(c) *Acceleration of S's intercompany items.* Under the acceleration rule of paragraph (d) of this section, S's $30 gain is taken into account in computing consolidated taxable income (and consolidated tax liability) immediately before the effect of treating S and B as divisions of a single corporation cannot be produced. Because the effect cannot be produced once S becomes a nonmember, S takes its $30 gain into account in Year 3 immediately before becoming a nonmember. S's gain is reflected under § 1.1502-32 in P's basis in the S stock immediately before P's sale of the stock. Under § 1.1502-32, P's basis in the S stock is increased by $30, and therefore P's gain is reduced (or loss is increased) by $18 (60% of $30). See also §§ 1.1502-33 and 1.1502-76(b). (The

results would be the same if S sold the land to B in an installment sale to which section 453 would otherwise apply, because S must take its intercompany gain into account under this section.)

(d) *B's corresponding items.* Notwithstanding the acceleration of S's gain, B continues to take its corresponding items into account under its accounting method. Thus, B's items from the land are taken into account based on subsequent events (e.g., its sale of the land).

(e) *Sale of B's stock.* The facts are the same as in paragraph (a) of this *Example 1*, except that P sells 60% of B's stock (rather than S stock) to X for $60 and, as a result, B becomes a nonmember. Because the effect of treating S and B as divisions of a single corporation cannot be produced once B becomes a nonmember, S takes its $30 gain into account under the acceleration rule immediately before B becomes a nonmember. (The results would be the same if S sold the land to B in an installment sale to which section 453 would otherwise apply, because S must take its intercompany gain into account under this section.)

(f) *Discontinue filing consolidated returns.* The facts are the same as in paragraph (a) of this *Example 1*, except that the P group receives permission under § 1.1502-75(c) to discontinue filing consolidated returns beginning in Year 3. Under the acceleration rule, S takes its $30 gain into account on December 31 of Year 2.

(g) *No subgroups.* The facts are the same as in paragraph (a) of this *Example 1*, except that P simultaneously sells all of the stock of both S and B to X (rather than 60% of S's stock), and S and B become members of the X consolidated group. Because the effect of treating S and B as divisions of a single corporation in the P group cannot be produced once S and B become nonmembers, S takes its $30 gain into account under the acceleration rule immediately before S and B become nonmembers. (Paragraph (j)(5) of this section does not apply to treat the X consolidated group as succeeding to the P group because the X group acquired only the stock of S and B.) However, so long as S and B continue to join with each other in the filing of consolidated returns, B continues to treat S and B as divisions of a single corporation for purposes of determining the attributes of B's corresponding items from the land.

Example 2. Becoming a nonmember—attributes. (a) *Facts.* S holds land for investment with a basis of $70. On January 1 of Year 1, S sells the land to B for $100. B holds the land for sale to customers in the ordinary course of business, and expends substantial resources over a two-year period subdividing, developing, and marketing the land. On July 1 of Year 3, before B has sold any of the land, P sells 60% of S's stock to X for $60 and, as a result, S becomes a nonmember.

(b) *Attributes.* Under the acceleration rule, the attributes of S's gain are redetermined under

Reg. § 1.1502-13(d)(3)

the principles of the matching rule as if B sold the land to an affiliated corporation that is not a member of the group for a cash payment equal to B's adjusted basis in the land (because the land continues to be held within the group). Thus, whether S's gain is capital gain or ordinary income depends on the activities of both S and B. Because S and B no longer join with each other in the filing of consolidated returns, the attributes of B's corresponding items (e.g., from its subsequent sale of the land) are redetermined under the principles of the matching rule as if the S division (but not the B division) were transferred by the single corporation to an unrelated person at the time of P's sale of the S stock. Thus, B continues to take into account the activities of S with respect to the land before the intercompany transaction.

(c) *Depreciable property.* The facts are the same as in paragraph (a) of this *Example 2*, except that the property sold by S to B is depreciable property. Section 1239 applies to treat all of S's gain as ordinary income because it is taken into account as a result of B's deemed sale of the property to a affiliated corporation that is not a member of the group (a related person within the meaning of section 1239(b)).

Example 3. Selling member's disposition of installment note. (a) *Facts.* S owns land with a basis of $70. On January 1 of Year 1, S sells the land to B in exchange for B's $110 note. The note bears a market rate of interest in excess of the applicable Federal rate, and provides for principal payments of $55 in Year 4 and $55 in Year 5. On July 1 of Year 3, S sells B's note to X for $110.

(b) *Timing.* S's intercompany gain is taken into account under this section, and not under the rules of section 453. Consequently, S's sale of B's note does not result in its intercompany gain from the land being taken into account (e.g., under section 453B). The sale does not prevent S's intercompany items and B's corresponding items from being taken into account in determining the group's consolidated taxable income under the matching rule, and X does not reflect any aspect of the intercompany transaction (X has its own cost basis in the note). S will take the intercompany gain into account under the matching rule or acceleration rule based on subsequent events (e.g., B's sale of the land). See also paragraph (g) of this section for additional rules applicable to B's note as an intercompany obligation.

Example 4. Cancellation of debt and attribute reduction under section 108(b). (a) *Facts.* S holds land for investment with a basis of $0. On January 1 of Year 1, S sells the land to B for $100. B also holds the land for investment. During Year 3, B is insolvent and B's nonmember creditors discharge $60 of B's indebtedness. Because of insolvency, B's $60 discharge is excluded from B's gross income under section 108(a), and B reduces the basis of the land by $60 under sections 108(b) and 1017.

(b) *Acceleration rule.* As a result of B's basis reduction under section 1017, $60 of S's intercompany gain will not be taken into account under the matching rule (because there is only a $40 difference between B's $40 basis in the land and the $0 basis the land would have if S and B were divisions of a single corporation). Accordingly, S takes $60 of its gain into account under the acceleration rule in Year 3. S's gain is long-term capital gain, determined under paragraph (d)(1)(ii) of this section as if B sold the land to an affiliated corporation that is not a member of the group for $100 immediately before the basis reduction.

(c) *Purchase price adjustment.* Assume instead that S sells the land to B in exchange for B's $100 purchase money note, B remains solvent, and S subsequently agrees to discharge $60 of the note as a purchase price adjustment to which section 108(e)(5) applies. Under applicable principles of tax law, $60 of S's gain and $60 of B's basis in the land are eliminated and never taken into account. Similarly, the note is not treated as satisfied and reissued under paragraph (g) of this section.

Example 5. Section 481. (a) *Facts.* S operates several trades or businesses, including a manufacturing business. S receives permission to change its method of accounting for valuing inventory for its manufacturing business. S increases the basis of its ending inventory by $100, and the related $100 positive section 481(a) adjustment is to be taken into account ratably over six taxable years, beginning in Year 1. During Year 3, S sells all of the assets used in its manufacturing business to B at a gain. Immediately after the transfer, B does not use the same inventory valuation method as S. On a separate entity basis, S's sale results in an acceleration of the balance of the section 481(a) adjustment to Year 3.

(b) *Timing and attributes.* Under paragraph (b)(2) of this section, the balance of S's section 481(a) adjustment accelerated to Year 3 is intercompany income. However, S's $100 basis increase before the intercompany transaction eliminates the related difference for this amount between B's corresponding items taken into account and the recomputed corresponding items in subsequent periods. Because the accelerated section 481(a) adjustment will not be taken into account in determining the group's consolidated taxable income (and consolidated tax liability) under the matching rule, the balance of S's section 481 adjustment is taken into account under the acceleration rule as ordinary income at the time of the intercompany transaction. (If S's sale had not resulted in accelerating S's section 481(a) adjustment on a separate entity basis, S would have no intercompany income to be taken into account under this section.)

(e) *Simplifying rules.*—(1) *Dollar-value LIFO inventory* methods.—(i) *In general.*—This paragraph (e)(1) applies if either S or B uses a dollar-value LIFO inventory method to account for intercompany transactions. Rather than applying the matching rule separately to each intercompany inventory transaction, this paragraph (e)(1) provides methods to apply an aggregate approach that is based on dollar-value LIFO inventory accounting. Any method selected under this paragraph (e)(1) must be applied consistently.

      (ii) *B uses dollar-value LIFO.*—(A) *In general.*—If B uses a dollar-value LIFO inventory method to account for its intercompany inventory purchases, and includes all of its inventory costs incurred for a year in its cost of goods sold for the year (that is, B has no inventory increment for the year), S takes into account all of its intercompany inventory items for the year. If B does not include all of its inventory costs incurred for the year in its cost of goods sold for the year (that is, B has an inventory increment for the year), S does not take all of its intercompany inventory income or loss into account. The amount not taken into account is determined under either the increment averaging method of paragraph (e)(1)(ii)(B) of this section or the increment valuation method of paragraph (e)(1)(ii)(C) of this section. Separate computations are made for each pool of B that receives intercompany purchases from S, and S's amount not taken into account is layered based on B's LIFO inventory layers.

      (B) *Increment averaging method.*—Under this paragraph (e)(1)(ii)(B), the amount not taken into account is the amount of S's intercompany inventory income or loss multiplied by the ratio of the LIFO value of B's current-year costs of its layer of increment to B's total inventory costs incurred for the year under its LIFO inventory method. If B includes more than its inventory costs incurred during any subsequent year in its cost of goods sold (a decrement), S takes into account the intercompany inventory income or loss layers in the same manner and proportion as B takes into account its inventory decrements.

      (C) *Increment valuation method.*—Under this paragraph (e)(1)(ii)(C), the amount not taken into account is the amount of S's intercompany inventory income or loss for the appropriate period multiplied by the ratio of the LIFO value of B's current-year costs of its layer of increment to B's total inventory costs incurred in the appropriate period under its LIFO inventory method. The principles of paragraph (e)(1)(ii)(B) of this section otherwise apply. The appropriate period is the period of B's year used to determine its current-year costs.

      (iii) *S uses dollar-value LIFO.*—If S uses a dollar-Value LIFO inventory method to account for its intercompany inventory sales, S may use any reasonable method of allocating its LIFO inventory costs to intercompany transactions. LIFO inventory costs include costs of prior layers if a decrement occurs. For example, a reasonable allocation of the most recent costs incurred during the consolidated return year can be used to compute S's intercompany inventory income or loss for the year if S has an inventory increment and uses the earliest acquisitions costs method, but S must apportion costs from the most recent appropriate layers of increment if an inventory decrement occurs for the year.

      (iv) *Other reasonable methods.*—S or B may use a method not specifically provided in this paragraph (e)(1) that is expected to reasonably take into account intercompany items and corresponding items from intercompany inventory transactions. However, if the method used results, for any year, in a cumulative amount of intercompany inventory items not taken into account by S that significantly exceeds the cumulative amount that would not be taken into account under paragraph (e)(1)(ii) or (iii) of this section, S must take into account for that year the amount necessary to eliminate the excess. The method is thereafter applied with appropriate adjustments to reflect the amount taken into account.

      (v) *Examples.*—The inventory rules of this paragraph (e)(1) are illustrated by the following examples.

      Example 1. Increment averaging method. (a) *Facts.* Both S and B use a double-extension, dollar-value LIFO inventory method, and both value inventory increments using the earliest acquisitions cost valuation method. During Year 2, S sells 25 units of product Q to B on January 15 at $10/unit. S sells another 25 units on April 15, on July 15, and on September 15, at $12/unit. S's earliest cost of product Q is $7.50/unit and S's most recent cost of product Q is $8.00/unit. Both S and B have an inventory increment for the year. B's total inventory costs incurred during Year 2 are $6,000 and the LIFO value of B's Year 2 layer of increment is $600.

      (b) *Intercompany inventory income.* Under paragraph (e)(1)(iii) of this section, S must use a reasonable method of allocating its LIFO inventory costs to intercompany transactions. Because S has an inventory increment for Year 2 and uses the earliest acquisitions cost method, a reasonable method of determining its intercompany cost of goods sold for product Q is to use its most recent costs. Thus, its intercompany cost of goods sold is $800 ($8.00 most recent cost, multiplied by 100 units sold to B), and its intercompany inventory income is $350 ($1,150 sales proceeds from B minus $800 cost).

      (c) *Timing.* (i) Under the increment averaging method of paragraph (e)(1)(ii)(B) of this section, $35 of S's $350 of intercompany inventory income is not taken into account in Year 2, computed as follows:

$$\frac{\text{LIFO value of B's Year 2 layer of increment}}{\text{B's total inventory costs for Year 2}} = \frac{\$600}{\$6,000} = 10\%$$

10% × S's $350 intercompany inventory income = $35

(ii) Thus, $315 of S's intercompany inventory income is taken into account in Year 2 ($350 of total intercompany inventory income minus $35 not taken into account).

(d) *S incurs a decrement.* The facts are the same as in paragraph (a) of this *Example 1*, except that in Year 2, S incurs a decrement equal to 50% of its Year 1 layer. Under paragraph (e)(1)(iii) of this section, S must reasonably allocate the LIFO cost of the decrement to the cost of goods sold to B to determine S's intercompany inventory income.

(e) *B incurs a decrement.* The facts are the same as in paragraph (a) of this *Example 1*, except that B incurs a decrement in Year 2. S must take into account the entire $350 of Year 2 intercompany inventory income because all 100 units of product Q are deemed sold by B in Year 2.

Example 2. Increment valuation method. (a) The facts are the same as in Example 1. In addition, B's use of the earliest acquisition's cost method of valuing its increments-results in B valuing its year-end inventory using costs incurred from January through March. B's costs incurred during the year are: $1,428 in the period January through March; $1,498 in the period April through June; $1,524 in the period July through September; and $1,550 in the period October through December. S's intercompany inventory income for these periods is: $50 in the period January through March ((25 × $10) – (25 × $8)); $100 in the period April through June ((25 × $12) – (25 × $8)); $100 in the period July through September ((25 × $12) – (25 × $8)); and $100 in the period October through December ((25 × $12) – (25 × $8)).

(b) *Timing.* (i) Under the increment valuation method of paragraph (e)(1)(ii)(C) of this section, $21 of S's $350 of intercompany inventory income is not taken into account in Year 2, computed as follows:

$$\frac{\text{LIFO value of B's Year 2 layer of increment}}{\substack{\text{B's total inventory costs from January through}\\\text{March of Year 2}}} = \frac{\$600}{\$1,428} = 42\%$$

42% × S's $50 intercompany inventory income for the period from
January through March　　　　　　　　= $21

(ii) Thus, $329 of S's intercompany inventory income is taken into account in Year 2 ($350 of total intercompany inventory income minus $21 not taken into account).

(c) *B incurs a subsequent decrement.* The facts are the same as in paragraph (a) of this *Example 2*. In addition, assume that in Year 3, B experiences a decrement in its pool that receives intercompany purchases from S. B's decrement equals 20% of the base-year costs for its Year 2 layer. The fact that B has incurred a decrement means that all of its inventory costs incurred for Year 3 are included in cost of goods sold. As a result, S takes into account its entire amount of intercompany inventory income from its Year 3 sales. In addition, S takes into account $4.20 of its Year 2 layer of intercompany inventory income not already taken into account (20% of $21).

Example 3. Other reasonable inventory methods. (a) *Facts.* Both S and B use a dollar-value LIFO inventory method for their inventory transactions. During Year 1, S sells inventory to B and to X. Under paragraph (e)(1)(iv) of this section, to compute its intercompany inventory income and the amount of this income not taken into account, S computes its intercompany inventory income using the transfer price of the inventory items less a FIFO cost for the goods, takes into account these items based on a FIFO cost flow assumption for B's corresponding items, and the LIFO methods used by S and B are ignored for these computations. These computations are comparable to the methods used by S and B for financial reporting purposes, and the book methods and results are used for tax purposes. S adjusts the amount of intercompany inventory items not taken into account as required by section 263A.

(b) *Reasonable method.* The method used by S is a reasonable method under paragraph (e)(1)(iv) of this section if the cumulative amount of intercompany inventory items not taken into account by S is not significantly greater than the cumulative amount that would not be taken into account under the methods specifically described in paragraph (e)(1) of this section. If, for any year, the method results in a cumulative amount of intercompany inventory items not taken into account by S that significantly exceeds the cumulative amount that would not be taken into account under the methods specifically provided, S must take into account for that year the amount necessary to eliminate the excess. The method is thereafter applied with appropriate adjustments to reflect the amount taken into ac-

Reg. § 1.1502-13(e)(1)(v)

count (e.g., to prevent the amount from being taken into account more than once).

(2) *Reserve accounting.*—(i) *Banks and thrifts.*—Except as provided in paragraph (g)(4)(v) of this section (deferral of items from an intercompany obligation), a member's addition to, or reduction of, a reserve for bad debts that is maintained under section 585 is taken into account on a separate entity basis. For example, if S makes a loan to a nonmember and subsequently sells the loan to B, any deduction for an addition to a bad debt reserve under section 585 and any recapture income (or reduced bad debt deductions) are taken into account on a separate entity basis rather than as intercompany items or corresponding items taken into account under this section. Any gain or loss of S from its sale of the loan to B is taken into account under this section, however, to the extent it is not attributable to recapture of the reserve.

(ii) *Insurance companies.*—(A) *Direct insurance.*—If a member provides insurance to another member in an intercompany transaction, the transaction is taken into account by both members on a separate entity basis. For example, if one member provides life insurance coverage for another member with respect to its employees, the premiums, reserve increases and decreases, and death benefit payments are determined and taken into account by both members on a separate entity basis rather than taken into account under this section as intercompany items and corresponding items.

(B) *Reinsurance.*—(1) *In general.*—Paragraph (e)(2)(ii)(A) of this section does not apply to a reinsurance transaction that is an intercompany transaction. For example, if a member assumes all or a portion of the risk on an insurance contract written by another member, the amounts transferred as reinsurance premiums, expense allowances, benefit reimbursements, reimbursed policyholder dividends, experience rating adjustments, and other similar items are taken into account under the matching rule and the acceleration rule. For purposes of this section, the assuming company is treated as B and the ceding company is treated as S.

(2) *Reserves determined on a separate entity basis.*—For purposes of determining the amount of a member's increase or decrease in reserves, the amount of any reserve item listed in section 807(c) or 832(b)(5) resulting from a reinsurance transaction that is an intercompany transaction is determined on a separate entity basis. But see section 845, under which the Commissioner may allocate between or among the members any items, recharacterize any such items, or make any other adjustments necessary to reflect the proper source and character of the separate taxable income of a member.

(3) *Consent to treat intercompany transactions on a separate entity basis.*—(i) *General rule.*—The common parent may request consent to take into account on a separate entity basis items from intercompany transactions other than intercompany transactions with respect to stock or obligations of members. Consent may be granted for all items, or for items from a class or classes of transactions. The consent is effective only if granted in writing by the Internal Revenue Service. Unless revoked with the written consent of the Internal Revenue Service, the separate entity treatment applies to all affected intercompany transactions in the consolidated return year for which consent is granted and in all subsequent consolidated return years. Consent under this paragraph (e)(3) does not apply for purposes of taking into account losses and deductions deferred under section 267(f).

(ii) *Time and manner for requesting consent.*—The request for consent described in paragraph (e)(3)(i) of this section must be made in the form of a ruling request. The request must be signed by the common parent, include any information required by the Internal Revenue Service, and be filed on or before the due date of the consolidated return (not including extensions of time) for the first consolidated return year to which the consent is to apply. The Internal Revenue Service may impose terms and conditions for granting consent. A copy of the consent must be attached to the group's consolidated returns (or amended returns) as required by the terms of the consent.

(iii) *Effect of consent on methods of accounting.*—A consent for separate entity accounting under this paragraph (e)(3), and a revocation of that consent, may require changes in members' methods of accounting for intercompany transactions. Because the consent, or a revocation of the consent, is effective for all intercompany transactions occurring in the consolidated return year for which the consent or revocation is first effective, any change in method is effected on a cut-off basis. Section 446(e) consent is granted for any changes in methods of accounting for intercompany transactions that are necessary solely to conform a member's methods to a binding consent with respect to the group under this paragraph (e)(3) or the revocation of that consent, provided the changes are made in the first consolidated return year for which the consent or revocation under this paragraph (e)(3) is effective. Therefore, section 446(e) consent must separately requested under applicable administrative procedures if a member has failed to conform its practices to the separate entity accounting provided under this paragraph (e)(3) or the revocation of that treatment in the first consolidated return year for which the consent to use separate entity accounting or revocation of that consent is effective.

Reg. §1.1502-13(e)(3)(iii)

(iv) *Consent to treat intercompany transactions on a separate entity basis under prior law.*—A group that has received consent that is in effect as of the first day of the first consolidated return year beginning on or after July 12, 1995 to treat certain intercompany transactions as provided in §1.1502-13(c)(3) of the regulations (as contained in the 26 CFR part 1 edition revised as of April 1, 1995) will be considered to have obtained the consent of the Commissioner to take items from intercompany transactions into account on a separate entity basis as provided in paragraph (e)(3)(i) of this section. This treatment is applicable only to the items, class or classes of transactions for which consent was granted under prior law.

(f) *Stock of members.*—(1) *In general.*—In addition to the general rules of this section, the rules of this paragraph (f) apply to stock of members.

(2) *Intercompany distributions to which section 301 applies.*—(i) *In general.*—This paragraph (f)(2) provides rules for intercompany transactions to which section 301 applies (intercompany distributions). For purposes of determining whether a distribution is an intercompany distribution, it is treated as occurring under the principles of the entitlement rule of paragraph (f)(2)(iv) of this section. A distribution is not an intercompany distribution to the extent it is deducted by the distributing member. See, for example, section 1382(c)(1).

(ii) *Distributee member.*—An intercompany distribution is not included in the gross income of the distributee member (B). However, this exclusion applies to a distribution only to the extent there is a corresponding negative adjustment reflected under §1.1502-32 in B's basis in the stock of the distributing member (S). For example, no amount is included in B's gross income under section 301(c)(3) from a distribution in excess of the basis of the stock of a subsidiary that results in an excess loss account under §1.1502-32(a) which is treated as negative basis under §1.1502-19. B's dividend received deduction under section 243(a)(3) is determined without regard to any intercompany distributions under this paragraph (f)(2) to the extent they are not included in gross income. See §1.1502-26(b) (applicability of the dividends received deduction to distributions not excluded from gross income, such as a distribution from the common parent to a subsidiary owning stock of the common parent).

(iii) *Distributing member.*—The principles of section 311(b) apply to S's loss, as well as gain, from an intercompany distribution of property. Thus, S's loss is taken into account under the matching rule if the property is subsequently sold to a nonmember. However, section 311(a) continues to apply to distributions to nonmembers (for example, loss is not recognized).

(iv) *Entitlement rule.*—(A) *In general.*—For all Federal income tax purposes, an intercompany distribution is treated as taken into account when the shareholding member becomes entitled to it (generally on the record date). For example, if B becomes entitled to a cash distribution before it is made, the distribution is treated as made when B becomes entitled to it. For this purpose, B is treated as entitled to a distribution no later than the time the distribution is taken into account under the Internal Revenue Code (e.g., under section 305(c)). To the extent a distribution is not made, appropriate adjustments must be made as of the date it was taken into account.

(B) *Nonmember shareholders.*—If nonmembers own stock of the distributing corporation at the time the distribution is treated as occurring under this paragraph (f)(2)(iv), appropriate adjustments must be made to prevent the acceleration of the distribution to members from affecting distributions to nonmembers.

(3) *Boot in an intercompany reorganization.*—(i) *Scope.*—This paragraph (f)(3) provides additional rules for an intercompany transaction in which the receipt of money or other property (nonqualifying property) results in the application of section 356. For example, the distribution of stock of a lower-tier member to a higher tier member in an intercompany transaction to which section 355 would apply but for the receipt of nonqualifying property is a transaction to which this paragraph (f)(3) applies. This paragraph (f)(3) does not apply if a party to the transaction becomes a member or nonmember as part of the same plan or arrangement. For example, if S merges into a nonmember in a transaction described in section 368(a)(1)(A), this paragraph (f)(3) does not apply.

(ii) *Treatment.*—Nonqualifying property received as part of a transaction described in this paragraph (f)(3) is treated as received by the member shareholder in a separate transaction. See, for example, sections 302 and 311 (rather than sections 356 and 361). The nonqualifying property is treated as taken into account immediately after the transaction if section 354 would apply but for the fact that nonqualifying property is received. It is treated as taken into account immediately before the transaction if section 355 would apply but for the fact that nonqualifying property is received. The treatment under this paragraph (f)(3)(ii) applies for all Federal income tax purposes.

(4) *Acquisition by issuer of its own stock.*—If a member acquires its own stock, or an option to buy or sell its own stock, in an intercompany transaction, the member's basis in that stock or option is treated as eliminated for all purposes. Accordingly, S's intercompany items from the stock or options of B are taken into account under this section if B acquires the stock or op-

Reg. §1.1502-13(e)(3)(iv)

tions in an intercompany transaction (unless, for example, B acquires the stock in exchange for successor property within the meaning of paragraph (j)(1)(1) of this section in a nonrecognition transaction). For example, if B redeems its stock from S in a transaction to which section 302(a) applies, S's gain from the transaction is taken into account immediately under the acceleration rule.

(5) *Certain liquidations and distributions.*—(i) *Netting allowed.*—S's intercompany item from a transfer to B of the stock of another corporation (T) is taken into account under this section in certain circumstances even though the T stock is never held by a nonmember after the intercompany transaction. For example, if S sells all of T's stock to B at a gain, and T subsequently liquidates into B in a separate transaction to which section 332 applies, S's gain is taken into account under the matching rule. Under paragraph (c)(6)(ii) of this section, S's intercompany gain taken into account as a result of a liquidation under section 332 or a comparable nonrecognition transaction is not redetermined to be excluded from gross income. Under this paragraph (f)(5)(i), if S has both intercompany income or gain and intercompany deduction or loss attributable to stock of the same corporation having the same material terms, only the income or gain in excess of the deduction or loss is subject to paragraph (c)(6)(ii) of this section. This paragraph (f)(5)(i) applies only to a transaction in which B's basis in its T stock is permanently eliminated in a liquidation under section 332 or any comparable nonrecognition transaction, including—

(A) A merger of B into T under section 368(a);

(B) A distribution by B of its T stock in a transaction described in section 355; or

(C) A deemed liquidation of T resulting from an election under section 338(h)(10).

(ii) *Elective relief.*—(A) *In general.*—If an election is made pursuant to this paragraph (f)(5)(ii), certain transactions are recharacterized to prevent S's items from being taken into account or to provide offsets to those items. This paragraph (f)(5)(ii) applies only if T is a member throughout the period beginning with S's transfer and ending with the completion of the nonrecognition transaction.

(B)(1) [Reserved]. For further guidance, see § 1.1502-13T(f)(5)(ii)(B)(1).

(2) [Reserved]. For further guidance, see § 1.1502-13T(f)(5)(ii)(B)(2).

(3) *Downstream merger, etc.*—The principles of this paragraph (f)(5)(ii)(B) apply, with appropriate adjustments, if B's basis in the T stock is eliminated in a transaction similar to a section 332 liquidation, such as a transaction described in section 368 in which B merges into T. For example, if S and B are subsidiaries, and S sells all of T's stock to B at a gain followed by B's

merger into T in a separate transaction described in section 368(a), S's gain is not taken into account solely as a result of the merger if T (as successor to B) forms new T with substantially all of T's former assets.

(C) *Section 338(h)(10).*—(1) *In general.*—This paragraph (f)(5)(ii)(C) applies to a deemed liquidation of T under section 332 as the result of an election under section 338(h)(10). This paragraph (f)(5)(ii)(C) does not apply if paragraph (f)(5)(ii)(B) of this section is applied to the deemed liquidation. Under this paragraph, B is treated with respect to each share of its T stock as recognizing as a corresponding item any loss or deduction it would recognize (determined after adjusting stock basis under § 1.1502-32) if section 331 applied to the deemed liquidation. For all other Federal income tax purposes, the deemed liquidation remains subject to section 332.

(2) *Limitation on amount of loss.*—The amount of B's loss or deduction under this paragraph (f)(5)(ii)(C) is limited as follows—

(i) The aggregate amount of loss recognized with respect to T stock cannot exceed the amount of S's intercompany income or gain that is in excess of S's intercompany deduction or loss with respect to shares of T stock having the same material terms as the shares giving rise to S's intercompany income or gain; and

(ii) The aggregate amount of loss recognized under this paragraph (f)(5)(ii)(C) from T's deemed liquidation cannot exceed the net amount of deduction or loss (if any) that would be taken into account from the deemed liquidation if section 331 applied with respect to all T shares.

(3) *Asset sale, etc.*—The principles of this paragraph (f)(5)(ii)(C) apply, with appropriate adjustments, if T transfers all of its assets to a nonmember and completely liquidates in a transaction comparable to the section 338(h)(10) transaction described in paragraph (f)(5)(ii)(C)(1) of this section. For example, if S sells all of T's stock to B at a gain followed by T's merger into a nonmember in exchange for a cash payment to B in a transaction treated for Federal income tax purposes as T's sale of its assets to the nonmember and complete liquidation, the merger is ordinarily treated as a comparable transaction.

(D) *Section 355.*—If B distributes the T stock in an intercompany transaction to which section 355 applies (including an intercompany transaction to which 355 applies because of the application of paragraph (f)(3) of this section), the redetermination of the basis of the T stock under section 358 could cause S's gain or loss to be taken into account under this section. This paragraph (f)(5)(ii)(D) applies to treat B's distribution as subject to section 301 and 311 (as modified by this paragraph (f)), rather than section 355. The election will prevent S's gain or loss

Reg. § 1.1502-13(f)(5)(ii)(D)

from being taken into account immediately to the extent matching remains possible, but B's gain or loss from the distribution will also be taken into account under this section.

(E) *Election.*—An election to apply paragraph (f)(5)(ii) of this section is made in a separate statement entitled, "[INSERT NAME AND EMPLOYER IDENTIFICATION NUMBER OF COMMON PARENT] HEREBY ELECTS THE APPLICATION OF § 1.1502-13(f)(5)(ii) FOR AN INTERCOMPANY TRANSACTION INVOLVING [INSERT NAME AND EMPLOYER IDENTIFICATION NUMBER OF S] AND [INSERT NAME AND EMPLOYER IDENTIFICATION NUMBER OF T]." A separate election must be made for each such application. The election must be filed by including the statement on or with the consolidated group's income tax return for the year of T's liquidation (or other transaction). The Commissioner may impose reasonable terms and conditions to the application of paragraph (f)(5)(ii) of this section that are consistent with the purposes of such section. The statement must—

(1) Identify S's intercompany transaction and T's liquidation (or other transaction); and

(2) Specify which provision of paragraph (f)(5)(ii) of this section applies and how it alters the otherwise applicable results under this section (including, for example, the amount of S's intercompany items and the amount deferred or offset as a result of paragraph (f)(5)(ii) of this section).

(6) *Stock of common parent.*—In addition to the general rules of this section, this paragraph (f)(6) applies to parent stock (P stock) and positions in P stock held or entered into by another member. For this purpose, P stock is any stock of the common parent held (directly or indirectly) by another member or any stock of a member (the issuer) that was the common parent if the stock was held (directly or indirectly) by another member while the issuer was the common parent.

(i) *Loss stock.*—(A) *Recognized loss.*—Any loss recognized, directly or indirectly, by a member with respect to P stock is permanently disallowed and does not reduce earnings and profits. See § 1.1502-32(b)(3)(iii)(A) for a corresponding reduction in the basis of the member's stock.

(B) *Other cases.*—If a member, M, owns P stock, the stock is subsequently owned by a nonmember, and, immediately before the stock is owned by the nonmember, M's basis in the share exceeds its fair market value, then, to the extent paragraph (f)(6)(i)(A) of this section does not apply, M's basis in the share is reduced to the share's fair market value immediately before the share is held by the nonmember. For example, if M owns shares of P stock with a $100x

basis and M becomes a nonmember at a time when the P shares have a value of $60x, M's basis in the P shares is reduced to $60x immediately before M becomes a nonmember. Similarly, if M contributes the P stock to a nonmember in a transaction subject to section 351, M's basis in the shares is reduced to $60x immediately before the contribution. See § 1.1502-32(b)(3)(iii)(B) for a corresponding reduction in the basis of M's stock.

(C) *Waiver of built-in loss on P stock.*—(1) *In general.*—If a nonmember that owns P stock with a basis in excess of its fair market value becomes a member of the P consolidated group in a qualifying cost basis transaction, the group may make an irrevocable election to reduce the basis of the P stock to its fair market value immediately before the nonmember becomes a member of the P group. If the nonmember was a member of another consolidated group immediately before becoming a member of the P group, the reduction in basis is treated as occurring immediately after it ceases to be a member of the prior group. A qualifying cost basis transaction is the purchase (i.e., a transaction in which basis is determined under section 1012) by members of the P consolidated group (while they are members) in a 12-month period of an amount of the nonmember's stock satisfying the requirements of section 1504(a)(2).

(2) *Election.*—The election described in paragraph (f)(6)(i)(C)(1) of this section must be made in a separate statement entitled, "ELECTION TO REDUCE BASIS OF P STOCK UNDER § 1.1502-13(f)(6) HELD BY [INSERT NAME AND EMPLOYER IDENTIFICATION NUMBER OF MEMBER WHOSE BASIS IN P STOCK IS REDUCED]." The election must be filed by including the statement on or with the consolidated group's income tax return for the year in which the nonmember becomes a member. The statement must identify the member's basis in the P stock (taking into account the effect of this election) and the number of shares of P stock held by the member.

(ii) *Gain stock.*—For dispositions of P stock occurring before May 16, 2000, see § 1.1502-13(f)(6)(ii) as contained in 26 CFR part 1 in effect on April 1, 2000. For dispositions of P stock occurring on or after May 16, 2000, see § 1.1032-3.

(iii) *Mark-to-market of P stock.*—Paragraphs (f)(6)(i) and (ii) of this section shall not apply to any gain or loss from a share of P stock held by a member, M, if—

(A) M regularly trades in P stock (of the same class) with customers in the ordinary course of its business as a dealer;

(B) The gain or loss on the share is taken into account by M pursuant to section 475(a);

(C) M's basis in the share is not adjusted by reference to the basis of any other property or by reference to income, gain, deduction, or loss from other property; and

(D) Neither M nor any other member of the group has structured or engaged in any transaction while a member (or in anticipation of becoming a member), during the taxable year or in any year within the preceding five taxable years that is open for assessment under section 6501, with a principal purpose of avoiding gain or creating loss on P stock subject to section 475(a).

(iv) *Options, warrants, and other positions.*—(A) *In general.*—This paragraph (f)(6) applies with appropriate adjustments to positions in P stock to the extent that P's gain or loss from an equivalent position would not be recognized under section 1032. Thus, if M purchases an option to buy or sell P stock and sells the option at a loss, the loss is permanently disallowed under paragraph (f)(6)(i)(A) of this section. Similarly, if M is the grantor of such an option and becomes a nonmember, then the principles of paragraph (f)(6)(i)(B) of this section apply to the extent that M would recognize loss from cash settlement of the option at its fair market value immediately before M becomes a nonmember, and proper adjustments must be made in the amount of any gain or loss subsequently realized from the position by M. If P grants M an option to acquire P stock in a transaction meeting the requirements of § 1.1032-3, M is treated as having purchased the option from P for fair market value with cash contributed to M by P.

(B) *Mark-to-market of positions in P stock.*—For purposes of paragraph (f)(6)(iii) of this section, gain or loss with respect to a position taken into account under section 1256(a) is treated as taken into account under section 475(a) to the extent that the gain or loss would be taken into account under the principles of section 475.

(v) *Effective date.*—This paragraph (f)(6) applies to gain or loss taken into account on or after July 12, 1995, and to transactions occurring on or after July 12, 1995. For example, if S sells P stock to B at a loss prior to July 12, 1995, and B sells the P stock to a nonmember after July 12, 1995, S's loss is disallowed because it is taken into account after July 12, 1995. If a taxpayer takes a gain or loss into account or engages in a transaction on or after July 12, 1995, during a tax year ending prior to December 31, 1995, the taxpayer may treat the gain or loss or the transaction under the rules of § 1.1502-13T(f)(6) (published in 1995-32 I.R.B. 47), instead of under the rules of this paragraph (f)(6).

(7) *Examples—In general.*—The application of this section to intercompany transactions with respect to stock of members is illustrated by the following examples.

Example 1. Dividend exclusion and property distribution. (a) *Facts.* S owns land with a $70 basis and $100 value. On January 1 of Year 1, P's basis in S's stock is $100. During Year 1, S declares and makes a dividend distribution of the land to P. Under section 311(b), S has a $30 gain. Under section 301(d), P's basis in the land is $100. On July 1 of Year 3, P sells the land to X for $110.

(b) *Dividend elimination and stock basis adjustments.* Under paragraph (b)(1) of this section, S's distribution to P is an intercompany distribution. Under paragraph (f)(2)(ii) of this section, P's $100 of dividend income is not included in gross income. Under § 1.1502-32, P's basis in S's stock is reduced from $100 to $0 in Year 1.

(c) *Matching rule and stock basis adjustments.* Under the matching rule (treating P as the buying member and S as the selling member), S takes its $30 gain into account in Year 3 to reflect the $30 difference between P's $10 gain taken into account and the $40 recomputed gain. Under § 1.1502-32, P's basis in S's stock is increased from $0 to $30 in Year 3.

(d) *Loss property.* The facts are the same as in paragraph (a) of this *Example except,* that S has a $130 (rather than $70) basis in the land. Under paragraph (f)(2)(iii) of this section, the principles of section 311(b) apply to S's loss from the intercompany distribution. Thus, S has a $30 loss that is taken into account under the matching rule in Year 3 to reflect the $30 difference between P's $10 gain taken into account and the $20 recomputed loss. (The results are the same under section 267(f).) Under § 1.1502-32, P's basis in S's stock is reduced from $100 to $0 in Year 1, and from $0 to a $30 excess loss account in Year 3. (If P had distributed the land to its shareholders, rather than selling the land to X, P would take its $10 gain under section 311(b) into account, and S would take its $30 loss into account under the matching rule with $10 offset by P's gain and $20 recharacterized as a noncapital, nondeductible amount.)

(e) *Entitlement rule.* The facts are the same as in paragraph (a) of this *Example 1,* except that, after P becomes entitled to the distribution but before the distribution is made, S issues additional stock to the public and becomes a nonmember. Under paragraph (f)(2)(i) of this section, the determination of whether a distribution is an intercompany distribution is made under the entitlement rule of paragraph (f)(2)(iv) of this section. Treating S's distribution as made when P becomes entitled to it results in the distribution being an intercompany distribution. Under paragraph (f)(2)(ii) of this section, the distribution is not included in P's gross income. S's $30 gain from the distribution is intercompany gain that is taken into account under the acceleration rule immediately before S becomes a nonmember. Thus, there is a net $70 decrease in P's basis in its S stock under § 1.1502-32 ($100 decrease for the distribution and a $30 increase for

S's $30 gain). Under paragraph (f)(2)(iv) of this section, P does not take the distribution into account again under separate return rules when received, and P is not entitled to a dividends received deduction.

Example 2. Excess loss accounts. (a) *Facts.* S owns all of T's only class of stock with a $10 basis and $100 value. S has substantial earnings and profits, and T has $10 of earnings and profits. On January 1 of Year 1, S declares and distributes a dividend of all of the T stock to P. Under section 311(b), S has a $90 gain. Under section 301(d), P's basis in the T stock is $100. During Year 3, T borrows $90 and declares and makes a $90 distribution to P to which section 301 applies, and P's basis in the T stock is reduced under § 1.1502-32 from $100 to $10. During Year 6, T has $5 of earnings that increase P's basis in the T stock under § 1.1502-32 from $10 to $15. On December 1 of Year 9, T issues additional stock to X and, as a result, T becomes a nonmember.

(b) *Dividend exclusion.* Under paragraph (f)(2)(ii) of this section, P's $100 of dividend income from S's distribution of the T stock, and its $10 of dividend income from T's $90 distribution, are not included in gross income.

(c) *Matching and acceleration rules.* Under § 1.1502-19(b)(1), when T becomes a nonmember P must include in income the amount of its excess loss account (if any) in T stock. P has no excess loss account in the T stock. Therefore P's corresponding item from the deconsolidation of T is $0. Treating S and P as divisions of a single corporation, the T stock would continue to have a $10 basis after the distribution, and the adjustments under § 1.1502-32 for T's $90 distribution and $5 of earnings would result in a $75 excess loss account. Thus, the recomputed corresponding item from the deconsolidation is $75. Under the matching rule, S takes $75 of its $90 gain into account in Year 9 as a result of T becoming a nonmember, to reflect the difference between P's $0 gain taken into account and the $75 recomputed gain. S's remaining $15 of gain is taken into account under the matching and acceleration rules based on subsequent events (for example, under the matching rule if P subsequently sells its T stock, or under the acceleration rule if S becomes a nonmember).

(d) *Reverse sequence.* The facts are the same as in paragraph (a) of this *Example 2,* except that T borrows $90 and makes its $90 distribution to S before S distributes T's stock to P. Under paragraph (f)(2)(ii) of this section, T's $90 distribution to S ($10 of which is a dividend) is not included in S's gross income. The corresponding negative adjustment under § 1.1502-32 reduces S's basis in the T stock from $10 to an $80 excess loss account. Under section 311(b), S has a $90 gain from the distribution of T stock to P. Under section 301(d) P's initial basis in the T stock is $10 (the stock's fair market value), and the basis increases to $15 under § 1.1502-32 as a result of

T's earnings in Year 6. The timing and attributes of S's gain are determined in the manner provided in paragraph (c) of this *Example 2.* Thus, $75 of S's gain is taken into account under the matching rule in Year 9 as a result of T becoming a nonmember, and the remaining $15 is taken into account under the matching and acceleration rules based on subsequent events.

(e) *Partial stock sale.* The facts are the same as in paragraph (a) of this *Example 2,* except that P sells 10% of T's stock to X on December 1 of Year 9 for $1.50 (rather than T's issuing additional stock and becoming a nonmember). Under the matching rule, S takes $9 of its gain into account to reflect the difference between P's $0 gain taken into account ($1,50 sale proceeds minus $1.50 basis) and the $9 recomputed gain ($1.50 sale proceeds plus $7.50 excess loss account).

(f) *Loss, rather than cash distribution.* The facts are the same as in paragraph (a) of this *Example 2,* except that T retains the loan proceeds and incurs a $90 loss in Year 3 that is absorbed by the group. The timing and attributes of S's gain are determined in the same manner provided in paragraph (c) of this *Example 2.* Under § 1.1502-32, the loss in Year 3 reduces P's basis in the T stock from $100 to $10, and T's $5 of earnings in Year 6 increase the basis to $15. Thus, $75 of S's gain is taken into account under the matching rule in Year 9 as a result of T becoming a nonmember, and the remaining $15 is taken into account under the matching and acceleration rules based on subsequent events. (The timing and attributes of S's gain would be determined in the same manner provided in paragraph (d) of this *Example 2* if T incurred the $90 loss before S's distribution of the T stock to P.)

(g) *Stock sale, rather than stock distribution.* The facts are the same as in paragraph (a) of this *Example except,* that S sells the T stock to P for $100 (rather than distributing the stock). The timing and attributes of S's gain are determined in the same manner provided in paragraph (c) of this *Example 2.* Thus, $75 of S's gain is taken into account under the matching rule in Year 9 as a result of T becoming a nonmember, and the remaining $15 is taken into account under the matching and acceleration rules based on subsequent events.

Example 3. Intercompany reorganization. (a) *Facts.* P forms S and B by contributing $200 to the capital of each. During Years 1 through 4, S and B each earn $50, and under § 1.1502-32 P adjusts its basis in the stock of each to $250. (See § 1.1502-33 for adjustments to earnings and profits.) On January 1 of Year 5, the fair market value of S's assets and its stock is $500, and S merges into B in a tax-free reorganization. Pursuant to the plan of reorganization, P receives B stock with a fair market value of $350 and $150 of cash.

(b) *Treatment as a section 301 distribution.* The merger of S into B is a transaction to which paragraph (f)(3) of this section applies. P is treated as receiving additional B stock with a fair market value of $500 and, under section 358, a basis of $250. Immediately after the merger, $150 of the stock received is treated as redeemed, and the redemption is treated under section 302(d) as a distribution to which section 301 applies. Because the $150 distribution is treated as not received as part of the merger, section 356 does not apply and no basis adjustments are required under section 358(a)(1)(A) and (B). Because B is treated under section 381(c)(2) as receiving S's earnings and profits and the redemption is treated as occurring after the merger, $100 of the distribution is treated as a dividend under section 301 and P's basis in the B stock is reduced correspondingly under §1.1502-32. The remaining $50 of the distribution reduces P's basis in the B stock. Section 301(c)(2) and §1.1502-32. Under paragraph (f)(2)(ii) of this section, P's $100 of dividend income is not included in gross income. Under §1.302-2(c), proper adjustments are made to P's basis in its B stock to reflect its basis in the B stock redeemed, with the result that P's basis in the B stock is reduced by the entire $150 distribution.

(c) *Depreciated property*. The facts are the same as in paragraph (a) of this *Example 3*, except that property of S with a $200 basis and $150 fair market value is distributed to p (rather than cash of B). As in paragraph (b) of this *Example 3*, P is treated as receiving additional B stock in the merger and a $150 distribution to which section 301 applies immediately after the merger. Under paragraph (f)(2)(iii) of this section, the principles of section 311(b) apply to B's $50 loss and the loss is taken into account under the matching and acceleration rules based on subsequent events (e.g., under the matching rule if P subsequently sells the property, or under the acceleration rule if B becomes a nonmember). The results are the same under section 267(f).

(d) *Divisive transaction*. Assume instead that, pursuant to a plan, S distributes the stock of a lower-tier subsidiary in a spin-off transaction to which section 355 applies together with $150 of cash. The distribution of stock is a transaction to which paragraph (f)(3) of this section applies. P is treated as receiving the $150 of cash immediately before the section 355 distribution, as a distribution to which section 301 applies. Section 356(b) does not apply and no basis adjustments are required under section 358(a)(1)(A) and (B). Because the $150 distribution is treated as made before the section 355 distribution, the distribution reduces P's basis in the S stock under §1.1502-32, and the basis allocated under section 358(c) between the S stock and the lower-tier subsidiary stock received reflects this basis reduction.

Example 4. All cash intercompany reorganization under section 368(a)(1)(D). (a) Facts. P owns all of the stock of M and B. M owns all of the stock of S with a basis of $25. On January 1 of Year 2, the fair market value of S's assets and its stock is $100, and S sells all of its assets to B for $100 cash and liquidates. The transaction qualifies as a reorganization described in section 368(a)(1)(D). Pursuant to §1.368-2(l), B will be deemed to issue a nominal share of B stock to S in addition to the $100 of cash actually exchanged for the S assets, and S will be deemed to distribute all of the consideration to M. M will be deemed to distribute the nominal share of B stock to P.

(b) *Treatment as a section 301 distribution.* The sale of S's assets to B is a transaction to which paragraph (f)(3) of this section applies. In addition to the nominal share issued by B to S under §1.368-2(l), S is treated as receiving additional B stock with a fair market value of $100 (in lieu of the $100) and, under section 358, a basis of $25 which S distributes to M in liquidation. Immediately after the sale, the B stock (with the exception of the nominal share which is still held by M) received by M is treated as redeemed for $100, and the redemption is treated under section 302(d) as a distribution to which section 301 applies. M's basis of $25 in the B stock is reduced under §1.1502-32(b)(3)(v), resulting in an excess loss account of $75 in the nominal share. (See §1.302-2(c)). M's deemed distribution of the nominal share of B stock to P under §1.368-2(l) will result in M generating an intercompany gain under section 311(b) of $75, to be subsequently taken into account under the matching and acceleration rules.

Example 5. Stock redemptions and distributions. (a) *Facts.* Before becoming a member of the P group, S owns P stock with a $30 basis. on January 1 of Year 1, P buys all of S's stock. On July 1 of Year 3, P redeems the P stock held by S for $100 in a transaction to which section 302(a) applies.

(b) *Gain under section 302.* Under paragraph (f)(4) of this section, P's basis in the P stock acquired from S is treated as eliminated. As a result of this elimination, S's intercompany item will never be taken into account under the matching rule because P's basis in the stock does not reflect S's intercompany item. Therefore, S's $70 gain is taken into account under the acceleration rule in Year 3. The attributes of S's item are determined under paragraph (d)(1)(ii) of this section by applying the matching rule as if p had sold the stock to an affiliated corporation that is not a member of the group at no gain or loss. Although P's corresponding item from a sale of its stock would have been excluded from gross income under section 1032, paragraph (c)(6)(ii) of this section prevents S's gain from being treated as excluded from gross income; instead S's gain is capital gain.

(c) *Gain under section 311.* The facts are the same as in paragraph (a) of this *Example except*, except that S distributes the P stock to P in a transaction to which section 301 applies (rather than the stock being redeemed), and S has a $70 gain under section 311(b). The timing and attributes of S's gain are determined in the manner provided in paragraph (b) of this *Example 4.*

(d) *Loss stock.* The facts are the same as in paragraph (a) of this *Example 4,* except that S has a $130 (rather than $30) basis in the P stock and has a $30 loss under section 302(a). The limitation under paragraph (c)(6)(ii) of this section does not apply to intercompany losses. Thus, S's loss is taken into account in Year 3 as a noncapital, nondeductible amount.

Example 6. Intercompany stock sale followed by section 332 liquidation. (a) *Facts.* S owns all of the stock of T, with a $70 basis and $100 value, and T's assets have a $10 basis and $100 value. On January 1 of Year 1, S sells all of T's stock to B for $100. On July 1 of Year 3, when T's assets are still worth $100, T distributes all of its assets to B in an unrelated complete liquidation to which section 332 applies.

(b) *Timing and attributes.* Under paragraph (b)(3)(ii) of this section, B's unrecognized gain or loss under section 332 is a corresponding item for purposes of applying the matching rule. In Year 3 when T liquidates, B has $0 of unrecognized gain or loss under section 332 because B has a $100 basis in the T stock and receives a $100 distribution with respect to its T stock. Treating S and B as divisions of a single corporation, the recomputed corresponding item would have been $30 of unrecognized gain under section 332 because B would have succeeded to S's $70 basis in the T stock. Thus, under the matching rule, S's $30 intercompany gain is taken into account in Year 3 as a result of T's liquidation. Under paragraph (c)(1)(i) of this section, the attributes of S's gain and B's corresponding item are redetermined as if S and B were divisions of a single corporation. Although S's gain ordinarily would be redetermined to be treated as excluded from gross income to reflect the nonrecognition of B's gain under section 332, S's gain remains capital gain because B's unrecognized gain under section 332 is not permanently and explicitly disallowed under the Code. See paragraph (c)(6)(ii) of this section. However, relief may be elected under paragraph (f)(5)(ii) of this section.

(c) *Intercompany sale at a loss.* The facts are the same as in paragraph (a) of this *Example 5,* except that S has a $130 (rather than $70) basis in the T stock. The limitation under paragraph (c)(6)(ii) of this section does not apply to intercompany losses. Thus, S's intercompany loss is taken into account in Year 3 as a noncapital, nondeductible amount. However, relief may be elected under paragraph (f)(5)(ii) of this section.

Example 7. Intercompany stock sale followed by section 355 distribution. (a) *Facts.* S owns all of the stock of T with a $70 basis and a $100 value. On January 1 of Year 1, S sells all of T's stock to M for $100. on June 1l of Year 6, M distributes all of its T stock to its nonmember shareholders in a transaction to which section 355 applies. At the time of the distribution, M has a basis in T stock of $100 and T has a value of $150.

(b) *Timing and attributes.* Under paragraph (b)(3)(ii) of this section, M's $50 gain not recognized on the distribution under section 355 is a corresponding item. Treating S and M as divisions of a single corporation, the recomputed corresponding item would be $80 of unrecognized gain under section 355 because M would have succeeded to S's $70 basis in the T stock. Thus, under the matching rule, S's $30 intercompany gain is taken into account in Year 6 as a result of the distribution. Under paragraph (c)(1)(i) of this section, the attributes of S's intercompany item and M's corresponding item are redetermined to produce the same effect on consolidated taxable income as if S and M were divisions of a single corporation. Although S's gain ordinarily would be redetermined to be treated as excluded from gross income to reflect the nonrecognition of M's gain under section 355(c), S's gain remains capital gain because M's unrecognized gain under section 355(c) is not permanently and explicitly disallowed under the Code. See paragraph (c)(6)(ii) of this section. Because M's distribution of the T stock is not an intercompany transaction, relief is not available under paragraph (f)(5)(ii) of this section.

(c) *Section 355 distribution within the group.* The facts are the same as under paragraph (a) of this *Example 6,* except that M distributes the T stock to B (another member of the group), and B takes a $75 basis in the T stock under section 358. Under paragraph (j)(2) of this section, B is a successor to M for purposes of taking S's intercompany gain into account, and therefore both M and B might have corresponding items with respect to S's intercompany gain. To the extent it is possible, matching with respect to B's corresponding items produces the result most consistent with treating S, M, and B as divisions of a single corporation. See paragraphs (j)(3) and (j)(4) of this section. However, because there is only $5 difference between B's $75 basis in the T stock and the $70 basis the stock would have if S, M, and B were divisions of a single corporation, only $5 can be taken into account under the matching rule with respect to B's corresponding items. (This $5 is taken into account with respect to B's corresponding items based on subsequent events.) The remaining $25 of S's $30 intercompany gain is taken into account in Year 6 under the matching rule with respect to M's corresponding item from its distribution of the T stock. The attributes of S's remaining $25 of gain are determined in the same manner as in paragraph (b) of this *Example 6.*

(d) *Relief elected.* The facts are the same as in paragraph (c) of this *Example 6* except that P elects relief pursuant to paragraph (f)(5)(ii)(D) of this section. As a result of the election, M's distribution of the T stock is treated as subject to sections 301 and 311 instead of section 355. Accordingly, M recognizes $50 of intercompany gain from the distribution, B takes a basis in the stock equal to its fair market value of $150, and S and M take their intercompany gains into account with respect to B's corresponding items based on subsequent events. (None of S's gain is taken into account in Year 6 as a result of M's distribution of the T stock.)

(g) *Obligations of members.*—(1) *In general.*—In addition to the general rules of this section, the rules of this paragraph (g) apply to intercompany obligations.

(2) *Definitions.*—For purposes of this section, the following definitions apply—

(i) *Obligation of a member* is a debt or security of a member.

(A) *Debt of a member* is any obligation of the member constituting indebtedness under general principles of Federal income tax law (for example, under nonstatutory authorities, or under section 108, section 163, or § 1.1275-1(d)), but not an executory obligation to purchase or provide goods or services.

(B) *Security of a member* is any security of the member described in section 475(c)(2)(D) or (E), and any commodity of the member described in section 475(e)(2)(A), (B), or (C), but not if the security or commodity is a position with respect to the member's stock. See paragraphs (f)(4) and (f)(6) of this section for special rules applicable to positions with respect to a member's stock.

(ii) *Intercompany obligation* is an obligation between members, but only for the period during which both parties are members.

(iii) *Intercompany obligation subgroup* is comprised of two or more members that include the creditor and debtor on an intercompany obligation if the creditor and debtor bear the relationship described in section 1504(a)(1) to each other through an intercompany obligation subgroup parent.

(iv) *Intercompany obligation subgroup parent* is the corporation (including either the creditor or debtor) that bears the same relationship to the other members of the intercompany obligation subgroup as a common parent bears to the members of a consolidated group. Any reference to an intercompany obligation subgroup parent includes, as the context may require, a reference to a predecessor or successor. For this purpose, a predecessor is a transferor of assets to a transferee (the successor) in a transaction to which section 381(a) applies.

(v) *Tax benefit* is the benefit of, for Federal tax purposes, a net reduction in income or gain, or a net increase in loss, deduction, credit, or allowance. A tax benefit includes, but is not limited to, the use of a built-in item or items from an intercompany obligation to reduce gain or increase loss on the sale of member stock, or to create or absorb a tax attribute of a member or subgroup.

(vi) *Eighty-percent chain* is a chain of two or more corporations in which stock meeting the requirements of section 1504(a)(2) of each lower-tier member is held directly by a higher-tier member of such chain.

(3) *Deemed satisfaction and reissuance of intercompany obligations in triggering transactions.*—(i) *Scope.*—(A) *Triggering transactions.*—For purposes of this paragraph (g)(3), a triggering transaction includes the following:

(1) *Assignment and extinguishment transactions.*—Any intercompany transaction in which a member realizes an amount, directly or indirectly, from the assignment or extinguishment of all or part of its remaining rights or obligations under an intercompany obligation or any comparable transaction in which a member realizes any such amount, directly or indirectly, from an intercompany obligation (for example, a mark to fair market value of an obligation or a bad debt deduction). However, a reduction of the basis of an intercompany obligation pursuant to § 1.1502-36(d) (attribute reduction to prevent duplication of loss), or pursuant to sections 108 and 1017 and § 1.1502-28 (basis reductions upon the exclusion from gross income of discharge of indebtedness) or any other provision that adjusts the basis of an intercompany obligation as a substitute for income, gain, deduction, or loss, is not a comparable transaction.

(2) *Outbound transactions.*—Any transaction in which an intercompany obligation becomes an obligation that is not an intercompany obligation.

(B) *Exceptions.*—Except as provided in paragraph (g)(3)(i)(C) of this section, a transaction is not a triggering transaction as described in paragraph (g)(3)(i)(A) of this section if any of the exceptions in this paragraph (g)(3)(i)(B) apply. In making this determination, if a creditor or debtor realizes an amount in a transaction in which a creditor assigns all or part of its rights under an intercompany obligation to the debtor, or a debtor assigns all or part of its obligations under an intercompany obligation to the creditor, the transaction will be treated as an extinguishment and will be excepted from the definition of "triggering transaction" only if either of the exceptions in paragraphs (g)(3)(i)(B)(5) or (6) of this section apply. The exceptions are as follows.

(1) *Intercompany section 361, 332, or 351 exchange.*—The transaction is an intercompany exchange to which section 361(a), sections 332 and 337(a), or (except as provided in the following sentence) section 351 applies in which no amount of income, gain, deduction or loss is recognized by the creditor or debtor. The assignment of an intercompany obligation by a creditor member in an intercompany exchange to which section 351 applies is a triggering transaction,

notwithstanding the preceding sentence, if a member of the group is described in, or engages in a transaction that is described in, any of the following paragraphs.

(i) The transferor or transferee member has a loss subject to a limitation (for example, a loss from a separate return limitation year that is subject to limitation under § 1.1502-21(c), or a dual consolidated loss that is subject to limitation under § 1.1503(d)-4), but only if the other member is not subject to a comparable limitation;

(ii) The transferor or transferee member has a special status within the meaning of § 1.1502-13(c)(5) (for example, a bank defined in section 581, or a life insurance company subject to tax under section 801) that the other member does not also possess;

(iii) A member of the group realizes discharge of indebtedness income that is excluded from gross income under section 108(a) within the same taxable year as that of the exchange, and the tax attributes attributable to either the transferor or the transferee member are reduced under sections 108, 1017, and § 1.1502-28 (except if the attribute reduction results solely from the application of § 1.1502-28(a)(4) (reduction of certain tax attributes attributable to other members));

(iv) The transferee member has a nonmember shareholder;

(v) The transferee member issues preferred stock to the transferor member in exchange for the assignment of the intercompany obligation; or

(vi) The stock of the transferee member (or a higher-tier member other than a higher-tier member of an 80-percent chain that includes the transferor and transferee) is disposed of within 12 months from the assignment of the intercompany obligation, unless at the time of the assignment, the transferor member, transferee member (or in the case of successive section 351 exchanges, each transferor and transferee member) and the debtor member are all in the same 80-percent chain; and all of the stock of the transferee (or in the case of successive section 351 exchanges, the lowest-tier transferee) held by members of the group is disposed of as part of the same plan or arrangement, either directly or indirectly, to persons that are not members of the group.

(2) *Intercompany assumption transaction.*—All of the debtor's obligations under an intercompany obligation are assumed in connection with the debtor's sale or other disposition of property (other than solely money) in an intercompany transaction in which gain or loss is recognized under section 1001.

(3) *Exception to the application of section 108(e)(4).*—The obligation became an intercompany obligation by reason of an event described in § 1.108-2(e)(2) (exception to the application of section 108(e)(4) in the case of acquisitions by securities dealers).

(4) *Reserve accounting.*—The amount realized is from reserve accounting under section 585 (see paragraph (g)(4)(v) of this section for special rules).

(5) *Intercompany extinguishment transaction.*—All or part of the rights and obligations under the intercompany obligation are extinguished in an intercompany transaction (other than an exchange or deemed exchange of an intercompany obligation for a newly issued intercompany obligation), the adjusted issue price of the obligation is equal to the creditor's basis in the obligation, and the debtor's corresponding item and the creditor's intercompany item (after taking into account the special rules of paragraph (g)(4)(i)(C) of this section) with respect to the obligation offset in amount.

(6) *Routine modification of intercompany obligation.*—All of the rights and obligations under the intercompany obligation are extinguished in an intercompany transaction that is an exchange (or deemed exchange) for a newly issued intercompany obligation, and the issue price of the newly issued obligation equals both the adjusted issue price of the extinguished obligation and the creditor's basis in the extinguished obligation. Solely for purposes of the preceding sentence, a newly issued intercompany obligation includes an obligation that is issued (or deemed issued) by a member other than the original debtor if such other member assumes the original debtor's obligations under the original obligation in a transaction that is described in either paragraph (g)(3)(i)(B)(1) or (g)(3)(i)(B)(2) of this section and the assumption results in a significant modification of the original obligation under § 1.1001-3(e)(4) and a deemed exchange under § 1.1001-3(b).

(7) *Outbound distribution of newly issued intercompany obligation.*—The intercompany obligation becomes an obligation that is not an intercompany obligation in a transaction in which a member that is a party to the reorganization exchanges property in pursuance of the plan of reorganization for a newly issued intercompany obligation of another member that is a party to the reorganization and distributes such intercompany obligation to a nonmember shareholder or nonmember creditor in a transaction to which section 361(c) applies.

(8) *Outbound subgroup exception.*—The intercompany obligation becomes an obligation that is not an intercompany obligation in a transaction in which the members of an intercompany obligation subgroup cease to be members of a consolidated group, neither the creditor nor the debtor recognize any income, gain, deduction, or loss with respect to the in-

tercompany obligation, and such members constitute an intercompany obligation subgroup of another consolidated group immediately after the transaction.

(C) *Tax benefit rule.*—If an assignment or extinguishment of an intercompany obligation in an intercompany transaction is otherwise excepted from the definition of triggering transaction under paragraph (g)(3)(i)(B)(1), (2), (5), or (6) of this section (and not also under paragraph (g)(3)(i)(B)(3) or (4) of this section), and the assignment or extinguishment is engaged in with a view to shift items of built-in gain, loss, income, or deduction from the obligation from one member to another member in order to secure a tax benefit (as defined in paragraph (g)(2)(v) of this section) that the group or its members would not otherwise enjoy in a consolidated or separate return year, then the assignment or extinguishment will be a triggering transaction to which paragraph (g)(3)(ii) of this section applies.

(ii) *Application of deemed satisfaction and reissuance.*—This paragraph (g)(3)(ii) applies if a triggering transaction occurs.

(A) *General rule.*—If the intercompany obligation is debt of a member, then (except as provided in the following sentence) the debt is treated for all Federal income tax purposes as having been satisfied by the debtor for cash in an amount equal to its fair market value, and then as having been reissued as a new obligation (with a new holding period but otherwise identical terms) for the same amount of cash, immediately before the triggering transaction. However, if the creditor realizes an amount with respect to the debt in the triggering transaction that differs from the debt's fair market value, and the triggering transaction is not an exchange (or deemed exchange) of debt of a member for newly issued debt of a member, then the debt is treated for all Federal income tax purposes as having been satisfied by the debtor for cash in an amount equal to such amount realized, and reissued as a new obligation (with a new holding period but otherwise identical terms) for the same amount of cash, immediately before the triggering transaction. If the triggering transaction is a mark to fair market value under section 475, then the intercompany obligation will be deemed satisfied and reissued for its fair market value (as determined under section 475 and applicable regulations) and section 475 will not otherwise apply with respect to that triggering transaction. If the intercompany obligation is a security of a member, similar principles apply (with appropriate adjustments) to treat the security as having been satisfied and reissued immediately before the triggering transaction.

(B) *Treatment as separate transaction.*—The deemed satisfaction and deemed reissuance are treated as transactions separate and apart from the triggering transaction. The deemed satisfaction and reissuance of a member's debt will not cause the debt to be recharacterized as other than debt for Federal income tax purposes.

(4) *Special rules.*—(i) *Timing and attributes.*—For purposes of applying the matching rule and the acceleration rule to a transaction involving an intercompany obligation (other than a transaction to which paragraph (g)(5) of this section applies)—

(A) Paragraph (c)(6)(i) of this section (treatment of intercompany items if corresponding items are excluded or nondeductible) will not apply to exclude any amount of income or gain attributable to a reduction of the basis of the intercompany obligation pursuant to § 1.1502-36(d), or pursuant to sections 108 and 1017 and § 1.1502-28 or any other provision that adjusts the basis of an intercompany obligation as a substitute for income or gain;

(B) Paragraph (c)(6)(ii) of this section (limitation on treatment of intercompany income or gain as excluded from gross income) does not apply to prevent any intercompany income or gain from the intercompany obligation from being excluded from gross income;

(C) Any income, gain, deduction, or loss from the intercompany obligation is not subject to section 108(a), section 354, section 355(a)(1), section 1091, or, in the case of an extinguishment of an intercompany obligation in a transaction in which the creditor transfers the obligation to the debtor in exchange for stock in such debtor, section 351(a); and

(D) Section 108(e)(7) does not apply upon the extinguishment of an intercompany obligation.

(ii) *Newly issued obligation in intercompany exchange.*—If an intercompany obligation is exchanged (or is deemed exchanged) for a newly issued intercompany obligation and the exchange (or deemed exchange) is not a routine modification of an intercompany obligation (as described in paragraph (g)(3)(i)(B)(6) of this section), then the newly issued obligation will be treated for all Federal income tax purposes as having an issue price equal to its fair market value.

(iii) *Off-market issuance.*—If an intercompany obligation is issued at a rate of interest that is materially off-market (off-market obligation) with a view to shift items of built-in gain, loss, income, or deduction from the obligation from one member to another member in order to secure a tax benefit (as defined in paragraph (g)(2)(v) of this section), then the intercompany obligation will be treated, for all Federal income tax purposes, as originally issued for its fair market value, and any difference between the amount loaned and the fair market value of the obligation will be treated as transferred between the creditor and the debtor at the time the obligation is issued. For example, if S lends $100 to B in

Reg. §1.1502-13(g)(4)(iii)

return for an off-market B note valued at $130, and the note is issued with a view to shift items from the note to secure a tax benefit, then the B note will be treated as issued for $130. The $30 difference will be treated as a distribution or capital contribution between S and B (as appropriate) at the time of issuance, and this amount will be reflected in future payments on the note as bond issuance premium. An adjustment to an off-market obligation under this paragraph (g)(4)(iii) will be made without regard to the application of, and in lieu of any adjustment under, section 467 (certain payments for the use of property or services), 482 (allocations among commonly controlled taxpayers), 483 (interest on certain deferred payments), 1274 (determination of issue price for certain debt instruments issued for property), or 7872 (treatment of loans with below-market interest rates).

(iv) *Deferral of loss or deduction with respect to nonmember indebtedness acquired in certain debt exchanges.*—If a creditor transfers an intercompany obligation to a nonmember (former intercompany obligation) in exchange for newly issued debt of a nonmember (nonmember debt), and the issue price of the nonmember debt is not determined by reference to its fair market value (for example, the issue price is determined under section 1273(b)(4) or 1274(a) or any other provision of applicable law), then any loss of the creditor otherwise allowable on the subsequent disposition of the nonmember debt, or any comparable tax benefit that would otherwise be available in any other transaction that directly or indirectly results from the disposition of the nonmember debt, is deferred until the date the debtor retires the former intercompany obligation.

(v) *Bad debt reserve.*—A member's deduction under section 585 for an addition to its reserve for bad debts with respect to an intercompany obligation is not taken into account, and is not treated as realized for purposes of paragraph (g)(3)(i)(A)(*1*) of this section, until the intercompany obligation is extinguished or becomes an obligation that is not an intercompany obligation.

(5) *Deemed satisfaction and reissuance of obligations becoming intercompany obligations.*— (i) *Application of deemed satisfaction and reissuance.*—(A) *In general.*—This paragraph (g)(5) applies if an obligation that is not an intercompany obligation becomes an intercompany obligation.

(B) *Exceptions.*—This paragraph (g)(5) does not apply to an intercompany obligation if either of the following exceptions apply.

(*1*) *Exception to the application of section 108(e)(4).*—The obligation becomes an intercompany obligation by reason of an event described in §1.108-2(e)(2) (exception to the ap-

plication of section 108(e)(4) in the case of acquisitions by securities dealers); or

(*2*) *Inbound subgroup exception.*—The obligation becomes an intercompany obligation in a transaction in which the members of an intercompany obligation subgroup cease to be members of a consolidated group, neither the creditor nor the debtor recognize any income, gain, deduction, or loss with respect to the intercompany obligation, and such members constitute an intercompany obligation subgroup of another consolidated group immediately after the transaction.

(ii) *Deemed satisfaction and reissuance.*— (A) *General rule.*—If the intercompany obligation is debt of a member, then the debt is treated for all Federal income tax purposes, immediately after it becomes an intercompany obligation, as having been satisfied by the debtor for cash in an amount determined under the principles of §1.108-2(f), and then as having been reissued as a new obligation (with a new holding period but otherwise identical terms) for the same amount of cash. If the intercompany obligation is a security of a member, similar principles apply (with appropriate adjustments) to treat the security, immediately after it becomes an intercompany obligation, as satisfied and reissued by the debtor for cash in an amount equal to its fair market value.

(B) *Treatment as separate transaction.*— The deemed satisfaction and deemed reissuance are treated as transactions separate and apart from the transaction in which the debt becomes an intercompany obligation, and the tax consequences of the transaction in which the debt becomes an intercompany obligation must be determined before the deemed satisfaction and reissuance occurs. (For example, if the debt becomes an intercompany obligation in a transaction to which section 351 applies, any limitation imposed by section 362(e) on the basis of the intercompany obligation in the hands of the transferee member is determined before the deemed satisfaction and reissuance.) The deemed satisfaction and reissuance of a member's debt will not cause the debt to be recharacterized as other than debt for Federal income tax purposes.

(6) *Special rules.*—(i) *Timing and attributes.*— If paragraph (g)(5) of this section applies to an intercompany obligation—

(A) Section 108(e)(4) does not apply;

(B) The attributes of all items taken into account from the satisfaction of the intercompany obligation are determined on a separate entity basis, rather than by treating S and B as divisions of a single corporation; and

(C) Any intercompany gain or loss realized by the creditor is not subject to section 354 or section 1091.

(ii) *Waiver of loss carryovers from separate return limitation years.*—Solely for purposes of § 1.1502-32(b)(4) and the effect of any election under that provision, any loss taken into account under paragraph (g)(5) of this section by a corporation that becomes a member as a result of the transaction in which the obligation becomes an intercompany obligation is treated as a loss carryover from a separate return limitation year.

(iii) *Deduction of repurchase premium in certain debt exchanges.*—If an obligation to which paragraph (g)(5) of this section applies is acquired in exchange for the issuance of an obligation to a nonmember and the issue price of this newly issued obligation is not determined by reference to its fair market value (for example, the issue price is determined under section 1273(b)(4) or 1274(a) or any other provision of applicable law), then, under the principles of § 1.163-7(c), any repurchase premium from the deemed satisfaction of the intercompany obligation under paragraph (g)(5)(ii) of this section will be amortized by the debtor over the term of the obligation issued to the nonmember in the same manner as if it were original issue discount and the obligation to the nonmember had been issued directly by the debtor.

(7) *Examples.*—(i) *In general.*—For purposes of the examples in this paragraph (g), unless otherwise stated, interest is qualified stated interest under § 1.1273-1(c), and the intercompany obligations are capital assets and are not subject to section 475.

(ii) The application of this section to obligations of members is illustrated by the following examples:

Example 1. Interest on intercompany obligation. (i) *Facts.* On January 1 of year 1, B borrows $100 from S in return for B's note providing for $10 of interest annually at the end of each year, and repayment of $100 at the end of year 5. B fully performs its obligations. Under their separate entity methods of accounting, B accrues a $10 interest deduction annually under section 163, and S accrues $10 of interest income annually under section 61(a)(4) and § 1.446-2.

(ii) *Matching rule.* Under paragraph (b)(1) of this section, the accrual of interest on B's note is an intercompany transaction. Under the matching rule, S takes its $10 of income into account in each of years 1 through 5 to reflect the $10 difference between B's $10 of interest expense taken into account and the $0 recomputed expense. S's income and B's deduction are ordinary items. (Because S's intercompany item and B's corresponding item would both be ordinary on a separate entity basis, the attributes are not redetermined under paragraph (c)(1)(i) of this section.)

(iii) *Original issue discount.* The facts are the same as in paragraph (i) of this *Example 1*, except that B borrows $90 (rather than $100) from S in return for B's note providing for $10 of interest annually and repayment of $100 at the end of year 5. The principles described in paragraph (ii) of this *Example 1* for stated interest also apply to the $10 of original issue discount. Thus, as B takes into account its corresponding expense under section 163(e), S takes into account its intercompany income under section 1272. S's income and B's deduction are ordinary items.

(iv) *Tax-exempt income.* The facts are the same as in paragraph (i) of this *Example 1*, except that B's borrowing from S is allocable under section 265 to B's purchase of state and local bonds to which section 103 applies. The timing of S's income is the same as in paragraph (ii) of this *Example 1*. Under paragraph (c)(4)(i) of this section, the attributes of B's corresponding item of disallowed interest expense control the attributes of S's offsetting intercompany interest income. Paragraph (c)(6) of this section does not prevent the redetermination of S's intercompany item as excluded from gross income because section 265(a)(2) permanently and explicitly disallows B's corresponding deduction and because, under paragraph (g)(4)(i)(B) of this section, paragraph (c)(6)(ii) of this section does not apply to prevent any intercompany income from the B note from being excluded from gross income. Accordingly, S's intercompany income is treated as excluded from gross income.

Example 2. Intercompany obligation becomes nonintercompany obligation. (i) *Facts.* On January 1 of year 1, B borrows $100 from S in return for B's note providing for $10 of interest annually at the end of each year, and repayment of $100 at the end of year 5. As of January 1 of year 3, B has paid the interest accruing under the note and S sells B's note to X for $70, reflecting an increase in prevailing market interest rates. B is never insolvent within the meaning of section 108(d)(3).

(ii) *Deemed satisfaction and reissuance.* Because the B note becomes an obligation that is not an intercompany obligation, the transaction is a triggering transaction under paragraph (g)(3)(i)(A)(2) of this section. Under paragraph (g)(3)(ii) of this section, B's note is treated as satisfied and reissued for its fair market value of $70 immediately before S's sale to X. As a result of the deemed satisfaction of the note for less than its adjusted issue price, B takes into account $30 of discharge of indebtedness income under § 1.61-12. On a separate entity basis, S's $30 loss would be a capital loss under section 1271(a)(1). Under the matching rule, however, the attributes of S's intercompany item and B's corresponding item must be redetermined to produce the same effect as if the transaction had occurred between divisions of a single corporation. Under paragraph (c)(4)(i) of this section, the attributes of B's $30 of discharge of indebtedness income control the attributes of S's loss. Thus, S's loss is treated as ordinary loss. B is also treated as reissuing, immediately after the satisfaction, a new note to S with a $70 issue price, a $100 stated redemption price at maturity, and a $70 basis in the hands of S. S is then treated as selling the new note to X for the $70 received by S in the actual transaction. Because S has a basis of $70 in the new note, S recognizes no gain or loss from the sale to X. After the sale, the new note held by X is not an intercompany obligation, it has a $70 issue price, a $100 stated redemption price at maturity, and a $70 basis. The $30 of original issue discount will be taken into account by B and X under sections 163(e) and 1272.

(iii) *Creditor deconsolidation.* The facts are the same as in paragraph (i) of this *Example 2*, except that P sells S's stock to X (rather than S selling B's note to X). Because the B note becomes an obligation that is not an intercompany obligation, the transaction is a triggering transaction under paragraph (g)(3)(i)(A)(2) of this section. Under paragraph (g)(3)(ii) of this section, B's note is treated as satisfied and reissued for its $70 fair market value immediately before S becomes a nonmember. The treatment of S's $30 of loss and B's $30 of discharge of indebtedness income is the same as in paragraph (ii) of this *Example 2*. The new note held by S upon deconsolidation is not an intercompany obligation, it has a $70 issue price, a $100 stated redemption price at maturity, and a $70 basis. The $30 of original issue discount will be taken into account by B and S under sections 163(e) and 1272.

(iv) *Debtor deconsolidation.* The facts are the same as in paragraph (i) of this *Example 2*, except that P sells S's stock to X (rather than S selling B's note to X). The results to S and B are the same as in paragraph (iii) of this *Example 2*.

(v) *Subgroup exception.* The facts are the same as in paragraph (i) of this *Example 2*, except that P owns all of the stock of S, S owns all of the stock of B, and P sells all of the S stock to X, the parent of another consolidated group. Because B and S, members of an intercompany obligation subgroup, cease to be members of the P group in a transaction that does not cause either member to recognize an item with respect to the B note, and such members constitute an intercompany obligation subgroup in the X group, P's sale of S stock is not a triggering transaction under paragraph (g)(3)(i)(B)(8) of this section, and the note is not treated as satisfied and reissued under paragraph (g)(3)(ii) of this section. After the sale, the note held by S has a $100 issue price, a $100 stated redemption price at maturity, and a $100 basis. The results are the same if the S stock is sold to an individual and the S-B affiliated group elects to file a consolidated return for the period beginning on the day after S and B cease to be members of the P group.

(vi) *Section 338 election.* The facts are the same as paragraph (i) of this *Example 2*, except that P sells S's stock to X and a section 338 election is made with respect to the stock sale. Under section 338, S is treated as selling all of its assets to new S, including the B note, at the close of the acquisition date. The aggregate deemed

sales price (within the meaning of § 1.338-4) allocated to the B note is $70. Because the B note becomes an obligation that is not an intercompany obligation, the transaction is a triggering transaction under paragraph (g)(3)(i)(A)(2) of this section. Under paragraph (g)(3)(ii) of this section, B's note is treated as satisfied and reissued immediately before S's deemed sale to new S for $70, the amount realized with respect to the note (the aggregate deemed sales price allocated to the note under § 1.338-6). The results to S and B are the same as in paragraph (ii) of this *Example 2*.

(vii) *Appreciated note.* The facts are the same as in paragraph (i) of this *Example 2*, except that S sells B's note to X for $130 (rather than $70), reflecting a decline in prevailing market interest rates. Because the B note becomes an obligation that is not an intercompany obligation, the transaction is a triggering transaction under paragraph (g)(3)(i)(A)(2) of this section. Under paragraph (g)(3)(ii) of this section, B's note is treated as satisfied and reissued for its fair market value of $130 immediately before S's sale to X. As a result of the deemed satisfaction of the note for more than its adjusted issue price, B takes into account $30 of repurchase premium under § 1.163-7(c). On a separate entity basis, S's $30 gain would be a capital gain under section 1271(a)(1). Under the matching rule, however, the attributes of S's intercompany item and B's corresponding item must be redetermined to produce the same effect as if the transaction had occurred between divisions of a single corporation. Under paragraph (c)(4)(i) of this section, the attributes of B's premium deduction control the attributes of S's gain. Accordingly, S's gain is treated as ordinary income. B is also treated as reissuing, immediately after the satisfaction, a new note to S with a $130 issue price, $100 stated redemption price at maturity, and $130 basis in the hands of S. S is then treated as selling the new note to X for the $130 received by S in the actual transaction. Because S has a basis of $130 in the new note, S recognizes no gain or loss from the sale to X. After the sale, the new note held by X is not an intercompany obligation, it has a $130 issue price, a $100 stated redemption price at maturity, and a $130 basis. The treatment of B's $30 of bond issuance premium under the new note is determined under § 1.163-13.

(viii) *Deferral of loss or deduction with respect to nonmember indebtedness acquired in debt exchange.* The facts are the same as in paragraph (i) of this *Example 2*, except that S sells B's note to X for a non-publicly traded X note with an issue price and face amount of $100 and a fair market value of $70, and that, subsequently, S sells the X note for $70. Because the B note becomes an obligation that is not an intercompany obligation, the transaction is a triggering transaction under paragraph (g)(3)(i)(A)(2) of this section. Under paragraph (g)(3)(ii) of this section, B's note is treated as satisfied and reissued immediately before S's sale to X for $100, the amount realized with respect to the note (determined under section 1274). As a result of the deemed satisfaction, neither S nor B take into account any items of income, gain, deduction, or loss. S is then treated as selling the new B note to X for the X note received by S in the actual transaction. Because S has a basis of $100 in the new note, S recognizes no gain or loss from the sale to X. After the sale, the new B note held by X is not an intercompany obligation, it has a $100 issue price, a $100 stated redemption price at maturity, and a $100 basis. S also holds an X note with a basis of $100 but a fair market value of $70. When S disposes of the X note, S's loss on the disposition is deferred under paragraph (g)(4)(iv) of this section, until B retires its note (the former intercompany obligation in the hands of X).

Example 3. Loss or bad debt deduction with respect to intercompany obligation. (i) *Facts.* On January 1 of year 1, B borrows $100 from S in return for B's note providing for $10 of interest annually at the end of each year, and repayment of $100 at the end of year 5. On January 1 of year 3, the fair market value of the B note has declined to $60 and S sells the B note to P for property with a fair market value of $60. B is never insolvent within the meaning of section 108(d)(3). The B note is not a security within the meaning of section 165(g)(2).

(ii) *Deemed satisfaction and reissuance.* Because S realizes an amount of loss from the assignment of the B note, the transaction is a triggering transaction under paragraph (g)(3)(i)(A)(1) of this section. Under paragraph (g)(3)(ii) of this section, B's note is treated as satisfied and reissued for its fair market value of $60 immediately before S's sale to P. As a result of the deemed satisfaction of the note for less than its adjusted issue price ($100), B takes into account $40 of discharge of indebtedness income under §1.61-12. On a separate entity basis, S's $40 loss would be a capital loss under section 1271(a)(1). Under the matching rule, however, the attributes of S's intercompany item and B's corresponding item must be redetermined to produce the same effect as if the transaction had occurred between divisions of a single corporation. Under paragraph (c)(4)(i) of this section, the attributes of B's $40 of discharge of indebtedness income control the attributes of S's loss. Thus, S's loss is treated as ordinary loss. B is also treated as reissuing, immediately after the satisfaction, a new note to S with a $60 issue price, $100 stated redemption price at maturity, and $60 basis in the hands of S. S is then treated as selling the new note to P for the $60 of property received by S in the actual transaction. Because S has a basis of $60 in the new note, S recognizes no gain or loss from the sale to P. After the sale, the note is an intercompany obligation, it has a $60 issue price and a $100 stated redemption price at maturity, and the $40 of original issue discount will

be taken into account by B and P under sections 163(e) and 1272.

(iii) *Partial bad debt deduction.* The facts are the same as in paragraph (i) of this *Example 3*, except that S claims a $40 partial bad debt deduction under section 166(a)(2) (rather than selling the note to P). Because S realizes a deduction from a transaction comparable to an assignment of the B note, the transaction is a triggering transaction under paragraph (g)(3)(i)(A)(1) of this section. Under paragraph (g)(3)(ii) of this section, B's note is treated as satisfied and reissued for its fair market value of $60 immediately before section 166(a)(2) applies. The treatment of S's $40 loss and B's $40 of discharge of indebtedness income are the same as in paragraph (ii) of this *Example 3.* After the reissuance, S has a basis of $60 in the new note. Accordingly, the application of section 166(a)(2) does not result in any additional deduction for S. The $40 of original issue discount on the new note will be taken into account by B and S under sections 163(e) and 1272.

(iv) *Insolvent debtor.* The facts are the same as in paragraph (i) of this *Example 3*, except that B is insolvent within the meaning of section 108(d)(3) at the time that S sells the note to P. As explained in paragraph (ii) of this *Example 3*, the transaction is a triggering transaction and the B note is treated as satisfied and reissued for its fair market value of $60 immediately before S's sale to P. On a separate entity basis, S's $40 loss would be capital, B's $40 income would be excluded from gross income under section 108(a), and B would reduce attributes under section 108(b) or section 1017 (see also §1.1502-28). However, under paragraph (g)(4)(i)(C) of this section, section 108(a) does not apply to characterize B's income as excluded from gross income. Accordingly, the attributes of S's loss and B's income are redetermined in the same manner as in paragraph (ii) of this *Example 3.*

Example 4. Intercompany nonrecognition transactions. (i) *Facts.* On January 1 of year 1, B borrows $100 from S in return for B's note providing for $10 of interest annually at the end of each year, and repayment of $100 at the end of year 5. As of January 1 of year 3, B has fully performed its obligations, but the note's fair market value is $130, reflecting a decline in prevailing market interest rates. On January 1 of year 3, S transfers the note and other assets to a newly formed corporation, Newco, for all of Newco's common stock in an exchange to which section 351 applies.

(ii) *No deemed satisfaction and reissuance.* Because the assignment of the B note is an exchange to which section 351 applies and neither S nor B recognize gain or loss, the transaction is not a triggering transaction under paragraph (g)(3)(i)(B)(1) of this section, and the note is not treated as satisfied and reissued under paragraph (g)(3)(ii) of this section.

(iii) *Receipt of other property.* The facts are the same as in paragraph (i) of this *Example 4*, except that the other assets transferred to Newco have a basis of $100 and a fair market value of $260, and S receives, in addition to Newco common stock, $15 of cash. Because S would recognize $15 of gain under section 351(b), the assignment of the B note is a triggering transaction under paragraph (g)(3)(i)(A)(*1*) of this section. Under paragraph (g)(3)(ii) of this section, B's note is treated as satisfied and reissued for its fair market value of $130 immediately before the transfer to Newco. As a result of the deemed satisfaction of the note for more than its adjusted issue price, B takes into account $30 of repurchase premium under § 1.163-7(c). On a separate entity basis, S's $30 gain would be a capital gain under section 1271(a)(1). Under the matching rule, however, the attributes of S's intercompany item and B's corresponding item must be redetermined to produce the same effect as if the transaction had occurred between divisions of a single corporation. Under paragraph (c)(4)(i) of this section, the attributes of B's premium deduction control the attributes of S's gain. Accordingly, S's gain is treated as ordinary income. B is also treated as reissuing, immediately after the satisfaction, a new note to S with a $130 issue price, $100 stated redemption price at maturity, and $130 basis in the hands of S. S is then treated as transferring the new note to Newco for the Newco stock and cash received by S in the actual transaction. Because S has a basis of $130 in the new B note, S recognizes no gain or loss with respect to the transfer of the note in the section 351 exchange, and S recognizes $10 of gain with respect to the transfer of the other assets under section 351(b). After the transfer, the note has a $130 issue price and a $100 stated redemption price at maturity. The treatment of B's $30 of bond issuance premium under the new note is determined under § 1.163-13.

(iv) *Transferee loss subject to limitation.* The facts are the same as in paragraph (i) of this *Example 4*, except that T is a member with a loss from a separate return limitation year that is subject to limitation under § 1.1502-21(c) (a SRLY loss), and on January 1 of year 3, S transfers the assets and the B note to T in an exchange to which section 351 applies. Because the transferee, T, has a loss that is subject to a limitation, the assignment of the B note is a triggering transaction under paragraph (g)(3)(i)(A)(*1*) of this section (the exception in paragraph (g)(3)(i)(B)(*1*) of this section does not apply). Under paragraph (g)(3)(ii) of this section, B's note is treated as satisfied and reissued for its fair market value, immediately before S's transfer to T. As a result of the deemed satisfaction of the note for more than its adjusted issue price, B takes into account $30 of repurchase premium under § 1.163-7(c). On a separate entity basis, S's $30 gain would be a capital gain under section 1271(a)(1). Under the matching rule, however, the attributes of S's in-

tercompany item and B's corresponding item must be redetermined to produce the same effect as if the transaction had occurred between divisions of a single corporation. Under paragraph (c)(4)(i) of this section, the attributes of B's premium deduction control the attributes of S's gain. Accordingly, S's gain is treated as ordinary income. B is also treated as reissuing, immediately after the satisfaction, a new note to S with a $130 issue price, $100 stated redemption price at maturity, and $130 basis in the hands of S. The treatment of B's $30 of bond issuance premium under the new note is determined under § 1.163-13. S is then treated as transferring the new note to T as part of the section 351 exchange. Because T will have a fair market value basis in the reissued B note immediately after the exchange, T's intercompany item from the subsequent retirement of the B note will not reflect any of S's built-in gain (and the amount of T's SRLY loss that may be absorbed by such item will be limited to any appreciation in the B note accruing after the exchange).

(v) *Intercompany obligation transferred in section 332 transaction.* The facts are the same as in paragraph (i) of this *Example 4*, except that S transfers the B note to P in complete liquidation under section 332. Because the transaction is an exchange to which section 332 and section 337(a) applies, and neither S nor B recognize gain or loss, the transaction is not a triggering transaction under paragraph (g)(3)(i)(B)(*1*) of this section, and the note is not treated as satisfied and reissued under paragraph (g)(3)(ii) of this section.

Example 5. Assumption of intercompany obligation. (i) *Facts.* On January 1 of year 1, B borrows $100 from S in return for B's note providing for $10 of interest annually at the end of each year, and repayment of $100 at the end of year 5. The note is fully recourse and is incurred for use in Business Z. As of January 1 of year 3, B has fully performed its obligations, but the note's fair market value is $110 reflecting a decline in prevailing market interest rates. Business Z has a fair market value of $95. On January 1 of year 3, B transfers all of the assets of Business Z and $15 of cash (substantially all of B's assets) to member T in exchange for the assumption by T of all of B's obligations under the note in a transaction in which gain or loss is recognized under section 1001. The terms and conditions of the note are not modified in connection with the sales transaction, the transaction does not result in a change in payment expectations, and no amount of income, gain, deduction, or loss is recognized by S, B, or T with respect to the note.

(ii) *No deemed satisfaction and reissuance.* Because all of B's obligations under the B note are assumed by T in connection with the sale of the Business Z assets, the assignment of B's obligations under the note is not a triggering transaction under paragraph (g)(3)(i)(B)(2) of this section, and the note is not treated as satisfied and reissued under paragraph (g)(3)(ii) of this section.

Example 6. Extinguishment of intercompany obligation. (i) *Facts.* On January 1 of year 1, B borrows $100 from S in return for B's note providing for $10 of interest annually at the end of each year, and repayment of $100 at the end of year 20. The note is a security within the meaning of section 351(d)(2). As of January 1 of year 3, B has fully performed its obligations, but the fair market value of the B note is $130, reflecting a decline in prevailing market interest rates, and S transfers the note to B in exchange for $130 of B stock in a transaction to which both section 351 and section 354 applies.

(ii) *No deemed satisfaction and reissuance.* As a result of the satisfaction of the note for more than its adjusted issue price, B takes into account $30 of repurchase premium under § 1.163-7(c). Although the transfer of the B note is a transaction to which both section 351 and section 354 applies, under paragraph (g)(4)(i)(C) of this section, any gain or loss from the intercompany obligation is not subject to either section 351(a) or section 354, and therefore, S has a $30 gain under section 1001. Because the note is extinguished in a transaction in which the adjusted issue price of the note is equal to the creditor's basis in the note, and the debtor's and creditor's items offset in amount, the transaction is not a triggering transaction under paragraph (g)(3)(i)(B)(5) of this section, and the note is not treated as satisfied and reissued under paragraph (g)(3)(ii) of this section. On a separate entity basis, S's $30 gain would be a capital gain under section 1271(a)(1). Under the matching rule, however, the attributes of S's intercompany item and B's corresponding item must be redetermined to produce the same effect as if the transaction had occurred between divisions of a single corporation. Under paragraph (c)(4)(i) of this section, the attributes of B's premium deduction control the attributes of S's gain. Accordingly, S's gain is treated as ordinary income. Under paragraph (g)(4)(i)(D) of this section, section 108(e)(7) does not apply upon the extinguishment of the B note, and therefore, the B stock received by S in the exchange will not be treated as section 1245 property.

Example 7. Exchange of intercompany obligations. (i) *Facts.* On January 1 of year 1, B borrows $100 from S in return for B's note providing for $10 of interest annually at the end of each year, and repayment of $100 at the end of year 20. As of January 1 of year 3, B has fully performed its obligations and, pursuant to a recapitalization to which section 368(a)(1)(E) applies, B issues a new note to S in exchange for the original B note. The new B note has an issue price, stated redemption price at maturity, and stated principal amount of $100, but contains terms that differ sufficiently from the terms of the original B note to cause a realization event under § 1.1001-3. The original B note and the new B note are both

securities (within the meaning of section 354(a)(1)).

(ii) *No deemed satisfaction and reissuance.* Because the original B note is extinguished in exchange for a newly issued B note and the issue price of the new B note is equal to both the adjusted issue price of the original B note and S's basis in the original B note, the transaction is not a triggering transaction under paragraph (g)(3)(i)(B)(6) of this section, and the note is not treated as satisfied and reissued under paragraph (g)(3)(ii) of this section. B has neither income from discharge of indebtedness under section 108(e)(10) nor a deduction for repurchase premium under § 1.163-7(c). Although the exchange of the original B note for the new B note is a transaction to which section 354 applies, under paragraph (g)(4)(i)(C) of this section, any gain or loss from the intercompany obligation is not subject to section 354. Under section 1001, S has no gain or loss from the exchange of notes.

Example 8. Tax benefit rule. (i) *Facts.* On January 1 of year 1, B borrows $100 from S in return for B's note providing for $10 of interest annually at the end of each year, and repayment of $100 at the end of year 5. As of January 1 of year 3, B has fully performed its obligations, but the note's fair market value has depreciated, reflecting an increase in prevailing market interest rates. On that date, S transfers the B note to member T as part of an exchange for T common stock which is intended to qualify for nonrecognition treatment under section 351 but with a view to sell the T stock at a reduced gain. On February 1 of year 4, all of the stock of T is sold at a reduced gain.

(ii) *Deemed satisfaction and reissuance.* Because the assignment of the B note does not occur within 12 months of the sale of T stock, paragraph (g)(3)(i)(B)(1)(vi) of this section does not apply to treat the assignment as a triggering transaction. However, because the assignment of the B note was engaged in with a view to shift built-in loss from the obligation in order to secure a tax benefit that the group or its members would not otherwise enjoy, under paragraph (g)(3)(i)(C) of this section, the assignment of the B note is a triggering transaction to which paragraph (g)(3)(ii) of this section applies. Under paragraph (g)(3)(ii) of this section, B's note is treated as satisfied and reissued for its fair market value, immediately before S's transfer to T. As a result of the deemed satisfaction of the note for less than its adjusted issue price, B takes into account discharge of indebtedness income and S has a corresponding loss which is treated as ordinary loss. B is also treated as reissuing, immediately after the deemed satisfaction, a new note to S with an issue price and basis equal to its fair market value. S is then treated as transferring the new note to T as part of the section 351 exchange. Because S's basis in the T stock received with respect to the transferred B note is equal to its fair market value, S's gain with respect to the

T stock will not reflect any of the built-in loss attributable to the B note. (This example does not address common law doctrines or other authorities that might apply to recharacterize the transaction or to otherwise affect the tax treatment of the transaction.)

Example 9. Issuance at off-market rate of interest. (i) *Facts.* T is a member with a SRLY loss. T's sole shareholder, P, borrows an amount of cash from T in return for a P note that provides for a materially above market rate of interest. The P note is issued with a view to generate additional interest income to T over the term of the note to facilitate the absorption of T's SRLY loss.

(ii) *With a view.* Because the P note is issued with a view to shift interest income from the off-market obligation in order to secure a tax benefit that the group or its members would not otherwise enjoy, under paragraph (g)(4)(iii) of this section, the intercompany obligation is treated, for all Federal income tax purposes, as originally issued for its fair market value so T is treated as purchasing the note at a premium. The difference between the amount loaned and the fair market value of the obligation is treated as transferred from P to T as a capital contribution at the time the note is issued. Throughout the term of the note, T takes into account interest income and bond premium and P takes into account interest deduction and bond issuance premium under generally applicable Internal Revenue Code sections. The adjustment under paragraph (g)(4)(iii) of this section is made without regard to the application of, and in lieu of any adjustment under, section 482 or 1274.

Example 10. Nonintercompany obligation becomes intercompany obligation. (i) *Facts.* On January 1 of year 1, B borrows $100 from X in return for B's note providing for $10 of interest annually at the end of each year, and repayment of $100 at the end of year 5. As of January 1 of year 3, B has fully performed its obligations, but the note's fair market value is $70, reflecting an increase in prevailing market interest rates. On January 1 of year 3, P buys all of X's stock. B is solvent within the meaning of section 108(d)(3).

(ii) *Deemed satisfaction and reissuance.* Under paragraph (g)(5)(ii) of this section, B's note is treated as satisfied for $70 (determined under the principles of §1.108-2(f)(2)) immediately after it becomes an intercompany obligation. Both X's $30 capital loss (under section 1271(a)(1)) and B's $30 of discharge of indebtedness income (under §1.61-12) are taken into account in determining consolidated taxable income for year 3. Under paragraph (g)(6)(i)(B) of this section, the attributes of items resulting from the satisfaction are determined on a separate entity basis. But see section 382 and §1.1502-15 (as appropriate). B is also treated as reissuing a new note to X. The new note is an intercompany obligation, it has a $70 issue price and $100 stated redemption price at maturity,

and the $30 of original issue discount will be taken into account by B and X in the same manner as provided in paragraph (iii) of *Example 1* of this paragraph (g)(7).

(iii) *Amortization of repurchase premium.* The facts are the same as in paragraph (i) of this *Example 10,* except that on January 1 of year 3, the B note has a fair market value of $130 and rather than P purchasing the X stock, P purchases the B note from X by issuing its own note. The P note has an issue price, stated redemption price at maturity, stated principal amount, and fair market value of $130. Under paragraph (g)(5)(ii) of this section, B's note is treated as satisfied for $130 (determined under the principles of §1.108-2(f)(1)) immediately after it becomes an intercompany obligation. As a result of the deemed satisfaction of the note, P has no gain or loss and B has $30 of repurchase premium. Under paragraph (g)(6)(iii) of this section, B's $30 of repurchase premium from the deemed satisfaction is amortized by B over the term of the newly issued P note in the same manner as if it were original issue discount and the newly issued P note had been issued directly by B. B is also treated as reissuing a new note to P. The new note is an intercompany obligation, it has a $130 issue price and $100 stated redemption price at maturity, and the treatment of B's $30 of bond issuance premium under the new B note is determined under §1.163-13.

(iv) *Election to file consolidated returns.* Assume instead that B borrows $100 from S during year 1, but the P group does not file consolidated returns until year 3. Under paragraph (g)(5)(ii) of this section, B's note is treated as satisfied and reissued as a new note immediately after the note becomes an intercompany obligation. The satisfaction and reissuance are deemed to occur on January 1 of year 3, for the fair market value of the obligation (determined under the principles of §1.108-2(f)(2)) at that time.

Example 11. Notional principal contracts. (i) *Facts.* On April 1 of year 1, M1 enters into a contract with counterparty M2 under which, for a term of five years, M1 is obligated to make a payment to M2 each April 1, beginning in year 2, in an amount equal to the London Interbank Offered Rate (LIBOR), as determined by reference to LIBOR on the day each payment is due, multiplied by a $1,000 notional principal amount. M2 is obligated to make a payment to M1 each April 1, beginning in year 2, in an amount equal to 8 percent multiplied by the same notional principal amount. LIBOR is 7.80 percent on April 1 of year 2, and therefore, M2 owes $2 to M1.

(ii) *Matching rule.* Under §1.446-3(d), the net income (or net deduction) from a notional principal contract for a taxable year is included in (or deducted from) gross income. Under §1.446-3(e), the ratable daily portion of M2's obligation to M1 as of December 31 of year 1 is $1.50 ($2 multiplied by 275/365). Under the

Reg. §1.1502-13(g)(7)(ii)

matching rule, M1's net income for year 1 of $1.50 is taken into account to reflect the difference between M2's net deduction of $1.50 taken into account and the $0 recomputed net deduction. Similarly, the $.50 balance of the $2 of net periodic payments made on April 1 of year 2 is taken into account for year 2 in M1's and M2's net income and net deduction from the contract. In addition, the attributes of M1's intercompany income and M2's corresponding deduction are redetermined to produce the same effect as if the transaction had occurred between divisions of a single corporation. Under paragraph (c)(4)(i) of this section, the attributes of M2's corresponding deduction control the attributes of M1's intercompany income. (Although M1 is the selling member with respect to the payment on April 1 of year 2, it might be the buying member in a subsequent period if it owes the net payment.)

(iii) *Dealer*. The facts are the same as in paragraph (i) of this *Example 11*, except that M2 is a dealer in securities, and the contract with M1 is not inventory in the hands of M2. Under section 475, M2 must mark its securities to fair market value at year-end. Assume that under section 475, M2's loss from marking to fair market value the contract with M1 is $10. Because M2 realizes an amount of loss from the mark to fair market value of the contract, the transaction is a triggering transaction under paragraph (g)(3)(i)(A)(*1*) of this section. Under paragraph (g)(3)(ii) of this section, M2 is treated as making a $10 payment to M1 to terminate the contract immediately before a new contract is treated as reissued with an up-front payment by M1 to M2 of $10. M1's $10 of income from the termination payment is taken into account under the matching rule to reflect M2's deduction under §1.446-3(h). The attributes of M1's intercompany income and M2's corresponding deduction are redetermined to produce the same effect as if the transaction had occurred between divisions of a single corporation. Under paragraph (c)(4)(i) of this section, the attributes of M2's corresponding deduction control the attributes of M1's intercompany income. Accordingly, M1's income is treated as ordinary income. Under §1.446-3(f), the deemed $10 up-front payment by M1 to M2 in connection with the issuance of a new contract is taken into account over the term of the new contract in a manner reflecting the economic substance of the contract (for example, allocating the payment in accordance with the forward rates of a series of cash-settled forward contracts that reflect the specified index and the $1,000 notional principal amount). (The timing of taking items into account is the same if M1, rather than M2, is the dealer subject to the mark-to-market requirement of section 475 at year-end. However in this case, because the attributes of the corresponding deduction control the attributes of the intercompany income, M1's income from the deemed termination payment from M2 might be ordinary or capital). Under paragraph

(g)(3)(ii)(A) of this section, section 475 does not apply to mark the notional principal contract to fair market value after its deemed satisfaction and reissuance.

(8) *Effective/applicability date.*—The rules of this paragraph (g) apply to transactions involving intercompany obligations occurring in consolidated return years beginning on or after December 24, 2008.

(h) *Anti-avoidance rules.*—(1) *In general.*—If a transaction is engaged in or structured with a principal purpose to avoid the purposes of this section (including, for example, by avoiding treatment as an intercompany transaction), adjustments must be made to carry out the purposes of this section.

(2) *Examples.*—The anti-avoidance rules of this paragraph (h) are illustrated by the following examples. The examples set forth below do not address common law doctrines or other authorities that might apply to recast a transaction or to otherwise affect the tax treatment of a transaction. Thus, in addition to adjustments under this paragraph (h), the Commissioner can, for example, apply the rules of section 269 or §1.701-2 to disallow a deduction or to recast a transaction.

Example 1. Sale of a partnership interest. (a) *Facts.* S owns land with a $10 basis and $100 value. B has net operating losses from separate return limitation years (SRLYs) subject to limitation under §1.1502-21(c). Pursuant to a plan to absorb the losses without limitation by the SRLY rules, S transfers the land to an unrelated, calendar-year partnership in exchange for a 10% interest in the capital and profits of the partnership in a transaction to which section 721 applies. The partnership does not have a section 754 election in effect. S later sells its partnership interest to B for $100. In the following year, the partnership sells the land to X for $100. Because the partnership does not have a section 754 election in effect, its $10 basis in the land does not reflect B's $100 basis in the partnership interest. Under section 704(c), the partnership's $90 built-in gain is allocated to B, and B's basis in the partnership interest increases to $190 under section 705. In a later year, B sells the partnership interest to a nonmember for $100.

(b) *Adjustments.* Under §1.1502-21(c), the partnership's $90 built-in gain allocated to B ordinarily increases the amount of B's SRLY limitation, and B's $90 loss from its sale of the partnership interest ordinarily is not subject to limitation under the SRLY rules. Because the contribution of property to the partnership and the sale of the partnership interest were part of a plan a principal purpose of which was to achieve a reduction in consolidated tax liability by creating offsetting gain and loss for B while deferring S's intercompany gain, B's allocable share of the partnership's gain from its sale of the land is treated under paragraph (h)(1) of this section as not increasing the amount of B's SRLY limitation.

Example 2. Transitory status as an intercompany obligation. (a) *Facts.* P historically has owned 70% of X's stock and the remaining 30% is owned by unrelated shareholders. On January 1 of Year 1, S borrows $100 from X in return for S's note requiring $10 of interest annually at the end of each year, and repayment of $100 at the end of Year 20. As of January 1 of Year 3, the P group has substantial net operating loss carryovers, and the fair market value of S's note falls to $70 due to an increase in prevailing market interest rates. X is not permitted under section 166(a)(2) to take into account a $30 loss with respect to the note. Pursuant to a plan to permit X to take into account its $30 loss without disposing of the note, P acquires an additional 10% of X's stock, causing X to become a member, and P subsequently resells the 10% interest. X's $30 loss with respect to the note is a net unrealized built-in loss within the meaning of § 1.1502-15.

(b) *Adjustments.* Under paragraph (g)(4) of this section, X ordinarily would take into account its $30 loss as a result of the note becoming an intercompany obligation, and S would take into account $30 of discharge of indebtedness income. Under § 1.1502-22, X's loss is not combined with items of the other members and the loss would be carried to X's separate return years as a result of X becoming a nonmember. However, the transitory status of S's indebtedness to X as an intercompany obligation is structured with a principal purpose to accelerate the recognition of X's loss. Thus, S's note is treated under paragraph (h)(1) of this section as not becoming an intercompany obligation.

Example 3. Corporate mixing bowl. (a) *Facts.* M1 and M2 are subsidiaries of P. M1 operates a manufacturing business on land it leases from M2. The land is the only asset held by M2. P intends to dispose of the M1 business, including the land owned by M2; P's basis in the M1 stock is equal to the stock's fair market value. M2's land has a value of $20 and a basis of $0 and P has a $0 basis in the stock of M2. In Year 1, with a principal purpose of avoiding gain from the sale of the land (by transferring the land to M1 with a carry-over basis without affecting P's basis in the stock of M1 or M2), M1 and M2 form corporation T; M1 contributes cash in exchange for 80% of the T stock and M2 contributes the land in exchange for 20% of the stock. In Year 3, T liquidates, distributing $20 cash to M2 and the land (plus $60 cash) to M1. Under § 1.1502-34, section 332 applies to both M1 and M2. Under section 337, T recognizes no gain or loss from its liquidating distribution of the land to M1. T has neither gain nor loss on its distribution of cash to M2. In Year 4, P sells all of the stock of M1 to X and liquidates M2.

(b) *Adjustments.* A principal purpose for the formation and liquidation of T was to avoid gain from the sale of M2's land. Thus, under paragraph (h)(1) of this section, M2 must take $20 of gain into account when the stock of M1 is sold to X.

Example 4. Partnership mixing bowl. (a) *Facts.* M1 owns a self-created intangible asset with a $0 basis and a fair market value of $100. M2 owns land with a basis of $100 and a fair market value of $100. In Year 1, with a principal purpose of creating basis in the intangible asset (which would be eligible for amortization under section 197), M1 and M2 form partnership PRS; M1 contributes the intangible asset and M2 contributes the land. X, an unrelated person, contributes cash to PRS in exchange for a substantial interest in the partnership. PRS uses the contributed assets in legitimate business activities. Five years and six months later, PRS liquidates, distributing the land to M1, the intangible to M2, and cash to X. The group reports no gain under sections 707(a)(2)(B) and 737(a) and claims that M2'S basis in the intangible asset is $100 under section 732 and that the asset is eligible for amortization under section 197.

(b) *Adjustments.* A principal purpose of the formation and liquidation of PRS was to create additional amortization without an offsetting increase in consolidated taxable income by avoiding treatment as an intercompany transaction. Thus, under paragraph (h)(1) of this section, appropriate adjustments must be made.

Example 5. Sale and leaseback. (a) *Facts.* S operates a factory with a $70 basis and $100 value, and has loss carryovers from SRLYS. Pursuant to a plan to take into account the $30 unrealized gain while continuing to operate the factory, S sells the factory to X for $100 and leases it back on a long-term basis. In the transaction, a substantial interest in the factory is transferred to X. The sale and leaseback are not recharacterized under general principles of Federal income tax law. As a result of S's sale to X, the $30 gain is taken into account and increases S's SRLY limitation.

(b) *No adjustments.* Although S's sale was pursuant to a plan to accelerate the $30 gain, it is not subject to adjustment under paragraph (h)(1) of this section. The sale is not treated as engaged in or structured with a principal purpose to avoid the purposes of this section.

(i) [Reserved]

(j) *Miscellaneous operating rules.*—For purposes of this section—

(1) *Successor assets.*—Any reference to an asset includes, as the context may require, a reference to any other asset the basis of which is determined, directly or indirectly, in whole or in part, by reference to the basis of the first asset.

(2) *Successor persons.*—(i) *In general.*—Any reference to a person includes, as the context may require, a reference to a predecessor or successor. For this purpose, a predecessor is a trans-

feror of assets to a transferee (the successor) in a transaction—

    (A) To which section 381(a) applies;

    (B) In which substantially all of the assets of the transferor are transferred to members in a complete liquidation;

    (C) In which the successor's basis in assets is determined (directly or indirectly, in whole or in part) by reference to the basis of the transferor, but the transferee is a successor only with respect to the assets the basis of which is so determined; or

    (D) Which is an intercompany transaction, but only with respect to assets that are being accounted for by the transferor in a prior intercompany transaction.

    (ii) *Intercompany items.*—If the assets of a predecessor are acquired by a successor member, the successor succeeds to, and takes into account (under the rules of this section), the predecessor's intercompany items. If two or more successor members acquire assets of the predecessor, the successors take into account the predecessor's intercompany items in a manner that is consistently applied and reasonably carries out the purposes of this section and applicable provisions of law.

    (3) *Multiple triggers.*—If more than one corresponding item can cause an intercompany item to be taken into account under the matching rule, the intercompany item is taken into account in connection with the corresponding item most consistent with the treatment of members as divisions of a single corporation. For example, if S sells a truck to B, its intercompany gain from the sale is not taken into account by reference to B's depreciation if the depreciation is capitalized under section 263A as part of B's cost for a building; instead, S's gain relating to the capitalized depreciation is taken into account when the building is sold or as it is depreciated. Similarly, if B purchases appreciated land from S and transfers the land to a lower-tier member in exchange for stock, thereby duplicating the basis of the land in the basis of the stock, items with respect to both the stock and the land can cause S's intercompany gain to be taken into account; if the lower-tier member becomes a nonmember as a result of the sale of its stock, the attributes of S's intercompany gain are determined with respect to the land rather than the stock.

    (4) *Multiple or successive intercompany transactions.*—If a member's intercompany item or corresponding item affects the accounting for more than one intercompany transaction, appropriate adjustments are made to treat all of the intercompany transactions as transactions between divisions of a single corporation. For example, if S sells property to M, and M sells the property to B, then S, M, and B are treated as divisions of a single corporation for purposes of applying the rules of this section. Similar princi-

ples apply with respect to intercompany transactions that are part of the same plan or arrangement. For example, if S sells separate properties to different members as part of the same plan or arrangement, all of the participating members are treated as divisions of a single corporation for purposes of determining the attributes (which might also affect timing) of the intercompany items and corresponding items from each of the properties.

    (5) *Acquisition of group.*—(i) *Scope.*—This paragraph (j)(5) applies only if a consolidated group (the terminating group) ceases to exist as a result of—

    (A) The acquisition of either the assets of the common parent of the terminating group in a reorganization described in section 381(a)(2), or the stock of the common parent of the terminating group; or

    (B) The application of the principles of § 1.1502-75(d)(2) or (d)(3).

    (ii) *Application.*—If the terminating group ceases to exist under circumstances described in paragraph (j)(5)(i) of this section, the surviving group is treated as the terminating group for purposes of applying this section to the intercompany transactions of the terminating group. For example, intercompany items and corresponding items from intercompany transactions between members of the terminating group are taken into account under the rules of this section by the surviving group. This treatment does not apply, however, to members of the terminating group that are not members of the surviving group immediately after the terminating group ceases to exist (for example, under section 1504(a)(3) relating to reconsolidation, or section 1504(c) relating to includible insurance companies).

    (6) *Former common parent treated as continuation of group.*—If a group terminates because the common parent is the only remaining member, the common parent succeeds to the treatment of the terminating group for purposes of applying this section so long as it neither becomes a member of an affiliated group filing separate returns nor becomes a corporation described in section 1504(b). For example, if the only subsidiary of the group liquidates into the common parent in a complete liquidation to which section 332 applies, or the common parent merges into the subsidiary and the subsidiary is treated as the common parent's successor under paragraph (j)(2)(i) of this section, the taxable income of the surviving corporation is treated as the group's consolidated taxable income in which the intercompany and corresponding items must be included. See § 1.267(f)-1 for additional rules applicable to intercompany losses or deductions.

    (7) *Becoming a nonmember.*—For purposes of this section, a member is treated as becoming a

nonmember if it has a separate return year (including another group's consolidated return year). A member is not treated as having a separate return year if its items are treated as taken into account in computing the group's consolidated taxable income under paragraph (j)(5) or (6) of this section.

(8) *Recordkeeping.*—Intercompany and corresponding items must be reflected on permanent records (including work papers). See also section 6001, requiring records to be maintained. The group must be able to identify from these permanent records the amount, location, timing, and attributes of the items, so as to permit the application of the rules of this section for each year.

(9) *Examples.*—The operating rules of this paragraph (j) are illustrated generally throughout this section, and by the following examples.

Example 1. Intercompany sale followed by section 351 transfer to member. (a) *Facts.* S holds land for investment with a basis of $70. On January 1 of Year 1, S sells the land to M for $100. M also holds the land for investment. On July 1 of Year 3, M transfers the land to B in exchange for all of B's stock in a transaction to which section 351 applies. Under section 358, M's basis in the B stock is $100. B holds the land for sale to customers in the ordinary course of business and, under section 362(b), B's basis in the land is $100. On December 1 of Year 5, M sells 20% of the B stock to X for $22. In an unrelated transaction on July 1 of Year 8, B sells 20% of the land for $22.

(b) *Definitions.* Under paragraph (b)(1) of this section, S's sale of the land to M and M's transfer of the land to B are both intercompany transactions. S is the selling member and M is the buying member in the first intercompany transaction, and M is the selling member and B is the buying member in the second intercompany transaction. M has no intercompany items under paragraph (b)(2) of this section. Because B acquired the land in an intercompany transaction, B's items from the land are corresponding items to be taken into account under this section. Under the successor asset rule of paragraph (j)(1) of this section, references to the land include references to M's B stock. Under the successor person rule of paragraph (j)(2) of this section, references to M include references to B with respect to the land.

(c) *Timing and attributes resulting from the stock sale.* Under paragraph (c)(3) of this section, M is treated as owning and selling B's stock for purposes of the matching rule even though, as divisions, M could not own and sell stock in B. Under paragraph (j)(3) of this section, both M's B stock and B's land can cause S's intercompany gain to be taken into account under the matching rule. Thus, S takes $6 of its gain into account in Year 5 to reflect the $6 difference between M's $2 gain taken into account from its sale of B stock and the $8 recomputed gain. Under paragraph (j)(4) of this section, the attributes of this gain are

determined by treating S, M, and B as divisions of a single corporation. Under paragraph (c)(1) of this section, S's $6 gain and M's $2 gain are treated as long-term capital gain. The gain would be capital on a separate entity basis (assuming that section 341 does not apply), and this treatment is not inconsistent with treating S, M, and B as divisions of a single corporation because the stock sale and subsequent land sale are unrelated transactions and B remains a member following the sale.

(d) *Timing and attributes resulting from the land sale.* Under paragraph (j)(3) of this section, S takes $6 of its gain into account in Year 8 under the matching rule to reflect the $6 difference between B's $2 gain taken into account from its sale of an interest in the land and the $8 recomputed gain. Under paragraph (j)(4) of this section, the attributes of this gain are determined by treating S, M, and B as divisions of a single corporation and taking into account the activities of S, M, and B with respect to the land. Thus, both S's gain and B's gain might be ordinary income as a result of B's activities. (If B subsequently sells the balance of the land, S's gain taken into account is limited to its remaining $18 of intercompany gain.)

(e) *Sale of successor stock resulting in deconsolidation.* The facts are the same as in paragraph (a) of this *Example 1,* except that M sells 60% of the B stock to X for $66 on December 1 of Year 5 and B becomes a nonmember. Under the matching rule, M's sale of B stock results in $18 of S's gain being taken into account (to reflect the difference between M's $6 gain taken into account and the $24 recomputed gain). Under the acceleration rule, however, the entire $30 gain is taken into account (to reflect B becoming a nonmember, because its basis in the land reflects M's $100 cost basis from the prior intercompany transaction). Under paragraph (j)(4) of this section, the attributes of S's gain are determined by treating S, M, and B as divisions of a single corporation. Because M's cost basis in the land will be reflected by B as a nonmember, all of S's gain is treated as from the land (rather than a portion being from B's stock), and B's activities with respect to the land might therefore result in S's gain being ordinary income.

Example 2. Intercompany sale of member stock followed by recapitalization. (a) *Facts.* Before becoming a member of the P group, S owns P stock with a basis of $70. On January 1 of Year 1, P buys all of S's stock. On July 1 of Year 3, S sells the P stock to M for $100. On December 1 of Year 5, P acquires M's original P stock in exchange for new P stock in a recapitalization described in section 368(a)(1)(E).

(b) *Timing and attributes.* Although P's basis in the stock acquired from M is eliminated under paragraph (f)(4) of this section, the new P stock received by M is exchanged basis property (within the meaning of section 7701(a)(44)) having a basis under section 358 equal to M's basis in the original P stock. Under the successor asset rule of paragraph (j)(1) of this section, references to M's original P stock include references to M's new P stock. Because it is still possible to take S's intercompany item into account under the matching rule with respect to the successor asset, S's gain is not taken into account under the acceleration rule as a result of the basis elimination under paragraph (f)(4) of this section. Instead, the gain is taken into account based on subsequent events with respect to M's new P stock (for example, a subsequent distribution or redemption of the new stock).

Example 3. Back-to-back intercompany transactions—matching. (a) *Facts.* S holds land for investment with a basis of $70. On January 1 of Year 1, S sells the land to M for $90. M also holds the land for investment. On July 1 of Year 3, M sells the land for $100 to B, and B holds the land for sale to customers in the ordinary course of business. During Year 5, B sells all of the land to customers for $105.

(b) *Timing.* Under paragraph (b)(1) of this section, S's sale of the land to M and M's sale of the land to B are both intercompany transactions. S is the selling member and M is the buying member in the first intercompany transaction, and M is the selling member and B is the buying member in the second intercompany transaction. Under paragraph (j)(4) of this section, S, M and B are treated as divisions of a single corporation for purposes of determining the timing of their items from the intercompany transactions. See also paragraph (j)(2) of this section (B is treated as a successor to M for purposes of taking S's intercompany gain into account). Thus, S's $20 gain and M's $10 gain are both taken into account in Year 5 to reflect the difference between B's $5 gain taken into account with respect to the land and the $35 recomputed gain (the gain that B would have taken into account if the intercompany sales had been transfers between divisions of a single corporation, and B succeeded to S's $70 basis).

(c) *Attributes.* Under paragraphs (j)(4) of this section, the attributes of the intercompany items and corresponding items of S, M, and B are also determined by treating S, M, and B as divisions of a single corporation. For example, the attributes of S's and M's intercompany items are determined by taking B's activities into account.

Example 4. Back-to-back intercompany transactions—acceleration. (a) *Facts.* During Year 1, S performs services for M in exchange for $10 from M. S incurs $8 of employee expenses. M capitalizes the $10 cost of S's services under section 263 as part of M's cost to acquire real property from X. Under its separate entity method of accounting, S would take its income and expenses into account in Year 1. M holds the real property for investment and, on July 1 of Year 5, M sells it to B at a gain. B also holds the real property for investment. On December 1 of Year 8, while B

still owns the real property, P sells all of M's stock to X and M becomes a nonmember.

(b) *M's items.* M takes its gain into account immediately before it becomes a nonmember. Because the real property stays in the group, the acceleration rule redetermines the attributes of M's gain under the principles of the matching rule as if B sold the real property to an affiliated corporation that is not a member of the group for a cash payment equal to B's adjusted basis in the real property, and S, M, and B were divisions of a single corporation. Thus, M's gain is capital gain.

(c) *S's items.* Under paragraph (b)(2)(ii) of this section, S includes the $8 of expenses in determining its $2 intercompany income. In Year 1, S takes into account $8 of income and $8 of expenses. Under paragraph (j)(4) of this section, appropriate adjustments must be made to treat both S's performance of services for M and M's sale to B as occurring between divisions of a single corporation. Thus, S's $2 of intercompany income is not taken into account as a result of M becoming a nonmember, but instead will be taken into account based on subsequent events (e.g., under the matching rule based on B's sale of the real property to a nonmember, or under the acceleration rule based on P's sale of the stock of S or B to a nonmember). See the successor person rules of paragraph (j)(2) of this section (B is treated as a successor to M for purposes of taking S's intercompany income into account).

(d) *Sale of S's stock.* The facts are the same as in paragraph (a) of this *Example 4*, except that P sells all of S's stock (rather than M's stock) and S becomes a nonmember on July 1 of Year 5. S's remaining $2 of intercompany income is taken into account immediately before S becomes a nonmember. Because S's intercompany income is not from an intercompany sale, exchange, or distribution of property, the attributes of the intercompany income are determined on a separate entity basis. Thus, S's $2 of intercompany income is ordinary income. M does not take any of its intercompany gain into account as a result of S becoming a nonmember.

(e) *Intercompany income followed by intercompany loss.* The facts are the same as in paragraph (a) of this *Example 4*, except that M sells the real property to B at a $1 loss (rather than a gain). M takes its $1 loss into account under the acceleration rule immediately before M becomes a nonmember. But see §1.267(f)-1 (which might further defer M's loss if M and B remain in a controlled group relationship after M becomes a nonmember). Under paragraph (j)(4) of this section appropriate adjustments must be made to treat the group as if both intercompany transactions occurred between divisions of a single corporation. Accordingly, P's sale of M stock also results in S taking into account $1 of intercompany income as capital gain to offset M's $1 of corresponding capital loss. The remaining $1 of

S's intercompany income is taken into account based on subsequent events.

Example 5. Successor group. (a) *Facts.* On January 1 of Year 1, B borrows $100 from S in return for B's note providing for $10 of interest annually at the end of each year, and repayment of $100 at the end of Year 20. As of January 1 of Year 3, B has paid the interest accruing under the note. On that date, X acquires all of P's stock and the former P group members become members of the X consolidated group.

(b) *Successor.* Under paragraph (j)(5) of this section; although B's note ceases to be an intercompany obligation of the P group, the note is not treated as satisfied and reissued under paragraph (g) of this section as a result of X's acquisition of P stock. Instead, the X consolidated group succeeds to the treatment of the P group for purposes of paragraph (g) of this section, and B's note is treated as an intercompany obligation of the X consolidated group.

Example 6. Liquidation—80% distributee. (a) *Facts.* X has had preferred stock described in section 1504(a)(4) outstanding for several years. On January 1 of Year 1, S buys all of X's common stock for $60, and B buys all of X's preferred stock for $40. X's assets have a $0 basis and $100 value. On July 1 of Year 3, X distributes all of its assets to S and B in a complete liquidation. Under § 1.1502-34, section 332 applies to both S and B. Under section 337, X has no gain or loss from its liquidating distribution to S. Under sections 336 and 337(c), X has a $40 gain from its liquidating distribution to B. B has a $40 basis under section 334(a) in the assets received from X, and S has a $0 basis under section 334(b) in the assets received from X.

(b) *Intercompany items from the liquidation.* Under the matching rule, X's $40 gain from its liquidating distribution to B is not taken into account under this section as a result of the liquidation (and therefore is not yet reflected under §§ 1.1502-32 and 1.1502-33). Under the successor person rule of paragraph (j)(2)(i) of this section, S and B are both successors to X. Under section 337(c), X recognizes gain or loss only with respect to the assets distributed to B. Under paragraph (j)(2)(ii) of this section, to be consistent with the purposes of this section, S succeeds to X's $40 intercompany gain. The gain will be taken into account by S under the matching and acceleration rules of this section based on subsequent events. (The allocation of the intercompany gain to S does not govern the allocation of any other attributes.)

Example 7. Liquidation—no 80% distributee. (a) *Facts.* X has only common stock outstanding. On January 1 of Year 1, S buys 60% of X's stock for $60, and B buys 40% of X's stock for $40. X's assets have a $0 basis and $100 value. On July 1 of Year 3, X distributes all of its assets to S and B in a complete liquidation. Under § 1.1502-34, section 332 applies to both S and B. Under sections 336 and 337(c), X has a $100 gain from its liqui-

dating distributions to S and B. Under section 334(b), S has a $60 basis in the assets received from X and B has a $40 basis in the assets received from X.

(b) *Intercompany items from the liquidation.* Under the matching rule, X's $100 intercompany gain from its liquidating distributions to S and B is not taken into account under this section as a result of the liquidation (and therefore is not yet reflected under §§ 1.1502-32 and 1.1502-33). Under the successor person rule of paragraph (j)(2)(i) of this section, S and B are both successors to X. Under paragraph (j)(2)(ii) of this section, to be consistent with the purposes of this section, S succeeds to X's $40 intercompany gain with respect to the assets distributed to B, and B succeeds to X's $60 intercompany gain with respect to the assets distributed to S. The gain will be taken into account by S and B under the matching and acceleration rules of this section based on subsequent events. (The allocation of the intercompany gain does not govern the allocation of any other attributes.)

(k) *Cross references.*—(1) *Section 108.*—See § 1.108-3 for the treatment of intercompany deductions and losses as subject to attribute reduction under section 108(b).

(2) *Section 263A(f).*—See section 263A(f) and § 1.263A9(g)(5) for special rules regarding interest from intercompany transactions.

(3) *Section 267(f).*—See section 267(f) and § 1.267(f)-1 for special rules applicable to certain losses and deductions from transactions between members of a controlled group.

(4) *Section 460.*—See § 1.460-4(j) for special rules regarding the application of section 460 to intercompany transactions.

(5) *Section 469.*—See § 1.469-1(h) for special rules regarding the application of section 469 to intercompany transactions.

(6) *§ 1.1502-80.*—See § 1.1502-80 for the non-application of certain Internal Revenue Code rules.

(l) *Effective/applicability dates.*—(1) *In general.*—This section applies with respect to transactions occurring in years beginning on or after July 12, 1995. If both this section and prior law apply to a transaction, or neither applies, with the result that items may be duplicated, omitted, or eliminated in determining taxable income (or tax liability), or items may be treated inconsistently, prior law (and not this section) applies to the transaction. For example, S's and B's items from S's sale of property to B which occurs in a consolidated return year beginning before July 12, 1995, are taken into account under prior law, even though B may dispose of the property in a consolidated return year beginning on or after July 12, 1995. Similarly, an intercompany distribution to which a shareholder becomes entitled in a consolidated return year beginning before July 12, 1995, but which is distributed in a consolidated return year beginning on or after that date is taken into account under prior law (generally when distributed), because this section generally takes dividends into account when the shareholder becomes entitled to them but this section does not apply at that time. If application of prior law to S's deferred gain or loss from a deferred intercompany transaction (as defined under prior law) occurring in a consolidated return year beginning prior to July 12, 1995, would be affected by an intercompany transaction (as defined under this section) occurring in a consolidated return year beginning on or after July 12, 1995, S's deferred gain or loss continues to be taken into account as provided under prior law, and the items from the subsequent intercompany transaction are taken into account under this section. Appropriate adjustments must be made to prevent items from being duplicated, omitted, or eliminated in determining taxable income as a result of the application of both this section and prior law to the successive transactions, and to ensure the proper application of prior law. Paragraphs (a)(4), (f)(6)(ii), (f)(6)(iv)(A), (g)(3)(ii)(B)(2), and (j)(5)(i)(A) of this section apply with respect to transactions occurring on or after September 17, 2008. However, taxpayers may apply paragraph (j)(5)(i)(A) of this section to transactions that occurred prior to September 17, 2008.

(2) *Avoidance transactions.*—This paragraph (1)(2) applies if a transaction is engaged in or structured on or after April 8, 1994, with a principal purpose to avoid the rules of this section (and instead to apply prior law). If this paragraph (1)(2) applies, appropriate adjustments must be made in years beginning on or after July 12, 1995, to prevent the avoidance, duplication, omission, or elimination of any item (or tax liability), or any other inconsistency with the rules of this section. For example, if S is a dealer in real property and sells land to B on March 16, 1995 with a principal purpose of converting any future appreciation in the land to capital gain, B's gain from the sale of the land on May 11, 1997 might be characterized as ordinary income under this paragraph (1)(2).

(3) *Election for certain stock elimination transactions.*—(i) *In general.*—A group may elect pursuant to this paragraph (1)(3) to apply this section (including the elections available under paragraph (f)(5)(ii) of this section) to stock elimination transactions to which prior law would otherwise apply. If an election is made, this section, and not prior law, applies to determine the timing and attributes of S's and B's gain or loss from stock with respect to all stock elimination transactions.

(ii) *Stock elimination transactions.*—For purposes of this paragraph (1)(3), a stock elimination transaction is a transaction in which stock transferred from S to B—

(A) Is cancelled or redeemed on or after July 12, 1995;

(B) Is treated as cancelled in a liquidation pursuant to an election under section 338(h)(10) with respect to a qualified stock purchase with an acquisition date on or after July 12, 1995;

(C) Is distributed on or after July 12, 1995; or

(D) Is exchanged on or after July 12, 1995 for stock of a member (determined immediately after the exchange) in a transaction that would cause S's gain or loss from the transfer to be taken into account under prior law.

(iii) *Time and manner of making election.*—An election under this paragraph (1)(3) is made by attaching to a timely filed original return (including extensions) for the consolidated return year including July 12, 1995 a statement entitled "[Insert Name and Employer Identification Number of Common Parent] HEREBY ELECTS THE APPLICATION OF § 1.1502-13(1)(3)." See paragraph (f)(5)(ii)(E) of this section for the manner of electing the relief provisions of paragraph (f)(5)(ii) of this section.

(4) *Prior law.*—For transactions occurring in S's years beginning before July 12, 1995, see the applicable regulations issued under section 1502. See § § 1.1502-13, 1.1502-13T, 1.1502-14, 1.1502-14T, 1.1502-31, and 1.1502-32 (as contained in the 26 CFR part 1 edition revised as of April 1, 1995).

(5) *Consent to adopt method of accounting.*—For intercompany transactions occurring in a consolidated group's first taxable year beginning on or after July 12, 1995, the Commissioner's consent under section 446(e) is hereby granted for any changes in methods of accounting that are necessary solely by reason of the timing rules of this section. Changes in method of accounting for these transactions are to be effected on a cut-off basis.

(6) *Effective/applicability date.*—(i) In general.—Paragraph (f)(7)(i) Example 4. applies to transactions occurring on or after December 18, 2009.

(ii) [Reserved]

(m) *Effective/applicability date.*—Paragraphs (f)(5)(ii)(E) and (f)(6)(i)(C)(2) of this section apply to any original consolidated Federal income tax return due (without extensions) after June 14, 2007. For original consolidated Federal income tax returns due (without extensions) after May 30, 2006, and on or before June 14, 2007, see § 1.1502-13T as contained in 26 CFR part 1 in effect on April 1, 2007. For original consolidated

Federal income tax returns due (without extensions) on or before May 30, 2006, see § 1.1502-13 as contained in 26 CFR part 1 in effect on April 1, 2006. [Reg. § 1.1502-13.]

☐ *[T.D. 6894, 9-7-66. Amended by T.D. 7246, 12-29-72; T.D. 8131, 3-24-87; T.D. 8196, 4-14-88; T.D. 8295, 3-9-90; T.D. 8478, 3-9-93; T.D. 8482, 8-6-93; T.D. 8560, 8-12-94; T.D. 8584, 12-28-94; T.D. 8597, 7-12-95; T.D. 8660, 3-13-96; T.D. 8677, 6-26-96; T.D. 8823, 6-25-99; T.D. 8883, 5-11-2000; T.D. 9025, 12-13-2002; T.D. 9048, 3-11-2003; T.D. 9117, 3-12-2004; T.D. 9192, 3-21-2005; T.D. 9261, 5-5-2006; T.D. 9264, 5-26-2006; T.D. 9329, 6-13-2007; T.D. 9383, 3-6-2008; T.D. 9424, 9-9-2008 (corrected 10-17-2008); T.D. 9442, 12-24-2008 (corrected 2-10-2009); T.D. 9458, 9-3-2009; T.D. 9475, 12-17-2009 (corrected 8-9-2011); and T.D. 9515, 3-3-2011 (corrected 3-30-2011).]*

[Reg. § 1.1502-13T]

§ 1.1502-13T. Intercompany transactions (temporary).—(a) through (f)(5)(ii)(A) [Reserved]. For further guidance, see § 1.1502-13(a) through (f)(5)(ii)(A).

(B) *Section 332.—(1) In general.*—If section 332 would otherwise apply to T's (old T's) liquidation into B, and B transfers substantially all of old T's assets to a new member (new T), and if a direct transfer of substantially all of old T's assets to new T would qualify as a reorganization described in section 368(a), then, for all Federal income tax purposes, T's liquidation into B and B's transfer of substantially all of old T's assets to new T will be disregarded and instead, the transaction will be treated as if old T transferred substantially all of its assets to new T in exchange for new T stock and the assumption of T's liabilities in a reorganization described in section 368(a). (Under § 1.1502-13(j)(1), B's stock in new T would be a successor asset to B's stock in old T, and S's gain would be taken into account based on the new T stock.)

(2) *Time limitation and adjustments.*—The transfer of old T's assets to new T qualifies under paragraph (f)(5)(ii)(B)(1) of this section only if B has entered into a written plan, on or before the due date of the group's consolidated income tax return (including extensions), to transfer the T assets to new T, and the statement described in paragraph (f)(5)(ii)(E) of this section is included on or with a timely filed consolidated tax return for the tax year that includes the date of the liquidation (including extensions). However, see paragraph (f)(5)(ii)(F) of this section for certain situations in which the plan may be entered into after the due date of the return and the statement described in paragraph (f)(5)(ii)(E) of this section may be included on either an original tax return or an amended tax return filed after the due date of the return. In either case, the transfer of substantially all of T's assets to

new T must be completed within 12 months of the filing of the return. Appropriate adjustments are made to reflect any events occurring before the formation of new T and to reflect any assets not transferred to new T, or liabilities not assumed by new T. For example, if B retains an asset of old T, the asset is treated under § 1.1502-13(f)(3) as acquired by new T but distributed to B immediately after the reorganization.

(f)(5)(ii)(B)(3) through (f)(5)(ii)(E) [Reserved]. For further guidance, see § 1.1502-13(f)(5)(ii)(B)(3) through (f)(5)(ii)(E).

(F) *Effective/Applicability date.—(1) General rule.*—Paragraphs (f)(5)(ii)(B)(1) and (f)(5)(ii)(B)(2) of this section apply to transactions in which old T's liquidation into B occurs on or after October 25, 2007.

(2) *Prior periods.*—For transactions in which old T's liquidation into B occurs before October 25, 2007, see 1.1502-13(f)(5)(ii)(B)(1) and (f)(5)(ii)(B)(2) in effect prior to October 25, 2007, as contained in 26 CFR part 1, revised April 1, 2009.

(3) *Special rule for tax returns filed before November 3, 2009.*—In the case of a liquidation on or after October 25, 2007, by a taxpayer whose original tax return for the year of liquidation was filed on or before November 3, 2009 then, notwithstanding paragraph (f)(5)(ii)(B)(2) of this section and § 1.1502-13(f)(5)(ii)(E), the election to apply paragraph (f)(5)(ii)(B) of this section may be made by entering into the written plan described in paragraph (f)(5)(ii)(B) of this section on or before November 3, 2009 including the statement described in § 1.1502-13(f)(5)(ii)(E) on or with an original tax return or an amended tax return for the tax year that includes the liquidation filed on or before November 3, 2009 and transferring substantially all of T's assets to new T within 12 months of the filing of such original or amended return.

(G) *Expiration date.*—These temporary regulations will expire on September 3, 2012. [Temporary Reg. § 1.1502-13T.]

☐ *[T.D. 9383, 3-6-2008 (corrected 4-2-2008). Amended by T.D. 9458, 9-3-2009 (corrected 1-12-2010) and T.D. 9515, 3-3-2011 (corrected 3-30-2011).]*

[Reg. § 1.1502-15]

§ 1.1502-15. SRLY limitation on built-in losses.—(a) *SRLY limitation.*—Except as provided in paragraph (f) of this section (relating to built-in losses of the common parent) and paragraph (g) of this section (relating to an overlap with section 382), built-in losses are subject to the SRLY limitation under § § 1.1502-21(c) and 1.1502-22(c) (including applicable subgroup principles). Built-in losses are treated as deductions or losses in the year recognized, except for the purpose of determining the amount of, and the extent to which the built-in loss is limited by, the SRLY limitation for the year in which it is recognized. Solely for such purpose, a built-in loss is treated as a hypothetical net operating loss carryover or net capital loss carryover arising in a SRLY, instead of as a deduction or loss in the year recognized. To the extent that a built-in loss is allowed as a deduction under this section in the year it is recognized, it offsets any consolidated taxable income for the year before any loss carryovers or carrybacks are allowed as a deduction. To the extent not so allowed, it is treated as a separate net operating loss or net capital loss carryover or carryback arising in the year of recognition and, under § 1.1502-21(c) or 1.1502-22(c), the year of recognition is treated as a SRLY.

(b) *Built-in losses.*—(1) *Defined.*—If a corporation has a net unrealized built-in loss under section 382(h)(3) (as modified by this section) on the day it becomes a member of the group (whether or not the group is a consolidated group), its deductions and losses are built-in losses under this section to the extent they are treated as recognized built-in losses under section 382(h)(2)(B) (as modified by this section). This paragraph (b) generally applies separately with respect to each member, but see paragraph (c) of this section for circumstances in which it is applied on a subgroup basis.

(2) *Operating rules.*—Solely for purposes of applying paragraph (b)(1) of this section, the principles of § 1.1502-94(c) apply with appropriate adjustments, including the following:

(i) *Stock acquisition.*—A corporation is treated as having an ownership change under section 382(g) on the day the corporation becomes a member of a group, and no other events (e.g., a subsequent ownership change under section 382(g) while it is a member) are treated as causing an ownership change.

(ii) *Asset acquisition.*—In the case of an asset acquisition by a group, the assets and liabilities acquired directly from the same transferor (whether corporate or non-corporate, foreign or domestic) pursuant to the same plan are treated as the assets and liabilities of a corporation that becomes a member of the group (and has an ownership change) on the date of the acquisition.

(iii) *Recognized built-in gain or loss.*—A loss that is included in the determination of net unrealized built-in gain or loss and that is recognized but disallowed or deferred (e.g., under §§ 1.337(d)-2, 1.1502-35, 1.1502-36, or section 267) is not treated as a built-in loss unless and until the loss would be allowed during the recognition period without regard to the application of this section. Section 382(h)(1)(B)(ii) does not apply to the extent it limits the amount of recognized

built-in loss that may be treated as a pre-change loss to the amount of the net unrealized built-in loss.

(c) *Built-in losses of subgroups.*—(1) *In general.*—In the case of a subgroup, the principles of paragraph (b) of this section apply to the subgroup, and not separately to its members. Thus, the net unrealized built-in loss and recognized built-in loss for purposes of paragraph (b) of this section are based on the aggregate amounts for each member of the subgroup.

(2) *Members of subgroups.*—A subgroup is composed of those members that have been continuously affiliated with each other for the 60 consecutive month period ending immediately before they become members of the group in which the loss is recognized. A member remains a member of the subgroup until it ceases to be affiliated with the loss member. For this purpose, the principles of § 1.1502-21(c)(2)(iv) through (vi) apply with appropriate adjustments.

(3) *Coordination of 60 month affiliation requirement with the overlap rule.*—If one or more corporations become members of a group and are included in the determination of a net unrealized built-in loss that is subject to the overlap rule described in paragraph (g)(1) of this section, then for purposes of paragraph (c)(2) of this section, such corporations that become members of the group are treated as having been affiliated for 60 consecutive months with the common parent of the group and are also treated as having been affiliated with any other members who have been affiliated or are treated as having been affiliated with the common parent at such time. The corporations are treated as having been affiliated with such other members for the same period of time that those members have been affiliated or are treated as having been affiliated with the common parent. If two or more corporations become members of the group at the same time, but this paragraph (c)(3) does not apply to every such corporation, then immediately after the corporations become members of the group, and solely for purposes of paragraph (c)(2) of this section, the corporations to which this paragraph (c)(3) applies are treated as having not been previously affiliated with the corporations to which this paragraph (c)(3) does not apply. If the common parent has become the common parent of an existing group within the previous five year period in a transaction described in § 1.1502-75(d)(2)(ii) or (3), the principles of §§ 1.1502-91(g)(6) and 1.1502-96(a)(2)(iii) shall apply.

(4) *Built-in amounts.*—Solely for purposes of determining whether the subgroup has a net unrealized built-in loss or whether it has a recognized built-in loss, the principles of § 1.1502-91(g) and (h) apply with appropriate adjustments.

Reg. § 1.1502-15(c)(4)

(d) *Examples.*—For purposes of the examples in this section, unless otherwise stated, all groups file consolidated returns, all corporations have calendar taxable years, the facts set forth the only corporate activity, value means fair market value and the adjusted basis of each asset equals its value, all transactions are with unrelated persons, and the application of any limitation or threshold under section 382 is disregarded. The principles of this section are illustrated by the following examples:

Example 1. Determination of recognized built-in loss. (i) Individual A owns all of the stock of P and T. T has two depreciable assets. Asset 1 has an unrealized loss of $55 (basis $75, value $20), and asset 2 has an unrealized gain of $20 (basis $30, value $50). P acquires all the stock of T from Individual A during Year 1, and T becomes a member of the P group. P's acquisition of T is not an ownership change as defined by section 382(g). Paragraph (g) of this section does not apply because there is not an overlap of the application of the rules contained in paragraph (a) of this section and section 382.

(ii) Under paragraph (b)(2)(i) of this section, and solely for purposes of applying paragraph (b)(1) of this section, T is treated as having an ownership change under section 382(g) on becoming a member of the P group. Under paragraph (b)(1) of this section, none of T's $55 of unrealized loss is treated as a built-in loss unless T has a net unrealized built-in loss under section 382(h)(3) on becoming a member of the P group.

(iii) Under section 382(h)(3)(A), T has a $35 net unrealized built-in loss on becoming a member of the P group ((\$55) + \$20 = (\$35)). Assume that this amount exceeds the threshold requirement in section 382(h)(3)(B). Under section 382(h)(2)(B), the entire amount of T's $55 unrealized loss is treated as a built-in loss to the extent it is recognized during the 5-year recognition period described in section 382(h)(7). Under paragraph (b)(2)(iii) of this section, the restriction under section 382(h)(1)(B)(ii), which limits the amount of recognized built-in loss that is treated as pre-change loss to the amount of the net unrealized built-in loss, is inapplicable for this purpose. Consequently, the entire $55 of unrealized loss (not just the $35 net unrealized loss) is treated under paragraph (b)(1) of this section as a built-in loss to the extent it is recognized within 5 years of T's becoming a member of the P group. Under paragraph (a) of this section, a built-in loss is subject to the SRLY limitation under § 1.1502-21(c)(1).

(iv) Under paragraph (b)(2)(ii) of this section, the builtin loss would similarly be subject to a SRLY limitation under § 1.1502-21(c)(1) if T transferred all of its assets and liabilities to a subsidiary of the P group in a single transaction described in section 351. To the extent the built-in loss is recognized within 5 years of T's transfer, all of the items contributed by the acquiring subsidiary to consolidated taxable income (and not just the items attributable to the assets and liabilities transferred by T) are included for purposes of determining the SRLY limitation under § 1.1502-21(c)(1).

Example 2. Actual application of section 382 not relevant. (i) Individual A owns all of the stock of P, and Individual B owns all of the stock of T. T has two depreciable assets. Asset 1 has an unrealized loss of $25 (basis $75, value $50), and asset 2 has an unrealized gain of $20 (basis $30, value $50). P buys 55 percent of the stock of T in January of Year 1, resulting in an ownership change of T under section 382(g). During March of Year 2, P buys the 45 percent balance of the T stock, and T becomes a member of the P group.

(ii) Although T has an ownership change for purposes of section 382 in Year 1 and not Year 2, T's joining the P group in Year 2 is treated as an ownership change under section 382(g) solely for purposes of this section. Consequently, for purposes of this section, whether T has a net unrealized built-in loss under section 382(h)(3) is determined as if the day T joined the P group were a change date.

Example 3. Determination of a recognized built-in loss of a subgroup. (i) Individual A owns all of the stock of P, S, and M. P and M are each the common parent of a consolidated group. During Year 1, P acquires all of the stock of S from Individual A, and S becomes a member of the P group. P's acquisition of S is not an ownership change as defined by section 382(g). At the beginning of Year 7, M acquires all of the stock of P from Individual A, and P and S become members of the M group. M's acquisitions of P and S are also not ownership changes as defined by section 382(g). At the time of M's acquisition of the P stock, P has (disregarding the stock of S) a $10 net unrealized built-in gain (two depreciable assets, asset 1 with a basis of $35 and a value of $55, and asset 2 with a basis of $55 and a value of $45), and S has a $75 net unrealized built-in loss (two depreciable assets, asset 3 with a basis of $95 and a value of $10, and asset 4 with a basis of $10 and a value of $20).

(ii) Under paragraph (c) of this section, P and S compose a subgroup on becoming members of the M group because P and S were continuously affiliated for the 60 month period ending immediately before they became members of the M group. Consequently, paragraph (b) of this section does not apply to P and S separately. Instead, their separately computed unrealized gains and losses are aggregated for purposes of determining whether, and the extent to which, any unrealized loss is treated as built-in loss under this section and is subject to the SRLY limitation under § 1.1502-21(c).

(iii) Under paragraph (c) of this section, the P subgroup has a net unrealized built-in loss on the day P and S become members of the M group, determined by treating the day they become members as a change date. The net unrealized built-in loss is the aggregate of P's net unrealized built-in gain of $10 and S's net unrealized built-in loss of $75, or an aggregate net unrealized built-in loss of $65. (The stock of S owned by P is disregarded for purposes of determining the net unrealized built-in loss. However, any loss allowed on the sale of the stock within the recognition period is taken into account in determining recognized loss.) Assume that the $65 net unrealized built-in loss exceeds the threshold requirement under section 382(h)(3)(B).

(iv) Under paragraphs (b)(1), (b)(2)(iii), and (c) of this section, a loss recognized during the 5-year recognition period on an asset of P or S held on the day that P and S became members of the M group is a built-in loss except to the extent the group establishes that such loss exceeds the amount by which the adjusted basis of such asset on the day the member became a member exceeded the fair market value of such asset on that same day. If P sells asset 2 for $45 in Year 7 and recognizes a $10 loss, the entire $10 loss is treated as a built-in loss under paragraphs (b)(2)(iii) and (c) of this section. If S sells asset 3 for $10 in Year 7 and recognizes an $85 loss, the entire $85 loss is treated as a built-in loss under paragraphs (b)(2)(iii) and (c) of this section (not just the $55 balance of the P subgroup's $65 net unrealized built-in loss).

(v) The determination of whether P and S constitute a SRLY subgroup for purposes of loss carryovers and carrybacks, and the extent to which built-in losses are not allowed under the SRLY limitation, is made under § 1.1502-21(c).

Example 4. Computation of SRLY limitation. (i) Individual A owns all of the stock of P, the common parent of a consolidated group. During Year 1, Individual A forms T by contributing $300 and T sustains a $100 net operating loss. During Year 2, T's assets decline in value to $100. At the beginning of Year 3, P acquires all the stock of T from Individual A, and T becomes a member of the P group with a net unrealized built-in loss of $100. P's acquisition of T is not an ownership change as defined by section 382(g). Assume that $100 exceeds the threshold requirements of section 382(h)(3)(B). During Year 3, T recognizes its unrealized built-in loss as a $100 ordinary loss. The members of the P group contribute the following net income to the consolidated taxable income of the P group (disregarding T's recognized built-in loss and any consolidated net operating loss deduction under § 1.1502-21) for Years 3 and 4:

	Year 3	Year 4	Total
P group (without T)	$100	$100	$200
T	$60	$40	$100
CTI	$160	$140	$300

(ii) Under paragraph (b) of this section, T's $100 ordinary loss in Year 3 (not taken into account in the consolidated taxable income computations above) is a built-in loss. Under paragraph (a) of this section, the built-in loss is treated as a net operating loss carryover for purposes of determining the SRLY limitation under § 1.1502-21(c).

(iii) For Year 3, § 1.1502-21(c) limits T's $100 built-in loss and $100 net operating loss carryover from Year 1 to the aggregate of the P group's consolidated taxable income through Year 3, determined by reference to only T's items. For this purpose, consolidated taxable income is determined without regard to any consolidated net operating loss deductions under § 1.1502-21(a).

(iv) The P group's consolidated taxable income through Year 3 is $60 when determined by reference to only T's items. Under § 1.1502-21(c), the SRLY limitation for Year 3 is therefore $60.

(v) Under paragraph (a) of this section, the $100 built-in loss is treated as a current deduction for all purposes other than determination of the SRLY limitation under § 1.1502-21(c). Consequently, a deduction for the built-in loss is allowed in Year 3 before T's loss carryover from Year 1 is allowed, but only to the extent of the $60 SRLY limitation. None of T's Year 1 loss carryover is allowed because the built-in loss ($100) exceeds the SRLY limitation for Year 3.

(vi) The $40 balance of the built-in loss that is not allowed in Year 3 because of the SRLY limitation is treated as a $40 net operating loss arising in Year 3 that is carried to other years in accordance with the rules of § 1.1502-21(b). The $40 net operating loss is treated under paragraph (a) of this section and § 1.1502-21(c)(1)(ii) as a loss carryover or carryback from Year 3 that arises in a SRLY, and is subject to the rules of § 1.1502-21 (including § 1.1502-21(c)) rather than this section. See also § 1.1502-21(c)(1)(iii) *Example 4.*

(vii) The facts are the same as in paragraphs (i) through (vi) of this *Example 4,* except that T has an additional built-in loss when it joins the P group which is recognized in Year 4. For purposes of determining the SRLY limitation for this additional loss in Year 4 (or any subsequent year), the $60 of built-in loss allowed as a deduction in Year 3 is treated under paragraph (a) of this section as a deduction in Year 3 that reduces the P group's consolidated taxable income when determined by reference to only T's items.

Example 5. Built-in loss exceeding consolidated taxable income in the year recognized. (i) Individual A owns all of the stock of P and T. During Year 1, P acquires all the stock of T from Individual A, and T becomes a member of the P group. P's acquisition of T was not an ownership change as defined by section 382(g). At the time of acquisition, T has a noncapital asset with an unrealized loss of $45 (basis $100, value $55), which exceeds the threshold requirements of section

382(h)(3)(B). During Year 2, T sells its asset for $55 and recognizes the unrealized built-in loss. The P group has $10 of consolidated taxable income in Year 2, computed by disregarding T's recognition of the $45 built-in loss and the consolidated net operating loss deduction, while the consolidated taxable income would be $25 if determined by reference to only T's items (other than the $45 loss).

(ii) T's $45 loss is recognized in Year 2 and, under paragraph (b) of this section, constitutes a built-in loss. Under paragraph (a) of this section and § 1.1502-21(c)(1)(ii), the loss is treated as a net operating loss carryover to Year 2 for purposes of applying the SRLY limitation under § 1.1502-21(c).

(iii) For Year 2, T's SRLY limitation is the aggregate of the P group's consolidated taxable income through Year 2 determined by reference to only T's items. For this purpose, consolidated taxable income is determined by disregarding any built-in loss that is treated as a net operating loss carryover, and any consolidated net operating loss deductions under § 1.1502-21(a). Consolidated taxable income so determined is $25.

(iv) Under § 1.1502-21(c), $25 of the $45 built-in loss could be deducted in Year 2. Because the P group has only $10 of consolidated taxable income (determined without regard to the $45), the $25 loss creates a consolidated net operating loss of $15. This loss is carried back or forward under the rules of § 1.1502-21(b) and absorbed under the rules of § 1.1502-21(a). This loss is not treated as arising in a SRLY (see § 1.1502-21(c)(1)(ii)) and therefore is not subject to the SRLY limitation under § 1.1502-21(c) in any consolidated return year of the group to which it is carried. The remaining $20 is treated as a loss carryover arising in a SRLY and is subject to the limitation of § 1.1502-21(c) in the year to which it is carried.

(e) *Predecessors and successors.*—For purposes of this section, any reference to a corporation or member includes, as the context may require, a reference to a successor or predecessor, as defined in § 1.1502-1(f)(4).

(f) *Built-in losses recognized by common parent of group.*—(1) *General rule.*—Paragraph (a) of this section does not apply to any loss recognized by the group on an asset held by the common parent on the date the group is formed. Following an acquisition described in § 1.1502-75(d)(2) or (3), references to the common parent are to the corporation that was the common parent immediately before the acquisition.

(2) *Anti-avoidance rule.*—If a corporation that becomes a common parent of a group acquires assets with a net unrealized built-in loss in excess of the threshold requirement of section 382(h)(3)(B) (and thereby increases its net unrealized built-in loss or decreases its net unrealized built-in gain) prior to, and in anticipation of, the formation of the group, paragraph (f)(1) of this section does not apply.

(g) *Overlap with section 382.*—(1) *General rule.*—The limitations provided in §§ 1.1502-21(c) and 1.1502-22(c) do not apply to recognized built-in losses or to loss carryovers or carrybacks attributable to recognized built-in losses when the application of paragraph (a) of this section results in an overlap with the application of section 382.

(2) *Definitions.*—(i) *Generally.*—For purposes of this paragraph (g), the definitions and nomenclature contained in section 382, the regulations thereunder, and §§ 1.1502-90 through 1.1502-99 apply.

(ii) *Overlap.*—(A) An overlap of the application of paragraph (a) of this section and the application of section 382 with respect to built-in losses occurs if a corporation becomes a member of a consolidated group (the SRLY event) within six months of the change date of an ownership change giving rise to a section 382(a) limitation that would apply with respect to the corporation's recognized built-in losses (the section 382 event). Except as provided in paragraph (g)(3) of this section, application of the overlap rule does not require that the size and composition of the corporation's net unrealized built-in loss is the same on the date of the section 382 event and the SRLY event.

(B) For special rules in the event that there is a SRLY subgroup and/or a loss subgroup as defined in § 1.1502-91(d)(2) with respect to built-in losses, see paragraph (g)(4) of this section.

(3) *Operating rules.*—(i) *Section 382 event before SRLY event.*—If a SRLY event occurs on the same date as a section 382 event or within the six month period beginning on the date of the section 382 event, paragraph (g)(1) of this section applies beginning with the tax year that includes the SRLY event. Paragraph (g)(1) of this section does not apply, however, if a corporation that would otherwise be subject to the overlap rule acquires assets from a person other than a member of the group with a net unrealized built-in loss in excess of the threshold requirement of section 382(h)(3)(B) (and thereby increases its net unrealized built-in loss) after the section 382 event, and before the SRLY event.

(ii) *SRLY event before section 382 event.*—If a section 382 event occurs within the period beginning the day after the SRLY event and ending six months after the SRLY event, paragraph (g)(1) of this section applies starting with the first tax year that begins after the section 382 event. However, paragraph (g)(1) of this section does not apply at any time if a corporation that otherwise would be subject to paragraph (g)(1) of this section transfers assets with an unrealized built-in loss to another member of the group after the SRLY event, but before the section 382 event, unless the corporation recognizes the built-in loss upon the transfer.

(4) *Subgroup rules.*—In general, in the case of built-in losses for which there is a SRLY subgroup and the corporations joining the group at the time of the SRLY event also constitute a loss subgroup (as defined in §1.1502-91(d)(2)), the principles of this paragraph (g) apply to the SRLY subgroup, and not separately to its members. However, paragraph (g)(1) of this section applies with respect to built-in losses only if—

(i) All members of the SRLY subgroup with respect to those built-in losses are also included in a loss subgroup (as defined in §1.1502-91(d)(2)); and

(ii) All members of a loss subgroup (as defined in §1.1502-91(d)(2)) are also members of a SRLY subgroup with respect to those built-in losses.

(5) *Asset acquisitions.*—Notwithstanding the application of this paragraph (g), paragraph (a) of this section applies to asset acquisitions by the corporation that occurs after the latter of the SRLY event and the section 382 event. See, paragraph (b)(2)(ii) of this section.

(6) *Examples.*—The principles of this paragraph (g) are illustrated by the following examples:

Example 1. Determination of subgroup. (i) Individual A owns all of the stock of P, P1, and S. In Year 1, P acquires all of the stock of P1, and they file a consolidated return. In Year 3, P acquires all of the stock of S, and S joins the P group. Individual B, unrelated to Individual A, owns all of the stock of M and K, each the common parent of a consolidated group. Individual C, unrelated to either Individual A or Individual B, owns all of the stock of T.

(ii) At the beginning of Year 7, M acquires all of the stock of P from Individual A, and, as a result, P, P1, and S become members of the M group. At the time of M's acquisition of the P stock, P has a $15 net unrealized built-in loss (disregarding the stock of P1), P1 has a net unrealized built-in gain of $10, and S has a net unrealized built-in gain of $5.

(iii) During Year 8, M acquires all of the stock of T, and T joins the M group. At the time of M's acquisition of the T stock, T had an unrealized built-in loss of $15. At the beginning of Year 9, K acquires all of the stock of M from Individual B, and the members of the M consolidated group including P, P1, S, and T become members of the K group. At the time of K's acquisition of the M stock, M has (disregarding the stock of P and T) a $15 net unrealized built-in loss, P has a $20 net unrealized built-in loss (disregarding the stock of P1), P1 has a net unrealized built-in gain of $5, S has a net unrealized built-in loss of $35, and T has a $15 net unrealized built-in loss.

(iv) M's acquisition of P in Year 7 results in P, P1, and S becoming members of the M group (the SRLY event). Under paragraph (c) of this section, P and P1 compose a SRLY built-in loss subgroup because they have been affiliated for the 60 consecutive month period immediately preceding joining the M group. S is not a member of the subgroup because on becoming a member of the M group it had not been continuously affiliated with P and P1 for the 60 month period ending immediately before it became a member of the M group. Consequently, §1.1502-15 applies to S separately from the P and P1 subgroup.

(v) Assuming that the $5 net unrealized built-in loss of the P/P1 subgroup exceeds the threshold requirement under section 382(h)(3)(B), M's acquisition of P resulted in an ownership change of P and P1 within the meaning of section 382(g) that subjects P and P1 to a limitation under section 382(a) (the section 382 event). Because, with respect to P and P1, the SRLY event and the change date of the section 382 event occur on the same date and because the loss subgroup and SRLY subgroup are coextensive, there is an overlap of the application of the SRLY rules and the application of section 382.

(vi) S was not a loss corporation because it did not have a net operating loss carryover, or a net unrealized built-in loss, and therefore, M's acquisition of P did not result in an ownership change of S within the meaning of section 382(g). S, therefore is not subject to the overlap rule of paragraph (g) of this section.

(vii) M's acquisition of T resulted in T becoming a member of the M group (the SRLY event). Assuming that T's $15 net unrealized built-in loss exceeds the threshold requirement under section 382(h)(3)(B), M's acquisition of T also resulted in an ownership change of T within the meaning of section 382(g) that subjects T to a limitation under section 382(a) (the section 382 event). Because, with respect to T, the SRLY event and the change date of the section 382 event occur on the same date, there is an overlap of the application of the SRLY rules and the application of section 382 within the meaning of paragraph (g) of this section.

(viii) K's acquisition of M results in the members of the M consolidated group, including T, P, P1, and S, becoming members of the K group (the SRLY event). Because T, P, and P1 were each included in the determination of a net unrealized built-in loss that was subject to the overlap rule described in paragraph (g)(1) of this section when they each became members of the M group, they are deemed under paragraph (c)(3) of this section to have been continuously affiliated with M for the 60 month period ending immediately before becoming a member of the M group, notwithstanding their actual affiliation history. As a result, M, T, P, and P1 compose a SRLY built-in loss subgroup under paragraph (c)(2) of this section. K's acquisition of M is not subject to paragraph (g) of this section because it does not result in a section 382 event.

(ix) S, however, is not a member of the subgroup under paragraph (c)(2) of this section. Because S was not included in the determination of a net unrealized built-in loss that was subject to the overlap rule described in paragraph (g)(1) of this section when it joined the M group, S is treated as becoming an affiliate of M on the date it joined the M group. Furthermore, under paragraph (c)(3) of this section, S is deemed to have begun its affiliation with P and P1 on the date it joined the M group. Consequently, § 1.1502-15 applies to S separately to the extent its built-in loss is recognized within the recognition period.

Example 2. Post-overlap acquisition of assets. (i) Individual A owns all of the stock of P, the common parent of a consolidated group. B, an individual unrelated to Individual A, owns all of the stock of T. T has two depreciable assets. Asset 1 has an unrealized built-in loss of $25 (basis $75, value $50), and asset 2 has an unrealized built-in gain of $20 (basis $30, value $50). During Year 3, P buys all of the stock of T from Individual B. On January 1, Year 4, P contributes $80 cash and Individual A contributes asset 3, a depreciable asset, with a net unrealized built-in loss of $45 (basis $65, value $20), in exchange for T stock in a transaction that is described in section 351.

(ii) P's acquisition of T results in T becoming a member of the P group (the SRLY event) and also results in an ownership change of T, within the meaning of section 382(g), that gives rise to a limitation under section 382(a) (the section 382 event).

(iii) Because the SRLY event and the change date of the section 382 event occur on the same date, there is an overlap of the application of the SRLY rules and the application of section 382. Consequently, under paragraph (g) of this section, the limitation under paragraph (a) of this section does not apply to T's net unrealized built-in loss when it joined the P group.

(iv) Individual A's Year 4 contribution of a depreciable asset occurred after T was a member of the P group. Assuming that the amount of the net unrealized built-in loss exceeds the threshold requirement of section 382(h)(3)(B), the sale of asset 3 within the recognition period is subject to the SRLY limitation of paragraphs (a) and (b)(2)(ii) of this section.

Example 3. Overlap rule. (i) Individual A owns all of the stock of P, the common parent of a consolidated group. B, an individual unrelated to Individual A, owns all of the stock of T. T has two depreciable assets. Asset 1 has an unrealized loss of $55 (basis $75, value $20), and asset 2 has an unrealized gain of $30 (basis $30, value $60). On February 28 of Year 2, P purchases 55% of T from Individual B. On June 30, of Year 2, P purchases an additional 35% of T from Individual B.

(ii) The February 28 purchase of 55% of T is a section 382 event because it results in an ownership change of T that gives rise to a section 382(a) limitation. The June 30 purchase of 35% of T results in T becoming a member of the P group and is therefore a SRLY event.

(iii) Because the SRLY event occurred within six months of the change date of the section 382 event, there is an overlap of the application of the SRLY rules and the application of section 382, and paragraph (a) of this section does not apply. Therefore, the SRLY limitation does not apply to any of the $55 loss in asset 1 recognized by T after T joined the P group. See § 1.1502-94 for rules relating to the application of section 382 with respect to T's $25 unrealized built-in loss.

Example 4. Overlap rule-Fluctuation in value. (i) The facts are the same as in *Example 3*, except that by June 30, of Year 2, asset 1 had declined in value by a further $10. Thus asset 1 had an unrealized loss of $65 (basis $75, value $10), and asset 2 had an unrealized gain of $30 (basis $30, value $60).

(ii) Because paragraph (a) of this section does not apply, the further decrease in asset 1's value is disregarded. Consequently, the results are the same as in *Example 3.*

(h) *Effective date.*—(1) *In general.*—This section generally applies to built-in losses recognized in taxable years for which the due date (without extensions) of the consolidated return is after June 25, 1999. However—

(i) In the event that paragraphs (f)(1) and (g)(1) of this section do not apply to a particular built-in loss in the current group, then solely for purposes of applying paragraph (a) of this section to determine a limitation with respect to that built-in loss and with respect to which the SRLY register (consolidated taxable income determined by reference to only the member's (or subgroup's) items of income, gain, deduction or loss) began in a taxable year for which the due date of the return was on or before June 25, 1999, paragraph (c)(3) of this section shall not apply; and

(ii) For purposes of paragraph (g) of this section, only an ownership change to which section 382(a) as amended by the Tax Reform Act of 1986 applies shall constitute a section 382 event.

(2) *Prior periods.*—For certain taxable years ending on or before June 25, 1999, see § 1.1502-15T in effect prior to June 25, 1999, as contained in 26 CFR part 1 revised April 1, 1999, as applicable. [Reg. § 1.1502-15.]

☐ [*T.D.* 8823, 6-25-99 (*corrected* 7-30-99). *Amended by T.D.* 9048, 3-11-2003 *T.D.* 9187, 3-2-2005; *T.D.* 9254, 3-9-2006 *and T.D.* 9424, 9-9-2008.]

[Reg. § 1.1502-15A]

§ 1.1502-15A. Limitations on the allowance of built-in deductions for consolidated return

years beginning before January 1, 1997.— (a) *Limitation on built-in deductions.*—(1) *General rule.*—Built-in deductions (as defined in subparagraph (2) of this paragraph) for a taxable year shall be subject to the limitation of §1.1502-21A(c) (determined without regard to such deductions and without regard to net operating loss carryovers to such year) and the limitation of §1.1502-22A(c) (determined without regard to such deductions and without regard to captial loss carryovers to such year). If as a result of applying such limitations, built-in deductions are not allowable in such consolidated return year, such deductions shall be treated as a net operating loss or net capital loss (as the case may be) sustained in such year and shall be carried to those taxable years (consolidated or separate) to which a consolidated net operating loss or a consolidated net capital loss could be carried under §§1.1502-21A, 1.1502-22A, and 1.1502-79A (or §§1.1502-21T and 1.1502-22T, as appropriate), except that such losses shall be treated as losses subject to the limitations contained in §1.1502-21T(c) or §1.1502-22T(c) (or §§1.1502-21A(c) or 1.1502-22A(c), as appropriate), as the case may be. Thus, for example, if member X sells a capital asset during a consolidated return year at a $1,000 loss and such loss is treated as a built-in deduction, then such loss shall be subject to the limitation contained in §1.1502-22(c), which, in general, would allow such loss to be offset only against X's own net capital gain. Assuming X had no capital gain net income (net capital gain for taxable years beginning before January 1, 1977) reflected in such year (after taking into account its capital losses, other than capital loss carryovers and the built-in deduction), such $1,000 loss shall be treated as a net capital loss and shall be carried over for 5 years under §1.1502-22, subject to the limitation contained in §1.1502-22(c) for consolidated return years.

(2) *Built-in deductions.*—(i) For purposes of this paragraph, the term "built-in deductions" for a consolidated return year means those deductions or losses of a corporation which are recognized in such year, or which are recognized in a separate return year and carried over in the form of a net operating or net capital loss to such year, but which are economically accrued in a separate return limitation year (as defined in §1.1502-1(f)). Such term does not include deductions or losses incurred in rehabilitating such corporation. Thus, for example, assume P is the common parent of a group filing consolidated returns on the basis of a calendar year and that P purchases all of the stock of S on December 31, 1966. Assume further that on December 31, 1966, S owns a capital asset with an adjusted basis of $100 and a fair market value of $50. If the group files a consolidated return for 1967, and S sells the asset for $30, $50 of the $70 loss is treated as a built-in deduction, since it was economically accrued in a separate return limitation year. If S

sells the asset for $80 instead of $30, the $20 loss is treated as a built-in deduction. On the other hand, if such asset is a depreciable asset and is not sold by S, depreciation deductions attributable to the $50 difference between basis and fair market value are treated as built-in deductions.

(ii) In determining, for purposes of subdivision (i) of this subparagraph, whether a deduction or loss with respect to any asset is economically accrued in a separate return limitation year, the term "predecessor" as used in §1.1502-1(f)(1) shall include any transferor of such asset if the basis of the asset in the hands of the transferee is determined (in whole or in part) by reference to its basis in the hands of such transferor.

(3) *Transitional rule.*—If the assets which produced the built-in deductions were acquired (either directly or by acquiring a new member) by the group on or before January 4, 1973, and the separate return limitation year in which such deductions were economically accrued ended before such date, then at the option of the taxpayer, the provisions of this paragraph before amendment by T.D. 7246 shall apply, and, in addition, if such assets were acquired on or before April 17, 1968, and the separate return limitation year in which the built-in deductions were economically accrued ended on or before such date, then at the option of the taxpayer, the provisions of §1.1502-31A(b)(9) (as contained in the 26 C.F.R. edition revised as of April 1, 1996) shall apply in lieu of this paragraph.

(4) *Exceptions.*—(i) Subparagraphs (1), (2), and (3) of this paragraph shall not limit built-in deductions in a taxable year with respect to assets acquired (either directly or by acquiring a new member) by the group if—

(a) The group acquired the assets more than 10 years before the first day of such taxable year, or

(b) Immediately before the group acquired the assets, the aggregate of the adjusted basis of all assets (other than cash, marketable securities, and goodwill) acquired from the transferor or owned by the new member did not exceed the fair market value of all such assets by more than 15 percent.

(ii) For purposes of subdivision (i)(b) of this subparagraph, a security is not a marketable security if immediately before the group acquired the assets—

(a) The fair market value of the security is less than 95 percent of its adjusted basis, or

(b) The transferor or new member had held the security for at least 24 months, or

(c) The security is stock in a corporation at least 50 percent of the fair market value of the outstanding stock of which is owned by the transferor or new member.

(b) *Effective date.*—This section applies to any consolidated return years to which §1.1.502-21T

Reg. §1.1502-15A(b)

does not apply. See § 1.1502-21T(g) for effective dates of that section. [Reg. § 1.1502-15A.]

□ [T.D. 6894, 9-7-66 and T.D. 6909, 12-29-66. Amended by T.D. 7246, 12-29-72 and T.D. 7728, 10-31-80. Redesignated as Reg. § 1.1502-15A and amended by T.D. 8677, 6-26-96.]

[Reg. § 1.1502-16]

§ 1.1502-16. Mine exploration expenditures.—(a) *Section 617.*—(1) *In general.*—If the aggregate amount of the expenditures to which section 617(a) applies, paid or incurred with respect to mines or deposits located outside the United States (as defined in section 638 and the regulations thereunder), does not exceed—

(i) $400,000 minus

(ii) all amounts deducted or deferred during the taxable year and all preceding taxable years under section 617 or section 615 of the Internal Revenue Code of 1954 and section 23(ff) of the Internal Revenue Code of 1939 by corporations which are members of the group during the taxable year (and individuals or corporations which have transferred any mineral property to any such member within the meaning of section 617(g)(2)(B)) for taxable years ending after December 31, 1950 and prior to the taxable year,

then the deduction under section 617 with respect to such foreign expenditures and paragraph (c) of § 1.1502-12 for each member shall be no greater than an allocable portion of such amount hereinafter referred to as the "consolidated foreign exploration limitation." Such allocable portion shall be determined under subparagraph (2) of this paragraph. If the amount of such expenditures exceeds the consolidated foreign exploration limitation, no deduction shall be allowed with respect to such excess.

(2) *Allocable portion of limitation.*—A member's allocable portion of the consolidated foreign exploration limitation for a consolidated return year shall be—

(i) The amount allocated by the common parent pursuant to an allocation plan adopted by the consolidated group, but in no event shall a member be allocated more than the amount it could have deducted had it filed a separate return. Such allocation plan must include a statement which also contains the total foreign exploration expenditures of each member which could have been deducted under section 617 if the member had filed a separate return. Such plan must be attached to a consolidated return filed on or before the due date of such return (including extensions of time), and may not be changed after such date, or

(ii) If no plan is filed in accordance with subdivision (i) of this subparagraph, then the portion of the consolidated foreign exploration limitation allocable to each member incurring such expenditures is an amount equal to such limitation multiplied by a fraction, the numera-

tor of which is the amount of foreign exploration expenditures which could have been deducted under section 617 by such member had it filed a separate return and the denominator of which is the aggregate of such amounts for all members of the group.

(b) *Section 615.*—(1) *In general.*—If the aggregate amount of the expenditures, to which section 615(a) applies, which are paid or incurred by the members of the group during any consolidated return year exceeds the lesser of—

(i) $100,000, or

(ii) $400,000 minus all such expenditures deducted (or deferred) by corporations which are members of the group during the taxable year (and individuals or corporations which have transferred any mineral property to any such member within the meaning of section 615(c)(2)(B)) for taxable years ending after December 31, 1950, and prior to the taxable year,

then the deduction (or amount deferrable) under section 615 and paragraph (c) of § 1.1502-12 for each member shall be no greater than an allocable portion of such lesser amount, hereinafter referred to as the "consolidated exploration limitation". Such allocable portion shall be determined under subparagraph (2) of this paragraph.

(2) *Allocable portion of limitation.*—A member's allocable portion of the consolidated exploration limitation for a consolidated return year shall be—

(i) The amount allocated by the common parent pursuant to an allocation plan adopted by the consolidated group, but in no event shall a member be allocated more than the amount it could have deducted (or deferred) had it filed a separate return. Such allocation plan must include a statement which also contains the total exploration expenditures of each member for the taxable year, and the expenditures of each member which could have been deducted (or deferred) under section 615 if the member had filed a separate return. Such plan must be attached to a consolidated return filed on or before the due date of such return (including extensions of time), and may not be changed after such date, or

(ii) If no plan is filed in accordance with subdivision (i) of this subparagraph, then the portion of the consolidated exploration limitation allocable to each member incurring such expenditures is an amount equal to such limitation multiplied by a fraction, the numerator of which is the amount which could have been deducted (or deferred) under section 615 by such member had it filed a separate return and the denominator of which is the aggregate of such amounts for all members of the group.

(c) *Examples.*—The provisions of this section may be illustrated by the following examples:

Example (1). Corporation X and its wholly-owned subsidiaries, corporations Y and Z, file a consolidated return for the calendar year 1971. None of the corporations have incurred exploration expenditures described in section 617 in previous years. During 1971, X incurred foreign exploration expenditures of $30,000, Y of $20,000 and Z of $40,000. The amount of foreign exploration expenditures deductible under section 617 for purposes of computing separate taxable income under §1.1502-12 will be the amount actually expended by each corporation.

Example (2). Assume the same facts as in example (1) except that prior to 1971, X, Y, and Z had deducted (or deferred) under section 615 and 617 a total of $300,000 of exploration expenditures.

Corporation	Expenditure
X	$25,000
Y	$75,000
Z	$125,000

The denominator of $200,000 was calculated as follows:

X = $ 25,000

Y = $ 75,000

Z = $100,000 (maximum amount allowed if filed separately)

Total $200,000

Example (3). Assume the same facts as in example (2) and that on January 1, 1971, X acquired all of the stock of corporation T which prior to its taxable year beginning January 1, 1971, had previously deducted (or deferred) $310,000 of exploration expenditures. Assume further that in 1971 X incurred $25,000 of foreign exploration expenditures, Y $50,000, T $50,000 and Z none. A consolidated return is filed for 1971. None of the expenditures may be deducted under section 617 since the consolidated exploration limitation is zero. The limitation is zero since the aggregate amount of previously deducted (or deferred) exploration expenditures by the members of the group exceeds $400,000. (The total of such expenditures is $410,000, of which $310,000 is attributable to T and, assuming the allocation of the limitation in example (2) is made under paragraph (a)(2)(ii) of this section, $12,500 is attributable to X, $37,500 to Y, and $50,000 to Z.)

Example (4). Assume the same facts as in example (3) except that on December 31, 1971, X sold all of the stock in Z to an unrelated party. The consolidated exploration limitation for 1972 will be $40,000, computed by subtracting from $400,000 the aggregate amount of previously deducted (or deferred) exploration expenditures incurred by the members of the group prior to 1972. (The total of such expenditures is $360,000, of which $12,500 is attributable to X, $37,500 to Y and $310,000 to T.) Amounts previously deducted (or deferred) by Z are not taken into account since it was not a member of the group at any time during 1972. Amounts previously deducted (or deferred) by Z shall be taken into account by it for subsequent separate return years. [Reg. §1.1502-16.]

☐ *[T.D. 6894, 9-7-66. Amended by T.D. 7192, 6-29-72.]*

During 1971, with respect to deposits located outside the United States X incurred exploration expenditures of $25,000, Y of $75,000 and Z of $125,000. The consolidated exploration limitation under paragraph (a) of this section with respect to the foreign deposits (there is no limitation with respect to the domestic expenditures) is $100,000. X may allocate the $100,000 in any manner among the three members, except that X may not be allocated more than $25,000 nor Y more than $75,000, the amount actually expended by X and Y and which they could have deducted had they each filed a separate return. If the allocation is not made in accordance with paragraph (a)(2)(i) of this section, the $100,000 limitation will be allocated under paragraph (a)(2)(ii) of this section as follows:

Fraction	Limitation	Allocable portion
$\dfrac{25,000}{200,000}$	× $100,000 =	$12,500
$\dfrac{75,000}{200,000}$	× $100,000 =	$37,500
$\dfrac{100,000}{200,000}$	× $100,000 =	$50,000

[Reg. §1.1502-17]

§1.1502-17. Methods of accounting.— (a) *General rule.*—The method of accounting to be used by each member of the group shall be determined in accordance with the provisions of section 446 as if such member filed a separate return. For treatment of depreciable property after a transfer within the group, see paragraph (g) of §1.1502-12.

(b) *Adjustments required if method of accounting changes.*—(1) *General rule.*—If a member of a group changes its method of accounting for a consolidated return year, the terms and conditions prescribed by the Commissioner under section 446(e), including section 481(a) where applicable, shall apply to the member. If the requirements of section 481(b) are met because applicable adjustments under section 481(a) are substantial, the increase in tax for any prior year shall be computed upon the basis of a consolidated return or a separate return, whichever was filed for such prior year.

(2) *Changes in method of accounting for intercompany transactions.*—If a member changes its method of accounting for intercompany transactions for a consolidated return year, the change in method generally will be effected on a cut-off basis.

(c) *Anti-avoidance rules.*—(1) *General rule.*—If one member (B) directly or indirectly acquires an activity of another member (S), or undertakes S's activity, with the principal purpose to avail the group of an accounting method that would be unavailable (or would be unavailable without securing consent from the Commissioner) if S and B were treated as divisions of a single corporation, B must use the accounting method for the acquired or undertaken activity determined under paragraph (c)(2) of this section or must secure consent from the Commissioner under applicable administrative procedures to use a different method.

(2) *Treatment as divisions of a single corporation.*—B must use the method of accounting that would be required if B acquired the activity from S in a transaction to which section 381 applied. Thus, the principles of section 381(c)(4) and (c)(5) apply to resolve any conflicts between the accounting methods of S and B, and the acquired or undertaken activity is treated as having the accounting method used by S. Appropriate adjustments are made to treat all acquisitions or undertakings that are part of the same plan or arrangement as a single acquisition or undertaking.

(d) *Examples.*—The provisions of this section are illustrated by the following examples:

Example 1. Separate return treatment generally. X and its wholly owned subsidiary Y filed separate returns for their calendar years ending December 31, 1965. During calendar year 1965, X employed an accrual method of accounting, established a reserve for bad debts, and elected under section 171 to amortize bond premiums with respect to its fully taxable bonds. During calendar year 1965, Y employed the cash receipts and disbursements method, used the specific charge-off method with respect to its bad debts, and did not elect to amortize bond premiums under section 171 with respect to its bonds. X and Y filed a consolidated return for 1966. For 1966 X and Y must continue to compute income under their respective methods of accounting (unless a change in method under section 446 is made).

Example 2. Adopting methods. Corporation P is a member of a consolidated group. P provides consulting services to customers under various agreements. For one type of customer, P's agreements require payment only when the contract is completed (payment-on-completion contracts). P uses an overall accrual method of accounting. Accordingly, P takes its income from consulting contracts into account when earned, received, or due, whichever is earlier. With the principal purpose to avoid seeking the consent of the Commissioner to change its method of accounting for the payment-on-completion contracts to the cash method, P forms corporation S, and S begins to render services to those customers subject to the payment-on-completion contracts. P continues to render services to those customers not subject to these contracts.

(b) Under paragraph (c) of this section, S must account for the consulting income under the payment-on-completion contracts on an accrual method rather than adopting the cash method contemplated by P.

Example 3. Changing inventory sub-method. (a) Corporation P is a member of a consolidated group. P operates a manufacturing business that uses dollar-value LIFO, and has built up a substantial LIFO reserve. P has historically manufactured all its inventory and has used one natural business unit pool. P begins purchasing goods identical to its own finished goods from a foreign supplier, and is concerned that it must establish a separate resale pool under §1.472-8(c). P anticipates that it will begin to purchase, rather than manufacture, a substantial portion of its inventory, resulting in a recapture of most of its LIFO reserve because of decrements in its manufacturing pool. With the principal purpose to avoid the decrements, P forms corporation S in Year 1. S operates as a distributor to nonmembers, and P sells all of its existing inventories to S. S adopts LIFO, and elects dollar-value LIFO with one resale pool. Thereafter, P continues to manufacture and purchase inventory, and to sell it to S for resale to nonmembers. P's intercompany gain from sales to S is taken into account under §1.1502-13. S maintains its Year 1 base dollar value of inventory so that P will not be required to take its intercompany items (which include the effects of the LIFO reserve recapture) into account.

(b) Under paragraph (c) of this section, S must maintain two pools (manufacturing and resale) to the same extent that P would be required to maintain those pools under §1.472-8 if it had not formed S.

(e) *Effective dates.*—Paragraph (b) of this section applies to changes in method of accounting effective for years beginning on or after July 12, 1995. For changes in method of accounting effective for years beginning before that date, see §1.1502-17 (as contained in the 26 CFR part 1 edition revised as of April 1, 1995). Paragraphs (c) and (d) apply with respect to acquisitions occurring or activities undertaken in years beginning on or after July 12, 1995. [Reg. §1.1502-17.]

☐ [*T.D. 6894, 9-7-66. Amended by T.D. 8597, 7-12-95.*]

[Reg. § 1.1502-18]

§ 1.1502-18. Inventory adjustments.—
(a) *Definition of intercompany profit amount.*—For purposes of this section, the term "intercompany profit amount" for a taxable year means an amount equal to the profits of a corporation (other than those profits which such corporation has elected not to defer pursuant to § 1.1502-13(c)(3) or which have been taken into account pursuant to § 1.1502-13(f)(1)(viii)) arising in transactions with other members of the group with respect to goods which are, at the close of such corporation's taxable year, included in the inventories of any member of the group. See § 1.1502-13(c)(2) with respect to the determination of profits. See the last sentence of § 1.1502-13(f)(1)(i) for rules for determining which goods are considered to be disposed of outside the group and therefore not included in inventories of members.

(b) *Addition of initial inventory amount to taxable income.*—If a corporation—

(1) Is a member of a group filing a consolidated return for the taxable year,

(2) Was a member of such group for its immediately preceding taxable year, and

(3) Filed a separate return for such preceding year,

then the intercompany profit amount of such corporation for such separate return year (hereinafter referred to as the "initial inventory amount") shall be added to the income of such corporation for the consolidated return year (or years) in which the goods to which the initial inventory amount is attributable are disposed of outside the group or such corporation becomes a nonmember. Such amount shall be treated as gain from the sale or exchange of property which is neither a capital asset nor property described in section 1231.

(c) *Recovery of initial inventory amount.*—(1) *Unrecovered inventory amount.*—The term "unrecovered inventory amount" for any consolidated return year means the lesser of—

(i) The intercompany profit amount for such year, or

(ii) The initial inventory amount.

However, if a corporation ceases to be a member of the group during a consolidated return year, its unrecovered inventory amount for such year shall be considered to be zero.

(2) *Recovery during consolidated return years.*—(i) To the extent that the unrecovered inventory amount of a corporation for a consolidated return year is less than such amount for its immediately preceding year, such decrease shall be treated for such year by such corporation as a loss from the sale or exchange of property which is neither a capital asset nor property described in section 1231.

(ii) To the extent that the unrecovered inventory amount for a consolidated return year exceeds such amount for the preceding year, such increase shall be treated as gain from the sale or exchange of property which is neither a capital asset nor property described in section 1231.

(3) *Recovery during first separate return year.*—For the first separate return year of a member following a consolidated return year, the unrecovered inventory amount for such consolidated return year (minus any part of the initial inventory amount which has not been added to income pursuant to paragraph (b) of this section) shall be treated as a loss from the sale or exchange of property which is neither a capital asset nor property described in section 1231.

(4) *Acquisition of group.*—For purposes of this section, a member of a group shall not become a nonmember or be considered as filing a separate return solely because of a termination of the group (hereinafter referred to as the "terminating group") resulting from—

(i) The acquisition by a nonmember corporation of (*a*) the assets of the common parent in a reorganization described in subparagraph (A), (C), or (D) (but only if the requirements of subparagraphs (A) and (B) of section 354(b)(1) are met) of section 368(a)(1), or (*b*) stock of the common parent, or

(ii) The acquisition (in a transaction to which § 1.1502-75(d)(3) applies) by a member of (*a*) the assets of a nonmember corporation in a reorganization referred to in subdivision (*i*) of this subparagraph, or (*b*) stock of a nonmember corporation,

if all the members of the terminating group (other than such common parent if its assets are acquired) immediately before the acquisition are members immediately after the acquisition of another group (hereinafter referred to as the "succeeding group") which files a consolidated return for the first taxable year ending after the date of acquisition. The members of the succeeding group shall succeed to any initial inventory amount and to any unrecovered inventory amount of members of the terminating group. This subparagraph shall not apply with respect to acquisitions occurring before August 25, 1971.

(d) *Examples.*—The provisions of paragraphs (a), (b), and (c) of this section may be illustrated by the following examples:

Example (1). Corporations P, S, and T report income on the basis of a calendar year. Such corporations file separate returns for 1965. P manufactures widgets which it sells to both S and T, who act as distributors. The inventories of S and T at the close of 1965 are comprised of widgets which they purchased from P and with respect to which P derived profits of $5,000 and $8,000, respectively. P, S, and T file a consolidated return for 1966. During 1966, P sells widgets to S and T with respect to which it derives profits of $7,000 and $10,000, respectively. The inventories of S and T as of December 31, 1966, are comprised of widgets on which P derived net profits of $4,000 and $8,000, respectively. P's initial inventory amount is $13,000, P's intercompany profit amount for 1965 (such $13,000 amount is the profits of P with respect to goods sold to S and T and included in their inventories at the close of 1965). Assuming that S and T identify their goods on a first-in, first-out basis, the entire opening inventory amount of $13,000 is added to P's income for 1966 as gain from the sale or exchange of property which is neither a capital asset nor property described in section 1231, since the goods to which the initial inventory amount is attributable were disposed of in 1966 outside the group. However, since P's unrecovered inventory amount for 1966, $12,000 (the intercompany profit amount for the year, which is less than the initial inventory amount), is less than the unrecovered inventory amount for 1965, $13,000, this decrease of $1,000 is treated by P for 1966 as a loss from the sale or exchange of property which is neither a capital asset nor property described in section 1231.

Example (2). Assume the same facts as in example (1) and that at the close of 1967, a consolidated return year, the inventories of S and T are comprised of widgets on which P derived profits of $5,000 and $3,000, respectively. Since P's unrecovered inventory amount for 1967, $8,000, is less than $12,000, the unrecovered inventory amount for 1966, this decrease of $4,000 is treated by P for 1967 as a loss from the sale or exchange of property which is neither a capital asset nor property described in section 1231.

Example (3). Assume the same facts as in examples (1) and (2) and that in 1968, a consolidated return year, P's intercompany profit amount is $11,000. P will report $3,000 (the excess of $11,000, P's unrecovered inventory amount for 1968, over $8,000, P's unrecovered inventory amount for 1967) for 1968 as a gain from the sale or exchange of property which is neither a capital asset nor property described in section 1231.

Example (4). Assume the same facts as in examples (1), (2), and (3) and that in 1969 P, S, and T file separate returns. P will report $11,000 (its unrecovered inventory amount for 1968, $11,000, minus the portion of the initial inventory amount which has not been added to income during 1966, 1967, and 1968, zero) as a loss from the sale or exchange of property which is neither a capital asset nor property described in section 1231.

Example (5). Corporations P and S file a consolidated return for the first time for the calendar year 1966. P manufactures machines and sells them to S, which sells them to users throughout the country. At the close of 1965, S has on hand 20 machines which it purchased from P and with

respect to which P derived profits of $3,500. During 1966, P sells 6 machines to S on which it derives profits of $1,300, and S sells 5 machines which it had on hand at the beginning of the year (S specifically identifies the machines which it sells) and on which P had derived profits of $900. P's initial inventory amount is $3,500, of which $900 is added to P's income in 1966 as gain from the sale or exchange of property which is neither a capital asset nor property described in section 1231, since such $900 amount is attributable to goods disposed of in 1966 outside the group, which goods were included in S's inventory at the close of 1965. If P and S continue to file consolidated returns, the remaining $2,600 of the initial inventory amount will be added to P's income as the machines on which such profits were derived are disposed of outside the group.

Example (6). Assume that in example (5) S had elected to inventory its goods under section 472 (relating to last-in, first-out inventories). None of P's initial inventory amount of $3,500 would be added to P's income in 1966, since none of the goods to which such amount is attributable would be considered to be disposed of during such year under the last-in, first-out method of identifying inventories.

(e) *Section 381 transfer.*—If a member of the group is a transferor or distributor of assets to another member of the group within the meaning of section 381(a), then the acquiring corporation shall be treated as succeeding to the initial inventory amount of the transferor or distributor corporation to the extent that as of the date of distribution or transfer such amount has not yet been added to income. Such amount shall then be added to the acquiring corporation's income under the provisions of paragraph (b) of this section. For purposes of applying paragraph (c) of this section—

(1) The initial inventory amount of the transferor or distributor corporation shall be added to such amount of the acquiring corporation as of the close of the acquiring corporation's taxable year in which the date of distribution or transfer occurs, and

(2) The unrecovered inventory amount of the transferor or distributor corporation for its taxable year preceding the taxable year of the group in which the date of distribution or transfer occurs shall be added to such amount of the acquiring corporation.

(f) *Transitional rules for years before 1966.*— (1) *In general.*—If—

(i) A group filed a consolidated return for the taxable year immediately preceding the first taxable year to which this section applies,

(ii) Any member of such group made an opening adjustment to its inventory pursuant to paragraph (b) of § 1.1502-39A (as contained in the 26 C.F.R. edition revised as of April 1, 1996), and

(iii) Paragraph (c) of §1.1502-39A (as contained in the 26 C.F.R. edition revised as of April 1, 1996) has not been applicable for any taxable year subsequent to the taxable year for which such adjustment was made,

then subparagraphs (2) and (3) of this paragraph shall apply.

(2) *Closing adjustment to inventory.*—(i) For the first consolidated return year to which this section applies, the increase in inventory prescribed in paragraph (c) of §1.1502-39A (as contained in the 26 C.F.R. edition revised as of April 1, 1996) shall be made as if such year were a separate return year.

(ii) For the first separate return year of a member to which this section applies, the adjustment to inventory (whether an increase or a decrease) prescribed in paragraph (c) of §1.1502-39A (as contained in the 26 C.F.R. edition revised as of April 1, 1996), minus any adjustment already made pursuant to subdivision (i) of this subparagraph, shall be made to the inventory of such member.

(3) *Addition and recovery of initial inventory amount.*—Each selling member shall treat as an initial inventory amount its share of the net amount by which the inventories of all members are increased pursuant to subparagraph (2)(i) of this paragraph for the first taxable year to which this section applies. A member's share shall be such net amount multiplied by a fraction, the numerator of which is its initial inventory amount (computed under paragraph (b) as if such taxable year were its first consolidated return year), and the denominator of which is the sum of such initial inventory amounts of all members. Such initial inventory amount shall be added to the income of such selling member and shall be recovered at the time and in the manner prescribed in paragraphs (b) and (c) of this section.

(4) *Example.*—The provisions of this paragraph may be illustrated by the following example:

Example. (i) Corporations P, S, and T file consolidated returns for calendar 1966, having filed consolidated returns continuously since 1962. P is a wholesale distributor of groceries selling to chains of supermarkets, including those owned by S and T. The opening inventories of S and T for 1962 were reduced by $40,000 and $80,000, respectively, pursuant to paragraph (b) of §1.1502-39A (as contained in the 26 C.F.R. edition revised as of April 1, 1996). At the close of 1965, S and T have on hand in their inventories goods on which P derived profits of $80,000 and $90,000, respectively. The inventories of S and T at the close of 1966 include goods which they purchased from P during the year on which P derived profits of $85,000 and $105,000, respectively.

(ii) The opening inventories of S and T for 1966, the first year to which this section applies, are increased by $40,000 and $80,000, respectively, pursuant to the provisions of subparagraph (2)(i) of this paragraph. P will take into account (as provided in paragraphs (b) and (c) of this section) an initial inventory amount of $120,000 as of the beginning of 1966, the net amount by which the inventories of S and T were increased in such year. Since the increases in the inventories of S and T are the maximum allowable under paragraph (c) of §1.1502-39A (as contained in the 26 C.F.R. edition revised as of April 1, 1996) (*i.e.*, the amount by which such inventories were originally decreased), no further adjustments will be made pursuant to subparagraph (2)(ii) of this paragraph to such inventories in the event that separate returns are subsequently filed.

(5) *Election not to eliminate.*—If a group filed a consolidated return for the taxable year immediately preceding the first taxable year to which this section applies, and for such preceding year the members of the group did not eliminate gain or loss on intercompany inventory transactions pursuant to the adoption under §1.1502-31A(b)(1) (as contained in the 26 C.F.R. edition revised as of April 1, 1996) of a consistent accounting practice taking into account such gain or loss, then for purposes of this section each member shall be treated as if it had filed a separate return for such immediately preceding year.

(g) *Transitional rules for years beginning on or after July 12, 1995.*—Paragraphs (a) through (f) of this section do not apply for taxable years beginning on or after July 12, 1995. Any remaining unrecovered inventory amount of a member under paragraph (c) of this section is recovered in the first taxable year beginning on or after July 12, 1995, under the principles of paragraph (c)(3) of this section by treating the first taxable year as the first separate return year of the member. The unrecovered inventory amount can be recovered only to the extent it was previously included in taxable income. The principles of this section apply, with appropriate adjustments, to comparable amounts under paragraph (f) of this section. [Reg. §1.1502-18.]

☐ [*T.D.* 6894, 9-7-66. *Amended by T.D.* 7246, 12-29-72; *T.D.* 8597, 7-12-95 *and T.D.* 8677, 6-26-96.]

[Reg. §1.1502-19]

§1.1502-19. Excess loss accounts.—(a) *In general.*—(1) *Purpose.*—This section provides rules for a member (M) to include in income its excess loss account in the stock of another member (S). The purpose of the excess loss account is to recapture in consolidated taxable income M's negative adjustments with respect to S's stock (e.g., under §1.1502-32 from S's deductions, losses, and distributions), to the extent the negative adjustments exceed M's basis in the stock. This section also provides rules for eliminating losses and other attributes attributable to S in certain cases in which S stock becomes worthless or S ceases to be a member and does not have a separate return year.

(2) *Excess loss accounts.*—(i) *In general.*—M's basis in S's stock is adjusted under the consolidated return regulations and other rules of law. Negative adjustments may exceed M's basis in S's stock. The resulting negative amount is M's excess loss account in S's stock. For example:

(A) Once M's negative adjustments under § 1.1502-32 exceed its basis in S's stock, the excess is M's excess loss account in the S stock. If M has further adjustments, they first increase or decrease the excess loss account.

(B) If M forms S by transferring property subject to liabilities in excess of basis, § 1.1502-80(d) provides for the nonapplicability of section 357(c) and the resulting negative basis under section 358 is M's excess loss account in the S stock.

(ii) *Treatment as negative basis.*—M's excess loss account is treated for all Federal income tax purposes as basis that is a negative amount, and a reference to M's basis in S's stock includes a reference to M's excess loss account.

(3) *Application of other rules of law, duplicative recapture.*—See § 1.1502-80(a) regarding the general applicability of other rules of law and a limitation on duplicative adjustments and recapture.

(b) *Excess loss account taken into account as income or gain.*—(1) *Operating rules.*—(i) *General rule.*—Except as provided in paragraph (b)(1)(ii) of this section, if M is treated as disposing of a share of S's stock, M takes into account its excess loss account in the share as income or gain from the disposition.

(ii) *Special limitation on amount taken into account.*—Notwithstanding paragraph (b)(1)(i) of this section, if M is treated as disposing of a share of S's stock as a result of the application of paragraph (c)(1)(iii)(B) of this section, the aggregate amount of its excess loss account in the shares of S's stock that M takes into account as income or gain from the disposition shall not exceed the amount of S's indebtedness that is discharged that is neither included in gross income nor treated as tax-exempt income under § 1.1502-32(b)(3)(ii)(C)(1). If more than one share of S's stock has an excess loss account, such excess loss accounts shall be taken into account pursuant to the preceding sentence, to the extent possible, in a manner that equalizes the excess loss accounts in S's shares that have an excess loss account.

(iii) *Treatment of disposition.*—Except as provided in paragraph (b)(4) of this section, the disposition is treated as a sale or exchange for purposes of determining the character of the income or gain.

(iv) *Reduction of attributes in the case of certain dispositions by worthlessness or where S ceases to be a member and does not become a nonmember.*—If this paragraph (b)(1)(iv) applies, any net operating or capital loss carryover that is attributable to S, including any losses that would be apportioned to S under the principles of § 1.1502-21(b)(2) if S had a separate return year, any deferred deductions attributable to S, including S's portion of such consolidated tax attributes (for example, consolidated excess charitable contributions that would be apportioned to S under the principles of § 1.1502-79(e) if S had a separate return year), and any credit carryover attributable to S, including any consolidated credits that would be apportioned to S under the principles of § 1.1502-79 if S had a separate return year, are eliminated. Attributes other than consolidated tax attributes (determined as of the disposition) are eliminated under this paragraph (b)(1)(iv) immediately before the disposition resulting in the application of this paragraph (b)(1)(iv). The elimination of attributes under this paragraph (b)(1)(iv) is not a noncapital, nondeductible expense described in § 1.1502-32(b)(2)(iii). This paragraph (b)(1)(iv) applies if—

(A) A share of S stock becomes worthless under section 165, the requirements of paragraph (c)(1)(iii) of this section are satisfied, M does not recognize a net deduction or loss on the S stock, and S is a member of the group on the day following the last day of the group's taxable year during which the share becomes worthless; or

(B) M recognizes any amount that is not a net deduction or loss on the stock of S in a transaction in which S ceases to be a member and does not become a nonmember.

(2) *Nonrecognition or deferral.*—(i) *In general.*—M's income or gain under paragraph (b)(1) of this section is subject to any nonrecognition or deferral rules applicable to the disposition. For example, if S liquidates and the exchange of M's stock in S is subject to section 332, or M transfers all of its assets (including S's stock) to S in a reorganization to which section 361(a) applies, M's income or gain from the excess loss account is not recognized under these rules.

(ii) *Nonrecognition or deferral inapplicable.*—If M's income or gain under paragraph (b)(1) of this section is from a disposition described in paragraph (c)(1)(ii) or (iii) of this section (relating to deconsolidations and worthlessness), the income or gain is taken into account notwithstanding any nonrecognition or deferral rules (even if the disposition is also described in paragraph (c)(1)(i) of this section). For example, if M transfers S's stock to a nonmember in a transaction to which section 351 applies, M's income or gain from the excess loss account is taken into account.

(3) *Tiering up in chains.*—If the stock of more than one subsidiary is disposed of in the same transaction, the income or gain under this section is taken into account in the order of the tiers, from the lowest to the highest.

(4) *Insolvency.*—(i) *In general.*—Gain under this section is treated as ordinary income to the extent of the amount by which S is insolvent (within the meaning of section 108(d)(3)) immediately before the disposition. For this purpose S's liabilities include any amount to which preferred stock would be entitled if S were liquidated immediately before the disposition, and any former liabilities that were discharged to the extent the discharge was treated as tax-exempt income under § 1.1502-32(b)(3(ii)(C) (special rule for discharges).

(ii) *Reduction for amount of distributions.*—The amount treated as ordinary income under this paragraph (b)(4) is reduced to the extent it exceeds the amount of M's excess loss account redetermined without taking into account S's distributions to M to which § 1.1502-32(b)(2)(iv) applies.

(c) *Disposition of stock.*—For purposes of this section:

(1) *In general.*—M is treated as disposing of a share of S's stock.

(i) *Transfer, cancellation, etc..*—At the time—

(A) M transfers or otherwise ceases to own the share for Federal income tax purposes, even if no gain or loss is taken into account; or

(B) M takes into account gain or loss (in whole or in part) with respect to the share.

(ii) *Deconsolidation.*—At the time—

(A) M becomes a nonmember, or a nonmember determines its basis in the share (or any other asset) by reference to M's basis in the share, directly or indirectly, in whole or in part (e.g., under section 362); or

(B) S becomes a nonmember, or M's basis in the share is reflected, directly or indirectly, in whole or in part, in the basis of any asset other than member stock (e.g., under section 1071).

(iii) *Worthlessness.*—At the time—

(A) All of S's assets (other than its corporate charter and those assets, if any, necessary to satisfy state law minimum capital requirements to maintain corporate existence) are treated as disposed of, abandoned, or destroyed for Federal income tax purposes (for example,

under section 165(a) or § 1.1502-80(c), or, if S's asset is stock of a lower-tier member, the stock is treated as disposed of under this paragraph (c)). An asset of S is not considered to be disposed of or abandoned to the extent the disposition is in complete liquidation of S under section 332 or is in exchange for consideration (other than relief from indebtedness);

(B) An indebtedness of S is discharged, if any part of the amount discharged is not included in gross income and is not treated as tax-exempt income under § 1.1502-32(b)(3)(ii)(C); or

(C) A member takes into account a deduction or loss for the uncollectibility of an indebtedness of S, and the deduction or loss is not matched in the same tax year by S's taking into account a corresponding amount of income or gain from the indebtedness in determining consolidated taxable income.

(2) *Becoming a nonmember.*—A member is treated as becoming a nonmember if it has a separate return year (including another group's consolidated return year). For example, S may become a nonmember if it issues additional stock to nonmembers, but S does not become a nonmember as a result of its complete liquidation. A disposition under paragraph (c)(1)(ii) of this section must be taken into account in the consolidated return of the group. For example, if a group ceases under § 1.1502-75(c) to file a consolidated return as of the close of its consolidated return year, the disposition under paragraph (c)(1)(ii) of this section is treated as occurring immediately before the close of the year. If S becomes a nonmember because M sells S's stock to a nonmember, M's sale is a disposition under both paragraphs (c)(1)(i) and (ii) of this section. If a group terminates under § 1.1502-75(d) because the common parent is the only remaining member, the common parent is not treated as having a deconsolidation event under paragraph (c)(1)(ii) of this section.

(3) *Exception for acquisition of group.*—(i) *Application.*—This paragraph (c)(3) applies only if a consolidated group (the terminating group) ceases to exist as a result of—

(A) The acquisition of either the assets of the common parent of the terminating group in a reorganization described in section 381(a)(2), or the stock of the common parent of the terminating group; or

(B) The application of the principles of § 1.1502-75(d)(2) or (d)(3).

(ii) *General rule.*—Paragraph (c)(1)(ii) of this section does not apply solely by reason of the termination of a group in a transaction to which this paragraph (c)(3) applies, if there is a surviving group that is, immediately thereafter, a consolidated group. Instead, the surviving group is treated as the terminating group for purposes of applying this section to the terminating group. This treatment does not apply,

Reg. § 1.1502-19(c)(3)(ii)

however, to members of the terminating group that are not members of the surviving group immediately after the terminating group ceases to exist (e.g., under section 1504(a)(3) relating to reconsolidation, or section 1504(c) relating to includible insurance companies).

(d) *Special allocation of basis in connection with an adjustment or determination.*—(1) *Excess loss account in original shares.*—If a member has an excess loss account in shares of a class of S's stock at the time of a basis adjustment or determination under the Internal Revenue Code with respect to shares of the same class of S's stock owned by the member, the adjustment or determination is allocated first to equalize and eliminate that member's excess loss account. See §1.1502-32(c) for similar allocations of investment adjustments to prevent or eliminate excess loss accounts.

(2) *Excess loss account in new S shares.*—If a member would otherwise determine shares of a class of S's stock (new shares) to have an excess loss account and such member owns one or more other shares of the same class of S's stock, the basis of such other shares is allocated to eliminate and equalize any excess loss account that would otherwise be in the new shares.

(e) *Anti-avoidance rule.*—If any person acts with a principal purpose contrary to the purposes of this section, to avoid the effect of the rules of this section or apply the rules of this section to avoid the effect of any other provision of the consolidated return regulations, adjustments must be made as necessary to carry out the purposes of this section.

(f) *Predecessors and successors.*—For purposes of this section, any reference to a corporation (or to a share of the corporation's stock) includes a reference to a successor or predecessor (or to a share of stock of a predecessor or successor), as the context may require.

(g) *Examples.*—For purposes of the examples in this section, unless otherwise stated, M owns all 100 shares of the only class of S's stock and S owns all 100 shares of the only class of T's stock, the stock is owned for the entire year, T owns no stock of lower-tier members, the tax year of all persons is the calendar year, all persons use the accrual method of accounting, the facts set forth the only corporate activity, all transactions are between unrelated persons, and tax liabilities are disregarded. The principles of this section are illustrated by the following examples.

Example 1. Taxable disposition of stock. (a) *Facts.* M has a $150 basis in S's stock, and S has a $100 basis in T's stock. For Year 1, M has $500 of ordinary income, S has no income or loss, and T has a $200 ordinary loss. S sells T's stock to a nonmember for $60 at the close of Year 1.

(b) *Analysis.* Under paragraph (c) of this section, the sale is a disposition of T's stock at the close of Year 1 (the day of the sale). Under §1.1502-32(b), T's loss results in S having a $100 excess loss account in T's stock immediately before the sale. Under paragraph (b)(1) of this section, S takes into account the $100 excess loss account as an additional $100 of gain from the sale. Consequently, S takes into account a $160 gain from the sale in determining the group's consolidated taxable income. Under §1.1502-32(b), T's $200 loss and S's $160 gain result in a net $40 decrease in M's basis in S's stock as of the close of Year 1, from $150 to $110.

(c) *Intercompany sale followed by sale to nonmember.* The facts are the same as in paragraph (a) of this *Example 1*, except that S sells T's stock to M for $60 at the close of Year 1, and M sells T's stock to a nonmember at a gain at the beginning of Year 5. Under paragraph (c) of this section, S's sale is treated as a disposition of T's stock at the close of Year 1 (the day of the sale). Under §1.1502-13 and paragraph (b)(2) of this section, S's $160 gain from the sale is deferred and taken into account in Year 5 as a result of M's sale of the T stock. Under §1.1502-32(b), the absorption of T's $200 loss in Year 1 results in M having a $50 excess loss account in S's stock at the close of Year 1. In Year 5, S's $160 gain taken into account eliminates M's excess loss account in S's stock and increases M's basis in the stock to $110.

(d) *Intercompany distribution followed by sale to a nonmember.* The facts are the same as in paragraph (a) of this *Example 1*, except that the value of the T stock is $60 and S declares and distributes a dividend of all of the T stock to M at the close of Year 1, and M sells the T stock to a nonmember at a gain at the beginning of Year 5. Under paragraph (c) of this section, S's distribution is treated as a disposition of T's stock at the close of Year 1 (the day of the distribution). S's $100 excess loss account in T's stock is treated as additional gain under section 311(b) from the distribution. Under section 301(d), M's basis in the T stock is $60. Under §1.1502-13, and paragraph (b)(2) of this section, S's $160 gain from the distribution is deferred and taken into account in Year 5 as a result of M's sale of the T stock. Under §1.1502-32(b), T's $200 loss and S's $60 distribution result in M having a $110 excess loss account in S's stock at the close of Year 1. In Year 5, S's $160 gain taken into account eliminates M's excess loss account in S's stock and increases M's basis in the stock to $50.

Example 2. Basis determinations under the Internal Revenue Code in intercompany reorganizations—transfer of shares without an excess loss account. (i) *Facts.* M owns all of the sole class of stock of each of S and T. M has 150 shares of S stock that it acquired on Date 1. Each S share has a $1 basis and a fair market value of $1. M has 100 shares of T stock that it acquired on Date 2. Each T share has a $1.20 excess loss account and a fair market value of $1. M transfers S's stock to T without receiving additional T stock. The transfer is an exchange described in both section 351 and section 354.

(ii) *Analysis.* Under sections 351 and 354, M does not recognize gain in connection with the transfer. Under § 1.358-2(a)(2)(iii), M is deemed to receive 150 shares of T stock of the same class. Without regard to the application of paragraph (d) of this section, under section 358 and § 1.358-2 (a) (2) (i), M would have a $1 basis in each such share. However, because the basis of the additional shares of T stock will be determined when M has an excess loss account in its original shares of T stock, under paragraph (d)(1) of this section, the basis that M would otherwise have in such additional shares will eliminate the excess loss account in M's original shares of T stock such that each original share of T stock will have a basis of $0 and each share of T stock deemed received will have a basis of $0.20. Then, under § 1.358-2(a) (2) (iii), the T stock is deemed to be recapitalized in a reorganization under section 368(a)(1)(E) in which M receives 100 shares of T stock (those shares M actually owns immediately after the transfer) in exchange for those 100 shares of T stock that M held immediately prior to the transfer and those 150 shares of T stock M is deemed to receive in the transfer. Under § 1.358-2(a)(2)(i), immediately after the transfer, M holds 100 shares of T stock, 60 of which take a basis of $0.50 each and 40 of which take a basis of $0 each. In addition, T takes a $1 basis in each share of S stock under section 362. (If M had actually received an additional 150 shares of T stock of the same class, paragraph (d)(1) of this section would apply to shift basis from such additional T shares to M's original T shares because the basis of the additional T stock would be determined when M had an excess loss account in its original T shares. M would have a basis of $0 in each of the original T shares and a basis of $0.20 in each of the additional T shares.)

(iii) *Transfer of shares with an excess loss account.* The facts are the same as in paragraph (i) of this *Example 2,* except that M transfers T's stock to S without receiving additional S stock. The transfer is an exchange described in both section 351 and section 354. Under paragraph (c) of this section, M's transfer is treated as a disposition of T's stock. Under sections 351 and 354 and paragraph (b)(2) of this section, M does not recognize gain from the disposition. Under § 1.358-2(a)(2)(iii), M is deemed to have received 100 shares of S stock of the same class. Without regard to the application of paragraph (d) of this section, M would have a $1.20 excess loss account in each such share. However, because M will have an excess loss account in such shares and M owns other shares of S stock of the same class, under paragraph (d)(2) of this section, the excess loss account that M would otherwise have in such shares will decrease M's basis in its original shares of S's stock such that each such original share will have a basis of $0.20 and each

share deemed received will have a basis of $0. Then, under § 1.358-2(a)(2)(iii), the S stock is deemed to be recapitalized in a reorganization under section 368(a)(1)(E) in which M receives 150 shares of S stock (those shares M actually owns immediately after the transfer) in exchange for those 150 shares of S stock that M held immediately prior to the transfer and those 100 shares of S stock that M is deemed to receive in connection with the transfer. Under § 1.358-2(a)(2)(i), immediately after the transfer, M holds 150 shares of S stock, 90 of which take a basis of $0.33 each and 60 of which take a basis of $0 each. In addition, S takes an excess loss account of $1.20 in each share of T stock under section 362. (If M had actually received 100 additional shares of S stock of the same class, paragraph (d)(2) of this section would apply to shift basis from M's original S stock because M would have otherwise had an excess loss account in such additional shares and M owned other shares of S stock of the same class. The excess loss account that M would otherwise had in such additional shares would have decreased M's basis in its original shares of S's stock. M would have had a basis of $0.20 in each of the original shares and a basis of $0 in each of the additional shares.)

(iv) *Intercompany merger—shares with excess loss account retained.* The facts are the same as in paragraph (i) of this *Example 2,* except that S merges into T in a reorganization described in section 368(a)(1)(A) (and in section 368(a)(1)(D)), and M receives 150 additional shares of T stock of the same class in the reorganization. Under section 354, M does not recognize gain. Without regard to the application of paragraph (d) of this section, under section 358 and § 1.358-2(a)(2)(i), M would have a $1 basis in each such share. However, because the basis of the additional shares of T stock will be determined when M has an excess loss account in its original shares of T stock, under paragraph (d)(1) of this section, the basis that M would otherwise have in such additional shares eliminates the excess loss account in M's original shares of T stock such that each original share of T stock has a basis of $0 and each additional share of T stock has a basis of $0.20.

(v) *Intercompany merger—shares with excess loss account surrendered.* The facts are the same as in paragraph (i) of this *Example 2,* except that T merges into S in a reorganization described in section 368(a)(1)(A) (and in section 368(a)(1)(D)), and M receives 100 additional shares of S stock of the same class in the reorganization. Under section 354 and paragraph (b)(2) of this section, M does not recognize gain from the disposition. Without regard to the application of paragraph (d) of this section, under section 358 and § 1.358-2(a)(2)(i), M would have a $1.20 excess loss account in each additional share of S stock received. However, because M would have an excess loss account in such shares and M owns other shares of S stock of the same class, under paragraph (d)(2) of this section, the excess loss account that M would otherwise have in such shares decreases M's basis in its original shares of S's stock such that each original share of S stock has a basis of $0.20 and each additional share of S stock has a basis of $0.

Example 3. Section 355 distribution of stock with an excess loss account. (a) *Facts.* M has a $30 excess loss account in S's stock, and S has a $90 excess loss account in T's stock. S distributes the T stock to M in a transaction to which section 355 applies, and neither M nor S recognizes any gain or loss. At the time of the distribution, the T stock represents 33% of the value of the S stock. Following the distribution, M's basis in the S stock is allocated under § 1.358-2 in proportion to the fair market values of the S stock and the T stock.

(b) *Analysis.* Under paragraph (c) of this section, S's distribution of the T stock is treated as a disposition. Under section 355(c) and paragraph (b)(2) of this section, S does not recognize any gain from the distribution. Under section 358, S's excess loss account in the T stock is eliminated, and M's $30 excess loss account in the S stock is treated as basis allocated between the S stock and the T stock based on their relative values. Consequently, M has a $20 excess loss account in the S stock and a $10 excess loss account in the T stock. (If M had a $30 basis rather than a $30 excess loss account in the S stock, S would not recognize gain, its excess loss account in the T stock would be eliminated, and M's basis in the stock of S and T would be $20 and $10, respectively.)

(c) *Section 355 distribution to nonmember.* The facts are the same as in paragraph (a) of this *Example 3,* except that M also distributes the T stock to its shareholders in a transaction to which section 355 applies. Under paragraph (c) of this section, M's distribution is treated as a disposition of T's stock. Under paragraph (b)(2) of this section, because M's disposition is described in paragraph (c)(1)(ii) of this section, M's $10 excess loss account in the T stock must be taken into account at the time of the distribution, notwithstanding the nonrecognition rules of section 355(c).

Example 4. Deconsolidation of a member. (a) *Facts.* M has a $50 excess loss account in S's stock, and S has a $100 excess loss account in T's stock. T issues additional stock to a nonmember and, as a consequence, T becomes a nonmember.

(b) *Analysis.* Under paragraph (c)(2) of this section, S is treated as disposing of each of its shares of T's stock immediately before T becomes a nonmember. Under paragraph (b)(1) of this section, S takes into account its $100 excess loss account as gain from the sale or exchange of T's stock. Under § 1.1502-32(b) of this section, S's $100 gain eliminates M's excess loss account in S's stock and increases M's basis in S's stock to $50.

(c) *Deconsolidation of a higher-tier member.* The facts are the same as in paragraph (a) of this *Example 4,* except that S (rather than T) issues the stock and, as a consequence, both S and T become nonmembers. Under paragraph (c)(2) of this section, M is treated as disposing of S's stock and S is treated as disposing of T's stock immediately before S and T become nonmembers. Under § 1.1502-32(b) and paragraph (b)(3) of this section, because S and T become nonmembers in the same transaction and T is the lower-tier member, S is first treated under paragraph (b)(1) of this section as taking into account its $100 excess loss account as gain from the sale or exchange of T's stock. Under § 1.1502-32(b), S's $100 gain eliminates M's excess loss account in S's stock and increases M's basis in S's stock to $50 immediately before S becomes a nonmember. Thus, only S's $100 gain is taken into account in the determination of the group's consolidated taxable income.

(d) *Intercompany gain and deconsolidation.* The facts are the same as in paragraph (c) of this *Example 4,* except that T has $30 of gain that is deferred under § 1.1502-13 and taken into account in determining consolidated taxable income immediately before T becomes a nonmember. Under § 1.1502-32(b), T's $30 gain decreases S's excess loss account in T's stock from $100 to $70 immediately before S is treated as disposing of T's stock. Under paragraph (b)(1) of this section, S is treated as taking into account its $70 excess loss account as gain from the disposition of T's stock. Under § 1.1502-32(b), S's $70 gain from the excess loss account and T's $30 deferred gain that is taken into account eliminate M's $50 excess loss account in S's stock and increase M's basis in S's stock to $50 immediately before S becomes a nonmember.

Example 5. Worthlessness. (a) *Facts.* M forms S with a $150 contribution, and S borrows $150. For Year 1, S has a $50 ordinary loss that is carried over as part of the group's consolidated net operating loss. For Year 2, M has $160 of ordinary income, and S has a $160 ordinary loss. Under § 1.1502-32(b), S's loss results in M having a $10 excess loss account in S's stock. During Year 3, the value of S's assets (without taking S's liabilities into account) continues to decline and S's stock becomes worthless within the meaning of section 165(g) (without taking into account § 1.1502-80(c)). For Year 4, S has $10 of ordinary income.

(b) *Analysis.* Under paragraph (c)(1)(iii)(A) of this section, M is not treated as disposing of S's stock in Year 3 solely because S's stock becomes worthless within the meaning of section 165(g) (taking S's liabilities into account). In addition, because S's stock is not treated as worthless, section 382(g)(4)(D) does not prevent the Year 1 consolidated net operating loss carryover from offsetting S's $10 of income in Year 4.

(c) *Discharge of indebtedness.* The facts are the same as in paragraph (a) of this *Example 5,* except that, instead of S's stock becoming worthless within the meaning of section 165(g), S's creditor discharges $40 of S's indebtedness during Year 3, S is insolvent by more than $40 before the discharge, the discharge is excluded from the M group's gross income under section 108(a), and $40 of the $50 consolidated net operating loss carryover attributable to S is eliminated under section 108(b). Under § 1.1502-32(b)(3)(ii)(C), S's $40 of discharge income is treated as tax-exempt income because there is a corresponding decrease under § 1.1502-32(b)(3)(iii) for elimination of the loss carryover. Under paragraph (c)(1)(iii)(B) of this section, M is treated as disposing of S's stock if the amount discharged is not included in gross income and is not treated as tax-exempt income under § 1.1502-32(b)(3)(ii)(C). Because the discharge is treated as tax-exempt income, M is not treated as disposing of S's stock by reason of the discharge.

Example 6. Avoiding worthlessness. (a) *Facts.* M forms S with a $100 contribution and S borrows $150. For Years 1 through 5, S has a $210 ordinary loss that is absorbed by the group. Under § 1.1502-32(b), S's loss results in M having a $110 excess loss account in S's stock. S defaults on the indebtedness, but the creditor does not discharge the debt (or initiate collection procedures). At the beginning of Year 6, S ceases any substantial operations with respect to the assets, but maintains their ownership with a principal purpose to avoid M's taking into account its excess loss account in S's stock.

(b) *Analysis.* Under paragraph (c)(1)(iii)(A) of this section, M's excess loss account on each of its shares of S's stock ordinarily is taken into account at the time substantially all of S's assets are treated as disposed of, abandoned, or destroyed for Federal income tax purposes. Under paragraph (e) of this section, however, S's assets are not taken into account at the beginning of Year 6 for purposes of applying paragraph (c)(1)(iii)(A) of this section. Consequently, S is treated as worthless at the beginning of Year 6, and M's $110 excess loss account is taken into account.

(h) *Effective/applicability dates.*—(1) *Application.*—This section applies with respect to determinations of the basis of (including an excess loss account in) the stock of a member in consolidated return years beginning on or after January 1, 1995. If this section applies, basis (and excess loss accounts) must be determined or redetermined as if this section were in effect for all years (including, for example, the consolidated return years of another consolidated group to the extent adjustments during those consolidated return years are still reflected). Any such determination or redetermination does not, however, affect any prior period. Paragraphs (a)(3), (c)(1)(iii)(A), and (c)(3)(i)(A) of this section apply with respect to determinations and transactions occurring on or after September 17, 2008. However, taxpayers

may apply paragraph (c)(3)(i)(A) of this section to transactions that occurred prior to September 17, 2008. The last sentence of paragraph (a)(1) and paragraph (b)(1)(iv) of this section applies with respect to dispositions on or after December 16, 2008.

(2) *Dispositions of stock.*—(i) *Dispositions of stock before effective date.*—If M was treated as disposing of stock of S in a tax year beginning before January 1, 1995 (including, for example, a deemed disposition because S was worthless) under the rules of this section then in effect, the amount of M's income, gain, deduction, or loss, and the stock basis reflected in that amount, are not redetermined under paragraph (h)(1) of this section. See paragraph (h)(3) of this section for the applicable rules.

(ii) *Application of special limitation.*—If M was treated as disposing of stock of S because S was treated as worthless as a result of the application of paragraph (c)(1)(iii)(B) of this section after August 29, 2003, the amount of M's income, gain, deduction, or loss, and the stock basis reflected in that amount, are determined or redetermined with regard to paragraph (b)(1)(ii) of this section. If M was treated as disposing of stock of S because S was treated as worthless as a result of the application of paragraph (c)(1)(iii)(B) of this section on or before August 29, 2003, the group may determine or redetermine the amount of M's income, gain, deduction, or loss, and the stock basis reflected in that amount with regard to paragraph (b)(1)(ii) of this section.

(iii) *Intercompany amounts.*—For purposes of this paragraph (h)(2), a disposition does not include a transaction to which § 1.1502-13, § 1.1502-13T, § 1.1502-14, or § 1.1502-14T applies. Instead, the transaction is deemed to occur as the income, gain, deduction, or loss (if any) is taken into account.

(iv) *Intercompany reorganizations.*—Paragraphs (d) and (g) *Example 2* of this section apply to transactions occurring on or after July 18, 2007. For transactions occurring on or after January 23, 2006, and before July 18, 2007, see § 1.1502-19T as contained in 26 CFR part 1 in effect April 1, 2007. For transactions occurring before January 23, 2006, see § 1.1502-19 as contained in 26 CFR part 1 in effect April 1, 2005.

(3) *Prior law.*—For prior determinations, see prior regulations under section 1502 as in effect with respect to the determination. See, e.g., § 1.1502-19 as contained in the 26 CFR part 1 edition revised as of April 1, 1994. For guidance regarding determinations of the basis of the stock of a subsidiary acquired in an intercompany reorganization before January 23, 2006, see paragraph (d) and (g) *Example 2* of § 1.1502-19 as contained in the 26 CFR part 1 edition revised as of April 1, 2005. [Reg. § 1.1502-19.]

Reg. § 1.1502-19(h)(3)

☐ [*T.D. 6909, 12-29-66. Amended by T.D. 7246, 12-29-72; T.D. 8364, 9-13-91; T.D. 8560, 8-12-94 (corrected 3-17-97); T.D. 9089, 8-29-2003; T.D. 9192, 3-21-2005; T.D. 9244, 1-23-2006; T.D. 9341, 7-17-2007 and T.D. 9424, 9-9-2008 (corrected 10-17-2008).*]

[Reg. § 1.1502-21]

§ 1.1502-21. Net operating losses.—
(a) *Consolidated net operating loss deduction.*—The consolidated net operating loss deduction (or CNOL deduction) for any consolidated return year is the aggregate of the net operating loss carryovers and carrybacks to the year. The net operating loss carryovers and carrybacks consist of—

(1) Any CNOLs (as defined in paragraph (e) of this section) of the consolidated group; and

(2) Any net operating losses of the members arising in separate return years.

(b) *Net operating loss carryovers and carrybacks to consolidated return and separate return years.*— Net operating losses of members arising during a consolidated return year are taken into account in determining the group's CNOL under paragraph (e) of this section for that year. Losses taken into account in determining the CNOL may be carried to other taxable years (whether consolidated or separate) only under this paragraph (b).

(1) *Carryovers and carrybacks generally.*—The net operating loss carryovers and carrybacks to a taxable year are determined under the principles of section 172 and this section. Thus, losses permitted to be absorbed in a consolidated return year generally are absorbed in the order of the taxable years in which they arose, and losses carried from taxable years ending on the same date, and which are available to offset consolidated taxable income for the year, generally are absorbed on a pro rata basis. In addition, the amount of any CNOL absorbed by the group in any year is apportioned among members based on the percentage of the CNOL attributable to each member as of the beginning of the year. The percentage of the CNOL attributable to a member is determined pursuant to paragraph (b)(2)(iv)(B) of this section. Additional rules provided under the Internal Revenue Code or regulations also apply. See, e.g., section 382(1)(2)(B) (if losses are carried from the same taxable year, losses subject to limitation under section 382 are absorbed before losses that are not subject to limitation under section 382). See paragraph (c)(1)(iii) of this section, *Example 2*, for an illustration of pro rata absorption of losses subject to a SRLY limitation.

(2) *Carryovers and carrybacks of CNOLs to separate return years.*—(i) *In general.*—If any CNOL that is attributable to a member may be carried to a separate return year of the member, the amount of the CNOL that is attributable to the

member is apportioned to the member (apportioned loss) and carried to the separate return year. If carried back to a separate return year, the apportioned loss may not be carried back to an equivalent, or earlier, consolidated return year of the group; if carried over to a separate return year, the apportioned loss may not be carried over to an equivalent, or later, consolidated return year of the group.

(ii) *Special rules.*—(A) *Year of departure from group.*—If a corporation ceases to be a member during a consolidated return year, net operating loss carryovers attributable to the corporation are first carried to the consolidated return year, then are subject to reduction under section 108 and § 1.1502-28 (regarding discharge of indebtedness income that is excluded from gross income under section 108(a)), and then are subject to reduction under § 1.1502-36 (regarding transfers of loss shares of subsidiary stock). Only the amount that is neither absorbed by the group in that year nor reduced under section 108 and § 1.1502-28 or under § 1.1502-36 may be carried to the corporation's first separate return year. For rules concerning a member departing a subgroup, see paragraph (c)(2)(vii) of this section.

(B) *Offspring rule.*—In the case of a member that has been a member continuously since its organization (determined without regard to whether the member is a successor to any other corporation), the CNOL attributable to the member is included in the carrybacks to consolidated return years before the member's existence. If the group did not file a consolidated return for a carryback year, the loss may be carried back to a separate return year of the common parent under paragraph (b)(2)(i) of this section, but only if the common parent was not a member of a different consolidated group or of an affiliated group filing separate returns for the year to which the loss is carried or any subsequent year in the carryback period. Following an acquisition described in § 1.1502-75(d)(2) or (3), references to the common parent are to the corporation that was the common parent immediately before the acquisition.

(iii) *Equivalent years.*—Taxable years are equivalent if they bear the same numerical relationship to the consolidated return year in which a CNOL arises, counting forward or backward from the year of the loss. For example, in the case of a member's third taxable year (which was a separate return year) that preceded the consolidated return year in which the loss arose, the equivalent year is the third consolidated return year preceding the consolidated return year in which the loss arose. See paragraph (b)(3)(iii) of this section for certain short taxable years that are disregarded in making this determination.

(iv) *Operating rules.*—(A) *Amount of CNOL attributable to a member.*—The amount of a CNOL that is attributable to a member shall equal the product of the CNOL and the percentage of the CNOL attributable to such member.

(B) *Percentage of CNOL attributable to a member.—(1) In general.*—Except as provided in paragraph (b)(2)(iv)(B)(2) of this section, the percentage of the CNOL attributable to a member shall equal the separate net operating loss of the member for the year of the loss divided by the sum of the separate net operating losses for that year of all members having such losses. For this purpose, the separate net operating loss of a member is determined by computing the CNOL by reference to only the member's items of income, gain, deduction, and loss, including the member's losses and deductions actually absorbed by the group in the taxable year (whether or not absorbed by the member).

(2) *Special rules.—(i) Carryback to a separate return year.*—If a portion of the CNOL attributable to a member for a taxable year is carried back to a separate return year, the percentage of the CNOL attributable to each member as of immediately after such portion of the CNOL is carried back shall be recomputed pursuant to paragraph (b)(2)(iv)(B)(2)(v) of this section.

(ii) *Excluded discharge of indebtedness income.*—If during a taxable year a member realizes discharge of indebtedness income that is excluded from gross income under section 108(a) and such amount reduces any portion of the CNOL attributable to any member pursuant to section 108 and § 1.1502-28, the percentage of the CNOL attributable to each member as of immediately after the reduction of attributes pursuant to sections 108 and 1017 and § 1.1502-28 shall be recomputed pursuant to paragraph (b)(2)(iv)(B)(2)(v) of this section.

(iii) *Departing member.*—If during a taxable year a member that had a separate net operating loss for the year of the CNOL ceases to be a member, the percentage of the CNOL attributable to each member as of the first day of the following consolidated return year shall be recomputed pursuant to paragraph (b)(2)(iv)(B)(2)(v) of this section.

(iv) *Reduction of attributes for stock loss.*—If during a taxable year a member does not cease to be a member of the group and any portion of the CNOL attributable to any member is reduced under § 1.1502-36, the percentage of the CNOL attributable to each member as of immediately after the reduction of attributes under § 1.1502-36 shall be recomputed pursuant to paragraph (b)(2)(iv)(B)(2)(v) of this section.

(v) *Recomputed percentage.*—The recomputed percentage of the CNOL attributable to each member shall equal the unabsorbed CNOL attributable to the member at the time of

the recomputation divided by the sum of the unabsorbed CNOL attributable to all of the members at the time of the recomputation. For purposes of the preceding sentence, a CNOL that is reduced under section 108 and § 1.1502-28, or under § 1.1502-36, or that is otherwise permanently disallowed or eliminated, shall be treated as absorbed.

(v) *Examples.*—For purposes of the examples in this section, unless otherwise stated, all groups file consolidated returns, all corporations have calendar taxable years, the facts set forth the only corporate activity, value means fair market value and the adjusted basis of each asset equals its value, all transactions are with unrelated persons, and the application of any limitation or threshold under section 382 is disregarded. The principles of this paragraph (b)(2) are illustrated by the following examples:

Example 1. Offspring rule. (i) During Year 1, Individual A forms P and T, and they each file a separate return. P forms S on March 15 of Year 2, and P and S file a consolidated return. P acquires all the stock of T from Individual A at the beginning of Year 3, and T becomes a member of the P group. P's acquisition of T is not an ownership change within the meaning of section 382. P, S, and T sustain a $1,100 CNOL in Year 3 and, under paragraph (b)(2)(iv) of this section, the loss is attributable $200 to P, $300 to S, and $600 to T.

(ii) Of the $1,100 CNOL in Year 3, the $500 amount of the CNOL that is attributable to P and S ($200 + $300) may be carried to P's separate return in Year 1. Even though S was not in existence in Year 1, the $300 amount of the CNOL attributable to S may be carried back to P's separate return in Year 1 because S (unlike T) has been a member of the P group since its organization and P is a qualified parent under paragraph (b)(2)(ii)(B) of this section. To the extent not absorbed in that year, the loss may then be carried to the P group's return in Year 2. The $600 amount of the CNOL attributable to T is a net operating loss carryback to T's separate return in Year 1, and if not absorbed in Year 1, then to Year 2.

Example 2. Departing members. (i) The facts are the same as in *Example 1.* In addition, on June 15 of Year 4, P sells all the stock of T. The P group's consolidated return for Year 4 includes the income of T through June 15. T files a separate return for the period from June 16 through December 31.

(ii) $600 of the Year 3 CNOL attributable to T is apportioned to T and is carried back to its separate return in Year 1. To the extent the $600 is not absorbed in T's separate return in Year 1 or Year 2, it is carried to the consolidated return in Year 4 before being carried to T's separate return in Year 4. Any portion of the loss not absorbed in T's Year 1 or Year 2 or in the P group's Year 4 is then carried to T's separate return in Year 4.

Reg. § 1.1502-21(b)(2)(v)

Example 3. Offspring rule following acquisition. (i) Individual A owns all of the stock of P, the common parent of a consolidated group. In Year 1, B, an individual unrelated to Individual A, forms T. P acquires all of the stock of T at the beginning of Year 3, and T becomes a member of the P group. The P group has $200 of consolidated taxable income in Year 2, and $300 of consolidated taxable income in Year 3 (computed without regard to the CNOL deduction). At the beginning of Year 4, T forms a subsidiary, Y, in a transaction described in section 351. The P group has a $300 consolidated net operating loss in Year 4, and under paragraph (b)(2)(iv) of this section, the loss is attributable entirely to Y.

(ii) Even though Y was not in existence in Year 2, $300, the amount of the consolidated net operating loss attributable to Y, may be carried back to the P group's Year 2 consolidated return under paragraph (b)(2)(ii)(B) of this section because Y has been a member of the P group since its organization. To the extent not absorbed in that year, the loss may then be carried to the P group's consolidated return in Year 3.

(3) *Special rules.*—(i) *Election to relinquish carryback.*—A group may make an irrevocable election under section 172(b)(3) to relinquish the entire carryback period with respect to a CNOL for any consolidated return year. Except as provided in § 1.1502-21(b)(3)(ii)(B), the election may not be made separately for any member (whether or not it remains a member), and must be made in a separate statement entitled "THIS IS AN ELECTION UNDER § 1.1502-21(b)(3)(i) TO WAIVE THE ENTIRE CARRYBACK PERIOD PURSUANT TO SECTION 172(b)(3) FOR THE [insert consolidated return year] CNOLs OF THE CONSOLIDATED GROUP OF WHICH [insert name and employer identification number of common parent] IS THE COMMON PARENT." The statement must be filed with the group's income tax return for the consolidated return year in which the loss arises. If the consolidated return year in which the loss arises begins before January 1, 2003, the statement making the election must be signed by the common parent. If the consolidated return year in which the loss arises begins after December 31, 2002, the election may be made in an unsigned statement.

(ii) *Special elections.*—(A) *Groups that include insolvent financial institutions.*—For rules applicable to relinquishing the entire carryback period with respect to losses attributable to insolvent financial institutions, see § 301.6402-7 of this chapter.

(B) *Acquisition of member from another consolidated group.*—If one or more members of a consolidated group becomes a member of another consolidated group, the acquiring group may make an irrevocable election to relinquish, with respect to all consolidated net operating losses attributable to the member, the portion of the carryback period for which the corporation was a member of another group, provided that any other corporation joining the acquiring group that was affiliated with the member immediately before it joined the acquiring group is also included in the waiver. This election is not a yearly election and applies to all losses that would otherwise be subject to a carryback to a former group under section 172. The election must be made in a separate statement entitled "THIS IS AN ELECTION UNDER § 1.1502-21(b)(3)(ii)(B)(2) TO WAIVE THE PRE-[insert first taxable year for which the member (or members) was not a member of another group] CARRYBACK PERIOD FOR THE CNOLs attributable to [insert names and employer identification number of members]." The statement must be filed with the acquiring consolidated group's original income tax return for the year the corporation (or corporations) became a member. If the year in which the corporation (or corporations) became a member begins before January 1, 2003, the statement must be signed by the common parent and each of the members to which it applies. If the year in which the corporation (or corporations) became a member begins after December 31, 2002, the election may be made in an unsigned statement.

(C) [Reserved]. For further guidance, see § 1.1502-21T(b)(3)(ii)(C).

(iii) *Short years in connection with transactions to which section 381(a) applies.*—If a member distributes or transfers assets to a corporation that is a member immediately after the distribution or transfer in a transaction to which section 381(a) applies, the transaction does not cause the distributor or transferor to have a short year within the consolidated return year of the group in which the transaction occurred that is counted as a separate year for purposes of determining the years to which a net operating loss may be carried.

(iv) *Special status losses.*—[Reserved].

(v) [Reserved]. For further guidance, see § 1.1502-21T(b)(3)(v).

(c) *Limitations on net operating loss carryovers and carrybacks from separate return limitation years.*—(1) *SRLY limitation.*—(i) *General rule.*—Except as provided in paragraph (g) of this section (relating to an overlap with section 382), the aggregate of the net operating loss carryovers and carrybacks of a member arising (or treated as arising) in SRLYs that are included in the CNOL deductions for all consolidated return years of the group under paragraph (a) of this section may not exceed the aggregate consolidated taxable income for all consolidated return years of the group determined by reference to only the member's items of income, gain, deduction, and loss. For this purpose—

(A) Consolidated taxable income is computed without regard to CNOL deductions;

(B) Consolidated taxable income takes into account the member's losses and deductions (including capital losses) actually absorbed by the group in consolidated return years (whether or not absorbed by the member);

(C) In computing consolidated taxable income, the consolidated return years of the group include only those years, including the year to which the loss is carried, that the member has been continuously included in the group's consolidated return but exclude—

(1) For carryovers, any years ending after the year to which the loss is carried; and

(2) For carrybacks, any years ending after the year in which the loss arose; and

(D) The treatment under § 1.1502-15 of a built-in loss as a hypothetical net operating loss carryover in the year recognized is solely for purposes of determining the limitation under this paragraph (c) with respect to the loss in that year and not for any other purpose. Thus, for purposes of determining consolidated taxable income for any other losses, a built-in loss allowed under this section in the year it arises is taken into account.

(ii) *Losses treated as arising in SRLYs.*—If a net operating loss carryover or carryback did not arise in a SRLY but is attributable to a built-in loss (as defined under § 1.1502-15), the carryover or carryback is treated for purposes of this paragraph (c) as arising in a SRLY if the built-in loss was not allowed, after application of the SRLY limitation, in the year it arose. For an illustration, see § 1.1502-15(d), *Example 5.* But see § 1.1502-15(g)(1).

(iii) *Examples.*—The principles of this paragraph (c)(1) are illustrated by the following examples:

Example 1. Determination of SRLY limitation. (i) Individual A owns P. In Year 1, Individual A forms T, and T sustains a $100 net operating loss that is carried forward. P acquires all the stock of T at the beginning of Year 2, and T becomes a member of the P group. The P group has $300 of consolidated taxable income in Year 2 (computed without regard to the CNOL deduction). Such consolidated taxable income would be $70 if determined by reference to only T's items.

(ii) T's $100 net operating loss carryover from Year 1 arose in a SRLY. See § 1.1502-1(f)(2)(iii). P's acquisition of T was not an ownership change as defined by section 382(g). Thus, the $100 net operating loss carryover is subject to the SRLY limitation in paragraph (c)(1) of this section. The SRLY limitation for Year 2 is consolidated taxable income determined by reference to only T's items, or $70. Thus, $70 of the loss is included under paragraph (a) of this section in the P group's CNOL deduction for Year 2.

(iii) The facts are the same as in paragraph (i) of this *Example 1*, except that such consolidated taxable income (computed without regard to the CNOL deduction and by reference to only T's items) for Year 2 is a loss (a CNOL) of $370. Because the SRLY limitation may not exceed the consolidated taxable income determined by reference to only T's items, and such items aggregate to a CNOL, T's $ 100 net operating loss carryover from Year 1 is not allowed under the SRLY limitation in Year 2. Moreover, if consolidated taxable income (computed without regard to the CNOL deduction and by reference to only T's items) did not exceed $370 in Year 3, the carryover would still be restricted under paragraph (c) of this section in Year 3, because the aggregate consolidated taxable income for all consolidated return years of the group computed by reference to only T's items would not be a positive amount.

Example 2. Net operating loss carryovers. (i) In Year 1, Individual A forms P, and P sustains a $40 net operating loss that is carried forward. P has no income in Year 2. Individual A also owns T which sustains a net operating loss of $50 in Year 2 that is carried forward. P acquires the stock of T from Individual A during Year 3, but T is not a member of the P group for each day of the year. P and T file separate returns and sustain net operating losses of $120 and $60, respectively, for Year 3. The P group files consolidated returns beginning in Year 4. During Year 4, the P group has $160 of consolidated taxable income (computed without regard to the CNOL deduction). Such consolidated taxable income would be $70 if determined by reference to only T's items. These results are summarized as follows:

	Separate Year 1	Separate Year 2	Separate/ Affiliated Year 3	Consolidated Year 4
P................	$(40)	$0	$(120)	$90
T................	0	(50)	(60)	70
CTI..............				160

(ii) P's Year 1, Year 2, and Year 3 are not SRLYs with respect to the P group. See § 1.1502-1(f)(2)(i). Thus, P's $ 40 net operating loss arising in Year 1 and $120 net operating loss arising in Year 3 are not subject to the SRLY limitation under paragraph (c) of this section.

Under the principles of section 172, paragraph (b) of this section requires that the loss arising in Year 1 be the first loss absorbed by the P group in Year 4. Absorption of this loss leaves $120 of the group's consolidated taxable income available for offset by other loss carryovers.

(iii) T's Year 2 and Year 3 are SRLYs with respect to the P group. See § 1.1502-1(f)(2)(ii). P's acquisition of T was not an ownership change as defined by section 382(g). Thus, T's $50 net operating loss arising in Year 2 and $60 net operating loss arising in Year 3 are subject to the SRLY limitation. Under paragraph (c)(1) of this section, the SRLY limitation for Year 4 is $70, and under paragraph (b) of this section, T's $50 loss from Year 2 must be included under paragraph (a) of this section in the P group's CNOL deduction for Year 4. The absorption of this loss leaves $70 of the group's consolidated taxable income available for offset by other loss carryovers.

(iv) P and T each carry over net operating losses to Year 4 from a taxable year ending on the same date (Year 3). The losses carried over from Year 3 total $180. Under paragraph (b) of this section, the losses carried over from Year 3 are absorbed on a pro rata basis, even though one arises in a SRLY and the other does not. However, the group cannot absorb more than $20 of T's $60 net operating loss arising in Year 3 because its $70 SRLY limitation for Year 4 is reduced by T's $50 Year 2 SRLY loss already included in the CNOL deduction for Year 4. Thus, the absorption of Year 3 losses is as follows:

	Year 1	Year 2	Year 3	Total
P	$100	$60	$80	$240
S	20	20	30	70
T	30	10	(50)	(10)
CTI	150	90	60	300

(ii) P sells all of the stock of T to Individual A at the beginning of Year 4. For its Year 4 separate return year, T has a net operating loss of $30.

(iii) T's Year 4 is a SRLY with respect to the P group. See § 1.1502-1(f)(1). T's $30 net operating loss carryback to the P group from Year 4 is not allowed under paragraph (c) of this section to be included in the CNOL deduction under paragraph (a) of this section for Year 1, 2, or 3, because the P group's consolidated taxable income would not be a positive amount if determined by reference to only T's items for all consolidated return years through Year 4 (without regard to the $30 net operating loss). The $30 loss is carried forward to T's Year 5 and succeeding taxable years as provided under the Internal Revenue Code.

	Year 3	Year 4	Total
P group (without T)	$100	$100	$200
T	$60	$40	$100
CTI	$160	$140	$300

(ii) Under § 1.1502-15(a), T's $100 of ordinary loss in Year 3 constitutes a built-in loss that is subject to the SRLY limitation under para-

Amount of P's Year 3 losses absorbed = $120 ÷ ($120 + $20) × $70 = $60.

Amount of T's Year 3 losses absorbed = $20 ÷ ($120 + $20) × $70 = $10.

(v) The absorption of $10 of T's Year 3 loss further reduces T's SRLY limitation to $10 ($70 of initial SRLY limitation, reduced by the $60 net operating loss already included in the CNOL deductions for Year 4 under paragraph (a) of this section).

(vi) P carries its remaining $60 Year 3 net operating loss and T carries its remaining $50 Year 3 net operating loss over to Year 5. Assume that, in Year 5, the P group has $90 of consolidated taxable income (computed without regard to the CNOL deduction). The group's CTI determined by reference to only T's items is a CNOL of $4. For Year 5, the CNOL deduction is $66, which includes $60 of P's Year 3 loss and $6 of T's Year 3 loss (the aggregate consolidated taxable income for Years 4 and 5 determined by reference to T's items, or $66, reduced by T's SRLY losses actually absorbed by the group in Year 4, or $60).

Example 3. Net operating loss carrybacks. (i) P owns all of the stock of S and T. The members of the P group contribute the following to consolidated taxable income of the P group for Years 1, 2, and 3:

Example 4. Computation of SRLY limitation for built-in losses treated as net operating loss carryovers. (i) Individual A owns P. In Year 1, Individual A forms T by contributing $300 and T sustains a $100 net operating loss. During Year 2, T's assets decline in value by $100. At the beginning of Year 3, P acquires all the stock of T from Individual A, and T becomes a member of the P group in a transaction that does not result in an ownership change under section 382(g). At the time of the acquisition, T has a $100 net unrealized built-in loss, which exceeds the threshold requirements of section 382(h)(3)(B). During Year 3, T recognizes its unrealized loss as a $100 ordinary loss. The members of the P group contribute the following to the consolidated taxable income of the P group for Years 3 and 4 (computed without regard to T's recognition of its unrealized loss and any CNOL deduction under this section):

graph (c) of this section. The amount of the limitation is determined by treating the deduction as a net operating loss carryover from a

SRLY. The built-in loss is therefore subject to a $60 SRLY limitation for Year 3. The built-in loss is treated as a net operating loss carryover solely for purposes of determining the extent to which the loss is not allowed by reason of the SRLY limitation, and for all other purposes the loss remains a loss arising in Year 3. Consequently, under paragraph (b) of this section, the $60 allowed under the SRLY limitation is absorbed by the P group before T's $100 net operating loss carryover from Year 1 is allowed.

(iii) Under § 1.1502-15(a), the $40 balance of the built-in loss that is not allowed in Year 3 because of the SRLY limitation is treated as a $40 net operating loss arising in Year 3 that is subject to the SRLY limitation because, under paragraph (c)(1)(ii) of this section, Year 3 is treated as a SRLY, and is carried to other years in accordance with the rules of paragraph (b) of this section. The SRLY limitation for Year 4 is the P group's consolidated taxable income for Year 3 and Year 4 determined by reference to only T's items and without regard to the group's CNOL deductions

($60 + $40), reduced by T's loss actually absorbed by the group in Year 3 ($60). The SRLY limitation for Year 4 is $40.

(iv) Under paragraph (c) of this section and the principles of section 172(b), $40 of T's $100 net operating loss carryover from Year 1 is included in the CNOL deduction under paragraph (a) of this section in Year 4.

Example 5. Dual SRLY registers and accounting for SRLY losses actually absorbed. (i) In Year 1, T sustains a $ 100 net operating loss and a $50 net capital loss. At the beginning of Year 2, T becomes a member of the P group in a transaction that does not result in an ownership change under section 382(g). Both of T's carryovers from Year 1 are subject to SRLY limits under this paragraph (c) and § 1.1502-22(c). The members of the P group contribute the following to the consolidated taxable income for Years 2 and 3 (computed without regard to T's CNOL deduction under this section or net capital loss carryover under § 1.1502-22):

	P	T
Year 1 (SRLY)		
Ordinary		(100)
Capital		(50)
Year 2		
Ordinary	30	60
Capital	0	(20)
Year 3		
Ordinary	10	40
Capital	0	30

(ii) For Year 2, the group computes separate SRLY limits for each of T's SRLY carryovers from Year 1. The group determines its ability to use its capital loss carryover before it determines its ability to use its ordinary loss carryover. Under section 1212, because the group has no Year 2 capital gain, it cannot absorb any capital losses in Year 2. T's Year 1 net capital loss and the group's Year 2 consolidated net capital loss (all of which is attributable to T) are carried over to Year 3.

(iii) Under this section, the aggregate amount of T's $100 net operating loss carryover from Year 1 that may be included in the CNOL deduction of the group for Year 2 may not exceed $60—the amount of the consolidated taxable income computed by reference only to T's items, including losses and deductions to the extent actually absorbed (i.e., $60 of T's ordinary income for Year 2). Thus, the group may include $60 of T's ordinary loss carryover from Year 1 in its Year 2 CNOL deduction. T carries over its remaining $40 of its Year 1 loss to Year 3.

(iv) For Year 3, the group again computes separate SRLY limits for each of T's SRLY carryovers from Year 1. The group has consolidated net capital gain (without taking into account a net capital loss carryover deduction) of $30. Under § 1.1502-22(c), the aggregate amount of

T's $50 capital loss carryover from Year 1 that may be included in computing the group's consolidated net capital gain for all years of the group (here Years 2 and 3) may not exceed $30 (the aggregate consolidated net capital gain computed by reference only to T's items, including losses and deductions actually absorbed (i.e., $30 of capital gain in Year 3)). Thus, the group may include $30 of T's Year 1 capital loss carryover in its computation of consolidated net capital gain for Year 3, which offsets the group's capital gains for Year 3. T carries over its remaining $20 of its Year 1 loss to Year 4. The group carries over the Year 2 consolidated net capital loss to Year 4.

(v) Under this section, the aggregate amount of T's net operating loss carryover from Year 1 that may be included in the CNOL deduction of the group for Years 2 and 3 may not exceed $100, which is the amount of the aggregate consolidated taxable income for Years 2 and 3 determined by reference only to T's items, including losses and deductions actually absorbed (i.e., $60 of ordinary income in Year 2 plus $40 of ordinary income, $30 of capital gain, and $30 of SRLY capital losses actually absorbed in Year 3). The group included $60 of T's ordinary loss carryover in its Year 2 CNOL deduction. It may include the remaining $40 of the carryover in its Year 3 CNOL deduction.

Reg. § 1.1502-21(c)(1)(iii)

(2) *SRLY subgroup limitation.*—In the case of a net operating loss carryover or carryback for which there is a SRLY subgroup, the principles of paragraph (c)(1) of this section apply to the SRLY subgroup, and not separately to its members. Thus, the contribution to consolidated taxable income and the net operating loss carryovers and carrybacks arising (or treated as arising) in SRLYs that are included in the CNOL deductions for all consolidated return years of the group under paragraph (a) of this section are based on the aggregate amounts of income, gain, deduction, and loss of the members of the SRLY subgroup for the relevant consolidated return years (as provided in paragraph (c)(1)(i)(C) of this section). For an illustration of aggregate amounts during the relevant consolidated return years following the year in which a member of a SRLY subgroup ceases to be a member of the group, see paragraph (c)(2)(viii) *Example 4* of this section. A SRLY subgroup may exist only for a carryover or carryback arising in a year that is not a SRLY (and is not treated as a SRLY under paragraph (c)(1)(ii) of this section) with respect to another group (the former group), whether or not the group is a consolidated group, or for a carryover that was subject to the overlap rule described in paragraph (g) of this section or § 1.1502-15(g) with respect to another group (the former group). A separate SRLY subgroup is determined for each such carryover or carryback. A consolidated group may include more than one SRLY subgroup and a member may be a member of more than one SRLY subgroup. Solely for purposes of determining the members of a SRLY subgroup with respect to a loss:

(i) *Carryovers.*—In the case of a carryover, the SRLY subgroup is composed of the member carrying over the loss (the loss member) and each other member that was a member of the former group that becomes a member of the group at the same time as the loss member. A member remains a member of the SRLY subgroup until it ceases to be affiliated with the loss member. The aggregate determination described in paragraph (c)(1) of this section and this paragraph (c)(2) includes the amounts of income, gain, deduction, and loss of each member of the SRLY subgroup for the consolidated return years during which it remains a member of the SRLY subgroup. For an illustration of the aggregate determination of a SRLY subgroup, see paragraph (c)(2)(viii) *Example 2* of this section.

(ii) *Carrybacks.*—In the case of a carryback, the SRLY subgroup is composed of the member carrying back the loss (the loss member) and each other member of the group from which the loss is carried back that has been continuously affiliated with the loss member from the year to which the loss is carried through the year in which the loss arises.

(iii) *Built-in losses.*—In the case of a built-in loss, the SRLY subgroup is composed of the member recognizing the loss (the loss member) and each other member that was part of the subgroup with respect to the loss determined under § 1.1502-15(c)(2) immediately before the members became members of the group. The principles of paragraphs (c)(2)(i) and (ii) of this section apply to determine the SRLY subgroup for the built-in loss that is, under paragraph (c)(1)(ii) of this section, treated as arising in a SRLY with respect to the group in which the loss is recognized. For this purpose and as the context requires, a reference in paragraphs (c)(2)(i) and (ii) of this section to a group or former group is a reference to the subgroup determined under § 1.1502-15(c)(2).

(iv) *Principal purpose of avoiding or increasing a SRLY limitation.*—The members composing a SRLY subgroup are not treated as a SRLY subgroup if any of them is formed, acquired, or availed of with a principal purpose of avoiding the application of, or increasing any limitation under, this paragraph (c). Any member excluded from a SRLY subgroup, if excluded with a principal purpose of so avoiding or increasing any SRLY limitation, is treated as included in the SRLY subgroup.

(v) *Coordination with other limitations.*—This paragraph (c) (2) does not allow a net operating loss to offset income to the extent inconsistent with other limitations or restrictions on the use of losses, such as a limitation based on the nature or activities of members. For example, any dual consolidated loss may not reduce the taxable income to an extent greater than that allowed under section 1503(d) and § § 1.1503(d)-1 through 1.1503(d)-8. See also § 1.1502-47(q) (relating to preemption of rules for life-nonlife groups).

(vi) *Anti-duplication.*—If the same item of income or deduction could be taken into account more than once in determining a limitation under this paragraph (c), or in a manner inconsistent with any other provision of the Internal Revenue Code or regulations incorporating this paragraph (c), the item of income or deduction is taken into account only once and in such manner that losses are absorbed in accordance with the ordering rules in paragraph (b) of this section and the underlying purposes of this section.

(vii) *Corporations that leave a SRLY subgroup.*—If a loss member ceases to be affiliated with a SRLY subgroup, the amount of the member's remaining SRLY loss from a specific year is determined pursuant to the principles of paragraphs (b)(2)(ii)(A) and (b)(2)(iv) of this section.

(viii) *Examples.*—The principles of this paragraph (c)(2) are illustrated by the following examples:

Example 1. Members of SRLY subgroups. (i) Individual A owns all of the stock of P, S, T, and M. P and M are each the common parent of a consolidated group. During Year 1, P sustains a $50 net operating loss. At the beginning of Year 2, P acquires all the stock of S at a time when the aggregate basis of S's assets exceeds their aggregate value by $70 and S becomes a member of the P group. At the beginning of Year 3, P acquires all the stock of T, T has a $60 net operating loss carryover at the time of the acquisition, and T becomes a member of the P group. During Year 4, S forms S1 and T forms T1, each by contributing assets with built-in gains which are, in the aggregate, material. S1 and T1 become members of the P group. During Year 7, M acquires all of the stock of P, and the members of the P group become members of the M group for the balance of Year 7. The $50 and $60 loss carryovers of P and T are carried to Year 7 of the M group, and the value and basis of S's assets did not change after it became a member of the former P group. None of the transactions described above resulted in an ownership change under section 382(g).

(ii) Under paragraph (c)(2) of this section, a separate SRLY subgroup is determined for each loss carryover and built-in loss. In the P group, P's $50 loss carryover is not treated as arising in a SRLY. See § 1.1502-1(f). Consequently, the carryover is not subject to limitation under paragraph (c) of this section in the P group.

(iii) In the M group, P's $50 loss carryover is treated as arising in a SRLY and is subject to the limitation under paragraph (c) of this section. A SRLY subgroup with respect to that loss is composed of members which were members of the P group, the group as to which the loss was not a SRLY. The SRLY subgroup is composed of P, the member carrying over the loss, and each other member of the P group that became a member of the M group at the same time as P. A member of the SRLY subgroup remains a member until it ceases to be affiliated with P. For Year 7, the SRLY subgroup is composed of P, S, T, S1, and T1.

(iv) In the P group, S's $70 unrealized loss, if recognized within the 5-year recognition period after S becomes a member of the P group, is subject to limitation under paragraph (c) of this section. See § 1.1502-15 and paragraph (c)(1)(ii) of this section. Because S was not continuously affiliated with P, T, or T1 for 60 consecutive months prior to joining the P group, these corporations cannot be included in a SRLY subgroup with respect to S's unrealized loss in the P group. See paragraph (c)(2)(iii) of this section. As a successor to S, S1 is included in a subgroup with S in the P group, and because 100 percent of S1's stock is owned directly by corporations that were members of the SRLY subgroup when the members of the SRLY subgroup became members of the P group, its net positive income is not excluded from the consolidated taxable income

of the P group that may be offset by the built-in loss. See paragraph (f) of this section.

(v) In the M group, S's $70 unrealized loss, if recognized within the 5-year recognition period after S becomes a member of the M group, is subject to limitation under paragraph (c) of this section. Prior to becoming a member of the M group, S had been continuously affiliated with P (but not T or T1) for 60 consecutive months and S1 is a successor that has remained continuously affiliated with S. Those members had a net unrealized built-in loss immediately before they became members of the group under § 1.1502-15(c). Consequently, in Year 7, S, S1, and P compose a subgroup in the M group with respect to S's unrealized loss. Because S1 was a member of the SRLY subgroup when it became a member of the M group and also because 100 percent of S1's stock is owned directly by corporations that were members of the SRLY subgroup when the members of the SRLY subgroup became members of the M group its net positive income is not excluded from the consolidated taxable income of the M group that may be offset by the recognized built-in loss. See paragraph (f) of this section.

(vi) In the P group, T's $60 loss carryover arose in a SRLY and is subject to limitation under paragraph (c) of this section. P, S, and S1 were not members of the group in which T's loss arose and T's loss carryover was not subject to the overlap rule described in paragraph (g) of this section with respect to the P group (the former group). Thus, P, S, and S1 are not members of a SRLY subgroup with respect to the T carryover in the P group. See paragraph (c)(2)(i) of this section. As a successor to T, T1 is included in a SRLY subgroup with T in the P group; and, because 100 percent of T1's stock is owned directly by corporations that were members of the SRLY subgroup when the members of the SRLY subgroup became members of the P group, its net positive income is not excluded from the consolidated taxable income of the P group that may be offset by the carryover. See paragraph (f) of this section.

(vii) In the M group, T's $60 loss carryover arose in a SRLY and is subject to limitation under paragraph (c) of this section. T and T1 remain the only members of a SRLY subgroup with respect to the carryover. Because T1 was a member of the SRLY subgroup when it became a member of the M group and also because 100 percent of T1's stock is owned directly by corporations that were members of the SRLY subgroup when the members of the SRLY subgroup became members of the M group, its net positive income is not excluded from the consolidated taxable income of the M group that may be offset by the carryover. See paragraph (f) of this section.

Example 2. Computation of SRLY subgroup limitation. (i) Individual A owns all of the stock of S, T, P, and M. P and M are each the common parent of a consolidated group. In Year 2, P acquires all the stock of S and T from Individual A, and S and T become members of the P group. For Year 3, the P group has a $45 CNOL, which is attributable to P, and which P carries forward. M is the common parent of another group. At the beginning of Year 4, M acquires all of the stock of P and the former members of the P group become members of the M group. None of the transactions described above resulted in an ownership change under section 382(g).

(ii) P's year to which the loss is attributable, Year 3, is a SRLY with respect to the M group. See §1.1502-1(f)(1). However, P, S, and T compose a SRLY subgroup with respect to the Year 3 loss under paragraph (c)(2)(i) of this section because Year 3 is not a SRLY (and is not treated as a SRLY) with respect to the P group. P's loss is carried over to the M group's Year 4 and is therefore subject to the SRLY subgroup limitation in paragraph (c)(2) of this section.

(iii) In Year 4, the M group has $10 of consolidated taxable income (computed without regard to the CNOL deduction for Year 4). Such consolidated taxable income would be $45 if determined by reference to only the items of P, S, and T, the members included in the SRLY subgroup with respect to P's loss carryover. Therefore, the SRLY subgroup limitation under paragraph (c)(2) of this section for P's net operating loss carryover from Year 3 is $45. Because the M group has only $10 of consolidated taxable income in Year 4, however, only $10 of P's net operating loss carryover is included in the CNOL deduction under paragraph (a) of this section in Year 4.

(iv) In Year 5, the M group has $100 of consolidated taxable income (computed without regard to the CNOL deduction for Year 5). Neither P, S, nor T has any items of income, gain, deduction, or loss in Year 5. Although the members of the SRLY subgroup do not contribute to the $100 of consolidated taxable income in Year 5, the SRLY subgroup limitation for Year 5 is $35 (the sum of SRLY subgroup consolidated taxable income of $45 in Year 4 and $0 in Year 5, less the $10 net operating loss carryover actually absorbed by the M group in Year 4). Therefore, $35 of P's net operating loss carryover is included in the CNOL deduction under paragraph (a) of this section in Year 5.

Example 3. Inclusion in more than one SRLY subgroup. (i) Individual A owns all of the stock of S, T, P, and M. S, P, and M are each the common parent of a consolidated group. At the beginning of Year 1, S acquires all the stock of T from Individual A, and T becomes a member of the S group. For Year 1, the S group has a CNOL of $10, all of which is attributable to S and is carried over to Year 2. At the beginning of Year 2, P acquires all the stock of S, and S and T become members of the P group. For Year 2, the P group has a CNOL of $35, all of which is attributable to P and is carried over to Year 3. At the beginning

of Year 3, M acquires all of the stock of P and the former members of the P group become members of the M group. None of the transactions described above resulted in an ownership change under section 382(g).

(ii) P's and S's net operating losses arising in SRLYs with respect to the M group are subject to limitation under paragraph (c) of this section. P, S, and T compose a SRLY subgroup for purposes of determining the limitation for P's $35 net operating loss carryover arising in Year 2 because, under paragraph (c)(2)(i) of this section, Year 2 is not a SRLY with respect to the P group. Similarly, S and T compose a SRLY subgroup for purposes of determining the limitation for S's $10 net operating loss carryover arising in Year 1 because Year 1 is not a SRLY with respect to the S group.

(iii) S and T are members of both the SRLY subgroup with respect to P's losses and the SRLY subgroup with respect to S's losses. Under paragraph (c)(2) of this section, S's and T's items cannot be included in the determination of the SRLY subgroup limitation for both SRLY subgroups for the same consolidated return year; paragraph (c)(2)(vi) of this section requires the M group to consider the items of S and T only once so that the losses are absorbed in the order of the taxable years in which they were sustained. Because S's loss was incurred in Year 1, while P's loss was incurred in Year 2, the items will be added in the determination of the consolidated taxable income of the S and T SRLY subgroup to enable S's loss to be absorbed first. The taxable income of the P, S, and T SRLY subgroup is then computed by including the consolidated taxable income for the S and T SRLY subgroup less the amount of any net operating loss carryover of S that is absorbed after applying this section to the S subgroup for the year.

Example 4. Corporation ceases to be affiliated with a SRLY subgroup. (i) Individual A owns all of the stock of P and M. P and S are members of the P group and the P group has a CNOL of $30 in Year 1, all of which is attributable to P and carried over to Year 2. At the beginning of Year 2, M acquires all of the stock of P, and P and S become members of the M group. P and S compose a SRLY subgroup with respect to P's net operating loss carryover. For Year 2, consolidated taxable income of the M group determined by reference to only the items of P (and without regard to the CNOL deduction for Year 2) is $40. However, such consolidated taxable income of the M group determined by reference to the items of both P and S is a loss of $20. Thus, the SRLY subgroup limitation under paragraph (c)(2) of this section prevents the M group from including any of P's net operating loss carryover in the CNOL deduction under paragraph (a) of this section in Year 2, and P carries the Year 1 loss to Year 3.

(ii) At the end of Year 2, P sells all of the S stock and S ceases to be a member of the M group and the P subgroup. For Year 3, consolidated taxable income of the M group is $50 (determined without regard to the CNOL deduction for Year 3), and such consolidated taxable income would be $10 if determined by reference to only items of P. However, the limitation under paragraph (c) of this section for Year 3 for P's net operating loss carryover still prevents the M group from including any of P's loss in the CNOL deduction under paragraph (a) of this section. The limitation results from the inclusion of S's items for Year 2 in the determination of the SRLY subgroup limitation for Year 3 even though S ceased to be a member of the M group (and the P subgroup) at the end of Year 2. Thus, the M group's consolidated taxable income determined by reference to only the SRLY subgroup members' items for all consolidated return years of the group through Year 3 (determined without regard to the CNOL deduction) is not a positive amount.

(ix) *Application to other than loss carryovers.*—Paragraph (g) of this section and the phrase "or for a carryover that was subject to the overlap rule described in paragraph (g) of this section or § 1.1502-15(g) with respect to another group (the former group)" in this paragraph (c)(2) apply only to carryovers of net operating losses, net capital losses, and for taxable years for which the due date (without extensions) of the consolidated return is after May 25, 2000, to carryovers of credits described in section 383(a)(2). Accordingly, as the context may require, if another regulation references this section and such other regulation does not concern a carryover of net operating losses, net capital losses, or for taxable years for which the due date (without extensions) of the consolidated return is after May 25, 2000, carryovers of credits described in section 383(a)(2), then such reference does not include a reference to such paragraph or phrase.

(d) *Coordination with consolidated return change of ownership limitation and transactions subject to old section 382.*—(1) *Consolidated return changes of ownership.*—If a consolidated return change of ownership occurred before January 1, 1997, the principles of § 1.1502-21A(d) apply to determine the amount of the aggregate of the net operating losses attributable to old members of the group that may be included in the consolidated net operating loss deduction under paragraph (a) of this section. For this purpose, § 1.1502-1(g) is applied by treating that date as the end of the year of change.

(2) *Old section 382.*—The principles of § 1.1502-21A(e) apply to disallow or reduce the amount of a net operating loss carryover of a member as a result of a transaction subject to old section 382.

(e) *Consolidated net operating loss.*—Any excess of deductions over gross income, as determined

under § 1.1502-11(a) (without regard to any consolidated net operating loss deduction), is also referred to as the consolidated net operating loss (or CNOL).

(f) *Predecessors and successors.*—(1) *In general.*—For purposes of this section, any reference to a corporation, member, common parent, or subsidiary, includes, as the context may require, a reference to a successor or predecessor, as defined in § 1.1502-1(f)(4).

(2) *Limitation on SRLY subgroups.*—(i) *General rule.*—Except as provided in paragraph (f)(2)(ii) of this section, if a successor's items of income and again exceed the successor's items of deduction and loss (net positive income), then the net positive income attributable to the successor is excluded from the computation of the consolidated taxable income of a SRLY subgroup.

(ii) *Exceptions.*—A successor's net positive income is not excluded from the consolidated taxable income of a SRLY subgroup if—

(A) The successor acquires substantially all the assets and liabilities of its predecessor and the predecessor ceases to exist;

(B) The successor was a member of the SRLY subgroup when the SRLY subgroup members became members of the group;

(C) 100 percent of the stock of the successor is owned directly by corporations that were members of the SRLY subgroup when the SRLY subgroup members became members of the group; or

(D) The Commissioner so determines

(g) *Overlap with section 382.*—(1) *General rule.*—The limitation provided in paragraph (c) of this section does not apply to net operating loss carryovers (other than a hypothetical carryover described in paragraph (c)(1)(i)(D) of this section and a carryover described in paragraph (c)(1)(ii) of this section) when the application of paragraph (c) of this section results in an overlap with the application of section 382. For a similar rule applying in the case of net operating loss carryovers described in paragraphs (c)(1)(i)(D) and (c)(1)(ii) of this section, see § 1.1502-15(g).

(2) *Definitions.*—(i) *Generally.*—For purposes of this paragraph (g), the definitions and nomenclature contained in section 382, the regulations thereunder, and § § 1.1502-90 through 1.1502-99 apply.

(ii) *Overlap.*—(A) An overlap of the application of paragraph (c) of this section and the application of section 382 with respect to a net operating loss carryover occurs if a corporation becomes a member of a consolidated group (the SRLY event) within six months of the change date of an ownership change giving rise to a section 382(a) limitation with respect to that carryover (the section 382 event).

Reg. § 1.1502-21(g)(2)(ii)(A)

(B) If an overlap described in paragraph (g)(2)(ii)(A) of this section occurs with respect to net operating loss carryovers of a corporation whose SRLY event occurs within the six month period beginning on the date of a section 382 event, then an overlap is treated as also occurring with respect to that corporation's net operating loss carryover that arises within the period beginning with the section 382 event and ending with the SRLY event.

(C) For special rules in the event that there is a SRLY subgroup and/or a loss subgroup as defined in § 1.1502-91(d)(1) with respect to a carryover, see paragraph (g)(4) of this section.

(3) *Operating rules.*—(i) *Section 382 event before SRLY event.*—If a SRLY event occurs on the same date as a section 382 event or within the six month period beginning on the date of the section 382 event, paragraph (g)(1) of this section applies beginning with the tax year that includes the SRLY event.

(ii) *SRLY event before section 382 event.*—If a section 382 event occurs within the period beginning the day after the SRLY event and ending six months after the SRLY event, paragraph (g)(1) of this section applies starting with the first tax year that begins after the section 382 event.

(4) *Subgroup rules.*—In general, in the case of a net operating loss carryover for which there is a SRLY subgroup and a loss subgroup (as defined in § 1.1502-91(d)(1)), the principles of this paragraph (g) apply to the SRLY subgroup, and not separately to its members. However, paragraph (g)(1) of this section applies—

(i) With respect to a carryover described in paragraph (g)(2)(ii)(A) of this section only if—

(A) All members of the SRLY subgroup with respect to that carryover are also included in a loss subgroup with respect to that carryover; and

(B) All members of a loss subgroup with respect to that carryover are also members of a SRLY subgroup with respect to that carryover; and

(ii) With respect to a carryover described in paragraph (g)(2)(ii)(B) of this section only if all members of the SRLY subgroup for that carryover are also members of a SRLY subgroup that has net operating loss carryovers described in paragraph (g)(2)(ii)(A) of this section that are subject to the overlap rule of paragraph (g)(1) of this section.

(5) *Examples.*—The principles of this paragraph (g) are illustrated by the following examples:

Example 1. Overlap—Simultaneous Acquisition. (i) Individual A owns all of the stock of P, which in turn owns all of the stock of S. P and S file a consolidated return. In Year 2, B, an indi-

vidual unrelated to Individual A, forms T which incurs a $100 net operating loss for that year. At the beginning of Year 3, S acquires T.

(ii) S's acquisition of T results in T becoming a member of the P group (the SRLY event) and also results in an ownership change of T, within the meaning of section 382(g), that gives rise to a limitation under section 382(a) (the section 382 event) with respect to the T carryover.

(iii) Because the SRLY event and the change date of the section 382 event occur on the same date, there is an overlap of the application of the SRLY rules and the application of section 382.

(iv) Consequently, under this paragraph (g), in Year 3 the SRLY limitation does not apply to the Year 2 $100 net operating loss.

Example 2. Overlap—Section 382 event before SRLY event. (i) Individual A owns all of the stock of P, which in turn owns all of the stock of S. P and S file a consolidated return. In Year 1, B, an individual unrelated to Individual A, forms T which incurs a $100 net operating loss for that year. On February 28 of Year 2, S purchases 55% of T from Individual B. On June 30, of Year 2, S purchases an additional 35% of T from Individual B.

(ii) The February 28 purchase of 55% of T is a section 382 event because it results in an ownership change of T, under section 382(g), that gives rise to a section 382(a) limitation with respect to the T carryover. The June 30 purchase of 35% of T results in T becoming a member of the P group and is therefore a SRLY event.

(iii) Because the SRLY event occurred within six months of the change date of the section 382 event, there is an overlap of the application of the SRLY rules and the application of section 382.

(iv) Consequently, under paragraph (g) of this section, in Year 2 the SRLY limitation does not apply to the Year 1 $100 net operating loss.

Example 3. No overlap—Section 382 event before SRLY event. (i) The facts are the same as in *Example 2* except that Individual B does not sell the additional 35% of T to S until September 30, Year 2.

(ii) The February 28 purchase of 55% of T is a section 382 event because it results in an ownership change of T, under section 382(g), that gives rise to a section 382(a) limitation with respect to the T carryover. The September 30 purchase of 35% of T results in T becoming a member of the P group and is therefore a SRLY event.

(iii) Because the SRLY event did not occur within six months of the change date of the section 382 event, there is no overlap of the application of the SRLY rules and the application of section 382. Consequently, the Year 1 net operating loss is subject to a SRLY limitation and a section 382 limitation.

Example 4. Overlap—SRLY event before section 382 event. (i) P and S file a consolidated return. S has owned 40% of T for 6 years. For Year 6, T has a net operating loss of $500 that is carried forward. On March 31, Year 7, S acquires an additional 40% of T, and on August 31, Year 7, S acquires the remaining 20% of T.

(ii) The March 31 purchase of 40% of T results in T becoming a member of the P group and is therefore a SRLY event. The August 31 purchase of 20% of T is a section 382 event because it results in an ownership change of T, under section 382(g), that gives rise to a section 382(a) limitation with respect to the T carryover.

(iii) Because the SRLY event occurred within six months of the change date of the section 382 event, there is an overlap of the application of the SRLY rules and the application of section 382 within the meaning of this paragraph (g).

(iv) Under this paragraph (g), the SRLY rules of paragraph (c) of this section will apply to the Year 7 tax year. Beginning in Year 8 (the year after the section 382 event), any unabsorbed portion of the Year 6 net operating loss will not be subject to a SRLY limitation.

Example 5. Overlap—Coextensive subgroups. (i) Individual A owns all of the stock of S, which in turn owns all of the stock of T. S and T file a consolidated return beginning in Year 1. B, an individual unrelated to Individual A, owns all of the stock of P, the common parent of a consolidated group. In Year 2, the S group has a $200 consolidated net operating loss which is carried forward, of which $100 is attributable to S, and $100 is attributable to T. At the beginning of Year 3, the P group acquires all of the stock of S from Individual A.

(ii) P's acquisition of S results in S and T becoming members of the P group (the SRLY event). With respect to the Year 2 net operating loss carryover, S and T compose a SRLY subgroup under paragraph (c)(2) of this section.

(iii) S and T also compose a loss subgroup under § 1.1502-91(d)(1) with respect to the Year 2 net operating loss carryover. P's acquisition also results in an ownership change of S, the subgroup parent, within the meaning of section 382(g), that gives rise to a limitation under section 382(a) (the section 382 event) with respect to the Year 2 carryover.

(iv) Because the SRLY event and the change date of the section 382 event occur on the same date, there is an overlap of the application of the SRLY rules and the application of section 382 within the meaning of paragraph (g) of this section. Because the SRLY subgroup and the loss subgroup are coextensive, under paragraph (g) of this section, the SRLY limitation does not apply to the Year 2 $200 net operating loss.

Example 6. No Overlap—Different subgroups. (i) Individual B owns all of the stock of P, the common parent of a consolidated group. P owns all of the stock of S and all of the stock of T. Individual A owns all of the stock of X, the common parent of another consolidated group. In Year 1, the P group has a $200 consolidated net operating loss, of which $100 is attributable

to S and $100 is attributable to T. At the beginning of Year 3, the X group acquires all of the stock of S and T from P and does not make an election under § 1.1502-91(d)(4) (concerning an election to treat the loss subgroup parent requirement as having been satisfied).

(ii) X's acquisition of S and T results in S and T becoming members of the X group (the SRLY event). With respect to the Year 1 net operating loss, S and T compose a SRLY subgrop under paragraph (c)(2) of this section.

(iii) S and T do not bear (and are not treated as bearing) a section 1504(a)(1) relationship. Therefore S and T do not qualify as a loss subgroup under § 1.1502-91(d)(1). X's acquisition of S and T results in separate ownership changes of S and T, that give rise to separate limitations under section 382(a) (the section 382 events) with respect to each of S and T's Year 1 net operating loss carryovers. See § 1.1502-94.

(iv) The SRLY event and the change dates of the section 382 events occur on the same date. However, paragraph (g)(1) of this section does not apply because the SRLY subgroup (composed of S and T) is not coextensive with a loss subgroup with respect to the Year 1 carryovers. Consequently, the Year 1 net operating loss is subject to both a SRLY subgroup limitation and also separate section 382 limitations for each of S and T.

Example 7. No Overlap—Different subgroups. (i) Individual A owns all of the stock of T and all of the stock of S, the common parent of a consolidated group. B, an individual unrelated to Individual A, owns all of the stock of P, the common parent of another consolidated group. In Year 1, T has a net operating loss of $100 that is carried forward. At the end of Year 2, S acquires all of the stock of T from Individual A. In Year 3, the S group sustains a $200 consolidated net operating loss that is carried forward. In Year 8, the P group acquires all of the stock of S from Individual A.

(ii) S's acquisition of T in Year 1 results in T becoming a member of the S group. The acquisition, however, did not result in an ownership change under section 382(g). As a result, T's Year 1 net operating loss is subject to SRLY within the S group. At the end of Year 7, § 1.1502-96(a) treats T's Year 1 net operating loss as not having arisen in a SRLY with respect to the S group. Section 1.1502-96(a), however, applies only for purposes of § § 1.1502-91 through 1.1502-96 and § 1.1502-98 but not for purposes of this section. See § 1.1502-96(a)(5).

(iii) P's acquisition of S in Year 8 results in S and T becoming members of the P group (the SRLY event). With respect to the Year 1 net operating loss, S and T do not compose a SRLY subgroup under paragraph (c)(2) of this section.

(iv) S and T compose a loss subgroup under § 1.1502-91(d)(1) with respect to the Year 1 net operating loss carryover. P's acquisition of S results in an ownership change of the loss subgroup, within the meaning of section 382(g), that gives rise to a subgroup limitation under section 382(a) (the section 382 event) with respect to that carryover.

(v) The SRLY event and the change date of the section 382 event occur on the same date. However, under paragraph (g)(4) of this section, because the SRLY subgroup and the loss subgroup are not coextensive, T's Year 1 net operating loss carryover is subject to a SRLY limitation.

(vi) With respect to the Year 3 net operating loss carryover, S and T compose both a SRLY subgroup and a loss subgroup under §1.1502-91(d)(1). Thus, paragraph (g)(1) of this section applies and the S group's Year 3 net operating loss carryover is not subject to a SRLY limitation.

Example 8. SRLY after overlap. (i) Individual A owns all of the stock of R and M, each the common parent of a consolidated group. B, an individual unrelated to Individual A, owns all of the stock of D. In Year 1, D incurs a $100 net operating loss that is carried forward. At the beginning of Year 3, R acquires all of the stock of D. In Year 5, M acquires all of the stock of R in a transaction that did not result in an ownership change of R.

(ii) R's Year 3 acquisition of D results in D becoming a member of the R group (the SRLY event) and also results in an ownership change of D, that gives rise to a limitation under section 382(a) (the section 382 event) with respect to D's net operating loss carryover.

(iii) Because the SRLY event and the change date of the section 382 event occur on the same date, there is an overlap of the application of paragraph (c) of this section and section 382 with respect to D's net operating loss. Consequently, under this paragraph (g), D's Year 1 $100 net operating loss is not subject to a SRLY limitation in the R group.

(iv) M's Year 5 acquisition of R results in R and D becoming members of the M group (the SRLY event), but does not result in an ownership change of R or D that gives rise to a limitation under section 382(a). Because there is no section 382 event, the application of the SRLY rules and section 382 do not overlap. Consequently, D's Year 1 $100 net operating loss is subject to a SRLY limitation in the M group.

(v) Because D's Year 1 net operating loss carryover was subject to the overlap rule of paragraph (g) of this section when it joined the R group, under §1.1502-21(c)(2) the SRLY subgroup with respect to that carryover includes all of the members of the R group that joined the M group at the same time as D.

Example 9. Overlap—Interim losses. (i) Individual A owns all of the stock of P and S, each the common parent of a consolidated group. S owns all of the stock of T, its only subsidiary. B, an individual unrelated to Individual A, owns all of the stock of M, the common parent of a consolidated group. In Year 1, the S group has a $100 consolidated net operating loss. On January 1 of Year 2, P acquires all of the stock of S from Individual A. On December 31 of Year 2, M acquires 51% of the stock of P from Individual A. On May 31 of Year 3, M acquires the remaining 49% of the stock of P from Individual A. The P group, for the Year 3 period prior to June 1 had a $50 consolidated net operating loss, and under paragraph (b)(2)(iv) of this section, the loss is attributable entirely to S. Other than the losses described above, the P group does not have any other consolidated net operating losses.

(ii) In the P group, S's $100 loss carryover is treated as arising in a SRLY and is subject to the limitation under paragraph (c) of this section. A SRLY subgroup with respect to that loss is composed of S and T, the members which were members of the S group as to which the loss was not a SRLY.

(iii) M's December 31 purchase of 51% of P is a section 382 event because it results in an ownership change of the S loss subgroup that gives rise to a section 382(a) limitation (the section 382 event) with respect to the Year 1 net operating loss carryover. The purchase, however, does not result in an ownership change of P because it is not a loss corporation under section 382(k)(1). M's May 31 purchase of 49% of P results in P, S, and T becoming members of the M group and is therefore a SRLY event.

(iv) With respect to the Year 1 net operating loss, S and T compose a SRLY subgroup under paragraph (c)(2) of this section and a loss subgroup under §1.1502-91(d)(1). The loss subgroup does not include P because the only loss at the time of the section 382 event was subject to SRLY with respect to the P group. See §1.1502-91(d)(1).

(v) Because the SRLY event occurred within six months of the change date of the section 382 event and the SRLY subgroup and loss subgroup are coextensive with respect to the Year 1 net operating loss carryover, there is an overlap of the application of the SRLY rules and the application of section 382 within the meaning of paragraph (g) of this section. Thus, the SRLY limitation does not apply to that carryover.

(vi) The Year 3 net operating loss, which arose between the section 382 event and the SRLY event, is a net operating loss described in paragraph (g)(2)(ii)(B) of this section because it is the net operating loss of a corporation whose SRLY event occurs within the six month period beginning on the date of a section 382 event.

(vii) With respect to the Year 3 net operating loss, P, S, and T compose a SRLY subgroup under paragraph (c)(2) of this section. Because P, a member of the SRLY subgroup for the Year 3 carryover, is not also a member of a SRLY subgroup that has net operating loss carryovers described in paragraph (g)(2)(ii)(A) of this section (the Year 1 net operating loss), the Year 3 carryover is subject to a SRLY limitation in the M group. See paragraph (g)(4)(ii) of this section.

(h) *Effective/applicability dates.*—(1) *In general.*—This section generally applies to taxable years for which the due date (without extensions) of the consolidated return is after June 25, 1999. However—

(i) In the event that paragraph (g)(1) of this section does not apply to a particular net operating loss carryover in the current group, then solely for purposes of applying paragraph (c) of this section to determine a limitation with respect to that carryover and with respect to which the SRLY register (consolidated taxable income determined by reference to only the member's or subgroup's items of income, gain, deduction or loss) began in a taxable year for which the due date of the return was on or before June 25, 1999, paragraph (c)(2) of this section shall be applied without regard to the phrase "or for a carryover that was subject to the overlap rule described in paragraph (g) of this section or § 1.1502-15(g) with respect to another group (the former group)"; and

(ii) For purposes of paragraph (g) of this section, only an ownership change to which section 382(a), as amended by the Tax Reform Act of 1986, applies shall constitute a section 382 event.

(iii) Paragraphs (b)(2)(ii)(A) and (b)(2)(iv)(B)(2) of this section apply to taxable years for which the due date of the original return (without regard to extensions) is on or after September 17, 2008.

(2) *SRLY limitation.*—Except in the case of those members (including members of a SRLY subgroup) described in paragraph (h)(3) of this section, a group does not take into account a consolidated taxable year beginning before January 1, 1997, in determining the aggregate of the consolidated taxable income under paragraph (c)(1) of this section (including for purposes of § 1.1502-15 and § 1.1502-22(c)) for the members (or SRLY subgroups).

(3) *Prior retroactive election.*—A consolidated group that applied the rules of § 1.1502-21T(g)(3) in effect prior to June 25, 1999, as contained in 26 CFR part 1 revised April 1, 1999, to all consolidated return years ending on or after January 29, 1991, and beginning before January 1, 1997, does not take into account a consolidated taxable year beginning before January 29, 1991, in determining the aggregate of the consolidated taxable income under paragraph (c)(1) of this section (including for purposes of § 1.1502-15 and § 1.1502-22(c)) for the members (or SRLY subgroups).

(4) *Offspring rule.*—Paragraph (b)(2)(ii)(B) of this section applies to net operating losses arising in taxable years ending on or after June 25, 1999.

(5) *Waiver of carrybacks.*—Paragraph (b)(3)(ii)(B) of this section (relating to the waiver of carrybacks for acquired members) applies to acquisitions occurring after June 25, 1999.

(6) *Certain prior periods.*—Paragraphs (b)(1), (b)(2)(iv)(A), (b)(2)(iv)(B)(1), and (c)(2)(vii) of this section apply to taxable years for which the due date of the original return (without regard to extensions) is after March 21, 2005. Paragraphs (b)(2)(ii)(A) and (b)(2)(iv)(B)(2) (as contained in 26 CFR part 1 revised as of April 1, 2008) apply to taxable years for which the due date of the original return (without regard to extensions) is on or after March 21, 2005, and before September 17, 2008. Paragraph (b)(2)(ii)(A) of this section and § 1.1502-21T(b)(1), (b)(2)(iv), and (c)(2)(vii), as contained in 26 CFR part 1 revised as of April 1, 2004, apply to taxable years for which the due date of the original return (without regard to extensions) is after August 29, 2003, and on or before March 21, 2005. For taxable years for which the due date of the original return (without regard to extensions) is on or before August 29, 2003, see paragraphs (b)(1), (b)(2)(ii)(A), (b)(2)(iv), and (c)(2)(vii) of this section and § 1.1502-21T(b)(1) as contained in 26 CFR part 1 revised as of April 1, 2003.

(7) *Prior periods.*—For certain taxable years ending on or before June 25, 1999, see § 1.1502-21T in effect prior to June 25, 1999, as contained in 26 CFR part 1 revised April 1, 1999, as applicable.

(8) *Losses treated as expired under § 1.1502-35(f)(1).*—For rules regarding losses treated as expired under § 1.1502-35(f) on or after March 10, 2006, see § 1.1502-21(b)(3)(v) as contained in 26 CFR part 1 in effect on April 1, 2006. For rules regarding losses treated as expired before March 10, 2006, see § 1.1502-21T(h)(8) as contained in 26 CFR part 1 in effect on January 1, 2006.

(9) [Reserved]. For further guidance, see § 1.1502-21T(h)(9). [Reg. § 1.1502-21.]

☐ [*T.D.* 8823, 6-25-99 (*corrected* 7-30-99). *Amended by T.D.* 8884, 5-24-2000; *T.D.* 8997, 5-30-2002; *T.D.* 9048, 3-11-2003; *T.D.* 9089, 8-29-2003; *T.D.* 9100, 12-18-2003 (*corrected* 2-2-2004) *T.D.* 9192, 3-21-2005; *T.D.* 9254, 3-9-2006; *T.D.* 9300, 12-7-2006; *T.D.* 9315, 3-19-2007; *T.D.* 9424, 9-9-2008 *and T.D.* 9490, 6-22-2010.]

[Reg. § 1.1502-21A]

§ 1.1502-21A. Consolidated net operating loss deduction generally applicable for consolidated return years beginning before January 1, 1997.—(a) *In general.*—The consolidated net operating loss deduction shall be an amount equal to the aggregate of the consolidated net operating loss carryovers and carrybacks to the taxable year (as determined under paragraph (b) of this section).

(b) *Consolidated net operating loss carryovers and carrybacks.*—(1) *In general.*—The consolidated net operating loss carryovers and carrybacks to the taxable year shall consist of any consolidated net operating losses (as determined under paragraph (f) of this section) of the group, plus any net operating losses sustained by members of the group in separate return years, which may be carried over or back to the taxable year under the principles of section 172(b). However, such consolidated carryovers and carrybacks shall not include any consolidated net operating loss apportioned to a corporation for a separate return year pursuant to § 1.1502-79A, and shall be subject to the limitations contained in paragraphs (c), (d), and (e) of this section and to the limitation contained in § 1.1502-15A (or § 1.1502-11(c), as appropriate).

(2) *Rules for applying section 172(b)(1).*—(i) *Regulated transportation corporations.*—For purposes of applying section 172(b)(1)(C) (relating to net operating losses sustained by regulated transportation corporations), in the case of a consolidated net operating loss sustained in a taxable year for which a member of the group was a regulated transportation corporation (as defined in section 172(j)(1)), the portion, if any, of such consolidated net operating loss which is attributable to such corporation (as determined under this paragraph) shall be a carryover to the sixth taxable year following the loss year only if such corporation is a regulated transportation corporation for such sixth year, and shall be a carryover to the seventh taxable year following the loss year only if such corporation is a regulated transportation corporation for both such sixth and seventh years.

(ii) *Trade expansion losses.*—In the case of a carryback of a consolidated net operating loss from a taxable year for which a member of the group has been issued a certification under section 317 of the Trade Expansion Act of 1962 and with respect to which the requirements of section 172(b)(3)(A) have been met, section 172(b)(1)(A)(ii) shall apply only to the portion of such consolidated net operating loss attributable to such member.

(iii) *Foreign expropriation losses.*—An election under section 172(b)(3)(C) (relating to 10-year carryover of portion of net operating loss attributable to a foreign expropriation loss) may be made for a consolidated return year only if the sum of the foreign expropriation losses (as defined in section 172(k)) of the members of the group for such year equals or exceeds 50 percent of the consolidated net operating loss for such year. If such election is made, the amount which may be carried over under section 172(b)(1)(D) is the smaller of (*a*) the sum of such foreign expropriation losses, or (*b*) the consolidated net operating loss.

(3) *Absorption rules.*—For purposes of determining the amount, if any, of a net operating loss (whether consolidated or separate) which can be carried to a taxable year (consolidated or separate), the amount of such net operating loss which is absorbed in a prior consolidated return year under section 172(b)(2) shall be determined by—

(i) Applying all net operating losses which can be carried to such prior year in the order of the taxable years in which such losses were sustained, beginning with the taxable year which ends earliest, and

(ii) Applying all such losses which can be carried to such prior year from taxable years ending on the same date on a pro rata basis, except that any portion of a net operating loss attributable to a foreign expropriation loss to which section 172(b)(1)(D) applies shall be applied last.

(c) *Limitation on net operating loss carryovers and carrybacks from separate return limitation years.*—(1) *General rule.*—In the case of a net operating loss of a member of the group arising in a separate return limitation year (as defined in paragraph (f) of § 1.1502-1) of such member (and in a separate return limitation year of any predecessor of such member), the amount which may be included under paragraph (b) of this section (computed without regard to the limitation contained in paragraph (d) of this section) in the consolidated net operating loss carryovers and carrybacks to a consolidated return year of the group shall not exceed the amount determined under subparagraph (2) of this paragraph.

(2) *Computation of limitation.*—The amount referred to in subparagraph (1) of this paragraph with respect to a member of the group is the excess, if any, of—

(i) Consolidated taxable income (computed without regard to the consolidated net operating loss deduction), minus such consolidated taxable income recomputed by excluding the items of income and deduction of such member, over

(ii) The net operating losses attributable to such member which may be carried to the consolidated return year arising in taxable years ending prior to the particular separate return limitation year.

(3) *Examples.*—The provisions of this paragraph and paragraphs (a) and (b) of this section may be illustrated by the following examples:

Example (1). (i) Corporation P formed corporations S and T on January 1, 1965. P, S, and T filed separate returns for the calendar year 1965, a year for which an election under section 1562 was effective. T's return for that year reflected a net operating loss of $10,000. The group filed a consolidated return for 1966 reflecting consolidated taxable income of $30,000 (computed without regard to the consolidated net operating loss deduction). Among the transactions occuring during 1966 were the following:

(*a*) P sold goods to T deriving deferred profits of $7,000 on such sales, $2,000 of which was restored to consolidated taxable income on the sale of such goods to outsiders:

(*b*) T sold a machine to S deriving a deferred profit of $5,000, $1,000 of which was restored to consolidated taxable income as a result of S's depreciation deductions;

(*c*) T distributed a $3,000 dividend to P; and

(*d*) In addition to the transactions described above, T had other taxable income of $6,000.

(ii) The carryover of T's 1965 net operating loss to 1966 is subject to the limitation contained in this paragraph, since 1965 was a separate return limitation year (an election under section 1562 was effective for such year). Thus, only $7,000 of T's $10,000 net operating loss is a consolidated net operating loss carryover to 1966, since such carryover is limited to consolidated taxable income (computed without regard to the consolidated net operating loss deduction), $30,000, minus such consolidated taxable income recomputed by excluding the items of income and deduction of T, $23,000 (*i.e.*, consolidated taxable income computed without regard to the $1,000 restoration of T's deferred gain and T's $6,000 of other income). In making such recomputation, no change is made in the effect on consolidated taxable income of P's sale to T, or of the dividend from T to P.

Example (2). (i) Corporation P was formed on January 1, 1966. P filed separate returns for the calendar years 1966 and 1967 reflecting net operating losses of $4,000 and $12,000, respectively. P purchased corporation S on March 15, 1967. S was formed on February 1, 1966, and filed a separate return for the taxable year ending January 31, 1967. S also filed a short period return for the period from February 1 to December 31, 1967, and joined with P in filing a consolidated return for 1968. S sustained net operating losses of $5,000 and $6,000 for its taxable years ending January 31, 1967 and December 31, 1967, respectively. An election under section 1562 was not effective for P and S during the period involved. Consolidated taxable income for 1968 (computed without regard to the consolidated net operating loss deduction) was $16,000; such consolidated taxable income recomputed by disregarding the items of income and deduction of S was $9,000.

(ii) In order of time, the following losses are absorbed in 1968:

(*a*) P's $4,000 net operating loss for the calendar year 1966 (such loss is not subject to the limitation contained in this paragraph since P is the common parent corporation for 1968);

(*b*) S's $5,000 net operating loss for the year ended January 31, 1967. Such loss is subject to the limitation contained in this paragraph, since S was not a member of the group on each day of

such year. However, such loss can be carried over and absorbed in full since such limitation is $7,000 (consolidated taxable income computed without regard to the consolidated net operating loss deduction, $16,000, minus such consolidated taxable income recomputed, $9,000); and

(*c*) $6,000 of P's net operating loss and $1,000 of S's net operating loss for the taxable years ending December 31, 1967. This is determined by applying the losses from such year which can be carried to 1968 (P's $12,000 loss and $2,000 of S's $6,000 loss, since such $6,000 loss is limited under this paragraph) on a pro rata basis against the amount of such losses which can be absorbed in that year, $7,000 (consolidated taxable income of $16,000 less the $9,000 of losses absorbed from prior years). The carryover of S's loss to 1968 is subject to the limitation contained in that paragraph, since S was not a member of the group on each day of its taxable year ending December 31, 1967. Such loss is limited to $2,000, the excess of $7,000 (as determined under (ii)(*b*)) over $5,000 (S's carryover from the year ended January 31, 1967). If a consolidated return is filed in 1969, the consolidated net operating loss carryovers will consist of P's unabsorbed loss of $6,000 ($12,000 minus $6,000) from 1967 and, subject to the limitation contained in this paragraph, S's unabsorbed loss of $5,000 ($6,000 minus $1,000) from its year ended December 31, 1967.

(d) *Limitations on carryovers where there has been a consolidated return change of ownership.—* (1) *General rule.—*If a consolidated return change of ownership (as defined in paragraph (g) of § 1.1502-1) occurs during the taxable year or an earlier taxable year, the amount which may be included under paragraph (b) of this section in the consolidated net operating loss carryovers to the taxable year with respect to the aggregate of the net operating losses attributable to old member of the group (as defined in paragraph (g)(3) of § 1.1502-1) arising in taxable years (consolidated or separate) ending on the same day and before the taxable year in which the consolidated return change of ownership occurred shall not exceed the amount determined under subparagraph (2) of this paragraph.

(2) *Computation of limitation.—*The amount referred to in subparagraph (1) of this paragraph shall be the excess of—

(i) The consolidated taxable income for the taxable year (determined without regard to the consolidated net operating loss deduction) recomputed by including only the items of income and deduction of the old members of the group, over

(ii) The sum of the net operating losses attributable to the old members of the group which may be carried to the taxable year arising in taxable years ending prior to the particular loss year or years.

Reg. § 1.1502-21A(d)(2)(ii)

(3) *Example.*—The provisions of this paragraph may be illustrated by the following example:

Example. (i) Corporation P is formed on January 1, 1967 and on the same day it forms corporation S. P and S file a consolidated return for the calendar year 1967, reflecting a consolidated net operating loss of $500,000. On January 1, 1968, individual X purchases all of the outstanding stock of P. X subsequently contributes $1,000,000 to P and P purchases the stock of corporation T. P, S, and T file a consolidated return for 1968 reflecting consolidated taxable income of $600,000 (computed without regard to the consolidated net operating loss deduction). Such consolidated taxable income recomputed by including only the items of income and deduction of P and S is $350,000.

(ii) Since a consolidated return change of ownership took place in 1968 (there was more than a 50 percent change of ownership of P), the amount of the consolidated net operating loss from 1967 which can be carried over to 1968 is limited to $350,000, the excess of $350,000 (consolidated taxable income recomputed by including only the items of income and deduction of the old members of the group, P and S) over zero (the amount of the consolidated net operating loss carryovers attributable to the old members of the group arising in taxable years ending before 1967).

(4) *Cross-reference.*—See § 1.1502-21T(d)(1) for the rule that applies the principles of this paragraph (d) in consolidated return years beginning on or after January 1, 1997, with respect to a consolidated return change of ownership occurring before January 1, 1997.

(e) *Limitations on net operating loss carryovers under section 382.*—(1) *Section 382(a).*—(i) If at the end of a taxable year (consolidated or separate) there has been an increase in ownership of the stock of the common parent of a group (within the meaning of section 382(a)(1)(A) and (B)), and any member of the group has not continued to carry on a trade or business substantially the same as that conducted before any such increase (within the meaning of section 382(a)(1)(C)), then the portion of any consolidated net operating loss sustained in prior taxable years attributable to such member (as determined under this paragraph) shall not be allowed as a carryover to such taxable year or to any subsequent taxable year.

(ii) If the provisions of section 382(a) disallow the deduction of a net operating loss carryover from a separate return year of a member of the group to a subsequent taxable year, no amount shall be included under paragraph (b) of this section as a consolidated net operating loss carryover to such a subsequent consolidated return year with respect to such separate return year of such member.

(iii) The provisions of this subparagraph may be illustrated by the following example:—
Example. P, S, and T file a consolidated return for the calendar year 1969, reflecting a consolidated net operating loss attributable in part to each member. P owns 80 percent of S's stock and S owns 80 percent of T's stock. On January 1, 1970, A purchases 50 percent of P's stock. During 1970 T's business is discontinued. Since there has been a 50 percentage point increase in ownership of P, the common parent of the group, and since T has not continued to carry on the same trade or business after such increase, the portion of the 1969 consolidated net operating loss attributable to T shall not be included in any net operating loss deduction for 1970 or for any subsequent taxable years, whether consolidated or separate.

(2) *Section 382(b).*—If a net operating loss carryover from a separate return year of a predecessor of a member of the group to the taxable year is reduced under the provisions of section 382(b), the amount included under paragraph (b) of this section with respect to such predecessor shall be so reduced.

(3) *Effective date.*—This paragraph (e) disallows or reduces the net operating loss carryovers of a member as a result of a transaction to which old section 382 (as defined in § 1.382-2T(f)(21)) applies. See § 1.1502-21T(d)(2) for the rule that applies the principles of this paragraph (e) in consolidated return years beginning on or after January 1, 1997, with respect to such a transaction.

(f) *Consolidated net operating loss.*—The consolidated net operating loss shall be determined by taking into account the following:

(1) The separate taxable income (as determined under § 1.1502-12) of each member of the group, computed without regard to any deduction under section 242;

(2) Any consolidated capital gain net income (net capital gain for taxable years beginning before January 1, 1977);

(3) Any consolidated section 1231 net loss;

(4) Any consolidated charitable contributions deduction;

(5) Any consolidated dividends received deduction (determined under § 1.1502-26 without regard to paragraph (a)(2) of that section); and

(6) Any consolidated section 247 deduction (determined under § 1.1502-27 without regard to paragraph (a)(1)(ii) of that section).

(g) *Groups that include insolvent financial institutions.*—For rules applicable to relinquishing the entire carryback period with respect to losses attributable to insolvent financial institutions, see § 301.6402-7 of this chapter.

(h) *Effective date.*—Except as provided in § 1.1502-21T(d)(1), (d)(2), and (g)(3), this section applies to consolidated return years beginning before January 1, 1997. [Reg. § 1.1502-21A.]

☐ [*T.D. 6894, 9-7-66. Amended by T.D. 7728, 10-31-80; T.D. 8387, 12-30-91 and T.D. 8446, 11-5-92. Redesignated as Reg. § 1.1502-21A and amended by T.D. 8677, 6-26-96.*]

[Reg. § 1.1502-21T]

§ 1.1502-21T. Net operating losses (temporary).—(a) through (b)(3)(ii)(B) [Reserved]. For further guidance, see § 1.1502-21(a) through (b)(3)(ii)(B).

(b)(3)(ii)(C) *Partial waiver of carryback period for an applicable consolidated net operating loss.*—*(1) Application.*—The acquiring group may make an election described in paragraph (b)(3)(ii)(C)(2) or (b)(3)(ii)(C)(3) of this section with respect to an acquired member or members only if it did not file a valid election described in § 1.1502-21(b)(3)(ii)(B) with respect to such acquired member or members on or before June 23, 2010.

(2) *Partial waiver of entire pre-acquisition carryback period.*—If one or more members of a consolidated group become members of another consolidated group, then, with respect to the consolidated net operating loss arising in a taxable year ending after December 31, 2007, and beginning before January 1, 2010 (Applicable CNOL) for which the group has made an election pursuant to section 172(b)(1)(H), the acquiring group may make an irrevocable election to relinquish, for the part of the Applicable CNOL attributable to such member, the portion of the carryback period during which the corporation was a member of another group. This election could thus operate to relinquish carryback for up to five taxable years, including the Extended Carryback Period (as defined in paragraph (b)(3)(v) of this section). However, any other corporation joining the acquiring group that was affiliated with the member immediately before it joined the acquiring group must also be included in the waiver, and the conditions of this paragraph (b)(3)(ii)(C)(2) must be satisfied. The acquiring group cannot make the election described in this paragraph (b)(3)(ii)(C)(2) with respect to any particular portion of an Applicable CNOL if any carryback is claimed, as provided in paragraph (b)(3)(ii)(C)(4) of this section, with respect to any such loss on a return or other filing by a group of which the acquired member was previously a member and such claim is filed on or before the date the election described in this paragraph (b)(3)(ii)(C)(2) is filed. The election must be made in a separate statement entitled "THIS IS AN ELECTION PURSUANT TO § 1.1502-21T(b)(3)(ii)(C)(2) TO WAIVE THE PRE-[insert the first day of the first taxable year for which the member (or members) was a member of the acquiring group] CARRYBACK PERIOD FOR THE CNOL ATTRIBUTABLE TO THE [in-

sert taxable year of loss] TAXABLE YEAR OF [insert names and employer identification numbers of members]." Such statement must be filed as provided in paragraph (b)(3)(ii)(C)(5) of this section.

(3) *Partial waiver of pre-acquisition Extended Carryback Period.*—If one or more members of a consolidated group become members of another consolidated group, then, with respect to the Applicable CNOL for which the acquiring group has made an election pursuant to section 172(b)(1)(H), the acquiring group may make an irrevocable election to relinquish, for the part of the Applicable CNOL attributable to such member, the portion of the Extended Carryback Period (as defined in paragraph (b)(3)(v) of this section) during which the corporation was a member of another group. This election could thus operate to relinquish carryback for up to three taxable years. However, any other corporation joining the acquiring group that was affiliated with the member immediately before it joined the acquiring group must also be included in the waiver, and the conditions of this paragraph (b)(3)(ii)(C)(3) must be satisfied. The acquiring group cannot make the election described in this paragraph (b)(3)(ii)(C)(3) with respect to any particular portion of an Applicable CNOL if a carryback to one or more taxable years that are prior to the taxable year that is two taxable years preceding the taxable year of the Applicable CNOL is claimed, as provided in paragraph (b)(3)(ii)(C)(4) of this section, with respect to any such loss on a return or other filing by a group of which the acquired member was previously a member, and such claim is filed on or before the date the election described in this paragraph (b)(3)(ii)(C)(3) is filed. The election must be made in a separate statement entitled "THIS IS AN ELECTION PURSUANT TO § 1.1502-21T(b)(3)(ii)(C)(3) TO WAIVE THE PRE-[insert the first day of the first taxable year for which the member (or members) was a member of the acquiring group] EXTENDED CARRYBACK PERIOD FOR THE CNOL ATTRIBUTABLE TO THE [insert taxable year of losses] TAXABLE YEAR OF [insert names and employer identification numbers of members]." Such statement must be filed as provided in paragraph (b)(3)(ii)(C)(5) of this section.

(4) *Claim for a carryback.*—For purposes of paragraphs (b)(3)(ii)(C)(2) and (b)(3)(ii)(C)(3) of this section, a carryback is claimed with respect to a net operating loss if there is a claim for refund, an amended return, an application for a tentative carryback adjustment, or any other filing that claims the benefit of the NOL or CNOL in a taxable year prior to the taxable year of the loss, whether or not subsequently revoked in favor of a claim based on an Extended Carryback Period provided under section 172(b)(1)(H).

Reg. § 1.1502-21T(b)(3)(ii)(C)(4)

(5) Time and manner for filing statement.—A statement described in paragraph (b)(3)(ii)(C)(2) or (b)(3)(ii)(C)(3) of this section that relates to an Applicable CNOL shall be made by the due date (including extension of time) for filing the return for the taxpayer's last taxable year beginning in 2009.

(6) Example.—(i) *Waiver in case of pre-consolidation separate return years.*—T was a separate corporation that was not part of a consolidated group, until December 31, 2004, when it was acquired by the X Group. On December 31, 2007, the X Group sold all of the stock of T to the P Group. P did not make the election described in § 1.1502-21(b)(3)(ii)(B) to relinquish, with respect to all CNOLs attributable to T, the portion of the carryback period for which T was a member of the X Group. In 2008, the P Group sustained a $1,000 CNOL, $600 of which was attributable to T under § 1.1502-21(b)(2)(iv)(A). P elected a Five-Year Carryback (as defined in paragraph (b)(3)(v) of this section) pursuant to section 172(b)(1)(H) with regard to the P Group's 2008 CNOL, and the P Group elected, pursuant to paragraph (b)(3)(ii)(C)(2) of this section, to waive the portion of the carryback period during which T was included in any other consolidated group. T's fifth and fourth taxable years preceding the year of the loss were its 2003 and 2004 separate return years. Due to the P Group's election pursuant to paragraph (b)(3)(ii)(C)(2) of this section, T's allocable portion of the P Group's 2008 CNOL will not be carried back to the years for which it was a member of the X Group. However, T's allocable portion of the P Group's 2008 CNOL will be carried back to T's non-consolidated taxable years (2003 and 2004), subject to the limitation provided in section 172(b)(1)(H)(iv).

(ii) *Split-waiver election made.*—The facts are the same as in paragraph (i) except that the group made the election described in § 1.1502-21(b)(3)(ii)(B) with regard to its acquisition of T in 2007. Due to the P Group's election pursuant to § 1.1502-21(b)(3)(ii)(B), T's allocable portion of the P Group's 2008 CNOL will not be carried back to the years for which T was a member of the X Group. However, T's allocable portion of the P Group's 2008 CNOL will be carried back to T's non-consolidated taxable years (2003 and 2004), subject to the limitation provided in section 172(b)(1)(H)(iv).

(b)(3)(iii) and (b)(3)(iv) [Reserved]. For further guidance, see § 1.1502-21(b)(3)(iii) and (b)(3)(iv).

(v) *Extended Carryback Period under section 172(b)(1)(H).*—Section 172(b)(1)(H) allows a taxpayer to elect to carry back a single net operating loss arising in a taxable year ending after December 31, 2007, and beginning before January 1, 2010 (Applicable NOL) to its third, fourth, or fifth taxable year preceding the taxable year of

the loss (Extended Carryback Period). As contemplated by section 172(b)(1)(H), the designated taxable year within the Extended Carryback Period may be the fifth taxable year preceding the year of the loss (Five-Year Carryback), and section 172(b)(1)(H)(iv) limits the amount of the Applicable NOL that may be carried back to 50 percent of the taxpayer's taxable income (computed without regard to any NOL deduction attributable to the loss year or any taxable year thereafter) for such fifth preceding taxable year. This paragraph (b)(3)(v) provides rules for computing the 50 percent limitation under section 172(b)(1)(H)(iv) where a Five-Year Carryback is made to a consolidated return year from any consolidated return year or separate return year.

(A) *Election.*—(1) *In general.*—Except as otherwise provided in this section, a consolidated group may elect an Extended Carryback Period pursuant to section 172(b)(1)(H) with regard to a consolidated net operating loss arising in a taxable year ending after December 31, 2007 and beginning before January 1, 2010 (Applicable CNOL). However, no election may be made under this paragraph for a taxpayer described in section 13(f) of the Worker, Homeownership, and Business Assistance Act of 2009, Public Law 111-92, 123 Stat. 2984 (November 6, 2009). The election pursuant to section 172(b)(1)(H) applies to the entire Applicable CNOL, except as otherwise provided in paragraph (b)(3)(ii)(C) of this section or in this paragraph (b)(3)(v). See also paragraph (c) of this section (SRLY limitation).

(2) *Revoking a previous carryback waiver.*—A consolidated group may revoke a prior election pursuant to § 1.1502-21(b)(3)(i) to relinquish the entire carryback period with respect to an Applicable CNOL, but only if the group makes the election pursuant to section 172(b)(1)(H) with regard to such Applicable CNOL.

(3) *Pre-acquisition electing member.*—If a member (Electing Member) of a consolidated group makes an Extended Carryback Period election pursuant to section 172(b)(1)(H) with regard to a loss from a separate return year ending before the Electing Member's inclusion in a consolidated group, the election will not disqualify the acquiring group from making an otherwise available election pursuant to section 172(b)(1)(H) with regard to an Applicable CNOL incurred in a consolidated return year that includes the Electing Member.

(B) *Taxpayer's taxable income.*—For purposes of computing the limitation under section 172(b)(1)(H)(iv) on a Five-Year Carryback to any consolidated return year from any consolidated return year or separate return year, *taxpayer's taxable income* as used in section 172(b)(1)(H)(iv)(I) means consolidated taxable income (CTI) in the consolidated return year that is the fifth taxable year preceding the year of the loss. For purposes of the preceding sentence, CTI is computed without regard to any CNOL deduction attributable to the particular Five-Year Carryback or any NOL from any member's taxable year ending on the same date as the taxable year in which the Five-Year Carryback arises, or any taxable year thereafter.

(C) *Limitation on Five-Year Carrybacks to a consolidated group.—(1) Annual limitation.—*The aggregate amount of Five-Year Carrybacks from years ending on the same date (Testing Date) to any consolidated return year may not exceed the excess of 50 percent of the CTI for that year over the total of Five-Year Carrybacks to that consolidated return year from years ending before the Testing Date (Annual Limitation). For purposes of the preceding sentence, CTI is computed without regard to—

(i) Any CNOL deduction attributable to Five-Year Carrybacks to such year; or

(ii) Any NOL from any member's taxable year ending on the Testing Date or any taxable year thereafter.

(2) *Pro rata absorption of limited and non-limited losses.*—Any Five-Year Carryback, and other net operating losses, from years ending on the same date that are available to offset CTI in the same year are absorbed on a pro rata basis. *See* § 1.1502-21(b)(1).

(D) *Election by small business.*—This paragraph (b)(3)(v) does not apply to any loss of an eligible small business as defined in section 172(b)(1)(H)(v)(II) with respect to any election made pursuant to section 172(b)(1)(H) as in effect on the day before the date of the enactment of the Worker, Homeownership, and Business Assistance Act of 2009.

(E) *Examples.*—The rules of this paragraph (b)(3)(v) are illustrated by the following examples. For purposes of the examples, all affiliated groups file consolidated returns, all corporations are includible corporations that have calendar taxable years, the facts set forth the only relevant corporate activity, and all transactions are with unrelated parties.

Example 1. Computation and Absorption of Five-Year Carrybacks. (i) *Facts.* P is the common parent of the P Group. On June 30, 2006, P acquired all of the stock of T from X, the common parent of the X Group. The X Group has been in existence since 1996. P did not make the election described in § 1.1502-21(b)(3)(ii)(B) to relinquish, with respect to all CNOLs attributable to T, the portion of the carryback period for which T was a member of the X Group. In 2008, the P Group sustained a $1,000 CNOL, $600 of which was attributable to T under § 1.1502-21(b)(2)(iv)(A). P elected a Five-Year Carryback pursuant to section 172(b)(1)(H) with regard to the P Group's 2008 CNOL. P did not make an election pursuant

to paragraph (b)(3)(ii)(C) of this section to waive any portion of the period during which T was included in the X Group. T's fifth taxable year preceding the year of the loss was the X Group's 2004 consolidated return year. For 2004, T's separate return limitation year (SRLY) limitation for losses carried into the X Group was $400. The X Group's CTI for 2004 is $200. The X Group did not make a Five-Year Carryback election for a CNOL from its 2008 or 2009 taxable year. There are no other NOL carrybacks into the X Group's 2004 consolidated taxable year.

(ii) *Five-Year Carryback from separate return year.* Pursuant to paragraph (b)(3)(v)(C)(1) of this section, the amount of T's apportioned loss that is eligible for Five-Year Carryback is limited to 50 percent of the X Group's CTI for 2004, or $100 ($200 × 50 percent). Therefore, $100 of T's apportioned loss will be carried into the X Group's 2004 consolidated return year. In addition, T's 2008 loss is subject to the SRLY limitation of $400 with respect to the X Group. Thus, the amount of T's portion of the P Group's 2008 CNOL that may offset the X Group's 2004 CTI is $100 (the lesser of $400 (T's SRLY limitation) or $100 (the amount of T's Five-Year Carryback)).

(iii) *Pro rata absorption of limited and non-limited losses within a single consolidated return year.* The facts are the same as in paragraph (i), except that the X Group sustained a $750 CNOL in 2008, which X elected to carry back four years to its 2004 consolidated return year (no Five-Year Carryback). Further, the X Group had CTI of $500 in 2004. Therefore, the X Group and the P Group both carry back CNOLs from years ending December 31, 2008, although only the P Group's CNOL (including the portion allocable to T) constitutes a Five-Year Carryback. The Annual Limitation on Five-Year Carrybacks will be $250 ($500 × 50 percent), with CTI determined without taking into account the portion of P's 2008 CNOL carried back to the X Group's 2004 consolidated return year or the X Group's 2008 CNOL, which arises from a taxable year ending on the same date as the Five-Year Carryback. The $750 CNOL carryback within the X Group is subject to no limitation. Under § 1.1502-21(b)(1), because the 2008 CNOL of the X Group and the 2008 SRLY loss of T are losses from years ending on the same date and are available to offset CTI in the same year, the two losses offset the X Group's $500 CTI on a pro rata basis. Accordingly, $375 of the X's Group's 2008 CNOL [$500 × $750/($750 + $250)] and $125 of T's portion of the P Group's 2008 CNOL [$500 × $250/($750 + $250)] offset the X Group's 2004 CTI.

Example 2. Multiple carryback years. (i) *Facts.* On January 1, 2004, Individual A formed X, which formed corporations S and T, and X elected to file a consolidated Federal income tax return. For its 2004 consolidated taxable year, the X Group's CTI was $1,100. For its 2005 consolidated taxable year, the X Group's CTI was $1,000. On June 30, 2007, the X Group sold all of the S stock to the Y Group and sold all of the T stock to the Z Group. The X Group terminated in 2007. Neither Y nor Z made the election described in § 1.1502-21(b)(3)(ii)(B) to relinquish, with respect to all CNOLs attributable to S and T, respectively, the portion of the carryback period for which S and T were members of the X Group. In 2008, the Y Group sustained an $800 CNOL, $400 of which was attributable to S under § 1.1502-21(b)(2)(iv)(A). Y elected a Five-Year Carryback with regard to the Y Group's 2008 CNOL pursuant to section 172(b)(1)(H). Y did not make an election pursuant to paragraph (b)(3)(ii)(C) of this section to waive any portion of the period during which S was included in the X Group. In 2009, the Z Group sustained a $1,000 CNOL, $600 of which was attributable to T under § 1.1502-21(b)(2)(iv)(A). Z elected a Five-Year Carryback with regard to the Z Group's 2009 CNOL pursuant to section 172(b)(1)(H). Z did not make an election pursuant to paragraph (b)(3)(ii)(C) of this section to waive any portion of the Extended Carryback Period during which T was included in the X Group.

(ii) *Analysis.* The $400 of Y Group's 2008 CNOL that is apportioned to S is carried back as a separate return year Five-Year Carryback to the X Group's 2004 consolidated return year. The $600 of Z Group's 2009 CNOL that is apportioned to T is also a separate return year Five-Year Carryback to the X Group's 2005 consolidated return year. The Annual Limitation on Five-Year Carryback to the X Group's 2004 consolidated return year computed under paragraph (b)(3)(v)(C)(*1*) of this section equals $550 ($1,100 of CTI x 50 percent). Because S is making the sole Five-Year Carryback to the X Group's 2004 consolidated return year, S will make a Five-Year Carryback of the full $400. Similarly, the Annual Limitation for Five-Year Carryback to the X Group's 2005 consolidated return year computed under paragraph (b)(3)(v)(C)(*1*) of this section equals $500 ($1,000 of CTI × 50 percent). Because T is making the sole Five-Year Carryback to the X Group's 2005 consolidated return year, T will make a Five-Year Carryback of the full $500. The SRLY limitations for S and T, respectively, may limit the absorption of the Five-Year Carrybacks within the X Group.

Example 3. Pre-acquisition election by T. P is the common parent of the P Group. On December 31, 2008, P acquired all of the stock of T from X, the common parent of the X Group. T had been a member of the X Group since 1999. P did not make the election described in § 1.1502-21(b)(3)(ii)(B) to relinquish, with respect to all CNOLs attributable to T, the portion of the carryback period for which T was a member of the X Group. Pursuant to section 172(b)(1)(H), the X Group elected to make a Five-Year Carryback of its 2008 CNOL back to 2003. A portion of this CNOL is attributable to T pursuant to § 1.1502-21(b)(2)(iv)(A). In 2009, the P Group incurred a CNOL of $1,000, $600 of which is attrib-

utable to T pursuant to § 1.1502-21(b)(2)(iv)(A). Pursuant to section 172(b)(1)(H), the P Group elected a Five-Year Carryback with regard to its 2009 CNOL. P did not make the election pursuant to paragraph (b)(3)(ii)(C) of this section to waive any portion of the period during which T was included in the X Group. The Five-Year Carryback election by the X Group with respect to its 2008 CNOL (which includes the portion of the CNOL attributable to T) does not disqualify the P Group from electing a Five-Year Carryback with regard to its 2009 CNOL. Therefore, the P Group may carry back its CNOL, including the portion attributable to T, in accordance with § 1.1502-21 and the rules of this section.

(c) through (h)(8) [Reserved]. For further guidance, see § 1.1502-21(c) through (h)(8).

(h)(9) *Section 172(b)(1)(H).*—(i) *Applicability date.*—This section applies to any consolidated Federal income tax return due (without extensions) after June 23, 2010, if such return was not filed on or before such date. However, a consolidated group may apply this section to any consolidated Federal income tax return that is not described in the preceding sentence.

(ii) *Expiration date.*—The applicability of this section will expire on June 21, 2013. [Temporary Reg. § 1.1502-21T.]

☐ [*T.D.* 8997, 5-30-2002. *Amended by T.D.* 9048, 3-11-2003 (*corrected* 4-3-2003); *T.D.* 9089, 8-29-2003; *T.D.* 9100, 12-18-2003 (*corrected* 2-2-2004) *T.D.* 9192, 3-21-2005; *T.D.* 9254, 3-9-2006; *T.D.* 9300, 12-7-2006 *and T.D.* 9490, 6-22-2010 (*corrected* 7-29-2010).]

[Reg. § 1.1502-22]

§ 1.1502-22. Consolidated capital gain and loss.—(a) *Capital gain.*—The determinations under section 1222, including capital gain net income, net long-term capital gain, and net capital gain, with respect to members during consolidated return years are not made separately. Instead, consolidated amounts are determined for the group as a whole. The consolidated capital gain net income for any consolidated return year is determined by reference to—

(1) The aggregate gains and losses of members from sales or exchanges of capital assets for the year (other than gains and losses to which section 1231 applies);

(2) The consolidated net section 1231 gain for the year (determined under § 1.1502-23); and

(3) The net capital loss carryovers or carrybacks to the year.

(b) *Net capital loss carryovers and carrybacks.*— (1) *In general.*—The determinations under section 1222, including net capital loss and net short-term capital loss, with respect to members during consolidated return years are not made separately. Instead, consolidated amounts are determined for the group as a whole. Losses included in the consolidated net capital loss may be carried to consolidated return years, and, after apportionment, may be carried to separate return years. The net capital loss carryovers and carrybacks consist of—

(i) Any consolidated net capital losses of the group; and

(ii) Any net capital losses of the members arising in separate return years.

(2) *Carryovers and carrybacks generally.*—The net capital loss carryovers and carrybacks to a taxable year are determined under the principles of section 1212 and this section. Thus, losses permitted to be absorbed in a consolidated return year generally are absorbed in the order of the taxable years in which they were sustained, and losses carried from taxable years ending on the same date, and which are available to offset consolidated capital gain net income, generally are absorbed on a pro rata basis. Additional rules provided under the Internal Revenue Code or regulations also apply, as well as the SRLY limitation under paragraph (c) of this section. See, e.g., section 382(l)(2)(B).

(3) *Carryovers and carrybacks of consolidated net capital losses to separate return years.*—If any consolidated net capital loss that is attributable to a member may be carried to a separate return year under the principles of § 1.1502-21(b)(2), the amount of the consolidated net capital loss that is attributable to the member is apportioned and carried to the separate return year (apportioned loss).

(4) *Special rules.*—(i) *Short years in connection with transactions to which section 381(a) applies.*—If a member distributes or transfers assets to a corporation that is a member immediately after the distribution or transfer in a transaction to which section 381(a) applies, the transaction does not cause the distributor or transferor to have a short year within the consolidated return year of the group in which the transaction occurred that is counted as a separate year for purposes of determining the years to which a net capital loss may be carried.

(ii) *Special status losses.*—[Reserved]

(c) *Limitations on net capital loss carryovers and carrybacks from separate return limitation years.*—The aggregate of the net capital losses of a member arising (or treated as arising) in SRLYs that are included in the determination of consolidated capital gain net income for all consolidated return years of the group under paragraph (a) of this section may not exceed the aggregate of the consolidated capital gain net income for all consolidated return years of the group determined by reference to only the member's items of gain and loss from capital assets as defined in section 1221 and trade or business assets defined in section 1231(b), including the member's losses actually absorbed by the group in the taxable

year (whether or not absorbed by the member). The principles of § 1.1502-21(c) (including the SRLY subgroup principles under § 1.1502-21(c)(2)) apply with appropriate adjustments for purposes of applying this paragraph (c).

(d) *Coordination with respect to consolidated return change of ownership limitation occurring in consolidated return years beginning before January 1, 1997.*—If a consolidated return change of ownership occurred before January 1, 1997, the principles of § 1.1502-22A(d) apply to determine the amount of the aggregate of the net capital loss attributable to old members of the group (as those terms are defined in § 1.1502-1(g)), that may be included in the net capital loss carryover under paragraph (b) of this section. For this purpose, § 1.1502-1(g) is applied by treating that date as the end of the year of change.

(e) *Consolidated net capital loss.*—Any excess of losses over gains, as determined under paragraph (a) of this section (without regard to any carryovers or carrybacks), is also referred to as the consolidated net capital loss.

(f) *Predecessors and successors.*—For purposes of this section, the principles of § 1.1502-21(f) apply with appropriate adjustments.

(g) *Overlap with section 383.*—(1) *General rule.*—The limitation provided in paragraph (c) of this section does not apply to net capital loss carryovers ((other than a hypothetical carryover like those described in § 1.1502-21(c)(1)(i)(D) and a carryover like those described in § 1.1502-21(c)(1)(ii)) when the application of paragraph (c) of this section results in an overlap with the application of section 383. For a similar rule applying in the case of net capital loss carryovers like those described in §§ 1.1502-21(c)(1)(i)(D) and (c)(1)(ii), see § 1.1502-15(g).

(2) *Definitions.*—(i) *Generally.*—For purposes of this paragraph (g), the definitions and nomenclature contained in sections 382 and 383, the regulations thereunder, and §§ 1.1502-90 through 1.1502-99 apply.

(ii) *Overlap.*—(A) An overlap of the application of paragraph (c) of this section and the application of section 383 with respect to a net capital loss carryover occurs if a corporation becomes a member of the consolidated group (the SRLY event) within six months of the change date of an ownership change giving rise to a section 382 limitation with respect to that carryover (the section 383 event).

(B) If an overlap described in paragraph (g)(2)(ii)(A) of this section occurs with respect to net capital loss carryovers of a corporation whose SRLY event occurs within the six month period beginning on the date of a section 383 event, then an overlap is treated as also occurring with respect to that corporation's net capital loss carryover that arises within the period beginning with the section 383 event and ending with the SRLY event.

(C) For special rules in the event that there is a SRLY subgroup and/or a loss subgroup as defined in § 1.1502-91(d)(1) with respect to a carryover, see paragraph (g)(4) of this section.

(3) *Operating rules.*—(i) *Section 383 event before SRLY event.*—If a SRLY event occurs on the same date as a section 383 event or within the six month period beginning on the date of the section 383 event, paragraph (g)(1) of this section applies beginning with the tax year that includes the SRLY event.

(ii) *SRLY event before section 383 event.*—If a section 383 event occurs within the period beginning the day after the SRLY event and ending six months after the SRLY event, paragraph (g)(1) of this section applies starting with the first tax year that begins after the section 383 event.

(4) *Subgroup rules.*—In general, in the case of a net capital loss carryover for which there is a SRLY subgroup and a loss subgroup (as defined in § 1.1502-91(d)(1)), the principles of this paragraph (g) apply to the SRLY subgroup, and not separately to its members. However, paragraph (g)(1) of this section applies—

(i) With respect to a carryover described in paragraph (g)(2)(ii)(A) of this section only if—

(A) All members of the SRLY subgroup with respect to that carryover are also included in a loss subgroup with respect to that carryover; and

(B) All members of a loss subgroup with respect to that carryover are also members of a SRLY subgroup with respect to that carryover; and

(ii) With respect to a carryover described in paragraph (g)(2)(ii)(B) of this section only if all members of the SRLY subgroup for that carryover are also members of a SRLY subgroup that has net capital loss carryovers described in paragraph (g)(2)(ii)(A) of this section that are subject to the overlap rule of paragraph (g)(1) of this section.

(h) *Effective date.*—(1) *In general.*—This section generally applies to taxable years for which the due date (without extensions) of the consolidated return is after June 25, 1999. However—

(i) In the event that paragraph (g)(1) of this section does not apply to a particular net capital loss carryover in the current group, then solely for purposes of applying paragraph (c) of this section to determine a limitation with respect to that carryover and with respect to which the SRLY register (consolidated taxable income determined by reference to only the member's or subgroup's items of income, gain, deduction or

loss) began in a taxable year for which the due date of the return was on or before June 25, 1999, the principles of § 1.1502-21(c)(2) shall be applied without regard to the phrase "or for a carryover that was subject to the overlap rule described in paragraph (g) of this section or § 1.1502-15(g) with respect to another group (the former group)"; and

(ii) For purposes of paragraph (g) of this section, only an ownership change to which section 383, as amended by the Tax Reform Act of 1986, applies and which results in a section 382 limitation shall constitute a section 383 event.

(2) *Prior periods.*—For certain taxable years ending on or before June 25, 1999, see § 1.1502-22T in effect prior to June 25, 1999, as contained in 26 CFR part 1 revised April 1, 1999, as applicable. [Reg. § 1.1502-22.]

☐ [*T.D.* 8823, 6-25-99.]

[Reg. § 1.1502-22A]

§ 1.1502-22A. Consolidated net capital gain or loss generally applicable for consolidated return years beginning before January 1, 1997.—(a) *Computation.*—(1) *Consolidated capital gain net income.*—The consolidated capital gain net income (net capital gain for taxable years beginning before January 1, 1977) for the taxable year shall be determined by taking into account—

(i) The aggregate of the capital gains and losses (determined without regard to gains or losses to which section 1231 applies or net capital loss carryovers or carrybacks) of the members of the group for the consolidated return year.

(ii) The consolidated section 1231 net gain for such year (computed in accordance with §§ 1.1502-23A or 1.1502-23T), and

(iii) The consolidated net capital loss carryovers or carrybacks to such year (as determined under paragraph (b) of this section).

(2) *Consolidated net capital loss.*—The consolidated net capital loss shall be determined under subparagraph (1) of this paragraph but without regard to subdivision (iii) thereof.

(3) *Special rules.*—For purposes of this section, capital gains and losses on intercompany transactions and transactions with respect to stock, bonds, and other obligations of a member of the group shall be reflected as provided in §§ 1.1502-13 and 1.1502-19, and capital losses shall be limited as provided in §§ 1.1502-15A and 1.1502-11(c).

(4) [Reserved]

(5) *Example.*—The provisions of this paragraph may be illustrated by the following example:

Example. (i) Corporations P, S, and T file consolidated returns on a calendar year basis for 1966 and 1967. The members had the following transactions involving capital assets during 1967: P sold an asset with a $10,000 basis to S for $17,000 and none of the circumstances of restoration described in § 1.1502-13 occurred by the end of the consolidated return year; S sold an asset to individual A for $7,000 which S had purchased during 1966 from P for $10,000, and with respect to which P had deferred a gain of $2,000; T sold an asset with a basis of $10,000 to individual B for $25,000. The group has a consolidated net capital loss carryover to the taxable year of $10,000.

(ii) The consolidated net capital gain of the group is $4,000, determined as follows: P's net capital gain of $2,000, representing the deferred gain on the sale to S during the taxable year 1966, restored into income during taxable year 1967 (the $7,000 gain on P's deferred intercompany transaction is not taken into account for the current year), plus T's net capital gain of $15,000, minus S's net capital loss of $3,000 and the consolidated net capital loss carryover of $10,000.

(b) *Consolidated net capital loss carryovers and carrybacks.*—(1) *In general.*—The consolidated net capital loss carryovers and carrybacks to the taxable year shall consist of any consolidated net capital losses of the group, plus any net capital losses of members of the group arising in separate return years of such members, which may be carried over or back to the taxable year under the principles of section 1212(a). However, such consolidated carryovers and carrybacks shall not include any consolidated net capital loss apportioned to a corporation for a separate return year pursuant to § 1.1502-79A(b) (or § 1.1502-22T(b), as appropriate) and shall be subject to the limitations contained in paragraphs (c) and (d) of this section. For purposes of section 1212(a)(1), the portion of any consolidated net capital loss for any taxable year attributable to a foreign expropriation capital loss is the amount of the foreign expropriation capital losses of all the members for such year (but not in excess of the consolidated net capital loss for such year).

(2) *Absorption rules.*—For purposes of determining the amount, if any, of a net capital loss (whether consolidated or separate) which can be carried to a taxable year (consolidated or separate), the amount of such net capital loss which is absorbed in a prior consolidated return year under section 1212(a)(1) shall be determined by—

(i) Applying all net capital losses which can be carried to such prior year in the order of the taxable years in which such losses were sustained, beginning with the taxable year which ends earliest, and

(ii) Applying all such losses which can be carried to such prior year from taxable years ending on the same date on a pro rata basis, except that any portion of a net capital loss attributable to a foreign expropriation capital loss

to which section 1212(a)(1)(B) applies shall be applied last.

(c) *Limitation on net capital loss carryovers and carrybacks from separate return limitation years.*—(1) *General rule.*—In the case of a net capital loss of a member of the group arising in a separate return limitation year (as defined in paragraph (f) of § 1.1502-1) of such member (and in a separate return limitation year of any predecessor of such member), the amount that may be included under paragraph (b) of this section (computed without regard to the limitation contained in paragraph (d) of this section) shall not exceed the amount determined under subparagraph (2) of this paragraph.

(2) *Computation of limitation.*—The amount referred to in subparagraph (1) of this paragraph with respect to a member of the group is the excess, if any, of—

(i) The consolidated capital gain net income (net capital gain for taxable years beginning before January 1, 1977) for the taxable year (computed without regard to any net capital loss carryovers or carrybacks), minus such consolidated capital gain net income (net capital gain for taxable years beginning before January 1, 1977) for the taxable year recomputed by excluding the capital gains and losses and the gains and losses to which section 1231 applies of such member, over

(ii) The net capital losses attributable to such member which can be carried to the taxable year arising in taxable years ending prior to the particular separate return limitation year.

(d) *Limitation on capital loss carryovers where there has been a consolidated return change of ownership.*—(1) *General rule.*—If a consolidated return change of ownership (as defined in paragraph (g) of § 1.1502-1) occurs during the taxable year or an earlier taxable year, the amount which may be included under paragraph (b) of this section in the consolidated net capital loss carryovers to the taxable year with respect to the aggregate of the net capital losses attributable to old members of the group (as defined in paragraph (g)(3) of § 1.1502-1) arising in taxable years (consolidated or separate) ending on the same day and before the taxable year in which the consolidated return change of ownership occurred shall not exceed the amount determined under subparagraph (2) of this paragraph.

(2) *Computation of limitation.*—The amount referred to in subparagraph (1) of this paragraph shall be the excess of—

(i) The consolidated capital gain net income (net capital gain for taxable years beginning before January 1, 1977) (determined without regard to any net capital loss carryovers for the taxable year) recomputed by including only capital gains and losses and gains and

Reg. § 1.1502-22A(d)(2)(i)

losses to which section 1231 applies of the old members of the group, over

(ii) The aggregate net capital losses attributable to the old members of the group which may be carried to the taxable year arising in taxable years ending prior to the particular loss year or years.

(3) *Cross-reference.*—See § 1.1502-22T(d) for the rule that applies the principles of this paragraph (d) in consolidated return years beginning on or after January 1, 1997, with respect to a consolidated return change of ownership occurring before January 1, 1997.

(e) *Effective date.*—This section applies to any consolidated return years to which § 1.1502-21T(g) does not apply. See § 1.1502-21T(g) for effective dates of that section. [Reg. § 1.1502-22A.]

□ [T.D. 6894, 9-7-66. *Amended by T.D. 7637,* 8-6-79; *T.D. 7728, 10-31-80 and T.D. 8597, 7-12-95.*

Redesignated as Reg. § 1.1502-22A and amended by T.D. 8677, 6-26-96.]

[Reg. § 1.1502-23]

§ 1.1502-23. Consolidated net section 1231 gain or loss.—(a) *In general.*—Net section 1231 gains and losses of members arising during consolidated return years are not determined separately. Instead, the consolidated net section 1231 gain or loss is determined under this section for the group as a whole.

(b) Example. The following example illustrates the provisions of this section:

Example. Use of SRLY registers with net gains and net losses under section 1231. (i) In Year 1, T sustains a $20 net capital loss. At the beginning of Year 2, T becomes a member of the P group. T's capital loss carryover from Year 1 is subject to SRLY limits under § 1.1502-22(c). The members of the P group contribute the following to the consolidated taxable income for Year 2 (computed without regard to T's net capital loss carryover under § 1.1502-22):

	P	T
Year 1 (SRLY)		
Ordinary		
Capital		(20)
Year 2		
Ordinary	10	20
Capital	70	0
§ 1231	(60)	30

(ii) Under section 1231, if the section 1231 losses for any taxable year exceed the section 1231 gains for such taxable year, such gains and losses are treated as ordinary gains or losses. Because the P group's section 1231 losses, $(60), exceed the section 1231 gains, $30, the P group's net loss is treated as an ordinary loss. T's net section 1231 gain has the same character as the P group's consolidated net section 1231 loss, so T's $30 of section 1231 income is treated as ordinary income for purposes of applying § 1.1502-22(c). Under § 1.1502-22(c), the group's consolidated net capital gain determined by reference only to T's items is $0. None of T's capital loss carryover from Year 1 may be taken into account in Year 2.

(c) *Recapture of ordinary loss.*—[Reserved]

(d) *Effective date.*—(1) *In general.*—This section applies to gains and losses arising in the determination of consolidated net section 1231 gain or loss for taxable years for which the due date (without extensions) of the consolidated return is after June 25, 1999.

(2) *Application to prior periods.*—See § 1.1502-21(h)(3) for rules applicable to groups that applied the rules of this section to consolidated return years ending on or after January 29, 1991, and beginning before January 1, 1997. [Reg. § 1.1502-23.]

□ [T.D. 8823, 6-25-99 (*corrected 7-30-99*).]

[Reg. § 1.1502-23A]

§ 1.1502-23A. Consolidated net section 1231 gain or loss generally applicable for consolidated return years beginning before January 1, 1997.—(a) The consolidated section 1231 net gain or loss for the taxable year shall be determined by taking into account the aggregate of the gains and losses to which section 1231 applies of the members of the group for the consolidated return year. Section 1231 gains and losses on intercompany transactions shall be reflected as provided in § 1.1502-13. Section 1231 losses that are "built-in deductions" shall be subject to the limitations of § § 1.1502-21A(c) and 1.1502-22A(c), as provided in § 1.1502-15A(a) (or § § (1.1502-21T(c) in effect prior to June 25, 1999, as contained in 26 CFR part 1 revised April 1, 1999 and 1.1502-22T(c) in effect prior to June 25, 1999, as contained in 26 CFR part 1 revised April 1, 1999, as provided in 1.1502-15T(a) in effect prior to June 25, 1999, as contained in 26 CFR part 1 revised April 1, 1999) or (1.1502-21(c) and 1.1502-22(c), as provided in 1.1502-15(a), as applicable), as appropriate).

(b) *Effective date.*—This section applies to any consolidated return years to which § 1.1502-21(h) or 1.1502-21T(g) in effect prior to June 25, 1999, as contained in 26 CFR part 1 revised April 1, 1999, as applicable does not apply. See § 1.1502-21(h) or 1.1502-21T(g) in effect prior to

June 25, 1999, as contained in 26 CFR part 1 revised April 1, 1999, as applicable for effective dates of these sections. [Reg. § 1.1502-23A.]

☐ [T.D. 6894, 9-7-66. *Amended by T.D. 7246, 12-29-72. Redesignated and amended by T.D. 8677, 6-26-96. Amended by T.D. 8823, 6-25-99.*]

[Reg. § 1.1502-24]

§ 1.1502-24. Consolidated charitable contributions deductions.—(a) *Determination of amount of consolidated charitable contributions deduction.*—The deduction allowed by section 170 for the taxable year shall be the lesser of—

(1) The aggregate deductions of the members of the group allowable under section 170 (determined without regard to section 170(b)(2)), plus the consolidated charitable contribution carryovers to such year, or

(2) Five percent of the adjusted consolidated taxable income as determined under paragraph (c) of this section.

(b) *Carryover of excess charitable contributions.*— The consolidated charitable contribution carryovers to any consolidated return year shall consist of any excess consolidated charitable contributions of the group, plus any excess charitable contributions of members of the group arising in separate return years of such members, which may be carried over to the taxable year under the principles of section 170(b)(2) and (3). However, such consolidated carryovers shall not include any excess charitable contributions apportioned to a corporation for a separate return year pursuant to paragraph (e) of § 1.1502-79.

(c) *Adjusted consolidated taxable income.*—For purposes of this section, the adjusted consolidated taxable income of the group for any consolidated return year shall be the consolidated taxable income computed without regard to this section, section 242, section 243(a)(2) and (3), §§ 1.1502-25, 1.1502-26, and 1.1502-27, and without regard to any consolidated net operating or net capital loss carrybacks to such year. [Reg. § 1.1502-24.]

☐ [T.D. 6894, 9-7-66. *Amended by T.D. 7637, 8-6-79.*]

[Reg. § 1.1502-26]

§ 1.1502-26. Consolidated dividends received deduction.—(a) *In general.*—(1) The consolidated dividends received deduction for the taxable year shall be the lesser of—

(i) The aggregate of the deduction of the members of the group allowable under sections 243(a)(1), 244(a) and 245 (computed without regard to the limitation provided in section 246(b)), or

(ii) 85 percent of the consolidated taxable income computed without regard to the consolidated net operating loss deduction, consolidated section 247 deduction, the consolidated dividends received deduction, and any consolidated net capital loss carryback to the taxable year.

Subdivision (ii) of this subparagraph shall not apply for any consolidated return year for which there is a consolidated net operating loss. (See §§ 1.1502-21(e) or 1.1502-21A(f), as appropriate for the definition of a consolidated net operating loss.)

(2) If any member computes a deduction under section 593(b)(2) for a taxable year beginning after July 11, 1969, and ending before August 30, 1975, the deduction otherwise computed under this section shall be reduced by an amount determined by multiplying the deduction (determined without regard to this sentence and without regard to dividends received by the common parent if such parent does not use the percentage of income method provided by section 593(b)(2)) by the applicable percentage of the member with the highest applicable percentage (determined under subparagraphs (A) and (B) of section 593(b)(2)).

(3) For taxable years ending on or after August 30, 1975, the deduction otherwise computed under this section shall be reduced by the sum of the amounts determined under paragraph (a)(4) of this section for each member that is a thrift institution that computes a deduction under section 593(b)(2).

(4) For each thrift institution, the amount determined under this subparagraph is the product of—

(i) The portion of the deduction determined with regard to the sum of the dividends received by (A) the thrift institution, and (B) any member in which that thrift institution owns, directly and with the application of paragraph (a)(5) of this section, 5 percent or more of the stock on any day during the consolidated return year, and

(ii) The thrift institution's applicable percentage determined under subparagraphs (A) and (B) of section 593(b)(2).

For purposes of this subparagraph, dividends allocated to a thrift institution under § 1.596-1(c) shall be considered received by the thrift institution.

(5) For purposes of paragraph (a)(4)(i) of this section, a member owning stock of another member (the "second member") shall be considered as owning its proportionate share of any stock of a member owned by the second member. Stock considered as being owned by reason of the preceding sentence shall, for purposes of applying that sentence, be treated as actually owned. The proportionate share of stock in a member owned by another member is the proportion which the value of the stock so owned bears to the value of all the outstanding stock in the member. For purposes of this paragraph the term "stock" includes nonvoting stock which is limited and preferred as to dividends.

(6) For purposes of paragraph (a)(4)(i) of this section, if two or more thrift institutions that are both members of the group each owns 5 percent or more of the same member's stock, the member's stock will be considered to be owned only by the thrift institution with the highest applicable percentage.

(b) *Intercompany dividends.*—The deduction determined under paragraph (a) of this section is determined without taking into account intercompany dividends to the extent that, under § 1.1502-13(f)(2), they are not included in gross income. See § 1.1502-13 for additional rules relating to intercompany dividends.

(c) *Examples.*—The provisions of this section may be illustrated by the following examples:

Example (1). Corporations P, S, and S-1 filed a consolidated return for the calendar year 1966 showing consolidated taxable income of $100,000 (determined without regard to the consolidated net operating loss deduction, consolidated dividends received deduction, and the consolidated section 247 deduction). Such corporations received dividends during such year from nonmember domestic corporations as follows:

Corporation	Dividends
P	$6,000
S	10,000
S-1	34,000
Total	$50,000

The dividends received deduction allowable to each member under section 243(a)(1) (computed without regard to the limitation in section 246(b)) is as follows: P has $5,100 (85 percent of $6,000), S has $8,500 (85 percent of $10,000), and S-1 has $28,900 (85 percent of $34,000), or a total of $42,500. Since $42,500 is less than $85,000 (85 percent of $100,000), the consolidated dividends received deduction is $42,500.

Example (2). Assume the same facts as in example (1) except that consolidated taxable income (computed without regard to the consolidated net operating loss deduction, consolidated dividends received deduction, and the consolidated section 247 deduction) was $40,000. The aggregate of the dividends received deductions, $42,500, computed without regard to section 246(b), results in a consolidated net operating loss of $2,500. See section 172(d)(6). Therefore, paragraph (a)(2) of this section does not apply and the consolidated dividends received deduction is $42,500. [Reg. § 1.1502-26.]

☐ [*T.D. 6894, 9-7-66. Amended by T.D. 7246, 12-29-72; T.D. 7631, 7-10-79; T.D. 8597, 7-12-95; T.D. 8677, 6-26-96 and T.D. 8823, 6-25-99.*]

[Reg. § 1.1502-27]

§ 1.1502-27. Consolidated section 247 deduction.—(a) *Amount of deduction.*—The consolidated section 247 deduction for the taxable year shall be an amount computed as follows:

(1) First, determine the amount which is the lesser of—

(i) The aggregate of the dividends paid (within the meaning of section 247(a)) during such year by members of the group which are public utilities (within the meaning of section 247(b)(1)) on preferred stock (within the meaning of section 247(b)(2)), other than dividends paid to other members of the group, or

(ii) The aggregate of the taxable income (or loss) (as determined under paragraph (b) of this section) of each such member which is a public utility.

(2) Then, multiply the amount determined under subparagraph (1) of this paragraph by the fraction specified in section 247(a)(2).

(b) *Computation of taxable income.*—For purposes of paragraph (a)(1)(ii) of this section, the taxable income (or loss) of a member of the group described in paragraph (a)(1)(i) shall be determined under § 1.1502-12, adjusted for the following items taken into account in the computation of consolidated taxable income:

(1) The portion of the consolidated net operating loss deduction, the consolidated charitable contributions deduction, and the consolidated dividends received deduction, attributable to such member;

(2) Such member's capital gain net income (net capital gain for taxable years beginning before January 1, 1977) (determined without regard to any net capital loss carryover or carryback attributable to such member);

(3) Such member's net capital loss and section 1231 net loss, reduced by the portion of the consolidated net capital loss attributable to such member; and

(4) The portion of any consolidated net capital loss carryover or carryback attributable to such member which is absorbed in the taxable year. [Reg. § 1.1502-27.]

☐ [*T.D. 6894, 9-7-66. Amended by T.D. 7637, 8-6-79 and T.D. 7728, 10-31-80.*]

[Reg. § 1.1502-28]

§ 1.1502-28. Consolidated section 108.—(a) *In general.*—This section sets forth rules for the application of section 108(a) and the reduction of tax attributes pursuant to section 108(b) when a member of the group realizes discharge of indebtedness income that is excluded from gross income under section 108(a) (excluded COD income).

(1) *Application of section 108(a).*—Section 108(a)(1)(A) and (B) is applied separately to each member that realizes excluded COD income. Therefore, the limitation of section 108(a)(3) on the amount of discharge of indebtedness income that is treated as excluded COD income is determined based on the assets (including stock and securities of other members) and liabilities (in-

cluding liabilities to other members) of only the member that realizes excluded COD income.

(2) *Reduction of tax attributes attributable to the debtor.*—(i) *In general.*—With respect to a member that realizes excluded COD income in a taxable year, the tax attributes attributable to that member (and its direct and indirect subsidiaries to the extent required by section 1017(b)(3)(D) and paragraph (a)(3) of this section), including basis of assets and losses and credits arising in separate return limitation years, shall be reduced as provided in sections 108 and 1017 and this section. Basis of subsidiary stock, however, shall not be reduced below zero pursuant to paragraph (a)(2) of this section (including when subsidiary stock is treated as depreciable property under section 1017(b)(3)(D) when there is an election under section 108(b)(5)).

(ii) *Consolidated tax attributes attributable to a member.*—For purposes of this section, the amount of a consolidated tax attribute (e.g., a consolidated net operating loss) that is attributable to a member shall be determined pursuant to the principles of § 1.1502-21(b)(2)(iv). In addition, if the member is a member of a separate return limitation year subgroup, the amount of a tax attribute that arose in a separate return limitation year that is attributable to that member shall also be determined pursuant to the principles of § 1.1502-21(b)(2)(iv).

(3) *Look-through rules.*—(i) *Priority of section 1017(b)(3)(D).*—If a member treats stock of a subsidiary as depreciable property pursuant to section 1017(b)(3)(D), the basis of the depreciable property of such subsidiary shall be reduced pursuant to section 1017(b)(3)(D) prior to the application of paragraph (a)(3)(ii) of this section.

(ii) *Application of additional look-through rule.*—If the basis of stock of a corporation (the lower-tier member) that is owned by another corporation (the higher-tier member) is reduced pursuant to sections 108 and 1017 and paragraph (a)(2) of this section (but not as a result of treating subsidiary stock as depreciable property pursuant to section 1017(b)(3)(D)), and both of such corporations are members of the same consolidated group on the last day of the higher-tier member's taxable year that includes the date on which the excluded COD income is realized or the first day of the higher-tier member's taxable year that follows the taxable year that includes the date on which the excluded COD income is realized, solely for purposes of sections 108 and 1017 and this section other than paragraphs (a)(4) and (b)(1) of this section, the lower-tier member shall be treated as realizing excluded COD income on the last day of the taxable year of the higher-tier member that includes the date on which the higher-tier member realized the excluded COD income. The amount of such ex-

cluded COD income shall be the amount of such basis reduction. Accordingly, the tax attributes attributable to such lower-tier member shall be reduced as provided in sections 108 and 1017 and this section. To the extent that the excluded COD income realized by the lower-tier member pursuant to this paragraph (a)(3) does not reduce a tax attribute attributable to the lower-tier member, such excluded COD income shall not be applied to reduce tax attributes attributable to any member under paragraph (a)(4) of this section and shall not cause an excess loss account to be taken into account under § 1.1502-19(b)(1) and (c)(1)(iii)(B).

(4) *Reduction of certain tax attributes attributable to other members.*—To the extent that, pursuant to paragraph (a)(2) of this section, the excluded COD income is not applied to reduce the tax attributes attributable to the member that realizes the excluded COD income, after the application of paragraph (a)(3) of this section, such amount shall be applied to reduce the remaining consolidated tax attributes of the group, other than consolidated tax attributes to which a SRLY limitation applies, as provided in section 108 and this section. Such amount also shall be applied to reduce the tax attributes attributable to members that arose (or are treated as arising) in a separate return limitation year to the extent that the member that realizes excluded COD income is a member of the separate return limitation year subgroup with respect to such attribute if a SRLY limitation applies to the use of such attribute. In addition, such amount shall be applied to reduce the tax attributes attributable to members that arose in a separate return year or that arose (or are treated as arising) in a separate return limitation year if no SRLY limitation applies to the use of such attribute. The reduction of each tax attribute pursuant to the three preceding sentences shall be made in the order prescribed in section 108(b)(2) and pursuant to the principles of § 1.1502-21(b)(1). Except as otherwise provided in this paragraph (a)(4), a tax attribute that arose in a separate return year or that arose (or is treated as arising) in a separate return limitation year is not subject to reduction pursuant to this paragraph (a)(4). Basis in assets is not subject to reduction pursuant to this paragraph (a)(4). Finally, to the extent that the realization of excluded COD income by a member pursuant to paragraph (a)(3) does not reduce a tax attribute attributable to such lower-tier member, such excess shall not be applied to reduce tax attributes attributable to any member pursuant to this paragraph (a)(4).

(b) *Special rules.*—(1) *Multiple debtor members.*—(i) *Reduction of tax attributes attributable to debtor members prior to reduction of consolidated tax attributes.*—If in a single taxable year multiple members realize excluded COD income, paragraphs (a)(2) and (3) of this section shall apply with respect to the excluded COD income of each such member before the application of paragraph (a)(4) of this section.

(ii) *Reduction of higher-tier debtor's tax attributes.*—If in a single taxable year multiple members realize excluded COD income and one such member is a higher-tier member of another such member, paragraphs (a)(2) and (3) of this section shall be applied with respect to the excluded COD income of the higher-tier member before such paragraphs are applied to the excluded COD income of the other such member. In applying the rules of paragraph (a)(2) and (3) of this section with respect to the excluded COD income of the higher-tier member, the liabilities that give rise to the excluded COD income of the other such member shall not be treated as discharged for purposes of computing the limitation on basis reduction under section 1017(b)(2). A member (the first member) is a higher-tier member of another member (the second member) if the first member is the common parent or investment adjustments under §1.1502-32 with respect to the stock of the second member would affect investment adjustments with respect to the stock of the first member.

(iii) *Reduction of additional tax attributes.*—If more than one member realizes excluded COD income that has not been applied to reduce a tax attribute attributable to such member (the remaining COD amount) and the remaining tax attributes available for reduction under paragraph (a)(4) of this section are less than the aggregate of the remaining COD amounts, after the application of paragraph (a)(2) of this section, each such member's remaining COD amount shall be applied on a pro rata basis (based on the relative remaining COD amounts), pursuant to paragraph (a)(4) of this section, to reduce such remaining available tax attributes.

(iv) *Ownership of lower-tier member by multiple higher-tier members.*—If stock of a corporation is held by more than one higher-tier member of the group and more than one such higher-tier member reduces its basis in such stock, then under paragraph (a)(3) of this section the excluded COD income resulting from the stock basis reductions shall be applied on a pro rata basis (based on the amount of excluded COD income caused by each basis reduction) to reduce the attributes of the corporation.

(v) *Ownership of lower-tier member by multiple higher-tier members in multiple groups.*—If a corporation is a member of one group (the first group) on the last day of the first group's higher-tier member's taxable year that includes the date on which that higher-tier member realizes excluded COD income and is a member of another group (the second group) on the following day and the first group's higher-tier member and the second group's higher-tier member both reduce their basis in the stock of such corporation pursuant to sections 108 and 1017 and this section,

paragraph (a)(3) of this section shall first be applied in respect of the excluded COD income that results from the reduction of the basis of the corporation's stock owned by the first group's higher-tier member and then shall be applied in respect of the excluded COD income that results from the reduction of the basis of the corporation's stock owned by the second group's higher-tier member.

(2) *Election under section 108(b)(5).*— (i) *Availability of election.*—The group may make the election described in section 108(b)(5) for any member that realizes excluded COD income. The election is made separately for each member. Therefore, an election may be made for one member that realizes excluded COD income (either actually or pursuant to paragraph (a)(3) of this section) while another election, or no election, may be made for another member that realizes excluded COD income (either actually or pursuant to paragraph (a)(3) of this section). See §1.108-4 for rules relating to the procedure for making an election under section 108(b)(5).

(ii) *Treatment of shares with an excess loss account.*—For purposes of applying section 108(b)(5)(B), the basis of stock of a subsidiary that has an excess loss account shall be treated as zero.

(3) *Application of section 1017.*—(i) *Timing of basis reduction.*—Basis of property shall be subject to reduction pursuant to the rules of sections 108 and 1017 and this section after the determination of the tax imposed by chapter 1 of the Internal Revenue Code for the taxable year during which the member realizes excluded COD income and any prior years and coincident with the reduction of other attributes pursuant to section 108 and this section. However, only the basis of property held as of the beginning of the taxable year following the taxable year during which the excluded COD income is realized is subject to reduction pursuant to sections 108 and 1017 and this section.

(ii) *Limitation of section 1017(b)(2).*—The limitation of section 1017(b)(2) on the reduction in basis of property shall be applied by reference to the aggregate of the basis of the property held by the member that realizes excluded COD income, not the aggregate of the basis of the property held by all of the members of the group, and the liabilities of such member, not the aggregate liabilities of all of the members of the group.

(iii) *Treatment of shares with an excess loss account.*—For purposes of applying section 1017(b)(2) and §1.1017-1, the basis of stock of a subsidiary that has an excess loss account shall be treated as zero.

(4) *Application of section 1245.*—Notwithstanding section 1017(d)(1)(B), a reduction of the basis of subsidiary stock is treated as a deduction

allowed for depreciation only to the extent that the amount by which the basis of the subsidiary stock is reduced exceeds the total amount of the attributes attributable to such subsidiary that are reduced pursuant to the subsidiary's consent under section 1017(b)(3)(D) or as a result of the application of paragraph (a)(3)(ii) of this section.

(5) *Reduction of basis of intercompany obligations and former intercompany obligations.*— (i) *Intercompany obligations that cease to be intercompany obligations.*—If excluded COD income is realized in a consolidated return year in which an intercompany obligation becomes an obligation that is not an intercompany obligation because the debtor or creditor becomes a nonmember, or because the assets of the debtor or the creditor are acquired by a nonmember in a transaction to which section 381 applies, then the basis of such intercompany obligation (or new obligation if the intercompany obligation is deemed reissued under § 1.1502-13(g)(3)) is available for reduction in respect of such excluded COD income pursuant to sections 108 and 1017 and this section.

(ii) *Intercompany obligations.*—The reduction of the basis of an intercompany obligation pursuant to sections 108 and 1017 and this section shall not result in the satisfaction and reissuance of the obligation under § 1.1502-13(g). Therefore, any income or gain (or reduction of loss or deduction) attributable to a reduction of the basis of an intercompany obligation will be taken into account when § 1.1502-13(g)(3) applies to such obligation. Furthermore, § 1.1502-13(c)(6)(i) (regarding the treatment of intercompany items if corresponding items are excluded or nondeductible) will not apply to exclude any amount of income or gain attributable to a reduction of the basis of an intercompany obligation pursuant to sections 108 and 1017 and this section. See § 1.1502-13(g)(3)(i)(A)(1) and (g)(4)(i)(A).

(6) *Taking into account of excess loss account.*— (i) *Determination of inclusion.*—The determination of whether any portion of an excess loss account in a share of stock of a subsidiary that realizes excluded COD income is required to be taken into account as a result of the application of § 1.1502-19(c)(1)(iii)(B) is made after the determination of the tax imposed by chapter 1 of the Internal Revenue Code for the year during which the member realizes excluded COD income (without regard to whether any portion of an excess loss account in a share of stock of the subsidiary is required to be taken into account) and any prior years, after the reduction of tax attributes pursuant to sections 108 and 1017 and this section, and after the adjustment of the basis of the share of stock of the subsidiary pursuant to § 1.1502-32 to reflect the amount of the subsidiary's deductions and losses that are absorbed in

the computation of taxable income (or loss) for the year of the disposition and any prior years, and the excluded COD income applied to reduce attributes and the attributes reduced in respect thereof. See § 1.1502-11(c) for special rules related to the computation of tax that apply when an excess loss account is required to be taken into account.

(ii) *Timing of inclusion.*—To the extent an excess loss account in a share of stock of a subsidiary that realizes excluded COD income is required to be taken into account as a result of the application of § 1.1502-19(c)(1)(iii)(B), such amount shall be included on the group's tax return for the taxable year that includes the date on which the subsidiary realizes such excluded COD income.

(7) *Dispositions of stock.*—See § 1.1502-11(c) for limitations on the reduction of tax attributes when a member disposes of stock of another member (including dispositions that result from the application of § 1.1502-19(c)(1)(iii)(B)) during a taxable year in which any member realizes excluded COD income.

(8) *Departure of member.*—If the taxable year of a member (the departing member) during which such member realizes excluded COD income ends on or prior to the last day of the consolidated return year and, on the first day of the taxable year of such member that follows the taxable year during which such member realizes excluded COD income, such member is not a member of the group and does not have a successor member (within the meaning of paragraph (b)(10) of this section), all tax attributes listed in section 108(b)(2) that remain after the determination of the tax imposed that belong to members of the group (including the departing member and subsidiaries of the departing member) shall be subject to reduction as provided in section 108 and the regulations promulgated thereunder (including § 1.108-7(c), if applicable) and this section.

(9) *Intragroup reorganization.*—(i) *In general.*—If the taxable year of a member during which such member realizes excluded COD income ends prior to the last day of the consolidated return year and, on the first day that follows the taxable year of such member during which such member realizes excluded COD income, such member has a successor member, for purposes of applying the rules of sections 108 and 1017 and this section, notwithstanding § 1.108-7, the successor member shall be treated as the member that realized the excluded COD income. Thus, all attributes attributable to the successor member listed in section 108(b)(2) (including attributes that were attributable to the successor member prior to the date such member became a successor member) are available for reduction under paragraph (a)(2) of this section.

Reg. § 1.1502-28(b)(9)(i)

(ii) *Group structure change.*—If a member that realizes excluded COD income acquires the assets of the common parent of the consolidated group in a transaction to which section 381(a) applies and succeeds such common parent under the principles of §1.1502-75(d)(2) as the common parent of the consolidated group, the member's attributes that remain after the determination of tax for the group for the consolidated return year during which the excluded COD income is realized (and any prior years) (including attributes that were attributable to the former common parent prior to the date of the transaction to which section 381(a) applies) shall be available for reduction under paragraph (a)(2) of this section.

(10) *Definition of successor member.*—A successor member means a person to which the member that realizes excluded COD income (or a successor member) transfers its assets in a transaction to which section 381(a) applies if such transferee is a member of the group immediately after the transaction.

(11) *Non-application of next day rule.*—For purposes of applying the rules of sections 108 and 1017 and this section, the next day rule of §1.1502-76(b)(1)(ii)(B) shall not apply to treat a member's excluded COD income as realized at the beginning of the day following the day on which such member's status as a member changes.

(c) *Examples.*—The principles of paragraphs (a) and (b) of this section are illustrated by the following examples. Unless otherwise indicated, no election under section 108(b)(5) has been made and the taxable year of all consolidated groups is the calendar year. The examples are as follows:

Example 1. (i) *Facts.* P is the common parent of a consolidated group that includes subsidiary S1. P owns 80 percent of the stock of S1. In Year 1, the P group sustained a $250 consolidated net operating loss. Under the principles of §1.1502-21(b)(2)(iv), of that amount, $125 was attributable to P and $125 was attributable to S1. On Day 1 of Year 2, P acquired 100 percent of the stock of S2, and S2 joined the P group. As of the beginning of Year 2, S2 had a $50 net operating loss carryover from Year 1, a separate return limitation year. In Year 2, the P group sustained a $200 consolidated net operating loss. Under the principles of §1.1502-21(b)(2)(iv), of that amount, $90 was attributable to P, $70 was attributable to S1, and $40 was attributable to S2. In Year 3, S2 realized $200 of excluded COD income from the discharge of non-intercompany indebtedness. In that same year, the P group sustained a $50 consolidated net operating loss, of which $40 was attributable to S1 and $10 was attributable to S2 under the principles of §1.1502-21(b)(2)(iv). As of the beginning of Year 4, S2 had Asset A with a fair market value of $10. After the compu-

tation of tax imposed for Year 3 and before the application of sections 108 and 1017 and this section, Asset A had a basis of $40 and S2 had no liabilities.

(ii) *Analysis*—(A) *Reduction of tax attributes attributable to debtor.* Pursuant to paragraph (a)(2) of this section, the tax attributes attributable to S2 must first be reduced to take into account its excluded COD income in the amount of $200.

(1) *Reduction of net operating losses.* Pursuant to section 108(b)(2)(A) and paragraph (a) of this section, the net operating loss and the net operating loss carryovers attributable to S2 under the principles of §1.1502-21(b)(2)(iv) are reduced in the order prescribed by section 108(b)(4)(B). Accordingly, the consolidated net operating loss for Year 3 is reduced by $10, the portion of the consolidated net operating loss attributable to S2, to $40. Then, again pursuant to section 108(b)(4)(B), S2's net operating loss carryover of $50 from its separate return limitation year is reduced to $0. Finally, the consolidated net operating loss carryover from Year 2 is reduced by $40, the portion of that consolidated net operating loss carryover attributable to S2, to $160.

(2) *Reduction of basis.* Following the reduction of the net operating loss and the net operating loss carryovers attributable to S2, S2 reduces its basis in its assets pursuant to section 1017 and §1.1017-1. Accordingly, S2 reduces its basis in Asset A by $40, from $40 to $0.

(B) *Reduction of remaining consolidated tax attributes.* The remaining $60 of excluded COD income then reduces consolidated tax attributes pursuant to paragraph (a)(4) of this section. In particular, the remaining $40 consolidated net operating loss for Year 3 is reduced to $0. Then, the consolidated net operating loss carryover from Year 1 is reduced by $20 from $250 to $230. Pursuant to paragraph (a)(4) of this section, a pro rata amount of the consolidated net operating loss carryover from Year 1 that is attributable to each of P and S1 is treated as reduced. Therefore, $10 of the consolidated net operating loss carryover from Year 1 that is attributable to each of P and S1 is treated as reduced.

Example 2. (i) *Facts.* P is the common parent of a consolidated group that includes subsidiaries S1 and S2. P owns 100 percent of the stock of S1 and S1 owns 100 percent of the stock of S2. None of P, S1, or S2 has a separate return limitation year. In Year 1, the P group sustained a $50 consolidated net operating loss. Under the principles of §1.1502-21(b)(2)(iv), of that amount, $10 was attributable to P, $20 was attributable to S1, and $20 was attributable to S2. In Year 2, the P group sustained a $70 consolidated net operating loss. Under the principles of §1.1502-21(b)(2)(iv), of that amount, $30 was attributable to P, $30 was attributable to S1, and $10 was attributable to S2. In Year 3, S1 realized $170 of excluded COD income from the discharge of non-intercompany indebtedness. In that same year, the P group sustained a $50 consolidated net operating loss, of which $10 was attributable to S1 and $40 was attributable to S2 under the principles of § 1.1502-21(b)(2)(iv). As of the beginning of Year 4, S1's sole asset was the stock of S2, and S2 had Asset A with a $10 value. After the computation of tax imposed for Year 3 and before the application of sections 108 and 1017 and this section, S1 had a $80 basis in the S2 stock, Asset A had a basis of $0, and neither S1 nor S2 had any liabilities.

(ii) *Analysis*—(A) *Reduction of tax attributes attributable to debtor.* Pursuant to paragraph (a)(2) of this section, the tax attributes attributable to S1 must first be reduced to take into account its excluded COD income in the amount of $170.

(*1*) *Reduction of net operating losses.* Pursuant to section 108(b)(2)(A) and paragraph (a) of this section, the net operating loss and the net operating loss carryovers attributable to S1 under the principles of § 1.1502-21(b)(2)(iv) are reduced in the order prescribed by section 108(b)(4)(B). Accordingly, the consolidated net operating loss for Year 3 is reduced by $10, the portion of the consolidated net operating loss for Year 3 attributable to S1, to $40. Then, the consolidated net operating loss carryover from Year 1 is reduced by $20, the portion of that consolidated net operating loss carryover attributable to S1, to $30, and the consolidated net operating loss carryover from Year 2 is reduced by $30, the portion of that consolidated net operating loss carryover attributable to S1, to $40.

(*2*) *Reduction of basis.* Following the reduction of the net operating loss and the net operating loss carryovers attributable to S1, S1 reduces its basis in its assets pursuant to section 1017 and § 1.1017-1. Accordingly, S1 reduces its basis in the stock of S2 by $80, from $80 to $0.

(*3*) *Tiering down of stock basis reduction.* Pursuant to paragraph (a)(3) of this section, for purposes of sections 108 and 1017 and this section, S2 is treated as realizing $80 of excluded COD income. Pursuant to section 108(b)(2)(A) and paragraph (a) of this section, therefore, the net operating loss and net operating loss carryovers attributable to S2 under the principles of § 1.1502-21(b)(2)(iv) are reduced in the order prescribed by section 108(b)(4)(B). Accordingly, the consolidated net operating loss for Year 3 is reduced by an additional $40, the portion of the consolidated net operating loss for Year 3 attributable to S2, to $0. Then, the consolidated net operating loss carryover from Year 1 is reduced by $20, the portion of that consolidated net operating loss carryover attributable to S2, to $10. Then, the consolidated net operating loss carryover from Year 2 is reduced by $10, the portion of that consolidated net operating loss carryover attributable to S2, to $30. S2's remaining $10 of excluded COD income does not reduce consolidated tax attributes attributable to P or S1 under paragraph (a)(4) of this section.

(B) *Reduction of remaining consolidated tax attributes.* Finally, pursuant to paragraph (a)(4) of this

section, S1's remaining $30 of excluded COD income reduces the remaining consolidated tax attributes. In particular, the remaining $10 consolidated net operating loss carryover from Year 1 is reduced by $10 to $0, and the remaining $30 consolidated net operating loss carryover from Year 2 is reduced by $20 to $10.

Example 3. (i) *Facts.* P is the common parent of a consolidated group that includes subsidiaries S1, S2, and S3. P owns 100 percent of the stock of S1, S1 owns 100 percent of the stock of S2, and S2 owns 100 percent of the stock of S3. None of P, S1, S2, or S3 had a separate return limitation year prior to Year 1. In Year 1, the P group sustained a $150 consolidated net operating loss. Under the principles of § 1.1502-21(b)(2)(iv), of that amount, $50 was attributable to S2, and $100 was attributable to S3. In Year 2, the P group sustained a $50 consolidated net operating loss. Under the principles of § 1.1502-21(b)(2)(iv), of that amount, $40 was attributable to S1 and $10 was attributable to S2. In Year 3, S1 realized $170 of excluded COD income from the discharge of non-intercompany indebtedness. In that same year, the P group sustained a $50 consolidated net operating loss, of which $10 was attributable to S1, $20 was attributable to S2, and $20 was attributable to S3 under the principles of § 1.1502-21(b)(2)(iv). At the beginning of Year 4, S1's only asset was the stock of S2, and S2's only asset was the stock of S3 with a value of $10. After the computation of tax imposed for Year 3 and before the application of sections 108 and 1017 and this section, S1's stock of S2 had a basis of $120 and S2's stock of S3 had a basis of $180. In addition, none of S1, S2, and S3 had any liabilities.

(ii) *Analysis*—(A) *Reduction of tax attributes attributable to debtor.* Pursuant to paragraph (a)(2) of this section, the tax attributes attributable to S1 must first be reduced to take into account its excluded COD income in the amount of $170.

(*1*) *Reduction of net operating losses.* Pursuant to section 108(b)(2)(A) and paragraph (a) of this section, the net operating loss and the net operating loss carryovers attributable to S1 under the principles of § 1.1502-21(b)(2)(iv) are reduced in the order prescribed by section 108(b)(4)(B). Accordingly, the consolidated net operating loss for Year 3 is reduced by $10, the portion of the consolidated net operating loss attributable to S1, to $40. Then, the consolidated net operating loss carryover from Year 2 is reduced by $40, the portion of that consolidated net operating loss carryover attributable to S1, to $10.

(*2*) *Reduction of basis.* Following the reduction of the net operating loss and the net operating loss carryovers attributable to S1, S1 reduces its basis in its assets pursuant to section 1017 and § 1.1017-1. Accordingly, S1 reduces its basis in the stock of S2 by $120, from $120 to $0.

(B) *Tiering down of stock basis reduction to S2.* Pursuant to paragraph (a)(3) of this section, for purposes of sections 108 and 1017 and this section, S2 is treated as realizing $120 of excluded

COD income. Pursuant to section 108(b)(2)(A) and paragraph (a) of this section, therefore, the net operating loss and net operating loss carryovers attributable to S2 under the principles of § 1.1502-21(b)(2)(iv) are reduced in the order prescribed by section 108(b)(4)(B). Accordingly, the consolidated net operating loss for Year 3 is further reduced by $20, the portion of the consolidated net operating loss attributable to S2, to $20. Then, the consolidated net operating loss carryover from Year 1 is reduced by $50, the portion of that consolidated net operating loss carryover attributable to S2, to $100. Then, the consolidated net operating loss carryover from Year 2 is further reduced by $10, the portion of that consolidated net operating loss carryover attributable to S2, to $0. Following the reduction of the net operating loss and the net operating loss carryovers attributable to S2, S2 reduces its basis in its assets pursuant to section 1017 and § 1.1017-1. Accordingly, S2 reduces its basis in its S3 stock by $40 to $140.

(C) *Tiering down of stock basis reduction to S3.* Pursuant to paragraph (a)(3) of this section, for purposes of sections 108 and 1017 and this section, S3 is treated as realizing $40 of excluded COD income. Pursuant to section 108(b)(2)(A) and paragraph (a) of this section, therefore, the net operating loss and the net operating loss carryovers attributable to S3 under the principles of § 1.1502-21(b)(2)(iv) are reduced in the order prescribed by section 108(b)(4)(B). Accordingly, the consolidated net operating loss for Year 3 is further reduced by $20, the portion of the consolidated net operating loss attributable to S3, to $0. Then, the consolidated net operating loss carryover from Year 1 is reduced by $20, the lesser of the portion of that consolidated net operating loss carryover attributable to S3 and the remaining excluded COD income, to $80.

Example 4. (i) *Facts.* P is the common parent of a consolidated group that includes subsidiaries S1, S2, and S3. P owns 100 percent of the stock of each of S1 and S2. Each of S1 and S2 owns stock of S3 that represents 50 percent of the value of the stock of S3. None of P, S1, S2, or S3 had a separate return limitation year prior to Year 1. In Year 1, the P group sustained a $160 consolidated net operating loss. Under the principles of § 1.1502-21(b)(2)(iv), of that amount, $10 was attributable to P, $50 was attributable to S2, and $100 was attributable to S3. In Year 2, the P group sustained a $110 consolidated net operating loss. Under the principles of § 1.1502-21(b)(2)(iv), of that amount, $40 was attributable to S1 and $70 was attributable to S2. In Year 3, S1 realized $200 of excluded COD income from the discharge of non-intercompany indebtedness, and S2 realized $270 of excluded COD income from the discharge of non-intercompany indebtedness. In that same year, the P group sustained a $50 consolidated net operating loss, of which $10 was attributable to S1, $20 was attributable to S2, and $20 was attributable to S3

under the principles of § 1.1502-21(b)(2)(iv). At the beginning of Year 4, S3 had one asset with a value of $10. After the computation of tax imposed for Year 3 and before the application of sections 108 and 1017 and this section, S1's basis in its S3 stock was $60, S2's basis in its S3 stock was $120, and S3's asset had a basis of $200. In addition, none of S1, S2, and S3 had any liabilities.

(ii) *Analysis*—(A) *Reduction of tax attributes attributable to debtors.* Pursuant to paragraph (b)(1)(i) of this section, the tax attributes attributable to each of S1 and S2 are reduced pursuant to paragraph (a)(2) of this section. Then, pursuant to paragraph (a)(3) of this section, the tax attributes attributable to S3 are reduced so as to reflect a reduction of S1's and S2's basis in the stock of S3. Then, paragraph (a)(4) is applied to reduce additional tax attributes.

(1) *Reduction of net operating losses generally.* Pursuant to section 108(b)(2)(A) and paragraph (a) of this section, the net operating losses and the net operating loss carryovers attributable to S1 and S2 under the principles of § 1.1502-21(b)(2)(iv) are reduced in the order prescribed by section 108(b)(4)(B).

(2) *Reduction of net operating losses attributable to S1.* The consolidated net operating loss for Year 3 is reduced by $10, the portion of the consolidated net operating loss attributable to S1, to $40. Then, the consolidated net operating loss carryover from Year 2 is reduced by $40, the portion of that consolidated net operating loss carryover attributable to S1, to $70.

(3) *Reduction of net operating losses attributable to S2.* The consolidated net operating loss for Year 3 is also reduced by $20, the portion of the consolidated net operating loss attributable to S2, to $20. Then, the consolidated net operating loss carryover from Year 1 is reduced by $50, the portion of that consolidated net operating loss carryover attributable to S2, to $110. Then, the consolidated net operating loss carryover from Year 2 is reduced by $70, the portion of that consolidated net operating loss carryover attributable to S2, to $0.

(4) *Reduction of basis.* Following the reduction of the net operating losses and the net operating loss carryovers attributable to S1 and S2, S1 and S2 must reduce their basis in their assets pursuant to section 1017 and § 1.1017-1. Accordingly, S1 reduces its basis in the stock of S3 by $60, from $60 to $0, and S2 reduces its basis in the stock of S3 by $120, from $120 to $0.

(B) *Tiering down of basis reduction.* Pursuant to paragraph (a)(3) of this section, for purposes of sections 108 and 1017 and this section, S3 is treated as realizing $180 of excluded COD income. Pursuant to section 108(b)(2)(A) and paragraph (a) of this section, therefore, the net operating loss and the net operating loss carryovers attributable to S3 under the principles of § 1.1502-21(b)(2)(iv) are reduced in the order prescribed by section 108(b)(4)(B). Accordingly, the consolidated net operating loss for Year 3 is further reduced by $20, the portion of the consolidated net operating loss attributable to S3, to $0. Then, the consolidated net operating loss carryover from Year 1 is reduced by $100, the portion of that consolidated net operating loss carryover attributable to S3, to $10. Following the reduction of the net operating loss and the net operating loss carryover attributable to S3, S3 reduces its basis in its asset pursuant to section 1017 and § 1.1017-1. Accordingly, S3 reduces its basis in its asset by $60, from $200 to $140.

(C) *Reduction of remaining consolidated tax attributes.* Finally, pursuant to paragraph (a)(4) of this section, the remaining $90 of S1's excluded COD income and the remaining $10 of S2's excluded COD income reduce the remaining consolidated tax attributes. In particular, the remaining $10 consolidated net operating loss carryover from Year 1 is reduced by $10 to $0. Because that amount is less than the aggregate amount of remaining excluded COD income, such income is applied on a pro rata basis to reduce the remaining consolidated tax attributes. Accordingly, $9 of S1's remaining excluded COD income and $1 of S2's remaining excluded COD income is applied to reduce the remaining consolidated net operating loss carryover from Year 1. Consequently, of S1's excluded COD income of $200, only $119 is applied to reduce tax attributes, and, of S2's excluded COD income of $270, only $261 is applied to reduce tax attributes.

Example 5. (i) *Facts.* P is the common parent of a consolidated group that includes subsidiaries S1, S2, and S3. P owns 100 percent of the stock of S1 and S2, and S1 owns 100 percent of the stock of S3. None of P, S1, S2, or S3 has a separate return limitation year prior to Year 1. In Year 1, the P group sustained a $90 consolidated net operating loss. Under the principles of § 1.1502-21(b)(2)(iv), of that amount, $10 was attributable to P, $15 was attributable to S1, $20 was attributable to S2, and $45 was attributable to S3. On January 1 of Year 2, P realized $140 of excluded COD income from the discharge of non-intercompany indebtedness. On December 31 of Year 2, S1 issued stock representing 50 percent of the vote and value of its outstanding stock to a person that was not a member of the group. As a result of the issuance of stock, S1 and S3 ceased to be members of the P group. For the consolidated return year of Year 2, the P group sustained a $60 consolidated net operating loss, of which $5 was attributable to S1, $40 was attributable to S2, and $15 was attributable to S3 under the principles of § 1.1502-21(b)(2)(iv). As of the beginning of Year 3, P's only assets were the stock of S1 and S2, S1's sole asset was the stock of S3, S2 had Asset A with a value of $10, and S3 had Asset B with a value of $10. After the computation of tax imposed for Year 2 and before the application of sections 108 and 1017 and this section, P had a $80 basis in the S1 stock and a $50 basis in the S2 stock, S1 had a $80 basis

in the S3 stock, and Asset A and B each had a basis of $10. In addition, none of P, S1, S2, and S3 had any liabilities.

(ii) *Analysis.* Pursuant to paragraph (a)(2) of this section, the tax attributes attributable to P must first be reduced to take into account its excluded COD income in the amount of $140.

(A) *Reduction of net operating losses.* Pursuant to section 108(b)(2)(A) and paragraph (a) of this section, the net operating loss and the net operating loss carryover attributable to P under the principles of § 1.1502-21(b)(2)(iv) are reduced in the order prescribed by section 108(b)(4)(B). Accordingly, the consolidated net operating loss carryover from Year 1 is reduced by $10, the portion of that consolidated net operating loss carryover attributable to P, to $80.

(B) *Reduction of basis.* Following the reduction of the net operating loss and the net operating loss carryover attributable to P, P reduces its basis in its assets pursuant to section 1017 and § 1.1017-1. Accordingly, P reduces its basis in the stock of S1 by $80, from $80 to $0, and its basis in the stock of S2 by $50, from $50 to $0.

(C) *Tiering down of stock basis reduction to S1.* Pursuant to paragraph (a)(3) of this section, for purposes of sections 108 and 1017 and this section, S1 is treated as realizing $80 of excluded COD income, despite the fact that it ceases to be a member of the group at the end of the day on December 31 of Year 2. Pursuant to section 108(b)(2)(A) and paragraph (a) of this section, therefore, the net operating loss and net operating loss carryovers attributable to S1 under the principles of § 1.1502-21(b)(2)(iv) are reduced in the order prescribed by section 108(b)(4)(B). Accordingly, the consolidated net operating loss for Year 2 is reduced by $5, the portion of the consolidated net operating loss for Year 2 attributable to S1, to $55. Then, the consolidated net operating loss carryover from Year 1 is reduced by an additional $15, the portion of that consolidated net operating loss carryover attributable to S1, to $65. Following the reduction of the net operating loss and the net operating loss carryover attributable to S1, S1 reduces its basis in its assets pursuant to section 1017 and § 1.1017-1. Accordingly, S1 reduces its basis in the stock of S3 by $60, from $80 to $20.

(D) *Tiering down of stock basis reduction to S2.* Pursuant to paragraph (a)(3) of this section, for purposes of sections 108 and 1017 and this section, S2 is treated as realizing $50 of excluded COD income. Pursuant to section 108(b)(2)(A) and paragraph (a) of this section, therefore, the net operating loss and net operating loss carryovers attributable to S2 under the principles of § 1.1502-21(b)(2)(iv) are reduced in the order prescribed by section 108(b)(4)(B). Accordingly, the consolidated net operating loss for Year 2 is reduced by an additional $40, the portion of the consolidated net operating loss for Year 2 attributable to S2, to $15. Then, the consolidated net operating loss carryover from Year 1 is reduced by an additional $10, a portion of the consolidated net operating loss carryover attributable to S2, to $55.

(E) *Tiering down of stock basis reduction to S3.* Pursuant to paragraph (a)(3) of this section, for purposes of sections 108 and 1017 and this section, S3 is treated as realizing $60 of excluded COD income (by reason of S1's reduction in its basis of its S3 stock). Pursuant to section 108(b)(2)(A) and paragraph (a) of this section, therefore, the net operating loss and net operating loss carryovers attributable to S3 under the principles of §1.1502-21(b)(2)(iv) are reduced in the order prescribed by section 108(b)(4)(B). Accordingly, the consolidated net operating loss for Year 2 is reduced by an additional $15, the portion of the consolidated net operating loss for Year 2 attributable to S3, to $0. Then, the consolidated net operating loss carryover from Year 1 is reduced by an additional $45, the portion of that consolidated net operating loss carryover attributable to S3, to $10.

Example 6. (i) *Facts.* P1 is the common parent of a consolidated group that includes subsidiaries S1, S2, and S3. P1 owns 100 percent of the stock of S1 and S2. S1 owns 100 percent of the stock of S3. None of P1, S1, S2, or S3 has a separate return limitation year prior to Year 1. In Year 1, the P1 group sustained a $120 consolidated net operating loss. Under the principles of §1.1502-21(b)(2)(iv), of that amount, $40 was attributable to P1, $35 was attributable to S1, $30 was attributable to S2, and $15 was attributable to S3. On January 1 of Year 2, S3 realized $65 of excluded COD income from the discharge of non-intercompany indebtedness. On June 30 of Year 2, S3 issued stock representing 80 percent of the vote and value of its outstanding stock to P2, the common parent of another group. As a result of the issuance of stock, S3 ceased to be a member of the P1 group and became a member of the P2 group. For the consolidated return year of Year 2, the P1 group sustained a $50 consolidated net operating loss, of which $5 was attributable to S1, $40 was attributable to S2, and $5 was attributable to S3 under the principles of §1.1502-21(b)(2)(iv). As of the beginning of its taxable year beginning on July 1 of Year 2, S3's sole asset was Asset A with a $10 value. After the computation of tax imposed for Year 2 on the P1 group and before the application of sections 108 and 1017 and this section and the computation of tax imposed for Year 2 on the P2 group, Asset A had a basis of $0. In addition, S3 had no liabilities. On January 1 of Year 3, P1 sold all of its stock of S1.

(ii) *Analysis*—(A) *Reduction of tax attributes attributable to debtor.* Pursuant to paragraph (a)(2) of this section, the tax attributes attributable to S3 must first be reduced to take into account its excluded COD income in the amount of $65. Pursuant to section 108(b)(2)(A) and paragraph (a) of this section, the net operating loss and the net operating loss carryover attributable to S3

under the principles of §1.1502-21(b)(2)(iv) are reduced in the order prescribed by section 108(b)(4)(B). Accordingly, the consolidated net operating loss for Year 2 is reduced by $5, the portion of the consolidated net operating loss for Year 2 attributable to S3, to $45. Then, the consolidated net operating loss carryover from Year 1 is reduced by $15, the portion of that consolidated net operating loss carryover attributable to S3, to $105.

(B) *Reduction of remaining consolidated tax attributes.* Pursuant to paragraphs (a)(4) and (b)(8) of this section, S3's remaining $45 of excluded COD income reduces the remaining consolidated tax attributes in the P1 group. In particular, the remaining $45 consolidated net operating loss for Year 2 is reduced by an additional $45 to $0.

(C) *Basis Adjustments.* For purposes of computing P1's gain or loss on the sale of the S1 stock in Year 3, P1's basis in its S1 stock will reflect a net positive adjustment of $40, which is the excess of the amount of S3's excluded COD income that is applied to reduce attributes ($65) over the reduction of S1's and S3's attributes in respect of such excluded COD income ($25).

Example 7. (i) *Facts.* P is the common parent of a consolidated group that includes subsidiaries S1 and S2. P owns 100 percent of the stock of S1, and S1 owns 100 percent of the stock of S2. None of P, S1, or S2 has a separate return limitation year prior to Year 1. In Year 1, the P group sustained a $50 consolidated net operating loss. Under the principles of §1.1502-21(b)(2)(iv), of that amount, $10 was attributable to P, $20 was attributable to S1, and $20 was attributable to S2. On January 1 of Year 2, S1 realized $55 of excluded COD income from the discharge of non-intercompany indebtedness. On June 30 of Year 2, P transferred all of its assets to S1 in a transaction to which section 381(a) applied. As a result of that transaction, pursuant to §1.1502-75(d)(2)(ii), S1 succeeded P as the common parent of the group. Pursuant to §1.1502-75(d)(2)(iii), S1's taxable year closed on the date of the acquisition. However, P's taxable year did not close. On the consolidated return for Year 2, the group sustained a $50 consolidated net operating loss. Under the principles of §1.1502-21(b)(2)(iv), of that amount, $10 was attributable to S1 for its taxable year that ended on June 30, $15 was attributable to S1 as the successor of P, and $25 was attributable to S2.

(ii) *Analysis.* Pursuant to paragraph (a)(2) of this section, the tax attributes attributable to S1 must first be reduced to take into account its excluded COD income in the amount of $55. For this purpose, S1's attributes that remain after the determination of tax for the group for Year 2 are subject to reduction. Pursuant to section 108(b)(2)(A) and paragraph (a) of this section, the net operating loss and the net operating loss carryover attributable to S1 under the principles of §1.1502-21(b)(2)(iv) are reduced. Accordingly, the consolidated net operating loss for Year 2 is reduced by $25, the portion of the consolidated net operating loss for Year 2 attributable to S1, to $25. Then, the consolidated net operating loss carryover from Year 1 is reduced by $30, the portion of that consolidated net operating loss carryover attributable to S1 (which includes the portion attributable to P), to $20.

(d) *Effective dates.*—This section applies to discharges of indebtedness that occur after March 21, 2005. Groups, however, may apply this section in whole, but not in part, to discharges of indebtedness that occur on or before March 21, 2005, and after August 29, 2003. For discharges of indebtedness occurring on or before March 21, 2005, and after August 29, 2003, with respect to which a group chooses not to apply this section, see § 1.1502-28T as contained in 26 CFR part 1 revised as of April 1, 2004. Furthermore, groups may apply paragraph (b)(4) of this section to discharges of indebtedness that occur on or before August 29, 2003, in cases in which section 1017(b)(3)(D) was applied. Paragraph (b)(5)(i) of this section and the last sentence of paragraph (b)(5)(ii) of this section applies to transactions occurring in consolidated return years beginning on or after December 24, 2008. [Reg. § 1.1502-28.]

☐ [*T.D.* 9192, 3-21-2005. *Amended by T.D.* 9442, 12-24-2008.]

[Reg. § 1.1502-30]

§ 1.1502-30. Stock basis after certain triangular reorganizations.—(a) *Scope.*—This section provides rules for determining the basis of the stock of an acquiring corporation as a result of a triangular reorganization. The definitions and nomenclature contained in § 1.358-6 apply to this section.

(b) *General rules.*—(1) *Forward triangular merger. triangular C reorganization, or triangular B reorganization.*—P adjusts its basis in the stock of S as a result of a forward triangular merger, triangular C reorganization, or triangular B reorganization under § 1.358-6(c) or (d). Sections § 1.358-6(c)(1)(ii) and (d)(2) do not apply. Instead, P adjusts such basis by taking into account the full amount of—

(i) T liabilities assumed by S or the amount of liabilities to which the T assets acquired by S are subject, and

(ii) The fair market value of any consideration not provided by P pursuant to the plan of reorganization.

(2) *Reverse triangular merger.*—If P adjusts its basis in the T stock acquired as a result of a reverse triangular merger under § 1.358-6(c)(2)(i) and (d), § 1.358-6(c)(1)(ii) and (d)(2) do not apply. Instead, P adjusts such basis by taking into account the full amount of—

(i) T liabilities deemed assumed by S or the amount of liabilities to which the T assets deemed acquired by S are subject, and

(ii) The fair market value of any consideration not provided by P pursuant to the plan of reorganization.

(3) *Excess loss accounts.*—Negative adjustments under this section may exceed P's basis in its S or T stock. The resulting negative amount is P's excess loss account in its S or T stock. See § 1.1502-19 for rules treating excess loss accounts as negative basis, and treating references to stock basis as including references to excess loss accounts.

(4) *Application of other rules of law.*—If a transaction otherwise subject to this section is also a group structure change subject to § 1.1502-31, the provisions of § 1.1502-31 and not this section apply to determine stock basis. See § 1.1502-80(a) regarding the general applicability of other rules of law and a limitation on duplicative adjustments. See § 1.1502-80(d) for the nonapplication of section 357(c) to P.

(5) *Examples.*—The rules of this paragraph (b) are illustrated by the following examples. For purposes of these examples, P, S, and T are domestic corporations, P and S file consolidated returns P owns all of the only class of S stock, the P stock exchanged in the transaction satisfies the requirements of the applicable triangular reorganization provisions, the facts set forth the only corporate activity, and tax liabilities are disregarded.

Example 1. Liabilities. (a) *Facts.* T has assets with an aggregate basis of $60 and fair market value of $100. T's assets are subject to $70 of liabilities. Pursuant to a plan, P forms S with $5 of cash (which S retains), and T merges into S. In the merger, the T shareholders receive P stock worth $30 in exchange for their T stock. The transaction is a reorganization to which sections 368(a)(1)(A) and (a)(2)(D) apply.

(b) *Basis adjustment.* Under § 1.358-6, P adjusts its $5 basis in the S stock as if P had acquired the T assets with a carryover basis under section 362 and transferred these assets to S in a transaction in which P determines its basis in the S stock under section 358. Under the rules of this section, the limitation described in § 1.358-6(c)(1)(ii) does not apply. Thus, P adjusts its basis in the S stock by –$10 (the aggregate adjusted basis of T's assets decreased by the amount of liabilities to which the T assets are subject). Consequently, as a result of the reorganization, P has an excess loss account of $5 in its S stock.

Example 2. Consideration not provided by P. (a) *Facts.* T has assets with an aggregate basis of $10 and fair market value of $100 and no liabilities. S is an operating company with substantial assets that has been in existence for several years. P has a $5 basis in its S stock. Pursuant to a plan, T merges into S and the T shareholders receive $70 of P stock provided by P pursuant to the plan of reorganization and $30 of cash provided by S in exchange for their T stock. The transaction is a reorganization to which sections 368(a)(1)(A) and (a)(2)(D) apply.

(b) *Basis adjustment.* Under §1.358-6, P adjusts its $5 basis in the S stock as if P had acquired the T assets with a carryover basis under section 362 and transferred these assets to S in a transaction in which P determines its basis in the S stock under section 358. Under the rules of this section, the limitation described in §1.358-6(d)(2) does not apply. Thus, P adjusts its basis in the S stock by –$20 (the aggregate adjusted basis of T's assets decreased by the fair market value of the consideration provided by S). As a result of the reorganization, P has an excess loss account of $15 in its S stock.

(c) *Appreciated asset.* The facts are the same as in paragraph (a) of this *Example 2*, except that in the reorganization S provides an asset with a $20 adjusted basis and $30 fair market value instead of $30 cash. The basis is adjusted in the same manner as in paragraph (b) of this *Example 2*. In addition, because S recognizes a $10 gain from the asset under section 1001, P's basis in its S stock is increased under §1.1502-32(b) by S's $10 gain. Consequently, as a result of the reorganization P has an excess loss account of $5 in its S stock. (The results would be the same if the appreciated asset provided by S was P stock with respect to which S recognized gain. See §1.1032-2(c)).

Example 3. Reverse triangular merger. (a) *Facts.* T has assets with an aggregate basis of $60 and fair market value of $100. T's assets are subject to $70 of liabilities. P owns all of the only class of S stock. P has a $5 basis in its S stock. Pursuant to a plan, S merges into T with T surviving. In the merger, the T shareholders exchange their T stock for $2 cash from P and $28 worth of P stock provided by P pursuant to the plan. The transaction is a reorganization to which sections 368(a)(1)(A) and (a)(2)(E) apply.

(b) *Basis adjustment.* Under §1.358-6, P's basis in the T stock acquired equals its $5 basis in its S stock immediately before the transaction adjusted by the $60 basis in the T assets deemed transferred, and the $70 of liabilities to which the T assets are subject. Under the rules of this section, the limitation described in §1.358-6(c)(1)(ii) does not apply. Consequently, P has an excess loss account of $5 in its T stock as a result of the transaction.

(c) *Effective/applicability date.*—This section applies to reorganizations occurring on or after December 21, 1995. However, paragraph (b)(4) of this section applies to reorganizations occurring on or after September 17, 2008. [Reg. §1.1502-30.]

☐ [T.D. 8648, 12-20-95. Amended by T.D. 9424, 9-9-2008.]

Reg. §1.1502-30(c)

[Reg. §1.1502-31]

§1.1502-31. Stock basis after a group structure change.—(a) *In general.*—(1) *Overview.*—If one corporation (P) succeeds another corporation (T) under the principles of §1.1502-75(d)(2) or (3) as the common parent of a consolidated group in a group structure change, the basis of members in the stock of the former common parent (or the stock of a successor) is adjusted or determined under this section. See §1.1502-33(f)(1) for the definition of group structure change. For example, if P owns all of the stock of another corporation (S), and T merges into S in a group structure change that is a reorganization described in section 368(a)(2)(D) in which P becomes the common parent of the T group, P's basis in S's stock must be adjusted to reflect the change in S's assets and liabilities. The rules of this section coordinate with the earnings and profits adjustments required under §1.1502-33(f)(1), generally conforming the results of transactions in which the T group continues under §1.1502-75 with P as the common parent. By preserving in P the relationship between T's earnings and profits and asset basis, these adjustments limit possible distortions under section 1502 (e.g., in the deconsolidation rules for earnings and profits under §1.1502-33(e), and the continued filing requirements under §1.1502-75(a)). This section applies whether or not T continues to exist after the group structure change.

(2) *Application of other rules of law.*—If a transaction subject to this section is also a triangular reorganization otherwise subject to §1.1502-30, the provisions of this section and not those of §1.1502-30 apply to determine stock basis. See §1.1502-80(a) regarding the general applicability of other rules of law and a limitation on duplicative adjustments.

(b) *General rules.*—Except as otherwise provided in this section—

(1) *Asset acquisitions.*—If a corporation acquires the former common parent's assets (and any liabilities assumed or to which the assets are subject) in a group structure change, the basis of members in the stock of the acquiring corporation is adjusted immediately after the group structure change to reflect the acquiring corporation's allocable share of the former common parent's net asset basis as determined under paragraph (c) of this section. For example, if S acquires all of T's assets in a group structure change that is a reorganization described in section 368(a)(2)(D), P's basis in S's stock is adjusted to reflect T's net asset basis. If P owned some of T's stock before the group structure change, the results would be the same because P's basis in the T stock is not taken into account in determining P's basis in S's stock. If T's net asset basis is a negative amount, it reduces P's basis in S's stock and, if the reduction exceeds P's basis in S's

stock, the excess is P's excess loss account in S's stock. See § 1.1502-19 for rules treating P's excess loss account as negative basis, and treating a reference to P's basis in S's stock as including an excess loss account.

(2) *Stock acquisitions.*—If a corporation acquires stock of the former common parent in a group structure change, the basis of the members in the former common parent's stock immediately after the group structure change (including any stock of the former common parent owned before the group structure change) that is, or would otherwise be, transferred basis property is redetermined in accordance with the results for an asset acquisition described in paragraph (b)(1) of this section. For example, if all of T's stock is contributed to P in a group structure change to which section 351 applies, P's basis in T's stock is T's net asset basis, rather than the amount determined under section 362. Similarly, if S merges into T in a group structure change described in section 368(a)(2)(E) and P acquires all of the T stock, P's basis in T's stock is the basis that P would have in S's stock under paragraph (b)(1) of this section if T had merged into S in a group structure change described in section 368(a)(2)(D).

(c) *Net asset basis.*—The former common parent's net asset basis is the basis it would have in the stock of a newly formed subsidiary, if—

(1) The former common parent transferred its assets (and any liabilities assumed or to which the assets are subject) to the subsidiary in a transaction to which section 351 applies;

(2) The former common parent and the subsidiary were members of the same consolidated group (see § 1.1502-80(d) for the non-application of section 357(c) to the transfer); and

(3) The asset basis taken into account is each asset's basis immediately after the group structure change (e.g., taking into account any income or gain recognized in the group structure change and reflected in the asset's basis).

(d) *Additional adjustments.*—In addition to the adjustments in paragraph (b) of this section, the following adjustments are made:

(1) *Consideration not provided by P.*—The basis is reduced to reflect the fair market value of any consideration not provided by the member. For example, if S acquires T's assets in a group structure change described in section 368(a)(2)(D), and S provides an appreciated asset (e.g., stock of P) as partial consideration in the transaction, P's basis in S's stock is reduced by the fair market value of the asset.

(2) *Allocable share.*—(i) *Asset acquisitions.*—If a corporation receives less than all of the former common parent's assets and liabilities in the group structure change, the former common parent's net asset basis taken into account under

paragraph (b)(1) of this section is adjusted accordingly.

(ii) *Stock acquisitions.*—If less than all of the former common parent's stock is subject to the redetermination described in paragraph (b)(2) of this section, the percentage of the former common parent's net asset basis taken into account in the redetermination equals the percentage (by fair market value) of the former common parent's stock subject to the redetermination. For example, if P owns less than all of the former common parent's stock immediately after the group structure change and such stock would otherwise be transferred basis property, only an allocable part of the basis determined under this section is reflected in the shares owned by P (and the amount allocable to shares owned by non-members has no effect on the basis of their shares). Alternatively, if P acquired 10 percent of the former common parent's stock in a transaction in which the stock basis was determined by P's cost, and P later acquires the remaining 90 percent of the former common parent's stock in a separate transaction that is described in paragraph (b)(2) of this section, P retains its cost basis in its original stock and the basis of P's newly acquired shares reflects only an allocable part of the former common parent's net asset basis.

(3) *Allocation among shares of stock.*—The basis determined under this section is allocated among shares under the principles of section 358. For example, if P owns multiple classes of the former common parent's stock immediately after the group structure change, only an allocable part of the basis determined under this section is reflected in the basis of each share. See § 1.1502-19(d), for special allocations with respect to excess loss accounts.

(4) *Higher-tier members.*—To the extent that the former common parent is owned by members other than the new common parent, the basis of members in the stock of all subsidiaries owning, directly or indirectly, in whole or in part, an interest in the former common parent's assets or liabilities is adjusted in accordance with the principles of this section. The adjustments are applied in the order of the tiers, from the lowest to the highest.

(e) *Waiver of loss carryovers of former common parent.*—(1) *General rule.*—An irrevocable election may be made to treat all or any portion of a loss carryover attributable to the common parent as expiring for all Federal income tax purposes immediately before the group structure change. Thus, if the loss carryover is treated as expiring under the election, it will not result in a negative adjustment to the basis of P's stock under § 1.1502-32(b).

(2) *Election.*—The election described in paragraph (e)(1) of this section must be made in a separate statement entitled, "ELECTION TO

TREAT LOSS CARRYOVER AS EXPIRING UNDER §1.1502-31(e)." The election must be filed by including the statement on or with the consolidated group's income tax return for the year that includes the group structure change. The statement must identify the amount of each loss carryover deemed to expire (or the amount of each loss carryover deemed not to expire, with any balance of any loss carryovers being deemed to expire).

(f) *Predecessors and successors.*—For purposes of this section, any reference to a corporation includes a reference to a successor or predecessor as the context may require. See §1.1502-32(f) for definitions of predecessor and successor.

(g) *Examples.*—For purposes of the examples in this section, unless otherwise stated, all corporations have only one class of stock outstanding, the tax year of all persons is the calendar year, all persons use the accrual method of accounting, the facts set forth the only corporate activity, all transactions are between unrelated persons, and tax liabilities are disregarded. The principles of this section are illustrated by the following examples:

Example 1. Forward triangular merger. (i) *Facts.* P is the common parent of one group and T is the common parent of another. T has assets with an aggregate basis of $60 and fair market value of $100 and no liabilities. T's shareholders have an aggregate basis of $50 in T's stock. In Year 1, pursuant to a plan, P forms S and T merges into S with the T shareholders receiving $100 of P stock in exchange for their T stock. The transaction is a reorganization described in section 368(a)(2)(D). The transaction is also a reverse acquisition under §1.1502-75(d)(3) because the T shareholders, as a result of owning T's stock, own more than 50% of the value of P's stock immediately after the transaction. Thus, the transaction is a group structure change under §1.1502-33(f)(1), and P's earnings and profits are adjusted to reflect T's earnings and profits immediately before T ceases to be the common parent of the T group.

(ii) *Analysis.* Under paragraph (b)(1) of this section, P's basis in S's stock is adjusted to reflect T's net asset basis. Under paragraph (c) of this section, T's net asset basis is $60, the basis T would have in the stock of a subsidiary under section 358 if T had transferred all of its assets and liabilities to the subsidiary in a transaction to which section 351 applies. Thus, P has a $60 basis in S's stock.

(iii) *Pre-existing S.* The facts are the same as in paragraph (i) of this *Example 1*, except that P has owned the stock of S for several years and P has a $50 basis in the S stock before the merger with T. Under paragraph (b)(1) of this section, P's $50 basis in S's stock is adjusted to reflect T's net asset basis. Thus, P's basis in S's stock is $110 ($50 plus $60).

(iv) *Excess loss account included in former common parent's net asset basis.* The facts are the same as in paragraph (i) of this *Example 1*, except that T has two assets, an operating asset with an $80 basis and $90 fair market value, and stock of a subsidiary with a $20 excess loss account and $10 fair market value. Under paragraph (c) of this section, T's net asset basis is $60 ($80 minus $20). See sections 351 and 358, and §1.1502-19. Consequently, P has a $60 basis in S's stock. Under section 362 and §1.1502-19, S has an $80 basis in the operating asset and a $20 excess loss account in the stock of the subsidiary.

(v) *Liabilities in excess of basis.* The facts are the same as in paragraph (i) of this *Example 1*, except that T's assets have a fair market value of $170 (and $60 basis) and are subject to $70 of liabilities. Under paragraph (c) of this section, T's net asset basis is negative $10 ($60 minus $70). See sections 351 and 358, and §§1.1502-19 and 1.1502-80(d). Thus, P has a $10 excess loss account in S's stock. Under section 362, S has a $60 basis in its assets (which are subject to $70 of liabilities). (Under paragraph (a)(2) of this section, because the liabilities are taken into account in determining net asset basis under paragraph (c) of this section, the liabilities are not also taken into account as consideration not provided by P under paragraph (d)(1) of this section.)

(vi) *Consideration provided by S.* The facts are the same as in paragraph (i) of this *Example 1*, except that P forms S with a $100 contribution at the beginning of Year 1, and during Year 6, pursuant to a plan, S purchases $100 of P stock and T merges into S with the T shareholders receiving P stock in exchange for their T stock. Under paragraph (b)(1) of this section, P's $100 basis in S's stock is increased by $60 to reflect T's net asset basis. Under paragraph (d)(1) of this section, P's basis in S's stock is decreased by $100 (the fair market value of the P stock) because the P stock purchased by S and used in the transaction is consideration not provided by P.

(vii) *Appreciated asset provided by S.* The facts are the same as in paragraph (i) of this *Example 1*, except that P has owned the stock of S for several years, and the shareholders of T receive $60 of P stock and an asset of S with a $30 adjusted basis and $40 fair market value. S recognizes a $10 gain from the asset under section 1001. Under paragraph (b)(1) of this section, P's basis in S's stock is increased by $60 to reflect T's net asset basis. Under paragraph (d)(1) of this section, P's basis in S's stock is decreased by $40 (the fair market value of the asset provided by S). In addition, P's basis in S's stock is increased under §1.1502-32(b) by S's $10 gain.

(viii) *Depreciated asset provided by S.* The facts are the same as in paragraph (i) of this *Example 1*, except that P has owned the stock of S for several years, and the shareholders of T receive $60 of P stock and an asset of S with a $50 adjusted basis and $40 fair market value. S recognizes a $10 loss from the asset under section 1001. Under paragraph (b)(1) of this section, P's basis in S's stock is increased by $60 to reflect T's net asset basis. Under paragraph (d)(1) of this section, P's basis in S's stock is decreased by $40 (the fair market value of the asset provided by S). In addition, S's $10 loss is taken into account under §1.1502-32(b) in determining P's basis adjustments under that section.

Example 2. Stock acquisition. (i) *Facts.* P is the common parent of one group and T is the common parent of another. T has assets with an aggregate basis of $60 and fair market value of $100 and no liabilities. T's shareholders have an aggregate basis of $50 in T's stock. Pursuant to a plan, P forms S and S acquires all of T's stock in exchange for P stock in a transaction described in section 368(a)(1)(B). The transaction is also a reverse acquisition under §1.1502-75(d)(3). Thus, the transaction is a group structure change under §1.1502-33(0(1), and the earnings and profits of P and S are adjusted to reflect T's earnings and profits immediately before T ceases to be the common parent of the T group.

(ii) *Analysis.* Under paragraph (d)(4) of this section, although S is not the new common parent of the T group, adjustments must be made to S's basis in T's stock in accordance with the principles of this section. Although S's basis in T's stock would ordinarily be determined under section 362 by reference to the basis of T's shareholders in T's stock immediately before the group structure change, under the principles of paragraph (b)(2) of this section, S's basis in T's stock is determined by reference to T's net asset basis. Thus, S's basis in T's stock is $60.

(iii) *Higher-tier adjustments.* Under paragraph (d)(4) of this section, P's basis in S's stock is increased by $60 (to be consistent with the adjustment to S's basis in T's stock).

(iv) *Cross ownership.* The facts are the same as in paragraph (i) of this *Example 2*, except S purchased 10% of T's stock from an unrelated person for cash. in an unrelated transaction, S acquires the remaining 90% of T's stock in exchange for P stock. S's basis in the initial 10% of T's stock is not redetermined under this section. However, S's basis in the additional 90% of T's stock is redetermined under this section. S's basis in that stock is adjusted to $54 (90% of T's net asset basis).

(v) *Allocable share.* The facts are the same as in paragraph (i) of this *Example 2*, except that P owns only 90% of S's stock immediately after the group structure change. S's basis in T's stock is the same as in paragraph (ii) of this *Example 2*. Under paragraph (d)(2) of this section, P's basis in its S stock is increased by $54 (90% of S's $60 adjustment).

Example 3. Taxable stock acquisition. (i) *Facts.* P is the common parent of one group and T is the common parent of another. T has assets with an aggregate basis of $60 and fair market value of $100 and no liabilities. T's shareholders have an aggregate basis of $50 in T's stock. Pursuant to a

plan, P acquires all of T's stock in exchange for $70 of P's stock and $30 in a transaction that is a group structure change under §1.1502-33(f)(1). P's acquired T stock is not transferred basis property. (Because of P's use of cash, the acquisition is not a transaction described in section 368(a)(1)(B).)

(ii) *Analysis.* The rules of this section do not apply to determine P's basis in T's stock. Therefore, P's basis in T's stock is $100.

(h) *Effective/applicability dates.*—(1) *General rule.*—This section applies to group structure changes that occur after April 26, 2004. However, a group may apply this section to group structure changes that occurred on or before April 26, 2004, and in consolidated return years beginning on or after January 1, 1995. In addition, paragraph (a)(2) of this section applies to group structure changes that occurred on or after September 17, 2008. Paragraph (e)(2) of this section applies to any original consolidated Federal income tax return due (without extensions) after June 14, 2007. For original consolidated Federal income tax returns due (without extensions) after May 30, 2006, and on or before June 14, 2007, see §1.1502-31T as contained in 26 CFR part 1 in effect on April 1, 2007. For original consolidated Federal income tax returns due (without extensions) on or before May 30, 2006, see §1.1502-31 as contained in 26 CFR part 1 in effect on April 1, 2006.

(2) *Prior law.*—For group structure changes that occur on or before April 26, 2004, and in consolidated return years beginning on or after January 1, 1995, with respect to which the group does not elect to apply the provisions of this section, see §1.1502-31 as contained in the 26 CFR part 1 edition revised as of April 1, 2003. For group structure changes that occur in consolidated return years beginning before January 1, 1995, see §1.1502-31T as contained in the 26 CFR part 1 edition revised as of April 1, 1994. [Reg. §1.1502-31.]

☐ [*T.D.* 6909, 12-29-66. *Amended by T.D.* 7246, 12-29-72; *T.D.* 8226, 9-7-88; *T.D.* 8560, 8-12-94; *T.D.* 9122, 4-23-2004; *T.D.* 9264, 5-26-2006; *T.D.* 9329, 6-13-2007 *and T.D.* 9424, 9-9-2008.]

[Reg. §1.1502-32]

§1.1502-32. Investment adjustments.—(a) *In general.*—(1) *Purpose.*—This section provides rules for adjusting the basis of the stock of a subsidiary (S) owned by another member (M). These rules modify the determination of M's basis in S's stock under applicable rules of law by adjusting M's basis to reflect S's distributions and S's items of income, gain, deduction, and loss taken into account for the period that S is a member of the consolidated group. The purpose of the adjustments is to treat M and S as a single entity so that consolidated taxable income reflects the group's income. For example, if M forms S with a $100 contribution, and S takes into account $10 of income, M's $100 basis in S's stock under section 358 is increased by $10 under this section to prevent S's income from being taken into account a second time on M's disposition of S's stock. Comparable adjustments are made for tax-exempt income and noncapital, nondeductible expenses that S takes into account, to preserve their treatment under the Internal Revenue Code.

(2) *Application of other rules of law, duplicative adjustments.*—See § 1.1502-80(a) regarding the general applicability of other rules of law and a limitation on duplicative adjustments. The rules of this section are in addition to other rules of law. See, e.g., section 358 (basis determinations for distributees), section 1016 (adjustments to basis), § 1.1502-11(b) (limitations on the use of losses), § 1.1502-19 (treatment of excess loss accounts), § 1.1502-31 (basis after a group structure change), and § 1.1502-35 (additional rules relating to stock loss, including losses attributable to worthlessness and certain dispositions not followed by a separate return year). M's basis in S's stock must not be adjusted under this section and other rules of law in a manner that has the effect of duplicating an adjustment.

(3) *Overview.*—(i) *In general.*—The amount of the stock basis adjustments and their timing are determined under paragraph (b) of this section. Under paragraph (c) of this section, the amount of the adjustment is allocated among the shares of S's stock. Paragraphs (d) through (g) of this section provide definitions, an anti-avoidance rule, successor rules, and recordkeeping requirements.

(ii) *Excess loss account.*—Negative adjustments under this section may exceed M's basis in S's stock. The resulting negative amount is M's excess loss account in S's stock. See § 1.1502-19 for rules treating excess loss accounts as negative basis, and treating references to stock basis as including references to excess loss accounts.

(iii) *Tiering up of adjustments.*—The adjustments to S's stock under this section are taken into account in determining adjustments to higher-tier stock. The adjustments are applied in the order of the tiers, from the lowest to the highest. For example, if M is also a subsidiary, M's adjustment to S's stock is taken into account in determining the adjustments to stock of M owned by other members.

(b) *Stock basis adjustments.*—(1) *Timing of adjustments.*—(i) *In general.*—Adjustments under this section are made as of the close of each consolidated return year, and as of any other time (an interim adjustment) if a determination at that time is necessary to determine a tax liability of any person. For example, adjustments are made as of M's sale of S's stock in order to measure M's gain or loss from the sale, and if

M's interest in S's stock is not uniform throughout the year (e.g., because M disposes of a portion of its S stock, or S issues additional shares to another person), the adjustments under this section are made by taking into account the varying interests. An interim adjustment may be necessary even if tax liability is not affected until a later time. For example, if M sells only 50% of S's stock and S becomes a nonmember, adjustments must be made for the retained stock as of the disposition (whether or not M has an excess loss account in that stock). Similarly, if S liquidates during a consolidated return year, adjustments must be made as of the liquidation (even if the liquidation is tax free under section 332).

(ii) *Special rule for discharge of indebtedness income.*—Adjustments under this section resulting from the realization of discharge of indebtedness income of a member that is excluded from gross income under section 108(a) (excluded COD income) and from the reduction of attributes in respect thereof pursuant to sections 108 and 1017 and § 1.1502-28 (including reductions in the basis of property) when a member (the departing member) ceases to be a member of the group on or prior to the last day of the consolidated return year that includes the date the excluded COD income is realized are made immediately after the determination of tax for the group for the taxable year during which the excluded COD income is realized (and any prior years) and are effective immediately before the beginning of the taxable year of the departing member following the taxable year during which the excluded COD income is realized. Such adjustments when a corporation (the new member) is not a member of the group on the last day of the consolidated return year that includes the date the excluded COD income is realized but is a member of the group at the beginning of the following consolidated return year are also made immediately after the determination of tax for the group for the taxable year during which the excluded COD income is realized (and any prior years) and are effective immediately before the beginning of the taxable year of the new member following the taxable year during which the excluded COD income is realized. If the new member was a member of another group immediately before it became a member of the group, such adjustments are treated as occurring immediately after it ceases to be a member of the prior group.

(iii) *Allocation of items.*—If § 1.1502-76(b) applies to S for purposes of an adjustment before the close of the group's consolidated return year, the amount of the adjustment is determined under that section. If § 1.1502-76(b) does not apply to the interim adjustment, the adjustment is determined under the principles of § 1.1502-76(b), consistently applied, and ratable allocation under the principles of § 1.1502-76(b)(2)(ii) or (iii) may be used without filing an election under § 1.1502-76(b)(2). The principles would apply, for example, if M becomes a nonmember but S remains a member.

(2) *Amount of adjustments.*—M's basis in S's stock is increased by positive adjustments and decreased by negative adjustments under this paragraph (b)(2). The amount of the adjustment, determined as of the time of the adjustment, is the net amount of S's—

(i) Taxable income or loss;

(ii) Tax-exempt income;

(iii) Noncapital, nondeductible expenses; and

(iv) Distributions with respect to S's stock.

(3) *Operating rules.*—For purposes of determining M's adjustments to the basis of S's stock under paragraph (b)(2) of this section—

(i) *Taxable income or loss.*—S's taxable income or loss is consolidated taxable income (or loss) determined by including only S's items of income, gain, deduction, and loss taken into account in determining consolidated taxable income (or loss), treating S's deductions and losses as taken into account to the extent they are absorbed by S or any other member. For this purpose:

(A) To the extent that S's deduction or loss is absorbed in the year it arises or is carried forward and absorbed in a subsequent year (e.g., under section 172, 465, or 1212), the deduction or loss is taken into account under paragraph (b)(2) of this section in the year in which it is absorbed.

(B) To the extent that S's deduction or loss is carried back and absorbed in a prior year (whether consolidated or separate), the deduction or loss is taken into account under paragraph (b)(2) of this section in the year in which it arises and not in the year in which it is absorbed.

(ii) *Tax-exempt income.*—(A) *In general.*—S's tax-exempt income is its income and gain which is taken into account but permanently excluded from its gross income under applicable law, and which increases, directly or indirectly, the basis of its assets (or an equivalent amount). For example, S's dividend income to which § 1.1502-13(f)(2)(ii) applies, and its interest excluded from gross income under section 103, are treated as tax-exempt income. However, S's income not recognized under section 1031 is not treated as tax-exempt income because the corresponding basis adjustments under section 1031(d) prevent S's nonrecognition from being permanent. Similarly, S's tax-exempt income does not include gain not recognized under section 332 from the liquidation of a lower-tier subsidiary, or not recognized under section 118 or section 351 from a transfer of assets to S.

(B) *Equivalent deductions.*—To the extent that S's taxable income or gain is permanently

offset by a deduction or loss that does not reduce, directly or indirectly, the basis of S's assets (or an equivalent amount), the income or gain is treated as tax-exempt income and is taken into account under paragraph (b)(3)(ii)(A) of this section. In addition, the income and the offsetting item are taken into account under paragraph (b)(3)(i) of this section. For example, if S receives a $100 dividend with respect to which a $70 dividends received deduction is allowed under section 243, $70 of the dividend is treated as tax-exempt income. Accordingly, M's basis in S's stock increases by $100 because the $100 dividend and $70 deduction are taken into account under paragraph (b)(3)(i) of this section (resulting in $30 of the increase), and $70 of the dividend is also taken into account under paragraph (b)(3)(ii)(A) of this section as tax-exempt income (resulting in $70 of the increase). (See paragraph (b)(3)(iii) of this section if there is a corresponding negative adjustment under section 1059.) Similarly, income from mineral properties is treated as tax-exempt income to the extent it is offset by deductions for depletion in excess of the basis of the property.

(C) *Discharge of indebtedness income.*—(1) *In general.*—Excluded COD income is treated as tax-exempt income only to the extent the discharge is applied to reduce tax attributes attributable to any member of the group under section 108, section 1017 or § 1.1502-28. However, if S is treated as realizing excluded COD income pursuant to § 1.1502-28(a)(3), S shall not be treated as realizing excluded COD income for purposes of the preceding sentence.

(2) *Expired loss carryovers.*—If the amount of the discharge exceeds the amount of the attribute reduction under sections 108 and 1017, and § 1.1502-28, the excess nevertheless is treated as applied to reduce tax attributes to the extent a loss carryover attributable to S expired without tax benefit, the expiration was taken into account as a noncapital, nondeductible expense under paragraph (b)(3)(iii) of this section, and the loss carryover would have been reduced had it not expired.

(D) *Basis shifts.*—An increase in the basis of S's assets (or an equivalent as described in paragraph (b)(3)(iv)(B) of this section) is treated as tax-exempt income to the extent that the increase is not otherwise taken into account in determining stock basis, it corresponds to a negative adjustment that is taken into account by the group under this paragraph (b) (or incurred by the common parent), and it has the effect (viewing the group in the aggregate) of a permanent recovery of the reduction. For example, S's basis increase under section 50(c)(2) is treated as tax-exempt income to the extent the preceding basis reduction under section 50(c)(1) is reflected in the basis of a member's stock. On the other hand, if S increases the basis of an asset as the result of an accounting method change, and the related positive section 481(a) adjustment is taken into account over time, the basis increase is not treated as tax-exempt income.

(iii) *Noncapital, nondeductible expenses.*— (A) *In general.*—S's noncapital, nondeductible expenses are its deductions and losses that are taken into account but permanently disallowed or eliminated under applicable law in determining its taxable income or loss, and that decrease, directly or indirectly, the basis of its assets (or an equivalent amount). For example, S's Federal taxes described in section 275 and loss not recognized under section 311(a) are noncapital, nondeductible expenses. Similarly, if a loss carryover (e.g., under section 172 or 1212) attributable to S expires or is reduced under section 108(b) and § 1.1502-28, it becomes a noncapital, nondeductible expense at the close of the last tax year to which it may be carried. However, when a tax attribute attributable to S is reduced as required pursuant to § 1.1502-28(a)(3), the reduction of the tax attribute is not treated as a noncapital, nondeductible expense of S. Finally, if S sells and repurchases a security subject to section 1091, the disallowed loss is not a noncapital, nondeductible expense because the corresponding basis adjustments under section 1091(d) prevent the disallowance from being permanent.

(B) *Nondeductible basis recovery.*—Any other decrease in the basis of S's assets (or an equivalent as described in paragraph (b)(3)(iv)(B) of this section) may be a noncapital, nondeductible expense to the extent that the decrease is not otherwise taken into account in determining stock basis and is permanently eliminated for purposes of determining S's taxable income or loss. Whether a decrease is so treated is determined by taking into account both the purposes of the Code or regulatory provision resulting in the decrease and the purposes of this section. For example, S's noncapital, nondeductible expenses include any basis reduction under section 50(c)(1), section 1017, section 1059, § 1.1502-35(b) or (f)(2). Also included as a noncapital, nondeductible expense is the amount of any gross-up for taxes paid by another taxpayer that S is treated as having paid (e.g., income included under section 78, or the portion of an undistributed capital gain dividend that is treated as tax deemed to have been paid by a shareholder under section 852(b)(3)(D)(ii), whether or not any corresponding amount is claimed as a tax credit). In contrast, a decrease generally is not a noncapital, nondeductible expense if it results because S redeems stock in a transaction to which section 302(a) applies, S receives assets in a liquidation to which section 332 applies and its basis in the assets is less than its basis in the stock canceled, or S distributes the stock of a subsidiary in a distribution to which section 355 applies.

(iv) *Special rules for tax-exempt income and noncapital, nondeductible expenses.*—For purposes of paragraphs (b)(3)(ii) and (iii) of this section:

(A) *Treatment as permanent.*—An amount is permanently excluded from gross income, or permanently disallowed or eliminated, if it is so treated by S even though another person may take a corresponding amount into account. For example, if S sells property to a nonmember at a loss that is disallowed under section 267(a), S's loss is a noncapital, nondeductible expense even though under section 267(d) the nonmember may treat a corresponding amount of gain as not recognized. (If the nonmember is a subsidiary in another consolidated group, its gain not recognized under section 267(d) is tax-exempt income under paragraph (b)(3)(ii)(A) of this section.)

(B) *Amounts equivalent to basis and adjustments to basis.*—Amounts equivalent to basis include the amount of money, the amount of a loss carryover, and the amount of an adjustment to gain or loss under section 475(a) for securities described in section 475(a)(2). An equivalent to a basis increase includes a decrease in an excess loss account, and an equivalent to a basis decrease includes the denial of basis for taxable income.

(C) *Timing.*—An amount is taken into account in the year in which it would be taken into account under paragraph (b)(3)(i) of this section if it were subject to Federal income taxation.

(D) *Tax sharing agreements.*—Taxes are taken into account by applying the principles of section 1552 and the percentage method under § 1.1502-33(d)(3) (and by assuming a 100% allocation of any decreased tax liability). The treatment of amounts allocated under this paragraph (b)(3)(iv)(D) is analogous to the treatment of allocations under § 1.1552-1(b)(2). For example, if one member owes a payment to a second member, the first member is treated as indebted to the second member. The right to receive payment is treated as a positive adjustment under paragraph (b)(3)(ii) of this section, and the obligation to make payment is treated as a negative adjustment under paragraph (b)(3)(iii) of this section. If the obligation is not paid, the amount not paid generally is treated as a distribution, contribution, or both, depending on the relationship between the members.

(v) *Distributions.*—Distributions taken into account under paragraph (b)(2) of this section are distributions with respect to S's stock to which section 301 applies and all other distributions treated as dividends (e.g., under section 356(a)(2)). See § 1.1502-13(f)(2)(iv) for taking into account distributions to which section 301 applies (but not other distributions treated as dividends) under the entitlement rule.

(4) *Waiver of loss carryovers from separate return limitation years.*—(i) *General rule.*—If S has a loss carryover from a separate return limitation year when it becomes a member of a consolidated group, the group may make an irrevocable election to treat all or any portion of the loss carryover as expiring for all Federal income tax purposes immediately before S becomes a member of the consolidated group (deemed expiration). If S was a member of another group immediately before it became a member of the consolidated group, the expiration is also treated as occurring immediately after it ceases to be a member of the prior group.

(ii) *Stock basis adjustments from a waiver.*—(A) *Qualifying transactions.*—If S becomes a member of the consolidated group in a qualifying cost basis transaction and an election under this paragraph (b)(4) is made, the noncapital, nondeductible expense resulting from the deemed expiration does not result in a corresponding stock basis adjustment for any member under this section. A qualifying cost basis transaction is the purchase (i.e., a transaction in which basis is determined under section 1012) by members of the acquiring consolidated group (while they are members) in a 12-month period of an amount of S's stock satisfying the requirements of section 1504(a)(2).

(B) *Nonqualifying transactions.*—If S becomes a member of the consolidated group other than in a qualifying cost basis transaction and an election under this paragraph (b)(4) is made, the basis of its stock that is owned by members immediately after it becomes a member is subject to reduction under the principles of this section to reflect the deemed expiration. The reduction occurs immediately before S becomes a member, but after it ceases to be a member of any prior group, and it therefore does not result in a corresponding stock basis adjustment for any higher-tier member of the transferring or acquiring consolidated group. Any basis reduction under this paragraph (b)(4)(ii)(B) is taken into account in making determinations of basis under the Code with respect to S's stock (e.g., a determination under section 362 because the stock is acquired in a transaction described in section 368(a)(1)(B)), but it does not result in corresponding stock basis adjustments under this section for any higher-tier member. If the basis reduction exceeds the basis of S's stock, the excess is treated as an excess loss account to which the members owning S's stock succeed.

(C) *Higher-tier corporations.*—If S becomes a member of the consolidated group as a result, in whole or in part, of a higher-tier corporation becoming a member (whether or not in a qualifying cost basis transaction), additional adjustments are required. The highest-tier corporation (T) whose becoming a member resulted in S becoming a member, and T's chain of lower-tier corporations that includes S, are subject to the adjustment. The deemed expiration of S's loss carryover that results in a negative adjustment for the first higher-tier corporation is treated as an expiring loss carryover of that higher-tier corporation for purposes of applying paragraph (b)(4)(ii)(B) of this section to that corporation. For example, if M purchases all of the stock of T, T owns all of the stock of T1, T1 owns all of the stock of S, S becomes a member as a result of T becoming a member, and the election under this paragraph (b)(4) is made, the basis of the S stock is reduced and the reduction tiers up to T1, T1 treats the negative adjustment to its basis in S's stock as an expiring loss carryover of T1, and T then adjusts its basis in T1's stock. In addition, if T becomes a member of the acquiring group in a transaction other than a qualifying cost basis transaction, the amount that tiers up to T also reduces the basis of its stock under paragraph (b)(4)(ii)(B) of this section (but the amount does not tier up to higher-tier members).

(iii) *Net asset basis limitation.*—Basis reduced under this paragraph (b)(4) is restored before S becomes a member (and before the basis of S's stock is taken into account in determining basis under the Code) to the extent necessary to conform a share's basis to its allocable portion of net asset basis. In the case of higher-tier corporations under paragraph (b)(4)(ii)(C) of this section, the restoration does not tier up but is instead applied separately to each higher-tier corporation. For purposes of determining each corporation's net asset basis (including the basis of stock in lower-tier corporations), the restoration is applied in the order of tiers, from the lowest to the highest. For purposes of the restoration:

(A) A member's net asset basis is the positive or negative difference between the adjusted basis of its assets (and the amount of any of its loss carryovers that are not deemed to expire) and its liabilities. Appropriate adjustments must be made, for example, to disregard liabilities that subsequently will give rise to deductions (e.g., liabilities to which section 461(h) applies).

(B) Within a class of stock, each share has the same allocable portion of net asset basis. If there is more than one class of common stock, the net asset basis is allocated to each class by taking into account the terms of each class and all other facts and circumstances relating to the overall economic arrangement.

(iv) *Election.*—The election described in paragraph (b)(4) of this section must be made in a separate statement entitled, "ELECTION TO TREAT LOSS CARRYOVER OF [INSERT NAME AND EMPLOYER IDENTIFICATION NUMBER OF S] AS EXPIRING UNDER §1.1502-32(b)(4)." The election must be filed by including a statement on or with the consolidated group's income tax return for the year S becomes a member. A separate statement must be made for each member whose loss carryover is deemed to expire. The statement must identify the amount of each loss carryover deemed to expire (or the amount of each loss carryover deemed not to expire, with any balance of any loss carryovers being deemed to expire) and the basis of any stock reduced as a result of the deemed expiration.

(v) *Special rule for loss carryovers of a subsidiary acquired in a transaction for which an election under §1.1502-20(i)(2) is made.*—(A) *Expired losses.*—Notwithstanding paragraph (b)(4)(iv) of this section, unless a group otherwise chooses, to the extent that S's loss carryovers are increased by reason of an election under §1.1502-20(i)(2) and such loss carryovers expire or would have been properly used to offset income in a taxable year for which the refund of an overpayment is prevented by any law or rule of law as of the date the group files its original return for the taxable year in which S receives the notification described in §1.1502-20(i)(3)(iv) and at all times thereafter, the group will be deemed to have made an election under paragraph (b)(4) of this section to treat all of such loss carryovers as expiring for all Federal income tax purposes immediately before S became a member of the consolidated group. A group may choose not to apply the rule of the previous sentence to all of such loss carryovers of S by taking a position on an original or amended tax return for each relevant taxable year that is consistent with having made such choice.

(B) *Available losses.*—Notwithstanding paragraph (b)(4)(iv) of this section, to the extent that S's loss carryovers are increased by reason of an election under §1.1502-20(i)(2) and such loss carryovers have not expired and would not have been properly used to offset income in a taxable year for which the refund of an overpayment is prevented by any law or rule of law as of the date the group files its original return for the taxable year in which S receives the notification described in §1.1502-20(i)(3)(iv) and at all times thereafter, the group may make an election under paragraph (b)(4) of this section to treat all or a portion of such loss carryovers as expiring for all Federal income tax purposes immediately before S became a member of the consolidated group. Such election must be filed with the group's original return for the taxable year in which S receives the notification described in §1.1502-20(i)(3)(iv).

(C) *Effective dates.*—Paragraph (b)(4)(v) of this section is applicable on and after March 3, 2005. For prior periods, see §1.1502-32T(b)(4)(v) as contained in the 26 CFR part 1 in effect on March 2, 2005.

(vi) *Special rules in the case of certain transactions subject to §1.1502-35.*—If a member of a consolidated group transfers stock of a subsidi-

ary and such stock has a basis that exceeds its value immediately before such transfer or a subsidiary is deconsolidated and any stock of such subsidiary owned by members of the group immediately before such deconsolidation has a basis that exceeds its value, all members of the group are subject to the provisions of §1.1502-35(b), which generally require a redetermination of members' basis in all shares of subsidiary stock.

(vii) *Special rules for amending waiver of loss carryovers from separate return limitation year.*—(A) *Waivers that increased allowable loss or reduced basis reduction required.*—If, in connection with the acquisition of S, the group made an election pursuant to paragraph (b)(4) of this section to treat all or any portion of S's loss carryovers as expiring, and the prior group elected to determine the amount of the allowable loss or the basis reduction required with respect to the stock of S or a higher-tier corporation of S by applying the provisions described in §1.1502-20(i)(2)(i) or (ii), then the group may reduce the amount of any loss carryover deemed to expire (or increase the amount of any loss carryover deemed not to expire) as a result of the election made pursuant to paragraph (b)(4) of this section. The aggregate amount of loss carryovers that may be treated as not expiring as a result of amendments made pursuant to this paragraph (b)(4)(vii)(A) with respect to S and any higher-and lower-tier corporation of S may not exceed the amount described in §1.1502-20(c)(1)(iii) with respect to the acquired stock (computed without regard to the effect of the group's election or elections pursuant to paragraph (b)(4) of this section, but with regard to the effect of the prior group's election pursuant to §1.1502-20(g), if any, prior to the application of §1.1502-20(i)(3)). For purposes of determining the aggregate amount of loss carryovers that may be treated as not expiring as a result of amendments made pursuant to this paragraph (b)(4)(vii)(A) with respect to S and any higher- and lower-tier corporation of S, the group may rely on a written notification provided by the prior group. Nothing in this paragraph shall be construed as permitting a group to increase the amount of any loss carryover deemed to expire (or reduce the amount of any loss carryover deemed not to expire) as a result of the election made pursuant to paragraph (b)(4) of this section.

(B) *Inadvertent waivers of loss carryovers previously subject to an election described in §1.1502-20(g).*—If, in connection with the acquisition of S, the group made an election pursuant to paragraph (b)(4) of this section to waive loss carryovers of S by identifying the amount of each loss carryover deemed not to expire, the prior group elected to determine the amount of the allowable loss or the basis reduction required with respect to the stock of S or a higher-tier corporation of S by applying the provisions described in §1.1502-20(i)(2)(i) or (ii), and the amount of S's loss carryovers treated as reattributed to the prior group pursuant to the election described in §1.1502-20(g) is reduced pursuant to §1.1502-20(i)(3), then the group may amend its election made pursuant to paragraph (b)(4) of this section to provide that all or a portion of the loss carryovers of S that are treated as loss carryovers of S as a result of the prior group's election to apply the provisions described in §1.1502-20(i)(2)(i) or (ii) are deemed not to expire. This paragraph (b)(4)(vii)(B), however, does not permit a group to reduce the amount of any loss carryover deemed not to expire as a result of the election made pursuant to paragraph (b)(4) of this section.

(C) *Time and manner of amending an election under §1.1502-32(b)(4).*—The amendment of an election made pursuant to paragraph (b)(4) of this section must be made in a statement entitled *Amendment of Election to Treat Loss Carryover as Expiring Under §1.1502-32(b)(4) Pursuant to §1.1502-32(b)(4)(vii).* The statement must be filed with or as part of any timely filed (including extensions) original return for the taxable year that includes August 26, 2004, or with or as part of an amended return filed before the date the original return for the taxable year that includes August 26, 2004, is due (with regard to extensions). A separate statement shall be filed for each election made pursuant to paragraph (b)(4) of this section that is being amended pursuant to this paragraph (b)(4)(vii). For purposes of making this statement, the group may rely on the statements set forth in a written notification provided by the prior group. The statement filed under this paragraph must include the following—

(1) The name and employer identification number (E.I.N.) of S;

(2) In the case of an amendment made pursuant to paragraph (b)(4)(vii)(A), a statement that the group has received a written notification from the prior group confirming that the group's prior election or elections pursuant to paragraph (b)(4) of this section had the effect of either increasing the prior group's allowable loss on the disposition of subsidiary stock or reducing the prior group's amount of basis reduction required;

(3) The amount of each loss carryover of S deemed to expire (or the amount of loss carryover deemed not to expire) as set forth in the election made pursuant to paragraph (b)(4) of this section;

(4) The amended amount of each loss carryover of S deemed to expire (or the amended amount of loss carryover deemed not to expire); and

(5) In the case of an amendment made pursuant to paragraph (b)(4)(vii)(A) of this section, a statement that the aggregate amount of loss carryovers of S and any higher- and lower-tier corporation of S that will be treated as not expiring as a result of amendments made pursuant to paragraph (b)(4)(vii)(A) of this section will not exceed the amount described in §1.1502-20(c)(1)(iii) with respect to the acquired stock (computed without regard to the effect of the group's election or elections pursuant to paragraph (b)(4) of this section, but with regard to the effect of the prior group's election pursuant to §1.1502-20(g), if any, prior to the application of §1.1502-20(i)(3)).

(D) *Items taken into account in open years.*—An amendment to an election made pursuant to paragraph (b)(4) of this section affects the group's items of income, gain, deduction, or loss only to the extent that the amendment gives rise, directly or indirectly, to items or amounts that would properly be taken into account in a year for which an assessment of deficiency or a refund for overpayment, as the case may be, is not prevented by any law or rule of law. Under this paragraph, if the year to which a loss previously deemed to expire as a result of an election made pursuant to paragraph (b)(4) of this section is deemed not to expire as a result of an election made pursuant to this paragraph would have been carried back or carried forward is a year for which a refund of overpayment is prevented by law, then to the extent that the absorption of such loss in such year would have affected the tax treatment of another item (e.g., another loss that was absorbed in such year) that has an effect in a year for which a refund of overpayment is not prevented by any law or rule of law, the amendment to the election made pursuant to paragraph (b)(4) of this section will affect the treatment of such other item. Therefore, if the absorption of such loss (the first loss) in a year for which a refund of overpayment is prevented by law would have prevented the absorption of another loss (the second loss) in such year and such second loss would have been carried to and used in a year for which a refund of overpayment is not prevented by any law or rule of law (the other year), the amendment of the election makes the second loss available for use in the other year.

(E) *Higher-and lower-tier corporations of S.*—A *higher-tier corporation of S* is a corporation that was a member of the prior group and, as a result of such higher-tier corporation becoming a member of the group, S became a member of the group. A *lower-tier corporation of S* is a corporation that was a member of the prior group and became a member of the group as a result of S becoming a member of the group.

(F) *Effective date.*—This paragraph (b)(4)(vii) is applicable on and after March 3, 2005. For prior periods, see §1.1502-32T(b)(4)(vii) as contained in the 26 CFR part 1 in effect on March 2, 2005.

Reg. §1.1502-32(b)(4)(vii)(F)

(5) *Examples.*—(i) *In general.*—For purposes of the examples in this section, unless otherwise stated, M owns all of the only class of S's stock, the stock is owned for the entire year, S owns no stock of lower-tier members, the tax year of all persons is the calendar year, all persons use the accrual method of accounting, the facts set forth the only corporate activity, preferred stock is described in section 1504(a)(4), all transactions are between unrelated persons, and tax liabilities are disregarded.

(ii) *Stock basis adjustments.*—The principles of this paragraph (b) are illustrated by the following examples.

Example 1. Taxable income. (a) *Current taxable income.* For Year 1, the M group has $100 of taxable income when determined by including only S's items of income, gain, deduction, and loss taken into account. Under paragraph (b)(1) of this section, M's basis in S's stock is adjusted under this section as of the close of Year 1. Under paragraph (b)(2) of this section, M's basis in S's stock is increased by the amount of the M group's taxable income determined by including only S's items taken into account. Thus, M's basis in S's stock is increased by $100 as of the close of Year 1.

(b) *Intercompany gain that is not taken into account.* The facts are the same as in paragraph (a) of this *Example 1,* except that S also sells property to another member at a $25 gain in Year 1, the gain is deferred under §1.1502-13 and taken into account in Year 3, and M sells 10% of S's stock to nonmembers in Year 2. Under paragraph (b)(3)(i) of this section, S's deferred gain is not additional taxable income for Year 1 or 2 because it is not taken into account in determining the M group's consolidated taxable income for either of those years. The deferred gain is not tax-exempt income under paragraph (b)(3)(ii) of this section because it is not permanently excluded from S's gross income. The deferred gain does not result in a basis adjustment until Year 3, when it is taken into account in determining the M group's consolidated taxable income. Consequently, M's basis in the S shares sold is not increased to reflect S's gain from the intercompany sale of the property. In Year 3, the deferred gain is taken into account, but the amount allocable to the shares sold by M does not increase their basis because these shares are held by nonmembers.

(c) *Intercompany gain taken into account.* The facts are the same as in paragraph (b) of this *Example 1,* except that M sells all of S's stock in Year 2 (rather than only 10%). Under §1.1502-13, S takes the $25 gain into account immediately before S becomes a nonmember. Thus, M's basis in S's stock is increased to reflect S's gain from the intercompany sale of the property.

Example 2. Tax loss. (a) *Current absorption.* For Year 2, the M group has a $50 consolidated net operating loss when determined by taking into account only S's items of income, gain, deduction, and loss. S's loss is absorbed by the M group in Year 2, offsetting M's income for that year. Under paragraph (b)(3)(i)(A) of this section, because S's loss is absorbed in the year it arises, M has a $50 negative adjustment with respect to S's stock. Under paragraph (b)(2) of this section, M reduces its basis in S's stock by $50. Under paragraph (a)(3)(ii) of this section, if the decrease exceeds M's basis in S's stock, the excess is M's excess loss account in S's stock.

(b) *Interim determination from stock sale.* The facts are the same as in paragraph (a) of this *Example 2,* except that S's Year 2 loss arises in the first half of the calendar year, M sells 50% of S's stock on July 1 of Year 2, and M's income for Year 2 does not arise until after the sale of S's stock. M's income for Year 2 (exclusive of the sale of S's stock) is offset by S's loss, even though the income arises after the stock sale, and no loss remains to be apportioned to S. See §§1.1502-11 and 1.1502-21(b). Under paragraph (b)(3)(i)(A) of this section, because S's $50 loss is absorbed in the year it arises, it reduces M's basis in the S shares sold by $25 immediately before the stock sale. Because S becomes a nonmember, the loss also reduces M's basis in the retained S shares by $25 immediately before S becomes a nonmember.

(c) *Loss carryback.* The facts are the same as in paragraph (a) of this *Example 2,* except that M has no income or loss for Year 2, S's $50 loss is carried back and absorbed by the M group in Year 1 (offsetting the income of M or S), and the M group receives a $17 tax refund in Year 2 that is paid to S. Under paragraph (b)(3)(i)(B) of this section, because the $50 loss is carried back and absorbed in Year 1, it is treated as a tax loss for Year 2 (the year in which it arises). Under paragraph (b)(3)(ii) of this section, the refund is treated as tax-exempt income of S. Under paragraph (b)(3)(iv)(C) of this section, the tax-exempt income is taken into account in Year 2 because that is the year it would be taken into account under S's method of accounting if it were subject to Federal income taxation. Thus, under paragraph (b)(2) of this section, M reduces its basis in S's stock by $33 as of the close of Year 2 (the $50 tax loss, less the $17 tax refund).

(d) *Loss carryforward.* The facts are the same as in paragraph (a) of this *Example 2,* except that M has no income or loss for Year 2, and S's loss is carried forward and absorbed by the M group in Year 3 (offsetting the income of M or S). Under paragraph (b)(3)(i)(A) of this section, the loss is not treated as a tax loss under paragraph (b)(2) of this section until Year 3.

Example 3. Tax-exempt income and noncapital, nondeductible expenses. (a) *Facts.* For Year 1, the M group has $500 of consolidated taxable income. However, the M group has a $100 consolidated net operating loss when determined by including only S's items of income, gain, deduction, and loss taken into account. Also for Year 1,

S has $80 of interest income that is permanently excluded from gross income under section 103, and S incurs $60 of related expense for which a deduction is permanently disallowed under section 265.

(b) *Analysis.* Under paragraph (b)(3)(i)(A) of this section, S has a $100 tax loss for Year 1. Under paragraph (b)(3)(ii)(A) of this section, S has $80 of tax-exempt income. Under paragraph (b)(3)(iii)(A) of this section, S has $60 of noncapital, nondeductible expense. Under paragraph (b)(3)(iv)(C) of this section, the tax-exempt income and noncapital, nondeductible expense are taken into account in Year 1 because that is the year they would be taken into account under S's method of accounting if they were subject to Federal income taxation. Thus, under paragraph (b) of this section, M reduces its basis in S's stock as of the close of Year 1 by an $80 net amount (the $100 tax loss, less $80 of tax-exempt income, plus $60 of noncapital, nondeductible expenses).

Example 4. Discharge of indebtedness. (a) *Facts.* M forms S on January 1 of Year 1 and S borrows $200. During Year 1, S's assets decline in value and the M group has a $100 consolidated net operating loss. Of that amount, $10 is attributable to M and $90 is attributable to S under the principles of §1.1502-21(b)(2)(iv). None of the loss is absorbed by the group in Year 1, and S is discharged from $100 of indebtedness at the close of Year 1. M has a $0 basis in the S stock. M and S have no attributes other than the consolidated net operating loss. Under section 108(a), S's $100 of discharge of indebtedness income is excluded from gross income because of insolvency. Under section 108(b) and §1.1502-28, the consolidated net operating loss is reduced to $0.

(b) *Analysis.* Under paragraph (b)(3)(iii)(A) of this section, the reduction of $90 of the consolidated net operating loss attributable to S is treated as a noncapital, nondeductible expense in Year 1 because that loss is permanently disallowed by section 108(b) and §1.1502-28. Under paragraph (b)(3)(ii)(C)(*1*) of this section, all $100 of S's discharge of indebtedness income is treated as tax-exempt income in Year 1 because the discharge results in a $100 reduction to the consolidated net operating loss. Consequently, the loss and the cancellation of the indebtedness result in a net positive $10 adjustment to M's basis in its S stock.

(c) *Insufficient attributes.* The facts are the same as in paragraph (a) of this *Example 4*, except that S is discharged from $120 of indebtedness at the close of Year 1. Under section 108(a), S's $120 of discharge of indebtedness income is excluded from gross income because of insolvency. Under section 108(b) and §1.1502-28, the consolidated net operating loss is reduced by $100 to $0 after the determination of tax for Year 1. Under paragraph (b)(3)(iii)(A) of this section, the reduction of $90 of the consolidated net operating loss attributable to S is treated as a noncapital, nondeductible expense. Under paragraph

(b)(3)(ii)(C)(*1*) of this section, only $100 of the discharge is treated as tax-exempt income because only that amount is applied to reduce tax attributes. The remaining $20 of discharge of indebtedness income excluded from gross income under section 108(a) has no effect on M's basis in S's stock.

(d) *Purchase price adjustment.* Assume instead that S buys land in Year 1 in exchange for S's $100 purchase money note (bearing interest at a market rate of interest in excess of the applicable Federal rate, and providing for a principal payment at the end of Year 10), and the seller agrees with S in Year 4 to discharge $60 of the note as a purchase price adjustment to which section 108(e)(5) applies. S has no discharge of indebtedness income that is treated as tax-exempt income under paragraph (b)(3)(ii) of this section. In addition, the $60 purchase price adjustment is not a noncapital, nondeductible expense under paragraph (b)(3)(iii) of this section. A purchase price adjustment is not equivalent to a discharge of indebtedness that is offset by a deduction or loss. Consequently, the purchase price adjustment results in no net adjustment to M's basis in S's stock under paragraph (b) of this section.

Example 5. Distributions. (a) *Amounts declared and distributed.* For Year 1, the M group has $120 of consolidated taxable income when determined by including only S's items of income, gain, deduction, and loss taken into account. S declares and makes a $10 dividend distribution to M at the close of Year 1. Under paragraph (b) of this section, M increases its basis in S's stock as of the close of Year 1 by a $110 net amount ($120 of taxable income, less a $10 distribution).

(b) *Distributions in later years.* The facts are the same as in paragraph (a) of this *Example 5*, except that S does not declare and distribute the $10 until Year 2. Under paragraph (b) of this section, M increases its basis in S's stock by $120 as of the close of Year 1, and decreases its basis by $10 as of the close of Year 2. (If M were also a subsidiary, the basis of its stock would also be increased in Year 1 to reflect M's $120 adjustment to basis of S's stock; the basis of M's stock would not be changed as a result of S's distribution in Year 2, because M's $10 of tax-exempt dividend income under paragraph (b)(3)(ii) of this section would be offset by the $10 negative adjustment to M's basis in S's stock for the distribution.)

(c) *Amounts declared but not distributed.* The facts are the same as in paragraph (a) of this *Example 5*, except that, during December of Year 1, S declares (and M becomes entitled to) another $70 dividend distribution with respect to its stock, but M does not receive the distribution until after it sells all of S's stock at the close of Year 1. Under §1.1502-13(f)(2)(iv), S is treated as making a $70 distribution to M at the time M becomes entitled to the distribution. (If S is distributing an appreciated asset, its gain under section 311 is also taken into account under para-

Reg. §1.1502-32(b)(5)(ii)

graph (b)(3)(i) of this section at the time M becomes entitled to the distribution.)
Consequently, under paragraph (b) of this section, M increases its basis in S's stock as of the
close of Year 1 by only a $40 net amount ($120 of
taxable income, less two distributions totalling
$80). Any further adjustments after S ceases to be
a member and the $70 distribution is made
would be duplicative, because the stock basis
has already been adjusted for the distribution.
Accordingly, the distribution will not result in
further adjustments or gain, even if the distribution is a payment to which section 301(c)(2) or (3)
applies.

　　Example 6. Reorganization with boot. (i)
Facts. M owns all the stock of S and T. M owns
ten shares of the same class of common stock of
S and ten shares of the same class of common
stock of T. The fair market value of each share of
S stock is $10 and the fair market value of each
share of T stock is $10. On January 1 of Year 1, M
has a $5 basis in each of its ten shares of S stock
and a $10 basis in each of its ten shares of T
stock. S and T have no items of income, gain,
deduction, or loss for Year 1. S and T each have
substantial earnings and profits. At the close of
Year 1, T merges into S in a reorganization described in section 368(a)(1)(A) (and in section
368(a)(1)(D)). M receives no additional S stock,
but does receive $10 which is treated as a divi-
dend under section 356(a)(2).

　　(ii) *Analysis.* The merger of T into S is a
transaction to which § 1.1502-13(f)(3) applies.
Under § 1.1502-13(f)(3) and § 1.358-2(a)(2)(iii), M
is deemed to receive ten additional shares of S
stock with a total fair market value of $100 (the
fair market value of the T stock surrendered by
M). Under § 1.358-2(a)(2)(i), M will have a basis
of $10 in each share of S stock deemed received
in the reorganization. Under § 1.358-2(a)(2)(iii),
M is deemed to surrender all twenty shares of its
S stock in a recapitalization under section
368(a)(1)(E) in exchange for the ten shares of S
stock, the number of shares of S stock held by M
immediately after the transaction. Thus, under
§ 1.358-2(a)(2)(i), M has five shares of S stock
each with a basis of $10 and five shares of S stock
each with a basis of $20. The $10 M received is
treated as a dividend distribution under section
301 and, under paragraph (b)(3)(v) of this section, the $10 is a distribution to which paragraph
(b)(2)(iv) of this section applies. Accordingly,
M's total basis in the S stock is decreased by the
$10 distribution.

　　Example 7. Tiering up of basis adjustments.
M owns all of S's stock, and S owns all of T's
stock. For Year 1, the M group has $100 of con-
solidated taxable income when determined by
including only T's items of income, gain, deduction, and loss taken into account, and $50 of
consolidated taxable income when determined
by including only S's items taken into account. S
increases its basis in T's stock by $100 under
paragraph (b) of this section. Under paragraph

(a)(3) of this section, this $100 basis adjustment is
taken into account in determining M's adjustments to its basis in S's stock. Thus, M increases
its basis in S's stock by $150 under paragraph (b)
of this section.

　　Example 8. Allocation of items. (a) *Acquisition in mid-year.* M is the common parent of a
consolidated group, and S is an unaffiliated corporation filing separate returns on a calendar-
year basis. M acquires all of S's stock and S
becomes a member of the M group on July 1 of
Year 1. For the entire calendar Year 1, S has $100
of ordinary income and under § 1.1502-76(b) $60
is allocated to the period from January 1 to June
30 and $40 to the period from July 1 to December
31. Under paragraph (b) of this section, M increases its basis in S's stock by $40.

　　(b) *Sale in mid-year.* The facts are the same
as in paragraph (a) of this *Example 8*, except that
S is a member of the M group at the beginning of
Year 1 but ceases to be a member on June 30 as a
result of M's sale of S's stock. Under paragraph
(b) of this section, M increases its basis in S's
stock by $60 immediately before the stock sale.
(M's basis increase would be the same if S became a nonmember because S issued additional
shares to nonmembers.)

　　(c) *Absorption of loss carryovers.* Assume
instead that S is a member of the M group at the
beginning of Year 1 but ceases to be a member on
June 30 as a result of M's sale of S's stock, and a
$100 consolidated net operating loss attributable
to S is carried over by the M group to Year 1. The
consolidated net operating loss may be apportioned to S for its first separate return year only
to the extent not absorbed by the M group during Year 1. Under paragraph (b)(3)(i) of this section, if the loss is absorbed by the M group in
Year 1, whether the offsetting income arises
before or after M's sale of S's stock, the absorption of the loss carryover is included in the determination of S's taxable income or loss for Year 1.
Thus, M's basis in S's stock is adjusted under
paragraph (b) of this section to reflect any absorption of the loss by the M group.

　　Example 9. Gross-ups. (a) *Facts.* M owns all
of the stock of S, and S owns all of the stock of T,
a newly formed controlled foreign corporation
that is not a passive foreign investment company. In Year 1, T has $100 of subpart F income
and pays $34 of foreign income tax, leaving T
with $66 of earnings and profits. The M group
has $100 of consolidated taxable income when
determined by taking into account only S's items
(the inclusion under section 951(a), taking into
account the section 78 gross-up). As a result of
the section 951(a) inclusion, S increases its basis
in T's stock by $66 under section 961(a).

　　(b) *Analysis.* Under paragraph (b)(3)(i) of
this section, S has $100 of taxable income. Under
paragraph (b)(3)(iii)(B) of this section, the $34
gross-up for taxes paid by T that S is treated as
having paid is a noncapital, nondeductible expense (whether or not any corresponding

amount is claimed by the M group as a tax credit). Thus, M increases it basis in S's stock under paragraph (b) of this section by the net adjustment of $66.

(c) *Subsequent distribution.* The facts are the same as in paragraph (a) of this *Example 9,* except that T distributes its $66 of earnings and profits in Year 2. The $66 distribution received by S is excluded from S's income under section 959(a) because the distribution represents earnings and profits attributable to amounts that were included in S's income under section 951(a) for Year 1. In addition, S's basis in T's stock is decreased by $66 under section 961(b). The excluded distribution is not tax-exempt income under paragraph (b)(3)(ii) of this section because of the corresponding reduction to S's basis in T's stock. Consequently, M's basis in S's stock is not adjusted under paragraph (b) of this section for Year 2.

Example 10. Recapture of tax-exempt items. (a) *Facts.* S is a life insurance company. For Year 1, the M group has $200 of consolidated taxable income, determined by including only S's items of income, gain, deduction, and loss taken into account (including a $300 small company deduction under section 806). In addition, S has $100 of tax-exempt interest income, $60 of which is S's *company share.* The remaining $40 of tax-exempt income is the *policyholders' share* that reduces S's deduction for increase in reserves.

(b) *Tax-exempt items generally.* Under paragraph (b)(3)(i) of this section, S has $200 of taxable income for Year 1. Also for Year 1, S has $100 of tax-exempt income under paragraph (b)(3)(ii)(A) of this section, and another $300 is treated as tax-exempt income under paragraph (b)(3)(ii)(B) of this section because of the deduction under section 806. Under paragraph (b)(3)(iii) of this section, S has $40 of noncapital, nondeductible expenses for Year 1 because S's deduction under section 807 for its increase in reserves has been permanently reduced by the $40 policyholders' share of the tax-exempt interest income. Thus, M increases its basis in S's stock by $560 under paragraph (b) of this section.

(c) *Recapture.* Assume instead that S is a property and casualty company and, for Year 1, S accrues $100 of estimated salvage recoverable under section 832. Of this amount, $87 (87% of $100) is excluded from gross income because of the "fresh start" provisions of Sec. 11305(c) of P.L. 101-508 (the Omnibus Budget Reconciliation Act of 1990). Thus, S has $87 of tax-exempt income under paragraph (b)(3)(ii)(A) of this section that increases M's basis in S's stock for Year 1. (S also has $13 of taxable income over the period of inclusion under section 481.) In Year 5, S determines that the $100 salvage recoverable was overestimated by $30 and deducts $30 for the reduction of the salvage recoverable. However, S has $26.10 (87% of $30) of taxable income in Year 5 due to the partial recapture of its fresh

start. Because S has no basis corresponding to this income, S is treated under paragraph (b)(3)(iii)(B) of this section as having a $26.10 noncapital, nondeductible expense in Year 5. This treatment is necessary to reflect the elimination of the erroneous fresh start in S's stock basis and causes a decreases in M's basis in S's stock by $30 for Year 5 (a $3.90 taxable loss and a $26.10 special adjustment).

(c) *Allocation of adjustments among shares of stock.*—(1) *In general.*—(i) *Distributions.*—The adjustment that is described in paragraph (b)(2)(iv) of this section (negative adjustments for distributions) is allocated to the shares of S stock to which the distribution relates.

(ii) *Special rules applicable in the case of certain loss transfers of subsidiary stock.*—(A) *Losses reattributed pursuant to an election under § 1.1502-36(d)(6).*—(1) *General rule.*—If a member transfers loss shares of S stock and the common parent elects under § 1.1502-36(d)(6) to reattribute all or a portion of S's attributes, S's resulting noncapital, nondeductible expense is allocated to all loss shares of S stock transferred by members in the transaction. The expense is allocated among those S shares in proportion to the loss in the shares. The tier-up of that expense is included in the remaining adjustment (see paragraph (c)(1)(iii) of this section).

(2) *Reattribution of attributes of a subsidiary that is lower-tier to S.*—If a member transfers loss shares of S stock and the common parent elects under § 1.1502-36(d)(6) to reattribute attributes of a subsidiary (S2) that is lower-tier to S, S2's resulting noncapital, nondeductible expense is allocated among S2 shares held by members as of the transaction, other than those transferred in the transaction and with respect to which gain or loss was recognized (recognition transfer), in a manner that permits the full amount of the expense to tier up and be applied to the bases of the loss shares of S stock transferred by members in the transaction. The expense is allocated among those S2 shares with positive basis in a manner that, first, reduces the bases of S2's preferred shares to equalize and then eliminate loss and, second, reduces the bases of S2's common shares in a manner that reduces disparity among the bases of those common shares to the greatest extent possible. The noncapital, nondeductible expense applied to the S2 shares tiers up and is applied to the stock of any subsidiaries that are lower-tier to S (middle-tier subsidiaries) in a manner that will permit the full amount of this expense to be applied to reduce the bases of the loss shares of S stock transferred by members in the transaction. Similar to the allocation among the S2 shares, the tierup of this expense is allocated among the middle-tier subsidiary shares held by members as of the transaction, other than those transferred in a recognition transfer, in a manner that per-

mits the full amount of the expense to tier up and be applied to the bases of the loss shares of S stock transferred by members in the transaction. The tierup of this expense is allocated among those middle-tier subsidiary shares with positive basis in a manner that, first, reduces the bases of the middle-tier subsidiary's preferred shares to equalize and then eliminate loss and, second, reduces the bases of the middle-tier subsidiary's common shares in a manner that reduces disparity among the bases of those common shares to the greatest extent possible. The tier-up of this expense is allocated to the loss shares of S stock transferred by members in the transaction in the same manner as provided in paragraph (c)(1)(ii)(A)(*1*) of this section, and thereafter the tier-up of that expense is included in the remaining adjustment (see paragraph (c)(1)(iii) of this section).

(3) *Example.*—The following example illustrates the rules of this paragraph (c)(1)(ii)(A).

Example. Assume P owns M1, P and M1 own M2, M2 owns S, M1 and S own S1, and M1 and S1 own S2. If S sells a portion of the S1 shares at a gain and M2 sells all of the S stock at a net loss (after adjusting the basis for the gain recognized by S on the sale of the S1 shares), and P elects under § 1.1502-36(d)(6) to reattribute attributes of S2, the resulting noncapital, nondeductible expense is allocated entirely to the S2 shares held by S1 with positive basis in a manner that reduces the disparity in those bases to the greatest extent possible. The tier-up of this amount is allocated entirely to the S1 shares held by S (excluding the S1 shares sold) with positive basis in a manner that reduces the disparity in those bases to the greatest extent possible. The tier-up of this amount is allocated to the loss shares of S stock sold by M2 in proportion to the loss in those shares. The tier-up of this amount is then included in the remaining adjustment and tiers up from M2 to M1 and P, and from M1 to P under the general rules of this section.

(B) *Tier-up of reallocated investment adjustments subject to prior use limitation.*—If the reallocation of an investment adjustment under § 1.1502-36(b)(2) is subject to the prior use limitation in § 1.1502-36(b)(2)(iii)(B)(*2*), no amount of the tier-up of such reallocated investment adjustment shall be allocated to any share whose prior use resulted in the application of the limitation. Thereafter, the tier-up of this amount is included in the remaining adjustment (see paragraph (c)(1)(iii) of this section).

(iii) *Remaining adjustment.*—The *remaining adjustment* is the adjustment that consists of the items described in paragraphs (b)(2)(i) through (b)(2)(iii) of this section (adjustments for taxable income or loss, tax-exempt income, and noncapital, nondeductible expenses), including adjustments to lower-tier stock basis that tier up under

paragraph (a)(3)(iii) of this section, but only to the extent not specially allocated under paragraph (c)(1)(ii) of this section. The remaining adjustment is allocated among the shares of S stock as provided in paragraphs (c)(2) through (c)(4) of this section. If the remaining adjustment is positive, it is allocated first to any preferred stock as provided in paragraph (c)(3) of this section, and then to the common stock as provided in paragraph (c)(2) of this section. If the remaining adjustment is negative, it is allocated only to common stock as provided in paragraph (c)(2) of this section.

(iv) *Nonmember shares.*—No adjustment under this section that is allocated to a share for the period it is owned by a nonmember affects the basis of the share.

(v) *Cross-references.*—See paragraph (c)(4) of this section for the reallocation of adjustments, and paragraph (d) of this section for definitions. See § 1.1502-19(d) for special allocations of basis determined or adjusted under the Internal Revenue Code (Code) with respect to excess loss accounts.

(2) *Common stock.*—(i) *Allocation within a class.*—The remaining adjustment described in paragraph (c)(1)(iii) of this section that is allocable to a class of common stock is generally allocated equally to each share within the class. However, if a member has an excess loss account in a share of a class of common stock at the time a positive remaining adjustment is to be allocated, the portion of the positive remaining adjustment allocable to the member with respect to the class is allocated first to equalize and then eliminate that member's excess loss accounts. It is then allocated equally among the members' shares in that class. Similarly, the portion of any negative remaining adjustment allocable to the member with respect to the class is allocated equally to the member's shares with positive bases, eliminating all positive basis in shares of the class before creating or increasing any excess loss accounts. After positive basis is eliminated, any remaining portion of the negative remaining adjustment is allocated to equalize the member's excess loss accounts in the shares of that class to the greatest extent possible. Distributions and any adjustments or determinations under the Internal Revenue Code (for example, under section 358, including any modifications under § 1.1502-19(d)) are taken into account before the allocation is made under this paragraph (c)(2)(i).

(ii) *Allocation among classes.*—(A) *General rule.*—If S has more than one class of common stock, the extent to which the remaining adjustment described in paragraph (c)(1)(iii) of this section is allocated to each class is determined, based on consistently applied assumptions, by taking into account the terms of each class and all other facts and circumstances relating to the overall economic arrangement. The allocation generally must reflect the manner in which the classes participate in the economic benefit or burden (if any) corresponding to the items of income, gain, deduction, or loss allocated. In determining participation, any differences in voting rights are not taken into account, and the following factors are among those to be considered—

    (1) The interest of each share in economic profits and losses (if different from the interest in taxable income);

    (2) The interest of each share in cash flow and other non-liquidating distributions; and

    (3) The interest of each share in distributions in liquidation.

    (B) *Distributions and Code adjustments.*— Distributions and any adjustments or determinations under the Internal Revenue Code are taken into account before the allocation is made under this paragraph (c)(2)(ii).

    (3) *Preferred stock.*—If the remaining adjustment described in paragraph (c)(1)(iii) of this section is positive, it is allocated to preferred stock to the extent required (when aggregated with prior allocations to the preferred stock during the period that S is a member of the consolidated group) to reflect distributions described in section 301 (and all other distributions treated as dividends) to which the preferred stock becomes entitled, and arrearages arising, during the period that S is a member of the consolidated group. For this purpose, the preferred stock is treated as entitled to a distribution no later than the time the distribution is taken into account under the Internal Revenue Code (e.g., under section 305). If the amount of distributions and arrearages exceeds the positive amount (when aggregated with prior allocations), the positive amount is first allocated among classes of preferred stock to reflect their relative priorities, and the amount allocated to each class is then allocated pro rata within the class. An allocation to a share with respect to arrearages and distributions for the period the share is owned by a nonmember is not reflected in the basis of the share under paragraph (b) of this section. However, if M and S cease to be members of one consolidated group and remain affiliated as members of another consolidated group, M's ownership of S's stock during consolidated return years of the prior group is treated for this purpose as ownership by a member to the extent that the the adjustments during the prior consolidated return years are still reflected in the basis of the preferred stock.

    (4) *Cumulative redetermination.*—(i) *General rule.*—A member's basis in each share of S preferred and common stock must be redetermined whenever necessary to determine the tax liability of any person. See paragraph (b)(1) of this sec-

tion. The redetermination is made by reallocating S's adjustments described in paragraphs (c)(1)(ii)(B) (specially allocated adjustments for tier-up of reallocated investment adjustments subject to prior use limitation) and (c)(1)(iii) (remaining adjustments) of this section for each consolidated return year (or other applicable period) of the group by taking into account all of the facts and circumstances affecting allocations under this paragraph (c) as of the redetermination date with respect to all of the S shares. For this purpose:

    (A) Amounts may be reallocated from one class of S's stock to another class, but not from one share of a class to another share of the same class.

    (B) If there is a change in the equity structure of S (e.g., as the result of S's issuance, redemption, or recapitalization of shares), a cumulative redetermination is made for the period before the change. If a reallocation is required by another redetermination after a change, amounts arising after the change are reallocated before amounts arising before the change.

    (C) If S becomes a nonmember as a result of a change in its equity structure, any reallocation is made only among the shares of S's stock immediately before the change. For example, if S issues stock to a nonmember creditor in exchange for its debt, and the exchange results in S becoming a nonmember, any reallocation is only among the shares of S's stock immediately before the exchange.

    (D) Any reallocation is treated for all purposes after it is made (including subsequent redeterminations) as the original allocation of an amount under this paragraph (c), but the reallocation does not affect any prior period.

    (ii) *Prior use of allocations.*—An amount may not be reallocated under paragraph (c)(4)(i) of this section to the extent that the amount has been used before the reallocation. For this purpose, an amount has been used to the extent it has been taken into account, directly or indirectly, by any member in determining income, gain, deduction, or loss, or in determining the basis of any property that is not subject to this section (e.g., stock of a corporation that has become a nonmember). For example, if M sells a share of S stock, an amount previously allocated to the share cannot be reallocated to another share of S stock, but an amount allocated to another share of S stock can still be reallocated to the sold share because the reallocated amount has not been taken into account; however, any adjustment reallocated to the sold share may effectively be eliminated, because the reallocation was not in effect when the share was previously sold and M's gain or loss from the sale is not redetermined. If, however, M sells the share of S stock to another member, the amount is not used until M's gain or loss is taken into account under § 1.1502-13.

(5) *Examples.*—The principles of this paragraph (c) are illustrated by the following examples.

Example 1. Ownership of less than all the stock. (a) *Facts.* M owns 80% of S's only class of stock with an $800 basis. For Year 1, S has $100 of taxable income.

(b) *Analysis.* Under paragraph (c)(1) of this section, the $100 positive adjustment under paragraph (b) of this section for S's taxable income is allocated among the shares of S's stock, including shares owned by nonmembers. Under paragraph (c)(2)(i) of this section, the adjustment is allocated equally to each share of S's stock. Thus, M increases its basis in S's stock under paragraph (b) of this section as of the close of Year 1 by $80. (The basis of the 20% of S's stock owned by nonmembers is not adjusted under this section.)

(c) *Varying interest.* The facts are the same as in paragraph (a) of this *Example 1*, except that M buys the remaining 20% of S's stock at the close of business on June 30 of Year 1 for $208. Under paragraph (b)(1) of this section and the principles of § 1.1502-76(b), S's $100 of taxable income is allocable $40 to the period from January 1 to June 30 and $60 to the period from July 1 to December 31. Thus, for the period ending June 30, M is treated as having a $32 adjustment with respect to the S stock that M has owned since January 1 (80% of $40) and, under paragraph (c)(2)(i) of this section, the adjustment is allocated equally among those shares. For the period ending December 31, M is treated as having a $60 adjustment (100% of $60) that is also allocated equally among M's shares of S's stock owned after June 30. M's basis in the shares owned as of the beginning of the year therefore increases by $80 (the sum of 80% of $40 and 80% of $60), from $800 to $880, and M's basis in the shares purchased on June 30 increases by $12 (20% of $60), from $208 to $220. Thus, M's aggregate basis in S's stock as of the end of Year 1 is $1,100.

(d) *Tax liability.* The facts are the same as in paragraph (a) of this *Example 1*, except that M pays S's $34 share of the group's consolidated tax liability resulting from S's taxable income, and S does not reimburse M. S's $100 of taxable income results in a positive adjustment under paragraph (b)(3)(i) of this section, and S's $34 of tax liability results in a negative adjustment under paragraph (b)(3)(iv)(D) of this section and the principles of section 1552. Because S does not make any payment in recognition of the additional tax liability, by analogy to the treatment under § 1.1552-1(b)(2), S is treated as having made a $34 payment that is described in paragraph (b)(3)(iii) of this section (noncapital, nondeductible expenses) and as having received an equal amount from M as a capital contribution. Thus, M increases its basis in its S stock by $52.80 (80% of the $100 of taxable income, less 80% of the $34 tax payment). In addition, M increases its

basis in S's stock by $34 under the Internal Revenue Code and paragraph (a)(2) of this section to reflect the capital contribution. In the aggregate, M increases its basis in S's stock by $86.80. (If, as in paragraph (c) of this *Example 1*, M buys the remaining 20% of S's stock at the close of business on June 30, M increases its basis in S's stock by another $7.90 for the additional 20% interest in S's income after June 30 ($60 multiplied by 20%, less 20% of the $20.40 tax payment on $60); the $34 capital contribution by M is reflected in all of its S shares (not just the original 80%), and M's aggregate basis adjustment under this section is $94.70 ($86.80 plus $7.90).)

Example 2. Preferred stock. (a) *Facts.* M owns all of S's common stock with an $800 basis, and nonmembers own all of S's preferred stock. The preferred stock was issued for $200, has a $20 annual, cumulative preference as to dividends, and has an initial liquidation preference of $200. For Year 1, S has $50 of taxable income and no distributions are declared or made.

(b) *Analysis of arrearages.* Under paragraphs (c)(1) and (3) of this section, $20 of the $50 positive adjustment under paragraph (b) of this section is allocated first to the preferred stock to reflect the dividend arrearage arising in Year 1. The remaining $30 of the positive adjustment is allocated to the common stock, increasing M's basis from $800 to $830 as of the close of Year 1. (The basis of the preferred stock owned by nonmembers is not adjusted under this section.)

(c) *Current distribution.* The facts are the same as in paragraph (a) of this *Example 2*, except that S declares and makes a $20 distribution with respect to the preferred stock during Year 1 in satisfaction of its preference. The results are the same as in paragraph (b) of this *Example 2*.

(d) *Varying interest.* The facts are the same as in paragraph (a) of this *Example 2*, except that S has no income or loss for Years 1 and 2, M purchases all of S's preferred stock at the beginning of Year 3 for $240, and S has $70 of taxable income for Year 3. Under paragraph (c)(3) of this section, $60 of the $70 positive adjustment under paragraph (b) of this section is allocated to the preferred stock to reflect the dividends arrearages for Years 1 through 3, but only the $20 for Year 3 is reflected in the basis of the preferred stock under paragraph (b) of this section. (The remaining $40 is not reflected because the preferred stock was owned by nonmembers during Years 1 and 2.) Thus, M increases its basis in S's preferred stock from $240 to $260, and its basis in S's common stock from $800 to $810, as of the close of Year 3. (If M had acquired all of S's preferred stock in a transaction to which section 351 applies, and M's initial basis in S's preferred stock was $200 under section 362, M's basis in S's preferred stock would increase from $200 to $220.)

(e) *Varying interest with current distributions.* The facts are the same as in paragraph (d) of this *Example 2*, except that S declares and makes a $20 distribution with respect to the preferred stock in each of Years 1 and 2 in satisfaction of its preference, and M purchases all of S's preferred stock at the beginning of Year 3 for $200. Under paragraph (c)(3) of this section, $40 of the $70 positive adjustment under paragraph (b) of this section is allocated to the preferred stock to reflect the distributions in Years 1 and 2, and $20 of the $70 is allocated to the preferred stock to reflect the arrearage for Year 3. However, as in paragraph (d) of this *Example 2*, only the $20 attributable to Year 3 is reflected in the basis of the preferred stock under paragraph (b) of this section. Thus, M increases its basis in S's preferred stock from $200 to $220, and M increases its basis in S's common stock from $800 to $810.

Example 3. Cumulative redetermination. (a) *Facts.* M owns all of S's common and preferred stock. The preferred stock has a $100 annual, cumulative preference as to dividends. For Year 1, S has $200 of taxable income, the first $100 of which is allocated to the preferred stock and the remaining $100 of which is allocated to the common stock. For Year 2, S has no adjustment under paragraph (b) of this section, and M sells all of S's common stock at the close of Year 2.

(b) *Analysis.* Under paragraph (c)(4) of this section, M's basis in S's common stock must be redetermined as of the sale of the stock. The redetermination is made by reallocating the $200 positive adjustment under paragraph (b) of this section for Year 1 by taking into account all of the facts and circumstances affecting allocations as of the sale. Thus, the $200 positive adjustment for Year 1 is reallocated entirely to the preferred stock to reflect the dividend arrearages for Years 1 and 2. The reallocation away from the common stock reflects the fact that, because of the additional amount of arrearage in Year 2, the common stock is not entitled to any part of the $200 of taxable income from Year 1. Thus, the common stock has no positive or negative adjustment, and the preferred stock has a $200 positive adjustment. These reallocations are treated as the original allocations for Years 1 and 2. (The results for the common stock would be the same if the common and preferred stock were not owned by the same member, or the preferred stock were owned by nonmembers.)

(c) *Preferred stock issued after adjustment arises.* The facts are the same as in paragraph (a) of this *Example 3*, except that S does not issue its preferred stock until the beginning of Year 2, S has no further adjustment under paragraph (b) of this section for Years 2 and 3, and M sells S's common stock at the close of Year 3. Under paragraphs (c)(1) and (2) of this section, the $200 positive adjustment for Year 1 is initially allocated entirely to the common stock. Under paragraph (c)(4) of this section, the $200 adjustment is reallocated to the preferred stock to reflect the arrearages for Years 2 and 3. Thus, the common stock has no positive or negative adjustment.

(d) *Common stock issued after adjustment arises.* The facts are the same as in paragraph (a) of this *Example 3*, except that S has no preferred stock, S issues additional common stock of the same class at the beginning of Year 2, S has no further adjustment under paragraph (b) of this section in Years 2 and 3, and M sells its S common stock at the close of Year 3. Under paragraphs (c)(1) and (2) of this section, the $200 positive adjustment for Year 1 is initially allocated entirely to the original common stock. Under paragraph (c)(4)(i)(A) of this section, the $200 adjustment is not reallocated among the original common stock and the additional stock. Unlike the preferred stock in paragraph (c) of this *Example 3*, the additional common stock is of the same class as the original stock, and there is no reallocation between shares of the same class.

(e) *Positive and negative adjustments.* The facts are the same as in paragraph (a) of this *Example 3*, except that S has a $200 loss for Year 2 that results in a negative adjustment to the common stock before any redetermination. For purposes of the basis redetermination under paragraph (c)(4) of this section, the Year 1 and 2 adjustments under paragraph (b) of this section are not netted. Thus, as in paragraph (b) of this *Example 3*, the redetermination is made by reallocating the $200 positive adjustment for Year 1 entirely to the preferred stock. The $200 negative adjustment for Year 2 is allocated entirely to the common stock. Consequently, the preferred stock has a $200 positive cumulative adjustment, and the common stock has a $200 negative cumulative adjustment. (The results would be the same if there were no other adjustments described in paragraph (b) of this section, M sells S's common stock at the close of Year 3 rather than Year 2, and an additional $100 arrearage arises in Year 3; only adjustments under paragraph (b) of this section may be reallocated, and there is no additional adjustment for Year 3.)

(f) *Current distributions.* The facts are the same as in paragraph (a) of this *Example 3*, except that, during Year 1, S declares and makes a distribution to M of $100 as a dividend on the preferred stock and $100 as a dividend on the common stock. The taxable income and distributions result in no Year 1 adjustment under paragraph (b) of this section for either the common or preferred stock. However, as in paragraph (b) of this *Example 3*, the redetermination under paragraph (c)(4) of this section is made by reallocating a $200 positive adjustment for Year 1 (S's net adjustment described in paragraph (b) of this section, determined without taking distributions into account) to the preferred stock. Consequently, the preferred stock has a $100 positive cumulative adjustment ($200 of taxable income, less a $100 distribution with respect to the preferred stock) and the common stock has a $100 negative cumulative adjustment (for the distribution).

Reg. § 1.1502-32(c)(5)

(g) *Convertible preferred stock.* The facts are the same as in paragraph (a) of this *Example 3*, except that the preferred stock is convertible into common stock that is identical to the common stock already outstanding, the holders of the preferred stock convert the stock at the close of Year 2, and no stock is sold until the close of Year 5. Under paragraph (c)(4) of this section, the $200 positive adjustment for Year 1 is reallocated entirely to the preferred stock immediately before the conversion. The newly issued common stock is treated as a second class of S common stock, and adjustments under paragraph (b) of this section are allocated between the original and the new common stock under paragraph (c)(2)(ii) of this section. Although the preferred stock is converted to common stock, the $200 adjustment to the preferred stock is not subsequently reallocated between the original and the new common stock. Because the original and the new stock are equivalent, adjustments under paragraph (b) of this section for subsequent periods are allocated equally to each share.

(h) *Prior use of allocations.* The facts are the same as in paragraph (a) of this *Example 3*, except that M sells 10% of S's common stock at the close of Year 1, and the remaining 90% at the close of Year 2. M's basis in the common stock sold in Year 1 reflects $10 of the adjustment allocated to the common stock for Year 1. Under paragraph (c)(4)(ii) of this section, because $10 of the Year 1 adjustment was used in determining M's gain or loss, only $90 is reallocated to the preferred stock, and $10 remains allocated to the common stock sold.

(i) *Lower-tier members.* The facts are the same as in paragraph (a) of this *Example 3*, except that M owns only S's common stock, and M is also a subsidiary. If there is a redetermination under paragraph (c)(4) of this section by a member owning M's stock, a redetermination with respect to S's stock must be made first, and the effect of that redetermination on M's adjustments is taken into account under paragraph (b) of this section. However, as in paragraph (h) of this *Example 3*, to the extent an amount of the initial adjustments with respect to S's common stock have already been tiered up and used by a member owning M's stock, that amount remains with S's common stock (and the higher-tier member using the adjustment with respect to M's stock), and may not be reallocated to S's preferred stock.

Example 4. Allocation to preferred stock between groups. (a) *Facts.* M owns all of S's only class of stock, and S owns all of T's common and preferred stock. The preferred stock has a $100 annual, cumulative preference as to dividends. For Year 1, T has $200 of taxable income, the first $100 of which is allocated to the preferred stock and the remaining $100 of which is allocated to the common stock, and S has no adjustments other than the amounts tiered up from T. S and T

have no adjustments under paragraph (b) of this section for Years 2 and 3. X, the common parent of another consolidated group, purchases all of S's stock at the close of Year 3, and S and T become members of the X group. For Year 4, T has $200 of taxable income, and S has no adjustments other than the amounts tiered up from T.

(b) *Analysis for Years 1 through 3.* Under paragraph (c)(4) of this section, the allocation of S's adjustments under paragraph (b) of this section (determined without taking distributions into account) must be redetermined as of the time M sells S's stock. As a result of this redetermination, T's common stock has no positive or negative adjustment and the preferred stock has a $200 positive adjustment.

(c) *Analysis for Year 4.* Under paragraph (c)(3) of this section, the allocation of T's $200 positive adjustment in Year 4 to T's preferred stock with respect to arrearages is made by taking into account the consolidated return years of both the M group and the X group. Thus, the allocation of the $200 positive adjustment for Year 4 to T's preferred stock is not treated as an allocation for a period for which the preferred stock is owned by a nonmember. Thus, the $200 adjustment is reflected in S's basis in T's preferred stock under paragraph (b) of this section.

(d) *Definitions.*—For purposes of this section—

(1) *Class.*—The shares of a member having the same material terms (without taking into account voting rights) are treated as a single class of stock.

(2) *Preferred stock.*—Preferred stock is stock that is limited and preferred as to dividends and has a liquidation preference. A class of stock that is not described in section 1504(a)(4), however, is not treated as preferred stock for purposes of paragraph (c) of this section if members own less than 80% of each class of common stock (determined without taking this paragraph (d)(2) into account).

(3) *Common stock.*—Common stock is stock that is not preferred stock.

(4) *Becoming a nonmember.*—A member is treated as becoming a nonmember if it has a separate return year (including another group's consolidated return year). For example, S may become a nonmember if it issues additional stock to nonmembers, but S does not become a nonmember as a result of its complete liquidation.

(e) *Anti-avoidance rule.*—(1) *General rule.*—If any person acts with a principal purpose contrary to the purposes of this section, to avoid the effect of the rules of this section or apply the rules of this section to avoid the effect of any other provision of the consolidated return regulations, adjustments must be made as necessary to carry out the purposes of this section.

(2) *Examples.*—The principles of this paragraph (e) are illustrated by the following examples.

Example 1. Preferred stock treated as common stock. (a) *Facts.* S has 100 shares of common stock and 100 shares of preferred stock described in section 1504(a)(4). M owns 80 shares of S's common stock and all of S's preferred stock. The shareholders expect that S will have negative adjustments under paragraph (b) of this section for Years 1 and 2 (all of which will be allocable to S's common stock), the negative adjustments will have no significant effect on the value of S's stock, and S will have offsetting positive adjustments thereafter. When the preferred stock was issued, M intended to cause S to recapitalize the preferred stock into additional common stock at the end of Year 2 in a transaction described in section 368(a)(1)(E). M's temporary ownership of the preferred stock is with a principal purpose to limit M's basis reductions under paragraph (b) of this section to 80% of the anticipated negative adjustments. The recapitalization is intended to cause significantly more than 80% of the anticipated positive adjustments to increase M's basis in S's stock because of M's increased ownership of S's common stock immediately after the recapitalization.

(b) *Analysis.* S has established a transitory capital structure with a principal purpose to enhance M's basis in S's stock under this section. Under paragraph (e)(1) of this section, all of S's common and preferred stock is treated as a single class of common stock in Years 1 and 2 for purposes of this section. Thus, S's items are allocated under the principles of paragraph (c)(2)(ii) of this section, and M decreases its basis in both the common and preferred stock accordingly.

Example 2. Contribution of appreciated property. (a) *Facts.* M owns all of the stock of S and T, and S and T each own 50% of the stock of U. M's S stock has a $150 basis and $200 value, and M's T stock has a $200 basis and $200 value. With a principal purpose to eliminate M's gain from an anticipated sale of S's stock, T contributes to U an asset with a $100 value and $0 basis, and S contributes $100 cash. U sells T's asset and recognizes a $100 gain that results in a $100 positive adjustment under paragraph (b) of this section.

(b) *Analysis.* Under paragraph (c)(2) of this section, U's adjustment ordinarily would be allocated equally to each share of U's stock. If so allocated, M's basis in S's stock would increase from $150 to $200 and M would recognize no gain from the sale of S's stock for $200. Under paragraph (e)(1) of this section, however, because T transferred an appreciated asset to U with a principal purpose to shift a portion of the stock basis increase from M's stock in T to M's stock in S, the allocation of the $100 positive adjustment under paragraph (c) of this section between the shares of U's stock must take into account the contribution. Consequently, all $100 of the positive adjustment is allocated to the U

stock owned by T, rather than $50 to the U stock owned by S and $50 to the U stock owned by T. M's basis in S's stock remains $150, and its basis in T's stock increases to $300. Thus, M recognizes a $50 gain from its sale of S's stock for $200.

Example 3. Reorganizations. (a) *Facts.* M forms S with an $800 contribution, $200 of which is in exchange for S's preferred stock described in section 1504(a)(4) and the balance of which is for S's common stock. For Years 1 through 3, S has a total of $160 of ordinary income, $60 of which is distributed with respect to the preferred stock in satisfaction of its $20 annual preference as to dividends. Under this section, M's basis in S's preferred stock is unchanged, and its basis in S's common stock is increased from $600 to $700. To reduce its gain from an anticipated sale of S's preferred stock, M forms T at the close of Year 3 with a contribution of all of S's stock in exchange for corresponding common and preferred stock of T in a transaction to which section 351 applies. At the time of the contribution, the fair market value of the common stock is $700 and the fair market value of the preferred stock is $300 (due to a decrease in prevailing market interest rates). M subsequently sells T's preferred stock for $300.

(b) *Analysis.* Under section 358(b), M ordinarily has a $630 basis in T's common stock (70% of the $900 aggregate stock basis) and a $270 basis in T's preferred stock (30% of the $900 aggregate stock basis). However, because M transferred S's stock to T with a principal purpose to shift the allocation of basis adjustments under this section, adjustments are made under paragraph (e)(1) of this section to preserve the allocation under this section. Thus, M has a $700 basis in T's common stock and a $200 basis in T's preferred stock. Consequently, M recognizes a $100 gain from the sale of T's preferred stock.

Example 4. Post-deconsolidation basis adjustments. (a) *Facts.* For Year 1, the M group has $40 of taxable income when determined by including only S's items of income, gain, deduction, and loss taken into account, and M increases its basis in S's stock by $40 under paragraph (b) of this section. M anticipates that S will have a $40 ordinary loss for Year 2 that will be carried back and offset S's income in Year 1 and result in a $40 reduction to M's basis in S's stock for Year 2 under paragraph (b) of this section. With a principal purpose to avoid the reduction, M causes S to issue voting preferred stock that results in S becoming a nonmember at the beginning of Year 2. As anticipated, S has a $40 loss for Year 2, which is carried back to Year 1 and offsets S's income from Year 1.

(b) *Analysis.* Under paragraph (e)(1) of this section, because M caused S to become a nonmember with a principal purpose to absorb S's loss but avoid the corresponding negative adjustment under this section, and M bears a substantial portion of the loss because of its continued ownership of S common stock, the basis of M's common stock in S is decreased by

$40 for Year 2. (If M has less than a $40 basis in the retained S stock, M must recognize income for Year 2 to the extent of the excess.) Section 1504(a)(3) limits the ability of S to subsequently rejoin the M group's consolidated return.

(c) *Carryback to pre-consolidation year.* The facts are the same as in paragraph (a) of this *Example 4*, except that M anticipates that S's loss will be carried back and absorbed in a separate return year of S before Year 1 (rather than to the M group's consolidated return for Year 1). Although M causes S to become a nonmember with a principal purpose to avoid the negative adjustment under this section, and M bears a substantial portion of the loss because of its continued ownership of S common stock, both S's income and loss are taken into account under the separate return rules. Consequently, no one has acted with a principal purpose contrary to the purposes of this section, and no adjustments are necessary to carry out the purposes of this section.

Example 5. Pre-consolidation basis adjustments. (a) *Facts.* M forms S with a $100 contribution, and S becomes a member of the M affiliated group which does not file consolidated returns. For Years 1 through 3, S earns $300. M anticipates that it will elect under section 1501 for the M group to begin filing consolidated returns in Year 5. In anticipation of filing consolidated returns, and to avoid the negative stock basis adjustment that would result under paragraph (b) of this section from distributing S's earnings after Year 5, M causes S to distribute $300 during Year 4 as a qualifying dividend within the meaning of section 243(b). There is no plan or intention to recontribute the funds to S after the distribution.

(b) *Analysis.* Although S's distribution of $300 is with a principal purpose to avoid a corresponding negative adjustment under this section, the $300 was both earned and distributed entirely under the separate return rules. Consequently, M and S have not acted with a principal purpose contrary to the purposes of this section, and no adjustments are necessary to carry out the purposes of this section.

(f) *Predecessors and successors.*—For purposes of this section, any reference to a corporation or to a share of stock includes a reference to a successor or predecessor as the context may require. A corporation is a successor if the basis of its assets is determined, directly or indirectly, in whole or in part, by reference to the basis of another corporation (the predecessor). For example, if T merges into S, S is treated, as the context may require, as a successor to T and as becoming a member of the group. A share is a successor if its basis is determined, directly or indirectly, in whole or in part, by reference to the basis of another share (the predecessor).

(g) *Recordkeeping.*—Adjustments under this section must be reflected annually on permanent records (including work papers). See also section 6001, requiring records to be maintained. The group must be able to identify from these permanent records the amount and allocation of adjustments, including the nature of any tax-exempt income and noncapital, nondeductible expenses, so as to permit the application of the rules of this section for each year.

(h) *Effective/applicability date.*—(1) *General rule.*—Except as provided in paragraph (h)(8) of this section, this section applies with respect to determinations of the basis of the stock of a subsidiary (e.g., for determining gain or loss from a disposition of stock), in consolidated return years beginning on or after January 1, 1995. If this section applies, basis must be determined or redetermined as if this section were in effect for all years (including, for example, the consolidated return years of another consolidated group to the extent adjustments from those years are still reflected). For example, if the portion of a consolidated net operating loss carryover attributable to S expired in 1990 and is treated as a noncapital, nondeductible expense under paragraph (b) of this section, it is taken into account in tax years beginning on or after January 1, 1995 as a negative adjustment for 1990. Any such determination or redetermination does not, however, affect any prior period. Thus, the negative adjustment for S's noncapital, nondeductible expense is not taken into account for tax years beginning before January 1, 1995.

(2) *Dispositions of stock before effective date.*—(i) *In general.*—If M disposes of stock of S in a consolidated return year beginning before January 1, 1995, the amount of M's income, gain, deduction, or loss, and the basis reflected in that amount, are not redetermined under this section. See §1.1502-19 as contained in the 26 CFR part 1 edition revised as of April 1, 1994 for the definition of disposition, and paragraph (h)(5) of this section for the rules applicable to such dispositions.

(ii) *Lower-tier members.*—Although M disposes of S's stock in a tax year beginning before January 1, 1995, S's determinations or adjustments with respect to the stock of a lower-tier member with which it continues to file a consolidated return are redetermined in accordance with the rules of this section (even if they were previously taken into account by M and reflected in income, gain, deduction, or loss from the disposition of S's stock). For example, assume that M owns all of S's stock, S owns all of T's stock, and T owns all of U's stock. If S sells 80% of T's stock in a tax year beginning before January 1, 1995 (the effective date), the amount of S's income, gain, deduction, or loss from the sale, and the stock basis adjustments reflected in that amount, are not redetermined if M sells S's stock after the effective date. If S sells the remaining 20% of T's stock after the effective date, S's stock basis adjustments with respect to that T stock are also not redetermined because T became a non-member before the effective date. However, if T and U continue to file a consolidated return with each other and T sells U's stock after the effective date, T's stock basis adjustments with respect to U's stock are redetermined (even though some of those adjustments may have been taken into account by S in its prior sale of T's stock before the effective date).

(iii) *Deferred amounts.*—For purposes of this paragraph (h)(2), a disposition does not include a transaction to which § 1.1502-13, § 1.1502-13T, § 1.1502-14, or § 1.1502-14T applies. Instead, the transaction is deemed to occur as the income, gain, deduction, or loss (if any) is taken into account.

(3) *Distributions.*—(i) *Deemed dividend elections.*—If there is a deemed distribution and recontribution pursuant to § 1.1502-32(f)(2) as contained in the 26 CFR part 1 edition revised as of April 1, 1994 in a consolidated return year beginning before January 1, 1995, the deemed distribution and recontribution under the election are treated as an actual distribution by S and recontribution by M as provided under the election.

(ii) *Affiliated earnings and profits.*—This section does not apply to reduce the basis in S's stock as a result of a distribution of earnings and profits accumulated in separate return years, if the distribution is made in a consolidated return year beginning before January 1, 1995, and the distribution does not cause a negative adjustment under the investment adjustment rules in effect at the time of the distribution. See paragraph (h)(5) of this section for the rules in effect with respect to the distribution.

(4) *Expiring loss carryovers.*—If S became a member of a consolidated group in a consolidated return year beginning before January 1, 1995, and S had a loss carryover from a separate return limitation year at that time, the group does not treat any expiration of the loss carryover (even if in a tax year beginning on or after January 1, 1995) as a noncapital, nondeductible expense resulting in a negative adjustment under this section. If S becomes a member of a consolidated group in a consolidated return year beginning on or after January 1, 1995, and S has a loss carryover from a separate return limitation year at that time, adjustments with respect to the expiration are determined under this section.

(5) *Prior law.*—(i) *In general.*—For prior determinations, see prior regulations under section 1502 as in effect with respect to the determination. See, e.g., § § 1.1502-32 and 1.1502-32T as contained in the 26 CFR part 1 edition revised as of April 1, 1994.

(ii) *Continuing basis reductions for certain deconsolidated subsidiaries.*—If a subsidiary ceases to be a member of a group in a consolidated return year beginning before January 1, 1995, and its basis was subject to reduction under § 1.1502-32T or § 1.1502-32(g) as contained in the 26 CFR part 1 edition revised as of April 1, 1994, its basis remains subject to reduction under those principles. For example, if S ceased to be a member in 1990, and M's basis in any retained S stock was subject to a basis reduction account, the basis remains subject to reduction. Similarly, if an election could be made to apply § 1.1502-32T instead of § 1.1502-32(g), the election remains available. However, § § 1.1502-32T and 1.1502-32(g) do not apply as a result of a subsidiary ceasing to be a member in tax years beginning on or after January 1, 1995.

(6) *Loss suspended under § 1.1502-35(c) or disallowed under § 1.1502-35(g)(3)(iii).*—Paragraphs (a)(2), (b)(3)(iii)(C), (b)(3)(iii)(D) and (b)(4)(vi) of this section are applicable on and after March 10, 2006. For rules applicable before March 10, 2006, see § 1.1502-32T(h)(6) as contained in 26 CFR part 1 in effect on January 1, 2006.

(7) *Rules related to discharge of indebtedness income excluded from gross income.*—Paragraphs (b)(1)(ii), (b)(3)(ii)(C)(*1*), (b)(3)(iii)(A), and (b)(5)(ii), *Example 4*, paragraphs (a), (b), and (c) of this section apply with respect to determinations of the basis of the stock of a subsidiary in consolidated return years the original return for which is due (without regard to extensions) after March 21, 2005. However, groups may apply those provisions with respect to determinations of the basis of the stock of a subsidiary in consolidated return years the original return for which is due (without regard to extensions) on or before March 21, 2005, and after August 29, 2003. For determinations of the basis of the stock of a subsidiary in consolidated return years the original return for which is due (without regard to extensions) on or before March 21, 2005, and after August 29, 2003, with respect to which a group chooses not to apply paragraphs (b)(1)(ii), (b)(3)(ii)(C)(*1*), (b)(3)(iii)(A), and (b)(5)(ii), *Example 4*, paragraphs (a), (b), and (c) of this section, see § 1.1502-32T(b)(3)(ii)(C)(*1*), (b)(3)(iii)(A), and (b)(5)(ii), *Example 4*, paragraphs (a), (b), and (c) as contained in 26 CFR part 1 revised as of April 1, 2004.

(8) Paragraph (b)(5)(ii) *Example 6* of this section applies only with respect to determinations of the basis of the stock of a subsidiary on or after January 23, 2006. For determinations of the basis of the stock of a subsidiary before January 23, 2006, see § 1.1502-32(b)(5)(ii) *Example 6* as contained in the 26 CFR part 1 edition revised as of April 1, 2005.

(9) *Allocations of investment adjustments, including adjustments attributable to certain loss transfers; certain conforming amendments.*—Paragraphs

(a)(2), (b)(3)(ii)(C)(2), (c)(1), (c)(2)(i), (c)(2)(ii)(A), (c)(3), and (c)(4)(i) of this section are applicable for determinations of the basis of stock of a subsidiary on or after September 17, 2008.

(i) [Reserved]. For further guidance, see § 1.1502-32T(i) through (j)(1).

(j) *Effective/applicability date.*—Paragraph (b)(4)(iv) of this section applies to any original consolidated Federal income tax return due (without extensions) after June 14, 2007. For original consolidated Federal income tax returns due (without extensions) after May 30, 2006, and on or before June 14, 2007, see § 1.1502-32T as contained in 26 CFR part 1 in effect on April 1, 2007. For original consolidated Federal income tax returns due (without extensions) on or before May 30, 2006, see § 1.1502-32 as contained in 26 CFR part 1 in effect on April 1, 2006.

(k) [Reserved]. For further guidance, see § 1.1502-32T(k). [Reg. § 1.1502-32.]

☐ [*T.D. 6909, 12-29-66. Amended by T.D. 7246, 12-29-72; T.D. 7637, 8-6-79; T.D. 7655, 11-28-79; T.D. 7947, 3-5-84; T.D. 8188, 3-14-88; T.D. 8245, 3-14-89; T.D. 8294, 3-9-90; T.D. 8319, 11-19-90; T.D. 8364, 9-13-91; T.D. 8401, 3-13-92; T.D. 8560, 8-12-94; T.D. 8677, 6-26-96; T.D. 8823, 6-25-99; T.D. 8984, 3-7-2002; T.D. 9048, 3-11-2003; T.D. 9089, 8-29-2003; T.D. 9187, 3-2-2005; T.D. 9192, 3-21-2005 T.D. 9244, 1-23-2006 (corrected 4-12-2006); T.D. 9254, 3-9-2006; T.D. 9264, 5-26-2006 (corrected 10-25-2006); T.D. 9322, 4-9-2007; T.D. 9329, 6-13-2007 and T.D. 9424, 9-9-2008.*]

[Reg. § 1.1502-33]

§ 1.1502-33. Earnings and profits.—(a) *In general.*—(1) *Purpose.*—This section provides rules for adjusting the earnings and profits of a subsidiary (S) and any member (P) owning S's stock. These rules modify the determination of P's earnings and profits under applicable rules of law, including section 312, by adjusting P's earnings and profits to reflect S's earnings and profits for the period that S is a member of the consolidated group. The purpose for modifying the determination of earnings and profits is to treat P and S as a single entity by reflecting the earnings and profits of lower-tier members in the earnings and profits of higher-tier members and consolidating the group's earnings and profits in the common parent. References in this section to earnings and profits include deficits in earnings and profits.

(2) *Application of other rules of law, duplicative adjustments.*—See § 1.1502-80(a) regarding the general applicability of other rules of law and a limitation on duplicative adjustments. The rules of this section are in addition to other rules of law. For example, the allowance for depreciation is determined in accordance with section 312(k). P's earnings and profits must not be adjusted under this section and other rules of law in a

manner that has the effect of duplicating an adjustment. For example, if S's earnings and profits are reflected in P's earnings and profits under paragraph (b) of this section, and S transfers its assets to P in a liquidation to which section 332 applies, S's earnings and profits that P succeeds to under section 381 must be adjusted to prevent duplication.

(b) *Tiering up earnings and profits.*—(1) *General rule.*—P's earnings and profits are adjusted under this section to reflect changes in S's earnings and profits in accordance with the applicable principles of § 1.1502-32, consistently applied, and an adjustment to P's earnings and profits for a tax year under this paragraph (b)(1) is treated as earnings and profits of P for the tax year in which the adjustment arises. Under these principles, for example, the adjustments are made as of the close of each consolidated return year, and as of any other time if a determination at that time is necessary to determine the earnings and profits of any person. Similarly, S's earnings and profits are allocated under the principles of § 1.1502-32(c), and the adjustments are applied in the order of the tiers, from the lowest to the highest. However, modifications to the principles include:

(i) The amount of P's adjustment is determined by reference to S's earnings and profits, rather than S's taxable and tax-exempt items (and therefore, for example, the deferral of a negative adjustment for S's unabsorbed losses does not apply).

(ii) The tax sharing rules under paragraph (d) of this section apply rather than those of § 1.1502-32(b)(3)(iv)(D).

(2) *Affiliated earnings and profits.*—The reduction in S's earnings and profits under section 312 from a distribution of earnings and profits accumulated in separate return years of S that are not separate return limitation years does not tier up to P's earnings and profits. Thus, the increase in P's earnings and profits under section 312 from receipt of the distribution is not offset by a corresponding reduction.

(3) *Examples.*—(i) *In general.*—For purposes of the examples in this section, unless otherwise stated, P owns all of the only class of S's stock, the stock is owned for the entire year, S owns no stock of lower-tier members, the tax year of all persons is the calendar year, all persons use the accrual method of accounting, the facts set forth the only corporate activity, preferred stock is described in section 1504(a)(4), all transactions are between unrelated persons, and tax liabilities are disregarded.

(ii) *Tiering up earnings and profits.*—The principles of this paragraph (b) are illustrated by the following examples.

Example 1. Tier-up and distribution of earnings and profits. (a) *Facts.* P forms S in Year 1 with a $100 contribution. S has $100 of earnings and profits for Year 1 and no earnings and profits for Year 2. During Year 2, S declares and distributes a $50 dividend to P.

(b) *Analysis.* Under paragraph (b)(1) of this section, S's $100 of earnings and profits for Year 1 increases P's earnings and profits for Year 1. P has no additional earnings and profits for Year 2 as a result of the $50 distribution in Year 2, because there is a $50 increase in P's earnings and profits as a result of the receipt of the dividend and a corresponding $50 decrease in S's earnings and profits under section 312(a) that is reflected in P's earnings and profits under paragraph (b)(1) of this section.

(c) *Distribution of current earnings and profits.* The facts are the same as in paragraph (a) of this *Example 1*, except that S distributes the $50 dividend at the end of Year 1 rather than during Year 2. Under paragraph (b)(1) of this section, P's earnings and profits are increased by $100 (S's $50 of undistributed earnings and profits, plus P's receipt of the $50 distribution). Thus, S's earnings and profits increase by $50 and P's earnings and profits increase by $100.

(d) *Affiliated earnings and profits.* The facts are the same as in paragraph (a) of this *Example 1*, except that P and S do not begin filing consolidated returns until Year 2. Because P and S file separate returns for Year 1, P's basis in S's stock remains $100 under §1.1502-32 and this section, S has $100 of earnings and profits, and none of S's earnings and profits is reflected in P's earnings and profits under paragraph (b) of this section. S's distribution in Year 2 ordinarily would reduce S's earnings and profits but not increase P's earnings and profits. (P's $50 of earnings and profits from the dividend would be offset by S's $50 reduction in earnings and profits that tiers up under paragraph (b) of this section.) However, under paragraph (b)(2) of this section, the negative adjustment for S's distribution to P does not apply. Thus, S's distribution reduces its earnings and profits by $50 but increases P's earnings and profits by $50. (If S's earnings and profits had been accumulated in a separate return limitation year, paragraph (b)(2) of this section would not apply and the distribution would reduce S's earnings and profits but not increase P's earnings and profits.)

(e) *Earnings and profits deficit.* Assume instead that after P forms S in Year 1 with a $100 contribution, S borrows additional funds and has a $150 deficit in earnings and profits for Year 1. The corresponding loss for tax purposes is not absorbed in Year 1, and is included in the group's consolidated net operating loss carried forward to Year 2. Under paragraph (b)(1) of this section, however, S's $150 deficit in earnings and profits decreases P's earnings and profits for Year 1 by $150. (Absorption of the loss in a later tax year has no effect on the earnings and profits of P and S.)

Example 2. Section 355 distribution. (a) *Facts.* P owns all of S's stock and S owns all of T's stock. For Year 1, T has $100 of earnings and profits. Under paragraph (b)(1) of this section, the earnings and profits of T tier up to S and to P. S and P have no other earnings and profits for Year 1. S distributes T's stock to P at the end of Year 1 in a distribution to which section 355 applies.

(b) *Analysis.* Because S's distribution of T's stock is a distribution to which section 355 applies, the applicable principles of §1.1502-32(b)(2)(iv) do not require P's earnings and profits to be adjusted by reason of the distribution. In addition, although S's earnings and profits may be reduced under section 312(h) as a result of the distribution, the applicable principles of §1.1502-32(b)(3)(iii) do not require P's earnings and profits to be adjusted to reflect this reduction in S's earnings and profits.

Example 3. Allocating earnings and profits among shares. P owns 80% of S's stock throughout Year 1. For Year 1, S has $100 of earnings and profits. Under paragraph (b)(1) of this section, $80 of S's earnings and profits is allocated to P based on P's ownership of S's stock. Accordingly, $80 of S's earnings and profits for Year 1 is reflected in P's earnings and profits for Year 1.

(c) *Special rules.*—For purposes of this section—

(1) *Stock of members.*—For purposes of determining P's earnings and profits from the disposition of S's stock, P's basis in S's stock is adjusted to reflect S's earnings and profits determined under paragraph (b) of this section, rather than under §1.1502-32. For example, P's basis in S's stock is increased by positive earnings and profits and decreased by deficits in earnings and profits. Similarly, P's basis in S's stock is not reduced for distributions to which paragraph (b)(2) of this section applies (affiliated earnings and profits). P may have an excess loss account in S's stock for earnings and profits purposes (whether or not there is an excess loss account under §1.1502-32), and the excess loss account is determined, adjusted, and taken into account in accordance with the principles of §§1.1502-19 and 1.1502-32.

(2) *Intercompany transactions.*—Intercompany items and corresponding items are not reflected in earnings and profits before they are taken into account under §1.1502-13. See §1.1502-13 for the applicable rules and definitions.

(3) *Example.*—The principles of this paragraph (c) are illustrated by the following example.

Example. Adjustments to stock basis. (a) *Facts.* P forms S in Year 1 with a $100 contribution. For Year 1, S has $75 of taxable income and $100 of earnings and profits. For Year 2, S has no taxable income or earnings and profits, and S declares and distributes a $50 dividend to P. P sells all of S's stock for $150 at the end of Year 2.

(b) *Analysis.* Under paragraph (c)(1) of this section, P's basis in S's stock for earnings and profits purposes immediately before the sale is $150 (the $100 initial basis, plus S's $100 of earnings and profits for Year 1, minus the $50 distribution of earnings and profits in Year 2). Thus, P recognizes no gain or loss from the sale of S's stock for earnings and profits purposes.

(c) *Earnings and profits deficit.* Assume instead that S has a $100 tax loss and earnings and profits deficit for Year 1. The tax loss is not absorbed in Year 1 and is included in the group's consolidated net operating loss carried forward to Year 2. Under paragraph (b) of this section, S's $100 deficit in earnings and profits decreases P's earnings and profits for Year 1. Under paragraph (c) of this section, P decreases its basis in S's stock for purposes of determining earnings and profits from $100 to $0. (If S had borrowed an additional $50 so that it also lost in Year 1, P would have decreased its earnings and profits for Year 1 by the additional $50, and P would have had a $50 excess loss account in S's stock for earnings and profits purposes, which would be taken into account in determining P's earnings and profits from its sale of S's stock.)

(d) *Affiliated earnings and profits.* Assume instead that P and S do not begin filing consolidated returns until Year 2. Under paragraph (b) of this section, the negative adjustment under §1.1502-32(b) for distributions does not apply to S's distribution of earnings and profits accumulated in a separate return year that is a not separate return limitation year. Thus, P's basis in S's stock for earnings and profits purposes remains $100, and P has $50 of earnings and profits from the sale of S's stock.

(d) *Federal income tax liability.*—(1) *In general.*—(i) *Extension of tax allocations.*—Section 1552 allocates the tax liability of a consolidated group among its members for purposes of determining the amounts by which their earnings and profits are reduced for taxes. Section 1552 does not reflect the absorption by one member of another member's tax attributes (e.g., losses, deductions and credits). For example, if P's $100 of income is offset by S's $100 of deductions, consolidated tax liability is $0 and no amount is allocated under section 1552. However, the group may elect under this paragraph (d) to allocate additional amounts to reflect the absorption by one member of the tax attributes of another member. Permissible methods are set forth in paragraphs (d)(2) through (4) of this section, and election procedures are provided in paragraph (d)(5) of this section. Allocations under this paragraph (d) must be reflected annually on permanent records (including work papers). Any computations of separate return tax liability are subject to the principles of section 1561.

(ii) *Effect of extended tax allocations.*—The amounts allocated under this paragraph (d) are treated as allocations of tax liability for purposes of §1.1552-1(b)(2). For example, if P's taxable income is offset by S's loss, and tax liability is allocated under the percentage method of paragraph (d)(3) of this section, P's earnings and profits are reduced as if its income were subject to tax, P is treated as liable to S for the amount of the tax, and corresponding adjustments are made to S's earnings and profits. If the liability of one member to another is not paid, the amount not paid generally is treated as a distribution, contribution, or both, depending on the relationship between the members.

(2) *Wait-and-see method.*—The wait-and-see method under this paragraph (d)(2) is derived from Securities and Exchange Commission procedures. In the year that a member's tax attribute is absorbed, the group's consolidated tax liability is allocated in accordance with the group's method under section 1552. When, in effect, the member with the tax attribute could have absorbed the attribute on a separate return basis in a later year, a portion of the group's consolidated tax liability for the later year that is otherwise allocated to members under section 1552 is reallocated. The reallocation takes into account all consolidated return years to which this paragraph (d) applies (the computation period), and is determined by comparing the tax allocated to a member during the computation period with the member's tax liability determined as if it had filed separate returns during the computation period.

(i) *Cap on allocation under section 1552.*—A member's allocation under section 1552 for a tax year may not exceed the excess, if any, of—

(A) The total of the tax liabilities of the member for the computation period (including the current year), determined as if the member had filed separate returns; over

(B) The total amount allocated to the member under section 1552 and this paragraph (d) for the computation period (except the current year).

(ii) *Reallocation of capped amounts.*—To the extent that the amount allocated to a member under section 1552 exceeds the limitation under paragraph (d)(2)(i) of this section, the excess is allocated among the remaining members in proportion to (but not to exceed the amount of) each member's excess, if any, of—

(A) The total of the tax liabilities of the member for the computation period (including the current year), determined as if the member had filed separate returns; over

(B) The total amount allocated to the member under section 1552 and this paragraph (d) for the computation period (including for the current year only the amount allocated under section 1552).

Reg. §1.1502-33(d)(1)

(iii) *Reallocation of excess capped amounts.*— If the reductions under paragraph (d)(2)(i) of this section exceed the amounts allocable under paragraph (d)(2)(ii) of this section, the excess is allocated among the members in accordance with the group's method under section 1552 without taking this paragraph (d)(2) into account.

(3) *Percentage method.*—The percentage method under this paragraph (d)(3) allocates tax liability based on the absorption of tax attributes, without taking into account the ability of any member to subsequently absorb its own tax attributes. The allocation under this method is in addition to the allocation under section 1552.

(i) *Decreased earnings and profits.*—A member's allocation under section 1552 for any year is increased, thereby decreasing its earnings and profits, by a fixed percentage (not to exceed 100%) of the excess, if any, of—

(A) The member's separate return tax liability for the consolidated return year as determined under § 1.1552-1(a)(2)(ii); over

(B) The amount allocated to the member under section 1552.

(ii) *Increased earnings and profits.*—An amount equal to the total decrease in earnings and profits under paragraph (d)(3)(i) of this section (including amounts allocated as a result of a carryback) increases the earnings and profits of the members whose attributes are absorbed, and is allocated among them in a manner that reasonably reflects the absorption of the tax attributes.

(4) *Additional methods.*—The absorption by one member of the tax attributes of another member may be reflected under any other method approved in writing by the Commissioner.

(5) *Election of allocation method.*—(i) *In general.*—Tax liability may be allocated under this paragraph (d) only if an election is filed with the group's first return. The election must—

(A) Be made in a separate statement entitled "ELECTION TO ALLOCATE TAX LIABILITY UNDER § 1.1502-33(d)";

(B) State the allocation method elected under § 1.1502-33(d) and under section 1552;

(C) If the percentage method is elected, state the percentage (not to exceed 100%) to be used; and

(D) If a method is permitted under paragraph (d)(4) of this section, provide the date and control number of the private letter ruling issued by the Internal Revenue Service approving such method.

(ii) *Consent.*—(A) *Electing or changing methods.*—An election for a later year, or an election to change methods, may be made only with the written consent of the Commissioner.

(B) *Prior law elections.*—An election in effect for the last tax year beginning before January 1, 1995, remains in effect under this section. However, a group may elect to conform its earnings and profits computations to the method described in § 1.1502-32(b)(3)(iv)(D) (the percentage method, using a 100% allocation), whether or not it has previously made an election for earnings and profits purposes. If a conforming election is made, the group must make all adjustments necessary to prevent amounts from being duplicated or omitted. The conforming election is made by attaching a statement entitled "ELECTION TO CONFORM TAX ALLOCATIONS UNDER §§ 1.1502-32 and 1.1502-33(d)" to the consolidated group's return for its first tax year beginning on or after January 1, 1995. The statement must be signed by the common parent, and must specify whether the method is conformed only for years beginning on or after January 1, 1995 or as if the method were in effect for all prior years. The statement must also describe the adjustments made by reason of the change (e.g., to reflect prior use of earnings and profits).

(6) *Examples.*—The principles of this paragraph (d) are illustrated by the following examples.

Example 1. Wait-and-see method. (a) *Facts.* P owns all of the stock of S1 and S2. The P group uses the wait-and-see method of allocation under paragraph (d)(2) of this section in conjunction with § 1.1552-1(a)(1). For Year 1, each member's taxable income, both for purposes of § 1.1552-1(a)(1) and redetermined as if the member had filed separate returns, is as follows: P $0, S1 $2,000, and S2 ($1,000). Thus, the P group's consolidated tax liability for Year 1 is $340 (assuming a 34% tax rate).

(b) *Analysis.* Under § 1.1552-1(a)(1)(i), the tax liability of the P group is allocated among the members in accordance with the portion of the consolidated taxable income attributable to each member having taxable income. Thus, all of the P group's $340 consolidated tax liability is allocated to S1. As a result, S1 decreases its earnings and profits under section 1552 by $340 (even if S1 does not pay the tax liability). No further allocations are made under paragraph (d)(2) of this section because S2 cannot yet absorb its loss on a separate return basis.

(c) *Payment of tax liability.* If S1 pays the $340 tax liability, there is no further effect on the income, earnings and profits, or stock basis of any member. If P pays the $340 tax liability (and the payment is not a loan from P to S1), P is treated as making a $340 contribution to the capital of S1; if S2 pays the $340 tax liability (and the payment is not a loan from S2 to S1), S2 is treated as making a $340 distribution to P with respect to its stock, and P is treated as making a $340 contribution to the capital of S1. See § 1.1552-1(b)(2).

Reg. § 1.1502-33(d)(6)

(d) *Year 2.* For Year 2, each member's taxable income, under §1.1552-1(a)(1)(ii) and redetermined as if the member had filed separate returns, without taking into account any carryover from Year 1, is as follows: P $0, S1 $1,000, and S2 $3,000. Thus, the P group's consolidated tax liability for Year 2 is $1,360 (assuming a 34% tax rate). Of this amount, section 1552 would allocate $340 to S1 and $1,020 to S2. However, under paragraph (d)(2)(i) of this section, no more than $680 may be allocated to S2. This is because S2 would have had an aggregate tax liability of $680 if it had filed separate returns for Years 1 and 2 (a $0 tax liability for Year 1, and a $680 tax liability for Year 2, taking into account a $1,000 net operating loss carryover from Year 1). Under paragraph (d)(2)(ii) of this section, the entire excess of $340 which would otherwise be allocated to S2 under §1.1552-1(a)(1) is allocated to S1. This is because S1 would have had an additional $340 of aggregate tax liability if it had filed separate returns for Years 1 and 2 (a $680 tax liability for Year 1, and a $340 tax liability for Year 2, not taking into account S2's $1,000 net operating loss for Year 1). The effect of the allocation of $680 to S1 and $680 to S2 is determined under §1.1552-1(b)(2).

Example 2. Percentage method. (a) *Facts.* The facts are the same as in *Example 1,* but the P group uses the percentage method of allocation under paragraph (d)(3) of this section, with a percentage of 100%. In addition, the taxable incomes and losses of the members are the same if computed as provided in §1.1552-1(a)(2)(ii).

(b) *Analysis.* Under §1.1552-1(a)(2)(ii), $340 of tax liability is allocated to S1 for Year 1. Under paragraph (d)(3)(i) of this section, S1 is allocated another $340 of tax liability because S1 would have had a $680 tax liability if it had filed separate returns but only $340 is allocated to S1 under section 1552. Thus, S1's earnings and profits are decreased by the $680 total. Under paragraph (d)(3)(ii) of this section, S2's earnings and profits are increased by $340 because the additional $340 allocated to S1 under paragraph (d)(3)(i) of this section is attributable to the absorption of S2's losses.

(c) *Payment of tax liability.* If S1 pays the $340 tax liability of the P group and pays $340 to S2, the Year 1 tax liability results in no further adjustments to the income, earnings and profits, or basis of any member's stock. If S1 pays the $340 tax liability of the P group and pays the other $340 to P instead of S2 because, for example, of an agreement among the members, S2 is treated as distributing $340 to P with respect to its stock in the year that S1 makes the payment to P. See §1.1552-1(b)(2).

(d) *Year 2.* For Year 2, $340 is allocated to S1 and $1,020 is allocated to S2 under section 1552. No additional amounts are allocated under paragraph (d)(3) of this section.

(e) *Deconsolidations.*—(1) *In general.*—Immediately before it becomes a nonmember, S's earnings and profits are eliminated to the extent they were taken into account by any member under this section. If S's earnings and profits are eliminated under this paragraph (e)(1), no corresponding adjustment is made to the earnings and profits of P (or any other member) under paragraph (b) of this section or to any basis in a member's stock under paragraph (c) of this section. For this purpose, S is treated as becoming a nonmember on the first day of its first separate return year (including another group's consolidated return year).

(2) *Acquisition of group.*—(i) *Application.*—This paragraph (e)(2) applies only if a consolidated group (the terminating group) ceases to exist as a result of—

(A) The acquisition of either the assets of the common parent of the terminating group in a reorganization described in section 381(a)(2), or the stock of the common parent of the terminating group; or

(B) The application of the principles of §1.1502-75(d)(2) or (d)(3).

(ii) *General rule.*—Paragraph (e)(1) of this section does not apply solely by reason of the termination of a group because it is acquired, if there is a surviving group that is, immediately thereafter, a consolidated group. Instead, the surviving group is treated as the terminating group for purposes of applying this paragraph (e) to the terminating group. This treatment does not apply, however, to members of the terminating group that are not members of the surviving consolidated group immediately after the terminating group ceases to exist (e.g., under section 1504(a)(3) relating to reconsolidation, or section 1504(c) relating to includible insurance companies).

(3) *Certain corporate separations and reorganizations.*—The adjustments under paragraph (e)(1) of this section must be modified to the extent necessary to effectuate the principles of section 312(h). Thus, P's earnings and profits rather than S's earnings and profits may be eliminated immediately before S becomes a nonmember. P's earnings and profits are eliminated to the extent that its earnings and profits reflect S's earnings and profits after applying section 312(h) immediately after S becomes a nonmember (determined without taking this paragraph (e) into account).

(4) *Special uses of earnings and profits.*—Paragraph (e)(1) of this section does not apply for purposes of determining—

(i) The extent to which a distribution is charged to reserve accounts under section 593(e);

(ii) The extent to which a distribution is taxable to the recipient under sections 805(a)(4) and 832; and

(iii) Any other special use identified in guidance published in the Internal Revenue Bulletin.

(5) *Example.*—The principles of this paragraph (e) are illustrated by the following example.

Example. (a) *Facts.* Individuals A and B own all of P's stock, and P owns all of the stock of S and T, each with a $500 basis. For Year 1, S has $100 of earnings and profits and T has $50 of earnings and profits. Under paragraph (b)(1) of this section, the earnings and profits of S and T tier up to P, and P has $150 of earnings and profits for Year 1. P sells all of S's stock for $600 at the close of Year 1.

(b) *Analysis.* Under paragraph (e)(1) of this section, S's $100 of earnings and profits is eliminated immediately before S becomes a nonmember because the earnings and profits are taken into account under paragraph (b) of this section in P's earnings and profits. However, no corresponding adjustment is made to P's earnings and profits or to P's basis in S's stock for purposes of earnings and profits. P's earnings and profits for Year 1 remain $150 following the sale of S's stock.

(c) *Forward merger.* The facts are the same as in paragraph (a) of this *Example*, except that, rather than P selling S's stock, S merges into a nonmember in a transaction described in section 368(a)(2)(D). Under paragraph (h) of this section, the nonmember is treated as a successor to S. Thus, as in paragraph (b) of this *Example*, S's $100 of earnings and profits is eliminated immediately before S ceases to be a member.

(d) *Acquisition of entire group.* The facts are the same as in paragraph (a) of this *Example*, except that X, the common parent of another consolidated group, purchases all of P's stock at the close of Year 1, and P sells S's stock during Year 3. Under paragraph (e)(2) of this section, the earnings and profits of S and T are not eliminated as a result of X purchasing P's stock. However, S's earnings and profits from consolidated return years of both the P group and the X group are eliminated immediately before S becomes a nonmember of the X group.

(e) *Earnings and profits deficit.* The facts are the same as in paragraph (d) of this *Example*, except that S has a $550 deficit in earnings and profits for Year 1. The effect of paragraph (e)(1) of this section is the same. Under paragraph (c)(1) of this section, P would have an excess loss account in S's stock for earnings and profits purposes under the principles of §§ 1.1502-19 and 1.1502-32, and, under the principles of § 1.1502-19(c)(2), the excess loss account is not taken into account as a result of X's purchase of P's stock. Under paragraph (e)(2) of this section, S's deficit is not eliminated under paragraph (e)(1) of this section immediately before X's purchase of P's stock. However, S's earnings and

profits (or deficit) is eliminated immediately before S becomes a nonmember of the X group.

(f) *Section 355 distribution.* The facts are the same as in paragraph (a) of this *Example*, except that, rather than selling S's stock, P distributes S's stock to A at the close of Year 1 in a distribution to which section 355 applies. Under paragraph (e)(3) of this section, P's earnings and profits may be reduced under section 312(h) as a result of the distribution. To the extent that P's earnings and profits are reduced, S's earnings and profits are not eliminated under paragraph (e)(1) of this section.

(f) *Changes in the structure of the group.*— (1) *Changes in the common parent.*—(i) *General rule.*—If P succeeds another corporation under the principles of § 1.1502-75(d)(2) or (3) as the common parent of a consolidated group (a group structure change), the earnings and profits of P are adjusted immediately after P becomes the new common parent to reflect the earnings and profits of the former common parent immediately before the former common parent ceases to be the common parent. The adjustment is made as if P succeeds to the earnings and profits of the former common parent in a transaction described in section 381(a). See § 1.1502-31 for the basis of the stock of members following a group structure change.

(ii) *Minority shareholders.*—If the former common parent's stock is not wholly owned by members of the consolidated group immediately after the former common parent ceases to be the common parent, appropriate adjustments must be made to reflect in the new common parent only an allocable part of the former common parent's earnings and profits.

(iii) *Higher-tier members.*—To the extent that earnings and profits are adjusted under this paragraph (f)(1), and the former common parent is owned by members other than P, the earnings and profits of the intermediate subsidiaries must be adjusted in accordance with the principles of this section.

(iv) *Example.*—The principles of this paragraph (f)(1) are illustrated by the following example.

Example. (a) *Facts.* X is the common parent of a consolidated group with $100 of earnings and profits, and P is the common parent of another consolidated group with $20 of earnings and profits. P acquires all of X's stock at the close of Year 1 in exchange for 70% of P's stock. The exchange is a reverse acquisition under § 1.1502-75(d)(3), and the X group is treated as remaining in existence with P as its new common parent.

(b) *Adjustments for X group earnings and profits.* Under paragraph (f)(1) of this section, P's earnings and profits are adjusted immediately after P becomes the new common parent, to reflect X's $100 of earnings and profits immediately before X ceases to be the common parent. The adjustment is made as if P succeeds to X's earnings and profits in a transaction described in section 381(a). Thus, immediately after the acquisition, P has $120 of accumulated earnings and profits and X continues to have $100 of accumulated earnings and profits.

(c) *Adjustments for P group earnings and profits.* Although the P group terminates on P's acquisition of X's stock, under paragraph (e)(2) of this section, no adjustments are made to the earnings and profits of any subsidiaries in the terminating P group.

(d) *Acquisition of separate return corporation.* The facts are the same as in paragraph (a) of this *Example*, except that, immediately before the acquisition of its stock by P, X is not affiliated with any other corporation. The exchange is a reverse acquisition under § 1.1502-75(d)(3), and P is treated as the common parent of the X group. Consequently, the results are the same as in paragraphs (b) and (c) of this *Example*:

(2) *Change in the location of subsidiaries.*—If the location of a member within a group changes, appropriate adjustments must be made to the earnings and profits of the members to prevent the earnings and profits from being eliminated. For example, if P transfers all of S's stock to another member in a transaction to which section 351 and § 1.1502-13 apply, the transferee's earnings and profits are adjusted immediately after the transfer to reflect S's earnings and profits immediately before the transfer from consolidated return years. On the other hand, if the transferee purchases S's stock from P, the transferee's earnings and profits are not adjusted.

(g) *Anti-avoidance rule.*—If any person acts with a principal purpose contrary to the purposes of this section, to avoid the effect of the rules of this section or apply the rules of this section to avoid the effect of any other provision of the consolidated return regulations, adjustments must be made as necessary to carry out the purposes of this section.

(h) *Predecessors and successors.*—For purposes of this section, any reference to a corporation or to a share includes a reference to a successor or predecessor as the context may require. A corporation is a successor if its earnings and profits are determined, directly or indirectly, in whole or in part, by reference to the earnings and profits of another corporation (the predecessor). A share is a successor if its basis is determined, directly or indirectly, in whole or in part, by reference to the basis of another share (the predecessor).

(i) [Reserved]

(j) *Effective/applicability date.*—(1) *General rule.*—This section applies with respect to determinations of the earnings and profits of a member (e.g., for purposes of a characterizing a distribution to which section 301 applies) in consolidated return years beginning on or after January 1, 1995. If this section applies, earnings and profits must be determined or redetermined as if this section were in effect for all years (including, for example, the consolidated return years of another consolidated group to the extent the earnings and profits from those years are still reflected). For example, if a distribution by P to a nonmember shareholder in 1990 was a dividend because of an unabsorbed loss carryover attributable to S, P's earnings and profits in tax years beginning after January 1, 1995 are redetermined by taking into account a negative adjustment in the tax year S's loss arose and in 1990 for P's distribution, and any subsequent absorption of the loss has no effect on earnings and profits. Any such determination or redetermination does not, however, affect any prior period. Thus, the shareholder's treatment in 1990 of the distribution as a dividend (and the effect of the distribution on stock basis) is not redetermined under this section. Paragraphs (a)(2) and (e)(2)(i)(A) of this section apply with respect to determinations of the earnings and profits of a member in consolidated return years beginning on or after September 17, 2008. However, taxpayers may apply paragraph (e)(2)(i)(A) of this section with respect to determinations of the earnings and profits of a member in consolidated return years beginning prior to September 17, 2008.

(2) *Dispositions of stock before effective date.*— (i) *In general.*—If P disposes of stock of S in a consolidated return year beginning before January 1, 1995, the amount of P's earnings and profits with respect to S are not redetermined under paragraph (j)(1) of this section. See § 1.1502-19 as contained in the 26 CFR part 1 edition revised as of April 1, 1994 for the definition of disposition, and paragraph (j)(5) of this section for the rules applicable to such dispositions.

(ii) *Lower-tier members.*—Although P disposes of S's stock in a tax year beginning before January 1, 1995, S's determinations or adjustments with respect to lower-tier members with which it continues to file a consolidated return are redetermined in accordance with the rules of this section (even if S's earnings and profits were previously taken into account by P). For example, assume that P owns all of S's stock, S owns all of T's stock, and T owns all of U's stock. If S sells 80% of T's stock in a tax year beginning before January 1, 1995 (the effective date), the amount of S's earnings and profits from the sale, and the adjustments to stock basis for earnings and profits purposes that are reflected in that amount, are not redetermined if P sells S's stock after the effective date. If S sells the remaining 20% of T's stock after the effective date, S's stock basis adjustments with respect to that T stock are also not redetermined because T became a nonmember before the effective date. However, if T and U continue to file a consolidated return with each other, paragraph (e)(1) of this section did not apply, and T sells U's stock after the effective date, T's earnings and profits with respect to U are redetermined (even though some of the earnings and profits may have been taken into account by S in its prior sale of T's stock before the effective date).

(iii) *Deferred amounts.*—For purposes of this paragraph (j)(2), a disposition does not include a transaction to which § 1.1502-13, § 1.1502-13T, § 1.1502-14, or § 1.1502-14T applies. Instead, the transaction is deemed to occur as the earnings and profits (if any) are taken into account.

(3) *Deconsolidations and group structure changes.*—(i) *In general.*—Paragraphs (e) and (f) of this section apply with respect to deconsolidations and group structure changes occurring in consolidated return years beginning on or after January 1, 1995.

(ii) *Prior period group structure changes.*—If there was a group structure change in a consolidated return year beginning before January 1, 1995, and earnings and profits were not determined under § 1.1502-33T(a) as contained in the 26 CFR part 1 edition revised as of April 1, 1994, a distribution in a tax year ending after September 7, 1988, of earnings and profits that are not reflected in the earnings and profits of the distributee member, but would have been so reflected if § 1.1502-33T(a) as contained in the 26 CFR part 1 edition revised as of April 1, 1994 had applied, the negative adjustment under paragraph (b) of this section for distributions does not apply (and there is therefore no offset to the increase in the earnings and profits of the distributee).

(4) *Deemed dividend elections.*—If there is a deemed distribution and recontribution pursuant to § 1.1502-32(f)(2) as contained in the 26 CFR part 1 edition revised as of April 1, 1994 in a consolidated return year beginning before January 1, 1995, the deemed distribution and recontribution under the election are treated as an actual distribution by S and recontribution by P as provided under the election.

(5) *Prior law.*—For prior determinations, see prior regulations under section 1502 as in effect with respect to the determination. See, e.g., §§ 1.1502-33 and 1.1502-33T as contained in the 26 CFR part 1 edition revised as of April 1, 1994.

(k) *Effective/applicability date.*—Paragraph (d)(5)(i)(D) of this section applies to any original consolidated Federal income tax return due (without extensions) after June 14, 2007. For original consolidated Federal income tax returns due (without extensions) after May 30, 2006, and on

or before June 14, 2007, see § 1.1502-33T as contained in 26 CFR part 1 in effect on April 1, 2007. For original consolidated Federal income tax returns due (without extensions) on or before May 30, 2006, see § 1.1502-33 as contained in 26 CFR part 1 in effect on April 1, 2006. [Reg. § 1.1502-33.]

☐ [*T.D.* 6909, 12-29-66. *Amended by T.D.* 6943, 1-15-68; *T.D.* 6962, 7-2-68; *T.D.* 7246, 12-29-72; *T.D.* 8226, 9-7-88; *T.D.* 8294, 3-9-90; *T.D.* 8319, 11-19-90, *T.D.* 8364, 9-13-91; *T.D.* 8560, 8-12-94; *T.D.* 8597, 7-12-9;5 *T.D.* 9264, 5-26-2006; *T.D.* 9329, 6-13-2007 and *T.D.* 9424, 9-9-2008 (*corrected* 10-17-2008).]

[Reg. § 1.1502-34]

§ 1.1502-34. Special aggregate stock ownership rules.—For purposes of §§ 1.1502-1 through 1.1502-80, in determining the stock ownership of a member of the group in another corporation (the "issuing corporation") for purposes of determining the application of section 165(g)(3)(A), 332(b)(1), 333(b), 351(a), 732(f), or 904(f), in a consolidated return year, there shall be included stock owned by all other members of the group in the issuing corporation. Thus, assume that members A, B, and C each own 33¹/₃ percent of the stock issued by D. In such case, A, B, and C shall each be treated as meeting the 80-percent stock ownership requirement for purposes of section 332, and no member can elect to have section 333 apply. Furthermore, the special rule for minority shareholders in section 337(d) cannot apply with respect to amounts received by A, B, or C in liquidation of D. [Reg. § 1.1502-34.]

☐ [*T.D.* 6894, 9-7-66. *Amended by T.D.* 8949, 6-18-2001.]

[Reg. § 1.1502-35]

§ 1.1502-35. Transfers of subsidiary stock and deconsolidations of subsidiaries.—(a) *In general.*—(1) *Purpose.*—The purpose of this section is to prevent a group from obtaining more than one tax benefit from a single economic loss. The provisions of this section shall be construed in a manner that is consistent with that purpose and in a manner that reasonably carries out that purpose.

(2) *Dates of applicability.*—This section applies if—

(i) On or after March 7, 2002, a member recognizes a loss on the disposition of a share of stock of a subsidiary (or, on or after April 10, 2007, a share of stock of a former subsidiary) or a carryover basis asset (subject to paragraph (c)(6) of this section),

(ii) The member's loss on the share of subsidiary stock or the carryover basis asset is allowed on or before the date that is ten years after the disposition of the share or carryover basis asset, and

(iii) If the disposition is of a share of subsidiary stock, it is not a transfer to which § 1.1502-36 applies.

(b) *Redetermination of basis on certain nondecon-solidating transfers of subsidiary stock and on certain deconsolidations of subsidiaries.*—(1) *Redetermination of basis on certain nondeconsolidating transfers of subsidiary stock.*—Except as provided in paragraph (b)(3)(i) of this section, if, immediately after a transfer of stock of a subsidiary that has a basis that exceeds its value, the subsidiary remains a member of the group, then the basis in each share of subsidiary stock owned by each member of the group shall be redetermined in accordance with the provisions of this paragraph (b)(1) immediately before such transfer. All of the members' bases in the shares of subsidiary stock immediately before such transfer shall be aggregated. Such aggregated basis shall be allocated first to the shares of the subsidiary's preferred stock that are owned by the members of the group immediately before such transfer, in proportion to, but not in excess of, the value of those shares at such time. After allocation of the aggregated basis to all shares of the preferred stock of the subsidiary pursuant to the preceding sentence, any remaining basis shall be allocated among all common shares of subsidiary stock held by members of the group immediately before the transfer, in proportion to the value of such shares at such time.

(2) *Redetermination of basis on certain deconsolidations of subsidiaries.*—(i) *Allocation of reallocable basis amount.*—Except as provided in paragraph (b)(3)(ii) of this section, if, immediately before a deconsolidation of a subsidiary, any share of stock of such subsidiary owned by a member of the group has a basis that exceeds its value, then the basis in each share of the subsidiary's stock owned by each member of the group shall be redetermined in accordance with the provisions of this paragraph (b)(2) immediately before such deconsolidation. The basis in each share of the subsidiary's stock held by members of the group immediately before the deconsolidation that has a basis in excess of value at such time shall be reduced, but not below such share's value, in a manner that, to the greatest extent possible, causes the ratio of the basis to the value of each such share to be the same; provided, however, that the aggregate amount of such reduction shall not exceed the reallocable basis amount (as computed pursuant to paragraph (b)(2)(ii) of this section). Then, to the extent of the reallocable basis amount, the basis of each share of the preferred stock of the subsidiary that are held by members of the group immediately before the deconsolidation shall be increased, but not above such share's value, in a manner that, to the greatest extent possible, causes the ratio of the basis to the value of each such share to be the same. Then, to the extent that the reallocable basis amount does not in-

crease the basis of shares of preferred stock of the subsidiary pursuant to the third sentence of this paragraph (b)(2)(i), such amount shall increase the basis of all common shares of the subsidiary's stock held by members of the group immediately before the deconsolidation in a manner that, to the greatest extent possible, causes the ratio of the basis to the value of each such share to be the same.

(ii) *Calculation of reallocable basis amount.*—The reallocable basis amount shall equal the lesser of—

(A) The aggregate of all amounts by which, immediately before the deconsolidation, the basis exceeds the value of a share of subsidiary stock owned by any member of the group at such time; and

(B) The total of the subsidiary's (and any predecessor's) items of deduction and loss, and the subsidiary's (and any predecessor's) allocable share of items of deduction and loss of all lower-tier subsidiaries, that were taken into account in computing the adjustment under § 1.1502-32 to the bases of shares of stock of the subsidiary (and any predecessor) held by members of the group immediately before the deconsolidation, other than shares that have bases in excess of value immediately before the deconsolidation.

(3) *Exceptions to application of redetermination rules.*—(i) Paragraph (b)(1) of this section shall not apply to a transfer of subsidiary stock if—

(A) During the taxable year of such transfer, in one or more fully taxable transactions, the members of the group dispose of all of the shares of the subsidiary stock that they own immediately before the transfer, other than the shares the transfer of which would otherwise trigger the application of paragraph (b)(1) of this section, to a person or persons that are not members of the group;

(B) During the taxable year of such transfer, the members of the group are allowed a worthless stock loss under section 165(g) (taking into account the provisions of § 1.1502-80(c)) with respect to all of the shares of subsidiary stock that they own immediately before the transfer, other than the shares the transfer of which would otherwise trigger the application of paragraph (b)(1) of this section; or

(C) Such transfer is to a member of the group and section 332 (provided the stock is transferred to an 80-percent distributee), section 351, section 354, or section 361 applies to such transfer.

(ii) Paragraph (b)(2) of this section shall not apply to a deconsolidation of a subsidiary if—

(A) During the taxable year of such deconsolidation, in one or more fully taxable transactions, the members of the group dispose of all of the shares of the subsidiary stock that they own immediately before the deconsolidation to a person or persons that are not members of the group;

    (B) Such deconsolidation results from a fully taxable disposition, to a person or persons that are not members of the group, of some of the shares of the subsidiary, and, during the taxable year of such deconsolidation, the members of the group are allowed a worthless stock loss under section 165(g) with respect to all of the shares of the subsidiary stock that they own immediately after the deconsolidation;

    (C) The members of the group are allowed a worthless stock loss under section 165(g) with respect to all of the shares of the subsidiary stock that they own immediately before the deconsolidation;

    (D) The deconsolidation of the subsidiary results from the deconsolidation of a higher-tier subsidiary and, immediately after the deconsolidation of the subsidiary, none of the stock of the subsidiary is owned by a group member; or

    (E) The deconsolidation of the subsidiary results from a termination of the group.

    (4) *Special rule for lower-tier subsidiaries.*—If, immediately after a transfer of subsidiary stock or a deconsolidation of a subsidiary, a lower-tier subsidiary some of the stock of which is owned by the subsidiary is a member of the group, then, for purposes of applying this paragraph (b), the subsidiary shall be treated as having transferred its stock of the lower-tier subsidiary. This principle shall apply to stock of subsidiaries that are owned by such lower-tier subsidiary.

    (5) *Stock basis adjustments for higher-tier stock.*—The basis adjustments required under this paragraph (b) result in basis adjustments to higher-tier member stock. The adjustments are applied in the order of the tiers, from the lowest to highest. For example, if a common parent owns stock of a subsidiary that owns stock of a lower-tier subsidiary and the subsidiary recognizes a loss on the disposition of a portion of its shares of the lower-tier subsidiary stock, the common parent must adjust its basis in its subsidiary stock under the principles of § 1.1502-32 to reflect the adjustments that the subsidiary must make to its basis in its stock of the lower-tier subsidiary.

    (6) *Ordering rules.*—(i) The rules of this paragraph (b) apply after the rules of § 1.1502-32 are applied.

    (ii) The rules of this paragraph (b) apply before the rules of § 1.337(d)-2 and paragraphs (c) and (f) of this section are applied.

    (iii) This paragraph (b)(and any resulting basis adjustments to higher-tier member stock made pursuant to paragraph (b)(5) of this section) applies to redetermine the basis of stock of a lower-tier subsidiary before this paragraph (b) applies to higher-tier member of such lower-tier subsidiary.

    (c) *Loss suspension.*—(1) *General rule.*—Any loss recognized by a member of a consolidated group with respect to the disposition of a share of subsidiary stock shall be suspended to the extent of the duplicated loss with respect to such share of stock if, immediately after the disposition, the subsidiary is a member of the consolidated group of which it was a member immediately prior to the disposition (or any successor group).

    (2) *Special rule for lower-tier subsidiaries.*—This paragraph (c)(2) applies if neither paragraph (c)(1) nor (f) of this section applies to a member's disposition of a share of stock of a subsidiary (the departing member), a loss is recognized on the disposition of such share, and the departing member owns stock of one or more other subsidiaries (a remaining member) that is a member of such group immediately after the disposition. In that case, such loss shall be suspended to the extent the duplicated loss with respect to the departing member stock disposed of is attributable to the remaining member or members.

    (3) *Treatment of suspended loss.*—(i) *General rule.*—For purposes of the rules of § 1.1502-32, any loss suspended pursuant to paragraph (c)(1) or (c)(2) of this section is treated as a noncapital, nondeductible expense of the member that disposes of subsidiary stock, incurred during the taxable year that includes the date of the disposition of stock to which paragraph (c)(1) or (c)(2) of this section applies. See § 1.1502-32(b)(3)(iii)(C). Consequently, the basis of a higher-tier member's stock of the member that disposes of subsidiary stock is reduced by the suspended loss in the year it is suspended.

    (ii) *Location of suspended loss following deconsolidation of selling member.*—If a member recognizes a loss that is suspended under this paragraph (c) but that member ceases to be a member of the group before the loss is allowable, the common parent is treated as succeeding to the loss in a transaction to which section 381(a) applies.

    (4) *Reduction of suspended loss.*—(i) *General rule.*—The amount of any loss suspended pursuant to paragraph (c)(1) or (c)(2) of § 1.1502-35 shall be reduced, but not below zero, by the subsidiary's (and any successor's) items of deduction and loss, and the subsidiary's (and any successor's) allocable share of items of deduction and loss of all lower-tier subsidiaries, that are allocable to the period beginning on the date of the disposition that gave rise to the suspended loss and ending on the day before the first date on which the subsidiary (and any successor) is not a member of the group of which it was a member immediately prior to the disposition (or any successor group), and that are taken into account in determining consolidated taxable income (or loss) of such group for any taxable year

Reg. § 1.1502-35(c)(4)(i)

that includes any date on or after the date of the disposition and before the first date on which the subsidiary (and any successor) is not a member of such group; provided, however, that such reduction shall not exceed the excess of the amount of such items over the amount of such items that are taken into account in determining the basis adjustments made under § 1.1502-32 to stock of the subsidiary (or any successor) owned by members of the group. The preceding sentence shall not apply to items of deduction and loss to the extent that the group can establish that all or a portion of such items was not reflected in the computation of the duplicated loss with respect to the subsidiary on the date of the disposition of stock that gave rise to the suspended loss.

(ii) *Operating rules.*—(A) *Year in which deduction or loss is taken into account.*—For purposes of paragraph (c)(4)(i) of this section, a subsidiary's (or any successor's) deductions and losses are treated as taken into account when and to the extent they are absorbed by the subsidiary (or any successor) or any other member. To the extent that the subsidiary's (or any successor's) deduction or loss is absorbed in the year it arises or is carried forward and absorbed in a subsequent year (e.g., under section 172, 465, or 1212), the deduction is treated as taken into account in the year in which it is absorbed. To the extent that a subsidiary's (or any successor's) deduction or loss is carried back and absorbed in a prior year (whether consolidated or separate), the deduction or loss is treated as taken into account in the year in which it arises and not in the year in which it is absorbed.

(B) *Determination of items that are allocable to the post-disposition, pre-deconsolidation period.*—For purposes of paragraph (c)(4)(i) of this section, the determination of whether a subsidiary's (or any successor's) items of deduction and loss and allocable share of items of deduction and loss of all lower-tier subsidiaries are allocable to the period beginning on the date of the disposition of subsidiary stock that gave rise to the suspended loss and ending on the day before the first date on which the subsidiary (or any successor) is not a member of the consolidated group of which it was a member immediately prior to the disposition (or any successor group) is determined pursuant to the rules of § 1.1502-76(b)(2), without regard to § 1.1502-76(b)(2)(ii)(D), as if the subsidiary ceased to be a member of the group at the end of the day before the disposition and filed separate returns for the period beginning on the date of the disposition and ending on the day before the first date on which it is not a member of such group.

(5) *Allowable loss.*—(i) *General rule.*—To the extent not reduced under paragraph (c)(4) of this section, any loss suspended pursuant to paragraph (c)(1) or (c)(2) of this section shall be allowed, to the extent otherwise allowable under applicable provisions of the Internal Revenue Code and regulations, on a return filed by the group of which the subsidiary was a member on the date of the disposition of subsidiary stock that gave rise to the suspended loss (or any successor group) for the taxable year that includes the earlier of—

(A) The day before the first date on which the subsidiary (and any successor) is not a member of such group or the date the group is allowed a worthless stock loss under section 165 (taking into account the provisions of § 1.1502-80(c)) with respect to all of the subsidiary stock owned by members and;

(B) The date that is ten years after the date of the disposition of subsidiary stock that gave rise to the suspended loss.

(ii) *No tiering up of certain adjustments.*—No adjustments shall be made to a member's basis of stock of a subsidiary (or any successor) for a suspended loss that is taken into account under paragraph (c)(5)(i) of this section. See § 1.1502-32(a)(2).

(iii) *Statement of allowed loss.*—Paragraph (c)(5)(i) of this section applies only if the separate statement required under this paragraph (c)(5)(iii) is filed with, or as part of, the taxpayer's return for the year in which the loss is allowable. The statement must be entitled "ALLOWED LOSS UNDER § 1.1502-35(c)(5)" and must contain the name and employer identification number of the subsidiary the stock of which gave rise to the loss.

(6) *Special rule for dispositions of certain carryover basis assets.*—If—

(i) A member of a group recognizes a loss on the disposition of an asset other than stock of a subsidiary;

(ii) Such member's basis in the asset disposed of was determined, directly or indirectly, in whole or in part, by reference to the basis of stock of a subsidiary and, at the time of the determination of the member's basis in the asset disposed of, there was a duplicated loss with respect to such stock of the subsidiary; and

(iii) Immediately after the disposition, the subsidiary is a member of such group, then such loss shall be suspended pursuant to the principles of paragraphs (c)(1) and (c)(2) of this section to the extent of the duplicated loss with respect to such stock at the time of the determination of basis of the asset disposed of. Principles similar to those set forth in paragraphs (c)(3), (c)(4), and (c)(5) of this section shall apply to a loss suspended pursuant to this paragraph (c)(6).

(7) *Coordination with loss deferral, loss disallowance, and other rules.*—(i) *In general.*—Loss recognized on the disposition of subsidiary stock or another asset is subject to redetermination, defer-

ral, or disallowance under other applicable provisions of the Internal Revenue Code and regulations thereunder, including sections 267(f) and 482. Paragraphs (c)(1), (c)(2), and (c)(6) of this section do not apply to a loss that is disallowed under any other provision. If loss is deferred under any other provision, paragraphs (c)(1), (c)(2), and (c)(6) of this section apply when the loss would otherwise be taken into account under such other provision. However, if an overriding event described in paragraph (c)(7)(ii) of this section occurs before the deferred loss is taken into account, paragraphs (c)(1), (c)(2), and (c)(6) of this section apply to the loss immediately before the event occurs, even though the loss may not be taken into account until a later time.

(ii) *Overriding events.*—For purposes of paragraph (c)(7)(i) of this section, the following are overriding events—

(A) The stock ceases to be owned by a member of the consolidated group;

(B) The stock is canceled or redeemed (regardless of whether it is retired or held as treasury stock); or

(C) The stock is treated as disposed of under § 1.1502-19(c)(1)(ii)(B) or (c)(1)(iii).

(8) *No elimination of economic loss.*—This paragraph (c) shall not be applied in a manner that permanently disallows a deduction for an economic loss, provided that such deduction is otherwise allowable. If the application of any provision of this paragraph (c) results in such a disallowance, proper adjustment may be made to prevent such a disallowance. Whether a provision of this paragraph (c) has resulted in such a disallowance is determined on the date on which the subsidiary (or any successor) the disposition of the stock of which gave rise to a suspended stock loss is not a member of the group or the date the group is allowed a worthless stock loss under section 165(g) (taking into account the provisions of § 1.1502-80(c)) with respect to all of such subsidiary stock owned by members. Proper adjustment in such cases shall be made by restoring the suspended stock loss immediately before the subsidiary ceases to be a member of the group or the group is allowed a worthless stock loss under section 165(g) (taking into account the provisions of § 1.1502-80(c)) with respect to all of such subsidiary stock owned by members, to the extent that its reduction pursuant to paragraph (c)(4) of this section had the result of permanently disallowing a deduction for an economic loss.

(9) *Ordering rule.*—The rules of this paragraph (c) apply after the rules of paragraph (b) of this section and § 1.337(d)-2 are applied.

(d) *Definitions.*—(1) *Disposition* means any event in which gain or loss is recognized, in whole or in part.

(2) *Deconsolidation* means any event that causes a subsidiary to no longer be a member of the consolidated group.

(3) *Value* means fair market value.

(4) *Duplicated loss.*—(i) *In general.*—Duplicated loss is determined immediately after a disposition and equals the excess, if any, of—

(A) The sum of—

(1) The aggregate adjusted basis of the subsidiary's assets other than any stock that subsidiary owns in another subsidiary;

(2) Any losses attributable to the subsidiary and carried to the subsidiary's first taxable year following the disposition; and

(3) Any deductions of the subsidiary that have been recognized but are deferred under a provision of the Internal Revenue Code (such as deductions deferred under section 469); over

(B) The sum of—

(1) The value of the subsidiary's stock; and

(2) Any liabilities of the subsidiary that have been taken into account for tax purposes.

(ii) *Special rules.*—(A) The amounts determined under paragraph (d)(4)(i) (other than amounts described in paragraph (d)(4)(i)(B)(1)) of this section with respect to a subsidiary include its allocable share of corresponding amounts with respect to all lower-tier subsidiaries. If 80 percent or more in value of the stock of a subsidiary is acquired by purchase in a single transaction (or in a series of related transactions during any 12-month period), the value of the subsidiary's stock may not exceed the purchase price of the stock divided by the percentage of the stock (by value) so purchased. For this purpose, stock is acquired by purchase if the transferee is not related to the transferor within the meaning of sections 267(b) and 707(b)(1), using the language "'10 percent'" instead of "'50 percent'" each place that it appears, and the transferee's basis in the stock is determined wholly by reference to the consideration paid for such stock.

(B) The amounts determined under paragraph (d)(4)(i) of this section are not applied more than once to suspend a loss under this section.

(5) *Predecessor and successor.*—A predecessor is a transferor of assets to a transferee (the successor) in a transaction—

(i) To which section 381(a) applies;

(ii) In which substantially all of the assets of the transferor are transferred to members in a complete liquidation;

(iii) In which the successor's basis in assets is determined (directly or indirectly, in whole or in part) by reference to the transferor's basis in such assets, but the transferee is a successor only with respect to the assets the basis of which is so determined; or

(iv) Which is an intercompany transaction, but only with respect to assets that are being accounted for by the transferor in a prior intercompany transaction.

(6) *Successor group.*—A surviving group is treated as a successor group of a consolidated group (the terminating group) that ceases to exist as a result of—

(i) The acquisition by a member of another consolidated group of either the assets of the common parent of the terminating group in a reorganization described in section 381(a)(2), or the stock of the common parent of the terminating group; or

(ii) The application of the principles of § 1.1502-75(d)(2) or (3).

(7) *Preferred stock, common stock.*—Preferred stock and common stock shall have the meanings set forth in § 1.1502-32(d)(2) and (3), respectively.

(8) *Higher-tier.*—A subsidiary is higher-tier with respect to a member if or to the extent investment adjustments under § 1.1502-32 with respect to the stock of the latter member would affect investment adjustments with respect to the stock of the former member.

(9) *Lower-tier.*—A subsidiary is lower-tier with respect to a member if or to the extent investment basis adjustments under § 1.1502-32 with respect to the stock of the former member would affect investment adjustments with respect to the stock of the latter member.

(e) *Examples.*—For purposes of the examples in this section, unless otherwise stated, all groups file consolidated returns on a calendar-year basis, the facts set forth the only corporate activity, all transactions are between unrelated persons, and tax liabilities are disregarded. In addition, all transactions described in section 362(a) are completed before October 22, 2004, and therefore are not subject to section 362(e)(2). The principles of paragraphs (a) through (d) of this section are illustrated by the following examples:

Example 1. Nondeconsolidating sale of preferred stock of lower-tier subsidiary— (i) *Facts.* P owns 100 percent of the common stock of each of S1 and S2. S1 and S2 each have only one class of stock outstanding. P's basis in the stock of S1 is $100 and the value of such stock is $130. P's basis in the stock of S2 is $120 and the value of such stock is $90. P, S1, and S2 are all members of the P group. S1 and S2 form S3. In year 1, in transfers to which section 351 applies, S1 contributes $100 to S3 in exchange for all of the common stock of S3 and S2 contributes an asset with a basis of $50 and a value of $20 to S3 in exchange for all of the preferred stock of S3. S3 becomes a member of the P group. In Year 3, in a transac-

tion that is not part of the plan that includes the contributions to S3, S2 sells the preferred stock of S3 for $20. Immediately after the sale, S3 is a member of the P group.

(ii) *Application of basis redetermination rule.* Because S2's basis in the preferred stock of S3 exceeds its value immediately prior to the sale and S3 is a member of the P group immediately after the sale, all of the P group members' bases in the stock of S3 is redetermined pursuant to paragraph (b)(1) of this section. Of the group members' total basis of $150 in the S3 stock, $20 is allocated to the preferred stock, the fair market value of the preferred stock on the date of the sale, and $130 is allocated to the common stock. S2's sale of the preferred stock results in the recognition of $0 of gain/loss. Pursuant to paragraph (b)(5) of this section, the redetermination of S1's and S2's bases in the stock of S3 results in adjustments to P's basis in the stock of S1 and S2. In particular, P's basis in the stock of S1 is increased by $30 to $130 and its basis in the stock of S2 is decreased by $30 to $90.

Example 2. Deconsolidating sale of common stock—(i) *Facts.* In Year 1, in a transfer to which section 351 applies, P contributes Asset A with a basis of $900 and a value of $200 to S in exchange for one share of S common stock (CS1). In Years 2 and 3, in successive but unrelated transfers to which section 351 applies, P transfers $200 to S in exchange for one share of S common stock (CS2), Asset B with a basis of $300 and a value of $200 in exchange for one share of S common stock (CS3), and Asset C with a basis of $1000 and a value of $200 in exchange for one share of S common stock (CS4). In Year 4, S sells Asset A for $200, recognizing $700 of loss that is used to offset income of P recognized during Year 4. As a result of the sale of Asset A, the basis of each of P's four shares of S common stock is reduced by $175. Therefore, the basis of CS1 is $725. The basis of CS2 is $25. The basis of CS3 is $125, and the basis of CS4 is $825. In Year 5 in a transaction that is not part of a plan that includes the Year 1 contribution, P sells CS4 for $200. Immediately after the sale of CS4, S is not a member of the P group.

(ii) *Application of basis redetermination rule.* Because P's basis in each of CS1 and CS4 exceeds its value immediately prior to the deconsolidation of S, P's basis in its shares of S common stock is redetermined pursuant to paragraph (b)(2) of this section. Pursuant to paragraph (b)(2)(ii) of this section, the reallocable basis amount is $350 (the lesser of $1150, the gross loss inherent in the stock of S owned by P immediately before the sale, and $350, the aggregate amount of S's items of deduction and loss that were previously taken into account in the computation of the adjustment to the basis of the stock of S that P did not hold at a loss immediately before the deconsolidation). Pursuant to paragraph (b)(2)(i) of this section, first, P's basis in CS1 is reduced from $725 to $600 and P's basis in CS4 is reduced from $825 to $600. Then, the reallocable basis amount increases P's basis in CS2 from $25 to $250 and P's basis in CS3 from $125 to $250. P recognizes $400 of loss on the sale of CS4. The loss suspension rule does not apply because S is no longer a member of the P group. Thus, the loss is allowable at that time.

Example 3. Nondeconsolidating sale of common stock—(i) *Facts.* In Year 1, P forms S with a contribution of $80 in exchange for 80 shares of the common stock of S, which at that time represents all of the outstanding stock of S. S becomes a member of the P group. In Year 2, P contributes Asset A with a basis of $50 and a value of $20 in exchange for 20 shares of the common stock of S in a transfer to which section 351 applies. In Year 4, in a transaction that is not part of the plan that includes the Year 2 contribution, P sells the 20 shares of the common stock of S that it acquired in Year 2 for $20. Immediately after the Year 4 stock sale, S is a member of the P group. At the time of the Year 4 stock sale, S has $80 and Asset A. In Year 5, S sells Asset A, the basis and value of which have not changed since its contribution to S. On the sale of Asset A for $20, S recognizes a $30 loss. The P group cannot establish that all or a portion of the $30 loss was not reflected in the calculation of the duplicated loss of S on the date of the Year 4 stock sale. The $30 loss is used on the P group return to offset income of P. In Year 6, P sells its remaining S common stock for $80.

(ii) *Application of basis redetermination and loss suspension rules.* Because P's basis in the common stock sold exceeds its value immediately prior to the sale and S is a member of the P group immediately after the sale, P's basis in all of the stock of S is redetermined pursuant to paragraph (b)(1) of this section. Of P's total basis of $130 in the S common stock, a proportionate amount is allocated to each of the 100 shares of S common stock. Accordingly, $26 is allocated to the common stock of S that is sold and $104 is allocated to the common stock of S that is retained. On P's sale of the 20 shares of the common stock of S for $20, P recognizes a loss of $6. Because the sale of the 20 shares of common stock of S does not result in the deconsolidation of S, under paragraph (c)(1) of this section, that loss is suspended to the extent of the duplicated loss with respect to the shares sold. The duplicated loss with respect to the shares sold is $6. Therefore, the entire $6 loss is suspended.

(iii) *Effect of subsequent asset sale on stock basis.* Of the $30 loss recognized on the sale of Asset A, $24 is taken into account in determining the basis adjustments made under § 1.1502-32 to the stock of S owned by P. Accordingly, P's basis in its S stock is reduced by $24 from $104 to $80.

(iv) *Effect of subsequent asset sale on suspended loss.* Because P cannot establish that all or a portion of the loss recognized on the sale of Asset A was not reflected in the calculation of the duplicated loss of S on the date of the Year 4

stock sale and such loss is allocable to the period beginning on the date of the Year 4 disposition of the S stock and ending on the day before the first date on which S is not a member of the P group and is taken into account in determining consolidated taxable income (or loss) of the P group for a taxable year that includes a date on or after the date of the Year 4 disposition and before the first date on which S is not a member of the P group, such asset loss reduces the suspended loss pursuant to paragraph (c)(4) of this section. The amount of such reduction, however, cannot exceed $6, the excess of the amount of such loss, $30, over the amount of such loss that is taken into account in determining the basis adjustment made to the stock of S owned by P, $24. Therefore, the suspended loss is reduced to zero.

(v) *Effect of subsequent stock sale.* P recognizes $0 gain/loss on the Year 6 sale of its remaining S common stock. No amount of suspended loss remains to be allowed under paragraph (c)(5) of this section.

Example 4. Nondeconsolidating sale of common stock of lower-tier subsidiary—(i) *Facts.* In Year 1, P forms S1 with a contribution of $200 in exchange for all of the common stock of S1, which represents all of the outstanding stock of S1. In the same year, S1 forms S2 with a contribution of $80 in exchange for 80 shares of the common stock of S2, which at that time represents all of the outstanding stock of S2. S1 and S2 become members of the P group. In the same year, S2 purchases Asset A for $80. In Year 2, S1 contributes Asset B with a basis of $50 and a value of $20 in exchange for 20 shares of the common stock of S2 in a transfer to which section 351 applies. In Year 4, S1 sells the 20 shares of the common stock of S2 that it acquired in Year 2 for $20. Immediately after the Year 4 stock sale, S2 is a member of the P group. At the time of the Year 4 stock sale, the bases and values of Asset A and Asset B are unchanged. In Year 5, S2 sells Asset B for $45, recognizing a $5 loss. The P group cannot establish that all or a portion of the $5 loss was not reflected in the calculation of the duplicated loss of S2 on the date of the Year 4 stock sale. The $5 loss is used on the P group return to offset income of P. In Year 6, S1 sells its remaining S2 common stock for $100.

(ii) *Application of basis redetermination and loss suspension rules.* Because S1's basis in the S2 common stock sold exceeds its value immediately prior to the sale and S2 is a member of the P group immediately after the sale, S1's basis in all of the stock of S2 is redetermined pursuant to paragraph (b)(1) of this section. Of S1's total basis of $130 in the S2 common stock, a proportionate amount is allocated to each of the 100 shares of S2 common stock. Accordingly, a total of $26 is allocated to the common stock of S2 that is sold and $104 is allocated to the common stock of S2 that is retained. On S1's sale of the 20 shares of the common stock of S2 for $20, S1 recognizes a loss of $6. Because the sale of the 20 shares of common stock of S2 does not result in the deconsolidation of S2, under paragraph (c)(1) of this section, that loss is suspended to the extent of the duplicated loss with respect to the shares sold. The duplicated loss with respect to the shares sold is $6. Therefore, the entire $6 loss is suspended. Pursuant to paragraph (c)(3) of this section and § 1.1502-32(b)(3)(iii)(C), the suspended loss is treated as a noncapital, nondeductible expense incurred by S1 during the tax year that includes the date of the disposition of stock to which paragraph (c)(1) of this section applies. Accordingly, P's basis in its S1 stock is reduced from $200 to $194.

(iii) *Effect of subsequent asset sale on stock basis.* Of the $5 loss recognized on the sale of Asset B, $4 is taken into account in determining the basis adjustments made under § 1.1502-32 to the stock of S2 owned by S1. Accordingly, S1's basis in its S2 stock is reduced by $4 from $104 to $100 and P's basis in its S1 stock is reduced by $4 from $194 to $190.

(iv) *Effect of subsequent asset sale on suspended loss.* Because P cannot establish that all or a portion of the loss recognized on the sale of Asset B was not reflected in the calculation of the duplicated loss of S2 on the date of the Year 4 stock sale and such loss is allocable to the period beginning on the date of the Year 4 disposition of the S2 stock and ending on the day before the first date on which S2 is not a member of the P group and is taken into account in determining consolidated taxable income (or loss) of the P group for a taxable year that includes a date on or after the date of the Year 4 disposition and before the first date on which S2 is not a member of the P group, such asset loss reduces the suspended loss pursuant to paragraph (c)(4) of this section. The amount of such reduction, however, cannot exceed $1, the excess of the amount of such loss, $5, over the amount of such loss that is taken into account in determining the basis adjustment made to the stock of S2 owned by members of the P group, $4. Therefore, the suspended loss is reduced to $5.

(v) *Effect of subsequent stock sale.* In year 6, when S1 sells its remaining S2 stock for $100, it recognizes $0 gain/loss. Pursuant to paragraph (c)(5) of this section, the remaining $5 of the suspended loss is allowed on the P group's return for Year 6 when S1 sells its remaining S2 stock.

Example 5. Deconsolidating sale of subsidiary owning stock of another subsidiary that remains in group—(i) *Facts.* In Year 1, P forms S1 with a contribution of Asset A with a basis of $50 and a value of $20 in exchange for 100 shares of common stock of S1 in a transfer to which section 351 applies. Also in Year 1, P and S1 form S2. P contributes $80 to S2 in exchange for 80 shares of common stock of S2. S1 contributes Asset A to S2 in exchange for 20 shares of common stock of S2 in a transfer to which section 351 applies. In Year 3, in a transaction that is not part of a plan that in-

includes the Year 1 contributions, P sells its 100 shares of S1 common stock for $20. Immediately after the Year 3 stock sale, S2 is a member of the P group. At the time of the Year 3 stock sale, S1 owns 20 shares of common stock of S2, and S2 has $80 and Asset A. In Year 4, S2 sells Asset A, the basis and value of which have not changed since its contribution to S2. On the sale of Asset A for $20, S2 recognizes a $30 loss. That $30 loss is used on the P group return to offset income of P. In Year 5, P sells its S2 common stock for $80.

(ii) *Application of basis redetermination and loss suspension rules.* Pursuant to paragraph (b)(4) of this section, because immediately before P's transfer of S1 stock S1 owns stock of S2 (another subsidiary of the same group) that has a basis that exceeds its value, paragraph (b) of this section applies as if S1 had transferred its stock of S2. Because S2 is a member of the group immediately after the transfer of the S1 stock, the group member's basis in the S2 stock is redetermined pursuant to paragraph (b)(1) of this section immediately prior to the sale of the S1 stock. Of the group members' total basis of $130 in the S2 stock, $26 is allocated to S1's 20 shares of S2 common stock and $104 is allocated to P's 80 shares of S2 common stock. Pursuant to paragraph (b)(5) of this section, the redetermination of S1's basis in the stock of S2 results in an adjustment to P's basis in the stock of S1. In particular, P's basis in the stock of S1 is decreased by $24 from $50 to $26. On P's sale of its 100 shares of S1 common stock for $20, P recognizes a loss of $6. Because S1 is not a member of the P group immediately after P's sale of the S1 stock, paragraph (c)(1) of this section does not apply to suspend such loss. However, because P recognizes a loss with respect to the disposition of the S1 stock and S1 owns stock of S2 (which is a member of the P group immediately after the disposition), paragraph (c)(2) of this section does apply to suspend up to $6 of that loss, an amount equal to the amount by which the duplicated loss with respect to the stock of S1 sold is attributable to S2's adjusted basis in its assets, loss carryforwards, and deferred deductions.

(iii) *Effect of subsequent asset sale on stock basis.* Of the $30 loss recognized on the sale of Asset A, $24 is taken into account in determining the basis adjustments made under § 1.1502-32 to the stock of S2 owned by P. Accordingly, P's basis in its S2 stock is reduced by $24 from $104 to $80.

(iv) *Effect of subsequent asset sale on suspended loss.* Because P cannot establish that all or a portion of the loss recognized on the sale of Asset A was not reflected in the calculation of the duplicated loss of S2 on the date of the Year 3 stock sale and such loss is allocable to the period beginning on the date of the Year 3 deemed disposition of the S2 stock and ending on the day before the first date on which S2 is not a member of the P group and is taken into account in determining consolidated taxable income (or loss) of the P group for a taxable year that includes a date on or after the date of the Year 3 deemed disposition and before the first date on which S2 is not a member of the P group, such asset loss reduces the suspended loss pursuant to paragraph (c)(4) of this section. The amount of such reduction, however, cannot exceed $6, the excess of the amount of such loss, $30, over the amount of such loss that is taken into account in determining the basis adjustment made to the stock of S2 owned by P, $24. Therefore, the suspended loss is reduced to zero.

(v) *Effect of subsequent stock sale.* P recognizes $0 gain/loss on the Year 5 sale of its remaining S2 common stock. No amount of suspended loss remains to be allowed under paragraph (c)(5) of this section.

Example 6. Loss recognized on asset with basis determined by reference to stock basis of subsidiary— (i) *Facts.* In Year 1, P forms S with a contribution of $80 in exchange for 80 shares of common stock of S which at that time represents all of the outstanding stock of S. S becomes a member of the P group. In Year 2, P contributes Asset A with a basis of $50 and a value of $20 in exchange for 20 shares of common stock of S in a transfer to which section 351 applies. In Year 4, in a transaction that is not part of a plan that includes the Year 1 and Year 2 contributions, P contributes the 20 shares of S common stock it acquired in Year 2 to PS, a partnership, in exchange for a 20 percent capital and profits interest in a transaction described in section 721. Immediately after the contribution to PS, S is a member of the P group. In Year 5, P sells its interest in PS for $20.

(ii) *Application of basis redetermination rule upon nonrecognition transfer.* Because P's basis in the S common stock contributed to PS exceeds its value immediately prior to the transfer and S is a member of the P group immediately after the transfer, P's basis in all of the S stock is redetermined pursuant to paragraph (b)(1) of this section. Of P's total basis of $130 in the common stock of S, a proportionate amount is allocated to each share of S common stock. Accordingly, $26 is allocated to the S common stock that is contributed to PS and, under section 722, P's basis in its interest in PS is $26.

(iii) *Application of loss suspension rule on disposition of asset with basis determined by reference to stock basis of subsidiary.* P recognizes a $6 loss on its disposition of its interest in PS. Because P's basis in its interest in PS was determined by reference to the basis of S stock and at the time of the determination of P's basis in its interest in PS such S stock had a duplicated loss of $6, and, immediately after the disposition, S is a member of the P group, such loss is suspended to the extent of such duplicated loss. Principles similar to those of paragraphs (c)(3), (c)(4), and (c)(5) of this section shall apply to such suspended loss.

(f) *Worthlessness not followed by separate return years.*—Notwithstanding any other provision in

the regulations under section 1502, if a member of a group (the claiming group) treats stock of a subsidiary as worthless under section 165 (taking into account the provisions of §1.1502-80(c)) and, on the day following the last day of the claiming group's taxable year in which the worthless stock deduction is claimed, the subsidiary (or its successor, determined without regard to paragraphs (d)(5)(iii) and (iv) of this section) is a member of a group that includes any corporation that, during that taxable year, was a member of the claiming group (other than a lower-tier subsidiary of the subsidiary) or is a successor (determined without regard to paragraphs (d)(5)(iii) and (iv) of this section) of such a member, then all losses treated as attributable to the subsidiary under the principles of §1.1502-21(b)(2)(iv) shall be treated as expired as of the beginning of the day following the last day of the claiming group's taxable year in which the worthless stock deduction is claimed. In addition, notwithstanding any other provision in the regulations under section 1502, if a member recognizes a loss with respect to subsidiary stock and on the following day the subsidiary is not a member of the group and does not have a separate return year, then all losses treated as attributable to the subsidiary under the principles of §1.1502-21(b)(2)(iv) shall be treated as expired as of the beginning of the day following the last day of the group's taxable year in which the stock loss is claimed. For purposes of this paragraph (f), the determination of the losses attributable to the subsidiary shall be made after computing the taxable income of the group for the taxable year in which the group treats the stock of the subsidiary as worthless or the subsidiary liquidates and after computing the taxable income for any taxable year to which such losses may be carried back. The loss treated as expired under this paragraph (f) shall not be treated as a noncapital, nondeductible expense under §1.1502-32(b)(2)(iii). This paragraph (f) applies to worthlessness determinations and liquidations that occur on or after March 10, 2006. For rules applicable to worthless determinations and liquidations before March 10, 2006, see §1.1502-35T(f)(1) and (2) as contained in 26 CFR part 1 in effect on January 1, 2006.

(g) *Anti-avoidance rules.*—(1) *Transfer of share without a loss in avoidance.*—If a share of subsidiary stock has a basis that does not exceed its value and the share is transferred with a view to avoiding application of the rules of paragraph (b) of this section prior to the transfer of a share of subsidiary stock that has a basis that does not exceed its value or a deconsolidation of a subsidiary, the rules of paragraph (b) of this section shall apply immediately prior to the transfer of stock that has a basis that does not exceed its value.

(2) *Transfers of loss property in avoidance.*—If a member of a consolidated group contributes an

Reg. §1.1502-35(g)(2)

asset with a basis that exceeds its value to a partnership in a transaction described in section 721 or a corporation that is not a member of such group in a transfer described in section 351, such partnership or corporation contributes such asset to a subsidiary in a transfer described in section 351, and such contributions are undertaken with a view to avoiding the rules of paragraph (b) or (c) of this section, adjustments must be made to carry out the purposes of this section.

(3) *Anti-loss reimportation rule.*— (i) *Conditions for application.*—This paragraph (g)(3) applies when—

(A) A member of a group (selling group) recognized and was allowed a loss with respect to a share of stock of S, a subsidiary or former subsidiary of the selling group;

(B) That stock loss was duplicated (in whole or in part) in S's attributes (duplicating items) at the earlier of the time that the loss was recognized or that S ceased to be a member; and

(C) Within ten years of the date that S ceased to be a member, there is a reimportation event. For this purpose, a reimportation event is any event after which a duplicating item is a reimported item. A reimported item is any duplicating item that is reflected in the attributes of any member of the selling group, including S, or, if not reflected in the attributes, would be properly taken into account by any member of the selling group (for example as the result of a carryback).

(ii) *Effect of application.*—Immediately before the time that a reimported item (or any portion of a reimported item) would be properly taken into account (but for the application of this paragraph (g)(3)), such item (or such portion of the item) is reduced to zero and no deduction or loss is allowed, directly or indirectly, with respect to that item.

(iii) *Operating rules.*—For purposes of this paragraph (g)(3)—

(A) The terms *member, subsidiary,* and *group* include their predecessors and successors to the extent necessary to effectuate the purposes of this section; and

(B) The reduction of a reimported item (other than duplicating items that are carried back to a consolidated return year of the selling group) is a noncapital, nondeductible expense within the meaning of § 1.1502-32(b)(3)(iii).

(4) *Avoidance of recognition of gain.*—(i) If a transaction is structured with a view to, and has the effect of, deferring or avoiding the recognition of gain on a disposition of stock by invoking the application of paragraph (b)(1) of this section to redetermine the basis of stock of a subsidiary, and the stock loss that gives rise to the application of paragraph (b)(1) of this section is not significant, paragraphs (b) and (c) of this section shall not apply.

(ii) If a transaction is structured with a view to, and has the effect of, deferring or avoiding the recognition of gain on a disposition of stock by invoking the application of paragraph (b)(2) of this section to redetermine the basis of stock of a subsidiary, and the duplicated loss of the subsidiary that is reflected in stock of the subsidiary owned by members of the group immediately before the deconsolidation is not significant, paragraphs (b) and (c) of this section shall not apply.

(5) *Examples.*—For purposes of the examples in this section, all transactions described in section 362(a) are completed before October 22, 2004, and therefore are not subject to section 362(e)(2). The principles of this paragraph (g) are illustrated by the following examples:

Example 1. Transfers of property in avoidance of basis redetermination rule—(i) *Facts.* In Year 1, P forms S with a contribution of $100 in exchange for 100 shares of common stock of S which at that time represents all of the outstanding stock of S. S becomes a member of the P group. In Year 2, P contributes 20 shares of common stock of S to PS, a partnership, in exchange for a 20 percent capital and profits interest in a transaction described in section 721. In Year 3, P contributes Asset A with a basis of $50 and a value of $20 to PS in exchange for an additional capital and profits interest in PS in a transaction described in section 721. Also in Year 3, PS contributes Asset A to S and P contributes an additional $80 to S in transfers to which section 351 applies. In Year 4, S sells Asset A for $20, recognizing a loss of $30. The P group uses that loss to offset income of P. In Year 5, P sells its entire interest in PS for $40.

(ii) *Analysis.* Pursuant to paragraph (g)(2) of this section, if P's contributions of S stock and Asset A to PS were undertaken with a view to avoiding the application of the basis redetermination or the loss suspension rule, adjustments must be made such that the group does not obtain more than one tax benefit from the $30 loss inherent in Asset A.

Example 2. Transfers effecting a reimportation of loss—(i) *Facts.* In Year 1, P forms S with a contribution of Asset A with a value of $100 and a basis of $120, Asset B with a value of $50 and a basis of $70, and Asset C with a value of $90 and a basis of $100 in exchange for all of the common stock of S and S becomes a member of the P group. In Year 2, in a transaction that is not part of a plan that includes the contribution, P sells the stock of S for $240, recognizing a loss of $50. At such time, the bases and values of Assets A, B, and C have not changed since their contribution to S. In Year 3, S sells Asset A, recognizing a $20 loss. In Year 3, S merges into M in a reorganization described in section 368(a)(1)(A). In Year 8, P purchases all of the stock of M for $300. At that time, M has a $10 net operating loss. In addition, M owns Asset D, which was acquired in an exchange described in section 1031 in connection with the surrender of Asset B. Asset C has a value of $80 and a basis of $100. Asset D has a value of $60 and a basis of $70. In Year 9, P has operating income of $100 and M recognizes $20 of loss on the sale of Asset C. In Year 10, P has operating income of $50 and M recognizes $50 of loss on the sale of Asset D.

(ii) *Analysis*. P's $50 loss on the sale of S stock is entirely attributable to duplicated loss. Therefore, pursuant to paragraph (g)(3) of this section, assuming the P group cannot establish otherwise, M's $10 net operating loss is treated as attributable to assets that were owned by S on the date of the disposition and that had bases in excess of value on such date. Without regard to any other limitations on the group's use of M's net operating loss, the P group cannot use M's $10 net operating loss pursuant to paragraph (g)(3)(iii)(D) of this section. Pursuant to paragraph (g)(3)(iv) of this section and §1.1502-32(b)(3)(iii)(D), such loss is treated as a noncapital, nondeductible expense of M incurred during the taxable year that it would otherwise be absorbed, namely in Year 9. In addition, the P group is denied the use of $10 of the loss recognized on the sale of Asset C. Finally, the P group is denied the use of $10 of the loss recognized on the sale of Asset D. Pursuant to paragraph (g)(3)(iv) of this section and §1.1502-32(b)(3)(iii)(D), each such disallowed loss is treated as a noncapital, nondeductible expense of M incurred during the taxable year that includes the date of the disposition of the asset with respect to which such loss was recognized.

Example 3. Transfers to avoid recognition of gain—(i) *Facts*. P owns all of the stock of S1 and S2. The S2 stock has a basis of $400 and a value of $500. S1 owns 50% of the S3 common stock with a basis of $150. S2 owns the remaining 50% of the S3 common stock with a basis of $100 and a value of $200 and one share of S3 preferred stock with a basis of $10 and a value of $9. P intends to sell all of its S2 stock to an unrelated buyer. P, therefore, engages in the following steps to dispose of S2 without recognizing a substantial portion of the built-in gain in S2. First, P causes a recapitalization of S3 in which S2's S3 common stock is exchanged for new S3 preferred shares. P then sells all of its S2 stock. Immediately after the sale of the S2 stock, S3 is a member of the P group.

(ii) *Analysis*. Pursuant to paragraph (b)(4) of this section, because S2 owns stock of S3 (another subsidiary of the same group) and, immediately after the sale of the S2 stock, S3 is a member of the group, then for purposes of applying paragraph (b) of this section, S2 is deemed to have transferred its S3 stock. Because S3 is a member of the group immediately after the transfer of the S2 stock and the S3 stock deemed transferred has a basis in excess of value, the group in the S3 stock is redetermined pursuant to paragraph (b)(1) of this section im-

mediately prior to the sale of the S2 stock. Accordingly, P would recognize only $1 of gain on the sale of its S2 stock. However, because the recapitalization of the S3 was structured with a view to, and has the effect of, avoiding the recognition of gain on a disposition of stock by invoking the application of paragraph (b) of this section, paragraph (g)(4)(i) of this section applies. Accordingly, paragraph (b) of this section does not apply upon P's disposition of the S2 stock and P recognizes $100 gain on the disposition of the S2 stock.

(6) *General anti-avoidance rule.*—If a taxpayer acts with a view to avoid the purposes of this section, appropriate adjustments will be made to carry out the purposes of this section.

(h) *Application of other rules of law.*—See §1.1502-80(a) regarding the general applicability of other rules of law.

(i) [Reserved].

(j) *Effective/applicability dates.*—This section applies after September 16, 2008. For prior law, see §§1.1502-35 and 1.1502-35T as contained in 26 CFR part 1 in effect on April 1, 2008 [Reg. §1.1502-35.]

☐ [*T.D.* 9254, 3-9-2006. *Amended by T.D.* 9264, 5-26-2006 (*corrected* 8-18-2006); *T.D.* 9322, 4-9-2007; *T.D.* 9342, 7-19-2007 *and T.D.* 9424, 9-9-2008 (*corrected* 3-4-2010).]

[Reg. §1.1502-36]

§1.1502-36. Unified loss rule.—(a) *In general.*—(1) *Scope.*—This section provides rules for adjusting members' bases in stock of a subsidiary (S) and for reducing S's attributes when a member (M) transfers a loss share of S stock. See paragraph (f) of this section for definitions of the terms used in this section, including *transfer* and *value*.

(2) *Purpose.*—The rules in this section have two principal purposes. The first is to prevent the consolidated return provisions from reducing a group's consolidated taxable income through the creation and recognition of noneconomic loss on S stock. The second is to prevent members (including former members) of the group from collectively obtaining more than one tax benefit from a single economic loss. Additional purposes are set forth in other paragraphs of this section. The rules of this section must be interpreted and applied in a manner that is consistent with and reasonably carries out the purposes of this section.

(3) *Overview.*—(i) *General application of section.*—This section applies when M transfers a share of S stock and, after taking into account the effects of all applicable rules of law (even if the adjustments required by such provisions are not deemed effective until after the transfer, such as certain adjustments required under sections 108

and 1017 and §1.1502-28), the share is a loss share. When this section applies, paragraph (b) of this section applies first and may redetermine members' bases in their shares of S stock. If the transferred share is a loss share after any basis redetermination under paragraph (b) of this section, paragraph (c) of this section applies and may reduce M's basis in the transferred loss share. If the transferred share is a loss share after any basis reduction required by paragraph (c) of this section, paragraph (d) of this section applies and may reduce attributes of S and subsidiaries that are lower-tier to S. Although the determination of whether there is a transfer of a loss share is made as of the transfer, this section applies, and any adjustments it requires are given effect, immediately before the transfer. Paragraphs (e), (f), and (g) of this section provide general operating rules (including rules for transfers of S stock between members), definitions, and an anti-abuse rule, respectively.

(ii) *Stock of multiple subsidiaries transferred in the transaction.*—(A) *Initial application of section to transferred shares in lowest tier.*—If shares of stock of more than one subsidiary are transferred in a transaction, the application of this section begins at the lowest tier. If no transferred shares of stock of the lowest-tier subsidiary (S2) are loss shares, any gain recognized with respect to the S2 shares immediately tiers up and adjusts members' bases in subsidiary stock under §1.1502-32. However, if any of the transferred S2 shares are loss shares, paragraph (b) of this section applies with respect to those shares. If, after the application of paragraph (b) of this section, any transferred S2 shares are still loss shares, paragraph (c) of this section applies with respect to those shares. If, after the application of paragraph (c) of this section, any transferred S2 shares are still loss shares and P makes an election under paragraph (d)(6) of this section with respect to those S2 shares, then paragraph (d) of this section applies with respect to those shares, but only to the extent necessary to give effect to the election. After taking into account the effects of any adjustments required by this initial application of this section, recognized gain or loss is computed on all transferred S2 shares. Any adjustments under paragraph (b) or (c) of this section, the effect of any election under paragraph (d)(6) of this section, any gain or loss recognized on the transferred S2 shares (whether allowed or disallowed), and any other related or resulting adjustments then tier-up and apply to adjust members' bases in subsidiary stock under §1.1502-32.

(B) *Initial application of section to transferred shares in higher tiers.*—After taking into account the effects of any adjustments described in paragraph (a)(3)(ii)(A) of this section, transferred shares in the next higher tier, and then in each next higher tier successively, other than the transferred loss shares at the highest tier, are

treated in the manner described in paragraph (a)(3)(ii)(A) of this section.

(C) *Application of section to transferred shares in highest tier.*—After paragraphs (b) and (c) of this section, and, to the extent necessary to give effect to any election under paragraph (d)(6) of this section, paragraph (d) of this section, have been applied to or with respect to all lower-tier transferred loss shares, and after all lower-tier adjustments have been taken into account (whether resulting from the application of paragraph (b) or (c) of this section, an election under paragraph (d)(6) of this section, the recognition of gain or loss on a transfer, or otherwise), paragraphs (b), then (c), and then (d) of this section apply with respect to the highest-tier shares that are transferred loss shares.

(D) *Final application of section to transferred shares in lower tiers.*—After paragraph (d) of this section has been applied with respect to transferred loss shares in the highest tier, it is applied with respect to transferred shares in each next lower tier, successively, to the extent such shares are loss shares after the application of paragraph (d) of this section.

(4) *Other rules of law and coordination with deferral and disallowance provisions.*—In general, this section applies and has effect immediately upon the transfer of a loss share even if the loss is deferred, disallowed, or otherwise not taken into account under any other applicable rules of law. However, see paragraph (e)(3) of this section for special rules applicable to shares of S stock transferred in an intercompany transaction. See section §1.1502-80(a) for the general applicability of other rules of law and a limitation on duplicative adjustments.

(5) *Nomenclature, factual assumptions adopted in this section.*—Unless otherwise stated, for purposes of this section, the following nomenclature and assumptions are adopted. P is the common parent of a consolidated group of which S, M, and M1 are members. X is not a member of the P group. If a corporation has preferred stock outstanding, it is stock described in section 1504(a)(4). The examples set forth the only facts, elections, and activities relevant to the example. All transactions are between unrelated persons and are independent of each other. Tax liabilities and their effect, and the application of any other loss disallowance or deferral provisions of the Internal Revenue Code (Code) or regulations, including but not limited to section 267, are disregarded. All persons report on a calendar year basis and use the accrual method of accounting. All parties comply with filing and other requirements of this section and all other provisions of the Code and regulations.

(b) *Basis redetermination to reduce disparity.*—(1) *In general.*—(i) *Purpose and scope.*—The rules of this paragraph (b) reduce the extent to which there is disparity in members' bases in shares of S stock. These rules supplement the operation of the investment adjustment system; their purpose is to prevent the realization of noneconomic loss and facilitate the elimination of duplicated loss when members hold S shares with disparate bases. The rules of this paragraph (b) only reallocate investment adjustments previously applied to members' bases in shares of S stock, thus they do not alter the aggregate amount of basis in shares of S stock held by members or the aggregate amount of investment adjustments applied to shares of S stock.

(ii) *Special rules for applicability of redetermination rule.*—Notwithstanding the general rule in paragraph (b)(2) of this section, members' bases in shares of S stock are not redetermined under this paragraph (b) if—

(A) There is no disparity among members' bases in shares of S common stock and no member owns a share of S preferred stock with respect to which there is unrecognized gain or loss; or

(B) All the shares of S stock held by members are transferred to one or more nonmembers, become worthless under section 165 (taking into account the provisions of § 1.1502-80(c)), or a combination thereof, in one fully taxable transaction. However, in such a case, P may elect to redetermine such bases under this paragraph (b). Such an election is made in the manner provided in paragraph (e)(5) of this section. If stock of more than one subsidiary is transferred in the transaction, the election may be made with respect to one or more of such subsidiaries.

(iii) *Investment adjustment.*—For purposes of this paragraph (b), the term *investment adjustment* includes adjustments specially allocated under § 1.1502-32(c)(1)(ii)(B) and remaining adjustments described in § 1.1502-32(c)(1)(iii). In applying any provision of this section, the term includes all such adjustments reflected in the basis of the share as of the application of the provision, whether originally allocated under § 1.1502-32 or otherwise. The term therefore includes adjustments previously reallocated to the share, and it does not include adjustments previously reallocated from the share, whether pursuant to this section or any other provision of law. It also includes the proportionate amount of adjustments reflected in the exchanged basis of a share, such as the basis determined under section 358 in connection with a reorganization or a transaction qualifying under section 355.

(2) *Basis redetermination rule.*—If M transfers a loss share of S stock, all members' bases in all their shares of S stock are subject to redetermination under this paragraph (b). The determination of whether a share is a loss share is made as of the transfer, taking into account the effects of all applicable rules of law. The redeterminations are made immediately before applying paragraph (c) of this section and in accordance with the following:

(i) *Decreasing the bases of transferred loss shares.*—(A) *Removing positive investment adjustments from transferred loss shares of common stock.*—M's basis in each of its transferred loss shares of S common stock is first reduced, but not below value, by removing positive investment adjustments previously applied to the basis of the share. The positive investment adjustments removed from transferred loss shares of S common stock are reallocated under paragraph (b)(2)(ii) of this section after negative investment adjustments are reallocated under paragraph (b)(2)(i)(B) of this section.

(B) *Reallocating negative investment adjustments from shares of S common stock.*—If a transferred share is still a loss share after applying paragraph (b)(2)(i)(A) of this section, M's basis in the share is reduced, but not below value, by reallocating negative investment adjustments to the transferred loss share (whether common or preferred stock) from members' shares of S common stock that are not transferred loss shares. The adjustments reallocated under this paragraph (b)(2)(i)(B) are reallocated and applied first to M's bases in transferred loss shares of S preferred stock and then to M's bases in transferred loss shares of S common stock. Reallocations under this paragraph (b)(2)(i)(B) are made in a manner that, to the greatest extent possible, reduces the disparity among members' bases in all transferred loss shares of S preferred stock, and reduces the disparity among members' bases in all shares of S common stock.

(ii) *Increasing the bases of gain preferred and all common shares.*—(A) *Preferred stock.*—After the application of paragraph (b)(2)(i) of this section, the positive investment adjustments removed from transferred loss shares of S common stock under paragraph (b)(2)(i)(A) of this section are reallocated and applied to increase, but not above value, members' bases in shares of S preferred stock (without regard to whether such shares are transferred in the transaction). Reallocations under this paragraph (b)(2)(ii)(A) are made in a manner that, to the greatest extent possible, reduces the disparity among members' bases in all shares of S preferred stock.

(B) *Common stock.*—Any positive investment adjustments removed from transferred loss shares of S common stock under paragraph (b)(2)(i)(A) of this section and not reallocated and applied to S preferred shares are reallocated and applied to increase members' bases in shares of S common stock. Reallocations are made to shares of S common stock without regard to whether a particular share is a loss share or a transferred share, and without regard to the share's value. Reallocations under this paragraph (b)(2)(ii)(B) are made in a manner that, to the greatest extent possible, reduces the disparity among members' bases in all shares of S common stock.

(iii) *Operating rules.*—(A) *Method.*—In general, reallocations should be made first with respect to the earliest available adjustments. However, the overall application of this paragraph (b) to a transaction must be made in a manner that, to the greatest extent possible, reduces basis disparity (as provided in paragraphs (b)(2)(i)(B) and (b)(2)(ii) of this section). The specific reallocation of an investment adjustment under this paragraph (b) may be made using any reasonable method or formula that is consistent with the provisions of this paragraph (b)(2) and furthers the purposes of this section.

(B) *Limits on reallocation.*—(1) *Restriction to members' outstanding shares.*—Investment adjustments can only be reallocated to shares that were held by members at the time the adjustment was originally applied.

(2) *Limitation by prior use.*—(i) *In general.*—In order to prevent the reallocation of investment adjustments from either increasing or decreasing members' aggregate bases in subsidiary stock, no investment adjustment (positive or negative) may be reallocated under this paragraph (b)(2) to the extent that it was (or would have been) used prior to the time that it would otherwise be reallocated under this paragraph (b)(2). For this purpose, an investment adjustment was used (or would have been used) to the extent that it was reflected in (or would have been reflected in) the basis of a share of subsidiary stock and the basis of that share has already been taken into account, directly or indirectly, in determining income, gain, deduction, or loss (including by affecting the application of this section to a prior transfer of subsidiary stock) or in determining the basis of any property that is not subject to § 1.1502-32. However, if the prior use was in an intercompany transaction, an investment adjustment may be reallocated to the extent that § 1.1502-13 has prevented the gain or loss on the transaction from being taken into account. (In that case, appropriate adjustments must be made to the intercompany item from the prior intercompany transaction that has not yet been taken into account.) Further, if an investment adjustment was reflected in (or would have been reflected in) the basis of a share that has been taken into account, the limitation on reallocation under this paragraph (b)(2)(iii)(B)(2) does not apply to the extent the basis of that share would not change as a result of the reallocation (for example, because the reallocation is between shares that are both lower-tier to the share with the previously used basis). See § 1.1502-32(c)(1)(ii)(B) regarding special allocations applicable to the tier-up of the reallocated investment adjustment if the reallocation is lim-

ited under this paragraph (b)(2)(iii)(B)(2) due to prior use at a higher tier.

(ii) *Example.*—The application of this paragraph (b)(2)(iii)(B)(2) is illustrated by the following example:

Example. (i) *Facts.* P owns all 20 shares of M stock, and 10 shares of S stock. M owns the remaining 10 shares of S stock. In year 1, S recognizes $200 of income that results in a $10 positive investment adjustment being allocated to each share of S stock. The group does not recognize any other items. The $100 positive adjustment to M's basis in the S stock tiers up, and results in a $5 positive adjustment to each share of M stock. In year 2, P sells one share of M stock and recognizes a gain. In year 3, M sells one loss share of S stock, and this paragraph (b) applies and requires a reallocation of the year 1 positive investment adjustment applied to the basis of the transferred S share.

(ii) *Application of limitation by prior use.* M's basis in the transferred loss share of S stock reflects a $10 positive investment adjustment attributable to S's year 1 income. Under the general rule of this paragraph (b), that $10 would be subject to reallocation to reduce basis disparity. However, that $10 adjustment had originally tiered up to adjust P's basis in its M shares and, as a result, $.50 of that adjustment was reflected in P's basis in each share of M stock. When P sold the share of M stock, the basis of that share (which included the tiered-up $.50) was used in determining the gain on the sale. Thus, $.50 of the $10 investment adjustment originally allocated to the transferred S share that tiered-up to the sold M share was previously used and, as such, cannot be reallocated in a manner that would (if it were the original allocation) affect the basis of the sold M share. Accordingly, no more than $9.50 of the adjustment to M's transferred S share could be reallocated to P's shares of S stock. If so, under the special allocation rule in § 1.1502-32(c)(1)(ii)(B), the tier-up of this $9.50 would only be allocated among P's remaining 19 shares of M stock. Alternatively, all $10 of the investment adjustment could be reallocated to M's other S shares (because the tier-up to P's M shares would have been the same regardless which of M's shares of S stock were adjusted).

(iii) *Application of limitation where adjustment would have been used.* The facts are the same as in paragraph (i) of this *Example* except that M does not sell any shares of S stock and, in year 3, P sells a loss share of S stock. As in paragraph (i) of this *Example,* when P sold the share of M stock, the basis of that share was used in determining the gain on the share. When P sells the loss share of S stock, the $10 positive investment adjustment from S's year 1 income cannot be reallocated in a manner that would (if it were the original adjustment) affect the basis of the sold M share. If this $10 positive investment adjustment had originally been allocated to the S shares held by M, $.50 of the $10 investment adjustment would have tiered up to the M share that P sold, would have been reflected in P's basis in that M share, and would have been used in determining P's gain or loss on the sale. Accordingly, up to $9.50 of the $10 investment adjustment applied to the basis of P's transferred S share could be reallocated to M's shares of S stock. If so, under the special allocation rule in §1.1502-32(c)(1)(ii)(B), the tier-up of this $9.50 would only be allocated among P's remaining 19 shares of M stock. Alternatively, all $10 of the investment adjustment could be reallocated to P's other S shares.

(3) *Examples.*—The general application of this paragraph (b) is illustrated by the following examples:

Example 1. Transfer of stock received in section 351 exchange. (i) *Redetermination to prevent noneconomic loss.* (A) *Facts.* For many years, M has owned two assets, Asset 1 and Asset 2. On January 1, year 1, M receives the only four outstanding shares of S common stock (Block 1 shares) in exchange for Asset 1, which has a basis and value of $80. Section 351 applies to the exchange and, therefore, under section 358, M's aggregate basis in the Block 1 shares is $80 ($20 per share). On July 1, year 2, M receives another share of S common stock (Block 2 share) in exchange for Asset 2, which has a basis of $0 and value of $20. Section 351 applies to this exchange and, under section 358, M's basis in the Block 2 share is $0. On October 1, year 3, S sells Asset 2 for $20, recognizing a $20 gain. On December 31, year 3, M sells one of its Block 1 shares to X for $20. After taking into account the effects of all applicable rules of law, M's basis in each Block 1 share is $24 (M's original $20 basis increased under §1.1502-32 by $4, the share's allocable portion of the $20 gain recognized on the sale of Asset 2). In addition, M's basis in its Block 2 share is $4 (M's original $0 basis increased under §1.1502-32 by $4 (the share's allocable portion of the $20 gain recognized on the sale of Asset 2)). M's sale of the Block 1 share is a transfer of a loss share and therefore subject to this section.

(B) *Basis redetermination under this paragraph (b).* Under this paragraph (b), M's bases in all its shares of S stock are subject to redetermination. First, paragraph (b)(2)(i)(A) of this section applies to reduce M's basis in the transferred loss share, but not below value, by removing positive investment adjustments applied to the basis of the share. Accordingly, M's basis in the transferred Block 1 share is reduced by $4 (the amount of the positive investment adjustment applied to the share), from $24 to $20. Even if there were negative investment adjustments applied to adjust the bases of nontransferred common shares, no further reduction to the basis of the share would be required under this paragraph (b) because the basis of the transferred share is then equal to the share's value. Under

paragraph (b)(2)(ii)(B) of this section, the positive investment adjustment removed from the transferred loss share is reallocated and applied to increase M's bases in its S common shares in a manner that reduces disparity in M's bases in all the S common shares, to the greatest extent possible. Accordingly, the $4 positive investment adjustment removed from the Block 1 share is reallocated and applied to the basis of the Block 2 share, increasing it from $4 to $8.

(C) *Application of paragraphs (c) and (d) of this section.* Because M's sale of the Block 1 share is not a transfer of a loss share after the application of this paragraph (b), neither paragraph (c) of this section nor paragraph (d) of this section applies to the transfer.

(ii) *Redetermination to eliminate duplicated loss.* (A) *Facts.* The facts are the same as in paragraph (i)(A) of this *Example 1,* except that, at the time of the second contribution, the value of Asset 1 had declined to $20 and so, instead of contributing Asset 2, M contributed Asset 3 to S in exchange for the Block 2 share. At the time of that exchange, Asset 3 had a basis and value of $5. On October 1, year 3, S sells Asset 1 for $20, recognizing a $60 loss that is absorbed by the group. On December 31, year 3, M sells one of its Block 1 shares to X for $5. After taking into account the effects of all applicable rules of law, M's basis in each Block 1 share is $8 (M's original $20 basis decreased under §1.1502-32 by $12 (the share's allocable portion of the $60 loss recognized on the sale of Asset 1)). M's basis in its Block 2 share is an excess loss account of $7 (M's original basis of $5 reduced under §1.1502-32 by $12, the share's allocable portion of the loss recognized on the sale of Asset 1). M's sale of the Block 1 share is a transfer of a loss share and therefore subject to this section.

(B) *Basis redetermination under this paragraph (b).* Under this paragraph (b), M's bases in all its shares of S stock are subject to redetermination. There are no positive investment adjustments and so there is no adjustment under paragraph (b)(2)(i)(A) of this section. However, under paragraph (b)(2)(i)(B) of this section, M's basis in the transferred Block 1 share is reduced, but not below value, by reallocating negative investment adjustments from common shares that are not transferred loss shares. In total, there were $48 of negative investment adjustments applied to common shares that are not transferred loss shares. Accordingly, M's basis in the Block 1 share is reduced by $3, from $8 to its value of $5. Under paragraph (b)(2)(i)(B) of this section, the negative investment adjustments applied to the transferred share are reallocated from (and therefore cause an increase in the basis of) S common shares that are not transferred loss shares in a manner that reduces disparity among members' bases in all S common shares to the greatest extent possible. Accordingly, the $3 negative investment adjustment reallocated and applied to the transferred Block 1 share is reallocated entirely from the Block 2 share, increasing the basis in the Block 2 share from an excess loss account of $7 to an excess loss account of $4.

(C) *Application of paragraphs (c) and (d) of this section.* Because M's sale of the Block 1 share is not a transfer of a loss share after the application of this paragraph (b), neither paragraph (c) of this section nor paragraph (d) of this section applies to the transfer.

(iii) *Nonapplicability of redetermination rule to sale of entire interest.* The facts are the same as in paragraph (ii)(A) of this *Example 1*, except that, on December 31, year 3, M sells all its shares of S stock to X for $25. M's sale of the S stock to X is a transfer of all of the shares of S stock held by members to one or more nonmembers in one fully taxable transaction and, therefore, basis is not redetermined under this paragraph (b). Accordingly, the sale of the Block 1 shares remains a transfer of loss shares and, as such, subject to paragraphs (c) and (d) of this section. However, paragraphs (c)(7) and (d)(3)(i)(A) of this section apply netting principles to prevent adjustments under either paragraph (c) or paragraph (d) of this section, respectively. Alternatively, the group could elect to apply this paragraph (b). In that case, the $12 negative adjustment applied to the Block 2 shares would be reallocated to the Block 1 shares with the result that there would be no loss (or gain) on any of the transferred shares following the application of this paragraph (b). In that case, there would be no further application of this section to the transfer.

(iv) *Transfer of entire interest, partially taxable.* The facts are the same as in paragraph (iii) of this *Example 1*, except that, instead of selling the Block 2 share to X, M contributes the share to a nonmember in a section 351 exchange that is part of the same transaction. Although all the S shares held by members are transferred in the transaction, not all the shares are transferred to one or more nonmembers in one fully taxable transaction. Therefore, paragraph (b)(1)(ii)(B) of this section does not apply and M must redetermine its bases in its shares of S stock under this paragraph (b). In total, there were $12 of negative investment adjustments applied to common shares that are not transferred loss shares (the Block 2 share, a gain share). Accordingly, M's basis in each of the Block 1 shares is reduced by $3, from $8 to its value of $5. Under paragraph (b)(2)(i)(B) of this section, the negative investment adjustments applied to the transferred shares are reallocated from (and therefore cause an increase in the basis of) S shares that are not transferred loss shares in a manner that reduces disparity among members' bases in all S common shares to the greatest extent possible. Accordingly, the $12 negative investment adjustment reallocated and applied to the transferred Block 1 shares is reallocated entirely from the Block 2 share, increasing the basis in the Block 2 share from an excess loss account of $7 to a basis of $5. Because M's transfer is not a trans-

fer of loss shares after the application of this paragraph (b), neither paragraph (c) of this section nor paragraph (d) of this section applies to the transfer.

Example 2. Redetermination increases basis of transferred loss share. (i) *Facts.* On January 1, year 1, M owns all 10 outstanding shares of S common stock. Five of the shares have a basis of $20 per share (Block 1 shares) and five of the shares have a basis of $10 per share (Block 2 shares). S's only asset, Asset 1, has a basis of $50. S has no other attributes. On October 1, year 1, S sells Asset 1 for $100, recognizing a $50 gain. On December 31, year 2, M sells one Block 1 share and one Block 2 share to X for $10 per share. After taking into account the effects of all applicable rules of law, M's basis in each Block 1 share is $25 (M's original $20 basis increased under § 1.1502-32 by $5, the share's allocable portion of the $50 gain recognized on the sale of Asset 1), and M's basis in each Block 2 share is $15 (M's original $10 basis increased under § 1.1502-32 by $5, the share's allocable portion of the $50 gain recognized on the sale of Asset 1). M's sale of the Block 1 and Block 2 shares is a transfer of loss shares and therefore subject to this section.

(ii) *Basis redetermination under this paragraph (b).* Under this paragraph (b), M's bases in all its shares of S stock are subject to redetermination. First, paragraph (b)(2)(i)(A) of this section applies to reduce M's basis in the transferred Block 1 and Block 2 shares, but not below value, by removing the positive investment adjustments applied to the bases of the transferred loss shares. Accordingly, the basis of the transferred Block 1 share is reduced by $5, from $25 to $20. The basis of the transferred Block 2 share is also reduced by $5, from $15 to $10. (Although the transferred Block 1 share is still a loss share, there is no reduction to its basis under paragraph (b)(2)(i)(B) of this section because there were no negative investment adjustments applied to the bases of the S common shares that are not transferred loss shares.) Next, paragraph (b)(2)(ii)(B) of this section applies to reallocate and apply the $10 of positive investment adjustments removed from the transferred loss shares to increase M's bases in its S common shares in a manner that reduces the disparity in its bases in all S common shares to the greatest extent possible. Accordingly, of the $10 of positive investment adjustments to be reallocated, $6 is reallocated and applied to the basis of the transferred Block 2 share (increasing it from $10 to $16) and $4 is reallocated and applied equally to the basis of each of the four retained Block 2 shares (increasing the basis of each from $15 to $16). After giving effect to the reallocations under this paragraph (b), M's basis in each retained Block 1 share is $25, M's basis in the transferred Block 1 share is $20, and M's basis in each Block 2 share is $16.

(iii) *Application of paragraph (c) of this section.* After the application of this paragraph (b), M's sale of the Block 1 and Block 2 shares is still a transfer of loss shares and, accordingly, subject to paragraph (c) of this section. No adjustment is required to the basis of the transferred Block 1 share under paragraph (c) of this section because, after its basis is redetermined under this paragraph (b), the net positive adjustment to the basis of the share is $0. See paragraph (c)(3) of this section. However, under paragraph (c) of this section M's basis in the transferred Block 2 share is reduced by $6 (the lesser of its net positive adjustment, $6, and its disconformity amount, $6), from $16 to $10, its value. See paragraph (c)(2) of this section.

(iv) *Application of paragraph (d) of this section.* After the application of paragraph (c) of this section, M's sale of the Block 1 share is still a transfer of a loss share and, accordingly, subject to paragraph (d) of this section. No adjustment is required under paragraph (d) of this section because there is no aggregate inside loss. See paragraph (d)(3)(iii) of this section. Because M's sale of the Block 2 share is no longer a transfer of a loss share after the application of paragraph (c) of this section, paragraph (d) of this section does not apply to the transfer of the Block 2 share.

Example 3. Tiered subsidiaries. (i) *Transfer of all shares of common stock.* (A) *Facts.* P owns the sole outstanding share of S stock with a basis of $100, and the sole outstanding share of M stock with a basis of $300. M has $200 and owns an asset with a basis of $0. S owns one asset, Asset 1, with a basis of $100. At a time when Asset 1 has a value of $200, S issues a second share of common stock to M in exchange for $200. Later S sells Asset 1 for $200, recognizing a $100 gain. After taking into account the effects of all applicable rules of law, P's basis in its S stock is $150 (P's original $100 basis increased under §1.1502-32 by $50, the share's allocable portion of the $100 gain recognized on the sale of Asset 1), M's basis in its S stock is $250 (M's original $200 basis increased under §1.1502-32 by $50, the share's allocable portion of the $100 gain recognized on the sale of Asset 1), and P's basis in its M stock is $350 (P's original $300 basis increased under §1.1502-32 by $50, the tier-up of M's increase in its basis in its S stock). P then sells its M share and its S share to X for $300 and $200, respectively. M and S are not members of the same consolidated group immediately after the sale. Therefore, the M share and both of the S shares are transferred in the transaction. Regarding P's sale of its share of S stock and its share of M stock, see paragraph (f)(10)(i)(A) of this section (ceasing to own a share in a taxable transaction) and paragraph (f)(10)(i)(C) of this section (nonmember acquires share); regarding M's share of S stock, see paragraph (f)(10)(i)(B) of this section (ceasing to be members of the same group). The application of this section begins with respect to the stock of S, the subsidiary at the lowest tier in which there is a transfer of subsidiary stock. See paragraph (a)(3)(ii) of this section. Although both P and M

transfer their S shares, only M's S share is a loss share. Thus, only M's transfer is a transfer of a loss share of S stock and only M's transfer is subject to this section.

(B) *Application of section to transferred S shares.* Although only M's transfer is subject to this section, all members' bases in their shares of S stock are subject to redetermination under this paragraph (b). First, paragraph (b)(2)(i)(A) of this section applies to reduce M's basis in its transferred S share, but not below value, by removing the positive investment adjustment applied to that share. Accordingly, the basis of M's S share is reduced by $50, from $250 to $200 (under §1.1502-32, that redetermination adjustment tiers up to reduce P's basis in its M stock by $50, from $350 to $300). Because there are no negative adjustments to reallocate under paragraph (b)(2)(i)(B) of this section, paragraph (b)(2)(ii)(B) of this section then applies to reallocate and apply the $50 positive investment adjustment removed from the transferred loss S share to increase P's basis in its S share in a manner that reduces disparity among members' bases in all S common shares to the greatest extent possible. Accordingly, all $50 of the positive investment adjustment is reallocated and applied to P's basis in its S share (increasing the basis from $150 to $200). Because M's transfer of its S share is not a transfer of a loss share after the application of this paragraph (b), neither paragraph (c) of this section nor paragraph (d) of this section applies to that transfer.

(C) *Application of section to transfers at next higher tier.* After the adjustments to M's share of S stock are given effect, P's transfer of its share of M stock is not a transfer of a loss share and so this section does not apply to that transfer.

(D) *Result of application of section.* After the application of this section, P recognizes no gain or loss on its sale of either the S share or the M share. In addition, the unrecognized (noneconomic) loss in M's basis in its S share is eliminated. The results would be the same if, in addition to the facts in paragraph (i)(A) of this *Example 3*, M transferred its S share to X in a fully taxable transaction and, as permitted under paragraph (b)(1)(ii)(B) of this section, P elected to redetermine basis under this paragraph (b).

(ii) *Transfer of less than all lower-tier shares of stock.* (A) *Facts.* The facts are the same as in paragraph (i)(A) of this *Example 1*, except that M and S are members of the same consolidated group immediately after the sale. Therefore, in this case, M's S share is not transferred and so this section has no application with respect to M's S share. P's transfer of its S share is not a transfer of a loss share and so is also not subject to this section. However, P's sale of its share of M stock is a transfer of a loss share and is subject to this section.

(B) *Basis redetermination under this paragraph (b).* Although P's transfer of its share of M stock is subject to this section, this paragraph (b) does not apply to the transfer because there is only one share of M stock outstanding (and so there can be no disparity among members' bases in common shares and there are no outstanding preferred shares with respect to which there can be unrecognized gain or loss). Accordingly, after the application of this paragraph (b), P's sale of its M share is still a transfer of a loss share and therefore subject to paragraph (c) of this section.

(C) *Application of paragraphs (c) and (d) of this section.* Under paragraph (c) of this section, P must reduce its basis in its M share by $50, the lesser of its net positive adjustment ($50, see paragraph (c)(3) of this section) and its disconformity amount ($150, see paragraphs (c)(4), (c)(5), and (c)(6) of this section). As a result, the share is no longer a loss share and the transfer is not subject to paragraph (d) of this section.

(D) *Result of application of section.* After the application of this section, P recognizes a $50 gain on its sale of the S share and no loss on its sale of the M share. Although there is unrecognized loss preserved in M's basis in its S share, if M later transfers the share when it is a loss share, that transfer will be subject to this section.

Example 4. Application to outstanding common and preferred shares. (i) *Facts.* P owns all the stock of M and all eight outstanding shares of S common stock. S also has two shares of nonvoting preferred stock outstanding; the preferred shares each have a $100 annual, cumulative preference as to dividends. M owns one of the preferred shares (PS1) and P owns the other (PS2). On January 1, year 1, the bases and values of the outstanding S shares are:

	Preferred				Common					
	PS1 (M)	PS2 (P)	CS1 (P)	CS2 (P)	CS3 (P)	CS4 (P)	CS5 (P)	CS6 (P)	CS7 (P)	CS8 (P)
Basis	1250	990	1025	710	550	400	375	250	215	100
Value	1000	1000	375	375	375	375	375	375	375	375

(A) As of January 1, year 1, there are no arrearages on the preferred stock. In year 1, S has a $1100 capital loss and $100 of ordinary income. The group absorbs the loss and the negative remaining adjustment of $1000 is allocable entirely to the common stock, equally to each common share ($125 per share). See § 1.1502-32(c)(1)(iii) and (c)(2).

(B) In year 2, S has $700 of ordinary income and a $100 ordinary loss. Also, on October 1, year 2, S declares and makes a $200 dividend distribution with respect to the preferred stock ($100 per share). Under § 1.1502-32(c)(1)(i), a negative adjustment of $100 is first allocated to each of the preferred shares to reflect the declara-

tion of the dividend. The $600 positive remaining adjustment determined under § 1.1502-32(c)(1)(iii) (reflecting S's net income reduced by the distribution) is then allocated to each of the preferred shares to the extent of its entitlement to dividends accruing in year 1 and year 2 ($200 per share). See § 1.1502-32(c)(1)(iii) and (c)(3). The $200 of the positive remaining adjustment not allocated to the preferred shares is then allocated to the common stock, equally to each common share ($25 per share). See § 1.1502-32(c)(1)(iii) and (c)(2). After taking into account the effects of all applicable rules of law, the adjusted bases and the values of the shares as of January 1, year 3, are:

	Preferred				Common					
	PS1 (M)	PS2 (P)	CS1 (P)	CS2 (P)	CS3 (P)	CS4 (P)	CS5 (P)	CS6 (P)	CS7 (P)	CS8 (P)
Basis	1250	990	1025	710	550	400	375	250	215	100
Year 1 § 1.1502-32 adjustments	N/A	N/A	-125	-125	-125	-125	-125	-125	-125	-125
Year 2 § 1.1502-32 adjustments	-100 +200 +100	-100 +200 +100	+25	+25	+25	+25	+25	+25	+25	+25
Adjusted basis	1350	1090	925	610	450	300	275	150	115	0
Value	1100	1100	275	275	275	275	275	275	275	275
Unrecognized gain/(loss)	(250)	10	(650)	(335)	(175)	(25)	0	125	160	275

(C) On January 1, year 3, M sells PS1 for $1100 and P sells CS2 for $275. The sales of PS1 and CS2 are transfers of loss shares and therefore subject to this section.

(ii) *Basis redetermination under this paragraph (b).* Under this paragraph (b), all members' bases

in shares of S stock are subject to redetermination in accordance with the following:

(A) *Removing positive investment adjustments from transferred loss common shares.* First, paragraph (b)(2)(i)(A) of this section applies to reduce P's basis in CS2, but not below value, by removing the positive investment adjustment applied to the basis of the share. Accordingly, P's basis in CS2 is reduced by $25, from $610 to $585.

(B) *Reallocating negative investment adjustments from common shares that are not transferred loss shares.* Because the transferred shares remain loss shares after the removal of positive investment adjustments, their bases are further reduced under paragraph (b)(2)(i)(B) of this section, but not below value, by reallocating negative investment adjustments applied to common shares that are not transferred loss shares. Reallocations are made first to preferred shares and then to the common shares, in a manner that reduces disparity among members' bases in transferred loss preferred shares, and reduces disparity among members' bases in all common shares, to the greatest extent possible. The loss on PS1 is $250, the remaining loss on CS2 is $310, and the total amount of negative investment adjustments applied to shares that are not transferred loss shares is $875 (the sum of the negative adjustments applied to all common shares other than CS2). Thus, $250 of negative investment adjustments are reallocated and applied to the basis of PS1, reducing it to the share's value, $1100. The negative investment adjustments are reallocated from the common shares that are not transferred loss shares in a manner that reduces disparity among members' bases in all common shares to the greatest extent possible. The negative investment adjustments may be reallocated to PS1 from the common shares that are not transferred loss shares as follows: $125 from each of CS7 and CS8. Such reallocations increase the basis of CS7 by $125, from $115 to $240, and increase the basis of CS8

by $125, from $0 to $125. Negative investment adjustments are then reallocated to CS2 from the common shares that are not transferred loss shares in a manner that reduces disparity among members' bases in all common shares to the greatest extent possible. The negative investment adjustments may be reallocated to CS2 from the other common shares as follows: $80 from CS4, $105 from CS5, and $125 from CS6. Such reallocations reduce the basis of CS2 by $310, from $585 to $275, increase the basis of CS4 by $80, from $300 to $380, increase the basis of CS5 by $105, from $275 to $380, and increase the basis of CS6 by $125, from $150 to $275. However, there may be other reasonable reallocations.

(C) *Increasing basis by reallocated positive investment adjustments.* Under paragraph (b)(2)(ii)(A) of this section, the $25 positive investment adjustment removed from CS2 (the transferred loss common share) is then reallocated and applied to increase the basis of preferred shares, but not above value. Accordingly, $10 of that amount is reallocated to PS2, increasing its basis from $1090 to $1100, its value. Under paragraph (b)(2)(ii)(B) of this section, the remaining $15 is reallocated and applied to the common shares in a manner that reduces disparity among members' bases in all common shares to the greatest extent possible. The $15 positive investment adjustment that is reallocated to common shares may be reallocated entirely to CS8, increasing its basis from $125 to $140. However, there may be other reasonable reallocations.

(D) *Summary of the reallocation of adjustments.* The adjustments made under this paragraph (b) are:

	Preferred		CS1 (P)	CS2 (P)	Common					
	PS1 (M)	PS2 (P)			CS3 (P)	CS4 (P)	CS5 (P)	CS6 (P)	CS7 (P)	CS8 (P)
Adjusted basis before redetermination	1350	1090	925	610	450	300	275	150	115	0
Removing positive adjustments from transferred loss shares				-25						
Reallocating negative adjustments	-250			-310		+80	+105	+125	+125	+125
Applying positive adjustments removed from transferred loss shares		+10								+15
Basis after redetermination	1100	1100	925	275	450	380	380	275	240	140
Value	1100	1100	275	275	275	275	275	275	275	275
Gain/(loss)	0	0	(650)	0	(175)	(105)	(105)	0	35	135

(iii) *Application of paragraphs (c) and (d) of this section.* Because M's sale of PS1 and P's sale of CS2 are not transfers of loss shares after the application of this paragraph (b), paragraphs (c) and (d) of this section do not apply.

(iv) *Higher-tier effects.* The $250 reduction in the basis of PS1 under this paragraph (b) is a noncapital, nondeductible expense under §1.1502-32(b)(3)(iii)(B) that will be included in the year 3 investment adjustment to be applied to P's basis in its M stock.

(c) *Stock basis reduction to prevent noneconomic loss.*—(1) *In general.*—The rules of this paragraph (c) reduce M's basis in a transferred share of S stock to prevent noneconomic stock loss and thus promote the clear reflection of the group's income. These rules limit the reduction to M's basis in the S share to the amount of net unrealized appreciation reflected in the share's basis as of the transfer (the disconformity amount). These rules also limit the reduction to M's basis in the S share to the portion of the share's basis that is attributable to investment adjustments made pursuant to the consolidated return regulations.

(2) *Basis reduction rule.*—This paragraph (c) applies if M transfers a share of S stock and, after taking into account the effects of all applicable rules of law, including any adjustments under paragraph (b) of this section, the share is a loss share. Under this paragraph (c), M's basis in the share is reduced, but not below value, by the lesser of—

(i) The share's net positive adjustment (as defined in paragraph (c)(3) of this section); and

(ii) The share's disconformity amount (as defined in paragraph (c)(4) of this section).

(3) *Net positive adjustment.*—A share's *net positive adjustment* is the greater of—

(i) Zero; and

(ii) The sum of all investment adjustments reflected in the basis of the share. The term *investment adjustment* has the same meaning as in paragraph (b)(1)(iii) of this section, except that it includes all adjustments specially allocated under §1.1502-32(c)(1)(ii).

(4) *Disconformity amount.*—A share's *disconformity amount* is the excess, if any, of—

(i) M's basis in the share; over

(ii) The share's allocable portion of S's net inside attribute amount (as defined in paragraph (c)(5) of this section).

(5) *Net inside attribute amount.*—S's *net inside attribute amount* is determined as of the transfer, taking into account all applicable rules of law (even if the adjustments required by such rules are not deemed effective until after the transfer, such as certain adjustments required under sections 108 and 1017 and §1.1502-28). S's net inside attribute amount is the sum of S's net operating and capital loss carryovers, deferred deductions,

money, and basis in assets other than money, reduced by the amount of S's liabilities. For this purpose, S's basis in any share of lower-tier subsidiary stock is generally S's basis in that share, adjusted to reflect any gain or loss recognized in the transaction with respect to the share and any other related or resulting adjustments to the basis of the share. However, see paragraph (c)(6) of this section for special rules regarding the computation of S's net inside attribute amount for purposes of this paragraph (c) if S holds stock of a subsidiary that is not transferred in the transaction. See paragraph (f) of this section for definitions of "allocable portion," "deferred deduction," "liability," "loss carryover," and other relevant terms.

(6) *Determination of S's net inside attribute amount if S owns stock of a lowertier subsidiary.*—(i) *Overview.*—If a loss share of S stock is transferred when S holds a share of stock of another subsidiary (S1) and the S1 share is not transferred in the same transaction, S's net inside attribute amount is determined by treating S's basis in its S1 share as tentatively reduced under this paragraph (c)(6). The purpose of this rule is to reduce the extent to which S1's investment adjustments increase noneconomic loss on S stock (as a result of S1's recognition of items that are indirectly reflected in a member's basis in a share of S stock).

(ii) *General rule for nontransferred shares of lower-tier subsidiary stock.*—For purposes of determining the disconformity amount of a share of S stock, S's basis in a nontransferred share of S1 stock is treated as reduced by the share's tentative reduction amount. The tentative reduction amount is the lesser of the S1 share's net positive adjustment and the S1 share's disconformity amount.

(iii) *Multiple tiers of nontransferred shares.*—If S directly or indirectly owns nontransferred shares of stock of subsidiaries in multiple tiers, then, subject to the limitations in paragraph (c)(6)(iv) of this section (regarding nontransferred shares that are lower-tier to transferred shares), the rules of this paragraph (c)(6) first apply to determine the tentatively reduced basis of stock of the subsidiary at the lowest tier. These rules then apply to determine the tentatively reduced basis of nontransferred shares of stock of subsidiaries successively at each next higher tier that is lower-tier to S. The tentative reductions at each tier are treated as noncapital, nondeductible expenses that tier up under the principles of §1.1502-32, and, as such, result in a tentative reduction of basis and any net positive adjustment of subsidiary shares that are lower-tier to S.

(iv) *Nonapplicability of tentative basis reduction rule to transferred shares.*—The tentative basis reduction rule in this paragraph (c)(6) does not apply to any share of stock of a lower-tier subsidiary (S1) that is transferred in the same transaction in which the S share is transferred. Further, for purposes of determining the S share's disconformity amount, the tentative basis reduction rule in this paragraph (c)(6) only applies with respect to stock of a lower-tier subsidiary if such stock is lower-tier to a nontransferred S1 share. The purpose of this rule is to prevent tentative adjustments to the bases of lower-tier shares if this paragraph (c) has already applied with respect to the shares, without regard to whether such application resulted in the reduction of the basis of any share.

(v) *Example.*—The rules of this paragraph (c)(6) are illustrated by the following example:

Example. (i) *Facts.* M owns the sole outstanding share of S stock, S owns the sole outstanding share of S1 stock, S1 owns all five outstanding shares of S2 stock (the bases of which are equal), and S2 owns the sole outstanding share of S3 stock. The basis of each of the shares reflects its allocable portion of a $5 positive investment adjustment attributable to income recognized by S3. The basis of the S share exceeds its value by $10 and the basis of the S1 share exceeds its value by $5. The basis of each S2 share is $1 less than its value. In one transaction, M sells its S share to X, S1 issues new shares in an amount that prevents S and S1 from being members of the same group, and S1 sells one of its S2 shares to an unrelated individual. S1, S2, and S3 elect to file a consolidated return following the transaction.

(ii) *General applicability of section.* As a result of the transaction, there is a transfer of the S share and the S2 share that was sold (because both shares were sold to nonmembers) and of the S1 share (because S and S1 cease to be members of the same group as a result of the stock issuance). The transfer of the S2 share is not a transfer of a loss share, and so this section does not apply to that transfer. The transfers of the S and S1 shares are transfers of loss shares, and so this section applies to those transfers. The S3 share and the four retained S2 shares are not transferred in the transaction. Under paragraph (a)(3)(ii)(A) of this section, this section applies first to the transfer of the S1 share because it is the lowest-tier transferred loss share.

(iii) *Application of paragraph (b) of this section and this paragraph (c) to transfer of S1 stock.* First, the $1 gain recognized on the transfer of the S2 share tiers up to adjust the basis of each upper-tier share. The transferred S1 share is still a loss share (by $4) and is therefore subject to this section. Although the transfer is subject to paragraph (b) of this section, there is no basis redetermination under paragraph (b) of this section because there is only one share of S1 stock outstanding (and so there can be no disparity among members' bases in common shares and there are no outstanding preferred shares with respect to which there can be unrecognized gain

or loss). See paragraph (b)(1)(ii)(A) of this section. Therefore, after the application of paragraph (b) of this section, the S1 share is still a loss share and, as such, subject to this paragraph (c). In determining the amount of any basis reduction under this paragraph (c), the disconformity amount of the S1 share is computed by comparing S's basis in its S1 share to S1's net inside attribute amount (because there is only one S1 share outstanding, the entire amount is allocable to that share). In determining S1's net inside attribute amount, the tentative reduction rule in this paragraph (c)(6) applies to nontransferred lower-tier shares (provided they are lower-tier to nontransferred shares). Thus, the rule applies to S1's four retained shares of S2 stock and to S2's share of S3 stock. The tentative reduction begins at the lowest level (S2's share of S3 stock) and any tentative reduction amount tiers up as a noncapital, nondeductible expense under the principles of § 1.1502-32, tentatively reducing the bases of any upper tier nontransferred shares that are lower-tier to the transferred loss share (the S1 share). Accordingly, each of S1s nontransferred share of S2 stock is tentatively reduced by its portion of the tentative reduction to S2's share of S3 stock. S1 then applies the tentative reduction rule to its four nontransferred S2 shares. S1's net inside attribute amount is the sum of its basis in each of its nontransferred S2 shares, as tentatively reduced under this paragraph (c)(6) and S1's actual basis in the transferred S2 share, increased to reflect the gain recognized on the sale of that share. After the application of this paragraph (c) to the transfer of the S1 share, paragraph (b) of this section applies to M's transfer of the S share.

(iv) *Application of section to transfer of S stock.* Because the S share is still a loss share after applying paragraph (b) of this section and this paragraph (c) to the transfer of the S1 stock, this section applies to M's transfer of the S share. Although paragraph (b) of this section applies to the transfer, there is no basis redetermination under paragraph (b) of this section because there is only one share of S stock outstanding (and so there can be no disparity among members' bases in common shares and there are no outstanding preferred shares with respect to which there can be unrecognized gain or loss). See paragraph (b)(1)(ii)(A) of this section. Therefore, after the application of paragraph (b) of this section, the share is still a loss share and, as such, subject to this paragraph (c). In determining the disconformity amount of the S share, S's net inside attribute amount is determined using S's actual basis in the transferred S1 stock (after any reduction under this paragraph (c)), because the tentative reduction rule in this paragraph (c)(6) does not apply to shares that are transferred in the transaction. All other shares are lower-tier to the transferred S1 share and are therefore also not subject to tentative reduction for purposes of determining the disconformity amount of the S share. After the application of this paragraph (c) to the transfer of the S share, paragraph (d) of this section applies with respect to M's transfer of the S share. After the application of paragraph (d) of this section with respect to the transfer of the S share, if the S1 share is still a loss share, paragraph (d) of this section applies with respect to S's transfer of the S1 share.

(7) *Netting of gains and losses taken into account.*—(i) *General rule.*—Solely for purposes of computing the basis reduction required under this paragraph (c), the basis of each transferred loss share of S stock is treated as reduced proportionately (as to loss) by the amount of income or gain taken into account by members with respect to transferred shares of S stock, provided that—

(A) The shares are transferred in one transaction; and

(B) The gain is taken into account as of the transaction.

(ii) *Example.*—The netting rule of this paragraph (c)(7) is illustrated by the following example:

Example. Disposition of gain and loss shares. (i) *Facts.* M owns the only three outstanding shares of S stock. Share A has a basis of $54, Share B has a basis of $100, and Share C has a basis of $80. In the same transaction, M sells all three S shares to X for $60 each. M realizes a gain of $6 on Share A, a loss of $40 on Share B, and a loss of $20 on Share C. M's sales of Share B and Share C are transfers of loss shares and therefore subject to this section. M's sale is a transfer of all of the shares of S stock held by members to one or more nonmembers in one fully taxable transaction and, therefore, basis is not redetermined under paragraph (b) of this section. See paragraph (b)(1)(ii)(B) of this section. The transfer is then subject to this paragraph (c). However, for this purpose, M treats its bases in Share B and Share C as reduced by the $6 gain taken into account on Share A. The gain is allocated to Share B and Share C proportionately based on the amount of loss in each share. Thus, $4 of gain ($40/$60 × $6) is treated as allocated to Share B and $2 of gain ($20/$60 × $6) is treated as allocated to Share C. Accordingly, M computes the basis reduction required under this paragraph (c) by treating its basis in Share B as $96 ($100 less $4) and its basis in Share C as $78 ($80 less $2). If, after the application of this paragraph (c), the sales of Share B and Share C are still transfers of loss shares, then the transfers are subject to paragraph (d) of this section. (Although the bases of Share B and Share C are not actually reduced by any portion of the gain, paragraph (d)(3)(i)(A) of this section applies netting principles to limit adjustments under paragraph (d) of this section.)

(ii) *Disposition of stock with deferred gain.* The facts are the same as in paragraph (i) of this *Example*, except that M sells the gain share to another member. Under § 1.1502-13, M's gain

recognized on Share A is not taken into account in the taxable year of the transfer and therefore cannot be treated as reducing M's loss recognized on Share B and Share C for purposes of this paragraph (c). The applicability of this section to the transfer of Share A is determined as of the time that the intercompany item (the gain on M's sale to the other member) is taken into account, see paragraph (e)(3) of this section. However, if Share B (instead of Share A) were sold to a member, the entire gain on Share A would be treated as reducing the loss on Share C for purposes of applying this paragraph (c), see paragraph (e)(3) of this section.

(8) *Examples.*—The application of this paragraph (c) is illustrated by the following examples.

Example 1. Appreciation reflected in stock basis at acquisition. (i) *Appreciation recognized as gain.* (A) *Facts.* On January 1, year 1, M purchases the sole outstanding share of S stock for $100. At that time, S owns two assets, Asset 1 with a basis of $0 and a value of $40, and Asset 2 with a basis and value of $60. In year 1, S sells Asset 1 for $40, recognizing a $40 gain. On December 31, year 1, M sells its S share for $100. After taking into account the effects of all applicable rules of law, M's basis in the S share is $140 (M's original $100 basis increased under § 1.1502-32 by $40, the share's allocable portion of the gain recognized on the sale of Asset 1). M's sale of the S share is a transfer of a loss share and therefore subject to this section.

(B) *Application of paragraph (b) of this section.* Although the transfer is subject to this section, there is no basis redetermination under paragraph (b) of this section because there is only one share of S stock outstanding (and so there can be no disparity among members' bases in common shares and there are no outstanding preferred shares with respect to which there can be unrecognized gain or loss). See paragraph (b)(1)(ii)(A) of this section. Therefore, after the application of paragraph (b) of this section, the share is still a loss share and, as such, subject to this paragraph (c).

(C) *Basis reduction under this paragraph (c).* Under this paragraph (c), M's basis in the S share, $140, is reduced, but not below value, $100, by the lesser of the share's net positive adjustment and disconformity amount. The share's net positive adjustment is the greater of zero and the sum of all investment adjustments (as defined in paragraph (b)(1)(iii) of this section) applied to the basis of the share. The only investment adjustment applied to the basis of the share is the $40 adjustment attributable to the gain recognized on the sale of Asset 1. Thus, the share's net positive adjustment is $40. The share's disconformity amount is the excess, if any, of its basis, $140, over its allocable portion of S's net inside attribute amount. S's net inside attribute amount is the sum of S's money ($40 from the sale of Asset 1) and S's basis in Asset 2, $60, or $100. The share is the only outstanding S share and so its allocable portion of the $100 net inside attribute amount is the entire $100. Thus, the share's disconformity amount is $40, the excess of $140 over $100. The lesser of the net positive adjustment, $40, and the share's disconformity amount, $40, is $40. Accordingly, immediately before the application of paragraph (d) of this section, M's basis in the share is reduced by $40, from $140 to $100.

(D) *Application of paragraph (d) of this section.* Because M's sale of the S share is not a transfer of a loss share after the application of this paragraph (c), paragraph (d) of this section does not apply to the transfer.

(ii) *Appreciation recognized as income earned in the consumption of built-in gain.* The facts are the same as in paragraph (i)(A) of this *Example 1,* except that, instead of selling Asset 1, the value of Asset 1 is consumed in the production of $40 of income in year 1 (reducing the value of Asset 1 to $0). Because the net positive adjustment includes items of income as well as items of gain, the results are the same as those described in paragraph (i) of this *Example 1.*

(iii) *Post-acquisition appreciation eliminates stock loss.* The facts are the same as in paragraph (i)(A) of this *Example 1* except that, in addition, the value of Asset 2 increases to $100 before the stock is sold. As a result, M sells the S share for $140. Because M's sale of the S share is not a transfer of a loss share, this section does not apply to the transfer, notwithstanding that P's basis in the S share was increased by the gain recognized on Asset 1.

(iv) *Distributions.* (A) *Facts.* The facts are the same as in paragraph (i)(A) of this *Example 1* except that, in addition, S declares and makes a $10 dividend distribution before the end of year 1. As a result, the value of the share decreases and M sells the share for $90. After taking into account the effects of all applicable rules of law, M's basis in the S share is $130 (M's original $100 basis increased under § 1.1502-32 by $30, the $10 distribution on the share reduced by the share's allocable portion of the $40 gain recognized on the sale of Asset 1). M's sale of the S share is a transfer of a loss share and therefore subject to this section.

(B) *Application of paragraph (b) of this section.* Although the transfer is subject to this section, there is no basis redetermination under paragraph (b) of this section for the reasons set forth in paragraph (i)(B) of this *Example 1.* Therefore, after the application of paragraph (b) of this section, the share is still a loss share and, as such, subject to this paragraph (c).

(C) *Basis reduction under this paragraph (c).* Under this paragraph (c), M's basis in the S share, $130, is reduced, but not below value, $90, by the lesser of the share's net positive adjustment and disconformity amount. The share's net

positive adjustment is $40 (the sum of all investment adjustments (as defined in paragraph (b)(1)(iii) of this section) applied to the basis of the share). The share's disconformity amount is the excess of its basis, $130, over its allocable portion of S's net inside attribute amount. S's net inside attribute amount is $90, the sum of S's money ($30, the $40 sale proceeds less the $10 distribution) and S's basis in Asset 2, $60. The share is the only outstanding S share and so its allocable portion of the $90 net inside attribute amount is the entire $90. The lesser of the share's net positive adjustment, $40, and its disconformity amount, $40, is $40. Accordingly, immediately before the application of paragraph (d) of this section, the basis in the share is reduced by $40, from $130 to $90.

(D) *Application of paragraph (d) of this section.* Because M's sale of the S share is not a transfer of a loss share after the application of this paragraph (c), paragraph (d) of this section does not apply to the transfer.

Example 2. Loss of appreciation reflected in basis. (i) *Facts.* On January 1, year 1, M purchases the sole outstanding share of S stock for $100. At that time, S owns two assets, Asset 1 with a basis of $0 and a value of $40, and Asset 2 with a basis and value of $60. The value of Asset 1 declines to $0 and M sells its S share for $60. After taking into account the effects of all applicable rules of law, M's basis in the S share is $100. M's sale of the S share is a transfer of a loss share and therefore subject to this section.

(ii) *Application of paragraph (b) of this section.* Although the transfer is subject to this section, there is no basis redetermination under paragraph (b) of this section because there is only one share of S stock outstanding (and so there can be no disparity among members' bases in common shares and there are no outstanding preferred shares with respect to which there can be unrecognized gain or loss). See paragraph (b)(1)(ii)(A) of this section. Therefore, after the application of paragraph (b) of this section, the share is still a loss share and, as such, subject to this paragraph (c).

(iii) *Basis reduction under this paragraph (c).* Under this paragraph (c), M's $100 basis in the S share is reduced, but not below its $60 value by the lesser of the share's net positive adjustment and disconformity amount. There were no investment adjustments applied to M's basis in the share and so the share's net positive adjustment is $0. Thus, although the share's disconformity amount is $40 (the excess of M's $100 basis in the share over the share's $60 allocable portion of S's net inside attribute amount), no basis reduction is required under this paragraph (c).

(iv) *Application of paragraph (d) of this section.* After the application of this paragraph (c), M's sale of the S share is still a transfer of a loss share, and, accordingly, subject to paragraph (d) of this section. No adjustment is required under paragraph (d) of this section because there is no aggregate inside loss. See paragraph (d)(3)(iii) of this section.

Example 3. Items accruing after S becomes a member. (i) *Recognition of loss accruing after S becomes a member.* (A) *Facts.* On January 1, year 1, M purchases the sole outstanding share of S stock for $100. At that time, S owns two assets, Asset 1, with a basis of $0 and a value of $40, and Asset 2, with a basis and value of $60. In year 1, S sells Asset 1 for $40, recognizing a $40 gain. Also in year 1, the value of Asset 2 declines and S sells Asset 2 for $20, recognizing a $40 loss that is absorbed by the group. On December 31, year 1, M sells its S share for $60. After taking into account the effects of all applicable rules of law, M's basis in the S share is $100 (M's original $100 basis, unadjusted under §1.1502-32 because the $40 gain recognized on the sale of Asset 1 and the $40 loss on the sale of Asset 2 net, resulting in an adjustment of $0). M's sale of the S share is a transfer of a loss share and therefore subject to this section.

(B) *Application of paragraph (b) of this section.* Although the transfer is subject to this section, there is no basis redetermination under paragraph (b) of this section because there is only one share of S stock outstanding (and so there can be no disparity among members' bases in common shares and there are no outstanding preferred shares with respect to which there can be unrecognized gain or loss). See paragraph (b)(1)(ii)(A) of this section. Therefore, after the application of paragraph (b) of this section, the share is still a loss share and, as such, subject to this paragraph (c).

(C) *Basis reduction under this paragraph (c).* Under this paragraph (c), M's basis in the S share is reduced, but not below the share's $60 value, by the lesser of the share's net positive adjustment and disconformity amount. The share's net positive adjustment is $0. Thus, although the share has a disconformity amount of $40 (the excess of M's basis in the share, $100, over the share's allocable portion of S's net inside attribute amount, $60), no basis reduction is required under this paragraph (c).

(D) *Application of paragraph (d) of this section.* After the application of this paragraph (c), M's sale of the S share is still a transfer of a loss share, and, accordingly, subject to paragraph (d) of this section. No adjustment is required under paragraph (d) of this section because there is no aggregate inside loss. See paragraph (d)(3)(iii) of this section.

(ii) *Recognition of gain accruing after S becomes a member.* (A) *Facts.* The facts are the same as in paragraph (i)(A) of this *Example 3,* except that M does not sell the S share and S does not sell either asset in year 1. In addition, in year 2, the value of Asset 1 declines to $0, the value of Asset 2 returns to $60, and S creates Asset 3 (with a basis of $0). In year 3, S sells Asset 3 for $40, recognizing a $40 gain. On December 31, year 3, M sells its S share for $100. After taking into account the effects of all applicable rules of law, M's basis in the S share is $140 (M's original $100 basis increased under §1.1502-32 by $40 (the share's allocable portion of the gain recognized on the sale of Asset 3 in year 3)). M's sale of the S share is a transfer of a loss share and therefore subject to this section.

(B) *Application of paragraph (b) of this section.* Although the transfer is subject to this section, there is no basis redetermination under paragraph (b) of this section for the reasons set forth in paragraph (i)(B) of this *Example 3.* Therefore, after the application of paragraph (b) of this section, the share is still a loss share and, as such, subject to this paragraph (c).

(C) *Basis reduction under this paragraph (c).* Under this paragraph (c), M's basis in the S share, $140, is reduced, but not below value, $100, by the lesser of the share's net positive adjustment and disconformity amount. The share's net positive adjustment is $40 (the year 3 investment adjustment). The share's disconformity amount is the excess of its basis, $140, over its allocable portion of S's net inside attribute amount. S's net inside attribute amount is $100, the sum of S's money ($40 from the sale of Asset 3) and its basis in its assets ($60 (the sum of Asset 1's basis of $0 and Asset 2's basis of $60)). S's $100 net inside attribute amount is allocable entirely to the sole outstanding S share. Thus, the share's disconformity amount is the excess of $140 over $100, or $40. The lesser of the share's net positive adjustment, $40, and its disconformity amount, $40, is $40. Accordingly, the basis in the share is reduced by $40, from $140 to $100.

(D) *Application of paragraph (d) of this section.* Because M's sale of the S share is not a transfer of a loss share after the application of this paragraph (c), paragraph (d) of this section does not apply to the transfer.

(iii) *Recognition of income earned after S becomes a member.* The facts are the same as in paragraph (ii)(A) of this *Example 3,* except that instead of creating Asset 3, S earns $40 of income from services provided in year 3. Because the net positive adjustment includes items of income as well as items of gain, the results are the same as those described in paragraph (ii) of this *Example 3.*

Example 4. Computing the disconformity amount. (i) *Unrecognized loss reflected in stock basis.* (A) *Facts.* M owns the sole outstanding share of S stock with a basis of $100. S owns two assets, Asset 1 with a basis of $20 and a value of $60, and Asset 2 with a basis of $60 and a value of $40. In year 1, S sells Asset 1 for $60, recognizing a $40 gain. On December 31, year 1, M sells the S share for $100. After taking into account the effects of all applicable rules of law, M's basis in the S share is $140 (M's original $100 basis increased under §1.1502-32 by $40, the share's allocable portion of the gain recognized on the sale of Asset 1). M's sale of the S share is a transfer of a loss share and therefore subject to this section.

(B) *Application of paragraph (b) of this section.* Although the transfer is subject to this section, there is no basis redetermination under paragraph (b) of this section because there is only one share of S stock outstanding (and so there can be no disparity among members' bases in common shares and there are no outstanding preferred shares with respect to which there can be unrecognized gain or loss). See paragraph (b)(1)(ii)(A) of this section. Therefore, after the application of paragraph (b) of this section, the share is still a loss share and, as such, subject to this paragraph (c).

(C) *Basis reduction under this paragraph (c).* Under this paragraph (c), M's basis in the S share, $140, is reduced, but not below the share's $100 value, by the lesser of the share's net positive adjustment and disconformity amount. The share's net positive adjustment is $40 (the year 1 investment adjustment). The share's disconformity amount is the excess of its basis, $140, over its allocable portion of S's net inside attribute amount. S's net inside attribute amount is $120, the sum of S's money ($60 from the sale of Asset 1) and S's basis in Asset 2, $60. S's net inside attribute amount is allocable entirely to the sole outstanding S share. Thus, the share's disconformity amount is $20, the excess of $140 over $120. The lesser of the share's net positive adjustment, $40, and its disconformity amount, $20, is $20. Accordingly, the basis in the share is reduced by $20, from $140 to $120.

(D) *Application of paragraph (d) of this section.* After the application of this paragraph (c), M's sale of the S share is still a transfer of a loss share, and, accordingly, S's attributes (to the extent of the $20 duplicated loss) are subject to reduction under paragraph (d) of this section.

(ii) *Loss carryover.* The facts are the same as in paragraph (i)(A) of this *Example 4*, except that Asset 2 has a basis of $0 (rather than $60) and S has a $60 loss carryover (as defined in paragraph (f)(6) of this section). The analysis is the same as paragraph (i) of this *Example 4*. Furthermore, the analysis of the application of this paragraph (c) would be the same if the $60 loss carryover were subject to a section 382 limitation from a prior ownership change, or if, instead, the $60 loss carryover were subject to the limitation in §1.1502-21(c) on losses carried from separate return limitation years.

(iii) *Liabilities.* The facts are the same as in paragraph (i)(A) of this *Example 4*, except that S borrows $100 before M sells the S share. S's net inside attribute amount remains $120, computed as the sum of S's money ($160, $60 from the sale of Asset 1 plus the $100 borrowed) and S's basis in Asset 2, $60, less its liabilities, $100. Thus, the S share's disconformity amount remains the excess of $140 over $120, or $20. The results are the same as in paragraph (i) of this *Example 4*.

Example 5. Computing the allocable portion of the net inside attribute amount. (i) *Facts.* On January 1, year 1, M owns all five outstanding shares

of S stock with a basis of $20 per share. S owns Asset with a basis of $0. In year 1, S sells Asset for $100, recognizing a $100 gain. On December 31, year 1, M sells one of the S shares, Share 1, for $20. After taking into account the effects of all applicable rules of law, M's basis in Share 1 is $40 (M's original $20 basis increased under §1.1502-32 by $20 (the share's allocable portion of the gain recognized on the sale of Asset)). M's sale of Share 1 is a transfer of a loss share and therefore subject to this section.

(ii) *Application of paragraph (b) of this section.* Although the transfer is subject to this section, basis is not redetermined under paragraph (b) of this section because there is no disparity among M's bases in shares of S common stock and there are no shares of S preferred stock outstanding (so there can be no unrecognized gain or loss with respect to preferred shares). See paragraph (b)(1)(ii)(A) of this section. After the application of paragraph (b) of this section, M's sale of Share 1 is still a transfer of a loss share and therefore subject to this paragraph (c).

(iii) *Basis reduction under this paragraph (c).* Under this paragraph (c), M's $40 basis in Share 1 is reduced, but not below its $20 value by the lesser of the share's net positive adjustment and disconformity amount. Share 1's net positive adjustment is $20 (the year 1 investment adjustment). Share 1's disconformity amount is the excess of its $40 basis over its allocable portion of S's net inside attribute amount. S's net inside attribute amount is equal to the amount of S's money ($100 from the sale of the asset). Share 1's allocable portion of S's $100 net inside attribute amount is $20 (1/5 × $100). Thus, Share 1's disconformity amount is the excess of $40 over $20, or $20. The lesser of the share's $20 net positive adjustment and its $20 disconformity amount is $20. Accordingly, the basis in the share is reduced by $20, from $40 to $20.

(iv) *Application of paragraph (d) of this section.* Because M's sale of Share 1 is not a transfer of a loss share after the application of this paragraph (c), paragraph (d) of this section does not apply to the transfer.

Example 6. Liabilities. (i) *In general.* (A) *Facts.* On January 1, year 1, M purchases the sole outstanding share of S stock for $100. At that time, S owns Asset, with a basis of $0 and value of $100, and $100 cash. S also has a $100 liability. In year 1, S declares and makes a $60 dividend distribution to M and recognizes $20 of income. The value of Asset declines to $60 and, on December 31, year 1, M sells the S share for $20. After taking into account the effects of all applicable rules of law, M's basis in the S share is $60 (M's original $100 basis decreased under §1.1502-32 by $40 (the net of the $60 distribution and the $20 income recognized)). M's sale of the S share is a transfer of a loss share and therefore subject to this section.

(B) *Application of paragraph (b) of this section.* Although the transfer is subject to this section, there is no basis redetermination under paragraph (b) of this section because there is only one share of S stock outstanding (and so there can be no disparity among members' bases in common shares and there are no outstanding preferred shares with respect to which there can be unrecognized gain or loss). See paragraph (b)(1)(ii)(A) of this section. Therefore, after the application of paragraph (b) of this section, the share is still a loss share and, as such, subject to this paragraph (c).

(C) *Basis reduction under this paragraph (c).* Under this paragraph (c), M's basis in the S share, $60, is reduced, but not below value, $20, by the lesser of the share's net positive adjustment and disconformity amount. The share's net positive adjustment is $20 (the year 1 investment adjustment, as defined in paragraph (b)(1)(iii) of this section). The share's disconformity amount is the excess of its basis, $60, over its allocable portion of S's net inside attribute amount. S's net inside attribute amount is negative $40, computed as the sum of S's money ($60 ($100 less the $60 distribution plus the $20 income recognized)) and S's basis in Asset, $0, less S's liability, $100. S's net inside attribute amount is allocable entirely to the sole outstanding S share. Thus, the share's disconformity amount is the excess of $60 over negative $40, or $100. The lesser of the share's net positive adjustment, $20, and its disconformity amount, $100, is $20. Accordingly, the basis in the share is reduced by $20, from $60 to $40.

(D) *Application of paragraph (d) of this section.* After the application of this paragraph (c), the S share is still a loss share and, accordingly, S's attributes are subject to reduction under paragraph (d) of this section. No adjustment is required under paragraph (d) of this section, however, because there is no aggregate inside loss. See paragraph (d)(3)(iii) of this section.

(ii) *Excluded cancellation of indebtedness income—insufficient attributes available for reduction under sections 108 and 1017, and §1.1502-28.* (A) *Facts.* The facts are the same as in paragraph (i)(A) of this *Example 6*, except that M does not sell the S share. Instead, in year 4, Asset is destroyed in a fire and S spends its $60 on deductible expenses that are not absorbed by the group. S's loss becomes part of the consolidated net operating loss (CNOL). In year 5, S becomes insolvent and S's debt is discharged. Because of S's insolvency, S's discharge of indebtedness income is excluded under section 108 and, as a result, S's attributes are subject to reduction under sections 108 and 1017, and §1.1502-28. S's only attribute is the portion of the CNOL attributable to S, $60, and it is reduced to $0. There are no other consolidated attributes. In year 5, the S stock (which is treated as a capital asset) becomes worthless under section 165, taking into account §1.1502-80(c). After taking into account the effects of all applicable rules of law, M's basis in the S share is $60 (M's original $100 basis

decreased under §1.1502-32 by the year 1 investment adjustment of $40 (the net of the $60 distribution and the $20 income recognized). The investment adjustment for year 5 is $0 (the net of the $60 tax exempt income from the excluded COD applied to reduce attributes and the $60 noncapital, nondeductible expense from the reduction of S's portion of the CNOL). Under paragraph (f)(10)(i)(D) of this section, a share is transferred on the last day of the taxable year during which it becomes worthless under section 165 if the share is treated as a capital asset, or the date the share becomes worthless if the share is not treated as a capital asset, taking into account §1.1502-80(c). Accordingly, M transfers the loss share of S stock on December 31, year 5, and the transfer is therefore subject to this section.

(B) *Application of paragraph (b) of this section.* Although the transfer is subject to this section, there is no basis redetermination under paragraph (b) of this section for the reasons set forth in paragraph (i)(B) of this *Example 6*. Therefore, after the application of paragraph (b) of this section, the share is still a loss share and, as such, subject to this paragraph (c).

(C) *Basis reduction under this paragraph (c).* Under this paragraph (c), M's basis in its S share, $60, is reduced, but not below value, $0, by the lesser of the share's net positive adjustment and disconformity amount. The share's net positive adjustment is $20 (the year 1 investment adjustment, as defined in paragraph (b)(1)(iii) of this section). The share's disconformity amount is the excess of its basis, $60, over its allocable portion of S's net inside attribute amount. S's net inside attribute amount is $0. (The effects of the attribute reduction required under sections 108 and 1017 and §1.1502-28 are taken into account in applying this section; therefore, for purposes of this section, S's portion of the CNOL is treated as eliminated under section 108 and §1.1502-28.) S's net inside attribute amount is allocable entirely to the sole outstanding S share. Thus, the share's disconformity amount is the excess of $60 over $0, or $60. The lesser of the share's net positive adjustment, $20, and its disconformity amount, $60, is $20. Accordingly, the basis in the share is reduced by $20, from $60 to $40, immediately before the transfer.

(D) *Application of paragraph (d) of this section.* After the application of this paragraph (c), the S share is still a loss share, and, accordingly, S's attributes are subject to reduction under paragraph (d) of this section. No adjustment is required under paragraph (d) of this section, however, because there is no aggregate inside loss. See paragraph (d)(3)(iii) of this section.

(iii) *Excluded cancellation of indebtedness income—full attribute reduction under sections 108 and 1017, and §1.1502-28 (using attributes attributable to another member).* (A) *Facts.* The facts are the same as in paragraph (ii)(A) of this *Example 6* except that M loses the $60 distributed in year 1 and the group does not absorb the loss. Thus, as of December 31, year 5, the CNOL is $120, attributable $60 to S and $60 to P. As a result, under § 1.1502-28(a)(4), after the portion of the CNOL attributable to S is reduced to $0, the remaining $40 of excluded COD applies to the portion of the CNOL attributable to P, reducing it from $60 to $20. After taking into account the effects of all applicable rules of law, M's basis in the S share at the end of year 5 is $100 (M's original $100 basis decreased under § 1.1502-32 by $40 at the end of year 1 and then increased under § 1.1502-32 by $40 at the end of year 5 (the net of the $100 tax exempt income from the excluded COD applied to reduce attributes and the $60 noncapital, nondeductible expense from the reduction of S's portion of the CNOL)). Under paragraph (f)(10)(i)(D) of this section, a share is transferred on the last day of the taxable year during which it becomes worthless under section 165 if the share is treated as a capital asset, or the date the share becomes worthless if the share is not treated as a capital asset, taking into account § 1.1502-80(c). Accordingly, M transfers the loss share of S stock on December 31, year 5, and the transfer is therefore subject to this section.

(B) *Application of paragraph (b) of this section.* Although the transfer is subject to this section, there is no basis redetermination under paragraph (b) of this section for the reasons set forth in paragraph (i)(B) of this *Example 6.* Therefore, after the application of paragraph (b) of this section, the share is still a loss share and, as such, subject to this paragraph (c).

(C) *Basis reduction under this paragraph (c).* Under this paragraph (c), M's basis in the S share, $100, is reduced, but not below value, $0, by the lesser of the share's net positive adjustment and disconformity amount. The share's net positive adjustment is $60 (the sum of the year 1 investment adjustment, as defined in paragraph (b)(1)(iii) of this section, $20, and the year 5 investment adjustment, $40). The share's disconformity amount is the excess of its basis, $100, over its allocable portion of S's net inside attribute amount. S's net inside attribute amount is $0 (taking into account the effects of the attribute reduction required under sections 108 and 1017 and § 1.1502-28). S's net inside attribute amount is allocable entirely to the sole outstanding S share. The share's disconformity amount is therefore $100. The lesser of the share's net positive adjustment, $60, and its disconformity amount, $100, is $60. Accordingly, M's basis in the share is reduced by $60, from $100 to $40, immediately before the transfer.

(D) *Application of paragraph (d) of this section.* After the application of this paragraph (c), the S share is still a loss share, and, accordingly, S's attributes are subject to reduction under paragraph (d) of this section. No adjustment is required under paragraph (d) of this section,

however, because there is no aggregate inside loss. See paragraph (d)(3)(iii) of this section.

Example 7. Lower-tier subsidiary (no transfer of lower-tier stock). (i) *Facts.* M owns the sole outstanding share of S stock with a basis of $160. S owns two assets, Asset 1 with a basis and value of $100, and the sole outstanding share of S1 stock with a basis of $60. S1 owns one asset, Asset 2, with a basis of $20 and value of $60. In year 1, S1 sells Asset 2 to X for $60, recognizing a $40 gain. On December 31, year 1, M sells its S share to Y, a member of another consolidated group, for $160. After taking into account the effects of all applicable rules of law, M's basis in the S share is $200 (M's original $160 basis increased under § 1.1502-32 by $40 (to reflect the tier-up of the adjustment to S's basis in the S1 stock for the gain recognized on S1's sale of Asset 2)). M's sale of the S share is a transfer of a loss share and therefore subject to this section. (S does not transfer the S1 share because S and S1 are members of the same group following the transfer. See paragraph (f)(10) of this section.)

(ii) *Application of paragraph (b) of this section.* Although the transfer is subject to this section, there is no basis redetermination under paragraph (b) of this section because there is only one share of S stock outstanding (and so there can be no disparity among members' bases in common shares and there are no outstanding preferred shares with respect to which there can be unrecognized gain or loss). See paragraph (b)(1)(ii)(A) of this section. Therefore, after the application of paragraph (b) of this section, the share is still a loss share and, as such, subject to this paragraph (c).

(iii) *Basis reduction under this paragraph (c).* (A) *In general.* Under this paragraph (c), M's basis in the S share, $200, is reduced, but not below value, $160, by the lesser of the share's net positive adjustment and disconformity amount. The S share's net positive adjustment is $40. The share's disconformity amount is the excess of its basis, $200, over the share's allocable portion of S's net inside attribute amount. S's net inside attribute amount is the sum of S's basis in Asset 1, $100, and S's basis in the S1 share.

(B) *S's basis in the S1 share.* Although S's actual basis in the S1 share is $100 (S's original $60 basis increased under § 1.1502-32 by $40 (the share's allocable portion of the gain recognized on the sale of Asset 2)), for purposes of computing the S share's disconformity amount, S's net inside attribute amount is determined by treating S's basis in the S1 share as tentatively reduced by the lesser of the S1 share's net positive adjustment and the S1 share's disconformity amount. The S1 share's net positive adjustment is $40 (the year 1 investment adjustment). The S1 share's disconformity amount is the excess of its basis, $100, over the share's allocable portion of S1's net inside attribute amount. S1's net inside attribute amount is equal to the amount of S1's money ($60 from the sale of Asset 2), and is

Reg. § 1.1502-36(c)(8)

56,884
        Consolidated Returns
See p. 20,601 for regulations not amended to reflect law changes

allocable entirely to the sole outstanding S1 share. Thus, the S1 share's disconformity amount is the excess of $100 over $60, or $40. The lesser of the S1 share's net positive adjustment, $40, and its disconformity amount, $40, is $40. Accordingly, for purposes of computing the disconformity amount of the S share, S's net inside attribute amount is determined by treating S's basis in its S1 share as tentatively reduced by $40, from $100 to $60.

(C) *The disconformity amount of M's S share.* S's net inside attribute amount is treated as the sum of its basis in Asset 1, $100, and its tentatively reduced basis in the S1 share, $60, or $160. S's net inside attribute amount is allocable entirely to the sole outstanding S share. Thus, the S share's disconformity amount is the excess of $200 over $160, or $40.

(D) *Amount of reduction.* M's basis in its S share is reduced by the lesser of the S share's net positive adjustment, $40, and disconformity amount, $40, or $40. Accordingly, M's basis in the S share is reduced by $40, from $200 to $160.

(E) *Effect on S's basis in its S1 share.* The tentative reduction under this paragraph (c) has no effect on S's actual basis in the S1 share. Thus, after the application of this paragraph (c), S owns the S1 share with a basis of $100 (S's original $60 basis increased under § 1.1502-32 by $40 (the share's allocable portion of the gain recognized on the sale of Asset 2)).

(iv) *Application of paragraph (d) of this section.* Because M's sale of the S share is not a transfer of a loss share after the application of this paragraph (c), paragraph (d) of this section does not apply to the transfer.

(d) *Attribute reduction to prevent duplication of loss.*—(1) *In general.*—The rules of this paragraph (d) reduce attributes of S and its lower-tier subsidiaries to the extent they duplicate a net loss on shares of S stock transferred by members in one transaction. This rule furthers single-entity principles by preventing S (or its lower-tier subsidiaries) from using deductions and losses to the extent that the group or its members (including former members) have either used, or preserved for later use, a corresponding loss in S shares.

(2) *Attribute reduction rule.*—(i) *General rule.*—If a transferred share is a loss share after taking into account the effects of all applicable rules of law, including any adjustments under paragraph (b), (c), or (d)(5)(iii) of this section, S's attributes are reduced by S's attribute reduction amount immediately before the transfer. S's attribute reduction amount is determined under paragraph (d)(3) of this section and applied in accordance with the provisions of paragraphs (d)(4), (d)(5), and (d)(6) of this section. In addition, paragraph (d)(7) of this section provides for additional attribute reduction in the case of certain transfers due to worthlessness and certain transfers not followed by a separate return year.

(ii) *Attribute reduction amount less than five percent of value.*—This paragraph (d) generally does not apply to a transaction if the aggregate attribute reduction amount in the transaction is less than five percent of the aggregate value of the shares transferred by members in the transaction. However, in such a case, P may elect to apply this paragraph (d) to the transaction. If such an election is made, this paragraph (d) will apply with respect to the entire aggregate attribute reduction amount determined in the transaction. Such an election is made in the manner provided in paragraph (e)(5) of this section.

(3) *Attribute reduction amount.*—(i) *In general.*—S's attribute reduction amount is the lesser of—

(A) The net stock loss (as defined in paragraph (d)(3)(ii) of this section); and

(B) S's aggregate inside loss (as defined in paragraph (d)(3)(iii) of this section).

(ii) *Net stock loss.*—The *net stock loss* is the excess, if any, of—

(A) The aggregate basis of all shares of S stock transferred by members in the transaction; over

(B) The aggregate value of those shares.

(iii) *Aggregate inside loss.*—(A) *In general.*—S's *aggregate inside loss* is the excess, if any, of—

(1) S's net inside attribute amount; over

(2) The value of all outstanding shares of S stock.

(B) *Net inside attribute amount.*—S's *net inside attribute amount* generally has the same meaning as in paragraph (c)(5) of this section. However, if S holds stock of a lower-tier subsidiary, the provisions of paragraph (d)(5) of this section (and not the provisions of paragraph (c)(6) of this section) modify the computation of S's net inside attribute amount for purposes of this paragraph (d).

(iv) *Lower-tier subsidiaries.*—See paragraph (d)(5) of this section for special rules relating to the application of this paragraph (d) if S owns shares of stock of a subsidiary.

(4) *Application of attribute reduction amount.*—(i) *Attributes available for reduction.*—S's attributes available for reduction under this paragraph (d) are—

(A) *Category A.*—Capital loss carryovers;

(B) *Category B.*—Net operating loss carryovers;

(C) *Category C.*—Deferred deductions; and

(D) *Category D.*—Basis of assets other than assets identified as Class I assets in § 1.338-6(b)(1).

(ii) *Rules of application.*—(A) *Category A, Category B, and Category C attributes.*—S's attribute reduction amount is first allocated and applied to reduce the attributes in Category A, Category B, and Category C.

(1) *Attribute reduction amount less than total attributes in Category A, Category B, and Category C.*—If S's attribute reduction amount is less than S's total attributes in Category A, Category B, and Category C, all of S's attribute reduction amount will be applied to reduce such attributes. However, P may specify the allocation of S's attribute reduction amount among such attributes. An election to specify the allocation of S's attribute reduction amount is made in the manner provided in paragraph (e)(5) of this section. To the extent that P does not specify an allocation of S's attribute reduction amount, S's attribute reduction amount will be applied to reduce any Category A attributes not reduced as a result of the specific allocation of S's attribute reduction amount, from oldest to newest, until they are eliminated. Then, any remaining attribute reduction amount will be applied to reduce any Category B attributes not reduced as a result of the specific allocation of S's attribute reduction amount, from oldest to newest, until they are eliminated. Finally, any remaining attribute reduction amount will be applied to reduce any Category C attributes not reduced as a result of the specific allocation of S's attribute reduction amount, proportionately.

(2) *Attribute reduction amount not less than the total attributes in Category A, Category B, and Category C.*—If S's attribute reduction amount equals or exceeds S's total attributes in Category A, Category B, and Category C, all such attributes are eliminated and any remaining attribute reduction amount is allocated and applied as provided in paragraphs (d)(4)(ii)(B) and (d)(4)(ii)(C) of this section.

(B) *Category D attributes.*—Any attribute reduction amount not applied to reduce S's Category A, Category B, and Category C attributes is allocated and applied as provided in this paragraph (d)(4)(ii)(B) and, to the extent applicable, paragraph (d)(5) of this section.

(1) *Allocation if S holds stock of another subsidiary.*—If S holds shares of stock of another subsidiary, the attribute reduction amount not applied to reduce S's Category A, Category B, and Category C attributes is first allocated between S's shares of lower-tier subsidiary stock and S's other Category D assets in the manner provided in paragraph (d)(5)(ii) of this section. S's attribute reduction amount allocated to shares of lower-tier subsidiary stock is applied to reduce S's bases in those shares, becomes an

attribute reduction amount of the lower-tier subsidiary, and, subject to certain limitations, reduces the lower-tier subsidiary's attributes. See paragraphs (d)(5)(iii) through (d)(5)(vi) of this section.

(2) *Allocation and application of attribute reduction amount not applied to lowertier subsidiary stock.*—Any portion of S's attribute reduction amount not applied to reduce S's Category A, Category B, and Category C attributes and not allocated to lower-tier subsidiary stock is allocated to S's Category D assets other than lower-tier subsidiary stock in the manner provided in this paragraph (d)(4)(ii)(B)(2). Such amount is first allocated to S's bases (if any) in its assets identified as Class VII assets in § 1.338-6(b)(2)(vii). If the attribute reduction amount allocated to Class VII assets is less than S's aggregate basis in those assets, it is applied proportionately (by basis) to reduce the bases of such assets. If the attribute reduction amount allocated to Class VII assets equals or exceeds S's aggregate basis in those assets, it is applied to reduce the bases of such assets to zero. Any remaining attribute reduction amount is then allocated and applied in the same manner to reduce S's bases (if any) in assets identified as Class VI assets in § 1.338-6(b)(2)(vi), and then to reduce S's bases (if any) in its assets identified in § 1.338-6(b)(2) as Class V, Class IV, Class III, and Class II, successively.

(C) *Attribute reduction amount exceeding attributes available for reduction.*—If the amount to be allocated and applied to attributes in Category D other than lower-tier subsidiary stock exceeds the amount of attributes in that category, then—

(1) To the extent of any liabilities of S that are not taken into account for tax purposes before the transfer, such excess amount is suspended. The suspended amount is applied proportionately to reduce any amounts attributable to S that would be deductible or capitalizable as a result of such liabilities being taken into account by S or any other person. Solely for purposes of this paragraph (d)(4)(ii)(C)(1) and paragraph (d)(5)(ii)(B) of this section, the term *liability* means any liability or obligation the satisfaction of which would be required to be capitalized as an assumed liability by a person that purchased all of S's assets and assumed all of S's liabilities in a single transaction.

(2) To the extent such excess amount is greater than any amount suspended under paragraph (d)(4)(ii)(C)(1) of this section, it is disregarded and has no further effect.

(iii) *Time and effect of attribute reduction.*— In general, the reduction of attributes is effective immediately before the transfer of a loss share of S stock. If the reduction to a member's basis in a share of lower-tier subsidiary stock exceeds the basis of that share, to the extent the excess is not restored under paragraph (d)(5)(vi) of this section it is an excess loss account in that share (and such excess loss account is not taken into account under § 1.1502-19 or otherwise as a result of the transaction). The reductions to attributes required under this paragraph (d)(4), including by reason of paragraph (d)(5)(v) of this section (tier down of attribute reduction amounts to lower-tier subsidiaries), are not noncapital, nondeductible expenses described in § 1.1502-32(b)(2)(iii).

(5) *Special rules applicable if S holds stock of another subsidiary.*—If S holds shares of stock of any other subsidiary (S1) as of a transfer of loss shares of S stock, the rules of this paragraph (d)(5) apply with respect to each such subsidiary.

(i) *Treatment of lower-tier subsidiary stock for computation of S's attribute reduction amount.*— For purposes of determining S's net inside attribute amount and attribute reduction amount under paragraph (d)(3) of this section—

(A) *Single share.*—All of S's shares of S1 stock held as of the transfer of S stock (whether or not transferred in, or held by S immediately after, the transaction) are treated as a single share of stock (generally referred to as the S1 stock); and

(B) *Deemed basis.*—S's basis in its S1 stock is treated as its *deemed basis* in the stock, which is equal to the greater of—

(1) The sum of S's basis in each share of S1 stock (adjusted to reflect any gain or loss recognized on the transfer of any S1 shares in the transaction, whether allowed or disallowed); and

(2) The portion of S1's net inside attribute amount allocable to S's shares of S1 stock.

(C) *Multiple tiers.*—For purposes of computing deemed basis under paragraph (d)(5)(i)(B) of this section, a subsidiary's basis in stock of a lower-tier subsidiary is the deemed basis in that lower-tier subsidiary stock. Thus, if stock is held in multiple tiers, the computation of deemed basis begins at the lowest tier, so that the computation of deemed basis at each tier takes into account the deemed basis of all lower-tier shares.

(ii) *Allocation of S's attribute reduction amount between lower-tier subsidiary stock and other Category D assets.*—The portion of S's attribute reduction amount that is not applied to reduce S's Category A, Category B, and Category C attributes must be allocated between each of S's deemed single shares of S1 stock and all of S's other Category D assets. For this purpose, S's Category D assets other than lower-tier subsidiary stock are treated as one asset with a basis equal to the aggregate bases of all Category D assets other than lower-tier subsidiary stock (non-stock Category D asset). S's attribute reduction amount is allocated proportionately (by basis) between (among) the non-stock Category D

asset and S's deemed single share(s) of subsidiary stock. (See paragraphs (d)(4)(ii)(B)(2) and (d)(4)(ii)(C) of this section regarding the portion of S's attribute reduction amount allocated to the Category D assets other than lower-tier subsidiary stock.) For allocation purposes, S's basis in each deemed single share of S1 stock is its deemed basis (determined under paragraphs (d)(5)(i)(B) and (d)(5)(i)(C) of this section), reduced by—

(A) The value of S's transferred shares of S1 stock; and

(B) The nontransferred S1 shares' allocable portion of the excess of S1's nonloss assets over S1's liabilities (including liabilities described in paragraph (d)(4)(ii)(C)(1) of this section). For this purpose, S1's non-loss assets are—

(1) S1's assets identified as Class I assets in § 1.338-6(b)(1),

(2) The value of S1's transferred shares of lower-tier subsidiary stock, and

(3) The nontransferred lower-tier subsidiary shares' allocable portions of lowertier non-loss assets (net of liabilities, including liabilities described in paragraph (d)(4)(ii)(C)(1) of this section) of all lower-tier subsidiaries.

(iii) *Application of attribute reduction amount to S's S1 stock.*—The portion of S's attribute reduction amount allocated under paragraph (d)(5)(ii) of this section to each deemed single share of S1 stock (allocated attribute reduction amount) is apportioned among, and applied to reduce S's bases in, individual S1 shares in accordance with the following—

(A) No portion of the allocated attribute reduction amount is apportioned to an individual share of transferred S1 stock if gain or loss is recognized on its transfer (recognition transfer);

(B) The allocated attribute reduction amount is apportioned among all of S's other shares of S1 stock in a manner that, first reduces the loss in and disparity among S's bases in loss shares of S1 preferred stock to the greatest extent possible, and then reduces the disparity among S's bases in the shares of S1 common stock (other than those transferred in a recognition transfer) to the greatest extent possible;

(C) The allocated attribute reduction amount apportioned to an individual S1 share is applied to reduce the basis of that share to, but not below, value if the share is either a preferred share or a common share that is transferred other than in a recognition transfer; and

(D) The allocated attribute reduction amount apportioned to an individual S1 share is applied to reduce the basis of that share without regard to value if the share is a common share that is not transferred in the transaction.

(iv) *Unapplied allocated attribute reduction amount.*—Any portion of the allocated attribute reduction amount that is not applied to reduce

S's basis in a share of S1 stock has no effect on any other attributes of S, it is not a noncapital, nondeductible expense of S, and it does not cause S to recognize income or gain. However, such amounts continue to be part of the allocated attribute reduction amount for purposes of the tier down rule in paragraph (d)(5)(v) of this section.

(v) *Tier down of attribute reduction amount.*—(A) *General rule.*—The allocated attribute reduction amount of each deemed single share of S1 stock is an attribute reduction amount of S1 (tier-down attribute reduction amount). Accordingly, the tierdown attribute reduction amount, in combination with any attribute reduction amount computed with respect to the transferred S1 shares (if any) (direct S1 attribute reduction amount), applies to reduce S1's attributes under the provisions of this paragraph (d). The tier-down attribute reduction amount is an attribute reduction amount of S1 that must be allocated to S1's assets, and may become an allocated attribute reduction amount of lower-tier subsidiary stock (and thus a tier-down attribute reduction amount of a lower-tier subsidiary), even if its application to S1's attributes is limited under paragraph (d)(5)(v)(B) of this section.

(B) *Conforming limitation on reduction of lower-tier subsidiary's attributes.*—Notwithstanding the general rule in paragraph (d)(5)(v)(A) of this section, and unless P elects otherwise in the manner provided in paragraph (e)(5) of this section, the application of S1's tier-down attribute reduction amount to S1's attributes is limited to an amount equal to the excess of the portion of S1's net inside attribute amount that is allocable to all S1 shares held by members as of the transaction (whether or not transferred in the transaction) over the sum of—

(1) Any direct S1 attribute reduction amount;

(2) The aggregate value of all S1 shares transferred by members in the transaction with respect to which gain or loss was recognized (recognition transfer);

(3) The sum of all members' bases (after any reduction under this section, including this paragraph (d)) in any shares of S1 stock transferred by members in the transaction (other than in a recognition transfer), reduced by any direct S1 attribute reduction amount computed with respect to the transfer of such S1 shares; and

(4) The sum of all members' bases (after any reduction under this section, including this paragraph (d)) in any nontransferred shares of S1 stock held as of the transaction.

(vi) *Stock basis restoration.*—(A) *In general.*—After paragraph (d)(5)(v) of this section has applied with respect to all shares of subsidiary stock transferred in the transaction, lower-tier subsidiary stock basis is restored under this paragraph (d)(5)(vi). Under this paragraph (d)(5)(vi), the reductions to members' bases in shares of lower-tier subsidiary stock under paragraph (d)(5)(iii) of this section are reversed to the extent necessary to restore such bases to an amount that conforms the basis of each such share to its allocable portion of the subsidiary's net inside attribute amount, taking into account any reductions under this paragraph (d). Restoration adjustments are first made at the lowest tier and then at each next higher tier successively. Restoration adjustments do not tier up to affect the bases of higher-tier shares. Rather, restoration is computed and applied separately at each tier. For purposes of this rule, when computing a subsidiary's net inside attribute amount—

(1) The subsidiary's basis in stock of a lower-tier subsidiary is the actual basis of the stock after application of this paragraph (d); and

(2) Any attribute reduction amount allocated to the subsidiary's Category D assets other than lower-tier subsidiary stock that is suspended under paragraph (d)(4)(ii)(C)(1) of this section is treated as reducing the subsidiary's net inside attribute amount.

(B) *Election not to restore basis.*—Notwithstanding paragraph (d)(5)(vi)(A) of this section, P may elect not to restore basis in stock of a lower-tier subsidiary that was reduced under paragraph (d)(5)(iii) of this section. An election not to restore lower-tier subsidiary stock basis is made in the manner provided in paragraph (e)(5) of this section.

(6) *Elections to reduce the potential for loss duplication.*—(i) *In general.*—Notwithstanding the general operation of this paragraph (d), P may elect to reduce the potential for loss duplication, and thereby reduce or avoid attribute reduction. To the extent of S's attribute reduction amount tentatively computed without regard to any election under this paragraph (d)(6), P may elect—

(A) To reduce all or any portion (including any portion in excess of a specified amount) of members' bases in transferred loss shares of S stock;

(B) To reattribute all or any portion (including any portion in excess of a specified amount) of S's Category A, Category B, and Category C attributes (including such attributes of lower-tier subsidiaries), to the extent they would otherwise be subject to reduction under this paragraph (d); or

(C) Any combination thereof.

(ii) *Manner and effect of election.*—An election to reduce loss duplication under this paragraph (d)(6) is made in the manner provided in paragraph (e)(5) of this section. Although such elections are irrevocable, they have no effect—

(A) If there is no attribute reduction amount; or

Reg. §1.1502-36(d)(6)(ii)(A)

(B) To the extent S's attribute reduction amount is less than the amount specified in the election.

(iii) *Order of application.*—(A) *Stock of one subsidiary transferred in the transaction.*—If shares of stock of only one subsidiary are transferred in the transaction, any stock basis reduction and reattribution of attributes (including from lower-tier subsidiaries) is deemed to occur immediately before the application of this paragraph (d). If a transferred share is still a loss share after giving effect to this election, the other provisions of this paragraph (d) then apply with respect to that share.

(B) *Stock of multiple subsidiaries transferred in the transaction.*—If shares of stock of more than one subsidiary are transferred in the transaction and elections under this paragraph (d)(6) are made with respect to transfers of stock of subsidiaries in multiple tiers, effect is given to the elections from the lowest tier to the highest tier in the manner provided in this paragraph (d)(6)(iii)(B). The amount of the election for the transfer at the lowest tier is determined by applying this paragraph (d) with respect to the transferred loss shares of this lowest-tier subsidiary immediately after applying paragraphs (b) and (c) of this section to the stock of such subsidiary. The effect of any stock basis reduction or reattribution of losses immediately tiers up under § 1.1502-32 to adjust members' bases in higher-tier shares. Elections and adjustments are then made with respect to transfers at each next higher tier successively.

(iv) *Special rules for reattribution elections.*—(A) *In general.*—Because the reattribution election is intended to provide the group a means to retain certain S attributes, and not to change the location of attributes where S continues to be a member of the same group as P, the election to reattribute attributes may only be made if S becomes a nonmember (within the meaning of § 1.1502-19(c)(2)) as a result of the transaction and S does not become a member of any group that includes P. The election to reattribute S's attributes can only be made for attributes in Category A, Category B, and Category C. The attributes that would otherwise be reduced under paragraph (d)(4) of this section may be reattributed to P. Accordingly, P may specify the attributes in Category A, Category B, and Category C to be reattributed. Such an election is made in the manner provided in paragraph (e)(5) of this section. To the extent that P elects to reattribute attributes but does not specify the attributes to be reattributed, any attributes not specifically reattributed will be reattributed in the default amount, order, and category described in paragraph (d)(4)(ii)(A)(*1*) of this section. P succeeds to reattributed attributes as if such attributes were succeeded to in a transaction to which section 381(a) applies. Any owner

shift of the subsidiary (including any deemed owner shift resulting from section 382(g)(4)(D) or section 382(l)(3)) in connection with the transaction is not taken into account under section 382 with respect to the reattributed attributes. (See § 1.1502-96(d) for rules relating to section 382 and the reattribution of losses under this paragraph (d)(6)). The reattribution of S's attributes is a noncapital, nondeductible expense described in § 1.1502-32(b)(2)(iii). See § 1.1502-32(c)(1)(ii)(A) regarding special allocations applicable to such noncapital, nondeductible expense. If P elects to reattribute S attributes (including attributes of a lower-tier subsidiary) and reduce S stock basis, the reattribution is given effect before the stock basis reduction.

(B) *Insolvency limitation.*—If S, or any higher-tier subsidiary, is insolvent within the meaning of section 108(d)(3) at the time of the transfer, S's losses may be reattributed only to the extent they exceed the sum of the separate insolvencies of any subsidiaries (taking into account only S and its higher-tier subsidiaries) that are insolvent. For purposes of determining insolvency, liabilities owed to higher-tier members are not taken into account, and stock of a subsidiary that is limited and preferred as to dividends and that is not owned by higher-tier members is treated as a liability to the extent of the amount of preferred distributions to which the stock would be entitled if the subsidiary were liquidated on the date of the transfer.

(C) *Limitation on reattribution from lower-tier subsidiaries.*—P's ability to reattribute attributes of lower-tier subsidiaries is limited under this paragraph (d)(6)(iv)(C) in order to prevent circular computations of the attribute reduction amount. Accordingly, attributes that would otherwise be reduced as a result of tier-down attribute reduction under paragraph (d)(5)(v) of this section may only be reattributed to the extent that the reduction in the basis of any lower-tier subsidiary stock resulting from the noncapital, nondeductible expense (as allocated under § 1.1502-32(c)(1)(ii)(A)(2)) will not create an excess loss account in any such stock.

(v) *Special rules for stock basis reduction elections.*—(A) *In general.*—An election to reduce basis in S stock is made with respect to all members' bases in loss shares of S stock that are transferred in the transaction. The reduction is allocated among all such shares in proportion to the amount of loss on each share. This reduction in S stock basis is a noncapital, nondeductible expense described in § 1.1502-32(b)(2)(iii) of the transferring member.

(B) *Adjustment to the attribute reduction amount.*—The attribute reduction amount (determined under paragraph (d)(3)(i) of this section) is treated as reduced by the amount of any elective reduction in the basis of the S stock under this paragraph (d)(6). Accordingly, the election to reduce stock basis under this paragraph (d)(6) is treated as reducing or eliminating the duplication even if the shares of S stock are loss shares after giving effect to the election.

(C) *Deemed stock basis reduction election in the case of certain disallowed stock losses.*—If there is a net stock loss in transferred shares after taking into account any actual elections under this paragraph (d)(6), and the stock loss would otherwise be permanently disallowed (for example, under section 311(a)), P will be deemed to have made a stock basis reduction election equal to such net stock loss.

(7) *Additional attribute reduction in the case of certain transfers due to worthlessness and certain transfers not followed by a separate return year.*—(i) *In general.*—Notwithstanding any other provision of this paragraph (d), if a transfer is subject to this paragraph (d)(7) any of S's Category A, Category B, and Category C attributes not otherwise reduced or reattributed under this paragraph (d), and any credit carryover attributable to S, including any consolidated credits that would be apportioned to S under the principles of § 1.1502-79 if S had a separate return year, are eliminated. Attributes other than consolidated tax attributes are eliminated under this paragraph (d)(7)(i) immediately before the transfer subject to this paragraph (d)(7)(i). The elimination of attributes under this paragraph (d)(7)(i) is not a noncapital, nondeductible expense described in § 1.1502-32(b)(2)(iii).

(ii) *Transfers subject to this paragraph (d)(7).*—A transfer is subject to this paragraph (d)(7) if—

(A) M transfers a share of S stock solely by reason of a transfer defined in paragraph (f)(10)(i)(D) of this section (worthlessness where the provisions of § 1.1502-80(c) are satisfied), M recognizes a net deduction or loss on the share, and S is a member of the group on the day following the last day of the group's taxable year during which the share becomes worthless under section 165 (taking into account the provisions of § 1.1502-80(c)), or

(B) M recognizes a net deduction or loss on the stock of S in a transaction in which S ceases to be a member and does not become a nonmember within the meaning of § 1.1502-19(c)(2).

(iii) *Example.*—The application of this paragraph (d) to transfers due to worthlessness and to loss transfers not followed by separate return years is illustrated by the following example.

Example. (i) *Worthlessness where S continues as a member.* M owns the sole share of S stock. The share is worthless under section 165. In addition, S has disposed of all its assets within the meaning of § 1.1502-19(c)(1)(iii)(A) and therefore satisfies the provisions of § 1.1502-80(c). M

claims a worthless securities deduction with respect to the share. The worthlessness is a transfer of the S share, a loss share, and therefore subject to this section. After the application of paragraphs (b) and (c) of this section, M's basis in the share (and therefore M's net stock loss) is $75. The portion of the consolidated net operating loss attributable to S is $100. Under the general rules of this paragraph (d), S's attribute reduction amount is $75 (the lesser of M's $75 net stock loss and S's $100 aggregate inside loss ($100 net inside attribute amount over $0 value of S share). S's attributes are reduced by $75, from $100 to $25. In addition, if S remains a member of the P group, this paragraph (d)(7) applies to eliminate the remaining $25 of the consolidated net operating loss attributable to S because the S share is worthless, and M recognizes a deduction (taking into account § 1.1502-80(c)) with respect to the share. Accordingly, after the application of this section, M recognizes a $75 worthless securities deduction, S has $0 net inside attributes, and the consolidated net operating loss is reduced by a total of $100.

(ii) *Dissolution of insolvent subsidiary.* The facts are the same as in paragraph (i) of this *Example,* except that S is insolvent, does not dispose of all its assets within the meaning of § 1.1502-19(c)(1)(iii)(A), M causes S to be legally dissolved, and the S share held by M is cancelled without consideration. Under paragraph (d)(7)(ii)(B) of this section, the dissolution of S is subject to this paragraph (d)(7) and the result is the same as in paragraph (i) of this *Example.* The result would also be the same if instead of being legally dissolved, S was converted into an entity that is disregarded as separate from M.

(iii) *Stock cancelled in connection with a section 381(a) transaction with another member.* M owns the sole share of S common stock with a basis of $75. M1 owns the sole share of S preferred stock. The value of S's assets (net of liabilities) is less than the liquidation preference on the S preferred stock. In a reorganization described in section 368(a)(1)(D), S transfers all of its assets to M2 in exchange for M2 common stock and M2's assumption of S's liabilities, S distributes all of the M2 common stock received in the exchange to M1 in exchange for M1's S preferred stock, the S common stock held by M is cancelled without consideration, and S ceases to exist. Notwithstanding that M is not entitled to treat its common share of S stock as worthless until § 1.1502-80(c) is satisfied, M's share is transferred within the meaning of paragraph (f)(10)(i)(A) of this section because M ceases to own the share in a transaction in which, but for this section (and notwithstanding the deferral of any amount recognized on the transfer, other than by reason of § 1.1502-13), M would recognize a loss or deduction with respect to the share. Accordingly, there is a transfer of the S common share and this section applies to the transfer. There are no ad-

Reg. § 1.1502-36(d)(7)(iii)

justments under paragraphs (b) or (c) of this section because no investment adjustments have been applied to the bases of the shares. The transfer of the S common stock is subject to the general rules of this paragraph (d), but is not subject to the additional attribute reduction under this paragraph (d)(7) because the transfer was not solely by reason of worthlessness where §1.1502-80(c) is satisfied, and S did not cease to be a member because M2 is a successor to S.

(iv) *Stock cancelled in connection with a section 381(a) transaction with a nonmember.* The facts are the same as in paragraph (iii) of this *Example*, except that the S preferred share is held by X, instead of M2 acquiring S's assets, S merges into Y in a reorganization described in section 368(a)(1)(A), M1 receives all of the Y stock issued in the merger in exchange for M1's S preferred stock, and Y does not become a member as a result of the transaction. M treats the cancelled S common stock as worthless, and §1.1502-80(c) is satisfied because S ceases to be a member. In this case, there is a transfer of M's S common share because it becomes worthless (taking into account §1.1502-80(c)); because M ceases to own the share in a transaction in which, but for this section (and notwithstanding the deferral of any amount recognized on the transfer, other than by reason of §1.1502-13), M would recognize a loss or deduction with respect to the share; and because M and S cease to be members of the same group. The transfer of the S common stock is subject to the general rules of this paragraph (d), but is not subject to the additional attribute reduction under this paragraph (d)(7) because the transfer was not solely by reason of worthlessness where §1.1502-80(c) is satisfied and, although S did cease to be a member, S became a nonmember within the meaning of §1.1502-19(c)(2) because Y is a successor to S.

(8) *Examples.*—The application of this paragraph (d) is illustrated by the following examples:

Example 1. Computation of attribute reduction amount. (i) *Transfer of all S shares.* (A) *Facts.* M owns all 100 of the outstanding shares of S stock with a basis of $2 per share. S owns land with a basis of $100, has a $120 loss carryover, and has no liabilities. Each share has a value of $1. M sells 30 of the S shares to X for $30. As a result of the sale, M and S cease to be members of the same group. Accordingly, all 100 of the S shares are transferred. See paragraphs (f)(10)(i)(A), (f)(10)(i)(B), and (f)(10)(i)(C) (with respect to the 30 S shares sold to X) of this section. M's transfer of the S shares is a transfer of loss shares and therefore subject to this section.

(B) *Application of paragraphs (b) and (c) of this section.* Although the transfer is subject to this section, there is no basis redetermination under paragraph (b) of this section because there is no disparity among M's bases in shares of S common stock and there are no shares of S preferred

stock outstanding (so there can be no unrecognized gain or loss on preferred stock). See paragraph (b)(1)(ii)(A) of this section. Therefore, after the application of paragraph (b) of this section, the share is still a loss share and, as such, subject to paragraph (c) of this section. No adjustment is required under paragraph (c) of this section because the net positive adjustment is $0. See paragraph (c)(3) of this section. Thus, after the application of paragraph (c) of this section, M's transfer of the S shares is still a transfer of loss shares and, accordingly, subject to this paragraph (d).

(C) *Attribute reduction under this paragraph (d).* Under this paragraph (d), S's attributes are reduced by S's attribute reduction amount. Paragraph (d)(3) of this section provides that S's attribute reduction amount is the lesser of the net stock loss and S's aggregate inside loss. The net stock loss is the excess of the $200 aggregate bases of the transferred shares over the $100 aggregate value of the transferred shares, or $100. S's aggregate inside loss is the excess of its $220 net inside attribute amount (the sum of the $100 basis in the land and the $120 loss carryover) over the $100 value of all outstanding S shares, or $120. The attribute reduction amount is therefore the lesser of the $100 net stock loss and the $120 aggregate inside loss, or $100. Under paragraph (d)(4) of this section, S's $100 attribute reduction amount is allocated and applied to reduce S's $120 loss carryover to $20. Under paragraph (d)(4)(iii) of this section, the reduction of the loss carryover is not a noncapital, nondeductible expense and has no effect on M's basis in the S stock.

(ii) *Transfer of less than all S shares.* (A) *Facts.* The facts are the same as in paragraph (i)(A) of this *Example 1*, except that M only sells 20 S shares to X. M's sale of the 20 S shares is a transfer of loss shares and therefore subject to this section. See paragraph (f)(10)(i)(A) and (f)(10)(i)(C) of this section. (There is no transfer of the remaining shares because S and M remain members of the same group.)

(B) *Application of paragraphs (b) and (c) of this section.* No adjustment is required under paragraph (b) or paragraph (c) of this section for the reasons set forth in paragraph (i)(B) of this *Example 1*. Thus, after the application of paragraph (c) of this section, M's transfer of the S shares is still a transfer of loss shares and, accordingly, subject to this paragraph (d).

(C) *Attribute reduction under this paragraph (d).* Under this paragraph (d), S's attributes are reduced by S's attribute reduction amount. Paragraph (d)(3) of this section provides that S's attribute reduction amount is the lesser of the net stock loss and S's aggregate inside loss. The net stock loss is $20, the excess of the $40 aggregate bases of the transferred shares over the $20 aggregate value of the transferred shares. S's aggregate inside loss is $120, the excess of its $220 net inside attribute amount (the sum of the $100

Reg. §1.1502-36(d)(8)

basis in the land and the $120 loss carryover) over the $100 value of all outstanding S shares. The attribute reduction amount is therefore $20, the lesser of the $20 net stock loss and the $120 aggregate inside loss. Under paragraph (d)(4) of this section, S's $20 attribute reduction amount is allocated and applied to reduce S's $120 loss carryover to $100.

Example 2. Proportionate allocation of attribute reduction amount. (i) *Facts.* M owns the sole outstanding share of S stock with a basis of $150. S owns land with a basis of $60, a factory with a basis of $30, publicly traded property with a basis of $30 and goodwill with a basis of $30. M sells its S share for $90. M's sale of the S share is a transfer of a loss share and therefore subject to this section. See paragraphs (f)(10)(i)(A), (f)(10)(i)(B), and (f)(10)(i)(C) of this section.

(ii) *Application of paragraphs (b) and (c) of this section.* Although the transfer is subject to this section, there is no basis redetermination under paragraph (b) of this section because there is only one share of S stock outstanding (and so there can be no disparity among members' bases in common shares and there are no outstanding preferred shares with respect to which there can

be unrecognized gain or loss). See paragraph (b)(1)(ii)(A) of this section. Therefore, after the application of paragraph (b) of this section, the share is still a loss share and, as such, subject to paragraph (c) of this section. No adjustment is required under paragraph (c) of this section because both the disconformity amount and the net positive adjustment are $0. See paragraph (c)(3) of this section. Thus, after the application of paragraph (c) of this section, M's sale of the S share is still a transfer of a loss share and, accordingly, subject to this paragraph (d).

(iii) *Attribute reduction under this paragraph (d).* Under paragraph (d)(3) of this section, S's attribute reduction amount is determined to be $60, the lesser of the $60 net stock loss ($150 basis over $90 value) and S's $60 aggregate inside loss (the excess of S's $150 net inside attribute amount (the $60 basis of the land, plus the $30 basis of the factory, plus the $30 basis of the publicly traded property, plus the $30 basis of the goodwill) over the $90 value of the S share). Under paragraph (d)(4)(ii)(B)(2) of this section, the $60 attribute reduction amount is allocated and applied to reduce S's bases in its Category D assets, S's only attributes available for reduction, as follows:

Available attributes, Basis in Category D assets	Attribute amount	Allocable portion of attribute reduction amount	Adjusted attribute amount
Class VII, Goodwill	$30	$30	$0
Class V			
Land	$60	(60/90 × $60) $40	$20
Factory	$30	(30/90 × $60) $20	$10
Total Class V	$90	$60	$30
Class II, publicly traded property	$30	$0	$30
Totals	$150	$60	$90

Example 3. Attribute reduction amount less than total attributes in Category, A, Category B, and Category C. (i) *No election to prescribe the allocation of S's attribute reduction amount.* (A) *Facts.* P owns the sole outstanding share of M stock with a basis of $1,000 and M owns the sole outstanding share of S stock with a basis of $210. M sells its S

share to X for $100. M's sale of the S share is a transfer of a loss share and therefore subject to this section. See paragraphs (f)(10)(i)(A), (f)(10)(i)(B), and (f)(10)(i)(C) of this section. At the time of the sale, S has no liabilities and the following attributes:

Category	Attribute	Attribute amount
Category A	Capital loss carryover	$10
Category B	NOL carryover	$200
Category C	Deferred deductions	$40
Category D, Class V	Basis in Land	$50
	Total Attributes	$300

(B) *Application of paragraphs (b) and (c) of this section.* Although the transfer is subject to this section, there is no basis redetermination under

paragraph (b) of this section because there is only one share of S stock outstanding (and so there can be no disparity among members' bases in common shares and there are no outstanding preferred shares with respect to which there can be unrecognized gain or loss). See paragraph (b)(1)(ii)(A) of this section. Therefore, after the application of paragraph (b) of this section, the share is still a loss share and, as such, subject to paragraph (c) of this section. No adjustment is required under paragraph (c) of this section because both the disconformity amount and the net positive adjustment are $0. See paragraph (c)(3) of this section. Thus, after the application of paragraph (c) of this section, M's transfer of the S share is still a transfer of a loss share and, accordingly, subject to this paragraph (d).

(C) *Attribute reduction under this paragraph (d).* (1) *Computation of attribute reduction amount.*

Under paragraph (d)(3) of this section, S's attribute reduction amount is the lesser of the $110 net stock loss ($210 basis over $100 value) and S's aggregate inside loss. S's aggregate inside loss is $200 (S's $300 net inside attribute amount (the $10 capital loss carryover, plus the $200 NOL carryover, plus the $40 deferred deductions, plus the $50 basis in land) less the $100 value of all outstanding S shares). Thus, the attribute reduction amount is $110, the lesser of the $110 net stock loss and S's $200 aggregate inside loss. Under paragraph (d)(4)(ii)(A)(*1*) of this section, the $110 attribute reduction amount is allocated and applied to reduce S's attributes as follows:

Category	Attribute	Attribute amount	Allocation of attribute reduction amount	Adjusted attribute amount
Category A	Capital loss carryover	$10	$10	$0
Category B	NOL carryover	$200	$100	$100
Category C	Deferred deductions	$40	$0	$40
Category D, Class V	Basis in land	$50	$0	$50
Totals		$300	$110	$190

(ii) *Election to prescribe the allocation of attribute reduction amount.* (A) *Facts.* The facts are the same as in paragraph (i)(A) of this *Example 3*, except that, P elects to allocate the attribute reduction amount to eliminate the Category C attributes, preserve the capital loss carryover, and reduce Category B attributes.

(B) *Application of paragraphs (b) and (c) of this section.* No adjustment is required under paragraph (b) or paragraph (c) of this section for the reasons set forth in paragraph (i)(B) of this *Exam-*

ple 3. Thus, after the application of paragraph (c) of this section, M's sale of the S share is still a transfer of a loss share, and accordingly, subject to this paragraph (d).

(C) *Attribute reduction under this paragraph (d).* For the reasons set forth in paragraph (i)(C) of this *Example 3*, under this paragraph (d)(3), S's attribute reduction amount is determined to be $110. M elects to apply S's $110 attribute reduction amount as follows:

Category	Attribute	Attribute amount	Allocation of attribute reduction amount	Adjusted attribute amount
Category A	Capital loss carryover	$10	$0	$10
Category B	NOL carryover	$200	$70	$130
Category C	Deferred deductions	$40	$40	$0
Category D, Class V	Basis of land	$50	$0	$50
Totals		$300	$110	$190

Example 4. Attributes attributable to liability not taken into account. (i) S *operates one business.* (A) *Facts.* On January 1, year 1, M forms S by exchanging $150 for the sole outstanding share of S stock. In year 1, S earns $500, purchases land for $50, spends $100 to build a factory on that land, and then purchases publicly traded property for $250. In year 2, S earns a section 38 general business credit of $50. However, pollution generated by S's business gives rise to an

environmental remediation liability under Federal law that would be required to be capitalized if a person purchased S's assets and assumed the liability. Before any amounts have been taken into account with respect to the environmental remediation liability, when the liability has a present value of $500, M sells its S share to X for $150. After giving effect to all other provisions of law, M's basis in the S share is $650 (the original basis of $150 increased under §1.1502-32 by $500 for the income earned). The sale is therefore a transfer of a loss share of subsidiary stock and subject to this section. See paragraphs (f)(10)(i)(A), (f)(10)(i)(B), and (f)(10)(i)(C) of this section.

(B) *Application of paragraphs (b) and (c) of this section.* Although the transfer is subject to this section, there is no basis redetermination under paragraph (b) of this section because there is only one share of S stock outstanding (and so there can be no disparity among members' bases in common shares and there are no outstanding preferred shares with respect to which there can be unrecognized gain or loss). See paragraph (b)(1)(ii)(A) of this section. Therefore, after the application of paragraph (b) of this section, the share is still a loss share and, as such, subject to paragraph (c) of this section. No adjustment to basis is made under paragraph (c) of this section because, although the net positive adjustment is $500, the disconformity amount is $0. See para-

graph (c)(3) of this section. Thus, after the application of paragraph (c) of this section, M's sale of the S share is still a transfer of a loss share and, accordingly, subject to this paragraph (d).

(C) *Attribute reduction under this paragraph (d).* (1) Under paragraph (d)(3) of this section, S's attribute reduction amount is the lesser of the $500 net stock loss ($650 basis over $150 value) and the aggregate inside loss. The aggregate inside loss is $500, computed as the excess of S's $650 net inside attribute amount (the sum of S's $100 basis in the factory, $50 basis in the land, $250 basis in the publicly traded property, and $250 cash remaining after the purchases) over the $150 value of the S share. Thus, S's attribute reduction amount is $500, the lesser of the $500 net stock loss and the $500 aggregate inside loss. Under paragraph (d)(4)(ii)(B)(2) of this section, S's $500 attribute reduction amount is allocated and applied to reduce S's attributes as follows:

Available attributes	Attribute amount	Allocable portion of attribute reduction amount	Adjusted attribute amount
Category D			
Class V Assets			
Basis of factory	$100	$100	$0
Basis of land	$50	$50	$0
Class II Assets			
Publicly traded property	$250	$250	$0

(2) The remaining $100 attribute reduction amount is not applied to S's $250 cash (Class I asset) or to S's $50 general business tax credit. Under the general rule of this paragraph (d), that remaining $100 attribute reduction amount would have no further effect on S's attributes. However, S has a $500 liability that has not been taken into account. Therefore, under paragraph (d)(4)(ii)(C)(1) of this section, the remaining $100 attribute reduction amount is suspended and will be allocated and applied to reduce any amounts that become deductible or capitalizable as a result of the environmental remediation liability later being taken into account. If the liability is satisfied for an amount that is less than $100, under paragraph (d)(4)(ii)(C)(2) of this section the remaining portion of that $100 suspended attribute reduction amount is disregarded and has no further effect.

(ii) *Lower-tier subsidiary with additional liability.* (A) *Facts.* The facts are the same as in paragraph (i)(A) of *Example 4*, except that, in addition, S exchanged $50 for the sole outstanding share of stock of S1. S1 has $50 and equipment with an aggregate basis of $0. S1 also has employee medical expense liabilities that have not been taken into account and that would be required to be capitalized if a person purchased S1's assets and assumed the liabilities. At the

time of the sale, S's environmental remediation liability had a present value of $475 and S1's employee medical expenses had a present value of $25. For the reasons set forth in paragraph (i)(A) of this *Example 4*, M's sale of the S share is a transfer of a loss share and therefore subject to this section.

(B) *Application of paragraphs (b) and (c) of this section.* No adjustment is made under paragraph (b) or paragraph (c) of this section for the reasons set forth in paragraph (i)(B) of this *Example 4*. Thus, after the application of paragraph (c) of this section, M's sale of the S share is still a transfer of a loss share and, accordingly, subject to this paragraph (d).

(C) *Attribute reduction under this paragraph (d).* (1) *Computation of attribute reduction amount.* Under paragraph (d)(3) of this section, S's attribute reduction amount is the lesser of the $500 net stock loss ($650 basis over $150 value) and the aggregate inside loss. The aggregate inside loss is the excess of S's net inside attribute amount over the value of the S share. Under paragraphs (d)(3)(iii)(B) and (d)(5)(i)(B) of this section, S's net inside attribute amount is determined by using S's $50 deemed basis in the S1 share (the greater of S's $50 actual basis in the share and S1's $50 net inside attribute amount). Accordingly, S's net inside attribute amount is

$650 (the sum of its $100 basis in the factory, $50 basis in the land, $250 basis in the publicly traded property, $200 cash, and $50 deemed basis in its S1 share). The aggregate inside loss is $500, the excess of S's $650 net inside attribute amount over the $150 value of the S share. Thus, S's attribute reduction amount is $500, the lesser of the $500 net stock loss and S's $500 aggregate inside loss.

(2) *Allocation, apportionment, and application of attribute reduction amount.* Under paragraphs (d)(4) and (d)(5)(ii) of this section, S's $500 attribute reduction amount is allocated proportionately (by basis) between its S1 share and its non-stock Category D asset (consisting of all S's Category D assets other than its share of S1 stock, with a basis equal to $600, the aggregate basis of S's non-stock assets). However, under paragraph (d)(5)(ii) of this section, for purposes of allocating S's attribute reduction amount between its non-stock Category D asset and the S1 share, S's $50 deemed basis in its S1 share is treated as reduced by S1's $25 net non-loss assets (its Class I asset, $50 cash over S1's liabilities (which, for this purpose include the $25 of employee medical expense liabilities not taken into account as of the transfer)). As a result, S's attribute reduction amount is allocated $480 (600/625 × 500) to S's non-stock Category D asset and $20 (25/625 × 500) to the S1 share. The $480 attribute reduction amount allocated to S's non-stock Category D asset produces the same reduction in the bases of S's assets (other than the S1 stock) as in paragraph (i)(C) of this *Example 4*; in addition, the $80 attribute reduction amount not applied to reduce S's attributes is suspended and applied to reduce any amounts that become deductible or capitalizable as a result of the environmental remediation liability later being taken into account. If the liability is satisfied for an amount that is less than $80, under paragraph (d)(4)(ii)(C)(2) of this section the remaining portion of that $80 suspended attribute reduction amount is disregarded and has no further effect. Because the S1 share is not transferred within the meaning of paragraph (f)(10) of this section, the allocated attribute reduction amount apportioned to the S1 share is applied fully to reduce the basis of the S1 share to $30. See paragraph (d)(5)(iii) of this section.

(D) *Tier down of S's attribute reduction amount.* The $20 portion of S's attribute reduction amount allocated to the S1 share is an attribute reduction amount of S1. Because S1 holds only cash, it has no attributes available for reduction under this paragraph (d). However, because S1 has a $25 liability not taken into account for tax purposes, paragraph (d)(4)(ii)(C)(1) of this section requires that $20 of the unapplied attribute reduction amount be suspended and then allocated and applied to reduce any amounts that become deductible or capitalizable as a result of the employee medical expense liabilities later being taken into account. If these liabilities are

satisfied for an amount that is less than $20, under paragraph (d)(4)(ii)(C)(2) of this section the remaining portion of that $20 suspended attribute reduction amount is disregarded and has no further effect.

Example 5. Wholly owned lower-tier subsidiary (no lower-tier transfer). (i) *Application of conforming limitation.* (A) *Facts.* M owns the sole outstanding share of S stock with a basis of $250. S owns Asset with a basis of $100 and the only two outstanding shares of S1 stock (Share A has a basis of $40 and Share B has a basis of $60). S1 owns Asset 1 with a basis of $50. M sells its S share to P1, the common parent of another consolidated group, for $50. The sale is a transfer of a loss share and therefore subject to this section. See paragraphs (f)(10)(i)(A), (f)(10)(i)(B), and (f)(10)(i)(C) of this section.

(B) *Application of paragraphs (b) and (c) of this section.* Although the transfer is subject to this section, there is no basis redetermination under paragraph (b) of this section because there is only one share of S stock outstanding (and so there can be no disparity among members' bases in common shares and there are no outstanding preferred shares with respect to which there can be unrecognized gain or loss). See paragraph (b)(1)(ii)(A) of this section. Therefore, after the application of paragraph (b) of this section, the share is still a loss share and, as such, subject to paragraph (c) of this section. No adjustment is required under paragraph (c) of this section because, although there is a $50 disconformity amount, the net positive adjustment is $0. See paragraph (c)(3) of this section. Thus, after the application of paragraph (c) of this section, M's sale of the S share is still a transfer of a loss share and, accordingly, subject to this paragraph (d).

(C) *Attribute reduction under this paragraph (d).* (1) *Computation of attribute reduction amount.* Under paragraph (d)(3) of this section, S's attribute reduction amount is the lesser of M's net stock loss and S's aggregate inside loss. M's net stock loss is $200 ($250 basis over $50 value). S's aggregate inside loss is the excess of S's net inside attribute amount over the value of the S share. Under paragraphs (d)(3)(iii)(B) and (d)(5)(i)(B) of this section, S's net inside attribute amount is $200, computed as the sum of S's $100 basis in Asset and its $100 deemed basis in the deemed single share of S1 stock (computed as the greater of S's $100 aggregate basis in the S1 shares and S1's $50 basis in Asset 1). S's aggregate inside loss is therefore $150, $200 net inside attribute amount over the $50 value of the S share. Accordingly, S's attribute reduction amount is $150, the lesser of the $200 net stock loss and the $150 aggregate inside loss.

(2) *Allocation, apportionment, and application of S's attribute reduction amount.* Under paragraphs (d)(4) and (d)(5)(ii) of this section, S's $150 attribute reduction amount is allocated proportionately (by basis) between Asset (non-stock Category D asset) with a basis of $100, and the

S1 stock (treated as a single share with a deemed basis of $100). Accordingly, $75 of the attribute reduction amount ($100/$200 × $150) is allocated to Asset and $75 of the attribute reduction amount ($100/$200 × $150) is allocated to the S1 stock. The $75 of the attribute reduction amount allocated to Asset is applied to reduce S's basis in Asset from $100 to $25. The $75 of the attribute reduction amount allocated to the S1 stock is first apportioned between the shares in a manner that reduces disparity to the greatest extent possible. Thus, of the total $75 allocated to the S1 stock, $27.50 is apportioned to Share A and $47.50 is apportioned to Share B. Because neither of the S1 shares is transferred within the meaning of paragraph (f)(10) of this section, the allocated attribute reduction amount apportioned to each of the individual S1 shares is applied fully to reduce the basis of each share to $12.50. See paragraph (d)(5)(iii) of this section. As a result, immediately after the allocation, apportionment, and application of S's attribute reduction amount, S's basis in Asset is $25 and S's basis in each of the S1 shares is $12.50.

(3) *Tier down of S's attribute reduction amount, application of conforming limitation.* Under paragraph (d)(5)(v)(A) of this section, the $75 portion of S's attribute reduction amount allocated to the S1 stock is an attribute reduction amount of S1 (regardless of the extent, if any, to which it is apportioned and applied to reduce the basis of any shares of S1 stock). Under the general rules of this paragraph (d), the $75 tier-down attribute reduction amount would be allocated and applied to reduce S1's basis in Asset 1 from $50 to $0. However, under paragraph (d)(5)(v)(B) of this section, S1's attributes can be reduced by only $25, the excess of the $50 portion of S1's net inside attribute amount that is allocable to all S1 shares held by members as of the transaction over $25, the aggregate amount of members' bases in nontransferred S1 shares after reduction under this paragraph (d). Thus, of S1's $75 tier-down attribute reduction amount, only $25 is applied to reduce S1's basis in Asset 1, from $50 to $25. The $50 unapplied portion of the tier-down attribute reduction amount subject to the conforming limitation has no further effect.

(ii) *Application of basis restoration rule.* (A) *Facts.* The facts are the same as in paragraph (i)(A) of this *Example 5,* except that S's basis in Share A is $15 and S's basis in Share B is $35, and S1's basis in Asset 1 is $100.

(B) *Basis redetermination and basis reduction under paragraphs (b) and (c) of this section.* No adjustment is required under paragraph (b) or paragraph (c) of this section for the reasons set forth in paragraph (i)(B) of this *Example 5.* Thus, after the application of paragraph (c) of this section, M's transfer of the S share is still a transfer of a loss share and, accordingly, subject to this paragraph (d).

(C) *Attribute reduction under this paragraph (d).* (1) *Computation of attribute reduction amount.*

Under paragraph (d)(3) of this section, S's attribute reduction amount is the lesser of M's net stock loss and S's aggregate inside loss. M's net stock loss is $200 ($250 basis over $50 value). S's aggregate inside loss is the excess of S's net inside attribute amount over the value of the S share. Under paragraphs (d)(3)(iii)(B) and (d)(5)(i)(B) of this section, S's net inside attribute amount is $200, the sum of S's $100 basis in Asset and its $100 deemed basis in the deemed single share of S1 stock (computed as the greater of S's $50 aggregate basis in the S1 shares and S1's $100 basis in Asset 1). S's aggregate inside loss is therefore $150, $200 net inside attribute amount over the $50 value of the S share. Accordingly, S's attribute reduction amount is $150, the lesser of the $200 net stock loss and the $150 aggregate inside loss.

(2) *Allocation, apportionment, and application of S's attribute reduction amount.* Under paragraphs (d)(4) and (d)(5)(ii) of this section, S's $150 attribute reduction amount is allocated proportionately (by basis) between Asset (non-stock Category D asset) with a basis of $100, and the S1 stock (treated as a single share with a deemed basis of $100). Accordingly, $75 of the attribute reduction amount ($100/$200 × $150) is allocated to Asset and $75 of the attribute reduction amount ($100/$200 × $150) is allocated to the S1 stock. The $75 of the attribute reduction amount allocated to Asset is applied to reduce S's basis in Asset from $100 to $25. The $75 of the attribute reduction amount allocated to the S1 stock is first apportioned between the shares in a manner that reduces disparity to the greatest extent possible. Thus, of the total $75 allocated to the S1 stock, $27.50 is apportioned to Share A and $47.50 is apportioned to Share B. Because neither of the S1 shares is transferred within the meaning of paragraph (f)(10) of this section, the allocated attribute reduction amount apportioned to each of the individual S1 shares is applied fully to reduce the basis of each share to an excess loss account of $12.50. See paragraph (d)(5)(iii) of this section. As a result, immediately after the allocation, apportionment, and application of S's attribute reduction amount, S's basis in Asset is $25 and S's basis in each of the S1 shares is an excess loss account of $12.50.

(3) *Tier down of S's attribute reduction amount.* Under paragraph (d)(5)(v)(A) of this section, the $75 portion of S's attribute reduction amount allocated to S1 stock is an attribute reduction amount of S1 (regardless of the extent, if any, to which it is apportioned and applied to reduce the basis of any shares of S1 stock). Accordingly, under the general rules of this paragraph (d), the $75 tier-down attribute reduction amount is applied to reduce S1's basis in Asset 1 from $100 to $25.

(4) *Basis restoration.* Under paragraph (d)(5)(vi)(A) of this section, after this paragraph (d) has been applied with respect to all transfers of subsidiary stock, any reduction made to the

basis of a share of lower-tier subsidiary stock under paragraph (d)(5)(iii) of this section is reversed to the extent necessary to conform the basis of that share to the share's allocable portion of the subsidiary's net inside attribute amount (after reduction). S1's net inside attribute amount after the application of this paragraph (d) is $25 and thus each of the two S1 share's allocable portion of S1's net inside attribute amount is $12.50. Accordingly, the reductions to Share A and to Share B under paragraph (d)(5)(iii) of this section are reversed to the extent necessary to restore the basis of each share to $12.50. Thus, $25 of the $27.50 of reduction to the basis of Share A, and $25 of the $47.50 of reduction to the basis of share B, is reversed, restoring the basis of each share to $12.50.

Example 6. Multiple blocks of lower-tier subsidiary stock outstanding. (i) *Excess loss account taken into account (transfer of upper-tier share causes disposition within the meaning of §1.1502-19(c)(1)(ii)(B)).* (A) *Facts.* M owns the sole outstanding share of S stock with a basis of $200. S holds all five outstanding shares of S1 common stock (Shares A, B, C, D, and E). S has an excess loss account of $20 in Share A and a positive basis of $20 in each of the other shares. The only investment adjustment applied to any S1 share was a negative $20 investment adjustment applied to Share A when it was the only outstanding share, and this amount tiered up and adjusted M's basis in the S share. S1 owns one asset with a basis of $250. M sells its S share to P1, the common parent of a consolidated group, for $20. The sale of the S share is a disposition of Share A under § 1.1502-19(c)(1)(ii)(B) (S1 becomes a nonmember because it will have a separate return year as a member of the P1 group). Accordingly, under § 1.1502-19(b)(1)(i) and paragraph (a)(3)(i) of this section, before the application of this section, S's excess loss account in Share A is taken into account, increasing S's basis in Share A to $0 and M's basis in its S share to $220. After giving effect to the recognition of the excess loss account, M's sale of the S share is a transfer of a loss share and therefore subject to this section. See paragraphs (f)(10)(i)(A), (f)(10)(i)(B), and (f)(10)(i)(C) of this section.

(B) *Basis redetermination and basis reduction under paragraphs (b) and (c) of this section.* Although the transfer is subject to this section, there is no basis redetermination under paragraph (b) of this section because there is only one share of S stock outstanding (and so there can be no disparity among members' bases in common shares and there are no outstanding preferred shares with respect to which there can be unrecognized gain or loss). See paragraph (b)(1)(ii)(A) of this section. Therefore, after the application of paragraph (b) of this section, the share is still a loss share and, as such, subject to paragraph (c) of this section. No adjustment is made under paragraph (c) of this section because, even though there is a disconformity amount of $140,

the net positive adjustment is $0. See paragraph (c)(3) of this section. Thus, after the application of paragraph (c) of this section, M's sale of the S share remains a transfer of a loss share and, accordingly, subject to this paragraph (d).

(C) *Attribute reduction under this paragraph (d).* (1) *Computation of attribute reduction amount.* Under paragraph (d)(3) of this section, S's attribute reduction amount is the lesser of M's net stock loss and S's aggregate inside loss. M's net stock loss is $200 ($220 basis over $20 value). S's aggregate inside loss is the excess of S's net inside attribute amount over the value of the S share. Under paragraphs (d)(3)(iii)(B) and (d)(5)(i)(B) of this section, S's net inside attribute amount is $250, S's $250 deemed basis in the deemed single share of S1 stock (computed as the greater of S's $80 aggregate basis in the S1 shares ($0 basis in Share A plus $20 basis in each of the four other shares) and S1's $250 basis in its asset). S's aggregate inside loss is therefore $230, $250 net inside attribute amount over the $20 value of the S share. Accordingly, S's attribute reduction amount is $200, the lesser of the $200 net stock loss and the $230 aggregate inside loss.

(2) *Allocation, apportionment, and application of S's attribute reduction amount.* Under paragraphs (d)(4) and (d)(5)(ii) of this section, S's $200 attribute reduction amount is allocated entirely to the S1 stock (treated as a single share) and then apportioned among the shares in a manner that reduces disparity to the greatest extent possible. Thus, $24 is apportioned to Share A and $44 is apportioned to each of the other shares. Because none of the S1 shares are transferred within the meaning of paragraph (f)(10) of this section (notwithstanding that there is a disposition under § 1.1502-19(c)(1)(ii)(B)), the allocated attribute reduction amount apportioned to each of the individual S1 shares is applied fully to reduce the basis of each share to an excess loss account of $24. See paragraph (d)(5)(iii) of this section.

(3) *Tier down of S's attribute reduction amount.* Under paragraph (d)(5)(v)(A) of this section, the $200 of S's attribute reduction amount allocated to the S1 shares is an attribute reduction amount of S1 (regardless of the extent, if any, to which it is apportioned and applied to reduce the basis of any shares of S1 stock). Under the general rules of this paragraph (d), S1's $200 tier-down attribute reduction amount is allocated and applied to reduce S1's basis in its asset from $250 to $50.

(4) *Basis restoration.* Under paragraph (d)(5)(vi)(A) of this section, after this paragraph (d) has been applied with respect to all transfers of subsidiary stock, any reduction made to the basis of a share of lower-tier subsidiary stock under paragraph (d)(5)(iii) of this section is reversed to the extent necessary to conform the basis of that share to the share's allocable portion of the subsidiary's net inside attribute amount (after reduction). S1's net inside attribute amount after the application of this paragraph (d) is $50 and thus each of the five S1 share's allocable

portion of S1's net inside attribute amount is $10. Accordingly, the reductions to the bases of S1 shares under paragraph (d)(5)(iii) of this section are reversed to the extent necessary to restore (to the extent possible) the basis of each share to $10. Thus, $24 of the $24 of reduction to the basis of Share A is reversed, restoring the basis of Share A to $0, and $34 of the $44 of reduction to the basis of each other share is reversed, restoring the basis of each of those shares to $10.

(ii) *Sale of gain share to member.* (A) *Facts.* The facts are the same as in paragraph (i)(A) of this *Example 6*, except that M owns Shares A, B, C, and D, S owns Share E, S has a liability of $20, and S1's basis in its asset is $500. Also, as part of the transaction, S sells Share E to M for $40. Unlike under the facts of paragraph (i)(A) of this *Example 6*, there is no disposition of Share A within the meaning of §1.1502-19(c)(1)(ii)(B) (S1 continues to be a member of the group, and thus does not have a separate return year). As a result, the Share A excess loss account is not taken into account. Although S's sale of Share E is a transfer of that share, the share is not a loss share and thus the transfer is not subject to this section. M's sale of the S share, however, is a transfer of a loss share and therefore subject to this section. See paragraphs (f)(10)(i)(A), (f)(10)(i)(B), and (f)(10)(i)(C) of this section.

(B) *Transfer in lowest tier (gain share).* S's sale of Share E is the lowest-tier transfer in the transaction. Under paragraph (a)(3)(ii)(A) of this section, because there are no transfers of loss shares at that tier, no adjustments are required under paragraph (b) or (c) of this section. However, S's gain recognized on the transfer of Share E is computed and immediately adjusts members' bases in subsidiary stock under §1.1502-32 (because M and S are not members of the same group immediately after the transaction, the sale is not an intercompany transaction subject to §1.1502-13). Accordingly, M's basis in its S share is increased by $20, from $200 to $220.

(C) *Transfers in next higher tier, application of paragraphs (b) and (c) of this section.* The next higher tier transfer is M's sale of the S stock. The sale is a transfer of a loss share and therefore subject to this section. Although the transfer is subject to this section, there is no basis redetermination under paragraph (b) of this section because there is only one share of S stock outstanding (and so there can be no disparity among members' bases in common shares and there are no outstanding preferred shares with respect to which there can be unrecognized gain or loss). See paragraph (b)(1)(ii)(A) of this section. Therefore, after the application of paragraph (b) of this section, the share is still a loss share and, as such, subject to paragraph (c) of this section. Under paragraph (c) of this section, M's basis in its S share is decreased by $20, the lesser of S's $200 disconformity amount (computed as the excess of M's $220 basis in the S stock over S's $20 net inside attribute amount

(computed as the $20 basis in Share E, increased by $20 to reflect the gain recognized with respect to the share, less the $20 liability)), and the $20 net positive adjustment. Thus, after the application of paragraph (c) of this section, M's basis in the S share is $200, and the sale remains a transfer of a loss share. There are no higher tier transfers and, therefore, M's transfer of the S share is then subject to this paragraph (d).

(D) *Attribute reduction under this paragraph (d).* (1) *Computation of attribute reduction amount.* Under paragraph (d)(3) of this section, S's attribute reduction amount is the lesser of M's net stock loss and S's aggregate inside loss. M's net stock loss is $180 ($200 basis over $20 value). S's aggregate inside loss is the excess of S's net inside attribute amount over the value of the S share. Under paragraphs (d)(3)(iii)(B) and (d)(5)(i)(B) of this section, S's net inside attribute amount is $80, computed as $100 (S's deemed basis in Share E (the greater of $40 (S's $20 basis in Share E, adjusted for the $20 gain recognized with respect to the share), and Share E's allocable portion of S1's net inside attribute amount of $100 (1/5 of S1's $500 basis in its asset)), less S's $20 liability. Accordingly, S's aggregate inside loss is $60 ($80 net inside attribute amount over the $20 value of the S stock). S's attribute reduction amount is therefore $60, the lesser of $180 net stock loss and $60 aggregate inside loss.

(2) *Allocation, apportionment, and application of S's attribute reduction amount.* Under paragraphs (d)(4) and (d)(5)(ii) of this section, S's $60 attribute reduction amount is allocated entirely to its S1 stock, Share E. However, because Share E was transferred within the meaning of paragraph (f)(10) of this section and gain was recognized on its transfer, none of the allocated amount is apportioned to, or applied to reduce the basis of Share E. See paragraph (d)(5)(iii)(A) of this section. Under paragraph (d)(5)(iv) of this section, the $60 allocated attribute reduction amount not apportioned or applied to Share E has no effect on S or S's attributes.

(3) *Tier down of S's attribute reduction amount.* Notwithstanding the fact that no portion of the allocated attribute reduction amount was apportioned to or applied to reduce the basis of Share E, the entire $60 allocated attribute reduction amount is an attribute reduction amount of S1. See paragraph (d)(5)(v)(A) of this section. Under the general rules of this paragraph (d), S1's $60 tier-down attribute reduction amount is allocated and applied to reduce S1's basis in its asset from $500 to $440.

(4) *Basis restoration.* Under paragraph (d)(5)(vi)(A) of this section, after this paragraph (d) has been applied with respect to all transfers of subsidiary stock, any reduction made to the basis of a share of subsidiary stock under paragraph (d)(5)(iii) of this section is reversed to the extent necessary to conform the basis of that share to the share's allocable portion of the subsidiary's net inside attribute amount. No reduc-

tion was made to the basis of the S1 stock under paragraph (d)(5)(iii) of this section. Therefore, no stock basis is increased under the basis restoration rule in paragraph (d)(5)(vi)(A) of this section.

Example 7. Allocation of attribute reduction if lower-tier subsidiary has non-loss assets or liabilities. (i) *S1 holds cash.* (A) *Facts.* M owns the sole outstanding share of S stock with a basis of $800. S owns Asset with a basis of $400 and the sole outstanding share of S1 stock with a basis of $300. S1 holds Asset 1 with a basis of $50, and $100 cash. M sells its S share to P1, the common parent of a consolidated group, for $100. The sale is not a transfer of the S1 share because S and S1 are members of the same group following the transaction. However, the sale is a transfer of the S share, a loss share, and therefore subject to this section. See paragraphs (f)(10)(i)(A), (f)(10)(i)(B), and (f)(10)(i)(C) of this section.

(B) *Application of paragraphs (b) and (c) of this section.* Although the transfer is subject to this section, there is no basis redetermination under paragraph (b) of this section because there is only one share of S stock outstanding (and so there can be no disparity among members' bases in common shares and there are no outstanding preferred shares with respect to which there can be unrecognized gain or loss). See paragraph (b)(1)(ii)(A) of this section. Therefore, after the application of paragraph (b) of this section, the share is still a loss share and, as such, subject to the provisions of this paragraph (c). No adjustment is required under paragraph (c) of this section because, even though there is a disconformity amount of $100, the net positive adjustment is $0. See paragraph (c)(3) of this section. Thus, after the application of paragraph (c) of this section, M's sale of the S share is still a transfer of a loss share and, accordingly, subject to this paragraph (d).

(C) *Attribute reduction under this paragraph (d).* (1) *Computation of attribute reduction amount.* Under paragraph (d)(3) of this section, S's attribute reduction amount is the lesser of M's net stock loss and S's aggregate inside loss. M's net stock loss is $700 ($800 basis over $100 value). S's aggregate inside loss is the excess of S's net inside attribute amount over the value of the S share. Under paragraphs (d)(3)(iii)(B) and (d)(5)(i)(B) of this section, S's net inside attribute amount is $700, the sum of its $400 basis in Asset and its $300 deemed basis in the S1 share (computed as the greater of S's $300 basis in the S1 share and S1's $150 net inside attribute amount (reflecting the sum of S1's $50 basis in Asset 1 and S1's $100 cash)). Therefore, S's aggregate inside loss is $600 ($700 net inside attribute amount over the $100 value of the S stock). S's attribute reduction amount is $600, the lesser of the $700 net stock loss and the $600 aggregate inside loss.

(2) *Allocation, apportionment, and application of S's attribute reduction amount.* Under paragraphs

(d)(4) and (d)(5)(ii) of this section, S's $600 attribute reduction amount is allocated proportionately (by basis) between S's $400 basis in Asset (nonstock Category D asset) and its deemed basis in the S1 share. However, under paragraph (d)(5)(ii) of this section, for purposes of allocating the attribute reduction amount, S's $300 deemed basis in the S1 share is treated as reduced by S1's net nonloss assets (its Class I asset, $100 cash) to $200. Thus, the $600 is allocated $400 to Asset ($400/$600 × $600) and $200 to the S1 share ($200/$600 × $600). The $400 allocated to Asset is applied to reduce S's basis in Asset from $400 to $0. Because the S1 share is not transferred within the meaning of paragraph (f)(10) of this section, the allocated attribute reduction amount apportioned to the S1 share is applied fully to reduce the basis of the S1 share to $100. See paragraph (d)(5)(iii) of this section.

(3) *Tier down of S's attribute reduction amount.* Under paragraph (d)(5)(v)(A) of this section, the $200 portion of S's attribute reduction amount allocated to the S1 stock is an attribute reduction amount of S1 (regardless of the extent, if any, to which it is apportioned and applied to reduce the basis of any shares of S1 stock). Under the general rules of this paragraph (d), S1's $200 tier-down attribute reduction amount is allocated and applied to reduce S1's basis in Asset 1 (S1's only attribute available for reduction) from $50 to $0. The $150 unapplied attribute reduction amount is disregarded and has no further effect.

(4) *Basis restoration.* Under paragraph (d)(5)(vi)(A) of this section, after this paragraph (d) has been applied with respect to all transfers of subsidiary stock, any reduction made to the basis of a share of subsidiary stock under paragraph (d)(5)(iii) of this section is reversed to the extent necessary to conform the basis of that share to the share's allocable portion of the subsidiary's net inside attribute amount. There is only one share of S1 stock outstanding and so S1's entire $100 net inside attribute amount is allocable to that share. Because S's $100 basis in the S1 share (as reduced under this paragraph (d)) is already conformed with its $100 allocable portion of S1's net inside attribute amount, there is no restoration under paragraph (d)(5)(vi)(A) of this section.

(ii) *S1 borrows cash.* The facts are the same as in paragraph (i)(A) of this *Example 7* except that, in addition, S1 borrows $50 from X immediately before M sells the S share. The computation of the attribute reduction amount is the same as in paragraph (i)(C) of this *Example 7* (the $50 cash from the loan proceeds and the $50 liability offset in the computation of S1's net inside attribute amount and so the net amount is unaffected, and the computation of S's deemed basis in the S1 stock is unaffected). Similarly, for purposes of allocating the attribute reduction amount between the non-stock Category D asset and the S1 stock, paragraph (d)(5)(ii) of this section requires S's deemed basis in the S1 share to be treated as reduced by S1's net nonloss assets (S1's non-loss assets over S1's liabilities). Accordingly, the additional $50 cash proceeds is offset by the $50 liability and there is no effect on the allocation of the attribute reduction amount. The results are the same as in paragraph (i) of this *Example 7*.

(iii) *S1 has a liability not taken into account for tax purposes.* (A) *Facts.* The facts are the same as in paragraph (ii) of this *Example 7* except that, in addition, S1 has a $40 liability that is not taken into account for tax purposes as of the transfer and that would be required to be capitalized if a person purchased S1's assets and assumed the liability.

(B) *Application of paragraphs (b) and (c) of this section.* No adjustment is required under paragraph (b) or paragraph (c) of this section for the reasons set forth in paragraph (i)(B) of this *Example 7*. Thus, after the application of paragraph (c) of this section, P's sale of the S share is still a transfer of a loss share and, accordingly, subject to this paragraph (d).

(C) *Attribute reduction under this paragraph (d).* (1) *Computation of attribute reduction amount.* The attribute reduction amount is the same as computed in paragraph (i)(C)(1) of this *Example 7* (under paragraph (f)(5) of this section, the term liability does not include liabilities not taken into account for tax purposes and so the additional $40 liability not yet taken into account for tax purposes does not affect the computation of S's attribute reduction amount).

(2) *Allocation, apportionment, and application of S's attribute reduction amount.* Under paragraphs (d)(4) and (d)(5)(ii) of this section, S's $600 attribute reduction amount is allocated proportionately (by basis) between S's $400 basis in Asset 1 (nonstock Category D asset) and its deemed basis in the S1 share. However, under paragraph (d)(5)(ii) of this section, for purposes of allocating the attribute reduction amount, S's $300 deemed basis in the S1 share is treated as reduced by S1's net nonloss assets (S1's non-loss assets over S1's liabilities). For this purpose, the term liabilities includes liabilities not taken into account for tax purposes, as described in paragraph (d)(4)(ii)(C)(1) of this section (generally, liabilities that, if assumed in a purchase, would give rise to a capitalized amount when satisfied). Thus, for this purpose, S's $300 deemed basis in the S1 share is reduced by S1's $60 net non-loss assets (the excess of S1's $150 non-loss assets (its Class I asset, $150 cash) over S1's $90 liabilities ($50 loan and $40 liability not yet taken into account for tax purposes)), to $240. Accordingly, S's $600 attribute reduction amount is allocated and applied $375 ($400/$640 × $600) to Asset (reducing S's basis in Asset from $400 to $25) and $225 ($240/$640 × $600) to the S1 share. Because the S1 share is not transferred within the meaning of paragraph (f)(10) of this section, the allocated attribute reduction amount apportioned to the S1 share is applied fully to reduce

the basis of the S1 share to $75. See paragraph (d)(5)(iii) of this section.

(3) *Tier down of S's attribute reduction amount, application of conforming limitation.* Under paragraph (d)(5)(v)(A) of this section, the $225 portion of S's attribute reduction amount allocated to the S1 stock is an attribute reduction amount of S1 (regardless of the extent, if any, to which it is apportioned and applied to reduce the basis of any shares of S1 stock). Under the general rules of this paragraph (d), S1's $225 tier-down attribute reduction amount would be allocated and applied to reduce S1's attributes. However, under paragraph (d)(5)(v)(B) of this section, S1's attributes can be reduced by only $75, the excess of the $150 portion of S1's net inside attribute amount that is allocable to all S1 shares held by members as of the transaction over $75, the aggregate amount of members' bases in nontransferred S1 shares, after reduction under this paragraph (d). Thus, of S1's $225 tier-down attribute reduction amount, $50 is applied to reduce S1's basis in Asset 1, from $50 to $0. Although the $25 unapplied attribute reduction amount not subject to the conforming limitation would generally be disregarded without further effect, because S1 has a $40 liability not taken into account for tax purposes, paragraph (d)(4)(ii)(C)(1) of this section requires that the $25 of the unapplied attribute reduction amount not subject to the conforming limitation be suspended and then allocated and applied to reduce any amounts that become deductible or capitalizable as a result of that liability later being taken into account. If the liability is satisfied for an amount that is less than $25, under paragraph (d)(4)(ii)(C)(2) of this section the remaining portion of that $25 suspended attribute reduction amount is disregarded and has no further effect. The $150 unapplied portion of the tier-down attribute reduction amount subject to the conforming limitation has no further effect.

(4) *Basis restoration.* Under paragraph (d)(5)(vi)(A) of this section, after this paragraph (d) has been applied with respect to all transfers of subsidiary stock, any reduction made to the basis of a share of lower-tier subsidiary stock under paragraph (d)(5)(iii) of this section is reversed to the extent necessary to conform the basis of that share to the share's allocable portion of the subsidiary's net inside attribute amount. Paragraph (d)(5)(vi)(A) provides that, for this purpose, S1's net inside attribute amount is its net inside attribute amount, taking into account any reductions under this paragraph (d) and treating it as reduced by any attribute reduction amount suspended under paragraph (d)(4)(ii)(C)(1) of this section. Because S's $75 basis in its S1 stock (after application of this paragraph (d)) is already conformed with its $75 allocable portion of S1's net inside attribute amount ($100 net inside attributes after reduction, reduced by S1's $25 suspended attribute

reduction amount), there is no restoration under paragraph (d)(5)(vi)(A) of this section.

Example 8. Election to reduce stock basis or reattribute attributes under paragraph (d)(6) of this section. (i) *Deconsolidating sale.* (A) *Facts.* P owns the sole outstanding share of M stock with a basis of $1,000. M owns all 100 outstanding shares of S stock with a basis of $2.10 per share ($210 total). M sells all its S shares to X for $1 per share ($100 total). M's sale of the S shares is a transfer of loss shares and therefore subject to this section. See paragraphs (f)(10)(i)(A), (f)(10)(i)(B), and (f)(10)(i)(C) of this section. At the time of the sale, S has no liabilities and the following:

Category	Attribute	Attribute amount
Category A	Capital loss carryover	$10
Category B	NOL carryover	$90
Category C	Deferred deduction	$40
	Total Category A, Category B, and Category C Attributes	$140
Category D, Class V	Basis in land	$70
	Total Attributes	$210

(B) *Application of paragraphs (b) and (c) of this section.* Although the transfer is subject to this section, there is no basis redetermination under paragraph (b) of this section because there is no disparity among M's bases in shares of S common stock and there are no shares of S preferred stock outstanding (so there can be no unrecognized gain or loss with respect to preferred shares). See paragraph (b)(1)(ii)(A) of this section. No adjustment is required under paragraph (c) of this section because both the disconformity amount and the net positive adjustment are $0. See paragraph (c)(3) of this section. Thus, after the application of paragraph (c) of this section, M's transfer of the S shares is still a transfer of loss shares and, accordingly, subject to this paragraph (d).

(C) *Attribute reduction under this paragraph (d).* (1) *Computation of attribute reduction amount.* Under paragraph (d)(3) of this section, S's attribute reduction amount is the lesser of the $110 net stock loss ($210 aggregate basis over the $100 aggregate value) and S's aggregate inside loss. S's aggregate inside loss is $110 (S's $210 net inside attribute amount (the $10 capital loss carryover, plus the $90 NOL carryover, plus the $40 deferred deduction, plus the $70 basis in the land) over the $100 value of all outstanding S shares). S's attribute reduction amount is $110, the lesser of the $110 net stock loss and the $110 aggregate inside loss.

(2) *Application of attribute reduction amount.* (i) S's $110 attribute reduction amount is applied as follows:

Category	Attribute	Attribute amount	Allocation of attribute reduction amount	Adjusted attribute amount
Category A	Capital loss carryover	$10	$10	$0
Category B	NOL carryover	$90	$90	$0
Category C	Deferred deduction	$40	$10	$30
Category D, Class V	Basis in land	$70	$0	$70
Totals		$210	$110	$100

(ii) Alternatively, under paragraph (d)(4)(ii)(A)(*1*) of this section, P could specify the allocation of S's $110 attribute reduction amount among S's $10 capital loss carryover, S's $90 NOL carryover, and S's $40 deferred deduction.

(D) *Results.* The P group recognizes a $110 loss on M's sale of the S shares that is absorbed by the group, which reduces P's basis in the M share under § 1.1502-32 from $1,000 to $890. Immediately after the transaction, the entities own the following:

Entity	Asset	Basis
P	M share	$890
X	100 S shares	$100

Entity	Asset	Basis
S	Category C, deferred deduction	$30
	Category D, Class V Asset (land)	$70

(E) *Election to reduce stock basis.* The facts are the same as in paragraph (i)(A) of this *Example 8* except that P elects under paragraph (d)(6) of this section to reduce M's basis in the S shares by the full attribute reduction amount of $110, in lieu of S reducing its attributes. The election is effective for all transferred loss shares and is allocated to those shares in proportion to the loss in each. See paragraph (d)(6)(v)(A) of this section. Accordingly, the basis of each of the 100 transferred shares is reduced from $2.10 to $1.00. After giving effect to the election, the S shares are not loss shares and this section has no further application to the transfer. The $110 reduction in M's basis in the S shares pursuant to the election under paragraph (d)(6) of this section is a noncapital, nondeductible expense of M that will reduce P's basis in the M share. See paragraph (d)(6)(v)(A) of this section. Immediately after the transaction, the entities own the following:

Entity	Asset	Basis/Attribute
P	M share	$890
X	100 S shares	$100
S	Category A, capital loss carryover	$10
	Category B, NOL carryover	$90
	Category C, deferred deduction	$40
	Category D, Class V Asset (land)	$70

(F) *Election to reattribute losses.* The facts are the same as in paragraph (i)(A) of this *Example 8* except that P elects under paragraph (d)(6) of this section to reattribute S's attributes. S's attribute reduction amount is $110, and P can reattribute all or any portion of the attributes in Category A, Category B, and Category C to the extent of $110. P elects to reattribute the $90 NOL, and, as a result, S's NOL is $0. Under paragraph (d)(6)(iv)(A) of this section, the reattribution of the $90 NOL is a noncapital, nondeductible expense of S. Under § 1.1502-32(c)(1)(ii)(A)(*1*) this $90 expense is allocated to the transferred loss shares of S stock in proportion to the loss in the shares, or $.90 per share. Further, this expense tiers up under § 1.1502-32 and reduces P's basis in the M stock by $90. After giving effect to the election, the P group would recognize a $20 loss on M's sale of the S shares, S would have an aggregate inside loss of $20 (S's $120 net inside attribute amount (the $10 capital loss carryover, plus the $40 deferred deduction, plus the $70 basis in the land) over the $100 value of all outstanding S shares), and S's attribute reduction amount would be $20 (applied $10 to the $10 capital loss carryover and $10 to the $40 deferred deduction). (Alternatively, under paragraph (d)(4)(ii)(A)(*1*) of this section, P could specify the allocation of S's $20 attribute reduction amount between S's $10 capi-

tal loss carryover and S's $40 deferred deduction. Further, P could elect to reduce M's remaining basis in the S shares by any amount up to the $20 attribute reduction amount, thereby reducing or eliminating S's attribute reduction amount.)

(ii) *Nonconsolidating sale.* (A) *Facts.* The facts are the same as in paragraph (i)(A) of this *Example 8,* except that M only sells 20 S shares ($20 total).

(B) *Application of paragraphs (b) and (c) of this section.* No adjustment is required under paragraph (b) or paragraph (c) of this section for the reasons set forth in paragraph (i)(B) of this *Example 8.* Thus, after the application of paragraph (c) of this section, M's sale of the S shares is still a transfer of loss shares and, accordingly, subject to this paragraph (d).

(C) *Attribute reduction under this paragraph (d).* (1) *Computation of attribute reduction amount.* Under paragraph (d)(3) of this section, S's attribute reduction amount is the lesser of the $22 net stock loss ($42 aggregate basis over $20 aggregate value) and S's $110 aggregate inside loss (as calculated in paragraph (i)(C)(*1*) of this *Example 8*). S's attribute reduction amount is $22, the lesser of the $22 net stock loss and the $110 aggregate inside loss.

(2) *Application of attribute reduction amount.* (i) S's $22 attribute reduction amount is applied as follows:

Category	Attribute	Attribute amount	Allocation of attribute reduction amount	Adjusted attribute amount
Category A	Capital loss carryover	$10	$10	$0
Category B	NOL carryover	$90	$12	$78

Reg. § 1.1502-36(d)(8)

Category	Attribute	Attribute amount	Allocation of attribute reduction amount	Adjusted attribute amount
Category C	Deferred deduction	$40	$0	$40
Category D, Class V	Land	$70	$0	$70

(*ii*) Alternatively, under paragraph (d)(4)(ii)(A)(*1*) of this section, P could specify the allocation of S's $22 attribute reduction amount among S's $10 capital loss carryover, S's $90 NOL carryover, and S's $40 deferred deduction.

(D) *Results.* The P group recognizes a $22 loss on M's sale of the S shares that is absorbed by the group, which reduces P's basis in the M share under § 1.1502-32 from $1,000 to $978. Immediately after the transaction, the entities have the following:

Entity	Asset	Basis
P	M share	$978
X	20 S shares	$20
S	Category B, NOL carryover	$78
	Category C, deferred deduction	$40
	Category D, Class V Asset (land)	$70

(E) *Election to reduce stock basis.* The facts are the same as in paragraph (ii)(A) of this *Example 8*, except that P elects under paragraph (d)(6) of this section to reduce M's basis in the S shares by the full attribute reduction amount of $22, in lieu of S reducing its attributes. The election is effective for all transferred loss shares and is allocated to such shares in proportion to the loss in each share. See paragraph (d)(6)(v)(A) of this section. Accordingly, the basis of each of the 20 transferred shares is reduced from $2.10 to $1.00.

After giving effect to the election, the transferred S shares are not loss shares and this section has no further application to the transfer. The $22 reduction in M's basis in the S shares pursuant to the election under paragraph (d)(6) of this section is a noncapital, nondeductible expense of M that will reduce P's basis in the M share. See paragraph (d)(6)(v)(A) of this section. Immediately after the transaction, the entities have the following:

Entity		Basis/ Attribute
P	M share	$978
M	80 S shares	$168
X	20 S shares	$20
S	Category A, capital loss carryover	$10
	Category B, NOL	$90
	Category C, deferred deduction	$40
	Category D Class V Asset (land)	$70

(F) *Election to reattribute attributes.* The facts are the same as in paragraph (ii)(A) of this *Example 8*. Because S remains a member of the same group as P following M's sale of S stock, P cannot elect under paragraph (d)(6) of this section to reattribute any portion of S's attributes in lieu of attribute reduction.

Example 9. Transfers at multiple tiers, gain and loss shares. (i) *Facts.* M owns the sole outstanding share of S stock with a basis of $700. S owns Asset 1 (basis of $170) and all ten outstanding shares of S1 common stock ($170 basis in share 1, $10 basis in share 2, and $15 basis in each of share 3 through share 10). S1 owns the sole outstanding share of S2 ($0 basis), the sole outstanding share of S3 ($60 basis), and the sole

outstanding share of S4 ($100 basis). S2's sole asset is Asset 2 ($75 basis). S3's sole asset is Asset 3 ($75 basis). S4's sole asset is Asset 4 ($80 basis). In one transaction, M sells its S share to P1 (the common parent of a consolidated group) for $240, S sells S1 share 1 to X for $20, S contributes S1 share 2 to a partnership in a section 721 transaction, and S1 sells its S2 share to Y for $50. M's sale of the S share and S1's sale of the S2 share are transfers under paragraphs (f)(10)(i)(A), (f)(10)(i)(B), and (f)(10)(i)(C) of this section. S's sale of S1 share 1 to X is a transfer under paragraphs (f)(10)(i)(A) and (f)(10)(i)(C) of this section. S's contribution of S1 share 2 to the partnership is a transfer under paragraph (f)(10)(i)(C) of this section.

(ii) *Transfer in lowest tier (gain share)*. S1's sale of the S2 share is the lowest tier transfer in the transaction. Under paragraph (a)(3)(ii)(A) of this section, because there are no transfers of loss shares at that tier, no adjustments are required under paragraph (b) or (c) of this section. However, S1's gain recognized on the transfer of the S2 share is computed and immediately adjusts members' bases in subsidiary stock under § 1.1502-32. Accordingly, $5 is allocated to each of 10 S1 shares, increasing the basis of share 1 to $175, the basis of share 2 to $15, and the basis of each other share to $20. The $50 applied to S's bases in the S1 shares then tiers up to increase P's basis in the S share from $700 to $750.

(iii) *Transfers in next highest tier (loss share)*. S's sale of the S1 share 1 and S's transfer of the S1 share 2 to a partnership are both transfers of stock in the next higher tier. However, only the S1 share 1 is a loss share and so this section only applies with respect to the transfer of that share.

(A) *Basis redetermination under paragraph (b) of this section*. Under paragraph (b)(2)(i)(A) of this section, members' bases in S1 shares are redetermined by first removing the positive investment adjustments applied to the bases of transferred loss common shares. Accordingly, the $5 positive investment adjustment applied to the basis of S1 share 1 is removed, reducing the basis of S1 share 1 from $175 to $170. Because there were no negative adjustments applied to the bases of S1 shares, there are no negative adjustments that can be reallocated to further reduce the basis of S1 share 1 under paragraph (b)(2)(i)(B) of this section. Finally, under paragraph (b)(2)(ii)(B) of this section, the $5 positive investment adjustment removed from S1 share 1 is reallocated and applied to increase the bases of other S1 common shares in a manner that reduces disparity to the greatest extent possible. Accordingly, the entire $5 investment adjustment removed from S1 share 1 is reallocated and applied to increase the basis of S1 share 2, from $15 to $20. After basis is redetermined under paragraph (b) of this section, the S1 share 1 is still a loss share and therefore subject to basis reduction under paragraph (c) of this section. (Because the S1 share 2 is not a loss share, this section does not apply with respect to the transfer of that share.)

(B) *Basis reduction under paragraph (c) of this section*. No adjustment is required to the basis of S1 share 1 under paragraph (c) of this section. The S1 share 1 has a disconformity amount of $149. This $149 disconformity amount is computed as the excess of the $170 basis in the S1 share 1 over the S1 share 1's $21 allocable portion (1/10) of S1's $210 net inside attribute amount. S1's $210 net inside attribute amount is determined under paragraph (c)(5) of this section as the sum of $50 (S1's $0 basis in the S2 share, adjusted for the $50 gain recognized with respect to that share), S1's $60 basis in the S3 stock, and S1's $100 basis in the S4 stock. (In computing the

disconformity amount, the basis of the S2 share is not treated as tentatively reduced because that share is transferred in the transaction, and the bases of the S3 and S4 shares are not treated as tentatively reduced because no positive investment adjustments were applied to the bases of those shares.) However, the S1 share 1's net positive adjustment is $0 because the $5 positive investment adjustment originally allocated to S1 share 1 was reallocated to S1 share 2 under paragraph (b) of this section. See paragraph (c)(3) of this section. No adjustment is required to the basis of S1 share 2 under paragraph (c) of this section because S1 share 2 is not a loss share.

(C) *Computation of loss, adjustments to stock basis*. S recognizes a loss of $150 on the sale of the S1 share 1 ($170 basis over $20 amount realized) that is absorbed by the group. Under § 1.1502-32, M's basis in its S share is therefore decreased by $100, the net of the $150 loss recognized by S on the sale of the S1 share, and the $50 gain that tiered up from S1 (as a result of S1's sale of the S2 share). Following these adjustments, M's basis in the S share is $600 and the sale of the S share is still a transfer of a loss share.

(iv) *Transfer in highest tier (loss share)*. The sale of the S share is a transfer in the next higher tier, which is the highest tier in this transaction. Because the sale is a transfer of a loss share, it is subject to this section.

(A) *Basis redetermination and basis reduction under paragraphs (b) and (c) of this section*. Although the transfer is subject to this section, there is no basis redetermination under paragraph (b) of this section because there is only one share of S stock outstanding (and so there can be no disparity among members' bases in common shares and there are no outstanding preferred shares with respect to which there can be unrecognized gain or loss). See paragraph (b)(1)(ii)(A) of this section. Therefore, after the application of paragraph (b) of this section, the share is still a loss share and, as such, subject to paragraph (c) of this section. In addition, no adjustment is required under paragraph (c) of this section. The S share has a disconformity amount of $230. This $230 disconformity amount is computed as the excess of the $600 basis in the S share over the S share's $370 allocable portion (1/1) of S's $370 net inside attribute amount. S's $370 net inside attribute amount is determined under paragraph (c)(5) of this section as the sum of $200 (S's $170 basis in the S1 share 1, adjusted for the $150 loss recognized with respect to that share, and S's $20 basis in each of S1 share 2 through share 10), and S's $170 basis in Asset 1. (In computing the disconformity amount, the bases of S1 share 1 and share 2 are not treated as tentatively reduced because those shares are transferred in the transaction, and the bases of S1 share 3 through share 10 are not treated as tentatively reduced because none of those shares have a disconformity amount -each share has a basis of $20 and a $21 allocable portion (1/10) of S1's $210 net inside attribute amount, as determined in paragraph (iii)(B) of this *Example 9.*) However, the S share's net positive adjustment is $0 (the S share's net adjustment is negative $100). See paragraph (c)(3) of this section. Accordingly, the sale of the S share is still a transfer of a loss share. Because there are no higher-tier loss shares transferred in the transaction, this paragraph (d) then applies with respect to the transfer of the S share.

(B) *Attribute reduction under this paragraph (d).* (1) *Computation of S's attribute reduction amount.* Under paragraph (d)(3) of this section, S's attribute reduction amount is the lesser of P's net stock loss and S's aggregate inside loss. P's net stock loss is $360 ($600 basis over $240 amount realized). S's aggregate inside loss is the excess of S's net inside attribute amount over the value of the S share. S's net inside attribute amount is the sum of its bases in its assets, treating its S1 shares as a single share (the S1 stock) and treating S's deemed basis in the S1 stock as its basis in that stock. Under paragraph (d)(5)(i)(C) of this section, when subsidiaries are owned in multiple tiers, deemed basis is first determined for shares at the lowest tier, and then for stock in each next higher tier. Under paragraph (d)(5)(i)(B) of this section, S1's deemed basis in the S2 stock is $75 (computed as the greater of $50 (S1's $0 basis in the S2 share, adjusted for the $50 gain recognized with respect to the share) and $75 (S2's net inside attribute amount, the basis in Asset 2)). S1's deemed basis in the S3 stock is $75 (computed as the greater of $60 (S1's basis in the S3 share) and $75 (S3's net inside attribute amount, the basis in Asset 3)). S1's deemed basis in the S4 stock is $100 (computed as the greater of $100 (S1's basis in the S4 share) and $80 (S4's net inside attribute amount, the basis in Asset 4)). Accordingly, S1's net inside attribute amount is $250 ($75 deemed basis in the S2 stock plus $75 deemed basis in the S3 stock plus $100 deemed basis in the S4 stock). S's deemed basis in the S1 stock is the greater of the sum of S's actual basis in each share of S1 stock (adjusted for any gain or loss recognized) and S1's net inside attribute amount. S's actual basis in the S1 stock, adjusted for the loss recognized, is $200 (the sum of S's $170 basis in the S1 share 1, adjusted by the $150 loss recognized with respect to the share, and S's $20 basis in each of S1 share 2 through share 10). Thus, S's deemed basis in the S1 stock is $250, the greater of $200 (aggregate basis in S1 shares, adjusted for loss recognized) and $250 (S1's net inside attribute amount). As a result, S's net inside attribute amount is $420, the sum of S's $250 deemed basis in the S1 stock and S's $170 basis in Asset 1. Accordingly, the aggregate inside loss is $180, the excess of S's $420 net inside attribute amount over the $240 value of all of the S stock. S's attribute reduction amount is therefore $180, the lesser of the $360 net stock loss and the $180 aggregate inside loss.

(2) *Allocation, apportionment, and application of S's attribute reduction amount.* Under paragraphs (d)(4) and (d)(5)(ii) of this section, S's $180 attribute reduction amount is allocated proportionately (by basis) between Asset 1 (non-stock Category D asset) and the S1 stock. However, under paragraph (d)(5)(ii) of this section, for purposes of allocating S's $180 attribute reduction amount between S's non-stock Category D asset and the S1 stock, S's $250 deemed basis in the S1 stock is reduced by the $40 value of the transferred S1 shares (S1 share 1 and share 2) and the nontransferred S1 shares' $40 allocable portion (8/10) of S1's $50 net non-loss assets. S1's net non-loss assets is the $50 value of S1's transferred S2 shares. (S1 has no other non-loss assets, and there are no non-loss assets held by lower-tier subsidiaries.) Accordingly, for this purpose, S's deemed basis in the S1 stock is reduced by $80, from $250 to $170. Thus, $90 of the attribute reduction amount ($170/$340 x $180) is allocated to Asset 1 (reducing S's basis in Asset 1 from $170 to $80) and $90 of the attribute reduction amount ($170/$340 × $180) is allocated to the S1 stock. Under paragraph (d)(5)(iii)(A) of this section, none of the $90 allocated attribute reduction amount is apportioned to S1 share 1 because loss is recognized on the transfer of S1 share 1. Under paragraph (d)(5)(iii)(B) of this section, the $90 allocated attribute reduction amount is apportioned among the other nine shares of S1 common stock in a manner that reduces disparity to the greatest extent possible. Accordingly, of the total $90 allocated amount, $10 is apportioned to each of the remaining nine shares of S1 stock. Under paragraph (d)(5)(iii)(C) of this section, the allocated attribute reduction amount apportioned to an individual share cannot be applied to reduce the basis of the share below its value if the share is transferred other than in a recognition transfer. Because the S1 share 2 is transferred (contributed to the partnership) and the basis of S1 share 2 is already equal to its value, none of the $10 allocated attribute reduction amount apportioned to S1 share 2 is applied to reduce its basis. Because none of S1 share 3 through share 10 are transferred within the meaning of paragraph (f)(10) of this section, the $10 allocated attribute reduction amount apportioned to each of S1 share 3 through share 10 is applied fully to reduce the basis of each of those shares from $20 to $10. As a result, immediately after the allocation and application of S's attribute reduction amount, S's basis in Asset 1 is $80 ($170 minus $90), its bases in S1 share 1 and share 2 are not adjusted under paragraph (d)(5)(iii), and its basis in each of S1 share 3 through share 10 is $10. Under paragraph (d)(5)(v)(A) of this section, the entire $90 of S's attribute reduction amount that was allocated to the S1 stock is an attribute reduction amount of S1, regardless of the fact that none of the allocated amount was apportioned to S1 share 1 and none of the amount apportioned to S1 share 2 was applied to reduce the basis of S1 share 2.

Reg. § 1.1502-36(d)(8)

(v) *Attribute reduction under this paragraph (d) in next lower tier.* (A) *Computation of S1's attribute reduction amount.* S's sale of S1 share 1 is a transfer of a loss share and it is in the next lower tier. Thus, this paragraph (d) next applies with respect to S's transfer of S1 share 1. S1's attribute reduction amount will include both the $90 attribute reduction amount that tiered down from S and any attribute reduction amount resulting from the application of this paragraph (d) with respect to S's transfer of S1 share 1 and share 2 (S1's direct attribute reduction amount). Under paragraph (d)(3) of this section, S1's direct attribute reduction amount is the lesser of the net stock loss on transferred S1 shares and S1's aggregate inside loss. The net stock loss on transferred S1 shares is $150, computed as the excess of S's $190 adjusted bases in transferred shares of S1 stock ($170 in S1 share 1 plus $20 in S1 share 2) over the $40 aggregate value of those shares. S1's aggregate inside loss is $50, the excess of S1's $250 net inside attribute amount (as calculated in paragraph (iv)(B)(1) of this *Example 9*) over the $200 value of all outstanding S1 shares. Therefore, S1's direct attribute reduction amount is $50, the lesser of the $150 net stock loss and S1's $50 aggregate inside loss. S1's total attribute reduction amount is thus $140, the sum of the $90 tierdown attribute reduction amount and the $50 direct attribute reduction amount.

(B) *Allocation, apportionment, and application of S1's attribute reduction amount.* Under paragraphs (d)(4) and (d)(5)(ii) of this section, S1's $140 attribute reduction amount is allocated proportionately (by basis) among the S2 stock, the S3 stock, and the S4 stock. However, under paragraph (d)(5)(ii) of this section, for purposes of allocating S1's $140 attribute reduction amount among S1's lower-tier subsidiary stock, S1's $75 deemed basis in the S2 stock is reduced by the $50 value of the transferred S2 share. Accordingly, for this purpose, S1's deemed basis in the S2 stock is reduced by $50, from $75 to $25. Thus, $17.50 of S1's attribute reduction amount ($25/$200 x $140) is allocated to the S2 stock, $52.50 of S1's attribute reduction amount ($75/$200 x $140) is allocated to the S3 stock, and $70 of S1's attribute reduction amount ($100/$200 × $140) is allocated to the S4 stock. Under paragraph (d)(5)(iii)(A) of this section, none of the $17.50 of S1's attribute reduction amount allocated to S2 stock is apportioned to the S2 share because gain was recognized on the transfer of the S2 share. Because neither the S3 share nor the S4 share is transferred within the meaning of paragraph (f)(10) of this section, the $52.50 of S1's attribute reduction amount allocated to the S3 stock, and the $70 of S1's attribute reduction amount allocated to the S4 stock, is apportioned to and applied fully to reduce the basis of such shares. Thus, S1's basis in the S3 share is reduced by $52.50, from $60 to $7.50, and S1's basis in the S4 stock is reduced by $70, from $100 to $30. (Note: The conforming limitation in

paragraph (d)(5)(v)(B) of this section limits the application of the $90 tier down attribute reduction amount to $80, the amount by which the portion (10/10) S1's $250 net inside attribute amount attributable to S1 shares held by members exceeds $170 (the sum of the $50 direct attribute reduction amount, the $20 value of the S1 share 1 transferred in a recognition transfer, the $20 basis (after reduction) in the S1 share 2 transferred other than in a recognition transfer, and the $80 aggregate basis (after reduction) in the nontransferred S1 shares held by members). However, the conforming limitation does not limit the application of S1's $90 tier-down attribute reduction amount because none of the $17.50 of S1's total attribute reduction amount allocated to the S2 share was applied to reduce the basis of the share. Accordingly, only $78.75 ($90 - ($17.50 × ($90/$140)) of the $90 tier-down attribute reduction was applied to reduce S1's attributes.) Under paragraph (d)(5)(v)(A) of this section, the attribute reduction amount allocated to the S2 stock, the S3 stock, and the S4 stock becomes an attribute reduction amount of S2, S3, and S4, respectively (even though the amount allocated to S2 stock was not apportioned to or applied to reduce the basis of the S2 share).

(vi) *Attribute reduction under this paragraph (d) in lowest tier.* Although the sale of the S2 share is a transfer of subsidiary stock at the next lower tier, the S2 share is not a loss share. Thus, this paragraph (d) does not apply with respect to that transfer. However, S2, S3, and S4 have attribute reduction amounts that tiered down from S1 and that are applied to reduce attributes under this paragraph (d).

(A) *Tier down of S1's attribute reduction amount to S2.* Under the general rules of this paragraph (d), S2's $17.50 tier-down attribute reduction amount is allocated and applied to reduce S2's basis in Asset 2 from $75 to $57.50.

(B) *Tier down of S1's attribute reduction amount to S3.* Under the general rules of this paragraph (d), S3's $52.50 tier-down attribute reduction amount is allocated and applied to reduce S3's basis in Asset 3 from $75 to $22.50.

(C) *Tier down of S1's attribute reduction amount to S4, application of conforming limitation.* Under the general rules of this paragraph (d), S4's $70 tier-down attribute reduction amount is allocated to, and would be applied to reduce, S4's basis in Asset 4. However, under paragraph (d)(5)(v)(B) of this section, the reduction is limited to the excess of S4's $80 net inside attribute amount over the $30 basis of the S4 share (after reduction under this paragraph (d)). As a result, only $50 (the excess of $80 over $30) of S4's $70 attribute reduction amount is applied to S4's basis in Asset 4, reducing it from $80 to $30. The $20 unapplied portion of S4's tier-down attribute reduction amount subject to the conforming limitation is disregarded and has no further effect.

(vii) *Application of basis restoration rule.* Under paragraph (d)(5)(vi)(A) of this section, after this paragraph (d) has been applied with respect to all transfers of subsidiary stock, any reduction made to the basis of a share of lower-tier subsidiary stock under paragraph (d)(5)(iii) of this section is reversed to the extent necessary to conform the basis of that share to the share's allocable portion of the subsidiary's net inside attribute amount. Restoration adjustments are first made at the lowest tier and then at each next higher tier successively.

(A) *Basis restoration at lowest tier.* The basis of the S2 share was not reduced under paragraph (d)(5)(iii) of this section and so there is no restoration of any basis in the S2 share. S3's $22.50 net inside attribute amount (after reduction under this paragraph (d)) exceeds S1's $7.50 basis in the S3 share (after reduction under this paragraph (d)) by $15. To conform S1's basis in the S3 share to S3's net inside attribute amount, the $52.50 reduction to the basis of the S3 share under paragraph (d)(5)(iii) of this section is reversed by $15 (restoring S1's basis in the S3 share to $22.50). The restoration of S1's basis in the S3 share does not tier up to affect the basis in stock of any other subsidiary. S1's $30 basis in the S4 share (after reduction under this paragraph (d)) is already conformed with S4's $30 net inside attribute amount (after reduction under this par-

agraph (d)) and so there is no restoration of any basis in the S4 share.

(B) *Basis restoration at next higher tier.* Each share of S1 stock has an allocable portion of S1's net inside attribute amount (after reduction) equal to $10.25 (1/10 x $102.50, the sum of S1's $0 basis in the S2 stock, adjusted for the $50 gain recognized with respect to the share, S1's $22.50 basis in the S3 stock (after restoration), and S1's $30 basis in the S4 stock). Neither S's basis in S1 share 1 nor S's basis in S1 share 2 was reduced under paragraph (d)(5)(iii) of this section. Accordingly, there is no restoration of any basis in either S1 share 1 or share 2. However, S's basis in each of S1 share 3 through share 10 was reduced under paragraph (d)(5)(iii) of this section by $10, from $20 to $10. Accordingly, the $10 reduction to the basis of each of those shares is reversed to the extent of $.25, to restore the basis of each such share to $10.25 (its allocable portion of S1's net inside attribute amount).

(viii) *Results.* After the application of this section, P recognizes a loss of $360 on the sale of the S share, S recognizes a loss of $150 on the sale of S1 share 1, and S1 recognizes a $50 gain on the sale of the S2 share. Immediately after the transaction, the entities each directly own the following:

Entity	Asset	Basis	Value
P1	S share	$240	$240
P	Proceeds of the sale of S share	$240	$240
S	Proceeds of sale of S1 share 1	$20	$20
	Partnership interest received for S1 share 2	$20	$20
	S1 share 3 through share 10	$82 ($10.25 per share)	
	Asset 1	$80	
S1	Proceeds of sale of S2 share	$50	$50
	The S3 share	$22.50	
	The S4 share	$30	
S2	Asset 2	$57.50	
S3	Asset 3	$22.50	
S4	Asset 4	$30	
X	S1 share 1	$20	$20
Partnership	S1 share 2	$20	$20
Y	The S2 share	$50	$50

(e) *Operating rules.*—(1) *Predecessors, successors.*—This section applies to predecessor or successor persons, groups, and assets to the extent necessary to effectuate the purposes of this section.

(2) *Adjustments for prior transactions that altered stock basis or other attributes.*—In certain situations, M's basis in S stock or S's attributes may be adjusted in a manner that alters the relationship between stock basis and inside attributes and prevents that relationship from identifying

the extent to which stock basis reflects unrecognized gain and duplicated loss. The provisions of this paragraph (e)(2) modify the computations in paragraphs (c) and (d) of this section to adjust for the effects of such adjustments.

(i) *Prior reductions to S's basis in assets or other attributes pursuant to section 362(e)(2)(A).*—If M transferred loss property to S in an intercompany transaction subject to section 362(e)(2) (for example, if the transfer was prior to September 17, 2008, no election was made to apply

§ 1.1502-80(h), and, as a result, S's attributes were reduced under section 362(e)(2)), then the disconformity amount of the S shares received in the section 362(e)(2) transaction is reduced by the amount that the basis in such shares would have been reduced under section 362(e)(2)(C) had such an election been made. In addition, for purposes of determining the attribute reduction amount under paragraph (d) of this section resulting from the transfer of any S shares received (or deemed received) in such a transfer, and for purposes of applying paragraph (d)(5)(v)(B) of this section (conforming limitation) to S, the bases in such shares is treated as reduced by the amount the bases in such shares would have been reduced under section 362(e)(2)(C) had such an election been made.

(ii) *Prior reductions to the basis of any share of S stock pursuant to an election under section 362(e)(2)(C).*—If M transferred loss property to S in an intercompany transaction subject to section 362(e)(2) and the basis of any share of S stock was reduced as the result of an election under section 362(e)(2)(C) (including in the hands of a predecessor, to the extent that the effect of the election remains reflected in the basis of the S stock), then, for purposes of computing either any S share's disconformity amount or S's aggregate inside loss, and for purposes of applying paragraph (d)(5)(vi)(A) of this section (stock basis restoration) to S, S's net inside attribute amount is treated as reduced by the amount that S's attributes would have been reduced under section 362(e)(2)(A) in the absence of an election under section 362(e)(2)(C). Notwithstanding the general rule of this paragraph (e)(2)(ii), no reduction will be required to the extent that the group can establish that the net loss in the S shares transferred by M is no longer reflected in S's net inside attributes.

(iii) *Other adjustments.*—Appropriate adjustments will be made in any other case in which an adjustment to S's net inside attributes or to M's basis in a share of S stock alters the relationship between such amounts, and the adjustment does not relate to the extent to which loss reflected in M's basis in S stock is noneconomic or duplicated within the meaning of this section.

(3) *Special rules for subsidiary stock transferred in an intercompany transaction.*—(i) *In general.*—This section applies with respect to M's transfer of a share of S stock to another member in an intercompany transaction in which M's intercompany item is deferred under § 1.1502-13 (and to any subsequent transfer of that share by a member) as of the time M's intercompany item is taken into account under § 1.1502-13. In determining the application of this section, all transferor-members are treated as divisions of a single corporation. Appropriate adjustments will be made to the intercompany item(s), any member's

basis in an S share, to S's attributes, or any combination thereof, to further the purposes of this section and § 1.1502-13.

(ii) *Certain prior intercompany transactions.*—If M transferred a share of S stock to another member before September 17, 2008 and M's intercompany item related to the transfer is taken into account on or after September 17, 2008, P may elect to apply this paragraph (e)(3) to the transfer. The election is made in the manner provided in paragraph (e)(5) of this section.

(iii) *Examples.*—The application of this paragraph (e)(3) is illustrated by the following examples:

Example 1. Intercompany sale with duplicated loss. (i) *Buying member later sells at gain.* (A) *Facts.* M owns the sole outstanding share of stock of S with a basis of $100. S has one asset with a basis of $100. M sells the S share to M1 for $70, recognizing a loss of $30. While owned by M1, S recognizes $10 of depreciation deductions that are absorbed by the group. S's basis in the asset is reduced by $10 (from $100 to $90), and M1's basis in the S stock is reduced under § 1.1502-32 by $10 (from $70 to $60). Later, M1 sells the S share to X, an unrelated person, for $80.

(B) *Analysis.* M's sale of its S share to M1 is a transfer of the share, but this section applies as of the time M's intercompany item is taken into account under § 1.1502-13, as if M and M1 were divisions of a single corporation. If M and M1 were divisions of a single corporation, the S share's basis would be $90 ($100 reduced by $10 for the depreciation deductions absorbed by the group) and the group would recognize a $10 loss on the sale of the share that is potentially subject to this section. Thus, the sale would be a transfer of a loss share (to the extent of $10) and would be subject to this section (to the extent of that $10). Although the transfer would be subject to this section, there would be no adjustment under paragraph (b) of this section (S has only one share outstanding and so there is no disparity in bases of common shares and no unrecognized gain or loss with respect to preferred) or under paragraph (c) of this section (S has no net positive adjustment). Thus, after the application of paragraph (c) of this section, the share would still be a loss share and would therefore be subject to paragraph (d) of this section. Under paragraph (d) of this section, S would be subject to $10 of attribute reduction (the lesser of the $10 net stock loss and S's $10 aggregate inside loss), allocable to the basis in S's asset. Accordingly, S's basis in its asset is reduced by $10, from $90 to $80, M takes its $30 intercompany stock loss into account, and M1 recognizes a $20 stock gain.

(ii) *Selling member deconsolidates.* Assume the same facts as in paragraph (i)(A) of this *Example 1,* except that M1 does not sell the S share and M ceases to be a member of the group when the value of the S share is $80. Under § 1.1502-13, M's deconsolidation causes M's intercompany loss to be taken into account and this section applies at that time. At the time that M deconsolidates, if M and M1 were divisions of a single corporation, the basis in the S share would be $90 ($100 reduced by $10 for the depreciation deductions absorbed by the group) and the group would recognize a $10 loss on the sale of the share that is potentially subject to this section. Such a sale would be a transfer of a loss share (to the extent of $10) and would be subject to this section (to the extent of that $10). The analysis is then the same as in paragraph (i)(B) of this *Example 1*. As a result, S's basis in its asset is reduced from $90 to $80, M takes its $30 intercompany stock loss into account, and M1 holds the S stock with a basis of $60 (and an unrecognized gain of $20).

(iii) *M1 sells the S share at a loss.* Assume the same facts as in paragraph (i)(A) of this *Example 1*, except that S declines in value and M1 sells the S share to X for $50, realizing a $10 loss. In this case, if M and M1 were divisions of a single corporation, the share's basis would be $90 ($100 reduced by $10 for the depreciation deductions absorbed by the group) and the group would recognize a $40 loss on the sale of the share that is potentially subject to this section. Thus, the sale would be a transfer of a loss share (to the extent of $40) and would be subject to this section (to the extent of that $40). Although the transfer would be subject to this section, for the reasons set forth in paragraph (i)(B) of this *Example 1*, there would be no adjustment under either paragraph (b) or paragraph (c) of this section. Thus, after the application of paragraph (c), the share would still be a loss share and would therefore be subject to paragraph (d) of this section. Under paragraph (d) of this section, S would be subject to $40 of attribute reduction (the lesser of the $40 net stock loss and S's $40 aggregate inside loss), allocable to the basis in S's asset. Accordingly, S's basis in its asset is reduced by $40, from $90 to $50, M takes its $30 intercompany stock loss into account, and M1 recognizes a $10 stock loss.

Example 2. Intercompany sale of built-in gain stock. (i) *Facts.* M owns the sole outstanding share of stock of S with a basis of $100. S's sole asset has a basis of $0. S sells its asset for $100 and recognizes a $100 gain that increases M's basis in its S share under § 1.1502-32 to $200. M sells the S share to M1 for $100 and recognizes a $100 intercompany loss. Later, M1 sells the S share to X, an unrelated person, for $120.

(ii) *Analysis.* M's sale of the S share to M1 is a transfer of the share, but this section applies as of the time M's intercompany item is taken into account under § 1.1502-13, as if M and M1 were divisions of a single corporation. If M and M1 were divisions of a single corporation, the S share's basis would be $200 ($100 increased by $100 for the gain recognized on the sale of the asset) and the group would recognize an $80 loss on the sale of the share that is potentially subject

to this section. Thus, the sale would be a transfer of a loss share (to the extent of $80) and would be subject to this section (to the extent of that $80). Although the transfer would be subject to this section, there would be no adjustment under paragraph (b) of this section (S has only one share outstanding and so there is no disparity in bases of common shares and no unrecognized gain or loss with respect to preferred). Thus, after the application of paragraph (b), the share would still be a loss share and would therefore be subject to paragraph (c) of this section. Under paragraph (c) of this section, the basis in the S share would be reduced, but not below its $120 value, by the lesser of the $100 disconformity amount and the $100 net positive adjustment that was applied to the share when held by M. Accordingly, the basis in the S share would be reduced by $80, to $120. Because the S share would not be a loss share after the application of paragraph (c) of this section, paragraph (d) of this section would not apply to the transfer. As a result, because the positive adjustment was applied to the share when held by M, M's intercompany item is adjusted to reflect what it would have been had M's basis in its S share been reduced by $80 immediately before its sale to M1. Thus, M's intercompany loss is reduced to $20 and M takes this loss into account, and M1 recognizes a gain of $20.

Example 3. Intercompany sale creates built-in gain stock. (i) *Facts.* M owns the sole outstanding share of stock of S with a basis of $0. S's sole asset has a basis of $0. M sells the S share to M1 for $100 and recognizes a $100 intercompany gain. While owned by M1, S sells its asset for $100, recognizing a $100 gain that increases M1's basis in the S share under § 1.1502-32 to $200. Later, M1 sells the S share to X for $120.

(ii) *Analysis.* M's sale of its S share to M1 is a transfer of the share, but this section applies as of the time M's intercompany item is taken into account under § 1.1502-13, as if M and M1 were divisions of a single corporation. If M and M1 were divisions of a single corporation, the S share's basis would be $100 ($0 increased by $100 for the gain recognized on the sale of the asset) and the group would recognize a $20 gain on the sale of the share. Thus, the sale would not be a transfer of a loss share and this section would not apply to the transfer. Accordingly, under this paragraph (e)(3), no portion of M1's $80 loss is subject to this section. M takes its $100 intercompany stock gain into account, and M1 recognizes an $80 loss.

Example 4. Disparate bases in members' shares. (i) *Facts.* M holds Share A, one of the two outstanding shares of S stock, with a basis of $50 and M1 holds Share B, the other outstanding share of S stock with a basis of $0. S has $50 cash and an asset with a basis of $0. S sells the asset for $50, recognizing a $50 gain that increases M's basis in its S share under § 1.1502-32 by $25 (from $50 to $75) and increases M1's basis under

§ 1.1502-32 by $25 (from $0 to $25). Later, M sells its Share A to M1 for $50 and recognizes a $25 intercompany loss. Later, M1 sells both S shares to X for $100.

(ii) *Analysis.* M's sale of its Share A to M1 is a transfer of the share, but this section applies as of the time M's intercompany item is taken into account under § 1.1502-13, as if M and M1 were divisions of a single corporation. If M and M1 were divisions of a single corporation, the basis of Share A would be $75 ($50 increased by $25 for its share of the gain recognized on the sale of the asset), the basis of Share B would be $25, and the group would recognize a $25 loss on the sale of Share A that is potentially subject to this section and a $25 gain on the sale of Share B. Thus, the sale would be a transfer of a loss share (to the extent of $25) and would be subject to this section (to the extent of that $25). Although the transfer is subject to this section, there would be no adjustment under paragraph (b) of this section (all S shares held by members are transferred to a nonmember in one taxable transaction). Thus, after the application of paragraph (b), Share A would still be a loss share and therefore subject to paragraph (c) of this section. Under paragraph (c)(7) of this section, the basis of Share A would be treated as reduced by the gain recognized and taken into account with respect to the transfer of Share B in the same transaction, and so Share A would not be a loss share for purposes of paragraph (c) of this section. Although the share would be a loss share after the application of paragraph (c) of this section, no adjustment would be required under paragraph (d) of this section because there would be no net stock loss in the transaction. Because no adjustment would be made under this section if M and M1 were divisions of a single corporation, M takes its $25 intercompany stock loss into account and M1 recognizes a gain of $25. Alternatively, if the group elects to apply paragraph (b) of this section, M's intercompany item would be adjusted to reflect what it would have been had the $25 investment adjustment applied to Share A been reallocated to Share B, and M1's basis in Share B would be increased by that amount. If so, M's $25 intercompany loss would be reduced to zero, M1's basis in Share B would be increased from $25 to $50, and there would be no gain or loss recognized on either share.

Example 5. Subsidiary with built-in gain and built-in loss assets. (i) *Facts.* M owns the sole outstanding share of stock of S with a basis of $100. S has two assets, Asset 1 with a basis of $0 and Asset 2 with a basis of $80. M sells the S share to M1 for $90 and recognizes a $10 intercompany loss. While owned by M1, S sells Asset 1 for $60, recognizing a $60 gain that increases M1's basis in the S share under § 1.1502-32 to $150. Later, M1 sells the S share to X for $90.

(ii) *Analysis.* M's sale of the S share to M1 is a transfer of the share, but this section applies as of the time M's intercompany item is taken into account under § 1.1502-13, as if M and M1 were divisions of a single corporation. If M and M1 were divisions of a single corporation, the S share's basis would be $160 ($100 increased by $60 for the gain recognized on the sale of Asset 1) and the group would recognize a $70 loss on the sale of the share that is potentially subject to this section. Thus, the sale would be a transfer of a loss share (to the extent of $70) and would be subject to this section (to the extent of that $70). Although the transfer is subject to this section, there would be no adjustment under paragraph (b) of this section (S has only one share outstanding and so there is no disparity in bases of common shares and no unrecognized gain or loss with respect to preferred). Thus, after the application of paragraph (b), the share would still be a loss share and would therefore be subject to paragraph (c) of this section. Under paragraph (c) of this section, the basis in the S share would be reduced, but not below its $90 value, by the lesser of the $20 disconformity amount ($160 stock basis over $140 net inside attribute amount) and the $60 net positive adjustment that was applied to the share when held by M1. Accordingly, the basis in the S share would be reduced by $20, to $140. Because the S share would still be a loss share after the application of paragraph (c) of this section, paragraph (d) of this section would apply to the transfer. Under paragraph (d) of this section, S would have an attribute reduction amount of $50, the lesser of the $50 net stock loss ($140 basis over $90 value) and S's $50 aggregate inside loss (the excess of the sum of S's $80 basis in Asset 2 and S's $60 cash from the sale of Asset 1, over the $90 value of the S share). The adjustments required under this section are applied as follows: because the positive adjustment was applied to the share when held by M1, the $20 basis reduction required under paragraph (c) of this section is applied to M1's basis in its S share immediately before its sale to X, reducing it from $150 to $130. In addition, pursuant to paragraph (d) of this section, S's basis in Asset 2 is reduced by $50, from $80 to $30. M takes its $10 intercompany stock loss into account and M1 recognizes a loss of $40.

(iii) *Allocation of basis reduction.* Assume the same facts as in paragraph (i) of this *Example 5*, except that, while S is held by M, S earns $30 (consuming a portion of Asset 1) and, while S is held by M1, S earns $20 (consuming a portion of Asset 1) and sells Asset 1 for $10. Thus, M's basis in the S share immediately before the sale to M1 is $130, and M recognizes a $40 intercompany stock loss, and M1's basis in the S share immediately before the sale to X is $120. The analysis regarding the application of this section is the same as in paragraph (ii) of this *Example 5*. On a separate entity basis, M's basis in the S share

Reg. § 1.1502-36(e)(3)(iii)

would be subject to a $20 reduction under paragraph (c) of this section (at the time M transferred the S share the share had a $30 net positive adjustment and a $20 disconformity amount), and M1's basis in the S share would not be subject to reduction under paragraph (c) of this section (at the time M1 transferred the S share the share had a $30 net positive adjustment and a $20 negative disconformity amount). Therefore, the $20 basis reduction required under paragraph (c) of this section is allocated entirely to M. Accordingly, M's intercompany item is adjusted to reflect what it would have been had the entire $20 basis reduction been applied to the S share while held by M, and M1's basis in the S share is not reduced. Thus, M's intercompany stock loss is reduced by $20 to $20 and M takes this loss into account, and M1 recognizes a $30 loss. S's basis in Asset 2 is reduced by $50, from $80 to $30.

(4) *Limited application to multiple-member section 332 liquidations.*—If more than one member owns shares of S stock, paragraphs (c) and (d) of this section do not apply to any transfer of S shares resulting from a liquidation of S to which section 332 applies.

(5) *Form and manner of election(s) under this section.*—The elections provided in this section are irrevocable and made in the form of a statement titled "Section 1.1502-36 Statement." The statement must be included on or with the group's timely filed return (original or amended, if filed by the due date for the return, including extensions) for the taxable year of the transfer of the subsidiary stock to which the election relates or, in the case of an intercompany transfer, the year in which the intercompany item from the transfer is taken into account. The statement must include—

(i) The name and employer identification number (E.I.N.) of each subsidiary with respect to which an election is being made;

(ii) If P is electing under paragraph (b)(1)(ii) of this section to redetermine basis with respect to the transfer of stock of one or more subsidiaries, a statement that members' bases in shares of [name of subsidiary or subsidiaries] stock are being redetermined notwithstanding that all members' shares of [name of subsidiary or subsidiaries] are being transferred to one or more nonmembers in one fully taxable transaction;

(iii) If P is electing under paragraph (d)(2)(ii) of this section (attribute reduction amount less than five percent of value) to apply the attribute reduction provisions, a statement that paragraph (d) of this section is being applied to the transfer of shares of stock of [names of all subsidiaries whose shares are transferred] notwithstanding that the aggregate attribute reduction amount in the transaction is less than five percent of the aggregate value of the stock of [names of all subsidiaries whose shares are

transferred] transferred by members in the transaction;

(iv) If P is electing under paragraph (d)(4)(ii)(A)(*1*) of this section to specify the allocation of the attribute reduction amount, a statement (for each subsidiary for which the election is being made) that the attribute reduction amount of [name of subsidiary] is being applied (or not applied) to reduce [identify the attributes in Category A, Category B, and Category C, and the amount of each, with respect to which the election is being made];

(v) If P is electing under paragraph (d)(5)(v)(B) of this section not to apply the conforming limitation on tier-down attribute reduction with respect to one or more subsidiaries, a statement that the conforming limitation in paragraph (d)(5)(v)(B) of this section is not being applied with respect to [name of subsidiary or subsidiaries];

(vi) If P is electing under paragraph (d)(5)(vi)(B) of this section not to restore lower-tier subsidiary stock basis with respect to one or more subsidiaries, a statement that members' bases in [name of subsidiary or subsidiaries] is not being restored under paragraph (d)(5)(vi)(A) of this section;

(vii) If P is electing under paragraph (d)(6) of this section to reattribute attributes, a statement (for each subsidiary for which the election is being made) that [identify the attributes in Category A, Category B, and Category C, and the amount of each or the amount in excess of an amount, with respect to which the election is being made] of [name of subsidiary] are being reattributed (or not) to P;

(viii) If P is electing under paragraph (d)(6) of this section to reduce stock basis, a statement (for each subsidiary for which the election is being made) that members' bases in shares of stock of [name of subsidiary] are being reduced by [specify amount or the amount in excess of an amount];

(ix) If P is electing under paragraph (e)(3)(ii) of this section to apply paragraph (e)(3) of this section to an intercompany transfer that occurred before September 17, 2008, a statement that paragraph (e)(3) of this section is being elected to apply to the transfer of stock of [name of subsidiary] by [name of transferor subsidiary] to [name of transferee subsidiary] on [date of transfer]; and

(x) If P is electing under § 1.1502-96(d)(5) to reattribute to itself all or any part of a section 382 limitation, a statement that P is electing to reattribute a section 382 limitation with respect to losses of [name of subsidiary or, if two or more subsidiaries are members of a loss subgroup, the name of each subsidiary in the loss subgroup]. A separate statement is made for each subsidiary or loss subgroup for which an election is being made. Each statement must include—

(A) The date of the ownership change giving rise to the separate section 382 limitation or subgroup section 382 limitation that is being apportioned;

(B) The amount of the separate (or subgroup) section 382 limitation for the taxable year in which the reattribution occurs (determined without reference to any apportionment under this section or §1.1502-95(c)); and

(C) The amount of each net operating loss carryover, capital loss carryover, or deferred deduction, and the year in which it arose, of the subsidiary (or subsidiaries) that is subject to the separate section 382 limitation or subgroup section 382 limitation that is being apportioned to the common parent, and the amount of the value element and adjustment element of that limitation that is apportioned to the common parent.

(f) *Definitions.*—In addition to the definitions in other paragraphs of this section and in other provisions of the regulations under section 1502, the following definitions apply for purposes of this section.

(1) *Allocable portion* has the same meaning as in §1.1502-32(b)(4)(iii)(B). Thus, for example, within a class of stock, each share has the same allocable portion of the net inside attribute amount and, if there is more than one class of stock, the net inside attribute amount is allocated to each class by taking into account the terms of each class and all other facts and circumstances relating to the overall economic arrangement.

(2) *Deferred deduction* means any deduction for expenses or loss that would be taken into account under general tax accounting principles as of the time of the transfer of the share, but that is nevertheless not taken into account immediately after the transfer by reason of the application of a deferral provision. Such provisions include, for example, sections 267(f) and 469, and §1.1502-13. "Deferred deduction" also includes S's portion of such consolidated tax attributes, for example consolidated excess charitable contributions that would be apportioned to S under the principles of §1.1502-79(e) if S had a separate return year. Additionally, it includes amounts equivalent to deductions, such as negative adjustments under section 475 (mark to market accounting method for dealers in securities) and section 481 (adjustments required by changes in method of accounting).

(3) *Distribution* has the same meaning as in §1.1502-32(b)(3)(v).

(4) *Higher-tier, lower-tier.*—A subsidiary (S1) (and its shares of stock) is "highertier" with respect to another subsidiary (S2) (and its shares of stock) if investment adjustments made to the bases of shares of S2 stock under §1.1502-32 affect the investment adjustments made to the bases of shares of S1 stock. A subsidiary (S1) (and its shares of stock) is "lower-tier" with respect to another subsidiary (S) (and its shares of

stock) if investment adjustments made to the bases of shares of S1 stock affect the investment adjustments made to the bases of shares of S stock. The term *lowest-tier subsidiary* generally refers to a subsidiary that owns no stock of another subsidiary. The term *highest-tier subsidiary* generally refers to a subsidiary the stock of which is not lower tier to any shares transferred in the transaction.

(5) *Liability* means a liability that has been incurred within the meaning of section 461(h), except to the extent otherwise provided in paragraph (d)(4)(ii)(C)(*1*) of this section.

(6) *Loss carryover* means any net operating or capital loss carryover that is attributable to S, including any losses that would be apportioned to S under the principles of §1.1502-21(b)(2) if S had a separate return year. However, solely for purposes of applying paragraph (d) of this section, loss carryovers do not include the amount of any losses waived under §1.1502-32(b)(4).

(7) *Loss share, gain share.*—A *loss share* is a share of stock with a basis that exceeds its value. A *gain share* is a share of stock with a value that exceeds its basis.

(8) *Preferred stock, common stock.*—Preferred *stock* and *common stock* have the same meanings as in §1.1502-32(d)(2) and (3), respectively.

(9) *Transaction* includes all the steps taken pursuant to the same plan or arrangement.

(10) *Transfer.*—(i) *Definition.*—Except as provided in paragraph (f)(10)(ii) of this section, for purposes of this section, M transfers a share of S stock on the earliest of—

(A) The date that M ceases to own the share as a result of a transaction in which, but for the application of this section (and notwithstanding the deferral of any amount recognized on the transfer, other than by reason of §1.1502-13), M would recognize income, gain, loss or deduction with respect to the share (see paragraph (e)(3) of this section in the case of a transfer in an intercompany transaction);

(B) The date that M and S cease to be members of the same group;

(C) The date that a nonmember acquires the share from M; and

(D) The last day of the taxable year during which the share becomes worthless under section 165 (taking into account the provisions of §1.1502-80(c)) if the share is treated as a capital asset, or the date the share becomes worthless (taking into account the provisions of §1.1502-80(c)) if the share is not treated as a capital asset.

(ii) *Excluded transactions.*—Notwithstanding paragraph (f)(10)(i) of this section, M does not transfer a share of S stock if—

(A) M ceases to own the share as a result of a transaction to which section 381(a) applies and in which either a member acquires

Reg. §1.1502-36(f)(10)(ii)(A)

assets from S or S acquires assets from M, provided that—

(1) M recognizes no income, gain, loss, or deduction with respect to the share, and

(2) If the transaction is a liquidation to which section 332 applies, M is the only member that owns shares of S stock (if another member owns shares of S stock, see paragraph (e)(4) of this section for a limitation on the application of this section); or

(B) M ceases to own the share as a result of a distribution of the share to a nonmember in a transaction to which section 355 applies, and in which the share is treated as qualified property for purposes of section 355(c) or section 361(c).

(11) *Value* means the amount realized, if any, or otherwise the fair market value.

(g) *Anti-abuse rule.*—(1) *General rule.*—If a taxpayer acts with a view to avoid the purposes of this section or to apply the rules of this section to avoid the purposes of any other rule of law, appropriate adjustments will be made to carry out the purposes of this section or such other rule of law.

(2) *Examples.*—The following examples illustrate the principles of the anti-abuse rule in this paragraph (g). No implication is intended regarding the potential applicability of any other anti-abuse rules:

Example 1. Loss Trafficking. (i) *Facts.* M purchases the sole outstanding share of S stock for $100. At that time, S owns Asset 1 with a basis of $0. S sells Asset 1 for $100. Later, S purchases the sole outstanding share of X stock, a corporation with losses, with a view to liquidating X in a transaction to which section 332 applies in order to reduce S's disconformity amount. S purchases the X share for $1, and X has a $100 NOL and an asset with a basis of $1. Subsequently, M sells its S share for $100. After taking into account the effects of all applicable rules of law, M's basis in the S share is $200 (M's original $100 basis, increased under §1.1502-32 to reflect the $100 gain recognized on the sale of Asset 1). M's sale of the S share is a transfer of a loss share and therefore subject to this section.

(ii) *Analysis.* Although M's transfer of the S share is subject to this section, there is no adjustment under paragraph (b) of this section (S has only one share outstanding and so there is no disparity in bases of common shares and no shares of S preferred stock outstanding (and so there is no unrecognized gain or loss on S preferred stock)). See paragraph (b)(1)(ii)(A) of this section. Accordingly, after the application of paragraph (b) of this section, M's sale of the S share is still a transfer of a loss share and therefore subject to paragraph (c) of this section. Under paragraph (c) of this section, M's $200 basis in the S share is reduced, but not below the share's $100 value, by the lesser of the share's net posi-

tive adjustment and disconformity amount. The share's net positive adjustment is $100, the positive adjustment attributable to the gain recognized on the sale of Asset 1. The share's disconformity amount is $0, the excess of M's $200 basis in the S share over S's $200 net inside attribute amount. Thus, the reduction to basis under paragraph (c) of this section would be $0. However, because S purchased the X stock and liquidated X with a view to avoiding the purposes of this section (by using X's attributes to minimize the disconformity amount of the S share), the attributes acquired from X are disregarded for purposes of applying this section. Accordingly, S's net inside attribute amount is limited to the $100 of attributes S would have had absent the purchase of the X stock, S's money ($100 from the sale of Asset 1). The loss share's disconformity amount is therefore the excess of $200 over $100, or $100. The lesser of the share's $100 net positive adjustment and $100 disconformity amount is $100. As a result, M's $200 basis in the S share is reduced by $100, to $100, and M recognizes no gain or loss on the sale of the S share.

Example 2. Use of a partnership to prevent current attribute reduction. (i) *Facts.* M owns all 5 outstanding shares of S common stock with a basis of $200 each. S owns Asset 1 with a basis of $1000. In year 1, with a view to preventing a current reduction in the basis of Asset 1, S contributes Asset 1 to a partnership in a transaction in which S recognizes no gain or loss. On December 31, year 2, M sells one S share for $20. After taking into account the effects of all applicable rules of law, M's basis in each S share is $200. M's sale of the S share is a transfer of a loss share and therefore subject to this section.

(ii) *Analysis.* Although M's transfer of the S share is subject to this section, there is no basis redetermination under paragraph (b) of this section because there is no disparity among M's bases in its shares of S common stock and there are no shares of S preferred stock outstanding (and so there is no unrecognized gain or loss on S preferred stock). See paragraph (b)(1)(ii)(A) of this section. Accordingly, after the application of paragraph (b) of this section, M's sale of the S share is still a transfer of a loss share and therefore subject to paragraph (c) of this section. However, no adjustment is required under paragraph (c) of this section because both the disconformity amount and the net positive adjustment are $0. See paragraph (c)(3) of this section. Under paragraph (d) of this section, S's attribute reduction amount is $180 (the lesser of the $180 net stock loss and S's $900 aggregate inside loss ($1000 of attributes over $100 value of all of the S shares)). Absent the application of this paragraph (g), the $180 attribute reduction amount would be applied to reduce S's basis in the partnership interest. However, because S acted with a view to avoiding a current reduction in the basis of Asset 1 under paragraph (d) of this section, this section is applied by treating S as if it held Asset 1 at the time of the stock sale. The basis of Asset 1 is reduced by $180, to $820, effective immediately before the transfer to the partnership and, as a result, S's basis in its partnership interest is $820.

Example 3. Creation of an intercompany receivable to mitigate attribute reduction. (i) *Facts.* M owns all five outstanding shares of S common stock each with equal basis that exceeds value. S holds cash and Asset 1 with a basis that exceeds value. In year 1, with a view to mitigating a reduction in the basis of Asset 1, S lends the cash to M1. Asset 1 and the intercompany note received from M1 are assets of the same class under § 1.338-6(b)(2). On December 31, year 2, M sells one of its S shares and, without regard to this section, recognizes a loss. M's sale of the S share is a transfer of a loss share and therefore subject to this section.

(ii) *Analysis.* Although M's transfer of the S share is subject to this section, no adjustment is required under paragraph (b) of this section because there is no disparity among M's bases in shares of S common stock and there are no shares of S preferred stock outstanding (and so there is no unrecognized gain or loss on S preferred stock). See paragraph (b)(1)(ii)(A) of this section. Accordingly, after the application of paragraph (b) of this section, M's sale of the S shares is still a transfer of a loss share and therefore subject to paragraph (c) of this section. However, there is no adjustment under paragraph (c) of this section because the net positive adjustment is $0. See paragraph (c)(3) of this section. Under paragraph (d) of this section, S's attribute reduction amount would be applied to reduce S's basis in Asset 1 and the intercompany receivable in proportion to basis. However, because S acted with a view to mitigating the reduction in the basis of Asset 1 under paragraph (d) of this section, this section is applied without regard to the intercompany receivable. Accordingly, S's basis in Asset 1 is reduced by the full attribute reduction amount.

Example 4. Use of a partnership to reduce net stock loss. (i) *Facts.* M owns all ten outstanding shares of S common stock, one share (Share 1) has a basis of $0, and one share (Share 2) has a basis of $160. S has an aggregate inside loss of $80. In one transaction and with a view to mitigating a reduction in S's attributes, M contributes Share 1 to a partnership, recognizing no gain or loss, and sells Share 2 for $80. M's contribution of Share 1 to the partnership is a transfer, but the share is not a loss share and so the transfer is not subject to this section. M's sale of Share 2 is a transfer of a loss share and is therefore subject to this section.

(ii) *Analysis.* Although M's transfer of Share 2 is subject to this section, there is no adjustment under paragraph (b) of this section because there are no investment adjustments that have been applied to the shares. Accordingly, after the ap-

plication of paragraph (b) of this section, M's sale of Share 2 is still a transfer of a loss share and therefore subject to paragraph (c) of this section. There is no adjustment under paragraph (c) of this section because the net positive adjustment is $0. See paragraph (c)(3) of this section. Accordingly, after the application of paragraph (c) of this section, M's sale of Share 2 is still a transfer of loss shares and therefore subject to paragraph (d) of this section. Under paragraph (d) of this section, the net stock loss would be determined to be $0, the excess of the $160 aggregate basis in all of the transferred shares over the $160 aggregate value of those shares. S's attribute reduction amount would be determined to be $0, the lesser of the $0 net stock loss and S's $80 aggregate inside loss. Thus, there would be no reduction of attributes under this paragraph (d) of this section. However, because M acted with a view to reducing the attribute reduction amount by transferring a gain share to a partnership while avoiding the recognition of the gain on the share, this section is applied without regard to the transfer of the gain share. Accordingly, the net stock loss is determined to be $80, and the attribute reduction amount is determined to be $80.

Example 5. Stuffing gain asset. (i) *Facts.* M owns the sole outstanding share of S stock (Share 1) with a basis of $100. S owns Asset 1 with a basis of $100 and a value of $20. With a view to avoid the purposes of this section, M transfers Asset 2 with a basis of $0 and a value of $80 to S in exchange for four additional shares of S stock (Share 2 through Share 5) in a transaction to which section 351 applies. M later sells Share 1 to X for $20. M's sale of Share 1 is a transfer of a loss share and therefore subject to this section.

(ii) *Analysis.* Although M's transfer of the Share 1 is subject to this section, there is no adjustment under paragraph (b) of this section because no investment adjustments have been applied to the basis of any S shares. Thus, after the application of paragraph (b) of this section, M's sale of the S share is still a transfer of a loss share and therefore subject to paragraph (c) of this section. There is no adjustment under paragraph (c) of this section because the net positive adjustment is $0. Accordingly, after the application of paragraph (c) of this section, M's sale of the S share is still a transfer of a loss share and therefore subject to paragraph (d) of this section. Under paragraph (d) of this section, S's attribute reduction amount would be $0, the lesser of the $80 net stock loss and S's $0 aggregate inside loss ($100 of attributes does not exceed the $100 value of all of the S shares). However, because M transferred Asset 2 to S with a view to avoid the purposes of this section, the application of this section to M's transfer of Share 1 is made without regard to the transfer of Asset 2. Accordingly, under paragraph (d) of this section, S's attribute reduction amount is $80, the lesser of the $80 net stock loss and S's $80 aggregate inside loss (computed without regard to Asset 2). S's basis in Asset 1 is therefore reduced by $80, from $100 to $20, under paragraph (d) of this section.

(iii) *Transfer of all S shares.* Assume the same facts as in paragraph (i) of this *Example 5*, except that M sells all five S shares to X, recognizing both the gain and the loss on the S shares. The transfer of Share 1 is still a transfer of a loss share and therefore subject to this section. However, because all the shares are transferred, the group's income is clearly reflected. Therefore, the purposes of this section are not avoided and this section applies without modification. S's attribute reduction amount is $0, the lesser of the $0 net stock loss and S's $0 aggregate inside loss.

(h) *Effective/applicability date.*—This section applies to transfers of shares of subsidiary stock on or after September 17, 2008 unless the transfer was made pursuant to a binding agreement that was in effect prior to September 17, 2008 and at all times thereafter. For transfers of shares of subsidiary stock that are not subject to this section, see §§ 1.337(d)-2 and 1.1502-35. [Reg. § 1.1502-36.]

□ [*T.D. 9424, 9-9-2008 (corrected 10-17-2008).*]

[Reg. § 1.1502-41A]

§ 1.1502-41A. Determination of consolidated net long-term capital gain and consolidated net short-term capital loss generally applicable for consolidated return years beginning before January 1, 1997.—(a) *Consolidated net long-term capital gain.*—The consolidated net long-term capital gain shall be determined by taking into account (1) those gains and losses to which § 1.1502-22A(a) applies which are treated as long term under section 1222, and (2) the consolidated section 1231 net gain (computed in accordance with § 1.1502-23A).

(b) *Consolidated net short term capital loss.*—The consolidated net short term capital loss shall be determined by taking into account (1) those gains and losses to which § 1.1502-22A(a) applies which are treated as short term under section 1222, and (2) the consolidated net capital loss carryovers and carrybacks to the taxable year (as determined under § 1.1502-22A(b)).

(c) *Effective date.*—This section applies to any consolidated return years to which § 1.1502-21(h) or 1.1502-21T(g) in effect prior to June 25, 1999, as contained in 26 CFR part 1 revised April 1, 1999, as applicable does not apply. See § 1.1502-21(h) or 1.1502-21T(g) in effect prior to June 25, 1999, as contained in 26 CFR part 1 revised April 1, 1999, as applicable for effective dates of these sections. [Reg. § 1.1502-41A.]

□ [*T.D. 6984, 9-7-66. Amended by T.D. 7637, 8-6-79; T.D. 8677, 6-26-96 and T.D. 8823, 6-25-99.*]

[Reg. § 1.1502-42]

§ 1.1502-42. Mutual savings banks, etc.— (a) *In general.*—This section applies to mutual savings banks and other institutions described in section 593(a).

(b) *Total deposits.*—In computing for purposes of section 593(b)(1)(B)(ii) total deposits or withdrawable accounts at the close of the taxable year, the total deposits or withdrawable accounts of other members shall be excluded.

(c) *Taxable income; taxable years for which the due date (without extensions) for filing returns is before March 15, 1983.*—For taxable years for which the due date (without extensions) for filing returns is before March 15, 1983, a member's taxable income for purposes of section 593(b)(2) is determined under § 1.1502-27(b) (computed without regard to any deduction under section 593(b)(2)). In addition, for taxable years beginning after July 11, 1969, taxable income as computed under the preceding sentence is subject to the adjustments provided in section 593(b)(2)(E). See § 1.593-6A(b)(5).

(d) *Taxable income; taxable years for which the due date (without extensions) for filing returns is after March 14, 1983.*—(1) *In general.*—For a taxable year for which the due date (without extensions) for filing returns is after March 14, 1983, a thrift's taxable income for purposes of section 593(b)(2) is its tentative taxable income (as defined in paragraph (e)(1) of this section).

(2) *Definitions.*—For purposes of this section—

(i) A "thrift" is a member described in section 593(a).

(ii) A "nonthrift" is a member that is not a thrift.

(e) *Tentative taxable income (or loss).*— (1) *Thrift.*—For purposes of this section, a thrift's tentative taxable income (or loss) is its separate taxable income (determined under § 1.1502-12 without paragraph (q) thereof and without any deduction under section 593(b)), subject to the following adjustments in the following order:

(i) the adjustments described in paragraph (e)(3) of this section;

(ii) the adjustments described in section 593(b)(2)(E) for those thrifts with separate taxable income greater than zero (determined after the adjustments under paragraph (e)(3) of this section); and

(iii) the adjustments described in paragraph (f) of this section.

(2) *Nonthrift.*—For purposes of this section, a nonthrift's tentative taxable income (or loss) is its separate taxable income (determined under § 1.1502-12), adjusted for the portion of the consolidated net operating loss deduction attributable to the member, the portion of the

consolidated net capital loss carryover or carryback attributable to the member, and further adjusted as described in paragraph (e)(3) of this section.

(3) *Adjustments for all members.*—For each member, the following adjustments taken into account in the computation of consolidated taxable income are included in determining its tentative taxable income (or loss) in order to adjust separate taxable income of the member to take into account certain consolidated items:

(i) The portions of the consolidated charitable contributions deduction and the consolidated dividends received deduction attributable to the member.

(ii) The member's capital gain net income, determined without any net capital loss carryover or carryback attributable to the member.

(iii) The member's net capital loss and section 1231 net loss, reduced by the portion of the consolidated net capital loss attributable to the member.

(f) *Adjustments for thrifts.*—(1) *Reductions.*—A thrift's separate taxable income (as adjusted under paragraph (e)(3) of this section) is reduced (but not below zero) by losses of thrifts and to the extent attributable to functionally related activities, losses of a nonthrift. Certain operating rules for determining the amount of the reductions are provided in paragraph (f)(4) of this section. The reductions are made in the following amounts in the following order:

(i) The thrift's allocable share (as determined under paragraph (h)(2) of this section) of another thrift's tentative taxable loss. That tentative taxable loss is determined by including a deduction under section 593(b) (other than paragraph (2) thereof) for the year in which the loss arises.

(ii) The thrift's allocable share (as determined under paragraph (h)(3) of this section) of the portion of the consolidated net operating loss deduction attributable to it or another thrift. That consolidated net operating loss deduction is determined by including a deduction under section 593(b) (other than paragraph (2) thereof) for the year in which the loss arose. The portion of a consolidated net operating loss deduction attributable to another thrift is computed by excluding losses arising in taxable years for which the due date (without extensions) for filing returns is before March 15, 1983.

(iii) The thrift's allocable share (as determined under paragraph (h)(4) of this section) of the loss attributable to functionally related activities of a nonthrift (as determined under paragraph (g) of this section). For a rule netting that share against certain income attributable to functionally related activities of that nonthrift, see paragraph (f)(4)(iv) of this section.

(iv) The thrift's allocable share (as determined under paragraph (h)(3) of this section) of the portion of the consolidated net operating loss deduction attributable to functionally related activities of a nonthrift (as determined under paragraph (h)(5) of this section). That consolidated net operating loss deduction is determined by excluding losses arising in taxable years for which the due date (without extensions) for filing returns is before March 15, 1983. For a rule netting that share against certain income attributable to functionally related activities of that nonthrift, see paragraph (f)(4)(iv) of this section.

(2) *Increases.*—(i) A thrift's separate taxable income (as adjusted under paragraphs (e)(3) and (f)(1) of this section) is increased in a subsequent consolidated return year to restore reductions made in a prior consolidated return year to a thrift's separate taxable income by reason of losses of a nonthrift. This increase is the amount of the thrift's allocable share (as determined under paragraph (h)(6) of this section) of the income attributable to functionally related activities of a nonthrift in a consolidated return year and is made only in that year. This increase is made only if both the thrift and the nonthrift were members of the group in the consolidated return years in which both the reduction and increase are made.

(ii) This subdivision (ii) limits the increases to a thrift's separate taxable income to assure that income of a particular nonthrift is used to restore reductions of a thrift only to the extent that such nonthrift's losses reduced the thrift's income. Therefore, as of the end of a consolidated return year, the cumulative increases to a thrift's separate taxable income (by reason of income attributable to functionally related activities of a nonthrift) may not exceed the cumulative reductions to the thrift's separate taxable income made (by reason of the nonthrift's functionally related activities) under paragraph (f)(1)(iii) and (iv) of this section in the current and all prior consolidated return years during which both the thrift institution and the nonthrift institution were members of the group.

(iii) For a netting rule, see paragraph (f)(4)(iv) of this section.

(3) *Special rule.*—(i) If a carryback to a thrift's separate taxable income diminishes the reduction to a thrift's separate taxable income for a prior consolidated return year otherwise required by paragraph (f)(1)(iii) or (iv) of this section, then any increase to a thrift's separate taxable income under paragraph (f)(2) of this section for an intervening consolidated return year must be recomputed to take into account the effect of such carryback. Thus, if a net operating loss attributable to a thrift is carried back and completely offsets the thrift's separate taxable income (before the reductions under paragraph (f)(1)(iii) or (iv) of this section), any increase to the thrift's separate taxable income under para-

graph (f)(2) of this section (attributable to a reduction in the year to which the loss is carried) for an intervening consolidated return year will be eliminated. The recomputation required by this subparagraph (3) must be reflected on an amended return for the intervening consolidated return year for which the increase was previously reported. See example (2) in paragraph (j) of this section.

(ii) If a deficiency for an intervening consolidated return year results from the application of paragraph (f)(3)(i) of this section with respect to an item to which section 6501(h) applies, the deficiency may be assessed at any time within the period described in section 6501(h).

(iii) For purposes of chapter 67 of the Code (relating to interest), the last date prescribed for payment of any tax owed as a result of the application of paragraph (f)(3)(i) of this section is deemed to be the last day of the taxable year for which the item carried back arose.

(4) *Operating rules.*—For purposes of paragraphs (d)-(j) of this section—

(i) The portion of a consolidated net operating loss deduction attributable to a member is determined as follows:

(A) First, determine under § 1.1502-21(b) (or § 1.1502-79A(a)(3), as appropriate) the portion of each consolidated net operating loss attributable to the member for the particular year in which the loss arose.

(B) Second, apply the anti-double-counting rule in paragraph (h)(3)(iii) of this section so as not to take the same loss into account twice.

(C) Finally, apply the loss absorption limit in paragraph (f)(4)(iii) of this section to the total amount of the consolidated net operating loss deduction from a particular loss year.

(ii) Capital loss carryovers and carrybacks shall be taken into account in a manner consistent with the principles of paragraphs (d)-(j) of this section.

(iii) This subdivision (iii) prescribes a loss absorption limit. The total amount of the consolidated net operating loss deduction from a given year (loss year) taken into account as reductions under paragraph (f)(1) of this section for another year (absorption year) shall not exceed the amount of the consolidated net operating loss deduction attributable to the loss year absorbed in computing consolidated taxable income for the absorption year. For this purpose, consolidated taxable income for the absorption year shall include a deduction under section 593(b) (other than paragraph (2) thereof) for each thrift member.

(iv) This subdivision (iv) prescribes a rule for netting in certain cases income attributable to functionally related activities of a nonthrift in a consolidated return year ("income year") against losses attributable to functionally related activities of that nonthrift which arise in a consolidated return year ("loss year"). That nonthrift's income is netted against the portion of that nonthrift's loss which would otherwise be applied in a consolidated return year ("reduction year") under paragraph (f)(1)(iii) or (iv) of this section to reduce a thrift's tentative taxable income, but—

(A) only if the income year is not later than the loss year and the reduction year, and

(B) only to the extent the income had not previously been taken into account under paragraph (f)(2) of this section or this subdivision (iv) as of the close of the later of the loss year and the reduction year.

(g) *Income (or loss) attributable to functionally related activities of a nonthrift.*—(1) *In general.*—For purposes of this section, the income (or loss) attributable to functionally related activities of a nonthrift is the income (or loss) of the nonthrift

(i) attributable to the provision of assets or the rendition of services to a thrift (such as the leasing of office space or providing computer or financial services), or

(ii) derived from the assets described in section 7701(a)(19)(C)(iii)-(x), but only if such assets comprise 5 percent or more of the gross assets of the nonthrift.

(2) *Amount of income (or loss).*—The amount of income (or loss) from such activities is the excess of (i) gross income from such activities over (ii) the deductions of the nonthrift allocable and apportionable to that gross income under the principles of § 1.861-8. The loss attributable to functionally related activities of a nonthrift is the excess (if any) of such deductions over such gross income. That loss, however, may not exceed the amount of the tentative taxable loss of that nonthrift (determined by excluding losses arising in taxable years for which the due date (without extensions) for filing returns is before March 15, 1983).

(h) *Allocation of income and losses.*—(1) *In general.*—Paragraph (h)(2)-(5) of this section provides rules for allocating different losses among thrifts that have tentative taxable income greater than zero. Generally, these allocations are made in the order listed in paragraph (f)(1) of this section and are based upon the relative tentative taxable income of the thrifts to which the particular loss is allocated. For purposes of each allocation under a subdivision of such paragraph (f)(1), the tentative taxable income of the thrifts used in making this allocation is reduced by the thrift's allocable share of losses allocated to the thrift under a prior subdivision of such paragraph (f)(1). Accordingly, for purposes of this paragraph (h), tentative taxable income is determined without regard to paragraph (f) of this section, except as otherwise provided. Paragraph (h)(6) of this section provides rules for allocating income attributable to functionally related activities of a nonthrift based upon the relative reductions to thrift income made on account of that nonthrift.

(2) *Allocation of tentative taxable loss of other thrifts.*—For purposes of paragraph (f)(1)(i) of this section, a thrift's allocable share of another thrift's tentative taxable loss is the loss multiplied by a fraction. The numerator of the fraction is the tentative taxable income (if greater than zero) of the thrift, and the denominator is the aggregate of such tentative taxable income of each thrift.

(3) *Allocation of portions of a consolidated net operating loss deduction.*—(i) For purposes of paragraph (f)(1)(ii) of this section, a first thrift's allocable share of the portion of the consolidated net operating loss deduction attributable to another thrift is determined under paragraph (h)(2) of this section as if that portion were a tentative taxable loss of that other thrift and by computing tentative taxable income under such paragraph (h)(2) by taking into account paragraph (f)(1)(i) of this section. A thrift's allocable share of the portion of the consolidated net operating loss deduction attributable to that thrift is equal to that entire portion.

(ii) For purposes of paragraph (f)(1)(iv) of this section, a thrift's allocable share of the portion of a consolidated net operating loss deduction attributable to functionally related activities of a nonthrift (determined under paragraph (h)(5) of this section) is determined under paragraph (h)(4) of this section as if that portion were a loss attributable to functionally related activities of the nonthrift and by computing tentative taxable income under such paragraph (h)(4) by taking into account paragraph (f)(1)(i), (ii), and (iii) of this section.

(iii) This subdivision (iii) prevents the "double-counting" of losses. The reduction to the tentative taxable income of a thrift is diminished to the extent the loss that gave rise to the reduction has previously been taken into account in reducing a thrift's tentative taxable income. Thus, any loss taken into account as a reduction to a thrift's separate taxable income under any subdivision of paragraph (f)(1) of this section shall be reduced (but not below zero) to the extent taken into account—

(A) in a prior consolidated return year under any subdivision of such paragraph (f)(1) or

(B) in the current consolidated return year under a previous subdivision of such paragraph (f)(1).

(4) *Allocation of loss attributable to functionally related activities of a nonthrift.*—For purposes of paragraph (f)(1)(iii) of this section, a thrift's allocable share of a loss attributable to functionally related activities of a nonthrift is determined by multiplying the loss by a fraction. The numerator of the fraction is the tentative taxable income (if

greater than zero) of the thrift (taking into account paragraph (f)(1)(i) and (ii) of this section) and the denominator is the aggregate of such tentative taxable income (so determined) of each thrift.

(5) *Portion of the consolidated net operating loss deduction attributable to functionally related activities of a particular nonthrift.*—The portion of the consolidated net operating loss deduction attributable to functionally related activities of a particular nonthrift is the lesser of the following two amounts:

(i) The portion of the consolidated net operating loss deduction attributable to that nonthrift.

(ii) The aggregate of the losses attributable to functionally related activities of that nonthrift for the taxable years in which the consolidated net operating loss deduction arose.

(6) *Allocation of income attributable to functionally related activities of a nonthrift.*—For purposes of paragraph (f)(2) of this section, a thrift institution's allocable share of the income attributable to functionally related activities of a nonthrift is determined by multiplying that income by a fraction. The numerator of the fraction is the amount of the cumulative reductions referred to in paragraph (f)(2)(ii) of this section (minus the cumulative increases under paragraph (f)(2) of this section) made on account of that nonthrift for the thrift and the denominator is the sum of such cumulative reductions (minus such cumulative increases) made on account of that nonthrift for all thrifts.

(7) *Proper accounting.*—The provisions of section 482 apply in determining a thrift institution's tentative taxable income, and in determining the gross income and deductions attributable to functionally related activities. For example, an expense such as the salary of an individual who performs services for both a thrift and a nonthrift must be allocated in a manner that fairly reflects the value of the services rendered to each.

(i) [Reserved]

(j) *Examples.*—The provisions of this section may be illustrated by the following examples. In each example the letter "T" for a member denotes a thrift and the letters "NT" denote a nonthrift. Also, in each example, a thrift loss includes a bad debt deduction under section 593(b) (other than paragraph (2) thereof) for such year and a thrift with income would have such a bad debt deduction of zero.

Example (1). (a) In 1983, corporations T1, T2, NT1, and NT2 are formed. These corporations constitute an affiliated group that files a consolidated return on the basis of a calendar year. For 1983, 1984, and 1985, the tentative taxable income (or loss) of each member (before the application of paragraph (f) of this section) is as follows:

Reg. §1.1502-42(j)

	1983	1984	1985
NT1	$(60)	$(140)	$15
T1	1,000	500	750
NT2	(90)	(220)	150
T2	(300)	400	250

In 1983, NT1, in addition to its other business activities, acted as a collection agency for T1. Deductions attributable to those collection activities exceeded gross income attributable to those activities by $70. NT1's other activities generated a $10 gain. In 1984 and 1985, NT1 acted as a collection agency for T1 as its sole activity.

(b) The tentative taxable incomes of T1 and T2 for 1983 (determined under paragraph (e) of this section) as of the close of that year are adjusted by paragraph (f) of this section as follows:

(i) T1's tentative taxable income:
T1's tentative taxable income (before the application of paragraph (f) of this section) $1,000
Less:
T2's tentative taxable loss .. $300
NT1's functionally related loss (limited by NT1's overall loss) .... 60 — 360
T1's tentative taxable income for 1983 640
(ii) T2's tentative taxable income for 1983 is zero.

(c) The tentative taxable incomes of T1 and T2 for 1984 (determined under paragraph (e) of this section) as of the close of that year are adjusted by paragraph (f) of this section as follows:

(i) T1's tentative taxable income:
T1's tentative taxable income (before the application of paragraph (f) of this section) $500
Less:
T1's allocable portion of NT1's functionally related loss (140 × 500/(500 + 400)) 78
T1's tentative taxable income for 1984 422

(ii) T2's tentative taxable income:
T2's tentative taxable income (before the application of paragraph (f) of this section 400
Less:
T2's allocable portion of NT1's functionally related loss (140 × 400/(500 + 400)) 62
T2's tentative taxable income for 1984 .... $338

(d) For 1985, the amount under paragraph (f)(2) of this section for both T1 and T2 is $15 (NT1's tentative taxable income from functionally related activities for 1985). For 1983 and

1984, T1's tentative taxable income was reduced by a total of $138 (i.e., $60 + $78) due to NT1's losses from functionally related activities. For 1984, T2's tentative taxable income was reduced by $62 due to those losses. Accordingly, under paragraph (f)(2) of this section, T1's tentative taxable income for 1983 is increased by $10 (i.e., $15 × $138/($138 + $62)) and T2's tentative taxable income is increased by $5 (i.e., $15 × $62/($138 + $62)).

Example (2). (a) In 1983, corporations T, NT1, and NT2 are formed. These corporations constitute an affiliated group. NT2 provides computer services to T as its sole activity. For the calendar years of 1983, 1984, and 1985, the group files a consolidated return. The tentative taxable income of each member (before the application of paragraph (f) of this section) is as follows:

	1983	1984	1985
T	$100	$0	$(200)
NT1	200	0	100
NT2	(20)	20	0

(b) Under paragraph (f)(1) of this section, T's tentative taxable income for 1983 (determined at the close of that year) is reduced to $80 (i.e., $100 less NT2's $20 loss). For 1984, under paragraph (f)(2) of this section, T's tentative taxable income is increased by $20. For 1985, the consolidated net operating loss of $100 (all of which is attributable to T) is carried back to 1983. That $100 carryback is not limited by paragraph (f)(4)(iii) of this section, since consolidated taxable income for 1983 available for absorption after a bad debt deduction of $0 under section 593(b) (other than paragraph (2) thereof) for that year is $280. Accordingly, under paragraph (f)(1)(ii) of this section, T's tentative taxable income is reduced by the full $100, which is taken into account before the previous reduction of T's tentative taxable income under paragraph (f)(1)(iii) of this section. In addition, under paragraph (f)(3)(i) of this section, the group must file an amended return for 1984 to eliminate the increase to T's bad debt deduction for 1984 by reason of the consolidated net operating loss carryback to 1983.

Example (3). (a) T and NT are formed in 1983 and are the only members of an affiliated group filing a consolidated return on a calendar year basis. NT provided computer services to T as its sole activity. For 1983, 1984, and 1985, the tentative taxable income of T and NT (before the application of paragraph (f) of this section) is as follows:

	1983	1984	1985
T	$100	$0	$0
NT	0	40	(40)

(b) At the close of 1983, T's tentative taxable income is $100. For 1985, however, the group has a consolidated net operating loss of $40, all of which is attributable to NT's functionally related activities and which is carried back to 1983. However, T's tentative taxable income for 1983 is not reduced under paragraph (f)(1)(iv) of this section, since, under paragraph (f)(4)(iv) of this section, NT's 1984 income attributable to functionally related activities of $40 is netted against that $40 carryback.

Example (4). (a) In 1983, corporations T1, T2, NT1, and NT2 are formed. For calendar years 1983, 1984, and 1985, the affiliated group consisting of T1, T2, NT1, and NT2 filed a consolidated return. NT1 provided computer services to T1 as its sole activity. The tentative taxable income of each member (before the application of paragraph (f) of this section) is as follows:

	1983	1984	1985
T1	($50)	$100	$30
T2	(50)	(80)	(25)
NT1	(50)	(40)	(99)
NT2	120	30	100

(b) For 1983, the group has a consolidated net operating loss of $30, apportioned $10 each to T1, T2, and NT1 under § 1.1502-79A(a)(3). For 1984, the only thrift with tentative taxable income greater than zero (before applying paragraph (f) of this section) is T1. That tentative taxable income of $100 is first reduced to $20 by T2's $80 1984 loss under paragraph (f)(1)(i) of this section. Next, T1's remaining tentative taxable income of $20 is reduced to $10 by the portions attributable to T1 and T2 of the 1983 consolidated net operating loss carryover to 1984 under paragraph (f)(1)(ii) of this section. The sum of those portions is limited to $10 (*i.e.*, $5 each) by paragraph (f)(4)(iii) of this section because 1984 consolidated taxable income available for absorption after a bad debt deduction under section 593(b) (other than paragraph (2) thereof) for each thrift member for that year is $10. For that reason, paragraph (f)(4)(iii) of this section also prevents any further portion of that carryover from being taken into account in 1984 as a reduction under paragraph (f)(1) of this section. T1's remaining tentative taxable income of $10 is reduced to zero, under paragraph (f)(1)(iii) of this section, by NT1's 1984 tentative taxable loss.

(c) For 1985, the only thrift with tentative taxable income greater than zero (before applying paragraph (f) of this section) is T1. T1's tentative taxable income for 1985 of $30 is reduced to $5 by T2's 1985 loss of $25 under paragraph (f)(1)(i) of this section. Next, the portions attributable to T1 and T2 of the consolidated net operating loss carryover from 1983 to 1985 for purposes of paragraph (f)(1)(ii) of this section must be determined. That determination is made without applying the rules for loss absorption in computing consolidated taxable income under § 1.1502-21A(b)(3). Those portions are instead determined in 3 steps under paragraph (f)(4)(i) of this section. The first of those steps is to determine each of T1's and T2's attributable portions of the 1983 consolidated net operating loss which under § 1.1502-79A(a)(3) is $10 or $20 for both thrifts. The second of those steps is to apply

the anti-double counting rule under paragraph (h)(3)(iii) of this section to reduce that $20 amount by the $10 total of the two $5 portions attributable to T1 and T2 of the consolidated net operating loss carryover from 1983 to 1984 taken into account as reductions to T1's tentative taxable income for 1984 under paragraph (f)(1)(ii) of this section. That leaves a $10 total amount available to be taken into account as reductions to T1's remaining tentative taxable income of $5 for 1985 under paragraph (f)(1)(ii) of this section. Under the third of those steps that $10 amount, however, is limited, under the loss absorption limit of paragraph (f)(4)(iii) of this section, to the $6 of the 1983 consolidated net operating loss carryover to 1985 which is absorbed in computing consolidated taxable income for 1985 since 1985 consolidated taxable income available for absorption after a bad debt deduction under section 593(b) (other than paragraph (2) thereof) for that year is $6 (*i.e.*, $30 + $100 − $99 − $25). Because separate taxable income cannot be reduced below zero under paragraph (f)(1) of this section, T1's remaining tentative taxable income of $5 if thus reduced to zero by the portions attributable to T1 and T2, respectively, of the consolidated net operating loss carryover from 1983 to 1985 under paragraph (f)(1)(ii) of this section. [Reg. § 1.1502-42.]

☐ [*T.D. 7246, 12-29-72. Amended by T.D. 7637, 8-6-79; T.D. 7815, 3-12-82; T.D. 7876, 3-14-83; T.D. 8677, 6-26-96 and T.D. 8823, 6-25-99.*]

[Reg. § 1.1502-43]

§ 1.1502-43. Consolidated accumulated earnings tax.—(a) *Group subject to tax.*—(1) *General rule.*—For a group filing a consolidated return for the taxable year, the accumulated earnings tax under section 531 is imposed on consolidated accumulated taxable income (as defined in paragraph (b) of this section). This tax applies to any group that is formed or availed of to avoid or prevent the imposition of the individual income tax on the shareholders of either any of its members or any other corporation by permitting earnings and profits to accumulate instead of dividing or distributing them. Section 531 and this section do not apply to a group that is treated as a "personal holding company" under section 542(a)(1) as a result of the application of section 542(b)(1). Special rules are provided in this section for other groups which include one or more personal holding companies.

(2) *Evidence of purpose to avoid income tax.*—(i) Under section 533(a), the fact that the group's earnings and profits are permitted to accumulate beyond the reasonable needs of its business is determinative of the purpose to avoid the income tax with respect to shareholders, unless the group by the preponderance of the evidence proves to the contrary.

(ii) The fact that a group is a mere holding or investment group is prima facie evidence of the group's purpose to avoid the income tax with respect to shareholders. The activities of a member which is a personal holding company are not taken into account in determining if the group is a mere holding or investment group.

(3) *Earnings and profits.*—For purposes of this paragraph (a) and paragraph (d) of this section, the following rules apply:

(i) If no member of the group is a personal holding company, the group's earnings and profits are the aggregate of the earnings and profits (or deficit) of each corporation that is a member at the close of the taxable year, determined in accordance with § 1.1502-33.

(ii) Earnings and profits resulting from the application of § 1.1502-33(b) are not taken into account.

(iii) Earnings and profits resulting from the disposition of a member's stock are determined without regard to the stock basis adjustments under § § 1.1502-32 and 1.1502-33(c)(1).

(4) *Reasonable needs of the business.*—The reasonable needs of the group's business include the reasonable needs of the business of any corporation (other than a personal holding company) that is a member at the close of the taxable year. Thus, the earnings and profits of one member may be accumulated with respect to the reasonable business needs of another member. If under § 1.537-3(b) the business of a nonmember corporation is considered the business of a member, then the earnings and profits of any member may be accumulated with respect to such nonmember's reasonable business needs.

(5) *Burden of proof.*—The notification described in section 534(b) and the statement described in section 534(c) are made to or by the common parent corporation in accordance with § 1.1502-77.

(b) *Consolidated accumulated taxable income.*—(1) *In general.*—"Consolidated accumulated taxable income" is the group's consolidated taxable income determined under § 1.1502-11 adjusted in the manner provided in paragraph (b)(2) of this section, minus the sum of—

(i) The consolidated dividends paid deduction determined under paragraph (c) of this section and

(ii) The consolidated accumulated earnings credit determined under paragraph (d) of this section.

(2) *Adjustments to consolidated taxable income.*—For purposes of paragraph (b)(1) of this section, consolidated taxable income is adjusted as follows:

(i) Under section 535(b)(1), the deduction for taxes is the excess of—

(A) The consolidated liability for tax determined without § 1.1502-2(b) through (d)

and without the foreign tax credit provided by section 33, over

(B) The consolidated foreign tax credit determined pursuant to § 1.1502-4.
Foreign taxes deductible under § 1.535-2(a)(2) are also allowed as a deduction under section 535(b)(1).

(ii) The consolidated charitable contributions deduction under § 1.1502-24 does not apply. Under section 535(b)(2), there shall be allowed the aggregate charitable contributions of the members allowable under section 170, determined without section 170(b)(2) and (d)(2).

(iii) Under section 535(b)(3), the deductions provided in § § 1.1502-26 and 1.1502-27 are not allowed.

(iv) Under section 535(b)(4), the consolidated net operating loss deduction described in § § 1.1502-21(a) or 1.1502-21A(a), as appropriate is not allowed.

(v) Under section 535(b)(5), there is allowed as a deduction the consolidated net capital loss, determined under § § 1.1502-22(a) or 1.1502A(a), as appropriate.

(vi) Under section 535(b)(6), there is allowed as a deduction an amount equal to (A) the excess of the consolidated net long-term capital gain (determined under § § 1.1502-22(a) or 1.1502-41A, as appropriate) over the consolidated net short-term capital loss (determined under § § 1.1502-22(a) or 1.1502-41A, as appropriate), minus (B) the taxes attributable to this excess. This consolidated net short-term capital loss is determined without the consolidated net capital loss carryovers or carrybacks to the taxable year.

(vii) Under section 535(b)(7), the consolidated net capital loss carryovers and carrybacks are not allowed. See § § 1.1502-22(b) or 1.1502-22A(b), as appropriate.

(viii) Sections 1.1502-15A (Limitations on built-in deductions not subject to § 1.1502-15) and 1.1502-15 do not apply.

(3) *Personal holding company a member.*—If a member is a personal holding company for the taxable year—

(i) [Reserved].

(ii) In applying paragraph (b)(2)(i) of this section, consolidated liability for tax (as determined under that paragraph (b)(2)(i)) is reduced by the portion thereof allocable to that member under section 1552(a)(1), (2), (3), or (4) (or § 1.1502-33(d)), whichever is applicable. The consolidated foreign tax credit is computed by excluding the taxable income and any foreign taxes paid or accrued by that member, and foreign taxes deductible under § 1.535-2(a)(2) do not include foreign taxes attributable to that member.

(c) *Consolidated dividends paid deduction.*—(1) *General rule.*—For purposes of this section, the consolidated dividends paid deduction is the aggregate of the members' deductions under section 561(a)(1) and (2). This deduction is determined by excluding deductions for dividends paid to other members.

(2) *Exception for certain personal holding companies.*—[Reserved].

(3) *Dividends paid defined.*—For purposes of this paragraph (c), "dividends paid" and "dividend (or portion thereof) paid" include amounts treated as dividends paid during the taxable year under sections 562(b)(1), 563, and 565 (relating respectively to liquidating distributions, dividends paid after year end, and consent dividends).

(4) *Examples.*—This paragraph (c) can be illustrated by the following examples:

Example (1). Corporations P and S constitute an affiliated group which files a consolidated return on a calendar year basis for 1984 and 1985. P owns all of S's stock and two individuals own all of P's stock. Neither member of the group is a personal holding company for 1984. Assume that on December 15, 1984, S pays a dividend (as defined in section 316(a)) of $2,000 to P, and P pays a dividend (as so defined) of $3,000 on January 15, 1985 to its individual shareholders. All dividends are paid in cash and are pro rata with no preference as to any shares or class of stock. For purposes of this paragraph (c), the consolidated dividends paid deduction for 1984 is $3,000, *i.e.,* the dividend paid on January 15, 1985, by P to its nonmember shareholders. See section 563(a). The $2,000 dividend paid by S to P is not taken into account in computing the consolidated dividends paid deduction.

Example (2). [Reserved].

(d) *Consolidated accumulated earnings credit.*—(1) *In general.*—[Reserved]

(2) *Special rule if a consolidated group is part of a controlled group.*—If a consolidated group is treated collectively as being one component member of a controlled group, or if each member of a consolidated group is treated as being a separate component member of a controlled group, see section 1561 for determining the portion of the accumulated earnings credit to be allocated to such group or to such members.

(e) *Effective/applicability date.*—This section applies to any consolidated Federal income tax return due (without extensions) on or after December 21, 2009. However, a consolidated group may apply this section to any consolidated Federal income tax return filed on or after December 21, 2009. For returns due before December 21, 2009, see § 1.1502-43T as contained in 26 CFR part 1 in effect on April 1, 2009. [Reg. § 1.1502-43.]

☐ [*T.D. 7937, 1-26-84. Amended by T.D. 8560, 8-12-94; T.D. 8677, 6-26-96; T.D. 8823, 6-25-99; T.D. 9304, 12-21-2006 and T.D. 9476, 12-22-2009.*]

[Reg. § 1.1502-44]

§ 1.1502-44. Percentage depletion for independent producers and royalty owners.—(a) *In general.*—The sum of the percentage depletion deductions for the taxable year for all oil or gas property owned by all members, plus any carryovers under section 613A(d)(1) or paragraph (d) of this section from a prior taxable year, may not exceed 65 percent of the group's adjusted consolidated taxable income (under paragraph (b) of this section) for the consolidated return year.

(b) *Adjusted consolidated taxable income.*—For purposes of this section, adjusted consolidated taxable income is an amount (not less than zero) equal to the group's consolidated taxable income determined without—

(1) Any depletion with respect to an oil or gas property (other than a gas property with respect to which the depletion allowance for all production is determined pursuant to section 613A(b)) for which percentage depletion would exceed cost depletion in the absence of the depletable quantity limitations contained in section 613A(c)(1) and (6) and the consolidated taxable income limitation contained in paragraph (a) of this section,

(2) Any consolidated net operating loss carryback to the consolidated return year under § § 1.1502-21 or 1.1502-21A (as appropriate), and

(3) Any consolidated net capital loss carryback to the consolidated return year under § § 1.1502-22 or 1.1502-22A (as appropriate).

(c) *Allocation to oil and gas properties.*—The maximum amount allowable as a deduction under section 613A(c), after the application of paragraph (a) of this section, is allocated to properties held by members in accordance with the regulations under section 613A(d). Those regulations provide for an initial allocation and possible reallocation of the maximum allowable percentage depletion deduction among oil and gas properties. Thus, if, after the initial allocation, cost depletion exceeds the percentage depletion that would be allowable for a particular oil or gas property, cost depletion must be used for that property and the maximum amount of percentage depletion allowable as a deduction for the group is reallocated among only the remaining properties held by all members.

(d) *Carryover for disallowed amounts.*—(1) If any amount is disallowed as a deduction for the taxable year by reason of section 613A(d)(1) or paragraph (a) of this section, the disallowed amount for each oil or gas property is treated as an amount allowed as a deduction under section 613A(c), for the following taxable year for the member that owned the property, in accordance with the regulations under section 613A and paragraphs (a) and (d)(2) of this section.

(2) Any amount that was disallowed as a deduction in a separate return limitation year of

a member may be carried to a consolidated return year only to the extent that 65 percent of the excess determined under paragraph (d)(3) of this section exceeds the sum of the otherwise allowable percentage depletion deductions for the member's oil and gas properties for the year.

(3) The excess determined in this subparagraph (3) for a member is the excess, if any, of adjusted consolidated taxable income for the year under paragraph (b) of this section over that income recomputed by excluding the items of income and deductions of the member.

(e) *Effective date.*—This section applies to taxable years for which the due date (without extensions) for filing returns is after September 30, 1980. [Reg. § 1.1502-44.]

☐ [*T.D. 7725, 9-30-80. Amended by T.D. 8677, 6-26-96 and T.D. 8823, 6-25-99.*]

[Reg. § 5.1502-45T]

§ 5.1502-45T. Limitation on losses to amount at risk (Temporary).—(a) *In general.*—(1) *Scope.*—This section applies to a loss of any subsidiary if the common parent's stock meets the stock ownership requirement described in section 465(a)(1)(C).

(2) *Limitation on use of losses.*—Except as provided in paragraph (a)(4) of this section, a loss from an activity of a subsidiary during a consolidated return year is includible in the computation of consolidated taxable income (or consolidated net operating loss) and consolidated capital gain net income (or consolidated net capital loss) only to the extent the loss does not exceed the amount that the parent is at risk in the activity at the close of that subsidiary's taxable year. In addition, the sum of a subsidiary's losses from all its activities is includible only to the extent that the parent is at risk in the subsidiary at the close of that year. Any excess may not be taken into account for the consolidated return year but will be treated as a deduction allocable to that activity of the subsidiary in the first succeeding taxable year.

(3) *Amount parent is at risk in subsidiary's activity.*—The amount the parent is at risk in an activity of a subsidiary is the lesser of (i) the amount the parent is at risk in the subsidiary or (ii) the amount the subsidiary is at risk in the activity. These amounts are determined under paragraph (b) of this section and the principles of section 465. See section 465 and the regulations thereunder and the examples in paragraph (e) of this section.

(4) *Excluded activities.*—The limitation on the use of losses in paragraph (a)(2) of this section does not apply to a loss attributable to an activity described in section 465 (c)(3)(D).

(5) *Substance over form.*—Any transaction or arrangement between members (or between a member and a person that is not a member) which does not cause the parent to be economically at risk in an activity of a subsidiary will be treated in accordance with the substance of the transaction or arrangement notwithstanding any other provision of this section.

(b) *Rules for determining amount at risk.*—(1) *Excluded amounts.*—The amount a parent is at risk in an activity of a subsidiary at the close of the subsidiary's taxable year does not include any amount which would not be taken into account under section 465 were the subsidiary not a separate corporation. Thus, for example, if the amount a parent is at risk in the activity of a subsidiary is attributable to nonrecourse financing, the amount at risk is not more than the fair market value of the property (other than the subsidiary's stock or debt or assets) pledged as security.

(2) *Guarantees.*—If a parent guarantees a loan by a person other than a member to a subsidiary, the loan increases the amount the parent is at risk in the activity of the subsidiary.

(c) *Application of section 465.*—This section applies in a manner consistent with the provisions of section 465. Thus, for example, the recapture of losses provided in section 465(e) applies if the amount the parent is at risk in the activity of a subsidiary is reduced below zero.

(d) *Other consolidated return provisions unaffected.*—This section limits only the extent to which losses of a subsidiary may be used in a consolidated return year. This section does not apply for other purposes, such as § 1.1502-32 and § 1.1502-19, relating to investment in stock of a subsidiary and excess loss accounts, respectively. Thus, a loss which reduces a subsidiary's earnings and profits in a consolidated return year, but is disallowed as a deduction for the year by reason of this section, may nonetheless result in a negative adjustment to the basis of an owning member's stock in the subsidiary or create (or increase) an excess loss account.

(e) *Examples.*—The provisions of this section may be illustrated by the examples in this paragraph (e). In each example, the stock ownership requirement of section 465(a)(1)(C) is met for the stock of the parent (P), and each affiliated group files a consolidated return on a calendar year basis and comprises only the members described.

Example (1). In 1979, P forms S with a contribution of $200 in exchange for all of S's stock. During the year, S borrows $400 from a commercial lender and P guarantees $100 of the loan. S uses $500 of its funds to acquire a motion picture film. S incurs a loss of $120 for the year with respect to the film. At the close of 1979, the amount P is at risk in S's activity is $300. If S has no gain or loss in 1980, and there are no contributions from or distributions to P, at the close of

1980 P's amount at risk in S's activity will be $180.

Example (2). P forms S-1 with a capital contribution of $1 on January 1, 1980. On February 1, 1980, S-1 borrows $100 with full recourse and contributes all $101 to its newly formed subsidiary S-2. S-2 uses the proceeds to explore for natural oil and gas resources. S-2 incurs neither gain nor loss from its explorations during the taxable year. As of December 31, 1980, P is at risk in the exploration activity of S-2 only to the extent of $1.

(f) *Effective date.*—This section applies to consolidated return years ending on or after December 31, 1979. [Temporary Reg. § 5.1502-45.]

☐ [*T.D.* 7685, 3-12-80.]

[Reg. § 1.1502-47]

§ 1.1502-47. Consolidated returns by life-nonlife groups.—(a) *Scope.*—(1) *In general.*— Under section 1504(b)(2), insurance companies that are taxed under section 802 or 821 (relating respectively to life insurance companies and to certain mutual insurance companies) are not treated as includible corporations for purposes of determining under section 1504(a) the existence of an affiliated group and the composition of its membership. Section 1504(c)(2) provides an election whereby certain life insurance companies and mutual insurance companies may be treated as includible corporations, and thus members, of a group composed of other includible corporations. This section provides regulations for the making of this election and for the determination of an electing group's composition and its consolidated tax liability.

(2) *General method of consolidation.*—(i) *Subgroup method.*—The regulations adopt a subgroup method to determine consolidated taxable income. One subgroup is the group's nonlife companies (including those taxable under section 821). The other subgroup is the group's life insurance companies. Initially, the nonlife subgroup computes nonlife consolidated taxable income and the life subgroup computes consolidated partial life insurance company taxable income. A subgroup's income may in effect be reduced by a loss of the other subgroup. The life subgroup losses consist of consolidated loss from operations and life consolidated net capital loss. The nonlife subgroup losses consist of nonlife consolidated net operating loss and nonlife consolidated net capital loss. Consolidated taxable income is therefore defined in pertinent part as the sum of nonlife consolidated taxable income and consolidated partial life insurance company taxable income reduced by life subgroup losses or nonlife subgroup losses.

(ii) *Subgroup loss.*—A subgroup loss does not actually affect the computation of nonlife consolidated taxable income or consolidated par-

tial life insurance company taxable income. It merely constitutes a bottom-line adjustment in reaching consolidated taxable income. Furthermore, one subgroup's loss must first be carried back against income of the same subgroup before it may be used as a setoff against the second subgroup income in the taxable year the loss arose. (See section 1503(c)(1)). The carryback of the losses from one subgroup may not be used to offset income of the other subgroup in the year to which the loss is to be carried. This carryback of the first subgroup's loss may "bump" the second subgroup's loss that in effect previously reduced the income of the first subgroup. The second subgroup's loss that is bumped in appropriate cases may in effect reduce a succeeding year's income of the second or first subgroup. This approach gives the group the tax savings of the use of losses but the bumping rule assures that insofar as possible life deductions will be matched against life income and nonlife deductions against nonlife income.

(iii) *Carryover of subgroup loss.*—A subgroup's loss may be used in a succeeding year, but in any particular succeeding year the loss must be used to reduce the income of the same subgroup before it may be used as a setoff against the other subgroup's income.

(3) *Authority.*—This section is prescribed under the authority of sections 1502, 1503(c), 1504(c)(2), and 7805(b).

(4) *Other provisions.*—The provisions of §§ 1.1502-1 through 1.1502-80 apply unless this section provides otherwise. Further, unless otherwise indicated in this section, a term used in this section has the same meaning as in sections 801-844.

(b) *Effective dates.*—(1) *General rule.*—This section is effective for taxable years for which the due date (without extensions) for filing returns is after March 14, 1983, except as provided in paragraph (b)(2) of this section.

(2) *Tacking rule effective dates.*—(i) *In general.* Paragraph (d)(12)(v) of this section applies to any original consolidated Federal income tax return due (without extensions) after July 20, 2007.

(ii) *Prior law.* For original consolidated Federal income tax returns due (without extensions) after April 25, 2006, and on or before July 20, 2007, see § 1.1502-47T as contained in 26 CFR part 1 in effect on April 1, 2007. For original consolidated Federal income tax returns due (without extensions) on or before April 25, 2006, see § 1.1502-47 as contained in 26 CFR part 1 in effect on April 1, 2006.

(c) *Cross references.*—The following table provides cross references for some of the definitions and operating rules that are relevant in making the election and determining the group's composition and its tax liability:

Item and Paragraph
— General definitions (d)
— Eligible corporation (Five-year rules) (d)(12)
— Election (e)
— Consolidated taxable income (g)
— Nonlife consolidated taxable income (h)
— Consolidated partial life insurance company taxable income (j)
— Nonlife subgroup losses (m)
— Life subgroup losses (n)
— Alternative tax (o)

(d) *Definitions.*—For purposes of this section—

(1) *Life insurance company.*—The term "life company" means a life insurance company as defined in section 801. Section 801 applies to each company separately.

(2) *Mutual insurance company.*—The term "mutual company" means a mutual insurance company taxable under section 821(a)(1).

(3) *Life insurance company taxable income.*—The term "life insurance company taxable income" is referred to as LICTI. The terms "TII", "GO", and "LO" refer, respectively, to taxable investment income (section 804), gain from operations (section 809), and loss from operations (section 812). The term "consolidated partial LICTI" refers to consolidated LICTI without section 802(b)(3).

(4) *Group.*—The term "group" means an affiliated group of corporations (as defined in section 1504(a)). Unless otherwise indicated in this section, a group's composition is determined without section 1504(b)(2).

(5) *Member.*—The term "member" means a corporation (including the common parent) that is an includible corporation in the group. A life company or mutual company is tentatively treated as a member for any taxable year for purposes of determining if it is an eligible corporation under paragraph (d)(12) of this section and therefore if it is an includible corporation under section 1504(c)(2). If such a company is eligible and includible (under section 1504(c)(2)), it will actually be treated as a member of the group.

(6) *Life member.*—A life member is a member of the group that is a life company.

(7) *Nonlife member.*—A nonlife member is a member of the group that is not a life company.

(8) *Life subgroup.*—A life subgroup is composed of those members that are life members. If the group has only one life member, it constitutes a life subgroup.

(9) *Nonlife subgroup.*—A nonlife subgroup is composed of those members that are nonlife members. If the group has only one nonlife member, it constitutes a nonlife subgroup.

(10) *Separate return year.*—The term "separate return year" means a taxable year of a corporation for which it files a separate return or for which it joins in the filing of a consolidated return by another group. For purposes of this subparagraph (10), the term "group" is defined with regard to section 1504(b)(2) for years in which an election under section 1504(c)(2) is not in effect. Thus, a separate return year includes a taxable year for which that election is not in effect.

(11) *Separate return limitation year.*—Section 1.1502-1(f)(2) provides exceptions to the definition of the term "separate return limitation year". For purposes of applying those exceptions to this section, for taxable years ending after December 31, 1980, the term "group" is defined without regard to section 1504(b)(2) and the definition in this subparagraph (11) applies separately to the nonlife subgroup in determining nonlife consolidated taxable income under paragraph (h) of this section and to the life subgroup in determining consolidated partial LICTI under paragraph (j) of this section. Paragraph (m)(3)(ix) of this section defines the term "separate return limitation year" for purposes of determining whether the losses of one subgroup may be used against the income of the other subgroup.

(12) *Eligible corporations.*—(i) *In general.*—A corporation is an eligible corporation for a taxable year of a group only if, throughout every day of the base period the corporation—

(A) Was in existence and a member of the group determined without the exclusions in section 1504(b)(2) (see paragraphs (d)(12)(iii)-(vi) of this section),

(B) Was engaged in the active conduct of a trade or business ("active business"),

(C) Did not experience a change in tax character (see paragraph (d)(12)(vii) of this section), and

(D) Did not undergo disproportionate asset acquisitions (see paragraph (d)(12)(viii) of this section).

(ii) *Base period.*—The base period consists of the common parent's five taxable years immediately preceding the group's taxable year for which the consolidated return and the determination of eligibility are made. Eligibility is determined for each consolidated return year beginning with the first year for which the election under section 1504(c)(2) is effective.

(iii) *In existence.*—Except as provided in paragraph (d)(12)(v) and (vi) of this section, a corporation organized after the base period begins is not eligible even though it is a member of the group immediately after its organization. For

Reg. §1.1502-47(d)

purposes of this subdivision (iii), a corporation that was a party to a reorganization described in section 368(a)(1)(F) shall be treated as the same entity both before and after the reorganization.

(iv) *Membership period.*—Except as provided in paragraph (d)(12)(v) and (vi) of this section, a corporation must have been a member of the group throughout the base period to be eligible. Thus, an ineligible corporation includes one whose stock was acquired from outside the group at any time during the base period or one which was a member of a different group (whether by application of reverse acquisition rules in §1.1502-75(d)(3) or otherwise) at any time during the base period. For purposes of this subdivision (iv), the common parent of a group is treated as constituting a group (and hence is a member) during any period when it was not a member of an affiliated group within the meaning of section 1504(a) (applied without section 1504(b)(2)).

(v) *Tacking rule.*—The period during which an old corporation is in existence and a member of the group engaged in active business is included in (or tacks onto) the period for the new corporation if the following four conditions listed in this paragraph (d)(12)(v) are met. For purposes of this paragraph (d)(12)(v), a new corporation is a corporation (whether or not newly organized) during the period its eligibility depends upon the tacking rule. The four conditions are as follows—

(A) The first condition is that, at any time, 80 percent or more of the new corporation's assets it acquired (other than in the ordinary course of its trade or business) were acquired from the old corporation in one or more transactions described in section 351(a) or 381(a). This asset test is applied by using the fair market values of assets on the date they were acquired and without regard to liabilities. Assets acquired in the ordinary course of business will be excluded from total assets only if they were acquired after the new corporation became a member of the group (determined without section 1504(b)(2)). In addition, assets that the old corporation acquired from outside the group in transactions not conducted in the ordinary course of its trade or business are not included in the 80 percent (but are included in total assets) if the old corporation acquired those assets within five calendar years before the date of their transfer to the new corporation.

(B) The second condition is that at the end of the taxable year during which the first condition is first met, the old corporation and the new corporation must both have the same tax character. For purposes of this paragraph (d)(12), a corporation's tax character is the section under which it would be taxed (i.e., sections 11, 802, 821, or 831) if it filed a separate return. If the old corporation is not in existence (or adopts a plan of complete liquidation) at the end of that taxa-

ble year, this paragraph (d)(12)(v)(B) will apply to the old corporation's taxable year immediately preceding the beginning of the taxable year during which the first condition is first met.

(C) The third condition is that, at the end of the taxable year during which the first condition is first met, the new corporation does not undergo a disproportionate asset acquisition under paragraph (d)(12)(viii) of this section.

(D) The fourth condition is that, if there is more than one old corporation, the first two conditions apply to all of the corporations. Thus, the second condition (tax character) must be met by all of the old corporations transferring assets taken into account in meeting the test in paragraph (d)(12)(v)(A) of this section.

(vi) *Old group remaining in existence.*—If the common parent of a group (or a new common parent) became the common parent in a transaction described in §1.1502-75(d)(2) or (3) where a group remained in existence, then paragraph (d)(12)(ii)-(iv) of this section apply by treating that common parent as if it were also the previous common parent of the group that remains in existence. If this subdivision (vi) applies to a transaction, the tacking rule in paragraph (d)(12)(v) of this section does not apply to the transaction.

(vii) *Change in tax character.*—A corporation must not experience during the base period a change in tax character (as defined in paragraph (d)(12)(v)(B) of this section) if the change is attributable to an acquisition of assets from outside the group in transactions not conducted in the ordinary course of its trade or business. However, if a new corporation relies on the tacking rules in paragraph (d)(12)(v) of this section, this subdivision (vii) shall apply during the base period and the current consolidated return year and even if the change in tax character is attributable to an asset acquisition from within the group.

(viii) *Disproportionate asset acquisition.*—To be eligible, a corporation must not undergo during the base period disproportionate asset acquisitions which are attributable to an acquisition (or a series of acquisitions) of assets from outside the group in transactions not conducted in the ordinary course of its trade or business (special acquisition). Whether special acquisitions are disproportionate is determined at the end of each base period. Whether an acquisition results in a disproportionate asset acquisition depends on all of the facts and circumstances including the following factors and rules:

(A) One factor is the portion of the insurance reserves (i.e., total reserves in section 801(c)) of the acquiring company at the end of the base period which is attributable to special acquisitions.

(B) A second factor is the portion of the fair market value of the assets (without reduc-

Reg. §1.1502-47(d)(12)(viii)(B)

tion for liabilities) of the acquiring company at the end of the base period that is attributable to special acquisitions.

(C) A third factor is the portion of the premiums generated during the last taxable year of the base period which are attributable to special acquisitions.

(D) A corporation will not experience a disproportionate asset acquisition unless 75 percent of one factor (whether or not listed in this subdivision (viii)) is attributable to special acquisitions.

(E) Money or other property contributed to a corporation by a shareholder that is not a member of the group (without section 1504(b)(2)) is not a special acquisition.

(F) If a new corporation relies on the tacking rules in paragraph (d)(12)(v) of this section, this subdivision (viii) applies to that corporation during a consolidated return year. Thus, if at any time during a consolidated return year, a new corporation undergoes a disproportionate asset acquisition, the corporation becomes ineligible at that time.

(13) *Ineligible corporation.*—A corporation that is not an eligible corporation is ineligible. If a life company or mutual company is ineligible, it is not treated under section 1504(c)(2) as an includible corporation. Losses of a nonlife member arising in years when it is ineligible may not be used under section 1503(c)(2) and paragraph (m) of this section to set off the income of a life member. If a life or mutual company is ineligible and is the common parent of the group (without section 1504(b)(2)), the election under section 1504(c)(2) may not be made.

(14) *Illustrations.*—The following examples illustrate this paragraph (d). In each example, L indicates a life company, another letter indicates a non-life company, and each corporation uses the calendar year as its taxable year.

Example (1). P has owned all of the stock of S since 1913. On January 1, 1980, P purchased all of the stock of L_1 which owns all of the stock of L_2 and S_2. L_1 and L_2 are treated as members for purposes of determining if they are eligible for 1982. However, for 1982, L_1, L_2, and S_2 are ineligible because none of them has been a member of the group for P's five taxable years preceding 1982. For 1982, L_1 and L_2 may elect to file a consolidated return because they constitute an affiliated group under section 1504(c)(1), and P and S may file a consolidated return.

Example (2). Since 1974, P has been a mutual insurance company owning all the stock of L_1. In 1980, P transfers assets to S_1, a new stock casualty company subject to taxation under section 831(a). For 1982, only P and L_1 are eligible corporations. The tacking rule in paragraph (d)(12)(v) of this section does not apply in 1982 because the old corporation (P) and the new corporation (S_1)

do not have the same tax character. The result would be the same if P were a life company.

Example (3). Since 1974, L has owned all the stock of L_1 which has owned all the stock of S_1, a stock casualty company. L_1 writes some accident and health insurance business. In 1980, L_1 transfers this business , and S_1 transfers some of its business, to a new stock casualty company, S_2, in a transaction described in section 351(a). The property transferred to S_2 by L_1 had a fair market value of $50 million. The property transferred by S_1 had a fair market value of $40 million. S_2 is ineligible for 1982 because the tacking rule in paragraph (d)(12)(v) of this section does not apply. The old corporations (L_1 and S_1) and the new corporation (S_2) do not all have the same tax character. See subparagraph (d)(12)(v)(B) and (E) of this section. The result would be the same if L_1 transferred other property (*e.g.*, stock and securities) with the same value, rather than accident and health insurance contracts, to S_2.

Example (4). Since 1974, P has owned all the stock of S and L_1. L_1 is a large life company engaged in active business since 1974. On January 1, 1982, L_1 transfers in a section 351(a) transaction assets (not acquired from outside the group) to a new life company, L_2. For 1982, L_2 is eligible because under paragraph (d)(12)(v) of this section, L_2 is considered to have been in existence and a member of the group engaged in the active business since 1974 which is the period L_1, the old corporation, was in existence and a member of the group so engaged.

Example (5). The facts are the same as in example (4). Assume that the fair market value of the assets L_1 transferred to L_2 was $10 million on January 1, 1982 and that L_2 acquired no other assets prior to June 30, 1983. Assume further that on January 1, 1983, L_1 acquires (other than in the ordinary course of its trade or business) assets having a fair market value of $40 million from L_3, an unrelated life company. On June 30, 1983, L_1 transfers those assets to L_2. L_2 becomes ineligible on June 30, 1983. Since by fair market values, 80 percent (*i.e.*, 40/50) of L_2's assets are attributable to special acquisitions, L_2 has undergone a disproportionate asset acquisition at that time. See paragraph (d)(12)(viii)(B), (D), and (F) of this section.

Example (6). The facts are the same as in example (5) except that L_1 transfers assets (other than life insurance contracts) having a fair market value of $40 million to L_2 and L_2 purchases the assets of L_3 on June 30, 1983. The result of the 1983 acquisition is the same as in example (5).

Example (7). The facts are the same as in example (5) except the acquired assets acquired by L_2 in 1983 from L_1 have a fair market value of $20 million. In 1983, L_2 had $1 million of premiums on its pre-existing contracts but premiums generated by the acquired business for the entire year would have been $2 million. L_2 is eligible in 1983 because it did not experience a disproportionate asset acquisition on June 30, 1983.

Example (8). Since 1974, L, a State A corporation, has owned all of the stock of L_1 and S_1. On January 1, 1982, L merges into L_3, a smaller State B corporation, which owns the stock of S_2. The transaction is a reverse acquisition described in § 1.1502-75(d)(3) and the group of which L was the common parent remains in existence. Under paragraph (d)(12)(vi) of this section, L_3 is eligible for 1982. However, S_2 is ineligible in 1982 under paragraph (d)(12)(iv) of this section.

Example (9). The facts are the same as in example (8) except that L acquires the stock of L_3. L_3 and S_2 are both ineligible for 1982. On January 1, 1983, the fair market value of L_3's assets are $5 million (without liabilities) and on that date L transfers assets (not acquired from outside the group) having a fair market value of $95 million (without liabilities) to L_3. L and L_3 are life companies at the end of 1983. L_3 is eligible in 1983 under the tacking rule in paragraph (d)(12)(v) of this section. S_2 is ineligible in that year. The result would be the same if L_3 was not a life company prior to January 1, 1983. See paragraph (d)(12)(v)(B) of this section.

Example (10). Since 1974, X, a foreign corporation, has owned all the stock of S_2 and S_1, and S_1 has owned all of the stock of L_1. On January 1, 1982, X incorporates a new U.S. company P, and transfers the stock of S_1 and S_2 to P. Assume that under § 1.1502-75(d)(3) (relating to reverse acquisitions), the S_1-L_1 affiliated group remains in existence. Under paragraph (d)(12)(vi) of this section, P, S_1, and L_1 are eligible but S_2 is ineligible. The result would be the same if X were an individual.

Example (11). The facts are the same as in *Example (10)* except that X owns all of the stock of S_1, L_1, and S_2. In addition, on January 1, 1982, X transfers the stock of S_1 and S_2 to L_1. L_1 is eligible in 1982 under paragraph (d)(12)(iv) of this section. L_1 would still be eligible even if it owned a subsidiary during the base period but sold the subsidiary prior to January 1, 1982. S_1 and S_2 are ineligible in 1982.

Example (12). Since 1974, S_1 has owned all of the stock of L_1. S_2, an unrelated company, has owned all of the stock of L_2 and S_3 for 10 years. S_1 and S_2 are active stock casualty companies and not holding companies. On January 1, 1982, S_1 and S_2 merge into a new casualty company, S, in a transaction described in § 1.1502-75(d)(3) so that the group of which S_1 was the common parent remains in existence. S and L_1 are eligible in 1982 under paragraph (d)(12)(vi) of this section. L_2 and S_3 are ineligible.

Example (13). The facts are the same as in *Example (12)* except that S_2 (the first corporation in § 1.1502-75(d)(3)) acquires the stock of S_1 in exchange for the stock of S_2. The result is that only S_2, S_1, and L_1 are eligible in 1982.

Example (14). Since 1974, S had owned all of the stock of L_1. L_1 is a large life company. On January 1, 1982, L_1 incorporates L_2 and transfers $ 40 million in cash and securities to L_2 in a

transaction described in section 351(a). On March 1, 1982, L_2 purchases the assets of L_3, an unrelated life company. The purchased assets have a fair market value (without liabilities) of $ 30 million on March 1, 1982. L_2 is ineligible for 1982 because the tacking rule in § 1.1502-47T(d)(12)(v) does not apply. L_2 experienced a disproportionate asset acquisition in 1982. See § 1.1502-47T(d)(12)(v)(C).

(e) *Election.*—(1) *In general.*—The election under section 1504(c)(2) may not be made if the group's common parent is an ineligible life company or an ineligible mutual company. The election under section 1504(c)(2) may only be made by the common parent of the group (as defined in section 1504(c)(2) without the exclusions in section 1504(b)(2)). For example, assume that P owns all of the stock of L_1, an eligible life company, which owns the stock of S_1. Assume further that P also owns the stock of L_2, an ineligible life member, which (for more than five years) has owned the stock of a nonlife company, S_2. Only P may make the election and, if it does so, P, L_1, and S_1 may file a consolidated return under this section. L_2 may not make the election under section 1504(c)(2) and may not file a consolidated return with S_2.

(2) *How election is made.*—(i) *General rule.*—The election under section 1504(c)(2) is generally made by the group's common parent in the same manner (and it has the same effect) as the election to file a consolidated return is made under § 1.1502-75(a) and (b) for a group which did not file a consolidated return for the immediately preceding taxable year. The procedure for making the election under section 1504(c)(2) is the same whether or not a consolidated return was filed by the life members or the nonlife members for the immediately preceding taxable year.

(ii) *Special rule.*—Notwithstanding the general rule, however, if the nonlife members in the group filed a consolidated return for the immediately preceding taxable year and had executed and filed a Form 1122 that is effective for the preceding year, then such members will be treated as if they filed a Form 1122 when they join in the filing of a consolidated return under section 1504(c)(2) and they will be deemed to consent to the regulations under this section. However, an affiliation schedule (Form 851) must be filed by the group and the life members must execute a Form 1122 in the manner prescribed in § 1.1502-75(h)(2).

(3) *Irrevocability.*—Except as provided in § 1.1502-75(c) and paragraph (e)(4) of this section, the election under section 1504(c)(2) is irrevocable.

(4) *Permission to discontinue.*—(i) *General rule.*—A "section 1504(c)(2) group" with a common parent that has made the election to file a consolidated return under section 1504(c)(2) in a

previous taxable year is granted permission to elect (under § 1.1502-75(c)(2)(ii)) to discontinue filing such a consolidated return for that group's first taxable year for which the regulations under this section are effective. This election to discontinue shall be exercised in the time and manner prescribed in § 1.1502-75(c)(3), except that the group's common parent shall exercise this election to discontinue (and the other members of the section 1504(c)(2) group must comply with this election) by filing appropriate returns. For purposes of this paragraph (e)(4), an appropriate return is either a separate return or a consolidated return that is filed by newly exercising the privilege under § 1.1502-75(a)(1).

(ii) *Types of groups.*—(A) A "section 1504(c)(2) group" is an affiliated group which files or filed a consolidated return pursuant to an election under section 1504(c)(2).

(B) A "limited group" is an affiliated group (determined without section 1504(c)(2)) having at least one member which was a member of a section 1504(c)(2) group on the date that the section 1504(c)(2) group elected to discontinue under paragraph (e)(4)(i) of this section.

(iii) *Effect on restoration rules.*—If a group ceases to file a consolidated return or terminates or if a member leaves the group, certain items of income, gain, or loss on transactions between members are taken into account under §§ 1.1502-13, 1.1502-18, and 1.1502-19 ("restoration rules"). For purposes of applying these restoration rules solely by reason of an election under paragraph (e)(4)(i) or (e)(4)(v)(A) of this section to discontinue filing consolidated returns as a section 1504(c)(2) group, the following rules apply:

(A) The section 1504(c)(2) group shall not be considered to terminate and no member of that group shall be treated as ceasing to be a member.

(B) Members of that section 1504(c)(2) group that are included in the consolidated return of a limited group for the first taxable year for which the discontinuance is effective shall be considered to be filing a consolidated return as a continuation of the section 1504(c)(2) group. However, a corporation that is not a member of a particular limited group for that taxable year is considered to have a separate return year (and, for purposes of § 1.1502-19(c), not to be a member of a group filing a consolidated return) with respect to that limited group's members.

(C) Section 1.1502-13 shall be applied without regard to paragraph (f)(1)(vii).

(iv) *Illustrations.*—The following examples illustrate paragraph (e)(4)(i)-(iii) of this section. In these examples, L indicates a life company and another letter indicates a nonlife company. All corporations use the calendar year as the taxable year. For all taxable years involved, P owns all the stock of L₁ and of S, L₁

owns all the stock of L₂, L₂ owns all the stock of L₃, and S owns all the stock of L₄. For 1981, P makes the life-nonlife election of section 1504(c)(2) and L₄ is an eligible corporation. For 1982, P makes the election to discontinue filing consolidated returns under section 1504(c)(2) in accordance with the permission granted in this paragraph (e)(4).

Example (1). L₁, L₂, and L₃ were eligible members. For 1982, P and S may either file separate returns or may file, as a limited group, a consolidated return. Similarly, L₁, L₂, and L₃ may either file separate returns or may file a consolidated return as a limited group under section 1504(c)(1). L₄ must file a separate return.

Example (2). For 1981, L₁ was an ineligible member and L₁, L₂, and L₃ filed a consolidated return under section 1504(c)(1). For 1982, L₁, L₂, and L₃ must continue filing a consolidated return under section 1504(c)(1).

Example (3). For 1981, L₁ was an eligible member and L₂ and L₃ were ineligible members. For 1982, L₁, L₂, and L₃ either must each file a separate return or must file a consolidated return as a limited group under section 1504(c)(1) having L₁ as the common parent.

Example (4). The facts are the same as in example (3). Assume further that for 1981, L₂ and L₃ file a consolidated return. During 1981, intercompany transactions (see § 1.1502-13) occur in the life-nonlife group between P and L₁, between P and S, and between S and L₄ and occur in the ineligible life subgroup between L₂ and L₃. For 1982, the restoration rules of § 1.1502-13, as modified by paragraph (e)(4)(iii)(B) of this section, will be applicable as indicated in the following table:

Intercompany transactions between:	§ 1.1502-13
P and L₁	Yes
P and S, if they file:	
Separate returns	Yes
A consolidated return	No
S and L₄	Yes
L₂ and L₃, if L₁, L₂, and L₃ file:	
Separate returns	Yes
A consolidated return	No

(v) *Additional rules.*—(A) If a group with a taxable year ending in the month of December, 1982, had made the election under section 1504(c)(2) for a taxable year ending prior to December 1, 1982, and if that group meets the conditions of subdivision (vi) of this paragraph (e)(4), then the common parent may elect to discontinue filing a consolidated return for its taxable year ending in the month of December, 1982 (and other members of the section 1504(c)(2) group must comply with this election) by filing appropriate returns (see paragraph (e)(4)(i) of this section) before September 16, 1983.

(B) If a group made the election under section 1504(c)(2) for its taxable year ending in the month of December, 1982, and if that group meets the conditions of subdivision (vi) of this paragraph (e)(4), then the common parent may elect to withdraw the section 1504(c)(2) election (and all other members of the group determined without section 1504(b)(2) comply with the election) by filing before September 16, 1983, any returns for the appropriate taxable years that would have been filed had the section 1504(c)(2) election never been made.

(vi) A group referred to at subdivision (v)(A) or (B) of this paragraph (e)(4) meets the conditions of this subdivision (vi) if it—

(A) filed before March 16, 1983, a return for its taxable year ending in the month of December, 1982, and

(B) had not been granted an extension of time beyond March 15, 1983, for the filing of that return.

(vii) *Interest.*—For purposes of section 6601(a), interest runs from the original due date (without extensions) for the filing of such returns as are filed pursuant to an election (to discontinue or withdraw as the case may be) under this paragraph (e)(4).

(5) *Consent to regulations.*—If a group does not discontinue filing a consolidated return under paragraph (e)(4) of this section but continues to file a consolidated return for the group's first taxable year for which the regulations under this section are first effective, the members of the group will be deemed to have consented to the regulations under this section.

(6) *Cross reference.*—If an election is made under section 1504(c)(2), see § 1.1502-75(e) and (f) for rules that apply for not including (or including) a member or a nonmember in the consolidated return.

(f) *Effect of election.*—If the common parent makes the election under section 1504(c)(2), the following rules apply:

(1) *Termination of group.*—A mere election under section 1504(c)(2) will not cause the creation of a new group or the termination of an affiliated group that files a consolidated return in the immediately preceding taxable year.

(2) *Effect of eligibility.*—If a life member is eligible after an election under section 1504(c)(2), it may not be included as a member of an affiliated group as defined in section 1504(c)(1).

(3) *Eligible and ineligible life companies.*—If any life company was a member of an affiliated group of life companies (as defined in section 1504(c)(1)) but is ineligible for a taxable year for which the election under section 1504(c)(2) is effective, that year is not a separate return year merely by reason of the election under section 1504(c)(2) in applying §§ 1.1502-13, 1.1502-18, and 1.1502-19 to transactions occurring in prior consolidated return years of that affiliated group. In addition, if more than one ineligible life member of the group (as defined in section 1504(c)(1)) joined in the filing of a consolidated return in the taxable year immediately preceding the year for which the election under section 1504(c)(2) is effective and, solely as a result of the election, one of the ineligible life members becomes the common parent of such a group (section 1504(c)(1)), the group must continue to file a consolidated return. For example, assume that L_1 owns all of the stock of S_1 and all of the stock of L_2. L_2 owns the stock of L_3. L_1, L_2, and L_3 are life companies and S_1 is a nonlife company. Assume further that in 1981, L_1, L_2, and L_3 file a consolidated return but L_1 makes the election under section 1504(c)(2) for 1982 and L_2 and L_3 are ineligible. L_2 and L_3 must continue to file a consolidated return in 1982. Moreover, L_2 could elect in 1982 to file a consolidated return (section 1504(c)(1)) with L_3 even if they did not file a consolidated return in 1981 with L_1.

(4) *Inclusion of life company.*—If a life company is ineligible in the consolidated return year for which the election is effective, it will be treated as an includible corporation for the common parent's first taxable year in which the company becomes eligible.

(5) *Dividends received deduction.*—Section 243(b)(5) defines the term affiliated group for purposes of the election to deduct 100 percent of the qualifying dividends received by a member from another member of the group. Section 246(b)(6) limits certain multiple tax benefits and the deduction itself. Section 243(b)(5) and (6) do not apply to the mutual companies and life companies that are eligible corporations. See section 1504(c)(2)(B)(i). Thus, the common parent of the group may elect to deduct 100 percent of the qualifying dividends received from an ineligible life company.

(6) *Controlled group.*—Sections 1563(a)(4), (b)(2)(D), and (b)(3)(C) (insofar as it applies to corporations described in section 1563(b)(2)(D)) do not apply to any eligible or ineligible life company that is a member of the group for a taxable year during which the election is effective. See paragraph (d)(4) of this section for the definition of group.

(7) *Consolidated tax.*—The tax liability of a group for a consolidated return year (before application of credits against that tax) is computed on a consolidated basis by adding together the following taxes:

(i) The tax imposed under section 11 on consolidated taxable income (as determined under paragraph (g) of this section). The taxes imposed under sections 802(a), 821(a), and 831(a) will each be treated as a tax imposed under section 11.

Reg. § 1.1502-47(f)(7)(i)

(ii) The tax imposed by section 1201 on consolidated net capital gain (as determined under paragraph (o) of this section) in lieu of the tax imposed under paragraph (f)(7)(i) of this section on that gain.

(iii) Any taxes described in § 1.1502-2 (other than by paragraphs (a), (f), and (h) thereof).

(g) *Consolidated taxable income.*—The consolidated taxable income is the sum of the following three amounts:

(1) *Nonlife consolidated taxable income.*—The nonlife consolidated taxable income (as defined in paragraph (h) of this section) of the nonlife subgroup, as set off by the life subgroup losses as provided in paragraph (n) of this section. The amount in this paragraph (g)(1) may not be less than zero.

(2) *Consolidated partial LICTI.*—The consolidated partial LICTI (as defined in paragraph (j) of this section) of the life subgroup, as set off by the nonlife subgroup losses as provided in paragraph (m) of this section. The amount in this paragraph (g)(2) may not be less than zero.

(3) *Surplus accounts.*—The sum of the amounts subtracted under section 815 from the policyholders' surplus accounts of the life members.

(h) *Nonlife consolidated taxable income.*—(1) *In general.*—Nonlife consolidated taxable income is the consolidated taxable income of the nonlife subgroup, computed under § 1.1502-11 as modified by this paragraph (h). For this purpose, separate taxable income of a member includes separate mutual insurance company taxable income (as defined in section 821(b)) and insurance company taxable income (as defined in section 832).

(2) *Nonlife consolidated net operating loss deduction.*—(i) *In general.*—In applying §§ 1.1502-21 or 1.1502-21A (as appropriate), the rules in this subparagraph (2) apply in determining for the nonlife subgroup the nonlife net operating loss and the portion of the nonlife net operating loss carryovers and carrybacks to the taxable year.

(ii) *Nonlife CNOL.*—The nonlife consolidated net operating loss is determined under §§ 1.1502-21(A)(f) or 1.1502-21(e) (as appropriate) by treating the nonlife subgroup as the group.

(iii) *Carryback.*—The nonlife consolidated net operating loss for the nonlife subgroup is carried back under §§ 1.1502-21A or 1.1502-21 (as appropriate) to the appropriate years (whether consolidated or separate) before the loss may be used as a nonlife subgroup loss under paragraphs (g)(2) and (m) of this section to set off consolidated partial LICTI in the year

the loss arose. The election under section 172(b)(3)(C) to relinquish the entire carryback period for the net operating loss of the nonlife subgroup may be made by the common parent of the group. Furthermore, the election may be made even though the election under section 812(b)(3) and paragraph (l)(3)(iii) of this section is not made.

(iv) *Subgroup rule.*—In determining the portion of the nonlife consolidated net operating loss that is absorbed when the loss is carried back to a consolidated return year beginning after December 31, 1981, §§ 1.1502-21A or 1.1502-21 (as appropriate) is applied by treating the nonlife subgroup as the group. Therefore, the absorption is determined without taking into account any life subgroup losses that were previously reported on a consolidated return as setting off nonlife consolidated taxable income for the year to which the nonlife loss is carried back.

(v) *Carryover.*—The portion of the nonlife consolidated net operating loss that is not absorbed in a prior year as a carryback, or as a nonlife subgroup loss that set off consolidated partial LICTI for the year the loss arose, constitutes a nonlife carryover under this subparagraph (2) to reduce nonlife consolidated taxable income before that portion may constitute a nonlife subgroup loss that sets off consolidated partial LICTI for a particular year.

(vi) *Transitional rules.*—The nonlife consolidated net operating loss deduction is subject to a transitional rule limitation in paragraph (h)(3) of this section.

(vii) *Example.*—The following example illustrates this paragraph (h)(2). In the example, L indicates a life company, another letter indicates a nonlife company, and each corporation uses the calendar year as its taxable year.

Example. P owns all of the stock of S and L_1. L_1 owns all of the stock of L_2. For 1982, the group first files a consolidated return for which the election under section 1504(c)(2) is effective. P and S filed consolidated returns for 1979 through 1981. In 1982, the P-S group sustains a nonlife consolidated net operating loss. The loss is carried back to the consolidated return years 1979, 1980, and 1981 of P and S by using the principles of §§ 1.1502-21A and 1.1502-79A and, because the election in 1982 under section 1504(c)(2) does not result under paragraph (f)(1) of this section in the creation of a new group or the termination of the P-S nonlife group, the loss is absorbed on the consolidated return in those years without regard to whether the loss in 1982 is attributable to P or S and without regard to their contribution to consolidated taxable income in 1979, 1980, or 1981. The portion of the loss not absorbed in 1979, 1980, and 1981 may serve as a nonlife subgroup loss in 1982 that may set off the

Reg. § 1.1502-47(f)(7)(ii)

consolidated partial LICTI of L_1 and L_2 under paragraphs (g)(2) and (m) of this section.

(3) *Transitional rule.*—(i) *In general.*—The portion of the nonlife consolidated net operating loss deduction in a consolidated return year beginning after December 31, 1980 (referred to as "post-1980 year") attributable to net operating losses sustained in separate return years ending before January 1, 1981 (referred to as "pre-1981 year"), is subject to the rules and limitations in this subparagraph (3).

(ii) *Separate nonlife groups.*—To determine the limitation, first, identify for the post-1980 year one or more separate affiliated groups of nonlife companies (as defined in section 1504 without section 1504(c)(2)). For this purpose, a single nonlife company may constitute a separate affiliated group if (A) it is not otherwise a member of a separate group or (B) it has a net operating loss sustained in the pre-1981 year that may be carried over and that year is a separate return limitation year (determined under §1.1502-1(f) without paragraph (d)(11) of this section).

(iii) *Carryover.*—Second, identify the pre-1981 year net operating losses that may be carried over and that are attributable to each separate affiliated group of nonlife companies. The separate return limitation year rules in §§1.1502-21A(c) or 1.1502-21(c) (as appropriate) do not apply to any of these carryovers.

(iv) *Limitation.*—Third, treat the last taxable year ending before January 1, 1981, as if in that year there was a consolidated return change of ownership of each such separate affiliated group of nonlife companies and apply the consolidated return change of ownership limitation in §1.1502-21A(d) to the losses of each group by treating the members of each separate group as old members.

(v) *Examples.*—The following examples illustrate this paragraph (h)(3). In the examples L indicates a life company, another letter indicates a nonlife company, and each corporation uses the calendar year as its taxable year.

Example (1). Throughout all of 1982, P owns all of the stock of S and L_1 and L_1 owns all of the stock of L_2 which in turn owns all of the stock of S_1. Thus, for 1982, there are two nonlife subgroups under this subparagraph (3), P-S and S_1. For 1981, P and S did not file a consolidated return and for 1980 P has a net operating loss of $200,000. Assume that P had no income in 1981. For 1982, the group makes an election under section 1504(c)(2) to file a consolidated return and all corporations are eligible corporations. The consolidated taxable income for the nonlife subgroup for 1982 (determined without the consolidated net operating loss deduction) recomputed by including only items of income and deduction of P and S is $120,000. If $120,000 is

the §1.1502-21A(d)(2) amount for P and S, then the amount of P's net operating loss for 1980 that may be carried over to P and S for 1982 cannot exceed $120,000.

Example (2). (a) P owns all of the stock of S_1. On January 1, 1979, P purchased all of the stock of L_1 which owns all of the stock of L_2 and S_2. Prior to 1984, all of the corporations filed separate returns. For 1984, the group makes an election under section 1504(c)(2) to file a consolidated return.

(b) 1981, 1982, and 1983 are not treated under paragraph (d)(11) of this section as separate return limitation years of the P_1, S_1, and S_2 nonlife subgroup. However, P and S_1 will be treated as old members under paragraph (h)(3)(iv) of this section and under §1.1502-21A(d) with respect to their losses in 1979 and 1980 (whether a consolidated return was filed or separate returns were filed) so that the portion of nonlife consolidated taxable income attributable to S_2 may not absorb the losses of P or S_1. The rules that apply to the P-S_1 nonlife subgroup for 1979 and 1980 apply in an identical way to S_2 by treating S_2 as a subgroup separate from the P-S_1 nonlife subgroup. See section 1507(c)(2)(A) of the Tax Reform Act of 1976.

(c) Similarly, L_1 and L_2 are treated as old members under paragraphs (l)(3) and (h)(3)(iv) of this section for losses arising in 1979 and 1980. However, since the L_1—L_2 subgroup is also the life subgroup under paragraph (d)(8) of this section, the limitation in paragraph (h)(3)(iv) of this section does not affect the computation of consolidated partial LICTI for the life subgroup.

(4) *Nonlife consolidated capital gain net income or loss.*—(i) *In general.*—In applying §§1.1502-22 or 1.1502-22A (as appropriate), the rules in this subparagraph (4) apply in determining for the nonlife subgroup the nonlife consolidated capital gain net income or loss and the portion of the nonlife net capital loss carryovers and carrybacks to the taxable year. In particular, the nonlife consolidated capital gain net income and nonlife consolidated net capital loss are determined under the principles of §§1.1502-22 or 1.1502-22A(a) (as appropriate) by treating the nonlife subgroup as the group.

(ii) *Additional principles.*—In applying §§1.1502-22A or 1.1502-22 to nonlife consolidated net capital loss carryovers and carrybacks, the principles set forth in paragraph (h)(2)(iii) through (v) for applying §§1.1502-21 or 1.1502-21A (as appropriate) to nonlife consolidated net operating loss carryovers and carrybacks shall also apply. Further, the portion of nonlife consolidated net capital loss carryovers attributable to losses sustained in taxable years ending before January 1, 1981, is subject to the limitations in paragraph (h)(3) of this section applied by substituting "net capital loss" for the term "net operating loss" and "§1.1502-22A(d)" for "§1.1502-21A(d)".

(iii) *Special rules.*—The nonlife consolidated net capital loss is reduced, for purposes of determining the carryovers and carrybacks under §§ 1.1502-22A(b)(1) or 1.1502-22(b) by the lesser of—

(A) The aggregate of the additional capital loss deductions allowed under section 822(c)(6) or section 832(c)(5), or

(B) The nonlife consolidated taxable income computed without capital gains and losses.

(i) [Reserved]

(j) *Consolidated partial LICTI.*—[Reserved]

(k) *Consolidated TII.*—(1) *General rule.*—[Reserved]

(2) *Separate TII.*—[Reserved]

(3) *Company's share of investment yield.*—[Reserved]

(4) *Life consolidated capital gain net income.*—[Reserved]

(5) *Life consolidated net capital loss carryovers and carrybacks.*—The life consolidated net capital loss carryovers and carrybacks for the life subgroup are determined by applying the principles of §§ 1.1502-22 or 1.1502-22A (as appropriate) as modified by the following rules in this subparagraph (5):

(i) Life consolidated net capital loss is first carried back (or apportioned to the life members for separate return years) to be absorbed by life consolidated capital gain net income without regard to any nonlife subgroup capital losses and before the life consolidated net capital loss may serve as a life subgroup capital loss that sets off nonlife consolidated capital gain net income in the year the life consolidated net capital loss arose.

(ii) If a life consolidated net capital loss is not carried back or is not a life subgroup loss that sets off nonlife consolidated capital gain net income in the year the life consolidated net capital loss arose, then it is carried over to the particular year under this paragraph (k)(5) first against life consolidated capital gain net income before it may serve as a life subgroup capital loss that sets off nonlife consolidated capital gain net income in that particular year.

(iii) *Section 818(f).*—Capital losses may not be deducted more than once and capital gain will not be included more than once. See section 818(e) and also section 818(f).

(iv) Capital loss carryovers are subject to the transitional rule in paragraph (k)(6) of this section.

(6) *Transitional rule.*—The portion of the life consolidated capital loss carryovers attributable to the net capital losses of the life members sustained in separate return years ending before January 1, 1981, is subject to the same limitations

as the capital losses of nonlife members in paragraph (h)(4)(iii) of this section by applying the principles of paragraph (h)(3) of this section to each separate affiliated group of life companies.

(l) *Consolidated GO or LO.*—(1) *General rule.*—[Reserved]

(2) *Separate GO.*—[Reserved]

(3) *Consolidated operations loss deduction.*—(i) *General rule.*—The consolidated operations loss deduction is an amount equal to the consolidated operations loss carryovers and carrybacks to the taxable year. The provisions of §§ 1.1502-21 or 1.1502-21A (as appropriate) and section 812 apply to the extent not inconsistent with this paragraph (l)(3).

(ii) *Consolidated offset.*—For purposes of applying section 812(b) and (d), the term "consolidated offset" means the increase in the consolidated operations loss deduction which reduces consolidated partial LICTI to zero. For setoff of consolidated LO against nonlife consolidated taxable income, see paragraph (n)(2) of this section.

(iii) *Carrybacks.*—A consolidated LO is first carried back to be absorbed by GO of a life member under section 809(d)(4) or consolidated partial LICTI (as the case may be under section 818(f)(2)) for prior consolidated return years (or apportioned to the life members for prior separate return years) without regard to any nonlife subgroup losses that were set off against consolidated partial LICTI and before the consolidated LO may serve as a life subgroup loss to be set off against nonlife consolidated taxable income in the year the consolidated LO arose. The election to relinquish the entire carryback period for the consolidated LO of the life subgroup may be made by the common parent of the group. See section 812(b)(3). Furthermore, the election may be made even though the election under section 172(b)(3)(C) and paragraph (h)(2)(iii) of this section is not made.

(iv) *Carryovers.*—If a consolidated LO is not carried back or is not applied as a life subgroup loss that set off nonlife consolidated taxable income in the year the consolidated LO arose, then it is carried over to a particular year under this paragraph (l)(3) first against the GO of a life member under section 809(d)(4) or consolidated partial LICTI (as the case may be under section 818(f)(2)) before it may serve as a life subgroup loss that may be set off against nonlife consolidated taxable income for that particular year.

(v) *Transitional rule.*—The portion of a consolidated operations loss deduction that is attributable to LOs sustained in separate return years ending before January 1, 1981, is subject to the same rules and limitations that the nonlife consolidated net operating loss deduction is subject to in paragraph (h)(3) of this section as applied by identifying separate affiliated groups of life companies.

(4) *Life consolidated capital gain net income or loss.*—Life consolidated capital gain net income or loss is determined in the same manner as under paragraph (k)(4) of this section. However, a life member's company share is determined under section 809(a) and (b)(3).

(m) *Consolidated partial LICTI setoff by nonlife subgroup losses.*—(1) *In general.*—The nonlife subgroup losses consist of the nonlife consolidated net operating loss and the nonlife consolidated net capital loss. Under paragraph (g)(2) of this section, consolidated partial LICTI is set off by the amounts of these two consolidated losses specified in paragraph (m)(2) of this section. The setoff is subject to the rules and limitations in paragraph (m)(3) of this section.

(2) *Amount of setoff.*—(i) *Current year.*—Consolidated partial LICTI for the current taxable year is set off by the portion of the nonlife consolidated net operating loss and nonlife consolidated net capital loss arising in that year that cannot be carried back under paragraph (h) of this section to prior taxable years (whether consolidated or separate return years) of the nonlife subgroup.

(ii) *Carryovers.*—The portion of the offsettable nonlife consolidated net operating loss or nonlife consolidated net capital loss that has not been used as a nonlife subgroup loss setoff against consolidated partial LICTI in the year it arose may be carried over to succeeding taxable years under the principles of §§ 1.1502-21 or 1.1502-21A (as appropriate) (relating to net operating loss deduction) or §§ 1.1502-22 or 1.1502-22A (as appropriate) (relating to net capital loss carryovers). However, in any particular succeeding year, the losses will be used under paragraph (h) of this section in computing nonlife consolidated taxable income before being used in that year as a nonlife subgroup loss that sets off consolidated partial LICTI.

(3) *Nonlife subgroup loss rules and limitations.*—The nonlife subgroup losses are subject to the following operating rules and limitations:

(i) *Separate return years.*—The carryovers in paragraph (m)(2)(ii) of this section may include net operating losses and net capital losses of the nonlife members arising in separate return years ending after December 31, 1980, that may be carried over to a succeeding year under the principles (including limitations) of §§ 1.1502-21 and 1.1502-22 (or §§ 1.1502-21A and 1.1502-22A, as appropriate). But see subdivision (ix) of this paragraph (m)(3).

(ii) *Capital loss.*—Nonlife consolidated net capital loss sets off consolidated partial LICTI only to the extent of life consolidated capital gain net income (as determined under paragraph

(l)(4) of this section) and this setoff applies before any nonlife consolidated net operating loss sets off consolidated partial LICTI.

(iii) *Capital gain.*—Life consolidated capital gain net income is zero in any taxable year in which the life subgroup has a consolidated LO and, in any taxable year, it may not exceed consolidated partial LICTI.

(iv) *Ordering rule.*—Consolidated partial LICTI for a consolidated return year is set off by nonlife subgroup losses for that year before being set off (under paragraph (m)(2)(ii) of this section) by a carryover of a nonlife subgroup loss to that year.

(v) *Setoff at bottom line.*—The setoff of nonlife subgroup losses against consolidated partial LICTI does not affect life member deductions that depend in whole or in part on GO or TII. Thus, the setoff does not affect the amount of consolidated partial LICTI (as determined under paragraph (j) of this section) for any taxable year but it merely constitutes an adjustment in arriving at the group's consolidated taxable income under paragraph (g) of this section.

(vi) *Ineligible nonlife member.*—(A) The offsetable nonlife consolidated net operating loss that arises in any consolidated return year (that may be set off against consolidated partial LICTI in the current taxable year or in a succeeding taxable year) is the amount computed under paragraph (h)(2)(ii) of this section reduced by the ineligible NOL. For purposes of this subparagraph (3), the "ineligible NOL" is in the year the loss arose the amount of the separate net operating loss (determined under §§ 1.1502-21(b)) of any nonlife member that is ineligible in that year (and not the portion of the nonlife consolidated net operating loss attributable under §§ 1.1502-21(b) to such a member). (B) The carryovers of offsetable nonlife net operating losses under paragraph (m)(2)(ii) of this section do not include an ineligible NOL arising in a consolidated return year or a loss attributable to an ineligible member arising in a separate return year. See section 1503(c)(2). (C) For absorption within the nonlife subgroup of an ineligible NOL arising in a consolidated return year or a loss of an ineligible member arising in a separate return year which is not a separate return limitation year under paragraph (m)(3)(ix) of this section, see paragraph (m)(3)(vii) of this section.

(vii) *Absorption of ineligible NOL.*—(A) If all or a portion of a nonlife member's ineligible NOL (determined under paragraph (m)(3)(vi)(A) of this section) may be carried back or carried over under paragraph (h)(2) of this section to a particular consolidated return year of the nonlife subgroup (absorption year), then notwithstanding § 1.1502-21A(b)(3)(ii) or 1.1502-21(b), the amount carried to the absorption year will be absorbed by that member's contribution (to the extent thereof) to nonlife consolidated taxable income for that year.

(B) For purposes of (A) of this subdivision (vii), a member's contribution to nonlife consolidated taxable income for an absorption year is the amount of such income (computed without the portion of the nonlife consolidated net operating loss deduction attributable to taxable years subsequent to the year the loss arose), minus such consolidated taxable income recomputed by excluding both that member's items of income and deductions for the absorption year. The deductions of the member include the prior application of this paragraph (m)(3)(vii) to the absorption of the nonlife consolidated net operating loss deduction for losses arising in taxable years prior to the particular loss year.

(viii) *Election to relinquish carryback.*—The offsetable nonlife consolidated net operating loss does not include the amount that could be carried back under paragraph (h)(2) of this section but for the common parent's election under section 172(b)(3)(C) to relinquish the carryback. See section 1503(c)(1).

(ix) *Separate return limitation year.*—The offsetable nonlife consolidated net operating and capital loss carryovers do not include any losses attributable to a nonlife member that were sustained (A) in a separate return limitation year (determined without section 1504(b)(2)) of that member (or a predecessor), or (B) in a separate return year ending after December 31, 1980, in which an election was in effect under neither section 1504(c)(2) nor section 243(b)(2). For purposes of this paragraph (m), a separate return limitation year includes a taxable year ending before January 1, 1981. See section 1507(c)(2)(A) of the Tax Reform Act of 1976 and §§ 1.1502-15 and 1.1502-15A (including applicable exceptions thereto).

(x) *Percentage limitation.*—The offsetable nonlife consolidated net operating losses that may be set off against consolidated partial LICTI in a particular year may not exceed a percentage limitation. This limitation is the applicable percentage in section 1503(c)(1) of the lesser of two amounts. The first amount is the sum of the offsetable nonlife consolidated net operating losses under paragraph (m)(2) of this section that may serve in the particular year (determined without this limitation) as a setoff against consolidated partial LICTI. The second amount is consolidated partial LICTI (as defined in paragraph (j) of this section) in the particular year reduced by any nonlife consolidated net capital loss that sets off consolidated partial LICTI in that year.

(xi) *Further limitation.*—Any offsetable nonlife consolidated net operating loss remaining after applying the percentage limitation that is carried over to a succeeding taxable year may not be set off against the consolidated partial LICTI attributable to a life member that was not

an eligible life member in the year the loss arose. See section 1503(c)(2).

(xii) *Restoration rule.*—The carryback of a consolidated LO or life consolidated net capital loss under paragraph (l) of this section that reduces consolidated partial LICTI (or life consolidated capital gain net income) for a prior year may reduce the amount of nonlife subgroup losses that would offset consolidated partial LICTI in that prior year. Thus, that amount may be carried over under paragraph (h)(2) or (4) of this section from that prior year in determining nonlife consolidated taxable income in a succeeding year or serve as offsetable nonlife subgroup losses in a succeeding year.

(4) *Acquired groups.*—[Reserved]

(5) *Illustrations.*—The following examples illustrate this paragraph (m). In the examples, L indicates a life company, another letter indicates a nonlife company, and each corporation uses the calendar year as its taxable year.

Example (1). P owns all of the stock of L and S. S owns all of the stock of I, a nonlife member that is an ineligible corporation for 1982 under paragraph (d)(13) of this section. For 1982, the group elects under section 1504(c)(2) to file a consolidated return. For 1982, assume that any nonlife consolidated net operating loss may not be carried back to a prior taxable year. Other facts are summarized in the following table:

	Separate taxable income (loss)
P	$100
S	(100)
I	(100)
Nonlife consolidated net operating loss	(100)

Under paragraph (m)(3)(vi) of this section, P's separate income is considered to absorb the loss of S, an eligible member, first and the offsetable nonlife consolidated net operating loss is zero, *i.e.*, the consolidated net operating loss ($100) reduced by I's loss ($100). The consolidated net operating loss ($100) may be carried over, but since it is entirely attributable to I (an ineligible member) its use is subject to the restrictions in paragraph (m)(3)(vi) of this section. The result would be the same if the group contained two additional members, S_1, an eligible member, and I_1, an ineligible member, where S_1 had a loss of ($100) and I_1 had income of $100.

Example (2). The facts are the same as in example (1) except that for 1982 S's separate net operating loss is $200. Assume further that L's consolidated partial LICTI is $200. Under paragraph (m)(3)(vi) of this section, the offsetable nonlife consolidated net operating loss is $100, *i.e.*, the nonlife consolidated net operating loss computed under paragraph (h)(2)(ii) of this section ($200), reduced by the separate net operating loss of I ($100). The offsetable nonlife consolidated net operating loss that may be set off against consolidated partial LICTI in 1982 is $30, *i.e.*, 30 percent of the lesser of the offsetable $100 or consolidated partial LICTI of $200. See paragraph (m)(3)(x) of this section. The nonlife subgroup may carry $170 to 1983 under para-

	Facts (a)	(Dollars omitted) Offsetable (b)	Limit (c)	Unused loss (d)
1. P.	100			
2. S.	(200)	(100)		(70)
3. I.	(100)			(100)
4. Nonlife subgroup	(200)	(100)	(100)	(170)
5. L.	200		200	
6. 30% of lower line 4(c) or 5(c)			30	
7. Unused offsetable loss				(70)

Accordingly, under paragraph (g) of this section (assuming no amount is withdrawn from L's surplus accounts), consolidated taxable income is $170, *i.e.*, line 5(a) minus line 6(c).

Example (3). The facts are the same as in example (2) with the following additions for 1983. The nonlife subgroup has nonlife consolidated taxable income of $50 (all of which is attributable to I) before the nonlife consolidated net operating loss deduction under paragraph (h)(2) of this section. Consolidated partial LICTI is $100. Under paragraph (h)(2) of this section, $50 of the nonlife consolidated net operating loss carryover ($170) is used in 1983 and, under paragraph (m)(3)(vi) and (vii) of this section, the portion used in 1982 is attributable to I, the ineligible nonlife member. Accordingly, the offsetable nonlife consolidated net operating loss from 1982 under paragraph (m)(3)(ii) of this section is $70, *i.e.*, the unused loss from 1982. The offsetable nonlife consolidated net operating loss in 1983 is $24.50, *i.e.*, 35 percent of the lesser of the offsetable loss of $70 or consolidated partial LICTI of $100. Accordingly, under paragraph (g) of this section (assuming no amount is withdrawn from L's surplus accounts), consolidated taxable income is $75.50, *i.e.*, consolidated partial LICTI of $100 minus the offsetable loss of $24.50.

Example (4). P owns all of the stock of S and L. For 1982, all corporations are eligible corporations, and the group elects under section 1504(c)(2) to file a consolidated return, the nonlife consolidated net operating loss is $100, and the nonlife consolidated net capital loss is $50. Assume that the losses may not be carried back and the capital losses are not attributable to built-in deductions under paragraph (m)(3)(ix) of this section or under § 1.1502-15A. Other facts and the results are set forth in the following table:

graph (h)(2) of this section against nonlife consolidated taxable income, *i.e.*, consolidated net operating loss ($200) less amount used in 1982 ($30). Under paragraph (m)(2)(ii) of this section, the offsetable nonlife consolidated net operating loss that may be carried to 1983 is $70, *i.e.*, $100 minus $30. The facts and results are summarized in the table below:

	P-S	L
1. Nonlife consolidated net operating loss	($100)	
2. Nonlife consolidated capital loss	(50)	
3. Consolidated partial LICTI		$100
4. Life consolidated capital gain net income included in line 3		50
5. Offsetable:		
(a) 30% of lower of line (1) or line (3) - (4)	(15)	
(b) Line 2	(50)	
(c) Total	(65)	
6. Unused losses available to be carried over:		
(a) From line 1 (line 1 minus line 5(a))	(85)	
(b) From line 2 (line 2 minus line 5(b))	0	

Accordingly, under paragraph (g) of this section consolidated taxable income is $35, *i.e.*, line 3 minus line 5(c).

Example (5). The facts are the same as in example (4). Assume further that for 1983 L has an LO that is carried back to 1982 and the LO is large enough to reduce consolidated partial LICTI for 1982 to zero as determined before any setoff for nonlife losses. Under paragraph (m)(3)(xii) of this section, the nonlife consolidated net operating loss of $15 and the nonlife consolidated net capital loss of $50 that were set off in 1982 respectively against consolidated partial LICTI and life consolidated capital gain net income are restored. These restored amounts may constitute part of the nonlife consolidated net operating loss carryover to 1983 under paragraph (h)(2) of this section or part of the nonlife net capital loss carryover to 1983 under paragraph (h)(4) of this section.

Reg. § 1.1502-47(m)(5)

Example (6). The facts are the same as in example (5) except that L's LO for 1983 as carried back reduces consolidated partial LICTI in 1982 from $100 to $25. Since consolidated partial LICTI of $100 in 1982 (before the carryback) included life consolidated capital gain net income of $50, under paragraph (m)(3)(iii) of this section, the life consolidated capital gain net income is $25, *i.e.,* $50 but not more than $25. Therefore, under paragraph (m)(3)(ii) of this section, the offsetable nonlife capital loss in 1982 is $25 and, under paragraph (m)(3)(xii) of this section, $25 of the $50 nonlife consolidated net capital loss in 1982 may be carried under paragraph (h)(4) of this section to 1983. No nonlife consolidated net operating loss is used as a setoff against consolidated partial LICTI in 1982 under paragraph (m)(3)(xii) of this section by reason of the carryback of the consolidated LO from 1983 to 1982.

(n) *Nonlife consolidated taxable income set off by life subgroup losses.*—(1) *In general.*—The life subgroup losses consist of the consolidated LO and the life consolidated net capital loss (as determined under paragraph (l)(4) of this section). Under paragraph (g)(1) of this section, nonlife consolidated taxable income is set off by the amounts of these two consolidated losses specified in paragraph (n)(2) of this section.

(2) *Amount of setoff.*—The portion of the consolidated LO or life consolidated net capital loss that may be set off against nonlife consolidated taxable income (determined under paragraph (h) of this section) is determined by applying the rules prescribed in paragraph (m)(2) and (3) of this section in the following manner:

(i) Substitute the term "life" for "nonlife", and vice versa.

(ii) Substitute the term "nonlife consolidated taxable income" for "consolidated partial LICTI", and vice versa.

(iii) Substitute the term "consolidated LO" for "non-life consolidated net operating loss", "paragraph (l)" or "paragraph (j)" for "paragraph (h)", and "section 812(b)(3)" for "section 172(b)(3)(C)".

(iv) Paragraphs (m)(3)(vi), (vii), (x), and (xi) of this section do not apply to a consolidated LO.

(v) Capital losses may not be deducted more than once. See section 818(e) and also the requirements in section 818(f).

(vi) The setoff of life subgroup losses against nonlife consolidated taxable income does not affect nonlife member deductions that depend in whole or in part on taxable income.

(3) *Illustrations.*—The following examples illustrate this paragraph (n). In the examples, L indicates a life company, another letter indicates a nonlife company, and each corporation uses the calendar year as its taxable year.

Example (1). P, S, L_1 and L_2 constitute a group that elects under section 1504(c)(2) to file a consolidated return for 1982. In 1982, the nonlife subgroup consolidated taxable income is $100 and there is $20 of nonlife consolidated net capital loss that cannot be carried back under paragraph (h) of this section to taxable years (whether consolidated or separate) preceding 1982. The nonlife subgroup has no carryover from years prior to 1982. Consolidated LO is $150 which under paragraph (l) of this section includes life consolidated capital gain net income of $25. The $150 LO is carried back under paragraph (l)(3) of this section to taxable years (whether consolidated or separate) preceding 1982 before it may offset in 1982 nonlife consolidated taxable income. Since life consolidated capital gain net income is zero for 1982, the nonlife capital loss offset is zero.

Example (2). The facts are the same as in example (1). Assume further that no part of the $150 consolidated LO for 1982 can be used by L_1 and L_2 in years prior to 1982. For 1982, $100 of consolidated LO sets off the $100 nonlife consolidated taxable income. The life subgroup carries under paragraph (l)(3) of this section to 1983 $50 of the consolidated LO ($150 minus $100). See paragraph (l)(3)(ii) of this section. The $50 carryover will be used in 1983 against life subgroup income before it may be used in 1983 to setoff nonlife consolidated taxable income.

Example (3). (a) The facts are the same as in example (1), except that for 1982 the nonlife consolidated taxable income is $150 and includes nonlife consolidated capital gain net income of $50, consolidated partial LICTI is $200, and a life consolidated net capital loss is $50. Assume that the $50 life consolidated net capital loss sets off the $50 nonlife consolidated capital gain net income. Consolidated taxable income under paragraph (g) of this section is $300, *i.e.,* nonlife consolidated taxable income ($150) minus the setoff of the life consolidated net capital loss ($50), plus consolidated partial LICTI ($200).

(b) Assume that for 1983 the nonlife consolidated net operating loss is $150. Under paragraph (h)(2) of this section, the loss may be carried back to 1982 against nonlife consolidated taxable income. If P, the common parent, does not elect to relinquish the carryback under section 172(b)(3)(C), the entire $150 must be carried back reducing 1982 nonlife consolidated taxable income to zero and nonlife consolidated capital gain net income to zero. Under paragraph (m)(3)(xii) of this section, the setoff in 1982 of the nonlife consolidated capital gain net income ($50) by the life consolidated net capital loss ($50) is restored. Accordingly, the 1982 life consolidated net capital loss may be carried over by the life subgroup to 1983. Under paragraph (g) of this section, after the carryback consolidated taxable income for 1982 is $200, *i.e.,* nonlife consolidated taxable income ($0) plus consolidated partial LICTI ($200).

Reg. §1.1502-47(n)

Example (4). The facts are the same as in example (3), except that P elects under section 172(b)(3)(C) to relinquish the carryback of $150 arising in 1983. The setoff in part (a) of example (3) is not restored. However, the offsetable nonlife consolidated net operating loss for 1983 (or that may be carried forward from 1983) is zero. See paragraph (m)(3)(viii) of this section. Nevertheless, the $150 nonlife consolidated net operating loss may be carried forward to be used by the nonlife group.

Example (5). P owns all of the stock of S_1 and of L_1. On January 1, 1978, L_1 purchases all of the stock of L_2. For 1982, the group elects under section 1504(c)(2) to file a consolidated return. For 1982, L_1 is an eligible corporation under paragraph (d)(12) of this section but L_2 is ineligible. Thus, L_1 but not L_2 is a member for 1982. For 1982, L_2 sustains an LO that cannot be carried back. For 1982, L_2 is treated under paragraph (f)(6) of this section as a member of a controlled group of corporations under section 1563 with P, S, and L_1. For 1983, L_2 is eligible and is included on the group's consolidated return. L_2's LO for 1982 that may be carried to 1983 is not treated under paragraph (d)(11) of this section as having been sustained in a separate return limitation year for purposes of computing consolidated partial LICTI of the L_1-L_2 life subgroup for 1983. Furthermore, the portion of L_2's LO not used under paragraph (l)(3) of this section against life subgroup income in 1983 may be included in offsetable consolidated operations loss under paragraph (n)(2) and (m)(3)(i) of this section that reduces in 1983 nonlife consolidated taxable income because L_2's loss in 1982 was not sustained in a separate return limitation year under paragraph (n)(2) and (m)(3)(ix)(A) of this section or in a separate return year (1982) when an election was in effect neither under section 1504(c)(2) nor section 243(b)(2).

(o) *Alternative tax.*—(1) *In general.*—For purposes of the alternative tax under paragraph (f)(7)(ii) of this section, consolidated net capital gain is the sum of the following two amounts.

(i) The nonlife consolidated net capital gain reduced by any setoff of a life consolidated net capital loss.

(ii) The life consolidated net capital gain reduced by any setoff of a nonlife consolidated net capital loss.

(2) *Net capital gain.*—For purposes of this paragraph (o)—

(i) Nonlife consolidated net capital gain is computed under §§ 1.1502-41A or 1,1502-22T (as appropriate) except that it may not exceed nonlife consolidated taxable income (computed under paragraph (h) of this section).

(ii) Life consolidated net capital gain is computed under §§ 1.1502-41A or 1.502-22T (as appropriate), applied in a manner consistent with paragraph (l)(4) of this section, except that

it may not exceed consolidated partial LICTI (as determined under paragraph (j) of this section).

(iii) *Setoffs.*—Setoffs are determined under paragraph (m) or (n) of this section (as the case may be).

(p) *Transitional rule for credit carryovers.*—For limitations on credits arising in taxable years ending before January 1, 1981, that may be carried over to taxable years beginning on or after that date, section 1507(c)(2)(A) of the Tax Reform Act of 1976 and the principles in paragraph (h)(3) of this section (relating to limitations on loss carryovers) apply.

(q) *Preemption.*—The rules in this section preempt any inconsistent rules in other sections (§ 1.1502-1 through 1.1502-80) of the consolidated return regulations. For example, the rules in paragraph (m)(3)(vi) apply notwithstanding §§ 1.1502-21A(b)(3) and 1.1502-79A(a)(3) (or § 1.1502-21, as appropriate).

(r) *Other consolidation principles.*—The fact that this section treats the life and nonlife members as separate groups in computing, respectively, consolidated partial LICTI (or LO) and nonlife consolidated taxable income (or loss) does not affect the usual rules in §§ 1.1502-0—1.1502-80 unless this section provides otherwise. Thus, the usual rules in § 1.1502-13 (relating to intercompany transactions) apply to both the life and nonlife members by treating them as members of one affiliated group.

(s) *Filing requirements.*—(1) *In general.*—To file a consolidated income tax return for a life-nonlife consolidated group, the common parent shall—

(i) File the applicable consolidated corporate income tax return: a Form 1120-L, "U.S. Life Insurance Company Income Tax Return," where the common parent is a life insurance company; a Form 1120-PC, "U.S. Property and Casualty Insurance Company Income Tax Return," where the common parent is an insurance company, other than a life insurance company; or a Form 1120, "U.S. Corporation Income Tax Return," where the common parent is any other type of corporation;

(ii) Indicate clearly on the face of this return that such corporate tax return is a life-nonlife return;

(iii) Show any set offs required by paragraphs (g), (m), and (n) of this section;

(iv) Report separately the nonlife consolidated taxable income or loss, determined under paragraph (h) of this section, on a Form 1120 or 1120-PC (whether filed by the common parent or as an attachment to the consolidated return), as the case may be, of all nonlife members of the consolidated group; and

(v) Report separately the consolidated partial Life Insurance Company Taxable Income

Reg. § 1.1502-47(s)(1)(v)

(as defined by paragraph (d)(3) of this section), determined under paragraph (j) of this section, on a Form 1120-L (whether filed by the common parent or as an attachment to the consolidated return), of all life members of the consolidated group.

(2) *Cross reference.*—See § 1.1502-75(j), regarding the inclusion in a corporate tax return of the required statements and schedules for subsidiaries.

(t) *Effective/applicability date.*—Paragraph (s) of this section applies to any consolidated Federal income tax return due (without extensions) on or after December 21, 2009. However, a consolidated group may apply paragraph (s) of this section to any consolidated Federal income tax return filed on or after December 21, 2009. For returns due before December 21, 2009, see § 1.1502-47T as contained in 26 CFR part 1 in effect on April 1, 2009. [Reg. § 1.1502-47.]

☐ [*T.D.* 7877, 3-14-83. *Amended by T.D.* 7912, 9-1-83; *T.D.* 8560, 8-12-94; *T.D.* 8597, 7-12-95; *T.D.* 8677, 6-26-96; *T.D.* 8823, 6-25-99; *T.D.* 9258, 4-24-2006; *T.D.* 9304, 12-21-2006; *T.D.* 9342, 7-19-2007 *and T.D.* 9476, 12-22-2009.]

[Reg. § 1.1502-55]

§ 1.1502-55. Computation of alternative minimum tax of consolidated groups.—(a) through (h)(3) [Reserved].

(h)(4) *Separate return year minimum tax credit.* (i) and (ii) [Reserved].

(iii)(A) *Limitation on portion of separate return year minimum tax credit arising in separate return limitation years.*—The aggregate of a member's minimum tax credits arising in SRLYs that are included in the consolidated minimum tax credits for all consolidated return years of the group may not exceed—

(1) The aggregate for all consolidated return years of the member's contributions to the consolidated section 53(c) limitation for each consolidated return year; reduced by

(2) The aggregate of the member's minimum tax credits arising and absorbed in all consolidated return years (whether or not absorbed by the member).

(B) *Computational rules.*—(1) *Member's contribution to the consolidated section 53(c) limitation.*—Except as provided in the special rule of paragraph (h)(4)(iii)(B)(2) of this section, a member's contribution to the consolidated section 53(c) limitation for a consolidated return year equals the member's share of the consolidated net regular tax liability minus its share of consolidated tentative minimum tax. The group computes the member's shares by applying to the respective consolidated amounts the principles of section 1552 and the percentage method under

§ 1.1502-33(d)(3), assuming a 100% allocation of any decreased tax liability. The group makes proper adjustments so that taxes and credits not taken into account in computing the limitation under section 53(c) are not taken into account in computing the member's share of the consolidated net regular tax, etc. (See, for example, the taxes described in section 26(b) that are disregarded in computing regular tax liability.)

(2) *Adjustment for year in which alternative minimum tax is paid.*—For a consolidated return year for which consolidated tentative minimum tax is greater than consolidated regular tax liability, the group reduces the member's share of the consolidated tentative minimum tax by the member's share of the consolidated alternative minimum tax for the year. The group determines the member's share of consolidated alternative minimum tax for a year using the same method it uses to determine the member's share of the consolidated minimum tax credits for the year.

(3) *Years included in computation.*—For purposes of computing the limitation under this paragraph (h)(4)(iii), the consolidated return years of the group include only those years, including the year to which a credit is carried, that the member has been continuously included in the group's consolidated return, but exclude any years after the year to which the credit is carried.

(4) *Subgroup principles.*—The SRLY subgroup principles under § 1.1502-21(c)(2) apply for purposes of this paragraph (h)(4)(iii). The predecessor and successor principles under § 1.1502-21(f) also apply for purposes of this paragraph (h)(4)(iii).

(5) *Overlap with section 383.*—The principles under § 1.1502-21(g) apply for purposes of this paragraph (h)(4)(iii). For example, an overlap of this paragraph (h)(4)(iii) and the application of section 383 with respect to a credit carryover occurs if a corporation becomes a member of a consolidated group (the SRLY event) within six months of the change date of an ownership change giving rise to a section 383 credit limitation with respect to that carryover (the section 383 event), with the result that the limitation of this paragraph (h)(4)(iii) does not apply. See §§ 1.1502-21(g)(2)(ii)(A) and 1.383-1; see also § 1.1502-21(g)(4) (subgroup rules).

(C) *Effective date.*—(1) *In general.*—This paragraph (h)(4)(iii) generally applies to consolidated return years for which the due date of the income tax return (without extensions) is after March 13, 1998. See § 1.1502-3(d)(4) for an optional effective date rule (generally making this paragraph (h)(4)(iii) also applicable to a consolidated return year beginning on or after January 1, 1997, if the due date of the income tax return (without extensions) was on or before March 13, 1998).

(i) *Contribution years.*—In general, a group does not take into account a consolidated taxable year for which the due date of the income tax return (without extensions) is on or before March 13, 1998, in determining a member's (or subgroup's) contributions to the consolidated section 53(c) limitation under this paragraph (h)(4)(iii). However, if a consolidated group chooses to apply the optional effective date rule, the consolidated group shall not take into account a consolidated taxable year beginning before January 1, 1997 in determining a member's (or subgroup's) contributions to the consolidated section 53(c) limitation under this paragraph (h)(4)(iii).

(ii) *Special subgroup rule.*—In the event that the principles of § 1.1502-21(g)(1) do not apply to a particular credit carryover in the current group, then solely for purposes of applying this paragraph (h)(4)(iii) to determine the limitation with respect to that carryover and with respect to which the SRLY register (the aggregate of the member's or subgroup's contribution to consolidated section 53(c) limitation reduced by the aggregate of the member's or subgroup's minimum tax credits arising and absorbed in all consolidated return years) began in a taxable year for which the due date of the return is on or before May 25, 2000, the principles of § 1.1502-21(c)(2) shall be applied without regard to the phrase "or for a carryover that was subject to the overlap rule described in paragraph (g) of this section or § 1.1502-15(g) with respect to another group (the former group)."

(2) *Overlap rule.*—Paragraph (h)(4)(iii)(B)(5) of this section (relating to overlap with section 383) applies to taxable years for which the due date (without extensions) of the consolidated return is after May 25, 2000. For purposes of paragraph (h)(4)(iii)(B)(5) of this section, only an ownership change to which section 383, as amended by the Tax Reform Act of 1986 (100 Stat. 2095), applies and which results, in a section 383 credit limitation shall constitute a section 383 event. The optional effective date rule of § 1.1502-3(d)(4) (generally making this paragraph (h)(4)(iii) also applicable to a consolidated return year beginning on or after January 1, 1997, if the due date of the income tax return (without extensions) was on or before March 13, 1998) does not apply with respect to paragraph (h)(4)(iii)(B)(5) of this section (relating to the overlap rule). [Reg. § 1.1502-55.]

☐ [*T.D. 8884, 5-24-2000.*]

[Reg. §1.1502-75]

§ 1.1502-75. Filing of consolidated returns.—(a) *Privilege of filing consolidated returns.*—(1) *Exercise of privilege for first consolidated return year.*—A group which did not file a consolidated return for the immediately preceding taxable year may file a consolidated return in lieu of separate returns for the taxable year, provided that each corporation which has been a member during any part of the taxable year for which the consolidated return is to be filed consents (in the manner provided in paragraph (b) of this section) to the regulations under section 1502. If a group wishes to exercise its privilege of filing a consolidated return, such consolidated return must be filed not later than the last day prescribed by law (including extensions of time) for the filing of the common parent's return. Such consolidated return may not be withdrawn after such last day (but the group may change the basis of its return at any time prior to such last day).

(2) *Continued filing requirement.*—A group which filed (or was required to file) a consolidated return for the immediately preceding taxable year is required to file a consolidated return for the taxable year unless it has an election to discontinue filing consolidated returns under paragraph (c) of this section.

(b) *How consent for first consolidated year exercised.*—(1) *General rule.*—The consent of a corporation referred to in paragraph (a)(1) of this section shall be made by such corporation joining in the making of the consolidated return for such year. A corporation shall be deemed to have joined in the making of such return for such year if it files a Form 1122 in the manner specified in paragraph (h)(2) of this section.

(2) *Consent under facts and circumstances.*—If a member of the group fails to file Form 1122, the Commissioner may under the facts and circumstances determine that such member has joined in the making of a consolidated return by such group. The following circumstances, among others, will be taken into account in making this determination:

(i) Whether or not the income and deductions of the member were included in the consolidated return;

(ii) Whether or not a separate return was filed by the member for that taxable year; and

(iii) Whether or not the member was included in the affiliations schedule, Form 851.

If the Commissioner determines that the member has joined in the making of the consolidated return, such member shall be treated as if it had filed a Form 1122 for such year for purposes of paragraph (h)(2) of this section.

(3) *Failure to consent due to mistake.*—If any member has failed to join in the making of a consolidated return under either subparagraph (1) or (2) of this paragraph, then the tax liability of each member of the group shall be determined on the basis of separate returns unless the common parent corporation establishes to the satisfaction of the Commissioner that the failure of such member to join in the making of the consolidated return was due to a mistake of law or fact, or to inadvertence. In such case, such

member shall be treated as if it had filed a Form 1122 for such year for purposes of paragraph (h)(2) of this section, and thus joined in the making of the consolidated return for such year.

(c) *Election to discontinue filing consolidated returns.*—(1) *Good cause.*—(i) *In general.*—Notwithstanding that a consolidated return is required for a taxable year, the Commissioner, upon application by the common parent, may for good cause shown grant permission to a group to discontinue filing consolidated returns. Any such application shall be made to the Commissioner of Internal Revenue, Washington, D.C. 20224, and shall be made not later than the 90th day before the due date for the filing of the consolidated return (including extensions of time). In addition, if an amendment of the Code, or other law affecting the computation of tax liability, is enacted and the enactment is effective for a taxable year ending before or within 90 days after the date of enactment, then application for such a taxable year may be made not later than the 180th day after the date of enactment, and if the application is approved the permission to discontinue filing consolidated returns will apply to such taxable year notwithstanding that a consolidated return has already been filed for such year.

(ii) *Substantial adverse change in law affecting tax liability.*—Ordinarily, the Commissioner will grant a group permission to discontinue filing consolidated returns if the net result of all amendments to the Code or regulations with effective dates commencing within the taxable year has a substantial adverse effect on the consolidated tax liability of the group for such year relative to what the aggregate tax liability would be if the members of the group filed separate returns for such year. Thus, for example, assume P and S filed a consolidated return for the calendar year 1966 and that the provisions of the Code have been amended by a bill which was enacted by Congress in 1966, but which is first effective for taxable years beginning on or after January 1, 1967. Assume further that P makes a timely application to discontinue filing consolidated returns. In order to determine whether the amendments have a substantial adverse effect on the consolidated tax liability for 1967, relative to what the aggregate tax liability would be if the members of the group filed separate returns for 1967, the difference between the tax liability of the group computed on a consolidated basis and taking into account the changes in the law effective for 1967 and the aggregate tax liability of the members of the group computed as if each such member filed separate returns for such year (also taking into account such changes) shall be compared with the difference between the tax liability of such group for 1967 computed on a consolidated basis without regard to the changes in the law effective in such year and the aggregate tax liability of the members of the group

computed as if separate returns had been filed by such members for such year without regard to the changes in the law effective in such year.

(iii) *Other factors.*—In addition, the Commissioner will take into account other factors in determining whether good cause exists for granting permission to discontinue filing consolidated returns beginning with the taxable year, including—

(a) Changes in law or circumstances, including changes which do not affect Federal income tax liability,

(b) Changes in law which are first effective in the taxable year and which result in a substantial reduction in the consolidated net operating loss (or consolidated unused investment credit) for such year relative to what the aggregate net operating losses (or investment credits) would be if the members of the group filed separate returns for such year, and

(c) Changes in the Code or regulations which are effective prior to the taxable year but which first have a substantial adverse effect on the filing of a consolidated return relative to the filing of separate returns by members of the group in such year.

(2) *Discretion of Commissioner to grant blanket permission.*—(i) *Permission to all groups.*—The Commissioner, in his discretion, may grant all groups permission to discontinue filing consolidated returns if any provision of the Code or regulations has been amended and such amendment is of the type which could have a substantial adverse effect on the filing of consolidated returns by substantially all groups, relative to the filing of separate returns. Ordinarily, the permission to discontinue shall apply with respect to the taxable year of each group which includes the effective date of such an amendment.

(ii) *Permission to a class of groups.*—The Commissioner, in his discretion, may grant a particular class of groups permission to discontinue filing consolidated returns if any provision of the Code or regulations has been amended and such amendment is of the type which could have a substantial adverse effect on the filing of consolidated returns by substantially all such groups relative to the filing of separate returns. Ordinarily, the permission to discontinue shall apply with respect to the taxable year of each group within the class which includes the effective date of such an amendment.

(3) *Time and manner for exercising election.*—If, under subparagraph (1) or (2) of this paragraph, a group has an election to discontinue filing consolidated returns for any taxable year and such group wishes to exercise such election, then the common parent must file a separate return for such year on or before the last day prescribed by law (including extensions of time) for the filing of the consolidated return for such

year. See section 6081 (relating to extensions of time for filing returns).

(d) *When a group remains in existence.*— (1) *General rule.*—A group remains in existence for a tax year if the common parent remains as the common parent and at least one subsidiary that was affiliated with it at the end of the prior year remains affiliated with it at the beginning of the year, whether or not one or more corporations have ceased to be subsidiaries at any time after the group was formed. Thus, for example, assume that corporation P acquires the sole outstanding share of stock of S on January 1, year 1, and that P and S file a consolidated return for the year 1 calendar year. On May 1, year 2, P acquires the sole outstanding share of stock of S1 and, on July 1, year 2, P sells the S share. The group (consisting originally of P and S) remains in existence in year 2 because P remained the common parent and, S, a subsidiary that was affiliated with P at the end of year 1, remained affiliated with P at the beginning of year 2.

(2) *Common parent no longer in existence.*— (i) *Mere change in identity.*—For purposes of this paragraph, the common parent corporation shall remain as the common parent irrespective of a mere change in identity, form, or place of organization of such common parent corporation (see section 368(a)(1)(F)).

(ii) *Transfer of assets to subsidiary.*—The group shall be considered as remaining in existence notwithstanding that the common parent is no longer in existence if the members of the affiliated group succeed to and become the owners of substantially all of the assets of such former parent and there remains one or more chains of includible corporations connected through stock ownership with a common parent corporation which is an includible corporation and which was a member of the group prior to the date such former parent ceases to exist. For purposes of applying paragraph (f)(2)(i) of § 1.1502-1 to separate return years ending on or before the date on which the former parent ceases to exist, such former parent, and not the new common parent, shall be considered to be the corporation described in such paragraph.

(iii) *Taxable years.*—If a transfer of assets described in subdivision (ii) of this subparagraph is an acquisition to which section 381(a) applies and if the group files a consolidated return for the taxable year in which the acquisition occurs, then for purposes of section 381—

(a) The former common parent shall not close its taxable year merely because of the acquisition, and all taxable years of such former parent ending on or before the date of acquisition shall be treated as taxable years of the acquiring corporation, and

(b) The corporation acquiring the assets shall close its taxable year as of the date of acquisition, and all taxable years of such corporation ending on or before the date of acquisition shall be treated as taxable years of the transferor corporation.

(iv) *Exception.*—With respect to acquisitions occurring before January 1, 1971, subdivision (iii) of this subparagraph shall not apply if the group, in its income tax return, treats the taxable year of the former common parent as having closed as of the date of acquisition.

(3) *Reverse acquisitions.*—(i) *In general.*—If a corporation (hereinafter referred to as the "first corporation") or any member of a group of which the first corporation is the common parent acquires after October 1, 1965—

(a) Stock of another corporation (hereinafter referred to as the second corporation), and as a result the second corporation becomes (or would become but for the application of this subparagraph) a member of a group of which the first corporation is the common parent, or

(b) Substantially all the assets of the second corporation,

in exchange (in whole or in part) for stock of the first corporation, and the stockholders (immediately before the acquisition) of the second corporation, as a result of owning stock of the second corporation, own (immediately after the acquisition) more than 50 percent of the fair market value of the outstanding stock of the first corporation, then any group of which the first corporation was the common parent immediately before the acquisition shall cease to exist as of the date of acquisition, and any group of which the second corporation was the common parent immediately before the acquisition shall be treated as remaining in existence (with the first corporation becoming the common parent of the group). Thus, assume that corporations P and S comprised groups PS (P being the common parent), that P was merged into corporation T (the common parent of a group composed of T and corporation U), and that the shareholders of P immediately before the merger, as a result of owning stock in P, own 90 percent of the fair market value of T's stock immediately after the merger. The group of which P was the common parent is treated as continuing in existence with T and U being added as members of the group, and T taking the place of P as the common parent.

For purposes of determining under (a) of this subdivision whether the second corporation becomes (or would become) a member of the group of which the first corporation is the common parent, and for purposes of determining whether the former stockholders of the second corporation own more than 50 percent of the outstanding stock of the first corporation, there shall be taken into account any acquisitions or redemptions of the stock of either corporation which are pursuant to a plan of acquisition described in (a) or (b) of this subdivision.

(ii) *Prior ownership of stock.*—For purposes of subdivision (i) of this subparagraph, if the first corporation, and any members of a group of which the first corporation is the common parent, have continuously owned for a period of at least five years ending on the date of the acquisition an aggregate of at least 25 percent of the fair market value of the outstanding stock of the second corporation, then the first corporation (and any subsidiary which owns stock of the second corporation immediately before the acquisition) shall, as a result of owning such stock, be treated as owning (immediately after the acquisition) a percentage of the fair market value of the first corporation's outstanding stock which bears the same ratio to (a) the percentage of the fair market value of all the stock of the second corporation owned immediately before the acquisition by the first corporation and its subsidiaries as (b) the fair market value of the total outstanding stock of the second corporation immediately before the acquisition bears to (c) the sum of (1) the fair market value, immediately before the acquisition, of the total outstanding stock of the first corporation, and (2) the fair market value, immediately before the acquisition, of the total outstanding stock of the second corporation (other than any such stock owned by the first corporation and any of its subsidiaries). For example, assume that corporation P owns stock in corporation T having a fair market value of $100,000, that P acquires the remaining stock of T from individuals in exchange for stock of P, that immediately before the acquisition the total outstanding stock of T had a fair market value of $150,000, and that immediately before the acquisition the total outstanding stock of P had a fair market value of $200,000. Assuming P owned at least 25 percent of the fair market value of T's stock for five years, then for purposes of this subparagraph, P is treated as owning (immediately after the acquisition) 40 percent of the fair market value of its own outstanding stock, determined as follows:

$$\frac{\$150,000}{\$200,000 + \$50,000} \times 66^2/3\% = 40\%$$

Thus, if the former individual stockholders of T own, immediately after the acquisition more than 10 percent of the fair market value of the outstanding stock of P as a result of owning stock of T, the group of which T was the common parent is treated as continuing in existence with P as the common parent, and the group of which P was the common parent before the acquisition ceases to exist.

(iii) *Election.*—The provisions of subdivision (ii) of this subparagraph shall not apply to any acquisition occurring in a taxable year ending after October 7, 1969, unless the first corporation elects to have such subdivision apply. The election shall be made by means of a statement, signed by any officer who is duly authorized to act on behalf of the first corporation, stating that the corporation elects to have the provisions of § 1.1502-75(d)(3)(ii) apply and identifying the acquisition to which such provisions will apply. The statement shall be filed, on or before the due date (including extensions of time) of the return for the group's first consolidated return year ending after the date of the acquisition, with the internal revenue officer with whom such return is required to be filed.

(iv) *Transfer of assets to subsidiary.*—This subparagraph shall not apply to a transaction to which subparagraph (2)(ii) of this paragraph applies.

(v) *Taxable years.*—If, in a transaction described in subdivision (i) of this subparagraph, the first corporation files a consolidated return for the first taxable year ending after the date of acquisition, then—

(a) The first corporation, and each corporation which, immediately before the acquisition, is a member of the group of which the first corporation is the common parent, shall close its taxable year as of the date of acquisition, and each such corporation shall, immediately after the acquisition, change to the taxable year of the second corporation, and

(b) If the acquisition is a transaction described in section 381(a)(2), then for purposes of section 381—

(1) All taxable years ending on or before the date of acquisition, of the first corporation and each corporation which, immediately before the acquisition, is a member of the group of which the first corporation is the common parent, shall be treated as taxable years of the transfer corporation, and

(2) The second corporation shall not close its taxable year merely because of such acquisition, and all taxable years ending on or before the date of acquisition, of the second corporation and each corporation which, immediately before the acquisition, is a member of any group of which the second corporation is the common parent, shall be treated as taxable years of the acquiring corporation.

(vi) *Exception.*—With respect to acquisitions occurring before April 17, 1968, subdivision (v) of this subparagraph shall not apply if the parties to the transaction, in their income tax returns, treat subdivision (i) as not affecting the closing of taxable years or the operation of section 381.

(4) [Reserved.]

(5) *Coordination with section 833.*— (i) *Election to continue old group.*—If, solely by reason of the enactment of section 833 (relating to certain Blue Cross or Blue Shield organizations and certain other health insurers), an organization to which section 833 applies (a "section 833 organization") became the new

common parent of an old group on January 1, 1987, the old group may elect to continue in existence with that section 833 organization as its new common parent, provided all the old groups having the same section 833 organization as their new common parent elect to continue in existence. To revoke this election, see paragraph (d)(5)(x) of this section. To file as a new group, see paragraph (d)(5)(v) of this section.

(ii) *Old group.*—For purposes of this paragraph (d)(5), an old group is a group which, for its last taxable year ending in 1986, either filed a consolidated return or was eligible to (but did not) file a consolidated return.

(iii) *Manner of electing to continue.*— (A) *Deemed election.*—If all the members of all the old groups having the same section 833 organization as their new common parent are included for the first taxable year beginning after December 31, 1986, on the same consolidated (or amended consolidated) return and a Form 1122 was not filed, the old groups are deemed to have elected under paragraph (d)(5)(i) of this section to continue in existence.

(B) *Delayed election.*—If a deemed election to continue in existence was not made under paragraph (d)(5)(iii)(A) of this section, all the members of all the old groups having the same section 833 organization as their new common parent may make a delayed election under paragraph (d)(5)(i) of this section to continue in existence by

(1) filing an appropriate consolidated (or amended consolidated) return or returns for each taxable year beginning after December 31, 1986, (notwithstanding § 1.1502-75(a)(1)) on or before January 3, 1991 and

(2) on the top of any such return prominently affixing a statement containing the following declaration: "THIS RETURN" (or, if applicable, "AMENDED RETURN") "REFLECTS A DELAYED ELECTION TO CONTINUE UNDER § 1.1502-75T(d)(5)(iii)(B)". A delayed election to continue in existence automatically revokes a deemed election to file as a new group which was made under paragraph (d)(5)(vi) of this section.

(iv) *Effects of election to continue in existence.*—If an old group or groups elect to continue in existence under paragraph (d)(5)(i) of this section, the following rules apply:

(A) *Taxable years.*—Each member that filed returns other than on a calendar year basis shall close its taxable year on December 31, 1986, and change to a calendar year beginning on January 1, 1987. See section 843 and § 1.1502-76(a)(1).

(B) *Carryovers from separate return limitation years.*—For purposes of applying the separate return limitation year rules to carryovers

from taxable years beginning before 1987 to taxable years beginning after 1986, the following rules apply:

(1) Any taxable year beginning before 1987 of a corporation that was not a member of an old group (including a section 833 organization) will be treated as a separate return limitation year;

(2) Any taxable year beginning before 1987 of a corporation that was a member of an old group that, without regard to this section and the enactment of section 833, was a separate return limitation year will continue to be treated as a separate return limitation year;

(3) Any taxable year beginning before 1987 of a member of an old group (other than a separate return limitation year described in paragraph (d)(5)(iv)(B)(2) of this section) will not be treated as a separate return limitation year with respect to any corporation that was a member of such group for each day of that taxable year; and

(4) Any taxable year beginning before 1987 of a member of an old group will be treated as a separate return limitation year with respect to any corporation that was not a member of such group for each day of that taxable year (*e.g.*, a corporation that was not a member of an old group, including a section 833 organization, or a corporation that was a member of another old group).

(C) *Five-year rules for life-nonlife groups.*—Any life-nonlife election under section 1504(c)(2) in effect for an old group remains in effect. Any old group which was eligible to make a life-nonlife election will remain eligible to make the election. For purposes of section 1503(c), a nonlife member is treated as ineligible under § 1.1502-47(d)(13) with respect to a life member, unless both were members of the same affiliated group (determined without regard to the exclusions in section 1504(b)(1) and (2)) for five taxable years immediately preceding the taxable year in which the loss arose. See paragraph (d)(5)(ix) of this section for a tacking rule.

(v) *Election to file as a new group.*—If, solely by reason of the enactment of section 833, a section 833 organization became the new common parent of an old group on January 1, 1987, the application of the five-year prohibition on reconsolidation in section 1504(a)(3)(A) to the old group is waived and the old group together with the new section 833 organization common parent may elect to file as a new group provided that all includible corporations elect to file a consolidated (or amended consolidated) return as a new group for the first taxable year beginning after December 31, 1986. To revoke this election, see paragraph (d)(5)(x) of this section.

(vi) *Manner of electing to file as a new group.*—(A) *Deemed election.*—The old group or groups and the section 833 organization are deemed to have elected under paragraph (d)(5)(v) of this section to file as a new group by filing, for the first taxable year beginning after December 31, 1986, a Form 1122 and a consolidated (or amended consolidated) tax return.

(B) *Delayed election.*—If a deemed election to file as a new group was not made pursuant to paragraph (d)(5)(vi)(A) of this section, the old group or groups and the section 833 organization may make a delayed election under paragraph (d)(5)(v) of this section to file as a new group by

(1) filing an appropriate consolidated (or amended consolidated) return or returns for each taxable year beginning after December 31, 1986, (notwithstanding § 1.1502-75(a)(1)) on or before January 3, 1991 and

(2) on the top of any such return prominently affixing a statement containing the following declaration: "THIS RETURN". (or, if applicable, "AMENDED RETURN") "REFLECTS A DELAYED ELECTION TO FILE AS A NEW GROUP UNDER § 1.1502-75T(d)(5)(vi)(B)". A delayed election to file as a new group automatically revokes any deemed election to continue in existence which was made under paragraph (d)(5)(iii) of this section.

(vii) *Effects of election to file as a new group.*—If an old group or groups elect to file as a new group under paragraph (d)(5)(v) of this section, the following rules apply:

(A) *Termination.*—Each old group is treated as if it terminated on January 1, 1987, and the termination is not treated as resulting from the acquisition by a nonmember of all of the stock of the common parent.

(B) *Taxable years.*—Each member that filed returns other than on a calendar year basis shall close its taxable year on December 31, 1986, and change to a calendar year beginning on January 1, 1987. See section 843 and § 1.1502-76(a)(1).

(C) *Separate return limitation year and life-nonlife groups.*—For purposes of § 1.1502-1(f), sections 1503(c) and 1504(c), and § 1.1502-47, the group is treated as coming into existence as a new group on January 1, 1987. Thus, for example, paragraphs (d)(5)(iv)(B) and (C) of this section do not apply.

(viii) *Earnings and profits.*—All distributions after January 1, 1987 by a corporation, whether or not such corporation was a member of an old group, to an existing Blue Cross or Blue Shield organization (as defined in section 833(c)(2)) out of earnings and profits accumulated before 1987 are deemed made out of earnings and profits accumulated in pre-affiliation years. See § 1.1502-32(h)(5).

(ix) *Five-year tacking rules for certain life-nonlife groups.*—For purposes of applying § 1.1502-47(d)(5) and (12) to any taxable year ending after 1986 to a corporation, whether or not the corporation was a member of an old group, (A) the determination of whether the corporation was in existence and a member or tentatively treated as a member of a group, for taxable years ending before 1987, is made without regard to the exclusions under section 1504(b)(1) and (2) of any section 833 organization or life insurance company (as the case may be) and (B) a section 833 organization is not treated as having a change in tax character solely by reason of the loss of its tax-exempt status due to the enactment of section 833. This paragraph (d)(5)(ix) does not apply if an election to file as a new group under paragraph (d)(5)(v) of this section is made.

(x) *Time to revoke elections made before September 5, 1990.*—An election by an old group to continue in existence or to file as a new group that was made (or deemed made) before September 5, 1990 may be revoked by filing an appropriate return (or returns) on or before January 3, 1991. For purposes of this paragraph (d)(5)(x), appropriate returns include separate returns filed by each member of the group or consolidated returns filed in accordance with a delayed election either under paragraph (d)(5)(iii)(B) or (vi)(B) of this section.

(xi) *Examples.*—The following examples illustrate this paragraph (d)(5). In these examples, each corporation uses the calendar year as its taxable year.

Example 1. B is a section 833 organization. For several years, B has owned all of the outstanding stock of X, Y, and Z. X has owned all the outstanding stock of X_1, throughout X_1's existence and Y has owned all of the outstanding stock of Y_1 throughout Y_1's existence. For 1986, X and X_1 filed a consolidated federal income tax return but Y and Y_1 filed separate returns. Under paragraph (d)(5)(ii) of this section, X and X_1 and Y and Y_1 each constitute an old group because they either filed a consolidated return or were eligible to file a consolidated return for 1986. The X and Y groups may elect under paragraph (d)(5)(i) of this section to continue in existence. If they elect to continue, under paragraph (d)(5)(iv)(B) of this section, the separate return limitation year rules apply as follows: any taxable year of B or Z beginning before 1987 is treated as a separate return limitation year with respect to each other and to all other members of the group; any taxable year of X or X_1 beginning before 1987 is treated as a separate return limitation year with respect to B, Z, Y and Y_1, but not with respect to each other; and any taxable year of Y or Y_1 beginning before 1987 is treated as a separate return limitation year with respect to B, Z, X and X_1, but not with respect to each other.

Example 2. The facts are the same as in Example 1 except that B is owned by C, another section 833 organization. If the X and Y groups elect to continue, the results are the same as in Example 1, except that, under paragraph (d)(5)(iv)(B)(1) of this section, for purposes of applying the separate return limitation year rules, any taxable year of C beginning before 1987 is also treated as a separate return limitation year with respect to all other members of the group.

Example 3. The facts are the same as in Example 1 except that Y purchased Y_1 on January 1, 1985. If the X and Y groups elect to continue, the results are the same as in Example 1, except that, under paragraph (d)(5)(iv)(B)(2) of this section, for purposes of applying the separate return limitation year rules, any taxable year of Y_1 beginning before 1985 is treated as a separate return limitation year with respect to Y as well as with respect to all other members of the group.

Example 4. B, a section 833 organization, has owned all the stock of X since November 1984. X has owned all the stock of L, a life insurance company, throughout L's existence. In 1986, X and L properly filed a life-nonlife consolidated return. Under paragraph (d)(5)(i) of this section, the X group elects to continue in existence. Under paragraph (d)(5)(iv)(C) of this section, the life-nonlife election will remain in effect. However, losses of B which arise before 1990 cannot be used to offset the income of L. See section 1503(c)(2) and §1.1502-47(d)(13) and paragraph (d)(5)(iv)(C) of this section. Under paragraph (d)(5)(iv)(B) of this section, the separate return limitation year rules apply as follows: any taxable year of B beginning before 1987 is treated as a separate return limitation year with respect to all other members of the group; and any taxable year of X or L beginning before 1987 is treated as a separate return limitation year with respect to B, but not with respect to each other.

Example 5. The facts are the same as [in] Example 4 except that, on January 1, 1984, B formed L_1, a life insurance company. Under paragraph (d)(5)(ix) of this section and section 1504(c), the first year L_1 is eligible to join in B's life-nonlife election is 1989.

Example 6. The facts are the same as in Example 4 except that B and the X group elect under paragraph (d)(5)(v) of this section to file as a new group. The X group will be considered to have terminated under §1.1502-75(d)(1) on December 31, 1986. X and L are each separately subject to the separate return limitation year rules of §1.1502-1(f). The first year L and L_1 are eligible to join the new group in a life-nonlife election is 1992 (five years after the new group is formed). See section 1504(c)(2) and paragraphs (d)(5)(vii)(C) and (ix) of this section.

(e) *Failure to include subsidiary.*—If a consolidated return is required for the taxable year

under the provisions of paragraph (a)(2) of this section, the tax liability of all members of the group for such year shall be computed on a consolidated basis even though—

(1) Separate returns are filed by one or more members of the group, or

(2) There has been a failure to include in the consolidated return the income of any member of the group.

If subparagraph (1) of this paragraph applies, the amounts assessed or paid upon the basis of separate returns shall be considered as having been assessed or paid upon the basis of a consolidated return.

(f) *Inclusion of one or more corporations not members of the group.*—(1) *Method of determining tax liability.*—If a consolidated return includes the income of a corporation which was not a member of the group at any time during the consolidated return year, the tax liability of such corporation will be determined upon the basis of a separate return (or a consolidated return of another group, if paragraph (a)(2) or (b)(3) of this section applies), and the consolidated return will be considered as including only the income of the corporations which were members of the group during that taxable year. If a consolidated return includes the income of two or more corporations which were not members of the group but which constitute another group, the tax liability of such corporations will be computed in the same manner as if separate returns had been made by such corporations unless the Commissioner upon application approves the making of a consolidated return for the other group or unless under paragraph (a)(2) of this section a consolidated return is required for the other group.

(2) *Allocation of tax liability.*—In any case in which amounts have been assessed and paid upon the basis of a consolidated return and the tax liability of one or more of the corporations included in the consolidated return is to be computed in the manner described in subparagraph (1) of this paragraph, the amounts so paid shall be allocated between the group composed of the corporations properly included in the consolidated return and each of the corporations the tax liability of which is to be computed on a separate basis (or on the basis of a consolidated return of another group) in such manner as the corporations which were included in the consolidated return may, subject to the approval of the Commissioner, agree upon or in the absence of an agreement upon the method used in allocating the tax liability of the members of the group under the provisions of section 1552(a).

(g) *Computing periods of limitation.*—(1) *Income incorrectly included in consolidated return.*—If—

(i) A consolidated return is filed by a group for the taxable year, and

(ii) The tax liability of a corporation whose income is included in such return must be

Reg. §1.1502-75(g)(1)(ii)

computed on the basis of a separate return (or on the basis of a consolidated return with another group),

then for the purpose of computing any period of limitation with respect to such separate return (or such other consolidated return), the filing of such consolidated return by the group shall be considered as the making of a return by such corporation.

(2) *Income incorrectly included in separate returns.*—If a consolidated return is required for the taxable year under the provisions of paragraph (a)(2) of this section, the filing of separate returns by the members of the group for such year shall not be considered as the making of a return for the purpose of computing any period of limitation with respect to such consolidated return unless there is attached to each such separate return a statement setting forth—

(i) The most recent taxable year of the member for which its income was included in a consolidated return, and

(ii) The reasons for the group's belief that a consolidated return is not required for the taxable year.

(h) *Method of filing return and forms.*—(1) *Consolidated return made by common parent corporation.*—The consolidated return shall be made on Form 1120 for the group by the common parent corporation. The consolidated return, with Form 851 (affiliations schedule) attached, shall be filed with the district director with whom the common parent would have filed a separate return.

(2) *Filing of Form 1122 for first year.*—If, under the provisions of paragraph (a)(1) of this section, a group wishes to file a consolidated return for a taxable year, then a Form 1122 ("Authorization and Consent of Subsidiary Corporation To Be Included in a Consolidated Income Tax Return") must be executed by each subsidiary. For taxable years beginning before January 1, 2003, the executed Forms 1122 must be attached to the consolidated return for the taxable year. For taxable years beginning after December 31, 2002, the group must attach either executed Forms 1122 or unsigned copies of the completed Forms 1122 to the consolidated return. If the group submits unsigned Forms 1122 with its return, it must retain the signed originals in its records in the manner required by §1.6001-1(e). Form 1122 is not required for a taxable year if a consolidated return was filed (or was required to be filed) by the group for the immediately preceding taxable year.

(3) *Persons qualified to execute returns and forms.*—Each return or form required to be made or prepared by a corporation must be executed by the person authorized under section 6062 to execute returns of separate corporations.

(i) [Reserved]

(j) *Statements and schedules for subsidiaries.*—The statement of gross income and deductions and the schedules required by the instructions on the return shall be prepared and filed in columnar form so that the details of the items of gross income, deductions, and credits for each member may be readily audited. Such statements and schedules shall include in columnar form a reconciliation of surplus for each corporation, and a reconciliation of consolidated surplus. Consolidated balance sheets as of the beginning and close of the taxable year of the group, taken from the books of the members, shall accompany the consolidated return and shall be prepared in a form similar to that required for reconciliation of surplus.

(k) *Cross-reference.*—See §1.338(h)(10)-1(d)(7) for special rules regarding filing consolidated returns when a section 338(h)(10) election is made for a target acquired from a selling consolidated group.

(l) *Effective/applicability dates.*—Paragraph (d)(1) of this section applies to taxable years for which the due date of the original return (without regard to extensions) is on or after September 17, 2008. [Reg. §1.1502-75.]

☐ [*T.D. 6894, 9-7-66. Amended by T.D. 7016, 10-6-69; T.D. 7024, 2-9-70; T.D. 7244, 12-29-72; T.D. 7246, 12-29-72; T.D. 8438, 9-24-92; T.D. 8515, 1-12-94; T.D. 8560, 8-12-94; T.D. 8858, 1-5-2000; T.D. 8940, 2-12-2001; T.D. 9100, 12-18-2003; T.D. 9300, 12-7-2006 and T.D. 9424, 9-9-2008.*]

[Reg. §1.1502-76]

§1.1502-76. Taxable year of members of group.—(a) *Taxable year of members of group.*—The consolidated return of a group must be filed on the basis of the common parent's taxable year, and each subsidiary must adopt the common parent's annual accounting period for the first consolidated return year for which the subsidiary's income is includible in the consolidated return. If any member is on a 52-53-week taxable year, the rule of the preceding sentence shall, with the advance consent of the Commissioner, be deemed satisfied if the taxable years of all members of the group end within the same 7-day period. Any request for such consent shall be filed with the Commissioner of Internal Revenue, Washington, DC 20224, not later than the 30th day before the due date (not including extensions of time) for the filing of the consolidated return.

(b) *Items included in the consolidated return.*—(1) *General rules.*—(i) *In general.*—A consolidated return must include the common parent's items of income, gain, deduction, loss, and credit for the entire consolidated return year, and each subsidiary's items for the portion of the year for which it is a member. If the consolidated return includes the items of a corporation for only a portion of its tax year determined without taking this section into account, items for the portion of the year not included in the consolidated return must be included in a separate return (including the consolidated return of another group). The rules of this paragraph (b) must be applied to prevent the duplication or elimination of the corporation's items.

(ii) *The day a corporation becomes or ceases to be a member.*—(A) *End of the day rule.*—(1) *In general.*—If a corporation (S), other than one described in paragraph (b)(1)(ii)(A)(2) of this section, becomes or ceases to be a member during a consolidated return year, it becomes or ceases to be a member at the end of the day on which its status as a member changes, and its tax year ends for all Federal income tax purposes at the end of that day. Appropriate adjustments must be made if another provision of the Internal Revenue Code or the regulations thereunder contemplates the event occurring before or after S's change in status. For example, S's items restored under § 1.1502-13 immediately before it becomes a nonmember are taken into account in determining the basis of S's stock under § 1.1502-32. On the other hand, if a section 338(g) election is made in connection with S becoming a member, the deemed asset sale under that section takes place before S becomes a member. See § 1.338-10(a)(5) (deemed sale excluded from purchasing corporation's consolidated return.)

(2) *Special rule for former S corporations.*—If S becomes a member in a transaction other than in a qualified stock purchase for which an election under section 338(g) is made, and immediately before becoming a member an election under section 1362(a) was in effect, then S will become a member at the beginning of the day the termination of its S corporation election is effective. S's tax year ends for all Federal income tax purposes at the end of the preceding day. This paragraph (b)(1)(ii)(A)(2) applies to transactions occurring after November 10, 1999.

(B) *Next day rule.*—If, on the day of S's change in status as a member, a transaction occurs that is properly allocable to the portion of S's day after the event resulting in the change, S and all persons related to S under section 267(b) immediately after the event must treat the transaction for all Federal income tax purposes as occurring at the beginning of the following day. A determination as to whether a transaction is properly allocable to the portion of S's day after the event will be respected if it is reasonable and consistently applied <u>by all affected persons</u>. In determining whether an allocation is reasonable, the following factors are among those to be considered—

(1) Whether income, gain, deduction, loss, and credit are allocated inconsistently (e.g., to maximize a seller's stock basis adjustments under § 1.1502-32);

(2) If the item is from a transaction with respect to S stock, whether it reflects ownership of the stock before or after the event (e.g., if a member transfers encumbered land to nonmember S in exchange for additional S stock in a transaction to which section 351 applies and the exchange results in S becoming a member of the consolidated group, the applicability of section 357(c) to the exchange must be determined under § 1.1502-80(d) by treating the exchange as occurring after the event; on the other hand, if S is a member but has a minority shareholder and becomes a nonmember as a result of its redemption of stock with appreciated property, S's gain under section 311 is treated as from a transaction occurring before the event);

(3) Whether the allocation is inconsistent with other requirements under the Internal Revenue Code and regulations promulgated thereunder (e.g., if a section 338(g) election is made in connection with a group's acquisition of S, the deemed asset sale must take place before S becomes a member and S's gain or loss with respect to its assets must be taken into account by S as a nonmember (but see § 1.338-1(d)), or if S realizes discharge of indebtedness income that is excluded from gross income under section 108(a) on the day it becomes a nonmember, the discharge of indebtedness income must be treated as realized by S as a member (see § 1.1502-28(b)(11))); and

(4) Whether other facts exist, such as a prearranged transaction or multiples changes in S's status, indicating that the transaction is not properly allocable to the portion of S's day after the event resulting in S's change.

(C) *Successor corporations.*—For purposes of this paragraph (b)(1)(ii), any reference to a corporation includes a reference to a successor or predecessor as the context may require. A corporation is a successor if the basis of its assets is determined, directly or indirectly, in whole or in part, by reference to the basis of the assets of another corporation (the predecessor). For example, if a member forms S, S is treated as a member from the beginning of its existence.

(iii) *Group structure changes.*—If the common parent ceases to be the common parent but the group remains in existence, adjustments must be made in accordance with the principles of § 1.1502-75(d)(2) and (3).

(2) *Determination of items included in separate and consolidated returns.*—(i) *In general.*—The returns for the years that end and begin with S becoming (or ceasing to be) a member are separate tax years for all Federal income tax purposes. The returns are subject to the rules of the Internal Revenue Code applicable to short periods, as if S ceased to exist on becoming a member (or first existed on becoming a nonmember). For example, cost recovery deductions under section 168 must be allocated for short periods.

Reg. § 1.1502-76(b)(2)(i)

On the other hand, annualization under section 443 is not required of S solely because it has a short year as a result of becoming a member. (Similarly, section 443 applies with respect to a consolidated return only to the extent that the group's return is for a short period and section 443 applies without taking this paragraph (b) into account.)

(ii) *Ratable allocation of a year's items.*—(A) *Application.*—Although the periods ending and beginning with S's change in status are different tax years, items (other than extraordinary items) may be ratably allocated between the periods if—

(1) S is not required to change its annual accounting period or its method of accounting as a result of its change in status (e.g., because its stock is sold between consolidated groups that have the same annual accounting periods); and

(2) An irrevocable ratable allocation election is made under paragraph (b)(2)(ii)(D) of this section.

(B) *General rule.*—(1) *Allocation within original year.*—Under a ratable allocation election, paragraph (b)(2) of this section applies by allocating to each day of S's original year (S's tax year determined without taking this section into account) an equal portion of S's items taken into account in the original year, except that extraordinary items must be allocated to the day that they are taken into account. All persons affected by the election must take into account S's extraordinary items and the ratable allocation of S's remaining items in a manner consistent with the election.

(2) *Items to be allocated.*—Under ratable allocation, the items to be allocated and their timing, location, character, and source are generally determined by treating the original year as a single tax year, and the items are not subject to the rules of the Internal Revenue Code applicable to short periods (unless the original year is a short period). However, the years ending and beginning with S's change in status are treated as different tax years (and as short periods) with respect to any item carried to or from these years (e.g., a net operating loss carried under section 172) and with respect to the application of section 481.

(3) *Multiple applications.*—If this paragraph (b) applies more than once with respect to an original year, adjustments must be made in accordance with the principles of this paragraph (b). For example, if S becomes a member of two different consolidated groups during the same original year and ratable allocation is elected with respect to both groups, ratable allocation is generally determined for both groups by treating the original year as a single tax year; however, if ratable allocation is elected only with respect to

the first group, the ratable allocation is determined by treating the original year as a short period that does not include the period that S is a member of the second group. Ratable allocation is not a method of accounting, and ratable allocation with respect to one application of this paragraph (b) to S does not require ratable allocation to be subsequently applied with respect to S.

(C) *Extraordinary items.*—An extraordinary item is—

(1) Any item from the disposition or abandonment of a capital asset as defined in section 1221 (determined without the application of any other rules of law);

(2) Any item from the disposition or abandonment of property used in a trade or business as defined in section 1231(b) (determined without the application of any holding period requirement);

(3) Any item from the disposition or abandonment of an asset described in section 1221(1), (3), (4), or (5), if substantially all the assets in the same category from the same trade or business are disposed of or abandoned in one transaction (or series of related transactions);

(4) Any item from assets disposed of in an applicable asset acquisition under section 1060(c);

(5) Any item carried to or from any portion of the original year (e.g., a net operating loss carried under section 172), and any section 481(a) adjustment;

(6) The effects of any change in accounting method initiated by the filing of the appropriate form after S's change in status;

(7) Any item from the discharge or retirement of indebtedness (e.g., cancellation of indebtedness income or a deduction for retirement at a premium);

(8) Any item from the settlement of a tort or similar third-party liability;

(9) Any compensation-related deduction in connection with S's change in status (including, for example, deductions from bonus, severance, and option cancellation payments made in connection with S's change in status);

(10) Any dividend income from a nonmember that S controls within the meaning of section 304 at the time the dividend is taken into account;

(11) Any deemed income inclusion from a foreign corporation, or any deferred tax amount on an excess distribution from a passive foreign investment company under section 1291;

(12) Any interest expense allocable under section 172(h) to a corporate equity reduction transaction causing this paragraph (b) to apply;

(13) Any credit, to the extent it arises from activities or items that are not ratably allo-

cated (e.g., the rehabilitation credit under section 47, which is based on placement in service); and

(14) Any item which, in the opinion of the Commissioner, would, if ratably allocated, result in a substantial distortion of income in any consolidated return or separate return in which the item is included.

(D) *Election.*—(1) *Statement.*—The election to ratably allocate items under this paragraph (b)(2)(ii) must be made in a separate statement entitled, "THIS IS AN ELECTION UNDER § 1.1502-76(b)(2)(ii) TO RATABLY ALLOCATE THE YEAR'S ITEMS OF [INSERT NAME AND EMPLOYER IDENTIFICATION NUMBER OF THE MEMBER]." The election must be filed by including a statement on or with the returns including the items for the years ending and beginning with S's change in status. If two or more members of the same consolidated group, as a consequence of the same plan or arrangement, cease to be members of that group and remain affiliated as members of another consolidated group, an election under this paragraph (b)(2)(ii)(D)(1) may be made only if it is made by each such member. Each statement must also indicate that an agreement, as described in paragraph (b)(2)(ii)(D)(2) of this section, has been entered into. Each party signing the agreement must retain either the original or a copy of the agreement as part of its records. See § 1.6001-1(e).

(2) *Agreement.*—For each election under this paragraph (b)(2)(ii), the member and the common parent of each affected group must sign and date an agreement. The agreement must—

(i) Identify the extraordinary items, their amounts, and the separate or consolidated returns in which they are included;

(ii) Identify the aggregate amount to be ratably allocated, and the portion of the amount included in the separate and consolidated returns; and

(iii) Include the name and employer identification number of the common parent (if any) of each group that must take the items into account.

(iii) *Ratable allocation of a month's items.*—If ratable allocation under paragraph (b)(2)(ii) of this section is not elected (e.g., because S is required to change its annual accounting period), this paragraph (b)(2)(iii) may be applied to ratably allocate only S's items taken into account in the month of its change in status, but only if the allocation is consistently applied by all affected persons. The ratable allocation is made by applying the principles of paragraph (b)(2)(ii) of this section under any reasonable method. For example, S may close its books both at the end of the preceding month and at the end of the month of the change, and allocate only its items (other than extraordinary items) from the month of the

change. See paragraph (b)(1)(ii)(B) of this section for factors to be considered in determining whether the method is reasonable.

(iv) *Taxes.*—To the extent properly taken into account during the member's tax year (determined without the application of this paragraph (b)), Federal, state, local, and foreign taxes are allocated under paragraph (b)(2) of this section on the basis of the items or activities to which the taxes relate. Thus, income tax is allocated based on the inclusion of the income (determined under the principles of this paragraph (b)) to which the tax relates. For example, if a calendar-year domestic corporation has $100 of foreign source dividend income (determined in accordance with United States tax accounting principles but without taking this paragraph (b) into account) that is passive income for purposes of section 904, and $60 of the income is allocated under this paragraph (b) to the period of the calendar year after it becomes a member of a consolidated group, then 60% of the corporation's deemed paid foreign tax credit associated with its dividend income for the calendar year is taken into account in computing the group's passive basket consolidated foreign tax credit. Similarly, property taxes relate to the ownership of property and are allocated over the period that the property is owned. This paragraph (b)(2)(iv) applies without regard to any determination or allocation by another taxing jurisdiction.

(v) *Acquisition of S corporation.*—If a corporation is acquired in a transaction to which paragraph (b)(1)(ii)(A)(2) of this section applies, then paragraphs (b)(2)(ii) and (iii) of this section do not apply and items of income, gain, loss, deduction, and credit are assigned to each short taxable year on the basis of the corporation's normal method of accounting as determined under section 446. This paragraph (b)(2)(v) applies to transactions occurring after November 10, 1999.

(vi) *Passthrough entities.*—(A) *In general.*—If S is a partner in a partnership or an owner of a similar interest with respect to which items of the entity are taken into account by S, S is treated, solely for purposes of determining the year to which the entity's items are allocated under paragraph (b)(2) of this section, as selling or exchanging its entire interest in the entity immediately before S's change in status.

(B) *Treatment as a conduit.*—For purposes of this paragraph (b)(2), if a member (together with other members) would be treated under section 318(a)(2) as owning an aggregate of at least 50% of any stock owned by the passthrough entity, the method that is used to determine the inclusion of the entity's items in the consolidated or separate return must be the same method that is used to determine the inclusion of the member's items in the consolidated or separate return.

Reg. § 1.1502-76(b)(2)(vi)(B)

(C) *Exception for certain foreign entities.*—This paragraph (b)(2)(v) does not apply to any foreign corporation generating the deemed inclusion of income, or to any passive foreign investment company generating a deferred tax amount on an excess distribution under section 1291.

(3) *Anti-avoidance rule.*—If any person acts with a principal purpose contrary to the purposes of this paragraph (b), to substantially reduce the Federal income tax liability of any person, adjustments must be made as necessary to carry out the purposes of this section.

(4) *Determination of due date for separate return.*—Paragraph (c) of this section contains rules for the filing of the separate return referred to in this paragraph (b). In applying paragraph (c) of this section, the due date for the filing of S's separate return shall also be determined without regard to the ending of the tax year under paragraph (b)(1)(ii) of this section or the deemed cessation of its existence under paragraph (b)(2)(i) of this section.

(5) *Examples.*—For purposes of the examples in this paragraph (b), unless otherwise stated, P and X are common parents of calendar-year consolidated groups, P owns all of the only class of T's stock, T owns no stock of lower-tier members, all persons use the accrual method of accounting, the facts set forth the only corporate activity, all transactions are between unrelated persons, tax liabilities are disregarded, and any election required under paragraph (b)(2) of this section is properly made. The principles of this paragraph (b) are illustrated by the following examples.

Example 1. Items allocated between consolidated and separate returns. (a) *Facts.* P and S are the only members of the P group. P sells all of S's stock to individual A on June 30, and therefore S becomes a nonmember on July 1 of Year 2.

(b) *Analysis.* Under paragraph (b)(1) of this section, the P group's consolidated return for Year 2 includes P's income for the entire tax year and S's income for the period from January 1 to June 30, and S must file a separate return for the period from July 1 to December 31.

(c) *Acquisition of another subsidiary before end of tax year.* The facts are the same as in paragraph (a) of this *Example 1,* except that on July 31 P acquires all the stock of T (which filed a separate return for its year ending on November 30 of Year 1) and T therefore becomes a member on August 1 of Year 2. Under § 1.1502-75(d) and paragraph (b)(1) of this section, the P group's consolidated return for Year 2 includes P's income for the entire year, S's income from January 1 to June 30, and T's income from August 1 to December 31. S must file a separate return that includes its income from July 1 to December 31, and T must file a separate return that includes its income from December 1 of Year 1 to July 31 of

Year 2. (If P had acquired T after December 31, the P group that included S is a different group from the P group that includes T, and, for example, the P group that includes T must make a separate election under section 1501 and § 1.1502-75 if consolidated returns are to be filed.)

Example 2. Group structure change. (a) *Facts.* P owns all of the stock of S and T. Shortly after the beginning of Year 1, P merges into T in a reorganization described in section 368(a)(1)(A) (and in section 368(a)(1)(D)), and P's shareholders receive T's stock in exchange for all of P's stock. The P group is treated under § 1.1502-75(d)(2)(ii) as remaining in existence with T as its common parent.

(b) *Analysis.* Under paragraph (b)(1) of this section, the P group's return must include the common parent's items for the entire consolidated return year and, if the common parent ceases to be the common parent but the group remains in existence, appropriate adjustments must be made. Consequently, although P did not exist for all of Year 1, P's items for the portion of Year 1 ending with the merger are treated as the items of the common parent that must be included in the P group's return for Year 1.

(c) *Reverse acquisition.* Assume instead that X acquires all of P's assets in exchange for more than 50% of X's stock in a reorganization described in section 368(a)(1)(D). The reorganization constitutes a reverse acquisition under § 1.1502-75(d)(3), with the X group terminating and the P group surviving with X as its common parent. Consequently, P's items for the portion of Year 1 ending with the acquisition are treated as the items of the common parent that must be included in the P group's return for Year 1, and X's items are treated for purposes of paragraph (b)(1) of this section as the items of a subsidiary included in the P group's return for the portion of Year 1 for which X is a member.

Example 3. Ratable allocation. (a) *Facts.* P sells all of T's stock to X, and T becomes a nonmember on July 1 of Year 1. T engages in the production and sale of merchandise throughout Year 1 and is required to use inventories. The sale is treated as causing T's tax year to end on June 30, and the periods beginning and ending with the sale are treated as two tax years for Federal income tax purposes.

(b) *Analysis.* If ratable allocation under paragraph (b)(2)(ii) of this section is not elected, T must perform an inventory valuation as of the acquisition and also as of the end of Year 1. If ratable allocation is elected, T must perform an inventory valuation only as of the close of Year 1, and T's income from inventory is ratably allocated, along with T's other items that are not extraordinary items, between the P and X consolidated returns.

(c) *Merger into nonmember.* Assume instead that T merges into a wholly owned subsidiary of X in a reorganization described in section

368(a)(2)(D), and P receives 10% of X's stock in exchange for all of T's stock. Under paragraph (b)(2)(ii)(B) of this section, because T's tax year ends on June 30 under section 381(b)(1), T's original year determined without taking paragraph (b) of this section into account also ends on June 30. Consequently, a ratable allocation under paragraph (b)(2)(ii) of this section is the same as an allocation based on closing the books.

Example 4. Net operating loss. P sells all of T's stock to X, T becomes a nonmember on June 30 of Year 1, and ratable allocation under paragraph (b)(2)(ii) of this section is elected. Under ratable allocation, the X group has a $100 consolidated net operating loss for Year 1, all of which is attributable to T. However, because of extraordinary items, T has $100 of income for the portion of Year 1 that T is a member of the P group. Under paragraph (b)(2)(ii)(B)(2) of this section, T's loss may be carried back from the X group to the portion of Year 1 that T was a member of the P group. See also section 172 and §1.1502-21(b). Under paragraph (b)(2)(ii)(C)(5) of this section, any item carried to or from any portion of the original year is an extraordinary item, and the loss therefore is not taken into account again in determining the ratable allocation under paragraph (b)(2)(ii) of this section.

Example 5. Employee benefit plans. (a) *Facts.* P sells all of T's stock to X, and T becomes a nonmember on June 30 of Year 1. On March 15 of Year 2, T contributes $100 to its retirement plan, which is a qualified plan under section 401(a). T is not required to make quarterly contributions to the plan for Year 1 under section 412(m). The contribution is made on account of T's taxable period beginning on July 1 of Year 1, and is deemed in accordance with section 404(a)(6) to have been made on the last day of T's taxable period beginning on July 1 of Year 1. Ratable allocation under paragraph (b)(2)(ii) of this section is not elected.

(b) *Analysis.* Under paragraph (b) of this section, the sale is treated as causing T's tax year to end on June 30, and the period beginning on July 1 is treated as a separate annual accounting period for all Federal income tax purposes. T's income from January 1 to June 30 is included in the P group's Year 1 return, and T's income from July 1 to December 31 is included in the X group's Year 1 return. Thus, the $100 contribution is deductible by T for the period of Year 1 that it is a member of the X group, subject to the applicable limitations of section 404, if a contribution on the last day of that period would otherwise be deductible.

(c) The facts are the same as in paragraph (a) of this *Example 5,* except that, in accordance with section 404(a)(6), $40 of the $100 contribution is made on account of T's taxable period beginning on January 1 of Year 1 and is deemed to be made on the last day of T's taxable period beginning on January 1 of Year 1. The remaining $60 is made on account of T's taxable period beginning

on July 1 of Year 1 and is deemed to be made on the last day of T's taxable period beginning on July 1 of Year 1. As in paragraph (b) of this *Example 5,* under paragraph (b) of this section, the sale is treated as causing T's tax year to end on June 30, and the period beginning on July 1 is treated as a separate annual accounting period for all Federal income tax purposes. The $40 portion of the contribution is deductible by T for the period of Year 1 that it is a member of the P group, subject to the applicable limitations of section 404 and provided that a $40 contribution on the last day of that period would otherwise be deductible for that period, and the $60 portion is deductible by T for the period of Year 1 that it is a member of the X group, subject to the same conditions.

(d) *Ratable allocation.* The facts are the same as in paragraph (a) of this *Example 5,* except that P, T, and X elect ratable allocation under paragraph (b)(2)(ii) of this section and T's deduction for the retirement plan contribution is not an extraordinary item. T's deduction may be ratably allocated, subject to the applicable limitations of section 404, and is allowable only if a contribution on the last day of Year 1 otherwise would be deductible for any period in the year. (The results would be the same if S were an unaffiliated corporation when acquired by X, and the due date of its last separate return (including extensions) were before the pension contribution was made on March 15 of Year 2.)

Example 6. Allocation of partnership items. (a) *Facts.* P sells all of T's stock to X, and T becomes a nonmember on June 30 of Year 1. T has a 10% interest in the capital and profits of a calendar-year partnership.

(b) *Analysis.* Under paragraph (b)(2)(vi)(A) of this section, T is treated, solely for purposes of determining T's tax year in which the partnership's items are included, as selling or exchanging its entire interest in the partnership as of P's sale of T's stock. Thus, the deemed disposition is not taken into account under section 708, it does not result in gain or loss being recognized by T, and T's holding period is unaffected. However, under section 706(a), in determining T's income, T is required to include its distributive share of partnership items for the partnership's year ending within or with T's tax year. Under section 706(c)(2), the partnership's tax year is treated as closing with respect to T for this purpose as of P's sale of T's stock. The allocation of T's distributive share of partnership items must be made under §1.706-1(c)(2)(ii).

(c) *Controlled partnership.* The facts are the same as in paragraph (a) of this *Example 6,* except that T has a 75% interest in the capital and profits of the partnership. Under paragraph (b)(2)(vi)(B) of this section, T's distributive share of the partnership items is treated as T's items for purposes of paragraph (b)(2) of this section. Thus, if ratable allocation under paragraph (b)(2)(ii) of this section is not elected, T's distributive share of the partnership's items must be determined under § 1.706-1(c)(2)(ii) by an interim closing of the partnership's books. Similarly, if ratable allocation is elected for T's items that are not extraordinary items, T's distributive share of the partnership's nonextraordinary items must also be ratably allocated under § 1.706-1(c)(2)(ii).

Example 7. Acquisition of S corporation. (a) *Facts.* Z is a small business corporation for which an election under section 1362(a) was in effect at all times since Year 1. At all times, Z had only 100 shares of stock outstanding, all of which were owned by individual A. On July 1 of Year 3, P acquired all of the Z stock. P does not make an election under section 338(g) with respect to its purchase of the Z stock.

(b) *Analysis.* As a result of P's acquisition of the Z stock, Z's election under section 1362(a) terminates. See sections 1361(b)(1)(B) and 1362(d)(2). Z is required to join in the filing of the P consolidated return. See § 1.1502-75. Z's tax year ends for all Federal income tax purposes on June 30 of Year 3. If no extension of time is sought, Z must file a separate return for the period from January 1 through June 30 of Year 3 on or before March 15 of Year 4. See paragraph (b)(4) of this section. Z will become a member of the P consolidated group as of July 1 of Year 3. See paragraph (b)(1)(ii)(A)(2) of this section. P group's Year 3 consolidated return will include Z's items from July 1 to December 31 of Year 3.

(6) *Effective date.*—(i) *General rule.*—Except as provided in paragraphs (b)(1)(ii)(A)(2) and (b)(2)(v) of this section, this paragraph (b) applies to corporations becoming or ceasing to be members of consolidated groups on or after January 1, 1995.

(ii) *Prior law.*—For prior transactions, see prior regulations under section 1502 as in effect with respect to the transaction. See, e.g., § 1.1502-76(b) and (d) as contained in the 26 CFR part 1 edition revised as of April 1, 1994. However, § 1.1502-76(b)(5) and (6) as contained in the 26 CFR part 1 edition revised as of April 1, 1994 do not apply with respect to corporations becoming or ceasing to be members of consolidated groups on or after January 1, 1995. If both this paragraph (b) and prior law may apply to determine the inclusion of any amount in a return, appropriate adjustments must be made to prevent the omission or duplication of the amount.

(c) *Time for making separate returns for periods not included in consolidated return.*—(1) *Consolidated return filed by due date for separate return.*—If the group has filed a consolidated return on or before the due date for the filing of a subsidiary's separate return (including extensions of time and determined without regard to any change of its taxable year required under paragraph (a) of this section), then the separate return for any portion of the subsidiary's taxable year for which its income is not included in the consolidated return of the group must be filed no later than the due date of such consolidated return (including extensions of time).

(2) *Consolidated return not filed by due date for separate return.*—If the group has not filed a consolidated return on or before the due date for the filing of a subsidiary corporation's separate return (including extensions of time and determined without regard to any change of its taxable year required under paragraph (a) of this section), then on or before such due date such subsidiary shall file a separate return either for the portion of its taxable year for which its income would not be included in a consolidated return if such a return were filed, or for its complete taxable year. However, if a separate return is filed for such portion of its taxable year and the group subsequently does not file a consolidated return, such subsidiary corporation shall file a substituted return for its complete taxable year not later than the due date (including extensions of time) prescribed for the filing of the common parent's return. On the other hand, if the return is filed for the subsidiary's complete taxable year and the group later files a consolidated return, such subsidiary must file an amended return not later than the due date (including extensions of time) for the filing of the consolidated return of the group. Such amended return shall be for that portion of such subsidiary's taxable year which is not included in the consolidated return. If, under this subparagraph, a substituted return must be filed, then the return previously filed shall not be considered a return within the meaning of section 6011. If, under this subparagraph, a substituted or amended return must be filed, then, for purposes of sections 6513(a) and 6601(a), the last date prescribed for payment of tax shall be the due date (not including extensions of time) for the filing of the subsidiary's separate return (determined without regard to this subparagraph and without regard to any change of its taxable year required under paragraph (a) of this section).

(3) *Examples.*—The provisions of this paragraph may be illustrated by the following examples:

Example (1). Corporation P, which filed a separate return for the calendar year 1966, acquires all of the stock of corporation S as of the close of December 31, 1966. Corporation S reports its income on the basis of a fiscal year ending March 31. On June 15, 1967, the due date for the filing of a separate return by S (assuming no extensions of time), a consolidated return has not been filed for the group (P and S). On such date S may either file a return for the period April 1, 1966, through December 31, 1966, or it may file a return for the complete fiscal year ending March 31, 1967. If S files a return for the short period ending December 31, 1966, and if the group elects not to file a consolidated return for the calendar year 1967, S, on or before March 15, 1968 (the due date of P's return, assuming no extensions of time) must file a substituted return for the complete fiscal year ending March 31, 1967, in lieu of the return previously filed for the short period. Interest is computed from June 15, 1967. If, however, S files a return for the complete fiscal year ending March 31, 1967, and the group elects to file a consolidated return for the calendar year 1967, then S must file an amended return covering the period from April 1, 1966, through December 31, 1966, in lieu of the return previously filed for the complete fiscal year. Interest is computed from June 15, 1967.

Example (2). Assume the same facts as in example (1) except that corporation P acquires all of the stock of corporation S at the close of September 30, 1967, and that P files a consolidated return for the group for 1967 on March 15, 1968 (not having obtained any extensions of time). Since a consolidated return has been filed on or before the due date (June 15, 1968) for the filing of the separate return for the taxable year ending March 31, 1968, the return of S for the short taxable year beginning April 1, 1967, and ending September 30, 1967, should be filed no later than March 15, 1968.

(d) *Effective/applicability date.*—(1) *Taxable years of members of group effective date.*—(i) *In general.*—Paragraph (a) of this section applies to any original consolidated Federal income tax return due (without extensions) after July 20, 2007.

(ii) *Prior law.*—For original consolidated Federal income tax returns due (without extensions) after April 25, 2006, and on or before July 20, 2007, see § 1.1502-76T as contained in 26 CFR part 1 in effect on April 1, 2007. For original consolidated Federal income tax returns due (without extensions) on or before April 25, 2006, see § 1.1502-76 as contained in 26 CFR part 1 in effect on April 1, 2006.

(2) *Election to ratably allocate items effective date.*—(i) *In general.*—Paragraph (b)(2)(ii)(D) of this section applies to any original consolidated Federal income tax return due (without extensions) after July 20, 2007.

(ii) *Prior law.*—For original consolidated Federal income tax returns due (without extensions) after May 30, 2006, and on or before July 20, 2007, see § 1.1502-76T as contained in 26 CFR part 1 in effect on April 1, 2007. For original consolidated Federal income tax returns due (without extensions) on or before May 30, 2006, see § 1.1502-76 as contained in 26 CFR part 1 in effect on April 1, 2006. [Reg. § 1.1502–76.]

□ [T.D. 6894, 9-7-66. Amended by T.D. 7244, 12-29-72; T.D. 7246, 12-29-72; T.D. 8560, 8-12-94; T.D. 8842, 11-9-99; T.D. 8858, 1-5-2000; T.D. 8940, 2-12-2001; T.D. 9192, 3-21-2005; T.D. 9258,

4-24-2006; T.D. 9264, 5-26-2006 and T.D. 9342, 7-19-2007.]

[Reg. § 1.1502-77]

§ 1.1502-77. Agent for the group.—(a) *Scope of agency.*—(1) *In general.*—(i) *Common parent.*—Except as provided in paragraphs (a)(3) and (6) of this section, the common parent (or a substitute agent described in paragraph (a)(1)(ii) of this section) for a consolidated return year is the sole agent (agent for the group) that is authorized to act in its own name with respect to all matters relating to the tax liability for that consolidated return year, for—

(A) Each member in the group; and

(B) Any successor (see paragraph (a)(1)(iii) of this section) of a member.

(ii) *Substitute agents.*—For purposes of this section, any corporation designated as a substitute agent pursuant to paragraph (d) of this section to replace the common parent or a previously designated substitute agent acts as agent for the group to the same extent and subject to the same limitations as are applicable to the common parent, and any reference in this section to the common parent includes any such substitute agent.

(iii) *Successor.*—For purposes of this section only, the term *successor* means an individual or entity (including a disregarded entity) that is primarily liable, pursuant to applicable law (including, for example, by operation of a state or Federal merger statute), for the tax liability of a member of the group. Such determination is made without regard to § 1.1502-1(f)(4) or 1.1502-6(a). (For inclusion of a successor in references to a subsidiary or member, see paragraph (c)(2) of this section.)

(iv) *Disregarded entity.*—If a subsidiary of a group becomes, or its successor is or becomes, a disregarded entity for Federal tax purposes, the common parent continues to serve as the agent with respect to that subsidiary's tax liability under § 1.1502-6 for consolidated return years during which it was included in the group, even though the entity generally is not treated as a person separate from its owner for Federal tax purposes.

(v) *Transferee liability.*—For purposes of assessing, paying and collecting transferee liability, any exercise of or reliance on the common parent's agency authority pursuant to this section is binding on a transferee (or subsequent transferees) of a member, regardless of whether the member's existence terminates prior to such exercise or reliance.

(vi) *Purported common parent.*—If any corporation files a consolidated return purporting to be the common parent of a consolidated group but is subsequently determined not to have been

Reg. § 1.1502-77(a)(1)(vi)

the common parent of the claimed group, that corporation is treated, to the extent necessary to avoid prejudice to the Commissioner, as if it were the common parent.

(2) *Examples of matters subject to agency.*— With respect to any consolidated return year for which it is the common parent—

(i) The common parent makes any election (or similar choice of a permissible option) that is available to a subsidiary in the computation of its separate taxable income, and any change in an election (or similar choice of a permissible option) previously made by or for a subsidiary, including, for example, a request to change a subsidiary's method or period of accounting;

(ii) All correspondence concerning the income tax liability for the consolidated return year is carried on directly with the common parent;

(iii) The common parent files for all extensions of time, including extensions of time for payment of tax under section 6164, and any extension so filed is considered as having been filed by each member;

(iv) The common parent gives waivers, gives bonds, and executes closing agreements, offers in compromise, and all other documents, and any waiver or bond so given, or agreement, offer in compromise, or any other document so executed, is considered as having also been given or executed by each member;

(v) The common parent files claims for refund, and any refund is made directly to and in the name of the common parent and discharges any liability of the Government to any member with respect to such refund;

(vi) The common parent takes any action on behalf of a member of the group with respect to a foreign corporation, for example, elections by, and changes to the method of accounting of, a controlled foreign corporation in accordance with § 1.964-1(c)(3);

(vii) Notices of claim disallowance are mailed only to the common parent, and the mailing to the common parent is considered as a mailing to each member;

(viii) Notices of deficiencies are mailed only to the common parent (except as provided in paragraph (b) of this section), and the mailing to the common parent is considered as a mailing to each member;

(ix) Notices of final partnership administrative adjustment under section 6223 with respect to any partnership in which a member of the group is a partner may be mailed to the common parent, and, if so, the mailing to the common parent is considered as a mailing to each member that is a partner entitled to receive such notice (for other rules regarding partnership proceedings, see paragraphs (a)(3)(v) and (a)(6)(iii) of this section);

(x) The common parent files petitions and conducts proceedings before the United States Tax Court, and any such petition is considered as also having been filed by each member;

(xi) Any assessment of tax may be made in the name of the common parent, and an assessment naming the common parent is considered as an assessment with respect to each member; and

(xii) Notice and demand for payment of taxes is given only to the common parent, and such notice and demand is considered as a notice and demand to each member.

(3) *Matters reserved to subsidiaries.*—Except as provided in this paragraph (a)(3) and paragraph (a)(6) of this section, no subsidiary has authority to act for or to represent itself in any matter related to the tax liability for the consolidated return year. The following matters, however, are reserved exclusively to each subsidiary—

(i) The making of the consent required by § 1.1502-75(a)(1);

(ii) Any action with respect to the subsidiary's liability for a federal tax other than the income tax imposed by chapter 1 of the Internal Revenue Code (including, for example, employment taxes under chapters 21 through 25 of the Internal Revenue Code, and miscellaneous excise taxes under chapters 31 through 47 of the Internal Revenue Code);

(iii) The making of an election under section 936(e);

(iv) The making of an election to be treated as a DISC under § 1.992-2; and

(v) Any actions by a subsidiary acting as tax matters partner under sections 6221 through 6234 and the accompanying regulations (but see paragraph (a)(2)(ix) of this section regarding the mailing of a final partnership administrative adjustment to the common parent).

(4) *Term of agency.*—(i) *In general.*—Except as provided in paragraph (a)(4)(iii) of this section, the common parent for the consolidated return year remains the agent for the group with respect to that year until the common parent's existence terminates, regardless of whether one or more subsidiaries in that year cease to be members of the group, whether the group files a consolidated return for any subsequent year, whether the common parent ceases to be the common parent or a member of the group in any subsequent year, or whether the group continues pursuant to § 1.1502-75(d) with a new common parent in any subsequent year.

(ii) *Replacement of substitute agent designated by Commissioner.*—If the Commissioner replaces a previously designated substitute agent pursuant to paragraph (d)(3)(ii) of this section, the replaced substitute agent ceases to be the agent after the Commissioner designates another substitute agent.

(iii) *New common parent after a group structure change.*—If the group continues in existence with a new common parent pursuant to §1.1502-75(d) during a consolidated return year, the common parent at the beginning of the year is the agent for the group through the date of the §1.1502-75(d) transaction, and the new common parent becomes the agent for the group beginning the day after the transaction, at which time it becomes the agent for the group with respect to the entire consolidated return year (including the period through the date of the transaction) and the former common parent is no longer the agent for that year.

(5) *Identifying members in notice of a lien.*—Notwithstanding any other provisions of this paragraph (a), any notice of a lien, any levy or any other proceeding to collect the amount of any assessment, after the assessment has been made, must name the entity from which such collection is to be made.

(6) *Direct dealing with a member.*—(i) *Several liability.*—The Commissioner may, upon issuing to the common parent written notice that expressly invokes the authority of this provision, deal directly with any member of the group with respect to its liability under §1.1502-6 for the consolidated tax of the group, in which event such member has sole authority to act for itself with respect to that liability. However, if the Commissioner believes or has reason to believe that the existence of the common parent has terminated, he may, if he deems it advisable, deal directly with any member with respect to that member's liability under §1.1502-6 without giving the notice required by this provision.

(ii) *Information requests.*—The Commissioner may, upon informing the common parent, request information relevant to the consolidated tax liability from any member of the group. However, if the Commissioner believes or has reason to believe that the existence of the common parent has terminated, he may request such information from any member of the group without informing the common parent.

(iii) *Members as partners in partnerships.*—The Commissioner generally will deal directly with any member in its capacity as a partner of a partnership that is subject to the provisions of sections 6221 through 6234 and the accompanying regulations (but see paragraph (a)(2)(ix) of this section regarding the mailing of a final partnership administrative adjustment to the common parent). However, if requested to do so in accordance with the provisions of §301.6223(c)-1(b) of this chapter, the Commissioner may deal with the common parent as agent for such member on any matter related to the partnership, except in regards to a settlement under section 6224(c) and except to the extent the member acts as tax matters partner of the partnership.

(b) *Copy of notice of deficiency to entity that has ceased to be a member of the group.*—An entity that ceases to be a member of the group during or after a consolidated return year may file a written notice of that fact with the Commissioner and request a copy of any notice of deficiency with respect to the tax for a consolidated return year during which the entity was a member, or a copy of any notice and demand for payment of such deficiency, or both. Such filing does not limit the scope of the agency of the common parent provided for in paragraph (a) of this section. Any failure by the Commissioner to comply with such request does not limit an entity's tax liability under §1.1502-6. For purposes of this paragraph (b), references to an entity include a successor of such entity.

(c) *References to member or subsidiary.*—For purposes of this section, all references to a member or subsidiary for a consolidated return year include—

(1) Each corporation that was a member of the group during any part of such year (except that any reference to a subsidiary does not include the common parent);

(2) Except as indicated otherwise, a successor (as defined in paragraph (a)(1)(iii) of this section) of any corporation described in paragraph (c)(1) of this section; and

(3) Each corporation whose income was included in the consolidated return for such year, notwithstanding that the tax liability of such corporation should have been computed on the basis of a separate return, or as a member of another consolidated group, under the provisions of §1.1502-75.

(d) *Termination of common parent.*—(1) *Designation of substitute agent by common parent.*—(i) If the common parent's existence terminates, it may designate a substitute agent for the group and notify the Commissioner, as provided in this paragraph (d)(1).

(A) Subject to the Commissioner's approval under paragraph (d)(1)(ii) of this section, before the common parent's existence terminates, the common parent may designate, for each consolidated return year for which it is the common parent and for which the period of limitations either for assessment, for collection after assessment, or for claiming a credit or refund has not expired, one of the following to act as substitute agent in its place—

(1) Any corporation that was a member of the group during any part of the consolidated return year and, except as provided in paragraph (e)(3)(ii) of this section, has not subsequently been disregarded as an entity separate from its owner or reclassified as a partnership for Federal tax purposes; or

(2) Any successor (as defined in paragraph (a)(1)(iii) of this section) of such a corporation or of the common parent that is a

domestic corporation (and, except as provided in paragraph (e)(3)(ii) of this section, is not disregarded as an entity separate from its owner or classified as a partnership for Federal tax purposes), including a corporation that will become a successor at the time that the common parent's existence terminates.

(B) The common parent must notify the Commissioner in writing (under procedures prescribed by the Commissioner) of the designation and provide the following—

(1) An agreement executed by the designated corporation agreeing to serve as the group's substitute agent; and

(2) If the designated corporation was not itself a member of the group during the consolidated return year (because the designated corporation is a successor of a member of the group for the consolidated return year), a statement by the designated corporation acknowledging that it is or will be primarily liable for the consolidated tax as a successor of a member.

(ii) A designation under paragraph (d)(1)(i)(A) of this section does not apply unless and until it is approved by the Commissioner. The Commissioner's approval of such a designation is not effective before the existence of the common parent terminates.

(2) *Default substitute agent.*—If the common parent fails to designate a substitute agent for the group before its existence terminates and if the common parent has a single successor that is a domestic corporation, such successor becomes the substitute agent for the group upon termination of the common parent's existence. However, see paragraph (d)(4) of this section regarding the consequences of the successor's failure to notify the Commissioner of its status as default substitute agent in accordance with procedures established by the Commissioner.

(3) *Designation by the Commissioner.*—(i) In the event the common parent's existence terminates and no designation is made and approved under paragraph (d)(1) of this section and the Commissioner believes or has reason to believe that there is no successor of the common parent that satisfies the requirements of paragraph (d)(2) of this section (or the Commissioner believes or has reason to believe there is such a successor but has no last known address on file for such successor), the Commissioner may, at any time, with or without a request from any member of the group, designate a corporation described in paragraph (d)(1)(i)(A) of this section to act as the substitute agent. The Commissioner will notify the designated substitute agent in writing of its designation, and the designation is effective upon receipt by the designated substitute agent of such notice. The designated substitute agent must give notice of the designation to each corporation that was a member of the group during any part of the consolidated return year, but a failure by the designated substitute

agent to notify any such member of the group does not invalidate the designation.

(ii) At the request of any member, the Commissioner may, but is not required to, replace a substitute agent previously designated under paragraph (d)(3)(i) of this section with another corporation described in paragraph (d)(1)(i)(A) of this section.

(4) *Absence of designation or notification of default substitute agent.*—Until a designation of a substitute agent for the group under paragraph (d)(1) of this section has become effective, the Commissioner has received notification in accordance with procedures established by the Commissioner that a successor qualifying under paragraph (d)(2) of this section has become the substitute agent by default, or the Commissioner has designated a substitute agent under paragraph (d)(3) of this section—

(i) Any notice of deficiency or other communication mailed to the common parent, even if no longer in existence, is considered as having been properly mailed to the agent for the group; and

(ii) The Commissioner is not required to act on any communication (including, for example, a claim for refund) submitted on behalf of the group by any person other than the common parent (including a successor of the common parent qualifying as a default substitute agent under paragraph (d)(2) of this section).

(e) *Termination of a corporation's existence.*—(1) *In general.*—For purposes of paragraphs (a)(1)(v), (a)(4)(i), (d), and (j) of this section, the existence of a corporation is deemed to terminate if—

(i) Its existence terminates under applicable law; or

(ii) Except as provided in paragraph (e)(3) of this section, it becomes, for Federal tax purposes, either—

(A) An entity that is disregarded as an entity separate from its owner; or

(B) An entity that is reclassified as a partnership.

(2) *Purported agency.*—If the existence of the agent for the group terminates under circumstances described in paragraph (e)(1)(ii) of this section, until the Commissioner has approved the designation of a substitute agent for the group pursuant to paragraph (d)(1) of this section or the Commissioner designates a substitute agent and notifies the designated substitute agent pursuant to paragraph (d)(3) of this section, any post-termination action by that purported agent on behalf of the group has the same effect, to the extent necessary to avoid prejudice to the Commissioner, as if the agent's corporate existence had not terminated.

(3) *Exceptions where no eligible corporation exists.*—(i) For purposes of the common parent's

term as agent under paragraph (a)(4)(i) of this section and the term as agent of the substitute agent designated under paragraph (d) of this section, if a corporation either becomes disregarded as an entity separate from its owner or is reclassified as a partnership for Federal tax purposes, its existence is not deemed to terminate if the effect of such termination would be that no corporation remains eligible to serve as the substitute agent for the group's consolidated return year.

(ii) Similarly, for purposes of paragraph (d) of this section, an entity that is either disregarded as an entity separate from its owner or reclassified as a partnership for Federal tax purposes is not precluded from designation as a substitute agent merely because of such classification if the effect of the inability to make such designation would be that no corporation remains eligible to serve as the substitute agent for the group's consolidated return year.

(iii) Any entity described in paragraphs (e)(3)(i) or (ii) of this section that remains or becomes the agent for the group is treated as a corporation for purposes of this section.

(4) *Exception for section 338 transactions.*—Notwithstanding section 338(a)(2), a target corporation for which an election is made under section 338 is not deemed to terminate for purposes of this section.

(f) *Examples.*—The following examples illustrate the principles of this section. Unless otherwise indicated, each example addresses the question of which corporation is the proper party to execute a consent to waive the statute of limitations for Years 1 and 2 or the more general question of which corporation may be designated as a substitute agent for the group for Years 1 and 2. In each example, as of January 1 of Year 1, the P group consists of P and its two subsidiaries, S and S-1. P, as the common parent of the P group, files consolidated returns for the P group in Years 1 and 2. On January 1 of Year 1, domestic corporations S-2, U, V, W, W-1, X, Y, Z and Z-1 are not related to P or the members of the P group. All corporations are calendar year taxpayers. For none of the tax years at issue does the Commissioner exercise the authority under paragraph (a)(6) of this section to deal with any member separately. Any surviving corporation in a merger is a successor as described in paragraph (a)(1)(iii) of this section. Any notification to the Commissioner of the designation of the P group's substitute agent also contains a statement signed on behalf of the designated agent that it agrees to act as the group's substitute agent and, in the case of a successor, that it is primarily liable as a successor of a member. The examples are as follows:

Example 1. Disposition of all group members. On December 31 of Year 1, P sells all the stock of S-1 to X. On December 31 of Year 2, P distributes all the stock of S to P's shareholders. P files a separate return for Year 3. Although P is no longer a common parent after Year 2, P remains the agent for the P group for Years 1 and 2. For as long as P remains in existence, only P may execute a waiver of the period of limitations on assessment on behalf of the group for Years 1 and 2.

Example 2. Acquisition of common parent by another group. The facts are the same as in *Example 1*, except on January 1 of Year 3, all of the outstanding stock of P is acquired by Y. P thereafter joins in the Y group consolidated return as a member of Y group. Although P is a member of Y group in Year 3, P remains the agent for the P group for Years 1 and 2. For as long as P remains in existence, only P may execute a waiver of the period of limitations on assessment on behalf of the P group for Years 1 and 2.

Example 3. Merger of common parent—designation of remaining member as substitute agent. On December 31 of Year 1, P sells all the stock of S-1 to X. On July 1 of Year 2, P acquires all the stock of S-2. On November 30 of Year 2, P distributes all the stock of S to P's shareholders. On January 1 of Year 3, P merges into Y corporation. Just before the merger, P notifies the Commissioner in writing of the planned merger and of its designation of S as the substitute agent for the P group for Years 1 and 2. S is the only member that P can designate as the substitute agent for both Years 1 and 2 because it is the only subsidiary that was a member of the P group during part of both years. Although S-2 is the only remaining subsidiary of the P group when P merges into Y, S-2 was a member of the P group only in Year 2. For that reason, S-2 cannot be the substitute agent for the P group for Year 1. Alternatively, P could designate a different substitute agent for each year, selecting S or S-1 as the substitute agent for Year 1, and S or S-2 as the substitute agent for Year 2. P could also designate its successor Y as the substitute agent for both Years 1 and 2.

Example 4. Forward triangular merger of common parent. On January 1 of Year 3, P merges with and into Z-1, a subsidiary of Z, in a forward triangular merger described in section 368(a)(1)(A) and (a)(2)(D). The transaction constitutes a reverse acquisition under § 1.1502-75(d)(3)(i) because P's shareholders receive more than 50% of Z's stock in exchange for all of P's stock. Just before the merger, P notifies the Commissioner in writing of the planned merger and its designation of Z-1, the corporation that will survive the planned merger, as the substitute agent of the P group for Years 1 and 2. Because Z-1 will be P's successor (within the meaning of paragraph (a)(1) of this section) after the planned merger, P may designate Z-1 as the substitute agent for the P group for Years 1 and 2, pursuant to paragraph (d)(1) of this section. Alternatively, P could have designated S or S-1 as the substitute agent for the P group for Years 1 and 2. Although Z is the new common parent of the P group, which continues pursuant to

§ 1.1502-75(d)(3)(i), P may not designate Z as the substitute agent for Years 1 and 2 because Z was not a member of the group during any part of Years 1 or 2 and is not a successor of P or any other member of P group.

Example 5. Reverse triangular merger of common parent. On March 1 of Year 3, W-1, a subsidiary of W, merges into P, in a reverse triangular merger described in section 368(a)(1)(A) and (a)(2)(E). P survives the merger with W-1. The transaction constitutes a reverse acquisition under § 1.1502-75(d)(3)(i) because P's shareholders receive more than 50% of W's stock in exchange for all of P's stock. Under paragraph (a) of this section, P remains the agent for the P group for Years 1 and 2, even though the P group continues with W as its new common parent pursuant to § 1.1502-75(d)(3)(i). Because the transaction constitutes a reverse acquisition, the P group is treated as remaining in existence with W as its common parent. Before March 2 of Year 3, P is the agent for the P group for Year 3. Beginning on March 2 of Year 3, W becomes the agent for the P group with respect to all of Year 3 (including the period through March 1) and subsequent consolidated return years. For as long as P remains in existence, P remains the agent of the P group under paragraph (a) of this section for Years 1 and 2, and therefore only P may execute a waiver of the period of limitations on assessment on behalf of the P group for Years 1 and 2.

Example 6. Reverse triangular merger of common parent-subsequent spinoff of common parent. The facts are the same as in *Example 5,* except that on April 1 of Year 4, in a transaction unrelated to the Year 3 reverse acquisition, P distributes the stock of its subsidiaries S and S-1 to W, and W then distributes the stock of P to the W shareholders. Beginning on March 2 of Year 3, W becomes the agent for the P group with respect to Year 3 (including the period through March 1) and subsequent consolidated return years. Although P is no longer a member of the P group after the Year 4 spinoff, P remains the agent for the P group under paragraph (a) of this section for Years 1 and 2. Thus, for as long as P remains in existence, only P may execute a waiver of the period of limitations on assessment on behalf of the P group for Years 1 and 2.

Example 7. Qualified stock purchase and section 338 election. On March 31 of Year 2, V purchases the stock of P in a qualified stock purchase (within the meaning of section 338(d)(3)), and V makes a timely election pursuant to section 338(g) with respect to P. Although section 338(a)(2) provides that P is treated as a new corporation as of the beginning of the day after the acquisition date for purposes of subtitle A, paragraph (e)(4) of this section provides that P's existence is not deemed to terminate for purposes of this section notwithstanding the general rule of section 338(a)(2). Therefore, the election under section 338(g) does not result in a termination of P under paragraph (e) of this section, and

new P remains the agent of the P group for Year 1 and the period ending March 31 of Year 2 (short Year 2). For as long as new P remains in existence, only new P may execute a waiver of the period of limitations on assessment on behalf of the P group for Year 1 and short Year 2.

Example 8. Fraudulent conveyance of assets. On March 15 of Year 2, P files a consolidated return that includes the income of S and S-1 for Year 1. On December 1 of Year 2, S-1 transfers assets having a fair market value of $100x to U in exchange for $10x. This transfer of assets for less than fair market value constitutes a fraudulent conveyance under applicable state law. On March 1 of Year 5, P executes a waiver extending to December 31 of Year 6 the period of limitations on assessment with respect to the group's Year 1 consolidated return. On February 1 of Year 6, the Commissioner issues a notice of deficiency to P asserting a deficiency of $30x for the P group's Year 1 consolidated tax liability. P does not file a petition for redetermination in the Tax Court, and the Commissioner makes a timely assessment against the P group. P, S and S-1 are all insolvent and are unable to pay the deficiency. On February 1 of Year 8, the Commissioner sends a notice of transferee liability to U, which does not file a petition in the Tax Court. On August 1 of Year 8, the Commissioner assesses the amount of the P group's deficiency against U. Under section 6901(c), the Commissioner may assess U's transferee liability within one year after the expiration of the period of limitations against the transferor S-1. By operation of section 6213(a) and 6503(a), the issuance of the notice of deficiency to P and the expiration of the 90-day period for filing a petition in the Tax Court have the effect of further extending by 150 days the P group's limitations period on assessment from the previously extended date of December 31 of Year 6 to May 30 of Year 7. Pursuant to paragraph (a)(1)(v) of this section, the waiver executed by P on March 1 of Year 5 to extend the period of limitations on assessment to December 31 of Year 6 and the further extension of the P group's limitations period to May 30 of Year 7 (by operation of sections 6213(a) and 6503(a)) have the derivative effect of extending the period of limitations on assessment of U's transferee liability to May 30 of Year 8. By operation of section 6901(f), the issuance of the notice of transferee liability to U and the expiration of the 90-day period for filing a petition in the Tax Court have the effect of further extending the limitations period on assessment of U's liability as a transferee by 150 days, from May 30 of Year 8 to October 27 of Year 8. Accordingly, the Commissioner may send a notice of transferee liability to U at any time on or before May 30 of Year 8 and assess the unpaid liability against U at any time on or before October 27 of Year 8. The result would be the same even if S-1 ceased to exist before March 1 of Year 5, the date P executed the waiver.

(g) *Cross-reference.*—For further rules applicable to groups that include insolvent financial institutions, see § 301.6402-7 of this chapter.

(h) *Effective date.*—(1) *Application.*—(i) *In general.*—This section applies with respect to taxable years beginning on or after June 28, 2002.

(ii) *Election to apply for prior taxable years.*—Notwithstanding paragraphs (h)(1)(i) and (h)(2) of this section, the common parent may elect to apply paragraph (d)(1) of this section in lieu of § 1.1502-77A(d) in designating a substitute agent for taxable years beginning before June 28, 2002. The common parent makes such an election by expressly referring to the election under this paragraph (h)(1)(ii) in notifying the Commissioner of the designation of the substitute agent. Once made, such election applies to any subsequent designation of a substitute agent for the consolidated return year(s) subject to the election.

(2) *Prior law.*—For taxable years beginning before June 28, 2002, see § 1.1502-77A.

(3) *Designation of a domestic substitute agent.*—(i) *In general.*—The provisions of paragraphs (e)(1) and (j) of this section apply to taxable years for which the consolidated Federal income tax return is due (without extensions) after July 23, 2007.

(ii) *Prior law.*—For taxable years for which the consolidated Federal income tax return is due (without extensions) on or before July 23, 2007, see Sec. 1.1502-77(e)(1) as contained in the 26 CFR part 1 edition revised as of April 1, 2007. For taxable years for which the consolidated Federal income tax return is due (without extensions) after March 14, 2006, and on or before July 23, 2007, see Sec. 1.1502-77T as contained in the 26 CFR part 1 edition revised as of April 1, 2007.

(i) [Reserved].

(j) *Designation by Commissioner if common parent is treated as a domestic corporation under section 7874 or section 953(d).*—(1) *In general.*—If the common parent is an entity created or organized under the law of a foreign country and is treated as a domestic corporation by reason of section 7874 (or regulations under that section) or a section 953(d) election (a foreign common parent), the Commissioner may at any time, with or without a request from any member of the group, designate another member of the group to act as the agent for the group (a domestic substitute agent) for any taxable year for which the consolidated Federal income tax return is due (without extensions) after July 23, 2007, and the foreign common parent would otherwise be the agent for the group. For each such year, the domestic substitute agent will be the sole agent for the group even though the foreign common parent remains in existence. The foreign com-

mon parent ceases to be the agent for the group when the Commissioner's designation of a domestic substitute agent becomes effective. The Commissioner may designate a domestic substitute agent for the term of a single taxable year, multiple years, or on a continuing basis.

(2) *Domestic substitute agent.*—The domestic substitute agent, by designation or by succession, shall be a domestic corporation described in paragraph (d)(1)(i)(A) of this section (determined without regard to section 7874, a section 953(d) election or section 1504(d)).

(3) *Designation by the Commissioner.*—The Commissioner will notify the domestic substitute agent in writing by mail or faxed transmission of the designation. The domestic substitute agent's designation is effective on the earliest of the 14th day following the date of a mailing, the 4th day following a faxed transmission, or the date the Commissioner receives written confirmation of the designation by a duly authorized officer of the domestic substitute agent (within the meaning of section 6062). The domestic substitute agent must give notice of its designation to the foreign common parent and each corporation that was a member of the group during any part of any consolidated return year for which the domestic substitute agent will be the agent. A failure of the domestic substitute agent to notify the foreign common parent or any member of the group does not invalidate the designation. The Commissioner will send a copy of the notification to the foreign common parent, and if applicable, to any domestic substitute agent the designation replaces; a failure to send a copy of the notification does not invalidate the designation.

(4) *Term of agency.*—(i) *Taxable years for which domestic substitute agent is the agent.*—If the Commissioner designates a domestic substitute agent for one or more taxable years, unless the designation is expressly limited to such term, such domestic substitute agent will continue as the group's sole agent for subsequent taxable years until the domestic substitute agent ceases to be a member of the continuing group, is replaced by a new domestic common parent (as provided in paragraph (j)(4)(iv)(A) of this section), is replaced by the Commissioner, or is replaced by a default substitute agent (as provided in paragraph (j)(5)(ii) of this section). If during the course of a consolidated return year the domestic substitute agent ceases to be a member of the continuing group or is replaced, it shall no longer act as agent for such taxable year or subsequent taxable years in any matter.

(ii) *Continuing agency for prior taxable years.*—Unless replaced by a default substitute agent (as provided in paragraph (j)(5)(ii) of this section) or by the Commissioner, the domestic substitute agent at the end of a taxable year of the group will remain the agent for such year until its existence terminates, even if the group subsequently ceases to exist or the domestic substitute agent subsequently ceases to be a member of the group.

(iii) *Replacement of a Sec. 1.1502-77(d)(1) agent.*—If, pursuant to paragraph (d)(1) of this section, the common parent of the group designates a foreign common parent as the agent for the group for any taxable year, the Commissioner may, at any time, designate a domestic substitute agent to replace the foreign common parent, even if the Commissioner approved the terminating common parent's designation.

(iv) *Group continues with a new common parent.*—(A) *Year the new common parent becomes the common parent.*—If the group has a domestic substitute agent and the group continues in existence with a new common parent during a consolidated return year, and such new common parent is a domestic corporation (determined without regard to section 7874 or a section 953(d) election), the domestic substitute agent at the beginning of the year is the agent for the group through the date of the transaction in which the new common parent becomes the common parent, and the new common parent becomes the agent for the group beginning the day after the transaction, at which time it becomes the agent for the group with respect to the entire consolidated return year (including the period through the date of the transaction) and the former domestic substitute agent will no longer be the agent for the group for that year.

(B) *Years preceding the year the new common parent becomes the common parent.*—If after the Commissioner's designation of a domestic substitute agent the group remains in existence with a new common parent, and such new common parent is a domestic corporation (determined without regard to section 7874 or a section 953(d) election), the Commissioner may designate the new common parent as the sole agent for the group for any of the group's prior taxable years (for which the consolidated Federal income tax return is due (without extensions) after July 23, 2007) in which the new common parent was a member of the group. For this purpose, the new common parent is treated as having been a member of the group for any taxable year it is primarily liable for the group's income tax liability.

(v) *Replacement of domestic substitute agent by the Commissioner.*—The Commissioner may at any time, with or without a request from any member of the group, designate a replacement for a domestic substitute agent (or a successor to such agent).

(5) *Deemed Sec. 1.1502-77(d) designation.*— (i) *In general.*—If the Commissioner designates a domestic substitute agent under this paragraph

(j), it will be treated as a designation of a substitute agent under paragraph (d) of this section.

(ii) *Default substitute agent.*—If the domestic substitute agent's existence terminates and it has a single successor that is a domestic corporation (without regard to section 269B) that is eligible to be a domestic substitute agent, such successor becomes the domestic substitute agent and is treated as a default substitute agent under paragraph (d)(2) of this section. See paragraph (d)(4) of this section regarding the consequences of the successor's failure to notify the Commissioner of its status as a default substitute agent. The default substitute agent shall use procedures in section 9 of Rev. Proc. 2002- 43 (2002-2 CB 99) or a corresponding provision of a successor revenue procedure for notification. (See Sec. 601.601(d)(2)(ii)(b) of this chapter.)

(6) *Request that IRS designate a domestic substitute agent.*—(i) *Original designation.*—If the common parent of the group is a foreign common parent, and the IRS has not designated a domestic substitute agent, one or more members of the group may request the IRS to make a designation for taxable years for which the consolidated Federal income tax return is due (without extensions) after July 23, 2007. Such request is deemed to be a request under paragraph (d)(3)(i) of this section. Members of the group shall use the procedures in section 10 of Rev. Proc. 2002-43 (2002-2 CB 99) or a corresponding provision of a successor revenue procedure for this purpose. (See Sec. 601.601(d)(2)(ii)(b) of this chapter.)

(ii) *Request that IRS replace a previously designated substitute agent.*—If the IRS designates a domestic substitute agent pursuant to this paragraph (j), one or more members of the group may request that the IRS replace the designated domestic substitute agent with another member (or successor to another member). Such a request is deemed to be a request pursuant to paragraph (d)(3)(ii) of this section. Members of the group shall use the procedures in section 11 of Rev. Proc. 2002-43 (2002-2 CB 99) or a corresponding provision of a successor revenue procedure for this purpose. (See Sec. 601.601(d)(2)(ii)(b) of this chapter.) [Reg. § 1.1502-77.]

☐ [T.D. 9002, 6-27-2002. *Amended by T.D. 9255, 3-9-2006 and T.D. 9343, 7-23-2007.*]

[Reg. § 1.1502-77A]

§ 1.1502-77A. Common parent agent for subsidiaries applicable for consolidated return years beginning before June 28, 2002.— (a) *Scope of agency of common parent corporation.*— The common parent, for all purposes other than the making of the consent required by paragraph (a)(1) of § 1.1502-75, the making of an election under section 936(e), the making of an election to be treated as a DISC under § 1.992-2 and a change of the annual accounting period pursuant to paragraph (b)(3)(ii) of §1.991-1, shall be the sole agent for each subsidiary in the group, duly authorized to act in its own name in all matters relating to the tax liability for the consolidated return year. Except as provided in the preceding sentence, no subsidiary shall have authority to act for or to represent itself in any such matter. For example, any election available to a subsidiary corporation in the computation of its separate taxable income must be made by the common parent, as must any change in an election previously made by the subsidiary corporation; all correspondence will be carried on directly with the common parent; the common parent shall file for all extensions of time including extensions of time for payment of tax under section 6164; notices of deficiencies will be mailed only to the common parent, and the mailing to the common parent shall be considered as a mailing to each subsidiary in the group; notice and demand for payment of taxes will be given only to the common parent and such notice and demand will be considered as a notice and demand to each subsidiary; the common parent will file petitions and conduct proceedings before the Tax Court of the United States, and any such petition shall be considered as also having been filed by each such subsidiary. The common parent will file claims for refund or credit, and any refund will be made directly to and in the name of the common parent and will discharge any liability of the Government in respect thereof to any such subsidiary; and the common parent in its name will give waivers, give bonds, and execute closing agreements, offers in compromise, and all other documents, and any waiver or bond so given, or agreement, offer in compromise, or any other document so executed, shall be considered as having also been given or executed by each such subsidiary. Notwithstanding the provisions of this paragraph, any notice of deficiency, in respect of the tax for a consolidated return year, will name each corporation which was a member of the group during any part of such period (but a failure to include the name of any such member will not affect the validity of the notice of deficiency as to the other members); any notice and demand for payment will name each corporation which was a member of the group during any part of such period (but a failure to include the name of any such member will not affect the validity of the notice and demand as to the other members); and any levy, any notice of a lien, or any other proceeding to collect the amount of any assessment, after the assessment has been made, will name the corporation from which such collection is to be made. The provisions of this paragraph shall apply whether or not a consolidated return is made for any subsequent year, and whether or not one or more subsidiaries have become or have ceased to be members of the group at any time. Notwithstanding the provisions of this paragraph, the Commissioner may, upon notifying the common parent, deal directly with any member of the group in respect of its liability, in which event such member shall have full authority to act for itself.

(b) *Notification of deficiency to corporation which has ceased to be a member of the group.*—If a subsidiary has ceased to be a member of the group and if such subsidiary files written notice of such cessation with the Commissioner, then the Commissioner upon request of such subsidiary will furnish it with a copy of any notice of deficiency in respect of the tax for a consolidated return year for which it was a member and a copy of any notice and demand for payment of such deficiency. The filing of such written notification and request by a corporation shall not have the effect of limiting the scope of the agency of the common parent provided for in paragraph (a) of this section and a failure by the Commissioner to comply with such written request shall not have the effect of limiting the tax liability of such corporation provided for in §1.1502-6.

(c) *Effect of waiver given by common parent.*— Unless the Commissioner agrees to the contrary, an agreement entered into by the common parent extending the time within which an assessment may be made or levy or proceeding in court begun in respect of the tax for a consolidated return year shall be applicable—

(1) To each corporation which was a member of the group during any part of such taxable year, and

(2) To each corporation the income of which was included in the consolidated return for such taxable year, notwithstanding that the tax liability of any such corporation is subsequently computed on the basis of a separate return under the provisions of §1.1502-75.

(d) *Effect of dissolution of common parent corporation.*—If the common parent corporation contemplates dissolution, or is about to be dissolved, or if for any other reason its existence is about to terminate, it shall forthwith notify the Commissioner of such fact and designate, subject to the approval of the Commissioner, another member to act as agent in its place to the same extent and subject to the same conditions and limitations as are applicable to the common parent. If the notice thus required is not given by the common parent, or the designation is not approved by the Commissioner, the remaining members may, subject to the approval of the Commissioner, designate another member to act as such agent, and notice of such designation shall be given to the Commissioner. Until a notice in writing designating a new agent has been approved by the Commissioner, any notice of deficiency or other communication mailed to the common parent shall be considered as having been properly mailed to the agent of the group; or, if the Commissioner has reason to believe that the existence of the common parent has terminated, he may, if he deems it advisable,

Reg. §1.1502-77A(d)

deal directly with any member in respect of its liability.

(e) *General rules.*—(1) *Scope.*—This section applies if the corporation that is the common parent of the group ceases to be the common parent, whether or not the group remains in existence under § 1.1502-75(d).

(2) *Notice of deficiency.*—A notice of deficiency mailed to any one or more corporations referred to in paragraph (a)(4) of this section is deemed for purposes of § 1.1502-77 to be mailed to the agent of the group. If the group has designated an agent that has been approved by the Commissioner under § 1.1502-77(d), a notice of deficiency shall be mailed to that designated agent in addition to any other corporation referred to in paragraph (a)(4) of this section. However, failure by the Commissioner to mail a notice of deficiency to that designated agent shall not invalidate the notice of deficiency mailed to any other corporation referred to in paragraph (a)(4) of this section.

(3) *Waiver of statute of limitations.*—A waiver of the statute of limitations with respect to the group given by any one or more corporations referred to in paragraph (a)(4) of this section is deemed to be given by the agent of the group.

(4) *Alternative agents.*—The corporations referred to in paragraph (a)(2) and (3) of this section are—

(i) The common parent of the group for all or any part of the year to which the notice or waiver applies,

(ii) A successor to the former common parent in a transaction to which section 381(a) applies,

(iii) The agent designated by the group under § 1.1502-77(d), or

(iv) If the group remains in existence under § 1.1502-75(d)(2) or (3), the common parent of the group at the time the notice is mailed or the waiver given.

(f) *Cross-reference.*—For further rules applicable to groups that include insolvent financial institutions, see § 301.6402-7 of this chapter.

(g) *Effective date.*—This section applies to taxable years beginning before June 28, 2002, except paragraph (e) of this section applies to statutory notices and waivers of the statute of limitations for taxable years for which the due date (without extensions) of the consolidated return is after September 7, 1988, and which begin before June 28, 2002. [Reg. § 1.1502-77A.]

☐ [*T.D. 6894, 9-7-66. Amended by T.D. 7323, 9-24-74; T.D. 7673, 2-7-80; T.D. 8226, 9-7-88; T.D. 8387, 12-30-91 and T.D. 8446, 11-5-92. Redesignated and amended by T.D. 9002, 6-27-2002.*]

[Reg. § 1.1502-78]

§ 1.1502-78. Tentative carryback adjustments.—(a) *General rule.*—If a group has a consolidated net operating loss, a consolidated net capital loss, or a consolidated unused business credit for any taxable year, then any application under section 6411 for a tentative carryback adjustment of the taxes for a consolidated return year or years preceding such year shall be made by the common parent corporation for the carryback year (or substitute agent designated under § 1.1502-77(d) for the carryback year) to the extent such loss or unused business credit is not apportioned to a corporation for a separate return year pursuant to § 1.1502-21(b), 1.1502-22(b), or 1.1502-79(c). In the case of the portion of a consolidated net operating loss or consolidated net capital loss or consolidated unused business credit to which the preceding sentence does not apply and that is to be carried back to a corporation that was not a member of a consolidated group in the carryback year, the corporation to which such loss or credit is attributable shall make any application under section 6411. In the case of a net capital loss or net operating loss or unused business credit arising in a separate return year that may be carried back to a consolidated return year, after taking into account the application of § 1.1502-21(b)(3)(ii)(B) with respect to any net operating loss arising in another consolidated group, the common parent for the carryback year (or substitute agent designated under § 1.1502-77(d) for the carryback year) shall make any application under section 6411.

(b) *Special rules.*—(1) *Payment of refund.*—Any refund allowable under an application referred to in paragraph (a) of this section shall be made directly to and in the name of the corporation filing the application, except that in all cases where a loss is deducted from the consolidated taxable income or a credit is allowed in computing the consolidated tax liability for a consolidated return year, any refund shall be made directly to and in the name of the common parent corporation for the carryback year (or substitute agent designated under § 1.1502-77(d) for the carryback year). The payment of any such refund shall discharge any liability of the Government with respect to such refund.

(2) *Several liability.*—If a group filed a consolidated return for a taxable year for which there was an adjustment by reason of an application under section 6411, and if a deficiency is assessed against such group under section 6213(b)(3), then each member of such group shall be severally liable for such deficiency including any interest or penalty assessed in connection with such deficiency.

(3) *Groups that include insolvent financial institutions.*—For further rules applicable to groups

that include insolvent financial institutions, see § 301.6402-7 of this chapter.

(c) *Examples.*—The provisions of paragraphs (a) and (b) of this section may be illustrated by the following examples:

Example (1). Corporations P, S, and S-1 filed a consolidated return for the calendar year 1966. P, S, and S-1 also filed a consolidated return for the calendar year 1969. The group incurred a consolidated net operating loss in 1969 attributable to S-1 which may be carried back to 1966 as a consolidated net operating loss carryback. If a tentative carryback adjustment is desired, P, the common parent for the carryback year, must file an application under section 6411 and any refund will be made to P.

Example (2). Assume the same facts as in example (1) except that P, S, and S-1 filed separate returns for the calendar year 1969, even though they were members of the same group for such year. S-1 incurred a net operating loss in 1969 which may be carried back to 1966. If a tentative carryback adjustment is desired, P must file an application under section 6411 and any refund from such application will be made to P.

Example (3). Corporations X, Y, and Z filed a consolidated return for the calendar year 1966. Z ceased to be a member of the group in 1967. Z filed a separate return for 1968 while X and Y filed a consolidated return for such year. The group incurred a consolidated net operating loss in 1968 attributable to Y, which may be carried back to 1966. Z also incurred a net operating loss for 1968 which may be carried back to 1966. If a tentative carryback adjustment is claimed with respect to the consolidated net operating loss, X, the common parent, must file an application under section 6411. If a tentative carryback adjustment is desired with respect to Z's loss, X must file an application. Any refunds attributable to either application will be made to X. If an assessment is made under section 6213(b)(3) to recover an excessive tentative allowance made with respect to calendar year 1966, X, Y, and Z are severally liable for such assessment.

Example (4). Corporations L and M filed a consolidated return for the calendar year 1966. Corporation N filed a separate return for such year. Later, N became a member of the group and filed a consolidated return with the group for the calendar year 1968. The group incurred a consolidated net operating loss in 1968 attributable to N which may be carried back to N's separate return for 1966. If a tentative carryback adjustment is desired, N must file an application under section 6411 and any refund will be made directly to N.

(d) *Adjustments of overpayments of estimated income tax.*—If a group paid its estimated income tax on a consolidated basis, then any application under section 6425 for an adjustment of overpayment of estimated income tax shall be made by the common parent corporation. If the members of a group paid estimated income taxes on a separate basis, then any application under section 6425 shall be made by the member of the group which claims an overpayment on a separate basis. Any refund allowable under an application under section 6425 shall be made directly to and in the name of the corporation filing the application.

(e) *Time for filing application.*—(1) *General rule.*—The provisions of section 6411(a) apply to the filing of an application for a tentative carryback adjustment by a consolidated group.

(2) *Special rule for new members.*—(i) *New member.*—A new member is a corporation that, in the preceding taxable year, did not qualify as a member, as defined in § 1.1502-1(b), of the consolidated group that it now joins.

(ii) *End of taxable year.*—Solely for the purpose of complying with the twelve-month requirement for making an application for a tentative carryback adjustment under section 6411(a), the separate return year of a qualified new member shall be treated as ending on the same date as the end of the current taxable year of the consolidated group that the qualified new member joins.

(iii) *Qualified new member.*—A new member of a consolidated group qualifies for purposes of the provisions of this paragraph (e)(2) if, immediately prior to becoming a new member, either—

(A) It was the common parent of a consolidated group; or

(B) It was not required to join in the filing of a consolidated return.

(iv) *Examples.*—The provisions of this paragraph (e)(2) may be illustrated by the following examples:

Example 1. Individual A owns 100 percent of the stock of X, a corporation that is not a member of a consolidated group and files separate tax returns on a calendar year basis. On January 31 of year 1, X becomes a member of the Y consolidated group, which also files returns on a calendar year basis. X is a qualified new member as defined in paragraph (e)(2)(iii)(B) of this section because, immediately prior to becoming a new member of the Y consolidated group, X was not required to join in the filing of a consolidated return. As a result of its becoming a new member of Group Y, X's separate return for the short taxable year (January 1 of year 1 through January 31 of year 1) is due September 15 of year 2 (with extensions). See § 1.1502-76(c). Group Y's consolidated return is also due September 15 of year 2 (with extensions). See '1.1502-76(c). Solely for the purpose of complying with the twelve-month requirement for making an application for a tentative carryback adjustment under section 6411(a), X's taxable year for the separate return year is treated as ending on December 31 of year 1. X's application for a tentative carryback adjustment is therefore due on or before December 31 of year 2.

Example 2. Assume the same facts as in *Example 1* except that immediately prior to becoming a new member of Group Y, X was a member of the Z consolidated group. Because X was required to join in the filing of the consolidated return for Group Z, X is not a qualified new member as defined in paragraph (e)(2)(iii) of this section. X's items for the one-month period will be included in the consolidated return for Group Z. Group Z's application for a tentative carryback adjustment, if any, continues to be due within 12 months of the end of its taxable year, which is not affected by X's change in status as a new member of Group Y.

(f) *Effective date.*—(1) *In general.*—This section applies to taxable years to which a loss or credit may be carried back and for which the due date (without extensions) of the original return is after June 28, 2002, except that the provisions of paragraph (e)(2) apply for applications by new members of consolidated groups for tentative carryback adjustments resulting from net operating losses, net capital losses, or unused business credits arising in separate return years of new members that begin on or after January 1, 2001.

(2) *Prior law.*—For taxable years to which a loss or credit may be carried back and for which the due date (without extensions) of the original return is on or before June 28, 2002, see §1.1502-78 in effect prior to June 28, 2002, as contained in 26 CFR part 1 revised April 1, 2002. [Reg. §1.1502-78.]

☐ [*T.D.* 6894, 9-7-66. *Amended by T.D.* 7059, 7-16-70; *T.D.* 7246, 12-29-72; *T.D.* 8387, 12-30-91; *T.D.* 8446, 11-5-92; *T.D.* 8677, 6-26-96; *T.D.* 8823, 6-25-99; *T.D.* 8950, 6-21-2001 *and T.D.* 9002, 6-27-2002 (*corrected* 12-18-2002).]

[Reg. §1.1502-79]

§1.1502-79. Separate return years.—
(a) *Carryover and carryback of consolidated net operating losses to separate return years.*—For losses arising in consolidated return years beginning before January 1, 1997, see §1.1502-79A(a). For later years, see §1.1502-21(b).

(b) *Carryover and carryback of consolidated net capital loss to separate return years.*—For losses arising in consolidated return years beginning before January 1, 1997, see §1.1502-79A(b). For later years, see §1.1502-22(b).

(c) *Carryover and carryback of consolidated unused investment credit to separate return years.*—(1) *In general.*—If a consolidated unused investment credit can be carried under the principles of section 46(b) and paragraph (b) of §1.1502-3 to a separate return year of a corporation (or could have been so carried if such corporation were in existence) which was a member of the group in

the year in which such unused credit arose, then the portion of such consolidated unused credit attributable to such corporation (as determined under subparagraph (2) of this paragraph) shall be apportioned to such corporation (and any successor to such corporation in a transaction to which section 381(a) applies) under the principles of §1.1502-21(b) (or §§1.1502-79A(a)(1) and (2), as appropriate) and shall be an investment credit carryover or carryback to such separate return year.

(2) *Portion of consolidated unused investment credit attributable to a member.*—(i) *Investment credit carryback.*—In the case of a consolidated unused credit which is an investment credit carryback, the portion of such consolidated unused credit attributable to a member of the group is an amount equal to such consolidated unused credit multiplied by a fraction, the numerator of which is the credit earned of such member for the consolidated unused credit year, and the denominator of which is the consolidated credit earned for such unused credit year.

(ii) *Investment credit carryover.*—In the case of a consolidated unused credit which is an investment credit carryover, the portion of such consolidated unused credit attributable to a member of the group is an amount equal to such consolidated unused credit multiplied by a fraction, the numerator of which is the credit earned with respect to any section 38 property placed in service in the consolidated unused credit year and owned by such member (whether or not placed in service by such member) at the close of the last day as of which the taxable income of such member is included in a consolidated return filed by the group, and the denominator of which is the consolidated credit earned for such unused credit year.

(d) *Carryover and carryback of consolidated unused foreign tax.*—(1) *In general.*—If a consolidated unused foreign tax can be carried under the principles of section 904(d) and paragraph (e) of §1.1502-4 to a separate return year of a corporation (or could have been so carried if such corporation were in existence) which was a member of the group in the year in which such unused foreign tax arose, then the portion of such consolidated unused foreign tax attributable to such corporation (as determined under subparagraph (2) of this paragraph) shall be apportioned to such corporation (and any successor to such corporation in a transaction to which section 381(a) applies) under the principles of §1.1502-21(b) (or §§1.1502-79A(a)(1) and (2), as appropriate) and shall be deemed paid or accrued in such separate return year to the extent provided in section 904(d).

(2) *Portion of consolidated unused foreign tax attributable to a member.*—The portion of a consolidated unused foreign tax for any year attributable to a member of a group is an amount equal to

such consolidated unused foreign tax multiplied by a fraction, the numerator of which is the foreign taxes paid or accrued for such year (including those taxes deemed paid or accrued, other than by reason of section 904(d)) to each foreign country or possession (or to all foreign countries or possessions if the overall limitation is effective) by such member, and the denominator of which is the aggregate of all such taxes paid or accrued for such year (including those taxes deemed paid or accrued, other than by reason of section 904(d)) to each such foreign country or possession (or to all foreign countries or possessions if the overall limitation is effective) by all the members of the group.

(e) *Carryover of consolidated excess charitable contributions to separate return years.*—(1) *In general.*—If the consolidated excess charitable contributions for any taxable year can be carried under the principles of section 170(b)(2) and paragraph (b) of § 1.1502-24 to a separate return year of a corporation (or could have been so carried if such corporation were in existence) which was a member of the group in the year in which such excess contributions arose, then the portion of such consolidated excess charitable contributions attributable to such corporation (as determined under subparagraph (2) of this paragraph) shall be apportioned to such corporation (and any successor to such corporation in a transaction to which section 381(a) applies) under the principles of § 1.1502-21(b) (or § § 1.1502-79A(a)(1) and (2), as appropriate) and shall be a charitable contribution carryover to such separate return year.

(2) *Portion of consolidated excess charitable contributions attributable to a member.*—The portion of the consolidated excess charitable contributions attributable to a member of a group is an amount equal to such consolidated excess contributions multiplied by a fraction, the numerator of which is the charitable contributions paid by such member for the taxable year, and the denominator of which is the aggregate of all such charitable contributions paid for such year by all the members of the group. [Reg. § 1.1502-79.]

☐ [*T.D. 6894, 9-7-66. Amended by T.D. 7637, 8-6-79; T.D. 7728, 10-31-80; T.D. 8294, 3-9-90; T.D. 8319, 11-19-90; T.D. 8364, 9-13-91; T.D. 8597, 7-12-95; T.D. 8677, 6-26-96 and T.D. 8823, 6-25-99.*]

[Reg. § 1.1502-79A]

§ 1.1502-79A. Separate return years generally applicable for consolidated return years beginning before January 1, 1997.—(a) *Carryover and carryback of consolidated net operating losses to separate return years.*—(1) *In general.*—(i) If a consolidated net operating loss can be carried under the principles of section 172(b) and paragraph (b) of § 1.1502-21A to a separate return year of a corporation (or could have been so carried if such

corporation were in existence) which was a member in the year in which such loss arose, then the portion of such consolidated net operating loss attributable to such corporation (as determined under subparagraph (3) of this paragraph) shall be apportioned to such corporation (and any successor to such corporation in a transaction to which section 381(a) applies) and shall be a net operating loss carryover or carryback to such separate return year; accordingly, such portion shall not be included in the consolidated net operating loss carryovers or carrybacks to the equivalent consolidated return year. Thus, for example, if a member filed a separate return for the third year preceding a consolidated return year in which a consolidated net operating loss was sustained and if any portion of such loss is apportioned to such member for such separate return year, such portion may not be carried back by the group to its third year preceding such consolidated return year.

(ii) If a corporation ceases to be a member during a consolidated return year, any consolidated net operating loss carryover from a prior taxable year must first be carried to such consolidated return year, notwithstanding that all or a portion of the consolidated net operating loss giving rise to the carryover is attributable to the corporation which ceases to be a member. To the extent not absorbed in such consolidated return year, the portion of the consolidated net operating loss attributable to the corporation ceasing to be a member shall then be carried to such corporation's first separate return year.

(iii) For rules permitting the reattribution of losses of a subsidiary to the common parent in the case of loss disallowance or basis reduction on the disposition or deconsolidation of stock of the subsidiary, see § 1.1502-20.

(2) *Nonapportionment to certain members not in existence.*—Notwithstanding subparagraph (1) of this paragraph, the portion of a consolidated net operating loss attributable to a member shall not be apportioned to a prior separate return year for which such member was not in existence and shall be included in the consolidated net operating loss carrybacks to the equivalent consolidated return year of the group (or, if such equivalent year is a separate return year, then to such separate return year), provided that such member was a member of the group immediately after its organization.

(3) *Portion of consolidated net operating loss attributable to a member.*—The portion of a consolidated net operating loss attributable to a member of a group is an amount equal to the consolidated net operating loss multiplied by a fraction, the numerator of which is the separate net operating loss of such corporation, and the denominator of which is the sum of the separate net operating losses of all members of the group in such year having such losses. For purposes of this subparagraph, the separate net operating

loss of a member of the group shall be determined under §1.1502-12 (except that no deduction shall be allowed under section 242), adjusted for the following items taken into account in the computation of the consolidated net operating loss:

(i) The portion of the consolidated dividends received deduction, the consolidated charitable contributions deductions, and the consolidated section 247 deduction, attributable to such member;

(ii) Such member's capital gain net income (net capital gain for taxable years beginning before January 1, 1977) (determined without regard to any net capital loss carryover attributable to such member);

(iii) Such member's net capital loss and section 1231 net loss, reduced by the portion of the consolidated net capital loss attributable to such member (as determined under paragraph (b)(2) of this section); and

(iv) The portion of any consolidated net capital loss carryover attributable to such member which is absorbed in the taxable year.

(4) *Examples.*—The provisions of this paragraph may be illustrated by the following examples:

Example (1). (i) Corporation P was formed on January 1, 1966. P filed a separate return for the calendar year 1966. On March 15, 1967, P formed corporation S. P and S filed a consolidated return for 1967. On January 1, 1968, P purchased all the stock of corporation T, which had been formed in 1967 and had filed a separate return for its taxable year ending December 31, 1967.

(ii) P, S, and T join in the filing of a consolidated return for 1968, which return reflects a consolidated net operating loss of $11,000. $2,000 of such consolidated net operating loss is attributable to P, $3,000 to S, and $6,000 to T. Such apportionment of the consolidated net operating loss was made on the basis of the separate net operating losses of each member as determined under subparagraph (3) of this paragraph.

(iii) $5,000 of the 1968 consolidated net operating loss can be carried back to P's separate return for 1966. Such amount is the portion of the consolidated net operating loss attributable to P and S. Even though S was not in existence in 1966, the portion attributable to S can be carried back to P's separate return year, since S (unlike T) was a member of the group immediately after its organization. The 1968 consolidated net operating loss can be carried back against the group's income in 1967 except to the extent (*i.e.,* $6,000) that it is apportioned to T for its 1967 separate return year and to the extent that it was absorbed in P's 1966 separate return year. The portion of the 1968 consolidated net operating loss attributable to T ($6,000) is a net operating loss carryback to its 1967 separate return.

Example (2). (i) Assume the same facts as in example (1). Assume further that on June 15, 1969, P sells all the stock of T to an outsider, that P and S file a consolidated return for 1969 (which includes the income of T for the period January 1 through June 15), and that T files a separate return for the period June 16 through December 31, 1969.

(ii) The 1968 consolidated net operating loss, to the extent not absorbed in prior years, must first be carried to the consolidated return year 1969. Any portion of the $6,000 amount attributable to T which is not absorbed in T's 1967 separate return year or in the 1969 consolidated return year shall then be carried to T's separate return year ending December 31, 1969.

(b) *Carryover and carryback of consolidated net capital loss to separate return years.*—(1) *In general.*—If a consolidated net capital loss can be carried under the principles of section 1212(a) and paragraph (b) of §1.1502-22A to a separate return year of a corporation (or could have been so carried if such corporation were in existence) which was a member of the group in the year in which such consolidated net capital loss arose, then the portion of such consolidated net capital loss attributable to such corporation (as determined under subparagraph (2) of this paragraph) shall be apportioned to such corporation (and any successor to such corporation in a transaction to which section 381(a) applies) under the principles of paragraph (a)(1), (2), and (3) of this section and shall be a net capital loss carryback or carryover to such separate return year.

(2) *Portion of consolidated net capital loss attributable to a member.*—The portion of a consolidated net capital loss attributable to a member of a group is an amount equal to such consolidated net capital loss multiplied by a fraction, the numerator of which is the net capital loss of such member, and the denominator of which is the sum of the net capital losses of those members of the group having net capital losses. For purposes of this subparagraph, the net capital loss of a member of the group shall be determined by taking into account the following:

(i) Such member's capital gain net income (net capital gain for taxable years beginning before January 1, 1977) or loss (determined without regard to any net capital loss carryover or carryback); and

(ii) Such member's section 1231 net loss, reduced by the portion of the consolidated section 1231 net loss attributable to such member.

(a)[(c)]through (e). [Reserved]

(f) *Effective date.*—Paragraphs (a) and (b) of this section apply to losses arising in consolidated return years to which §1.1502-21T(g) does not apply for this purpose net operating loss deductions, carryovers, and carrybacks arise in the year from which they are carried. See

§ 1.1502-21T(g) for effective dates of that section. [Reg. § 1.1502-79A.]

☐ [*T.D. 8677, 6-26-96.*]

[Reg. § 1.1502-80]

§ 1.1502-80. Applicability of other provisions of law.—(a) *In general.*—(1) *Application of other provisions.*—The Internal Revenue Code (Code), or other law, shall be applicable to the group to the extent the regulations do not exclude its application. To the extent not excluded, other rules operate in addition to, and may be modified by, these regulations. Thus, for example, in a transaction to which section 381(a) applies, the acquiring corporation will succeed to the tax attributes described in section 381(c). Furthermore, sections 269 and 482 apply for any consolidated return year. However, in a recognition transaction otherwise subject to section 1001, for example, the rules of section 1001 continue to apply, but may be modified by the intercompany transaction regulations under § 1.1502-13.

(2) *No duplicative adjustments.*—Nothing in these regulations shall be interpreted or applied to require an adjustment, inclusion, or other item to the extent it would have the effect of duplicating any other adjustment, inclusion, or other item required under the Code or other rule of law, including other provisions of these regulations.

(3) *Application of single-entity principles.*—If two or more adjustments, inclusions, or other items are subject to paragraph (a)(2) of this section, the determination of which adjustment, inclusion, or other item is treated as applied or taken into account is made by taking into account the purposes of the provisions and applying single-entity principles as appropriate.

(4) *Effective/applicability dates.*—This paragraph (a) is applicable with respect to transactions and determinations on or after September 17, 2008.

(b) *Non-applicability of section 304.*—Section 304 does not apply to any acquisition of stock of a corporation in an intercompany transaction or to any intercompany item from such transaction occurring on or after July 24, 1991.

(c) *Deferral of section 165.*—(1) *General rule.*—Subsidiary stock is not treated as worthless under section 165 until immediately before the earlier of the time—

(i) The stock is worthless within the meaning of § 1.1502-19(c)(1)(iii); or

(ii) The subsidiary for any reason ceases to be a member of the group.

(2) *Cross reference.*—See § 1.1502-36 for additional rules relating to worthlessness of subsidiary stock on or after September 17, 2008.

(3) *Effective/applicability date.*—This paragraph (c) applies to taxable years for which the original consolidated Federal income tax return is due (without extensions) after July 18, 2007. However, taxpayers may apply this paragraph (c) to taxable years beginning on or after January 1, 1995.

(d) *Non-applicability of section 357(c).*—(1) *In general.*—Section 357(c) does not apply to any transaction to which § 1.1502-13, § 1.1502-13T, § 1.1502-14, or § 1.1502-14T applies, if it occurs in a consolidated return year beginning on or after January 1, 1995. For example, P, S, and T are members of a consolidated group, P owns all of the stock of S and T with bases of $30 and $20, respectively, S has a $30 basis in its assets and $40 of liabilities, and S merges into T in a transaction described in section 368(a)(1)(A) (and in section 368(a)(1)(D)); section 357(c) does not apply to the merger, P's basis in T's stock increases to $50 ($30 plus $20), and T succeeds to S's $30 basis in the assets transferred subject to the $40 liability. Similarly, if S instead transferred its assets and liabilities to a newly formed subsidiary in a transaction to which section 351 applies, section 357(c) does not apply and S's basis in the subsidiary's stock is a $10 excess loss account. This paragraph (d) does not apply to a transaction if the transferor or transferee becomes a nonmember as part of the same plan or arrangement. The transferor (or transferee) is treated as becoming a nonmember once it is no longer a member of a consolidated group that includes the transferee (or transferor). For purposes of this paragraph (d), any reference to a transferor or transferee includes, as the context may require, a reference to a successor or predecessor.

(2) *Prior period transactions.*—If, in a tax year beginning before January 1, 1995, a member's stock with an excess loss account is transferred in a transaction to which § 1.1502-13, § 1.1502-13T, § 1.1502-14, or § 1.1502-14T applies, paragraph (d)(1) of this section applies to the stock transfer to the extent that the income, gain, deduction, or loss (if any) is not taken into account in a tax year beginning before January 1, 1995. For example, if P, S, and T, are members of a consolidated group, T's stock has an excess loss account, and P transfers the T stock to S in 1993 in a transaction to which section 351 and § 1.1502-13 apply, section 357(c) applies to the transfer only to the extent P's gain is taken into account in tax years beginning before January 1, 1995.

(e) *Non-applicability of section 163(e)(5).*—Section 163(e)(5) does not apply to any intercompany obligation (within the meaning of § 1.1502-13(g)) issued in a consolidated return year beginning on or after July 12, 1995.

(f) *Non-applicability of section 1031.*—Section 1031 does not apply to any intercompany transaction occurring in consolidated return years beginning on or after July 12, 1995.

(g) *Special rules for liquidations to which section 332 applies.*—Notwithstanding the general rule of section 381, if multiple members (distributee members) acquire assets of a corporation in a liquidation to which section 332 applies (regardless of whether any single member owns stock in the liquidating corporation meeting the requirements of section 1504(a)(2)), such members succeed to and take into account the items of the liquidating corporation (including items described in section 381(c), but excluding intercompany items under § 1.1502-13) as provided in this paragraph (g) to the extent not otherwise prohibited by any applicable provision of law. This paragraph (g) does not apply to the intercompany items of the liquidating corporation. See § 1.1502-13(j)(2)(ii).

(1) *Income offset items and deferred income.*— Except as otherwise provided in this paragraph (g)(1), each distributee member succeeds to and takes into account the items of the liquidating corporation that could be used to offset the income of the group or any member (including deferred deductions, net operating loss carryovers, and capital loss carryovers) (income offset items) to the extent that such items would have been reflected in investment adjustments to the stock of the liquidating corporation owned by such distributee member under § 1.1502-32(c) if, immediately prior to the liquidation, any stock of the liquidating corporation owned by nonmembers had been redeemed and then such items had been taken into account. However, each distributee member succeeds to the full amount of any deferred deduction or deferred income item attributable to the particular property or business operations distributed to such distributee in the liquidation to the extent that such item is not taken into account in the determination of the income or loss of the liquidating corporation with regard to the liquidation under chapter 1 of the Internal Revenue Code (Code). If the liquidating corporation is not a member of the group at the time of the liquidation, the rules of this paragraph (g)(1) are applied as if the liquidating corporation had been a member of the group.

(2) *Accounting for deferred income items.*— Solely for the purpose of determining whether deferred income items of a liquidating corporation are taken into account under applicable principles of law as a result of a liquidation to which section 332 applies, the transfer of property to, and the assumption of liabilities by, a distributee member that does not own stock in the liquidating corporation meeting the requirements of section 1504(a)(2) without regard to the application of § 1.1502-34 immediately prior to the liquidation is not treated as part of a transaction to which section 381(a) applies. In addition,

section 332(a) does not apply in determining the recognition or nonrecognition of any income realized by the distributee member under applicable principles of law on account of consideration received (or deemed received) on the assumption of the liquidating corporation's obligation or liability attributable to any deferred income item.

(3) *Credits and earnings and profits.*—Each distributee member succeeds to and takes into account a percentage of each credit of the liquidating corporation equal to the value of the stock of the liquidating corporation owned by such distributee at the time of the liquidation divided by the total value of all the stock of the liquidating corporation owned by members of the group at the time of the liquidation. Except to the extent that the distributee member's earnings and profits already reflect the liquidating corporation's earnings and profits, each distributee member succeeds to and takes into account under the principles of § 1.1502-32(c) the earnings and profits, or deficit in earnings and profits, of the liquidating corporation (determined after taking into account the amount of earnings and profits properly applicable to distributions to non-member shareholders under § 1.381(c)(2)-1(c)(2)). If the liquidating corporation is not a member of the group at the time of the liquidation, the rules of this paragraph (g)(3) are applied as if the liquidating corporation had been a member of the group.

(4) *Other items.*—With regard to items to which neither paragraph (g)(1) nor (g)(3) of this section applies, a distributee member that, immediately prior to the liquidation, owns stock in the liquidating corporation meeting the requirements of section 1504(a)(2) without regard to the application of § 1.1502-34 succeeds to the items of the liquidating corporation in accordance with section 381 and other applicable principles. A distributee member that, immediately prior to the liquidation, does not own stock in the liquidating corporation meeting the requirements of section 1504(a)(2) without regard to the application of § 1.1502-34 succeeds to the items of the liquidating corporation to the extent that it would have succeeded to those items if it had purchased, in a taxable transaction, the assets or businesses of the liquidating corporation that it received in the liquidation and had assumed the liabilities that it assumed in the liquidation.

(5) *Determination of the items of a liquidating subsidiary.*—For purposes of this section, the items of a liquidating subsidiary include the amount of any consolidated tax attribute attributable to the liquidating subsidiary that is determined pursuant to the principles of § 1.1502-21(b)(2)(iv). In addition, if the liquidating subsidiary is a member of a separate return limitation year subgroup, the amount of a tax attribute that arose in a separate return limita-

tion year that is attributable to that member shall also be determined pursuant to the principles of § 1.1502-21(b)(2)(iv).

(6) *Examples.*—The following examples illustrate the application of this paragraph (g):

Example 1. Liquidation-80 percent distributee. (i) *Facts.* X has only common stock outstanding. On January 1 of year 1, X acquired equipment with a 10-year recovery period and elected to depreciate the equipment using the straight-line method of depreciation. On January 1 of year 7, M1 and M2 own 80 percent and 20 percent, respectively, of X's stock. X is a domestic corporation but is not a member of the group that includes M1 and M2. On that date, X distributes all of its assets to M1 and M2 in complete liquidation. The equipment is distributed to M1. Under section 334(b), M1's basis in the equipment is the same as it would be in X's hands. After computing its tax liability for the taxable year that includes the liquidation, X has net operating losses of $100, business credits of $40, and earnings and profits of $80.

(ii) *Succession to items described in section 381(c).* (A) *Losses.* Under paragraph (g)(1) of this section, each distributee member succeeds to X's items that could be used to offset the income of the group or any member to the extent that such items would have been reflected in investment adjustments to the stock of X it owned under § 1.1502-32(c) if, immediately prior to the liquidation, such items had been taken into account. Accordingly, M1 and M2 succeed to $80 and $20, respectively, of X's net operating loss.

(B) *Credits and earnings and profits.* Under paragraph (g)(3) of this section, because, immediately prior to the liquidation, M1 and M2 hold 80 percent and 20 percent, respectively, of the value of the stock of X, M1 and M2 succeed to $32 and $8, respectively, of X's $40 of business credits. In addition, because M1's and M2's earnings and profits do not reflect X's earnings and profits, X's earnings and profits are allocated to M1 and M2 under the principles of § 1.1502-32(c). Therefore, M1 and M2 succeed to $64 and $16, respectively, of X's earnings and profits.

(C) *Depreciation of equipment's basis.* Under paragraph (g)(4) of this section, because M1 owns stock in X meeting the requirements of section 1504(a)(2) without regard to the application of § 1.1502-34, M1 is required to continue to depreciate the equipment using the straight-line method of depreciation over the remaining recovery period of 4.5 years (assuming X used a half-year convention).

Example 2. Liquidation-no 80 percent distributee. (i) *Facts.* The facts are the same as in *Example 1* except that M1 and M2 own 60 percent and 40 percent, respectively, of X's stock. In addition, on January 1 of year 6, X entered into a long-term contract with Y, an unrelated party. The total contract price is $1000, and X estimates the total

allocable contract costs to be $500. At the time of the liquidation, X had received $250 in progress payments under the contract and incurred costs of $125. X accounted for the contract under the percentage of completion method described in section 460(b). In the liquidation, M1 assumes X's contract obligations and rights.

(ii) *Succession to items described in section 381(c).* (A) *Losses.* Under paragraph (g)(1) of this section, each distributee member succeeds to X's items that could be used to offset the income of the group or any member to the extent that such items would have been reflected in investment adjustments to the stock of X it owned under § 1.1502-32(c) if, immediately prior to the liquidation, such items had been taken into account. Accordingly, M1 and M2 succeed to $60 and $40, respectively, of X's net operating loss.

(B) *Credits and earnings and profits.* Under paragraph (g)(3) of this section, because, immediately prior to the liquidation, M1 and M2 hold 60 percent and 40 percent, respectively, of the value of the stock of X, M1 and M2 succeed to $24 and $16, respectively, of X's $40 of business credits. In addition, because M1's and M2's earnings and profits do not reflect X's earnings and profits, X's earnings and profits are allocated to M1 and M2 under the principles of § 1.1502-32(c). Therefore, M1 and M2 succeed to $48 and $32, respectively, of X's earnings and profits.

(C) *Depreciation of equipment's basis.* Under section 334(a), M1's basis in the equipment is its fair market value at the time of the distribution. Pursuant to section 168(i)(7), to the extent that M1's basis in the equipment does not exceed X's adjusted basis in the equipment at the time of the transfer, M1 is required to continue to depreciate the equipment using the straight-line method of depreciation over the remaining recovery period of 4.5 years (assuming X used a half-year convention). Any portion of M1's basis in the equipment that exceeds X's adjusted basis in the equipment at the time of the transfer is treated as being placed in service by M1 in the year of the transfer. Thus, M1 may choose any applicable depreciation method, recovery period, and convention under section 168 for such excess basis.

(D) *Method of accounting for long-term contract.* Under paragraph (g)(4) of this section, M1 does not succeed to X's method of accounting for the contract. Rather, under § 1.460-4(k)(2), M1 is treated as having entered into a new contract on the date of the liquidation. Under § 1.460-4(k)(2)(iii), M1 must evaluate whether the new contract should be classified as a long-term contract within the meaning of § 1.460-1(b) and account for the contract under a permissible method of accounting.

Example 3. Liquidation—deferred items. (i) *Facts.* X has only common stock outstanding, and M1 and M2 (who are members of the same group) own 80 percent and 20 percent, respectively, of X's stock. X operates two divisions, each of which defers prepaid subscription income pursuant to an election under section 455. X distributes all of its assets in complete liquidation. M1 receives all of the assets of Division 1, including prepaid subscription income, and assumes X's liability to furnish or deliver the newspaper, magazine, or other periodical to which the prepaid subscription income received by M1 relates. M2 receives all of the assets of Division 2, including prepaid subscription income, and assumes X's liability to furnish or deliver the newspaper, magazine, or other periodical to which the prepaid subscription income received by M2 relates.

(ii) *Acceleration of deferred income items and succession to other deferred items.* Under paragraph (g)(1) of this section, M1 succeeds to the full amount of the deferred prepaid subscription income of X attributable to Division 1. Under applicable law, X does not recognize the deferred prepaid subscription income attributable to Division 1 because X's liability to furnish or deliver the newspaper, magazine, or other periodical ends as a result of a transaction to which section 381(a) applies. Under paragraph (g)(2) of this section, solely for purposes of determining whether the deferred income items of X attributable to Division 2 are taken into account as a result of the liquidation, the distribution of property to M2 is not treated as a transaction to which section 381(a) applies. Therefore, under applicable law, X's deferred prepaid subscription income attributable to Division 2 is taken into account in the determination of X's income or loss with regard to the liquidation. Further, under paragraph (g)(2) of this section, section 332(a) does not apply in determining the recognition or nonrecognition of any income that M2 realizes on account of consideration received (or deemed received) on its assumption of X's liability to furnish or deliver the newspaper, magazine, or other periodical to which the prepaid subscription income relates.

(7) *Effective/applicability date.*—This paragraph (g) applies to transactions occurring after April 14, 2008.

(h) *Non-applicability of section 362(e)(2).*—(1) *General rule.*—Section 362(e)(2) does not apply to any intercompany transaction occurring on or after September 17, 2008. Taxpayers may apply this paragraph (h) to intercompany transactions occurring on or after October 22, 2004, and in such case, any election made under section 362(e)(2)(C) will have no effect. The purpose of this paragraph (h) is to facilitate the application of the consolidated return provisions addressing the duplication of loss between members of a consolidated group.

(2) *Anti-abuse rule.*—(i) *General rule.*—If a taxpayer engages in a transaction to which section 362(e)(2) would apply but for the application of paragraph (h)(1) of this section, and acts

with a view to prevent the consolidated return provisions from properly addressing loss duplication, appropriate adjustments will be made to clearly reflect the income of the group.

(ii) *Example.*—The following example illustrates the principle of the anti-abuse rule in this paragraph (h)(2).

Example. (A) *Facts.* P, the common parent of a consolidated group, owns the four outstanding shares of S stock (Share 1 through Share 4) with an aggregate basis of $0 and value of $80. S owns Asset 1 with a basis of $0 and a value of $80. With a view to prevent the consolidated return provisions from addressing the duplication of loss, P transfers Asset 2 with a basis of $100 and a value of $20 to S in exchange for an additional share of S stock (Share 5) in a transaction to which section 351 applies. P later sells Share 5 to X, an unrelated person, for $20 at a time when S's basis in Asset 2 was still $100. The sale is a transfer of a loss share and therefore subject to § 1.1502-36.

(B) *Analysis.* Although the sale would be subject to § 1.1502-36, that section would not prevent the stock loss or reduce S's attributes (to prevent duplication of the stock loss) because neither § 1.1502-36(b) nor § 1.1502-36(c) would adjust the basis of the transferred share (because there are no investment adjustments) and § 1.1502-36(d) would not reduce S's attributes (because S's aggregate inside loss is $0). However, because P acted with a view to prevent the consolidated return provisions from addressing the duplication of the loss on Asset 2, P's transfer of Asset 2 to S is subject to the anti-abuse rule in this paragraph (h)(2). Accordingly, effective immediately before the transfer of Share 5 to X, either P's basis in Share 5 or S's basis in Asset 2 must be adjusted to reflect what it would have been had section 362(e)(2) been applied at the time P transferred Asset 2 to S (taking into account the interim facts and circumstances). Accordingly, S must either reduce its basis in Asset 2 by $80 to $20 (eliminating the duplicated loss) or P must reduce its basis in Share 5 by $80 to $20 (eliminating the duplicated loss).

(C) *Transfer of all S shares.* Assume the same facts as those in paragraph (A) of this *Example,* except that P sells all five S shares to X. Although P's transfer of Asset 2 to S results in the duplication of an $80 loss, because all the shares are transferred, the transaction does not prevent the consolidated return provisions from properly addressing loss duplication. P's $80 duplicated loss is offset by an $80 duplicated gain, and the group recognizes the offsetting stock gain and loss. Accordingly, this paragraph (h)(2) does not apply to P's transfer of Asset 2 to S. [Reg. § 1.1502-80.]

☐ [*T.D.* 6894, 9-7-66. *Amended by T.D.* 8402, 3-13-92; *T.D.* 8560, 8-12-94; *T.D.* 8597, 7-12-95; *T.D.* 8677, 6-26-96; *T.D.* 9048, 3-11-2003; *T.D.* 9118, 3-17-2004 *T.D.* 9192, 3-21-2005; *T.D.* 9254,

3-9-2006; *T.D. 9341, 7-17-2007; T.D. 9376, 1-14-2008 and T.D. 9424, 9-9-2008.*]

[Reg. §1.1502-81T]

§1.1502-81T. Alaska Native Corporations (Temporary).—(a) *General Rule.*—The application of section 60(b)(5) of the Tax Reform Act of 1984 and section 1804(e)(4) of the Tax Reform Act of 1986 (relating to Native Corporations established under the Alaska Native Claims Settlement Act (43 U.S.C. 1601 *et seq.*)) is limited to the use on a consolidated return of losses and credits of a Native Corporation, and of a corporation all of whose stock is owned directly by a Native Corporation, during any taxable year (beginning after the effective date of such sections and before 1992), or any part thereof, against the income and tax liability of a corporation affiliated with the Native Corporation. Thus, no other tax saving, tax benefit, or tax loss is intended to result from the application of section 60(b)(5) of the Tax Reform Act of 1984 and section 1804(e)(4) of the Tax Reform Act of 1986 to any person (whether or not such person is a member of an affiliated group of which a Native Corporation is the common parent). In particular, except as approved by the Secretary, no positive adjustment under §1.1502-32(b) will be made with respect to the basis of stock of a corporation that is affiliated with a Native Corporation through application of section 60(b)(5) of the Tax Reform Act of 1984 and section 1804(e)(4) of the Tax Reform Act of 1986.

(b) *Effective dates.*—This section applies to taxable years beginning after December 31, 1984. [Temporary Reg. §1.1502-81T.]

☐ [*T.D. 8130, 3-13-87. Amended by T.D. 8560, 8-12-94.*]

[Reg. §1.1502-90]

§1.1502-90. Table of contents.—The following list contains the major headings in §§1.1502-91 through 1.1502-99:

(4) End of separate tracking of certain losses.

(c) Supplemental rules for determining ownership change.

(1) Scope.

(2) Cause for applying supplemental rule.

(3) Operating rules.

(4) Supplemental ownership change rules.

(i) Additional testing dates for the common parent (or loss subgroup parent).

(ii) Treatment of subsidiary stock as stock of the common parent (or loss subgroup parent).

(iii) Different testing periods.

(iv) Disaffiliation of a subsidiary.

(v) Subsidiary stock acquired first.

(vi) Anti-duplication rule.

(5) Examples.

(d) Testing period following ownership change under this section.

(e) Information statements.

(1) Common parent of a loss group.

(2) Abbreviated statement with respect to loss subgroups.

§1.1502-93 *Consolidated section 382 limitation (or subgroup section 382 limitation).*

(a) Determination of the consolidated section 382 limitation (or subgroup section 382 limitation).

(1) In general.

(2) Coordination with apportionment rule.

(b) Value of the loss group (or loss subgroup).

(1) Stock value immediately before ownership change.

(2) Adjustment to value.

(i) In general.

(ii) Anti-duplication.

(3) Examples.

(c) Recognized built-in gain of a loss group or loss subgroup.

(1) In general.

(2) Adjustments.

(d) Continuity of business.

(1) In general.

(2) Example.

(e) Limitations of losses under other rules.

§1.502-94 *Coordination with section 382 and the regulations thereunder when a corporation becomes a member of a consolidated group.*

(a) Scope.

(1) In general.

(2) Successor corporation as new loss member.

(3) Coordination in the case of a loss subgroup.

(4) End of separate tracking of certain losses.

(5) Cross-reference.

(b) Application of section 382 to a new loss member.

(1) In general.

(2) Adjustment to value.

(3) Pre-change separate attribute defined.

(4) Examples.

(c) Built-in gains and losses.

(d) Information statements.

§1.1502-95 *Rules on ceasing to be a member of a consolidated group (or loss subgroup).*

(a) In general.

(1) Consolidated group.

(2) Election by common parent.

(3) Coordination with §§1.1502-91 through 1.1502-93.

(b) Separate application of section 382 when a member leaves a consolidated group.

(1) In general.

(2) Effect of a prior ownership change of the group.

(3) Application in the case of a loss subgroup.

(4) Examples.

(c) Apportionment of a consolidated section 382 limitation.

(1) In general.

(2) Amount which may be apportioned.

(i) Consolidated section 382 limitation.

(ii) Net unrealized built-in gain.

(3) Effect of apportionment on the consolidated group.

(i) Consolidated section 382 limitation.

(ii) Net unrealized built-in gain.

(4) Effect on corporations to which an apportionment is made.

(i) Consolidated section 382 limitation.

(ii) Net unrealized built-in gain.

(5) Deemed apportionment when loss group terminates.

(6) Appropriate adjustments when former member leaves during the year.

(7) Examples.

(d) Rules pertaining to ceasing to be a member of a loss subgroup.

(1) In general.

(2) Exceptions.

(3) Examples.

(e) Allocation of net unrealized built-in loss.

(1) In general.

(2) Amount of allocation.

(i) In general.

(ii) Transferred basis property and deferred gain or loss.

(iii) Assets for which gain or loss has been recognized.

(iv) Exchanged basis property.

(v) Two or more members depart during the same year.

(vi) Anti-abuse rule.

(3) Effect of the allocation on the consolidated group.

(4) Effect on corporations to which the allocation is made.

(5) Subgroup principles.

(6) Apportionment of consolidated section 382 limitation (or subgroup section 382 limitation).

(i) In general.

(ii) Special rule for former members that become members of the same consolidated group.

(7) Examples.

(8) Reporting requirements.

(i) Common Parent.

(ii) Former Member.

(iii) Exception.

(f) Filing the election to apportion the section 382 limitation and net unrealized built-in gain.

(1) Form of the election to apportion.

(i) Statement.

(ii) Agreement.

(2) Signing the agreement.

(3) Filing the election.

(i) Filing by the common parent.

(ii) Filing by the former member.

(4) Revocation of election.

(g) Effective/applicability date.

§ 1.1502-96 Rules on ceasing to be a member of a consolidated group (or loss subgroup) (temporary).

(a) End of separate tracking of losses.

(1) Application.

(2) Effect of end of separate tracking.

(i) Net operating loss carryovers.

(ii) Net unrealized built-in losses.

(iii) Common parent not common parent for five years.

(3) Continuing effect of end of separate tracking.

(i) In general.

(ii) Example.

(4) Special rule for testing period.

(5) Limits on effects of end of separate tracking.

(b) Ownership change of subsidiary.

(1) Ownership change of a subsidiary because of options or plan or arrangement.

(2) Effect of the ownership change.

(i) In general.

(ii) Pre-change losses.

(3) Coordination with §§ 1.1502-91, 1.1502-92, and 1.1502-94.

(4) Example.

(c) Continuing effect of an ownership change.

(d) Losses reattributed under § 1.1502-36(d)(6).

(1) In general.

(2) Deemed section 381(a) transaction.

(3) Rules relating to owner shifts.

(i) In general.

(ii) Examples.

(4) Rules relating to the section 382 limitation.

(i) Reattributed loss is a pre-change separate attribute of a new loss member.

(ii) Reattributed loss is a pre-change subgroup attribute.

(iii) Potential application of section 382(l)(1).

(iv) Duplication or omission of value.

(v) Special rule for continuity of business requirement.

(5) Election to reattribute section 382 limitation.

(i) Effect of election.

(ii) Examples.

(e) Time and manner of making election under § 1.1502-91(d)(4).

(1) In general.

(2) Election statement.

§ 1.1502-97 Special rules under section 382 for members under the jurisdiction of a court in a title 11 or similar case.

[Reserved].

§ 1.1502-98 Coordination with section 383.

§ 1.1502-99 Effective dates.

(a) Effective date.

(b) Special rules.

(1) Election to treat subgroup parent requirement as satisfied.

(2) Principal purpose of avoiding a limitation.

(3) Ceasing to be a member of a loss subgroup.

(i) Ownership change of a loss subgroup.

(ii) Expiration of 5-year period.

(4) Reattribution of net operating loss carryovers under § 1.1502-36(d)(6).

(5) Election to apportion net unrealized built-in gain.

(c) Testing period may include a period beginning before June 25, 1999.

(1) In general.

(2) Transition rule for net unrealized built-in losses.

[Reg. § 1.1502-90.]

☐ [*T.D.* 8824, 6-25-99. *Amended by T.D. 9304,* 12-21-2006; *T.D.* 9329, 6-13-2007 *and T.D. 9424,* 9-9-2008.]

[Reg. §1.1502-90A]

§1.1502-90A. Table of contents.—The following list contains the major headings in §§1.1502-91A through 1.1502-99A:

§1.1502-91A Application of section 382 with respect to a consolidated group generally applicable for testing dates before June 25, 1999.

(a) Determination and effect of an ownership change.

(1) In general.

(2) Special rule for post-change year that includes the change date.

(3) Cross reference.

(b) Definitions and nomenclature.

(c) Loss group.

(1) Defined.

(2) Coordination with rule that ends separate tracking.

(3) Example.

(d) Loss subgroup.

(1) Net operating loss carryovers.

(2) Net unrealized built-in loss.

(3) Loss subgroup parent.

(4) Principal purpose of avoiding a limitation.

(5) Special rules.

(6) Examples.

(e) Pre-change consolidated attribute.

(1) Defined.

(2) Example.

(f) Pre-change subgroup attribute.

(1) Defined.

(2) Example.

(g) Net unrealized built-in gain and loss.

(1) In general.

(2) Members included.

(i) Consolidated group.

(ii) Loss subgroup.

(3) Acquisitions of built-in gain or loss assets.

(4) Indirect ownership.

(h) Recognized built-in gain or loss.

(1) In general. [Reserved]

(2) Disposition of stock or an intercompany obligation of a member.

(3) Deferred gain or loss.

(4) Exchanged basis property.

(i) [Reserved]

(j) Predecessor and successor corporations.

§1.1502-92A Ownership change of a loss group or a loss subgroup generally applicable for testing dates before June 25, 1999.

(a) Scope.

(b) Determination of an ownership change.

(1) Parent change method.

(i) Loss group.

(ii) Loss subgroup.

(2) Examples.

(3) Special adjustments.

(i) Common parent succeeded by a new common parent.

(ii) Newly created loss subgroup parent.

(iii) Examples.

(4) End of separate tracking of certain losses.

(c) Supplemental rules for determining ownership change.

(1) Scope.

(2) Cause for applying supplemental rule.

(3) Operating rules.

(4) Supplemental ownership change rules.

(i) Additional testing dates for the common parent (or loss subgroup parent).

(ii) Treatment of subsidiary stock as stock of the common parent (or loss subgroup parent).

(iii) 5-percent shareholder of the common parent (or loss subgroup parent).

(5) Examples.

(d) Testing period following ownership change under this section.

(e) Information statements.

(1) Common parent of a loss group.

(2) Abbreviated statement with respect to loss subgroups.

§1.1502-93A Consolidated section 382 limitation (or subgroup section 382 limitation) generally applicable for testing dates before June 25, 1999.

(a) Determination of the consolidated section 382 limitation (or subgroup section 382 limitation).

(1) In general.

(2) Coordination with apportionment rule.

(b) Value of the loss group (or loss subgroup).

(1) Stock value immediately before ownership change.

(2) Adjustment to value.

(3) Examples.

(c) Recognized built-in gain of a loss group or loss subgroup.

(d) Continuity of business.

(1) In general.

(2) Example.

(e) Limitations of losses under other rules.

§1.1502-94A Coordination with section 382 and the regulations thereunder when a corporation becomes a member of a consolidated group generally applicable for corporations becoming members of a group before June 25, 1999.

(a) Scope.

(1) In general.

(2) Successor corporation as new loss member.

(3) Coordination in the case of a loss subgroup.

(4) End of separate tracking of certain losses.

(5) Cross-reference.

(b) Application of section 382 to a new loss member.

(1) In general.

(2) Adjustment to value.

(3) Pre-change separate attribute defined.

(4) Examples.

(c) Built-in gains and losses.

(d) Information statements.

§ 1.1502-95A Rules on ceasing to be a member of a consolidated group (or loss subgroup) generally applicable for corporations ceasing to be members before June 25, 1999.

(a) In general.

(1) Consolidated group.

(2) Election by common parent.

(3) Coordination with §§ 1.1502-91T through 1.1502-93T.

(b) Separate application of section 382 when a member leaves a consolidated group.

(1) In general.

(2) Effect of a prior ownership change of the group.

(3) Application in the case of a loss subgroup.

(4) Examples.

(c) Apportionment of a consolidated section 382 limitation.

(1) In general.

(2) Amount of apportionment.

(3) Effect of apportionment on the consolidated section 382 limitation.

(4) Effect on corporations to which the consolidated section 382 limitation is apportioned.

(5) Deemed apportionment when loss group terminates.

(6) Appropriate adjustments when former member leaves during the year.

(7) Examples.

(d) Rules pertaining to ceasing to be a member of a loss subgroup.

(1) In general.

(2) Examples.

(e) Filing the election to apportion.

(1) Form of the election to apportion.

(2) Signing of the election.

(3) Filing of the election.

(4) Revocation of election.

§ 1.1502-96A Miscellaneous rules generally applicable for testing dates before June 25, 1999.

(a) End of separate tracking of losses.

(1) Application.

(2) Effect of end of separate tracking.

(3) Continuing effect of end of separate tracking.

(4) Special rule for testing period.

(5) Limits on effects of end of separate tracking.

(b) Ownership change of subsidiary.

(1) Ownership change of a subsidiary because of options or plan or arrangement.

(2) Effect of the ownership change.

(i) In general.

(ii) Pre-change losses.

(3) Coordination with §§ 1.1502-91T, 1.1502-92T, and 1.1502-94T.

(4) Example.

(c) Continuing effect of an ownership change.

§ 1.1502-97A Special rules under section 382 for members under the jurisdiction of a court in a title 11 or similar case

[Reserved]

§ 1.1502-98A Coordination with section 383 generally applicable for testing dates (or members joining or leaving a group) before June 25, 1999.

§ 1.1502-99A Effective dates.

(a) Effective date.

(1) In general.

(2) Anti-duplication rules for recognized built-in gain.

(b) Testing period may include a period beginning before January 1, 1997.

(c) Transition rules.

(1) Methods permitted.

(i) In general.

(ii) Adjustments to offset excess limitation.

(iii) Coordination with effective date.

(2) Permitted methods.

(d) Amended returns.

(e) Section 383.

[Reg. § 1.1502-90A.]

☐ [*T.D. 8678, 6-26-96. Amended and redesignated by T.D. 8824, 6-25-99.*]

[Reg. § 1.1502-91]

§ 1.1502-91. Application of section 382 with respect to a consolidated group.— (a) *Determination and effect of an ownership change.*—(1) *In general.*—This section and §§ 1.1502-92 and 1.1502-93 set forth the rules for determining an ownership change under section 382 for members of consolidated groups and the section 382 limitations with respect to attributes described in paragraphs (e) and (f) of this section. These rules generally provide that an ownership change and the section 382 limitation are determined with respect to these attributes for the group (or loss subgroup) on a single entity basis and not for its members separately. Following an ownership change of a loss group (or a loss subgroup) under § 1.1502-92, the amount of consolidated taxable income for any post-change year which may be offset by pre-change consolidated attributes (or pre-change subgroup attributes) shall not exceed the consolidated section 382 limitation (or subgroup section 382 limitation) for such year as determined under § 1.1502-93.

(2) *Special rule for post-change year that includes the change date.*—If the post-change year includes the change date, section 382(b)(3)(A) is applied so that the consolidated section 382 limitation (or subgroup section 382 limitation) does not apply to the portion of consolidated taxable income that is allocable to the period in the year on or before the change date. See generally § 1.382-6 (relating to the allocation of income and loss). The allocation of consolidated taxable income for the post-change year that includes the change date must be made before taking into account any consolidated net operating loss deduction (as defined in § 1.1502-21(a)).

(3) *Cross-reference.*—See § § 1.1502-94 and 1.1502-95 for rules that apply section 382 to a corporation that becomes or ceases to be a member of a group or loss subgroup.

(b) *Definitions and nomenclature.*—For purposes of this section and § § 1.1502-92 through 1.1502-99, unless otherwise stated:

(1) The definitions and nomenclature contained in section 382 and the regulations thereunder (including the nomenclature and assumptions relating to the examples in § 1.382-2T(b)) and this section and § § 1.1502-92 through 1.1502-99 apply.

(2) In all examples, all groups file consolidated returns, all corporations file their income tax returns on a calendar year basis, the only 5-percent shareholder of a corporation is a public group, the facts set forth the only owner shifts during the testing period, no election is made

under paragraph (d)(4) of this section, and each asset of a corporation has a value equal to its adjusted basis.

(3) As the context requires, references to § § 1.1502-91 through 1.1502-96 include references to corresponding provisions of § § 1.1502-91A through 1.1502-96A. For example, a reference to an ownership change under § 1.1502-92 in § 1.1502-95(b) can include a reference to an ownership change under § 1.1502-92A.

(c) *Loss group.*—(1) *Defined.*—A loss group is a consolidated group that—

(i) Is entitled to use a net operating loss carryover to the taxable year that did not arise (and is not treated under § 1.1502-21(c) as arising) in a SRLY;

(ii) Has a consolidated net operating loss for the taxable year in which a testing date of the common parent occurs (determined by treating the common parent as a loss corporation); or

(iii) Has a net unrealized built-in loss (determined under paragraph (g) of this section by treating the date on which the determination is made as though it were a change date).

(2) *Coordination with rule that ends separate tracking.*—A consolidated group may be a loss group because a member's losses that arose in (or are treated as arising in) a SRLY are treated as described in paragraph (c)(1)(i) of this section. See § 1.1502-96(a).

(3) *Example.*—The following example illustrates the principles of this paragraph (c):

Example. Loss group. (i) L and L1 file separate returns and each has a net operating loss carryover arising in Year 1 that is carried over to Year 2. A owns 40 shares and L owns 60 shares of the 100 outstanding shares of L1 stock. At the close of Year 1, L buys the 40 shares of L1 stock from A. For Year 2, L and L1 file a consolidated return. The following is a graphic illustration of these facts:

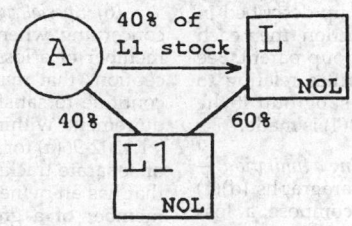

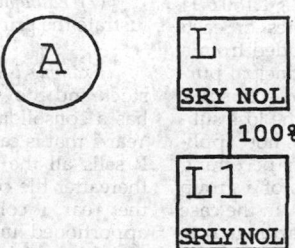

(ii) L and L1 become a loss group at the beginning of Year 2 because the group is entitled to use the Year 1 net operating loss carryover of L, the common parent, which did not arise (and is not treated under §1.1502-21(c) as arising) in a SRLY. See §1.1502-94 for rules relating to the application of section 382 with respect to Ll's net operating loss carryover from Year 1 which did arise in a SRLY.

(d) *Loss subgroup.*—(1) *Net operating loss carryovers.*—Two or more corporations that become members of a consolidated group (the current group) compose a loss subgroup if—

(i) They were affiliated with each other in another group (the former group), whether or not the group was a consolidated group;

(ii) They bear the relationship described in section 1504(a)(1) to each other through a loss subgroup parent immediately after they become members of the current group (or are deemed to bear that relationship as a result of an election described in paragraph (d)(4) of this section); and

(iii) At least one of the members carries over a net operating loss that did not arise (and is not treated under §1.1502-21(c) as arising) in a SRLY with respect to the former group.

(2) *Net unrealized built-in loss.*—Two or more corporations that become members of a consolidated group compose a loss subgroup if they—

(i) Have been continuously affiliated with each other for the 5 consecutive year period ending immediately before they become members of the group;

(ii) Bear the relationship described in section 1504(a)(1) to each other through a loss subgroup parent immediately after they become

members of the current group (or are deemed to bear that relationship as a result of an election described in paragraph (d)(4) of this section); and

(iii) Have a net unrealized built-in loss (determined under paragraph (g) of this section on the day they become members of the group by treating that day as though it were a change date).

(3) *Loss subgroup parent.*—A loss subgroup parent is the corporation that bears the same relationship to the other members of the loss subgroup as a common parent bears to the members of a group.

(4) *Election to treat loss subgroup parent requirement as satisfied.*—(i) *In general.*—Solely for purposes of paragraphs (d)(1)(i) and (2)(ii) of this section, two or more corporations that become members of a consolidated group at the same time and that were affiliated with each other immediately before becoming members of the group are deemed to bear a section 1504(a)(1) relationship to each other immediately after they become members of the group if the common parent of that group makes an election under this paragraph (d)(4) with respect to those members. See §1.1502-96(e) for the time and manner of making the election.

(ii) *Members included.*—An election under this paragraph (d)(4) includes all corporations that become members of the current group at the same time and that were affiliated with each other immediately before they become members of the current group.

(iii) *Each member included treated as loss subgroup parent.*—If the members to which this election applies are a loss subgroup described in paragraph (d)(1) or (2) of this section, then each member is treated as a loss subgroup parent. See § 1.1502-92(b)(1)(iii) for special rules relating to an ownership change of a loss subgroup if the election under this paragraph (d)(4) is made.

(5) *Principal purpose of avoiding a limitation.*—The corporations described in paragraphs (d)(1) or (2) of this section do not compose a loss subgroup if any one of them is formed, acquired, or availed of with a principal purpose of avoiding the application of, or increasing any limitation under, section 382. Instead, § 1.1502-94 applies with respect to the attributes of each such corporation. Any member excluded from a loss subgroup, if excluded with a principal purpose of so avoiding or increasing any section 382 limitation, is treated as included in the loss subgroup. This paragraph (d)(5) does not apply solely because, in connection with becoming members of the group, the members of a group (or loss subgroup) are rearranged (or, in the case of the preceding sentence, are not rearranged) to bear a relationship to the other members described in section 1504(a)(1).

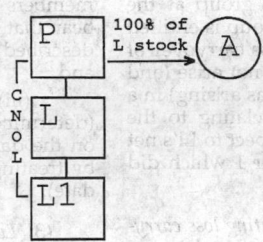

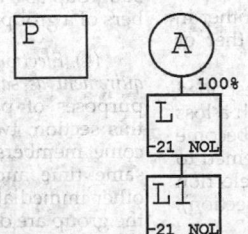

(ii) (a) L and L1 compose a loss subgroup within the meaning of paragraph (d)(1) of this section because—

(A) They were affiliated with each other in the P group (the former group);

(B) They bear a relationship described in section 1504(a)(1) to each other through a loss subgroup parent (L) immediately after they became members of the L group; and

(C) At least one of the members (here, both L and L1) carries over a net operating loss to the L group (the current group) that did not arise in a SRLY with respect to the P group.

(6) *Special rules.*—See § 1.1502-95(d) for rules concerning when a corporation ceases to be a member of a loss subgroup, and for certain exceptions that may apply if a member does not continue to satisfy the loss subgroup parent requirement within the current group. See also § 1.1502-96(a) for a special rule regarding the end of separate tracking of SRLY losses of a member that has an ownership change or that has been a member of a group for at least 5 consecutive years.

(7) *Examples.*—The following examples illustrate the principles of this paragraph (d):

Example 1. Loss subgroup. (i) P owns all the L stock and L owns all the L1 stock. The P group has a consolidated net operating loss arising in Year 1 that is carried to Year 2. On May 2, Year 2, P sells all the stock of L to A, and L and L1 thereafter file consolidated returns. A portion of the Year 1 consolidated net operating loss is apportioned under § 1.1502-21(b) to each of L and L1, which they carry over to Year 2. The following is a graphic illustration of these facts:

(b) Under paragraph (d)(3) of this section, L is the loss subgroup parent of the L loss subgroup.

Example 2. Loss subgroup—section 1504(a)(1) relationship. (i) P owns all the stock of L and L1. L owns all the stock of L2. L1 and L2 own 40 percent and 60 percent of the stock of L3, respectively. The P group has a consolidated net operating loss arising in Year 1 that is carried over to Year 2. On May 22, Year 2, P sells all the stock of L and L1 to P1, the common parent of another consolidated group. The Year 1 consolidated net operating loss is apportioned under § 1.1502-21(b), and each of L, L2, L2, and L3 carries over a portion of such loss to the first consolidated return year of the P1 group ending after the acquisition. The following is a graphic illustration of these facts:

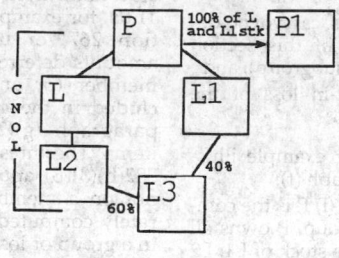

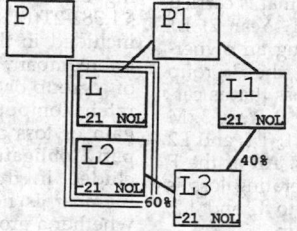

(ii) L and L2 compose a loss subgroup within the meaning of paragraph (d)(1) of this section. Neither L1 nor L3 is included in a loss subgroup because neither bears a relationship described in section 1504(a)(1) through a loss subgroup parent to any other member of the former group immediately after becoming members of the P1 group.

Example 3. Loss subgroup—section 1504(a)(1) relationship. The facts are the same as in *Example 2*, except that the stock of L1 is transferred to L in connection with the sale of the L stock to P1. L, L1, L2, and L3 compose a loss subgroup within the meaning of paragraph (d)(1) of this section because—

(i) They were affiliated with each other in the P group (the former group);

(ii) They bear a relationship described in section 1504(a)(1) to each other through a loss subgroup parent (L) immediately after they become members of the P1 group; and

(iii) At least one of the members (here, each of L, L1, L2, and L3) carries over a net operating loss to the P1 group (the current group).

Example 4. Loss subgroup—elective section 1504(a)(1) relationship. The facts are the same as in *Example 2*, except that P1 makes the election under paragraph (d)(4) of this section. The election includes L, L1, L2, and L3 (even though L and L2 would compose a loss subgroup without regard to the election) because they become members of the current group (the P1 group) at the same time and were affiliated with each other in the P group immediately before they became members of the P1 group. As a result of the election, L, L1, L2, and L3 are treated as satisfying the requirement that they bear the relationship described in section 1504(a)(1) to each other through a loss subgroup parent immediately after they become members of the P1 group. L, L1, L2, and L3 compose a loss subgroup within the meaning of paragraph (d)(1) of this section.

(e) *Pre-change consolidated attribute.*—(1) *Defined.*—A pre-change consolidated attribute of a loss group is—

(i) Any loss described in paragraph (c)(1)(i) or (ii) of this section (relating to the definition of loss group) that is allocable to the period ending on or before the change date; and

(ii) Any recognized built-in loss of the loss group.

(2) *Example.*—The following example illustrates the principle of this paragraph (e):

Example. Pre-change consolidated attribute. (i) The L group has a consolidated net operating loss arising in Year 1 that is carried over to Year 2. The L loss group has an ownership change at the beginning of Year 2.

(ii) The net operating loss carryover of the L loss group from Year 1 is a pre-change consolidated attribute because the L group was entitled to use the loss in Year 2 and therefore the loss was described in paragraph (c)(1)(i) of this section. Under paragraph (a)(2)(i) of this section, the amount of consolidated taxable income of the L group for Year 2 that may be offset by this loss carryover may not exceed the consolidated section 382 limitation of the L group for that year. See § 1.1502-93 for rules relating to the computation of the consolidated section 382 limitation.

Reg. § 1.1502-91(e)(2)

(f) *Pre-change subgroup attribute.*—(1) *Defined.*—A pre-change subgroup attribute of a loss subgroup is—

(i) Any net operating loss carryover described in paragraph (d)(1)(iii) of this section (relating to the definition of loss subgroup); and

(ii) Any recognized built-in loss of the loss subgroup.

(2) *Example.*—The following example illustrates the principle of this paragraph (f):

Pre-change subgroup attribute. (i) P is the common parent of a consolidated group. P owns all the stock of L, and L owns all the stock of L1. L2 is not a member of an affiliated group, and has a net operating loss arising in Year 1 that is carried over to Year 2. On December 11, Year 2, L1 acquires all the stock of L2, causing an ownership change of L2. During Year 2, the P group has a consolidated net operating loss that is carried over to Year 3. On November 2, Year 3, M acquires all the L stock from P. M, L, L1, and L2 thereafter file consolidated returns. All of the P group Year 2 consolidated net operating loss is apportioned under § 1.1502-21(b) to L and L2, which they carry over to the M group.

(ii)(a) L, L1, and L2 compose a loss subgroup because—

(1) They were affiliated with each other in the P group (the former group);

(2) They bear a relationship described in section 1504(a)(1) to each other through a loss subgroup parent (L) immediately after they became members of the L group; and

(3) At least one of the members (here, both L and L2) carries over a net operating loss to the M group (the current group) that is described in paragraph (d)(1)(iii) of this section.

(b) For this purpose, L2's loss from Year 1 that was a SRLY loss with respect to the P group (the former group) is described in paragraph (d)(1)(iii) of this section because L2 had an ownership change on becoming a member of the P group (see § 1.1502-96(a)) on December 11, Year 2. Starting on December 12, Year 2, the P group no longer separately tracked owner shifts of the stock of L1 with respect to the Year 1 loss. M's acquisition results in an ownership change of L, and therefore the L loss subgroup under § 1.1502-92(a)(2). See § 1.1502-93 for rules governing the computation of the subgroup section 382 limitation.

(iii) In the M group, L2's Year 1 loss continues to be subject to a section 382 limitation resulting from the ownership change that occurred on December 11, Year 2. See § 1.1502-96(c).

(g) *Net unrealized built-in gain and loss.*—(1) *In general.*—The determination whether a consolidated group (or loss subgroup) has a net unrealized built-in gain or loss under section 382(h)(3) is based on the aggregate amount of the separately computed net unrealized built-in gains or losses of each member that is included in the group (or loss subgroup) under paragraph (g)(2) of this section, including items of built-in income and deduction described in section 382(h)(6). Thus, for example, amounts deferred under section 267, or under § 1.1502-13 (other than amounts deferred with respect to the stock of a member (or an intercompany obligation) included in the group (or loss subgroup) under paragraph (g)(2) of this section) are built-in items. The threshold requirement under section 382(h)(3)(B) applies on an aggregate basis and not on a member-by-member basis. The separately computed amount of a member included in a group or loss subgroup does not include any unrealized built-in gain or loss on stock (including stock described in section 1504(a)(4) and § 1.382-2T(f)(18)(ii) and (iii)) of another member included in the group or loss subgroup (or an intercompany obligation). However, a member of a group or loss subgroup includes in its separately computed amount the unrealized built-in gain or loss on stock (but not on an intercompany obligation) of another member not included in the group or loss subgroup. If a member is not included in the determination whether a group (or subgroup) has a net unrealized built-in loss under paragraph (g)(2)(ii) or (iv) of this section, that member is not included in the loss group or loss subgroup. See § 1.1502-94(c) (relating to built-in gain or loss of a new loss member) and § 1.1502-96(a) (relating to the end of separate tracking of certain losses).

(2) *Members included.*—(i) *Consolidated group with a net operating loss.*—The members included in the determination whether a consolidated group described in paragraph (c)(1)(i) or (ii) of this section (relating to loss groups with net operating losses) has a net unrealized built-in gain are all members of the consolidated group on the day that the determination is made.

(ii) *Determination whether a consolidated group has a net unrealized built-in loss.*—The members included in the determination whether a consolidated group is a loss group described in paragraph (c)(1)(iii) of this section are—

(A) The common parent and all other members that have been affiliated with the common parent for the 5 consecutive year period ending on the day that the determination is made;

(B) Any other member that has a net unrealized built-in loss determined under paragraph (g)(1) of this section on the date that the determination is made, and that is neither a new loss member described in § 1.1502-94(a)(1)(ii) nor a member of a loss subgroup described in paragraph (d)(2) of this section;

(C) Any new loss member described in § 1.1502-94(a)(1)(ii) that has a net unrealized built-in gain determined under paragraph (g)(1) of this section on the day that the determination is made; and

(D) The members of a loss subgroup described in paragraph (d)(2) of this section if the members of the subgroup have, in the aggregate, a net unrealized built-in gain on the day that the determination is made.

(iii) *Loss subgroup with net operating loss carryovers.*—The members included in the determination whether a loss subgroup described in paragraph (d)(1) of this section (relating to loss subgroups with net operating loss carryovers) has a net unrealized built-in gain are all members of the loss subgroup on the day that the determination is made.

(iv) *Determination whether subgroup has a net unrealized built-in loss.*—The members included in the determination whether a subgroup has a net unrealized built-in loss are those members described in paragraphs (d)(2)(i) and (ii) of this section.

(v) *Separate determination of section 382 limitation for recognized built-in losses and net operating losses.*—In determining whether a loss group described in paragraph (c)(1)(i) or (ii) of this section (relating to loss groups that have net operating loss carryovers) has a net unrealized built-in gain which, if recognized, increases the consolidated section 382 limitation, the group includes, under paragraph (g)(2)(i) of this section, all of its members on the day the determination is made. Under paragraph (g)(2)(ii) of this section, however, for purposes of determining whether a group has a net unrealized built-in loss described in paragraph (c)(1)(iii) of this section, not all members of the consolidated group may be included. Thus, a consolidated group may have recognized built-in gains that increase the amount of consolidated taxable income that may be offset by its pre-change net operating loss carryovers that did not arise (and are not treated as arising) in a SRLY, and also may have recognized built-in losses the absorption of which is limited. Similar results may obtain for loss subgroups under paragraphs (g)(2)(iii) and (iv) of this section. See § 1.1502-93(c)(2) for rules prohibiting the use of recognized built-in gains to increase the amount of consolidated taxable income that can be offset by recognized built-in losses.

(3) *Coordination with rule that ends separate tracking.*—See § 1.1502-96(a) for special rules relating to members (or loss subgroups) that have an ownership change within six months before, on, or after becoming a member of the group.

(4) *Acquisitions of built-in gain or loss assets.*— A member of a consolidated group (or loss subgroup) may not, in determining its separately computed net unrealized built-in gain or loss, include any gain or loss with respect to assets acquired with a principal purpose to affect the amount of its net unrealized built-in gain or loss. A group (or loss subgroup) may not, in determining its net unrealized built-in gain or loss, include any gain or loss of a member acquired with a principal purpose to affect the amount of its net unrealized built-in gain or loss.

(5) *Indirect ownership.*—A member's separately computed net unrealized built-in gain or loss is adjusted to the extent necessary to prevent any duplication of unrealized gain or loss attributable to the member's indirect ownership interest in another member through a nonmember if the member has a 5-percent or greater ownership interest in the nonmember.

(6) *Common parent not common parent for five years.*—If the common parent has become the common parent of an existing group within the previous 5 year period in a transaction described in § 1.1502-75(d)(2)(ii) or (3), appropriate adjustments must be made in applying paragraph (g)(2)(ii)(A) of this section so that corporations that have not been members of the group for five years are not included. In such a case, references to the common parent in paragraph (g)(2)(ii)(A) of this section are to the former common parent. Thus, members of the group remaining in existence (including the new common parent) that have not been affiliated with the former common parent (or that have not been members of that group) for the five consecutive year period ending on the day that the determination is made are not included under paragraph (g)(2)(ii)(A) of this section. See, however, § 1.1502-96(a)(2) for special rules relating to members (or loss subgroups) that have an ownership change within six months before, on, or after the time that the member becomes a member of the group.

(h) *Recognized built-in gain or loss.*—(1) *In general.*—[Reserved].

(2) *Disposition of stock or an intercompany obligation of a member.*—Gain or loss recognized by a member on the disposition of stock (including stock described in section 1504(a)(4) and § 1.382-2T(f)(18)(ii) and (iii)) of another member is treated as a recognized gain or loss for purposes of section 382(h)(2) (unless disallowed) even though gain or loss on such stock was not included in the determination of a net unrealized built-in gain or loss under paragraph (g)(1) of this section. Gain or loss recognized by a member with respect to an intercompany obligation is treated as recognized gain or loss only to the extent (if any) the transaction gives rise to aggregate income or loss within the consolidated group. The first sentence of this paragraph (h)(2) is applicable on or after September 17, 2008.

(3) *Intercompany transactions.*—Gain or loss that is deferred under provisions such as section 267 and § 1.1502-13 is treated as recognized built-in gain or loss only to the extent taken into account by the group during the recognition period. See also § 1.1502-13(c)(7) *Example 10.*

Reg. § 1.1502-91(h)(3)

(4) *Exchanged basis property.*—If the adjusted basis of any asset is determined, directly or indirectly, in whole or in part, by reference to the adjusted basis of another asset held by the member a: the beginning of the recognition period, the asset is treated, with appropriate adjustments, as held by the member at the beginning of the recognition period.

(i) [Reserved]

(j) *Predecessor and successor corporations.*—A reference in this section and §§1.1502-92 through 1.1502-99 to a corporation, member, common parent, loss subgroup parent, or subsidiary includes, as the context may require, a reference to a predecessor or successor corporation as defined in §1.1502-1(f)(4). For example, the determination whether a successor satisfies the continuous affiliation requirement of paragraph (d)(2)(i) or (g)(2)(ii) of this section is made by reference to its predecessor. [Reg. §1.1502-91.]

☐ [*T.D.* 8824, 6-25-99. *Amended by T.D.* 9048, 3-11-2003 *T.D.* 9187, 3-2-2005; *T.D.* 9254, 3-9-2006 *and T.D.* 9424, 9-9-2008.]

[Reg. §1.1502-91A]

§1.1502-91A. Application of section 382 with respect to a consolidated group generally applicable for testing dates before June 25, 1999.— (a) *Determination and effect of an ownership change.*—(1) *In general.*—This section and §§1.1502-92A and 1.1502-93A set forth the rules for determining an ownership change under section 382 for members of consolidated groups and the section 382 limitations with respect to attributes described in paragraphs (e) and (f) of this section. These rules generally provide that an ownership change and the section 382 limitation are determined with respect to these attributes for the group (or loss subgroup) on a single entity basis and not for its members separately. Following an ownership change of a loss group (or a loss subgroup) under §1.1502-92A, the amount of consolidated taxable income for any post-change year which may be offset by pre-change consolidated attributes (or pre-change subgroup attributes) shall not exceed the consolidated section 382 limitation (or subgroup section 382 limitation) for such year as determined under §1.1502-93A.

(2) *Special rule for post-change year that includes the change date.*—If the post-change year includes the change date, section 382(b)(3)(A) is applied so that the consolidated section 382 limitation (or subgroup section 382 limitation) does not apply to the portion of consolidated taxable income that is allocable to the period in the year on or before the change date. See generally §1.382-6 (relating to the allocation of income and loss). The allocation of consolidated taxable income for the post-change year that includes the

change date must be made before taking into account any consolidated net operating loss deduction (as defined in §1.1502-21(a) or 1.1502-21T(a) in effect prior to June 25, 1999, as contained in 26 CFR part 1 revised April 1, 1999, as applicable).

(3) *Cross reference.*—See §§1.1502-94A and 1.1502-95A for rules that apply section 382 to a corporation that becomes or ceases to be a member of a group or loss subgroup.

(b) *Definitions and nomenclature.*—For purposes of this section and §§1.1502-92A through 1.1502-99A, unless otherwise stated:

(1) The definitions and nomenclature contained in section 382 and the regulations thereunder (including the nomenclature and assumptions relating to the examples in §1.382-2T(b)) and this section and §§1.1502-92A through 1.1502-99A apply; and

(2) In all examples, all groups file consolidated returns, all corporations file their income tax returns on a calendar year basis, the only 5-percent shareholder of a corporation is a public group, the facts set forth the only owner shifts during the testing period, and each asset of a corporation has a value equal to its adjusted basis.

(c) *Loss group.*—(1) *Defined.*—A loss group is a consolidated group that:

(i) Is entitled to use a net operating loss carryover to the taxable year that did not arise (and is not treated under §1.1502-21T(c) as arising) in a SRLY;

(ii) Has a consolidated net operating loss for the taxable year in which a testing date of the common parent occurs (determined by treating the common parent as a loss corporation); or

(iii) Has a net unrealized built-in loss (determined under paragraph (g) of this section by treating the date on which the determination is made as though it were a change date).

(2) *Coordination with rule that ends separate tracking.*—A consolidated group may be a loss group because a member's losses that arose in (or are treated as arising in) a SRLY are treated as described in paragraph (c)(1)(i) of this section. See §1.1502-96A(a).

(3) *Example.*—The following example illustrates the principles of this paragraph (c).

Example. Loss group. (a) L and L1 file separate returns and each has a net operating loss carryover arising in Year 1 that is carried over to Year 2. A owns 40 shares and L owns 60 shares of the 100 outstanding shares of L1 stock. At the close of Year 1, L buys the 40 shares of L1 stock from A. For Year 2, L and L1 file a consolidated return. The following is a graphic illustration of these facts:

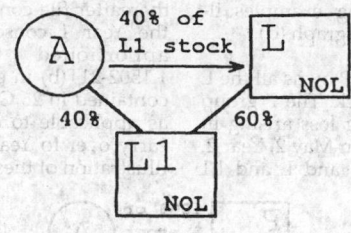

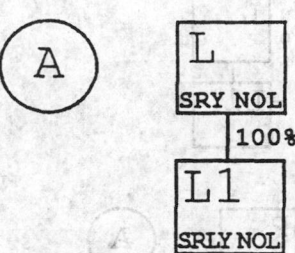

(b) L and L1 become a loss group at the beginning of Year 2 because the group is entitled to use the Year 1 net operating loss carryover of L, the common parent, which did not arise (and is not treated under §1.1502-21(c) or 1.1502-21T(c) in effect prior to June 25, 1999, as contained in 26 CFR part 1 revised April 1, 1999, as applicable as arising) in a SRLY. See §1.1502-94A for rules relating to the application of section 382 with respect to L1's net operating loss carryover from Year 1 which did arise in a SRLY.

(d) *Loss subgroup.*—(1) *Net operating loss carryovers.*—Two or more corporations that become members of a consolidated group (the current group) compose a loss subgroup if:

(i) They were affiliated with each other in another group (the former group), whether or not the group was a consolidated group;

(ii) They bear the relationship described in section 1504(a)(1) to each other through a loss subgroup parent immediately after they become members of the current group; and

(iii) At least one of the members carries over a net operating loss that did not arise (and is not treated under §1.1502-21(c) or 1.1502-21T(c) in effect prior to June 25, 1999, as contained in 26 CFR part 1 revised April 1, 1999, as applicable as arising) in a SRLY with respect to the former group.

(2) *Net unrealized built-in loss.*—Two or more corporations that become members of a consolidated group compose a loss subgroup if they:

(i) Have been continuously affiliated with each other for the 5 consecutive year period ending immediately before they become members of the group;

(ii) Bear the relationship described in section 1504(a)(1) to each other through a loss subgroup parent immediately after they become members of the current group; and

(iii) Have a net unrealized built-in loss (determined under paragraph (g) of this section on the day they become members of the group by treating that day as though it were a change date).

(3) *Loss subgroup parent.*—A loss subgroup parent is the corporation that bears the same relationship to the other members of the loss subgroup as a common parent bears to the members of a group.

(4) *Principal purpose of avoiding a limitation.*—The corporations described in paragraph (d)(1) or (2) of this section do not compose a loss subgroup if any one of them is formed, acquired, or availed of with a principal purpose of avoiding the application of, or increasing any limitation under, section 382. Instead, §1.1502-94A applies with respect to the attributes of each such corporation. This paragraph (d)(4) does not apply solely because, in connection with becoming members of the group, the members of a group (or loss subgroup) are rearranged to bear a relationship to the other members described in section 1504(a)(1).

(5) *Special rules.*—See §1.1502-95A(d) for rules concerning when a corporation ceases to be a member of a loss subgroup. See also §1.1502-96A(a) for a special rule regarding the end of separate tracking of SRLY losses of a member that has an ownership change or that has been a member of a group for at least 5 consecutive years.

Reg. §1.1502-91A(d)(5)

(6) *Examples.*—The following examples illustrate the principles of this paragraph (d).

Example 1. Loss subgroup. (a) P owns all the L stock and L owns all the L1 stock. The P group has a consolidated net operating loss arising in Year 1 that is carried to Year 2. On May 2, Year 2, P sells all the stock of L to A, and L and L1

thereafter file consolidated returns. A portion of the Year 1 consolidated net operating loss is apportioned under § 1.1502-21(b) or 1.1502-21T(b) in effect prior to June 25, 1999, as contained in 26 CFR part 1 revised April 1, 1999, as applicable to each of L and L1, which they carry over to Year 2. The following is a graphic illustration of these facts:

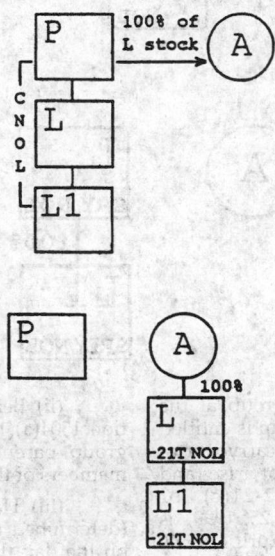

(b) (1) L and L1 compose a loss subgroup within the meaning of paragraph (d)(1) of this section because—

(i) They were affiliated with each other in the P group (the former group);

(ii) They bear a relationship described in section 1504(a)(1) to each other through a loss subgroup parent (L) immediately after they became members of the L group; and

(iii) At least one of the members (here, both L and L1) carries over a net operating loss to the L group (the current group) that did not arise in a SRLY with respect to the P group.

(2) Under paragraph (d)(3) of this section, L is the loss subgroup parent of the L loss subgroup.

Example 2. Loss subgroup—section 1504(a)(1) relationship. (a) P owns all the stock of L and L1. L owns all the stock of L2. L1 and L2 own 40 percent and 60 percent of the stock of L3, respectively. The P group has a consolidated net operating loss arising in Year 1 that is carried over to Year 2. On May 22, Year 2, P sells all the stock of L and L1 to P1, the common parent of another consolidated group. The Year 1 consolidated net operating loss is apportioned under § 1.1502-21(b) or 1.1502-21T(b) in effect prior to June 25, 1999, as contained in 26 CFR part 1 revised April 1, 1999, as applicable, and each of L, L1, L2, and L3 carries over a portion of such loss to the first consolidated return year of the P1 group ending after the acquisition. The following is a graphic illustration of these facts:

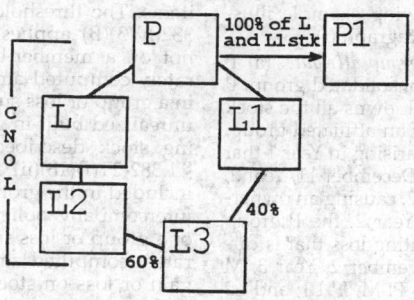

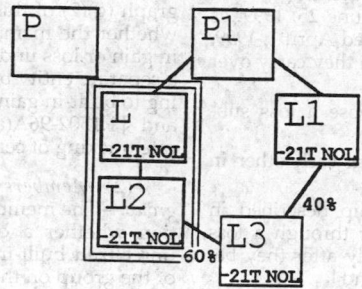

(b) L and L2 compose a loss subgroup within the meaning of paragraph (d)(1) of this section. Neither L1 nor L3 is included in a loss subgroup because neither bears a relationship described in section 1504(a)(1) through a loss subgroup parent to any other member of the former group immediately after becoming members of the P1 group.

Example 3. Loss subgroup—section 1504(a)(1) relationship. The facts are the same as in *Example 2,* except that the stock of L1 is transferred to L in connection with the sale of the L stock to P1. L, L1, L2, and L3 compose a loss subgroup within the meaning of paragraph (d)(1) of this section because—

(1) They were affiliated with each other in the P group (the former group);

(2) They bear a relationship described in section 1504(a)(1) to each other through a loss subgroup parent (L) immediately after they become members of the P1 group; and

(3) At least one of the members (here, each of L, L1, L2, and L3) carries over to the P1 group (the current group) a net operating loss that did not arise in a SRLY with respect to the P group (the former group).

(e) *Pre-change consolidated attribute.*—(1) *Defined.*—A pre-change consolidated attribute of a loss group is—

(i) Any loss described in paragraph (c)(1)(i) or (ii) of this section (relating to the definition of loss group) that is allocable to the period ending on or before the change date; and

(ii) Any recognized built-in loss of the loss group.

(2) *Example.*—The following example illustrates the principle of this paragraph (e).

Example. Pre-change consolidated attribute. (a) The L group has a consolidated net operating loss arising in Year 1 that is carried over to Year 2. The L loss group has an ownership change at the beginning of Year 2.

(b) The net operating loss carryover of the L loss group from Year 1 is a pre-change consolidated attribute because the L group was entitled to use the loss in Year 2, the loss did not arise in a SRLY with respect to the L group, and therefore the loss was described in paragraph (c)(1)(i) of this section. Under paragraph (a) of this section, the amount of consolidated taxable income of the L group for Year 2 that may be offset by this loss carryover may not exceed the consolidated section 382 limitation of the L group for that year. See § 1.1502-93A for rules relating to the computation of the consolidated section 382 limitation.

(f) *Pre-change subgroup attribute.*—(1) *Defined.*—A pre-change subgroup attribute of a loss subgroup is—

(i) Any net operating loss carryover described in paragraph (d)(1)(iii) of this section (relating to the definition of loss subgroup); and

(ii) Any recognized built-in loss of the loss subgroup.

(2) *Example.*—The following example illustrates the principle of this paragraph (f).

Example. Pre-change subgroup attribute. (a) P is the common parent of a consolidated group. P owns all the stock of L, and L owns all the stock of L1. L2 is not a member of an affiliated group, and has a net operating loss arising in Year 1 that is carried over to Year 2. On December 11, Year 2, L1 acquires all the stock of L2, causing an ownership change of L2. During Year 2, the P group has a consolidated net operating loss that is carried over to Year 3. On November 2, Year 3, M acquires all the L stock from P. M, L, L1, and L2 thereafter file consolidated returns. All of the P group Year 2 consolidated net operating loss is apportioned under § 1.1502-21(b) or 1.1502-21T(b) in effect prior to June 25, 1999, as contained in 26 CFR part 1 revised April 1, 1999, as applicable to L and L2, which they carry over to the M group.

(b)(1) L, L1, and L2 compose a loss subgroup because—

(i) They were affiliated with each other in the P group (the former group);

(ii) They bore a relationship described in section 1504(a)(1) to each other through a loss subgroup parent (L) immediately after they became members of the L group; and

(iii) At least one of the members (here, both L and L2) carries over a net operating loss to the M group (the current group) that is described in paragraph (d)(1)(iii) of this section.

(2) For this purpose, L2's loss from Year 1 that was a SRLY loss with respect to the P group (the former group) is treated as described in paragraph (d)(1)(iii) of this section because of the application of the principles of § 1.1502-96A(a). See paragraph (d)(5) of this section. M's acquisition results in an ownership change of L, and therefore the L loss subgroup under § 1.1502-92A(a)(2). See § 1.1502-93A for rules governing the computation of the subgroup section 382 limitation.

(c) In the M group, L2's Year 1 loss continues to be subject to a section 382 limitation resulting from the ownership change that occurred on December 11, Year 2. See § 1.1502-96A(c).

(g) *Net unrealized built-in gain and loss.*—(1) *In general.*—The determination whether a consolidated group (or loss subgroup) has a net unrealized built-in gain or loss under section 382(h)(3) is based on the aggregate amount of the separately computed net unrealized built-in gains or losses of each member that is included in the group (or loss subgroup) under paragraph (g)(2) of this section, including items of built-in income and deduction described in section 382(h)(6). Thus, for example, amounts deferred under section 267, or under § 1.1502-13 (other than amounts deferred with respect to the stock of a member (or an intercompany obligation) included in the group (or loss subgroup) under paragraph (g)(2) of this section) are built-in

items. The threshold requirement under section 382(h)(3)(B) applies on an aggregate basis and not on a member-by-member basis. The separately computed amount of a member included in a group or loss subgroup does not include any unrealized built-in gain or loss on stock (including stock described in section 1504(a)(4) and § 1.382-2T(f)(18)(ii) and (iii)) of another member included in the group or loss subgroup (or on an intercompany obligation). However, a member of a group or loss subgroup includes in its separately computed amount the unrealized built-in gain or loss on stock of another member (or on an intercompany obligation) not included in the group or loss subgroup. If a member is not included in a group (or loss subgroup) under paragraph (g)(2) of this section, the determination of whether the member has a net unrealized built-in gain or loss under section 382(h)(3) is made on a separate entity basis. See § 1.1502-94A(c) (relating to built-in gain or loss of a new loss member) and § 1.1502-96A(a) (relating to the end of separate tracking of certain losses).

(2) *Members included.*—(i) *Consolidated group.*—The members included in the determination whether a consolidated group has a net unrealized built-in gain or loss are all members of the group on the day that the determination is made other than—

(A) A new loss member with a net unrealized built-in loss described in § 1.1502-94A(a)(1)(ii); and

(B) Members included in a loss subgroup described in § 1.1502-91A(d)(2).

(ii) *Loss subgroup.*—The members included in the determination whether a loss subgroup has a net unrealized built-in gain or loss are those members described in paragraphs (d)(2)(i) and (ii) of this section.

(3) *Acquisitions of built-in gain or loss assets.*—A member of a consolidated group (or loss subgroup) may not, in determining its separately computed net unrealized built-in gain or loss, include any gain or loss with respect to assets acquired with a principal purpose to affect the amount of its net unrealized built-in gain or loss. A group (or loss subgroup) may not, in determining its net unrealized built-in gain or loss, include any gain or loss of a member acquired with a principal purpose to affect the amount of its net unrealized built-in gain or loss.

(4) *Indirect ownership.*—A member's separately computed net unrealized built-in gain or loss is adjusted to the extent necessary to prevent any duplication of unrealized gain or loss attributable to the member's indirect ownership interest in another member through a nonmember if the member has a 5-percent or greater ownership interest in the nonmember.

(h) *Recognized built-in gain or loss.*—(1) *In general.*—[Reserved]

(2) *Disposition of stock or an intercompany obligation of a member.*—Gain or loss recognized by a member on the disposition of stock (including stock described in section 1504(a)(4) and § 1.382-2T(f)(18)(ii) and (iii)) of another member (or an intercompany obligation disposed of before June 25, 1999) is treated as a recognized built-in gain or loss under section 382(h)(2) (unless disallowed under § 1.1502-20 or otherwise), even though gain or loss on such stock or obligation was not included in the determination of a net unrealized built-in gain or loss under paragraph (g)(1) of this section.

(3) *Deferred gain or loss.*—Gain or loss that is deferred under provisions such as section 267 and § 1.1502-13 is treated as recognized built-in gain or loss only to the extent taken into account by the group during the recognition period.

(4) *Exchanged basis property.*—If the adjusted basis of any asset is determined, directly or indirectly, in whole or in part, by reference to the adjusted basis of another asset held by the member at the beginning of the recognition period, the asset is treated, with appropriate adjustments, as held by the member at the beginning of the recognition period.

(i) [Reserved]

(j) *Predecessor and successor corporations.*—A reference in this section and §§ 1.1502-92A through 1.1502-99A to a corporation, member, common parent, loss subgroup parent, or subsidiary includes, as the context may require, a reference to a predecessor or successor corporation. For example, the determination whether a successor satisfies the continuous affiliation requirement of paragraph (d)(2)(i) of this section is made by reference to its predecessor. [Reg. § 1.1502-91A.]

☐ [T.D. 8678, 6-26-96. *Amended by T.D. 8823, 6-25-99 and amended and redesignated by T.D. 8824, 6-25-99.*]

[Reg. § 1.1502-92]

§ 1.1502-92. Ownership change of a loss group or a loss subgroup.—(a) *Scope.*—This section provides rules for determining if there is an ownership change for purposes of section 382 with respect to a loss group or a loss subgroup. See § 1.1502-94 for special rules for determining if there is an ownership change with respect to a new loss member and § 1.1502-96(b) for special rules for determining if there is an ownership change of a subsidiary.

(b) *Determination of an ownership change.*—(1) *Parent change method.*—(i) *Loss group.*—A loss group has an ownership change if the loss group's common parent has an ownership change under section 382 and the regulations thereunder. Solely for purposes of determining whether the common parent has an ownership change—

(A) The losses described in § 1.1502-91(c) are treated as net operating losses (or a net unrealized built-in loss) of the common parent; and

(B) The common parent determines the earliest day that its testing period can begin by reference to only the attributes that make the group a loss group under § 1.1502-91(c).

(ii) *Loss subgroup.*—A loss subgroup has an ownership change if the loss subgroup parent has an ownership change under section 382 and the regulations thereunder. The principles of § 1.1502-95(b) (relating to ceasing to be a member of a consolidated group) apply in determining whether the loss subgroup parent has an ownership change. Solely for purposes of determining whether the loss subgroup parent has an ownership change—

(A) The losses described in § 1.1502-91(d) are treated as net operating losses (or a net unrealized built-in loss) of the loss subgroup parent;

(B) The day that the members of the loss subgroup become members of the group (or a loss subgroup) is treated as a testing date within the meaning of § 1.382-2(a)(4); and

(C) The loss subgroup parent determines the earliest day that its testing period can begin under § 1.382-2T(d)(3) by reference to only the attributes that make the members a loss subgroup under § 1.1502-91(d).

(iii) *Special rule if election regarding section 1504(a)(1) relationship is made.*—(A) *Ownership change of deemed loss subgroup parent is an ownership change of loss subgroup.*—If the common parent makes an election under § 1.1502-91(d)(4), each of the members in the loss subgroup is treated as the loss subgroup parent for purposes of determining whether the loss subgroup has an ownership change under section 382 and the regulations thereunder on or after the day the members become members of the group.

(B) *Exception.*—Paragraph (b)(1)(iii)(A) of this section does not apply to cause an ownership change of a loss subgroup if a deemed loss subgroup parent has an ownership change upon (or after) ceasing to be a member of the current group.

(2) *Examples.*—The following examples illustrate the principles of this paragraph (b):

Example 1. Loss group—ownership change of the common parent. (i) A owns all the L stock. L owns 80 percent and B owns 20 percent of the L1 stock. For Year 1, the L group has a consolidated net operating loss that resulted from the operations of L1 and that is carried over to Year 2. The value of the L stock is $1000. The total value of the L1 stock is $600 and the value of the L1 stock held by B is $120. The L group is a loss group under § 1.1502-91(c)(1) because it is entitled to use its net operating loss carryover from Year 1.

On August 15, Year 2, A sells 51 percent of the L stock to C. The following is a graphic illustration of these facts:

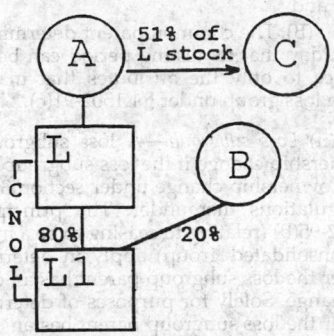

(ii) Under paragraph (b)(1)(i) of this section, section 382 and the regulations thereunder are applied to L to determine whether it (and therefore the L loss group) has an ownership change with respect to its net operating loss carryover from Year 1 attributable to L1 on August 15, Year 2. The sale of the L stock to C causes an ownership change of L under § 1.382-2T and of the L loss group under paragraph (b)(1)(i) of this section. The amount of consolidated taxable income of the L loss group for any post-change taxable year that may be offset by its pre-change consolidated attributes (that is, the net operating loss carryover from Year 1 attributable to L1) may not exceed the consolidated section 382 limitation for the L loss group for the taxable year.

Example 2. Loss group—owner shifts of subsidiaries disregarded. (i) The facts are the same as in *Example 1*, except that on August 15, Year 2, A sells only 49 percent of the L stock to C and, on December 12, Year 3, in an unrelated transaction, B sells the 20 percent of the L1 stock to D. A's sale of the L stock to C does not cause an ownership change of L under § 1.382-2T nor of the L

loss group under paragraph (b)(1)(i) of this section. The following is a graphic illustration of these facts:

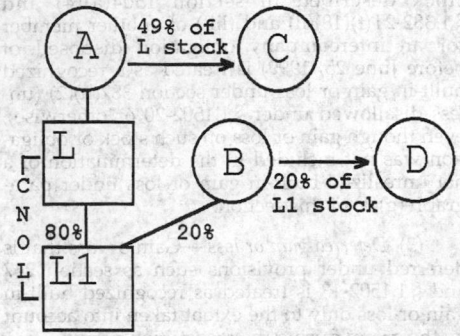

(ii) B's subsequent sale of L1 stock is not taken into account for purposes of determining whether the L loss group has an ownership change under paragraph (b)(1)(i) of this section, and, accordingly, there is no ownership change of the L loss group. See paragraph (c) of this section, however, for a supplemental ownership change method that would apply to cause an ownership change if the purchases by C and D were pursuant to a plan or arrangement and certain other conditions are satisfied.

Example 3. Loss subgroup—ownership change of loss subgroup parent controls. (i) P owns all the L stock. L owns 80 percent and A owns 20 percent of the L1 stock. The P group has a consolidated net operating loss arising in Year 1 that is carried over to Year 2. On September 9, Year 2, P sells 51 percent of the L stock to B, and L1 is apportioned a portion of the Year 1 consolidated net operating loss under § 1.1502-21(b), which it carries over to its next taxable year. L and L1 file a consolidated return for their first taxable year ending after the sale to B. The following is a graphic illustration of these facts:

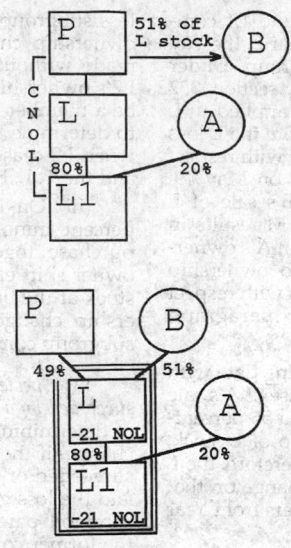

(ii) Under § 1.1502-91(d)(1), L and L1 compose a loss subgroup on September 9, Year 2, the day that they become members of the L group. Under paragraph (b)(1)(ii) of this section, section 382 and the regulations thereunder are applied to L to determine whether it (and therefore the L loss subgroup) has an ownership change with respect to the portion of the Year 1 consolidated net operating loss that is apportioned to L1 on September 9, Year 2. L has an ownership change resulting from P's sale of 51 percent of the L stock to A. Therefore, the L loss subgroup has an ownership change with respect to that loss.

Example 4. Loss group and loss subgroup—contemporaneous ownership changes. (i) A owns all

the stock of corporation M, M owns 35 percent and B owns 65 percent of the L stock, and L owns all the L1 stock. The L group has a consolidated net operating loss arising in Year 1 that is carried over to Year 2. On May 19, Year 2, B sells 45 percent of the L stock to M for cash. M, L, and L1 thereafter file consolidated returns. L and L1 are each apportioned a portion of the Year 1 consolidated net operating loss, which they carry over to the M group's Year 2 and Year 3 consolidated return years. The M group has a consolidated net operating loss arising in Year 2 that is carried over to Year 3. On June 9, Year 3, A sells 70 percent of the M stock to C. The following is a graphic illustration of these facts:

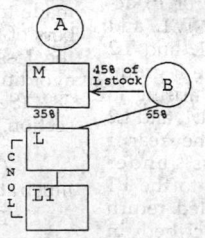

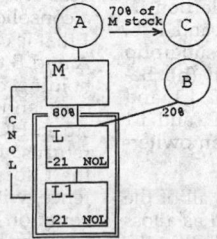

(ii) Under § 1.1502-91(d)(1), L and L1 compose a loss subgroup on May 19, Year 2, the day they become members of the M group. Under paragraph (b)(1)(ii) of this section, section 382 and the regulations thereunder are applied to L to determine whether L (and therefore the L loss subgroup) has an ownership change with respect to the loss carryovers from Year 1 on May 19, Year 2, a testing date because of B's sale of L stock to M. The sale of L stock to M results in only a 45 percentage point increase in A's ownership of L stock. Thus, there is no ownership change of L (or the L loss subgroup) with respect to those loss carryovers under paragraph (b)(1)(ii) of this section on that day.

(iii) June 9, Year 3, is also a testing date with respect to the L loss subgroup because of A's sale of M stock to C. The sale results in a 56 percentage point increase in C's ownership of L stock, and L has an ownership change. Therefore, the L loss subgroup has an ownership change on that day with respect to the loss carryovers from Year 1.

(iv) Paragraph (b)(1)(i) of this section requires that section 382 and the regulations thereunder be applied to M to determine whether M (and therefore the M loss group) has an ownership change with respect to the net operating loss carryover from Year 2 on June 9, Year 3, a testing date because of A's sale of M stock to C. The sale results in a 70 percentage point increase in C's ownership of M stock, and M has an ownership change. Therefore, the M loss group has an ownership change on that day with respect to that loss carryover.

Example 5—Deemed subgroup parent. (i) P owns all the stock of L and L1 and 80 percent of the stock of T. A owns the remaining 20 percent of the stock of T. L1 owns all the stock of L2. P1, which owns 60 percent of the stock of P, acquires, at the beginning of Year 2, the T, L, and L1 stock owned by P, and T, L, L1, and L2 become members of the P1 group. The P group has a consolidated net operating loss arising in Year 1 that is carried over to Year 2. L, L1, L2 are each apportioned a portion of the Year 1 consolidated net operating loss under § 1.1502-21(b), which they carry over to the P1 group's Year 2 and Year 3 consolidated return years. P1 makes the election described in § 1.1502-91(d)(4) to treat T, L, L1 and L2 as meeting the section 1504(a)(1) requirement of § 1.1502-91(d)(1)(ii). As a result of the election, T, L, L1 and L2 compose a loss subgroup and T, L, L1, and L2 are each treated as the loss subgroup parent for purposes of this paragraph (b). Because of P1's indirect ownership of T, L, L1, and L2 prior to P1's acquisition of the T, L, and L1 stock, P1's acquisition does not cause an ownership change of the loss subgroup.

(ii) On February 2, Year 3, L1 sells all of the stock of L2 to B. Although L2 is treated as a loss subgroup parent, the determination whether the loss subgroup comprised of T, L, and L1 has an ownership change under this paragraph (b) is made without regard to the sale of L2 because L2's ownership change occurred upon ceasing to be a member of the P1 group. See § 1.1502-95(b) to determine the application of section 382 to L2 when L2 ceases to be a member of the P1 group and the T, L, L1 and L2 loss subgroup.

(iii) On March 26, Year 3, A sells her 20 percent minority stock interest in T to C. C's purchase, together with the 32 percentage point owner shift effected by P1's acquisition of the T stock at the beginning of Year 2, causes an ownership change of T, and therefore of the loss subgroup comprised of T, L, and L1.

(3) *Special adjustments.*—(i) *Common parent succeeded by a new common parent.*—For purposes of determining if a loss group has an ownership change, if the common parent of a loss group is succeeded or acquired by a new common parent and the loss group remains in existence, the new common parent is treated as a continuation of the former common parent with appropriate adjustments to take into account shifts in ownership of the former common parent during the testing period (including shifts that occur incident to the common parent's becoming the former common parent). A new common parent may be a continuation of the former common parent even if, under § 1.1502-91(g)(2)(ii), the new common parent is not included in determining whether the group has a net unrealized built-in loss.

(ii) *Newly created loss subgroup parent.*— For purposes of determining if a loss subgroup has an ownership change, if the member that is the loss subgroup parent has not been the loss subgroup parent for at least 3 years as of a testing date, appropriate adjustments must be made to take into account owner shifts of members of the loss subgroup so that the structure of the loss subgroup does not have the effect of avoiding an ownership change under section 382. (See paragraph (b)(3)(iii), *Example 3* of this section.)

(iii) *Examples.*—The following examples illustrate the principles of this paragraph (b)(3):

Example 1. New common parent acquires old common parent. (i) A, who owns all the L stock, sells 30 percent of the L stock to B on August 26, Year 1. L owns all the L1 stock. The L group has a consolidated net operating loss arising in Year 1 that is carried over to Year 3. On July 16, Year 2, A and B transfer their L stock to a newly created holding company, HC, in exchange for 70 percent and 30 percent, respectively, of the HC stock. HC, L, and L1 thereafter file consolidated returns. Under the principles of § 1.1502-75(d), the L loss group is treated as remaining in existence, with HC taking the place of L as the new common parent of the loss group. The following is a graphic illustration of these facts:

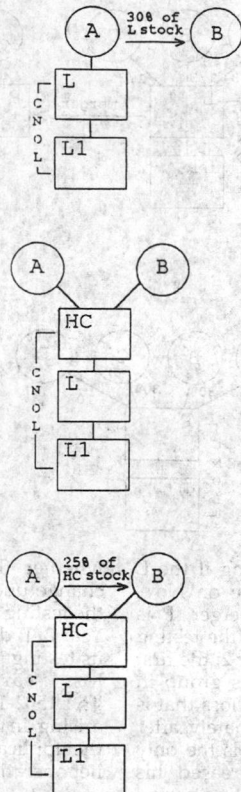

(ii) On November 11, Year 3, A sells 25 percent of the HC stock to B. For purposes of determining if the L loss group has an ownership change under paragraph (b)(1)(i) of this section on November 11, Year 3, HC is treated as a continuation of L under paragraph (b)(4)(i) of this section because it acquired L and became the common parent without terminating the L loss group. Accordingly, HC's testing period commences on January 1, Year 1, the first day of the taxable year of the L loss group in which the consolidated net operating loss that is carried over to Year 3 arose (see § 1.382-2T(d)(3)(i)). Immediately after the close of November 11, Year 3, B's percentage ownership interest in the common parent of the loss group (HC) has increased by 55 percentage points over its lowest percentage ownership during the testing period (zero percent). Accordingly, HC and the L loss group have an ownership change on that day.

Example 2. New common parent in case in which common parent ceases to exist. (i) A, B, and C each own one-third of the L stock. L owns all the L1 stock. The L group has a consolidated net operating loss arising in Year 2 that is carried over to Year 3. On November 22, Year 3, L is merged into P, a corporation owned by D, and L1 thereafter files consolidated returns with P. A, B, and C, as a result of owning stock of L, own 90 percent of P's stock after the merger. D owns the remaining 10 percent of P's stock. The merger of L into P qualifies as a reverse acquisition of the L group under § 1.1502-75(d)(3)(i), and the L loss group is treated as remaining in existence, with P taking the place of L as the new common parent of the L group. The following is a graphic illustration of these facts:

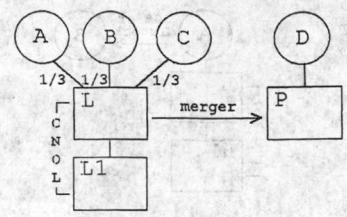

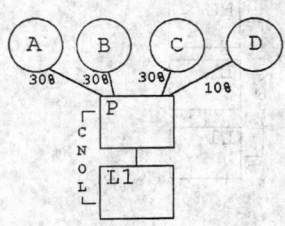

(ii) For purposes of determining if the L loss group has an ownership change on November 22, Year 3, the day of the merger, P is treated as a continuation of L so that the testing period for P begins on January 1, Year 2, the first day of the taxable year of the L loss group in which the consolidated net operating loss that is carried over to Year 3 arose. Immediately after the close of November 22, Year 3, D is the only 5-percent shareholder that has increased his ownership interest in P during the testing period (from zero to 10 percentage points).

(iii) The facts are the same as in paragraph (i) of this *Example 2*, except that A has held 23 $^1/_3$ shares (23 $^1/_3$ percent) of L's stock for five years, and A purchased an additional 10 shares of L stock from E two years before the merger. Immediately after the close of the day of the merger (a testing date), A's ownership interest in P, the common parent of the L loss group, has increased by 6 $^2/_3$ percentage points over A's lowest percentage ownership during the testing period (23 $^1/_3$ percent to 30 percent).

(iv) The facts are the same as in (i) of this *Example 2*, except that P has a net operating loss arising in Year 1 that is carried to the first consolidated return year ending after the day of the merger. Solely for purposes of determining

whether the L loss group has an ownership change under paragraph (b)(1)(i) of this section, the testing period for P commences on January 1, Year 2. P does not determine the earliest day for its testing period by reference to its net operating loss carryover from Year 1, which §§ 1.1502-1(f)(3) and 1.1502-75(d)(3)(i) treat as arising in a SRLY. See § 1.1502-94 to determine the application of section 382 with respect to P's net operating loss carryover.

Example 3. Newly acquired loss subgroup parent. (i) P owns all the L stock and L owns all the L1 stock. The P group has a consolidated net operating loss arising in Year 1 that is carried over to Year 3. On January 19, Year 2, L issues a 20 percent stock interest to B. On February 5, Year 3, P contributes its L stock to a newly formed subsidiary, HC, in exchange for all the HC stock, and distributes the HC stock to its sole shareholder A. HC, L, and L1 thereafter file consolidated returns. A portion of the P group's Year 1 consolidated net operating loss is apportioned to L and L1 under § 1.1502-21(b) and is carried over to the HC group's year ending after February 5, Year 3. HC, L, and L1 compose a loss subgroup within the meaning of § 1.1502-91(d) with respect to the net operating loss carryovers from Year 1. The following is a graphic illustration of these facts:

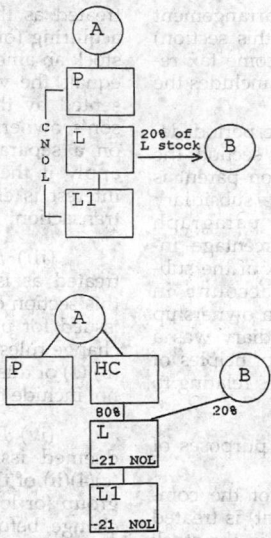

(ii) February 5, Year 3, is a testing date for HC as the loss subgroup parent with respect to the net operating loss carryovers of L and L1 from Year 1. See paragraph (b)(1)(ii)(B) of this section. For purposes of determining whether HC has an ownership change on the testing date, appropriate adjustments must be made with respect to the changes in the percentage ownership of the stock of HC because HC was not the loss subgroup parent for at least 3 years prior to the day on which it became a member of the HC loss subgroup (a testing date). The appropriate adjustments include adjustments so that HC succeeds to the owner shifts of other members of the former group. Thus, HC succeeds to the owner shift of L that resulted from the sale of the 20 percent interest to B in determining whether the HC loss subgroup has an ownership change on February 5, Year 3, and on any subsequent testing date that includes January 19, Year 2.

(4) *End of separate tracking of certain losses.*— If § 1.1502-96(a) (relating to the end of separate tracking of attributes) applies to a loss subgroup, then, while one or more members that were included in the loss subgroup remain members of the consolidated group, there is an ownership change with respect to their attributes described in § 1.1502-96(a)(2) only if the consolidated group is a loss group and has an ownership change under paragraph (b)(1)(i) of this section (or such a member has an ownership change under § 1.1502-96(b) (relating to ownership changes of subsidiaries)). If, however, the loss subgroup has had an ownership change before § 1.1502-96(a) applies, see § 1.1502-96(c) for the continuing application of the subgroup's section 382 limitation with respect to its pre-change subgroup attributes.

(c) *Supplemental rules for determining ownership change.*—(1) *Scope.*—This paragraph (c) contains a supplemental rule for determining whether there is an ownership change of a loss group (or loss subgroup). It applies in addition to, and not instead of, the rules of paragraph (b) of this section. Thus, for example, if the common parent of the loss group has an ownership change under paragraph (b) of this section, the loss group has an ownership change even if, by applying this paragraph (c), the common parent would not have an ownership change. This paragraph (c) does not apply in determining an ownership change of a loss subgroup for which an election under § 1.1502-91(d)(4) is made.

(2) *Cause for applying supplemental rule.*— This paragraph (c) applies to a loss group (or loss subgroup) if—

(i) Any 5-percent shareholder of the common parent (or loss subgroup parent) increases its percentage ownership interest in the stock of both—

(A) A subsidiary of the loss group (or loss subgroup) other than by a direct or indirect acquisition of stock of the common parent (or loss subgroup parent); and

(B) The common parent (or loss subgroup parent);

(ii) Those increases occur within a 3 year period ending on any day of a consolidated return year or, if shorter, the period beginning on the first day following the most recent ownership change of the loss group (or loss subgroup); and

(iii) Either—

(A) The common parent (or loss subgroup parent) has actual knowledge of the increase in the 5-percent shareholder's ownership interest in the stock of the subsidiary (or has

Reg. § 1.1502-92(c)(2)(iii)(A)

actual knowledge of the plan or arrangement described in paragraph (c)(3)(i) of this section) before the date that the group's income tax return is filed for the taxable year that includes the date of that increase; or

(B) At any time during the period described in paragraph (c)(2)(ii) of this section, the 5-percent shareholder of the common parent is also a 5-percent shareholder of the subsidiary (determined without regard to paragraph (c)(3)(i) of this section) whose percentage increase in the ownership of the stock of the subsidiary would be taken into account in determining if the subsidiary has an ownership change (determined as if the subsidiary was a loss corporation and applying the principles of § 1.382-2T(k), including the principles relating to duty to inquire).

(3) *Operating rules.*—Solely for purposes of this paragraph (c)—

(i) A 5-percent shareholder of the common parent (or loss subgroup, parent) is treated as increasing its ownership interest in the stock of a subsidiary to the extent, if any, that another person or persons increases its percentage ownership interest in the stock of a subsidiary pursuant to a plan or arrangement under which the 5-percent shareholder increases its percentage ownership interest in the common parent (or loss subgroup parent);

(ii) The rules in section 382(l)(3) and §§ 1.382-2T(h) and 1.382-4(d) (relating to constructive ownership) apply with respect to the stock of the subsidiary by treating such stock as stock of a loss corporation; and

(iii) In the case of a loss subgroup, a subsidiary includes any member of the loss subgroup other than the loss subgroup parent. (A loss subgroup parent is, however, a subsidiary of the loss group of which it is a member.)

(4) *Supplemental ownership change rules.*— The determination whether the common parent (or loss subgroup parent) has an ownership change is made by applying paragraph (b)(1) of this section as modified by the following additional rules:

(i) *Additional testing dates for the common parent (or loss subgroup parent).*—A testing date for the common parent (or loss subgroup parent) also includes—

(A) Each day on which there is an increase in the percentage ownership of stock of a subsidiary as described in paragraph (c)(2) of this section; and

(B) The first day of the first consolidated return year for which the group is a loss group (or the members compose a loss subgroup).

(ii) *Treatment of subsidiary stock as stock of the common parent (or loss subgroup parent).*—The common parent (or loss subgroup parent) is

treated as though it had issued to the person acquiring (or deemed to acquire) the subsidiary stock an amount of its own stock (by value) that equals the value of the subsidiary stock represented by the percentage increase in that person's ownership of the subsidiary (determined on a separate entity basis). Similar principles apply if the increase in percentage ownership interest is effected by a redemption or similar transaction.

(iii) *Different testing periods.*—Stock treated as issued under paragraph (c)(4)(ii) of this section on a testing date is not treated as so issued for purposes of applying the ownership change rules of this paragraph (c) and paragraph (b) (1) of this section in a testing period that does not include that testing date.

(iv) *Disaffiliation of a subsidiary.*—If a deemed issuance of stock under paragraph (c)(4)(ii) of this section would not cause the loss group (or loss subgroup) to have an ownership change before the day (if any) on which the subsidiary ceases to be a member of the loss group (or subgroup), then paragraph (c)(4) of this section shall not apply.

(v) *Subsidiary stock acquired first.*—If an increase of subsidiary stock described in paragraph (c)(2)(i)(A) of this section occurs before the date that the 5-percent shareholder increases its percentage ownership interest in the stock of the common parent (or loss subgroup parent), then the deemed issuance of stock is treated as occurring on that later date, but in an amount equal to the value of the subsidiary stock on the date it was acquired.

(vi) *Anti-duplication rule.*—If two or more 5-percent shareholders are treated as increasing their percentage ownership interests pursuant to the same plan or arrangement described in paragraph (c)(3)(i) of this section, appropriate adjustments must be made so that the amount of stock treated as issued is not taken into account more than once.

(5) *Examples.*—The following examples illustrate the principles of this paragraph (c):

Example 1. Stock of the common parent under supplemental rules. (i) A owns all the L stock. L is not a member of an affiliated group and has a net operating loss carryover arising in Year 1 that is carried over to Year 6. On September 20, Year 6, L transfers all of its assets and liabilities to a newly created subsidiary, S, in exchange for S stock. L and S thereafter file consolidated returns. On November 23, Year 6, B contributes cash to L in exchange for a 45 percent ownership interest in L and contributes cash to S for a 20 percent ownership interest in S.

(ii) During the 3 year period ending on November 23, Year 6, B is a 5% shareholder of L and of S that increases its ownership interest in L and S during that period. Under paragraph (c)(4)(ii) of this section, the determination whether L (the common parent of a loss group) has an ownership change on November 23, Year 6 (or, subject to paragraph (c)(4)(iv) of this section, on any testing date in the testing period which includes November 23, Year 6), is made by applying paragraph (b)(1)(i) of this section and by treating the value of B's 20 percent ownership interest in S as if it were L stock issued to B. Because B is a 5% shareholder of both L and S during the 3 year period ending on November 23, Year 6, and B's increase in its percentage ownership in the stock of S would be taken into account in determining if S (if it were a loss corporation) had an owner-

ship change, it is not relevant whether L has actual knowledge of B's acquisition of S stock.

Example 2. Plan or arrangement—public offering of subsidiary stock. (i) A owns all the stock of L and L owns all the stock of L1. The L group has a consolidated net operating loss arising in Year 1 that resulted from the operations of L1 and that is carried over to Year 2. On October 7, Year 2, A sells 49 percent of the L stock to B. As part of a plan that includes the sale of L stock, A causes a public offering of L1 stock on November 6, Year 2. L has actual knowledge of the plan. The following is a graphic illustration of these facts:

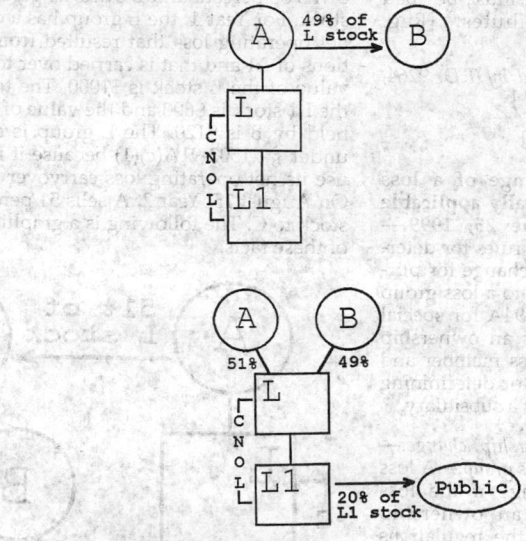

(ii) A's sale of the L stock to B does not cause an ownership change of the L loss group on October 7, Year 2, under the rules of § 1.382-2T and paragraph (b)(1)(i) of this section.

(iii) Because the issuance of L1 stock to the public occurs as part of the same plan as B's acquisition of L stock, and L has knowledge of the plan, paragraph (c)(4) of this section applies to determine whether the L loss group has an ownership change on November 6, Year 2 (or, subject to paragraph (c)(4)(iv) of this section, on any testing date for which the testing period includes November 6, Year 2).

(d) *Testing period following ownership change under this section.*—If a loss group (or a loss subgroup) has had an ownership change under this section, the testing period for determining a subsequent ownership change with respect to prechange consolidated attributes (or pre-change subgroup attributes) begins no earlier than the first day following the loss group's (or loss subgroup's) most recent change date.

(e) *Information statements.*—(1) *Common parent of a loss group.*—The common parent of a loss

group must file the information statement required by § 1.382-11(a) for a consolidated return year because of any owner shift, equity structure shift, or other transaction described in § 1.382-2T(a)(2)(i)—

(i) With respect to the common parent and with respect to any subsidiary stock subject to paragraph (c) of this section; and

(ii) With respect to an ownership change described in § 1.1502-96(b) (relating to ownership changes of subsidiaries).

(2) *Abbreviated statement with respect to loss subgroups.*—The common parent of a consolidated group that has a loss subgroup during a consolidated return year must file the information statement required by § 1.382-11(a) because of any owner shift, equity structure shift, or other transaction described in § 1.382-2T(a)(2)(i) with respect to the loss subgroup parent and with respect to any subsidiary stock subject to paragraph (c) of this section. Instead of filing a separate statement for each loss subgroup parent, the common parent (which is treated as a loss corporation) may file the single statement described in paragraph (e)(1) of this section. In

addition to the information concerning stock ownership of the common parent, the single statement must identify each loss subgroup parent and state which loss subgroups, if any, have had ownership changes during the consolidated return year. The loss subgroup parent is, however, still required to maintain the records necessary to determine if the loss subgroup has an ownership change. This paragraph (e)(2) applies with respect to the attributes of a loss subgroup until, under §1.1502-96(a), the attributes are no longer treated as described in §1.1502-91(d) (relating to the definition of loss subgroup). After that time, the information statement described in paragraph (e)(1) of this section must be filed with respect to those attributes. [Reg. §1.1502-92.]

☐ [*T.D. 8824, 6-25-99. Amended by T.D. 9264, 5-26-2006 and T.D. 9329, 6-13-2007.*]

[Reg. §1.1502-92A]

§1.1502-92A. Ownership change of a loss group or a loss subgroup generally applicable for testing dates before June 25, 1999.— (a) *Scope.*—This section provides rules for determining if there is an ownership change for purposes of section 382 with respect to a loss group or a loss subgroup. See §1.1502-94A for special rules for determining if there is an ownership change with respect to a new loss member and §1.1502-96A(b) for special rules for determining if there is an ownership change of a subsidiary.

(b) *Determination of an ownership change.*— (1) *Parent change method.*—(i) *Loss group.*—A loss group has an ownership change if the loss group's common parent has an ownership change under section 382 and the regulations thereunder. Solely for purposes of determining whether the common parent has an ownership change—

(A) The losses described in §1.1502-91A(c) are treated as net operating losses (or a net unrealized built-in loss) of the common parent; and

(B) The common parent determines the earliest day that its testing period can begin by reference to only the attributes that make the group a loss group under §1.1502-91A(c).

(ii) *Loss subgroup.*—A loss subgroup has an ownership change if the loss subgroup parent has an ownership change under section 382 and the regulations thereunder. The principles of §1.1502-95A(b) (relating to ceasing to be a member of a consolidated group) apply in determining whether the loss subgroup parent has an ownership change. Solely for purposes of determining whether the loss subgroup parent has an ownership change—

(A) The losses described in §1.1502-91A(d) are treated as net operating losses (or a net unrealized built-in loss) of the loss subgroup parent;

(B) The day that the members of the loss subgroup become members of the group (or a loss subgroup) is treated as a testing date within the meaning of §1.382-2(a)(4); and

(C) The loss subgroup parent determines the earliest day that its testing period can begin under §1.382-2T(d)(3) by reference to only the attributes that make the members a loss subgroup under §1.1502-91A(d).

(2) *Examples.*—The following examples illustrate the principles of this paragraph (b).

Example 1. Loss group—ownership change of the common parent. (a) A owns all the L stock. L owns 80 percent and B owns 20 percent of the L1 stock. For Year 1, the L group has a consolidated net operating loss that resulted from the operations of L1 and that is carried over to Year 2. The value of the L stock is $1000. The total value of the L1 stock is $600 and the value of the L1 stock held by B is $120. The L group is a loss group under §1.1502-91A(c)(1) because it is entitled to use its net operating loss carryover from Year 1. On August 15, Year 2, A sells 51 percent of the L stock to C. The following is a graphic illustration of these facts:

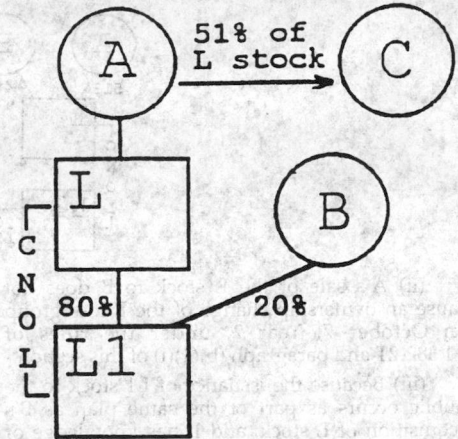

(b) Under paragraph (b)(1)(i) of this section, section 382 and the regulations thereunder are applied to L to determine whether it (and therefore the L loss group) has an ownership change with respect to its net operating loss carryover from Year 1 attributable to L1 on August 15, Year 2. The sale of the L stock to C causes an ownership change of L under §1.382-2T and of the L loss group under paragraph (b)(1)(i) of this section. The amount of consolidated taxable income of the L loss group for any post-change taxable year that may be offset by its pre-change consolidated attributes (that is, the net operating loss carryover from Year 1 attributable to L1) may not exceed the consolidated section 382 limitation for the L loss group for the taxable year.

Example 2. Loss group—owner shifts of subsidiaries disregarded. (a) The facts are the same as in

Example 1, except that on August 15, Year 2, A sells only 49 percent of the L stock to C and, on December 12, Year 3, in an unrelated transaction, B sells the 20 percent of the L1 stock to D. A's sale of the L stock to C does not cause an ownership change of L under §1.382-2T nor of the L loss group under paragraph (b)(1)(i) of this section. The following is a graphic illustration of these facts:

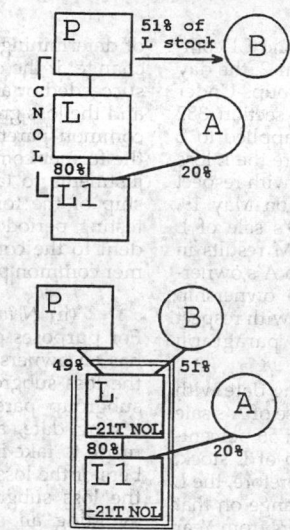

(b) Under §1.1502-91A(d)(1), L and L1 compose a loss subgroup on September 9, Year 2, the day that they become members of the L group. Under paragraph (b)(1)(ii) of this section, section 382 and the regulations thereunder are applied to L to determine whether it (and therefore the L loss subgroup) has an ownership change with respect to the portion of the Year 1 consolidated net operating loss that is apportioned to L1 on September 9, Year 2. L has an ownership change resulting from P's sale of 51 percent of the L stock to A. Therefore, the L loss subgroup has an ownership change with respect to that loss.

(b) B's subsequent sale of L1 stock is not taken into account for purposes of determining whether the L loss group has an ownership change under paragraph (b)(1)(i) of this section, and, accordingly, there is no ownership change of the L loss group. See paragraph (c) of this section, however, for a supplemental ownership change method that would apply to cause an ownership change if the purchases by C and D were pursuant to a plan or arrangement.

Example 3. Loss subgroup—ownership change of loss subgroup parent controls. (a) P owns all the L stock. L owns 80 percent and A owns 20 percent of the L1 stock. The P group has a consolidated net operating loss arising in Year 1 that is carried over to Year 2. On September 9, Year 2, P sells 51 percent of the L stock to B, and L1 is apportioned a portion of the Year 1 consolidated net operating loss under §1.1502-21(b) or 1.1502-21T(b) in effect prior to June 25, 1999, as contained in 26 CFR part 1 revised April 1, 1999, as applicable, which it carries over to its next taxable year. L and L1 file a consolidated return for their first taxable year ending after the sale to B. The following is a graphic illustration of these facts:

Example 4. Loss group and loss subgroup— contemporaneous ownership changes. (a) A owns all the stock of corporation M, M owns 35 percent and B owns 65 percent of the L stock, and L owns all the L1 stock. The L group has a consolidated net operating loss arising in Year 1 that is carried over to Year 2. On May 19, Year 2, B sells 45 percent of the L stock to M for cash. M, L, and L1 thereafter file consolidated returns. L and L1 are each apportioned a portion of the Year 1 consolidated net operating loss, which they carry over to the M group's Year 2 and Year 3 consolidated return years. The M group has a consolidated net operating loss arising in Year 2 that is carried over to Year 3. On June 9, Year 3, A sells

70 percent of the M stock to C. The following is a graphic illustration of these facts:

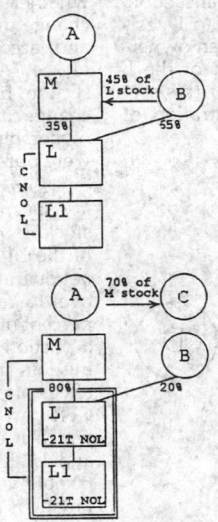

(b) Under § 1.1502-91A(d)(1), L and L1 compose a loss subgroup on May 19, Year 2, the day they become members of the M group. Under paragraph (b)(1)(ii) of this section, section 382 and the regulations thereunder are applied to L to determine whether L (and therefore the L loss subgroup) has an ownership change with respect to the loss carryovers from Year 1 on May 19, Year 2, a testing date because of B's sale of L stock to M. The sale of L stock to M results in only a 45 percentage point increase in A's ownership of L stock. Thus, there is no ownership change of L (or the L loss subgroup) with respect to those loss carryovers under paragraph (b)(1)(ii) of this section on that day.

(c) June 9, Year 3, is also a testing date with respect to the L loss subgroup because of A's sale of M stock to C. The sale results in a 56 percentage point increase in C's ownership of L stock, and L has an ownership change. Therefore, the L loss subgroup has an ownership change on that day with respect to the loss carryovers from Year 1.

(d) Paragraph (b)(1)(i) of this section requires that section 382 and the regulations thereunder be applied to M to determine whether M (and therefore the M loss group) has an ownership change with respect to the net operating loss carryover from Year 2 on June 9, Year 3, a testing date because of A's sale of M stock to C. The sale results in a 70 percentage point increase in C's ownership of M stock, and M has an ownership change. Therefore, the M loss group has an ownership change on that day with respect to that loss carryover.

(3) *Special adjustments.*—(i) *Common parent succeeded by a new common parent.*—For purposes

of determining if a loss group has an ownership change, if the common parent of a loss group is succeeded or acquired by a new common parent and the loss group remains in existence, the new common parent is treated as a continuation of the former common parent with appropriate adjustments to take into account shifts in ownership of the former common parent during the testing period (including shifts that occur incident to the common parent's becoming the former common parent).

(ii) *Newly created loss subgroup parent.*—For purposes of determining if a loss subgroup has an ownership change, if the member that is the loss subgroup parent has not been the loss subgroup parent for at least 3 years as of a testing date, appropriate adjustments must be made to take into account owner shifts of members of the loss subgroup so that the structure of the loss subgroup does not have the effect of avoiding an ownership change under section 382. (See paragraph (b)(3)(iii) *Example 3* of this section.)

(iii) *Examples.*—The following examples illustrate the principles of this paragraph (b)(3).

Example 1. New common parent acquires old common parent. (a) A, who owns all the L stock, sells 30 percent of the L stock to B on August 26, Year 1. L owns all the L1 stock. The L group has a consolidated net operating loss arising in Year 1 that is carried over to Year 3. On July 16, Year 2, A and B transfer their L stock to a newly created holding company, HC, in exchange for 70 percent and 30 percent, respectively, of the HC stock. HC, L, and L1 thereafter file consolidated returns. Under the principles of § 1.1502-75(d), the L loss group is treated as remaining in existence, with HC taking the place of L as the new

common parent of the loss group. The following is a graphic illustration of these facts:

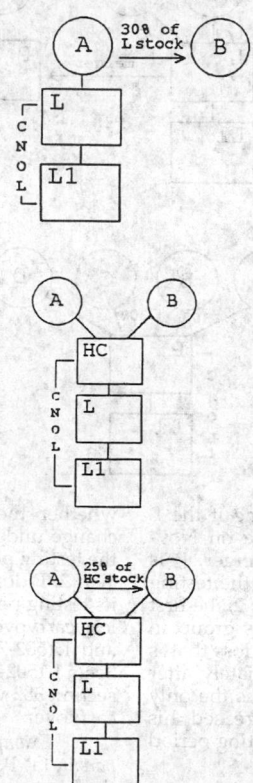

(b) On November 11, Year 3, A sells 25 percent of the HC stock to B. For purposes of determining if the L loss group has an ownership change under paragraph (b)(1)(i) of this section on November 11, Year 3, HC is treated as a continuation of L under paragraph (b)(3)(i) of this section because it acquired L and became the common parent without terminating the L loss group. Accordingly, HC's testing period commences on January 1, Year 1, the first day of the taxable year of the L loss group in which the consolidated net operating loss that is carried over to Year 3 arose (see § 1.382-2T(d)(3)(i)). Immediately after the close of November 11, Year 3, B's percentage ownership interest in the common parent of the loss group (HC) has increased by 55 percentage points over its lowest percentage ownership during the testing period (zero

percent). Accordingly, HC and the L loss group have an ownership change on that day.

Example 2. New common parent in case in which common parent ceases to exist. (a) A, B, and C each own one-third of the L1 stock. L owns all the L1 stock. The L group has a consolidated net operating loss arising in Year 2 that is carried over to Year 3. On November 22, Year 3, L is merged into P, a corporation owned by D, and L1 thereafter files consolidated returns with P. A, B, and C, as a result of owning stock of L, own 90 percent of P's stock after the merger. D owns the remaining 10 percent of P's stock. The merger of L into P qualifies as a reverse acquisition of the L group under § 1.1502-75(d)(3)(i), and the L loss group is treated as remaining in existence, with P taking the place of L as the new common parent of the L group. The following is a graphic illustration of these facts:

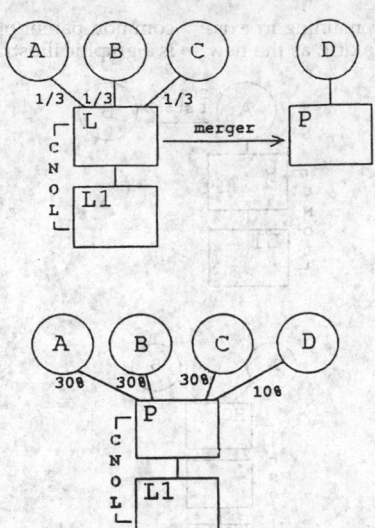

(b) For purposes of determining if the L loss group has an ownership change on November 22, Year 3, the day of the merger, P is treated as a continuation of L so that the testing period for P begins on January 2, the first day of the taxable year of the L loss group in which the consolidated net operating loss that is carried over to Year 3 arose. Immediately after the close of November 22, Year 3, D is the only 5-percent shareholder that has increased his ownership interest in P during the testing period (from zero to 10 percentage points).

(c) The facts are the same as in paragraph (a) of this *Example* 2, except that A has held $23^1/3$ shares ($23^1/3$ percent) of L's stock for five years, and A purchased an additional 10 shares of L stock from E two years before the merger. Immediately after the close of the day of the merger (a testing date), A's ownership interest in P, the common parent of the L loss group, has increased by $6^2/3$ percentage points over her lowest percentage ownership during the testing period ($23^1/3$ percent to 30 percent).

(d) The facts are the same as in (a) of this *Example* 2, except that P has a net operating loss arising in Year 1 that is carried to the first consolidated return year ending after the day of the merger. Solely for purposes of determining

whether the L loss group has an ownership change under paragraph (b)(1)(i) of this section, the testing period for P commences on January 1, Year 2. P does not determine the earliest day for its testing period by reference to its net operating loss carryover from Year 1, which §§ 1502-1(f)(3) and 1.1502-75(d)(3)(i) treat as arising in a SRLY. See § 1.1502-94A to determine the application of section 382 with respect to P's net operating loss carryover.

Example 3. Newly acquired loss subgroup parent. (a) P owns all the L stock and L owns all the L1 stock. The P group has a consolidated net operating loss arising in Year 1 that is carried over to Year 3. On January 19, Year 2, L issues a 20 percent stock interest to B. On February 5, Year 3, P contributes its L stock to a newly formed subsidiary, HC, in exchange for all the HC stock, and distributes the HC stock to its sole shareholder A. HC, L, and L1 thereafter file consolidated returns. A portion of the P group's Year 1 consolidated net operating loss is apportioned to L and L1 under § 1.1502-21T(b) and is carried over to the HC group's year ending after February 5, Year 3. HC, L, and L1 compose a loss subgroup within the meaning of § 1.1502-91A(d) with respect to the net operating loss carryovers from Year 1. The following is a graphic illustration of these facts:

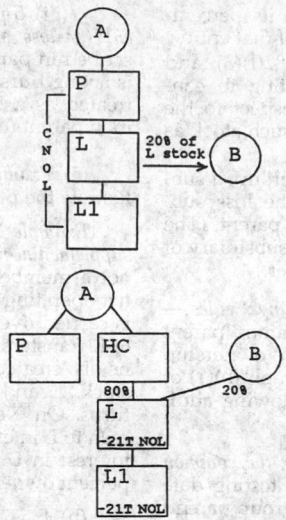

(b) February 5, Year 3, is a testing date for HC as the loss subgroup parent with respect to the net operating loss carryovers of L and L1 from Year 1. See paragraph (b)(1)(ii)(B) of this section. For purposes of determining whether HC has an ownership change on the testing date, appropriate adjustments must be made with respect to the changes in the percentage ownership of the stock of HC because HC was not the loss subgroup parent for at least 3 years prior to the day on which it became a member of the HC loss subgroup (a testing date). The appropriate adjustments include adjustments so that HC succeeds to the owner shifts of other members of the former group. Thus, HC succeeds to the owner shift of L that resulted from the sale of the 20 percent interest to B in determining whether the HC loss subgroup has an ownership change on February 5, Year 3, and on any subsequent testing date that includes January 19, Year 2.

(4) *End of separate tracking of certain losses.*— If §1.1502-96A(a) (relating to the end of separate tracking of attributes) applies to a loss subgroup, then, while one or more members that were included in the loss subgroup remain members of the consolidated group, there is an ownership change with respect to their attributes described in §1.1502-96A(a)(2) only if the consolidated group is a loss group and has an ownership change under paragraph (b)(1)(i) of this section (or such a member has an ownership change under §1.1502-96A(b) (relating to ownership changes of subsidiaries)). If, however, the loss subgroup has had an ownership change before §1.1502-96A(a) applies, see §1.1502-96A(c) for the continuing application of the subgroup's section 382 limitation with respect to its pre-change subgroup attributes.

(c) *Supplemental rules for determining ownership change.*—(1) *Scope.*—This paragraph (c) contains a supplemental rule for determining whether there is an ownership change of a loss group (or loss subgroup). It applies in addition to, and not instead of, the rules of paragraph (b) of this section. Thus, for example, if the common parent of the loss group has an ownership change under paragraph (b) of this section, the loss group has an ownership change even if, by applying this paragraph (c), the common parent would not have an ownership change.

(2) *Cause for applying supplemental rule.*— This paragraph (c) applies to a loss group (or loss subgroup) if—

(i) Any 5-percent shareholder of the common parent (or loss subgroup parent) increases its percentage ownership interest in the stock of both—

(A) A subsidiary of the loss group (or loss subgroup) other than by a direct or indirect acquisition of stock of the common parent (or loss subgroup parent); and

(B) The common parent (or loss subgroup parent); and

(ii) Those increases occur within a 3 year period ending on any day of a consolidated return year or, if shorter, the period beginning on the first day following the most recent ownership change of the loss group (or loss subgroup).

(3) *Operating rules.*—Solely for purposes of this paragraph (c)—

(i) A 5-percent shareholder of the common parent (or loss subgroup parent) is treated as increasing its percentage ownership interest in the common parent (or loss subgroup parent) or a subsidiary to the extent, if any, that any person acting pursuant to a plan or arrangement with

Reg. §1.1502-92A(c)(3)(i)

the 5-percent shareholder increases its percentage ownership interest in the stock of that entity;

(ii) The rules in section 382(l)(3) and §§ 1.382-2T(h) and 1.382-4(d) (relating to constructive ownership) apply with respect to the stock of the subsidiary by treating such stock as stock of a loss corporation; and

(iii) In the case of a loss subgroup, a subsidiary includes any member of the loss subgroup other than the loss subgroup parent. (The loss subgroup parent is, however, a subsidiary of the loss group of which it is a member.)

(4) *Supplemental ownership change rules.*— The determination whether the common parent (or loss subgroup parent) has an ownership change is made by applying paragraph (b)(1) of this section as modified by the following additional rules—

(i) *Additional testing dates for the common parent (or loss subgroup parent).*—A testing date for the common parent (or loss subgroup parent) also includes—

(A) Each day on which there is an increase in the percentage ownership of stock of a subsidiary as described in paragraph (c)(2) of this section; and

(B) The first day of the first consolidated return year for which the group is a loss group (or the members compose a loss subgroup);

(ii) *Treatment of subsidiary stock as stock of the common parent (or loss subgroup parent).*—The common parent (or loss subgroup parent) is treated as though it had issued to the person acquiring (or deemed to acquire) the subsidiary stock an amount of its own stock (by value) that equals the value of the subsidiary stock represented by the percentage increase in that person's ownership of the subsidiary (determined on a separate entity basis). A similar principle applies if the increase in percentage ownership interest is effected by a redemption or similar transaction; and

(iii) *5-percent shareholder of the common parent (or loss subgroup parent).*—Any person described in paragraph (c)(3)(i) of this section who is acting pursuant to the plan or arrangement is treated as a 5-percent shareholder of the common parent (or loss subgroup parent).

(5) *Examples.*—The following examples illustrate the principles of this paragraph (c).

Example 1. Stock of the common parent under supplemental rules. (a) A owns all the L stock. L is not a member of an affiliated group and has a net operating loss carryover arising in Year 1 that is carried over to Year 6. On September 20, Year 6, L transfers all of its assets and liabilities to a newly created subsidiary, S, in exchange for S stock. L and S thereafter file consolidated returns. On November 23, Year 6, B contributes cash to L in exchange for a 45 percent ownership interest in L and contributes cash to S for a 20 percent ownership interest in S.

(b) B is a 5-percent shareholder of L who increases his percentage ownership interest in L and S during the 3 year period ending on November 23, Year 6. Under paragraph (c)(4)(ii) of this section, the determination whether L (the common parent of a loss group) has an ownership change on November 23, Year 6 (or on any testing date in the testing period which includes November 23, Year 6), is made by applying paragraph (b)(1)(i) of this section and by treating the value of B's 20 percent ownership interest in S as if it were L stock issued to B.

Example 2. Plan or arrangement—public offering of subsidiary stock. (a) A owns all the stock of L and L owns all the stock of L1. The L group has a consolidated net operating loss arising in Year 1 that resulted from the operations of L1 and that is carried over to Year 2. As part of a plan, A sells 49 percent of the L stock to B on October 7, Year 2, and L1 issues new stock representing a 20 percent ownership interest in L1 to the public on November 6, Year 2. The following is a graphic illustration of these facts:

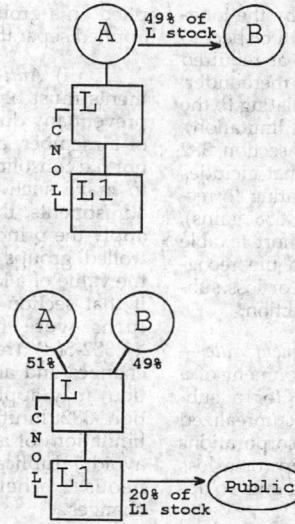

(b) A's sale of the L stock to B does not cause an ownership change of the L loss group on October 7, Year 2, under the rules of § 1.382-2T and paragraph (b)(1)(i) of this section.

(c) Because the issuance of L1 stock to the public occurs in connection with B's acquisition of L stock pursuant to a plan, paragraph (c)(4) of this section applies to determine whether the L loss group has an ownership change on November 6, Year 2 (or on any testing date for which the testing period includes November 6, Year 2).

(d) *Testing period following ownership change under this section.*—If a loss group (or a loss subgroup) has had an ownership change under this section, the testing period for determining a subsequent ownership change with respect to pre-change consolidated attributes (or pre-change subgroup attributes) begins no earlier than the first day following the loss group's (or loss subgroup's) most recent change date.

(e) *Information statements.*—(1) *Common parent of a loss group.*—The common parent of a loss group must file the information statement required by § 1.382-2T(a)(2)(ii) for a consolidated return year because of any owner shift, equity structure shift, or the issuance or transfer of an option—

(i) With respect to the common parent and with respect to any subsidiary stock subject to paragraph (c) of this section; and

(ii) With respect to an ownership change described in § 1.1502-96A(b) (relating to ownership changes of subsidiaries).

(2) *Abbreviated statement with respect to loss subgroups.*—The common parent of a consolidated group that has a loss subgroup during a consolidated return year must file the information statement required by § 1.382-2T(a)(2)(ii) be-

cause of any owner shift, equity structure shift, or issuance or transfer of an option with respect to the loss subgroup parent and with respect to any subsidiary stock subject to paragraph (c) of this section. Instead of filing a separate statement for each loss subgroup parent, the common parent (which is treated as a loss corporation) may file the single statement described in paragraph (e)(1) of this section. In addition to the information concerning stock ownership of the common parent, the single statement must identify each loss subgroup parent and state which loss subgroups, if any, have had ownership changes during the consolidated return year. The loss subgroup parent is, however, still required to maintain the records necessary to determine if the loss subgroup has an ownership change. This paragraph (e)(2) applies with respect to the attributes of a loss subgroup until, under § 1.1502-96A(a), the attributes are no longer treated as described in § 1.1502-91A(d) (relating to the definition of loss subgroup). After that time, the information statement described in paragraph (e)(1) of this section must be filed with respect to those attributes. [Reg. § 1.1502-92A.]

☐ [*T.D. 8678, 6-26-96. Amended by T.D. 8823, 6-25-99 and amended and redesignated by T.D. 8824, 6-25-99.*]

[Reg. § 1.1502-93]

§ 1.1502-93. Consolidated section 382 limitation (or subgroup section 382 limitation).—(a) *Determination of the consolidated section 382 limitation (or subgroup section 382 limitation.*—(1) *In general.*—Following an ownership change, the consolidated section 382 limitation (or subgroup section 382 limitation) for any post-change year is an amount equal to the value of the loss group (or loss subgroup), as defined in paragraph (b) of this section, multiplied by the long-term tax-exempt rate that applies with respect to the ownership change, and adjusted as required by section 382 and the regulations thereunder. See, for example, section 382(b)(2) (relating to the carryforward of unused section 382 limitation), section 382(b)(3)(B) (relating to the section 382 limitation for the post-change year that includes the change date), section 382(h) (relating to recognized built-in gains and section 338 gains), and section 382(m)(2) (relating to short taxable years). For special rules relating to the recognized built-in gains of a loss group (or loss subgroup), see paragraph (c)(2) of this section.

(2) *Coordination with apportionment rule.*— For special rules relating to apportionment of a consolidated section 382 limitation (or a subgroup section 382 limitation) or net unrealized built-in gain when one or more corporations cease to be members of a loss group (or a loss subgroup) and to aggregation of amounts so apportioned, see § 1.1502-95(c).

(b) *Value of the loss group (or loss subgroup).*— (1) *Stock value immediately before ownership change.*—Subject to any adjustment under paragraph (b)(2) of this section, the value of the loss group (or loss subgroup) is the value, immediately before the ownership change, of the stock of each member, other than stock that is owned directly or indirectly by another member. For this purpose—

(i) Ownership is determined under § 1.382-2T;

(ii) A member is considered to indirectly own stock of another member through a nonmember only if the member has a 5-percent or greater ownership interest in the nonmember; and

(iii) Stock includes stock described in section 1504(a)(4) and § 1.382-2T(f)(18)(ii) and (iii).

(2) *Adjustment to value.*—(i) *In general.*—The value of the loss group (or loss subgroup), as determined under paragraph (b)(1) of this section, is adjusted under any rule in section 382 or the regulations thereunder requiring an adjustment to such value for purposes of computing the amount of the section 382 limitation. See, for example, section 382(e)(2) (redemptions and corporate contractions), section 382(l)(1) (certain capital contributions) and section 382(l)(4) (ownership of substantial nonbusiness assets). For purposes of section 382(e)(2), redemptions and corporate contractions that do not effect a transfer of value outside of the loss group (or loss subgroup) are disregarded. For purposes of section 382(l)(1), capital contributions between members of the loss group (or loss subgroup) (or a contribution of stock to a member made solely to satisfy the loss subgroup parent requirement of paragraph (d)(1)(ii) or (2)(ii) of this section), are not taken into account. Also, the substantial nonbusiness asset test of section 382(l)(4) is ap-

plied on a group (or subgroup) basis, and is not applied separately to its members.

(ii) *Anti-duplication.*—Appropriate adjustments must be made to the extent necessary to prevent any duplication of the value of the stock of a member, even though corporations that do not file consolidated returns may not be required to make such an adjustment. In making these adjustments, the group (or loss subgroup) may apply the principles of § 1.382-8 (relating to controlled groups of corporations) in determining the value of a loss group (or loss subgroup) even if that section would not apply if separate returns were filed. Also, the principles of § 1.382-5(d) (relating to successive ownership changes and absorption of a section 382 limitation) may apply to adjust the consolidated section 382 limitation (or subgroup section 382 limitation) of a loss group (or loss subgroup) to avoid a duplication of value if there are simultaneous (rather than successive) ownership changes.

(3) *Examples.*—The following examples illustrate the principles of this paragraph (b):

Example 1. Basic case. (i) L, L1, and L2 compose a loss group. L has outstanding common stock, the value of which is $100. L1 has outstanding common stock and preferred stock that is described in section 1504(a)(4). L owns 90 percent of the L1 common stock, and A owns the remaining 10 percent of the L1 common stock plus all the preferred stock. The value of the L1 common stock is $40, and the value of the L1 preferred stock is $30. L2 has outstanding common stock, 50 percent of which is owned by L and 50 percent by L1. The L group has an ownership change. The following is a graphic illustration of these facts:

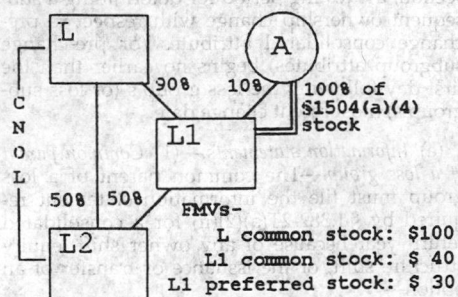

(ii) Under paragraph (b)(1) of this section, the L group does not include the value of the stock of any member that is owned directly or indirectly by another member in computing its consolidated section 382 limitation. Accordingly, the value of the stock of the loss group is $134, the sum of the value of—

(a) The common stock of L ($100);

(b) The 10 percent of the L1 common stock ($4) owned by A; and

(c) The L1 preferred stock ($30) owned by A.

Example 2—Indirect ownership. (i) L and L1 compose a consolidated group. L's stock has a value of $100. L owns 80 shares (worth $80) and corporation M owns 20 shares (worth $20) of the L1 stock. L also owns 79 percent of the stock of corporation M. The L group has an ownership change. The following is a graphic illustration of these facts:

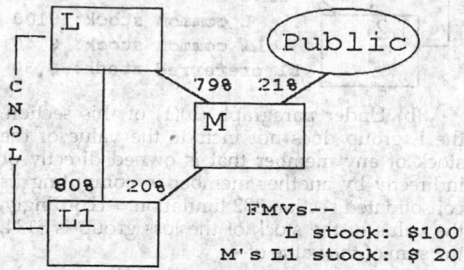

(ii) Under paragraph (b)(1) of this section, because of L's more than 5 percent ownership interest in M, a nonmember, L is considered to indirectly own 15.8 shares of the L1 stock held by M (79%×20 shares). The value of the L loss group is $104.20, the sum of the values of—

(a) The L stock ($100); and

(b) The L1 stock not owned directly or indirectly by L (21%×$20, or $4.20).

(c) *Recognized built-in gain of a loss group or loss subgroup.*—(1) *In general.*—If a loss group (or loss subgroup) has a net unrealized built-in gain, any recognized built-in gain of the loss group (or loss subgroup) is taken into account under section 382(h) in determining the consolidated section 382 limitation (or subgroup section 382 limitation).

(2) *Adjustments.*—Appropriate adjustments must be made so that any recognized built-in gain of a member that increases more than one section 382 limitation (whether consolidated, subgroup, or separate) does not effect a duplication in the amount of consolidated taxable income that can be offset by pre-change net operating losses. For example, a consolidated section 382 limitation that is increased by recognized built-in gains is reduced to the extent that pre-change net operating losses of a loss subgroup absorb additional consolidated taxable income because the same recognized built-in gains caused an increase in that loss subgroup's section 382 limitation. In addition, recognized built-in gain may not increase the amount of consolidated taxable income that can be offset by recognized built-in losses.

(d) *Continuity of business.*—(1) *In general.*—A loss group (or a loss subgroup) is treated as a single entity for purposes of determining whether it satisfies the continuity of business enterprise requirement of section 382(c)(1).

(2) *Example.*—The following example illustrates the principle of this paragraph (d):

Example. Continuity of business enterprise. L owns all the stock of' two subsidiaries, L1 and L2. The L group has an ownership change. It has pre-change consolidated attributes attributable to L2. Each of the members has historically conducted a separate line of business. Each line of business is approximately equal in value. One year after the ownership change, L discontinues its separate business and the business of L2. The separate business of L1 is continued for the remainder of the 2 year period following the ownership change. The continuity of business enterprise requirement of section 382(c)(1) is met even though the separate businesses of L and L2 are discontinued.

(e) *Limitations of losses under other rules.*—If a section 382 limitation for a post-change year exceeds the consolidated taxable income that may be offset by pre-change attributes for any reason, including the application of the limitation of § 1.1502-21(c), the amount of the excess is carried forward under section 382(b)(2) (relating to the carryforward of unused section 382 limitation). [Reg. § 1.1502-93.]

☐ [*T.D.* 8824, 6-25-99.]

[Reg. § 1.1502-93A]

§ 1.1502-93A. Consolidated section 382 limitation (or subgroup section 382 limitation) generally applicable for testing dates before June 25, 1999.—(a) *Determination of the consolidated section 382 limitation (or subgroup section 382 limitation).*—(1) *In general.*—Following an ownership change, the consolidated section 382 limitation (or subgroup section 382 limitation) for any post-change year is an amount equal to the value of the loss group (or loss subgroup), as defined in paragraph (b) of this section, multiplied by the long-term tax-exempt rate that applies with respect to the ownership change, and adjusted as required by section 382 and the regulations thereunder. See, for example, section 382(b)(2) (relating to the carryforward of unused section 382 limitation), section 382(b)(3)(B) (relating to the section 382 limitation for the post-change year that includes the change date), section 382(m)(2) (relating to short taxable years), and section 382(h) (relating to recognized built-in gains and section 338 gains).

(2) *Coordination with apportionment rule.*—For special rules relating to apportionment of a consolidated section 382 limitation (or a subgroup section 382 limitation) when one or more corporations cease to be members of a loss group (or a loss subgroup) and to aggregation of amounts so apportioned, see § 1.1502-95A(c).

(b) *Value of the loss group (or loss subgroup).*—(1) *Stock value immediately before ownership change.*—Subject to any adjustment under paragraph (b)(2) of this section, the value of the loss group (or loss subgroup) is the value, immediately before the ownership change, of the stock of each member, other than stock that is owned directly or indirectly by another member. For this purpose—

(i) Ownership is determined under § 1.382-2T;

(ii) A member is considered to indirectly own stock of another member through a nonmember only if the member has a 5-percent or greater ownership interest in the nonmember; and

(iii) Stock includes stock described in section 1504(a)(4) and § 1.382-2T(f)(18)(ii) and (iii).

(2) *Adjustment to value.*—The value of the loss group (or loss subgroup), as determined under paragraph (b)(1) of this section, is adjusted under any rule in section 382 or the regulations thereunder requiring an adjustment to such value for purposes of computing the amount of the section 382 limitation. See, for example, section 382(e)(2) (redemptions and corporate contractions), section 382(l)(1) (certain capital contributions) and section 382(l)(4) (ownership of substantial nonbusiness assets). The value of the loss group (or loss subgroup) determined under this paragraph (b) is also adjusted to the extent necessary to prevent any duplication of the value of the stock of a member. For example, the principles of § 1.382-8 (relating to controlled groups of corporations) apply in determining the value of a loss group (or loss subgroup) if, under § 1.1502-91A(g)(2), members are not included in the determination whether the group (or loss subgroup) has a net unrealized built-in loss.

(3) *Examples.*—The following examples illustrate the principles of this paragraph (b).

Example 1. Basic case. (a) L, L1, and L2 compose a loss group. L has outstanding common stock, the value of which is $100. L1 has outstanding common stock and preferred stock that is described in section 1504(a)(4). L owns 90 percent of the L1 common stock, and A owns the remaining 10 percent of the L1 common stock plus all the preferred stock. The value of the L1 common stock is $40, and the value of the L1 preferred stock is $30. L2 has outstanding common stock, 50 percent of which is owned by L and 50 percent by L1. The L group has an ownership change. The following is a graphic illustration of these facts:

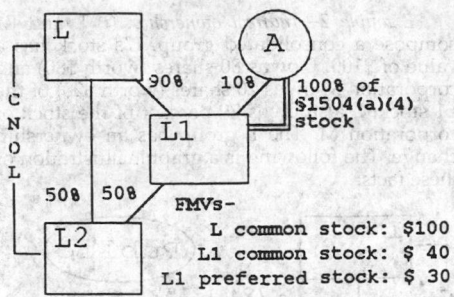

FMVs—
L common stock: $100
L1 common stock: $ 40
L1 preferred stock: $ 30

(b) Under paragraph (b)(1) of this section, the L group does not include the value of the stock of any member that is owned directly or indirectly by another member in computing its consolidated section 382 limitation. Accordingly, the value of the stock of the loss group is $134, the sum of the value of—

(1) The common stock of L ($100);

(2) the 10 percent of the L1 common stock ($4) owned by A; and

(3) The L1 preferred stock ($30) owned by A.

Example 2. Indirect ownership. (a) L and L1 compose a consolidated group. L's stock has a value of $100. L owns 80 shares (worth $80) and corporation M owns 20 shares (worth $20) of the L1 stock. L also owns 79 percent of the stock of corporation M. The L group has an ownership change. The following is a graphic illustration of these facts:

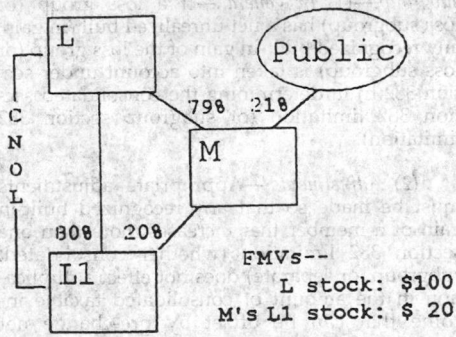

FMVs—
L stock: $100
M's L1 stock: $ 20

(b) Under paragraph (b)(1) of this section, because of L's more than 5 percent ownership interest in M, a nonmember, L is considered to indirectly own 15.8 shares of the L1 stock held by M (79% × 20 shares). The value of the L loss group is $104.20, the sum of the values of—

(1) The L stock ($100); and

(2) The L1 stock not owned directly or indirectly by L (21% × $20, or $4.20).

(c) *Recognized built-in gain of a loss group or loss subgroup.*—If a loss group (or loss subgroup) has a net unrealized built-in gain, any recognized built-in gain of the loss group (or loss subgroup) is taken into account under section 382(h) in determining the consolidated section 382 limitation (or subgroup section 382 limitation). See § 1.1502-99A(a)(2) for a special rule relating to the application of § 1.502-93(c)(2) to consolidated return years for which the due date of the return is after June 25, 1999.

(d) *Continuity of business.*—(1) *In general.*—A loss group (or a loss subgroup) is treated as a single entity for purposes of determining whether it satisfies the continuity of business enterprise requirement of section 382(c)(1).

(2) *Example.*—The following example illustrates the principle of this paragraph (d).

Example. Continuity of business enterprise. L owns all the stock of two subsidiaries, L1 and L2. The L group has an ownership change. It has pre-change consolidated attributes attributable to L2. Each of the members has historically conducted a separate line of business. Each line of business is approximately equal in value. One year after the ownership change, L discontinues its separate business and the business of L2. The separate business of L1 is continued for the remainder of the 2 year period following the ownership change. The continuity of business enterprise requirement of section 382(c)(1) is met even though the separate businesses of L and L2 are discontinued.

(e) *Limitations of losses under other rules.*—If a section 382 limitation for a post-change year exceeds the consolidated taxable income that may be offset by pre-change attributes for any reason, including the application of the limitation of § 1.1502-21(c) or 1.1502-21T(c) in effect prior to June 25, 1999, as contained in 26 CFR part 1 revised April 1, 1999, as applicable, the amount of the excess is carried forward under section 382(b)(2) (relating to the carryforward of unused section 382 limitation). [Reg. § 1.1502-93A.]

☐ [T.D. 8678, 6-26-96. *Amended by T.D. 8823, 6-25-99 and amended and redesignated by T.D. 8824, 6-25-99.*]

[Reg. § 1.1502-94]

§ 1.1502-94. Coordination with section 382 and the regulations thereunder when a corporation becomes a member of a consolidated group.—(a) *Scope.*—(1) *In general.*—This section applies section 382 and the regulations thereunder to a corporation that is a new loss member of a consolidated group. A corporation is a new loss member if it—

(i) Carries over a net operating loss that arose (or is treated under § 1.1502-21(c) as arising) in a SRLY with respect to the current group, and that is not described in § 1.1502-91(d)(1); or

(ii) Has a net unrealized built-in loss (determined under paragraph (c) of this section immediately before it becomes a member of the current group by treating that day as a change date) that is not taken into account under

§ 1.1502-91(d)(2) in determining whether two or more corporations compose a loss subgroup.

(2) *Successor corporation as new loss member.*—A new loss member also includes any successor to a corporation that has a net operating loss carryover arising in a SRLY and that is treated as remaining in existence under § 1.382-2(a)(1)(ii) following a transaction described in section 381(a).

(3) *Coordination in the case of a loss subgroup.*—For rules regarding the determination of whether there is an ownership change of a loss subgroup with respect to a net operating loss or a net unrealized built-in loss described in § 1.1502-91(d) (relating to the definition of loss subgroup) and the computation of a subgroup section 382 limitation following such an ownership change, see § § 1.1502-92 and 1.1502-93.

(4) *End of separate tracking of certain losses.*—If § 1.1502-96(a) (relating to the end of separate tracking of attributes) applies to a new loss member, then, while that member remains a member of the consolidated group, there is an ownership change with respect to its attributes described in § 1.1502-96(a)(2) only if the consolidated group is a loss group and has an ownership change under § 1.1502-92(b)(1)(i) (or that member has an ownership change under § 1.1502-96(b) (relating to ownership changes of subsidiaries)). If, however, the new loss member has had an ownership change before § 1.1502-96(a) applies, see § 1.1502-96(c) for the continuing application of the section 382 limitation with respect to the member's pre-change losses.

(5) *Cross-reference.*—See section 382(a) and § 1.1502-96(c) for the continuing effect of an ownership change after a corporation becomes or ceases to be a member.

(b) *Application of section 382 to a new loss member.*—(1) *In general.*—Section 382 and the regulations thereunder apply to a new loss member to determine, on a separate entity basis, whether and to what extent a section 382 limitation applies to limit the amount of consolidated taxable income that may be offset by the new loss member's pre-change separate attributes. For example, if an ownership change with respect to the new loss member occurs under section 382 and the regulations thereunder, the amount of consolidated taxable income for any post-change year that may be offset by the new loss member's pre-change separate attributes shall not exceed the section 382 limitation as determined separately under section 382(b) with respect to that member for such year. If the post-change year includes the change date, section 382(b)(3)(A) is applied so that the section 382 limitation of the new loss member does not apply to the portion of the taxable income for such year that is allocable to the period in such year on or before the change date. See generally § 1.382-6 (relating to the allocation of income and loss).

(2) *Adjustment to value.*—Appropriate adjustments must be made to the extent necessary to prevent any duplication of the value of the stock of a member, even though corporations that do not file consolidated returns may not be required to make such an adjustment. For example, the principles of § 1.1502-93(b)(2)(ii) (relating to adjustments to value) apply in determining the value of a new loss member.

(3) *Pre-change separate attribute defined.*—A pre-change separate attribute of a new loss member is—

(i) Any net operating loss carryover of the new loss member described in paragraph (a)(1) of this section; and

(ii) Any recognized built-in loss of the new loss member.

(4) *Examples.*—The following examples illustrate the principles of this paragraph (b):

Example 1. Basic case. (i) A and P each own 50 percent of the L stock. On December 19, Year 6, P purchases 30 percent of the L stock from A for cash. L has net operating losses arising in Year 1 and Year 2 that it carries over to Year 6 and Year 7. The following is a graphic illustration of these facts:

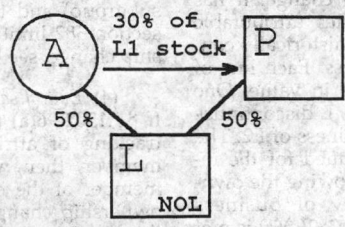

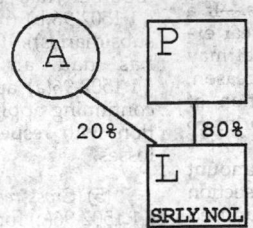

(ii) L is a new loss member because it has net operating loss carryovers that arose in a SRLY with respect to the P group and L is not a member of a loss subgroup under § 1.1502-91(d). Under section 382 and the regulations thereunder, L is a loss corporation on December 19, Year 6, that day is a testing date for L, and the testing period for L commences on December 20, Year 3.

(iii) P's purchase of L stock does not cause an ownership change of L on December 19, Year 6, with respect to the net operating loss carry-

overs from Year 1 and Year 2 under section 382 and § 1.382-2T. The use of the loss carryovers, however, is subject to limitation under § 1.1502-21(c).

Example 2. Multiple new loss members. (i) The facts are the same as in *Example 1*, and, on December 31, Year 6, L purchases all the stock of L1 from B for cash. L1 has a net operating loss of $40 arising in Year 3 that it carries over to Year 7. The following is a graphic illustration of these facts:

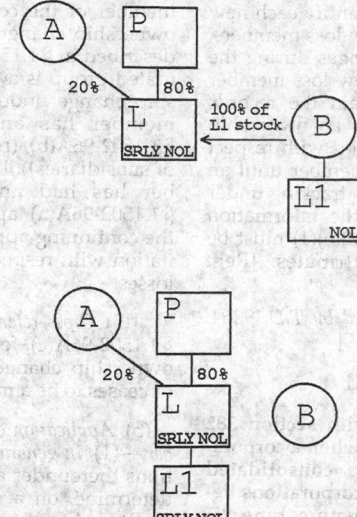

(ii) L1 is a new loss member because it has a net operating loss carryover from Year 3 that arose in a SRLY with respect to the P group and L1 is not a member of a loss subgroup under § 1.1502-91(d)(1).

(iii) L's purchase of all the stock of L1 causes an ownership change of L1 on December 31, Year 6, under section 382 and § 1.382-2T. Accordingly, a section 382 limitation based on the value of the L1 stock immediately before the ownership change limits the amount of consolidated taxable income of the P group for any post-change year that may be offset by L1's loss from Year 3.

(iv) L1's ownership change upon becoming a member of the P group is an ownership change described in § 1.1502-96(a). Thus, starting on January 1, Year 7, the P group no longer separately tracks owner shifts of the stock of L1 with respect to L1's loss from Year 3, and the P group is a loss group because L1's Year 3 loss is treated as a loss described in § 1.1502-91(c).

Example 3. Ownership changes of new loss members. (i) The facts are the same as in *Example 2*, and, on July 30, Year 7, C purchases all the stock of P for cash.

(ii) L is a new loss member on July 30, Year 7, because its Year 1 and Year 2 losses arose in SRLYs with respect to the P group and it is not a member of a loss subgroup under § 1.1502-91(d)(1). The testing period for L commences on August 1, Year 4. C's purchase of all the P stock causes an ownership change of L on July 30, Year 7, under section 382 and § 1.382-2T with respect to its Year 1 and Year 2 losses. Accordingly, a section 382 limitation based on the value of the L stock immediately before the ownership change limits the amount of consolidated taxable income of the P group for any post-change year that may be offset by L's Year 1

and Year 2 losses. See § 1.1502-21(c) for rules relating to an additional limitation.

(iii) The P group is a loss group on July 30, Year 7, because it is entitled to use L1's loss from Year 3, and such loss is no longer treated as a loss of a new loss member starting the day after L1's ownership change on December 31, Year 6. See § § 1.1502-96(a) and 1.1502-91(c)(2). C's purchase of all the P stock causes an ownership change of P, and therefore the P loss group, on July 30, Year 7, with respect to L1's Year 3 loss. Accordingly, a consolidated section 382 limitation based on the value of the P stock immediately before the ownership change limits the amount of consolidated taxable income of the P group for any post-change year that may be offset by L1's Year 3 loss.

(c) *Built-in gains and losses.*—As the context may require, the principles of § § 1.1502-91(g) and (h) and 1.1502-93(c) (relating to built-in gains and losses) apply to a new loss member on a separate entity basis. See § 1.1502-91(g)(4). See § 1.1502-13 (including *Example 10* of § 1.1502-13(c)(7)) for rules relating to the treatment of intercompany transactions.

(d) *Information statements.*—The common parent of a consolidated group that has a new loss member subject to paragraph (b)(1) of this section during a consolidated return year must file the information statement required by § 1.382-11(a) because of any owner shift, equity structure shift, or other transaction described in § 1.382-2T(a)(2)(i). Instead of filing a separate statement for each new loss member, the common parent may file a single statement described in § 1.382-11(a) with respect to the stock ownership of the common parent (which is treated as a loss corporation). In addition to the information concerning stock ownership of the common parent, the single statement must identify each new loss member and state which new loss members, if any, have had ownership changes during the consolidated return year. The new loss member is, however, required to maintain the records necessary to determine if it has an ownership change. This paragraph (d) applies with respect to the attributes of a new loss member until an event occurs which ends separate tracking under §1.1502-96(a). After that time, the information statement described in §1.1502-92(e)(1) must be filed with respect to these attributes. [Reg. §1.1502-94.]

□ [*T.D. 8824, 6-25-99. Amended by T.D. 9264, 5-26-2006 and T.D. 9329, 6-13-2007.*]

[Reg. §1.1502-94A]

§1.1502-94A. Coordination with section 382 and the regulations thereunder when a corporation becomes a member of a consolidated group generally applicable for corporations becoming members of a group before June 25, 1999.—(a) *Scope.*—(1) *In general.*—This section applies section 382 and the regulations thereunder to a corporation that is a new loss member of a consolidated group. A corporation is a new loss member if it—

(i) Carries over a net operating loss that arose (or is treated under §1.1502-21(c) or 1.1502-21T(c) in effect prior to June 25, 1999, as contained in 26 CFR part 1 revised April 1, 1999, as applicable as arising) in a SRLY with respect to the current group, and that is not described in §1.1502-91A(d)(1); or

(ii) Has a net unrealized built-in loss (determined under paragraph (c) of this section on the day it becomes a member of the current group by treating that day as a change date) that is not taken into account under §1.1502-91A(d)(2) in determining whether two or more corporations compose a loss subgroup.

(2) *Successor corporation as new loss member.*—A new loss member also includes any successor to a corporation that has a net operating loss carryover arising in a SRLY and that is treated as remaining in existence under §1.382-2(a)(1)(ii) following a transaction described in section 381(a).

(3) *Coordination in the case of a loss subgroup.*—For rules regarding the determination of whether there is an ownership change of a loss subgroup with respect to a net operating loss or a net unrealized built-in loss described in §1.1502-91A(d) (relating to the definition of loss subgroup) and the computation of a subgroup section 382 limitation following such an ownership change, see §§1.1502-92A and 1.1502-93A.

(4) *End of separate tracking of certain losses.*—If §1.1502-96A(a) (relating to the end of separate tracking of attributes) applies to a new loss member, then, while that member remains a

member of the consolidated group, there is an ownership change with respect to its attributes described in §1.1502-96A(a)(2) only if the consolidated group is a loss group and has an ownership change under §1.1502-92A(b)(1)(i) (or that member has an ownership change under §1.1502-96A(b) (relating to ownership changes of subsidiaries)). If, however, the new loss member has had an ownership change before §1.1502-96A(a) applies, see §1.1502-96A(c) for the continuing application of the section 382 limitation with respect to the member's pre-change losses.

(5) *Cross-reference.*—See section 382(a) and §1.1502-96A(c) for the continuing effect of an ownership change after a corporation becomes or ceases to be a member.

(b) *Application of section 382 to a new loss member.*—(1) *In general.*—Section 382 and the regulations thereunder apply to a new loss member to determine, on a separate entity basis, whether and to what extent a section 382 limitation applies to limit the amount of consolidated taxable income that may be offset by the new loss member's pre-change separate attributes. For example, if an ownership change with respect to the new loss member occurs under section 382 and the regulations thereunder, the amount of consolidated taxable income for any post-change year that may be offset by the new loss member's pre-change separate attributes shall not exceed the section 382 limitation as determined separately under section 382(b) with respect to that member for such year. If the post-change year includes the change date, section 382(b)(3)(A) is applied so that the section 382 limitation of the new loss member does not apply to the portion of the taxable income for such year that is allocable to the period in such year on or before the change date. See generally §1.382-6 (relating to the allocation of income and loss).

(2) *Adjustment to value.*—The value of the new loss member is adjusted to the extent necessary to prevent any duplication of the value of the stock of a member. For example, the principles of §1.382-8T (relating to controlled groups of corporations) apply in determining the value of a new loss member.

(3) *Pre-change separate attribute defined.*—A pre-change separate attribute of a new loss member is—

(i) Any net operating loss carryover of the new loss member described in paragraph (a)(1) of this section; and

(ii) Any recognized built-in loss of the new loss member.

(4) *Examples.*—The following examples illustrate the principles of this paragraph (b).

Example 1. Basic case. (a) A and P each own 50 percent of the L stock. On December 19, Year

Reg. §1.1502-94A

6, P purchases 30 percent of the L stock from A for cash. L has net operating losses arising in Year 1 and Year 2 that it carries over to Year 6 and Year 7. The following is a graphic illustration of these facts:

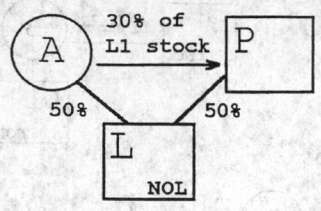

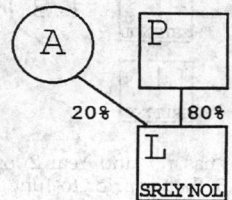

(b) L is a new loss member because it has net operating loss carryovers that arose in a SRLY with respect to the P group and L is not a member of a loss subgroup under § 1.1502-91A(d). Under section 382 and the regulations thereunder, L is a loss corporation on December 19, Year 6, that day is a testing date for L, and the testing period for L commences on December 20, Year 3.

(c) P's purchase of L stock does not cause an ownership change of L on December 19, Year 6, with respect to the net operating loss carryovers from Year 1 and Year 2 under section 382 and § 1.382-2T. The use of the loss carryovers, however, is subject to limitation under § 1.1502-21(c) or 1.1502-21T(c) in effect prior to June 25, 1999, as contained in 26 CFR part 1 revised April 1, 1999, as applicable.

Example 2. Multiple new loss members. (a) The facts are the same as in *Example 1*, and, on December 31, Year 6, L purchases all the stock of L1 from B for cash. L1 has a net operating loss of $40 arising in Year 3 that it carries over to Year 7. The following is a graphic illustration of these facts:

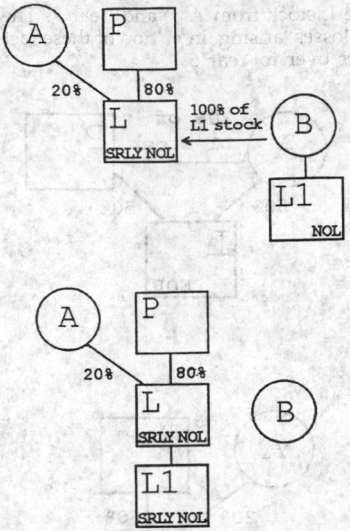

(b) L1 is a new loss member because it has a net operating loss carryover from Year 3 that arose in a SRLY with respect to the P group and L1 is not a member of a loss subgroup under §1.1502-91A(d)(1).

(c) L's purchase of all the stock of L1 causes an ownership change of L1 on December 31, Year 6, under section 382 and §1.382-2T. Accordingly, a section 382 limitation based on the value of the L1 stock immediately before the ownership change limits the amount of consolidated taxable income of the P group for any post-change year that may be offset by L1's loss from Year 3.

(d) L1's ownership change in connection with its becoming a member of the P group is an ownership change described in §1.1502-96A(a). Thus, starting on January 1, Year 7, the P group no longer separately tracks owner shifts of the stock of L1 with respect to L1's loss from Year 3. Instead, the P group is a loss group because of such loss under §1.1502-91A(c).

Example 3. Ownership changes of new loss members. (a) The facts are the same as in *Example 2,* and, on April 30, Year 7, C purchases all the stock of P for cash.

(b) L is a new loss member on April 30, Year 7, because its Year 1 and Year 2 losses arose in SRLYs with respect to the P group and it is not a member of a loss subgroup under §1.1502-91A(d)(1). The testing period for L commences on May 1, Year 4. C's purchase of all the P stock causes an ownership change of L on April 30, Year 7, under section 382 and §1.382-2T with respect to its Year 1 and Year 2 losses. Accordingly, a section 382 limitation based on the value of the L stock immediately before the ownership change limits the amount of consolidated taxable income of the P group for any post-change year that may be offset by L's Year 1 and Year 2 losses. See also §1.1502-21T in effect prior to June 25, 1999, contained in 26 CFR Part 1, revised April 1, 1999, or §1.1502-21, as applicable.

(c) The P group is a loss group on April 30, Year 7, because it is entitled to use L1's loss from Year 3, and such loss is no longer treated as a loss of a new loss member starting the day after L1's ownership change on December 31, Year 6. See §§1.1502-96A(a) and 1.1502-91A(c)(2). C's purchase of all the P stock causes an ownership change of P, and therefore the P loss group, on April 30, Year 7, with respect to L1's Year 3 loss. Accordingly, a consolidated section 382 limitation based on the value of the P stock immediately before the ownership change limits the amount of consolidated taxable income of the P group for any post-change year that may be offset by L1's Year 3 loss.

(c) *Built-in gains and losses.*—As the context may require, the principles of §§1.1502-91A(g) and (h) and 1.1502-93A(c) (relating to built-in gains and losses) apply to a new loss member on a separate entity basis. See §1.1502-91A(g)(3).

(d) *Information statements.*—The common parent of a consolidated group that has a new loss member subject to paragraph (b)(1) of this section during a consolidated return year must file the information statement required by §1.382-2T(a)(2)(ii) because of any owner shift, equity structure shift, or issuance or transfer of an option with respect to the new loss member. Instead of filing a separate statement for each new loss member the common parent may file a single statement described in §1.382-2T(a)(2)(ii) with respect to the stock ownership of the common parent (which is treated as a loss corporation). In addition to the information concerning stock ownership of the common parent, the sin-

Reg. §1.1502-94A(c)

gle statement must identify each new loss member and state which new loss members, if any, have had ownership changes during the consolidated return year. The new loss member is, however, required to maintain the records necessary to determine if it has an ownership change. This paragraph (d) applies with respect to the attributes of a new loss member until an event occurs which ends separate tracking under §1.1502-96A(a). After that time, the information statement described in §1.1502-92A(e)(1) must be filed with respect to these attributes. [Reg. §1.1502-94A.]

☐ [*T.D. 8678, 6-26-96. Amended by T.D. 8823, 6-25-99 and amended and redesignated by T.D. 8824, 6-25-99.*]

[Reg. §1.1502-95]

§1.1502-95. Rules on ceasing to be a member of a consolidated group (or loss subgroup).— (a) *In general.*—(1) *Consolidated group.*—This section provides rules for applying section 382 on or after the day that a member ceases to be a member of a consolidated group (or loss subgroup). The rules concern how to determine whether an ownership change occurs with respect to losses of the member, and how a consolidated section 382 limitation (or subgroup section 382 limitation) and a loss group's (or loss subgroup's) net unrealized built-in gain or loss is apportioned to the member. As the context requires, a reference in this section to a loss group, a member, or a corporation also includes a reference to a loss subgroup, and a reference to a consolidated section 382 limitation also includes a reference to a subgroup section 382 limitation.

(2) *Election by common parent.*—Only the common parent (not the loss subgroup parent) may make the election under paragraph (c) of this section to apportion a consolidated section 382 limitation (or subgroup section 382 limitation) or a loss group's (or loss subgroup's) net unrealized built-in gain.

(3) *Coordination with §§1.1502-91 through 1.1502-93.*—For rules regarding the determination of whether there is an ownership change of a loss subgroup and the computation of a subgroup section 382 limitation following such an ownership change, see §§1.1502-91 through 1.1502-93.

(b) *Separate application of section 382 when a member leaves a consolidated group.*—(1) *In general.*—Except as provided in §§1.1502-91 through 1.1502-93 (relating to rules applicable to loss groups and loss subgroups), section 382 and the regulations thereunder apply to a corporation on a separate entity basis after it ceases to be a member of a consolidated group (or loss subgroup). Solely for purposes of determining whether a corporation has an ownership change—

(i) Any portion of a consolidated net operating loss that is apportioned to the corporation under §1.1502-21(b) is treated as a net operating loss of the corporation beginning on the first day of the taxable year in which the loss arose;

(ii) The testing period may include the period during which (or before which) the corporation was a member of the group (or loss subgroup); and

(iii) Except to the extent provided in §1.1502-96(d) (relating to reattributed losses), the day it ceases to be a member of a consolidated group is treated as a testing date of the corporation within the meaning of §1.382-2(a)(4).

(2) *Effect of a prior ownership change of the group.*—If a loss group has had an ownership change under §1.1502-92 before a corporation ceases to be a member of a consolidated group (the former member)—

(i) Any pre-change consolidated attribute that is subject to a consolidated section 382 limitation continues to be treated as a pre-change loss with respect to the former member after it is apportioned to the former member and, if any net unrealized built-in loss is allocated to the former member under paragraph (e) of this section, any recognized built-in loss of the former member is a pre-change loss of the member;

(ii) The section 382 limitation with respect to such pre-change attribute is zero unless the common parent, under paragraph (c) of this section, apportions to the former member all or part of the consolidated section 382 limitation applicable to such attribute. The limitation applicable to a pre-change attribute other than a recognized built-in loss may be increased to the extent that the common parent has apportioned all or part of the loss group's net unrealized built-in gain to the former member, and the former member recognizes built-in gain during the recognition period;

(iii) The testing period for determining a subsequent ownership change with respect to such pre-change attribute (or such net unrealized built-in loss, if any) begins no earlier than the first day following the loss group's most recent change date; and

(iv) As generally provided under section 382, an ownership change of the former member that occurs on or after the day it ceases to be a member of a loss group may result in an additional, lesser limitation amount with respect to such losses.

(3) *Application in the case of a loss subgroup.*—If two or more former members are included in the same loss subgroup immediately after they cease to be members of a consolidated group, the principles of paragraphs (b), (c) and (e) of this section apply to the loss subgroup. Therefore, for example, an apportionment by the common parent under paragraph (c) of this section is made to

the loss subgroup rather than separately to its members. If the common parent of the consolidated group apportions all or part of a limitation (or net unrealized built-in gain) separately to one or more former members that are included in a loss subgroup because the common parent of the acquiring group makes an election under § 1.1502-91(d)(4) with respect to those members, the aggregate of those separate amounts is treated as the amount apportioned to the loss subgroup. Such separate apportionment may occur, for example, because the election under § 1.1502-91(d)(4) has not been filed at the time that the election of apportionment is made under paragraph (f) of this section.

(4) *Examples.*—The following examples illustrate the principles of this paragraph (b):

Example 1. Treatment of departing member as a separate corporation throughout the testing period. (i) A owns all the L stock. L owns all the stock of L1 and L2. The L group has a consolidated net operating loss arising in Year 1 that is carried over to Year 3. On January 12, Year 2, A sells 30 percent of the L stock to B. On February 7, Year 3, L sells 40 percent of the L2 stock to C, and L2 ceases to be a member of the group. A portion of the Year 1 consolidated net operating loss apportioned to L2 under § 1.1502-21(b) and is carried to L2's first separate return year, which ends December 31, Year 3. The following is a graphic illustration of these facts:

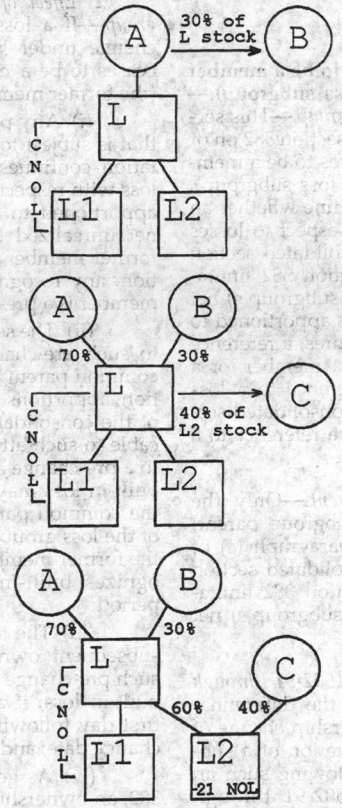

(ii) Under paragraph (b)(1) of this section, L2 is a loss corporation on February 7, Year 3. Under paragraph (b)(1)(iii) of this section, February 7, Year 3, is a testing date. Under paragraph (b)(1)(ii) of this section, the testing period for L2 with respect to this testing date commences on January 1, Year 1, the first day of the taxable year in which the portion of the consolidated net operating loss apportioned to L2 arose. Therefore, in determining whether L2 has an ownership change on February 7, Year 3, B's purchase of 30 percent of the L stock and C's purchase of 40 percent of the L2 stock are each owner shifts. L2 has an ownership change under section 382(g) and § 1.382-2T because B and C have increased their ownership interests in L2 by 18 and 40 percentage points, respectively, during the testing period.

Example 2. Effect of prior ownership change of loss group. (i) L owns all the L1 stock and L1 owns all the L2 stock. The L loss group had an ownership change under § 1.1502-92 in Year 2 with respect to a consolidated net operating loss arising in Year 1 and carried over to Year 2 and

Year 3. The consolidated section 382 limitation computed solely on the basis of the value of the stock of L is $100. On December 31, Year 2, L1 sells 25 percent of the stock of L2 to B. L2 is apportioned a portion of the Year 1 consolidated net operating loss which it carries over to its first separate return year ending after December 31, Year 2. L2's separate section 382 limitation with respect to this loss is zero unless L elects to apportion all or a part of the consolidated section 382 limitation to L2. (See paragraph (c) of this section for rules regarding the apportionment of a consolidated section 382 limitation.) L apportions $50 of the consolidated section 382 limitation to L2, and the remaining $50 of the consolidated section 382 limitation stays with the loss group composed of L and L1.

(ii) On December 31, Year 3, L1 sells its remaining 75 percent stock interest in L2 to C, resulting in an ownership change of L2. L2's section 382 limitation computed on the change date with respect to the value of its stock is $30. Accordingly, L2's section 382 limitation for post-change years ending after December 31, Year 3, with respect to its pre-change losses, including the consolidated net operating losses apportioned to it from the L group, is $30, adjusted for a short taxable year, carryforward of unused limitation, or any other adjustment required under section 382.

(c) *Apportionment of a consolidated section 382 limitation.*—(1) *In general.*—The common parent may elect to apportion all or any part of a consolidated section 382 limitation to a former member (or loss subgroup). The common parent also may elect to apportion all or any part of the loss group's net unrealized built-in gain to a former member (or loss subgroup).

(2) *Amount which may be apportioned.*—(i) *Consolidated section 382 limitation.*—The common parent may apportion all or part of each element of the consolidated section 382 limitation determined under § 1-1502-93. For this purpose, the consolidated section 382 limitation consists of two elements—

(A) The value element, which is the element of the limitation determined under section 382(b)(1) (relating to value multiplied by the long-term tax-exempt rate) without regard to such adjustments as those described in section 382(b)(2) (relating to the carryforward of unused section 382 limitation), section 382(b)(3)(B) (relating to the section 382 limitation for the post-change year that includes the change date), section 382(h) (relating to built-in gains and section 338 gains), and section 382(m)(2) (relating to short taxable years); and

(B) The adjustment element, which is so much (if any) of the limitation for the taxable year during which the former member ceases to be a member of the consolidated group that is attributable to a carryover of unused limitation

under section 382(b)(2) or to recognized built-in gains under 382(h).

(ii) *Net unrealized built-in gain.*—The aggregate amount of the loss group's net unrealized built-in gain that may be apportioned to one or more former members that cease to be members during the same consolidated return year cannot exceed the loss group's excess, immediately after the close of that year, of net unrealized built-in gain over recognized built-in gain, determined under section 382(h)(1)(A)(ii) (relating to a limitation on recognized built-in gain). For this purpose, net unrealized built-in gain apportioned to former members in prior consolidated return years is treated as recognized built-in gain in those years.

(3) *Effect of apportionment on the consolidated group.*—(i) *Consolidated section 382 limitation.*—The value element of the consolidated section 382 limitation for any post-change year ending after the day that a former member (or loss subgroup) ceases to be a member(s) is reduced to the extent that it is apportioned under this paragraph (c). The consolidated section 382 limitation for the post-change year in which the former member (or loss subgroup) ceases to be a member(s) is also reduced to the extent that the adjustment element for that year is apportioned under this paragraph (c).

(ii) *Net unrealized built-in gain.*—The amount of the loss group's net unrealized built-in gain that is apportioned to the former member (or loss subgroup) is treated as recognized built-in gain for a prior taxable year ending in the recognition period for purposes of applying the limitation of section 382(h)(1)(A)(ii) to the loss group's recognition period taxable years beginning after the consolidated return year in which the former member (or loss subgroup) ceases to be a member.

(4) *Effect on corporations to which an apportionment is made.*—(i) *Consolidated section 382 limitation.*—The amount of the value element that is apportioned to a former member (or loss subgroup) is treated as the amount determined under section 382(b)(1) for purposes of determining the amount of that corporation's (or loss subgroup's) section 382 limitation for any taxable year ending after the former member (or loss subgroup) ceases to be a member(s). Appropriate adjustments must be made to the limitation based on the value element so apportioned for a short taxable year, carryforward of unused limitation, or any other adjustment required under section 382. The adjustment element apportioned to a former member (or loss subgroup) is treated as an adjustment under section 382(b)(2) or section 382(h), as appropriate, for the first taxable year after the member (or members) ceases to be a member (or members).

(ii) *Net unrealized built-in gain.*—For purposes of determining the amount by which the former member's (or loss subgroup's) section 382 limitation for any taxable year beginning after the former member (or loss subgroup), ceases to be a member(s) is increased by its recognized built-in gain—

(A) The amount of net unrealized built-in gain apportioned to a former member (or loss subgroup) is treated as if it were an amount of net unrealized built-in gain determined under section 382(h)(1)(A)(i) (without regard to the threshold of section 382(h)(3)(B)) with respect to such member or loss subgroup, and that amount is not reduced under section 382(h)(1)(A)(ii) by the loss group's recognized built-in gain;

(B) The former member's (or loss subgroup's) 5 year recognition period begins on the loss group's change date;

(C) In applying section 382(h)(1)(A)(ii), the former member (or loss subgroup) takes into account only its prior taxable years that begin after it ceases to be a member of the loss group; and

(D) The former member's (or loss subgroup's) recognized built-in gain on the disposition of an asset is determined under section 382(h)(2)(A), treating references to the change date in that section as references to the loss group's change date.

(5) *Deemed apportionment when loss group terminates.*—If a loss group terminates, to the extent the consolidated section 382 limitation or net unrealized built-in gain is not apportioned under paragraph (c)(1) of this section, the consolidated section 382 limitation or net unrealized built-in gain is deemed to be apportioned to the loss subgroup that includes the common parent, or, if there is no loss subgroup that includes the common parent immediately after the loss group terminates, to the common parent. A loss group terminates on the first day of the first taxable year that is a separate return year with respect to each member of the former loss group.

(6) *Appropriate adjustments when former member leaves during the year.*—Appropriate adjustments are made to the consolidated section 382 limitation for the consolidated return year during which the former member (or loss subgroup) ceases to be a member(s) to reflect the inclusion of the former member in the loss group for a portion of that year.

(7) *Examples.*—The following examples illustrate the principles of this paragraph (c):

Example 1. Consequence of apportionment. (i) L owns all the L1 stock and L1 owns all the L2 stock. The L group has a $200 consolidated net operating loss arising in Year 1 that is carried over to Year 2. At the close of December 31, Year 1, the group has an ownership change under § 1.1502-92. The ownership change results in a consolidated section 382 limitation of $10 based

on the value of the stock of the group. On August 29, Year 2, L1 sells 30 percent of the stock of L2 to A. L2 is apportioned $90 of the group's $200 consolidated net operating loss under § 1.1502-21(b). L, the common parent, elects to apportion $6 of the consolidated section 382 limitation to L2. The following is a graphic illustration of these facts:

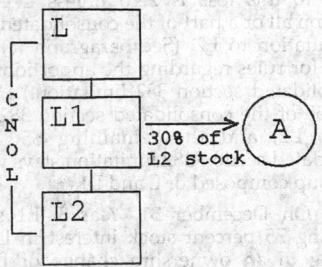

(ii) For its separate return years ending after December 31, Year 2, L2's section 382 limitation with respect to the $90 of the group's net operating loss apportioned to it is $6, adjusted, as appropriate, for any short taxable year, unused section 382 limitation, or other adjustment. For its consolidated return year ending December 31, Year 2 the L group's consolidated section 382 limitation with respect to the remaining $110 of pre-change consolidated attribute is $4 ($10 minus the $6 value element apportioned to L2), adjusted, as appropriate, for any short taxable year, unused section 382 limitation, or other adjustment.

(iii) For the L group's consolidated return year ending December 31, Year 2, the value element of its consolidated section 382 limitation is increased by $4 (rounded to the nearest dollar), to account for the period during which L2 was a member of the L group ($6, the consolidated section 382 limitation apportioned to L2, times 241/365, the ratio of the number of days during Year 2 that L2 is a member of the group to the number of days in the group's consolidated return year). See paragraph (c)(6) of this section. Therefore, the value element of the consolidated section 382 limitation for Year 2 of the L group is $8 (rounded to the nearest dollar).

(iv) The section 382 limitation for L2's short taxable year ending December 31, Year 2, is $2 (rounded to the nearest dollar), which is the amount that bears the same relationship to $6, the value element of the consolidated section 382 limitation apportioned to L2, as the number of days during that short taxable year, 124 days, bears to 365. See § 1.382-5(c).

Example 2. Consequence of no apportionment. The facts are the same as in *Example 1*, except that L does not elect to apportion any portion of the consolidated section 382 limitation to L2. For its separate return years ending after August 29, Year 2, L2's section 382 limitation with respect to the $90 of the group's pre-change consolidated attribute apportioned to L2 is zero under paragraph (b)(2)(ii) of this section. Thus, the $90 consolidated net operating loss apportioned to L2 cannot offset L2's taxable income in any of its separate return years ending after August 29, Year 2. For its consolidated return years ending after August 29, Year 2, the L group's consolidated section 382 limitation with respect to the remaining $110 of pre-change consolidated attribute is $10, adjusted, as appropriate, for any short taxable year, unused section 382 limitation, or other adjustment.

Example 3. Apportionment of adjustment element. The facts are the same as in *Example 1*, except that L2 ceases to be a member of the L group on August 29, Year 3, and the L group has a $4 carryforward of an unused consolidated section 382 limitation (under section 382(b)(2)) to the Year 3 consolidated return year. The carryover of unused limitation increases the consolidated section 382 limitation for the Year 3 consolidated return year from $10 to $14. L may elect to apportion all or any portion of the $10 value element and all or any portion of the $4 adjustment element to L2.

(d) *Rules pertaining to ceasing to be a member of a loss subgroup.*—(1) *In general.*—A corporation ceases to be a member of a loss subgroup on the earlier of—

(i) The first day of the first taxable year for which it files a separate return; or

(ii) The first day that it ceases to bear a relationship described in section 1504(a)(1) to the loss subgroup parent (treating for this purpose the loss subgroup parent as the common parent described in section 1504(a)(1)(A)).

(2) *Exceptions.*—Paragraph (d)(1)(ii) of this section does not apply to a member of a loss subgroup while that member remains a member of the current group—

(i) If an election under § 1.1502-91(d)(4)(relating to treating the subgroup parent requirement as satisfied) applies to the members of the loss subgroup;

(ii) Starting on the day after the change date (but not earlier than the date the loss subgroup becomes a member of the group), if there is an ownership change of the loss subgroup within six months before, on, or after becoming members of the group; or

(iii) Starting the day after the period of 5 consecutive years following the day that the loss subgroup become members of the group during which the loss subgroup has not had an ownership change.

(3) *Examples.*—The principles of this paragraph (d) are illustrated by the following examples:

Example 1. Basic case. (i) P owns all the L stock, L owns all the L1 stock and L1 owns all the L2 stock. The P group has a consolidated net operating loss arising in Year 1 that is carried over to Year 2. On December 11, Year 2, P sells all the stock of L to corporation M. Each of L, L1, and L2 is apportioned a portion of the Year 1 consolidated net operating loss, and thereafter each joins with M in filing consolidated returns. Under § 1.1502-92, the L loss subgroup has an ownership change on December 11, Year 2. The L loss subgroup has a subgroup section 382 limitation of $100. The following is a graphic illustration of these facts:

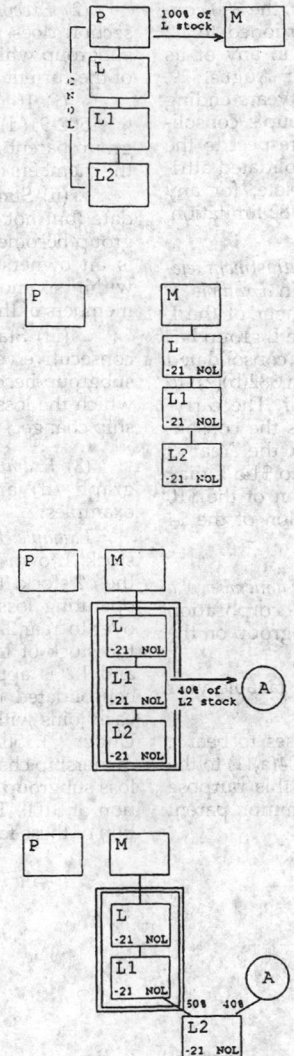

(ii) On May 22, Year 3, L1 sells 40 percent of the L2 stock to A. L2 carries over a portion of the P group's net operating loss from Year 1 to its separate return year ending December 31, Year 3. Under paragraph (d)(1) of this section, L2 ceases to be a member of the L loss subgroup on May 22, Year 3, which is both (1) the first day of the first taxable year for which it files a separate return and (2) the day it ceases to bear a relationship described in section 1504(a)(1) to the loss subgroup parent, L. The net operating loss of L2 that is carried over from the P group is treated as a pre-change loss of L2 for its separate return years ending after May 22, Year 3. Under paragraphs (a)(2) and (b)(2) of this section, the separate section 382 limitation with respect to this loss is zero unless M elects to apportion all

or a part of the subgroup section 382 limitation of the L loss subgroup to L2.

Example 2. Formation of a new loss subgroup. The facts are the same as in *Example 1*, except that A purchases 40 percent of the L1 stock from L rather than purchasing L2 stock from L1. L1 and L2 file a consolidated return for their first taxable year ending after May 22, Year 3, and each of L1 and L2 carries over a part of the net operating loss of the P group that arose in Year 1. Under paragraph (d)(1) of this section, L1 and L2 cease to be members of the L loss subgroup on May 22, Year 3. The net operating losses carried over from the P group are treated as pre-change subgroup attributes of the loss subgroup composed of L1 and L2. The subgroup section 382 limitation with respect to those losses is zero unless M elects to apportion all or part of the subgroup section 382 limitation of the L loss subgroup to the L1 loss subgroup. The following is a graphic illustration of these facts:

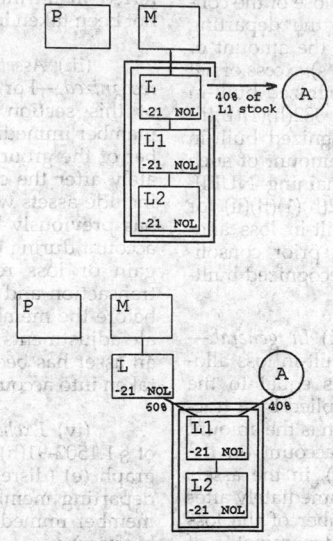

Example 3. Ownership change upon becoming members of the group. (i) A owns all the stock of P, and P owns all the stock of L1 and L2. The P group has a consolidated net operating loss arising in Year 1 that is carried over to Year 3 and Year 4. Corporation M acquires all the stock of P on November 11, Year 3, and P, L1, and L2 thereafter file consolidated returns with M. M's acquisition results in an ownership change of the P loss subgroup under § 1.1502-92(b)(1)(ii).

(ii) P distributes the L2 stock to M on October 7, Year 4, and L2 ceases to bear the relationship described in section 1504(a)(1) to P, the P loss subgroup parent. However, under paragraph (d)(2) of this section, L2 does not cease to be a member of the P loss subgroup because the P loss subgroup had an ownership change upon becoming members of the M group and L2 remains in the M group.

Example 4. Ceasing to bear a section 1504(a)(1) to the loss subgroup parent. (i) A owns all the stock of P, and P owns all the stock of L1 and L2. The P group has a consolidated net operating loss arising in Year 1 that is carried over to Year 7. At the close of Year 2, X acquires all of the stock of P, causing an ownership change of the loss subgroup composed of P, L1 and L2 under § 1.1502-92(b)(1)(ii). In Year 4, M, which is owned by the same person that owns X, acquires all of the stock of P, and the M acquisition does not cause a second ownership change of the P loss subgroup.

(ii) P distributes the L2 stock to M on February 3, Year 6 (less than 5 years after the P loss subgroup became members of the M group) and L2 ceases to bear the relationship described in section 1504(a)(1) to P, the loss subgroup parent.

Thus, the section 382 limitation from the Year 2 ownership change that applies with respect to the pre-change attributes attributable to L2 is zero except to the extent M elects to apportion all or part of the P loss subgroup section 382 limitation to L2.

Example 5. Relationship through a successor. The facts are the same as in *Example 3*, except that M's acquisition of the P stock does not result in an ownership change of the P loss subgroup, and, instead of P's distributing the stock of L2, L2 merges into L1 on October 7, Year 4. L1 (as successor to L2 in the merger within the meaning of § 1.1502-1(f)(4)) continues to bear a relationship described in section 1504(a)(1) to P, the loss subgroup parent. Thus, L2 does not cease to be a member of the P loss subgroup as a result of the merger.

Example 6. Reattribution of net operating loss carryover under § 1.1502-36(d)(6). The facts are the same as in *Example 3*, except that, instead of distributing the L2 stock to M, P sells that stock to B, and, under § 1.1502-36(d)(6), M reattributes $10 of L2's net operating loss carryover to itself. Under § 1.1502-36(d)(6)(iv)(A), M succeeds to the reattributed loss as if the loss were succeeded to in a transaction to which section 381(a) applies. M, as successor to L2, does not cease to be a member of the P loss subgroup.

(e) *Allocation of net unrealized built-in loss.*— (1) *In general.*—This paragraph (e) provides rules for the allocation of a loss group's (or loss subgroup's) net unrealized built-in loss if a member ceases to be a member of a loss group (or loss subgroup). This paragraph (e) applies if—

Reg. § 1.1502-95(e)(1)

(i) A loss group (or loss subgroup) has a net unrealized built-in loss on a change date; and

(ii) Immediately after the close of the consolidated return year in which the departing member ceases to be a member, the amount of the loss group's (or loss subgroup's) excess of net unrealized built-in loss over recognized built-in loss, determined under section 382(h)(1)(B)(ii) (relating to a limitation on recognized built-in loss), is greater than zero. (The amount of such excess is referred to as the remaining NUBIL balance.) In applying section 382(h)(1)(B)(ii) for this purpose, net unrealized built-in loss allocated to departing members in prior consolidated return years is treated as recognized built-in loss in those years.

(2) *Amount of allocation.*—(i) *In general.*—The amount of net unrealized built-in loss allocated to a departing member is equal to the remaining NUBIL balance, multiplied by a fraction. The numerator of the fraction is the amount of the built-in loss, taken into account on the change date under §1.1502-91(g), in the assets held by the departing member immediately after the member ceases to be a member of the loss group (or loss subgroup). The denominator of the fraction is the sum of the numerator, plus the amount of the built-in loss, taken into account under §1.1502-91(g) on the change date, in the assets held by the loss group (or loss subgroup) immediately after the close of the taxable year in which the departing member ceases to be a member. (Fluctuations in value of the assets between the change date and the date that the member ceases to be a member of the group (or loss subgroup), or the close of the taxable year in which the member ceases to be a member of the loss group, are disregarded.) Because the amount of built-in loss on the change date with respect to a departing member's assets is taken into account (rather than that member's separately computed net unrealized built-in loss on the change date), a departing member can be apportioned all or part of the loss group's net unrealized built-in loss, even if the departing member had a separately computed net unrealized built-in gain on the change date. Amounts taken into account under section 382(h)(6)(C) (relating to certain deduction items) are treated as if they were assets in determining the numerator and denominator of the fraction.

(ii) *Transferred basis property and deferred gain or loss.*—For purposes of paragraph (b)(2)(i) of this section, assets held by the departing member immediately after it ceases to be a member of the group (or by other members immediately after the close of the taxable year) include—

(A) Assets held at that time that are transferred basis property that was held by any member of the group (or loss subgroup) on the change date; and

(B) Assets held at that time by any member of the consolidated group with respect to which gain or loss of the group member or loss subgroup member at issue has been deferred in an intercompany transaction and has not been taken into account.

(iii) *Assets for which gain or loss has been recognized.*—For purposes of paragraph (b)(2)(i) of this section, assets held by the departing member immediately after it ceases to be a member of the group (or by other members immediately after the close of the taxable year) do not include assets with respect to which gain or loss has previously been recognized and taken into account during the recognition period (including gain or loss recognized in an intercompany transaction and taken into account immediately before the member leaves the group). Appropriate adjustments must be made if gain or loss on an asset has been only partially recognized and taken into account.

(iv) *Exchanged basis property.*—The rules of §1.1502-91(h) apply for purposes of this paragraph (e) (disregarding stock received from the departing member or another member that is a member immediately after the close of the taxable year).

(v) *Two or more members depart during the same year.*—If two or more members cease to be members during the same consolidated return year, appropriate adjustments must be made to the denominator of the fraction for each departing member by treating the other departing members during that year as if they had not ceased to be members during that year and as if the assets held by those other departing members immediately after they cease to be members of the group (or loss subgroup) are assets held by the group immediately after the close of the taxable year.

(vi) *Anti-abuse rule.*—If assets are transferred between members or a member ceases to be a member with a principal purpose of causing or affecting the allocation of amounts under this paragraph (e), appropriate adjustments must be made to eliminate any benefit of such acquisition, disposition, or allocation.

(3) *Effect of allocation on the consolidated group.*—The amount of the net unrealized built-in loss that is allocated to the former member is treated as recognized built-in loss for a prior taxable year ending in the recognition period for purposes applying the limitation of section 382(h)(1)(B)(ii) to a loss group's (or loss subgroup's) recognition period taxable years beginning after the consolidated return year in which the former member ceases to be a member.

(4) *Effect on corporations to which the allocation is made.*—For purposes of determining the amount of the former member's recognized built-in losses in any taxable year beginning after the former member ceases to be a member—

(i) The amount of the loss group's (or loss subgroup's) net unrealized built-in loss that is allocated to the former member is treated as if it were an amount of net unrealized built-in loss determined under section 382(h)(1)(B)(i)(without regard to the threshold of section 382(h)(3)(B)) with respect to such member or loss subgroup, and that amount is not reduced under section 382(h)(1)(B)(ii) by the loss group's (or loss subgroup's) recognized built-in losses;

(ii) The former member's 5 year recognition period begins on the loss group's (or loss subgroup's) change date;

(iii) In applying section 382(h)(1)(B)(ii), the former member takes into account only its prior taxable years that begin after it ceases to be a member of the loss group (or loss subgroup); and

(iv) The former member's recognized built-in loss on the disposition of an asset is determined under section 382(h)(2)(B), treating references to the change date in that section as references to the loss group's (or loss subgroup's) change date.

(5) *Subgroup principles.*—If two or more former members are members of the same consolidated group (the second group) immediately after they cease to be members of the current group, the principles of paragraphs (e)(1), (2) and (4) of this section apply to those former members on an aggregate basis. Thus, for example, the amount of net unrealized built-in loss allocated to those members is based on the assets held by those members immediately after they cease to be members of the current group and the limitation of section 382(h)(1)(B)(ii) on recognized built-in losses is applied by taking into account the aggregate amount of net unrealized built-in loss allocated to the former members and the aggregate recognized losses of those members in taxable years beginning after they cease to be members of the current group. If one or more of such members cease to be members of the second group, the principles of this paragraph (e) are applied with respect to those members to allocate to them all or part of any remaining unrecognized amount of net unrealized built-in loss allocated to the members that became members of the second group.

(6) *Apportionment of consolidated section 382 limitation (or subgroup section 382 limitation).*— (i) *In general.*—For rules relating to the apportionment of a consolidated section 382 limitation (or subgroup section 382 limitation) to a former member, see paragraph (c) of this section.

(ii) *Special rule for former members that become members of the same consolidated group.*—If recognized built-in losses of one or more former members would be subject to a consolidated section 382 limitation (or subgroup section 382 limitation) if recognized immediately before the member (or members) cease to be members of the group, an apportionment of that limitation may be made, under paragraph (c) of this section, to a loss subgroup that includes such member (or members), and the recognized built-in losses (if any) of that member (or members) will be subject to that apportioned limitation. If two or more of such former members are not included in a loss subgroup immediately after they cease to be members of the group (for example, because they do not have net operating loss carryovers or, in the aggregate, a net unrealized built-in loss), but are members of the same consolidated group, an apportionment of the consolidated section 382 limitation (or subgroup section 382 limitation) may be made to them as if they were a loss subgroup.

(7) *Examples.*—The following examples illustrate the principles of this paragraph (e):

Example 1. Basic allocation case. (i) P owns all of the stock of L1 and L2. On September 4, Year 1, A purchases all of the P stock, causing an ownership change of the P group. On that date P has two assets (other than the L1 and L2 stock), asset 1 with an adjusted basis of $40 and a fair market value of $15 and asset 2 with an adjusted basis of $50 and a fair market value of $100. L1 has two assets, asset 3, with a fair market value of $50 and an adjusted basis of $100, and asset 4, with an adjusted basis of $125 and a fair market value of $75. L2 has two assets, asset 5, with a fair market value of $150 and an adjusted basis of $100, and asset 6, with an adjusted basis of $90 and a fair market value of $40. Thus, the P loss group has a net unrealized built-in loss of $75.

(ii) On March 19, Year 3, P sells all of the L2 stock to M. At that time, asset 5, which has appreciated in value, has a fair market value of $250 and an adjusted basis of $100. Asset 6, which has declined in value, has an adjusted basis of $90 and a fair market value of $10.

(iii) On April 8, Year 3, P sells asset 1, and has a recognized built-in loss of $25 that is subject to the P group's section 382 limitation. On November 11, Year 4, L2 sells asset 6 for its then fair market value, $10, recognizing a loss of $80. On June 3, Year 5, L1 sells asset 4, recognizing a loss of $50.

(iv) Immediately after the close of Year 3, the P loss group's remaining NUBIL balance is $50 ($75 net unrealized built-in loss reduced by the $25 recognized built-in loss of P). The portion of the remaining NUBIL balance that is allocated to L2 is $17 (rounded to the nearest dollar). Seventeen dollars is the product obtained by multiplying $50 (the remaining NUBIL balance) by $50/$150. The numerator of the fraction ($50) is the amount of built-in loss in asset 6, taken into account on the change date under § 1.1502-91(g). The denominator ($150) is the sum of the numerator ($50) and the amount of built-in loss in assets 3 and 4, taken into account on the change date under § 1.1502-91(g) ($100). The built-in loss in asset 1 is not included in the denominator of the fraction because it is not held by the P group immediately after the close of Year 3.

(v) Seventeen dollars of L2's $80 loss on the sale of asset 6 is a recognized built-in loss and subject to a section 382 limitation of zero, unless P apportions some or all of the P group's consolidated section 382 limitation to L2 (adjusted for a short taxable year, carryover of unused limitation, or any other adjustment required under section 382).

(vi) Thirty-three dollars of L1's $50 loss on the sale of asset 4 is subject to the P group's consolidated section 382 limitation, reduced by the amount of such limitation apportioned to L2, and adjusted for any short taxable year, a carryforward of unused limitation, or other adjustment. (In applying section 382(h)(1)(B)(ii) with respect to Year 5, the P group's net unrealized built-in loss is reduced by P's $25 recognized built-in loss in Year 3 and the $17 of net unrealized built-in loss allocated to L2, thus limiting the P group's recognized built-in loss in Year 5 to $33.)

Example 2. Two members depart in the same year. The facts are the same as in *Example 1,* except that P sells all of the stock of L1 to C on November 1, Year 3. The amount of net unrealized built-in loss apportioned to L2 (rounded to the nearest dollar) is $17 ($50 remaining NUBIL balance × $50/$150). The amount of net unrealized built-in loss apportioned to L1 (rounded to the nearest dollar) is $33 ($50 remaining NUBIL balance × $100/$150).

(8) *Reporting requirements.*—(i) *Common Parent.*—Except as provided in paragraph (e)(8)(iii) of this section, if a net unrealized built-in loss is allocated under paragraph (e) of this section, the common parent must include a statement entitled, "STATEMENT OF NET UNREALIZED BUILT-IN LOSS ALLOCATION PURSUANT TO § 1.1502-95(e)," on or with its income tax return for the taxable year in which the former member(s) (or a new loss subgroup that includes that member) ceases to be a member. The statement must include—

(A) The name and employer identification number of the departing member;

(B) The amount of the remaining NUBIL balance for the taxable year in which the member departs;

(C) The amount of the net unrealized built-in loss allocated to the departing member; and

(D) A representation that the common parent has delivered a copy of the statement to the former member (or the common parent of the group of which the former member is a member) on or before the day the group files its income tax return for the consolidated return year that the former member ceases to be a member.

(ii) *Former Member.*—Except as provided in paragraph (e)(8)(iii) of this section, the former member must include a statement on or with its first income tax return (or the first return in which the former member joins) that is filed after the close of the consolidated return year of the group of which the former member (or a new loss subgroup that includes that member) ceases to be a member. The statement will be identical to the statement filed by the common parent under paragraph (e)(8)(i) of this section except that instead of including the information described in paragraph (e)(8)(i)(A) of this section the former member must provide the name, employer identification number and tax year of the former common parent, and instead of the representation described in paragraph (e)(8)(i)(D) of this section the former member must represent that it has received and retained the copy of the statement delivered by the common parent as part of its records. See § 1.6001-1(e).

(iii) *Exception.*—This paragraph (e)(8) does not apply if the required information (other than the amount of the remaining NUBIL balance) is included in a statement of election under paragraph (f) of this section (relating to apportioning a section 382 limitation).

(f) *Filing the election to apportion the section 382 limitation and net unrealized built-in gain.*—(1) *Form of the election to apportion.*—(i) *Statement.*—An election under paragraph (c) of this section must be made in the form set forth in this paragraph (f)(1)(i). The election must be made by the common parent and the party described in paragraph (f)(2) of this section. It must be filed in accordance with paragraph (f)(3) of this section and be entitled, "THIS IS AN ELECTION UNDER § 1.1502-95 TO APPORTION ALL OR PART OF THE [INSERT THE CONSOLIDATED SECTION 382 LIMITATION, THE SUBGROUP SECTION 382 LIMITATION, THE LOSS GROUP'S NET UNREALIZED BUILT-IN GAIN, OR THE LOSS SUBGROUP'S NET UNREALIZED BUILT-IN GAIN, AS APPROPRIATE] IN THE AMOUNT OF [INSERT THE AMOUNT OF THE LOSS LIMITATION OR NET UNREALIZED BUILT-IN GAIN] TO [INSERT NAME(S) AND EMPLOYER IDENTIFICATION NUMBER(S) OF THE CORPORATION (OR THE CORPORATIONS THAT COMPOSE A NEW LOSS SUBGROUP) TO WHICH ALLOCATION IS MADE]." The statement must also indicate that an agreement, as described in paragraph (f)(1)(ii) of this section, has been entered into.

(ii) *Agreement.*—Both the common parent and the party described in paragraph (f)(2) of this section must sign and date the agreement. The agreement must include, as appropriate—

(A) The date of the ownership change that resulted in the consolidated section 382 limitation (or subgroup section 382 limitation) or the loss group's (or loss subgroup's) net unrealized built-in gain;

(B) The amount of the departing member's (or loss subgroup's) pre-change net operating loss carryovers and the taxable years in which they arose that will be subject to the limitation that is being apportioned to that member (or loss subgroup);

(C) The amount of any net unrealized built-in loss allocated to the departing member (or loss subgroup) under paragraph (e) of this section, which, if recognized, can be a pre-change attribute subject to the limitation that is being apportioned;

(D) If a consolidated section 382 limitation (or subgroup section 382 limitation) is being apportioned, the amount of the consolidated section 382 limitation (or subgroup section 382 limitation) for the taxable year during which the former member (or new loss subgroup) ceases to be a member of the consolidated group (determined without regard to any apportionment under this section);

(E) If any net unrealized built-in gain is being apportioned, the amount of the loss group's (or loss subgroup's) net unrealized built-in gain (as determined under paragraph (c)(2)(ii) of this section) that may be apportioned to members that ceased to be members during the consolidated return year;

(F) The amount of the value element and adjustment element of the consolidated section 382 limitation (or subgroup section 382 limitation) that is apportioned to the former member (or new loss subgroup) pursuant to paragraph (c) of this section;

(G) The amount of the loss group's (or loss subgroup's) net unrealized built-in gain that is apportioned to the former member (or new loss subgroup) pursuant to paragraph (c) of this section;

(H) If the former member is allocated any net unrealized built-in loss under paragraph (e) of this section, the amount of any adjustment element apportioned to the former member that is attributable to recognized built-in gains (determined in a manner that will enable both the group and the former member to apply the principles of § 1.1502-93(c)); and

(I) The name and employer identification number of the common parent making the apportionment.

(2) *Signing the agreement.*—The agreement must be signed by both the common parent and the former member (or, in the case of a loss subgroup, the common parent and the loss subgroup parent) by persons authorized to sign their respective income tax returns. If the allocation is made to a loss subgroup for which an election under § 1.1502-91(d)(4) is made, and not separately to its members, the agreement under this paragraph (f) must be signed by the common parent and any member of the new loss

subgroup by persons authorized to sign their respective income tax returns. Each party signing the agreement must retain either the original or a copy of the agreement as part of its records. See § 1.6001-1(e).

(3) *Filing of the election.*—(i) *Filing by the common parent.*—The election must be filed by the common parent of the group that is apportioning the consolidated section 382 limitation (or the subgroup section 382 limitation) or the loss group's net unrealized built-in gain (or loss subgroup's net unrealized built-in gain) by including the statement on or with its income tax return for the taxable year in which the former member (or new loss subgroup) ceases to be a member.

(ii) *Filing by the former member.*—An identical statement must be included on or with the first return of the former member (or the first return in which the former member, or the members of a new loss subgroup, join) that is filed after the close of the consolidated return year of the group of which the former member (or the members of a new loss subgroup) ceases to be a member.

(4) *Revocation of election.*—An election statement made under paragraph (c) of this section is revocable only with the consent of the Commissioner.

(g) *Effective/applicability date.*—Paragraphs (e)(8) and (f) of this section apply to any original consolidated Federal income tax return due (without extensions) after June 14, 2007. For original consolidated Federal income tax returns due (without extensions) after May 30, 2006, and on or before June 14, 2007, see § 1.1502-95T as contained in 26 CFR part 1 in effect on April 1, 2007. For original consolidated Federal income tax returns due (without extensions) on or before May 30, 2006, see § 1.1502-95 as contained in 26 CFR part 1 in effect on April 1, 2006. [Reg. § 1.1502-95.]

☐ [*T.D.* 8824, 6-25-99. *Amended by T.D.* 9264, 5-26-2006; *T.D.* 9329, 6-13-2007 *and T.D.* 9424, 9-9-2008.]

[Reg. § 1.1502-95A]

§ 1.1502-95A. Rules on ceasing to be a member of a consolidated group generally applicable for corporations ceasing to be members before June 25, 1999.—(a) *In general.*—(1) *Consolidated group.*—This section provides rules for applying section 382 on or after the day that a member ceases to be a member of a consolidated group (or loss subgroup). The rules concern how to determine whether an ownership change occurs with respect to losses of the member, and how a consolidated section 382 limitation (or subgroup section 382 limitation) is apportioned to the member. As the context requires, a reference in this section to a loss group, a member, or a corporation also includes a reference to a loss subgroup, and a reference to a consolidated section 382 limitation also includes a reference to a subgroup section 382 limitation.

(2) *Election by common parent.*—Only the common parent (not the loss subgroup parent) may make the election under paragraph (c) of this section to apportion either a consolidated section 382 limitation or a subgroup section 382 limitation.

(3) *Coordination with §§1.1502-91A through 1.1502-93A.*—For rules regarding the determination of whether there is an ownership change of a loss subgroup and the computation of a subgroup section 382 limitation following such an ownership change, see §§1.1502-91A through 1.1502-93A.

(b) *Separate application of section 382 when a member leaves a consolidated group.*—(1) *In general.*—Except as provided in §§1.1502-91A through 1.1502-93A (relating to rules applicable to loss groups and loss subgroups), section 382 and the regulations thereunder apply to a corporation on a separate entity basis after it ceases to be a member of a consolidated group (or loss subgroup). Solely for purposes of determining whether a corporation has an ownership change—

(i) Any portion of a consolidated net operating loss that is apportioned to the corporation under §1.1502-21(b) or 1.1502-21T(b) in effect prior to June 25, 1999, as contained in 26 CFR part 1 revised April 1, 1999, as applicable is treated as a net operating loss of the corporation beginning on the first day of the taxable year in which the loss arose;

(ii) The testing period may include the period during which (or before which) the corporation was a member of the group (or loss subgroup); and

(iii) Except to the extent provided in §1.1502-20(g) (relating to reattributed losses), the day it ceases to be a member of a consolidated group is treated as a testing date of the corporation within the meaning of §1.382-2(a)(4).

(2) *Effect of a prior ownership change of the group.*—If a loss group has had an ownership change under §1.1502-92A before a corporation ceases to be a member of a consolidated group (the former member)—

(i) Any pre-change consolidated attribute that is subject to a consolidated section 382 limitation continues to be treated as a pre-change loss with respect to the former member after the attribute is apportioned to the former member;

(ii) The former member's section 382 limitation with respect to such attribute is zero except to the extent the common parent apportions under paragraph (c) of this section all or a part of the consolidated section 382 limitation to the former member;

(iii) The testing period for determining a subsequent ownership change with respect to such attribute begins no earlier than the first day following the loss group's most recent change date; and

(iv) As generally provided under section 382, an ownership change of the former member that occurs on or after the day it ceases to be a member of a loss group may result in an additional, lesser limitation amount with respect to such loss.

(3) *Application in the case of a loss subgroup.*— If two or more former members are included in the same loss subgroup immediately after they cease to be members of a consolidated group, the principles of paragraphs (b) and (c) of this section apply to the loss subgroup. Therefore, for example, an apportionment by the common parent under paragraph (c) of this section is made to the loss subgroup rather than separately to its members.

(4) *Examples.*—The following examples illustrate the principles of this paragraph (b).

Example 1. Treatment of departing member as a separate corporation throughout the testing period. (a) A owns all the L stock. L owns all the stock of L1 and L2. The L group has a consolidated net operating loss arising in Year 1 that is carried over to Year 3. On January 12, Year 2, A sells 30 percent of the L stock to B. On February 7, Year 3, L sells 40 percent of the L2 stock to C, and L2 ceases to be a member of the group. A portion of the Year 1 consolidated net operating loss is apportioned to L2 under §1.1502-21(b) or 1.1502-21T(b) in effect prior to June 25, 1999, as contained in 26 CFR part 1 revised April 1, 1999, as applicable and is carried to L2's first separate return year, which ends December 31, Year 3. The following is a graphic illustration of these facts:

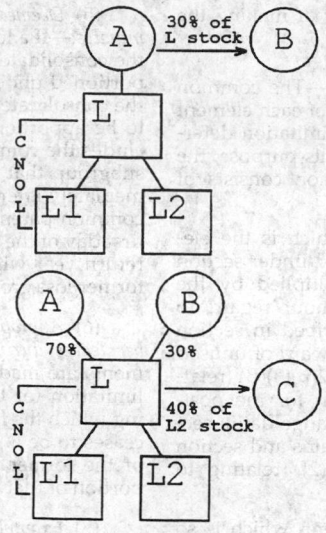

(b) Under paragraph (b)(1) of this section, L2 is a loss corporation on February 7, Year 3. Under paragraph (b)(1)(iii) of this section, February 7, Year 3, is a testing date. Under paragraph (b)(1)(ii) of this section, the testing period for L2 with respect to this testing date commences on January 1, Year 1, the first day of the taxable year in which the portion of the consolidated net operating loss apportioned to L2 arose. Therefore, in determining whether L2 has an ownership change on February 7, Year 3, B's purchase of 30 percent of the L stock and C's purchase of 40 percent of the L2 stock are each owner shifts. L2 has an ownership change under section 382(g) and §1.382-2T because B and C have increased their ownership interests in L2 by 18 and 40 percentage points, respectively, during the testing period.

Example 2. Effect of prior ownership change of loss group. (a) L owns all the L1 stock and L1 owns all the L2 stock. The L loss group had an ownership change under §1.1502-92A in Year 2 with respect to a consolidated net operating loss arising in Year 1 and carried over to Year 2 and Year 3. The consolidated section 382 limitation computed solely on the basis of the value of the stock of L is $100. On December 31, Year 2, L1 sells 25 percent of the stock of L2 to B. L2 is

apportioned a portion of the Year 1 consolidated net operating loss which it carries over to its first separate return year ending after December 31, Year 2. L2's separate section 382 limitation with respect to this loss is zero unless L elects to apportion all or a part of the consolidated section 382 limitation to L2. (See paragraph (c) of this section for rules regarding the apportionment of a consolidated section 382 limitation.) L apportions $50 of the consolidated section 382 limitation to L2.

(b) On December 31, Year 3, L1 sells its remaining 75 percent stock interest in L2 to C, resulting in an ownership change of L2. L2's section 382 limitation computed on the change date with respect to the value of its stock is $30. Accordingly, L2's section 382 limitation for post-change years ending after December 31, Year 3, with respect to its pre-change losses, including the consolidated net operating losses apportioned to it from the L group, is $30, adjusted as required by section 382 and the regulations thereunder.

(c) *Apportionment of a consolidated section 382 limitation.*—(1) *In general.*—The common parent may elect to apportion all or any part of a consolidated section 382 limitation to a former member (or loss subgroup). See paragraph (e) of this section for the time and manner of making the election to apportion.

(2) *Amount of apportionment.*—The common parent may apportion all or part of each element of the consolidated section 382 limitation determined under §1.1502-93A. For this purpose, the consolidated section 382 limitation consists of two elements —

(i) The value element, which is the element of the limitation determined under section 382(b)(1) (relating to value multiplied by the long-term tax-exempt rate) without regard to such adjustments as those described in section 382(b)(2) (relating to the carryforward of unused section 382 limitation), section 382(b)(3)(B) (relating to the section 382 limitation for the post-change year that includes the change date), section 382(h) (relating to built-in gains and section 338 gains), and section 382(m)(2) (relating to short taxable years); and

(ii) The adjustment element, which is so much (if any) of the limitation for the taxable year during which the former member ceases to be a member of the consolidated group that is attributable to a carryover of unused limitation under section 382(b)(2) or to recognized built-in gains under 382(h).

(3) *Effect of apportionment on the consolidated section 382 limitation.*—The value element of the consolidated section 382 limitation for any post-change year ending after the day that a former member (or loss subgroup) ceases to be a member(s) is reduced to the extent that it is apportioned under this paragraph (c). The consolidated section 382 limitation for the post-change year in which the former member (or loss subgroup) ceases to be a member(s) is also reduced to the extent that the adjustment element for that year is apportioned under this paragraph (c).

(4) *Effect on corporations to which the consolidated section 382 limitation is apportioned.*—The amount of the value element that is apportioned to a former member (or loss subgroup) is treated as the amount determined under section 382(b)(1) for purposes of determining the amount of that corporation's (or loss subgroup's) section 382 limitation for any taxable year ending after the former member (or loss subgroup) ceases to be a member(s). Appropriate adjustments must be made to the limitation based on the value element so apportioned for a short taxable year, carryforward of unused limitation, or any other adjustment required under section 382. The adjustment element apportioned to a former member (or loss subgroup) is treated as an adjustment under section 382(b)(2) or section 382(h), as appropriate, for the first taxable year after the member (or members) ceases to be a member (or members).

(5) *Deemed apportionment when loss group terminates.*—If a loss group terminates, to the extent the consolidated section 382 limitation is not apportioned under paragraph (c)(1) of this section, the consolidated section 382 limitation is deemed to be apportioned to the loss subgroup that includes the common parent, or, if there is no loss subgroup that includes the common parent immediately after the loss group terminates, to the common parent. A loss group terminates on the first day of the first taxable year that is a separate return year with respect to each member of the former loss group.

(6) *Appropriate adjustments when former member leaves during the year.*—Appropriate adjustments are made to the consolidated section 382 limitation for the consolidated return year during which the former member (or loss subgroup) ceases to be a member(s) to reflect the inclusion of the former member in the loss group for a portion of that year.

(7) *Examples.*—The following examples illustrate the principles of this paragraph (c).

Example 1. Consequence of apportionment. (a) L owns all the L1 stock and L1 owns all the L2 stock. The L group has a $200 consolidated net operating loss arising in Year 1 that is carried over to Year 2. At the close of December 31, Year 1, the group has an ownership change under §1.1502-92A. The ownership change results in a consolidated section 382 limitation of $10 based on the value of the stock of the group. On August 29, Year 2, L1 sells 30 percent of the stock of L2 to A. L2 is apportioned $90 of the group's $200 consolidated net operating loss under §1.1502-21(b) or 1.1502-21T(b) in effect prior to June 25, 1999, as contained in 26 CFR part 1 revised April 1, 1999, as applicable. L, the common parent, elects to apportion $6 of the consolidated section 382 limitation to L2. The following is a graphic illustration of these facts:

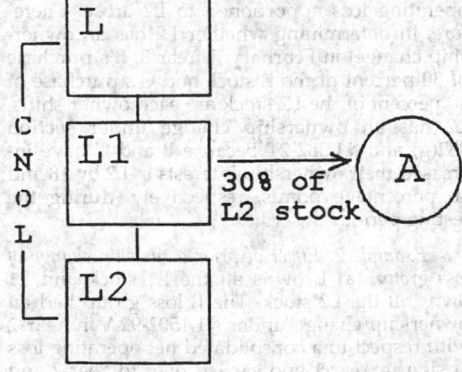

(b) For its separate return years ending after August 29, Year 2 (other than the taxable year ending December 31, Year 2), L2's section 382 limitation with respect to the $90 of the group's net operating loss apportioned to it is $6, adjusted, as appropriate, for any short taxable year, unused section 382 limitation, or other adjustment. For its consolidated return years ending after August 29, Year 2, (other than the year ending December 31, Year 2) the L group's consolidated section 382 limitation with respect to the remaining $110 of pre-change consolidated attribute is $4 ($10 minus the $6 value element apportioned to L2), adjusted, as appropriate, for any short taxable year, unused section 382 limitation, or other adjustment.

(c) For the L group's consolidated return year ending December 31, Year 2, the value element of its consolidated section 382 limitation is increased by $4 (rounded to the nearest dollar), to account for the period during which L2 was a member of the L group ($6, the consolidated section 382 limitation apportioned to L2, times 241/365, the ratio of the number of days during Year 2 that L2 is a member of the group to the number of days in the group's consolidated return year). See paragraph (c)(6) of this section. Therefore, the value element of the consolidated section 382 limitation for Year 2 of the L group is $8 (rounded to the nearest dollar).

(d) The section 382 limitation for L2's short taxable year ending December 31, Year 2, is $2 (rounded to the nearest dollar), which is the amount that bears the same relationship to $6, the value element of the consolidated section 382 limitation apportioned to L2, as the number of days during that short taxable year, 124 days, bears to 365. See § 1.382-4(c).

Example 2. Consequence of no apportionment. The facts are the same as in *Example 1*, except that L does not elect to apportion any portion of the consolidated section 382 limitation to L2. For its separate return years ending after August 29, Year 2, L2's section 382 limitation with respect to the $90 of the group's pre-change consolidated attribute apportioned to L2 is zero under paragraph (b)(2)(ii) of this section. Thus, the $90 consolidated net operating loss apportioned to L2 cannot offset L2's taxable income in any of its separate return years ending after August 29, Year 2. For its consolidated return years ending

after August 29, Year 2, the L group's consolidated section 382 limitation with respect to the remaining $110 of pre-change consolidated attribute is $10, adjusted, as appropriate, for any short taxable year, unused section 382 limitation, or other adjustment.

Example 3. Apportionment of adjustment element. The facts are the same as in *Example 1*, except that L2 ceases to be a member of the L group on August 29, Year 3, and the L group has a $4 carryforward of an unused consolidated section 382 limitation (under section 382(b)(2)) to the 1993 consolidated return year. The carryover of unused limitation increases the consolidated section 382 limitation for the Year 3 consolidated return year from $10 to $14. L may elect to apportion all or any portion of the $10 value element and all or any portion of the $4 adjustment element to L2.

(d) *Rules pertaining to ceasing to be a member of a loss subgroup.*—(1) *In general.*—A corporation ceases to be a member of a loss subgroup—

(i) On the first day of the first taxable year for which it files a separate return; or

(ii) The first day that it ceases to bear a relationship described in section 1504(a)(1) to the loss subgroup parent (treating for this purpose the loss subgroup parent as the common parent described in section 1504(a)(1)(A)).

(2) *Examples.*—The principles of this paragraph (d) are illustrated by the following examples.

Example 1. Basic case. (a) P owns all the L stock, L owns all the L1 stock and L1 owns all the L2 stock. The P group has a consolidated net operating loss arising in Year 1 that is carried over to Year 2. On December 11, Year 2, P sells all the stock of L to corporation M. Each of L, L1, and L2 is apportioned a portion of the Year 1 consolidated net operating loss, and thereafter each joins with M in filing consolidated returns. Under § 1.1502-92A, the L loss subgroup has an ownership change on December 11, Year 2. The L loss subgroup has a subgroup section 382 limitation of $100. The following is a graphic illustration of these facts:

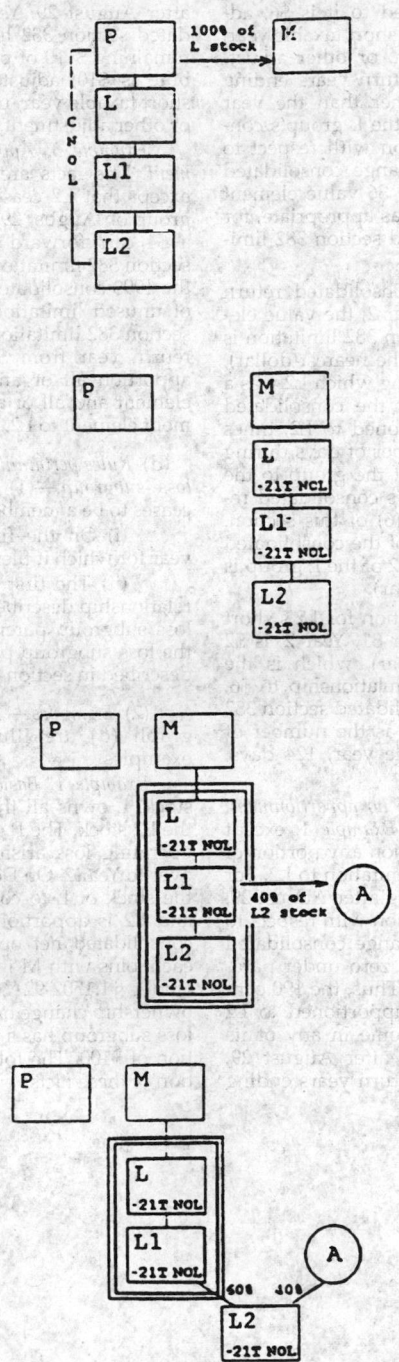

(b) On May 22, Year 3, L1 sells 40 percent of the L2 stock to A. L2 carries over a portion of the P group's net operating loss from Year 1 to its separate return year ending December 31, Year 3. Under paragraph (d)(1) of this section, L2 ceases to be a member of the L loss subgroup on May

22, Year 3, which is both (1) the first day of the first taxable year for which it files a separate return and (2) the day it ceases to bear a relationship described in section 1504(a)(1) to the loss subgroup parent, L. The net operating loss of L2 that is carried over from the P group is treated as a pre-change loss of L2 for its separate return years ending after May 22, Year 3. Under paragraphs (a)(2) and (b)(2) of this section, the separate section 382 limitation with respect to this loss is zero unless M elects to apportion all or a part of the subgroup section 382 limitation of the L loss subgroup to L2.

Example 2. Formation of a new loss subgroup. The facts are the same as in *Example 1*, except that A purchases 40 percent of the L1 stock from

L rather than purchasing L2 stock from L1. L1 and L2 file a consolidated return for their first taxable year ending after May 22, Year 3, and each of L1 and L2 carries over a part of the net operating loss of the P group that arose in Year 1. Under paragraph (d)(1) of this section, L1 and L2 cease to be members of the L loss subgroup on May 22, Year 3. The net operating losses carried over from the P group are treated as pre-change subgroup attributes of the loss subgroup composed of L1 and L2. The subgroup section 382 limitation with respect to those losses is zero unless M elects to apportion all or part of the subgroup section 382 limitation of the L loss subgroup to the L1 loss subgroup. The following is a graphic illustration of these facts:

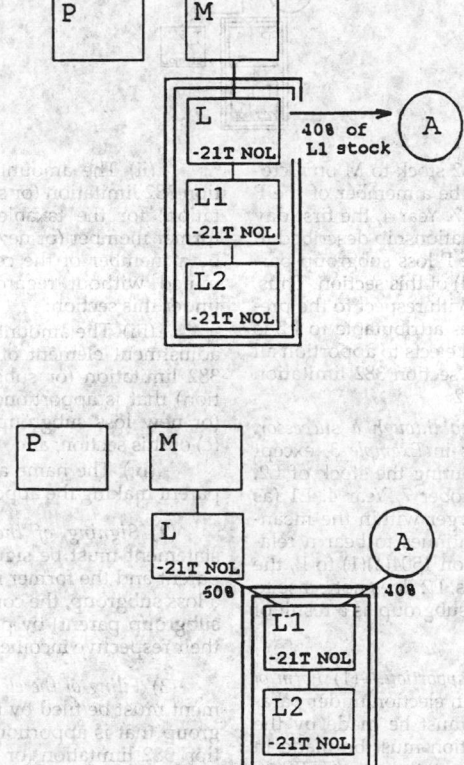

Example 3. Ceasing to bear a section 1504(a)(1) relationship to a loss subgroup parent. (a) A owns all the stock of P, and P owns all the stock of L1 and L2. The P group has a consolidated net operating loss arising in Year 1 that is carried over to Year 3 and Year 4. Corporation M ac-

quires all the stock of P on November 11, Year 3, and P, L1, and L2 thereafter file consolidated returns with M. M's acquisition results in an ownership change of the P loss subgroup under § 1.1502-92A(b)(1)(ii). The following is a graphic illustration of these facts:

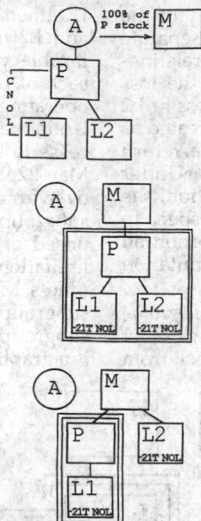

(b) P distributes the L2 stock to M on October 7, Year 4. L2 ceases to be a member of the P loss subgroup on October 7, Year 4, the first day that it ceases to bear the relationship described in section 1504(a)(1) to P, the P loss subgroup parent. See paragraph (d)(1)(ii) of this section. Thus, the section 382 limitation with respect to the pre-change subgroup attributes attributable to L2 is zero except to the extent M elects to apportion all or a part of the subgroup section 382 limitation of the P loss subgroup to L2.

Example 4. Relationship through a successor. The facts are the same as in *Example 3*, except that, instead of P's distributing the stock of L2, L2 merges into L1 on October 7, Year 4. L1 (as successor to L2 in the merger within the meaning of §1.382-2T(f)(4)) continues to bear a relationship described in section 1504(a)(1) to P, the loss subgroup parent. Thus, L2 does not cease to be a member of the P loss subgroup as a result of the merger.

(e) *Filing the election to apportion.*—(1) *Form of the election to apportion.*—An election under paragraph (c) of this section must be made by the common parent. The election must be made in the form of the following statement: "THIS IS AN ELECTION UNDER §1.1502-95A OF THE INCOME TAX REGULATIONS TO APPORTION ALL OR PART OF THE [insert either CONSOLIDATED SECTION 382 LIMITATION or SUBGROUP SECTION 382 LIMITATION, as appropriate] TO [insert name and E.I.N. of the corporation (or the corporations that compose a new loss subgroup) to which allocation is made]. The declaration must also include the following information, as appropriate—

(i) The date of the ownership change that resulted in the consolidated section 382 limitation (or subgroup section 382 limitation);

(ii) The amount of the consolidated section 382 limitation (or subgroup section 382 limitation) for the taxable year during which the former member (or new loss subgroup) ceases to be a member of the consolidated group (determined without regard to any apportionment under this section;

(iii) The amount of the value element and adjustment element of the consolidated section 382 limitation (or subgroup section 382 limitation) that is apportioned to the former member (or new loss subgroup) pursuant to paragraph (c) of this section; and

(iv) The name and E.I.N. of the common parent making the apportionment.

(2) *Signing of the election.*—The election statement must be signed by both the common parent and the former member (or, in the case of a loss subgroup, the common parent and the loss subgroup parent) by persons authorized to sign their respective income tax returns.

(3) *Filing of the election.*—The election statement must be filed by the common parent of the group that is apportioning the consolidated section 382 limitation (or the subgroup section 382 limitation) with its income tax return for the taxable year in which the former member (or new loss subgroup) ceases to be a member. The common parent must also deliver a copy of the statement to the former member (or the members of the new loss subgroup) on or before the day the group files its income tax return for the consolidated return year that the former member (or new loss subgroup) ceases to be a member. A copy of the statement must be attached to the first return of the former member (or the first return in which the members of a new loss subgroup join) that is filed after the close of the consolidated return year of the group of which

the former member (or the members of a new loss subgroup) ceases to be a member.

(4) *Revocation of election.*—An election statement made under paragraph (c) of this section is revocable only with the consent of the Commissioner. [Reg. § 1.1502-95A.]

☐ [*T.D. 8678, 6-26-96. Amended by T.D. 8823, 6-25-99 and amended and redesignated by T.D. 8824, 6-25-99.*]

[Reg. § 1.1502-96]

§ 1.1502-96. Miscellaneous rules.—(a) *End of separate tracking of losses.*—(1) *Application.*—This paragraph (a) applies to a member (or a loss subgroup) with a net operating loss carryover that arose (or is treated under § 1.1502-21(c) as arising) in a SRLY, or a member (or loss subgroup) with a net unrealized built-in loss determined at the time that the member (or loss subgroup) becomes a member of the consolidated group if there is—

(i) An ownership change of the member (or loss subgroup) within six months before, on, or after becoming a member of the group; or

(ii) A period of 5 consecutive years following the day that the member (or loss subgroup) becomes a member of a group during which the member (or loss subgroup) has not had an ownership change.

(2) *Effect of end of separate tracking.*—(i) *Net operating loss carryovers.*—If this paragraph (a) applies with respect to a member (or loss subgroup) with a net operating loss carryover, then, starting on the day after the earlier of the change date (but not earlier than the day the member (or loss subgroup) becomes a member of the consolidated group) or the last day of the 5 consecutive year period described in paragraph (a)(1)(ii) of this section, such loss carryover is treated as described in § 1.1502-91(c)(1)(i). The preceding sentence also applies for purposes of determining whether there is an ownership change with respect to such loss carryover following such change date or 5 consecutive year period. Thus, for example, starting the day after the change date (but not earlier than the day the member (or loss subgroup) becomes a member of the consolidated group) or the end of the 5 consecutive year period—

(A) The consolidated group which includes the new loss member or loss subgroup is no longer required to separately track owner shifts of the stock of the new loss member or subgroup parent to determine if an ownership change occurs with respect to the loss carryover of the new loss member or members included in the loss subgroup;

(B) The group is a loss group because the member's loss carryover is treated as a loss described in § 1.1502-91(c)(1)(i);

(C) There is an ownership change with respect to such loss carryover only if the group has an ownership change; and

(D) If the group has an ownership change, such loss carryover is a pre-change consolidated attribute subject to the loss group's consolidated section 382 limitation.

(ii) *Net unrealized built-in losses.*—If this paragraph (a) applies with respect to a new loss member described in § 1.1502-94(a)(1)(ii) (or a loss subgroup described in § 1.1502-91(d)(2)) then, starting on the day after the earlier of the change date (but not earlier than the day the member (or loss subgroup) becomes a member of the group) or the last day of the 5 consecutive year period described in paragraph (a)(1)(ii) of this section, the member (or members of the loss subgroup) are treated, for purposes of applying § 1.1502-91(g)(2)(ii), as if they have been affiliated with the common parent for 5 consecutive years. Starting on that day, the member's (or the members of the loss subgroup's) separately computed net unrealized built-in loss is included in the determination whether the group has a net unrealized built-in loss, and there is an ownership change with respect to the member's separately computed net unrealized built-in loss only if the group (including the member) has a net unrealized built-in loss and has an ownership change. Thus, for example, starting the day after the change date (but not earlier than the day the member (or loss subgroup) becomes a member of the consolidated group), or the end of the 5 consecutive period—

(A) The consolidated group which includes the new loss member or loss subgroup is no longer required to separately track owner shifts of the stock of the new loss member or subgroup parent to determine if an ownership change occurs with respect to the net unrealized built-in loss of the new loss member or members of the loss subgroup;

(B) The group includes the member's (or the loss subgroup members') separately computed net unrealized built-in loss in determining whether it is a loss group under § 1.1502-91(c)(1)(iii);

(C) There is an ownership change with respect to such net unrealized built-in loss only if the group is a loss group and has an ownership change; and

(D) If the group has an ownership change, the member's separately computed net unrealized built-in loss and its assets are taken into account in determining the group's pre-change consolidated attributes described in § 1.1502-91(e)(1) (relating to recognized built-in losses) that are subject to the group's consolidated section 382 limitation.

(iii) *Common parent not common parent for five years.*—If the common parent has become the common parent of an existing group within the previous 5-year period in a transaction described in § 1.1502-75(d)(2)(ii) or (3), appropriate adjustments must be made in applying paragraphs (a)(2)(ii) and (3) of this section. In such a case, as the context requires, references to the common parent are to the former common parent.

(3) *Continuing effect of end of separate tracking.*—(i) *In general.*—As the context may require, a current group determines which of its members are included in a loss subgroup on any testing date by taking into account the application of this section in the former group. See the example in § 1.1502-91(f)(2). For this purpose, corporations that are treated under paragraph (a)(2)(ii) of this section as having been affiliated with the common parent of the former group for 5 consecutive years are also treated as having been affiliated with any other members that have been (or are treated as having been) affiliated with the common parent. The corporations are treated as having been affiliated with such other members for the same period of time that those members have been (or are treated as having been) affiliated with the common parent. If two or more corporations become members of the group at the same time, but paragraph (a)(1) of this section does not apply to every such corporation, then immediately after the corporations become members of the group, the corporations to which paragraph (a)(1) of this section applied are treated as not having been previously affiliated, for purposes of applying this paragraph (a)(3), with the corporations to which paragraph (a)(2)(ii) of this section did not apply.

(ii) *Example.*—The following example illustrates the principles of this paragraph (a)(3):

Example. (i) L has owned all the stock of L1 for three years. At the close of December 31, Year 1, the M group purchases all the L stock, and L and L1 become members of the M group. Other than the stock of L1, L has one asset (the L loss asset) with a net unrealized built-in loss of $200 on this date. L1 has one asset with a net unrealized built-in gain of $50 (the L1 gain asset). L and L1 do not compose a loss subgroup because they do not meet the five year affiliation requirement of § 1.1502-91(d)(2)(i). L is a new loss member, and M's purchase of L causes an ownership change of L. At the close of December 31, Year 4, at a time when L1 has been affiliated with the M group for three years and has been affiliated with L for six years, the S group purchases all the M stock. On this date, the L loss asset has a net unrealized built-in loss of $300, the L1 gain asset has a net unrealized built-in gain of $80, and M, the common parent of the M group, has one asset with a net unrealized built-in gain of $200.

(ii) Paragraph (a)(1) of this section applies to L because L is a new loss member described in § 1.1502-94(a)(1)(ii) that has an ownership change upon becoming a member of the M group on December 31, Year 1. Accordingly, L is treated as having been affiliated with M for 5

consecutive years, and the L loss asset with a net unrealized built-in loss of $300 is included in the determination whether the M group has a net unrealized built-in loss.

(iii) The S group determines which of its members are included in a loss subgroup by taking into account application of paragraph (a) of this section in the M group. For this purpose, application of paragraph (a) of this section causes L to be treated as having been affiliated with M (or as having been a member of the M group) for 5 consecutive years as of January 1, Year 2. Therefore, the S group includes L in the determination whether the M subgroup acquired by S on December 31, Year 4, has a net unrealized built-in loss.

(iv) Because paragraph (a)(1) of this section applied to L when L became a member of the M group, but did not apply to L1, L is treated as not having been affiliated with L1 before L and L1 joined the M group. Also, L1 is not included in the determination whether the M subgroup has a net unrealized built-in loss because L1 has not been continuously affiliated with members of the M group for the five consecutive year period ending immediately before they become members of the S group. See § 1.1502-91(g)(2).

(4) *Special rule for testing period.*—For purposes of determining the beginning of the testing period for a loss group, the member's (or loss subgroup's) net operating loss carryovers (or net unrealized built-in loss) described in paragraph (a)(2) of this section are considered to arise—

(i) In a case described in paragraph (a)(1)(i) of this section, in a taxable year that begins not earlier than the later of the day following the change date or the day that the member becomes a member of the group; and

(ii) In a case described in paragraph (a)(1)(ii) of this section, in a taxable year that begins 3 years before the end of the 5 consecutive year period.

(5) *Limits on effects of end of separate tracking.*—The rule contained in this paragraph (a) applies solely for purposes of § § 1.1502-91 through 1.1502-95 and this section (other than paragraph (b)(2)(ii)(B) of this section (relating to the definition of pre-change attributes of a subsidiary)) and § 1.1502-98, and not for purposes of other provisions of the consolidated return regulations. However, the rule contained in this paragraph (a) does apply in § § 1.1502-15(g), 1.1502-21(g) and 1.1502-22(g) for purposes of determining the composition of loss subgroups defined in § 1.1502-91(d). See also paragraph (c) of this section for the continuing effect of an ownership change with respect to pre-change attributes.

(b) *Ownership change of subsidiary.*—(1) *Ownership change of a subsidiary because of options or plan or arrangement.*—Notwithstanding

§ 1.1502-92, a subsidiary may have an ownership change for purposes of section 382 with respect to its attributes which a group or loss subgroup includes in making a determination under § 1.1502-91(c)(1) (relating to the definition of loss group) or § 1.1502-91(d) (relating to the definition of loss subgroup). The subsidiary has such an ownership change if it has an ownership change under the principles of § 1.1502-95(b) and section 382 and the regulations thereunder (determined on a separate entity basis by treating the subsidiary as not being a member of a consolidated group) in the event of—

(i) The deemed exercise under § 1.382-4(d) of an option or options (other than an option with respect to stock of the common parent) held by a person (or persons acting pursuant to a plan or arrangement) to acquire more than 20 percent of the stock of the subsidiary; or

(ii) An increase by 1 or more 5-percent shareholders, acting pursuant to a plan or arrangement to avoid an ownership change of a subsidiary, in their percentage ownership interest in the subsidiary by more than 50 percentage points during the testing period of the subsidiary through the acquisition (or deemed acquisition pursuant to § 1.382-4(d)) of ownership interests in the subsidiary and in higher-tier members with respect to the subsidiary.

(2) *Effect of the ownership change.*—(i) *In general.*—If a subsidiary has an ownership change under paragraph (b)(1) of this section, the amount of consolidated taxable income for any post-change year that may be offset by the pre-change losses of the subsidiary shall not exceed the section 382 limitation for the subsidiary. For purposes of this limitation, the value of the subsidiary is determined solely by reference to the value of the subsidiary's stock.

(ii) *Pre-change losses.*—The pre-change losses of a subsidiary are—

(A) Its allocable part of any consolidated net operating loss which is attributable to it under § 1.1502-21(b) (determined on the last day of the consolidated return year that includes the change date) that is not carried back and absorbed in a taxable year prior to the year including the change date;

(B) Its net operating loss carryovers that arose (or are treated under § 1.1502-21(c) as having arisen) in a SRLY; and

(C) Its recognized built-in loss with respect to its separately computed net unrealized built-in loss, if any, determined on the change date.

(3) *Coordination with §§ 1.1502-91, 1.1502-92, and 1.1502-94.*—If an increase in percentage ownership interest causes an ownership change with respect to an attribute under this paragraph (b) and under § 1.1502-92 on the same day, the ownership change is considered to occur only under § 1.1502-92 and not under this paragraph (b). See § 1.1502-94 for anti-duplication rules relating to value.

(4) *Example.*—The following example illustrates paragraph (b)(1)(ii) of this section:

Example. Plan to avoid an ownership change of a subsidiary. (i) L owns all the stock of L1, L1 owns all the stock of L2, L2 owns all the stock of L3, and L3 owns all the stock of L4. The L group has a consolidated net operating loss arising in Year 1 that is carried over to Year 2. L has assets other than its L1 stock with a value of $900. L1, L2, and L3 own no assets other than their L2, L3, and L4 stock. L4 has assets with a value of $100. During Year 2, A, B, C, and D, acting pursuant to a plan to avoid an ownership change of L4, acquire the following ownership interests in the members of the L loss group: (A) on September 11, Year 2, A acquires 20 percent of the L1 stock from L and B acquires 20 percent of the L2 stock from L1; and (B) on September 20, Year 2, C acquires 20 percent of the stock of L3 from L2 and D acquires 20 percent of the stock of L4 from L3.

(ii) The acquisitions by A, B, C, and D pursuant to the plan have increased their respective percentage ownership interests in L4 by approximately 10, 13, 16, and 20 percentage points, for a total of approximately 59 percentage points during the testing period. This more than 50 percentage point increase in the percentage ownership interest in L4 causes an ownership change of L4 under paragraph (b)(2) of this section.

(c) *Continuing effect of an ownership change.*—A loss corporation (or loss subgroup) that is subject to a limitation under section 382 with respect to its pre-change losses continues to be subject to the limitation regardless of whether it becomes a member or ceases to be a member of a consolidated group. See § 1.382-5(d) (relating to successive ownership changes and absorption of a section 382 limitation).

(d) *Losses reattributed under § 1.1502-36(d)(6).*—(1) *In general.*—This paragraph (d) contains rules relating to net operating carryovers, capital loss carryovers, and deferred deductions (collectively, loss or losses) that are reattributed to the common parent under § 1.1502-36(d)(6). References in this paragraph (d) to a subsidiary are references to the subsidiary (or lower-tier subsidiary) whose loss is reattributed to the common parent.

(2) *Deemed section 381(a) transaction.*—Under § 1.1502-36(d)(6)(iv)(A), the common parent succeeds to the reattributed losses as if the losses were succeeded to in a transaction to which section 381(a) applies. In general, §§ 1.1502-91 through 1.1502-95, this section, and § 1.1502-98 are applied to the reattributed losses in accordance with that characterization. See generally, § 1.382-2(a)(1)(ii) (relating to distributor or transferor loss corporations in transactions under sec-

tion 381), §1.1502-1(f)(4) (relating to the definition of predecessor and successor) and §1.1502-91(j) (relating to predecessor and successor corporations). For example, if the reattributed loss is a pre-change attribute subject to a section 382 limitation, it remains subject to that limitation following the reattribution. In certain cases, the limitation applicable to the reattributed loss is zero unless the common parent apportions all or part of the limitation to itself. (See paragraph (d)(4) of this section.)

(3) *Rules relating to owner shifts.*—(i) *In general.*—Any owner shift of the subsidiary (including any deemed owner shift resulting from section 382(g)(4)(D) or 382(l)(3)) in connection with the disposition of the stock of the subsidiary is not taken into account in determining whether there is an ownership change with respect to the reattributed loss. However, any owner shift with respect to the successor corporation that is treated as continuing in existence under §1.382-2(a)(1)(ii) must be taken into account for such purpose if such owner shift is effected by the reattribution and an owner shift of the stock of the subsidiary not held directly or indirectly by the common parent would have been taken into account if such shift had occurred immediately before the reattribution. See paragraph (d)(3)(ii) *Example 2* of this section.

(ii) *Examples.*—The following examples illustrate the principles of this paragraph (d)(3):

Example 1. No owner shift for reattributed loss. (i) *Facts.* P, the common parent of a consolidated group, owns 60% of the stock of L, and B owns the remaining 40%. L has a net operating loss carryover of $100 from year 1 that it carries over to years 2, 3, and 4. At the beginning of year 2, P purchases 40% of the L stock from B, which does not cause an ownership change of L. On December 31, year 3, P sells all of the L stock to M. Pursuant to §1.1502-36(d)(6), P reattributes $10 of L's $100 net operating loss carryover to itself, and L carries $90 of its net operating loss carryover to its year 4.

(ii) *Analysis.* The sale of the L stock to M does not cause an owner shift that is taken into account in determining if there is an ownership change with respect to the $10 reattributed loss. Following the reattribution, §1.1502-94(b) continues to apply to determine if there is an ownership change with respect to the $10 reattributed loss, until, under paragraph (a) of this section, the loss is treated as described in §1.1502-91(c)(1)(i). In applying §1.1502-94(b), the 40 percentage point increase by the P shareholders prior to the reattribution is taken into account. The sale of the L stock to M does cause an ownership change of L with respect to the $90 of its net operating loss that it carries over to year 4.

Example 2. Owner shift for reattributed loss. The facts are the same as in Example 1, except that P only purchases 20% of the L stock from B and sells 80% of the L stock to M. L is a new loss member, and, under §1.1502-94(b)(1), an owner shift of the stock of L not held directly or indirectly by the common parent (the 20% of L stock still held by B) would have been taken into account if such shift had occurred immediately before the reattribution. Following the reattribution, §1.1502-94(b) continues to apply to determine if there is an ownership change with respect to the $10 reattributed loss, until, under paragraph (a) of this section, the loss is treated as described in §1.1502-91(c)(1)(i). With respect to the $10 reattributed loss, the P shareholders have increased their percentage ownership interest by 40 percentage points. The P shareholders have increased their ownership interests by 20 percentage points as a result of P's purchase of stock from B, and, under §1.382-2(a)(1)(ii), are treated as increasing their interests by an additional 20 percentage points as a result of the reattribution. (The acquisition of the L stock by M does not, however, effect an owner shift for the $10 of reattributed loss.) The sale of the L stock to M causes an ownership change of L with respect to the $90 of net operating loss that L carries over to Year 4.

(4) *Rules relating to the section 382 limitation.*—(i) *Reattributed loss is a prechange separate attribute of a new loss member.*—If the reattributed loss is a prechange separate attribute of a new loss member that is subject to a separate section 382 limitation prior to the disposition of subsidiary stock, the common parent's limitation with respect to that loss is zero, except to the extent that the common parent apportions to itself, under paragraph (d)(5) of this section, all or part of such limitation. A separate section 382 limitation is the limitation described in §1.1502-94(b) that applies to a prechange separate attribute.

(ii) *Reattributed loss is a pre-change subgroup attribute.*—If the reattributed loss is a pre-change subgroup attribute subject to a subgroup section 382 limitation prior to the disposition of subsidiary stock, and, immediately after the reattribution, the common parent is not a member of the loss subgroup, the section 382 limitation with respect to that loss is zero, except to the extent that the common parent apportions to itself, under paragraph (d)(5) of this section, all or part of the subgroup section 382 limitation. See, however, §1.1502-95(d)(3) *Example 6*, for an illustration of a case where the common parent, as successor to the subsidiary, is a member of the loss subgroup immediately after the reattribution.

(iii) *Potential application of section 382(l)(1).*—In general, the value of the stock of the common parent is used to determine the section 382 limitation for an ownership change with respect to the reattributed loss that occurs at the time of, or after, the reattribution. For example, if the loss is a pre-change consolidated attribute, the value of the stock of the common parent is used to determine the section 382 limitation, and no adjustment to that value is required because of the deemed section 381(a) transaction. However, if the loss is a pre-change separate attribute of a new loss member (or is a pre-change attribute of a loss subgroup member and the common parent was not the loss subgroup parent immediately before the reattribution), the deemed section 381(a) transaction is considered to constitute a capital contribution with respect to the new loss member (or loss subgroup member) for purposes of section 382(l)(1). Accordingly, if that section applies because the deemed capital contribution is (or is considered under section 382(l)(1)(B) to be) part of a plan described in section 382(l)(1)(A), the value of the stock of the common parent after the deemed section 381(a) transaction must be adjusted to reflect the capital contribution. Ordinarily, this will require the value of the stock of the common parent to be reduced to an amount that represents the value of the stock of the subsidiary (or loss subgroup of which the subsidiary was a member) when the reattribution occurred.

(iv) *Duplication or omission of value.*—In determining any section 382 limitation with respect to the reattributed loss and with respect to other pre-change losses, appropriate adjustments must be made so that value is not improperly omitted or duplicated as a result of the reattribution. For example, if the subsidiary has an ownership change upon its departure, and the common parent (as successor) has an ownership change with respect to the reattributed pre-change separate attribute upon its reattribution under paragraph (d)(3)(i) of this section, proper adjustments must be made so that the value of the subsidiary is not taken into account more than once in determining the section 382 limitation for the reattributed loss and the loss that is not reattributed.

(v) *Special rule for continuity of business requirement.*—If the reattributed loss is a pre-change attribute of new loss member and the reattribution occurs within the two-year period beginning on the change date, then, starting immediately after the reattribution, the continuity of business requirement of section 382(c)(1) is applied with respect to the business enterprise of the common parent. Similar principles apply if the reattributed loss is a pre-change subgroup attribute and, on the day after the reattribution, the common parent is not a member of the loss subgroup.

(5) *Election to reattribute section 382 limitation.*—(i) *Effect of election.*—The common parent may elect to apportion to itself all or part of any separate section 382 limitation or subgroup section 382 limitation to which the loss is subject immediately before the reattribution. However, no net unrealized built-in gain of the member (or loss subgroup) whose loss is reattributed can be apportioned to the common parent. The principles of § 1.1502-95(c) apply to the apportionment, treating, as the context requires, references to the former member as references to the common parent, and references to the consolidated section 382 limitation as references to the separate section 382 limitation (or subgroup section 382 limitation) that is being apportioned. Thus, for example, the common parent can reattribute to itself all or part of the value element or adjustment element of the limitation, and any part of such element that is apportioned requires a corresponding reduction in such element of the separate section 382 limitation of the subsidiary whose loss is reattributed (or in the subgroup section 382 limitation if the reattributed loss is a pre-change subgroup attribute). Appropriate adjustments must be made to the separate section 382 limitation (or subgroup section 382 limitation) for the consolidated return year in which the reattribution is made to reflect that the reattributed loss is an attribute acquired by the common parent during the year in a transaction to which section 381(a) applies. The election is made by the common parent as part of the election to reattribute the loss. See § 1.1502-36(e)(5)(x) for the time and manner of making the election.

(ii) *Examples.*—The following examples illustrate the principles of this paragraph (d)(5):

Example 1. Consequence of apportionment. (i) *Facts.* P, the common parent of a consolidated group, purchases all of the stock of L on December 31, year 1. L carries over a net operating loss arising in year 1 to each of the next 5 taxable years. The purchase of the L stock causes an ownership change of L, and results in a separate section 382 limitation of $10 for L's net operating loss carryover based on the value of the L stock. On July 2, year 3, P sells 30% of the L stock to A. Under § 1.1502-36(d)(6), P elects to reattribute to itself $110 of L's $200 net operating loss carryover. P also elects to apportion to itself $6 of the $10 value element of the separate section 382 limitation.

(ii) *Analysis.* (A) *P's separate section 382 limitation.* For the consolidated return years ending after December 31, year 3, P's separate section 382 limitation with respect to the reattributed net operating loss carryover is $6, adjusted as appropriate for any short taxable year, unused section 382 limitation, or other adjustment. For the P group's consolidated return year ending December 31, year 3, the separate section 382 limitation for L's net operating loss carryover is $8, the sum of $5 and $3. Five dollars of the limitation is the amount that bears the same relationship to $10 as the number of days in the period ending with the deemed section 381(a) transaction, 183 days, bears to 365. Three dollars of the limitation is the amount that bears the same relationship to $6 as the number of days in the period between July 3 and December 31, 182, bears to 365.

Reg. § 1.1502-96(d)(5)(ii)

(B) *L's separate section 382 limitation.* For L's taxable years ending after December 31, year 3, L's separate section 382 limitation for its $90 of net operating loss carryover that was not reattributed to P is $4, adjusted as appropriate for any short taxable year, unused section 382 limitation, or other adjustment. For L's short taxable year ending December 31, year 3, the section 382 limitation for its $90 of net operating loss carryover is $2, the amount that bears the same relationship to $4 (the portion of the value element that was not apportioned to P), as the number of days during the short taxable year, 182 days, bears to 365. See § 1.382-5(c).

Example 2. No apportionment required for consolidated pre-change attribute. (i) *Facts.* P, the common parent of a consolidated group, forms L. For year 1, L has an operating loss of $70 that is not absorbed and is included in the group's consolidated net operating loss that is carried over to subsequent years. On January 1 of year 3, A buys all of the P stock and the P group has an ownership change. The consolidated section 382 limitation based on the value of the P stock is $10.

(ii) *Analysis.* On April 13 of year 4, P sells all of the stock of L to B and, under § 1.1502-36(d)(6), elects to reattribute to itself $45 of L's net operating loss carryover. Following the reattribution, the $45 portion of the year 1 net operating loss carryover retains its character as a pre-change consolidated attribute, and remains subject to so much of the $10 consolidated section 382 limitation as P does not elect to apportion to L under § 1.1502-95(c).

(e) *Time and manner of making election under § 1.1502-91(d)(4).*—(1) *In general.*—This paragraph (e) prescribes the time and manner of making the election under § 1.1502-91(d)(4), relating to treating two or more corporations as treating the section 1504(a)(1) requirement of § 1.1502-91(d)(1)(ii) and (d) (2)(ii) as satisfied.

(2) *Election statement.*—An election under § 1.1502-91(d)(4) must be made by the common parent. The election must be made in the form of the following statement: "THIS IS AN ELECTION UNDER § 1.1502-91(d)(4) TO TREAT THE FOLLOWING CORPORATIONS AS MEETING THE REQUIREMENTS OF § 1.1502-91(d)(1)(ii) AND (d)(2)(ii) IMMEDIATELY AFTER THEY BECAME MEMBERS OF THE GROUP." [List separately the name of each corporation, its E.I.N., and the date that it became a member of the group]. If separate elections are being made for corporations that became members at different times or that were acquired from different affiliated groups, provide a separate statement and list for each election.

(3) The election statement must be filed by the common parent with its income tax return for the consolidated return year in which the members with respect to which the election is made become members of the group. Such election must be filed on or before the due date for such income tax return, including extensions.

(4) An election made under this paragraph (e) is irrevocable. [Reg. § 1.1502-96.]

☐ [*T.D.* 8824, 6-25-99. *Amended by T.D.* 9424, 9-9-2008.]

[Reg. § 1.1502-96A]

§ 1.1502-96A. Miscellaneous rules generally applicable for testing dates before June 25, 1999.—(a) *End of separate tracking of losses.*— (1) *Application.*—This paragraph (a) applies to a member (or a loss subgroup) with a net operating loss carryover that arose (or is treated under § 1.1502-21(c) or 1.1502-21T(c) in effect prior to June 25, 1999, as contained in 26 CFR part 1 revised April 1, 1999, as applicable as arising) in a SRLY (or a net unrealized built-in gain or loss determined at the time that the member (or loss subgroup) becomes a member of the consolidated group if there is—

(i) An ownership change of the member (or loss subgroup in connection with, or after, becoming a member of the group; or

(ii) A period of 5 consecutive years following the day that the member (or loss subgroup) becomes a member of a group during which the member (or loss subgroup) has not had an ownership change.

(2) *Effect of end of separate tracking.*—If this paragraph (a) applies with respect to a member (or loss subgroup), then, starting on the day after the earlier of the change date (but not earlier than the day the member (or loss subgroup) becomes a member of the consolidated group) or the last day of the 5 consecutive year period described in paragraph (a)(1)(ii) of this section, the member's net operating loss carryover that arose (or is treated under § 1.1502-21(c) or 1.1502-21T(c) in effect prior to June 25, 1999, as contained in 26 CFR part 1 revised April 1, 1999, as applicable as arising) in a SRLY, is treated as described in § 1.1502-91A(c)(1)(i). Also, the member's separately computed net unrealized built-in gain or loss is included in the determination whether the group has a net unrealized built-in gain or loss. The preceding sentences also apply for purposes of determining whether there is an ownership change with respect to such attributes following such change date (or earlier day) or 5 consecutive year period. Thus, for example, starting the day after the change date or the end of the 5 consecutive year period—

(i) The consolidated group which includes the new loss member or loss subgroup is no longer required to separately track owner shifts of the stock of the new loss member or loss subgroup parent to determine if an ownership change occurs with respect to the attributes of the new loss member or members included in the loss subgroup;

(ii) The group includes the member's attributes in determining whether it is a loss group under § 1.1502-91A(c);

(iii) There is an ownership change with respect to such attributes only if the group is a loss group and has an ownership change; and

(iv) If the group has an ownership change, such attributes are pre-change consolidated attributes subject to the loss group's consolidated section 382 limitation.

(3) *Continuing effect of end of separate tracking.*—As the context may require, a current group determines which of its members are included in a loss subgroup on any testing date by taking into account the application of this section in the former group. See the example in § 1.1502-91A(f)(2).

(4) *Special rule for testing period.*—For purposes of determining the beginning of the testing period for a loss group, the member's (or loss subgroup's) net operating loss carryovers (or net unrealized built-in gain or loss) described in paragraph (a)(2) of this section are considered to arise—

(i) in a case described in paragraph (a)(1)(i) of this section, in a taxable year that begins not earlier than the later of the day following the change date or the day that the member becomes a member of the group; and

(ii) in a case described in paragraph (a)(1)(ii) of this section, in a taxable year that begins 3 years before the end of the 5 consecutive year period.

(5) *Limits on effects of end of separate tracking.*—The rule contained in this paragraph (a) applies solely for purposes of §§ 1.1502-91A through 1.1502-95A and this section (other than paragraph (b)(2)(ii)(B) of this section (relating to the definition of pre-change attributes of a subsidiary)) and § 1.1502-98A, and not for purposes of other provisions of the consolidated return regulations, including, for example, §§ 1.1502-15 and 1.1502-21 (or § 1.1502-15T in effect prior to June 25, 1999, as contained in 26 CFR part 1 revised April 1, 1999 and 1.1502-21T in effect prior to June 25, 1999, as contained in 26 CFR part 1 revised April 1, 1999, as applicable) (relating to the consolidated net operating loss deduction). See also paragraph (c) of this section for the continuing effect of an ownership change with respect to pre-change attributes.

(b) *Ownership change of subsidiary.*—(1) *Ownership change of a subsidiary because of options or plan or arrangement.*—Notwithstanding § 1.1502-92A, a subsidiary may have an ownership change for purposes of section 382 with respect to its attributes which a group or loss subgroup includes in making a determination under § 1.1502-91A(c)(1) (relating to the definition of loss group) or § 1.1502-91A(d) (relating to the definition of loss subgroup). The subsidiary has such an ownership change if it has an ownership change under the principles of § 1.1502-95A(b) and section 382 and the regulations thereunder (determined on a separate entity basis by treating the subsidiary as not being a member of a consolidated group) in the event of—

(i) The deemed exercise under § 1.382-4(d) of an option or options (other than an option with respect to stock of the common parent) held by a person (or persons acting pursuant to a plan or arrangement) to acquire more than 20 percent of the stock of the subsidiary; or

(ii) An increase by 1 or more 5-percent shareholders, acting pursuant to a plan or arrangement to avoid an ownership change of a subsidiary, in their percentage ownership interest in the subsidiary by more than 50 percentage points during the testing period of the subsidiary through the acquisition (or deemed acquisition pursuant to § 1.382-4(d)) of ownership interests in the subsidiary and in higher-tier members with respect to the subsidiary.

(2) *Effect of the ownership change.*—(i) *In general.*—If a subsidiary has an ownership change under paragraph (b)(1) of this section, the amount of consolidated taxable income for any post-change year that may be offset by the pre-change losses of the subsidiary shall not exceed the section 382 limitation for the subsidiary. For purposes of this limitation, the value of the subsidiary is determined solely by reference to the value of the subsidiary's stock.

(ii) *Pre-change losses.*—The pre-change losses of a subsidiary are—

(A) Its allocable part of any consolidated net operating loss which is attributable to it under § 1.1502-21(b) or 1.1502-21T(b) in effect prior to June 25, 1999, as contained in 26 CFR part 1 revised April 1, 1999, as applicable (determined on the last day of the consolidated return year that includes the change date) that is not carried back and absorbed in a taxable year prior to the year including the change date;

(B) Its net operating loss carryovers that arose (or are treated under § 1.1502-21(c) or 1.1502-21T(c) in effect prior to June 25, 1999, as contained in 26 CFR part 1 revised April 1, 1999, as applicable as having arisen) in a SRLY; and

(C) Its recognized built-in loss with respect to its separately computed net unrealized built-in loss, if any, determined on the change date.

(3) *Coordination with §§ 1.1502-91A, 1.1502-92A, and 1.1502-94A.*—If an increase in percentage ownership interest causes an ownership change with respect to an attribute under this paragraph (b) and under § 1.1502-92A on the same day, the ownership change is considered to occur only under § 1.1502-92A and not under this paragraph (b). See § 1.1502-94A for anti-duplication rules relating to value.

Reg. § 1.1502-96A(b)(3)

(4) *Example.*—The following example illustrates paragraph (b)(1)(ii) of this section.

Example. Plan to avoid an ownership change of a subsidiary. (a) L owns all the stock of L1, L1 owns all the stock of L2, L2 owns all the stock of L3, and L3 owns all the stock of L4. The L group has a consolidated net operating loss arising in Year 1 that is carried over to Year 2. L has assets other than its L1 stock with a value of $900. L1, L2, and L3 own no assets other than their L2, L3, and L4

stock. L4 has assets with a value of $100. During Year 2, A, B, C, and D, acting pursuant to a plan to avoid an ownership change of L4, acquire the following ownership interests in the members of the L loss group: (A) on September 11, Year 2, A acquires 20 percent of the L1 stock from L and B acquires 20 percent of the L2 stock from L1; and (B) on September 20, Year 2, C acquires 20 percent of the stock of L3 from L2 and D acquires 20 percent of the stock of L4 from L3. The following is a graphic illustration of these facts:

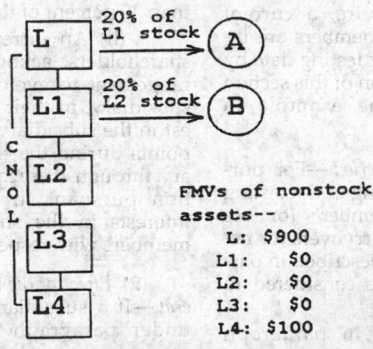

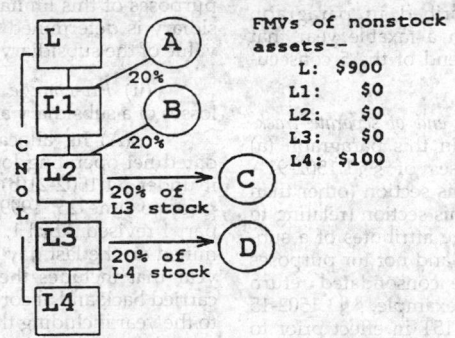

(b) The acquisitions by A, B, C, and D pursuant to the plan have increased their respective percentage ownership interests in L4 by approximately 10, 13, 16, and 20 percentage points, for a total of approximately 59 percentage points during the testing period. This more than 50 percentage point increase in the percentage ownership interest in L4 causes an ownership change of L4 under paragraph (b)(2) of this section.

(c) *Continuing effect of an ownership change.*—A loss corporation (or loss subgroup) that is subject to a limitation under section 382 with respect to its pre-change losses continues to be subject to

the limitation regardless of whether it becomes a member or ceases to be a member of a consolidated group. See § 1.382-5(d) (relating to successive ownership changes and absorption of a section 382 limitation). [Reg. § 1.1502-96A.]

☐ [*T.D. 8678, 6-26-96. Amended by T.D. 8823, 6-25-99 and amended and redesignated by T.D. 8824, 6-25-99.*]

[Reg. § 1.1502-97]

§ 1.1502-97. Special rules under section 382 for members under the jurisdiction of a court in a title 11 or similar case.—[Reserved]

☐ [*T.D. 8824, 6-25-99.*]

[Reg. §1.1502-97A]

§1.1502-97A. Special rules under section 382 for members under the jurisdiction of a court in a title 11 or similar case.—[Reserved]

☐ [*T.D. 8678, 6-26-96. Amended and redesignated by T.D. 8824, 6-25-99.*]

[Reg. §1.1502-98]

§1.1502-98. Coordination with section 383.— The rules contained in §§1.1502-91 through 1.1502-96 also apply for purposes of section 383, with appropriate adjustments to reflect that section 383 applies to credits and net capital losses. For example, subgroups with respect to the carryover of general business credits, minimum tax credits, unused foreign tax, and net capital loss are determined by applying the principles of §1.1502-91(d)(1). Similarly, in the case of net capital losses, general business credits, and excess foreign taxes that are pre-change attributes, §1.383-1 applies the principles of §§1.1502-91 through 1.1502-96. For example, if a loss group has an ownership change under §1.1502-92 and has a carryover of unused general business credits from a pre-change consolidated return year to a post-change consolidated return year, the amount of the group's regular tax liability for the post-change year that can be offset by the carryover cannot exceed the consolidated section 383 credit limitation for that post-change year, determined by applying the principles of §§1.383-1(c)(6) and 1.1502-93 (relating to the computation of the consolidated section 382 limitation). [Reg. §1.1502-98.]

☐ [*T.D. 8824, 6-25-99. Amended by T.D. 8884, 5-24-2000.*]

[Reg. §1.1502-98A]

§1.1502-98A. Coordination with section 383 generally applicable for testing dates (or members joining or leaving a group) before June 25, 1999.—The rules contained in §§1.1502-91A through 1.1502-96A also apply for purposes of section 383, with appropriate adjustments to reflect that section 383 applies to credits and net capital losses. Similarly, in the case of net capital losses, general business credits, and excess foreign taxes that are pre-change attributes, §1.383-1 applies the principles of §§1.1502-91A through 1.1502-96A. For example, if a loss group has an ownership change under §1.1502-92A and has a carryover of unused general business credits from a pre-change consolidated return year to a post-change consolidated return year, the amount of the group's regular tax liability for the post-change year that can be offset by the carryover cannot exceed the consolidated section 383 credit limitation for that post-change year, determined by applying the principles of §§1.3831(c)(6) and 1.1502-93A (relating to the computation of the consolidated section 382 limitation). [Reg. §1.1502-98A.]

☐ [*T.D. 8678, 6-26-96. Amended and redesignated by T.D. 8824, 6-25-99.*]

[Reg. §1.1502-99]

§1.1502-99. Effective/applicability dates.— (a) *In general.*—Except as provided in paragraphs (b) and (c) of this section, §§1.1502-91 through 1.1502-96 and §1.1502-98 apply to any testing date on or after June 25, 1999. Sections 1.1502-94 through 1.1502-96 also apply to a corporation that becomes a member of a group or ceases to be a member of a group (or loss subgroup) on any date on or after June 25, 1999.

(b) *Special rules.*—(1) *Election to treat subgroup parent requirement as satisfied.*—Section 1.1502-91(d)(4), §1.1502-91(d)(7), Example 4, §1.1502-92(b)(1)(iii), §1.1502-92(b)(2), Example 5, the last two sentences of §1.1502-95(b)(3), §1.1502-95(d)(2)(i), and §1.1502-96(e)(all of which relate to the election under §1.1502-91(d)(4) to treat the loss subgroup parent requirement as satisfied) apply to corporations that become members of a consolidated group in taxable years for which the due date of the income tax return (without extensions) is after June 25, 1999.

(2) *Principal purpose of avoiding a limitation.*— The third sentence of §1.1502-91(d)(5) (relating to members excluded from a loss subgroup) applies to corporations that become members of a consolidated group on or after June 25, 1999.

(3) *Ceasing to be a member of a loss subgroup.*—(i) *Ownership change of a loss subgroup.*— Section 1.1502-95(d)(2)(ii) and §1.1502-95(d)(3), Example 3 apply to corporations that cease to bear a relationship described in section 1504(a)(1) to a loss subgroup parent in taxable years for which the due date of the income tax return (without extensions) is after June 25, 1999.

(ii) *Expiration of 5-year period.*—Section 1.1502-95(d)(2)(iii) applies with respect to the day after the last day of any 5 consecutive year period described in that section that ends in a taxable year for which the due date of the income tax return (without extensions) is after June 25, 1999.

(4) *Reattribution of losses under §1.1502-36(d)(6).*—Section 1.1502-96(d) applies to reattributions of net operating loss carryovers, capital loss carryovers, and deferred deductions in connection with a transfer of stock to which §1.1502-36 applies, and the election under §1.1502-96(d)(5) (relating to an election to reattribute section 382 limitation) can be made with an election under §1.1502-36(d)(6) to reattribute a loss to the common parent that is filed at the time and in the manner provided in §1.1502-36(e)(5)(x).

(5) *Election to apportion net unrealized built-in gain.*—In the case of corporations that cease to be members of a loss group (or loss subgroup) before June 25, 1999 in a taxable year for which the due date of the income tax return (without extensions) is after June 25, 1999, § 1.1502-95(a), (b), (c), and (f) apply to those corporations if the common parent makes the election described in the second sentence of paragraph (c)(1) of § 1.1502-95 in the time and manner prescribed in paragraph (f) of § 1.1502-95.

(c) *Testing period may include a period beginning before June 25, 1999.*—(1) *In general.*—A testing period for purposes of §§ 1.1502-91 through 1.1502-96 and 1.1502-98 may include a period beginning before June 25, 1999. Thus, for example, in applying § 1.1502-92(b)(1)(i)(relating to the determination of an ownership change of a loss group), the determination of the lowest percentage of ownership interest of any 5-percent shareholder of the common parent during a testing period ending on a testing date occurring on or after June 25, 1999 takes into account the period beginning before June 25, 1999, except the extent that the period is more than 3 years before the testing date or is otherwise before the beginning of the testing period. See § 1.1502-92(b)(1).

(2) *Transition rule for net unrealized built-in loss.*—A loss group (or loss subgroup) that has a net unrealized built-in loss on a testing date on or after June 25, 1999 may apply § 1.1502-91A(g) (and § 1.1502-96A(a) as it relates to § 1.1502-91A(g)) for the period ending on the day before June 25, 1999 to determine under § 1.382-2T(d)(ii)(A) the earliest date that its testing period begins (treating the day before June 25, 1999 as the end of a taxable year.) Thus, for example, if a consolidated group with no net operating losses has a net unrealized built-in loss determined under § 1.1502-91(g) on a testing date after June 25, 1999, but, under § 1.1502-91A(g), does not have a net unrealized built-in loss for the period ending on the day before June 25, 1999, the group's testing period begins no earlier than June 25, 1999. [Reg. § 1.1502-99.]

□ [*T.D. 8824, 6-25-99. Amended by T.D. 9424, 9-9-2008.*]

[Reg. § 1.1502-99A]

§ 1.1502-99A. Effective dates.—(a) *Effective date.*—(1) *In general.*—Except as provided in § 1.1502-99(b), §§ 1.1502-91A through 1.1502-96A and 1.1502-98A apply to any testing date on or after January 1, 1997, and before June 25, 1999. Sections 1.1502-94A through 1.1502-96A also apply on any date on or after January 1, 1997, and before June 25, 1999, on which a corporation becomes a member of a group or on which a corporation ceases to be a member of a loss group (or a loss subgroup).

(2) *Anti-duplication rules for recognized built-in gain.*—Section 1.1502-93(c)(2) (relating to recognized built-in gain of a loss group or loss subgroup) applies to taxable years for which the due date for income tax returns (without extensions) is after June 25, 1999.

(b) *Testing period may include a period beginning before January 1, 1997.*—A testing period for purposes of §§ 1.1502-91A through 1.1502-96A and 1.1502-98A may include a period beginning before January 1, 1997. Thus, for example, in applying § 1.1502-92A(b)(1)(i) (relating to the determination of an ownership change of a loss group), the determination of the lowest percentage ownership interest of any 5-percent shareholder of the common parent during a testing period ending on a testing date occurring on or after January 1, 1997, takes into account the period beginning before January 1, 1997, except to the extent that the period is more than 3 years before the testing date or is otherwise before the beginning of the testing period. See § 1.1502-92A(b)(1).

(c) *Transition rules.*—(1) *Methods permitted.*—(i) *In general.*—For the period ending before January 1, 1997, a consolidated group is permitted to use any method described in paragraph (c)(2) of this section which is consistently applied to determine if an ownership change occurred with respect to a consolidated net operating loss, a net operating loss carryover (including net operating loss carryovers arising in SRLYs), or a net unrealized built-in loss. If an ownership change occurred during that period, the group is also permitted to use any method described in paragraph (c)(2) of this section which is consistently applied to compute the amount of the section 382 limitation that applies to limit the use of taxable income in any post-change year ending before, on, or after January 1, 1997. The preceding sentence does not preclude the imposition of an additional, lesser limitation due to a subsequent ownership change nor, except as provided in paragraph (c)(1)(iii) of this section, does it permit the beginning of a new testing period for the loss group.

(ii) *Adjustments to offset excess limitation.*—If an ownership change occurred during the period ending before January 1, 1997, and a method described in paragraph (c)(2) of this section was not used for a post-change year, the members (or group) must reduce the section 382 limitation for post-change years for which an income tax return is filed after January 1, 1997, to offset, as quickly as possible, the effects of any section 382 limitation that members took into account in excess of the amount that would have been allowable under §§ 1.1502-91A through 1.1502-96A and 1.1502-98A.

(iii) *Coordination with effective date.*—Notwithstanding that a group may have used a method described in paragraph (c)(2)(ii) or (iii) of this section for the period before January 1, 1997, §§ 1.1502-91A through 1.1502-96A and 1.1502-98A apply to any testing date occurring on or after January 1, 1997, for purposes of determining whether there is an ownership change with respect to any losses and, if so, the collateral consequences. Any ownership change of a member other than the common parent pursuant to a method described in paragraph (c)(2)(ii) or (iii) of this section does not cause a new testing period of the loss group to begin for purposes of applying § 1.1502-92A on or after January 1, 1997.

(2) *Permitted methods.*—The methods described in this paragraph (c)(2) are:

(i) A method that does not materially differ from the rules in §§ 1.1502-91A through 1.1502-96A and 1.1502-98A (other than those in § 1.1502-95A(c) and (b)(2)(ii) (relating to the apportionment of a section 382 limitation) as they would apply to a corporation that ceases to be a member of the group before January 1, 1997). As the context requires, the method must treat references to rules in current regulations as references to rules in regulations generally effective for taxable years before January 1, 1997. Thus, for example, the taxpayer must treat a reference to § 1.382-4(d) (relating to options) as a reference to § 1.382-2T(h)(4) for any testing date to which § 1.382-2T(h)(4) applies. Similarly, a reference to § 1.1502-21(c) or 1.1502-21T(c) in effect prior to June 25, 1999, as contained in 26 CFR part 1 revised April 1, 1999, as applicable may be a reference to § 1.1502-21A(c), as appropriate. Furthermore, the method must treat all corporations that were affiliated on January 1, 1987, and continuously thereafter as having met the 5 consecutive year requirement of § 1.1502-91A(d)(2)(i) on any day before January 1, 1992, on which the determination of net unrealized built-in gain or loss of a loss subgroup is made;

(ii) A reasonable application of the rules in section 382 and the regulations thereunder applied to each member on a separate entity basis, treating each member's allocable part of a consolidated net operating loss which is attributable to it under § 1.1502-21(b) or 1.1502-21T(b) in effect prior to June 25, 1999, as contained in 26 CFR part 1 revised April 1, 1999, as applicable as a net operating loss of that member and applying rules similar to § 1.382-8 to avoid duplication of value in computing the section 382 limitation for the member (see § 1.382-8(h) (relating to the effective date and transition rules regarding controlled groups)); or

(iii) A method approved by the Commissioner upon application by the common parent.

(d) *Amended returns.*—A group may file an amended return in connection with an ownership change occurring before January 1, 1997, to modify the amount of a section 382 limitation with respect to a consolidated net operating loss, a net operating loss carryover (including net op-

erating loss carryovers arising in SRLYs), or a recognized built-in loss (or gain) only if it files amended returns:

(1) For the earliest taxable year ending after December 31, 1986, in which it had an ownership change, if any, under § 1.1502-92A;

(2) For all subsequent taxable years for which returns have already been filed as of the date of the amended return;

(3) The modification with respect to all members for all taxable years ending in 1987 and thereafter complies with §§ 1.1502-91A through 1.1502-96A and 1.1502-98A; and

(4) The amended return(s) permitted by the applicable statute of limitations is/are filed before March 26, 1997.

(e) *Section 383.*—This section also applies for the purposes of section 383, with appropriate adjustments to reflect that section 383 applies to credits and net capital losses. [Reg. § 1.1502-99A.]

☐ [*T.D. 8678, 6-26-96. Amended by T.D. 8823, 6-25-99 and amended and redesignated by T.D. 8824, 6-25-99.*]

[Reg. § 1.1502-100]

§ 1.1502-100. Corporations exempt from tax.—(a) *In general.*—(1) *Computation of tax liability.*—The tax liability for a consolidated return year of a group of two or more corporations described in section 1504(e) which are exempt from taxation under section 501 (hereinafter referred to in this section as "exempt group") shall be determined on a consolidated basis by applying the provisions of subchapter F of chapter 1 of the Code in the manner provided in this section. See section 1504(e) for tax-exempt corporations eligible to file a consolidated return.

(2) *Applicability of other consolidated return provisions.*—The provisions of § 1.1502-1 through § 1.1502-80 shall be applicable to an exempt group to the extent they are not inconsistent with the provisions of this section or the provisions of subchapter F of chapter 1 of the Code. For purposes of applying the provisions of § 1.1502-1 through § 1.1502-80 to an exempt group, the following substitutions shall be made—

(i) The term "exempt group" shall be substituted for the term "group",

(ii) The terms "unrelated business taxable income", "separate unrelated business taxable income", and "consolidated unrelated business taxable income" shall be substituted for the terms "taxable income", "separate taxable income", and "consolidated taxable income", and

(iii) The term "consolidated liability for tax determined under § 1.1502-2" (or an equivalent term) shall mean the consolidated liability for tax of an exempt group determined under paragraph (b) of this section.

(b) *Consolidated liability for tax.*—The tax liability for a consolidated return year of an exempt group is the tax imposed by section 511(a) or section 1201(a) on the consolidated unrelated business taxable income for the year (determined under paragraph (c) of this section), and by allowing the credits and surtax exemption provided in § 1.1502-2.

(c) *Consolidated unrelated business taxable income.*—The consolidated unrelated business taxable income for a consolidated return year shall be determined by taking into account—

(1) The separate unrelated business taxable income of each member of the exempt group (determined under paragraph (d) of this section);

(2) Any consolidated net operating loss deduction (determined under § 1.1502-21A or 1.1502-21 (as appropriate)) subject to the limitations provided in section 512(b)(6);

(3) Any consolidated charitable contribution deduction (determined under § 1.1502-24) subject to the limitations provided in section 512(b)(10); and

(4) Any consolidated net gain or net loss from the disposition of debt-financed property (as defined in section 514(b)) taken into account as provided by section 514(a), or from the cutting of timber to which section 631 applies.

(d) *Separate unrelated business taxable income.*— The separate unrelated business taxable income of a member of an exempt group shall be computed in accordance with the provisions of section 512 covering the determination of unrelated business taxable income of separate corporations, except that—

(1) The provisions of paragraphs (a) through (k) and (o) of § 1.1502-12 shall apply; and

(2) No charitable contributions deduction shall be taken into account under section 512(b)(10).

See sections 511(c) and 512(a)(3)(C) for special rules applicable to organizations described in section 501(c)(2). [Reg. § 1.1502-100.]

[T.D. 7183, 4-30-72. *Amended by T.D.* 2-16-79; *T.D.* 8677, 6-26-96 *and T.D.* 8823, 6-25-99.]

[Reg. § 1.1503-1]

§ 1.1503-1. Computation and payment of tax.—(a) *General rule.*—In any case in which a consolidated return is filed or required to be filed, the tax shall be determined, computed, assessed, collected, and adjusted in accordance with the regulations prescribed under section 1502 promulgated prior to the last date prescribed by law for the filing of such return.

(b) *Limitation.*—If the affiliated group includes one or more Western Hemisphere trade corporations (as defined in section 921) or one or more regulated public utilities (as defined in section 1503(c)) the increase in tax described in section 1503(a) shall be applied in a manner provided in the regulations under section 1502. [Reg. § 1.1503-1.]

[T.D. 6140, 8-29-55. *Amended by T.D.* 7244, 12-29-72.]

[Reg. § 1.1503-2]

§ 1.1503-2. Dual consolidated loss.— (a) *Purpose and scope.*—This section provides rules for the application of section 1503(d), concerning the determination and use of dual consolidated losses. Paragraph (b) of this section provides a general rule prohibiting a dual consolidated loss from offsetting the taxable income of a domestic affiliate. Paragraph (c) of this section provides definitions of the terms used in this section. Paragraph (d) of this section provides rules for calculating the amount of a dual consolidated loss and for adjusting the basis of stock of a dual resident corporation. Paragraph (e) of this section contains an anti-avoidance provision. Paragraph (f) of this section applies the rules of paragraph (d) of this section to the computation of foreign tax credit limitations. Paragraph (g) of this section provides certain exceptions to the limitation rule of paragraph (b) of this section. Finally, paragraph (h) of this section provides the effective date of the regulations and a provision for the retroactive application of the regulations to qualifying taxpayers.

(b) *In general.*—(1) *Limitation on the use of a dual consolidated loss to offset income of a domestic affiliate.*—Except as otherwise provided in this section, a dual consolidated loss of a dual resident corporation cannot offset the taxable income of any domestic affiliate in the taxable year in which the loss is recognized or in any other taxable year, regardless of whether the loss offsets income of another person under the income tax laws of a foreign country and regardless of whether the income that the loss may offset in the foreign country is, has been, or will be subject to tax in the United States. Pursuant to paragraph (c)(1) and (2) of this section, the same limitation shall apply to a dual consolidated loss of a separate unit of a domestic corporation as if the separate unit were a wholly owned subsidiary of such corporation.

(2) *Limitation on the use of a dual consolidated loss to offset income of a successor-in-interest.*—A dual consolidated loss of a dual resident corporation also cannot be used to offset the taxable income of another corporation by means of a transaction in which the other corporation succeeds to the tax attributes of the dual resident corporation under section 381 of the Code. Similarly, a dual consolidated loss of a separate unit of a domestic corporation cannot be used to offset income of the domestic corporation following the termination, liquidation, sale, or other disposition of the separate unit. However, if a dual resident corporation transfers its assets to another corporation in a transaction subject to

section 381, and the acquiring corporation is a dual resident corporation of the same foreign country of which the transferor dual resident corporation is a resident, or a domestic corporation that carries on the business activities of the transferor dual resident corporation as a separate unit, then income generated by the transferee dual resident corporation, or separate unit, may be offset by the carryover losses of the transferor dual resident corporation. In addition, if a domestic corporation transfers a separate unit to another domestic corporation in a transaction subject to section 381, the income generated by the separate unit following the transfer may be offset by the carryover losses of the separate unit.

(3) *Application of rules to multiple tiers of separate units.*—If a separate unit of a domestic corporation is owned indirectly through another separate unit, the principles of paragraph (b)(1) and (2) of this section shall apply as if the upper-tier separate unit were a subsidiary of the domestic corporation and the lower-tier separate unit were a lower-tier subsidiary.

(4) *Examples.*—The following examples illustrate the application of this paragraph (b).

Example 1. P, a domestic corporation, owns all of the outstanding stock of DRC, a domestic corporation. P and DRC file a consolidated U.S. income tax return. DRC is managed and controlled in Country W, a country that determines the tax residence of corporations according to their place of management and control. Therefore, DRC is a dual resident corporation and any net operating loss it incurs is a dual consolidated loss. In Years 1 through 3, DRC incurs dual consolidated losses. Under this paragraph (b), the dual consolidated losses may not be used to offset P's income on the group's consolidated U.S. income tax return. At the end of Year 3, DRC sells all of its assets and discontinues its business operations. DRC is then liquidated into P, pursuant to the provisions of section 332. Normally, under section 381, P would succeed to, and be permitted to utilize, DRC's net operating loss carryovers. However, this paragraph (b) prohibits the dual consolidated losses of DRC from reducing P's income for U.S. tax purposes. Therefore, DRC's net operating loss carryovers will not be available to offset P's income.

Example 2. The facts are the same as in *Example 1*, except that DRC does not sell its assets and, following the liquidation of DRC, P continues to operate DRC's business as a separate unit (*e.g.,* a branch). DRC's loss carryovers are available to offset P's income generated by the assets previously owned by DRC and now held by the separate unit.

(c) *Definitions.*—The following definitions shall apply for purposes of this section.

(1) *Domestic corporation.*—The term "domestic corporation" has the meaning assigned to it by section 7701(a)(3) and (4). The term also includes any corporation otherwise treated as a domestic corporation by the Code, including, but not limited to, sections 269B, 953(d), and 1504(d). For purposes of this section, any separate unit of a domestic corporation, as defined in paragraph (c)(3) and (4) of this section, shall be treated as a separate domestic corporation.

(2) *Dual resident corporation.*—A dual resident corporation is a domestic corporation that is subject to the income tax of a foreign country on its worldwide income or on a residence basis. A corporation is taxed on a residence basis if it is taxed as a resident under the laws of the foreign country. An S corporation, as defined in section 1361, is not a dual resident corporation. For purposes of this section, any separate unit of a domestic corporation, as defined in paragraph (c)(3) and (4) of this section, shall be treated as a dual resident corporation. Unless otherwise indicated, any reference in this section to a dual resident corporation refers also to a separate unit.

(3) *Separate unit.*—(i) The term "separate unit" shall mean any of the following:

(A) A foreign branch, as defined in § 1.367(a)-6T(g) (or a successor regulation), that is owned either directly by a domestic corporation or indirectly by a domestic corporation through ownership of a partnership or trust interest (regardless of whether the partnership or trust is a United States person);

(B) an interest in a partnership; or

(C) an interest in a trust.

(ii) If two or more foreign branches located in the same foreign country are owned by a single domestic corporation and the losses of each branch are made available to offset the income of the other branches under the tax laws of the foreign country, within the meaning of paragraph (c)(15)(ii) of this section, then the branches shall be treated as one separate unit.

(4) *Hybrid entity separate unit.*—The term "separate unit" includes an interest in an entity that is not taxable as an association for U.S. income tax purposes but is subject to income tax in a foreign country as a corporation (or otherwise at the entity level) either on its worldwide income or on a residence basis.

(5) *Dual consolidated loss.*—(i) *In general.*—The term "dual consolidated loss" means the net operating loss (as defined in section 172(c) and the regulations thereunder) of a domestic corporation incurred in a year in which the corporation is a dual resident corporation. The dual consolidated loss shall be computed under paragraph (d)(1) of this section. The fact that a particular item taken into account in computing a dual resident corporation's net operating loss is not

taken into account in computing income subject to a foreign country's income tax shall not cause such item to be excluded from the calculation of the dual consolidated loss.

(ii) *Exceptions.*—A dual consolidated loss shall not include the following—

(A) A net operating loss incurred by a dual resident corporation in a foreign country whose income tax laws—

(1) Do not permit the dual resident corporation to use its losses, expenses or deductions to offset the income of any other person that is recognized in the same taxable year in which the losses, expenses or deductions are incurred; and

(2) Do not permit the losses, expenses or deductions of the dual resident corporation to be carried over or back to be used, by any means, to offset the income of any other person in other taxable years; or

(B) A net operating loss incurred during that portion of the taxable year prior to the date on which the domestic corporation becomes a dual resident corporation or subsequent to the date on which the domestic corporation ceases to be a dual resident corporation. For purposes of determining the amount of the net operating loss incurred in that portion of the taxable year prior to the date on which the domestic corporation becomes a dual resident corporation or subsequent to the date on which the domestic corporation ceases to be a dual resident corporation, in no event shall more than the aggregate of the equal daily portion of the net operating loss commensurate with the portion of the taxable year during which the domestic corporation was not a dual resident corporation be allocated to that portion of the taxable year in which the domestic corporation was not a dual resident corporation.

(iii) *Dual consolidated losses of separate units that are partnership interests, including interests in hybrid entities.*—[Reserved]

(6) *Subject to tax.*—For purposes of determining whether a domestic corporation is subject to the income tax of a foreign country on its income, the fact that the corporation has no actual income tax liability to the foreign country for a particular taxable year shall not be taken into account.

(7) *Foreign country.*—For purposes of this section, possessions of the United States shall be considered foreign countries.

(8) *Consolidated group.*—The term "consolidated group" means an affiliated group, as defined in section 1504(a), with which a dual resident corporation or domestic owner files a consolidated U.S. income tax return.

(9) *Domestic owner.*—The term "domestic owner" means a domestic corporation that owns one or more separate units.

(10) *Affiliated dual resident corporation or affiliated domestic owner.*—The term "affiliated dual resident corporation" or "affiliated domestic owner" means a dual resident corporation or domestic owner that is a member of a consolidated group.

(11) *Unaffiliated dual resident corporation or unaffiliated domestic owner.*—The term "unaffiliated dual resident corporation" or "unaffiliated domestic owner" means a dual resident corporation or domestic owner that is an unaffiliated domestic corporation.

(12) *Successor-in-interest.*—The term "successor-in-interest" means an acquiring corporation that succeeds to the tax attributes of an acquired corporation by means of a transaction subject to section 381.

(13) *Domestic affiliate.*—The term "domestic affiliate" means any member of an affiliated group, without regard to the exceptions contained in section 1504(b) (other than section 1504(b)(3)) relating to includible corporations.

(14) *Unaffiliated domestic corporation.*—The term "unaffiliated domestic corporation" means a domestic corporation that is not a member of an affiliated group.

(15) *Use of loss to offset income of a domestic affiliate or another person.*—(i) A dual consolidated loss shall be deemed to offset income of a domestic affiliate in the year it is included in the computation of the consolidated taxable income of a consolidated group. The fact that no tax benefit results from the inclusion of the dual consolidated loss in the computation of the group's consolidated taxable income in the taxable year shall not be taken into account.

(ii) Except as provided in paragraph (c)(15)(iii) of this section, a loss, expense, or deduction taken into account in computing a dual consolidated loss shall be deemed to offset income of another person under the income tax laws of a foreign country in the year it is made available for such offset. The fact that the other person does not have sufficient income in that year to benefit from such an offset shall not be taken into account. However, where the laws of a foreign country provide an election that would enable a dual resident corporation or separate unit to use its losses, expenses, or deductions to offset income of another person, the losses, expenses, or deductions shall be considered to offset such income only if the election is made.

(iii) The losses, expenses, or deductions taken into account in computing a dual resident corporation's or separate unit's dual consolidated loss shall not be deemed to offset income of another person under the income tax laws of a foreign country for purposes of this section, if under the laws of the foreign country the losses, expenses, or deductions of the dual resident corporation or separate unit are used to offset the income of another dual resident corporation or separate unit within the same consolidated group (or income of another separate unit that is owned by the unaffiliated domestic owner of the first separate unit). If the losses, expenses, or deductions of a dual resident corporation or separate unit are made available under the laws of a foreign country to offset the income of other dual resident corporations or separate units within the same consolidated group (or other separate units owned by the unaffiliated domestic owner of the first separate unit), as well as the income of another person, and the laws of the foreign country do not provide applicable rules for determining which person's income is offset by the losses, expenses, or deductions, then for purposes of this section, the losses, expenses or deductions shall be deemed to offset the income of the other dual resident corporations or separate units, to the extent of such income, before being considered to offset the income of the other person.

(iv) Except to the extent paragraph (g)(1) of this section applies, where the income tax laws of a foreign country deny the use of losses, expenses, or deductions of a dual resident corporation to offset the income of another person because the dual resident corporation is also subject to income taxation by another country on its worldwide income or on a residence basis, the dual resident corporation shall be treated as if it actually had offset its dual consolidated loss against the income of another person in such foreign country.

(16) *Examples.*—The following examples illustrate this paragraph (c).

Example 1. X, a member of a consolidated group, conducts business through a branch in Country Y. Under Country Y's income tax laws, the branch is taxed as a permanent establishment and its losses may be used under the Country Y form of consolidation to offset the income of Z, a Country Y affiliate of X. In Year 1, the branch of X incurs an overall loss that would be treated as a net operating loss if the branch were a separate domestic corporation. Under paragraph (c)(3) of this section, the branch of X is treated as a separate domestic corporation and a dual resident corporation. Thus, under paragraph (c)(5), its loss constitutes a dual consolidated loss. Unless X qualifies for an exception under paragraph (g) of this section, paragraph (b) of this section precludes the use of the branch's loss to offset any income of X not derived from the branch operations or any income of a domestic affiliate of X.

Example 2. A and B are members of a consolidated group. FC is a Country X corporation that is wholly owned by B. A and B organize a partnership, P, under the laws of Country X. P con-

ducts business in Country X and its business activity constitutes a foreign branch within the meaning of paragraph (c)(3)(i)(A) of this section. P also earns U.S. source income that is unconnected with the branch operations and, therefore, is not subject to tax by Country X. Under the laws of Country X, the branch can consolidate with FC. The interests in P held by A and B are each treated as a dual resident corporation. The branch is also treated as a separate dual resident corporation. Unless an exception under paragraph (g) of this section applies, any dual consolidated loss incurred by P's branch cannot offset the U.S. source income earned by P or any other income of A or B.

Example 3. X is classified as a partnership for U.S. income tax purposes. A, B and C are the sole partners of X. A and B are domestic corporations and C is a Country Y corporation. For U.S. income tax purposes, each partner has an equal interest in each item of partnership profit or loss. Under Country Y's law, X is classified as a corporation and its income and losses may be used under the Country Y form of consolidation to offset the income of companies that are affiliates of X. Under paragraph (c)(3) and (4) of this section, the partnership interests held by A and B are treated as separate domestic corporations and as dual resident corporations. Unless an exception under paragraph (g) of this section applies, losses allocated to A and B can only be used to offset profits of X allocated to A and B, respectively.

Example 4. P, a domestic corporation, files a consolidated U.S. income tax return with its two wholly-owned domestic subsidiaries, DRC1 and DRC2. Each subsidiary is also treated as a Country Y resident for Country Y tax purposes. Thus, DRC1 and DRC2 are dual resident corporations. DRC1 owns FC, a Country Y corporation. Country Y's tax laws permit affiliated resident corporations to file a form of consolidated return. In Year 1, DRC1 incurs a $200 net operating loss for both U.S. and Country Y tax purposes, while DRC2 recognizes $200 of income under the tax laws of each country. FC also earns $200 of income for Country Y tax purposes. DRC1, DRC2, and FC file a Country Y consolidated return. However, Country Y has no applicable rules for determining which income is offset by DRC1's $200 loss. Under paragraph (c)(15)(iii) of this section, the loss shall be treated as offsetting DRC2's $200 of income. Because DRC1 and DRC2 are members of the same consolidated group, for purposes of this section, the offset of DRC1's loss against the income of DRC2 is not considered a use of the loss against the income of another person under the laws of a foreign country.

Example 5. DRC, a domestic corporation, files a consolidated U.S. income tax return with its parent, P. DRC is also subject to tax in Country Y on its worldwide income. Therefore, DRC is a dual resident corporation and any net operating loss incurred by DRC is a dual consolidated loss. Country Y's tax laws permit corporations that are subject to tax on their worldwide income to use the Country Y form of consolidation, thus enabling eligible corporations to use their losses to offset income of affiliates. However, to prevent corporations like DRC from offsetting losses against income of affiliates in Country Y and then again offsetting the losses against income of foreign affiliates under the tax laws of another country, Country Y prevents a corporation that is also subject to the income tax of another country on its worldwide income or on a residence basis from using the Country Y form of consolidation. There is no agreement, as described in paragraph (g)(1) of this section, between the United States and Country Y. Because of Country Y's statute, DRC will be treated as having actually offset its losses against the income of affiliates in Country Y under paragraph (c)(15)(iv) of this section. Therefore, DRC will not be able to file an agreement described in paragraph (g)(2) of this section and offset its losses against the income of P or any other domestic affiliate.

(d) *Special rules for accounting for dual consolidated losses.*—(1) *Determination of amount of dual consolidated loss.*—(i) *Dual resident corporation that is a member of a consolidated group.*—For purposes of determining whether a dual resident corporation that is a member of a consolidated group has a dual consolidated loss for the taxable year, the dual resident corporation shall compute its taxable income (or loss) in accordance with the rules set forth in the regulations under section 1502 governing the computation of consolidated taxable income, taking into account only the dual resident corporation's items of income, gain, deduction, and loss for the year. However, for purposes of this computation, the following items shall not be taken into account:

(A) Any net capital loss of the dual resident corporation; and

(B) Any carryover or carryback losses.

(ii) *Dual resident corporation that is a separate unit of a domestic corporation.*—For purposes of determining whether a separate unit has a dual consolidated loss for the taxable year, the separate unit shall compute its taxable income (or loss) as if it were a separate domestic corporation and a dual resident corporation in accordance with the provisions of paragraph (d)(1)(i) of this section, using only those items of income, expense, deduction, and loss that are otherwise attributable to such separate unit.

(2) *Effect of a dual consolidated loss.*—For any taxable year in which a dual resident corporation or separate unit has a dual consolidated loss to which paragraph (b) of this section applies, the following rules shall apply.

(i) If the dual resident corporation is a member of a consolidated group, the group shall compute its consolidated taxable income without taking into account the items of income, loss, or deduction taken into account in computing the dual consolidated loss. The dual consolidated loss may be carried over or back for use in other taxable years as a separate net operating loss carryover or carryback of the dual resident corporation arising in the year incurred. It shall be treated as a loss incurred by the dual resident corporation in a separate return limitation year and (without regard to whether the dual resident corporation is a common parent) shall be subject to all of the limitations of §1.1502-21A(c) or 1.1502-21(c), as appropriate (relating to limitations on net operating loss carryovers and carrybacks from separate return limitation years).

(ii) The unaffiliated domestic owner of a separate unit, or the consolidated group of an affiliated domestic owner, shall compute its taxable income without taking into account the items of income, loss or deduction taken into account in computing the separate unit's dual consolidated loss. The dual consolidated loss shall be treated as a loss incurred by a separate corporation and its use shall be subject to all of the limitations of §1.1502-21A(c) or 1.1502-21(c), as appropriate, as if the separate unit were filing a consolidated return with the unaffiliated domestic owner or with the consolidated group of the affiliated domestic owner.

(3) *Basis adjustments for dual consolidated losses.*—(i) *Dual resident corporation that is a member of an affiliated group.*—When a dual resident corporation is a member of a consolidated group, each other member owning stock in the dual resident corporation shall adjust the basis of the stock in the following manner.

(A) *Positive adjustments.*—Positive adjustments shall be made in accordance with the principles of §1.1502-32(b)(1), except that there shall be no positive adjustment under §1.1502-32(b)(1)(ii) for any amount of the dual consolidated loss that is not absorbed as a result of the application of paragraph (b) of this section. In addition, there shall be no positive adjustment for any amount included in income pursuant to paragraph (g)(2)(vii) of this section.

(B) *Negative adjustments.*—Negative adjustments shall be made in accordance with the principles of §1.1502-32(b)(2), except that there shall be no negative adjustment under §1.1502-32(b)(2)(ii) for the amount of the dual consolidated loss subject to paragraph (b) of this section that is absorbed in a carryover year.

(ii) *Dual resident corporation that is a separate unit arising from an interest in a partnership.*—Where a separate unit is an interest in a partnership, the domestic owner shall adjust its basis in the separate unit in accordance with section 705, except that no increase in basis shall be permitted for any amount included as income pursuant to paragraph (g)(2)(vii) of this section.

(4) *Examples.*—The following examples illustrate this paragraph (d).

Example 1. (i) P, S1, S2, and T are domestic corporations. P owns all of the stock of S1 and S2. S2 owns all of the stock of T. T is a resident of Country FC for Country FC income tax purposes. Therefore, T is a dual resident corporation. P, S1, S2, and T file a consolidated U.S. income tax return. X and Y are corporations that are not members of the consolidated group.

(ii) At the beginning of Year 1, P has a basis of $1,000 in the stock of S2. S2 has a $500 basis in the stock of T.

(iii) In Year 1, T incurs interest expense in the amount of $100. In addition, T sells a noncapital asset, *u*, in which it has a basis of $10, to S1 for $50. T also sells a noncapital asset, *v*, in which it has a basis of $200, to S1 for $100. The sales of *u* and *v* are intercompany transactions described in § 1.1502-13. T also sells a capital asset, *z*, in which it has a basis of $180, to Y for $90. In Year 1, S1 earns $200 of separate taxable income, calculated in accordance with § 1.1502-12, as well as $90 of capital gain from a sale of an asset to X. P and S2 have no items of income, loss, or deduction for Year 1.

(iv) In Year 1, T has a dual consolidated loss of $100 (attributable to its interest expense). T's $90 capital loss is not included in the computation of the dual consolidated loss. Instead, T's capital loss is included in the computation of the consolidated group's capital gain net income under § 1.1502-22(c) and is used to offset S1's $90 capital gain.

(v) No elective agreement, as described in paragraph (g)(1) of this section, exists between the United States and Country FC. For Country FC tax purposes, T's $100 loss is offset against the income of a Country FC affiliate. Therefore, T is not eligible for the exception provided in paragraph (g)(2) of this section.

(vi) Because T has a dual consolidated loss for the year, the consolidated taxable income of the consolidated group is calculated without regard to T's items of income, loss or deduction taken into account in computing the dual consolidated loss. Therefore, the consolidated taxable income of the consolidated group is $200 (the sum of $200 of separate taxable income earned by S1 plus $90 of capital gain earned by S1 minus $90 of capital loss incurred by T). The $40 gain recognized by T upon the sale of item *u* to S1 and the $100 loss recognized by T upon the sale of Item *v* to S1 are deferred pursuant to § 1.1502-13(c)(1).

(vii) S2 may not make the positive adjustment provided for in § 1.1502-32(b)(1)(ii) to its basis in the stock of T for the $100 dual consolidated loss incurred by T. In addition, no positive adjustment in the basis of the stock is required for T's $90 capital loss because the loss has been absorbed by the consolidated group. S2, however, must make the negative adjustment provided for in § 1.1502-32(b)(2)(i) for its allocable

part of T's deficit in earnings and profits for the taxable year attributable to both T's $100 dual consolidated loss and T's $90 capital loss. Thus, as provided in § 1.1502-32(e)(1), S2 must make a $190 net negative adjustment to its basis in the stock of T, reducing its basis to $310. As provided in § 1.1502-33(c)(4)(ii) (a), S2's earnings and profits for Year 1 will reflect S2's decrease in its basis in T stock for the taxable year. Since S2 has no other earnings and profits for the taxable year, S2 has a $190 deficit in earnings and profits for the year. As provided in § 1.1502-32(b)(2)(i), P must make a negative adjustment to its basis in the stock of S2 for its allocable part of S2's deficit in earnings and profits for the taxable year. Thus, P must make a $190 net negative adjustment to its basis in S2 stock, reducing its basis to $810.

Example 2. (i) The facts are the same as in *Example 1*, except that in Year 2, S1 sells items *u* and *v* to X for no gain or loss. The disposition of items *u* and *v* outside of the consolidated group restores the deferred loss and gain to T. T also incurs $100 of interest expense in Year 2. In addition, T sells a noncapital asset, *r*, in which it has a basis of $100, to Y for $300. P and S2 have no items of income, loss, or deduction for Year 2.

(ii) T has $40 of separate taxable income in Year 2, computed as follows:

($100)	interest expense
($100)	sale of item *v* to S1
$ 40	sale of item *u* to S1
$200	sale of item *r* to Y
$ 40	

Thus, T has no dual consolidated loss for the year.

(iii) Since T does not have a dual consolidated loss for the taxable year, the group's consolidated taxable income is calculated in accordance with the general rule of § 1.1502-11 and not in accordance with paragraph (d)(2) of this section. T is the only member of the consolidated group that has any income or loss for the taxable year. Thus, the consolidated taxable income of the group, computed without regard to T's dual consolidated loss carryover, is $40.

(iv) As provided by § 1.1502-21A(c), the amount of the dual consolidated loss arising in Year 1 that is included in the group's consolidated net operating loss deduction for Year 2 is $40 (that is, the consolidated taxable income computed without regard to the consolidated net operating loss deduction minus such consolidated taxable income recomputed by excluding the items of income and deduction of T). Thus, the group has no consolidated taxable income for the year.

(v) S2 must make the positive adjustment provided for in § 1.1502-32(b)(1)(i) to its basis in T stock for its allocable part of T's undistributed earnings and profits for the taxable year. S2 cannot make the negative adjustment provided for in § 1.1502-32(b)(2)(ii) for the dual consolidated loss of T incurred in Year 1 and absorbed in Year 2. Thus, as provided in § 1.1502-32(e)(2), S2 must make a $40 net positive adjustment to its basis in T stock, increasing its basis to $350. As provided in § 1.1502-33(c)(4)(ii)(a), S2's earnings and profits for Year 2 will reflect S2's increase in its basis in T stock for the taxable year. Since S2 has no other earnings and profits for the taxable year, S2 has $40 of earnings and profits for the year. As provided in § 1.1502-32(b)(1)(i), P must make a positive adjustment to its basis in the stock of S2 for its allocable part of the undistributed earnings and profits of S2 for the taxable year. Thus, P must make a $40 net positive adjustment to its basis in S2 stock, increasing its basis to $850.

(e) *Special rule for use of dual consolidated loss to offset tainted income.*—(1) *In general.*—The dual consolidated loss of any dual resident corporation that ceases to be a dual resident corporation shall not be used to offset income of such corporation to the extent that such income is tainted income, as defined in paragraph (e)(2) of this section.

(2) *Tainted income defined.*—Tainted income is any income derived from tainted assets, as defined in paragraph (e)(3) of this section, beginning on the date such assets are acquired by the dual resident corporation. In the absence of evidence establishing the actual amount of income that is attributable to the tainted assets, the portion of a corporation's income in a particular taxable year that is treated as tainted income shall be an amount equal to the corporation's taxable income for the year multiplied by a fraction, the numerator of which is the fair market value of the tainted asset at the end of the taxable year and the denominator of which is the fair market value of the total assets owned by the corporation at the end of the taxable year. Documentation submitted to establish the actual amount of income that is attributable to the tainted assets must be attached to the consolidated group's or unaffiliated dual resident corporation's timely filed tax return for the taxable year in which the income is recognized.

(3) *Tainted assets defined.*—Tainted assets are any assets acquired by a dual resident corporation in a nonrecognition transaction, as defined in section 7701(a)(45), or any assets otherwise transferred to the corporation as a contribution to capital, at any time during the three taxable years immediately preceding the taxable year in which the corporation ceases to be a dual resident corporation or at any time thereafter. Tainted assets shall not include assets that were acquired by such dual resident corporation on or before December 31, 1986.

(4) *Exceptions.*—Income derived from assets acquired by a dual resident corporation shall not be subject to the limitation described in paragraph (e)(1) of this section, if—

(i) For the taxable year in which the assets were acquired, the corporation did not have a dual consolidated loss (or a carry forward of a dual consolidated loss to such year); or

(ii) The assets were acquired as replacement property in the ordinary course of business.

(f) *Computation of foreign tax credit limitations.*—If a dual resident corporation or separate unit is subject to paragraph (d)(2) of this section, the consolidated group or unaffiliated domestic owner shall compute its foreign tax credit limitation by applying the limitations of paragraph (d)(2). Thus, the dual consolidated loss is not taken into account until the year in which it is absorbed.

(g) *Exception.*—(1) *Elective agreement in place between the United States and a foreign country.*—Paragraph (b) of this section shall not apply to a dual consolidated loss to the extent the dual resident corporation, or domestic owner of a separate unit, elects to deduct the loss in the United States pursuant to an agreement entered into between the United States and a foreign country that puts into place an elective procedure through which losses offset income in only one country.

(2) *Elective relief provision.*—(i) *In general.*—Paragraph (b) of this section shall not apply to a dual consolidated loss if the consolidated group, unaffiliated dual resident corporation, or unaffiliated domestic owner elects to be bound by the provisions of this paragraph (g)(2). In order to elect relief under this paragraph (g)(2), the consolidated group, unaffiliated dual resident corporation, or unaffiliated domestic owner must attach to its timely filed (including extensions) U.S. income tax return for the taxable year in which the dual consolidated loss is incurred an agreement described in paragraph (g)(2)(i)(A) of this section. The agreement must be signed under penalties of perjury by the person who signs the return. For taxable years beginning after December 31, 2002, the agreement attached to the income tax return of the consolidated group, unaffiliated dual resident corporation or unaffiliated domestic owner pursuant to the preceding sentence may be an unsigned copy. If an unsigned copy is attached to the return, the consolidated group, unaffiliated dual resident corporation, or unaffiliated domestic owner must retain the original in its records in the manner specified by § 1.6001-1(e). The agreement must include the following items, in paragraphs labeled to correspond with the items set forth in paragraph (g)(2)(i)(A) through (F) of this section.

(A) A statement that the document submitted is an election and an agreement under the provisions of paragraph (g)(2) of this section.

(B) The name, address, identifying number, and place and date of incorporation of the dual resident corporation, and the country or countries that tax the dual resident corporation on its worldwide income or on a residence basis, or, in the case of a separate unit, identification of the separate unit, including the name under which it conducts business, its principal activity, and the country in which its principal place of business is located.

(C) An agreement by the consolidated group, unaffiliated dual resident corporation, or unaffiliated domestic owner to comply with all of the provisions of § 1.1503-2(g)(2)(iii)-(vii).

(D) A statement of the amount of the dual consolidated loss covered by the agreement.

(E) A certification that no portion of the dual resident corporation's or separate unit's losses, expenses, or deductions taken into account in computing the dual consolidated loss has been, or will be, used to offset the income of any other person under the income tax laws of a foreign country.

(F) A certification that arrangements have been made to ensure that no portion of the dual consolidated loss will be used to offset the income of another person under the laws of a foreign country and that the consolidated group, unaffiliated dual resident corporation, or unaffiliated domestic owner will be informed of any such foreign use of any portion of the dual consolidated loss.

(ii) *Consistency rule.*—(A) If any loss, expense, or deduction taken into account in computing the dual consolidated loss of a dual resident corporation or separate unit is used under the laws of a foreign country to offset the income of another person, then the following other dual consolidated losses (if any) shall be treated as also having been used to offset income of another person under the laws of such foreign country, but only if the income tax laws of the foreign country permit any loss, expense, or deduction taken into account in computing the other dual consolidated loss to be used to offset the income of another person in the same taxable year:

(1) Any dual consolidated loss of a dual resident corporation that is a member of the same consolidated group of which the first dual resident corporation or domestic owner is a member, if any loss, expense, or deduction taken into account in computing such dual consolidated loss is recognized under the income tax laws of such country in the same taxable year; and

(2) Any dual consolidated loss of a separate unit that is owned by the same domestic owner that owns the first separate unit, or that is owned by any member of the same consolidated group of which the first dual resident corporation or domestic owner is a member, if any loss, expense, or deduction taken into account in computing such dual consolidated loss is recognized under the income tax laws of such country in the same taxable year.

(B) The following examples illustrate the application of this paragraph (g)(2)(ii).

Example 1. P, a domestic corporation, owns A and B, which are domestic corporations, and C, a Country X corporation. A is subject to the income tax laws of Country X on a residence basis and, thus, is a dual resident corporation. B conducts business in Country X through a branch, which is a separate unit under paragraph (c)(3) of this section. The income tax laws of Country X permit branches of foreign corporations to elect to file consolidated returns with Country X affiliates. In Year 1, A incurs a dual consolidated loss, which is used to offset the income of C under the Country X form of consolidation. The branch of B also incurs a net operating loss. However, B elects not to use the loss on a Country X consolidated return to offset the income of foreign affiliates. The use of A's loss to offset the income of C in Country X will cause the separate unit of B to be treated as if it too had used its dual consolidated loss to offset the income of an affiliate in Country X. Therefore, an election and agreement under this paragraph (g)(2) cannot be made with respect to the separate unit's dual consolidated loss.

Example 2. The facts are the same as in *Example 1*, except that the income tax laws of Country X do not permit branches of foreign corporations to file consolidated income tax returns with Country X affiliates. Therefore, an election and agreement described in this paragraph (g)(2) may be made for the dual consolidated loss incurred by the separate unit of B.

(iii) *Triggering events requiring the recapture of dual consolidated losses.*—(A) The consolidated group, unaffiliated dual resident corporation, or unaffiliated domestic owner must agree that, if there is a triggering event described in this paragraph (g)(2)(iii), and no exception applies under paragraph (g)(2)(iv) of this section, the consolidated group, unaffiliated dual resident corporation, or unaffiliated domestic owner will recapture and report as income the amount of the dual consolidated loss provided in paragraph (g)(2)(vii) of this section on its tax return for the taxable year in which the triggering event occurs (or, when the triggering event is a use of the loss for foreign purposes, the taxable year that includes the last day of the foreign tax year during which such use occurs). In addition, the consolidated group, unaffiliated dual resident corporation, or unaffiliated domestic owner must pay any applicable interest charge provided by paragraph (g)(2)(vii) of this section. For purposes of this section, any of the following events shall constitute a triggering event:

(1) In any taxable year up to and including the 15th taxable year following the year in which the dual consolidated loss that is the subject of the agreement filed under this paragraph (g)(2) was incurred, any portion of the losses, expenses, or deductions taken into ac-

count in computing the dual consolidated loss is used by any means to offset the income of any other person under the income tax laws of a foreign country;

(2) An affiliated dual resident corporation or affiliated domestic owner ceases to be a member of the consolidated group that filed the election. For purposes of this paragraph (g)(2)(iii)(A)(2), a dual resident corporation or domestic owner shall be considered to cease to be a member of the consolidated group if it is no longer a member of the group within the meaning of § 1.1502-1(b), or if the group ceases to exist because the common parent is no longer in existence or is no longer a common parent or the group no longer files on the basis of a consolidated return. Such disaffiliation, however, shall not constitute a triggering event if the taxpayer demonstrates, to the satisfaction of the Commissioner, that the dual resident corporation's or separate unit's losses, expenses, or deductions cannot be used to offset income of another person under the laws of a foreign country at any time after the affiliated dual resident corporation or affiliated domestic owner ceases to be a member of the consolidated group;

(3) An unaffiliated dual resident corporation or unaffiliated domestic owner becomes a member of a consolidated group. Such affiliation of the dual resident corporation or domestic owner, however, shall not constitute a triggering event if the taxpayer demonstrates, to the satisfaction of the Commissioner, that the losses, expenses, or deductions of the dual resident corporation or separate unit cannot be used to offset the income of another person under the laws of a foreign country at any time after the dual resident corporation or domestic owner becomes a member of the consolidated group.

(4) A dual resident corporation transfers assets in a transaction that results, under the laws of a foreign country, in a carryover of its losses, expenses, or deductions. For purposes of this paragraph (g)(2)(iii) (A)(4), a transfer, either in a single transaction or a series of transactions within a twelve-month period, of 50% or more of the dual resident corporation's assets (measured by the fair market value of the assets at the time of such transfer (or for multiple transactions, at the time of the first transfer)) shall be deemed a triggering event, unless the taxpayer demonstrates, to the satisfaction of the Commissioner, that the transfer of assets did not result in a carryover under foreign law of the dual resident corporation's losses, expenses, or deductions to the transferee of the assets;

(5) A domestic owner of a separate unit transfers assets of the separate unit in a transaction that results, under the laws of a foreign country, in a carryover of the separate unit's losses, expenses, or deductions. For purposes of this paragraph (g)(2)(iii)(A)(5), a transfer, either in a single transaction or a series of transactions over a twelve-month period, of 50% or more of the separate unit's assets (measured by the fair market value of the assets at the time of the transfer (or for multiple transfers, at the time of the first transfer)), shall be deemed a triggering event, unless the taxpayer demonstrates, to the satisfaction of the Commissioner, that the transfer of assets did not result in a carryover under foreign law of the separate unit's losses, expenses, or deductions to the transferee of the assets;

(6) An unaffiliated dual resident corporation or unaffiliated domestic owner becomes a foreign corporation by means of a transaction (e.g., a reorganization) that, for foreign tax purposes, is not treated as involving a transfer of assets (and carryover of losses) to a new entity. Such a transaction, however, shall not constitute a triggering event if the taxpayer demonstrates, to the satisfaction of the Commissioner, that the dual resident corporation's or separate unit's losses, expenses, or deductions cannot be used to offset income of another person under the laws of the foreign country at any time after the unaffiliated dual resident corporation or unaffiliated domestic owner becomes a foreign corporation.

(7) A domestic owner of a separate unit, either in a single transaction or a series of transactions within a twelve-month period, sells, or otherwise disposes of, 50% or more of the interest in the separate unit (measured by voting power or value) owned by the domestic owner on the last day of the taxable year in which the dual consolidated loss was incurred. For purposes of this paragraph (g)(2)(iii)(A)(7), the domestic owner shall be deemed to have disposed of its entire interest in a hybrid entity separate unit if such hybrid entity becomes classified as a foreign corporation for U.S. tax purposes. The disposition of 50% or more of the interest in a separate unit, however, shall not constitute a triggering event if the taxpayer demonstrates, to the satisfaction of the Commissioner, that the losses, expenses, or deductions of the separate unit cannot be used to offset income of another person under the laws of the foreign country at any time after the disposition of the interest in the separate unit; or

(8) The consolidated group, unaffiliated dual resident corporation, or unaffiliated domestic owner fails to file a certification required under paragraph (g)(2)(vi)(B) of this section.

(B) A taxpayer wishing to rebut the presumption of a triggering event described in paragraphs (g)(2)(iii)(A) (2) through (7) of this section, by demonstrating that the losses, expenses, or deductions of the dual resident corporation or separate unit cannot be carried over or otherwise used under the laws of the foreign country, must attach documents demonstrating such facts to its timely filed U.S. income tax return for the year in which the presumed triggering event occurs.

Reg. § 1.1503-2(g)(2)(iii)(A)(2)

(C) The following example illustrates this paragraph (g)(2)(iii).

Example. DRC, a domestic corporation, is a member of CG, a consolidated group. DRC is a resident of Country Y for Country Y income tax purposes. Therefore, DRC is a dual resident corporation. In Year 1, DRC incurs a dual consolidated loss of $100. CG files an agreement described in paragraph (g)(2) of this section and, thus, the $100 dual consolidated loss is included in the computation of CG's consolidated taxable income. In Year 6, all of the stock of DRC is sold to P, a domestic corporation that is a member of NG, another consolidated group. The sale of DRC to P is a triggering event under paragraph (g)(2)(iii)(A) of this section, requiring the recapture of the dual consolidated loss. However, the laws of Country Y provide for a five-year carryover period for losses. At the time of DRC's disaffiliation from CG, the losses, expenses and deductions that were included in the computation of the dual consolidated loss had expired for Country Y purposes. Therefore, upon adequate documentation that the losses, expenses, or deductions have expired for Country Y purposes, CG can rebut the presumption that a triggering event has occurred.

(iv) *Exceptions.*—(A) *Acquisition by a member of the consolidated group.*—The following events shall not constitute triggering events, requiring the recapture of the dual consolidated loss under paragraph (g)(2)(vii) of this section:

(1) An affiliated dual resident corporation or affiliated domestic owner ceases to be a member of a consolidated group solely by reason of a transaction in which a member of the same consolidated group succeeds to the tax attributes of the dual resident corporation or domestic owner under the provisions of section 381;

(2) Assets of an affiliated dual resident corporation or assets of a separate unit of an affiliated domestic owner are acquired by a member of its consolidated group in any other transaction; or

(3) An affiliated domestic owner of a separate unit transfers its interest in the separate unit to another member of its consolidated group.

(B) *Acquisition by an unaffiliated domestic corporation or a new consolidated group.*—(1) If all the requirements of paragraph (g)(2)(iv)(B)(3) of this section are met, the following events shall not constitute triggering events requiring the recapture of the dual consolidated loss under paragraph (g)(2)(vii) of this section:

(i) An affiliated dual resident corporation or affiliated domestic owner becomes an unaffiliated domestic corporation or a member of a new consolidated group (other than in a transaction described in paragraph (g)(2)(iv)(B)(2)(ii) of this section);

(ii) Assets of a dual resident corporation or a separate unit are acquired by an unaffiliated domestic corporation or a member of a new consolidated group; or

(iii) A domestic owner of a separate unit transfers its interest in the separate unit to an unaffiliated domestic corporation or to a member of a new consolidated group.

(2) If the requirements of paragraph (g)(2)(iv)(B)(3)(iii) of this section are met, the following events shall not constitute triggering events requiring the recapture of the dual consolidated loss under paragraph (g)(2)(vii) of this section—

(i) An unaffiliated dual resident corporation or unaffiliated domestic owner becomes a member of a consolidated group;

(ii) A consolidated group that filed an agreement under this paragraph (g)(2) ceases to exist as a result of a transaction described in §1.1502-13(j)(5)(i) (other than a transaction in which any member of the terminating group, or the successor-in-interest of such member, is not a member of the surviving group immediately after the terminating group ceases to exist).

(3) If the following requirements (as applicable) are satisfied, the events listed in paragraphs (g)(2)(iv)(B)(1) and (2) of this section shall not constitute triggering events requiring recapture under paragraph (g)(2)(vii) of this section.

(i) The consolidated group, unaffiliated dual resident corporation, or unaffiliated domestic owner that filed the agreement under this paragraph (g)(2) and the unaffiliated domestic corporation or new consolidated group must enter into a closing agreement with the Internal Revenue Service providing that the consolidated group, unaffiliated dual resident corporation, or unaffiliated domestic owner and the unaffiliated domestic corporation or new consolidated group will be jointly and severally liable for the total amount of the recapture of dual consolidated loss and interest charge required in paragraph (g)(2)(vii) of this section, if there is a triggering event described in paragraph (g)(2)(iii) of this section;

(ii) The unaffiliated domestic corporation or new consolidated group must agree to treat any potential recapture amount under paragraph (g)(2)(vii) of this section as unrealized built-in gain for purposes of section 384(a), subject to any applicable exceptions thereunder;

(iii) The unaffiliated domestic corporation or new consolidated group must file, with its timely filed (including extensions) income tax return for the taxable year in which the event described in paragraph (g)(2)(iv)(B)(1) or (2) of this section occurs, an agreement described in paragraph (g)(2)(i) of this section (new (g)(2)(i) agreement), whereby it assumes the same obligations with respect to the dual consolidated loss as the corporation or consolidated group that filed the original (g)(2)(i) agreement

Reg. §1.1503-2(g)(2)(iv)(B)(3)(iii)

with respect to that loss. The new (g)(2)(i) agreement must be signed under penalties of perjury by the person who signs the return and must include a reference to this paragraph (g)(2)(iv)(B)(3)(iii). For taxable years beginning after December 31, 2002, the agreement attached to the return pursuant to the preceding sentence may be an unsigned copy. If an unsigned copy is attached to the return, the corporation or consolidated group must retain the original in its records in the manner specified by § 1.6001-1(e).

(C) *Subsequent triggering events.*—Any triggering event described in paragraph (g)(2)(iii) of this section that occurs subsequent to one of the transactions described in paragraph (g)(2)(iv)(A) or (B) of this section and does not fall within the exceptions provided in paragraph (g)(2)(iv)(A) or (B) of this section shall require recapture under paragraph (g)(2)(vii) of this section.

(D) Example. The following example illustrates the application of paragraph (g)(2)(iv)(B)(2)(ii) of this section:

Example. (i) Facts. C is the common parent of a consolidated group (the C Group) that includes DRC, a domestic corporation. DRC is a dual resident corporation and incurs a dual consolidated loss in its taxable year ending December 31, Year 1. The C Group elects to be bound by the provisions of this paragraph (g)(2) with respect to the Year 1 dual consolidated loss. No member of the C Group incurs a dual consolidated loss in Year 2. On December 31, Year 2, stock of C is acquired by D in a transaction described in § 1.1502-13(j)(5)(i). As a result of the acquisition, all the C Group members, including DRC, become members of a consolidated group of which D is the common parent (the D Group).

(ii) Acquisition not a triggering event. Under paragraph (g)(2)(iv)(B)(2)(ii) of this section, the acquisition by D of the C Group is not an event requiring the recapture of the Year 1 dual consolidated loss of DRC, or the payment of an interest charge, as described in paragraph (g)(2)(vii) of this section, provided that the D Group files the new (g)(2)(i) agreement described in paragraph (g)(2)(iv)(B)(3)(iii) of this section.

(iii) Subsequent event. A triggering event occurs on December 31, Year 3, that requires recapture by the D Group of the dual consolidated loss that DRC incurred in Year 1, as well as the payment of an interest charge, as provided in paragraph (g)(2)(vii) of this section. Each member of the D Group, including DRC and the other former members of the C Group, is severally liable for the additional tax (and the interest charge) due upon the recapture of the dual consolidated loss of DRC.

(v) *Ordering rules for determining the foreign use of losses.*—If the laws of a foreign country provide for the use of losses of a dual resident corporation to offset the income of another per-

son but do not provide applicable rules for determining the order in which such losses are used to offset the income of another person in a taxable year, then for purposes of this section, the following rules shall govern:

(A) If under the laws of the foreign country the dual resident corporation has losses from different taxable years, the dual resident corporation shall be deemed to use first the losses from the earliest taxable year from which a loss may be carried forward or back for foreign law purposes.

(B) Any net loss, or income, that the dual resident corporation has in a taxable year shall first be used to offset net income, or loss, recognized by affiliates of the dual resident corporation in the same taxable year before any carryover of the dual resident corporation's losses is considered to be used to offset any income from the taxable year.

(C) Where different losses, expenses, or deductions (*e.g.*, capital losses and ordinary losses) of a dual resident corporation incurred in the same taxable year are available to offset the income of another person, the different losses shall be deemed to offset such income on a pro rata basis.

Example. DRC, a domestic corporation, is taxed as a resident under the tax laws of Country Y. Therefore, DRC is a dual resident corporation. FA is a Country Y affiliate of DRC. Country Y's tax laws permit affiliated corporations to file a form of consolidated return. In Year 1, DRC incurs a capital loss of $80 which, for Country Y purposes, offsets completely $30 of capital gain recognized by FA. Neither corporation has any other taxable income or loss for the year. In Year 1 (and in other years), DRC recognizes the same amount of income for U.S. purposes as it does for Country Y purposes. Under paragraph (d)(1)(i) of this section, however, DRC's $80 capital loss is not a dual consolidated loss. In Year 2, DRC incurs a net operating loss of $100, while FA incurs a net operating loss of $50. DRC's $100 loss is a dual consolidated loss. Since the dual consolidated loss is not used to offset the income of another person under Country Y law, DRC is permitted to file an agreement described in this paragraph (g)(2). In Year 3, DRC has a net operating loss of $10 and FA has capital gains of $60. For Country Y purposes, DRC's $10 net operating loss is used to offset $10 of FA's $60 capital gain. DRC's $10 loss is a dual consolidated loss. Because the loss is used to offset FA's income, DRC will not be able to file an agreement under this paragraph (g)(2) with respect to the loss. Country Y permits FA's remaining $50 of Year 3 income to be offset by carryover losses. However, Country Y has no applicable rules for determining which carryover losses from Years 1 and 2 are used to offset such income. Under the ordering rules of paragraph (g)(2)(v)(A) of this section, none of DRC's $100 Year 2 loss will be deemed to offset FA's remaining $50 of Year 3 income. Instead, the $50 of capital loss carryover from Year 1 will be considered to offset the income.

(vi) *Reporting requirements.*—(A) *In general.*—The consolidated group, unaffiliated dual resident corporation, or unaffiliated domestic owner must answer the applicable questions regarding dual consolidated losses on its U.S. income tax return filed for the year in which the dual consolidated loss is incurred and for each of the following fifteen taxable years.

(B) *Annual certification.*—Except as provided in §1.1503-2(g)(2)(vi)(C), until and unless Form 1120 or the Schedules thereto contain questions pertaining to dual consolidated losses, the consolidated group, unaffiliated dual resident corporation, or unaffiliated domestic owner must file with its income tax return for each of the 15 taxable years following the taxable year in which the dual consolidated loss is incurred a certification that the losses, expenses, or deductions that make up the dual consolidated loss have not been used to offset the income of another person under the tax laws of a foreign country. For taxable years beginning before January 1, 2003, the annual certification must be signed under penalties of perjury by a person authorized to sign the agreement described in §1.1503-2(g)(2)(i). For taxable years beginning after December 31, 2002, the certification is verified by signing the return with which the certification is filed. The certification for a taxable year must identify the dual consolidated loss to which it pertains by setting forth the taxpayer's year in which the loss was incurred and the amount of such loss. In addition, the certification must warrant that arrangements have been made to ensure that the loss will not be used to offset the income of another person under the laws of a foreign country and that the taxpayer will be informed of any such foreign use of any portion of the loss. If dual consolidated losses of more than one taxable year are subject to the rules of this paragraph (g)(2)(vi)(B), the certifications for those years may be combined in a single document but each dual consolidated loss must be separately identified.

(C) *Exception.*—A consolidated group or unaffiliated domestic owner is not required to file annual certifications under paragraph (g)(2)(vi)(B) of this section with respect to a dual consolidated loss of any separate unit other than a hybrid entity separate unit.

(vii) *Recapture of loss and interest charge.*—(A) *Presumptive rule.*—(1) *Amount of recapture.*—Except as otherwise provided in this paragraph (g)(2)(vii), upon the occurrence of a triggering event described in paragraph (g)(2)(iii) of this section, the taxpayer shall recapture and report as gross income the total amount of the dual consolidated loss to which the triggering event applies on its income tax return for the taxable year in which the triggering event occurs (or, when the triggering event is a use of the loss for foreign tax purposes, the taxable year that includes the last day of the foreign tax year during which such use occurs).

(2) *Interest charge.*—In connection with the recapture, the taxpayer shall pay an interest charge. Except as otherwise provided in this paragraph (g)(2)(vii), such interest shall be determined under the rules of section 6601(a) as if the additional tax owed as a result of the recapture had accrued and been due and owing for the taxable year in which the losses, expenses, or deductions taken into account in computing the dual consolidated loss gave rise to a tax benefit for U.S. income tax purposes. For purposes of this paragraph (g)(2)(vii)(A)(2), a tax benefit shall be considered to have arisen in a taxable year in which such losses, expenses or deductions reduced U.S. taxable income.

(B) *Rebuttal of presumptive rule.*—(1) *Amount of recapture.*—The amount of dual consolidated loss that must be recaptured under this paragraph (g)(2)(vii) may be reduced if the taxpayer demonstrates, to the satisfaction of the Commissioner, the offset permitted by this paragraph (g)(2)(vii)(B). The reduction in the amount of recapture is the amount by which the dual consolidated loss would have offset other taxable income reported on a timely filed U.S. income tax return for any taxable year up to and including the year of the triggering event if such loss had been subject to the restrictions of paragraph (b) of this section (and therefore had been subject to the separate return limitation year restrictions of §1.1502-21A(c) or 1.1502-21(c) (as appropriate)) commencing in the taxable year in which the loss was incurred. A taxpayer utilizing this rebuttal rule must attach to its timely filed U.S. income tax return a separate accounting showing that the income for each year that offsets the dual resident corporation's or separate unit's recapture amount is attributable only to the dual resident corporation or separate unit.

(2) *Interest charge.*—The interest charge imposed under this paragraph (g)(2)(vii) may be appropriately reduced if the taxpayer demonstrates, to the satisfaction of the Commissioner, that the net interest owed would have been less than that provided in paragraph (g)(2)(vii)(A)(2) of this section if the taxpayer had filed an amended return for the year in which the loss was incurred, and for any other affected years up to and including the year of recapture, treating the dual consolidated loss as a loss subject to the restrictions of paragraph (b) of this section (and therefore subject to the separate return limitation year restrictions of §1.1502-21A(c) or 1.1502-21(c) (as appropriate)). A taxpayer utilizing this rebuttal rule must attach to its timely filed U.S. income tax return a computation demonstrating the reduction in the

net interest owed as a result of treating the dual consolidated loss as a loss subject to the restrictions of paragraph (b) of this section.

(C) *Computation of taxable income in year of recapture.*—*(1) Presumptive rule.*—Except as otherwise provided in paragraph (g)(2)(vii)(C)(2) of this section, for purposes of computing the taxable income for the year of recapture, no current, carryover or carryback losses of the dual resident corporation or separate unit, of other members of the consolidated group, or of the domestic owner that are not attributable to the separate unit, may offset and absorb the recapture amount.

(2) *Rebuttal of presumptive rule.*— The recapture amount included in gross income may be offset and absorbed by that portion of the taxpayer's (consolidated or separate) net operating loss carryover that is attributable to the dual consolidated loss being recaptured, if the taxpayer demonstrates, to the satisfaction of the Commissioner, the amount of such portion of the carryover. A taxpayer utilizing this rebuttal rule must attach to its timely filed U.S. income tax return a computation demonstrating the amount of net operating loss carryover that, under this paragraph (g)(2)(vii)(C)(2), may absorb the recapture amount included in gross income.

(D) *Character and source of recapture income.*—The amount recaptured under this paragraph (g)(2)(vii) shall be treated as ordinary income in the year of recapture. The amount recaptured shall be treated as income having the same source and falling within the same separate category for purposes of section 904 as the dual consolidated loss being recaptured.

(E) *Reconstituted net operating loss.*— Commencing in the taxable year immediately following the year in which the dual consolidated loss is recaptured, the dual resident corporation or separate unit shall be treated as having a net operating loss in an amount equal to the amount actually recaptured under paragraph (g)(2)(vii)(A) or (B) of this section. This reconstituted net operating loss shall be subject to the restrictions of paragraph (b) of this section (and therefore, the separate return limitation year restrictions of §§ 1.1502-21A(c) or 1.1502-21T(c) (as appropriate)). The net operating loss shall be available only for carryover, under section 172(b), to taxable years following the taxable year of recapture. For purposes of determining the remaining carryover period, the loss shall be treated as if it had been recognized in the taxable year in which the dual consolidated loss that is the basis of the recapture amount was incurred.

(F) *Consequences of failing to comply with recapture provisions.*—*(1) In general.*—If the taxpayer fails to comply with the recapture provisions of this paragraph (g)(2)(vii) upon the occurrence of a triggering event, then the dual resident corporation or separate unit that incurred the dual consolidated loss (or a successor-in-interest) shall not be eligible for the relief provided in paragraph (g)(2) of this section with respect to any dual consolidated losses incurred in the five taxable years beginning with the taxable year in which recapture is required.

(2) *Exceptions.*—In the case of a triggering event other than a use of the losses, expenses, or deductions taken into account in computing the dual consolidated loss to offset income of another person under the income tax laws of a foreign country, this rule shall not apply in the following circumstances:

(i) The failure to recapture is due to reasonable cause; or

(ii) A taxpayer seeking to rebut the presumption of a triggering event satisfies the filing requirements of paragraph (g)(2)(iii)(B) of this section.

(G) *Examples.*—The following examples illustrate this paragraph (g)(2)(vii).

Example 1. P, a domestic corporation, files a consolidated return with DRC, a dual resident corporation. In Year 1, DRC incurs a dual consolidated loss of $100 and P earns $100. P files an agreement under this paragraph (g)(2). Therefore, the consolidated group is permitted to offset P's $100 of income with DRC's $100 loss. In Year 2, DRC earns $30, which is completely offset by a $30 net operating loss incurred by P. In Year 3, DRC earns income of $25 while P recognizes no income or loss. In addition, there is a triggering event in Year 3. Therefore, under the presumptive rule of paragraph (g)(2)(vii)(A) of this section, DRC must recapture $100. However, the $100 recapture amount may be reduced by $25 (the amount by which the dual consolidated loss would have offset other taxable income if it had been subject to the separate return limitation year restrictions from Year 1) upon adequate documentation of such offset under paragraph (g)(2)(vii)(B)(1) of this section. Commencing in Year 4, the $100 (or $75) recapture amount is treated as a loss incurred by DRC in a separate return limitation year, subject to the restrictions of § 1.1502-21A(c) or 1.1502-21(c), as appropriate. The carryover period of the loss, for purposes of section 172(b), will start from Year 1, when the dual consolidated loss was incurred.

Example 2. The facts are the same as in *Example 1,* except that in Year 2, DRC earns $75 and P earns $50. In Year 3, DRC earns $25 while P earns $30. A triggering event occurs in Year 3. The $100 presumptive amount of recapture can be reduced to zero by the $75 and $25 earned by DRC in Years 2 and 3, respectively, upon adequate documentation of such offset under paragraph (g)(2)(vii)(B)(1) of this section. Nevertheless, an interest charge will be owed. Under the presumptive rule of paragraph (g)(2)(vii)(A)(2) of this section, interest will be charged on the additional tax owed on the $100 of recapture income as if the tax had accrued in Year 1 (the year in which the dual consolidated loss reduced the income of P). However, the net interest will be reduced to the amount that would have been owed if the consolidated group had filed amended returns, treating the dual consolidated loss as a loss subject to the separate return limitation year restrictions of § 1.1502-21A(c) or 1.1502-21(c), as appropriate, upon adequate documentation of such reduction of interest under paragraph (g)(2)(vii)(B)(2) of this section.

Example 3. P, a domestic corporation, owns DRC, a domestic corporation that is subject to the income tax laws of Country Z on a residence basis. DRC owns FE, a Country Z corporation. In Year 1, DRC incurs a net operating loss for U.S. tax purposes. Under the tax laws of Country Z, the loss is not recognized until Year 3. The Year 1 net operating loss is a dual consolidated loss under paragraph (c)(5) of this section. The consolidated group elects relief under paragraph (g)(2) of this section by filing the appropriate agreement and uses the dual consolidated loss on its U.S. income tax return. In Year 3, the dual consolidated loss is used under the laws of Country Z to offset the income of FE, which is a triggering event under paragraph (g)(2)(iii) of this section. However, the consolidated group does not recapture the dual consolidated loss. The consolidated group's failure to comply with the recapture provisions of this paragraph (g)(2)(vii) prevents DRC from being eligible for the relief provided under paragraph (g)(2) of this section for any dual consolidated losses incurred in Years 3 through 7, inclusive.

(h) *Effective date.*—(1) *In general.*—These regulations are effective for taxable years beginning on or after October 1, 1992. Section 1.1503-2A is effective for taxable years beginning after December 31, 1986, and before October 1, 1992. Paragraph (g)(2)(iv)(B)(2) of this section shall apply with respect to transactions otherwise constituting triggering events occurring on or after January 1, 2002.

(2) *Taxpayers that have filed for relief under § 1.1503-2A.*—(i) *In general.*—Except as provided in paragraph (h)(ii)(b) of this section, taxpayers that have filed agreements described in § 1.1503-2A(c)(3) or certifications described in § 1.1503-2A(d)(3) shall continue to be subject to the provisions of such agreements or certifications, including the amended return or recapture requirements applicable in the event of a triggering event, for the remaining term of such agreements or certifications.

(ii) *Special transition rule.*—A taxpayer that has filed an agreement described in § 1.1503-2A(c)(3) or a certification described in § 1.1503-2A(d)(3) and that is in compliance with the provisions of § 1.1503-2A may elect to replace

such agreement or certification with an agreement described in paragraph (g)(2)(i) of this section. However, a taxpayer making this election must replace all agreements and certifications filed under § 1.1503-2A. If the taxpayer is a consolidated group, the election must be made with respect to all dual resident corporations or separate units within the group. Likewise, if the taxpayer is an unaffiliated domestic owner, the election must be made with respect to all separate units of the domestic owner. The taxpayer must file the replacement agreement with its timely filed income tax return for its first taxable year commencing on or after October 1, 1992, stating that such agreement is a replacement for the agreement filed under § 1.1503-2A(c)(3) or the certification filed under § 1.1503-2A(d)(3) and identifying the taxable year for which the original agreement or certification was filed. A single agreement described in paragraph (g)(2)(i) of this section may be filed to replace more than one agreement or certification filed under § 1.1503-2A; however, each dual consolidated loss must be separately identified. A taxpayer may also elect to apply § 1.1503-2 for all open years, with respect to agreements filed under § 1.1503-2A(c)(3) or certifications filed under § 1.1503-2A(d)(3), in cases where the agreement or certification is no longer in effect and the taxpayer has complied with the provisions of § 1.1503-2A. For example, a taxpayer may have had a triggering event under § 1.1503-2A that is not a triggering event under § 1.1503-2. If the taxpayer fully complied with the requirements of the agreement entered into under § 1.1503-2A(c)(3) and filed amended U.S. income tax returns within the time required under § 1.1503-2A(c)(3), the taxpayer may file amended U.S. income tax returns consistent with the position that the earlier triggering event is no longer a triggering event.

(3) *Taxpayers that are in compliance with § 1.1503-2A but have not filed for relief thereunder.*—A taxpayer that is in compliance with the provisions of § 1.1503-2A but has not filed an agreement described in § 1.1503-2A(c)(3) or a certification described in § 1.1503-2A(d)(3) may elect to have the provisions of § 1.1503-2 apply for any open year. In particular, a taxpayer may elect to apply the provisions of § 1.1503-2 in a case where the dual consolidated loss has been subjected to the separate return limitation year restrictions of § 1.1502-21A(c) or 1.1502-21(c) (as appropriate) but the losses, expenses, or deductions taken into account in computing the dual consolidated loss have not been used to offset the income of another person for foreign tax purposes. However, if a taxpayer is a consolidated group, the election must be made with respect to all dual resident corporations or separate units within the group. Likewise, if the taxpayer is an unaffiliated domestic owner, the election must be made with respect to all sepa-

rate units of the domestic owner. [Reg. § 1.1503-2.]

☐ [*T.D. 8434, 9-4-92. Amended by T.D. 8597, 7-12-95; T.D. 8677, 6-26-96; T.D. 8823, 6-25-99; T.D. 9084, 7-29-2003; T.D. 9100, 12-18-2003 and T.D. 9300, 12-7-2006.*]

[Reg. § 1.1503(d)-0]

§ 1.1503(d)-0. Table of contents.—This section lists the captions contained in § § 1.1503(d)-1 through 1.1503(d)-8.

(i) Transactions described in section 381(a).

(ii) Cessation of separate unit status.

(2) Exceptions.

(i) Certain section 368(a)(1)(F) reorganizations.

(ii) Acquisition of a dual resident corporation by another dual resident corporation.

(iii) Acquisition of a separate unit by a domestic corporation.

(A) Acquisition by a corporation that is not a member of the same consolidated group.

(B) Acquisition by a member of the same consolidated group.

(iv) Special rules for foreign insurance companies.

(e) Special rule denying the use of a dual consolidated loss to offset tainted income.

(1) In general.

(2) Tainted income.

(i) Definition.

(ii) Income presumed to be derived from holding tainted assets.

(3) Tainted assets defined.

(4) Exceptions.

(f) Computation of foreign tax credit limitation.

§ 1.1503(d)-5. Attribution of items and basis adjustments.

(a) In general.

(b) Determination of amount of income or dual consolidated loss of a dual resident corporation.

(1) In general.

(2) Exceptions.

(c) Determination of amount of income or dual consolidated loss attributable to a separate unit, and income or loss attributable to an interest in a transparent entity.

(1) In general.

(i) Scope and purpose.

(ii) Only items of domestic owner taken into account.

(iii) Separate application.

(2) Foreign branch separate unit.

(i) In general.

(ii) Principles of § 1.882-5.

(iii) Exception where foreign country attributes interest expense solely by reference to books and records.

(3) Hybrid entity separate unit and an interest in a transparent entity.

(i) General rule.

(ii) Interests in certain disregarded entities, partnerships, and grantor trusts owned by a hybrid entity or transparent entity.

(4) Special rules.

(i) Allocation of items between certain tiered separate units and interests in transparent entities.

(A) Foreign branch separate unit.

(B) Hybrid entity separate unit or interest in a transparent entity.

(ii) Combined separate unit.

(iii) Gain or loss on the direct or indirect disposition of a separate unit or an interest in a transparent entity.

(A) In general.

(B) Multiple separate units or interests in transparent entities.

(iv) Inclusions on stock.

(v) Foreign currency gain or loss recognized under section 987.

(vi) Recapture of dual consolidated loss.

(d) Foreign tax treatment disregarded.

(e) Items generated or incurred while a dual resident corporation, a separate unit, or a transparent entity.

(f) Assets and liabilities of a separate unit or an interest in a transparent entity.

(g) Basis adjustments.

(1) Affiliated dual resident corporation or affiliated domestic owner.

(2) Interests in hybrid entities that are partnerships or interests in partnerships through which a separate unit is owned indirectly.

(i) Scope.

(ii) Determination of basis of partner's interest.

(3) Combined separate units.

§ 1.1503(d)-6. Exceptions to the domestic use limitation rule.

(a) In general.

(1) Scope and purpose.

(2) Absence of foreign affiliate or foreign consolidation regime.

(3) Foreign insurance companies treated as domestic corporations.

(b) Elective agreement in place between the United States and a foreign country.

(1) In general.

(2) Application to combined separate units.

(c) No possibility of foreign use.

(1) In general.

(2) Statement.

(d) Domestic use election.

(1) In general.

(2) No domestic use election available if there is a triggering event in the year the dual consolidated loss is incurred.

(e) Triggering events requiring the recapture of a dual consolidated loss.

(1) Events.

(i) Foreign use.

(ii) Disaffiliation.

(iii) Affiliation.

(iv) Transfer of assets.

Reg. § 1.1503(d)-0

(v) Transfer of an interest in a separate unit.

(vi) Conversion to a foreign corporation.

(vii) Conversion to a regulated investment company, a real estate investment trust, or an S corporation.

(viii) Failure to certify.

(ix) Cessation of stand-alone status.

(2) Rebuttal.

(i) General rule.

(ii) Certain asset transfers.

(iii) Reporting.

(iv) Examples.

(f) Triggering event exceptions.

(1) Continuing ownership of assets or interests.

(i) Disaffiliation as a result of a transaction described in section 381.

(ii) Continuing ownership by consolidated group.

(iii) Continuing ownership by unaffiliated dual resident corporation or unaffiliated domestic owner.

(2) Transactions requiring a new domestic use agreement.

(i) Multiple-party events.

(ii) Events resulting in a single consolidated group.

(iii) Requirements.

(A) New domestic use agreement.

(B) Statement filed by original elector.

(3) Certain transfers qualifying for the de minimis exception to foreign use.

(4) Deemed transactions as a result of certain transfers that do not result in a foreign use.

(5) Compulsory transfers.

(6) Subsequent triggering events.

(g) Annual certification reporting requirement.

(h) Recapture of dual consolidated loss and interest charge.

(1) Presumptive rules.

(i) Amount of recapture.

(ii) Interest charge.

(2) Reduction of presumptive recapture amount and presumptive interest charge.

(i) Amount of recapture.

(ii) Interest charge.

(3) Rules regarding multiple-party event exceptions to triggering events.

(i) Scope.

(ii) Original elector and prior subsequent electors not subject to recapture or interest charge.

(iii) Recapture tax amount and required statement.

(A) In general.

(B) Recapture tax amount.

(iv) Tax assessment and collection procedures.

(A) In general.

(B) Collection from original elector and prior subsequent electors; joint and several liability.

(C) Allocation of partial payments of tax.

(D) Refund.

(v) Definition of income tax liability.

(vi) Example.

(4) Computation of taxable income in year of recapture.

(i) Presumptive rule.

(ii) Exception to presumptive rule.

(5) Character and source of recapture income.

(6) Reconstituted net operating loss.

(i) General rule.

(ii) Exception.

(iii) Special rule for recapture following multiple-party event exception to a triggering event.

(i) [Reserved]

(j) Termination of domestic use agreement and annual certifications.

(1) Rebuttals, exceptions to triggering events, and recapture.

(2) Termination of ability for foreign use.

(i) In general.

(ii) Statement.

(3) Agreements filed in connection with stand-alone exception.

§ 1.1503(d)-7. Examples.

(a) In general.

(b) Presumed facts for examples.

(c) Examples.

§ 1.1503(d)-8. Effective dates.

(a) General rule.

(b) Special rules.

(1) Reduction of term of agreements filed under §§ 1.1503-2A(c)(3), 1.1503-2A(d)(3), 1.1503-2(g)(2)(i), or 1.1503-2T(g)(2)(i).

(2) Reduction of term of agreements filed under §§ 1.1503-2(g)(2)(iv)(B)(2)(*i*) (1992), 1.1503-2(g)(2)(iv)(B)(3)(*i*), or Rev. Proc. 2000-42.

(3) Relief for untimely filings.

(i) General rule.

(ii) Closing agreements.

(iii) Pending requests for relief.

(4) Multiple-party event exception to triggering events.

(5) Basis adjustment rules.

[Reg. § 1.1503(d)-0.]

☐ [*T.D. 9315, 3-16-2007 (corrected 4–24–2007).*]

Reg. § 1.1503(d)-0

[Reg. § 1.1503(d)-1]

§ 1.1503(d)-1. Definitions and special rules for filings under section 1503(d).—(a) *In general.*—This section and § § 1.1503(d)-2 through 1.1503(d)-8 provide rules concerning the determination and use of dual consolidated losses pursuant to section 1503(d). Paragraph (b) of this section provides definitions that apply for purposes of this section and § § 1.1503(d)-2 through 1.1503(d)-8. Paragraph (c) of this section provides a reasonable cause exception and a signature requirement for filings.

(b) *Definitions.*—The following definitions apply for purposes of this section and § § 1.1503(d)-2 through 1.1503(d)-8:

(1) Domestic corporation means an entity classified as a domestic corporation under section 7701(a)(3) and (4) or otherwise treated as a domestic corporation by the Internal Revenue Code, including, but not limited to, sections 269B, 953(d), 1504(d), and 7874. However, solely for purposes of section 1503(d), the term domestic corporation shall not include a regulated investment company as defined in section 851, a real estate investment trust as defined in section 856, or an S corporation as defined in section 1361.

(2) Dual resident corporation means—

(i) A domestic corporation that is subject to an income tax of a foreign country on its worldwide income or on a residence basis. A corporation is taxed on a residence basis if it is taxed as a resident under the laws of the foreign country; and

(ii) A foreign insurance company that makes an election to be treated as a domestic corporation pursuant to section 953(d) and is treated as a member of an affiliated group for purposes of chapter 6, even if such company is not subject to an income tax of a foreign country on its worldwide income or on a residence basis. See section 953(d)(3).

(3) Hybrid entity means an entity that is not taxable as an association for Federal tax purposes, but is subject to an income tax of a foreign country as a corporation (or otherwise at the entity level) either on its worldwide income or on a residence basis.

(4) *Separate unit.*—(i) *In general.*—The term separate unit means either of the following that is carried on or owned, as applicable, directly or indirectly, by a domestic corporation (including a dual resident corporation):

(A) Except to the extent provided in paragraph (b)(4)(iii) of this section, a business operation outside the United States that, if carried on by a U.S. person, would constitute a foreign branch as defined in § 1.367(a)-6T(g)(1) (foreign branch separate unit).

(B) An interest in a hybrid entity (hybrid entity separate unit).

(ii) *Separate unit combination rule..*—Except as otherwise provided in this paragraph, if a domestic owner, or two or more domestic owners that are members of the same consolidated group, have two or more separate units (individual separate units), then all such individual separate units that are located (in the case of a foreign branch separate unit) or subject to an income tax either on their worldwide income or on a residence basis (in the case of a hybrid entity an interest in which is a hybrid entity separate unit) in the same foreign country shall be treated as one separate unit (combined separate unit). See § 1.1503(d)-7(c) *Example 1.* Separate units of a foreign insurance company that is a dual resident corporation under paragraph (b)(2)(ii) of this section, however, shall not be combined with separate units of any other domestic corporation. Except as specifically provided in this section or § § 1.1503(d)-2 through 1.1503(d)-8, any individual separate unit composing a combined separate unit loses its character as an individual separate unit.

(iii) Business operations that do not constitute a permanent establishment. A business operation carried on by a domestic corporation that is not a dual resident corporation shall not constitute a foreign branch separate unit, provided the business operation:

(A) Is not carried on indirectly through a hybrid entity or a transparent entity; and

(B) Is conducted in a country with which the United States has entered into an income tax convention and is not treated as a permanent establishment pursuant to that convention, or is not otherwise subject to tax on a net basis under that convention. See § 1.1503(d)-7(c) *Example 2.*

(iv) Foreign branch separate units held by dual resident corporations or hybrid entities in the same foreign country. A foreign branch separate unit may be owned by a dual resident corporation, or through a hybrid entity (an interest in which is a separate unit), even where the foreign branch is located in the same foreign country that subjects such dual resident corporation or hybrid entity to tax on its worldwide income or on a residence basis. But see the rule under paragraph (b)(4)(ii) of this section that combines certain same-country hybrid entity separate units and foreign branch separate units. See also § 1.1503(d)-7(c) *Example 1.*

(5) Dual consolidated loss means—

(i) In the case of a dual resident corporation, and except to the extent provided in § 1.1503(d)-5(b), the net operating loss (as defined in section 172(c) and the related regulations) incurred in a year in which the corporation is a dual resident corporation; and

(ii) In the case of a separate unit, the net loss attributable to the separate unit under § 1.1503(d)-5(c) through (e).

(6) *Subject to tax.*—For purposes of determining whether a domestic corporation or another entity is subject to an income tax of a foreign country on its income, the fact that it has no actual income tax liability to the foreign country for a particular taxable year shall not be taken into account.

(7) Foreign country includes any possession of the United States.

(8) Consolidated group has the meaning provided in § 1.1502-1(h).

(9) Domestic owner means—

(i) A domestic corporation (including a dual resident corporation) that has one or more separate units or interests in a transparent entity; and

(ii) In the case of a combined separate unit, a domestic corporation (including a dual resident corporation) that has one or more individual separate units that are treated as part of the combined separate unit under paragraph (b)(4)(ii) of this section.

(10) Affiliated dual resident corporation and affiliated domestic owner mean a dual resident corporation and a domestic owner, respectively, that is a member of a consolidated group.

(11) Unaffiliated dual resident corporation, unaffiliated domestic corporation, and unaffiliated domestic owner mean a dual resident corporation, domestic corporation, and domestic owner, respectively, that is not a member of a consolidated group.

(12) Domestic affiliate means—

(i) A member of an affiliated group, without regard to the exceptions contained in section 1504(b) (other than section 1504(b)(3)) relating to includible corporations;

(ii) A domestic owner;

(iii) A separate unit; or

(iv) An interest in a transparent entity, as defined in paragraph (b)(16) of this section.

(13) *Domestic use.*—See § 1.1503(d)-2.

(14) *Foreign use.*—See § 1.1503(d)-3.

(15) Grantor trust means a trust, any portion of which is treated as being owned by the grantor or another person under subpart E of subchapter J of this chapter.

(16) *Transparent entity.*—(i) *In general.*—The term transparent entity means an entity described in this paragraph (b)(16) where all or a portion of its interests are owned, directly or indirectly, by a domestic corporation. An entity is described in this paragraph (b)(16) if the entity—

(A) Is not taxable as an association for Federal tax purposes;

(B) Is not subject to income tax in a foreign country as a corporation (or otherwise at the entity level) either on its worldwide income or on a residence basis; and

(C) Is not a pass-through entity under the laws of the applicable foreign country. For purposes of applying the preceding sentence, the applicable foreign country is the foreign country in which the relevant foreign branch separate unit is located, or the foreign country that subjects the relevant hybrid entity (an interest in which is a separate unit) or dual resident corporation to an income tax either on its worldwide income or on a residence basis.

(ii) *Example.*—A U.S. limited liability company (LLC) does not elect to be taxed as an association for Federal tax purposes and is not subject to income tax in a foreign country as a corporation (or otherwise at the entity level) either on its worldwide income or on a residence basis. The LLC is owned by a hybrid entity (an interest in which is a separate unit) that is the relevant hybrid entity. Provided the LLC is not treated as a pass-through entity by the applicable foreign country that subjects the relevant hybrid entity to an income tax either on its worldwide income or on a residence basis, the LLC would qualify as a transparent entity. See also § 1.1503(d)-7(c) *Example 26.*

(17) Disregarded entity means an entity that is disregarded as an entity separate from its owner, under §§ 301.7701-1 through 301.7701-3 of this chapter, for Federal tax purposes.

(18) Partnership means an entity that is classified as a partnership, under §§ 301.7701-1 through 301.7701-3 of this chapter, for Federal tax purposes.

(19) Indirectly, when used in reference to ownership, means ownership through a partnership, a disregarded entity, or a grantor trust, regardless of whether the partnership, disregarded entity, or grantor trust is a U.S. person.

(20) Certification period means the period of time up to and including the fifth taxable year following the year in which the dual consolidated loss that is the subject of a domestic use agreement (as described in § 1.1503(d)-6(d)(1)) was incurred.

(c) Special rules for filings under section 1503(d)

(1) *Reasonable cause exception.*—A person that is permitted or required to file an election, agreement, statement, rebuttal, computation, or other information pursuant to section 1503(d) and these regulations, that fails to make such filing in a timely manner, shall be considered to have satisfied the timeliness requirement with respect to such filing if the person is able to demonstrate, to the Area Director, Field Examination, Small Business/Self Employed or the Director of Field Operations, Large and Mid-Size Business (Director) having jurisdiction of the taxpayer's tax return for the taxable year, that such failure was due to reasonable cause and not willful neglect. In determining whether the taxpayer has reasonable cause, the Director shall consider whether the taxpayer acted reasonably and in

good faith. In general, the taxpayer must demonstrate that it exercised ordinary care and prudence in meeting its tax obligations but nonetheless did not comply with the prescribed duty within the prescribed time. Whether the taxpayer acted reasonably and in good faith will be determined after considering all the facts and circumstances. The Director shall notify the person in writing within 120 days of the filing if it is determined that the failure to comply was not due to reasonable cause, or if additional time will be needed to make such determination. For this purpose, the 120-day period shall begin on the date the taxpayer is notified in writing that the request has been received and assigned for review. If, once such period commences, the taxpayer is not again notified within 120 days, then the taxpayer shall be deemed to have established reasonable cause. The reasonable cause exception of this paragraph (c) shall only apply if, once the person becomes aware of its failure to file the election, agreement, statement, rebuttal, computation or other information in a timely manner, the person complies with the requirements of paragraph (c)(2) of this section.

(2) *Requirements for reasonable cause relief.*— (i) *Time of submission.*—Requests for reasonable cause relief will only be considered if once the person becomes aware of the failure to file the election, agreement, statement, rebuttal, computation or other information, the person attaches all the documents that should have been filed, as well as a written statement setting forth the reasons for the failure to timely comply, to an amended return that amends the return to which the documents should have been attached pursuant to the rules of section 1503(d) and these regulations.

(ii) *Notice requirement.*—In addition to the requirements of paragraph (c)(2)(i) of this section, the taxpayer must provide a copy of the amended return and all required attachments to the Director as follows:

(A) If the taxpayer is under examination for any taxable year when the taxpayer requests relief, the taxpayer must provide a copy of the amended return and attachments to the personnel conducting the examination.

(B) If the taxpayer is not under examination for any taxable year when the taxpayer requests relief, the taxpayer must provide a copy of the amended return and attachments to the Director having jurisdiction of the taxpayer's return.

(3) *Signature requirement.*—When an election, agreement, statement, rebuttal, computation, or other information is required pursuant to section 1503(d) and these regulations to be attached to and filed by the due date (including extensions) of a U.S. tax return and signed under penalties of perjury by the person who signs the return, the attachment and filing of an unsigned

copy is considered to satisfy such requirement, provided the taxpayer retains the original in its records in the manner specified by § 1.6001-1(e). [Reg. § 1.1503(d)-1.]

☐ [*T.D.* 9315, 3-16-2007.]

[Reg. § 1.1503(d)-2]

§ 1.1503(d)-2. Domestic use.—A domestic use of a dual consolidated loss shall be deemed to occur when the dual consolidated loss is made available to offset, directly or indirectly, the income of a domestic affiliate (other than the dual resident corporation or separate unit that, in each case, incurred the dual consolidated loss) in the taxable year in which the dual consolidated loss is recognized, or in any other taxable year, regardless of whether the dual consolidated loss offsets income under the income tax laws of a foreign country and regardless of whether any income that the dual consolidated loss may offset in the foreign country is, has been, or will be subject to tax in the United States. A domestic use shall be deemed to occur in the year the dual consolidated loss is included in the computation of the taxable income of a consolidated group, unaffiliated dual resident corporation, or an unaffiliated domestic owner, as applicable, even if no tax benefit results from such inclusion in that year. See § 1.1503(d)-7(c) *Examples 2 through 4*. [Reg. § 1.1503(d)-2.]

☐ [*T.D.* 9315, 3-16-2007.]

[Reg. § 1.1503(d)-3]

§ 1.1503(d)-3. Foreign use.—(a) *Foreign use.*— (1) *In general.*—Except as provided in paragraph (c) of this section, a foreign use of a dual consolidated loss shall be deemed to occur when any portion of a deduction or loss taken into account in computing the dual consolidated loss is made available under the income tax laws of a foreign country to offset or reduce, directly or indirectly, any item that is recognized as income or gain under such laws and that is, or would be, considered under U.S. tax principles to be an item of—

(i) A foreign corporation as defined in section 7701(a)(3) and (a)(5); or

(ii) A direct or indirect owner of an interest in a hybrid entity, provided such interest is not a separate unit. See § 1.1503(d)-7(c) *Examples 5 through 10* and 37.

(2) *Indirect use.*—(i) *General rule.*—Except to the extent provided in paragraph (a)(2)(ii) of this section, an item of deduction or loss shall be deemed to be made available indirectly if—

(A) One or more items are taken into account as deductions or losses for foreign tax purposes, but do not give rise to corresponding items of income or gain for U.S. tax purposes; and

(B) The item or items described in paragraph (a)(2)(i)(A) of this section have the effect

Reg. § 1.1503(d)-3(a)(2)(i)(B)

of making an item of deduction or loss composing the dual consolidated loss available for a foreign use as described in paragraph (a)(1) of this section.

(ii) *Exception.*—The general rule provided in paragraph (a)(2)(i) of this section shall not apply if the consolidated group, unaffiliated domestic owner, or unaffiliated dual resident corporation demonstrates, to the satisfaction of the Commissioner, that the item or items described in paragraph (a)(2)(i)(A) of this section that gave rise to the indirect foreign use—

(A) Were not incurred, or taken into account, with a principal purpose of avoiding the provisions of section 1503(d). For purposes of this paragraph (a)(2)(ii), an item incurred or taken into account as interest for foreign tax purposes, but disregarded for U.S. tax purposes, shall be deemed to have been incurred, or taken into account, with a principal purpose of avoiding the provisions of section 1503(d). Similarly, for purposes of this paragraph (a)(2)(ii), an item incurred or taken into account as the result of an instrument that is treated as debt for foreign tax purposes and equity for U.S. tax purposes, shall be deemed to have been incurred, or taken into account, with a principal purpose of avoiding the provisions of section 1503(d); and

(B) Were incurred, or taken into account, in the ordinary course of the dual resident corporation's or separate unit's trade or business.

(iii) *Examples.*—See § 1.1503(d)-7(c) *Examples 6* through *8.*

(3) *Deemed use.*—See paragraph (e) of this section for a deemed foreign use pursuant to the mirror legislation rule.

(b) *Available for use.*—A foreign use shall be deemed to occur in the year in which any portion of a deduction or loss taken into account in computing the dual consolidated loss is made available for an offset described in paragraph (a) of this section, regardless of whether it actually offsets or reduces any items of income or gain under the income tax laws of the foreign country in such year, and regardless of whether any of the items that may be so offset or reduced are regarded as income under U.S. tax principles.

(c) *Exceptions.*—(1) *In general.*—Paragraphs (c)(2) through (9) of this section provide exceptions to the general definition of foreign use set forth in paragraphs (a) and (b) of this section. These exceptions only apply to a foreign use that occurs solely as a result of the conditions or circumstances described therein, and do not apply if a foreign use occurs in any other case or by any other means. For example, the exception under paragraph (c)(4) of this section (regarding certain interests in partnerships or grantor trusts) shall not apply where the item of deduction or loss is made available through a foreign consolidation regime (or similar method). In addition, these exceptions do not apply when attempting to demonstrate that no foreign use of a dual consolidated loss can occur in any other year by any means under § 1.1503(d)-6(c), (e)(2)(i), or (j)(2). But see § 1.1503(d)-6(e)(2)(ii), which takes into account the exception under paragraph (c)(7) of this section for purposes of rebutting certain asset transfers.

(2) *Election or merger required to enable foreign use.*—Where the laws of a foreign country provide an election that would enable a foreign use, a foreign use shall be considered to occur only if the election is made. Similarly, where the laws of a foreign country would enable a foreign use through a sale, merger, or similar transaction, a foreign use shall be considered to occur only if the sale, merger, or similar transaction occurs.

(3) *Presumed use where no foreign country rule for determining use.*—This paragraph (c)(3) applies if the losses or deductions composing the dual consolidated loss are made available under the laws of a foreign country both to offset income that would constitute a foreign use and to offset income that would not constitute a foreign use, and the laws of the foreign country do not provide applicable rules for determining which income is offset by the losses or deductions. In such a case, the losses or deductions shall be deemed to be made available to offset the income that does not constitute a foreign use, to the extent of such income, before being considered to be made available to offset the income that does constitute a foreign use. See § 1.1503(d)-7(c) *Example 11.*

(4) *Certain interests in partnerships or grantor trusts.*—(i) *General rule.*—Except to the extent provided in paragraph (c)(4)(iii) of this section, this paragraph (c)(4)(i) applies to a dual consolidated loss attributable to an interest in a hybrid entity partnership or a hybrid entity grantor trust, or to a separate unit owned indirectly through a partnership or grantor trust. In such a case, a foreign use will not be considered to occur if the foreign use is solely the result of another person's ownership of an interest in the partnership or grantor trust, as applicable, and the allocation or carry forward of an item of deduction or loss composing such dual consolidated loss as a result of such ownership. See § 1.1503(d)-7(c) *Example 13.*

(ii) *Combined separate unit.*—This paragraph applies to a dual consolidated loss attributable to a combined separate unit that includes an individual separate unit to which paragraph (c)(4)(i) of this section would apply, but for the application of the separate unit combination rule provided under § 1.1503(d)-1(b)(4)(ii). In such a case, paragraph (c)(4)(i) of this section shall apply to the portion of the dual consolidated loss of such combined separate unit that is attributable, as provided under § 1.1503(d)-5(c) through (e), to the individual separate unit (otherwise described in paragraph (c)(4)(i) of this section) that is a component of the combined separate unit. See § 1.1503(d)-7(c) *Example 14.*

(iii) *Reduction in interest.*—The exception under paragraph (c)(4)(i) of this section shall not apply if, at any time following the year in which the dual consolidated loss is incurred, there is more than a de minimis reduction in the domestic owner's percentage interest in the partnership or grantor trust, as applicable, as described in paragraph (c)(5) of this section. In such a case, a foreign use shall be deemed to occur at the time the reduction in interest exceeds the de minimis amount. See § 1.1503(d)-7(c) *Example 13.*

(5) *De minimis reduction of an interest in a separate unit.*—(i) *General rule.*—This paragraph applies to a de minimis reduction of a domestic owner's interest in a separate unit (including an interest described in paragraph (c)(4)(i) of this section). Except to the extent provided in paragraph (c)(5)(ii) of this section, no foreign use shall be considered to occur with respect to a dual consolidated loss as a result of an item of deduction or loss composing such dual consolidated loss being made available solely as a result of a reduction in the domestic owner's interest in the separate unit, as provided under paragraph (c)(5)(iii) of this section. See § 1.1503(d)-7(c) *Example 5.*

(ii) *Limitations.*—The exception provided in paragraph (c)(5)(i) of this section shall not apply if—

(A) During any 12-month period the domestic owner's percentage interest in the separate unit is reduced by 10 percent or more, as determined by reference to the domestic owner's interest at the beginning of the 12-month period; or

(B) At any time the domestic owner's percentage interest in the separate unit is reduced by 30 percent or more, as determined by reference to the domestic owner's interest at the end of the taxable year in which the dual consolidated loss was incurred.

(iii) *Reduction in interest.*—The following rules apply for purposes of paragraphs (c)(4) and (5) of this section. A reduction of a domestic owner's interest in a separate unit shall include a reduction resulting from another person acquiring through sale, exchange, contribution, or other means, an interest in the foreign branch or hybrid entity, as applicable. A reduction may occur either directly or indirectly, including through an interest in a partnership, a disregarded entity, or a grantor trust through which a separate unit is carried on or owned. In the case of an interest in a hybrid entity partnership or a separate unit all or a portion of which is carried on or owned through a partnership, an interest in such separate unit (or portion of such separate

unit) is determined by reference to the owner's interest in the profits or the capital in the separate unit. In the case of an interest in a hybrid entity grantor trust or a separate unit all or a portion of which is carried on or owned through a grantor trust, an interest in such separate unit (or portion of such separate unit) is determined by reference to the domestic owner's share of the assets and liabilities of the separate unit.

(iv) *Examples and coordination with exceptions to other triggering events.*—See § 1.1503(d)-7(c) *Examples 5, 13, and 14.* See also § 1.1503(d)-6(f)(3) and (f)(5) for rules that coordinate the the de minimis exception to foreign use with exceptions to other triggering events described in § 1.1503(d)-6(e)(1), and provide an exception to foreign use following certain compulsory transfers.

(6) *Certain asset basis carryovers.*—No foreign use shall be considered to occur with respect to a dual consolidated loss solely as a result of items of deduction or loss composing such dual consolidated loss being made available as a result of the transfer of assets of a dual resident corporation or separate unit, provided—

(i) Such items of loss and deduction are made available solely as a result of the basis of the transferred assets being determined, under foreign law, in whole or in part by reference to the basis of the assets in the hands of the dual resident corporation or separate unit;

(ii) The aggregate adjusted basis, as determined under U.S. tax principles, of all the assets so transferred during any 12-month period is less than 10 percent of the aggregate adjusted basis, as determined under U.S. tax principles, of all the dual resident corporation's or separate unit's assets, determined by reference to the assets held at the beginning of such 12-month period; and

(iii) The aggregate adjusted basis, as determined under U.S. tax principles, of all the assets so transferred at any time is less than 30 percent of the aggregate adjusted basis, as determined under U.S. tax principles, of all the dual resident corporation's or separate unit's assets, determined by reference to the assets held at the end of the taxable year in which the dual consolidated loss was generated. See § 1.1503(d)-7(c) *Example 15.*

(7) *Assumption of certain liabilities.*—(i) *In general.*—Except to the extent provided in paragraph (c)(7)(ii) of this section, no foreign use shall be considered to occur with respect to any dual consolidated loss solely as a result of an item of deduction or loss composing such dual consolidated loss being made available following the assumption of liabilities of a dual resident corporation or separate unit, provided such availability arises solely as the result of an item of deduction or loss incurred with respect to, or

as a result of, such liabilities. See § 1.1503(d)-7(c) *Example 16*.

(ii) *Ordinary course limitation.*—Paragraph (c)(7)(i) of this section shall apply only to the extent the liabilities assumed were incurred in the ordinary course of the dual resident corporation's, or separate unit's, trade or business. For purposes of this paragraph, liabilities incurred in the ordinary course of a trade or business shall include debt incurred to finance the trade or business of the dual resident corporation or separate unit.

(8) *Multiple-party events.*—This paragraph applies to a transaction that qualifies for the triggering event exception described in § 1.1503(d)-6(f)(2)(i)(B) where the acquiring unaffiliated domestic corporation or consolidated group owns, directly or indirectly, more than 90 percent, but less than 100 percent, of the transferred assets or interests immediately after the transaction. In such a case, no foreign use shall be considered to occur with respect to a dual consolidated loss of the dual resident corporation or separate unit whose assets or interests were acquired, solely as a result of the less than 10 percent direct or indirect ownership of the acquired assets or interests by persons other than the acquiring unaffiliated domestic corporation or consolidated group, as applicable, immediately after the transaction. See § 1.1503(d)-7(c) *Example 37*.

(9) *Additional guidance.*—The Commissioner may provide, by guidance published in the Internal Revenue Bulletin, that certain events or transactions do or do not result in a foreign use. Such guidance may also modify the triggering events and rebuttals described in § 1.1503(d)-6(e), and the exceptions thereto under § 1.1503(d)-6(f), as appropriate.

(d) *Ordering rules for determining the foreign use of losses.*—If the laws of a foreign country provide for the foreign use of losses of a dual resident corporation or a separate unit, but do not provide applicable rules for determining the order in which such losses are used in a taxable year, the following rules shall apply:

(1) Any net loss, or net income, that the dual resident corporation or separate unit has in a taxable year shall first be used to offset net income, or loss, recognized by its affiliates in the same taxable year before any carry over of its losses is considered to be used to offset any income from the taxable year.

(2) If under the laws of the foreign country the dual resident corporation or separate unit has losses from different taxable years, it shall be deemed to use first the losses which would not constitute a triggering event that would result in the recapture of a dual consolidated loss pursuant to § 1.1503(d)-6(h). Thereafter, it shall be deemed to use first the losses from the most

recent taxable year from which a loss may be carried forward or back for foreign law purposes.

(3) Where different losses or deductions (for example, capital losses and ordinary losses) of a dual resident corporation or separate unit incurred in the same taxable year are available for foreign use, the different losses shall be deemed to be used on a pro rata basis. See § 1.1503(d)-7(c) *Example 12*.

(e) *Mirror legislation rule.*—(1) *In general.*—Except as provided in paragraph (e)(2) of this section and § 1.1503(d)-6(b) (relating to agreements entered into between the United States and a foreign country), a foreign use shall be deemed to occur if the income tax laws of a foreign country would deny any opportunity for the foreign use of the dual consolidated loss in the year in which the dual consolidated loss is incurred (mirror legislation), determined by assuming that such foreign country had recognized the dual consolidated loss in such year, for any of the following reasons:

(i) The dual resident corporation or separate unit that incurred the loss is subject to income taxation by another country (for example, the United States) on its worldwide income or on a residence basis.

(ii) The loss may be available to offset income (other than income of the dual resident corporation or separate unit) under the laws of another country (for example, the United States).

(iii) The deductibility of any portion of a deduction or loss taken into account in computing the dual consolidated loss depends on whether such amount is deductible under the laws of another country (for example, the United States). See § 1.1503(d)-7(c) *Examples 17* through *19*.

(2) *Stand-alone exception.*—(i) *In general.*—This paragraph (e)(2) applies if, in the absence of the mirror legislation described in paragraph (e)(1) of this section, no item of deduction or loss composing the dual consolidated loss of such dual resident corporation or separate unit would otherwise be available for a foreign use in the taxable year in which such dual consolidated loss is incurred. This determination is made without regard to whether such availability is limited by election (or other similar procedure). However, for purposes of this paragraph (e)(2)(i), no item of deduction or loss composing the dual consolidated loss of a dual resident corporation or separate unit is considered to be made available for foreign use solely because the laws of a foreign country would enable a foreign use through a sale, merger, or similar transaction (provided no such sale, merger, or similar transaction actually occurs). In such a case, no foreign use shall be considered to occur pursuant to paragraph (e)(1) of this section with respect to the dual consolidated loss, provided the requirements of paragraph (e)(2)(ii) of this section are

satisfied. See § 1.1503(d)-7(c) *Examples 17 through 19.*

(ii) *Stand-alone domestic use agreement.*—In order to qualify for the exception under paragraph (e)(2)(i) of this section, the consolidated group, unaffiliated dual resident corporation, or unaffiliated domestic owner, as the case may be, must enter into a domestic use agreement in accordance with the provisions of § 1.1503(d)-6(d) and, in addition, must include the following items in such domestic use agreement:

(A) A statement that the document is also being submitted under the provisions of paragraph (e)(2) of this section.

(B) A certification that the conditions of paragraph (e)(2)(i) of this section are satisfied during the taxable year in which the dual consolidated loss is incurred.

(C) An agreement to include with each annual certification required under § 1.1503(d)-6(g), a certification that the conditions described in paragraph (e)(2)(i) of this section are satisfied during the taxable year of each such certification.

(iii) *Termination of stand-alone domestic use agreement.*—This paragraph (e)(2)(iii) applies to a consolidated group, unaffiliated dual resident corporation, or unaffiliated domestic owner, as the case may be, that entered into a domestic use agreement pursuant to paragraph (e)(2)(ii) of this section, with respect to a dual consolidated loss, and which subsequently makes an election pursuant to § 1.1503(d)-6(b) (relating to agreements entered into between the United States and a foreign country) with respect to such dual consolidated loss. In such a case, the dual consolidated loss shall be subject to the election under § 1.1503(d)-6(b) (and any related agreements, representations and conditions), and the domestic use agreement entered into pursuant to paragraph (e)(2)(ii) of this section shall terminate and have no further effect. [Reg. § 1.1503(d)-3.]

☐ [*T.D.* 9315, 3-16-2007.]

[Reg. § 1.1503(d)-4]

§ 1.1503(d)-4. Domestic use limitation and related operating rules.—(a) *Scope.*—This section prescribes rules that apply when the general limitation on the domestic use of a dual consolidated loss under paragraph (b) of this section applies. Thus, the rules of this section do not apply when an exception to the domestic use limitation applies (for example, as a result of a domestic use election under § 1.1503(d)-6(d)). In general, when the domestic use limitation applies, the dual consolidated loss of a dual resident corporation or separate unit is subject to the separate return limitation year (SRLY) provisions of § 1.1502-21(c), as modified under this section. Paragraph (c) of this section provides rules that determine the effect of a dual consolidated loss

on a consolidated group, an unaffiliated dual resident corporation, or an unaffiliated domestic owner. Paragraph (d) of this section provides rules that eliminate dual consolidated losses following certain transactions or events. Paragraph (e) of this section contains provisions that prevent dual consolidated losses from offsetting tainted income. Finally, paragraph (f) of this section provides rules for computing foreign tax credits.

(b) *Limitation on domestic use of a dual consolidated loss.*—Except as provided in § 1.1503(d)-6, the domestic use of a dual consolidated loss is not permitted. See § 1.1503(d)-2 for the definition of a domestic use. See also § 1.1503(d)-7(c) *Examples 2 through 4.*

(c) *Effect of a dual consolidated loss on a consolidated group, unaffiliated dual resident corporation, or unaffiliated domestic owner.* For any taxable year in which a dual resident corporation or separate unit has a dual consolidated loss that is subject to the domestic use limitation of paragraph (b) of this section, the following rules shall apply:

(1) *Dual resident corporation.*—This paragraph (c)(1) applies to a dual consolidated loss of a dual resident corporation. The unaffiliated dual resident corporation, or consolidated group that includes the dual resident corporation, shall compute its taxable income (or loss), or consolidated taxable income (or loss), respectively, without taking into account those items of deduction and loss that compose the dual resident corporation's dual consolidated loss. For this purpose, the dual consolidated loss shall be treated as composed of a pro rata portion of each item of deduction and loss of the dual resident corporation taken into account in calculating the dual consolidated loss. The dual consolidated loss is subject to the limitations on its use contained in paragraph (c)(3) of this section and, subject to such limitations, may be carried over or back for use in other taxable years as a separate net operating loss carryover or carryback of the dual resident corporation arising in the year incurred. If the dual resident corporation owns a separate unit or an interest in a transparent entity, the limitations contained in paragraph (c)(3) of this section shall apply to the dual resident corporation as if the separate unit or interest in a transparent entity were a separate domestic corporation that filed a consolidated return with the unaffiliated dual resident corporation, or with the consolidated group of the affiliated dual resident corporation, as applicable.

(2) *Separate unit.*—This paragraph (c)(2) applies to a dual consolidated loss that is attributable to a separate unit. The unaffiliated domestic owner of a separate unit, or the consolidated group of an affiliated domestic owner of a separate unit, shall compute its taxable income (or loss) or consolidated taxable income (or loss),

respectively, without taking into account those items of deduction and loss that compose the separate unit's dual consolidated loss. For this purpose, the dual consolidated loss shall be treated as composed of a pro rata portion of each item of deduction and loss of the separate unit taken into account in calculating the dual consolidated loss. The dual consolidated loss is subject to the limitations contained in paragraph (c)(3) of this section as if the separate unit to which the dual consolidated loss is attributable were a separate domestic corporation that filed a consolidated return with its unaffiliated domestic owner or with the consolidated group of its affiliated domestic owner, as applicable. Subject to such limitations, the dual consolidated loss may be carried over or back for use in other taxable years as a separate net operating loss carryover or carryback of the separate unit arising in the year incurred. See § 1.1503(d)-7(c) *Examples 29 and 38*.

(3) *SRLY limitation.*—The dual consolidated loss shall be treated as a loss incurred by the dual resident corporation or separate unit in a separate return limitation year and shall be subject to all of the limitations of § 1.1502-21(c) (SRLY limitation), subject to the following modifications—

(i) Notwithstanding § 1.1502-1(f)(2)(i), the SRLY limitation is applied to any dual consolidated loss of a common parent that is a dual resident corporation, or any dual consolidated loss attributable to a separate unit of a common parent;

(ii) The SRLY limitation is applied without regard to § 1.1502-21(c)(2) (SRLY subgroup limitation) and 1.1502-21(g) (overlap with section 382);

(iii) For purposes of calculating the general SRLY limitation under § 1.1502-21(c)(1)(i), the calculation of aggregate consolidated taxable income shall only include items of income, gain, deduction, and loss generated—

(A) In the case of a hybrid entity separate unit, in years in which the hybrid entity (an interest in which is a separate unit) is taxed as a corporation (or otherwise at the entity level) either on its worldwide income or as a resident in the same foreign country in which it was so taxed during the year in which the dual consolidated loss was generated; and

(B) In the case of a foreign branch separate unit, in years in which the foreign branch qualified as a separate unit in the same foreign country in which it so qualified during the year in which the dual consolidated loss was generated.

(iv) For purposes of calculating the general SRLY limitation under § 1.1502-21(c)(1)(i), the calculation of aggregate consolidated taxable income shall not include any amount included in income pursuant to § 1.1503(d)-6(h) (relating to the recapture of a dual consolidated loss).

(4) *Items of a dual consolidated loss used in other taxable years.*—A pro rata portion of each item of deduction or loss that composes the dual consolidated loss shall be considered to be used when the dual consolidated loss is used in other taxable years. See § 1.1503(d)-7(c) *Examples 29 and 38*.

(5) *Reconstituted net operating losses.*—For additional rules and limitations that apply to reconstituted net operating losses, see § 1.1503(d)-6(h)(6).

(d) *Elimination of a dual consolidated loss after certain transactions.*—(1) *General rule.*—In general, a dual resident corporation has a net operating loss (and, therefore, a dual consolidated loss) only if it sustains such loss, or succeeds to such loss as a result of acquiring the assets of a corporation that sustained the loss in a transaction described in section 381(a). Similarly, a net loss generally is attributable to a separate unit of a domestic owner (and therefore is a dual consolidated loss) only if the domestic owner incurs the deductions or losses, or succeeds to such deductions or losses in a transaction described in section 381(a). Except as provided in § 1.1503(d)-6(h)(6)(iii), section 1503(d) and these regulations do not alter these general rules. Thus, the provisions of §§ 1.1503(d)-1 through 1.1503(d)-8 generally do not cause a corporation to have a dual consolidated loss if it did not sustain (or inherit) the loss. Instead, these regulations either eliminate a dual consolidated loss that a corporation sustained (or inherited), or prevent the carryover of a dual consolidated loss under section 381 that would ordinarily occur, as a result of certain transactions.

(i) *Transactions described in section 381(a).*—This paragraph (d)(1)(i) applies to a dual consolidated loss of a dual resident corporation, or of a domestic owner attributable to a separate unit, that is subject to the domestic use limitation rule of paragraph (b) of this section. In such a case, and except as provided in paragraph (d)(2) of this section, the dual consolidated loss shall not carry over to another corporation in a transaction described in section 381(a) and, as a result, shall be eliminated. See § 1.1503(d)-7(c) *Example 20*.

(ii) *Cessation of separate unit status.*—This paragraph (d)(1)(ii) applies when a separate unit of an unaffiliated domestic owner ceases to be a separate unit of its domestic owner, or when a separate unit of an affiliated domestic owner ceases to be a separate unit with respect to its domestic owner and all other members of the affiliated domestic owner's consolidated group. In such a case, and except as provided in paragraph (d)(2)(iii) of this section, a dual consolidated loss of the domestic owner attributable to such separate unit, that is subject to the domestic use limitation of paragraph (b) of this section, shall be eliminated. For purposes of this para-

Reg. § 1.1503(d)-4(c)(3)

graph (d)(1)(ii), a separate unit may cease to be a separate unit if, for example, such separate unit is terminated, dissolved, liquidated, sold, or otherwise disposed of. See § 1.1503(d)-7(c) *Example 21.*

(2) *Exceptions.*—(i) *Certain section 368(a)(1)(F) reorganizations.*—Paragraph (d)(1)(i) of this section (relating to transactions described in section 381(a)) shall not apply to a dual consolidated loss of a dual resident corporation that undergoes a reorganization described in section 368(a)(1)(F) in which the resulting corporation is a domestic corporation. In such a case, the dual consolidated loss of the resulting corporation continues to be subject to the limitations of paragraphs (b) and (c) of this section, applied as if the resulting corporation incurred the dual consolidated loss.

(ii) *Acquisition of a dual resident corporation by another dual resident corporation.*—If a dual resident corporation transfers its assets to another dual resident corporation in a transaction described in section 381(a), and the transferee corporation is a resident of (or is taxed on its worldwide income by) the same foreign country of which the transferor was a resident (or was taxed on its worldwide income), then paragraph (d)(1)(i) of this section shall not apply with respect to dual consolidated losses of the dual resident corporation, and income generated by the transferee may be offset by the carryover dual consolidated losses of the transferor, subject to the limitations of paragraphs (b) and (c) of this section applied as if the transferee incurred the dual consolidated loss. Dual consolidated losses of the transferor dual resident corporation may not, however, be used to offset income attributable to separate units or interests in transparent entities owned by the transferee because they constitute domestic affiliates under § 1.1503(d)-1(b)(12)(iii) and (iv), respectively.

(iii) *Acquisition of a separate unit by a domestic corporation.*—This paragraph (d)(2)(iii) provides exceptions to the general rules in paragraphs (d)(1)(i) and (ii) of this section that eliminate the dual consolidated loss of a domestic owner that is attributable to a separate unit following certain transactions or events. The exceptions set forth in this paragraph (d)(2)(iii) shall only apply where a domestic owner transfers its assets to a domestic corporation (transferee corporation) in a transaction described in section 381(a).

(A) *Acquisition by a corporation that is not a member of the same consolidated group.*—(1) *General rule.*—If a domestic owner transfers either an individual separate unit or a combined separate unit to a transferee corporation that is not a member of its consolidated group in a transaction described in section 381(a), and the transferee corporation, or a member of the transferee's consolidated group, is a domestic owner

of the transferred separate unit immediately after the transaction, then paragraphs (d)(1)(i) and (ii) of this section shall not apply to such transfer. In addition, income of the transferee, or a member of the transferee's consolidated group, that is attributable to the transferred separate unit may be offset by the carryover dual consolidated losses of the transferor domestic owner that were attributable to the transferred separate unit, subject to the limitations of paragraphs (b) and (c) of this section applied as if the transferee incurred the dual consolidated losses and such losses were attributable to the separate unit. See § 1.1503(d)-7(c) *Example 21.*

(2) *Combination with separate units of the transferee.*—This paragraph (d)(2)(iii)(A)(2) applies to a transaction described in paragraph (d)(2)(iii)(A)(1) of this section where the transferred separate unit is combined with another separate unit of the transferee, or another member of the transferee's consolidated group, immediately after the transfer as provided under § 1.1503(d)-1(b)(4)(ii). In such a case, income generated by the transferee, or another member of the transferee's consolidated group, that is attributable to the combined separate unit may be offset by the carryover dual consolidated losses that were attributable to the transferred separate unit, subject to the limitations of paragraphs (b) and (c) of this section, applied as if the transferee incurred the dual consolidated losses and such losses were attributable to the combined separate unit.

(B) *Acquisition by a member of the same consolidated group.*—If an affiliated domestic owner transfers its assets to another member of its consolidated group in a transaction described in section 381(a), and the transferee corporation or another member of such consolidated group is a domestic owner of the separate unit to which the dual consolidated loss was attributable, then paragraphs (d)(1)(i) and (ii) of this section shall not apply. In addition, income generated by the transferee that is attributable to the transferred separate unit may be offset by the carryover dual consolidated losses that were attributable to the transferred separate unit, subject to the limitations of paragraphs (b) and (c) of this section, applied as if the transferee incurred the dual consolidated losses and such losses were attributable to the separate unit. See § 1.1503(d)-7(c) *Example 21.*

(iv) *Special rules for foreign insurance companies.*—See § 1.1503(d)-6(a) for additional limitations that apply where the transferor is a foreign insurance company that is a dual resident corporation under § 1.1503(d)-1(b)(2)(ii).

(e) *Special rule denying the use of a dual consolidated loss to offset tainted income.*—(1) *In general.*—Dual consolidated losses incurred by a dual resident corporation that are subject to the domestic use limitation rule under paragraph (b) of this section shall not be used to offset income it earns after it ceases to be a dual resident corporation to the extent that such income is tainted income.

(2) *Tainted income.*—(i) *Definition.*—For purposes of paragraph (e)(1) of this section, the term tainted income means—

(A) Income or gain recognized on the sale or other disposition of tainted assets; and

(B) Income derived as a result of holding tainted assets.

(ii) *Income presumed to be derived from holding tainted assets.*—In the absence of evidence establishing the actual amount of income that is attributable to holding tainted assets, the portion of a corporation's income in a particular taxable year that is treated as tainted income derived as a result of holding tainted assets shall be an amount equal to the corporation's taxable income for the year (other than income described in paragraph (e)(2)(i)(A) of this section) multiplied by a fraction, the numerator of which is the fair market value of all tainted assets acquired by the corporation (determined at the time such assets were so acquired) and the denominator of which is the fair market value of the total assets owned by the corporation at the end of such taxable year. To establish the actual amount of income that is attributable to holding tainted assets, documentation must be attached to, and filed by the due date (including extensions) of, the domestic corporation's tax return or the consolidated tax return of an affiliated group of which it is a member, as the case may be, for the taxable year in which the income is generated. See § 1.1503(d)-7(c) *Example 22.*

(3) *Tainted assets defined.*—For purposes of paragraph (e)(2) of this section, tainted assets are any assets acquired by a domestic corporation in a nonrecognition transaction, as defined in section 7701(a)(45), any assets otherwise transferred to the corporation as a contribution to capital, or any assets otherwise received from a separate unit or a transparent entity owned by such domestic corporation, at any time during the three taxable years immediately preceding the taxable year in which the corporation ceases to be a dual resident corporation or at any time thereafter.

(4) *Exceptions.*—Income derived from assets acquired by a domestic corporation shall not be subject to the limitation described in paragraph (e)(1) of this section, and in addition shall not be treated as tainted assets as defined in paragraph (e)(3) of this section, if—

(i) For the taxable year in which the assets were acquired, the corporation did not have a dual consolidated loss (or a carryforward of a dual consolidated loss to such year); or

(ii) The assets were acquired as replacement property in the ordinary course of business.

(f) *Computation of foreign tax credit limitation.*— If a dual consolidated loss is subject to the domestic use limitation rule under paragraph (b) of this section, the consolidated group, unaffiliated dual resident corporation, or unaffiliated domestic owner shall compute its foreign tax credit limitation by applying the limitations of paragraph (c) of this section. Thus, the items constituting the dual consolidated loss are not taken into account until the year in which such items are absorbed. [Reg. § 1.1503(d)-4.]

☐ [*T.D.* 9315, 3-16-2007.]

[Reg. § 1.1503(d)-5]

§ 1.1503(d)-5. Attribution of items and basis adjustments.—(a) *In general.*—This section provides rules for determining the amount of income or dual consolidated loss of a dual resident corporation. This section also provides rules for determining the income or dual consolidated loss attributable to a separate unit, as well as the income or loss attributable to an interest in a transparent entity. Paragraph (b) of this section provides rules with respect to dual resident corporations. Paragraph (c) of this section provides rules with respect to separate units and interests in transparent entities. These determinations are required for various purposes under section 1503(d). For example, it is necessary for purposes of applying the domestic use limitation rule under § 1.1503(d)-4(b) to a dual consolidated loss, and for determining the extent to which a dual consolidated loss is available to offset income as provided under § 1.1503(d)-4(c). These determinations are also necessary for purposes of determining whether the amount subject to recapture may be reduced pursuant to § 1.1503(d)-6(h)(2). Paragraph (d) of this section provides rules with respect to the foreign tax treatment of items. Paragraph (e) of this section provides rules regarding the treatment of items where a dual resident corporation, separate unit, or transparent entity only qualified as such during a portion of a taxable year. Paragraph (f) of this section provides rules for determining the assets and liabilities of a separate unit. Finally, paragraph (g) of this section provides rules for making basis adjustments to stock of certain members of a consolidated group and to certain interests in partnerships. The rules in this section apply for purposes of § § 1.1503(d)-1 through 1.1503(d)-7.

(b) *Determination of amount of income or dual consolidated loss of a dual resident corporation.*— (1) *In general.*—For purposes of determining whether a dual resident corporation has income or a dual consolidated loss for the taxable year, and except as provided in paragraph (b)(2) of this section, the dual resident corporation shall compute its income or dual consolidated loss taking into account only those items of income, gain, deduction, and loss from such year (including any items recognized by such corporation as a result of an election under section 338). In the case of an affiliated dual resident corporation, such calculation shall be made in accordance with the rules set forth in the regulations under section 1502 governing the computation of consolidated taxable income. See also paragraphs (d) and (e) of this section.

(2) *Exceptions.*—For purposes of determining the income or dual consolidated loss of a dual resident corporation, the following shall not be taken into account—

(i) Any net capital loss of the dual resident corporation;

(ii) Any carryover or carryback losses; or

(iii) Any items of income, gain, deduction, and loss that are attributable to a separate unit or an interest in a transparent entity of the dual resident corporation.

(c) *Determination of amount of income or dual consolidated loss attributable to a separate unit, and income or loss attributable to an interest in a transparent entity.*—(1) *In general.*—(i) *Scope and purpose.*—Paragraphs (c) through (e) of this section apply for purposes of determining the income or dual consolidated loss attributable to a separate unit, and the income or loss attributable to an interest in a transparent entity, for the taxable year. In the case of an affiliated domestic owner, this determination shall be made in accordance with the rules set forth in the regulations under section 1502 governing the computation of consolidated taxable income. These rules apply solely for purposes of section 1503(d).

(ii) *Only items of domestic owner taken into account.*—The computation made under paragraphs (c) through (e) of this section shall be made using only those existing items of income, gain, deduction, and loss of the separate unit's or transparent entity's domestic owner (or owners, in the case of certain combined separate units), as determined for U.S. tax purposes. These items must be translated into U.S. dollars (if necessary) at the appropriate exchange rate provided under section 989(b), as modified by regulations. The computation shall be made as if the separate unit or interest in a transparent entity were a domestic corporation, using items that are attributable to the separate unit or interest in a transparent entity. However, for purposes of making this computation, net capital losses, and carryover or carryback losses, of the domestic owner shall not be taken into account. Items of income, gain, deduction, and loss that are otherwise disregarded for U.S. tax purposes shall not be regarded or taken into account for purposes of this section. See § 1.1503(d)-7(c) *Examples 6 and 23 through 25.*

(iii) *Separate application.*—The attribution rules of this section shall apply separately to each separate unit or interest in a transparent entity. Thus, an item of income, gain, deduction, or loss shall not be considered attributable to more than one separate unit or interest in a transparent entity. In addition, for purposes of this section items of income, gain, deduction, and loss attributable to a separate unit or an interest in a transparent entity shall not offset items of income, gain, deduction, and loss of another separate unit or interest in a transparent entity. See § 1.1503(d)-7(c) *Example 24.* See also the separate unit combination rule in § 1.1503(d)-1(b)(4)(ii).

(2) *Foreign branch separate unit.*—(i) *In general.*—Except to the extent provided in paragraph (c)(4) of this section, for purposes of determining the items of income, gain, deduction (other than interest), and loss of a domestic owner that are attributable to the domestic owner's foreign branch separate unit, the principles of section 864(c)(2), (c)(4), and (c)(5), as set forth in § 1.864-4(c), and § § 1.864-5 through 1.864-7, shall apply. The principles apply without regard to limitations imposed on the effectively connected treatment of income, gain, or loss under the trade or business safe harbors in section 864(b) and the limitations for treating foreign source income as effectively connected under section 864(c)(4)(D). Except as provided in paragraph (c)(2)(iii) of this section, for purposes of determining the domestic owner's interest expense that is attributable to a foreign branch separate unit, the principles of § 1.882-5, as modified in paragraph (c)(2)(ii) of this section, shall apply. When applying the principles of section 864(c) (as modified by this paragraph) and § 1.882-5 (as modified in paragraph (c)(2)(ii) of this section), the foreign branch separate unit's domestic owner shall be treated as a foreign corporation, the foreign branch separate unit shall be treated as a trade or business within the United States, and the other assets of the domestic owner shall be treated as assets that are not U.S. assets.

(ii) *Principles of § 1.882-5.*—For purposes of paragraph (c)(2)(i) of this section, the principles of § 1.882-5 shall be applied, subject to the following modifications—

(A) Except as otherwise provided in this section, only the assets, liabilities, and interest expense of the domestic owner shall be taken into account in the § 1.882-5 formula;

(B) Except as provided under paragraph (c)(2)(ii)(C) of this section, a taxpayer may use the alternative tax book value method under § 1.861-9(i) for purposes of determining the value of its U.S. assets pursuant to § 1.882-5(b)(2) and its worldwide assets pursuant to § 1.882-5(c)(2);

(C) For purposes of determining the value of a U.S. asset pursuant to § 1.882-5(b)(2), and worldwide assets pursuant to § 1.882-5(c)(2), the taxpayer must use the same methodology under § 1.861-9T(g) (that is, tax book value, alternative tax book value, or fair market value) that the taxpayer uses for purposes of allocating and apportioning interest expense for the taxable year under section 864(e);

(D) Asset values shall be determined pursuant to § 1.861-9T(g)(2); and

(E) For purposes of determining the step-two U.S. connected liabilities, the amounts of worldwide assets and liabilities under § 1.882-5(c)(2)(iii) and (iv) must be determined in accordance with U.S. tax principles, rather than substantially in accordance with U.S. tax principles.

(iii) *Exception where foreign country attributes interest expense solely by reference to books and records.*—The principles of § 1.882-5 shall not apply if the foreign country in which the foreign branch separate unit is located determines, for purposes of computing taxable income (or loss) of a permanent establishment or branch of a nonresident corporation under the laws of the foreign country, the interest expense of the foreign branch separate unit by taking into account only the items of interest expense reflected on the foreign branch separate unit's books and records. In such a case, only those items of the domestic owner's interest expense reflected on the foreign branch separate unit's books and records (as provided in paragraph (c)(3)(i) of this section), adjusted to conform to U.S. tax principles, shall be attributable to the foreign branch separate unit. This paragraph shall not apply where the foreign country does not use a method of attributing interest based solely on the interest that is reflected on the books and records. For example, this paragraph does not apply if the foreign country uses a method for attributing interest expense similar to § 1.882-5 or that set forth in the Organization for Economic Co-operation and Development Report on the Attribution of Profits to Permanent Establishments, Part II (Banks), December 2006. See http://www.oecd.org.

(3) *Hybrid entity separate unit and an interest in a transparent entity.*—(i) *General rule.*—This paragraph (c)(3) applies to determine the items of income, gain, deduction, and loss of a domestic owner that are attributable to a hybrid entity separate unit, or an interest in a transparent entity, of such domestic owner. Except to the extent provided in paragraph (c)(4) of this section, the domestic owner's items of income, gain, deduction, and loss are attributable to the extent they are reflected on the books and records of the hybrid entity or transparent entity, as applicable, as adjusted to conform to U.S. tax principles. See § 1.1503(d)-7(c) *Examples* 23 through 26. For purposes of this paragraph (c)(3), the term "books and records" has the meaning provided under § 1.989(a)-1(d). The treatment of items for foreign tax purposes, including under any type of foreign anti-deferral regime, is not relevant for purposes of determining whether items are reflected on the books and records of the entity, or for purposes of making adjustments to such items to conform to U.S. tax principles. The method described in the second sentence of this paragraph shall not apply to the extent that the Commissioner determines that booking practices are employed with a principal purpose of avoiding the principles of section 1503(d), including inconsistently treating the same or similar items of income, gain, deduction, and loss. In such a case, the Commissioner may reallocate the items of income, gain, deduction, and loss between or among a domestic owner, its hybrid entities, its transparent entities (and interests therein), its separate units, or any other entity, as applicable, in a manner consistent with the principles of section 1503(d) and which properly reflects income (or loss).

(ii) *Interests in certain disregarded entities, partnerships, and grantor trusts owned by a hybrid entity or transparent entity.*—This paragraph (c)(3)(ii) applies if a hybrid entity or transparent entity to which paragraph (c)(3)(i) of this section applies owns, directly or indirectly (other than through a hybrid entity or transparent entity), an interest in an entity that is treated as a disregarded entity, partnership, or grantor trust for U.S. tax purposes, but is not a hybrid entity or a transparent entity. For example, the rules of this paragraph would apply when a hybrid entity holds an interest in a limited partnership created in the United States and, for both U.S. and foreign tax purposes the entity is considered a partnership. In such a case, and except to the extent provided in paragraph (c)(4) of this section, items of income, gain, deduction, and loss that are reflected on the books and records of such disregarded entity, partnership or grantor trust, as determined under paragraph (c)(3)(i) of this section, shall be treated as being reflected on the books and records of the hybrid entity or transparent entity for purposes of applying paragraph (c)(3)(i) of this section. See § 1.1503(d)-7(c) *Example 26.*

(4) *Special rules.*—The following special rules shall apply for purposes of attributing items to separate units or interests in transparent entities under this section:

(i) *Allocation of items between certain tiered separate units and interests in transparent entities.*—(A) *Foreign branch separate unit.*—This paragraph (c)(4)(i) applies where a hybrid entity or transparent entity owns directly or indirectly (other than through a hybrid entity or a transparent entity), a foreign branch separate unit. For purposes of determining items of income, gain, deduction, and loss of the domestic owner that are attributable to the domestic owner's foreign branch separate unit described in the preceding sentence, only items of income, gain, deduction, and loss that are attributable to the domestic owner's interest in the hybrid entity, or transparent entity, as provided in paragraph (c)(3) of this section, shall be taken into account. Further, only assets, liabilities, and activities of the domestic owner's interest in the hybrid entity or the transparent entity shall be taken into account under paragraph (c)(2) of this section when applying the principles of 864(c)(2), (c)(4), (c)(5) (as set forth in § 1.864-4(c), and § § 1.864-5 through 1.864-7), and § 1.882-5 (as modified in paragraph (c)(2)(ii) of this section). See § 1.1503(d)-7(c) *Examples 25 and 26.*

(B) *Hybrid entity separate unit or interest in a transparent entity..*—For purposes of determining items of income, gain, deduction, and loss that are attributable to a hybrid entity separate unit or an interest in a transparent entity described in paragraph (c)(3) of this section, such items shall not be taken into account to the extent they are attributable to a foreign branch separate unit pursuant to paragraph (c)(4)(i)(A) of this section. See § 1.1503(d)-7(c) *Examples 25 and 26.*

(ii) *Combined separate unit.*—If two or more individual separate units defined in § 1.1503(d)-1(b)(4)(i) are treated as one combined separate unit pursuant to § 1.1503(d)-1(b)(4)(ii), the items of income, gain, deduction, and loss that are attributable to the combined separate unit shall be determined as follows:

(A) Items of income, gain, deduction, and loss are first attributed to each individual separate unit without regard to § 1.1503(d)-1(b)(4)(ii), pursuant to the rules of paragraphs (c) through (e) of this section.

(B) The combined separate unit then takes into account all of the items of income, gain, deduction, and loss attributable to its individual separate units pursuant to paragraph (c)(4)(ii)(A) of this section. See § 1.1503(d)-7(c) *Examples 25 and 26.*

(iii) *Gain or loss on the direct or indirect disposition of a separate unit or an interest in a transparent entity.*—(A) *In general.*—This paragraph (c)(4)(iii) applies for purposes of attributing items of income, gain, deduction, and loss that are recognized on the sale, exchange, or other disposition of a separate unit or an interest in a transparent entity (or an interest in a disregarded entity, partnership, or grantor trust that owns, directly or indirectly, a separate unit or an interest in a transparent entity). For purposes of this paragraph (c)(4)(iii), items taken into account on the sale, exchange, or other disposition include loss recapture income or gain under section 367(a)(3)(C) or 904(f)(3), and gain or loss recognized by the domestic owner as the result of an election under section 338. In cases where this paragraph (c)(4)(iii)(A) applies, items taken into account on the sale, exchange, or other disposition shall be attributable to the separate unit or the interest in the transparent entity to the extent of gain or loss that would have been recognized had the separate unit or transparent entity sold all its assets (as determined in para-graph (f) of this section) in a taxable exchange, immediately before the sale, exchange, or other disposition (deemed sale). For purposes of a deemed sale described in this paragraph (c)(4)(iii), the assets are treated as being sold for an amount equal to their fair market value, plus the assumption of the liabilities of the separate unit or interest in a transparent entity (as determined in paragraph (f) of this section). See § 1.1503(d)-7(c) *Example 27.*

(B) *Multiple separate units or interests in transparent entities.*—This paragraph (c)(4)(iii)(B) applies to a sale, exchange, or other disposition described in paragraph (c)(4)(iii)(A) of this section that results in more than one separate unit or interest in a transparent entity being, directly or indirectly, disposed of. In such a case, items of income, gain, deduction, and loss recognized on such sale, exchange, or other disposition are allocated and attributed to each separate unit or interest in a transparent entity, based on the relative gain or loss that would have been recognized by each separate unit or interest in a transparent entity pursuant to a deemed sale of their assets. See § 1.1503(d)-7(c) *Example 28.*

(iv) *Inclusions on stock.*—Any amount included in income of a domestic owner arising from ownership of stock in a foreign corporation (for example, under sections 78, 951, or 986(c)) through a separate unit, or interest in a transparent entity, shall be attributable to the separate unit or interest in a transparent entity, if an actual dividend from such foreign corporation would have been so attributed. See § 1.1503(d)-7(c) *Example 24.*

(v) *Foreign currency gain or loss recognized under section 987.*—Foreign currency gain or loss of a domestic owner recognized under section 987 as a result of a transfer or remittance shall not be attributable to a separate unit or an interest in a transparent entity.

(vi) *Recapture of dual consolidated loss.*—If all or a portion of a dual consolidated loss that was attributable to a separate unit is included in the gross income of a domestic owner under the recapture provisions of § 1.1503(d)-6(h), such amount shall be attributable to the separate unit that incurred the dual consolidated loss being recaptured. See § 1.1503(d)-7(c) *Examples 38 and 40.*

(d) *Foreign tax treatment disregarded.*—The fact that a particular item taken into account in computing the income or dual consolidated loss of a dual resident corporation or a separate unit, or the income or loss of an interest in a transparent entity, is not taken into account in computing income (or loss) subject to a foreign country's income tax shall not cause such item to be excluded from being taken into account under paragraph (b), (c), or (e) of this section.

(e) *Items generated or incurred while a dual resident corporation, a separate unit, or a transparent entity.*—For purposes of determining the amount of the dual consolidated loss of a dual resident corporation for the taxable year, only the items of income, gain, deduction, and loss generated or incurred during the period the dual resident corporation qualified as such shall be taken into account. For purposes of determining the amount of income of a dual resident corporation for the taxable year, all the items of income, gain, deduction, and loss generated or incurred during the year shall be taken into account. For purposes of determining the amount of the income or dual consolidated loss attributable to a separate unit, or the income or loss attributable to an interest in a transparent entity, for the taxable year, only the items of income, gain, deduction, and loss generated or incurred during the period the separate unit or the interest in the transparent entity qualified as such shall be taken into account. For purposes of this paragraph (e), the allocation of items to periods shall be made under the principles of § 1.1502-76(b).

(f) *Assets and liabilities of a separate unit or an interest in a transparent entity.*—A separate unit or an interest in a transparent entity shall be treated as owning assets to the extent items of income, gain, deduction, and loss from such assets would be attributable to the separate unit or interest in the transparent entity under paragraphs (c) through (e) of this section. Similarly, liabilities shall be treated as liabilities of a separate unit, or an interest in a transparent entity, to the extent interest expense incurred on such liabilities would be attributable to the separate unit, or the interest in a transparent entity, under paragraphs (c) through (e) of this section.

(g) *Basis adjustments.*—(1) *Affiliated dual resident corporation or affiliated domestic owner.*—If a member of a consolidated group owns stock in an affiliated dual resident corporation or an affiliated domestic owner that is a member of the same consolidated group, the member shall adjust the basis of the stock in accordance with the provisions of § 1.1502-32. Corresponding adjustments shall be made to the stock of other members in accordance with the provisions of § 1.1502-32. In the case where two or more individual separate units are treated as a combined separate unit pursuant to § 1.1503(d)-1(b)(4)(ii), see paragraph (g)(3) of this section.

(2) *Interests in hybrid entities that are partnerships or interests in partnerships through which a separate unit is owned indirectly.*—(i) *Scope.*—This paragraph (g)(2) applies for purposes of determining the adjusted basis of an interest in—

(A) A hybrid entity that is a partnership; and

(B) A partnership through which a domestic owner indirectly owns a separate unit.

(ii) *Determination of basis of partner's interest.*—The adjusted basis of an interest described in paragraph (g)(2)(i) of this section shall be adjusted in accordance with section 705 and this paragraph (g)(2). The adjusted basis shall not be decreased for any amount of a dual consolidated loss that is attributable to the partnership interest, or separate unit owned indirectly through the partnership interest, as applicable, that is not absorbed as a result of the application of § 1.1503(d)-4(b) and (c). The adjusted basis shall, however, be decreased for the amount of such dual consolidated loss that is absorbed in a carryover or carryback taxable year. The adjusted basis shall be increased for any amount included in income pursuant to § 1.1503(d)-6(h) as a result of the recapture of a dual consolidated loss that was attributable to the interest in the hybrid partnership, or separate unit owned indirectly through the partnership interest, as applicable.

(3) *Combined separate units.*—This paragraph (g)(3) applies where two or more individual separate units of one or more affiliated domestic owners are treated as one combined separate unit pursuant to § 1.1503(d)-1(b)(4)(ii). In such a case, a member owning stock in an affiliated domestic owner of the combined separate unit shall adjust the basis in the stock of such domestic owner as provided in paragraph (g)(1) of this section, and an affiliated domestic owner shall adjust its basis in a partnership, as provided in paragraph (g)(2) of this section, taking into account only those items of income, gain, deduction, or loss attributable to each individual separate unit, prior to combination. For purposes of this rule, if the dual consolidated loss attributable to a combined separate unit is subject to the domestic use limitation of § 1.1503(d)-4(b), then for purposes of this paragraph (g) and § 1.1502-32, the dual consolidated loss shall be allocated to an individual separate unit to the extent such individual separate unit contributed items of deduction or loss giving rise to the dual consolidated loss. In addition, if one or more affiliated domestic owners are required to recapture all or a portion of a dual consolidated loss pursuant to paragraph (h) of this section, such recapture amount shall be allocated to the affiliated domestic owner of the individual separate units composing the combined separate unit, to the extent such individual separate units contributed items of deduction or loss giving rise to the recaptured dual consolidated loss. [Reg. § 1.1503(d)-5.]

☐ [T.D. 9315, 3-16-2007 (*corrected* 4-24-2007).]

[Reg. § 1.1503(d)-6]

§ 1.1503(d)-6. Exceptions to the domestic use limitation rule.—(a) *In general.*—(1) *Scope and purpose.*—This section provides certain exceptions to the domestic use limitation rule of § 1.1503(d)-4(b). Paragraph (b) of this section provides an exception for bilateral elective agreements. Paragraph (c) of this section provides rules regarding an exception that applies when there is no possibility of a foreign use. Paragraphs (d) through (h) of this section provide rules for an exception where a domestic use election is made. Paragraph (e) of this section provides rules with respect to triggering events, and paragraph (f) of this section provides rules regarding exceptions to triggering events. Paragraph (g) of this section provides rules with respect to the annual certification reporting requirement. Paragraph (h) of this section provides rules regarding the recapture of dual consolidated losses. Finally, paragraph (j) of this section provides rules regarding the termination of domestic use agreements and the annual certification requirement.

(2) *Absence of foreign affiliate or foreign consolidation regime.*—The absence of a foreign affiliate or a foreign consolidation regime alone does not constitute an exception to the domestic use limitation rule. This is the case because it is still possible that all or a portion of the dual consolidated loss may be put to a foreign use. For example, there may be a foreign use with respect to an affiliate acquired in a year subsequent to the year in which the dual consolidated loss was incurred. In addition, a foreign use may occur in the absence of a foreign consolidation regime through a sale, merger, or similar transaction. See § 1.1503(d)-7(c) *Example 2.*

(3) *Foreign insurance companies treated as domestic corporations.*—The exceptions contained in this section shall not apply to losses of a foreign insurance company that is a dual resident corporation under § 1.1503(d)-1(b)(2)(ii), or to losses attributable to any separate unit of such foreign insurance company. In addition, these exceptions shall not apply to losses described in the preceding sentence that, subject to the rules of § 1.1503(d)-4(d), carry over to a domestic corporation pursuant to a transaction described in section 381(a).

(b) *Elective agreement in place between the United States and a foreign country.*—(1) *In general.*—The domestic use limitation rule of § 1.1503(d)-4(b) shall not apply to a dual consolidated loss to the extent the consolidated group, unaffiliated dual resident corporation, or unaffiliated domestic owner, as the case may be, elects to deduct the loss in the United States pursuant to an agreement entered into between the United States and a foreign country that puts into place an elective procedure through which losses in a particular year may be used to offset income in only one country. This exception shall apply only if all the terms and conditions required under such agreement are satisfied, including any reporting or filing requirements. See § 1.1503(d)-3(e)(2)(iii) for the effect of an agreement described in this paragraph on a stand-alone domestic use agreement.

(2) *Application to combined separate units.*—This paragraph (b)(2) applies where two or more individual separate units are treated as one combined separate unit pursuant to § 1.1503(d)-1(b)(4)(ii), and an agreement described in paragraph (b)(1) of this section would apply to at least one of the individual separate units. In such a case, and except to the extent provided in the agreement, the consolidated group, unaffiliated dual resident corporation, or unaffiliated domestic owner, as the case may be, may apply the agreement to the individual separate units, as applicable, provided the terms and conditions of the agreement are otherwise satisfied. See § 1.1503(d)-7(c) *Example 19.*

(c) *No possibility of foreign use.*—(1) *In general.*—The domestic use limitation rule of § 1.1503(d)-4(b) shall not apply to a dual consolidated loss if the consolidated group, unaffiliated dual resident corporation, or unaffiliated domestic owner, as the case may be—

(i) Demonstrates, to the satisfaction of the Commissioner, that no foreign use (as defined in § 1.1503(d)-3) of the dual consolidated loss occurred in the year in which it was incurred, and that no foreign use can occur in any other year by any means; and

(ii) Prepares a statement described in paragraph (c)(2) of this section that is attached to, and filed by the due date (including extensions) of, its U.S. income tax return for the taxable year in which the dual consolidated loss is incurred. See § 1.1503(d)-7(c) *Examples 2, 30, and 31.*

(2) *Statement.*—The statement described in this paragraph (c)(2) must be signed under penalties of perjury by the person who signs the tax return. The statement must be labeled "No Possibility of Foreign Use of Dual Consolidated Loss Statement" at the top of the page and must include the following items, in paragraphs labeled to correspond with the items set forth in paragraphs (c)(2)(i) through (iv) of this section:

(i) A statement that the document is submitted under the provisions of paragraph (c) of this section.

(ii) The name, address, taxpayer identification number, and place and date of incorporation of the dual resident corporation, and the country or countries that tax the dual resident corporation on its worldwide income or on a residence basis, or, in the case of a separate unit, identification of the separate unit, including the name under which it conducts business, its principal activity, and the country in which its principal place of business is located. In the case of a combined separate unit, such information must be provided for each individual separate unit that is treated as part of the combined separate unit under § 1.1503(d)-1(b)(4)(ii).

(iii) A statement of the amount of the dual consolidated loss at issue.

(iv) An analysis, in reasonable detail and specificity, of the treatment of the losses and deductions composing the dual consolidated loss under the relevant facts. The analysis must include the reasons supporting the conclusion that no foreign use of the dual consolidated loss can occur as described in paragraph (c)(1)(i) of this section. The analysis must be supported with official or certified English translations of the relevant provisions of foreign law. The analysis may, for example, be based on the taxpayer's interpretation of foreign law, on advice received from local tax advisers in an opinion, or on a ruling from local country tax authorities. In all cases, however, the determination must be made to the satisfaction of the Commissioner.

(d) *Domestic use election.*—(1) *In general.*—The domestic use limitation rule of § 1.1503(d)-4(b) shall not apply to a dual consolidated loss if an election to be bound by the provisions of paragraphs (d) through (j) of this section is made by the consolidated group, unaffiliated dual resident corporation, or unaffiliated domestic owner, as the case may be (elector). In order to elect such relief, an agreement described in this paragraph (d)(1) (domestic use agreement) must be attached to, and filed by the due date (including extensions) of, the U.S. income tax return of the elector for the taxable year in which the dual consolidated loss is incurred. The domestic use agreement must be signed under penalties of perjury by the person who signs the return. If dual consolidated losses of more than one dual resident corporation or separate unit requires the filing of domestic use agreements by the same elector, the agreements may be combined in a single document, but the information required by paragraphs (d)(1)(ii) and (iv) of this section must be provided separately with respect to each dual consolidated loss. The domestic use agreement must be labeled "Domestic Use Election and Agreement" at the top of the page and must include the following items, in paragraphs labeled to correspond with the following:

(i) A statement that the document submitted is an election and an agreement under the provisions of paragraph (d) of this section.

(ii) The information required by paragraph (c)(2)(ii) of this section.

(iii) An agreement by the elector to comply with all of the provisions of paragraphs (d) through (j) of this section, as applicable.

(iv) A statement of the amount of the dual consolidated loss at issue.

(v) A certification that there has not been, and will not be, a foreign use (as defined in § 1.1503(d)-3) during the certification period (as defined in § 1.1503(d)-1(b)(20)).

(vi) A certification that arrangements have been made to ensure that there will be no foreign use of the dual consolidated loss during the certification period, and that the elector will be informed of any such foreign use of the dual consolidated loss during such period.

(vii) If applicable, a notification that an excepted triggering event under paragraph (f)(2) of this section has occurred with respect to the dual consolidated loss within the taxable year in which the loss is incurred. See paragraph (g) of this section for notification of excepted triggering events occurring during the certification period.

(2) *No domestic use election available if there is a triggering event in the year the dual consolidated loss is incurred.*—Except as otherwise provided in this section, if a dual resident corporation or separate unit incurs a dual consolidated loss in a taxable year and a triggering event, as described in paragraph (e)(1) of this section, occurs (and no exception applies) with respect to the dual consolidated loss in such taxable year, then the consolidated group, unaffiliated dual resident corporation, or unaffiliated domestic owner, as the case may be, may not make a domestic use election with respect to such dual consolidated loss and the loss will be subject to the domestic use limitation rule of § 1.1503(d)-4(b). See § 1.1503(d)-7(c) *Examples 5* through *7*. See also § 1.1503(d)-4(d) for rules that eliminate a dual consolidated loss after certain transactions.

(e) *Triggering events requiring the recapture of a dual consolidated loss.*—(1) *Events.*—Except as provided under paragraphs (e)(2) (rebuttal of triggering events) and (f) (exceptions to triggering events) of this section, if there is a triggering event described in this paragraph (e)(1) with respect to a dual consolidated loss of a dual resident corporation or a separate unit during the certification period (as defined in § 1.1503(d)-1(b)(20)), the elector will recapture and report as ordinary income the amount of such dual consolidated loss as provided in paragraph (h) of this section on its tax return for the taxable year in which the triggering event occurs (or, when the triggering event is a foreign use of the dual consolidated loss, the taxable year that includes the last day of the foreign taxable year during which such use occurs). In addition, the elector must pay any applicable interest charge required by paragraph (h) of this section. For purposes of this section, any of the following events shall constitute a triggering event:

(i) *Foreign use.*—A foreign use (as defined in § 1.1503(d)-3) of the dual consolidated loss. See § 1.1503(d)-3(c) for exceptions to foreign use.

(ii) *Disaffiliation.*—An affiliated dual resident corporation or affiliated domestic owner that incurred directly or through a separate unit, respectively, a dual consolidated loss that is subject to a domestic use election, ceases to be a member of the consolidated group that made the domestic use election. For purposes of this paragraph (e)(1)(ii), an affiliated dual resident corporation or affiliated domestic owner shall be considered to cease to be a member of the consolidated group if it is no longer a member of the group within the meaning of §1.1502-1(b), or if the group ceases to exist (for example, when the group no longer files a consolidated return). See §1.1503(d)-7(c) *Example 34*. Any consequences resulting from this triggering event (for example, recapture of a dual consolidated loss) shall be taken into account on the tax return of the consolidated group for the taxable year that includes the date on which the affiliated dual resident corporation or affiliated domestic owner ceases to be a member of the consolidated group. This paragraph (e)(1)(ii) shall not apply to an acquisition described in §1.1502-75(d)(3) where the consolidated group that includes the affiliated dual resident corporation or affiliated domestic owner, as applicable, is treated as remaining in existence.

(iii) *Affiliation.*—An unaffiliated dual resident corporation or unaffiliated domestic owner becomes a member of a consolidated group. Any consequences resulting from this triggering event (for example, recapture of a dual consolidated loss) shall be taken into account on the tax return of the unaffiliated dual resident corporation or unaffiliated domestic owner for the taxable year that ends at the end of the day on which such corporation becomes a member of the consolidated group.

(iv) *Transfer of assets.*—Fifty percent or more of the dual resident corporation's or separate unit's gross assets (measured by the fair market value of the assets at the time of such transaction or, for multiple transactions, at the time of the first transaction) is sold or otherwise disposed of in either a single transaction or a series of transactions within a twelve-month period. See §1.1503(d)-7(c) *Examples 5* and *35 through 37*. In determining whether fifty percent or more of such assets is sold or otherwise disposed of, any dispositions occurring in the ordinary course of the dual resident corporation's or separate unit's trade or business shall be disregarded. In addition, for purposes of this paragraph (e)(1)(iv), an interest in another separate unit and the shares of a dual resident corporation shall not be treated as assets of a separate unit or a dual resident corporation.

(v) *Transfer of an interest in a separate unit.*—Fifty percent or more of the interest in a separate unit (measured by voting power or value at the time of such transaction, or for multiple transactions, at the time of the first transaction) of the domestic owner, as determined by reference to such domestic owner's percentage interest on the last day of the taxable year in which the dual consolidated loss was incurred, is sold or otherwise disposed of either in a single transaction or a series of transactions within a twelve-month period. See §1.1503(d)-7(c) *Examples 5* and *35 through 37*.

(vi) *Conversion to a foreign corporation.*—An unaffiliated dual resident corporation, unaffiliated domestic owner, or hybrid entity an interest in which is a separate unit, that incurred the dual consolidated loss, becomes a foreign corporation (for example, as a result of a reorganization or an election to be classified as a corporation under §301.7701-3(c) of this chapter).

(vii) *Conversion to a regulated investment company, a real estate investment trust, or an S corporation.*—An unaffiliated dual resident corporation or unaffiliated domestic owner elects to be a regulated investment company pursuant to section 851(b)(1), a real estate investment trust pursuant to section 856(c)(1), or an S corporation pursuant to section 1362(a).

(viii) *Failure to certify.*—The elector fails to file a certification with respect to a dual consolidated loss as required under paragraph (g) of this section.

(ix) *Cessation of stand-alone status.*—In the case of a dual consolidated loss that is subject to the stand-alone exception described in §1.1503(d)-3(e)(2), the conditions described in §1.1503(d)-3(e)(2)(i) are no longer satisfied. See §1.1503(d)-7(c) *Example 18*.

(2) *Rebuttal.*—(i) *General rule.*—An event described in paragraph (e)(1) of this section shall not constitute a triggering event if the elector demonstrates, to the satisfaction of the Commissioner, that there can be no foreign use (as defined in §1.1503(d)-3) of the dual consolidated loss during the remaining certification period by any means. See paragraph (j)(1) of this section for rules regarding the termination of domestic use agreements and annual certifications following rebuttals under this general rule.

(ii) *Certain asset transfers.*—An event described in paragraph (e)(1)(iv) of this section shall not constitute a triggering event if the elector demonstrates, to the satisfaction of the Commissioner, that the transfer of assets did not result in a carryover under foreign law of the dual resident corporation's, or separate unit's, losses, expenses, or deductions to the transferee of the assets. For purposes of this determination, the exception to foreign use in §1.1503(d)-3(c)(7) shall be taken into account. Following rebuttal under this paragraph (e)(2)(ii), the domestic use agreement continues in effect.

(iii) *Reporting.*—In order to satisfy the requirements of paragraph (e)(2)(i) or (ii) of this section, the elector must prepare a statement, labeled "Rebuttal of Triggering Event" at the top of the page, that indicates that it is submitted under the provisions of this paragraph (e)(2). The statement must include the information described in paragraphs (c)(2)(ii) and (iii) of this section. The statement must also include the information described in paragraph (c)(2)(iv) of this section that supports the conclusions under paragraph (e)(2)(i) or (ii) of this section, as applicable. The statement must be attached to, and filed by the due date (including extensions) of, the elector's income tax return for the taxable year in which the presumed triggering event occurs.

(iv) *Examples.*—See § 1.1503(d)-7(c) *Examples 32 and 33.*

(f) *Triggering event exceptions.*—(1) *Continuing ownership of assets or interests.*—The following events shall not constitute triggering events, requiring the recapture of the dual consolidated loss under paragraph (h) of this section:

(i) *Disaffiliation as a result of a transaction described in section 381.*—An affiliated dual resident corporation or affiliated domestic owner ceases to be a member of a consolidated group solely by reason of a transaction in which a member of the same consolidated group succeeds to the tax attributes of the dual resident corporation or domestic owner under the provisions of section 381.

(ii) *Continuing ownership by consolidated group.*—This paragraph (f)(1)(ii) applies when assets of an affiliated dual resident corporation, or assets of, or interests in, a separate unit of an affiliated domestic owner are sold or otherwise disposed of. In such a case, the sale or disposition shall not be treated as a triggering event to the extent the assets or interests are acquired by one or more members of the consolidated group that includes the affiliated dual resident corporation or affiliated domestic owner, or by a partnership or a grantor trust, but only if immediately after the acquisition more than 90 percent of the partnership's or grantor trust's interests is owned, directly or indirectly, by members of such consolidated group.

(iii) *Continuing ownership by unaffiliated dual resident corporation or unaffiliated domestic owner.*—This paragraph (f)(1)(iii) applies when assets of an unaffiliated dual resident corporation, or assets of, or interests in, a separate unit of an unaffiliated domestic owner, are sold or otherwise disposed of. In such a case, the sale or disposition shall not be a triggering event to the extent such assets or interests are acquired by the unaffiliated dual resident corporation, or unaffiliated domestic owner, as applicable, or by a partnership or grantor trust, but only if immediately after the acquisition more than 90 percent of the partnership's or grantor trust's interests is owned, directly or indirectly, by the unaffiliated dual resident corporation or unaffiliated domestic owner. For example, this paragraph (f)(1)(iii) applies when an unaffiliated domestic owner acquires direct ownership of the assets of a separate unit that it had immediately before owned indirectly through a partnership.

(2) *Transactions requiring a new domestic use agreement.*—(i) *Multiple-party events.*—If all the requirements of paragraph (f)(2)(iii) of this section are satisfied, the following events shall not constitute triggering events requiring the recapture of the dual consolidated loss under paragraph (h) of this section:

(A) An affiliated dual resident corporation or affiliated domestic owner becomes an unaffiliated domestic corporation or a member of a new consolidated group (other than in a transaction described in paragraph (f)(2)(ii)(B) of this section).

(B) Assets of a dual resident corporation or assets of, or interests in, a separate unit, are sold or otherwise disposed of in a transaction in which such assets or interests are acquired by an unaffiliated domestic corporation, one or more members of a new consolidated group, or by a partnership or grantor trust, but only if immediately after the sale or disposition more than 90 percent of the partnership's or grantor trust's interests is owned, directly or indirectly, by the unaffiliated domestic owner or by members of a new consolidated group, as applicable. See the related exception to foreign use provided under § 1.1503(d)-3(c)(8). See also § 1.1503(d)-7(c) *Examples 36 and 37.*

(ii) *Events resulting in a single consolidated group.*—If the requirements of paragraph (f)(2)(iii)(A) of this section are satisfied, the following events shall not constitute triggering events requiring the recapture of the dual consolidated loss under paragraph (h) of this section:

(A) An unaffiliated dual resident corporation or unaffiliated domestic owner becomes a member of a consolidated group.

(B) A consolidated group ceases to exist as a result of a transaction described in § 1.1502-13(j)(5)(i) (relating to acquisitions of the common parent of the consolidated group), other than a transaction in which any member of the terminating group, or the successor-in-interest of such member, is not a member of the surviving group immediately after the terminating group ceases to exist. See § 1.1503(d)-7(c) *Example 34.*

(iii) *Requirements.*—(A) *New domestic use agreement.*—The unaffiliated domestic corporation or new consolidated group (subsequent elector) must file an agreement described in paragraph (d)(1) of this section (new domestic use agreement). The new domestic use agreement must be labeled "New Domestic Use Agreement" at the top of the page, and must be attached to and filed by the due date (including extensions) of, the subsequent elector's income tax return for the taxable year in which the event described in paragraph (f)(2)(i) or (f)(2)(ii) of this section occurs. The new domestic use agreement must be signed under penalties of perjury by the person who signs the return and must include the following items:

(1) A statement that the document submitted is an election and agreement under the provisions of paragraph (f)(2) of this section.

(2) An agreement to assume the same obligations with respect to the dual consolidated loss as the unaffiliated dual resident corporation, unaffiliated domestic owner, or consolidated group, as applicable, that filed the original domestic use agreement (original elector) with respect to that loss. In such a case, obligations of an elector provided under this section shall also be considered to be obligations of a subsequent elector.

(3) In the event of a transaction described in section 384(a) involving the subsequent elector, an agreement to treat any potential recapture amount under paragraph (h) of this section with respect to the dual consolidated loss as unrealized built-in gain for purposes of section 384(a), subject to any applicable exceptions (for example, the threshold requirements under section 382(h)(3)(B)). The potential recapture amount treated as unrealized built-in gain under this paragraph (f)(2)(iii)(A)(3) may be reduced to the extent permitted by paragraph (h)(2)(i) of this section.

(4) In the case of a multiple-party event described in paragraph (f)(2)(i) of this section, an agreement to be subject to the rules provided in paragraph (h)(3) of this section.

(5) The name, U.S. taxpayer identification number, and address of the original elector and prior subsequent electors, if any, with respect to the dual consolidated loss.

(B) *Statement filed by original elector.*—In the case of a multiple-party event described in paragraph (f)(2)(i) of this section, the original elector must file a statement that is attached to and filed by the due date (including extensions) of its income tax return for the taxable year in which the event occurs. The statement must be labeled "Original Elector Statement" at the top of the page, must be signed under penalties of perjury by the person who signs the tax return, and must include the following items:

(1) A statement that the document submitted is an election and agreement under the provisions of paragraph (f)(2) of this section.

(2) An agreement to be subject to the rules provided in paragraph (h)(3) of this section.

(3) The name, U.S. taxpayer identification number, and address of the subsequent elector.

(3) *Certain transfers qualifying for the de minimis exception to foreign use.*—If a transaction or event qualifies for the de minimis exception to foreign use described in § 1.1503(d)-3(c)(5), the transaction or event shall not constitute a triggering event under paragraph (e)(1)(iv) (transfers of assets) or (v) (transfers of an interest in a separate unit) of this section. For purposes of the preceding sentence, the transaction or event shall include deemed transfers that occur as a result of the transaction or event. See, for example, deemed transfers occurring pursuant to Rev. Rul. 99-5 (1999-1 CB 434), see § 601.601(d)(2)(ii)(b), and section 708 and the related regulations. See also § 1.1503(d)-7 *Example 5.* This paragraph (f)(3) only applies if the entire transaction or event qualifies for the de minimis exception to foreign use. For example, if a domestic owner sells five percent of a separate unit to a foreign corporation, which would qualify for the de minimis exception to foreign use if it were the only transfer, but pursuant to the same transaction also sells 70 percent of the same separate unit to another corporation in a manner that results in a triggering event under paragraph (e)(1)(v) of this section, this paragraph shall not apply to prevent the transaction from resulting in a triggering event.

(4) *Deemed transactions as a result of certain transfers that do not result in a foreign use.*—The rules in this paragraph (f)(4) apply where the assets of, or the interests in, a separate unit are transferred in a transaction that would not result in a foreign use and, but for resulting deemed transactions or events, would not result in a triggering event described in paragraph (e)(1) of this section. For purposes of this paragraph (f)(4), deemed transactions or events shall include transactions or events that are deemed to occur pursuant to Rev. Rul. 99-5 and section 708 and the related regulations. In such a case, the deemed transactions shall not result in a triggering event under paragraph (e)(1)(iv) (transfers of assets) or (v) (transfers of an interest in a separate unit) of this section. See also § 1.1503(d)-7 *Example 35.*

(5) *Compulsory transfers.*—Transfers of the assets or stock of a dual resident corporation, or of the assets or interests in a separate unit, shall not constitute a triggering event (including a foreign use that occurs as a result of, or following, the transfer) if such transfers are—

(i) Legally required by a foreign government as a necessary condition of doing business in a foreign country;

(ii) Compelled by a genuine threat of immediate expropriation by a foreign government; or

(iii) The result of the expropriation of assets by the foreign government.

(6) *Subsequent triggering events.*—Any triggering event described in paragraph (e) of this section that occurs subsequent to one of the transactions described in this paragraph (f), and that itself does not meet any of the exceptions provided in this paragraph (f), shall require recapture under paragraph (h) of this section by the elector or subsequent elector, as applicable.

(g) *Annual certification reporting requirement.*— Unless and until the domestic use agreement is terminated pursuant to paragraph (j) of this section, the elector must file a certification, labeled "Certification of Dual Consolidated Loss" at the top of the page, that is attached to, and filed by the due date (including extensions) of, its income tax return for each taxable year during the certification period. The certification must provide that there has been no foreign use of the dual consolidated loss. The certification must identify the dual consolidated loss to which it pertains by setting forth the elector's year in which the loss was incurred and the amount of such loss. In addition, the certification must warrant that arrangements have been made to ensure that there will be no foreign use of the dual consolidated loss and that the elector will be informed of any such foreign use. If applicable, the certification must include a notification that an excepted triggering event under paragraph (f)(2) of this section has occurred with respect to the dual consolidated loss within the taxable year being certified. If dual consolidated losses of more than one taxable year are subject to the rules of this paragraph (g), the certification for those years may be combined in a single document, but each dual consolidated loss must be separately identified. See § 1.1503(d)-3(e)(2)(ii) for additional certifications required where taxpayers elect the stand-alone exception of § 1.1503(d)-3(e)(2).

(h) *Recapture of dual consolidated loss and interest charge.*—(1) *Presumptive rules.*—(i) *Amount of recapture.*—Except as otherwise provided in this section, upon the occurrence of a triggering event described in paragraph (e) of this section that does not meet any of the exceptions provided in paragraph (f) of this section, the dual resident corporation or domestic owner of the separate unit shall recapture as gross income the total amount of the dual consolidated loss to which the triggering event applies on its income tax return for the taxable year in which the triggering event occurs (or, when the triggering event is a foreign use of the dual consolidated loss, the taxable year that includes the last day of the foreign taxable year during which such foreign use occurs). See § 1.1503(d)-5(c)(4)(vi) for rules with respect to the attribution of recapture income to a separate unit. See also § 1.1503(d)-7 *Examples 38* through *40*.

(ii) *Interest charge.*—In connection with the recapture, the elector shall pay an interest charge. An interest charge may be due even if the amount of recapture income is reduced to zero pursuant to paragraph (h)(2)(i) of this section. See § 1.1503(d)-7(c) *Example 39*. Except as otherwise provided in this section, the amount of the interest shall be computed under the rules of section 6601(a) by treating the additional tax resulting from the recapture as though it had been due and unpaid as of the date for payment of the tax for the taxable year in which the taxpayer

received a tax benefit from the dual consolidated loss. For purposes of this paragraph (h)(1)(ii), a tax benefit shall be considered to have arisen in a taxable year in which the losses or deductions taken into account in computing the dual consolidated loss reduced U.S. taxable income. For the purpose of computing the interest charge, the additional tax resulting from the recapture is determined by treating the recapture income as the last income earned in the year of recapture. The interest shall be computed to the date for payment of the tax for the year of recapture and the interest thus computed becomes a part of the tax liability for that taxable year. See section 6601 for the computation of interest on a tax liability that it is not paid timely. The recapture interest charge shall be deductible to the same extent as interest under section 6601.

(2) *Reduction of presumptive recapture amount and presumptive interest charge.*—(i) *Amount of recapture.*—The dual resident corporation or domestic owner may recapture an amount less than the total dual consolidated loss if the elector demonstrates, to the satisfaction of the Commissioner, the lesser amount described in this paragraph (h)(2)(i). The reduction in the amount of recapture is the amount by which the dual consolidated loss would have offset other taxable income reported on a timely filed U.S. income tax return for any taxable year up to and including the taxable year of the triggering event (or, when the triggering event is a foreign use of the dual consolidated loss, the taxable year that includes the last day of the foreign taxable year during which such foreign use occurs) if no domestic use election had been made for the loss such that it was subject to the domestic use limitation of § 1.1503(d)-4(b) (and therefore subject to the limitation under § 1.1503(d)-4(c)). For this purpose, the rules for attributing items of income, gain, deduction, and loss under § 1.1503(d)-5 shall apply. An elector using this rebuttal rule must prepare a separate accounting showing the income for each year that would have offset the dual resident corporation's or separate unit's recapture amount if no domestic use election had been made for the dual consolidated loss. The separate accounting must be signed under penalties of perjury by the person who signs the elector's tax return, must be labeled "Reduction of Recapture Amount" at the top of the page, and must indicate that it is submitted under the provisions of this paragraph (h)(2)(i). The accounting must be attached to, and filed by the due date (including extensions) of, the elector's income tax return for the taxable year in which the triggering event occurs. See § 1.1503(d)-7(c) *Examples 38* through *40*.

(ii) *Interest charge.*—The interest charge imposed under this section may be reduced if the elector demonstrates, to the satisfaction of the Commissioner, that the net interest owed would have been less than that provided in paragraph (h)(1)(ii) of this section if the elector had filed an amended return for the taxable year in which the recaptured dual consolidated loss was incurred, and for any other affected taxable years up to and including the taxable year of recapture, if no domestic use election had been made for the dual consolidated loss such that it had been subject to the restrictions of § 1.1503(d)-4(b) (and therefore subject to the limitations under § 1.1503(d)-4(c)). An elector using this rebuttal rule must prepare a computation demonstrating the reduction in the net interest owed as a result of treating the dual consolidated loss as a loss subject to the restrictions of § 1.1503(d)-4(b) (and therefore subject to the limitations under § 1.1503(d)-4(c)). The computation must be labeled "Reduction of Interest Charge" at the top of the page and must indicate that it is submitted under the provisions of this paragraph (h)(2)(ii). The computation must be signed under penalties of perjury by the person who signs the elector's tax return, and must be attached to, and filed by the due date (including extensions) of, the elector's income tax return for the taxable year in which the triggering event occurs. See § 1.1503(d)-7(c) *Examples 39 and 40.*

(3) *Rules regarding multiple-party event exceptions to triggering events.*—(i) *Scope.*—The rules of this paragraph (h)(3) apply when, after a triggering event described in paragraph (e) of this section with respect to which the requirements of paragraph (f)(2)(i) of this section were met (excepted event), a triggering event under paragraph (e) of this section occurs, and no exception applies to such triggering event under paragraph (f) of this section (subsequent triggering event). See § 1.1503(d)-7(c) *Examples 36 and 37.*

(ii) *Original elector and prior subsequent electors not subject to recapture or interest charge.*—(A) Except to the extent otherwise provided in this paragraph (h)(3), neither the original elector nor any prior subsequent elector shall be subject to the rules of this paragraph (h) with respect to dual consolidated losses subject to the original domestic use agreement.

(B) In the case of a dual consolidated loss with respect to which multiple excepted events have occurred, only the subsequent elector that owns the dual resident corporation or separate unit at the time of the subsequent triggering event shall be subject to the recapture rules of this paragraph (h). For purposes of this paragraph (h), the term prior subsequent elector refers to all other subsequent electors.

(iii) *Recapture tax amount and required statement.*—(A) *In general.*—If a subsequent triggering event occurs, the subsequent elector shall take into account the recapture tax amount as determined under paragraph (h)(3)(iii)(B) of this section. The subsequent elector must prepare a statement that computes the recapture tax amount, as provided under paragraph

(h)(3)(iii)(B) of this section, with respect to the dual consolidated loss subject to the new domestic use agreement. This statement must be attached to, and filed by the due date (including extensions) of, the subsequent elector's income tax return for the taxable year in which the subsequent triggering event occurs (or, when the subsequent triggering event is a foreign use of the dual consolidated loss, the taxable year that includes the last day of the foreign taxable year during which such foreign use occurs). The statement must be signed under penalties of perjury by the person who signs the return. The statement must be labeled "Statement Identifying Liability" at the top and, in addition to the calculation of the recapture tax amount, must include the following items, in paragraphs labeled to correspond with the items set forth in paragraphs (h)(3)(iii)(A)(1) through (3) of this section:

(1) A statement that the document is submitted under the provisions of § 1.1503(d)-6(h)(3)(iii).

(2) A statement identifying the amount of the dual consolidated losses at issue and the taxable years in which they were used.

(3) The name, address, and taxpayer identification number of the original elector and all prior subsequent electors.

(B) *Recapture tax amount.*—The recapture tax amount equals the excess (if any) of—

(1) The income tax liability of the subsequent elector for the taxable year that includes the amount of recapture and related interest charge with respect to the dual consolidated losses that are recaptured as a result of the subsequent triggering event, as provided under paragraphs (h)(1) and (h)(2) of this section; over

(2) The income tax liability of the subsequent elector for such taxable year, computed by excluding the amount of recapture and related interest charge described in paragraph (h)(3)(iii)(B)(1) of this section.

(iv) *Tax assessment and collection procedures.*—(A) *In general.*—(1) *Subsequent elector.*—An assessment identifying an income tax liability of the subsequent elector is considered an assessment of the recapture tax amount where the recapture tax amount is part of the income tax liability being assessed and the recapture tax amount is reflected in a statement attached to the subsequent elector's income tax return as provided under paragraph (h)(3)(iii) of this section.

(2) *Original elector and prior subsequent electors.*—The assessment of the recapture tax amount as set forth in paragraph (h)(3)(iv)(A)(1) of this section shall be considered as having been properly assessed as an income tax liability of the original elector and of each prior subsequent elector, if any. The date of such assessment shall be the date the income tax liability of the subsequent elector was properly

assessed. The Commissioner may collect all or a portion of such recapture tax amount from the original elector and/or the prior subsequent electors under the circumstances set forth in paragraph (h)(3)(iv)(B) of this section.

(B) *Collection from original elector and prior subsequent electors; joint and several liability.*—(1) *In general.*—If the subsequent elector does not pay in full the income tax liability that includes a recapture tax amount, the Commissioner may collect that portion of the unpaid balance of such income tax liability attributable to the recapture tax amount in full or in part from the original elector and/or from any prior subsequent elector, provided that the following conditions are satisfied with respect to such elector:

(i) The Commissioner properly has assessed the recapture tax amount pursuant to paragraph (h)(3)(iv)(A)(1) of this section.

(ii) The Commissioner has issued a notice and demand for payment of the recapture tax amount to the subsequent elector in accordance with § 301.6303-1 of this chapter.

(iii) The subsequent elector has failed to pay all of the recapture tax amount by the date specified in such notice and demand.

(iv) The Commissioner has issued a notice and demand for payment of the unpaid portion of the recapture tax amount to the original elector, or prior subsequent elector (as the case may be), in accordance with § 301.6303-1 of this chapter.

(2) *Joint and several liability.*—The liability imposed under this paragraph (h)(3)(iv)(B) on the original elector and each prior subsequent elector shall be joint and several.

(C) *Allocation of partial payments of tax.*—If the subsequent elector's income tax liability for a taxable period includes a recapture tax amount, and if such income tax liability is satisfied in part by payment, credit, or offset, such payment, credit or offset shall be allocated first to that portion of the income tax liability that is not attributable to the recapture tax amount, and then to that portion of the income tax liability that is attributable to the recapture tax amount.

(D) *Refund.*—If the Commissioner makes a refund of any income tax liability that includes a recapture tax amount, the Commissioner shall allocate and pay the refund to each elector who paid a portion of such income tax liability as follows:

(1) The Commissioner shall first determine the total amount of recapture tax paid by and/or collected from the original elector and from any prior subsequent electors. The Commissioner shall then allocate and pay such refund to the original elector and prior subsequent electors, with each such elector receiving an amount of such refund on a pro rata basis, not to exceed the amount of recapture tax paid by and/or collected from such elector.

(2) The Commissioner shall pay the balance of such refund, if any, to the subsequent elector.

(v) *Definition of income tax liability.*— Solely for purposes of paragraph (h)(3) of this section, the term income tax liability means the income tax liability imposed on a domestic corporation under Title 26 of the United States Code for a taxable year, including additions to tax, additional amounts, penalties, and any interest charge related to such income tax liability.

(vi) *Example.*—See § 1.1503(d)-7(c) Example 36.

(4) *Computation of taxable income in year of recapture.*—(i) *Presumptive rule.*—Except to the extent provided in paragraph (h)(4)(ii) of this section, for purposes of computing the taxable income for the year of recapture, no current, carryover or carryback losses may offset and absorb the recapture amount.

(ii) *Exception to presumptive rule.*—The recapture amount included in gross income may be offset and absorbed by that portion of the elector's net operating loss carryover that is attributable to the dual resident corporation or separate unit that incurred the dual consolidated loss being recaptured, if the elector demonstrates, to the satisfaction of the Commissioner, the amount of such portion of the carryover. The principles of § 1.1502-21(b)(2)(iv) shall apply for purposes of determining whether any portion of a net operating loss carryover is attributable to the dual resident corporation or separate unit. In the case of a separate unit, such determination shall be made by treating the separate unit as a domestic corporation and a member of the consolidated group composing its unaffiliated domestic owner, or members of the consolidated group of which its affiliated domestic owner is a member, as appropriate. An elector utilizing this rebuttal rule must prepare a computation demonstrating the amount of net operating loss carryover that, under this paragraph (h)(4)(ii), may absorb the recapture amount included in gross income. Such computation must be signed under penalties of perjury and attached to and filed by the due date (including extensions) of, the income tax return for the taxable year in which the triggering event occurs (or, when the triggering event is a foreign use of the dual consolidated loss, the taxable year that includes the last day of the foreign taxable year during which such foreign use occurs).

(5) *Character and source of recapture income.*— The amount recaptured under this paragraph (h) shall be treated as ordinary income. Except as provided in the prior sentence, such income shall be treated, as applicable, as income from the

same source, having the same character, and falling within the same separate category, for all purposes, including sections 904(d) and 907, to which the items of deduction or loss composing the dual consolidated loss were allocated and apportioned, as provided under sections 861(b), 862(b), 863(a), 864(e), 865, and the related regulations. For this determination, the pro rata computation of the items of deduction or loss composing the dual consolidated loss as described in § 1.1503(d)-4(c)(4) shall apply. See § 1.1503(d)-7(c) *Example 38.*

(6) *Reconstituted net operating loss.*— (i) *General rule.*—Except as provided in paragraphs (h)(6)(ii) and (iii) of this section, commencing in the year immediately following the year in which the dual consolidated loss is recaptured, the dual resident corporation, or the domestic owner of the separate unit, that incurred the dual consolidated loss that is recaptured shall be treated as having a net operating loss (reconstituted net operating loss) in an amount equal to the amount actually recaptured under this paragraph (h). If a domestic corporation (transferee) acquires the assets of the dual resident corporation or domestic owner in a transaction described in section 381(a), the preceding sentence shall be applied by treating the transferee as the dual resident corporation or domestic owner, as applicable. In a case to which this paragraph (h)(6) applies, the transferee corporation shall be treated as having a reconstituted net operating loss in an amount equal to the amount actually recaptured under this paragraph (h). In no event, however, shall more than one corporation be treated as having a reconstituted net operating loss as a result of a single dual consolidated loss being recaptured. A reconstituted net operating loss of a domestic owner shall be attributable under § 1.1503(d)-5 to the separate unit that incurred the dual consolidated loss that was recaptured. Moreover, a reconstituted net operating loss shall be subject to the domestic use limitation of § 1.1503(d)-4(b) (and therefore subject to the limitation under § 1.1503(d)-4(c)), without regard to the exceptions contained in paragraphs (b) through (d) of this section (relating to elective agreements in place between the United States and a foreign country, the ability to demonstrate no possibility of a foreign use, and a domestic use election, respectively). The reconstituted net operating loss shall be available only for carryover, under section 172(b), to taxable years following the taxable year of recapture. For purposes of determining the remaining carryover period, the reconstituted net operating loss shall be treated as if it had been recognized in the taxable year in which the dual consolidated loss that is the basis of the recapture amount was incurred. See § 1.1503(d)-7(c) *Examples 36, 38, and 40.*

(ii) *Exception.*—Paragraph (h)(6)(i) of this section shall not apply to the extent the dual consolidated loss that is the basis of the recapture amount would have been eliminated pursuant to § 1.1503(d)-4(d) if no domestic use election had been made for such loss. See § 1.1503(d)-7(c) *Example 40.*

(iii) *Special rule for recapture following multiple-party event exception to a triggering event.*— This paragraph applies to an excepted event described in paragraph (f)(2)(i)(B) of this section that is followed by a subsequent triggering event requiring recapture as described in paragraph (f)(6) of this section. In such a case, the domestic corporation that owns, directly or indirectly, the assets of the dual resident corporation, or the assets of or the interests in a separate unit, immediately following the excepted event shall be treated as if it incurred the dual consolidated loss that is recaptured for purposes of applying paragraph (h)(6)(i) of this section. See § 1.1503(d)-7(c) *Example 36.*

(i) *[Reserved].*

(j) *Termination of domestic use agreement and annual certifications.*—(1) *Rebuttals, exceptions to triggering events, and recapture.*—The domestic use agreement filed with respect to a dual consolidated loss shall terminate prior to the end of the certification period and have no further effect if—

(i) An elector is able to rebut the presumption of a triggering event pursuant to the general rule in paragraph (e)(2)(i) of this section;

(ii) An event described in paragraph (e)(1) of this section is not a triggering event as a result of the application of paragraphs (f)(2)(i) or (ii) (relating to events requiring a new domestic use agreement) of this section; this paragraph (j)(1)(ii) does not, however, apply to terminate the new domestic use agreement filed in connection with the event pursuant to paragraph (f)(2)(iii)(A) of this section. See also paragraph (h)(3)(iv) of this section regarding collection from the original elector and prior subsequent electors in certain cases; or

(iii) A dual consolidated loss is recaptured pursuant to paragraph (h) of this section. See § 1.1503(d)-7(c) *Examples 32* through 34.

(2) *Termination of ability for foreign use.*— (i) *In general.*—A domestic use agreement filed with respect to a dual consolidated loss shall terminate and have no further effect as of the end of a taxable year if the elector—

(A) Demonstrates, to the satisfaction of the Commissioner, that as of the end of such taxable year no foreign use (as defined in § 1.1503(d)-3) of the dual consolidated loss can occur in any other year by any means; and

(B) Prepares a statement described in paragraph (j)(2)(ii) of this section that is attached to, and filed by the due date (including extensions) of, its U.S. income tax return for such taxable year.

(ii) *Statement.*—The statement described in this paragraph (j)(2)(ii) must be signed under penalties of perjury by the person who signs the return. The statement must be labeled "Termination of Ability for Foreign Use" at the top of the page and must include the following information, in paragraphs labeled to correspond with the following:

(A) A statement that the document is submitted under the provisions of paragraph (j)(2) of this section.

(B) The information required by paragraph (c)(2)(ii) of this section.

(C) A statement of the amount of the dual consolidated loss at issue and the year in which such dual consolidated loss was incurred.

(D) The information described in paragraph (c)(2)(iv) of this section that supports the conclusion that no foreign use can occur as provided in paragraph (j)(2)(i)(A) of this section.

(3) *Agreements filed in connection with stand-alone exception.*—See § 1.1503(d)-3(e)(2)(iii) for the termination of domestic use agreements filed in connection with the stand-alone exception to the mirror legislation rule when a subsequent election is made under paragraph (b) of this section (relating to agreements entered into between the United States and a foreign country). [Reg. § 1.1503(d)-6.]

☐ [*T.D.* 9315, 3-16-2007.]

[Reg. § 1.1503(d)-7]

§ 1.1503(d)-7. Examples.—(a) *In general.*—This section provides examples that illustrate the application of §§ 1.1503(d)-1 through 1.1503(d)-6. This section also provides facts that are presumed for such examples.

(b) *Presumed facts for examples.*—For purposes of the examples in this section, unless otherwise indicated, the following facts are presumed:

(1) Each entity has only a single class of equity outstanding, all of which is held by a single owner.

(2) P, a domestic corporation and the common parent of the P consolidated group, owns S, a domestic corporation and a member of the P consolidated group.

(3) DRCX, a domestic corporation, is subject to Country X tax on its worldwide income or on a residence basis, and is a dual resident corporation.

(4) DE1X and DE2X are both Country X entities, subject to Country X tax on their worldwide income or on a residence basis, and disregarded as entities separate from their owners for U.S. tax purposes. DE3Y is a Country Y entity, subject to Country Y tax on its worldwide income or on a residence basis, and disregarded as an entity separate from its owner for U.S. tax purposes. All the interests in DE1X, DE2X, and DE3Y constitute hybrid entity separate units.

(5) FBX is a Country X business operation that, if carried on by a U.S. person, would constitute a foreign branch, as defined in § 1.367(a)-6T(g)(1), and is a Country X foreign branch separate unit.

(6) Neither the assets nor the activities of an entity constitute a foreign branch separate unit.

(7) FSX is a Country X entity that is subject to Country X tax on its worldwide income or on a residence basis and is classified as a foreign corporation for U.S. tax purposes.

(8) The applicable foreign country has a consolidation regime that—

(i) Includes as members of a consolidated group any commonly controlled branches and permanent establishments in such jurisdiction, and entities that are subject to tax in such jurisdiction on their worldwide income or on a residence basis; and

(ii) Allows the losses of members of consolidated groups to offset income of other members.

(9) There is no mirror legislation, within the meaning of § 1.1503(d)-3(e)(1), in the applicable foreign country.

(10) There is no elective agreement described in § 1.1503(d)-6(b) between the United States and the applicable foreign country.

(11) There is no income tax convention between the United States and the applicable foreign country.

(12) If a domestic use election, within the meaning of § 1.1503(d)-6(d), is made, all the necessary filings related to such election are properly completed on a timely basis.

(13) If there is a triggering event requiring recapture of a dual consolidated loss, the amount of recapture is not reduced pursuant to § 1.1503(d)-6(h)(2).

(14) There are no other items of income, gain, deduction, and loss. In addition, the United States and the applicable foreign country recognize the same items of income, gain, deduction, and loss in each taxable year.

(15) All taxpayers use the calendar year as their taxable year.

(c) *Examples.*—The following examples illustrate the application of §§ 1.1503(d)-1 through 1.1503(d)-6:

Example 1. Separate unit combination rule. (i) *Facts.* P owns DE3Y which, in turn, owns DE1X. DE1X owns FBX. PRS, an entity treated as a partnership for both U.S. and Country X tax purposes, is owned 50 percent by P and 50 percent by an unrelated foreign person. PRS carries on a business operation in Country X that, if carried on by a U.S. person, would constitute a foreign branch within the meaning of § 1.367(a)-6T(g)(1). In addition, P owns DRCX, a member of the consolidated group of which P is the parent, which carries on business operations in Country X that constitute a foreign branch within the meaning of §1.367(a)-6T(g)(1). S owns DE2X.

(ii) *Result.* Pursuant to §1.1503(d)-1(b)(4)(ii), the interest in DE1X, the interest in DE2X, FBX, P's share of the Country X business operations carried on by PRS (which is owned by P indirectly through its interest in PRS), and DRCX's Country X business operations are combined and treated as a single separate unit of the consolidated group of which P is the parent. This is the case regardless of whether the losses of each individual separate unit are made available to offset the income of the other individual separate units under Country X tax laws. Because DRCX is a dual resident corporation, it is not combined and treated as part of this combined separate unit and, as a result, DRCx's income or dual consolidated loss is not taken into account in determining the income or dual consolidated loss of the combined separate unit. In addition, P's interest in DE3Y is not combined and is another separate unit because it is subject to tax in Country Y, rather than Country X.

Example 2. Definition of a separate unit and application of domestic use limitation—foreign branch separate unit. (i) *Facts.* P carries on business operations in Country X that constitute a permanent establishment under the U.S.-Country X income tax convention. In year 1, a loss is attributable to P's Country X permanent establishment, as determined under §1.1503(d)-5.

(ii) *Result.* Under §§1.1503(d)-1(b)(4)(i)(A) and 1.367(a)-6T(g)(1), P's Country X permanent establishment constitutes a foreign branch separate unit. Therefore, the year 1 loss attributable to the foreign branch separate unit constitutes a dual consolidated loss pursuant to §1.1503(d)-1(b)(5)(ii). The dual consolidated loss rules apply to the dual consolidated loss even though there is no affiliate of the foreign branch separate unit in Country X, because it is still possible that all or a portion of the dual consolidated loss can be put to a foreign use. For example, there may be a foreign use with respect to a Country X affiliate acquired in a year subsequent to the year in which the dual consolidated loss was incurred. See §1.1503(d)-6(a)(2). Accordingly, unless an exception under §1.1503(d)-6 applies (such as a domestic use election), the year 1 dual consolidated loss attributable to P's Country X permanent establishment is subject to the domestic use limitation rule of §1.1503(d)-4(b). As a result, pursuant to §1.1503(d)-4(c), the year 1 dual consolidated loss cannot offset income of P that is not attributable to its Country X foreign branch separate unit, nor can it offset income of any other domestic affiliate. The loss can, however, offset income of the Country X foreign branch separate unit, subject to the application of §1.1503(d)-4(c). The result would be the same even if Country X did not have a consolidation regime that includes as members of consolidated groups Country X branches or permanent establishments of nonres-

ident corporations. The dual consolidated loss rules apply even in the absence of a consolidation regime in the foreign country because it is possible that all or a portion of a dual consolidated loss can be put to a foreign use by other means, such as through a sale, merger, or similar transaction. See §1.1503(d)-6(a)(2).

(iii) *Alternative facts.* The facts are the same as in paragraph (i) of this *Example 2*, except that P's Country X business operations constitute a foreign branch as defined in §1.367(a)-6T(g)(1), but do not constitute a permanent establishment under the U.S.-Country X income tax convention. Although the activities carried on by P in Country X would otherwise constitute a foreign branch separate unit as described in §1.1503(d)-1(b)(4)(i)(A), the exception under §1.1503(d)-1(b)(4)(iii) applies because the activities do not constitute a permanent establishment under the U.S.-Country X income tax convention. Thus, the Country X business operations do not constitute a foreign branch separate unit, and the year 1 loss is not subject to the dual consolidated loss rules. If P instead carried on its Country X business operations through DE1X, then the exception under §1.1503(d)-1(b)(4)(iii) would not apply because P carries on the business operations through a hybrid entity and, as a result, the business operations would constitute a foreign branch separate unit. Thus, in such a case the year 1 loss would be subject to the dual consolidated loss rules.

Example 3. Domestic use limitation—foreign branch separate unit owned through a partnership. (i) *Facts.* P and S organize a partnership, PRSX, under the laws of Country X. PRSX is treated as a partnership for both U.S. and Country X tax purposes. PRSX owns FBX. PRSX earns U.S. source income that is unconnected with its FBX branch operations, and such income is not subject to tax by Country X. In addition, such U.S. source income is not attributable to FBX under §1.1503(d)-5.

(ii) *Result.* Under §1.1503(d)-1(b)(4)(i)(A), P's and S's shares of FBX owned indirectly through their interests in PRSX are individual foreign branch separate units. Pursuant to §1.1503(b)-1(b)(4)(ii), these individual separate units are combined and treated as a single separate unit of the consolidated group of which P is the parent. Unless an exception under §1.1503(d)-6 applies, any dual consolidated loss attributable to FBX cannot offset income of P or S (other than income attributable to FBX, subject to the application of §1.1503(d)-4(c)), including their distributive share of the U.S. source income earned through their interests in PRSX, nor can it offset income of any other domestic affiliates.

Example 4. Definition of a separate unit and domestic use limitation—interest in hybrid entity partnership and indirectly owned foreign branch separate unit. (i) *Facts.* HPSX is a Country X entity that is subject to Country X tax on its worldwide income. HPSX is classified as a partnership for

Federal tax purposes. P, S, and FSX, are the sole partners of HPSX. For U.S. tax purposes, P, S, and FSX each has an equal interest in each item of HPSX's profit or loss. HPSX carries on operations in Country Y that, if carried on by a U.S. person, would constitute a foreign branch within the meaning of § 1.367(a)-6T(g)(1).

(ii) *Result*. Under § 1.1503(d)-1(b)(4)(i)(B), the partnership interests in HPSX held by P and S are individual hybrid entity separate units. These individual separate units are combined into a single separate unit under § 1.1503(d)-1(b)(4)(ii). In addition, P's and S's share of the Country Y operations owned indirectly through their interests in HPSX are individual foreign branch separate units under § 1.1503(d)-1(b)(4)(i)(B). These individual separate units are also combined into a single separate unit under § 1.1503(d)-1(b)(4)(ii). Unless an exception under § 1.1503(d)-6 applies, dual consolidated losses attributable to P's and S's combined interests in HPSX can only be used to offset income attributable to their combined interests in HPSX (other than income attributable to P's and S's combined interests in the Country Y foreign branch separate unit), subject to the application of § 1.1503(d)-4(c). Similarly, dual consolidated losses attributable to P's and S's combined interests in the Country Y operations of HPSX can only be used to offset income attributable to their combined interests in such Country Y operations, subject to the application of § 1.1503(d)-4(c). Neither FSX's interest in HPSX, nor its share of the Country Y operations owned by HPSX, is a separate unit because FSX is not a domestic corporation.

Example 5. Foreign use—general rule and de minimis reduction exception. (i) *Facts*. P owns DE1X. DE1X owns FSX. In year 1, there is a $100x loss attributable to P's interest in DE1X that is a dual consolidated loss. Also in year 1, FSX earns $200x of income. DE1X and FSX file a Country X consolidated tax return. For Country X tax purposes, the year 1 $100x loss of DE1X is used to offset $100x of year 1 income generated by FSX. Under Country X tax law, unused losses are carried forward and available to offset income in subsequent taxable years.

(ii) *Result*. The $100x loss attributable to P's interest in DE1X is available to, and in fact does, offset FSX's income under the laws of Country X. In addition, under U.S. tax principles, such income is considered to be an item of FSX, a foreign corporation. As a result, under § 1.1503(d)-3(a), there has been a foreign use of the year 1 dual consolidated loss attributable to P's interest in DE1X. Therefore, P cannot make a domestic use election with respect to the loss as provided under § 1.1503(d)-6(d)(2), and such loss will be subject to the domestic use limitation rule of § 1.1503(d)-4(b). The result would be the same even if FSX, under Country X tax law, had no income against which the dual consolidated loss of DE1X could be offset (unless FSX's ability to

use the loss under Country X tax law requires an election, and no such election is made).

(iii) *Alternative facts*. The facts are the same as in paragraph (i) of this *Example 5*, except that FSX cannot use the loss of DE1X under Country X tax law without an election, and no such election is made. Pursuant to the exception in § 1.1503(d)-3(c)(2), there is no foreign use of the year 1 dual consolidated loss attributable to P's interest in DE1X. In addition, P files a domestic use election with respect to the year 1 dual consolidated loss attributable to its interest in DE1X and, at the beginning of year 3, P sells its interest in DE1X to F, a Country Y entity that is a foreign corporation. The sale of the interest in DE1X to F results in a foreign use triggering event pursuant to § 1.1503(d)-6(e)(1)(i) because, immediately after the sale, the loss attributable to the interest in DE1X carries over under Country X law and, therefore, is available under U.S. tax principles to offset income of the owner of the interest in DE1X which, in the hands of F, is not a separate unit. It is also a foreign use because the loss is available under U.S. tax principles to offset the income of F, a foreign corporation. See § 1.1503(d)-3(a)(1). Finally, the transfer is a triggering event pursuant to § 1.1503(d)-6(e)(1)(iv) and (v).

(iv) *Alternative facts*. The facts are the same as in paragraph (iii), of this *Example 5*, except that P only sells 5 percent of its interest in DE1X to F. Pursuant to Rev. Rul. 99-5 (1999-1 CB 434), see § 601.601(d)(2)(ii)(b) of this chapter, the transaction is treated as if P sold 5 percent of its interest in each of DE1X's assets to F, and then immediately thereafter P and F transferred their interests in the assets of DE1X to a partnership in exchange for an ownership interest therein. The sale of the 5 percent interest in DE1X generally results in a foreign use triggering event because a portion of the dual consolidated loss carries over under Country X tax law and is available under U.S. tax principles to offset income of the owner of the interest in DE1X, a hybrid entity, which in the hands of F is not a separate unit. It is also a foreign use because the loss is available under U.S. tax principles to offset the income of F, a foreign corporation. See § 1.1503(d)-3(a)(1). However, pursuant to the exception under § 1.1503(d)-3(c)(5) (relating to a de minimis reduction of an interest in a separate unit), such availability does not result in a foreign use. In addition, pursuant to § 1.1503(d)-6(f)(1) and (3) , the deemed transfers pursuant to Rev. Rul. 99-5 as a result of the sale are not treated as triggering events described in § 1.1503(d)-6(e)(1)(iv) or (v).

Example 6. Foreign use and indirect foreign use—foreign reverse hybrid structure and disregarded payments. (i) *Facts*. P owns DE1X. DE1X owns 99 percent and S owns 1 percent of FRHX, a Country X partnership that elected to be treated as a corporation for U.S. tax purposes. FRHX conducts a trade or business in Country X. In year 1, DE1X incurs interest expense on a third-party loan, which constitutes a dual consolidated loss attributable to P's interest in DE1X. In year 1, for Country X tax purposes, DE1X takes into account its distributive share of income generated by FRHX and offsets such income with its interest expense.

(ii) *Result*. In year 1, the dual consolidated loss attributable to P's interest in DE1X is available to, and in fact does, offset income recognized in Country X and, under U.S. tax principles, the income is considered to be income of FRHX, a foreign corporation. Accordingly, pursuant to § 1.1503(d)-3(a)(1), there is a foreign use of the dual consolidated loss. Therefore, P cannot make a domestic use election with respect to the year 1 dual consolidated loss attributable to its interest in DE1X, as provided under § 1.1503(d)-6(d)(2), and such loss will be subject to the domestic use limitation rule of § 1.1503(d)-4(b).

(iii) *Alternative facts*. (A) The facts are the same as in paragraph (i) of this *Example 6*, except as follows. Instead of owning DE1X, P owns DE3Y which, in turn, owns DE1X. In addition, DE3Y, rather than DE1X, is the obligor on the third-party loan and therefore incurs the interest expense on such loan. Finally, DE3Y on-lends the loan proceeds from the third-party loan to DE1X, and DE1X pays interest to DE3Y on such loan that is generally disregarded for U.S. tax purposes.

(B) Pursuant to § 1.1503(d)-5(c)(1)(ii), for purposes of calculating income or a dual consolidated loss, DE3Y and DE1X do not take into account interest income or interest expense, respectively, with respect to amounts paid on the disregarded loan from DE3Y to DE1X. As a result, such items neither create a dual consolidated loss with respect to the interest in DE1X, nor do they reduce (or eliminate) the dual consolidated loss attributable to the interest in DE3Y. Thus, in year 1, there is a dual consolidated loss attributable to P's interest in DE3Y, but not to P's indirect interest in DE1X.

(C) In year 1, interest expense paid by DE1X to DE3Y on the disregarded loan is taken into account as a deduction in computing DE1X's taxable income for Country X tax purposes, but does not give rise to a corresponding item of income or gain for U.S. tax purposes (because it is generally disregarded). In addition, such interest has the effect of making an item of deduction or loss composing the dual consolidated loss attributable to P's interest in DE3Y available for a foreign use. This is the case because it may reduce or offset items of deduction or loss composing the dual consolidated loss for foreign tax purposes, and creates another deduction or loss that may reduce or offset income of DE1X for foreign tax purposes that, under U.S. tax principles, is treated as income of FRHX, a foreign corporation. Moreover, because the disregarded item is incurred or taken into account as interest for foreign tax purposes, it is deemed to have been incurred or taken into account with a principal

purpose of avoiding the provisions of section 1503(d). Accordingly, there is an indirect foreign use of the year 1 dual consolidated loss attributable to P's interest in DE3Y, and P cannot make a domestic use election with respect to such loss as provided under § 1.1503(d)-6(d)(2). Thus, the loss will be subject to the domestic use limitation rule of § 1.1503(d)-4(b).

Example 7. Indirect foreign use—hybrid instrument. (i) *Facts*. P owns DE1X which, in turn, owns FSX. DE1X borrows cash from an unrelated lender and transfers the cash to FSX in exchange for an instrument (hybrid instrument). The hybrid instrument is treated as equity for U.S. tax purposes and debt for Country X tax purposes. Interest expense on the loan from the unrelated lender results in a dual consolidated loss being attributable to P's interest in DE1X in year 1. DE1X does not elect under Country X law to consolidate with FSX. In year 1, FSX distributes its stock as a payment on the hybrid instrument to DE1X. For U.S. tax purposes, such payment is excluded from P's gross income under section 305. However, for Country X tax purposes, such payment is treated as interest and gives rise to a deduction taken into account in computing FSX's Country X tax liability; the payment also gives rise to interest income to DE1X for Country X tax purposes.

(ii) *Result*. The payment on the hybrid instrument does not give rise to an item of income or gain for U.S. tax purposes and therefore does not reduce (or eliminate) the dual consolidated loss attributable to P's interest in DE1X. In addition, such payment is taken into account as a deduction in computing FSX's taxable income for Country X tax purposes. Moreover, such payment has the effect of making an item of deduction or loss composing the dual consolidated loss attributable to P's interest in DE1X available for a foreign use. This is the case because it may reduce or offset items of deduction or loss composing the dual consolidated loss for foreign tax purposes, and creates a deduction that reduces or offsets income of FSX for foreign tax purposes that, under U.S. tax principles, is income of a foreign corporation. Further, because the item is incurred, or taken into account, using an instrument that is treated as equity for U.S. tax purposes and debt for foreign tax purposes, it is deemed to have been engaged in with the principal purpose of avoiding the provisions of section 1503(d). As a result, there has been an indirect foreign use of the year 1 dual consolidated loss, and P cannot make a domestic use election with respect to such loss, as provided under § 1.1503(d)-6(d)(2). Thus, the year 1 dual consolidated loss will be subject to the domestic use limitation rule of § 1.1503(d)-4(b).

Example 8. No indirect foreign use—transaction entered into in the ordinary course of business. (i) *Facts*. P owns DE1X and FBY. FBY is a foreign branch separate unit located in Country Y. DE1X owns FBX and FSX. P's interest in DE1X and FBX are combined and treated as a single separate unit (Country X separate unit) pursuant to § 1.1503(d)-1(b)(4)(ii). Under Country X tax laws, DE1X elects to consolidate with FSX. FBY engages in the business of providing services and, in connection with its ordinary course of business, provides services to unrelated third parties and to DE1X. As compensation for services, DE1X makes a payment to FBY. Under Country X tax law, the payment is deductible. However, the payment is generally disregarded for U.S. tax purposes and, pursuant to § 1.1503(d)-5(c)(1)(ii), is not taken into account in calculating the income or dual consolidated loss attributable to the Country X separate unit or FBY. In year 1, the Country X separate unit and FBY each has a dual consolidated loss. The dual consolidated loss attributable to the Country X separate unit is subject to the domestic use limitation under § 1.1503(d)-4(b) because DE1X and FSX elect to consolidate and, as a result, the dual consolidated loss is put to a foreign use.

(ii) *Result.* The payment made by DE1X to FBY in connection with the performance of services is taken into account as a deduction in computing DE1X's taxable income for Country X tax purposes, but does not give rise to an item of income or gain for U.S. tax purposes. In addition, such payment has the effect of making an item of deduction or loss composing the dual consolidated loss attributable to FBY available for a foreign use. This is the case because it may reduce or offset items of deduction or loss composing the dual consolidated loss of FBY for foreign tax purposes, and creates another deduction for that reduces or offsets income of FSX for foreign tax purposes (because DE1X and FSX elect to file a consolidated return) that, under U.S. tax principles, is income of a foreign corporation. However, the transaction between DE1X and FBY was entered into in the ordinary course of FBY's trade or business. As a result, if P can demonstrate to the satisfaction of the Commissioner that the transaction was not entered into with a principal purpose of avoiding the provisions of section 1503(d), FBY's year 1 dual consolidated loss will not be treated as having been made available for an indirect foreign use. In such a case, P would be entitled to make a domestic use election with respect to such loss.

Example 9. Foreign use—dual resident corporation with hybrid entity joint venture. (i) *Facts.* P owns DRCX, a member of the P consolidated group. DRCX owns 80 percent of HPSX, a Country X entity that is subject to Country X tax on its worldwide income. HPSX is classified as a partnership for U.S. tax purposes. FSX owns the remaining 20 percent of HPSX. In year 1, DRCX generates a $100x net operating loss (without regard to items attributable to DRCX's interest in HPSX). Also in year 1, HPSX generates $100x of income, $80x of which is attributable to DRCX's interest in HPSX. DRCX and HPSX file a consolidated tax return for Country X tax purposes, and

HPSX offsets its $100x of income with the $100x loss generated by DRCX.

(ii) *Result.* DRCX and its interest in HPSX are not combined because DRCX is a dual resident corporation and the combination rule under § 1.1503(d)-1(b)(4)(ii) only applies to separate units. The $100x year 1 net operating loss incurred by DRCX (without regard to items attributable to DRCX's interest in HPSX) is a dual consolidated loss. In addition, HPSX is a hybrid entity and DRCX's interest in HPSX is a hybrid entity separate unit; however, there is no dual consolidated loss attributable to such separate unit in year 1 (instead, there is $80x of income attributable to such separate unit). DRCX's year 1 dual consolidated loss offsets $100x of income for Country X purposes, and $20x of such income is, under U.S. tax principles, income of FSX, which owns an interest in HPSX that is not a separate unit (in addition, FSX is a foreign corporation). As a result, pursuant to § 1.1503(d)-3(a), there is a foreign use of the year 1 dual consolidated loss of DRCX, and P cannot make a domestic use election with respect to such loss pursuant to § 1.1503(d)-6(d)(2). Therefore, such loss will be subject to the domestic use limitation rule of § 1.1503(d)-4(b). The result would be the same even if HPSX, under Country X laws, had no income against which the dual consolidated loss could be offset (unless the ability to use the loss under Country X laws required an election, and no such election is made).

Example 10. Foreign use—foreign parent corporation. (i) *Facts.* F1 and F2, nonresident alien individuals, each owns 50 percent of FPX, a Country X entity that is subject to Country X tax on its worldwide income. FPX is classified as a foreign corporation for U.S. tax purposes. FPX owns DRCX. DRCX is the parent of a consolidated group that includes as a member DS, a domestic corporation. In year 1, DRCX incurs a dual consolidated loss of $100x and, for Country X tax purposes, FPX generates $100x of income. In year 1, FPX elects to consolidate with DRCX for Country X tax purposes, and the $100x year 1 loss of DRCX is used to offset the income of FPX under the laws of Country X. For U.S. tax purposes, the items of FPX do not constitute items of income in year 1.

(ii) *Result.* The year 1 dual consolidated loss of DRCX offsets the income of FPX under the laws of Country X. Pursuant to § 1.1503(d)-3(a), the offset constitutes a foreign use because the items constituting such income are considered under U.S. tax principles to be items of a foreign corporation. This is the case even though the United States does not recognize such items as income in year 1. Therefore, DRCX cannot make a domestic use election with respect to its year 1 dual consolidated loss pursuant to § 1.1503(d)-6(d)(2). As a result, such loss will be subject to the domestic use limitation rule of § 1.1503(d)-4(b).

(iii) *Alternative facts.* The facts are the same as in paragraph (i) of this *Example 10,* except that

FPX is classified as a partnership for U.S. tax purposes. The result would be the same as in paragraph (ii) of this *Example 10*, because the offset of the income generated by FPX is a foreign use pursuant to § 1.1503(d)-3(a). This is the case because the items constituting such income are considered under U.S. tax principles to be items of F1 and F2, the owners of interests in FPX (a hybrid entity), that are not separate units. Moreover, the result would be the same if F1 and F2 owned their interests in FPX indirectly through another partnership.

Example 11. No foreign use—absence of foreign loss allocation rules. (i) *Facts.* P owns DE1X and DRCX. DRCX is a member of the P consolidated group and owns FSX. DE1X owns FBX. P's interest in DE1X and P's indirect interest in FBX are individual separate units that are combined into a single separate unit (Country X separate unit) pursuant to § 1.1503(d)-1(b)(4)(ii). In year 1, DRCX incurs a $200x net operating loss and $200x of income is attributable to P's Country X separate unit. The $200x net operating loss incurred by DRCX is a dual consolidated loss. FSX also earns $200x of income in year 1. DRCX, DE1X, and FSX file a Country X consolidated tax return. However, Country X has no applicable rules for determining which income is offset by DRCX's year 1 $200x loss.

(ii) *Result.* Under § 1.1503(d)-3(c)(3), DRCX's $200x loss shall be treated as having been made available to offset the $200x of income attributable to P's Country X separate unit. P's Country X separate unit is not, under U.S. tax principles, a foreign corporation, and there is no interest in DE1X (which is a hybrid entity) that is not a separate unit. As a result, DRCX's loss being made available to offset the income attributable to P's Country X separate unit is not considered a foreign use of such loss. Therefore, P can make a domestic use election with respect to DRCX's year 1 dual consolidated loss.

(iii) *Alternative facts.* The facts are the same as in paragraph (i) of this *Example 11*, except that in year 1 only $150x of income is attributable to P's Country X separate unit. Because only $150x of income is attributed to P's Country X separate unit, $50x of DRCX's year 1 dual consolidated loss is treated as being made available to offset the income of FSX, a foreign corporation, and therefore constitutes a foreign use. As a result, DRCX cannot make a domestic use election with respect to its year 1 dual consolidated loss pursuant to § 1.1503(d)-6(d)(2), and such loss will be subject to the domestic use limitation rule of § 1.1503(d)-4(b).

Example 12. No foreign use—absence of foreign loss usage ordering rules. (i) *Facts.* (A) P owns DRCX, a member of the P consolidated group. DRCX owns FSX. Under the Country X consolidation regime, a consolidated group may elect in any given year to use all or a portion of the losses of one consolidated group member to offset income of other consolidated group mem-

bers. If no such election is made in a year in which losses are generated by a consolidated member, such losses carry forward and are available, at the election of the consolidated group, to offset income of consolidated group members in subsequent taxable years. Country X law does not provide ordering rules for determining when a loss from a particular taxable year is used because, under Country X law, losses never expire. In addition, Country X law does not provide ordering rules for determining when a particular type of loss (for example, capital or ordinary) is used.

(B) In year 1, DRCX incurs a capital loss of $80x which, under § 1.1503(d)-5(b)(2), is not a dual consolidated loss. DRCX also incurs a net operating loss of $80x in year 1 which is a dual consolidated loss. FSX generates $60x of capital gain in year 1 which, for Country X purposes, can be offset by capital losses and net operating losses. Under the laws of Country X, DRCX elects to use $60x of its total year 1 loss of $160x to offset the $60x of capital gain generated by FSX in year 1; the remaining $100x of year 1 loss carries forward. In both year 2 and year 3, DRCX incurs a net operating loss of $100x, while FSX incurs no income or loss in years 2 and 3. DRCX's $100x losses incurred in year 2 and year 3 are dual consolidated losses. Because DRCX does not elect under the laws of Country X to use all or a portion of its year 2 or year 3 net operating losses of $100x to offset the income of other members of the Country X consolidated group, P is permitted to make (and in fact does make) a domestic use election with respect to both the year 2 and year 3 dual consolidated losses of DRCX. In year 4, DRCX has a net operating loss of $10x and FSX generates $125x of income. Country X law permits, upon an election, FSX's $125x of income generated in year 4 to be offset by losses (including carryover losses from prior years) of other group members. Accordingly, in year 4, DRCX elects to use $125x of its accumulated losses to offset the $125x of year 4 income generated by FSX.

(ii) *Result.* (A) Under the ordering rules of § 1.1503(d)-3(d)(3), a pro rata amount of DRCX's year 1 net operating loss ($30x) and capital loss ($30x) is considered to be used to offset FSX's year 1 $60x capital gain. As a result, P cannot make a domestic use election with respect to DRCX's year 1 $80x dual consolidated loss because a portion of such loss is put to a foreign use.

(B) DRCX's $10x year 4 net operating loss is also a dual consolidated loss. Under the ordering rules of § 1.1503(d)-3(d)(1), such loss is considered to be used to offset $10x of FSX's year 4 $125x of income. Consequently, P cannot make a domestic use election with respect to such loss. Under the ordering rules of § 1.1503(d)-3(d)(2), $50x of capital loss carryover and $50x of ordinary loss from year 1 will be considered to offset $100x of FSX's year 4 income because the income is first deemed to have been offset by losses the use of which would not constitute a triggering event that would result in the recapture of a dual consolidated loss. The remaining $15x of FSX's year 4 income is considered to be offset by losses from year 3 because it is the most recent taxable year from which a loss may be carried forward. Thus, a portion of the year 3 dual consolidated loss has been put to a foreign use and the entire year 3 dual consolidated loss is recaptured. However, none of DRCX's $100x year 2 net operating loss will be deemed to offset FSX's year 4 income. As a result, DRCX's year 2 dual consolidated loss will not be recaptured.

Example 13. Exception to foreign use through partnership interest. (i) *Facts.* (A) P owns 80 percent of HPSX, a Country X entity subject to Country X tax on its worldwide income. FSZ, an unrelated foreign corporation, owns the remaining 20 percent of HPSX. HPSX is classified as a partnership for Federal tax purposes and carries on operations in Country X that, if carried on by a U.S. person, would constitute a foreign branch within the meaning of § 1.367(a)-6T(g)(1). P's interest in HPSX and P's indirect interest in the Country X branch are individual separate units that are combined into a single separate unit (Country X separate unit) pursuant to § 1.1503(d)-1(b)(4)(ii).

(B) In year 1, HPSX incurs a loss of $100x, $80x of which is attributable to P's Country X separate unit. The $80x of loss attributable to P's Country X separate unit constitutes a dual consolidated loss and P makes a domestic use election with respect to such loss. In year 2, HPSX generates $50x of income, $40x of which is attributable to P's interest in the Country X separate unit. Under Country X income tax laws, the $100x of year 1 loss incurred by HPSX is carried forward and offsets the $50x of income generated by HPSX in year 2; the remaining $50x of loss is carried forward and is available to offset income generated by HPSX in subsequent years. P and FSZ maintain their ownership interests in HPSX throughout years 1 and 2.

(ii) *Result.* In year 2, under the laws of Country X, the $100x of year 1 loss, which includes the $80x dual consolidated loss attributable to P's Country X separate unit, is made available to offset income of HPSX. Such income is attributable to P's interest in HPSX, which is a separate unit. Such income also is income of FSZ, a foreign corporation that is an owner of an interest in HPSX, which is not a separate unit. However, pursuant to § 1.1503(d)-3(c)(4), there is no foreign use of the year 1 dual consolidated loss in year 2. This is the case because P's interest in HPSX as of the end of year 1 has not been reduced by more than a de minimis amount, and the portion of the $80x dual consolidated loss was made available for a foreign use in year 2 solely as a result of FSZ's ownership in HPSX and the allocation or carry forward of the dual consolidated loss as a result of such ownership.

(iii) *Alternative facts.* The facts are the same as in paragraph (i) of this *Example 13*, except that P also owns FSX. In addition, FSX and HPSX elect to file a consolidated return under Country X law. The exception to foreign use under § 1.1503(d)-3(c)(4) does not apply because there is a foreign use other than by reason of the dual consolidated loss being made available as a result of FSZ's ownership in HPSX and the allocation or carry forward of the dual consolidated loss as a result of such ownership. That is, the exception does not apply because there is also a foreign use of the dual consolidated loss as a result of FSX and HPSX filing a consolidated return under Country X law.

(iv) *Alternative facts.* The facts are the same as in paragraph (i) of this *Example 13*, except that at the end of year 2, FSZ contributes cash to HPSX in exchange for additional equity of HPSX. As a result of the contribution, FSZ's interest in HPSX increases from 20 percent to 30 percent, and P's interest in HPSX decreases from 80 percent to 70 percent. P's interest in HPSX is reduced within a single 12-month period by 12.5 percent (10/80), as compared to P's interest in HPSX as of the beginning of such 12-month period. Accordingly, pursuant to § 1.1503(d)-3(c)(4)(iii), the exception to foreign use provided under § 1.1503(d)-3(c)(4)(i) does not apply. Therefore, in year 2 there is a foreign use of the $80x year 1 dual consolidated loss attributable to P's Country X separate unit. Such foreign use constitutes a triggering event in year 2 and the $80x year 1 dual consolidated loss is recaptured. Alternatively, if FSZ were a domestic corporation, there would not be a foreign use of the $80x year 1 dual consolidated loss because the loss would not be available to offset income that, under U.S. tax principles, is income of a foreign corporation or a direct or indirect owner of an interest in a hybrid entity that is not a separate unit.

Example 14. Exception to foreign use through partnership interest—combination rule. (i) *Facts.* (A) P and FSX form PRSX. P and FSX each own 50 percent of PRSX throughout years 1 and 2. PRSX is treated as a partnership for both U.S. and Country X tax purposes. PRSX owns DEY. DEY is a Country Y entity subject to Country Y tax on its worldwide income and disregarded as an entity separate from its owner for U.S. tax purposes. DEY conducts business operations in Country Y that, if carried on by a U.S. person, would constitute a foreign branch as defined in § 1.367(a)-6T(g)(1). P's interest in the Country Y operations conducted by DEY is an individual foreign branch separate unit. P's interest in DEY, owned indirectly through PRSX, is a hybrid entity individual separate unit. P also owns FBY, a Country Y foreign branch individual separate unit. Under § 1.1503(d)-1(b)(4)(ii), FBY and P's indirect interests in DEY and DEY's Country Y business operations are treated as a combined separate unit (Country Y separate unit).

(B) In year 1, there is a $100x loss attributable to the Country Y business operations conducted by DEY. Thus, there is a $50x loss attributable to P's interest in DEY's Country Y business operations in year 1. Also in year 1, there is a $200x loss attributable to FBY. No income or loss is attributable to P's interest in DEY in year 1. Under § 1.1503(d)-5(c)(4)(ii), the dual consolidated loss attributable to P's combined Country Y separate unit is $250x ($50x loss attributable to P's indirect interest in DEY's Country Y operations, plus $200x loss attributable to FBY). In year 2, neither DEY nor DEY's Country Y operations generates income or loss. Under Country Y law, the $100x of year 1 loss incurred by DEY is carried forward and is available to offset income of DEY in year 2.

(ii) *Result.* As a result of the carryover of the year 1 $100x loss (which includes $50x of the year 1 dual consolidated loss) under Country Y law, a portion of such loss will be available to offset income of DEY that is attributable to P's interest in DEY owned indirectly through PRSX. A portion of such loss will also be available to offset income of DEY that is attributable to FSX's indirect ownership of DEY. Accordingly, under § 1.1503(d)-3(a), there would be a foreign use of a portion of P's $250x year 1 dual consolidated loss because it is available to offset an item of income of the owner of an interest in a hybrid entity, which is not a separate unit (there would also be a foreign use in this case because FSX is a foreign corporation). However, there has not been a reduction of P's interest in DEY, DEY has not consolidated under the laws of Country Y, and there has not been any other foreign use of the dual consolidated losses. As a result, no foreign use occurs as a result of the carryforward pursuant to § 1.1503(d)-3(c)(4)(i) and (ii).

Example 15. No foreign use—asset basis carryover exception. (i) *Facts.* P owns FBX and FSX. In year 1, there is a dual consolidated loss attributable to FBX. P's items of income, gain, deduction, and loss that are taken into account in calculating FBX's dual consolidated loss include depreciation deductions attributable to FBX's assets. P makes a domestic use election under § 1.1503(d)-6(d) with respect to the year 1 dual consolidated loss of FBX. At the end of year 2, P contributes a portion of FBX's assets to FSX, in exchange for stock in FSX. The aggregate adjusted basis of the assets transferred by P to FSX is less than 10 percent of the aggregate adjusted basis of all of FBX's assets held at the beginning of year 2. In addition, no other assets of FBX are transferred during the certification period. Under Country X law, FSX's basis in the transferred assets is determined by reference to P's basis in such assets. In addition, under Country X law, a portion of the depreciation deductions that were taken into account in year 1 for U.S. tax purposes, are taken into account in year 2 for Country X tax purposes.

(ii) *Result.* As a result of the transfer of assets from P to FSX, a portion of the year 1 dual consolidated loss is available for a foreign use. This is the case because a portion of the basis in FBX's assets, which gave rise to depreciation deductions that were taken into account in computing the year 1 dual consolidated loss, will give rise to a depreciation deduction under Country X laws that will be available, under U.S. tax principles, to offset the income of FSX, a foreign corporation, in year 2. However, the aggregate adjusted basis of all the assets transferred by P to FSX, within the 12-month period ending at the end of year 2, is less than 10 percent of the aggregate adjusted basis of all of FBX's assets at the beginning of such 12-month period. Moreover, the aggregate adjusted basis of the assets transferred by P to FSX at any time during the certification period is less than 30 percent of the aggregate adjusted basis of FBX's assets held at the end of year 1. In addition, the item of deduction giving rise to the foreign use is being made available solely as a result of the adjusted basis of the transferred assets being determined in whole, or in part, by reference to the adjusted basis of such transferred assets in the hands of FBX. As a result, this transfer will not result in a foreign use pursuant to § 1.1503(d)-3(c)(6).

Example 16. No foreign use—liability assumption exception. (i) *Facts.* P owns FBX. In year 1, there is a dual consolidated loss attributable to FBX for which P makes a domestic use election under § 1.1503(d)-6(d). The dual consolidated loss includes a deduction for salary expense that was deductible for U.S. tax purposes at the end of year 1, even though it was not paid until year 2. The deduction was incurred in the ordinary course of FBX's trade or business. During year 2, and before the accrued salary expense liability was paid, P sells all the assets of FBX to FSX in exchange for cash and FSX's assumption of the liabilities of the FBX trade or business, including the obligation to pay the accrued salary expense. Under Country X law, the accrued salary expense of FBX is deductible, and is taken into account for purposes of computing the taxable income of FBX, when paid. FBX pays the accrued salary expense after the sale of FBX to FSX.

(ii) *Result.* (A) As a result of FSX's assumption of the FBX liabilities, including the accrued salary expense, a portion of the dual consolidated loss is available for a foreign use in year 2. This is the case because the deduction that was taken into account in year 1 in computing the dual consolidated loss under U.S. tax principles will, under Country X tax law, be taken into account and will be available to offset the income of FSX, a foreign corporation, in year 2. However, because this item of expense is made available solely as a result of the assumption of a liability of FBX, and such liability was incurred in the ordinary course of FBX's trade or business, there will not be a foreign use of the year 1 dual consolidated loss pursuant to § 1.1503(d)-3(c)(7).

(B) The transfer of all the assets of FBX to FSX is a triggering event under § 1.1503(d)-6(e)(1)(iv), unless P can rebut the triggering event under § 1.1503(d)-6(e)(2). For purposes of determining whether, under § 1.1503(d)-6(e)(2)(ii), the transfer of assets resulted in a carryover under foreign law of FBX's losses, expenses, or deductions, the exception to foreign use for the assumption of liabilities is taken into account. However, the other exceptions to foreign use do not apply for this purpose (or for purposes of demonstrating that no foreign use of a dual consolidated loss can occur in any other year under § 1.1503(d)-6(c), (e)(2)(i) or (j)(2)). See § 1.1503(d)-3(c)(1). Provided the other requirements of § 1.1503(d)-6(e)(2)(ii) and (iii) are satisfied, P may be able to rebut the occurrence of a triggering event upon the transfer of FBX's assets to FSX.

Example 17. Mirror legislation rule—dual resident corporation and hybrid entity separate unit. (i) *Facts.* P owns DRCX, a member of the P consolidated group. DRCX owns FSX. In year 1, DRCX incurs a $100x net operating loss that is a dual consolidated loss. To prevent corporations like DRCX from offsetting losses both against income of affiliates in Country X and against income of foreign affiliates under the tax laws of another country, Country X mirror legislation prevents a corporation that is subject to the income tax of another country on its worldwide income or on a residence basis from using the Country X form of consolidation. Accordingly, the Country X mirror legislation prevents the loss of DRCX from being made available to offset income of FSX.

(ii) *Result.* Under § 1.1503(d)-3(e), because the losses of DRCX are subject to Country X's mirror legislation, there is a deemed foreign use of DRCX's year 1 dual consolidated loss. The standalone exception to the mirror rule in § 1.1503(d)-3(e)(2) does not apply because, absent the mirror legislation, DRCX's year 1 consolidated loss would be available for a foreign use (as defined in § 1.1503(d)-3), without regard to whether such availability is limited by election or similar procedure. That is, absent the mirror legislation, all or a portion of the dual consolidated loss would be available to offset the income of FSX under the Country X consolidation regime. This is the case even if Country X did not recognize DRCX as having a loss in year 1. Therefore, P may not make a domestic use election with respect to DRCX's year 1 dual consolidated loss pursuant to § 1.1503(d)-6(d)(2).

(iii) *Alternative facts.* The facts are the same as in paragraph (i) of this *Example 17*, except that P owns DE1X (rather than DRCX) and, in year 1, there is a $100 dual consolidated loss attributable to P's interest in DE1X (rather than of DRCX). The Country X mirror legislation only applies to Country X dual resident corporations and, there-

fore, does not apply to losses attributable to P's interest in DE1X. As a result, the mirror legislation rule under § 1.1503(d)-3(e) would not deny the opportunity of such loss from being put to a foreign use (for example, by offsetting the income of FSX through the Country X consolidation regime). Therefore, a domestic use election can be made with respect to the dual consolidated loss (provided the conditions for such an election are otherwise satisfied).

Example 18. Mirror legislation rule—standalone foreign branch separate unit. (i) *Facts.* P owns FBX. In year 1, there is a $100x dual consolidated loss attributable to FBX. Country X enacted mirror legislation to prevent Country X branches and permanent establishments of nonresident corporations from offsetting losses both against income of Country X affiliates and against other income of its owner (or foreign affiliates thereof) under the tax laws of another country. The Country X mirror legislation prevents a Country X branch or permanent establishment of a nonresident corporation from offsetting its losses against the income of Country X affiliates if such losses may be deductible against income (other than income of the Country X branch or permanent establishment) under the laws of another country.

(ii) *Result.* In general, under § 1.1503(d)-3(e), because the losses of FBX are subject to Country X's mirror legislation, there is a deemed foreign use of FBX's year 1 dual consolidated loss. However, in the absence of the Country X mirror legislation, no item of deduction or loss composing FBX's year 1 dual consolidated loss would be available in the year incurred for a foreign use (as defined in § 1.1503(d)-3), without regard to whether such availability is limited by election or otherwise. This is the case because there is no Country X entity through which the dual consolidated loss could be put to a foreign use (absent a sale, merger, or similar transaction involving FBX). As a result, the stand-alone exception in § 1.1503(d)-3(e)(2) may apply, provided P complies with the requirements of § 1.1503(d)-3(e)(2)(ii). Accordingly, P may make a domestic use election with respect to the year 1 dual consolidated loss of FBX pursuant to § 1.1503(d)-6(d). If, however, any item of the dual consolidated loss would otherwise be available for a foreign use during the certification period (for example, as a result of P acquiring a foreign corporation that is organized under the laws of Country X such that losses of FBX could be put to a foreign use through consolidation or similar means), then such loss would be recaptured pursuant to § 1.1503(d)-6(e)(1)(ix).

(iii) *Alternative facts.* The facts are the same as in paragraph (i) of this *Example 18*, except that the Country X mirror legislation operates in a manner similar to the rules under section 1503(d). That is, it allows the taxpayer to elect to use the loss to either offset income of an affiliate in Country X, or income of an affiliate (or other income of the owner of the Country X branch or permanent establishment) in the other country, but not both. Because the Country X mirror legislation permits the taxpayer to choose to put the dual consolidated loss to a foreign use, it does not deny the opportunity to put the loss to a foreign use. Therefore, there is no deemed foreign use of the dual consolidated loss pursuant to § 1.1503(d)-4(e) and a domestic use election can be made for such loss.

Example 19. Application of mirror legislation rule to combined separate unit. (i) *Facts.* P owns FBX, FSX, and DE1X. In year 1, there is a $50x dual consolidated loss attributable to FBX and $10x of income attributable to P's interest in DE1X. FSX has income of $100x. Pursuant to § 1.1503(d)-1(b)(4)(ii), FBX and P's interest in DE1X are combined and treated as a single separate unit (Country X separate unit) which has a year 1 dual consolidated loss of $40x. Country X enacted mirror legislation to prevent Country X branches or permanent establishments of nonresident corporations from offsetting losses both against income of Country X affiliates and against other income of its owner (or foreign affiliates thereof) under the tax laws of another country. The Country X mirror legislation prevents a Country X branch or permanent establishment of a nonresident corporation from offsetting its losses against the income of Country X affiliates if such losses may be deductible against income (other than income of the Country X branch or permanent establishment) under the laws of another country. However, the United States and Country X have entered into an agreement described in § 1.1503(d)-6(b) pursuant to the U.S.-Country X income tax convention (mirror agreement). The mirror agreement applies to Country X foreign branch separate units of domestic corporations, but not to Country X hybrid entity separate units. The mirror agreement provides that neither the Country X mirror legislation nor the mirror legislation rule under § 1.1503(d)-3(e) will apply to losses attributable to Country X foreign branch separate units, provided certain conditions and reporting requirements are satisfied (including a domestic use election, if the loss is to be used to offset income of a domestic affiliate). Thus, losses attributable to Country X foreign branch separate units can, subject to the requirements of the mirror agreement, be used to offset income of a domestic affiliate or a Country X affiliate (but not both).

(ii) *Result.* The Country X mirror legislation only applies to Country X foreign branch separate units and does not apply to hybrid entity separate units. In addition, if P complies with the terms and conditions of the mirror agreement, the Country X mirror legislation would not apply to FBX. As a result, the income tax laws of Country X would not deny the opportunity of a loss of either individual separate unit that composes P's combined Country X separate unit

from being put to a foreign use. Therefore, notwithstanding § 1.1503(d)-3(e), a domestic use election can be made with respect to the dual consolidated loss attributable to P's Country X separate unit, provided the terms and conditions of the mirror agreement are satisfied. See § 1.1503(d)-6(b)(2).

(iii) *Alternative facts.* The facts are the same as in paragraph (i) of this *Example 19*, except that the Country X mirror legislation also applies to losses attributable to DE1X, but the mirror agreement does not apply to such losses. The mirror legislation rule would apply with respect to P's interest in DE1X and, as a result, there is a deemed foreign use of the dual consolidated loss attributable to the Country X separate unit and a domestic use election cannot be made for such loss. This is the case even though, pursuant to § 1.1503(d)-5(c)(4)(ii)(A), P's interest in DE1X (which is subject to the Country X mirror legislation) does not, as an individual separate unit, have a dual consolidated loss in year 1. Further, the stand-alone exception to the mirror legislation rule in § 1.1503(d)-3(e)(2) does not apply because, absent the mirror legislation, the Country X combined separate unit's dual consolidated loss would be available in the year incurred for a foreign use (as defined in § 1.1503(d)-3) because it could be used to offset income of FSX under the Country X consolidation regime. This is the case even if Country X requires an election to consolidate and no such election is made. The result would be the same even if Country X did not recognize DE1X as having a loss.

Example 20. Dual consolidated loss limitation after section 381 transaction—disposition of assets and subsequent liquidation of dual resident corporation. (i) *Facts.* P owns DRCX, a member of the P consolidated group. In year 1, DRCX incurs a dual consolidated loss and P does not make a domestic use election with respect to such loss. Under § 1.1503(d)-4(b), DRCX's year 1 dual consolidated loss is subject to the limitations under § 1.1503(d)-4(c) and, therefore, may not be used to offset the income of P or S (or any other domestic affiliate) on the group's U.S. income tax return. At the beginning of year 2, DRCX sells all of its assets for cash and distributes the cash to P pursuant to a liquidation that qualifies under section 332.

(ii) *Result.* In general, under section 381, P would succeed to, and be permitted to use, DRCX's net operating loss carryover. However, § 1.1503(d)-4(d)(1)(i) prohibits the dual consolidated loss of DRCX from carrying over to P. Therefore, DRCX's year 1 net operating loss carryover is eliminated.

Example 21. Dual consolidated loss limitation applied to a separate unit transferred in a section 381 transaction. (i) *Facts.* S owns DE1X which, in turn, owns FBX. S's interest in DE1X and its indirect interest in FBX are combined and treated as a single separate unit (Country X separate unit) pursuant to § 1.1503(d)-1(b)(4)(ii). In year 1, a dual consolidated loss is attributable to the Country X separate unit, and P does not make a domestic use election with respect to such loss. Under § 1.1503(d)-4(b), the year 1 dual consolidated loss attributable to the Country X separate unit may not be used to offset the income of P or S (other than income attributable to the Country X separate unit, subject to the application of § 1.1503(d)-4(c)) on the group's consolidated U.S. income tax return (nor may it be used to offset the income of any other domestic affiliates). At the beginning of year 2, S transfers its entire interest in DE1X, and thus its entire indirect interest in FBX, to FSX in a transaction described in section 381.

(ii) *Result.* Section 1.1503(d)-4(d)(1)(ii) provides that the dual consolidated loss attributable to a separate unit that is subject to the domestic use limitation under § 1.1503(d)-4(b) is eliminated if the separate unit ceases to be a separate unit of its affiliated domestic owner and all other members of the affiliated domestic owner's separate group. As a result of the transfer of the Country X separate unit to FSx, the Country X separate unit ceases to be a separate unit of S, and is not a separate unit of any other member of the P consolidated group. In addition, the exceptions in § 1.1503(d)-4(d)(2)(iii) do not apply because FSX is not a domestic corporation. Thus, the year 1 dual consolidated loss attributable to the Country X separate unit is eliminated.

(iii) *Alternative facts.* Assume the same facts as in paragraph (i) of this *Example 21*, except S transfers its assets to DC, a domestic corporation that is not a member of the P consolidated group, in a transaction described in section 381(a). Immediately after the transaction, the Country X separate unit is a separate unit of DC. Under § 1.1503(d)-4(d)(1)(ii), the year 1 dual consolidated loss of the Country X separate unit would be eliminated because it ceases to be a separate unit of S, and is not a separate unit of any other member of the P consolidated group. However, because the transferee is a domestic corporation and the Country X separate unit is a separate unit in the hands of DC immediately after the transaction, the exception under § 1.1503(d)-4(d)(2)(iii)(A) applies. As a result, the year 1 dual consolidated loss of the Country X separate unit is not eliminated and any income generated by DC that is attributable to the Country X separate unit following the transfer may be offset by the carryover dual consolidated losses attributable to the Country X separate unit, subject to the limitations of § 1.1503(d)-4(b) and (c) applied as if DC generated the dual consolidated loss and such loss was attributable to the Country X separate unit.

(iv) *Alternative facts.* Assume the same facts as in paragraph (iii) of this *Example 21*, except that P owns DE2X and the interest in DE2X is combined with and therefore included in the Country X separate unit. In addition, a portion of the dual consolidated loss of the Country X separate unit is attributable to P's interest in DE2X. Pursuant to § 1.1503(d)-4(d)(2)(iii)(A), the result would be the same as in paragraph (iii) of this *Example 21*, with respect to the portion of the dual consolidated loss attributable to the combined separate unit that is succeeded to and taken into account by DC pursuant to section 381. The portion of the dual consolidated loss attributable to P's interest in DE2X, however, does not carry over to DC but is retained by P and continues to be subject to the limitations of § 1.1503(d)-4(b) and (c) with respect to P's interest in DE2X.

(v) *Alternative facts.* Assume the same facts as in paragraph (iv) of this *Example 21*, except that DC is a member of the P consolidated group. Pursuant to § 1.1503(d)-4(d)(2)(iii)(B), the dual consolidated loss of the Country X separate unit is not eliminated and income attributable to the Country X separate unit may continue to be offset by the dual consolidated loss that is succeeded to and taken into account by DC pursuant to section 381, subject to the limitations of § 1.1503(d)-4(b) and (c). The result would be the same even if the interest in DE1X ceased to be a separate unit in the hands of DC (for example, because it dissolved under Country X law in connection with the transaction), provided P, or another member of the P consolidated group, continued to own a portion of the Country X separate unit.

Example 22. Tainted income. (i) *Facts.* P owns 100 percent of DRCZ, a domestic corporation that is included as a member of the P consolidated group. DRCZ conducts a business in the United States. During year 1, DRCZ was managed and controlled in Country Z and therefore was subject to tax as a resident of Country Z and was a dual resident corporation. In year 1, DRCZ incurred a dual consolidated loss of $200x, and P did not make a domestic use election with respect to such loss. As a result, such loss is subject to the domestic use limitation rule of § 1.1503(d)-4(b). At the end of year 1, DRCZ moved its management and control to the United States and, as a result, ceased being a dual resident corporation. At the beginning of year 2, P transferred asset A, a non-depreciable asset, to DRCZ in exchange for common stock in a transaction that qualified for nonrecognition under section 351. At the time of the transfer, P's tax basis in asset A equaled $50x and the fair market value of asset A equaled $100x. The tax basis of asset A in the hands of DRCZ immediately after the transfer equaled $50x pursuant to section 362. Asset A did not constitute replacement property acquired in the ordinary course of business. DRCZ did not generate income or gain during years 2, 3, or 4. On June 30, year 5, DRCZ sold asset A to a third party for $100x, its fair market value at the time of the sale, and recognized $50x of income on such sale. In addition to the $50x income generated on the sale of asset A, DRCZ generated $100x of operating income in year 5. At the end of year 5, the fair market value of all the assets of DRCZ was $400x.

(ii) *Result*. DRCZ ceased being a dual resident corporation at the end of year 1. Therefore, its year 1 dual consolidated loss cannot be offset by tainted income. Asset A is a tainted asset because it was acquired in a nonrecognition transaction after DRCZ ceased being a dual resident corporation (and was not replacement property acquired in the ordinary course of business). As a result, the $50x of income recognized by DRCZ on the disposition of asset A is tainted income and cannot be offset by the year 1 dual consolidated loss of DRCZ. In addition, absent evidence establishing the actual amount of tainted income, $25x of the $100x year 5 operating income of DRCZ (($100x/$400x) × $100x) also is treated as tainted income and cannot be offset by the year 1 dual consolidated loss of DRCZ under § 1.1503(d)-4(e)(2)(ii). Therefore, $75x of the $150x year 5 income of DRCZ constitutes tainted income and may not be offset by the year 1 dual consolidated loss of DRCZ; however, the remaining $75x of year 5 income of DRCZ may be offset by such dual consolidated loss. The result would be the same if, instead of P transferring asset A to DRCZ, such asset was received from a separate unit or a transparent entity of DRCZ.

Example 23. Treatment of disregarded item and books and records of a hybrid entity. (i) *Facts*. P owns DE1X which, in turn, owns FSX. In year 1, P borrows from a third party and on-lends the proceeds to DE1X. In year 1, P incurs interest expense attributable to the third-party loan. Also in year 1, DE1X incurs interest expense attributable to its loan from P, but such expense is generally disregarded for U.S. tax purposes because DE1X is disregarded as an entity separate from P. The third-party loan and related interest expense are reflected on the books and records of P (and not on the books and records of DE1X). The loan from P to DE1X and related interest expense are reflected on the books and records of DE1X. There are no other items of income, gain, deduction, or loss reflected on the books and records of DE1X in year 1.

(ii) *Result*. Because the interest expense on P's third-party loan is not reflected on the books and records of DE1X, no portion of such expense is attributable to P's interest in DE1X pursuant to § 1.1503(d)-5(c)(3) for purposes of calculating the year 1 dual consolidated loss, if any, attributable to such interest. In addition, even though P's interest in DE1X is treated as a separate domestic corporation for purposes of determining the amount of income or dual consolidated loss attributable to it pursuant to § 1.1503(d)-5(c)(1)(ii), such treatment does not cause the interest expense incurred on the loan from P to DE1X that is generally disregarded for U.S. tax purposes to be regarded for purposes of calculating the year 1 dual consolidated loss, if any, attributable to P's interest in DE1X. As a result, even though the disregarded interest expense is reflected on the

books and records of DE1X, it is not taken into account for purposes of calculating income or a dual consolidated loss. Therefore, there is no dual consolidated loss attributable to P's interest in DE1X in year 1.

Example 24. Dividend income attributable to a separate unit. (i) *Facts*. P owns DE1X which, in turn, owns FBX. P's interest in DE1X and its indirect interest in FBX are combined and treated as a single separate unit (Country X separate unit) pursuant to § 1.1503(d)-1(b)(4)(ii). DE1X owns DE3Y. DE3Y owns the stock of FSX. P's Country X separate unit would, without regard to year 1 dividend income (or related section 78 gross-up) received from FSX, have a dual consolidated loss of $75x in year 1. In year 1, FSX distributes $50x to DE3Y that is taxable as a dividend. DE3Y distributes the same amount to DE1X. P computes foreign taxes deemed paid on the dividend under section 902 of $25x and includes that amount in gross income under section 78.

(ii) *Result*. The $50x dividend is reflected on the books and records of DE3Y and, therefore, is attributable to P's interest in DE3Y pursuant to § 1.1503(d)-5(c)(3)(i). In addition, the $25x section 78 gross-up is attributable to P's interest in DE3Y pursuant to § 1.1503(d)-5(c)(4)(iv). The distribution of $50x from DE3Y to DE1X is generally disregarded for U.S. tax purposes and, therefore, does not give rise to an item that is taken into account for purposes of calculating income or a dual consolidated loss. This is the case even though the item would be reflected on the books and records of DE1X. In addition, pursuant to § 1.1503(d)-5(c)(1)(iii), each separate unit must calculate its own income or dual consolidated loss, and each item of income, gain, deduction, and loss must be taken into account only once. As a result, the dual consolidated loss of $75x attributable to P's Country X separate unit in year 1 is not reduced by the amount of dividend income attributable to P's indirect interest in DE3Y.

Example 25. Items reflected on books and records of a combined separate unit. (i) *Facts*. P owns DE1X which, in turn, owns FBX. P's interest in DE1X and its indirect interest in FBX are combined and treated as a single separate unit (Country X separate unit) pursuant to § 1.1503(d)-1(b)(4)(ii). The following items are reflected on the books and records of DE1X in year 1: sales, depreciation expense, a political contribution, royalty expense paid to P, repairs and maintenance expense paid to a third party, and Country X income tax expense. The amount of sales under U.S. tax principles equals the amount of sales reported for accounting purposes. The depreciation expense is calculated on a straight-line basis over the useful life of the asset for accounting purposes, but is subject to accelerated depreciation for U.S. tax purposes. In addition, the repairs and maintenance expense, which is deducted when paid for accounting purposes, is properly capitalized and amortized over five years for U.S. tax purposes. Finally, P elects to claim as a credit under section 901 the Country X income tax expense that was paid in year 1.

(ii) *Result.* (A) For purposes of determining the income or dual consolidated loss attributable to P's Country X separate unit, items of income, gain, deduction, and loss must first be attributed to the individual separate units (that is, P's interest in DE1X and its indirect interest in FBX). For purposes of attributing items to P's interest in DE1X, P's items that are reflected on DE1X's books and records, as adjusted to conform to U.S. tax principles, are taken into account. See § 1.1503(d)-5(c)(3)(i). For purposes of attributing items (other than interest expense) to FBX, the principles of section 864(c)(2), (c)(4), and (c)(5) (as set forth in § 1.864-4(c) and § § 1.864-5 through 1.864-7) must be applied and, for interest expense, the principles of § 1.882-5, as modified under § 1.1503(d)-5(c)(2)(ii), must be applied; however, for these purposes, pursuant to § 1.1503(d)-5(c)(4)(i)(A), FBX only takes into account items attributable to P's interest in DE1X and the assets, liabilities, and activities of such interest. In addition, to the extent such items are taken into account by FBX, they are not taken into account in determining the items attributable to P's interest in DE1X. § 1.1503(d)-5(c)(4)(i)(B). Because P's interest in DE1X has no assets or liabilities, and conducts no activities, other than through its ownership of FBX, all of the items that are reflected on the books and records of DE1X, as adjusted to conform to U.S. tax principles, are attributable to FBX; no items are attributable to P's interest in DE1X.

(B) The items reflected on the books and records of DE1X must be adjusted to conform to U.S. tax principles. No adjustment is required to sales because the amount of sales under U.S. tax principles equals the amount of sales for accounting purposes. The amount of straight-line depreciation expense reflected on DE1X's books and records must be adjusted to reflect the amount of depreciation on the asset that is allowable for U.S. tax purposes. The political contribution is not taken into account because it is not deductible for U.S. tax purposes. Similarly, because the royalty expense is paid to P, and therefore is generally disregarded for U.S. tax purposes, it is not taken into account. The repair and maintenance expense that is deducted in year 1 for accounting purposes also must be adjusted to conform to U.S. tax principles. Thus, the repair and maintenance expense will be taken into account in computing the income or dual consolidated loss attributable to P's Country X separate unit over five years (even though no item related to such expense would be reflected on the books and records of DE1X for years 2 through 5). Finally, because P elected to claim as a credit the Country X foreign taxes paid during year 1, no deduction is allowed for

such amount pursuant to section 275(a)(4) and, therefore, the Country X tax expense is not taken into account.

(C) Pursuant to § 1.1503(d)-5(c)(4)(ii)(B), the combined Country X separate unit of P calculates its income or dual consolidated loss by taking into account all the items of income, gain, deduction, and loss that were separately attributable to P's interest in DE1X and FBX. However, in this case, there are no items attributable to P's interest in DE1X. Therefore, the items attributable to the Country X separate unit are the items attributable to FBX.

Example 26. Items attributable to a combined separate unit. (i) *Facts.* P owns DE1X. DE1X owns a 50 percent interest in PRSZ, a Country Z entity that is classified as a partnership both for Country Z tax purposes and for U.S. tax purposes. FSX, which is unrelated to P, owns the remaining 50 percent interest in PRSZ. PRSZ carries on operations in Country X that, if carried on by a U.S. person, would constitute a foreign branch as defined in § 1.367(a)-6T(g)(1). Therefore, P's share of the Country X operations carried on by PRSZ constitutes a foreign branch separate unit. PRSZ also owns assets that do not constitute a part of its Country X branch, including all of the interests in TET, a disregarded entity. TET is an entity incorporated under the laws of Country T, a country that does not have an income tax. Under the laws of Country X, an interest holder of TET does not take into account on a current basis the interest holder's share of items of income, gain, deduction, and loss of TET.

(ii) *Result.* (A) Pursuant to § 1.1503(d)-1(b)(4)(ii), P's interest in DE1X, and P's indirect ownership of a portion of the Country X operations carried on by PRSZ, are combined and treated as a single separate unit (Country X separate unit). Pursuant to § 1.1503(d)-5(c)(4)(ii)(A), for purposes of determining P's items of income, gain, deduction, and loss attributable to the Country X separate unit, the items of P are first attributed to each separate unit that composes the Country X separate unit.

(B) Pursuant to § 1.1503(d)-5(c)(2)(i), the principles of section 864(c)(2), (c)(4), and (c)(5) (as set forth in § 1.864-4(c) and § § 1.864-5 through 1.864-7), apply for purposes of determining P's items of income, gain, deduction (other than interest expense), and loss that are attributable to P's indirect interest in the Country X operations carried on by PRSZ. For purposes of determining P's interest expense that is attributable to P's indirect interest in the Country X operations carried on by PRSZ, the principles of § 1.882-5, as modified under § 1.1503(d)-5(c)(2)(ii), shall apply. For purposes of applying these rules, P is treated as a foreign corporation, the Country X operations carried on by PRSZ are treated as a trade or business within the United States, and the assets of P (including its share of the PRSZ assets, other than those of the Country X operations) are treated as assets that are not U.S. assets. In addition, because P carries on its share of the Country X operations through DE1X, a hybrid entity, § 1.1503(d)-5(c)(4)(i)(A) provides that only the items attributable to P's interest in DE1X, and only the assets, liabilities, and activities of P's interest in DE1X, are taken into account for purposes of this determination.

(C) TET is a transparent entity as defined in § 1.1503(d)-1(b)(16) because it is not taxable as an association for Federal tax purposes, is not subject to income tax in a foreign country as a corporation (or otherwise at the entity level) either on its worldwide income or on a residence basis, and is not treated as a pass-through entity under the laws of Country X (the applicable foreign country). TET is not a pass-through entity under the laws of Country X because a Country X holder of an interest in TET does not take into account on a current basis the interest holder's share of items of income, gain, deduction, and loss of TET. For purposes of determining P's items of income, gain, deduction, and loss that are attributable to P's interest in TET, only those items of P that are reflected on the books and records of TET, as adjusted to conform to U.S. tax principles, are taken into account. § 1.1503(d)-5(c)(3)(i). Because the interest in TET is not a separate unit, a loss attributable to such interest is not a dual consolidated loss and is not subject to section 1503(d) and these regulations. Items must nevertheless be attributed to the interests in TET. For example, such attribution is required for purposes of calculating the income or dual consolidated loss attributable to the Country X separate unit, and for purposes of applying the domestic use limitation under § 1.1503(d)-4(b) to a dual consolidated loss attributable to the Country X separate unit.

(D) For purposes of determining P's items of income, gain, deduction, and loss that are attributable to P's interest in DE1X, only those items of P that are reflected on the books and records of DE1X, as adjusted to conform to U.S. tax principles, are taken into account. § 1.1503(d)-5(c)(3)(i). For this purpose, DE1X's distributive share of the items of income, gain, deduction, and loss that are reflected on the books and records of PRSZ, as adjusted to conform to U.S. tax principles, are treated as being reflected on the books and records of DE1X, except to the extent such items are taken into account by the Country X operations of PRSZ. See § 1.1503(d)-5(c)(3)(ii) and (4)(i)(B). Because TET is a transparent entity, the items reflected on its books and records are not treated as being reflected on the books and records of DE1X.

(E) Pursuant to § 1.1503(d)-5(c)(4)(ii)(B), the combined Country X separate unit of P calculates its income or dual consolidated loss by taking into account all the items of income, gain, deduction, and loss that were separately attributable to P's interest in DE1X and the Country X operations of PRSZ owned indirectly by P.

Example 27. Sale of separate unit by another separate unit. (i) *Facts.* P owns DE3Y which, in turn, owns DE1X. DE3Y also owns other assets that do not constitute a foreign branch separate unit. DE1X owns FBX. Pursuant to § 1.1503(d)-1(b)(4)(ii), P's indirect interests in DE1X and FBX are combined and treated as one Country X separate unit (Country X separate unit). DE3Y sells its interest in DE1X at the end of year 1 to an unrelated foreign person for cash. The sale results in an ordinary loss of $30x. Items of income, gain, deduction, and loss derived from the assets that gave rise to the $30x loss would be attributable to the Country X separate unit under § 1.1503(d)-5(c) through (e). Without regard to the sale of DE1X, no items of income, gain, deduction, and loss are attributable to P's Country X separate unit in year 1.

(ii) *Result.* Pursuant to § 1.1503(d)-5(c)(4)(iii)(A), the $30x ordinary loss recognized on the sale is attributable to the Country X separate unit, and not P's interest in DE3Y. This is the case because the Country X separate unit is treated as owning the assets that gave rise to the loss under § 1.1503(d)-5(f). Thus, the loss attributable to the sale creates a year 1 dual consolidated loss attributable to the Country X separate unit. In addition, pursuant to § 1.1503(d)-6(d)(2), P cannot make a domestic use election with respect to the dual consolidated loss because the sale of the interest in DE1X is a triggering event described in § 1.1503(d)-6(e)(1)(iv) and (v). Further, although the year 1 dual consolidated loss would otherwise be subject to the domestic use limitation rule of § 1.1503(d)-4(b), it is eliminated pursuant to § 1.1503(d)-4(d)(1)(ii). Finally, if there were a dual consolidated loss attributable to P's interest in DE3Y, the sale of the interest in DE1X would not be taken into account for purposes of determining whether there is an asset triggering event with respect to such dual consolidated loss under § 1.1503(d)-6(e)(1)(iv).

Example 28. Gain on sale of tiered separate units. (i) *Facts.* P owns 75 percent of HPSX, a Country X entity subject to Country X tax on its worldwide income. FSX owns the remaining 25 percent of HPSX. HPSX is classified as a partnership for Federal tax purposes. HPSX carries on operations in Country Y that, if carried on by a U.S. person, would constitute a foreign branch within the meaning of § 1.367(a)-6T(g)(1). HPSX also owns assets that do not constitute a part of its Country Y operations and would not themselves constitute a foreign branch within the meaning of § 1.367(a)-6T(g)(1) if owned by a U.S. person. Neither HPSX nor the Country Y operations has liabilities. P's indirect interest in the Country Y operations carried on by HPSX, and P's interest in HPSX, are each separate units. P sells its interest in HPSX and recognizes a gain of $150x on such sale. Immediately prior to P's sale of its interest in HPSX, P's portion of the assets of the Country Y operations (that is, assets the income, gain, deduction and loss from which would be attributable to P's Country Y foreign branch separate unit) had a built-in gain of $200x, and P's portion of HPSX's other assets (that is, assets the income, gain, deduction and loss from which would be attributable to P's interest in HPSX) had a built-in gain of $100x.

(ii) *Result*. Pursuant to §1.1503(d)-5(c)(4)(iii)(B), $100x of the total $150x of gain recognized ($200x/$300x × $150x) is attributable to P's indirect interest in its share of the Country Y operations carried on by HPSX.

Item	Year 1	Year 2
Sales Income	$100x	$160x
Salary expense	($75x)	($75x)
Research and experimental expense	($50x)	($50x)
Interest expense	($25x)	($25x)
Income/(dual consolidated loss)	($50x)	$10x

(B) P does not make a domestic use election with respect to the year 1 dual consolidated loss attributable to its Country X separate unit. Pursuant to §1.1503(d)-4(b) and (c)(2), the year 1 dual consolidated loss of $50x is treated as a loss incurred by a separate domestic corporation and is subject to the limitations under §1.1503(d)-4(c)(3). The P consolidated group has $100x of consolidated taxable income in year 2.

(ii) *Result*. (A) P must compute its taxable income for year 1 without taking into account the $50x dual consolidated loss, pursuant to §1.1503(d)-4(c)(2). Such amount consists of a pro rata portion of the expenses that were taken into account in calculating the year 1 dual consolidated loss. Thus, the items of the dual consolidated loss that are not taken into account by P in computing its taxable income are as follows: $25x of salary expense ($75x/$150x × $50x); $16.67x of research and experimental expense ($50x/$150x × $50x); and $8.33x of interest expense ($25x/$150x × $50x). The remaining amounts of each of these items, together with the $100x of sales income, are taken into account by P in computing its taxable income for year 1 as follows: $50x of salary expense ($75x − $25x); $33.33x of research and experimental expense ($50x − $16.67x); and $16.67x of interest expense ($25x − $8.33x).

(B) Subject to the limitations provided under §1.1503(d)-4(c), the year 1 $50x dual consolidated loss is carried forward and is available to offset the $10x of income attributable to the Country X separate unit in year 2. Pursuant to §1.1503(d)-4(c)(4), a pro rata portion of each item of deduction or loss included in such dual consolidated loss is considered to be used to offset the $10x of income, as follows: $5x of salary expense ($25x/$50x × $10x); $3.33x of research and experimental expense ($16.67x/$50x × $10x); and $1.67x of interest expense ($8.33x/$50x × $10x). The remaining amount of each item shall continue to be subject to the limitations under §1.1503(d)-4(c).

Similarly, $50x of such gain ($100x/$300x × $150x) is attributable to P's interest in HPSX.

Example 29. Effect on domestic affiliate. (i) *Facts.* (A) P owns DE1X which, in turn, owns FBX. P's interest in DE1X and its indirect interest in FBX are combined and treated as a single separate unit (Country X separate unit) pursuant to §1.1503(d)-1(b)(4)(ii). In years 1 and 2, the items of income, gain, deduction, and loss that are attributable to P's Country X separate unit pursuant to §1.1503(d)-5 are as follows:

Example 30. Exception to domestic use limitation—no possibility of foreign use because items are not deducted or capitalized under foreign law. (i) Facts. P owns DE1X which, in turn, owns FSX. In year 1, the sole item of income, gain, deduction, and loss attributable to P's interest in DE1X, as provided under §1.1503(d)-5, is $100x of interest expense paid on a loan to an unrelated lender. For Country X tax purposes, the $100x interest expense attributable to P's interest in DE1X in year 1 is treated as a repayment of principal and therefore cannot be deducted (at any time) or capitalized.

(ii) *Result*. The $100x of interest expense attributable to P's interest in DE1X constitutes a dual consolidated loss. However, because the sole item constituting the dual consolidated loss cannot be deducted or capitalized (at any time) for Country X tax purposes, P can demonstrate that there can be no foreign use of the dual consolidated loss at any time. As a result, pursuant to §1.1503(d)-6(c)(1), if P prepares a statement described in §1.1503(d)-6(c)(2) and attaches it to its timely filed tax return, the year 1 dual consolidated loss attributable to P's interest in DE1X will not be subject to the domestic use limitation rule of §1.1503(d)-4(b).

Example 31. No exception to domestic use limitation—inability to demonstrate no possibility of foreign use. (i) Facts. P owns DE1X which, in turn, owns FBX. P's interest in DE1X and its indirect interest in FBX are combined and treated as a single separate unit (Country X separate unit) pursuant to §1.1503(d)-1(b)(4)(ii). In year 1, the sole items of income, gain, deduction, and loss attributable to P's Country X separate unit, as provided under §1.1503(d)-5, are $75x of sales income and $100x of depreciation expense. For Country X tax purposes, DE1X also generates $75x of sales income in year 1, but the $100x of depreciation expense is not deductible until year 2.

(ii) *Result*. The year 1 $25x net loss attributable to P's interest in the Country X separate unit constitutes a dual consolidated loss. In addition, even though DE1X has positive income in year 1 for Country X tax purposes, P cannot demonstrate that there is no possibility of foreign use with respect to the Country X separate unit's dual consolidated loss as provided under §1.1503(d)-6(c)(1)(i). P cannot make such a demonstration because the depreciation expense, an item composing the year 1 dual consolidated loss, is deductible (in a later year) for Country X tax purposes and, therefore, may be available to offset or reduce income for Country X purposes that would constitute a foreign use. For example, if DE1X elected to be classified as a corporation pursuant to §301.7701-3(c) of this chapter effective as of the end of year 1, and the deferred depreciation expense were available for Country X tax purposes to offset year 2 income of DE1X, an entity treated as a foreign corporation in year 2 for U.S. tax purposes, there would be a foreign use.

(iii) *Alternative facts.* (A) The facts are the same as in paragraph (i) of this *Example 31*, except as follows. In year 1, the sole items of income, gain, deduction, and loss attributable to P's Country X separate unit, as provided in §1.1503(d)-5, are $75x of sales income, $100x of interest expense, and $25x of depreciation expense. For Country X tax purposes, DE1X generates $75x of sales income in year 1; the $100x interest expense is treated as a repayment of principal and therefore cannot be deducted or capitalized (at any time); and the $25x of depreciation expense is not deductible in year 1, but is deductible in year 2.

(B) In year 1, the $50x net loss attributable to P's Country X separate unit constitutes a dual consolidated loss. Even though the $100x interest expense, a nondeductible and noncapital item for Country X tax purposes, exceeds the $50x year 1 dual consolidated loss attributable to P's Country X separate unit, P cannot demonstrate that there is no possibility of foreign use of the dual consolidated loss as provided under §1.1503(d)-6(c)(1)(i). P cannot make such a demonstration because the $25x depreciation expense, an item of deduction or loss composing the year 1 dual consolidated loss, is deductible under Country X law (in year 2) and, therefore, may be available to offset or reduce income for Country X tax purposes that would constitute a foreign use.

Example 32. Triggering event rebuttal—expiration of losses in foreign country. (i) *Facts.* P owns DRCX, a member of the P consolidated group. In year 1, DRCX incurs a dual consolidated loss of $100x. P makes a domestic use election with respect to DRCX's year 1 dual consolidated loss and such loss therefore is included in the computation of the P group's consolidated taxable income. DRCX has no income or loss in year 2 through year 5. In year 5, P sells the stock of DRCX to FSX. At the time of the sale of the stock of DRCX, all of the losses and deductions that were included in the computation of the year 1 dual consolidated loss of DRCX had expired for

Country X tax purposes because the laws of Country X only provide for a three-year carryover period for such items.

(ii) *Result.* The sale of DRCX to FSX generally would be a triggering event under §1.1503(d)-6(e)(1)(ii), which would require DRCX to recapture the year 1 dual consolidated loss (and pay an applicable interest charge) on the P consolidated group's tax return for the year that includes the date on which DRCX ceases to be a member of the P consolidated group. However, upon adequate documentation that the losses and deductions have expired for Country X tax purposes, P can rebut the presumption that a triggering event has occurred pursuant to §1.1503(d)-6(e)(2)(i). If the triggering event presumption is rebutted, the domestic use agreement filed by the P consolidated group with respect to the year 1 dual consolidated loss of DRCX is terminated and has no further effect pursuant to §1.1503(d)-6(j)(1)(i). If the presumptive triggering event is not rebutted, the domestic use agreement would terminate and have no further effect pursuant to §1.1503(d)-6(j)(1)(iii) because the dual consolidated loss would be recaptured.

Example 33. Triggering events and rebuttals—tax basis carryover transaction. (i) *Facts.* (A) P owns DE1X. DE1X's sole asset is A, which it acquired at the beginning of year 1 for $100x. DE1X does not have any liabilities. For U.S. tax purposes, DE1X's tax basis in A at the beginning of year 1 is $100x and DE1X's sole item of income, gain, deduction, and loss for year 1 is a $20x depreciation deduction attributable to A. As a result, the $20x depreciation deduction constitutes a dual consolidated loss attributable to P's interest in DE1X. P makes a domestic use election with respect to the year 1 dual consolidated loss.

(B) For Country X tax purposes, DE1X has a $100x tax basis in A at the beginning of year 1, but A is not a depreciable asset. As a result, DE1X does not have any items of income, gain, deduction, and loss in year 1 for Country X tax purposes.

(C) During year 2, P sells its interest in DE1X to FSX for $80x. P's disposition of its interest in DE1X constitutes a presumptive triggering event under §1.1503(d)-6(e)(1)(iv) and (v) requiring the recapture of the year 1 $20x dual consolidated loss (plus the applicable interest charge). For Country X tax purposes, DE1X retains its tax basis of $100x in A following the sale.

(ii) *Result.* The year 1 dual consolidated loss is a result of the $20x depreciation deduction attributable to A. Although no item of deduction or loss was recognized by DE1X at the time of the sale for Country X tax purposes, the deduction composing the dual consolidated loss was retained by DE1X after the sale in the form of tax basis in A. As a result, a portion of the dual consolidated loss may be available to offset income for Country X tax purposes in a manner that would constitute a foreign use. For example, if DE1X were to dispose of A, the amount of gain recognized by DE1X would be reduced (or an amount of loss recognized by DE1X would be increased) and, therefore, an item composing the dual consolidated loss would be available, under U.S. tax principles, to reduce income of a foreign corporation (and an owner of an interest in a hybrid entity that is not a separate unit). Thus, P cannot demonstrate pursuant to § 1.1503(d)-6(e)(2)(i) that there can be no foreign use of the year 1 dual consolidated loss following the triggering event, and must recapture the year 1 dual consolidated loss. Pursuant to § 1.1503(d)-6(j)(1)(iii), the domestic use agreement filed by the P consolidated group with respect to the year 1 dual consolidated loss is terminated and has no further effect.

(iii) *Alternative facts.* The facts are the same as paragraph (i) of this *Example 33*, except that instead of P selling its interest in DE1X to FSX, DE1X sells asset A to FSX for $80x and, for Country X tax purposes, FSX's tax basis in A immediately after the sale is $80x. P's disposition of Asset A constitutes a presumptive triggering event under § 1.1503(d)-6(e)(1)(iv) requiring the recapture of the year 1 $20x dual consolidated loss (plus the applicable interest charge). For Country X tax purposes, FSX's tax basis in A was not determined, in whole or in part, by reference to the basis of A in the hands of DE1X. As a result, the deduction composing the dual consolidated loss will not give rise to an item of deduction or loss in the form of tax basis for Country X tax purposes (for example, when FSX disposes of A). Therefore, P may be able to demonstrate (for example, by obtaining the opinion of a Country X tax advisor) pursuant to § 1.1503(d)-6(e)(2)(i) that there can be no foreign use of the year 1 dual consolidated loss and, thus, would not be required to recapture the year 1 dual consolidated loss.

Example 34. Triggering event resulting in a single consolidated group where acquirer files a new domestic use agreement. (i) *Facts.* P owns DRCX, a member of the P consolidated group. In year 1, DRCX incurs a dual consolidated loss and P makes a domestic use election with respect to such loss. No member of the P consolidated group incurs a dual consolidated loss in year 2. At the end of year 2, T, the parent of the T consolidated group, acquires all the stock of P, and all the members of the P group, including DRCX, become members of a consolidated group of which T is the common parent.

(ii) *Result.* (A) Under § 1.1503(d)-6(f)(2)(ii)(B), the acquisition by T of the P consolidated group is not an event described in § 1.1503(d)-6(e)(1)(ii) requiring the recapture of the year 1 dual consolidated loss of DRCX (and the payment of an interest charge), provided that the T consolidated group files a new domestic use agreement described in § 1.1503(d)-6(f)(2)(iii)(A). If a new domestic use agreement is filed, then pursuant to § 1.1503(d)-6(j)(1)(ii), the domestic use agreement filed by the P consolidated group with respect to the year 1 dual consolidated loss of DRCX is terminated and has no further effect.

(B) Assume that T files a new domestic use agreement and a triggering event occurs at the end of year 3. As a result, the T consolidated group must recapture the dual consolidated loss that DRCX incurred in year 1 (and pay an interest charge), as provided in § 1.1503(d)-6(h). Each member of the T consolidated group, including DRCX and any former members of the P consolidated group, is severally liable for the additional tax (and the interest charge) due upon the recapture of the dual consolidated loss of DRCX. In addition, pursuant to § 1.1503(d)-6(j)(1)(iii), the new domestic use agreement filed by the T group with respect to the year 1 dual consolidated loss of DRCX is terminated and has no further effect.

Example 35. Triggering event exceptions for certain deemed transfers. (i) *Facts.* P owns DE1X. In year 1, there is a $100x dual consolidated loss attributable to P's interest in DE1X. P files a domestic use agreement under § 1.1503(d)-6(d) with respect to such loss. During year 2, P sells 33 percent of its interest in DE1X to T, an unrelated domestic corporation.

(ii) *Result.* Pursuant to Rev. Rul. 99-5, the transaction is treated as if P sold 33 percent of its interest in each of DE1X's assets to T and then immediately thereafter P and T transferred their interests in the assets of DE1X to a partnership in exchange for an ownership interest therein. Upon the transfer of 33 percent of P's interest to T, a domestic corporation, no foreign use occurs and, therefore, there is no foreign use triggering event. However, P's deemed transfer of 67 percent of its interest in the assets of DE1X to a partnership is nominally a triggering event under § 1.1503(d)-6(e)(1)(iv). Because the initial transfer of 33 percent of DE1X's interest was to a domestic corporation and there is only a triggering event because of the deemed transfer under Rev. Rul. 99-5, the deemed asset transfer is not treated as resulting in a triggering event pursuant to § 1.1503(d)-6(f)(4).

(iii) *Alternative facts.* The facts are the same as in paragraph (i) of this *Example 35*, except that P sells 60 percent (rather than 33 percent) of its interest in DE1X to T. The sale is a triggering event under § 1.1503(d)-6(e)(1)(iv) and (v) without regard to the occurrence of a deemed transaction. Therefore, § 1.1503(d)-6(f)(4) does not apply.

Example 36. Triggering event exception involving multiple parties. (i) *Facts.* P owns DE1X which, in turn, owns FBX. P's interest in DE1X and its indirect interest in FBX are combined and treated as a single separate unit (Country X separate unit) pursuant to § 1.1503(d)-1(b)(4)(ii). In year 1, there is a $100x dual consolidated loss attributable to P's Country X separate unit and P makes a domestic use election with respect to such loss. No member of the P consolidated group incurs a dual consolidated loss in year 2. At the end of year 2, T, the parent of the T consolidated group, acquires all of P's interest in DE1X for cash.

(ii) *Result.* (A) Under § 1.1503(d)-6(f)(2)(i)(B), the acquisition by T of the interest in DE1X is not an event described in § 1.1503(d)-6(e)(1)(iv) or (v) requiring the recapture of the year 1 dual consolidated loss attributable to the Country X separate unit (and the payment of an interest charge), provided: (1) the T consolidated group files a new domestic use agreement described in § 1.1503(d)-6(f)(2)(iii)(A) with respect to the year 1 dual consolidated loss of the Country X separate unit; and (2) the P consolidated group files a statement described in § 1.1503(d)-6(f)(2)(iii)(B) with respect to the year 1 dual consolidated loss. If these requirements are satisfied, then pursuant to § 1.1503(d)-6(j)(1)(ii) the domestic use agreement filed by the P consolidated group with respect to the year 1 dual consolidated loss is terminated and has no further effect (if these requirements are not satisfied such that the P consolidated group recaptures the dual consolidated loss, the domestic use agreement would terminate pursuant to § 1.1503(d)-6(j)(1)(iii)).

(B) Assume a triggering event occurs at the end of year 3 that requires recapture by the T consolidated group of the year 1 dual consolidated loss, as well as the payment of an interest charge, as provided in § 1.1503(d)-6(h). T continues to own the Country X separate unit after the triggering event. In that case, each member of the T consolidated group is severally liable for the additional tax (and the interest charge) due upon the recapture of the year 1 dual consolidated loss. The T consolidated group must prepare a statement that computes the recapture tax amount as provided under § 1.1503(d)-6(h)(3)(iii). Pursuant to § 1.1503(d)-6(h)(3)(iv)(A), the recapture tax amount is assessed as an income tax liability of the T consolidated group and is considered as having been properly assessed as an income tax liability of the P consolidated group. If the T consolidated group does not pay in full the income tax liability attributable to the recapture tax amount, the unpaid balance of such recapture tax amount may be collected from the P consolidated group in accordance with the provisions of § 1.1503(d)-6(h)(3)(iv)(B). Pursuant to § 1.1503(d)-6(j)(1)(iii), the new domestic use agreement filed by the T consolidated group is terminated and has no further effect. Finally, pursuant to § 1.1503(d)-6(h)(6)(iii), T is treated as if it incurred the dual consolidated loss that is recaptured for purposes of applying

Sales Income	. . . .	$100x
Salary Expense	. . . .	($75x)
Interest expense	. . . .	($50x)
Dual consolidated loss	. . . .	($25x)

(B) P makes a domestic use election with respect to the year 1 dual consolidated loss attributable to FBX and, thus, the $25x dual

§ 1.1503(d)-6(h)(6)(i). Thus, T has a reconstituted net operating loss equal to the amount of the year 1 dual consolidated loss that was recaptured, and such loss is attributable to the Country X separate unit (and subject to the rules and limitations under § 1.1503(d)-6(h)(6)(i)). Because T is treated as if it incurred the year 1 dual consolidated loss, P shall not be treated as having a net operating loss under § 1.1503(d)-6(h)(6)(i).

Example 37. No foreign use following multiple-party event exception to triggering event. (i) *Facts.* P owns DE1X which, in turn, owns FBX. P's interest in DE1X and its indirect interest in FBX are combined and treated as a single separate unit (Country X separate unit) pursuant to § 1.1503(d)-1(b)(4)(ii). In year 1, there is a $100x dual consolidated loss attributable to P's Country X separate unit and P makes a domestic use election with respect to such loss. T, a domestic corporation unrelated to P, owns 95 percent of PRS, a partnership. FSX owns the remaining 5 percent of PRS. At the beginning of year 3, PRS purchases 100 percent of the interest in DE1X from P for cash. For Country X tax purposes, the $100x loss incurred by DE1X in year 1 carries forward and is available to offset income of DE1X in subsequent years.

(ii) *Result.* P's sale of its interest in DE1X is a triggering event under § 1.1503(d)-6(e)(1)(iv) and (v). However, if P and T comply with the requirements under § 1.1503(d)-6(f)(2)(iii), the sale would qualify for the multiple-party exception under § 1.1503(d)-6(f)(2)(i). In addition, because the $100x loss of DE1X carries forward to subsequent years for Country X purposes and is available to offset income of DE1X, there would be a foreign use of the dual consolidated loss immediately after the sale pursuant to § 1.1503(d)-3(a)(1). This is the case because the dual consolidated loss would be available to offset or reduce income that is considered, under U.S. tax principles, to be an item of FSX, a foreign corporation (it would also be a foreign use because FSX is an indirect owner of an interest in a hybrid entity that is not a separate unit). However, there is no foreign use in this case as a result of FSX's 5 percent interest in DE1X pursuant to § 1.1503(d)-3(c)(8).

Example 38. Character and source of recapture income. (i) *Facts.* (A) P owns FBX. In year 1, the items of income, gain, deduction, and loss that are attributable to FBX for purposes of determining whether it has a dual consolidated loss are as follows:

consolidated loss is used to offset the P group's consolidated taxable income.

(C) Pursuant to §1.861-8, the $75x of salary expense incurred by FBX is allocated and apportioned entirely to foreign source general limitation income. Pursuant to §1.861-9T, $25x of the $50x interest expense attributable to FBX is allocated and apportioned to domestic source income, $15x of such interest expense is allocated and apportioned to foreign source general limitation income, and the remaining $10x of such interest expense is allocated and apportioned to foreign source passive income.

(D) During year 2, $5x of income is attributable to FBX under the rules of §1.1503(d)-5, and the P consolidated group has $100x of consolidated taxable income. At the end of year 2, FBX undergoes a triggering event described in §1.1503(d)-6(e)(1), and P continues to own FBX following the triggering event. Pursuant to §1.1503(d)-6(h)(2)(i), P is able to demonstrate to the satisfaction of the Commissioner that the $25x dual consolidated loss attributable to FBX in year 1 would have offset the $5x of income attributable to FBX in year 2, if no domestic use election were made with respect to the year 1 loss such that it was subject to the limitations of §1.1503(d)-4(b) and (c).

(ii) *Result.* P must recapture and report as ordinary income $20x ($25x - $5x) of FBX's year 1 dual consolidated loss, plus applicable interest. The $20x recapture income is attributable to FBX pursuant to §1.1503(d)-5(c)(4)(vi). Pursuant to §1.1503(d)-6(h)(5), the recapture income is treated as ordinary income whose source and character (including section 904 separate limitation character) is determined by reference to the manner in which the recaptured items of expense or loss taken into account in calculating the dual consolidated loss were allocated and apportioned. Further, pursuant to §1.1503(d)-6(h)(5), the pro rata computation described in §1.1503(d)-4(c)(4) shall apply. Thus, the character and source of the recapture income is determined in the same proportion as each item of deduction or loss that contributed to the dual consolidated loss being recaptured. Accordingly, P's $20x of recapture income is characterized and sourced as follows: $4x of domestic source income (($25x/$125x) x $20x); $14.4x of foreign source general limitation income (($75x + $15x)/$125x) x $20x); and $1.6x of foreign source passive income (($10x/$125x) x $20x). Pursuant to §1.1503(d)-6(h)(6)(i), commencing in year 3, the $20x recapture amount is reconstituted and treated as a net operating loss incurred by FBX in a separate return limitation year, subject to the limitation under §1.1503(d)-4(b) (and therefore subject to the restrictions of §1.1503(d)-4(c)). Pursuant to §1.1503(d)-6(j)(1)(iii), the domestic use agreement filed by the P consolidated group with respect to the year 1 dual consolidated loss of FBX is terminated and has no further effect.

Example 39. Interest charge without recapture. (i) *Facts.* P owns DE1X which, in turn, owns FBX. P's interest in DE1X and its indirect interest in FBX are combined and treated as a single separate unit (Country X separate unit) pursuant to §1.1503(d)-1(b)(4)(ii). In year 1, a dual consolidated loss of $100x is attributable to P's Country X separate unit. P makes a domestic use election with respect to such loss and uses the loss to offset the P group's consolidated taxable income. In year 2, there is $100x of income attributable to P's Country X separate unit and the P consolidated group has $200x of consolidated taxable income. At the end of year 2, the Country X separate unit undergoes a triggering event within the meaning of §1.1503(d)-6(e)(1). P demonstrates, to the satisfaction of the Commissioner, that if no domestic use election were made with respect to the year 1 dual consolidated loss such that it was subject to the limitations of §1.1503(d)-4(b) and (c), the year 1 $100x dual consolidated loss would have been offset by the $100x of year 2 income.

(ii) *Result.* There is no recapture of the year 1 dual consolidated loss attributable to P's Country X separate unit because it is reduced to zero under §1.1503(d)-6(h)(2)(i). However, P is liable for one year of interest charge under §1.1503(d)-6(h)(1)(ii), even though P's recapture amount is zero. This is the case because the P consolidated group had the benefit of the dual consolidated loss in year 1, and the income that offset the recapture income was not recognized until year 2. Pursuant to §1.1503(d)-6(j)(1)(iii), the domestic use agreement filed by the P consolidated group with respect to the year 1 dual consolidated loss is terminated and has no further effect.

Example 40. Reduced recapture and interest charge, and reconstituted dual consolidated loss. (i) *Facts.* S owns DE1X which, in turn, owns FBX. S's interest in DE1X and its indirect interest in FBX are combined and treated as a single separate unit (Country X separate unit) pursuant to §1.1503(d)-1(b)(4)(ii). In year 1, there is a $100x dual consolidated loss attributable to S's Country X separate unit, and P earns $100x. P makes a domestic use election with respect to the Country X separate unit's year 1 dual consolidated loss. Therefore, the consolidated group is permitted to offset P's $100x of income with the Country X separate unit's $100x dual consolidated loss. In year 2, $30x of income is attributable to the Country X separate unit under the rules of §1.1503(d)-5 and such income is offset by a $30x net operating loss incurred by P in such year. In year 3, $25x of income is attributable to the Country X separate unit under the rules of §1.1503(d)-5, and P earns $15x of income. In addition, at the end of year 3 there is a foreign use of the year 1 dual consolidated loss that constitutes a triggering event. S continues to own the Country X separate unit after the triggering event.

(ii) *Result.* (A) Under the presumptive rule of §1.1503(d)-6(h)(1)(i), S must recapture $100x (plus applicable interest). However, under

§ 1.1503(d)-6(h)(2)(i), S may be able to demonstrate that a lesser amount is subject to recapture. The lesser amount is the amount of the $100x dual consolidated loss that would have remained subject to § 1.1503(d)-4(c) at the time of the foreign use triggering event if a domestic use election had not been made for such loss.

(B) Although the combined separate unit earned $30x of income in year 2, there was no consolidated taxable income in such year. As a result, as of the end of year 2 the $100x dual consolidated loss would continue to be subject to § 1.1503(d)-4(c) if a domestic use election had not been made for such loss. However, the $30x earned in year 2 can be carried forward to subsequent taxable years and may reduce the recapture income to the extent of consolidated taxable income generated in subsequent years. In year 3, $25x of income was attributable to the Country X separate unit and P earns $15x of income. Thus, the P consolidated group has $40x of consolidated taxable income in year 3. As a result, the $100x of recapture income can be reduced by $40x. This is the case because if a domestic use election had not been made for the $100x year 1 dual consolidated loss such that it was subject to the limitations of § 1.1503(d)-4(b) and (c), only $60x of the loss would have remained subject to such limitations at the time of the foreign use triggering event. Accordingly, if S can adequately document the lesser amount, the amount of recapture income is $60x ($100x - $40x). The $60x recapture income is attributable to the Country X separate unit pursuant to § 1.1503(d)-5(c)(4)(vi).

(C) Pursuant to § 1.1503(d)-6(h)(6)(i), commencing in year 4, the $60x recapture amount is reconstituted and treated as a net operating loss incurred by the Country X separate unit of S in a separate return limitation year, subject to the limitation under § 1.1503(d)-4(b) (and therefore subject to the restrictions of § 1.1503(d)-4(c)). The loss is only available for carryover to taxable years after year 3 (and is not available for carryback). The carryover period of the loss, for purposes of section 172(b), will start from year 1, when the dual consolidated loss that was subject to recapture was incurred. In addition, such reconstituted net operating loss is not eligible for the exceptions contained in § 1.1503(d)-6(b) through (d). Pursuant to § 1.1503(d)-6(j)(1)(iii), the domestic use agreement filed by the P consolidated group with respect to the year 1 dual consolidated loss of the Country X separate unit is terminated and has no further effect.

(iii) *Alternative facts.* The facts are the same as in paragraph (i) of this *Example 40*, except that the triggering event that occurs at the end of year 3 is a sale by S of its entire interest in DE1X to B, an unrelated domestic corporation. The sale does not qualify as a transaction described in section 381. The results are the same as in paragraph (ii) of this *Example 40*, except that pursuant to § 1.1503(d)-6(h)(6)(ii) the $60x net operating

loss is not reconstituted (with respect to either S or B). The loss is not reconstituted with respect to S because the Country X separate unit ceases to be a separate unit of S (or any other member of the consolidated group that includes S) and therefore would have been eliminated pursuant to § 1.1503(d)-4(d)(1)(ii) if no domestic use election had been made with respect to such loss. The loss is not reconstituted with respect to B because B was not the domestic owner of the combined separate unit when the dual consolidated loss that is recaptured was incurred, and B did not acquire the Country X separate unit in a section 381 transaction. [Reg. § 1.1503(d)-7.]

☐ [*T.D.* 9315, 3-16-2007 (*corrected* 4-24-2007).]

[Reg. § 1.1503(d)-8]

§ 1.1503(d)-8. Effective dates.—(a) *General rule.*—Except as provided in paragraph (b) of this section, this paragraph (a) provides the dates of applicability of §§ 1.1503(d)-1 through 1.1503(d)-7. Sections 1.1503(d)-1 through 1.1503(d)-7 shall apply to dual consolidated losses incurred in taxable years beginning on or after April 18, 2007. However, a taxpayer may apply §§ 1.1503(d)-1 through 1.1503(d)-7, in their entirety, to dual consolidated losses incurred in taxable years beginning on or after January 1, 2007, by filing its return and attaching to such return the domestic use agreements, certifications, or other information in accordance with these regulations. For purposes of this section, the term application date means either April 18, 2007, or, if the taxpayer applies these regulations pursuant to the preceding sentence, January 1, 2007. Section 1.1503-2 applies for dual consolidated losses incurred in taxable years beginning on or after October 1, 1992, and before the application date.

(b) *Special rules.*—(1) *Reduction of term of agreements filed under* §§ *1.1503-2A(c)(3), 1.1503-2A(d)(3), 1.1503-2(g)(2)(i),* or *1.1503-2T(g)(i).*—If an agreement is filed in accordance with §§ 1.1503-2A(c)(3), 1.1503-2A(d)(3), 1.1503-2(g)(2)(i), or 1.1503-2T(g)(2)(i) with respect to a dual consolidated loss incurred in a taxable year beginning prior to the application date and an event requiring recapture with respect to the dual consolidated loss subject to the agreement has not occurred as of the application date, then such agreement will be considered by the Internal Revenue Service to apply only for any taxable year up to and including the fifth taxable year following the year in which the dual consolidated loss that is the subject of the agreement was incurred and thereafter will have no effect.

(2) *Reduction of term of agreements filed under* §§ *1.1503-2(g)(2)(iv)(B)(2)(i)* (1992), *1.1503-2(g)(2)(iv)(B)(3)(i), or Rev. Proc. 2000-42.*—Taxpayers subject to the terms of a closing agreement entered into with the Internal Revenue Ser-

vice pursuant to §§1.1503-2(g)(2)(iv)(B)(2)(*i*) (1992), 1.1503-2(g)(2)(iv)(B)(3)(*i*), or Rev. Proc. 2000-42 (2000-2 CB 394), see §601.601(d)(2)(ii)(*b*) of this chapter, will be deemed to have satisfied the closing agreement's fifteen-year certification period requirement if the five-year certification period specified in §1.1503(d)-1(b)(20) has elapsed, provided such closing agreement is still in effect as of the application date, and provided the dual consolidated losses have not been recaptured. For example, if a calendar year taxpayer that has a January 1, 2007, application date entered into a closing agreement with respect to a dual consolidated loss incurred in 2003 and, as of January 1, 2007, the closing agreement is still in effect and the dual consolidated loss subject to the closing agreement has not been recaptured, then the closing agreement's fifteen-year certification period will be deemed satisfied when the five-year certification period described in §1.1503(d)-1(b)(20) has elapsed. Thus, the dual consolidated loss will be subject to the recapture and certification provisions of the closing agreement in such a case only through December 31, 2008. Alternatively, if a calendar year taxpayer that has a January 1, 2007, application date entered into a closing agreement with respect to a dual consolidated loss incurred in 2000 and, as of January 1, 2007, the closing agreement is still in effect and the dual consolidated loss subject to the closing agreement has not been recaptured, then the certification period is deemed to be satisfied.

(3) Relief for untimely filings.— Paragraphs (b)(3)(i) through (iii) of this section set forth the effective dates for rules that provide relief for the failure to make timely filings of an election, agreement, statement, rebuttal, computation, closing agreement, or other information, pursuant to section 1503(d) and these regulations.

(i) *General rule.*—Except as provided in paragraphs (b)(3)(ii) and (iii) of this section, the reasonable cause relief standard of §1.1503(d)-1(c) applies for all untimely filings with respect to dual consolidated losses, including with respect to dual consolidated losses incurred in taxable years beginning before the application date.

(ii) *Closing agreements.*—Solely with respect to closing agreements described in §1.1503-2(g)(2)(iv)(B)(3)(i) and Rev. Proc. 2000-42, taxpayers must request relief for untimely requests through the process provided under §§301.9100-1 through 301.9100-3 of this chapter. See paragraph (b)(4) of this section for rules that permit the multiple-party event exception, rather than closing agreements, for certain triggering events.

(iii) *Pending requests for relief.*—Taxpayers that have letter ruling requests under §§301.9100-1 through 301.9100-3 of this chapter pending as of March 19, 2007 (other than requests under paragraph (b)(3)(ii) of this section) are not required to use the reasonable cause procedure under §1.1503(d)-1(c); however, if such taxpayers have not yet received a determination of their request, they may withdraw their request consistent with the procedures contained in Rev. Proc. 2007-1 (2007-1 IRB 1), see §601.601(d)(2)(ii)(b) of this chapter, (or any succeeding document) and use the reasonable cause procedure set forth in §1.1503(d)-1(c). In that event, the Internal Revenue Service will refund the taxpayer's user fee.

(4) *Multiple-party event exception to triggering events.*—This paragraph (b)(4) applies to events described in §1.1503-2(g)(2)(iv)(B)(1)(i) through (iii) that occur after April 18, 2007 and that are with respect to dual consolidated losses that were incurred in taxable years beginning on or after October 1, 1992, and before the application date. The events described in the previous sentence are not eligible for the exception described in §1.1503-2(g)(2)(iv)(B)(1), but instead are eligible for the multiple-party event exception described in §1.1503(d)-6(f)(2)(i), as modified by this paragraph (b)(4). Thus, such events are not eligible for a closing agreement described in §1.1503-2(g)(2)(iv)(B)(3)(i) and Rev. Proc. 2000-42. For purposes of applying §1.1503(d)-6(f)(2)(i) to transactions covered by this paragraph, agreements described in §1.1503-2(g)(2)(i) (rather than domestic use agreements) shall be filed, and subsequent triggering events and exceptions thereto have the meaning provided in §1.1503-2(g)(2)(iii)(A) and (iv) (other than the exception provided under §1.1503-2(g)(2)(iv)(B)(1)). For example, if a calendar year taxpayer that has a January 1, 2007, application date filed an election under §1.1503-2(g)(2)(i) with respect to a dual consolidated loss that was incurred in 2004, and a triggering event described in §1.1503-2(g)(2)(iv)(B)(1)(ii) occurs with respect to such dual consolidated loss after April 18, 2007, then the event is eligible for the multiple-party event exception under §1.1503(d)-6(f)(2)(i) (and not the exception under §1.1503-2(g)(2)(iv)(B)(1)). However, in order to comply with §1.1503(d)-6(f)(2)(iii)(A), the subsequent elector must file a new agreement described in §1.1503-2(g)(2)(i) (rather than a new domestic use agreement). In addition, for purposes of determining whether there is a subsequent triggering event, and exceptions thereto, pursuant to such new agreement, §1.1503-2(g)(2)(iii)(A) and (iv) (other than the exception provided under §1.1503-2(g)(2)(iv)(B)(1)) shall apply. Notwithstanding the general application of this paragraph (b)(4) to events described in §1.1503-2(g)(2)(iv)(B)(1)(i) through (iii) that occur after April 18, 2007, a taxpayer may choose to apply this paragraph (b)(4) to events described in §1.1503-2(g)(2)(iv)(B)(1)(i) through (iii)

that occur after March 19, 2007 and on or before April 18, 2007.

(5) *Basis adjustment rules.*—Taxpayers may apply the basis adjustment rules of §1.1503(d)-5(g) for all open years in which such basis is relevant, even if the basis adjustment is attributable to a dual consolidated loss incurred (or recaptured) in a closed taxable year. Taxpayers applying the provisions of §1.1503(d)-5(g), however, must do so consistently for all open years. [Reg. §1.1503(d)-8.]

☐ [*T.D.* 9315, 3-16-2007 (*corrected* 4-24-2007).]

[Reg. §1.1504-0]

§1.1504-0. Outline of provisions.—In order to facilitate the use of §§1.1504-1 through 1.1504-4, this section lists the captions contained in §§1.1504-1 through 1.1504-4.

§1.1504-1. Definitions.

§1.1504-2. [Reserved].

§1.1504-3. [Reserved].

§1.1504-4. Treatment of warrants, options, convertible obligations, and other similar interests.—
  (a) Introduction.
    (1) General rule.
    (2) Exceptions.
  (b) Options not treated as stock or as exercised.
    (1) General rule.
    (2) Options treated as exercised.
      (i) In general.
      (ii) Aggregation of options.
      (iii) Effect of treating option as exercised.
        (A) In general.
        (B) Cash settlement options, phantom stock, stock appreciation rights, or similar interests.
      (iv) Valuation.
    (3) Example.
  (c) Definitions.
    (1) Issuing corporation.
    (2) Related or sequential option.
    (3) Related persons.
    (4) Measurement date.
      (i) General rule.
      (ii) Issuances, transfers, or adjustments not treated as measurement dates.
      (iii) Transactions increasing likelihood of exercise.
      (iv) Measurement date for options issued pursuant to a plan.
      (v) Measurement date for related or sequential options.
      (vi) Example.
    (5) In-the-money.
  (d) Options.
    (1) Instruments treated as options.

    (2) Instruments generally not treated as options.
      (i) Options on section 1504(a)(4) stock.
      (ii) Certain publicly traded options.
        (A) General rule.
        (B) Exception.
      (iii) Stock purchase agreements.
      (iv) Escrow, pledge, or other security agreements.
      (v) Compensatory options.
        (A) General rule.
        (B) Exceptions.
      (vi) Options granted in connection with a loan.
      (vii) Options created pursuant to a title 11 or similar case.
      (viii) Convertible preferred stock.
      (ix) Other enumerated instruments.
  (e) Elimination of federal income tax liability.
  (f) Substantial amount of federal income tax liability.
  (g) Reasonable certainty of exercise.
    (1) Generally.
      (i) Purchase price.
      (ii) In-the-money option.
      (iii) Not in-the-money option.
      (iv) Exercise price.
      (v) Time of exercise.
      (vi) Related or sequential options.
      (vii) Stockholder rights.
      (viii) Restrictive covenants.
      (ix) Intention to alter value.
      (x) Contingencies.
    (2) Cash settlement options, phantom stock, stock appreciation rights, or similar interests.
    (3) Safe harbors.
      (i) Options to acquire stock.
      (ii) Options to sell stock.
      (iii) Options exercisable at fair market value.
      (iv) Exceptions.
      (v) Failure to satisfy safe harbor.
  (h) Examples.
  (i) Effective date.
[Reg. §1.1504-0.]

☐ [*T.D.* 8462, 12-28-92.]

[Reg. §1.1504-1]

§1.1504-1. Definitions.—The privilege of filing consolidated returns is extended to all includible corporations constituting affiliated groups as defined in section 1504. See the regulations under §1.1502 for a description of an affiliated group and the corporations which may be considered as includible corporations. [Reg. §1.1504-1.]

☐ [*T.D.* 6140, 8-29-55.]

[Reg. §1.1504-2]

§1.1504-2. [Reserved].

[Reg. §1.1504-3]

§1.1504-3. [Reserved].

[Reg. §1.1504-4]

§1.1504-4. Treatment of warrants, options, convertible obligations, and other similar interests.—(a) *Introduction.*—(1) *General rule.*—This section provides regulations under section 1504(a)(5)(A) and (B) regarding the circumstances in which warrants, options, obligations convertible into stock, and other similar interests are treated as exercised for purposes of determining whether a corporation is a member of an affiliated group. The fact that an instrument may be treated as an option under these regulations does not prevent such instrument from being treated as stock under general principles of law. Except as provided in paragraph (a)(2) of this section, this section applies to all provisions under the Internal Revenue Code and the regulations to which affiliation within the meaning of section 1504(a) (with or without the exceptions in section 1504(b)) is relevant, including those provisions that refer to section 1504(a)(2) (with or without the exceptions in section 1504(b)) without referring to affiliation, provided that the 80 percent voting power and 80 percent value requirements of section 1504(a)(2) are not modified therein.

(2) *Exceptions.*—This section does not apply to sections 163(j), 864(e), or 904(i) or to the regulations thereunder. This section also does not apply to any other provision specified by the Internal Revenue Service in regulations, a revenue ruling, or revenue procedure. See § 601.601(d)(2)(ii)(b) of this chapter.

(b) *Options not treated as stock or as exercised.*—(1) *General rule.*—Except as provided in paragraph (b)(2) of this section, an option is not considered either as stock or as exercised. Thus, options are disregarded in determining whether a corporation is a member of an affiliated group unless they are described in paragraph (b)(2) of this section.

(2) *Options treated as exercised.*—(i) *In general.*—Solely for purposes of determining whether a corporation is a member of an affiliated group, an option is treated as exercised if, on a measurement date with respect to such option—

(A) It could reasonably be anticipated that, if not for this section, the issuance or transfer of the option in lieu of the issuance, redemption, or transfer of the underlying stock would result in the elimination of a substantial amount of federal income tax liability (as described in paragraphs (e) and (f) of this section); and

(B) It is reasonably certain that the option will be exercised (as described in paragraph (g) of this section).

(ii) *Aggregation of options.*—All options with the same measurement date are aggregated in determining whether the issuance or transfer of an option in lieu of the issuance, redemption, or transfer of the underlying stock would result in the elimination of a substantial amount of federal income tax liability.

(iii) *Effect of treating option as exercised.*—(A) *In general.*—An option that is treated as exercised is treated as exercised for purposes of determining the percentage of the value of stock owned by the holder and other parties, but is not treated as exercised for purposes of determining the percentage of the voting power of stock owned by the holder and other parties.

(B) *Cash settlement options, phantom stock, stock appreciation rights, or similar interests.*—If a cash settlement option, phantom stock, stock appreciation right, or similar interest is treated as exercised, the option is treated as having been converted into stock of the issuing corporation. If the amount to be received upon the exercise of such an option is determined by reference to a multiple of the increase in the value of a share of the issuing corporation's stock on the exercise date over the value of a share of the stock on the date the option is issued, the option is treated as converted into a corresponding number of shares of such stock. Appropriate adjustments must be made in any situation in which the amount to be received upon exercise of the option is determined in another manner.

(iv) *Valuation.*—For purposes of section 1504(a)(2)(B) and this section, all shares of stock within a single class are considered to have the same value. Thus, control premiums and minority and blockage discounts within a single class are not taken into account.

(3) *Example.*—The provisions of paragraph (b)(2) of this section may be illustrated by the following example:

Example. (i) Corporation P owns all 100 shares of the common stock of Corporation S, the only class of S stock outstanding. Each share of S stock has a fair market value of $10 and has one vote. On June 30, 1992, P issues to Corporation X an option to acquire 80 shares of the S stock from P.

(ii) If, under the provisions of this section, the option is treated as exercised, then, solely for purposes of determining affiliation, P is treated as owning only 20 percent of the value of the outstanding S stock and X is treated as owing the remaining 80 percent of the value of the S stock. P is still treated as owning all of the voting power of S. Accordingly, because P is treated as owning less than 80 percent of the value of the outstanding S stock, P and S are no longer affiliated. However, because X is not treated as owning any of the voting power of S, X and S are also not affiliated.

(c) *Definitions.*—For purposes of this section—

(1) *Issuing corporation.*—"Issuing corporation" means the corporation whose stock is subject to an option.

(2) *Related or sequential option.*—"Related or sequential option" means an option that is one of a series of options issued to the same or related persons. For purposes of this section, any options issued to the same person or related persons within a two year period are presumed to be part of a series of options. This presumption may be rebutted if the facts and circumstances clearly establish that the options are not part of a series of options. Any options issued to the same person or related persons more than two years apart are presumed not to be part of a series of options. This presumption may be rebutted if the facts and circumstances clearly establish that the options are part of a series of options.

(3) *Related persons.*—Persons are related if they are related within the meaning of section 267(b) (without the application of sections 267(c) and 1563(e)(1)) or 707(b)(1), substituting "10 percent" for "50 percent" wherever it appears.

(4) *Measurement date.*—(i) *General rule.*—"Measurement date" means a date on which an option is issued or transferred or on which the terms of an existing option or the underlying stock are adjusted (including an adjustment pursuant to the terms of the option or the underlying stock).

(ii) *Issuances, transfers, or adjustments not treated as measurement dates.*—A measurement date does not include a date on which—

(A) An option is issued or transferred by gift, at death, or between spouses or former spouses under section 1041;

(B) An option is issued or transferred—

(1) Between members of an affiliated group (determined with the exceptions in section 1504(b) and without the application of this section); or

(2) Between persons none of which is a member of the affiliated group (determined without the exceptions in section 1504(b) and without the application of this section), if any, of which the issuing corporation is a member, unless—

(i) Any such person is related to (or acting in concert with) the issuing corporation or any member of its affiliated group; and

(ii) The issuance or transfer is pursuant to a plan a principal purpose of which is to avoid the application of section 1504 and this section;

(C) An adjustment occurs in the terms or pursuant to the terms of an option or the underlying stock that does not materially increase the likelihood that the option will be exercised; or

(D) A change occurs in the exercise price of an option or in the number of shares that may be issued or transferred pursuant to the option as determined by a bona fide, reasonable, adjustment formula that has the effect of preventing dilution of the interests of the holders of the options.

(iii) *Transactions increasing likelihood of exercise.*—If a change or alteration referred to in this paragraph (c)(4)(iii) is made for a principal purpose of increasing the likelihood that an option will be exercised, a measurement date also includes any date on which—

(A) The capital structure of the issuing corporation is changed; or

(B) The fair market value of the stock of the issuing corporation is altered through a transfer of assets to or from the issuing corporation (other than regular, ordinary dividends) or by any other means.

(iv) *Measurement date for options issued pursuant to a plan.*—In the case of options issued pursuant to a plan, a measurement date for any of the options constitutes a measurement date for all options issued pursuant to the plan that are outstanding on the measurement date.

(v) *Measurement date for related or sequential options.*—In the case of related or sequential options, a measurement date for any of the options constitutes a measurement date for all related or sequential options that are outstanding on the measurement date.

(vi) *Example.*—The provisions of paragraph (c)(4)(v) of this section may be illustrated by the following example.

Example. (i) Corporation P owns all 80 shares of the common stock of Corporation S, the only class of S stock outstanding. On January 1, 1992, S issues a warrant, exercisable within 3 years, to U, an unrelated corporation, to acquire 10 newly issued shares of S common stock. On July 1, 1992, S issues a second warrant to U to acquire 10 additional newly issued shares of S common stock. On January 1, 1993, S issues a third warrant to T, a wholly owned subsidiary of U, to acquire 10 newly issued shares of S common stock. Assume that the facts and circumstances do not clearly establish that the options are not part of a series of options.

(ii) January 1, 1992, July 1, 1992, and January 1, 1993, constitute measurement dates for the first warrant, the second warrant, and the third warrant, respectively, because the warrants were issued on those dates.

(iii) Because the first and second warrants were issued within two years of each other, and

Reg. §1.1504-4(c)(4)(vi)

both warrants were issued to U, the warrants constitute related or sequential options. Accordingly, July 1, 1992, constitutes a measurement date for the first warrant as well as for the second warrant.

(iv) Because the first, second, and third warrants were all issued within two years of each other, and were all issued to the same or related persons, the warrants constitute related or sequential options. Accordingly, January 1, 1993, constitutes a measurement date for the first and second warrants, as well as for the third warrant.

(5) *In-the-money.*—"In-the-money" means the exercise price of the option is less than (or in the case of an option to sell stock, greater than) the fair market value of the underlying stock.

(d) *Options.*—(1) *Instruments treated as options.*—For purposes of this section, except to the extent otherwise provided in this paragraph (d), the following are treated as options:

(i) A call option, warrant, convertible obligation, put option, redemption agreement (including a right to cause the redemption of stock), or any other instrument that provides for the right to issue, redeem, or transfer stock (including an option on an option); and

(ii) A cash settlement option, phantom stock, stock appreciation right, or any other similar interest (except for stock).

(2) *Instruments generally not treated as options.*—For purposes of this section, the following will not be treated as options:

(i) *Options on section 1504(a)(4) stock.*—Options on stock described in section 1504(a)(4);

(ii) *Certain publicly traded options.*—(A) *General rule.*—Options which on the measurement date are traded on (or subject to the rules of) a qualified board or exchange as defined in section 1256(g)(7), or on any other exchange, board of trade, or market specified by the Internal Revenue Service in regulations, a revenue ruling, or revenue procedure. See § 601.601(d)(2)(ii)(*b*) of this chapter;

(B) *Exception.*—Paragraph (d)(2)(ii)(A) of this section does not apply to options issued, transferred, or listed with a principal purpose of avoiding the application of section 1504 and this section. For example, a principal purpose of avoiding the application of section 1504 and this section may exist if warrants, convertible or exchangeable debt instruments, or other similar instruments have an exercise price (or, in the case of convertible or exchangeable instruments, a conversion or exchange premium) that is materially less than, or a term that is materially longer than, those that are customary for publicly traded instruments of their type. A principal purpose may also exist if a large percentage

of an issuance of an instrument is placed with one investor (or group of investors) and a very small percentage of the issuance is traded on a qualified board or exchange;

(iii) *Stock purchase agreements.*—Stock purchase agreements or similar arrangements whose terms are commercially reasonable and in which the parties' obligations to complete the transaction are subject only to reasonable closing conditions;

(iv) *Escrow, pledge, or other security agreements.*—Agreements for holding stock in escrow or under a pledge or other security agreement that are part of a typical commercial transaction and that are subject to customary commercial conditions;

(v) *Compensatory options.*—(A) *General rule.*—Stock appreciation rights, warrants, stock options, phantom stock, or other similar instruments provided to employees, directors, or independent contractors in connection with the performance of services for the corporation or a related corporation (and that is not excessive by reference to the services performed) and which—

(1) Are nontransferable within the meaning of § 1.83-3(d); and

(2) Do not have a readily ascertainable fair market value as defined in § 1.83-7(b) on the measurement date;

(B) *Exceptions.*—(1) Paragraph (d)(2)(v)(A) of this section does not apply to options issued or transferred with a principal purpose of avoiding the application of section 1504 and this section; and

(2) Paragraph (d)(2)(v)(A) of this section ceases to apply to options that become transferable;

(vi) *Options granted in connection with a loan.*—Options granted in connection with a loan if the lender is actively and regularly engaged in the business of lending and the options are issued in connection with a loan to the issuing corporation that is commercially reasonable. This paragraph (d)(2)(vi) continues to apply if the option is transferred with the loan (or if a portion of the option is transferred with a corresponding portion of the loan). However, if the option is transferred without a corresponding portion of the loan, this paragraph (d)(2)(vi) ceases to apply;

(vii) *Options created pursuant to a title 11 or similar case.*—Options created by the solicitation or receipt of acceptances to a plan of reorganization in a title 11 or similar case (within the meaning of section 368(a)(3)(A)), the option created by the confirmation of the plan, and any option created under the plan prior to the time the plan becomes effective;

(viii) *Convertible preferred stock.*—Convertible preferred stock, provided the terms of the conversion feature do not permit or require the tender of any consideration other than the stock being converted; and

(ix) *Other enumerated instruments.*—Any other instruments specified by the Internal Revenue Service in regulations, a revenue ruling, or revenue procedure. See §601.601(d)(2)(ii)(*b*) of this chapter.

(e) *Elimination of federal income tax liability.*—For purposes of this section, the elimination of federal income tax liability includes the elimination or deferral of federal income tax liability. In determining whether there is an elimination of federal income tax liability, the tax consequences to all involved parties are considered. Examples of elimination of federal income tax liability include the use of a loss or deduction that would not otherwise be utilized, the acceleration of a loss or deduction to a year earlier than the year in which the loss or deduction would otherwise be utilized, the deferral of gain or income to a year later than the year in which the gain or income would otherwise be reported, and the acceleration of gain or income to a year earlier than the year in which the gain or income would otherwise be reported, if such gain or income is offset by a net operating loss or net capital loss that would otherwise expire unused. The elimination of federal income tax liability does not include the deferral of gain with respect to the stock subject to the option that would be recognized if such stock were sold on a measurement date.

(f) *Substantial amount of federal income tax liability.*—The determination of what constitutes a substantial amount of federal income tax liability is based on all the facts and circumstances, including the absolute amount of the elimination, the amount of the elimination relative to overall tax liability, and the timing of items of income and deductions, taking into account present value concepts.

(g) *Reasonable certainty of exercise.*—(1) *Generally.*—The determination of whether, as of a measurement date, an option is reasonably certain to be exercised is based on all the facts and circumstances, including:

(i) *Purchase price.*—The purchase price of the option in absolute terms and in relation to the fair market value of the stock or the exercise price of the option;

(ii) *In-the-money option.*—Whether and to what extent the option is in-the-money on the measurement date;

(iii) *Not in-the-money option.*—If the option is not in-the-money on the measurement date, the amount or percentage by which the exercise price of the option is greater than (or in the case of an option to sell stock, is less than) the fair market value of the underlying stock;

(iv) *Exercise price.*—Whether the exercise price of the option is fixed or fluctuates depending on the earnings, value, or other indication of economic performance of the issuing corporation;

(v) *Time of exercise.*—The time at which, or the period of time during which, the option can be exercised;

(vi) *Related or sequential options.*—Whether the option is one in a series of related or sequential options;

(vii) *Stockholder rights.*—The existence of an arrangement (either within the option agreement or in a related agreement) that, directly or indirectly, affords managerial or economic rights in the issuing corporation that ordinarily would be afforded to owners of the issuing corporation's stock (*e.g.*, voting rights, dividend rights, or rights to proceeds on liquidation) to the person who would acquire the stock upon exercise of the option or a person related to such person. For this purpose, managerial or economic rights in the issuing corporation possessed because of actual stock ownership in the issuing corporation are not taken into account;

(viii) *Restrictive covenants.*—The existence of restrictive covenants or similar arrangements (either within the option agreement or in a related agreement) that, directly or indirectly, prevent or limit the ability of the issuing corporation to undertake certain activities while the option is outstanding (*e.g.*, covenants limiting the payment of dividends or borrowing of funds);

(ix) *Intention to alter value.*—Whether it was intended that through a change in the capital structure of the issuing corporation or a transfer of assets to or from the issuing corporation (other than regular, ordinary dividends) or by any other means, the fair market value of the stock of the issuing corporation would be altered for a principal purpose of increasing the likelihood that the option would be exercised; and

(x) *Contingencies.*—Any contingency (other than the mere passage of time) to which the exercise of the option is subject (*e.g.*, a public offering of the issuing corporation's stock or reaching a certain level of earnings).

(2) *Cash settlement options, phantom stock, stock appreciation rights, or similar interests.*—A cash settlement option, phantom stock, stock appreciation right, or similar interest is treated as reasonably certain to be exercised if it is reasonably certain that the option will have value at some time during the period in which the option may be exercised.

Reg. §1.1504-4(g)(2)

(3) *Safe harbors.*—(i) *Options to acquire stock.*—Except as provided in paragraph (g)(3)(iv) of this section, an option to acquire stock is not considered reasonably certain, as of a measurement date, to be exercised if—

(A) The option may be exercised no more than 24 months after the measurement date and the exercise price is equal to or greater than 90 percent of the fair market value of the underlying stock on the measurement date; or

(B) The terms of the option provide that the exercise price of the option is equal to or greater than the fair market value of the underlying stock on the exercise date.

(ii) *Options to sell stock.*—Except as provided in paragraph (g)(3)(iv) of this section, an option to sell stock is not considered reasonably certain, as of a measurement date, to be exercised if—

(A) The option may be exercised no more than 24 months after the measurement date and the exercise price is equal to or less than 110 percent of the fair market value of the underlying stock on the measurement date; or

(B) The terms of the option provide that the exercise price of the option is equal to or less than the fair market value of the underlying stock on the exercise date.

(iii) *Options exercisable at fair market value.*—For purposes of paragraphs (g)(3)(i)(B) and (g)(3)(ii)(B) of this section, an option whose exercise price is determined by a formula is considered to have an exercise price equal to the fair market value of the underlying stock on the exercise date if the formula is agreed upon by the parties when the option is issued in a bona fide attempt to arrive at fair market value on the exercise date and is to be applied based upon the facts in existence on the exercise date.

(iv) *Exceptions.*—The safe harbors of this paragraph (g)(3) do not apply if—

(A) An arrangement exists that provides the holder or a related party with stockholder rights described in paragraph (g)(1)(vii) of this section (except for rights arising upon a default under the option or a related agreement);

(B) It is intended that through a change in the capital structure of the issuing corporation or a transfer of assets to or from the issuing corporation (other than regular, ordinary dividends) or by any other means, the fair market value of the stock of the issuing corporation will be altered for a principal purpose of increasing the likelihood that the option will be exercised; or

(C) The option is one in a series of related or sequential options, unless all such options satisfy paragraph (g)(3)(i) or (ii) of this section.

(v) *Failure to satisfy safe harbor.*—Failure of an option to satisfy one of the safe harbors of this paragraph (g)(3) does not affect the determination of whether an option is treated as reasonably certain to be exercised.

(h) *Examples.*—The provisions of this section may be illustrated by the following examples. These examples assume that the measurement dates set forth in the examples are the only measurement dates that have taken place or will take place.

Example 1. (i) P is the common parent of a consolidated group, consisting of P, S, and T. P owns all 100 shares of S's only class of stock, which is voting common stock. P also owns all the stock of T. On June 30, 1992, when the fair market value of the S stock is $40 per share, P sells to U, an unrelated corporation, an option to acquire 40 shares of the S stock that P owns at an exercise price of $30 per share, exercisable at any time within 3 years after the granting of the option. P and T have had substantial losses for 5 consecutive years while S has had substantial income during the same period. Because P, S, and T have been filing consolidated returns, P and T have been able to use all of their losses to offset S's income. It is anticipated that P, S, and T will continue their earnings histories for several more years. On July 31, 1992, S declares and pays a dividend of $1 per share to P.

(ii) If P, S, and T continue to file consolidated returns after June 30, 1992, it could reasonably be anticipated that P, S, and T would eliminate a substantial amount of federal income tax liability by using P's and T's future losses to offset S's income in consolidated returns. Furthermore, based on the difference between the exercise price of the option and the fair market value of the S stock, it is reasonably certain, on June 30, 1992, a measurement date, that the option will be exercised. Therefore, the option held by U is treated as exercised. As a result, for purposes of determining whether P and S are affiliated, P is treated as owning only 60 percent of the value of outstanding shares of S stock and U is treated as owning the remaining 40 percent. P is still treated as owning 100 percent of the voting power. Because members of the P group are no longer treated as owning stock possessing 80 percent of the total value of the S stock as of June 30, 1992, S is no longer a member of the P group. Additionally, P is not entitled to a 100 percent dividends received deduction under section 243(a)(3) because P and S are also treated as not affiliated for purposes of section 243. P is only entitled to an 80 percent dividends received deduction under section 243(c).

Example 2. (i) The facts are the same as in *Example 1* except that rather than P issuing an option to acquire 40 shares of S stock to U on June 30, 1992, P, pursuant to a plan, issues an option to U1 on July 1, 1992, to acquire 20 shares of S stock, and issues an option to U2 on July 2, 1992, to acquire 20 shares of S stock.

(ii) Because the options issued to U1 and U2 were issued pursuant to a plan, July 2, 1992, constitutes a measurement date for both options. Therefore, both options are aggregated in determining whether the issuance of the options, rather than the sale of the S stock, would result in the elimination of a substantial amount of federal income tax liability. Accordingly, as in *Example 1*, because the continued affiliation of P, S, and T could reasonably be anticipated to result in the elimination of a substantial amount of federal income tax liability and the options are reasonably certain to be exercised, the options are treated as exercised for purposes of determining whether P and S are affiliated, and P and S are no longer affiliated as of July 2, 1992.

Example 3. (i) The facts are the same as in *Example 1* except that the option gives U the right to acquire all 100 shares of the S stock, and U is the common parent of a consolidated group. The U group has had substantial losses for 5 consecutive years and it is anticipated that the U group will continue its earnings history for several more years.

(ii) If P sold the S stock, in lieu of the option, to U, S would become a member of the U group. Because the U group files consolidated returns, if P sold the S stock to U, U would be able to use its future losses to offset future income of S. When viewing the transaction from the effect on all parties, the sale of the option, in lieu of the underlying S stock, does not result in the elimination of federal income tax liability because S's income would be offset by the losses of members of either the P or U group. Accordingly, the option is disregarded and S remains a member of the P group.

Example 4. (i) P is the common parent of a consolidated group, consisting of P and S. P owns 90 of the 100 outstanding shares of S's only class of stock, which is voting common stock, and U, an unrelated corporation, owns the remaining 10 shares. On August 31, 1992, when the fair market value of the S stock is $100 per share, P sells a call option to U that entitles U to purchase 20 shares of S stock from P, at any time before August 31, 1993, at an exercise price of $115 per share. The call option does not provide U with any voting rights, dividend rights, or any other managerial or economic rights ordinarily afforded to owners of the S stock. There is no intention on August 31, 1992, to alter the value of S to increase the likelihood of the exercise of the call option.

(ii) Because the exercise price of the call option is equal to or greater than 90 percent of the fair market value of the S stock on August 31, 1992, a measurement date, the option may be exercised no more than 24 months after the measurement date, and none of the items described in paragraph (g)(3)(iv) of this section that preclude application of the safe harbor are present, the safe harbor of paragraph (g)(3)(i) of this section applies and the call option is treated as if it is not reasonably certain to be exercised. Therefore, regardless of whether the continued affiliation of P and S would result in the elimination of a substantial amount of federal income tax liability, the call option is disregarded in determining whether S remains a member of the P group.

Example 5. (i) The facts are the same as in *Example 4* except that the call option gives U the right to vote similar to that of a shareholder.

(ii) Under paragraph (g)(3)(iv) of this section, the safe harbor of paragraph (g)(3)(i) of this section does not apply because the call option entitles U to voting rights equivalent to that of a shareholder. Accordingly, all of the facts and circumstances surrounding the sale of the call option must be taken into consideration in determining whether it is reasonably certain that the call option will be exercised.

Example 6. (i) In 1992, two unrelated corporations, X and Y, decide to engage jointly in a new business venture. To accomplish this purpose, X organizes a new corporation, S, on September 30, 1992. X acquires 100 shares of the voting common stock of S, which are the only shares of S stock outstanding. Y acquires a debenture of S which is convertible, on September 30, 1995, into 100 shares of S common stock. If the conversion right is not exercised, X will have the right, on September 30, 1995, to put 50 shares of its S stock to Y in exchange for 50 percent of the debenture held by Y. The likelihood of the success of the venture is uncertain. It is anticipated that S will generate substantial losses in its early years of operation. X expects to have substantial taxable income during the three years following the organization of S.

(ii) Under the terms of this arrangement, it is reasonably certain, on September 30, 1992, a measurement date, that on September 30, 1995, either through Y's exercise of its conversion right or X's right to put S stock to Y, that Y will own 50 percent of the S stock. Additionally, it will reasonably be anticipated, on September 30, 1992, a measurement date, that the affiliation of X and S would result in the elimination of a substantial amount of federal income tax liability. Accordingly, for purposes of determining whether X and S are affiliated, X is treated as owning only 50 percent of the value of the S stock as of September 30, 1992, a measurement date, and S is not a member of the X affiliated group.

Example 7. (i) The facts are the same as in *Example 6* except that rather than acquiring 100 percent of the S stock and the right to put S stock to Y, X acquires only 80 percent of the S stock, while S, rather than acquiring a convertible debenture, acquires 20 percent of the S stock, and an option to acquire an additional 30 percent of the S stock. The terms of the option are such that the option will only be exercised if the new business venture succeeds.

(ii) In contrast to *Example 6*, because of the true business risks involved in the start-up of S and

Reg. §1.1504-4(h)

whether the business venture will ultimately succeed, along with the fact that X does not have an option to put S stock to Y, it is not reasonably certain on September 30, 1992, a measurement date, that the option will be exercised and that X will only own 50 percent of the S stock on September 30, 1995. Accordingly, the option is disregarded in determining whether S is a member of the X group.

(i) *Effective date.*—This section applies, generally, to options with a measurement date on or after February 28, 1992. This section does not apply to options issued prior to February 28, 1992, which have a measurement date on or after February 28, 1992, if the measurement date for the option occurs solely because of an adjustment in the terms of the option pursuant to the terms of the option as it existed on February 28, 1992. Paragraph (b)(2)(iv) of this section applies to stock outstanding on or after February 28, 1992. [Reg. § 1.1504-4.]

☐ [*T.D.* 8462, 12-28-92.]

RELATED RULES

In General

[Reg. § 1.1551-1]

§ 1.1551-1. Disallowance of surtax exemption and accumulated earnings credit.—(a) *In general.*—If—

(1) Any corporation transfers, on or after January 1, 1951, and before June 13, 1963, all or part of its property (other than money) to a transferee corporation,

(2) Any corporation transfers, directly or indirectly, after June 12, 1963, all or part of its property (other than money) to a transferee corporation, or

(3) Five or fewer individuals are in control of a corporation and one or more of them transfer, directly or indirectly, after June 12, 1963, property (other than money) to a transferee corporation,

and the transferee was created for the purpose of acquiring such property or was not actively engaged in business at the time of such acquisition, and if after such transfer the transferor or transferors are in control of the transferee during any part of the taxable year of the transferee, then for such taxable year of the transferee the Secretary or his delegate may disallow the surtax exemption defined in section 11(d) or the accumulated earnings credit of $150,000 ($100,000 in the case of taxable years beginning before January 1, 1975) provided in paragraph (2) or (3) of section 535(c), unless the transferee establishes by the clear preponderance of the evidence that the securing of such exemption or credit was not a major purpose of the transfer.

(b) *Purpose of section 1551.*—The purpose of section 1551 is to prevent avoidance or evasion of the surtax imposed by section 11(c) or of the accumulated earnings tax imposed by section 531. It is not intended, however, that section 1551 be interpreted as delimiting or abrogating any principle of law established by judicial decision, or any existing provisions of the Code, such as sections 269 and 482, which have the effect of preventing the avoidance or evasion of income taxes. Such principles of law and such provisions of the Code, including section 1551, are not mutually exclusive, and in appropriate cases they may operate together or they may operate separately.

(c) *Application of section 269(b) to cases covered by section 1551.*—The provisions of section 269(b) and the authority of the district director thereunder, to the extent not inconsistent with the provisions of section 1551, are applicable to cases covered by section 1551. Pursuant to the authority provided in section 269(b) the district director may allow to the transferee any part of a surtax exemption or accumulated earnings credit for a taxable year for which such exemption or credit would otherwise be disallowed under section 1551(a); or he may apportion such exemption or credit among the corporations involved. For example, corporation A transfers on January 1, 1955, all of its property to corporations B and C in exchange for all of the stock of such corporations. Immediately thereafter, corporation A is dissolved and its stockholders become the sole stockholders of corporations B and C. Assuming that corporations B and C are unable to establish by the clear preponderance of the evidence that the securing of the surtax exemption defined in section 11(d) or the accumulated earnings credit provided in section 535, or both, was not a major purpose of the transfer, the district director is authorized under sections 1551(c) and 269(b) to allow one such exemption and credit and to apportion such exemption and credit between corporations B and C.

(d) *Actively engaged in business.*—For purposes of this section, a corporation maintaining an office for the purpose of preserving its corporate existence is not considered to be "actively engaged in business" even though such corporation may be deemed to be "doing business" for other purposes. Similarly, for purposes of this section, a corporation engaged in winding up its affairs, prior to an acquisition to which section 1551 is applicable, is not considered to be "actively engaged in business."

(e) *Meaning and application of the term "control".*—(1) *In general.*—For purposes of this section, the term "control" means—

(i) With respect to a transferee corporation described in paragraph (a)(1) or (2) of this section, the ownership by the transferor corporation, its shareholders, or both, of stock possessing either (*a*) at least 80 percent of the total combined voting power of all classes of stock entitled to vote, or (*b*) at least 80 percent of the total value of shares of all classes of stock.

(ii) With respect to each corporation described in paragraph (a)(3) of this section, the ownership by five or fewer individuals of stock possessing (*a*) at least 80 percent of the total combined voting power of all classes of stock entitled to vote or at least 80 percent of the total value of shares of all classes of the stock of each corporation, and (*b*) more than 50 percent of the total combined voting power of all classes of stock entitled to vote or more than 50 percent of the total value of shares of all classes of stock of each corporation, taking into account the stock ownership of each such individual only to the extent such stock ownership is identical with respect to each such corporation.

(2) *Special rules.*—In determining for purposes of this section whether stock possessing at least 80 percent (or more than 50 percent in the case of subparagraph (1)(ii)(*b*) of this paragraph) of the total combined voting power of all classes of stock entitled to vote is owned, all classes of such stock shall be considered together; it is not necessary that at least 80 percent (or more than 50 percent) of each class of voting stock be owned. Likewise, in determining for purposes of this section whether stock possessing at least 80 percent (or more than 50 percent) of the total value of shares of all classes of stock is owned, all classes of stock of the corporation shall be considered together; it is not necessary that at least 80 percent (or more than 50 percent) of the value of shares of each class be owned. The fair market value of a share shall be considered as the value to be used for purposes of this computation. With respect to transfers described in paragraph (a)(2) or (3) of this section, the ownership of stock shall be determined in accordance with the provisions of section 1563(e) and the regulations thereunder. With respect to transfers described in paragraph (a)(1) of this section, the ownership of stock shall be determined in accordance with the provisions of section 544 and the regulations thereunder, except that constructive ownership under section 544(a)(2) shall be determined only with respect to the individual's spouse and minor children. In determining control, no stock shall be excluded because such stock was acquired before January 1, 1951 (the effective date of section 1551(a)(1)), or June 13, 1963 (the effective date of section 1551(a)(2) and (3)).

(3) *Example.*—This paragraph may be illustrated by the following example:

Example. On January 1, 1964, individual A, who owns 50 percent of the voting stock of corporation X, and individual B, who owns 30 percent of such voting stock, transfer property (other than money) to corporation Y (newly created for the purpose of acquiring such property) in exchange for all of Y's voting stock. After the transfer, A and B own the voting stock of corporations X and Y in the following proportions:

Individual	Corporation X	Corporation Y	Identical Ownership
A	50	30	30
B	30	50	30
Total	80	80	60

The transfer of property by A and B to corporation Y is a transfer described in paragraph (a)(3) of this section since (i) A and B own at least 80 percent of the voting stock of corporations X and Y, and (ii) taking into account each such individual's stock ownership only to the extent such ownership is identical with respect to each such corporation, A and B own more than 50 percent of the voting stock of corporations X and Y.

(f) *Taxable year of allowance or disallowance.*—(1) *In general.*—The district director's authority with respect to cases covered by section 1551 is not limited to the taxable year of the transferee corporation in which the transfer of property occurs. Such authority extends to the taxable year in which the transfer occurs or any subsequent taxable year of the transferee corporation if, during any part of such year, the transferor or transferors are in control of the transferee.

(2) *Examples.*—This paragraph may be illustrated by the following examples:

Example (1). On January 1, 1955, corporation D transfers property (other than money) to corporation E, a corporation not actively engaged in business at the time of the acquisition of such property, in exchange for 60 percent of the voting stock of E. During a later taxable year of E, corporation D acquires an additional 20 percent of such voting stock. As a result of such additional acquisition, D owns 80 percent of the voting stock of E. Accordingly, section 1551(a)(1) is applicable for the taxable year in which the later acquisition of stock occurred and for each taxable year thereafter in which the requisite control continues.

Example (2). On June 20, 1963, individual A, who owns all of the stock of corporation X, transfers property (other than money) to corporation Y, a corporation not actively engaged in business at the time of the acquisition of such property, in exchange for 60 percent of the voting stock of Y. During a later taxable year of Y, A acquires an additional 20 percent of such voting stock. After such acquisition A owns at least 80 percent of the voting stock of corporations X and

Y. Accordingly, section 1551(a)(3) is applicable for the taxable year in which the later acquisition of stock occurred and for each taxable year thereafter in which the requisite control continues.

Example (3). Individuals A and B each owns 50 percent of the stock of corporation X. On January 15, 1964, A transfers property (other than money) to corporation Y (newly created by A for the purpose of acquiring such property) in exchange for all the stock of Y. In a subsequent taxable year of Y, individual B buys 50 percent of the stock which A owns in Y (or he transfers money to Y in exchange for its stock, as a result of which he owns 50 percent of Y's stock). Immediately thereafter the stock ownership of A and B in corporation Y is identical to their stock ownership in corporation X. Accordingly, section 1551(a)(3) is applicable for the taxable year in which B acquires stock in corporation Y (see paragraph (g)(3) of this section) and for each taxable year thereafter in which the requisite control continues. Moreover, if B's acquisition of stock in Y is pursuant to a preexisting agreement with A, A's transfer to Y and B's acquisition of Y's stock are considered a single transaction and section 1551(a)(3) also would be applicable for the taxable year in which A's transfer to Y took place and for each taxable year thereafter in which the requisite control continues.

(g) *Nature of transfer.*—(1) *Corporate transfers before June 13, 1963.*—A transfer made before June 13, 1963, by any corporation of all or part of its assets, whether or not such transfer qualifies as a reorganization under section 368, is within the scope of section 1551(a)(1), except that section 1551(a)(1) does not apply to a transfer of money only. For example, the transfer of cash for the purpose of expanding the business of the transferor corporation through the formation of a new corporation is not a transfer within the scope of section 1551(a)(1), irrespective of whether the new corporation uses the cash to purchase from the transferor corporation stock in trade or similar property.

(2) *Corporate transfers after June 12, 1963.*—A direct or indirect transfer made after June 12, 1963, by any corporation of all or part of its assets to a transferee corporation, whether or not such transfer qualifies as a reorganization under section 368, is within the scope of section 1551(a)(2) except that section 1551(a)(2) does not apply to a transfer of money only. For example, if a transferor corporation transfers property to its shareholders or to a subsidiary, the transfer of that property by the shareholders or the subsidiary to a transferee corporation as part of the same transaction is a transfer of property by the transferor corporation to which section 1551(a)(2) applies. A transfer of property pursuant to a purchase by a transferee corporation from a transferor corporation controlling the transferee is within the scope of section

1551(a)(2), whether or not the purchase follows a transfer of cash from the controlling corporation.

(3) *Other transfers after June 12, 1963.*—A direct or indirect transfer made after June 12, 1963, by five or fewer individuals to a transferee corporation, whether or not such transfer qualifies under one or more other provisions of the Code (for example, section 351), is within the scope of section 1551(a)(3) except that section 1551(a)(3) does not apply to a transfer of money only. Thus, if one of five or fewer individuals who are in control of a corporation transfers property (other than money) to a controlled transferee corporation, the transfer is within the scope of section 1551(a)(3) notwithstanding that the other individuals transfer nothing or transfer only money.

(4) *Examples.*—This paragraph may be illustrated by the following examples:

Example (1). Individuals A and B each owns 50 percent of the voting stock of corporation X. On January 15, 1964, A and B each acquires property (other than money) from X and, as part of the same transaction, each transfers such property to his wholly owned corporation (newly created for the purpose of acquiring such property). A and B retain substantial continuing interests in corporation X. The transfers to the two newly created corporations are within the scope of section 1551(a)(2).

Example (2). Corporation W organizes corporation X, a wholly owned subsidiary, for the purpose of acquiring the properties of corporation Y. Pursuant to a reorganization qualifying under section 368(a)(1)(C), substantially all of the properties of corporation Y are transferred on June 15, 1963, to corporation X solely in exchange for voting stock of corporation W. There is a transfer of property from W to X within the meaning of section 1551(a)(2).

Example (3). Individuals A and B, each owning 50 percent of the voting stock of corporation X, organize corporation Y to which each transfers money only in exchange for 50 percent of the stock of Y. Subsequently, Y uses such money to acquire other property from A and B after June 12, 1963. Such acquisition is within the scope of section 1551(a)(3).

Example (4). Individual A owns 55 percent of the stock of corporation X. Another 25 percent of corporation X's stock is owned in the aggregate by individuals B, C, D, and E. On June 15, 1963, individual A transfers property to corporation Y (newly created for the purpose of acquiring such property) in exchange for 60 percent of the stock of Y, and B, C, and D acquire all of the remaining stock of Y. The transfer is within the scope of section 1551(a)(3).

(h) *Purpose of transfer.*—In determining, for purposes of this section, whether the securing of the surtax exemption or accumulated earnings credit constituted "a major purpose" of the transfer, all circumstances relevant to the transfer shall be considered. "A major purpose" will not be inferred from the mere purchase of inventory by a subsidiary from a centralized warehouse maintained by its parent corporation or by another subsidiary of the parent corporation. For disallowance of the surtax exemption and accumulated earnings credit under section 1551, it is not necessary that the obtaining of either such credit or exemption, or both, have been the sole or principal purpose of the transfer of the property. It is sufficient if it appears, in the light of all the facts and circumstances, that the obtaining of such exemption or credit, or both, was one of the major considerations that prompted the transfer. Thus, the securing of the surtax exemption or the accumulated earnings credit may constitute "a major purpose" of the transfer, notwithstanding that such transfer was effected for a valid business purpose and qualified as a reorganization within the meaning of section 368. The taxpayer's burden of establishing by the clear preponderance of the evidence that the securing of either such exemption or credit or both was not "a major purpose" of the transfer may be met, for example, by showing that the obtaining of such exemption, or credit, or both, was not a major factor in relationship to the other consideration or considerations which prompted the transfer. [Reg. § 1.1551-1.]

☐ [*T.D.* 6140, 8-29-55. *Amended by T.D.* 6377, 5-12-59; *T.D.* 6412, 9-10-59; *T.D.* 6911, 2-23-67 *and T.D.* 7376, 9-15-75.]

[Reg. § 1.1552-1]

§ 1.1552-1. Earnings and profits.—(a) *General rule.*—For the purpose of determining the earnings and profits of each member of an affiliated group which is required to be included in a consolidated return for such group filed for a taxable year beginning after December 31, 1953, and ending after August 16, 1954, the tax liability of the group shall be allocated among the members of the group in accordance with one of the following methods, pursuant to an election under paragraph (c) of this section:

(1)(i) The tax liability of the group shall be apportioned among the members of the group in accordance with the ratio which that portion of the consolidated taxable income attributable to each member of the group having taxable income bears to the consolidated taxable income.

(ii) For consolidated return years beginning after December 31, 1965, a member's portion of the tax liability of the group under the method of allocation provided by subdivision (i) of this subparagraph is an amount equal to the tax liability of the group multiplied by a fraction, the numerator of which is the taxable income of such member, and the denominator of which is the sum of the taxable incomes of all the members. For purposes of this subdivision the taxable income of a member shall be the separate taxable income determined under § 1.1502-12, adjusted

for the following items taken into account in the computation of consolidated taxable income:

(a) The portion of the consolidated net operating loss deduction, the consolidated charitable contributions deduction, the consolidated dividends received deduction, the consolidated section 247 deduction, the consolidated section 582(c) net loss, and the consolidated section 922 deduction, attributable to such member;

(b) Such member's capital gain net income (net capital gain for taxable years beginning before January 1, 1977) (determined without regard to any net capital loss carryover attributable to such member);

(c) Such member's net capital loss and section 1231 net loss, reduced by the portion of the consolidated net capital loss attributable to such member; and

(d) The portion of any consolidated net capital loss carryover attributable to such member which is absorbed in the taxable year.

If the computation of the taxable income of a member under this subdivision results in an excess of deductions over gross income, then for purposes of this subdivision such member's taxable income shall be zero.

(2)(i) The tax liability of the group shall be allocated to the several members of the group on the basis of the percentage of the total tax which the tax of such member if computed on a separate return would bear to the total amount of the taxes for all members of the group so computed.

(ii) For consolidated return years beginning after December 31, 1965, a member's portion of the tax liability of the group under the method of allocation provided by subdivision (i) of this subparagraph is an amount equal to the tax liability of the group multiplied by a fraction, the numerator of which is the separate return tax liability of such member, and the denominator of which is the sum of the separate return tax liabilities of all the members. For purposes of this subdivision the separate return tax liability of a member is its tax liability computed as if it has filed a separate return for the year except that—

(a) Gains and losses on intercompany transactions shall be taken into account as provided in § 1.1502-13 as if a consolidated return had been filed for the year;

(b) Gains and losses relating to inventory adjustments shall be taken into account as provided in § 1.1502-18 as if a consolidated return had been filed for the year;

(c) Transactions with respect to stock, bonds, or other obligations of members shall be reflected as provided in § 1.1502-13(f) and (g) as if a consolidated return had been filed for the year;

(d) Excess losses shall be included in income as provided in § 1.1502-19 as if a consolidated return had been filed for the year;

(e) In the computation of the deduction under section 167, property shall not lose its character as new property as a result of a transfer from one member to another member during the year;

(f) A dividend distributed by one member to another member during the year shall not be taken into account in computing the deductions under section 243(a)(1), 244(a), 245, or 247 (relating to deductions with respect to dividends received and dividends paid);

(g) Basis shall be determined under §§1.1502-31 and 1.1502-32, and earnings and profits shall be determined under §1.1502-33, as if a consolidated return had been filed for the year;

(h) Subparagraph (2) of §1.1502-3(f) shall apply as if a consolidated return had been filed for the year; and

(i) For purposes of subtitle A of the Code, the surtax exemption of the member shall be an amount equal to $25,000 ($50,000 in the case of a taxable year ending in 1975), divided by the number of members (or such portion of $25,000 or $50,000 which is apportioned to the member pursuant to a schedule attached to the consolidated return for the taxable year). (However, if for the taxable year some or all of the members are component members of a controlled group of corporations (within the meaning of section 1563) and if there are other such component members which do not join in filing the consolidated return for such year, the amount to be divided among the members filing the consolidated return shall be (in lieu of $25,000 or $50,000) the sum of the amounts apportioned to the component members which join in filing the consolidated return (as determined for taxable years beginning after December 31, 1974, under §1.1561-2(a)(2) or §1.1561-3, whichever is applicable, and for taxable years beginning before January 1, 1975, under §1.1561-2A(a)(2) or §1.1561-3A, whichever is applicable).)

If the computation of the separate return tax liability of a member under this subdivision does not result in a positive tax liability, then for purposes of this subdivision such member's separate return tax liability shall be zero.

(3)(i) The tax liability of the group (excluding the tax increases arising from the consolidation) shall be allocated on the basis of the contribution of each member of the group to the consolidated taxable income of the group. Any tax increases arising from the consolidation shall be distributed to the several members in direct proportion to the reduction in tax liability resulting to such members from the filing of the consolidated return as measured by the difference between their tax liabilities determined on a separate return basis and their tax liabilities (determined without regard to the 2-percent increase provided by section 1503(a) and paragraph (a) of §1.1502-30A (as contained in the 26 C.F.R. edition revised as of April 1, 1996) for taxable years

beginning before Jan. 1, 1964) based on their contributions to the consolidated taxable income.

(ii) For consolidated return years beginning after December 31, 1965, a member's portion of the tax liability of the group under the method of allocation provided by subdivision (i) of this subparagraph shall be determined by—

(a) Allocating the tax liability of the group in accordance with subparagraph (1)(ii) of this paragraph, but

(b) The amount of tax liability allocated to any member shall not exceed the separate return tax liability of such member, determined in accordance with subparagraph (2)(ii) of this paragraph, and

(c) The sum of the amounts which would be allocated to the members but for (b) of this subdivision (ii) shall be apportioned among the other members in direct proportion to, but limited to, the reduction in tax liability resulting to such other members. Such reduction for any member shall be the excess, if any, of

(1) its separate return tax liability determined in accordance with subparagraph (2)(ii) of this paragraph, over

(2) the amount allocated to such member under (a) of this subdivision (ii).

If any amount remains after being apportioned among members with a reduction in tax liability to the extent of such reduction, as provided in (c) of this subdivision (ii), such remaining amount shall, notwithstanding (b) of this subdivision (ii), be allocated to the members in accordance with the fractions determined under subparagraph (1)(ii) of this paragraph.

(4) The tax liability of the group shall be allocated in accordance with any other method selected by the group with the approval of the Commissioner. No method of allocation may be approved under this subparagraph which may result in the allocation of a positive tax liability for a taxable year, among the members who are allocated a positive tax liability for such year, in a total amount which is more or less than the tax liability of the group for such year. (However, see paragraph (d) of §1.1502-33.)

(b) *Application of rules.*—(1) *Tax liability of the group.*—For purposes of section 1552 and this section, the tax liability of the group for a taxable year shall consist of the Federal income tax liability of the group for such year determined in accordance with §1.1502-2 or §1.1502-30A (as contained in the 26 C.F.R. edition revised as of April 1, 1996), whichever is applicable. Thus, in the case of a carryback of a loss or credit to such year, although the earnings and profits of the members of the group may not be adjusted until the subsequent taxable year from which the loss or credit was carried back, the effect of the carryback, for purposes of this section, shall be determined by allocating the amount of the adjustment as a part of the tax liability of the group for the taxable year to which the loss or credit is carried. For example, if a consolidated net operating loss is carried back from 1969 to 1967, the allocation of the tax liability of the group for 1967 shall be recomputed in accordance with the method of allocation used for 1967, and the changes resulting from such recomputation shall, for accrual method taxpayers, be reflected in the earnings and profits of the appropriate members in 1969.

(2) *Effect of allocation.*—The amount of tax liability allocated to a corporation as its share of the tax liability of the group, pursuant to this section, shall (i) result in a decrease in the earnings and profits of such corporation in such amount, and (ii) be treated as a liability of such corporation for such amount. If the full amount of such liability is not paid by such corporation, pursuant to an agreement among the members of the group or otherwise, the amount which is not paid will generally be treated as a distribution with respect to stock, a contribution to capital, or a combination thereof, as the case may be.

(c) *Method of election.*—(1) The election under paragraph (a)(1), (2), or (3) of this section shall be made not later than the time prescribed by law for filing the first consolidated return of the group for a taxable year beginning after December 31, 1953, and ending after August 16, 1954 (including extensions thereof). If the group elects to allocate its tax liability in accordance with the method prescribed in paragraph (a)(1), (2), or (3) of this section, a statement shall be attached to the return stating which method is elected. Such statement shall be made by the common parent corporation and shall be binding upon all members of the group. In the event that the group desires to allocate its tax liability in accordance with any other method pursuant to paragraph (a)(4) of this section, approval of such method by the Commissioner must be obtained within the time prescribed above. If such approval is not obtained in such time, the group shall allocate in accordance with the method prescribed in paragraph (a)(1) of this section. The request shall state fully the method which the group wishes to apply in apportioning the tax liability. Except as provided in subparagraph (2) of this paragraph, an election once made shall be irrevocable and shall be binding upon the group with respect to the year for which made and for all future years for which a consolidated return is filed or required to be filed unless the Commissioner authorizes a change to another method prior to the time prescribed by law for filing the return for the year in which such change is to be effective.

(2) Each group may make a new election to use any one of the methods prescribed in paragraph (a)(1), (2), or (3) of this section for its first consolidated return year beginning after December 31, 1965, or in conjunction with an election under paragraph (d) of § 1.1502-33, or may request the Commissioner's approval of a method under paragraph (a)(4) of this section for its first

consolidated return year beginning after December 31, 1965, irrespective of its previous method of allocation under this section. If such new election is not made in conjunction with an election under paragraph (d) of § 1.1502-33, it shall be effective for the first consolidated return year beginning after December 31, 1965, and all succeeding years. (See § 1.1502-33 for the method of making such new election in conjunction with an election under paragraph (d) of § 1.1502-33.) Any other such new election (or request for the Commissioner's approval of a method under paragraph (a)(4) of this section) shall be made within the time prescribed by law for filing the consolidated return for the first taxable year beginning after December 31, 1965 (including extensions thereof), or within 60 days after July 3, 1968, whichever is later. Such new election shall be made by attaching a statement to the consolidated return for the first taxable year beginning after December 31, 1965, or if such election is made within the time prescribed above but after such return is filed, by filing a statement with the internal revenue officer with whom such return was filed.

(d) *Failure to elect.*—If a group fails to make an election in its first consolidated return, or any other election, in accordance with paragraph (c) of this section, the method prescribed under paragraph (a)(1) of this section shall be applicable and shall be binding upon the group in the same manner as if an election had been made to so allocate.

(e) *Definitions.*—Except as otherwise provided in this section, the terms used in this section shall have the same meaning as provided in the regulations under section 1502.

(f) *Example.*—The provisions of this section may be illustrated by the following example:

Example. Corporation P is the common parent owning all of the stock of corporations S1 and S2, members of an affiliated group. A consolidated return is filed for the taxable year ending December 31, 1966, by P, S1, and S2. For 1966 such corporations had the following taxable incomes or losses computed in accordance with paragraph (a)(1)(ii) of this section:

P	$0
S1	2,000
S2	(1,000)

The group has not made an election under paragraph (c) of this section or paragraph (d) of § 1.1502-33. Accordingly, the method of allocation provided by paragraph (a)(1) of this section is in effect for the group. Assuming that the consolidated taxable income is equal to the sum of the members' taxable income and losses, or $1,000, the tax liability of the group for the year (assuming a 22-percent rate) is $220, all of which is allocated to S1. S1 accordingly reduces its earnings and profits in the amount of $220, irrespective of who actually pays the tax liability. If S1 pays the $220 tax liability there will be no further effect upon the income, earnings and profits, or the basis of stock of any member. If, however, P pays the $220 tax liability (and such payment is not in fact a loan from P to S1), then P shall be treated as having made a contribution to the capital of S1 in the amount of $220. On the other hand, if S2 pays the $220 tax liability (and such payment is not in fact a loan from S2), then S2 shall be treated as having made a distribution with respect to its stock to P in the amount of $220, and P shall be treated as having made a contribution to the capital of S1 in the amount of $220. [Reg. § 1.1552-1.]

☐ [*T.D. 6140, 8-29-55. Amended by T.D. 6962, 7-2-68; T.D. 7528, 12-27-77; T.D. 7728, 10-31-80; T.D. 8560, 8-12-94; T.D. 8597, 7-12-95 and T.D. 8677, 6-26-96.*]

Certain Controlled Corporations

[Reg. § 1.1561-0]

§ 1.1561-0. Table of contents.—This section lists the table of contents for § § 1.1561-1 through 1.1561-3.

§ 1.1561-1 General rules regarding certain tax benefits available to the component members of a controlled group of corporations.

☐ [*T.D. 9476, 12-22-2009.*]

[Reg. § 1.1561-1]

§ 1.1561-1. General rules regarding certain tax benefits available to the component members of a controlled group of corporations.— (a) *In general.*—(1) *Limitation.*—Part II (section 1561 and following) of subchapter B of chapter 6 of the Internal Revenue Code (Code) (part II) provides rules to limit the amounts of certain specified tax benefit items of component members of a controlled group of corporations for their tax years which include a particular December 31st date; or, in the case of a short taxable year member (see section 1561(b) and § 1.1561-2(e)), the date substituted for that December 31st date. The amount of the tax items enumerated in section 1561(a) available to any of the component members of a controlled group shall be determined for purposes of subtitle A of the Code as if the component members were a single corporation. Certain other tax items also set forth in section 1561(a) (for example, the additional tax imposed by section 11(b)(1) and the section 55(d)(3) phase out of the alternative minimum tax exemption amount) will be determined by combining the positive taxable income or positive alternative minimum taxable income of the component members of such a group and then allocating the amount of such items among those members.

(2) *Definitions.*—For certain definitions (including the definition of a *controlled group of corporations* and a *component member*) and special rules for purposes of this part II see section 1563.

(b) *Special rules.*—(1) *S Corporation.*—For purposes of this part II, the term *corporation* includes a small business corporation (as defined in section 1361). However, for the treatment of such a corporation as an *excluded member* of a controlled group of corporations see § 1.1563-1(b)(2)(ii)(C).

(2) *52-53-week taxable year.*—In the case of corporations electing a 52-53-week taxable year under section 441(f)(1), the provisions of this

part II shall be applied in accordance with the special rule of section 441(f)(2)(A). See § 1.441-2.

(c) *Tax avoidance.*—The provisions of this part II do not delimit or abrogate any principle of law established by judicial decision, or any existing provisions of the Code, such as sections 269, 482, and 1551, which serve to prevent any avoidance or evasion of income taxes.

(d) *Effective/applicability date.*—This section applies to any tax year beginning on or after December 21, 2009. However, taxpayers may apply this section to any Federal income tax return filed on or after December 21, 2009. For tax years beginning before December 21, 2009, see § 1.1561-1T as contained in 26 CFR part 1 in effect on April 1, 2009. [Reg. § 1.1561-1.]

☐ [*T.D.* 9476, 12-22-2009.]

[Reg. § 1.1561-2]

§ 1.1561-2. Special rules for allocating reductions of certain section 1561(a) tax-benefit items.—(a) *Additional tax.*—(1) *Calculation.*—(i) *In general.*—For the purpose of determining the amount, if any, of the additional tax imposed by section 11(b)(1) (the additional tax), the taxable incomes of all of the component members of a controlled group of corporations shall be combined to determine whether either of the income thresholds for imposing the additional tax have been attained.

(ii) *Special rules.*—For purposes of paragraph (a)(1)(i) of this section—

(A) *Component member* means a corporation that is apportioned some part of any applicable tax bracket amount; and

(B) *Taxable income* means the positive taxable income of a component member for its entire tax year (even if it was not a member of the group for each day of that tax year) that includes the same December 31st testing date, which is also applicable to the other component members of that same controlled group.

(2) *Apportionment.*—(i) *General rule.*—Any additional tax determined under paragraph (a)(1) of this section shall be apportioned among such members in the same manner as the corresponding tax bracket of section 11(b)(1) is apportioned. For rules to apportion the section 11(b)(1) tax brackets among the component members of a controlled group, see § 1.1561-3(b) or (c).

(ii) *Apportionment methods.*—Unless the component members of a controlled group elect to use the first-in-first-out (FIFO) method described in paragraph (a)(2)(ii)(B) of this section, such members are required to apportion the amount of the additional tax using the proportionate method described in paragraph (a)(2)(ii)(A) of this section. These component members may elect the FIFO method by specifi-

cally adopting such method in their apportionment plan.

(A) *Proportionate method.*—Under the proportionate method, the additional tax is allocated to each component member in the same proportion as the portion of the taxbenefit amount that inured to a member from utilizing lower tax brackets bears to the amount of the group's total tax-benefit amount inuring to it from utilizing those lower tax brackets. The tax-benefit amount that inures to a corporation from using a particular tax bracket is the tax savings that such corporation realizes from having a portion of its taxable income taxed at the lower rate attributed to that tax bracket instead of the high tax rates to which it would otherwise be subject. The steps for applying the proportionate method of allocation are as follows:

(1) *Step 1.*—The regular tax (not including the additional tax) owed by a component member under a particular tax bracket is divided by the total tax owed by all component members under that tax bracket;

(2) *Step 2.*—The percentage calculated under *Step 1* is multiplied by the total taxbenefit amount inuring to all the members of the group from their use of this tax bracket. This computed amount equals the portion of the group's tax-benefit amount that inured to such member from using its portion of this tax bracket;

(3) *Step 3.*—The amount determined under *Step 2* is divided by the total taxbenefit amount, inuring to all the component members of the group from using all the tax brackets to which any component member's income was subject;

(4) *Step 4.*—The percentage calculated under *Step 3* is multiplied by the amount of the group's additional tax. The amount determined under this *Step 4* equals the amount of the additional tax apportioned to such member for that tax bracket; and

(5) *Step 5.*—If a component member is liable for regular tax (not including the additional tax) under more than one tax bracket, that member must calculate the amount of the additional tax apportioned to it with respect to each tax bracket. Accordingly, steps 1 through 4 must be applied for each tax bracket applicable to that member. The sum of all the apportioned amounts of additional tax from each tax bracket for which the member is subject is the total amount of the additional tax apportioned to that member.

(B) *FIFO method.*—Under the FIFO method, the first dollars of the additional tax are to be allocated proportionately to the members starting with the lowest tax bracket (that is, the first tax bracket), up to the amount of the tax benefit inuring to those members from using that tax bracket. Any remaining amount of additional tax is then allocated proportionately among the component members who use the next higher tax bracket, and so on, until the entire amount of the additional tax has been fully apportioned among the members. For example, the first $9,500 of the additional tax liability of a controlled group is apportioned entirely to the member(s) that availed themselves of the benefit of the 15 percent tax bracket.

(3) *Examples.*—The provisions of this paragraph (a) may be illustrated by the following examples:

Example 1. (i) *Facts.* A controlled group of corporations consists of three members: X, Y and Z. X owns all the stock of Y and Z. Each corporation files its separate return on a calendar year basis. For calendar year 2007, the component members of the controlled group have an apportionment plan in effect. The members apportioned 80% of the 15 percent tax-bracket amount ($40,000) to X and the remaining 10% ($10,000) to Y. The members apportioned 100% of the 25 percent taxbracket amount ($25,000) to Y. However, these members have not adopted the FIFO method for apportioning the additional taxes. Therefore, they must follow the proportionate method. For 2007, X had taxable income (TI) of $40,000, Y had TI of $60,000 and Z had TI of $100,000. Thus the total TI of the group is $200,000.

(ii) *Calculating the tax from the tax brackets and the tax benefit derived from such tax.* (A) *Regular tax of group subject to a 15 percent tax rate.* (1) *Calculating the group's tax which resulted from applying a 15 percent tax rate.* The amount of tax under the 15 percent tax bracket is $7,500 (15% × $50,000).

(2) *The tax-benefit amount inuring to the group from using the 15 percent tax bracket.* A tax benefit inures to those members of the group who avail themselves of the 15 percent tax bracket. That tax benefit results from having the first $50,000 of its income taxed at the 15 percent tax rate, instead of at the 34 percent tax rate. Thus, the tax-benefit

amount inuring to this group from using the 15 percent tax bracket is $9,500 ($17,000 (34% × $50,000) minus $7,500 (15% × $50,000)).

(B) *Regular tax of group subject to a 25 percent tax rate.* (1) *Calculating the group's tax which resulted from applying a 25 percent tax rate.* The amount of tax under the 25 percent tax bracket is $6,250 (25% × $25,000 ($75,000 - $50,000)).

(2) *The tax-benefit amount inuring to the group from using the 25 percent tax bracket.* A tax benefit inures to those members of the group who avail themselves of the 25 percent tax bracket. That tax benefit results from having $25,000 of its income taxed at the 25 percent tax rate, instead of at the 34 percent tax rate. Thus, the taxbenefit amount inuring to this group from using the 25 percent tax bracket is $2,250 ($8,500 (34% × $25,000) minus $6,250 (25% × $25,000)).

(C) *Regular tax of group subject to a 34 percent tax rate.* (1) *Calculating the group's tax which resulted from applying a 34 percent tax rate.* The amount of tax under the 34 percent tax bracket is $42,500 (34% × $125,000 ($200,000 (total TI) - $75,000) (amount taxed at lower rates)).

(2) *The tax-benefit amount inuring to the group from using the 34 percent tax bracket.* The group's total TI of $200,000 is less than the $15,000,000 income threshold for imposing any 3 percent additional tax on the group. Therefore, there is no tax benefit inuring to the members of this group for using the 34 percent tax bracket.

(D) *The computation of the additional tax.* Since the combined TI of the group exceeds $100,000, a 5 percent additional tax is imposed on the group. That 5 percent additional tax is the lesser amount of 5 percent of the group's taxable income exceeding $100,000 or $11,750. Five percent of that excess amount of taxable income is $5,000 (5% × $100,000 ($200,000 - $100,000)). Since $5,000 is less than $11,750, the group's 5 percent additional tax is $5,000.

(iii) *Apportioning the amount of additional tax to each applicable tax bracket.* (A) *The apportioned tax under each bracket.* The amount of tax owed by each member under each tax bracket pursuant to the apportionment plan is as follows:

Name of Component Member	Amount of tax owed under the 15% tax bracket	Amount of tax owed under the 25% tax bracket	Amount of tax owed under the 34% tax bracket
X	$6,000	0	0
Y	$1,500	$6,250	$8,500
Z	0	0	$34,000

(B) *Apportioning the 5 percent additional tax among the component members of the controlled group.* Since the group did not elect to adopt the FIFO method of apportionment, it is required to apportion the $5,000 of its 5 percent additional tax pursuant to the proportionate method in the following manner:

(1) *Amount of the additional tax apportioned to X.* Pursuant to the plan, X was liable for $6,000 of the group's $7,500 regular tax (80%) owed under

the 15 percent tax bracket (and X is not liable for any regular tax under any higher tax bracket). See *Step 1* of paragraph (a)(2)(ii)(A) of this section. X's portion of the group's tax benefit which it derived from using the 15 percent tax rate is $7,600 (0.8 × $9,500). See *Step 2.* The tax benefit inuring to the entire group from using the 15 percent and 25 percent tax brackets is $11,750 ($9,500 (from the 15 percent tax bracket) + $2,250 (from the 25 percent tax bracket)). So, X's percentage portion of the group's total tax benefit is $7,600/$11,750 (64.68%). See *Step 3*. Thus, X's allocated portion of the 5 percent additional tax from using the 15 percent tax bracket is $3,234 (0.6468 x $5,000). See *Step 4*.

(2) *Amount of the additional tax apportioned to Y*. (i) *Regular tax apportioned to Y from using the 15 percent tax bracket*. Pursuant to the plan, Y was liable for the remaining $1,500 of the group's $7,500 regular tax (20%) owed under the 15 percent tax bracket. See *Step 1*. Y's portion of the group's tax benefit which it derived from using the 15 percent tax rate is $1,900 ($9,500 - $7,600, or 0.2 × $9,500). See *Step 2*. So, Y's percentage portion of the group's total tax benefit is $1,900/$11,750 (16.17%). See *Step 3*. Thus, Y's allocated portion of the 5 percent additional tax from using the 15 percent tax bracket is $809 (0.1617 × $5,000). See *Step 4*.

(ii) *Regular tax apportioned to Y from using the 25 percent tax bracket*. Pursuant to the plan, Y was liable for 100% of the group's regular tax owed under the 25 percent tax bracket, an amount of $6,250. See *Step 1*. Y is, therefore, entitled to 100% of the group's tax benefit which it derived from using this tax bracket, an amount of $2,250. See *Step 2*. So, Y's percentage portion of the group's total tax benefit is $2,250/$11,750 (19.15%). See *Step 3*. Thus, Y's allocated portion of the 5 percent additional tax from using the 25 percent tax bracket is $957 (0.1915 × $5,000). See *Step 4*. Y's total allocated portion of the additional tax is $1,766 ($809 + $957). See *Step 5*.

Example 2. (i) *Facts*. The facts are the same as in *Example 1*, except that on August 31, 2007, X of the X-Y-Z controlled group sold all of the stock of Z to M of the MN controlled group, a pair of corporations unrelated to the X-Y group. Pursuant to the terms of the sales agreement, the members of the M-N group properly notified the members of the X-Y group on a timely basis that Z's taxable income for its 2007 tax year, as based on the group's December 31st testing date, was $100,000.

(ii) *Controlled group analysis*. On December 31st, 2007, X and Y are members of the selling controlled group and M, N and Z are members of the buying controlled group. However, pursuant to section 1563(b)(3), Z is treated as an additional member of the X-Y group on December 31st 2007, since it was a member for at least one-half the number of days (243 out of 364) during the period beginning on January 1 and ending on December 30, 2007. Conversely, pursuant to section 1563(b)(2)(A), Z is treated as an excluded member of the M-N controlled group. Therefore, on December 31st, 2007, X, Y and Z qualify as component members of the selling group, and only M and N qualify as component members of the buying group.

(iii) *Additional tax analysis*. With regard to X and Y's 2007 tax years, X and Y together owed $5,000 of additional tax, as calculated in *Example 1*. X's allocated portion of the additional tax is $3,234, as calculated in the manner set forth in *Example 1*. Y's allocated portion of the additional tax is $1,766, also as calculated in the manner set forth in *Example 1*.

Example 3. (i) *Facts*. The facts are the same as in *Example 2*, except that in 2012, pursuant to an IRS audit, Z's 2007 taxable income was re-determined. It was adjusted by an income increase of $10,000. Pursuant to the terms of the sales agreement, the members of the M-N group timely notified the members of the X-Y group of Z's income adjustment.

(ii) *Additional tax analysis*. For 2007 the X-Y-Z group owed a revised additional tax in the amount of $5,500, allocated as follows: $3,557.40 to X and $1,942.60 to Y. X and Y each filed an amended 2007 tax return to report their portions of the $500 increase to the group's additional tax. Pursuant to their apportionment plan for allocating their regular tax, and as a result of defaulting to the proportionate method for allocating the group's additional tax, X reported $323.40 as its share of the group's increase to its additional tax and Y reported $176.60 as its share of the group's increase to its additional tax.

Example 4. The facts are the same as in *Example 1*, except that the members elected in their apportionment plan to adopt the FIFO method for apportioning the additional tax. Under the FIFO method, the 5 percent additional tax amount of $5,000 will be apportioned entirely to those members who would benefit from using the 15 percent tax bracket, by reason that $5,000 of the group's additional tax is less than $9,500, which is the full tax-benefit amount inuring to a controlled group from having a 15 percent tax rate applied to the full income bracket subject to that rate. Since X derived 80 percent of the group's tax benefit by its use of the 15 percent tax bracket, its share of the group's 5 percent additional tax is $4,000 (80% × $5,000), and Y's share of the group's 5 percent additional tax is, therefore, $1,000, which is the remaining amount of the group's 5 percent additional tax, attributable to the 15 percent tax bracket.

(b) *Reduction to the amount exempted from the alternative minimum tax*.—(1) *Calculation*.—The alternative minimum taxable incomes of the component members of a controlled group of corporations shall be taken into account in calculating the reduction set forth in section 55(d)(3) to the amount exempted from the alternative minimum tax (the exemption amount). For purposes of the preceding sentence, *alternative minimum taxable income* means the positive alternative minimum taxable income of a component member for its entire tax year (even if it was not a member of the group for each day of that tax year) that includes the same December 31st testing date, which is also applicable to the other component members of that same controlled group.

(2) *Apportionment.*—Any reduction to the exemption amount shall be apportioned to the component members of a controlled group in the same manner that the amount of the exemption (provided in section 55(d)(2)) to the alternative minimum tax was allocated under section 1561(a). For rules to apportion the section 55(d)(2) exemption amount among the component members of a controlled group, see § 1.1561-3(b) or (c).

(3) *Examples.*—The provisions of this paragraph (b) may be illustrated by the following example:

Example. (i) *Facts.* A controlled group of corporations consists of three members: X, Y and Z. X owns all of the stock of Y and Z. Each corporation files its separate return on a calendar year basis. For calendar year 2007, the component members of this controlled group have an apportionment plan in effect. The group has chosen to apportion the entire section 55(d)(2) exemption amount of $40,000 to Z. For 2007, X had alternative minimum taxable income (AMTI) of $40,000, Y had AMTI of $60,000 and Z had AMTI of $100,000. Thus the total AMTI of the group is $200,000.

(ii) *Calculating the reduction to the exemption amount.* Section 55(d)(3)(A) provides that the section 55(d)(2) exemption amount shall be reduced (but not below zero) by an amount equal to 25 percent of the amount by which the AMTI of a corporation exceeds $150,000. For the purpose of computing the group's AMTI, the AMTI of each of the component members, for their tax years that have the same December 31st testing date, shall be taken into account. In accordance with these provisions, the $40,000 exemption amount is reduced by $12,500 (25% x $50,000 ($200,000 - $150,000)). Pursuant to the group's allocation plan, the entire $12,500 reduction to the exemption amount is allocated to Z. Thus, after such allocation, Z's $40,000 exemption amount is reduced to $27,500 ($40,000 - $12,500).

(c) *Accumulated earnings credit.*—The component members of a controlled group of corporations are permitted to allocate the amount of the accumulated earnings credit unequally if they have an apportionment plan in effect.

(d) [Reserved].

(e) *Short taxable years not including a December 31st date.*—(1) *General rule.*—If a corporation has a short taxable year not including a December 31st date and, after applying the rules of section 1561(b) and paragraph (e)(2)(i) of this section, it qualifies as a component member of the group with respect to its short taxable year (short-year member), then, for purposes of subtitle A of the Internal Revenue Code, the amount of any tax-benefit item described in section 1561(b) allocated to that component member's short taxable year shall be the amount specified in section 1561(a) for that item, divided by the number of corporations which are component members of that group on the last day of that component member's short taxable year. The component members of such group may not apportion, by an apportionment plan, an amount of such tax-benefit item to any short-year member that differs from equal apportionment of that item.

(2) *Additional rules.*—For purposes of paragraph (e)(1) of this section—

(i) Section 1563(b) shall be applied as if the last day of the taxable year of a short-year member were substituted for December 31st; and

(ii) The term *short taxable year* does not refer to any portion of a tax year of a corporation for which its income is required to be included in a consolidated return pursuant to § 1.1502-76(b).

(3) *Calculation of the additional tax.*—A short-year member (as defined in paragraph (e)(1) of this section) for its short taxable year calculates its additional tax liability imposed by section 11(b)(1) only on its own income, and therefore the subsequent calculation of the additional tax liability with regard to the remaining members of the group will not include the income of this short-year member.

(4) *Calculation of the alternative minimum tax.*—If a component member has a tax year of less than 12 months, whether or not such tax year includes a December 31st date, see section 443(d) for the annualization method required for calculating the alternative minimum tax.

(5) *Examples.*—The provisions of this paragraph (e) may be illustrated by the following examples:

Example 1. Formation of a new member of a controlled group. (i) *Facts.* On January 2, 2007, corporation X transfers cash to newly formed corporation Y (which begins business on that date) and receives all of the stock of Y in return. X also owns all of the stock of corporation Z on each day of 2006 and 2007. X, Y and Z have an apportionment plan in effect, apportioning the 15 percent tax-bracket amount as follows: 40% ($20,000) to each of X and Y and 20% ($10,000) to Z. X, Y and Z each file a separate return with respect to the group's December 31st 2007 testing date. X is on a calendar tax year and Z is on a fiscal tax year ending on March 31. Y adopts a fiscal year ending on June 30 and timely files a tax return for its short taxable year beginning on January 2, 2007, and ending on June 30, 2007.

(ii) *Y's short taxable year.* On June 30, 2007, Y is a component member of a parent-subsidiary controlled group of corporations composed of X, Y and Z. Pursuant to paragraph (e)(1) of this section, the group may not apportion any amount of the 15 percent tax bracket to Y's short taxable year ending on June 30, 2007. Rather, Y is entitled to exactly $1/3$ of such bracket amount, or $16,667.

Reg. § 1.1561-2(b)(2)

(iii) *The members' subsequent tax years.* On December 31st, 2007, X, Y and Z are component members of a parent-subsidiary controlled group of corporations. For their tax years that include December 31st, 2007 (X's calendar year ending December 31st, 2007, Z's fiscal year ending March 31, 2008 and Y's fiscal year ending June 30, 2008), X, Y and Z apportion among themselves the full amount of all of the applicable tax brackets pursuant to their apportionment plan. For example, 40% of the 15 percent tax-bracket amount, or $20,000, was apportioned to each of X and Y, and the remaining 10%, or $10,000, was apportioned to Z.

Example 2. Allocating a tax bracket to the short taxable year of a liquidated member of a controlled group (i) *Facts.* On January 1, 2007, corporation P owns all of the stock of corporations S_1, S_2 and S_3 (the P group). Each of these four component members of the P group, with respect to the group's December 31st, 2007 testing date, files its separate return on a calendar year basis. These members have an apportionment plan in effect (the P group plan) under which S_1 and S_2 are each entitled to 40% of the 15 percent tax-bracket amount ($20,000), and P and S_3 are each entitled to 10% of the 15 percent tax-bracket amount ($5,000). On May 31, 2007, S_1 liquidates and therefore files a return for the short taxable year beginning on January 1, 2007, and ending on May 31, 2007. On July 31, 2007, S_2 liquidates and therefore files a return for the short taxable year beginning on January 1, 2007 and ending on July 31, 2007. P and S_3 each file a return for their 2007 calendar tax years.

(ii) *Apportionment of the 15 percent tax bracket to S₁ for its short taxable year.* On May 31, 2007, S_1 is a component member of the P group composed of P, S_1, S_2 and S_3. Pursuant to paragraph (e)(1) of this section, the group may not apportion any amount of the 15 percent tax bracket to S_1's short taxable year ending on June 30, 2007. Rather, S_1 is entitled to exactly $^1/_4$ of such bracket amount, or $12,500.

(iii) *Apportionment of the 15 percent tax bracket to S₂ for its short taxable year.* On July 31, 2007, S_2 is a component member of the P group composed of P, S_2 and S_3. Pursuant to paragraph (e)(1) of this section, the group may not apportion any amount of the 15 percent tax bracket to S_2's short taxable year ending on June 30, 2007. Rather, S_2 is entitled to exactly of such bracket amount, or $16,667.

(iv) *Apportionment of the 15 percent tax bracket to P and S₃ for each of their calendar tax years.* On December 31st, 2007, P and S_3 are component members of the P group. Accordingly, for P and S_3's 2007 calendar tax year, they are each apportioned $25,000 of the 15 percent tax bracket, pursuant to the applicable P group plan.

Example 3. Liquidation of member after its transfer to another controlled group. (i) *Facts.* The facts are the same as in *Example 2*, except that P, on April 30, 2007, sold all of the stock of S_2 to the M-N controlled group. At the time of the sale, M and N are both unrelated to any members of the P group. As in *Example 2*, S_2 liquidates on July 31, 2007, and therefore files a tax return for its short taxable year beginning on January 1, 2007, and ending on July 31, 2007. Pursuant to the sales agreement, the N-M group timely notified P that S_2 had liquidated.

(ii) *Controlled group analysis.* On April 30, 2007, the date of the sale of S_2, the P group reasonably expected that S_2 would be treated as an excluded member with respect to its December 31st, 2007 testing date. On that April 30th date, S_2 had been a member of the P group for less than one-half the number of days of what it expected would be a full 2007 calendar tax year preceding December 31st, 2007 (120 days (January 1-April 30) out of 364 days (January 1-December 30)). Yet, as a result of S_2's subsequent liquidation by the M-N group prior to December 31st, 2007, S_2 became a component member of the P group with respect to the P group's December 31st, 2007 testing date. With respect to that December 31st testing date, S_2 thus was a member of the P group for more than one-half of the number of days of its tax year ending on July 31, 2007, which days proceeded December 31st, 2007 (120 days (January 1-April 30 of 2007) out of 211 days (January 1-July 30 of 2007)). The allocation of the 15 percent tax-bracket amount to the P group members is determined in the same manner as in *Example 2* and, therefore, the bracket amounts allocated to P, S_1, S_2 and S_3 are the same as determined in *Example 2*. The allocation of the bracket amounts would be the same if, at the time P sold all of the S_2 stock, the parties had made a section 338(h)(10) election.

Example 4. Short tax year including a December 31st date. Corporation X owns all of the stock of corporations Y and Z. X, Y and Z each file separate returns. X and Y are on a calendar tax year and Z is on a fiscal tax year beginning October 1 and ending September 30. On January 2, 2007, Z liquidates. Because Z's final tax year (beginning on October 1, 2006 and ending on January 2, 2007) includes a December 31st date, that is, December 31, 2006, it is therefore not subject to the short taxable year rule provided by section 1561(b) and paragraph (e) of this section. Accordingly, Z is a component member of the X-Y-Z group, for the group's December 31st, 2006 testing date. Thus, the rules of this paragraph (e) do not limit the amount of any of the tax-benefit items of section 1561(a) available to Z or to this controlled group.

(f) *Effective/applicability date.*—This section applies to any tax year beginning on or after December 21, 2009. However, taxpayers may apply this section to any Federal income tax return filed on or after December 21, 2009. For tax years beginning before December 21, 2009, see §1.1561-2T as contained in 26 CFR part 1 in effect on April 1, 2009. [Reg. §1.1561-2.]

☐ [T.D. 9476, 12-22-2009.]

[Reg. §1.1561-3]

§1.1561-3. Allocation of the section 1561(a) tax items.—(a) *Filing of form.*—(1) *In general.*—For each tax year that a corporation is a component member of the same controlled group of corporations on a December 31st (its testing date), or, in the case of a short-year member (see section 1561(b) and §1.1561-2(e)), the date substituted for that December 31st date (its testing date), such corporation and all the other component members of such group each must file the required form (that is, Schedule O or any successor form) with the Federal income tax return for that component member's tax year that includes a particular testing date. Each such corporation must file that form with its return whether or not—

(i) An apportionment plan is in effect; or

(ii) Any change is made to the group's apportionment of its section 1561(a) tax benefit items from the previous year.

(2) *Exception for component members that are members of a consolidated group.*—If any of the component members of a controlled group of corporations are also members of a consolidated group, the parent of such consolidated group shall file only one form on behalf of all such members. Such form shall contain the information required for each such member.

(b) *No apportionment plan in effect.*—If the component members of a controlled group of corporations do not have an apportionment plan in effect, the amounts of the section 1561(a) items must be divided equally among all such members. For purposes of the preceding sentence, if any of the component members of a controlled group of corporations are also members of a consolidated group, such members will each be treated as a separate component member of the controlled group.

(c) *Apportionment plan in effect.*—(1) *Adoption of plan.*—The component members of a controlled group of corporations consent to the adoption (or amendment) of an apportionment plan by checking the box to that effect on such form. For purposes of this paragraph (c)—

(i) An apportionment plan that is adopted (including a plan that has been amended) continues in effect until it is terminated;

(ii) A consolidated group is treated collectively as one component member of such group. This treatment occurs even where a member of that consolidated group has joined or left the group, if after such corporation joins or leaves the consolidated group, that group remains in existence, pursuant to §1.1502-75(d); and

(iii) The members must allocate the amounts of the section 1561(a) items between/among themselves as described in the plan.

(2) *Limitation on adopting a plan.*—(i) *Sufficient statute of limitations period for making an assessment of tax.*—The members may only adopt or amend such a plan if there is at least one year remaining in the statutory period (including any extensions thereof) for the assessment of a deficiency against every member the tax liability of which would be increased by the adoption of such a plan.

(ii) *Insufficient statute of limitations period for making an assessment of tax.*—If any member cannot satisfy the requirement of paragraph (c)(2)(i) of this section, the members may not adopt or amend such a plan unless the member not satisfying such requirement has entered into an agreement with the Internal Revenue Service to extend the statute of limitations for the limited purpose of assessing any deficiency against such member attributable to the adoption of such a plan.

(3) *Termination of plan.*—An apportionment plan that is in effect for the component members of a controlled group with respect to a preceding December 31st is terminated with respect to the current December 31st if—

(i) Each member of such group consents to the termination of such a plan for the current December 31st by checking the box to that effect on its form;

(ii) The controlled group ceases to remain in existence (within the meaning of section 1563(a)) during the calendar year ending on the current December 31st;

(iii) Any corporation which was a component member of such group on the preceding December 31st is not a component member of such group on the current December 31st; or

(iv) Any corporation which was not a component member of such group on the preceding December 31st is a component member of such group on the current December 31st.

(d) *Effective/applicability date.*—This section applies to any tax year beginning on or after December 21, 2009. However, taxpayers may apply this section to any Federal income tax return filed on or after December 21, 2009. For tax years beginning before December 21, 2009, see §1.1561-3T as contained in 26 CFR part 1 in effect on April 1, 2009. [Reg. §1.1561-3.]

☐ [T.D. 9476, 12-22-2009.]

[Reg. §1.1563-1]

§1.1563-1. Definition of controlled group of corporations and component members and related concepts.—(a) *Controlled group of corporations.*—(1) *In general.*—(i) *Types of controlled groups.*—For purposes of sections 1561 through

1563, the term *controlled group of corporations* means any group of corporations which is—

    (A) A *parent-subsidiary controlled group* (as defined in paragraph (a)(2) of this section);

    (B) A *brother-sister controlled group* (as defined in paragraph (a)(3)(i) of this section);

    (C) A *combined group* (as defined in paragraph (a)(4) of this section); or

    (D) A *life insurance controlled group* (as defined in paragraph (a)(5) of this section).

    (ii) *Special rules.*—In determining whether a corporation is included in a controlled group of corporations, section 1563(b) and paragraph (b) of this section shall not be taken into account. For rules defining a component member of a controlled group of corporations, including rules defining an excluded member and an additional member, see section 1563(b) and paragraph (b) of this section.

    (iii) *Cross reference.*—For the exclusion of certain stock for purposes of applying the definitions contained in this paragraph, see section 1563(c) and § 1.1563-2.

    (2) *Parent-subsidiary controlled group.*—(i) *Definition.*—The term *parent-subsidiary controlled group* means one or more chains of corporations connected through stock ownership with a common parent corporation if—

    (A) Stock possessing at least 80 percent of the total combined voting power of all classes of stock entitled to vote or at least 80 percent of the total value of shares of all classes of stock of each of the corporations, except the common parent corporation, is owned (directly and with the application of § 1.1563-3(b)(1), relating to options) by one or more of the other corporations; and

    (B) The common parent corporation owns (directly and with the application of § 1.1563-3(b)(1), relating to options) stock possessing at least 80 percent of the total combined voting power of all classes of stock entitled to vote or at least 80 percent of the total value of shares of all classes of stock of at least one of the other corporations, excluding, in computing such voting power or value, stock owned directly by such other corporations.

    (ii) *Examples.*—The definition of a parent-subsidiary controlled group of corporations may be illustrated by the following examples:

    Example 1. P Corporation owns stock possessing 80 percent of the total combined voting power of all classes of stock entitled to vote of S Corporation. P is the common parent of a parent-subsidiary controlled group consisting of member corporations P and S.

    Example 2. Assume the same facts as in *Example 1.* Assume further that S owns stock possessing 80 percent of the total value of shares of all classes of stock of X Corporation. P is the common parent of a parent-subsidiary controlled group consisting of member corporations P, S, and X. The result would be the same if P, rather than S, owned the X stock.

    Example 3. P Corporation owns 80 percent of the only class of stock of S Corporation and S, in turn, owns 40 percent of the only class of stock of X Corporation. P also owns 80 percent of the only class of stock of Y Corporation and Y, in turn, owns 40 percent of the only class of stock of X. P is the common parent of a parent-subsidiary controlled group consisting of member corporations P, S, X, and Y.

    Example 4. P Corporation owns 75 percent of the only class of stock of Y and Z Corporations; Y owns all the remaining stock of Z; and Z owns all the remaining stock of Y. Since intercompany stockholdings are excluded (that is, are not treated as outstanding) for purposes of determining whether P owns stock possessing at least 80 percent of the voting power or value of at least one of the other corporations, P is treated as the owner of stock possessing 100 percent of the voting power and value of Y and of Z for purposes of paragraph (a)(2)(i)(B) of this section. Also, stock possessing 100 percent of the voting power and value of Y and Z is owned by the other corporations in the group within the meaning of paragraph (a)(2)(i)(A) of this section. (P and Y together own stock possessing 100 percent of the voting power and value of Z, and P and Z together own stock possessing 100 percent of the voting power and value of Y.) Therefore, P is the common parent of a parent-subsidiary controlled group of corporations consisting of member corporations P, Y, and Z.

    (3) *Brother-sister controlled group.*—(i) *Definition.*—The term *brother-sister controlled group* means two or more corporations if the same five or fewer persons who are individuals, estates, or trusts own (directly and with the application of the rules contained in § 1.1563-3(b)) stock possessing more than 50 percent of the total combined voting power of all classes of stock entitled to vote or more than 50 percent of the total value of shares of all classes of stock of each corporation, taking into account the stock ownership of each such person only to the extent such stock ownership is identical with respect to each such corporation.

    (ii) *Additional stock ownership requirement for purposes of certain other provisions of law.*—For purposes of any provision of law (other than sections 1561 through 1563) that incorporates the section 1563(a) definition of a controlled group, the term *brother-sister controlled group* means two or more corporations if the same five or fewer persons who are individuals, estates, or trusts own (directly and with the application of the rules contained in § 1.1563-3(b)) stock possessing—

    (A) At least 80 percent of the total combined voting power of all classes of stock entitled to vote or at least 80 percent of the total value of

Reg. § 1.1563-1(a)(3)(ii)(A)

shares of all classes of stock of each corporation (the 80 percent requirement);

(B) More than 50 percent of the total combined voting power of all classes of stock entitled to vote or more than 50 percent of the total value of shares of all classes of stock of each corporation, taking into account the stock ownership of each such person only to the extent such stock ownership is identical with respect to each such corporation (the more-than-50 percent identical ownership requirement); and

(C) The five or fewer persons whose stock ownership is considered for purposes of the 80 percent requirement must be the same persons whose stock ownership is considered for purposes of the more-than-50 percent identical ownership requirement.

(iii) *Examples.*—The principles of paragraph (a)(3)(ii) of this section may be illustrated by the following examples:

Example 1. (i) The outstanding stock of corporations P, W, X, Y, and Z, which have only one class of stock outstanding, is owned by the following unrelated individuals:

Individuals	P (%)	W (%)	X (%)	Y (%)	Z (%)	Identical Ownership
A	55	51	55	55	55	51
B	45	49				(45% in P and W)
C			45			
D				45		
E					45	
Total	100	100	100	100	100	

(ii) Corporations P and W are members of a brother-sister controlled group of corporations. Although the more-than-50 percent identical ownership requirement is met for all 5 corporations, corporations X, Y, and Z are not members because at least 80 percent of the stock of each of those corporations is not owned by the same 5 or fewer persons whose stock ownership is considered for purposes of the more-than-50 percent identical ownership requirement.

Example 2. (i) The outstanding stock of corporations X and Y, which have only one class of stock outstanding, is owned by the following unrelated individuals:

Individuals	Corporations	
	X (%)	Y (%)
A	12	12
B	12	12
C	12	12
D	12	12
E	13	13
F	13	13
G	13	13
H	13	13
Total	100	100

(ii) Any group of five of the shareholders will own more than 50 percent of the stock in each corporation, in identical holdings. However, X and Y are not members of a brother-sister controlled group because at least 80 percent of the stock of each corporation is not owned by the same five or fewer persons.

Example 3. (i) Corporation X and Y each have two classes of stock outstanding, voting common and non-voting common. (None of this stock is excluded from the definition of stock under section 1563(c).) Unrelated individuals A and B own the following percentages of the class of stock entitled to vote (voting) and of the total value of shares of all classes of stock (value) in each of corporations X and Y:

Individuals	Corporations	
	X	Y
A	100% voting; 60% value	75% voting; 60% value
B	0% voting; 10% value	25% voting; 10% value

Reg. §1.1563-1(a)(3)(ii)(B)

(ii) No other shareholder of X owns (or is considered to own) any stock in Y. X and Y are a brother-sister controlled group of corporations. The group meets the more-than-50 percent identical ownership requirement because A and B own more than 50 percent of the total value of shares of all classes of stock of X and Y in identical holdings. (The group also meets the more-than-50 percent identical ownership requirement because of A's voting stock ownership.) The group meets the 80 percent requirement because A and B own at least 80 percent of the total combined voting power of all classes of stock entitled to vote.

Example 4. Assume the same facts as in *Example 3* except that the value of the stock owned by A and B is not more than 50 percent of the total value of shares of all classes of stock of each corporation in identical holdings. X and Y are not a brother-sister controlled group of corporations. The group meets the more-than-50 percent identical ownership requirement because A owns more than 50 percent of the total combined voting power of the voting stock of each corporation. For purposes of the 80 percent requirement, B's voting stock in Y cannot be combined with A's voting stock in Y since B, who does not own any voting stock in X, is not a person whose ownership is considered for purposes of the more-than-50 percent identical ownership requirement. Because no other shareholder owns stock in both X and Y, these other shareholders' stock ownership is not counted towards meeting either the more-than-50 percent identical ownership requirement or the 80 percent ownership requirement.

(iv) *Special rule if prior law applies.*—Paragraph (a)(3)(ii) of this section, as amended by TD 8179, applies to taxable years ending on or after December 31, 1970. See, however, the transitional rule in paragraph (d) of this section.

(4) *Combined group.*—(i) *Definition.*—The term *combined group* means any group of three or more corporations if—

(A) Each such corporation is a member of either a parent-subsidiary controlled group of corporations or a brother-sister controlled group of corporations; and

(B) At least one of such corporations is the common parent of a parent-subsidiary controlled group and also is a member of a brother-sister controlled group.

(ii) *Examples.*—The definition of a combined group of corporations may be illustrated by the following examples:

Example 1. A, an individual, owns stock possessing 80 percent of the total combined voting power of all classes of the stock of corporations X and Y. Y, in turn, owns stock possessing 80 percent of the total combined voting power of all classes of the stock of corporation Z. X, Y, and Z are members of the same combined group since—

(i) X, Y, and Z are each members of either a parent-subsidiary or brother-sister controlled group of corporations; and

(ii) Y is the common parent of a parent-subsidiary controlled group of corporations consisting of Y and Z, and also is a member of a brother-sister controlled group of corporations consisting of X and Y.

Example 2. Assume the same facts as in *Example 1*, and further assume that corporation X owns 80 percent of the total value of shares of all classes of stock of corporation S. X, Y, Z, and S are members of the same combined group.

(5) *Life insurance controlled group.*—(i) *Definition.*—The term *life insurance controlled group* means two or more life insurance companies each of which is a member of a controlled group of corporations described in paragraph (a)(2), (a)(3)(i), or (a)(4) of this section and to which § 1.1502-47(f)(6) does not apply. Such insurance companies shall be treated as a controlled group of corporations separate from any other corporations which are members of a controlled group described in such paragraph (a)(2), (a)(3)(i), or (a)(4) of this section. For purposes of this section, the common parent of the controlled group described in paragraph (a)(2) of this section shall be referred to as the common parent of the life insurance controlled group.

(ii) *Examples.*—The following examples illustrate the definition of a *life insurance controlled group.* In these examples, L indicates a life company, another letter indicates a nonlife company and each corporation uses the calendar year as its taxable year:

Example 1. Since January 1, 1999, corporation P has owned all the stock of corporations L_1 and Y, and L_1 has owned all the stock of corporation X. On January 1, 2005, Y acquired all of the stock of corporation L_2. Since L_1 and L_2 are members of a parent-subsidiary controlled group of corporations, such companies are treated as members of a life insurance controlled group separate from the parent-subsidiary controlled group consisting of P, X and Y. For purposes of this section, P is referred to as the common parent of the life insurance controlled group even though P is not a member of such group.

Example 2. The facts are the same as in *Example 1*, except that, beginning with the 2005 tax year, the P affiliated group elected to file a consolidated return and P made a section 1504(c)(2) election. Pursuant to paragraph (a)(5)(i) of this section, L_1 and L_2 are not members of a separate life insurance controlled group. Instead, P, X, Y, L_1 and L_2 constitute one controlled group. See § 1.1502-47(f)(6).

(6) *Voting power of stock.*—For purposes of this section, and § § 1.1563-2 and 1.1563-3, in determining whether the stock owned by a person

(or persons) possesses a certain percentage of the total combined voting power of all classes of stock entitled to vote of a corporation, consideration will be given to all the facts and circumstances of each case. A share of stock will generally be considered as possessing the voting power accorded to such share by the corporate charter, by-laws, or share certificate. On the other hand, if there is any agreement, whether express or implied, that a shareholder will not vote his stock in a corporation, the formal voting rights possessed by his stock may be disregarded in determining the percentage of the total combined voting power possessed by the stock owned by other shareholders in the corporation, if the result is that the corporation becomes a component member of a controlled group of corporations. Moreover, if a shareholder agrees to vote his stock in a corporation in the manner specified by another shareholder in the corporation, the voting rights possessed by the stock owned by the first shareholder may be considered to be possessed by the stock owned by such other shareholder if the result is that the corporation becomes a component member of a controlled group of corporations.

(b) *Component members.*—(1) *In general.*—(i) *Definition.*—For purposes of sections 1561 through 1563, a corporation is with respect to its taxable year a component member of a controlled group of corporations for the group's testing date if such corporation—

(A) Is a member of such controlled group on such testing date and is not treated as an excluded member under paragraph (b)(2) of this section; or

(B) Is not a member of such controlled group on such testing date but is treated as an additional member under paragraph (b)(3) of this section.

(ii) *Member of a controlled group of corporations.*—For purposes of sections 1561 through 1563, a member of a controlled group is a corporation connected with other member(s) of a controlled group under the stock ownership rules and the stock qualification rules set forth in section 1563. Under these rules, for a corporation to qualify as a component member of the group with respect to a group's December 31st testing date (or the short-year testing date for a short-year testing date), that corporation does not have to be a member of that group on that group's testing date. In addition, a corporation that is a member of a controlled group on the group's testing date does not necessarily qualify as a component member of that group with respect to that testing date.

(iii) *Additional concepts used in applying the controlled group rules.*

(A) The term *testing date* means the date used for determining the status of controlled group members as either component

members or excluded members. That testing date is then also used to determine which taxable years of those component members are to be subjected to the controlled group rules. Generally, a member's testing date is the December 31st date included within that member's taxable year, whether such member is on a calendar or fiscal taxable year. However, if a component member of a controlled group has a short taxable year that does not include a December 31st date, then the last day of that short taxable year becomes that member's testing date.

(B) The term *testing period* means the time period used for determining the status of controlled group members as either component members or excluded members. The testing period begins on the first day of a member's taxable year and ends on the day before its testing date. (Generally, the testing date is December 31st, but for a component member having a short taxable year not ending on December 31st, the testing date for the short taxable year of that member (and only that member) becomes the last day of that member's short taxable year.) Thus, for a member on a fiscal taxable year, the portion of its taxable year beginning on December 31st and ending on the last day of its taxable year is not taken into account for determining its status as a component member or an excluded member.

(2) *Excluded members.*—(i) *Temporal test.*—A corporation, which is a member of a controlled group of corporations on the group's testing date, a date included within that member's taxable year, but who was a member of such group for less than one-half of the number of days of its testing period, shall be treated as an excluded member of such group for that group's testing date.

(ii) *Qualification test.*—A corporation which is a member of a controlled group of corporations on a testing date shall be treated as an excluded member of such group on such date if, for its taxable year including such date, such corporation is—

(A) Exempt from taxation under section 501(a) (except a corporation which is subject to tax on its unrelated business taxable income under section 511) or 521 for such taxable year;

(B) A foreign corporation not subject to taxation under section 882(a) for the taxable year;

(C) An S corporation (as defined in section 1361) for purposes of any tax benefit item described in section 1561(a) to which it is not subject;

(D) A franchised corporation (as defined in section 1563(f)(4) and § 1.1563-4); or

(E) An insurance company subject to taxation under section 801, unless such insurance company (without regard to this paragraph (b)(2)(ii)(E)) is a component member of a life

Reg. §1.1563-1(b)(1)

insurance controlled group described in paragraph (a)(5)(i) of this section or unless § 1.1502-47(f)(6) applies (which treats a life insurance company, for which a section 1504(c)(2) election is effective, as a member (whether eligible or ineligible) of a life-nonlife affiliated group).

(3) *Additional members.*—A corporation shall be treated as an additional member of a controlled group of corporations, that is, an additional component member, on the group's testing date if it—

(i) Is not a member of such group on such date;

(ii) Is not described, with respect to such taxable year, in paragraph (b)(2)(ii)(A), (b)(2)(ii)(B), (b)(2)(ii)(C), (b)(2)(ii)(D), or (b)(2)(ii)(E) of this section; and

(iii) Was a member of such group for one-half (or more) of the number of days in its testing period.

(4) *Examples.*—The provisions of this paragraph (b) may be illustrated by the following examples:

Example 1. B, an individual, owns all of the stock of corporations W and X on each day of 1964. W and X each use the calendar year as their taxable year. On January 1, 1964, B also owns all the stock of corporation Y (a fiscal year corporation with a taxable year beginning on July 1, 1964, and ending on June 30, 1965), which stock he sells on October 15, 1964. On December 1, 1964, B purchases all the stock of corporation Z (a fiscal year corporation with a taxable year beginning on September 1, 1964, and ending on August 31, 1965). On December 31, 1964, W, X, and Z are members of the same controlled group. However, the component members of the group on such December 31st are W, X, and Y. Under paragraph (b)(2)(i) of this section, Z is treated as an excluded member of the group on December 31, 1964, since Z was a member of the group for less than one-half of the number of days (29 out of 121 days) during the period beginning on September 1, 1964 (the first day of its taxable year) and ending on December 30, 1964. Under paragraph (b)(3) of this section, Y is treated as an additional member of the group on December 31, 1964, since Y was a member of the group for at least one-half of the number of days (107 out of 183 days) during the period beginning on July 1, 1964 (the first day of its taxable year) and ending on December 30, 1964.

Example 2. On January 1, 1964, corporation P owns all the stock of corporation S, which in turn owns all the stock of corporation S-1. On November 1, 1964, P purchases all of the stock of corporation X from the public and sells all of the stock of S to the public. Corporation X owns all the stock of corporation Y during 1964. P, S, S-1, X, and Y file their returns on the basis of the calendar year. On December 31, 1964, P, X, and Y are members of a parent-subsidiary controlled

group of corporations; also, corporations S and S-1 are members of a different parent-subsidiary controlled group on such date. However, since X and Y have been members of the parent-subsidiary controlled group of which P is the common parent for less than one-half the number of days during the period January 1 through December 30, 1964, they are not component members of such group on such date. On the other hand, X and Y have been members of a parent-subsidiary controlled group of which X is the common parent for at least one-half the number of days during the period January 1 through December 30, 1964, and therefore they are component members of such group on December 31, 1964. Also since S and S-1 were members of the parent-subsidiary controlled group of which P is the common parent for at least one-half the number of days in the taxable years of each such corporation during the period January 1 through December 30, 1964, P, S, and S-1 are component members of such group on December 31, 1964.

Example 3. Throughout 1964, corporation M owns all the stock of corporation F which, in turn, owns all the stock of corporations L_1, L_2, X, and Y. M is a domestic mutual insurance company subject to taxation under section 821, F is a foreign corporation not engaged in a trade or business within the United States, L_1 and L_2 are domestic life insurance companies subject to taxation under section 802, and X and Y are domestic corporations subject to tax under section 11 of the Code. Each corporation uses the calendar year as its taxable year. On December 31, 1964, M, F, L_1, L_2, X, and Y are members of a parent-subsidiary controlled group of corporations. However, under paragraph (b)(2)(ii) of this section, M, F, L_1, and L_2 are treated as excluded members of the group on December 31, 1964. Thus, on December 31, 1964, the component members of the parent-subsidiary controlled group of which M is the common parent include only X and Y. Furthermore, since paragraph (b)(2)(ii)(E) of this section does not result in L_1 and L_2 being treated as excluded members of a life insurance controlled group, L_1 and L_2 are component members of a life insurance controlled group on December 31, 1964.

Example 4. Individual A owns all of the stock of corporations X, Y and Z. Each of these corporations is an S corporation. X, Y, and Z are each members of a brother-sister controlled group, even though each such corporation is treated as an excluded member of such group. See § 1.1563-1(b)(2)(ii)(C).

(5) *Application of constructive ownership rules.*—For purposes of paragraphs (b)(2)(i) and (b)(3)(iii) of this section, it is necessary to determine whether a corporation was a member of a controlled group of corporations for one-half (or more) of the number of days in its taxable year which precede the December 31st falling within such taxable year. Therefore, the constructive ownership rules contained in § 1.1563-3(b) (to the

extent applicable in making such determination) must be applied on a day-by-day basis. For example, if P Corporation owns all the stock of X Corporation on each day of 1964, and on December 30, 1964, acquires an option to purchase all the stock of Y Corporation (a calendar-year taxpayer which has been in existence on each day of 1964), the application of §1.1563-3(b)(1) on a day-by-day basis results in Y being a member of the brother- sister controlled group on only one day of Y's 1964 year which precedes December 31, 1964. Accordingly, since Y is not a member of such group for one-half or more of the number of days in its 1964 year preceding December 31, 1964, Y is treated as an excluded member of such group on December 31, 1964.

(c) *Overlapping groups.*—(1) *In general.*—If on a December 31st a corporation is a component member of a controlled group of corporations by reason of ownership of stock possessing at least 80 percent of the total value of shares of all classes of stock of the corporation, and if on such December 31st such corporation is also a component member of another controlled group of corporations by reason of ownership of other stock (that is, stock not used to satisfy the at-least-80 percent total value test) possessing at least 80 percent of the total combined voting power of all classes of stock of the corporation entitled to vote, then such corporation shall be treated as a component member only of the controlled group of which it is a component member by reason of the ownership of at least 80 percent of the total value of its shares.

(2) *Brother-sister controlled groups.*—(i) *One corporation.*—If on a December 31st, a corporation would, without the application of this paragraph (c)(2), be a component member of more than one brother-sister controlled group on such date, the corporation will be treated as a component member of only one such group on such date. Such corporation may elect the group in which it is to be included by including on or with its income tax return for the taxable year that includes such date a statement entitled, "STATEMENT TO ELECT CONTROLLED GROUP PURSUANT TO §1.1563-1(c)(2)." This statement must include—

(A) A description of each of the controlled groups in which the corporation could be included. The description must include the name and employer identification number of each component member of each such group and the stock ownership of the component members of each such group; and

(B) The following representation: [INSERT NAME AND EMPLOYER IDENTIFICA-

TION NUMBER OF CORPORATION] ELECTS TO BE TREATED AS A COMPONENT MEMBER OF THE [INSERT DESIGNATION OF GROUP].

(ii) *Multiple corporations.*—If more than one corporation would, without the application of this paragraph (c)(2), be a component member of more than one controlled group, those corporations electing to be component members of the same group must file a single statement. The statement must contain the information described in paragraph (c)(2)(i) of this section, plus the names and employer identification numbers of all other corporations designating the same group. The original statement must be included on or with the original Federal income tax return (including any amended return filed on or before the due date (including extensions) of such return) of the corporation that, among those corporations which would (without the application of this paragraph (c)(2)) belong to more than one group, has the taxable year including such December 31st which ends on the earliest date. That corporation must provide a copy of the statement to each other corporation included in the statement and represent in its statement that it has done so. Either the original or a copy of the statement must be retained by each corporation as part of its records. See §1.6001-1(e) of this chapter.

(iii) *Election.*—(A) An election filed under this paragraph (c)(2) is irrevocable and effective until a change in the stock ownership of the corporation results in termination of membership in the controlled group in which such corporation has been included.

(B) In the event no election is filed in accordance with the provisions of this paragraph (c)(2), then the Internal Revenue Service will determine the group in which such corporation is to be included. Such determination will be binding for all subsequent years unless the corporation files a valid election with respect to any such subsequent year or until a change in the stock ownership of the corporation results in termination of membership in the controlled group in which such corporation has been included.

(iv) *Examples.*—The provisions of this paragraph (c)(2) may be illustrated by the following examples (in which it is assumed that all the individuals are unrelated):

Example 1. (i) On each day of 1970 all the outstanding stock of corporations X, Y, and Z is held in the following manner:

Individuals	Corporations		
	X (%)	Y (%)	Z (%)
A	55	40	5
B	40	20	40
C	5	40	55

(ii) Since the more-than-50 percent identical ownership requirement of section 1563(a)(2) is met with respect to corporations X and Y and with respect to corporations Y and Z, but not with respect to corporations X, Y, and Z, corporation Y would, without the application of this paragraph (c)(2), be a component member on December 31, 1970, of overlapping groups consisting of X and Y and of Y and Z. If Y does not file an election in accordance with paragraph (c)(2)(i) of this section, the Internal Revenue Service will determine the group in which Y is to be included.

Example 2. (i) On each day of 1970, all the outstanding stock of corporations V, W, X, Y, and Z is held in the following manner:

Individuals	Corporations				
	V	W	X	Y	Z
D	52	52	52	52	52
E	40	2	2	2	2
F	2	40	2	2	2
G	2	2	40	2	2
H	2	2	2	40	2
I	2	2	2	2	40

(ii) On December 31, 1970, the more-than-50 percent identical ownership requirement of section 1563(a)(2) may be met with regard to any combination of the corporations but all five corporations cannot be included as component members of a single controlled group because the inclusion of all the corporations in a single group would be dependent upon taking into account the stock ownership of more than five persons. Therefore, if the corporations do not file a statement in accordance with paragraph (c)(2)(ii) of this section, the Internal Revenue Service will determine the group in which each corporation is to be included. The corporations or the Internal Revenue Service, as the case may be, may designate that three corporations be included in one group and two corporations in another, or that any four corporations be included in one group and that the remaining corporation not be included in any group.

(d) *Transitional rules.*—(1) *In general.*—Treasury decision 8179 amended paragraph (a)(3)(ii) of this section to revise the definition of a brother-sister controlled group of corporations. In general, those amendments are effective for taxable years ending on or after December 31, 1970.

(2) *Limited nonretroactivity.*—(i) *Old group.*—Under the authority of section 7805(b), the Internal Revenue Service will treat an old group as a brother-sister controlled group corporations for purposes of applying sections 401, 404(a), 408(k), 409A, 410, 411, 412, 414, 415, and 4971 of the Internal Revenue Code (Code) and sections 202, 203, 204, and 302 of the Employment Retirement Income Security Act of 1974 (ERISA) in a plan year or taxable year beginning before March 2, 1988, to the extent necessary to prevent an adverse effect on any old member (or any other corporation), or on any plan or other entity described in such sections (including plans, etc., of corporations not part of such old group), that would result solely from the retroactive effect of

the amendment to this section by TD 8179. An adverse effect includes the disqualification of a plan or the disallowance of a deduction or credit for a contribution to a plan. The Internal Revenue Service, however, will not treat an old member as a member of an old group to the extent that such treatment will have an adverse effect on that old member.

(ii) *Old member of old group.*—Section 7805(b) will not be applied pursuant to paragraph (d)(2)(i) of this section to treat an old member of an old group as a member of a brother-sister controlled group to prevent an adverse effect for a taxable year if, for that taxable year, that old member treats or has treated itself as not being a member of that old group for purposes of sections 401, 404(a), 408(k), 409A, 410, 411, 412, 414, 415, and 4971 of the Code and sections 202, 203, 204, and 302 and Title IV of ERISA for such taxable year (such as by filing, with respect to such taxable year, a return, amended return, or claim for credit or refund in which the amount of any deduction, credit, limitation, or tax due is determined by treating itself as not being a member of the old group for purposes of those sections). However, the fact that one or more (but not all) of the old members do not qualify for section 7805(b) treatment because of the preceding sentence will not preclude that old member (or members) from being treated as a member of the old group under paragraph (d)(2)(i) of this section in order to prevent the disallowance of a deduction or credit of another old member (or other corporation) or to prevent the disqualification of, or other adverse effect on, another old member's plan (or other entity) described in the sections of the Code and ERISA enumerated in such paragraph.

(3) *Election of general nonretroactivity.*—In the case of a taxable year ending on or after December 31, 1970, and before March 2, 1988, an old group will be treated as a brother-sister con-

Reg. § 1.1563-1(d)(3)

trolled group of corporations for all purposes of the Code for such taxable year if—

(i) Each old member files a statement consenting to such treatment for such taxable year with the District Director having audit jurisdiction over its return within six months after March 2, 1988; and

(ii) No old member—

(A) Files or has filed, with respect to such taxable year, a return, amended return, or claim for credit or refund in which the amount of any deduction, credit, limitation, or tax due is determined by treating any old member as not a member of the old group; or

(B) Treats the employees of all members of the old group as not being employed by a single employer for purposes of sections 401, 404(a), 408(k), 409A, 410, 411, 412, 414, 415, and 4971 of the Code and sections 202, 203, 204, and 302 of ERISA for such taxable year.

(4) *Definitions.*—For purposes of this paragraph (d)—

(i) An *old group* is a brother-sister controlled group of corporations, determined by applying paragraph (a)(3)(ii) of this section as in effect before the amendments made by TD 8179, that is not a brother-sister controlled group of corporations, determined by applying paragraph (a)(3)(ii) of this section as amended by such Treasury decision; and

(ii) An *old member* is any corporation that is a member of an old group.

(5) *Election to choose between membership in more than one controlled group.*—(i) *In general.*—A corporation may make an election under paragraph (c)(2) of this section by filing an amended return on or before September 2, 1988 if—

(A) An old member has filed an election under paragraph (c)(2) of this section to be treated as a component member of an old group for a December 31st before March 2, 1988; and

(B) That corporation would (without regard to such paragraph (c)(2)) be a component member of more than one brother-sister controlled group (not including an old group) on the December 31st.

(ii) *Exception.*—This paragraph (d)(5) does not apply to a corporation that is treated as a member of an old group under paragraph (d)(3) of this section.

(6) *Refunds.*—See section 6511(a) for period of limitation on filing claims for credit or refund.

(e) *Effective/applicability date.*—This section applies to taxable years beginning on or after May 26, 2009. However, taxpayers may apply this section to taxable years beginning before May 26, 2009. For taxable years beginning before May 26, 2009, see §1.1563-1T as contained in 26 CFR part 1 in effect on April 1, 2009. Paragraph (a)(1)(ii) of this section applies to taxable years beginning on or after April 11, 2011. [Reg. §1.1563-1.]

☐ [*T.D.* 9451, 5-26-2009. *Amended by T.D.* 9522, 4-8-2011.]

[Reg. §1.1563-2]

§1.1563-2. Excluded stock.—(a) *Certain stock excluded.*—For purposes of sections 1561 through 1563 and the regulations thereunder, the term "stock" does not include—

(1) Nonvoting stock which is limited and preferred as to dividends, and

(2) Treasury stock.

(b) *Stock treated as excluded stock.*—(1) *Parent-subsidiary controlled group.*—If a corporation (hereinafter in this paragraph referred to as "parent corporation") owns 50 percent or more of the total combined voting power of all classes of stock entitled to vote or 50 percent or more of the total value of shares of all classes of stock in another corporation (hereinafter in this paragraph referred to as "subsidiary corporation"), the provisions of subparagraph (2) of this paragraph shall apply. For purposes of this subparagraph, stock owned by a corporation means stock owned directly plus stock owned with the application of the constructive ownership rules of paragraph (b)(1) and (4) of §1.1563-3, relating to options and attribution from corporations. In determining whether the stock owned by a corporation possesses the requisite percentage of the total combined voting power of all classes of stock entitled to vote of another corporation, see paragraph (a)(6) of §1.1563-1.

(2) *Stock treated as not outstanding.*—If the provisions of this subparagraph apply, then for purposes of determining whether the parent corporation or the subsidiary corporation is a member of a parent-subsidiary controlled group of corporations within the meaning of paragraph (a)(2) of §1.1563-1, the following stock of the subsidiary corporation shall, except as otherwise provided in paragraph (c) of this section, be treated as if it were not outstanding:

(i) *Plan of deferred compensation.*—Stock in the subsidiary corporation held by a trust which is part of a plan of deferred compensation for the benefit of the employees of the parent corporation or the subsidiary corporation. The term "plan of deferred compensation" shall have the same meaning such term has in section 406(a)(3) and the regulations thereunder.

(ii) *Principal stockholders and officers.*—Stock in the subsidiary corporation owned (directly and with the application of the rules contained in paragraph (b) of §1.1563-3) by an individual who is a principal stockholder or officer of the parent corporation. A principal stockholder of the parent corporation is an individual who owns (directly and with the application of the rules contained in paragraph (b) of §1.1563-3) 5 percent or more of the total combined voting power of all classes of stock entitled to vote or 5 percent or more of the total value of shares of all classes of stock of the parent corporation. An officer of the parent corporation includes the president, vice-presidents, general manager, treasurer, secretary, and comptroller of such corporation, and any other person who performs duties corresponding to those normally performed by persons occupying such positions.

(iii) *Employees.*—Stock in the subsidiary corporation owned (directly and with the application of the rules contained in paragraph (b) of § 1.1563-3) by an employee of the subsidiary corporation if such stock is subject to conditions which substantially restrict or limit the employee's right (or if the employee constructively owns such stock, the direct owner's right) to dispose of such stock and which run in favor of the parent or subsidiary corporation. In general, any condition which extends, directly or indirectly, to the parent corporation or the subsidiary corporation preferential rights with respect to the acquisition of the employee's (or direct owner's) stock will be considered to be a condition described in the preceding sentence. It is not necessary, in order for a condition to be considered to be in favor of the parent corporation or the subsidiary corporation, that the parent or subsidiary be extended a discriminatory concession with respect to the price of the stock. For example, a condition whereby the parent corporation is given a right of first refusal with respect to any stock of the subsidiary corporation offered by an employee for sale is a condition which substantially restricts or limits the employee's right to dispose of such stock and runs in favor of the parent corporation. Moreover, any legally enforceable condition which prohibits the employee from disposing of his stock without the consent of the parent (or a subsidiary of the parent) will be considered to be a substantial limitation running in favor of the parent corporation.

(iv) *Controlled exempt organization.*—Stock in the subsidiary corporation owned (directly and with the application of the rules contained in paragraph (b) of § 1.1563-3) by an organization (other than the parent corporation)—

(*a*) To which section 501 (relating to certain educational and charitable organizations which are exempt from tax) applies, and

(*b*) Which is controlled directly or indirectly by the parent corporation or subsidiary corporation, by an individual, estate, or trust that is a principal stockholder of the parent corporation, by an officer of the parent corporation, or by any combination thereof.

The terms "principal stockholder of the parent corporation" and "officer of the parent corpora-

tion" shall have the same meanings in this subdivision as in subdivision (ii) of this subparagraph. The term "control" as used in this subdivision means control in fact and the determination of whether the control requirement of (*b*) of this subdivision is met will depend upon all the facts and circumstances of each case, without regard to whether such control is legally enforceable and irrespective of the method by which such control is exercised or exercisable.

(3) *Brother-sister controlled group.*—If 5 or fewer persons (hereinafter referred to as common owners) who are individuals, estates, or trusts own (directly and with the application of the rules contained in paragraph (b) of § 1.1563-3) stock possessing 50 percent or more of the total combined voting power of all classes of stock entitled to vote or 50 percent or more of the total value of shares of all classes of stock in a corporation, the provisions of subparagraph (4) of this paragraph shall apply. In determining whether the stock owned by such person or persons possesses the requisite percentage of the total combined voting power of all classes of stock entitled to vote of a corporation, see paragraph (a)(6) of § 1.1563-1.

(4) *Stock treated as not outstanding.*—If the provisions of this subparagraph apply, then for purposes of determining whether a corporation is a member of a brother-sister controlled group of corporations within the meaning of paragraph (a)(3) of § 1.1563-1, the following stock of such corporation shall, except as otherwise provided in paragraph (c) of this section, be treated as if it were not outstanding:

(i) *Exempt employees' trust.*—Stock in such corporation held by an employees' trust described in section 401(a) which is exempt from tax under section 501(a), if such trust is for the benefit of the employees of such corporation.

(ii) *Employees.*—Stock in such corporation owned (directly and with the application of the rules contained in paragraph (b) of § 1.1563-3) by an employee of such corporation if such stock is subject to conditions which run in favor of a common owner of such corporation (or in favor of such corporation) and which substantially restrict or limit the employee's right (or if the employee constructively owns such stock, the record owner's right) to dispose of such stock. The principles of subparagraph (2)(iii) of this paragraph shall apply in determining whether a condition satisfies the requirements of the preceding sentence. Thus, in general, a condition which extends, directly or indirectly, to a common owner or such corporation preferential rights with respect to the acquisition of the employee's (or record owner's) stock will be considered to be a condition which satisfies such requirements. For purposes of this subdivision, if a condition which restricts or limits an employee's right (or record owner's right) to dispose of his stock also applies to the stock in such corporation held by such common owner pursuant to a bona fide reciprocal stock purchase arrangement, such condition shall not be treated as one which restricts or limits the employee's (or record owner's) right to dispose of such stock. An example of a reciprocal stock purchase arrangement is an agreement whereby a common owner and the employee are given a right of first refusal with respect to stock of the employer corporation owned by the other party. If, however, the agreement also provides that the common owner has the right to purchase the stock of the employer corporation owned by the employee in the event that the corporation should discharge the employee for reasonable cause, the purchase arrangement would not be reciprocal within the meaning of this subdivision.

(iii) *Controlled exempt organization.*—Stock in such corporation owned (directly and with the application of the rules contained in paragraph (b) of § 1.1563-3) by an organization—

(a) To which section 501(c)(3) (relating to certain educational and charitable organizations which are exempt from tax) applies, and

(b) Which is controlled directly or indirectly by such corporation, by an individual, estate, or trust that is a principal stockholder of such corporation, by an officer of such corporation, or by any combination thereof. The terms "principal stockholder" and "officer" shall have the same meanings in this subdivision as in subparagraph (2)(ii) of this paragraph. The term "control" as used in this subdivision means control in fact and the determination of whether the control requirement of (b) of this subdivision is met will depend upon all the facts and circumstances of each case, without regard to whether such control is legally enforceable and irrespective of the method by which such control is exercised or exercisable.

(5) *Other controlled groups.*—The provisions of subparagraphs (1), (2), (3), and (4) of this paragraph shall apply in determining whether a corporation is a member of a combined group (within the meaning of paragraph (a)(4) of § 1.1563-1) or an insurance group (within the meaning of paragraph (a)(5) of § 1.1563-1). For example, under paragraph (a)(4) of § 1.1563-1, in order for a corporation to be a member of a combined group such corporation must be a member of a parent-subsidiary group or a brother-sister group. Accordingly, the excluded stock rules provided by this paragraph are applicable in determining whether the corporation is a member of such group.

(6) *Meaning of employee.*—For purposes of this section, § § 1.1563-3 and 1.1563-4, the term "employee" has the same meaning such term is given in section 3306(i) of the Code (relating to definitions for purposes of the Federal Unemployment Tax Act). Accordingly, the term employee as used in such sections includes an officer of a corporation.

(7) *Examples.*—The provisions of this paragraph may be illustrated by the following examples:

Example (1). Corporation P owns 70 of the 100 shares of the only class of stock of corporation S. The remaining shares of S are owned as follows: 4 shares by Jones (the general manager of P), and 26 shares by Smith (who also owns 5 percent of the total combined voting power of the stock of P). P satisfies the 50 percent stock ownership requirement of subparagraph (1) of this paragraph with respect to S. Since Jones is an officer of P and Smith is a principal stockholder of P, under subparagraph (2)(ii) of this paragraph the S stock owned by Jones and Smith is treated as not outstanding for purposes of determining whether P and S are members of a parent-subsidiary controlled group of corporations within the meaning of paragraph (a)(2) of § 1.1563-1. Thus, P is considered to own stock possessing 100 percent (70 ÷ 70) of the total voting power and value of all the S stock. Accordingly, P and S are members of a parent-subsidiary controlled group of corporations.

Example (2). Assume the same facts as in example (1) and further assume that Jones owns 15 shares of the 100 shares of the only class of stock of corporation S-1, and corporation S owns 75 shares of such stock. P satisfies the 50 percent stock ownership requirement of subparagraph (1) of this paragraph with respect to S-1 since P is considered as owning 52.5 percent (70 percent × 75 percent) of the S-1 stock with the application of paragraph (b)(4) of § 1.1563-3. Since Jones is an officer of P, under subparagraph (2)(ii) of this paragraph, the S-1 stock owned by Jones is treated as not outstanding for purposes of determining whether S-1 is a member of the parent-subsidiary controlled group of corporations. Thus, S is considered to own stock possessing 88.2 percent (75 ÷ 85) of the voting power and value of the S-1 stock. Accordingly, P, S, and S-1 are members of a parent-subsidiary controlled group of corporations.

Example (3). Corporation X owns 60 percent of the only class of stock of corporation Y. Davis, the president of Y, owns the remaining 40 percent of the stock of Y. Davis has agreed that if he offers his stock in Y for sale he will first offer the stock to X at a price equal to the fair market value of the stock on the first date the stock is offered for sale. Since Davis is an employee of Y within the meaning of section 3306(i) of the Code, and his stock in Y is subject to a condition which substantially restricts or limits his right to dispose of such stock and runs in favor of X, under subparagraph (2)(iii) of this paragraph such stock is treated as if it were not outstanding for purposes of determining whether X and Y are members of a parent subsidiary controlled group of corporations. Thus, X is considered to own stock possessing 100 percent of the voting power and value of the stock of Y. Accordingly, X and Y are members of a parent-subsidiary controlled group of corporations. The result would be the same if Davis's wife, instead of Davis, owned directly the 40 percent stock interest in Y and such stock was subject to a right of first refusal running in favor of X.

(c) *Exception.*—(1) *General.*—If stock of a corporation is owned by a person directly or with the application of the rules contained in paragraph (b) of § 1.1563-3 and such ownership results in the corporation being a component member of a controlled group of corporations on a December 31, then the stock shall not be treated as excluded stock under the provisions of paragraph (b) of this section if the result of applying such provisions is that such corporation is not a component member of a controlled group of corporations on such December 31.

(2) *Illustration.*—The provisions of this paragraph may be illustrated by the following example:

Example. On each day of 1965, corporation P owns directly 50 of the 100 shares of the only class of stock of corporation S. Jones, an officer of P, owns directly 30 shares of S stock and P has an option to acquire such 30 shares from Jones. The remaining shares of S are owned by unrelated persons. If, pursuant to the provisions of paragraph (b)(2)(ii) of this section, the 30 shares of S stock owned directly by Jones is treated as not outstanding, the result is that P would be treated as owning stock possessing only 71 percent (50 ÷ 70) of the total voting power and value of S stock, and S would not be a component member of a controlled group of corporations on December 31, 1965. However, since P is considered as owning the 30 shares of S stock with the application of paragraph (b)(1) of this section, and such ownership plus the S stock directly owned by P (50 shares) results in S being a component member of a controlled group of corporations on December 31, 1965, the provisions of this paragraph apply. Therefore, the provisions of paragraph (b)(2)(ii) of this section do not apply with respect to the 30 shares of S stock, and on December 31, 1965, S is a component member of a controlled group of corporations consisting of P and S. [Reg. § 1.1563-2.]

☐ [T.D. 6845, 8-4-65. *Amended by T.D.* 7181, 4-24-72.]

[Reg. § 1.1563-3]

§ 1.1563-3. Rules for determining stock ownership.—(a) *In general.*—In determining stock ownership for purposes of §§ 1.1562-5, 1.1563-1, 1.1563-2, and this section, the constructive ownership rules of paragraph (b) of this section apply to the extent such rules are referred to in such sections. The application of such rules shall be subject to the operating rules and special rules contained in paragraphs (c) and (d) of this section.

(b) *Constructive ownership.*—(1) *Options.*—If a person has an option to acquire any outstanding stock of a corporation, such stock shall be considered as owned by such person. For purposes of this subparagraph, an option to acquire such an option, and each one of a series of such options, shall be considered as an option to acquire such stock. For example, assume Smith owns an option to purchase 100 shares of the outstanding stock of M Corporation. Under this subparagraph, Smith is considered to own such 100 shares. The result would be the same if Smith owned an option to acquire the option (or one of a series of options) to purchase 100 shares of M stock.

(2) *Attribution from partnerships.*—(i) Stock owned, directly or indirectly, by or for a partnership shall be considered as owned by any partner having an interest of 5 percent or more in either the capital or profits of the partnership in proportion to his interest in capital or profits, whichever such proportion is the greater.

(ii) The provisions of this subparagraph may be illustrated by the following example:

Example. Green, Jones, and White, unrelated individuals, are partners in the GJW partnership. The partners' interests in the capital and profits of the partnership are as follows:

Partner	Capital	Profits
Green	36 %	25 %
Jones	60	71
White	4	4

The GJW partnership owns the entire outstanding stock (100 shares) of X Corporation. Under this subparagraph, Green is considered to own the X stock owned by the partnership in proportion to his interest in capital (36 percent) or profits (25 percent), whichever such proportion is the greater. Therefore, Green is considered to own 36 shares of the X stock. However, since Jones has a greater interest in the profits of the partnership, he is considered to own the X stock in proportion to his interest in such profits. Therefore, Jones is considered to own 71 shares of the X stock. Since White does not have an interest of 5 percent or more in either the capital or profits of the partnership, he is not considered to own any shares of the X stock.

(3) *Attribution from estates or trusts.*—(i) Stock owned, directly or indirectly, by or for an estate or trust shall be considered as owned by any beneficiary who has an actuarial interest of 5 percent or more in such stock, to the extent

of such actuarial interest. For purposes of this subparagraph, the actuarial interest of each beneficiary shall be determined by assuming the maximum exercise of discretion by the fiduciary in favor of such beneficiary and the maximum use of such stock to satisfy his rights as a beneficiary. A beneficiary of an estate or trust who cannot under any circumstances receive any interest in stock held by the estate or trust, including the proceeds from the disposition thereof, or the income therefrom, does not have an actuarial interest in such stock. Thus, where stock owned by a decedent's estate has been specifically bequeathed to certain beneficiaries and the remainder of the estate is bequeathed to other beneficiaries, the stock is attributable only to the beneficiaries to whom it is specifically bequeathed. Similarly, a remainderman of a trust who cannot under any circumstances receive any interest in the stock of a corporation which is a part of the corpus of the trust (including any accumulated income therefrom or the proceeds from a disposition thereof) does not have an actuarial interest in such stock. However, an income beneficiary of a trust does have an actuarial interest in stock if he has any right to the income from such stock even though under the terms of the trust instrument such stock can never be distributed to him. The factors and methods prescribed in § 20.2031-7 of this chapter (Estate Tax Regulations) [Reg. § 20.2031-7 of this chapter is reproduced at ¶ 2391.05.—CCH.] for use in ascertaining the value of an interest in property for estate tax purposes shall be used for purposes of this subdivision in determining a beneficiary's actuarial interest in stock owned directly or indirectly by or for a trust.

(ii) For the purposes of this subparagraph, property of a decedent shall be considered as owned by his estate if such property is subject to administration by the executor or administrator for the purposes of paying claims against the estate and expenses of administration notwithstanding that, under local law, legal title to such property vests in the decedent's heirs, legatees or devisees immediately upon death. With respect to an estate, the term "beneficiary" includes any person entitled to receive property of the decedent pursuant to a will or pursuant to laws of descent and distribution. A person shall no longer be considered a beneficiary of an estate when all the property to which he is entitled has been received by him, when he no longer has a claim against the estate arising out of having been a beneficiary, and when there is only a remote possibility that it will be necessary for the estate to seek the return of property or to seek payment from him by contribution or otherwise to satisfy claims against the estate or expenses of administration. When pursuant to the preceding sentence, a person ceases to be a beneficiary, stock owned by the estate shall not thereafter be considered owned by him.

(iii) Stock owned, directly or indirectly, by or for any portion of a trust of which a person is considered the owner under subpart E, part I, subchapter J of the Code (relating to grantors and others treated as substantial owners) is considered as owned by such person.

(iv) This subparagraph does not apply to stock owned by any employees' trust described in section 401(a) which is exempt from tax under section 501(a).

(4) *Attribution from corporations.*—(i) Stock owned, directly or indirectly, by or for a corporation shall be considered as owned by any person who owns (within the meaning of section 1563(d)) 5 percent or more in value of its stock in that proportion which the value of the stock which such person so owns bears to the value of all the stock in such corporation.

(ii) The provisions of this subparagraph may be illustrated by the following example:

Example. Brown, an individual, owns 60 shares of the 100 shares of the only class of outstanding stock of corporation P. Smith, an individual, owns 4 shares of the P stock, and corporation X owns 36 shares of the P stock. Corporation P owns, directly and indirectly, 50 shares of the stock of corporation S. Under this subparagraph, Brown is considered to own 30 shares of the S stock ($60/100 \times 50$), and X is considered to own 18 shares of the S stock ($36/100 \times 50$). Since Smith does not own 5 percent or more in value of the P stock, he is not considered as owning any of the S stock owned by P. If, in this example, Smith's wife had owned directly 1 share of the P stock, Smith (and his wife) would each own 5 shares of the P stock, and therefore Smith (and his wife) would be considered as owning 2.5 shares of the S stock ($5/100 \times 50$).

(5) *Spouse.*—(i) Except as provided in subdivision (ii) of this subparagraph, an individual shall be considered to own the stock owned, directly or indirectly, by or for his spouse, other than a spouse who is legally separated from the individual under a decree of divorce, whether interlocutory or final, or a decree of separate maintenance.

(ii) An individual shall not be considered to own stock in a corporation owned, directly or indirectly, by or for his spouse on any day of a taxable year of such corporation, provided that each of the following conditions are satisfied with respect to such taxable year:

(*a*) Such individual does not, at any time during such taxable year, own directly any stock in such corporation.

(*b*) Such individual is not a member of the board of directors or an employee of such corporation and does not participate in the management of such corporation at any time during such taxable year.

Reg. § 1.1563-3(b)(3)(ii)

(c) Not more than 50 percent of such corporation's gross income for such taxable year was derived from royalties, rents, dividends, interest, and annuities.

(d) Such stock in such corporation is not, at any time during such taxable year, subject to conditions which substantially restrict or limit the spouse's right to dispose of such stock and which run in favor of the individual or his children who have not attained the age of 21 years. The principles of paragraph (b)(2)(iii) of § 1.1563-2 shall apply in determining whether a condition is a condition described in the preceding sentence.

(iii) For purposes of subdivision (ii)(c) of this subparagraph, the gross income of a corporation for a taxable year shall be determined under section 61 and the regulations thereunder. The terms "royalties", "rents", "dividends", "interest", and "annuities" shall have the same meanings such terms are given for purposes of section 1244(c). See paragraph (e)(1)(ii), (iii), (iv), (v), and (vi) of § 1.1244(c)-1.

(6) *Children, grandchildren, parents, and grandparents.*—(i) An individual shall be considered to own the stock owned, directly or indirectly, by or for his children who have not attained the age of 21 years, and, if the individual has not attained the age of 21 years, the stock owned, directly or indirectly, by or for his parents.

(ii) If an individual owns (directly, and with the application of the rules of this paragraph but without regard to this subdivision) stock possessing more than 50 percent of the total combined voting power of all classes of stock entitled to vote or more than 50 percent of the total value of shares of all classes of stock in a corporation, then such individual shall be considered to own the stock in such corporation owned, directly or indirectly, by or for his parents, grandparents, grandchildren, and children who have attained the age of 21 years. In determining whether the stock owned by an individual possesses the requisite percentage of the total combined voting power of all classes of stock entitled to vote of a corporation, see paragraph (a)(6) of § 1.1563-1.

(iii) For purposes of section 1563, and §§ 1.1563-1 through 1.1563-4, a legally adopted child of an individual shall be treated as a child of such individual by blood.

(iv) The provisions of this subparagraph may be illustrated by the following example:

Example—(a) *Facts.* Individual F owns directly 40 shares of the 100 shares of the only class of stock of Z Corporation. His son, M (20 years of age), owns directly 30 shares of such stock, and his son, A (30 years of age), owns directly 20 shares of such stock. The remaining 10 shares of the Z stock are owned by an unrelated person.

(b) *F's ownership.* Individual F owns 40 shares of the Z stock directly and is considered to own the 30 shares of Z stock owned directly by M. Since, for purposes of the more-than-50-percent stock ownership test contained in subdivision (ii) of this subparagraph, F is treated as owning 70 shares or 70 percent of the total voting power and value of the Z stock, he is also considered as owning the 20 shares owned by his adult son, A. Accordingly, F is considered as owning a total of 90 shares of the Z stock.

(c) *M's ownership.* Minor son, M, owns 30 shares of the Z stock directly, and is considered to own the 40 shares of Z stock owned directly by his father, F. However, M is not considered to own the 20 shares of Z stock owned directly by his brother, A, and constructively by F, because stock constructively owned by F by reason of family attribution is not considered as owned by him for purposes of making another member of his family the constructive owner of such stock. See paragraph (c)(2) of this section. Accordingly, M owns and is considered as owning a total of 70 shares of the Z stock.

(d) *A's ownership.* Adult son, A, owns 20 shares of the Z stock directly. Since, for purposes of the more-than-50-percent stock ownership test contained in subdivision (ii) of this subparagraph, A is treated as owning only the Z stock which he owns directly, he does not satisfy the condition precedent for the attribution of Z stock from his father. Accordingly, A is treated as owning only the 20 shares of Z stock which he owns directly.

(c) *Operating rules and special rules.*—(1) *In general.*—Except as provided in subparagraph (2) of this paragraph, stock constructively owned by a person by reason of the application of subparagraph (1), (2), (3), (4), (5), or (6) of paragraph (b) of this section shall, for purposes of applying such subparagraphs, be treated as actually owned by such person.

(2) *Members of family.*—Stock constructively owned by an individual by reason of the application of subparagraph (5) or (6) of paragraph (b) of this section shall not be treated as owned by him for purposes of again applying such subparagraphs in order to make another the constructive owner of such stock.

(3) *Precedence of option attribution.*—For purposes of this section, if stock may be considered as owned by a person under subparagraph (1) of paragraph (b) of this section (relating to option attribution) and under any other subparagraph of such paragraph, such stock shall be considered as owned by such person under subparagraph (1) of such paragraph.

(4) *Examples.*—The provisions of this paragraph may be illustrated by the following examples:

Example (1). A, 30 years of age, has a 90 percent interest in the capital and profits of a partnership. The partnership owns all the outstanding stock of corporation X and X owns 60 shares of the 100 outstanding shares of corporation Y. Under subparagraph (1) of this paragraph, the 60 shares of Y constructively owned by the partnership by reason of subparagraph (4) of paragraph (b) of this section is treated as actually owned by the partnership for purposes of applying subparagraph (2) of paragraph (b) of this section. Therefore, A is considered as owning 54 shares of the Y stock (90 percent of 60 shares).

Example (2). Assume the same facts as in example (1). Assume further that B, who is 20 years of age and the brother of A, directly owns 40 shares of Y stock. Although the stock of Y owned by B is considered as owned by C (the father of A and B) under paragraph (b)(6)(i) of this section, under subparagraph (2) of this paragraph such stock may not be treated as owned by C for purposes of applying paragraph (b)(6)(ii) of this section in order to make A the constructive owner of such stock.

Example (3). Assume the same facts assumed for purposes of example (2), and further assume that C has an option to acquire the 40 shares of Y stock owned by his son, B. The rule contained in subparagraph (2) of this paragraph does not prevent the reattribution of such 40 shares to A because, under subparagraph (3) of this paragraph, C is considered as owning the 40 shares by reason of option attribution and not by reason of family attribution. Therefore, since A satisfies the more-than-50-percent stock ownership test contained in paragraph (b)(6)(ii) of this section with respect to Y, the 40 shares of Y stock constructively owned by C are reattributed to A, and A is considered as owning a total of 94 shares of Y stock.

(d) *Special rule of section 1563(f)(3)(B).*—(1) *In general.*—If the same stock of a corporation is owned (within the meaning of section 1563(d)) by two or more persons, then such stock shall be treated as owned by the person whose ownership of such stock results in the corporation being a component member of a controlled group on a December 31 which has at least one other component member on such date.

(2) *Component member of more than one group.*—(i) If, by reason of subparagraph (1) of this paragraph, a corporation would (but for this subparagraph) become a component member of more than one controlled group on a December 31, such corporation shall be treated as a component member of only one such controlled group on such date. The determination as to which group such corporation is treated as a component member of shall be made in accordance with the rules contained in paragraphs (d)(2)(ii), (iii) and (iv) of the section.

(ii) In any case in which a corporation is a component member of a controlled group of corporations on a December 31 as a result of treating each share of its stock as owned only by the person who owns such share directly, then each such share shall be treated as owned by the person who owns such share directly.

(iii) If the application of subdivision (ii) of this subparagraph does not result in a corporation being treated as a component member of only one controlled group on a December 31, then the stock of such corporation described in subparagraph (1) of this paragraph shall be treated as owned by the one person described in such subparagraph who owns, directly and with the application of the rules contained in paragraph (b)(1), (2), (3), and (4) of this section, the stock possessing the greatest percentage of the total value of shares of all classes of stock of the corporation.

(iv) *Statement.*—If the application of paragraph (d)(2)(ii) or (iii) of this section does not result in a corporation being treated as a component member of only one controlled group of corporations on a December 31, then such corporation will be treated as a component member of only one such group on such date. Such corporation may elect the group in which it is to be included by including on or with its income tax return a statement entitled, "STATEMENT TO ELECT CONTROLLED GROUP PURSUANT TO § 1.1563-3(d)(2)(iv)." The statement must include—

(A) A description of each of the controlled groups in which the corporation could be included. The description must include the name and employer identification number of each component member of each such group and the stock ownership of the component members of each such group; and

(B) The following representation: [INSERT NAME AND EMPLOYER IDENTIFICATION NUMBER OF CORPORATION] ELECTS TO BE TREATED AS A COMPONENT MEMBER OF THE [INSERT DESIGNATION OF GROUP].

(v) *Election.*—(A) *Election filed.*—An election filed under paragraph (d)(2)(iv) of this section is irrevocable and effective until paragraph (d)(2)(ii) or (iii) of this section applies or until a change in the stock ownership of the corporation results in termination of membership in the controlled group in which such corporation has been included.

(B) *Election not filed.*—In the event no election is filed in accordance with the provisions of paragraph (d)(2)(iv) of this section, then the Internal Revenue Service will determine the group in which such corporation is to be included. Such determination will be binding for all subsequent years unless the corporation files a valid election with respect to any such subsequent year or until a change in the stock ownership of the corporation results in termination of membership in the controlled group in which such corporation has been included.

(3) *Examples.*—The provisions of this paragraph may be illustrated by the following examples, in which each corporation referred to uses the calendar year as its taxable year and the stated facts are assumed to exist on each day of 1970 (unless otherwise provided in the example):

Example (1). Jones owns all the stock of corporation X and has an option to purchase from Smith all the outstanding stock of corporation Y. Smith owns all the outstanding stock of corporation Z. Since the Y stock is considered as owned by two or more persons, under subparagraph (2)(ii) of this paragraph the Y stock is treated as owned only by Smith since he has direct ownership of such stock. Therefore, on December 31, 1970, Y and Z are component members of the same brother-sister controlled group. If, however, Smith had owned his stock in corporation Z for less than one-half of the number of days of Z's 1970 taxable year, then under subparagraph (1) of this paragraph the Y stock would be treated as owned only by Jones since his ownership results in Y being a component member of a controlled group on December 31, 1970.

Example (2). Individual H owns directly all the outstanding stock of corporation M. W (the wife of H) owns directly all the outstanding stock of corporation N. Neither spouse is considered as owning the stock directly owned by the other because each of the conditions prescribed in paragraph (b)(5)(ii) of this section is satisfied with respect to each corporation's 1970 taxable year. H owns directly 60 percent of the only class of stock of corporation P and W owns the remaining 40 percent of the P stock. Under subparagraph (2)(iii) of this paragraph, the stock of P is treated as owned only by H since H owns (directly and with the application of the rules contained in paragraph (b)(1), (2), (3), and (4) of this section) the stock possessing the greatest percentage of the total value of shares of all classes of stock of P. Accordingly, on December 31, 1970, P is treated as a component member of a brother-sister group consisting of M and P.

Example (3). Unrelated individuals A and B each own 49 percent of all the outstanding stock of corporation R, which in turn owns 70 percent of the only class of outstanding stock of corporation S. The remaining 30 percent of the stock of corporation S is owned by unrelated individual C. C also owns the remaining 2 percent of the stock of corporation R. Under the attribution rule of paragraph (b)(4) of this section A and B are each considered to own 34.3 percent of the stock of corporation S. Accordingly, since five or fewer persons own at least 80 percent of the stock of corporations R and S and also own more than 50 percent identically (A's and B's identical ownership each is 34.3 percent, C's identical ownership is 2 percent), on December 31, 1970, corporations R and S are treated as component members of the same brother-sister controlled group for purposes of paragraph (a)(3)(ii) of § 1.1563-1.

(e) *Effective/applicability date.*—Paragraph (d)(2)(iv) and (v) of this section apply to any taxable year beginning on or after May 30, 2006. However, taxpayers may apply paragraph (d)(2)(iv) and (v) of this section to any original Federal income tax return (including any amended return filed on or before the due date (including extensions) of such original return) timely filed on or after May 30, 2006. For taxable years beginning before May 30, 2006, see § 1.1563-3 as contained in 26 CFR part 1 in effect on April 1, 2006. [Reg. § 1.1563-3.]

☐ [*T.D. 6845, 8-4-65. Amended by T.D. 7181, 4-24-72; T.D. 7779, 6-1-81; T.D. 8179, 3-1-88; T.D. 9264, 5-26-2006; T.D. 9304, 12-21-2006; T.D. 9329, 6-13-2007 and T.D. 9451, 5-26-2009.*]

[Reg. § 1.1563-4]

§ 1.1563-4. **Franchised corporations.**—(a) *In general.*—For purposes of paragraph (b)(2)(ii)(*d*) of § 1.1563-1, a member of a controlled group of corporations shall be considered to be a franchised corporation for a taxable year if each of the following conditions is satisfied for one-half (or more) of the number of days preceding the December 31 included within such taxable year (or, if such taxable year does not include a December 31, for one-half or more of the number of days in such taxable year preceding the last day of such year):

(1) Such member is franchised to sell the products of another member, or the common owner, of such controlled group.

(2) More than 50 percent (determined on the basis of cost) of all the goods held by such member primarily for sale to its customers are acquired from members or the common owner of the controlled group, or both.

(3) The stock of such member is to be sold to an employee (or employees) of such member pursuant to a bona fide plan designed to eliminate the stock ownership of the parent corporation (as defined in paragraph (b)(1) of § 1.1563-2) or of the common owner (as defined in paragraph (b)(3) of § 1.1563-2) in such member.

(4) Such employee owns (or such employees in the aggregate own) directly more than 20 percent of the total value of shares of all classes of stock of such member. For purposes of this subparagraph, the determination of whether an employee (or employees) owns the requisite percentage of the total value of the stock of the member shall be made without regard to paragraph (b) of § 1.1563-2, relating to certain stock treated as excluded stock. Furthermore, if the corporation has more than one class of stock outstanding, the relative voting rights as between each such class of stock shall be disregarded in making such determination.

(b) *Plan for elimination of stock ownership.*—(1) A plan referred to in paragraph (a)(3) of this section must—

(i) Provide a reasonable selling price for the stock of the member, and

(ii) Require that a portion of the employee's compensation or dividends, or both, from such member be applied to the purchase of such stock (or to the purchase of notes, bonds, debentures, or similar evidences of indebtedness of such member held by the parent corporation or the common owner).

It is not necessary, in order to satisfy the requirements of subdivision (ii) of this subparagraph, that the plan require that a percentage of every dollar of the compensation and dividends be applied to the purchase of the stock (or the indebtedness). The requirements of such subdivision are satisfied if an otherwise qualified plan provides that under certain specified conditions (such as a requirement that the member earn a specified profit) no portion of the compensation and/or dividends need be applied to the purchase of the stock (or indebtedness), provided such conditions are reasonable.

(2) A plan for the elimination of the stock ownership of the parent corporation or of the common owner will satisfy the requirements of paragraph (a)(3) of this section and subparagraph (1) of this paragraph even though it does not require that the stock of the member be sold to an employee (or employees) if it provides for the redemption of the stock of the member held by the parent or common owner and under the plan the amount of such stock to be redeemed during any period is calculated by reference to the profits of such member during such period. [Reg. § 1.1563-4.]

☐ [*T.D.* 6845, 8-4-65.]

[The next page is 58,501.]

ESTATE AND GIFT TAXES

Estate Tax

ESTATES OF CITIZENS OR RESIDENTS

Tax Imposed

See p. 20,601 for regulations not amended to reflect law changes

[Reg. § 20.0-1]

§ 20.0-1. Introduction.—(a) *In general.*—(1) The regulations in this part (Part 20, Subchapter B, Chapter I, Title 26, Code of Federal Regulations) are designated "Estate Tax Regulations". These regulations pertain to (i) the Federal estate tax imposed by chapter 11 of subtitle B of the Internal Revenue Code on the transfer of estates of decedents dying after August 16, 1954, and (ii) certain related administrative provisions of subtitle F of the Code. It should be noted that the application of many of the provisions of these regulations may be affected by the provisions of an applicable death tax convention with a foreign country. Unless otherwise indicated, references in the regulations to the "Internal Revenue Code" or the "Code" are references to the Internal Revenue Code of 1954, as amended, and references to a section or other provision of law are references to a section or other provision of the Internal Revenue Code of 1954, as amended. Unless otherwise provided, the Estate Tax Regulations are applicable to the estates of decedents dying after August 16, 1954, and supersede the regulations contained in Part 81 of this chapter (1939) (Regulations 105, Estate Tax), as prescribed and made applicable to the Internal Revenue Code of 1954 by Treasury Decision 6091, signed August 16, 1954 (19 F.R. 5167, August 17, 1954).

(2) Section 2208 makes the provisions of chapter 11 of the Code apply to the transfer of the estates of certain decedents dying after September 2, 1958, who were citizens of the United States and residents of a possession thereof at the time of death. Section 2209 makes the provisions of chapter 11 apply to the transfer of the estates of certain other decedents dying after September 14, 1960, who were citizens of the United States and residents of a possession thereof at the time of death. See §§ 20.2208-1 and 20.2209-1. Except as otherwise provided in §§ 20.2208-1 and 20.2209-1, the provisions of these regulations do not apply to the estates of such decedents.

(b) *Scope of regulations.*—(1) *Estates of citizens or residents.*—Subchapter A of chapter 11 of the Code pertains to the taxation of the estate of a person who was a citizen or a resident of the United States at the time of his death. A "resident" decedent is a decedent who, at the time of his death, had his domicile in the United States. The term "United States," as used in the Estate Tax Regulations, includes only the States and the District of Columbia. The term also includes the Territories of Alaska and Hawaii prior to their admission as States. See section 7701(a)(9). A person acquires a domicile in a place by living there, for even a brief period of time, with no definite present intention of later removing therefrom. Residence without the requisite intention to remain indefinitely will not suffice to constitute domicile, nor will intention to change domicile effect such a change unless accompanied by actual removal. For the meaning of the term "citizen of the United States" as applied in a case where the decedent was a resident of a possession of the United States, see § 20.2208-1. The regulations pursuant to subchapter A are set forth in §§ 20.2001 to 20.2056(d)-1.

(2) *Estates of nonresidents not citizens.*—Subchapter B of Chapter 11 of the Code pertains to the taxation of the estate of a person who was a nonresident not a citizen of the United States at the time of his death. A "nonresident" decedent is a decedent who, at the time of his death, had his domicile outside the United States under the principles set forth in subparagraph (1) of this paragraph. (See, however, section 2202 with respect to missionaries in foreign service.) The regulations pursuant to subchapter B are set forth in §§ 20.2101 to 20.2108.

(3) *Miscellaneous substantive provisions.*—Subchapter C of chapter 11 of the Code contains a number of miscellaneous substantive provisions. The regulations pursuant to subchapter C are set forth in §§ 20.2201-1 to 20.2209-1.

(4) *Procedure and administration provisions.*—Subtitle F of the Internal Revenue Code contains some sections which are applicable to the Federal estate tax. The regulations pursuant to those sections are set forth in §§ 20.6001 to 20.7404. Such regulations do not purport to be all the regulations on procedure and administration which are pertinent to estate tax matters. For the remainder of the regulations on procedure and administration which are pertinent to estate tax matters, see Part 301 (Procedure and Administration Regulations) of this chapter.

(c) *Arrangement and numbering.*—Each section of the regulations in this part (other than this section and § 20.0-2) is designated by a number composed of the part number followed by a decimal point (20.); the section of the Internal Revenue Code which it interprets; a hyphen (-); and a number identifying the section. By use of these designations one can ascertain the sections of the regulations relating to a provision of the Code. For example, the regulations pertaining to section 2012 of the Code are designated §20.2012-1. [Reg. §20.0-1.]

☐ [*T.D. 6296, 6-23-58. Amended by T.D. 6526, 1-18-61; T.D. 7238, 12-28-72; T.D. 7296, 12-11-73; T.D. 7665, 1-24-80 and T.D. 8522, 2-28-94.*]

[Reg. §20.0-2]

§20.0-2. General description of tax.— (a) *Nature of tax.*—The Federal estate tax is neither a property tax nor an inheritance tax. It is a tax imposed upon the transfer of the entire taxable estate and not upon any particular legacy, devise, or distributive share. Escheat of a decedent's property to the State for lack of heirs is a transfer which causes the property to be included in the decedent's gross estate.

(b) *Method of determining tax; estate of citizen or resident.*—(1) *In general.*—Subparagraphs (2) to (5) of this paragraph contain a general description of the method to be used in determining the Federal estate tax imposed upon the transfer of the estate of a decedent who was a citizen or resident of the United States at the time of his death.

(2) *Gross estate.*—The first step in determining the tax is to ascertain the total value of the decedent's gross estate. The value of the gross estate includes the value of all property to the extent of the interest therein of the decedent at the time of his death. (For certain exceptions in the case of real property situated outside the United States, see paragraphs (a) and (c) of §20.2031-1.) In addition, the gross estate may include property in which the decedent did not have an interest at the time of his death. A decedent's gross estate for Federal estate tax purposes may therefore be very different from the decedent's estate for local probate purposes. Examples of items which may be included in a decedent's gross estate and not in his probate estate are the following: certain property transferred by the decedent during his lifetime without adequate consideration; property held jointly by the decedent and others; property over which the decedent had a general power of appointment; proceeds of certain policies of insurance on the decedent's life; annuities; and dower or curtesy of a surviving spouse or a statutory estate in lieu thereof. For a detailed explanation of the method of ascertaining the value of the gross estate, see sections 2031 through 2044, and the regulations thereunder.

(3) *Taxable estate.*—The second step in determining the tax is to ascertain the value of the decedent's taxable estate. The value of the taxable estate is determined by subtracting from the value of the gross estate the authorized exemption and deductions. Under various conditions and limitations, deductions are allowable for expenses, indebtedness, taxes, losses, charitable transfers, and transfers to a surviving spouse. For a detailed explanation of the method of ascertaining the value of the taxable estate, see sections 2051 through 2056, and the regulations thereunder.

(4) *Gross estate tax.*—The third step is the determination of the gross estate tax. This is accomplished by the application of certain rates to the value of the decedent's taxable estate. In this connection, see section 2001 and the regulations thereunder.

(5) *Net estate tax payable.*—The final step is the determination of the net estate tax payable. This is done by subtracting from the gross estate tax the authorized credits against tax. Under certain conditions and limitations, credits are allowable for the following (computed in the order stated below):

   (i) State death taxes paid in connection with the decedent's estate (section 2011);

   (ii) Gift taxes paid on inter-vivos transfers by the decedent of property included in his gross estate (section 2012);

   (iii) Foreign death taxes paid in connection with the decedent's estate (section 2014); and

   (iv) Federal estate taxes paid on transfers of property to the decedent (section 2013).

Sections 2015 and 2016 contain certain further rules for the application of the credits for State and foreign death taxes.

Sections 25.2701-5 and 25.2702-6 of this chapter contain rules that provide additional adjustments to mitigate double taxation in cases where the amount of the decedent's gift was previously determined under the special valuation provisions of section 2701 and 2702. For a detailed explanation of the credits against tax, see sections 2011 through 2016 and the regulations thereunder.

(c) *Method of determining tax; estate of nonresident not a citizen.*—In general, the method to be used in determining the Federal estate tax imposed upon the transfer of an estate of a decedent who was a nonresident not a citizen of the United States is similar to that described in paragraph (b) of this section with respect to the estate of a citizen or resident. Briefly stated, the steps are as follows: First, ascertain the sum of the value of that part of the decedent's "entire gross estate" which at the time of his death was situated in the United States (see §§20.2103-1 and 20.2014-1) and, in the case of an estate of an expatriate to which section 2107 applies, any amounts includible in his gross estate under section 2107(b) (see paragraph (b) of §20.2107-1); second, determine the value of the taxable estate by subtracting from the amount determined under the first step the amount of the allowable deductions (see § 20.2106-1); third, compute the gross estate tax on the taxable estate (see § 20.2106-1); and fourth, subtract from the gross estate tax the total amount of any allowable credits in order to arrive at the net estate tax payable (see § 20.2102-1 and paragraph (c) of § 20.2107-1). [Reg. § 20.0-2.]

☐ [*T.D.* 6296, 6-23-58. *Amended by T.D.* 6684, 10-23-63; *T.D.* 7296, 12-11-73 *and T.D.* 8395, 1-28-92.]

[Reg. § 20.2001-1]

§ 20.2001-1. Valuation of adjusted taxable gifts and section 2701(d)taxable events.— (a) *Adjusted taxable gifts made prior to August 6, 1997.—*For purposes of determining the value of adjusted taxable gifts as defined in section 2001(b), if the gift was made prior to August 6, 1997, the value of the gift may be adjusted at any time, even if the time within which a gift tax may be assessed has expired under section 6501. This paragraph (a) also applies to adjustments involving issues other than valuation for gifts made prior to August 6, 1997.

(b) *Adjusted taxable gifts and section 2701(d) taxable events occurring after August 5, 1997.—*For purposes of determining the amount of adjusted taxable gifts as defined in section 2001(b), if, under section 6501, the time has expired within which a gift tax may be assessed under chapter 12 of the Internal Revenue Code (or under corresponding provisions of prior laws) with respect to a gift made after August 5, 1997, or with respect to an increase in taxable gifts required under section 2701(d) and § 25.2701-4 of this chapter, then the amount of the taxable gift will be the amount as finally determined for gift tax purposes under chapter 12 of the Internal Revenue Code and the amount of the taxable gift may not thereafter be adjusted. The rule of this paragraph (b) applies to adjustments involving all issues relating to the gift, including valuation issues and legal issues involving the interpretation of the gift tax law.

(c) *Finally determined.—*For purposes of paragraph (b) of this section, the amount of a taxable gift as finally determined for gift tax purposes is—

(1) The amount of the taxable gift as shown on a gift tax return, or on a statement attached to the return, if the Internal Revenue Service does not contest such amount before the time has expired under section 6501 within which gift taxes may be assessed;

(2) The amount as specified by the Internal Revenue Service before the time has expired under section 6501 within which gift taxes may be assessed on the gift, if such specified amount is not timely contested by the taxpayer;

(3) The amount as finally determined by a court of competent jurisdiction; or

(4) The amount as determined pursuant to a settlement agreement entered into between the taxpayer and the Internal Revenue Service.

(d) *Definitions.—*For purposes of paragraph (b) of this section, the amount is finally determined by a court of competent jurisdiction when the court enters a final decision, judgment, decree or other order with respect to the amount of the taxable gift that is not subject to appeal. See, for example, section 7481 regarding the finality of a decision by the U.S. Tax Court. Also, for purposes of paragraph (b) of this section, a settlement agreement means any agreement entered into by the Internal Revenue Service and the taxpayer that is binding on both. The term includes a closing agreement under section 7121, a compromise under section 7122, and an agreement entered into in settlement of litigation involving the amount of the taxable gift.

(e) *Expiration of period of assessment.—*For purposes of determining if the time has expired within which a tax may be assessed under chapter 12 of the Internal Revenue Code, see § 301.6501(c)-1(e) and (f) of this chapter.

(f) *Effective dates.—*Paragraph (a) of this section applies to transfers of property by gift made prior to August 6, 1997, if the estate tax return for the donor/decedent's estate is filed after December 3, 1999. Paragraphs (b) through (e) of this section apply to transfers of property by gift made after August 5, 1997, if the gift tax return for the calendar period in which the gift is made is filed after December 3, 1999. [Reg. § 20.2001-1.]

☐ [*T.D.* 6296, 6-23-58. *Amended by T.D.* 8845, 12-2-99.]

[Reg. § 20.2002-1]

§ 20.2002-1. Liability for payment of tax.— The Federal estate tax imposed both with respect to the estates of citizens or residents and with respect to estates of nonresidents not citizens is payable by the executor or administrator of the decedent's estate. This duty applies to the entire tax, regardless of the fact that the gross estate consists in part of property which does not come within the possession of the executor or administrator. If there is no executor or administrator appointed, qualified, and acting in the United States, any person in actual or constructive possession of any property of the decedent is required to pay the entire tax to the extent of the value of the property in his possession. See section 2203, defining the term "executor". The personal liability of the executor or such other person is described in section 3467 of the Revised Statutes (31 U.S.C. 192) as follows:

Every executor, administrator, or assignee, or other person, who pays, in whole or in part, any debt due by the person or estate for whom or for which he acts before he satisfies and pays the debts due to the United States from such person or estate, shall become answerable in his own person and estate to the extent of such payments for the debts so due to the United States, or for so much thereof as may remain due and unpaid.

As used in said section, the word "debt" includes a beneficiary's distributive share of an estate. Thus, if the executor pays a debt due by the decedent's estate or distributes any portion of the estate before all the estate tax is paid, he is personally liable, to the extent of the payment or distribution, for so much of the estate tax as remains due and unpaid. In addition, section 6324(a)(2) provides that if the estate tax is not paid when due, then the spouse, transferee, trustee (except the trustee of an employee's trust which meets the requirements of section 401(a)), surviving tenant, person in possession of the property by reason of the exercise, nonexercise, or release of a power of appointment, or beneficiary, who receives, or has on the date of the decedent's death, property included in the gross estate under sections 2034 through 2042, is personally liable for the tax to the extent of the value, at the time of the decedent's death, of such property. See also the following related sections of the Internal Revenue Code: section 2204, discharge of executor from personal liability; section 2205, reimbursement out of estate; sections 2206 and 2207, liability of life insurance beneficiaries and recipients of property over which decedent had power of appointment; sections 6321 through 6325, concerning liens for taxes; and section 6901(a)(1), concerning the liabilities of transferees and fiduciaries. [Reg. § 20.2002-1.]

☐ [T.D. 6296, 6-23-58.]

Credits Against Tax

[Reg. § 20.2011-1]

§ 20.2011-1. Credit for State death taxes.— (a) *In general.*—A credit is allowed under section 2011 against the Federal estate tax for estate, inheritance, legacy or succession taxes actually paid to any State, Territory, or the District of Columbia, or in the case of decedents dying before September 3, 1958, any possession of the United States (hereafter referred to as "State death taxes"). The credit, however, is allowed only for State death taxes paid (1) with respect to property included in the decedent's gross estate, and (2) with respect to the decedent's estate. The amount of the credit is subject to the limitation described in paragraph (b) of this section. It is subject to further limitations described in § 20.2011-2 if a deduction is allowed under section 2053(d) for State death taxes paid with respect to a charitable gift. See paragraph (a) of § 20.2014-1 as to the allowance of a credit for death taxes paid to a possession of the United States in a case where the decedent died after September 2, 1958.

(b) *Amount of credit.*—(1) If the decedent's taxable estate does not exceed $40,000, the credit for State death taxes is zero. If the decedent's taxable estate does exceed $40,000, the credit for State death taxes is limited to an amount computed in accordance with the following table:

TABLE FOR COMPUTATION OF MAXIMUM CREDIT FOR STATE DEATH TAXES

(A) Taxable estate equal to or more than—	(B) Taxable estate less than—	(C) Credit on amount in column (A)	(D) Rates of credit on excess over amount in column (A)
			Percent
$40,000	$90,000	. . . . .	.8
90,000	140,000	$400	1.6
140,000	240,000	1,200	2.4
240,000	440,000	3,600	3.2
440,000	640,000	10,000	4.0
640,000	840,000	18,000	4.8
840,000	1,040,000	27,600	5.6
1,040,000	1,540,000	38,800	6.4
1,540,000	2,040,000	70,800	7.2
2,040,000	2,540,000	106,800	8.0
2,540,000	3,040,000	146,800	8.8
3,040,000	3,540,000	190,800	9.6
3,540,000	4,040,000	238,800	10.4
4,040,000	5,040,000	290,800	11.2
5,040,000	6,040,000	402,800	12.0
6,040,000	7,040,000	522,800	12.8
7,040,000	8,040,000	650,800	13.6
8,040,000	9,040,000	786,800	14.4
9,040,000	10,040,000	930,800	15.2
10,040,000	. . . .	1,082,800	16.0

(2) Subparagraph (1) of this paragraph may be illustrated by the following example:

Example. (i) The decedent died January 1, 1955, leaving a taxable estate of $150,000. On January 1, 1956, inheritance taxes totaling $2,500 were actually paid to a State with respect to property included in the decedent's gross estate. Reference to the table discloses that the specified amount in column (A) nearest to but less than the value of the decedent's taxable estate is $140,000. The maximum credit in respect of this amount, as indicated in column (C), is $1,200. The amount by which the taxable estate exceeds the same specified amount is $10,000. The maximum credit in respect of this amount, computed at the rate of 2.4 percent indicated in column (D), is $240. Thus, the maximum credit in respect of the decedent's taxable estate of $150,000 is $1,440, even though $2,500 in inheritance taxes was actually paid to the State.

(ii) If, in subdivision (i) of this example, the amount actually paid to the State was $950, the credit for State death taxes would be limited to $950. If, in subdivision (i) of this example, the decedent's taxable estate was $35,000, no credit for State death taxes would be allowed.

(c) *Miscellaneous limitations and conditions to credit.*—(1) *Period of limitations.*—The credit for State death taxes is limited under section 2011(c) to those taxes which were actually paid and for which a credit was claimed within four years after the filing of the estate tax return for the decedent's estate. If, however, a petition has been filed with the Tax Court of the United States for the redetermination of a deficiency within the time prescribed in section 6213(a), the credit is limited to those taxes which were actually paid and for which a credit was claimed within four years after the filing of the return or within 60 days after the decision of the Tax Court becomes final, whichever period is the last to expire. Similarly, if an extension of time has been granted under section 6161 for payment of the tax shown on the return, or of a deficiency, the credit is limited to those taxes which were actually paid and for which a credit was claimed within four years after the filing of the return, or before the date of the expiration of the period of the extension, whichever period is last to expire. If a claim for refund or credit of an overpayment of the Federal estate tax is filed within the time prescribed in section 6511, the credit for State death taxes is limited to such taxes as were actually paid and credit therefor claimed within four years after the filing of the return or before the expiration of 60 days from the date of mailing by certified or registered mail by the district director to the taxpayer of a notice of disallowance of any part of the claim, or before the expiration of 60 days after a decision by any court of competent jurisdiction becomes final with respect to a timely suit instituted upon the claim, whichever period is the last to expire. See section 2015 for the applicable period of limitations for credit for State death taxes on reversionary or remainder interests if an election is made under section

6163(a) to postpone payment of the estate tax attributable to reversionary or remainder interests. If a claim for refund based on the credit for State death taxes is filed within the applicable period described in this subparagraph, a refund may be made despite the general limitation provisions of sections 6511 and 6512. Any refund based on the credit described in this section shall be made without interest.

(2) *Submission of evidence.*—Before the credit for State death taxes is allowed, evidence that such taxes have been paid must be submitted to the district director. The district director may require the submission of a certificate from the proper officer of the taxing State, Territory, or possession of the United States, or the District of Columbia, showing: (i) the total amount of tax imposed (before adding interest and penalties and before allowing discount); (ii) the amount of any discount allowed; (iii) the amount of any penalties and interest imposed or charged; (iv) the total amount actually paid in cash; and (v) the date or dates of payment. If the amount of these taxes has been redetermined, the amount finally determined should be stated. The required evidence should be filed with the return, but if that is not convenient or possible, then it should be submitted as soon thereafter as practicable. The district director may require the submission of such additional proof as is deemed necessary to establish the right to the credit. For example, he may require the submission of a certificate of the proper officer of the taxing jurisdiction showing (vi) whether a claim for refund of any part of the State death tax is pending and (vii) whether a refund of any part thereof has been authorized, and if a refund has been made, its date and amount, and a description of the property or interest in respect of which the refund was made. The district director may also require an itemized list of the property in respect of which State death taxes were imposed certified by the officer having custody of the records pertaining to those taxes. In addition, he may require the executor to submit a written statement (containing a declaration that it is made under penalties of perjury) stating whether, to his knowledge, any person has instituted litigation or taken an appeal (or contemplates doing so), the final determination of which may affect the amount of those taxes. See section 2016 concerning the redetermination of the estate tax if State death taxes claimed as credit are refunded.

(d) *Definition of "basic estate tax".*—Section 2011(d) provides definitions of the terms "basic estate tax" and "additional estate tax", used in the Internal Revenue Code of 1939, and "estate tax imposed by the Revenue Act of 1926", for the purpose of supplying a means of computing State death taxes under local statutes using those terms, and for use in determining the exemption provided for in section 2201 for estates of certain members of the Armed Forces. See section 2011(e)(3) for a modification of these definitions if a deduction is allowed under section 2053(d)

Reg. § 20.2011-1(d)

for State death taxes paid with respect to a charitable gift. [Reg. § 20.2011-1.]

☐ [*T.D. 6296, 6-23-58. Amended by T.D. 6526, 1-18-61.*]

[Reg. § 20.2011-2]

§ 20.2011-2. Limitation on credit if a deduction for State death taxes is allowed under section 2053(d).—If a deduction is allowed under section 2053(d) for State death taxes paid with respect to a charitable gift, the credit for State death taxes is subject to special limitations. Under these limitations, the credit cannot exceed the least of the following:

(a) The amount of State death taxes paid other than those for which a deduction is allowed under section 2053(d);

(b) The amount indicated in section 2011(b) to be the maximum credit allowable with respect to the decedent's taxable estate; or

(c) An amount, A, which bears the same ratio to B (the amount which would be the maximum credit allowable under section 2011(b) if the deduction under section 2053(d) for State death taxes were not allowed in computing the decedent's taxable estate) as C (the amount of State death taxes paid other than those for which a deduction is allowed under section 2053(d))

bears to D (the total amount of State death taxes paid). For the purpose of this computation, in determining what the decedent's taxable estate would be if the deduction for State death taxes under section 2053(d) were not allowed, adjustment must be made for the decrease in the deduction for charitable gifts under section 2055 or 2106(a)(2) (for estates of nonresidents not citizens) by reason of any increase in Federal estate tax which would be charged against the charitable gifts.

The application of this section may be illustrated by the following example:

Example. The decedent died January 1, 1955, leaving a gross estate of $925,000. Expenses, indebtedness, etc., amounted to $25,000. The decedent bequeathed $400,000 to his son with the direction that the son bear the State death taxes on the bequest. The residuary estate was left to a charitable organization. Except as noted above, all Federal and State death taxes were payable out of the residuary estate. The State imposed death taxes of $60,000 on the son's bequest and death taxes of $75,000 on the bequest to charity. No death taxes were imposed by a foreign country with respect to any property in the gross estate. The decedent's taxable estate (determined without regard to the limitation imposed by section 2011(e)(2)(B)) is computed as follows:

Gross estate				$925,000.00
Expenses, indebtedness, etc.		$25,000.00		
Exemption		60,000.00		
Deduction under section 2053(d)		75,000.00		
Charitable deduction:				
Gross estate		$925,000.00		
Expenses, etc.	$25,000.00			
Bequest to son	400,000.00			
State death tax paid from residue	75,000.00			
Federal estate tax paid from residue	122,916.67	622,916.67	302,083.33	462,083.33
Taxable estate				$462,916.67

If the deduction under section 2053(d) were not allowed, the decedent's taxable estate would be computed as follows:

Gross estate				$925,000.00
Expenses, indebtedness, etc.		$25,000.00		
Exemption		$60,000.00		
Charitable deduction:				
Gross estate		$925,000.00		
Expenses, etc.	$25,000.00			
Bequest to son	400,000.00			
State death tax paid from residue	75,000.00			
Federal estate tax paid from residue	155,000.00	655,000.00	270,000.00	$355,000.00
Taxable estate				$570,000.00

On a taxable estate of $570,000, the maximum credit allowable under section 2011(b) would be $15,200. Under these facts, the credit for State death taxes is determined as follows:

(1)   Amount of State death taxes paid other than those for which a deduction is allowed under section 2053(d) ($135,000 – $75,000) $60,000.00

(2)   Amount indicated in section 2011(b) to be the maximum credit allowable with respect to the decedent's taxable estate of $462,916.67 . . . .   10,916.67

(3)   Amount determined by use of the ratio described in paragraph (c) above

$$\frac{\$60,000}{\$135,000} \times \$15,200 \dots\dots\dots\dots\dots\dots\dots\dots\dots\dots\dots\dots\dots \quad 6{,}755.56$$

(4)   Credit for State death taxes (least of subparagraphs (1) through (3) above) . .   6,755.56

[Reg. § 20.2011-2]

☐ [T.D. 6296, 6-23-58. Amended by T.D. 6600, 5-28-62.]

[Reg. § 20.2012-1]

§ 20.2012-1. Credit for gift tax.—(a) In general.—With respect to gifts made before 1977, a credit is allowed under section 2012 against the Federal estate tax for gift tax paid under chapter 12 of the Internal Revenue Code, or corresponding provisions of prior law, on a gift by the decedent of property subsequently included in the decedent's gross estate. The credit is allowable even though the gift tax is paid after the decedent's death and the amount of the gift tax is deductible from the gross estate as a debt of the decedent.

(b) Limitations on credit.—The credit for gift tax is limited to the smaller of the following amounts:

(1) The amount of gift tax paid on the gift, computed as set forth in paragraph (c) of this section, or

(2) The amount of the estate tax attributable to the inclusion of the gift in the gross estate, computed as set forth in paragraph (d) of this section.

When more than one gift is included in the gross estate, a separate computation of the two limitations on the credit is to be made for each gift.

(c) "First limitation".—The amount of the gift tax paid on the gift is the "first limitation." Thus, if only one gift was made during a certain calendar quarter or calendar year if the gift was made before January 1, 1971, and the gift is wholly included in the decedent's gross estate for the purpose of the estate tax, the credit with respect to the gift is limited to the amount of the gift tax paid for that calendar quarter or calendar year. On the other hand, if more than one gift was made during a certain calendar quarter or calendar year, the credit with respect to any such gift which is included in the decedent's gross estate is limited under section 2012(d) to an amount, A, which bears the same ratio to B (the total gift tax paid for that calendar quarter or calendar year) as C (the "amount of the gift," computed as described below) bears to D (the total taxable gifts for the calendar quarter or the calendar year, computed without deduction of the gift tax specific exemption). Stated algebraically, the "first limitation" (A) equals

$$\frac{\text{"amount of the gift" (C)}}{\substack{\text{total taxable gifts,} \\ \text{plus specific} \\ \text{exemption allowed} \\ \text{(D)}}} \times \substack{\text{total gift} \\ \text{tax paid} \\ \text{(B).}}$$

For purposes of the ratio stated above, the "amount of the gift" referred to as factor "C" is the value of the gift reduced by any portion excluded or deducted under section 2503(b) (annual exclusion), 2522 (charitable deduction), or 2523 (marital deduction) of the Internal Revenue Code or corresponding provisions of prior law. In making the computations described in this paragraph, the values to be used are those finally determined for the purpose of the gift tax, irrespective of the values determined for the purpose of the estate tax. A similar computation is made in case only a portion of any gift is included in the decedent's gross estate. The application of this paragraph may be illustrated by the following example:

Example. The donor made gifts during the calendar year 1955 on which a gift tax was determined as shown below:

Gift of property to son on February 1 . . . $13,000
Gift of property to wife on May 1 86,000
Gift of property to charitable
organization on May 15 10,000

Total gifts 109,000
Less exclusions ($3,000 for each gift) 9,000

Total included amount of gifts 100,000
Marital deduction (for gift to
wife) $43,000
Charitable deduction 7,000

Specific exemption ($30,000 less
$20,000 used in prior years) 10,000

Total deductions 60,000

Taxable gifts 40,000
Total gift tax paid for calendar year 1955 $ 3,600

$$\frac{\$86,000 - \$3,000 - \$43,000 \quad \begin{array}{l}\text{(gift to wife, less annual}\\ \text{exclusion and marital}\\ \text{deduction)}\end{array}}{\$40,000 + \$10,000 \quad \begin{array}{l}\text{(taxable gifts, plus spe-}\\ \text{cific exemption}\\ \text{allowed)}\end{array}} \times \$3,600 \text{ (total gift tax paid)} = \$2,880.$$

(d) *"Second limitation"*.—(1) The amount of the estate tax attributable to the inclusion of the gift in the gross estate is the "second limitation". Thus, the credit with respect to any gift of property included in the gross estate is limited to an amount, E, which bears the same ratio to F (the gross estate tax, reduced by any credit for State death taxes under section 2011) as G (the "value

$$(E) \text{ equals} \quad \frac{\text{"value of the gift" (G)}}{\begin{array}{c}\text{value of gross estate, less marital}\\ \text{and charitable deductions (H)}\end{array}} \times$$

(2) For purposes of the ratio stated in subparagraph (1) of this paragraph, the "value of the gift" referred to as factor "G" is the value of the property transferred by gift and included in the gross estate, as determined for the purpose of the gift tax or for the purpose of the estate tax, whichever is lower, and adjusted as follows:

(i) The appropriate value is reduced by all or a portion of any annual exclusion allowed for gift tax purposes under section 2503(b) of the Internal Revenue Code or corresponding provisions of prior law. If the gift tax value is lower than the estate tax value, it is reduced by the

$$\frac{\$15,000 \quad \text{(annual exclusions allowed)}}{\$300,000 \quad \begin{array}{c}\text{(value of transferred property for the}\\ \text{purpose of the gift tax)}\end{array}} \times \$270,000 \quad \begin{array}{l}\text{(value of transferred}\\ \text{property}\\ \text{for the purpose of the estate}\\ \text{tax)} = \$13,500.\end{array}$$

(ii) The appropriate value is further reduced if any portion of the value of the property is allowed as a marital deduction under section 2056 or as a charitable deduction under section 2055 or section 2106(a)(2) (for estates of nonresidents not citizens). The amount of the reduction is an amount which bears the same ratio to the value determined under subdivision (i) of this subparagraph as the portion of the property allowed as a marital deduction or as a charitable deduction bears to the total value of the property as determined for the purpose of the estate tax.

The donor's gift to his wife was made in contemplation of death and was thereafter included in his gross estate. Under the "first limitation," the credit with respect to that gift cannot exceed

of the gift," computed as described in subparagraph (2) of this paragraph) bears to H (the value of the entire gross estate, reduced by the total deductions allowed under sections 2055 or 2106(a)(2) (charitable deduction) and 2056 (marital deduction)). Stated algebraically, the "second limitation"

gross estate tax, less credit for State death taxes (F).

entire amount of the exclusion. If the estate tax value is lower than the gift tax value, it is reduced by an amount which bears the same ratio to the estate tax value as the annual exclusion bears to the total value of the property as determined for gift tax purposes. To illustrate: In 1955, a donor, in contemplation of death, transferred certain property to his five children which was valued at $300,000 for the purpose of gift tax. Thereafter, the same property was included in his gross estate at a value of $270,000. In computing his gift tax, the donor was allowed annual exclusions totalling $15,000. The reduction provided for in this subdivision is

Thus, if a gift is made solely to the decedent's surviving spouse and is subsequently included in the decedent's gross estate as having been made in contemplation of death, but a marital deduction is allowed under section 2056 for the full value of the gift, no credit for gift tax on the gift will be allowed since the reduction under this subdivision together with the reduction under subdivision (i) of this subparagraph will have the effect of reducing the factor "G" of the ratio in subparagraph (1) of this paragraph to zero.

Reg. §20.2012-1(d)(1)

(e) *Credit for "split gifts".*—If a decedent made a gift of property which is thereafter included in his gross estate, and, under the provisions of section 2513 of the Internal Revenue Code of 1954 or section 1000(f) of the Internal Revenue Code of 1939, the gift was considered as made one-half by the decedent and one-half by his spouse, credit against the estate tax is allowed for the gift tax paid with respect to both halves of the gift. The "first limitation" is to be separately computed with respect to each half of the gift in accordance with the principles stated in paragraph (c) of this section. The "second limitation" is to be computed with respect to the entire gift in accordance with the principles stated in paragraph (d) of this section. To illustrate: A donor, in contemplation of death, transferred property valued at $106,000 to his son on January 1, 1955, and he and his wife consented that the gift should be considered as made one-half by him and one-half by her. The property was thereafter included in the donor's gross estate. Under the "first limitation", the amount of the gift tax of the donor paid with respect to the one-half of the gift considered as made by him is determined to be $11,250, and the amount of the gift tax of his wife paid with respect to the one-half of the gift considered as made by her is determined to be $1,200. Under the "second limitation", the amount of the estate tax attributable to the property is determined to be $28,914. Therefore, the credit for gift tax allowed is $12,450 ($11,250 plus $1,200). [Reg. § 20.2012-1.]

☐ [*T.D.* 6296, 6-23-58. *Amended by T.D.* 7238, 12-28-72 *and T.D.* 8522, 2-28-94.]

[Reg. § 20.2013-1]

§ 20.2013-1. **Credit for tax on prior transfers.**—(a) *In general.*—A credit is allowed under section 2013 against the Federal estate tax imposed on the present decedent's estate for Federal estate tax paid on the transfer of property to the present decedent from a transferor who died within ten years before, or within two years after, the present decedent's death. See § 20.2013-5 for definition of the terms "property" and "transfer." There is no requirement that the transferred property be identified in the estate of the present decedent or that the property be in existence at the time of the decedent's death. It is sufficient that the transfer of the property was subjected to Federal estate tax in the estate of the transferor and that the transferor died within the prescribed period of time. The executor must submit such proof as may be requested by the district director in order to establish the right of the estate to the credit.

(b) *Limitations on credit.*—The credit for tax on prior transfers is limited to the smaller of the following amounts:

(1) The amount of the Federal estate tax attributable to the transferred property in the transferor's estate, computed as set forth in § 20.2013-2; or

(2) The amount of the Federal estate tax attributable to the transferred property in the decedent's estate, computed as set forth in § 20.2013-3. Rules for valuing property for purposes of the credit are contained in § 20.2013-4.

(c) *Percentage reduction.*—If the transferor died within the two years before, or within the two years after, the present decedent's death, the credit is the smaller of the two limitations described in paragraph (b) of this section. If the transferor predeceased the present decedent by more than two years, the credit is a certain percentage of the smaller of the two limitations described in paragraph (b) of this section, determined as follows:

(1) 80 percent, if the transferor died within the third or fourth years preceding the present decedent's death;

(2) 60 percent, if the transferor died within the fifth or sixth years preceding the present decedent's death;

(3) 40 percent, if the transferor died within the seventh or eighth years preceding the present decedent's death; and

(4) 20 percent, if the transferor died within the ninth or tenth years preceding the present decedent's death.

The word "within" as used in this paragraph means "during". Therefore, if a death occurs on the second anniversary of another death, the first death is considered to have occurred within the two years before the second death. If the credit for tax on prior transfers relates to property received from two or more transferors, the provisions of this paragraph are to be applied separately with respect to the property received from each transferor. See paragraph (d) of example (2) in § 20.2013-6.

(d) *Examples.*—For illustrations of the application of this section, see examples (1) and (2) set forth in § 20.2013-6. [Reg. § 20.2013-1.]

☐ [*T.D.* 6296, 6-23-58.]

[Reg. § 20.2013-2]

§ 20.2013-2. **"First limitation."**—(a) The amount of the Federal estate tax attributable to the transferred property in the transferor's estate is the "first limitation." Thus, the credit is limited to an amount, A, which bears the same ratio to B (the "transferor's adjusted Federal estate tax," computed as described in paragraph (b) of this section) as C (the value of the property transferred (see § 20.2013-4)) bears to D (the "transferor's adjusted taxable estate," computed as described in paragraph (c) of this section). Stated algebraically, the "first limitation" (A) equals

$$\frac{\text{value of transferred property (C)}}{\text{"transferor's adjusted taxable estate" (D)}} \times \frac{\text{"transferor's adjusted Federal}}{\text{estate tax" (B).}}$$

(b) For purposes of the ratio stated in paragraph (a) of this section, the "transferor's adjusted Federal estate tax" referred to as factor "B" is the amount of the Federal estate tax paid with respect to the transferor's estate plus:

(1) Any credit allowed the transferor's estate for gift tax under section 2012, or the corresponding provisions of prior law; and

(2) Any credit allowed the transferor's estate, under section 2013, for tax on prior transfers, but only if the transferor acquired property from a person who died within 10 years before the death of the present decedent.

(c)(1) For purposes of the ratio stated in paragraph (a) of this section, the "transferor's adjusted taxable estate" referred to as factor "D" is the amount of the transferor's taxable estate (or net estate) decreased by the amount of any "death taxes" paid with respect to his gross estate and increased by the amount of the exemption allowed in computing his taxable estate (or net estate). The amount of the transferor's taxable estate (or net estate) is determined in accordance with the provisions of §20.2051-1 in the case of a citizen or resident of the United States or of §20.2106-1 in the case of a nonresident not a citizen of the United States (or the corresponding provisions of prior regulations). The term "death taxes" means the Federal estate tax plus all other estate, inheritance, legacy, succession, or similar death taxes imposed by, and paid to, any taxing authority, whether within or without the United States. However, only the net amount of such taxes paid is taken into consideration.

(2) The amount of the exemption depends upon the citizenship and residence of the transferor at the time of his death. Except in the case of a decedent described in section 2209 (relating to certain residents of possessions of the United States who are considered nonresidents not citizens), if the decedent was a citizen or resident of the United States, the exemption is the $60,000 authorized by section 2052 (or the corresponding provisions of prior law). If the decedent was a nonresident not a citizen of the United States, or is considered under section 2209 to have been such a nonresident, the exemption is the $30,000 or $2,000, as the case may be, authorized by section 2106(a)(3) (or the corresponding provisions of prior law), or such larger amount as is authorized by section 2106(a)(3)(B) or may have been allowed as an exemption pursuant to the prorated exemption provisions of an applicable death tax convention. See §20.2052-1 and paragraph (a)(3) of §20.2106-1.

(d) If the credit for tax on prior transfers relates to property received from two or more transferors, the provisions of this section are to be applied separately with respect to the property received from each transferor. See paragraph (b) of example (2) in §20.2013-6.

(e) For illustrations of the application of this section, see examples (1) and (2) set forth in §20.2013-6. [Reg. §20.2013-2.]

☐ [T.D. 6296, 6-23-58. *Amended by T.D. 7296,* 12-11-73.]

[Reg. §20.2013-3]

§20.2013-3. "Second limitation.".—(a) The amount of the Federal estate tax attributable to the transferred property in the present decedent's estate is the "second limitation." Thus, the credit is limited to the difference between—

(1) The net estate tax payable (see paragraph (b)(5) or (c), as the case may be, of §20.0-2) with respect to the present decedent's estate, determined without regard to any credit for tax on prior transfers under section 2013 or any credit for foreign death taxes claimed under the provisions of a death tax convention, and

(2) The net estate tax determined as provided in paragraph (1) of this section, but computed by subtracting from the present decedent's gross estate the value of the property transferred (see §20.2013-4), and by making only the adjustment indicated in paragraph (b) of this section if a charitable deduction is allowable to the estate of the present decedent.

(b) If a charitable deduction is allowable to the estate of the present decedent under the provisions of section 2055 or section 2106(a)(2) (for estates of nonresidents not citizens), for purposes of determining the tax described in paragraph (a)(2) of this section, the charitable deduction otherwise allowable is reduced by an amount, E, which bears the same ratio to F (the charitable deduction otherwise allowable) as G (the value of the transferred property (see §20.2013-4)) bears to H (the value of the present decedent's gross estate reduced by the amount of the deductions for expenses, indebtedness, taxes, losses, etc., allowed under the provisions of sections 2053 and 2054 or section 2106(a)(1) (for estates of nonresidents not citizens)). See paragraph (c)(2) of example (1) and paragraph (c)(2) of example (2) in §20.2013-6.

(c) If the credit for tax on prior transfers relates to property received from two or more transferors, the property received from all transferors is aggregated in determining the limitation on credit under this section (the "second limitation"). However, the limitation so determined is apportioned to the property received from each transferor in the ratio that the property received from each transferor bears to the total property received from all transferors. See paragraph (c) of example (2) in § 20.2013-6.

(d) For illustrations of the application of this section, see examples (1) and (2) set forth in § 20.2013-6. [Reg. § 20.2013-3.]

☐ [*T.D. 6296, 6-23-58. Amended by T.D. 7296,* 12-11-73.]

[Reg. § 20.2013-4]

§ 20.2013-4. Valuation of property transferred.—(a) For purposes of section 2013 and §§ § 20.2013-1 to 20.2013-6, the value of the property transferred to the decedent is the value at which the property was included in the transferor's gross estate for the purpose of the Federal estate tax (see sections 2031, 2032, 2103, and 2107, and the regulations thereunder) reduced as indicated in paragraph (b) of this section. If the decedent received a life estate or a remainder or other limited interest in property that was included in a transferor decedent's gross estate, the value of the interest is determined as of the date of the transferor's death on the basis of recognized valuation principles (see §§ § 20.2031-7 (or, for certain prior periods, § 20.2031-7A) and 20.7520-1 through 20.7520-4). The application of this paragraph may be illustrated by the following examples:

Example (1). A died on January 1, 1953, leaving Blackacre to B. The property was included in A's gross estate at a value of $100,000. On January 1, 1955, B sold Blackacre to C for $150,000. B died on February 1, 1955. For purposes of computing the credit against the tax imposed on B's estate, the value of the property transferred to B is $100,000.

Example (2). A died on January 1, 1953, leaving Blackacre to B for life and, upon B's death, remainder to C. At the time of A's death, B was 56 years of age. The property was included in A's gross estate at a value of $100,000. The part of that value attributable to the life estate is $44,688 and the part of that value attributable to the remainder is $55,312 (see § 20.2031-7A(b)). B died on January 1, 1955, and C died on January 1, 1956. For purposes of computing the credit against the tax imposed on B's estate, the value of the property transferred to B is $44,688. For purposes of computing the credit against the tax imposed on C's estate, the value of the property transferred to C is $55,312.

(b) In arriving at the value of the property transferred to the decedent, the value at which the property was included in the transferor's gross estate (see paragraph (a) of this section) is reduced as follows:

(1) By the amount of the Federal estate tax and any other estate, inheritance, legacy, or succession taxes which were payable out of the property transferred to the decedent or which were payable by the decedent in connection with the property transferred to him. For example, if under the transferor's will or local law all death taxes are to be paid out of other property with the result that the decedent receives a bequest free and clear of all death taxes, no reduction is to be made under this subparagraph;

(2) By the amount of any marital deduction allowed the transferor's estate under section 2056 (or under section 812(e) of the Internal Revenue Code of 1939) if the decedent was the spouse of the transferor at the time of the transferor's death;

(3)(i) By the amount of administration expenses in accordance with the principles of § 20.2056(b)-4(d).

(ii) This paragraph (b)(3) applies to transfers from estates of decedents dying on or after December 3, 1999; and

(4)(i) By the amount of any encumbrance on the property or by the amount of any obligation imposed by the transferor and incurred by the decedent with respect to the property, to the extent such charges would be taken into account if the amount of a gift to the decedent of such property were being determined.

(ii) For purposes of this subparagraph, an obligation imposed by the transferor and incurred by the decedent with respect to the property includes a bequest, etc., in lieu of the interest of the surviving spouse under community property laws, unless the interest was, immediately prior to the transferor's death, a mere expectancy. However, an obligation imposed by the transferor and incurred by the decedent with respect to the property does not include a bequest, devise, or other transfer in lieu of dower, curtesy, or of a statutory estate created in lieu of dower or curtesy, or of other marital rights in the transferor's property or estate.

(iii) The application of this subparagraph may be illustrated by the following examples:

Example (1). The transferor devised to the decedent real estate subject to a mortgage. The value of the property transferred to the decedent does not include the amount of the mortgage. If, however, the transferor by his will directs the executor to pay off the mortgage, such payment constitutes an additional amount transferred to the decedent.

Example (2). The transferor bequeathed certain property to the decedent with a direction that the decedent pay $1,000 to X. The value of the property transferred to the decedent is the value of the property reduced by $1,000.

Example (3). The transferor bequeathed certain property to his wife, the decedent, in lieu of her interest in property held by them as community property under the law of the State of their residence. The wife elected to relinquish her community property interest and to take the bequest. The value of the property transferred to the decedent is the value of the property reduced by the value of the community property interest relinquished by the wife.

Example (4). The transferor bequeathed to the decedent his entire residuary estate, out of which certain claims were to be satisfied. The entire distributable income of the transferor's estate (during the period of its administration) was applied toward the satisfaction of these claims and the remaining portion of the claims was satisfied by the decedent out of his own funds. Thus, the decedent received a larger sum upon settlement of the transferor's estate than he was actually bequeathed. The value of the property transferred to the decedent is the value at which such property was included in the transferor's gross estate, reduced by the amount of the estate income and the decedent's own funds paid out in satisfaction of the claims. [Reg. § 20.2013-4.]

☐ [*T.D.* 6296, 6-23-58. *Amended by T.D.* 7077, 12-1-70; *T.D.* 7296, 12-11-73; *T.D.* 8522, 2-28-94; *T.D.* 8540, 6-9-94 *and T.D.* 8846, 12-2-99.]

[Reg. § 20.2013-5]

§ 20.2013-5. "Property" and "transfer" defined.—(a) For purposes of section 2013 and §§ 20.2013-1 through 20.2013-6, the term "property" means any beneficial interest in property, including a general power of appointment (as defined in section 2041) over property. Thus, the term does not include an interest in property consisting merely of a bare legal title, such as that of a trustee. Nor does the term include a power of appointment over property which is not a general power of appointment (as defined in section 2041). Examples of property, as described in this paragraph, are annuities, life estates, estates for terms of years, vested or contingent remainders and other future interests.

(b) In order to obtain the credit for tax on prior transfers, there must be a transfer of property described in paragraph (a) of this section by or from the transferor to the decedent. The term "transfer" of property by or from a transferor means any passing of property or an interest in property under circumstances which were such that the property or interest was included in the gross estate of the transferor. In this connection, if the decedent receives property as a result of the exercise or nonexercise of a power of appointment, the donee of the power (and not the creator) is deemed to be the transferor of the property subject to the power if the property subject to the power is includible in the donee's gross estate under section 2041 (relating to powers of appointment). Thus, notwithstanding the designation by local law of the capacity in which the decedent takes, property received from the transferor includes interests in property held by or devolving upon the decedent: (1) as spouse under dower or curtesy laws or laws creating an estate in lieu of dower or curtesy; (2) as surviving tenant of a tenancy by the entirety or joint tenancy with survivorship rights; (3) as beneficiary of the proceeds of life insurance; (4) as survivor under an annuity contract; (5) as donee (possessor) of a general power of appointment (as defined in section 2041); (6) as appointee under the exercise of a general power of appointment (as defined in section 2041); or (7) as remainderman under the release or nonexercise of a power of appointment by reason of which the property is included in the gross estate of the donee of the power under section 2041.

(c) The application of this section may be illustrated by the following example:

Example. A devises Blackacre to B, as trustee, with directions to pay the income therefrom to C, his son, for life. Upon C's death, Blackacre is to be sold. C is given a general testamentary power to appoint one-third of the proceeds, and a testamentary power, which is not a general power, to appoint the remaining two-thirds of the proceeds, to such of the issue of his sister D as he should choose. D has a daughter, E, and a son, F. Upon his death, C exercised his general power by appointing one-third of the proceeds to D and his special power by appointing two-thirds of the proceeds to E. Since B's interest in Blackacre as a trustee is not a beneficial interest, no part of it is "property" for purpose of the credit in B's estate. On the other hand, C's life estate and his testamentary power over the one-third interest in the remainder constitute "property" received from A for purpose of the credit in C's estate. Likewise, D's one-third interest in the remainder received through the exercise of C's general power of appointment is "property" received from C for purpose of the credit in D's estate. No credit is allowed E's estate for the property which passed to her from C since the property was not included in C's gross estate. On the other hand, no credit is allowed in E's estate for property passing to her from A since her interest was not susceptible of valuation at the time of A's death (see § 20.2013-4). [Reg. § 20.2013-5.]

☐ [*T.D.* 6296, 6-23-58.]

[Reg. § 20.2013-6]

§ 20.2013-6. Examples.—The application of §§ 20.2013-1 through 20.2013-5 may be further illustrated by the following examples:

Example (1). (a) A died December 1, 1953, leaving a gross estate of $1,000,000. Expenses, indebtedness, etc., amounted to $90,000. A bequeathed $200,000 to B, his wife, $100,000 of which qualifies for the marital deduction. B died November 1, 1954, leaving a gross estate of $500,000. Expenses, indebtedness, etc., amounted to $40,000. B bequeathed $150,000 to charity. A and B were both citizens of the United States. The estates of A and B both paid State death taxes equal to the maximum credit allowable for State death taxes. Death taxes were not a charge on the bequest to B.

(b) "First limitation" on credit for B's estate (§ 20.2013-2):

A's gross estate		$1,000,000.00
Expenses, indebtedness, etc.		90,000.00
A's adjusted gross estate		$910,000.00
Marital deduction	$100,000.00	
Exemption	60,000.00	160,000.00
A's taxable estate		750,000.00
A's gross estate tax		233,200.00
Credit for State death taxes		23,280.00
A's net estate tax payable		$209,920.00

"First limitation" = $209,920.00 (§ 20.2013-2(b)) × [($200,000.00 − $100,000.00) (§ 20.2013-4) ÷ ($750,000.00 − $209,920.00 − $23,280.00 + $60,000.00) (§ 20.2013-2(c))]   = $36,393.90

(c) "Second limitation" on credit for B's estate (§ 20.2013-3):

(1) B's net estate tax payable as described in § 20.2013-3(a)(1) (previously taxed transfer included):

B's gross estate	$500,000.00	
Expenses, indebtedness, etc.	$40,000.00	
Charitable deduction	150,000.00	
Exemption	60,000.00	250,000.00
B's taxable estate		$250,000.00
B's gross estate tax		$65,700.00
Credit for State death taxes		3,920.00
B's net estate tax payable		$61,780.00

(2) B's net estate tax payable as described in § 20.2013-3(a)(2) (previously taxed transfer excluded):

B's gross estate		$400,000.00
Expenses, indebtedness, etc.	$ 40,000.00	
Charitable deduction (§ 20.2013-3(b)) = $150,000.00 − [$150,000.00 × ($200,000.00 − $100,000.00 ÷ $500,000.00 − $ 40,000.00)] =	$117,391.30	
Exemption	60,000.00	217,391.30
B's taxable estate		$182,608.70
B's gross estate tax		$45,482.61
Credit for State death taxes		2,221.61
B's net estate tax payable		$43,260.00

(3) "Second limitation":

Subparagraph (1)	$61,780.00	
Less: Subparagraph (2)	43,260.00	$18,520.00

(d) Credit of B's estate for tax on prior transfers (§ 20.2013-1(c)):

Credit for tax on prior transfers = $18,520.00 (lower of paragraphs (b) and (c)) × 100% (percentage to be taken into account under § 20.2013-1(c))	$18,520.00

Example (2). (a) The facts are the same as those contained in example (1) of this paragraph with the following additions. C died December 1, 1950, leaving a gross estate of $250,000. Expenses, indebtedness, etc., amounted to $50,000. C bequeathed $50,000 to B. C was a citizen of the United States. His estate paid State death taxes equal to the maximum credit allowable for State death taxes. Death taxes were not a charge on the bequest to B.

(b) "First limitation" on credit for B's estate (§ 20.2013-2(d))—

(1) With respect to the property received from A:

"First limitation" = $36,393.90 (this computation is identical with the one contained in paragraph (b) of example (1) of this section).

(2) With respect to the property received from C:

C's gross estate		$250,000.00
Expenses, indebtedness, etc.	$50,000.00	
Exemption	60,000.00	110,000.00
C's taxable estate		$140,000.00
C's gross estate tax		$32,700.00
Credit for State death taxes		1,200.00
C's net estate tax payable		$31,500.00

"First limitation" = $31,500.00 (§ 20.2013-2(b)) ×
[$50,000.00 (§ 20.2013-4) ÷
($140,000.00 − $31,500.00 − $1,200.00 + $60,000.00)
(§ 20.2013-2(c))]   = $9,414.23

(c) "Second limitation" on credit for B's estate (§ 20.2013-3(c)):

(1) B's net estate tax payable as described in § 20.2013-3(a)(1) (previously taxed transfers included) = $61,780.00 (this computation is identical with the one contained in paragraph (c)(1) of example (1) of this section).

(2) B's net estate tax payable as described in § 20.2013-3(a)(2) (previously taxed transfers excluded):

B's gross estate		$350,000.00
Expenses, indebtedness, etc.	$40,000.00	
Charitable deduction (§ 20.2013-3(b)) =		
$150,000.00 − [$150,000.00 ×		
($200,000.00 − $100,000.00 + $50,000.00) ÷		
($500,000.00 − $40,000.00)] = ...	101,086.96	
Exemption	60,000.00	201,086.96
B's taxable estate		$148,913.04
B's gross estate tax		$35,373.91
Credit for State death taxes		1,413.91
B's net estate tax payable		$33,960.00

(3) "Second limitation":

Subparagraph (1)	$61,780.00	
Less: Subparagraph (2)	33,960.00	$27,820.00

(4) Apportionment of "second limitation" on credit:

Transfer from A (§ 20.2013-4)	$100,000.00
Transfer from C (§ 20.2013-4)	50,000.00
Total	$150,000.00
Portion of "second limitation" attributable to transfer from A (100/150 of $27,820.00)	18,546.67
Portion of "second limitation" attributable to transfer from C (50/150 of $27,820.00)	9,273.33

(d) Credit of B's estate for tax on prior transfers (§ 20.2013-1(c)):

Credit for tax on transfer from A = $18,546.67 (lower of "first limitation" computed in paragraph (b)(1) and "second limitation" apportioned to A's transfer in paragraph (c)(4)) × 100% (percentage to be taken into account under § 20.2013-1(c))	$18,546.67
Credit for tax on transfer from C = $9,273.33 (lower of "first limitation" computed in paragraph (b)(2) and "second limitation" apportioned to B's transfer in paragraph (c)(4)) × 80% (percentage to be taken into account under § 20.2013-1(c))	7,418.66
Total credit for tax on prior transfers	$ 25,965.33

[Reg. § 20.2013-6.]

☐ [T.D. 6296, 6-23-58.]

[Reg. § 20.2014-1]

§ 20.2014-1. Credit for foreign death taxes.— (a) *In general.*—(1) A credit is allowed under section 2014 against the Federal estate tax for any estate, inheritance, legacy, or succession taxes actually paid to any foreign country (hereinafter referred to as "foreign death taxes"). The credit is allowed only for foreign death taxes paid (i) with respect to property situated within the country to which the tax is paid, (ii) with respect to property included in the decedent's gross estate, and (iii) with respect to the decedent's estate. The credit is allowable to the estate of a decedent who was a citizen of the United States at the time of his death. The credit is also allowable, as provided in paragraph (c) of this section, to the estate of a decedent who was a resident but not a citizen of the United States at the time of his death. The credit is not allowable to the estate of a decedent who was neither a citizen nor a resident of the United States at the time of his death. See paragraph(b)(1) of § 20.0-1 for the meaning of the term "resident" as applied to a decedent. The credit is allowable not only for death taxes paid to foreign countries which are states in the international sense, but also for death taxes paid to possessions or political subdivisions of foreign states. With respect to the estate of a decedent dying after September 2, 1958, the term "foreign country", as used in this section and § § 20.2014-2 to 20.2014-6, includes a possession of the United States. See § § 20.2011-1 and 20.2011-2 for the allowance of a credit for death taxes paid to a possession of the United States in the case of a decedent dying before September 3, 1958. No credit is allowable for interest or penalties paid in connection with foreign death taxes.

(2) In addition to the credit for foreign death taxes under section 2014, similar credits are allowed under death tax conventions with certain foreign countries. If credits against the Federal estate tax are allowable under section 2014, or under section 2014 and one or more death tax conventions, for death taxes paid to more than one country, the credits are combined and the aggregate amount is credited against the Federal estate tax, subject to the limitation provided for in paragraph (c) of § 20.2014-4. For application of the credit in cases involving a death tax convention, see § 20.2014-4.

(3) No credit is allowable under section 2014 in connection with property situated outside of the foreign country imposing the tax for which credit is claimed. However, such a credit may be allowable under certain death tax conventions. In the case of a tax imposed by a political subdivision of a foreign country, credit for the tax shall be allowed with respect to property having a situs in that foreign country, even though, under the principles described in this subparagraph, the property has a situs in a political subdivision different from the one imposing the tax. Whether or not particular property of a decedent is situated in the foreign country imposing the tax is determined in accordance with the same principles that would be applied in determining whether or not similar property of a nonresident decedent not a citizen of the United States is situated within the United States for Federal estate tax purposes. See § § 20.2104-1 and 20.2105-1. For example, under § 20.2104-1 shares of stock are deemed to be situated in the United States only if issued by a domestic corporation. Thus, a share of corporate stock is regarded as situated in the foreign country imposing the tax only if the issuing corporation is incorporated in that country. Further, under § 20.2105-1 amounts receivable as insurance on the life of a nonresident not a citizen of the United States at the time

of his death are not deemed situated in the United States. Therefore, in determining the credit under section 2014 in the case of a decedent who was a citizen or resident of the United States, amounts receivable as insurance on the life of the decedent and payable under a policy issued by a corporation incorporated in a foreign country are not deemed situated in such foreign country. In addition, under § 20.2105-1 in the case of an estate of a nonresident not a citizen of the United States who died on or after November 14, 1966, a debt obligation of a domestic corporation is not considered to be situated in the United States if any interest thereon would be treated under section 862(a)(1) as income from sources without the United States by reason of section 861(a)(1)(B) (relating to interest received from a domestic corporation less than 20 percent of whose gross income for a 3-year period was derived from sources within the United States). Accordingly, a debt obligation the primary obligor on which is a corporation incorporated in the foreign country imposing the tax is not considered to be situated in that country if, under circumstances corresponding to those described in § 20.2105-1 less than 20 percent of the gross income of the corporation for the 3-year period was derived from sources within that country. Further, under § 20.2104-1 in the case of an estate of a nonresident not a citizen of the United States who died before November 14, 1966, a bond for the payment of money is not situated within the United States unless it is physically located in the United States. Accordingly, in the case of the estate of a decedent dying before November 14, 1966, a bond is deemed situated in the foreign country imposing the tax only if it is physically located in that country. Finally, under § 20.2105-1 moneys deposited in the United States with any person carrying on the banking business by or for a nonresident not a citizen of the United States who died before November 14, 1966, and who was not engaged in business in the United States at the time of death are not deemed situated in the United States. Therefore, an account with a foreign bank in the foreign country imposing the tax is not considered to be situated in that country under corresponding circumstances.

(4) Where a deduction is allowed under section 2053(d) for foreign death taxes paid with respect to a charitable gift, the credit for foreign death taxes is subject to further limitations as explained in § 20.2014-7.

(b) *Limitations on credit.*—The credit for foreign death taxes is limited to the smaller of the following amounts:

(1) The amount of a particular foreign death tax attributable to property situated in the country imposing the tax and included in the decedent's gross estate for Federal estate tax purposes, computed as set forth in § 20.2014-2; or

(2) The amount of the Federal estate tax attributable to particular property situated in a

foreign country, subjected to foreign death tax in that country, and included in the decedent's gross estate for Federal estate tax purposes, computed as set forth in § 20.2014-3.

(c) *Credit allowable to estate of resident not a citizen.*—(1) In the case of an estate of a decedent dying before November 14, 1966, who was a resident but not a citizen of the United States, a credit is allowed to the estate under section 2014 only if the foreign country of which the decedent was a citizen or subject, in imposing foreign death taxes, allows a similar credit to the estates of citizens of the United States who were resident in that foreign country at the time of death.

(2) In the case of an estate of a decedent dying on or after November 14, 1966, who was a resident but not a citizen of the United States, a credit is allowed to the estate under section 2014 without regard to the similar credit requirement of subparagraph (1) of this paragraph unless the decedent was a citizen or subject of a foreign country with respect to which there is in effect at the time of the decedent's death a Presidential proclamation, as authorized by section 2014(h), reinstating the similar credit requirement. In the case of an estate of a decedent who was a resident of the United States and a citizen or subject of a foreign country with respect to which such a proclamation has been made, and who dies while the proclamation is in effect, a credit is allowed under section 2014 only if that foreign country, in imposing foreign death taxes, allows a similar credit to the estates of citizens of the United States who were resident in that foreign country at the time of death. The proclamation authorized by section 2014(h) for the reinstatement of the similar credit requirement with respect to the estates of citizens or subjects of a specific foreign country may be made by the President whenever he finds that—

(i) The foreign country, in imposing foreign death taxes, does not allow a similar credit to the estates of citizens of the United States who were resident in the foreign country at the time of death,

(ii) The foreign country, after having been requested to do so, has not acted to provide a similar credit to the estates of such citizens, and

(iii) It is in the public interest to allow the credit under section 2014 to the estates of citizens or subjects of the foreign country only if the foreign country allows a similar credit to the estates of citizens of the United States who were resident in the foreign country at the time of death. The proclamation for the reinstatement of the similar credit requirement with respect to the estates of citizens or subjects of a specific foreign country may be revoked by the President. In that case, a credit is allowed under section 2014, to the estate of a decedent who was a citizen or subject of that foreign country and a resident of the United States at the time of death, without regard to the similar credit requirement if the decedent dies after the proclamation reinstating the similar credit requirement has been revoked. [Reg. § 20.2014-1.]

☐ [*T.D. 6296, 6-23-58. Amended by T.D. 6526, 1-18-61, T.D. 6600, 5-28-62 and T.D. 7296, 12-11-73.*]

[Reg. § 20.2014-2]

§ 20.2014-2. **"First limitation".**—(a) The amount of a particular foreign death tax attributable to property situated in the country imposing the tax and included in the decedent's gross estate for Federal estate tax purposes is the "first limitation." Thus, the credit for any foreign death tax is limited to an amount, A, which bears the same ratio to B (the amount of the foreign death tax without allowance of credit, if any, for Federal estate tax) as C (the value of the property situated in the country imposing the foreign death tax, subjected to the foreign death tax, included in the gross estate and for which a deduction is not allowed under section 2053(d)) bears to D (the value of all property subjected to the foreign death tax). Stated algebraically, the "first limitation"(A) equals

$$\frac{\text{Value of property in foreign country subjected to foreign death tax, in- cluded in gross estate and for which a deduction is not allowed under section 2053(d) (C)}}{\text{Value of all property subjected to foreign death tax (D)}} \times \text{Amount of foreign death tax (B)}$$

The values used in this proportion are the values determined for the purpose of the foreign death tax. The amount of the foreign death tax for which credit is allowable must be converted into United States money. The application of this paragraph may be illustrated by the following example:

Example. At the time of his death on June 1, 1966, the decedent, a citizen of the United States, owned stock in X Corp. (a corporation organized under the laws of Country Y) valued at $80,000. In addition, he owned bonds issued by Country

Y valued at $80,000. The stock and bond certificates were in the United States. Decedent left by will $20,000 of the stock and $50,000 of the Country Y bonds to his surviving spouse. He left the rest of the stock and bonds to his son. Under the situs rules referred to in paragraph (a)(3) of § 20.2014-1 the stock is deemed situated in Country Y while the bonds are deemed to have their situs in the United States. (The bonds would be deemed to have their situs in Country Y if the decedent had died on or after November 14, 1966.) There is no death tax convention in existence between the United States and Country Y. The laws of Country Y provide for inheritance taxes computed as follows:

Inheritance tax of surviving spouse:

Value of stock	$20,000
Value of bonds	50,000
Total value	70,000
Tax (16 percent rate)	$11,200

Inheritance tax of son:

Value of stock	$60,000
Value of bonds	30,000
Total value	$90,000
Tax (16 percent rate)	$14,400

The "first limitation" on the credit for foreign death taxes is:

$$\frac{\$20,000 + \$60,000 \text{ (factor C of the ratio stated at §20.2014-2(a))}}{\$70,000 + \$90,000 \text{ (factor D of the ratio stated at §20.2014-2(a))}} \times \begin{array}{c} (\$11,200 + \$14,400) \\ \text{(factor B of the ratio stated at} \\ \text{§20.2014-2(a))} \end{array} = \$12,800$$

(b) If a foreign country imposes more than one kind of death tax or imposes taxes at different rates upon the several shares of an estate, or if a foreign country and a political subdivision or possession thereof each imposes a death tax, a "first limitation" is to be computed separately for each tax or rate and the results added in order to determine the total "first limitation." The application of this paragraph may be illustrated by the following example:

Example. The facts are the same as those contained in the example set forth in paragraph (a) of this section, except that the tax of the surviving spouse was computed at a 10-percent rate and amounted to $7,000, and the tax of the son was computed at a 20-percent rate and amounted to $18,000. In this case, the "first limitation" on the credit for foreign death taxes is computed as follows:

"First limitation" with respect to inheritance tax of surviving spouse =

$$\frac{\$20,000 \text{ (factor C of the ratio stated at §20.2014-2(a))}}{\$70,000 \text{ (factor D of the ratio stated at §20.2014-2(a))}} \times \begin{array}{c} \$7,000 \\ \text{(factor B of the ratio} \\ \text{stated at §20.2014-2(a))} \end{array} = \$2,000$$

"First limitation" with respect to inheritance tax of son =

$$\frac{\$60,000 \text{ (factor C of the ratio stated at §20.2014-2(a))}}{\$90,000 \text{ (factor D of the ratio stated at §20.2014-2(a))}} \times \begin{array}{c} \$18,000 \\ \text{(factor B of the ratio} \\ \text{stated at §20.2014-2(a))} \end{array} = \$12,000$$

Total "first limitation" on the credit for foreign death taxes $14,000

[Reg. §20.2014-2.]

[Reg. §20.2014-3]

□ [T.D. 6296, 6-23-58. *Amended by T.D. 6600,* 5-28-62; *T.D. 6684, 10-23-63 and T.D. 7296,* 12-11-73.]

§20.2014-3. "Second limitation".—(a) The amount of the Federal estate tax attributable to particular property situated in a foreign country, subjected to foreign death tax in that country, and included in the decedent's gross estate for Federal estate tax purposes is the "second limitation." Thus, the credit is limited to an amount, E, which bears the same ratio to F (the gross Federal estate tax, reduced by any credit for State death taxes under section 2011 and by any credit for gift tax under section 2012) as G (the "adjusted value of the property situated in the for-

$$\frac{\text{"adjusted value of the property situated in the foreign country, subjected to foreign death taxes, and included in the gross estate" (G)}}{\text{value of entire gross estate, less charitable and marital deductions (H)}}$$

The values used in this proportion are the values determined for the purpose of the Federal estate tax.

(b) Adjustment is required to factor "G" of the ratio stated in paragraph (a) of this section if a deduction for foreign death taxes under section 2053(d), a charitable deduction under section 2055, or a marital deduction under section 2056 is allowed with respect to the foreign property. If a deduction for foreign death taxes is allowed, the value of the property situated in the foreign country, subjected to foreign death tax, and included in the gross estate does not include the value of any property in respect of which the deduction for foreign death taxes is allowed. See § 20.2014-7. If a charitable deduction or a marital deduction is allowed, the value of such foreign property (after exclusion of the value of any property in respect of which the deduction for foreign death taxes is allowed) is reduced as follows:

(1) If a charitable deduction or a marital deduction is allowed to a decedent's estate with respect to any part of the foreign property, except foreign property in respect of which a deduction for foreign death taxes is allowed, specifically bequeathed, devised, or otherwise specifically passing to a charitable organization or to the decedent's spouse, the value of the foreign property is reduced by the amount of the charitable deduction or marital deduction allowed with respect to such specific transfer. See example (1) of paragraph (c) of this section.

(2) If a charitable deduction or a marital deduction is allowed to a decedent's estate with respect to a bequest, devise or other transfer of an interest in a group of assets including both the foreign property and other property, the value of the foreign property is reduced by an amount, I, which bears the same ratio to J (the amount of the charitable deduction or marital deduction allowed with respect to such transfer of an interest in a group of assets) as K (the value of the foreign property, except foreign property in respect of which a deduction for foreign death taxes is allowed, included in the group of assets)

eign country, subjected to foreign death tax, and included in the gross estate," computed as described in paragraph (b) of this section) bears to H (the value of the entire gross estate, reduced by the total amount of the deductions allowed under sections 2055 (charitable deduction) and 2056 (marital deduction)). Stated algebraically, the "second limitation" (E) equals

$$\frac{G}{H} \times \text{gross Federal estate tax, less credits for State death taxes and gift tax (F).}$$

bears to L (the value of the entire group of assets). As used in this subparagraph, the term "group of assets" has reference to those assets which, under applicable law, are chargeable with the charitable or marital transfer. See example (2) of paragraph (c) of this section.

Any reduction described in paragraph (b)(1) or (b)(2) of this section on account of the marital deduction must proportionately take into account, if applicable, the limitation on the aggregate amount of the marital deduction contained in § 20.2056(a)-1(c). See § 20.2014-3(c), *Example 3*.

(c) The application of paragraphs (a) and (b) of this section may be illustrated by the following examples. In each case, the computations relate to the amount of credit under section 2014 without regard to the amount of credit which may be allowable under an applicable death tax convention.

Example (1). (i) Decedent, a citizen and resident of the United States at the time of his death on February 1, 1967, left a gross estate of $1,000,000 which includes the following: shares of stock issued by a domestic corporation, valued at $750,000; bonds issued in 1960 by the United States and physically located in foreign Country X, valued at $50,000; and shares of stock issued by a Country X corporation, valued at $200,000, with respect to which death taxes were paid to Country X. Expenses, indebtedness, etc., amounted to $60,000. Decedent specifically bequeathed $40,000 of the stock issued by the Country X corporation to a U. S. charity and left the residue of his estate, in equal shares, to his son and daughter. The gross Federal estate tax is $266,500, and the credit for State death taxes is $27,600. Under the situs rules referred to in paragraph (a)(3) of § 20.2014-1, the shares of stock issued by the Country X corporation comprise the only property deemed to be situated in Country X. (The bonds also would be deemed to have their situs in Country X if the decedent had died before November 14, 1966.)

(ii) The "second limitation" on the credit for foreign death taxes is

$$\frac{\begin{array}{c}\$200{,}000 - \$40{,}000\\ \text{(factor G of the ratio}\\ \text{stated at § 20.2014-3(a);}\\ \text{see also § 20.2014-3(b)(1))}\end{array}}{\begin{array}{c}\$1{,}000{,}000 - \$40{,}000\\ \text{(factor H of the ratio}\\ \text{stated at § 20.2014-3(a))}\end{array}} \times \begin{array}{c}(\$266{,}500 - \$27{,}600) = \$39{,}816.67\\ \text{(factor F of the ratio stated at}\\ \text{§ 20.2014-3(a))}\end{array}$$

The lesser of this amount and the amount of the "first limitation" (computed under § 20.2014-2) is the credit for foreign death taxes.

Example (2). (i) Decedent, a citizen and resident of the United States at the time of his death, left a gross estate of $1,000,000 which includes: shares of stock issued by a United States corporation, valued at $650,000; shares of stock issued by a Country X corporation, valued at $200,000; and life insurance, in the amount of $150,000, payable to a son. Expenses, indebtedness, etc., amounted to $40,000. The decedent made a specific bequest of $25,000 of the Country X corporation stock to Charity A and a general bequest of $100,000 to Charity B. The residue of his estate was left to his daughter. The gross Federal estate tax is $242,450 and the credit for State death taxes is $24,480. Under these facts and applicable law, neither the stock of the Country X corporation specifically bequeathed to Charity A nor the insurance payable to the son could be charged with satisfying the bequest to Charity B. Therefore, the "group of assets" which could be so charged is limited to stock of the Country X corporation valued at $175,000 and stock of the United States corporation valued at $650,000.

(ii) Factor "G" of the ratio which is used in determining the "second limitation" is computed as follows:

Value of property situated in Country X				$200,000.00
Less: Reduction described in § 20.2014-3(b)(1)		$25,000.00		

$$\frac{\begin{array}{c}\text{Reduction described in § 20.2014-3(b)(2) =}\\ \$175{,}000\\ \text{(factor K of the}\\ \text{ratio stated at}\\ \text{§ 20.2014-3(b)(2))}\end{array}}{\begin{array}{c}\$175{,}000 + \$650{,}000\\ \text{(factor L of the}\\ \text{ratio stated at}\\ \text{§ 20.2014-3(b)(2))}\end{array}} \times \begin{array}{c}\$100{,}000 = \ldots..\\ \text{(factor J of the ratio}\\ \text{stated at}\\ \text{§ 20.2014-3(b)(2))}\end{array} \quad \underline{21{,}212.12} \quad \underline{46{,}212.12}$$

Factor "G" of the ratio $153,787.88

(iii) In this case, the "second limitation" on the credit for foreign death taxes is

$$\frac{\begin{array}{c}\$153{,}787.88\\ \text{(factor G of the ratio}\\ \text{stated at § 20.2014-3(a);}\\ \text{see also subdivision (ii)}\\ \text{above)}\end{array}}{\begin{array}{c}\$1{,}000{,}000 - \$125{,}000\\ \text{(factor H of the ratio}\\ \text{stated at § 20.2014-3(a))}\end{array}} \times \begin{array}{c}(\$242{,}450 - \$24{,}480) = \$38{,}309.88\\ \text{(factor F of the ratio stated at § 20.2014-3(a))}\end{array}$$

Example (3). (i) Decedent, a citizen and resident of the United States at the time of his death, left a gross estate of $850,000 which includes: shares of stock issued by United States corporations, valued at $440,000; real estate located in the United States, valued at $110,000; and shares of stock issued by Country X corporations, valued at $300,000. Expenses, indebtedness, etc., amounted to $50,000. Decedent devised $40,000 in real estate to a United States charity. In addition, he bequeathed to his wife $200,000 in United States stocks and $300,000 in Country X stocks. The residue of his estate passed to his children. The gross Federal estate tax is $81,700 and the credit for State death taxes is $5,520.

(ii) Decedent's adjusted gross estate is $800,000 (i.e., $850,000, gross estate less $50,000, expenses, indebtedness, etc.). Assume that the limitation imposed by section 2056(c), as in effect before 1982, is applicable so that the aggregate allowable marital deduction is limited to one-half the adjusted gross estate, or $400,000 (which is 50 percent of $800,000). Factor "G" of the ratio which is used in determining the "second limitation" is computed as follows:

Value of property situated in Country X	$300,000

Less: Reduction described in § 20.2014-3(b)(1) determined as follows
(see also end of § 20.2014-3(b))—
Total amount of bequests which qualify for the marital
deduction: . . . .

Specific bequest of Country X stock	$300,000
Specific bequest of United States stock	200,000
	500,000

Limitation on aggregate marital deduction under section 2056(c)	$400,000

Part of specific bequest of Country X stock with respect to
which the marital deduction is allowed—

$$\frac{\$400,000}{\$500,000} \times \$300,000 \quad \dots \dots \dots \dots \qquad \$240,000$$

Factor "G" of the ratio	60,000

(iii) Thus, the "second limitation" on the credit for foreign death taxes is

$$\frac{\$60,000 \;\text{(factor G of the ratio stated at § 20.2014-3(a); see also subdivision (ii) above)}}{\$850,000 - \$40,000 - \$400,000 \;\text{(factor H of the ratio stated at § 20.2014-3(a))}} \times \frac{(\$81,700 - \$5,520) = \$11,148.29.}{\text{(factor F of the ratio stated at § 20.2014-3(a))}}$$

(d) If the foreign country imposes more than one kind of death tax or imposes taxes at different rates upon the several shares of an estate, or if the foreign country and a political subdivision or possession thereof each imposes a death tax the "second limitation" is still computed by applying the ratio set forth in paragraph (a) of § 20.2014-3. Factor "G" of the ratio is determined by taking into consideration the combined value of the foreign property which is subjected to each different tax or different rate. The combined value, however, cannot exceed the value at which such property was included in the gross estate for Federal estate tax purposes. Thus, if Country X imposes a tax on the inheritance of a surviving spouse at a 10-percent rate and on the inheritance of a son at a 20-percent rate, the combined value of their inheritances is taken into consideration in determining factor "G" of the ratio, which is then used in computing the "second limitation." However, the "first limitation" is computed as provided in paragraph (b) of § 20.2014-2. The lesser of the "first limitation" and the "second limitation" is the credit for foreign death taxes. [Reg. § 20.2014-3.]

☐ [T.D. 6296, 6-23-58. Amended by T.D. 6600, 5-28-62; T.D. 7296, 12-11-73 and T.D. 8522, 2-28-94.]

[Reg. § 20.2014-4]

§ 20.2014-4. Application of credit in cases involving a death tax convention.—(a) In general.—(1) If credit for a particular foreign death tax is authorized by a death tax convention, there is allowed either the credit provided for by the convention or the credit provided for by section 2014, whichever is the more beneficial to the estate. For cases where credit may be taken under both the death tax convention and section 2014, see paragraph (b) of this section. The application of this paragraph may be illustrated by the following example:

Example. (i) Decedent, a citizen of the United States and a domiciliary of foreign Country X at the time of his death on December 1, 1966, left a gross estate of $1,000,000 which includes the following: shares of stock issued by a Country X corporation, valued at $400,000; bonds issued in 1962 by the United States and physically located in Country X, valued at $350,000; and real estate located in the United States, valued at $250,000. Expenses, indebtedness, etc., amounted to $50,000. Decedent left his entire estate to his son. There is in effect a death tax convention between the United States and Country X which provides for the allowance of credit by the United States for succession duties imposed by the national government of Country X. The gross Federal estate tax is $307,200, and the credit for State death taxes is $33,760. Country X imposed a net succession duty on the stocks and bonds of $180,000. Under the situs rules referred to in paragraph (a)(3) of § 20.2014-1, the shares of stock comprise the only property deemed to be situated in Country X. (If the decedent had died before November 14, 1966, the bonds also would be deemed to have their situs in Country X.) Under the convention, both the stocks and the bonds are deemed to be situated in Country X. In this example all figures are rounded to the nearest dollar.

(ii)(a) The credit authorized by the convention for death taxes imposed by Country X is computed as follows:

(1) Country X tax attributable to property situated in Country X and subjected to tax by both countries

$$\frac{(\$750,000}{(\$750,000} \times \$180,000) \dots\dots\dots\dots\dots\dots\dots\dots\dots\dots\dots\dots \quad \$180,000$$

(2) Federal estate tax attributable to property situated in Country X and subjected to tax by both countries

$$\frac{(\$750,000}{(\$1,000,000} \times \$273,440) \dots\dots\dots\dots\dots\dots\dots\dots\dots\dots\dots \quad 205,080$$

(3) Credit (subdivision (1) or (2), whichever is less) $180,000

(b) The credit authorized by section 2014 for death taxes imposed by Country X is computed as follows:

(1) "First limitation" computed under § 20.2014-2

$$\frac{(\$400,000}{(\$750,000} \times \$180,000) \dots\dots\dots\dots\dots\dots\dots\dots\dots\dots\dots \quad \$96,000$$

(2) "Second limitation" computed under § 20.2014-3

$$\frac{(\$400,000}{(\$1,000,000} \times \$273,440) \dots\dots\dots\dots\dots\dots\dots\dots\dots\dots\dots \quad 109,376$$

(3) Credit (subdivision (1) or (2), whichever is less) $96,000

(iii) On the basis of the facts contained in this example, the credit of $180,000 authorized by the convention is the more beneficial to the estate.

(2) It should be noted that the greater of the treaty credit and the statutory credit is not necessarily the more beneficial to the estate. Such is the situation, for example, in those cases which involve both a foreign death tax credit and a credit under section 2013 for tax on prior transfers. The reason is that the amount of the credit for tax on prior transfers may differ depending upon whether the credit for foreign death tax is taken under the treaty or under the statute. Therefore, under certain circumstances, the advantage of taking the greater of the treaty credit and the statutory credit may be more than offset by a resultant smaller credit for tax on prior transfers. The solution is to compute the net estate tax payable first on the assumption that the treaty credit will be taken and then on the assumption that the statutory credit will be taken. Such computations will indicate whether the treaty credit or the statutory credit is in fact the more beneficial to the estate.

(b) *Taxes imposed by both a foreign country and a political subdivision thereof.*—If death taxes are imposed by both a foreign country with which the United States has entered into a death tax convention and one or more of its possessions or political subdivisions, there is allowed, against the tax imposed by section 2001—

(1) A credit for the combined death taxes paid to the foreign country and its political sub-divisions or possessions as provided for by the convention, or

(2) A credit for the combined death taxes paid to the foreign country and its political subdivisions or possessions as determined under section 2014, or

(3)(i) A credit for that amount of the combined death taxes paid to the foreign country and its political subdivisions or possessions as is allowable under the convention, and

(ii) A credit under section 2014 for the death taxes paid to each political subdivision or possession, but only to the extent such death taxes are not directly or indirectly creditable under the convention, whichever is the most beneficial to the estate. The application of this paragraph may be illustrated by the following example:

Example. (1) Decedent, a citizen of the United States and a domiciliary of Province Y of foreign Country X at the time of his death on February 1, 1966, left a gross estate of $250,000 which includes the following: bonds issued by Country X physically located in Province Y, valued at $75,000; bonds issued by Province Z of Country X and physically located in the United States, valued at $50,000; and shares of stock issued by a domestic corporation, valued at $125,000. Decedent left his entire estate to his son. Expenses, indebtedness, etc., amounted to $26,000. The Federal estate tax after allowance of the credit for State death taxes is $38,124. Province Y imposed a death tax of 8 percent on the Country X bonds located therein which amounted to $6,000. No death tax was imposed by Province Z. Country X imposed a death tax of 15 percent on the Country X bonds and the Province Z bonds which amounted to $18,750 before allowance of any credit for the death tax of Province Y. Country X allows against its death taxes a credit for death taxes paid to any of its provinces on property which it also taxes, but only to the extent of one-half of the Country X death tax attributable to the property, or the amount of death taxes paid to its province, whichever is less. Country X, therefore, allowed a credit of $5,625 for the death taxes paid to Province Y. There is in effect a death tax convention between the United States and Country X which provides for allowance of credit by the United States for death taxes imposed by the national government of Country X. The death tax convention provides that in computing the "first limitation" for the credit under the convention, the tax of Country X is not to be reduced by the amount of the credit allowed for provincial taxes. Under the situs rules described in paragraph (a)(3) of § 20.2014-1, only the Country X bonds located in Province Y are deemed situated in Country X. (The bonds issued by Province Z also would be deemed to have their situs in Country X if the decedent had died on or after November 14, 1966.) Under the convention, both the Country X bonds and the Province Z bonds are deemed to be situated in Country X. In this example all figures are rounded to the nearest dollar.

(2)(i) The credit authorized by section 2014 for death taxes imposed by Country X (which includes death taxes imposed by Province Y according to § 20.2014-1(a)(1)) is computed as follows:

(a) "First limitation" with respect to tax imposed by national government of Country X (computed under paragraph (b) of § 20.2014-2)

(1) Gross Country X death tax attributable to Country X bonds (before allowance of provincial death taxes)

$$\frac{\$75,000}{\$125,000} \times \$18,750 \dots \dots \quad \$11,250$$

(2) Less credit for Province Y death taxes on such bonds .

. . . .   5,625

(3) Net Country X death tax attributable to such bonds   5,625

(b) "First limitation" with respect to tax imposed by Province Y (computed under paragraph (b) of § 20.2014-2)

$$\frac{\$75,000}{\$75,000} \times \$6,000 \dots \dots \quad \$6,000$$

(c) Total "first limitation" . . .   11,625

(d) "Second limitation" (computed under paragraph (d) of § 20.2014-3)

$$\frac{\$75,000}{\$250,000} \times \$38,124 \dots \dots \quad \$11,437$$

(e) Credit (subdivision (c) or (d), whichever is less) . . .   11,437

(ii) The credit authorized under the death tax convention between the United States and Country X is computed as follows:

(a) Country X tax attributable to property situated in Country X and subject to tax by both countries

$$\frac{\$125,000}{\$125,000} \times \$18,750 \dots \dots \quad \$18,750$$

(b) Federal estate tax attributable to property situated in Country X and subjected to tax by both countries:

$$\frac{\$125,000}{\$250,000} \times \$38,124 \dots \dots \quad \$19,062$$

(c) Credit (subdivision (a) or (b), whichever is less) $18,750

(3) If the estate takes a credit for death taxes under the convention, it would receive a credit of $18,750 which would include an indirect credit of $5,625 for death taxes paid to Province Y. The death tax of Province Y which was not directly or indirectly creditable under the convention is $375 ($6,000–$5,625). A credit for this tax would also be allowed under section 2014 but only to the extent of $187, as the amount of credit for the combined foreign death taxes is limited to the amount of Federal estate tax attributable to the property, determined in accordance with the rules prescribed for computing the "second limitation" under section 2014. In this case, the "second limitation" under section 2014 on the taxes attributable to the Country X bonds is $11,437 (see computation set forth in (2)(i)(d) of this example). The amount of credit under the convention for taxes attributable to Country X bonds is $11,250 ($75,000 ÷ $125,000 × $18,750). Inasmuch as the "second limitation" under section 2014 in respect of the Country X bonds ($11,437) exceeds the amount of the credit allowed under the convention in respect of the Country X bonds ($11,250) by $187, the additional credit allowable under section 2014 for the death taxes paid to Province Y not directly or indirectly creditable under the convention is limited to $187.

(c) *Taxes imposed by two foreign countries with respect to the same property.*—It is stated as a general rule in paragraph (a)(2) of § 20.2014-1 that if credits against the Federal estate tax are allowable under section 2014, or under section 2014 and one or more death tax conventions, for death taxes paid to more than one country, the credits are combined and the aggregate amount is credited against the Federal estate tax. This rule may result in credit being allowed for taxes imposed by two different countries upon the same item of property. If such is the case, the total amount of the credits with respect to such property is limited to the amount of the Federal estate tax attributable to the property, determined in accordance with the rules prescribed for computing the "second limitation" set forth in §20.2014-3. The application of this section may be illustrated by the following example:

Example. The decedent, a citizen of the United States and a domiciliary of Country X at the time of his death on May 1, 1967, left a taxable estate which included bonds issued by Country Z and physically located in Country X. Each of the three countries involved imposed death taxes on the Country Z bonds. Assume that under the provisions of a treaty between the United States and Country X the estate is entitled to a credit against the Federal estate tax for death taxes imposed by Country X on the bonds in the maximum amount of $20,000. Assume, also, that since the decedent died after November 13, 1966, so that under the situs rules referred to in paragraph (a)(3) of §20.2014-1 the bonds are deemed to have their situs in Country Z, the estate is entitled to a credit against the Federal estate tax for death taxes imposed by Country Z on the bonds in the maximum amount of $10,000. Finally, assume that the Federal estate tax attributable to the bonds is $25,000. Under these circumstances, the credit allowed the estate with respect to the bonds would be limited to $25,000. [Reg. §20.2014-4.]

☐ [*T.D. 6296, 6-23-58. Amended by T.D. 6742, 6-22-64 and T.D. 7296, 12-11-73.*]

[Reg. §20.2014-5]

§20.2014-5. **Proof of credit.**—(a) If the foreign death tax has not been determined and paid by the time the Federal estate tax return required by section 6018 is filed, credit may be claimed on the return in an estimated amount. However, before credit for the foreign death tax is finally allowed, satisfactory evidence, such as a statement by an authorized official of each country, possession or political subdivision thereof imposing the tax, must be submitted on Form 706CE certifying: (1) the full amount of the tax (exclusive of any interest or penalties), as computed before allowance of any credit, remission, or relief; (2) the amount of any credit, allowance, remission, or relief, and other pertinent information, including the nature of the allowance and a description of the property to which it pertains; (3) the net foreign death tax payable after any such allowance; (4) the date on which the death tax was paid, or if not all paid at one time, the date and amount of each partial payment; and (5) a list of the property situated in the foreign country and subjected to its tax, showing a description and the value of the property. Satisfactory evidence must also be submitted showing that no refund of the death tax is pending and none is authorized or, if any refund is pending or has been authorized, its amount and other pertinent information. See also section 2016 and §20.2016-1 for requirements if foreign death taxes claimed as a credit are subsequently recovered.

(b) The following information must also be submitted whenever applicable:

(1) If any of the property subjected to the foreign death tax was situated outside of the country imposing the tax, the description of each item of such property and its value.

(2) If more than one inheritance or succession is involved with respect to which credit is claimed, or if the foreign country, possession or political subdivision thereof imposes more than one kind of death tax, or if both the foreign country and a possession or political subdivision thereof each imposes a death tax, a separate computation with respect to each inheritance or succession tax.

(c) In addition to the information required under paragraphs (a) and (b) of this section, the district director may require the submission of any further proof deemed necessary to establish the right to the credit. [Reg. §20.2014-5.]

☐ [*T.D. 6296, 6-23-58.*]

[Reg. §20.2014-6]

§20.2014-6. **Period of limitations on credit.**— The credit for foreign death taxes under section 2014 is limited to those taxes which were actually paid and for which a credit was claimed within four years after the filing of the estate tax return for the decedent's estate. If, however, a petition has been filed with the The Tax Court of the United States for the redetermination of a deficiency within the time prescribed in section 6213(a), the credit is limited to those taxes which were actually paid and for which a credit was claimed within four years after the filing of the return, or before the expiration of 60 days after the decision of The Tax Court becomes final, whichever period is the last to expire. Similarly, if an extension of time has been granted under section 6161 for payment of the tax shown on the return, or of a deficiency, the credit is limited to those taxes which were actually paid and for which a credit was claimed within four years after the filing of the return, or before the date of the expiration of the period of the extension, whichever period is the last to expire. See section 2015 for the applicable period of limitations for credit for foreign death taxes on reversionary or remainder interests if an election is made under section 6163(a) to postpone payment of the estate tax attributable to reversionary or remainder interests. If a claim for refund based on the credit for foreign death taxes is filed within the applicable period described in this section, a refund may be made despite the general limitation provisions of sections 6511 and 6512. Any refund based on the credit for foreign death taxes shall be made without interest. [Reg. § 20.2014-6.]

☐ [*T.D.* 6296, 6-23-58.]

[Reg. § 20.2014-7]

§ 20.2014-7. Limitation on credit if a deduction for foreign death taxes is allowed under section 2053(d).—If a deduction is allowed under section 2053(d) for foreign death taxes paid with respect to a charitable gift, the credit for foreign death taxes is subject to special limitations. In such a case the property described in subparagraphs(A), (B), and (C) of paragraphs (1) and (2) of section 2014(b) shall not include any property with respect to which a deduction is allowed under section 2053(d). The application of this section may be illustrated by the following example:

Example. The decedent, a citizen of the United States, died July 1, 1955, leaving a gross estate of $1,200,000 consisting of: Shares of stock issued by United States corporations, valued at $600,000; bonds issued by the United States Government physically located in the United States, valued at $300,000; and shares of stock issued by a Country X corporation, valued at $300,000. Expenses, indebtedness, etc., amounted to $40,000. The decedent made specific bequests of $400,000 of the United States corporation stock to a niece and $100,000 of the Country X corporation stock to a nephew. The residue of his estate was left to charity. There is no death tax convention in existence between the United States and Country X. The Country X tax imposed was at a 50-percent rate on all beneficiaries. A State inheritance tax of $20,000 was imposed on the niece and nephew. The decedent did not provide in his will for the payment of the death taxes, and under local law the Federal estate tax is payable from the general estate, the same as administration expenses.

Distribution of the Estate

Gross estate		$1,200,000.00
Debts and charges	$40,000.00	
Bequest of United States corporation stock to niece .	400,000.00	
Bequest of Country X corporation stock to nephew .	100,000.00	
Net Federal estate tax	136,917.88	$676,917.88
Residue before Country X tax		523,082.12
Country X succession tax on charity		100,000.00
Charitable deduction		$423,082.12

Taxable Estate and Federal Estate Tax

Gross estate		$1,200,000.00
Debts and charges	$40,000.00	
Deduction of foreign death tax under section 2053(d)	100,000.00	
Charitable deduction	423,082.12	
Exemption	60,000.00	623,082.12
Taxable estate		$576,917.88
Gross estate tax		$172,621.26
Credit for State death taxes		15,476.72
Gross estate tax less credit for State death taxes		$157,144.54
Credit for foreign death taxes		20,226.66
Net Federal estate tax		$136,917.88

Credit for Foreign Death Taxes

Country X tax	
Succession tax on nephew:	
Value of stock of Country X corporation	$100,000.00
Tax (50% rate)	50,000.00
Succession tax on charity:	
Value of stock of Country X corporation	200,000.00
Tax (50% rate)	100,000.00

Computation of exclusion under section 2014(b)

Value of property situated in Country X	$300,000.00
Value of property in respect of which a deduction is allowed under section 2053(d)	200,000.00
Value of property situated within Country X, subjected to tax, and included in gross estate as limited by section 2014(f)	$100,000.00

$$\frac{\text{First limitation, §20.2014-2(a) } \$100,000 \text{ (factor C of the ratio stated at §20.2014-2(a))}}{\$100,000 + \$200,000 \text{ (factor D of the ratio stated at §20.2014-2(a))}} \times \begin{array}{c}(\$50,000.00 + \$100,000.00) \\ \text{(factor B of the ratio stated at} \\ \text{§20.2014-2(a))} = \$50,000.00\end{array}$$

$$\frac{\text{Second limitation, §20.2014-3(a) } \$100,000 \text{ (factor G of the ratio stated at §20.2014-3(a)) (as limited by section 2014(f))}}{\$1,200,000 - \$423,082.12 \text{ (factor H of the ratio stated at §20.2014-3(a))}} \times \begin{array}{c}(\$172,621.26 - \$15,476.72) \\ \text{(factor F of the ratio stated} \\ \text{at §20.2014-3(a))} = \\ \$20,226.66\end{array}$$

[Reg. §20.2014-7.]

☐ [T.D. 6600, 5-28-62.]

[Reg. §20.2015-1]

§ 20.2015-1. Credit for death taxes on remainders.—(a) If the executor of an estate elects under section 6163(a) to postpone the time for payment of any portion of the Federal estate tax attributable to a reversionary or remainder interest in property, credit is allowed under sections 2011 and 2014 against that portion of the Federal estate tax for State death taxes and foreign death taxes attributable to the reversionary or remainder interest if the State death taxes or foreign death taxes are paid and if credit therefor is claimed either—

(1) Within the time provided for in sections 2011 and 2014, or

(2) Within the time for payment of the tax imposed by section 2001 or 2101 as postponed under section 6163(a) and as extended under section 6163(b) (on account of undue hardship) or, if the precedent interest terminated before July 5, 1958, within 60 days after the termination of the preceding interest or interests in the property.

The allowance of credit, however, is subject to the other limitations contained in sections 2011 and 2014 and, in the case of the estate of a decedent who was a nonresident not a citizen of the United States, in section 2102(b).

(b) In applying the rule stated in paragraph (a) of this section, credit for State death taxes or foreign death taxes paid within the time provided in sections 2011 and 2014 is applied first to the portion of the Federal estate tax payment of which is not postponed, and any excess is applied to the balance of the Federal estate tax. However, credit for State death taxes or foreign death taxes not paid within the time provided in sections 2011 and 2014 is allowable only against the portion of the Federal estate tax attributable to the reversionary or remainder interest, and only for State or foreign death taxes attributable to that interest. If a State death tax or a foreign death tax is imposed upon both a reversionary or remainder interest and upon other property, without a definite apportionment of the tax, the amount of the tax deemed attributable to the reversionary or remainder interest is an amount which bears the same ratio to the total tax as the value of the reversionary or remainder interest bears to the value of the entire property with respect to which the tax was imposed. In applying this ratio, adjustments consistent with those required under paragraph (c) of §20.6163-1 must be made.

(c) The application of this section may be illustrated by the following examples:

Example (1). One-third of the Federal estate tax was attributable to a remainder interest in real property located in State Y, and two-thirds of the Federal estate tax was attributable to other property located in State X. The payment of the tax attributable to the remainder interest was postponed under the provisions of section 6163(a). The maximum credit allowable for State death taxes under the provisions of section 2011 is $12,000. Therefore, of the maximum credit allowable, $4,000 is attributable to the remainder interest and $8,000 is attributable to the other property. Within the 4-year period provided for in section 2011, inheritance tax in the amount of $9,000 was paid to State X in connection with the other property. With respect to this $9,000, $8,000 (the maximum amount allowable) is allowed as a credit against the Federal estate tax attributable to the other property, and $1,000 is allowed as a credit against the postponed tax. The life estate or other precedent interest expired after July 4, 1958. After the expiration of the 4-year period but before the expiration of the period of postponement elected under section 6163(a) and of the period of extension granted under section 6163(b) for payment of the tax, inheritance tax in the amount of $5,000 was paid to State Y in connection with the remainder interest. As the maximum credit allowable with respect to the remainder interest is $4,000 and $1,000 has already been allowed as a credit, an additional $3,000 will be credited against the Federal estate tax attributable to the remainder interest. It should be noted that if the life estate or other precedent interest had expired after the expiration of the 4-year period but before July 5, 1958, the same result would be reached only if the inheritance tax had been paid to State Y before the expiration of 60 days after the termination of the life estate or other precedent interest.

Example (2). The facts are the same as in example (1), except that within the 4-year period inheritance tax in the amount of $2,500 was paid to State Y with respect to the remainder interest and inheritance tax in the amount of $7,500 was paid to State X with respect to the other property. The amount of $8,000 is allowed as a credit against the Federal estate tax attributable to the other property and the amount of $2,000 is allowed as a credit against the postponed tax. The life estate or other precedent interest expired after July 4, 1958. After the expiration of the 4-year period but before the expiration of the period of postponement elected under section 6163(a) and of the period of extension granted under section 6163(b) for payment of the tax, inheritance tax in the amount of $5,000 was paid to State Y in connection with the remainder interest. As the maximum credit allowable with respect to the remainder interest is $4,000 and $2,000 already has been allowed as a credit, an additional $2,000 will be credited against the Federal estate tax attributable to the remainder interest. It should be noted that if the life estate or other precedent interest had expired after the expiration of the 4-year period but before July 5, 1958, the same result would be reached only if the inheritance tax had been paid to State Y before the expiration of 60 days after the termination of the life estate or other precedent interest.

Example (3). The facts are the same as in example (2), except that no payment was made to State Y within the 4-year period. The amount of $7,500 is allowed as a credit against the Federal estate tax attributable to the other property. After termination of the life interest additional

credit will be allowed in the amount of $4,000 against the Federal estate tax attributable to the remainder interest. Since the payment of $5,000 was made to State Y following the expiration of the 4-year period, no part of the payment may be allowed as a credit against the Federal estate tax attributable to the other property. [Reg. §20.2015-1.]

☐ [T.D. 6296, 6-23-58. *Amended by T.D. 6526,* 1-18-61 *and T.D. 7296,* 12-11-73.]

[Reg. §20.2016-1]

§20.2016-1. Recovery of death taxes claimed as credit.—In accordance with the provisions of section 2016, the executor (or any other person) receiving a refund of any State death taxes or foreign death taxes claimed as a credit under section 2011 or section 2014 shall notify the district director of the refund within 30 days of its receipt. The notice shall contain the following information:

(a) The name of the decedent;

(b) The date of the decedent's death;

(c) The property with respect to which the refund was made;

(d) The amount of the refund, exclusive of interest;

(e) The date of the refund; and

(f) The name and address of the person receiving the refund.

If the refund was in connection with foreign death taxes claimed as a credit under section 2014, the notice shall also contain a statement showing the amount of interest, if any, paid by the foreign country on the refund. Finally, the person filing the notice shall furnish the district director such additional information as he may request. Any Federal estate tax found to be due by reason of the refund is payable by the person or persons receiving it, upon notice and demand, even though the refund is received after the expiration of the period of limitations set forth in section 6501 (see section 6501(c)(5)). If the tax found to be due results from a refund of foreign death tax claimed as a credit under section 2014, such tax shall not bear interest for any period before the receipt of the refund, except to the extent that interest was paid by the foreign country on the refund. [Reg. §20.2016-1.]

☐ [T.D. 6296, 6-23-58.]

Gross Estate

[Reg. §20.2031-0]

§20.2031-0. Table of contents.—This section lists the section headings and undesignated

center headings that appear in the regulations under section 2031.

§ 20.2031-1 Definition of gross estate; valuation of property.

§ 20.2031-2 Valuation of stocks and bonds.

§ 20.2031-3 Valuation of interests in businesses.

§ 20.2031-4 Valuation of notes.

§ 20.2031-5 Valuation of cash on hand or on deposit.

§ 20.2031-6 Valuation of household and personal effects..

§ 20.2031-7 Valuation of annuities, interests for life or term of years, and remainder or reversionary interests.

§ 20.2031-8 Valuation of certain life insurance and annuity contracts; valuation of shares in an open-end investment company.

§ 20.2031-9 Valuation of other property.
Actuarial Tables Applicable Before May 1, 2009.

§ 20.2031-7A Valuation of annuities, interests for life or term of years, and remainder or reversionary interests for estates of decedents for which the valuation date of the gross estate is before May 1, 2009.

[Reg. § 20.2031-0.]

☐ [*T.D. 8540, 6-9-94. Amended by T.D. 8819, 4-29-99; T.D. 8886, 6-9-2000; T.D. 9448, 5-1-2009 and T.D. 9540, 8-9-2011.*]

[Reg. § 20.2031-1]

§ 20.2031-1. Definition of gross estate; valuation of property.—(a) *Definition of gross estate.*—Except as otherwise provided in this paragraph the value of the gross estate of a decedent who was a citizen or resident of the United States at the time of his death is the total value of the interests described in sections 2033 through 2044. The gross estate of a decedent who died before October 17, 1962, does not include real property situated outside the United States (as defined in paragraph (b)(1) of § 20.0-1). Except as provided in paragraph (c) of this section (relating to the estates of decedents dying after October 16, 1962, and before July 1, 1964), in the case of a decedent dying after October 16, 1962, real property situated outside the United States which comes within the scope of sections 2033 through 2044 is included in the gross estate to the same extent as any other property coming within the scope of those sections. In arriving at the value of the gross estate the interests described in sections 2033 through 2044 are valued as described in this section, § § 20.2031-2 through 20.2031-9 and § 20.2032-1. The contents of sections 2033 through 2044 are, in general, as follows:

(1) Sections 2033 and 2034 are concerned mainly with interests in property passing through the decedent's probate estate. Section 2033 includes in the decedent's gross estate any interest that the decedent has in property at the time of his death. Section 2034 provides that any interest of the decedent's surviving spouse in the decedent's property, such as dower or curtesy, does not prevent the inclusion of such property in the decedent's gross estate.

(2) Sections 2035 through 2038 deal with interests in property transferred by the decedent during his life under such circumstances as to bring the interests within the decedent's gross estate. Section 2035 includes in the decedent's gross estate property transferred in contemplation of death, even though the decedent had no interest in, or control over, the property at the time of his death. Section 2036 provides for the inclusion of transferred property with respect to which the decedent retained the income or the power to designate who shall enjoy the income. Section 2037 includes in the decedent's gross estate certain transfers under which the beneficial enjoyment of the property could be obtained only by surviving the decedent. Section 2038 provides for the inclusion of transferred property if the decedent had at the time of his death the power to change the beneficial enjoyment of the property. It should be noted that there is a considerable overlap in the application of sections 2036 through 2038 with respect to reserved powers, so that transferred property may be includible in the decedent's gross estate in varying degrees under more than one of those sections.

(3) Sections 2039 through 2042 deal with special kinds of property and powers. Sections 2039 and 2040 concern annuities and jointly held property, respectively. Section 2041 deals with powers held by the decedent over the beneficial enjoyment of property not originating with the decedent. Section 2042 concerns insurance under policies on the life of the decedent.

(4) Section 2043 concerns the sufficiency of consideration for transfers made by the decedent during his life. This has a bearing on the amount to be included in the decedent's gross estate under sections 2035 through 2038, and 2041. Section 2044 deals with retroactivity.

(b) *Valuation of property in general.*—The value of every item of property includible in a decedent's gross estate under sections 2031 through 2044 is its fair market value at the time of the decedent's death, except that if the executor elects the alternate valuation method under section 2032, it is the fair market value thereof at the date, and with the adjustments, prescribed in that section. The fair market value is the price at which the property would change hands between a willing buyer and a willing seller, neither being under any compulsion to buy or to sell and both having reasonable knowledge of relevant facts. The fair market value of a particular item of property includible in the decedent's gross estate is not to be determined by a forced sale price. Nor is the fair market value of an item of property to be determined by the sale price of

Reg. § 20.2031-1(b)

the item in a market other than that in which such item is most commonly sold to the public, taking into account the location of the item wherever appropriate. Thus, in the case of an item of property includible in the decedent's gross estate, which is generally obtained by the public in the retail market, the fair market value of such an item of property is the price at which the item or a comparable item would be sold at retail. For example, the fair market value of an automobile (an article generally obtained by the public in the retail market) includible in the decedent's gross estate is the price for which an automobile of the same or approximately the same description, make, model, age, condition, etc., could be purchased by a member of the general public and not the price for which the particular automobile of the decedent would be purchased by a dealer in used automobiles. Examples of items of property which are generally sold to the public at retail may be found in §§ 20.2031-6 and 20.2031-8. The value is generally to be determined by ascertaining as a basis the fair market value as of the applicable valuation date of each unit of property. For example, in the case of shares of stock or bonds, such unit of property is generally a share of stock or a bond. Livestock, farm machinery, harvested and growing crops must generally be itemized and the value of each item separately returned. Property shall not be returned at the value at which it is assessed for local tax purposes unless that value represents the fair market value as of the applicable valuation date. All relevant facts and elements of value as of the applicable valuation date shall be considered in every case. The value of items of property which were held by the decedent for sale in the course of a business generally should be reflected in the value of the business. For valuation of interests in businesses, see § 20.2031-3. See § 20.2031-2 and §§ 20.2031-4 through 20.2031-8 for further information concerning the valuation of other particular kinds of property. For certain circumstances under which the sale of an item of property at a price below its fair market value may result in a deduction for the estate, see paragraph (d)(2) of § 20.2053-3.

(c) *Real property situated outside the United States; gross estate of decedent dying after October 16, 1962, and before July 1, 1964.*—(1) *In general.*— In the case of a decedent dying after October 16, 1962, and before July 1, 1964, the value of real property situated outside the United States (as defined in paragraph (b)(1) of § 20.0-1) is not included in the gross estate of the decedent—

(i) Under section 2033, 2034, 2035(a), 2036(a), 2037(a), or 2038(a) to the extent the real property, or the decedent's interest in it, was acquired by the decedent before February 1, 1962;

(ii) Under section 2040 to the extent such property or interest was acquired by the decedent before February 1, 1962, or was held by the decedent and the survivor in a joint tenancy or

tenancy by the entirety before February 1, 1962; or

(iii) Under section 2041(a) to the extent that before February 1, 1962, such property or interest was subject to a general power of appointment (as defined in section 2041) possessed by the decedent.

(2) *Certain property treated as acquired before February 1, 1962.*—For purposes of this paragraph real property situated outside the United States (including property held by the decedent and the survivor in a joint tenancy or tenancy by the entirety), or an interest in such property or a general power of appointment in respect of such property, which was acquired by the decedent after January 31, 1962, is treated as acquired by the decedent before February 1, 1962, if

(i) Such property, interest, or power was acquired by the decedent by gift within the meaning of section 2511, or from a prior decedent by devise or inheritance, or by reason of death, form of ownership, or other conditions (including the exercise or nonexercise of a power of appointment); and

(ii) Before February 1, 1962, the donor or prior decedent had acquired the property or his interest therein or had possessed a power of appointment in respect thereof.

(3) *Certain property treated as acquired after January 31, 1962.*—For purposes of this paragraph that portion of capital additions or improvements made after January 31, 1962, to real property situated outside the United States is, to the extent that it materially increases the value of the property, treated as real property acquired after January 31, 1962. Accordingly, the gross estate may include the value of improvements on unimproved real property, such as office buildings, factories, houses, fences, drainage ditches, and other capital items, and the value of capital additions and improvements placed on real property after January 31, 1962, whether or not the value of such real property or existing improvements is included in the gross estate. [Reg. § 20.2031-1.]

[T.D. 6296, 6-23-58. Amended by T.D. 6684, 10-23-63 and T.D. 6826, 6-14-65.]

[Reg. § 20.2031-2]

§ 20.2031-2. **Valuation of stocks and bonds.**— (a) *In general.*—The value of stocks and bonds is the fair market value per share or bond on the applicable valuation date.

(b) *Based on selling prices.*—(1) In general, if there is a market for stocks or bonds, on a stock exchange, in an over-the-counter market, or otherwise, the mean between the highest and lowest quoted selling prices on the valuation date is the fair market value per share or bond. If there were no sales on the valuation date but there were sales on dates within a reasonable period both before and after the valuation date, the fair market value is determined by taking a weighted average of the means between the highest and lowest sales on the nearest date before and the nearest date after the valuation date. The average is to be weighted inversely by the respective numbers of trading days between the selling dates and the valuation date. If the stocks or bonds are listed on more than one exchange, the records of the exchange where the stocks or bonds are principally dealt in should be employed if such records are available in a generally available listing or publication of general circulation. In the event that such records are not so available and such stocks or bonds are listed on a composite listing of combined exchanges in a generally available listing or publication of general circulation, the records of such combined exchanges should be employed. In valuing listed securities, the executor should be careful to consult accurate records to obtain values as of the applicable valuation date. If quotations of unlisted securities are obtained from brokers, or evidence as to their sale is obtained from officers of the issuing companies, copies of the letters furnishing such quotations or evidence of sale should be attached to the return.

(2) If it is established with respect to bonds for which there is a market on a stock exchange, that the highest and lowest selling prices are not available for the valuation date in a generally available listing or publication of general circulation but that closing selling prices are so available, the fair market value per bond is the mean between the quoted closing selling price on the valuation date and the quoted closing selling price on the trading day before the valuation date. If there were no sales on the trading day before the valuation date but there were sales on a date within a reasonable period before the valuation date, the fair market value is determined by taking a weighted average of the quoted closing selling price on the valuation date and the quoted closing selling price on the nearest date before the valuation date. The closing selling price for the valuation date is to be weighted by the number of trading days between the previous selling date and the valuation date. If there were no sales within a reasonable period before the valuation date but there were sales on the valuation date, the fair market value is the closing selling price on such valuation date. If there were no sales on the valuation date but there were sales on dates within a reasonable period both before and after the valuation date, the fair market value is determined by taking a weighted average of the quoted closing selling prices on the nearest date before and the nearest date after the valuation date. The average is to be weighted inversely by the respective numbers of trading days between the selling dates and the valuation date. If the bonds are listed on more than one exchange, the records of the exchange where the bonds are

principally dealt in should be employed. In valuing listed securities, the executor should be careful to consult accurate records to obtain values as of the applicable valuation date.

(3) The application of this paragraph may be illustrated by the following examples:

Example (1). Assume that sales of X Company common stock nearest the valuation date (Friday, June 15) occurred two trading days before (Wednesday, June 13) and three trading days after (Wednesday, June 20) and on these days the mean sale prices per share were $10 and $15, respectively. The price of $12 is taken as representing the fair market value of a share of X Company common stock as of the valuation date

$$\frac{(3 \times 10) + (2 \times 15)}{5}$$

Example (2). Assume the same facts as in example (1) except that the mean sale prices per share on June 13 and June 20 were $15 and $10, respectively. The price of $13 is taken as representing the fair market value of a share of X Company common stock as of the valuation date

$$\frac{(3 \times 15) + (2 \times 10)}{5}$$

Example (3). Assume the decedent died on Sunday, October 7, and that Saturday and Sunday were not trading days. If sales of X Company common stock occurred on Friday, October 5, at mean sale prices per share of $20 and on Monday, October 8, at mean sale prices per share of $23, the price of $21.50 is taken as representing the fair market value of a share of X Company common stock as of the valuation date

$$\frac{(1 \times 20) + (23 \times 1)}{2}$$

Example (4). Assume that on the valuation date (Tuesday, April 3, 1973) the closing selling price of a listed bond was $25 per bond and that the highest and lowest selling prices are not available in a generally available listing or publication of general circulation for that date. Assume further, that the closing selling price of the same listed bond was $21 per bond on the day before the valuation date (Monday, April 2, 1973). Thus, under paragraph (b)(2) of this section the price of $23 is taken as representing the fair market value per bond as of the valuation date

$$\frac{(25 + 21)}{2}$$

Example (5). Assume the same facts as in example (4) except that there were no sales on the day before the valuation date. Assume further, that there were sales on Thursday, March 29, 1973 and that the closing selling price on that day was $23. The price of $24.50 is taken as representing the fair market value per bond as of the valuation date

$$\frac{((1 \times 23) + (3 \times 25))}{4}$$

Example (6). Assume that no bonds were traded on the valuation date (Friday, April 20). Assume further, that sales of bonds nearest the valuation date occurred two trading days before (Wednesday, April 18) and three trading days after (Wednesday, April 25) the valuation date and that on these two days the closing selling prices per bond were $29 and $22, respectively. The highest and lowest selling prices are not available for these dates in a generally available listing or publication of general circulation. Thus, under paragraph (b)(2) of this section, the price of $26.20 is taken as representing the fair market value of a bond as of the valuation date

$$\frac{((3 \times 29) + (2 \times 22))}{5}$$

(c) *Based on bid and asked prices.*—If the provisions of paragraph (b) of this section are inapplicable because actual sales are not available during a reasonable period beginning before and ending after the valuation date, the fair market value may be determined by taking the mean between the bona fide bid and asked prices on the valuation date, or if none, by taking a weighted average of the means between the bona fide bid and asked prices on the nearest trading date before and the nearest trading date after the valuation date, if both such nearest dates are within a reasonable period. The average is to be determined in the manner described in paragraph (b) of this section.

(d) *Based on incomplete selling prices or bid and asked prices.*—If the provisions of paragraphs (b) and (c) of this section are inapplicable because no actual sale prices or bona fide bid and asked prices are available on a date within a reasonable period before the valuation date, but such prices are available on a date within a reasonable period after the valuation date, or vice versa, then the mean between the highest and lowest available sale prices or bid and asked prices may be taken as the value.

(e) *Where selling prices or bid and asked prices do not reflect fair market value.*—If it is established that the value of any bond or share of stock determined on the basis of selling or bid and asked prices as provided under paragraphs (b), (c), and (d) of this section does not reflect the fair market value thereof, then some reasonable modification of that basis or other relevant facts and elements of value are considered in determining the fair market value.

Where sales at or near the date of death are few or of a sporadic nature, such sales alone may not indicate fair market value. In certain exceptional cases, the size of the block of stock to be valued in relation to the number of shares changing hands in sales may be relevant in determining whether selling prices reflect the fair market value of the block of stock to be valued. If the executor can show that the block of stock to be valued is so large in relation to the actual sales on the existing market that it could not be liquidated in a reasonable time without depressing the market, the price at which the block could be sold as such outside the usual market, as through an underwriter, may be a more accurate indication of value than market quotations. Complete data in support of any allowance claimed due to the size of the block of stock being valued shall be submitted with the return. On the other hand, if the block of stock to be valued represents a controlling interest, either actual or effective, in a going business, the price at which other lots change hands may have little relation to its true value.

(f) *Where selling prices or bid and asked prices are unavailable.*—If the provisions of paragraphs (b), (c), and (d) of this section are inapplicable because actual sale prices and bona fide bid and asked prices are lacking, then the fair market value is to be determined by taking the following factors into consideration:

(1) In the case of corporate or other bonds, the soundness of the security, the interest yield, the date of maturity, and other relevant factors; and

(2) In the case of shares of stock, the company's net worth, prospective earning power and dividend-paying capacity, and other relevant factors.

Some of the "other relevant factors" referred to in subparagraphs (1) and (2) of this paragraph are: the good will of the business; the economic outlook in the particular industry; the company's position in the industry and its management; the degree of control of the business represented by the block of stock to be valued; and the values of securities of corporations engaged in the same or similar lines of business which are listed on a stock exchange. However, the weight to be accorded such comparisons or any other evidentiary factors considered in the determination of a value depends upon the facts of each case. In addition to the relevant factors described above, consideration shall also be given to nonoperating assets, including proceeds of life insurance policies payable to or for the benefit of the company, to the extent such nonoperating assets have not been taken into account in the determination of net worth, prospective earning power and dividend-earning capacity. Complete financial and other data upon which the valuation is based should be submitted with the return, including copies of reports of any examinations of the company made by accountants, engineers, or any technical experts as of or near the applicable valuation date.

(g) *Pledged securities.*—The full value of securities pledged to secure an indebtedness of the decedent is included in the gross estate. If the decedent had a trading account with a broker, all securities belonging to the decedent and held by the broker at the date of death must be included at their fair market value as of the applicable valuation date. Securities purchased on margin for the decedent's account and held by a broker must also be returned at their fair market value as of the applicable valuation date. The amount of the decedent's indebtedness to a broker or other person with whom securities were pledged is allowed as a deduction from the gross estate in accordance with the provisions of § 20.2053-1 or § 20.2106-1 (for estates of nonresidents not citizens).

(h) *Securities subject to an option or contract to purchase.*—Another person may hold an option or a contract to purchase securities owned by a decedent at the time of his death. The effect, if any, that is given to the option or contract price in determining the value of the securities for estate tax purposes depends upon the circumstances of the particular case. Little weight will be accorded a price contained in an option or contract under which the decedent is free to dispose of the underlying securities at any price he chooses during his lifetime. Such is the effect, for example, of an agreement on the part of a shareholder to purchase whatever shares of stock the decedent may own at the time of his death. Even if the decedent is not free to dispose of the underlying securities at other than the option or contract price, such price will be disregarded in determining the value of the securities unless it is determined under the circumstances of the particular case that the agreement represents a bona fide business arrangement and not a device to pass the decedent's shares to the natural objects of his bounty for less than an adequate and full consideration in money or money's worth. See section 2703 and the regulations at § 25.2703 of this chapter for special rules involving options and agreements (including contracts to purchase) entered into (or substantially modified after) October 8, 1990.

(i) *Stock sold "ex-dividend.".*—In any case where a dividend is declared on a share of stock before the decedent's death but payable to stockholders of record on a date after his death and the stock is selling "ex-dividend" on the date of the decedent's death, the amount of the dividend is added to the ex-dividend quotation in determining the fair market value of the stock as of the date of the decedent's death.

(j) *Application of chapter 14.*—See section 2701 and the regulations at § 25.2701 of this chapter for special rules for valuing the transfer of an interest in a corporation and for the treatment of

unpaid qualified payments at the death of the transferor or an applicable family member. See section 2704(b) and the regulations at § 25.2704-2 of this chapter for special valuation rules involving certain restrictions on liquidation rights created after October 8, 1990. [Reg. § 20.2031-2]

☐ [*T.D. 6296, 6-23-58. Amended by T.D. 6826, 6-14-65; T.D. 7312, 4-26-74; T.D. 7327, 9-30-74; T.D. 7432, 9-13-76 and T.D. 8395, 1-28-92.*]

[Reg. § 20.2031-3]

§ 20.2031-3. Valuation of interests in businesses.—The fair market value of any interest of a decedent in a business, whether a partnership or a proprietorship, is the net amount which a willing purchaser, whether an individual or a corporation, would pay for the interest to a willing seller, neither being under any compulsion to buy or to sell and both having reasonable knowledge of relevant facts. The net value is determined on the basis of all relevant factors including—

(a) A fair appraisal as of the applicable valuation date of all the assets of the business, tangible and intangible, including good will;

(b) The demonstrated earning capacity of the business; and

(c) The other factors set forth in paragraphs (f) and (h) of § 20.2031-2 relating to the valuation of corporate stock, to the extent applicable.

Special attention should be given to determining an adequate value of the good will of the business in all cases in which the decedent has not agreed, for an adequate and full consideration in money or money's worth, that his interest passes at his death to, for example, his surviving partner or partners. Complete financial and other data upon which the valuation is based should be submitted with the return, including copies of reports of examinations of the business made by accountants, engineers, or any technical experts as of or near the applicable valuation date. See section 2701 and the regulations at § 25.2701 of this chapter for special rules for valuing the transfer of an interest in a partnership and for the treatment of unpaid qualified payments at the death of the transferor or an applicable family member. See section 2703 and the regulations at § 25.2703 of this chapter for special rules involving options and agreements (including contracts to purchase) entered into (or substantially modified after) October 8, 1990. See section 2704(b) and the regulations at § 25.2704-2 of this chapter for special valuation rules involving certain restrictions on liquidation rights created after October 8, 1990. [Reg. § 20.2031-3.]

☐ [*T.D. 6296, 6-23-58. Amended by T.D. 8395, 1-28-92.*]

[Reg. § 20.2031-4]

§ 20.2031-4. Valuation of notes.—The fair market value of notes, secured or unsecured, is presumed to be the amount of unpaid principal, plus interest accrued to the date of death, unless the executor establishes that the value is lower or that the notes are worthless. However, items of interest shall be separately stated on the estate tax return. If not returned at face value, plus accrued interest, satisfactory evidence must be submitted that the note is worth less than the unpaid amount (because of the interest rate, date of maturity, or other cause), or that the note is uncollectible, either in whole or in part (by reason of the insolvency of the party or parties liable, or for other cause), and that any property pledged or mortgaged as security is insufficient to satisfy the obligation. [Reg. § 20.2031-4.]

☐ [T.D. 6296, 6-23-58.]

[Reg. § 20.2031-5]

§ 20.2031-5. Valuation of cash on hand or on deposit.—The amount of cash belonging to the decedent at the date of his death, whether in his possession or in the possession of another, or deposited with a bank, is included in the decedent's gross estate. If bank checks outstanding at the time of the decedent's death and given in discharge of bona fide legal obligations of the decedent incurred for an adequate and full consideration in money or money's worth are subsequently honored by the bank and charged to the decedent's account, the balance remaining in the account may be returned, but only if the obligations are not claimed as deductions from the gross estate. [Reg. § 20.2031-5.]

☐ [T.D. 6926, 6-23-58.]

[Reg. § 20.2031-6]

§ 20.2031-6. Valuation of household and personal effects.—(a) *General rule.*—The fair market value of the decedent's household and personal effects is the price which a willing buyer would pay to a willing seller, neither being under any compulsion to buy or to sell and both having reasonable knowledge of relevant facts. A room by room itemization of household and personal effects is desirable. All the articles should be named specifically, except that a number of articles contained in the same room, none of which has a value in excess of $100, may be grouped. A separate value should be given for each article named. In lieu of an itemized list, the executor may furnish a written statement, containing a declaration that it is made under penalties of perjury, setting forth the aggregate value as appraised by a competent appraiser or appraisers of recognized standing and ability, or by a dealer or dealers in the class of personalty involved.

(b) *Special rule in cases involving a substantial amount of valuable articles.*—Notwithstanding the provisions of paragraph (a) of this section, if there are included among the household and personal effects articles having marked artistic or intrinsic value of a total value in excess of $3,000 (e.g., jewelry, furs, silverware, paintings, etch-ings, engravings, antiques, books, statuary, vases, oriental rugs, coin or stamp collections), the appraisal of an expert or experts, under oath, shall be filed with the return. The appraisal shall be accompanied by a written statement of the executor containing a declaration that it is made under the penalties of perjury as to the completeness of the itemized list of such property and as to the disinterested character and the qualifications of the appraiser or appraisers.

(c) *Disposition of household effects prior to investigation.*—If it is desired to effect distribution or sale of any portion of the household or personal effects of the decedent in advance of an investigation by an officer of the Internal Revenue Service, information to that effect shall be given to the district director. The statement to the district director shall be accompanied by an appraisal of such property, under oath, and by a written statement of the executor, containing a declaration that it is made under the penalties of perjury, regarding the completeness of the list of such property and the qualifications of the appraiser, as heretofore described. If a personal inspection by an officer of the Internal Revenue Service is not deemed necessary, the executor will be so advised. This procedure is designed to facilitate disposition of such property and to obviate future expense and inconvenience to the estate by affording the district director an opportunity to make an investigation should one be deemed necessary prior to sale or distribution.

(d) *Additional rules if an appraisal involved.*—If, pursuant to paragraphs (a), (b), and (c) of this section, expert appraisers are employed, care shall be taken to see that they are reputable and of recognized competency to appraise the particular class of property involved. In the appraisal, books in sets by standard authors shall be listed in separate groups. In listing paintings having artistic value, the size, subject, and artist's name shall be stated. In the case of oriental rugs, the size, make, and general condition shall be given. Sets of silverware shall be listed in separate groups. Groups or individual pieces of silverware shall be weighed and the weights given in troy ounces. In arriving at the value of silverware, the appraisers shall take into consideration its antiquity, utility, desirability, condition, and obsolescence. [Reg. § 20.2031-6.]

☐ [T.D. 6296, 6-23-58.]

[Reg. § 20.2031-7]

§ 20.2031-7. Valuation of annuities, interests for life or term of years, and remainder or reversionary interests.—(a) *In general.*—Except as otherwise provided in paragraph (b) of this section and § 20.7520-3(b) (pertaining to certain limitations on the use of prescribed tables), the fair market value of annuities, life estates, terms of years, remainders, and reversionary interests for estates of decedents is the present value of such interests, determined under paragraph (d) of this section. The regulations in this and in related sections provide tables with standard actuarial factors and examples that illustrate how to use the tables to compute the present value of ordinary annuity, life, and remainder interests in property. These sections also refer to standard and special actuarial factors that may be necessary to compute the present value of similar interests in more unusual fact situations.

(b) *Commercial annuities and insurance contracts.*—The value of annuities issued by companies regularly engaged in their sale, and of insurance policies on the lives of persons other

Valuation Date		Applicable
After	Before	Regulations
-	01-01-52	20.2031-7A(a)
12-31-51	01-01-71	20.2031-7A(b)
12-31-70	12-01-83	20.2031-7A(c)
11-30-83	05-01-89	20.2031-7A(d)
04-30-89	05-01-99	20.2031-7A(e)
04-30-99	05-01-09	20.2031-7A(f)

(d) *Actuarial valuations on or after May 1, 2009.*—(1) *In general.*—Except as otherwise provided in paragraph (b) of this section and § 20.7520-3(b) (pertaining to certain limitations on the use of prescribed tables), if the valuation date for the gross estate of the decedent is on or after May 1, 2009, the fair market value of annuities, life estates, terms of years, remainders, and reversionary interests is the present value determined by use of standard or special section 7520 actuarial factors. These factors are derived by using the appropriate section 7520 interest rate and, if applicable, the mortality component for the valuation date of the interest that is being valued. For purposes of the computations described in this section, the age of an individual is the age of that individual at the individual's nearest birthday. See § § 20.7520-1 through 20.7520-4.

(2) *Specific interests.*—(i) *Charitable remainder trusts.*—The fair market value of a remainder interest in a pooled income fund, as defined in § 1.642(c)-5 of this chapter, is its value determined under § 1.642(c)-6(e). The fair market value of a remainder interest in a charitable remainder annuity trust, as defined in § 1.664-2(a), is the present value determined under § 1.664-2(c). The fair market value of a remainder interest in a charitable remainder unitrust, as defined in § 1.664-3, is its present value determined under § 1.664-4(e). The fair market value of a life interest or term of years in a charitable remainder unitrust is the fair market value of the property as of the date of valuation less the fair market value of the remainder interest on that date determined under § 1.664-4(e)(4) and (5).

(ii) *Ordinary remainder and reversionary interests.*—If the interest to be valued is to take effect after a definite number of years or after the

than the decedent, is determined under § 20.2031-8. See § 20.2042-1 with respect to insurance policies on the decedent's life.

(c) *Actuarial valuations.*—The present value of annuities, life estates, terms of years, remainders, and reversions for estates of decedents for which the valuation date of the gross estate is on or after May 1, 2009, is determined under paragraph (d) of this section. The present value of annuities, life estates, terms of years, remainders, and reversions for estates of decedents for which the valuation date of the gross estate is before May 1, 2009, is determined under the following sections:

death of one individual, the present value of the interest is computed by multiplying the value of the property by the appropriate remainder interest actuarial factor (that corresponds to the applicable section 7520 interest rate and remainder interest period) in Table B (for a term certain) or in Table S (for one measuring life), as the case may be. Table B is contained in paragraph (d)(6) of this section and Table S (for one measuring life when the valuation date is on or after May 1, 2009) is contained in paragraph (d)(7) of this section and in Internal Revenue Service Publication 1457. See § 20.2031-7A containing Table S for valuation of interests before May 1, 2009. For information about obtaining actuarial factors for other types of remainder interests, see paragraph (d)(4) of this section.

(iii) *Ordinary term-of-years and life interests.*—If the interest to be valued is the right of a person to receive the income of certain property, or to use certain nonincome-producing property, for a term of years or for the life of one individual, the present value of the interest is computed by multiplying the value of the property by the appropriate term-of-years or life interest actuarial factor (that corresponds to the applicable section 7520 interest rate and term-of-years or life interest period). Internal Revenue Service Publication 1457 includes actuarial factors for a remainder interest after a term of years in Table B and after the life of one individual in Table S (for one measuring life when the valuation date is on or after May 1, 2009). However, term-of-years and life interest actuarial factors are not included in Table B in paragraph (d)(6) of this section or Table S in paragraph (d)(7) of this section (or in § 20.2031-7A). If Internal Revenue Service Publication 1457 (or any other reliable source of term-of-years and life interest actuarial factors) is not conveniently available, an actuarial factor for the interest may be derived mathematically. This actuarial factor may be derived by subtracting the correlative remainder factor (that corresponds to the applicable section 7520 interest rate and the term of years or the life) in Table B (for a term of years) in paragraph (d)(6) of this section or in Table S (for the life of one individual) in paragraph (d)(7) of this section, as the case may be, from 1.000000. For information about obtaining actuarial factors for other types of term-of-years and life interests, see paragraph (d)(4) of this section.

(iv) *Annuities.*—(A) If the interest to be valued is the right of a person to receive an annuity that is payable at the end of each year for a term of years or for the life of one individual, the present value of the interest is computed by multiplying the aggregate amount payable annually by the appropriate annuity actuarial factor (that corresponds to the applicable section 7520 interest rate and annuity period). Internal Revenue Publication 1457 includes actuarial factors for a remainder interest in Table B (after an annuity payable for a term of years) and in Table S (after an annuity payable for the life of one individual when the valuation date is on or after May 1, 2009). However, annuity actuarial factors are not included in Table B in paragraph (d)(6) of this section or Table S in paragraph (d)(7) of this section (or in § 20.2031-7A). If Internal Revenue Service Publication 1457 (or any other reliable source of annuity actuarial factors) is not conveniently available, a required annuity factor for a term of years or for one life may be mathematically derived. This annuity factor may be derived by subtracting the applicable remainder factor (that corresponds to the applicable section 7520 interest rate and annuity period) in Table B (in the case of a term-of-years annuity) in paragraph (d)(6) of this section or in Table S (in the case of a one-life annuity when the valuation date is on or after May 1, 2009) in paragraph (d)(7) of this section, as the case may be, from 1.000000 and then dividing the result by the applicable section 7520 interest rate expressed as a decimal number.

(B) If the annuity is payable at the end of semiannual, quarterly, monthly, or weekly periods, the product obtained by multiplying the annuity factor by the aggregate amount payable annually is then multiplied by the applicable adjustment factor as contained in Table K in paragraph (d)(6) of this section for payments made at the end of the specified periods. The provisions of this paragraph (d)(2)(iv)(B) are illustrated by the following example:

Example. At the time of the decedent's death, the survivor/annuitant, age 72, is entitled to receive an annuity of $15,000 a year for life payable in equal monthly installments at the end of each period. The section 7520 rate for the month in which the decedent died is 5.6 percent. Under Table S in paragraph (d)(7) of this section, the remainder factor at 5.6 percent for an indi-

vidual aged 72 is .53243. By converting the remainder factor to an annuity factor, as described above, the annuity factor at 5.6 percent for an individual aged 72 is 8.3495 (1.000000 minus .53243, divided by .056). Under Table K in paragraph (d)(6) of this section, the adjustment factor under the column for payments made at the end of each monthly period at the rate of 5.6 percent is 1.0254. The aggregate annual amount, $15,000, is multiplied by the factor 8.3495 and the product is multiplied by 1.0254. The present value of the annuity at the date of the decedent's death is, therefore, $128,423.66 ($15,000 x 8.3495 × 1.0254).

(C) If an annuity is payable at the beginning of annual, semiannual, quarterly, monthly, or weekly periods for a term of years, the value of the annuity is computed by multiplying the aggregate amount payable annually by the annuity factor described in paragraph (d)(2)(iv)(A) of this section, and the product so obtained is then multiplied by the adjustment factor in Table J in paragraph (d)(6) of this section at the appropriate interest rate component for payments made at the beginning of specified periods. If an annuity is payable at the beginning of annual, semiannual, quarterly, monthly, or weekly periods for one or more lives, the value of the annuity is the sum of the first payment plus the present value of a similar annuity, the first payment of which is not to be made until the end of the payment period, determined as provided in this paragraph (d)(2)(iv).

(v) *Annuity and unitrust interests for a term of years or until the prior death of an individual.*— See § 25.2512-5(d)(2)(v) of this chapter for examples explaining how to compute the present value of an annuity or unitrust interest that is payable until the earlier of the lapse of a specific number of years or the death of an individual.

(3) *Transitional rule.*—(i) If a decedent dies on or after May 1, 2009, and if on May 1, 2009, the decedent was mentally incompetent so that the disposition of the decedent's property could not be changed, and the decedent dies without having regained competency to dispose of the decedent's property or dies within 90 days of the date on which the decedent first regains competency, the fair market value of annuities, life estates, terms for years, remainders, and reversions included in the gross estate of the decedent is their present value determined either under this section or under the corresponding section applicable at the time the decedent became mentally incompetent, at the option of the decedent's executor. For examples, see § 20.2031-7A(d).

(ii) If a decedent dies on or after May 1, 2009, and before July 1, 2009, the fair market value of annuities, life estates, remainders, and reversions based on one or more measuring lives included in the gross estate of the decedent is their present value determined under this section by use of the section 7520 interest rate for the month in which the valuation date occurs (see §§ 20.7520-1(b) and 20.7520-2(a)(2)) and the appropriate actuarial tables under either paragraph (d)(7) of this section or § 20.2031-7A(f)(4), at the option of the decedent's executor.

(iii) For purposes of paragraphs (d)(3)(i) and (d)(3)(ii) of this section, where the decedent's executor is given the option to use the appropriate actuarial tables under either paragraph (d)(7) of this section or § 20.2031-7A(f)(4), the decedent's executor must use the same actuarial table with respect to each individual transaction and with respect to all transfers occurring on the valuation date. For example, gift and income tax charitable deductions with respect to the same transfer must be determined based on the same tables, and all assets includible in the gross estate and/or estate tax deductions claimed must be valued based on the same tables.

(4) *Publications and actuarial computations by the Internal Revenue Service.*—Many standard actuarial factors not included in paragraph (d)(6) or (d)(7) of this section are included in Internal Revenue Service Publication 1457, "Actuarial Valuations Version 3A" (2009). Publication 1457 also includes examples that illustrate how to compute many special factors for more unusual situations. This publication is available, at no charge, electronically via the Internal Revenue Service Internet site at *www.irs.gov*. If a special factor is required in the case of an actual decedent, the Internal Revenue Service may furnish the factor to the executor upon a request for a ruling. The request for a ruling must be accompanied by a recitation of the facts including a statement of the date of birth for each measuring life, the date of the decedent's death, any other applicable dates, and a copy of the will, trust, or other relevant documents. A request for a ruling must comply with the instructions for requesting a ruling published periodically in the Internal Revenue Bulletin (see §§ 601.201 and 601.601(d)(2)(ii)(b) of this chapter) and must include payment of the required user fee.

(5) *Examples.*—The provisions of this section are illustrated by the following examples:

Example 1. Remainder payable at an individual's death. The decedent, or the decedent's estate, was entitled to receive certain property worth $50,000 upon the death of A, to whom the income was bequeathed for life. At the time of the decedent's death, A was 47 years and 5 months old. In the month in which the decedent died, the section 7520 rate was 6.2 percent. Under Table S in paragraph (d)(7) of this section, the remainder factor at 6.2 percent for determining the present value of the remainder interest due at the death of a person aged 47, the number of years nearest A's actual age at the decedent's death, is .18672. The present value of the remainder interest at the date of the decedent's death is, therefore, $9,336.00 ($50,000 X .18672).

Example 2. Income payable for an individual's life. A's parent bequeathed an income interest in property to A for life, with the remainder interest passing to B at A's death. At the time of the parent's death, the value of the property was $50,000 and A was 30 years and 10 months old. The section 7520 rate at the time of the parent's death was 6.2 percent. Under Table S in paragraph (d)(7) of this section, the remainder factor at 6.2 percent for determining the present value of the remainder interest due at the death of a person aged 31, the number of years closest to A's age at the decedent's death, is .08697. Converting this remainder factor to an income factor, as described in paragraph (d)(2)(iii) of this section, the factor for determining the present value of an income interest for the life of a person aged 31 is .91303. The present value of A's interest at the time of the parent's death is, therefore, $45,651.50 ($50,000 X .91303).

Example 3. Annuity payable for an individual's life. A purchased an annuity for the benefit of both A and B. Under the terms of the annuity contract, at A's death, a survivor annuity of $10,000 per year payable in equal semiannual installments made at the end of each interval is payable to B for life. At A's death, B was 45 years and 7 months old. Also, at A's death, the section 7520 rate was 4.8 percent. Under Table S in paragraph (d)(7) of this section, the factor at 4.8 percent for determining the present value of the remainder interest at the death of a person age 46 (the number of years nearest B's actual age) is .24774. By converting the factor to an annuity factor, as described in paragraph (d)(2)(iv)(A) of this section, the factor for the present value of an annuity payable until the death of a person age 46 is 15.6721 (1.000000 minus .24774, divided by .048). The adjustment factor from Table K in paragraph (d)(6) of this section at an interest rate of 4.8 percent for semiannual annuity payments made at the end of the period is 1.0119. The present value of the annuity at the date of A's death is, therefore, $158,585.98 ($10,000 X 15.6721 X 1.0119).

Example 4. Annuity payable for a term of years. The decedent, or the decedent's estate, was entitled to receive an annuity of $10,000 per year payable in equal quarterly installments at the end of each quarter throughout a term certain. At the time of the decedent's death, the section 7520 rate was 9.8 percent. A quarterly payment had been made immediately prior to the decedent's death and payments were to continue for 5 more years. Under Table B in paragraph (d)(6) of this section for the interest rate of 9.8 percent, the factor for the present value of a remainder interest due after a term of 5 years is .626597. Converting the factor to an annuity factor, as described in paragraph (d)(2)(iv)(A) of this section, the factor for the present value of an annuity for a term of 5 years is 3.8102 (1.000000 minus .626597, divided by .098). The adjustment factor from Table K in paragraph (d)(6) of this section at an interest rate of 9.8 percent for quarterly annuity payments made at the end of the period is 1.0360. The present value of the annuity is, therefore, $39,473.67 ($10,000 X 3.8102 X 1.0360).

(6) *Actuarial Table B, Table J, and Table K where the valuation date is after April 30, 1989.*—Except as provided in § 20.7520-3(b) (pertaining to cer-

tain limitations on prescribed tables), for determination of the present value of an interest that is dependent on a term of years, the tables in this paragraph (d)(6) must be used in the application of the provisions of this section when the section 7520 interest rate component is between 4.2 and 14 percent.

TABLE B
TERM CERTAIN REMAINDER FACTORS
APPLICABLE AFTER APRIL 30, 1989

INTEREST RATE

YEARS	4.2%	4.4%	4.6%	4.8%	5.0%	5.2%	5.4%	5.6%	5.8%	6.0%
1	.959693	.957854	.956023	.954198	.952381	.950570	.948767	.946970	.945180	.943396
2	.921010	.917485	.913980	.910495	.907029	.903584	.900158	.896752	.893364	.889996
3	.883887	.878817	.873786	.868793	.863838	.858920	.854040	.849197	.844390	.839619
4	.848260	.841779	.835359	.829001	.822702	.816464	.810285	.804163	.798100	.792094
5	.814069	.806302	.798623	.791031	.783526	.776106	.768771	.761518	.754348	.747258
6	.781257	.772320	.763501	.754801	.746215	.737744	.729384	.721135	.712994	.704961
7	.749766	.739770	.729925	.720230	.710681	.701277	.692015	.682893	.673908	.665057
8	.719545	.708592	.697825	.687242	.676839	.666613	.656561	.646679	.636964	.627412
9	.690543	.678728	.667137	.655765	.644609	.633663	.622923	.612385	.602045	.591898
10	.662709	.650122	.637798	.625730	.613913	.602341	.591009	.579910	.569041	.558395
11	.635997	.622722	.609750	.597071	.584679	.572568	.560729	.549157	.537846	.526788
12	.610362	.596477	.582935	.569724	.556837	.544266	.532001	.520035	.508361	.496969
13	.585760	.571339	.557299	.543630	.530321	.517363	.504745	.492458	.480492	.468839
14	.562150	.547259	.532790	.518731	.505068	.491790	.478885	.466343	.454151	.442301
15	.539491	.524195	.509360	.494972	.481017	.467481	.454350	.441612	.429255	.417265
16	.517746	.502102	.486960	.472302	.458112	.444374	.431072	.418194	.405723	.393646
17	.496877	.480941	.465545	.450670	.436297	.422408	.408987	.396017	.383481	.371364
18	.476849	.460671	.445071	.430028	.415521	.401529	.388033	.375016	.362458	.350344
19	.457629	.441256	.425498	.410332	.395734	.381681	.368153	.355129	.342588	.330513
20	.439183	.422659	.406786	.391538	.376889	.362815	.349291	.336296	.323807	.311805
21	.421481	.404846	.388897	.373605	.358942	.344881	.331396	.318462	.306056	.294155
22	.404492	.387783	.371794	.356494	.341850	.327834	.314417	.301574	.289278	.277505
23	.388188	.371440	.355444	.340166	.325571	.311629	.298309	.285581	.273420	.261797
24	.372542	.355785	.339813	.324586	.310068	.296225	.283025	.270437	.258431	.246979
25	.357526	.340791	.324869	.309719	.295303	.281583	.268525	.256096	.244263	.232999
26	.343115	.326428	.310582	.295533	.281241	.267664	.254768	.242515	.230873	.219810
27	.329285	.312670	.296923	.281998	.267848	.254434	.241715	.229654	.218216	.207368
28	.316012	.299493	.283866	.269082	.255094	.241857	.229331	.217475	.206253	.195630
29	.303275	.286870	.271382	.256757	.242946	.229902	.217582	.205943	.194947	.184557
30	.291051	.274780	.259447	.244997	.231377	.218538	.206434	.195021	.184260	.174110
31	.279319	.263199	.248038	.233776	.220359	.207736	.195858	.184679	.174158	.164255
32	.268061	.252106	.237130	.223069	.209866	.197468	.185823	.174886	.164611	.154957
33	.257256	.241481	.226702	.212852	.199873	.187707	.176303	.165612	.155587	.146186
34	.246887	.231304	.216732	.203103	.190355	.178429	.167270	.156829	.147058	.137912
35	.236935	.221556	.207201	.193801	.181290	.169609	.158701	.148512	.138996	.130105
36	.227385	.212218	.198089	.184924	.172657	.161225	.150570	.140637	.131376	.122741
37	.218220	.203274	.189377	.176454	.164436	.153256	.142856	.133179	.124174	.115793
38	.209424	.194707	.181049	.168373	.156605	.145681	.135537	.126116	.117367	.109239
39	.200983	.186501	.173087	.160661	.149148	.138480	.128593	.119428	.110933	.103056
40	.192882	.178641	.165475	.153302	.142046	.131635	.122004	.113095	.104851	.097222
41	.185107	.171112	.158198	.146281	.135282	.125128	.115754	.107098	.099103	.091719
42	.177646	.163900	.151241	.139581	.128840	.118943	.109823	.101418	.093670	.086527

Reg. § 20.2031-7(d)(6)

YEARS	4.2%	4.4%	4.6%	4.8%	5.0%	5.2%	5.4%	5.6%	5.8%	6.0%
43	.170486	.156992	.144590	.133188	.122704	.113064	.104197	.096040	.088535	.081630
44	.163614	.150376	.138231	.127088	.116861	.107475	.098858	.090947	.083682	.077009
45	.157019	.144038	.132152	.121267	.111297	.102163	.093793	.086124	.079094	.072650
46	.150690	.137968	.126340	.115713	.105997	.097113	.088988	.081557	.074758	.068538
47	.144616	.132153	.120784	.110413	.100949	.092312	.084429	.077232	.070660	.064658
48	.138787	.126583	.115473	.105356	.096142	.087749	.080103	.073136	.066786	.060998
49	.133193	.121248	.110395	.100530	.091564	.083412	.075999	.069258	.063125	.057546
50	.127824	.116138	.105540	.095926	.087204	.079289	.072106	.065585	.059665	.054288
51	.122672	.111243	.100898	.091532	.083051	.075370	.068411	.062107	.056394	.051215
52	.117728	.106555	.096461	.087340	.079096	.071644	.064907	.058813	.053302	.048316
53	.112982	.102064	.092219	.083340	.075330	.068103	.061581	.055695	.050380	.045582
54	.108428	.097763	.088164	.079523	.071743	.064737	.058426	.052741	.047618	.043001
55	.104058	.093642	.084286	.075880	.068326	.061537	.055433	.049944	.045008	.040567
56	.099864	.089696	.080580	.072405	.065073	.058495	.052593	.047296	.042541	.038271
57	.095839	.085916	.077036	.069089	.061974	.055604	.049898	.044787	.040208	.036105
58	.091976	.082295	.073648	.065924	.059023	.052855	.047342	.042412	.038004	.034061
59	.088268	.078826	.070409	.062905	.056212	.050243	.044916	.040163	.035921	.032133
60	.084710	.075504	.067313	.060024	.053536	.047759	.042615	.038033	.033952	.030314

TABLE B
TERM CERTAIN REMAINDER FACTORS
APPLICABLE AFTER APRIL 30, 1989

INTEREST RATE

YEARS	6.2%	6.4%	6.6%	6.8%	7.0%	7.2%	7.4%	7.6%	7.8%	8.0%
1	.941620	.939850	.938086	.936330	.934579	.932836	.931099	.929368	.927644	.925926
2	.886647	.883317	.880006	.876713	.873439	.870183	.866945	.863725	.860523	.857339
3	.834885	.830185	.825521	.820892	.816298	.811738	.807211	.802718	.798259	.793832
4	.786144	.780249	.774410	.768626	.762895	.757218	.751593	.746021	.740500	.735030
5	.740248	.733317	.726464	.719687	.712986	.706360	.699808	.693328	.686920	.680583
6	.697032	.689208	.681486	.673864	.666342	.658918	.651590	.644357	.637217	.630170
7	.656339	.647752	.639292	.630959	.622750	.614662	.606694	.598845	.591111	.583490
8	.618022	.608789	.599711	.590786	.582009	.573379	.564892	.556547	.548340	.540269
9	.581942	.572170	.562581	.553170	.543934	.534868	.525971	.517237	.508664	.500249
10	.547968	.537754	.527750	.517950	.508349	.498944	.489731	.480704	.471859	.463193
11	.515977	.505408	.495075	.484972	.475093	.465433	.455987	.446750	.437717	.428883
12	.485854	.475007	.464423	.454093	.444012	.434173	.424569	.415196	.406046	.397114
13	.457490	.446436	.435669	.425181	.414964	.405012	.395316	.385870	.376666	.367698
14	.430781	.419582	.408695	.398109	.387817	.377810	.368078	.358615	.349412	.340461
15	.405632	.394344	.383391	.372762	.362446	.352434	.342717	.333285	.324130	.315242
16	.381951	.370624	.359654	.349028	.338735	.328763	.319103	.309745	.300677	.291890
17	.359653	.348331	.337386	.326805	.316574	.306682	.297117	.287867	.278921	.270269
18	.338656	.327379	.316498	.305997	.295864	.286084	.276645	.267534	.258739	.250249
19	.318885	.307687	.296902	.286514	.276508	.266870	.257584	.248638	.240018	.231712
20	.300268	.289179	.278520	.268272	.258419	.248946	.239836	.231076	.222651	.214548
21	.282739	.271785	.261276	.251191	.241513	.232225	.223311	.214755	.206541	.198656
22	.266232	.255437	.245099	.235197	.225713	.216628	.207925	.199586	.191596	.183941
23	.250689	.240073	.229924	.220222	.210947	.202078	.193598	.185489	.177733	.170315
24	.236054	.225632	.215689	.206201	.197147	.188506	.180259	.172387	.164873	.157699
25	.222273	.212060	.202334	.193072	.184249	.175845	.167839	.160211	.152943	.146018
26	.209297	.199305	.189807	.180779	.172195	.164035	.156275	.148895	.141877	.135202
27	.197078	.187317	.178056	.169269	.160930	.153017	.145507	.138379	.131611	.125187
28	.185572	.176049	.167031	.158491	.150402	.142740	.135482	.128605	.122088	.115914
29	.174739	.165460	.156690	.148400	.140563	.133153	.126147	.119521	.113255	.107328
30	.164537	.155507	.146989	.138951	.131367	.124210	.117455	.111079	.105060	.099377
31	.154932	.146154	.137888	.130104	.122773	.115868	.109362	.103233	.097458	.092016
32	.145887	.137362	.129351	.121820	.114741	.108085	.101827	.095942	.090406	.085200
33	.137370	.129100	.121342	.114064	.107235	.100826	.094811	.089165	.083865	.078889
34	.129350	.121335	.113830	.106802	.100219	.094054	.088278	.082867	.077797	.073045
35	.121798	.114036	.106782	.100001	.093663	.087737	.082196	.077014	.072168	.067635
36	.114688	.107177	.100171	.093634	.087535	.081844	.076532	.071574	.066946	.062625
37	.107992	.100730	.093969	.087673	.081809	.076347	.071259	.066519	.062102	.057986
38	.101688	.094671	.088151	.082090	.076457	.071219	.066349	.061821	.057609	.053690
39	.095751	.088977	.082693	.076864	.071455	.066436	.061778	.057454	.053440	.049713
40	.090161	.083625	.077573	.071970	.066780	.061974	.057521	.053396	.049573	.046031
41	.084897	.078595	.072770	.067387	.062412	.057811	.053558	.049625	.045987	.042621
42	.079941	.073867	.068265	.063097	.058329	.053929	.049868	.046120	.042659	.039464
43	.075274	.069424	.064038	.059079	.054513	.050307	.046432	.042862	.039572	.036541
44	.070880	.065248	.060074	.055318	.050946	.046928	.043233	.039835	.036709	.033834
45	.066742	.061323	.056354	.051796	.047613	.043776	.040254	.037021	.034053	.031328
46	.062845	.057635	.052865	.048498	.044499	.040836	.037480	.034406	.031589	.029007
47	.059176	.054168	.049592	.045410	.041587	.038093	.034898	.031976	.029303	.026859
48	.055722	.050910	.046522	.042519	.038867	.035535	.032493	.029717	.027183	.024869

YEARS	6.2%	6.4%	6.6%	6.8%	7.0%	7.2%	7.4%	7.6%	7.8%	8.0%
49	.052469	.047848	.043641	.039812	.036324	.033148	.030255	.027618	.025216	.023027
50	.049405	.044970	.040939	.037277	.033948	.030922	.028170	.025668	.023392	.021321
51	.046521	.042265	.038405	.034903	.031727	.028845	.026229	.023855	.021699	.019742
52	.043805	.039722	.036027	.032681	.029651	.026907	.024422	.022170	.020129	.018280
53	.041248	.037333	.033796	.030600	.027711	.025100	.022739	.020604	.018673	.016925
54	.038840	.035087	.031704	.028652	.025899	.023414	.021172	.019149	.017322	.015672
55	.036572	.032977	.029741	.026828	.024204	.021842	.019714	.017796	.016068	.014511
56	.034437	.030993	.027900	.025119	.022621	.020375	.018355	.016539	.014906	.013436
57	.032427	.029129	.026172	.023520	.021141	.019006	.017091	.015371	.013827	.012441
58	.030534	.027377	.024552	.022023	.019758	.017730	.015913	.014285	.012827	.011519
59	.028751	.025730	.023032	.020620	.018465	.016539	.014817	.013276	.011899	.010666
60	.027073	.024183	.021606	.019307	.017257	.015428	.013796	.012339	.011038	.009876

TABLE B
TERM CERTAIN REMAINDER FACTORS
APPLICABLE AFTER APRIL 30, 1989

INTEREST RATE

YEARS	8.2%	8.4%	8.6%	8.8%	9.0%	9.2%	9.4%	9.6%	9.8%	10.0%
1	.924214	.922509	.920810	.919118	.917431	.915751	.914077	.912409	.910747	.909091
2	.854172	.851023	.847892	.844777	.841680	.838600	.835536	.832490	.829460	.826446
3	.789438	.785077	.780747	.776450	.772183	.767948	.763744	.759571	.755428	.751315
4	.729610	.724241	.718920	.713649	.708425	.703250	.698121	.693039	.688003	.683013
5	.674316	.668119	.661989	.655927	.649931	.644001	.638136	.632335	.626597	.620921
6	.623213	.616346	.609566	.602874	.596267	.589745	.583305	.576948	.570671	.564474
7	.575982	.568585	.561295	.554112	.547034	.540059	.533186	.526412	.519737	.513158
8	.532331	.524524	.516846	.509294	.501866	.494560	.487373	.480303	.473349	.466507
9	.491988	.483879	.475917	.468101	.460428	.452894	.445496	.438233	.431101	.424098
10	.454703	.446383	.438230	.430240	.422411	.414738	.407218	.399848	.392624	.385543
11	.420243	.411792	.403526	.395441	.387533	.379797	.372228	.364824	.357581	.350494
12	.388394	.379882	.371571	.363457	.355535	.347799	.340245	.332869	.325666	.318631
13	.358960	.350445	.342147	.334060	.326179	.318497	.311010	.303713	.296599	.289664
14	.331756	.323288	.315052	.307040	.299246	.291664	.284287	.277110	.270127	.263331
15	.306613	.298236	.290103	.282206	.274538	.267092	.259860	.252838	.246017	.239392
16	.283376	.275126	.267130	.259381	.251870	.244589	.237532	.230691	.224059	.217629
17	.261901	.253806	.245976	.238401	.231073	.223983	.217123	.210485	.204061	.197845
18	.242052	.234139	.226497	.219119	.211994	.205113	.198467	.192048	.185848	.179859
19	.223708	.215995	.208561	.201396	.194490	.187832	.181414	.175226	.169260	.163508
20	.206754	.199257	.192045	.185107	.178431	.172007	.165826	.159878	.154153	.148644
21	.191085	.183817	.176837	.170135	.163698	.157516	.151578	.145874	.140395	.135131
22	.176604	.169573	.162834	.156374	.150182	.144245	.138554	.133097	.127864	.122846
23	.163220	.156432	.149939	.143726	.137781	.132093	.126649	.121439	.116452	.111678
24	.150850	.144310	.138065	.132101	.126405	.120964	.115767	.110802	.106058	.101526
25	.139418	.133128	.127132	.121416	.115968	.110773	.105820	.101097	.096592	.092296
26	.128852	.122811	.117064	.111596	.106393	.101441	.096727	.092241	.087971	.083905
27	.119087	.113295	.107794	.102570	.097608	.092894	.088416	.084162	.080119	.076278
28	.110062	.104515	.099258	.094274	.089548	.085068	.080819	.076790	.072968	.069343
29	.101721	.096416	.091398	.086649	.082155	.077901	.073875	.070064	.066456	.063039
30	.094012	.088945	.084160	.079640	.075371	.071338	.067527	.063927	.060524	.057309
31	.086887	.082053	.077495	.073199	.069148	.065328	.061725	.058327	.055122	.052099
32	.080302	.075694	.071358	.067278	.063438	.059824	.056422	.053218	.050202	.047362
33	.074216	.069829	.065708	.061837	.058200	.054784	.051574	.048557	.045722	.043057
34	.068592	.064418	.060504	.056835	.053395	.050168	.047142	.044304	.041641	.039143
35	.063394	.059426	.055713	.052238	.048986	.045942	.043092	.040423	.037924	.035584
36	.058589	.054821	.051301	.048013	.044941	.042071	.039389	.036882	.034539	.032349
37	.054149	.050573	.047239	.044130	.041231	.038527	.036005	.033652	.031457	.029408
38	.050045	.046654	.043498	.040560	.037826	.035281	.032911	.030704	.028649	.026735
39	.046253	.043039	.040053	.037280	.034703	.032309	.030083	.028015	.026092	.024304
40	.042747	.039703	.036881	.034264	.031838	.029587	.027498	.025561	.023763	.022095
41	.039508	.036627	.033961	.031493	.029209	.027094	.025136	.023322	.021642	.020086
42	.036514	.033789	.031271	.028946	.026797	.024811	.022976	.021279	.019711	.018260
43	.033746	.031170	.028795	.026605	.024584	.022721	.021002	.019415	.017951	.016600
44	.031189	.028755	.026515	.024453	.022555	.020807	.019197	.017715	.016349	.015091
45	.028825	.026527	.024415	.022475	.020692	.019054	.017548	.016163	.014890	.013719
46	.026641	.024471	.022482	.020657	.018984	.017449	.016040	.014747	.013561	.012472
47	.024622	.022575	.020701	.018986	.017416	.015978	.014662	.013456	.012351	.011338
48	.022756	.020825	.019062	.017451	.015978	.014632	.013402	.012277	.011248	.010307

Reg. §20.2031-7(d)(6)

YEARS	8.2%	8.4%	8.6%	8.8%	9.0%	9.2%	9.4%	9.6%	9.8%	10.0%
49	.021031	.019212	.017552	.016039	.014659	.013400	.012250	.011202	.010244	.009370
50	.019437	.017723	.016163	.014742	.013449	.012271	.011198	.010221	.009330	.008519
51	.017964	.016350	.014883	.013550	.012338	.011237	.010236	.009325	.008497	.007744
52	.016603	.015083	.013704	.012454	.011319	.010290	.009356	.008508	.007739	.007040
53	.015345	.013914	.012619	.011446	.010385	.009423	.008552	.007763	.007048	.006400
54	.014182	.012836	.011620	.010521	.009527	.008629	.007817	.007083	.006419	.005818
55	.013107	.011841	.010699	.009670	.008741	.007902	.007146	.006463	.005846	.005289
56	.012114	.010923	.009852	.008888	.008019	.007237	.006532	.005897	.005324	.004809
57	.011196	.010077	.009072	.008169	.007357	.006627	.005971	.005380	.004849	.004371
58	.010347	.009296	.008354	.007508	.006749	.006069	.005458	.004909	.004416	.003974
59	.009563	.008576	.007692	.006901	.006192	.005557	.004989	.004479	.004022	.003613
60	.008838	.007911	.007083	.006343	.005681	.005089	.004560	.004087	.003663	.003284

TABLE B
TERM CERTAIN REMAINDER FACTORS
APPLICABLE AFTER APRIL 30, 1989

INTEREST RATE

YEARS	10.2%	10.4%	10.6%	10.8%	11.0%	11.2%	11.4%	11.6%	11.8%	12.0%
1	.907441	.905797	.904159	.902527	.900901	.899281	.897666	.896057	.894454	.892857
2	.823449	.820468	.817504	.814555	.811622	.808706	.805804	.802919	.800049	.797194
3	.747232	.743178	.739153	.735158	.731191	.727253	.723343	.719461	.715607	.711780
4	.678069	.673168	.668312	.663500	.658731	.654005	.649321	.644679	.640078	.635518
5	.615307	.609754	.604261	.598827	.593451	.588134	.582873	.577669	.572520	.567427
6	.558355	.552313	.546348	.540457	.534641	.528897	.523225	.517625	.512093	.506631
7	.506674	.500284	.493985	.487777	.481658	.475627	.469682	.463821	.458044	.452349
8	.459777	.453156	.446641	.440232	.433926	.427722	.421617	.415610	.409700	.403883
9	.417221	.410467	.403835	.397322	.390925	.384642	.378472	.372411	.366458	.360610
10	.378603	.371800	.365131	.358593	.352184	.345901	.339741	.333701	.327780	.321973
11	.343560	.336775	.330137	.323640	.317283	.311062	.304974	.299016	.293184	.287476
12	.311760	.305050	.298496	.292094	.285841	.279732	.273765	.267935	.262240	.256675
13	.282904	.276313	.269888	.263623	.257514	.251558	.245749	.240085	.234561	.229174
14	.256719	.250284	.244022	.237927	.231995	.226221	.220601	.215130	.209804	.204620
15	.232957	.226706	.220634	.214735	.209004	.203436	.198026	.192769	.187661	.182696
16	.211395	.205350	.199489	.193804	.188292	.182946	.177761	.172732	.167854	.163122
17	.191828	.186005	.180369	.174914	.169633	.164520	.159570	.154778	.150138	.145644
18	.174073	.168483	.163083	.157864	.152822	.147950	.143241	.138690	.134291	.130040
19	.157961	.152612	.147453	.142477	.137678	.133048	.128582	.124274	.120117	.116107
20	.143340	.138235	.133321	.128589	.124034	.119648	.115424	.111357	.107439	.103667
21	.130073	.125213	.120543	.116055	.111742	.107597	.103612	.099782	.096100	.092560
22	.118033	.113418	.108990	.104743	.100669	.096760	.093009	.089410	.085957	.082643
23	.107108	.102733	.098544	.094533	.090693	.087014	.083491	.080117	.076884	.073788
24	.097195	.093056	.089100	.085319	.081705	.078250	.074947	.071789	.068770	.065882
25	.088198	.084289	.080560	.077003	.073608	.070369	.067278	.064327	.061511	.058823
26	.080035	.076349	.072839	.069497	.066314	.063281	.060393	.057641	.055019	.052521
27	.072627	.069157	.065858	.062723	.059742	.056908	.054213	.051650	.049212	.046894
28	.065905	.062642	.059547	.056609	.053822	.051176	.048665	.046281	.044018	.041869
29	.059804	.056741	.053840	.051091	.048488	.046022	.043685	.041470	.039372	.037383
30	.054269	.051396	.048680	.046111	.043683	.041386	.039214	.037160	.035216	.033378
31	.049246	.046554	.044014	.041617	.039354	.037218	.035201	.033297	.031500	.029802
32	.044688	.042169	.039796	.037560	.035454	.033469	.031599	.029836	.028175	.026609
33	.040552	.038196	.035982	.033899	.031940	.030098	.028365	.026735	.025201	.023758
34	.036798	.034598	.032533	.030595	.028775	.027067	.025463	.023956	.022541	.021212
35	.033392	.031339	.029415	.027613	.025924	.024341	.022857	.021466	.020162	.018940
36	.030301	.028387	.026596	.024921	.023355	.021889	.020518	.019235	.018034	.016910
37	.027497	.025712	.024047	.022492	.021040	.019684	.018418	.017236	.016131	.015098
38	.024952	.023290	.021742	.020300	.018955	.017702	.016533	.015444	.014428	.013481
39	.022642	.021096	.019658	.018321	.017077	.015919	.014841	.013839	.012905	.012036
40	.020546	.019109	.017774	.016535	.015384	.014316	.013323	.012400	.011543	.010747
41	.018645	.017309	.016071	.014923	.013860	.012874	.011959	.011111	.010325	.009595
42	.016919	.015678	.014531	.013469	.012486	.011577	.010735	.009956	.009235	.008567
43	.015353	.014201	.013138	.012156	.011249	.010411	.009637	.008922	.008260	.007649
44	.013932	.012864	.011879	.010971	.010134	.009362	.008651	.007994	.007389	.006830
45	.012642	.011652	.010740	.009902	.009130	.008419	.007765	.007163	.006609	.006098
46	.011472	.010554	.009711	.008937	.008225	.007571	.006971	.006419	.005911	.005445
47	.010410	.009560	.008780	.008065	.007410	.006809	.006257	.005752	.005287	.004861
48	.009447	.008659	.007939	.007279	.006676	.006123	.005617	.005154	.004729	.004340

YEARS	10.2%	10.4%	10.6%	10.8%	11.0%	11.2%	11.4%	11.6%	11.8%	12.0%
49	.008572	.007844	.007178	.006570	.006014	.005506	.005042	.004618	.004230	.003875
50	.007779	.007105	.006490	.005929	.005418	.004952	.004526	.004138	.003784	.003460
51	.007059	.006435	.005868	.005351	.004881	.004453	.004063	.003708	.003384	.003089
52	.006406	.005829	.005306	.004830	.004397	.004005	.003647	.003322	.003027	.002758
53	.005813	.005280	.004797	.004359	.003962	.003601	.003274	.002977	.002708	.002463
54	.005275	.004783	.004337	.003934	.003569	.003238	.002939	.002668	.002422	.002199
55	.004786	.004332	.003922	.003551	.003215	.002912	.002638	.002390	.002166	.001963
56	.004343	.003924	.003546	.003205	.002897	.002619	.002368	.002142	.001938	.001753
57	.003941	.003554	.003206	.002892	.002610	.002355	.002126	.001919	.001733	.001565
58	.003577	.003220	.002899	.002610	.002351	.002118	.001908	.001720	.001550	.001398
59	.003246	.002916	.002621	.002356	.002118	.001905	.001713	.001541	.001387	.001248
60	.002945	.002642	.002370	.002126	.001908	.001713	.001538	.001381	.001240	.001114

TABLE B
TERM CERTAIN REMAINDER FACTORS
APPLICABLE AFTER APRIL 30, 1989

INTEREST RATE

YEARS	12.2%	12.4%	12.6%	12.8%	13.0%	13.2%	13.4%	13.6%	13.8%	14.0%
1	.891266	.889680	.888099	.886525	.884956	.883392	.881834	.880282	.878735	.877193
2	.794354	.791530	.788721	.785926	.783147	.780382	.777632	.774896	.772175	.769468
3	.707981	.704208	.700462	.696743	.693050	.689383	.685742	.682127	.678536	.674972
4	.630999	.626520	.622080	.617680	.613319	.608996	.604711	.600464	.596254	.592080
5	.562388	.557402	.552469	.547589	.542760	.537982	.533255	.528577	.523949	.519369
6	.501237	.495909	.490648	.485451	.480319	.475249	.470242	.465297	.460412	.455587
7	.446735	.441200	.435744	.430364	.425061	.419831	.414676	.409592	.404580	.399637
8	.398160	.392527	.386984	.381529	.376160	.370876	.365675	.360557	.355518	.350559
9	.354866	.349223	.343680	.338235	.332885	.327629	.322465	.317391	.312406	.307508
10	.316280	.310697	.305222	.299853	.294588	.289425	.284361	.279394	.274522	.269744
11	.281889	.276421	.271068	.265827	.260698	.255676	.250759	.245945	.241232	.236617
12	.251238	.245926	.240735	.235663	.230706	.225862	.221128	.216501	.211979	.207559
13	.223920	.218795	.213797	.208921	.204165	.199525	.194998	.190582	.186273	.182069
14	.199572	.194658	.189873	.185213	.180677	.176258	.171956	.167766	.163685	.159710
15	.177872	.173183	.168626	.164196	.159891	.155705	.151637	.147681	.143835	.140096
16	.158531	.154077	.149757	.145564	.141496	.137549	.133718	.130001	.126393	.122892
17	.141293	.137080	.132999	.129046	.125218	.121510	.117917	.114438	.111066	.107800
18	.125930	.121957	.118116	.114403	.110812	.107341	.103984	.100737	.097598	.094561
19	.112237	.108503	.104899	.101421	.098064	.094824	.091696	.088677	.085762	.082948
20	.100033	.096533	.093161	.089912	.086782	.083767	.080861	.078061	.075362	.072762
21	.089156	.085883	.082736	.079709	.076798	.073999	.071306	.068716	.066224	.063826
22	.079462	.076408	.073478	.070664	.067963	.065370	.062880	.060489	.058193	.055988
23	.070821	.067979	.065255	.062646	.060144	.057747	.055450	.053247	.051136	.049112
24	.063121	.060480	.057953	.055537	.053225	.051014	.048898	.046873	.044935	.043081
25	.056257	.053807	.051468	.049235	.047102	.045065	.043119	.041261	.039486	.037790
26	.050140	.047871	.045709	.043648	.041683	.039810	.038024	.036321	.034698	.033149
27	.044688	.042590	.040594	.038695	.036888	.035168	.033531	.031973	.030490	.029078
28	.039829	.037892	.036052	.034304	.032644	.031067	.029569	.028145	.026793	.025507
29	.035498	.033711	.032017	.030411	.028889	.027444	.026075	.024776	.023544	.022375
30	.031638	.029992	.028435	.026960	.025565	.024244	.022994	.021810	.020689	.019627
31	.028198	.026684	.025253	.023901	.022624	.021417	.020277	.019199	.018180	.017217
32	.025132	.023740	.022427	.021189	.020021	.018920	.017881	.016900	.015975	.015102
33	.022399	.021121	.019917	.018785	.017718	.016714	.015768	.014877	.014038	.013248
34	.019964	.018791	.017689	.016653	.015680	.014765	.013905	.013096	.012336	.011621
35	.017793	.016718	.015709	.014763	.013876	.013043	.012261	.011528	.010840	.010194
36	.015858	.014873	.013951	.013088	.012279	.011522	.010813	.010148	.009525	.008942
37	.014134	.013233	.012390	.011603	.010867	.010178	.009535	.008933	.008370	.007844
38	.012597	.011773	.011004	.010286	.009617	.008992	.008408	.007864	.007355	.006880
39	.011227	.010474	.009772	.009119	.008510	.007943	.007415	.006922	.006463	.006035
40	.010007	.009319	.008679	.008084	.007531	.007017	.006538	.006093	.005679	.005294
41	.008919	.008291	.007708	.007167	.006665	.006199	.005766	.005364	.004991	.004644
42	.007949	.007376	.006845	.006354	.005898	.005476	.005085	.004722	.004386	.004074
43	.007084	.006562	.006079	.005633	.005219	.004837	.004484	.004157	.003854	.003573
44	.006314	.005838	.005399	.004993	.004619	.004273	.003954	.003659	.003386	.003135
45	.005628	.005194	.004795	.004427	.004088	.003775	.003487	.003221	.002976	.002750
46	.005016	.004621	.004258	.003924	.003617	.003335	.003075	.002835	.002615	.002412
47	.004470	.004111	.003782	.003479	.003201	.002946	.002711	.002496	.002298	.002116
48	.003984	.003658	.003359	.003084	.002833	.002602	.002391	.002197	.002019	.001856

Reg. § 20.2031-7(d)(6)

YEARS	12.2%	12.4%	12.6%	12.8%	13.0%	13.2%	13.4%	13.6%	13.8%	14.0%
49	.003551	.003254	.002983	.002734	.002507	:002299	.002108	.001934	.001774	.001628
50	.003165	.002895	.002649	.002424	.002219	.002031	.001859	.001702	.001559	.001428
51	.002821	.002576	.002353	.002149	.001963	.001794	.001640	.001499	.001370	.001253
52	.002514	.002292	.002089	.001905	.001737	.001585	.001446	.001319	.001204	.001099
53	.002241	.002039	.001856	.001689	.001538	.001400	.001275	.001161	.001058	.000964
54	.001997	.001814	.001648	.001497	.001361	.001237	.001124	.001022	.000930	.000846
55	.001780	.001614	.001463	.001327	.001204	.001093	.000991	.000900	.000817	.000742
56	.001586	.001436	.001300	.001177	.001066	.000965	.000874	.000792	.000718	.000651
57	.001414	.001277	.001154	.001043	.000943	.000853	.000771	.000697	.000631	.000571
58	.001260	.001136	.001025	.000925	.000835	.000753	.000680	.000614	.000554	.000501
59	.001123	.001011	.000910	.000820	.000739	.000665	.000600	.000540	.000487	.000439
60	.001001	.000900	.000809	.000727	.000654	.000588	.000529	.000476	.000428	.000385

Reg. § 20.2031-7(d)(6)

TABLE J
ADJUSTMENT FACTORS FOR TERM CERTAIN ANNUITIES
PAYABLE AT THE BEGINNING OF EACH INTERVAL
APPLICABLE AFTER APRIL 30, 1989
FREQUENCY OF PAYMENTS

INTEREST RATE	ANNUALLY	SEMI ANNUALLY	QUARTERLY	MONTHLY	WEEKLY
4.2	1.0420	1.0314	1.0261	1.0226	1.0213
4.4	1.0440	1.0329	1.0274	1.0237	1.0223
4.6	1.0460	1.0344	1.0286	1.0247	1.0233
4.8	1.0480	1.0359	1.0298	1.0258	1.0243
5.0	1.0500	1.0373	1.0311	1.0269	1.0253
5.2	1.0520	1.0388	1.0323	1.0279	1.0263
5.4	1.0540	1.0403	1.0335	1.0290	1.0273
5.6	1.0560	1.0418	1.0348	1.0301	1.0283
5.8	1.0580	1.0433	1.0360	1.0311	1.0293
6.0	1.0600	1.0448	1.0372	1.0322	1.0303
6.2	1.0620	1.0463	1.0385	1.0333	1.0313
6.4	1.0640	1.0478	1.0397	1.0343	1.0323
6.6	1.0660	1.0492	1.0409	1.0354	1.0333
6.8	1.0680	1.0507	1.0422	1.0365	1.0343
7.0	1.0700	1.0522	1.0434	1.0375	1.0353
7.2	1.0720	1.0537	1.0446	1.0386	1.0363
7.4	1.0740	1.0552	1.0458	1.0396	1.0373
7.6	1.0760	1.0567	1.0471	1.0407	1.0383
7.8	1.0780	1.0581	1.0483	1.0418	1.0393
8.0	1.0800	1.0596	1.0495	1.0428	1.0403
8.2	1.0820	1.0611	1.0507	1.0439	1.0413
8.4	1.0840	1.0626	1.0520	1.0449	1.0422
8.6	1.0860	1.0641	1.0532	1.0460	1.0432
8.8	1.0880	1.0655	1.0544	1.0471	1.0442
9.0	1.0900	1.0670	1.0556	1.0481	1.0452
9.2	1.0920	1.0685	1.0569	1.0492	1.0462
9.4	1.0940	1.0700	1.0581	1.0502	1.0472
9.6	1.0960	1.0715	1.0593	1.0513	1.0482
9.8	1.0980	1.0729	1.0605	1.0523	1.0492
10.0	1.1000	1.0744	1.0618	1.0534	1.0502
10.2	1.1020	1.0759	1.0630	1.0544	1.0512
10.4	1.1040	1.0774	1.0642	1.0555	1.0521
10.6	1.1060	1.0788	1.0654	1.0565	1.0531
10.8	1.1080	1.0803	1.0666	1.0576	1.0541
11.0	1.1100	1.0818	1.0679	1.0586	1.0551
11.2	1.1120	1.0833	1.0691	1.0597	1.0561
11.4	1.1140	1.0847	1.0703	1.0607	1.0571
11.6	1.1160	1.0862	1.0715	1.0618	1.0581
11.8	1.1180	1.0877	1.0727	1.0628	1.0590
12.0	1.1200	1.0892	1.0739	1.0639	1.0600
12.2	1.1220	1.0906	1.0752	1.0649	1.0610
12.4	1.1240	1.0921	1.0764	1.0660	1.0620
12.6	1.1260	1.0936	1.0776	1.0670	1.0630
12.8	1.1280	1.0950	1.0788	1.0681	1.0639
13.0	1.1300	1.0965	1.0800	1.0691	1.0649
13.2	1.1320	1.0980	1.0812	1.0701	1.0659
13.4	1.1340	1.0994	1.0824	1.0712	1.0669
13.6	1.1360	1.1009	1.0836	1.0722	1.0679

Reg. § 20.2031-7(d)(6)

INTEREST RATE	ANNUALLY	SEMI ANNUALLY	QUARTERLY	MONTHLY	WEEKLY
13.8	1.1380	1.1024	1.0849	1.0733	1.0688
14.0	1.1400	1.1039	1.0861	1.0743	1.0698

TABLE K
ADJUSTMENT FACTORS FOR ANNUITIES
PAYABLE AT THE END OF EACH INTERVAL
APPLICABLE AFTER APRIL 30, 1989
FREQUENCY OF PAYMENTS

INTEREST RATE	ANNUALLY	SEMI ANNUALLY	QUARTERLY	MONTHLY	WEEKLY
4.2	1.0000	1.0104	1.0156	1.0191	1.0205
4.4	1.0000	1.0109	1.0164	1.0200	1.0214
4.6	1.0000	1.0114	1.0171	1.0209	1.0224
4.8	1.0000	1.0119	1.0178	1.0218	1.0234
5.0	1.0000	1.0123	1.0186	1.0227	1.0243
5.2	1.0000	1.0128	1.0193	1.0236	1.0253
5.4	1.0000	1.0133	1.0200	1.0245	1.0262
5.6	1.0000	1.0138	1.0208	1.0254	1.0272
5.8	1.0000	1.0143	1.0215	1.0263	1.0282
6.0	1.0000	1.0148	1.0222	1.0272	1.0291
6.2	1.0000	1.0153	1.0230	1.0281	1.0301
6.4	1.0000	1.0158	1.0237	1.0290	1.0311
6.6	1.0000	1.0162	1.0244	1.0299	1.0320
6.8	1.0000	1.0167	1.0252	1.0308	1.0330
7.0	1.0000	1.0172	1.0259	1.0317	1.0339
7.2	1.0000	1.0177	1.0266	1.0326	1.0349
7.4	1.0000	1.0182	1.0273	1.0335	1.0358
7.6	1.0000	1.0187	1.0281	1.0344	1.0368
7.8	1.0000	1.0191	1.0288	1.0353	1.0378
8.0	1.0000	1.0196	1.0295	1.0362	1.0387
8.2	1.0000	1.0201	1.0302	1.0370	1.0397
8.4	1.0000	1.0206	1.0310	1.0379	1.0406
8.6	1.0000	1.0211	1.0317	1.0388	1.0416
8.8	1.0000	1.0215	1.0324	1.0397	1.0425
9.0	1.0000	1.0220	1.0331	1.0406	1.0435
9.2	1.0000	1.0225	1.0339	1.0415	1.0444
9.4	1.0000	1.0230	1.0346	1.0424	1.0454
9.6	1.0000	1.0235	1.0353	1.0433	1.0463
9.8	1.0000	1.0239	1.0360	1.0442	1.0473
10.0	1.0000	1.0244	1.0368	1.0450	1.0482
10.2	1.0000	1.0249	1.0375	1.0459	1.0492
10.4	1.0000	1.0254	1.0382	1.0468	1.0501
10.6	1.0000	1.0258	1.0389	1.0477	1.0511
10.8	1.0000	1.0263	1.0396	1.0486	1.0520
11.0	1.0000	1.0268	1.0404	1.0495	1.0530
11.2	1.0000	1.0273	1.0411	1.0503	1.0539
11.4	1.0000	1.0277	1.0418	1.0512	1.0549
11.6	1.0000	1.0282	1.0425	1.0521	1.0558
11.8	1.0000	1.0287	1.0432	1.0530	1.0568
12.0	1.0000	1.0292	1.0439	1.0539	1.0577

INTEREST RATE	ANNUALLY	SEMI ANNUALLY	QUARTERLY	MONTHLY	WEEKLY
12.2	1.0000	1.0296	1.0447	1.0548	1.0587
12.4	1.0000	1.0301	1.0454	1.0556	1.0596
12.6	1.0000	1.0306	1.0461	1.0565	1.0605
12.8	1.0000	1.0310	1.0468	1.0574	1.0615
13.0	1.0000	1.0315	1.0475	1.0583	1.0624
13.2	1.0000	1.0320	1.0482	1.0591	1.0634
13.4	1.0000	1.0324	1.0489	1.0600	1.0643
13.6	1.0000	1.0329	1.0496	1.0609	1.0652
13.8	1.0000	1.0334	1.0504	1.0618	1.0662
14.0	1.0000	1.0339	1.0511	1.0626	1.0671

(7) *Actuarial Table S and Table 2000CM where the valuation date is on or after May 1, 2009.*— Except as provided in § 20.7520-2(b) (pertaining to certain limitations on the use of prescribed tables), for determination of the present value of an interest that is dependent on the termination of a life interest, Table 2000CM and Table S (single life remainder factors applicable where the valuation date is on or after May 1, 2009) contained in this paragraph (d)(7) and Table J and Table K contained in paragraph (d)(6) of this section, must be used in the application of the provisions of this section when the section 7520 interest rate component is between 0.2 and 14 percent.

Table S
Based on Life Table 2000CM
Single Life Remainder Factors
Applicable On or After May 1, 2009

Interest Rate

AGE	0.2%	0.4%	0.6%	0.8%	1.0%	1.2%	1.4%	1.6%	1.8%	2.0%
0	.85816	.73751	.63478	.54723	.47252	.40872	.35416	.30747	.26745	.23313
1	.85889	.73863	.63604	.54844	.47355	.40948	.35459	.30752	.26711	.23239
2	.86054	.74145	.63968	.55260	.47802	.41409	.35922	.31209	.27155	.23664
3	.86221	.74433	.64339	.55687	.48263	.41887	.36404	.31685	.27619	.24112
4	.86390	.74725	.64716	.56121	.48733	.42374	.36898	.32175	.28098	.24575
5	.86560	.75018	.65097	.56561	.49209	.42871	.37401	.32675	.28588	.25050
6	.86731	.75314	.65482	.57006	.49692	.43375	.37913	.33186	.29090	.25538
7	.86902	.75611	.65868	.57454	.50180	.43885	.38432	.33704	.29601	.26035
8	.87073	.75909	.66258	.57907	.50674	.44403	.38960	.34233	.30122	.26544
9	.87246	.76209	.66651	.58364	.51173	.44928	.39497	.34771	.30654	.27064
10	.87419	.76511	.67046	.58826	.51679	.45459	.40042	.35319	.31197	.27596
11	.87592	.76814	.67445	.59291	.52190	.45998	.40596	.35876	.31750	.28139
12	.87766	.77119	.67845	.59761	.52706	.46544	.41157	.36443	.32313	.28693
13	.87939	.77424	.68247	.60232	.53225	.47094	.41723	.37015	.32884	.29255
14	.88112	.77728	.68649	.60704	.53746	.47646	.42293	.37592	.33460	.29823
15	.88284	.78031	.69050	.61176	.54267	.48199	.42865	.38172	.34038	.30394
16	.88455	.78333	.69449	.61647	.54788	.48752	.43437	.38752	.34619	.30968
17	.88625	.78633	.69848	.62117	.55309	.49307	.44012	.39336	.35203	.31546
18	.88795	.78933	.70246	.62588	.55830	.49863	.44589	.39923	.35791	.32129
19	.88964	.79232	.70644	.63059	.56354	.50422	.45170	.40514	.36385	.32719
20	.89132	.79532	.71044	.63534	.56882	.50987	.45757	.41114	.36987	.33317
21	.89301	.79832	.71445	.64010	.57413	.51555	.46350	.41719	.37597	.33925
22	.89470	.80133	.71847	.64488	.57947	.52129	.46948	.42332	.38216	.34541
23	.89639	.80434	.72251	.64970	.58486	.52708	.47554	.42954	.38844	.35168
24	.89808	.80737	.72658	.65456	.59031	.53295	.48169	.43586	.39484	.35809
25	.89978	.81042	.73068	.65947	.59583	.53890	.48795	.44230	.40137	.36464
26	.90149	.81349	.73482	.66443	.60141	.54494	.49430	.44886	.40804	.37134
27	.90320	.81657	.73899	.66944	.60707	.55107	.50076	.45554	.41484	.37819
28	.90492	.81968	.74319	.67450	.61278	.55728	.50733	.46233	.42178	.38520
29	.90665	.82279	.74741	.67960	.61856	.56356	.51398	.46924	.42884	.39233

AGE	0.2%	0.4%	0.6%	0.8%	1.0%	1.2%	1.4%	1.6%	1.8%	2.0%
30	.90837	.82591	.75165	.68473	.62438	.56990	.52070	.47623	.43601	.39959
31	.91010	.82904	.75592	.68989	.63024	.57631	.52751	.48333	.44329	.40698
32	.91182	.83218	.76020	.69509	.63616	.58278	.53440	.49052	.45068	.41449
33	.91355	.83532	.76449	.70031	.64212	.58931	.54137	.49780	.45818	.42213
34	.91527	.83847	.76880	.70556	.64811	.59589	.54839	.50516	.46578	.42988
35	.91700	.84162	.77312	.71082	.65414	.60253	.55549	.51261	.47347	.43774
36	.91872	.84477	.77744	.71611	.66021	.60921	.56266	.52014	.48127	.44572
37	.92043	.84792	.78178	.72142	.66631	.61594	.56989	.52774	.48916	.45381
38	.92215	.85107	.78613	.72675	.67244	.62272	.57718	.53544	.49715	.46201
39	.92386	.85422	.79048	.73210	.67860	.62955	.58453	.54320	.50523	.47032
40	.92557	.85736	.79483	.73746	.68479	.63641	.59194	.55104	.51340	.47873
41	.92727	.86050	.79918	.74283	.69100	.64331	.59940	.55894	.52165	.48724
42	.92896	.86364	.80354	.74820	.69723	.65024	.60690	.56691	.52998	.49585
43	.93065	.86677	.80789	.75359	.70348	.65721	.61447	.57495	.53840	.50457
44	.93234	.86990	.81225	.75899	.70976	.66422	.62208	.58305	.54690	.51338
45	.93402	.87302	.81660	.76439	.71605	.67125	.62973	.59122	.55547	.52228
46	.93569	.87613	.82095	.76980	.72236	.67832	.63743	.59945	.56413	.53129
47	.93735	.87924	.82530	.77521	.72867	.68541	.64517	.60773	.57286	.54037
48	.93901	.88233	.82964	.78062	.73501	.69253	.65295	.61606	.58166	.54955
49	.94065	.88541	.83397	.78604	.74135	.69967	.66077	.62446	.59053	.55882
50	.94229	.88849	.83830	.79145	.74771	.70684	.66864	.63292	.59949	.56819
51	.94393	.89156	.84263	.79688	.75409	.71404	.67655	.64143	.60852	.57766
52	.94556	.89462	.84695	.80230	.76048	.72127	.68450	.65001	.61763	.58722
53	.94717	.89767	.85126	.80772	.76687	.72852	.69249	.65863	.62680	.59687
54	.94878	.90070	.85555	.81313	.77326	.73577	.70050	.66730	.63603	.60658
55	.95037	.90371	.85983	.81853	.77964	.74302	.70851	.67598	.64530	.61635
56	.95195	.90670	.86406	.82388	.78599	.75024	.71651	.68465	.65457	.62613
57	.95351	.90965	.86827	.82920	.79230	.75744	.72448	.69332	.66384	.63593
58	.95505	.91257	.87243	.83447	.79857	.76459	.73242	.70195	.67309	.64573
59	.95657	.91546	.87655	.83970	.80479	.77170	.74033	.71057	.68233	.65553
60	.95807	.91832	.88064	.84490	.81098	.77879	.74822	.71918	.69158	.66534
61	.95955	.92115	.88469	.85005	.81713	.78584	.75608	.72776	.70081	.67515
62	.96101	.92395	.88869	.85515	.82323	.79283	.76388	.73630	.71001	.68494
63	.96245	.92670	.89265	.86020	.82926	.79977	.77164	.74479	.71917	.69470
64	.96387	.92942	.89655	.86518	.83524	.80665	.77933	.75323	.72828	.70443
65	.96527	.93210	.90040	.87011	.84116	.81346	.78697	.76162	.73735	.71411
66	.96665	.93476	.90423	.87502	.84706	.82027	.79461	.77002	.74645	.72385
67	.96802	.93739	.90803	.87990	.85292	.82705	.80223	.77841	.75554	.73359
68	.96937	.93999	.91179	.88472	.85874	.83378	.80980	.78676	.76461	.74331
69	.97070	.94255	.91549	.88949	.86449	.84044	.81731	.79504	.77362	.75299
70	.97200	.94506	.91914	.89419	.87016	.84702	.82473	.80326	.78256	.76260
71	.97328	.94754	.92273	.89882	.87577	.85353	.83209	.81140	.79143	.77215
72	.97453	.94997	.92626	.90338	.88129	.85996	.83935	.81945	.80021	.78162
73	.97576	.95234	.92972	.90785	.88671	.86627	.84651	.82739	.80888	.79098
74	.97695	.95466	.93310	.91223	.89202	.87247	.85353	.83518	.81741	.80019
75	.97811	.95692	.93638	.91649	.89720	.87851	.86039	.84281	.82577	.80923
76	.97924	.95910	.93957	.92063	.90224	.88440	.86708	.85026	.83393	.81807
77	.98033	.96122	.94267	.92465	.90715	.89013	.87360	.85753	.84191	.82671
78	.98138	.96327	.94567	.92855	.91190	.89571	.87995	.86461	.84968	.83515
79	.98239	.96526	.94857	.93233	.91652	.90112	.88611	.87149	.85725	.84337
80	.98337	.96717	.95138	.93598	.92098	.90635	.89208	.87817	.86460	.85135
81	.98431	.96901	.95408	.93951	.92529	.91141	.89786	.88463	.87172	.85910
82	.98521	.97077	.95667	.94290	.92944	.91629	.90344	.89088	.87861	.86660

Reg. § 20.2031-7(d)(7)

AGE	0.2%	0.4%	0.6%	0.8%	1.0%	1.2%	1.4%	1.6%	1.8%	2.0%
83	.98608	.97247	.95917	.94616	.93343	.92099	.90882	.89691	.88526	.87385
84	.98691	.97409	.96156	.94928	.93727	.92551	.91399	.90271	.89166	.88084
85	.98770	.97565	.96384	.95228	.94094	.92984	.91895	.90828	.89782	.88757
86	.98845	.97713	.96602	.95514	.94446	.93398	.92371	.91362	.90373	.89402
87	.98917	.97854	.96810	.95786	.94781	.93794	.92825	.91873	.90939	.90021
88	.98985	.97988	.97008	.96046	.95100	.94171	.93258	.92361	.91479	.90612
89	.99049	.98115	.97196	.96292	.95404	.94530	.93671	.92826	.91994	.91176
90	.99110	.98235	.97373	.96526	.95691	.94871	.94062	.93267	.92484	.91713
91	.99168	.98348	.97541	.96747	.95964	.95193	.94434	.93686	.92949	.92223
92	.99222	.98455	.97700	.96955	.96222	.95498	.94785	.94083	.93390	.92707
93	.99273	.98556	.97849	.97152	.96464	.95786	.95117	.94457	.93806	.93163
94	.99321	.98651	.97989	.97337	.96692	.96057	.95429	.94810	.94199	.93595
95	.99366	.98739	.98121	.97510	.96907	.96312	.95724	.95143	.94569	.94002
96	.99408	.98822	.98244	.97673	.97108	.96551	.95999	.95454	.94916	.94384
97	.99447	.98900	.98359	.97825	.97297	.96774	.96258	.95747	.95242	.94742
98	.99483	.98973	.98467	.97967	.97473	.96984	.96500	.96021	.95547	.95078
99	.99518	.99040	.98568	.98101	.97638	.97180	.96727	.96278	.95834	.95394
100	.99549	.99103	.98661	.98224	.97791	.97362	.96937	.96516	.96100	.95687
101	.99579	.99162	.98750	.98340	.97935	.97534	.97136	.96742	.96351	.95964
102	.99607	.99217	.98831	.98448	.98068	.97692	.97319	.96950	.96583	.96220
103	.99634	.99271	.98911	.98553	.98199	.97848	.97500	.97155	.96812	.96473
104	.99659	.99320	.98984	.98651	.98320	.97992	.97666	.97344	.97023	.96705
105	.99683	.99369	.99056	.98747	.98439	.98134	.97830	.97530	.97231	.96934
106	.99713	.99429	.99146	.98865	.98586	.98309	.98033	.97760	.97488	.97218
107	.99747	.99496	.99246	.98998	.98751	.98506	.98262	.98020	.97779	.97539
108	.99800	.99602	.99404	.99208	.99012	.98818	.98624	.98431	.98240	.98049
109	.99900	.99801	.99702	.99603	.99505	.99407	.99310	.99213	.99116	.99020

Table S
Based on Life Table 2000CM
Single Life Remainder Factors
Applicable On or After May 1, 2009

Interest Rate

AGE	2.2%	2.4%	2.6%	2.8%	3.0%	3.2%	3.4%	3.6%	3.8%	4.0%
0	.20365	.17830	.15648	.13767	.12144	.10741	.09528	.08476	.07564	.06772
1	.20251	.17677	.15458	.13542	.11885	.10451	.09209	.08131	.07194	.06379
2	.20656	.18060	.15817	.13877	.12197	.10740	.09476	.08376	.07420	.06586
3	.21084	.18466	.16200	.14236	.12533	.11054	.09767	.08647	.07670	.06817
4	.21527	.18888	.16600	.14613	.12887	.11385	.10076	.08935	.07938	.07066
5	.21984	.19324	.17013	.15004	.13255	.11730	.10399	.09237	.08220	.07329
6	.22454	.19773	.17440	.15408	.13636	.12089	.10736	.09553	.08515	.07605
7	.22933	.20233	.17879	.15824	.14030	.12460	.11085	.09880	.08822	.07892
8	.23425	.20705	.18330	.16254	.14436	.12844	.11447	.10221	.09142	.08193
9	.23930	.21191	.18795	.16697	.14857	.13243	.11824	.10576	.09476	.08507
10	.24446	.21689	.19273	.17153	.15292	.13655	.12214	.10945	.09824	.08835
11	.24975	.22200	.19764	.17623	.15740	.14081	.12619	.11328	.10187	.09177
12	.25515	.22724	.20268	.18107	.16202	.14521	.13037	.11724	.10563	.09533
13	.26064	.23256	.20782	.18600	.16674	.14972	.13466	.12132	.10949	.09900
14	.26620	.23796	.21303	.19101	.17154	.15430	.13903	.12547	.11344	.10273
15	.27179	.24340	.21829	.19607	.17639	.15894	.14344	.12968	.11743	.10652
16	.27742	.24887	.22358	.20117	.18128	.16361	.14790	.13391	.12145	.11034
17	.28309	.25439	.22893	.20632	.18622	.16834	.15241	.13821	.12554	.11421
18	.28881	.25997	.23434	.21154	.19123	.17314	.15699	.14258	.12969	.11815
19	.29461	.26563	.23983	.21684	.19633	.17803	.16167	.14703	.13393	.12218

Reg. § 20.2031-7(d)(7)

AGE	2.2%	2.4%	2.6%	2.8%	3.0%	3.2%	3.4%	3.6%	3.8%	4.0%
20	.30050	.27139	.24543	.22226	.20156	.18304	.16646	.15161	.13829	.12633
21	.30649	.27726	.25114	.22779	.20689	.18817	.17138	.15631	.14277	.13060
22	.31259	.28323	.25697	.23344	.21235	.19342	.17642	.16114	.14739	.13500
23	.31879	.28934	.26293	.23923	.21795	.19882	.18161	.16612	.15215	.13955
24	.32515	.29559	.26904	.24519	.22372	.20440	.18699	.17128	.15710	.14429
25	.33166	.30201	.27534	.25133	.22969	.21018	.19256	.17665	.16226	.14924
26	.33833	.30861	.28182	.25767	.23586	.21616	.19835	.18224	.16764	.15440
27	.34517	.31538	.28849	.26420	.24224	.22236	.20436	.18804	.17324	.15980
28	.35217	.32233	.29535	.27093	.24882	.22877	.21058	.19407	.17907	.16542
29	.35932	.32944	.30237	.27784	.25558	.23537	.21701	.20031	.18511	.17126
30	.36661	.33670	.30956	.28492	.26253	.24216	.22362	.20674	.19135	.17730
31	.37403	.34411	.31691	.29217	.26965	.24914	.23044	.21338	.19779	.18355
32	.38160	.35167	.32442	.29960	.27697	.25631	.23745	.22022	.20445	.19002
33	.38930	.35939	.33211	.30721	.28447	.26368	.24467	.22727	.21133	.19671
34	.39713	.36724	.33993	.31497	.29213	.27123	.25207	.23451	.21839	.20360
35	.40509	.37523	.34792	.32290	.29998	.27896	.25967	.24195	.22567	.21070
36	.41318	.38337	.35606	.33100	.30800	.28688	.26746	.24961	.23317	.21803
37	.42139	.39165	.36435	.33927	.31621	.29499	.27546	.25746	.24087	.22557
38	.42974	.40008	.37281	.34771	.32460	.30330	.28366	.26554	.24880	.23334
39	.43821	.40864	.38141	.35631	.33316	.31179	.29205	.27381	.25694	.24133
40	.44679	.41734	.39016	.36507	.34189	.32046	.30064	.28229	.26529	.24954
41	.45549	.42616	.39906	.37399	.35080	.32932	.30942	.29097	.27386	.25797
42	.46430	.43511	.40809	.38307	.35987	.33836	.31840	.29986	.28264	.26662
43	.47324	.44421	.41729	.39232	.36913	.34760	.32758	.30897	.29165	.27552
44	.48229	.45343	.42663	.40172	.37857	.35702	.33697	.31829	.30088	.28465
45	.49144	.46277	.43611	.41128	.38817	.36663	.34655	.32782	.31033	.29400
46	.50072	.47225	.44574	.42101	.39796	.37644	.35634	.33757	.32002	.30360
47	.51009	.48185	.45550	.43089	.40791	.38642	.36633	.34753	.32992	.31343
48	.51958	.49158	.46540	.44093	.41803	.39660	.37652	.35770	.34006	.32351
49	.52917	.50143	.47545	.45113	.42833	.40696	.38691	.36810	.35043	.33383
50	.53888	.51141	.48566	.46150	.43883	.41754	.39754	.37874	.36106	.34442
51	.54871	.52153	.49602	.47204	.44951	.42832	.40838	.38961	.37194	.35528
52	.55865	.53179	.50653	.48276	.46038	.43931	.41945	.40073	.38307	.36641
53	.56869	.54217	.51718	.49363	.47143	.45050	.43074	.41208	.39446	.37781
54	.57882	.55265	.52796	.50465	.48265	.46186	.44222	.42364	.40607	.38945
55	.58902	.56322	.53884	.51579	.49400	.47338	.45387	.43540	.41789	.40131
56	.59926	.57383	.54978	.52701	.50544	.48501	.46565	.44729	.42987	.41335
57	.60951	.58449	.56078	.53830	.51698	.49675	.47755	.45932	.44201	.42555
58	.61978	.59517	.57182	.54964	.52858	.50858	.48956	.47147	.45427	.43790
59	.63007	.60589	.58290	.56105	.54027	.52050	.50167	.48375	.46668	.45041
60	.64039	.61665	.59405	.57254	.55205	.53253	.51392	.49617	.47925	.46310
61	.65072	.62743	.60524	.58409	.56390	.54465	.52627	.50872	.49196	.47595
62	.66104	.63822	.61645	.59566	.57581	.55683	.53870	.52136	.50478	.48892
63	.67133	.64900	.62766	.60726	.58774	.56907	.55120	.53409	.51770	.50200
64	.68161	.65977	.63887	.61887	.59970	.58134	.56375	.54688	.53071	.51519
65	.69186	.67053	.65009	.63049	.61170	.59367	.57637	.55976	.54381	.52849
66	.70216	.68136	.66140	.64223	.62383	.60615	.58916	.57283	.55713	.54203
67	.71250	.69224	.67277	.65405	.63605	.61874	.60208	.58605	.57062	.55575
68	.72283	.70312	.68416	.66590	.64833	.63140	.61509	.59938	.58423	.56963
69	.73312	.71398	.69553	.67776	.66062	.64409	.62815	.61277	.59793	.58360
70	.74335	.72479	.70688	.68959	.67291	.65680	.64124	.62621	.61168	.59764
71	.75353	.73556	.71819	.70141	.68519	.66951	.65434	.63968	.62549	.61176

AGE	2.2%	2.4%	2.6%	2.8%	3.0%	3.2%	3.4%	3.6%	3.8%	4.0%
72	.76364	.74626	.72945	.71318	.69744	.68220	.66745	.65317	.63933	.62593
73	.77365	.75686	.74061	.72487	.70962	.69484	.68051	.66662	.65315	.64009
74	.78350	.76733	.75164	.73643	.72167	.70735	.69346	.67997	.66688	.65417
75	.79318	.77761	.76249	.74781	.73355	.71971	.70625	.69318	.68048	.66813
76	.80266	.78769	.77314	.75899	.74524	.73187	.71886	.70621	.69390	.68192
77	.81194	.79756	.78358	.76997	.75672	.74382	.73127	.71904	.70713	.69553
78	.82100	.80722	.79380	.78072	.76798	.75556	.74346	.73166	.72016	.70894
79	.82984	.81664	.80378	.79124	.77900	.76706	.75542	.74405	.73296	.72213
80	.83843	.82582	.81351	.80149	.78976	.77830	.76711	.75618	.74550	.73507
81	.84678	.83474	.82298	.81148	.80025	.78927	.77853	.76803	.75777	.74773
82	.85487	.84339	.83217	.82119	.81045	.79994	.78966	.77959	.76974	.76009
83	.86269	.85177	.84107	.83060	.82035	.81030	.80047	.79083	.78139	.77214
84	.87024	.85986	.84968	.83970	.82993	.82035	.81095	.80174	.79271	.78385
85	.87751	.86765	.85798	.84849	.83919	.83005	.82110	.81230	.80368	.79521
86	.88450	.87515	.86597	.85696	.84811	.83942	.83089	.82251	.81428	.80619
87	.89119	.88234	.87363	.86508	.85668	.84843	.84031	.83234	.82450	.81679
88	.89760	.88922	.88099	.87289	.86492	.85708	.84938	.84180	.83434	.82700
89	.90372	.89580	.88801	.88034	.87280	.86537	.85806	.85087	.84378	.83681
90	.90954	.90207	.89471	.88746	.88032	.87329	.86637	.85954	.85282	.84620
91	.91508	.90803	.90109	.89424	.88750	.88085	.87429	.86783	.86146	.85518
92	.92033	.91369	.90714	.90068	.89432	.88803	.88184	.87572	.86969	.86374
93	.92530	.91904	.91287	.90678	.90078	.89484	.88899	.88321	.87751	.87188
94	.92999	.92411	.91830	.91256	.90690	.90130	.89578	.89032	.88493	.87961
95	.93442	.92889	.92342	.91802	.91269	.90741	.90220	.89706	.89197	.88694
96	.93858	.93338	.92824	.92316	.91813	.91316	.90825	.90340	.89859	.89385
97	.94248	.93759	.93276	.92798	.92325	.91857	.91395	.90937	.90484	.90036
98	.94614	.94155	.93701	.93252	.92807	.92367	.91931	.91500	.91073	.90650
99	.94959	.94528	.94101	.93679	.93260	.92846	.92436	.92030	.91628	.91229
100	.95278	.94874	.94473	.94075	.93682	.93292	.92906	.92523	.92144	.91769
101	.95581	.95201	.94824	.94451	.94081	.93715	.93352	.92992	.92635	.92281
102	.95860	.95503	.95149	.94798	.94450	.94105	.93763	.93424	.93088	.92754
103	.96136	.95802	.95470	.95142	.94816	.94492	.94171	.93853	.93538	.93224
104	.96390	.96077	.95766	.95458	.95152	.94848	.94547	.94248	.93951	.93657
105	.96640	.96347	.96057	.95769	.95483	.95199	.94917	.94637	.94359	.94083
106	.96950	.96684	.96420	.96157	.95896	.95636	.95379	.95123	.94868	.94616
107	.97301	.97064	.96829	.96595	.96362	.96131	.95901	.95672	.95445	.95219
108	.97859	.97670	.97482	.97295	.97109	.96923	.96739	.96555	.96373	.96191
109	.98924	.98828	.98733	.98638	.98544	.98450	.98356	.98263	.98170	.98077

Table S
Based on Life Table 2000CM
Single Life Remainder Factors
Applicable On or After May 1, 2009

				Interest Rate					
AGE	4.2%	4.4%	4.6%	4.8%	5.0%	5.2%	5.4%	5.6%	5.8%	6.0%
0	.06083	.05483	.04959	.04501	.04101	.03749	.03441	.03170	.02931	.02721
1	.05668	.05049	.04507	.04034	.03618	.03254	.02934	.02652	.02403	.02183
2	.05858	.05222	.04665	.04178	.03750	.03373	.03042	.02750	.02492	.02264
3	.06072	.05420	.04848	.04346	.03904	.03516	.03173	.02871	.02603	.02366
4	.06303	.05634	.05046	.04530	.04075	.03674	.03319	.03006	.02729	.02483
5	.06547	.05861	.05258	.04726	.04258	.03844	.03478	.03153	.02866	.02610
6	.06805	.06102	.05482	.04935	.04453	.04026	.03647	.03312	.03014	.02749

AGE	4.2%	4.4%	4.6%	4.8%	5.0%	5.2%	5.4%	5.6%	5.8%	6.0%
7	.07074	.06353	.05717	.05155	.04658	.04217	.03826	.03479	.03171	.02895
8	.07356	.06617	.05964	.05386	.04875	.04421	.04017	.03658	.03338	.03053
9	.07651	.06895	.06225	.05631	.05105	.04637	.04220	.03849	.03518	.03222
10	.07960	.07185	.06499	.05889	.05347	.04865	.04435	.04052	.03709	.03402
11	.08283	.07490	.06786	.06160	.05603	.05106	.04663	.04267	.03912	.03594
12	.08620	.07808	.07087	.06444	.05871	.05360	.04903	.04494	.04127	.03798
13	.08967	.08137	.07397	.06738	.06149	.05623	.05152	.04729	.04351	.04010
14	.09321	.08472	.07715	.07038	.06433	.05892	.05406	.04971	.04579	.04227
15	.09680	.08812	.08036	.07342	.06721	.06164	.05664	.05214	.04810	.04445
16	.10041	.09154	.08360	.07649	.07011	.06438	.05923	.05459	.05041	.04664
17	.10409	.09502	.08689	.07960	.07305	.06716	.06185	.05707	.05276	.04886
18	.10782	.09855	.09024	.08276	.07604	.06998	.06452	.05959	.05514	.05111
19	.11164	.10217	.09366	.08600	.07910	.07288	.06726	.06218	.05758	.05341
20	.11559	.10592	.09721	.08937	.08228	.07589	.07010	.06487	.06012	.05582
21	.11965	.10977	.10087	.09283	.08557	.07900	.07305	.06765	.06276	.05831
22	.12383	.11376	.10465	.09642	.08897	.08223	.07610	.07055	.06550	.06090
23	.12817	.11789	.10859	.10016	.09252	.08559	.07930	.07358	.06837	.06363
24	.13270	.12221	.11270	.10408	.09625	.08914	.08267	.07678	.07141	.06651
25	.13744	.12674	.11703	.10821	.10019	.09289	.08625	.08018	.07465	.06960
26	.14239	.13149	.12158	.11256	.10435	.09686	.09003	.08380	.07810	.07288
27	.14758	.13647	.12636	.11714	.10873	.10106	.09405	.08764	.08177	.07639
28	.15300	.14169	.13137	.12195	.11335	.10549	.09829	.09171	.08567	.08012
29	.15864	.14712	.13660	.12698	.11819	.11013	.10275	.09598	.08977	.08406
30	.16448	.15275	.14203	.13222	.12323	.11498	.10742	.10047	.09408	.08820
31	.17053	.15861	.14769	.13768	.12849	.12006	.11230	.10517	.09860	.09255
32	.17680	.16468	.15357	.14336	.13398	.12535	.11741	.11009	.10335	.09712
33	.18330	.17099	.15968	.14927	.13970	.13088	.12275	.11525	.10832	.10192
34	.19000	.17750	.16599	.15539	.14562	.13661	.12829	.12061	.11350	.10693
35	.19692	.18423	.17253	.16174	.15178	.14258	.13408	.12621	.11892	.11217
36	.20407	.19119	.17931	.16833	.15818	.14879	.14009	.13204	.12457	.11764
37	.21144	.19838	.18631	.17515	.16481	.15523	.14635	.13811	.13046	.12335
38	.21904	.20582	.19357	.18222	.17170	.16193	.15287	.14444	.13661	.12932
39	.22687	.21348	.20105	.18952	.17882	.16887	.15962	.15102	.14300	.13554
40	.23493	.22137	.20878	.19707	.18619	.17606	.16663	.15784	.14965	.14201
41	.24322	.22950	.21674	.20487	.19381	.18350	.17390	.16493	.15656	.14873
42	.25173	.23786	.22494	.21290	.20168	.19120	.18141	.17227	.16372	.15572
43	.26049	.24648	.23342	.22122	.20982	.19918	.18922	.17990	.17118	.16301
44	.26950	.25535	.24214	.22979	.21824	.20742	.19730	.18781	.17892	.17057
45	.27874	.26447	.25112	.23862	.22692	.21595	.20566	.19600	.18694	.17843
46	.28824	.27385	.26038	.24774	.23589	.22476	.21431	.20450	.19527	.18659
47	.29798	.28349	.26989	.25712	.24513	.23386	.22326	.21328	.20390	.19505
48	.30797	.29338	.27967	.26678	.25466	.24325	.23250	.22238	.21283	.20383
49	.31822	.30355	.28974	.27674	.26449	.25294	.24206	.23179	.22210	.21294
50	.32876	.31401	.30011	.28701	.27465	.26298	.25196	.24156	.23172	.22242
51	.33958	.32477	.31079	.29759	.28513	.27335	.26221	.25168	.24170	.23226
52	.35068	.33582	.32178	.30851	.29595	.28407	.27282	.26216	.25206	.24249
53	.36206	.34717	.33308	.31974	.30710	.29513	.28378	.27301	.26279	.25309
54	.37371	.35880	.34467	.33127	.31857	.30651	.29507	.28420	.27388	.26406
55	.38559	.37067	.35652	.34308	.33032	.31820	.30668	.29572	.28529	.27537
56	.39765	.38275	.36859	.35512	.34232	.33014	.31855	.30751	.29699	.28697
57	.40990	.39502	.38086	.36739	.35455	.34233	.33068	.31957	.30898	.29887
58	.42231	.40747	.39333	.37985	.36700	.35474	.34304	.33188	.32121	.31103
59	.43490	.42011	.40600	.39253	.37968	.36740	.35567	.34446	.33374	.32348

Reg. §20.2031-7(d)(7)

AGE	4.2%	4.4%	4.6%	4.8%	5.0%	5.2%	5.4%	5.6%	5.8%	6.0%
60	.44768	.43296	.41890	.40546	.39261	.38033	.36858	.35733	.34656	.33625
61	.46064	.44600	.43200	.41860	.40578	.39351	.38175	.37048	.35968	.34933
62	.47373	.45920	.44527	.43194	.41915	.40690	.39514	.38387	.37305	.36267
63	.48696	.47253	.45870	.44544	.43271	.42049	.40876	.39749	.38666	.37625
64	.50030	.48601	.47229	.45911	.44645	.43428	.42258	.41133	.40051	.39010
65	.51377	.49963	.48603	.47295	.46037	.44827	.43662	.42540	.41460	.40420
66	.52750	.51352	.50007	.48711	.47464	.46262	.45103	.43987	.42911	.41872
67	.54144	.52765	.51436	.50154	.48919	.47727	.46578	.45468	.44397	.43363
68	.55554	.54196	.52885	.51619	.50398	.49218	.48079	.46978	.45915	.44887
69	.56976	.55640	.54349	.53102	.51896	.50731	.49603	.48513	.47458	.46438
70	.58407	.57095	.55826	.54598	.53410	.52260	.51147	.50069	.49025	.48013
71	.59848	.58561	.57316	.56109	.54940	.53808	.52710	.51646	.50615	.49614
72	.61294	.60035	.58815	.57632	.56484	.55371	.54291	.53243	.52225	.51237
73	.62741	.61512	.60318	.59160	.58035	.56943	.55882	.54851	.53849	.52876
74	.64183	.62983	.61818	.60686	.59586	.58516	.57476	.56464	.55480	.54523
75	.65612	.64444	.63309	.62204	.61129	.60083	.59065	.58074	.57109	.56169
76	.67026	.65891	.64786	.63710	.62661	.61640	.60646	.59676	.58731	.57810
77	.68423	.67321	.66248	.65201	.64181	.63186	.62215	.61269	.60345	.59444
78	.69800	.68733	.67692	.66676	.65684	.64717	.63772	.62849	.61948	.61068
79	.71156	.70124	.69116	.68132	.67170	.66230	.65312	.64414	.63537	.62680
80	.72487	.71490	.70516	.69563	.68632	.67721	.66830	.65959	.65106	.64272
81	.73791	.72830	.71890	.70970	.70069	.69188	.68325	.67481	.66654	.65844
82	.75065	.74140	.73235	.72348	.71479	.70628	.69794	.68977	.68176	.67391
83	.76308	.75419	.74548	.73695	.72858	.72037	.71232	.70443	.69669	.68909
84	.77516	.76664	.75828	.75008	.74203	.73413	.72638	.71877	.71130	.70396
85	.78689	.77873	.77072	.76285	.75512	.74753	.74008	.73275	.72556	.71849
86	.79825	.79044	.78278	.77524	.76783	.76055	.75340	.74636	.73944	.73264
87	.80921	.80176	.79443	.78722	.78014	.77316	.76630	.75956	.75292	.74638
88	.81978	.81268	.80569	.79880	.79203	.78536	.77880	.77234	.76598	.75971
89	.82994	.82317	.81651	.80995	.80349	.79712	.79085	.78467	.77859	.77259
90	.83967	.83324	.82690	.82065	.81450	.80843	.80244	.79655	.79073	.78500
91	.84898	.84288	.83685	.83091	.82505	.81928	.81358	.80795	.80241	.79693
92	.85787	.85208	.84636	.84072	.83515	.82966	.82423	.81888	.81360	.80838
93	.86632	.86083	.85541	.85006	.84477	.83955	.83440	.82931	.82428	.81931
94	.87435	.86915	.86402	.85894	.85393	.84898	.84409	.83925	.83447	.82975
95	.88197	.87705	.87219	.86739	.86265	.85795	.85331	.84872	.84419	.83970
96	.88915	.88451	.87991	.87537	.87088	.86643	.86203	.85768	.85338	.84912
97	.89593	.89154	.88720	.88290	.87865	.87444	.87028	.86616	.86208	.85804
98	.90232	.89818	.89408	.89002	.88600	.88202	.87808	.87418	.87031	.86649
99	.90835	.90444	.90057	.89674	.89294	.88918	.88546	.88177	.87811	.87449
100	.91397	.91028	.90663	.90301	.89942	.89587	.89234	.88885	.88539	.88196
101	.91930	.91583	.91238	.90897	.90558	.90223	.89890	.89560	.89233	.88908
102	.92424	.92096	.91771	.91448	.91128	.90811	.90496	.90184	.89875	.89568
103	.92914	.92605	.92300	.91996	.91695	.91397	.91100	.90806	.90514	.90225
104	.93364	.93074	.92786	.92501	.92217	.91935	.91656	.91379	.91103	.90830
105	.93809	.93537	.93266	.92998	.92731	.92467	.92204	.91943	.91683	.91426
106	.94365	.94115	.93867	.93621	.93376	.93133	.92892	.92651	.92413	.92176
107	.94994	.94771	.94549	.94328	.94108	.93890	.93673	.93457	.93242	.93028
108	.96010	.95830	.95651	.95472	.95295	.95118	.94942	.94767	.94593	.94420
109	.97985	.97893	.97801	.97710	.97619	.97529	.97438	.97348	.97259	.97170

Reg. § 20.2031-7(d)(7)

Table S
Based on Life Table 2000CM
Single Life Remainder Factors
Applicable On or After May 1, 2009

					Interest Rate					
AGE	6.2%	6.4%	6.6%	6.8%	7.0%	7.2%	7.4%	7.6%	7.8%	8.0%
0	.02534	.02370	.02223	.02093	.01978	.01874	.01782	.01699	.01625	.01559
1	.01989	.01817	.01664	.01528	.01406	.01298	.01202	.01115	.01037	.00967
2	.02061	.01882	.01722	.01580	.01454	.01340	.01239	.01148	.01066	.00993
3	.02156	.01969	.01802	.01654	.01521	.01403	.01297	.01201	.01115	.01038
4	.02264	.02069	.01896	.01741	.01602	.01478	.01367	.01267	.01176	.01095
5	.02383	.02180	.01999	.01838	.01693	.01563	.01446	.01341	.01246	.01161
6	.02512	.02301	.02113	.01944	.01793	.01657	.01535	.01424	.01325	.01235
7	.02650	.02430	.02234	.02058	.01900	.01758	.01630	.01514	.01410	.01315
8	.02798	.02570	.02365	.02182	.02017	.01868	.01734	.01613	.01503	.01404
9	.02957	.02720	.02507	.02316	.02143	.01988	.01848	.01721	.01606	.01502
10	.03128	.02881	.02659	.02460	.02280	.02118	.01971	.01838	.01718	.01608
11	.03309	.03053	.02823	.02615	.02428	.02258	.02105	.01966	.01839	.01725
12	.03503	.03237	.02997	.02781	.02585	.02408	.02248	.02103	.01971	.01850
13	.03704	.03428	.03179	.02954	.02750	.02565	.02398	.02246	.02108	.01982
14	.03909	.03623	.03364	.03130	.02918	.02726	.02551	.02392	.02248	.02116
15	.04117	.03820	.03551	.03308	.03087	.02886	.02704	.02538	.02387	.02249
16	.04324	.04016	.03737	.03484	.03254	.03046	.02855	.02682	.02524	.02379
17	.04533	.04214	.03924	.03661	.03422	.03205	.03007	.02826	.02661	.02509
18	.04746	.04415	.04114	.03841	.03592	.03366	.03159	.02970	.02798	.02639
19	.04963	.04620	.04309	.04025	.03766	.03530	.03315	.03117	.02937	.02772
20	.05191	.04835	.04512	.04217	.03948	.03702	.03478	.03272	.03083	.02910
21	.05427	.05058	.04723	.04416	.04137	.03881	.03647	.03432	.03235	.03054
22	.05672	.05291	.04943	.04625	.04334	.04067	.03823	.03599	.03394	.03205
23	.05930	.05535	.05174	.04844	.04542	.04265	.04010	.03777	.03562	.03364
24	.06204	.05795	.05421	.05078	.04764	.04476	.04211	.03967	.03743	.03536
25	.06497	.06074	.05687	.05331	.05005	.04705	.04429	.04174	.03940	.03724
26	.06811	.06373	.05972	.05603	.05264	.04952	.04665	.04400	.04155	.03929
27	.07146	.06694	.06278	.05895	.05543	.05219	.04920	.04644	.04389	.04153
28	.07503	.07036	.06605	.06209	.05844	.05507	.05196	.04908	.04642	.04396
29	.07881	.07398	.06953	.06542	.06163	.05814	.05490	.05191	.04913	.04656
30	.08279	.07780	.07319	.06894	.06502	.06138	.05802	.05491	.05202	.04933
31	.08697	.08182	.07707	.07267	.06860	.06483	.06134	.05810	.05509	.05229
32	.09137	.08606	.08115	.07660	.07239	.06848	.06485	.06148	.05835	.05543
33	.09601	.09053	.08546	.08075	.07639	.07234	.06858	.06508	.06182	.05878
34	.10084	.09520	.08996	.08511	.08059	.07640	.07249	.06886	.06547	.06231
35	.10590	.10009	.09470	.08968	.08501	.08067	.07662	.07285	.06933	.06605
36	.11120	.10522	.09966	.09448	.08966	.08517	.08098	.07706	.07341	.06999
37	.11674	.11059	.10486	.09952	.09454	.08990	.08556	.08150	.07771	.07416
38	.12254	.11621	.11032	.10481	.09968	.09487	.09039	.08618	.08225	.07856
39	.12857	.12208	.11601	.11035	.10505	.10009	.09545	.09110	.08702	.08320
40	.13487	.12820	.12196	.11613	.11067	.10555	.10076	.09626	.09204	.08807
41	.14142	.13458	.12817	.12217	.11655	.11127	.10632	.10167	.09730	.09319
42	.14823	.14122	.13464	.12848	.12269	.11725	.11214	.10734	.10282	.09856
43	.15535	.14816	.14141	.13508	.12913	.12353	.11826	.11330	.10863	.10422
44	.16274	.15538	.14847	.14196	.13585	.13008	.12466	.11954	.11472	.11016
45	.17042	.16290	.15581	.14914	.14286	.13694	.13135	.12608	.12110	.11640
46	.17842	.17073	.16348	.15664	.15020	.14411	.13836	.13293	.12780	.12294
47	.18672	.17886	.17145	.16445	.15784	.15159	.14568	.14010	.13481	.12980

Reg. § 20.2031-7(d)(7)

AGE	6.2%	6.4%	6.6%	6.8%	7.0%	7.2%	7.4%	7.6%	7.8%	8.0%
48	.19534	.18732	.17974	.17258	.16581	.15940	.15334	.14759	.14215	.13699
49	.20429	.19612	.18838	.18106	.17413	.16757	.16134	.15544	.14984	.14453
50	.21362	.20529	.19740	.18993	.18284	.17612	.16974	.16368	.15793	.15247
51	.22332	.21484	.20680	.19917	.19194	.18506	.17853	.17232	.16642	.16080
52	.23341	.22479	.21660	.20883	.20144	.19442	.18774	.18138	.17533	.16957
53	.24388	.23513	.22681	.21889	.21136	.20419	.19737	.19087	.18467	.17876
54	.25473	.24585	.23739	.22935	.22168	.21437	.20741	.20076	.19442	.18837
55	.26593	.25693	.24835	.24017	.23238	.22494	.21784	.21105	.20458	.19838
56	.27742	.26831	.25962	.25132	.24340	.23583	.22860	.22169	.21508	.20875
57	.28922	.28001	.27121	.26280	.25476	.24707	.23971	.23267	.22593	.21947
58	.30129	.29199	.28309	.27457	.26642	.25862	.25114	.24398	.23712	.23053
59	.31367	.30428	.29529	.28667	.27842	.27051	.26293	.25565	.24867	.24197
60	.32638	.31691	.30784	.29914	.29079	.28278	.27509	.26771	.26062	.25380
61	.33940	.32987	.32073	.31195	.30352	.29542	.28763	.28015	.27295	.26603
62	.35269	.34311	.33391	.32506	.31656	.30837	.30050	.29293	.28564	.27862
63	.36625	.35663	.34738	.33847	.32990	.32165	.31370	.30604	.29867	.29155
64	.38007	.37043	.36113	.35218	.34356	.33524	.32723	.31950	.31204	.30484
65	.39417	.38451	.37519	.36620	.35753	.34917	.34110	.33330	.32577	.31850
66	.40871	.39905	.38972	.38071	.37201	.36361	.35550	.34765	.34006	.33273
67	.42365	.41400	.40468	.39567	.38696	.37853	.37038	.36250	.35487	.34749
68	.43892	.42931	.42001	.41101	.40230	.39387	.38570	.37780	.37014	.36272
69	.45450	.44493	.43567	.42670	.41800	.40958	.40141	.39350	.38582	.37837
70	.47033	.46083	.45162	.44269	.43403	.42563	.41748	.40957	.40189	.39443
71	.48644	.47702	.46788	.45901	.45040	.44203	.43391	.42602	.41835	.41090
72	.50278	.49347	.48441	.47562	.46707	.45877	.45069	.44284	.43520	.42776
73	.51930	.51010	.50115	.49245	.48399	.47575	.46774	.45994	.45234	.44494
74	.53591	.52684	.51802	.50943	.50106	.49291	.48497	.47724	.46970	.46235
75	.55253	.54361	.53492	.52645	.51820	.51015	.50230	.49465	.48719	.47991
76	.56912	.56036	.55182	.54349	.53536	.52742	.51968	.51213	.50475	.49754
77	.58565	.57706	.56868	.56050	.55251	.54471	.53708	.52964	.52236	.51525
78	.60209	.59369	.58549	.57747	.56963	.56197	.55448	.54715	.53999	.53298
79	.61841	.61021	.60219	.59435	.58668	.57917	.57182	.56463	.55760	.55071
80	.63456	.62657	.61875	.61109	.60359	.59625	.58906	.58202	.57512	.56836
81	.65050	.64273	.63512	.62766	.62034	.61318	.60616	.59927	.59252	.58590
82	.66621	.65867	.65127	.64401	.63690	.62992	.62308	.61636	.60977	.60330
83	.68164	.67433	.66716	.66012	.65321	.64642	.63976	.63322	.62680	.62050
84	.69676	.68969	.68275	.67593	.66923	.66265	.65618	.64983	.64358	.63745
85	.71154	.70472	.69801	.69141	.68493	.67856	.67229	.66613	.66007	.65412
86	.72595	.71937	.71290	.70654	.70028	.69412	.68806	.68210	.67623	.67046
87	.73995	.73362	.72740	.72127	.71523	.70929	.70344	.69768	.69201	.68642
88	.75354	.74746	.74148	.73558	.72978	.72406	.71842	.71287	.70739	.70200
89	.76668	.76085	.75511	.74945	.74387	.73837	.73295	.72761	.72234	.71714
90	.77934	.77377	.76827	.76284	.75749	.75222	.74701	.74188	.73681	.73181
91	.79153	.78620	.78094	.77575	.77063	.76558	.76059	.75566	.75080	.74600
92	.80323	.79814	.79312	.78816	.78326	.77843	.77365	.76894	.76428	.75967
93	.81440	.80956	.80477	.80004	.79536	.79074	.78618	.78166	.77721	.77280
94	.82508	.82047	.81591	.81140	.80694	.80253	.79817	.79387	.78961	.78539
95	.83526	.83088	.82654	.82225	.81800	.81380	.80965	.80554	.80148	.79746
96	.84491	.84074	.83662	.83254	.82850	.82450	.82055	.81663	.81276	.80892
97	.85405	.85009	.84617	.84230	.83846	.83466	.83089	.82717	.82348	.81982
98	.86270	.85895	.85523	.85155	.84791	.84430	.84072	.83718	.83367	.83019
99	.87090	.86735	.86382	.86033	.85687	.85345	.85005	.84668	.84335	.84004

Reg. §20.2031-7(d)(7)

AGE	6.2%	6.4%	6.6%	6.8%	7.0%	7.2%	7.4%	7.6%	7.8%	8.0%
100	.87856	.87519	.87185	.86854	.86526	.86201	.85878	.85559	.85242	.84927
101	.88587	.88268	.87952	.87638	.87327	.87019	.86713	.86409	.86109	.85810
102	.89263	.88961	.88662	.88364	.88069	.87777	.87487	.87199	.86913	.86629
103	.89938	.89653	.89370	.89089	.88810	.88534	.88259	.87987	.87717	.87448
104	.90558	.90289	.90021	.89756	.89492	.89231	.88971	.88713	.88456	.88202
105	.91170	.90916	.90664	.90413	.90164	.89917	.89672	.89428	.89186	.88945
106	.91940	.91706	.91474	.91242	.91013	.90784	.90558	.90332	.90108	.89885
107	.92816	.92605	.92395	.92186	.91978	.91772	.91567	.91362	.91159	.90957
108	.94247	.94075	.93904	.93734	.93565	.93396	.93229	.93062	.92895	.92730
109	.97081	.96992	.96904	.96816	.96729	.96642	.96555	.96468	.96382	.96296

Table S
Based on Life Table 2000CM
Single Life Remainder Factors
Applicable On or After May 1, 2009

Interest Rate

AGE	8.2%	8.4%	8.6%	8.8%	9.0%	9.2%	9.4%	9.6%	9.8%	10.0%
0	.01498	.01444	.01395	.01351	.01310	.01273	.01240	.01209	.01181	.01155
1	.00904	.00847	.00796	.00749	.00707	.00668	.00633	.00601	.00572	.00545
2	.00926	.00866	.00812	.00763	.00718	.00677	.00640	.00606	.00575	.00547
3	.00968	.00905	.00848	.00796	.00748	.00705	.00666	.00630	.00597	.00567
4	.01021	.00955	.00894	.00839	.00789	.00744	.00702	.00664	.00629	.00597
5	.01083	.01013	.00949	.00891	.00839	.00790	.00746	.00706	.00669	.00635
6	.01153	.01080	.01012	.00951	.00895	.00844	.00798	.00755	.00715	.00679
7	.01229	.01151	.01081	.01016	.00957	.00903	.00854	.00808	.00767	.00728
8	.01314	.01232	.01157	.01089	.01026	.00969	.00917	.00869	.00825	.00784
9	.01407	.01321	.01242	.01170	.01104	.01044	.00989	.00938	.00891	.00848
10	.01509	.01418	.01335	.01259	.01190	.01126	.01068	.01014	.00965	.00919
11	.01620	.01525	.01437	.01358	.01285	.01218	.01156	.01099	.01047	.00998
12	.01740	.01640	.01549	.01465	.01388	.01317	.01252	.01192	.01137	.01086
13	.01867	.01762	.01665	.01577	.01496	.01422	.01353	.01290	.01231	.01177
14	.01995	.01885	.01784	.01691	.01606	.01527	.01455	.01389	.01327	.01270
15	.02123	.02007	.01901	.01803	.01714	.01632	.01556	.01485	.01420	.01360
16	.02247	.02126	.02015	.01913	.01818	.01732	.01652	.01578	.01509	.01446
17	.02371	.02244	.02127	.02020	.01921	.01830	.01746	.01668	.01596	.01529
18	.02494	.02361	.02239	.02126	.02022	.01926	.01838	.01756	.01680	.01610
19	.02620	.02480	.02352	.02234	.02125	.02024	.01931	.01844	.01764	.01690
20	.02751	.02605	.02471	.02346	.02232	.02126	.02028	.01937	.01853	.01775
21	.02888	.02735	.02593	.02463	.02343	.02231	.02128	.02032	.01944	.01861
22	.03030	.02870	.02722	.02585	.02458	.02341	.02233	.02132	.02038	.01951
23	.03181	.03013	.02858	.02714	.02581	.02458	.02344	.02237	.02139	.02047
24	.03345	.03169	.03006	.02855	.02715	.02586	.02465	.02353	.02249	.02152
25	.03524	.03340	.03169	.03010	.02863	.02727	.02600	.02482	.02373	.02270
26	.03720	.03527	.03348	.03181	.03027	.02884	.02750	.02626	.02510	.02402
27	.03934	.03732	.03544	.03370	.03208	.03057	.02916	.02786	.02664	.02549
28	.04167	.03955	.03759	.03576	.03406	.03247	.03099	.02962	.02833	.02713
29	.04417	.04196	.03990	.03798	.03619	.03453	.03298	.03153	.03017	.02890
30	.04684	.04452	.04237	.04036	.03848	.03674	.03510	.03358	.03215	.03081
31	.04969	.04727	.04501	.04291	.04094	.03911	.03739	.03579	.03428	.03287
32	.05272	.05019	.04783	.04563	.04357	.04165	.03984	.03816	.03657	.03509
33	.05595	.05331	.05085	.04854	.04639	.04437	.04248	.04070	.03904	.03748
34	.05936	.05661	.05403	.05162	.04936	.04725	.04527	.04341	.04166	.04001
35	.06297	.06010	.05741	.05489	.05253	.05032	.04824	.04629	.04445	.04272
36	.06679	.06380	.06100	.05837	.05590	.05358	.05140	.04935	.04742	.04561

Reg. §20.2031-7(d)(7)

AGE	8.2%	8.4%	8.6%	8.8%	9.0%	9.2%	9.4%	9.6%	9.8%	10.0%
37	.07083	.06771	.06479	.06204	.05947	.05704	.05476	.05261	.05059	.04868
38	.07511	.07186	.06881	.06595	.06326	.06072	.05834	.05609	.05397	.05196
39	.07961	.07623	.07306	.07007	.06726	.06462	.06212	.05977	.05754	.05544
40	.08434	.08083	.07753	.07442	.07149	.06873	.06612	.06366	.06133	.05913
41	.08932	.08568	.08225	.07901	.07596	.07308	.07035	.06778	.06534	.06304
42	.09455	.09077	.08720	.08384	.08066	.07766	.07481	.07213	.06958	.06717
43	.10007	.09615	.09245	.08895	.08564	.08251	.07955	.07674	.07408	.07156
44	.10586	.10180	.09796	.09433	.09089	.08763	.08454	.08162	.07884	.07621
45	.11195	.10774	.10376	.09999	.09642	.09303	.08982	.08677	.08387	.08112
46	.11835	.11400	.10987	.10596	.10225	.09873	.09539	.09222	.08920	.08633
47	.12505	.12055	.11629	.11224	.10839	.10474	.10126	.09796	.09482	.09182
48	.13209	.12745	.12303	.11884	.11485	.11106	.10746	.10402	.10075	.09764
49	.13948	.13469	.13013	.12579	.12167	.11774	.11400	.11043	.10703	.10379
50	.14727	.14233	.13762	.13314	.12887	.12481	.12093	.11723	.11370	.11033
51	.15546	.15037	.14551	.14089	.13648	.13228	.12826	.12443	.12077	.11726
52	.16407	.15884	.15384	.14907	.14452	.14018	.13603	.13206	.12826	.12463
53	.17312	.16774	.16260	.15769	.15300	.14852	.14423	.14012	.13620	.13243
54	.18259	.17707	.17179	.16674	.16191	.15729	.15286	.14862	.14456	.14067
55	.19247	.18680	.18139	.17620	.17123	.16648	.16192	.15755	.15335	.14933
56	.20270	.19690	.19135	.18602	.18092	.17603	.17134	.16684	.16251	.15836
57	.21329	.20736	.20167	.19622	.19099	.18596	.18114	.17650	.17205	.16777
58	.22422	.21816	.21235	.20677	.20140	.19625	.19130	.18653	.18195	.17754
59	.23553	.22935	.22341	.21770	.21221	.20693	.20185	.19696	.19225	.18772
60	.24725	.24095	.23489	.22906	.22345	.21805	.21285	.20783	.20300	.19834
61	.25937	.25296	.24679	.24084	.23511	.22959	.22427	.21914	.21419	.20941
62	.27185	.26534	.25906	.25300	.24716	.24153	.23609	.23084	.22577	.22088
63	.28469	.27808	.27169	.26553	.25959	.25384	.24830	.24294	.23776	.23275
64	.29789	.29119	.28471	.27845	.27240	.26656	.26091	.25544	.25016	.24504
65	.31148	.30468	.29812	.29177	.28563	.27969	.27394	.26837	.26299	.25777
66	.32564	.31877	.31213	.30570	.29948	.29345	.28761	.28195	.27647	.27115
67	.34034	.33341	.32671	.32021	.31391	.30780	.30188	.29614	.29057	.28517
68	.35552	.34855	.34179	.33523	.32887	.32270	.31671	.31089	.30524	.29976
69	.37115	.36414	.35734	.35073	.34432	.33809	.33204	.32616	.32045	.31489
70	.38719	.38016	.37332	.36668	.36023	.35396	.34786	.34193	.33616	.33054
71	.40366	.39662	.38977	.38311	.37663	.37032	.36419	.35821	.35240	.34674
72	.42053	.41350	.40665	.39998	.39349	.38716	.38100	.37500	.36916	.36346
73	.43774	.43073	.42389	.41723	.41074	.40441	.39824	.39222	.38636	.38063
74	.45519	.44821	.44140	.43476	.42829	.42197	.41580	.40979	.40391	.39818
75	.47280	.46587	.45910	.45250	.44605	.43975	.43360	.42759	.42173	.41599
76	.49051	.48364	.47693	.47037	.46396	.45770	.45158	.44560	.43975	.43403
77	.50830	.50150	.49486	.48836	.48201	.47580	.46972	.46377	.45795	.45225
78	.52613	.51942	.51286	.50644	.50015	.49400	.48797	.48208	.47630	.47064
79	.54396	.53736	.53089	.52456	.51835	.51227	.50632	.50048	.49476	.48915
80	.56174	.55525	.54888	.54265	.53653	.53054	.52466	.51890	.51325	.50770
81	.57941	.57305	.56681	.56068	.55467	.54878	.54299	.53731	.53174	.52627
82	.59696	.59073	.58461	.57861	.57272	.56693	.56125	.55566	.55018	.54480
83	.61430	.60822	.60224	.59637	.59061	.58494	.57937	.57389	.56851	.56322
84	.63142	.62549	.61966	.61393	.60830	.60276	.59731	.59196	.58669	.58150
85	.64825	.64249	.63682	.63124	.62575	.62035	.61503	.60980	.60465	.59958
86	.66477	.65918	.65367	.64825	.64291	.63765	.63248	.62738	.62236	.61741
87	.68092	.67550	.67016	.66490	.65972	.65462	.64959	.64463	.63975	.63493
88	.69669	.69145	.68628	.68119	.67618	.67123	.66635	.66154	.65680	.65212
89	.71201	.70696	.70198	.69706	.69221	.68742	.68270	.67805	.67345	.66892

Reg. § 20.2031-7(d)(7)

AGE	8.2%	8.4%	8.6%	8.8%	9.0%	9.2%	9.4%	9.6%	9.8%	10.0%
90	.72688	.72201	.71721	.71246	.70779	.70317	.69861	.69411	.68966	.68528
91	.74126	.73658	.73196	.72739	.72289	.71844	.71404	.70970	.70541	.70117
92	.75513	.75063	.74620	.74181	.73748	.73320	.72897	.72479	.72066	.71657
93	.76844	.76414	.75988	.75568	.75152	.74741	.74334	.73932	.73535	.73142
94	.78123	.77711	.77303	.76901	.76502	.76108	.75718	.75332	.74951	.74573
95	.79348	.78954	.78565	.78179	.77798	.77421	.77047	.76677	.76312	.75950
96	.80513	.80137	.79765	.79397	.79032	.78671	.78314	.77960	.77610	.77263
97	.81621	.81262	.80908	.80556	.80208	.79864	.79522	.79184	.78849	.78517
98	.82674	.82333	.81995	.81660	.81328	.80999	.80673	.80351	.80031	.79713
99	.83677	.83352	.83030	.82711	.82395	.82082	.81771	.81463	.81158	.80855
100	.84616	.84307	.84001	.83697	.83396	.83097	.82801	.82507	.82216	.81927
101	.85514	.85221	.84930	.84641	.84355	.84070	.83788	.83509	.83231	.82956
102	.86348	.86069	.85792	.85517	.85245	.84974	.84706	.84439	.84175	.83912
103	.87182	.86918	.86655	.86395	.86136	.85880	.85625	.85372	.85121	.84872
104	.87950	.87699	.87450	.87203	.86957	.86713	.86471	.86231	.85992	.85755
105	.88706	.88468	.88232	.87998	.87765	.87534	.87304	.87076	.86849	.86624
106	.89664	.89444	.89225	.89008	.88792	.88577	.88364	.88152	.87941	.87731
107	.90756	.90557	.90358	.90160	.89964	.89768	.89574	.89380	.89188	.88997
108	.92565	.92401	.92238	.92075	.91914	.91753	.91592	.91433	.91274	.91116
109	.96211	.96125	.96041	.95956	.95872	.95788	.95704	.95620	.95537	.95455

Table S
Based on Life Table 2000CM
Single Life Remainder Factors
Applicable On or After May 1, 2009

Interest Rate

AGE	10.2%	10.4%	10.6%	10.8%	11.0%	11.2%	11.4%	11.6%	11.8%	12.0%
0	.01132	.01110	.01089	.01071	.01053	.01037	.01022	.01008	.00995	.00983
1	.00520	.00497	.00476	.00457	.00439	.00423	.00407	.00393	.00379	.00367
2	.00521	.00496	.00474	.00454	.00435	.00417	.00401	.00385	.00371	.00358
3	.00539	.00513	.00490	.00468	.00447	.00429	.00411	.00395	.00380	.00366
4	.00567	.00540	.00515	.00492	.00470	.00450	.00432	.00414	.00398	.00383
5	.00603	.00574	.00547	.00523	.00500	.00478	.00459	.00440	.00423	.00407
6	.00646	.00615	.00587	.00560	.00536	.00513	.00492	.00472	.00453	.00436
7	.00693	.00660	.00630	.00602	.00576	.00551	.00529	.00508	.00488	.00469
8	.00747	.00712	.00680	.00650	.00622	.00596	.00572	.00549	.00528	.00509
9	.00808	.00771	.00737	.00705	.00675	.00648	.00622	.00598	.00576	.00555
10	.00877	.00838	.00801	.00767	.00736	.00707	.00679	.00654	.00630	.00608
11	.00954	.00912	.00873	.00838	.00804	.00773	.00744	.00717	.00692	.00668
12	.01038	.00994	.00953	.00915	.00880	.00847	.00816	.00788	.00761	.00735
13	.01127	.01081	.01038	.00998	.00960	.00925	.00893	.00862	.00833	.00806
14	.01217	.01168	.01122	.01080	.01040	.01003	.00969	.00937	.00906	.00878
15	.01305	.01253	.01205	.01160	.01118	.01079	.01042	.01008	.00976	.00946
16	.01387	.01333	.01282	.01234	.01190	.01149	.01110	.01074	.01040	.01009
17	.01467	.01409	.01356	.01306	.01259	.01216	.01175	.01137	.01101	.01067
18	.01544	.01484	.01427	.01374	.01325	.01279	.01236	.01195	.01157	.01122
19	.01621	.01557	.01497	.01442	.01390	.01341	.01295	.01253	.01213	.01175
20	.01702	.01634	.01571	.01512	.01457	.01406	.01357	.01312	.01270	.01230
21	.01784	.01713	.01646	.01584	.01526	.01471	.01420	.01372	.01327	.01285
22	.01870	.01794	.01724	.01658	.01596	.01539	.01485	.01434	.01386	.01342
23	.01961	.01881	.01807	.01737	.01672	.01611	.01554	.01500	.01449	.01402
24	.02062	.01977	.01899	.01825	.01756	.01691	.01630	.01573	.01520	.01469
25	.02175	.02085	.02002	.01924	.01851	.01782	.01718	.01657	.01600	.01547

AGE	10.2%	10.4%	10.6%	10.8%	11.0%	11.2%	11.4%	11.6%	11.8%	12.0%
26	.02301	.02207	.02119	.02036	.01958	.01886	.01817	.01753	.01692	.01635
27	.02443	.02343	.02250	.02162	.02080	.02003	.01930	.01862	.01798	.01737
28	.02600	.02495	.02396	.02303	.02216	.02134	.02057	.01985	.01916	.01852
29	.02771	.02660	.02555	.02457	.02365	.02278	.02197	.02120	.02047	.01979
30	.02956	.02838	.02728	.02624	.02526	.02434	.02348	.02266	.02189	.02116
31	.03155	.03031	.02914	.02804	.02701	.02604	.02512	.02425	.02344	.02266
32	.03370	.03239	.03115	.02999	.02890	.02787	.02690	.02598	.02511	.02429
33	.03601	.03463	.03333	.03210	.03095	.02985	.02883	.02785	.02693	.02606
34	.03847	.03701	.03564	.03434	.03312	.03197	.03088	.02985	.02887	.02795
35	.04109	.03956	.03811	.03675	.03546	.03424	.03308	.03199	.03096	.02998
36	.04390	.04228	.04076	.03932	.03795	.03667	.03545	.03429	.03320	.03216
37	.04688	.04518	.04358	.04206	.04062	.03926	.03798	.03676	.03560	.03450
38	.05007	.04829	.04660	.04500	.04349	.04205	.04069	.03940	.03818	.03701
39	.05346	.05158	.04981	.04812	.04653	.04502	.04358	.04222	.04092	.03969
40	.05705	.05508	.05321	.05144	.04976	.04817	.04666	.04522	.04385	.04255
41	.06086	.05879	.05683	.05497	.05320	.05152	.04993	.04841	.04697	.04559
42	.06488	.06271	.06066	.05870	.05684	.05508	.05340	.05180	.05028	.04882
43	.06917	.06690	.06474	.06269	.06074	.05888	.05711	.05543	.05382	.05229
44	.07370	.07132	.06906	.06691	.06486	.06291	.06105	.05928	.05759	.05598
45	.07850	.07602	.07365	.07139	.06924	.06719	.06524	.06338	.06160	.05990
46	.08360	.08100	.07852	.07616	.07390	.07176	.06970	.06775	.06587	.06409
47	.08897	.08626	.08367	.08120	.07884	.07659	.07443	.07238	.07041	.06853
48	.09466	.09183	.08912	.08654	.08407	.08172	.07946	.07730	.07524	.07326
49	.10069	.09774	.09492	.09222	.08964	.08717	.08481	.08255	.08038	.07831
50	.10711	.10403	.10109	.09827	.09558	.09300	.09053	.08816	.08589	.08371
51	.11392	.11072	.10765	.10472	.10191	.09921	.09663	.09415	.09178	.08950
52	.12116	.11783	.11464	.11159	.10866	.10585	.10315	.10057	.09808	.09569
53	.12883	.12538	.12206	.11889	.11584	.11291	.11010	.10740	.10481	.10231
54	.13694	.13336	.12992	.12662	.12345	.12041	.11748	.11467	.11196	.10936
55	.14547	.14176	.13820	.13478	.13149	.12832	.12528	.12235	.11953	.11682
56	.15437	.15054	.14685	.14330	.13989	.13661	.13345	.13040	.12747	.12464
57	.16365	.15969	.15588	.15221	.14868	.14527	.14199	.13883	.13578	.13284
58	.17330	.16921	.16528	.16149	.15783	.15431	.15091	.14763	.14447	.14141
59	.18335	.17914	.17508	.17117	.16739	.16375	.16023	.15684	.15356	.15039
60	.19385	.18952	.18534	.18131	.17741	.17365	.17001	.16650	.16311	.15982
61	.20480	.20035	.19605	.19189	.18788	.18400	.18025	.17662	.17311	.16971
62	.21615	.21158	.20717	.20290	.19877	.19477	.19090	.18716	.18354	.18003
63	.22791	.22323	.21870	.21431	.21007	.20596	.20198	.19812	.19439	.19077
64	.24009	.23530	.23066	.22616	.22181	.21758	.21349	.20953	.20568	.20195
65	.25271	.24781	.24306	.23846	.23400	.22967	.22547	.22139	.21744	.21360
66	.26600	.26100	.25615	.25145	.24688	.24245	.23814	.23396	.22990	.22596
67	.27992	.27483	.26989	.26509	.26043	.25590	.25150	.24722	.24306	.23901
68	.29443	.28926	.28423	.27934	.27459	.26997	.26548	.26110	.25685	.25271
69	.30950	.30424	.29914	.29417	.28934	.28463	.28005	.27559	.27125	.26703
70	.32508	.31976	.31459	.30955	.30464	.29986	.29520	.29067	.28625	.28194
71	.34122	.33585	.33062	.32552	.32054	.31570	.31097	.30637	.30187	.29749
72	.35790	.35249	.34721	.34205	.33703	.33213	.32734	.32268	.31812	.31367
73	.37505	.36960	.36428	.35909	.35403	.34908	.34425	.33953	.33492	.33042
74	.39258	.38711	.38177	.37655	.37145	.36647	.36160	.35684	.35219	.34764
75	.41039	.40491	.39956	.39432	.38921	.38420	.37931	.37452	.36983	.36525
76	.42843	.42296	.41760	.41236	.40724	.40222	.39731	.39250	.38779	.38318

Reg. §20.2031-7(d)(7)

AGE	10.2%	10.4%	10.6%	10.8%	11.0%	11.2%	11.4%	11.6%	11.8%	12.0%
77	.44668	.44122	.43588	.43065	.42552	.42050	.41559	.41077	.40605	.40143
78	.46510	.45967	.45435	.44914	.44403	.43902	.43411	.42930	.42458	.41995
79	.48365	.47826	.47298	.46780	.46271	.45773	.45284	.44804	.44333	.43871
80	.50226	.49693	.49169	.48655	.48150	.47655	.47169	.46692	.46224	.45763
81	.52090	.51562	.51044	.50536	.50036	.49546	.49064	.48590	.48125	.47668
82	.53951	.53431	.52920	.52418	.51924	.51439	.50963	.50494	.50033	.49580
83	.55802	.55291	.54788	.54294	.53808	.53329	.52859	.52396	.51941	.51493
84	.57640	.57139	.56645	.56159	.55681	.55210	.54747	.54291	.53843	.53401
85	.59459	.58968	.58484	.58008	.57539	.57077	.56623	.56175	.55733	.55298
86	.61254	.60774	.60302	.59836	.59377	.58925	.58479	.58040	.57607	.57180
87	.63019	.62551	.62090	.61635	.61187	.60745	.60309	.59880	.59456	.59038
88	.64751	.64296	.63847	.63405	.62968	.62537	.62112	.61693	.61279	.60871
89	.66444	.66003	.65567	.65137	.64712	.64293	.63880	.63471	.63068	.62670
90	.68094	.67667	.67244	.66827	.66415	.66009	.65607	.65210	.64818	.64431
91	.69699	.69285	.68877	.68473	.68074	.67680	.67291	.66906	.66526	.66150
92	.71254	.70855	.70460	.70071	.69685	.69304	.68928	.68555	.68187	.67823
93	.72753	.72369	.71989	.71613	.71242	.70874	.70510	.70150	.69794	.69442
94	.74200	.73830	.73464	.73103	.72745	.72390	.72040	.71693	.71350	.71010
95	.75591	.75236	.74885	.74538	.74194	.73853	.73516	.73182	.72851	.72524
96	.76920	.76580	.76243	.75909	.75579	.75252	.74928	.74607	.74289	.73974
97	.78188	.77863	.77540	.77220	.76904	.76590	.76279	.75971	.75665	.75363
98	.79399	.79088	.78779	.78473	.78170	.77869	.77571	.77276	.76983	.76693
99	.80555	.80257	.79962	.79670	.79380	.79092	.78807	.78525	.78244	.77966
100	.81641	.81357	.81075	.80796	.80518	.80243	.79971	.79700	.79432	.79165
101	.82683	.82412	.82144	.81877	.81612	.81350	.81089	.80831	.80574	.80320
102	.83652	.83394	.83137	.82882	.82630	.82379	.82130	.81883	.81637	.81394
103	.84624	.84379	.84135	.83892	.83652	.83413	.83176	.82941	.82707	.82475
104	.85519	.85285	.85053	.84822	.84593	.84365	.84139	.83915	.83692	.83470
105	.86400	.86178	.85957	.85737	.85519	.85302	.85087	.84873	.84660	.84449
106	.87523	.87316	.87110	.86905	.86702	.86500	.86299	.86099	.85900	.85703
107	.88806	.88617	.88429	.88242	.88055	.87870	.87686	.87502	.87320	.87139
108	.90958	.90802	.90646	.90490	.90336	.90182	.90028	.89876	.89724	.89573
109	.95372	.95290	.95208	.95126	.95045	.94964	.94883	.94803	.94723	.94643

Table S
Based on Life Table 2000CM
Single Life Remainder Factors
Applicable On or After May 1, 2009

Interest Rate

AGE	12.2%	12.4%	12.6%	12.8%	13.0%	13.2%	13.4%	13.6%	13.8%	14.0%
0	.00972	.00961	.00951	.00941	.00932	.00924	.00916	.00908	.00901	.00894
1	.00355	.00345	.00334	.00325	.00316	.00307	.00299	.00292	.00285	.00278
2	.00346	.00334	.00323	.00313	.00303	.00294	.00286	.00278	.00270	.00263
3	.00353	.00340	.00329	.00318	.00307	.00298	.00289	.00280	.00272	.00264
4	.00369	.00356	.00343	.00332	.00321	.00310	.00300	.00291	.00283	.00274
5	.00392	.00377	.00364	.00352	.00340	.00329	.00318	.00308	.00299	.00290
6	.00420	.00405	.00391	.00377	.00365	.00353	.00342	.00331	.00321	.00311
7	.00452	.00436	.00421	.00406	.00393	.00380	.00368	.00357	.00346	.00336
8	.00490	.00473	.00457	.00441	.00427	.00413	.00400	.00388	.00376	.00365
9	.00535	.00517	.00499	.00483	.00467	.00453	.00439	.00426	.00413	.00402
10	.00587	.00567	.00548	.00531	.00514	.00499	.00484	.00470	.00456	.00444
11	.00645	.00624	.00605	.00586	.00568	.00551	.00536	.00521	.00506	.00493
12	.00711	.00689	.00668	.00648	.00629	.00611	.00595	.00579	.00563	.00549

AGE	12.2%	12.4%	12.6%	12.8%	13.0%	13.2%	13.4%	13.6%	13.8%	14.0%
13	.00781	.00757	.00735	.00714	.00694	.00675	.00657	.00640	.00624	.00609
14	.00851	.00826	.00802	.00780	.00759	.00739	.00720	.00702	.00684	.00668
15	.00918	.00891	.00866	.00842	.00820	.00799	.00779	.00759	.00741	.00724
16	.00979	.00950	.00924	.00899	.00875	.00853	.00832	.00811	.00792	.00774
17	.01035	.01006	.00978	.00951	.00926	.00902	.00880	.00859	.00838	.00819
18	.01088	.01057	.01027	.00999	.00973	.00948	.00924	.00901	.00880	.00860
19	.01139	.01106	.01075	.01045	.01017	.00990	.00965	.00942	.00919	.00898
20	.01192	.01157	.01124	.01092	.01063	.01035	.01008	.00983	.00959	.00936
21	.01245	.01208	.01173	.01139	.01108	.01078	.01050	.01023	.00998	.00974
22	.01300	.01260	.01222	.01187	.01154	.01122	.01092	.01064	.01037	.01011
23	.01357	.01315	.01275	.01238	.01202	.01168	.01137	.01106	.01078	.01051
24	.01422	.01377	.01334	.01294	.01257	.01221	.01187	.01155	.01124	.01095
25	.01496	.01448	.01403	.01361	.01320	.01282	.01246	.01212	.01180	.01149
26	.01582	.01531	.01483	.01438	.01395	.01354	.01316	.01279	.01244	.01211
27	.01680	.01626	.01575	.01527	.01481	.01437	.01396	.01357	.01320	.01285
28	.01791	.01734	.01679	.01628	.01579	.01533	.01489	.01447	.01408	.01370
29	.01914	.01853	.01795	.01740	.01688	.01639	.01592	.01548	.01505	.01465
30	.02048	.01982	.01921	.01862	.01807	.01754	.01704	.01657	.01612	.01569
31	.02193	.02124	.02058	.01996	.01937	.01881	.01828	.01777	.01729	.01683
32	.02351	.02278	.02208	.02142	.02079	.02019	.01962	.01908	.01857	.01808
33	.02523	.02445	.02371	.02300	.02234	.02170	.02109	.02052	.01997	.01944
34	.02707	.02624	.02545	.02470	.02399	.02331	.02267	.02205	.02146	.02091
35	.02905	.02817	.02733	.02653	.02577	.02505	.02436	.02371	.02308	.02249
36	.03117	.03024	.02935	.02850	.02769	.02693	.02619	.02550	.02483	.02419
37	.03345	.03246	.03151	.03061	.02976	.02894	.02816	.02742	.02671	.02603
38	.03590	.03485	.03385	.03289	.03198	.03112	.03029	.02950	.02874	.02802
39	.03852	.03740	.03634	.03533	.03436	.03344	.03256	.03172	.03092	.03015
40	.04131	.04013	.03900	.03793	.03690	.03593	.03499	.03410	.03324	.03242
41	.04428	.04303	.04184	.04070	.03962	.03858	.03759	.03664	.03573	.03486
42	.04744	.04612	.04486	.04366	.04250	.04140	.04035	.03934	.03838	.03745
43	.05083	.04943	.04810	.04683	.04561	.04444	.04333	.04226	.04123	.04025
44	.05443	.05296	.05155	.05021	.04892	.04768	.04650	.04537	.04428	.04324
45	.05827	.05672	.05523	.05381	.05245	.05114	.04989	.04869	.04754	.04643
46	.06237	.06074	.05917	.05767	.05623	.05485	.05352	.05225	.05103	.04986
47	.06673	.06500	.06335	.06177	.06025	.05879	.05739	.05605	.05475	.05351
48	.07137	.06955	.06781	.06614	.06454	.06300	.06152	.06010	.05874	.05742
49	.07632	.07441	.07258	.07082	.06913	.06750	.06595	.06444	.06300	.06161
50	.08162	.07962	.07769	.07584	.07407	.07236	.07071	.06913	.06760	.06614
51	.08731	.08520	.08318	.08124	.07937	.07757	.07583	.07416	.07256	.07101
52	.09340	.09119	.08907	.08703	.08507	.08317	.08135	.07959	.07790	.07627
53	.09991	.09760	.09538	.09324	.09118	.08919	.08728	.08543	.08365	.08193
54	.10685	.10443	.10211	.09987	.09771	.09562	.09361	.09167	.08980	.08799
55	.11420	.11168	.10925	.10690	.10464	.10246	.10035	.09832	.09635	.09445
56	.12191	.11928	.11675	.11430	.11193	.10965	.10745	.10531	.10325	.10126
57	.13001	.12727	.12462	.12207	.11960	.11721	.11491	.11268	.11052	.10843
58	.13846	.13561	.13286	.13020	.12762	.12513	.12273	.12040	.11814	.11595
59	.14732	.14436	.14150	.13873	.13605	.13346	.13095	.12851	.12616	.12388
60	.15665	.15358	.15060	.14772	.14494	.14224	.13962	.13709	.13463	.13225
61	.16642	.16324	.16016	.15717	.15428	.15147	.14875	.14611	.14355	.14107
62	.17663	.17333	.17014	.16704	.16404	.16113	.15830	.15556	.15290	.15031
63	.18726	.18385	.18055	.17734	.17423	.17121	.16828	.16544	.16267	.15999
64	.19833	.19481	.19140	.18809	.18487	.18175	.17871	.17576	.17289	.17010

Reg. § 20.2031-7(d)(7)

AGE	12.2%	12.4%	12.6%	12.8%	13.0%	13.2%	13.4%	13.6%	13.8%	14.0%
65	.20987	.20624	.20273	.19931	.19598	.19275	.18961	.18656	.18358	.18069
66	.22213	.21840	.21478	.21125	.20783	.20449	.20125	.19809	.19501	.19202
67	.23508	.23125	.22753	.22390	.22037	.21694	.21360	.21034	.20716	.20407
68	.24868	.24476	.24094	.23722	.23359	.23006	.22662	.22327	.22000	.21681
69	.26291	.25889	.25498	.25117	.24745	.24383	.24030	.23685	.23349	.23020
70	.27773	.27364	.26964	.26574	.26194	.25823	.25461	.25107	.24762	.24425
71	.29321	.28904	.28496	.28099	.27710	.27331	.26961	.26599	.26246	.25900
72	.30933	.30508	.30094	.29689	.29294	.28907	.28530	.28160	.27799	.27446
73	.32602	.32171	.31751	.31340	.30938	.30545	.30160	.29784	.29416	.29056
74	.34319	.33884	.33458	.33042	.32634	.32236	.31845	.31463	.31089	.30723
75	.36076	.35637	.35207	.34786	.34374	.33970	.33575	.33188	.32808	.32437
76	.37867	.37425	.36991	.36567	.36151	.35744	.35344	.34953	.34569	.34192
77	.39690	.39245	.38810	.38383	.37964	.37554	.37151	.36756	.36369	.35989
78	.41541	.41096	.40659	.40231	.39811	.39398	.38993	.38596	.38206	.37823
79	.43418	.42973	.42536	.42107	.41686	.41272	.40866	.40467	.40075	.39691
80	.45311	.44868	.44432	.44003	.43582	.43169	.42763	.42363	.41971	.41585
81	.47219	.46777	.46343	.45916	.45497	.45084	.44679	.44280	.43888	.43502
82	.49135	.48696	.48265	.47841	.47424	.47014	.46610	.46213	.45822	.45437
83	.51052	.50618	.50191	.49771	.49357	.48950	.48549	.48154	.47766	.47383
84	.52966	.52537	.52115	.51700	.51291	.50887	.50490	.50099	.49714	.49334
85	.54870	.54448	.54032	.53622	.53218	.52820	.52428	.52041	.51660	.51284
86	.56759	.56344	.55935	.55532	.55135	.54742	.54356	.53974	.53598	.53227
87	.58626	.58219	.57818	.57422	.57031	.56646	.56266	.55891	.55521	.55155
88	.60468	.60070	.59677	.59290	.58907	.58529	.58157	.57788	.57425	.57066
89	.62277	.61888	.61505	.61126	.60753	.60383	.60018	.59658	.59302	.58950
90	.64048	.63670	.63296	.62927	.62563	.62202	.61846	.61494	.61146	.60803
91	.65778	.65411	.65048	.64689	.64334	.63983	.63636	.63293	.62954	.62619
92	.67462	.67106	.66754	.66406	.66061	.65720	.65383	.65050	.64720	.64393
93	.69094	.68749	.68408	.68071	.67737	.67406	.67079	.66756	.66435	.66118
94	.70673	.70340	.70011	.69685	.69362	.69042	.68725	.68412	.68102	.67794
95	.72199	.71878	.71560	.71246	.70934	.70625	.70319	.70016	.69716	.69419
96	.73662	.73353	.73047	.72743	.72443	.72145	.71850	.71557	.71268	.70981
97	.75063	.74766	.74471	.74180	.73890	.73604	.73319	.73038	.72758	.72482
98	.76405	.76120	.75837	.75557	.75279	.75003	.74730	.74459	.74190	.73923
99	.77690	.77417	.77146	.76877	.76610	.76345	.76083	.75822	.75564	.75308
100	.78901	.78639	.78379	.78121	.77866	.77612	.77360	.77110	.76862	.76616
101	.80067	.79816	.79568	.79321	.79076	.78832	.78591	.78351	.78114	.77877
102	.81152	.80912	.80674	.80438	.80203	.79970	.79738	.79508	.79280	.79054
103	.82245	.82016	.81789	.81563	.81339	.81116	.80895	.80676	.80458	.80241
104	.83250	.83031	.82814	.82599	.82384	.82171	.81960	.81750	.81541	.81334
105	.84239	.84030	.83823	.83617	.83412	.83209	.83006	.82806	.82606	.82407
106	.85507	.85311	.85117	.84924	.84733	.84542	.84352	.84164	.83976	.83790
107	.86958	.86779	.86600	.86422	.86246	.86070	.85895	.85721	.85548	.85376
108	.89422	.89272	.89123	.88974	.88826	.88679	.88533	.88386	.88241	.88096
109	.94563	.94484	.94405	.94326	.94248	.94170	.94092	.94014	.93937	.93860

Reg. § 20.2031-7(d)(7)

Table 2000CM

Age x	l_x	Age x	l_x	Age x	l_x
0	100000	37	96921	74	66882
1	99305	38	96767	75	64561
2	99255	39	96600	76	62091
3	99222	40	96419	77	59476
4	99197	41	96223	78	56721
5	99176	42	96010	79	53833
6	99158	43	95782	80	50819
7	99140	44	95535	81	47694
8	99124	45	95268	82	44475
9	99110	46	94981	83	41181
10	99097	47	94670	84	37837
11	99085	48	94335	85	34471
12	99073	49	93975	86	31114
13	99057	50	93591	87	27799
14	99033	51	93180	88	24564
15	98998	52	92741	89	21443
16	98950	53	92270	90	18472
17	98891	54	91762	91	15685
18	98822	55	91211	92	13111
19	98745	56	90607	93	10773
20	98664	57	89947	94	8690
21	98577	58	89225	95	6871
22	98485	59	88441	96	5315
23	98390	60	87595	97	4016
24	98295	61	86681	98	2959
25	98202	62	85691	99	2122
26	98111	63	84620	100	1477
27	98022	64	83465	101	997
28	97934	65	82224	102	650
29	97844	66	80916	103	410
30	97750	67	79530	104	248
31	97652	68	78054	105	144
32	97549	69	76478	106	81
33	97441	70	74794	107	43
34	97324	71	73001	108	22
35	97199	72	71092	109	11
36	97065	73	69056	110	0

(e) *Effective/applicability dates.*—This section applies on and after May 1, 2009. [Reg. §20.2031-7.]

☐ [*T.D.* 8540, 6-10-94. *Amended by T.D.* 8819, 4-29-99; *T.D.* 8886, 6-9-2000; *T.D.* 9448, 5-1-2009 *and T.D.* 9540, 8-9-2011.]

[Reg. §20.2031-7A]

§20.2031-7A. Valuation of annuities, interests for life or term of years, and remainder or reversionary interests for estates of decedents for which the valuation date of the gross estate is before May 1, 2009.—(a) *Valuation of annuities, interests for life or term of years, and remainder or reversionary interests for estates of decedents for which the valuation date of the gross estate is before January 1, 1952.*—Except as otherwise provided in §20.2031-7(b), if the valuation date of the decedent's gross estate is before January 1, 1952, the present value of annuities, life estates, terms for years, remainders, and reversions is their present value determined under this section. If the valuation of the interest involved is dependent upon the continuation or termination of one or more lives or upon a term certain concurrent with one or more lives, the factor for the present value is computed on the basis of interest at the rate of 4 percent a year, compounded annually, and life contingencies as to each life involved from values that are based on the Actuaries' or Combined Experience Table of Mortality, as extended. This table and related factors are described in former § 81.10 (as contained in the 26 CFR Part 81 edition revised as of April 1, 1958). The present value of an interest measured by a term of years is computed on the basis of interest at the rate of 4 percent a year.

(b) *Valuation of annuities, interests for life or term of years, and remainder or reversionary interests for estates of decedents for which the valuation date of the gross estate is after December 31, 1951, and before January 1, 1971.*—Except as otherwise provided in § 20.2031-7(b), if the valuation date for the decedent's gross estate is after December 31, 1951, and before January 1, 1971, the present value of annuities, life estates, terms of years, remainders, and reversions is their present value determined under this section. If the valuation of the interest involved is dependent upon the continuation or termination of one or more lives, or upon a term certain concurrent with one or more lives, the factor for the present value is computed on the basis of interest at the rate of 3 1/2 percent a year, compounded annually, and life contingencies as to each life involved are taken from U.S. Life Table 38. This table and related factors are set forth in former § 20.2031-7 (as contained in the 26 CFR Part 20 edition revised as of April 1, 1984). Special factors involving one and two lives may be found in or computed with the use of tables contained in the publication entitled "Actuarial Values for Estate and Gift Tax," Internal Revenue Service Publication Number 11 (Rev. 5-59). This publication is no longer available for purchase from the Superintendent of Documents. However, it may be obtained by requesting a copy from: CC:DOM:CORP:T:R (IRS Publication 11), room 5228, Internal Revenue Service, POB 7604, Ben Franklin Station, Washington, DC 20044. The present value of an interest measured by a term of years is computed on the basis of interest at the rate of 3 1/2 percent a year.

(c) *Valuation of annuities, interests for life or term of years, and remainder or reversionary interests for estates of decedents for which the valuation date of the gross estate is after December 31, 1970, and before December 1, 1983.*—Except as otherwise provided in § 20.2031-7(b), if the valuation date of the decedent's gross estate is after December 31, 1970, and before December 1, 1983, the present value of annuities, life estates, terms of years, remainders, and reversions is their present value determined under this section. If the valuation of the interest involved is dependent upon the continuation of or termination of one or more lives or upon a term certain concurrent with one or more lives, the factor for the present value is computed on the basis of interest at the rate of 6 percent a year, compounded annually, and life contingencies are determined as to each male and female life involved, from values that are set forth in Table LN. Table LN contains values that are taken from the life table for total males and

the life table for total females appearing as Tables 2 and 3, respectively, in United States Life Tables: 1959-1960, published by the Department of Health and Human Services, Public Health Service. Table LN and related factors are set forth in former § 20.2031-10 (as contained in the 26 CFR Part 20 edition revised as of April 1, 1994 (see FEGT ¶ 6435)). Special factors involving one and two lives may be found in or computed with the use of tables contained in Internal Revenue Service Publication 723, "Actuarial Values I: Valuation of Last Survivor Charitable Remainders," (12-70), and Internal Revenue Service Publication 723A, "Actuarial Values II: Factors at 6 Percent Involving One and Two Lives," (12-70). These publications are no longer available for purchase from the Superintendent of Documents. However, a copy of each may be obtained from: CC:DOM:CORP:T:R (IRS Publication 723/723A), room 5228, Internal Revenue Service, POB 7604, Ben Franklin Station, Washington, DC 20044.

(d) *Valuation of annuities, interests for life or term of years, and remainder or reversionary interests for estates of decedents for which the valuation date of the gross estate is after November 30, 1983, and before May 1, 1989.*—(1) MDULIn general.—(i) Except as otherwise provided in § 20.2031-7(b), if the decedent died after November 30, 1983, and the valuation date for the gross estate is before May 1, 1989, the fair market value of annuities, life estates, terms of years, remainders, and reversions is their present value determined under this section. If the decedent died after November 30, 1983, and before August 9, 1984, or, in cases where the valuation date of the decedent's gross estate is before May 1, 1989, if, on December 1, 1983, the decedent was mentally incompetent so that the disposition of the decedent's property could not be changed, and the decedent died on or after December 1, 1983, without having regained competency to dispose of the decedent's property, or if the decedent died within 90 days of the date on which the decedent first regained competency, the fair market value of annuities, life estates, terms for years, remainders, and reversions included in the gross estate of such decedent is their present value determined under either this section or § 20.2031-7A(c), at the option of the taxpayer. The value of annuities issued by companies regularly engaged in their sale, and of insurance policies on the lives of persons other than decedent, is determined under § 20.2031-8. The fair market value of a remainder interest in a charitable remainder unitrust, as defined in § 1.664-3 of this chapter, is its present value determined under § 1.664-4 of this chapter. The fair market value of a life interest or term for years in a charitable remainder unitrust is the fair market value of the property as of the date of valuation less the fair market value of the remainder interest on such date determined under § 1.664-4 of this chapter. The fair market value of the interests in a pooled income fund, as defined in

58,566
                  Gross Estate
See p. 20,601 for regulations not amended to reflect law changes

§ 1.642(c)-5 of this chapter, is their value determined under § 1.642(c)-6 of this chapter.

    (ii) The present value of an annuity, life estate, remainder, or reversion determined under this section which is dependent on the continuation or termination of the life of one person is computed by the use of Table A in paragraph (d)(6) of this section. The present value of an annuity, term for years, remainder, or reversion dependent on a term certain is computed by the use of Table B in paragraph (d)(6) of this section. If the interest to be valued is dependent upon more than one life or there is a term certain concurrent with one or more lives, see paragraph (d)(5) of this section. For purposes of the computations described in this section, the age of a person is to be taken as the age of that person at his or her nearest birthday.

    (iii) In all examples set forth in this section, the decedent is assumed to have died on or after August 9, 1984, with the valuation date of the decedent's gross estate before May 1, 1989, and to have been competent to change the disposition of the property on December 1, 1983.

    (2) *Annuities.*—(i) If an annuity is payable annually at the end of each year during the life of an individual (as for example if the first payment is due one year after the decedent's death), the amount payable annually is multiplied by the figure in column 2 of Table A opposite the number of years in column 1 nearest the age of the individual whose life measures the duration of the annuity. If the annuity is payable annually at the end of each year for a definite number of years, the amount payable annually is multiplied by the figure in column 2 of Table B opposite the number of years in column 1 representing the duration of the annuity. The application of this paragraph (d)(2)(i) may be illustrated by the following examples:

    Example (1). The decedent received, under the terms of the decedent's father's will an annuity of $10,000 a year payable annually for the life of the decedent's elder brother. At the time the decedent died, an annual payment had just been made. The brother at the decedent's death was 40 years eight months old. By reference to Table A, the figure in column 2 opposite 41 years, the number nearest to the brother's actual age, is found to be 9.1030. The present value of the annuity at the date of the decedent's death is, therefore, $91,030 ($10,000 × 9.1030).

    Example (2). The decedent was entitled to receive an annuity of $10,000 a year payable annually throughout a term certain. At the time the decedent died, the annual payment had just been made and five more annual payments were still to be made. By reference to Table B, it is found that the figure in column 2 opposite five years is 3.7908. The present value of the annuity is, therefore, $37,908 ($10,000 × 3.7908).

    (ii) If an annuity is payable at the end of semiannual, quarterly, monthly, or weekly periods during the life of an individual (as for example if the first payment is due one month after the decedent's death), the aggregate amount to be paid within a year is first multiplied by the figure in column 2 of Table A opposite the number of years in column 1 nearest the age of the individual whose life measures the duration of the annuity. The product so obtained is then multiplied by whichever of the following factors is appropriate:

1.0244 for semiannual payments,

1.0368 for quarterly payments,

1.0450 for monthly payments,

1.0482 for weekly payments.

If the annuity is payable at the end of semiannual, quarterly, monthly or weekly periods for a definite number of years, the aggregate amount to be paid within a year is first multiplied by the figure in column 2 of Table B opposite the number of years in column 1 representing the duration of the annuity. The product so obtained is then multiplied by whichever of the above factors is appropriate. The application of this paragraph (d)(2)(ii) may be illustrated by the following example.

    Example. The facts are the same as those contained in example (1) set forth in paragraph (d)(2)(i) of this section, except that the annuity is payable semiannually. The aggregate annual amount, $10,000, is multiplied by the factor 9.1030 and the product multiplied by 1.0244. The present value of the annuity at the date of the decedent's death is, therefore, $93,251.13 ($10,000 × 9.1030 × 1.0244).

    (iii)(A) If the first payment of an annuity for the life of an individual is due at the beginning of the annual or other payment period rather than at the end (as for example if the first payment is to be made immediately after the decedent's death), the value of the annuity is the sum of (A) the first payment plus (B) the present value of a similar annuity, the first payment of which is not to be made until the end of the payment period, determined as provided in paragraphs (d)(2)(i) or (ii) of this section, the application of this paragraph (d)(2)(iii)(A) may be illustrated by the following example:

    Example. The decedent was entitled to receive an annuity of $50 a month during the life of another person. The decedent died on the date the payment was due. At the date of the decedent's death, the person whose life measures the duration of the annuity was 50 years of age. The value of the annuity at the date of the decedent's death is $50 plus the product of $50 × 12 × 8.4743 (see Table A) × 1.0450 (See paragraph (d)(2)(ii) of this section). That is $50 plus $5,313.39, or $5,363.39.

    (B) If the first payment of an annuity for a definite number of years is due at the beginning of the annual or other payment period, the applicable factor is the product of the factor shown in Table B multiplied by whichever of the following factors is appropriate:

1.1000 for annual payments,
1.0744 for semiannual payments,
1.0618 for quarterly payments,
1.0534 for monthly payments,
1.0502 for weekly payments.

The application of this paragraph (d)(2)(iii)(B) may be illustrated by the following example:

Example. The decedent was the beneficiary of an annuity of $50 a month. On the day a payment was due, the decedent died. There were 300 payments to be made, including the payment due. The value of the annuity as of the date of decedent's death is the product of $50 × 12 × 9.0770 (see Table B) × 1.0534, or $5,737.03.

(3) *Life estates and terms for years.*—If the interest to be valued is the right of a person for his or her life, or for the life of another person, to receive the income of certain property or to use nonincome-producing property, the value of the interest is the value of the property multiplied by the figure in column 3 of Table A opposite the number of years nearest to the actual age of the measuring life. If the interest to be valued is the right to receive income of property or to use nonincome-producing property for a term of years, column 3 of Table B is used. The application of this paragraph (d)(3) may be illustrated by the following example:

Example. The decedent or the decedent's estate was entitled to receive the income from a fund of $50,000 during the life of the decedent's elder brother. Upon the brother's death, the remainder is to go to B. The brother was 31 years, five months old at the time of the decedent's death. By reference to Table A the figure in column 3 opposite 31 years is found to be 0.95254. The present value of the decedent's interest is, therefore, $47,627 ($50,000 × 0.95254).

(4) *Remainders or reversionary interests.*—If a decedent had, at the time of the decedent's death, a remainder or a reversionary interest in property to take effect after an estate for the life of another, the present value of the decedent's interest is obtained by multiplying the value of the property by the figure in column 4 of Table A opposite the number of years nearest to the actual age of the person whose life measures the preceding estate. If the remainder or reversion is to take effect at the end of the term for years,

column 4 of Table B is used. The application of this paragraph (d)(4) may be illustrated by the following example:

Example. The decedent was entitled to receive certain property worth $50,000 upon the death of the decedent's elder sister, to whom the income was bequeathed for life. At the time of the decedent's death, the elder sister was 31 years five months old. By reference to Table A the figure in column 4 opposite 31 years is found to be .04746. The present value of the remainder interest at the date of the decedent's death is, therefore, $2,373 ($50,000 × .04746).

(5) *Actuarial computation by the Internal Revenue Service.*—If the valuation of the interest involved is dependent upon the continuation or the termination of more than one life or upon a term certain concurrent with one or more lives a special factor must be used. The factor is to be computed on the basis of interest at the rate of 10 percent a year, compounded annually, and life contingencies determined, as to each person involved, from the values of $1x$ that are set forth in column 2 of Table LN of paragraph (d)(6). Table LN contains values of lx taken from the life table for the total population appearing as Table 1 of United States Life Tables: 1969-71, published by the Department of Health and Human Services, Public Health Service. Many special factors involving one and two lives may be found in or computed with the use of the tables contained in Internal Revenue Service Publication 723E, "Actuarial Values II: Factors at 10 Percent Involving One and Two Lives," (12-83). This publication is no longer available for purchase from the Superintendent of Documents. However, it may be obtained by requesting a copy from: CC:DOM:CORP:T:R (IRS Publication 723E), room 5228, Internal Revenue Service, POB 7604, Ben Franklin Station, Washington, DC 20044. However, if a special factor is required in the case of an actual decedent, the Commission will furnish the factor to the executor upon request. The request must be accompanied by a statement of the date of birth of each person, the duration of whose life may affect the value of interest, and by copies of the relevant instruments. Special factors are not furnished for prospective transfers.

(6) *Tables.*—The following tables shall be used in the application of the provisions of this section:

TABLE A

TABLE A—SINGLE LIFE, UNISEX, 10 PERCENT—TABLE SHOWING THE PRESENT WORTH OF AN ANNUITY, OF A LIFE ESTATE, AND A REMAINDER INTEREST—APPLICABLE FOR TRANSFERS AFTER NOVEMBER 30, 1983, AND BEFORE MAY 1, 1989

Age (1)	Annuity (2)	Life Estate (3)	Remainder (4)	Age (1)	Annuity (2)	Life Estate (3)	Remainder (4)
0	9.7188	.97188	.02812	55	8.0046	.80046	.19954
1	9.8988	.98988	.01012	56	7.9006	.79006	.20994
2	9.9017	.99017	.00983	57	7.7931	.77931	.22069
3	9.9008	.99008	.00992	58	7.6822	.76822	.23178
4	9.8981	.98981	.01019	59	7.5675	.75675	.24325
5	9.8938	.98938	.01062	60	7.4491	.74491	.25509
6	9.8884	.98884	.01116	61	7.3267	.73267	.26733
7	9.8822	.98822	.01178	62	7.2002	.72002	.27998
8	9.8748	.98748	.01252	63	7.0696	.70696	.29304
9	9.8663	.98663	.01337	64	6.9352	.69352	.30648
10	9.8565	.98565	.01435	65	6.7970	.67970	.32030
11	9.8453	.98453	.01547	66	6.6551	.66551	.33449
12	9.8329	.98329	.01671	67	6.5098	.65098	.34902
13	9.8198	.98198	.01802	68	6.3610	.63610	.36390
14	9.8066	.98066	.01934	69	6.2086	.62086	.37914
15	9.7937	.97937	.02063	70	6.0522	.60522	.39478
16	9.7815	.97815	.02185	71	5.8914	.58914	.41086
17	9.7700	.97700	.02300	72	5.7261	.57261	.42739
18	9.7590	.97590	.02410	73	5.5571	.55571	.44429
19	9.7480	.97480	.02520	74	5.3862	.53862	.46138
20	9.7365	.97365	.02635	75	5.2149	.52149	.47851
21	9.7245	.97245	.02755	76	5.0441	.50441	.49559
22	9.7120	.97120	.02880	77	4.8742	.48742	.51258
23	9.6986	.96986	.03014	78	4.7049	.47049	.52951
24	9.6841	.96841	.03159	79	4.5357	.45357	.54643
25	9.6678	.96678	.03322	80	4.3659	.43659	.56341
26	9.6495	.96495	.03505	81	4.1967	.41967	.58033
27	9.6290	.96290	.03710	82	4.0295	.40295	.59705
28	9.6062	.96062	.03938	83	3.8642	.38642	.61358
29	9.5813	.95813	.04187	84	3.6998	.36998	.63002
30	9.5543	.95543	.04457	85	3.5359	.35359	.64641
31	9.5254	.95254	.04746	86	3.3764	.33764	.66236
32	9.4942	.94942	.05058	87	3.2262	.32262	.67738
33	9.4608	.94608	.05392	88	3.0859	.30859	.69141
34	9.4250	.94250	.05750	89	2.9526	.29526	.70474
35	9.3868	.93868	.06132	90	2.8221	.28221	.71779
36	9.3460	.93460	.06540	91	2.6955	.26955	.73045
37	9.3026	.93026	.06974	92	2.5771	.25771	.74229
38	9.2567	.92567	.07433	93	2.4692	.24692	.75308
39	9.2083	.92083	.07917	94	2.3728	.23728	.76272
40	9.1571	.91571	.08429	95	2.2887	.22887	.77113
41	9.1030	.91030	.08970	96	2.2181	.22181	.77819
42	9.0457	.90457	.09543	97	2.1550	.21550	.78450
43	8.9855	.89855	.10145	98	2.1000	.21000	.79000
44	8.9221	.89221	.10779	99	2.0486	.20486	.79514
45	8.8558	.88558	.11442	100	1.9975	.19975	.80025
46	8.7863	.87863	.12137	101	1.9532	.19532	.80468
47	8.7137	.87137	.12863	102	1.9054	.19054	.80946
48	8.6374	.86374	.13626	103	1.8437	.18437	.81563
49	8.5578	.85578	.14422	104	1.7856	.17856	.82144
50	8.4743	.84743	.15257	105	1.6962	.16962	.83038
51	8.3874	.83874	.16126	106	1.5488	.15488	.84512
52	8.2969	.82969	.17031	107	1.3409	.13409	.86591
53	8.2028	.82028	.17972	108	1.0068	.10068	.89932
54	8.1054	.81054	.18946	109	0.4545	.04545	.95455

TABLE B

TABLE B—TERM CERTAIN, UNISEX, 10 PERCENT—TABLE SHOWING THE PRESENT WORTH OF AN ANNUITY FOR A TERM CERTAIN, OF AN INCOME INTEREST FOR A TERM CERTAIN, AND OF A REMAINDER INTEREST POSTPONED FOR A TERM CERTAIN—APPLICABLE FOR TRANSFERS AFTER NOVEMBER 30, 1983, AND BEFORE MAY 1, 1989

(1) Number of Years	(2) Annuity	(3) Term Certain	(4) Remainder	(1) Number of Years	(2) Annuity	(3) Term Certain	(4) Remainder
1	0.9091	.090909	.909091	31	9.4790	.947901	.052099
2	1.7355	.173554	.826446	32	9.5264	.952638	.047362
3	2.4869	.248685	.751315	33	9.5694	.956943	.043057
4	3.1699	.316987	.683013	34	9.6086	.960857	.039143
5	3.7908	.379079	.620921	35	9.6442	.964416	.035584
6	4.3553	.435526	.564474	36	9.6765	.967651	.032349
7	4.8684	.486842	.513158	37	9.7059	.970592	.029408
8	5.3349	.533493	.466507	38	9.7327	.973265	.026735
9	5.7590	.575902	.424098	39	9.7570	.975686	.024304
10	6.1446	.614457	.385543	40	9.7791	.977905	.022095
11	6.4951	.649506	.350494	41	9.7991	.979914	.020096
12	6.8137	.681369	.318631	42	9.8174	.981740	.018260
13	7.1034	.710336	.289664	43	9.8340	.983400	.016600
14	7.3667	.736669	.263331	44	9.8491	.984909	.015091
15	7.6061	.760608	.239392	45	9.8628	.986281	.013718
16	7.8237	.782371	.217629	46	9.8753	.987528	.012472
17	8.0216	.802155	.197845	47	9.8866	.988662	.011338
18	8.2014	.820141	.179859	48	9.8969	.989693	.010307
19	8.3649	.836492	.163508	49	9.9063	.990630	.009370
20	8.5136	.851356	.148644	50	9.9148	.991481	.008519
21	8.6487	.864869	.135131	51	9.9226	.992256	.007744
22	8.7715	.877154	.122846	52	9.9296	.992960	.007040
23	8.8832	.888322	.111678	53	9.9360	.993600	.006400
24	8.9847	.898474	.101526	54	9.9418	.994182	.005818
25	9.0770	.907704	.092296	55	9.9471	.994711	.005289
26	9.1609	.916095	.083905	56	9.9519	.995191	.004809
27	9.2372	.923722	.076278	57	9.9563	.995629	.004371
28	9.3066	.930657	.069343	58	9.9603	.996026	.003974
29	9.3696	.936961	.063039	59	9.9639	.996387	.003613
30	9.4269	.942691	.057309	60	9.9672	.996716	.003284

TABLE LN

TABLE LN—APPLICABLE FOR TRANSFERS AFTER NOVEMBER 30, 1983, AND BEFORE MAY 1, 1989

Age X (1)	lx (2)	Age X (1)	lx (2)	Age X (1)	lx (2)	Age X (1)	lx (2)	Age X (1)	lx (2)	Age X (1)	lx (2)
0	100000	19	96846	38	93843	57	83103	76	46946	95	2786
1	97998	20	96716	39	93593	58	81988	77	44101	96	2068
2	97876	21	96580	40	93322	59	80798	78	41192	97	1511
3	97792	22	96438	41	93028	60	79529	79	38245	98	1087
4	97724	23	96292	42	92712	61	78181	80	35285	99	772
5	97668	24	96145	43	92368	62	76751	81	32323	100	542
6	97619	25	96000	44	91995	63	75236	82	29375	101	375
7	97573	26	95859	45	91587	64	73631	83	26469	102	257
8	97531	27	95721	46	91144	65	71933	84	23638	103	175
9	97494	28	95586	47	90662	66	70139	85	20908	104	117
10	97460	29	95448	48	90142	67	68246	86	18282	105	78
11	97430	30	95307	49	89579	68	66254	87	15769	106	52
12	97401	31	95158	50	88972	69	64166	88	13407	107	34
13	97367	32	95003	51	88315	70	61984	89	11240	108	22
14	97322	33	94840	52	87605	71	59715	90	9297	109	14
15	97261	34	94666	53	86838	72	57360	91	7577	110	0
16	97181	35	94482	54	86007	73	54913	92	6070		
17	97083	36	94285	55	85110	74	52363	93	4773		
18	96970	37	94073	56	84142	75	49705	94	3682		

(e) *Valuation of annuities, interests for life or term of years, and remainder or reversionary interests for estates of decedents for which the valuation date of the gross estate is after April 30,1989, and before May 1, 1999.*—(1) *In general.*—Except as otherwise provided in § 20.2031-7(b) and § 20.7520-3(b) (pertaining to certain limitations on the use of prescribed tables), if the valuation date for the gross estate of the decedent is after April 30, 1989, and before May 1, 1999, the fair market value of annuities, life estates, terms of years, remainders, and reversionary interests is the present value of the interests determined by use of standard or special section 7520 actuarial factors and the valuation methodology described in § 20.2031-7(d). These factors are derived by using the appropriate section 7520 interest rate and, if applicable, the mortality component for the valuation date of the interest that is being valued. See §§ 20.7520-1 through 20.7520-4. See paragraph (e)(4) of this section for determination of the appropriate table for use in valuing these interests.

(2) *Transitional rule.*—(i) If the valuation date is after April 30, 1989, and before June 10, 1994, a taxpayer can rely on Notice 89-24 (1989-1 C.B. 660), or Notice 89-60 (1989-1 C.B. 700). See § 601.601(d)(2)(ii)(b) of this chapter.

(ii) If a decedent dies after April 30, 1989, and if on May 1, 1989, the decedent was mentally incompetent so that the disposition of the decedent's property could not be changed, and the decedent dies without having regained competency to dispose of the decedent's property or dies within 90 days of the date on which the decedent first regains competency, the fair market value of annuities, life estates, terms for years, remainders, and reversions included in the gross estate of the decedent is their present value determined either under this section or under the corresponding section applicable at the time the decedent became mentally incompetent, at the option of the decedent's executor. For example, see paragraph (d) of this section.

(3) *Publications and actuarial computations by the Internal Revenue Service.*—Many standard actuarial factors not included in paragraph (e)(4) of this section or in § 20.2031-7(d)(6) are included in Internal Revenue Service Publication 1457, "Actuarial Values, Alpha Volume," (8-89). Publication 1457 also includes examples that illustrate how to compute many special factors for more unusual situations. Publication 1457 is no longer available for purchase from the Superintendent of Documents, United States Government Printing Office, Washington, DC 20402. However, pertinent factors in this publication may be obtained from: CC:DOM:CORP:R (IRS Publication 1457), room 5226, Internal Revenue Service, POB 7604, Ben Franklin Station, Washington, DC 20044. If a special factor is required in the case of an actual decedent, the Internal Revenue Service may furnish the factor to the executor upon a request for a ruling. The request for a ruling must be accompanied by a recitation of the facts including a statement of the date of birth for each measuring life, the date of the decedent's death, any other applicable dates, and a copy of the will, trust, or other relevant documents. A request for a ruling must comply with the instructions for requesting a ruling published periodically in the Internal Revenue Bulletin (see §§ 601.201 and 601.601(d)(2)(ii)(b) of this chapter) and include payment of the required user fee.

(4) *Actuarial tables.*—Except as provided in § 20.7520-3(b) (pertaining to certain limitations on the use of prescribed tables), Life Table 80CNSMT and Table S (Single life remainder factors applicable where the valuation date is after April 30, 1989, and before May 1, 1999), contained in this paragraph (e)(4), and Table B, Table J, and Table K set forth in § 20.2031-7(d)(6) must be used in the application of the provisions of this section when the section 7520 interest rate component is between 4.2 and 14 percent. Table S and Table 80CNSMT are as follows:

TABLE S
BASED ON LIFE TABLE 80CNSMT
SINGLE LIFE REMAINDER FACTORS
APPLICABLE AFTER APRIL 30, 1989,
AND BEFORE MAY 1, 1999
INTEREST RATE

AGE	4.2%	4.4%	4.6%	4.8%	5.0%	5.2%	5.4%	5.6%	5.8%	6.0%
0	.07389	.06749	.06188	.05695	.05261	.04879	.04541	.04243	.03978	.03744
1	.06494	.05832	.05250	.04738	.04287	.03889	.03537	.03226	.02950	.02705
2	.06678	.05999	.05401	.04874	.04410	.03999	.03636	.03314	.03028	.02773
3	.06897	.06200	.05587	.05045	.04567	.04143	.03768	.03435	.03139	.02875
4	.07139	.06425	.05796	.05239	.04746	.04310	.03922	.03578	.03271	.02998
5	.07401	.06669	.06023	.05451	.04944	.04494	.04094	.03738	.03421	.03137
6	.07677	.06928	.06265	.05677	.05156	.04692	.04279	.03911	.03583	.03289
7	.07968	.07201	.06521	.05918	.05381	.04903	.04477	.04097	.03757	.03453
8	.08274	.07489	.06792	.06172	.05621	.05129	.04689	.04297	.03945	.03630
9	.08597	.07794	.07079	.06443	.05876	.05370	.04917	.04511	.04148	.03821
10	.08936	.08115	.07383	.06730	.06147	.05626	.05159	.04741	.04365	.04027
11	.09293	.08453	.07704	.07035	.06436	.05900	.05419	.04988	.04599	.04250
12	.09666	.08807	.08040	.07354	.06739	.06188	.05693	.05248	.04847	.04486
13	.10049	.09172	.08387	.07684	.07053	.06487	.05977	.05518	.05104	.04731
14	.10437	.09541	.08738	.08017	.07370	.06788	.06263	.05791	.05364	.04978
15	.10827	.09912	.09090	.08352	.07688	.07090	.06551	.06064	.05623	.05225
16	.11220	.10285	.09445	.08689	.08008	.07394	.06839	.06337	.05883	.05472
17	.11615	.10661	.09802	.09028	.08330	.07699	.07129	.06612	.06144	.05719
18	.12017	.11043	.10165	.09373	.08656	.08009	.07422	.06890	.06408	.05969
19	.12428	.11434	.10537	.09726	.08992	.08327	.07724	.07177	.06679	.06226
20	.12850	.11836	.10919	.10089	.09337	.08654	.08035	.07471	.06959	.06492
21	.13282	.12248	.11311	.10462	.09692	.08991	.08355	.07775	.07247	.06765
22	.13728	.12673	.11717	.10848	.10059	.09341	.08686	.08090	.07546	.07049
23	.14188	.13113	.12136	.11248	.10440	.09703	.09032	.08418	.07858	.07345
24	.14667	.13572	.12575	.11667	.10839	.10084	.09395	.08764	.08187	.07659
25	.15167	.14051	.13034	.12106	.11259	.10486	.09778	.09130	.08536	.07991
26	.15690	.14554	.13517	.12569	.11703	.10910	.10184	.09518	.08907	.08346
27	.16237	.15081	.14024	.13056	.12171	.11359	.10614	.09930	.09302	.08724
28	.16808	.15632	.14555	.13567	.12662	.11831	.11068	.10366	.09720	.09125
29	.17404	.16208	.15110	.14104	.13179	.12329	.11547	.10827	.10163	.09551
30	.18025	.16808	.15692	.14665	.13721	.12852	.12051	.11313	.10631	.10002
31	.18672	.17436	.16300	.15255	.14291	.13403	.12584	.11827	.11127	.10480
32	.19344	.18090	.16935	.15870	.14888	.13980	.13142	.12367	.11650	.10985
33	.20044	.18772	.17598	.16514	.15513	.14587	.13730	.12936	.12201	.11519
34	.20770	.19480	.18287	.17185	.16165	.15221	.14345	.13533	.12780	.12080
35	.21522	.20215	.19005	.17884	.16846	.15883	.14989	.14159	.13388	.12670
36	.22299	.20974	.19747	.18609	.17552	.16571	.15660	.14812	.14022	.13287
37	.23101	.21760	.20516	.19360	.18286	.17288	.16358	.15492	.14685	.13933
38	.23928	.22572	.21311	.20139	.19048	.18032	.17085	.16201	.15377	.14607
39	.24780	.23409	.22133	.20945	.19837	.18804	.17840	.16939	.16097	.15310
40	.25658	.24273	.22982	.21778	.20654	.19605	.18624	.17706	.16847	.16043
41	.26560	.25163	.23858	.22639	.21499	.20434	.19436	.18502	.17627	.16806
42	.27486	.26076	.24758	.23525	.22370	.21289	.20276	.19326	.18434	.17597
43	.28435	.27013	.25683	.24436	.23268	.22172	.21143	.20177	.19270	.18416
44	.29407	.27975	.26633	.25373	.24191	.23081	.22038	.21057	.20134	.19265
45	.30402	.28961	.27608	.26337	.25142	.24019	.22962	.21966	.21028	.20144
46	.31420	.29970	.28608	.27326	.26120	.24983	.23913	.22904	.21951	.21053
47	.32460	.31004	.29632	.28341	.27123	.25975	.24892	.23870	.22904	.21991
48	.33521	.32058	.30679	.29379	.28151	.26992	.25897	.24862	.23883	.22957

AGE	4.2%	4.4%	4.6%	4.8%	5.0%	5.2%	5.4%	5.6%	5.8%	6.0%
49	.34599	.33132	.31746	.30438	.29201	.28032	.26926	.25879	.24888	.23949
50	.35695	.34224	.32833	.31518	.30273	.29094	.27978	.26921	.25918	.24966
51	.36809	.35335	.33940	.32619	.31367	.30180	.29055	.27987	.26973	.26010
52	.37944	.36468	.35070	.33744	.32486	.31292	.30158	.29081	.28057	.27083
53	.39098	.37622	.36222	.34892	.33629	.32429	.31288	.30203	.29170	.28186
54	.40269	.38794	.37393	.36062	.34795	.33590	.32442	.31349	.30308	.29316
55	.41457	.39985	.38585	.37252	.35983	.34774	.33621	.32522	.31474	.30473
56	.42662	.41194	.39796	.38464	.37193	.35981	.34824	.33720	.32666	.31658
57	.43884	.42422	.41028	.39697	.38426	.37213	.36053	.34945	.33885	.32872
58	.45123	.43668	.42279	.40951	.39682	.38468	.37307	.36196	.35132	.34114
59	.46377	.44931	.43547	.42224	.40958	.39745	.38584	.37471	.36405	.35383
60	.47643	.46206	.44830	.43513	.42250	.41040	.39880	.38767	.37699	.36674
61	.48916	.47491	.46124	.44814	.43556	.42350	.41192	.40080	.39012	.37985
62	.50196	.48783	.47427	.46124	.44874	.43672	.42518	.41408	.40340	.39314
63	.51480	.50081	.48736	.47444	.46201	.45006	.43856	.42749	.41684	.40658
64	.52770	.51386	.50054	.48773	.47540	.46352	.45208	.44105	.43043	.42019
65	.54069	.52701	.51384	.50115	.48892	.47713	.46577	.45480	.44422	.43401
66	.55378	.54029	.52727	.51472	.50262	.49093	.47965	.46876	.45824	.44808
67	.56697	.55368	.54084	.52845	.51648	.50491	.49373	.48293	.47248	.46238
68	.58026	.56717	.55453	.54231	.53049	.51905	.50800	.49729	.48694	.47691
69	.59358	.58072	.56828	.55624	.54459	.53330	.52238	.51179	.50154	.49160
70	.60689	.59427	.58205	.57021	.55874	.54762	.53683	.52638	.51624	.50641
71	.62014	.60778	.59578	.58415	.57287	.56193	.55131	.54100	.53099	.52126
72	.63334	.62123	.60948	.59808	.58700	.57624	.56579	.55563	.54577	.53617
73	.64648	.63465	.62315	.61198	.60112	.59056	.58029	.57030	.56059	.55113
74	.65961	.64806	.63682	.62590	.61527	.60492	.59485	.58504	.57550	.56620
75	.67274	.66149	.65054	.63987	.62948	.61936	.60950	.59990	.59053	.58140
76	.68589	.67495	.66429	.65390	.64377	.63390	.62427	.61487	.60570	.59676
77	.69903	.68841	.67806	.66796	.65811	.64849	.63910	.62993	.62097	.61223
78	.71209	.70182	.69179	.68199	.67242	.66307	.65393	.64501	.63628	.62775
79	.72500	.71507	.70537	.69588	.68660	.67754	.66867	.65999	.65151	.64321
80	.73768	.72809	.71872	.70955	.70058	.69180	.68320	.67479	.66655	.65849
81	.75001	.74077	.73173	.72288	.71422	.70573	.69741	.68926	.68128	.67345
82	.76195	.75306	.74435	.73582	.72746	.71926	.71123	.70335	.69562	.68804
83	.77346	.76491	.75654	.74832	.74026	.73236	.72460	.71699	.70952	.70219
84	.78456	.77636	.76831	.76041	.75265	.74503	.73756	.73021	.72300	.71592
85	.79530	.78743	.77971	.77212	.76466	.75733	.75014	.74306	.73611	.72928
86	.80560	.79806	.79065	.78337	.77621	.76917	.76225	.75544	.74875	.74216
87	.81535	.80813	.80103	.79404	.78717	.78041	.77375	.76720	.76076	.75442
88	.82462	.81771	.81090	.80420	.79760	.79111	.78472	.77842	.77223	.76612
89	.83356	.82694	.82043	.81401	.80769	.80147	.79533	.78929	.78334	.77747
90	.84225	.83593	.82971	.82357	.81753	.81157	.80570	.79991	.79420	.78857
91	.85058	.84455	.83861	.83276	.82698	.82129	.81567	.81013	.80466	.79927
92	.85838	.85263	.84696	.84137	.83585	.83040	.82503	.81973	.81449	.80933
93	.86557	.86009	.85467	.84932	.84405	.83884	.83370	.82862	.82360	.81865
94	.87212	.86687	.86169	.85657	.85152	.84653	.84160	.83673	.83192	.82717
95	.87801	.87298	.86801	.86310	.85825	.85345	.84872	.84404	.83941	.83484
96	.88322	.87838	.87360	.86888	.86420	.85959	.85502	.85051	.84605	.84165
97	.88795	.88328	.87867	.87411	.86961	.86515	.86074	.85639	.85208	.84782
98	.89220	.88769	.88323	.87883	.87447	.87016	.86589	.86167	.85750	.85337
99	.89612	.89176	.88745	.88318	.87895	.87478	.87064	.86656	.86251	.85850
100	.89977	.89555	.89136	.88722	.88313	.87908	.87506	.87109	.86716	.86327
101	.90326	.89917	.89511	.89110	.88712	.88318	.87929	.87543	.87161	.86783
102	.90690	.90294	.89901	.89513	.89128	.88746	.88369	.87995	.87624	.87257
103	.91076	.90694	.90315	.89940	.89569	.89200	.88835	.88474	.88116	.87760
104	.91504	.91138	.90775	.90415	.90058	.89704	.89354	.89006	.88661	.88319
105	.92027	.91681	.91337	.90996	.90658	.90322	.89989	.89659	.89331	.89006
106	.92763	.92445	.92130	.91816	.91506	.91197	.90890	.90586	.90284	.89983
107	.93799	.93523	.93249	.92977	.92707	.92438	.92170	.91905	.91641	.91378
108	.95429	.95223	.95018	.94814	.94611	.94409	.94208	.94008	.93809	.93611
109	.97985	.97893	.97801	.97710	.97619	.97529	.97438	.97348	.97259	.97170

Reg. §20.2031-7A(e)(4)

TABLE S
BASED ON LIFE TABLE 80CNSMT
SINGLE LIFE REMAINDER FACTORS
APPLICABLE AFTER APRIL 30, 1989,
AND BEFORE MAY 1, 1999
INTEREST RATE

AGE	6.2%	6.4%	6.6%	6.8%	7.0%	7.2%	7.4%	7.6%	7.8%	8.0%
0	.03535	.03349	.03183	.03035	.02902	.02783	.02676	.02579	.02492	.02413
1	.02486	.02292	.02119	.01963	.01824	.01699	.01587	.01486	.01395	.01312
2	.02547	.02345	.02164	.02002	.01857	.01727	.01609	.01504	.01408	.01321
3	.02640	.02429	.02241	.02073	.01921	.01785	.01662	.01552	.01451	.01361
4	.02753	.02535	.02339	.02163	.02005	.01863	.01735	.01619	.01514	.01418
5	.02883	.02656	.02453	.02269	.02105	.01956	.01822	.01700	.01590	.01490
6	.03026	.02790	.02578	.02387	.02215	.02060	.01919	.01792	.01677	.01572
7	.03180	.02935	.02714	.02515	.02336	.02174	.02027	.01894	.01773	.01664
8	.03347	.03092	.02863	.02656	.02469	.02300	.02146	.02007	.01881	.01766
9	.03528	.03263	.03025	.02810	.02615	.02438	.02278	.02133	.02000	.01880
10	.03723	.03449	.03201	.02977	.02774	.02590	.02423	.02271	.02133	.02006
11	.03935	.03650	.03393	.03160	.02949	.02757	.02583	.02424	.02279	.02147
12	.04160	.03865	.03598	.03356	.03136	.02936	.02755	.02589	.02438	.02299
13	.04394	.04088	.03811	.03560	.03331	.03123	.02934	.02761	.02603	.02458
14	.04629	.04312	.04025	.03764	.03527	.03311	.03113	.02933	.02768	.02617
15	.04864	.04536	.04238	.03968	.03721	.03496	.03290	.03103	.02930	.02773
16	.05099	.04759	.04451	.04170	.03913	.03679	.03466	.03270	.03090	.02926
17	.05333	.04982	.04662	.04370	.04104	.03861	.03638	.03434	.03247	.03075
18	.05570	.05207	.04875	.04573	.04296	.04044	.03812	.03599	.03404	.03225
19	.05814	.05438	.05095	.04781	.04494	.04231	.03990	.03769	.03565	.03378
20	.06065	.05677	.05321	.04996	.04698	.04424	.04173	.03943	.03731	.03535
21	.06325	.05922	.05554	.05217	.04907	.04623	.04362	.04122	.03901	.03697
22	.06594	.06178	.05797	.05447	.05126	.04831	.04559	.04309	.04078	.03865
23	.06876	.06446	.06051	.05688	.05355	.05048	.04766	.04505	.04265	.04042
24	.07174	.06729	.06321	.05945	.05599	.05281	.04987	.04715	.04465	.04233
25	.07491	.07031	.06609	.06219	.05861	.05530	.05224	.04941	.04680	.04438
26	.07830	.07355	.06918	.06515	.06142	.05799	.05481	.05187	.04915	.04662
27	.08192	.07702	.07250	.06832	.06446	.06090	.05759	.05454	.05170	.04906
28	.08577	.08071	.07603	.07171	.06772	.06402	.06059	.05740	.05445	.05170
29	.08986	.08464	.07981	.07534	.07120	.06736	.06380	.06049	.05742	.05456
30	.09420	.08882	.08383	.07921	.07492	.07095	.06725	.06381	.06061	.05763
31	.09881	.09327	.08812	.08335	.07891	.07479	.07095	.06738	.06405	.06095
32	.10369	.09797	.09267	.08774	.08315	.07888	.07491	.07120	.06774	.06451
33	.10885	.10297	.09750	.09241	.08767	.08325	.07913	.07529	.07170	.06834
34	.11430	.10824	.10261	.09736	.09246	.08790	.08363	.07964	.07592	.07243
35	.12002	.11380	.10800	.10259	.09754	.09282	.08841	.08428	.08041	.07679
36	.12602	.11963	.11366	.10809	.10288	.09800	.09344	.08917	.08516	.08140
37	.13230	.12574	.11961	.11387	.10850	.10347	.09876	.09433	.09018	.08628
38	.13887	.13214	.12584	.11994	.11441	.10922	.10436	.09978	.09549	.09145
39	.14573	.13883	.13237	.12630	.12061	.11527	.11025	.10553	.10109	.09690
40	.15290	.14583	.13920	.13297	.12712	.12162	.11644	.11157	.10698	.10266
41	.16036	.15312	.14633	.13994	.13393	.12827	.12294	.11792	.11318	.10871
42	.16810	.16071	.15375	.14720	.14103	.13522	.12973	.12456	.11967	.11505
43	.17614	.16858	.16146	.15475	.14842	.14245	.13682	.13149	.12645	.12169
44	.18447	.17675	.16948	.16261	.15613	.15000	.14421	.13873	.13355	.12864
45	.19310	.18524	.17780	.17078	.16414	.15787	.15192	.14630	.14096	.13591
46	.20204	.19402	.18644	.17926	.17247	.16604	.15995	.15418	.14870	.14350
47	.21128	.20311	.19538	.18806	.18112	.17454	.16830	.16238	.15676	.15141
48	.22080	.21249	.20462	.19716	.19007	.18335	.17696	.17090	.16513	.15964
49	.23059	.22214	.21413	.20653	.19930	.19244	.18591	.17970	.17379	.16816
50	.24063	.23206	.22391	.21617	.20881	.20180	.19514	.18879	.18274	.17697
51	.25095	.24225	.23398	.22610	.21861	.21147	.20466	.19818	.19199	.18609
52	.26157	.25275	.24436	.23636	.22874	.22147	.21453	.20791	.20159	.19556
53	.27249	.26357	.25505	.24694	.23919	.23180	.22474	.21799	.21154	.20537
54	.28369	.27466	.26604	.25782	.24995	.24244	.23526	.22839	.22181	.21552
55	.29518	.28605	.27734	.26900	.26103	.25341	.24611	.23912	.23243	.22601

Reg. §20.2031-7A(e)(4)

AGE	6.2%	6.4%	6.6%	6.8%	7.0%	7.2%	7.4%	7.6%	7.8%	8.0%
56	.30695	.29774	.28893	.28050	.27242	.26469	.25728	.25019	.24338	.23685
57	.31902	.30973	.30084	.29232	.28415	.27632	.26881	.26161	.25469	.24805
58	.33138	.32203	.31306	.30446	.29621	.28829	.28069	.27339	.26637	.25962
59	.34402	.33461	.32558	.31691	.30859	.30059	.29290	.28550	.27839	.27155
60	.35690	.34745	.33836	.32963	.32124	.31317	.30540	.29792	.29073	.28379
61	.36999	.36050	.35137	.34259	.33414	.32601	.31817	.31062	.30334	.29633
62	.38325	.37374	.36458	.35576	.34726	.33907	.33117	.32356	.31621	.30912
63	.39669	.38717	.37799	.36913	.36060	.35236	.34441	.33674	.32933	.32217
64	.41031	.40078	.39159	.38272	.37415	.36588	.35789	.35016	.34270	.33548
65	.42416	.41464	.40545	.39656	.38798	.37968	.37166	.36390	.35639	.34912
66	.43825	.42876	.41958	.41070	.40211	.39380	.38576	.37797	.37043	.36312
67	.45260	.44315	.43399	.42513	.41655	.40824	.40019	.39238	.38482	.37749
68	.46720	.45779	.44868	.43985	.43129	.42299	.41494	.40713	.39956	.39221
69	.48197	.47263	.46357	.45478	.44625	.43798	.42995	.42215	.41458	.40722
70	.49686	.48760	.47861	.46988	.46140	.45316	.44516	.43738	.42983	.42248
71	.51182	.50265	.49374	.48508	.47666	.46847	.46051	.45276	.44523	.43790
72	.52685	.51778	.50896	.50038	.49203	.48390	.47599	.46829	.46079	.45349
73	.54194	.53298	.52426	.51578	.50751	.49946	.49161	.48397	.47652	.46926
74	.55714	.54832	.53972	.53134	.52317	.51520	.50744	.49986	.49247	.48527
75	.57250	.56382	.55536	.54710	.53904	.53118	.52351	.51601	.50870	.50156
76	.58803	.57951	.57120	.56308	.55515	.54740	.53984	.53245	.52522	.51817
77	.60369	.59535	.58720	.57923	.57144	.56383	.55639	.54912	.54200	.53504
78	.61942	.61126	.60329	.59549	.58787	.58040	.57310	.56596	.55896	.55212
79	.63508	.62713	.61935	.61174	.60428	.59698	.58983	.58283	.57597	.56925
80	.65059	.64285	.63527	.62785	.62058	.61345	.60646	.59961	.59290	.58632
81	.66579	.65827	.65090	.64368	.63659	.62965	.62283	.61615	.60959	.60316
82	.68061	.67332	.66616	.65914	.65226	.64550	.63886	.63235	.62595	.61968
83	.69499	.68793	.68099	.67418	.66749	.66092	.65447	.64813	.64191	.63579
84	.70896	.70213	.69541	.68881	.68233	.67595	.66969	.66353	.65748	.65153
85	.72256	.71596	.70947	.70308	.69681	.69063	.68456	.67859	.67271	.66693
86	.73569	.72931	.72305	.71688	.71081	.70484	.69896	.69318	.68748	.68188
87	.74818	.74204	.73599	.73003	.72417	.71839	.71271	.70711	.70159	.69616
88	.76011	.75419	.74836	.74261	.73695	.73137	.72588	.72046	.71512	.70986
89	.77169	.76599	.76037	.75484	.74938	.74400	.73870	.73347	.72831	.72323
90	.78302	.77755	.77215	.76683	.76158	.75640	.75129	.74625	.74128	.73638
91	.79395	.78870	.78352	.77842	.77337	.76840	.76349	.75864	.75385	.74913
92	.80423	.79920	.79423	.78933	.78449	.77971	.77499	.77033	.76572	.76118
93	.81377	.80894	.80417	.79946	.79481	.79022	.78568	.78120	.77677	.77239
94	.82247	.81784	.81325	.80873	.80425	.79983	.79547	.79115	.78688	.78266
95	.83033	.82586	.82145	.81709	.81278	.80852	.80431	.80014	.79602	.79195
96	.83729	.83298	.82872	.82451	.82034	.81622	.81215	.80812	.80414	.80019
97	.84361	.83944	.83532	.83124	.82721	.82322	.81927	.81537	.81151	.80769
98	.84929	.84525	.84126	.83730	.83339	.82952	.82569	.82190	.81815	.81443
99	.85454	.85062	.84674	.84290	.83910	.83534	.83161	.82792	.82427	.82066
100	.85942	.85561	.85184	.84810	.84440	.84074	.83711	.83352	.82997	.82644
101	.86408	.86037	.85670	.85306	.84946	.84589	.84236	.83886	.83539	.83196
102	.86894	.86534	.86177	.85823	.85473	.85126	.84782	.84442	.84104	.83770
103	.87408	.87060	.86714	.86371	.86032	.85695	.85362	.85031	.84703	.84378
104	.87980	.87644	.87311	.86980	.86653	.86328	.86005	.85686	.85369	.85054
105	.88684	.88363	.88046	.87731	.87418	.87108	.86800	.86494	.86191	.85890
106	.89685	.89389	.89095	.88804	.88514	.88226	.87940	.87656	.87374	.87094
107	.91117	.90858	.90600	.90344	.90089	.89836	.89584	.89334	.89085	.88838
108	.93414	.93217	.93022	.92828	.92634	.92442	.92250	.92060	.91870	.91681
109	.97081	.96992	.96904	.96816	.96729	.96642	.96555	.96468	.96382	.96296

Reg. § 20.2031-7A(e)(4)

TABLE S
BASED ON LIFE TABLE 80CNSMT
SINGLE LIFE REMAINDER FACTORS
APPLICABLE AFTER APRIL 30, 1989,
AND BEFORE MAY 1, 1999
INTEREST RATE

AGE	8.2%	8.4%	8.6%	8.8%	9.0%	9.2%	9.4%	9.6%	9.8%	10.0%
0	.02341	.02276	.02217	.02163	.02114	.02069	.02027	.01989	.01954	.01922
1	.01237	.01170	.01108	.01052	.01000	.00953	.00910	.00871	.00834	.00801
2	.01243	.01172	.01107	.01048	.00994	.00944	.00899	.00857	.00819	.00784
3	.01278	.01203	.01135	.01073	.01016	.00964	.00916	.00872	.00832	.00795
4	.01332	.01253	.01182	.01116	.01056	.01001	.00951	.00904	.00862	.00822
5	.01400	.01317	.01241	.01172	.01109	.01051	.00998	.00949	.00904	.00862
6	.01477	.01390	.01310	.01238	.01171	.01110	.01054	.01002	.00954	.00910
7	.01563	.01472	.01389	.01312	.01242	.01178	.01118	.01064	.01013	.00966
8	.01660	.01564	.01477	.01396	.01322	.01254	.01192	.01134	.01081	.01031
9	.01770	.01669	.01577	.01492	.01414	.01342	.01276	.01216	.01159	.01107
10	.01891	.01785	.01688	.01599	.01517	.01442	.01372	.01308	.01249	.01194
11	.02026	.01915	.01814	.01720	.01634	.01555	.01481	.01414	.01351	.01293
12	.02173	.02056	.01950	.01852	.01761	.01678	.01601	.01529	.01463	.01402
13	.02326	.02204	.02092	.01989	.01895	.01807	.01726	.01651	.01582	.01517
14	.02478	.02351	.02234	.02126	.02027	.01935	.01850	.01771	.01698	.01630
15	.02628	.02495	.02372	.02259	.02155	.02058	.01969	.01886	.01810	.01738
16	.02774	.02635	.02507	.02388	.02279	.02178	.02084	.01997	.01917	.01842
17	.02917	.02772	.02637	.02513	.02399	.02293	.02194	.02103	.02018	.01940
18	.03059	.02907	.02767	.02637	.02517	.02406	.02302	.02207	.02118	.02035
19	.03205	.03046	.02899	.02763	.02637	.02521	.02412	.02312	.02218	.02131
20	.03355	.03188	.03035	.02892	.02760	.02638	.02524	.02419	.02320	.02229
21	.03509	.03334	.03173	.03024	.02886	.02758	.02638	.02527	.02424	.02328
22	.03669	.03487	.03318	.03162	.03017	.02882	.02757	.02640	.02532	.02430
23	.03837	.03646	.03470	.03306	.03154	.03013	.02881	.02759	.02644	.02538
24	.04018	.03819	.03634	.03463	.03303	.03155	.03016	.02888	.02767	.02655
25	.04214	.04006	.03812	.03633	.03465	.03309	.03164	.03029	.02902	.02784
26	.04428	.04210	.04008	.03820	.03644	.03481	.03328	.03186	.03052	.02928
27	.04662	.04434	.04223	.04025	.03841	.03670	.03509	.03360	.03219	.03088
28	.04915	.04677	.04456	.04249	.04056	.03876	.03708	.03550	.03403	.03264
29	.05189	.04941	.04709	.04493	.04291	.04102	.03925	.03760	.03604	.03458
30	.05485	.05226	.04984	.04757	.04546	.04348	.04162	.03988	.03825	.03671
31	.05805	.05535	.05282	.05045	.04824	.04616	.04421	.04238	.04067	.03905
32	.06149	.05867	.05603	.05356	.05124	.04906	.04702	.04510	.04329	.04160
33	.06520	.06226	.05950	.05692	.05449	.05221	.05007	.04806	.04616	.04438
34	.06916	.06609	.06322	.06052	.05799	.05560	.05336	.05125	.04926	.04738
35	.07339	.07020	.06720	.06439	.06174	.05925	.05690	.05469	.05260	.05063
36	.07787	.07455	.07143	.06850	.06573	.06313	.06068	.05836	.05617	.05411
37	.08262	.07917	.07593	.07287	.06999	.06727	.06470	.06228	.05999	.05783
38	.08765	.08407	.08069	.07751	.07451	.07167	.06899	.06646	.06407	.06180
39	.09296	.08925	.08574	.08243	.07931	.07635	.07356	.07092	.06841	.06604
40	.09858	.09472	.09109	.08765	.08440	.08132	.07841	.07565	.07303	.07055
41	.10449	.10050	.09673	.09316	.08978	.08658	.08355	.08067	.07794	.07535
42	.11069	.10656	.10265	.09895	.09544	.09212	.08896	.08596	.08312	.08041
43	.11718	.11291	.10887	.10503	.10140	.09794	.09466	.09154	.08858	.08576
44	.12399	.11958	.11540	.11143	.10766	.10407	.10067	.09743	.09434	.09141
45	.13111	.12656	.12224	.11814	.11423	.11052	.10699	.10362	.10042	.09736
46	.13856	.13387	.12941	.12516	.12113	.11728	.11362	.11013	.10680	.10363
47	.14633	.14150	.13690	.13252	.12835	.12438	.12059	.11697	.11352	.11022
48	.15442	.14945	.14471	.14020	.13589	.13179	.12787	.12412	.12055	.11713
49	.16280	.15769	.15281	.14816	.14373	.13949	.13544	.13157	.12787	.12433
50	.17147	.16622	.16121	.15643	.15186	.14749	.14331	.13931	.13548	.13182
51	.18045	.17507	.16993	.16501	.16030	.15580	.15150	.14737	.14342	.13963
52	.18979	.18427	.17899	.17394	.16911	.16448	.16004	.15579	.15172	.14780
53	.19947	.19383	.18842	.18324	.17828	.17352	.16896	.16458	.16038	.15635
54	.20950	.20372	.19819	.19288	.18779	.18291	.17822	.17372	.16940	.16524
55	.21986	.21397	.20831	.20288	.19767	.19266	.18785	.18322	.17878	.17450

Reg. §20.2031-7A(e)(4)

AGE	8.2%	8.4%	8.6%	8.8%	9.0%	9.2%	9.4%	9.6%	9.8%	10.0%
56	.23058	.22457	.21879	.21324	.20791	.20278	.19785	.19310	.18854	.18414
57	.24167	.23554	.22965	.22399	.21854	.21329	.20824	.20338	.19870	.19419
58	.25314	.24690	.24090	.23512	.22956	.22420	.21904	.21407	.20927	.20464
59	.26497	.25863	.25252	.24664	.24097	.23550	.23023	.22515	.22024	.21551
60	.27712	.27068	.26448	.25849	.25272	.24716	.24178	.23659	.23158	.22674
61	.28956	.28304	.27674	.27067	.26480	.25913	.25366	.24837	.24325	.23831
62	.30228	.29567	.28929	.28312	.27717	.27141	.26584	.26045	.25524	.25020
63	.31525	.30857	.30211	.29586	.28982	.28397	.27832	.27284	.26754	.26240
64	.32851	.32176	.31522	.30890	.30278	.29685	.29111	.28555	.28016	.27493
65	.34209	.33528	.32868	.32229	.31610	.31010	.30429	.29865	.29317	.28787
66	.35604	.34918	.34253	.33609	.32983	.32377	.31788	.31217	.30663	.30124
67	.37037	.36347	.35678	.35028	.34398	.33786	.33191	.32614	.32053	.31508
68	.38508	.37815	.37142	.36489	.35854	.35237	.34638	.34055	.33488	.32937
69	.40008	.39313	.38638	.37982	.37344	.36724	.36120	.35533	.34961	.34405
70	.41533	.40838	.40162	.39504	.38864	.38241	.37634	.37043	.36468	.35907
71	.43076	.42382	.41705	.41047	.40405	.39780	.39171	.38578	.38000	.37436
72	.44638	.43945	.43269	.42611	.41969	.41344	.40733	.40138	.39558	.38991
73	.46218	.45527	.44854	.44197	.43556	.42931	.42321	.41725	.41143	.40575
74	.47823	.47137	.46466	.45812	.45173	.44549	.43940	.43345	.42763	.42195
75	.49459	.48777	.48112	.47462	.46826	.46205	.45598	.45004	.44424	.43856
76	.51127	.50452	.49793	.49148	.48517	.47900	.47297	.46706	.46129	.45563
77	.52823	.52157	.51505	.50867	.50243	.49632	.49033	.48447	.47873	.47311
78	.54541	.53885	.53242	.52613	.51996	.51392	.50800	.50220	.49652	.49094
79	.56267	.55621	.54989	.54369	.53762	.53166	.52582	.52009	.51448	.50897
80	.57987	.57354	.56733	.56125	.55527	.54941	.54366	.53802	.53248	.52705
81	.59685	.59065	.58457	.57860	.57274	.56699	.56134	.55579	.55035	.54499
82	.61351	.60746	.60151	.59567	.58993	.58429	.57875	.57331	.56796	.56270
83	.62978	.62387	.61806	.61236	.60675	.60123	.59581	.59047	.58523	.58007
84	.64567	.63992	.63426	.62869	.62321	.61783	.61253	.60731	.60218	.59713
85	.66125	.65565	.65014	.64472	.63938	.63413	.62896	.62387	.61886	.61392
86	.67636	.67092	.66557	.66030	.65511	.65000	.64496	.64000	.63511	.63030
87	.69081	.68554	.68034	.67522	.67018	.66520	.66031	.65548	.65071	.64602
88	.70468	.69957	.69453	.68956	.68466	.67983	.67507	.67037	.66574	.66117
89	.71821	.71326	.70838	.70357	.69882	.69414	.68952	.68495	.68045	.67601
90	.73153	.72676	.72204	.71739	.71280	.70827	.70379	.69938	.69502	.69071
91	.74447	.73986	.73532	.73083	.72640	.72202	.71770	.71343	.70921	.70504
92	.75669	.75225	.74787	.74354	.73927	.73504	.73087	.72674	.72267	.71864
93	.76807	.76379	.75957	.75540	.75127	.74719	.74317	.73918	.73524	.73135
94	.77849	.77437	.77030	.76627	.76229	.75835	.75446	.75061	.74680	.74303
95	.78792	.78394	.78001	.77611	.77226	.76845	.76468	.76096	.75727	.75362
96	.79630	.79244	.78863	.78485	.78112	.77742	.77377	.77015	.76657	.76303
97	.80391	.80016	.79646	.79280	.78917	.78559	.78203	.77852	.77504	.77160
98	.81076	.80712	.80352	.79996	.79643	.79294	.78948	.78606	.78267	.77931
99	.81709	.81354	.81004	.80657	.80313	.79972	.79635	.79302	.78971	.78644
100	.82296	.81950	.81609	.81270	.80934	.80602	.80273	.79947	.79624	.79304
101	.82855	.82518	.82185	.81854	.81526	.81201	.80880	.80561	.80245	.79932
102	.83438	.83110	.82785	.82462	.82142	.81826	.81512	.81200	.80892	.80586
103	.84056	.83737	.83420	.83106	.82795	.82487	.82181	.81878	.81577	.81279
104	.84743	.84433	.84127	.83822	.83521	.83221	.82924	.82630	.82338	.82048
105	.85591	.85295	.85001	.84709	.84419	.84132	.83846	.83563	.83282	.83003
106	.86816	.86540	.86266	.85993	.85723	.85454	.85187	.84922	.84659	.84397
107	.88592	.88348	.88105	.87863	.87623	.87384	.87147	.86911	.86676	.86443
108	.91493	.91306	.91119	.90934	.90749	.90566	.90383	.90201	.90020	.89840
109	.96211	.96125	.96041	.95956	.95872	.95788	.95704	.95620	.95537	.95455

Reg. §20.2031-7A(e)(4)

TABLE S
BASED ON LIFE TABLE 80CNSMT
SINGLE LIFE REMAINDER FACTORS
APPLICABLE AFTER APRIL 30, 1989,
AND BEFORE MAY 1, 1999
INTEREST RATE

AGE	10.2%	10.4%	10.6%	10.8%	11.0%	11.2%	11.4%	11.6%	11.8%	12.0%
0	.01891	.01864	.01838	.01814	.01791	.01770	.01750	.01732	.01715	.01698
1	.00770	.00741	.00715	.00690	.00667	.00646	.00626	.00608	.00590	.00574
2	.00751	.00721	.00693	.00667	.00643	.00620	.00600	.00580	.00562	.00544
3	.00760	.00728	.00699	.00671	.00646	.00622	.00600	.00579	.00560	.00541
4	.00786	.00752	.00721	.00692	.00665	.00639	.00616	.00594	.00573	.00554
5	.00824	.00788	.00755	.00724	.00695	.00668	.00643	.00620	.00598	.00578
6	.00869	.00832	.00796	.00764	.00733	.00705	.00678	.00654	.00630	.00608
7	.00923	.00883	.00846	.00811	.00779	.00749	.00720	.00694	.00669	.00646
8	.00986	.00943	.00904	.00867	.00833	.00801	.00771	.00743	.00716	.00692
9	.01059	.01014	.00972	.00933	.00897	.00863	.00831	.00801	.00773	.00747
10	.01142	.01095	.01051	.01009	.00971	.00935	.00901	.00869	.00840	.00812
11	.01239	.01189	.01142	.01098	.01057	.01019	.00983	.00950	.00918	.00889
12	.01345	.01292	.01243	.01197	.01154	.01113	.01075	.01040	.01007	.00975
13	.01457	.01401	.01349	.01300	.01255	.01212	.01172	.01135	.01100	.01067
14	.01567	.01508	.01453	.01402	.01354	.01309	.01267	.01227	.01190	.01155
15	.01672	.01610	.01552	.01498	.01448	.01400	.01356	.01314	.01275	.01238
16	.01772	.01707	.01646	.01589	.01536	.01486	.01439	.01396	.01354	.01315
17	.01866	.01798	.01734	.01674	.01618	.01566	.01516	.01470	.01427	.01386
18	.01958	.01886	.01818	.01755	.01697	.01641	.01590	.01541	.01495	.01452
19	.02050	.01974	.01903	.01837	.01775	.01717	.01662	.01611	.01563	.01517
20	.02143	.02064	.01989	.01919	.01854	.01793	.01735	.01681	.01630	.01582
21	.02238	.02154	.02075	.02002	.01933	.01868	.01807	.01750	.01696	.01646
22	.02336	.02247	.02164	.02087	.02014	.01946	.01882	.01821	.01764	.01711
23	.02438	.02345	.02257	.02176	.02099	.02027	.01959	.01895	.01835	.01778
24	.02550	.02451	.02359	.02273	.02192	.02115	.02044	.01976	.01913	.01853
25	.02673	.02569	.02472	.02381	.02295	.02214	.02138	.02067	.01999	.01936
26	.02811	.02701	.02598	.02502	.02411	.02326	.02246	.02170	.02098	.02031
27	.02965	.02849	.02741	.02639	.02543	.02452	.02367	.02287	.02211	.02140
28	.03134	.03013	.02898	.02790	.02689	.02593	.02503	.02418	.02338	.02262
29	.03322	.03193	.03072	.02958	.02851	.02750	.02654	.02564	.02479	.02398
30	.03527	.03391	.03264	.03143	.03030	.02923	.02821	.02726	.02635	.02550
31	.03753	.03610	.03475	.03348	.03228	.03115	.03008	.02907	.02811	.02720
32	.04000	.03849	.03707	.03573	.03446	.03326	.03213	.03105	.03004	.02907
33	.04269	.04111	.03961	.03819	.03685	.03558	.03438	.03325	.03217	.03115
34	.04561	.04394	.04236	.04087	.03946	.03812	.03685	.03565	.03451	.03342
35	.04877	.04702	.04535	.04378	.04229	.04087	.03953	.03826	.03706	.03591
36	.05215	.05031	.04856	.04690	.04533	.04384	.04242	.04108	.03980	.03859
37	.05578	.05384	.05200	.05025	.04860	.04703	.04553	.04411	.04276	.04148
38	.05965	.05761	.05568	.05385	.05211	.05045	.04888	.04738	.04595	.04460
39	.06379	.06165	.05962	.05770	.05587	.05412	.05247	.05089	.04939	.04795
40	.06820	.06596	.06383	.06181	.05989	.05806	.05631	.05465	.05307	.05155
41	.07288	.07054	.06832	.06620	.06418	.06226	.06042	.05868	.05701	.05541
42	.07784	.07539	.07306	.07085	.06873	.06671	.06479	.06295	.06119	.05952
43	.08308	.08052	.07808	.07576	.07355	.07143	.06941	.06748	.06564	.06387
44	.08861	.08594	.08340	.08097	.07865	.07644	.07432	.07230	.07036	.06851
45	.09445	.09167	.08901	.08648	.08406	.08174	.07953	.07741	.07538	.07343
46	.10060	.09770	.09494	.09230	.08977	.08735	.08503	.08281	.08068	.07865
47	.10707	.10406	.10119	.09843	.09579	.09327	.09085	.08853	.08630	.08417
48	.11386	.11073	.10774	.10487	.10213	.09949	.09697	.09455	.09222	.08999
49	.12094	.11769	.11458	.11160	.10874	.10600	.10337	.10084	.09842	.09609
50	.12831	.12494	.12172	.11862	.11565	.11280	.11006	.10743	.10490	.10247
51	.13600	.13251	.12917	.12596	.12288	.11991	.11706	.11432	.11169	.10915
52	.14405	.14044	.13698	.13366	.13046	.12738	.12442	.12157	.11883	.11619
53	.15247	.14875	.14517	.14172	.13841	.13522	.13215	.12919	.12635	.12360
54	.16124	.15740	.15370	.15014	.14671	.14341	.14023	.13717	.13421	.13136
55	.17039	.16642	.16261	.15893	.15539	.15198	.14868	.14551	.14244	.13948

Reg. § 20.2031-7A(e)(4)

AGE	10.2%	10.4%	10.6%	10.8%	11.0%	11.2%	11.4%	11.6%	11.8%	12.0%
56	.17991	.17583	.17190	.16811	.16445	.16092	.15752	.15423	.15106	.14799
57	.18984	.18564	.18160	.17769	.17392	.17029	.16677	.16338	.16010	.15692
58	.20018	.19587	.19172	.18770	.18382	.18007	.17645	.17295	.16956	.16628
59	.21093	.20652	.20225	.19812	.19414	.19028	.18655	.18294	.17945	.17606
60	.22206	.21753	.21316	.20893	.20483	.20087	.19703	.19332	.18972	.18624
61	.23353	.22890	.22442	.22009	.21589	.21182	.20788	.20407	.20037	.19678
62	.24532	.24059	.23601	.23158	.22728	.22311	.21907	.21515	.21135	.20767
63	.25742	.25260	.24793	.24339	.23900	.23473	.23060	.22658	.22268	.21890
64	.26987	.26495	.26019	.25556	.25107	.24671	.24248	.23837	.23438	.23050
65	.28271	.27771	.27286	.26815	.26357	.25912	.25480	.25059	.24651	.24254
66	.29601	.29093	.28600	.28120	.27654	.27200	.26760	.26331	.25913	.25507
67	.30978	.30462	.29961	.29474	.29000	.28539	.28090	.27653	.27227	.26813
68	.32401	.31879	.31371	.30877	.30396	.29927	.29471	.29027	.28593	.28171
69	.33863	.33336	.32822	.32322	.31835	.31359	.30896	.30445	.30005	.29576
70	.35361	.34829	.34310	.33804	.33311	.32830	.32361	.31903	.31457	.31021
71	.36886	.36349	.35826	.35316	.34818	.34332	.33858	.33394	.32942	.32500
72	.38439	.37899	.37373	.36858	.36356	.35866	.35387	.34919	.34461	.34015
73	.40021	.39479	.38950	.38432	.37927	.37433	.36950	.36478	.36016	.35565
74	.41639	.41096	.40565	.40046	.39538	.39042	.38556	.38081	.37616	.37161
75	.43301	.42758	.42226	.41706	.41198	.40699	.40212	.39734	.39267	.38809
76	.45009	.44467	.43937	.43417	.42908	.42410	.41921	.41443	.40974	.40514
77	.46761	.46221	.45693	.45175	.44667	.44170	.43682	.43203	.42734	.42274
78	.48548	.48013	.47488	.46973	.46468	.45972	.45486	.45009	.44541	.44082
79	.50356	.49826	.49306	.48795	.48294	.47802	.47319	.46845	.46379	.45922
80	.52171	.51647	.51133	.50628	.50132	.49644	.49166	.48695	.48233	.47779
81	.53974	.53457	.52950	.52451	.51961	.51479	.51006	.50541	.50083	.49633
82	.55753	.55245	.54745	.54254	.53771	.53296	.52828	.52369	.51917	.51472
83	.57500	.57001	.56510	.56026	.55551	.55083	.54623	.54170	.53724	.53285
84	.59216	.58726	.58245	.57770	.57304	.56844	.56391	.55945	.55506	.55074
85	.60906	.60428	.59956	.59492	.59034	.58583	.58139	.57702	.57270	.56845
86	.62555	.62088	.61627	.61173	.60725	.60284	.59849	.59420	.58997	.58580
87	.64139	.63683	.63233	.62790	.62352	.61921	.61495	.61076	.60661	.60253
88	.65666	.65221	.64783	.64350	.63923	.63502	.63086	.62675	.62270	.61871
89	.67163	.66730	.66304	.65882	.65466	.65055	.64650	.64249	.63854	.63463
90	.68646	.68226	.67812	.67402	.66998	.66599	.66204	.65814	.65430	.65049
91	.70093	.69686	.69285	.68888	.68496	.68108	.67725	.67347	.66973	.66604
92	.71466	.71073	.70684	.70300	.69920	.69545	.69173	.68806	.68444	.68085
93	.72750	.72370	.71994	.71622	.71254	.70890	.70530	.70174	.69822	.69474
94	.73931	.73562	.73198	.72838	.72481	.72129	.71780	.71434	.71093	.70755
95	.75001	.74644	.74291	.73941	.73595	.73253	.72914	.72579	.72247	.71919
96	.75953	.75606	.75262	.74923	.74586	.74253	.73924	.73598	.73275	.72955
97	.76819	.76481	.76147	.75816	.75489	.75165	.74844	.74526	.74211	.73899
98	.77599	.77270	.76944	.76621	.76302	.75986	.75672	.75362	.75054	.74750
99	.78319	.77998	.77680	.77365	.77053	.76744	.76437	.76134	.75833	.75535
100	.78987	.78673	.78362	.78054	.77748	.77446	.77146	.76849	.76555	.76263
101	.79622	.79315	.79010	.78708	.78409	.78113	.77819	.77528	.77239	.76953
102	.80283	.79983	.79685	.79390	.79097	.78807	.78519	.78234	.77951	.77671
103	.80983	.80690	.80399	.80111	.79825	.79541	.79260	.78981	.78705	.78430
104	.81760	.81475	.81192	.80912	.80633	.80357	.80083	.79810	.79541	.79273
105	.82726	.82451	.82178	.81907	.81638	.81371	.81106	.80843	.80582	.80322
106	.84137	.83879	.83623	.83368	.83115	.82863	.82614	.82366	.82119	.81874
107	.86211	.85981	.85751	.85523	.85297	.85071	.84847	.84624	.84403	.84182
108	.89660	.89481	.89304	.89127	.88950	.88775	.88601	.88427	.88254	.88081
109	.95372	.95290	.95208	.95126	.95045	.94964	.94883	.94803	.94723	.94643

TABLE S
BASED ON LIFE TABLE 80CNSMT
SINGLE LIFE REMAINDER FACTORS
APPLICABLE AFTER APRIL 30, 1989,
AND BEFORE MAY 1, 1999
INTEREST RATE

AGE	12.2%	12.4%	12.6%	12.8%	13.0%	13.2%	13.4%	13.6%	13.8%	14.0%
0	.01683	.01669	.01655	.01642	.01630	.01618	.01607	.01596	.01586	.01576
1	.00559	.00544	.00531	.00518	.00506	.00494	.00484	.00473	.00464	.00454
2	.00528	.00513	.00499	.00485	.00473	.00461	.00449	.00439	.00428	.00419
3	.00524	.00508	.00493	.00479	.00465	.00453	.00441	.00429	.00419	.00408
4	.00536	.00519	.00503	.00488	.00473	.00460	.00447	.00435	.00423	.00412
5	.00558	.00540	.00523	.00507	.00492	.00477	.00464	.00451	.00439	.00427
6	.00588	.00569	.00550	.00533	.00517	.00502	.00487	.00473	.00460	.00448
7	.00624	.00604	.00584	.00566	.00549	.00532	.00517	.00502	.00488	.00475
8	.00668	.00646	.00626	.00606	.00588	.00570	.00554	.00538	.00523	.00509
9	.00722	.00699	.00677	.00656	.00636	.00617	.00600	.00583	.00567	.00552
10	.00785	.00761	.00737	.00715	.00694	.00674	.00655	.00637	.00620	.00604
11	.00861	.00835	.00810	.00786	.00764	.00743	.00723	.00704	.00686	.00668
12	.00946	.00918	.00891	.00866	.00843	.00820	.00799	.00779	.00760	.00741
13	.01035	.01006	.00978	.00951	.00927	.00903	.00880	.00859	.00839	.00819
14	.01122	.01091	.01061	.01034	.01007	.00982	.00958	.00936	.00914	.00894
15	.01203	.01171	.01140	.01110	.01082	.01056	.01031	.01007	.00985	.00963
16	.01279	.01244	.01211	.01181	.01151	.01123	.01097	.01072	.01048	.01025
17	.01347	.01311	.01276	.01244	.01213	.01184	.01156	.01130	.01104	.01081
18	.01411	.01373	.01336	.01302	.01270	.01239	.01210	.01182	.01155	.01130
19	.01474	.01434	.01396	.01359	.01325	.01293	.01262	.01233	.01205	.01178
20	.01537	.01494	.01454	.01415	.01379	.01345	.01313	.01282	.01252	.01224
21	.01598	.01553	.01510	.01470	.01432	.01396	.01361	.01329	.01298	.01268
22	.01660	.01613	.01568	.01525	.01485	.01446	.01410	.01375	.01343	.01312
23	.01725	.01674	.01627	.01581	.01539	.01498	.01460	.01423	.01388	.01355
24	.01796	.01742	.01692	.01644	.01599	.01556	.01515	.01476	.01439	.01404
25	.01876	.01819	.01765	.01714	.01666	.01621	.01577	.01536	.01497	.01460
26	.01967	.01907	.01850	.01796	.01745	.01696	.01650	.01606	.01565	.01525
27	.02072	.02008	.01948	.01890	.01836	.01784	.01735	.01688	.01644	.01601
28	.02190	.02122	.02057	.01996	.01938	.01883	.01831	.01781	.01734	.01689
29	.02322	.02249	.02181	.02116	.02054	.01996	.01940	.01887	.01836	.01788
30	.02469	.02392	.02319	.02250	.02184	.02122	.02062	.02006	.01952	.01900
31	.02634	.02552	.02475	.02401	.02331	.02264	.02201	.02140	.02083	.02028
32	.02816	.02729	.02647	.02568	.02494	.02423	.02355	.02291	.02229	.02170
33	.03018	.02926	.02838	.02755	.02675	.02600	.02528	.02459	.02393	.02331
34	.03239	.03142	.03048	.02960	.02875	.02795	.02718	.02645	.02575	.02508
35	.03482	.03378	.03279	.03185	.03095	.03009	.02928	.02850	.02775	.02704
36	.03743	.03633	.03528	.03428	.03333	.03242	.03155	.03072	.02992	.02916
37	.04026	.03909	.03798	.03692	.03591	.03494	.03401	.03313	.03228	.03147
38	.04330	.04207	.04089	.03977	.03869	.03767	.03668	.03574	.03484	.03398
39	.04658	.04528	.04403	.04284	.04170	.04061	.03957	.03857	.03762	.03670
40	.05011	.04873	.04741	.04615	.04495	.04379	.04269	.04163	.04061	.03964
41	.05389	.05244	.05104	.04971	.04844	.04721	.04604	.04492	.04384	.04281
42	.05791	.05638	.05491	.05350	.05216	.05086	.04962	.04844	.04729	.04620
43	.06219	.06057	.05902	.05754	.05612	.05475	.05344	.05218	.05098	.04981
44	.06673	.06503	.06340	.06184	.06034	.05890	.05752	.05619	.05491	.05368
45	.07157	.06978	.06806	.06642	.06484	.06332	.06186	.06046	.05911	.05781
46	.07669	.07481	.07301	.07128	.06962	.06802	.06649	.06501	.06358	.06221
47	.08212	.08015	.07826	.07645	.07470	.07302	.07140	.06984	.06834	.06690
48	.08784	.08578	.08380	.08190	.08006	.07830	.07660	.07496	.07338	.07186
49	.09384	.09169	.08961	.08762	.08570	.08384	.08206	.08034	.07868	.07708
50	.10013	.09787	.09570	.09361	.09160	.08966	.08779	.08598	.08424	.08256
51	.10671	.10436	.10209	.09991	.09780	.09577	.09381	.09192	.09009	.08832
52	.11365	.11120	.10883	.10655	.10435	.10222	.10017	.09819	.09628	.09442
53	.12095	.11840	.11593	.11355	.11126	.10904	.10689	.10482	.10282	.10088
54	.12860	.12595	.12338	.12090	.11851	.11619	.11396	.11179	.10970	.10767
55	.13663	.13386	.13120	.12862	.12613	.12372	.12138	.11912	.11694	.11482

Reg. §20.2031-7A(e)(4)

AGE	12.2%	12.4%	12.6%	12.8%	13.0%	13.2%	13.4%	13.6%	13.8%	14.0%
56	.14503	.14217	.13940	.13672	.13413	.13162	.12919	.12683	.12456	.12235
57	.15385	.15089	.14801	.14523	.14254	.13994	.13741	.13496	.13259	.13029
58	.16311	.16004	.15706	.15418	.15139	.14868	.14606	.14352	.14105	.13866
59	.17279	.16961	.16654	.16355	.16066	.15786	.15514	.15250	.14994	.14745
60	.18286	.17958	.17640	.17332	.17033	.16743	.16462	.16188	.15922	.15664
61	.19330	.18992	.18665	.18347	.18038	.17738	.17447	.17164	.16889	.16622
62	.20409	.20061	.19724	.19396	.19078	.18768	.18467	.18175	.17891	.17614
63	.21522	.21165	.20818	.20480	.20152	.19833	.19523	.19221	.18928	.18642
64	.22672	.22306	.21949	.21602	.21265	.20937	.20617	.20306	.20003	.19708
65	.23867	.23491	.23125	.22769	.22423	.22085	.21757	.21437	.21125	.20821
66	.25112	.24727	.24353	.23988	.23632	.23286	.22948	.22619	.22299	.21986
67	.26409	.26016	.25633	.25260	.24896	.24541	.24195	.23857	.23528	.23206
68	.27760	.27359	.26968	.26586	.26214	.25851	.25497	.25151	.24814	.24484
69	.29157	.28748	.28350	.27961	.27581	.27211	.26849	.26495	.26150	.25812
70	.30596	.30181	.29775	.29379	.28992	.28614	.28245	.27884	.27532	.27187
71	.32069	.31648	.31236	.30833	.30440	.30055	.29679	.29312	.28952	.28600
72	.33578	.33151	.32733	.32325	.31925	.31535	.31152	.30778	.30412	.30054
73	.35123	.34691	.34269	.33855	.33450	.33054	.32666	.32286	.31914	.31550
74	.36715	.36279	.35852	.35434	.35024	.34623	.34230	.33845	.33468	.33098
75	.38360	.37921	.37491	.37069	.36656	.36250	.35853	.35464	.35082	.34708
76	.40064	.39623	.39190	.38765	.38349	.37941	.37540	.37148	.36762	.36384
77	.41823	.41381	.40947	.40521	.40103	.39692	.39290	.38895	.38507	.38126
78	.43632	.43189	.42755	.42329	.41910	.41499	.41095	.40698	.40309	.39926
79	.45473	.45032	.44599	.44173	.43755	.43344	.42940	.42543	.42153	.41770
80	.47333	.46894	.46463	.46040	.45623	.45213	.44811	.44414	.44025	.43642
81	.49191	.48755	.48328	.47907	.47493	.47085	.46684	.46290	.45902	.45520
82	.51034	.50603	.50179	.49762	.49351	.48947	.48549	.48157	.47772	.47392
83	.52852	.52427	.52008	.51595	.51189	.50788	.50394	.50006	.49623	.49246
84	.54648	.54228	.53815	.53407	.53006	.52610	.52221	.51836	.51458	.51084
85	.56426	.56013	.55606	.55205	.54810	.54420	.54035	.53656	.53282	.52913
86	.58169	.57764	.57364	.56970	.56581	.56197	.55818	.55445	.55076	.54713
87	.59850	.59452	.59060	.58673	.58291	.57913	.57541	.57174	.56811	.56453
88	.61476	.61086	.60702	.60322	.59947	.59577	.59212	.58851	.58494	.58142
89	.63078	.62697	.62321	.61950	.61583	.61220	.60862	.60508	.60159	.59813
90	.64674	.64302	.63935	.63573	.63215	.62861	.62511	.62165	.61823	.61485
91	.66238	.65877	.65520	.65167	.64819	.64474	.64133	.63795	.63462	.63132
92	.67730	.67379	.67032	.66689	.66350	.66014	.65682	.65354	.65029	.64708
93	.69130	.68789	.68452	.68119	.67789	.67463	.67140	.66820	.66504	.66191
94	.70421	.70090	.69762	.69438	.69118	.68800	.68486	.68175	.67867	.67563
95	.71594	.71272	.70954	.70639	.70326	.70017	.69712	.69409	.69109	.68812
96	.72638	.72325	.72014	.71707	.71403	.71101	.70803	.70507	.70215	.69925
97	.73590	.73285	.72982	.72682	.72385	.72090	.71799	.71510	.71224	.70941
98	.74448	.74149	.73853	.73560	.73269	.72981	.72696	.72414	.72134	.71856
99	.75240	.74948	.74658	.74371	.74086	.73805	.73525	.73248	.72974	.72702
100	.75974	.75687	.75403	.75121	.74842	.74566	.74292	.74020	.73751	.73484
101	.76669	.76388	.76109	.75833	.75559	.75287	.75018	.74751	.74486	.74223
102	.77393	.77117	.76844	.76573	.76304	.76037	.75773	.75511	.75251	.74993
103	.78158	.77888	.77620	.77355	.77091	.76830	.76571	.76313	.76058	.75805
104	.79007	.78743	.78482	.78222	.77964	.77709	.77455	.77203	.76953	.76705
105	.80065	.79809	.79556	.79304	.79054	.78805	.78559	.78314	.78071	.77829
106	.81631	.81389	.81149	.80911	.80674	.80438	.80204	.79972	.79741	.79511
107	.83963	.83745	.83529	.83313	.83099	.82886	.82674	.82463	.82254	.82045
108	.87910	.87739	.87569	.87400	.87232	.87064	.86897	.86731	.86566	.86401
109	.94563	.94484	.94405	.94326	.94248	.94170	.94092	.94014	.93937	.93860

TABLE 80CNSMT
APPLICABLE AFTER APRIL 30, 1989,
AND BEFORE MAY 1, 1999

Age x	1(x)	Age x	1(x)	Age x	1(x)
(1)	(2)	(1)	(2)	(1)	(2)
0	100000	37	95492	74	59279
1	98740	38	95317	75	56799
2	98648	39	95129	76	54239
3	98584	40	94926	77	51599
4	98535	41	94706	78	48878
5	98495	42	94465	79	46071
6	98459	43	94201	80	43180
7	98426	44	93913	81	40208
8	98396	45	93599	82	37172
9	98370	46	93256	83	34095
10	98347	47	92882	84	31012
11	98328	48	92472	85	27960
12	98309	49	92021	86	24961
13	98285	50	91526	87	22038
14	98248	51	90986	88	19235
15	98196	52	90402	89	16598
16	98129	53	89771	90	14154
17	98047	54	89087	91	11908
18	97953	55	88348	92	9863
19	97851	56	87551	93	8032
20	97741	57	86695	94	6424
21	97623	58	85776	95	5043
22	97499	59	84789	96	3884
23	97370	60	83726	97	2939
24	97240	61	82581	98	2185
25	97110	62	81348	99	1598
26	96982	63	80024	100	1150
27	96856	64	78609	101	815
28	96730	65	77107	102	570
29	96604	66	75520	103	393
30	96477	67	73846	104	267
31	96350	68	72082	105	179
32	96220	69	70218	106	119
33	96088	70	68248	107	78
34	95951	71	66165	108	51
35	95808	72	63972	109	33
36	95655	73	61673	110	0

(f) *Valuation of annuities, interests for life or term of years, and remainder or reversionary interests for estates of decedents for which the valuation date of the gross estate is after April 30,1999, and before May 1, 2009.*—(1) *In general.*—Except as otherwise provided in §20.2031-7(b) and §20.7520-3(b) (pertaining to certain limitations on the use of prescribed tables), if the valuation date for the gross estate of the decedent is after April 30, 1999, and before May 1, 2009, the fair market value of annuities, life estates, terms of years, remainders, and reversionary interests is the present value of the interests determined by use of standard or special section 7520 actuarial factors and the valuation methodology described in §20.2031-7(d). These factors are derived by using the appropriate section 7520 interest rate and, if applicable, the mortality component for the valuation date of the interest that is being valued. See §§20.7520-1 through 20.7520-4. See paragraph (f)(4) of this section for determination of the appropriate table for use in valuing these interests.

(2) *Transitional rule.*—(i) If a decedent dies after April 30, 1999, and if on May 1, 1999, the decedent was mentally incompetent so that the disposition of the decedent's property could not be changed, and the decedent dies without having regained competency to dispose of the decedent's property or dies within 90 days of the date on which the decedent first regains competency, the fair market value of annuities, life estates, terms for years, remainders, and reversions included in the gross estate of the decedent is their present value determined either under this section or under the corresponding section applicable at the time the decedent became mentally incompetent, at the option of the decedent's

Reg. §20.2031-7A(f)(2)(i)

executor. For example, see paragraph (d) of this section.

(ii) If a decedent dies after April 30, 1999, and before July 1, 1999, the fair market value of annuities, life estates, remainders, and reversions based on one or more measuring lives included in the gross estate of the decedent is their present value determined under this section by use of the section 7520 interest rate for the month in which the valuation date occurs (see §§ 20.7520-1(b) and 20.7520-2(a)(2) and the appropriate actuarial tables under either paragraph (e)(4) or paragraph (f)(4) of this section, at the option of the decedent's executor.

(iii) For purposes of paragraphs (f)(2)(i) and (f)(2)(ii) of this section, where the decedent's executor is given the option to use the appropriate actuarial tables under either paragraph (e)(4) or paragraph (f)(4) of this section, the decedent's executor must use the same actuarial table with respect to each individual transaction and with respect to all transfers occurring on the valuation date (for example, gift and income tax charitable deductions with respect to the same transfer must be determined based on the same tables, and all assets includible in the gross estate and/or estate tax deductions claimed must be valued based on the same tables).

(3) *Publications and actuarial computations by the Internal Revenue Service.*—Many standard actuarial factors not included in paragraph (f)(4) of this section or in § 20.2031-7(d)(6) are included in Internal Revenue Service Publication 1457, "Actuarial Values, Book Aleph," (7-99). Publication 1457 also includes examples that illustrate how

to compute many special factors for more unusual situations. Publication 1457 is no longer available for purchase from the Superintendent of Documents, United States Government Printing Office. However, pertinent factors in this publication may be obtained from: CC:PA:LPD:PR (IRS Publication 1457), Room 5205, Internal Revenue Service, P.O.Box 7604, Ben Franklin Station, Washington, DC 20044. If a special factor is required in the case of an actual decedent, the Internal Revenue Service may furnish the factor to the executor upon a request for a ruling. The request for a ruling must be accompanied by a recitation of the facts including a statement of the date of birth for each measuring life, the date of the decedent's death, any other applicable dates, and a copy of the will, trust, or other relevant documents. A request for a ruling must comply with the instructions for requesting a ruling published periodically in the Internal Revenue Bulletin (see §§ 601.201 and 601.601(d)(2)(ii)(b)) and include payment of the required user fee.

(4) *Actuarial tables.*—Except as provided in § 20.7520-3(b) (pertaining to certain limitations on the use of prescribed tables), Life Table 90CM and Table S (Single life remainder factors applicable where the valuation date is after April 30, 1999, and before May 1, 2009), contained in this paragraph (f)(4), and Table B, Table J, and Table K set forth in § 20.2031-7(d)(6) must be used in the application of the provisions of this section when the section 7520 interest rate component is between 4.2 and 14 percent. Table S and Table 90CM are as follows:

TABLE S
BASED ON LIFE TABLE 90CM
SINGLE LIFE REMAINDER FACTORS
[APPLICABLE AFTER APRIL 30, 1999, AND BEFORE MAY 1, 2009]

INTEREST RATE

AGE	4.2%	4.4%	4.6%	4.8%	5.0%	5.2%	5.4%	5.6%	5.8%	6.0%
0	.06752	.06130	.05586	.05109	.04691	.04322	.03998	.03711	.03458	.03233
1	.06137	.05495	.04932	.04438	.04003	.03620	.03283	.02985	.02721	.02487
2	.06325	.05667	.05088	.04580	.04132	.03737	.03388	.03079	.02806	.02563
3	.06545	.05869	.05275	.04752	.04291	.03883	.03523	.03203	.02920	.02668
4	.06784	.06092	.05482	.04944	.04469	.04048	.03676	.03346	.03052	.02791
5	.07040	.06331	.05705	.05152	.04662	.04229	.03845	.03503	.03199	.02928
6	.07310	.06583	.05941	.05372	.04869	.04422	.04025	.03672	.03357	.03076
7	.07594	.06849	.06191	.05607	.05089	.04628	.04219	.03854	.03528	.03236
8	.07891	.07129	.06453	.05853	.05321	.04846	.04424	.04046	.03709	.03407
9	.08203	.07423	.06731	.06115	.05567	.05079	.04643	.04253	.03904	.03592
10	.08532	.07734	.07024	.06392	.05829	.05326	.04877	.04474	.04114	.03790
11	.08875	.08059	.07331	.06683	.06104	.05587	.05124	.04709	.04336	.04002
12	.09233	.08398	.07653	.06989	.06394	.05862	.05385	.04957	.04572	.04226
13	.09601	.08748	.07985	.07304	.06693	.06146	.05655	.05214	.04816	.04458
14	.09974	.09102	.08322	.07624	.06997	.06435	.05929	.05474	.05064	.04694
15	.10350	.09460	.08661	.07946	.07303	.06725	.06204	.05735	.05312	.04930
16	.10728	.09818	.09001	.08268	.07608	.07014	.06479	.05996	.05559	.05164
17	.11108	.10179	.09344	.08592	.07916	.07306	.06755	.06257	.05807	.05399
18	.11494	.10545	.09691	.08921	.08227	.07601	.07034	.06521	.06057	.05636
19	.11889	.10921	.10047	.09259	.08548	.07904	.07322	.06794	.06315	.05880
20	.12298	.11310	.10417	.09610	.08881	.08220	.07622	.07078	.06584	.06135
21	.12722	.11713	.10801	.09976	.09228	.08550	.07935	.07375	.06866	.06403
22	.13159	.12130	.11199	.10354	.09588	.08893	.08260	.07685	.07160	.06682
23	.13613	.12563	.11612	.10748	.09964	.09250	.08601	.08009	.07468	.06975
24	.14084	.13014	.12043	.11160	.10357	.09625	.08958	.08349	.07793	.07284
25	.14574	.13484	.12493	.11591	.10768	.10018	.09334	.08708	.08135	.07611
26	.15084	.13974	.12963	.12041	.11199	.10431	.09728	.09085	.08496	.07956
27	.15615	.14485	.13454	.12513	.11652	.10865	.10144	.09484	.08878	.08322
28	.16166	.15016	.13965	.13004	.12124	.11319	.10580	.09901	.09279	.08706
29	.16737	.15567	.14497	.13516	.12617	.11792	.11035	.10339	.09699	.09109
30	.17328	.16138	.15048	.14047	.13129	.12286	.11510	.10796	.10138	.09532
31	.17938	.16728	.15618	.14599	.13661	.12799	.12004	.11272	.10597	.09974
32	.18568	.17339	.16210	.15171	.14214	.13333	.12520	.11769	.11076	.10435
33	.19220	.17972	.16824	.15766	.14790	.13889	.13058	.12289	.11578	.10920
34	.19894	.18627	.17460	.16383	.15388	.14468	.13618	.12831	.12102	.11426
35	.20592	.19307	.18121	.17025	.16011	.15073	.14204	.13399	.12652	.11958
36	.21312	.20010	.18805	.17691	.16658	.15701	.14814	.13990	.13225	.12514
37	.22057	.20737	.19514	.18382	.17331	.16356	.15450	.14608	.13825	.13096
38	.22827	.21490	.20251	.19100	.18031	.17038	.16113	.15253	.14452	.13705
39	.23623	.22270	.21013	.19845	.18759	.17747	.16805	.15927	.15108	.14344
40	.24446	.23078	.21805	.20620	.19516	.18487	.17527	.16631	.15795	.15013
41	.25298	.23915	.22626	.21425	.20305	.19259	.18282	.17368	.16514	.15715
42	.26178	.24782	.23478	.22262	.21125	.20062	.19069	.18138	.17267	.16450
43	.27087	.25678	.24360	.23129	.21977	.20898	.19888	.18941	.18053	.17220
44	.28025	.26603	.25273	.24027	.22860	.21766	.20740	.19777	.18873	.18023
45	.28987	.27555	.26212	.24953	.23772	.22664	.21622	.20644	.19724	.18858
46	.29976	.28533	.27179	.25908	.24714	.23591	.22536	.21542	.20606	.19725

AGE	4.2%	4.4%	4.6%	4.8%	5.0%	5.2%	5.4%	5.6%	5.8%	6.0%
47	.30987	.29535	.28171	.26889	.25682	.24546	.23476	.22468	.21518	.20621
48	.32023	.30563	.29190	.27897	.26678	.25530	.24447	.23425	.22460	.21549
49	.33082	.31615	.30234	.28931	.27702	.26543	.25447	.24412	.23434	.22509
50	.34166	.32694	.31306	.29995	.28756	.27586	.26479	.25432	.24441	.23502
51	.35274	.33798	.32404	.31085	.29838	.28658	.27541	.26482	.25479	.24528
52	.36402	.34924	.33525	.32200	.30946	.29757	.28630	.27561	.26547	.25584
53	.37550	.36070	.34668	.33339	.32078	.30882	.29746	.28667	.27643	.26669
54	.38717	.37237	.35833	.34500	.33234	.32031	.30888	.29801	.28766	.27782
55	.39903	.38424	.37019	.35683	.34413	.33205	.32056	.30961	.29918	.28925
56	.41108	.39631	.38227	.36890	.35617	.34405	.33250	.32149	.31099	.30097
57	.42330	.40857	.39455	.38118	.36844	.35629	.34469	.33363	.32306	.31297
58	.43566	.42098	.40699	.39364	.38089	.36873	.35710	.34600	.33538	.32522
59	.44811	.43351	.41956	.40623	.39350	.38133	.36968	.35855	.34789	.33768
60	.46066	.44613	.43224	.41896	.40624	.39408	.38243	.37127	.36058	.35033
61	.47330	.45887	.44505	.43182	.41914	.40699	.39535	.38418	.37347	.36318
62	.48608	.47175	.45802	.44485	.43223	.42011	.40848	.39732	.38660	.37629
63	.49898	.48478	.47115	.45807	.44550	.43343	.42184	.41069	.39997	.38966
64	.51200	.49793	.48442	.47143	.45895	.44694	.43539	.42427	.41357	.40326
65	.52512	.51121	.49782	.48495	.47255	.46062	.44912	.43805	.42738	.41709
66	.53835	.52461	.51137	.49862	.48634	.47449	.46307	.45206	.44143	.43118
67	.55174	.53818	.52511	.51250	.50034	.48860	.47727	.46633	.45576	.44556
68	.56524	.55188	.53899	.52654	.51452	.50291	.49168	.48083	.47034	.46020
69	.57882	.56568	.55299	.54071	.52885	.51737	.50627	.49552	.48513	.47506
70	.59242	.57951	.56703	.55495	.54325	.53193	.52096	.51034	.50004	.49007
71	.60598	.59332	.58106	.56918	.55767	.54651	.53569	.52520	.51503	.50516
72	.61948	.60707	.59504	.58338	.57206	.56108	.55043	.54009	.53004	.52029
73	.63287	.62073	.60895	.59751	.58640	.57561	.56513	.55495	.54505	.53543
74	.64621	.63435	.62282	.61162	.60073	.59015	.57985	.56984	.56009	.55061
75	.65953	.64796	.63671	.62575	.61510	.60473	.59463	.58480	.57523	.56591
76	.67287	.66160	.65063	.63995	.62954	.61940	.60952	.59989	.59050	.58135
77	.68622	.67526	.66459	.65419	.64404	.63415	.62450	.61509	.60590	.59694
78	.69954	.68892	.67856	.66845	.65858	.64895	.63955	.63036	.62140	.61264
79	.71278	.70250	.69246	.68265	.67308	.66372	.65457	.64563	.63690	.62836
80	.72581	.71588	.70618	.69668	.68740	.67833	.66945	.66077	.65227	.64396
81	.73857	.72899	.71962	.71045	.70147	.69268	.68408	.67566	.66741	.65933
82	.75101	.74178	.73274	.72389	.71522	.70672	.69840	.69024	.68225	.67441
83	.76311	.75423	.74553	.73700	.72864	.72044	.71240	.70451	.69678	.68919
84	.77497	.76645	.75809	.74988	.74183	.73393	.72618	.71857	.71110	.70377
85	.78665	.77848	.77047	.76260	.75487	.74728	.73982	.73250	.72530	.71823
86	.79805	.79025	.78258	.77504	.76764	.76036	.75320	.74617	.73925	.73245
87	.80904	.80159	.79427	.78706	.77998	.77301	.76615	.75940	.75277	.74624
88	.81962	.81251	.80552	.79865	.79188	.78521	.77865	.77220	.76584	.75958
89	.82978	.82302	.81636	.80980	.80335	.79699	.79072	.78455	.77847	.77248
90	.83952	.83309	.82676	.82052	.81437	.80831	.80234	.79645	.79064	.78492
91	.84870	.84260	.83658	.83064	.82479	.81902	.81332	.80771	.80217	.79671
92	.85716	.85136	.84563	.83998	.83441	.82891	.82348	.81812	.81283	.80761
93	.86494	.85942	.85396	.84858	.84326	.83801	.83283	.82771	.82266	.81767
94	.87216	.86690	.86170	.85657	.85149	.84648	.84153	.83664	.83181	.82704
95	.87898	.87397	.86902	.86412	.85928	.85450	.84977	.84510	.84049	.83592
96	.88537	.88060	.87587	.87121	.86659	.86203	.85751	.85305	.84864	.84427
97	.89127	.88672	.88221	.87775	.87335	.86898	.86467	.86040	.85618	.85200
98	.89680	.89245	.88815	.88389	.87968	.87551	.87138	.86730	.86326	.85926
99	.90217	.89803	.89393	.88987	.88585	.88187	.87793	.87402	.87016	.86633

Reg. § 20.2031-7A(f)(4)

AGE	4.2%	4.4%	4.6%	4.8%	5.0%	5.2%	5.4%	5.6%	5.8%	6.0%
100	.90738	.90344	.89953	.89567	.89183	.88804	.88428	.88056	.87687	.87322
101	.91250	.90876	.90504	.90137	.89772	.89412	.89054	.88699	.88348	.88000
102	.91751	.91396	.91045	.90696	.90350	.90007	.89668	.89331	.88997	.88666
103	.92247	.91912	.91579	.91249	.90922	.90598	.90276	.89957	.89640	.89326
104	.92775	.92460	.92148	.91839	.91532	.91227	.90924	.90624	.90326	.90031
105	.93290	.92996	.92704	.92415	.92127	.91841	.91558	.91276	.90997	.90719
106	.93948	.93680	.93415	.93151	.92889	.92628	.92370	.92113	.91857	.91604
107	.94739	.94504	.94271	.94039	.93808	.93579	.93351	.93124	.92899	.92675
108	.95950	.95767	.95585	.95404	.95224	.95045	.94867	.94689	.94512	.94336
109	.97985	.97893	.97801	.97710	.97619	.97529	.97438	.97348	.97259	.97170

TABLE S
BASED ON LIFE TABLE 90CM
SINGLE LIFE REMAINDER FACTORS
[APPLICABLE AFTER APRIL 30, 1999, AND BEFORE MAY 1, 2009]

INTEREST RATE

AGE	6.2%	6.4%	6.6%	6.8%	7.0%	7.2%	7.4%	7.6%	7.8%	8.0%
0	.03034	.02857	.02700	.02559	.02433	.02321	.02220	.02129	.02047	.01973
1	.02279	.02094	.01929	.01782	.01650	.01533	.01427	.01331	.01246	.01168
2	.02347	.02155	.01983	.01829	.01692	.01569	.01458	.01358	.01268	.01187
3	.02444	.02243	.02065	.01905	.01761	.01632	.01516	.01412	.01317	.01232
4	.02558	.02349	.02163	.01996	.01846	.01712	.01590	.01481	.01382	.01292
5	.02686	.02469	.02275	.02101	.01945	.01804	.01677	.01562	.01458	.01364
6	.02825	.02600	.02398	.02217	.02053	.01906	.01773	.01653	.01544	.01445
7	.02976	.02742	.02532	.02343	.02172	.02019	.01880	.01754	.01640	.01536
8	.03137	.02894	.02675	.02479	.02301	.02140	.01995	.01864	.01744	.01635
9	.03311	.03059	.02832	.02627	.02442	.02274	.02122	.01985	.01859	.01745
10	.03499	.03237	.03001	.02788	.02595	.02420	.02262	.02118	.01987	.01867
11	.03700	.03428	.03183	.02961	.02760	.02578	.02413	.02262	.02125	.02000
12	.03913	.03632	.03377	.03146	.02937	.02748	.02575	.02418	.02275	.02144
13	.04135	.03843	.03579	.03339	.03122	.02924	.02744	.02580	.02431	.02294
14	.04359	.04057	.03783	.03534	.03308	.03102	.02915	.02744	.02587	.02444
15	.04584	.04270	.03986	.03728	.03493	.03279	.03083	.02905	.02742	.02593
16	.04806	.04482	.04187	.03919	.03674	.03452	.03248	.03063	.02892	.02736
17	.05029	.04692	.04387	.04108	.03855	.03623	.03411	.03218	.03040	.02877
18	.05253	.04905	.04588	.04299	.04036	.03795	.03574	.03373	.03187	.03017
19	.05484	.05124	.04796	.04496	.04222	.03972	.03742	.03532	.03339	.03161
20	.05726	.05354	.05013	.04702	.04418	.04158	.03919	.03700	.03498	.03313
21	.05980	.05595	.05242	.04920	.04625	.04354	.04105	.03877	.03667	.03473
22	.06246	.05847	.05482	.05147	.04841	.04559	.04301	.04063	.03844	.03642
23	.06524	.06112	.05734	.05387	.05069	.04777	.04508	.04260	.04032	.03821
24	.06819	.06392	.06001	.05642	.05312	.05008	.04728	.04470	.04232	.04012
25	.07131	.06690	.06285	.05913	.05570	.05255	.04964	.04695	.04447	.04218
26	.07460	.07005	.06586	.06200	.05845	.05518	.05215	.04936	.04677	.04438
27	.07810	.07340	.06907	.06508	.06140	.05800	.05485	.05195	.04925	.04676
28	.08179	.07693	.07246	.06833	.06451	.06098	.05772	.05469	.05189	.04929
29	.08566	.08065	.07603	.07176	.06780	.06414	.06075	.05761	.05469	.05198
30	.08973	.08456	.07978	.07536	.07127	.06748	.06396	.06069	.05766	.05483
31	.09398	.08865	.08372	.07915	.07491	.07098	.06733	.06394	.06078	.05785
32	.09843	.09294	.08785	.08313	.07875	.07468	.07089	.06737	.06409	.06103
33	.10310	.09745	.09220	.08732	.08279	.07858	.07466	.07100	.06759	.06441
34	.10799	.10217	.09676	.09173	.08705	.08269	.07862	.07483	.07129	.06798
35	.11314	.10715	.10157	.09638	.09155	.08704	.08283	.07890	.07522	.07179
36	.11852	.11236	.10662	.10127	.09628	.09162	.08726	.08319	.07938	.07581
37	.12416	.11783	.11193	.10641	.10126	.09645	.09194	.08772	.08377	.08006
38	.13009	.12359	.11751	.11183	.10652	.10155	.09689	.09253	.08843	.08459
39	.13629	.12962	.12338	.11753	.11206	.10693	.10212	.09761	.09337	.08938
40	.14281	.13597	.12955	.12355	.11791	.11262	.10766	.10299	.09860	.09447
41	.14966	.14264	.13606	.12989	.12409	.11864	.11352	.10870	.10417	.09989
42	.15685	.14966	.14291	.13657	.13061	.12500	.11972	.11475	.11006	.10564
43	.16437	.15702	.15010	.14360	.13747	.13171	.12627	.12115	.11631	.11174
44	.17224	.16472	.15764	.15098	.14469	.13876	.13317	.12789	.12290	.11819
45	.18042	.17274	.16550	.15867	.15223	.14615	.14040	.13496	.12982	.12496
46	.18893	.18110	.17370	.16671	.16011	.15387	.14796	.14238	.13708	.13207
47	.19775	.18975	.18220	.17505	.16830	.16190	.15584	.15010	.14466	.13950

Reg. § 20.2031-7A(f)(4)

AGE	6.2%	6.4%	6.6%	6.8%	7.0%	7.2%	7.4%	7.6%	7.8%	8.0%
48	.20688	.19873	.19102	.18373	.17682	.17027	.16406	.15817	.15258	.14727
49	.21633	.20804	.20018	.19274	.18568	.17898	.17262	.16658	.16084	.15539
50	.22612	.21769	.20969	.20210	.19490	.18805	.18155	.17536	.16948	.16388
51	.23625	.22769	.21955	.21182	.20448	.19749	.19084	.18452	.17849	.17275
52	.24669	.23799	.22973	.22186	.21438	.20726	.20047	.19400	.18784	.18196
53	.25742	.24861	.24022	.23222	.22461	.21735	.21043	.20383	.19753	.19151
54	.26845	.25952	.25101	.24290	.23516	.22777	.22072	.21399	.20756	.20140
55	.27978	.27074	.26212	.25389	.24604	.23853	.23136	.22450	.21793	.21166
56	.29140	.28227	.27355	.26522	.25725	.24963	.24233	.23535	.22867	.22227
57	.30333	.29411	.28529	.27686	.26879	.26106	.25365	.24656	.23976	.23324
58	.31551	.30621	.29731	.28878	.28061	.27278	.26528	.25807	.25116	.24453
59	.32790	.31854	.30956	.30095	.29269	.28477	.27716	.26986	.26284	.25610
60	.34050	.33107	.32202	.31334	.30500	.29699	.28929	.28190	.27478	.26794
61	.35331	.34384	.33473	.32598	.31757	.30948	.30170	.29422	.28701	.28007
62	.36639	.35688	.34772	.33892	.33044	.32229	.31443	.30687	.29958	.29255
63	.37974	.37020	.36101	.35216	.34363	.33542	.32750	.31986	.31250	.30539
64	.39334	.38378	.37456	.36568	.35711	.34884	.34087	.33317	.32574	.31857
65	.40718	.39761	.38838	.37947	.37087	.36257	.35455	.34681	.33932	.33208
66	.42128	.41172	.40249	.39357	.38496	.37663	.36858	.36079	.35326	.34597
67	.43569	.42616	.41694	.40803	.39941	.39107	.38299	.37518	.36761	.36028
68	.45038	.44089	.43170	.42281	.41419	.40585	.39777	.38994	.38235	.37499
69	.46531	.45587	.44672	.43786	.42927	.42094	.41286	.40503	.39743	.39006
70	.48040	.47103	.46194	.45312	.44456	.43626	.42820	.42038	.41278	.40540
71	.49558	.48629	.47727	.46851	.46000	.45174	.44371	.43591	.42832	.42095
72	.51082	.50162	.49268	.48399	.47554	.46733	.45934	.45157	.44401	.43666
73	.52607	.51697	.50813	.49952	.49114	.48299	.47506	.46733	.45981	.45249
74	.54139	.53241	.52367	.51515	.50686	.49879	.49092	.48325	.47578	.46849
75	.55683	.54798	.53936	.53095	.52276	.51477	.50698	.49938	.49197	.48474
76	.57243	.56373	.55524	.54696	.53888	.53100	.52330	.51579	.50846	.50130
77	.58819	.57965	.57132	.56318	.55523	.54747	.53988	.53247	.52523	.51815
78	.60408	.59572	.58755	.57957	.57177	.56414	.55668	.54939	.54225	.53527
79	.62001	.61184	.60385	.59604	.58840	.58092	.57360	.56644	.55943	.55256
80	.63582	.62786	.62007	.61244	.60497	.59765	.59048	.58347	.57659	.56985
81	.65142	.64367	.63608	.62864	.62135	.61421	.60721	.60034	.59361	.58701
82	.66673	.65920	.65182	.64458	.63748	.63052	.62368	.61698	.61041	.60395
83	.68175	.67444	.66728	.66024	.65334	.64656	.63991	.63338	.62696	.62066
84	.69657	.68950	.68256	.67574	.66904	.66246	.65599	.64964	.64340	.63727
85	.71128	.70446	.69775	.69116	.68467	.67830	.67204	.66587	.65982	.65386
86	.72576	.71919	.71272	.70636	.70010	.69394	.68789	.68193	.67606	.67029
87	.73981	.73349	.72726	.72114	.71511	.70917	.70333	.69757	.69190	.68632
88	.75342	.74735	.74137	.73548	.72968	.72396	.71833	.71279	.70732	.70194
89	.76658	.76076	.75503	.74938	.74381	.73832	.73290	.72757	.72231	.71712
90	.77928	.77371	.76823	.76281	.75748	.75221	.74702	.74190	.73684	.73186
91	.79131	.78600	.78075	.77557	.77046	.76542	.76044	.75553	.75068	.74589
92	.80246	.79737	.79235	.78740	.78250	.77767	.77290	.76818	.76353	.75893
93	.81274	.80788	.80307	.79832	.79363	.78899	.78441	.77989	.77542	.77100
94	.82232	.81766	.81306	.80850	.80401	.79956	.79517	.79082	.78653	.78228
95	.83141	.82695	.82254	.81818	.81387	.80961	.80539	.80122	.79710	.79302
96	.83996	.83569	.83147	.82729	.82316	.81907	.81503	.81103	.80707	.80315
97	.84787	.84378	.83973	.83573	.83176	.82784	.82396	.82012	.81632	.81255
98	.85530	.85138	.84750	.84366	.83985	.83609	.83236	.82867	.82502	.82140
99	.86255	.85880	.85508	.85140	.84776	.84415	.84057	.83703	.83353	.83005

Reg. §20.2031-7A(f)(4)

AGE	6.2%	6.4%	6.6%	6.8%	7.0%	7.2%	7.4%	7.6%	7.8%	8.0%
100	.86960	.86601	.86246	.85894	.85546	.85200	.84858	.84519	.84183	.83849
101	.87655	.87313	.86974	.86638	.86305	.85975	.85648	.85324	.85003	.84684
102	.88338	.88012	.87689	.87369	.87052	.86738	.86426	.86116	.85809	.85505
103	.89015	.88706	.88399	.88095	.87793	.87494	.87197	.86903	.86611	.86321
104	.89737	.89446	.89157	.88871	.88586	.88304	.88024	.87745	.87469	.87195
105	.90443	.90170	.89898	.89628	.89360	.89094	.88830	.88568	.88307	.88049
106	.91351	.91101	.90852	.90605	.90359	.90115	.89873	.89632	.89392	.89154
107	.92452	.92230	.92010	.91791	.91573	.91356	.91141	.90927	.90714	.90502
108	.94161	.93987	.93814	.93641	.93469	.93298	.93128	.92958	.92790	.92622
109	.97081	.96992	.96904	.96816	.96729	.96642	.96555	.96468	.96382	.96296

TABLE S
BASED ON LIFE TABLE 90CM
SINGLE LIFE REMAINDER FACTORS
[APPLICABLE AFTER APRIL 30, 1999, AND BEFORE MAY 1, 2009]

INTEREST RATE

AGE	8.2%	8.4%	8.6%	8.8%	9.0%	9.2%	9.4%	9.6%	9.8%	10.0%
0	.01906	.01845	.01790	.01740	.01694	.01652	.01613	.01578	.01546	.01516
1	.01098	.01034	.00977	.00924	.00876	.00833	.00793	.00756	.00722	.00691
2	.01113	.01046	.00986	.00930	.00880	.00834	.00791	.00753	.00717	.00684
3	.01155	.01084	.01020	.00962	.00909	.00860	.00816	.00775	.00737	.00702
4	.01211	.01137	.01069	.01008	.00952	.00900	.00853	.00810	.00770	.00733
5	.01279	.01201	.01130	.01065	.01006	.00952	.00902	.00856	.00814	.00775
6	.01356	.01274	.01199	.01131	.01068	.01011	.00959	.00910	.00865	.00824
7	.01442	.01356	.01277	.01205	.01140	.01079	.01023	.00972	.00925	.00881
8	.01536	.01446	.01363	.01287	.01218	.01154	.01096	.01041	.00991	.00945
9	.01641	.01546	.01460	.01380	.01307	.01240	.01178	.01120	.01068	.01019
10	.01758	.01659	.01567	.01484	.01407	.01336	.01270	.01210	.01154	.01103
11	.01886	.01781	.01686	.01598	.01517	.01442	.01373	.01310	.01251	.01196
12	.02024	.01915	.01814	.01721	.01636	.01558	.01485	.01419	.01357	.01299
13	.02168	.02054	.01948	.01851	.01762	.01679	.01603	.01533	.01467	.01407
14	.02313	.02193	.02083	.01981	.01887	.01801	.01721	.01646	.01578	.01514
15	.02456	.02330	.02214	.02107	.02009	.01918	.01834	.01756	.01684	.01617
16	.02593	.02462	.02340	.02229	.02126	.02030	.01942	.01860	.01785	.01714
17	.02728	.02590	.02463	.02346	.02238	.02138	.02046	.01960	.01880	.01806
18	.02861	.02717	.02584	.02462	.02348	.02243	.02146	.02056	.01972	.01894
19	.02998	.02847	.02708	.02580	.02461	.02351	.02249	.02154	.02066	.01984
20	.03142	.02984	.02839	.02704	.02580	.02465	.02357	.02258	.02165	.02079
21	.03295	.03130	.02978	.02837	.02706	.02585	.02473	.02368	.02271	.02180
22	.03455	.03283	.03124	.02976	.02839	.02712	.02594	.02484	.02382	.02286
23	.03626	.03446	.03279	.03124	.02981	.02847	.02723	.02608	.02500	.02400
24	.03809	.03620	.03446	.03283	.03133	.02993	.02863	.02741	.02628	.02522
25	.04005	.03808	.03625	.03456	.03298	.03151	.03014	.02887	.02768	.02656
26	.04216	.04010	.03819	.03641	.03476	.03322	.03178	.03044	.02919	.02802
27	.04444	.04229	.04029	.03843	.03670	.03508	.03357	.03217	.03085	.02962
28	.04687	.04463	.04254	.04059	.03877	.03708	.03550	.03402	.03263	.03133
29	.04946	.04712	.04493	.04289	.04099	.03922	.03756	.03600	.03455	.03318
30	.05221	.04976	.04748	.04534	.04335	.04149	.03975	.03812	.03659	.03515
31	.05511	.05255	.05017	.04794	.04585	.04390	.04208	.04037	.03876	.03725
32	.05818	.05551	.05302	.05069	.04851	.04647	.04455	.04276	.04107	.03948
33	.06144	.05866	.05606	.05363	.05135	.04921	.04720	.04532	.04355	.04188
34	.06489	.06200	.05928	.05674	.05436	.05212	.05002	.04805	.04619	.04444
35	.06857	.06555	.06273	.06007	.05758	.05524	.05304	.05097	.04902	.04718
36	.07246	.06932	.06638	.06361	.06101	.05856	.05626	.05409	.05205	.05012
37	.07659	.07332	.07025	.06737	.06466	.06210	.05969	.05742	.05528	.05325
38	.08098	.07758	.07439	.07138	.06855	.06588	.06336	.06099	.05874	.05662
39	.08563	.08210	.07878	.07565	.07270	.06992	.06729	.06480	.06245	.06023
40	.09059	.08692	.08347	.08021	.07714	.07423	.07149	.06889	.06643	.06411
41	.09586	.09206	.08848	.08509	.08189	.07886	.07600	.07329	.07072	.06828
42	.10147	.09753	.09381	.09029	.08696	.08381	.08083	.07800	.07531	.07277
43	.10742	.10334	.09948	.09583	.09237	.08909	.08598	.08304	.08024	.07758
44	.11373	.10950	.10551	.10172	.09813	.09472	.09148	.08841	.08549	.08272
45	.12035	.11599	.11185	.10792	.10420	.10066	.09730	.09410	.09106	.08817
46	.12732	.12281	.11853	.11447	.11061	.10694	.10345	.10013	.09696	.09395
47	.13460	.12995	.12553	.12133	.11733	.11353	.10991	.10646	.10317	.10004

Reg. §20.2031-7A(f)(4)

AGE	8.2%	8.4%	8.6%	8.8%	9.0%	9.2%	9.4%	9.6%	9.8%	10.0%
48	.14223	.13743	.13287	.12853	.12439	.12046	.11671	.11313	.10972	.10646
49	.15020	.14526	.14056	.13608	.13181	.12774	.12385	.12015	.11661	.11322
50	.15855	.15347	.14862	.14401	.13960	.13540	.13138	.12754	.12388	.12037
51	.16727	.16205	.15707	.15232	.14777	.14344	.13929	.13532	.13153	.12789
52	.17634	.17098	.16587	.16097	.15630	.15183	.14755	.14345	.13953	.13577
53	.18576	.18027	.17501	.16999	.16518	.16057	.15616	.15194	.14789	.14400
54	.19552	.18990	.18451	.17935	.17441	.16968	.16514	.16078	.15661	.15260
55	.20564	.19989	.19437	.18908	.18402	.17915	.17449	.17001	.16571	.16157
56	.21613	.21025	.20461	.19919	.19400	.18901	.18422	.17962	.17519	.17093
57	.22698	.22098	.21522	.20968	.20436	.19925	.19434	.18961	.18507	.18069
58	.23816	.23204	.22616	.22051	.21507	.20984	.20481	.19996	.19530	.19080
59	.24962	.24339	.23740	.23163	.22608	.22073	.21558	.21062	.20584	.20123
60	.26136	.25502	.24892	.24304	.23738	.23192	.22666	.22158	.21669	.21196
61	.27339	.26695	.26075	.25477	.24900	.24343	.23806	.23288	.22787	.22304
62	.28578	.27925	.27295	.26687	.26100	.25533	.24985	.24456	.23945	.23451
63	.29854	.29192	.28553	.27935	.27339	.26762	.26205	.25666	.25145	.24641
64	.31164	.30494	.29846	.29221	.28615	.28030	.27463	.26915	.26384	.25870
65	.32508	.31831	.31177	.30543	.29930	.29336	.28761	.28203	.27663	.27140
66	.33891	.33208	.32547	.31906	.31285	.30684	.30101	.29536	.28987	.28456
67	.35318	.34630	.33963	.33316	.32689	.32081	.31491	.30918	.30363	.29823
68	.36785	.36093	.35422	.34770	.34138	.33524	.32928	.32349	.31787	.31240
69	.38290	.37595	.36920	.36265	.35628	.35009	.34408	.33824	.33256	.32703
70	.39823	.39127	.38450	.37791	.37151	.36529	.35924	.35335	.34762	.34204
71	.41378	.40681	.40003	.39343	.38701	.38076	.37467	.36875	.36298	.35736
72	.42950	.42253	.41575	.40914	.40271	.39644	.39034	.38438	.37858	.37293
73	.44535	.43840	.43162	.42502	.41858	.41231	.40619	.40022	.39440	.38872
74	.46139	.45446	.44771	.44112	.43469	.42842	.42230	.41632	.41049	.40479
75	.47769	.47080	.46408	.45752	.45111	.44485	.43874	.43277	.42693	.42123
76	.49430	.48747	.48079	.47427	.46790	.46167	.45558	.44963	.44380	.43811
77	.51123	.50447	.49786	.49139	.48506	.47888	.47282	.46690	.46111	.45543
78	.52845	.52177	.51523	.50884	.50257	.49645	.49044	.48457	.47881	.47317
79	.54584	.53926	.53282	.52650	.52032	.51426	.50833	.50251	.49681	.49122
80	.56325	.55678	.55044	.54423	.53813	.53216	.52630	.52056	.51492	.50939
81	.58054	.57419	.56797	.56186	.55587	.54999	.54422	.53856	.53300	.52754
82	.59762	.59140	.58530	.57931	.57343	.56766	.56198	.55641	.55094	.54557
83	.61448	.60840	.60243	.59657	.59081	.58515	.57958	.57411	.56874	.56346
84	.63124	.62531	.61949	.61376	.60813	.60259	.59715	.59179	.58652	.58134
85	.64800	.64224	.63657	.63099	.62550	.62010	.61478	.60955	.60441	.59934
86	.66461	.65902	.65351	.64810	.64276	.63751	.63233	.62724	.62222	.61728
87	.68083	.67541	.67008	.66483	.65965	.65455	.64953	.64458	.63970	.63489
88	.69663	.69140	.68624	.68116	.67615	.67121	.66634	.66154	.65680	.65213
89	.71201	.70696	.70199	.69708	.69224	.68747	.68276	.67811	.67353	.66900
90	.72694	.72209	.71730	.71257	.70791	.70330	.69876	.69427	.68984	.68547
91	.74117	.73650	.73190	.72735	.72286	.71842	.71404	.70972	.70545	.70123
92	.75439	.74991	.74548	.74110	.73678	.73251	.72829	.72412	.72000	.71593
93	.76664	.76233	.75806	.75385	.74969	.74557	.74150	.73748	.73350	.72957
94	.77809	.77394	.76983	.76578	.76177	.75780	.75388	.75000	.74616	.74237
95	.78899	.78500	.78106	.77715	.77329	.76947	.76569	.76195	.75826	.75460
96	.79928	.79544	.79165	.78790	.78418	.78050	.77686	.77326	.76970	.76617
97	.80883	.80514	.80149	.79787	.79430	.79075	.78725	.78377	.78033	.77693
98	.81781	.81427	.81075	.80727	.80382	.80041	.79703	.79368	.79036	.78708
99	.82661	.82320	.81982	.81648	.81316	.80988	.80662	.80340	.80020	.79704

Reg. § 20.2031-7A(f)(4)

AGE	8.2%	8.4%	8.6%	8.8%	9.0%	9.2%	9.4%	9.6%	9.8%	10.0%
100	.83519	.83192	.82868	.82547	.82228	.81913	.81600	.81290	.80982	.80678
101	.84368	.84055	.83744	.83437	.83131	.82829	.82529	.82231	.81936	.81643
102	.85203	.84904	.84607	.84313	.84021	.83731	.83444	.83159	.82876	.82596
103	.86034	.85748	.85465	.85184	.84906	.84629	.84355	.84082	.83812	.83544
104	.86923	.86653	.86385	.86119	.85855	.85593	.85333	.85074	.84818	.84563
105	.87792	.87537	.87283	.87032	.86782	.86534	.86287	.86042	.85799	.85557
106	.88918	.88683	.88450	.88218	.87987	.87758	.87530	.87304	.87079	.86855
107	.90291	.90082	.89873	.89666	.89460	.89255	.89051	.88849	.88647	.88447
108	.92455	.92288	.92123	.91958	.91794	.91630	.91468	.91306	.91145	.90984
109	.96211	.96125	.96041	.95956	.95872	.95788	.95704	.95620	.95537	.95455

TABLE S
BASED ON LIFE TABLE 90CM
SINGLE LIFE REMAINDER FACTORS
[APPLICABLE AFTER APRIL 30, 1999, AND BEFORE MAY 1, 2009]

INTEREST RATE

AGE	10.2%	10.4%	10.6%	10.8%	11.0%	11.2%	11.4%	11.6%	11.8%	12.0%
0	.01488	.01463	.01439	.01417	.01396	.01377	.01359	.01343	.01327	.01312
1	.00662	.00636	.00612	.00589	.00568	.00548	.00530	.00513	.00497	.00482
2	.00654	.00626	.00600	.00576	.00554	.00533	.00514	.00496	.00479	.00463
3	.00670	.00641	.00613	.00588	.00564	.00542	.00522	.00502	.00484	.00468
4	.00699	.00668	.00639	.00612	.00587	.00563	.00542	.00521	.00502	.00484
5	.00739	.00706	.00675	.00646	.00620	.00595	.00571	.00550	.00529	.00510
6	.00786	.00751	.00718	.00687	.00659	.00633	.00608	.00585	.00563	.00543
7	.00841	.00803	.00769	.00736	.00706	.00678	.00652	.00627	.00604	.00582
8	.00902	.00863	.00826	.00791	.00759	.00730	.00702	.00675	.00651	.00628
9	.00973	.00931	.00892	.00856	.00822	.00790	.00760	.00733	.00706	.00682
10	.01055	.01010	.00969	.00930	.00894	.00861	.00829	.00799	.00772	.00746
11	.01146	.01099	.01055	.01014	.00976	.00940	.00907	.00875	.00846	.00818
12	.01246	.01196	.01150	.01106	.01066	.01028	.00993	.00960	.00928	.00899
13	.01351	.01298	.01249	.01204	.01161	.01121	.01084	.01049	.01016	.00985
14	.01455	.01400	.01348	.01300	.01255	.01213	.01173	.01136	.01102	.01069
15	.01555	.01497	.01443	.01392	.01345	.01300	.01259	.01220	.01183	.01148
16	.01648	.01587	.01530	.01477	.01427	.01380	.01336	.01295	.01257	.01220
17	.01737	.01673	.01612	.01556	.01504	.01455	.01408	.01365	.01324	.01286
18	.01822	.01754	.01691	.01632	.01576	.01525	.01476	.01430	.01387	.01347
19	.01908	.01837	.01770	.01708	.01650	.01595	.01544	.01495	.01450	.01407
20	.01999	.01924	.01854	.01788	.01726	.01669	.01615	.01564	.01516	.01471
21	.02096	.02017	.01943	.01874	.01809	.01748	.01691	.01637	.01586	.01539
22	.02197	.02114	.02036	.01963	.01895	.01830	.01770	.01713	.01660	.01610
23	.02306	.02218	.02136	.02059	.01987	.01919	.01855	.01795	.01739	.01686
24	.02424	.02331	.02245	.02163	.02087	.02016	.01948	.01885	.01825	.01769
25	.02552	.02455	.02364	.02278	.02197	.02122	.02051	.01984	.01920	.01861
26	.02692	.02589	.02493	.02403	.02318	.02238	.02162	.02091	.02025	.01961
27	.02846	.02738	.02636	.02541	.02451	.02367	.02287	.02212	.02141	.02074
28	.03012	.02898	.02791	.02690	.02595	.02506	.02422	.02342	.02267	.02196
29	.03190	.03070	.02957	.02851	.02751	.02656	.02567	.02483	.02404	.02329
30	.03381	.03254	.03135	.03023	.02917	.02817	.02723	.02634	.02551	.02471
31	.03583	.03450	.03324	.03206	.03094	.02989	.02890	.02796	.02707	.02623
32	.03799	.03659	.03527	.03402	.03284	.03173	.03068	.02968	.02874	.02785
33	.04031	.03883	.03744	.03612	.03488	.03371	.03260	.03155	.03055	.02961
34	.04279	.04123	.03976	.03838	.03707	.03583	.03465	.03354	.03249	.03149
35	.04545	.04382	.04227	.04081	.03943	.03812	.03688	.03571	.03459	.03354
36	.04830	.04658	.04495	.04341	.04196	.04058	.03927	.03803	.03685	.03573
37	.05134	.04953	.04782	.04620	.04467	.04321	.04183	.04052	.03928	.03809
38	.05462	.05272	.05092	.04921	.04760	.04606	.04461	.04322	.04191	.04066
39	.05812	.05613	.05424	.05245	.05075	.04913	.04760	.04614	.04475	.04343
40	.06190	.05981	.05782	.05594	.05415	.05245	.05083	.04929	.04783	.04643
41	.06597	.06378	.06170	.05972	.05784	.05605	.05435	.05272	.05118	.04970
42	.07035	.06806	.06587	.06380	.06182	.05994	.05815	.05644	.05481	.05326
43	.07505	.07265	.07036	.06818	.06611	.06414	.06225	.06045	.05874	.05710
44	.08008	.07757	.07518	.07290	.07072	.06865	.06667	.06478	.06298	.06125
45	.08542	.08279	.08029	.07791	.07563	.07346	.07138	.06940	.06750	.06569
46	.09108	.08834	.08573	.08324	.08085	.07858	.07640	.07432	.07233	.07043
47	.09705	.09419	.09147	.08886	.08637	.08399	.08172	.07954	.07745	.07545

AGE	10.2%	10.4%	10.6%	10.8%	11.0%	11.2%	11.4%	11.6%	11.8%	12.0%
48	.10335	.10038	.09754	.09482	.09222	.08973	.08735	.08507	.08288	.08078
49	.10999	.10690	.10394	.10111	.09840	.09581	.09332	.09093	.08864	.08644
50	.11701	.11380	.11073	.10778	.10496	.10225	.09965	.09716	.09477	.09247
51	.12441	.12108	.11789	.11482	.11189	.10907	.10636	.10376	.10126	.09886
52	.13217	.12871	.12540	.12222	.11916	.11623	.11341	.11071	.10810	.10560
53	.14028	.13670	.13327	.12997	.12680	.12375	.12082	.11801	.11529	.11268
54	.14875	.14505	.14150	.13808	.13480	.13163	.12859	.12566	.12284	.12012
55	.15760	.15378	.15011	.14657	.14317	.13989	.13674	.13370	.13077	.12794
56	.16684	.16290	.15911	.15546	.15194	.14855	.14528	.14213	.13909	.13615
57	.17648	.17242	.16851	.16474	.16111	.15760	.15422	.15096	.14781	.14477
58	.18647	.18229	.17827	.17438	.17064	.16702	.16353	.16015	.15689	.15374
59	.19678	.19249	.18835	.18435	.18049	.17676	.17316	.16968	.16631	.16305
60	.20740	.20300	.19875	.19464	.19066	.18682	.18311	.17952	.17604	.17268
61	.21837	.21385	.20949	.20527	.20119	.19724	.19341	.18971	.18613	.18266
62	.22973	.22511	.22064	.21631	.21212	.20807	.20414	.20033	.19664	.19306
63	.24152	.23680	.23222	.22779	.22350	.21934	.21530	.21139	.20760	.20392
64	.25372	.24890	.24422	.23969	.23529	.23103	.22690	.22289	.21899	.21521
65	.26633	.26141	.25664	.25201	.24752	.24316	.23893	.23482	.23083	.22695
66	.27940	.27439	.26953	.26481	.26023	.25577	.25145	.24724	.24316	.23918
67	.29299	.28790	.28296	.27815	.27348	.26894	.26453	.26024	.25606	.25200
68	.30709	.30193	.29691	.29202	.28728	.28265	.27816	.27378	.26952	.26537
69	.32166	.31643	.31134	.30639	.30157	.29687	.29230	.28785	.28351	.27928
70	.33661	.33133	.32618	.32116	.31628	.31152	.30688	.30235	.29794	.29364
71	.35188	.34654	.34134	.33627	.33133	.32651	.32181	.31722	.31275	.30838
72	.36742	.36204	.35679	.35168	.34668	.34181	.33706	.33241	.32788	.32345
73	.38317	.37776	.37248	.36733	.36229	.35738	.35257	.34788	.34330	.33882
74	.39923	.39380	.38849	.38330	.37823	.37328	.36844	.36370	.35908	.35455
75	.41566	.41021	.40489	.39968	.39459	.38961	.38474	.37997	.37531	.37074
76	.43254	.42709	.42176	.41655	.41144	.40645	.40156	.39677	.39208	.38749
77	.44988	.44444	.43912	.43391	.42880	.42380	.41891	.41411	.40940	.40479
78	.46765	.46224	.45694	.45174	.44665	.44166	.43677	.43197	.42726	.42265
79	.48574	.48037	.47510	.46993	.46487	.45990	.45502	.45024	.44554	.44094
80	.50397	.49865	.49343	.48830	.48327	.47834	.47349	.46873	.46406	.45947
81	.52219	.51693	.51176	.50669	.50171	.49682	.49201	.48729	.48265	.47809
82	.54029	.53510	.53000	.52499	.52007	.51523	.51047	.50580	.50120	.49667
83	.55826	.55315	.54813	.54319	.53834	.53356	.52886	.52424	.51969	.51522
84	.57624	.57123	.56629	.56144	.55666	.55195	.54732	.54277	.53828	.53386
85	.59435	.58944	.58460	.57984	.57516	.57054	.56599	.56151	.55710	.55275
86	.61241	.60762	.60289	.59824	.59365	.58913	.58468	.58029	.57596	.57170
87	.63015	.62548	.62087	.61633	.61185	.60744	.60309	.59880	.59456	.59039
88	.64753	.64299	.63851	.63409	.62973	.62543	.62118	.61700	.61287	.60879
89	.66454	.66013	.65579	.65150	.64726	.64308	.63895	.63488	.63086	.62689
90	.68115	.67689	.67268	.66853	.66442	.66037	.65637	.65241	.64851	.64465
91	.69706	.69294	.68887	.68486	.68089	.67696	.67309	.66925	.66547	.66173
92	.71190	.70792	.70399	.70011	.69627	.69247	.68872	.68501	.68134	.67771
93	.72569	.72184	.71804	.71429	.71057	.70689	.70326	.69967	.69611	.69259
94	.73861	.73490	.73123	.72759	.72400	.72044	.71692	.71344	.71000	.70659
95	.75097	.74739	.74384	.74033	.73686	.73342	.73002	.72665	.72331	.72001
96	.76267	.75922	.75579	.75240	.74905	.74572	.74243	.73917	.73595	.73275
97	.77356	.77022	.76691	.76363	.76039	.75718	.75399	.75084	.74772	.74463
98	.78382	.78059	.77740	.77423	.77110	.76799	.76491	.76186	.75884	.75584
99	.79390	.79079	.78771	.78465	.78162	.77862	.77565	.77270	.76978	.76688

AGE	10.2%	10.4%	10.6%	10.8%	11.0%	11.2%	11.4%	11.6%	11.8%	12.0%
100	.80376	.80076	.79779	.79485	.79193	.78904	.78617	.78333	.78051	.77771
101	.81353	.81066	.80780	.80497	.80217	.79938	.79662	.79388	.79117	.78847
102	.82318	.82042	.81768	.81496	.81227	.80960	.80694	.80431	.80170	.79911
103	.83278	.83014	.82752	.82491	.82233	.81977	.81723	.81470	.81220	.80971
104	.84310	.84059	.83810	.83563	.83317	.83073	.82831	.82591	.82352	.82115
105	.85318	.85079	.84843	.84607	.84374	.84142	.83911	.83682	.83455	.83229
106	.86633	.86413	.86193	.85975	.85758	.85543	.85329	.85116	.84904	.84694
107	.88247	.88049	.87852	.87656	.87460	.87266	.87073	.86881	.86690	.86500
108	.90825	.90666	.90507	.90350	.90193	.90037	.89881	.89727	.89572	.89419
109	.95372	.95290	.95208	.95126	.95045	.94964	.94883	.94803	.94723	.94643

TABLE S
BASED ON LIFE TABLE 90CM
SINGLE LIFE REMAINDER FACTORS
[APPLICABLE AFTER APRIL 30, 1999, AND BEFORE MAY 1, 2009]

INTEREST RATE

AGE	12.2%	12.4%	12.6%	12.8%	13.0%	13.2%	13.4%	13.6%	13.8%	14.0%
0	.01298	.01285	.01273	.01261	.01250	.01240	.01230	.01221	.01212	.01203
1	.00468	.00455	.00443	.00431	.00420	.00410	.00400	.00391	.00382	.00374
2	.00448	.00435	.00421	.00409	.00398	.00387	.00376	.00366	.00357	.00348
3	.00452	.00437	.00423	.00410	.00398	.00386	.00375	.00365	.00355	.00345
4	.00468	.00452	.00437	.00423	.00410	.00397	.00386	.00375	.00364	.00354
5	.00493	.00476	.00460	.00445	.00431	.00418	.00405	.00393	.00382	.00371
6	.00524	.00506	.00489	.00473	.00458	.00444	.00430	.00418	.00406	.00394
7	.00562	.00543	.00525	.00508	.00492	.00477	.00462	.00449	.00436	.00423
8	.00606	.00586	.00566	.00548	.00531	.00515	.00499	.00485	.00471	.00458
9	.00659	.00637	.00616	.00597	.00579	.00561	.00545	.00529	.00514	.00500
10	.00721	.00698	.00676	.00655	.00636	.00617	.00600	.00583	.00567	.00552
11	.00792	.00767	.00744	.00722	.00701	.00682	.00663	.00645	.00628	.00612
12	.00871	.00845	.00821	.00797	.00775	.00754	.00735	.00716	.00698	.00681
13	.00955	.00928	.00902	.00877	.00854	.00831	.00810	.00790	.00771	.00753
14	.01038	.01009	.00981	.00955	.00930	.00907	.00885	.00864	.00843	.00824
15	.01116	.01085	.01056	.01028	.01002	.00977	.00954	.00932	.00910	.00890
16	.01186	.01153	.01123	.01094	.01066	.01040	.01015	.00992	.00969	.00948
17	.01250	.01215	.01183	.01152	.01124	.01096	.01070	.01045	.01022	.00999
18	.01308	.01272	.01238	.01206	.01175	.01147	.01119	.01093	.01068	.01044
19	.01367	.01329	.01293	.01259	.01227	.01196	.01167	.01140	.01113	.01088
20	.01428	.01388	.01350	.01314	.01280	.01248	.01217	.01188	.01161	.01134
21	.01494	.01451	.01411	.01373	.01337	.01303	.01271	.01240	.01211	.01183
22	.01562	.01517	.01475	.01435	.01397	.01361	.01326	.01294	.01263	.01233
23	.01635	.01588	.01543	.01501	.01460	.01422	.01386	.01351	.01319	.01287
24	.01716	.01665	.01618	.01573	.01530	.01489	.01451	.01415	.01380	.01347
25	.01804	.01751	.01701	.01653	.01608	.01565	.01524	.01485	.01448	.01413
26	.01902	.01845	.01792	.01741	.01693	.01648	.01604	.01563	.01524	.01487
27	.02011	.01951	.01895	.01841	.01790	.01742	.01696	.01652	.01610	.01571
28	.02129	.02066	.02006	.01949	.01895	.01844	.01795	.01748	.01704	.01662
29	.02258	.02191	.02127	.02067	.02009	.01955	.01903	.01853	.01806	.01762
30	.02396	.02325	.02257	.02193	.02132	.02074	.02019	.01966	.01916	.01869
31	.02543	.02467	.02396	.02328	.02263	.02201	.02143	.02087	.02034	.01983
32	.02701	.02621	.02545	.02472	.02404	.02338	.02276	.02217	.02160	.02106
33	.02871	.02786	.02706	.02629	.02556	.02487	.02420	.02357	.02297	.02240
34	.03054	.02964	.02879	.02797	.02720	.02646	.02576	.02509	.02445	.02383
35	.03253	.03158	.03067	.02981	.02898	.02820	.02745	.02674	.02606	.02541
36	.03467	.03366	.03269	.03178	.03090	.03007	.02928	.02852	.02779	.02710
37	.03697	.03590	.03488	.03391	.03298	.03209	.03125	.03044	.02967	.02893
38	.03947	.03833	.03725	.03622	.03524	.03430	.03340	.03254	.03172	.03094
39	.04217	.04096	.03982	.03873	.03768	.03669	.03573	.03482	.03395	.03312
40	.04510	.04383	.04262	.04146	.04035	.03930	.03828	.03732	.03639	.03550
41	.04830	.04695	.04567	.04445	.04327	.04215	.04108	.04005	.03907	.03812
42	.05177	.05035	.04900	.04770	.04646	.04527	.04413	.04304	.04200	.04100
43	.05553	.05404	.05261	.05123	.04992	.04866	.04746	.04630	.04520	.04413
44	.05960	.05802	.05651	.05506	.05368	.05235	.05107	.04985	.04867	.04754
45	.06395	.06229	.06069	.05917	.05770	.05630	.05495	.05365	.05241	.05121
46	.06860	.06685	.06517	.06356	.06202	.06053	.05911	.05774	.05643	.05516
47	.07353	.07169	.06992	.06823	.06660	.06504	.06353	.06209	.06070	.05936

AGE	12.2%	12.4%	12.6%	12.8%	13.0%	13.2%	13.4%	13.6%	13.8%	14.0%
48	.07877	.07684	.07498	.07320	.07149	.06984	.06826	.06673	.06527	.06385
49	.08433	.08231	.08036	.07849	.07669	.07495	.07329	.07168	.07013	.06864
50	.09026	.08814	.08609	.08413	.08224	.08042	.07867	.07698	.07535	.07378
51	.09655	.09433	.09219	.09013	.08815	.08624	.08440	.08262	.08091	.07926
52	.10318	.10086	.09863	.09647	.09439	.09239	.09046	.08860	.08680	.08506
53	.11017	.10774	.10541	.10315	.10098	.09888	.09686	.09491	.09302	.09120
54	.11750	.11498	.11254	.11019	.10792	.10572	.10361	.10156	.09958	.09767
55	.12522	.12258	.12005	.11759	.11522	.11294	.11072	.10859	.10652	.10451
56	.13332	.13059	.12794	.12539	.12292	.12054	.11823	.11599	.11383	.11174
57	.14183	.13899	.13624	.13359	.13102	.12853	.12613	.12380	.12154	.11936
58	.15070	.14775	.14490	.14215	.13948	.13689	.13439	.13197	.12962	.12734
59	.15990	.15685	.15389	.15103	.14826	.14558	.14298	.14046	.13801	.13564
60	.16942	.16626	.16321	.16024	.15737	.15459	.15189	.14927	.14673	.14426
61	.17929	.17603	.17287	.16981	.16684	.16395	.16115	.15844	.15580	.15324
62	.18960	.18623	.18297	.17980	.17673	.17375	.17085	.16803	.16530	.16264
63	.20035	.19688	.19352	.19025	.18708	.18400	.18100	.17809	.17525	.17250
64	.21154	.20797	.20451	.20114	.19787	.19469	.19159	.18859	.18566	.18281
65	.22318	.21951	.21595	.21249	.20912	.20584	.20265	.19955	.19652	.19358
66	.23532	.23156	.22790	.22434	.22088	.21751	.21422	.21102	.20791	.20487
67	.24804	.24419	.24044	.23679	.23324	.22977	.22640	.22311	.21990	.21678
68	.26133	.25740	.25356	.24983	.24618	.24263	.23917	.23579	.23250	.22929
69	.27516	.27114	.26723	.26341	.25969	.25605	.25251	.24905	.24567	.24237
70	.28945	.28536	.28137	.27747	.27367	.26996	.26633	.26279	.25934	.25596
71	.30412	.29996	.29590	.29193	.28806	.28427	.28057	.27696	.27343	.26998
72	.31913	.31491	.31078	.30675	.30281	.29895	.29519	.29150	.28790	.28438
73	.33444	.33016	.32597	.32188	.31788	.31396	.31013	.30638	.30271	.29913
74	.35012	.34579	.34155	.33741	.33335	.32938	.32549	.32168	.31795	.31430
75	.36628	.36190	.35762	.35343	.34932	.34530	.34136	.33750	.33372	.33001
76	.38299	.37858	.37427	.37004	.36589	.36183	.35784	.35394	.35011	.34636
77	.40028	.39585	.39151	.38725	.38307	.37898	.37496	.37103	.36716	.36337
78	.41812	.41368	.40933	.40506	.40086	.39675	.39271	.38874	.38485	.38103
79	.43641	.43198	.42762	.42334	.41914	.41502	.41096	.40698	.40308	.39924
80	.45496	.45054	.44619	.44192	.43772	.43360	.42954	.42556	.42164	.41779
81	.47360	.46920	.46487	.46061	.45643	.45231	.44827	.44429	.44038	.43653
82	.49223	.48785	.48355	.47932	.47516	.47106	.46703	.46307	.45916	.45532
83	.51081	.50648	.50221	.49802	.49388	.48982	.48581	.48187	.47799	.47416
84	.52951	.52523	.52101	.51686	.51277	.50874	.50477	.50086	.49701	.49321
85	.54847	.54425	.54009	.53600	.53196	.52798	.52406	.52019	.51638	.51262
86	.56749	.56335	.55926	.55523	.55126	.54734	.54348	.53966	.53591	.53220
87	.58627	.58221	.57820	.57425	.57035	.56650	.56270	.55895	.55526	.55161
88	.60477	.60079	.59688	.59301	.58919	.58542	.58170	.57802	.57439	.57081
89	.62297	.61909	.61527	.61149	.60776	.60408	.60044	.59685	.59330	.58979
90	.64084	.63707	.63335	.62968	.62604	.62246	.61891	.61540	.61194	.60851
91	.65803	.65437	.65076	.64719	.64366	.64017	.63672	.63330	.62993	.62659
92	.67412	.67058	.66707	.66360	.66017	.65678	.65342	.65010	.64682	.64357
93	.68911	.68567	.68227	.67890	.67557	.67227	.66901	.66578	.66258	.65942
94	.70321	.69988	.69657	.69330	.69006	.68686	.68369	.68055	.67744	.67437
95	.71674	.71351	.71031	.70713	.70399	.70088	.69781	.69476	.69174	.68875
96	.72959	.72646	.72335	.72028	.71724	.71422	.71123	.70828	.70534	.70244
97	.74156	.73853	.73552	.73254	.72959	.72666	.72376	.72089	.71804	.71522
98	.75287	.74993	.74702	.74413	.74126	.73842	.73561	.73282	.73006	.72732
99	.76401	.76117	.75834	.75555	.75277	.75002	.74730	.74459	.74191	.73926

Reg. § 20.2031-7A(f)(4)

AGE	12.2%	12.4%	12.6%	12.8%	13.0%	13.2%	13.4%	13.6%	13.8%	14.0%
100	.77494	.77219	.76946	.76676	.76408	.76142	.75878	.75616	.75357	.75099
101	.78580	.78315	.78052	.77791	.77532	.77275	.77021	.76768	.76517	.76268
102	.79654	.79399	.79146	.78894	.78645	.78397	.78152	.77908	.77666	.77426
103	.80724	.80479	.80236	.79994	.79755	.79517	.79280	.79046	.78813	.78582
104	.81879	.81646	.81413	.81183	.80954	.80726	.80501	.80276	.80054	.79832
105	.83005	.82782	.82560	.82340	.82121	.81904	.81688	.81474	.81260	.81049
106	.84485	.84277	.84071	.83866	.83662	.83459	.83257	.83057	.82857	.82659
107	.86311	.86124	.85937	.85751	.85566	.85382	.85199	.85017	.84835	.84655
108	.89266	.89114	.88963	.88812	.88662	.88513	.88364	.88216	.88068	.87922
109	.94563	.94484	.94405	.94326	.94248	.94170	.94092	.94014	.93937	.93860

LIFE TABLE
TABLE 90CM
APPLICABLE AFTER APRIL 30, 1999, AND BEFORE MAY 1, 2009

Age x	l(x)	Age x	l(x)	Age x	l(x)
(1)	(2)	(1)	(2)	(1)	(2)
0	100000	37	95969	74	62852
1	99064	38	95780	75	60449
2	98992	39	95581	76	57955
3	98944	40	95373	77	55373
4	98907	41	95156	78	52704
5	98877	42	94928	79	49943
6	98850	43	94687	80	47084
7	98826	44	94431	81	44129
8	98803	45	94154	82	41091
9	98783	46	93855	83	37994
10	98766	47	93528	84	34876
11	98750	48	93173	85	31770
12	98734	49	92787	86	28687
13	98713	50	92370	87	25638
14	98681	51	91918	88	22658
15	98635	52	91424	89	19783
16	98573	53	90885	90	17046
17	98497	54	90297	91	14466
18	98409	55	89658	92	12066
19	98314	56	88965	93	9884
20	98215	57	88214	94	7951
21	98113	58	87397	95	6282
22	98006	59	86506	96	4868
23	97896	60	85537	97	3694
24	97784	61	84490	98	2745
25	97671	62	83368	99	1999
26	97556	63	82169	100	1424
27	97441	64	80887	101	991
28	97322	65	79519	102	672
29	97199	66	78066	103	443
30	97070	67	76531	104	284
31	96934	68	74907	105	175
32	96791	69	73186	106	105
33	96642	70	71357	107	60
34	96485	71	69411	108	33
35	96322	72	67344	109	17
36	96150	73	65154	110	0

(5) *Effective/applicability dates.*—Paragraphs (f)(1) through (f)(4) apply after April 30, 1999, and before May 1, 2009. [Reg. § 20.2031-7A.]

□ [T.D. 6296, 6-23-58. *Amended by T.D. 7077,* 12-1-70 and T.D. 7955, 5-10-84. Reg. § 20.2031-7 was redesignated Reg. § 20.2031-7A(d) and amended by T.D. 8540, 6-9-94. Amended by T.D. 8819, 4-29-99 (corrected 6-21-99); T.D. 8886, 6-9-2000; T.D. 9448, 5-1-2009 and T.D. 9540, 8-9-2011.]

[Reg. § 20.2031-8]

§ 20.2031-8. Valuation of certain life insurance and annuity contracts; valuation of shares in an open-end investment company.— (a) *Valuation of certain life insurance and annuity contracts.*—(1) The value of a contract for the payment of an annuity, or an insurance policy on the life of a person other than the decedent, issued by a company regularly engaged in the selling of contracts of that character is established through the sale by that company of comparable contracts. An annuity payable under a combination annuity contract and life insurance policy on the decedent's life (e.g., a "retirement income" policy with death benefit) under which there was no insurance element at the time of the decedent's death (see paragraph (d) of § 20.2039-1) is treated like a contract for the payment of an annuity for purposes of this section.

(2) As valuation of an insurance policy through sale of comparable contracts is not readily ascertainable when, at the date of the decedent's death, the contract has been in force for some time and further premium payments are to be made, the value may be approximated by adding to the interpolated terminal reserve at the date of the decedent's death the proportionate part of the gross premium last paid before the date of the decedent's death which covers the period extending beyond that date. If, however, because of the unusual nature of the contract such an approximation is not reasonably close to

the full value of the contract, this method may not be used.

(3) The application of this section may be illustrated by the following examples. In each case involving an insurance contract, it is assumed that there are no accrued dividends or outstanding indebtedness on the contract.

Example (1). X purchased from a life insurance company a joint and survivor annuity contract under the terms of which X was to receive payments of $1,200 annually for his life and, upon X's death, his wife was to receive payments of $1,200 annually for her life. Five years after such purchase, when his wife was 50 years of age, X died. The value of the annuity contract at the date of X's death is the amount which the company would charge for an annuity providing for the payment of $1,200 annually for the life of a female 50 years of age.

Example (2). Y died holding the incidents of ownership in a life insurance policy on the life of his wife. The policy was one on which no further payments were to be made to the company (e.g., a single premium policy or a paid-up policy). The value of the insurance policy at the date of Y's death is the amount which the company would charge for a single premium contract of the same specified amount on the life of a person of the age of the insured.

Example (3). Z died holding the incidents of ownership in a life insurance policy on the life of his wife. The policy was an ordinary life policy issued nine years and four months prior to Z's death and at a time when Z's wife was 35 years of age. The gross annual premium is $2,811 and the decedent died four months after the last premium due date. The value of the insurance policy at the date of Z's death is computed as follows:

Terminal reserve at end of tenth year	$14,601.00
Terminal reserve at end of ninth year	12,965.00
Increase	$1,636.00
One-third of such increase (Z having died four months following the last preceding premium due date) is........................	$545.33
Terminal reserve at end of ninth year	12,965.00
Interpolated terminal reserve at date of Z's death...............	13,510.33
Two-thirds of gross premium ($2/3 \times \$2,811$)	1,874.00
Value of the insurance policy................................	$15,384.33

(b) *Valuation of shares in an open-end investment company.*—(1) The fair market value of a share in an open-end investment company (commonly known as a "mutual fund") is the public redemption price of a share. In the absence of an affirmative showing of the public redemption price in effect at the time of death, the last public redemption price quoted by the company for the date of death shall be presumed to be the applicable public redemption price. If the alternate valuation method under 2032 is elected, the last public redemption price quoted by the company for the alternate valuation date shall be the applicable redemption price. If there is no public redemption price quoted by the company for the applicable valuation date (e.g., the valuation date is a Saturday, Sunday, or holiday), the fair market value of the mutual fund share is the last public redemption price quoted by the company for the first day preceding the applicable valuation date for which there is a quotation. In any case where a dividend is declared on a share in an open-end investment company before the decedent's death but payable to shareholders of record on a date after his death and the share is quoted "ex-dividend" on the date of the decedent's death, the amount of the dividend is added to the ex-dividend quotation in determining the fair market value of the share as of the date of the decedent's death. As used in this paragraph, the term "open-end investment company" includes only a company which on the applicable valuation date was engaged in offering its shares to the public in the capacity of an open-end investment company.

(2) The provisions of this paragraph shall apply with respect to estates of decedents dying after August 16, 1954. [Reg. § 20.2031-8.]

☐ [*T.D.* 6296, 6-23-58. *Amended by T.D.* 6680, 10-9-63 *and T.D.* 7319, 7-22-74.]

[Reg. § 20.2031-9]

§ 20.2031-9. Valuation of other property.— The valuation of any property not specifically described in §§ 20.2031-2 through 20.2031-8 is made in accordance with the general principles set forth in § 20.2031-1. For example, a future interest in property not subject to valuation in accordance with the actuarial principles set forth in § 20.2031-7 is to be valued in accordance with the general principles set forth in § 20.2031-1. [Reg. § 20.2031-9.]

☐ [*T.D.* 6296, 6-23-58.]

[Reg. § 20.2032-1]

§ 20.2032-1. Alternate valuation.—(a) *In general.*—In general, section 2032 provides for the valuation of a decedent's gross estate at a date other than the date of the decedent's death. More specifically, if an executor elects the alternate valuation method under section 2032, the property included in the decedent's gross estate on the date of his death is valued as of whichever of the following dates is applicable:

(1) Any property distributed, sold, exchanged, or otherwise disposed of within 6 months (1 year, if the decedent died on or before December 31, 1970) after the decedent's death is valued as of the date on which it is first distributed, sold, exchanged, or otherwise disposed of;

(2) Any property not distributed, sold, exchanged, or otherwise disposed of within 6 months (1 year, if the decedent died on or before December 31, 1970) after the decedent's death is valued as of the date 6 months (1 year, if the decedent died on or before December 31, 1970) after the date of the decedent's death;

(3) Any property, interest, or estate which is affected by mere lapse of time is valued as of the date of the decedent's death, but adjusted for any difference in its value not due to mere lapse of time as of the date 6 months (1 year, if the decedent died on or before December 31, 1970) after the decedent's death, or as of the date of its distribution, sale, exchange, or other disposition, whichever date first occurs.

(b) *Method and effect of election.*—(1) *In general.*—The election to use the alternate valuation method is made on the return of tax imposed by section 2001. For purposes of this paragraph (b), the term *return of tax imposed by section 2001* means the last estate tax return filed by the executor on or before the due date of the return (including extensions of time to file actually granted) or, if a timely return is not filed, the first estate tax return filed by the executor after the due date, provided the return is filed no later than 1 year after the due date (including extensions of time to file actually granted). Once the election is made, it is irrevocable, provided that an election may be revoked on a subsequent return filed on or before the due date of the return (including extensions of time to file actually granted). The election may be made only if it will decrease both the value of the gross estate and the sum (reduced by allowable credits) of the estate tax and the generation-skipping transfer tax payable by reason of the decedent's death with respect to the property includible in the decedent's gross estate. If the election is made, the alternate valuation method applies to all property included in the gross estate and cannot be applied to only a portion of the property.

(2) *Protective election.*—If, based on the return of tax as filed, use of the alternate valuation method would not result in a decrease in both the value of the gross estate and the sum (reduced by allowable credits) of the estate tax and the generation-skipping transfer tax liability payable by reason of the decedent's death with respect to the property includible in the decedent's gross estate, a protective election may be made to use the alternate valuation method if it is subsequently determined that such a decrease would occur. A protective election is made on the return of tax imposed by section 2001. The protective election is irrevocable as of the due date of the return (including extensions of time actually granted). The protective election becomes effective on the date on which it is determined that use of the alternate valuation method would result in a decrease in both the value of the gross estate and in the sum (reduced by allowable credits) of the estate tax and generation-skipping transfer tax liability payable by reason of the decedent's death with respect to the property includible in the decedent's gross estate.

(3) *Requests for extension of time to make the election.*—A request for an extension of time to make the election or protective election pursuant to §§301.9100-1 and 301.9100-3 of this chapter will not be granted unless the return of tax imposed by section 2001 is filed no later than 1 year after the due date of the return (including extensions of time actually granted).

(c) *Meaning of "distributed, sold, exchanged, or otherwise disposed of".*—(1) The phrase "distributed, sold, exchanged, or otherwise disposed of" comprehends all possible ways by which property ceases to form a part of the gross estate. For example, money on hand at the date of the decedent's death which is thereafter used in the payment of funeral expenses, or which is thereafter invested, falls within the term "otherwise disposed of." The term also includes the surrender of a stock certificate for corporate assets in complete or partial liquidation of a corporation pursuant to section 331. The term does not, however, extend to transactions which are mere changes in form. Thus, it does not include a transfer of assets to a corporation in exchange for its stock in a transaction with respect to which no gain or loss would be recognizable for income tax purposes under section 351. Nor does it include an exchange of stock or securities in a corporation for stock or securities in the same corporation or another corporation in a transaction, such as a merger, recapitalization, reorganization or other transaction described in section 368(a) or 355, with respect to which no gain or loss is recognizable for income tax purposes under section 354 or 355.

(2) Property may be "distributed" either by the executor, or by a trustee of property included in the gross estate under sections 2035 through 2038, or section 2041. Property is considered as "distributed" upon the first to occur of the following:

(i) The entry of an order or decree of distribution, if the order or decree subsequently becomes final;

(ii) The segregation or separation of the property from the estate or trust so that it becomes unqualifiedly subject to the demand or disposition of the distributee; or

(iii) The actual paying over or delivery of the property to the distributee.

(3) Property may be "sold, exchanged, or otherwise disposed of" by:

(i) The executor;

(ii) A trustee or other donee to whom the decedent during his lifetime transferred property included in his gross estate under sections 2035 through 2038, or section 2041;

(iii) An heir or devisee to whom title to property passes directly under local law;

(iv) A surviving joint tenant or tenant by the entirety; or

(v) Any other person.

If a binding contract for the sale, exchange, or other disposition of property is entered into, the property is considered as sold, exchanged, or otherwise disposed of on the effective date of the contract, unless the contract is not subsequently carried out substantially in accordance with its terms. The effective date of a contract is normally the date it is entered into (and not the date it is consummated, or the date legal title to the property passes) unless the contract specifies a different effective date.

(d) *"Included property" and "excluded property".*—If the executor elects the alternate valuation method under section 2032, all property interests existing at the date of decedent's death which form a part of his gross estate as determined under sections 2033 through 2044 are valued in accordance with the provisions of this section. Such property interests are referred to in this section as "included property". Furthermore, such property interests remain "included property" for the purpose of valuing the gross estate under the alternate valuation method even though they change in form during the alternate valuation period by being actually received, or disposed of, in whole or in part, by the estate. On the other hand, property earned or accrued (whether received or not) after the date of the decedent's death and during the alternate valuation period with respect to any property interest existing at the date of the decedent's death, which does not represent a form of "included property" itself or the receipt of "included property" is excluded in valuing the gross estate under the alternate valuation method. Such property is referred to in this section as "excluded property". Illustrations of "included property" and "excluded property" are contained in the subparagraphs (1) to (4) of this paragraph:

(1) *Interest-bearing obligations.*—Interest-bearing obligations, such as bonds or notes, may comprise two elements of "included property" at the date of the decedent's death, namely, (i) the principal of the obligation itself, and (ii) interest accrued to the date of death. Each of these elements is to be separately valued as of the applicable valuation date. Interest accrued after the date of death and before the subsequent valuation date constitutes "excluded property". How-

ever, any part payment of principal made between the date of death and the subsequent valuation date, or any advance payment of interest for a period after the subsequent valuation date made during the alternate valuation period which has the effect of reducing the value of the principal obligation as of the subsequent valuation date, will be included in the gross estate, and valued as of the date of such payment.

(2) *Leased property.*—The principles set forth in subparagraph (1) of this paragraph with respect to interest-bearing obligations also apply to leased realty or personalty which is included in the gross estate and with respect to which an obligation to pay rent has been reserved. Both the realty or personalty itself and the rents accrued to the date of death constitute "included property", and each is to be separately valued as of the applicable valuation date. Any rent accrued after the date of death and before the subsequent valuation date is "excluded property". Similarly, the principle applicable with respect to interest paid in advance is equally applicable with respect to advance payments of rent.

(3) *Noninterest-bearing obligations.*—In the case of noninterest-bearing obligations sold at a discount, such as savings bonds, the principal obligation and the discount amortized to the date of death are property interests existing at the date of death and constitute "included property". The obligation itself is to be valued at the subsequent valuation date without regard to any further increase in value due to amortized discount. The additional discount amortized after death and during the alternate valuation period is the equivalent of interest accruing during that period and is, therefore, not to be included in the gross estate under the alternate valuation method.

(4) *Stock of a corporation.*—Shares of stock in a corporation and dividends declared to stockholders of record on or before the date of the decedent's death and not collected at the date of death constitute "included property" of the estate. On the other hand, ordinary dividends out of earnings and profits (whether in cash, shares of the corporation, or other property) declared to stockholders of record after the date of the decedent's death are "excluded property" and are not to be valued under the alternate valuation method. If, however, dividends are declared to stockholders of record after the date of the decedent's death with the effect that the shares of stock at the subsequent valuation date do not reasonably represent the same "included property" of the gross estate as existed at the date of the decedent's death, the dividends are "included property", except to the extent that they are out of earnings of the corporation after the date of the decedent's death. For example, if a corporation makes a distribution in partial liqui-

dation to stockholders of record during the alternate valuation period which is not accompanied by a surrender of a stock certificate for cancellation, the amount of the distribution received on stock included in the gross estate is itself "included property", except to the extent that the distribution was out of earnings and profits since the date of the decedent's death. Similarly, if a corporation, in which the decedent owned a substantial interest and which possessed at the date of the decedent's death accumulated earnings and profits equal to its paid-in capital, distributed all of its accumulated earnings and profits as a cash dividend to shareholders of record during the alternate valuation period, the amount of the dividends received on stock includible in the gross estate will be included in the gross estate under the alternate valuation method. Likewise, a stock dividend distributed under such circumstances is "included property".

(e) *Illustrations of "included property" and "excluded property".*—The application of paragraph (d) of this section may be further illustrated by the following example in which it is assumed that the decedent died on January 1, 1955:

Description	Subsequent valuation date	Alternate value	Value at date of death
Bond, par value $1,000, bearing interest at 4% payable quarterly on Feb. 1, May 1, Aug. 1, and Nov. 1. Bond distributed to legatee on Mar. 1, 1955	Mar. 1, 1955	$1,000.00	$1,000.00
Interest coupon of $10 attached to bond and not cashed at date of death although due and payable Nov. 1, 1954. Cashed by executor on Feb. 1, 1955	Feb. 1, 1955	10.00	10.00
Interest accrued from Nov. 1, 1954, to Jan. 1, 1955, collected on Feb. 1, 1955	Feb. 1, 1955	6.67	6.67
Real estate, not disposed of within year following death. Rent of $300 due at the end of each quarter, Feb. 1, May 1, Aug. 1, and Nov. 1	Jan. 1, 1956	11,000.00	12,000.00
Rent due for quarter ending Nov. 1, 1954, but not collected until Feb. 1, 1955	Feb. 1, 1955	300.00	300.00
Rent accrued for November and December 1954, collected on Feb. 1, 1955	Feb. 1, 1955	200.00	200.00
Common stock, X Corporation, 500 shares, not disposed of within year following decedent's death	Jan. 1, 1956	47,500.00	50,000.00
Dividend of $2 per share declared Dec. 10, 1954, and paid on Jan. 10, 1955, to holders of record on Dec. 30, 1954	Jan. 10, 1955	$1,000.00	$1,000.00

(f) *Mere lapse of time.*—In order to eliminate changes in value due only to mere lapse of time, section 2032(a)(3) provides that any interest or estate "affected by mere lapse of time" is included in a decedent's gross estate under the alternate valuation method at its value as of the date of the decedent's death, but with adjustment for any difference in its value as of the subsequent valuation date not due to mere lapse of time. Properties, interests, or estates which are "affected by mere lapse of time" include patents, estates for the life of a person other than the decedent, remainders, reversions, and other like properties, interests, or estates. The phrase "affected by mere lapse of time" has no reference to obligations for the payment of money, whether or not interest-bearing, the value of which changes with the passing of time. However, such an obligation, like any other property, may become affected by lapse of time when made the subject of a bequest or transfer which itself is creative of an interest or estate so affected. The application of this paragraph is illustrated in subparagraphs (1) and (2) of this paragraph:

(1) [Reserved]. For guidance, see §20.2032-1T(f)(1).

(2) *Patents.*—To illustrate the alternate valuation of a patent, assume that the decedent owned a patent which, on the date of the decedent's death, had an unexpired term of ten years and a value of $78,000. Six months after the date of the decedent's death, the patent was sold, because of lapse of time and other causes, for $60,000. The alternate value thereof would be obtained by dividing $60,000 by 0.95 (ratio of the remaining life of the patent at the alternate date to the remaining life of the patent at the date of

the decedent's death), and would, therefore, be $63,157.89.

(g) *Effect of election on deductions.*—If the executor elects the alternate valuation method under section 2032, any deduction for administration expenses under section 2053(b) (pertaining to property not subject to claims) or losses under section 2054 (or section 2106(a)(1), relating to estates of nonresidents not citizens) is allowed only to the extent that it is not otherwise in effect allowed in determining the value of the gross estate. Furthermore, the amount of any charitable deduction under section 2055 (or section 2106(a)(2), relating to the estates of nonresidents not citizens) or the amount of any marital deduction under section 2056 is determined by the value of the property with respect to which the deduction is allowed as of the date of the decedent's death, adjusted, however, for any difference in its value as of the date 6 months (1 year, if the decedent died on or before December 31, 1970) after death, or as of the date of its distribution, sale, exchange, or other disposition, whichever first occurs. However, no such adjustment may take into account any difference in value due to lapse of time or to the occurrence or nonoccurrence of a contingency.

(h) *Effective date.*—Paragraph (b) of this section is applicable to decedents dying on or after January 4, 2005. However, pursuant to section 7805(b)(7), taxpayers may elect to apply paragraph (b) of this section retroactively if the period of limitations for filing a claim for a credit or refund of Federal estate or generation-skipping transfer tax under section 6511 has not expired. [Reg. § 20.2032-1.]

☐ *[T.D. 6296, 6-23-58. Amended by T.D. 7238, 12-28-72, T.D. 7955, 5-10-84; T.D. 8540, 6-9-94; T.D. 8819, 4-29-99; T.D. 9172, 1-3-2005 and T.D. 9448, 5-1-2009 (corrected 6-5-2009).]*

[Reg. § 20.2032-1T]

§ 20.2032-1T. Alternate Valuation (temporary).—(a) through (e) [Reserved]. For further guidance, see § 20.2032-1(a) through (e).

(f) [Reserved]. For further guidance, see § 20.2032-1(f).

(1) *Life estates, remainders, and similar interests.*—The values of life estates, remainders, and similar interests are to be obtained by applying the methods prescribed in § 20.2031-7, using (i) the age of each person, the duration of whose life may affect the value of the interest, as of the date of the decedent's death, and (ii) the value of the property as of the alternate valuation date. For example, assume that the decedent, or the decedent's estate, was entitled to receive certain property worth $50,000 upon the death of A, who was entitled to the income for life. At the time of the decedent's death, on or after May 1, 2009, A was 47 years and 5 months old. In the month in which the decedent died, the section

7520 rate was 6.2 percent. The value of the decedent's remainder interest at the date of the decedent's death would, as illustrated in *Example 1* of § 20.2031-7T(d)(5), be $9,336.00 ($50,000 × .18672). If, because of economic conditions, the property declined in value and was worth only $40,000 on the date that was 6 months after the date of the decedent's death, the value of the remainder interest would be $7,468.80 ($40,000 × .18672), even though A would be 48 years old on the alternate valuation date.

(f)(2) through (g) [Reserved]. For further guidance, see § 20.2032-1(f)(2) through (g).

(h) *Effective/applicability date.*—Paragraph (f)(1) applies on or after May 1, 2009.

(i) *Expiration date.*—Paragraph (f)(1) expires on or before May 1, 2012. [Temporary Reg. § 20.2032-1T.]

☐ *[T.D. 9448, 5-1-2009.]*

[Reg. § 20.2032A-3]

§ 20.2032A-3. Material participation requirements for valuation of certain farm and closely-held business real property.—(a) *In general.*—Under section 2032A, an executor may, for estate tax purposes, make a special election concerning valuation of qualified real property (as defined in section 2032A(b)) used as a farm for farming purposes or in another trade or business. If this election is made, the property will be valued on the basis of its value for its qualified use in farming or the other trade or business, rather than its fair market value determined on the basis of highest and best use (irrespective of whether its highest and best use is the use in farming or other business). For the special valuation rules of section 2032A to apply, the deceased owner and/or a member of the owner's family (as defined in section 2032A(e)(2)) must materially participate in the operation of the farm or other business. Whether the required material participation occurs is a factual determination, and the types of activities and financial risks which will support such a finding will vary with the mode of ownership of both the property itself and of any business in which it is used. Passively collecting rents, salaries, draws, dividends, or other income from the farm or other business is not sufficient for material participation, nor is merely advancing capital and reviewing a crop plan or other business proposal and financial reports each season or business year.

(b) *Types of qualified property.*—(1) *In general.*—Real property valued under section 2032A must pass from the decedent to a qualified heir or be acquired from the decedent by a qualified heir. The real property may be owned directly or may be owned indirectly through ownership of an interest in a corporation, a partnership, or a trust. Where the ownership is indirect, however, the decedent's interest in the business must, in addition to meeting the tests for qualification under section 2032A, qualify under the tests of section 6166(b)(1) as an interest in a closely-held business on the date of the decedent's death and for sufficient other time (combined with periods of direct ownership) to equal at least 5 years of the 8 year period preceding the death. All specially valued property must be used in a trade or business. Directly owned real property that is leased by a decedent to a separate closely held business is considered to be qualified real property, but only if the separate business qualifies as a closely held business under section 6166(b)(1) with respect to the decedent on the date of his or her death and for sufficient other time (combined with periods during which the property was operated as a proprietorship) to equal at least 5 years of the 8 year period preceding the death. For example, real property owned by the decedent and leased to a farming corporation or partnership owned and operated entirely by the decedent and fewer than 15 members of the decedent's family is eligible for special use valuation. Under section 2032A, the term trade or business applies only to an active business such as a manufacturing, mercantile, or service enterprise, or to the raising of agricultural or horticultural commodities, as distinguished from passive investment activities. The mere passive rental of property to a party other than a member of the decedent's family will not qualify. The decedent or a member of the decedent's family must own an equity interest in the farm operation. A trade or business is not necessarily present even though an office and regular hours are maintained for management of income producing assets, as the term "business" is not as broad under section 2032A as under section 162. Additionally, no trade or business is present in the case of activities not engaged in for profit. *See* section 183.

(2) *Structures and other real property improvements.*—Qualified real property includes residential buildings and other structures and real property improvements occupied or used on a regular basis by the owner or lessee of real property (or by employees of the owner or lessee) for the purpose of operating the farm or other closely held business. A farm residence occupied by the decedent owner of the specially valued property is considered to be occupied for the purpose of operating the farm even though a family member (not the decedent) was the person materially participating in the operation of the farm as required under section 2032A(b)(1)(C).

(c) *Period material participation must last.*—The required participation must last—

(1) For periods totalling 5 years or more during the 8 years immediately preceding the date of the decedent's death; and

(2) For periods totalling 5 years or more during any 8 year period ending after the date of the decedent's death (up to a maximum of 15

years after decedent's death, when the additional estate tax provisions of section 2032A(c) cease to apply).

In determining whether the material participation requirement is satisfied, no exception is made for periods during which real property is held by the decedent's estate. Additionally, contemporaneous material participation by 2 or more family members during a period totalling a year will not result in that year being counted as 2 or more years for purposes of satisfying the requirements of this paragraph (c). Death of a qualified heir (as defined in section 2032A(e)(1)) before the requisite time has passed ends any material participation requirement for that heir's portion of the property as to the original decedent's estate if the heir received a separate, joint or other undivided property interest from the decedent. If qualified heirs receive successive interests in specially valued property (e.g., life estate and remainder interests) from the decedent, the material participation requirement does not end with respect to any part of the property until the death of the last qualified heir (or, if earlier, the expiration of 15 years from the date of the decedent's death). The requirements of section 2032A will fully apply to an heir's estate if an election under this section is made for the same property by the heir's executor. In general, to determine whether the required participation has occurred, brief periods (*e. g.*, periods of 30 days or less) during which there was no material participation may be disregarded. This is so only if these periods were both preceded and followed by substantial periods (*e. g.*, periods of more than 120 days) in which there was uninterrupted material participation. *See* paragraph (e)(1) of this section which provides a special rule for periods when little or no activity is necessary to manage fully a farm.

(d) *Period property must be owned by decedent and family members.*—Only real property which is actually owned by any combination of the decedent, members of the decedent's family, and qualified closely held businesses for periods totalling at least 5 of the 8 years preceding the date of decedent's death may be valued under section 2032A. For example, replacement property acquired in [a] like-kind exchange under section 1031 is considered to be owned only from the date on which the replacement property is actually acquired. On the other hand, replacement property acquired as a result of an involuntary conversion in a transfer that would meet the requirements of section 2032A(h) if it occurred after the date of the decedent's death is considered to have been owned from the date in which the involuntarily converted property was acquired. Property transferred from a proprietorship to a corporation or a partnership during the 8-year period ending on the date of the decedent's death is considered to be continuously owned to the extent of the decedent's equity interest in the corporation or partnership if, (1) the transfer meets the requirements of section 351 or 721, respectively, and (2) the decedent's interest in the corporation or partnership meets the requirements for indirectly held property contained in paragraph (b)(1) of this section. Likewise, property transferred to a trust is considered to be continuously owned if the beneficial ownership of the trust property is such that the requirements of section 6166(b)(1)(C) would be so satisfied if the property were owned by a corporation and all beneficiaries having vested interests in the trust were shareholders in the corporation. Any periods following the transfer during which the interest in the corporation, partnership, or trust does not meet the requirements of section 6166(b)(1) may not be counted for purposes of satisfying the ownership requirement of this paragraph (d).

(e) *Required activities.*—(1) *In general.*—Actual employment of the decedent (or of a member of the decedent's family) on a substantially full-time basis (35 hours a week or more) or to any lesser extent necessary personally to manage fully the farm or business in which the real property to be valued under section 2032A is used constitutes material participation. For example, many farming operations require only seasonal activity. Material participation is present as long as all necessary functions are performed even though little or no actual activity occurs during nonproducing seasons. In the absence of this direct involvement in the farm or other business, the activities of either the decedent or family members must meet the standards prescribed in this paragraph and those prescribed in the regulations issued under section 1402(a)(1). Therefore, if the participant (or participants) is self-employed with respect to the farm or other trade or business, his or her income from the farm or other business must be earned income for purposes of the tax on self-employment income before the participant is considered to be materially participating under section 2032A. Payment of the self-employment tax is not conclusive as to the presence of material participation. If no self-employment taxes have been paid, however, material participation is presumed not to have occurred unless the executor demonstrates to the satisfaction of the Internal Revenue Service that material participation did in fact occur and informs the Service of the reason no such tax was paid. In addition, all such taxes (including interest and penalties) determined to be due must be paid. In determining whether the material participation requirement is satisfied, the activities of each participant are viewed separately from the activities of all other participants, and at any given time, the activities of at least one participant must be material. If the involvement is less than full-time, it must be pursuant to an arrangement providing for actual participation in the production or management of production where the land is used by any nonfamily member, or any trust or business entity, in farming or an-

other business. The arrangement may be oral or written, but must be formalized in some manner capable of proof. Activities not contemplated by the arrangement will not support a finding of material participation under section 2032A, and activities of any agent or employee other than a family member may not be considered in determining the presence of material participation. Activities of family members are considered only if the family relationship existed at the time the activities occurred.

(2) *Factors considered.*—No single factor is determinative of the presence of material participation, but physical work and participation in management decisions are the principal factors to be considered. As a minimum, the decedent and/or a family member must regularly advise or consult with the other managing party on the operation of the business. While they need not make all final management decisions alone, the decedent and/or family members must participate in making a substantial number of these decisions. Additionally, production activities on the land should be inspected regularly by the family participant, and funds should be advanced and financial responsibility assumed for a substantial portion of the expense involved in the operation of the farm or other business in which the real property is used. In the case of a farm, the furnishing by the owner or other family members of a substantial portion of the machinery, implements, and livestock used in the production activities is an important factor to consider in finding material participation. With farms, hotels, or apartment buildings, the operation of which qualifies as a trade or business, the participating decedent or heir's maintaining his or her principal place of residence on the premises is a factor to consider in determining whether the overall participation is material. Retention of a professional farm manager will not by itself prevent satisfaction of the material participation requirement by the decedent and family members. However, the decedent and/or a family member must personally materially participate under the terms of arrangement with the professional farm manager to satisfy this requirement.

(f) *Special rules for corporations, partnerships, and trusts.*—(1) *Required arrangement.*—With indirectly owned property as with property that is directly owned, there must be an arrangement calling for material participation in the business by the decedent owner or a family member. Where the real property is indirectly owned, however, even full-time involvement must be pursuant to an arrangement between the entity and the decedent or family member specifying the services to be performed. Holding an office in which certain material functions are inherent may constitute the necessary arrangement for material participation. Where property is owned by a trust, the arrangement will generally be found in one or more of four situations. First, the arrangement may result from appointment as a trustee. Second, the arrangement may result from an employer-employee relationship in which the participant is employed by a qualified closely held business owned by the trust in a position requiring his or her material participation in its activities. Third, the participants may enter into a contract with the trustees to manage, or take part in managing, the real property for the trust. Fourth, where the trust agreement expressly grants the management rights to the beneficial owner, that grant is sufficient to constitute the arrangement required under this section.

(2) *Required activities.*—The same participation standards apply under section 2032A where property is owned by a qualified closely held business as where the property is directly owned. In the case of a corporation, a partnership, or a trust where the participating decedent and/or family members are employees and thereby not subject to self-employment income taxes, they are to be viewed as if they were self-employed, and their activities must be activities that would subject them to self-employment income taxes were they so. Where property is owned by a corporation, a partnership or a trust, participation in the management and operation of the real property itself as a component of the closely held business is the determinative factor. Nominally holding positions as a corporate officer or director and receiving a salary therefrom or merely being listed as a partner and sharing in profits and losses will not alone support a finding of material participation. This is so even though, as partners, the participants pay self-employment income taxes on their distributive shares of partnership earnings under § 1.1402(a)-2. Further, it is especially true for corporate directors in states where the board of directors need not be an actively functioning entity or need only act informally. Corporate offices held by an owner are, however, factors to be considered with all other relevant facts in judging the degree of participation. When real property is directly owned and is leased to a corporation or partnership in which the decedent owns an interest which qualifies as an interest in a trade or business within the meaning of section 6166(b)(1), the presence of material participation is determined by looking at the activities of the participant with regard to the property in whatever capacity rendered. During any periods when qualified real property is held by an estate, material participation is to be determined in the same manner as if the property were owned by a trust.

(g) *Examples.*—The rules for determining material participation may be illustrated by the following examples. Additional illustrations may be found in examples (1) through (6) in § 1.1402(a)-4.

Example (1). A, the decedent, actively operated his 100-acre farm on a full-time basis for 20 years. He then leased it to B for the 10 years immediately preceding his death. By the terms of the lease, A was to consult with B on where crops were to be planted, to supervise marketing of the crop, and to share equally with B in expenses and earnings. A was present on the farm each spring for consultation; however, once planting was complete, he left for his retirement cottage where he remained until late summer, at which time he returned to the farm to supervise the marketing operations. A at all times maintained the farm home in which he had lived for the time he had owned the farm and lived there when at the farm. In light of his activities, assumption of risks, and valuable knowledge of proper techniques for the particular land gained over 20 years of full-time farming on the land involved, A is deemed to have materially participated in the farming business.

Example (2). D is the 70-year old widow of farmer C. She lives on a farm for which special valuation has been elected and has lived there for 20 years. D leases the land to E under an arrangement calling for her participation in the operation of the farm. D annually raises a vegetable garden, chickens, and hogs. She also inspects the tobacco fields (which produce approximately 50 percent of farm income) weekly and informs E if she finds any work that needs to be done. D and E share expenses and income equally. Other decisions such as what fields to plant and when to plant and harvest crops are left to E, but D does occasionally make suggestions. During the harvest season, D prepares and serves meals for all temporary farm help. D is deemed to participate materially in the farm operation based on her farm residence and her involvement with the main money crop.

Example (3). Assume that D in example (2) moved to a nursing home 1 year after her husband's death. E completely operated the farm for her for 6 years following her move. If E is not a member of D's family, material participation ceases when D moves; however, if E is a member of D's family, E's material participation will prevent disqualification even if D owns the property. Further, upon D's death, the section 2032A valuation could be elected for her estate if E were a member of her family and the other requirements of section 2032A were satisfied.

Example (4). F, a qualified heir, owned a specially valued farm. He contracted with G to manage the farm for him as F, a lawyer, lived and worked 15 miles away in a nearby town. F supplied all machinery and equipment and assumed financial responsibility for the expenses of the farm operation. The contract specified that G was to submit a crop plan and a list of expenses and earnings for F's approval. It also called for F to inspect the farm regularly and to approve all expenditures over $100. In practice, F visited the farm weekly during the growing season to inspect and discuss operations. He actively participated in making important management decisions such as what fields to plant or pasture and how to utilize the subsidy program. F is deemed to have materially participated in the farm operation as his personal involvement amounted to more than managing an investment. Had F not regularly inspected the farm and participated in management decisions, however, he would not be considered to be materially participating. This would be true even though F did assume financial responsibility for the operation and did review annual crop plans.

Example (5). Decedent I owned 90 percent of all outstanding stock of X Corporation, a qualified closely-held business which owns real property to be specially valued. I held no formal position in the corporation and there was no arrangement for him to participate in daily business operations. I regularly spent several hours each day at the corporate offices and made decisions on many routine matters. I is not deemed to have materially participated in the X Corporation despite his activity because there was no arrangement requiring him to act in the manner in which he did.

Example (6). Decedent J was a senior partner in the law firm of X, Y and Z, which is a qualified closely held business owning the building in which its offices are located. J ceased to practice law actively 5 years before his death in 1977; however, he remained a full partner and annually received a share of firm profits. J is not deemed to have materially participated under section 2032A even though he still may have reported his distributive share of partnership income for self-employment income tax purposes if the payments were not made pursuant to any retirement agreement. This is so because J does not meet the requirement of actual personal material participation.

Example (7). K, the decedent, owned a tree farm. He contracted with L, a professional forester, to manage the property for him as K, a doctor, lived and worked in a town 50 miles away. The activities of L are not considered in determining whether K materially participated in the tree farm operation. During the 5 years preceding K's death, there was no need for frequent inspections of the property or consultation concerning it, inasmuch as most of the land had been reforested and the trees were in the beginning stages of their growing cycle. However, once every year, L submitted for K's approval a proposed plan for the management of the property over the next year. K actively participated in making important management decisions, such as where and whether a pre-commercial thinning should be conducted, whether the timber was adequately protected from fire and disease, whether fire lines needed to be plowed around the new trees, and whether boundary lines were properly maintained around the property. K inspected the property at least twice every year and assumed financial responsibility for the expenses of the tree farm. K also reported his income from the tree farm as earned income for purposes of the tax on self-employment income. Over a period of several years, K had harvested and marketed timber from certain tracts of the tree farm and had supervised replanting of the areas where trees were removed. K's history of harvesting, marketing, and replanting of trees showed him to be in the business of tree farming rather than merely passively investing in timber land. If the history of K's tree farm did not show such an active business operation, however, the tree farm would not qualify for special use valuation. In light of all these facts, K is deemed to have materially participated in the farm as his personal involvement amounted to more than managing an investment.

Example (8). Decedent M died on January 1, 1978, owning a farm for which special use valuation under section 2032A has been elected. M owned the farm real property for 15 years before his death. During the 4 years preceding M's death (January 1, 1974 through December 31, 1977), the farm was rented to N, a non-family member, and neither M nor any member of his family materially participated in the farming operation. From January 1, 1970, until December 31, 1973, both M and his daughter, O, materially participated in the farming operation. The material participation requirement of section 2032A(b)(1)(C)(ii) is not satisfied because material participation did not occur for periods aggregating at least 5 different years of the 8 years preceding M's death. [Reg. § 20.2032A-3.]

☐ [*T.D. 7710, 7-28-80. Amended by T.D. 7786, 8-25-81.*]

[Reg. § 20.2032A-4]

§ 20.2032A-4. Method of valuing farm real property.—(a) *In general.*—Unless the executor of the decedent's estate elects otherwise under section 2032A(e)(7)(B)(ii) or fails to document comparable rented farm property meeting the requirements of this section, the value of the property which is used for farming purposes and which is subject to an election under section 2032A is determined by—

(1) Subtracting the average annual state and local real estate taxes on actual tracts of comparable real property in the same locality from the average annual gross cash rental for that same comparable property, and

(2) Dividing the results so obtained by the average annual effective interest rate charged on new Federal land bank loans.

The computation of each average annual amount is to be based on the 5 most recent calendar years ending before the date of the decedent's death.

(b) *Gross cash rental.*—(1) *Generally.*—Gross cash rental is the total amount of cash received for the use of actual tracts of comparable farm real property in the same locality as the property being specially valued during the period of one calendar year. This amount is not diminished by the amount of any expenses or liabilities associated with the farm operation or the lease. *See,* paragraph (d) of this section for a definition of comparable property and rules for property on which buildings or other improvements are located and farms including multiple property types. Only rentals from tracts of comparable farm property which are rented solely for an amount of cash which is not contingent upon production are acceptable for use in valuing real property under section 2032A(e)(7). The rentals considered must result from an arm's-length transaction as defined in this section. Additionally, rentals received under leases which provide for payment solely in cash are not acceptable as accurate measures of cash rental value if involvement by the lessor (or a member of the lessor's family who is other than a lessee) in the management or operation of the farm to an extent which amounts to material participation under the rules of section 2032A is contemplated or actually occurs. In general, therefore, rentals for any property which qualifies for special use valuation cannot be used to compute gross cash rentals under this section because the total amount received by the lessor does not reflect the true cash rental value of the real property.

(2) *Special rules.*—(i) *Documentation required of executor.*—The executor must identify to the Internal Revenue Service actual comparable property for all specially valued property and cash rentals from that property if the decedent's real property is valued under section 2032A(e)(7). If the executor does not identify such property and cash rentals, all specially valued real property must be valued under the rules of section 2032A(e)(8) if special use valuation has been elected. *See,* however, §20.2032A-8(d) for a special rule for estates electing section 2032A treatment on or before August 30, 1980.

(ii) *Arm's-length transaction required.*— Only those cash rentals which result from a lease entered into in an arm's-length transaction are acceptable under section 2032A(e)(7). For these purposes, lands leased from the Federal government, or any state or local government, which are leased for less than the amount that would be demanded by a private individual leasing for profit are not leased in an arm's-length transaction. Additionally, leases between family members (as defined in section 2032A(e)(2)) which do not provide a return on the property commensurate with that received under leases between unrelated parties in the locality are not acceptable under this section.

(iii) *In-kind rents, statements of appraised rental value, and area averages.*—Rents which are paid wholly or partly in kind (*e.g.,* crop shares)

may not be used to determine the value of real property under section 2032A(e)(7). Likewise, appraisals or other statements regarding rental value as well as area-wide averages of rentals (*i.e.,* those compiled by the United States Department of Agriculture) may not be used under section 2032A(e)(7) because they are not true measures of the actual cash rental value of comparable property in the same locality as the specially valued property.

(iv) *Period for which comparable real property must have been rented solely for cash.*—Comparable real property rented solely for cash must be identified for each of the five calendar years preceding the year of the decedent's death if section 2032A(e)(7) is used to value the decedent's real property. Rentals from the same tract of comparable property need not be used for each of these 5 years, however, provided an actual tract of property meeting the requirements of this section is identified for each year.

(v) *Leases under which rental of personal property is included.*—No adjustment to the rents actually received by the lessor is made for the use of any farm equipment or other personal property the use of which is included under a lease for comparable real property unless the lease specifies the amount of the total rental attributable to the personal property and that amount is reasonable under the circumstances.

(c) *State and local real estate taxes.*—For purposes of the farm valuation formula under section 2032A(e)(7) state and local taxes are taxes which are assessed by a state or local government and which are allowable deductions under section 164. However, only those taxes on the comparable real property from which cash rentals are determined may be used in the formula valuation.

(d) *Comparable real property defined.*—Comparable real property must be situated in the same locality as the specially valued property. This requirement is not to be viewed in terms of mileage or political divisions alone, but rather is to be judged according to generally accepted real property valuation rules. The determination of properties which are comparable is a factual one and must be based on numerous factors, no one of which is determinative. It will, therefore, frequently be necessary to value farm property in segments where there are different uses or land characteristics included in the specially valued farm. For example, if section 2032A(e)(7) is used, rented property on which comparable buildings or improvements are located must be identified for specially valued property on which buildings or other real property improvements are located. In cases involving multiple areas or land characteristics, actual comparable property for each segment must be used, and the rentals and taxes from all such properties combined (using generally accepted real property valuation rules) for use in the valuation formula given in this section. However, any premium or discount resulting from the presence of multiple uses or other characteristics in one farm is also to be reflected. All factors generally considered in real estate valuation are to be considered in determining comparability under section 2032A. While not intended as an exclusive list, the following factors are among those to be considered in determining comparability—

(1) Similarity of soil as determined by any objective means, including an official soil survey reflected in a soil productivity index;

(2) Whether the crops grown are such as would deplete the soil in a similar manner;

(3) The types of soil conservation techniques that have been practiced on the two properties;

(4) Whether the two properties are subject to flooding;

(5) The slope of the land;

(6) In the case of livestock operations, the carrying capacity of the land;

(7) Where the land is timbered, whether the timber is comparable to that on the subject property;

(8) Whether the property as a whole is unified or whether it is segmented, and where segmented, the availability of the means necessary for movement among the different segments;

(9) The number, types, and conditions of all buildings and other fixed improvements located on the properties and their location as it affects efficient management and use of property and value per se; and

(10) Availability of, and type of, transportation facilities in terms of costs and of proximity of the properties to local markets.

(e) *Effective interest rate defined.*—(1) *Generally.*—The annual effective interest rate on new Federal land bank loans is the average billing rate charged on new agricultural loans to farmers and ranchers in the farm credit district in which the real property to be valued under section 2032A is located, adjusted as provided in paragraph (e)(2) of this section. This rate is to be a single rate for each district covering the period of one calendar year and is to be computed to the nearest one-hundredth of one percent. In the event that the district billing rates of interest on such new agricultural loans change during a year, the rate for that year is to be weighted to reflect the portion of the year during which each such rate was charged. If a district's billing rate on such new agricultural loans varies according to the amount of the loan, the rate applicable to a loan in an amount resulting from dividing the total dollar amount of such loans closed during the year by the total number of the loans closed is to be used under section 2032A. Applicable rates may be obtained from the district director of internal revenue.

(2) *Adjustment to billing rate of interest.*—The billing rate of interest determined under this paragraph is to be adjusted to reflect the increased cost of borrowing resulting from the required purchase of land bank association stock. For section 2032A purposes, the rate of required stock investment is the average of the percentages of the face amount of new agricultural loans to farmers and ranchers required to be invested in such stock by the applicable district bank during the year. If this percentage changes during a year, the average is to be adjusted to reflect the period when each percentage requirement was effective. The percentage is viewed as a reduction in the loan proceeds actually received from the amount upon which interest is charged.

(3) *Example.*—The determination of the effective interest rate for any year may be illustrated as follows:

Example. District X of the Federal land bank system charged an 8 percent billed interest rate on new agricultural loans for 8 months of the year, 1976, and an 8.75 percent rate for 4 months of the year. The average billing rate was, therefore, 8.25 percent $[(1.08 \times {}^8/_{12}) + (1.0875 \times {}^4/_{12}) = 1.0825]$. The district required stock equal to 5 percent of the face amount of the loan to be purchased as a precondition to receiving a loan. Thus, the borrower only received 95 percent of the funds upon which he paid interest. The applicable annual interest rate for 1976 of 8.68 percent is computed as follows:

8.25 percent $\times$ 1.00 (total loan amount) = 8.25 percent (billed interest rate) divided by 0.95 (percent of loan proceeds received by borrower) = 8.68 percent (effective interest rate for 1976).

[Reg. § 20.2032A-4.]

☐ [T.D. 7710, 7-28-80.]

[Reg. § 20.2032A-8]

§ 20.2032A-8. Election and agreement to have certain property valued under section 2032A for estate tax purposes.—(a) *Election of special use valuation.*—(1) *In general.*—An election under section 2032A is made as prescribed in paragraph (a)(3) of this section and on Form 706, United States Estate Tax Return. Once made, this election is irrevocable; however, see paragraph(d) of this section for a special rule for estates for which elections are made on or before August 30, 1980. Under section 2032A(a)(2), special use valuation may not reduce the value of the decedent's estate by more than $500,000. This election is available only if, at the time of death, the decedent was a citizen or resident of the United States.

(2) *Elections to specially value less than all qualified real property included in an estate.*—An election under section 2032A need not include all real property included in an estate which is eligible for special use valuation, but sufficient property to satisfy the threshold requirements of

section 2032A(b)(1)(B) must be specially valued under the election. If joint or undivided interests (e.g. interests as joint tenants or tenants in common) in the same property are received from a decedent by qualified heirs, an election with respect to one heir's joint or undivided interest need not include any other heir's interest in the same property if the electing heir's interest plus other property to be specially valued satisfy the requirements of section 2032A(b)(1)(B). If successive interests (e.g. life estates and remainder interests) are created by a decedent in otherwise qualified property, an election under section 2032A is available only with respect to that property (or portion thereof) in which qualified heirs of the decedent receive all of the successive interests, and such an election must include the interests of all of those heirs. For example, if a surviving spouse receives a life estate in otherwise qualified property and the spouse's brother receives a remainder interest in fee, no part of the property may be valued pursuant to an election under section 2032A. Where successive interests in specially valued property are created, remainder interests are treated as being received by qualified heirs only if such remainder interests are not contingent upon surviving a nonfamily member or are not subject to divestment in favor of a nonfamily member.

(3) *Time and manner of making election.*—An election under this section is made by attaching to a timely filed estate tax return the agreement described in paragraph (c)(1) of this section and a notice of election which contains the following information:

(i) The decedent's name and taxpayer identification number as they appear on the estate tax return;

(ii) The relevant qualified use;

(iii) The items of real property shown on the estate tax return to be specially valued pursuant to the election (identified by schedule and item number);

(iv) The fair market value of the real property to be specially valued under section 2032A and its value based on its qualified use (both values determined without regard to the adjustments provided by section 2032A(b)(3)(B));

(v) The adjusted value (as defined in section 2032A(b)(3)(B)) of all real property which is used in a qualified use and which passes from the decedent to a qualified heir and the adjusted value of all real property to be specially valued;

(vi) The items of personal property shown on the estate tax return that pass from the decedent to a qualified heir and are used in a qualified use under section 2032A (identified by schedule and item number) and the total value of such personal property adjusted as provided under section 2032A(b)(3)(B);

(vii) The adjusted value of the gross estate, as defined in section 2032A(b)(3)(A);

(viii) The method used in determining the special value based on use;

(ix) Copies of written appraisals of the fair market value of the real property;

(x) A statement that the decedent and/or a member of his or her family has owned all specially valued real property for at least 5 years of the 8 years immediately preceding the date of the decedent's death;

(xi) Any periods during the 8-year period preceding the date of the decedent's death during which the decedent or a member of his or her family did not own the property, use it in a qualified use, or materially participate in the operation of the farm or other business within the meaning of section 2032A(e)(6);

(xii) The name, address, taxpayer identification number, and relationship to the decedent of each person taking an interest in each item of specially valued property, and the value of property interests passing to each such person based on both fair market value and qualified use;

(xiii) Affidavits describing the activities constituting material participation and the identity of the material participant or participants; and

(xiv) A legal description of the specially valued property.

If neither an election nor a protective election is timely made, special use valuation is not available to the estate. *See* sections 2032A(d)(1), 6075(a), and 6081(a).

(b) *Protective election.*—A protective election may be made to specially value qualified real property. The availability of special use valuation pursuant to this election is contingent upon values as finally determined (or agreed to following examination of a return) meeting the requirements of section 2032A. A protective election does not, however, extend the time for payment of any amount of tax. Rules for such extensions are contained in sections 6161, 6163, 6166, and 6166A. The protective election is to be made by a notice of election filed with a timely estate tax return stating that a protective election under section 2032A is being made pending final determination of values. This notice is to include the following information:

(1) The decedent's name and taxpayer identification number as they appear on the estate tax return;

(2) The relevant qualified use; and

(3) The items of real and personal property shown on the estate tax return which are used in a qualified use, and which pass to qualified heirs (identified by schedule and item number).

If it is found that the estate qualifies for special use valuation based upon values as finally determined (or agreed to following examination of a return), an additional notice of election must be filed within 60 days after the date of such determination. This notice must set forth the information required under paragraph (a)(3) of this section and is to be attached, together with the agreement described in paragraph (c)(1) of this section, to an amended estate tax return. The new return is to be filed with the Internal Revenue Service office where the original return was filed.

(c) *Agreement to special valuation by persons with an interest in property.*—(1) *In general.*—The agreement required under section 2032A(a)(1)(B) and (d)(2) must be executed by all parties who have any interest in the property being valued based on its qualified use as of the date of the decedent's death. In the case of a qualified heir, the agreement must express consent to personal liability under section 2032A(c) in the event of certain early dispositions of the property or early cessation of the qualified use. See section 2032A(c)(6). In the case of parties (other than qualified heirs) with interests in the property, the agreement must express consent to collection of any additional estate tax imposed under section 2032A(c) from the qualified property. The agreement is to be in a form that is binding on all parties having an interest in the property. It must designate an agent with satisfactory evidence of authority to act for the parties to the agreement in all dealings with the Internal Revenue Service on matters arising under section 2032A and must indicate the address of that agent.

(2) *Persons having an interest in designated property.*—An interest in property is an interest which, as of the date of the decedent's death, can be asserted under applicable local law so as to affect the disposition of the specially valued property by the estate. Any person in being at the death of the decedent who has any such interest in the property, whether present or future, or vested or contingent, must enter into the agreement. Included among such persons are owners of remainder and executory interests, the holders of general or special powers of appointment, beneficiaries of a gift over in default of exercise of any such power, co-tenants, joint tenants and holders of other undivided interests when the decedent held only a joint or undivided interest in the property or when only an undivided interest is specially valued, and trustees of trusts holding any interest in the property. An heir who has the power under local law to caveat (challenge) a will and thereby affect disposition of the property is not, however, considered to be a person with an interest in property under section 2032A solely by reason of that right. Likewise, creditors of an estate are not such persons solely by reason of their status as creditors.

(3) *Consent on behalf of interested party.*—If any person required to enter into the agreement provided for by paragraph (c)(1) either desires that an agent act for him or her or cannot legally bind himself or herself due to infancy or other

incompetency, or to death before the election under section 2032A is timely exercised, a representative authorized under local law to bind such person in an agreement of this nature is permitted to sign the agreement on his or her behalf.

(4) *Duties of agent designated in agreement.*—The Internal Revenue Service will contact the agent designated in the agreement under paragraph (c)(1) on all matters relating to continued qualification under section 2032A of the specially valued real property and on all matters relating to the special lien arising under section 6324B. It is the duty of the agent as attorney-in-fact for the parties with interests in the specially valued property to furnish the Service with any requested information and to notify the Service of any disposition or cessation of qualified use of any part of the property.

(d) *Special rule for estates for which elections under section 2032A are made on or before August 30, 1980.*—An election to specially value real property under section 2032A that is made on or before August 30, 1980, may be revoked. To revoke an election, the executor must file a notice of revocation with the Internal Revenue Service office where the original estate tax return was filed on or before January 31, 1981 (or if earlier, the date on which the period of limitation for assessment expires). This notice of revocation must contain the decedent's name, date of death, and taxpayer identification number, and is to be accompanied by remittance of any additional amount of estate tax and interest determined to be due as a result of valuation of the qualified property based upon its fair market value. Elections that are made on or before August 30, 1980, that do not comply with this section as proposed on July 13, 1978 (43 FR 30070), and amended on December 21, 1978 (43 FR 59517), must be conformed to this final regulation by means of an amended return before the original estate tax return can be finally accepted by the Internal Revenue Service. [Reg. § 20.2032A-8.]

☐ [*T.D. 7710, 7-28-80. Amended by T.D. 7786,* 8-25-81.]

[Reg. § 22.0]

§ 22.0. Certain elections under the Economic Recovery Tax Act of 1981.—(a) *Election of special rules for woodlands.*

(1) *In general.*—This paragraph applies to the election of special rules for woodlands under section 2032A(e)(13) of the Code, as added by section 421(h) of the Economic Recovery Tax Act of 1981. The executor shall make this election for an estate by attaching to the estate tax return a statement that—

(i) Contains the decedent's name and taxpayer identification number as they appear on the estate tax return,

(ii) Identifies the election as an election under section 2032A(e)(13) of the Code,

(iii) Specifies the property with respect to which the election is made, and

(iv) Provides all information necessary to show that the executor is entitled to make the election.

(2) *Additional information required.*—If later regulations issued under section 2032A(e)(13) require the executor to furnish information in addition to that required under paragraph (a)(1) of this section and an office of the Internal Revenue Service requests the executor to furnish the additional information, the executor shall furnish the additional information in a statement filed with that office of the Internal Revenue Service within 60 days after the request is made. The statement shall also contain the information required by paragraph (a)(1)(i), (ii), and (iii) of this section. If the additional information is not provided within 60 days after the request is made, the election may, at the discretion of the Commissioner, be held invalid.

(b) *Election of special use valuation for qualified real property.*—This paragraph applies to the election of special use valuation for qualified real property under section 2032A(d)(1) of the Code, as amended by section 421(j)(3) of the Economic Recovery Tax Act of 1981. This election shall be made in the manner prescribed in §20.2032A-8(a)(3), except that the election shall be valid even if the estate tax return is not timely filed.

(c) *Elections irrevocable.*—Elections to which this section applies may not be revoked.

(d) *Effective date.*—The elections described in this section are available with respect to the estate of decedents dying after 1981. [Temporary Reg. §22.0.]

☐ [*T.D. 7793, 10-29-81.*]

[Reg. §20.2033-1]

§20.2033-1. Property in which the decedent had an interest.—(a) *In general.*—The gross estate of a decedent who was a citizen or resident of the United States at the time of his death includes under section 2033 the value of all property, whether real or personal, tangible or intangible, and wherever situated, beneficially owned by the decedent at the time of his death. (For certain exceptions in the case of real property situated outside the United States, see paragraphs (a) and (c) of §20.2031-1.) Real property is included whether it came into the possession and control of the executor or administrator or passed directly to heirs or devisees. Various statutory provisions which exempt bonds, notes, bills, and certificates of indebtedness of the Federal Government or its agencies and the interest thereon from taxation are generally not applicable to the estate tax, since such tax is an excise tax on the transfer of property at death and is not a tax on the property transferred.

(b) *Miscellaneous examples.*—A cemetery lot owned by the decedent is part of his gross estate, but its value is limited to the salable value of that part of the lot which is not designed for the interment of the decedent and the members of his family. Property subject to homestead or other exemptions under local law is included in the gross estate. Notes or other claims held by the decedent are likewise included even though they are cancelled by the decedent's will. Interest and rents accrued at the date of the decedent's death constitute a part of the gross estate. Similarly, dividends which are payable to the decedent or his estate by reason of the fact that on or before the date of the decedent's death he was a stockholder of record (but which have not been collected at death) constitute a part of the gross estate. [Reg. §20.2033-1.]

☐ [*T.D. 6296, 6-23-58. Amended by T.D. 6684,* 10-23-63.]

[Reg. §20.2034-1]

§20.2034-1. Dower or curtesy interests.—A decedent's gross estate includes under section 2034 any interest in property of the decedent's surviving spouse existing at the time of the decedent's death as dower or curtesy, or any interest created by statute in lieu thereof (although such other interest may differ in character from dower or curtesy). Thus, the full value of property is included in the decedent's gross estate, without deduction of such an interest of the surviving husband or wife, and without regard to when the right to such an interest arose. [Reg. §20.2034-1.]

☐ [*T.D. 6296, 6-23-58.*]

[Reg. §20.2036-1]

§20.2036-1. Transfers with retained life estate.—(a) *In general.*—A decedent's gross estate includes under section 2036 the value of any interest in property transferred by the decedent after March 3, 1931, whether in trust or otherwise, except to the extent that the transfer was for an adequate and full consideration in money or money's worth (see §20.2043-1), if the decedent retained or reserved—

(1) For his life;

(2) For any period not ascertainable without reference to his death (if the transfer was made after June 6, 1932); or

(3) For any period which does not in fact end before his death:

(i) The use, possession, right to income, or other enjoyment of the transferred property.

(ii) The right, either alone or in conjunction with any other person or persons, to designate the person or persons who shall possess or enjoy the transferred property or its income (except that, if the transfer was made before June 7,

1932, the right to designate must be retained by or reserved to the decedent alone).

(b) *Meaning of terms.*—(1) A reservation by the decedent "for any period not ascertainable without reference to his death" may be illustrated by the following examples:

(i) A decedent reserved the right to receive the income from transferred property in quarterly payments, with the proviso that no part of the income between the last quarterly payment and the date of the decedent's death was to be received by the decedent or his estate; and

(ii) A decedent reserved the right to receive the income, annuity, or other payment from transferred property after the death of another person who was in fact enjoying the income, annuity, or other payment at the time of the decedent's death. In such a case, the amount to be included in the decedent's gross estate under this section does not include the value of the outstanding interest of the other person as determined in paragraphs (c)(1)(i) and (c)(2)(ii) of this section. See also, paragraphs (c)(1)(ii) *Example 1* and (c)(2)(iv) *Example 8* of this section. If the other person predeceased the decedent, the reservation by the decedent may be considered to be either for life, or for a period that does not in fact end before death.

(2) The "use, possession, right to the income, or other enjoyment of the transferred property" is considered as having been retained by or reserved to the decedent to the extent that the use, possession, right to the income, or other enjoyment is to be applied toward the discharge of a legal obligation of the decedent, or otherwise for his pecuniary benefit. The term "legal obligation" includes a legal obligation to support a dependent during the decedent's lifetime.

(3) The phrase "right . . . to designate the person or persons who shall possess or enjoy the transferred property or the income therefrom" includes a reserved power to designate the person or persons to receive the income from the transferred property, or to possess or enjoy non-income-producing property, during the decedent's life or during any other period described in paragraph (a) of this section. With respect to such a power, it is immaterial (i) whether the power was exercisable alone or only in conjunction with another person or persons, whether or not having an adverse interest; (ii) in what capacity the power was exercisable by the decedent or by another person or persons in conjunction with the decedent; and (iii) whether the exercise of the power was subject to a contingency beyond the decedent's control which did not occur before his death (e.g., the death of another person during the decedent's lifetime). The phrase, however, does not include a power over the transferred property itself which does not affect the enjoyment of the income received or earned during the decedent's life. (See, however, section 2038 for the inclusion of property in the gross estate on account of such a power.) Nor does the phrase apply to a power held solely by a person other than the decedent. But, for example, if the decedent reserved the unrestricted power to remove or discharge a trustee at any time and appoint himself as trustee, the decedent is considered as having the powers of the trustee.

(c) *Retained or reserved interest.*—(1) *Amount included in gross estate.*—(i) *In general.*—If the decedent retained or reserved an interest or right with respect to all of the property transferred by him, the amount to be included in his gross estate under section 2036 is the value of the entire property, less only the value of any outstanding income interest which is not subject to the decedent's interest or right and which is actually being enjoyed by another person at the time of the decedent's death. If the decedent retained or reserved an interest or right with respect to a part only of the property transferred by him, the amount to be included in his gross estate under section 2036 is only a corresponding proportion of the amount described in the preceding sentence. An interest or right is treated as having been retained or reserved if at the time of the transfer there was an understanding, express or implied, that the interest or right would later be conferred. If this section applies to an interest retained by the decedent in a trust or otherwise and the terms of the trust or other governing instrument provide that, after the decedent's death, payments the decedent was receiving during life are to continue to be made to the decedent's estate for a specified period (as opposed to payments that were payable to the decedent prior to the decedent's death but were not actually paid until after the decedent's death), such payments that become payable after the decedent's death are not includible in the decedent's gross estate under section 2033 because they are properly reflected in the value of the trust corpus included under this section. Payments that become payable to the decedent prior to the decedent's date of death, but are not paid until after the decedent's date of death, are includible in the decedent's gross estate under section 2033.

(ii) *Examples.*—The application of paragraph (c)(1)(i) of this section is illustrated in the following examples:

Example 1. Decedent (D) creates an irrevocable inter vivos trust. The terms of the trust provide that all of the trust income is to be paid to D and D's child, C, in equal shares during their joint lives and, on the death of the first to die of D and C, all of the trust income is to be paid to the survivor. On the death of the survivor of D and C, the remainder is to be paid to another individual, F. Subsequently, D dies survived by C. Fifty percent of the value of the trust corpus is includible in D's gross estate under

Reg. §20.2036-1(c)(1)(ii)

section 2036(a)(1) because, under the terms of the trust, D retained the right to receive one-half of the trust income for D's life. In addition, the excess (if any) of the value of the remaining 50 percent of the trust corpus, over the present value of C's outstanding life estate in that 50 percent of trust corpus, also is includible in D's gross estate under section 2036(a)(1), because D retained the right to receive all of the trust income for such time as D survived C. If C had predeceased D, then 100 percent of the trust corpus would have been includible in D's gross estate.

Example 2. D transferred D's personal residence to D's child (C), but retained the right to use the residence for a term of years. D dies during the term. At D's death, the fair market value of the personal residence is includible in D's gross estate under section 2036(a)(1) because D retained the right to use the residence for a period that did not in fact end before D's death.

(2) *Retained annuity, unitrust, and other income interests in trusts.*—(i) *In general.*—This paragraph (c)(2) applies to a grantor's retained use of an asset held in trust or a retained annuity, unitrust, or other interest in any trust (other than a trust constituting an employee benefit) including without limitation the following (collectively referred to in this paragraph (c)(2) as "trusts"): certain charitable remainder trusts (collectively CRTs) such as a charitable remainder annuity trust (CRAT) within the meaning of section 664(d)(1), a charitable remainder unitrust (CRUT) within the meaning of section 664(d)(2) or (d)(3), and any charitable remainder trust that does not qualify under section 664(d), whether because the CRT was created prior to 1969, there was a defect in the drafting of the CRT, there was no intention to qualify the CRT for the charitable deduction, or otherwise; other trusts established by a grantor (collectively GRTs) such as a grantor retained annuity trust (GRAT) paying out a qualified annuity interest within the meaning of § 25.2702-3(b) of this chapter, a grantor retained unitrust (GRUT) paying out a qualified unitrust interest within the meaning of § 25.2702-3(c) of this chapter; and various other forms of grantor retained income trusts (GRITs) whether or not the grantor's retained interest is a qualified interest as defined in section 2702(b), including without limitation a qualified personal residence trust (QPRT) within the meaning of § 25.2702-5(c) of this chapter and a personal residence trust (PRT) within the meaning of § 25.2702-5(b) of this chapter. If a decedent transferred property into such a trust and retained or reserved the right to use such property, or the right to an annuity, unitrust, or other interest in such trust with respect to the property decedent so transferred for decedent's life, any period not ascertainable without reference to the decedent's death, or for a period that does not in fact end before the decedent's death, then the decedent's right to use the property or the retained annuity,

unitrust, or other interest (whether payable from income and/or principal) constitutes the retention of the possession or enjoyment of, or the right to the income from, the property for purposes of section 2036. The portion of the trust's corpus includible in the decedent's gross estate for Federal estate tax purposes is that portion of the trust corpus necessary to provide the decedent's retained use or retained annuity, unitrust, or other payment (without reducing or invading principal). In the case of a retained annuity or unitrust, the portion of the trust's corpus includible in the decedent's gross estate is that portion of the trust corpus necessary to generate sufficient income to satisfy the retained annuity or unitrust (without reducing or invading principal), using the interest rates provided in section 7520 and the adjustment factors prescribed in § 20.2031-7 (or § 20.2031-7A), if applicable. The computation is illustrated in paragraph (c)(2)(iv), *Examples 1, 2,* and *3* of this section. The portion of the trust's corpus includible in the decedent's gross estate under section 2036, however, shall not exceed the fair market value of the trust's corpus at the decedent's date of death.

(ii) *Decedent's retained annuity following a current annuity interest of another person.*—If the decedent retained the right to receive an annuity or other payment (rather than income) after the death of the current recipient of that interest, then the amount includible in the decedent's gross estate under this section is the amount of trust corpus required to produce sufficient income to satisfy the entire annuity or other payment the decedent would have been entitled to receive if the decedent had survived the current recipient (thus, also including the portion of that entire amount payable to the decedent before the current recipient's death), reduced by the present value of the current recipient's interest. However, the amount includible shall not be less than the amount of corpus required to produce sufficient income to satisfy the annuity or other payment the decedent was entitled, at the time of the decedent's death, to receive for each year. In addition, in no event shall the amount includible exceed the value of the trust corpus on the date of death. Finally, in calculating the present value of the current recipient's interest, the exhaustion of trust corpus test described in § 20.7520-3(b)(2) (exhaustion test) is not to be applied, even in cases where § 20.7520-3(b)(2) would otherwise require it to be applied. The following steps implement this computation.

(A) *Step 1:* Determine the fair market value of the trust corpus on the decedent's date of death.

(B) *Step 2:* Determine, in accordance with paragraph (c)(2)(i) of this section, the amount of corpus required to generate sufficient income to pay the annuity, unitrust, or other payment (determined on the date of the decedent's death) payable to the decedent for the trust year in which the decedent's death occurred.

(C) *Step 3*: Determine, in accordance with paragraph (c)(2)(i) of this section, the amount of corpus required to generate sufficient income to pay the annuity, unitrust, or other payment that the decedent would have been entitled to receive for each trust year if the decedent had survived the current recipient.

(D) *Step 4*: Determine the present value of the current recipient's annuity, unitrust, or other payment (without applying the exhaustion test).

(E) *Step 5*: Reduce the amount determined in Step 3 by the amount determined in Step 4, but not to below the amount determined in Step 2.

(F) *Step 6*: The amount includible in the decedent's gross estate under this section is the lesser of the amounts determined in Step 5 and Step 1.

(iii) *Graduated retained interests.*—(A) *In general.*—For purposes of this section, a *graduated retained interest* is the grantor's reservation of a right to receive an annuity, unitrust, or other payment as described in paragraph (c)(2)(i) of this section, payable at least annually, that increases (but does not decrease) over a period of time, not more often than annually.

(B) *Other definitions.*—(1) *Base amount.*—The *base amount* is the amount of corpus required to generate the annuity, unitrust, or other payment payable for the trust year in which the decedent's death occurs. See paragraph (c)(2)(i) of this section for the calculation of the base amount.

(2) *Periodic addition.*—The *periodic addition* in a graduated retained interest for each year after the year in which decedent's death occurs is the amount (if any) by which the annuity, unitrust, or other payment that would have been payable for that year if the decedent had survived exceeds the total amount of payments that would have been payable for the year immediately preceding that year. For example, assume the trust instrument provides that the grantor is to receive an annual annuity payable to the grantor or the grantor's estate for a 5-year term. The initial annual payment is $100,000, and each succeeding annual payment is to be 120 percent of the amount payable for the preceding year. Assuming the grantor dies in the second year of the trust (whether before or after the due date of the second annual payment), the periodic additions for years 3, 4, and 5 of the trust are as follows:

	(1) Annual Payment	(2) Prior Year Payment	(1 - 2) Periodic Addition
Year 3	144,000	120,000	24,000
Year 4	172,800	144,000	28,800
Year 5	207,360	172,800	34,560

(3) *Corpus amount.*—For each trust year in which a periodic addition occurs (increase year), the *corpus amount* is the amount of trust corpus which, starting from the decedent's date of death, is necessary to generate an amount of income sufficient to pay the periodic addition, beginning in the increase year and continuing in perpetuity, without reducing or invading principal. For each year with a periodic addition, the corpus amount required as of the decedent's date of death is the product of two factors: the first is the result of dividing the periodic addition (adjusted for payments made more frequently than annually, if applicable, and for

$$\frac{\text{(Periodic Addition)} \times \text{(Adjustment Factor)}}{\text{Section 7520 Rate}}$$

(ii) The adjustment factor, if applicable, is the factor for payments made more frequently than annually and for payments due at the beginning, rather than the end, of a calendar period (see Table K or J of § 20.2031-7(d)(6)). T equals the time period in years from the decedent's date of death through the last day of the trust year immediately before the year for which the periodic addition is first payable.

payments due at the beginning, rather than the end, of a payment period (see Table K or J of § 20.2031-7(d)(6)) by the section 7520 rate (periodic addition / rate)); and the second is 1 divided by the sum of 1 and the section 7520 rate raised to the T power $(1 / (1 + \text{rate})^\wedge T)$. The second factor applies a present value discount to reflect the period beginning with the date of death and ending on the last day of the trust year immediately before the year for which periodic addition is first payable.

(i) The corpus amount is determined as follows:

$$\times \quad \frac{1}{(1+ \text{Section 7520 Rate})^T}$$

(C) *Amount includible.*—The amount includible in the gross estate in the case of a graduated retained interest is the sum of the base amount and the corpus amount for each year for which a periodic addition is first payable. The sum of these amounts represents the amount of trust principal that would be necessary to generate the annual payments that would have been paid to the decedent if the decedent had sur-

Reg. § 20.2036-1(c)(2)(iii)(C)

vived and had continued to receive the graduated retained interest. The amount of trust corpus includible in a decedent's gross estate under this section, however, shall not exceed the fair market value of the trust corpus on the decedent's date of death. The provisions of this section also apply to graduated retained interests in transferred property not held in trust.

(iv) *Examples.*—The application of paragraphs (c)(2)(i), (c)(2)(ii), and (c)(2)(iii) of this section is illustrated in the following examples:

Example 1. (i) Decedent (D) transferred $100,000 to an inter vivos trust that qualifies as a CRAT under section 664(d)(1). The trust agreement provides for an annuity of $7,500 to be paid each year to D for D's life, then to D's child (C) for C's life, with the remainder to be distributed upon the survivor's death to N, a charitable organization described in sections 170(c), 2055(a), and 2522(a). The annuity is payable to D or C, as the case may be, annually on each December 31st. D dies in September 2006, survived by C who was then age 40. On D's death, the value of the trust assets was $300,000 and the section 7520 interest rate was 6 percent. D's executor does not elect to use the alternate valuation date.

(ii) The amount of corpus with respect to which D retained the right to the income, and thus the amount includible in D's gross estate under section 2036, is that amount of corpus necessary to yield the annual annuity payment to D (without reducing or invading principal). In this case, the formula for determining the amount of corpus necessary to yield the annual annuity payment to D is: annual annuity / section 7520 interest rate = amount includible under section 2036. The amount of corpus necessary to yield the annual annuity is $7,500 / .06 = $125,000. Therefore, $125,000 is includible in D's gross estate under section 2036(a)(1). (The result would be the same if D had retained an interest in the CRAT for a term of years and had died during the term. The result also would be the same if D had irrevocably relinquished D's annuity interest less than 3 years prior to D's death because of the application of section 2035.) If, instead, the trust agreement had provided that D could revoke C's annuity interest or change the identity of the charitable remainderman, see section 2038 with regard to the portion of the trust to be included in the gross estate on account of such a retained power to revoke. Under the facts presented, section 2039 does not apply to include any amount in D's gross estate by reason of this retained annuity. See § 20.2039-1(e).

Example 2. (i) D transferred $100,000 to a GRAT in which D's annuity is a qualified interest described in section 2702(b). The trust agreement provides for an annuity of $12,000 per year to be paid to D for a term of ten years or until D's earlier death. The annuity amount is payable in twelve equal installments at the end of each month. At the expiration of the term of years or on D's earlier death, the remainder is to be distributed to D's child (C). D dies prior to the expiration of the ten-year term. On the date of D's death, the value of the trust assets is $300,000 and the section 7520 interest rate is 6 percent. D's executor does not elect to use the alternate valuation date.

(ii) The amount of corpus with respect to which D retained the right to the income, and thus the amount includible in D's gross estate under section 2036, is that amount of corpus necessary to yield the annual annuity payment to D (without reducing or invading principal). In this case, the formula for determining the amount of corpus necessary to yield the annual annuity payment to D is: annual annuity (adjusted for monthly payments) / section 7520 interest rate = amount includible under section 2036. The Table K adjustment factor for monthly annuity payments in this case is 1.0272. Thus, the amount of corpus necessary to yield the annual annuity is ($12,000 × 1.0272) / .06 = $205,440. Therefore, $205,440 is includible in D's gross estate under section 2036(a)(1). If, instead, the trust agreement had provided that the annuity was to be paid to D during D's life and to D's estate for the balance of the 10-year term if D died during that term, then the portion of trust corpus includible in D's gross estate would still be as calculated in this paragraph. It is not material whether payments are made to D's estate after D's death. Under the facts presented, section 2039 does not apply to include any amount in D's gross estate by reason of this retained annuity. See § 20.2039-1(e).

Example 3. (i) In 2000, D created a CRUT within the meaning of section 664(d)(2). The trust instrument directs the trustee to hold, invest, and reinvest the corpus of the trust and to pay to D for D's life, and then to D's child (C) for C's life, in equal quarterly installments payable at the end of each calendar quarter, an amount equal to 6 percent of the fair market value of the trust as valued on December 15 of the prior taxable year of the trust. At the termination of the trust, the then-remaining corpus, together with any and all accrued income, is to be distributed to N, a charitable organization described in sections 170(c), 2055(a), and 2522(a). D dies in 2006, survived by C, who was then age 55. The value of the trust assets on D's death was $300,000. D's executor does not elect to use the alternate valuation date and, as a result, D's executor does not choose to use the section 7520 interest rate for either of the two months prior to D's death.

(ii) The amount of the corpus with respect to which D retained the right to the income, and thus the amount includible in D's gross estate under section 2036(a)(1), is that amount of corpus necessary to yield the unitrust payments. In this case, such amount of corpus is determined by dividing the trust's equivalent income interest rate by the section 7520 rate (which was 6 percent at the time of D's death). The equivalent income interest rate is determined by dividing the trust's adjusted payout rate by the excess of 1 over the adjusted payout rate. Based on § 1.664-4(e)(3) of this chapter, the appropriate adjusted payout rate for the trust at D's death is 5.786 percent (6 percent x .964365). Thus, the equivalent income interest rate is 6.141 percent (5.786 percent / (1 - 5.786 percent)). The ratio of the equivalent interest rate to the assumed interest rate under section 7520 is 102.35 percent (6.141 percent / 6 percent). Because this exceeds 100 percent, D's retained payout interest exceeds a full income interest in the trust, and D effectively retained the income from all the assets transferred to the trust. Accordingly, because D retained for life an interest at least equal to the right to all income from all the property transferred by D to the CRUT, the entire value of the corpus of the CRUT is includible in D's gross estate under section 2036(a)(1). (The result would be the same if D had retained, instead, an interest in the CRUT for a term of years and had died during the term.) Under the facts presented, section 2039 does not apply to include any amount in D's gross estate by reason of D's retained unitrust interest. See § 20.2039-1(e).

(iii) If, instead, D had retained the right to a unitrust amount having an adjusted payout for which the corresponding equivalent interest rate would have been less than the 6 percent assumed interest rate of section 7520, then a correspondingly reduced proportion of the trust corpus would be includible in D's gross estate under section 2036(a)(1). Alternatively, if the interest retained by D was instead only one-half of the 6 percent unitrust interest, then the amount included in D's estate would be the amount needed to produce a 3 percent unitrust interest. All of the results in this *Example 3* would be the same if the trust had been a GRUT instead of a CRUT.

Example 4. During life, D established a 15-year GRIT for the benefit of individuals who are not members of D's family within the meaning of section 2704(c)(2). D retained the right to receive all of the net income from the GRIT, payable annually, during the GRIT's term. D dies during the GRIT's term. D's executor does not elect to use the alternate valuation date. In this case, the GRIT's corpus is includible in D's gross estate under section 2036(a)(1) because D retained the right to receive all of the income from the GRIT for a period that did not in fact end before D's death. If, instead, D had retained the right to receive 60 percent of the GRIT's net income, then 60 percent of the GRIT's corpus would have been includible in D's gross estate under section 2036. Under the facts presented,

section 2039 does not apply to include any amount in D's gross estate by reason of D's retained interest. See § 20.2039-1(e).

Example 5. In 2003, D transferred $10X to a pooled income fund that conforms to Rev. Proc. 88-53, 1988-2 CB 712 (1988) in exchange for 1 unit in the fund. D is to receive all of the income from that 1 unit during D's life. Upon D's death, D's child (C), is to receive D's income interest for C's life. In 2008, D dies. D's executor does not elect to use the alternate valuation date. In this case, the fair market value of D's 1 unit in the pooled income fund is includible in D's gross estate under section 2036(a)(1) because D retained the right to receive all of the income from that unit for a period that did not in fact end before D's death. See § 601.601(d)(2)(ii)(b) of this chapter.

Example 6. D transferred D's personal residence to a trust that met the requirements of a qualified personal residence trust (QPRT) as set forth in § 25.2702-5(c) of this chapter. Pursuant to the terms of the QPRT, D retained the right to use the residence for 10 years or until D's prior death. D dies before the end of the term. D's executor does not elect to use the alternate valuation date. In this case, the fair market value of the QPRT's assets on the date of D's death are includible in D's gross estate under section 2036(a)(1) because D retained the right to use the residence for a period that did not in fact end before D's death.

Example 7. (i) On November 1, year N, D transfers assets valued at $2,000,000 to a GRAT. Under the terms of the GRAT, the trustee is to pay to D an annuity for a 5-year term that is a qualified interest described in section 2702(b). The annuity amount is to be paid annually at the end of each trust year, on October 31st. The first annual payment is to be $100,000. Each succeeding payment is to be 120 percent of the amount paid in the preceding year. Income not distributed in any year is to be added to principal. If D dies during the 5-year term, the payments are to be made to D's estate for the balance of the GRAT term. At the end of the 5-year term, the trust is to terminate and the corpus is to be distributed to C, D's child. D dies on January 31st of the third year of the GRAT term. On the date of D's death, the value of the trust corpus is $3,200,000, the section 7520 interest rate is 6.8 percent, and the adjustment factor from Table K of § 20.2031-7 is 1.0000. D's executor does not elect to value the gross estate as of the alternate valuation date pursuant to section 2032.

(ii) The amount includible in D's gross estate under section 2036(a)(1) as described in paragraph (c)(2)(iii)(C) of this section is determined and illustrated as follows:

A	B	C	D	E	F	G
			Required Principal:			Corpus or Base
	Annual		C × Adj.			Amount At Death:
GRAT	Annuity	Periodic	Factor /	Deferral Period:	Present Value Factor:	D × F
Year	Payment	Addition	0.068	Death to GRAT Year	1/(1+.068) E	
3	144,000	n/a	2,117,647	n/a	n/a	2,117,647
4	172,800	28,800	423,529	0.747945	0.951985	403,193
5	207,360	34,560	508,235	1.747945	0.891372	453,026
					Total:	2,973,866

(iii) Specifically:

(A) *Column A.* First, determine the year of the trust term during which the decedent's death occurs, and the number of subsequent years remaining in the trust term for which the decedent retained or reserved an interest. In this example, D dies during year 3, with two additional years remaining in the term.

(B) *Column B.* Under the formula specified in the trust, the annuity payment to be made on October 31st of the 3rd year of the trust term is $144,000. Using that same formula, determine the annuity amounts for years 4 and 5.

(C) *Column C.* Determine the periodic addition for year 4 and year 5 by subtracting the annuity amount for the preceding year from the annuity amount for that year; the periodic addition for that year is the amount of the increase in the annuity amount for that year.

(D) *Columns D through G for year 3.* For the year of the decedent's death (year 3), determine the principal required to produce the annuity amount (Column D) by multiplying the annuity amount (Column B) by the adjustment factor (in this case 1.0000) and by dividing the product by the applicable interest rate under section 7520. Because this is the year of decedent's death and reflects the annuity amount payable to the dece-

dent in that year, there is no deferral, so this is also the Base Amount (the amount of corpus required to produce the annuity for year 3) (Column G).

(E) *Columns D through G for years 4 and 5.* For each succeeding year of the trust term during which the periodic addition will not be payable until a year subsequent to the year of the decedent's death, determine the principal required to produce the periodic addition payable for that year (Column D) by multiplying the periodic addition (Column C) by the adjustment factor and by dividing the product by the applicable interest rate under section 7520. Compute the factors to reflect the length of the deferral period (Column E) and the present value (Column F) as described in paragraph (c)(2)(iii)(B)(3) of this section. Multiply the amount of corpus in Column D by the factors in Columns E and F to determine the Corpus Amount for that year (Column G).

(F) *Column G total.* The sum of the amounts in Column G represents the total amount includable in the gross estate (but not in excess of the fair market value of the trust on the decedent's date of death).

(iv) An illustration of the amount of trust corpus (as of the decedent's death) necessary to produce the scheduled payments is as follows:

	Year 3	Year 4	Year 5	Corpus Amount
2nd Periodic Addition	$34,560	___Deferral Period___	$453,026	$453,026
1st Periodic Addition	$28,800	*Deferral Period* ___$403,193___		$403,193
Annuity in year of death	$144,000	___$2,117,647___		$2,117,647
	Total amount (sum) included in gross estate			$2,973,866

(v) A total corpus amount (as defined in paragraph (c)(2)(iii)(B)(3) of this section) of $2,973,866 constitutes the principal required as of decedent's date of death to produce (without reducing or invading principal) the annual payments that D would have received if D had survived and had continued to receive the retained annuity. Therefore, $2,973,866 of the trust corpus is includible in D's gross estate under section 2036(a)(1). The remaining $226,134 of the trust corpus is not includible in D's gross estate under section 2036(a)(1). The result would be the

same if D's retained annuity instead had been payable to D for a term of 5 years, or until D's prior death, at which time the GRAT would have terminated and the trust corpus would have become payable to another.

(vi) If, instead, D's annuity was to have been paid on a monthly or quarterly basis, then the periodic addition would have to be adjusted as provided in paragraph (c)(2)(iii)(B)(3) of this section. Specifically, in Column D of the Table for years 4 and 5 in this example, the amount of the principal required would be computed by multiplying the periodic addition by the appropriate factor from Table K or J of § 20.2031-7(d)(6) before dividing as indicated and computing the amounts in Columns E through G. In addition, Column D in year 3 also would have to be so adjusted. Under the facts presented, section 2039 does not apply to include any amount in D's gross estate by reason of this retained interest. See § 20.2039-1(e).

Example 8. (i) D creates an irrevocable inter vivos trust. The terms of the trust provide that an annuity of $10,000 per year is to be paid to D and C, D's child, in equal shares during their joint lives. On the death of the first to die of D and C, the entire $10,000 annuity is to be paid to the survivor for life. On the death of the survivor of D and C, the remainder is to be paid to another individual, F. Subsequently, D dies survived by C. On D's date of death, the fair market value of the trust is $120,000 and the section 7520 rate is 7 percent. At the date of D's death, the amount of trust corpus needed to produce D's annuity interest ($5,000 per year) is $71,429 ($5,000/0.07). In addition, assume the present value of C's right to receive $5,000 annually for the remainder of C's life is $40,000. The portion of the trust corpus includible in D's gross estate under section 2036(a)(1) is $102,857, determined as follows:

(ii) *Step 1*: Fair market value of corpus.	$120,000
(iii) *Step 2*: Corpus required to produce D's date of death annuity ($5,000/0.07).	$71,429
(iv) *Step 3*: Corpus required to produce D's annuity if D had survived C ($10,000/0.07).	$142,857
(v) *Step 4*: Present value of C's interest.	$40,000
(vi) *Step 5*: The amount determined in Step 3, reduced by the amount determined in Step 4, but not to below the amount determined in Step 2 ($142,857 - $40,000, but not less than $71,429).	$102,857
(vii) *Step 6*: The lesser of the amounts determined in Steps 5 and 1 ($102,857 or $120,000).	$102,857.

(3) *Effective/applicability dates.*—Paragraphs (a) and (c)(1)(i) of this section are applicable to the estates of decedents dying after August 16, 1954. Paragraphs (c)(1)(ii) and (c)(2) of this section apply to the estates of decedents dying on or after July 14, 2008. All but the last two sentences at the end of paragraph (c)(1)(i) of this section are applicable to the estates of decedents dying after August 16, 1954. The first, second, and sixth sentences in paragraph (c)(2)(i) of this section and all but the introductory text, *Example 7*, and *Example 8* of paragraph (c)(2)(iv) of this section are applicable to the estates of decedent's dying on or after July 14, 2008. Paragraph (b)(1)(ii) of this section, the last two sentences at the end of paragraph (c)(1)(i) of this section, *Example 1* of paragraph (c)(1)(ii) of this section, the third, fourth, and fifth sentences in paragraph (c)(2)(i) of this section; paragraph (c)(2)(ii) of this section; paragraph (c)(2)(iii) of this section; and the introductory text, *Example 7*, and *Example 8* of paragraph (c)(2)(iv) of this section are applicable to the estates of decedents dying on or after November 8, 2011. [Reg. § 20.2036-1.]

☐ [*T.D.* 6296, 6-23-58. *Amended by T.D.* 6501, 11-15-60; *T.D.* 9414, 7-11-2008 (*corrected* 7-30-2008) *and T.D.* 9555, 11-7-2011.]

[Reg. § 20.2037-1]

§ 20.2037-1. Transfers taking effect at death.—(a) *In general.*—A decedent's gross estate includes under section 2037 the value of any interest in property transferred by the decedent after September 7, 1916, whether in trust or otherwise, except to the extent that the transfer was for an adequate and full consideration in money or money's worth (see § 20.2043-1), if—

(1) Possession or enjoyment of the property could, through ownership of the interest, have been obtained only by surviving the decedent,

(2) The decedent had retained a possibility (hereinafter referred to as a "reversionary interest") that the property, other than the income alone, would return to the decedent or his estate or would be subject to a power of disposition by him, and

(3) The value of the reversionary interest immediately before the decedent's death exceeded 5 percent of the value of the entire property.

However, if the transfer was made before October 8, 1949, section 2037 is applicable only if the reversionary interest arose by the express terms of the instrument of transfer and not by operation of law (see paragraph (f) of this section). See also paragraph (g) of this section with respect to transfers made between November 11, 1935, and January 29, 1940. The provisions of section 2037 do not apply to transfers made before September 8, 1916.

(b) *Condition of survivorship.*—As indicated in paragraph (a) of this section, the value of an interest in transferred property is not included in a decedent's gross estate under section 2037 unless possession or enjoyment of the property could, through ownership of such interest, have been obtained only by surviving the decedent. Thus, property is not included in the decedent's gross estate if, immediately before the decedent's death, possession or enjoyment of the property could have been obtained by any beneficiary either by surviving the decedent or through the occurrence of some other event such as the expiration of a term of years. However, if a consideration of the terms and circumstances of the transfer as a whole indicates that the "other event" is unreal and if the death of the decedent does, in fact, occur before the "other event," the beneficiary will be considered able to possess or enjoy the property only by surviving the decedent. Notwithstanding the foregoing, an interest in transferred property is not includible in a decedent's gross estate under section 2037 if possession or enjoyment of the property could have been obtained by any beneficiary during the decedent's life through the exercise of a general power of appointment (as defined in section 2041) which in fact was exercisable immediately before the decedent's death. See examples (5) and (6) in paragraph (e) of this section.

(c) *Retention of reversionary interest.*—(1) As indicated in paragraph (a) of this section, the value of an interest in transferred property is not included in a decedent's gross estate under section 2037 unless the decedent had retained a reversionary interest in the property, and the value of the reversionary interest immediately before the death of the decedent exceeded 5 percent of the value of the property.

(2) For purposes of section 2037, the term "reversionary interest" includes a possibility that property transferred by the decedent may return to him or his estate and a possibility that property transferred by the decedent may become subject to a power of disposition by him. The term is not used in a technical sense, but has reference to any reserved right under which the transferred property shall or may be returned to the grantor. Thus, it encompasses an interest arising either by the express terms of the instrument of transfer or by operation of law. (See, however, paragraph (f) of this section with respect to transfers made before October 8, 1949.) The term "reversionary interest" does not include rights to income only, such as the right to receive the income from a trust after the death of another person. (However, see section 2036 for the inclusion of property in the gross estate on account of such rights.) Nor does the term "reversionary interest" include the possibility that the decedent during his lifetime might have received back an interest in transferred property by inheritance through the estate of another person. Similarly, a statutory right of a spouse to receive a portion of whatever estate a decedent may leave at the time of his death is not a "reversionary interest".

(3) For purposes of this section, the value of the decedent's reversionary interest is computed as of the moment immediately before his death, without regard to whether or not the executor elects the alternate valuation method under section 2032 and without regard to the fact of the decedent's death. The value is ascertained in accordance with recognized valuation principles for determining the value for estate tax purposes of future or conditional interests in property. (See §§ 20.2031-1, 20.2031-7, and 20.2031-9.) For

example, if the decedent's reversionary interest was subject to an outstanding life estate in his wife, his interest is valued according to the actuarial rules set forth in § 20.2031-7. On the other hand, if the decedent's reversionary interest was contingent on the death of his wife without issue surviving and if it cannot be shown that his wife is incapable of having issue (so that his interest is not subject to valuation according to the actuarial rules in § 20.2031-7), his interest is valued according to the general rules set forth in § 20.2031-1. A possibility that the decedent may be able to dispose of property under certain conditions is considered to have the same value as a right of the decedent to the return of the property under those same conditions.

(4) In order to determine whether or not the decedent retained a reversionary interest in transferred property of a value in excess of 5 percent, the value of the reversionary interest is compared with the value of the transferred property, including interests therein which are not dependent upon survivorship of the decedent. For example, assume that the decedent, A, transferred property in trust with the income payable to B for life and with the remainder payable to C if A predeceases B, but with the property to revert to A if B predeceases A. Assume further that A does, in fact, predecease B. The value of A's reversionary interest immediately before his death is compared with the value of the trust corpus, without deduction of the value of B's outstanding life estate. If, in the above example, A had retained a reversionary interest in one-half only of the trust corpus, the value of his reversionary interest would be compared with the value of one-half of the trust corpus, again without deduction of any part of the value of B's outstanding life estate.

(d) *Transfers partly taking effect at death.*—If separate interests in property are transferred to one or more beneficiaries, paragraphs (a) through (c) of this section are to be separately applied with respect to each interest. For example, assume that the decedent transferred an interest in Blackacre to A which could be possessed or enjoyed only by surviving the decedent, and that the decedent transferred an interest in Blackacre to B which could be possessed or enjoyed only on the occurrence of some event unrelated to the decedent's death. Assume further that the decedent retained a reversionary interest in Blackacre of a value in excess of 5 percent. Only the value of the interest transferred to A is includible in the decedent's gross estate. Similar results would obtain if possession or enjoyment of the entire property could have been obtained only by surviving the decedent, but the decedent had retained a reversionary interest in a part only of such property.

(e) *Examples.*—The provisions of paragraphs (a) through (d) of this section may be further illustrated by the following examples. It is assumed that the transfers were made on or after October 8, 1949; for the significance of this date, see paragraphs (f) and (g) of this section:

Example (1). The decedent transferred property in trust with the income payable to his wife for life and, at her death, remainder to the decedent's then surviving children, or if none, to the decedent or his estate. Since each beneficiary can possess or enjoy the property without surviving the decedent, no part of the property is includible in the decedent's gross estate under section 2037, regardless of the value of the decedent's reversionary interest. (However, see section 2033 for inclusion of the value of the reversionary interest in the decedent's gross estate.)

Example (2). The decedent transferred property in trust with the income to be accumulated for the decedent's life, and at his death, principal and accumulated income to be paid to the decedent's then surviving issue, or, if none, to A or A's estate. Since the decedent retained no reversionary interest in the property, no part of the property is includible in the decedent's gross estate, even though possession or enjoyment of the property could be obtained by the issue only by surviving the decedent.

Example (3). The decedent transferred property in trust with the income payable to his wife for life and with the remainder payable to the decedent or, if he is not living at his wife's death, to his daughter or her estate. The daughter cannot obtain possession or enjoyment of the property without surviving the decedent. Therefore, if the decedent's reversionary interest immediately before his death exceeded 5 percent of the value of the property, the value of the property, less the value of the wife's outstanding life estate, is includible in the decedent's gross estate.

Example (4). The decedent transferred property in trust with the income payable to his wife for life and with the remainder payable to his son or, if the son is not living at the wife's death, to the decedent or, if the decedent is not then living, to X or X's estate. Assume that the decedent was survived by his wife, his son, and X. Only X cannot obtain possession or enjoyment of the property without surviving the decedent. Therefore, if the decedent's reversionary interest immediately before his death exceeded 5 percent of the value of the property, the value of X's remainder interest (with reference to the time immediately after the decedent's death) is includible in the decedent's gross estate.

Example (5). The decedent transferred property in trust with the income to be accumulated for a period of 20 years or until the decedent's prior death, at which time the principal and accumulated income was to be paid to the decedent's son if then surviving. Assume that the decedent does, in fact, die before the expiration of the 20-year period. If, at the time of the transfer, the decedent was 30 years of age, in good health, etc., the son will be considered able to possess or enjoy the property without surviving the dece-

dent. If, on the other hand, the decedent was 70 years of age at the time of the transfer, the son will not be considered able to possess or enjoy the property without surviving the decedent. In this latter case, if the value of the decedent's reversionary interest (arising by operation of law) immediately before his death exceeded 5 percent of the value of the property, the value of the property is includible in the decedent's gross estate.

Example (6). The decedent transferred property in trust with the income to be accumulated for his life and, at his death, the principal and accumulated income to be paid to the decedent's then surviving children. The decedent's wife was given the unrestricted power to alter, amend, or revoke the trust. Assume that the wife survived the decedent but did not, in fact, exercise her power during the decedent's lifetime. Since possession or enjoyment of the property could have been obtained by the wife during the decedent's lifetime under the exercise of a general power of appointment, which was, in fact, exercisable immediately before the decedent's death, no part of the property is includible in the decedent's gross estate.

(f) *Transfers made before October 8, 1949.*—(1) Notwithstanding any provisions to the contrary contained in paragraphs (a) to (e) of this section, the value of an interest in property transferred by a decedent before October 8, 1949, is included in his gross estate under section 2037 only if the decedent's reversionary interest arose by the express terms of the instrument and not by operation of law. For example, assume that the decedent, on January 1, 1947, transferred property in trust with the income payable to his wife for the decedent's life and, at his death, remainder to his then surviving descendants. Since no provision was made for the contingency that no descendants of the decedent might survive him, a reversion to the decedent's estate existed by operation of law. The descendants cannot obtain possession or enjoyment of the property without surviving the decedent. However, since the decedent's reversionary interest arose by operation of law, no part of the property is includible in the decedent's gross estate under section 2037. If, in the above example, the transfer had been made on or after October 8, 1949, and if the decedent's reversionary interest immediately before his death exceeded 5 percent of the value of the property, the value of the property would be includible in the decedent's gross estate.

(2) The decedent's reversionary interest will be considered to have arisen by the express terms of the instrument of transfer and not by operation of law if the instrument contains an express disposition which affirmatively creates the reversionary interest, even though the terms of the disposition do not refer to the decedent or his estate, as such. For example, where the disposition is, in its terms, to the next of kin of the

decedent and such a disposition, under applicable local law, constitutes a reversionary interest in the decedent's estate, the decedent's reversionary interest will be considered to have arisen by the express terms of the instrument of transfer and not by operation of law.

(g) *Transfers made after November 11, 1935, and before January 29, 1940.*—The provisions of paragraphs (a) to (f) of this section are fully applicable to transfers made after November 11, 1935 (the date on which the Supreme Court decided *Helvering v. St. Louis Union Trust Co.* (296 U. S. 39) and *Becker v. St. Louis Union Trust Co.* (296 U. S. 48)), and before January 29, 1940 (the date on which the Supreme Court decided *Helvering v. Hallock* and companion cases (309 U. S. 106)), except that the value of an interest in property transferred between these dates is not included in a decedent's gross estate under section 2037 if—

(1) The Commissioner, whose determination shall be final, determines that the transfer is classifiable with the transfers involved in the *St. Louis Union Trust Co.* cases, rather than with the transfer involved in the case of *Klein v. United States* (283 U. S. 231), previously decided by the Supreme Court, and

(2) The transfer shall have been finally treated for all gift tax purposes, both as to the calendar year of the transfer and as to subsequent calendar years, as a gift in an amount measured by the value of the property undiminished by reason of a provision in the instrument of transfer by which the property, in whole or in part, is to revert to the decedent should he survive the donee or another person, or the reversion is conditioned upon some other contingency terminable by the decedent's death. [Reg. § 20.2037-1.]

☐ [T.D. 6296, 6-23-58.]

[Reg. § 20.2038-1]

§ 20.2038-1. Revocable transfers.—(a) *In general.*—A decedent's gross estate includes under section 2038 the value of any interest in property transferred by the decedent, whether in trust or otherwise, if the enjoyment of the interest was subject at the date of the decedent's death to any change through the exercise of a power by the decedent to alter, amend revoke, or terminate, or if the decedent relinquished such a power in contemplation of death. However, section 2038 does not apply—

(1) To the extent that the transfer was for an adequate and full consideration in money or money's worth (see § 20.2043-1);

(2) If the decedent's power could be exercised only with the consent of all parties having an interest (vested or contingent) in the transferred property, and if the power adds nothing to the rights of the parties under local law; or

(3) To a power held solely by a person other than the decedent. But, for example, if the decedent had the unrestricted power to remove or discharge a trustee at any time and appoint himself trustee, the decedent is considered as having the powers of the trustee. However, this result would not follow if he only had the power to appoint himself trustee under limited conditions which did not exist at the time of his death. (See last two sentences of paragraph (b) of this section.)

Except as provided in this paragraph, it is immaterial in what capacity the power was exercisable by the decedent or by another person or persons in conjunction with the decedent; whether the power was exercisable alone or only in conjunction with another person or persons, whether or not having an adverse interest (unless the transfer was made before June 2, 1924; see paragraph (d) of this section); and at what time or from what source the decedent acquired his power (unless the transfer was made before June 23, 1936; see paragraph (c) of this section). Section 2038 is applicable to any power affecting the time or manner of enjoyment of property or its income, even though the identity of the beneficiary is not affected. For example, section 2038 is applicable to a power reserved by the grantor of a trust to accumulate income or distribute it to A, and to distribute corpus to A, even though the remainder is vested in A or his estate, and no other person has any beneficial interest in the trust. However, only the value of an interest in property subject to a power to which section 2038 applies is included in the decedent's gross estate under section 2038.

(b) *Date of existence of power.*—A power to alter, amend, revoke, or terminate will be considered to have existed at the date of the decedent's death even though the exercise of the power was subject to a precedent giving of notice or even though the alteration, amendment, revocation, or termination would have taken effect only on the expiration of a stated period after the exercise of the power, whether or not on or before the date of the decedent's death notice had been given or the power had been exercised. In determining the value of the gross estate in such cases, the full value of the property transferred subject to the power is discounted for the period required to elapse between the date of the decedent's death and the date upon which the alteration, amendment, revocation, or termination could take effect. In this connection, see especially § 20.2031-7. However, section 2038 is not applicable to a power the exercise of which was subject to a contingency beyond the decedent's control which did not occur before his death (e.g., the death of another person during the decedent's life). See, however, section 2036(a)(2) for the inclusion of property in the decedent's gross estate on account of such a power.

(c) *Transfers made before June 23, 1936.*—Notwithstanding anything to the contrary in paragraphs (a) and (b) of this section, the value of an interest in property transferred by a decedent before June 23, 1936, is not included in his gross estate under section 2038 unless the power to alter, amend, revoke, or terminate was reserved at the time of the transfer. For purposes of this paragraph, the phrase "reserved at the time of the transfer" has reference to a power (arising either by the express terms of the instrument of transfer or by operation of law) to which the transfer was subject when made and which continued to the date of the decedent's death (see paragraph (b) of this section) to be exercisable by the decedent alone or by the decedent in conjunction with any other person or persons. The phrase also has reference to any understanding, express or implied, had in connection with the making of the transfer that the power would later be created or conferred.

(d) *Transfers made before June 2, 1924.*—Notwithstanding anything to the contrary in paragraphs (a) to (c) of this section, if an interest in property was transferred by a decedent before the enactment of the Revenue Act of 1924 (June 2, 1924, 4:01 p.m., eastern standard time), and if a power reserved by the decedent to alter, amend, revoke, or terminate was exercisable by the decedent only in conjunction with a person having a substantial adverse interest in the transferred property, or in conjunction with several persons some or all of whom held such an adverse interest, there is included in the decedent's gross estate only the value of any interest or interests held by a person or persons not required to join in the exercise of the power plus the value of any insubstantial adverse interest or interests of a person or persons required to join in the exercise of the power.

(e) *Powers relinquished in contemplation of death.*—(1) *In general.*—If a power to alter, amend, revoke, or terminate would have resulted in the inclusion of an interest in property in a decedent's gross estate under section 2038 if it had been held until the decedent's death, the relinquishment of the power in contemplation of the decedent's death within 3 years before his death results in the inclusion of the same interest in property in the decedent's gross estate, except to the extent that the power was relinquished for an adequate and full consideration in money or money's worth (see § 20.2043-1). For the meaning of the phrase "in contemplation of death", see paragraph (c) of § 20.2035-1.

(2) *Transfers before June 23, 1936.*—In the case of a transfer made before June 23, 1936, section 2038 applies only to a relinquishment made by the decedent. However, in the case of a transfer made after June 22, 1936, section 2038 also applies to a relinquishment made by a person or persons holding the power in conjunction with the decedent, if the relinquishment was made in contemplation of the decedent's death and had the effect of extinguishing the power.

(f) *Effect of disability to relinquish power in certain cases.*—Notwithstanding anything to the contrary in paragraphs (a) through (e) of this section the provisions of this section do not apply to a transfer if—

(1) The relinquishment on or after January 1, 1940, and on or before December 31, 1947, of the power would, by reason of section 1000(e), of the Internal Revenue Code of 1939, be deemed not a transfer of property for the purpose of the gift tax under chapter 4 of the Internal Revenue Code of 1939, and

(2) The decedent was, for a continuous period beginning on or before September 30, 1947, and ending with his death, after August 16, 1954, under a mental disability to relinquish a power.

For the purpose of the foregoing provision, the term "mental disability" means mental incompetence, in fact, to release the power whether or not there was an adjudication of incompetence. Such provision shall apply even though a guardian could have released the power for the decedent. No interest shall be allowed or paid on any overpayment allowable under section 2038(c) with respect to amounts paid before August 7, 1959. [Reg. § 20.2038-1.]

☐ [*T.D. 6296, 6-23-58. Amended by T.D. 6600, 5-28-62.*]

[Reg. § 20.2039-1]

§ 20.2039-1. Annuities.—(a) *In general.*—A decedent's gross estate includes under section 2039(a) and (b) the value of an annuity or other payment receivable by any beneficiary by reason of surviving the decedent under certain agreements or plans to the extent that the value of the annuity or other payment is attributable to contributions made by the decedent or his employer. Sections 2039(a) and (b), however, have no application to an amount which constitutes the proceeds of insurance under a policy on the decedent's life. Paragraph (b) of this section describes the agreements or plans to which section 2039(a) and (b) applies; paragraph (c) of this section provides rules for determining the amount includible in the decedent's gross estate; paragraph (d) of this section distinguishes proceeds of life insurance; and paragraph (e) of this section distinguishes annuity, unitrust, and other interests retained by a decedent in certain trusts. The fact that an annuity or other payment is not includible in a decedent's gross estate under section 2039(a) and (b) does not mean that it is not includible under some other section of part III of subchapter A of chapter 11. However, see section 2039(c) and (d) and § 20.2039-2 for rules relating to the exclusion from a decedent's gross estate of annuities and other payments under certain "qualified plans." Further, the fact that an annuity or other payment may be includible under section 2039(a) will not preclude the application of another section of chapter 11 with regard to that interest. For annuity interests in trust, see paragraph (e)(1) of this section.

(b) *Agreements or plans to which section 2039(a) and (b) applies.*—(1) Section 2039(a) and (b) applies to the value of an annuity or other payment receivable by any beneficiary under any form of contract or agreement entered into after March 3, 1931, under which—

(i) An annuity or other payment was payable to the decedent, either alone or in conjunction with another person or persons, for his life or for any period not ascertainable without reference to his death or for any period which does not in fact end before his death, or

(ii) The decedent possessed, for his life or for any period not ascertainable without reference to his death or for any period which does not in fact end before his death, the right to receive such an annuity or other payment, either alone or in conjunction with another person or persons.

The term "annuity or other payment" as used with respect to both the decedent and the beneficiary has reference to one or more payments extending over any period of time. The payments may be equal or unequal, conditional or unconditional, periodic or sporadic. The term "contract or agreement" includes any arrangement, understanding or plan, or any combination of arrangements, understandings or plans arising by reason of the decedent's employment. An annuity or other payment "was payable" to the decedent if, at the time of his death, the decedent was in fact receiving an annuity or other payment, whether or not he had an enforceable right to have payments continued. The decedent "possessed the right to receive" an annuity or other payment if, immediately before his death, the decedent had an enforceable right to receive payments at some time in the future, whether or not, at the time of his death, he had a present right to receive payments. In connection with the preceding sentence, the decedent will be regarded as having had "an enforceable right to receive payments at some time in the future" so long as he had complied with his obligations under the contract or agreement up to the time of his death. For the meaning of the phrase "for his life or for any period not ascertainable without reference to his death or for any period which does not in fact end before his death", see section 2036 and § 20.2036-1.

(2) The application of this paragraph is illustrated and more fully explained in the following examples. In each example: (i) It is assumed that all transactions occurred after March 3, 1931, and (ii) the amount stated to be includible in the decedent's gross estate is determined in accordance with the provisions of paragraph (c) of this section.

Example (1). The decedent purchased an annuity contract under the terms of which the issuing company agreed to pay an annuity to the decedent for his life and, upon his death, to pay a specified lump sum to his designated beneficiary. The decedent was drawing his annuity at the time of his death. The amount of the lump sum payment to the beneficiary is includible in the decedent's gross estate under section 2039(a) and (b).

Example (2). Pursuant to a retirement plan, the employer made contributions to a fund which was to provide the employee, upon his retirement at age 60, with an annuity for life, and which was to provide the employee's wife, upon his death after retirement, with a similar annuity for life. The benefits under the plan were completely forfeitable during the employee's life, but, upon his death after retirement, the benefits to the wife were forfeitable only upon her remarriage. The employee had no right originally to designate or ever to change the employer's designation of the surviving beneficiary. The retirement plan at no time met the requirements of section 401(a) (relating to qualified plans). Assume that the employee died at age 61 after the employer started payment of his annuity as described above. The value of the wife's annuity is includible in the decedent's gross estate under section 2039(a) and (b). Includibility in this case is based on the fact that the annuity to the decedent "was payable" at the time of his death. The fact that the decedent's annuity was forfeitable is of no consequence since, at the time of his death, he was in fact receiving payments under the plan. Nor is it important that the decedent had no right to choose the surviving beneficiary. The element of forfeitability in the wife's annuity may be taken into account only with respect to the valuation of the annuity in the decedent's gross estate.

Example (3). Pursuant to a retirement plan, the employer made contributions to a fund which was to provide the employee, upon his retirement at age 60, with an annuity of $100 per month for life, and which was to provide his designated beneficiary, upon the employee's death after retirement, with a similar annuity for life. The plan also provided that (a) upon the employee's separation from service before retirement, he would have a nonforfeitable right to receive a reduced annuity starting at age 60, and (b) upon the employee's death before retirement, a lump sum payment representing the amount of the employer's contributions credited to the employee's account would be paid to the designated beneficiary. The plan at no time met the requirements of section 401(a) (relating to qualified plans). Assume that the employee died at age 49 and that the designated beneficiary was paid the specified lump sum payment. Such amount is includible in the decedent's gross estate under section 2039(a) and (b). Since, immediately before his death, the employee had an enforceable right to receive an annuity commencing at age 60, he is considered to have "possessed the right to receive" an annuity as that term is used in section 2039(a). If, in this example, the employee would not be entitled to any benefits in the event of his separation from service before retirement for any reason other than death, the result would be the same so long as the decedent had complied with his obligations under the contract up to the time of his death. In such case, he is considered to have had, immediatley before his death, an enforceable right to receive an annuity commencing at age 60.

Example (4). Pursuant to a retirement plan, the employer made contributions to a fund which was to provide the employee, upon his retirement at age 60, with an annuity for life, and which was to provide his designated beneficiary, upon the employee's death after retirement, with a similar annuity for life. The plan provided, however, that no benefits were payable in the event of the employee's death before retirement. The retirement plan at no time met the requirements of section 401(a) (relating to qualified plans). Assume that the employee died at age 59 but that the employer nevertheless started payment of an annuity in a slightly reduced amount to the designated beneficiary. The value of the annuity is not includible in the decedent's gross estate under section 2039(a) and (b). Since the employee died before reaching the retirement age, the employer was under no obligation to pay the annuity to the employee's designated beneficiary. Therefore, the annuity was not paid under a "contract or agreement" as that term is used in section 2039(a). If, however, it can be established that the employer has consistently paid an annuity under such circumstances, the annuity will be considered as having been paid under a "contract or agreement."

Example (5). The employer made contributions to a retirement fund which were credited to the employee's individual account. Under the plan, the employee was to receive one-half the amount credited to his account upon his retirement at age 60, and his designated beneficiary was to receive the other one-half upon the employee's death after retirement. If the employee should die before reaching the retirement age, the entire amount credited to his account at such time was to be paid to the designated beneficiary. The retirement plan at no time met the requirements of section 401(a) (relating to qualified plans). Assume that the employee received one-half the amount credited to his account upon reaching the retirement age and that he died shortly thereafter. Since the employee received all that he was entitled to receive under the plan before his death, no amount was payable to him for his life or for any period not ascertainable without reference to his death, or for any period which did not in fact end before his death. Thus, the amount of the payment to the designated beneficiary is not includible in the decedent's gross estate under section 2039(a) and (b). If, in this example, the employee died before reaching the retirement age, the amount of the payment to the designated beneficiary would be includible in the decedent's gross estate under section 2039(a) and (b). In this latter case, the decedent possessed the right to receive a lump sum payment for a period which did not in fact end before his death.

Example (6). The employer made contributions to two different funds set up under two different plans. One plan was to provide the employee, upon his retirement at age 60, with an annuity for life, and the other plan was to provide the employee's designated beneficiary, upon the employee's death, with a similar annuity for life. Each plan was established at a different time and each plan was administered separately in every respect. Neither plan at any time met the requirements of section 401(a) (relating to qualified plans). The value of the designated beneficiary's annuity is includible in the employee's gross estate. All rights and benefits accruing to an employee and to others by reason of the employment (except rights and benefits accruing under certain plans meeting the requirements of section 401(a) (see § 20.2039-2)) are considered together in determining whether or not section 2039(a) and (b) applies. The scope of section 2039(a) and (b) cannot be limited by indirection.

(c) *Amount includible in the gross estate.*—The amount to be included in a decedent's gross estate under section 2039(a) and (b) is an amount which bears the same ratio to the value at the decedent's death of the annuity or other payment receivable by the beneficiary as the contribution made by the decedent, or made by his employer (or former employer) for any reason connected with his employment, to the cost of the contract or agreement bears to its total cost. In applying this ratio, the value at the decedent's death of the annuity or other payment is determined in accordance with the rules set forth in §§ 20.2031-1, 20.2031-7, 20.2031-8, and 20.2031-9. The application of this paragraph may be illustrated by the following examples:

Example (1). On January 1, 1945, the decedent and his wife each contributed $15,000 to the purchase price of an annuity contract under the terms of which the issuing company agreed to pay an annuity to the decedent and his wife for their joint lives and to continue the annuity to the survivor for his life. Assume that the value of the survivor's annuity at the decedent's death (computed under § 20.2031-8) is $20,000. Since the decedent contributed one-half of the cost of the contract, the amount to be included in his gross estate under section 2039(a) and (b) is $10,000.

Example (2). Under the terms of an employment contract entered into on January 1, 1945, the employer and the employee made contributions to a fund which was to provide the employee, upon his retirement at age 60, with an annuity for life, and which was to provide his designated beneficiary, upon the employee's death after retirement, with a similar annuity for life. The retirement fund at no time formed part of a plan meeting the requirements of section 401(a) (relating to qualified plans). Assume that the employer and the employee each contributed $5,000 to the retirement fund. Assume, further, that the employee died after retirement at which time the value of the survivor's annuity was $8,000. Since the employer's contributions were made by reason of the decedent's employment, the amount to be included in his gross estate under section 2039(a) and (b) is the entire $8,000. If, in the above example, only the employer made contributions to the fund, the amount to be included in the gross estate would still be $8,000.

(d) *Insurance under policies on the life of the decedent.*—If an annuity or other payment receivable by a beneficiary under a contract or agreement is in substance the proceeds of insurance under a policy on the life of the decedent, section 2039(a) and (b) does not apply. For the extent to which such an annuity or other payment is includible in a decedent's gross estate, see section 2042 and § 20.2042-1. A combination annuity contract and life insurance policy on the decedent's life (e. g., a "retirement income" policy with death benefits) which matured during the decedent's lifetime so that there was no longer an insurance element under the contract at the time of the decedent's death is subject to the provisions of section 2039(a) and (b). On the other hand, the treatment of a combination annuity contract and life insurance policy on the decedent's life which did not mature during the decedent's lifetime depends upon the nature of the contract at the time of the decedent's death. The nature of the contract is generally determined by the relation of the reserve value of the policy to the value of the death benefit at the time of the decedent's death. If the decedent dies before the reserve value equals the death benefit, there is still an insurance element under the contract. The contract is therefore considered, for estate tax purposes, to be an insurance policy subject to the provisions of section 2042. However, if the decedent dies after the reserve value equals the death benefit, there is no longer an insurance element under the contract. The contract is therefore considered to be a contract for an annuity or other payment subject to the provisions of section 2039(a) and (b) or some other section of part III of subchapter A of chapter 11. Notwithstanding the relation of the reserve value to the value of the death benefit, a contract under which the death benefit could never exceed the total premiums paid, plus interest, contains no insurance element.

Example. Pursuant to a retirement plan established January 1, 1945, the employer purchased a contract from an insurance company which was to provide the employee, upon his retirement at age 65, with an annuity of $100 per month for life, and which was to provide his designated beneficiary, upon the employee's death after retirement, with a similar annuity for life. The contract further provided that if the employee should die before reaching the retirement age, a lump sum payment of $20,000 would be paid to his designated beneficiary in lieu of the annuity described above. The plan at no time met the requirements of section 401(a) (relating to qualified plans). Assume that the reserve value of the contract at the retirement age would be $20,000. If the employee died after reaching the retirement age, the death benefit to the designated beneficiary would constitute an annuity, the value of which would be includible in the employee's gross estate under section 2039(a) and (b). If, on the other hand, the employee died before reaching his retirement age, the death benefit to the designated beneficiary would constitute insurance under a policy on the life of the decedent since the reserve value would be less than the death benefit. Accordingly, its includibility would depend upon section 2042 and § 20.2042-1.

(e) *No application to certain trusts.*—Section 2039 shall not be applied to include in a decedent's gross estate all or any portion of a trust (other than a trust constituting an employee benefit, but including those described in the following sentence) if the decedent retained a right to use property of the trust or retained an annuity, unitrust, or other interest in the trust, in either case as described in section 2036. Such trusts include without limitation the following (collectively referred to in this paragraph (e) as "trusts"): certain charitable remainder trusts (collectively CRTs) such as a charitable remainder annuity trust (CRAT) within the meaning of section 664(d)(1), a charitable remainder unitrust (CRUT) within the meaning of section 664(d)(2) or (d)(3), and any other charitable remainder trust that does not qualify under section 664(d), whether because the CRT was created prior to 1969, there was a defect in the drafting of the CRT, there was no intention to qualify the CRT for the charitable deduction, or otherwise; other trusts established by a grantor (collectively GRTs) such as a grantor retained annuity trust (GRAT) paying out a qualified annuity interest within the meaning of § 25.2702-3(b) of this chapter, a grantor retained unitrust (GRUT) paying out a qualified unitrust interest within the meaning of § 25.2702-3(c) of this chapter; and various forms of grantor retained income trusts (GRITs) whether or not the grantor's retained interest is a qualified interest as defined in section 2702(b), including without limitation a qualified personal residence trust (QPRT) within the meaning of § 25.2702-5(c) of this chapter and a personal residence trust (PRT) within the meaning of § 25.2702-5(b) of this chapter. For purposes of determining the extent to which a retained interest causes all or a portion of a trust to be included in a decedent's gross estate, see § 20.2036-1(c)(1), (2), and (3).

(f) *Effective/applicability dates.*—The first, second, and fourth sentences in paragraph (a) of this section are applicable to the estates of decedents dying after August 16, 1954. The fifth sentence of paragraph (a) of this section is applicable to the estates of decedents dying on or after October 27, 1972, and to the estates of decedents for which the period for filing a claim for credit or refund of an estate tax overpayment ends on or after October 27, 1972. The third, sixth, and seventh sentences of paragraph (a) of this section and all of paragraph (e) of this section are applicable to the estates of decedents dying on or after July 14, 2008. [Reg. § 20.2039-1.]

☐ *[T.D. 6296, 6-23-58. Amended by T.D. 7416, 4-5-76 and T.D. 9414, 7-11-2008*

[Reg. § 20.2039-1T]

§ 20.2039-1T. Limitations and repeal of estate tax exclusion for qualified plans and individual retirement plans (IRAs) (Temporary).

Q-1: Are there any exceptions to the general effective dates of the $100,000 limitation and the repeal of the estate tax exclusion for the value of interests under qualified plans and IRAs described in section 2039(c) and (e)?

A-1: (a) Yes. Section 245 of the Tax Equity and Fiscal Responsibility Act of 1982 (TEFRA) limited the estate tax exclusion to $100,000 for estates of decedents dying after December 31, 1982. Section 525 of the Tax Reform Act of 1984 (TRA of 1984) repealed the exclusion for estates of decedents dying after December 31, 1984.

(b) Section 525(b)(3) of the TRA of 1984 amended section 245 of TEFRA to provide that the $100,000 limitation on the exclusion for the value of a decedent's interest in a plan or IRA will not apply to the estate of any decedent dying after December 31, 1982, to the extent that the decedent-participant was in pay status on December 31, 1982, with respect to such interest and irrevocably elected the form of benefit payable under the plan or IRA (including the form of any survivor benefits) with respect to such interest before January 1, 1983.

(c) Similarly, the TRA of 1984 provides that the repeal of the estate tax exclusion for the value of a decedent's interest in a plan or IRA will not apply to the estate of a decedent dying after December 31, 1984, to the extent that the decedent-participant was in pay status on December 31, 1984, with respect to such interest and irrevocably elected the form of benefit payable under the plan or IRA (including the form of any survivor benefits) with respect to such interest before July 18, 1984.

Q-2: What is the meaning of "in pay status" on the applicable date?

A-2: A participant was in pay status on the applicable date with respect to a portion of his or her interest in a plan or IRA if such portion is to be paid in a benefit form that has been elected on or before such date and the participant has received, on or before such date, at least one payment under such benefit form.

Q-3: What is required for an election of the form of benefit payable under the plan to have been irrevocable as of any applicable date?

A-3: As of any applicable date, an election of the form of benefit payable under a plan is irrevocable if, as of such date, it was a written irrevocable election that, with respect to all payments to be received after such date, specified the form of distribution (e.g., lump sum, level dollar annuity, formula annuity) and the period over which the distribution would be made (e.g., single life, joint and survivor, term certain). An election is not irrevocable as of any applicable date if, on or after such date, the form or period of the distribution could be determined or altered by any person or persons. An election does not fail to be irrevocable as of an applicable date merely because the beneficiaries were not designated as of such date or could be changed after such date. If any interest in any IRA may not, by law or contract, be subject to an irrevocable election described in this section, any election of the form of benefit payable under the IRA does not satisfy the requirement that an irrevocable election have been made. [Temporary Reg. § 20.2039-1T.]

☐ *[T.D. 8073, 1-29-86.]*

[Reg. § 20.2039-2]

§ 20.2039-2. Annuities under "qualified plans" and section 403(b) annuity contracts.—
(a) *Section 2039(c) exclusion.*—In general, in the case of a decedent dying after December 31, 1953, the value of an annuity or other payment receivable under a plan or annuity contract described in paragraph (b) of this section is excluded from the decedent's gross estate to the extent provided in paragraph (c) of this section. In the case of a plan described in paragraph (b) (1) or (2) of this section(a "qualified plan"), the exclusion is subject to the limitation described in § 20.2039-3 (relating to lump sum distributions paid with respect to a decedent dying after December 31, 1976, and before January 1, 1979) or § 20.2039-4 (relating to lump sum distributions paid with respect to a decedent dying after December 31, 1978).

(b) *Plans and annuity contracts to which section 2039(c) applies.*—Section 2039(c) excludes from a decedent's gross estate, to the extent provided in paragraph (c) of this section, the value of an annuity or other payment receivable by any beneficiary (except the value of an annuity or other payment receivable by or for the benefit of the decedent's estate) under—

(1) An employees' trust (or under a contract purchased by an employees' trust) forming part of a pension, stock bonus, or profit-sharing plan which, at the time of the decedent's separation from employment (whether by death or otherwise), or at the time of the earlier termination of the plan, met the requirements of section 401(a);

(2) A retirement annuity contract purchased by an employer (and not by an employees' trust) pursuant to a plan which, at the time of decedent's separation from employment (by death or otherwise), or at the time of the earlier termination of the plan, was described in section 403(a);

(3) In the case of a decedent dying after December 31, 1957, a retirement annuity contract purchased for an employee by an employer which, for its taxable year in which the purchase occurred, is an organization referred to in section 170(b)(1)(A)(ii) or (vi) or which is a religious organization (other than a trust), and is exempt from tax under section 501(a);

(4) In the case of a decedent dying after December 31, 1965, an annuity under chapter 73 of title 10 of the United States Code, (10 U. S. C. 1431, *et seq.*); or

(5) In the case of a decedent dying after December 31, 1962, a bond purchase plan described in section 405.

For the meaning of the term "annuity or other payment", see paragraph (b) of §20.2039-1. For the meaning of the phrase "receivable by or for the benefit of the decedent's estate", see paragraph (b) of §20.2042-1. The application of this paragraph may be illustrated by the following examples in each of which it is assumed that the amount stated to be excludable from the decedent's gross estate is determined in accordance with paragraph (c) of this section:

Example (1). Pursuant to a pension plan, the employer made contributions to a trust which was to provide the employee, upon his retirement at age 60, with an annuity for life, and which was to provide his wife, upon the employee's death after retirement, with a similar annuity for life. At the time of the employee's retirement, the pension trust formed part of a plan meeting the requirements of section 401(a). Assume that the employee died at age 61 after the trustee started payment of his annuity as described above. Since the wife's annuity was receivable under a qualified pension plan, no part of the value of such annuity is includible in the decedent's gross estate by reason of the provisions of section 2039(c). If, in this example, the employer provided other benefits under nonqualified plans, the result would be the same since the exclusion under section 2039(c) is confined to the benefits provided for under the qualified plan.

Example (2). Pursuant to a profit-sharing plan, the employer made contributions to a trust which were allocated to the employee's individual account. Under the plan, the employee would, upon retirement at age 60, receive a distribution of the entire amount credited to the account. If the employee should die before reaching retirement age, the amount credited to the account would be distributed to the employee's designated beneficiary. Assume that the employee died before reaching the retirement age and that at such time the plan met the requirements of section 401(a). Since the payment to the designated beneficiary is receivable under a qualified profit-sharing plan, the provisions of section 2039(c) apply. However, if the payment is a lump sum distribution to which §20.2039-3 or §20.2039-4 applies, the payment is excludable from the decedent's gross estate only as provided in such section.

Example (3). Pursuant to a pension plan, the employer made contributions to a trust which were used by the trustee to purchase a contract from an insurance company for the benefit of an employee. The contract was to provide the employee, upon retirement at age 65, with an annuity of $100 per month for life, and was to provide the employee's designated beneficiary upon the employee's death after retirement, with a similar annuity for life. The contract further provided that if the employee should die before reaching retirement age, a lump sum payment equal to the greater of (a) $10,000 or (b) the reserve value of the policy would be paid to the designated beneficiary in lieu of the annuity. Assume that the employee died before reaching the retirement age and that at such time the plan met the requirements of section 401(a). Since the payment to the designated beneficiary is receivable under a qualified pension plan, the provisions of section 2039(c) apply. However, if the payment is a lump sum distribution to which §20.2039-3 or §20.2039-4 applies, the payment is excludable from decedent's gross estate only as provided in such section. It should be noted that for purposes of the exclusion under section 2039(c) it is immaterial whether or not the payment constitutes the proceeds of life insurance under the principles set forth in §20.2039-1(d).

Example (4). Pursuant to a profit-sharing plan, the employer made contributions to a trust which were allocated to the employee's individual account. Under the plan, the employee would, upon his retirement at age 60, be given the option to have the amount credited to his account (a) paid to him in a lump sum, (b) used to purchase a joint and survivor annuity for him and his designated beneficiary, or (c) left with the trustee under an arrangement whereby interest would be paid to him for his lifetime with the principal to be paid, at his death, to his designated beneficiary. The plan further provided that, if the third method of settlement were selected, the employee would retain the right to have the principal paid to himself in a lump sum up to the time of his death. At the time of the employee's retirement, the profit-sharing plan met the requirements of section 401(a). Assume that the employee, upon reaching his retirement age, elected to have the amount credited to his account left with the trustee under the interest arrangement. Assume, further, that the employee did not exercise his right to have such amount paid to him before his death. Under such circumstances, the employee is considered as having constructively received the amount credited to his account upon his retirement. Thus, such amount is not considered as receivable by the designated beneficiary under the profit-sharing plan and the exclusion of section 2039(c) is not applicable.

Example (5). An employer purchased a retirement annuity contract for an employee which was to provide the employee, upon his retirement at age 60, with an annuity for life and which was to provide his wife, upon the employee's death after retirement, with a similar annuity for life. The employer, for its taxable year in which the annuity contract was purchased, was an organization referred to in section 170(b)(1)(A)(ii), and was exempt from tax under section 501(a). The entire amount of the purchase price of the annuity contract was excluded from the employee's gross income under section 403(b). No part of the value of the survivor annuity payable after the employee's death is includible in the decedent's gross estate by reason of the provisions of section 2039(c).

(c) *Amounts excludable from the gross estate.*— (1) The amount to be excluded from a decedent's gross estate under section 2039(c) is an amount which bears the same ratio to the value at the decedent's death of an annuity or other payment receivable by the beneficiary as the employer's contribution (or a contribution made on the employer's behalf) on the employee's account to the plan or towards the purchase of the annuity contract bears to the total contributions on the employee's account to the plan or towards the purchase of the annuity contract. In applying this ratio—

(i) Payments or contributions made by or on behalf of the employer towards the purchase of an annuity contract described in paragraph (b)(3) of this section are considered to include only such payments or contributions as are, or were, excludable from the employee's gross income under section 403(b).

(ii) In the case of a decedent dying before January 1, 1977, payments or contributions made under a plan described in paragraph (b)(1), (2) or (5) of this section on behalf of the decedent for a period for which the decedent was self-employed, within the meaning of section 401(c)(1), with respect to the plan are considered payments or contributions made by the decedent and not by the employer.

(iii) In the case of a decedent dying after December 31, 1976, however, payments or contributions made under a plan described in para-

graph (b)(1), (2) or (5) of this section on behalf of the decedent for a period for which the decedent was self-employed, within the meaning of section 401(c)(1), with respect to the plan are considered payments or contributions made by the employer to the extent the pay ments or contributions are, or were, deductible under section 404 or 405(c). Contributions or payments attributable to that period which are not, or were not, so deductible are considered made by the decedent.

(iv) In the case of a plan described in paragraph (b)(1) or (2) of this section, a rollover contribution described in section 402(a)(5), 403(a)(4), 408(d)(3)(A)(ii) or 409(b)(3)(C) is considered an amount contributed by the employer.

(v) In the case of an annuity contract described in paragraph (b)(3) of this section, a rollover contribution described in section 403(b)(8) is considered an amount contributed by the employer.

(vi) In the case of a plan described in paragraph (b)(1), (2) or (5) of this section, an amount includable in the gross income of an employer under section 1379(b) (relating to shareholder-employee beneficiaries under certain qualified plans) is considered an amount paid or contributed by the decedent.

(vii) Amounts payable under paragraph (b)(4) of this section are attributable to payments or contributions made by the decedent only to the extent of amounts deposited by the decedent pursuant to section 1438 or 1452(d) of Title 10 of the United States Code.

(viii) The value at the decedent's death of the annuity or other payment is determined under the rules of §§ 20.2031-1 and 20.2031-7 or, for certain prior periods, § 20.2031-7A.

(2) In certain cases, the employer's contribution (or a contribution made on his behalf) to a plan on the employee's account and thus the total contributions to the plan on the employee's account cannot be readily ascertained. In order to apply the ratio stated in subparagraph (1) of this paragraph in such a case, the method outlined in the following two sentences must be used unless a more precise method is presented. In such a case, the total contributions to the plan on the employee's account is the value of any annuity or other payment payable to the decedent and his survivor computed as of the time the decedent's rights first mature (or as of the time the survivor's rights first mature if the decedent's rights never mature) and computed in accordance with the rules set forth in §§ 20.2031-1, 20.2031-7, 20.2031-8, and 20.2031.9. By subtracting from such value the amount of the employee's contribution to the plan, the amount of the employer's contribution to the plan on the employee's account may be obtained. The application of this paragraph may be illustrated by the following example:

Example. Pursuant to a pension plan, the employer and the employee contributed to a trust which was to provide the employee, upon his retirement at age 60, with an annuity for life, and which was to provide his wife, upon the employee's death after retirement, with a similar annuity for life. At the time of the employee's retirement, the pension trust formed part of a plan meeting the requirements of section 401(a). Assume the following: (i) that the employer's contributions to the fund were not credited to the accounts of individual employees; (ii) that the value of the employee's annuity and his wife's annuity, computed as of the time of the decedent's retirement, was $40,000; (iii) that the

$$\text{employer's contributions} \left(\frac{\$30,000}{\$40,000} \times \$16,000, \text{ or } \$12,000 \right) \text{ is excludable from}$$

the decedent's gross estate by reason of the provisions of section 2039(c). Compare this result with the results reached in the examples set forth in paragraph (b) of this section in which all contributions to the plans were made by the employer.

(d) *Exclusion of certain annuity interests created by community property laws.*—(1) In the case of an employee on whose behalf contributions or payments were made by his employer or former employer under an employees' trust forming part of a pension, stock bonus, or profit-sharing plan described in section 2039(c)(1), under an employee's retirement annuity contract described in section 2039(c)(2), or toward the purchase of an employee's retirement annuity contract described in section 2039(c)(3), which under section 2039(c) are not considered as contributed by the employee, if the spouse of such employee predeceases him, then, notwithstanding the provisions of section 2039 or of any other provision of law, there shall be excluded from the gross estate of such spouse the value of any interest of such spouse in such plan or trust or such contract, to the extent such interest—

(i) Is attributable to such contributions or payments, and

(ii) Arises solely by reason of such spouse's interest in community income under the community property laws of a State.

(2) Section 2039(d) and this paragraph do not provide any exclusion for such spouse's property interest in the plan, trust or contract to the extent it is attributable to the contributions of the employee spouse. Thus, the decedent's community property interest in the plan, trust, or contract which is attributable to contributions made by the employee spouse are includible in the decedent's gross estate. See paragraph (c) of this section.

(3) Section 2039(d) and this paragraph apply to the estate of a decedent who dies on or after October 27, 1972, and to the estate of a decedent who died before October 27, 1972, if the period for filing a claim for credit or refund of an overpayment of the estate tax ends on or

employee contributed $10,000 to the plan; and (iv) that the value at the decedent's death of the wife's annuity was $16,000. On the basis of these facts, the total contributions to the fund on the employee's account are presumed to be $40,000 and the employer's contribution to the plan on the employee's account is presumed to be $30,000 ($40,000 less $10,000). Since the wife's annuity was receivable under a qualified pension plan, that part of the value of such annuity which is attributable to the

after October 27, 1972. Interest will not be allowed or paid on any overpayment of tax resulting from the application of section 2039(d) and this paragraph for any period prior to April 26, 1973. [Reg. § 20.2039-2.]

☐ [*T.D.* 6296, 6-23-58. *Amended by T.D.* 6526, 1-18-61, *T.D.* 6666, 7-15-63, *T.D.* 7043, 6-1-70, *T.D.* 7416, 4-5-76, *T.D.* 7428, 8-13-76, *T.D.* 7761, 1-21-81 *and T.D.* 8540, 6-9-94.]

[Reg. § 20.2039-3]

§ 20.2039-3. Lump sum distributions under "qualified plans"; decedents dying after December 31, 1976, and before January 1, 1979.— (a) *Limitation of section 2039(c) exclusion.*—This section applies in the case of a decedent dying after December 31, 1976, and before January 1, 1979. If a lump sum distribution is paid with respect to the decedent under a plan described in § 20.2039-2(b)(1) or (2) (a "qualified plan"), no amount payable with respect to the decedent under the plan is excludable from the decedent's gross estate under § 20.2039-2.

(b) *"Lump sum distribution" defined.*—For purposes of this section the term "lump sum distribution" means a lump sum distribution defined in section 402(e)(4)(A) that satisfies the requirements of section 402(e)(4)(C), relating to the aggregation of certain trusts and plans. The distribution of an annuity contract is not a lump sum distribution for purposes of this section, and § 20.2039-2 will apply with respect to the distribution of an annuity contract without regard to whether the contract is included in a distribution that is otherwise a lump sum distribution under this paragraph (b). A distribution is a lump sum distribution for purposes of this section without regard to the election described in section 402(e)(4)(B).

(c) *Amounts payable as a lump sum distribution.*—If on the date the estate tax return is filed, an amount under a qualified plan is payable with respect to the decedent as a lump sum distribution (whether at the election of a beneficiary or otherwise), for purposes of this section the amount is deemed paid as a lump sum distribution no later than on such date. Accordingly, no portion of the amount payable under the plan is excludable from the value of the decedent's gross estate under § 20.2039-2. If, however, the amount payable as a lump sum distribution is not, in fact, thereafter paid as a lump sum distribution, there shall be allowed a credit or refund of any tax paid which is attributable to treating such amount as a lump sum distribution under this paragraph. Any claim for credit or refund filed under this paragraph must be filed within the time prescribed by section 6511, and must provide satisfactory evidence that the amount originally payable as a lump sum distribution is no longer payable in such form.

(d) *Filing date.*—For purposes of paragraph (c) of this section, "the date the estate tax return is filed" means the earlier of—

(1) The date the estate tax return is actually filed, or

(2) The date nine months after the decedent's death, plus any extension of time for filing the estate tax return granted under section 6081. [Reg. § 20.2039-3.]

☐ [*T.D.* 7761, 1-21-81.]

[Reg. § 20.2039-4]

§ 20.2039-4. Lump sum distributions from "qualified plans"; decedents dying after December 31, 1978.—(a) *Limitation on section 2039(c) exclusion.*—This section applies in the case of a decedent dying after December 31, 1978. If a lump sum distribution is paid or payable with respect to a decedent under a plan described in § 20.2039-2(b)(1) or (2) (a "qualified plan"), no amount paid or payable with respect to the decedent under the plan is excludable from the decedent's gross estate under § 20.2039-2, unless the recipient of the distribution makes the section 402(a)/403(a) taxation election described in paragraph(c) of this section. For purposes of this section, an amount is payable as a lump sum distribution under a plan if, as of the date the estate tax return is filed (as determined under § 20.2039-3(d)), it is payable as a lump sum distribution at the election of the recipient or otherwise.

(b) *"Lump sum distribution" defined; treatment of annuity contracts.*—For purposes of this section the term "lump sum distribution" means a lump sum distribution defined in section 402(e)(4)(A) that satisfies the requirements of section 402(e)(4)(C), relating to the aggregation of certain trusts and plans. A distribution is a lump sum distribution for purposes of this section without regard to the election described in section 402(e)(4)(B). The distribution of an annuity contract is not a lump sum distribution for purposes of this section, and the limitation described in this section does not apply to an annuity contract distributed under a plan. Ac-

cordingly, if the amount payable with respect to a decedent under a plan is paid to a recipient partly by the distribution of an annuity contract, and partly by the distribution of an amount that is a lump sum distribution within the meaning of this paragraph (b), § 20.2039-2 shall apply with respect to the annuity contract without regard to whether the recipient makes the section 402(a)/403(a) taxation election with respect to the remainder of the distribution.

(c) *Recipient's section 402(a)/403(a) taxation election.*—The section 402(a)/403(a) taxation election is the election by the recipient of a lump sum distribution to treat the distribution as—

(1) Taxable under section 402(a), without regard to section 402(a)(2), to the extent includable in gross income (in the case of a distribution under a qualified plan described in § 20.2039-2(b)(1)),

(2) Taxable under section 403(a), without regard to section 403(a)(2), to the extent includable in gross income (in the case of a distribution under a qualified annuity contract described in § 20.2039-2(b)(2)), or

(3) A rollover contribution, in whole or in part, under section 402(a)(7) (relating to rollovers by a decedent's surviving spouse).

Accordingly, if a recipient makes the election, no portion of the distribution is taxable to the recipient under the 10-year averaging provisions of section 402(e) or as long-term capital gain under section 402(a)(2). However, a recipient's election under this paragraph (c) does not preclude the application of section 402(e)(4)(J) to any securities of the employer corporation included in the distribution.

(d) *Method of election.*—(1) *General rule.*—The recipient of a lump sum distribution shall make the section 402(a)/403(a) taxation election by:

(i) Determining the income tax liability on the income tax return (or amended return) for the taxable year of the distribution in a manner consistent with paragraph (c)(1) or (2) of this section,

(ii) Rolling over all or any part of the distribution under section 402(a)(7), or

(iii) Filing a section 2039(f)(2) election statement described in paragraph (d)(2) of this section.

(2) *Election statement.*—A recipient may file a section 2039(f)(2) election statement indicating that the recipient elects to treat a lump sum distribution in the manner described in paragraph (c) of this section. The statement must be filed where the recipient would file the income tax return for the taxable year of the distribution. The statement must be signed by the recipient and include the individual's name, address, social security number, the name of the decedent, and a statement indicating the election is being made. A section 2039(f)(2) election statement may be filed at any time prior to making the

election under paragraph (d)(1)(i) or (ii) of this section.

(3) *Effect on estate tax return.*—If the date the estate tax return is filed precedes the date on which the recipient makes the section 402(a)/403(a) taxation election with respect to a lump sum distribution, the estate tax return may not reflect the election. However, if after the estate tax return is filed, the recipient makes the section 402(a)/403(a) taxation election, the executor of the estate may file a claim for refund or credit of an overpayment of the Federal estate tax within the time prescribed in section 6511. See also, § 20.6081-1 for rules relating to obtaining an extension of time for filing the estate tax return.

(e) *Election irrevocable.*—If a recipient of a lump sum distribution files a section 2039(f)(2) election statement, an income tax return (or amended return) or makes a rollover contribution that constitutes the section 402(a)/403(a) taxation election described in paragraphs (c) and (d), the election may not be revoked. Accordingly, a subsequent and amended income tax return filed by the recipient that is inconsistent with the prior election will not be given effect for purposes of section 2039 and section 402 or 403.

(f) *Lump sum distribution to multiple recipients.*—In the case of a lump sum distribution paid or payable under a qualified plan with respect to the decedent to more than one recipient, the exclusion under § 20.2039-2 applies to so much of the distribution as is paid or payable to a recipient who makes the section 402(a)/403(a) taxation election.

(g) *Distributions of annuity contracts included multiple distributions.*—Notwithstanding that a recipient makes the section 402(a)/403(a) taxation election with respect to a lump sum distribution that includes the distribution of an annuity contract, the distribution of an annuity contract is to be taken into account by the recipient for purposes of the multiple distribution rules under section 402(e). [Reg. § 20.2039-4.]

☐ [*T.D. 7761*, 1-21-81. *Amended by T.D. 7956*, 5-11-84.]

[Reg. § 20.2039-5]

§ 20.2039-5. Annuities under individual retirement plans.—(a) *Section 2039(e) exclusion.*—(1) *In general.*—In the case of a decedent dying after December 31, 1976, section 2039(e) excludes from the decedent's gross estate, to the extent provided in paragraph (c) of this section, the value of a "qualifying annuity" receivable by a beneficiary under an individual retirement plan. The term "individual retirement plan" means—

(i) An individual retirement account described in section 408(a),

(ii) An individual retirement annuity described in section 408(b), or

(iii) A retirement bond described in section 409(a).

(2) *Limitations.*—(i) Section 2039(e) applies only with respect to the gross estate of a decedent on whose behalf the individual retirement plan was established. Accordingly, section 2039(e) does not apply with respect to the estate of a decedent who was only a beneficiary under the plan.

(ii) Section 2039(e) does not apply to an annuity receivable by or for the benefit of the decedent's estate. For the meaning of the term "receivable by or for the benefit of the decedent's estate," see § 20.2042-1(b).

(b) *Qualifying annuity.*—For purposes of this section, the term "qualifying annuity" means an annuity contract or other arrangement providing for a series of substantially equal periodic payments to be made to a beneficiary for the beneficiary's life or over a period ending at least 36 months after the decedent's death. The term "annuity contract" includes an annuity purchased for a beneficiary and distributed to the beneficiary, if under section 408 the contract is not included in the gross income of the beneficiary upon distribution. The term "other arrangement" includes any arrangement arising by reason of the decedent's participation in the program providing the individual retirement plan. Payments shall be considered "periodic" if under the arrangement or contract (including a distributed contract) payments are to be made to the beneficiary at regular intervals. If the contract or arrangement provides optional payment provisions, not all of which provide for periodic payments, payments shall be considered periodic only if an option providing periodic payments is elected not later than the date the estate tax return is filed (as determined under § 20.2039-3(d)). For this purpose, the right to surrender a contract (including a distributed contract) for a cash surrender value will not be considered an optional payment provision. Payments shall be considered "substantially equal" even though the amounts receivable by the beneficiary may vary. Payments shall not be considered substantially equal, however, if more than 40% of the total amount payable to the beneficiary under the individual retirement plan, determined as of the date of the decedent's death and excluding any postmortem increase, is payable to the beneficiary in any 12-month period.

(c) *Amount excludible from gross estate.*—(1) *In general.*—Except as otherwise described in this paragraph (c), the amount excluded from the decedent's gross estate under section 2039(e) is the entire value of the qualifying annuity (as determined under §§ 20.2031-1 and 20.2031-7 or, for certain prior periods, § 20.2031-7A) payable under the individual retirement plan.

(2) *Excess contribution.*—In any case in which there exists, on the date of the decedent's

death, an excess contribution (as defined in section 4973(b)) with respect to the individual retirement plan, the amount excluded from the value of the decedent's gross estate is determined under the following formula:

$$E = A - A \left(\frac{X}{C - R} \right)$$

Where:

E = the amount excluded from the decedent's gross estate under section 2039(e),

A = the value of the qualifying annuity at the decedent's death (as determined under §§ 20.2031-1 and 20.2031-7 or, for certain prior periods, § 20.2031-7A),

X = the amount which is an excess contribution at the decedent's death (as determined under section 4973(b)),

C = the total amount contributed by or on behalf of the decedent to the individual retirement plan, and

R = the total of amounts paid or distributed from the individual retirement plan before the death of the decedent which were either includable in the gross income of the recipient under section 408(d)(1) and represented the payment or distribution of an excess contribution, or were payments or distributions described in section 408(d)(4) or (5) (relating to returned excess contributions).

(3) *Certain section 403(b)(8) rollover contributions.*—This subparagraph (3) applies if the decedent made a rollover contribution to the individual retirement plan under section 403(b)(8), and the contribution was attributable to a distribution under an annuity contract other than an annuity contract described in § 20.2039-2(b)(3). If such a rollover contribution was the only contribution made to the plan, no part of the value of the qualifying annuity payable under the plan is excluded from the decedent's gross estate under section 2039(e). If a contribution other than such a rollover contribution was made to the plan, the amount excluded from the decedent's gross estate is determined under the formula described in subparagraph (2) of this paragraph, except that for purposes of that formula, X includes the amount that was a rollover contribution under section 403(b)(8) attributable to a distribution under an annuity contract not described in § 20.2039-2(b)(3).

(4) *Surviving spouse's rollover contribution.*— This subparagraph (4) applies if the decedent made a rollover contribution to the individual retirement plan under section 402(a)(7), relating to rollovers by a surviving spouse. If the rollover contribution under section 402(a)(7) was the only contribution made by the decedent to the plan, no part of the value of the qualifying annuity payable under the plan is excluded from the decedent's gross estate under section 2039(e). If a contribution other than a rollover contribution under section 402(a)(7) was made by the decedent to the plan, the amount excluded from the decedent's gross estate is determined under the formula described in subparagraph (2) of this paragraph, except that for purposes of that formula, X includes the amount that was a rollover contribution under section 402(a)(7).

(5) *Election under § 1.408-2(b)(7)(ii).*—This subparagraph (5) applies if the decedent at any time made the election described in § 1.408-2(b)(7)(ii) with respect to an amount in the individual retirement plan. If this subparagraph (5) applies, the amount excluded from the decedent's gross estate is determined under the formula described in subparagraph (2), except that for purposes of that formula, X and C include the amount with respect to which the election was made.

(6) *Plan-to-plan rollovers.*—(i) This subparagraph (6) applies if the individual retirement plan is a transferee plan. A "transferee plan" is a plan that was the recipient of a contribution described in section 408(d)(3)(A)(i) or 409(b)(3)(C) (relating to rollovers from one individual retirement plan to another) made by the decedent. The amount of the contribution described in section 408(d)(3)(A)(i) or 409(b)(3)(C) is the "rollover amount." The plan from which the rollover amount was paid or distributed to the decedent is the "transferor plan."

(ii) If the decedent made a contribution described in subparagraph (3) or (4) to the transferor plan, the amount excluded from the decedent's gross estate with respect to the transferee plan is determined under the formula described in subparagraph (2), except that for purposes of that formula, X includes so much of the rollover amount as was attributable to the contribution to the transferor plan that was described in subparagraph (3) or (4). The extent to which a rollover amount is attributable to a contribution described in subparagraph (3) or (4) that was made to the transferor plan is determined by multiplying the rollover amount by a fraction, the numerator of which is the amount of such contribution, and the denominator of which is the sum of all amounts contributed by the decedent to the transferor plan (if not returned as described under R in subparagraph (2)), and any amount in the transferor plan to which the election described in subparagraph (5) applied.

(iii) If the decedent made the election described in subparagraph (5) with respect to an amount in the transferor plan, the amount excluded from the decedent's gross estate with respect to the transferee plan is determined under the formula described in subparagraph (2), except that for purposes of that formula, X includes so much of the rollover amount as was attributable to the amount in the transferor plan to which the election applied. The extent to which a rollover amount is attributable to an

Reg. § 20.2039-5(c)(6)(iii)

amount in the transferor plan to which the election applied is determined by multiplying the rollover amount by a fraction, the numerator of which is the amount to which the election applied, and the denominator of which is the sum of all amounts contributed by the decedent to the transferor plan (if not returned as described under R in subparagraph (2)), and the amount in the transferor plan to which the election applied.

(iv) If a transferor plan described in this subparagraph (6) was also a transferee plan, then the rules described in this subparagraph (6) are to be applied with respect to both the rollover amount paid to the plan and the rollover amount thereafter paid from the plan.

(d) *Examples.*—The provisions of this section are illustrated by the following examples:

Example (1). (1) A establishes an individual retirement account described in section 408(a) on January 1, 1976, when A is age 65. A's only contribution to the account is a rollover contribution described in section 402(a)(5). The trust agreement provides that A may at any time elect to have the balance in the account distributed in one of the following methods:

(i) A single sum payment of the account,

(ii) Equal or substantially equal semiannual payments over a period equal to A's life expectancy, or

(iii) Equal or substantially equal semiannual payments over a period equal to the life expectancy of A and A's spouse.

(2) The trust agreement further provides that although semiannual payments have commenced under option (ii) or (iii), A (or A's surviving spouse) may, by written notice to the trustee, receive all or a part of the balance remaining in the account. In addition, under option (ii), any balance remaining in the account at A's death is payable in a single sum to A's designated beneficiary. Under option (iii), any balance remaining in the account at the death of the survivor of A or A's spouse is payable in a single sum to a beneficiary designated by A or A's surviving spouse.

(3) A elects option (iii), and the first semiannual payment is made to A on July 1, 1976. On that date, A's life expectancy is 15 years, and that of A's spouse is 22 years. Under option (iii), the semiannual payments to A or A's surviving spouse will continue until July 1, 1998.

(4) A dies on November 20, 1978. On December 15, 1978, the trust agreement is modified so that A's surviving spouse no longer may elect to receive all or part of the balance remaining in the account. The value of the semiannual payments payable to A's spouse is excluded from A's gross estate under section 2039(e).

(5) A's spouse dies July 12, 1981, and the single sum payment payable on account of the death of A's spouse is paid to the designated beneficiary on August 1, 1981. Notwithstanding that the balance in the account was paid to the designated beneficiary within 36 months after A's death, the value of the semiannual payments payable to A's spouse are excluded from A's gross estate, since at A's death those semiannual payments were to be paid over a period extending beyond 36 months. Section 2039(e) does not apply to exclude any amount from the estate of A's spouse, because A's spouse was only a beneficiary and not the individual on whose behalf the account was established.

Example (2). Assume the same facts as in example (1), except that the trust agreement is not modified so that A's surviving spouse no longer may elect to receive all or part of the balance remaining in the account (see (2) and (4) in example (1)). Instead, the balance of the account is applied toward the purchase of a contract providing an immediate annuity, the contract is distributed to A's surviving spouse on December 15, 1978, and under section 408 the contract is not included in the gross income of the spouse upon its distribution. The value of the annuity contract is excluded from A's gross estate, if the contract provides for a series of substantially equal periodic payments (within the meaning of paragraph (b) of this section) to be made over the life of A's surviving spouse or over a period not ending before the date 36 months after A's death.

Example (3). (1) B establishes an individual retirement plan described in section 408(a) ("IRA B") on February 6, 1981, in order to receive a $220,000 rollover contribution from a qualified plan, as described in section 402(a)(5). B dies August 14, 1981. C, an individual, is the sole beneficiary under IRA B. The amount in IRA B ($238,000) is payable to C in whole or part as C may elect. Because the amount in IRA B is payable to C as other than a qualifying annuity, within the meaning of paragraph (b) of this section, no amount is excluded from B's gross estate under section 2039(e).

(2) On October 17, 1981, C contributes $1,500 on C's own behalf to IRA B. Under § 1.408-2(b)(7)(ii), C's contribution will cause IRA B to be treated as being maintained by and on behalf of C ("IRA C") and C's making the contribution constitutes an election to which paragraph (c)(5) of this section applies. The balance in IRA C immediately before C's contribution is $240,000. Accordingly, the amount with respect to which C made the election is $240,000.

(3) C dies January 19, 1982. E, an individual, is the sole beneficiary under the plan, and the amounts payable to E ($242,000) are payable as a qualifying annuity, within the meaning of paragraph (b) of this section.

(4) The rules described in section 2039(e) and this section are applied with respect to the gross estate of C without regard to whether amounts now payable under IRA C were or were not excluded from B's gross estate. Under paragraph (c) of this section, the amount not excluded from C's gross estate is the value of the qualifying

annuity payable to E ($242,000), multiplied by the fraction $240,000/($240,000 + $1,500). Thus, the amount not excluded from C's gross estate is $240,497. [($242,000) ($240,000 ÷ ($240,000 + $1,500)) = $240,497.]The amount excluded is therefore $1,503 ($242,000 – $240,497).

Example (4). (1) F, an individual, establishes an individual retirement plan ("IRA F1") in 1977 and makes $1,250 annual contributions for 1977, 1978, 1979 and 1980 (4 × $1,250 = $5,000), each of which is deducted by F under section 219. In February 1980, F receives an $85,000 distribution on account of the death of G, F's spouse, from the qualified plan of G's former employer, and rolls it over into IRA F1, under section 402(a)(7). Because IRA F1 includes a rollover contribution under section 402(a)(7), paragraph (c)(4) of this section applies. In 1981, F's entire interest in IRA F1, $100,000, is paid to F and contributed to another individual retirement plan ("IRA F2") under section 408(d)(3)(A)(i). IRA F2 is a transferee plan to which paragraph (c)(6) of this section applies because of the rollover. F makes a $1,500 deductible contribution to IRA F2 for 1981.

(2) F dies in 1984. The balance in IRA F2 ($146,000) is payable to G, an individual, as a qualifying annuity, within the meaning of paragraph (b) of this section.

(3) Under paragraph (c) of this section, the amount *not* excluded from F's gross estate is the value of the qualifying annuity payable under IRA F2 multiplied by the fraction $96,700/$101,500. Accordingly, the amount not excluded is $139,096. [($146,000) ($96,700/$101,500) = $139,096.] The amount excluded is $6,904 ($146,000 – $139,096).

(4) The numerator of the fraction ($96,700) is determined by multiplying the amount rolled over from IRA F1 to IRA F2 ($100,000) by a fraction, the numerator of which is the amount of the rollover contribution to IRA F1 ($85,000), and the denominator of which is the total contributions to IRA F1 ($85,000 + $5,000 = $90,000). [($100,000) ($85,000/$90,000) = $96,700.]

(5) The denominator of the fraction ($101,500) is the sum of the contributions to IRA F2 (the $100,000 rollover contribution from IRA F1, and the $1,500 annual contribution to IRA F2). [Reg. § 20.2039-5.]

☐ [T.D. 7761, 1-21-81. *Amended by T.D. 8540,* 6-9-94.]

[Reg. § 20.2040-1]

§ 20.2040-1. Joint interests.—(a) *In general.*— A decedent's gross estate includes under section 2040 the value of property held jointly at the time of the decedent's death by the decedent and another person or persons with right of survivorship, as follows:

(1) To the extent that the property was acquired by the decedent and the other joint owner or owners by gift, devise, bequest, or inheritance, the decedent's fractional share of the property is included.

(2) In all other cases, the entire value of the property is included except such part of the entire value as is attributable to the amount of the consideration in money or money's worth furnished by the other joint owner or owners. See § 20.2043-1 with respect to adequacy of consideration. Such part of the entire value is that portion of the entire value of the property at the decedent's death (or at the alternate valuation date described in section 2032) which the consideration in money or money's worth furnished by the other joint owner or owners bears to the total cost of acquisition and capital additions. In determining the consideration furnished by the other joint owner or owners, there is taken into account only that portion of such consideration which is shown not to be attributable to money or other property acquired by the other joint owner or owners from the decedent for less than a full and adequate consideration in money or money's worth.

The entire value of jointly held property is included in a decedent's gross estate unless the executor submits facts sufficient to show that property was not acquired entirely with consideration furnished by the decedent, or was acquired by the decedent and the other joint owner or owners by gift, bequest, devise, or inheritance.

(b) *Meaning of "property held jointly.".*—Section 2040 specifically covers property held jointly by the decedent and any other person (or persons), property held by the decedent and spouse as tenants by the entirety, and a deposit of money, or a bond or other instrument, in the name of the decedent and any other person and payable to either or the survivor. The section applies to all classes of property, whether real or personal, and regardless of when the joint interests were created. Furthermore, it makes no difference that the survivor takes the entire interest in the property by right of survivorship and that no interest therein forms a part of the decedent's estate for purposes of administration. The section has no application to property held by the decedent and any other person (or persons) as tenants in common.

(c) *Examples.*—The application of this section may be explained in the following examples in each of which it is assumed that the other joint owner or owners survived the decedent:

(1) If the decedent furnished the entire purchase price of the jointly held property, the value of the entire property is included in his gross estate;

(2) If the decedent furnished only a part of the purchase price, only a corresponding portion of the value of the property is so included;

(3) If the decedent furnished no part of the purchase price, no part of the value of the property is so included;

(4) If the decedent, before the acquisition of the property by himself and the other joint owner, gave the latter a sum of money or other property which thereafter became the other joint owner's entire contribution to the purchase price then the value of the entire property is so included, notwithstanding the fact that the other property may have appreciated in value due to market conditions between the time of the gift and the time of the acquisition of the jointly held property;

(5) If the decedent, before the acquisition of the property by himself and the other joint owner, transferred to the latter for less than an adequate and full consideration in money or money's worth other income-producing property, the income from which belonged to and became the other joint owner's entire contribution to the purchase price, then the value of the jointly held property less that portion attributable to the income which the other joint owner did furnish is included in the decedent's gross estate;

(6) If the property originally belonged to the other joint owner and the decedent purchased his interest from the other joint owner, only that portion of the value of the property attributable to the consideration paid by the decedent is included;

(7) If the decedent and his spouse acquired the property by will or gift as tenants by the entirety, one-half of the value of the property is included in the decedent's gross estate; and

(8) If the decedent and his two brothers acquired the property by will or gift as joint tenants, one-third of the value of the property is so included. [Reg. § 20.2040-1.]

☐ [*T.D. 6296, 6-23-58.*]

[Reg. § 20.2041-1]

§ 20.2041-1. Powers of appointment; in general.—(a) *Introduction.*—A decedent's gross estate includes under section 2041 the value of property in respect of which the decedent possessed, exercised, or released certain powers of appointment. This section contains rules of general application; § 20.2041-2 contains rules specifically applicable to general powers of appointment created on or before October 21, 1942; and § 20.2041-3 sets forth specific rules applicable to powers of appointment created after October 21, 1942.

(b) *Definition of "power of appointment".*—(1) *In general.*—The term "power of appointment" includes all powers which are in substance and effect powers of appointment regardless of the nomenclature used in creating the power and regardless of local property law connotations. For example, if a trust instrument provides that the beneficiary may appropriate or consume the principal of the trust, the power to consume or appropriate is a power of appointment. Similarly, a power given to a decedent to affect the beneficial enjoyment of trust property or its income by altering, amending, or revoking the trust instrument or terminating the trust is a power of appointment. If the community property laws of a State confer upon the wife a power of testamentary disposition over property in which she does not have a vested interest she is considered as having a power of appointment. A power in a donee to remove or discharge a trustee and appoint himself may be a power of appointment. For example, if under the terms of a trust instrument, the trustee or his successor has the power to appoint the principal of the trust for the benefit of individuals including himself, and the decedent has the unrestricted power to remove or discharge the trustee at any time and appoint any other person including himself, the decedent is considered as having a power of appointment. However, the decedent is not considered to have a power of appointment if he only had the power to appoint a successor, including himself, under limited conditions which did not exist at the time of his death, without an accompanying unrestricted power of removal. Similarly, a power to amend only the administrative provisions of a trust instrument, which cannot substantially affect the beneficial enjoyment of the trust property or income, is not a power of appointment. The mere power of management, investment, custody of assets, or the power to allocate receipts and disbursements as between income and principal, exercisable in a fiduciary capacity, whereby the holder has no power to enlarge or shift any of the beneficial interests therein except as an incidental consequence of the discharge of such fiduciary duties is not a power of appointment. Further, the right in a beneficiary of a trust to assent to a periodic accounting, thereby relieving the trustee from further accountability, is not a power of appointment if the right of assent does not consist of any power or right to enlarge or shift the beneficial interest of any beneficiary therein.

(2) *Relation to other sections.*—For purposes of §§ 20.2041-1 to 20.2041-3, the term "power of appointment" does not include powers reserved by the decedent to himself within the concept of sections 2036 to 2038. (See §§ 20.2036-1 to 20.2038-1.) No provision of section 2041 or of §§ 20.2041-1 to 20.2041-3 is to be construed as in any way limiting the application of any other section of the Internal Revenue Code or of these regulations. The power of the owner of a property interest already possessed by him to dispose of his interest, and nothing more, is not a power of appointment, and the interest is includible in his gross estate to the extent it would be includible under section 2033 or some other provision of part III of subchapter A of chapter 11. For example, if a trust created by S provides for payment of the income to A for life with power in A to appoint the remainder by will and, in default of such appointment for payment of the income to A's widow, W, for her life and for

payment of the remainder to A's estate, the value of A's interest in the remainder is includible in his gross estate under section 2033 regardless of its includibility under section 2041.

(3) *Powers over a portion of property.*—If a power of appointment exists as to part of an entire group of assets or only over a limited interest in property, section 2041 applies only to such part or interest. For example, if a trust created by S provides for the payment of income to A for life, then to W for life, with power in A to appoint the remainder by will and in default of appointment for payment of the remainder to B or his estate, and if A dies before W, section 2041 applies only to the value of the remainder interest excluding W's life estate. If A dies after W, section 2041 would apply to the value of the entire property. If the power were only over one-half the remainder interest, section 2041 would apply only to one-half the value of the amounts described above.

(c) *Definition of "general power of appointment".*—(1) *In general.*—The term "general power of appointment" as defined in section 2041(b)(1) means any power of appointment exercisable in favor of the decedent, his estate, his creditors, or the creditors of his estate, except (i) joint powers, to the extent provided in §§ 20.2041-2 and 20.2041-3, and (ii) certain powers limited by an ascertainable standard, to the extent provided in subparagraph (2) of this paragraph. A power of appointment exercisable to meet the estate tax, or any other taxes, debts, or charges which are enforceable against the estate, is included within the meaning of a power of appointment exercisable in favor of the decedent's estate, his creditors, or the creditors of his estate. A power of appointment exercisable for the purpose of discharging a legal obligation of the decedent or for his pecuniary benefit is considered a power of appointment exercisable in favor of the decedent or his creditors. However, for purposes of §§ 20.2041-1 to 20.2041-3, a power of appointment not otherwise considered to be a general power of appointment is not treated as a general power of appointment merely by reason of the fact that an appointee may, in fact, be a creditor of the decedent or his estate. A power of appointment is not a general power if by its terms it is either—

(a) Exercisable only in favor of one or more designated persons or classes other than the decedent or his creditors, or the decedent's estate or the creditors of his estate, or

(b) Expressly not exercisable in favor of the decedent or his creditors, or the decedent's estate or the creditors of his estate.

A decedent may have two powers under the same instrument, one of which is a general power of appointment and the other of which is not. For example, a beneficiary may have a power to withdraw trust corpus during his life,

and a testamentary power to appoint the corpus among his descendants. The testamentary power is not a general power of appointment.

(2) *Powers limited by an ascertainable standard.*—A power to consume, invade, or appropriate income or corpus, or both, for the benefit of the decedent which is limited by an ascertainable standard relating to the health, education, support, or maintenance of the decedent is, by reason of section 2041(b)(1)(A), not a general power of appointment. A power is limited by such a standard if the extent of the holder's duty to exercise and not to exercise the power is reasonably measurable in terms of his needs for health, education, or support (or any combination of them). As used in this subparagraph, the words "support" and "maintenance" are synonymous and their meaning is not limited to the bare necessities of life. A power to use property for the comfort, welfare, or happiness of the holder of the power is not limited by the requisite standard. Examples of powers which are limited by the requisite standard are powers exercisable for the holder's "support," "support in reasonable comfort," "maintenance in health and reasonable comfort" "support in his accustomed manner of living," "education, including college and professional education," "health," and "medical, dental, hospital and nursing expenses and expenses of invalidism." In determining whether a power is limited by an ascertainable standard, it is immaterial whether the beneficiary is required to exhaust his other income before the power can be exercised.

(3) *Certain powers under wills of decedents dying between January 1 and April 2, 1948.*—Section 210 of the Technical Changes Act of 1953 provides that if a decedent died after December 31, 1947, but before April 3, 1948, certain property interests described therein may, if the decedent's surviving spouse so elects, be accorded special treatment in the determination of the marital deduction to be allowed the decedent's estate under the provisions of section 812(e) of the Internal Revenue Code of 1939. See § 81.47a(h) of Regulations 105 (26 CFR (1939) 81.47a(h)). The section further provides that property affected by the election shall, for the purpose of inclusion in the surviving spouse's gross estate, be considered property with respect to which she has a general power of appointment. Therefore, notwithstanding any other provision of law or of §§ 20.2041-1 to 20.2041-3, if the present decedent (in her capacity as surviving spouse of a prior decedent) has made an election under section 210 of the Technical Changes Act of 1953, the property which was the subject of the election shall be considered as property with respect to which the present decedent has a general power of appointment created after October 21, 1942, exercisable by deed or will, to the extent it was treated as an interest passing to the surviving spouse and not passing to any other person for

Reg. § 20.2041-1(c)(3)

the purpose of the marital deduction in the prior decedent's estate.

(d) *Definition of "exercise.".*—Whether a power of appointment is in fact exercised may depend upon local law. For example, the residuary clause of a will may be considered under local law as an exercise of a testamentary power of appointment in the absence of evidence of a contrary intention drawn from the whole of the testator's will. However, regardless of local law, a power of appointment is considered as exercised for purposes of section 2041 even though the exercise is in favor of the taker in default of appointment, and irrespective of whether the appointed interest and the interest in default of appointment are identical or whether the appointee renounces any right to take under the appointment. A power of appointment is also considered as exercised even though the disposition cannot take effect until the occurrence of an event after the exercise takes place, if the exercise is irrevocable and, as of the time of the exercise, the condition was not impossible of occurrence. For example, if property is left in trust to A for life, with a power in B to appoint the remainder by will, and B dies before A, exercising his power by appointing the remainder to C if C survives A, B is considered to have exercised his power if C is living at B's death. On the other hand, a testamentary power of appointment is not considered as exercised if it is exercised subject to the occurrence during the decedent's life of an express or implied condition which did not in fact occur. Thus, if in the preceding example, C dies before B, B's power of appointment would not be considered to have been exercised. Similarly, if a trust provides for income to A for life, remainder as A appoints by will, and A appoints a life estate in the property to B and does not otherwise exercise his power, but B dies before A, A's power is not considered to have been exercised.

(e) *Time of creation of power.*—A power of appointment created by will is, in general, considered as created on the date of the testator's death. However, section 2041(b)(3) provides that a power of appointment created by a will executed on or before October 21, 1942, is considered a power created on or before that date if the testator dies before July 1, 1949, without having republished the will, by codicil or otherwise, after October 21, 1942. A power of appointment created by an inter vivos instrument is considered as created on the date the instrument takes effect. Such a power is not considered as created at some future date merely because it is not exercisable on the date the instrument takes effect, or because it is revocable, or because the identity of its holders is not ascertainable until after the date the instrument takes effect. However, if the holder of a power exercises it by creating a second power, the second power is considered as created at the time of the exercise

of the first. The application of this paragraph may be illustrated by the following examples:

Example (1). A created a revocable trust before October 22, 1942, providing for payment of income to B for life with remainder as B shall appoint by will. Even though A dies after October 21, 1942, without having exercised his power of revocation, B's power of appointment is considered a power created before October 22, 1942.

Example (2). C created an irrevocable inter vivos trust before October 22, 1942, naming T as trustee and providing for payment of income to D for life with remainder to E. T was given the power to pay corpus to D and the power to appoint a successor trustee. If T resigns after October 21, 1942, and appoints D as successor trustee, D is considered to have a power of appointment created before October 22, 1942.

Example (3). F created an irrevocable inter vivos trust before October 22, 1942, providing for payment of income to G for life with remainder as G shall appoint by will, but in default of appointment income to H for life with remainder as H shall appoint by will. If G died after October 21, 1942, without having exercised his power of appointment, H's power of appointment is considered a power created before October 22, 1942, even though it was only a contingent interest until G's death.

Example (4). If in example (3) above G had exercised his power of appointment by creating a similar power in J, J's power of appointment would be considered a power created after October 21, 1942. [Reg. § 20.2041-1.]

□ [*T.D. 6296, 6-23-58. Amended by T.D. 6582, 12/11/61.*]

[Reg. § 20.2041-2]

§ 20.2041-2. Powers of appointment created on or before October 21, 1942.—(a) *In general.*—Property subject to a general power of appointment created on or before October 21, 1942, is includible in the gross estate of the holder of the power under section 2041 only if he exercised the power under specified circumstances. Section 2041(a)(1) requires that there be included in the gross estate of a decedent the value of property subject to such a power only if the power is exercised by the decedent either (1) by will, or (2) by a disposition which is of such nature that if it were a transfer of property owned by the decedent, the property would be includible in the decedent's gross estate under section 2035 (relating to transfers in contemplation of death), 2036 (relating to transfers with retained life estate), 2037 (relating to transfers taking effect at death), or 2038 (relating to revocable transfers). See paragraphs (b), (c), and (d) of § 20.2041-1 for the definition of various terms used in this section.

(b) *Joint powers created on or before October 21, 1942.*—Section 2041(b)(1)(B) provides that a power created on or before October 21, 1942, which at the time of the exercise is not exercisable by the decedent except in conjunction with another person, is not deemed a general power of appointment.

(c) *Exercise during life.*—The circumstances under which section 2041 applies to the exercise other than by will of a general power of appointment created on or before October 21, 1942, are set forth in paragraph (a) of this section. In this connection, the rules of sections 2035 through 2038 which are to be applied are those in effect on the date of the decedent's death which are applicable to transfers made on the date when the exercise of the power occurred. Those rules are to be applied in determining the extent to which and the conditions under which a disposition is considered a transfer of property. The application of this paragraph may be illustrated by the following examples:

Example (1). A decedent in 1951 exercised a general power of appointment created in 1940, reserving no interest in or power over the property subject to the general power. The decedent died in 1956. Since the exercise was not made within three years before the decedent's death, no part of the property is includible in his gross estate. See section 2035(b), relating to transfers in contemplation of death.

Example (2). S created a trust in 1930 to pay the income to A for life, remainder as B appoints by an instrument filed with the trustee during B's lifetime, and in default of appointment remainder to C. B exercised the power in 1955 by directing that after A's death the income be paid to himself for life with remainder to C. If B dies after A, the entire value of the trust property would be included in B's gross estate, since such a disposition if it were a transfer of property owned by B would cause the property to be included in his gross estate under section 2036(a)(1). If B dies before A, the value of the trust property less the value of A's life estate would be included in B's gross estate for the same reason.

Example (3). S created a trust in 1940 to pay the income to A for life, remainder as A appoints by an instrument filed with the trustee during A's lifetime. A exercised the power in 1955, five years before his death, reserving the right of revocation. The exercise, if not revoked before death, will cause the property subject to the power to be included in A's gross estate under section 2041(a)(1), since such a disposition if it were a transfer of property owned by A would cause the property to be included in his gross estate under section 2038. However, if the exercise were completely revoked, so that A died still possessed of the power, the property would not be included in A's gross estate for the reason that the power will not be treated as having been exercised.

Example (4). A decedent exercised a general power of appointment created in 1940 by making a disposition in trust under which possession

or enjoyment of the property subject to the exercise could be obtained only by surviving the decedent and under which the decedent retained a reversionary interest in the property of a value of more than five percent. The exercise will cause the property subject to the power to be included in the decedent's gross estate, since such a disposition if it were a transfer of property owned by the decedent would cause the property to be included in his gross estate under section 2037.

(d) *Release or lapse.*—A failure to exercise a general power of appointment created on or before October 21, 1942, or a complete release of such a power is not considered to be an exercise of a general power of appointment. The phrase "a complete release" means a release of all powers over all or a portion of the property subject to a power of appointment, as distinguished from the reduction of a power of appointment to a lesser power. Thus, if the decedent completely relinquished all powers over one-half of the property subject to a power of appointment, the power is completely released as to that one-half. If at or before the time a power of appointment is relinquished, the holder of the power exercises the power in such a manner or to such an extent that the relinquishment results in the reduction, enlargement, or shift in a beneficial interest in property, the relinquishment will be considered to be an exercise and not a release of the power. For example, assume that A created a trust in 1940 providing for payment of the income to B for life and, upon B's death, remainder to C. Assume further that B was given the unlimited power to amend the trust instrument during his lifetime. If B amended the trust in 1948 by providing that upon his death the remainder was to be paid to D, and if he further amended the trust in 1950 by deleting his power to amend the trust, such relinquishment will be considered an exercise and not a release of a general power of appointment. On the other hand, if the 1948 amendment became ineffective before or at the time of the 1950 amendment, or if B in 1948 merely amended the trust by changing the purely ministerial powers of the trustee, his relinquishment of the power in 1950 will be considered as a release of a power of appointment.

(e) *Partial release.*—If a general power of appointment created on or before October 21, 1942, is partially released so that it is not thereafter a general power of appointment, a subsequent exercise of the partially released power is not an exercise of a general power of appointment if the partial release occurs before whichever is the later of the following dates:

(1) November 1, 1951, or

(2) If the decedent was under a legal disability to release the power on October 21, 1942, the day after the expiration of 6 months following the termination of such legal disability.

However, if a general power created on or before October 21, 1942, is partially released on or after the later of these dates, a subsequent exercise of the power will cause the property subject to the power to be included in the holder's gross estate, if the exercise is such that if it were a disposition of property owned by the decedent it would cause the property to be included in his gross estate. The legal disability referred to in this paragraph is determined under local law and may include the disability of an insane person, a minor, or an unborn child. The fact that the type of general power of appointment possessed by the decedent actually was not generally releasable under the local law does not place the decedent under a legal disability within the meaning of this paragraph. In general, however, it is assumed that all general powers of appointment are releasable, unless the local law on the subject is to the contrary, and it is presumed that the method employed to release the power is effective, unless it is not in accordance with the local law relating specifically to releases or, in the absence of such local law, is not in accordance with the local law relating to similar transactions.

(f) *Partial exercise.*—If a general power of appointment created on or before October 21, 1942, is exercised only as to a portion of the property subject to the power, section 2041 is applicable only to the value of that portion. For example, if a decedent had a general power of appointment exercisable by will created on or before October 21, 1942, over a trust fund valued at $200,000 at the date of his death, and if the decedent exercised his power either to the extent of directing the distribution of one-half of the trust property to B or of directing the payment of $100,000 to B, the trust property would be includible in the decedent's gross estate only to the extent of $100,000. [Reg. § 20.2041-2.]

☐ [*T. D.* 6296, 6/23/58.]

[Reg. § 20.2041-3]

§ 20.2041-3. Powers of appointment created after October 21, 1942.—(a) *In general.*—(1) Property subject to a power of appointment created after October 21, 1942, is includible in the gross estate of the holder of the power under varying conditions depending on whether the power is (i) general in nature, (ii) possessed at death, or (iii) exercised or released. See paragraphs (b), (c), and (d) of § 20.2041-1 for the definition of various terms used in this section. See paragraph (c) of this section for the rules applicable to determine the extent to which joint powers created after October 21, 1942, are to be treated as general powers of appointment.

(2) If the power is a general power of appointment, the value of an interest in property subject to such a power is includible in a decedent's gross estate under section 2041(a)(2) if either—

(i) The decedent has the power at the time of his death (and the interest exists at the time of his death), or

(ii) The decedent exercised or released the power, or the power lapsed, under the circumstances and to the extent described in paragraph (d) of this section.

(3) If the power is not a general power of appointment, the value of property subject to the power is includible in the holder's gross estate under section 2041(a)(3) only if it is exercised to create a further power under certain circumstances (see paragraph (e) of this section).

(b) *Existence of power at death.*—For purposes of section 2041(a)(2), a power of appointment is considered to exist on the date of a decedent's death even though the exercise of the power is subject to the precedent giving of notice, or even though the exercise of the power takes effect only on the expiration of a stated period after its exercise, whether or not on or before the decedent's death notice has been given or the power has been exercised. However, a power which by its terms is exercisable only upon the occurrence during the decedent's lifetime of an event or a contingency which did not in fact take place or occur during such time is not a power in existence on the date of the decedent's death. For example, if a decedent was given a general power of appointment exercisable only after he reached a certain age, only if he survived another person, or only if he died without descendants, the power would not be in existence on the date of the decedent's death if the condition precedent to its exercise had not occurred.

(c) *Joint powers created after October 21, 1942.*—The treatment of a power of appointment created after October 21, 1942, which is exercisable only in conjunction with another person is governed by section 2041(b)(1)(C), which provides as follows:

(1) Such a power is not considered a general power of appointment if it is not exercisable by the decedent except with the consent or joinder of the creator of the power.

(2) Such power is not considered a general power of appointment if it is not exercisable by the decedent except with the consent or joinder of a person having a substantial interest in the property subject to the power which is adverse to the exercise of the power in favor of the decedent, his estate, his creditors, or the creditors of his estate. An interest adverse to the exercise of a power is considered as substantial if its value in relation to the total value of the property subject to the power is not insignificant. For this purpose, the interest is to be valued in accordance with the actuarial principles set forth in § 20.2031-7 or, if it is not susceptible to valuation under those provisions, in accordance with the general principles set forth in § 20.2031-1. A taker in default of appointment under a power has an interest which is adverse to an exercise of

the power. A coholder of the power has no adverse interest merely because of his joint possession of the power nor merely because he is a permissible appointee under a power. However, a coholder of a power is considered as having an adverse interest where he may possess the power after the decedent's death and may exercise it at that time in favor of himself, his estate, his creditors, or the creditors of his estate. Thus, for example, if X, Y, and Z held a power jointly to appoint among a group of persons which includes themselves and if on the death of X the power will pass to Y and Z jointly, then Y and Z are considered to have interests adverse to the exercise of the power in favor of X. Similarly, if on Y's death the power will pass to Z, Z is considered to have an interest adverse to the exercise of the power in favor of Y. The application of this subparagraph may be further illustrated by the following additional examples in each of which it is assumed that the value of the interest in question is substantial:

Example (1). The decedent and R were trustees of a trust under the terms of which the income was to be paid to the decedent for life and then to M for life, and the remainder was to be paid to R. The trustees had power to distribute corpus to the decedent. Since R's interest was substantially adverse to an exercise of the power in favor of the decedent the latter did not have a general power of appointment. If M and the decedent were the trustees, M's interest would likewise have been adverse.

Example (2). The decedent and L were trustees of a trust under the terms of which the income was to be paid to L for life and then to M for life, and the remainder was to be paid to the decedent. The trustees had power to distribute corpus to the decedent during L's life. Since L's interest was adverse to an exercise of the power in favor of the decedent, the decedent did not have a general power of appointment. If the decedent and M were the trustees, M's interest would likewise have been adverse.

Example (3). The decedent and L were trustees of a trust under the terms of which the income was to be paid to L for life. The trustees could designate whether corpus was to be distributed to the decedent or to A after L's death. L's interest was not adverse to an exercise of the power in favor of the decedent, and the decedent therefore had a general power of appointment.

(3) A power which is exercisable only in conjunction with another person, and which after application of the rules set forth in subparagraphs (1) and (2) of this paragraph constitutes a general power of appointment, will be treated as though the holders of the power who are permissible appointees of the property subject to the power, were joint owners of property subject to the power. The decedent, under this rule, will be treated as possessed of a general power of appointment over an aliquot share of the property to be determined with reference to the number of joint holders,

including the decedent, who (or whose estates or creditors) are permissible appointees. Thus, for example, if X, Y, and Z hold an unlimited power jointly to appoint among a group of persons, including themselves, but on the death of X the power does not pass to Y and Z jointly, then Y and Z are not considered to have interests adverse to the exercise of the power in favor of X. In this case X is considered to possess a general power of appointment as to one-third of the property subject to the power.

(d) *Releases, lapses, and disclaimers of general powers of appointment.*—(1) Property subject to a general power of appointment created after October 21, 1942, is includible in the gross estate of a decedent under section 2041(a)(2) even though he does not have the power at the date of his death, if during his life he exercised or released the power under circumstances such that, if the property subject to the power had been owned and transferred by the decedent, the property would be includible in the decedent's gross estate under section 2035, 2036, 2037, or 2038. Further, section 2041(b)(2) provides that the lapse of a power of appointment is considered to be a release of the power to the extent set forth in subparagraph (3) of this paragraph. A release of a power of appointment need not be formal or express in character. The principles set forth in § 20.2041-2 for determining the application of the pertinent provisions of sections 2035 through 2038 to a particular exercise of a power of appointment are applicable for purposes of determining whether or not an exercise or release of a power of appointment created after October 21, 1942, causes the property to be included in a decedent's gross estate under section 2041(a)(2). If a general power of appointment created after October 21, 1942, is partially released, a subsequent exercise or release of the power under circumstances described in the first sentence of this subparagraph, or its possession at death, will nevertheless cause the property subject to the power to be included in the gross estate of the holder of the power.

(2) Section 2041(a)(2) is not applicable to the complete release of a general power of appointment created after October 21, 1942, whether exercisable during life or by will, if the release was not made in contemplation of death within the meaning of section 2035, and if after the release the holder of the power retained no interest in or control over the property subject to the power which would cause the property to be included in his gross estate under sections 2036 through 2038 if the property had been transferred by the holder.

(3) The failure to exercise a power of appointment created after October 21, 1942, within a specified time, so that the power lapses, constitutes a release of the power. However, section 2041(b)(2) provides that such a lapse of a power of appointment during any calendar year during the decedent's life is treated as a release for

purposes of inclusion of property in the gross estate under section 2041(a)(2) only to the extent that the property which could have been appointed by exercise of the lapsed power exceeds the greater of (i) $5,000 or (ii) 5 percent of the aggregate value, at the time of the lapse, of the assets out of which, or the proceeds of which, the exercise of the lapsed power could have been satisfied. For example, assume that A transferred $200,000 worth of securities in trust providing for payment of income to B for life with remainder to B's issue. Assume further that B was given a non-cumulative right to withdraw $10,000 a year from the principal of the trust fund (which neither increased nor decreased in value prior to B's death). In such case, the failure of B to exercise his right of withdrawal will not result in estate tax with respect to the power to withdraw $10,000 which lapses each year before the year of B's death. At B's death there will be included in his gross estate the $10,000 which he was entitled to withdraw for the year in which his death occurs less any amount which he may have taken during that year. However, if in the above example B had possessed the right to withdraw $15,000 of the principal annually, the failure to exercise such power in any year will be considered a release of the power to the extent of the excess of the amount subject to withdrawal over 5 percent of the trust fund (in this example, $5,000, assuming that the trust fund is worth $200,000 at the time of the lapse). Since each lapse is treated as though B had exercised dominion over the trust property by making a transfer of principal reserving the income therefrom for his life, the value of the trust property (but only to the extent of the excess of the amount subject to withdrawal over 5 percent of the trust fund) is includible in B's gross estate (unless before B's death he has disposed of his right to the income under circumstances to which sections 2035 through 2038 would not be applicable). The extent to which the value of the trust property is included in the decedent's gross estate is determined as provided in subparagraph (4) of this paragraph.

(4) The purpose of section 2041(b)(2) is to provide a determination, as of the date of the lapse of the power, of the proportion of the property over which the power lapsed which is an exempt disposition for estate tax purposes and the proportion which, if the other requirements of sections 2035 through 2038 are satisfied, will be considered as a taxable disposition. Once the taxable proportion of any disposition at the date of lapse has been determined, the valuation of that proportion as of the date of the decedent's death (or, if the executor has elected the alternate valuation method under section 2032, the value as of the date therein provided), is to be ascertained in accordance with the principles which are applicable to the valuation of transfers of property by the decedent under the corresponding provisions of sections 2035 through

2038. For example, if the life beneficiary of a trust had a right exercisable only during one calendar year to draw down $50,000 from the corpus of a trust, which he did not exercise, and if at the end of the year the corpus was worth $800,000, the taxable portion over which the power lapsed is $10,000 (the excess of $50,000 over 5 percent of the corpus), or $1/80$ of the total value. On the decedent's death, if the total value of the corpus of the trust (excluding income accumulated after the lapse of the power) on the applicable valuation date was $1,200,000, $15,000 ($1/80$ of $1,200,000) would be includible in the decedent's gross estate. However, if the total value was then $600,000, only $7,500 ($1/80$ of $600,000) would be includible.

(5) If the failure to exercise a power, such as a right of withdrawal, occurs in more than a single year, the proportion of the property over which the power lapsed which is treated as a taxable disposition will be determined separately for each such year. The aggregate of the taxable proportions for all such years, valued in accordance with the above principles, will be includible in the gross estate by reason of the lapse. The includible amount, however, shall not exceed the aggregate value of the assets out of which, or the proceeds of which, the exercise of the power could have been satisfied, valued as of the date of the decedent's death (or, if the executor has elected the alternate valuation method under section 2032, the value as of the date therein provided).

(6)(i) A disclaimer or renunciation of a general power of appointment created in a transfer made after December 31, 1976, is not considered to be the release of the power if the disclaimer or renunciation is a qualified disclaimer as described in section 2518 and the corresponding regulations. For rules relating to when the transfer creating the power occurs, see § 25.2518-2(c)(3) of this chapter. If the disclaimer or renunciation is not a qualified disclaimer, it is considered a release of the power by the disclaimant.

(ii) The disclaimer or renunciation of a general power of appointment created in a taxable transfer before January 1, 1977, in the person disclaiming is not considered to be a release of the power. The disclaimer or renunciation must be unequivocal and effective under local law. A disclaimer is a complete and unqualified refusal to accept the rights to which one is entitled. There can be no disclaimer or renunciation of a power after its acceptance. In the absence of facts to the contrary, the failure to renounce or disclaim within a reasonable time after learning of its existence will be presumed to constitute an acceptance of the power. In any case where a power is purported to be disclaimed or renounced as to only a portion of the property subject to the power, the determination as to whether or not there has been a complete and unqualified refusal to accept the rights to which one is entitled will depend on all the facts and circumstances of the particular case, taking into account the recognition and effectiveness of such a disclaimer under local law. Such rights refer to the incidents of the power and not to other interests of the decedent in the property. If effective under local law, the power may be disclaimed or renounced without disclaiming or renouncing such other interests.

(iii) The first and second sentences of paragraph (d)(6)(i) of this section are applicable for transfers creating the power to be disclaimed made on or after December 31, 1997.

(e) *Successive powers.*—(1) Property subject to a power of appointment created after October 21, 1942, which is not a general power, is includible in the gross estate of the holder of the power under section 2041(a)(3) if the power is exercised, and if both of the following conditions are met:

(i) If the exercise is *(a)* by will, or *(b)* by a disposition which is of such nature that if it were a transfer of property owned by the decedent, the property would be includible in the decedent's gross estate under sections 2035 through 2037; and

(ii) If the power is exercised by creating another power of appointment which, under the terms of the instruments creating and exercising the first power and under applicable local law, can be validly exercised so as to *(a)* postpone the vesting of any estate or interest in the property for a period ascertainable without regard to the date of the creation of the first power, or *(b)* (if the applicable rule against perpetuities is stated in terms of suspension of ownership or of the power of alienation, rather than of vesting) suspend the absolute ownership or the power of alienation of the property for a period ascertainable without regard to the date of the creation of the first power.

(2) For purposes of the application of section 2041(a)(3), the value of the property subject to the second power of appointment is considered to be its value unreduced by any precedent or subsequent interest which is not subject to the second power. Thus, if a decedent has a power to appoint by will $100,000 to a group of persons consisting of his children and grandchildren and exercises the power by making an outright appointment of $75,000 and by giving one appointee a power to appoint $25,000, no more than $25,000 will be includible in the decedent's gross estate under section 2041(a)(3). If, however, the decedent appoints the income from the entire fund to a beneficiary for life with power in the beneficiary to appoint the remainder by will, the entire $100,000 will be includible in the decedent's gross estate under section 2041(a)(3) if the exercise of the second power can validly postpone the vesting of any estate or interest in the property or can suspend the absolute ownership or power of alienation of the property for a

period ascertainable without regard to the date of the creation of the first power.

(f) *Examples.*—The application of this section may be further illustrated by the following examples, in each of which it is assumed, unless otherwise stated, that S has transferred property in trust after October 21, 1942, with the remainder payable to R at L's death, and that neither L nor R has any interest in or power over the enjoyment of the trust property except as is indicated separately in each example:

Example (1). Income is directed to be paid to L during his lifetime at the end of each year, if living. L has an unrestricted power during his lifetime to cause the income to be distributed to any other person, but no power to cause it to be accumulated. At L's death, no part of the trust property is includible in L's gross estate since L had a power to dispose of only his income interest, a right otherwise possessed by him.

Example (2). Income is directed to be accumulated during L's life but L has a noncumulative power to distribute $10,000 of each year's income to himself. Unless L's power is limited by an ascertainable standard (relating to his health, etc.), as defined in paragraph (c)(2) of §20.2041-1, he has a general power of appointment over $10,000 of each year's income, the lapse of which may cause a portion of any income not distributed to be included in his gross estate under section 2041. See subparagraphs (3), (4), and (5) of paragraph (d) of this section. Thus, if the trust income during the year amounts to $20,000, L's failure to distribute any of the income to himself constitutes a lapse as to $5,000 (i.e., the amount by which $10,000 exceeds $5,000). If L's power were cumulative (i.e., if the power did not lapse at the end of each year but lapsed only by reason of L's death), the total accumulations which L chose not to distribute to himself immediately before his death would be includible in his gross estate under section 2041.

Example (3). L is entitled to all the income during his lifetime and has an unrestricted power to cause corpus to be distributed to himself. L had a general power of appointment over the corpus of the trust, and the entire corpus as of the time of his death is includible in his gross estate under section 2041.

Example (4). Income was payable to L during his lifetime. R has an unrestricted power to cause corpus to be distributed to L. R dies before L. In such case, R has only a power to dispose of his remainder interest, the value of which is includible in his gross estate under section 2033, and nothing in addition would be includible under section 2041. If in this example R's remainder were contingent on his surviving L, nothing would be includible in his gross estate under either section 2033 or 2041. While R would have a power of appointment, it would not be a general power.

Reg. §20.2041-3(f)

Example (5). Income was payable to L during his lifetime. R has an unrestricted power to cause corpus to be distributed to himself. R dies before L. While the value of R's remainder interest is includible in his gross estate under section 2033, R also has a general power of appointment over the entire trust corpus. Under such circumstances, the entire value of the trust corpus is includible in R's gross estate under section 2041. [Reg. § 20.2041-3.]

☐ [*T.D. 6296, 6-23-58. Amended by T.D. 8095, 8-6-86 and T.D. 8744, 12-30-97.*]

[Reg. § 20.2042-1]

§ 20.2042-1. Proceeds of life insurance.— (a) *In general.*—(1) Section 2042 provides for the inclusion in a decedent's gross estate of the proceeds of insurance on the decedent's life (i) receivable by or for the benefit of the estate (see paragraph (b) of this section), and (ii) receivable by other beneficiaries(see paragraph (c) of this section). The term "insurance" refers to life insurance of every description, including death benefits paid by fraternal beneficial societies operating under the lodge system.

(2) Proceeds of life insurance which are not includible in the gross estate under section 2042 may, depending upon the facts of the particular case, be includible under some other section of part III of subchapter A of chapter 11. For example, if the decedent possessed incidents of ownership in an insurance policy on his life but gratuitously transferred all rights in the policy in contemplation of death, the proceeds would be includible under section 2035. Section 2042 has no application to the inclusion in the gross estate of the value of rights in an insurance policy on the life of a person other than the decedent, or the value of rights in a combination annuity contract and life insurance policy on the decedent's life (i.e., a "retirement income" policy with death benefit or an "endowment" policy) under which there was no insurance element at the time of the decedent's death (see paragraph (d) of § 20.2039-1).

(3) Except as provided in paragraph (c)(6), the amount to be included in the gross estate under section 2042 is the full amount receivable under the policy. If the proceeds of the policy are made payable to a beneficiary in the form of an annuity for life or for a term of years, the amount to be included in the gross estate is the one sum payable at death under an option which could have been exercised either by the insured or by the beneficiary, or if no option was granted, the sum used by the insurance company in determining the amount of the annuity.

(b) *Receivable by or for the benefit of the estate.—* (1) Section 2042 requires the inclusion in the gross estate of the proceeds of insurance on the decedent's life receivable by the executor or administrator, or payable to the decedent's estate.

It makes no difference whether or not the estate is specifically named as the beneficiary under the terms of the policy. Thus, if under the terms of an insurance policy the proceeds are receivable by another beneficiary but are subject to an obligation, legally binding upon the other beneficiary, to pay taxes, debts, or other charges enforceable against the estate, then the amount of such proceeds required for the payment in full (to the extent of the beneficiary's obligation) of such taxes, debts, or other charges is includible in the gross estate. Similarly, if the decedent purchased an insurance policy in favor of another person or a corporation as collateral security for a loan or other accommodation, its proceeds are considered to be receivable for the benefit of the estate. The amount of the loan outstanding at the date of the decedent's death, with interest accrued to that date, will be deductible in determining the taxable estate. See § 20.2053-4.

(2) If the proceeds of an insurance policy made payable to the decedent's estate are community assets under the local community property law and, as a result, one-half of the proceeds belongs to the decedent's spouse, then only one-half of the proceeds is considered to be receivable by or for the benefit of the decedent's estate.

(c) *Receivable by other beneficiaries.*—(1) Section 2042 requires the inclusion in the gross estate of the proceeds of insurance on the decedent's life not receivable by or for the benefit of the estate if the decedent possessed at the date of his death any of the incidents of ownership in the policy, exercisable either alone or in conjunction with any other person. However, if the decedent did not possess any of such incidents of ownership at the time of his death nor transfer them in contemplation of death, no part of the proceeds would be includible in his gross estate under section 2042. Thus, if the decedent owned a policy of insurance on his life and, 4 years before his death, irrevocably assigned his entire interest in the policy to his wife retaining no reversionary interest therein (see subparagraph (3) of this paragraph), the proceeds of the policy would not be includible in his gross estate under section 2042.

(2) For purposes of this paragraph, the term "incidents of ownership" is not limited in its meaning to ownership of the policy in the technical legal sense. Generally speaking, the term has reference to the right of the insured or his estate to the economic benefits of the policy. Thus, it includes the power to change the beneficiary, to surrender or cancel the policy, to assign the policy, to revoke an assignment, to pledge the policy for a loan, or to obtain from the insurer a loan against the surrender value of the policy, etc. See subparagraph (6) of this paragraph for rules relating to the circumstances under which incidents of ownership held by a corporation are attributable to a decedent through his stock ownership.

(3) The term "incidents of ownership" also includes a reversionary interest in the policy or its proceeds, whether arising by the express terms of the policy or other instrument or by operation of law, but only if the value of the reversionary interest immediately before the death of the decedent exceeded 5 percent of the value of the policy. As used in this subparagraph, the term "reversionary interest" includes a possibility that the policy or its proceeds may return to the decedent or his estate and a possibility that the policy or its proceeds may become subject to a power of disposition by him. In order to determine whether or not the value of a reversionary interest immediately before the death of the decedent exceeded 5 percent of the value of the policy, the principles contained in paragraph (c)(3) and (4) of § 20.2037-1 insofar as applicable, shall be followed under this subparagraph. In that connection, there must be specifically taken into consideration any incidents of ownership held by others immediately before the decedent's death which would affect the value of the reversionary interest. For example, the decedent would not be considered to have a reversionary interest in the policy of a value in excess of 5 percent if the power to obtain the cash surrender value existed in some other person immediately before the decedent's death and was exercisable by such other person alone and in all events. The terms "reversionary interest" and "incidents of ownership" do not include the possibility that the decedent might receive a policy or its proceeds by inheritance through the estate of another person, or as a surviving spouse under a statutory right of election or a similar right.

(4) A decedent is considered to have an "incident of ownership" in an insurance policy on his life held in trust if, under the terms of the policy, the decedent (either alone or in conjunction with another person or persons) has the power (as trustee or otherwise) to change the beneficial ownership in the policy or its proceeds, or the time or manner of enjoyment thereof, even though the decedent has no beneficial interest in the trust. Moreover, assuming the decedent created the trust, such a power may result in the inclusion in the decedent's gross estate under section 2036 or 2038 of other property transferred by the decedent to the trust if, for example, the decedent has the power to surrender the insurance policy and if the income otherwise used to pay premiums on the policy would become currently payable to a beneficiary of the trust in the event that the policy were surrendered.

(5) As an additional step in determining whether or not a decedent possessed any incidents of ownership in a policy or any part of a policy, regard must be given to the effect of the State or other applicable law upon the terms of the policy. For example, assume that the decedent purchased a policy of insurance on his life with funds held by him and his surviving wife as community property, designating their son as beneficiary but retaining the right to surrender the policy. Under the local law, the proceeds upon surrender would have inured to the marital community. Assuming that the policy is not surrendered and that the son receives the proceeds on the decedent's death, the wife's transfer of her one-half interest in the policy was not considered absolute before the decedent's death. Upon the wife's prior death, one-half of the value of the policy would have been included in her gross estate. Under these circumstances, the power of surrender possessed by the decedent as agent for his wife with respect to one-half of the policy is not, for purposes of this section, an "incident of ownership", and the decedent is, therefore, deemed to possess an incident of ownership in only one-half of the policy.

(6) In the case of economic benefits of a life insurance policy on the decedent's life that are reserved to a corporation of which the decedent is the sole or controlling stockholder, the corporation's incidents of ownership will not be attributed to the decedent through his stock ownership to the extent the proceeds of the policy are payable to the corporation. Any proceeds payable to a third party for a valid business purpose, such as in satisfaction of a business debt of the corporation, so that the net worth of the corporation is increased by the amount of such proceeds, shall be deemed to be payable to the corporation for purposes of the preceding sentence. See § 20.2031-2(f) for a rule providing that the proceeds of certain life insurance policies shall be considered in determining the value of the decedent's stock. Except as hereinafter provided with respect to a group-term life insurance policy, if any part of the proceeds of the policy are not payable to or for the benefit of the corporation, and thus are not taken into account in valuing the decedent's stock holdings in the corporation for purposes of section 2031, any incidents of ownership held by the corporation as to that part of the proceeds will be attributed to the decedent through his stock ownership where the decedent is the sole or controlling stockholder. Thus, for example, if the decedent is the controlling stockholder in a corporation, and the corporation owns a life insurance policy on his life, the proceeds of which are payable to the decedent's spouse, the incidents of ownership held by the corporation will be attributed to the decedent through his stock ownership and the proceeds will be included in his gross estate under section 2042. If in this example the policy proceeds had been payable 40 percent to decedent's spouse and 60 percent to the corporation, only 40 percent of the proceeds would be included in decedent's gross estate under section 2042. For purposes of this subparagraph, the decedent will not be deemed to be the controlling stockholder of a corporation unless, at the time of his death, he owned stock possessing

more than 50 percent of the total combined voting power of the corporation. Solely for purposes of the preceding sentence, a decedent shall be considered to be the owner of only the stock with respect to which legal title was held, at the time of his death, by (i) the decedent (or his agent or nominee); [(ii)] the decedent and another person jointly (but only the proportionate number of shares which corresponds to the portion of the total consideration which is considered to be furnished by the decedent for purposes of section 2040 and the regulations thereunder); and (iii) by a trustee of a voting trust (to the extent of the decedent's beneficial interest therein) or any other trust with respect to which the decedent was treated as an owner under subpart E, part I, subchapter J, chapter 1 of the Code immediately prior to his death. In the case of group-term life insurance, as defined the regulations under section 79, the power to surrender or cancel a policy held by a corporation shall not be attributed to any decedent through his stock ownership. [Reg. § 20.2042-1.]

☐ [*T.D. 6296, 6-23-58. Amended by T.D. 7312, 4-26-74 and T.D. 7623, 5-14-79.*]

[Reg. § 20.2043-1]

§ 20.2043-1. Transfers for insufficient consideration.—(a) *In general.*—The transfers, trusts, interests, rights or powers enumerated and described in sections 2035 through 2038 and section 2041 are not subject to the Federal estate tax if made, created, exercised, or relinquished in a transaction which constituted a bona fide sale for an adequate and full consideration in money or money's worth. To constitute a bona fide sale for an adequate and full consideration in money or money's worth, the transfer must have been made in good faith, and the price must have been an adequate and full equivalent reducible to a money value. If the price was less than such a consideration, only the excess of the fair market value of the property (as of the applicable valuation date) over the price received by the decedent is included in ascertaining the value of his gross estate.

(b) *Marital rights and support obligations.*—For purposes of chapter 11, a relinquishment or promised relinquishment of dower, curtesy, or of a statutory estate created in lieu of dower or curtesy, or of other marital rights in the decedent's property or estate, is not to support obligations. For purposes of chapter 11, a relinquishment or promised relinquishment of dower, curtesy, or of a statutory estate created in lieu of dower or curtesy, or of other marital rights in the decedent's property or estate, is not to any extent a consideration in "money or money's worth." [Reg. § 20.2043-1.]

☐ [*T.D. 6296, 6-23-58.*]

[Reg. § 20.2044-1]

§ 20.2044-1. Certain property for which marital deduction was previously allowed.—(a) *In general.*—Section 2044 generally provides for the inclusion in the gross estate of property in which the decedent had a qualifying income interest for life and for which a deduction was allowed under section 2056(b)(7) or 2523(f). The value of the property included in the gross estate under section 2044 is not reduced by the amount of any section 2503(b) exclusion that applied to the transfer creating the interest. See section 2207A, regarding the right of recovery against the persons receiving the property that is applicable in certain cases.

(b) *Passed from.*—For purposes of section 1014 and chapters 11 and 13 of subtitle B of the Internal Revenue Code, property included in a decedent's gross estate under section 2044 is considered to have been acquired from or to have passed from the decedent to the person receiving the property upon the decedent's death. Thus, for example, the property is treated as passing from the decedent for purposes of determining the availability of the charitable deduction under section 2055, the marital deduction under section 2056, and special use valuation under section 2032A. In addition, the tax imposed on property includible under section 2044 is eligible for the installment payment of estate tax under section 6166.

(c) *Presumption.*—Unless established to the contrary, section 2044 applies to the entire value of the trust at the surviving spouse's death. If a marital deduction is taken on either the estate or gift tax return with respect to the transfer which created the qualifying income interest, it is presumed that the deduction was allowed for purposes of section 2044. To avoid the inclusion of property in the decedent-spouse's gross estate under this section, the executor of the spouse's estate must establish that a deduction was not taken for the transfer which created the qualifying income interest. For example, to establish that a deduction was not taken, the executor may produce a copy of the estate or gift tax return filed with respect to the transfer by the first spouse or the first spouse's estate establishing that no deduction was taken under section 2523(f) or section 2056(b)(7). In addition, the executor may establish that no return was filed on the original transfer by the decedent because the value of the first spouse's gross estate was below the threshold requirement for filing under section 6018. Similarly, the executor could establish that the transfer creating the decedent's qualifying income interest for life was made before the effective date of section 2056(b)(7) or section 2523(f).

(d) *Amount included.*—(1) *In general.*—The amount included under this section is the value of the entire interest in which the decedent had a qualifying income interest for life, determined as of the date of the decedent's death (or the alternate valuation date, if applicable). If, in connection with the transfer of property that created the decedent's qualifying income interest for life, a deduction was allowed under section 2056(b)(7) or section 2523(f) for less than the entire interest in the property (i.e., for a fractional or percentage share of the entire interest in the transferred property), the amount includible in the decedent's gross estate under this section is equal to the fair market value of the entire interest in the property on the date of the decedent's death (or the alternate valuation date, if applicable) multiplied by the fractional or percentage share of the interest for which the deduction was taken.

(2) *Inclusion of income.*—If any income from the property for the period between the date of the transfer creating the decedent-spouse's interest and the date of the decedent-spouse's death has not been distributed before the decedent-spouse's death, the undistributed income is included in the decedent-spouse's gross estate under this section to the extent that the income is not so included under any other section of the Internal Revenue Code.

(3) *Reduction of includible share in certain cases.*—If only a fractional or percentage share is includible under this section, the includible share is appropriately reduced if—

(i) The decedent-spouse's interest was in a trust and distributions of principal were made to the spouse during the spouse's lifetime;

(ii) The trust provides that the distributions are to be made from the qualified terminable interest share of the trust; and

(iii) The executor of the decedent-spouse's estate can establish the reduction in that share based on the fair market value of the trust assets at the time of each distribution.

(4) *Interest in previously severed trust.*—If the decedent-spouse's interest was in a trust consisting of only qualified terminable interest property and the trust was severed (in compliance with § 20.2056(b)-7(b) or § 25.2523(f)-1(b) of this chapter) from a trust that, after the severance, held only property that was not qualified terminable interest property, only the value of the property in the severed portion of the trust is includible in the decedent-spouse's gross estate.

(e) *Examples.*—The following examples illustrate the principles in paragraphs (a) through (d) of this section, where the decedent, D, was survived by spouse, S.

Example 1. Inclusion of trust subject to election. Under D's will, assets valued at $800,000 in D's gross estate (net of debts, expenses and other charges, including death taxes, payable from the property) passed in trust with income payable to S for life. Upon S's death, the trust principal is to be distributed to D's children. D's executor

elected under section 2056(b)(7) to treat the entire trust property as qualified terminable interest property and claimed a marital deduction of $800,000. S made no disposition of the income interest during S's lifetime under section 2519. On the date of S's death, the fair market value of the trust property was $740,000. S's executor did not elect the alternate valuation date. The amount included in S's gross estate pursuant to section 2044 is $740,000.

Example 2. Inclusion of trust subject to partial election. The facts are the same as in *Example 1*, except that D's executor elected under section 2056(b)(7) with respect to only 50 percent of the value of the trust ($400,000). Consequently, only the equivalent portion of the trust is included in S's gross estate; i.e., $370,000 (50 percent of $740,000).

Example 3. Spouse receives qualifying income interest in a fraction of trust income. Under D's will, assets valued at $800,000 in D's gross estate (net of debts, expenses and other charges, including death taxes, payable from the property) passed in trust with 20 percent of the trust income payable to S for S's life. The will provides that the trust principal is to be distributed to D's children upon S's death. D's executor elected to deduct, pursuant to section 2056(b)(7), 50 percent of the amount for which the election could be made; i.e., $80,000 (50 percent of 20 percent of $800,000). Consequently, on the death of S, only the equivalent portion of the trust is included in S's gross estate; i.e., $74,000 (50 percent of 20 percent of $740,000).

Example 4. Distribution of corpus during spouse's lifetime. The facts are the same as in *Example 3*, except that S was entitled to receive all the trust income but the executor of D's estate elected under section 2056(b)(7) with respect to only 50 percent of the value of the trust ($400,000). Pursuant to authority in the will, the trustee made a discretionary distribution of $100,000 of principal to S in 1995 and charged the entire distribution to the qualified terminable interest share. Immediately prior to the distribution, the fair market value of the trust property was $1,100,000 and the qualified terminable interest portion of the trust was 50 percent. Immediately after the distribution, the qualified terminable interest portion of the trust was 45 percent ($450,000 divided by $1,000,000). Provided S's executor can establish the relevant facts, the amount included in S's gross estate is $333,000 (45 percent of $740,000).

Example 5. Spouse assigns a portion of income interest during life. Under D's will, assets valued at $800,000 in D's gross estate (net of debts, expenses and other charges, including death taxes, payable from the property) passed in trust with all the income payable to S, for S's life. The will provides that the trust principal is to be distributed to D's children upon S's death. D's executor elected under section 2056(b)(7) to treat the entire trust property as qualified terminable interest property and claimed a marital deduction of $800,000. During the term of the trust, S transfers to C the right to 40 percent of the income from the trust for S's life. Because S is treated as transferring the entire remainder interest in the trust corpus under section 2519 (as well as 40 percent of the income interest under section 2511), no part of the trust is includible in S's gross estate under section 2044. However, if S retains until death an income interest in 60 percent of the trust corpus (which corpus is treated pursuant to section 2519 as having been transferred by S for both gift and estate tax purposes), 60 percent of the property will be includible in S's gross estate under section 2036(a) and a corresponding adjustment is made in S's adjusted taxable gifts.

Example 6. Inter vivos trust subject to election under section 2523(f). D transferred $800,000 to a trust providing that trust income is to be paid annually to S, for S's life. The trust provides that upon S's death, $100,000 of principal is to be paid to X charity and the remaining principal distributed to D's children. D elected to treat all of the property transferred to the trust as qualified terminable interest property under section 2523(f). At the time of S's death, the fair market value of the trust is $1,000,000. S's executor does not elect the alternate valuation date. The amount included in S's gross estate is $1,000,000; i.e., the fair market value at S's death of the entire trust property. The $100,000 that passes to X charity on S's death is treated as a transfer by S to X charity for purposes of section 2055. Therefore, S's estate is allowed a charitable deduction for the $100,000 transferred from the trust to the charity to the same extent that a deduction would be allowed by section 2055 for a bequest by S to X charity.

Example 7. Spousal interest in the form of an annuity. D died prior to October 24, 1992, the effective date of the Energy Policy Act of 1992 (Pub. L. 102-486). See § 20.2056(b)-7(e). Under D's will, assets valued at $500,000 in D's gross estate (net of debts, expenses and other charges, including death taxes, payable from the property) passed in trust pursuant to which an annuity of $20,000 a year was payable to S for S's life. Trust income not paid to S as an annuity is to be accumulated in the trust and may not be distributed during S's lifetime. D's estate deducted $200,000 under section 2056(b)(7) and § 20.2056(b)-7(e)(2). S did not assign any portion of S's interest during S's life. At the time of S's death, the value of the trust property is $800,000. S's executor does not elect the alternate valuation date. The amount included in S's gross estate pursuant to section 2044 is $320,000 ([$200,000/$500,000] × $800,000).

Example 8. Inclusion of trust property when surviving spouse dies before first decedent's estate tax return is filed. D dies on July 1, 1997. Under the terms of D's will, a trust is established for the benefit of D's spouse, S. The will provides that S

is entitled to receive the income from that portion of the trust that the executor elects to treat as qualified terminable interest property. The remaining portion of the trust passes as of D's date of death to a trust for the benefit of C, D's child. The trust terms otherwise provide S with a qualifying income interest for life under section 2056(b)(7)(B)(ii). S dies on February 10, 1998. On April 1, 1998, D's executor files D's estate tax return on which an election is made to treat a portion of the trust as qualified terminable interest property under section 2056(b)(7). S's estate tax return is filed on November 10, 1998. The value on the date of S's death of the portion of the trust for which D's executor made a QTIP election is includible in S's gross estate under section 2044.

[Reg. § 20.2044-1.]

☐ [*T.D. 8522, 2-28-94. Amended by T.D. 8779,* 8-18-98.]

[Reg. § 20.2044-2]

§ 20.2044-2. Effective dates.—Except as specifically provided in *Example 7* of § 20.2044-1(e), the provisions of § 20.2044-1 are effective with respect to estates of a decedent-spouse dying after March 1, 1994. With respect to estates of decedent-spouses dying on or before such date, taxpayers may rely on any reasonable interpretation of the statutory provisions. For these purposes, the provisions of § 20.2044-1 (as well as project LR-211-76, 1984-1 C.B., page 598, see § 601.601(d)(2)(ii)(b) of this chapter) are considered a reasonable interpretation of the statutory provisions. [Reg. § 20.2044-2.]

☐ [*T.D. 8522, 2-28-94.*]

[Reg. § 20.2045-1]

§ 20.2045-1. Applicability to pre-existing transfers or interests.—Sections 2034 through 2042 are applicable regardless of when the interests and events referred to in those sections were created or took place, except as otherwise provided in those sections and the regulations thereunder. [Reg. § 20.2045-1.]

☐ [*T.D. 6296, 6-23-58. Redesignated by T.D.* 8522, 2-28-94.]

[Reg. § 20.2046-1]

§ 20.2046-1. Disclaimed property.—(a) This section shall apply to the disclaimer or renunciation of an interest in the person disclaiming by a transfer made after December 31, 1976. For rules relating to when the transfer creating the interest occurs, see § 25.2518-2(c)(3) and (c)(4) of this chapter. If a qualified disclaimer is made with respect to such a transfer, the Federal estate tax provisions are to apply with respect to the property interest disclaimed as if the interest had never been transferred to the person making the disclaimer. See section 2518 and the corresponding regulations for rules relating to a qualified disclaimer.

(b) The first and second sentences of this section are applicable for transfers creating the in-

terest to be disclaimed made on or after December 31, 1997. [Reg. § 20.2046-1.]

☐ *[T.D. 8095, 8-6-86. Amended by T.D. 8744, 12-30-97.]*

Taxable Estate

[Reg. § 20.2051-1]

§ 20.2051-1. Definition of taxable estate.— (a) *General rule.*—The taxable estate of a decedent who was a citizen or resident (see § 20.0-1(b)(1)) of the United States at death is determined by subtracting the total amount of the deductions authorized by sections 2053 through 2058 from the total amount which must be included in the gross estate under sections 2031 through 2044. These deductions are in general as follows—

(1) Funeral and administration expenses and claims against the estate (including certain taxes and charitable pledges) (section 2053).

(2) Losses from casualty or theft during the administration of the estate (section 2054).

(3) Charitable transfers (section 2055).

(4) The marital deduction (section 2056).

(5) Qualified domestic trusts (section 2056A).

(6) Family-owned business interests (section 2057) to the extent applicable to estates of decedents.

(7) State death taxes (section 2058) to the extent applicable to estates of decedents.

(b) *Special rules.*—See section 2106 and the corresponding regulations for special rules regarding the computation of the taxable estate of a decedent who was not a citizen or resident of the United States. See also § 1.642(g)-1 of this chapter concerning the disallowance for income tax purposes of certain deductions allowed for estate tax purposes.

(c) *Effective/applicability date.*—This section applies to the estates of decedents dying on or after October 20, 2009. [Reg. § 20.2051-1.]

☐ *[T.D. 6296, 6-23-58. Amended by T.D. 9468, 10-16-2009.]*

[Reg. § 20.2053-1]

§ 20.2053-1. Deductions for expenses, indebtedness, and taxes; in general.—(a) *General rule.*—In determining the taxable estate of a decedent who was a citizen or resident of the United States at death, there are allowed as deductions under section 2053(a) and (b) amounts falling within the following two categories (subject to the limitations contained in this section and in § § 20.2053-2 through 20.2053-10)—

(1) *First category.*—Amounts which are payable out of property subject to claims and which are allowable by the law of the jurisdiction, whether within or without the United States,

under which the estate is being administered for—

(i) Funeral expenses;

(ii) Administration expenses;

(iii) Claims against the estate (including taxes to the extent set forth in § 20.2053-6 and charitable pledges to the extent set forth in § 20.2053-5); and

(iv) Unpaid mortgages on, or any indebtedness in respect of, property, the value of the decedent's interest in which is included in the value of the gross estate undiminished by the mortgage or indebtedness.

As used in this subparagraph, the phrase "allowable by the law of the jurisdiction" means allowable by the law governing the administration of decedents' estates. The phrase has no reference to amounts allowable as deductions under a law which imposes a State death tax. See further § § 20.2053-2 through 20.2053-7.

(2) *Second category.*—Amounts representing expenses incurred in administering property which is included in the gross estate but which is not subject to claims and which—

(i) Would be allowed as deductions in the first category if the property being administered were subject to claims; and

(ii) Were paid before the expiration of the period of limitation for assessment provided in section 6501.

See further § 20.2053-8.

(b) *Provisions applicable to both categories.*— (1) *In general.*—If the item is not one of those described in paragraph (a) of this section, it is not deductible merely because payment is allowed by the local law. If the amount which may be expended for the particular purpose is limited by the local law, no deduction in excess of that limitation is permissible.

(2) *Bona fide requirement.*—(i) *In general.*— Amounts allowed as deductions under section 2053(a) and (b) must be expenses and claims that are bona fide in nature. No deduction is permissible to the extent it is founded on a transfer that is essentially donative in character (a mere cloak for a gift or bequest) except to the extent the deduction is for a claim that would be allowable as a deduction under section 2055 as a charitable bequest.

(ii) *Claims and expenses involving family members.*—Factors indicative (but not necessarily determinative) of the bona fide nature of a claim or expense involving a family member of a decedent, a related entity, or a beneficiary of a decedent's estate or revocable trust, in relevant instances, may include, but are not limited to, the following—

(A) The transaction underlying the claim or expense occurs in the ordinary course of business, is negotiated at arm's length, and is free from donative intent.

(B) The nature of the claim or expense is not related to an expectation or claim of inheritance.

(C) The claim or expense originates pursuant to an agreement between the decedent and the family member, related entity, or beneficiary, and the agreement is substantiated with contemporaneous evidence.

(D) Performance by the claimant is pursuant to the terms of an agreement between the decedent and the family member, related entity, or beneficiary and the performance and the agreement can be substantiated.

(E) All amounts paid in satisfaction or settlement of a claim or expense are reported by each party for Federal income and employment tax purposes, to the extent appropriate, in a manner that is consistent with the reported nature of the claim or expense.

(iii) *Definitions.*—The following definitions apply for purposes of this paragraph (b)(2):

(A) *Family members* include the spouse of the decedent; the grandparents, parents, siblings, and lineal descendants of the decedent or of the decedent's spouse; and the spouse and lineal descendants of any such grandparent, parent, and sibling. Family members include adopted individuals.

(B) A *related entity* is an entity in which the decedent, either directly or indirectly, had a beneficial ownership interest at the time of the decedent's death or at any time during the three-year period ending on the decedent's date of death. Such an entity, however, shall not include a publicly-traded entity nor shall it include a closely-held entity in which the combined beneficial interest, either direct or indirect, of the decedent and the decedent's family members, collectively, is less than 30 percent of the beneficial ownership interests (whether voting or non-voting and whether an interest in stock, capital and/or profits), as determined at the time a claim described in this section is being asserted. Notwithstanding the foregoing, an entity in which the decedent, directly or indirectly, had any managing interest (for example, as a general partner of a partnership or as a managing member of a limited liability company) at the time of the decedent's death shall be considered a related entity.

(C) *Beneficiaries* of a decedent's estate include beneficiaries of a trust of the decedent.

(3) *Court decrees and settlements.*—(i) *Court decree.*—If a court of competent jurisdiction over the administration of an estate reviews and approves expenditures for funeral expenses, administration expenses, claims against the estate, or unpaid mortgages (referred to in this section as a "claim or expense"), a final judicial decision in that matter may be relied upon to establish the amount of a claim or expense that is otherwise deductible under section 2053 and these regulations provided that the court actually passes upon the facts on which deductibility depends. If the court does not pass upon those facts, its decree may not be relied upon to establish the amount of the claim or expense that is otherwise deductible under section 2053. It must appear that the court actually passed upon the merits of the claim. This will be presumed in all cases of an active and genuine contest. If the result reached appears to be unreasonable, this is some evidence that there was not such a contest, but it may be rebutted by proof to the contrary. Any amount meeting the requirements of this paragraph (b)(3)(i) is deductible to the extent it actually has been paid or will be paid, subject to any applicable limitations in this section.

(ii) *Claims and expenses where court approval not required under local law.*—A deduction for the amount of a claim or expense that is otherwise deductible under section 2053 and these regulations will not be denied under section 2053 solely because a local court decree has not been entered with respect to such amount, provided that no court decree is required under applicable law to determine the amount or allowability of the claim or expense.

(iii) *Consent decree.*—A local court decree rendered by consent may be relied on to establish the amount of a claim or expense that is otherwise deductible under section 2053 and these regulations provided that the consent resolves a bona fide issue in a genuine contest. Consent given by all parties having interests adverse to that of the claimant will be presumed to resolve a bona fide issue in a genuine contest. Any amount meeting the requirements of this paragraph (b)(3)(iii) is deductible to the extent it actually has been paid or will be paid, subject to any applicable limitations in this section.

(iv) *Settlements.*—A settlement may be relied on to establish the amount of a claim or expense (whether contingent or noncontingent) that is otherwise deductible under section 2053 and these regulations, provided that the settlement resolves a bona fide issue in a genuine contest and is the product of arm's-length negotiations by parties having adverse interests with respect to the claim or expense. A deduction will not be denied for a settlement amount paid by an estate if the estate can establish that the cost of defending or contesting the claim or expense, or the delay associated with litigating the claim or expense, would impose a higher burden on the estate than the payment of the amount paid to settle the claim or expense. Nevertheless, no deduction will be allowed for amounts paid in settlement of an unenforceable claim. For this purpose, to the extent a claim exceeds an applicable limit under local law, the claim is deemed to be unenforceable. However, as long as the enforceability of the claim is at issue in a bona fide dispute, the claim will not be deemed to be unenforceable for this purpose. Any amount meeting the requirements of this paragraph (b)(3)(iv) is deductible to the extent it actually has been paid or will be paid, subject to any applicable limitations in this section.

(v) *Additional rules.*—Notwithstanding paragraph (b)(3)(i) through (iv) of this section, additional rules may apply to the deductibility of certain claims and expenses. See §20.2053-2 for additional rules regarding the deductibility of funeral expenses. See §20.2053-3 for additional rules regarding the deductibility of administration expenses. See §20.2053-4 for additional rules regarding the deductibility of claims against the estate. See §20.2053-7 for additional rules regarding the deductibility of unpaid mortgages.

(4) *Examples.*—Unless otherwise provided, assume that the amount of any claim or expense is paid out of property subject to claims and is paid within the time prescribed for filing the "United States Estate (and Generation-Skipping Transfer) Tax Return," Form 706. The following examples illustrate the application of this paragraph (b):

Example 1. Consent decree at variance with the law of the State. Decedent's (D's) estate is probated in State. D's probate estate is valued at $100x. State law provides that the executor's commission shall not exceed 3 percent of the probate estate. A consent decree is entered allowing the executor's commission in the amount of $5x. The estate pays the executor's commission in the amount of $5x. For purposes of section 2053, the executor may deduct only $3x of the $5x expense paid for the executor's commission because the amount approved by the consent decree in excess of $3x is in excess of the applicable limit for executor's commissions under local law. Therefore, for purposes of section 2053, the consent decree may not be relied upon to establish the amount of the expense for the executor's commission.

Example 2. Decedent's (D's) estate is probated in State. State law grants authority to an executor to administer an estate without court approval, so long as notice of and a right to object to a proposed action is provided to interested persons. The executor of D's estate (E) proposes to sell property of the estate in order to pay the debts of D. E gives requisite notice to all interested parties and no interested person objects. E sells the real estate and pays a real estate commission of $20x to a professional real estate agent. The amount of the real estate commission paid does not exceed the applicable limit under State law. Provided that the sale of the property was necessary to pay D's debts, expenses of administration, or taxes, to preserve the estate, or to effect distribution, the executor may deduct the $20x expense for the real estate commission under section 2053 even though no court decree was entered approving the expense.

Example 3. Claim by family member. For a period of three years prior to D's death, D's niece (N) provides accounting and bookkeeping services on D's behalf. N is a CPA and provides similar accounting and bookkeeping services to unrelated clients. At the end of each month, N presents an itemized bill to D for services rendered. The fees charged by N conform to the prevailing market rate for the services rendered and are comparable to the fees N charges other clients for similar services. The amount due is timely paid each month by D and is properly reported for Federal income and employment tax purposes by N. In the six months prior to D's death, D's poor health prevents D from making payments to N for the amount due. After D's death, N asserts a claim against the estate for $25x, an amount representing the amount due for the sixmonth period prior to D's death. D's estate pays $25x to N in satisfaction of the claim before the return is timely filed and N properly reports the $25x received by E for income tax purposes. Barring any other relevant facts or circumstances, E may rely on the following factors to establish that the claim is bona fide: (1) N's claim for services rendered arose in the ordinary course of business, as N is a CPA performing similar services for other clients; (2) the fees charged were deemed to be negotiated at arm's length, as the fees were consistent with the fees N charged for similar services to unrelated clients; (3) the billing records and the records of D's timely payments to N constitute contemporaneous evidence of an agreement between D and N for N's bookkeeping services; and (4) the amount of the payments to N is properly reported by N for Federal income and employment tax purposes. E may deduct the amount paid to N in satisfaction of the claim.

(c) *Provision applicable to first category only.*— Deductions of the first category (described in paragraph (a)(1) of this section) are limited under section 2053(a) to amounts which would be properly allowable out of property subject to claims by the law of the jurisdiction under which the decedent's estate is being administered. Further, the total allowable amount of deductions of the first category is limited by section 2053(c)(2) to the sum of—

(1) The value of property included in the decedent's gross estate and subject to claims, plus

(2) Amounts paid, out of property not subject to claims against the decedent's estate, within 9 months (15 months in the case of the

estate of a decedent dying before January 1, 1971) after the decedent's death (the period within which the estate tax return must be filed under section 6075), or within any extension of time for filing the return granted under section 6081. The term "property subject to claims" is defined in section 2053(c)(2) as meaning the property includible in the gross estate which, or the avails of which, under the applicable law, would bear the burden of the payment of these deductions in the final adjustment and settlement of the decedent's estate. However, for the purposes of this definition, the value of property subject to claims is first reduced by the amount of any deduction allowed under section 2054 for any losses from casualty or theft incurred during the settlement of the estate attributable to such property. The application of this paragraph may be illustrated by the following examples:

Example (1). The only item in the gross estate is real property valued at $250,000 which the decedent and his surviving spouse held as tenants by the entirety. Under the local law, this real property is not subject to claims. Funeral expenses of $1,200 and debts of the decedent in the amount of $1,500 are allowable under local law. Before the prescribed date for filing the estate tax return, the surviving spouse paid the funeral expenses and $1,000 of the debts. The remaining $500 of the debts was paid by her after the prescribed date for filing the return. The total amount allowable as deductions under section 2053 is limited to $2,200, the amount paid prior to the prescribed date for filing the return.

Example (2). The only two items in the gross estate were a bank deposit of $20,000 and insurance in the amount of $150,000. The insurance was payable to the decedent's surviving spouse and under local law was not subject to claims. Funeral expenses of $1,000 and debts in the amount of $29,000 were allowable under local law. A son was executor of the estate and before the prescribed date for filing the estate tax return he paid the funeral expenses and $9,000 of the debts, using therefor $5,000 of the bank deposit and $5,000 supplied by the surviving spouse. After the prescribed date for filing the return, the executor paid the remaining $20,000 of the debts, using for that purpose the $15,000 left in the bank account plus an additional $5,000 supplied by the surviving spouse. The total amount allowable as deductions under section 2053 is limited to $25,000 ($20,000 of property subject to claims plus the $5,000 additional amount which, before the prescribed date for filing the return, was paid out of property not subject to claims).

(d) *Amount deductible.*—(1) *General rule.*—To take into account properly events occurring after the date of a decedent's death in determining the amount deductible under section 2053 and these regulations, the deduction for any claim or expense described in paragraph (a) of this section is limited to the total amount actually paid in settlement or satisfaction of that item (subject to any applicable limitations in this section). However, see paragraph (d)(4) of this section for the rules for deducting certain ascertainable amounts; see § 20.2053-4(b) and (c) for the rules regarding the deductibility of certain claims against the estate; and see § 20.2053-7 for the rules regarding the deductibility of unpaid mortgages and other indebtedness.

(2) *Application of post-death events.*—In determining whether and to what extent a deduction under section 2053 is allowable, events occurring after the date of a decedent's death will be taken into consideration—

(i) Until the expiration of the applicable period of limitations on assessment prescribed in section 6501 (including without limitation at all times during which the running of the period of limitations is suspended); and

(ii) During subsequent periods, in determining the amount (if any) of an overpayment of estate tax due in connection with a claim for refund filed within the time prescribed in section 6511(a).

(3) *Reimbursements.*—A deduction is not allowed to the extent that a claim or expense described in paragraph (a) of this section is or could be compensated for by insurance or otherwise could be reimbursed. If the executor is able to establish that only a partial reimbursement could be collected, then only that portion of the potential reimbursement that reasonably could have been expected to be collected will reduce the estate's deductible portion of the total claim or expense. An executor may certify that the executor neither knows nor reasonably should have known of any available reimbursement for a claim or expense described in section 2053(a) or (b) on the estate's United States Estate (and Generation-Skipping Transfer) Tax Return (Form 706), in accordance with the instructions for that form. A potential reimbursement will not reduce the deductible amount of a claim or expense to the extent that the executor, on Form 706 and in accordance with the instructions for that form, provides a reasonable explanation for his or her reasonable determination that the burden of necessary collection efforts in pursuit of a right of reimbursement would outweigh the anticipated benefit from those efforts. Nevertheless, even if a reasonable explanation is provided, subsequent events (including without limitation an actual reimbursement) occurring within the period described in § 20.2053-1(d)(2) will be considered in determining the amount (if any) of a reduction under this paragraph (d)(3) in the deductible amount of a claim or expense.

(4) *Exception for certain ascertainable amounts.*—(i) *General rule.*—A deduction will be allowed for a claim or expense that satisfies all applicable requirements even though it is not yet paid, provided that the amount to be paid is ascertainable with reasonable certainty and will

be paid. For example, executors' commissions and attorneys' fees that are not yet paid, and that meet the requirements for deductibility under § 20.2053-3(b) and (c), respectively, are deemed to be ascertainable with reasonable certainty and may be deducted if such expenses will be paid. However, no deduction may be taken upon the basis of a vague or uncertain estimate. To the extent a claim or expense is contested or contingent, such a claim or expense cannot be ascertained with reasonable certainty.

(ii) *Effect of post-death events.*—A deduction under this paragraph (d)(4) will be allowed to the extent the Commissioner is reasonably satisfied that the amount to be paid is ascertainable with reasonable certainty and will be paid. In making this determination, the Commissioner will take into account events occurring after the date of a decedent's death. To the extent the amount for which a deduction was claimed does not satisfy the requirements of this paragraph (d)(4), and is not otherwise deductible, the deduction will be disallowed by the Commissioner. If a deduction is claimed on Form 706 for an amount that is not yet paid and the deduction is disallowed in whole or in part (or if no deduction is claimed on Form 706), then if the claim or expense subsequently satisfies the requirements of this paragraph (d)(4) or is paid, relief may be sought by filing a claim for refund. To preserve the estate's right to claim a refund for amounts becoming deductible after the expiration of the period of limitation for the filing of a claim for refund, a protective claim for refund may be filed in accordance with paragraph (d)(5) of this section.

(5) *Protective claim for refund.*—(i) *In general.*—A protective claim for refund under this section may be filed at any time before the expiration of the period of limitation prescribed in section 6511(a) for the filing of a claim for refund to preserve the estate's right to claim a refund by reason of claims or expenses that are not paid or do not otherwise meet the requirements of deductibility under section 2053 and these regulations until after the expiration of the period of limitation for filing a claim for refund. Such a protective claim shall be made in accordance with guidance that may be provided from time to time by publication in the Internal Revenue Bulletin (see § 601.601(d)(2)(ii)(*b*)). Although the protective claim need not state a particular dollar amount or demand an immediate refund, a protective claim must identify each outstanding claim or expense that would have been deductible under section 2053(a) or (b) if such item already had been paid and must describe the reasons and contingencies delaying the actual payment of the claim or expense. Action on protective claims will proceed after the executor has notified the Commissioner within a reasonable period that the contingency has been resolved

and that the amount deductible under § 20.2053-1 has been established.

(ii) *Effect on marital and charitable deduction.*—To the extent that a protective claim for refund is filed with respect to a claim or expense that would have been deductible under section 2053(a) or (b) if such item already had been paid and that is payable out of a share that meets the requirements for a charitable deduction under section 2055 or a marital deduction under section 2056 or section 2056A, or from a combination thereof, neither the charitable deduction nor the marital deduction shall be reduced by the amount of such claim or expense until the amount is actually paid or meets the requirements of paragraph (d)(4) of this section for deducting certain ascertainable amounts or the requirements of § 20.2053-4(b) or (c) for deducting certain claims against the estate.

(6) [Reserved].

(7) *Examples.*—Assume that the amounts described in section 2053(a) are payable out of property subject to claims and are allowable by the law of the jurisdiction governing the administration of the estate, whether the applicable jurisdiction is within or outside of the United States. Assume that the claims against the estate are not deductible under § 20.2053-4(b) or (c). Also assume, unless otherwise provided, that none of the limitations on the amount of the deduction described in this section apply to the deduction claimed under section 2053. The following examples illustrate the application of this paragraph (d):

Example 1. Amount of expense ascertainable. Decedent's (D's) estate was probated in State. State law provides that the personal representative shall receive compensation equal to 2.5 percent of the value of the probate estate. The executor (E) may claim a deduction for estimated fees equal to 2.5 percent of D's probate estate on the Form 706 filed for D's estate under the rule for deducting certain ascertainable amounts set forth in paragraph (d)(4) of this section, provided that the estimated amount will be paid. However, the Commissioner will disallow the deduction upon examination of the estate's Form 706 to the extent that the amount for which a deduction was claimed no longer satisfies the requirements of paragraph (d)(4) of this section. If this occurs, E may file a protective claim for refund in accordance with paragraph (d)(5) of this section in order to preserve the estate's right to claim a refund for the amount of the fee that is subsequently paid or that subsequently meets the requirements of paragraph (d)(4) of this section for deducting certain ascertainable amounts.

Example 2. Amount of claim not ascertainable. Prior to death, Decedent (D) is sued by Claimant (C) for $100x in a tort proceeding and responds asserting affirmative defenses available to D under applicable local law. C and D are unrelated. D subsequently dies and D's Form 706 is due before a final judgment is entered in the case. The executor of D's estate (E) may not claim a deduction with respect to C's claim on D's Form 706 under the special rule contained in paragraph (d)(4) of this section because the deductible amount cannot be ascertained with reasonable certainty. However, E may file a timely protective claim for refund in accordance with paragraph (d)(5) of this section in order to preserve the estate's right to subsequently claim a refund at the time a final judgment is entered in the case and the claim is either paid or meets the requirements of paragraph (d)(4) of this section for deducting certain ascertainable amounts.

Example 3. Amount of claim payable out of property qualifying for marital deduction. The facts are the same as in *Example 2* except that the applicable credit amount, under section 2010, against the estate tax was fully consumed by D's lifetime gifts, D is survived by Spouse (S), and D's estate passes entirely to S in a bequest that qualifies for the marital deduction under section 2056. Even though any amount D's estate ultimately pays with respect to C's claim will be paid from the assets qualifying for the marital deduction, in filing Form 706, E need not reduce the amount of the marital deduction claimed on D's Form 706. Instead, pursuant to the protective claim for refund filed by E, the marital deduction will be reduced by the claim once a final judgment is entered in the case. At that time, a deduction will be allowed for the amount that is either paid or meets the requirements of paragraph (d)(4) of this section for deducting certain ascertainable amounts.

(e) *Disallowance of double deductions.*—See section 642(g) and § 1.642(g)-1 with respect to the disallowance for income tax purposes of certain deductions unless the right to take such deductions for estate tax purposes is waived.

(f) *Effective/applicability date.*—This section applies to the estates of decedents dying on or after October 20, 2009. [Reg. § 20.2053-1.]

☐ [*T.D.* 6296, 6-23-58. *Amended by T.D.* 7238, 12-28-72 *and T.D.* 9468, 10-16-2009 (*corrected* 11-24-2009).]

[Reg. § 20.2053-2]

§ 20.2053-2. Deduction for funeral expenses.—Such amounts for funeral expenses are allowed as deductions from a decedent's gross estate as (a) are actually expended, (b) would be properly allowable out of property subject to claims under the laws of the local jurisdiction, and (c) satisfy the requirements of paragraph (c) of § 20.2053-1. A reasonable expenditure for a tombstone, monument, or mausoleum, or for a burial lot, either for the decedent or his family, including a reasonable expenditure for its future care, may be deducted under this heading, provided such an expenditure is allowable by the local law. Included in funeral expenses is the

cost of transportation of the person bringing the body to the place of burial. [Reg. § 20.2053-2.]

☐ [*T.D.* 6296, 6-23-58.]

[Reg. § 20.2053-3]

§ 20.2053-3. Deduction for expenses of administering estate.—(a) *In general.*—The amounts deductible from a decedent's gross estate as "administration expenses" of the first category (see paragraphs (a) and (c) of § 20.2053-1) are limited to such expenses as are actually and necessarily incurred in the administration of the decedent's estate; that is, in the collection of assets, payment of debts, and distribution of property to the persons entitled to it. The expenses contemplated in the law are such only as attend the settlement of an estate and the transfer of the property of the estate to individual beneficiaries or to a trustee, whether the trustee is the executor or some other person. Expenditures not essential to the proper settlement of the estate, but incurred for the individual benefit of the heirs, legatees, or devisees, may not be taken as deductions. Administration expenses include (1) executor's commissions; (2) attorney's fees; and (3) miscellaneous expenses. Each of these classes is considered separately in paragraphs (b) through (d) of this section.

(b) *Executor's commissions.*—(1) Executors' commissions are deductible to the extent permitted by § 20.2053-1 and this section, but no deduction may be taken if no commissions are to be paid. In addition, the amount of the commissions claimed as a deduction must be in accordance with the usually accepted standards and practice of allowing such an amount in estates of similar size and character in the jurisdiction in which the estate is being administered, or any deviation from the usually accepted standards or range of amounts (permissible under applicable local law) must be justified to the satisfaction of the Commissioner.

(2) A bequest or devise to the executor in lieu of commissions is not deductible. If, however, the terms of the will set forth the compensation payable to the executor for services to be rendered in the administration of the estate, a deduction may be taken to the extent that the amount so fixed does not exceed the compensation allowable by the local law or practice and to the extent permitted by § 20.2053-1.

(3) Except to the extent that a trustee is in fact performing services with respect to property subject to claims which would normally be performed by an executor, amounts paid as trustees' commissions do not constitute expenses of administration under the first category, and are only deductible as expenses of the second category to the extent provided in § 20.2053-8.

(c) *Attorney's fees.*—(1) Attorney's fees are deductible to the extent permitted by § 20.2053-1 and this section. Further, the amount of the fees claimed as a deduction may not exceed a reasonable remuneration for the services rendered, taking into account the size and character of the estate, the law and practice in the jurisdiction in which the estate is being administered, and the skill and expertise of the attorneys.

(2) A deduction for attorneys' fees incurred in contesting an asserted deficiency or in prosecuting a claim for refund should be claimed at the time the deficiency is contested or the refund claim is prosecuted. A deduction for reasonable attorney's fees actually incurred in contesting an asserted deficiency or in prosecuting a claim for refund will be allowed to the extent permitted by § 20.2053-1 even though the deduction, as such, was not claimed on the estate tax return or in the claim for refund. A deduction for these fees shall not be denied, and the sufficiency of a claim for refund shall not be questioned, solely by reason of the fact that the amount of the fees to be paid was not established at the time that the right to the deduction was claimed.

(3) Attorneys' fees incurred by beneficiaries incident to litigation as to their respective interests are not deductible if the litigation is not essential to the proper settlement of the estate within the meaning of paragraph (a) of this section. An attorney's fee not meeting this test is not deductible as an administration expense under section 2053 and this section, even if it is approved by a probate court as an expense payable or reimbursable by the estate.

(d) *Miscellaneous administration expenses.*— (1) Miscellaneous administration expenses include such expenses as court costs, surrogates' fees, accountants' fees, appraisers' fees, clerk hire, etc. Expenses necessarily incurred in preserving and distributing the estate, including the cost of storing or maintaining property of the estate if it is impossible to effect immediate distribution to the beneficiaries, are deductible to the extent permitted by § 20.2053-1. Expenses for preserving and caring for the property may not include outlays for additions or improvements; nor will such expenses be allowed for a longer period than the executor is reasonably required to retain the property.

(2) Expenses for selling property of the estate are deductible to the extent permitted by § 20.2053-1 if the sale is necessary in order to pay the decedent's debts, expenses of administration, or taxes, to preserve the estate, or to effect distribution. The phrase "expenses for selling property" includes brokerage fees and other expenses attending the sale, such as the fees of an auctioneer if it is reasonably necessary to employ one. Where an item included in the gross estate is disposed of in a bona fide sale (including a redemption) to a dealer in such items at a price below its fair market value, for purposes of this paragraph there shall be treated as an expense for selling the item whichever of the following amounts is the lesser: (i) the amount by which

the fair market value of the property on the applicable valuation date exceeds the proceeds of the sale, or (ii) the amount by which the fair market value of the property on the date of the sale exceeds the proceeds of the sale. The principles used in determining the value at which an item of property is included in the gross estate shall be followed in arriving at the fair market value of the property for purposes of this paragraph. See § § 20.2031-1 through 20.2031-9.

(3) Expenses incurred in defending the estate against claims described in section 2053(a)(3) are deductible to the extent permitted by § 20.2053-1 if the expenses are incurred incident to the assertion of defenses to the claim available under the applicable law, even if the estate ultimately does not prevail. For purposes of this paragraph (d)(3), "expenses incurred in defending the estate against claims" include costs relating to the arbitration and mediation of contested issues, costs associated with defending the estate against claims (whether or not enforceable), and costs associated with reaching a negotiated settlement of the issues.

(e) *Effective/applicability date.*—This section applies to the estates of decedents dying on or after October 20, 2009. [Reg. § 20.2053-3.]

☐ *[T.D. 6296, 6-23-58. Amended by T.D. 6826, 6-14-65; T.D. 7612, 4-19-79 and T.D. 9468, 10-16-2009.]*

[Reg. § 20.2053-4]

§ 20.2053-4. Deduction for claims against the estate.—(a) *In general.*—(1) *General rule.*—For purposes of this section, liabilities imposed by law or arising out of contracts or torts are deductible if they meet the applicable requirements set forth in § 20.2053-1 and this section. To be deductible, a claim against a decedent's estate must represent a personal obligation of the decedent existing at the time of the decedent's death. Except as otherwise provided in paragraphs (b) and (c) of this section and to the extent permitted by § 20.2053-1, the amounts that may be deducted as claims against a decedent's estate are limited to the amounts of bona fide claims that are enforceable against the decedent's estate (and are not unenforceable when paid) and claims that—

(i) Are actually paid by the estate in satisfaction of the claim; or

(ii) Meet the requirements of § 20.2053-1(d)(4) for deducting certain ascertainable amounts.

(2) *Effect of post-death events.*—Events occurring after the date of a decedent's death shall be considered in determining whether and to what extent a deduction is allowable under section 2053. See § 20.2053-1(d)(2).

(b) *Exception for claims and counterclaims in related matter.*—(1) *General rule.*—If a decedent's gross estate includes one or more claims or causes of action and there are one or more claims against the decedent's estate in the same or a substantiallyrelated matter, or, if a decedent's gross estate includes a particular asset and there are one or more claims against the decedent's estate integrally related to that particular asset, the executor may deduct on the estate's United States Estate (and Generation-Skipping Transfer) Tax Return (Form 706) the current value of the claim or claims against the estate, even though payment has not been made, provided that—

(i) Each such claim against the estate otherwise satisfies the applicable requirements set forth in § 20.2053-1;

(ii) Each such claim against the estate represents a personal obligation of the decedent existing at the time of the decedent's death;

(iii) Each such claim is enforceable against the decedent's estate (and is not unenforceable when paid);

(iv) The value of each such claim against the estate is determined from a "qualified appraisal" performed by a "qualified appraiser" within the meaning of section 170 of the Internal Revenue Code and the corresponding regulations;

(v) The value of each such claim against the estate is subject to adjustment for post-death events; and

(vi) The aggregate value of the related claims or assets included in the decedent's gross estate exceeds 10 percent of the decedent's gross estate.

(2) *Limitation on deduction.*—The deduction under this paragraph (b) is limited to the value of the related claims or particular assets included in decedent's gross estate.

(3) *Effect of post-death events.*—If, under this paragraph (b), a deduction is claimed on Form 706 for a claim against the estate and, during the period described in § 20.2053-1(d)(2), the claim is paid or meets the requirements of § 20.2053-1(d)(4) for deducting certain ascertainable amounts, the claimed deduction is subject to adjustment to reflect, and may not exceed, the amount paid on the claim or the amount meeting the requirements of § 20.2053-1(d)(4). If, under this paragraph (b), a deduction is claimed on Form 706 for a claim against the estate and, during the period described in § 20.2053-1(d)(2), the claim remains unpaid (and does not meet the requirements of § 20.2053-1(d)(4) for deducting certain ascertainable amounts), the claimed deduction is subject to adjustment to reflect, and may not exceed, the current valuation of the claim. A valuation of the claim will be considered current if it reflects events occurring after the decedent's death. With regard to any amount in excess of the amount deductible under this paragraph (b), an estate may preserve the estate's right to claim a refund for claims that are

paid or that meet the requirements of § 20.2053-(1)(d)(4) after the expiration of the period of limitation for filing a claim for refund by filing a protective claim for refund in accordance with the rules in § 20.2053-1(d)(5).

(c) *Exception for claims totaling not more than $500,000.*—(1) *General rule.*—An executor may deduct on Form 706 the current value of one or more claims against the estate even though payment has not been made on the claim or claims to the extent that—

(i) Each such claim against the estate otherwise satisfies the applicable requirements for deductibility set forth in § 20.2053-1;

(ii) Each such claim against the estate represents a personal obligation of the decedent existing at the time of the decedent's death;

(iii) Each such claim is enforceable against the decedent's estate (and is not unenforceable when paid);

(iv) The value of each such claim against the estate is determined from a "qualified appraisal" performed by a "qualified appraiser" within the meaning of section 170 of the Internal Revenue Code and the corresponding regulations;

(v) The total amount deducted by the estate under this paragraph (c) does not exceed $500,000;

(vi) The full value of each claim, rather than just a portion of that amount, must be deductible under this paragraph (c) and, for this purpose, the full value of each such claim is deemed to be the unpaid amount of that claim that is not deductible after the application of §§ 20.2053-1 and 20.2053-4(b); and

(vii) The value of each claim deducted under this paragraph (c) is subject to adjustment for post-death events.

(2) *Effect of post-death events.*—If, under this paragraph (c), a deduction is claimed for a claim against the estate and, during the period described in § 20.2053-1(d)(2), the claim is paid or meets the requirements of § 20.2053-1(d)(4) for deducting certain ascertainable amounts, the amount of the allowable deduction for that claim is subject to adjustment to reflect, and may not exceed, the amount paid on the claim or the amount meeting the requirements of § 20.2053-1(d)(4). If, under this paragraph (c), a deduction is claimed for a claim against the estate and, during the period described in § 20.2053-1(d)(2), the claim remains unpaid (and does not meet the requirements of § 20.2053-1(d)(4) for deducting certain ascertainable amounts), the amount of the allowable deduction for that claim is subject to adjustment to reflect, and may not exceed, the current value of the claim. The value of the claim will be considered current if it reflects events occurring after the decedent's death. To claim a deduction for amounts in excess of the amount deductible

under this paragraph (c), the estate may preserve the estate's right to claim a refund for claims that are not paid or that do not meet the requirements of § 20.2053-1(d)(4) until after the expiration of the period of limitation for the filing of a claim for refund by filing a protective claim for refund in accordance with the rules in § 20.2053-1(d)(5).

(3) *Examples.*—The following examples illustrate the application of this paragraph (c). Assume that the value of each claim is determined from a "qualified appraisal" performed by a "qualified appraiser" and reflects events occurring after the death of the decedent (D). Also assume that each claim represents a personal obligation of D that existed at D's death, that each claim is enforceable against the decedent's estate (and is not unenforceable when paid), and that each claim otherwise satisfies the requirements for deductibility of § 20.2053-1.

Example 1. There are three claims against the estate of the decedent (D) that are not paid and are not deductible under § 20.2053-1(d)(4) or paragraph (b) of this section: $25,000 of Claimant A, $35,000 of Claimant B, and $1,000,000 of Claimant C. The executor of D's estate (E) may not claim a deduction under this paragraph with respect to any portion of the claim of Claimant C because the value of that claim exceeds $500,000. E may claim a deduction under this paragraph for the total amount of the claims filed by Claimant A and Claimant B ($60,000) because the aggregate value of the full amount of those claims does not exceed $500,000.

Example 2. There are three claims against the estate of the decedent (D) that are not paid and are not deductible under § 20.2053-1(d)(4) or paragraph (b) of this section; specifically, a separate $200,000 claim of each of three claimants, A, B and C. The executor of D's estate (E) may claim a deduction under this paragraph for any two of these three claims because the aggregate value of the full amount of any two of the claims does not exceed $500,000. E may not deduct any part of the value of the remaining claim under this paragraph because the aggregate value of the full amount of all three claims would exceed $500,000.

Example 3. As a result of an automobile accident involving the decedent (D) and A, D's gross estate includes a claim against A that is valued at $750,000. In the same matter, A files a counterclaim against D's estate that is valued at $1,000,000. A's claim against D's estate is not paid and is not deductible under § 20.2053-1(d)(4). All other section 2053 claims and expenses of D's estate have been paid and are deductible. The executor of D's estate (E) deducts $750,000 of A's claim against the estate under § 20.2053-4(b). E may claim a deduction under this paragraph (c) for the total value of A's claim not deducted under § 20.2053-4(b), or $250,000. If, instead, the value of A's claim

against D's estate is $1,500,000, so that the amount not deductible under § 20.2053-4(b) exceeds $500,000, no deduction is available under this paragraph (c).

(d) *Special rules.*—(1) *Potential and unmatured claims.*—Except as provided in § 20.2053-1(d)(4) and in paragraphs (b) and (c) of this section, no estate tax deduction may be taken for a claim against the decedent's estate while it remains a potential or unmatured claim. Claims that later mature may be deducted (to the extent permitted by § 20.2053-1) in connection with a timely claim for refund. To preserve the estate's right to claim a refund for claims that mature and become deductible after the expiration of the period of limitation for filing a claim for refund, a protective claim for refund may be filed in accordance with § 20.2053-1(d)(5). See § 20.2053-1(b)(3) for rules relating to the treatment of court decrees and settlements.

(2) *Contested claims.*—Except as provided in paragraphs (b) and (c) of this section, no estate tax deduction may be taken for a claim against the decedent's estate to the extent the estate is contesting the decedent's liability. Contested claims that later mature may be deducted (to the extent permitted by § 20.2053-1) in connection with a claim for refund filed within the time prescribed in section 6511(a). To preserve the estate's right to claim a refund for claims that mature and become deductible after the expiration of the period of limitation for the filing a claim for refund, a protective claim for refund may be filed in accordance with § 20.2053-1(d)(5). See § 20.2053-1(b)(3) for rules relating to the treatment of court decrees and settlements.

(3) *Claims against multiple parties.*—If the decedent or the decedent's estate is one of two or more parties against whom the claim is being asserted, the estate may deduct only the portion of the total claim due from and paid by the estate, reduced by the total of any reimbursement received from another party, insurance, or otherwise. The estate's deductible portion also will be reduced by the contribution or other amount the estate could have collected from another party or an insurer but which the estate declines or fails to attempt to collect. See further § 20.2053-1(d)(3).

(4) *Unenforceable claims.*—Claims that are unenforceable prior to or at the decedent's death are not deductible, even if they are actually paid. Claims that become unenforceable during the administration of the estate are not deductible to the extent that they are paid (or will be paid) after they become unenforceable. However, see § 20.2053-1(b)(3)(iv) regarding a claim whose enforceability is at issue.

(5) *Claims founded upon a promise.*—Except with regard to pledges or subscriptions (see

§ 20.2053-5), section 2053(c)(1)(A) provides that the deduction for a claim founded upon a promise or agreement is limited to the extent that the promise or agreement was bona fide and in exchange for adequate and full consideration in money or money's worth; that is, the promise or agreement must have been bargained for at arm's length and the price must have been an adequate and full equivalent reducible to a money value.

(6) *Recurring payments.*—(i) *Noncontingent obligations.*—If a decedent is obligated to make recurring payments on an enforceable and certain claim that satisfies the requirements for deductibility under this section and the payments are not subject to a contingency, the amount of the claim will be deemed ascertainable with reasonable certainty for purposes of the rule for deducting certain ascertainable amounts set forth in § 20.2053-1(d)(4). If the recurring payments will be paid, a deduction will be allowed under the rule for deducting certain ascertainable amounts set forth in § 20.2053-1(d)(4) (subject to any applicable limitations in § 20.2053-1). Recurring payments for purposes of this section exclude those payments made in connection with a mortgage or indebtedness described in and governed by § 20.2053-7. If a decedent's obligation to make a recurring payment is contingent on the death or remarriage of the claimant and otherwise satisfies the requirements of this paragraph (d)(6)(i), the amount of the claim (measured according to actuarial principles, using factors set forth in the transfer tax regulations or otherwise provided by the IRS) will be deemed ascertainable with reasonable certainty for purposes of the rule for deducting certain ascertainable amounts set forth in § 20.2053-1(d)(4).

(ii) *Contingent obligations.*—If a decedent has a recurring obligation to pay an enforceable and certain claim but the decedent's obligation is subject to a contingency or is not otherwise described in paragraph (d)(6)(i) of this section, the amount of the claim is not ascertainable with reasonable certainty for purposes of the rule for deducting certain ascertainable amounts set forth in § 20.2053-1(d)(4). Accordingly, the amount deductible is limited to amounts actually paid by the estate in satisfaction of the claim in accordance with § 20.2053-1(d)(1) (subject to any applicable limitations in § 20.2053-1).

(iii) *Purchase of commercial annuity to satisfy recurring obligation to pay.*—If a decedent has a recurring obligation (whether or not contingent) to pay an enforceable and certain claim and the estate purchases a commercial annuity from an unrelated dealer in commercial annuities in an arm's-length transaction to satisfy the obligation, the amount deductible by the estate (subject to any applicable limitations in § 20.2053-1) is the sum of—

(A) The amount paid for the commercial annuity, to the extent that the amount paid is not refunded, or expected to be refunded, to the estate;

(B) Any amount actually paid to the claimant by the estate prior to the purchase of the commercial annuity; and

(C) Any amount actually paid to the claimant by the estate in excess of the annuity amount as is necessary to satisfy the recurring obligation.

(7) *Examples.*—The following examples illustrate the application of paragraph (d) of this section. Except as is otherwise provided in the examples, assume—

(i) A claim satisfies the applicable requirements set forth in § 20.2053-1 and paragraph (a) of this section, is payable from property subject to claims, and the amount of the claim is not subject to any other applicable limitations in § 20.2053-1;

(ii) A claim is not deductible under paragraphs (b) or (c) of this section as an exception to the general rule contained in paragraph (a) of this section; and

(iii) The claimant (C) is not a family member, related entity or beneficiary of the estate of decedent (D) and is not the executor (E).

Example 1. Contested claim, single defendant, no decision. D is sued by C for $100x in a tort proceeding and responds asserting affirmative defenses available to D under applicable local law. D dies and E is substituted as defendant in the suit. D's Form 706 is due before a judgment is reached in the case. D's gross estate exceeds $100x. E may not take a deduction on Form 706 for the claim against the estate. However, E may claim a deduction under § 20.2053-3(c) or § 20.2053-3(d)(3) for expenses incurred in defending the estate against the claim if the expenses have been paid in accordance with § 20.2053-1(d)(1) or if the expenses meet the requirements of § 20.2053-1(d)(4) for deducting certain ascertainable amounts. E may file a protective claim for refund before the expiration of the period of limitation prescribed in section 6511(a) in order to preserve the estate's right to claim a refund, if the amount of the claim will not be paid or cannot be ascertained with reasonable certainty by the expiration of this limitation period. If payment is subsequently made pursuant to a court decision or a settlement, the payment, as well as expenses incurred incident to the claim and not previously deducted, may be deducted and relief may be sought in connection with a timely-filed claim for refund.

Example 2. Contested claim, single defendant, final court decree and payment. The facts are the same as in *Example 1* except that, before the Form 706 is timely filed, the court enters a decision in favor of C, no timely appeal is filed, and payment is made. E may claim a deduction on Form 706 for the amount paid in satisfaction of the claim against the estate pursuant to the final decision of the local court, including any interest accrued prior to D's death. In addition, E may claim a deduction under § 20.2053-3(c) or § 20.2053-3(d)(3) for expenses incurred in defending the estate against the claim and in processing payment of the claim if the expenses have been paid in accordance with § 20.2053-1(d)(1) or if the expenses meet the requirements of § 20.2053-1(d)(4) for deducting certain ascertainable amounts.

Example 3. Contested claim, single defendant, settlement and payment. The facts are the same as in *Example 1* except that a settlement is reached between E and C for $80x and payment is made before Form 706 is timely filed. E may claim a deduction on Form 706 for the amount paid to C ($80x) in satisfaction of the claim against the estate. In addition, E may claim a deduction under § 20.2053-3(c) or § 20.2053-3(d)(3) for expenses incurred in defending the estate, reaching a settlement, and processing payment of the claim if the expenses have been paid in accordance with § 20.2053-1(d)(1) or if the expenses meet the requirements of § 20.2053-1(d)(4) for deducting certain ascertainable amounts.

Example 4. Contested claim, multiple defendants. The facts are the same as in *Example 1* except that the suit filed by C lists D and an unrelated third-party (K) as defendants. If the claim against the estate is not resolved prior to the time the Form 706 is filed, E may not take a deduction for the claim on Form 706. If payment is subsequently made of D's share of the claim pursuant to a court decision holding D liable for 40 percent of the amount due and K liable for 60 percent of the amount due, then E may claim a deduction for the amount paid in satisfaction of the claim against the estate representing D's share of the liability as assigned by the court decree ($40x), plus any interest on that share accrued prior to D's death. If the court decision finds D and K jointly and severally liable for the entire $100x and D's estate pays the entire $100x but could have reasonably collected $50x from K in reimbursement, E may claim a deduction of $50x together with the interest on $50x accrued prior to D's death. In both instances, E also may claim a deduction under § 20.2053-3(c) or § 20.2053-3(d)(3) for expenses incurred and not previously deducted in defending the estate against the claim and processing payment of the amount due from D if the expenses have been paid in accordance with § 20.2053-1(d)(1) or if the expenses meet the requirements of § 20.2053-1(d)(4) for deducting certain ascertainable amounts.

Example 5. Contested claim, multiple defendants, settlement and payment. The facts are the same as in *Example 1* except that the suit filed by C lists D and an unrelated third-party (K) as defendants. D's estate settles with C for $10x and payment is made before Form 706 is timely filed. E may take a deduction on Form 706 for the amount paid to C ($10x) in satisfaction of the claim against the estate. In addition, E may claim a deduction under § 20.2053-3(c) or § 20.2053-3(d)(3) for expenses incurred in defending the estate, reaching a settlement, and processing payment of the claim if the expenses have been paid in accordance with § 20.2053-1(d)(1) or if the expenses meet the requirements of § 20.2053-1(d)(4) for deducting certain ascertainable amounts.

Example 6. Mixed claims. During life, D contracts with C to perform specific work on D's home for $75x. Under the contract, additional work must be approved in advance by D. C performs additional work and sues D for $100x for work completed including the $75x agreed to in the contract. D dies and D's Form 706 is due before a judgment is reached in the case. E accepts liability of $75x but contests liability of $25x. E may take a deduction of $75x on Form 706 if the amount has been paid or meets the requirements of § 20.2053-1(d)(4) for deducting certain ascertainable amounts. In addition, E may claim a deduction under § 20.2053-3(c) or § 20.2053-3(d)(3) for expenses incurred in defending the estate against the claim if the expenses have been paid or if the expenses meet the requirements of § 20.2053-1(d)(4) for deducting certain ascertainable amounts. E may file a protective claim for refund before the expiration of the period of limitation prescribed in section 6511(a) in order to preserve the estate's right to claim a refund for any amount in excess of $75x that is subsequently paid to resolve the claim against the estate. To the extent that any unpaid expenses incurred in defending the estate against the claim are not deducted as an ascertainable amount pursuant to § 20.2053-1(d)(4), they may be included in the protective claim for refund.

Example 7. Claim having issue of enforceability. D is sued by C for $100x in a tort proceeding in which there is an issue as to whether the claim is barred by the applicable period of limitations. After D's death but prior to the decision of the court, a settlement meeting the requirements of § 20.2053-1(b)(3)(iv) is reached between E and C in the amount of $50x. E pays C this amount before the Form 706 is timely filed. E may take a deduction on Form 706 for the amount paid to C ($50x) in satisfaction of the claim. If, subsequent to E's payment to C, facts develop to indicate that the claim was, in fact, unenforceable, the deduction will not be denied provided the enforceability of the claim was at issue in a bona dispute at the time of the payment. See § 20.2053-1(b)(3)(iv). A deduction may be available under § 20.2053-3(d)(3) for expenses incurred in defending the estate, reaching a settlement, and processing payment of the claim if the expenses have been paid in accordance with § 20.2053-1(d)(1) or if the expenses meet the requirements of § 20.2053-1(d)(4) for deducting certain ascertainable amounts.

Example 8. Noncontingent and recurring obligation to pay, binding on estate. D's property settlement agreement incident to D's divorce, signed three years prior to D's death, obligates D or D's estate to pay to S, D's former spouse, $20x per year until S's death or remarriage. Prior to D's death, D made payments in accordance with the agreement and, after D's death, E continues to make the payments in accordance with the agreement. D's obligation to pay S under the property settlement agreement is deemed to be a claim against the estate that is ascertainable with reasonable certainty for purposes of §20.2053-1(d)(4). To the extent the obligation to make the recurring payment is a claim that will be paid, E may deduct the amount of the claim (measured according to actuarial principles, using factors set forth in the transfer tax regulations or otherwise provided by the IRS) under the rule for deducting certain ascertainable amounts set forth in §20.2053-1(d)(4).

Example 9. Recurring obligation to pay, estate purchases a commercial annuity in satisfaction. D's settlement agreement with T, the claimant in a suit against D, signed three years prior to D's death, obligates D or D's estate to pay to T $20x per year for 10 years, provided that T does not reveal the details of the claim or of the settlement during that period. D dies in Year 1. In Year 2, D's estate purchases a commercial annuity from an unrelated issuer of commercial annuities, XYZ, to fund the obligation to T. E may deduct the entire amount paid to XYZ to obtain the annuity, even though the obligation to T was contingent.

(e) *Interest on claim.*—(1) Subject to any applicable limitations in §20.2053-1, the interest on a deductible claim is itself deductible as a claim under section 2053 to the extent of the amount of interest accrued at the decedent's death (even if the executor elects the alternate valuation method under section 2032), but only to the extent of the amount of interest actually paid or meeting the requirements of §20.2053-1(d)(4) for deducting certain ascertainable amounts.

(2) Post-death accrued interest may be deductible in appropriate circumstances either as an estate tax administration expense under section 2053 or as an income tax deduction.

(f) *Effective/applicability date.*—This section applies to the estates of decedents dying on or after October 20, 2009. [Reg. §20.2053-4.]

☐ [*T.D.* 6296, 6-23-58. *Amended by T.D.* 9468, 10-16-2009 (*corrected* 11-24-2009).]

[Reg. §20.2053-5]

§20.2053-5. Deductions for charitable, etc., pledges or subscriptions.—(a) A pledge or a subscription, evidenced by a promissory note or otherwise, even though enforceable against the estate, is deductible (subject to any applicable limitations in §20.2053-1) only to the extent that—

(1) Liability therefore was contracted bona fide and for an adequate and full consideration in cash or its equivalent, or

(2) It would have constituted an allowable deduction under section 2055 (relating to charitable, etc., deductions) if it had been a bequest.

(b) *Effective/applicability date.*—This section applies to the estates of decedents dying on or after October 20, 2009. [Reg. §20.2053-5.]

☐ [*T.D.* 6296, 6-23-58. *Amended by T.D.* 9468, 10-16-2009.]

[Reg. §20.2053-6]

§20.2053-6. Deduction for taxes.—(a) *In general.*—(1) Taxes are deductible in computing a decedent's gross estate—

(i) Only as claims against the estate (except to the extent that excise taxes may be allowable as administration expenses);

(ii) Only to the extent not disallowed by section 2053(c)(1)(B) and this section; and

(iii) Subject to any applicable limitations in §20.2053-1.

(2) See §§20.2053-9 and 20.2053-10 with respect to the deduction allowed for certain state and foreign death taxes.

(b) *Property taxes.*—Property taxes are not deductible unless they accrued before the decedent's death. However, they are not deductible merely because they have accrued in an accounting sense. Property taxes in order to be deductible must be an enforceable obligation of the decedent at the time of his death.

(c) *Death taxes.*—(1) For the estates of decedents dying on or before December 31, 2004, no estate, succession, legacy or inheritance tax payable by reason of the decedent's death is deductible, except as provided in §§20.2053-9 and 20.2053-10 with respect to certain state and foreign death taxes on transfers for charitable, etc., uses. However, see sections 2011 and 2014 and the corresponding regulations with respect to credits for death taxes.

(2) For the estates of decedents dying after December 31, 2004, see section 2058 to determine the deductibility of state death taxes.

(d) *Gift taxes.*—Unpaid gift taxes on gifts made by a decedent before his death are deductible. If a gift is considered as made one-half by the decedent and one-half by his spouse under section 2513, the entire amount of the gift tax, unpaid at the decedent's death, attributable to a gift in fact made by the decedent is deductible. No portion of the tax attributable to a gift in fact made by the decedent's spouse is deductible except to the extent that the obligation is enforced against the decedent's estate and his estate has no effective right of contribution against his spouse. (See section 2012 and § 20.2012-1 with respect to credit for gift taxes paid upon gifts of property included in a decedent's gross estate.)

(e) *Excise taxes.*—Excise taxes incurred in selling property of a decedent's estate are deductible as an expense of administration if the sale is necessary in order to (1) pay the decedent's debts, expenses of administration, or taxes, (2) preserve the estate, or (3) effect distribution. Excise taxes incurred in distributing property of the estate in kind are also deductible.

(f) *Income taxes.*—Unpaid income taxes are deductible if they are on income properly includible in an income tax return of the decedent for a period before his death. Taxes on income received after the decedent's death are not deductible. If income received by a decedent during his lifetime is included in a joint income tax return filed by the decedent and his spouse, or by the decedent's estate and his surviving spouse, the portion of the joint liability for the period covered by the return for which a deduction would be allowed is the amount for which the decedent's estate would be liable under local law, as between the decedent and his spouse, after enforcement of any effective right of reimbursement or contribution. In the absence of evidence to the contrary, the deductible amount is presumed to be an amount bearing the same ratio to the total joint tax liability for the period covered by the return that the amount of income tax for which the decedent would have been liable if he had filed a separate return for that period bears to the total of the amounts for which the decedent and his spouse would have been liable if they had both filed separate returns for that period. Thus, in the absence of evidence to the contrary, the deductible amount equals

$$\frac{\text{decedent's separate tax}}{\text{both separate taxes}} \times \text{joint tax.}$$

However, the deduction cannot in any event exceed the lesser of—

(1) The decedent's liability for the period (as determined in this paragraph) reduced by the amounts already contributed by the decedent toward payment of the joint liability, or

(2) If there is an enforceable agreement between the decedent and his spouse or between the executor and the spouse relative to the payment of the joint liability, the amount which pursuant to the agreement is to be contributed by the estate toward payment of the joint liability.

If the decedent's estate and his surviving spouse are entitled to a refund on account of an overpayment of a joint income tax liability, the overpayment is an asset includible in the decedent's gross estate under section 2033 in the amount to which the estate would be entitled under local

law, as between the estate and the surviving spouse. In the absence of evidence to the contrary, the includible amount is presumed to be the amount by which the decedent's contributions toward payment of the joint tax exceeds his liability determined in accordance with the principles set forth in this paragraph (other than subparagraph (1) of this paragraph).

(g) *Post-death adjustments of deductible tax liability.*—Post-death adjustments increasing a tax liability accrued prior to the decedent's death, including increases of taxes deducted under this section, will increase the amount of the deduction available under section 2053(a)(3) for that tax liability. Similarly, any refund subsequently determined to be due to and received by the estate or its successor in interest with respect to taxes deducted by the estate under this section reduce the amount of the deduction taken for that tax liability under section 2053(a)(3). Expenses associated with defending the estate against the increase in tax liability or with obtaining the refund may be deductible under § 20.2053-3(d)(3). A protective claim for refund of estate taxes may be filed before the expiration of the period of limitation for filing a claim for refund in order to preserve the estate's right to claim a refund if the amount of a deductible tax liability may be affected by such an adjustment or refund. The application of this section may be illustrated by the following examples:

Example 1. Increase in tax due. After the decedent's death, the Internal Revenue Service examines the gift tax return filed by the decedent in the year before the decedent's death and asserts a deficiency of $100x. The estate pays attorney's fees of $30x in a non-frivolous defense against the increased deficiency. The final determination of the deficiency, in the amount of $90x, is paid by the estate prior to the expiration of the limitation period for filing a claim for refund. The estate may deduct $90x under section 2053(a)(3) and $30x under § 20.2053-3(c)(2) or (d)(3) in connection with a timely claim for refund.

Example 2. Refund of taxes paid. Decedent's estate timely files D's individual income tax return for the year in which the decedent died. The estate timely pays the entire amount of the tax due, $50x, as shown on that return. The entire $50x was attributable to income received prior to the decedent's death. Decedent's estate subsequently discovers an error on the income tax return and timely files a claim for refund of income tax. Decedent's estate receives a refund of $10x. The estate is allowed a deduction of only $40x under section 2053(a)(3) for the income tax liability accrued prior to the decedent's death. If D's estate had claimed a deduction of $50x on D's United States Estate (and Generation-Skipping Transfer) Tax Return (Form 706), the deduction claimed under section 2053(a)(3) will be allowed only to the extent of $40x upon examination by the Commissioner.

(h) *Effective/applicability date.*—This section applies to the estates of decedents dying on or after October 20, 2009. [Reg. § 20.2053-6.]

☐ [*T.D. 6296, 6-23-58. Amended by T.D. 9468, 10-16-2009.*]

[Reg. § 20.2053-7]

§ 20.2053-7. Deduction for unpaid mortgages.—A deduction is allowed from a decedent's gross estate of the full unpaid amount of a mortgage upon, or of any other indebtedness in respect of, any property of the gross estate, including interest which had accrued thereon to the date of death, provided the value of the property, undiminished by the amount of the mortgage or indebtedness, is included in the value of the gross estate. If the decedent's estate is liable for the amount of the mortgage or indebtedness, the full value of the property subject to the mortgage or indebtedness must be included as part of the value of the gross estate; the amount of the mortgage or indebtedness being in such case allowed as a deduction. But if the decedent's estate is not so liable, only the value of the equity of redemption (or the value of the property, less the mortgage or indebtedness) need be returned as part of the value of the gross estate. In no case may the deduction on account of the mortgage or indebtedness exceed the liability therefor contracted bona fide and for an adequate and full consideration in money or money's worth. See § 20.2043-1. Only interest accrued to the date of the decedent's death is allowable even though the alternate valuation method under section 2032 is selected. In any case where real property situated outside the United States does not form a part of the gross estate, no deduction may be taken of any mortgage thereon or any other indebtedness in respect thereof. [Reg. § 20.2053-7.]

☐ [*T.D. 6296, 6-23-58. Amended by T.D. 6684, 10-23-63.*]

[Reg. § 20.2053-8]

§ 20.2053-8. Deduction for expenses in administering property not subject to claims.— (a) Expenses incurred in administering property included in a decedent's gross estate but not subject to claims fall within the second category of deductions set forth in § 20.2053-1, and may be allowed as deductions if they—

(1) Would be allowed as deductions in the first category if the property being administered were subject to claims; and

(2) Were paid before the expiration of the period of limitation for assessment provided in section 6501.

Usually, these expenses are incurred in connection with the administration of a trust established by a decedent during his lifetime. They may also be incurred in connection with the collection of other assets or the transfer or clearance of title to other property included in a decedent's gross estate for estate tax purposes but not included in his probate estate.

(b) These expenses may be allowed as deductions only to the extent that they would be allowed as deductions under the first category if the property were subject to claims. See § 20.2053-3. The only expenses in administering property not subject to claims which are allowed as deductions are those occasioned by the decedent's death and incurred in settling the decedent's interest in the property or vesting good title to the property in the beneficiaries. Expenses not coming within the description in the preceding sentence but incurred on behalf of the transferees are not deductible.

(c) The principles set forth in paragraphs (b), (c), and (d) of § 20.2053-3 (relating to the allowance of executor's commissions, attorney's fees, and miscellaneous administration expenses of the first category) are applied in determining the extent to which trustee's commissions, attorney's and accountant's fees, and miscellaneous administration expenses are allowed in connection with the administration of property not subject to claims.

(d) The application of this section may be illustrated by the following examples:

Example (1). In 1940, the decedent made an irrevocable transfer of property to the X Trust Company, as trustee. The instrument of transfer provided that the trustee should pay the income from the property to the decedent for the duration of his life and, upon his death, distribute the corpus of the trust among designated beneficiaries. The property was included in the decedent's gross estate under the provisions of section 2036. Three months after the date of death, the trustee distributed the trust corpus among the beneficiaries, except for $6,000 which it withheld. The amount withheld represented $5,000 which it retained as trustee's commissions in connection with the termination of the trust and $1,000 which it had paid to an attorney for representing it in connection with the termination. Both the trustee's commissions and the attorney's fees were allowable under the law of the jurisdiction in which the trust was being administered, were reasonable in amount, and were in accord with local custom. Under these circumstances, the estate is allowed a deduction of $6,000.

Example (2). In 1945, the decedent made an irrevocable transfer of property to Y Trust Company, as trustee. The instrument of transfer provided that the trustee should pay the income from the property to the decedent during his life. If the decedent's wife survived him, the trust was to continue for the duration of her life, with Y Trust Company and the decedent's son as co-trustees, and with income payable to the decedent's wife for the duration of her life. Upon the death of both the decedent and his wife, the corpus is to be distributed among designated remaindermen. The decedent was survived by his wife. The property was included in the decedent's gross estate under the provisions of section 2036. In accordance with local custom, the trustee made an accounting to the court as of the date of the decedent's death. Following the death of the decedent, a controversy arose among the remaindermen as to their respective rights under the instrument of transfer, and a suit was brought in court to which the trustee was made a party. As a part of the accounting, the court approved the following expenses which the trustee had paid within 3 years following the date of death: $10,000, trustee's commissions; $5,000, accountant's fees; $25,000, attorney's fees; and $2,500, representing fees paid to the guardian of a remainderman who was a minor. The trustee's commissions and accountant's fees were for services in connection with the usual issues involved in a trust accounting as also were one-half of the attorney's and guardian's fees. The remainder of the attorney's and guardian's fees were for services performed in connection with the suit brought by the remaindermen. The amount allowed as a deduction is the $28,750 ($10,000, trustee's commissions; $5,000, accountant's fees; $12,500, attorney's fees; and $1,250, guardian's fees) incurred as expenses in connection with the usual issues involved in a trust accounting. The remaining expenses are not allowed as deductions since they were incurred on behalf of the transferees.

Example (3). Decedent in 1950 made an irrevocable transfer of property to the Z Trust Company, as trustee. The instrument of transfer provided that the trustee should pay the income from the property to the decedent's wife for the duration of her life. If the decedent survived his wife the trust corpus was to be returned to him but if he did not survive her, then upon the death of the wife, the trust corpus was to be distributed among their children. The decedent predeceased his wife and the transferred property, less the value of the wife's outstanding life estate, was included in his gross estate under the provisions of section 2037 since his reversionary interest therein immediately before his death was in excess of 5 percent of the value of the property. At the wife's request, the court ordered the trustee to render an accounting of the trust property as of the date of the decedent's death. No deduction will be allowed the decedent's estate for any of the expenses incurred in connection with the trust accounting, since the expenses were incurred on behalf of the wife.

Example (4). If, in the preceding example, the decedent died without other property and no executor or administrator of his estate was appointed, so that it was necessary for the trustee to prepare an estate tax return and participate in its audit, or if the trustee required accounting proceedings for its own protection in accordance with local custom, trustees', attorneys', and guardians' fees in connection with the estate tax

or accounting proceedings would be deductible to the same extent that they would be deductible if the property were subject to claims. Deductions incurred under similar circumstances by a surviving joint tenant or the recipient of life insurance proceeds would also be deductible. [Reg. § 20.2053-8.]

[*T.D.* 6296, 6-23-58.]

[Reg. § 20.2053-9]

§ 20.2053-9. Deduction for certain State death taxes.—(a) *General rule.*—A deduction is allowed a decedent's estate under section 2053(d) for the amount of any estate, succession, legacy, or inheritance tax imposed by a State, Territory, or the District of Columbia, or, in the case of a decedent dying before September 3, 1958, a possession of the United States upon a transfer by the decedent for charitable, etc., uses described in section 2055 or 2106(a)(2) (relating to the estates of nonresidents not citizens), but only if (1) the conditions stated in paragraph (b) of this section are met, and (2) an election is made in accordance with the provisions of paragraph (c) of this section. See section 2011(e) and § 20.2011-2 for the effect which the allowance of this deduction has upon the credit for State death taxes. However, see section 2058 to determine the deductibility of state death taxes by estates to which section 2058 is applicable.

(b) *Condition for allowance of deduction.*—(1) The deduction is not allowed unless either—

(i) The entire decrease in the Federal estate tax resulting from the allowance of the deduction inures solely to the benefit of a charitable, etc., transferee described in section 2055 or 2106(a)(2), or

(ii) The Federal estate tax is equitably apportioned among all the transferees (including the decedent's surviving spouse and the charitable, etc., transferees) of property included in the decedent's gross estate.

For allowance of the credit, it is sufficient if either of these conditions is satisfied. Thus, in a case where the entire decrease in Federal estate tax inures to the benefit of a charitable transferee, the deduction is allowable even though the Federal estate tax is not equitably apportioned among all the transferees of property included in the decedent's gross estate. Similarly, if the Federal estate tax is equitably apportioned among all the transferees of property included in the decedent's gross estate, the deduction is allowable even though a noncharitable transferee receives some benefit from the allowance of the deduction.

(2) For purposes of this paragraph, the Federal estate tax is considered to be equitably apportioned among all the transferees (including the decedent's surviving spouse and the charitable, etc., transferees) of property included in the decedent's gross estate only if each transferee's share of the tax is based upon the net amount of

his transfer subjected to the tax (taking into account any exemptions, credits, or deductions allowed by chapter 11). See examples (2) through (5) of paragraph (e) of this section.

(c) *Exercise of election.*—The election to take a deduction for a state death tax imposed upon a transfer for charitable, etc., uses shall be exercised by the executor by the filing of a written notification to that effect with the Commissioner. The notification shall be filed before the expiration of the period of limitation for assessment provided in section 6501 (usually 3 years from the last day for filing the return). The election may be revoked by the executor by the filing of a written notification to that effect with the Commissioner at any time before the expiration of such period.

(d) *Amount of State death tax imposed upon a transfer.*—If a State death tax is imposed upon the transfer of the decedent's entire estate and not upon the transfer of a particular share thereof, the State death tax imposed upon a transfer for charitable, etc., uses is deemed to be an amount, E, which bears the same ratio to F (the amount of the State death tax imposed with respect to the transfer of the entire estate) as G (the value of the charitable, etc., transfer, reduced as provided in the next sentence) bears to H (the total value of the properties, interests, and benefits subjected to the State death tax received by all persons interested in the estate, reduced as provided in the last sentence of this paragraph). In arriving at amount G of the ratio, the value of the charitable, etc., transfer is reduced by the amount of any deduction or exclusion allowed with respect to such property in determining the amount of the State death tax. In arriving at amount H of the ratio, the total value of the properties, interests, and benefits subjected to State death tax received by all persons interested in the estate is reduced by the amount of all deductions and exclusions allowed in determining the amount of the State death tax on account of the nature of a beneficiary or a beneficiary's relationship to the decedent.

(e) *Examples.*—The application of this section may be illustrated by the following examples:

Example (1). The decedent's gross estate was valued at $200,000. He bequeathed $90,000 to a newphew, $10,000 to Charity A, and the remainder of his estate to Charity B. State inheritance tax in the amount of $13,500 was imposed upon the bequest to the nephew, $1,500 upon the bequest to Charity A, and $15,000 upon the bequest to Charity B. Under the will and local law, each legatee is required to pay the State inheritance tax on his bequest, and the Federal estate tax is to be paid out of the residuary estate. Since the entire burden of paying the Federal estate tax falls on Charity B, it follows that the decrease in the Federal estate tax resulting from the allowance of deductions for State death taxes in the

amounts of $1,500 and $15,000 would inure solely for the benefit of Charity B. Therefore, deductions of $1,500 and $15,000 are allowable under section 2053(d). If, in this example, the State death taxes as well as the Federal estate tax were to be paid out of the residuary estate, the result would be the same.

Example (2). The decedent's gross estate was valued at $350,000. Expenses, indebtedness, etc., amounted to $50,000. The entire estate was bequeathed in equal shares to a son, a daughter, and Charity C. State inheritance tax in the amount of $2,000 was imposed upon the bequest to the son, $2,000 upon the bequest to the daughter, and $5,000 upon the bequest to Charity C. Under the will and local law, each legatee is required to pay his own State inheritance tax and his proportionate share of the Federal estate tax determined by taking into consideration the net amount of his bequest subjected to the tax. Since each legatee's share of the Federal estate tax is based upon the net amount of his bequest subjected to the tax (note that the deductions under sections 2053(d) and 2055 will have the effect of reducing Charity C's proportionate share of the tax), the tax is considered to be equitably apportioned. Thus, a deduction of $5,000 is allowable under section 2053(d). This deduction together with a deduction of $95,000 under section 2055 (charitable deduction) will mean that none of Charity C's bequest is subjected to Federal estate tax. Hence, the son and the daughter will bear the entire estate tax.

Example (3). The decedent bequeathed his property in equal shares, after payment of all expenses, to a son, a daughter, and a charity. State inheritance tax of $2,000 was imposed upon the bequest to the son, $2,000 upon the bequest to the daughter, and $15,000 upon the bequest to the charity. Under the will and local law, each beneficiary pays the State inheritance tax on his bequest and the Federal estate tax is to be paid out of the estate as an administration expense. If the deduction for State death tax on the charitable bequest is allowed in this case, some portion of the decrease in the Federal estate tax would inure to the benefit of the son and the daughter. The Federal estate tax is not considered to be equitably apportioned in this case since each legatee's share of the Federal estate tax is not based upon the net amount of his bequest subjected to the tax (note that the deductions under sections 2053(d) and 2055 will not have the effect of reducing the charity's proportionate share of the tax). Inasmuch as some of the decrease in the Federal estate tax payable would inure to the benefit of the son and the daughter, and inasmuch as there is no equitable apportionment of the tax, no deduction is allowable under section 2053(d).

Example (4). The decedent bequeathed his entire residuary estate in trust to pay the income to X for life with remainder to charity. The State imposed inheritance taxes of $2,000 upon the bequest to X and $10,000 upon the bequest to charity. Under the will and local law, all State and Federal taxes are payable out of the residuary estate and therefore they would reduce the amount which would become the corpus of the trust. If the deduction for the State death tax on the charitable bequest is allowed in this case, some portion of the decrease in the Federal estate tax would inure to the benefit of X since the allowance of the deduction would increase the size of the corpus from which X is to receive the income for life. Also, the Federal estate tax is not considered to be equitably apportioned in this case since each legatee's share of the Federal estate tax is not based upon the net amount of his bequest subjected to the tax (note that the deductions under sections 2053(d) and 2055 will not have the effect of reducing the charity's proportionate share of the tax). Inasmuch as some of the decrease in the Federal estate tax payable would inure to the benefit of X, and inasmuch as there is no equitable apportionment of the tax, no deduction is allowable under section 2053(d).

Example (5). The decedent's gross estate was valued at $750,000. Expenses, indebtedness, etc., amounted to $50,000. The decedent bequeathed $350,000 of his estate to his surviving spouse and the remainder of his estate equally to his son and Charity D. State inheritance tax in the amount of $7,000 was imposed upon the bequest to the surviving spouse, $26,250 upon the bequest to the son, and $26,250 upon the bequest to Charity D. The will was silent concerning the payment of taxes. In such a case, the local law provides that each legatee shall pay his own State inheritance tax. The local law further provides for an apportionment of the Federal estate tax among the legatees of the estate. Under the apportionment provisions, the surviving spouse is not required to bear any part of the Federal estate tax with respect to her $350,000 bequest. It should be noted, however, that the marital deduction allowed to the decedent's estate by reason of the bequest to the surviving spouse is limited to $343,000 ($350,000 bequest less $7,000 State inheritance tax payable by the surviving spouse). Thus, the bequest to the surviving spouse is subjected to the Federal estate tax in the net amount of $7,000. If the deduction for State death tax on the charitable bequest is allowed in this case, some portion of the decrease in the Federal estate tax would inure to the benefit of the son. The Federal estate tax is not considered to be equitably apportioned in this case since each legatee's share of the Federal estate tax is not based upon the net amount of his bequest subjected to the tax (note that the surviving spouse is to pay no tax). Inasmuch as some of the decrease in the Federal estate tax payable would inure to the benefit of the son, and inasmuch as there is no equitable apportionment of the tax, no deduction is allowable under section 2053(d).

(f) *Effective/applicability date.*—(1) The last sentence of paragraph (a) of this section applies to the estates of decedents dying on or after October 20, 2009, to which section 2058 is applicable.

(2) The other provisions of this section apply to the estates of decedents dying on or after October 20, 2009, to which section 2058 is not applicable. [Reg. § 20.2053-9.]

☐ [*T.D.* 6296, 6-23-58. *Amended by T.D.* 6526, 1-18-61 *and T.D.* 9468, 10-16-2009.]

[Reg. § 20.2053-10]

§ 20.2053-10. Deduction for certain foreign death taxes.—(a) *General rule.*—A deduction is allowed the estate of a decedent dying on or after July 1, 1955, under section 2053(d) for the amount of any estate, succession, legacy, or inheritance tax imposed by and actually paid to any foreign country, in respect of any property situated within such foreign country and included in the gross estate of a citizen or resident of the United States, upon a transfer by the decedent for charitable, etc., uses described in section 2055, but only if (1) the conditions stated in paragraph (b) of this section are met, and (2) an election is made in accordance with the provisions of paragraph(c) of this section. The determination of the country within which property is situated is made in accordance with the rules contained in sections 2104 and 2105 in determining whether property is situated within or without the United States. See section 2014(f) and § 20.2014-7 for the effect which the allowance of this deduction has upon the credit for foreign death taxes.

(b) *Condition for allowance of deduction.*— (1) The deduction is not allowed unless either—

(i) The entire decrease in the Federal estate tax resulting from the allowance of the deduction inures solely to the benefit of a charitable, etc., transferee described in section 2055, or

(ii) The Federal estate tax is equitably apportioned among all the transferees (including the decedent's surviving spouse and the charitable, etc., transferees) of property included in the decedent's gross estate.

For allowance of the deduction, it is sufficient if either of these conditions is satisfied. Thus, in a case where the entire decrease in Federal estate tax inures to the benefit of a charitable transferee, the deduction is allowable even though the Federal estate tax is not equitably apportioned among all the transferees of property included in the decedent's gross estate. Similarly, if the Federal estate tax is equitably apportioned among all the transferees of property included in the decedent's gross estate, the deduction is allowable even though a noncharitable transferee receives some benefit from the allowance of the deduction.

(2) For purposes of this paragraph, the Federal estate tax is considered to be equitably apportioned among all the transferees (including

the decedent's surviving spouse and the charitable, etc., transferees) of property included in the decedent's gross estate only if each transferee's share of the tax is based upon the net amount of his transfer subjected to the tax (taking into account any exemptions, credits, or deductions allowed by chapter 11). See examples (2) through (5) of paragraph (e) of § 20.2053-9.

(c) *Exercise of election.*—The election to take a deduction for a foreign death tax imposed upon a transfer for charitable, etc., uses shall be exercised by the executor by the filing of a written notification to that effect with the Commissioner of internal revenue in whose district the estate tax return for the decedent's estate was filed. An election to take the deduction for foreign death taxes is deemed to be a waiver of the right to claim a credit under a treaty with any foreign country for any tax or portion thereof claimed as a deduction under this section. The notification shall be filed before the expiration of the period of limitation for assessment provided in section 6501 (usually 3 years from the last day for filing the return). The election may be revoked by the executor by the filing of a written notification to that effect with the Commissioner at any time before the expiration of such period.

(d) *Amount of foreign death tax imposed upon a transfer.*—If a foreign death tax is imposed upon the transfer of the entire part of the decedent's estate subject to such tax and not upon the transfer of a particular share thereof, the foreign death tax imposed upon a transfer for charitable, etc., uses is deemed to be an amount, J, which bears the same ratio to K (the amount of the foreign death tax imposed with respect to the transfer of the entire part of the decedent's estate subject to such tax) as M (the value of the charitable, etc., transfer, reduced as provided in the next sentence) bears to N (the total value of the properties, interests, and benefits subjected to the foreign death tax received by all persons interested in the estate, reduced as provided in the last sentence of this paragraph). In arriving at amount M of the ratio, the value of the charitable, etc., transfer is reduced by the amount of any deduction or exclusion allowed with respect to such property in determining the amount of the foreign death tax. In arriving at amount N of the ratio, the total value of the properties, interests, and benefits subjected to foreign death tax received by all persons interested in the estate is reduced by the amount of all deductions and exclusions allowed in determining the amount of the foreign death tax on account of the nature of a beneficiary or a beneficiary's relationship to the decedent.

(e) *Effective/applicability date.*—This section applies to the estates of decedents dying on or after October 20, 2009. [Reg. § 20.2053-10.]

☐ [*T.D.* 6600, 5-28-62. *Amended by T.D.* 9468, 10-16-2009.]

[Reg. § 20.2054-1]

§ 20.2054-1. Deduction for losses from casualties or theft.—A deduction is allowed for losses incurred during the settlement of the estate arising from fires, storms, shipwrecks, or other casualties, or from theft, if the losses are not compensated for by insurance or otherwise. If the loss is partly compensated for, the excess of the loss over the compensation may be deducted. Losses which are not of the nature described are not deductible. In order to be deductible a loss must occur during the settlement of the estate. If a loss with respect to an asset occurs after its distribution to the distributee it may not be deducted. Notwithstanding the foregoing, no deduction is allowed under this section if the estate has waived its right to take such a deduction pursuant to the provisions of section 642(g) in order to permit its allowance for income tax purposes. See further § 1.642(g)-1. [Reg. § 20.2054-1.]

☐ [*T.D.* 6296, 6-23-58.]

[Reg. § 20.2055-1]

§ 20.2055-1. Deduction for transfers for public, charitable, and religious uses; in general.—(a) *General rule.*—A deduction is allowed under section 2055(a) from the gross estate of a decedent who was a citizen or resident of the United States at the time of his death for the value of property included in the decedent's gross estate and transferred by the decedent during his lifetime or by will—

(1) To or for the use of the United States, any State, Territory, any political subdivision thereof, or the District of Columbia, for exclusively public purposes;

(2) To or for the use of any corporation or association organized and operated exclusively for religious, charitable, scientific, literary, or educational purposes (including the encouragement of art and the prevention of cruelty to children or animals), if no part of the net earnings of the corporation or association inures to the benefit of any private stockholder or individual (other than as a legitimate object of such purposes), if the organization is not disqualified for tax exemption under section 501(c)(3) by reason of attempting to influence legislation, and if, in the case of transfers made after December 31, 1969, it does not participate in, or intervene in (including the publishing or distributing of statements), any political campaign on behalf of or in opposition to any candidate for public office;

(3) To a trustee or trustees, or a fraternal society, order, or association operating under the lodge system, if the transferred property is to be used exclusively for religious, charitable, scientific, literary, or educational purposes (or for the prevention of cruelty to children or animals), if no substantial part of the activities of such transferee is carrying on propaganda, or otherwise attempting, to influence legislation, and if, in the

case of transfers made after December 31, 1969, such transferee does not participate in, or intervene in (including the publishing or distributing of statements), any political campaign on behalf of any candidate for public office; or

(4) To or for the use of any veterans' organization incorporated by act of Congress, or of any of its departments, local chapters, or posts, no part of the net earnings of which inures to the benefit of any private shareholder or individual.

The deduction is not limited, in the case of estates of citizens or residents of the United States, to transfers to domestic corporations or associations, or to trustees for use within the United States.

Nor is the deduction subject to percentage limitations such as are applicable to the charitable deduction under the income tax. An organization will not be considered to meet the requirements of subparagraph (2) or (3) of this paragraph if such organization engages in any activity which would cause it to be classified as an "action" organization under paragraph (c)(3) of § 1.501(c)(3)-1 of this chapter (Income Tax Regulations). See § 20.2055-4 and § 20.2055-5 for rules relating to the disallowance of deductions to trusts and organizations which engage in certain prohibited transactions or whose governing instruments do not contain certain specified requirements.

(b) *Powers of appointment.*—(1) *General rule.*— A deduction is allowable under section 2055(b) for the value of property passing to or for the use of a transferee described in paragraph (a) of this section by the exercise, failure to exercise, release or lapse of a power of appointment by reason of which the property is includible in the decedent's gross estate under section 2041.

(2) *Certain bequests subject to power of appointment.*—For the allowance of a deduction in the case of a bequest in trust where the decedent's surviving spouse (i) was over 80 years of age at the date of decedent's death, (ii) was entitled for life to all of the net income from the trust, and (iii) had a power of appointment over the corpus of the trust exercisable by will in favor of, among others, a charitable organization, see section 2055(b)(2). See also section 6503(e) for suspension of the period of limitations for assessment or collection of any deficiency attributable to the allowance of the deduction.

(c) *Submission of evidence.*—In establishing the right of the estate to the deduction authorized by section 2055, the executor should submit the following with the return:

(1) A copy of any instrument in writing by which the decedent made a transfer of property in his lifetime the value of which is required by statute to be included in his gross estate, for which a deduction under section 2055 is claimed. If the instrument is of record the copy should be certified, and if not of record, the copy should be verified.

(2) A written statement by the executor containing a declaration that it is made under penalties of perjury and stating whether any action has been instituted to construe or to contest the decedent's will or any provision thereof affecting the charitable deduction claimed and whether, according to his information and belief, any such action is designed or contemplated.

The executor shall also submit such other documents or evidence as may be requested by the district director.

(d) *Cross references.*—(1) See section 2055(f) for certain cross references relating to section 2055.

(2) For treatment of bequests accepted by the Secretary of State or the Secretary of Commerce, for the purpose of organizing and holding an international conference to negotiate a Patent Corporation Treaty, as bequests to or for the use of the United States, see section 3 of Joint Resolution of December 24, 1969 (P.L. 91-160, 83 Stat. 443).

(3) For treatment of bequests accepted by the Secretary of the Department of Housing and Urban Development, for the purpose of aiding or facilitating the work of the Department, as bequests to or for the use of the United States, see section 7(k) of the Department of Housing and Urban Development Act (42 U.S.C. 3535), as added by section 905 of P.L. 91-609 (84 Stat. 1809).

(4) For treatment of certain property accepted by the Chairman of the Administrative Conference of the United States, for the purpose of aiding and facilitating the work of the Conference, as a devise or bequest to the United States, see 5 U.S.C. 575(c)(12), as added by section 1(b) of the Act of October 21, 1972 (Public Law 92-526, 86 Stat. 1048).

(5) For treatment of the Board for International Broadcasting as a corporation described in section 2055(a)(2), see section 7 of the Board for International Broadcasting Act of 1973 (Public Law 93-129, 87 Stat. 459). [Reg. § 20.2055-1.]

☐ [*T.D. 6296, 6-23-58. Amended by T.D. 7318, 7-10-74 and T.D. 8308, 8-30-90.*]

[Reg. § 20.2055-2]

§ 20.2055-2. Transfers not exclusively for charitable purposes.—(a) *Remainders and similar interests.*—If a trust is created or property is transferred for both a charitable and a private purpose, deduction may be taken of the value of the charitable beneficial interest only insofar as that interest is presently ascertainable, and hence severable from the noncharitable interest. Thus, in the case of decedents dying before January 1, 1970, if money or property is placed in trust to pay the income to an individual during his life, or for a term of years, and then to pay the principal to a charitable organization, the present value of the remainder is deductible. See paragraph (e) of this section for limitations applicable to decedents dying after December 31, 1969. See paragraph (f) of this section for rules relating to valuation of partial interests in property passing for charitable purposes.

(b) *Transfers subject to a condition or a power.*— (1) If, as of the date of a decedent's death, a transfer for charitable purposes is dependent upon the performance of some act or the happening of a precedent event in order that it might become effective, no deduction is allowable unless the possibility that the charitable transfer will not become effective is so remote as to be negligible. If an estate or interest has passed to, or is vested in, charity at the time of a decedent's death and the estate or interest would be defeated by the subsequent performance of some act or the happening of some event, the possibility of occurrence of which appeared at the time of the decedent's death to be so remote as to be negligible, the deduction is allowable. If the legatee, devisee, donee, or trustee is empowered to divert the property or fund, in whole or in part, to a use or purpose which would have rendered it, to the extent that it is subject to such power, not deductible had it been directly so bequeathed, devised, or given by the decedent, the deduction will be limited to that portion, if any, of the property or fund which is exempt from an exercise of the power.

(2) The application of this paragraph may be illustrated by the following examples:

Example (1). In 1965, A dies leaving certain property in trust in which charity is to receive the income for the life of his widow. The assets placed in trust by the decedent consist of stock in a corporation the fiscal policies of which are controlled by the decedent and his family. The trustees of the trust and the remaindermen are members of the decedent's family, and the governing instrument contains no adequate guarantee of the requisite income to the charitable organization. Under such circumstances, no deduction will be allowed. Similarly, if the trustees are not members of the decedent's family but have no power to sell or otherwise dispose of the closely held stock, or otherwise insure the requisite enjoyment of income to the charitable organization, no deduction will be allowed.

Example (2). C dies leaving a tract of land to a city government for as long as the land is used by the city for a public park. If the city accepts the tract and if, on the date of C's death, the possibility that the city will not use the land for a public park is so remote as to be negligible, a deduction will be allowed.

(c) *Disclaimers.*—(1) *Decedents dying after December 31, 1976.*—In the case of a bequest, devise, or transfer made by a decedent dying after December 31, 1976, the amount of a bequest, devise or transfer for which a deduction is allowable under section 2055 includes an interest which

falls into the bequest, devise or transfer as the result of either—

(i) A qualified disclaimer (see section 2518 and the corresponding regulations for rules relating to a qualified disclaimer), or

(ii) The complete termination of a power to consume, invade, or appropriate property for the benefit of an individual by reason of the death of such individual or for any other reason, if the termination occurs within the period of time (including extensions) for filing the decedent's Federal estate tax return and before such power has been exercised.

(2) *Decedents dying before January 1, 1977.*— In the case of a bequest, devise or transfer made by a decedent dying before January 1, 1977, the amount of a bequest, devise or transfer for which a deduction is allowable under section 2055 includes an interest which falls into the bequest, devise or transfer as a result of either—

(i) A disclaimer of a bequest, devise, transfer, or power, if the disclaimer is made within 9 months (15 months if the decedent died on or before December 31, 1970) after the decedent's death (the period of time within which the estate tax return must be filed under section 6075) or within any extension of time for filing the return granted pursuant to section 6081, and the disclaimer is irrevocable at the time the deduction is allowed, or

(ii) The complete termination of a power to consume, invade, or appropriate property for the benefit of an individual (whether the termination occurs by reason of the death of the individual, or otherwise) if the termination occurs within the period described in paragraph (c)(2)(i) of this section and before the power has been exercised. Ordinarily, a disclaimer made by a person not under any legal disability will be considered irrevocable when filed with the probate court. A disclaimer is a complete and unqualified refusal to accept the rights to which one is entitled. Thus, if a beneficiary uses these rights for his own purposes, as by receiving a consideration for his formal disclaimer, he has not refused the rights to which he was entitled. There can be no disclaimer after an acceptance of these rights, expressly or impliedly. The disclaimer of a power is to be distinguished from the release or exercise of a power. The release or exercise of a power by the donee of the power in favor of a person or object described in paragraph (a) of §20.2055-1 does not result in any deduction under section 2055 in the estate of the donor of a power (but see paragraph (b)(1) of §20.2055-1 with respect to the donee's estate).

(d) *Payments in compromise.*—If a charitable organization assigns or surrenders a part of a transfer to it pursuant to a compromise agreement in settlement of a controversy, the amount so assigned or surrendered is not deductible as a transfer to that charitable organization.

(e) *Limitation applicable to decedents dying after December 31, 1969.*—(1) *Disallowance of deduction.*—(i) *In general.*—In the case of decedents dying after December 31, 1969, where an interest in property passes or has passed from the decedent for charitable purposes and an interest (other than an interest which is extinguished upon the decedent's death) in the same property passes or has passed from the decedent for private purposes (for less than an adequate and full consideration in money or money's worth) after October 9, 1969, no deduction is allowed under section 2055 for the value of the interest which passes or has passed for charitable purposes unless the interest in property is a deductible interest described in subparagraph (2) of this paragraph. The principles of section 2056 and the regulations thereunder shall apply for purposes of determining under this subparagraph whether an interest in property passes or has passed from the decedent. If however, as of the date of a decedent's death, a transfer for a private purpose is dependent upon the performance of some act or the happening of a precedent event in order that it might become effective, an interest in property will be considered to pass for a private purpose unless the possibility of occurrence of such act or event is so remote as to be negligible. The application of this subparagraph may be illustrated by the following examples, in each of which it is assumed that the interest in property which passes for private purposes does not pass for an adequate and full consideration in money or money's worth:

Example (1). In 1973, H creates a trust which is to pay the income of the trust to W for her life, the reversionary interest in the trust being retained by H. H predeceases W in 1975. H's will provides that the residue of his estate (including the reversionary interest in the trust) is to be transferred to charity. For purposes of this paragraph (e)(1)(i), interests in the same property have passed from H for charitable purposes and for private purposes.

Example (2). In 1973, H creates a trust which is to pay the income of the trust to W for her life and upon termination of the life estate to transfer the remainder to S. S predeceases W in 1975. S's will provides that the residue of his estate (including the remainder interest in the trust) is to be transferred to charity. For purposes of this paragraph (e)(1)(i), interests in the same property have not passed from H or S for charitable purposes and for private purposes.

Example (3). H transfers Blackacre to A by gift, reserving the right to the rentals of Blackacre for a term of 20 years. H dies within the 20-year term, bequeathing the right to the remaining rentals to charity. For purposes of this paragraph (e)(1)(i) the term "property" refers to Blackacre, and the right to rentals from Blackacre consist of an interest in Blackacre. An interest in Blackacre has passed from H for charitable purposes and for private purposes.

Example (4). H bequeaths the residue of his estate in trust for the benefit of A and a charity. An annuity of $5,000 a year is to be paid to charity for 20 years. Upon termination of the 20-year term the corpus is to be distributed to A if living. However, if A should die during the 20-year term, the corpus is to be distributed to charity upon termination of the term. An interest in the residue of the estate has passed from H for charitable purposes. In addition, an interest in the residue of the estate has passed from H for private purposes, unless the possibility that A will survive the 20-year term is so remote as to be negligible.

Example (5). H bequeaths the residue of his estate in trust. Under the terms of the trust an annuity of $5,000 a year is to be paid to charity for 20 years. Upon termination of the term, the corpus is to pass to such of A's children and their issue as A may appoint. However, if A should die during the 20-year term without exercising the power of appointment, the corpus is to be distributed to charity upon termination of the term. Since the possible appointees include private persons, an interest in the residue of the estate is considered to have passed from H for private purposes.

Example (6). H devises Blackacre to X Charity. Under applicable local law, W, H's widow, is entitled to elect a dower interest in Blackacre. W elects to take her dower interest in Blackacre. For purposes of this paragraph (e)(1)(i), interests in the same property have passed from H for charitable purposes and for private purposes. If, however, W does not elect to take her dower interest in Blackacre, then, for purposes of this paragraph (e)(1)(i), interests in the same property have not passed from H for charitable purposes and for private purposes.

(ii) *Works of art and copyrights treated as separate properties.*—(a) *In general.*—For purposes of paragraphs (e)(1)(i) and (e)(2) of this section, in the case of decedents dying after December 31, 1981, if a decedent makes a qualified contribution of a work of art, the work of art and the copyright on such work of art shall be treated as separate properties. Thus, a deduction is allowable under section 2055 for a qualified contribution of a work of art, whether or not the related copyright is simultaneously transferred to a charitable organization.

(b) *Work of art defined.*—For purposes of paragraph (e)(1)(ii)(a) of this section, the term "work of art" means any tangible personal property with respect to which a copyright exists under Federal law.

(c) *Qualified contribution defined.*—For purposes of paragraph (e)(1)(ii)(a) of this section, the term "qualified contribution" means any transfer of property to a qualified organization (as defined in paragraph (e)(1)(ii)(d) of this section) if the use of the property by the organiza-

Reg. § 20.2055-2(e)(1)(ii)(c)

tion is related to the purpose or function constituting the basis for its exemption under section 501. The rules contained in §1.170A-4 (b)(3) shall apply in determining if the use of property by an organization is related to such purpose or function.

(d) Qualified organization defined.—For purposes of paragraph (e)(1)(ii)(c) of this section, the term "qualified organization" means any organization described in section 501(c)(3) other than a private foundation (as defined in section 509). A private operating foundation (as defined in section 4042(j)(3)) shall be considered a qualified organization under this paragraph.

(e) Examples.—The application of paragraphs (e)(1)(i) and (e)(1)(ii)(a) through (d) of this section may be illustrated by the following examples:

Example (1). A, an artist, died in 1983. A work of art created by A and the copyright interest in that work of art were included in A's estate. Under the terms of A's will, the work of art is transferred to X charity, the only charitable beneficiary under A's will. X has no suitable use for the work of art and sells it. It is determined under the rules of §1.170A-4 (b)(3) that the property is put to an unrelated use by X charity. Therefore, the rule of paragraph (e)(1)(ii)(a), which treats works of art and their copyrights as separate properties, does not apply because the transfer of the work of art to X is not a qualified contribution. To determine whether paragraph (e)(1)(i) of this section applies to disallow a deduction under section 2055, it must be determined which interests are treated as passing to X under local law.

(i) If under local law A's will is treated as fully transferring both the work of art and the copyright interest to X, then paragraph (e)(1)(i) of this section does not apply to disallow a deduction under section 2055 for the value of the work of art and the copyright interest.

(ii) If under local law A's will is treated as transferring only the work of art to X, and the copyright interest is treated as part of the residue of the estate, no deduction is allowable under section 2055 to A's estate for the value of the work of art because the transfer of the work of art is not a qualified contribution and paragraph (e)(1)(i) of this section applies to disallow the deduction.

Example (2). B, a collector of art, purchased a work of art from an artist who retained the copyright interest. B died in 1983. Under the terms of B's will the work of art is given to Y charity. Since B did not own the copyright interest, paragraph (e)(1)(i) of this section does not apply to disallow a deduction under section 2055 for the value of the work of art, regardless of whether or not the contribution is a qualified contribution under paragraph (e)(1)(ii)(c) of this section.

(iii) The rule in paragraphs (e)(2)(vi)(a) and (e)(2)(vii)(a) of this section that guaranteed annuity interests or unitrust interests, respectively, may be payable for a specified term of years or for the life or lives of only certain individuals is generally effective in the case of transfers pursuant to wills and revocable trusts when the decedent dies on or after April 4, 2000. Two exceptions from the application of this rule in paragraphs (e)(2)(vi)(a) and(e)(2)(vii)(a) of this section are provided in the case of transfers pursuant to a will or revocable trust executed before April 4, 2000. One exception is for a decedent who dies on or before July 5, 2001, without having republished the will (or amended the trust) by codicil or otherwise. The other exception is for a decedent who was on April 4, 2000, under a mental disability that prevented a change in the disposition of the decedent's property, and who either does not regain competence to dispose of such property before the date of death, or dies prior to the later of 90 days after the date on which the decedent first regains competence, or July 5, 2001, without having republished the will (or amended the trust) by codicil or otherwise. If a guaranteed annuity interest or unitrust interest created pursuant to a will or revocable trust of a decedent dying on or after April 4, 2000, uses an individual other than one permitted in paragraphs (e)(2)(vi)(a) and (e)(2)(vii)(a) of this section, and the interest does not qualify for this transitional relief, the interest may be reformed into a lead interest payable for a specified term of years. The term of years is determined by taking the factor for valuing the annuity or unitrust interest for the named individual measuring life and identifying the term of years (rounded up to the next whole year) that corresponds to the equivalent term of years factor for an annuity or unitrust interest. For example, in the case of an annuity interest payable for the life of an individual age 40 at the time of the transfer on or after May 1, 2009, assuming an interest rate of 7.4 percent under section 7520, the annuity factor from column 1 of Table S(7.4), contained in IRS Publication 1457, "Actuarial Valuations Version 3A", for the life of an individual age 40 is 12.1519 (1.000000 minus .10076, divided by .074). Based on Table B(7.4), contained in Publication 1457, "Actuarial Valuations Version 3A", the factor 12.1519 corresponds to a term of years between 32 and 33 years. Accordingly, the annuity interest must be reformed into an interest payable for a term of 33 years. A judicial reformation must be commenced prior to the later of July 5, 2001, or the date prescribed by section 2055(e)(3)(C)(iii). Any judicial reformation must be completed within a reasonable time after it is commenced. A non-judicial reformation is permitted if effective under state law, provided it is completed by the date on which a judicial reformation must be commenced. In the alternative, if a court, in a proceeding that is commenced on or before July 5, 2001, declares any transfer made pursuant to a will or revocable trust where the

Reg. §20.2055-2(e)(1)(ii)(d)

decedent dies on or after April 4, 2000, and on or before March 6, 2001, null and void ab initio, the Internal Revenue Service will treat such transfers in a manner similar to that described in section 2055(e)(3)(J).

* * *

(2) *Deductible interests.*—A deductible interest for purposes of subparagraph (1) of this paragraph is a charitable interest in property where—

(i) *Undivided portion of decedent's entire interest.*—The charitable interest is an undivided portion, not in trust, of the decedent's entire interest in property. An undivided portion of a decedent's entire interest in property must consist of a fraction or percentage of each and every substantial interest or right owned by the decedent in such property and must extend over the entire term of the decedent's interest in such property and in other property into which such property is converted. For example, if the decedent transferred a life estate in an office building to his wife for her life and retained a reversionary interest in the office building, the devise by the decedent of one-half of that reversionary interest to charity while his wife is still alive will not be considered the transfer of a deductible interest; because an interest in the same property has already passed from the decedent for private purposes, the reversionary interest will not be considered the decedent's entire interest in the property. If, on the other hand, the decedent had been given a life estate in Blackacre for the life of his wife and the decedent had no other interest in Blackacre at any time during his life, the devise by the decedent of one-half of that life estate to charity would be considered the transfer of a deductible interest; because the life estate would be considered the decedent's entire interest in the property, the devise would be of an undivided portion of such entire interest. An undivided portion of a decedent's entire interest in the property includes an interest in property whereby the charity is given the right, as a tenant in common with the decedent's devisee or legatee, to possession, dominion, and control of the property for a portion of each year appropriate to its interest in such property. However, except as provided in paragraphs (e)(2)(ii), (iii), and (iv) of this section, for purposes of this subdivision a charitable contribution of an interest in property not in trust where the decedent transfers some specific rights to one party and transfers other substantial rights to another party will not be considered a contribution of an undivided portion of the decedent's entire interest in property. A bequest to charity made on or before December 17, 1980, of an open space easement in gross in perpetuity shall be considered the transfer to charity of an undivided portion of the decedent's entire interest in the property. For the definition of an open space easement in gross in perpetuity, see §1.170A-7(b)(1)(ii) of this chapter (Income Tax Regulations).

(ii) *Remainder interest in personal residence.*—The charitable interest is a remainder interest, not in trust, in a personal residence. Thus, for example, if the decedent devises to charity a remainder interest in a personal residence and bequeaths to his surviving spouse a life estate in such property, the value of the remainder interest is deductible under section 2055. For purposes of this subdivision, the term "personal residence" means any property which was used by the decedent as his personal residence even though it was not used as his principal residence. For example, a decedent's vacation home may be a personal residence for purposes of this subdivision. The term "personal residence" also includes stock owned by the decedent as a tenant-stockholder in a cooperative housing corporation (as those terms are defined in section 216(b)(1) and (2)) if the dwelling which the decedent was entitled to occupy as such stockholder was used by him as his personal residence.

(iii) *Remainder interest in a farm.*—The charitable interest is a remainder interest, not in trust, in a farm. Thus, for example, if the decedent devises to charity a remainder interest in a farm and bequeaths to his daughter a life estate in such property, the value of the remainder interest is deductible under section 2055. For purposes of this subdivision, the term "farm" means any land used by the decedent or his tenant for the production of crops, fruits, or other agricultural products or for the sustenance of livestock. The term "livestock" includes cattle, hogs, horses, mules, donkeys, sheep, goats, captive fur-bearing animals, chickens, turkeys, pigeons, and other poultry. A farm includes the improvements thereon.

(iv) *Qualified conservation contribution.*—The charitable interest is a qualified conservation contribution. For the definition of a qualified conservation contribution, see §1.170A-14.

(v) *Charitable remainder trusts and pooled income funds.*—The charitable interest is a remainder interest in a trust which is a charitable remainder annuity trust, as defined in section 664(d)(1) and §1.664-2 of this chapter; a charitable remainder unitrust, as defined in section 664(d)(2) and (3) and §1.664-3 of this chapter; or a pooled income fund, as defined in section 642(c)(5) and §1.642(c)-5 of this chapter. The charitable organization to or for the use of which the remainder interest passes must meet the requirements of both section 2055(a) and section 642(c)(5)(A), section 664(d)(1)(C), or section 664(d)(2)(C), whichever applies. For example, the charitable organization to which the remainder interest in a charitable remainder annuity trust passes may not be a foreign corporation.

(vi) *Guaranteed annuity interest.*—(a) The charitable interest is a guaranteed annuity interest, whether or not such interest is in trust. For purposes of this subdivision (vi), the term "guaranteed annuity interest" means the right pursuant to the instrument of transfer to receive a guaranteed annuity. A guaranteed annuity is an arrangement under which a determinable amount is paid periodically, but not less often than annually, for a specified term of years or for the life or lives of certain individuals, each of whom must be living at the date of death of the decedent and can be ascertained at such date. Only one or more of the following individuals may be used as measuring lives: the decedent's spouse, and an individual who, with respect to all remainder beneficiaries (other than charitable organizations described in section 170, 2055, or 2522), is either a lineal ancestor or the spouse of a lineal ancestor of those beneficiaries. A trust will satisfy the requirement that all noncharitable remainder beneficiaries are lineal descendants of the individual who is the measuring life, or that individual's spouse, if there is less than a 15% probability that individuals who are not lineal descendants will receive any trust corpus. This probability must be computed, based on the current applicable Life Table contained in § 20.2031-7, as of the date of the decedent's death taking into account the interests of all primary and contingent remainder beneficiaries who are living at that time. An interest payable for a specified term of years can qualify as a guaranteed annuity interest even if the governing instrument contains a savings clause intended to ensure compliance with a rule against perpetuities. The savings clause must utilize a period for vesting of 21 years after the deaths of measuring lives who are selected to maximize, rather than limit, the term of the trust. The rule in this paragraph that a charitable interest may be payable for the life or lives of only certain specified individuals does not apply in the case of a charitable guaranteed annuity interest payable under a charitable remainder trust described in section 664. An amount is determinable if the exact amount which must be paid under the conditions specified in the instrument of transfer can be ascertained as of the appropriate valuation date. For example, the amount to be paid may be a stated sum for a term of years, or for the life of the decedent's spouse, at the expiration of which it may be changed by a specified amount, but it may not be redetermined by reference to a fluctuating index such as the cost of living index. In further illustration, the amount to be paid may be expressed in terms of a fraction or a percentage of the net fair market value, as finally determined for Federal estate tax purposes, of the residue of the estate on the appropriate valuation date, or it may be expressed in terms of a fraction or percentage of the cost of living index on the appropriate valuation date.

(b) A charitable interest is a guaranteed annuity interest only if it is a guaranteed annuity interest in every respect. For example, if the charitable interest is the right to receive from a trust each year a payment equal to the lesser of a sum certain or a fixed percentage of the net fair market value of the trust assets, determined annually, such interest is not a guaranteed annuity interest.

(c) Where a charitable interest in the form of a guaranteed annuity interest is not in trust, the interest will be considered a guaranteed annuity interest only if it is to be paid by an insurance company or by an organization regularly engaged in issuing annuity contracts.

(d) Where a charitable interest in the form of a guaranteed annuity interest is in trust, the governing instrument of the trust may provide that income of the trust which is in excess of the amount required to pay the guaranteed annuity interest shall be paid to or for the use of a charity. Nevertheless, the amount of the deduction under section 2055 shall be limited to the fair market value of the guaranteed annuity interest as determined under paragraph (f)(2)(iv) of this section.

(e) Where a charitable interest in the form of a guaranteed annuity interest is in trust and the present value, on the appropriate valuation date, of all the income interests for a charitable purpose exceeds 60 percent of the aggregate fair market value of all amounts in such trust (after the payment of estate taxes and all other liabilities), the charitable interest will not be considered a guaranteed annuity interest unless the governing instrument of the trust prohibits both the acquisition and the retention of assets which would give rise to a tax under section 4944 if the trustee had acquired such assets.

(f) Where a charitable interest in the form of a guaranteed annuity interest is in trust, the charitable interest generally is not a guaranteed annuity interest if any amount may be paid by the trust for a private purpose before the expiration of all the charitable annuity interests. There are two exceptions to this general rule. First, the charitable interest is a guaranteed annuity interest if the amount payable for a private purpose is in the form of a guaranteed annuity interest and the trust's governing instrument does not provide for any preference or priority in the payment of the private annuity as opposed to the charitable annuity. Second, the charitable interest is a guaranteed annuity interest if under the trust's governing instrument the amount that may be paid for a private purpose is payable only from a group of assets that are devoted exclusively to private purposes and to which section 4947(a)(2) is inapplicable by reason of section 4947(a)(2)(B). For purposes of this paragraph (e)(2)(vi)(f), an amount is not paid for a private purpose if it is paid for an adequate and full consideration in money or money's worth. See § 53.4947-1(c) of this chapter for rules relating to the inapplicability of section 4947(a)(2) to segregated amounts in a split-interest trust.

(g) Neither the requirement in (e) of this subdivision (v) for a prohibition in the governing instrument against the retention of assets which would give rise to a tax under section 4944 if the trustee had acquired the assets nor the provisions of (f) of this subdivision (vi) shall apply to—

(1) A trust executed on or before May 21, 1972, if—

(i) The trust is irrevocable on such date,

(ii) The trust is revocable on such date and the decedent dies within 3 years after such date without having amended any dispositive provision of the trust after such date, or

(iii) The trust is revocable on such date and no dispositive provision of the trust is amended within a period ending 3 years after such date and the decedent is, at the end of such 3-year period and at all times thereafter, under a mental disability (as defined in § 1.642(c)-2(b)(3)(ii) of this chapter) to amend the trust, or

(2) A will executed on or before May 21, 1972, if—

(i) The testator dies within 3 years after such date without having amended any dispositive provision of the will after such date, by codicil or otherwise,

(ii) The testator at no time after such date has the right to change the provisions of the will which pertain to the trust, or

(iii) No dispositive provision of the will is amended by the decedent, by codicil or otherwise, within a period ending 3 years after such date and the decedent is, at the end of such 3-year period and at all times thereafter, under a mental disability (as defined in § 1.642(c)-2(b)(3)(ii) of this chapter) to amend the will by codicil or otherwise.

(h) For purposes of this subdivision (vi) and paragraph (f) of this section, the term "appropriate valuation date" means the date of death or the alternate valuation date determined pursuant to an election under section 2032.

(i) For rules relating to certain governing instrument requirements and to the imposition of certain excise taxes where the guaranteed annuity interest is in trust and for rules governing payment of private income interests by split-interest trusts, see section 4947(a)(2) and (b)(3)(A), and the regulations thereunder.

(vii) *Unitrust interest.*—(a) The charitable interest is a unitrust interest, whether or not such interest is in trust. For purposes of this subdivision (vii), the term "unitrust interest" means the right pursuant to the instrument of transfer to receive payment, not less often than annually, of a fixed percentage of the net fair market value, determined annually, of the property which funds the unitrust interest. In computing the net fair market value of the property which funds the unitrust interest, all assets and liabilities shall be taken into account without regard to whether particular items are taken into account in deter-

mining the income from the property. The net fair market value of the property which funds the unitrust interest may be determined on any one date during the year or by taking the average of valuations made on more than one date during the year, provided that the same valuation date or dates and valuation methods are used each year. Where the charitable interest is a unitrust interest to be paid by a trust and the governing instrument of the trust does not specify the valuation date or dates, the trustee shall select such date or dates and shall indicate his selection on the first return on Form 1041 which the trust is required to file. Payments under a unitrust interest may be paid for a specified term of years or for the life or lives of certain individuals, each of whom must be living at the date of death of the decedent and can be ascertained at such date. Only one or more of the following individuals may be used as measuring lives: the decedent's spouse, and an individual who, with respect to all remainder beneficiaries (other than charitable organizations described in section 170, 2055, or 2522), is either a lineal ancestor or the spouse of a lineal ancestor of those beneficiaries. A trust will satisfy the requirement that all noncharitable remainder beneficiaries are lineal descendants of the individual who is the measuring life, or that individual's spouse, if there is less than a 15% probability that individuals who are not lineal descendants will receive any trust corpus. This probability must be computed, based on the current applicable Life Table contained in § 20.2031-7, as of the date of the decedent's death taking into account the interests of all primary and contingent remainder beneficiaries who are living at that time. An interest payable for a specified term of years can qualify as a unitrust interest even if the governing instrument contains a savings clause intended to ensure compliance with a rule against perpetuities. The savings clause must utilize a period for vesting of 21 years after the deaths of measuring lives who are selected to maximize, rather than limit, the term of the trust. The rule in this paragraph that a charitable interest may be payable for the life or lives of only certain specified individuals does not apply in the case of a charitable unitrust interest payable under a charitable remainder trust described in section 664.

(b) A charitable interest is a unitrust interest only if it is a unitrust interest in every respect. For example, if the charitable interest is the right to receive from a trust each year a payment equal to the lesser of a sum certain or a fixed percentage of the net fair market value of the trust assets, determined annually, such interest is not a unitrust interest.

(c) Where a charitable interest in the form of a unitrust interest is not in trust, the interest will be considered a unitrust interest only if it is to be paid by an insurance company or by an organization regularly engaged in issuing interests otherwise meeting the requirements of a unitrust interest.

(d) Where a charitable interest in the form of a unitrust interest is in trust, the governing instrument of the trust may provide that income of the trust which is in excess of the amount required to pay the unitrust interest shall be paid to or for the use of a charity. Nevertheless, the amount of the deduction under section 2055 shall be limited to the fair market value of the unitrust interest as determined under paragraph (f)(2)(v) of this section.

(e) Where a charitable interest in the form of a unitrust interest is in trust, the charitable interest generally is not a unitrust interest if any amount may be paid by the trust for a private purpose before the expiration of all the charitable unitrust interests. There are two exceptions to this general rule. First, the charitable interest is a unitrust interest if the amount payable for a private purpose is in the form of a unitrust interest and the trust's governing instrument does not provide for any preference or priority in the payment of the private unitrust interest as opposed to the charitable unitrust interest. Second, the charitable interest is a unitrust interest if under the trust's governing instrument the amount that may be paid for a private purpose is payable only from a group of assets that are devoted exclusively to private purposes and to which section 4947(a)(2) is inapplicable by reason of section 4947(a)(2)(B). For purposes of this paragraph (e)(2)(vii)(e), an amount is not paid for a private purpose if it is paid for an adequate and full consideration in money or money's worth. See §53.4947-1(c) of this chapter for rules relating to the inapplicability of section 4947(a)(2) to segregated amounts in a split-interest trust.

(f) For rules relating to certain governing instrument requirements and to the imposition of certain excise taxes where the unitrust interest is in trust and for rules governing payment of private income interests by a split-interest trust, see section 4947(a)(2) and (b)(3)(A), and the regulations thereunder.

(3) *Effective/applicability date.*—The provisions of this paragraph apply only in the case of decedents dying after December 31, 1969, except that they do not apply—

(i) In the case of property passing under the terms of a will executed on or before October 9, 1969—

(a) If the decedent dies after October 9, 1969, but before October 9, 1972, without having amended any dispositive provision of the will after October 9, 1969, by codicil or otherwise,

(b) If the decedent dies after October 9, 1969, and at no time after that date had the right to change the portions of the will which pertain to the passing of the property to, or for the use of, an organization described in section 2055(a), or

(c) If no dispositive provision of the will is amended by the decedent, by codicil or otherwise, after October 9, 1969, and before October 9, 1972, and the decedent is on October 9, 1972, and at all times thereafter under a mental disability (as defined in §1.642(c)-2(b)(3)(ii) of this chapter (Income Tax Regulations)) to amend the will by codicil or otherwise, or

(ii) In the case of property transferred in trust on or before October 9, 1969—

(a) If the decedent dies after October 9, 1969, but before October 9, 1972, without having amended, after October 9, 1969, any dispositive provision of the instrument governing the disposition of the property,

(b) If the property transferred was an irrevocable interest to, or for the use of, an organization described in section 2055(a), or

(c) If no dispositive provision of the instrument governing the disposition of the property is amended by the decedent after October 9, 1969, and before October 9, 1972, and the decedent is on October 9, 1972, and at all times thereafter under a mental disability (as defined in §1.642(c)-2(b)(3)(ii) of this chapter) to change the disposition of the property, and

(iii) The rule in paragraphs (e)(2)(vi)(a) and (e)(2)(vii)(a) of this section that guaranteed annuity interests or unitrust interests, respectively, may be payable for a specified term of years or for the life or lives of only certain individuals is generally effective in the case of transfers pursuant to wills and revocable trusts when the decedent dies on or after April 4, 2000. Two exceptions from the application of this rule in paragraphs (e)(2)(vi)(a) and(e)(2)(vii)(a) of this section are provided in the case of transfers pursuant to a will or revocable trust executed before April 4, 2000. One exception is for a decedent who dies on or before July 5, 2001, without having republished the will (or amended the trust) by codicil or otherwise. The other exception is for a decedent who was on April 4, 2000, under a mental disability that prevented a change in the disposition of the decedent's property, and who either does not regain competence to dispose of such property before the date of death, or dies prior to the later of 90 days after the date on which the decedent first regains competence, or July 5, 2001, without having republished the will (or amended the trust) by codicil or otherwise. If a guaranteed annuity interest or unitrust interest created pursuant to a will or revocable trust of a decedent dying on or after April 4, 2000, uses an individual other than one permitted in paragraphs (e)(2)(vi)(a) and (e)(2)(vii)(a) of this section, and the interest does not qualify for this transitional relief, the interest may be reformed into a lead interest payable for a specified term of years. The term of years is determined by taking the factor for valuing the annuity or unitrust interest for the named individual measuring life and identifying the term of years (rounded up to the next whole year) that corresponds to the equivalent term of years factor for an annuity or unitrust interest. For example, in the case of an annuity interest payable for the life of an individual age 40 at the time of the transfer on or after May 1, 2009, assuming an interest rate of 7.4 percent under section 7520, the annuity factor from column 1 of Table S(7.4), contained in IRS Publication 1457, "Actuarial Valuations Version 3A", for the life of an individual age 40 is 12.1519 (1.000000 minus .10076, divided by .074). Based on Table B(7.4), contained in Publication 1457, "Actuarial Valuations Version 3A", the factor 12.1519 corresponds to a term of years between 32 and 33 years. Accordingly, the annuity interest must be reformed into an interest payable for a term of 33 years. A judicial reformation must be commenced prior to the later of July 5, 2001, or the date prescribed by section 2055(e)(3)(C)(iii). Any judicial reformation must be completed within a reasonable time after it is commenced. A non-judicial reformation is permitted if effective under state law, provided it is completed by the date on which a judicial reformation must be commenced. In the alternative, if a court, in a proceeding that is commenced on or before July 5, 2001, declares any transfer made pursuant to a will or revocable trust where the decedent dies on or after April 4, 2000, and on or before March 6, 2001, null and void ab initio, the Internal Revenue Service will treat such transfers in a manner similar to that described in section 2055(e)(3)(J).

(4) *Amendment of dispositive provisions.*—For purposes of subparagraphs (2) and (3) of this paragraph, an amendment shall generally be considered as one which amends the dispositive provisions of a will or trust if it results in a change in the persons to whom the funds are to be given or makes changes in the conditions under which the funds are given. Examples of amendments which do not amend the dispositive provisions of a will or trust include the substitution of one fiduciary for another to act in the capacity of executor or trustee and the change in the name of a legatee or beneficiary by reason of the legatee's or beneficiary's marriage. On the other hand, examples of amendments which do amend the dispositive provisions of a will or trust include an increase or decrease in the amount of a general bequest, an amendment which increases or decreases the power of a trustee to determine an allocation of income or corpus in such a way as to change the beneficiaries of the funds or a beneficiary's share of the funds, or a change in the allocation of, or in the right to allocate, receipts and expenditures between income and principal in such a way as to change the beneficiaries of the funds or a beneficiary's share of the funds.

(5) *Amendment of wills providing for pour-over into trusts.*—For purposes of subparagraphs (2) and (3) of this paragraph, an amendment of a dispositive provision of a trust to which assets are to be transferred under a will shall be considered a dispositive amendment of such will.

(f) *Valuation of charitable interest.*—(1) *In general.*—The amount of the deduction in the case of a contribution of a partial interest in property to which this section applies is the fair market value of the partial interest at the appropriate valuation date, as defined in paragraph (e)(2)(vi)(*h*) of this section. The fair market value of an annuity, life estate, term for years, remainder, reversion, or unitrust interest is its present value.

(2) *Certain decedents dying after July 31, 1969.*—In the case of a transfer of an interest described in subdivision (v), (vi), or (vii) of paragraph (e)(2) of this section by decedents dying after July 31, 1969, the present value of such interest is to be determined under the following rules:

(i) The present value of a remainder interest in a charitable remainder annuity trust is to be determined under § 1.664-2(c) of this chapter (Income Tax Regulations).

(ii) The present value of a remainder interest in a charitable remainder unitrust is to be determined under § 1.664-4 of this chapter.

(iii) The present value of a remainder interest in a pooled income fund is to be determined under § 1.642(c)-6 of this chapter.

(iv) The present value of a guaranteed annuity interest described in paragraph (e)(2)(vi) of this section is to be determined under § 20.2031-7 or, for certain prior periods, § 20.2031-7A, except that, if the annuity is issued by a company regularly engaged in the sale of annuities, the present value is to be determined under § 20.2031-8. If by reason of all the conditions and circumstances surrounding a transfer of an income interest in property in trust it appears that the charity may not receive the beneficial enjoyment of the interest, a deduction will be allowed under section 2055 only for the minimum amount it is evident the charity will receive.

Example (1). In 1975, B dies bequeathing $20,000 in trust with the requirement that a designated charity be paid a guaranteed annuity interest (as defined in paragraph (e)(2)(vi) of this section) of $4,100 a year, payable annually at the end of each year, for a period of 6 years and that the remainder be paid to his children. The fair market value of an annuity of $4,100 a year for a period of 6 years is $20,160.93 ($4,100 × 4.9173), as determined under Table B in § 20.2031-7A(d). The deduction with respect to the guaranteed annuity interest will be limited to $20,000, which is the minimum amount it is evident the charity will receive.

Example (2). In 1975, C dies bequeathing $40,000 in trust with the requirement that D, an individual, and X Charity be paid simultaneously guaranteed annuity interests (as defined in paragraph (e)(2)(vi) of this section) of $5,000 a year each, payable annually at the end of each year, for a period of 5 years and that the remainder be paid to C's children. The fair market value of two annuities of $5,000 each a year for a period of 5 years is $42,124 ([$5,000 × 4.2124] × 2), as determined under Table B in §20.2031-7A(d). The trust instrument provides that in the event the trust fund is insufficient to pay both annuities in a given year, the trust fund will be evenly divided between the charitable and private annuitants. The deduction with respect to the charitable annuity will be limited to $20,000, which is the minimum amount it is evident the charity will receive.

Example (3). In 1975, D dies bequeathing $65,000 in trust with the requirement that a guaranteed annuity interest (as defined in paragraph (e)(2)(vi) of this section) of $5,000 a year, payable annually at the end of each year, be paid to Y Charity for a period of 10 years and that a guaranteed annuity interest (as defined in paragraph (e)(2)(vi) of this section) of $5,000 a year, payable annually at the end of each year, be paid to W, his widow, aged 62, for 10 years or until her prior death. The annuities are to be paid simultaneously, and the remainder is to be paid to D's children. The fair market value of the private annuity is $33,877 ($5,000 × 6.7754), as determined pursuant to §20.2031-7A(c) and by the use of factors involving one life and a term of years as published in Publication 723A (12-70). The fair market value of the charitable annuity is $36,800.50 ($5,000 × 7.3601), as determined under Table B in §20.2031-7A(d). It is not evident from the governing instrument of the trust or from local law that the trustee would be required to apportion the trust fund between the widow and charity in the event the fund were insufficient to pay both annuities in a given year. Accordingly, the deduction with respect to the charitable annuity will be limited to $31,123 ($65,000 less $33,877 [the value of the private annuity]), which is the minimum amount it is evident the charity will receive.

(v) The present value of a unitrust interest described in paragraph (e)(2)(vii) of this section is to be determined by subtracting the present value of all interests in the transferred property other than the unitrust interest from the fair market value of the transferred property.

(4) *Other decedents.*—The present value of an interest not described in paragraph (f)(2) of this section is to be determined under §20.2031-7(d) in the case of decedents where the valuation date of the gross estate is on or after May 1, 2009, or under §20.2031-7A in the case of decedents where the valuation date of the gross estate is before May 1, 2009.

(5) *Special computations.*—If the interest transferred is such that its present value is to be determined by a special computation, a request for a special factor, accompanied by a statement of the date of birth and sex of each individual the duration of whose life may affect the value of the interest, and by copies of the relevant instruments, may be submitted by the fiduciary to the Commissioner who may, if conditions permit, supply the factor requested. If the Commissioner furnishes the factor, a copy of the letter supplying the factor must be attached to the tax return in which the deduction is claimed. If the Commissioner does not furnish the factor, the claim for deduction must be supported by a full statement of the computation of the present value made in accordance with the principles set forth in this paragraph.

(6) *Effective/applicability date.*—Paragraphs (e)(3)(iii) and (f)(4) of this section apply on and after May 1, 2009. [Reg. §20.2055-2.]

☐ [*T.D. 6296, 6-23-58. Amended by T.D. 7238, 12-28-72; T.D. 7318, 7-10-74; T.D. 7340, 1-6-75; T.D. 7955, 5-10-84; T.D. 7957, 5-16-84; T.D. 8069, 1-13-86; T.D. 8095, 8-6-86; T.D. 8540, 6-9-94; T.D. 8819, 4-29-99; T.D. 8886, 6-9-2000; T.D. 8923, 1-4-2001; T.D. 9068, 7-3-2003; T.D. 9448, 5-1-2009 and T.D. 9540, 8-9-2011.*]

[Reg. §20.2055-3]

§20.2055-3. Effect of death taxes and administration expenses.—(a) *Death taxes.*—(1) If under the terms of the will or other governing instrument, the law of the jurisdiction under which the estate is administered, or the law of the jurisdiction imposing the particular tax, the Federal estate tax, or any estate, succession, legacy, or inheritance tax is payable in whole or in part out of any property the transfer of which would otherwise be allowable as a deduction under section 2055, section 2055(c) provides that the sum deductible is the amount of the transferred property reduced by the amount of the tax. Section 2055(c) in effect provides that the deduction is based on the amount actually available for charitable uses, that is, the amount of the fund remaining after the payment of all death taxes. Thus, if $50,000 is bequeathed for a charitable purpose and is subjected to a State inheritance tax of $5,000, payable out of the $50,000, the amount deductible is $45,000. If a life estate is bequeathed to an individual with remainder over to a charitable organization, and by the local law the inheritance tax upon the life estate is paid out of the corpus with the result that the charitable organization will be entitled to receive only the amount of the fund less the tax, the deduction is limited to the present value, as of the date of the testator's death, of the remainder of the fund so reduced. If a testator bequeaths his residuary estate, or a portion of it, to charity, and his will contains a direction that certain inheritance taxes, otherwise payable from legacies upon which they were imposed, shall be payable out of the residuary estate, the deduction may not exceed the bequest to charity thus reduced pursuant to the direction of the will. If a residuary estate, or a portion of it, is bequeathed to charity, and by the local law the Federal estate tax is payable out of the residuary estate, the deduction may not exceed that portion of the residuary estate bequeathed to charity as reduced by the Federal estate tax. The return should fully disclose the computation of the amount to be deducted. If the amount to be deducted is dependent upon the amount of any death tax which has not been paid before the filing of the return, there should be submitted with the return a computation of that tax.

(2) It should be noted that if the Federal estate tax is payable out of a charitable transfer so that the amount of the transfer otherwise passing to charity is reduced by the amount of the tax, the resultant decrease in the amount passing to charity will further reduce the allowable deduction. In such a case, the amount of the charitable deduction can be obtained only by a series of trial-and-error computations, or by a formula. If, in addition, interdependent State and Federal taxes are involved, the computation becomes highly complicated. Examples of methods of computation of the charitable deduction and the marital deduction (with which similar problems are encountered) in various situations are contained in supplemental instructions to the estate tax return.

(3) For the allowance of a deduction to a decedent's estate for certain State death taxes imposed upon charitable transfers, see section 2053(d) and § 20.2053-9.

(b) *Administration expenses.*—(1) *Definitions.*— (i) *Management expenses.*—Estate management expenses are expenses that are incurred in connection with the investment of estate assets or with their preservation or maintenance during a reasonable period of administration. Examples of these expenses could include investment advisory fees, stock brokerage commissions, custodial fees, and interest.

(ii) *Transmission expenses.*—Estate transmission expenses are expenses that would not have been incurred but for the decedent's death and the consequent necessity of collecting the decedent's assets, paying the decedent's debts and death taxes, and distributing the decedent's property to those who are entitled to receive it. Estate transmission expenses include any administration expense that is not a management expense. Examples of these expenses could include executor commissions and attorney fees (except to the extent of commissions or fees specifically related to investment, preservation, or maintenance of the assets), probate fees, expenses incurred in construction proceedings and defending against will contests, and appraisal fees.

(iii) *Charitable share.*—The charitable share is the property or interest in property that passed from the decedent for which a deduction is allowable under section 2055(a) with respect to all or part of the property interest. The charitable share includes, for example, bequests to charitable organizations and bequests to a charitable lead unitrust or annuity trust, a charitable remainder unitrust or annuity trust, and a pooled income fund, described in section 2055(e)(2). The charitable share also includes the income produced by the property or interest in property during the period of administration if the income, under the terms of the governing instrument or applicable local law, is payable to the charitable organization or is to be added to the principal of the property interest passing in whole or in part to the charitable organization.

(2) *Effect of transmission expenses.*—For purposes of determining the charitable deduction, the value of the charitable share shall be reduced by the amount of the estate transmission expenses paid from the charitable share.

(3) *Effect of management expenses attributable to the charitable share.*—For purposes of determining the charitable deduction, the value of the charitable share shall not be reduced by the amount of the estate management expenses attributable to and paid from the charitable share. Pursuant to section 2056(b)(9), however, the amount of the allowable charitable deduction shall be reduced by the amount of any such management expenses that are deducted under section 2053 on the decedent's federal estate tax return.

(4) *Effect of management expenses not attributable to the charitable share.*—For purposes of determining the charitable deduction, the value of the charitable share shall be reduced by the amount of the estate management expenses paid from the charitable share but attributable to a property interest not included in the charitable share.

(5) *Example.*—The following example illustrates the application of this paragraph (b):

Example. The decedent, who dies in 2000, leaves his residuary estate, after the payment of debts, expenses, and estate taxes, to a charitable remainder unitrust that satisfies the requirements of section 664(d). During the period of administration, the estate incurs estate transmission expenses of $400,000. The residue of the estate (the charitable share) must be reduced by the $400,000 of transmission expenses and by the Federal and State estate taxes before the present value of the remainder interest passing to charity can be determined in accordance with the provisions of § 1.664-4 of this chapter. Because the estate taxes are payable out of the residue, the computation of the estate taxes and the allowable charitable deduction are interrelated. See paragraph (a)(2) of this section.

(6) *Cross reference.*—See § 20.2056(b)-4(d) for additional examples applicable to the treatment

of administration expenses under this paragraph (b).

(7) *Effective date.*—The provisions of this paragraph (b) apply to estates of decedents dying on or after December 3, 1999. [Reg. § 20.2055-3.]

☐ [*T.D.* 6296, 6-23-58. *Amended by T.D.* 8846, 12-2-99 (*corrected* 12-17-99).]

[Reg. § 20.2055-4]

§ 20.2055-4. Disallowance of charitable, etc., deductions because of "prohibited transactions" in the case of decedents dying before January 1, 1970.—(a) Sections 503(e) and 681(b)(5) provide that no deduction which would otherwise be allowable under section 2055 for the value of property transferred by the decedent during his lifetime or by will for religious, charitable, scientific, literary, or educational purposes (including the encouragement of art and the prevention of cruelty to children or animals) is allowed if (1) the transfer is made in trust, and, for income tax purposes for the taxable year of the trust in which the transfer is made, the deduction otherwise allowable to the trust under section 642(c) is limited by section 681(b)(1) by reason of the trust having engaged in a prohibited transaction described in section 681(b)(2), or (2) the transfer is made to a corporation, community chest, fund or foundation which, for its taxable year in which the transfer is made, is not exempt from income tax under section 501(a) by reason of having engaged in a prohibited transaction described in section 503(c).

(b) For purposes of section 681(b)(5) and section 503(e), the term "transfer" includes any gift, contribution, bequest, devise, legacy, or other disposition. In applying such sections for estate tax purposes, a transfer, whether made during the decedent's lifetime or by will, is considered as having been made at the moment of the decedent's death.

(c) The income tax regulations contain the rules for the determination of the taxable year of the trust for which the deduction under section 642(c) is limited by section 681(b) and for the determination of the taxable year of the organization for which an exemption is denied under section 503(a). Generally, such taxable year is a taxable year subsequent to the taxable year during which the trust or organization has been notified by the Commissioner of Internal Revenue that it has engaged in a prohibited transaction. However, if the trust or organization during or prior to the taxable year entered into the prohibited transaction for the purpose of diverting its corpus or income from the charitable or other purposes by reason of which it is entitled to a deduction or exemption, and the transaction involves a substantial part of the income or corpus, then the deduction of the trust under section 642(c) for such taxable year is limited by

section 681(b), or exemption of the organization for such taxable year is denied under section 503(a), whether or not the organization has previously received notification by the Commissioner of Internal Revenue that it is engaged in a prohibited transaction. In certain cases, the limitation of sections 681 or 503 may be removed or the exemption may be reinstated for certain subsequent taxable years under the rules set forth in the income tax regulations under sections 681 and 503. In cases in which prior notification by the Commissioner of Internal Revenue is not required in order to limit the deduction of the trust under section 681(b) or to deny exemption of the organization under section 503, the deduction otherwise allowable under section 2055 is not disallowed in respect of transfers made during the same taxable year of the trust or organization in which a prohibited transaction occurred or in a prior taxable year unless the decedent or a member of his family was a party to the prohibited transaction. For the purpose of the preceding sentence, the members of the decedent's family include only his brothers and sisters, whether by whole or half blood, spouse, ancestors, and lineal descendants.

(d) This section applies only in the case of decedents dying before January 1, 1970. In the case of decedents dying after December 31, 1969, see § 20.2055-5. [Reg. § 20.2055-4.]

☐ [*T.D.* 6296, 6-23-58. *Amended by T.D.* 7318, 7-10-74.]

[Reg. § 20.2055-5]

§ 20.2055-5. Disallowance of charitable, etc., deductions in the case of decedents dying after December 31, 1969.—(a) *Organizations subject to section 507(c) tax.*—Section 508(d)(1) provides that, in the case of decedents dying after December 31, 1969, a deduction which would otherwise be allowable under section 2055 for the value of property transferred by the decedent to or for the use of an organization upon which the tax provided by section 507(c) has been imposed shall not be allowed if the transfer is made by the decedent after notification is made under section 507(a) or if the decedent is a substantial contributor (as defined in section 507(d)(2)) who dies on or after the first day on which action is taken by such organization that culminates in the imposition of the tax under section 507(c). This paragraph does not apply if the entire amount of the unpaid portion of the tax imposed by section 507(c) is abated under section 507(g) by the Commissioner or his delegate.

(b) *Taxable private foundations, section 4947 trusts, etc.*—(1) *In general.*—Section 508(d)(2) provides that, in the case of decedents dying after December 31, 1969, a deduction which would otherwise be allowable under section 2055 for the value of property transferred by the decedent shall not be allowed if the transfer is made to or for the use of—

(i) A private foundation or a trust described in section 4947(a)(2) in a taxable year of such organization for which such organization fails to meet the governing instrument requirements of section 508(e) (determined without regard to section 508(e)(2)(B) and (C)), or

(ii) Any organization in a period for which it is not treated as an organization described in section 501(c)(3) by reason of its failure to give notification under section 508(a) of its status to the Commissioner.

For additional rules, see § 1.508-2(b)(1) of this chapter (Income Tax Regulations).

(2) *Transfers not covered by section 508(d)(2)(A).*—(i) *In general.*—Any deduction which would otherwise be allowable under section 2055 for the value of property transferred by a decedent dying after December 31, 1969, will not be disallowed under section 508(d)(2)(A) and subparagraph (1)(i) of this paragraph—

(*a*) In the case of property passing under the terms of a will executed on or before October 9, 1969—

(*1*) If the decedent dies after October 9, 1969, but before October 9, 1972, without having amended any dispositive provision of the will after October 9, 1969, by codicil or otherwise,

(*2*) If the decedent dies after October 9, 1969, and at no time after that date had the right to change the portions of the will which pertain to the passing of the property to, or for the use of, an organization described in section 2055(a), or

(*3*) If no dispositive provision of the will is amended by the decedent, by codicil or otherwise, after October 9, 1969, and before October 9, 1972, and the decedent is on October 9, 1972, and at all times thereafter under a mental disability (as defined in § 1.642(c)-2(b)(3)(ii) of this chapter) to amend the will by codicil or otherwise, or

(*b*) In the case of property transferred in trust on or before October 9, 1969—

(*1*) If the decedent dies after October 9, 1969, but before October 9, 1972, without having amended, after October 9, 1969, any dispositive provision of the instrument governing the disposition of the property,

(*2*) If the property transferred was an irrevocable interest to, or for the use of, an organization described in section 2055(a), or

(*3*) If no dispositive provision of the instrument governing the disposition of the property is amended by the decedent after October 9, 1969, and before October 9, 1972, and the decedent is on October 9, 1972, and at all times thereafter under a mental disability (as defined in § 1.642(c)-2(b)(3)(ii) of this chapter) to change the disposition of the property.

(ii) *Amendment of dispositive provisions.*—For purposes of subdivision (i) of this subparagraph, the provisions of paragraph (e)(4) and (5) of § 20.2055-2 shall apply in determining whether an amendment will be considered as one which amends the dispositive provisions of a will or trust.

(c) *Foreign organization with substantial support from foreign sources.*—Section 4948(c)(4) provides that, in the case of decedents dying after December 31, 1969, a deduction which would otherwise be allowable under section 2055 for the value of property transferred by the decedent to or for the use of a foreign organization which has received substantially all of its support (other than gross investment income) from sources without the United States shall not be allowed if the transfer is made (1) after the date on which the Commissioner has published notice that he has notified such organization that it has engaged in a prohibited transaction, or (2) in a taxable year of such organization for which it is not exempt from taxation under section 501(a) because it has engaged in a prohibited transaction after December 31, 1969. [Reg. § 20.2055-5.]

☐ [T.D. 7318, 7-10-74.]

[Reg. § 20.2055-6]

§ 20.2055-6. Disallowance of double deduction in the case of qualified terminable interest property.—No deduction is allowed from the decedent's gross estate under section 2055 for property with respect to which a deduction is allowed by reason of section 2056(b)(7). See section 2056(b)(9) and § 20.2056(b)-9. [Reg. § 20.2055-6.]

☐ [T.D. 8522, 2-28-94.]

[Reg. § 20.2056-0]

§ 20.2056-0. Table of contents.—This section lists the captions that appear in the regulations under § § 20.2056(a)-1 through 20.2056(d)-2.

§ 20.2056(c)-2. Marital deduction; definition of "passed from the decedent to his surviving spouse."

  (a) In general.

  (b) Examples.

  (c) Effect of election by surviving spouse.

  (d) Will contests.

  (e) Survivorship.

§ 20.2056(e)-3. Marital deduction; definition of passed from the decedent to a person other than his surviving spouse.

§ 20.2056(d)-1. Marital deduction; special rules for marital deduction if surviving spouse is not a United States citizen.

§ 20.2056(d)-2. Marital deduction; effect of disclaimers of post-December 31,1976 transfers.

  (a) Disclaimer by a surviving spouse.

  (b) Disclaimer by a person other than a surviving spouse.

§ 20.2056(d)-3. Marital deduction; effect of disclaimers of pre-January 1, 1977 transfers.

  (a) Disclaimers by a surviving spouse.

  (b) Disclaimer by a person other than a surviving spouse.

    (1) Decedents dying after October 3, 1966, and before January 1, 1977.

    (2) Decedents dying after September 30, 1963, and before October 4, 1966.

    (3) Decedents dying before October 4, 1966.

[Reg. § 20.2056-0.]

  ☐ *[T.D. 8522, 2-28-94. Amended by T.D. 8612, 8-21-95.]*

[Reg. § 20.2056(a)-1]

§ 20.2056(a)-1. Marital deduction; in general.—(a) *In general.*—A deduction is allowed under section 2056 from the gross estate of a decedent for the value of any property interest which passes from the decedent to the decedent's surviving spouse if the interest is a *deductible interest* as defined in § 20.2056(a)-2. With respect to decedents dying in certain years, a deduction is allowed under section 2056 only to the extent that the total of the deductible interests does not exceed the applicable limitations set forth in paragraph(c) of this section. The deduction allowed under section 2056 is referred to as the *marital deduction.* See also sections 2056(d) and 2056A for special rules applicable in the case of decedents dying after November 10, 1988, if the decedent's surviving spouse is not a citizen of the United States at the time of the decedent's death. In such cases, the marital deduction may not be allowed unless the property passes to a qualified domestic trust as described in section 2056A(a).

  (b) *Requirements for marital deduction.*—(1) *In general.*—To obtain the marital deduction with respect to any property interest, the executor must establish the following facts—

    (i) The decedent was survived by a spouse (see § 20.2056(c)-2(e));

    (ii) The property interest passed from the decedent to the spouse (see § § 20.2056(b)-5 through 20.2056(b)-8 and 20.2056(c)-1 through 20.2056(c)-3);

    (iii) The property interest is a *deductible interest* (see § 20.2056(a)-2); and

    (iv) The value of the property interest (see § 20.2056(b)-4).

  (2) *Burden of establishing requisite facts.*—The executor must provide the facts relating to any applicable limitation on the amount of the allowable marital deduction under § 20.2056(a)-1(c), and must submit proof necessary to establish any fact required under paragraph (b)(1), including any evidence requested by the district director.

  (c) *Marital deduction; limitation on aggregate deductions.*—(1) *Estates of decedents dying before 1977.*—In the case of estates of decedents dying before January 1, 1977, the marital deduction is limited to one-half of the value of the *adjusted gross estate,* as that term was defined under section 2056(c)(2) prior to repeal by the Economic Recovery Tax Act of 1981.

  (2) *Estates of decedents dying after December 31, 1976, and before January 1, 1982.*—Except as provided in § 2002(d)(1) of the Tax Reform Act of 1976 (Pub. L. 94-455), in the case of decedents dying after December 31, 1976, and before January 1, 1982, the marital deduction is limited to the greater of—

    (i) $250,000; or

    (ii) One-half of the value of the decedent's adjusted gross estate, adjusted for intervivos gifts to the spouse as prescribed by section 2056(c)(1)(B) prior to repeal by the Economic Recovery Tax Act of 1981 (Pub. L. 97-34).

  (3) *Estates of decedents dying after December 31, 1981.*—In the case of estates of decedents dying after December 31, 1981, the marital deduction is limited as prescribed in paragraph (c)(2) of this section if the provisions of section 403(e)(3) of Pub. L. 97-34 are satisfied. [Reg. § 20.2056(a)-1.]

  ☐ *[T.D. 6296, 6-23-58. Amended by T.D. 8095, 8-6-86 and T.D. 8522, 2-28-94.]*

[Reg. § 20.2056(a)-2]

§ 20.2056(a)-2. Marital deduction; deductible interests and nondeductible interests.—(a) *In general.*—Property interests which passed from a decedent to his surviving spouse fall within two general categories: (1) those with respect to which the marital deduction is authorized, and (2) those with respect to which the marital deduction is not authorized. These categories are referred to in this section and other sections of the regulations under section 2056 as "deductible interests" and "nondeductible interests," respectively (see paragraph (b) of this section). Subject to any applicable limitations set forth in § 20.2056(a)-1(c), the amount of the marital deduction is the aggregate value of the *deductible interests*.

(b) *Deductible interests.*—An interest passing to a decedent's surviving spouse is a "deductible interest" if it does not fall within one of the following categories of "nondeductible interests":

(1) Any property interest which passed from the decedent to his surviving spouse is a "nondeductible interest" to the extent it is not included in the decedent's gross estate.

(2) If a deduction is allowed under section 2053 (relating to deductions for expenses and indebtedness) by reason of the passing of a property interest from the decedent to his surviving spouse, such interest is, to the extent of the deduction under section 2053, a "nondeductible interest." Thus, a property interest which passed from the decedent to his surviving spouse in satisfaction of a deductible claim of the spouse against the estate is, to the extent of the claim, a "nondeductible interest" (see § 20.2056(b)-4). Similarly, amounts deducted under section 2053(a)(2) for commissions allowed to the surviving spouse as executor are "nondeductible interests." As to the valuation, for the purpose of the marital deduction, of any property interest which passed from the decedent to his surviving spouse subject to a mortgage or other encumbrance, see § 20.2056(b)-4.

(3) If during settlement of the estate a loss deductible under section 2054 occurs with respect to a property interest, then that interest is, to the extent of the deductible loss, a "nondeductible interest" for the purpose of the marital deduction.

(4) A property interest passing to a decedent's surviving spouse which is a "terminable interest," as defined in § 20.2056(b)-1, is a "nondeductible interest" to the extent specified in that section. [Reg. § 20.2056(a)-2.]

☐ [*T.D.* 6296, 6-23-58. *Amended by T.D.* 8522, 2-28-94.]

[Reg. § 20.2056(b)-1]

§ 20.2056(b)-1. Marital deduction; limitation in case of life estate or other terminable interest.—(a) *In general.*—Section 2056(b) provides that no marital deduction is allowed with respect to certain property interests, referred to generally as "terminable interests," passing from a decedent to his surviving spouse. The phrase "terminable interest" is defined in paragraph (b) of this section. However, the fact that an interest in property passing to a decedent's surviving spouse is a "terminable interest" makes it nondeductible only (1) under the circumstances de-

scribed in paragraph (c) of this section, and (2) if it does not come within one of the exceptions referred to in paragraph (d) of this section.

(b) *"Terminable interests.".*—A "terminable interest" in property is an interest which will terminate or fail on the lapse of time or on the occurrence or the failure to occur of some contingency. Life estates, terms for years, annuities, patents, and copyrights are therefore terminable interests. However, a bond, note, or similar contractual obligation, the discharge of which would not have the effect of an annuity or a term for years, is not a terminable interest.

(c) *Nondeductible terminable interests.*—(1) A property interest which constitutes a terminable interest, as defined in paragraph (b) of this section, is nondeductible if—

(i) Another interest in the same property passed from the decedent to some other person for less than an adequate and full consideration in money or money's worth, and

(ii) By reason of its passing, the other person or his heirs or assigns may possess or enjoy any part of the property after the termination or failure of the spouse's interest.

(2) Even though a property interest which constitutes a terminable interest is not nondeductible by reason of the rules stated in subparagraph (1) of this paragraph, such an interest is nondeductible if—

(i) The decedent has directed his executor or a trustee to acquire such an interest for the decedent's surviving spouse (see further paragraph (f) of this section), or

(ii) Such an interest passing to the decedent's surviving spouse may be satisfied out of a group of assets which includes a nondeductible interest (see further § 20.2056(b)-2). In this case, however, full nondeductibility may not result.

(d) *Exceptions.*—A property interest passing to a decedent's surviving spouse is deductible (if it is not otherwise disqualified under § 20.2056(a)-2) even though it is a terminable interest, and even though an interest therein passed from the decedent to another person, if it is a terminable interest only because—

(1) It is conditioned on the spouse's surviving for a limited period, in the manner described in § 20.2056(b)-3;

(2) It is a right to income for life with a general power of appointment, meeting the requirements set forth in § 20.2056(b)-5;

(3) It consists of life insurance or annuity payments held by the insurer with a general power of appointment in the spouse, meeting the requirements set forth in § 20.2056(b)-6;

(4) It is qualified terminable interest property, meeting the requirements set forth in § 20.2056(b)-7; or

(5) It is an interest in a qualified charitable remainder trust in which the spouse is the only

noncharitable beneficiary, meeting the requirements set forth in § 20.2056(b)-8.

(e) *Miscellaneous principles.*—(1) In determining whether an interest passed from the decedent to some other person, it is immaterial whether interests in the same property passed to the decedent's spouse and another person at the same time, or under the same instrument.

(2) In determining whether an interest in the same property passed from the decedent both to his surviving spouse and to some other person, a distinction is to be drawn between "property," as such term is used in section 2056, and an "interest in property." The term "property" refers to the underlying property in which various interests exist; each such interest is not for this purpose to be considered as "property."

(3) Whether or not an interest is nondeductible because it is a terminable interest is to be determined by reference to the property interests which actually passed from the decedent. Subsequent conversions of the property are immaterial for this purpose. Thus, where a decedent bequeathed his estate to his wife for life with remainder to his children, the interest which passed to his wife is a nondeductible interest, even though the wife agrees with the children to take a fractional share of the estate in fee in lieu of the life interest in the whole, or sells the life estate for cash, or acquires the remainder interest of the children either by purchase or gift.

(4) The terms *passed from the decedent, passed from the decedent to his surviving spouse,* and *passed from the decedent to a person other than his surviving spouse* are defined in §§ 20.2056(c)-1 through 20.2056(c)-3.

(f) *Direction to acquire a terminable interest.*—No marital deduction is allowed with respect to a property interest which a decedent directs his executor or a trustee to convert after his death into a terminable interest for his surviving spouse. The marital deduction is not allowed even though no interest in the property subject to the terminable interest passes to another person and even though the interest would otherwise come within the exceptions described in §§ 20.2056(b)-5 and 20.2056(b)-6 (relating to life estates and life insurance and annuity payments with powers of appointment). However, a general investment power, authorizing investments in both terminable interests and other property, is not a direction to invest in a terminable interest.

(g) *Examples.*—The application of this section may be illustrated by the following examples. In each example, it is assumed that the executor made no election under section 2056(b)(7) (even if under the specific facts the election would have been available), that any property interest passing from the decedent to a person other than the surviving spouse passed for less than full and adequate consideration in money or

money's worth, and that section 2056(b)(8) is inapplicable.

Example (1). H (the decedent) devised real property to W (his surviving wife) for life, with remainder to A and his heirs. The interest which passed from H to W is a nondeductible interest since it will terminate upon her death and A (or his heirs or assigns) will thereafter possess or enjoy the property.

Example (2). H bequeathed the residue of his estate in trust for the benefit of W and A. The trust income is to be paid to W for life, and upon her death the corpus is to be distributed to A or his issue. However, if A should die without issue, leaving W surviving, the corpus is then to be distributed to W. The interest which passed from H to W is a nondeductible interest since it will terminate in the event of her death if A or his issue survive, and A or his issue will thereafter possess or enjoy the property.

Example (3). H during his lifetime purchased an annuity contract providing for payments to himself for life and then to W for life if she should survive him. Upon the death of the survivor of H and W, the excess, if any, of the cost of the contract over the annuity payments theretofore made was to be refunded to A. The interest which passed from H to W is a nondeductible interest since A may possess or enjoy a part of the property following the termination of the interest of W. If, however, the contract provided for no refund upon the death of the survivor of H and W, or provided that any refund was to go to the estate of the survivor, then the interest which passed from H to W is (to the extent it is included in H's gross estate) a deductible interest.

Example (4). H, in contemplation of death, transferred a residence to A for life with remainder to W provided W survives A, but if W predeceases A, the property is to pass to A's heirs. If it is assumed that H died during A's lifetime, and the value of the residence was included in determining the value of his gross estate, the interest which passed from H to W is a nondeductible interest since it will terminate if W predeceases A and the property will thereafter be possessed or enjoyed by B (or his heirs or assigns). This result is not affected by B's assignment of his interest during H's lifetime, whether made in favor of W or another person, since the term "assigns" (as used in section 2056(b)(1)(B)) includes such an assignee. However, if it is assumed that A predeceased H, the interest of B in the property was extinguished, and, viewed as of the time of the subsequent death of H, the interest which passed from him to W is the entire interest in the property and, therefore, a deductible interest.

Example (5). H transferred real property to A by gift, reserving the right to the rentals of the property for a term of 20 years. H died within the 20-year term, bequeathing the right to the remaining rentals to a trust for the benefit of W.

Reg. § 20.2056(b)-1(g)

The terms of the trust satisfy the five conditions stated in §20.2056(b)-5, so that the property interest which passed in trust is considered to have passed from H to W. However, the interest is a nondeductible interest since it will terminate upon the expiration of the term and A will thereafter possess or enjoy the property.

Example (6). H bequeathed a patent to W and A as tenants in common. In this case, the interest of W will terminate upon the expiration of the term of the patent, but possession or enjoyment of the property by A must necessarily cease at the same time. Therefore, since A's possession or enjoyment cannot outlast the termination of W's interest, the latter is a deductible interest.

Example (7). A decedent bequeathed $100,000 to his wife, subject to a direction to his executor to use the bequest for the purchase of an annuity for the wife. The bequest is a nondeductible interest.

Example (8). Assume that pursuant to local law an allowance for support is payable to the decedent's surviving spouse during the period of the administration of the decedent's estate, but that upon her death or remarriage during such period her right to any further allowance will terminate. Assume further that the surviving spouse is sole beneficiary of the decedent's estate. Under such circumstances, the allowance constitutes a deductible interest since any part of the allowance not receivable by the surviving spouse during her lifetime will pass to her estate under the terms of the decedent's will. If, in this example, the decedent bequeathed only one-third of his residuary estate to his surviving spouse, then two-thirds of the allowance for support would constitute a nondeductible terminable interest. [Reg. §20.2056(b)-1.]

☐ *[T.D. 6296, 6-23-58. Amended by T.D. 8522, 2-28-94.]*

[Reg. §20.2056(b)-2]

§20.2056(b)-2. Marital deduction; interest in unidentified assets.—(a) *In general.*—Section 2056(b)(2) provides that if an interest passing to a decedent's surviving spouse may be satisfied out of assets (or their proceeds) which include a particular asset that would be a nondeductible interest if it passed from the decedent to his spouse, the value of the interest passing to the spouse is reduced, for the purpose of the marital deduction, by the value of the particular asset.

(b) *Application of section 2056(b)(2).*—In order for section 2056(b)(2) to apply, two circumstances must coexist, as follows:

(1) The property interest which passed from the decedent to his surviving spouse must be payable out of a group of assets included in the gross estate. Examples of property interests payable out of a group of assets are a general legacy, a bequest of the residue of the decedent's estate or of a portion of the residue, and a right to a share of the corpus of a trust upon its termination.

(2) The group of assets out of which the property interest is payable must include one or more particular assets which, if passing specifically to the surviving spouse, would be nondeductible interests. Therefore, section 2056(b)(2) is not applicable merely because the group of assets includes a terminable interest, but would only be applicable if the terminable interest were nondeductible under the provisions of §20.2056(b)-1.

(c) *Interest nondeductible if circumstances present.*—If both of the circumstances set forth in paragraph (b) of this section are present, the property interest payable out of the group of assets is (except as to any excess of its value over the aggregate value of the particular asset or assets which would not be deductible if passing specifically to the surviving spouse) a nondeductible interest.

(d) The application of this section may be illustrated by the following example:

Example. A decedent bequeathed one-third of the residue of his estate to his wife. The property passing under the decedent's will included a right to the rentals of an office building for a term of years, reserved by the decedent under a deed of the building by way of gift to his son. The decedent did not make a specific bequest of the right to such rentals. Such right, if passing specifically to the wife, would be a nondeductible interest (see example (5) of paragraph (g) of §20.2056(b)-1). It is assumed that the value of the bequest of one-third of the residue of the estate to the wife was $85,000, and that the right to the rentals was included in the gross estate at a value of $60,000. If the decedent's executor had the right under the decedent's will or local law to assign the entire lease in satisfaction of the bequest, the bequest is a nondeductible interest to the extent of $60,000. If the executor could only assign a one-third interest in the lease in satisfaction of the bequest, the bequest is a nondeductible interest to the extent of $20,000. If the decedent's will provided that his wife's bequest could not be satisfied with a nondeductible interest, the entire bequest is a deductible interest. If, in this example, the asset in question had been foreign real estate not included in the decedent's gross estate, the results would be the same. [Reg. §20.2056(b)-2.]

☐ *[T.D. 6296, 6-23-58. Amended by T.D. 8522, 2-28-94.]*

[Reg. §20.2056(b)-3]

§20.2056(b)-3. Marital deduction; interest of spouse conditioned on survival for limited period.—(a) *In general.*—Generally, no marital deduction is allowable if the interest passing to the surviving spouse is a terminable interest as defined in paragraph (b) of §20.2056(b)-1. However, section 2056(b)(3) provides an exception to this rule so as to allow a deduction if (1) the only condition under which it will terminate is the death of the surviving spouse within 6 months after the decedent's death, or her death as a result of a common disaster which also resulted in the decedent's death, and (2) the condition does not in fact occur.

(b) *Six months' survival.*—If the only condition which will cause the interest taken by the surviving spouse to terminate is the death of the surviving spouse and the condition is of such nature that it can occur only within 6 months following the decedent's death, the exception provided by section 2056(b)(3) will apply, provided the condition does not in fact occur. However, if the condition (unless it relates to death as a result of a common disaster) is one which may occur either within the 6-month period or thereafter, the exception provided by section 2056(b)(3) will not apply.

(c) *Common disaster.*—If a property interest passed from the decedent to his surviving spouse subject to the condition that she does not die as a result of a common disaster which also resulted in the decedent's death, the exception provided by section 2056(b)(3) will not be applied in the final audit of the return if there is still a possibility that the surviving spouse may be deprived of the property interest by operation of the common disaster provision as given effect by the local law.

(d) *Examples.*—The application of this section may be illustrated by the following examples:

Example (1). A decedent bequeathed his entire estate to his spouse on condition that she survive him by 6 months. In the event his spouse failed to survive him by 6 months, his estate was to go to his niece and her heirs. The decedent was survived by his spouse. It will be observed that, as of the time of the decedent's death, it was possible that the niece would, by reason of the interest which passed to her from the decedent, possess or enjoy the estate after the termination of the interest which passed to the spouse. Hence, under the general rule set forth in §20.2056(b)-1, the interest which passed to the spouse would be regarded as a nondeductible interest. If the surviving spouse in fact died within 6 months after the decedent's death, that general rule is to be applied, and the interest which passed to the spouse is a nondeductible interest. However, if the spouse in fact survived the decedent by 6 months, thus extinguishing the interest of the niece, the case comes within the exception provided by section 2056(b)(3), and the interest which passed to the spouse is a deductible interest. (It is assumed for the purpose of this example that no other factor which would cause the interest to be nondeductible is present.)

Example (2). The facts are the same as in example (1) except that the will provided that the

estate was to go to the niece either in case the decedent and his spouse should both die as a result of a common disaster, or in case the spouse should fail to survive the decedent by 3 months. It is assumed that the decedent was survived by his spouse. In this example, the interest which passed from the decedent to his surviving spouse is to be regarded as a nondeductible interest if the surviving spouse in fact died either within 3 months after the decedent's death or as a result of a common disaster which also resulted in the decedent's death. However, if the spouse in fact survived the decedent by 3 months, and did not thereafter die as a result of a common disaster which also resulted in the decedent's death, the exception provided under section 2056(b)(3) will apply and the interest will be deductible.

Example (3). The facts are the same as in example (1) except that the will provided that the estate was to go to the niece if the decedent and his spouse should both die as a result of a common disaster and if the spouse failed to survive the decedent by 3 months. If the spouse in fact survived the decedent by 3 months, the interest of the niece is extinguished, and the interest passing to the spouse is a deductible interest.

Example (4). A decedent devised and bequeathed his residuary estate to his wife if she was living on the date of distribution of his estate. The devise and bequest is a nondeductible interest even though distribution took place within 6 months after the decedent's death and the surviving spouse in fact survived the date of distribution. [Reg. § 20.2056(b)-3.]

☐ [*T.D.* 6296, 6-23-58.]

[Reg. § 20.2056(b)-4]

§ 20.2056(b)-4. **Marital deduction; valuation of interest passing to surviving spouse.**—(a) *In general.*—The value, for the purpose of the marital deduction, of any deductible interest which passed from the decedent to his surviving spouse is to be determined as of the date of the decedent's death, except that if the executor elects the alternate valuation method under section 2032 the valuation is to be determined as of the date of the decedent's death but with the adjustment described in paragraph (a)(3) of § 20.2032-1. The marital deduction may be taken only with respect to the net value of any deductible interest which passed from the decedent to his surviving spouse, the same principles being applicable as if the amount of a gift to the spouse were being determined.

(b) *Property interest subject to an encumbrance or obligation.*—If a property interest passed from the decedent to his surviving spouse subject to a mortgage or other encumbrance, or if an obligation is imposed upon the surviving spouse by the decedent in connection with the passing of a property interest, the value of the property interest is to be reduced by the amount of the mortgage, other encumbrance, or obligation. However, if under the terms of the decedent's will or under local law the executor is required to discharge, out of other assets of the decedent's estate, a mortgage or other encumbrance on property passing from the decedent to his surviving spouse, or is required to reimburse the surviving spouse for the amount of the mortgage or other encumbrance, the payment or reimbursement constitutes an additional interest passing to the surviving spouse. The passing of a property interest subject to the imposition of an obligation by the decedent does not include a bequest, devise, or transfer in lieu of dower, curtesy, or of a statutory estate created in lieu of dower or curtesy, or of other marital rights in the decedent's property or estate. The passing of a property interest subject to the imposition of an obligation by the decedent does, however, include a bequest, etc., in lieu of the interest of his surviving spouse under community property laws unless such interest was, immediately prior to the decedent's death, a mere expectancy. The following examples are illustrative of property interests which passed from the decedent to his surviving spouse subject to the imposition of an obligation by the decedent:

Example (1). A decedent devised a residence valued at $25,000 to his wife, with a direction that she pay $5,000 to his sister. For the purpose of the marital deduction, the value of the property interest passing to the wife is only $20,000.

Example (2). A decedent devised real property to his wife in satisfaction of a debt owing to her. The debt is a deductible claim under section 2053. Since the wife is obligated to relinquish the claim as a condition to acceptance of the devise, the value of the devise is, for the purpose of the marital deduction, to be reduced by the amount of the claim.

Example (3). A decedent bequeathed certain securities to his wife in lieu of her interest in property held by them as community property under the law of the State of their residence. The wife elected to relinquish her community property interest and to take the bequest. For the purpose of the marital deduction, the value of the bequest is to be reduced by the value of the community property interest relinquished by the wife.

(c) *Effect of death taxes.*—(1) In the determination of the value of any property interest which passed from the decedent to his surviving spouse, there must be taken into account the effect which the Federal estate tax, or any estate, succession, legacy, or inheritance tax, has upon the net value to the surviving spouse of the property interest.

(2) For example, assume that the only bequest to the surviving spouse is $100,000 and the spouse is required to pay a State inheritance tax in the amount of $1,500. If no other death taxes affect the net value of the bequest, the value, for the purpose of the marital deduction, is $98,500.

(3) As another example, assume that a decedent devised real property to his wife having a value for Federal estate tax purposes of $100,000 and also bequeathed to her a nondeductible interest for life under a trust. The State of residence valued the real property at $90,000 and the life interest at $30,000, and imposed an inheritance tax (at graduated rates) of $4,800 with respect to the two interests. If it is assumed that the inheritance tax on the devise is required to be paid by the wife, the amount of tax to be ascribed to the devise is

$$\frac{90,000}{120,000} \times \$4,800 = \$3,600.$$

Accordingly, if no other death taxes affect the net value of the bequest, the value, for the purpose of the marital deduction, is $100,000 less $3,600, or $96,400.

(4) If the decedent bequeaths his residuary estate, or a portion of it, to his surviving spouse, and his will contains a direction that all death taxes shall be payable out of the residuary estate, the value of the bequest, for the purpose of the marital deduction, is based upon the amount of the residue as reduced pursuant to such direction. If the residuary estate, or a portion of it, is bequeathed to the surviving spouse, and by the local law the Federal estate tax is payable out of the residuary estate, the value of the bequest, for the purpose of the marital deduction, may not exceed its value as reduced by the Federal estate tax. Methods of computing the deduction, under such circumstances, are set forth in supplemental instructions to the estate tax return.

(d) *Effect of administration expenses.*—(1) *Definitions.*—(i) *Management expenses.*—Estate management expenses are expenses that are incurred in connection with the investment of estate assets or with their preservation or maintenance during a reasonable period of administration. Examples of these expenses could include investment advisory fees, stock brokerage commissions, custodial fees, and interest.

(ii) *Transmission expenses.*—Estate transmission expenses are expenses that would not have been incurred but for the decedent's death and the consequent necessity of collecting the decedent's assets, paying the decedent's debts and death taxes, and distributing the decedent's property to those who are entitled to receive it. Estate transmission expenses include any administration expense that is not a management expense. Examples of these expenses could include executor commissions and attorney fees (except to the extent of commissions or fees specifically related to investment, preservation, or maintenance of the assets), probate fees, expenses incurred in construction proceedings and defending against will contests, and appraisal fees.

(iii) *Marital share.*—The marital share is the property or interest in property that passed from the decedent for which a deduction is allowable under section 2056(a). The marital share includes the income produced by the property or interest in property during the period of administration if the income, under the terms of the governing instrument or applicable local law, is payable to the surviving spouse or is to be added to the principal of the property interest passing to, or for the benefit of, the surviving spouse.

(2) *Effect of transmission expenses.*—For purposes of determining the marital deduction, the value of the marital share shall be reduced by the amount of the estate transmission expenses paid from the marital share.

(3) *Effect of management expenses attributable to the marital share.*—For purposes of determining the marital deduction, the value of the marital share shall not be reduced by the amount of estate management expenses attributable to and paid from the marital share. Pursuant to section 2056(b)(9), however, the amount of the allowable marital deduction shall be reduced by the amount of any such management expenses that are deducted under section 2053 on the decedent's Federal estate tax return.

(4) *Effect of management expenses not attributable to the marital share.*—For purposes of determining the marital deduction, the value of the marital share shall be reduced by the amount of the estate management expenses paid from the marital share but attributable to a property interest not included in the marital share.

(5) *Examples.*—The following examples illustrate the application of this paragraph (d):

Example 1. The decedent dies after 2006 having made no lifetime gifts. The decedent makes a bequest of shares of ABC Corporation stock to the decedent's child. The bequest provides that the child is to receive the income from the shares from the date of the decedent's death. The value of the bequeathed shares on the decedent's date of death is $3,000,000. The residue of the estate is bequeathed to a trust for which the executor properly makes an election under section 2056(b)(7) to treat as qualified terminable interest property. The value of the residue on the decedent's date of death, before the payment of administration expenses and Federal and State estate taxes, is $6,000,000. Under applicable local law, the executor has the discretion to pay administration expenses from the income or principal of the residuary estate. All estate taxes are to be paid from the residue. The State estate tax equals the State death tax credit available under section 2011. During the period of administration, the estate incurs estate transmission expenses of $400,000, which the executor charges

to the residue. For purposes of determining the marital deduction, the value of the residue is reduced by the Federal and State estate taxes and by the estate transmission expenses. If the transmission expenses are deducted on the Federal estate tax return, the marital deduction is $3,500,000 ($6,000,000 minus $400,000 transmission expenses and minus $2,100,000 Federal and State estate taxes). If the transmission expenses are deducted on the estate's Federal income tax return rather than on the estate tax return, the marital deduction is $3,011,111 ($6,000,000 minus $400,000 transmission expenses and minus $2,588,889 Federal and State estate taxes).

Example 2. The facts are the same as in *Example 1*, except that, instead of incurring estate transmission expenses, the estate incurs estate management expenses of $400,000 in connection with the residue property passing for the benefit of the spouse. The executor charges these management expenses to the residue. In determining the value of the residue passing to the spouse for marital deduction purposes, a reduction is made for Federal and State estate taxes payable from the residue but no reduction is made for the estate management expenses. If the management expenses are deducted on the estate's income tax return, the net value of the property passing to the spouse is $3,900,000 ($6,000,000 minus $2,100,000 Federal and State estate taxes). A marital deduction is claimed for that amount, and the taxable estate is $5,100,000.

Example 3. The facts are the same as in *Example 1*, except that the estate management expenses of $400,000 are incurred in connection with the bequest of ABC Corporation stock to the decedent's child. The executor charges these management expenses to the residue. For purposes of determining the marital deduction, the value of the residue is reduced by the Federal and State estate taxes and by the management expenses. The management expenses reduce the value of the residue because they are charged to the property passing to the spouse even though they were incurred with respect to stock passing to the child. If the management expenses are deducted on the estate's Federal income tax return, the marital deduction is $3,011,111 ($6,000,000 minus $400,000 management expenses and minus $2,588,889 Federal and State estate taxes). If the management expenses are deducted on the estate's Federal estate tax return, rather than on the estate's Federal income tax return, the marital deduction is $3,500,000 ($6,000,000 minus $400,000 management expenses and minus $2,100,000 in Federal and State estate taxes).

Example 4. The decedent, who dies in 2000, has a gross estate of $3,000,000. Included in the gross estate are proceeds of $150,000 from a policy insuring the decedent's life and payable to the decedent's child as beneficiary. The applicable credit amount against the tax was fully consumed by the decedent's lifetime gifts.

Applicable State law requires the child to pay any estate taxes attributable to the life insurance policy. Pursuant to the decedent's will, the rest of the decedent's estate passes outright to the surviving spouse. During the period of administration, the estate incurs estate-management expenses of $150,000 in connection with the property passing to the spouse. The value of the property passing to the spouse is $2,850,000 ($3,000,000 less the insurance proceeds of $150,000 passing to the child). For purposes of determining the marital deduction, if the management expenses are deducted on the estate's income tax return, the marital deduction is $2,850,000 ($3,000,000 less $150,000) and there is a resulting taxable estate of $150,000 ($3,000,000 less a marital deduction of $2,850,000). Suppose, instead, the management expenses of $150,000 are deducted on the estate's estate tax return under section 2053 as expenses of administration. In such a situation, claiming a marital deduction of $2,850,000 would be taking a deduction for the same $150,000 in property under both sections 2053 and 2056 and would shield from estate taxes the $150,000 in insurance proceeds passing to the decedent's child. Therefore, in accordance with section 2056(b)(9), the marital deduction is limited to $2,700,000, and the resulting taxable estate is $150,000.

Example 5. The decedent dies after 2006 having made no lifetime gifts. The value of the decedent's residuary estate on the decedent's date of death is $3,000,000, before the payment of administration expenses and Federal and State estate taxes. The decedent's will provides a formula for dividing the decedent's residuary estate between two trusts to reduce the estate's Federal estate taxes to zero. Under the formula, one trust, for the benefit of the decedent's child, is to be funded with that amount of property equal in value to so much of the applicable exclusion amount under section 2010 that would reduce the estate's Federal estate tax to zero. The other trust, for the benefit of the surviving spouse, satisfies the requirements of section 2056(b)(7) and is to be funded with the remaining property in the estate. The State estate tax equals the State death tax credit available under section 2011. During the period of administration, the estate incurs transmission expenses of $200,000. The transmission expenses of $200,000 reduce the value of the residue to $2,800,000. If the transmission expenses are deducted on the Federal estate tax return, then the formula divides the residue so that the value of the property passing to the child's trust is $1,000,000 and the value of the property passing to the marital trust is $1,800,000. The allowable marital deduction is $1,800,000. The applicable exclusion amount shields from Federal estate tax the entire $1,000,000 passing to the child's trust so that the amount of Federal and State estate taxes is zero. Alternatively, if the transmission expenses are deducted on the estate's Federal income tax return, the formula divides the residue so that the value of the property passing to the child's trust is $800,000 and the value of the property passing to the marital trust is $2,000,000. The allowable marital deduction is $2,000,000. The applicable exclusion amount shields from Federal estate tax the entire $800,000 passing to the child's trust so that the amount of Federal and State estate taxes remains zero.

Example 6. The facts are the same as in *Example 5,* except that the decedent's will provides that the child's trust is to be funded with that amount of property equal in value to the applicable exclusion amount under section 2010 allowable to the decedent's estate. The residue of the estate, after the payment of any debts, expenses, and Federal and State estate taxes, is to pass to the marital trust. The applicable exclusion amount in this case is $1,000,000, so the value of the property passing to the child's trust is $1,000,000. After deducting the $200,000 of transmission expenses, the residue of the estate is $1,800,000 less any estate taxes. If the transmission expenses are deducted on the Federal estate tax return, the allowable marital deduction is $1,800,000, the taxable estate is zero, and the Federal and State estate taxes are zero. Alternatively, if the transmission expenses are deducted on the estate's Federal income tax return, the net value of the property passing to the spouse is $1,657,874 ($1,800,000 minus $142,106 estate taxes). A marital deduction is claimed for that amount, the taxable estate is $1,342,106, and the Federal and State estate taxes total $142,106.

Example 7. The decedent, who dies in 2000, makes an outright pecuniary bequest of $3,000,000 to the decedent's surviving spouse, and the residue of the estate, after the payment of all debts, expenses, and Federal and State estate taxes, passes to the decedent's child. Under the terms of the governing instrument and applicable local law, a beneficiary of a pecuniary bequest is not entitled to any income on the bequest. During the period of administration, the estate pays estate transmission expenses from the income earned by the property that will be distributed to the surviving spouse in satisfaction of the pecuniary bequest. The income earned on this property is not part of the marital share. Therefore, the allowable marital deduction is $3,000,000, unreduced by the amount of the estate transmission expenses.

(6). *Effective date.*—The provisions of this paragraph (d) apply to estates of decedents dying on or after December 3, 1999.

(e) *Remainder interests.*—If the income from property is made payable to another individual for life, or for a term of years, with remainder absolutely to the surviving spouse or to her estate, the marital deduction is based upon the present value of the remainder. The present value of the remainder is to be determined in accordance with the rules stated in §20.2031-7.

For example, if the surviving spouse is to receive $50,000 upon the death of a person aged 31 years, the present value of the remainder is $14,466. If the remainder is such that its value is to be determined by a special computation (see paragraph (b) of § 20.2031-7), a request for a specific factor may be submitted to the Commissioner. The request should be accompanied by a statement of the date of birth of each person, the duration of whose life may affect the value of the remainder, and copies of the relevant instruments. The Commissioner may, if conditions permit, supply the factor requested. If the Commissioner does not furnish the factor, the claim for deduction must be supported by a full statement of the computation of the present value made in accordance with the principles set forth in the applicable paragraphs of § 20.2031-7. [Reg. § 20.2056(b)-4.]

☐ [*T.D. 6296, 6-23-58. Amended by T.D. 8522, 2-28-94; T.D. 8540, 6-9-94 and T.D. 8846, 12-2-99 (corrected 12-17-99).*]

[Reg. § 20.2056(b)-5]

§ 20.2056(b)-5. Marital deduction; life estate with power of appointment in surviving spouse.—(a) *In general.*—Section 2056(b)(5) provides that if an interest in property passes from the decedent to his surviving spouse (whether or not in trust) and the spouse is entitled for life to all the income from the entire interest or all the income from a specific portion of the entire interest, with a power in her to appoint the entire interest or the specific portion, the interest which passes to her is a deductible interest, to the extent that it satisfies all five of the conditions set forth below (see paragraph (b) of this section if one or more of the conditions is satisfied as to only a portion of the interest):

(1) The surviving spouse must be entitled for life to all of the income from the entire interest or a specific portion of the entire interest, or to a specific portion of all the income from the entire interest.

(2) The income payable to the surviving spouse must be payable annually or at more frequent intervals.

(3) The surviving spouse must have the power to appoint the entire interest or the specific portion to either herself or her estate.

(4) The power in the surviving spouse must be exercisable by her alone and (whether exercisable by will or during life) must be exercisable in all events.

(5) The entire interest or the specific portion must not be subject to a power in any other person to appoint any part to any person other than the surviving spouse.

(b) *Specific portion; deductible amount.*—If either the right to income or the power of appointment passing to the surviving spouse pertains only to a specific portion of a property interest passing from the decedent, the marital deduction is allowed only to the extent that the rights in the surviving spouse meet all of the five conditions described in paragraph (a) of this section. While the rights over the income and the power must coexist as to the same interest in property, it is not necessary that the rights over the income or the power as to such interest be in the same proportion. However, if the rights over income meeting the required conditions set forth in paragraph (a)(1) and (2) of this section extend over a smaller share of the property interest than the share with respect to which the power of appointment requirements set forth in paragraph (a)(3) through (5) of this section are satisfied, the deductible interest is limited to the smaller share. Correspondingly, if a power of appointment meeting all the requirements extends to a smaller portion of the property interest than the portion over which the income rights pertain, the deductible interest cannot exceed the value of the portion to which such power of appointment applies. Thus, if the decedent leaves to his surviving spouse the right to receive annually all of the income from a particular property interest and a power of appointment meeting the specifications prescribed in paragraph (a)(3) through (5) of this section as to only one-half of the property interest, then only one-half of the property interest is treated as a deductible interest. Correspondingly, if the income interest of the spouse satisfying the requirements extends to only one-fourth of the property interest and a testamentary power of appointment satisfying the requirements extends to all of the property interest, then only one-fourth of the interest in the spouse qualifies as a deductible interest. Further, if the surviving spouse has no right to income from a specific portion of a property interest but a testamentary power of appointment which meets the necessary conditions over the entire interest, then none of the interest qualifies for the deduction. In addition, if, from the time of the decedent's death, the surviving spouse has a power of appointment meeting all of the required conditions over three-fourths of the entire property interest and the prescribed income rights over the entire interest, but with a power in another person to appoint one-half of the entire interest, the value of the interest in the surviving spouse over only one-half of the property interest will qualify as a deductible interest.

(c) *Meaning of specific portion.*—(1) *In general.*—Except as provided in paragraphs (c)(2) and (c)(3) of this section, a partial interest in property is not treated as a specific portion of the entire interest. In addition, any specific portion of an entire interest in property is nondeductible to the extent the specific portion is subject to invasion for the benefit of any person other than the surviving spouse, except in the case of a deduction allowable under section 2056(b)(5), relating to the exercise of a general power of appointment by the surviving spouse.

(2) *Fraction or percentage share.*—Under section 2056(b)(10), a partial interest in property is treated as a specific portion of the entire interest if the rights of the surviving spouse in income, and the required rights as to the power described in § 20.2056(b)-5(a), constitute a fractional or percentage share of the entire property interest, so that the surviving spouse's interest reflects its proportionate share of the increase or decrease in the value of the entire property interest to which the income rights and the power relate. Thus, if the spouse's right to income and the spouse's power extend to a specified fraction or percentage of the property, or the equivalent, the interest is in a specific portion of the property. In accordance with paragraph (b) of this section, if the spouse has the right to receive the income from a specific portion of the trust property (after applying paragraph (c)(3) of this section) but has a power of appointment over a different specific portion of the property (after applying paragraph (c)(3) of this section), the marital deduction is limited to the lesser specific portion.

(3) *Special rule in the case of estates of decedents dying on or before October 24, 1992, and certain decedents dying after October 24, 1992, with wills or revocable trusts executed on or prior to that date.*

(i) In the case of estates of decedents within the purview of the effective date and transitional rules contained in paragraphs (c)(3)(ii) and (iii) of this section:

(A) A specific sum payable annually, or at more frequent intervals, out of the property and its income that is not limited by the income of the property is treated as the right to receive the income from a specific portion of the property. The specific portion, for purposes of paragraph (c)(2) of this section, is the portion of the property that, assuming the interest rate generally applicable for the valuation of annuities at the time of the decedent's death, would produce income equal to such payments. However, a pecuniary amount payable annually to a surviving spouse is not treated as a right to the income from a specific portion of the trust property for purposes of this paragraph (c)(3)(i)(A) if any person other than the surviving spouse may receive, during the surviving spouse's lifetime, any distribution of the property. To determine the applicable interest rate for valuing annuities, see sections 2031 and 7520 and the regulations under those sections.

(B) The right to appoint a pecuniary amount out of a larger fund (or trust corpus) is considered the right to appoint a specific portion of such fund or trust for purposes of paragraph (c)(2) in an amount equal to such pecuniary amount.

(ii) The rules contained in paragraphs (c)(3)(i)(A) and (B) of this section apply with respect to estates of decedents dying on or before October 24, 1992.

(iii) The rules contained in paragraphs (c)(3)(i)(A) and (B) of this section apply in the case of decedents dying after October 24, 1992, if property passes to the spouse pursuant to a will or revocable trust agreement executed on or before October 24, 1992, and either—

(A) On that date, the decedent was under a mental disability to change the disposition of the property and did not regain competence to dispose of such property before the date of death; or

(B) The decedent dies prior to October 24, 1995.

(iv) Notwithstanding paragraph (c)(3)(iii) of this section, paragraphs (c)(3)(i)(A) and (B) of this section do not apply if the will or revocable trust is amended after October 24, 1992, in any respect that increases the amount of the transfer qualifying for the marital deduction or alters the terms by which the interest so passes to the surviving spouse of the decedent.

(4) *Local law.*—A partial interest in property is treated as a specific portion of the entire interest if it is shown that the surviving spouse has rights under local law that are identical to those the surviving spouse would have acquired had the partial interest been expressed in terms satisfying the requirements of paragraph (c)(2) (or paragraph (c)(3) if applicable) of this section.

(5) *Examples.*—The following examples illustrate the application of paragraphs (a) through (c)(4) of this section:

Example 1. Spouse entitled to the lesser of an annuity or a fraction of trust income. The decedent, D, died prior to October 24, 1992. D bequeathed in trust 500 identical shares of X company stock, valued for estate tax purposes at $500,000. The trust provides that during the lifetime of D's spouse, S, the trustee is to pay annually to S the lesser of one-half of the trust income or $20,000. Any trust income not paid to S is to be accumulated in the trust and may not be distributed during S's lifetime. S has a testamentary general power of appointment over the entire trust principal. The applicable interest rate for valuing annuities as of D's date of death under section 7520 is 10 percent. For purposes of paragraphs (a) through (c) of this section, S is treated as receiving all of the income from the lesser of—

(i) One half of the stock ($250,000); or

(ii) $200,000, the specific portion of the stock which, as determined in accordance with § 20.2056(b)-5(c)(3)(i)(A), would produce annual income of $20,000 (20,000/.10). Accordingly, the marital deduction is limited to $200,000 (200,000/500,000 or 2/5th of the value of the trust).

Example 2. Spouse possesses power and income interest over different specific portions of trust. The facts are the same as in *Example 1* except that S's testamentary general power of appointment is exercisable over only 1/4th of the trust principal.

Consequently, under section 2056(b)(5), the marital deduction is allowable only for the value of 1/4th of the trust ($125,000); i.e., the lesser of the value of the portion with respect to which S is deemed to be entitled to all of the income (2/5th of the trust or $200,000), or the value of the portion with respect to which S possesses the requisite power of appointment (1/4th of the trust or $125,000).

Example 3. Power of appointment over pecuniary amount. The decedent, D, died prior to October 24, 1992. D bequeathed property valued at $400,000 for estate tax purposes in trust. The trustee is to pay annually to D's spouse, S, one-fourth of the trust income. Any trust income not paid to S is to be accumulated in the trust and may not be distributed during S's lifetime. The will gives S a testamentary general power of appointment over the sum of $160,000. Because D died prior to October 24, 1992, S's power of appointment over $160,000 is treated as a power of appointment over a specific portion of the entire trust interest. The marital deduction allowable under section 2056(b)(5) is limited to $100,000; that is, the lesser of—

(1) The value of the trust corpus ($400,000);

(2) The value of the trust corpus over which S has a power of appointment ($160,000); or

(3) That specific portion of the trust with respect to which S is entitled to all the income ($100,000).

Example 4. Power of appointment over shares of stock constitutes a power over a specific portion. Under D's will, 250 shares of Y company stock were bequeathed in trust pursuant to which all trust income was payable annually to S, D's spouse, for life. S was given a testamentary general power of appointment over 100 shares of stock. The trust provides that if the trustee sells the Y company stock, S's general power of appointment is exercisable with respect to the sale proceeds or the property in which the proceeds are reinvested. Because the amount of property represented by a single share of stock would be altered if the corporation split its stock, issued stock dividends, made a distribution of capital, etc., a power to appoint 100 shares at the time of S's death is not necessarily a power to appoint the entire interest that the 100 shares represented on the date of D's death. If it is shown that, under local law, S has a general power to appoint not only the 100 shares designated by D but also 100/250 of any distributions by the corporation that are included in trust principal, the requirements of paragraph (c)(2) of this section are satisfied and S is treated as having a general power to appoint 100/250 of the entire interest in the 250 shares. In that case, the marital deduction is limited to 40 percent of the trust principal. If local law does not give S that power, the 100 shares would not constitute a specific portion under §20.2056(b)-5(c) (including §20.2056(b)-5(c)(3)(i)(B)). The nature of the asset is such that a change in the capitalization of the corporation could cause an alteration in the original value represented by the shares at the time of D's death and, thus, it does not represent a specific portion of the trust.

(d) *Meaning of entire interest.*—Because a marital deduction is allowed for each separate qualifying interest in property passing from the decedent to the decedent's surviving spouse (subject to any applicable limitations in §20.2056(a)-1(c)), for purposes of paragraphs (a) and (b) of this section, each property interest with respect to which the surviving spouse received any rights is considered separately in determining whether the surviving spouse's rights extend to the entire interest or to a specific portion of the entire interest. A property interest which consists of several identical units of property (such as a block of 250 shares of stock, whether the ownership is evidenced by one or several certificates) is considered one property interest, unless certain of the units are to be segregated and accorded different treatment, in which case each segregated group of items is considered a separate property interest. The bequest of a specified sum of money constitutes the bequest of a separate property interest if immediately following distribution by the executor and thenceforth it, and the investments made with it, must be so segregated or accounted for as to permit its identification as a separate item of property. The application of this paragraph may be illustrated by the following examples:

Example (1). The decedent transferred to a trustee three adjoining farms, Blackacre, Whiteacre, and Greenacre. His will provided that during the lifetime of the surviving spouse the trustee should pay her all of the income from the trust. Upon her death, all of Blackacre, a one-half interest in Whiteacre, and a one-third interest in Greenacre were to be distributed to the person or persons appointed by her in her will. The surviving spouse is considered as being entitled to all of the income from the entire interest in Blackacre, all of the income from the entire interest in Whiteacre, and all of the income from the entire interest in Greenacre. She also is considered as having a power of appointment over the entire interest in Blackacre, over one-half of the entire interest in Whiteacre, and over one-third of the entire interest in Greenacre.

Example (2). The decedent bequeathed $250,000 to C, as trustee. C is to invest the money and pay all of the income from the investments to W, the decedent's surviving spouse, annually. W was given a general power, exercisable by will, to appoint one-half of the corpus of the trust. Here, immediately following distribution by the executor the $250,000 will be sufficiently segregated to permit its identification as a separate item, and the $250,000 will constitute an entire property interest. Therefore, W has a right to income and a power of appointment such that one-half of the entire interest is a deductible interest.

Example (3). The decedent bequeathed 100 shares of Z Corporation stock to D, as trustee. W, the decedent's surviving spouse, is to receive all of the income of the trust annually and is given a general power, exercisable by will, to appoint out of the trust corpus the sum of $25,000. In this case the $25,000 is not, immediately following distribution, sufficiently segregated to permit its identification as a separate item of property in which the surviving spouse has the entire interest. Therefore, the $25,000 does not constitute the entire interest in a property for the purpose of paragraphs (a) and (b) of this section.

(e) *Application of local law.*—In determining whether or not the conditions set forth in paragraph (a)(1) through (5) of this section are satisfied by the instrument of transfer, regard is to be had to the applicable provisions of the law of the jurisdiction under which the interest passes and, if the transfer is in trust, the applicable provisions of the law governing the administration of the trust. For example, silence of a trust instrument as to the frequency of payment will not be regarded as a failure to satisfy the condition set forth in paragraph (a)(2) of this section that income must be payable to the surviving spouse annually or more frequently unless the applicable law permits payment to be made less frequently than annually. The principles outlined in this paragraph and paragraphs (f) and (g) of this section which are applied in determining whether transfers in trust meet such conditions are equally applicable in ascertaining whether, in the case of interests not in trust, the surviving spouse has the equivalent in rights over income and over the property.

(f) *Right to income.*—(1) If an interest is transferred in trust, the surviving spouse is "entitled for life to all of the income from the entire interest or a specific portion of the entire interest," for the purpose of the condition set forth in paragraph (a)(1) of this section, if the effect of the trust is to give her substantially that degree of beneficial enjoyment of the trust property during her life which the principles of the law of trusts accord to a person who is unqualifiedly designated as the life beneficiary of a trust. Such degree of enjoyment is given only if it was the decedent's intention, as manifested by the terms of the trust instrument and the surrounding circumstances, that the trust should produce for the surviving spouse during her life such an income, or that the spouse should have such use of the trust property as is consistent with the value of the trust corpus and with its preservation. The designation of the spouse as sole income beneficiary for life of the entire interest or a specific portion of the entire interest will be sufficient to qualify the trust unless the terms of the trust and the surrounding circumstances considered as a whole evidence an intention to deprive the spouse of the requisite degree of enjoyment. In determining whether a trust evidences that intention, the treatment required or permitted with respect to individual items must be considered in relation to the entire system provided for the administration of the trust. In addition, the surviving spouse's interest shall meet the condition set forth in paragraph (a)(1) of this section if the spouse is entitled to income as determined by applicable local law that provides for a reasonable apportionment between the income and remainder beneficiaries of the total return of the trust and that meets the requirements of § 1.643(b)-1 of this chapter.

(2) If the over-all effect of a trust is to give to the surviving spouse such enforceable rights as will preserve to her the requisite degree of enjoyment, it is immaterial whether that result is effected by rules specifically stated in the trust instrument, or, in their absence, by the rules for the management of the trust property and the allocation of receipts and expenditures supplied by the State law. For example, a provision in the trust instrument for amortization of bond premium by appropriate periodic charges to interest will not disqualify the interest passing in trust even though there is no State law specifically authorizing amortization, or there is a State law denying amortization which is applicable only in the absence of such a provision in the trust instrument.

(3) In the case of a trust, the rules to be applied by the trustee in allocation of receipts and expenses between income and corpus must be considered in relation to the nature and expected productivity of the assets passing in trust, the nature and frequency of occurrence of the expected receipts, and any provisions as to change in the form of investments. If it is evident from the nature of the trust assets and the rules provided for management of the trust that the allocation to income of such receipts as rents, ordinary cash dividends, and interest will give to the spouse the substantial enjoyment during life required by the statute, provisions that such receipts as stock dividends and proceeds from the conversion of trust assets shall be treated as corpus will not disqualify the interest passing in trust. Similarly, provision for a depletion charge against income in the case of trust assets which are subject to depletion will not disqualify the interest passing in trust, unless the effect is to deprive the spouse of the requisite beneficial enjoyment. The same principle is applicable in the case of depreciation, trustees' commissions, and other charges.

(4) Provisions granting administrative powers to the trustee will not have the effect of disqualifying an interest passing in trust unless the grant of powers evidences the intention to deprive the surviving spouse of the beneficial enjoyment required by the statute. Such an intention will not be considered to exist if the entire terms of the instrument are such that the local courts will impose reasonable limitations upon the exercise of the powers. Among the powers

which if subject to reasonable limitations will not disqualify the interest passing in trust are the power to determine the allocation or apportionment of receipts and disbursements between income and corpus, the power to apply the income or corpus for the benefit of the spouse, and the power to retain the assets passing to the trust. For example, a power to retain trust assets which consist substantially of unproductive property will not disqualify the interest if the applicable rules for the administration of the trust require, or permit the spouse to require, that the trustee either make the property productive or convert it within a reasonable time. Nor will such a power disqualify the interest if the applicable rules for administration of the trust require the trustee to use the degree of judgment and care in the exercise of the power which a prudent man would use if he were owner of the trust assets. Further, a power to retain a residence or other property for the personal use of the spouse will not disqualify the interest passing in trust.

(5) An interest passing in trust will not satisfy the condition set forth in paragraph (a)(1) of this section that the surviving spouse be entitled to all the income if the primary purpose of the trust is to safeguard property without providing the spouse with the required beneficial enjoyment. Such trusts include not only trusts which expressly provide for the accumulation of the income but also trusts which indirectly accomplish a similar purpose. For example, assume that the corpus of a trust consists substantially of property which is not likely to be income producing during the life of the surviving spouse and that the spouse cannot compel the trustee to convert or otherwise deal with the property as described in subparagraph (4) of this paragraph. An interest passing to such a trust will not qualify unless the applicable rules for the administration require, or permit the spouse to require, that the trustee provide the required beneficial enjoyment, such as by payments to the spouse out of other assets of the trust.

(6) If a trust is created during the decedent's life, it is immaterial whether or not the interest passing in trust satisfied the conditions set forth in paragraph (a)(1) through (5) of this section prior to the decedent's death. If a trust may be terminated during the life of the surviving spouse, under her exercise of a power of appointment or by distribution of the corpus to her, the interest passing in trust satisfies the condition set forth in paragraph (a)(1) of this section (that the spouse be entitled to all the income) if she (i) is entitled to the income until the trust terminates, or (ii) has the right, exercisable in all events, to have the corpus distributed to her at any time during her life.

(7) An interest passing in trust fails to satisfy the condition set forth in paragraph (a)(1) of this section, that the spouse be entitled to all the income, to the extent that the income is required to be accumulated in whole or in part or may be accumulated in the discretion of any person other than the surviving spouse; to the extent that the consent of any person other than the surviving spouse is required as a condition precedent to distribution of the income; or to the extent that any person other than the surviving spouse has the power to alter the terms of the trust so as to deprive her of her right to the income. An interest passing in trust will not fail to satisfy the condition that the spouse be entitled to all the income merely because its terms provide that the right of the surviving spouse to the income shall not be subject to assignment, alienation, pledge, attachment or claims of creditors.

(8) In the case of an interest passing in trust, the terms "entitled for life" and "payable annually or at more frequent intervals", as used in the conditions set forth in paragraph (a)(1) and (2) of this section, require that under the terms of the trust the income referred to must be currently (at least annually; see paragraph (e) of this section) distributable to the spouse or that she must have such command over the income that it is virtually hers. Thus, the conditions in paragraph (a)(1) and (2) of this section are satisfied in this respect if, under the terms of the trust instrument, the spouse has the right exercisable annually (or more frequently) to require distribution to herself of the trust income, and otherwise the trust income is to be accumulated and added to corpus. Similarly, as respects the income for the period between the last distribution date and the date of the spouse's death, it is sufficient if that income is subject to the spouse's power to appoint. Thus, if the trust instrument provides that income accrued or undistributed on the date of the spouse's death is to be disposed of as if it had been received after her death, and if the spouse has a power of appointment over the trust corpus, the power necessarily extends to the undistributed income.

(9) An interest is not to be regarded as failing to satisfy the conditions set forth in paragraph (a)(1) and (2) of this section (that the spouse be entitled to all the income and that it be payable annually or more frequently) merely because the spouse is not entitled to the income from estate assets for the period before distribution of those assets by the executor, unless the executor is, by the decedent's will, authorized or directed to delay distribution beyond the period reasonably required for administration of the decedent's estate. As to the valuation of the property interest passing to the spouse in trust where the right to income is expressly postponed, see § 20.2056(b)-4.

(g) *Power of appointment in surviving spouse.*— (1) The conditions set forth in paragraph (a)(3) and (4) of this section, that is, that the surviving spouse must have a power of appointment exercisable in favor of herself or her estate and exercisable alone and in all events, are not met unless the power of the surviving spouse to appoint the entire interest or a specific portion of it falls within one of the following categories:

(i) A power so to appoint fully exercisable in her own favor at any time following the decedent's death (as, for example, an unlimited power to invade); or

(ii) A power so to appoint exercisable in favor of her estate. Such a power, if exercisable during life, must be fully exercisable at any time during life, or, if exercisable by will, must be fully exercisable irrespective of the time of her death (subject in either case to the provisions of §20.2056(b)-3, relating to interests condi tioned on survival for a limited period); or

(iii) A combination of the powers described under subparagraphs (i) and (ii) of this subparagraph. For example, the surviving spouse may, until she attains the age of 50 years, have a power to appoint to herself and thereafter have a power to appoint to her estate. However, the condition that the spouse's power must be exercisable in all events is not satisfied unless irrespective of when the surviving spouse may die the entire interest or a specific portion of it will at the time of her death be subject to one power or the other (subject to the exception in §20.2056(b)-3, relating to interests contingent on survival for a limited period).

(2) The power of the surviving spouse must be a power to appoint the entire interest or a specific portion of it as unqualified owner (and free of the trust if a trust is involved, or free of the joint tenancy if a joint tenancy is involved) or to appoint the entire interest or a specific portion of it as a part of her estate (and free of the trust if a trust is involved), that is, in effect, to dispose of it to whomsoever she pleases. Thus, if the decedent devised property to a son and the surviving spouse as joint tenants with right of survivorship and under local law the surviving spouse has a power of severance exercisable without consent of the other joint tenant, and by exercising this power could acquire a one-half interest in the property as a tenant in common, her power of severance will satisfy the condition set forth in paragraph (a)(3) of this section that she have a power of appointment in favor of herself or her estate. However, if the surviving spouse entered into a binding agreement with the decedent to exercise the power only in favor of their issue, that condition is not met. An interest passing in trust will not be regarded as failing to satisfy the condition merely because takers in default of the surviving spouse's exercise of the power are designated by the decedent. The decedent may provide that, in default of exercise of the power, the trust shall continue for an additional period.

(3) A power is not considered to be a power exercisable by a surviving spouse alone and in all events as required by paragraph (a)(4) of this section if the exercise of the power in the surviving spouse to appoint the entire interest or a specific portion of it to herself or to her estate requires the joinder or consent of any other person. The power is not "exercisable in all events", if it can be terminated during the life of the surviving spouse by any event other than her complete exercise or release of it. Further, a power is not "exercisable in all events" if it may be exercised for a limited purpose only. For example, a power which is not exercisable in the event of the spouse's remarriage is not exercisable in all events. Likewise, if there are any restrictions, either by the terms of the instrument or under applicable local law, on the exercise of a power to consume property (whether or not held in trust) for the benefit of the spouse, the power is not exercisable in all events. Thus, if a power of invasion is exercisable only for the spouse's support, or only for her limited use, the power is not exercisable in all events. In order for a power of invasion to be exercisable in all events, the surviving spouse must have the unrestricted power exercisable at any time during her life to use all or any part of the property subject to the power, and to dispose of it in any manner, including the power to dispose of it by gift (whether or not she has power to dispose of it by will).

(4) The power in the surviving spouse is exercisable in all events only if it exists immediately following the decedent's death. For example, if the power given to the surviving spouse is exercisable during life, but cannot be effectively exercised before distribution of the assets by the executor, the power is not exercisable in all events. Similarly, if the power is exercisable by will, but cannot be effectively exercised in the event the surviving spouse dies before distribution of the assets by the executor, the power is not exercisable in all events. However, an interest will not be disqualified by the mere fact that, in the event the power is exercised during administration of the estate, distribution of the property to the appointee will be delayed for the period of administration. If the power is in existence at all times following the decedent's death, limitations of a formal nature will not disqualify an interest. Examples of formal limitations on a power exercisable during life are requirements that an exercise must be in a particular form, that it must be filed with a trustee during the spouse's life, that reasonable notice must be given, or that reasonable intervals must elapse between successive partial exercises. Examples of formal limitations on a power exercisable by will are that it must be exercised by a will executed by the surviving spouse after the decedent's death or that exercise must be by specific reference to the power.

(5) If the surviving spouse has the requisite power to appoint to herself or her estate, it is immaterial that she also has one or more lesser powers. Thus, if she has a testamentary power to appoint to her estate, she may also have a limited power of withdrawal or of appointment during her life. Similarly, if she has an unlimited

power of withdrawal, she may have a limited testamentary power.

(h) *Requirement of survival for a limited period.*— A power of appointment in the surviving spouse will not be treated as failing to meet the requirements of paragraph (a)(3) of this section even though the power may terminate, if the only conditions which would cause the termination are those described in paragraph (a) of §20.2056(b)-3, and if those conditions do not in fact occur. Thus, the entire interest or a specific portion of it will not be disqualified by reason of the fact that the exercise of the power in the spouse is subject to a condition of survivorship described in §20.2056(b)-3 if the terms of the condition, that is, the survivorship of the surviving spouse, or the failure to die in a common disaster, are fulfilled.

(i) [Reserved].

(j) *Existence of a power in another.*—Paragraph (a)(5) of this section provides that a transfer described in paragraph (a) is nondeductible to the extent that the decedent created a power in the trustee or in any other person to appoint a part of the interest to any person other than the surviving spouse. However, only powers in other persons which are in opposition to that of the surviving spouse will cause a portion of the interest to fail to satisfy the condition set forth in paragraph (a)(5) of this section. Thus, a power in a trustee to distribute corpus to or for the benefit of a surviving spouse will not disqualify the trust. Similarly, a power to distribute corpus to the spouse for the support of minor children will not disqualify the trust if she is legally obligated to support such children. The application of this paragraph may be illustrated by the following examples:

Example (1). Assume that a decedent created a trust, designating his surviving spouse as income beneficiary for life with an unrestricted power in the spouse to appoint the corpus during her life. The decedent further provided that in the event the surviving spouse should die without having exercised the power, the trust should continue for the life of his son with a power in the son to appoint the corpus. Since the power in the son could become exercisable only after the death of the surviving spouse, the interest is not regarded as failing to satisfy the condition set forth in paragraph (a)(5) of this section.

Example (2). Assume that the decedent created a trust, designating his surviving spouse as income beneficiary for life and as donee of a power to appoint by will the entire corpus. The decedent further provided that the trustee could distribute 30 percent of the corpus to the decedent's son when he reached the age of 35 years. Since the trustee has a power to appoint 30 percent of the entire interest for the benefit of a person other than the surviving spouse, only 70 percent of the interest placed in trust satisfied the condition set forth in paragraph (a)(5) of this section.

If, in this case, the surviving spouse had a power, exercisable by her will, to appoint only one-half of the corpus as it was constituted at the time of her death, it should be noted that only 35 percent of the interest placed in the trust would satisfy the condition set forth in paragraph (a)(3) of this section. [Reg. § 20.2056(b)-5.]

☐ [*T.D. 6296, 6-23-58. Amended by T.D. 8522, 2-28-94 and T.D. 9102, 12-30-2003.*]

[Reg. § 20.2056(b)-6]

§ 20.2056(b)-6. Marital deduction; life insurance or annuity payments with power of appointment in surviving spouse.—(a) *In general.*—Section 2056(b)(6) provides that an interest in property passing from a decedent to his surviving spouse, which consists of proceeds held by an insurer under the terms of a life insurance, endowment, or annuity contract, is a "deductible interest" to the extent that it satisfied all five of the following conditions (see paragraph (b) of this section if one or more of the conditions is satisfied as to only a portion of the proceeds):

(1) The proceeds, or a specific portion of the proceeds, must be held by the insurer subject to an agreement either to pay the entire proceeds or a specific portion thereof in installments, or to pay interest thereon, and all or a specific portion of the installments or interest payable during the life of the surviving spouse must be payable only to her.

(2) The installments or interest payable to the surviving spouse must be payable annually, or more frequently, commencing not later than 13 months after the decedent's death.

(3) The surviving spouse must have the power to appoint all or a specific portion of the amounts so held by the insurer to either herself or her estate.

(4) The power in the surviving spouse must be exercisable by her alone and (whether exercisable by will or during life) must be exercisable in all events.

(5) The amounts or the specific portion of the amounts payable under such contract must not be subject to a power in any other person to appoint any part thereof to any person other than the surviving spouse.

(b) *Specific portion; deductible interest.*—If the right to receive interest or installment payments or the power of appointment passing to the surviving spouse pertains only to a specific portion of the proceeds held by the insurer, the marital deduction is allowed only to the extent that the rights of the surviving spouse in the specific portion meet the five conditions described in paragraph (a) of this section. While the rights to interest, or to receive payment in installments, and the power must coexist as to the proceeds of the same contract, it is not necessary that the rights to each be in the same proportion. If the rights to interest meeting the required conditions set forth in paragraph (a)(1) and (2) of this section extend over a smaller share of the proceeds than the share with respect to which the power of appointment requirements set forth in paragraph (a)(3) through (5) of this section are satisfied, the deductible interest is limited to the smaller share. Similarly, if the portion of the proceeds payable in installments is a smaller portion of the proceeds than the portion to which the power of appointment meeting such requirements relates, the deduction is limited to the smaller portion. In addition, if a power of appointment meeting all the requirements extends to a smaller portion of the proceeds than the portion over which the interest or installment rights pertain, the deductible interest cannot exceed the value of the portion to which such power of appointment applies. Thus, if the contract provides that the insurer is to retain the entire proceeds and pay all of the interest thereon annually to the surviving spouse and if the surviving spouse has a power of appointment meeting the specifications prescribed in paragraph (a)(3) through (5) of this section, as to only one-half of the proceeds held, then only one-half of the proceeds may be treated as a deductible interest. Correspondingly, if the rights of the spouse to receive installment payments or interest satisfying the requirements extend to only one-fourth of the proceeds and a testamentary power of appointment satisfying the requirements of paragraph (a)(3) through (5) of this section extends to all of the proceeds, then only one-fourth of the proceeds qualifies as a deductible interest. Further, if the surviving spouse has no right to installment payments (or interest) over any portion of the proceeds but a testamentary power of appointment which meets the necessary conditions over the entire remaining proceeds, then none of the proceeds qualifies for the deduction. In addition, if, from the time of the decedent's death, the surviving spouse has a power of appointment meeting all of the required conditions over three-fourths of the proceeds and the right to receive interest from the entire proceeds, but with a power in another person to appoint one-half of the entire proceeds, the value of the interest in the surviving spouse over only one-half of the proceeds will qualify as a deductible interest.

(c) *Applicable principles.*—(1) The principles set forth in paragraph (c) of § 20.2056(b)-5 for determining what constitutes a "specific portion of the entire interest" for the purpose of section 2056(b)(5) are applicable in determining what constitutes a "specific portion of all such amounts" for the purpose of section 2056(b)(6). However, the interest in the proceeds passing to the surviving spouse will not be disqualified by the fact that the installment payments or interest to which the spouse is entitled or the amount of the proceeds over which the power of appointment is exercisable may be expressed in terms of

a specific sum rather than a fraction or a percentage of the proceeds provided it is shown that such sums are a definite or fixed percentage or fraction of the total proceeds.

(2) The provisions of paragraph (a) of this section are applicable with respect to a property interest which passed from the decedent in the form of proceeds of a policy of insurance upon the decedent's life, a policy of insurance upon the life of a person who predeceased the decedent, a matured endowment policy, or an annuity contract, but only in case the proceeds are to be held by the insurer. With respect to proceeds under any such contract which are to be held by a trustee, with power of appointment in the surviving spouse, see § 20.2056(b)-5. As to the treatment of proceeds not meeting the requirements of § 20.2056(b)-5 or of this section, see § 20.2056(a)-2.

(3) In the case of a contract under which payments by the insurer commenced during the decedent's life, it is immaterial whether or not the conditions in subparagraphs (1) through (5) of paragraph (a) of this section were satisfied prior to the decedent's death.

(d) *Payments of installments or interest.*—The conditions in subparagraphs (1) and (2) of paragraph (a) of this section relative to the payments of installments or interest to the surviving spouse are satisfied if, under the terms of the contract, the spouse has the right exercisable annually (or more frequently) to require distribution to herself of installments of the proceeds or a specific portion thereof, as the case may be, and otherwise such proceeds or interest are to be accumulated and held by the insurer pursuant to the terms of the contract. A contract which otherwise requires the insurer to make annual or more frequent payments to the surviving spouse following the decedent's death, will not be disqualified merely because the surviving spouse must comply with certain formalities in order to obtain the first payment. For example, the contract may satisfy the conditions in subparagraphs (1) and (2) of paragraph (a) of this section even though it requires the surviving spouse to furnish proof of death before the first payment is made. The condition in paragraph (a)(1) of this section is satisfied where interest on the proceeds or a specific portion thereof is payable, annually or more frequently, for a term, or until the occurrence of a specified event, following which the proceeds or a specific portion thereof are to be paid in annual or more frequent installments.

(e) *Powers of appointment.*—(1) In determining whether the terms of the contract satisfy the conditions in subparagraph (3), (4), or (5) of paragraph (a) of this section relating to a power of appointment in the surviving spouse or any other person, the principles stated in § 20.2056(b)-5 are applicable. As stated in § 20.2056(b)-5, the surviving spouse's power to appoint is "exercisable in all events" only if it is in existence immediately following the decedent's death, subject, however, to the operation of § 20.2056(b)-3 relating to interests conditioned on survival for a limited period.

(2) For examples of formal limitations on the power which will not disqualify the contract, see paragraph (g)(4) of § 20.2056(b)-5. If the power is exercisable from the moment of the decedent's death, the contract is not disqualified merely because the insurer may require proof of the decedent's death as a condition to making payment to the appointee. If the submission of proof of the decedent's death is a condition to the exercise of the power, the power will not be considered "exercisable in all events" unless in the event the surviving spouse had died immediately following the decedent, her power to appoint would have been considered to exist at the time of her death, within the meaning of section 2041(a)(2). See paragraph (b) of § 20.2041-3.

(3) It is sufficient for the purposes of the condition in paragraph (a)(3) of this section that the surviving spouse have the power to appoint amounts held by the insurer to herself or her estate if the surviving spouse has the unqualified power, exercisable in favor of herself or her estate, to appoint amounts held by the insurer which are payable after her death. Such power to appoint need not extend to installments or interest which will be paid to the spouse during her life. Further, the power to appoint need not be a power to require payment in a single sum. For example, if the proceeds of a policy are payable in installments, and if the surviving spouse has the power to direct that all installments payable after her death be paid to her estate, she has the requisite power.

(4) It is not necessary that the phrase "power to appoint" be used in the contract. For example, the condition in paragraph (a)(3) of this section that the surviving spouse have the power to appoint amounts held by the insurer to herself or her estate is satisfied by terms of a contract which give the surviving spouse a right which is, in substance and effect, a power to appoint to herself or her estate, such as a right to withdraw the amount remaining in the fund held by the insurer, or a right to direct that any amount held by the insurer under the contract at her death shall be paid to her estate. [Reg. § 20.2056(b)-6.]

☐ [*T.D.* 6296, 6-23-58.]

[Reg. § 20.2056(b)-7]

§ 20.2056(b)-7. Election with respect to life estate for surviving spouse.—(a) *In general.*— Subject to section 2056(d), a marital deduction is allowed under section 2056(b)(7) with respect to estates of decedents dying after December 31, 1981, for qualified terminable interest property as defined in paragraph (b) of this section. All of the property for which a deduction is allowed under this paragraph (a) is treated as passing to the surviving spouse (for purposes of § 20.2056(a)-1), and no part of the property is treated as passing to any person other than the surviving spouse (for purposes of § 20.2056(b)-1).

(b) *Qualified terminable interest property.*— (1) *In general.*—Section 2056(b)(7)(B)(i) provides the definition of *qualified terminable interest property.*

(i) Terminable interests described in section 2056(b)(1)(C) cannot qualify as qualified terminable interest property. Thus, if the decedent directs the executor to purchase a terminable interest with estate assets, the terminable interest acquired will not qualify as qualified terminable interest property.

(ii) For purposes of section 2056(b)(7)(B)(i), the term *property* generally means the *entire interest in property* (within the meaning of § 20.2056(b)-5(d)) or a *specific portion of the entire interest* (within the meaning of § 20.2056(b)-5(c)).

(2) *Property for which an election may be made.*—(i) *In general.*—The election may relate to all or any part of property that meets the requirements of section 2056(b)(7)(B)(i), provided that any partial election must be made with respect to a fractional or percentage share of the property so that the elective portion reflects its proportionate share of the increase or decrease in value of the entire property for purposes of applying sections 2044 or 2519. The fraction or percentage may be defined by formula.

(ii) *Division of trusts.*—(A) *In general.*—A trust may be divided into separate trusts to reflect a partial election that has been made, or is to be made, if authorized under the governing instrument or otherwise permissible under local law. Any such division must be accomplished no later than the end of the period of estate administration. If, at the time of the filing of the estate tax return, the trust has not yet been divided, the intent to divide the trust must be unequivocally signified on the estate tax return.

(B) *Manner of dividing and funding trust.*—The division of the trust must be done on a fractional or percentage basis to reflect the partial election. However, the separate trusts do not have to be funded with a pro rata portion of each asset held by the undivided trust.

(C) *Local law.*—A trust may be divided only if the fiduciary is required, either by applicable local law or by the express or implied provisions of the governing instrument, to divide the trust on the basis of the fair market value of the assets of the trust at the time of the division.

(3) *Persons permitted to make the election.*— The election referred to in section 2056(b)(7)(B)(i)(III) must be made by the executor that is appointed, qualified, and acting

within the United States, within the meaning of section 2203, regardless of whether the property with respect to which the election is to be made is in the executor's possession. If there is no executor appointed, qualified, and acting within the United States, the election may be made by any person with respect to property in the actual or constructive possession of that person and may also be made by that person with respect to other property not in the actual or constructive possession of that person if the person in actual or constructive possession of such other property does not make the election. For example, in the absence of an appointed executor, the trustee of an intervivos trust (that is included in the gross estate of the decedent) can make the election.

(4) *Manner and time of making the election.*— (i) *In general.*—The election referred to in section 2056(b)(7)(B)(i)(III) and (v) is made on the return of tax imposed by section 2001 (or section 2101). For purposes of this paragraph, the term *return of tax imposed by section 2001* means the last estate tax return filed by the executor on or before the due date of the return, including extensions or, if a timely return is not filed, the first estate tax return filed by the executor after the due date.

(ii) *Election irrevocable.*—The election, once made, is irrevocable, provided that an election may be revoked or modified on a subsequent return filed on or before the due date of the return, including extensions actually granted. If an executor appointed under local law has made an election on the return of tax imposed by section 2001 (or section 2101) with respect to one or more properties, no subsequent election may be made with respect to other properties included in the gross estate after the return of tax imposed by section 2001 is filed. An election under section 2056(b)(7)(B)(v) is separate from any elections made under section 2056A(a)(3).

(c) *Protective elections.*—(1) *In general.*—A protective election may be made to treat property as qualified terminable interest property only if, at the time the federal estate tax return is filed, the executor of the decedent's estate reasonably believes that there is a bona fide issue that concerns whether an asset is includible in the decedent's gross estate, or the amount or nature of the property the surviving spouse is entitled to receive, i.e., whether property that is includible is eligible for the qualified terminable interest property election. The protective election must identify either the specific asset, group of assets, or trust to which the election applies and the specific basis for the protective election.

(2) *Protective election irrevocable.*—The protective election, once made on the return of tax imposed by section 2001, cannot be revoked. For example, if a protective election is made on the basis that a bona fide question exists regarding the inclusion of a trust corpus in the gross estate

and it is later determined that the trust corpus is so includible, the protective election becomes effective with respect to the trust corpus and cannot thereafter be revoked.

(d) *Qualifying income interest for life.*—(1) *In general.*—Section 2056(b)(7)(B)(ii) provides the definition of *qualifying income interest for life.* For purposes of section 2056(b)(7)(B)(ii)(II), the surviving spouse is included within the prohibited class of powerholders referred to therein. A power under applicable local law that permits the trustee to adjust between income and principal to fulfill the trustee's duty of impartiality between the income and remainder beneficiaries that meets the requirements of § 1.643(b)-1 of this chapter will not be considered a power to appoint trust property to a person other than the surviving spouse.

(2) *Entitled for life to all income.*—The principles of § 20.2056(b)-5(f), relating to whether the spouse is entitled for life to all of the income from the entire interest, or a specific portion of the entire interest, apply in determining whether the surviving spouse is entitled for life to all of the income from the property regardless of whether the interest passing to the spouse is in trust.

(3) *Contingent income interests.*—(i) An income interest for a term of years, or a life estate subject to termination upon the occurrence of a specified event (e.g., remarriage), is not a qualifying income interest for life. However, a qualifying income interest for life that is contingent upon the executor's election under section 2056(b)(7)(B)(v) will not fail to be a qualifying income interest for life because of such contingency or because the portion of the property for which the election is not made passes to or for the benefit of persons other than the surviving spouse. This paragraph (d)(3)(i) applies with respect to estates of decedents whose estate tax returns are due after February 18, 1997. This paragraph (d)(3)(i) also applies to estates of decedents whose estate tax returns were due on or before February 18, 1997, that meet the requirements of paragraph (d)(3)(ii) of this section.

(ii) Estates of decedents whose estate tax returns were due on or before February 18, 1997, that did not make the election under section 2056(b)(7)(B)(v) because the surviving spouse's income interest in the property was contingent upon the election or because the nonelected portion of the property was to pass to a beneficiary other than the surviving spouse are granted an extension of time to make the QTIP election if the following requirements are satisfied:

(A) The period of limitations on filing a claim for credit or refund under section 6511(a) has not expired.

(B) A claim for credit or refund is filed on Form 843 with a revised Recapitulation and Schedule M, Form 706 (or 706NA) that signifies the QTIP election. Reference to this section should be made on the Form 843.

(C) The following statement is included with the Form 843: "The undersigned certifies that the property with respect to which the QTIP election is being made will be included in the gross estate of the surviving spouse as provided in section 2044 of the Internal Revenue Code, in determining the federal estate tax liability on the spouse's death." The statement must be signed, under penalties of perjury, by the surviving spouse, the surviving spouse's legal representative (if the surviving spouse is legally incompetent), or the surviving spouse's executor (if the surviving spouse is deceased).

(4) *Income between last distribution date and date of spouse's death.*—An income interest does not fail to constitute a qualifying income interest for life solely because income between the last distribution date and the date of the surviving spouse's death is not required to be distributed to the surviving spouse or to the estate of the surviving spouse. See § 20.2044-1 relating to the inclusion of such undistributed income in the gross estate of the surviving spouse.

(5) *Pooled income funds.*—An income interest in a pooled income fund described in section 642(c)(5) constitutes a qualifying income interest for life for purposes of section 2056(b)(7)(B)(ii).

(6) *Power to distribute principal to spouse.*—An income interest in a trust will not fail to constitute a qualifying income interest for life solely because the trustee has a power to distribute principal to or for the benefit of the surviving spouse. The fact that property distributed to a surviving spouse may be transferred by the spouse to another person does not result in a failure to satisfy the requirement of section 2056(b)(7)(B)(ii)(II). However, if the surviving spouse is legally bound to transfer the distributed property to another person without full and adequate consideration in money or money's worth, the requirement of section 2056(b)(7)(B)(ii)(II) is not satisfied.

(e) *Annuities payable from trusts in the case of estates of decedents dying on or before October 24, 1992, and certain decedents dying after October 24, 1992, with wills or revocable trusts executed on or prior to that date.*—(1) *In general.*—In the case of estates of decedents within the purview of the effective date and transitional rules contained in § 20.2056(b)-7(e)(5), a surviving spouse's lifetime annuity interest payable from a trust or other group of assets passing from the decedent is treated as a qualifying income interest for life for purposes of section 2056(b)(7)(B)(ii).

(2) *Deductible interest.*—The deductible interest, for purposes of § 20.2056(a)-2(b), is the specific portion of the property that, assuming the applicable interest rate for valuing annuities, would produce income equal to the minimum amount payable annually to the surviving spouse. If, based on the applicable interest rate, the entire property from which the annuity may be satisfied is insufficient to produce income equal to the minimum annual payment, the value of the deductible interest is the entire value of the property. The value of the deductible interest may not exceed the value of the property from which the annuity is payable. If the annual payment may increase, the increased amount is not taken into account in valuing the deductible interest.

(3) *Distributions permissible only to surviving spouse.*—An annuity interest is not treated as a qualifying income interest for life for purposes of section 2056(b)(7)(B)(ii) if any person other than the surviving spouse may receive, during the surviving spouse's lifetime, any distribution of the property or its income (including any distribution under an annuity contract) from which the annuity is payable.

(4) *Applicable interest rate.*—To determine the applicable interest rate for valuing annuities, see sections 2031 and 7520 and the regulations under those sections.

(5) *Effective dates.*—(i) The rules contained in § 20.2056(b)-7(e) apply with respect to estates of decedents dying on or before October 24, 1992.

(ii) The rules contained in § 20.2056(b)-7(e) apply in the case of decedents dying after October 24, 1992, if property passes to the spouse pursuant to a will or revocable trust executed on or before October 24, 1992, and either—

(A) On that date, the decedent was under a mental disability to change the disposition of his property and did not regain his competence to dispose of such property before the date of death; or

(B) The decedent dies prior to October 24, 1995.

(iii) Notwithstanding the foregoing, the rules contained in § 20.2056(b)-7(e) do not apply if the will or revocable trust is amended after October 24, 1992, in any respect that increases the amount of the transfer qualifying for the marital deduction or alters the terms by which the interest so passes to the surviving spouse.

(f) *Joint and survivor annuities.*—[Reserved]

(g) *Application of local law.*—The provisions of local law are taken into account in determining whether the conditions of section 2056(b)(7)(B)(ii)(I) are satisfied. For example, silence of a trust instrument as to the frequency of payment is not regarded as a failure to satisfy the requirement that the income must be payable to the surviving spouse annually or more frequently unless applicable local law permits payments less frequently.

Reg. § 20.2056(b)-7(g)

(h) *Examples.*—The following examples illustrate the application of paragraphs (a) through (g) of this section. In each example, it is assumed that the decedent, D, was survived by S, D's spouse and that, unless stated otherwise, S is not the trustee of any trust established for S's benefit.

Example 1. Life estate in residence. D owned a personal residence valued at $250,000 for estate tax purposes. Under D's will, the exclusive and unrestricted right to use the residence (including the right to continue to occupy the property as a personal residence or to rent the property and receive the income) passes to S for life. At S's death, the property passes to D's children. Under applicable local law, S must consent to any sale of the property. If the executor elects to treat all of the personal residence as qualified terminable interest property, the deductible interest is $250,000, the value of the residence for estate tax purposes.

Example 2. Power to make property productive. D's will established a trust funded with property valued for estate tax purposes at $500,000. The assets include both income producing assets and non-productive assets. S was given the power, exercisable annually, to require distribution of all of the trust income to herself. No trust property may be distributed during S's lifetime to any person other than S. Applicable local law permits S to require that the trustee either make the trust property productive or sell the property and reinvest in productive property within a reasonable time after D's death. If the executor elects to treat all of the trust as qualified terminable interest property, the deductible interest is $500,000. If the executor elects to treat only 20 percent of the trust as qualified terminable interest property, the deductible interest is $100,000, i.e., 20 percent of $500,000.

Example 3. Power of distribution over fraction of trust income. The facts are the same as in *Example 2* except that S is given the right exercisable annually for S's lifetime to require distribution to herself of only 50 percent of the trust income for life. The remaining trust income is to be accumulated or distributed among S and the decedent's children in the trustee's discretion. The maximum amount that D's executor may elect to treat as qualified terminable interest property is $250,000; i.e., the estate tax value of the trust ($500,000) multiplied by the percentage of the trust in which S has a qualifying income interest for life (50 percent). If D's executor elects to treat only 20 percent of the portion of the trust in which S has a qualifying income interest as qualified terminable interest property, the deductible interest is $50,000, i.e., 20 percent of $250,000.

Example 4. Power to distribute trust corpus to other beneficiaries. D's will established a trust providing that S is entitled to receive at least annually all the trust income. The trustee is given the power to use annually during S's lifetime $5,000 from the trust for the maintenance and support of S's minor child, C. Any such distribution does not necessarily relieve S of S's obligation to support and maintain C. S does not have a qualifying income interest for life in any portion of the trust because the bequest fails to satisfy the condition that no person have a power, other than a power the exercise of which takes effect only at or after S's death, to appoint any part of the property to any person other than S. The trust would also be nondeductible under section 2056(b)(7) if S, rather than the trustee, held the power to appoint a portion of the principal to C. However, in the latter case, if S made a qualified disclaimer (within the meaning of section 2518) of the power to appoint to C, the trust could qualify for the marital deduction pursuant to section 2056(b)(7), assuming that the power is personal to S and S's disclaimer terminates the power. Similarly, in either case, if C made a qualified disclaimer of C's right to receive distributions from the trust, the trust would qualify under section 2056(b)(7), assuming that C's disclaimer effectively negates the trustee's power under local law.

Example 5. Spouse's income interest terminable on remarriage. D's will established a trust providing that all of the trust income is payable at least annually to S for S's lifetime, provided that, if S remarries, S's interest in the trust will pass to X. The trust is not deductible under section 2056(b)(7). S's income interest is not a *qualifying income interest for life* because it is not for life but, rather, is terminable upon S's remarriage.

Example 6. Spouse's qualifying income interest for life contingent on executor's election. D's will established a trust providing that S is entitled to receive the income, payable at least annually, from that portion of the trust that the executor elects to treat as qualified terminable interest property. The portion of the trust which the executor does not elect to treat as qualified terminable interest property passes as of D's date of death to a trust for the benefit of C, D's child. Under these facts, the executor is not considered to have a power to appoint any part of the trust property to any person other than S during S's life.

Example 7. Formula partial election. D's will established a trust funded with the residue of D's estate. Trust income is to be paid annually to S for life, and the principal is to be distributed to D's children upon S's death. S has the power to require that all the trust property be made productive. There is no power to distribute trust property during S's lifetime to any person other than S. D's executor elects to deduct a fractional share of the residuary estate under section 2056(b)(7). The election specifies that the numerator of the fraction is the amount of deduction necessary to reduce the Federal estate tax to zero (taking into account final estate tax values) and the denominator of the fraction is the final estate tax value of the residuary estate (taking into account any specific bequests or liabilities of the estate paid out of the residuary estate). The formula election is of a fractional share. The value of the share qualifies for the marital deduction even though the executor's determinations to claim administration expenses as estate or income tax deductions and the final estate tax values will affect the size of the fractional share.

Example 8. Formula partial election. The facts are the same as in *Example 7* except that, rather than defining a fraction, the executor's formula states: "I elect to treat as qualified terminable interest property that portion of the residuary trust, up to 100 percent, necessary to reduce the Federal estate tax to zero, after taking into account the available unified credit, final estate tax values and any liabilities and specific bequests paid from the residuary estate." The formula election is of a fractional share. The share is equivalent to the fractional share determined in *Example 7.*

Example 9. Severance of QTIP trust. D's will established a trust funded with the residue of D's estate. Trust income is to be paid annually to S for life, and the principal is to be distributed to D's children upon S's death. S has the power to require that all of the trust property be made productive. There is no power to distribute trust property during S's lifetime to any person other than S. D's will authorizes the executor to make the election under section 2056(b)(7) only with respect to the minimum amount of property necessary to reduce estate taxes on D's estate to zero, authorizes the executor to divide the residuary estate into two separate trusts to reflect the election, and authorizes the executor to charge any payment of principal to S to the qualified terminable interest trust. S is the sole beneficiary of both trusts during S's lifetime. The authorizations in the will do not adversely affect the allowance of the marital deduction. Only the property remaining in the marital deduction trust, after payment of principal to S, is subject to inclusion in S's gross estate under section 2044 or subject to gift tax under section 2519.

Example 10. Payments to spouse from individual retirement account. S is the life beneficiary of sixteen remaining annual installments payable from D's individual retirement account. The terms of the account provide for the payment of the account balance in nineteen annual installments that commenced when D reached age $70^{1}/_{2}$. Each installment is equal to all the income earned on the remaining principal in the account plus a share of the remaining principal equal to 1/19 in the first year, 1/18 in the second year, 1/17 in the third year, etc. Under the terms of the account, S has no right to withdraw any other amounts from the account. Any payments remaining after S's death pass to D's children. S's interest in the account qualifies as a qualifying income interest for life under section 2056(b)(7)(B)(ii), without regard to the provisions of section 2056(b)(7)(C).

Example 11. Spouse's interest in trust in the form of an annuity. D died prior to October 24, 1992. D's will established a trust funded with income producing property valued at $500,000 for estate tax purposes. The trustee is required by the trust instrument to pay $20,000 a year to S for life. Trust income in excess of the annuity amount is to be accumulated in the trust and may not be distributed during S's lifetime. S's lifetime annuity interest is treated as a qualifying income interest for life. If the executor elects to treat the entire portion of the trust in which S has a qualifying income interest as qualified terminable interest property, the value of the deductible interest is (assuming that 10 percent is the applicable interest rate under section 7520 for valuing annuities on the appropriate valuation date) $200,000, because that amount would yield an income to S of $20,000 a year.

Example 12. Value of spouse's annuity exceeds value of trust corpus. The facts are the same as in *Example 11* except that the trustee is required to pay S $70,000 a year for life. If the executor elects to treat the entire portion of the trust in which S has a qualifying income interest as qualified terminable interest property, the value of the deductible interest is $500,000, which is the lesser of the entire value of the property ($500,000), or the amount of property that (assuming a 10 percent interest rate) would yield an income to S of $70,000 a year ($700,000).

Example 13. Pooled income fund. D's will provides for a bequest of $200,000 to a pooled income fund described in section 642(c)(5), designating S as the income beneficiary for life. If D's executor elects to treat the entire $200,000 as qualified terminable interest property, the deductible interest is $200,000.

Example 14. Funding severed QTIP trusts. D's will established a trust satisfying the requirements of section 2056(b)(7). Pursuant to the authority in D's will and § 20.2056(b)-7(b)(2)(ii), D's executor indicates on the Federal estate tax return that an election under section 2056(b)(7) is being made with respect to 50 percent of the trust, and that the trust will subsequently be divided to reflect the partial election on the basis of the fair market value of the property at the time of the division. D's executor funds the trust at the end of the period of estate administration. At that time, the property available to fund the trusts consists of 100 shares of X Corporation stock with a current value of $400,000 and 200 shares of Y Corporation stock with a current value of $400,000. D may fund each trust with the stock of either or both corporations, in any combination, provided that the aggregate value of the stock allocated to each trust is $400,000. [Reg. § 20.2056(b)-7.]

☐ [*T.D.* 8522, 2-28-94. *Amended by T.D.* 8779, 8-18-98 *and T.D.* 9102, 12-30-2003.]

[Reg. § 20.2056(b)-8]

§ 20.2056(b)-8. Special rule for charitable remainder trusts.—(a) *In general.*—(1) *Surviving spouse only noncharitable beneficiary.*—With respect to estates of decedents dying after December 31, 1981, subject to section 2056(d), if the surviving spouse of the decedent is the only noncharitable beneficiary of a charitable remainder annuity trust or a charitable remainder unitrust described in section 664 (qualified charitable remainder trust), section 2056(b)(1) does not apply to the interest in the trust that is transferred to the surviving spouse. Thus, the value of the annuity or unitrust interest passing to the spouse qualifies for a marital deduction under section 2056(b)(8) and the value of the remainder interest qualifies for a charitable deduction under section 2055. If an interest in property qualifies for a marital deduction under section 2056(b)(8), no election may be made with respect to the property under section 2056(b)(7). For purposes of this section, the term *noncharitable beneficiary* means any beneficiary of the qualified charitable remainder trust other than an organization described in section 170(c).

(2) *Interest for life or term of years.*—The surviving spouse's interest need not be an interest for life to qualify for a marital deduction under section 2056(b)(8). However, for purposes of section 664, an annuity or unitrust interest payable to the spouse for a term of years cannot be payable for a term that exceeds 20 years.

(3) *Payment of state death taxes.*—A deduction is allowed under section 2056(b)(8) even if the transfer to the surviving spouse is conditioned on the spouse's payment of state death taxes, if any, attributable to the qualified charitable remainder trust. See § 20.2056(b)-4(c) for the effect of such a condition on the amount of the deduction allowable.

(b) *Charitable remainder trusts where the surviving spouse is not the only noncharitable beneficiary.*—In the case of a charitable remainder trust where the decedent's spouse is not the only noncharitable beneficiary (for example, where the noncharitable interest is payable to the decedent's spouse for life and then to another individual for life), the qualification of the interest as qualified terminable interest property is determined solely under section 2056(b)(7) and not under section 2056(b)(8). Accordingly, if the decedent died on or before October 24, 1992, or the trust otherwise comes within the purview of the transitional rules contained in § 20.2056(b)-7(e)(5), the spousal annuity or unitrust interest may qualify under § 20.2056(b)-(7)(e) as a qualifying income interest for life. [Reg. § 20.2056(b)-8.]

☐ [*T.D.* 8522, 2-28-94.]

[Reg. § 20.2056(b)-9]

§ 20.2056(b)-9. Denial of double deduction..—The value of an interest in property may not be deducted for Federal estate tax purposes more than once with respect to the same decedent. For example, where a decedent transfers a life estate in a farm to the spouse with a remain-

der to charity, the entire property is, pursuant to the executor's election under section 2056(b)(7), treated as passing to the spouse. The entire value of the property qualifies for the marital deduction. No part of the value of the property qualifies for a charitable deduction under section 2055 in the decedent's estate. [Reg. § 20.2056(b)-9.]

☐ [*T.D.* 8522, 2-28-94.]

[Reg. § 20.2056(b)-10]

§ 20.2056(b)-10. Effective dates..—Except as specifically provided in § § 20.2056(b)-5(c)(3)(ii) and (iii), 20.2056(b)-7(d)(3), 20.2056(b)-7(e)(5), and 20.2056(b)-8(b), the provisions of § § 20.2056(b)-5(c), 20.2056(b)-7, 20.2056(b)-8, and 20.2056(b)-9 are applicable with respect to estates of decedents dying after March 1, 1994. With respect to decedents dying on or before such date, the executor of the decedent's estate may rely on any reasonable interpretation of the statutory provisions. In addition, the rule in the last sentence of § 20.2056(b)-5(f)(1) and the rule in the last sentence of § 20.2056(b)-7(d)(1) regarding the effect on the spouse's right to income if applicable local law provides for the reasonable apportionment between the income and remainder beneficiaries of the total return of the trust are applicable with respect to trusts for taxable years ending after January 2, 2004. [Reg. § 20.2056(b)-10.]

☐ [*T.D.* 8522, 2-28-94. *Amended by T.D.* 8779, 8-18-98 *and T.D.* 9102, 12-30-2003.]

[Reg. § 20.2056(c)-1]

§ 20.2056(c)-1. Marital deduction; definition of passed from the decedent..—(a) *In general.*— The following rules are applicable in determining the person to whom any property interest "passed from the decedent":

(1) Property interests devolving upon any person (or persons) as surviving co-owner with the decedent under any form of joint ownership under which the right of survivorship existed are considered as having passed from the decedent to such person (or persons).

(2) Property interests at any time subject to the decedent's power to appoint (whether alone or in conjunction with any person) are considered as having passed from the decedent to the appointee under his exercise of the power, or, in case of the lapse, release or nonexercise of the power, as having passed from the decedent to the taker in default of exercise.

(3) The dower or curtesy interest (or statutory interest in lieu thereof) of the decedent's surviving spouse is considered as having passed from the decedent to his spouse.

(4) The proceeds of insurance upon the life of the decedent are considered as having passed from the decedent to the person who, at the time of the decedent's death, was entitled to receive the proceeds.

(5) Any property interest transferred during life, bequeathed or devised by the decedent, or inherited from the decedent, is considered as having passed to the person to whom he transferred, bequeathed, or devised the interest, or to the person who inherited the interest from him.

(6) The survivor's interest in an annuity or other payment described in section 2039 (see §§ 20.2039-1 and 20.2039-2) is considered as having passed from the decedent to the survivor only to the extent that the value of such interest is included in the decedent's gross estate under that section. If only a portion of the entire annuity or other payment is included in the decedent's gross estate and the annuity or other payment is payable to more than one beneficiary, then the value of the interest considered to have passed to each beneficiary is that portion of the amount payable to each beneficiary that the amount of the annuity or other payment included in the decedent's gross estate bears to the total value of the annuity or other payment payable to all beneficiaries.

(b) *Expectant interest in property under community property laws.*—If before the decedent's death the decedent's surviving spouse had merely an expectant interest in property held by her and the decedent under community property laws, that interest is considered as having passed from the decedent to the spouse. [Reg. § 20.2056(c)-1.]

☐ [*T.D. 6296, 6-23-58. Redesignated and amended by T.D. 8522, 2-28-94.*]

[Reg. § 20.2056(c)-2]

§ 20.2056(c)-2. Marital deduction; definition of passed from the decedent to his surviving spouse.—(a) *In general.*—In general, the definition stated in § 20.2056(c)-1 is applicable in determining the property interests which "passed from the decedent to his surviving spouse." Special rules are provided, however, for the following:

(1) In the case of certain interests with income for life to the surviving spouse with power of appointment in her (see § 20.2056(b)-5);

(2) In the case of certain interests with income for life to the surviving spouse that the executor elects to treat as qualified terminable interest property (see § 20.2056(b)-7);

(3) In the case of proceeds held by the insurer under a life insurance, endowment, or annuity contract with power of appointment in the surviving spouse (see § 20.2056(b)-6);

(4) In case of the disclaimer of an interest by the surviving spouse or by any other person (see § 20.2056(d)-1);

(5) In case of an election by the surviving spouse (see paragraph (c) of this section); and

(6) In case of a controversy involving the decedent's will, see paragraph (d) of this section.

A property interest is considered as passing to the surviving spouse only if it passes to the spouse as beneficial owner, except to the extent otherwise provided in §§ 20.2056(b)-5 through 20.2056(b)-7 in the case of certain life estates and insurance and annuity contracts with powers of appointment. For this purpose, where a property interest passed from the decedent in trust, such interest is considered to have passed from him to his surviving spouse to the extent of her beneficial interest therein. The deduction may not be taken with respect to a property interest which passed to such spouse merely as trustee, or subject to a binding agreement by the spouse to dispose of the interest in favor of a third person. An allowance or award paid to a surviving spouse pursuant to local law for her support during the administration of the decedent's estate constitutes a property interest passing from the decedent to his surviving spouse. In determining whether or not such an interest is deductible, however, see generally the terminable interest rules of § 20.2056(b)-1 and especially example (8) of paragraph (g) of that section.

(b) *Examples.*—The following illustrate the provisions of paragraph (a) of this section:

(1) A property interest bequeathed in trust by H (the decedent) is considered as having passed from him to W (his surviving spouse)—

(i) If the trust income is payable to W for life and upon her death the corpus is distributable to her executors or administrators;

(ii) If W is entitled to the trust income for a term of years following which the corpus is to be paid to W or her estate;

(iii) If the trust income is to be accumulated for a term of years or for W's life and the augmented fund paid to W or her estate; or

(iv) If the terms of the transfer satisfy the requirements of § 20.2056(b)-5 or 20.2056(b)-7.

(2) If H devised property—

(i) To A for life with remainder absolutely to W or her estate, the remainder interest is considered to have passed from H to W;

(ii) To W for life with remainder to her estate, the entire property is considered as having passed from H to W; or

(iii) Under conditions which satisfy the provisions of § 20.2056(b)-5 or 20.2056(b)-7, the entire property is considered as having passed from H to W.

(3) Proceeds of insurance upon the life of H are considered as having passed from H to W if the terms of the contract—

(i) Meet the requirements of § 20.2056(b)-6;

(ii) Provide that the proceeds are payable to W in a lump sum;

(iii) Provide that the proceeds are payable in installments to W for life and after her death any remaining installments are payable to her estate;

(iv) Provide that interest on the proceeds is payable to W for life and upon her death the principal amount is payable to her estate; or

(v) Provide that the proceeds are payable to a trustee under an arrangement whereby the requirements of § 2056 (b)(5) or 20.2056(b)-7 are satisfied.

(c) *Effect of election by surviving spouse.*—This paragraph contains rules applicable if the surviving spouse may elect between a property interest offered to her under the decedent's will or other instrument and a property interest to which she is otherwise entitled (such as dower, a right in the decedent's estate, or her interest under community property laws) of which adverse disposition was attempted by the decedent under the will or other instrument. If the surviving spouse elects to take against the will or other instrument, then the property interests offered thereunder are not considered as having "passed from the decedent to his surviving spouse" and the dower or other property interest retained by her is considered as having so passed (if it otherwise so qualifies under this section). If the surviving spouse elects to take under the will or other instrument, then the dower or other property interest relinquished by her is not considered as having "passed from the decedent to his surviving spouse" (irrespective of whether it otherwise comes within the definition stated in paragraph (a) of this section) and the interest taken under the will or other instrument is considered as having so passed (if it otherwise so qualifies). As to the valuation of the property interest taken under the will or other instrument, see paragraph (b) of § 20.2056(b)-4.

(d) *Will contests.*—(1) If as a result of a controversy involving the decedent's will, or involving any bequest or devise thereunder, his surviving spouse assigns or surrenders a property interest in settlement of the controversy, the interest so assigned or surrendered is not considered as having "passed from the decedent to his surviving spouse."

(2) If as a result of the controversy involving the decedent's will, or involving any bequest or devise thereunder, a property interest is assigned or surrendered to the surviving spouse, the interest so acquired will be regarded as having "passed from the decedent to his surviving spouse" only if the assignment or surrender was a bona fide recognition of enforceable rights of the surviving spouse in the decedent's estate. Such a bona fide recognition will be presumed where the assignment or surrender was pursuant to a decision of a local court upon the merits in an adversary proceeding following a genuine and active contest. However, such a decree will be accepted only to the extent that the court passed upon the facts upon which deductibility of the property interests depends. If the assignment or surrender was pursuant to a decree rendered by consent, or pursuant to an agreement not to contest the will or not to probate the will, it will not necessarily be accepted as a bona fide evaluation of the rights of the spouse.

(e) *Survivorship.*—If the order of deaths of the decedent and his spouse cannot be established by proof, a presumption (whether supplied by local law, the decedent's will, or otherwise) that the decedent was survived by his spouse will be recognized as satisfying paragraph (b)(1) of § 20.2056(a)-1, but only to the extent that it has the effect of giving to the spouse an interest in property includible in her gross estate under part III of subchapter A of chapter 11. Under these circumstances, if an estate tax return is required to be filed for the estate of the decedent's spouse, the marital deduction will not be allowed in the final audit of the estate tax return of the decedent's estate with respect to any property interest which has not been finally determined to be includible in the gross estate of his spouse. [Reg. § 20.2056(c)-2.]

☐ [*T.D. 6296, 6-23-58. Redesignated and amended by T.D. 8522, 2-28-94.*]

[Reg. § 20.2056(c)-3]

§ 20.2056(c)-3. Marital deduction; definition of passed from the decedent to a person other than his surviving spouse.—The expression "passed from the decedent to a person other than his surviving spouse" refers to any property interest which, under the definition stated in § 20.2056(c)-1 is considered as having "passed from the decedent" and which under the rules referred to in § 20.2056(c)-2 is not considered as having "passed from the decedent to his surviving spouse." Interests which passed to a person other than the surviving spouse include interests so passing under the decedent's exercise, release, or nonexercise of a nontaxable power to appoint. It is immaterial whether the property interest which passed from the decedent to a person other than his surviving spouse is included in the decedent's gross estate. The term "person other than his surviving spouse" includes the possible unascertained takers of a property interest, as, for example, the members of a class to be ascertained in the future. As another example, assume that the decedent created a power of appointment over a property interest, which does not come within the purview of § 20.2056(b)-5 or § 20.2056(b)-6. In such a case, the term "person other than his surviving spouse" refers to the possible appointees and possible takers in default (other than the spouse) of such property interest. Whether or not there is a possibility that the "person other than his surviving spouse" (or the heirs or assigns of such person) may possess or enjoy the property following termination or failure of the interest therein which passed from the decedent to his surviving spouse is to be determined as of the time of the decedent's death. [Reg. § 20.2056(c)-3.]

□ [*T.D.* 6296, 6-23-58. *Redesignated and amended by T.D.* 8522, 2-28-94.]

[Reg. § 20.2056(d)-1]

§ 20.2056(d)-1. Marital deduction; special rules for marital deduction if surviving spouse is not a United States citizen.—Rules pertaining to the application of section 2056(d), including certain transition rules, are contained in § § 20.2056A-1 through 20.2056A-13. [Reg. § 20.2056(d)-1.]

□ [*T.D.* 8612, 8-21-95.]

[Reg. § 20.2056(d)-2]

§ 20.2056(d)-2. Marital deduction; effect of disclaimers of post-December 31, 1976 transfers.—(a) *Disclaimer by a surviving spouse.*—If a surviving spouse disclaims an interest in property passing to such spouse from the decedent, which interest was created in a transfer made after December 31, 1976, the effectiveness of the disclaimer will be determined by section 2518 and the corresponding regulations. For rules relating to when the transfer creating the interest occurs, see § 25.2518-2(c)(3) and (c)(4) of this chapter. If a qualified disclaimer is determined to have been made by the surviving spouse, the property interest disclaimed is treated as if such interest had never been transferred to the surviving spouse.

(b) *Disclaimer by a person other than a surviving spouse.*—If an interest in property passes from a decedent to a person other than the surviving spouse, and the interest is created in a transfer made after December 31, 1976, and—

(1) The person other than the surviving spouse makes a qualified disclaimer with respect to such interest; and

(2) The surviving spouse is entitled to such interest in property as a result of such disclaimer, the disclaimed interest is treated as passing directly from the decedent to the surviving spouse. For rules relating to when the transfer creating the interest occurs, see § 25.2518-2(c)(3) and (c)(4) of this chapter.

(c) *Effective date.*—The first and second sentences of paragraphs (a) and (b) of this section are applicable for transfers creating the interest to be disclaimed made on or after December 31, 1997. [Reg. § 20.2056(d)-2.]

□ [*T.D.* 6296, 6-23-58. *Amended by T.D.* 8095, 8-6-86. *Redesignated by T.D.* 8612, 8-21-95. *Amended by T.D.* 8744, 12-30-97.]

[Reg. § 20.2056(d)-3]

§ 20.2056(d)-3. Marital deduction; effect of disclaimers of pre-January 1, 1977 transfers.—(a) *Disclaimer by a surviving spouse.*—If an interest in property passes to a decedent's surviving spouse in a taxable transfer made by a decedent dying before January 1, 1977, and the decedent's surviving spouse makes a disclaimer of this property interest, the disclaimed interest is considered as passing from the decedent to the person or persons entitled to receive the interest as a result of the disclaimer. A disclaimer is a complete and unqualified refusal to accept the rights to which one is entitled. It is, therefore, necessary to distinguish between the surviving spouse's disclaimer of a property interest and such surviving spouse's acceptance and subsequent disposal of a property interest. For example, if proceeds of insurance are payable to the surviving spouse and the proceeds are refused so that they consequently pass to an alternate beneficiary designated by the decedent, the proceeds are considered as having passed from the decedent to the alternate beneficiary. On the other hand, if the insurance company is directed by the surviving spouse to hold the proceeds at interest during such spouse's life and, upon this spouse's death, to pay the principal sum to another person designated by the surviving spouse, thus effecting a transfer of a remainder interest, the proceeds are considered as having passed from the decedent to the surviving spouse. See paragraph(c) of § 20.2056(e)-2 with respect to a spouse's exercise or failure to exercise a right to take against a decedent's will.

(b) *Disclaimer by a person other than a surviving spouse.*—(1) *Decedents dying after October 3, 1966 and before January 1, 1977.*—This paragraph (b)(1) applies in the case of a disclaimer of property passing to one other than the surviving spouse from a decedent dying after October 3, 1966 and before January 1, 1977. If a surviving spouse is entitled to receive property from the decedent as a result of the timely disclaimer made by the disclaimant, the property received by the surviving spouse is to be treated as passing to the surviving spouse from the decedent. Both a disclaimer of property passing by the laws of intestacy or otherwise, as by insurance or by trust, and a disclaimer of bequests and devises under the will of a decedent are to be fully effective for purposes of computing the marital deduction under section 2056. A disclaimer is a complete and unqualified refusal to accept some or all of the rights to which one is entitled. It must be a valid refusal under State law and must be made without consideration. For example, a disclaimer for the benefit of a surviving spouse who promises to give or bequeath property to a child of the person who disclaims is not a disclaimer within the meaning of this paragraph (b)(1). The disclaimer must be made before the person disclaiming accepts any property under the disclaimed interest. In the case of property transferred by a decedent dying after December 31, 1970, and before January 1, 1977, the disclaimer must be made within 9 months after the decedent's death (or within any extension of time for filing the estate tax return granted pursuant to section 6081). In the case of property transferred by a decedent dying after October 3,

1966, and before January 1, 1971, the disclaimer must be made within 15 months after the decedent's death (or within any extension of time for filing the estate's tax return granted pursuant to section 6081). If the disclaimer does not satisfy the requirements of this paragraph (b)(1), for the purpose of the marital deduction, the property is considered as passing from the decedent to the person who made the disclaimer as if the disclaimer had not been made.

(2) *Decedents dying after September 30, 1963 and before October 4, 1966.*—This paragraph (b)(2) applies in the case of a disclaimer of property passing to one other than the surviving spouse from a decedent dying after September 30, 1963 and before October 4, 1966. If, as a result of the disclaimer by the disclaimant, the surviving spouse is entitled to receive the disclaimed property interest, then such interest shall, for the purposes of this paragraph (b)(2), be considered as passing from the decedent to the surviving spouse if the following conditions are met. First, the interest disclaimed was bequeathed or devised to the disclaimant. Second, the disclaimant disclaimed all bequests and devises under the will before the date prescribed for the filing of the estate tax return. Third, the disclaimant did not accept any property under the bequest or devise before making the disclaimer. The interests passing by disclaimer to the surviving spouse under this paragraph (b)(2) are to qualify for the marital deduction only to the extent that, when added to any other allowable marital deduction without regard to this paragraph (b)(2), they do not exceed the greater of the deductions which would be allowable for the marital deduction without regard to the disclaimer if the surviving spouse exercised the election under State law to take against the will, or an amount equal to one-third of the decedent's adjusted gross estate. If the disclaimer does not satisfy the requirements of this paragraph (b)(2), the property is treated as passing from the decedent to the person who made the disclaimer, in the same manner as if the disclaimer had not been made.

(3) *Decedents dying before October 4, 1966.*— Unless the rule of paragraph (b)(2) of this section applies, this paragraph (b)(3) applies in the case of a disclaimer of property passing to one other than the surviving spouse from a decedent dying before October 4, 1966. For the purpose of these transfers, it is unnecessary to distinguish for the purpose of the marital deduction between a disclaimer by a person other than the surviving spouse and a transfer by such person. If the surviving spouse becomes entitled to receive an interest in property from the decedent as a result of a disclaimer made by some other person, the interest is, nevertheless, considered as having passed from the decedent, not to the surviving spouse, but to the person who made the disclaimer, as though the disclaimer had not been

made. If, as a result of a disclaimer made by a person other than the surviving spouse, a property interest passes to the surviving spouse under circumstances which meet the conditions set forth in § 20.2056(b)-5 (relating to a life estate with a power of appointment), the rule stated in the preceding sentence applies, not only with respect to the portion of the interest which beneficially vests in the surviving spouse, but also with respect to the portion over which such spouse acquires a power to appoint. The rule applies also in the case of proceeds under a life insurance, endowment, or annuity contract which, as a result of a disclaimer made by a person other than the surviving spouse, are held by the insurer subject to the conditions set forth in § 20.2056(b)-6. [Reg. § 20.2056(d)-3.]

☐ [*T.D.* 8095, 8-6-86. *Redesignated by T.D.* 8612, 8-21-95.]

[Reg. § 20.2056A-0]

§ 20.2056A-0. Table of contents.—This section lists the captions that appear in the final regulations under § § 20.2056A-1 through 20.2056A-13.

§ 20.2056A-4. *Procedures for conforming marital trusts and nontrust marital transfers to the requirements of a qualified domestic trust.*

(a) Marital trusts.

    (1) In general.

    (2) Judicial reformations.

    (3) Tolling of statutory assessment period.

(b) Nontrust marital transfers.

    (1) In general.

    (2) Form of transfer or assignment.

    (3) Assets eligible for transfer or assignment.

    (4) Pecuniary assignment - special rules.

    (5) Transfer tax treatment of transfer or assignment.

    (6) Period for completion of transfer.

    (7) Retirement accounts and annuities.

    (8) Protective assignment.

(c) Nonassignable annuities and other arrangements.

    (1) Definition and general rule.

    (2) Agreement to remit section 2056A estate tax on corpus portion of each annuity payment.

    (3) Agreement to roll over corpus portion of annuity payment to QDOT.

    (4) Determination of corpus portion.

    (5) Information Statement.

    (6) Agreement to pay section 2056A estate tax.

    (7) Agreement to roll over annuity payments.

(d) Examples.

§ 20.2056A-5. *Imposition of section 2056A estate tax.*

(a) In general.

(b) Amounts subject to tax.

    (1) Distribution of principal during the spouse's lifetime.

    (2) Death of surviving spouse.

    (3) Trust ceases to qualify as QDOT.

(c) Distributions and dispositions not subject to tax.

    (1) Distributions of principal on account of hardship.

    (2) Distributions of income to the surviving spouse.

    (3) Certain miscellaneous distributions and dispositions.

§ 20.2056A-6. *Amount of tax.*

(a) Definition of tax.

(b) Benefits allowed in determining amount of section 2056A estate tax.

    (1) General rule.

    (2) Treatment as resident.

    (3) Special rule in the case of trusts described in section 2056(b)(8).

    (4) Credit for state and foreign death taxes.

    (5) Alternate valuation and special use valuation.

    (c) Miscellaneous rules.

    (d) Examples.

§ 20.2056A-7. *Allowance of prior transfer credit under section 2013.*

(a) Property subject to QDOT election.

(b) Property not subject to QDOT election.

(c) Example.

§ 20.2056A-8. *Special rules for joint property.*

(a) Inclusion in gross estate.

    (1) General rule.

    (2) Consideration furnished by surviving spouse.

    (3) Amount allowed to be transferred to QDOT.

(b) Surviving spouse becomes citizen.

(c) Examples.

§ 20.2056A-9. *Designated Filer.*

§ 20.2056A-10. *Surviving spouse becomes citizen after QDOT established.*

(a) Section 2056A estate tax no longer imposed under certain circumstances.

(b) Special election by spouse.

§ 20.2056A-11. *Filing requirements and payment of the section 2056A estate tax.*

(a) Distributions during surviving spouse's life.

(b) Tax at death of surviving spouse.

(c) Extension of time for paying section 2056A estate tax.

    (1) Extension of time for paying tax under section 6161(a)(2).

    (2) Extension of time for paying tax under section 6161(a)(1).

(d) Liability for tax.

§ 20.2056A-12. *Increased basis for section 2056A estate tax paid with respect to distribution from a QDOT.*

§ 20.2056A-13. *Effective date.*

[Reg. § 20.2056A-0.]

☐ [*T.D.* 8612, 8-21-95. *Amended by T.D.* 8686, 11-27-96.]

[Reg. § 20.2056A-1]

§ 20.2056A-1. Restrictions on allowance of marital deduction if surviving spouse is not a United States citizen.—(a) *General rule.*—Subject to the special rules provided in section 7815(d)(14) of the Omnibus Budget Reconciliation Act of 1989 (Pub. L. 101-239; 103 Stat. 2106), in the case of a decedent dying after November 10, 1988, the federal estate tax marital deduction is not allowed for property passing to or for the benefit of a surviving spouse who is not a United States citizen at the date of the decedent's death (whether or not the surviving spouse is a resident of the United States) unless—

(1) The property passes from the decedent to (or pursuant to)—

(i) A qualified domestic trust (QDOT) described in section 2056A and § 20.2056A-2;

(ii) A trust that, although not meeting all of the requirements for a QDOT, is reformed after the decedent's death to meet the requirements of a QDOT (see § 20.2056A-4(a));

(iii) The surviving spouse not in trust (e.g., by outright bequest or devise, by operation of law, or pursuant to the terms of an annuity or other similar plan or arrangement) and, prior to the date that the estate tax return is filed and on or before the last date prescribed by law that the QDOT election may be made (no more than one year after the time prescribed by law, including extensions, for filing the return), the surviving spouse either actually transfers the property to a QDOT or irrevocably assigns the property to a QDOT (see § 20.2056A-4(b)); or

(iv) A plan or other arrangement that would have qualified for the marital deduction but for section 2056(d)(1)(A), and whose payments are not assignable or transferable to a QDOT, if the requirements of § 20.2056A-4(c) are met; and

(2) The executor makes a timely QDOT election under § 20.2056A-3.

(b) *Marital deduction allowed if resident spouse becomes citizen.*—For purposes of section 2056(d)(1) and paragraph (a) of this section, the surviving spouse is treated as a citizen of the United States at the date of the decedent's death if the requirements of section 2056(d)(4) are satisfied. For purposes of section 2056(d)(4)(A) and notwithstanding § 20.2056A-3(a), a return filed prior to the due date (including extensions) is considered filed on the last date that the return is required to be filed (including extensions), and a late return filed at any time after the due date is considered filed on the date that it is actually filed. A surviving spouse is a resident only if the spouse is a resident under chapter 11 of the Internal Revenue Code. See § 20.0-1(b)(1). The status of the spouse as a resident under section 7701(b) is not relevant to this determination except to the extent that the income tax residency of the spouse is pertinent in applying § 20.0-1(b)(1).

(c) *Special rules in the case of certain transfers subject to estate and gift tax treaties.*—Under section 7815(d)(14) of the Omnibus Budget Reconciliation Act of 1989 (Pub. L. 101-239, 103 Stat. 2106) certain special rules apply in the case of transfers governed by certain estate and gift tax treaties to which the United States is a party. In the case of the estate of, or gift by, an individual who was not a citizen or resident of the United States but was a resident of a foreign country with which the United States has a tax treaty with respect to estate, inheritance, or gift taxes, the amendments made by section 5033 of the Technical and Miscellaneous Revenue Act of 1988 (Pub. L. 100-647, 102 Stat. 3342) do not apply to the extent such amendments would be inconsistent with the provisions of such treaty relating to estate, inheritance, or gift tax marital deductions. Under this rule, the estate may choose either the statutory deduction under section 2056A or the marital deduction allowed under the treaty. Thus, the estate may not avail itself of both the marital deduction under the treaty and the marital deduction under the QDOT provisions of section 2056A and chapter 11 of the Internal Revenue Code with respect to the remainder of the marital property that is not deductible under the treaty. [Reg. § 20.2056A-1.]

☐ [*T.D.* 8612, 8-21-95.]

[Reg. § 20.2056A-2]

§ 20.2056A-2. Requirements for qualified domestic trust.—(a) *In general.*—In order to qualify as a qualified domestic trust (QDOT), the requirements of paragraphs (b) and (c) of this section, and the requirements of § 20.2056A-2T(d), must be satisfied. The executor of the decedent's estate and the U.S. Trustee shall establish in such manner as may be prescribed by the Commissioner on the estate tax return and applicable instructions that these requirements have been satisfied or are being complied with. In order to constitute a QDOT, the trust must be maintained under the laws of a state of the United States or the District of Columbia, and the administration of the trust must be governed by the laws of a particular state of the United States or the District of Columbia. For purposes of this paragraph, a trust is maintained under the laws of a state of the United States or the District of Columbia if the records of the trust (or copies thereof) are kept in that state (or the District of Columbia). The trust may be established pursuant to an instrument executed under either the laws of a state of the United States or the District of Columbia or pursuant to an instrument executed under the laws of a foreign jurisdiction, such as a foreign will or trust, provided that such foreign instrument designates the law of a particular state of the United States or the District of Columbia as governing the administration of the trust, and such designation is effective under the law of the designated jurisdiction. In addition, the trust must constitute an ordinary trust, as defined in § 301.7701-4(a) of this chapter, and not any other type of entity. For purposes of this paragraph (a), a trust will not fail to constitute an ordinary trust solely because of the nature of the assets transferred to that trust, regardless of its classification under §§ 301.7701-2 through 301.7701-4 of this chapter.

(b) *Qualified marital interest requirements.*—(1) *Property passing to QDOT.*—If property passes from a decedent to a QDOT, the trust must qualify for the federal estate tax marital deduction under section 2056(b)(5) (life estate with power of appointment), section 2056(b)(7) (qualified terminable interest property, including joint and survivor annuities under section 2056(b)(7)(C)), or section 2056(b)(8) (surviving spouse is the only noncharitable beneficiary of a charitable remainder trust), or meet the requirements of an estate trust as defined in § 20.2056(c)-2(b)(1)(i) through (iii).

(2) *Property passing outright to spouse.*—If property does not pass from a decedent to a QDOT, but passes to a noncitizen surviving spouse in a form that meets the requirements for a marital deduction without regard to section 2056(d)(1)(A), and that is not described in paragraph (b)(1) of this section, the surviving spouse must either actually transfer the property, or irrevocably assign the property, to a trust (whether created by the decedent, the decedent's executor or by the surviving spouse) that meets the requirements of paragraph (c) of this section and the requirements of § 20.2056A-2T(d) (pertaining, respectively, to statutory requirements and regulatory requirements imposed to ensure collection of tax) prior to the filing of the estate tax return for the decedent's estate and on or before the last date prescribed by law that the QDOT election may be made (see § 20.2056A-3(a)).

(3) *Property passing under a nontransferable plan or arrangement.*—If property does not pass from a decedent to a QDOT, but passes under a plan or other arrangement that meets the requirements for a marital deduction without regard to section 2056(d)(1)(A) and whose payments are not assignable or transferable (see § 20.2056A-4(c)), the property is treated as meeting the requirements of this section, and the requirements of § 20.2056A-2T(d), if the requirements of § 20.2056A-4(c) are satisfied. In addition, where an annuity or similar arrangement is described above except that it is assignable or transferable, see § 20.2056A-4(b)(7).

(c) *Statutory requirements.*—The requirements of section 2056A(a)(1)(A) and (B) must be satisfied. For purposes of that section, a domestic corporation is a corporation that is created or organized under the laws of the United States or under the laws of any state of the United States or the District of Columbia. The trustee required under that section is referred to herein as the "U.S. Trustee".

(d) *Additional requirements to ensure collection of the section 2056A estate tax.*—(1) *Security and other arrangements for payment of estate tax imposed under section 2056A(b)(1).*—(i) *QDOTs with assets in excess of $2 million.*—If the fair market value of the assets passing, treated, or deemed to have passed to the QDOT (or in the form of a QDOT), determined without reduction for any indebtedness with respect to the assets, as finally deter-

mined for federal estate tax purposes, exceeds $2 million as of the date of the decedent's death or, if applicable, the alternate valuation date (adjusted as provided in paragraph (d)(1)(iii) of this section), the trust instrument must meet the requirements of either paragraph (d)(1)(i)(A), (B), or (C) of this section at all times during the term of the QDOT. The QDOT may alternate between any of the arrangements provided in paragraphs (d)(1)(i)(A), (B), and (C) of this section provided that, at any given time, one of the arrangements must be operative. See paragraph (d)(1)(iii) of this section for the definition of finally determined. The QDOT may provide that the trustee has the discretion to use any one of the security arrangements or may provide that the trustee is limited to using only one or two of the arrangements specified in the trust instrument. A trust instrument that specifically states that the trust must be administered in compliance with paragraph (d)(1)(i)(A), (B), or (C) of this section is treated as meeting the requirements of paragraphs (d)(1)(i)(A), (B), or (C) for purposes of paragraphs (d)(1)(i) and, if applicable, (d)(1)(ii) of this section.

(A) *Bank Trustee.*—Except as otherwise provided in paragraph (d)(6)(ii) or (iii) of this section, the trust instrument must provide that whenever the Bank Trustee security alternative is used for the QDOT, at least one U.S. Trustee must be a bank as defined in section 581. Alternatively, except as otherwise provided in paragraph (d)(6)(ii) or (iii) of this section, at least one trustee must be a United States branch of a foreign bank, provided that, in such cases, during the entire term of the QDOT a U.S. Trustee must act as a trustee with the foreign bank trustee.

(B) *Bond.*—Except as otherwise provided in paragraph (d)(6)(ii) or (iii) of this section, the trust instrument must provide that whenever the bond security arrangement alternative is used for the QDOT, the U.S. Trustee must furnish a bond in favor of the Internal Revenue Service in an amount equal to 65 percent of the fair market value of the trust assets (determined without regard to any indebtedness with respect to the assets) as of the date of the decedent's death (or alternate valuation date, if applicable), as finally determined for federal estate tax purposes (and as further adjusted as provided in paragraph (d)(1)(iv) of this section). If, after examination of the estate tax return, the fair market value of the trust assets, as originally reported on the estate tax return, is adjusted (pursuant to a judicial proceeding or otherwise) resulting in a final determination of the value of the assets as reported on the return, the U.S. Trustee has a reasonable period of time (not exceeding sixty days after the conclusion of the proceeding or other action resulting in a final determination of the value of the assets) to adjust the amount of the bond accordingly. But see, paragraph (d)(1)(i)(D) of this section for a special rule in the case of a substantial undervaluation of QDOT assets. Unless an alternate arrangement under paragraph (d)(1)(i)(A), (B), or (C) of this section, or an arrangement prescribed under paragraph (d)(4) of this section, is provided, or the trust is otherwise no longer subject to the requirements of section 2056A pursuant to section 2056A(b)(12), the bond must remain in effect until the trust ceases to function as a QDOT and any tax liability finally determined to be due under section 2056A(b) is paid, or is finally determined to be zero.

(1) *Requirements for the bond.*—The bond must be with a satisfactory surety, as prescribed under section 7101 and § 301.7101-1 of this chapter (Regulations on Procedure and Administration), and is subject to Internal Revenue Service review as may be prescribed by the Commissioner. The bond may not be cancelled. The bond must be for a term of at least one year and must be automatically renewable at the end of that term, on an annual basis thereafter, unless notice of failure to renew is mailed to the U.S. Trustee and the Internal Revenue Service at least 60 days prior to the end of the term, including periods of automatic extensions. Any notice of failure to renew required to be sent to the Internal Revenue Service must be sent to the Estate and Gift Tax Group in the District Office of the Internal Revenue Service that has examination jurisdiction over the decedent's estate (Internal Revenue Service, District Director, *[specify location]* District Office, Estate and Gift Tax Examination Group, [specify Street Address, City, State, Zip Code]) (or in the case of noncitizen decedents and United States citizens who die domiciled outside the United States, Estate Tax Group, Assistant Commissioner (International), 950 L'Enfant Plaza, CP:IN:D:C:EX:HQ:1114, Washington, DC 20024). The Internal Revenue Service will not draw on the bond if, within 30 days of receipt of the notice of failure to renew, the U.S. Trustee notifies the Internal Revenue Service (at the same address to which notice of failure to renew is to be sent) that an alternate arrangement under paragraph (d)(1)(i)(A), (B), or (C) or (d)(4) of this section, has been secured and that the arrangement will take effect immediately prior to or upon expiration of the bond.

(2) *Form of bond.*—The bond must be in the following form (or in a form that is the same as the following form in all material respects), or in such alternative form as the Commissioner may prescribe by guidance published in the Internal Revenue Bulletin (see § 601.601(d)(2) of this chapter):

Bond in Favor of the Internal Revenue Service To Secure Payment of Section 2056A Estate Tax Imposed Under Section 2056A(b) of the Internal Revenue Code.

KNOW ALL PERSONS BY THESE PRESENTS, That the undersigned, _____, the SURETY, and _____, the PRINCIPAL, are irrev-ocably held and firmly bound to pay the Internal Revenue Service upon written demand that amount of any tax up to $*[amount determined under paragraph (d)(1)(i)(B) of this section]*, imposed under section 2056A(b)(1) of the Internal Revenue Code (including penalties and interest on said tax) determined by the Internal Revenue Service to be payable with respect to the principal as trustee for: *[Identify trust and governing instrument, name and address of trustee]*, a qualified domestic trust as defined in section 2056A(a) of the Internal Revenue Code, for the payment of which the said Principal and said Surety, bind themselves, their heirs, executors, administrators, successors and assigns, jointly and severally, firmly by these presents.

WHEREAS, The Internal Revenue Service may demand payment under this bond at any time if the Internal Revenue Service in its sole discretion determines that a taxable event with respect to the trust has occurred; the trust no longer qualifies as a qualified domestic trust as described in section 2056A(a) of the Internal Revenue Code and the regulations promulgated thereunder, or a distribution subject to the tax imposed under section 2056A(b)(1) has been made. Demand by the Internal Revenue Service for payment may be made whether or not the tax and tax return (Form 706-QDT) with respect to the taxable event is due at the time of such demand, or an assessment has been made by the Internal Revenue Service with respect to the tax.

NOW THEREFORE, The condition of this obligation is such that it must not be cancelled and, if payment of all tax liability finally determined to be imposed under section 2056A(b) is made, then this obligation is null and void; otherwise, this obligation is to remain in full force and effect for one year from its effective date and is to be automatically renewable on an annual basis unless, at least 60 days prior to the expiration date, including periods of automatic renewals, the surety mails to the U.S. Trustee and the Internal Revenue Service by Registered or Certified Mail, return receipt requested, notice of the failure to renew. Receipt of this notice of failure to renew by the Internal Revenue Service may be considered a taxable event. The Internal Revenue Service will not draw upon the bond if, within 30 days of receipt of the notice of failure to renew, the trustee notifies the Internal Revenue Service that an alternate security arrangement has been secured and that the arrangement will take effect immediately prior to or upon expiration of the bond. The surety remains liable for all taxable events occurring prior to the date of expiration. All notices required to be sent to the Internal Revenue Service under this instrument should be sent to District Director, *[specify location]* District Office, Estate and Gift Tax Examination Group, Street Address, City, State, Zip Code. (In the case of nonresident noncitizen decedents and United States citizens who die domiciled outside the United States, all notices should be sent to Estate Tax Group, Assistant Commissioner (International), 950 L'Enfant Plaza, CP:IN:D:C:EX:HQ:1114, Washington, DC 20024).

This bond shall be effective as of _____.

Principal _____

Date _____

Surety _____

Date _____

(3) Additional governing instrument requirements.—The trust instrument must provide that in the event the Internal Revenue Service draws on the bond, in accordance with its terms, neither the U.S. Trustee nor any other person will seek a return of any part of the remittance until after April 15th of the calendar year following the year in which the bond is drawn upon. After that date, any such remittance will be treated as a deposit and returned (without interest) upon request of the U.S. Trustee, unless it is determined that assessment or collection of the tax imposed by section 2056A(b)(1) is in jeopardy, within the meaning of section 6861. If an assessment under section 6861 is made, the remittance will first be credited to any tax liability reported on the Form 706-QDT, then to any unpaid balance of a section 2056A(b)(1)(A) tax liability (plus interest and penalties) for any prior taxable years, and any balance will then be returned to the U.S. Trustee.

(4) Procedure.—The bond is to be filed with the decedent's federal estate tax return, Form 706 or 706NA (unless an extension for filing the bond is granted under § 301.9100 of this chapter). The U.S. Trustee must provide a written statement with the bond that provides a list of the assets that will be used to fund the QDOT and the respective values of the assets. The written statement must also indicate whether any exclusions under paragraph (d)(1)(iv) of this section are claimed.

(C) *Letter of credit.*—Except as otherwise provided in paragraph (d)(6)(ii) or (iii) of this section, the trust instrument must provide that whenever the letter of credit security arrangement is used for the QDOT, the U.S. Trustee must furnish an irrevocable letter of credit issued by a bank as defined in section 581, a United States branch of a foreign bank, or a foreign bank with a confirmation by a bank as defined in section 581. The letter of credit must be for an amount equal to 65 percent of the fair market value of the trust assets (determined without regard to any indebtedness with respect to the assets) as of the date of the decedent's death (or alternate valuation date, if applicable), as finally determined for federal estate tax purposes (and as further adjusted as provided in paragraph (d)(1)(iv) of this section). If, after examination of the estate tax return, the fair market value of the trust assets, as originally reported

on the estate tax return, is adjusted (pursuant to a judicial proceeding or otherwise) resulting in a final determination of the value of the assets as reported on the return, the U.S. Trustee has a reasonable period of time (not exceeding 60 days after the conclusion of the proceeding or other action resulting in a final determination of the value of the assets) to adjust the amount of the letter of credit accordingly. But see, paragraph (d)(1)(i)(D) of this section for a special rule in the case of a substantial undervaluation of QDOT assets. Unless an alternate arrangement under paragraph (d)(1)(i)(A), (B), or (C) of this section, or an arrangement prescribed under paragraph (d)(4) of this section, is provided, or the trust is otherwise no longer subject to the requirements of section 2056A pursuant to section 2056A(b)(12), the letter of credit must remain in effect until the trust ceases to function as a QDOT and any tax liability finally determined to be due under section 2056A(b) is paid or is finally determined to be zero.

(1) Requirements for the letter of credit.—The letter of credit must be irrevocable and provide for sight payment. The letter of credit must have a term of at least one year and must be automatically renewable at the end of the term, at least on an annual basis, unless notice of failure to renew is mailed to the U.S. Trustee and the Internal Revenue Service at least sixty days prior to the end of the term, including periods of automatic renewals. If the letter of credit is issued by the U.S. branch of a foreign bank and the U.S. branch is closing, the branch (or foreign bank) must notify the U.S. Trustee and the Internal Revenue Service of the closure and the notice of closure must be mailed at least 60 days prior to the date of closure. Any notice of failure to renew or closure of a U.S. branch of a foreign bank required to be sent to the Internal Revenue Service must be sent to the Estate and Gift Tax Group in the District Office of the Internal Revenue Service that has examination jurisdiction over the decedent's estate (Internal Revenue Service, District Director, [*specify location*] District Office, Estate and Gift Tax Examination Group, [Street Address, City State, Zip Code]) (or in the case of noncitizen decedents and United States citizens who die domiciled outside the United States, Estate Tax, Assistant Commissioner (International), 950 L'Enfant Plaza, CP:IN:D:C:EX:HQ:1114, Washington, DC 20024). The Internal Revenue Service will not draw on the letter of credit if, within 30 days of receipt of the notice of failure to renew or closure of the U.S. branch of a foreign bank, the U.S. Trustee notifies the Internal Revenue Service (at the same address to which notice is to be sent) that an alternate arrangement under paragraph (d)(1)(i)(A), (B), or (C), or (d)(4) of this section, has been secured and that the arrangement will take effect immediately prior to or upon expiration of the letter of credit or closure of the U.S. branch of the foreign bank.

Reg. § 20.2056A-2(d)(1)(i)(C)(1)

(2) Form of letter of credit.—The letter of credit must be made in the following form (or in a form that is the same as the following form in all material respects), or an alternative form that the Commissioner prescribes by guidance published in the Internal Revenue Bulletin (see § 601.601(d)(2) of this chapter):

[Issue Date]

To: Internal Revenue Service
Attention: District Director, *[specify location]* District Office
Estate and Gift Tax Examination Group
[Street Address, City, State, ZIP Code]
[Or in the case of nonresident noncitizen decedents and United States citizens who die domiciled outside the United States,

To: Estate Tax Group,
Assistant Commissioner (International)
950 L'Enfant Plaza
CP:IN:D:C:EX:HQ:1114
Washington, DC 20024].

Dear Sirs:

We hereby establish our irrevocable Letter of Credit No.—in your favor for drawings up to U.S. $[Applicant should provide bank with amount which Applicant determined under paragraph (d)(1)(i)(C)] effective immediately. This Letter of Credit is issued, presentable and payable at our office at _____ and expires at 3:00 p.m. [EDT, EST, CDT, CST, MDT, MST, PDT, PST]on _____ at said office.

For information and reference only, we are informed that this Letter of Credit relates to *[Applicant should provide bank with the identity of qualified domestic trust and governing instrument]*, and the name, address, and identifying number of the trustee is *[Applicant should provide bank with the trustee name, address and the QDOT's TIN number, if any]*.

Drawings on this Letter of Credit are available upon presentation of the following documents:

1. Your draft drawn at sight on us bearing our Letter of Credit No. _____; and

2. Your signed statement as follows:

The amount of the accompanying draft is payable under *[identify bank]* irrevocable Letter of Credit No. _____ pursuant to section 2056A of the Internal Revenue Code and the regulations promulgated thereunder, because the Internal Revenue Service in its sole discretion has determined that a "taxable event" with respect to the trust has occurred; e.g., the trust no longer qualifies as a qualified domestic trust as described in section 2056A of the Internal Revenue Code and regulations promulgated thereunder, or a distribution subject to the tax imposed under section 2056A(b)(1) of the Internal Revenue Code has been made.

Except as expressly stated herein, this undertaking is not subject to any agreement, requirement or qualification. The obligation of

[Name of Issuing Bank] under this Letter of Credit is the individual obligation of [Name of Issuing Bank] and is in no way contingent upon reimbursement with respect thereto.

It is a condition of this Letter of Credit that it is deemed to be automatically extended without amendment for a period of one year from the expiration date hereof, or any future expiration date, unless at least 60 days prior to any expiration date, we mail to you and to the U.S. Trustee notice by Registered Mail or Certified Mail, return receipt requested, or by courier to your and the trustee's address indicated above, that we elect not to consider this Letter of Credit renewed for any such additional period. Upon receipt of this notice, you may draw hereunder on or before the then current expiration date, by presentation of your draft and statement as stipulated above.

[In the case of a letter of credit issued by a U.S. branch of a foreign bank the following language must be added]. It is a further condition of this Letter of Credit that if the U.S. branch of [name of foreign bank] is to be closed, that at least sixty days prior to closing, we mail to you and the U.S. Trustee notice by Registered Mail or Certified Mail, return receipt requested, or by courier to your and the U.S. Trustee's address indicated above, that this branch will be closing. This notice will specify the actual date of closing. Upon receipt of the notice, you may draw hereunder on or before the date of closure, by presentation of your draft and statement as stipulated above.

Except where otherwise stated herein, this Letter of Credit is subject to the Uniform Customs and Practice for Documentary Credits, 1993 Revision, ICC Publication No. 500. If we notify you of our election not to consider this Letter of Credit renewed and the expiration date occurs during an interruption of business described in Article 17 of said Publication 500, unless you had consented to cancellation prior to the expiration date, the bank hereby specifically agrees to effect payment if this Letter of Credit is drawn against within 30 days after the resumption of business.

Except as stated herein, this Letter of Credit cannot be modified or revoked without your consent.

Authorized Signature _____
Date _____

(3) Form of confirmation.—If the requirements of this paragraph (d)(1)(i)(C) are satisfied by the issuance of a letter of credit by a foreign bank with confirmation by a bank as defined in section 581, the confirmation must be made in the following form (or in a form that is the same as the following form in all material respects), or an alternative form as the Commissioner prescribes by guidance published in the Internal Revenue Bulletin (see § 602.101(d)(2) of this chapter):

[Issue Date]
To: Internal Revenue Service
Attention: District Director, *[specify location]* District Office
Estate and Gift Tax Examination Group
[State Address, City, State, ZIP Code]
[or in the case of nonresident noncitizen decedents and United States citizens who die domiciled outside the United States,

To: Estate Tax Group,
Assistant Commissioner (International)
950 L'Enfant Plaza
CP:IN:D:C:EX:HQ:1114
Washington, DC 20024].
Dear Sirs:

We hereby confirm the enclosed irrevocable Letter of Credit No. _____, and amendments thereto, if any, in your favor by _____ [Issuing Bank] for drawings up to U.S. $_____ [same amount as in initial Letter of Credit] effective immediately. This confirmation is issued, presentable and payable at our office at _____ and expires at 3:00 p.m. [EDT, EST, CDT, CST, MDT, MST, PDT, PST]on _____ at said office.

For information and reference only, we are informed that this Confirmation relates to [Applicant should provide bank with the identity of qualified domestic trust and governing instrument], and the name, address, and identifying number of the trustee is [Applicant should provide bank with the trustee name, address and the QDOT's TIN number, if any].

We hereby undertake to honor your sight draft(s) drawn as specified in the Letter of Credit.

Except as expressly stated herein, this undertaking is not subject to any agreement, condition or qualification. The obligation of *[Name of Confirming Bank]* under this Confirmation is the individual obligation of *[Name of Confirming Bank]* and is in no way contingent upon reimbursement with respect thereto.

It is a condition of this Confirmation that it is deemed to be automatically extended without amendment for a period of one year from the expiry date hereof, or any future expiration date, unless at least sixty days prior to the expiration date, we send to you and to the U.S. Trustee notice by Registered Mail or Certified Mail, return receipt requested, or by courier to your and the trustee's addresses, respectively, indicated above, that we elect not to consider this Confirmation renewed for any additional period. Upon receipt of this notice by you, you may draw hereunder on or before the then current expiration date, by presentation of your draft and statement as stipulated above.

Except where otherwise stated herein, this Confirmation is subject to the Uniform Customs and Practice for Documentary Credits, 1993 Revision, ICC Publication No. 500.

If we notify you of our election not to consider this Confirmation renewed and the expiration date occurs during an interruption of business described in Article 17 of said Publication 500, unless you had consented to cancellation prior to the expiration date, the bank hereby specifically agrees to effect payment if this Confirmation is drawn against within 30 days after the resumption of business.

Except as stated herein, this Confirmation cannot be modified or revoked without your consent.

Authorized Signature _____
Date _____

(4) *Additional governing instrument requirements.*—The trust instrument must provide that if the Internal Revenue Service draws on the letter of credit (or confirmation) in accordance with its terms, neither the U.S. Trustee nor any other person will seek a return of any part of the remittance until April 15th of the calendar year following the year in which the letter of credit (or confirmation) is drawn upon. After that date, any such remittance will be treated as a deposit and returned (without interest) upon request of the U.S. Trustee after the date specified above, unless it is determined that assessment or collection of the tax imposed by section 2056A(b)(1) is in jeopardy, within the meaning of section 6861. If an assessment under section 6861 is made, the remittance will first be credited to any tax liability reported on the Form 706-QDT, then to any unpaid balance of a section 2056A(b)(1)(A) tax liability (plus interest and penalties) for any prior taxable years, and any balance will then be returned to the U.S. Trustee.

(5) *Procedure.*—The letter of credit (and confirmation, if applicable) is to be filed with the decedent's federal estate tax return, Form 706 or 706NA (unless an extension for filing the letter of credit is granted under §301.9100 of this chapter). The U.S. Trustee must provide a written statement with the letter of credit that provides a list of the assets that will be used to fund the QDOT and the respective values of the assets. The written statement must also indicate whether any exclusions under paragraph (d)(1)(iv) of this section are claimed.

(D) *Disallowance of marital deduction for substantial undervaluation of QDOT property in certain situations.*—(1) If either—

(i) The bond or letter of credit security arrangement under paragraph (d)(1)(i)(B) or (C) of this section is chosen by the U.S. Trustee; or

(ii) The QDOT property as originally reported on the decedent's estate tax return is valued at $2 million or less but, as finally determined for federal estate tax purposes, the QDOT property is determined to be in excess of $2 million, then the marital deduction will be disallowed in its entirety for failure to comply

Reg. §20.2056A-2(d)(1)(i)(D)(1)(ii)

with the requirements of section 2056A if the value of the QDOT property reported on the estate tax return is 50 percent or less of the amount finally determined to be the correct value of the property for federal estate tax purposes.

(2) The preceding sentence does not apply if—

(i) There was reasonable cause for the undervaluation; and

(ii) The fiduciary of the estate acted in good faith with respect to the undervaluation. For this purpose, § 1.6664-4(b) of this chapter applies, to the extent applicable, with respect to the facts and circumstances to be taken into account in making this determination.

(ii) *QDOTs with assets of $2 million or less.*—If the fair market value of the assets passing, treated, or deemed to have passed to the QDOT (or in the form of a QDOT), determined without reduction for any indebtedness with respect to the assets, as finally determined for federal estate tax purposes, is $2 million or less as of the date of the decedent's death or, if applicable, the alternate valuation date (adjusted as provided in paragraph (d)(1)(iv) of this section), the trust instrument must provide that either no more than 35 percent of the fair market value of the trust assets, determined annually on the last day of the taxable year of the trust (or on the last day of the calendar year if the QDOT does not have a taxable year), will consist of real property located outside of the United States, or the trust will meet the requirements prescribed by paragraph (d)(1)(i)(A), (B), or (C) of this section. See paragraph (d)(1)(ii)(D) of this section for special rules in the case of principal distributions from a QDOT, fluctuations in the value of foreign real property held by a QDOT due to changes in value of foreign currency, and fluctuations in the fair market value of assets held by the QDOT. See paragraph (d)(1)(iv) of this section for a special rule for personal residences. If the fair market value, as originally reported on the decedent's estate tax return, of the assets passing or deemed to have passed to the QDOT (determined without reduction for any indebtedness with respect to the assets) is $2 million or less, but the fair market value of the assets as finally determined for federal estate tax purposes is more than $2 million, the U.S. Trustee has a reasonable period of time (not exceeding sixty days after the conclusion of the proceeding or other action resulting in a final determination of the value of the assets) to meet the requirements prescribed by paragraph (d)(1)(i)(A), (B), or (C) of this section. However, see paragraph (d)(1)(i)(D) of this section in the case of a substantial undervaluation of QDOT assets. See § 20.2056A-2(d)(1)(iii) for the definition of finally determined.

(A) *Multiple QDOTs.*—For purposes of this paragraph (d)(1)(ii), if more than one QDOT

is established for the benefit of the surviving spouse, the fair market value of all the QDOTs are aggregated in determining whether the $2 million threshold under this paragraph (d)(1)(ii) is exceeded.

(B) *Look-through rule.*—For purposes of determining whether no more than 35 percent of the fair market value of the QDOT assets consists of foreign real property, if the QDOT owns more than 20% of the voting stock or value in a corporation with 15 or fewer shareholders, or more than 20% of the capital interest of a partnership with 15 or fewer partners, then all assets owned by the corporation or partnership are deemed to be owned directly by the QDOT to the extent of the QDOT's pro rata share of the assets of that corporation or partnership. For a partnership, the QDOT partner's pro rata share is based on the greater of its interest in the capital or profits of the partnership. For purposes of this paragraph, all stock in the corporation, or interests in the partnership, as the case may be, owned by or held for the benefit of the surviving spouse, or any members of the surviving spouse's family (within the meaning of section 267(c)(4)), are treated as owned by the QDOT solely for purposes of determining the number of partners or shareholders in the entity and the QDOT's percentage voting interest or value in the corporation or capital interest in the partnership, but not for the purpose of determining the QDOT's pro rata share of the assets of the entity.

(C) *Interests in other entities.*—Interests owned by the QDOT in other entities (such as an interest in a trust) are accorded treatment consistent with that described in paragraph (d)(1)(ii)(B) of this section.

(D) *Special rule for foreign real property.*—For purposes of this paragraph (d)(1)(ii), if, on the last day of any taxable year during the term of the QDOT (or the last day of the calendar year if the QDOT does not have a taxable year), the value of foreign real property owned by the QDOT exceeds 35 percent of the fair market value of the trust assets due to: distributions of QDOT principal during that year; fluctuations in the value of the foreign currency in the jurisdiction where the real estate is located; or fluctuations in the fair market value of any assets held in the QDOT, then the QDOT will not be treated as failing to meet the requirements of this paragraph (d)(1). Accordingly, the QDOT will not cease to be a QDOT within the meaning of § 20.2056A-5(b)(3) if, by the end of the taxable year (or the last day of the calendar year if the QDOT does not have a taxable year) of the QDOT immediately following the year in which the 35 percent limit was exceeded, the value of the foreign real property held by the QDOT does not exceed 35 percent of the fair market value of the trust assets or, alternatively, the QDOT meets the requirements of either paragraph (d)(1)(i)(A),

(B), or (C) of this section on or before the close of that succeeding year.

(iii) *Definition of finally determined.*—For purposes of § 20.2056A-2(d)(1)(i) and (ii), the fair market value of assets will be treated as finally determined on the earliest to occur of—

(A) The entry of a decision, judgment, decree, or other order by any court of competent jurisdiction that has become final;

(B) The execution of a closing agreement made under section 7121;

(C) Any final disposition by the Internal Revenue Service of a claim for refund;

(D) The issuance of an estate tax closing letter (Form L-154 or equivalent) if no claim for refund is filed; or

(E) The expiration of the period of assessment.

(iv) *Special rules for personal residence and related personal effects.*—(A) *Two million dollar threshold.*—For purposes of determining whether the $2 million threshold under paragraphs (d)(1)(i) and (ii) of this section has been exceeded, the executor of the estate may elect to exclude up to $600,000 in value attributable to real property (and related furnishings) owned directly by the QDOT that is used by, or held for the use of the surviving spouse as a personal residence and that passes, or is treated as passing, to the QDOT under section 2056(d). The election may be made regardless of whether the real property is situated within or without the United States. The election is made by attaching to the estate tax return on which the QDOT election is made a written statement claiming the exclusion. The statement must clearly identify the property or properties (i.e. address and location) for which the election is being made.

(B) *Security requirement.*—For purposes of determining the amount of the bond or letter of credit required when paragraph (d)(1)(i)(B) or (C) of this section applies, the executor of the estate may elect to exclude, during the term of the QDOT, up to $600,000 in value attributable to real property (and related furnishings) owned directly by the QDOT that is used by, or held for the use of the surviving spouse as a personal residence and that passes, or is treated as passing, to the QDOT under section 2056(d). The election may be made regardless of whether the real property is situated within or without the United States. The election is made by attaching to the estate tax return on which the QDOT election is made a written statement claiming the exclusion. If an election is not made on the decedent's estate tax return, the election may be made, prospectively, at any time, during the term of the QDOT, by attaching to the Form 706-QDT a written statement claiming the exclusion. A statement may also be attached to the Form 706-QDT that cancels a prior election of the personal residence exclusion that was made

under this paragraph, either on the decedent's estate tax return or on a Form 706-QDT.

(C) *Foreign real property limitation.*—The special rules of this paragraph (d)(1)(iv) do not apply for purposes of determining whether more than 35 percent of the QDOT assets consist of foreign real property under paragraph (d)(1)(ii) of this section.

(D) *Personal residence.*—For purposes of this paragraph (d)(1)(iv), a *personal residence* is either the principal residence of the surviving spouse within the meaning of section 1034 or one other residence of the surviving spouse. In order to be used by or held for the use of the spouse as a personal residence, the residence must be available at all times for use by the surviving spouse. The residence may not be rented to another party, even when not occupied by the spouse. A personal residence may include appurtenant structures used by the surviving spouse for residential purposes and adjacent land not in excess of that which is reasonably appropriate for residential purposes (taking into account the residence's size and location).

(E) *Related furnishings.*—The term *related furnishings* means furniture and commonly included items such as appliances, fixtures, decorative items and china, that are not beyond the value associated with normal household and decorative use. Rare artwork, valuable antiques, and automobiles of any kind or class are not within the meaning of this term.

(F) *Required statement.*—If one or both of the exclusions provided in paragraph (d)(1)(iv)(A) or (B) of this section are elected by the executor of the estate and the personal residence is later sold or ceases to be used, or held for use as a personal residence, the U.S. Trustee must file the statement that is required under paragraph (d)(3) of this section at the time and in the manner provided in paragraphs (d)(3)(ii) and (iii) of this section.

(G) *Cessation of use.*—Except as provided in this paragraph (d)(1)(iv)(G), if the residence ceases to be used by, or held for the use of, the spouse as a personal residence of the spouse, or if the residence is sold during the term of the QDOT, the exclusions provided in paragraphs (d)(1)(iv)(A) and (B) of this section cease to apply. However, if the residence is sold, the exclusion continues to apply if, within 12 months of the date of sale, the amount of the adjusted sales price (as defined in section 1034(b)(1)) is reinvested to purchase a new personal residence for the spouse. If less than the amount of the adjusted sales price is reinvested, the amount of the exclusion equals the amount reinvested in the new residence plus any amount previously allocated to a residence that continues to qualify for the exclusion, up to a total of $600,000. If the QDOT ceases to qualify for all or any portion of the initially claimed exclusions, paragraph (d)(1)(i) of this section, if applicable (determined as if the portion of the exclusions disallowed had not been initially claimed by the QDOT), must be complied with no later than 120 days after the effective date of the cessation. In addition, if a residence ceases to be used by, or held for the use of the spouse as a personal residence of the spouse or if the personal residence is sold during the term of the QDOT, the personal residence exclusion may be allocated to another residence that is held in either the same QDOT or in another QDOT that is established for the surviving spouse, if the other residence qualifies as being used by, or held for the use of the spouse as a personal residence. The trustee may allocate up to $600,000 to the new personal residence (less the amount previously allocated to a residence that continues to qualify for the exclusion) even if the entire $600,000 exclusion was not previously utilized with respect to the original personal residence(s).

(v) *Anti-abuse rule.*—Regardless of whether the QDOT designates a bank as the U.S. Trustee under paragraph (d)(1)(i)(A) of this section (or otherwise complies with paragraph (d)(1)(i)(A) of this section by naming a foreign bank with a United States branch as a trustee to serve with the U.S. Trustee), complies with paragraph (d)(1)(i)(B) or (C) of this section, or is subject to and complies with the foreign real property requirements of paragraph (d)(1)(ii) of this section, the trust immediately ceases to qualify as a QDOT if the trust utilizes any device or arrangement that has, as a principal purpose, the avoidance of liability for the estate tax imposed under section 2056A(b)(1), or the prevention of the collection of the tax. For example, the trust may become subject to this paragraph (d)(1)(v) if the U.S. Trustee that is selected is a domestic corporation established with insubstantial capitalization by the surviving spouse or members of the spouse's family.

(2) *Individual trustees.*—If the U.S. Trustee is an individual United States citizen, the individual must have a tax home (as defined in section 911(d)(3)) in the United States.

(3) *Annual reporting requirements.*—(i) *In general.*—The U.S. Trustee must file a written statement described in paragraph (d)(3)(iii) of this section, if the QDOT satisfies any one of the following criteria for the applicable reporting years—

(A) The QDOT directly owns any foreign real property on the last day of its taxable year (or the last day of the calendar year if it has no taxable year), and the QDOT does not satisfy the requirements of paragraph (d)(1)(i)(A), (B), or (C) or (d)(4) of this section by employing a bank as trustee or providing security; or

(B) The personal residence previously subject to the exclusion under paragraph

(d)(1)(iv) of this section is sold, or that personal residence ceases to be used, or held for use, as a personal residence, during the taxable year (or during the calendar year if the QDOT does not have a taxable year); or

(C) After the application of the look-through rule contained in paragraph (d)(1)(ii)(B) of this section, the QDOT is treated as owning any foreign real property on the last day of the taxable year (or the last day of the calendar year if the QDOT has no taxable year), and the QDOT does not satisfy the requirements of paragraph (d)(1)(A), (B), (C) or (d)(4) of this section by employing a bank as trustee or providing security.

(ii) *Time and manner of filing.*—The written statement, containing the information described in paragraph (d)(3)(iii) of this section, is to be filed for the taxable year of the QDOT (calendar year if the QDOT does not have a taxable year) for which any of the events or conditions requiring the filing of a statement under paragraph (d)(3)(i) of this section have occurred or have been satisfied. The written statement is to be submitted to the Internal Revenue Service by filing a Form 706-QDT, with the statement attached, no later than April 15th of the calendar year following the calendar year in which or with which the taxable year of the QDOT ends (or by April 15th of the following year if the QDOT has no taxable year), unless an extension of time is obtained under §20.2056A-11(a). The Form 706-QDT, with attached statement, must be filed regardless of whether the Form 706-QDT is otherwise required to be filed under the provisions of this chapter. Failure to file timely the statement may subject the QDOT to the rules of paragraph (d)(1)(v) of this section.

(iii) *Contents of statement.*—The written statement must contain the following information—

(A) The name, address, and taxpayer identification number, if any, of the U.S. Trustee and the QDOT; and

(B) A list summarizing the assets held by the QDOT, together with the fair market value of each listed QDOT asset, determined as of the last day of the taxable year (December 31 if the QDOT does not have a taxable year) for which the written statement is filed. If the look-through rule contained in paragraph (d)(1)(ii)(B) of this section applies, then the partnership, corporation, trust or other entity must be identified and the QDOT's pro rata share of the foreign real property and other assets owned by that entity must be listed on the statement as if directly owned by the QDOT; and

(C) If a personal residence previously subject to the exclusion under paragraph (d)(1)(iv) of this section is sold during the taxable year (or during the calendar year if the QDOT does not have a taxable year), the statement must provide the date of sale, the adjusted sales price (as defined in section 1034(b)(1)), the extent to which the amount of the adjusted sales price has been or will be used to purchase a new personal residence and, if not timely reinvested, the steps that will or have been taken to comply with paragraph (d)(1)(i) of this section, if applicable; and

(D) If the personal residence ceases to be used, or held for use, as a personal residence by the surviving spouse during the taxable year (or during the calendar year if the QDOT does not have a taxable year), the written statement must describe the steps that will or have been taken to comply with paragraph (d)(1)(i) of this section, if applicable.

(4) *Request for alternate arrangement or waiver.*—If the Commissioner provides guidance published in the Internal Revenue Bulletin (see §601.601(d)(2) of this chapter) pursuant to which a testator, executor, or the U.S. Trustee may adopt an alternate plan or arrangement to assure collection of the section 2056A estate tax, and if the alternate plan or arrangement is adopted in accordance with the published guidance, then the QDOT will be treated, subject to paragraph (d)(1)(v) of this section, as meeting the requirements of paragraph (d)(1) of this section. Until this guidance is published in the Internal Revenue Bulletin (see §601.601(d)(2) of this chapter), taxpayers may submit a request for a private letter ruling for the approval of an alternate plan or arrangement proposed to be adopted to assure collection of the section 2056A estate tax in lieu of the requirements prescribed in this paragraph (d)(4).

(5) *Adjustment of dollar threshold and exclusion.*—The Commissioner may increase or decrease the dollar amounts referred to in paragraph (d)(1)(i), (ii) or (iv) of this section in accordance with guidance published in the Internal Revenue Bulletin (see §601.601(d)(2) of this chapter).

(6) *Effective date and special rules.*—(i) This paragraph (d) is effective for estates of decedents dying after February 19, 1996.

(ii) *Special rule in the case of incompetency.*—A revocable trust or a trust created under the terms of a will is deemed to meet the governing instrument requirements of this paragraph (d) notwithstanding that the requirements are not contained in the governing instrument (or otherwise incorporated by reference) if the trust instrument (or will) was executed on or before November 20, 1995, and—

(A) The testator or settlor dies after February 19, 1996;

(B) The testator or settlor is, on November 20, 1995, and at all times thereafter, under a legal disability to amend the will or trust instrument;

(C) The will or trust instrument does not provide the executor or the U.S. Trustee with a power to amend the instrument in order to meet the requirements of section 2056A; and

(D) The U.S. Trustee provides a written statement with the federal estate tax return (Form 706 or 706NA) that the trust is being administered (or will be administered) so as to be in actual compliance with the requirements of this paragraph (d) and will continue to be administered so as to be in actual compliance with this paragraph (d) for the duration of the trust. This statement must be binding on all successor trustees.

(iii) *Special rule in the case of certain irrevocable trusts.*—An irrevocable trust is deemed to meet the governing instrument requirements of this paragraph (d) notwithstanding that the requirements are not contained in the governing instrument (or otherwise incorporated by reference) if the trust was executed on or before November 20, 1995, and:

(A) The settlor dies after February 19, 1996;

(B) The trust instrument does not provide the U.S. Trustee with a power to amend the trust instrument in order to meet the requirements of section 2056A; and

(C) The U.S. Trustee provides a written statement with the decedent's federal estate tax return (Form 706 or 706NA) that the trust is being administered in actual compliance with the requirements of this paragraph (d) and will continue to be administered so as to be in actual compliance with this paragraph (d) for the duration of the trust. This statement must be binding on all successor trustees. [Reg. §20.2056A-2.]

□ *[T.D. 8612, 8-21-95. Amended by T.D. 8686, 11-27-96.]*

[Reg. §20.2056A-3]

§20.2056A-3. QDOT election.—(a) *General rule.*—Subject to the time period prescribed in section 2056A(d), the election to treat a trust as a QDOT must be made on the last federal estate tax return filed before the due date (including extensions of time to file actually granted) or, if a timely return is not filed, on the first federal estate tax return filed after the due date. The election, once made, is irrevocable.

(b) *No partial elections.*—An election to treat a trust as a QDOT may not be made with respect to a specific portion of an entire trust that would otherwise qualify for the marital deduction but for the application of section 2056(d). However, if the trust is actually severed in accordance with the applicable requirements of §20.2056(b)-7(b)(2)(ii) prior to the due date for the election, a QDOT election may be made for any one or more of the severed trusts.

Reg. §20.2056A-3(b)

(c) *Protective elections.*—A protective election may be made to treat a trust as a QDOT only if at the time the federal estate tax return is filed, the executor of the decedent's estate reasonably believes that there is a bona fide issue that concerns either the residency or citizenship of the decedent, the citizenship of the surviving spouse, whether an asset is includible in the decedent's gross estate, or the amount or nature of the property the surviving spouse is entitled to receive. For example, if at the time the federal estate tax return is filed either the estate is involved in a bona fide will contest, there is uncertainty regarding the inclusion in the gross estate of an asset which, if includible, would be eligible for the QDOT election, or there is uncertainty regarding the status of the decedent as a resident alien or a nonresident alien for estate tax purposes, or a similar uncertainty regarding the citizenship status of the surviving spouse, a protective QDOT election may be made. The protective election is in addition to, and is not in lieu of, the requirements set forth in § 20.2056A-4. The protective QDOT election must be made on a written statement signed by the executor under penalties of perjury and must be attached to the return described in paragraph (a) of this section, and must identify the specific assets to which the protective election refers and the specific basis for the protective election. However, the protective election may otherwise be defined by means of a formula (such as the minimum amount necessary to reduce the estate tax to zero). Once made, the protective election is irrevocable. For example, if a protective election is made because a bona fide question exists as to the includibility of an asset in the decedent's gross estate and it is later finally determined that the asset is so includible, the protective election becomes effective with respect to the asset and cannot thereafter be revoked.

(d) *Manner of election.*—The QDOT election under paragraph (a) of this section is made in the form and manner set forth in the decedent's estate tax return, including applicable instructions. [Reg. § 20.2056A-3.]

☐ [*T.D.* 8612, 8-21-95.]

[Reg. § 20.2056A-4]

§ 20.2056A-4. Procedures for conforming marital trusts and nontrust marital transfers to the requirements of a qualified domestic trust.—(a) *Marital trusts.*—(1) *In general.*—If an interest in property passes from the decedent to a trust for the benefit of a noncitizen surviving spouse and if the trust otherwise qualifies for a marital deduction but for the provisions of section 2056(d)(1)(A), the property interest is treated as passing to the surviving spouse in a QDOT if the trust is reformed, either in accordance with the terms of the decedent's will or trust agreement or pursuant to a judicial proceeding, to meet the requirements of a QDOT. For this pur-

pose, the requirements of a QDOT include all of the applicable requirements set forth in § 20.2056A-2, and the requirements of § 20.2056A-2T(d). A reformation pursuant to the terms of the decedent's will or trust instrument must be completed by the time prescribed (including extensions) for filing the decedent's estate tax return. For purposes of this paragraph (a), a return filed prior to the due date (including extensions) is considered filed on the last date that the return is required to be filed (including extensions), and a late return filed at any time after the due date is considered filed on the date that it is actually filed.

(2) *Judicial reformations.*—In general, a reformation pursuant to a judicial proceeding is permitted under this section if the reformation is commenced on or before the due date (determined with regard to extensions actually granted) for filing the return of tax imposed by chapter 11 of the Internal Revenue Code, regardless of the date that the return is actually filed. The reformation (either pursuant to a judicial proceeding or otherwise) must result in a trust that is effective under local law. The reformed trust may be revocable by the spouse, or otherwise be subject to the spouse's general power of appointment, provided that no person (including the spouse) has the power to amend the trust during the continued existence of the trust such that it would no longer qualify as a QDOT. Prior to the time that the judicial reformation is completed, the trust must be treated as a QDOT. Thus, the trustee of the trust is responsible for filing the Form 706-QDT, paying any section 2056A estate tax that becomes due, and filing the annual statement required under § 20.2056A-2T(d)(3), if applicable. Failure to comply with these requirements may cause the trust to be subject to the anti-abuse rule under § 20.2056A-2T(d)(1)(iv). In addition, if the judicial reformation is terminated prior to the time that the reformation is completed, the estate of the decedent is required to pay the increased estate tax imposed on the decedent's estate (plus interest and any applicable penalties) that becomes due at the time of such termination as a result of the failure of the trust to comply with section 2056(d). See section 6511 as to applicable time periods for credit or refund of tax.

(3) *Tolling of statutory assessment period.*—For the tolling of the statute of limitations in the case of a judicial reformation, see section 2056(d)(5)(B).

(b) *Nontrust marital transfers.*—(1) *In general.*—Under section 2056(d)(2)(B), if an interest in property passes outright from a decedent to a noncitizen surviving spouse either by testamentary bequest or devise, by operation of law, or pursuant to an annuity or other similar plan or arrangement, and such property interest otherwise qualifies for a marital deduction except that it does not pass in a QDOT, solely for purposes of section 2056(d)(2)(A), the property is treated as passing to the surviving spouse in a QDOT if the property interest is either actually transferred to a QDOT before the estate tax return is filed and on or before the last date prescribed by law that the QDOT election may be made, or is assigned to a QDOT under an enforceable and irrevocable written assignment made on or before the date on which the return is filed and on or before the last date prescribed by law that the QDOT election may be made. The transfer or assignment of property to a QDOT may be made by the surviving spouse, the surviving spouse's legal representative (if the surviving spouse is incompetent), or the personal representative of the surviving spouse's estate (if the surviving spouse has died). The QDOT to which the property is transferred may be created by the decedent (during life or by will), by the surviving spouse, or by the executor. For purposes of section 2056(d)(2)(B), if no property other than the property passing to the surviving spouse from the decedent is transferred to the QDOT, the transferee QDOT need not be in a form such that the property transferred to the QDOT would qualify for a marital deduction under section 2056(a). However, if other property is or has been transferred to the QDOT, 100 percent of the value of the transferee QDOT must qualify for the marital deduction under section 2056. For example, if the decedent, a U.S. citizen, bequeaths property to a trust that does not satisfy the requirements of section 2056(b)(5) or (7), or to a trust that does not qualify as an estate trust under § 20.2056(c)-2(b)(1)(i)-(iii), that trust cannot be used as a transferee QDOT by the surviving spouse, since after that trust is fully funded the portion of the value of the trust attributable to property bequeathed to the trust by the decedent will not qualify for a marital deduction under section 2056. Similarly, if the decedent, a nonresident not a citizen of the United States, bequeaths foreign situs assets to a trust created under his will, the surviving spouse may not transfer U.S. situs assets passing to the spouse outside of the will to that trust under this paragraph. See § 20.2056A-3(c) with respect to protective elections. See § 20.2056A-3(a) with respect to the time limitations for making the QDOT election.

(2) *Form of transfer or assignment.*—A transfer or assignment of property to a QDOT must be in writing and otherwise be in accordance with all local law requirements for such assignment or transfer. The transfer or assignment may be of a specific asset or a group of assets, or a fractional share of either, or may be of a pecuniary amount. A transfer or assignment of less than an entire interest in an asset or a group of assets may be expressed by means of a formula (such as the minimum amount necessary to reduce the estate tax to zero). In the case of a transfer, a copy of the trust instrument evidenc-

ing the transfer must be submitted with the decedent's estate tax return. In the case of an assignment, a copy of the assignment must be submitted with the decedent's estate tax return.

(3) *Assets eligible for transfer or assignment.*— If a transfer or assignment is of a specific asset or group of assets, only assets included in the decedent's gross estate and passing from the decedent to the spouse (or the proceeds from the sale, exchange or conversion of such assets) may be transferred or assigned to the QDOT. The noncitizen surviving spouse may not transfer or assign to the QDOT property owned by the surviving spouse at the time of the decedent's death in lieu of property included in the decedent's gross estate that passes to the spouse (or in lieu of the proceeds from the sale, exchange or conversion of such includible assets). In addition, if only a portion of an asset is includible in the decedent's gross estate, the spouse may only transfer the portion that is so includible to the transferee trust under this paragraph (b)(3).

(4) *Pecuniary assignment—special rules.*—If the assignment is expressed in the form of a pecuniary amount (such as a fixed dollar amount or a formula designed to reduce the decedent's estate tax to zero), the assignment must specify that—

(i) Assets actually transferred to the QDOT in satisfaction of the assignment have an aggregate fair market value on the date of actual transfer to the QDOT amounting to no less than the amount of the pecuniary transfer or assignment; or

(ii) The assets actually transferred to the QDOT be fairly representative of appreciation or depreciation in the value of all property available for transfer to the QDOT between the valuation date and the date of actual transfer to the QDOT, if the assignment is to be satisfied by accounting for the assets on the basis of their fair market value as of some date before the date of actual transfer to the QDOT.

(5) *Transfer tax treatment of transfer or assignment.*—Property assigned or transferred to a QDOT pursuant to section 2056(d)(2)(B) is treated as passing from the decedent to a QDOT solely for purposes of section 2056(d)(2)(A). For all other purposes (e.g., income, gift, estate, generation-skipping transfer tax, and section 1491 excise tax), the surviving spouse is treated as the transferor of the property to the QDOT. However, the spouse is not considered the transferor of property to a QDOT if the transfer by the spouse constitutes a transfer that satisfies the requirements of section 2518(c)(3). For a special exception to the valuation rules of section 2702 in the case of a transfer by the surviving spouse to a QDOT, see § 25.2702-1(c)(8) of this chapter.

(6) *Period for completion of transfer.*—Property irrevocably assigned but not actually trans-

ferred to the QDOT before the estate tax return is filed must actually be conveyed and transferred to the QDOT under applicable local law before the administration of the decedent's estate is completed. If there is no administration of the decedent's estate (because for example, none of the decedent's assets are subject to probate under local law), the conveyance must be made on or before the date that is one year after the due date (including extensions) for filing the decedent's estate tax return. If an actual transfer to the QDOT is not timely made, section 2056(d)(1)(A) applies and the marital deduction is not allowed. The executor of the decedent's estate (or other authorized legal representative) may request a private letter ruling from the Internal Revenue Service requesting an extension of the time for completing the conveyance or waiving the actual conveyance under specified circumstances under § 301.9100-1(a) of this chapter.

(7) *Retirement accounts and annuities.*—(i) *In general.*—An assignment otherwise in compliance with this paragraph (b) of rights under annuities or other similar arrangements that are assignable and thus, are not described in paragraph (c) of this section, is treated as a transfer of such property to the QDOT regardless of the method of payment actually elected under such annuity or plan.

(ii) *Individual retirement annuities.*—Individual retirement annuities described in section 408(b) are not assignable pursuant to section 408(b)(1) and thus, do not come within the purview of this paragraph (b)(7). See the procedures provided in paragragh (c) of this section.

(iii) *Individual retirement accounts.*—Unless the terms of the account provide otherwise, individual retirement accounts described in section 408(a) are assignable and subject to the provisions of this paragraph (b)(7). However, under paragraph (c) of this section, the surviving spouse may treat an individual retirement account as nonassignable and, therefore, eligible for the procedures in paragraph (c) of this section if the spouse timely complies with the requirements in paragraph (c) of this section.

(iv) *Other effects of assignment.*—The provisions of this paragraph (b)(7) apply solely for purposes of qualifying the annuity or account under the rules of § 20.2056A-2 and this section. See, for example, section 408(d) and 4980A regarding the consequences of an assignment for purposes other than this paragraph (b)(7).

(8) *Protective assignment.*—A protective assignment of property to a QDOT may be made only if, at the time the federal estate tax return is filed, the executor of the decedent's estate reasonably believes that there is a bona fide issue that concerns either the residency or citizenship of the decedent, the citizenship of the surviving spouse, whether all or a portion of an asset is includible in the decedent's gross estate, or the amount or nature of the property the surviving spouse is entitled to receive. For example, if at the time the federal estate tax return is filed, either the estate is involved in a bona fide will contest, there is uncertainty regarding the inclusion in the gross estate of an asset which, if includible, would be eligible for the QDOT election, or there is uncertainty regarding the status of the decedent as a resident alien or a nonresident alien for estate tax purposes, or a similar uncertainty regarding the citizenship status of the surviving spouse, a protective assignment may be made. The protective assignment must be made on a written statement signed by the assignor under penalties of perjury on or before the date prescribed under paragraph (b)(1) of this section, and must identify the specific assets to which the assignment refers and the specific basis for the protective assignment. However, the protective assignment may otherwise be defined by means of a formula (such as the minimum amount necessary to reduce the estate tax to zero). Once made, the protective assignment cannot be revoked. For example, if a protective assignment is made because a bona fide question exists as to the includibility of an asset in the decedent's gross estate and it is later finally determined that the asset is so includible, the protective assignment becomes effective with respect to the asset and cannot thereafter be revoked. Protective assignments are, in all events, subject to paragraph (b)(6) of this section. A copy of the protective assignment must be submitted with the decedent's estate tax return.

(c) *Nonassignable annuities and other arrangements.*—(1) *Definition and general rule.*—For purposes of this section, a *nonassignable annuity or other arrangement* means a plan, annuity, or other arrangement (whether qualified or not qualified under part I of subchapter D of chapter 1 of subtitle A of the Internal Revenue Code) that qualifies for the marital deduction but for section 2056(d)(1)(A), and whose payments are not assignable or transferable to the QDOT under either federal law (see, e.g., section 401(a)(13)), state law, foreign law, or the terms of the plan or arrangement itself. For purposes of this paragraph (c), a surviving spouse's interest as beneficiary of an individual retirement annuity described in section 408(b) is a nonassignable annuity or other arrangement. See section 408(b)(1). For purposes of this paragraph (c), a surviving spouse's interest as beneficiary of an individual retirement account described in section 408(a), although assignable under that section, is considered to be a nonassignable annuity or other arrangement eligible for the procedures contained in this paragraph (c), at the option of the surviving spouse, if the requirements of this paragraph are otherwise satisfied. See paragraph (b)(7) of this section if the spouse elects to treat the account as assignable. In the case of a plan, annuity, or other arrangement which is not assignable or transferable (or is treated as such), the property passing under the plan from the decedent is treated as meeting the requirements § 20.2056A-2, and the requirements of § 20.2056A-2T(d) (pertaining, respectively, to general requirements, qualified marital interest requirements, statutory requirements, and requirements to ensure collection of the tax) if the requirements of either paragraph (c)(2) or (3) of this section are satisfied. Thus, the property will be treated as passing in the form of a QDOT, notwithstanding that the spouse does not irrevocably transfer or assign the annuity or other payment to the QDOT as provided in paragraph (b) of this section. The Commissioner will prescribe by administrative guidance the extent, if any, to which the provisions of this paragraph (c) apply to a rollover from a qualified trust to an eligible retirement plan within the meaning of section 402(c) or a distribution from an individual retirement account or an individual retirement annuity that is paid into an individual retirement account or an individual retirement annuity within the meaning of section 408(d)(3).

(2) *Agreement to remit section 2056A estate tax on corpus portion of each annuity payment.*—The requirements of this paragraph (c)(2) are satisfied if—

(i) The noncitizen surviving spouse agrees to pay on an annual basis, as described in paragraph (c)(6)(i) of this section, the estate tax imposed under section 2056A(b)(1) due on the corpus portion, as defined in paragraph (c)(4) of this section, of each nonassignable annuity or other payment received under the plan or arrangement. However, for purposes of this paragraph (c)(2), if the financial circumstances of the spouse are such that an amount equal to all or a portion of the corpus portion of a nonassignable annuity payment received by the spouse would be subject to a hardship exemption (as defined in § 20.2056A-5(c)) if paid from a QDOT, then all or a corresponding part of the corpus portion will be exempt from the tax payment requirement under this paragraph (c)(2);

(ii) The executor of the decedent's estate files with the estate tax return the Information Statement described in paragraph (c)(5) of this section;

(iii) The executor files with the estate tax return the Agreement To Pay Section 2056A Estate Tax described in paragraph (c)(6) of this section; and

(iv) The executor makes the election under § 20.2056A-3 with respect to the nonassignable annuity or other payment.

(3) *Agreement to roll over corpus portion of annuity payment to QDOT.*—The requirements of this paragraph (c)(3) are satisfied if—

(i) The noncitizen surviving spouse agrees to roll over and transfer, within the time prescribed under paragraph (c)(7)(i) of this section, the corpus portion of each annuity payment to a QDOT, whether the QDOT is created by the decedent's will, the executor of the decedent's estate, or the surviving spouse. However, for purposes of this section, if the financial circumstances of the spouse are such that an amount equal to all or a portion of the corpus portion of a nonassignable annuity payment received by the spouse would be subject to a hardship exemption (as defined in § 20.2056A-5(c)) if paid from a QDOT, then all or a corresponding part of the corpus portion will be exempt from the rollover requirement under this paragraph (c)(3);

(ii) A QDOT for the benefit of the surviving spouse is established prior to the date that the estate tax return is filed and on or prior to the last date prescribed by law that the QDOT election may be made;

(iii) The executor of the decedent's estate files with the estate tax return the Information Statement described in paragraph (c)(5) of this section;

(iv) The executor files with the estate tax return the Agreement To Roll Over Annuity Payments described in paragraph (c)(7) of this section; and

(v) The executor makes the election under § 20.2056A-3 with respect to the nonassignable annuity or other payment. See § 20.2056A-5(c)(3)(iv)(A), regarding distributions from the QDOT reimbursing the spouse for income taxes paid (either by actual payment or withholding) by the spouse with respect to amounts transferred to the QDOT pursuant to this paragraph (c)(3).

(4) *Determination of corpus portion.*—(i) *Corpus portion.*—For purposes of this paragraph (c), the corpus portion of each nonassignable annuity or other payment is the corpus amount of the annual payment divided by the total annual payment.

(ii) *Corpus amount.*—(A) The corpus amount of the annual payment is determined in accordance with the following formula:

$$\text{Corpus Amount} = \frac{\text{Total present value of annuity or other payment}}{\text{Expected annuity term}}$$

(B) The total present value of the annuity or other payment is the present value of the nonassignable annuity or other payment as of the date of the decedent's death, determined

in accordance with the interest rates and mortality data prescribed by section 7520. The expected annuity term is the number of years that would be required for the scheduled payments to ex-

Reg. § 20.2056A-4(c)(4)(ii)(B)

haust a hypothetical fund equal to the present value of the scheduled payments. This is determined by first dividing the total present value of the payments by the annual payment. From the quotient so obtained, the expected annuity term is derived by identifying the term of years that corresponds to the annuity factor equal to the quotient. This is determined by using column 1 of Table B, for the applicable interest rate, contained in Publication 1457, "Actuarial Valuations Version 3A". A copy of this publication is available, at no charge, electronically via the IRS Internet site at *www.irs.gov*. If the quotient obtained falls between two terms, the longer term is used.

(5) *Information Statement.*—(i) *In general.*—In order for a nonassignable annuity or other payment described in this paragraph (c) to qualify under either paragraph (c)(2) or (3) of this section, the Information Statement described in paragraph (c)(5)(ii) of this section must be filed with the decedent's federal estate tax return. The Information Statement must be signed under penalties of perjury by both the executor of the decedent's estate and by the surviving spouse of the decedent (or by the legal representative of the surviving spouse if the surviving spouse is legally incompetent to sign the statement). The Statement must contain all of the information prescribed by this paragraph (c)(5).

(ii) *Annuity source information.*—(A) *Employment-related annuity.*—If the nonassignable annuity or other payment is employment-related, the following information must be provided—

(1) The name and address of the employer;

(2) The date of retirement or other separation from employment of the decedent;

(3) The name and address of the pension fund, insurance company, or other obligor that is paying the annuity (or similar payment); and

(4) The identification number, if any, that the obligor has assigned to the annuity or other payment.

(B) *Annuity not employment-related.*—If the nonassignable annuity or other payment is not employment-related, the following information must be provided—

(1) The name and address of the person or entity paying the nonassignable annuity or other payment;

(2) The date of acquisition of the nonassignable annuity contract by the decedent or by the decedent and the surviving spouse; and

(3) The identification number, if any, that the obligor has assigned to the nonassignable annuity or other payment.

(iii) *The total annuity amount payable each year.*—The total amount payable annually under the nonassignable annuity or other arrangement, including a description of whether the annuity is payable monthly, quarterly, or at some other interval, and a description of any scheduled changes in the annuity payout amount.

(iv) *The duration of the annuity.*—A description of the term of the nonassignable annuity or other payment in years, if it is determined by a term certain, and the name, address, and birthdate of any measuring life if the nonassignable annuity or other payment is determined by one or more lives.

(v) *The market interest rate under section 7520.*—The applicable interest rate as determined under section 7520.

(vi) *Determination of corpus portion of each payment (in accordance with paragraph (c)(4) of this section).*—The following items are required in order to determine the corpus portion of each payment—

(A) The present value of the nonassignable annuity or other payment as of the decedent's death;

(B) The expected annuity term;

(C) The corpus amount of the annual annuity payments (paragraph (c)(5)(vi)(A) of this section divided by paragraph (c)(5)(vi)(B) of this section); and

(D) The corpus portion of the annual payments (paragraph (c)(5)(vi)(C) of this section divided by the total amount payable annually).

(vii) *Recipient QDOT.*—In the case of an agreement to rollover under paragraph (c)(3) of this section, the following must be provided—

(A) The name and address of the trustee of the QDOT who is the U.S. Trustee; and

(B) The name and taxpayer identification number of the QDOT.

(viii) *Certification statement.*—The executor of the decedent's estate and the surviving spouse of the decedent (or the legal representative of the surviving spouse if the surviving spouse is legally incompetent to so certify) must each sign a Certification Statement as follows:

Under penalties of perjury, I hereby certify that, to the best of my knowledge and belief, the information reported in this Information Statement is true, correct and complete.

(6) *Agreement to pay section 2056A estate tax.*—(i) *Payment of section 2056A estate tax.*—The tax payable under paragraph (c)(2) of this section is payable on an annual basis, commencing in the calendar year following the calendar year of the receipt by the surviving spouse of the spouse's first annuity payment. Form 706QDT and the payment are due on April 15th of each year following the calendar year in which an

annuity payment is received except that, in the year of the deceased spouse's death, the Form 706-QDT and the payment are not due prior to the due date, including extensions, for filing the deceased spouse's estate tax return, or if no return is filed, no later than 9 months from the date of the deceased spouse's death; and, in the year of the surviving spouse's death, the Form 706-QDT must be filed and the payment made no later than 9 months from the date of the surviving spouse's death. See §20.2056A-11 for extensions of time for filing Form 706-QDT and paying the section 2056A estate tax.

(ii) *Agreement.*—In order for a nonassignable annuity or other payment described in this paragraph (c) to qualify under paragraph (c)(2) of this section, the executor of the decedent's estate must file with the estate tax return the following Agreement To Pay Section 2056A Estate Tax, which must be signed by the surviving spouse of the decedent (or by the surviving spouse's legal representative if the surviving spouse is legally incompetent to sign the agreement):

I [*name*] hereby agree that I will report all annuity payments received under the [*name of plan or arrangement*]on Form 706-QDT for the calendar year and remit, on an annual basis, to the Internal Revenue Service the estate tax that is imposed under section 2056A(b)(1) of the Internal Revenue Code on the corpus portion of each annuity payment (as defined in §20.2056A-4(c)(4) of the Estate Tax Regulations) received under the plan during the calendar year. I also agree that Form 706-QDT is to be filed no later than April 15th of the year following the calendar year in which any annuity payments are received except that: in the case of annuity payments received in the year of my spouse's death, Form 706-QDT and the payment shall not be due prior to the due date, including extensions, for filing my spouse's estate tax return or, if no return is filed, no later than 9 months from the date of my spouse's death (except if I am granted an extension of time to file Form 706-QDT under the provisions of §20.2056A-11); and in the year of my death, the Form 706-QDT must be filed and the payment made no later than the date my estate tax return is filed (or if no return is filed, no later than 9 months from the date of my death). I further agree that if I fail to timely file Form 706-QDT or to timely pay the tax imposed on the corpus portion of any annuity payment (determined after any extensions of time to pay granted to me under the provisions of §20.2056A-11), I may become immediately liable to pay the amount of the tax determined by application of section 2056A(b)(1) on the entire remaining present value of the annuity, calculated as of the beginning of the year in which the payment was received with respect to which I failed to timely pay the tax or failed to timely file the return. However, I may make an application for relief

under §301.9100-1 of the Procedure and Administration Regualations, from the consequences of failing to timely file the Form 706-QDT or failing to timely pay the tax on the corpus portion. [The following sentence is applicable only in cases where the plan or arrangement is established and administered by a person or an entity that is located outside of the United States.] I agree, at the request of the District Director, [or the Assistant Commissioner (International) in the case of a surviving spouse of a nonresident noncitizen decedent or a surviving spouse of a United States citizen who died domiciled outside the United States] to enter into a security agreement to secure my undertakings under this agreement.

(7) *Agreement to roll over annuity payments.*—(i) *Roll over of corpus portion.*—Beginning in the calendar year of the receipt by the surviving spouse of the spouse's first annuity payment, the corpus portion of each annuity payment, as determined under paragraph (c)(4) of this section, must, within 60 days of receipt, be transferred to a QDOT. In addition, all annuity payments received during the calendar year must be reported on Form 706-QDT no later than April 15th of the year following the year in which the annuity payments are received, except that in the year of the surviving spouse's death, the Form 706-QDT must be filed no later than the date the estate tax return is filed (or if no return is filed, no later than 9 months from the date of the surviving spouse's death). See §20.2056A-11 for extensions of time for filing Form 706-QDT.

(ii) *Agreement.*—In order for a nonassignable annuity or other payment described in this paragraph (c) to qualify under paragraph (c)(3) of this section, the executor of the decedent's estate must file with the estate tax return the following Agreement To Roll Over Annuity Payments, which must be signed by the surviving spouse of the decedent (or by the legal representative of the surviving spouse if the surviving spouse is legally incompetent to sign the agreement):

I [*name*] hereby agree that within 60 days of receipt of each annuity payment paid under the [*name of plan or arrangement*], I will transfer an amount equal to percent (the corpus portion determined under §20.2056A-4(c)(4) of the Estate Tax Regulations) of each annuity payment to [*identify the QDOT*]. Further, I will report all annuity payments received during the calendar year under the [*name of plan or arrangement*]on Form 706-QDT including a schedule of transfers to the [*identify the QDOT*]. I also agree that Form 706-QDT is to be filed no later than April 15th of the year following the year in which any annuity payments are received except that: in the case of annuity payments received in the year of my spouse's death, Form 706-QDT shall not be due prior to the due date, including extensions, for filing my spouse's estate tax return, or, if no return is filed, no later than 9 months from the date of my spouse's death (except if I am granted an extension of time to file Form 706-QDT under the provisions of § 20.2056A-11); and in the year of my death, the Form 706-QDT must be filed no later than the date my estate tax return is filed (or if no return is filed, no later than 9 months from the date of my death), and except if I am granted an extension of time to file Form 706-QDT under the provisions of § 20.2056A-11. I further agree that if I fail to timely transfer any required amount with respect to any annuity payment, or fail to timely file Form 706-QDT reporting the transfers for any year, I may become immediately liable to pay the amount of the tax determined by application of section 2056A(b)(1) on the entire remaining present value of the annuity, calculated as of the beginning of the year in which the payment was received with respect to which I failed to make the timely transfer or timely file a return. However, I may make an application for relief under § 301.9100-1 of the Procedure and Administration Regulations, from the consequences of failing to timely file Form 706-QDT or failing to

timely transfer the corpus portion of any annuity payment to the QDOT. [The following sentence is applicable only in cases where the plan or arrangement is established and administered by a person or an entity that is located outside of the United States.] I agree, at the request of the District Director [or the Assistant Commissioner (International) in the case of a surviving spouse of a nonresident noncitizen decedent or a surviving spouse of a United States citizen who died domiciled outside the United States] to enter into a security agreement to secure my undertakings under this agreement.

(d) *Examples.*—The provisions of this section are illustrated by the following examples. In each of the following examples the decedent, *D*, a citizen of the United States, died after August 22, 1995, and *D*'s surviving spouse, *S*, is not a United States citizen at the time of *D*'s death.

Example 1. Transfer and assignment of probate and nonprobate property to QDOT.—(i) *S* is the beneficiary of the following probate and nonprobate assets included in *D*'s gross estate:

Pecuniary bequest under will	$400,000
Proceeds of life insurance	200,000
D's interest in property owned jointly with S includible in the gross estate under § 2040(a)	300,000
Devise of real property under will	100,000
Total	$1,000,000

(ii) Before the estate tax return for *D*'s estate is filed and before the date that the QDOT election must be made, *S* creates a QDOT pursuant to which all income is payable to *S* for life and the remainder is distributable to *S*'s children. *S* retains a power of appointment over the disposition of the remainder to ensure that *S* does not make an immediate gift of the remainder of the trust. Also, before the estate tax return is filed and before the date that the QDOT election must be made, *S* transfers the life insurance proceeds and the specifically devised real property to the QDOT. *S* decides not to transfer the property that had been jointly owned to the QDOT. Because *S* has not received distribution of the pecuniary bequest before *D*'s estate tax return is filed and before the date that the QDOT election must be made, *S* irrevocably assigns the interest in the pecuniary bequest to the QDOT. Assume that the pecuniary bequest is in fact transferred by *S* to the QDOT before the estate administration is concluded. *D*'s executor makes a QDOT election on the estate tax return for the $700,000 in property that *S* has transferred and assigned to the QDOT. A marital deduction of $700,000 is allowed to *D*'s estate assuming the estate tax return is filed and the QDOT election is made within the time limitation prescribed in § 20.2056A-3(a). No marital deduction is allowed for the $300,000 interest in jointly-owned property not transferred to the QDOT.

Example 2. Formula assignment. Under the terms of *D*'s will, the entire probate estate passes

outright to *S*. Prior to the date *D*'s estate tax return is filed and before the date that the QDOT election must be made, *S* establishes a QDOT and *S* executes an irrevocable assignment in which *S* assigns to the QDOT, "that portion of the gross estate necessary to reduce the estate tax to zero, taking into account all available credits and deductions." The assignment meets the requirements of paragraph (b) of this section, assuming that the QDOT is funded by the time that administration of *D*'s estate is completed.

Example 3. Jointly owned property. At the time of *D*'s death, *D* and *S* hold real property as joint tenants with right of survivorship. In accordance with section 2056(d)(1)(B), section 2040(a), and § 20.2056A-8(a), 60 percent of the value of the property is included in *D*'s gross estate. *S* establishes a QDOT and, prior to the date the estate tax return is filed and before the date that the QDOT election must be made, *S* transfers a 60 percent interest in the real property to the QDOT. The transfer satisfies the requirements of paragraph (b) of this section.

Example 4. Computation of corpus portion of annuity payment. (i) At the time of *D*'s death on or after May 1, 2009, *D* is a participant in an employees' pension plan described in section 401(a). On *D*'s death, *D*'s spouse S, a resident of the United States, becomes entitled to receive a survivor's annuity of $72,000 per year, payable monthly, for life. At the time of *D*'s death, *S* is age 60. Assume that under section 7520, the appropriate discount rate to be used for valuing annuities in the case of this decedent is 6.0 percent. The annuity factor at 6.0 percent for a person age 60 is 11.0625 (1.000000 minus .33625, divided by .06). The adjustment factor at 6.0 percent in Table K for monthly payments is 1.0272. Accordingly, the right to receive $72,000 per year on a monthly basis is equal to the right to receive $73,958.40 ($72,000 × 1.0272) on an annual basis.

(ii) The corpus portion of each annuity payment received by S is determined as follows. The first step is to determine the annuity factor for the number of years that would be required to exhaust a hypothetical fund that has a present value and a payout corresponding to S's interest in the payments under the plan, determined as follows:

(A) Present value of S's annuity: $73,958.40 × 11.0625 = $818,164.80.

(B) Annuity Factor for Expected Annuity Term: $818,164.80 / $73,958.40 = 11.0625.

(iii) The second step is to determine the number of years that would be required for S 's annuity to exhaust a hypothetical fund of $818,164.80. The term certain annuity factor of 11.0625 falls between the annuity factors for 18 and 19 years in a 6.0 percent term certain annuity table (Column 1 of Table B, Publication 1457 Actuarial Valuations Version 3A, which may be obtained on the IRS Internet site). Accordingly, the expected annuity term is 19 years.

(iv) The third step is to determine the corpus amount by dividing the expected term of 19 years into the present value of the hypothetical fund as follows:

(A) Corpus amount of annual payment: $818,164.80/19 = $43,061.31.

(B) [Reserved].

(v) In the fourth step, the corpus portion of each annuity payment is determined by dividing the corpus amount of each annual payment by the annual annuity payment (adjusted for payments more frequently than annually as in (i) of this *Example 4*) as follows:

(A) Corpus portion of each annuity payment: $43,061.31/$73,958.40 = .58.

(B) [Reserved].

(vi) Accordingly, 58 percent of each payment to S is deemed to be a distribution of corpus. A marital deduction is allowed for $818,164.80, the present value of the annuity as of D's date of death, if either: S agrees to roll over the corpus portion of each payment to a QDOT and the executor files the Information Statement described in paragraph (c)(5) of this section and the Roll Over Agreement described in paragraph (c)(7) of this section; or S agrees to pay the tax due on the corpus portion of each payment and the executor files the Information Statement described in paragraph (c)(5) of this section and the Payment Agreement described in paragraph (c)(6) of this section.

Example 5. Transfer to QDOT subject to gift tax. D's will bequeaths $700,000 outright to S. The bequest qualifies for a marital deduction under section 2056(a) except that it does not pass in a QDOT. S creates an irrevocable trust that meets the requirements for a QDOT and transfers the $700,000 to the QDOT. The QDOT instrument provides that S is entitled to all the income from the QDOT payable at least annually and that, upon the death of S, the property remaining in the QDOT is to be distributed to the grandchildren of D and S in equal shares. The trust instrument contains all other provisions required to qualify as a QDOT. On D's estate tax return, D's executor makes a QDOT election under section 2056A(a)(3). Solely for purposes of the marital deduction, the property is deemed to pass from D to the QDOT. D's estate is entitled to a marital deduction for the $700,000 value of the property passing from D to S. S's transfer of property to the QDOT is treated as a gift of the remainder interest for gift tax purposes because S's transfer creates a vested remainder interest in the grandchildren of D and S. Accordingly, as of the date that S transfers the property to the QDOT, a gift tax is imposed on the present value of the remainder interest. See § 25.2702-1(c)(8) of this chapter exempting S's transfer from the special valuation rules contained in section 2702. At S's death, S is treated as the transferor of the property into the trust for estate tax and generation-skipping transfer tax purposes. See, e.g., sections 2036 and 2652(a)(1). The trust is not eligible for a reverse QTIP election by D's estate under section 2652(a)(3) because a QTIP election cannot be made for the QDOT. This is so because the marital deduction is allowed under section 2056(a) for the outright bequest to the spouse and the spouse is then separately treated as the transferor of the property to the QDOT.

(e) *Effective/applicability date.*—Paragraph (c)(4)(ii)(B) and *Example 4* in paragraph (d) of this section are applicable with respect to decedents dying on or after May 1, 2009. [Reg. § 20.2056A-4.]

☐ [*T.D. 8612, 8-21-95. Amended by T.D. 8819, 4-29-99; T.D. 9448, 5-1-2009; and T.D. 9540, 8-9-2011.*]

[Reg. § 20.2056A-5]

§ 20.2056A-5. Imposition of section 2056A estate tax.—(a) *In general.*—An estate tax is imposed under section 2056A(b)(1) on the occurrence of a taxable event, as defined in section 2056A(b)(9). The tax is generally equal to the amount of estate tax that would have been imposed if the amount involved in the taxable event had been included in the decedent's taxable estate and had not been deductible under section 2056. See section 2056A(b)(3) and paragraph (c) of this section for certain exceptions from taxable events.

(b) *Amounts subject to tax.*—(1) *Distribution of principal during the spouse's lifetime.*—If a taxable event occurs during the noncitizen surviving spouse's lifetime, the amount on which the section 2056A estate tax is imposed is the amount of money and the fair market value of the property that is the subject of the distribution (including property distributed from the trust pursuant to the exercise of a power of appointment), including any amount withheld from the distribution by the U.S. Trustee to pay the tax. If, however, the tax is not withheld by the U.S. Trustee but is paid by the U.S. Trustee out of other assets of the QDOT, an amount equal to the tax so paid is treated as an additional distribution to the spouse in the year that the tax is paid.

(2) *Death of surviving spouse.*—If a taxable event occurs as a result of the death of the surviving spouse, the amount subject to tax is the fair market value of the trust assets on the date of the spouse's death (or alternate valuation date if applicable). See also section 2032A. Any corpus portion amounts, within the meaning of § 20.2056A-4(c)(4)(i), remaining in a QDOT upon the surviving spouse's death, are subject to tax under section 2056A(b)(1)(B), as well as any residual payments resulting from a nonassignable plan or arrangement that, upon the surviving spouse's death, are payable to the spouse's estate or to successor beneficiaries.

(3) *Trust ceases to qualify as QDOT.*—If a taxable event occurs as a result of the trust ceasing to qualify as a QDOT (for example, the trust ceases to have at least one U.S. Trustee), the amount subject to tax is the fair market value of the trust assets on the date of disqualification.

(c) *Distributions and dispositions not subject to tax.*—(1) *Distributions of principal on account of hardship.*—Section 2056A(b)(3)(B) provides an exemption from the section 2056A estate tax for distributions to the surviving spouse on account of hardship. A distribution of principal is treated as made on account of hardship if the distribution is made to the spouse from the QDOT in response to an immediate and substantial financial need relating to the spouse's health, maintenance, education, or support, or the health, maintenance, education, or support of any person that the surviving spouse is legally obligated to support. A distribution is not treated as made on account of hardship if the amount distributed may be obtained from other sources that are reasonably available to the surviving spouse; e.g., the sale by the surviving spouse of personally owned, publicly traded stock or the cashing in of a certificate of deposit owned by the surviving spouse. Assets such as closely held business interests, real estate and tangible personalty are not considered sources that are reasonably available to the surviving spouse. Although a hardship distribution of principal is exempt from the section 2056A estate tax, it must be reported on

Form 706-QDT even if it is the only distribution that occurred during the filing period. See § 20.2056A-11 regarding filing requirements for Form 706-QDT.

(2) *Distributions of income to the surviving spouse.*—Section 2056A(b)(3)(A) provides an exemption from the section 2056A estate tax for distributions of income to the surviving spouse. In general, for purposes of section 2056A(b)(3)(A), the term *income* has the same meaning as is provided in section 643(b), except that income does not include capital gains. In addition, income does not include any other item that would be allocated to corpus under applicable local law governing the administration of trusts irrespective of any specific trust provision to the contrary. However, distributions made to the surviving spouse as the income beneficiary in conformance with applicable local law that defines the term income as a unitrust amount (or permits a right to income to be satisfied by such an amount), or that permits the trustee to adjust between principal and income to fulfill the trustee's duty of impartiality between income and principal beneficiaries, will be considered distributions of trust income if applicable local law provides for a reasonable apportionment between the income and remainder beneficiaries of the total return of the trust and meets the requirements of § 1.643(b)-1 of this chapter. In cases where there is no specific statutory or case law regarding the allocation of such items under the law governing the administration of the QDOT, the allocation under this paragraph (c)(2) will be governed by general principles of law (including but not limited to any uniform state acts, such as the Uniform Principal and Income Act, or any Restatements of applicable law). Further, except as provided in this paragraph (c)(2) or in administrative guidance published by the Internal Revenue Service, income does not include items constituting income in respect of a decedent (IRD) under section 691. However, in cases where a QDOT is designated by the decedent as a beneficiary of a pension or profit sharing plan described in section 401(a) or an individual retirement account or annuity described in section 408, the proceeds of which are payable to the QDOT in the form of an annuity, any payments received by the QDOT may be allocated between income and corpus using the method prescribed under § 20.2056A-4(c) for determining the corpus and income portion of an annuity payment.

(3) *Certain miscellaneous distributions and dispositions.*—Certain miscellaneous distributions and dispositions of trust assets are exempt from the section 2056A estate tax, including but not limited to the following—

(i) Payments for ordinary and necessary expenses of the QDOT (including bond premiums and letter of credit fees);

(ii) Payments to applicable governmental authorities for income tax or any other applicable tax imposed on the QDOT (other than a payment of the section 2056A estate tax due on the occurrence of a taxable event as described in paragraph (b) of this section);

(iii) Dispositions of trust assets by the trustees (such as sales, exchanges, or pledging as collateral) for full and adequate consideration in money or money's worth; and

(iv) Pursuant to section 2056A(b)(15), amounts paid from the QDOT to reimburse the surviving spouse for any tax imposed on the spouse under Subtitle A of the Internal Revenue Code on any item of income of the QDOT to which the surviving spouse is not entitled under the terms of the trust. Such distributions include (but are not limited to) amounts paid from the QDOT to reimburse the spouse for income taxes paid by the spouse (either by actual payment or through withholding) with respect to amounts received from a nonassignable annuity or other arrangement that are transferred by the spouse to a QDOT pursuant to §20.2056A-4(c)(3); and income taxes paid by the spouse (either by actual payment or through withholding) with respect to amounts received in a lump sum distribution from a qualified plan if the lump sum distribution is assigned by the surviving spouse to a QDOT. For purposes of this paragraph (c)(3)(iv), the amount of attributable tax eligible for reimbursement is the difference between the actual income tax liability of the spouse and the spouse's income tax liability determined as if the item had not been included in the spouse's gross income in the applicable taxable year. [Reg. §20.2056A-5.]

☐ [T.D. 8612, 8-21-95. Amended by T.D. 9102, 12-30-2003.]

[Reg. §20.2056A-6]

§20.2056A-6. Amount of tax.—(a) *Definition of tax.*—Section 2056A(b)(2) provides for the computation of the section 2056A estate tax. For purposes of sections 2056A(b)(2)(A)(i) and (ii), in determining the tax that would have been imposed under section 2001 on the estate of the first decedent, the rates in effect on the date of the first decedent's death are used. For this purpose, the provisions of section 2001(c)(2) (pertaining to phaseout of graduated rates and unified credit) apply. In addition, for purposes of sections 2056A(b)(2)(A)(i) and (ii), *the tax which would have been imposed by section 2001 on the estate of the decedent* means the net tax determined under section 2001 or 2101, as the case may be, after allowance of any allowable credits, including the unified credit allowable under section 2010, the credit for state death taxes under section 2011, the credit for tax on prior transfers under section 2013, and the credit for foreign death taxes under section 2014. See paragraph (b)(4) of this section regarding the application of the credits under sections 2011 and 2014. In the

case of a decedent nonresident not a citizen of the United States, the applicable credits are determined under section 2102. The estate tax (net of any applicable credits) imposed under section 2056A(b)(1) constitutes an estate tax for purposes of section 691(c)(2)(A).

(b) *Benefits allowed in determining amount of section 2056A estate tax.*—(1) *General rule.*—Section 2056A(b)(10) provides for the allowance of certain benefits in computing the section 2056A estate tax. Except as provided in this section, the rules of each of the credit, deduction and deferral provisions, as provided in the Internal Revenue Code must be complied with.

(2) *Treatment as resident.*—For purposes of section 2056A(b)(10)(A), a noncitizen spouse is treated as a resident of the United States for purposes of determining whether the QDOT property is includible in the spouse's gross estate under chapter 11 of the Internal Revenue Code, and for purposes of determining whether any of the credits, deductions or deferral provisions are allowable with respect to the QDOT property to the estate of the spouse.

(3) *Special rule in the case of trusts described in section 2056(b)(8).*—In the case of a QDOT in which the spouse's interest qualifies for a marital deduction under section 2056(b)(8), the provisions of section 2056A(b)(10)(A) apply in determining the allowance of a charitable deduction in computing the section 2056A estate tax, notwithstanding that the QDOT is not includible in the spouse's gross estate.

(4) *Credit for state and foreign death taxes.*—If the assets of the QDOT are included in the surviving spouse's gross estate for federal estate tax purposes, or would have been so includible if the spouse had been a United States resident, and state or foreign death taxes are paid by the spouse's estate with respect to the QDOT, the taxes paid by the spouse's estate with respect to the QDOT are creditable, to the extent allowable under section 2011 or 2014, as applicable, in computing the section 2056A estate tax. In addition, state or foreign death taxes previously paid by the decedent/transferor's estate are also creditable in computing the section 2056A estate tax to the extent allowable under sections 2011 and 2014. Specifically, the tax that would have been imposed on the decedent's estate if the taxable estate had been increased by the value of the QDOT assets on the spouse's death plus the amount involved in prior taxable events (section 2056A(b)(2)(A)(i)), is determined after allowance of a credit equal to the lesser of the state or foreign death tax previously paid by the decedent's estate, or the amount prescribed under section 2011(b) or 2014(b) computed based on a taxable estate increased by such amounts. Similarly, the tax that would have been imposed on the decedent's estate if the taxable estate had been increased only by the amount involved in

prior taxable events (section 2056A(b)(2)(A)(ii)) is determined after allowance of a credit equal to the lesser of the state or foreign death tax previously paid by the decedent's estate, or the amount prescribed under section 2011(b) or 2014(b) computed based on a taxable estate increased by the amount involved in such prior taxable events. See paragraph (d), *Example 2*, of this section.

(5) *Alternate valuation and special use valuation.*—(i) *In general.*—In order to claim the benefits of alternate valuation under section 2032, or special use valuation under section 2032A, for purposes of computing the section 2056A estate tax, an election must be made on the Form 706-QDT that is filed with respect to the balance remaining in the QDOT upon the death of the surviving spouse. In addition, the separate requirements for making the section 2032 and/or section 2032A elections under those sections and the regulations thereunder must be complied with except that, for this purpose, the surviving spouse is treated as a resident of the United States regardless of the surviving spouse's actual residency status. Solely for purposes of this paragraph (b)(5), the citizenship of the first decedent is immaterial.

(ii) *Alternate valuation.*—For purposes of the alternate valuation election under section 2032, the election may not be made unless the election decreases both the value of the property remaining in the QDOT upon the death of the surviving spouse and the net amount of section 2056A estate tax due. Once made, the election is irrevocable.

(iii) *Special use valuation.*—For purposes of section 2032A, the Designated Filer (in the case of multiple QDOTs) or the U.S. Trustee may elect to value certain farm and closely held business real property at its farm or business use value, rather than its fair market value, if all of the requirements under section 2032A and the applicable regulations are met, except that, for this purpose, the surviving spouse is treated as a resident of the United States regardless of the spouse's actual residency status. The total value of property valued under section 2032A in the QDOT cannot be decreased from fair market value by more than $750,000.

(c) *Miscellaneous rules.*—See sections 2056A(b)(2)(B)(i) and 2056A(b)(2)(C) for special rules regarding the appropriate rate of tax. See section 2056A(b)(2)(B)(ii) for provisions regarding a credit or refund with respect to the section 2056A estate tax.

(d) *Examples.*—The rules of this section are illustrated by the following examples.

Example 1. (i) *D*, a United States citizen, dies in 1995 a resident of State X, with a gross estate of $1,200,000. Under *D*'s will, a pecuniary bequest of $700,000 passes to a QDOT for the benefit of *D*'s spouse *S*, who is a resident but not a citizen of the United States. *D*'s estate tax is computed as follows:

Gross estate	$1,200,000	
Marital Deduction	(700,000)	
Taxable Estate	$500,000	
Gross Tax		$155,800
Less: Unified Credit		(155,800)
Net Tax		0

(ii) *S* dies in 1997 at which time *S* is still a resident of the United States and the value of the assets of the QDOT is $700,000. Assuming there were no taxable events during *S*'s lifetime with respect to the QDOT, the estate tax imposed under section 2056A(b)(1)(B) is $235,000, computed as follows:

D's actual taxable estate	$500,000	
QDOT property	700,000	
Total	$1,200,000	
Gross Tax		$427,800
Less: Unified Credit		(192,800)
Net Tax		$235,000
Less: Tax that would have been imposed on *D*'s actual taxable estate of $500,000		0
Section 2056A Estate Tax		$235,000

Example 2. (i) The facts are the same as in *Example 1*, except that *D*'s gross estate was $2,000,000 and *D*'s estate paid $70,000 in state death taxes to State X. *D*'s estate tax is computed as follows:

Gross Estate	$2,000,000
Marital Deduction	(700,000)
Taxable Estate	$1,300,000

Gross Tax		$469,800
Less: Unified Credit	192,800	
State Death Tax Credit Limitation (lesser of $51,600 or $70,000 tax paid)	51,600	(244,400)
Estate Tax		$225,400

(ii) *S* dies in 1997 at which time *S* is still a resident of the United States and the value of the assets of the QDOT is $800,000. *S*'s estate pays $40,000 in State X death taxes with respect to the inclusion of the QDOT in *S*'s gross estate for state death tax purposes. Assuming there were no taxable events during *S*'s lifetime with respect to the QDOT, the estate tax imposed under section 2056A(b)(1)(B) is $ 304,800 computed as follows:

D's Actual Taxable Estate	$1,300,000	
QDOT Property	800,000	
Total	$2,100,000	
Gross Tax		$829,800
Less: Unified Credit		(192,800)
Pre-2011 section 2056A estate tax		$637,000

(A) State Death Tax Credit Computation:

(1) State death tax paid by *S*'s estate with respect to the QDOT [$40,000] plus state death tax previously paid by *D*'s estate [$70,000] = $110,000.

(2) Credit limit under section 2011(b) (based on *D*'s adjusted taxable estate of $ 2,040,000 under sections 2056A(b)(2)(A) and 2011(b)) = $106,800.

(B) State death tax credit allowable against section 2056A estate tax (lesser of paragraph (ii)(A)(1) or (2) of this *Example 2* . . . . (106,800)

Net Tax	$530,200
Less: Tax that would have been imposed on D's taxable estate of $1,300,000 . .	225,400
Section 2056A Estate Tax	$304,800

[Reg. § 20.2056A-6.]

☐ [T.D. 8612, 8-21-95.]

[Reg. § 20.2056A-7]

§ 20.2056A-7. Allowance of prior transfer credit under section 2013.—(a) *Property subject to QDOT election.*—Section 2056(d)(3) provides special rules for computing the section 2013 credit allowed with respect to property subject to a QDOT election. In computing the credit under section 2013, the amount of the credit is determined under section 2013 and the regulations thereunder, except that—

(1) The first limitation as described in section 2013(b) and § 20.2013-2 is the amount of the estate tax imposed under section 2056A(b)(1)(A), with respect to distributions during the spouse's life, and under section 2056A(b)(1)(B), with respect to the value of the QDOT assets on the spouse's death;

(2) In computing the second limitation as described in section 2013(c) and § 20.2013-3, the value of the property transferred to the decedent (as defined in section 2013(d) and § 20.2013-4) is deemed to be the value of the QDOT assets on the date of death of the surviving spouse. The value as so determined is not reduced by the section 2056A estate tax imposed at the time of the spouse's death; and

(3) The amount of the credit is determined without regard to the percentage limitations contained in section 2013(a).

(b) *Property not subject to QDOT election.*—If property includible in a decedent's gross estate passes to a noncitizen surviving spouse (the transferee) and no deduction is allowed to the decedent's estate for that interest in property under section 2056(a) solely because the requirements of section 2056(d)(2) are not satisfied, and the transferee spouse dies with an estate that is subject to tax under section 2001 or 2101, as the case may be, any credit for tax on prior transfers allowable to the estate of the transferee spouse under section 2013 with respect to such interest in property is determined in accordance with the rules of section 2013 and the regulations thereunder, except that the amount of the credit is determined without regard to the percentage limitations contained in section 2013(a).

(c) *Example.*—The application of this section may be illustrated by the following example:

Example. The facts are the same as in § 20.2056A-6, *Example* 2(ii). *D*, a United States citizen, dies in 1994, a resident of State X, with a gross estate of $2,000,000. Under *D*'s will, a pecuniary bequest of $700,000 passes to a QDOT for the benefit of *D*'s spouse *S*, who is a resident but not a citizen of the United States. *S* dies in 1997 at which time *S* is still a resident of the United States and the value of the assets of the QDOT is $800,000. There were no taxable events during *S*'s lifetime. An estate tax of $304,800 is imposed under section 2056A(b)(1)(B). *S*'s taxable estate, including the value of the QDOT ($800,000), is $1,500,000.

(i) Under paragraph (a)(1) of this section, the first limitation for purposes of section 2013(b) is

Taxable estate		$1,500,000
Gross estate tax		555,800
Less: Unified credit	$192,800	
Credit for state death taxes	64,400	257,200
Pre-2013 net estate tax payable		$298,600

(B) *S*'s net estate tax payable under §20.2013-3(a)(2), as modified under paragraph (a)(2) of this section, is computed as follows:

Taxable estate		$700,000
Gross estate tax		229,800
Less: Unified credit	$192,800	
Credit for state death taxes	18,000	210,800
Net tax payable		$19,000
(C) *Second Limitation:*		
Paragraph (ii)(A) of this *Example*	$298,600	
Less: Paragraph (ii)(B) of this *Example*	19,000	$279,600

(iii) Credit for tax on prior transfers = $279,600 (lesser of paragraphs (i) or (ii) of this *Example*. [Reg. §20.2056A-7.]

☐ [*T.D.* 8612, 8-21-95.]

[Reg. §20.2056A-8]

§20.2056A-8. Special rules for joint property.—(a) *Inclusion in gross estate.*—(1) *General rule.*—If property is held by the decedent and the surviving spouse of the decedent as joint tenants with right of survivorship, or as tenants by the entirety, and the surviving spouse is not a United States citizen (or treated as a United States citizen) at the time of the decedent's death, the property is subject to inclusion in the decedent's gross estate in accordance with the rules of section 2040(a) (general rule for includibility of joint interests), and section 2040(b) (special rule for includibility of certain joint interests of husbands and wives) does not apply. Accordingly, the rules contained in section 2040(a) and §20.2040-1 govern the extent to which such joint interests are includible in the gross estate of a decedent who was a citizen or resident of the United States. Under §20.2040-1(a)(2), the entire value of jointly held property is included in the decedent's gross estate unless the executor submits facts sufficient to show that property was not entirely acquired with consideration furnished by the decedent, or was acquired by the decedent and the other joint owner by gift, bequest, devise or inheritance. If the decedent is a nonresident not a citizen of the United States, the

$304,800, the amount of the section 2056A estate tax.

(ii) Under paragraph (a)(2) of this section, the second limitation for purposes of section 2013(c) is computed as follows:

(A) *S*'s net estate tax payable under §20.2013-3(a)(1), as modified under paragraph (a)(2) of this section, is computed as follows:

rules of this paragraph (a)(1) apply pursuant to sections 2103, 2031, 2040(a), and 2056(d)(1)(B).

(2) *Consideration furnished by surviving spouse.*—For purposes of applying section 2040(a), in determining the amount of consideration furnished by the surviving spouse, any consideration furnished by the decedent with respect to the property before July 14, 1988, is treated as consideration furnished by the surviving spouse to the extent that the consideration was treated as a gift to the spouse under section 2511, or to the extent that the decedent elected to treat the transfer as a gift to the spouse under section 2515 (to the extent applicable). For purposes of determining whether the consideration was a gift by the decedent under section 2511, it is presumed that the decedent was a citizen of the United States at the time the consideration was so furnished to the spouse. The special rule of this paragraph (a)(2) is applicable only if the donor spouse predeceases the donee spouse and not if the donee spouse predeceases the donor spouse. In cases where the donee spouse predeceases the donor spouse, any portion of the consideration treated as a gift to the donee spouse/decedent on the creation of the tenancy (or subsequently thereafter), regardless of the date the tenancy was created, is not treated as consideration furnished by the donee spouse/decedent for purposes of section 2040(a).

(3) *Amount allowed to be transferred to QDOT.*—If, as a result of the application of the rules described above, only a portion of the

value of a jointly-held property interest is includible in a decedent's gross estate, only that portion that is so includible may be transferred to a QDOT under section 2056(d)(2). See § 20.2056A-4(b)(1) and (d), *Example 3*.

(b) *Surviving spouse becomes citizen.*—Paragraph (a) of this section does not apply if the surviving spouse meets the requirements of section 2056(d)(4). For the definition of resident in applying section 2056(d)(4), see § 20.0-1(b).

(c) *Examples.*—The provisions of this section are illustrated by the following examples:

Example 1. In 1987, D, a United States citizen, purchases real property and takes title in the names of D and S, D's spouse (a noncitizen, but a United States resident), as joint tenants with right of survivorship. In accordance with § 25.2511-1(h)(5) of this chapter, one-half of the value of the property is a gift to S. D dies in 1995. Because S is not a United States citizen, the provisions of section 2040(a) are determinative of the extent to which the real property is includible in D's gross estate. Because the joint tenancy was established before July 14, 1988, and under the applicable provisions of the Internal Revenue Code and regulations the transfer was treated as a gift of one-half of the property, one-half of the value of the property is deemed attributable to consideration furnished by S for purposes of section 2040(a). Accordingly, only one-half of the value of the property is includible in D's gross estate under section 2040(a).

Example 2. The facts are the same as in *Example 1*, except that S dies in 1995 survived by D who is not a citizen of the United States. For purposes of applying section 2040(a), D's gift to S on the creation of the tenancy is not treated as consideration furnished by S toward the acquisition of the property. Accordingly, since S made no other contributions with respect to the property, no portion of the property is includible in S's gross estate.

Example 3. The facts are the same as in *Example 1*, except that D and S purchase real property in 1990 making the down payment with funds from a joint bank account. All subsequent mortgage payments and improvements are paid from the joint bank account. The only funds deposited in the joint bank account are the earnings of D and S. It is established that D earned approximately 60% of the funds and S earned approximately 40% of the funds. D dies in 1995. The establishment of S's contribution to the joint bank account is sufficient to show that S contributed 40% of the consideration for the property. Thus, under paragraph § 20.2040-1(a)(2), 60% of the value of the property is includible in D's gross estate. [Reg. § 20.2056A-8.]

☐ [*T.D.* 8612, 8-21-95.]

[Reg. § 20.2056A-9]

§ 20.2056A-9. Designated Filer.—Section 2056A(b)(2)(C) provides special rules where more than one QDOT is established with respect to a decedent. The designation of a person responsible for filing a return under section 2056A(b)(2)(C)(i) (the Designated Filer) must be made on the decedent's federal estate tax return, or on the first Form 706-QDT that is due and is filed by its prescribed date, including extensions. The Designated Filer must be a U.S. Trustee. If the U.S. Trustee is an individual, that individual must have a tax home (as defined in section 911(d)(3)) in the United States. At least sixty days before the due date for filing the tax returns for all of the QDOTs, the U.S. Trustee(s) of each of the QDOTs must provide to the Designated Filer all of the necessary information relating to distributions from their respective QDOTs. The section 2056A estate tax due from each QDOT is allocated on a pro rata basis (based on the ratio of the amount of each respective distribution constituting a taxable event to the amount of all such distributions), unless a different allocation is required under the terms of the governing instrument or under local law. Unless the decedent has provided for a successor Designated Filer, if the Designated Filer ceases to qualify as a U.S. Trustee, or otherwise becomes unable to serve as the Designated Filer, the remaining trustees of each QDOT must select a qualifying successor Designated Filer (who is also a U.S. Trustee) prior to the due date for the filing of Form 706-QDT (including extensions). The selection is to be indicated on the Form 706-QDT. Failure to select a successor Designated Filer will result in the application of section 2056A(b)(2)(C). [Reg. § 20.2056A-9.]

☐ [*T.D.* 8612, 8-21-95.]

[Reg. § 20.2056A-10]

§ 20.2056A-10. Surviving spouse becomes citizen after QDOT established.—(a) *Section 2056A estate tax no longer imposed under certain circumstances.*—Section 2056A(b)(12) provides that a QDOT is no longer subject to the imposition of the section 2056A estate tax if the surviving spouse becomes a citizen of the United States and the following conditions are satisfied—

(1) The spouse either was a United States resident (for the definition of resident for this purpose, see § 20.2056A-1(b)) at all times after the death of the decedent and before becoming a United States citizen, or no taxable distributions are made from the QDOT before the spouse becomes a United States citizen (regardless of the residency status of the spouse); and

(2) The U.S. Trustee(s) of the QDOT notifies the Internal Revenue Service and certifies in writing that the surviving spouse has become a United States citizen. Notice is to be made by filing a final Form 706-QDT on or before April 15th of the calendar year following the year in

which the surviving spouse becomes a United States citizen, unless an extension of time for filing is granted under section 6081.

(b) *Special election by spouse.*—If the surviving spouse becomes a United States citizen and the spouse is not a United States resident at all times after the death of the decedent and before becoming a United States citizen, and a tax was previously imposed under section 2056A(b)(1)(A) with respect to any distribution from the QDOT before the surviving spouse becomes a United States citizen, the estate tax imposed under section 2056A(b)(1) does not apply to distributions after the spouse becomes a citizen if—

(1) The spouse elects to treat any taxable distribution from the QDOT prior to the spouse's election as a taxable gift made by the spouse for purposes of section 2001(b)(1)(B) (referring to adjusted taxable gifts), and for purposes of determining the amount of the tax imposed by section 2501 on actual taxable gifts made by the spouse during the year in which the spouse becomes a citizen or in any subsequent year;

(2) The spouse elects to treat any previous reduction in the section 2056A estate tax by reason of the decedent's unified credit (under either section 2010 or section 2102(c)) as a reduction in the spouse's unified credit under section 2505 for purposes of determining the amount of the credit allowable with respect to taxable gifts made by the surviving spouse during the taxable year in which the spouse becomes a citizen, or in any subsequent year; and

(3) The elections referred to in this paragraph (b) are made by timely filing a Form 706-QDT on or before April 15th of the year following the year in which the surviving spouse becomes a citizen (unless an extension of time for filing is granted under section 6081) and attaching notification of the election to the return. [Reg. § 20.2056A-10.]

☐ [*T.D.* 8612, 8-21-95.]

[Reg. § 20.2056A-11]

§ 20.2056A-11. Filing requirements and payment of the section 2056A estate tax.— (a) *Distributions during surviving spouse's life.*— Section 2056A(b)(5)(A) provides the due date for payment of the section 2056A estate tax imposed on distributions during the spouse's lifetime. An extension of not more than 6 months may be obtained for the filing of Form 706-QDT under section 6081(a) if the conditions specified therein are satisfied. See also § 20.2056A-5(c)(1) regarding the requirements for filing a Form 706-QDT in the case of a distribution to the surviving spouse on account of hardship, and § 20.2056A-2T(d)(3) regarding the requirements for filing Form 706-QDT in the case of the required annual statement.

(b) *Tax at death of surviving spouse.*—Section 2056A(b)(5)(B) provides the due date for payment of the section 2056A estate tax imposed on the death of the spouse under section 2056A(b)(1)(B). An extension of not more than 6 months may be obtained for the filing of the Form 706-QDT under section 6081(a), if the conditions specified therein are satisfied. The obtaining of an extension of time to file under section 6081(a) does not extend the time to pay the section 2056A estate tax as prescribed under section 2056A(b)(5)(B).

(c) *Extension of time for paying section 2056A estate tax.*—(1) *Extension of time for paying tax under section 6161(a)(2).*—Pursuant to sections 2056A(b)(10)(C) and 6161(a)(2), upon a showing of reasonable cause, an extension of time for a reasonable period beyond the due date may be granted to pay any part of the estate tax that is imposed upon the surviving spouse's death under section 2056A(b)(1)(B) and shown on the final Form 706-QDT, or any part of any installments of such tax payable under section 6166 (including any part of a deficiency prorated to any installment under such section). The extension may not exceed 10 years from the date prescribed for payment of the tax (or in the case of an installment or part of a deficiency prorated to an installment, if later, not beyond the date that is 12 months after the due date for the last installment). Such extension may be granted by the district director or the director of the service center where the Form 706-QDT is filed.

(2) *Extension of time for paying tax under section 6161(a)(1).*—An extension of time beyond the due date to pay any part of the estate tax imposed on lifetime distributions under section 2056A(b)(1)(A), or imposed at the death of the surviving spouse under section 2056A(b)(1)(B), may be granted for a reasonable period of time, not to exceed 6 months (12 months in the case of the estate tax imposed under section 2056A(b)(1)(B) at the surviving spouse's death), by the district director or the director of the service center where the Form 706-QDT is filed.

(d) *Liability for tax.*—Under section 2056A(b)(6), each trustee (and not solely the U.S. Trustee(s)) of a QDOT is personally liable for the amount of the estate tax imposed in the case of any taxable event under section 2056A(b)(1). In the case of multiple QDOTs with respect to the same decedent, each trustee of a QDOT is personally liable for the amount of the section 2056A estate tax imposed on any taxable event with respect to that trustee's QDOT, but is not personally liable for tax imposed with respect to taxable events involving QDOTs of which that person is not a trustee. However, the assets of any QDOT are subject to collection by the Internal Revenue Service for any tax resulting from a taxable event with respect to any other QDOT established with respect to the same decedent.

The trustee may also be personally liable as a withholding agent under section 1461 or other applicable provisions of the Internal Revenue Code. [Reg. § 20.2056A-11.]

☐ [*T.D.* 8612, 8-21-95.]

[Reg. § 20.2056A-12]

§ 20.2056A-12. Increased basis for section 2056A estate tax paid with respect to distribution from a QDOT.—Under section 2056A(b)(13), in the case of any distribution from a QDOT on which an estate tax is imposed under section 2056A(b)(1)(A), the distribution is treated as a transfer by gift for purposes of section 1015, and any estate tax paid under section 2056A(b)(1)(A) is treated as a gift tax. See § 1.1015-5(c)(4) and (5) of this chapter for rules for determining the amount by which the basis

of the distributed property is increased. [Reg. § 20.2056A-12.]

☐ [*T.D.* 8612, 8-21-95.]

[Reg. § 20.2056A-13]

§ 20.2056A-13. Effective date.—Except as provided in this section, the provisions of §§ 20.2056A-1 through 20.2056A-12 are applicable with respect to estates of decedents dying after August 22, 1995. The rule in the fourth sentence of § 20.2056A-5(c)(2) regarding unitrusts and distributions of income to the surviving spouse in conformance with applicable local law is applicable to trusts for taxable years ending after January 2, 2004. [Reg. § 20.2056A-13.]

☐ [*T.D.* 8612, 8-21-95. *Amended by T.D.* 9102, 12-30-2003.]

Estates of Nonresidents Not Citizens

See p. 20,601 for regulations not amended to reflect law changes

[Reg. § 20.2101-1]

§ 20.2101-1. Estates of nonresidents not citizens; tax imposed.—(a) *Imposition of tax.*—Section 2101 imposes a tax on the transfer of the taxable estate of a nonresident who is not a citizen of the United States at the time of death. In the case of estates of decedents dying after November 10, 1988, the tax is computed at the same rates as the tax that is imposed on the transfer of the taxable estate of a citizen or resident of the United States in accordance with the provisions of sections 2101(b) and (c). For the meaning of the terms *resident*, *nonresident*, and *United States*, as applied to a decedent for purposes of the estate tax, see § 20.0-1(b)(1) and (2). For the liability of the executor for the payment

of the tax, see section 2002. For special rules as to the phaseout of the graduated rates and unified credit, see sections 2001(c)(2) and 2101(b).

(b) *Special rates in the case of certain decedents.*—In the case of an estate of a nonresident who was not a citizen of the United States and who died after December 31, 1976, and on or before November 10, 1988, the tax on the nonresident's taxable estate is computed using the formula provided under section 2101(b), except that the rate schedule in paragraph (c) of this section is to be used in lieu of the rate schedule in section 2001(c).

(c) *Rate schedule for decedents dying after December 31, 1976 and on or before November 10, 1988.*

If the amount for which the tentative tax to be computed is:	The tentative tax is:
Not over $100,000	6% of such amount.
Over $100,000 but not over $500,000	$6,000, plus 12% of excess over $100,000.
Over $500,000 but not over $1,000,000	$54,000, plus 18% of excess over $500,000.
Over $1,000,000 but not over $2,000,000	$144,000, plus 24% of excess over $1,000,000
Over $2,000,000	$384,000, plus 30% of excess over $2,000,000.

[Reg. § 20.2101-1.]

☐ [*T.D.* 6296, 6-23-58. *Amended by T.D.* 7296, 12-11-73 *and T.D.* 8612, 8-21-95.]

[Reg. § 20.2102-1]

§ 20.2102-1. Estates of nonresidents not citizens; credits against tax.—(a) *In general.*—In arriving at the net estate tax payable with respect

to the transfer of an estate of a nonresident who was not a citizen of the United States at the time of his death, the following credits are subtracted from the tax imposed by section 2101:

(1) The State death tax credit under section 2011, to the extent permitted by section 2102(b) and paragraph (b) of this section;

(2) The gift tax credit under section 2012; and

(3) The credit under section 2013 for tax on prior transfers.

Except as provided in section 2102(b) and paragraph (b) of this section (relating to a special limitation on the amount of the credit for State death taxes), the amount of each of these credits is determined in the same manner as that prescribed for its determination in the case of estates of citizens or residents of the United States. See §§ 20.2011 through 20.2013-6. Subject to the additional special limitation contained in section 2102(b) in the case of section 2015, the provisions of sections 2015 and 2016, relating respectively to the credit for death taxes on remainders and the recovery of taxes claimed as a credit, are applicable with respect to the credit for State death taxes in the case of the estates of nonresidents not citizens. However, no credit is allowed under section 2014 for foreign death taxes.

(b) *Special limitation.*—(1) *In general.*—In the case of estates of decedents dying on or after November 14, 1966, other than estates the estate tax treatment of which is subject to a Presidential proclamation made pursuant to section 2108(a), the maximum credit allowable under section 2011 for State death taxes against the tax imposed by section 2101 on the transfer of estates of nonresidents not citizens of the United States is an amount which bears the same ratio to the maximum credit computed as provided in section 2011(b) (and without regard to this special limitation) as the value of the property (determined in the same manner as that prescribed in paragraph (b) of § 20.2031-1 for the estates of citizens or residents of the United States) in respect of which a State death tax was actually paid and which is included in the gross estate under section 2103 or, if applicable, section 2107(b) bears to the value (as so determined) of the total gross estate under section 2103 or 2107(b). For purposes of this special limitation, the term "State death taxes" means the taxes described in section 2011(a) and paragraph (a) of § 20.2011-1.

(2) *Illustrations.*—The application of this paragraph may be illustrated by the following examples:

Example (1). A, a nonresident not a citizen of the United States, died on February 15, 1967, owning real property in State Z valued at $50,000 and stock in various domestic corporations valued at $100,000 and not subject to death taxes in any State. State Z's inheritance tax actually paid with respect to the real property in State Z is $2,000. A's taxable estate for Federal estate tax purposes is $110,000, in respect of which the maximum credit under section 2011 would be $720 in the absence of the special limitation contained in section 2102(b). However, under section 2102(b) and this paragraph the amount of the maximum credit allowable in respect to A's estate for State death taxes is limited to the amount which bears the same ratio to $720 (the maximum credit computed as provided in section 2011(b)) as $50,000 (the value of the property in respect of which a State death tax was actually paid and which is included in A's gross estate under section 2103) bears to $150,000 (the value of A's total gross estate under section 2103). Accordingly, the maximum credit allowable under section 2102 and this section for all State death taxes actually paid is $240 ($720 × $50,000/$150,000).

Example (2). B, a nonresident not a citizen of the United States, died on January 15, 1967, owning real property in State X valued at $100,000, real property in State Y valued at $200,000, and stock in various domestic corporations valued at $300,000 and not subject to death taxes in any State. States X and Y both impose inheritance taxes. State X has, in addition to its inheritance tax, an estate tax equal to the amount by which the maximum State death tax credit allowable to an estate against its Federal estate tax exceeds the amount of the inheritance tax imposed by State X plus the amount of death taxes paid to other States. State Y has no estate tax. The amount of the inheritance tax actually paid to State X with respect to the real property situated in State X is $4,000; the amount of the inheritance tax actually paid to State Y with respect to the real property situated in State Y is $9,000. B's taxable estate for Federal estate tax purposes is $550,000, in respect of which the maximum credit under section 2011 would be $14,400 in the absence of the special limitation contained in section 2102(b). However, under section 2102(b) and this paragraph the amount of the maximum credit allowable in respect of B's estate for State death taxes is limited to the amount which bears the same ratio to $14,400 (the maximum credit computed as provided in section 2011(b)) as $300,000 (the value of the property in respect of which a State death tax was actually paid and which is included in B's gross estate under section 2103) bears to $600,000 (the value of B's total gross estate under section 2103). Accordingly, the maximum credit allowable under section 2102 and this section for all State death taxes actually paid is $7,200 ($14,400 × $300,000/$600,000), and the estate tax of State X is not applicable to B's estate.

(c) *Unified credit.*—(1) *In general.*—Subject to paragraph (c)(2) of this section, in the case of estates of decedents dying after November 10, 1988, a unified credit of $13,000 is allowed against the tax imposed by section 2101 subject to the limitations of section 2102(c).

(2) *When treaty is applicable.*—To the extent required under any treaty obligation of the United States, the estate of a nonresident not a citizen of the United States is allowed the unified credit permitted to a United States citizen or resident of $192,800, multiplied by the proportion that the total gross estate of the decedent

situated in the United States bears to the decedent's total gross estate wherever situated.

(3) *Certain residents of possessions.*—In the case of a decedent who is considered to be a nonresident not a citizen of the United States under section 2209, there is allowed a unified credit equal to the greater of $13,000, or $46,800 multiplied by the proportion that the decedent's gross estate situated in the United States bears to the total gross estate of the decedent wherever situated. [Reg. § 20.2102-1.]

☐ [*T.D. 6296, 6-23-58. Amended by T.D. 7296, 12-11-73 and T.D. 8612, 8-21-95.*]

[Reg. § 20.2103-1]

§ 20.2103-1. Estates of nonresidents not citizens; "entire gross estate.".—The "entire gross estate" wherever situated of a nonresident who was not a citizen of the United States at the time of his death is made up in the same way as the "gross estate" of a citizen or resident of the United States. See § § 20.2031 through 20.2044-1. See paragraphs (a) and (c) of § 20.2031-1 for the circumstances under which real property situated outside the United States is excluded from the gross estate of a citizen or resident of the United States. However, except as provided in section 2107(b) with respect to the estates of certain expatriates, in the case of a nonresident not a citizen, only that part of the entire gross estate which on the date of the decedent's death is situated in the United States is included in his taxable estate. In fact, property situated outside the United States need not be disclosed on the return unless section 2107 is applicable, certain deductions are claimed, or information is specifically requested. See § § 20.2106-1, 20.2106-2, and 20.2107-1. For a description of property considered to be situated in the United States, see § 20.2104-1. For a description of property considered to be situated outside the United States, see § 20.2105-1. [Reg. § 20.2103-1.]

☐ [*T.D. 6296, 6-23-58. Amended by T.D. 6684, 10-23-63 and T.D. 7296, 12-11-73.*]

[Reg. § 20.2104-1]

§ 20.2104-1. Estates of nonresidents not citizens; property within the United States.—(a) *In general.*—Property of a nonresident who was not a citizen of the United States at the time of his death is considered to be situated in the United States if it is—

(1) Real property located in the United States.

(2) Tangible personal property located in the United States, except certain works of art on loan for exhibition (see paragraph (b) of § 20.2105-1).

(3) In the case of an estate of a decedent dying before November 14, 1966, written evidence of intangible personal property which is treated as being the property itself, such as a bond for the payment of money, if it is physically located in the United States; except that this subparagraph shall not apply to obligations of the United States (but not its instrumentalities) issued before March 1, 1941, if the decedent was not engaged in business in the United States at the time of his death. See section 2106(c).

(4) Except as specifically provided otherwise in this section or in § 20.2105-1 (which specific exceptions, in the case of estates of decedents dying on or after November 14, 1966, cause this subparagraph to have relatively limited applicability), intangible personal property the written evidence of which is not treated as being the property itself, if it is issued by or enforceable against a resident of the United States or a domestic corporation or governmental unit.

(5) Shares of stock issued by a domestic corporation, irrespective of the location of the certificates (see, however, paragraph (i) of § 20.2105-1 for a special rule with respect to certain withdrawable accounts in savings and loan or similar associations).

(6) In the case of an estate of a decedent dying before November 14, 1966, moneys deposited in the United States by or for the decedent with any person carrying on the banking business, if the decedent was engaged in business in the United States at the time of his death.

(7) In the case of an estate of a decedent dying on or after November 14, 1966, except as specifically provided otherwise in paragraph (d), (i), (j), (l), or (m) of § 20.2105-1, any debt obligation, including a bank deposit, the primary obligor of which is—

(i) A United States person (as defined in section 7701(a)(30)), or

(ii) The United States, a State or any political subdivision thereof, the District of Columbia, or any agency or instrumentality of any such government.

This subparagraph applies irrespective of whether the written evidence of the debt obligation is treated as being the property itself or whether the decedent was engaged in business in the United States at the time of his death. For purposes of this subparagraph and paragraphs (k), (l), and (m) of § 20.2105-1, a debt obligation on which there are two or more primary obligors shall be apportioned among such obligors, taking into account to the extent appropriate under all the facts and circumstances any choate or inchoate rights of contribution existing among such obligors with respect to the indebtedness. The term "agency or instrumentality", as used in subdivision (ii) of this subparagraph, does not include a possession of the United States or an agency or instrumentality of a possession. Currency is not a debt obligation for purposes of this subparagraph.

(8) In the case of an estate of a decedent dying on or after January 1, 1970, except as specifically provided otherwise in paragraph (i) or

(l) of §20.2105-1, deposits with a branch in the United States of a foreign corporation, if the branch is engaged in the commercial banking business, whether or not the decedent was engaged in business in the United States at the time of his death.

(b) *Transfers.*—Property of which the decedent has made a transfer taxable under sections 2035 through 2038 is deemed to be situated in the United States if it is determined, under the provisions of paragraph (a) of this section, to be so situated either at the time of the transfer or at the time of the decedent's death. See §§ 20.2035-1 through 20.2038-1.

(c) *Death tax convention.*—It should be noted that the situs rules described in this section may be modified for various purposes under the provisions of an applicable death tax convention with a foreign country. [Reg. § 20.2104-1.]

☐ [*T.D.* 6296, 6-23-58. *Amended by T.D.* 7296, 12-11-73 *and T.D.* 7321, 8-15-74.]

[Reg. § 20.2105-1]

§ 20.2105-1. Estates of nonresidents not citizens; property without the United States.— Property of a nonresident who was not a citizen of the United States at the time of his death is considered to be situated outside the United States if it is—

(a)(1) Real property located outside the United States, except to the extent excludable from the entire gross estate wherever situated under § 20.2103-1.

(2) Tangible personal property located outside the United States.

(b) Works of art owned by the decedent if they were—

(1) Imported into the United States solely for exhibition purposes,

(2) Loaned for those purposes to a public gallery or museum, no part of the net earnings of which inures to the benefit of any private shareholder or individual, and

(3) At the time of the death of the owner, on exhibition, or en route to or from exhibition, in such a public gallery or museum.

(c) In the case of an estate of a decedent dying before November 14, 1966, written evidence of intangible personal property which is treated as being the property itself, such as a bond for the payment of money, if it is not physically located in the United States.

(d) Obligations of the United States issued before March 1, 1941, even though physically located in the United States, if the decedent was not engaged in business in the United States at the time of his death.

(e) Except as specifically provided otherwise in this section or in § 20.2104-1, intangible personal property the written evidence of which is not treated as being the property itself, if it is not

issued by or enforceable against a resident of the United States or a domestic corporation or governmental unit.

(f) Shares of stock issued by a corporation which is not a domestic corporation, regardless of the location of the certificates.

(g) Amounts receivable as insurance on the decedent's life.

(h) In the case of an estate of a decedent dying before November 14, 1966, moneys deposited in the United States by or for the decedent with any person carrying on the banking business, if the decedent was not engaged in business in the United States at the time of his death.

(i) In the case of an estate of a decedent dying on or after November 14, 1966, and before January 1, 1976, any amount deposited in the United States which is described in section 861(c) (relating to certain bank deposits, withdrawable accounts, and amounts held by an insurance company under an agreement to pay interest), if any interest thereon, were such interest received by the decedent at the time of his death, would be treated under section 862(a)(1) as income from sources without the United States by reason of section 861(a)(1)(A) (relating to interest on amounts described in section 861(c) which is not effectively connected with the conduct of a trade or business within the United States) and the regulations thereunder. If such interest would be treated by reason of those provisions as income from sources without the United States only in part, the amount described in section 861(c) shall be considered situated outside the United States in the same proportion as the part of the interest which would be treated as income from sources without the United States bears to the total amount of the interest. This paragraph applies whether or not the decedent was engaged in business in the United States at the time of his death, and, except with respect to amounts described in section 861(c)(3) (relating to amounts held by an insurance company under an agreement to pay interest), whether or not the deposit or other amount is in fact interest bearing.

(j) In the case of an estate of a decedent dying on or after November 14, 1966, deposits with a branch outside of the United States of a domestic corporation or domestic partnership, if the branch is engaged in the commercial banking business. This paragraph applies whether or not the decedent was engaged in business in the United States at the time of his death, and whether or not the deposits, upon withdrawal, are payable in currency of the United States.

(k) In the case of an estate of a decedent dying on or after November 14, 1966, except as specifically provided otherwise in paragraph (a)(8) of § 20.2104-1 with respect to estates of decedents dying on or after January 1, 1970, any debt obligation, including a bank deposit, the primary obligor of which is neither—

(1) A United States person (as defined in section 7701(a)(30)), nor

(2) The United States, a State or any political subdivision thereof, the District of Columbia, or any agency or instrumentality of any such government.

This paragraph applies irrespective of whether the written evidence of the debt obligation is treated as being the property itself or whether the decedent was engaged in business in the United States at the time of his death. See paragraph (a)(7) of §20.2104-1 for the treatment of a debt obligation on which there are two or more primary obligors. The term "agency or instrumentality", as used in subparagraph (2) of this paragraph, does not include a possession of the United States or an agency or instrumentality of a possession. Currency is not a debt obligation for purposes of this paragraph.

(l) In the case of an estate of a decedent dying on or after November 14, 1966, any debt obligation to the extent that the primary obligor on the debt obligation is a domestic corporation, if any interest thereon, were the interest received from such obligor by the decedent at the time of his death, would be treated under section 862(a)(1) as income from sources without the United States by reason of section 861(a)(1)(B) (relating to interest received from a domestic corporation less than 20 percent of whose gross income for a 3-year period was derived from sources within the United States) and the regulations thereunder. For such purposes the 3-year period referred to in section 861(a)(1)(B) is the period of 3 years ending with the close of the domestic corporation's last taxable year terminating before the decedent's death. This paragraph applies whether or not (1) the obligation is in fact interest-bearing, (2) the written evidence of the debt obligation is treated as being the property itself, or (3) the decedent was engaged in business in the United States at the time of his death. See paragraph (a)(7) of §20.2104-1 for the treatment of a debt obligation on which there are two or more primary obligors.

(m)(1) In the case of an estate of a decedent dying after December 31, 1972, except as otherwise provided in subparagraph (2) of this paragraph, any debt obligation to the extent that the primary obligor on the debt obligation is a domestic corporation or domestic partnership, if any interest thereon, were the interest received from such obligor by the decedent at the time of his death, would be treated under section 862(a)(1) as income from sources without the United States by reason of section 861(a)(1)(G) (relating to interest received on certain debt obligations with respect to which elections have been made under section 4912(c)) and the regulations thereunder. This paragraph applies whether or not (i) the obligation is in fact interest bearing, (ii) the written evidence of the debt obligation is treated as being the property itself, or (iii) the decedent was engaged in business in the United States at the time of his death. See paragraph (a)(7) of §20.2104-1 for the treatment

of a debt obligation on which there are two or more primary obligors.

(2) In the case of an estate of a decedent dying before January 1, 1974, this paragraph does not apply to any debt obligation of a foreign corporation assumed by a domestic corporation which is treated under section 4912(c)(2) as issued by such domestic corporation during 1973. [Reg. §20.2105-1.]

☐ [T.D. 6296, 6-23-58. *Amended by* T.D. 6684, 10-23-63; T.D. 7296, 12-11-73; *and* T.D. 7321, 8-15-74.]

[Reg. §20.2106-1]

§20.2106-1. Estates of nonresidents not citizens; taxable estate; deductions in general.— (a) The taxable estate of a nonresident who was not a citizen of the United States at the time of his death is determined by adding the value of that part of his gross estate which, at the time of his death, is situated in the United States and, in the case of an estate to which section 2107 (relating to expatriation to avoid taxes) applies, any amounts includible in his gross estate under section 2107(b), and then subtracting from the sum thereof the total amount of the following deductions:

(1) The deductions allowed in the case of estates of decedents who were citizens or residents of the United States under sections 2053 and 2054 (see §§20.2053-1 through 20.2053-9 and §20.2054-1) for expenses, indebtedness and taxes, and for losses, to the extent provided in §20.2106-2.

(2) A deduction computed in the same manner as the one allowed under section 2055 (see §§20.2055-1 through 20.2055-5) for charitable, etc., transfers, except—

(i) That the deduction is allowed only for transfers to corporations and associations created or organized in the United States, and to trustees for use within the United States, and

(ii) That the provisions contained in paragraph (c)(2) of §20.2055-2 relating to termination of a power to consume are not applicable.

(3) Subject to the special rules set forth at §20.2056A-1(c), the amount which would be deductible with respect to property situated in the United States at the time of the decedent's death under the principles of section 2056. Thus, if the surviving spouse of the decedent is a citizen of the United States at the time of the decedent's death, a marital deduction is allowed with respect to the estate of the decedent if all other applicable requirements of section 2056 are satisfied. If the surviving spouse of the decedent is not a citizen of the United States at the time of the decedent's death, the provisions of section 2056, including specifically the provisions of section 2056(d) and (unless section 2056(d)(4) applies) the provisions of section 2056A (QDOTs) must be satisfied.

(b) Section 2106(b) provides that no deduction is allowed under paragraph (a)(1) or (2) of this section unless the executor discloses in the estate tax return the value of that part of the gross estate not situated in the United States. See §20.2105-1. Such part must be valued as of the date of the decedent's death, or if the alternate valuation method under section 2032 is elected, as of the applicable valuation date. [Reg. §20.2106-1.]

☐ [T.D. 6296, 6-23-58. Amended by T.D. 6526, 1-18-61; T.D. 7296, 12-11-73; T.D. 7318, 7-10-74 and T.D. 8612, 8-21-95.]

[Reg. §20.2106-2]

§20.2106-2. Estates of nonresidents not citizens; deductions for expenses, losses, etc.— (a) In computing the taxable estate of a nonresident who was not a citizen of the United States at the time of his death, deductions are allowed under sections 2053 and 2054 for expenses, indebtedness and taxes, and for losses, to the following extent:

(1) A pledge or subscription is deductible if it is an enforceable claim against the estate and if it would constitute an allowable deduction under paragraph (a)(2) of §20.2106-1, relating to charitable, etc., transfers, if it had been a bequest.

(2) That proportion of other deductions under sections 2053 and 2054 is allowed which the value of that part of the decedent's gross estate situated in the United States at the time of his death bears to the value of the decedent's entire gross estate wherever situated. It is immaterial whether the amounts to be deducted were incurred or expended within or without the United States. For purposes of this subparagraph, an amount which is includible in the decedent's gross estate under section 2107(b) with respect to stock in a foreign corporation shall be included in the value of the decedent's gross estate situated in the United States.

No deduction is allowed under this paragraph unless the value of the decedent's entire gross estate is disclosed in the estate tax return. See paragraph (b) of §20.2106-1.

(b) In order that the Internal Revenue Service may properly pass upon the items claimed as deductions, the executor should submit a certified copy of the schedule of liabilities, claims against the estate, and expenses of administration filed under any applicable foreign death duty act. If no such schedule was filed, the executor should submit a certified copy of the schedule of these liabilities, claims and expenses filed with the foreign court in which administration was had. If the items of deduction allowable under section 2106(a)(1) were not included in either such schedule, or if no such schedules were filed, then there should be submitted a written statement of the foreign executor containing a declaration that it is made under the penalties of perjury setting forth the facts relied upon as entitling the estate to the benefit of the particular deduction or deductions.

(c) [Reserved][Reg. §20.2106-2.]

☐ [T.D. 6296, 6-23-58. Amended by T.D. 7296, 12-11-73 and T.D. 8612, 8-21-95.]

[Reg. §20.2107-1]

§20.2107-1. Expatriation to avoid tax.— (a) Rate of tax.—The tax imposed by section 2107(a) on the transfer of the taxable estates of certain nonresident expatriate decedents who were formerly citizens of the United States is computed in accordance with the table contained in section 2001, relating to the rate of the tax imposed on the transfer of the taxable estates of decedents who were citizens or residents of the United States. Except for any amounts included in the gross estate solely by reason of section 2107(b) and paragraph (b)(1)(ii) and (iii) of this section, the value of the taxable estate to be used in this computation is determined as provided in section 2106 and §20.2106-1. The decedents to which section 2107(a) and this section apply are described in paragraph (d) of this section.

(b) Gross estate.—(1) Determination of value.— (i) General rule.—Except as provided in subdivision (ii) of this subparagraph with respect to stock in certain foreign corporations, for purposes of the tax imposed by section 2107(a) the value of the gross estate of every estate the transfer of which is subject to the tax imposed by that section is determined as provided in section 2103 and §20.2103-1.

(ii) Amount includible with respect to stock in certain foreign corporations.—If at the time of his death a nonresident expatriate decedent the transfer of whose estate is subject to the tax imposed by section 2107(a)—

(a) Owned (within the meaning of section 958(a) and the regulations thereunder) 10 percent or more of the total combined voting power of all classes of stock entitled to vote in a foreign corporation, and

(b) Owned (within the meaning of section 958(a) and the regulations thereunder), or is considered to have owned (by applying the ownership rules of section 958(b) and the regulations thereunder), more than 50 percent of the total combined voting power of all classes of stock entitled to vote in such foreign corporation, then section 2107(b) requires the inclusion in the decedent's gross estate, in addition to amounts otherwise includible therein under subdivision (i) of this subparagraph, of an amount equal to that proportion of the fair market value (determined at the time of the decedent's death or, if so elected by the executor of the decedent's estate, on the alternate valuation date as provided in section 2032) of the stock in such foreign corporation owned (within the meaning of section 958(a) and the regulations thereunder) by the decedent at the time of his death, which the fair market value of any assets owned by such foreign corporation and situated in the United States, at the time of his death, bears to the total fair market value of all assets owned by such foreign corporation at the time of his death.

(iii) *Rules of application.*—*(a)* In determining the proportion of the fair market value of the stock which is includible in the gross estate under subdivision (ii) of this subparagraph, the fair market value of the foreign corporation's assets situated in the United States and of its total assets shall be determined without reduction for any outstanding liabilities of the corporation.

(b) For purposes of subdivision (ii) of this subparagraph, the foreign corporation's assets which are situated in the United States shall be all its property which, by applying the provisions of sections 2104, 2105, and §§ 20.2104-1 and 20.2105-1, would be considered to be situated in the United States if such property were property of a nonresident who was not a citizen of the United States.

(c) For purposes of subdivision (ii)*(a)* of this subparagraph, a decedent is treated as owning stock in a foreign corporation at the time of his death to the extent he owned (within the meaning of section 958(a) and the regulations thereunder) the stock at the time he made a transfer of the stock in a transfer described in sections 2035 to 2038, inclusive (relating respectively to transfers made in contemplation of death, transfers with a retained life estate, transfers taking effect at death, and revocable transfers). For purposes of subdivision (ii)*(b)* of this subparagraph, a decedent is treated as owning stock in a foreign corporation at the time of his death to the extent he owned (within the meaning of section 958(a) and the regulations thereunder), or is considered to have owned (by applying the ownership rules of section 958(b) and the regulations thereunder), the stock at the time he made a transfer of the stock in a transfer described in sections 2035 to 2038, inclusive. In applying the proportion rule of section 2107(b) and subdivision (ii) of this subparagraph where a decedent is treated as owning stock in a foreign corporation at the time of his death by reason of having transferred his interest in such stock in a transfer described in sections 2035 to 2038, inclusive, the proportionate value of the interest includible in his gross estate is based upon the value as of the applicable valuation date described in section 2031 or 2032 of the amount, determined as of the date of transfer, of his interest in the stock. See example (2) in subparagraph (2) of this paragraph.

(d) For purposes of applying subdivision (ii) *(b)* of this subparagraph, the same shares of stock may not be counted more than once. See example (2) in subparagraph (2) of this paragraph.

(e) The principles applied in paragraph (b) of § 1.957-1 of this chapter (Income Tax Regulations) for determining what constitutes total combined voting power of all classes of stock entitled to vote in a foreign corporation for purposes of section 957(a) shall be applied in determining what constitutes total combined voting power of all classes of stock entitled to vote in a foreign corporation for purposes of section 2107(b) and subdivision (ii) of this subparagraph. In applying such principles under this paragraph changes in language shall be made, where necessary, in order to treat the nonresident expatriate decedent, rather than U. S. shareholders, as owning such total combined voting power.

(2) *Illustrations.*—The application of this paragraph may be illustrated by the following examples:

Example (1). (a) At the time of his death, H, a nonresident expatriate decedent the transfer of whose estate is subject to the tax imposed by section 2107(a), owned a 60-percent interest in M Company, a foreign partnership, which in turn owned stock issued by N Corporation, a foreign corporation. The stock in N Corporation held by M Company, which constituted 50 percent of the total combined voting power of all classes of stock entitled to vote in N Corporation, was valued at $50,000 at the time of H's death. In addition, W, H's wife, also a nonresident not a citizen of the United States, owned at the time of H's death stock in N Corporation constituting 25 percent of the total combined voting power of all classes of stock entitled to vote in that corporation. The fair market value of the assets of N Corporation which, at the time of H's death, were situated in the United States constituted 40 percent of the fair market value of all assets of that corporation. It is assumed for purposes of this example that the executor of H's estate has not elected to value the estate on the alternate valuation date provided in section 2032.

(b) The test contained in subparagraph (1)(ii)*(a)* of this paragraph is met since at the time of his death H indirectly owned (within the meaning of section 958(a) and the regulations thereunder) 30 percent (60% of 50%) of the total combined voting power of all classes of stock entitled to vote in N Corporation; and the test contained in subparagraph (1)(ii)*(b)* of this paragraph is met since at such time H owned or is considered to have owned (within the meaning of section 958(a) and (b) and the regulations thereunder) 55 percent of the total combined voting power of all classes of stock entitled to vote in N Corporation (having constructive ownership of his wife's 25 percent, in addition to his own indirect ownership of 30 percent, of the total combined voting power). Accordingly, $12,000 is included in H's gross estate by reason of section 2107(b) and this paragraph. This $12,000 is the amount which is equal to 40 percent (the percentage of the fair market value of N

Corporation's assets which were situated within the United States at H's death) of $30,000 (the fair market value of the stock then owned by H within the meaning of section 958(a) and the regulations thereunder, i. e., H's 60-percent interest in the $50,000 fair market value of stock held by M Company).

Example (2). (a) Assume the same facts as those given in example (1) except that H made a transfer to W in contemplation of his death (within the meaning of section 2035) of his 60-percent interest in M Company, that on the date of the transfer M Company held stock in N Corporation constituting 80 percent of the total combined voting power of all classes of stock entitled to vote in that corporation (rather than the 50 percent of total combined voting power held by M Company on the date of H's death), and that the 80 percent of total combined voting power owned by M Company on the date of the transfer is valued at $70,000 on that date and at $85,000 at the time of H's death. It is assumed for purposes of this example that the 60-percent interest in M Company was held by W at the time of H's death.

(b) The test contained in subparagraph (1)(ii)(*a*) of this paragraph is met since, under subparagraph (1)(iii)(*c*) of this paragraph, H is treated as owning (within the meaning of section 958(a) and the regulations thereunder), at the time of his death, the 48 percent (60% of 80%) of the total combined voting power of all classes of stock entitled to vote in N Corporation represented by his transferred interest in M Company; and the test contained in subparagraph (1)(ii)(*b*) of this paragraph is met since, under that subparagraph and subparagraph (1)(iii)(*c*) of this paragraph, H is treated as owning (within the meaning of section 958(a) or (b)), at the time of his death, 73 percent (48% plus 25%) of the total combined voting power of all classes of stock entitled to vote in N Corporation. Accordingly, $20,400 is included in H's gross estate by reason of section 2107(b) and this paragraph. This $20,400 is the amount which is equal to 40 percent (the percentage of the fair market value of N Corporation's assets which were situated within the United States at H's death) of $51,000 (the fair market value at the time of H's death of the transferred interest which under subparagraph (1)(iii)(*c*) of this paragraph H is considered to own within the meaning of section 958(a) and the regulations thereunder at that time, i. e., the 60-percent interest in the $85,000 fair market value at that time of the 80-percent total combined voting power held by M Company on the date of transfer).

(c) The fact that the stock in N Corporation owned by M Company is considered under subparagraph (1)(ii)(*b*) of this paragraph to be owned by H for two independent reasons (i. e., under section 958(a) and the regulations thereunder, because H transferred his 60-percent interest in M Company to W in contemplation of death,

and under section 958(b) and the regulations thereunder, because H is considered to own the stock in N Corporation indirectly owned by his wife, W, by reason of her ownership of such transferred interest) does not cause the shares of stock represented by the transferred interest in M Company to be counted twice in determining whether the test contained in that subparagraph is met. See subparagraph (1)(iii)(*d*) of this paragraph.

Example (3). (a) At the time of his death, H, a nonresident expatriate decedent the transfer of whose estate is subject to the tax imposed by section 2107(a), owned a 40-percent beneficial interest in a domestic trust; at that time he also directly owned stock in P Corporation, a foreign corporation, constituting 15 percent of the total combined voting power of all classes of stock entitled to vote in that corporation. The trust owned stock in P Corporation constituting 51 percent of the total combined voting power of all classes of stock entitled to vote in that corporation. The stock in P Corporation owned directly by H was valued at $20,000 on the alternate valuation date determined pursuant to an election under section 2032. The fair market value of the assets of P Corporation which, at the time of H's death, were situated in the United States constituted 20 percent of the fair market value of all assets of that corporation.

(b) By reason of section 958(b)(2) and the regulations thereunder, the trust is considered to own all the stock entitled to vote in P Corporation since it owns more than 50 percent of the total combined voting power of all classes of stock entitled to vote in that corporation. The test contained in subparagraph (1)(ii)(*a*) of this paragraph is met since at the time of his death H owned (within the meaning of section 958(a) and the regulations thereunder) 15 percent of the total combined voting power of all classes of stock entitled to vote in P Corporation; the stock in P Corporation owned by the trust is not considered to have been owned by H under section 958(a)(2) since the trust is not a foreign corporation. In addition, the test contained in subparagraph (1)(ii)(*b*) of this paragraph is met since at the time of his death H owned or is considered to have owned (within the meaning of section 958(a) and (b) and the regulations thereunder) 55 percent of the total combined voting power of all classes of stock entitled to vote in that corporation (his 15 percent directly owned plus his 40 percent (40% of 100%) considered to be owned). Accordingly, $4,000 is included in H's gross estate by reason of section 2107(b) of this paragraph. This $4,000 is the amount which is equal to 20 percent (the percentage of the fair market value of P Corporation's assets which were situated within the United States at H's death) of $20,000 (the fair market value of the stock then owned by H within the meaning of section 958(a) and the regulations thereunder). In addition, the value of H's interest in the domestic trust is included in his gross estate under section 2103 to the extent it constitutes property having a situs in the United States.

(c) *Credits.*—Credits against the tax imposed by section 2107(a) are allowed for any amounts determined in accordance with section 2102 and §20.2102–1 (relating to credits against the estate tax for State death taxes, gift tax, and tax on prior transfers). In computing the special limitation on the credit for State death taxes contained in section 2102(b) and paragraph (b) of §20.2102–1, amounts included in the gross estate under section 2107(b) and paragraph (b)(1) of this section are to be taken into account.

(d) *Decedents to whom the tax imposed by section 2107(a) applies.*—(1) *General rule.*—The tax imposed by section 2107(a) applies to the transfer of the taxable estate of every decedent nonresident not a citizen of the United States dying on or after November 14, 1966, who lost his U. S. citizenship after March 8, 1965, and within the 10-year period ending with the date of his death, except in the case of the estate of a decedent whose loss of U. S. citizenship either—

(i) Resulted from the application of section 301(b), 350, or 355 of the Immigration and Nationality Act, as amended (8 U. S. C. 1401(b), 1482, or 1487); or

(ii) Did not have for one of its principal purposes (but not necessarily its only principal purpose) the avoidance of Federal income, estate, or gift tax.

Section 301(b) of the Immigration and Nationality Act provides generally that a U. S. citizen, who is born outside the United States of parents one of whom is an alien and the other is a U. S. citizen who was physically present in the United States for a specified period, shall lose his U. S. citizenship if, within a specified period preceding the age of 28 years, he fails to be continuously physically present in the United States for at least 5 years. Section 350 of that Act provides that under certain circumstances a person, who at birth acquired the nationality of the United States and of a foreign country and who has voluntarily sought or claimed benefits of the nationality of any foreign country, shall lose his U. S. nationality if, after attaining the age of 22 years, he has a continuous residence for 3 years in the foreign country of which he is a national by birth. Section 355 of that Act provides that a person having U. S. nationality, who is under 21 years of age and whose residence is in a foreign country with or under the legal custody of a parent who loses his U. S. nationality under specified circumstances, shall lose his U. S. nationality if he has or acquires the nationality of that foreign country and attains the age of 25 years without having established his residence in the United States. Section 2107 and this section do not apply to the transfer of any estate the estate tax treatment of which is subject to a Presidential proclamation made pursuant to section 2108(a) (relating to the application of pre-1967 estate tax provisions in the case of a foreign country which imposes a more burdensome tax than the United States).

(2) *Burden of proof.*—(i) *General rule.*—In determining for purposes of subparagraph (1)(ii) of this paragraph whether a principal purpose for the loss of U. S. citizenship by a decedent was the avoidance of Federal income, estate, or gift tax, the Commissioner must first establish that it is reasonable to believe that the decedent's loss of U. S. citizenship would, but for section 2107 and this section, result in a substantial reduction in the sum of (a) the Federal estate tax and (b) all estate, inheritance, legacy, and succession taxes imposed by foreign countries and political subdivisions thereof, in respect of the transfer of the decedent's estate. Once the Commissioner has so established, the burden of proving that the loss of citizenship by the decedent did not have for one of its principal purposes the avoidance of Federal income, estate, or gift tax shall be on the executor of the decedent's estate.

(ii) *Tentative determination of substantial reduction in Federal and foreign death taxes.*—In the absence of complete factual information, the Commissioner may make a tentative determination, based on the information available, that the decedent's loss of U. S. citizenship would, but for section 2107 and this section, result in a substantial reduction in the sum of the Federal and foreign death taxes described in subdivision (i)*(a)* and *(b)* of this subparagraph. This tentative determination may be based upon the fact that the laws of the foreign country of which the decedent became a citizen and the laws of the foreign country of which the decedent was a resident at the time of his death, including the laws of any political subdivisions of those foreign countries, would ordinarily result, in the case of an estate of a nonexpatriate decedent having the same citizenship and residence as the decedent, in liability for total death taxes under such laws substantially lower than the amount of the Federal estate tax which would be imposed on the transfer of a comparable estate of a citizen of the United States. In the absence of a preponderance of evidence to the contrary, this tentative determination shall be sufficient to establish that it is reasonable to believe that the decedent's loss of U. S. citizenship would, but for section 2107 and this section, result in a substantial reduction in the sum of the Federal and foreign death taxes described in subdivision (i)*(a)* and *(b)* of this subparagraph. [Reg. §20.2107–1.]

☐ [*T.D. 7296*, 12-11-73.]

Miscellaneous

See p. 20,601 for regulations not amended to reflect law changes

[Reg. § 20.2201-1]

§ 20.2201-1. Members of the Armed Forces dying during an induction period.—(a) The additional estate tax as defined in section 2011(d) does not apply to the transfer of the taxable estate of a citizen or resident of the United States dying during an induction period as defined in section 112(c)(5) (see paragraph (b) of this section) and while in active service as a member of the Armed Forces of the United States, if the decedent—

(1) Was killed in action while serving in a combat zone, as determined under section 112(c)(2) and (3) (see paragraph (c) of this section), or

(2) Died as a result of wounds, disease, or injury suffered while serving in such a combat zone and while in line of duty, by reason of a hazard to which he was subject as an incident of such service.

(b) Section 112(c)(5) defines the term "induction period" as meaning any period during which individuals are liable for induction, for reasons other than prior deferment, for training and service in the Armed Forces of the United States.

(c) Section 112(c)(2) and (3) provides that service is performed in a combat zone only—

(1) If it is performed in an area which the President of the United States has designated by Executive order for purposes of section 112(c) as an area in which the Armed Forces of the United States are, or have, engaged in combat, and

(2) If it is performed on or after the date designated by the President by Executive order as the date of the commencing of combatant activities in such zone and on or before the date designated by the President by Executive order as the date of termination of combatant activities in such zone.

(d) If the official record of the branch of the Armed Forces of which the decedent was a member at the time of his death states that the decedent was killed in action while serving in a combat zone, or that death resulted from wounds or injuries received or disease contracted while in line of duty in a combat zone, this fact shall, in the absence of evidence establishing to the contrary, be presumed to be established for the purposes of the exemption. Moreover, wounds, injuries or disease suffered while in line of duty will be considered to have been caused by a hazard to which the decedent was subjected as an incident of service as a member of the Armed Forces, unless the hazard which caused the wounds, injuries, or disease was clearly unrelated to such service.

(e) A person was in active service as a member of the Armed Forces of the United States if he was at the time of his death actually serving in such forces. A member of the Armed Forces in active service in a combat zone who thereafter becomes a prisoner of war or missing in action, and occupies such status at death or when the wounds, disease, or injury resulting in death were incurred, is considered for purposes of this section as serving in a combat zone.

(f) The exemption from tax granted by section 2201 does not apply to the basic estate tax as defined in section 2011(d). [Reg. § 20.2201-1.]

□ [T.D. 6296, 6-23-58.]

[Reg. § 20.2203-1]

§ 20.2203-1. Definition of executor.—The term "executor" means the executor or administrator of the decedent's estate. However, if there is no executor or administrator appointed, qualified and acting within the United States, the term means any person in actual or constructive possession of any property of the decedent. The term "person in actual or constructive possession of any property of the decedent" includes, among others, the decedent's agents and representatives; safe-deposit companies, warehouse companies, and other custodians of property in this country; brokers holding, as collateral, securities belonging to the decedent; and debtors of the decedent in this country. [Reg. § 20.2203-1.]

□ [T.D. 6296, 6-23-58.]

[Reg. § 20.2204-1]

§ 20.2204-1. Discharge of executor from personal liability.—(a) *General rule.*—The executor of a decedent's estate may make written application to the applicable internal revenue officer with whom the estate tax return is required to be filed, as provided in § 20.6091-1, for a determination of the Federal estate tax and for a discharge of personal liability therefrom. Within 9 months after receipt of the application, or if the application is made before the return is filed then within 9 months after the return is filed, the executor will be notified of the amount of the tax and, upon payment thereof, he will be discharged from personal liability for any deficiency in the tax thereafter found to be due. If no such notification is received, the executor is discharged at the end of such 9-month period from personal liability for any deficiency thereafter found to be due. The discharge of the executor from personal liability under this section applies only to him in his personal capacity and to his personal assets. The discharge is not applicable to his liability as executor to the extent of the assets of the estate in his possession or control. Further, the discharge is not to operate as a release of any part of the gross estate from the lien for estate tax for any deficiency that may thereafter be determined to be due.

(b) *Special rule in the case of extension of time for payment of tax.*—In addition to the provisions of paragraph (a) of this section, an executor of the estate of a decedent dying after December 31, 1970, may make written application to be discharged from personal liability for the amount of Federal estate tax for which the time for payment has been extended under section 6161, 6163, or 6166. In such a case, the executor will be notified of the amount of bond, if any, to be furnished within 9 months after receipt of the application, or, if the application is made before the return is filed, within 9 months after the return is filed. The amount of any bond required under the provisions of this paragraph shall not exceed the amount of tax the payment of which has been extended. Upon furnishing the bond in the form required under § 301.7101-1 of this chapter (Regulations on Procedure and Administration), or upon receipt of the notification that no bond is required, the executor will be discharged from personal liability for the tax the payment of which has been extended. If no notification is received, the executor is discharged at the end of such 9-month period from personal liability for the tax the payment of which has been extended. [Reg. § 20.2204-1.]

☐ [*T.D. 6296, 6-23-58. Amended by T.D. 7238, 12-28-72, and T.D. 7941, 2-6-84.*]

[Reg. § 20.2204-2]

§ 20.2204-2. Discharge of fiduciary other than executor from personal liability.—(a) A fiduciary (not including a fiduciary of the estate of a nonresident decedent), other than the executor, who as a fiduciary holds, or has held at any time since the decedent's death, property transferred to the fiduciary from a decedent dying after December 31, 1970, or his estate, may make written application to the applicable internal revenue officer with whom the estate tax return is required to be filed, as provided in § 20.6091-1, for a determination of the Federal estate tax liability with respect to such property and for a discharge of personal liability therefrom. The application must be accompanied by a copy of the instrument, if any, under which the fiduciary is acting, a description of all the property transferred to the fiduciary from the decedent or his estate, and any other information that would be relevant to a determination of the fiduciary's tax liability.

(b) Upon the discharge of the executor from personal liability under § 20.2204-1, or, if later, within 6 months after the receipt of the application filed by a fiduciary pursuant to the provisions of paragraph (a) of this section, such fiduciary will be notified either (1) of the amount of tax for which it has been determined the fiduciary is liable, or (2) that it has been determined that the fiduciary is not liable for any such tax. The fiduciary will also be notified of the amount of bond, if any, to be furnished for any Federal estate tax for which the time for payment has been extended under section 6161,

6163, or 6166. The amount of any bond required under the provisions of this paragraph shall not exceed the amount of tax the payment of which has been so extended. Upon payment of the amount for which it has been determined the fiduciary is liable, and upon furnishing any bond required under this paragraph in the form specified under § 301.7101-1 of this chapter (Regulations on Procedure and Administration), or upon receipt by the fiduciary of notification of a determination that he is not liable for such tax or that a bond is not required, the fiduciary will be discharged from personal liability for any deficiency in the tax thereafter found to be due. If no such notification is received, the fiduciary is discharged at the end of such 6 months (or upon discharge of the executor, if later) from personal liability for any deficiency thereafter found to be due. The discharge of the fiduciary from personal liability under this section applies only to him in his personal capacity and to his personal assets. The discharge is not applicable to his liability as a fiduciary (such as a trustee) to the extent of the assets of the estate in his possession or control. Further, the discharge is not to operate as a release of any part of the gross estate from the lien for estate tax for any deficiency that may thereafter be determined to be due. [Reg. § 20.2204-2.]

☐ [*T.D. 7238, 12-28-72.*]

[Reg. § 20.2204-3]

§ 20.2204-3. Special rules for estates of decedents dying after December 31, 1976; special lien under section 6324A.—For purposes of §§ 20.2204-1(b) and 20.2204-2(b), in the case of a decedent dying after December 31, 1976, if the executor elects a special lien in favor of the United States under section 6324A, relating to special lien for estate taxes deferred under section 6166 or 6166A (as in effect prior to its repeal by the Economic Recovery Tax Act of 1981), such lien shall be treated as the furnishing of a bond with respect to the amount for which the time for payment has been extended under section 6166. If an election has been made under section 6324A, the executor may not thereafter substitute a bond pursuant to section 2204 in lieu of that lien. If a bond has been supplied under section 2204, however, the executor may, by filing a proper notice of election and agreement, substitute a lien under section 6324A for any part or all of such bond. See §§ 20.6324A-1 and 301.6324A-1 for rules relating to a special lien under section 6324A. [Reg. § 20.2204-3.]

☐ [*T.D. 7941, 2-6-84.*]

[Reg. § 20.2205-1]

§ 20.2205-1. Reimbursement out of estate.—If any portion of the tax is paid by or collected out of that part of the estate passing to, or in the possession of, any person other than the duly qualified executor or administrator, that person may be entitled to reimbursement, either out of the undistributed estate or by contribution from other beneficiaries whose shares or interests in the estate would have been reduced had the tax been paid before distribution of the estate, or whose shares or interests are subject either to an equal or prior liability for the payment of taxes, debts, or other charges against the estate. For specific provisions giving the executor the right to reimbursement from life insurance beneficiaries and from recipients of property over which the decedent had a power of appointment, see sections 2206 and 2207. These provisions, however, are not designed to curtail the right of the district director to collect the tax from any person, or out of any property, liable for its payment. The district director cannot be required to apportion the tax among the persons liable nor to enforce any right of reimbursement or contribution. [Reg. § 20.2205-1.]

☐ [T.D. 6296, 6-23-58.]

[Reg. § 20.2206-1]

§ 20.2206-1. Liability of life insurance beneficiaries.—With respect to the right of the district director to collect the tax without regard to the provisions of section 2206, see § 20.2205-1. [Reg. § 20.2206-1.]

☐ [T.D. 6296, 6-23-58.]

[Reg. § 20.2207-1]

§ 20.2207-1. Liability of recipient of property over which decedent had power of appointment.—With respect to the right of the district director to collect the tax without regard to the provisions of section 2207, see § 20.2205-1. [Reg. § 20.2207-1.]

☐ [T.D. 6296, 6-23-58.]

[Reg. § 20.2207A-1]

§ 20.2207A-1. Right of recovery of estate taxes in the case of certain marital deduction property.—(a) *In general.*—(1) *Right of recovery from person receiving the property.*—If the gross estate includes the value of property that is includible by reason of section 2044 (relating to certain property in which the decedent had a qualifying income interest for life under sections 2056(b)(7) or 2523(f)), the estate of the surviving spouse is entitled to recover from the *person receiving the property* (as defined in paragraph (d) of this section) the amount of Federal estate tax attributable to that property. The right of recovery arises when the Federal estate tax with respect to the property includible in the gross estate by reason of section 2044 is paid by the estate. There is no right of recovery from any person for the property received by that person for which a deduction was allowed from the gross estate if no tax is attributable to that property.

(2) *Failure to exercise right of recovery.*—Failure of an estate to exercise a right of recovery under this section upon a transfer subject to section 2044 is treated as a transfer for Federal gift tax purposes of the unrecovered amounts from the persons who would benefit from the recovery to the persons from whom the recovery could have been obtained. See § 25.2511-1 of this chapter. The transfer is considered made when the right of recovery is no longer enforceable under applicable law. A delay in the exercise of the right of recovery without payment of sufficient interest is a below-market loan. Section 1.7872-5T of the Temporary Income Tax regulations describes factors that are used to determine, based on the facts and circumstances of a particular case, whether a loan otherwise subject to imputation under section 7872 (relating to the treatment of below-market loans) is exempted from its provisions.

(3) *Waiver of right of recovery.*—The provisions of § 20.2207A-1(a)(2) do not apply to the extent that the surviving spouse's will provides that a recovery shall not be made or to the extent that the beneficiaries cannot otherwise compel recovery. Thus, e.g., if the surviving spouse gives the executor of the estate discretion to waive the right of recovery and the executor waives the right, no gift occurs under § 25.2511-1 of this chapter if the persons who would benefit from the recovery cannot compel the executor to exercise the right of recovery.

(b) *Amount of estate tax attributable to property includible under section 2044.*—The amount of Federal estate tax attributable to property includible in the gross estate under section 2044 is the amount by which the total Federal estate tax (including penalties and interest attributable to the tax) under chapter 11 of the Internal Revenue Code that has been paid, exceeds the total Federal estate tax (including penalties and interest attributable to the tax) under chapter 11 of the Internal Revenue Code that would have been paid if the value of the property includible in the gross estate by reason of section 2044 had not been so included.

(c) *Amount of estate tax attributable to a particular property.*—An estate's right of recovery with respect to a particular property is an amount equal to the amount determined in paragraph (b) of this section multiplied by a fraction. The numerator of the fraction is the value for Federal estate tax purposes of the particular property included in the gross estate by reason of section 2044, less any deduction allowed with respect to the property. The denominator of the fraction is the total value of all properties included in the gross estate by reason of section 2044, less any deductions allowed with respect to those properties.

(d) *Person receiving the property.*—If the property is in a trust at the time of the decedent's death, the *person receiving the property* is the trustee and any person who has received a distribution of the property prior to the expiration of the right of recovery if the property does not remain in trust. This paragraph (d) does not affect the right, if any, under local law, of any person with an interest in property to reimbursement or contribution from another person with an interest in the property.

(e) *Example.*—The following example illustrates the application of paragraphs (a) through (d) of this section.

Example. D died in 1994. D's will created a trust funded with certain income producing assets included in D's gross estate at $1,000,000. The trust provides that all the income is payable to D's wife, S, for life, remainder to be divided equally among their four children. In computing D's taxable estate, D's executor deducted, pursuant to section 2056(b)(7), $1,000,000. Assume that S received no other property from D and that S died in 1996. Assume further that S made no section 2519 disposition of the property, that the property was included in S's gross estate at a value of $1,080,000, and that S's will contained no provision regarding section 2207A(a). The tax attributable to the property is equal to the amount by which the total Federal estate tax (including penalties and interest) paid by S's estate exceeds the Federal estate tax (including penalties and interest) that would have been paid if S's gross estate had been reduced by $1,080,000. That amount of tax may be recovered by S's estate from the trust. If, at the time S's estate seeks reimbursement, the trust has been distributed to the four children, S's estate is also entitled to recover the tax from the children. [Reg. § 20.2207A-1.]

☐ [*T.D.* 8522, 2-28-94. *Amended by T.D.* 9077, 7-17-2003.]

[Reg. § 20.2207A-2]

§ 20.2207A-2. Effective date.—The provisions of § 20.2207A-1 are effective with respect to estates of decedents dying after March 1, 1994. With respect to estates of decedent dying on or before such date, the executor of the decedent's estate may rely on any reasonable interpretation of the statutory provisions. For these purposes, the provisions of § 20.2207A-1 (as well as project LR-211-76, 1984-1 C.B., page 598, see § 601.601(d)(2)(ii)(*b*) of this chapter), are considered a reasonable interpretation of the statutory provisions. [Reg. § 20.2207A-2.]

☐ [*T.D.* 8522, 2-28-94.]

[Reg. § 20.2208-1]

§ 20.2208-1. Certain residents of possessions considered citizens of the United States.—As used in this part, the term "citizen of the United States" is considered to include a decedent dying after September 2, 1958, who, at the time of his death, was domiciled in a possession of the United States and was a United States citizen, and who did not acquire his United States citizenship solely by reason of his being a citizen of such possession or by reason of his birth or residence within such possession. The estate of such a decedent is, therefore, subject to the tax imposed by section 2001. See paragraph (a)(2) of § 20.0-1 and § 20.2209-1 for further information relating to the application of the Federal estate tax to the estates of decedents who were residents of possessions of the United States. The application of this section may be illustrated by the following example and the examples set forth in § 20.2209-1:

Example. A, a citizen of the United States by reason of his birth in the United States at San Francisco, established residence in Puerto Rico and acquired a Puerto Rican citizenship. A died on September 4, 1958, while a citizen and domiciliary of Puerto Rico. A's estate is, by reason of the provisions of section 2208, subject to the tax imposed by section 2001 inasmuch as his United States citizenship is based on birth in the United States and is not based solely on being a citizen of a possession or solely on birth or residence in a possession. [Reg. § 20.2208-1.]

☐ [*T.D.* 6526, 1-18-61.]

[Reg. § 20.2209-1]

§ 20.2209-1. Certain residents of possessions considered nonresidents not citizens of the United States.—As used in this part, the term "nonresident not a citizen of the United States" is considered to include a decedent dying after September 14, 1960, who, at the time of his death, was domiciled in a possession of the United States and was a United States citizen, and who acquired his United States citizenship solely by reason of his being a citizen of such possession or by reason of his birth or residence within such possession. The estate of such a decedent is, therefore, subject to the tax imposed by section 2101 which is the tax applicable in the case of a "nonresident not a citizen of the United States." See paragraph (a)(2) of § 20.0-1 and § 20.2208-1 for further information relating to the application of the Federal estate tax to the estates of decedents who were residents of possessions of the United States. The application of this section may be illustrated by the following examples and the example set forth in § 20.2208-1. In each of the following examples the decedent is deemed a "nonresident not a citizen of the United States" and his estate is subject to the tax imposed by section 2101 since the decedent died after September 14, 1960, but would not have been so deemed and subject to such tax if the decedent had died on or before September 14, 1960.

Example (1). C, who acquired his United States citizenship under section 5 of the Act of March 2, 1917 (39 Stat. 953), by reason of being a citizen of Puerto Rico, died in Puerto Rico on October 1,

1960, while domiciled therein. C is considered to have acquired his United States citizenship solely by reason of his being a citizen of Puerto Rico.

Example (2). E, whose parents were United States citizens by reason of their birth in Boston, was born in the Virgin Islands on March 1, 1927. On September 30, 1960, he died in the Virgin Islands while domiciled therein. E is considered to have acquired his United States citizenship solely by reason of his birth in the Virgin Islands (section 306 of the Immigration and Nationality Act (66 Stat. 237, 8 U. S. C. 1406)).

Example (3). N, who acquired United States citizenship by reason of being a native of the Virgin Islands and a resident thereof on June 28, 1932 (section 306 of the Immigration and Nationality Act (66 Stat. 237, 8 U. S. C. 1406)), died on October 1, 1960, while domiciled in the Virgin Islands. N is considered to have acquired his United States citizenship solely by reason of his birth or residence in the Virgin Islands.

Example (4). P, a former Danish citizen, who on January 17, 1917, resided in the Virgin Islands,

made the declaration to preserve his Danish citizenship required by Article 6 of the treaty entered into on August 4, 1916, between the United States and Denmark. Subsequently P acquired United States citizenship when he renounced such declaration before a court of record (section 306 of the Immigration and Nationality Act (66 Stat. 237, 8 U. S. C. 1406)). P died on October 1, 1960, while domiciled in the Virgin Islands. P is considered to have acquired his United States citizenship solely by reason of his birth or residence in the Virgin Islands.

Example (5). R, a former French citizen, acquired his United States citizenship through naturalization proceedings in a court located in the Virgin Islands after having qualified for citizenship by residing in the Virgin Islands for 5 years. R died on October 1, 1960, while domiciled in the Virgin Islands. R is considered to have acquired his United States citizenship solely by reason of his birth or residence within the Virgin Islands. [Reg. § 20.2209-1.]

☐ *[T.D. 6526, 1-18-61.]*

→ *Caution: Reg. §§ 20.6001-1, 20.6011-1, 20.6018-1—20.6018-4, 20.6036-1—20.6036-2, 20.6061-1, 20.6065-1, 20.6071-1, 20.6075-1, 20.6081-1, 20.6091-1—20.6091-2, 20.6151-1, 20.6161-1—20.6161-2, 20.6163-1, 20.6165-1, 20.6166-1—20.6166A-4, 20.6314-1, 20.6321-1, 20.6323-1, 20.6324-1, 20.6324A-1— 20.6324B-1, 20.6325-1, 20.6601-1, 20.6905-1, and 20.7101-1, dealing with administration of the estate tax, are reproduced in Code section numerical order.*

Gift Tax

DETERMINATION OF TAX LIABILITY

See p. 20,601 for regulations not amended to reflect law changes

[Reg. § 25.0-1]

§ 25.0-1. Introduction.—(a) *In general.*— (1) The regulations in this part are designated "Gift Tax Regulations." These regulations pertain to (i) the gift tax imposed by chapter 12 of subtitle B of the Internal Revenue Code on the transfer of property by gift by individuals in the calendar year 1955, in subsequent calendar years beginning before the calendar year 1971, in calendar quarters beginning with the first calendar quarter of calendar year 1971 through the last calendar quarter of the calendar year 1981, and in calendar years beginning with the calendar year 1982, and (ii) certain related administrative provisions of subtitle F of the Code. It should be noted that the application of some of the provisions of these regulations may be affected by the provisions of an applicable gift tax convention with a foreign country. Unless otherwise indicated, references in these regulations to the "Internal Revenue Code" or the "Code" are references to the Internal Revenue Code of 1954, as amended, and references to a section or other provision of law are references to a section or other provision of the Internal Revenue Code of

1954, as amended. The Gift Tax Regulations are applicable to the transfer of property by gift by individuals in calendar years 1955 through 1970, in calendar quarters beginning with the first calendar quarter of calendar year 1971 through the last calendar quarter of the calendar year 1981, and in calendar years beginning with the calendar year 1982, and supersede the regulations contained in Part 86, Subchapter B, Chapter 1, Title 26, Code of Federal Regulations (1939) (Regulations 108, Gift Tax (8 F. R. 10858)), as prescribed and made applicable to the Internal Revenue Code of 1954 by Treasury Decision 6091, signed August 16, 1954 (19 F. R. 5167, Aug. 17, 1954).

(2) Section 2501(b) makes the provisions of chapter 12 of the Code apply in the case of gifts made after September 2, 1958, by certain citizens of the United States who were residents of a possession thereof at the time the gifts were made. Section 2501(c) makes the provisions of chapter 12 apply in the case of gifts made after September 14, 1960, by certain other citizens of the United States who were residents of a possession thereof at the time the gifts were made. See paragraphs (c) and (d) of § 25.2501-1. Except

as otherwise provided in paragraphs (c) and (d) of § 25.2501-1, the provisions of these regulations do not apply to the making of gifts by such citizens.

(b) *Nature of tax.*—The gift tax is not a property tax. It is a tax imposed upon the transfer of property by individuals. It is not applicable to transfers by corporations or persons other than individuals. However, see paragraph (h)(1) of § 25.2511-1 with respect to the extent to which a transfer by or to a corporation is considered a transfer by or to its shareholders.

(c) *Scope of regulations.*—(1) *Determination of tax liability.*—Subchapter A of chapter 12 of the Code pertains to the determination of tax liability. The regulations pursuant to subchapter A are set forth in § § 25.2501-1 through 25.2504-2 of this part. Sections 25.2701-5 and 25.2702-6 contain rules that provide additional adjustments to mitigate double taxation where the amount of the transferor's property was previously determined under the special valuation provisions of sections 2701 and 2702.

(2) *Transfer.*—Subchapter B of chapter 12 and chapter 14 of the Internal Revenue Code pertain to the transfers which constitute the making of gifts and the valuation of those transfers. The regulations pursuant to subchapter B are set forth in § § 25.2511-1 through 25.2518-3. The regulations pursuant to chapter 14 are set forth in § § 25.2701-1 through 25.2704-3.

(3) *Deductions.*—Subchapter C of chapter 12 of the Code pertains to the deductions which are allowed in determining the amount of taxable gifts. The regulations pursuant to subchapter C are set forth in § § 25.2521-1 through 25.2524-1 of this part.

(4) *Procedure and administration provisions.*—Subtitle F of the Internal Revenue Code contains some sections which are applicable to the gift tax. The regulations pursuant to those sections are set forth in § § 25.6001-1 through 25.7101-1. Such regulations do not purport to be all the regulations on procedure and administration which are pertinent to gift tax matters. For the remainder of the regulations on procedure and administration which are pertinent to gift tax matters, see part 301 of this chapter (Regulations on Procedure and Administration).

(d) *Arrangement and numbering.*—Each section of the regulations in this part (other than this section) is designated by a number composed of the part number followed by a decimal point (25.); the section of the Internal Revenue Code which it interprets; a hyphen (-); and a number identifying the section. By use of these designations one can ascertain the sections of the regulations relating to a provision of the Code. For example, the regulations pertaining to section 2521 of the Code are designated § 25.2521-1. [Reg. § 25.0-1.]

☐ [*T.D.* 6334, 11-14-58. *Amended by T.D.* 6542, 1-19-61; *T.D.* 7238, 12-28-72; *T.D.* 7296, 12-11-73; *T.D.* 7665, 1-24-80; *T.D.* 7910, 9-6-83 *and T.D.* 8395, 1-28-92.]

[Reg. § 25.2207A-1]

§ 25.2207A-1. Right of recovery of gift taxes in the case of certain marital deduction property.—(a) *In general.*—If an individual is treated as transferring an interest in property by reason of section 2519, the individual or the individual's estate is entitled to recover from the *person receiving the property* (as defined in paragraph (e) of this section) the amount of gift tax attributable to that property. The value of property to which this paragraph (a) applies is the value of all interests in the property other than the qualifying income interest. There is no right of recovery from any person for the property received by that person for which a deduction was allowed from the total amount of gifts, if no Federal gift tax is attributable to the property. The right of recovery arises at the time the Federal gift tax is actually paid by the transferor subject to section 2519.

(b) *Failure of a person to exercise the right of recovery.*—(1) The failure of a person to exercise a right of recovery provided by section 2207A(b) upon a lifetime transfer subject to section 2519 is treated as a transfer for Federal gift tax purposes of the unrecovered amounts to the person(s) from whom the recovery could have been obtained. See § 25.2511-1. The transfer is considered to be made when the right to recovery is no longer enforceable under applicable law and is treated as a gift even if recovery is impossible. A delay in the exercise of the right of recovery without payment of sufficient interest is a below-market loan. Section 1.7872-5T of this chapter describes factors that are used to determine, based on the facts and circumstances of a particular case, whether a loan otherwise subject to imputation under section 7872 (relating to the treatment of below-market loans) is exempted from its provisions.

(2) The transferor subject to section 2519 may execute a written waiver of the right of recovery arising under section 2207A before that right of recovery becomes unenforceable. If a waiver is executed, the transfer of the unrecovered amounts by the transferor is considered to be made on the later of—

(i) The date of the valid and irrevocable waiver rendering the right of recovery no longer enforceable; or

(ii) The date of the payment of the tax by the transferor.

(c) *Amount of gift tax attributable to all properties.*—The amount of Federal gift tax attributable to all properties includible in the total amount of gifts under section 2519 made during the calendar year is the amount by which the total Federal gift tax for the calendar year (including penalties and interest attributable to the tax) under chapter 12 of the Internal Revenue Code which has been paid, exceeds the total Federal gift tax for the calendar year (including penalties and interest attributable to the tax) under chapter 12 of the Internal Revenue Code which would have been paid if the value of the properties includible in the total amount of gifts by reason of section 2519 had not been included.

(d) *Amount of gift tax attributable to a particular property.*—A person's right of recovery with respect to a particular property is an amount equal to the amount determined in paragraph (c) of this section multiplied by a fraction. The numerator of the fraction is the value of the particular property included in the total amount of gifts made during the calendar year by reason of section 2519, less any deduction allowed with respect to the property. The denominator of the fraction is the total value of all properties included in the total amount of gifts made during the calendar year by reason of section 2519, less any deductions allowed with respect to those properties.

(e) *Person receiving the property.*—If the property is in a trust at the time of the transfer, the *person receiving the property* is the trustee, and any person who has received a distribution of the property prior to the expiration of the right of recovery if the property does not remain in trust. This paragraph (e) does not affect the right, if any, under local law, of any person with an interest in property to reimbursement or contribution from another person with an interest in the property.

(f) *Example.*—The following example illustrates the application of paragraphs (a) through (e) of this section.

Example. D created an inter vivos trust during 1994 with certain income producing assets valued at $1,000,000. The trust provides that all income is payable to D's wife, S, for S's life, with the remainder at S's death to be divided equally among their four children. In computing taxable gifts during calendar year 1994, D deducted, pursuant to section 2523(f), $1,000,000 from the total amount of gifts made. In addition, assume that S received no other transfers from D and that S made a gift during 1996 of the entire life interest to one of the children, at which time the value of trust assets was $1,080,000 and the value of S's life interest was $400,000. Although the entire value of the trust assets ($1,080,000) is, pursuant to sections 2511 and 2519, included in the total amount of S's gifts for calendar year 1996, S is only entitled to reimbursement for the Federal gift tax attributable to the value of the remainder interest, that is, the Federal gift tax attributable to $680,000 ($1,080,000 less

$400,000). The Federal gift tax attributable to $680,000 is equal to the amount by which the total Federal gift tax (including penalties and interest) paid for the calendar year exceeds the federal gift tax (including penalties and interest) that would have been paid if the total amount of gifts during 1996 had been reduced by $680,000. That amount of tax may be recovered by S from the trust. [Reg. § 25.2207A-1.]

□ [*T.D.* 8522, 2-28-94. *Amended by T.D.* 9077, 7-17-2003.]

[Reg. § 25.2207A-2]

§ 25.2207A-2. Effective date.—The provisions of § 25.2207A-1 are effective with respect to dispositions made after March 1, 1994. With respect to gifts made on or before such date, the donor may rely on any reasonable interpretation of the statutory provisions. For these purposes, the provisions of § 25.2207A-1 (as well as project LR-211-76, 1984-1 C.B., page 598, see § 601.601(d)(2)(ii)(*b*) of this chapter), are considered a reasonable interpretation of the statutory provisions. [Reg. § 25.2207A-2.]

□ [*T.D.* 8522, 2-28-94.]

[Reg. § 25.2501-1]

§ 25.2501-1. Imposition of tax.—(a) *In general.*—(1) The tax applies to all transfers by gift of property, wherever situated, by an individual who is a citizen or resident of the United States, to the extent the value of the transfers exceeds the amount of the exclusions authorized by section 2503 and the deductions authorized by sections 2521 (as in effect prior to its repeal by the Tax Reform Act of 1976), 2522, and 2523. For each "calendar period" (as defined in § 25.2502-1(c)(1)), the tax described in this paragraph (a) is imposed on the transfer of property by gift during such calendar quarter. For calendar years after 1954 and before 1971, the tax described in this subparagraph is imposed on the transfer of property by gift during such calendar period.

(2) The tax does not apply to a transfer by gift of intangible property before January 1, 1967, by a nonresident not a citizen of the United States, unless the donor was engaged in business in the United States during the calendar year in which the transfer was made.

(3)(i) The tax does not apply to any transfer by gift of intangible property on or after January 1, 1967, by a nonresident not a citizen of the United States (whether or not he was engaged in business in the United States), unless the donor is an expatriate who lost his U. S. citizenship after March 8, 1965, and within the 10-year period ending with the date of transfer, and the loss of citizenship—

(*a*) Did not result from the application of section 301(b), 350, or 355 of the Immigration and Nationality Act, as amended (8 U. S. C. 1401(b), 1482, or 1487) (For a summary of these

Reg. § 25.2207A-1(d)

sections, see paragraph (d)(1) of § 20.2107-1 of this chapter (Estate Tax Regulations)), and

(b) Had for one of its principal purposes (but not necessarily its only principal purpose) the avoidance of Federal income, estate, or gift tax.

(ii) In determining for purposes of subdivision (i)(b) of this subparagraph whether a principal purpose for the loss of U. S. citizenship by a donor was the avoidance of Federal income, estate, or gift tax, the Commissioner must first establish that it is reasonable to believe that the donor's loss of U. S. citizenship would, but for section 2501(a)(3) and this subparagraph, result in a substantial reduction for the "calendar period" (as defined in § 25.2502-1(c)(1)), in the sum of (a) the Federal gift tax and (b) all gift taxes imposed by foreign countries and political subdivisions thereof, in respect of the transfer of property by gift. Once the Commissioner has so established, the burden of proving that the loss of citizenship by the donor did not have for one of its principal purposes the avoidance of Federal income, estate, or gift tax shall be on the donor. In the absence of complete factual information, the Commissioner may make a tentative determination, based on the information available, that the donor's loss of U. S. citizenship would, but for section 2501(a)(3) and this subparagraph, result in a substantial reduction for the calendar period in the sum of the Federal and foreign gift taxes described in (a) and (b) of this subdivision on the transfer of property by gift. This tentative determination may be based upon the fact that the laws of the foreign country of which the donor became a citizen and the laws of the foreign country of which the donor was a resident at the time of the transfer, including the laws of any political subdivision of those foreign countries, would ordinarily result, in the case of a nonexpatriate donor having the same citizenship and residence as the donor, in liability for total gift taxes under such laws for the calendar period substantially lower than the amount of the Federal gift tax which would be imposed for such period on an amount of comparable gifts by a citizen of the United States. In the absence of a preponderance of evidence to the contrary, this tentative determination shall be sufficient to establish that it is reasonable to believe that the donor's loss of U. S. citizenship would, but for section 2501(a)(3) and this subparagraph, result in a substantial reduction for the calendar period in the sum of the Federal and foreign gift taxes described in (a) and (b) of this subdivision on the transfer of property by gift.

(4) For additional rules relating to the application of the tax to transfers by nonresidents not citizens of the United States, see section 2511 and § 25.2511-3.

(5) The general rule of this paragraph (a) shall not apply to a transfer after May 7, 1974, of money or other property to a political organiza-

tion for the use of that organization. However, this exception to the general rule applies solely to a transfer to a political organization as defined in section 527(e)(1) and including a newsletter fund to the extent provided under section 527(g). The general rule governs a transfer of property to an organization other than a political organization as so defined.

(b) *Resident.*—A resident is an individual who has his domicile in the United States at the time of the gift. For this purpose the United States includes the States and the District of Columbia. The term also includes the Territories of Alaska and Hawaii prior to admission as a State. See section 7701(a)(9). All other individuals are nonresidents. A person acquires a domicile in a place by living there, for even a brief period of time, with no definite present intention of moving therefrom. Residence without the requisite intention to remain indefinitely will not constitute domicile, nor will intention to change domicile effect such a change unless accompanied by actual removal.

(c) *Certain residents of possessions considered citizens of the United States.*—As used in this part, the term "citizen of the United States" includes a person who makes a gift after September 2, 1958 and who, at the time of making the gift, was domiciled in a possession of the United States and was a United States citizen, and who did not acquire his United States citizenship solely by reason of his being a citizen of such possession or by reason of his birth or residence within such possession. The gift of such a person is, therefore, subject to the tax imposed by section 2501 in the same manner in which a gift made by a resident of the United States is subject to the tax. See paragraph (a) of § 25.01 and paragraph (d) of this section for further information relating to the application of the Federal gift tax to gifts made by persons who were residents of possessions of the United States. The application of this paragraph may be illustrated by the following example and the examples set forth in paragraph (d) of this section:

Example. A, a citizen of the United States by reason of his birth in the United States at San Francisco, established residence in Puerto Rico and acquired Puerto Rican citizenship. A makes a gift of stock of a Spanish corporation on September 4, 1958, while a citizen and domiciliary of Puerto Rico. A's gift is, by reason of the provisions of section 2501(b) subject to the tax imposed by section 2501 inasmuch as his United States citizenship is based on birth in the United States and is not based solely on being a citizen of a possession or solely on birth or residence in a possession.

(d) *Certain residents of possessions considered nonresidents not citizens of the United States.*—As used in this part, the term "nonresident not a citizen of the United States" includes a person who makes a gift after September 14, 1960, and who at the time of making the gift, was domiciled in a possession of the United States and was a United States citizen, and who acquired his United States citizenship solely by reason of his being a citizen of such possession or by reason of his birth or residence within such possession. The gift of such a person is, therefore, subject to the tax imposed by section 2501 in the same manner in which a gift is subject to the tax when made by a donor who is a "nonresident not a citizen of the United States." See paragraph (a) of § 25.01 and paragraph (c) of this section for further information relating to the application of the Federal gift tax to gifts made by persons who were residents of possessions of the United States. The application of this paragraph may be illustrated by the following examples and the example set forth in paragraph (c) of this section. In each of the following examples the person who makes the gift is deemed a "nonresident not a citizen of the United States" and his gift is subject to the tax imposed by section 2501 in the same manner in which a gift is subject to the tax when made by a donor who is a nonresident not a citizen of the United States, since he made the gift after September 14, 1960, but would not have been so deemed and subject to such tax if the person who made the gift had made it on or before September 14, 1960.

Example (1). C, who acquired his United States citizenship under section 5 of the Act of March 2, 1917 (39 Stat. 953), by reason of being a citizen of Puerto Rico, while domiciled in Puerto Rico makes a gift on October 1, 1960, of real estate located in New York. C is considered to have acquired his United States citizenship solely by reason of his being a citizen of Puerto Rico.

Example (2). E, whose parents were United States citizens by reason of their birth in Boston, was born in the Virgin Islands on March 1, 1927. On September 30, 1960, while domiciled in the Virgin Islands, he made a gift of tangible personal property situated in Kansas. E is considered to have acquired his United States citizenship solely by reason of his birth in the Virgin Islands (section 306 of the Immigration and Nationality Act (66 Stat. 237, 8 U. S. C. 1406)).

Example (3). N, who acquired United States citizenship by reason of being a native of the Virgin Islands and a resident thereof on June 28, 1932 (section 306 of the Immigration and Nationality Act (66 Stat. 237, 8 U. S. C. 1406)), made a gift on October 1, 1960, at which time he was domiciled in the Virgin Islands, of tangible personal property situated in Wisconsin. N is considered to have acquired his United States citizenship solely by reason of his birth or residence in the Virgin Islands.

Example (4). P, a former Danish citizen, who on January 17, 1917 resided in the Virgin Islands, made the declaration to preserve his Danish citizenship required by Article 6 of the treaty entered into on August 14, 1916, between the United States and Denmark. Subsequently P acquired United States citizenship when he renounced such declaration before a court of record (section 306 of the Immigration and Nationality Act (66 Stat. 237, 8 U. S. C. 1406)). P, while domiciled in the Virgin Islands, made a gift on October 1, 1960, of tangible personal property situated in California. P is considered to have acquired his United States citizenship solely by reason of his birth or residence in the Virgin Islands.

Example (5). R, a former French citizen, acquired his United States citizenship through naturalization proceedings in a court located in the Virgin Islands after having qualified for citizenship by residing in the Virgin Islands for 5 years. R, while domiciled in the Virgin Islands, made a gift of tangible personal property situated in Hawaii on October 1, 1960. R is considered to have acquired his United States citizenship solely by reason of his birth or residence within the Virgin Islands. [Reg. § 25.2501-1.]

☐ [*T.D.* 6334, 11-14-58. *Amended by T.D.* 6542, 1-19-61; *T.D.* 7238, 12-28-72; *T.D.* 7296, 12-11-73; *T.D.* 7671, 2-5-80 *and T.D.* 7910, 9-6-83.]

[Reg. § 25.2502-1]

§ 25.2502-1. Rate of tax.—(a) *Computation of tax.*—The rate of tax is determined by the total of all gifts made by the donor during the calendar period and all the preceding calendar periods since June 6, 1932. See § 25.2502-1(c)(1) for the definition of "calendar period" and § 25.2502-1(c)(2) for the definition of "preceding calendar periods." The following six steps are to be followed in computing the tax:

(1) *First step.*—Ascertain the amount of the "taxable gifts" (as defined in § 25.2503-1) for the calendar period for which the return is being prepared.

(2) *Second step.*—Ascertain "the aggregate sum of the taxable gifts for each of the preceding "calendar periods" (as defined in § 25.2504-1), considering only those gifts made after June 6, 1932.

(3) *Third step.*—Ascertain the total amount of the taxable gifts, which is the sum of the amounts determined in the first and second steps. See § 25.2702-6 for an adjustment to the total amount of an individual's taxable gifts where the individual's current taxable gifts include the transfer of certain interests in trust that were previously valued under the provisions of section 2702.

(4) *Fourth step.*—Compute the tentative tax on the total amount of taxable gifts (as determined in the third step) using the rate schedule in effect at the time the gift (for which the return is being filed) is made.

(5) *Fifth step.*—Compute the tentative tax on the aggregate sum of the taxable gifts for each of the preceding calendar periods (as determined in the second step), using the same rate schedule set forth in the fourth step of this paragraph (a).

(6) *Sixth step.*—Subtract the amount determined in the fifth step from the amount determined in the fourth step. The amount remaining is the gift tax for the calendar period for which the return is being prepared.

(b) *Rate of tax.*—The tax is computed in accordance with the rate schedule in effect at the time the gift was made as set forth in section 2001(c) or corresponding provisions of prior law.

(c) *Definitions.*—(1) The term "calendar period" means:

(i) Each calendar year for the calendar years 1932 (but only that portion of such year after June 6, 1932) through 1970;

(ii) Each calendar quarter for the first calendar quarter of the calendar year 1971 through the last calendar quarter of calendar year 1981; or

(iii) Each calendar year for the calendar year 1982 and each succeeding calendar year.

(2) The term "preceding calendar periods" means all calendar periods ending prior to the calendar period for which the tax is being computed.

(d) *Examples.*—The following examples illustrate the application of this section with respect to gifts made by citizens or residents of the United States:

Example (1). Assume that in 1955 the donor made taxable gifts, as ascertained under the first step (paragraph (a)(2) of this section), of $62,500 and that there were no taxable gifts for prior years, with the result that the amount ascertaina-

ble under the third step is $62,500. Under the fourth step a tax is computed on this amount. Reference to the tax rate schedule in effect in the year 1955 discloses that the tax on this amount is $7,650.

Example (2). A donor makes gifts (other than gifts of future interests in property) during the calendar year 1955 of $30,000 to A and $33,000 to B. Two exclusions of $3,000 each are allowable, in accordance with the provisions of section 2503(b), which results in included gifts for 1955 of $57,000. Specific exemption was claimed and allowed in a total amount of $50,000 in the donor's gift tax returns for the calendar years 1934 and 1935 so there remains no specific exemption available for the donor to claim for 1955. The total amount of gifts made by the donor during preceding years, after excluding $5,000 for each donee for each calendar year in accordance with the provisions of section 1003(b)(1) of the 1939 Code, is computed as follows:

Calendar year 1934	$120,000
Calendar year 1935	25,000
Total amount of included gifts for preceding calendar years	$145,000

The aggregate sum of the taxable gifts for preceding calendar years is $115,000, which is determined by deducting a specific exemption of $30,000 from $145,000, the total amount of included gifts for preceding calendar years. The deduction from the 1934 and 1935 gifts for the specific exemption cannot exceed $30,000 for purposes of computing the tax on the 1955 gifts even though a specific exemption in a total amount of $50,000 was allowed in computing the donor's gift tax liability for 1934 and 1935. See paragraph (b) of § 25.2504-1. The computation of the tax for the calendar year 1955 (following the steps set forth in paragraph (a) of this section) is shown below:

(1)	Amount of taxable gifts for year	$57,000
(2)	Total amount of taxable gifts for preceding years	$115,000
(3)	Total taxable gifts	$172,000
(4)	Tax computed on item 3 in accordance with the rate schedule in effect for the year 1955	$31,725
(5)	Tax computed on item 2 (using same rate schedule)	18,900
(6)	Tax for year 1955 (item 4 minus item 5)	$12,825

Example (3). (i) *Facts.* During the calendar year 1955, H makes the following gifts of present interests:

To his daughter	$ 40,000
To his son	5,000
To W, his wife	5,000
To a charitable organization	10,000

The gifts to W qualify for the marital deduction, and, pursuant to the provisions of section 2513 (see § 25.2513-1), H and W consent to treat the

gifts to third parties as having been made one-half by each spouse. The amount of H's taxable gifts for preceding years is $50,000. Only $25,000 of H's specific exemption provided under section 2521, which was in effect at the time, was claimed and allowed in preceding years. H's remaining specific exemption of $5,000 is claimed for the calendar year 1955. See § 25.2521-1. W made no gifts during the calendar year 1955 nor during any preceding calendar year. W claims sufficient specific exemption on her return to eliminate tax liability.

Reg. § 25.2502-1(d)

(ii) *Computation of H's tax for the calendar year 1955—(a) H's taxable gifts for year*

Total gifts of H	$60,000
Less: Portion of items to be reported by spouse (one-half of total gifts to daughter, son and charity)	27,500
Balance	$32,500
Less: Exclusions (three of $3,000 each for daughter, wife and charity and one of $2,500 for son)	11,500
Total included amount of gifts for year	$21,000
Less: Deductions:	
Charity $2,000	
Marital 2,000	
Specific exemption 5,000	
Total deductions	9,000
Amount of taxable gifts for year	$12,000

(b) *Computation of tax.* The steps set forth in paragraph (a) of this section are followed.

(1)	Amount of taxable gifts for year	$12,000
(2)	Total taxable gifts for preceding years	50,000
(3)	Total taxable gifts (item (1) plus item (2))	$62,000
(4)	Tax computed on item 3 in accordance with the rate schedule in effect for the year 1955	$7,545
(5)	Tax computed on item 2 in accordance with the rate schedule in effect for the year 1955	5,250
(6)	Tax for calendar year (item (4) minus item (5))	$2,295

(iii) *Computation of W's tax for calendar year 1955—(a) W's taxable gifts for year*

Total gifts of W	$0
Less: Portion of items to be reported by spouse	0
Balance	$0
Gifts of spouse to be included	27,500
Total gifts for year	$27,500
Less: Exclusions (two of $3,000 each for daughter and charity and one of $2,500 for son)	8,500
Balance	$19,000
Less: Deductions:	
Charity .... $ 2,000	
Marital 0	
Specific exemption 17,000	
Total deductions	19,000
Amount of taxable gifts for year	$ 0

(b) *Computation of tax.*—Since W had no "taxable gifts" during the year, there is no tax.

Example (4). (i) *Facts.* The facts are the same as in example (3) except that W made outright gifts of $10,000 to her niece and $20,000 to H at various times during the year. The amount of taxable gifts made by W in preceding calendar years is $75,000, and only $20,000 of her specific exemp-

tion provided under section 2521, which was in effect at the time, was claimed and allowed for preceding years. See §25.2521-1. The remaining specific exemption of $10,000 is claimed for the calendar year 1955.

(ii) *Computation of H's tax for the calendar year 1955—(a) H's taxable gifts for year.*

Total gifts of H	$60,000
Less: Portion of items to be reported by spouse	27,500
Balance	$32,500
Gifts of spouse to be included	5,000
Total gifts for year	$37,500

Less: Exclusions ($11,500) as shown in example (3) plus $3,000 exclusion for gift to niece)			14,500
Total included amount of gifts for year			$23,000
Deductions:			
Charity		$2,000	
Marital		2,000	
Specific exemption		5,000	
Total deductions			9,000
Amount of taxable gifts for year			$14,000

(b) Computation of tax.

(1)	Amount of taxable gifts for year	$14,000
(2)	Total taxable gifts for preceding years	50,000
(3)	Total taxable gifts (item *(1)* plus item *(2)*)	$64,000
(4)	Tax computed on item 3	$7,965
(5)	Tax computed on item 2	$5,250
(6)	Tax for year (item *(4)* minus item *(5)*)	$2,715

(iii) Computation of W's tax for the calendar year 1955—(a) W's taxable gifts for year

Total gifts of W			$30,000
Less: Portion of items to be reported by spouse (one-half of gift to niece) . .			5,000
Balance			$25,000
Gifts of spouse to be included			27,500
Total gifts for year			$52,500
Less: Exclusions (four of $3,000 each for daughter, husband, niece and charity, and one of $2,500 for son)			14,500
Total included amount of gifts for year			$38,000
Deductions:			
Charity		$2,000	
Marital		10,000	
Specific exemption		10,000	
Total deductions			22,000
Amount of taxable gifts for year			$16,000

(b) Computation of tax.

(1)	Amount of taxable gifts for year	$16,000
(2)	Total taxable gifts for preceding years	75,000
(3)	Total taxable gifts	$91,000
(4)	Tax computed on item 3	13,635
(5)	Tax computed on item 2	10,275
(6)	Tax for year (item 4 minus item 5)	$ 3,360

Example (5). A makes gifts (other than gifts of future interests in property) to B in the first quarter of 1971 of $43,000 and in the second quarter of 1971 of $60,000. A gave to C in the second quarter of 1971 land valued at $11,000. The full amount of A's specific exemption provided under section 2521 was claimed and allowed in 1956. In 1966, A made taxable gifts totaling $21,000 on which gift tax was timely paid and no other taxable gifts were made by A in any other year preceding 1971. The gift tax return due for the first calendar quarter of 1971 was timely filed and the tax paid. With respect to the gifts made to B in 1971, the $3,000 annual gift tax exclusion provided by section 2503(b) is applied in its entirety against the $43,000 gift made to B in the first quarter and therefore is not available to offset the $60,000 gift made to B in the second quarter. (See § 25.2503-2(b).) A further $3,000 annual gift tax exclusion is available, however, to offset the $11,000 gift made to C in the second quarter of 1971. The computation of the gift tax for the second calendar quarter of 1971 due on August 15, 1971 (following the steps set forth in paragraph (a) of this section) is shown below:

(1)	Amount of taxable gifts for the second calendar quarter of 1971 ($60,000 + $11,000 − $3,000)	$ 68,000
(2)	Total amount of taxable gifts for preceding calendar periods ($43,000 − $3,000 + $21,000)	61,000
(3)	Total taxable gifts	$129,000
(4)	Tax computed on item 3 in accordance with rate schedule in effect for the year 1971	$ 22,050
(5)	Tax computed on item 2 (using same rate schedule)	$ 7,335
(6)	Tax for second calendar quarter of 1971 (item 4 minus item 5)	$ 14,715

Example (6). A makes gifts (other than gifts of future interests in property) during the calendar year 1982 of $160,000 to B and $100,000 to C. Two exclusions of $10,000 each are allowable, in accordance with the provisions of section 2503(b), which results in taxable gifts for 1982 of $240,000. In the first calendar quarter of 1978, A made taxable gifts totaling $100,000 on which gift tax was paid. For the calendar year 1969, A made taxable gifts totaling $50,000. The full amount of A's specific exemption provided under section 2521, which was in effect at the time, was claimed and allowed in 1968. The computation of the gift tax for the calendar period 1982 (following the steps set forth in paragraph (a) of this section) is shown below.

(1) Amount of taxable gifts for the calendar year 1982, $240,000.

(2) Total amount of taxable gifts for preceding calendar periods ($100,000 + $50,000), $150,000.

(3) Total taxable gifts, $390,000.

(4) Tax computed on item 3 (in accordance with the rate schedule in effect for the year 1982), $118,400.

(5) Tax computed on item 2 (using same rate schedule), $38,800.

(6) Tax for year 1982 (Item 4 minus item 5), $79,600.

[Reg. § 25.2502-1.]

☐ [*T.D.* 6334, 11-14-58. *Amended by T.D.* 7238, 12-28-72; *T.D.* 7910, 9-6-83 *and T.D.* 8395, 1-28-92.]

[Reg. § 25.2502-2]

§ 25.2502-2. Donor primarily liable for tax.—
Section 2502(d) provides that the donor shall pay the tax. If the donor dies before the tax is paid the amount of the tax is a debt due the United States from the decedent's estate and his executor or administrator is responsible for its payment out of the estate. (See § 25.6151-1 for the time and place for paying the tax.) If there is no duly qualified executor or administrator, the heirs, legatees, devisees and distributees are liable for and required to pay the tax to the extent of the value of their inheritances, bequests, devises or distributive shares of the donor's estate. If a husband and wife effectively signify consent, under section 2513, to have gifts made to a third party during any "calendar period" (as defined

in § 25.2502-1(c)(1)) considered as made one-half by each, the liability with respect to the gift tax of each spouse for that calendar period is joint and several (see § 25.2513-4). As to the personal liability of the donee, see paragraph (b) of § 301.6324-1 of this chapter (Regulations on Procedure and Administration). As to the personal liability of the executor or administrator, see section 3467 of the Revised Statutes (31 U. S. C. 192), which reads as follows:

Every executor, administrator, or assignee, or other person, who pays, in whole or in part, any debt due by the person or estate for whom or for which he acts before he satisfies and pays the debts due to the United States from such person or estate, shall become answerable in his own person and estate to the extent of such payments for the debts so due to the United States, or for so much thereof as may remain due and unpaid.

As used in such section 3467, the word "debt" includes a beneficiary's distributive share of an estate. Thus if an executor pays a debt due by the estate which is being administered by him or distributes any portion of the estate before there is paid all of the gift tax which he has a duty to pay, the executor is personally liable, to the extent of the payment or distribution, for so much of the gift tax as remains due and unpaid. [Reg. § 25.2502-2.]

☐ [*T.D.* 6334, 11-14-58. *Amended by T.D.* 7238, 12-38-72 *and T.D.* 7910, 9-6-83.]

[Reg. § 25.2503-1]

§ 25.2503-1. General definitions of "taxable gifts" and of "total amount of gifts.".—The term "taxable gifts" means the "total amount of gifts" made by the donor during the "calendar period" (as defined in § 25.2502-1(c)(1)) less the deductions provided for in sections 2521 (as in effect before its repeal by the Tax Reform Act of 1976), 2522, and 2523 (specific exemption, charitable, etc., gifts and the marital deduction, respectively). The term "total amount of gifts" means the sum of the values of the gifts made during the calendar period less the amounts excludable under section 2503(b). See § 25.2503-2. The entire value of any gift of a future interest in property must be included in the total amount of gifts for the calendar period in which the gift is made. See § 25.2503-3. [Reg. § 25.2503-1.]

☐ [*T.D. 6334, 11-14-58. Amended by T.D. 7238, 12-28-72 and T.D. 7910, 9-6-83.*]

[Reg. § 25.2503-2]

§ 25.2503-2. Exclusions from gifts.—(a) *Gifts made after December 31, 1981.*—Except as provided in paragraph (f) of this section (involving gifts to a noncitizen spouse), the first $10,000 of gifts made to any one donee during the calendar year 1982 or any calendar year thereafter, except gifts of future interests in property as defined in §§ 25.2503-3 and 25.2503-4, is excluded in determining the total amount of gifts for the calendar year. In the case of a gift in trust the beneficiary of the trust is the donee.

(b) *Gifts made after December 31, 1970 and before January 1, 1982.*—In computing taxable gifts for the calendar quarter, in the case of gifts (other than gifts of future interests in property) made to any person by the donor during any calendar quarter of the calendar year 1971 or any subsequent calendar year, $3,000 of such gifts to such person less the aggregate of the amounts of such gifts to such person during all preceding calendar quarters of any such calendar year shall not be included in the total amount of gifts made during such quarter. Thus, the first $3,000 of gifts made to any one donee during the calendar year 1971 or any calendar year thereafter, except gifts of future interests in property as defined in §§ 25.2503-3 and 25.2503-4, is excluded in determining the total amount of gifts for a calendar quarter. In the case of a gift in trust the beneficiary of the trust is the donee. The application of this paragraph may be illustrated by the following examples:

Example (1). A made a gift of $3,000 to B on January 8, 1971, and on April 20, 1971, gave B an additional gift of $10,000. A made no other gifts in 1971. The total amount of gifts made by A during the second quarter of 1971 is $10,000 because the $3,000 exclusion provided by section 2503(b) is first applied to the January 8 gift.

Example (2). A gave $2,000 to B on January 8, 1971, and on April 20, 1971, gave him $10,000. The total amount of gifts made by A during the second quarter of 1971 is $9,000 because only $2,000 of the $3,000 exclusion provided by section 2503(b) was applied against the January 8 gift; $1,000 was available to offset other gifts (except gifts of a future interest) made to B during 1971.

(c) *Gifts made before January 1, 1971.*—The first $3,000 of gifts made to any one donee during the calendar year 1955, or 1970, or any calendar year intervening between calendar year 1955 and calendar year 1970, except gifts of future interests in property as defined in §§ 25.2503-3 and 25.2503-4, is excluded in determining the total amount of gifts for the calendar year. In the case of a gift in trust the beneficiary of the trust is the donee.

(d) *Transitional rule.*—The increased annual gift tax exclusion as defined in section 2503(b) shall not apply to any gift subject to a power of appointment granted under an instrument executed before September 12, 1981, and not amended on or after that date, provided that: (1) The power is exercisable after December 31, 1981, (2) the power is expressly defined in terms of, or by reference to, the amount of the gift tax exclusion under section 2503(b) (or the corresponding provision of prior law), and (3) there is not enacted a State law applicable to such instrument which construes the power of appointment as referring to the increased annual gift tax exclusion provided by the Economic Recovery Tax Act of 1981.

(e) *Examples.*—The provisions of paragraph (d) of this section may be illustrated by the following examples:

Example (1). A executed an instrument to create a trust for the benefit of B on July 2, 1981. The trust granted to B the power, for a period of 90 days after any transfer of cash to the trust, to withdraw from the trust the lesser of the amount of the transferred cash or the amount equal to the section 2503(b) annual gift tax exclusion. The trust was not amended on or after September 12, 1981. No state statute has been enacted which construes the power of appointment as referring to the increased annual gift tax exclusion provided by the Economic Recovery Tax Act of 1981. Accordingly, the maximum annual gift tax exclusion applicable to any gift subject to the exercise of the power of appointment is $3,000.

Example (2). Assume the same facts as in example (1) except that the power of appointment granted in the trust refers to section 2503(b) as amended at any time. The maximum annual gift tax exclusion applicable to any gift subject to the exercise of the power of appointment is $10,000.

(f) *Special rule in the case of gifts made on or after July 14, 1988, to a spouse who is not a United States citizen.*—(1) *In general.*—Subject to the special rules set forth at § 20.2056A-1(c) of this chapter, in the case of gifts made on or after July 14, 1988, if the donee of the gift is the donor's spouse and the donee spouse is not a citizen of the United States at the time of the gift, the first $100,000 of gifts made during the calendar year to the donee spouse (except gifts of future interests) is excluded in determining the total amount of gifts for the calendar year. The rule of this paragraph (f) applies regardless of whether the donor is a citizen or resident of the United States for purposes of chapter 12 of the Internal Revenue Code.

(2) *Gifts made after June 29, 1989.*—In the case of gifts made after June 29, 1989, the $100,000 exclusion provided in paragraph (f)(1) of this section applies only if the gift in excess of the otherwise applicable annual exclusion is in a form that qualifies for the gift tax marital deduc-

tion under section 2523(a) but for the provisions of section 2523(i)(1) (disallowing the marital deduction if the donee spouse is not a United States citizen.) See § 25.2523(i)-1(d), *Example 4*.

(3) *Effective date.*—This paragraph (f) is effective with respect to gifts made after August 22, 1995. [Reg. § 25.2503-2.]

☐ [*T.D. 6334, 11-14-58. Amended by T.D. 7238, 12-28-72; T.D. 7910, 9-6-83; T.D. 7978, 9-28-84 and T.D. 8612, 8-21-95.*]

[Reg. § 25.2503-3]

§ 25.2503-3. Future interests in property.—(a) No part of the value of a gift of a future interest may be excluded in determining the total amount of gifts made during the "calendar period"(as defined § 25.2502-1(c)(1)). "Future interest" is a legal term, and includes reversions, remainders, and other interests or estates, whether vested or contingent, and whether or not supported by a particular interest or estate, which are limited to commence in use, possession, or enjoyment at some future date or time. The term has no reference to such contractual rights as exist in a bond, note (though bearing no interest until maturity), or in a policy of life insurance, the obligations of which are to be discharged by payments in the future. But a future interest or interests in such contractual obligations may be created by the limitations contained in a trust or other instrument of transfer used in effecting a gift.

(b) An unrestricted right to the immediate use, possession, or enjoyment of property or the income from property (such as a life estate or term certain) is a present interest in property. An exclusion is allowable with respect to a gift of such an interest (but not in excess of the value of the interest). If a donee has received a present interest in property, the possibility that such interest may be diminished by the transfer of a greater interest in the same property to the donee through the exercise of a power is disregarded in computing the value of the present interest, to the extent that no part of such interest will at any time pass to any other person (see example (4) of paragraph (c) of this section). For an exception to the rule disallowing an exclusion for gifts of future interests in the case of certain gifts to minors, see § 25.2503-4.

(c) The operation of this section may be illustrated by the following examples:

Example (1). Under the terms of a trust created by A the trustee is directed to pay the net income to B, so long as B shall live. The trustee is authorized in his discretion to withhold payments of income during any period he deems advisable and add such income to the trust corpus. Since B's right to receive the income payments is subject to the trustee's discretion, it is not a present interest and no exclusion is allowable with respect to the transfer in trust.

Example (2). C transfers certain insurance policies on his own life to a trust created for the benefit of D. Upon C's death the proceeds of the policies are to be invested and the net income therefrom paid to D during his lifetime. Since the income payments to D will not begin until after C's death the transfer in trust represents a gift of a future interest in property against which no exclusion is allowable.

Example (3). Under the terms of a trust created by E the net income is to be distributed to E's three children in such shares as the trustee, in his uncontrolled discretion, deems advisable. While the terms of the trust provide that all of the net income is to be distributed, the amount of income any one of the three beneficiaries will receive rests entirely within the trustee's discretion and cannot be presently ascertained. Accordingly, no exclusions are allowable with respect to the transfers to the trust.

Example (4). Under the terms of a trust the net income is to be paid to F for life, with the remainder payable to G on F's death. The trustee has the uncontrolled power to pay over the corpus to F at any time. Although F's present right to receive the income may be terminated, no other person has the right to such income interest. Accordingly, the power in the trustee is disregarded in determining the value of F's present interest. The power would not be disregarded to the extent that the trustee during F's life could distribute corpus to persons other than F.

Example (5). The corpus of a trust created by J consists of certain real property, subject to a mortgage. The terms of the trust provide that the net income from the property is to be used to pay the mortgage. After the mortgage is paid in full the net income is to be paid to K during his lifetime. Since K's right to receive the income payments will not begin until after the mortgage is paid in full the transfer in trust represents a gift of a future interest in property against which no exclusion is allowable.

Example (6). L pays premiums on a policy of insurance on his life. All the incidents of ownership in the policy (including the right to surrender the policy) are vested in M. The payment of premiums by L constitutes a gift of a present interest in property. [Reg. § 25.2503-3.]

☐ [*T.D. 6334, 11-14-58. Amended by T.D. 7238, 12-28-72 and T.D. 7910, 9-6-83.*]

[Reg. § 25.2503-4]

§ 25.2503-4. Transfer for the benefit of a minor.—(a) Section 2503(c) provides that no part of a transfer for the benefit of a donee who has not attained the age of 21 years on the date of the gift will be considered a gift of a future interest in property if the terms of the transfer satisfy all of the following conditions:

(1) Both the property itself and its income may be expended by or for the benefit of the donee before he attains the age of 21 years;

(2) Any portion of the property and its income not disposed of under (1) will pass to the donee when he attains the age of 21 years; and

(3) Any portion of the property and its income not disposed of under (1) will be payable either to the estate of the donee or as he may appoint under a general power of appointment as defined in section 2514(c) if he dies before attaining the age of 21 years.

(b) Either a power of appointment exercisable by the donee by will or a power of appointment exercisable by the donee during his lifetime will satisfy the conditions set forth in paragraph (a)(3) of this section. However, if the transfer is to qualify for the exclusion under this section, there must be no restrictions of substance (as distinguished from formal restrictions of the type described in paragraph (g)(4) of § 25.2523(e)-1) by the terms of the instrument of transfer on the exercise of the power by the donee. However, if the minor is given a power of appointment exercisable during lifetime or is given a power of appointment exercisable by will, the fact that under the local law a minor is under a disability to exercise an inter vivos power or to execute a will does not cause the transfer to fail to satisfy the conditions of section 2503(c). Further, a transfer does not fail to satisfy the conditions of section 2503(c) by reason of the mere fact that—

(1) There is left to the discretion of a trustee the determination of the amounts, if any, of the income or property to be expended for the benefit of the minor and the purpose for which the expenditure is to be made, provided there are no substantial restrictions under the terms of the trust instrument on the exercise of such discretion;

(2) The donee, upon reaching age 21, has the right to extend the term of the trust; or

(3) The governing instrument contains a disposition of the property or income not expended during the donee's minority to persons other than the donee's estate in the event of the default of appointment by the donee.

(c) A gift to a minor which does not satisfy the requirements of section 2503(c) may be either a present or a future interest under the general rules of § 25.2503-3. Thus, for example, a transfer of property in trust with income required to be paid annually to a minor beneficiary and corpus to be distributed to him upon his attaining the age of 25 is a gift of a present interest with respect to the right to income but is a gift of a future interest with respect to the right to corpus. [Reg. § 25.2503-4.]

☐ [*T.D.* 6334, 11-14-58.]

[Reg. § 25.2503-6]

§ 25.2503-6. Exclusion for certain qualified transfers to tuition or medical expenses.—(a) *In general.*—Section 2503(e) provides that any qualified transfer after December 31, 1981, shall not be treated as a transfer of property by gift for purposes of chapter 12 of subtitle B of the Code. Thus, a qualified transfer on behalf of any individual is excluded in determining the total amount of gifts in calendar year 1982 and subsequent years. This exclusion is available in addition to the $10,000 annual gift tax exclusion. Furthermore, an exclusion for a qualified transfer is permitted without regard to the relationship between the donor and the donee.

(b) *Qualified transfers.*—(1) *Definition.*—For purposes of this paragraph, the term "qualified transfer" means any amount paid on behalf of an individual—

(i) As tuition to a qualifying educational organization for the education or training of that individual, or

(ii) To any person who provides medical care with respect to that individual as payment for the qualifying medical expenses arising from such medical care.

(2) *Tuition expenses.*—For purposes of paragraph (b)(1)(i) of this section, a qualifying educational organization is one which normally maintains a regular faculty and curriculum and normally has a regularly enrolled body of pupils or students in attendance at the place where its educational activities are regularly carried on. See section 170(b)(1)(A)(ii) and the regulations thereunder. The unlimited exclusion is permitted for tuition expenses of full-time or part-time students paid directly to the qualifying educational organization providing the education. No unlimited exclusion is permitted for amounts paid for books, supplies, dormitory fees, board, or other similar expenses which do not constitute direct tuition costs.

(3) *Medical expenses.*—For purposes of paragraph (b)(1)(ii) of this section, qualifying medical expenses are limited to those expenses defined in section 213(d) (section 213(e) prior to January 1, 1984) and include expenses incurred for the diagnosis, cure, mitigation, treatment or prevention of disease, or for the purpose of affecting any structure or function of the body or for transportation primarily for and essential to medical care. In addition, the unlimited exclusion from the gift tax includes amounts paid for medical insurance on behalf of any individual. The unlimited exclusion from the gift tax does not apply to amounts paid for medical care that are reimbursed by the donee's insurance. Thus, if payment for a medical expense is reimbursed by the donee's insurance company, the donor's payment for that expense, to the extent of the reimbursed amount, is not eligible for the unlimited

exclusion from the gift tax and the gift is treated as having been made on the date the reimbursement is received by the donee.

(c) *Examples.*—The provisions of paragraph (b) of this section may be illustrated by the following examples.

Example (1). In 1982, A made a tuition payment directly to a foreign univerity on behalf of B. A had no legal obligation to make this payment. The foreign university is described in section 170(b)(1)(A)(ii) of the Code. A's tuition payment is exempt from the gift tax under section 2503(e) of the Code.

Example (2). A transfers $100,000 to a trust the provisions of which state that the funds are to be used for tuition expenses incurred by A's grandchildren. A's transfer to the trust is a completed gift for Federal gift tax purposes and is not a direct transfer to an educational organization as provided in paragraph (b)(2) of this section and does not qualify for the unlimited exclusion from gift tax under section 2503(e).

Example (3). C was seriously injured in an automobile accident in 1982. D, who is unrelated to C, paid C's various medical expenses by checks made payable to the physician. D also paid the hospital for C's hospital bills. These medical and hospital expenses were types described in section 213 of the Code and were not reimbursed by insurance or otherwise. Because the medical and hospital bills paid in 1982 for C were medical expenses within the meaning of section 213 of the Code, and since they were paid directly by D to the person rendering the medical care, they are not treated as transfers subject to the gift tax.

Example (4). Assume the same facts as in example (2) except that instead of making the payments directly to the medical service provider, D reimbursed C for the medical expenses which C had previously paid. The payments made by D to C do not qualify for the exclusion under section 2503(e) of the Code and are subject to the gift tax on the date the reimbursement is received by C to the extent the reimbursement and all other gifts from D to C during the year of the reimbursement exceed the $10,000 annual exclusion provided in section 2503(b). [Reg. § 25.2503-6.]

☐ [*T.D. 7978, 9-28-84.*]

[Reg. § 25.2504-1]

§ 25.2504-1. Taxable gifts for preceding calendar periods.—(a) In order to determine the correct gift tax liability for any calendar period it is necessary to ascertain the correct amount, if any, of the aggregate sum of the taxable gifts for each of the "preceding calendar periods" (as defined in § 25.2502-1(c)(2)). See paragraph (a) of § 25.2502-1. The term aggregate sum of the taxable gifts for each of the preceding calendar periods means the correct aggregate of such gifts, not necessarily that returned for those calendar periods and in respect of which tax was paid. All

transfers that constituted gifts in prior calendar periods under the laws, including the provisions of law relating to exclusions from gifts, in effect at the time the transfers were made are included in determining the amount of taxable gifts for preceding calendar periods. The deductions other than for the specific exemption (see paragraph (b) of this section) allowed by the laws in effect at the time the transfers were made also are taken into account in determining the aggregate sum of the taxable gifts for preceding calendar periods. (The allowable exclusion from a gift is $5,000 for years before 1939, $4,000 for the calendar years 1939 through 1942, $3,000 for the calendar years 1943 through 1981, and $10,000 thereafter.)

(b) In determining the aggregate sum of the taxable gifts for the "preceding calendar periods" (as defined in § 25.2502-1(c)(2)), the total of the amounts allowed as deductions for the specific exemption, under section 2521 (as in effect prior to its repeal by the Tax Reform Act of 1976) and the corresponding provisions of prior laws, shall not exceed $30,000. Thus, if the only prior gifts by a donor were made in 1940 and 1941 (at which time the specific exemption allowable was $40,000), and if in the donor's returns for those years the donor claimed deductions totaling $40,000 for the specific exemption and reported taxable gifts totaling $110,000, then in determining the aggregate sum of the taxable gifts for the preceding calendar period: the deductions for the specific exemption cannot exceed $30,000, and the donor's taxable gifts for such periods will be $120,000 (instead of the $110,000 reported on his returns). (The allowable deduction for the specific exemption was $50,000 for calendar years before 1936, $40,000 for calendar years 1936 through 1942, and $30,000 for 1943 through 1976.)

(c) If the donor and the donor's spouse consented to have gifts made to third parties considered as made one-half by each spouse, pursuant to the provisions of section 2513 or section 1000(f) of the Internal Revenue Code of 1939 (which corresponds to section 2513), these provisions shall be taken into account in determining the aggregate sum of the taxable gifts for the preceding calendar periods (under paragraph (a) of this section).

(d) If interpretations of the gift tax law in preceding calendar periods resulted in the erroneous inclusion of property for gift tax purposes that should have been excluded, or the erroneous exclusion of property that should have been included, adjustments must be made in order to arrive at the correct aggregate of taxable gifts for the preceding calendar periods (under paragraph (a) of this section). However, see § 25.2504-2(b) regarding certain gifts made after August 5, 1997. [Reg. § 25.2504-1.]

☐ [*T.D. 6334, 11-14-58. Amended by T.D. 7238, 12-28-72; T.D. 7910, 9-6-83 and T.D. 8845, 12-2-99.*]

[Reg. § 25.2504-2]

§ 25.2504-2. Determination of gifts for preceding calendar periods.—(a) *Gifts made before August 6, 1997.*—If the time has expired within which a tax may be assessed under chapter 12 of the Internal Revenue Code (or under corresponding provisions of prior laws) on the transfer of property by gift made during a preceding calendar period, as defined in § 25.2502-1(c)(2), the gift was made prior to August 6, 1997, and a tax has been assessed or paid for such prior calendar period, the value of the gift, for purposes of arriving at the correct amount of the taxable gifts for the preceding calendar periods (as defined under § 25.2504-1(a)), is the value used in computing the tax for the last preceding calendar period for which a tax was assessed or paid under chapter 12 of the Internal Revenue Code or the corresponding provisions of prior laws. However, this rule does not apply where no tax was paid or assessed for the prior calendar period. Furthermore, this rule does not apply to adjustments involving issues other than valuation. See § 25.2504-1(d).

(b) *Gifts made or section 2701(d) taxable events occurring after August 5, 1997.*—If the time has expired under section 6501 within which a gift tax may be assessed under chapter 12 of the Internal Revenue Code (or under corresponding provisions of prior laws) on the transfer of property by gift made during a preceding calendar period, as defined in § 25.2502-1(c)(2), or with respect to an increase in taxable gifts required under section 2701(d) and § 25.2701-4, and the gift was made, or the section 2701(d) taxable event occurred, after August 5, 1997, the amount of the taxable gift or the amount of the increase in taxable gifts, for purposes of determining the correct amount of taxable gifts for the preceding calendar periods (as defined in § 25.2504-1(a)), is the amount that is finally determined for gift tax purposes (within the meaning of § 20.2001-1(c) of this chapter) and such amount may not be thereafter adjusted. The rule of this paragraph (b) applies to adjustments involving all issues relating to the gift including valuation issues and legal issues involving the interpretation of the gift tax law. For purposes of determining if the time has expired within which a gift tax may be assessed, see § 301.6501(c)-1(e) and (f) of this chapter.

(c) *Examples.*—The following examples illustrate the rules of paragraphs (a) and (b) of this section:

Example 1. (i) *Facts.* In 1996, A transferred closely-held stock in trust for the benefit of B, A's child. A timely filed a Federal gift tax return reporting the 1996 transfer to B. No gift tax was assessed or paid as a result of the gift tax annual exclusion and the application of A's available unified credit. In 2001, A transferred additional closely-held stock to the trust. A's Federal gift

tax return reporting the 2001 transfer was timely filed and the transfer was adequately disclosed under § 301.6501(c)-1(f)(2) of this chapter. In computing the amount of taxable gifts, A claimed annual exclusions with respect to the transfers in 1996 and 2001. In 2003, A transfers additional property to B and timely files a Federal gift tax return reporting the gift.

(ii) *Application of the rule limiting adjustments to prior gifts.* Under section 2504(c), in determining A's 2003 gift tax liability, the amount of A's 1996 gift can be adjusted for purposes of computing prior taxable gifts, since that gift was made prior to August 6, 1997, and therefore, the provisions of paragraph (a) of this section apply. Adjustments can be made with respect to the valuation of the gift and legal issues presented (for example, the availability of the annual exclusion with respect to the gift). However, A's 2001 transfer was adequately disclosed on a timely filed gift tax return and, thus, under paragraph (b) of this section, the amount of the 2001 taxable gift by A may not be adjusted (either with respect to the valuation of the gift or any legal issue) for purposes of computing prior taxable gifts in determining A's 2003 gift tax liability.

Example 2. (i) *Facts.* In 1996, A transferred closely-held stock to B, A's child. A timely filed a Federal gift tax return reporting the 1996 transfer to B and paid gift tax on the value of the gift reported on the return. On August 1, 1997, A transferred additional closely-held stock to B in exchange for a promissory note signed by B. Also, on September 10, 1997, A transferred closely-held stock to C, A's other child. On April 15, 1998, A timely filed a gift tax return for 1997 reporting the September 10, 1997, transfer to C and, under § 301.6501(c)-1(f)(2) of this chapter, adequately disclosed that transfer and paid gift tax with respect to the transfer. However, A believed that the transfer to B on August 1, 1997, was for full and adequate consideration and A did not report the transfer to B on the 1997 Federal gift tax return. In 2002, A transfers additional property to B and timely files a Federal gift tax return reporting the gift.

(ii) *Application of the rule limiting adjustments to prior gifts.* Under section 2504(c), in determining A's 2002 gift tax liability, the value of A's 1996 gift cannot be adjusted for purposes of computing the value of prior taxable gifts, since that gift was made prior to August 6, 1997, and a timely filed Federal gift tax return was filed on which a gift tax was assessed and paid. However, A's prior taxable gifts can be adjusted to reflect the August 1, 1997, transfer because, although a gift tax return for 1997 was timely filed and gift tax was paid, under § 301.6501(c)-1(f) of this chapter the period for assessing gift tax with respect to the August 1, 1997, transfer did not commence to run since that transfer was not adequately disclosed on the 1997 gift tax return. Accordingly, a gift tax may be assessed with respect to the August 1, 1997, transfer and the amount of the gift would be reflected in prior taxable gifts for purposes of computing A's gift tax liability for 2002. A's September 10, 1997, transfer to C was adequately disclosed on a timely filed gift tax return and, thus, under paragraph (b) of this section, the amount of the September 10, 1997, taxable gift by A may not be adjusted for purposes of computing prior taxable gifts in determining A's 2002 gift tax liability.

Example 3. (i) *Facts.* In 1994, A transferred closely-held stock to B and C, A's children. A timely filed a Federal gift tax return reporting the 1994 transfers to B and C and paid gift tax on the value of the gifts reported on the return. Also in 1994, A transferred closely-held stock to B in exchange for a bona fide promissory note signed by B. A believed that the transfer to B in exchange for the promissory note was for full and adequate consideration and A did not report that transfer to B on the 1994 Federal gift tax return. In 2002, A transfers additional property to B and timely files a Federal gift tax return reporting the gift.

(ii) *Application of the rule limiting adjustments to prior gifts.* Under section 2504(c), in determining A's 2002 gift tax liability, the value of A's 1994 gifts cannot be adjusted for purposes of computing prior taxable gifts because those gifts were made prior to August 6, 1997, and a timely filed Federal gift tax return was filed with respect to which a gift tax was assessed and paid, and the period of limitations on assessment has expired. The provisions of paragraph (a) of this section apply to the 1994 transfers. However, for purposes of determining A's adjusted taxable gifts in computing A's estate tax liability, the gifts may be adjusted. See § 20.2001-1(a) of this chapter.

(d) *Effective dates.*—Paragraph (a) of this section applies to transfers of property by gift made prior to August 6, 1997. Paragraphs (b) and (c) of this section apply to transfers of property by gift made after August 5, 1997, if the gift tax return for the calendar period in which the transfer is reported is filed after December 3, 1999. [Reg. § 25.2504-2.]

☐ [*T.D.* 6334, 11-14-58. *Amended by T.D.* 7238, 12-28-72; *T.D.* 7910, 9-6-83 *and T.D.* 8845, 12-2-99.]

TRANSFERS

§ 25.2511-1. Transfers in general.—(a) The gift tax applies to a transfer by way of gift whether the transfer is in trust or otherwise, whether the gift is direct or indirect, and whether the property is real or personal, tangible or intangible. For example, a taxable transfer may be effected by the creation of a trust, the forgiving of a debt, the assignment of a judgment, the assignment of the benefits of an insurance policy, or the transfer of cash, certificates of deposit, or Federal, State or municipal bonds. Statutory provisions which exempt bonds, notes, bills and certificates of indebtedness of the Federal Government or its agencies and the interest thereon from taxation are not applicable to the gift tax, since the gift tax is an excise tax on the transfer, and is not a tax on the subject of the gift.

(b) In the case of a gift by a nonresident not a citizen of the United States—

(1) If the gift was made on or after January 1, 1967, by a donor who was not an expatriate to whom section 2501(a)(2) was inapplicable on the date of the gift by reason of section 2501(a)(3) and paragraph (a)(3) of § 25.2501-1, or

(2) If the gift was made before January 1, 1967, by a donor who was not engaged in business in the United States during the calendar year in which the gift was made,

the gift tax applies only if the gift consisted of real property or tangible personal property situated within the United States at the time of the transfer. See § § 25.2501-1 and 25.2511-3.

(c)(1) The gift tax also applies to gifts indirectly made. Thus, any transaction in which an interest in property is gratuitously passed or conferred upon another, regardless of the means or device employed, constitutes a gift subject to tax. See further § 25.2512-8 relating to transfers for insufficient consideration. However, in the case of a transfer creating an interest in property (within the meaning of § 25.2518-2(c)(3) and (c)(4)) made after December 31, 1976, this paragraph (c)(1) shall not apply to the donee if, as a result of a qualified disclaimer by the donee, the interest passes to a different donee. Nor shall it apply to a donor if, as a result of a qualified disclaimer by the donee, a completed transfer of an interest in property is not effected. See section 2518 and the corresponding regulations for rules relating to a qualified disclaimer.

(2) In the case of taxable transfers creating an interest in the person disclaiming made before January 1, 1977, where the law governing the administration of the decedent's estate gives a beneficiary, heir, or next-of-kin a right completely and unqualifiedly to refuse to accept ownership of property transferred from a decedent (whether the transfer is effected by the decedent's will or by the law of descent and distribution), a refusal to accept ownership does not constitute the making of a gift if the refusal is made within a reasonable time after knowledge of the existence of the transfer. The refusal must be unequivocal and effective under the local law. There can be no refusal of ownership of property after its acceptance. In the absence of the facts to the contrary, if a person fails to refuse to accept a transfer to him of ownership of a decedent's property within a reasonable time after learning of the existence of the transfer, he will be pre-

sumed to have accepted the property. Where the local law does not permit such a refusal, any disposition by the beneficiary, heir, or next-of-kin whereby ownership is transferred gratuitously to another constitutes the making of a gift by the beneficiary, heir, or next-of-kin. In any case where a refusal is purported to relate to only a part of the property, the determination of whether or not there has been a complete and unqualified refusal to accept ownership will depend on all of the facts and circumstances in each particular case, taking into account the recognition and effectiveness of such a purported refusal under the local law. In illustration, if Blackacre was devised to A under the decedent's will (which also provided that all lapsed legacies and devises shall go to B, the residuary beneficiary), and under the local law A could refuse to accept ownership in which case title would be considered as never having passed to A, A's refusal to accept Blackacre within a reasonable time of learning of the devise will not constitute the making of a gift by A to B. However, if a decedent who owned Greenacre died intestate with C and D as his only heirs, and under local law the heir of a decedent cannot, by refusal to accept, prevent himself from becoming an owner of intestate property, any gratuitous disposition by C (by whatever term it is known) whereby he gives up his ownership of a portion of Greenacre and D acquires the whole thereof constitutes the making of a gift by C to D.

(3) The fourth sentence of paragraph (c)(1) of this section is applicable for transfers creating an interest to be disclaimed made on or after December 31, 1997.

(d) If a joint income tax return is filed by a husband and wife for a taxable year, the payment by one spouse of all or part of the income tax liability for such year is not treated as resulting in a transfer which is subject to gift tax. The same rule is applicable to the payment of gift tax for a "calendar period" (as defined in § 25.2502-1(c)(1)) in the case of a husband and wife who have consented to have the gifts made considered as made half by each of them in accordance with the provisions of section 2513.

(e) If a donor transfers by gift less than his entire interest in property, the gift tax is applicable to the interest transferred. The tax is applicable, for example, to the transfer of an undivided half interest in property, or to the transfer of a life estate when the grantor retains the remainder interest, or vice versa. However, if the donor's retained interest is not susceptible of measurement on the basis of generally accepted valuation principles, the gift tax is applicable to the entire value of the property subject to the gift. Thus, if a donor, aged 65 years, transfers a life estate in property to A, aged 25 years, with remainder to A's issue, or in default of issue, with reversion to the donor, the gift tax will normally be applicable to the entire value of the property.

(f) If a donor is the owner of only a limited interest in property, and transfers his entire interest, the interest is in every case to be valued by the rules set forth in §§ 25.2512-1 through 25.2512-7. If the interest is a remainder or reversion or other future interest, it is to be valued on the basis of actuarial principles set forth in § 25.2512-5, or if it is not susceptible of valuation in that manner, in accordance with the principles set forth in § 25.2512-1.

(g)(1) Donative intent on the part of the transferor is not an essential element in the application of the gift tax to the transfer. The application of the tax is based on the objective facts of the transfer and the circumstances under which it is made, rather than on the subjective motives of the donor. However, there are certain types of transfers to which the tax is not applicable. It is applicable only to a transfer of a beneficial interest in property. It is not applicable to a transfer of bare legal title to a trustee. A transfer by a trustee of trust property in which he has no beneficial interest does not constitute a gift by the trustee (but such a transfer may constitute a gift by the creator of the trust, if until the transfer he had the power to change the beneficiaries by amending or revoking the trust). The gift tax is not applicable to a transfer for a full and adequate consideration in money or money's worth, or to ordinary business transactions, described in § 25.2512-8.

(2) If a trustee has a beneficial interest in trust property, a transfer of the property by the trustee is not a taxable transfer if it is made pursuant to a fiduciary power the exercise or nonexercise of which is limited by a reasonably fixed or ascertainable standard which is set forth in the trust instrument. A clearly measurable standard under which the holder of a power is legally accountable is such a standard for this purpose. For instance, a power to distribute corpus for the education, support, maintenance, or health of the beneficiary; for his reasonable support and comfort; to enable him to maintain his accustomed standard of living; or to meet an emergency, would be such a standard. However, a power to distribute corpus for the pleasure, desire, or happiness of a beneficiary is not such a standard. The entire context of a provision of a trust instrument granting a power must be considered in determining whether the power is limited by a reasonably definite standard. For example, if a trust instrument provides that the determination of the trustee shall be conclusive with respect to the exercise or nonexercise of a power, the power is not limited by a reasonably definite standard. However, the fact that the governing instrument is phrased in discretionary terms is not in itself an indication that no such a standard exists.

(h) The following are examples of transactions resulting in taxable gifts and in each case it is assumed that the transfers were not made for an adequate and full consideration in money or money's worth:

(1) A transfer of property by a corporation to B is a gift to B from the stockholders of the corporation. If B himself is a stockholder, the transfer is a gift to him from the other stockholders but only to the extent it exceeds B's own interest in such amount as a shareholder. A transfer of property by B to a corporation generally represents gifts by B to the other individual shareholders of the corporation to the extent of their proportionate interests in the corporation. However, there may be an exception to this rule, such as a transfer made by an individual to a charitable, public, political or similar organization which may constitute a gift to the organization as a single entity, depending upon the facts and circumstances in the particular case.

(2) The transfer of property to B if there is imposed upon B the obligation of paying a commensurate annuity to C is a gift to C.

(3) The payment of money or the transfer of property to B in consideration of B's promise to render a service to C is a gift to C, or to both B and C, depending on whether the service to be rendered to C is or is not an adequate and full consideration in money or money's worth for that which is received by B. See section 2512(b) and the regulations thereunder.

(4) If A creates a joint bank account for himself and B (or a similar type of ownership by which A can regain the entire fund without B's consent), there is a gift to B when B draws upon the account for his own benefit, to the extent of the amount drawn without any obligation to account for a part of the proceeds to A. Similarly, if A purchases a United States savings bond, registered as payable to "A or B," there is a gift to B when B surrenders the bond for cash without any obligation to account for a part of the proceeds to A.

(5) If A with his own funds purchases property and has the title conveyed to himself and B as joint owners, with rights of survivorship (other than a joint ownership described in example (4)) but which rights may be defeated by either party severing his interest, there is a gift to B in the amount of half the value of the property. However, see § 25.2515-1 relative to the creation of a joint tenancy (or tenancy by the entirety) between husband and wife in real property with rights of survivorship which, unless the donor elects otherwise, is not considered as a transfer includible for Federal gift tax purposes at the time of the creation of the joint tenancy. See § 25.2515-2 with respect to determining the extent to which the creation of a tenancy by the entirety constitutes a taxable gift if the donor elects to have the creation of the tenancy so treated. See also § 25.2523(d)-1 with respect to the marital deduction allowed in the case of the creation of a joint tenancy or a tenancy by the entirety.

(6) If A is possessed of a vested remainder interest in property, subject to being divested only in the event he should fail to survive one or more individuals or the happening of some other event, an irrevocable assignment of all or any part of his interest would result in a transfer includible for Federal gift tax purposes. See especially § 25.2512-5 for the valuation of an interest of this type.

(7) If A, without retaining a power to revoke the trust or to change the beneficial interests therein, transfers property in trust whereby B is to receive the income for life and at his death the trust is to terminate and the corpus is to be returned to A, provided A survives, but if A predeceases B the corpus is to pass to C, A has made a gift equal to the total value of the property less the value of his retained interest. See § 25.2512-5 for the valuation of the donor's retained interest.

(8) If the insured purchases a life insurance policy, or pays a premium on a previously issued policy, the proceeds of which are payable to a beneficiary or beneficiaries other than his estate, and with respect to which the insured retains no reversionary interest in himself or his estate and no power to revest the economic benefits in himself or his estate or to change the beneficiaries or their proportionate benefits (or if the insured relinquishes by assignment, by designation of a new beneficiary or otherwise, every such power that was retained in a previously issued policy), the insured has made a gift of the value of the policy, or to the extent of the premium paid, even though the right of the assignee or beneficiary to receive the benefits is conditioned upon his surviving the insured. For the valuation of life insurance policies see § 25.2512-6.

(9) Where property held by a husband and wife as community property is used to purchase insurance upon the husband's life and a third person is revocably designated as beneficiary and under the State law the husband's death is considered to make absolute the transfer by the wife, there is a gift by the wife at the time of the husband's death of half the amount of the proceeds of such insurance.

(10) If under a pension plan (pursuant to which he has an unqualified right to an annuity) an employee has an option to take either a retirement annuity for himself alone or a smaller annuity for himself with a survivorship annuity payable to his wife, an irrevocable election by the employee to take the reduced annuity in order that an annuity may be paid, after the employee's death, to his wife results in the making of a gift. However, see section 2517 and the regulations thereunder for the exemption from gift tax of amounts attributable to employers' contributions under qualified plans and certain other contracts. [Reg. § 25.2511-1.]

☐ [T.D. 6334, 11-14-58. *Amended by T.D.* 6542, 1-19-61; T.D. 7150, 12-1-71; T.D. 7238, 12-28-72;

T.D. 7296, 12-11-73; T.D. 7910, 9-6-83; T.D. 8095, 8-6-86; T.D. 8540, 6-9-94 and T.D. 8744, 12-30-97.]

[Reg. §25.2511-2]

§25.2511-2. Cessation of donor's dominion and control.—(a) The gift tax is not imposed upon the receipt of the property by the donee, nor is it necessarily determined by the measure of enrichment resulting to the donee from the transfer, nor is it conditioned upon ability to identify the donee at the time of the transfer. On the contrary, the tax is a primary and personal liability of the donor, is an excise upon his act of making the transfer, is measured by the value of the property passing from the donor, and attaches regardless of the fact that the identity of the donee may not then be known or ascertainable.

(b) As to any property, or part thereof or interest therein, of which the donor has so parted with dominion and control as to leave in him no power to change its disposition, whether for his own benefit or for the benefit of another, the gift is complete. But if upon a transfer of property (whether in trust or otherwise) the donor reserves any power over its disposition, the gift may be wholly incomplete, or may be partially complete and partially incomplete, depending upon all the facts in the particular case. Accordingly, in every case of a transfer of property subject to a reserved power, the terms of the power must be examined and its scope determined. For example, if a donor transfers property to another in trust to pay the income to the donor or accumulate it in the discretion of the trustee, and the donor retains a testamentary power to appoint the remainder among his descendants, no portion of the transfer is a completed gift. On the other hand, if the donor had not retained the testamentary power of appointment, but instead provided that the remainder should go to X or his heirs, the entire transfer would be a completed gift. However, if the exercise of the trustee's power in favor of the grantor is limited by a fixed or ascertainable standard (see paragraph (g)(2) of §25.2511-1), enforceable by or on behalf of the grantor, then the gift is incomplete to the extent of the ascertainable value of any rights thus retained by the grantor.

(c) A gift is incomplete in every instance in which a donor reserves the power to revest the beneficial title to the property in himself. A gift is also incomplete if and to the extent that a reserved power gives the donor the power to name new beneficiaries or to change the interests of the beneficiaries as between themselves unless the power is a fiduciary power limited by a fixed or ascertainable standard. Thus, if an estate for life is transferred but, by an exercise of a power, the estate may be terminated or cut down by the donor to one of less value, and without restriction upon the extent to which the estate may be so cut down, the transfer constitutes an incomplete gift. If in this example the power was confined to the right to cut down the estate for life to one for a term of five years, the certainty of an estate for not less than that term results in a gift to that extent complete.

(d) A gift is not considered incomplete, however, merely because the donor reserves the power to change the manner or time of enjoyment. Thus, the creation of a trust the income of which is to be paid annually to the donee for a period of years, the corpus being distributable to him at the end of the period, and the power reserved by the donor being limited to a right to require that, instead of the income being so payable, it should be accumulated and distributed with the corpus to the donee at the termination of the period, constitutes a completed gift.

(e) A donor is considered as himself having a power if it is exercisable by him in conjunction with any person not having a substantial adverse interest in the disposition of the transferred property or the income therefrom. A trustee, as such, is not a person having an adverse interest in the disposition of the trust property or its income.

(f) The relinquishment or termination of a power to change the beneficiaries of transferred property, occurring otherwise than by the death of the donor (the statute being confined to transfers by living donors), is regarded as the event which completes the gift and causes the tax to apply. For example, if A transfers property in trust for the benefit of B and C but reserves the power as trustee to change the proportionate interests of B and C, and if A thereafter has another person appointed trustee in place of himself, such later relinquishment of the power by A to the new trustee completes the gift of the transferred property, whether or not the new trustee has a substantial adverse interest. The receipt of income or of other enjoyment of the transferred property by the transferee or by the beneficiary (other than by the donor himself) during the interim between the making of the initial transfer and the relinquishment or termination of the power operates to free such income or other enjoyment from the power, and constitutes a gift of such income or of such other enjoyment taxable as of the "calendar period" (as defined in §25.2502-1(c)(1). If property is transferred in trust to pay the income to A for life with remainder to B, powers to distribute corpus to A, and to withhold income from A for future distribution to B, are powers to change the beneficiaries of the transferred property.

(g) If a donor transfers property to himself as trustee (or to himself and some other person, not possessing a substantial adverse interest, as trustees), and retains no beneficial interest in the trust property and no power over it except fiduciary powers, the exercise or nonexercise of which is limited by a fixed or ascertainable standard, to change the beneficiaries of the transferred property, the donor has made a completed gift and the entire value of the transferred property is subject to the gift tax.

(h) If a donor delivers a properly indorsed stock certificate to the donee or the donee's agent, the gift is completed for gift tax purposes on the date of delivery. If the donor delivers the certificate to his bank or broker as his agent, or to the issuing corporation or its transfer agent, for transfer into the name of the donee, the gift is completed on the date the stock is transferred on the books of the corporation.

(i) [Reserved]

(j) If the donor contends that a power is of such nature as to render the gift incomplete, and hence not subject to the tax as of the calendar period (as defined in § 25.2502-1(c)(1)) of the initial transfer, see § 301.6501(c)-1(f)(5) of this chapter. [Reg. § 25.2511-2.]

☐ [*T.D.* 6334, 11-14-58. *Amended by T.D.* 7238, 12-28-72; *T.D.* 7910, 9-6-83 *and T.D.* 8845, 12-2-99.]

[Reg. § 25.2511-3]

§ 25.2511-3. Transfers by nonresidents not citizens.—(a) *In general.*—Sections 2501 and 2511 contain rules relating to the taxation of transfers of property by gift by a donor who is a nonresident not a citizen of the United States. (See paragraph(b) of § 25.2501-1 for the definition of the term "resident" for purposes of the gift tax.) As combined these rules are:

(1) The gift tax applies only to the transfer of real property and tangible personal property situated in the United States at the time of the transfer if either—

(i) The gift was made on or after January 1, 1967, by a nonresident not a citizen of the United States who was not an expatriate to whom section 2501(a)(2) was inapplicable on the date of the gift by reason of section 2501(a)(3) and paragraph (a)(3) of § 25.2501-1, or

(ii) The gift was made before January 1, 1967, by a nonresident not a citizen of the United States who was not engaged in business in the United States during the calendar year in which the gift was made.

(2) The gift tax applies to the transfer of all property (whether real or personal, tangible or intangible) situated in the United States at the time of the transfer if either—

(i) The gift was made on or after January 1, 1967, by a nonresident not a citizen of the United States who was an expatriate to whom section 2501(a)(2) was inapplicable on the date of the gift by reason of section 2501(a)(3) and paragraph (a)(3) of § 25.2501-1, or

(ii) The gift was made before January 1, 1967, by a nonresident not a citizen of the United States who was engaged in business in the United States during the calendar year in which the gift was made.

(b) *Situs of property.*—For purposes of applying the gift tax to the transfer of property owned and held by a nonresident not a citizen of the United States at the time of the transfer—

(1) *Real property and tangible personal property.*—Real property and tangible personal property constitute property within the United States only if they are physically situated therein.

(2) *Intangible personal property.*—Except as provided otherwise in subparagraphs (3) and (4) of this paragraph, intangible personal property constitutes property within the United States if it consists of a property right issued by or enforceable against a resident of the United States or a domestic corporation (public or private), irrespective of where the written evidence of the property is physically located at the time of the transfer.

(3) *Shares of stock.*—Irrespective of where the stock certificates are physically located at the time of the transfer—

(i) Shares of stock issued by a domestic corporation constitute property within the United States, and

(ii) Shares of stock issued by a corporation which is not a domestic corporation constitute property situated outside the United States.

(4) *Debt obligations.*—

(i) In the case of gifts made on or after January 1, 1967, a debt obligation, including a bank deposit, the primary obligor of which is a United States person (as defined in section 7701(a)(30)), the United States, a State, or any political subdivision thereof, the District of Columbia, or any agency or instrumentality of any such government constitutes property situated within the United States. This subdivision applies—

(*a*) In the case of a debt obligation of a domestic corporation, whether or not any interest on the obligation would be treated under section 862(a)(1) as income from sources without the United States by reason of section 861(a)(1)(B) (relating to interest received from a domestic corporation less than 20 percent of whose gross income for a 3-year period was derived from sources within the United States) and the regulations thereunder;

(*b*) In the case of an amount described in section 861(c) (relating to certain bank deposits, withdrawable accounts, and amounts held by an insurance company under an agreement to pay interest), whether or not any interest thereon would be treated under section 862(a)(1) as income from sources without the United States, by reason of section 861(a)(1)(A) (relating to interest on amounts described in section 861(c) which is not effectively connected with the conduct of a trade or business within the United States) and the regulations thereunder;

(c) In the case of a deposit with a domestic corporation or domestic partnership, whether or not the deposit is with a foreign branch thereof engaged in the commercial banking business; and

(d) Irrespective of where the written evidence of the debt obligation is physically located at the time of the transfer.

For purposes of this subdivision, a debt obligation on which there are two or more primary obligors shall be apportioned among such obligors, taking into account to the extent appropriate under all the facts and circumstances any choate or inchoate rights of contribution existing among such obligors with respect to the indebtedness. The term "agency or instrumentality," as used in this subdivision, does not include a possession of the United States or an agency or instrumentality of a possession.

(ii) In the case of gifts made on or after January 1, 1967, a debt obligation, including a bank deposit, not deemed under subdivision (i) of this subparagraph to be situated within the United States, constitutes property situated outside the United States.

(iii) In the case of gifts made before January 1, 1967, a debt obligation the written evidence of which is treated as being the property itself constitutes property situated within the United States if the written evidence of the obligation is physically located in the United States at the time of the transfer, irrespective of who is the primary obligor on the debt. If the written evidence of the obligation is physically located outside the United States, the debt obligation constitutes property situated outside the United States.

(iv) Currency is not a debt obligation for purposes of this subparagraph. [Reg. § 25.2511-3.]

☐ [*T.D. 6334, 11-14-58. Amended by T.D. 6542, 1-19-61; T.D. 7238, 12-28-72 and T.D. 7296, 12-11-73.*]

[Reg. § 25.2512-0]

§ 25.2512-0. Table of contents.—This section lists the section headings that appear in the regulations under section 2512.

[Reg. § 25.2512-0.]

☐ [*T.D. 8540, 6-9-94. Amended by T.D. 8819, 4-29-99; T.D. 8886, 6-9-2000; T.D. 9448, 5-1-2009 and T.D. 9540, 8-9-2011.*]

[Reg. § 25.2512-1]

§ 25.2512-1. Valuation of property; in general.—Section 2512 provides that if a gift is made in property, its value at the date of the gift shall be considered the amount of the gift. The value of the property is the price at which such property would change hands between a willing buyer and a willing seller, neither being under any compulsion to buy or to sell, and both having reasonable knowledge of relevant facts. The value of a particular kind of property is not the price that a forced sale of the property would produce. Nor is the fair market value of an item of property the sale price in a market other than that in which such item is most commonly sold to the public, taking into account, the location of the item wherever appropriate. Thus, in the case of an item of property made the subject of a gift, which is generally obtained by the public in the retail market, the fair market value of such an item of property is the price at which the item or a comparable item would be sold at retail. For example, the value of an automobile (an article generally obtained by the public in the retail market) which is the subject of a gift, is the price for which an automobile of the same or approximately the same description, make, model, age, condition, etc., could be purchased by a member of the general public and not the price for which the particular automobile of the donor would be purchased by a dealer in used automobiles. Examples of items of property which are generally sold to the public at retail may be found in

§ 25.2512-6. The value is generally to be determined by ascertaining as a basis the fair market value at the time of the gift of each unit of the property. For example, in the case of shares of stocks or bonds, such unit of property is generally a share or a bond. Property shall not be returned at the value at which it is assessed for local tax purposes unless that value represents the fair market value thereof on the date of the gift. All relevant facts and elements of value as of the time of the gift shall be considered. Where the subject of a gift is an interest in a business, the value of items of property in the inventory of the business generally should be reflected in the value of the business. For valuation of interests in businesses, see § 25.2512-3. See § 25.2512-2 and §§ 25.2512-4 through 25.2512-6 for further information concerning the valuation of other particular kinds of property. See section 2701 and the regulations at § 25.2701 for special rules for valuing transfers of an interest in a corporation or a partnership and for the treatment of unpaid qualified payments at the subsequent transfer of an applicable retained interest by the transferor or by an applicable family member. See section 2704(b) and the regulations at § 25.2704-2 for special valuation rules where an interest in property is subject to an applicable restriction. [Reg. § 25.2512-1.]

☐ [*T.D.* 6334, 11-14-58. *Amended by T.D.* 6826, 6-14-65 *and T.D.* 8395, 1-28-92.]

[Reg. § 25.2512-2]

§ 25.2512-2. **Stocks and bonds.**—(a) *In general.*—The value of stocks and bonds is the fair market value per share or bond on the date of the gift.

(b) *Based on selling prices.*—(1) In general, if there is a market for stocks or bonds, on a stock exchange, in an over-the-counter market or otherwise, the mean between the highest and lowest quoted selling prices on the date of the gift is the fair market value per share or bond. If there were no sales on the date of the gift but there were sales on dates within a reasonable period both before and after the date of the gift, the fair market value is determined by taking a weighted average of the means between the highest and lowest sales on the nearest date before and the nearest date after the date of the gift. The average is to be weighted inversely by the respective numbers of trading days between the selling dates and the date of the gift. If the stocks or bonds are listed on more than one exchange, the records of the exchange where the stocks or bonds are principally dealt in should be employed if such records are available in a generally available listing or publication of general circulation. In the event such records are not so available and such stocks or bonds are listed on a composite listing of combined exchanges available in a generally available listing or publication

of general circulation, the records of such combined exchanges should be employed. In valuing listed securities, the donor should be careful to consult accurate records to obtain values as of the date of the gift. If quotations of unlisted securities are obtained from brokers, or evidence as to their sale is obtained from the officers of the issuing companies, copies of letters furnishing such quotations or evidence of sale should be attached to the return.

(2) If it is established with respect to bonds for which there is a market on a stock exchange, that the highest and lowest selling prices are not available for the date of the gift in a generally available listing or publication of general circulation but that closing prices are so available, the fair market value per bond is the mean between the quoted closing selling price on the date of the gift and the quoted closing selling price on the trading day before the date of the gift. If there were no sales on the trading day before the date of the gift but there were sales on dates within a reasonable period before the date of the gift, the fair market value is determined by taking a weighted average of the quoted closing selling prices on the date of the gift and the nearest date before the date of the gift. The closing selling price for the date of the gift is to be weighted by the respective number of trading days between the previous selling date and the date of the gift. If there were no sales within a reasonable period before the date of the gift but there were sales on the date of the gift, the fair market value is the closing selling price on the date of the gift. If there were no sales on the date of the gift but there were sales within a reasonable period both before and after the date of the gift, the fair market value is determined by taking a weighted average of the quoted closing selling prices on the nearest date before and the nearest date after the date of the gift. The average is to be weighted inversely by the respective numbers of trading days between the selling dates and the date of the gift. If the bonds are listed on more than one exchange, the records of the exchange where the bonds are principally dealt in should be employed. In valuing listed securities, the donor should be careful to consult accurate records to obtain values as of the date of the gift.

(3) The application of this paragraph may be illustrated by the following examples:

Example (1). Assume that sales of stock nearest the date of the gift (Friday, June 15) occurred two trading days before (Wednesday, June 13) and three trading days after (Wednesday, June 20) and on these days the mean sale prices per share were $10 and $15, respectively. The price of $12 is taken as representing the fair market value of a share of stock as of the date of the gift

$$\frac{((3 \times 10) + (2 \times 15))}{5}.$$

Example (2). Assume the same facts as in example 1 except that the mean sale prices per share on June 13 and June 20 were $15 and $10 respectively. The price of $13 is taken as representing the fair market value of a share of stock as of the date of the gift

$$\frac{(3 \times 15) + (2 \times 10)}{5}$$

Example (3). Assume that on the date of the gift (Tuesday, April 3, 1973) the closing selling price of certain listed bonds was $25 per bond and that the highest and lowest selling prices are not available in a generally available listing or publication of general circulation for that date. Assume further, that the closing selling price of such bonds was $21 per bond on the day before the date of the gift (Monday, April 2, 1973). Thus, under paragraph (b)(2) of this section, the price of $23 is taken as representing the fair market value per bond as of the date of the gift

$$\frac{(25 + 21)}{2}$$

Example (4). Assume the same facts as in example 3 except that there were no sales on the day before the date of the gift. Assume further, that there were sales on Thursday, March 29, 1973, and that the closing selling price on that day was $23. The price of $24.50 is taken as representing the fair market value per bond as of the date of the gift

$$\frac{((1 \times 23) + (3 \times 25))}{4}$$

Example (5). Assume that no bonds were traded on the date of the gift (Friday, April 20). Assume further, that sales of bonds nearest the date of the gift occurred two trading days before (Wednesday, April 18) and three trading days after (Wednesday, April 25) the date of the gift and that on these two days the closing selling prices per bond were $29 and $22, respectively. The highest and lowest selling prices are not available for these dates in a generally available listing or publication of general circulation. Thus, under paragraph (b)(2) of this section the price of $26.20 is taken as representing the fair market value of a bond as of the date of the gift

$$\frac{((3 \times 29) + (2 \times 22))}{5}$$

(c) *Based on bid and asked prices.*—If the provisions of paragraph (b) of this section are inapplicable because actual sales are not available during a reasonable period beginning before and ending after the date of the gift, the fair market value may be determined by taking the mean between the bona fide bid and asked prices on the date of the gift, or if none, by taking a weighted average of the means between the bona fide bid and asked prices on the nearest trading date before and the nearest trading date after the date of the gift, if both such nearest dates are within a reasonable period. The average is to be determined in the manner described in paragraph (b) of this section.

(d) *Where selling prices and bid and asked prices are not available for dates both before and after the date of gift.*—If the provisions of paragraphs (b) and (c) of this section are inapplicable because no actual sale prices or quoted bona fide bid and asked prices are available on a date within a reasonable period before the date of the gift, but such prices are available on a date within a reasonable period after the date of the gift, or vice versa, then the mean between the highest and lowest available sale prices or bid and asked prices may be taken as the value.

(e) *Where selling prices or bid and asked prices do not represent fair market value.*—In cases in which it is established that the value per bond or share of any security determined on the basis of the selling or bid and asked prices as provided under paragraphs (b), (c), and (d) of this section does not represent the fair market value thereof, then some reasonable modification of the value determined on that basis or other relevant facts and elements of value shall be considered in determining fair market value. Where sales at or near the date of the gift are few or of a sporadic nature, such sales alone may not indicate fair market value. In certain exceptional cases, the size of the block of securities made the subject of each separate gift in relation to the number of shares changing hands in sales may be relevant in determining whether selling prices reflect the fair market value of the block of stock to be valued. If the donor can show that the block of stock to be valued, with reference to each separate gift, is so large in relation to the actual sales on the existing market that it could not be liquidated in a reasonable time without depressing the market, the price at which the block could be sold as such outside the usual market, as through an underwriter, may be a more accurate indication of value than market quotations. Complete data in support of any allowance claimed due to the size of the block of stock being valued should be submitted with the return. On the other hand, if the block of stock to be valued represents a controlling interest, either actual or effective, in a going business, the price at which other lots change hands may have little relation to its true value.

(f) *Where selling prices or bid and asked prices are unavailable.*—If the provisions of paragraphs (b), (c), and (d) of this section are inapplicable because actual sale prices and bona fide bid and asked prices are lacking, then the fair market value is to be determined by taking the following factors into consideration:

Reg. §25.2512-2(f)

(1) In the case of corporate or other bonds, the soundness of the security, the interest yield, the date of maturity, and other relevant factors; and

(2) In the case of shares of stock, the company's net worth, prospective earning power and dividend-paying capacity, and other relevant factors.

Some of the "other relevant factors" referred to in subparagraphs (1) and (2) of this paragraph are: the good will of the business; the economic outlook in the particular industry; the company's position in the industry and its management; the degree of control of the business represented by the block of stock to be valued; and the values of securities of corporations engaged in the same or similar lines of business which are listed on a stock exchange. However, the weight to be accorded such comparisons or any other evidentiary factors considered in the determination of a value depends upon the facts of each case. Complete financial and other data upon which the valuation is based should be submitted with the return, including copies of reports of any examinations of the company have been made by accountants, engineers, or any technical experts as of or near the date of the gift. [Reg. § 25.2512-2.]

☐ [*T.D.* 6334, 11-14-58. *Amended by T.D.* 7327, 9-30-74 *and by T.D.* 7432, 9-10-76.]

[Reg. § 25.2512-3]

§ 25.2512-3. Valuation of interests in businesses.—(a) Care should be taken to arrive at an accurate valuation of any interest in a business which the donor transfers without an adequate and full consideration in money or money's worth. The fair market value of any interest in a business, whether a partnership or a proprietorship, is the net amount which a willing purchaser, whether an individual or a corporation, would pay for the interest to a willing seller, neither being under any compulsion to buy or to sell and both having reasonable knowledge of the relevant facts. The net value is determined on the basis of all relevant factors including—

(1) A fair appraisal as of the date of the gift of all the assets of the business, tangible and intangible, including good will;

(2) The demonstrated earning capacity of the business; and

(3) The other factors set forth in paragraph (f) of § 25.2512-2 relating to the valuation of corporate stock, to the extent applicable.

Special attention should be given to determining an adequate value of the good will of the business. Complete financial and other data upon which the valuation is based should be submitted with the return, including copies of reports of examinations of the business made by accountants, engineers, or any technical experts as of or near the date of the gift. [Reg. § 25.2512-3.]

☐ [*T.D.* 6334, 11-14-58.]

[Reg. § 25.2512-4]

§ 25.2512-4. Valuation of notes.—The fair market value of notes, secured or unsecured, is presumed to be the amount of unpaid principal, plus accrued interest to the date of the gift, unless the donor establishes a lower value. Unless returned at face value, plus accrued interest, it must be shown by satisfactory evidence that the note is worth less than the unpaid amount (because of the interest rate, or date of maturity, or other cause), or that the note is uncollectible in part (by reason of the insolvency of the party or parties liable, or for other cause), and that the property, if any, pledged or mortgaged as security is insufficient to satisfy it. [Reg. § 25.2512-4.]

☐ [*T.D.* 6334, 11-14-58.]

[Reg. § 25.2512-5]

§ 25.2512-5. Valuation of annuities, unitrust interests, interests for life or term of years, and remainder or reversionary interests.—(a) *In general.*—Except as otherwise provided in paragraph(b) of this section and § 25.7520-3(b), the fair market value of annuities, unitrust interests, life estates, terms of years, remainders, and reversions transferred by gift is the present value of the interests determined under paragraph (d) of this section. Section 20.2031-7 of this chapter (Estate Tax Regulations) and related sections provide tables with standard actuarial factors and examples that illustrate how to use the tables to compute the present value of ordinary annuity, life, and remainder interests in property. These sections also refer to standard and special actuarial factors that may be necessary to compute the present value of similar interests in more unusual fact situations. These factors and examples are also generally applicable for gift tax purposes in computing the values of taxable gifts.

(b) *Commercial annuities and insurance contracts.*—The value of life insurance contracts and contracts for the payment of annuities issued by companies regularly engaged in their sale is determined under § 25.2512-6.

(c) *Actuarial valuations.*—The present value of annuities, unitrust interests, life estates, terms of years, remainders, and reversions transferred by gift on or after May 1, 2009, is determined under paragraph (d) of this section. The present value of annuities, unitrust interests, life estates, terms of years, remainders, and reversions transferred by gift before May 1, 2009, is determined under the following sections:

Transfers		Applicable
After	Before	Regulations
-	01-01-52	25.2512-5A(a)
12-31-51	01-01-71	25.2512-5A(b)

| Transfers | | Applicable |
After	Before	Regulations
12-31-70	12-01-83	25.2512-5A(c)
11-30-83	05-01-89	25.2512-5A(d)
04-30-89	05-01-99	25.2512-5A(e)
04-30-99	05-01-09	25.2512-5A(f)

(d) *Actuarial valuations on or after May 1, 2009.*—(1) *In general.*—Except as otherwise provided in paragraph (b) of this section and §25.7520-3(b) (relating to exceptions to the use of prescribed tables under certain circumstances), if the valuation date for the gift is on or after May 1, 2009, the fair market value of annuities, life estates, terms of years, remainders, and reversions transferred on or after May 1, 2009, is the present value of such interests determined under paragraph (d)(2) of this section and by use of standard or special section 7520 actuarial factors. These factors are derived by using the appropriate section 7520 interest rate and, if applicable, the mortality component for the valuation date of the interest that is being valued. See §§25.7520-1 through 25.7520-4. The fair market value of a qualified annuity interest described in section 2702(b)(1) and a qualified unitrust interest described in section 2702(b)(2) is the present value of such interests determined under §25.7520-1(c).

(2) *Specific interests.*—When the donor transfers property in trust or otherwise and retains an interest therein, generally, the value of the gift is the value of the property transferred less the value of the donor's retained interest. However, if the donor transfers property after October 8, 1990, to or for the benefit of a member of the donor's family, the value of the gift is the value of the property transferred less the value of the donor's retained interest as determined under section 2702. If the donor assigns or relinquishes an annuity, life estate, remainder, or reversion that the donor holds by virtue of a transfer previously made by the donor or another, the value of the gift is the value of the interest transferred. However, see section 2519 for a special rule in the case of the assignment of an income interest by a person who received the interest from a spouse.

(i) *Charitable remainder trusts.*—The fair market value of a remainder interest in a pooled income fund, as defined in §1.642(c)-5 of this chapter, is its value determined under §1.642(c)-6(e) (see §1.642(c)-6A for certain prior periods). The fair market value of a remainder interest in a charitable remainder annuity trust, as described in §1.664-2(a), is its present value determined under §1.664-2(c). The fair market value of a remainder interest in a charitable remainder unitrust, as defined in §1.664-3, is its present value determined under §1.664-4(e). The fair market value of a life interest or term for years in a charitable remainder unitrust is the fair market value of the property as of the date of

transfer less the fair market value of the remainder interest, determined under §1.664-4(e)(4) and (e)(5).

(ii) *Ordinary remainder and reversionary interests.*—If the interest to be valued is to take effect after a definite number of years or after the death of one individual, the present value of the interest is computed by multiplying the value of the property by the appropriate remainder interest actuarial factor (that corresponds to the applicable section 7520 interest rate and remainder interest period) in Table B (for a term certain) or in Table S (for one measuring life), as the case may be. Table B is contained in §20.2031-7(d)(6) of this chapter and Table S (for one measuring life when the valuation date is on or after May 1, 2009) is included in §20.2031-7(d)(7) and Internal Revenue Service Publication 1457. See §20.2031-7A containing Table S for valuation of interests before May 1, 2009. For information about obtaining actuarial factors for other types of remainder interests, see paragraph (d)(4) of this section.

(iii) *Ordinary term-of-years and life interests.*—If the interest to be valued is the right of a person to receive the income of certain property, or to use certain nonincome-producing property, for a term of years or for the life of one individual, the present value of the interest is computed by multiplying the value of the property by the appropriate term-of-years or life interest actuarial factor (that corresponds to the applicable section 7520 interest rate and term-of-years or life interest period). Internal Revenue Service Publication 1457 includes actuarial factors for a remainder interest after a term of years in Table B and after the life of one individual in Table S (for one measuring life when the valuation date is on or after May 1, 2009). However, term-of-years and life interest actuarial factors are not included in Table B in §20.2031-7(d)(6) of this chapter or Table S in §20.2031-7(d)(7) (or in §20.2031-7A). If Internal Revenue Service Publication 1457 (or any other reliable source of term-of-years and life interest actuarial factors) is not conveniently available, an actuarial factor for the interest may be derived mathematically. This actuarial factor may be derived by subtracting the correlative remainder factor (that corresponds to the applicable section 7520 interest rate) in Table B (for a term of years) in §20.2031-7(d)(6) or in Table S (for the life of one individual) in §20.2031-7(d)(7), as the case may be, from 1.000000. For information about obtaining actuarial factors for other types of term-of-years and life interests, see paragraph (d)(4) of this section.

Reg. §25.2512-5(d)(2)(iii)

(iv) *Annuities.*—(A) If the interest to be valued is the right of a person to receive an annuity that is payable at the end of each year for a term of years or for the life of one individual, the present value of the interest is computed by multiplying the aggregate amount payable annually by the appropriate annuity actuarial factor (that corresponds to the applicable section 7520 interest rate and annuity period). Internal Revenue Service Publication 1457 includes actuarial factors in Table B (for a remainder interest after an annuity payable for a term of years) and in Table S (for a remainder interest after an annuity payable for the life of one individual when the valuation date is on or after May 1, 2009). However, annuity actuarial factors are not included in Table B in §20.2031-7(d)(6) of this chapter or Table S in §20.2031-7(d)(7) (or in §20.2031-7A). If Internal Revenue Service Publication 1457 (or any other reliable source of annuity actuarial factors) is not conveniently available, an annuity factor for a term of years or for one life may be derived mathematically. This annuity factor may be derived by subtracting the applicable remainder factor (that corresponds to the applicable section 7520 interest rate and annuity period) in Table B (in the case of a term-of-years annuity) in §20.2031-7(d)(6) or in Table S (in the case of a one-life annuity) in §20.2031-7(d)(7), as the case may be, from 1.000000 and then dividing the result by the applicable section 7520 interest rate expressed as a decimal number. See §20.2031-7(d)(2)(iv) for an example that illustrates the computation of the present value of an annuity.

(B) If the annuity is payable at the end of semiannual, quarterly, monthly, or weekly periods, the product obtained by multiplying the annuity factor by the aggregate amount payable annually is then multiplied by the applicable adjustment factor set forth in Table K in §20.2031-7(d)(6) at the appropriate interest rate component for payments made at the end of the specified periods. The provisions of this paragraph (d)(2)(iv)(B) are illustrated by the following example:

Example. In July of a year after 2009 but before 2019, the donor agreed to pay the annuitant the sum of $10,000 per year, payable in equal semiannual installments at the end of each period. The semiannual installments are to be made on each December 31st and June 30th. The annuity is payable until the annuitant's death. On the date of the agreement, the annuitant is 68 years and 5 months old. The donee annuitant's age is treated as 68 for purposes of computing the present value of the annuity. The section 7520 rate on the date of the agreement is 6.6 percent. Under Table S in §20.2031-7(d)(7), the factor at 6.6 percent for determining the present

value of a remainder interest payable at the death of an individual aged 68 is .42001. Converting the remainder factor to an annuity factor, as described above, the annuity factor for determining the present value of an annuity transferred to an individual age 68 is 8.7877 (1.000000 minus .42001 divided by .066). The adjustment factor from Table K in §20.2031-7(d)(6) in the column for payments made at the end of each semiannual period at the rate of 6.6 percent is 1.0162. The aggregate annual amount of the annuity, $10,000, is multiplied by the factor 8.7877 and the product is multiplied by 1.0162. The present value of the donee's annuity is, therefore, $89,300.61 ($10,000 × 8.7877 × 1.0162).

(C) If an annuity is payable at the beginning of annual, semiannual, quarterly, monthly, or weekly periods for a term of years, the value of the annuity is computed by multiplying the aggregate amount payable annually by the annuity factor described in paragraph (d)(2)(iv)(A) of this section; and the product so obtained is then multiplied by the adjustment factor in Table J in §20.2031-7(d)(6) of this chapter at the appropriate interest rate component for payments made at the beginning of specified periods. If an annuity is payable at the beginning of annual, semiannual, quarterly, monthly, or weekly periods for one or more lives, the value of the annuity is the sum of the first payment and the present value of a similar annuity, the first payment of which is not to be made until the end of the payment period, determined as provided in paragraph (d)(2)(iv)(B) of this section.

(v) *Annuity and unitrust interests for a term of years or until the prior death of an individual.*—(A) *Annuity interests.*—The present value of an annuity interest that is payable until the earlier to occur of the lapse of a specific number of years or the death of an individual may be computed with values from the tables in §§20.2031-7(d)(6) and 20.2031-7(d)(7) of this chapter as described in the following example:

Example. The donor transfers $100,000 into a trust early in 2010, and retains the right to receive an annuity from the trust in the amount of $6,000 per year, payable in equal semiannual installments at the end of each period. The semiannual installments are to be made on each June 30th and December 31st. The annuity is payable for 10 years or until the donor's prior death. At the time of the transfer, the donor is 59 years and 6 months old. The donor's age is deemed to be 60 for purposes of computing the present value of the retained annuity. If the section 7520 rate for the month in which the transfer occurs is 5.8 percent, the present value of the donor's retained interest would be $42,575.65, determined as follows:

TABLE S value at 5.8 percent, age 60 34656
TABLE S value at 5.8 percent, age 70 49025

Reg. §25.2512-5(d)(2)(iv)(A)

TABLE 2000CM value at age 70	74794
TABLE 2000CM value at age 60	87595
TABLE B value at 5.8 percent, 10 years	.569041
TABLE K value at 5.8 percent	1.0143

Factor for donor's retained interest at 5.8 percent:

$$\frac{(1.00000 - .34656) - (.569041 \times (74794/87595) \times (1.00000 - .49025))}{.058} = 6.9959$$

Present value of donor's retained interest:

($6,000 × 6.9959 × 1.0143) $42,575.65

(B) *Unitrust interests.*—The present value of a unitrust interest that is payable until the earlier to occur of the lapse of a specific number of years or the death of an individual may be computed with values from the tables in §§ 1.664-4(e)(6) and 1.664-4(e)(7) of this chapter as described in the following example:

Example. The donor who, as of the nearest birthday, is 60 years old, transfers $100,000 to a unitrust on January 1st of a year after 2009 but before 2019. The trust instrument requires that each year the trust pay to the donor, in equal semiannual installments on June 30th and December 31st, 6 percent of the fair market value of the trust assets, valued as of January 1st each year, for 10 years or until the prior death of the donor. The section 7520 rate for the January in which the transfer occurs is 6.6 percent. Under Table F(6.6) in § 1.664-4(e)(6), the appropriate adjustment factor is .953317 for semiannual payments payable at the end of the semiannual period. The adjusted payout rate is 5.720 percent (6% × .953317). The present value of the donor's retained interest is $41,920.00 determined as follows:

TABLE U(1) value at 5.6 percent, age 60	.33970
TABLE U(1) value at 5.6 percent, age 70	.48352
TABLE 2000CM value at age 70	74794
TABLE 2000CM value at age 60	87595
TABLE D value at 5.6 percent, 10 years	.561979

Factor for donor's retained interest at 5.6 percent:

(1.000000 −.33970) − (.561979 × (74794/87595) × (1.000000 − .48352)) = .41247

TABLE U(1) value at 5.8 percent, age 60	.32846
TABLE U(1) value at 5.8 percent, age 70	.47241
TABLE 2000CM value at age 70	74794
TABLE 2000CM value at age 60	87595
TABLE D value at 5.8 percent, 10 years	.550185

Factor for donor's retained interest at 5.8 percent:

(1.000000 − .32846) − (.550185 × (74974/87595) × (1.000000 − .47241)) = .42369

Difference .... .01122

Interpolation adjustment:

$$\frac{5.720\% - 5.6\%}{0.2\%} = \frac{\times}{.01122}$$

x = .00673

Factor at 5.6 percent, age 60	.41247
Plus: Interpolation adjustment	.00673
Interpolated Factor	.41920

Present value of donor's retained interest:

($100,000 × .41920) $41,920.00

(3) *Transitional rule.*—If the valuation date of a transfer of property by gift is on or after May 1, 2009, and before July 1, 2009, the fair market value of the interest transferred is determined by use of the section 7520 interest rate for the month in which the valuation date occurs (see §§ 25.7520-1(b) and 25.7520-2(a)(2)) and the appropriate actuarial tables under either § 20.2031-7(d)(7) or § 20.2031-7A(f)(4) of this chapter, at the option of the donor. However, with respect to each individual transaction and with respect to all transfers occurring on the valuation date, the donor must use the same actuarial tables (for example, gift and income tax charitable deductions with respect to the same transfer must be determined based on the same tables, and all transfers made on the same date must be valued based on the same tables).

(4) *Publications and actuarial computations by the Internal Revenue Service.*—Many standard actuarial factors not included in § 20.2031-7(d)(6) or § 20.2031-7(d)(7) of this chapter are included in Internal Revenue Service Publication 1457, "Actuarial Valuations Version 3A" (2009). Internal Revenue Service Publication 1457 also includes examples that illustrate how to compute many special factors for more unusual situations. A copy of this publication is available, at no charge, electronically via the IRS Internet site at *www.irs.gov*. If a special factor is required in the case of a completed gift, the Internal Revenue Service may furnish the factor to the donor upon a request for a ruling. The request for a ruling must be accompanied by a recitation of the facts including a statement of the date of birth for each measuring life, the date of the gift, any other applicable dates, and a copy of the will, trust, or other relevant documents. A request for a ruling must comply with the instructions for requesting a ruling published periodically in the Internal Revenue Bulletin (see §§ 601.201 and 601.601(d)(2)(ii)(b) of this chapter) and include payment of the required user fee.

(e) *Effective/applicability dates.*—This section applies on and after May 1, 2009. [Reg. § 25.2512-5.]

☐ [*T.D.* 8540, 6-9-94. *Amended by T.D.* 8819, 4-29-99; *T.D.* 8886, 6-9-2000 (*corrected 9-27-2000*); *T.D.* 9448-5-1-2009 *and T.D.* 9540, 8-9-2011.]

[Reg. § 25.2512-5A]

§ 25.2512-5A. Valuation of annuities, unitrust interests, interests for life or term of years, and remainder or reversionary interests transferred before May 1, 2009.—(a) *Valuation of annuities, interests for life or term of years, and remainder or reversionary interests transferred before January 1, 1952.*—Except as otherwise provided in § 25.2512-5(b), if the transfer was made before January 1, 1952, the present value of annuities, life estates, terms of years, remainders, and reversions is their present value determined under this section. If the valuation of the interest involved is dependent upon the continuation or termination of one or more lives or upon a term certain concurrent with one or more lives, the factor for the present value is computed on the basis of interest at the rate of 4 percent a year, compounded annually, and life contingencies for each life involved from values that are based upon the "Actuaries' or Combined Experience Table of Mortality, as extended." This table and many additional factors are described in former § 86.19 (as contained in the 26 CFR Part 81 edition revised as of April 1, 1958). The present value of an interest measured by a term of years is computed on the basis of interest at the rate of 4 percent a year.

(b) *Valuation of annuities, interests for life or term of years, and remainder or reversionary interests transferred after December 31, 1951, and before January 1, 1971.*—Except as otherwise provided in § 25.2512-5(b), the present value of annuities, life estates, terms of years, remainders, and reversions transferred after December 31, 1951, and before January 1, 1971, is the present value of such interests determined under this section. If the value of the interest involved is dependent upon the continuation or termination of one or more lives, the factor for the present value is computed on the basis of interest at the rate of $3^1/_2$ percent a year, compounded annually, and life contingencies for each life involved from U.S. Life Table 38. This table and many accompanying factors are set forth in former § 25.2512-5 (as contained in the 26 CFR Part 25 edition revised as of April 1, 1984). Special factors involving one and two lives may be found in or computed with the use of tables contained in Internal Revenue Service Publication Number 11, "Actuarial Values for Estate and Gift Tax," (Rev. 5-59). This publication is no longer available for purchase from the Superintendent of Documents. However, it may be obtained by requesting a copy from: CC:DOM:CORP:T:R (IRS Publication 11), room 5228, Internal Revenue Service, POB 7604, Ben Franklin Station, Washington, DC 20044. The present value of an interest measured by a term of years is computed on the basis of interest at the rate of $3^1/_2$ percent a year.

(c) *Valuation of annuities, interests for life or term of years, and remainder or reversionary interests transferred after December 31, 1970, and before December 1, 1983.*—Except as otherwise provided in § 25.2512-5(b), the present value of annuities, life estates, terms of years, remainders, and reversions transferred after December 31, 1970, and before December 1, 1983, is the present value of such interests determined under this section. If the interest to be valued is dependent upon the continuation or termination of one or more lives or upon a term certain concurrent with one or more lives, the factor for the present value is computed on the basis of interest at the rate of 6 percent a year, compounded annually, and life contingencies determined for each male and female life involved, from the values that are set forth in Table LN. Table LN contains values that are taken from the life table for total males and the life table for total females appearing as Tables 2 and 3, respectively, in United States Life Tables: 1959-61, published by the Department of Health and Human Services, Public Health Service. Table LN and accompanying factors are set forth in former § 25.2512-9 (as contained in the 26 CFR Part 25 edition revised as of April 1, 1994). Special factors involving one and two lives may be found in or computed with the use of tables contained in Internal Revenue Service Publication 723, entitled "Actuarial Values I: Valuation of Last Survivor Charitable Remainders" (12-70), and Internal Revenue Service Publication 723A, entitled "Actuarial Values II: Factors at 6 Percent Involving One and Two Lives" (12-70). These publications are no longer available for purchase from the Superintendent of Documents. However, a copy of each may be obtained from: CC:DOM:CORP:T:R (IRS Publication 723/723A), room 5228, Internal Revenue Service, POB 7604, Ben Franklin Station, Washington, DC 20044. The present value of an interest measured by a term of years is computed on the basis of interest at the rate of 6 percent a year.

(d) *Valuation of annuities, interests for life or term of years, and remainder or reversionary interests transferred after November 30, 1983, and before May 1, 1989.*—(1) *In general.*—(i)(A) Except as otherwise provided in § 25.2512-5(b) and in this paragraph (d)(1)(i)(A), the fair market value of annuities, life estates, terms of years, remainders, and reversions transferred after November 30, 1983, and before May 1, 1989, is the present value of such interests determined under this section. The value of annuities issued by companies regularly engaged in their sale and of insurance policies issued by companies regularly engaged in their sale is determined under § 25.2512-6. The fair market value of a remainder interest in a charitable remainder unitrust, as defined in § 1.664-3, is its present value determined under § 1.664-4. The fair market value of a life interest or term for years in a charitable remainder unitrust is the fair market value of the property as of the date of transfer less the fair market value of the remainder interest on such date determined under § 1.664-4. The fair market value of interests in a pooled income fund, as defined in § 1.642(c)-5, is their value determined under § 1.642(c)-6. Where the donor transfers property in trust or otherwise and retains an interest therein, the value of the gift is the value of the property transferred less the value of the donor's retained interest. See section 2702 and the regulations at § 25.2702 for special rules for valuing transfers of interests in trust after October 8, 1990. See § 25.2512-9 with respect to the valuation of annuities, life estates, terms for years, remainders, and reversions transferred after December 31, 1970, and before December 1, 1983.

(B) If the donor transfers in December of 1983, either—

(1) A remainder or a reversion subject to a life interest or a term for years where the life interest or term for years was transferred by the donor after December 31, 1982, and before December 1, 1983, or

(2) A life interest or term for years, the remainder interest of which was transferred by the donor after December 31, 1982, and before December 1, 1983,

the donor shall make an election. The donor may elect to value both interests transferred in 1983 under § 25.2512-5A(c) as if such section applied to all transfers made before January 1, 1984, or the donor may elect to have both interests transferred valued under this section. The donor shall indicate the election being made in a statement attached to the donor's gift tax return for 1983.

(C) If the donor transfers in calendar year 1984, either—

(1) A remainder on [or] a reversion subject to a life interest or a term for years where the life interest or term for years was transferred by the donor in the first eleven months of 1983, or

(2) A life interest or term for years, the remainder interest of which was transferred by the donor in the first eleven months of 1983,

the donor shall make an election. The donor may elect to value the interest transferred in 1984 under § 25.2512-5A(c) as if such section applied to all transfers made before January 1, 1985, or the donor may elect to have the transfer valued under this section. If the donor elects to value the interest transferred in 1984 under § 25.2512-5A(c), the donor shall indicate that the election is being made by attaching a statement to the donor's gift tax return for 1984. If the donor elects to value the interest transferred in 1984 under this section the election shall not be effective unless the donor declares, in a statement attached to the donor's gift tax return for 1984, that the donor has filed an amended gift tax return for 1983, in which the donor has revalued the transfers made in the first eleven months of 1983 under this section as if this section applied to transfers made after December 31, 1982.

(ii) The present value of an annuity, life estate, remainder, or reversion determined under this section which is dependent on the continuation or termination of the life of one person is computed by the use of Table A in paragraph (d)(6) of this section. The present value of an annuity, term for years, remainder, or reversion dependent on a term certain is computed by the use of Table B in paragraph (d)(6) of this section. If the interest to be valued is dependent upon more than one life or there is a term certain concurrent with one or more lives, see paragraph (d)(5) of this section. For purposes of the computations described in this section, the age of the person is to be taken at his or her nearest birthday.

(iii) In all examples set forth in this section, the interest is assumed to have been transferred after November 30, 1983 and before May 1, 1989.

(2) *Annuities.*—(i) If an annuity is payable annually at the end of each year during the life of an individual (as for example if the first payment is due one year after the date of the gift), the amount payable annually is multiplied by the figure in column 2 of Table A opposite the number of years in column 1 nearest the age of the individual whose life measures the duration of the annuity. If the annuity is payable annually at the end of each year for a definite number of years, the amount payable annually is multiplied by the figure in column 2 of Table B opposite the number of years in column 1 representing the duration of the annuity.

The application of this paragraph (d)(2)(i) may be illustrated by the following examples:

Example (1). The donor assigns an annuity of $10,000 a year payable annually during the donor's life immediately after an annual payment has been made. The age of the donor on the date of assignment is 40 years and eight months. By reference to Table A, it is found that the figure in column 2 opposite 41 years is 9.1030. The value of the gift is, therefore, $91,030 ($10,000 multiplied by 9.1030).

Example (2). The donor was entitled to receive an annuity of $10,000 a year payable annually at the end of annual periods throughout a term of 20 years. The donor, when 15 years have elapsed, makes a gift thereof to the donor's son. By reference to Table B, it is found that the figure in column 2 opposite five years, the unexpired portion of the 20-year period, is 3.7906. The present value of the annuity is, therefore, $37,908 ($10,000 multiplied by 3.7908).

(ii) If an annuity is payable at the end of semiannual, quarterly, monthly, or weekly periods during the life of an individual (as for example if the first payment is due one month after the date of the gift), the aggregate amount to be paid within a year is first multiplied by the figure in column 2 of Table A opposite the number of years in column 1 nearest the age of the individual whose life measures the duration of the annuity. The product so obtained is then multiplied by whichever of the following factors is appropriate:

1.0244 for semiannual payments,
1.0368 for quarterly payments,

1.0450 for monthly payments,
1.0482 for weekly payments.

If the annuity is payable at the end of semiannual, quarterly, monthly, or weekly periods for a definite number of years the aggregate amount to be paid within a year is first multiplied by the figure in column 2 of Table B opposite the number of years in column 1 representing the duration of the annuity. The product so obtained is then multiplied by whichever of the above factors is appropriate. The application of this paragraph (d)(2)(ii) may be illustrated by the following example:

Example. The facts are the same as those contained in example (1) set forth in paragraph (d)(2)(i) above, except that the annuity is payable semiannually. The aggregate annual amount, $10,000[,] is multiplied by the factor 9.1030, and the product multiplied by 1.0244. The value of the gift is, therefore, $93,251.13 ($10,000 × 9.1030 ×1.0244).

(iii)(A) If the first payment of an annuity for the life of an individual is due at the beginning of the annual or other payment period rather than at the end (as for example if the first payment is to be made immediately after the date of the gift), the value of the annuity is the sum of (A) the first payment plus (B) the present value of a similar annuity, the first payment of which is not to be made until the end of the payment period, determined as provided in paragraphs (d)(2)(i) or (ii) of this section. The application of this paragraph (d)(2)(iii)(A) may be illustrated by the following example:

Example. The donee is made the beneficiary for life of an annuity of $50 a month from the income of a trust, subject to the right reserved by the donor to cause the annuity to be paid for the donor's own benefit or for the benefit of another. On the day a payment is due, the donor relinquishes the reserved power. The donee is then 50 years of age. The value of the gift is $50 plus the product of $50 × 12 × 8.4743 (see Table A) × 1.0450. That is, $50 plus $5,313.39, or $5,363.39.

(B) If the first payment of an annuity for a definite number of years is due at the beginning of the annual or other payment period, the applicable factor is the product of the factor shown in Table B multiplied by whichever of the following factors is appropriate:

1.1000 for annual payments,
1.0744 for semiannual payments,
1.0618 for quarterly payments,
1.0534 for monthly payments,or
1.0502 for weekly payments.

The application of this paragraph (d)(2)(iii)(B) may be illustrated by the following example:

Example. The donee is the beneficiary of an annuity of $50 a month, subject to a reserved right in the donor to cause the annuity or the cash value thereof to be paid for the donor's own benefit or the benefit of another. On the day a payment is due, the donor relinquishes the power. There are 308 payments to be made covering a period of 25 years, including the payment due. The value of the gift is the product of $50 × 12 × 9,0770 (factor for 25 years Table B) × 1.0534, or $5,737.03.

(3) *Life estates and terms for years.*—If the interest to be valued is the right of a person for his or her life, or for the life of another person, to receive the income of certain property or to use non-income-producing property, the value of the interest is the value of the property multiplied by the figure in column 3 of Table A opposite the number of years nearest to the actual age of the measuring life. If the interest to be valued is the right to receive income of property or to use non-income-producing property for a term of years, column 3 of Table B is used. The application of this paragraph (c) may be illustrated by the following example:

Example. The donor who during the donor's life is entitled to receive the income from property worth $50,000, makes a gift of such interest. The donor is 31 years old on the date of the gift. The value of the gift is $47,627 ($50,000 × .95254).

(4) *Remainders or reversionary interests.*—If the interest to be valued is a remainder or reversionary interest subject to a life estate, the value of the interest should be obtained by multiplying the value of the property at the date of the gift by the figure in column 4 of Table A opposite the number of years nearest the age of the life tenant. If the remainder or reversion is to take effect at the end of a term for years, column 4 of Table B should be used. The application of this paragraph (d) may be illustrated by the following example:

Example. The donor transfers by gift a remainder interest in property worth $50,000, subject to the donor's sister's right to receive the income therefrom for her life. The sister at the date of the gift is 31 years of age. By reference to Table A it is found that the figure in column 4 opposite age 31 is .04746. The value of the gift is, therefore, $2,373 ($50,000 × .04746).

(5) *Actuarial computations by the Internal Revenue Service.*—If the interest to be valued is dependent upon the continuation or termination of more than one life, or there is a term certain concurrent with one or more lives, or if the retained interest of the donor is conditioned upon survivorship, a special factor is necessary. The factor is to be computed on the basis of interest at the rate of 10 percent a year, compounded annually, and life contingencies are determined for each person involved from the values of lx that are set forth in column 2 of Table LN in §20.2031-7A(d)(6) of this chapter. Table LN contains values of lx taken from the life table for the total population appearing as Table 1 in United States Life Tables: 1969-71, published by the Department of Health and Human Services, Public

Health Service. A copy of the publication containing many such special factors, may be purchased from the Superintendent of Documents, United States Government Printing Office, Washington, D.C. 20402. However, if a special factor is required in the case of an actual gift, the Commissioner will furnish the factor to the donor upon request. The request must be accompanied by a statement of the date of birth of each person the duration of whose life may affect the value of the interest, and by copies of the relevant instruments. Special factors are not furnished for prospective transfers.

(6) *Tables.*—(i) For actuarial factors showing the present worth at 10 percent of a single life annuity, a life interest, and a remainder interest postponed for a single life, see §20.2031-7A(d)(6) of this chapter, Table A, of the Estate Tax Regulations.

(ii) For actuarial factors showing the present worth at 10 percent of an annuity for a term certain, an income interest for a term certain, and a remainder interest postponed for a term certain, see §20.2031-7A(d)(6) of this chapter, Table B, of the Estate Tax Regulations.

(e) *Valuation of annuities, unitrust interests, interests for life or term of years, and remainder or reversionary interests transferred after April 30, 1989, and before May 1, 1999.*—(1) *In general.*— Except as otherwise provided in §§25.2512-5(b) and 25.7520-3(b) (pertaining to certain limitations on the use of prescribed tables), if the valuation date of the transferred interest is after April 30, 1989, and before May 1, 1999, the fair market value of annuities, unitrust interests, life estates, terms of years, remainders, and reversions transferred by gift is the present value of the interests determined by use of standard or special section 7520 actuarial factors and the valuation methodology described in §25.2512-5(d). Sections 20.2031-7(d)(6) and 20.2031-7A(e)(4) of this chapter and related sections provide tables with standard actuarial factors and examples that illustrate how to use the tables to compute the present value of ordinary annuity, life, and remainder interests in property. These sections also refer to standard and special actuarial factors that may be necessary to compute the present value of similar interests in more unusual fact situations. These factors and examples are also generally applicable for gift tax purposes in computing the values of taxable gifts.

(2) *Transitional rule.*—(i) If the valuation date of a transfer of an interest in property by gift is after April 30, 1989, and before June 10, 1994, a donor can rely on Notice 89-24 (1989-1 C.B. 660), or Notice 89-60 (1989-1 C.B. 700), in valuing the transferred interest. (See §601.601(d)(2)(ii)(*b*) of this chapter.)

(ii) If a donor transferred an interest in property by gift after December 31, 1988, and before May 1, 1989, retaining an interest in the same property, and after April 30, 1989, and before January 1, 1990, transferred the retained interest in property, the donor may, at the option of the donor, value the transfer of the retained interest under this paragraph (e) or paragraph (d) of this section.

(3) *Publications and actuarial computations by the Internal Revenue Service.*—Many standard actuarial factors not included in §§ 20.2031-7(d)(6) and 20.2031-7A(e)(4) of this chapter are included in Internal Revenue Service Publication 1457, "Actuarial Values, Alpha Volume," (8-89). Internal Revenue Service Publication 1457 also includes examples that illustrate how to compute many special factors for more unusual situations. Publication 1457 is no longer available for purchase from the Superintendent of Documents, United States Government Printing Office, Washington, DC 20402. However, pertinent factors in this publication may be obtained from: CC:DOM:CORP:R (IRS Publication 1457), room 5226, Internal Revenue Service, POB 7604, Ben Franklin Station, Washington, DC 20044. If a special factor is required in the case of a completed gift, the Internal Revenue Service may furnish the factor to the donor upon a request for a ruling. The request for a ruling must be accompanied by a recitation of the facts including a statement of the date of birth for each measuring life, the date of the gift, any other applicable dates, and a copy of the will, trust, or other relevant documents. A request for a ruling must comply with the instructions for requesting a ruling published periodically in the Internal Revenue Bulletin (see §§ 601.201 and 601.601(d)(2)(ii)(*b*) of this chapter) and include payment of the required user fee.

(f) *Valuation of annuities, unitrust interests, interests for life or term of years, and remainder or reversionary interests transferred after April 30, 1999, and before May 1, 2009.*—(1) *In general.*— Except as otherwise provided in §§ 25.2512-5(b) and 25.7520-3(b) (pertaining to certain limitations on the use of prescribed tables), if the valuation date of the transferred interest is after April 30, 1999, and before May 1, 2009, the fair market value of annuities, unitrust interests, life estates, terms of years, remainders, and reversions transferred by gift is the present value of the interests determined by use of standard or special section 7520 actuarial factors and the valuation methodology described in § 25.2512-5(d). Sections 20.2031-7(d)(6) and 20.2031-7A(f)(4) and related sections provide tables with standard actuarial factors and examples that illustrate how to use the tables to compute the present value of ordinary annuity, life, and remainder interests in property. These sections also refer to standard and special actuarial factors that may be necessary to compute the present value of similar interests in more unusual fact situations. These

factors and examples are also generally applicable for gift tax purposes in computing the values of taxable gifts.

(2) *Transitional rule.*—If the valuation date of a transfer of property by gift is after April 30, 1999, and before July 1, 1999, the fair market value of the interest transferred is determined by use of the section 7520 interest rate for the month in which the valuation date occurs (see §§ 25.7520-1(b) and 25.7520-2(a)(2) and the appropriate actuarial tables under either § 20.2031-7A(e)(4) or § 20.2031-7A(f)(4), at the option of the donor. However, with respect to each individual transaction and with respect to all transfers occurring on the valuation date, the donor must use the same actuarial tables (for example, gift and income tax charitable deductions with respect to the same transfer must be determined based on the same tables, and all transfers made on the same date must be valued based on the same tables).

(3) *Publications and actuarial computations by the Internal Revenue Service.*—Many standard actuarial factors not included in §§ 20.2031-7(d)(6) and 20.2031-7A(f)(4) are included in Internal Revenue Service Publication 1457, "Actuarial Values, Book Aleph," (7-99). Internal Revenue Service Publication 1457 also includes examples that illustrate how to compute many special factors for more unusual situations. Publication 1457 is no longer available for purchase from the Superintendent of Documents, United States Government Printing Office. However, pertinent factors in this publication may be obtained from: CC:PA:LPD:PR (IRS Publication 1457), Room 5205, Internal Revenue Service, P.O.Box 7604, Ben Franklin Station, Washington, DC 20044. If a special factor is required in the case of a completed gift, the Internal Revenue Service may furnish the factor to the donor upon a request for a ruling. The request for a ruling must be accompanied by a recitation of the facts including a statement of the date of birth for each measuring life, the date of the gift, any other applicable dates, and a copy of the will, trust, or other relevant documents. A request for a ruling must comply with the instructions for requesting a ruling published periodically in the Internal Revenue Bulletin (see §§ 601.201 and 601.601(d)(2)(ii)(*b*)) and include payment of the required user fee.

(4) *Effective/applicability dates.*—Paragraphs (f)(1) through (f)(3) apply after April 30, 1999, and before May 1, 2009. [Reg. § 25.2512-5A.]

☐ [*T.D. 6334, 11-14-58. Amended by T.D. 7955, 5-10-84, T.D. 8395, 1-28-92. Reg. § 25.2512-5 was redesignated Reg. § 25.2512-5A(d) and amended by T.D. 8540, 6-9-94. Amended by T.D. 8819, 4-29-99; T.D. 8886, 6-9-2000; T.D. 9448, 5-1-2009 and T.D. 9540, 8-9-2011.]*

[Reg. §25.2512-6]

§25.2512-6. Valuation of certain life insurance and annuity contracts; valuation of shares in an open-end investment company.—
(a) *Valuation of certain life insurance and annuity contracts.*—The value of a life insurance contract or of a contract for the payment of an annuity issued by a company regularly engaged in the selling of contracts of that character is established through the sale of the particular contract by the company, or through the sale by the company of comparable contracts. As valuation of an insurance policy through sale of comparable contracts is not readily ascertainable when the gift is of a contract which has been in force for some time and on which further premium payments are to be made, the value may be approximated by adding to the interpolated terminal reserve at the date of the gift the proportionate part of the gross premium last paid before the date of the gift which covers the period extending beyond that date. If, however, because of the unusual nature of the contract such approximation is not reasonably close to the full value, this method may not be used.

The following examples, so far as relating to life insurance contracts, are of gifts of such contracts on which there are no accrued dividends or outstanding indebtedness.

Example (1). A donor purchases from a life insurance company for the benefit of another a life insurance contract or a contract for the payment of an annuity. The value of the gift is the cost of the contract.

Example (2). An annuitant purchased from a life insurance company a single payment annuity contract by the terms of which he was entitled to receive payments of $1,200 annually for the duration of his life. Five years subsequent to such purchase, and when the age of 50 years, he gratuitously assigns the contract. The value of the gift is the amount which the company would charge for an annuity contract providing for the payment of $1,200 annually for the life of a person 50 years of age.

Example (3). A donor owning a life insurance policy on which no further payments are to be made to the company (e.g., a single premium policy or paid-up policy) makes a gift of the contract. The value of the gift is the amount which the company would charge for a single premium contract of the same specified amount on the life of a person of the age of the insured.

Example (4). A gift is made four months after the last premium due date of an ordinary life insurance policy issued nine years and four months prior to the gift thereof by the insured, who was 35 years of age at date of issue. The gross annual premium is $2,811. The computation follows:

Terminal reserve at end of tenth year	$14,601.00
Terminal reserve at end of ninth year	12,965.00
Increase	$1,636.00
One-third of such increase (the gift having been made four months following the last preceding premium due date), is	$545.33
Terminal reserve at end of ninth year	12,965.00
Interpolated terminal reserve at the date of gift	$13,510.33
Two-thirds of gross premium ($2,811)	1,874.00
Value of the gift	$15,384.33

Example (5). A donor purchases from a life insurance company for $15,198 a joint and survivor annuity contract which provides for the payment of $60 a month to the donor during his lifetime, and then to his sister for such time as she may survive him. The premium which would have been charged by the company for an annuity of $60 monthly payable during the life of the donor alone is $10,690. The value of the gift is $4,508 ($15,198 less $10,690).

(b) *Valuation of shares in an open-end investment company.*—(1) The fair market value of a share in an open-end investment company (commonly known as a "mutual fund") is the public redemption price of a share. In the absence of an affirmative showing of the public redemption price in effect at the time of the gift, the last public redemption price quoted by the company for the date of the gift shall be presumed to be the applicable public redemption price. If there is no public redemption price quoted by the company for the date of the gift (e.g., the date of the gift is a Saturday, Sunday, or holiday), the fair market value of the mutual fund share is the last public redemption price quoted by the company for the first day preceding the date of the gift for which there is a quotation. As used in this paragraph the term "open-end investment company" includes only a company which on the date of the gift was engaged in offering its shares to the public in the capacity of an open-end investment company.

(2) The provisions of this paragraph shall apply with respect to gifts made after December 31, 1954. [Reg. §25.2512-6.]

☐ [*T.D.* 6334, 11-14-58. *Amended by T.D.* 6542, 1-19-61; *T.D.* 6680, 10-9-63 *and T.D.* 7319, 7-22-74.]

[Reg. § 25.2512-7]

§ 25.2512-7. Effect of excise tax.—If jewelry, furs or other property, the purchase of which is subject to an excise tax, is purchased at retail by a taxpayer and made the subject of gifts within a reasonable time after purchase, the purchase price, including the excise tax, is considered to be the fair market value of the property on the date of the gift, in the absence of evidence that the market price of similar articles has increased or decreased in the meantime. Under other circumstances, the excise tax is taken into account in determining the fair market value of property to the extent, and only to the extent, that it affects the price at which the property would change hands between a willing buyer and a willing seller, as provided in § 25.2512-1. [Reg. § 25.2512-7.]

☐ [*T.D.* 6334, 11-14-58.]

[Reg. § 25.2512-8]

§ 25.2512-8. Transfers for insufficient consideration.—Transfers reached by the gift tax are not confined to those only which, being without a valuable consideration, accord with the common law concept of gifts, but embrace as well sales, exchanges, and other dispositions of property for a consideration to the extent that the value of the property transferred by the donor exceeds the value in money or money's worth of the consideration given therefor. However, a sale, exchange, or other transfer of property made in the ordinary course of business (a transaction which is bona fide, at arm's length, and free from any donative intent), will be considered as made for an adequate and full consideration in money or money's worth. A consideration not reducible to a value in money or money's worth, as love and affection, promise of marriage, etc., is to be wholly disregarded, and the entire value of the property transferred constitutes the amount of the gift. Similarly, a relinquishment or promised relinquishment of dower or curtesy, or of a statutory estate created in lieu of dower or curtesy, or of other marital rights in the spouse's property or estate, shall not be considered to any extent a consideration "in money or money's worth." See, however, section 2516 and the regulations thereunder with respect to certain transfers incident to a divorce. See also sections 2701, 2702, 2703 and 2704 and the regulations at §§ 25.2701-0 through 25.2704-3 for special rules for valuing transfers of business interests, transfers in trust, and transfers pursuant to options and purchase agreements. [Reg. § 25.2512-8.]

☐ [*T.D.* 6334, 11-14-58. *Amended by T.D.* 8395, 1-28-92.]

[Reg. § 25.2513-1]

§ 25.2513-1. Gifts by husband or wife to third party considered as made one-half by each.—

(a) A gift made by one spouse to a person other than his (or her) spouse may, for the purpose of the gift tax, be considered as made one-half by him and one-half by his spouse, but only if at the time of the gift each spouse was a citizen or resident of the United States. For purposes of this section, an individual is to be considered as the spouse of another individual only if he was married to such individual at the time of the gift and does not remarry during the remainder of the "calendar period" (as defined in § 25.2502-1(c)(1)).

(b) The provisions of this section will apply to gifts made during a particular "calendar period" (as defined in § 25.2502-1(c)(1)) only if both spouses signify their consent to treat all gifts made to third parties during that calendar period by both spouses while married to each other as having been made one-half by each spouse. As to the manner and time for signifying consent, see § 25.2513-2. Such consent, if signified with respect to any calendar period, is effective with respect to all gifts made to third parties during such calendar period except as follows:

(1) If the consenting spouses were not married to each other during a portion of the calendar period, the consent is not effective with respect to any gifts made during such portion of the calendar period. Where the consent is signified by an executor or administrator of a deceased spouse, the consent is not effective with respect to gifts made by the surviving spouse during the portion of the calendar period that his spouse was deceased.

(2) If either spouse was a nonresident not a citizen of the United States during any portion of the calendar period, the consent is not effective with respect to any gift made during that portion of the calendar year.

(3) The consent is not effective with respect to a gift by one spouse of a property interest over which he created in his spouse a general power of appointment (as defined in section 2514(c)).

(4) If one spouse transferred property in part to his spouse and in part to third parties, the consent is effective with respect to the interest transferred to third parties only insofar as such interest is ascertainable at the time of the gift and hence severable from the interest transferred to his spouse. See § 25.2512-5 for the principles to be applied in the valuation of annuities, life estates, terms for years, remainders and reversions.

(5) The consent applies alike to gifts made by one spouse alone and to gifts made partly by each spouse, provided such gifts were to third parties and do not fall within any of the exceptions set forth in subparagraphs (1) through (4) of this paragraph. The consent may not be applied only to a portion of the property interest constituting such gifts. For example, a wife may not treat gifts made by her spouse from his separate property to third parties as having been made one-half by her if her spouse does not consent to treat gifts made by her to third parties

during the same calendar period as having been made one-half by him. If the consent is effectively signified on either the husband's return or the wife's return, all gifts made by the spouses to third parties (except as described in subparagraphs (1) through (4) of this paragraph), during the calendar period will be treated as having been made one-half by each spouse.

(c) If a husband and wife consent to have the gifts made to third party donees considered as made one-half by each spouse, and only one spouse makes gifts during the "calendar period" (as defined in § 25.2502-1(c)(1)), the other spouse is not required to file a gift tax return provided: (1) The total value of the gifts made to each third party donee since the beginning of the calendar year is not in excess of $20,000 ($6,000 for calendar years prior to 1982), and (2) no portion of the property transferred constitutes a gift of a future interest. If a transfer made by either spouse during the calendar period to a third party represents a gift of a future interest in property and the spouses consent to have the gifts considered as made one-half by each, a gift tax return for such calendar period must be filed by each spouse regardless of the value of the transfer. (See § 25.2503-3 for the definition of a future interest.)

(d) The following examples illustrate the application of this section relative to the requirements for the filing of a return, assuming that a consent was effectively signified:

(1) A husband made gifts valued at $7,000 during the second quarter of 1971 to a third party and his wife made no gifts during this time. Each spouse is required to file a return for the second calendar quarter of 1971.

(2) A husband made gifts valued at $5,000 to each of two third parties during the year 1970 and his wife made no gifts. Only the husband is required to file a return. (See § 25.6019-2.)

(3) During the third quarter of 1971, a husband made gifts valued at $5,000 to a third party, and his wife made gifts valued at $2,000 to the same third party. Each spouse is required to file a return for the third calendar quarter of 1971.

(4) A husband made gifts valued at $5,000 to a third party and his wife made gifts valued at $3,000 to another third party during the year 1970. Only the husband is required to file a return for the calendar year 1970. (See § 25.6019-2.)

(5) A husband made gifts valued at $2,000 during the first quarter of 1971 to third parties which represented gifts of future interests in property (see § 25.2503-3), and his wife made no gifts during such calendar quarter. Each spouse is required to file a return for the first calendar quarter of 1971. [Reg. § 25.2513-1.]

☐ [T.D. 6334, 11-14-58. *Amended by* T.D. 7238, 12-28-72 *and* T.D. 7910, 9-6-83.]

[Reg. § 25.2513-2]

§ 25.2513-2. Manner and time of signifying consent.—(a)(1) Consent to the application of the provisions of section 2513 with respect to a "calendar period" (as defined in § 25.2502-1(c)(1)) shall, in order to be effective, be signified by both spouses. If both spouses file gift tax returns within the time for signifying consent, it is sufficient if—

(i) The consent of the husband is signified on the wife's return, and the consent of the wife is signified on the husband's return;

(ii) The consent of each spouse is signified on his own return; or

(iii) The consent of both spouses is signified on one of the returns.

If only one spouse files a gift tax return within the time provided for signifying consent, the consent of both spouses shall be signified on that return. However, wherever possible, the notice of the consent is to be shown on both returns and it is preferred that the notice be executed in the manner described in subdivision (i) of this subparagraph. The consent may be revoked only as provided in § 25.2513-3. If one spouse files more than one gift tax return for a calendar period on or before the due date of the return, the last return so filed shall, for the purpose of determining whether a consent has been signified, be considered as that return. (See §§ 25.6075-1 and 25.6075-2 for the due date of a gift tax return.)

(2) For gifts made after December 31, 1970, and before January 1, 1982, subject to the limitations of paragraph (b) of this section, the consent signified on a return filed for a calendar quarter will be effective for a previous calendar quarter of the same calendar year for which no return was filed because the gifts made during such previous calendar quarter did not exceed the annual exclusion provided by section 2503(b), if the gifts in such previous calendar quarter are listed on that return. Thus, for example, if A gave $2,000 to his son in the first quarter of 1972 (and filed no return because of section 2503(b)) and gave a further $4,000 to such son in the last quarter of the year, A and his spouse could signify consent to the application of section 2513 on the return filed for the fourth quarter and have it apply to the first quarter as well, provided that the $2,000 gift is listed on such return.

(b)(1) With respect to gifts made after December 31, 1981, or before January 1, 1971, the consent may be signified at any time following the close of the calendar year, subject to the following limitations:

(i) The consent may not be signified after the 15th day of April following the close of the calendar year, unless before such 15th day, no return has been filed for the year by either spouse, in which case the consent may not be signified after a return for the year is filed by either spouse; and

(ii) The consent may not be signified for a calendar year after a notice of deficiency in gift tax for that year has been sent to either spouse in accordance with section 6212(a).

(2) With respect to gifts made after December 31, 1970 and before January 1, 1982, the consent may be signified at any time following the close of the calendar quarter in which the gift was made, subject to the following limitations:

(i) The consent may not be signified after the 15th day of the second month following the close of the calendar quarter, unless before such 15th day, no return has been filed for such quarter by either spouse, in which case the consent may not be signified after a return for such calendar quarter is filed by either spouse; and

(ii) The consent may not be signified after a notice of deficiency with respect to the tax for such calendar quarter has been sent to either spouse in accordance with section 6212(a).

(c) The executor or administrator of a deceased spouse, or the guardian or committee of a legally incompetent spouse, as the case may be, may signify the consent.

(d) If the donor and spouse consent to the application of section 2513, the return or returns for the "calendar period" [as defined in §25.2502-1(c)(1)] must set forth, to the extent provided thereon, information relative to the transfers made by each spouse. [Reg. §25.2513-2.]

☐ [*T.D.* 6334, 11-14-58. *Amended by T.D.* 7238, 12-28-72 *and T.D.* 7910, 9-6-83.]

[Reg. §25.2513-3]

§25.2513-3. Revocation of consent.— (a)(1) With respect to gifts made after December 31, 1981, or before January 1, 1971, if the consent to the application of the provisions of section 2513 for a calendar year was effectively signified on or before the 15th day of April following the close of the calendar year, either spouse may revoke the consent by filing in duplicate a signed statement of revocation, but only if the statement is filed on or before such 15th day of April. Therefore, a consent that was not effectively signified until after the 15th day of April following the close of the calendar year to which it applies may not be revoked.

(2) With respect to gifts made after December 31, 1970, and before January 1, 1982, if the consent to the application of the provisions of section 2513 for a calendar quarter was effectively signified on or before the 15th day of the second month following the close of such calendar quarter, either spouse may revoke the consent by filing in duplicate a signed statement of revocation, but only if the statement is filed on or before such 15th day of the second month following the close of such calendar quarter. Therefore, a consent that was not effectively signified until after the 15th day of the second month

following the close of the calendar quarter to which it applies may not be revoked.

(b) Except as provided in paragraph (b) of §301.6091-1 of this chapter (relating to hand-carried documents), the statement referred to in paragraph (a) of this section shall be filed with the internal revenue officer with whom the gift tax return is required to be filed, or with whom the gift tax return would be required to be filed if a return were required. [Reg. §25.2513-3.]

☐ [*T.D.* 6334, 11-14-58. *Amended by T.D.* 7012, 5-14-64; *T.D.* 7238, 12-28-72 *and T.D.* 7910, 9-6-83.]

[Reg. §25.2513-4]

§25.2513-4. Joint and several liability for tax.— If consent to the application of the provisions of section 2513 is signified as provided in §25.2513-2, and not revoked as provided in §25.2513-3, the liability with respect to the entire gift tax of each spouse for such "calendar period" (as defined in §25.2502-1(c)(1)) is joint and several. See paragraph (d) of §25.2511-1. [Reg. §25.2513-4.]

☐ [*T.D.* 6334, 11-14-58. *Amended by T.D.* 7238, 12-28-72 *and T.D.* 7910, 9-6-83.]

[Reg. §25.2514-1]

§25.2514-1. Transfers under power of appointment.— (a) *Introductory.—*(1) Section 2514 treats the exercise of a general power of appointment created on or before October 21, 1942, as a transfer of property for purposes of the gift tax. The section also treats as a transfer of property the exercise or complete release of a general power of appointment created after October 21, 1942, and under certain circumstances the exercise of a power of appointment (not a general power of appointment) created after October 21, 1942, by the creation of another power of appointment. See paragraph (d) of §25.2514-3. Under certain circumstances, also, the failure to exercise a power of appointment created after October 21, 1942, within a specified time, so that the power lapses, constitutes a transfer of property. Paragraphs (b) through (e) of this section contain definitions of certain terms used in §§25.2514-2 and 25.2514-3. See §25.2514-2 for specific rules applicable to certain powers created on or before October 21, 1942. See §25.2514-3 for specific rules applicable to powers created after October 21, 1942.

(b) *Definition of "power of appointment".—*(1) *In general.—*The term "power of appointment" includes all powers which are in substance and effect powers of appointment received by the donee of the power from another person, regardless of the nomenclature used in creating the power and regardless of local property law connotations. For example, if a trust instrument provides that the beneficiary may appropriate or consume the principal of the trust, the power to consume or appropriate is a power of appointment. Similarly, a power given to a donee to affect the beneficial enjoyment of a trust property or its income by altering, amending or revoking the trust instrument or terminating the trust is a power of appointment. A power in a donee to remove or discharge a trustee and appoint himself may be a power of appointment. For example, if under the terms of a trust instrument, the trustee or his successor has the power to appoint the principal of the trust for the benefit of individuals including himself, and A, another person, has the unrestricted power to remove or discharge the trustee at any time and appoint any other person including himself, A is considered as having a power of appointment. However, he would not be considered to have a power of appointment if he only had the power to appoint a successor, including himself, under limited conditions which did not exist at the time of exercise, release or lapse of the trustee's power, without an accompanying unrestricted power of removal. Similarly, a power to amend only the administrative provisions of a trust instrument, which cannot substantially affect the beneficial enjoyment of the trust property or income, is not a power of appointment. The mere power of management, investment, custody of assets, or the power to allocate receipts and disbursements as between income and principal, exercisable in a fiduciary capacity, whereby the holder has no power to enlarge or shift any of the beneficial interests therein except as an incidental consequence of the discharge of such fiduciary duties is not a power of appointment. Further, the right in a beneficiary of a trust to assent to a periodic accounting, thereby relieving the trustee from further accountability, is not a power of appointment if the right of assent does not consist of any power or right to enlarge or shift the beneficial interest of any beneficiary therein.

(2) *Relation to other sections.*—For purposes of §§25.2514-1 through 25.2514-3, the term "power of appointment" does not include powers reserved by a donor to himself. No provision of section 2514 or of §§25.2514-1 through 25.2514-3 is to be construed as in any way limiting the application of any other section of the Internal Revenue Code or of these regulations. The power of the owner of a property interest already possessed by him to dispose of his interest, and nothing more, is not a power of appointment, and the interest is includible in the amount of his gifts to the extent it would be includible under section 2511 or other provisions of the Internal Revenue Code. For example, if a trust created by S provides for payment of the income to A for life with power in A to appoint the entire trust property by deed during her lifetime to a class consisting of her children, and a further power to dispose of the entire corpus by will to anyone, including her estate, and A exercises the inter vivos power in favor of her children, she

has necessarily made a transfer of her income interest which constitutes a taxable gift under section 2511(a), without regard to section 2514. This transfer also results in a relinquishment of her general power to appoint by will, which constitutes a transfer under section 2514 if the power was created after October 21, 1942.

(3) *Powers over a portion of property.*—If a power of appointment exists as to part of an entire group of assets or only over a limited interest in property, section 2514 applies only to such part or interest.

(c) *Definition of "general power of appointment".*—(1) *In general.*—The term "general power of appointment" as defined in section 2514(c) means any power of appointment exercisable in favor of the person possessing the power (referred to as the "possessor"), his estate, his creditors, or the creditors of his estate, except (i) joint powers, to the extent provided in §§25.2514-2 and 25.2514-3 and (ii) certain powers limited by an ascertainable standard, to the extent provided in subparagraph (2) of this paragraph. A power of appointment exercisable to meet the estate tax, or any other taxes, debts, or charges which are enforceable against the possessor or his estate, is included within the meaning of a power of appointment exercisable in favor of the possessor, his estate, his creditors, or the creditors of his estate. A power of appointment exercisable for the purpose of discharging a legal obligation of the possessor for his pecuniary benefit is considered a power of appointment exercisable in favor of the possessor or his creditors. However, for purposes of §§25.2514-1 through 25.2514-3, a power of appointment not otherwise considered to be a general power of appointment is not treated as a general power of appointment merely by reason of the fact that an appointee may, in fact, be a creditor of the possessor or his estate. A power of appointment is not a general power if by its terms it is either—

(a) Exercisable only in favor of one or more designated persons or classes other than the possessor or his creditors, or the possessor's estate or the creditors of his estate, or

(b) Expressly not exercisable in favor of the possessor or his creditors, the possessor's estate or the creditors of his estate.

A beneficiary may have two powers under the same instrument, one of which is a general power of appointment and the other of which is not. For example, a beneficiary may have a general power to withdraw a limited portion of trust corpus during his life, and a further power exercisable during his lifetime to appoint the corpus among his children. The latter power is not a general power of appointment (but its exercise may result in the exercise of the former power; see paragraph (d) of this section).

(2) *Powers limited by an ascertainable standard.*—A power to consume, invade, or appro-

Reg. §25.2514-1(c)(2)

priate income or corpus, or both, for the benefit of the possessor which is limited by an ascertainable standard relating to the health, education, support, or maintenance of the possessor is, by reason of section 2514(c)(1), not a general power of appointment. A power is limited by such a standard if the extent of the possessor's duty to exercise and not to exercise the power is reasonably measurable in terms of his needs for health, education, or support (or any combination of them). As used in this subparagraph, the words "support" and "maintenance" are synonymous and their meaning is not limited to the bare necessities of life. A power to use property for the comfort, welfare, or happiness of the holder of the power is not limited by the requisite standard. Examples of powers which are limited by the requisite standard are powers exercisable for the holder's "support," "support in reasonable comfort," "maintenance in health and reasonable comfort," "support in his accustomed manner of living," "education, including college and professional education," "health," and "medical, dental, hospital and nursing expenses and expenses of invalidism." In determining whether a power is limited by an ascertainable standard, it is immaterial whether the beneficiary is required to exhaust his other income before the power can be exercised.

(3) *Certain powers under wills of decedents dying between January 1 and April 2, 1948.*—Section 210 of the Technical Changes Act of 1953 provides that if a decedent died after December 31, 1947, but before April 3, 1948, certain property interests described therein may, if the decedent's surviving spouse so elects, be accorded special treatment in the determination of the marital deduction to be allowed the decedent's estate under the provisions of section 812(e) of the Internal Revenue Code of 1939. See paragraph (h) of §81.47a of Regulations 105 (26 CFR (1939) 81.47a(h)). The section further provides that property affected by the election shall be considered property with respect to which the surviving spouse has a general power of appointment. Therefore, notwithstanding any other provision of law or of §§25.2514-1 through 25.2514-3, if the surviving spouse has made an election under section 210 of the Technical Changes Act of 1953, the property which was the subject of the election shall be considered as property with respect to which she has a general power of appointment created after October 21, 1942, exercisable by deed or will, to the extent it was treated as an interest passing to the surviving spouse and not passing to any other person for the purpose of the marital deduction in the prior decedent's estate.

(d) *Definition of "exercise.".*—Whether a power of appointment is in fact exercised may depend upon local law. However, regardless of local law, a power of appointment is considered as exercised for purposes of section 2514 even though the exercise is in favor of the taker in default of appointment, and irrespective of whether the appointed interest and the interest in default of appointment are identical or whether the appointee renounces any right to take under the appointment. A power of appointment is also considered as exercised even though the disposition cannot take effect until the occurrence of an event after the exercise takes place, if the exercise is irrevocable and, as of the time of the exercise, the condition was not impossible of occurrence. For example, if property is left in trust to A for life, with a power in A to appoint the remainder by an instrument filed with the trustee during his life, and A exercises his power by appointing the remainder to B in the event that B survives A, A is considered to have exercised his power if the exercise was irrevocable. Furthermore, if a person holds both a presently exercisable general power of appointment and a presently exercisable nongeneral power of appointment over the same property, the exercise of the nongeneral power is considered the exercise of the general power only to the extent that immediately after the exercise of the nongeneral power the amount of money or property subject to being transferred by the exercise of the general power is decreased. For example, assume A has a noncumulative annual power to withdraw the greater of $5,000 or 5 percent of the value of a trust having a value of $300,000 and a lifetime nongeneral power to appoint all or a portion of the trust corpus to A's child or grandchildren. If A exercises the nongeneral power by appointing $150,000 to A's child, the exercise of the nongeneral power is treated as the exercise of the general power to the extent of $7,500 (maximum exercise of general power before the exercise of the nongeneral power, 5% of $300,000 or $15,000, less maximum exercise of the general power after the exercise of the nongeneral power, 5% of $150,000 or $7,500).

(e) *Time of creation of power.*—A power of appointment created by will is, in general, considered as created on the date of the testator's death. However, section 2514(f) provides that a power of appointment created by a will executed on or before October 21, 1942, is considered a power created on or before that date if the testator dies before July 1, 1949, without having republished the will, by codicil or otherwise, after October 21, 1942. A power of appointment created by an inter vivos instrument is considered as created on the date the instrument takes effect. Such a power is not considered as created at some future date merely because it is not exercisable on the date the instrument takes effect, or because it is revocable, or because the identity of its holders is not ascertainable until after the date the instrument takes effect. However, if the holder of a power exercises it by creating a second power, the second power is considered as created at the time of the exercise of the first. The application of this paragraph may be illustrated by the following examples:

Example (1). A created a revocable trust before October 22, 1942, providing for payment of income to B for life with remainder as B shall appoint by deed or will. Even though A dies after October 21, 1942, without having exercised his power of revocation, B's power of appointment is considered a power created before October 22, 1942.

Example (2). C created an irrevocable inter vivos trust before October 22, 1942, naming T as trustee and providing for payment of income to D for life with remainder to E. T was given the power to pay corpus to D and the power to appoint a successor trustee. If T resigns after October 21, 1942, and appoints D as successor trustee, D is considered to have a power of appointment created before October 22, 1942.

Example (3). F created an irrevocable inter vivos trust before October 22, 1942, providing for payment of income to G for life with remainder as G shall appoint by deed or will, but in default of appointment income to H for life with remainder as H shall appoint by deed or will. If G died after October 21, 1942, without having exercised his power of appointment, H's power of appointment is considered a power created before October 22, 1942, even though it was only a contingent interest until G's death.

Example (4). If in example (3) above G had exercised by will his power of appointment, by creating a similar power in J, J's power of appointment would be considered a power created after October 21, 1942. [Reg. § 25.2514-1.]

☐ [*T.D.* 6334, 11-14-58. *Amended by T.D.* 6582, 12-11-61 *and T.D.* 7757, 1-16-81.]

[Reg. § 25.2514-2]

§ 25.2514-2. Powers of appointment created on or before October 21, 1942.—(a) *In general.*— The exercise of a general power of appointment created on or before October 21, 1942, is deemed to be a transfer of property by the individual possessing the power.

(b) *Joint powers created on or before October 21, 1942.*—Section 2514(c)(2) provides that a power created on or before October 21, 1942, which at the time of the exercise is not exercisable by the possessor except in conjunction with another person, is not deemed a general power of appointment.

(c) *Release or lapse.*—A failure to exercise a general power of appointment created on or before October 21, 1942, or a complete release of such a power is not considered to be an exercise of a general power of appointment. The phrase "a complete release" means a release of all powers over all or a portion of the property subject to a power of appointment, as distinguished from the reduction of a power of appointment to a lesser power. Thus, if the possessor completely relinquished all powers over one-half of the property subject to a power of appointment, the power is completely released as to that one-half. If at or before the time a power of appointment is relinquished, the holder of the power exercises the power in such a manner or to such an extent that the relinquishment results in the reduction, enlargement, or shift in a beneficial interest in property, the relinquishment will be considered to be an exercise and not a release of the power. For example, assume that A created a trust in 1940 providing for payment of the income to B for life with the power in B to amend the trust, and for payment of the remainder to such persons as B shall appoint or, upon default of appointment, to C. If B amended the trust in 1948 by providing that upon his death the remainder was to be paid to D, and if he further amended the trust in 1955 by deleting his power to amend the trust, such relinquishment will be considered an exercise and not a release of a general power of appointment. On the other hand, if the 1948 amendment became ineffective before or at the time of the 1955 amendment, or if B in 1948 merely amended the trust by changing the purely ministerial powers of the trustee, his relinquishment of the power in 1955 will be considered as release of a power of appointment.

(d) *Partial release.*—If a general power of appointment created on or before October 21, 1942, is partially released so that it is not thereafter a general power of appointment, a subsequent exercise of the partially released power is not an exercise of a general power of appointment if the partial release occurs before whichever is the later of the following dates:

(1) November 1, 1951; or

(2) If the possessor was under a legal disability to release the power on October 21, 1942, the day after the expiration of 6 months following the termination of such legal disability.

However, if a general power created on or before October 21, 1942, is partially released on or after the later of those dates, a subsequent exercise of the power will constitute an exercise of a general power of appointment. The legal disability referred to in this paragraph is determined under local law and may include the disability of an insane person, a minor, or an unborn child. The fact that the type of general power of appointment possessed by the holder actually was not generally releasable under the local law does not place the holder under a legal disability within the meaning of this paragraph. In general, however, it is assumed that all general powers of appointment are releasable, unless the local law on the subject is to the contrary, and it is presumed that the method employed to release the power is effective, unless it is not in accordance with the local law relating specifically to releases or, in the absence of such local law, is not in accordance with the local law relating to similar transactions.

(e) *Partial exercise.*—If a general power of appointment created on or before October 21, 1942, is exercised only as to a portion of the property subject to the power, the exercise is considered to be a transfer only as to the value of that portion. [Reg. § 25.2514-2.]

☐ [*T.D.* 6334, 11-14-58.]

[Reg. § 25.2514-3]

§ 25.2514-3. Powers of appointment created after October 21, 1942.—(a) *In general.*—The exercise, release, or lapse (except as provided in paragraph(c) of this section) of a general power of appointment created after October 21, 1942, is deemed to be a transfer of property by the individual possessing the power. The exercise of a power of appointment that is not a general power is considered to be a transfer if it is exercised to create a further power under certain circumstances(see paragraph (d) of this section). See paragraph (c) of § 25.2514-1 for the definition of various terms used in this section. See paragraph (b) of this section for the rules applicable to determine the extent to which joint powers created after October 21, 1942, are to be treated as general powers of appointment.

(b) *Joint powers created after October 21, 1942.*—The treatment of a power of appointment created after October 21, 1942, which is exercisable only in conjunction with another person is governed by section 2514(c)(3), which provides as follows:

(1) Such a power is not considered as a general power of appointment if it is not exercisable by the possessor except with the consent or joinder of the creator of the power.

(2) Such power is not considered as a general power of appointment if it is not exercisable by the possessor except with the consent or joinder of a person having a substantial interest in the property subject to the power which is adverse to the exercise of the power in favor of the possessor, his estate, his creditors, or the creditors of his estate. An interest adverse to the exercise of a power is considered as substantial if its value in relation to the total value of the property subject to the power is not insignificant. For this purpose, the interest is to be valued in accordance with the actuarial principles set forth in § 25.2512-5 or, if it is not susceptible to valuation under those provisions, in accordance with the general principles set forth in § 25.2512-1. A taker in default of appointment under a power has an interest which is adverse to an exercise of the power. A coholder of the power has no adverse interest merely because of his joint possession of the power nor merely because he is a permissible appointee under a power. However, a coholder of a power is considered as having an adverse interest where he may possess the power after the possessor's death and may exercise it at that time in favor of himself, his estate, his creditors, or the creditors of his estate. Thus,

for example, if X, Y, and Z held a power jointly to appoint among a group of persons which includes themselves and if on the death of X the power will pass to Y and Z jointly, then Y and Z are considered to have interests adverse to the exercise of the power in favor of X. Similarly, if on Y's death the power will pass to Z, Z is considered to have an interest adverse to the exercise of the power in favor of Y. The application of this subparagraph may be further illustrated by the following examples in each of which it is assumed that the value of the interest in question is substantial:

Example (1). The taxpayer and R are trustees of a trust under which the income is to be paid to the taxpayer for life and then to M for life, and R is remainderman. The trustees have power to distribute corpus to the taxpayer. Since R's interest is substantially adverse to an exercise of the power in favor of the taxpayer, the latter does not have a general power of appointment. If M and the taxpayer were trustees, M's interest would likewise be adverse.

Example (2). The taxpayer and L are trustees of a trust under which the income is to be paid to L for life and then to M for life, and the taxpayer is remainderman. The trustees have power to distribute corpus to the taxpayer during L's life. Since L's interest is adverse to an exercise of the power in favor of the taxpayer, the taxpayer does not have a general power of appointment. If the taxpayer and M were trustees, M's interest would likewise be adverse.

Example (3). The taxpayer and L are trustees of a trust under which the income is to be paid to L for life. The trustees can designate whether corpus is to be distributed to the taxpayer or to A after L's death. L's interest is not adverse to an exercise of the power in favor of the taxpayer, and the taxpayer therefore has a general power of appointment.

(3) A power which is exercisable only in conjunction with another person, and which after application of the rules set forth in subparagraphs (1) and (2) of this paragraph, constitutes a general power of appointment, will be treated as though the holders of the power who are permissible appointees of the property were joint owners of property subject to the power. The possessor, under this rule, will be treated as possessed of a general power of appointment over an aliquot share of the property to be determined with reference to the number of joint holders, including the possessor, who (or whose estates or creditors) are permissible appointees. Thus, for example, if X, Y, and Z hold an unlimited power jointly to appoint among a group of persons, including themselves, but on the death of X the power does not pass to Y and Z jointly, then Y and Z are not considered to have interests adverse to the exercise of the power in favor of X. In this case, X is considered to possess a general power of appointment as to one-third of the property subject to the power.

(c) *Partial releases, lapses and disclaimers of general powers of appointment created after October 21, 1942.*—(1) *Partial release of power.*—The general principles set forth in § 25.2511-2 for determining whether a donor of property (or of a property right or interest) has divested himself of all or any portion of his interest therein to the extent necessary to effect a completed gift are applicable in determining whether a partial release of a power of appointment constitutes a taxable gift. Thus, if a general power of appointment is partially released so that thereafter the donor may still appoint among a limited class of persons not including himself the partial release does not effect a complete gift, since the possessor of the power has retained the right to designate the ultimate beneficiaries of the property over which he holds the power and since it is only the termination of such control which completes a gift.

(2) *Power partially released before June 1, 1951.*—If a general power of appointment created after October 21, 1942, was partially released prior to June 1, 1951, so that it no longer represented a general power of appointment, as defined in paragraph (c) of § 25.2514-1, the subsequent exercise, release, or lapse of the partially released power at any time thereafter will not constitute the exercise or release of a general power of appointment. For example, assume that A created a trust in 1943 under which B possessed a general power of appointment. By an instrument executed in 1948 such general power of appointment was reduced in scope by B to an excepted power. The inter vivos exercise in 1955, or in any "calendar period" (as defined in § 25.2502-1(c)(1)) thereafter, of such excepted power is not considered an exercise or release of a general power of appointment for purposes of the gift tax.

(3) *Power partially released after May 31, 1951.*—If a general power of appointment created after October 21, 1942, was partially released after May 31, 1951, the subsequent exercise, release or a lapse of the power at any time thereafter, will constitute the exercise or release of a general power of appointment for gift tax purposes.

(4) *Release or lapse of power.*—A release of a power of appointment need not be formal or express in character. For example, the failure to exercise a general power of appointment created after October 21, 1942, within a specified time so that the power lapses, constitutes a release of the power. In any case where the possessor of a general power of appointment is incapable of validly exercising or releasing a power, by reason of minority, or otherwise, and the power may not be validly exercised or released on his behalf, the failure to exercise or release the power is not a lapse of the power. If a trustee has in his capacity as trustee a power which is con-

sidered as a general power of appointment, his resignation or removal as trustee will cause a lapse of his power. However, section 2514(e) provides that a lapse during any calendar year is considered as a release so as to be subject to the gift tax only to the extent that the property which could have been appointed by exercise of the lapsed power of appointment exceeds the greater of (i) $5,000, or (ii) 5 percent of the aggregate value, at the time of the lapse, of the assets out of which, or the proceeds of which, the exercise of the lapsed power could be satisfied. For example, if an individual has a noncumulative right to withdraw $10,000 a year from the principal of a trust fund, the failure to exercise this right of withdrawal in a particular year will not constitute a gift if the fund at the end of the year equals or exceeds $200,000. If, however, at the end of the particular year the fund should be worth only $100,000, the failure to exercise the power will be considered a gift to the extent of $5,000, the excess of $10,000 over 5 percent of a fund of $100,000. Where the failure to exercise the power, such as the right of withdrawal, occurs in more than a single year, the value of the taxable transfer will be determined separately for each year.

(5) *Disclaimer of power created after December 31, 1976.*—A disclaimer or renunciation of a general power of appointment created in a transfer made after December 31, 1976, is not considered a release of the power for gift tax purposes if the disclaimer or renunciation is a qualified disclaimer as described in section 2518 and the corresponding regulations. For rules relating to when a transfer creating the power occurs, see § 25.2518-2(c)(3). If the disclaimer or renunciation is not a qualified disclaimer, it is considered a release of the power.

(6) *Disclaimer of power created before January 1, 1977.*—A disclaimer or renunciation of a general power of appointment created in a taxable transfer before January 1, 1977, in the person disclaiming is not considered a release of the power. The disclaimer or renunciation must be unequivocal and effective under local law. A disclaimer is a complete and unqualified refusal to accept the rights to which one is entitled. There can be no disclaimer or renunciation of a power after its acceptance. In the absence of facts to the contrary, the failure to renounce or disclaim within a reasonable time after learning of the existence of a power shall be presumed to constitute an acceptance of the power. In any case where a power is purported to be disclaimed or renounced as to only a portion of the property subject to the power, the determination as to whether there has been a complete and unqualified refusal to accept the rights to which one is entitled will depend on all the facts and circumstances of the particular case, taking into account the recognition and effectiveness of such a disclaimer under local law. Such rights refer to

the incidents of the power and not to other interests of the possessor of the power in the property. If effective under local law, the power may be disclaimed or renounced without disclaiming or renouncing such other interests.

(7) The first and second sentences of paragraph (c)(5) of this section are applicable for transfers creating the power to be disclaimed made on or after December 31, 1997.

(d) *Creation of another power in certain cases.*— Paragraph (d) of section 2514 provides that there is a transfer for purposes of the gift tax of the value of property (or of property rights or interests) with respect to which a power of appointment, which is not a general power of appointment, created after October 21, 1942, is exercised by creating another power of appointment, which under the terms of the instruments creating and exercising the first power and under applicable local law, can be validly exercised so as to (1) postpone the vesting of any estate or interest in the property for a period ascertainable without regard to the date of the creation of the first power, or (2) (if the applicable rule against perpetuities is stated in terms of suspension of ownership or of the power of alienation, rather than of vesting) suspend the absolute ownership or the power of alienation of the property for a period ascertainable without regard to the date of the creation of the first power. For the purpose of section 2514(d), the value of the property subject to the second power of appointment is considered to be its value unreduced by any precedent or subsequent interest which is not subject to the second power. Thus, if a donor has a power to appoint $100,000 among a group consisting of his children or grandchildren and during his lifetime exercises the power by making an outright appointment of $75,000 and by giving one appointee a power to appoint $25,000, no more than $25,000 will be considered a gift under section 2514(d). If, however, the donor appoints the income from the entire fund to a beneficiary for life with power in the beneficiary to appoint the remainder, the entire $100,000 will be considered a gift under section 2514(d), if the exercise of the second power can validly postpone the vesting of any estate or interest in the property or can suspend the absolute ownership or power of alienation of the property for a period ascertainable without regard to the date of the creation of the first power.

(e) *Examples.*—The application of this section may be further illustrated by the following examples in each of which it is assumed, unless otherwise stated, that S has transferred property in trust after October 21, 1942, with the remainder payable to R at L's death, and that neither L nor R has any interest in or power over the enjoyment of the trust property except as is indicated separately in each example:

Example (1). The income is payable to L for life. L has the power to cause the income to be paid to R. The exercise of the right constitutes the making of a transfer of property under section 2511. L's power does not constitute a power of appointment since it is only a power to dispose of his income interest, a right otherwise possessed by him.

Example (2). The income is to be accumulated during L's life. L has the power to have the income distributed to himself. If L's power is limited by an ascertainable standard (relating to health, etc.) as defined in paragraph (c)(2) of § 25.2514-1, the lapse of such power will not constitute a transfer of property for gift tax purposes. If L's power is not so limited, its lapse or release during L's lifetime may constitute a transfer of property for gift tax purposes. See especially paragraph (c)(4) of § 25.2514-3.

Example (3). The income is to be paid to L for life. L has a power, exercisable at any time, to cause corpus to be distributed to himself. L has a general power of appointment over the remainder interest, the release of which constitutes a transfer for gift tax purposes of the remainder interest. If in this example L had a power to cause the corpus to be distributed only to X, L would have a power of appointment which is not a general power of appointment, the exercise or release of which would not constitute a transfer of property for purposes of the gift tax. Although the exercise or release of the nongeneral power is not taxable under this section, see § 25.2514-1(b)(2) for the gift tax consequences of the transfer of the life income interest.

Example (4). The income is payable to L for life. R has the right to cause the corpus to be distributed to L at any time. R's power is not a power of appointment, but merely a right to dispose of his remainder interest, a right already possessed by him. In such a case, the exercise of the right constitutes the making of a transfer of property under section 2511 of the value, if any, of his remainder interest. See paragraph (e) of § 25.2511-1.

Example (5). The income is to be paid to L. R has the right to appoint the corpus to himself at any time. R's general power of appointment over the corpus includes a general power to dispose of L's income interest therein. The lapse or release of R's general power over the income interest during his life may constitute the making of a transfer of property. See especially paragraph (c)(4) of § 25.2514-3. [Reg. § 25.2514-3.]

☐ [*T.D. 6334, 11-14-68. Amended by T.D. 7238, 12-28-72, T.D. 7776, 5-20-81; T.D. 7910, 9-6-83; T.D. 8095, 8-6-86 and T.D. 8744, 12-30-97.*]

[Reg. § 25.2515-1]

§ 25.2515-1. Tenancies by the entirety; in general.—(a) *Scope.*—(1) *In general.*—This section and § § 25.2515-2 through 25.2515-4 do not apply to the creation of a tenancy by the entirety after

December 31, 1981, and do not reflect changes made to the Internal Revenue Code by sections 702(k)(1)(A) of the Revenue Act of 1978, or section 2002(c)(2) of the Tax Reform Act of 1976.

(2) *Special rule in the case of tenancies created after July 13, 1988, if the donee spouse is not a United States citizen.*—Under section 2523(i)(3), applicable (subject to the special treaty rule contained in Pub. L. 101-239, section 7815(d)(14)) in the case of tenancies by the entirety and joint tenancies created between spouses after July 13, 1988, if the donee spouse is not a citizen of the United States, the principles contained in section 2515 and §§ 25.2515-1 through 25.2515-4 apply in determining the gift tax consequences with respect to the creation and termination of the tenancy, except that the election provided in section 2515(a) (prior to repeal by the Economic Recovery Tax Act of 1981) and § 25.2515-2 (relating to the donor's election to treat the creation of the tenancy as a transfer for gift tax purposes) does not apply.

(3) *Nature of.*—An estate by the entirety in real property is essentially a joint tenancy between husband and wife with the right of survivorship. As used in this section and §§ 25.2515-2 through 25.2515-4, the term "tenancy by the entirety" includes a joint tenancy between husband and wife in real property with right of survivorship, or a tenancy which accords to the spouses rights equivalent thereto regardless of the term by which such a tenancy is described in local property law.

(b) *Gift upon creation of tenancy by the entirety; in general.*—During calendar years prior to 1955 the contribution made by a husband or wife in the creation of a tenancy by the entirety constituted a gift to the extent that the consideration furnished by either spouse exceeded the value of the rights retained by that spouse. The contribution made by either or both spouses in the creation of such a tenancy during the calendar year 1955, any calendar year beginning before January 1, 1971, or any calendar quarter beginning after December 31, 1970, is not deemed a gift by either spouse, regardless of the proportion of the total consideration furnished by either spouse, unless the donor spouse elects (see § 25.2515-2) under section 2515(c) to treat such transaction as a gift in the calendar quarter or calendar year in which the transaction is effected. See § 25.2502-1(c)(1) for the definition of calendar quarter. However, there is a gift upon the termination of such a tenancy, other than by the death of a spouse, if the proceeds received by one spouse on termination of the tenancy are larger than the proceeds allocable to the consideration furnished by that spouse to the tenancy. The creation of a tenancy by the entirety takes place if (1) a husband or his wife purchases property and causes the title thereto to be conveyed to themselves as tenants by the entirety, (2) both

join in such a purchase, or (3) either or both cause to be created such a tenancy in property already owned by either or both of them. The rule prescribed herein with respect to the creation of a tenancy by the entirety applies also to contributions made in the making of additions to the value of such a tenancy (in the form of improvements, reductions in the indebtedness, or otherwise), regardless of the proportion of the consideration furnished by each spouse. See § 25.2516-1 for transfers made pursuant to a property settlement agreement incident to divorce.

(c) *Consideration.*—(1) *In general.*—(i) The consideration furnished by a person in the creation of a tenancy by the entirety or the making of additions to the value thereof is the amount contributed by him in connection therewith. The contribution may be made by either spouse or by a third party. It may be furnished in the form of money, other property, or an interest in property. If it is furnished in the form of other property or an interest in property, the amount of the contribution is the fair market value of the property or interest at the time it was transferred to the tenancy or was exchanged for the property which became the subject of the tenancy. For example, if a decedent devised real property to the spouses as tenants by the entirety and the fair market value of the property was $30,000 at the time of the decedent's death, the amount of the decedent's contribution to the creation of the tenancy was $30,000. As another example, assume that in 1950 the husband purchased real property for $25,000, taking it in his own name as sole owner, and that in 1956 when the property had a fair market value of $40,000 he caused it to be transferred to himself and his wife as tenants by the entirety. Here, the amount of the husband's contribution to the creation of the tenancy was $40,000 (the fair market value of the property at the time it was transferred to the tenancy). Similarly, assume that in 1950 the husband purchased, as sole owner, corporate shares for $25,000 and in 1956, when the shares had a fair market value of $35,000, he exchanged them for real property which was transferred to the husband and his wife as tenants by the entirety. The amount of the husband's contribution to the creation of the tenancy was $35,000 (the fair market value of the shares at the time he exchanged them for the real property which became the subject of the tenancy).

(ii) Whether consideration derived from third-party sources is deemed to have been furnished by a third party or to have been furnished by the spouses will depend upon the terms under which the transfer is made. If a decedent devises real property to the spouses as tenants by the entirety, the decedent, and not the spouses, is the person who furnished the consideration for the creation of the tenancy. Likewise, if a decedent in his will directs his executor to discharge an indebtedness of the tenancy, the decedent, and not the spouses, is the person who furnished the consideration for the addition to the value of the tenancy. However, if the decedent bequeathed a general legacy to the husband and the wife and they used the legacy to discharge an indebtedness of the tenancy, the spouses, and not the decedent, are the persons who furnished the consideration for the addition to the value of the tenancy. The principles set forth in this subdivision with respect to transfers by decedents apply equally well to inter vivos transfers by third parties.

(iii) Where a tenancy is terminated in part (*e.g.*, where a portion of the property subject to the tenancy is sold to a third party, or where the original property is disposed of and in its place there is substituted other property of lesser value acquired through reinvestment under circumstances which satisfy the requirements of paragraph (d)(2)(ii) of this section), the proportionate contribution of each person to the remaining tenancy is in general the same as his proportionate contribution to the original tenancy, and the character of his contribution remains the same. These proportions are applied to the cost of the remaining or substituted property. Thus, if the total contribution to the cost of the property was $20,000 and a fourth of the property was sold, the contribution to the remaining portion of the tenancy is normally $15,000. However, if it is shown that at the time of the contribution more or less than one-fourth thereof was attributable to the portion sold, the contribution is divided between the portion sold and the portion retained in the proper proportion. If the portion sold was acquired as a separate tract, it is treated as a separate tenancy. As another example of the application of this subdivision, assume that in 1950 X (a third party) gave to H and W (H's wife), as tenants by the entirety, real property then having a value of $15,000. In 1955, H spent $5,000 thereon in improvements and under section 2515(c) elected to treat his contribution as a gift. In 1956, W spent $10,000 in improving the property but did not elect to treat her contribution as a gift. Between 1957 and 1960 the property appreciated in value by $30,000. In 1960, the property was sold for $60,000, and $45,000 of the proceeds of the sale were, under circumstances that satisfy the requirements of paragraph (d)(2)(ii) of this section, reinvested in other real property. Since X contributed one-half of the total consideration for the original property and the additions to its value, he is considered as having furnished $22,500 (one-half of $45,000) toward the creation of the remaining portion of the tenancy and the making of additions to the value thereof. Similarly, H is considered as having furnished $7,500 (one-sixth of $45,000) which was treated as a gift in the year furnished, and W is considered as having furnished $15,000 (one-third of $45,000) which was not treated as a gift in the year furnished.

(2) *Proportion of consideration attributable to appreciation.*—Any general appreciation (appreciation due to fluctuations in market value) in the value of the property occurring between two successive contribution dates which can readily be measured and which can be determined with reasonable certainty to be allocable to any particular contribution or contributions previously furnished is to be treated, for the purpose of the computations in §§ 25.2515-3 and 25.2515-4, as though it were additional consideration furnished by the person who furnished the prior consideration. Any general depreciation in value is treated in a comparable manner. For the purpose of the first sentence of this subparagraph, successive contribution dates are the two consecutive dates on which any contributions to the tenancy are made, not necessarily by the same party. Further, appreciation allocable to the prior consideration falls in the same class as the prior consideration to which it relates. The application of this subparagraph may be illustrated by the following examples:

Example (1). In 1940, H purchased real property for $15,000 which he caused to be transferred to himself and W (his wife) as tenants by the entirety. In 1956 when the fair market value of the property was $30,000, W made $5,000 improvements to the property. In 1957 the property was sold for $35,000. The general appreciation of $15,000 which occurred between the date of purchase and the date of W's improvements to the property constitutes an additional contribution by H, having the same characteristics as his original contribution of $15,000.

Example (2). In 1955 real property was purchased by H and W and conveyed to them as tenants by the entirety. The purchase price of the property was $15,000 of which H contributed $10,000 and W, $5,000. In 1960 when the fair market value of the property is $21,000, W makes improvements thereto of $5,000. The property then is sold for $26,000. The appreciation in value of $6,000 results in an additional contribution of $4,000 ($10,000/15,000 × $6,000) by H, and an additional contribution by W of $2,000 ($5,000/15,000 × $6,000). H's total contribution to the tenancy is $14,000 ($10,000 + $4,000) and W's total contribution is $12,000 ($5,000 + $2,000 + $5,000).

Example (3). In 1956 real property was purchased by H and W and conveyed to them as tenants by the entirety. The purchase price of the property was $15,000, on which a down payment of $3,000 was made. The remaining $12,000 was to be paid in monthly installments over a period of 15 years. H furnished $2,000 of the down payment and W, $1,000. H paid all the monthly installments. During the period 1956 to 1971 the property gradually appreciates in value to $24,000. Here, the appreciation is so gradual and the contributions so numerous that the amount allocable to any particular contribution cannot be ascertained with any reasonable certainty. Accordingly, in such a case the appreciation in value may be disregarded in determining the amount of consideration furnished in making the computations provided for in §§ 25.2515-3 and 25.2515-4.

(d) *Gift upon termination of tenancy by the entirety.*—(1) *In general.*—Upon the termination of the tenancy, whether created before, during, or subsequent to the calendar year 1955, a gift may result, depending upon the disposition made of the proceeds of the termination (whether the proceeds be in the form of cash, property, or interests in property). A gift may result notwithstanding the fact that the contribution of either spouse to the tenancy was treated as a gift. See § 25.2515-3 for the method of determining the amount of any gift that may result from the termination of the tenancy in those cases in which no portion of the consideration contributed was treated as a gift by the spouses in the calendar quarter or calendar year in which it was furnished. See § 25.2515-4 for the method of determining the amount of any gift that may result from the termination of the tenancy in those cases in which all or a portion of the consideration contributed was treated as constituting a gift by the spouses in the calendar quarter or calendar year in which it was furnished. See § 25.2515-2 for the procedure to be followed by a donor who elects under section 2515(c) to treat the creation of a tenancy by the entirety (or the making of additions to its value) as a transfer subject to the gift tax in the calendar quarter (calendar year with respect to such transfers made before January 1, 1971) in which the transfer is made, and for the method of determining the amount of the gift. See § 25.2502-1(c)(1) for the definition of calendar quarter.

(2) *Termination.*—(i) *In general.*—Except as indicated in subdivision (ii) of this subparagraph, a termination of a tenancy is effected when all or a portion of the property so held by the spouses is sold, exchanged, or otherwise disposed of, by gift or in any other manner, or when the spouses through any form of conveyance or agreement become tenants in common of the property or otherwise alter the nature of their respective interests in the property formerly held by them as tenants by the entirety. In general, any increase in the indebtedness on a tenancy constitutes a termination of the tenancy to the extent of the increase in the indebtedness. However, such an increase will not constitute a termination of the tenancy to the extent that the increase is offset by additions to the tenancy within a reasonable time after such increase. Such additions (to the extent of the increase in the indebtedness) shall not be treated by the spouses as contributions within the meaning of paragraph (c) of this section.

(ii) *Exchange or reinvestment.*—A termination is not considered as effected to the extent that the property subject to the tenancy is exchanged for other real property, the title of which is held by the spouses in an identical tenancy. For this purpose, a tenancy is considered identical if the proportionate values of the spouses' respective rights (other than any change in the proportionate values resulting solely from the passing of time) are identical to those held in the property which was sold. In addition the sale, exchange (other than an exchange described above), or other disposition of property held as tenants by the entirety is not considered as a termination if all three of the following conditions are satisfied:

(a) There is no division of the proceeds of the sale, exchange or other disposition of the property held as tenants by the entirety;

(b) On or before the due date for the filing of a gift tax return for the calendar quarter or calendar year (see § 25.6075-1 for the time for filing gift tax returns) in which the property held as tenants by the entirety was sold, exchanged, or otherwise disposed of, the spouses enter into a binding contract for the purchase of other real property; and

(c) After the sale, exchange or other disposition of the former property and within a reasonable time after the date of the contract referred to in (b) of this subdivision, such other real property actually is acquired by the spouses and held by them in an identical tenancy.

To the extent that all three of the conditions set forth in this subdivision are not met (whether by reason of the death of one of the spouses or for any other reason), the provisions of the preceding sentence shall not apply, and the sale, exchange or other disposition of the property will constitute a termination of the tenancy. As used in subdivision (c) the expression "a reasonable time" means the time which, under the particular facts in each case, is needed for those matters which are incident to the acquisition of the other property (*i.e.*, perfecting of title, arranging for financing, construction, etc.). The fact that proceeds of a sale are deposited in the name of one tenant or of both tenants separately or jointly as a convenience does not constitute a division within the meaning of subdivision (a) if the other requirements of this subdivision are met. The proceeds of a sale, exchange or other disposition of the property held as tenants by the entirety will be deemed to have been used for the purchase of other real property if applied to the purchase or construction of improvements which themselves constitute real property and which are additions to other real property held by the spouses in a tenancy identical to that in which they held the property which was sold, exchanged, or otherwise disposed of.

(3) *Proceeds of termination.*—(i) The proceeds of termination may be received by a spouse in the form of money, property, or an interest in property. Where the proceeds are re-

Reg. §25.2515-1(d)(3)(i)

ceived in the form of property (other than money) or an interest in property, the value of the proceeds received by that spouse is the fair market value, on the date of termination of the tenancy by the entirety, of the property or interest received. Thus, if a tenancy by the entirety is terminated so that thereafter each spouse owns an undivided half interest in the property as tenant in common, the value of the proceeds of termination received by each spouse is one-half the value of the property at the time of the termination of the tenancy by the entirety. If under local law one spouse, without the consent of the other, can bring about a severance of his or her interest in a tenancy by the entirety and does so by making a gift of his or her interest to a third party, that spouse is considered as having received proceeds of termination in the amount of the fair market value, at the time of the termination, of his severable interest determined in accordance with the rules prescribed in § 25.2512-5. He has, in addition, made a gift to the third party of the fair market value of the interest conveyed to the third party. In such a case, the other spouse also is considered as having received as proceeds of termination the fair market value, at the time of termination, of the interest which she thereafter holds in the property as tenant in common with the third party. However, since section 2515(b) contemplates that the spouses may divide the proceeds of termination in some proportion other than that represented by the values of their respective legal interests in the property, if both spouses join together in making a gift to a third party of property held by them as tenants by the entirety, the value of the proceeds of termination which will be treated as received by each is the amount which each reports (on his or her gift tax return filed for the calendar quarter or calendar year in which the termination occurs) as the value of his or her gift to the third party. This amount is the amount which each reports without regard to whether the spouses elect under section 2513 to treat the gifts as made one-half by each. For example, assume that H and W (his wife) hold real property as tenants by the entirety; that in the first calendar quarter of 1972, when the property has a fair market value of $60,000, they give it to their son; and that on their gift tax returns for such calendar quarter, H reports himself as having made a gift to the son of $36,000 and W reports herself as having made a gift to the son of $24,000. Under these circumstances, H is considered as having received proceeds of termination valued at $36,000, and W is considered as having received proceeds of termination valued at $24,000.

(ii) Except as provided otherwise in subparagraph (2)(ii) of this paragraph (under which certain tenancies by the entirety are considered not to be terminated), where the proceeds of a sale, exchange, or other disposition of the property are not actually divided between the spouses but are held (whether in a bank account or otherwise) in their joint names or in the name of one spouse as custodian or trustee for their joint interests, each spouse is presumed, in the absence of a showing to the contrary, to have received, as of the date of termination, proceeds of termination equal in value to the value of his or her enforceable property rights in respect of the proceeds. [Reg. § 25.2515-1.]

☐ [T.D. 6334, 11-15-58. *Amended by T.D. 7238,* 12-29-72 *and T.D. 8522,* 2-28-94.]

[Reg. § 25.2515-2]

§ 25.2515-2. Tenancies by the entirety; transfers treated as gifts; manner of election and valuation.—(a) The election to treat the creation of a tenancy by the entirety in real property, or additions made to its value, as constituting a gift in the calendar quarter or calendar year in which effected, shall be exercised by including the value of such gifts in the gift tax return of the donor for such calendar quarter or calendar year in which the tenancy was created, or the additions in value were made to the property. See section 6019 and the regulations thereunder. The election may be exercised only in a return filed within the time prescribed by law, or before the expiration of any extension of time granted pursuant to law for the filing of the return. See section 6075 for the time for filing the gift tax return and section 6081 for extensions of time for filing the return, together with the regulations thereunder. In order to make the election, a gift tax return must be filed for the calendar quarter or calendar year in which the tenancy was created, or additions in value thereto made, even though the value of the gift involved does not exceed the amount of the exclusion provided by section 2503(b). See § 25.2502-1(c)(1) for the definition of calendar quarter.

(b) If the donor spouse exercises the election as provided in paragraph (a) of this section, the amount of the gift at the creation of the tenancy is the amount of his contribution to the tenancy less the value of his retained interest in it, determined as follows:

(1) If under the law of the jurisdiction governing the rights of the spouses, either spouse, acting alone, can bring about a severance of his or her interest in the property, the value of the donor's retained interest is one-half the value of the property.

(2) If, under the law of the jurisdiction governing the rights of the spouses each is entitled to share in the income or other enjoyment of the property but neither, acting alone, may defeat the right of the survivor of them to the whole of the property, the amount of retained interest of the donor is determined by use of the appropriate actuarial factors for the spouses at their respective attained ages at the time the transaction is effected.

(c) Factors representing the respective interests of the spouses, under a tenancy by the entirety, at their attained ages at the time of the transaction may be readily computed based on the method described in § 25.2512-5. State law may provide that the husband only is entitled to all of the income or other enjoyment of the real property held as tenants by the entirety, and the wife's interest consists only of the right of survivorship with no right of severance. In such a case, a special factor may be needed to determine the value of the interests of the respective spouses. See § 25.2512-5(d)(4) for the procedure for obtaining special factors from the Internal Revenue Service in appropriate cases.

(d) The application of this paragraph may be illustrated by the following example:

Example. A husband with his own funds acquires real property valued at $10,000 and has it conveyed to himself and his wife as tenants by the entirety. Under the law of the jurisdiction governing the rights of the parties, each spouse is entitled to share in the income from the property but neither spouse acting alone could bring about a severance of his or her interest. The husband elects to treat the transfer as a gift in the year in which effected. At the time of transfer, the ages of the husband and wife are 45 and 40, respectively, on their birthdays nearest to the date of transfer. The value of the gift to the wife is $5,502.90, computed as follows:

Value of property transferred	$10,000.00
Less $10,000 × 0.44971 (factor for value of donor's retained rights) . . .	4,497.10
Value of gift	5,502.90

[Reg. § 25.2515-2.]

□ [T.D. 6334, 11-15-58. *Amended by T.D.* 7150, 12-2-71, *T.D.* 7238, 12-29-72 *and T.D.* 8540, 6-9-94.]

[Reg. § 25.2515-3]

§ 25.2515-3. Termination of tenancy by the entirety; cases in which entire value of gift is determined under section 2515(b).—(a) *In any case in which.*—(1) The creation of a tenancy by the entirety (including additions in value thereto) was not treated as a gift, and

(2) The entire consideration for the creation of the tenancy, and any additions in value thereto, was furnished solely by the spouses (see paragraph (c)(1)(ii) of § 25.2515-1), the termination of the tenancy (other than by the death of a spouse) always results in the making of a gift by a spouse who receives a smaller share of the proceeds of the termination (whether received in cash, property or interests in property) than the share of the proceeds attributable to the total consideration furnished by him. See paragraph (c) of § 25.2515-1 for a discussion of what constitutes consideration and the value thereof. Thus, a gift is effected at the time of termination of the tenancy by the spouse receiving less than one-half of the proceeds of termination if such spouse (regardless of age) furnished one-half or more of the total consideration for the purchase and improvements, if any, of the property held in the tenancy. Also, if one spouse furnished the entire consideration, a gift is made by such spouse to the extent that the other spouse receives any portion of the proceeds of termination. See § 25.2515-4 for determination of the amount of the gift, if any, in cases in which the creation of the tenancy was treated as a gift or a portion of the consideration was furnished by a third person. See paragraph (d)(2) of § 25.2515-1 as to the acts which effect a termination of the tenancy.

(b) In computing the value of the gift under the circumstances described in paragraph (a) of this section, it is first necessary to determine the spouse's share of the proceeds attributable to the consideration furnished by him. This share is computed by multiplying the total value of the proceeds of the termination by a fraction, the numerator of which is the total consideration furnished by the donor spouse and the denominator of which is the total consideration furnished by both spouses. From this amount there is subtracted the value of the proceeds of termination received by the donor spouse. The amount remaining is the value of the gift. In arriving at the "total consideration furnished by the donor spouse" and the "total consideration furnished by both spouses", for purposes of the computation provided for in this paragraph, the consideration furnished (see paragraph (c) of § 25.2515-1) is not reduced by any amounts which otherwise would have been excludable under section 2503(b) in determining the amounts of taxable gifts for calendar quarters or calendar years in which the consideration was furnished. (See § 25.2502-1(c)(1) for the definition of calendar quarter.) As an example assume that in 1955, real property was purchased for $30,000, the husband and wife each contributing $12,000 and the remaining $6,000 being obtained through a mortgage on the property. In each of the years 1956 and 1957, the husband paid $3,000 on the principal of the indebtedness, but did not disclose the value of these transfers on his gift tax returns for those years. The total consideration furnished by the husband is $18,000, the total consideration furnished by the wife is $12,000, and the total consideration furnished by both spouses is $30,000.

(c) The application of this section may be illustrated by the following examples:

Example (1). In 1956 the husband furnished $30,000 and his wife furnished $10,000 of the consideration for the purchase and subsequent improvement of real property held by them as tenants by the entirety. The husband did not elect to treat the consideration furnished as a gift. The property later is sold for $60,000, the husband receiving $35,000 and his wife receiving $25,000 of the proceeds of the termination. The termination of the tenancy results in a gift of $10,000 by the husband to his wife, computed as follows:

[$30,000 (consideration furnished by husband) ÷ $40,000 (total consideration furnished by both spouses)] × $60,000 (proceeds of termination) = $45,000
$45,000 – $35,000 (proceeds received by husband) = $10,000 gift by husband to wife.

Example (2). In 1950 the husband purchased shares of X Company for $10,000. In 1955 when those shares had a fair market value of $30,000, he and his wife purchased real property from A and had it conveyed to them as tenants by the entirety. In payment for the real property, the husband transferred his shares of X Company to A and the wife paid A the sum of $10,000. They later sold the real property for $60,000, divided $24,000 (each taking $12,000) and reinvested the remaining $36,000 in other real property under circumstances that satisfied the conditions set forth in paragraph (d)(2)(ii) of § 25.2515-1. The tenancy was terminated only with respect to the $24,000 divided between them. This termination of the tenancy resulted in a gift of $6,000 by the husband to the wife, computed as follows:

[$30,000 (consid eration furnished by husband) ÷ $40,000 (total consideration furnished by both spouses)] × $24,000 (proceeds of termination) = $18,000
$18,000 – $12,000 (proceeds received by husband) = $6,000 gift by husband to wife.

Since the tenancy was terminated only in part, with respect to the remaining portion of the tenancy each spouse is considered as having furnished that proportion of the total consideration for the remaining portion of the tenancy as the consideration furnished by him before the sale bears to the total consideration furnished by both spouses before the sale. See paragraph (c) of § 25.2515-1. The consideration furnished by the husband for the reduced tenancy is $27,000, computed as follows:

[$30,000 (consid eration furnished by husband before sale) ÷ $40,000 (total consideration furnished by both spouses before sale)]× $36,000 (consideration for reduced tenancy) = $27,000

The consideration furnished by the wife is $9,000, computed in a similar manner. [Reg. § 25.2515-3.]

☐ [*T.D.* 6334, 11-15-58. *Amended by T.D.* 7238, 12-29-72.]

[Reg. § 25.2515-4]

§ 25.2515-4. Termination of tenancy by entirety; cases in which none, or a portion only, of value of gift is determined under section 2515(b).—(a) *In general.*—The rules provided in section 2515(b) (see § 25.2515-3) are not applied in determining whether a gift has been made at

the termination of a tenancy to the extent that the consideration furnished for the creation of the tenancy was treated as a gift or if the consideration for the creation of the tenancy was furnished by a third party. Consideration furnished for the creation of the tenancy was treated as a gift if it was furnished either (1) during calendar years prior to 1955, or (2) during the calendar year 1955 and subsequent calendar years and calendar quarters and the donor spouse exercised the election to treat the furnishing of consideration as a gift. (For the definition of calendar quarter see § 25.2502-1(c)(1).) See paragraph (b) of this section for the manner of computing the value of gifts resulting from the termination of the tenancy under these circumstances. See paragraph (c) of this section for the rules to be applied where part of the total consideration for the creation of the tenancy and additions to the value thereof was not treated as a gift and part either was treated as a gift or was furnished by a third party.

(b) *Value of gift when entire consideration is of the type described in paragraph (a) of this section.*—If the entire consideration for the creation of a tenancy by the entirety was treated as a gift or contributed by a third party, the determination of the amount, if any, of a gift made at the termination of the tenancy will be made by the application of the general principles set forth in § 25.2511-1. Under those principles, when a spouse surrenders a property interest in a tenancy, the creation of which was treated as a gift, and in return receives an amount (whether in the form of cash, property, or an interest in property) less than the value of the property interest surrendered, that spouse is deemed to have made a gift in an amount equal to the difference between the value at the time of termination, of the property interest surrendered by such spouse and the amount received in exchange. Thus, if the husband's interest in such a tenancy at the time of termination is worth $44,971 and the wife's interest therein at the time is worth $55,029, the property is sold for $100,000, and each spouse received $50,000 out of the proceeds of the sale, the wife has made a gift to the husband of $5,029. The principles applied in paragraph (c) of § 25.2515-2 for the method of determining the value of the respective interests of the spouses at the time of the creation of a tenancy by the entirety are equally applicable in determining the value of each spouse's interest in the tenancy at termination, except that the actuarial factors to be applied are those for the respective spouses at the ages attained at the date of termination.

(c) *Valuation of gift where both types of consideration are involved.*—If the consideration furnished consists in part of the type described in paragraph (a) of § 25.2515-3 (consideration furnished by the spouses after 1954, and not treated as a gift in the calendar quarter or calendar year in which it was furnished) and in part of the type described in paragraph (a) of this section (consideration furnished by the spouses and treated as a gift or furnished by a third party), the amount of the gift is determined as follows:

(1) By applying the principles set forth in paragraph (b) of § 25.2515-3 to that portion of the total proceeds of termination which the consideration described in paragraph (a) of § 25.2515-3 bears to the total consideration furnished;

(2) By applying the principles set forth in paragraph (b) of this section to the remaining portion of the total proceeds of termination; and

(3) By subtracting the proceeds of termination received by the donor from the total of the amounts which under the principles referred to in subparagraphs (1) and (2) of this paragraph are to be compared with the proceeds of termination received by a spouse in determining whether a gift was made by that spouse. For example, assume that consideration of $30,000 was furnished by the husband in 1954. Assume also that on February 1, 1955, the husband contributed $12,000 and the wife $8,000, the husband's contribution not being treated as a gift (see paragraph (b) of § 25.2515-1). Assume further that between 1957 and 1965 the property appreciated in value by $40,000 and was sold in 1965 for $90,000 (of which the husband received $40,000 and the wife $50,000). The principles set forth in paragraph (b) of § 25.2515-3 are applied to $36,000 (20,000/50,000 × $90,000) in arriving at the amount which is compared with the proceeds of termination received by a spouse. Applying the principles set forth in paragraph (b) of § 25.2515-3, this amount in the case of the husband is $21,600 (12,000/20,000 × $36,000). Similarly, the principles set forth in paragraph (b) of this section are applied to $54,000 ($90,000 − 36,000), the remaining portion of the proceeds of termination, in arriving at the amount which is compared with the proceeds of termination received by a spouse. If in this case either spouse, without the consent of the other spouse, can bring about a severance of his interest in the tenancy, the amount determined under paragraph (b) of this section in the case of the husband would be $27,000 (¹/₂ of $54,000). The total of the two amounts which are to be compared with the proceeds of termination received by the husband is $48,600 ($21,600 + 27,000). This sum of $48,600 is then compared with the $40,000 proceeds received by the husband, and the termination of the tenancy has resulted, for gift tax purposes, in a transfer of $8,600 by the husband to his wife in 1965. See paragraph (d) of this section for an additional example illustrating the application of this paragraph.

(d) The application of paragraph (c) of this section may further be illustrated by the following example:

Example. X died in 1948 and devised real property to Y and Z (Y's wife) as tenant by the entirety. Under the law of the jurisdiction, both spouses are entitled to share equally in the income from, or the enjoyment of, the property, but neither spouse, acting along, may defeat the right of the survivor of them to the whole of the property. The fair market value of the property at the time of X's death was $100,000 and this amount is the consideration which X furnished toward the creation of the tenancy. In 1955, at which time the fair market value of the property was the same as at the time of X's death, improvements of $50,000 were made to the property, of which Y furnished $40,000 out of his own funds and Z furnished $10,000 out of her own funds. Y did not elect to treat his transfer to the tenancy as resulting in the making of a gift in 1955. In 1956 the property was sold for $300,000 and Y and Z each received $150,000 of the proceeds. At the time the property was sold Y and Z were 45 and 40 years of age, respectively, on their birthdays nearest the date of sale. The value of the gift made by Y to Z is $19,942, computed as follows:

Amount determined under principles set forth in § 25.2515-3:
$50,000 (consideration not treated as gift in year furnished) ÷ $150,000 (total consideration furnished) × $300,000 (proceeds of termination) = $100,000 (proceeds of termination to which principles set forth in § 25.2515-3 apply)
$40,000 (consideration furnished by H and not treated as gift) ÷ $50,000 (total consideration not treated as gift) × $100,000 = $80,000
Amount determined under principles set forth in paragraph (b) of this section:
$300,000 (total proceeds of termination) − $100,000 (proceeds to which principles set forth in § 25.2515-3 apply) = $200,000 (proceeds to which principles set forth in paragraph (b) apply) 0.44971 (factor for Y's latest) × $200,000 = $89,942

Amount of gift:
Amount determined under § 25.2515-3	$80,000
Amount determined under paragraph (b)	89,942
Total	169,942
Less: Proceeds received by Y	150,000
Amount of gift made by Y to Z . . .	19,942

[Reg. § 25.2515-4.]

☐ [*T.D.* 6334, 11-15-58. *Amended by T.D.* 7238, 12-29-72.]

[Reg. § 25.2516-1]

§ 25.2516-1. Certain property settlements.—
(a) Section 2516 provides that transfers of property or interests in property made under the terms of a written agreement between spouses in settlement of their marital or property rights are deemed to be for an adequate and full consideration in money or money's worth and, therefore, exempt from the gift tax (whether or not such

58,794
                  Transfers
See p. 20,601 for regulations not amended to reflect law changes

agreement is approved by a divorce decree), if the spouses obtain a final decree of divorce from each other within two years after entering into the agreement.

(b) See paragraph (b) of § 25.6019-3 for the circumstances under which information relating to property settlements must be disclosed on the transferor's gift tax return for the "calendar period" (as defined in § 25.2502-1(c)(1)) in which the agreement becomes effective. [Reg. § 25.2516-1.]

☐ [*T.D.* 6334, 11-14-58. *Amended by T.D.* 7238, 12-28-72 *and T.D.* 7910, 9-6-83.]

[Reg. § 25.2516-2]

§ 25.2516-2. Transfers in settlement of support obligations.—Transfers to provide a reasonable allowance for the support of children (including legally adopted children) of a marriage during minority are not subject to the gift tax if made pursuant to an agreement which satisfies the requirements of section 2516. [Reg. § 25.2516-2.]

☐ [*T.D.* 6334, 11-14-58.]

[Reg. § 25.2518-1]

§ 25.2518-1. Qualified disclaimers of property; In general.—(a) *Applicability.*—(1) *In general.*—The rules described in this section, § 25.2518-2, and § 25.2518-3 apply to the qualified disclaimer of an interest in property which is created in the person disclaiming by a transfer made after December 31, 1976. In general, a qualified disclaimer is an irrevocable and unqualified refusal to accept the ownership of an interest in property. For rules relating to the determination of when a transfer creating an interest occurs, see § 25.2518-2(c)(3) and (4).

(2) *Example.*—The provisions of paragraph (a)(1) of this section may be illustrated by the following example:

Example. W creates an irrevocable trust on December 10, 1968, and retains the right to receive the income for life. Upon the death of W, which occurs after December 31, 1976, the trust property is distributable to W's surviving issue, *per stirpes.* The transfer creating the remainder interest in the trust occurred in 1968. See § 25.2511-1(c)(2). Therefore, section 2518 does not apply to the disclaimer of the remainder interest because the transfer creating the interest was made prior to January 1, 1977. If, however, W had caused the gift to be incomplete by also retaining the power to designate the person or persons to receive the trust principal at death, and, as a result, no transfer (within the meaning of § 25.2511-1(c)(2)) of the remainder interest was made at the time of the creation of the trust, section 2518 would apply to any disclaimer made after W's death with respect to an interest in the trust property.

(3) Paragraph (a)(1) of this section is applicable for transfers creating the interest to be disclaimed made on or after December 31, 1997.

(b) *Effect of a qualified disclaimer.*—If a person makes a qualified disclaimer as described in section 2518(b) and § 25.2518-2, for purposes of the Federal estate, gift, and generation-skipping transfer tax provisions, the disclaimed interest in property is treated as if it had never been transferred to the person making the qualified disclaimer. Instead, it is considered as passing directly from the transferor of the property to the person entitled to receive the property as a result of the disclaimer. Accordingly, a person making a qualified disclaimer is not treated as making a gift. Similarly, the value of a decedent's gross estate for purposes of the Federal estate tax does not include the value of property with respect to which the decedent, or the decedent's executor or administrator on behalf of the decedent, has made a qualified disclaimer. If the disclaimer is not a qualified disclaimer, for the purposes of the Federal estate, gift, and generation-skipping transfer tax provisions, the disclaimer is disregarded and the disclaimant is treated as having received the interest.

(c) *Effect of local law.*—(1) *In general.*—(i) *Interests created before 1982.*—A disclaimer of an interest created in a taxable transfer before 1982 which otherwise meets the requirements of a qualified disclaimer under section 2518 and the corresponding regulations but which, by itself, is not effective under applicable local law to divest ownership of the disclaimed property from the disclaimant and vest it in another, is nevertheless treated as a qualified disclaimer under section 2518 if, under applicable local law, the disclaimed interest in property is transferred, as a result of attempting the disclaimer, to another person without any direction on the part of the disclaimant. An interest in property will not be considered to be transferred without any direction on the part of the disclaimant if, under applicable local law, the disclaimant has any discretion (whether or not such discretion is exercised) to determine who will receive such interest. Actions by the disclaimant which are required under local law merely to divest ownership of the property from the disclaimant and vest ownership in another person will not disqualify the disclaimer for purposes of section 2518(a). See § 25.2518-2(d)(1) for rules relating to the immediate vesting of title in the disclaimant.

(ii) *Interests created after 1981.*—[Reserved].

(2) *Creditor's claims.*—The fact that a disclaimer is voidable by the disclaimant's creditors has no effect on the determination of whether such disclaimer constitutes a qualified disclaimer. However, a disclaimer that is wholly void or that is voided by the disclaimant's creditors cannot be a qualified disclaimer.

(3) *Examples.*—The provisions of paragraphs (c)(1) and (2) of this section may be illustrated by the following examples:

Example (1). F dies testate in State Y on June 17, 1978. G and H are beneficiaries under the will. The will provides that any disclaimed property is to pass to the residuary estate. H has no interest in the residuary estate. Under the applicable laws of State Y, a disclaimer must be made within 6 months of the death of the testator. Seven months after F's death, H disclaimed the real property H received under the will. The disclaimer statute of State Y has a provision stating that an untimely disclaimer will be treated as an assignment of the interest disclaimed to those persons who would have taken had the disclaimer been valid. Pursuant to this provision, the disclaimed property became part of the residuary estate. Assuming the remaining requirements of section 2518 are met, H has made a qualified disclaimer for purposes of section 2518(a).

Example (2). Assume the same facts as in example (1) except that the law of State Y does not treat an ineffective disclaimer as a transfer to alternative takers. H assigns the disclaimed interest by deed to those who would have taken had the disclaimer been valid. Under these circumstances, H has not made a qualified disclaimer for purposes of section 2518(a) because the disclaimant directed who would receive the property.

Example (3). Assume the same facts as in example (1) except that the law of State Y requires H to pay a transfer tax in order to effectuate the transfer under the ineffective disclaimer provision. H pays the transfer tax. H has made a qualified disclaimer for purposes of section 2518(a).

(d) *Cross-reference.*—For rules relating to the effect of qualified disclaimers on the estate tax charitable and marital deductions, see §§ 20.2055-2(c) and 20.2056(d)-1 respectively. For rules relating to the effect of a qualified disclaimer of a general power of appointment, see § 20.2041-3(d). [Reg. § 25.2518-1.]

☐ [*T.D.* 8095, 8-6-89. *Amended by T.D.* 8744, 12-30-97.]

[Reg § 25.2518-2]

§ 25.2518-2. Requirements for a qualified disclaimer.—(a) *In general.*—For the purposes of section 2518(a), a disclaimer shall be a qualified disclaimer only if it satisfies the requirements of this section. In general, to be a qualified disclaimer—

(1) The disclaimer must be irrevocable and unqualified;

(2) The disclaimer must be in writing;

(3) The writing must be delivered to the person specified in paragraph (b)(2) of this sec-

tion within the time limitations specified in paragraph (c)(1) of this section;

(4) The disclaimant must not have accepted the interest disclaimed or any of its benefits; and

(5) The interest disclaimed must pass either to the spouse of the decedent or to a person other than the disclaimant without any direction on the part of the person making the disclaimer.

(b) *Writing.*—(1) *Requirements.*—A disclaimer is a qualified disclaimer only if it is in writing. The writing must identify the interest in property disclaimed and be signed either by the disclaimant or by the disclaimant's legal representative.

(2) *Delivery.*—The writing described in paragraph (b)(1) of this section must be delivered to the transferor of the interest, the transferor's legal representative, the holder of the legal title to the property to which the interest relates, or the person in possession of such property.

(c) *Time limit.*—(1) *In general.*—A disclaimer is a qualified disclaimer only if the writing described in paragraph (b)(1) of this section is delivered to the persons described in paragraph (b)(2) of this section no later than the date which is 9 months after the later of—

(i) The date on which the transfer creating the interest in the disclaimant is made, or

(ii) The day on which the disclaimant attains age 21.

(2) *A timely mailing of a disclaimer treated as a timely delivery.*—Although section 7502 and the regulations under that section apply only to documents to be filed with the Service, a timely mailing of a disclaimer to the person described in paragraph (b)(2) of this section is treated as a timely delivery if the mailing requirements under paragraphs (c)(1), (c)(2) and (d) of § 301.7502-1 are met. Further, if the last day of the period specified in paragraph (c)(1) of this section falls on Saturday, Sunday or a legal holiday (as defined in paragraph (b) of § 301.7503-1), then the delivery of the writing described in paragraph (b)(1) of this section shall be considered timely if delivery is made on the first succeeding day which is not Saturday, Sunday or a legal holiday. See paragraph (d)(3) of this section for rules applicable to the exception for individuals under 21 years of age.

(3) *Transfer.*—(i) For purposes of the time limitation described in paragraph (c)(1)(i) of this section, the 9-month period for making a disclaimer generally is to be determined with reference to the transfer creating the interest in the disclaimant. With respect to inter vivos transfers, a transfer creating an interest occurs when there is a completed gift for Federal gift tax purposes regardless of whether a gift tax is imposed on the completed gift. Thus, gifts qualifying for the gift tax annual exclusion under section 2503(b) are regarded as transfers creating an interest for this

Reg. § 25.2518-2(c)(3)(i)

purpose. With respect to transfers made by a decedent at death or transfers that become irrevocable at death, the transfer creating the interest occurs on the date of the decedent's death, even if an estate tax is not imposed on the transfer. For example, a bequest of foreign-situs property by a nonresident alien decedent is regarded as a transfer creating an interest in property even if the transfer would not be subject to estate tax. If there is a transfer creating an interest in property during the transferor's lifetime and such interest is later included in the transferor's gross estate for estate tax purposes (or would have been included if such interest were subject to estate tax), the 9-month period for making the qualified disclaimer is determined with reference to the earlier transfer creating the interest. In the case of a general power of appointment, the holder of the power has a 9-month period after the transfer creating the power in which to disclaim. If a person to whom any interest in property passes by reason of the exercise, release, or lapse of a general power desires to make a qualified disclaimer, the disclaimer must be made within a 9-month period after the exercise, release, or lapse regardless of whether the exercise, release, or lapse is subject to estate or gift tax. In the case of a nongeneral power of appointment, the holder of the power, permissible appointees, or takers in default of appointment must disclaim within a 9-month period after the original transfer that created or authorized the creation of the power. If the transfer is for the life of an income beneficiary with succeeding interests to other persons, both the life tenant and the other remaindermen, whether their interests are vested or contingent, must disclaim no later than 9 months after the original transfer creating an interest. In the case of a remainder interest in property which an executor elects to treat as qualified terminable interest property under section 2056(b)(7), the remainderman must disclaim within 9 months of the transfer creating the interest, rather than 9 months from the date such interest is subject to tax under section 2044 or 2519. A person who receives an interest in property as the result of a qualified disclaimer of the interest must disclaim the previously disclaimed interest no later than 9 months after the date of the transfer creating the interest in the preceding disclaimant. Thus, if A were to make a qualified disclaimer of a specific bequest and as a result of the qualified disclaimer the property passed as part of the residue, the beneficiary of the residue could make a qualified disclaimer no later than 9 months after the date of the testator's death. See paragraph (d)(3) of this section for the time limitation rule with reference to recipients who are under 21 years of age.

(ii) Sentences 1 through 10 and 12 of paragraph (c)(3)(i) of this section are applicable for transfers creating the interest to be disclaimed made on or after December 31, 1997.

(4) *Joint property.*—(i) *Interests in joint tenancy with right of survivorship or tenancies by the entirety.*—Except as provided in paragraph (c)(4)(iii) of this section (with respect to joint bank, brokerage, and other investment accounts), in the case of an interest in a joint tenancy with right of survivorship or a tenancy by the entirety, a qualified disclaimer of the interest to which the disclaimant succeeds upon creation of the tenancy must be made no later than 9 months after the creation of the tenancy regardless of whether such interest can be unilaterally severed under local law. A qualified disclaimer of the survivorship interest to which the survivor succeeds by operation of law upon the death of the first joint tenant to die must be made no later than 9 months after the death of the first joint tenant to die regardless of whether such interest can be unilaterally severed under local law and, except as provided in paragraph (c)(4)(ii) of this section (with respect to certain tenancies created on or after July 14, 1988), such interest is deemed to be a one-half interest in the property. (See, however, section 2518(b)(2)(B) for a special rule in the case of disclaimers by persons under age 21.) This is the case regardless of the portion of the property attributable to consideration furnished by the disclaimant and regardless of the portion of the property that is included in the decedent's gross estate under section 2040 and regardless of whether the interest can be unilaterally severed under local law. See paragraph (c)(5), Examples *(7)* and *(8)*, of this section.

(ii) *Certain tenancies in real property between spouses created on or after July 14, 1988.*—In the case of a joint tenancy between spouses or a tenancy by the entirety in real property created on or after July 14, 1988, to which section 2523(i)(3) applies (relating to the creation of a tenancy where the spouse of the donor is not a United States citizen), the surviving spouse may disclaim any portion of the joint interest that is includible in the decedent's gross estate under section 2040. See paragraph (c)(5), *Example (9)*, of this section.

(iii) *Special rule for joint bank, brokerage, and other investment accounts (e.g., accounts held at mutual funds) established between spouses or between persons other than husband and wife.*—In the case of a transfer to a joint bank, brokerage, or other investment account (e.g., an account held at a mutual fund), if a transferor may unilaterally regain the transferor's own contributions to the account without the consent of the other cotenant, such that the transfer is not a completed gift under § 25.2511-1(h)(4), the transfer creating the survivor's interest in the decedent's share of the account occurs on the death of the deceased cotenant. Accordingly, if a surviving joint tenant desires to make a qualified disclaimer with respect to funds contributed by a deceased cotenant, the disclaimer must be made within 9 months of the cotenant's death. The surviving joint tenant may not disclaim any portion of the joint account attributable to consideration furnished by that surviving joint tenant. See paragraph (c)(5), *Examples(12)*, *(13)*, and *(14)*, of this section, regarding the treatment of disclaimed interests under sections 2518, 2033 and 2040.

(iv) *Effective date*.—This paragraph (c)(4) is applicable for disclaimers made on or after December 31, 1997.

(5) *Examples*.—The provisions of paragraphs (c)(1) through (c)(4) of this section may be illustrated by the following examples. For purposes of the following examples, assume that all beneficiaries are over 21 years of age.

Example (1). On May 13, 1978, in a transfer which constitutes a completed gift for Federal gift tax purposes, A creates a trust in which B is given a lifetime interest in the income from the trust. B is also given a nongeneral testamentary power of appointment over the corpus of the trust. The power of appointment may be exercised in favor of any of the issue of A and B. If there are no surviving issue at B's death or if the power is not exercised, the corpus is to pass to E. On May 13, 1978, A and B have two surviving children, C and D. If A, B, C or D wishes to make a qualified disclaimer, the disclaimer must be made no later than 9 months after May 13, 1978.

Example (2). Assume the same facts as in example (1) except that B is given a general power of appointment over the corpus of the trust. B exercises the general power of appointment in favor of C upon B's death on June 17, 1989. C may make a qualified disclaimer no later than 9 months after June 17, 1989. If B had died without exercising the general power of appointment, E could have made a qualified disclaimer no later than 9 months after June 17, 1989.

Example (3). F creates a trust on April 1, 1978, in which F's child G is to receive the income from the trust for life. Upon G's death, the corpus of the trust is to pass to G's child H. If either G or H wishes to make a qualified disclaimer, it must be made no later than 9 months after April 1, 1978.

Example (4). A creates a trust on February 15, 1978, in which B is named the income beneficiary for life. The trust further provides that upon B's death the proceeds of the trust are to pass to C, if then living. If C predeceases D, the proceeds shall pass to D or D's estate. To have timely disclaimers for purposes of section 2518, B, C, and D must disclaim their respective interests no later than 9 months after February 15, 1978.

Example (5). A, a resident of State Q, dies on January 10, 1979, devising certain real property to B. The disclaimer laws of State Q require that a disclaimer be made within a reasonable time after a transfer. B disclaims the entire interest in real property on November 10, 1979. Although B's disclaimer may be effective under State Q law, it is not a qualified disclaimer under section

2518 because the disclaimer was made later than 9 months after the taxable transfer to B.

Example (6). A creates a revocable trust on June 1, 1980, in which B and C are given the income interest for life. Upon the death of the last income beneficiary, the remainder interest is to pass to D. The creation of the trust is not a completed gift for Federal gift tax purposes, but each distribution of trust income to B and C is a completed gift at the date of distribution. B and C must disclaim each income distribution no later than 9 months after the date of the particular distribution. In order to disclaim an income distribution in the form of a check, the recipient must return the check to the trustee uncashed along with a written disclaimer. A dies on September 1, 1982, causing the trust to become irrevocable, and the trust corpus is includible in A's gross estate for Federal estate tax purposes under section 2038. If B or C wishes to make a qualified disclaimer of his income interest, he must do so no later than 9 months after September 1, 1982. If D wishes to make a qualified disclaimer of his remainder interest, he must do so no later than 9 months after September 1, 1982.

Example (7). On February 1, 1990, A purchased real property with A's funds. Title to the property was conveyed to "A and B, as joint tenants with right of survivorship." Under applicable state law, the joint interest is unilaterally severable by either tenant. B dies on May 1, 1998, and is survived by A. On January 1, 1999, A disclaims the one-half survivorship interest in the property to which A succeeds as a result of B's death. Assuming that the other requirements of section 2518(b) are satisfied, A has made a qualified disclaimer of the one-half survivorship interest (but not the interest retained by A upon the creation of the tenancy, which may not be disclaimed by A). The result is the same whether or not A and B are married and regardless of the proportion of consideration furnished by A and B in purchasing the property.

Example (8). Assume the same facts as in *Example (7)* except that A and B are married and title to the property was conveyed to "A and B, as tenants by the entirety." Under applicable state law, the tenancy cannot be unilaterally severed by either tenant. Assuming that the other requirements of section 2518(b) are satisfied, A has made a qualified disclaimer of the one-half survivorship interest (but not the interest retained by A upon the creation of the tenancy, which may not be disclaimed by A). The result is the same regardless of the proportion of consideration furnished by A and B in purchasing the property.

Example (9). On March 1, 1989, H and W purchase a tract of vacant land which is conveyed to them as tenants by the entirety. The entire consideration is paid by H. W is not a United States citizen. H dies on June 1, 1998. W can disclaim the entire joint interest because this is the interest includible in H's gross estate under section 2040(a). Assuming that W's disclaimer is received by the executor of H's estate no later than 9 months after June 1, 1998, and the other requirements of section 2518(b) are satisfied, W's disclaimer of the property would be a qualified disclaimer. The result would be the same if the property was held in joint tenancy with right of survivorship that was unilaterally severable under local law.

Example (10). In 1986, spouses A and B purchased a personal residence taking title as tenants by the entirety. B dies on July 10, 1998. A wishes to disclaim the one-half undivided interest to which A would succeed by right of survivorship. If A makes the disclaimer, the property interest would pass under B's will to their child C. C, an adult, and A resided in the residence at B's death and will continue to reside there in the future. A continues to own a one-half undivided interest in the property. Assuming that the other requirements of section 2518(b) are satisfied, A may make a qualified disclaimer with respect to the one-half undivided survivorship interest in the residence if A delivers the written disclaimer to the personal representative of B's estate by April 10, 1999, since A is not deemed to have accepted the interest or any of its benefits prior to that time and A's occupancy of the residence after B's death is consistent with A's retained undivided ownership interest. The result would be the same if the property was held in joint tenancy with right of survivorship that was unilaterally severable under local law.

Example (11). H and W, husband and wife, reside in state X, a community property state. On April 1, 1978, H and W purchase real property with community funds. The property is not held by H and W as jointly owned property with rights of survivorship. H and W hold the property until January 3, 1985, when H dies. H devises his portion of the property to W. On March 15, 1985, W disclaims the portion of the property devised to her by H. Assuming all the other requirements of section 2518(b) have been met, W has made a qualified disclaimer of the interest devised to her by H. However, W could not disclaim the interest in the property that she acquired on April 1, 1978.

Example (12). On July 1, 1990, A opens a bank account that is held jointly with B, A's spouse, and transfers $50,000 of A's money to the account. A and B are United States citizens. A can regain the entire account without B's consent, such that the transfer is not a completed gift under § 25.2511-1(h)(4). A dies on August 15, 1998, and B disclaims the entire amount in the bank account on October 15, 1998. Assuming that the remaining requirements of section 2518(b) are satisfied, B made a qualified disclaimer under section 2518(a) because the disclaimer was made within 9 months after A's death at which time B had succeeded to full dominion and control over the account. Under

state law, B is treated as predeceasing A with respect to the disclaimed interest. The disclaimed account balance passes through A's probate estate and is no longer joint property includible in A's gross estate under section 2040. The entire account is, instead, includible in A's gross estate under section 2033. The result would be the same if A and B were not married.

Example (13). The facts are the same as *Example (12),* except that B, rather than A, dies on August 15, 1998. A may not make a qualified disclaimer with respect to any of the funds in the bank account, because A furnished the funds for the entire account and A did not relinquish dominion and control over the funds.

Example (14). The facts are the same as *Example (12),* except that B disclaims 40 percent of the funds in the account. Since, under state law, B is treated as predeceasing A with respect to the disclaimed interest, the 40 percent portion of the account balance that was disclaimed passes as part of A's probate estate, and is no longer characterized as joint property. This 40 percent portion of the account balance is, therefore, includible in A's gross estate under section 2033. The remaining 60 percent of the account balance that was not disclaimed retains its character as joint property and, therefore, is includible in A's gross estate as provided in section 2040(b). Therefore, 30 percent (1/2 x 60 percent) of the account balance is includible in A's gross estate under section 2040(b), and a total of 70 percent of the aggregate account balance is includible in A's gross estate. If A and B were not married, then the 40 percent portion of the account subject to the disclaimer would be includible in A's gross estate as provided in section 2033 and the 60 percent portion of the account not subject to the disclaimer would be includible in A's gross estate as provided in section 2040(a), because A furnished all of the funds with respect to the account.

(d) *No acceptance of benefits.*—(1) *Acceptance.*—A qualified disclaimer cannot be made with respect to an interest in property if the disclaimant has accepted the interest or any of its benefits, expressly or impliedly, prior to making the disclaimer. Acceptance is manifested by an affirmative act which is consistent with ownership of the interest in property. Acts indicative of acceptance include using the property or the interest in property; accepting dividends, interest, or rents from the property; and directing others to act with respect to the property or interest in property. However, merely taking delivery of an instrument of title, without more, does not constitute acceptance. Moreover, a disclaimant is not considered to have accepted property merely because under applicable local law title to the property vests immediately in the disclaimant upon the death of a decedent. The acceptance of one interest in property will not, by itself, constitute an acceptance of any other separate interests created by the transferor and held by the disclaimant in the same property. In the case of residential property, held in joint tenancy by some or all of the residents, a joint tenant will not be considered to have accepted the joint interest merely because the tenant resided on the property prior to disclaiming his interest in the property. The exercise of a power of appointment to any extent by the donee of the power is an acceptance of its benefits. In addition, the acceptance of any consideration in return for making the disclaimer is an acceptance of the benefits of the entire interest disclaimed.

(2) *Fiduciaries.*—If a beneficiary who disclaims an interest in property is also a fiduciary, actions taken by such person in the exercise of fiduciary powers to preserve or maintain the disclaimed property shall not be treated as an acceptance of such property or any of its benefits. Under this rule, for example, an executor who is also a beneficiary may direct the harvesting of a crop or the general maintenance of a home. A fiduciary, however, cannot retain a wholly discretionary power to direct the enjoyment of the disclaimed interest. For example, a fiduciary's disclaimer of a beneficial interest does not meet the requirements of a qualified disclaimer if the fiduciary exercised or retains a discretionary power to allocate enjoyment of that interest among members of a designated class. See paragraph (e) of this section for rules relating to the effect of directing the redistribution of disclaimed property.

(3) *Under 21 years of age.*—A beneficiary who is under 21 years of age has until 9 months after his twenty-first birthday in which to make a qualified disclaimer of his interest in property. Any actions taken with regard to an interest in property by a beneficiary or a custodian prior to the beneficiary's twenty-first birthday will not be an acceptance by the beneficiary of the interest.

(4) *Examples.*—The provisions of paragraphs (d)(1), (2) and (3) of this section may be illustrated by the following examples:

Example (1). On April 9, 1977, A established a trust for the benefit of B, then age 22. Under the terms of the trust, the current income of the trust is to be paid quarterly to B. Additionally, one half the principal is to be distributed to B when B attains the age of 30 years. The balance of the principal is to be distributed to B when B attains the age of 40 years. Pursuant to the terms of the trust, B received a distribution of income on June 30, 1977. On August 1, 1977, B disclaimed B's right to receive both the income from the trust and the principal of the trust. B's disclaimer of the income interest is not a qualified disclaimer for purposes of section 2518(a) because B accepted income prior to making the disclaimer. B's disclaimer of the principal, however, does satisfy section 2518(b)(3). See also § 25.2518-3 for rules relating to the disclaimer of less than an entire interest in property.

Example (2). B is the recipient of certain property devised to B under the will of A. The will stated that any disclaimed property was to pass to C. B and C entered into negotiations in which it was decided that B would disclaim all interest in the real property that was devised to B. In exchange, C promised to let B live in the family home for life. B's disclaimer is not a qualified disclaimer for purposes of section 2518(a) because B accepted consideration for making the disclaimer.

Example (3). A received a gift of Blackacre on December 25, 1978. A never resided on Blackacre but when property taxes on Blackacre became due on July 1, 1979, A paid them out of personal funds. On August 15, 1979, A disclaimed the gift of Blackacre. Assuming all the requirements of section 2518(b) have been met, A has made a qualified disclaimer of Blackacre. Merely paying the property taxes does not constitute an acceptance of Blackacre even though A's personal funds were used to pay the taxes.

Example (4). A died on February 15, 1978. Pursuant to A's will, B received a farm in State Z. B requested the executor to sell the farm and to give the proceeds to B. The executor then sold the farm pursuant to B's request. B then disclaimed $50,000 of the proceeds from the sale of the farm. B's disclaimer is not a qualified disclaimer. By requesting the executor to sell the farm B accepted the farm even though the executor may not have been legally obligated to comply with B's request. See also § 25.2518-3 for rules relating to the disclaimer of less than an entire interest in property.

Example (5). Assume the same facts as in example (4) except that instead of requesting the executor to sell the farm, B pledged the farm as security for a short-term loan which was paid off prior to distribution of the estate. B then disclaimed his interest in the farm. B's disclaimer is not a qualified disclaimer. By pledging the farm as security for the loan, B accepted the farm.

Example (6). A delivered 1,000 shares of stock in Corporation X to B as a gift on February 1, 1980. A had the shares registered in B's name on that date. On April 1, 1980, B disclaimed the interest in the 1,000 shares. Prior to making the disclaimer, B did not pledge the shares, accept any dividends or otherwise commit any acts indicative of acceptance. Assuming the remaining requirements of section 2518 are satisfied, B's disclaimer is a qualified disclaimer.

Example (7). On January 1, 1980, A created an irrevocable trust in which B was given a testamentary general power of appointment over the trust's corpus. B executed a will on June 1, 1980, in which B provided for the exercise of the power of appointment. On September 1, 1980, B disclaimed the testamentary power of appointment. Assuming the remaining requirements of section 2518(b) are satisfied, B's disclaimer of the testamentary power of appointment is a qualified disclaimer.

Reg. § 25.2518-2(d)(4)

Example (8). H and W reside in X, a community property state. On January 1, 1981, H and W purchase a residence with community funds. They continue to reside in the house until H dies testate on February 1, 1990. Although H could devise his portion of the residence to any person, H devised his portion of the residence to W. On September 1, 1990, W disclaims the portion of the residence devised to her pursuant to H's will but continues to live in the residence. Assuming the remaining requirements of section 2518(b) are satisfied, W's disclaimer is a qualified disclaimer under section 2518(a). W's continued occupancy of the house prior to making the disclaimer will not by itself be treated as an acceptance of the benefits of the portion of the residence devised to her by H.

Example (9). In 1979, D established a trust for the benefit of D's minor children E and F. Under the terms of the trust, the trustee is given the power to make discretionary distributions of current income and corpus to both children. The corpus of the trust is to be distributed equally between E and F when E becomes 35 years of age. Prior to attaining the age of 21 years on April 8, 1982, E receives several distributions of income from the trust. E receives no distributions of income between April 8, 1982 and August 15, 1982, which is the date on which E disclaims all interest in the income from the trust. As a result of the disclaimer the income will be distributed to F. If the remaining requirements of section 2518 are met, E's disclaimer is a qualified disclaimer under section 2518(a). To have a qualified disclaimer of the interest in corpus, E must disclaim the interest no later than 9 months after April 8, 1982, E's 21st birthday.

Example (10). Assume the same facts as in example (9) except that E accepted a distribution of income on May 13, 1982. E's disclaimer is not a qualified disclaimer under section 2518 because by accepting an income distribution after attaining the age of 21, E accepted benefits from the income interest.

Example (11). F made a gift of 10 shares of stock to G as custodian for H under the State X Uniform Gifts to Minors Act. At the time of the gift, H was 15 years old. At age 18, the local age of majority, the 10 shares were delivered to and registered in the name of H. Between the receipt of the shares and H's 21st birthday, H received dividends from the shares. Within 9 months of attaining age 21, H disclaimed the 10 shares. Assuming H did not accept any dividends from the shares after attaining age 21, the disclaimer by H is a qualified disclaimer under section 2518.

(e) *Passage without direction by the disclaimant of beneficial enjoyment of disclaimed interest.*—(1) *In general.*—A disclaimer is not a qualified disclaimer unless the disclaimed interest passes without any direction on the part of the disclaimant to a person other than the disclaimant (except as provided in paragraph (e)(2) of this

section). If there is an express or implied agreement that the disclaimed interest in property is to be given or bequeathed to a person specified by the disclaimant, the disclaimant shall be treated as directing the transfer of the property interest. The requirements of a qualified disclaimer under section 2518 are not satisfied if—

(i) The disclaimant, either alone or in conjunction with another, directs the redistribution or transfer of the property or interest in property to another person (or has the power to direct the redistribution or transfer of the property or interest in property to another person unless such power is limited by an ascertainable standard); or

(ii) The disclaimed property or interest in property passes to or for the benefit of the disclaimant as a result of the disclaimer (except as provided in paragraph (e)(2) of this section).

If a power of appointment is disclaimed, the requirements of this paragraph (e)(1) are satisfied so long as there is no direction on the part of the disclaimant with respect to the transfer of the interest subject to the power or with respect to the transfer of the power to another person. A person may make a qualified disclaimer of a beneficial interest in property even if after such disclaimer the disclaimant has a fiduciary power to distribute to designated beneficiaries, but only if the power is subject to an ascertainable standard. See examples (11) and (12) of paragraph (e)(5) of this section.

(2) *Disclaimer by surviving spouse.*—In the case of a disclaimer made by a decedent's surviving spouse with respect to property transferred by the decedent, the disclaimer satisfies the requirements of this paragraph (e)(2) if the interest passes as a result of the disclaimer without direction on the part of the surviving spouse either to the surviving spouse or to another person. If the surviving spouse, however, retains the right to direct the beneficial enjoyment of the disclaimed property in a transfer that is not subject to Federal estate and gift tax (whether as trustee or otherwise), such spouse will be treated as directing the beneficial enjoyment of the disclaimed property, unless such power is limited by an ascertainable standard. See examples (4), (5), and (6) in paragraph (e)(5) of this section.

(3) *Partial failure of disclaimer.*—If a disclaimer made by a person other than the surviving spouse is not effective to pass completely an interest in property to a person other than the disclaimant because—

(i) The disclaimant also has a right to receive such property as an heir at law, residuary beneficiary, or by any other means; and

(ii) The disclaimant does not effectively disclaim these rights,

the disclaimer is not a qualified disclaimer with respect to the portion of the disclaimed property which the disclaimant has a right to receive. If the portion of the disclaimed interest in property which the disclaimant has a right to receive is not severable property or an undivided portion of the property, then the disclaimer is not a qualified disclaimer with respect to any portion of the property. Thus, for example, if a disclaimant who is not a surviving spouse receives a specific bequest of a fee simple interest in property and as a result of the disclaimer of the entire interest, the property passes to a trust in which the disclaimant has a remainder interest, then the disclaimer will not be a qualified disclaimer unless the remainder interest in the property is also disclaimed. See § 25.2518-3(a)(1)(ii) for the definition of severable property.

(4) *Effect of precatory language.*—Precatory language in a disclaimer naming takers of disclaimed property will not be considered as directing the redistribution or transfer of the property or interest in property to such persons if the applicable State law gives the language no legal effect.

(5) *Examples.*—The provisions of this paragraph (e) may be illustrated by the following examples:

Example (1). A, a resident of State X, died on July 30, 1978. Pursuant to A's will, B, A's son and heir at law, received the family home. In addition, B and C each received 50 percent of A's residuary estate. B disclaimed the home. A's will made no provision for the distribution of property in the case of a beneficiary's disclaimer. Therefore, pursuant to the disclaimer laws of State X, the disclaimed property became part of the residuary estate. Because B's 50 percent share of the residuary estate will be increased by 50 percent of the value of the family home, the disclaimed property will not pass solely to another person. Consequently, B's disclaimer of the family home is a qualified disclaimer only with respect to the 50 percent portion ($60,000) that passes solely to C. Had B also disclaimed B's 50 percent interest in the residuary estate, the disclaimer would have been a qualified disclaimer under section 2518 of the entire interest in the home (assuming the remaining requirements of a qualified disclaimer were satisfied). Similarly, if under the laws of State X, the disclaimer has the effect of divesting B of all interest in the home, both as devisee and as a beneficiary of the residuary estate, including any property resulting from its sale, the disclaimer would be a qualified disclaimer of B's entire interest in the home.

Example (2). D, a resident of State Y, died testate on June 30, 1978. E, an heir at law of D, received specific bequests of certain severable personal property from D. E disclaimed the property transferred by D under the will. The will had no residuary clause and made no provision for the distribution of property in the case of a beneficiary's disclaimer. The disclaimer laws of State Y provide that such property shall pass to the decedent's heirs at law in the same manner

as if the disclaiming beneficiary had died immediately before the testator's death. Because State Y's law treats E as predeceasing D, the property disclaimed by E does not pass to E as an heir at law or otherwise. Consequently, if the remaining requirements of section 2518(b) are satisfied, E's disclaimer is a qualified disclaimer under section 2518(a).

Example (3). Assume the same facts as in example (2) except that State Y has no provision treating the disclaimant as predeceasing the testator. E's disclaimer satisfies section 2518(b)(4) only to the extent that E does not have a right to receive the property as an heir at law. Had E disclaimed both the share E received under D's will and E's intestate share, the requirement of section 2518(b)(4) would have been satisfied.

Example (4). B died testate on February 13, 1980. B's will established both a marital trust and a nonmarital trust. The decedent's surviving spouse, A, is an income beneficiary of the marital trust and has a testamentary general power of appointment over its assets. A is also an income beneficiary of the nonmarital trust, but has no power to appoint or invade the corpus. The provisions of the will specify that any portion of the marital trust disclaimed is to be added to the nonmarital trust. A disclaimed 30 percent of the marital trust. (See § 25.2518-3(b) for rules relating to the disclaimer of an undivided portion of an interest in property.) Pursuant to the will, this portion of the marital trust property was transferred to the nonmarital trust without any direction on the part of A. This disclaimer by A satisfies section 2518(b)(4).

Example (5). Assume the same facts as in example (4) except that A, the surviving spouse, has both an income interest in the nonmarital trust and a testamentary nongeneral power to appoint among designated beneficiaries. This power is not limited by an ascertainable standard. The requirements of section 2518(b)(4) are not satisfied unless A also disclaims the nongeneral power to appoint the portion of the trust corpus that is attributable to the property that passed to the nonmarital trust as a result of A's disclaimer. Assuming that the fair market value of the disclaimed property on the date of the disclaimer is $250,000 and that the fair market value of the nonmarital trust (including the disclaimed property) immediately after the disclaimer is $750,000, A must disclaim the power to appoint one-third of the nonmarital trust's corpus. The result is the same regardless of whether the nongeneral power is testamentary or inter vivos.

Example (6). Assume the same facts as in example (4) except that A has both an income interest in the nonmarital trust and a power to invade corpus if needed for A's health or maintenance. In addition, an independent trustee has power to distribute to A any portion of the corpus which the trustee determines to be desirable for A's happiness. Assuming the other requirements of section 2518 are satisfied, A may make a qualified disclaimer of interests in the marital trust without disclaiming any of A's interests in the nonmarital trust.

Example (7). B died testate on June 1, 1980. B's will created both a marital trust and a nonmarital trust. The decedent's surviving spouse, C, is an income beneficiary of the marital trust and has a testamentary general power of appointment over its assets. C is an income beneficiary of the nonmarital trust, and additionally has the noncumulative right to withdraw yearly the greater of $5,000 or 5 percent of the aggregate value of the principal. The provisions of the will specify that any portion of the marital trust disclaimed is to be added to the nonmarital trust. C disclaims 50 percent of the marital trust corpus. Pursuant to the will, this amount is transferred to the nonmarital trust. Assuming the remaining requirements of section 2518(b) are satisfied, C's disclaimer is a qualified disclaimer.

Example (8). A, a resident of State X, died on July 19, 1979. A was survived by a spouse B, and three children, C, D, and E. Pursuant to A's will, B received one-half of A's estate and the children received equal shares of the remaining one-half of the estate. B disclaimed the entire interest B had received. The will made no provisions for the distribution of property in the case of a beneficiary's disclaimer. The disclaimer laws of State X provide that under these circumstances disclaimed property passes to the decedent's heirs at law in the same manner as if the disclaiming beneficiary had died immediately before the testator's death. As a result, C, D, and E are A's only remaining heirs at law, and will divide the disclaimed property equally among themselves. B's disclaimer includes language stating that "it is my intention that C, D, and E will share equally in the division of this property as a result of my disclaimer." State X considers these to be precatory words and gives them no legal effect. B's disclaimer meets all other requirements imposed by State X on disclaimers, and is considered an effective disclaimer under which the property will vest solely in C, D, and E in equal shares without any further action required by B. Therefore, B is not treated as directing the redistribution or transfer of the property. If the remaining requirements of section 2518 are met, B's disclaimer is a qualified disclaimer.

Example (9). C died testate on January 1, 1979. According to C's will, D was to receive 1/3 of the residuary estate with any disclaimed property going to E. D was also to receive a second 1/3 of the residuary estate with any disclaimed property going to F. Finally, D was to receive a final 1/3 of the residuary estate with any disclaimed property going to G. D specifically states that he is disclaiming the interest in which the disclaimed property is designated to pass to E. D has effectively directed that the disclaimed property will pass to E and therefore D's disclaimer is not a qualified disclaimer under section 2518(a).

Example (10). Assume the same facts as in example (9) except that C's will also states that D was to receive Blackacre and Whiteacre. C's will further provides that if D disclaimed Blackacre then such property was to pass to E and that if D disclaimed Whiteacre then Whiteacre was to pass to F. D specifically disclaims Blackacre with the intention that it pass to E. Assuming the other requirements of section 2518 are met, D has made a qualified disclaimer of Blackacre. Alternatively, D could disclaim an undivided portion of both Blackacre and Whiteacre. Assuming the other requirements of section 2518 are met, this would also be a qualified disclaimer.

Example (11). G creates an irrevocable trust on February 16, 1983, naming H, I and J as the income beneficiaries for life and F as the remainderman. F is also named the trustee and as trustee has the discretionary power to invade the corpus and make discretionary distributions to H, I or J during their lives. F disclaims the remainder interest on August 8, 1983, but retains his discretionary power to invade the corpus. F has not made a qualified disclaimer because F retains the power to direct enjoyment of the corpus and the retained fiduciary power is not limited by an ascertainable standard.

Example (12). Assume the same facts as in example (11) except that F may only invade the corpus to make distributions for the health, maintenance or support of H, I or J during their lives. If the other requirements of section 2518(b) are met, F has made a qualified disclaimer of the remainder interest because the retained fiduciary power is limited by an ascertainable standard.

[Reg. § 25.2518-2.]

☐ [T.D. 8095, 8-6-86. *Amended by T.D. 8744,* 12-30-97.]

[Reg. § 25.2518-3]

§ 25.2518-3. Disclaimer of less than an entire interest.—(a) *Disclaimer of a partial interest.*—(1) *In general.*—(i) *Interest.*—If the requirements of this section are met, the disclaimer of all or an undivided portion of any separate interest in property may be a qualified disclaimer even if the disclaimant has another interest in the same property. In general, each interest in property that is separately created by the transferor is treated as a separate interest. For example, if an income interest in securities is bequeathed to A for life, then to B for life, with the remainder interest in such securities bequeathed to A's estate, and if the remaining requirements of section 2518(b) are met, A could make a qualified disclaimer of either the income interest or the remainder, or an undivided portion of either interest. A could not, however, make a qualified disclaimer of the income interest for a certain number of years. Further, where local law merges interests separately created by the transferor, a qualified disclaimer will be allowed only if there is a disclaimer of the entire merged interest or an undivided portion of such merged interest. See example (12) in paragraph(d) of this section. See § 25.2518-3(b) for rules relating to the disclaimer of an undivided portion. Where the merger of separate interests would occur but for the creation by the transferor of a nominal interest (as defined in paragraph (a)(1)(iv) of this section), a qualified disclaimer will be allowed only if there is a disclaimer of all the separate interests, or an undivided portion of all such interests, which would have merged but for the nominal interest.

(ii) *Severable property.*—A disclaimant shall be treated as making a qualified disclaimer of a separate interest in property if the disclaimer relates to severable property and the disclaimant makes a disclaimer which would be a qualified disclaimer if such property were the only property in which the disclaimant had an interest. If applicable local law does not recognize a purported disclaimer of severable property, the disclaimant must comply with the requirements of paragraph (c)(1) of § 25.2518-1 in order to make a qualified disclaimer of the severable property. Severable property is property which can be divided into separate parts each of which, after severance, maintains a complete and independent existence. For example, a legatee of shares of corporate stock may accept some shares of the stock and make a qualified disclaimer of the remaining shares.

(iii) *Powers of appointment.*—A power of appointment with respect to property is treated as a separate interest in such property and such power of appointment with respect to all or an undivided portion of such property may be disclaimed independently from any other interests separately created by the transferor in the property if the requirements of section 2518(b) are met. See example (21) of paragraph (d) of this section. Further, a disclaimer of a power of appointment with respect to property is a qualified disclaimer only if any right to direct the beneficial enjoyment of the property which is retained by the disclaimant is limited by an ascertainable standard. See example (9) of paragraph (d) of this section.

(iv) *Nominal interest.*—A nominal interest is an interest in property created by the transferor that—

(A) Has an actuarial value (as determined under § 20.2031-7) of less than 5 percent of the total value of the property at the time of the taxable transfer creating the interest,

(B) Prevents the merger under local law of two or more other interests created by the transferor, and

(C) Can be clearly shown from all the facts and circumstances to have been created primarily for the purpose of preventing merger of such other interests.

Factors to be considered in determining whether an interest is created primarily for the purpose of preventing merger include (but are not limited to) the following: the relationship between the transferor and the interest holder; the age difference between the interest holder and the beneficiary whose interests would have merged; the interest holder's state of health at the time of the taxable transfer; and, in the case of a contingent remainder, any other factors which indicate that the possibility of the interest vesting as a fee simple is so remote as to be negligible.

(2) *In trust.*—A disclaimer is not a qualified disclaimer under section 2518 if the beneficiary disclaims income derived from specific property transferred in trust while continuing to accept income derived from the remaining properties in the same trust unless the disclaimer results in such property being removed from the trust and passing, without any direction on the part of the disclaimant, to persons other than the disclaimant or to the spouse of the decedent. Moreover, a disclaimer of both an income interest and a remainder interest in specific trust assets is not a qualified disclaimer if the beneficiary retains interests in other trust property unless, as a result of the disclaimer, such assets are removed from the trust and pass, without any direction on the part of the disclaimant, to persons other than the disclaimant or to the spouse of the decedent. The disclaimer of an undivided portion of an interest in a trust may be a qualified disclaimer. See also paragraph (b) of this section for rules relating to the disclaimer of an undivided portion of an interest in property.

(b) *Disclaimer of undivided portion.*—A disclaimer of an undivided portion of a separate interest in property which meets the other requirements of a qualified disclaimer under section 2518(b) and the corresponding regulations is a qualified disclaimer. An undivided portion of a disclaimant's separate interest in property must consist of a fraction or percentage of each and every substantial interest or right owned by the disclaimant in such property and must extend over the entire term of the disclaimant's interest in such property and in other property into which such property is converted. A disclaimer of some specific rights while retaining other rights with respect to an interest in the property is not a qualified disclaimer of an undivided portion of the disclaimant's interest in property. Thus, for example, a disclaimer made by the devisee of a fee simple interest in Blackacre is not a qualified disclaimer if the disclaimant disclaims a remainder interest in Blackacre but retains a life estate.

(c) *Disclaimer of a pecuniary amount.*—A disclaimer of a specific pecuniary amount out of a pecuniary or nonpecuniary bequest or gift which satisfies the other requirements of a qualified disclaimer under section 2518(b) and the corre-

Reg. §25.2518-3(c)

sponding regulations is a qualified disclaimer provided that no income or other benefit of the disclaimed amount inures to the benefit of the disclaimant either prior to or subsequent to the disclaimer. Thus, following the disclaimer of a specific pecuniary amount from a bequest or gift, the amount disclaimed and any income attributable to such amount must be segregated from the portion of the gift or bequest that was not disclaimed. Such a segregation of assets making up the disclaimer of a pecuniary amount must be made on the basis of the fair market value of the assets on the date of the disclaimer or on a basis that is fairly representative of value changes that may have occurred between the date of transfer and the date of the disclaimer. A pecuniary amount distributed to the disclaimant from the bequest or gift prior to the disclaimer shall be treated as a distribution of corpus from the bequest or gift. However, the acceptance of a distribution from the gift or bequest shall also be considered to be an acceptance of a proportionate amount of income earned by the bequest or gift. The proportionate share of income considered to be accepted by the disclaimant shall be determined at the time of the disclaimer according to the following formula:

$$\frac{\text{total amount of distributions received by the disclaimant out of the gift or bequest}}{\text{total value of the gift or bequest on the date of transfer}} \times \begin{array}{c}\text{total amount of income}\\\text{earned by the gift or}\\\text{bequest between date of}\\\text{transfer and date of}\\\text{disclaimer.}\end{array}$$

See examples (17), (18), and (19) in § 25.2518-3 (d) for illustrations of the rules set forth in this paragraph (c).

(d) *Examples.*—The provisions of this section may be illustrated by the following examples:

Example (1). A, resident of State Q, died on August 1, 1978. A's will included specific bequests of 100 shares of stock in X corporation; 200 shares of stock in Y corporation; 500 shares of stock in Z corporation; personal effects consisting of paintings, home furnishings, jewelry, and silver; and a 500 acre farm consisting of a residence, various outbuildings, and 500 head of cattle. The laws of State Q provide that a disclaimed interest passes in the same manner as if the disclaiming beneficiary had died immediately before the testator's death. Pursuant to A's will, B was to receive both the personal effects and the farm. C was to receive all the shares of stock in Corporation X and Y and D was to receive all the shares of stock in Corporation Z. B disclaimed 2 of the paintings and all the jewelry, C disclaimed 50 shares of Y corporation stock, and D disclaimed 100 shares of Z corporation stock. If the remaining requirements of section 2518(b) and the corresponding regulations are met, each of these disclaimers is a qualified disclaimer for purposes of section 2518(a).

Example (2). Assume the same facts as in example (1) except that D disclaimed the income interest in the shares of Z corporation stock while retaining the remainder interest in such shares. D's disclaimer is not a qualified disclaimer.

Example (3). Assume the same facts as in example (1) except that B disclaimed 300 identified acres of the 500 acres. Assuming that B's disclaimer meets the remaining requirements of section 2518(b), it is a qualified disclaimer.

Example (4). Assume the same facts as in example (1) except that A devised the income from the farm to B for life and the remainder interest to C. B disclaimed 40 percent of the income from the farm. Assuming that it meets the remaining requirements of section 2518(b), B's disclaimer of an undivided portion of the income is a qualified disclaimer.

Example (5). E died on September 13, 1978. Under the provisions of E's will, E's shares of stock in X, Y, and Z corporations were to be transferred to a trust. The trust provides that all income is to be distributed currently to F and G in equal parts until F attains the age of 45 years. At that time the corpus of the trust is to be divided equally between F and G. F disclaimed the income arising from the shares of X stock. G disclaimed 20 percent of G's interest in the trust. F's disclaimer is not a qualified disclaimer because the X stock remains in the trust. If the remaining requirements of section 2518(b) are met, G's disclaimer is a qualified disclaimer.

Example (6). Assume the same facts as in example (5) except that F disclaimed both the income interest and the remainder interest in the shares of X stock. F's disclaimer results in the X stock being transferred out of the trust to G without any direction on F's part. F's disclaimer is a qualified disclaimer under section 2518(b).

Example (7). Assume the same facts as in example (5) except that F is only an income beneficiary of the trust. The X stock remains in the trust after F's disclaimer of the income arising from the shares of X stock. F's disclaimer is not a qualified disclaimer under section 2518.

Example (8). Assume the same facts as in example (5) except that F disclaimed the entire income interest in the trust while retaining the interest F has in corpus. Alternatively, assume that G disclaimed G's entire corpus interest while retaining G's interest in the income from the trust. If the remaining requirements of section 2518(b) are met, either disclaimer will be a qualified disclaimer.

Example (9). G creates an irrevocable trust on May 13, 1980, with H, I, and J as the income beneficiaries. In addition, H, who is the trustee, holds the power to invade corpus for H's health, maintenance, support and happiness and a testamentary power of appointment over the corpus. In the absence of the exercise of the power of appointment, the property passes to I and J in equal shares. H disclaimed the power to invade corpus for H's health, maintenance, support and happiness. Because H retained the testamentary power to appoint the property in the corpus, H's disclaimer is not a qualified disclaimer. If H also disclaimed the testamentary power of appointment, H's disclaimer would have been a qualified disclaimer.

Example (10). E creates an irrevocable trust on May 1, 1980, in which D is the income beneficiary for life. Subject to the trustee's discretion, E's children, A, B, and C, have the right to receive corpus during D's lifetime. The remainder passes to D if D survives A, B, C, and all their issue. D also holds an inter vivos power to appoint the trust corpus to A, B, and C. On September 1, 1980, D disclaimed the remainder interest. D's disclaimer is not a qualified disclaimer because D retained the power to direct the use and enjoyment of corpus during D's life.

Example (11). Under H's will, a trust is created from which W is to receive all of the income for life. The trustee has the power to invade the trust corpus for the support or maintenance of D during the life of W. The trust is to terminate at W's death, at which time the trust property is to be distributed to D. D makes a timely disclaimer of the right to corpus during W's lifetime, but does not disclaim the remainder interest. D's disclaimer is a qualified disclaimer assuming the remaining requirements of section 2518 are met.

Example (12). Under the provisions of G's will A received a life estate in a farm, and was the sole beneficiary of property in the residuary estate. The will also provided that the remainder interest in the farm pass to the residuary estate. Under local law A's interests merged to give A a fee simple in the farm. A made a timely disclaimer of the life estate. A's disclaimer of a partial interest is not a qualified disclaimer under section 2518(a). If A makes a disclaimer of the entire merged interest in the farm or an undivided portion of such merged interest then A would be making a qualified disclaimer assuming all the other requirements of section 2518(b) are met.

Example (13). A, a resident of State Z, dies on September 3, 1980. Under A's will, Blackacre is devised to C for life, then to D for 1 month, remainder to C. Had A not created D's interest, State Z law would have merged C's life estate and the remainder to C to create a fee simple interest in C. Assume that the actuarial value of D's interest is less than 5 percent of the total value of Blackacre on the date of A's death. Further assume that facts and circumstances (particularly the duration of D's interest) clearly indicate that D's interest was created primarily for the purpose of preventing the merger of C's two interests in Blackacre. D's interest in Black-

acre is a nominal interest and C's two interests will, for purposes of making a qualified disclaimer, be considered to have merged. Thus, C cannot make a qualified disclaimer of his remainder while retaining the life estate. C can, however, make a qualified disclaimer of both of these interests entirely or an undivided portion of both.

Example (14). A, a resident of State X, dies on October 12, 1978. Under A's will, Blackacre was devised to B for life, then to C for life if C survives B, remainder to B's estate. On the date of A's death, B and C are both 8 year old grandchildren of A. In addition, C is in good health. The actual value of C's interest is less than 5 percent of the total value of Blackacre on the date of A's death. No facts are present which would indicate that the possibility of C's contingent interest vesting is so remote as to be negligible. Had C's contingent life estate not been created, B's life estate and remainder interests would have merged under local law to give B a fee simple interest in Blackacre. Although C's interest prevents the merger of B's two interests and has an actual value of less than 5 percent, C's interest is not a nominal interest within the meaning of § 25.2518-3(a)(1)(iv) because the facts and circumstances do not clearly indicate that the interest was created primarily for the purpose of preventing the merger of other interests in the property. Assuming all the other requirements of section 2518(b) are met, B can make a qualified disclaimer of the remainder while retaining his life estate.

Example (15). In 1981, A transfers $60,000 to a trust created for the benefit of B who was given the income interest for life and who also has a testamentary nongeneral power of appointment over the corpus. A transfers an additional $25,000 to the trust on June 1, 1984. At that time the trust corpus (exclusive of the $25,000 transfer) has a fair market value of $75,000. On January 1, 1985, B disclaims the right to receive income attributable to 25 percent of the corpus

$$\frac{\$25,000 \quad \text{(1984 transfer)}}{\$100,000 \quad \begin{array}{l}\text{(Fair market value of} \\ \text{corpus immediately} \\ \text{after the 1984} \\ \text{transfer)}\end{array}} = 25\%.$$

Assuming that no distributions were made to B attributable to the $25,000, B's disclaimer is a qualified disclaimer for purposes of section 2518(a) if all the remaining requirements of section 2518(b) are met.

Example (16). Under the provisions of B's will, A is left an outright cash legacy of $50,000 and has no other interest in B's estate. A timely disclaimer by A of any stated dollar amount is a qualified disclaimer under section 2518(a).

Example (17). D bequeaths his brokerage account to E. The account consists of stocks and bonds and a cash amount earning interest. The total value of the cash and assets in the account on the date of D's death is $100,000. Four months after D's death, E makes a withdrawal of cash from the account for personal use amounting to $40,000. Eight months after D's death, E disclaims $60,000 of the account without specifying any particular assets or cash. The cumulative fair market value of the stocks and bonds in the account on the date of the disclaimer is equal to the value of such stocks and bonds on the date of D's death. The income earned by the account between the date of D's death and the date of E's disclaimer was $20,000. The amount of income earned by the account that E accepted by withdrawing $40,000 from the account prior to the disclaimer is determined by applying the formula set forth in § 25.2518-3(c) as follows:

$$\frac{\$40,000}{\$100,000} \times \$20,000 = \$8,000$$

E is considered to have accepted $8,000 of the income earned by the account. If (i) the $60,000 disclaimed by E and the $12,000 of income earned prior to the disclaimer which is attributable to that amount are segregated from the $8,000 of income E is considered to have accepted, (ii) E does not accept any benefits of the $72,000 so segregated, and (iii) the other requirements of section 2518(b) are met, then E's disclaimer of $60,000 from the account is a qualified disclaimer.

Example (18). A bequeathed his residuary estate to B. The residuary estate had a value of $1 million on the date of A's death. Six months later, B disclaimed $200,000 out of this bequest. B received distributions of all the income from the entire estate during the period of administration. When the estate was distributed, B received the entire residuary estate except for $200,000 in cash. B did not make a qualified disclaimer since he accepted the benefits of the $200,000 during the period of estate administration.

Example (19). Assume the same facts as in example (18) except that no income was paid to B and the value of the residuary estate on the date of the disclaimer (including interest earned from date of death) was $1.5 million. In addition, as soon as B's disclaimer was made, the executor of A's estate set aside assets worth $300,000

$$\frac{\$200,000}{\$1,000,000} \times \$1,500,000$$

and the interest earned after the disclaimer on that amount in a separate fund so that none of the income was paid to B. B's disclaimer is a qualified disclaimer under section 2518(a).

Example (20). A bequeathed his residuary estate to B. B disclaims a fractional share of the residuary estate. Any disclaimed property will pass to A's surviving spouse, W. The numerator of the fraction disclaimed is the smallest amount which will allow A's estate to pass free of Federal estate tax and the denominator is the value of the residuary estate. B's disclaimer is a qualified disclaimer.

Example (21). A created a trust on July 1, 1979. The trust provides that all current income is to be distributed equally between B and C for the life of B. B also is given a testamentary general power of appointment over the corpus. If the power is not exercised, the corpus passes to C or C's heirs. B disclaimed the testamentary power to appoint an undivided one-half of the trust corpus. Assuming the remaining requirements of section 2518(b) are satisfied, B's disclaimer is a qualified disclaimer under section 2518(a). [Reg. § 25.2518-3.]

☐ [*T.D.* 8095, 8-6-86. *Amended by T.D.* 8540, 6-9-94.]

[Reg. § 25.2519-1]

§ 25.2519-1. Dispositions of certain life estates.—(a) *In general.*—If a donee spouse makes a disposition of all or part of a qualifying income interest for life in any property for which a deduction was allowed under section 2056(b)(7) or section 2523(f) for the transfer creating the qualifying income interest, the donee spouse is treated for purposes of chapters 11 and 12 of subtitle B of the Internal Revenue Code as transferring all interests in property other than the qualifying income interest. For example, if the donee spouse makes a disposition of part of a qualifying income interest for life in trust corpus, the spouse is treated under section 2519 as making a transfer subject to chapters 11 and 12 of the entire trust other than the qualifying income interest for life. Therefore, the donee spouse is treated as making a gift under section 2519 of the entire trust less the qualifying income interest, and is treated for purposes of section 2036 as having transferred the entire trust corpus, including that portion of the trust corpus from which the retained income interest is payable. A transfer of all or a portion of the income interest of the spouse is a transfer by the spouse under section 2511. See also section 2702 for special rules applicable in valuing the gift made by the spouse under section 2519.

(b) *Presumption.*—Unless the donee spouse establishes to the contrary, section 2519 applies to the entire trust at the time of the disposition. If a deduction is taken on either the estate or gift tax return with respect to the transfer which created the qualifying income interest, it is presumed that the deduction was allowed for purposes of section 2519. To avoid the application of section 2519 upon a transfer of all or part of the donee spouse's income interest, the donee spouse must establish that a deduction was not taken for the transfer of property which created the qualifying income interest. For example, to establish that a deduction was not taken, the donee spouse may produce a copy of the estate or gift tax return filed with respect to the transfer creating the qualifying income interest for life establishing that no deduction was taken under section 2056(b)(7) or section 2523(f). In addition, the donee spouse may establish that no return was filed on the original transfer by the donor spouse because the value of the first spouse's gross estate was below the threshold requirement for filing under section 6018. Similarly, the donee spouse could establish that the transfer creating the qualifying income interest for life was made before the effective date of section 2056(b)(7) or section 2523(f), whichever is applicable.

(c) *Amount treated as a transfer.*—(1) *In general.*—The amount treated as a transfer under this section upon a disposition of all or part of a qualifying income interest for life in qualified terminable interest property is equal to the fair market value of the entire property subject to the qualifying income interest, determined on the date of the disposition (including any accumulated income and not reduced by any amount excluded from total gifts under section 2503(b) with respect to the transfer creating the interest), less the value of the qualifying income interest in the property on the date of the disposition. The gift tax consequences of the disposition of the qualifying income interest are determined separately under § 25.2511-2. See paragraph (c)(4) of this section for the effect of gift tax that the donee spouse is entitled to recover under section 2207A.

(2) *Disposition of interest in property with respect to which a partial election was made.*—If, in connection with the transfer of property that created the spouse's qualifying income interest for life, a deduction was allowed under section 2056(b)(7) or section 2523(f) for less than the entire interest in the property (i.e., for a fractional or percentage share of the entire interest in the transferred property) the amount treated as a transfer by the donee spouse under this section is equal to the fair market value of the entire property subject to the qualifying income interest on the date of the disposition, less the value of the qualifying income interest for life, multiplied by the fractional or percentage share of the interest for which the deduction was taken.

(3) *Reduction for distributions charged to nonelective portion of trust.*—The amount determined under paragraph (c)(2) of this section (if applicable) is appropriately reduced if—

(i) The donee spouse's interest is in a trust and distributions of principal have been made to the donee spouse;

(ii) The trust provides that distributions of principal are made first from the qualified terminable interest share of the trust; and

(iii) The donee spouse establishes the reduction in that share based on the fair market value of the trust assets at the time of each distribution.

(4) *Effect of gift tax entitled to be recovered under section 2207A on the amount of the transfer.*—The amount treated as a transfer under paragraph (c)(1) of this section is further reduced by the amount the donee spouse is entitled to recover under section 2207A(b) (relating to the right to recover gift tax attributable to the remainder interest). If the donee spouse is entitled to recover gift tax under section 2207A(b), the amount of gift tax recoverable and the value of the remainder interest treated as transferred under section 2519 are determined by using the same interrelated computation applicable for other transfers in which the transferee assumes the gift tax liability. The gift tax consequences of failing to exercise the right of recovery are determined separately under § 25.2207A-1(b).

(5) *Interest in previously severed trust.*—If the donee spouse's interest is in a trust consisting of only qualified terminable interest property, and the trust was previously severed (in compliance with § 20.2056(b)-7(b)(2)(ii) of this chapter or § 25.2523(f)-1(b)(3)(ii) from a trust that, after the severance, held only property that was not qualified terminable interest property, only the value of the property in the severed portion of the trust at the time of the disposition is treated as transferred under this section.

(d) *Identification of property transferred.*—If only part of the property in which a donee spouse has a qualifying income interest for life is qualified terminable interest property, the donee spouse is, in the case of a disposition of all or part of the income interest within the meaning of section 2519, deemed to have transferred a pro rata portion of the entire qualified terminable interest property for purposes of this section.

(e) *Exercise of power of appointment.*—The exercise by any person of a power to appoint qualified terminable interest property to the donee spouse is not treated as a disposition under section 2519, even though the donee spouse subsequently disposes of the appointed property.

(f) *Conversion of qualified terminable interest property.*—The conversion of qualified terminable interest property into other property in which the donee spouse has a qualifying income interest for life is not, for purposes of this section, treated as a disposition of the qualifying income interest. Thus, the sale and reinvestment of assets of a trust holding qualified terminable interest property is not a disposition of the qualifying income interest, provided that the donee spouse continues to have a qualifying income interest for life in the trust after the sale and reinvestment. Similarly, the sale of real property in which the spouse possesses a legal life estate and thus meets the requirements of qualified terminable interest property, followed by the transfer of the proceeds into a trust which also meets the requirements of qualified terminable interest property, or by the reinvestment of the

Reg. § 25.2519-1(f)

proceeds in income producing property in which the donee spouse has a qualifying income interest for life, is not considered a disposition of the qualifying income interest. On the other hand, the sale of qualified terminable interest property, followed by the payment to the donee spouse of a portion of the proceeds equal to the value of the donee spouse's income interest, is considered a disposition of the qualifying income interest.

(g) *Examples.*—The following examples illustrate the application of paragraphs (a) through (f) of this section. Except as provided otherwise in the examples, assume that the decedent, D, was survived by spouse, S, that in each example the section 2503(b) exclusion has already been fully utilized for each year with respect to the donee in question, that section 2503(e) is not applicable to the amount deemed transferred, and that the gift taxes on the amount treated as transferred under paragraph (c) are offset by S's unified credit. The examples are as follows:

Example 1. Transfer of the spouse's life estate in residence. Under D's will, a personal residence valued for estate tax purposes at $250,000 passes to S for life, and after S's death to D's children. D's executor made a valid election to treat the property as qualified terminable interest property. During 1995, when the fair market value of the property is $300,000 and the value of S's life interest in the property is $100,000, S makes a gift of S's entire interest in the property to D's children. Pursuant to section 2519, S makes a gift in the amount of $200,000 (i.e., the fair market value of the qualified terminable interest property of $300,000 less the fair market value of S's qualifying income interest in the property of $100,000). In addition, under section 2511, S makes a gift of $100,000 (i.e., the fair market value of S's income interest in the property). See § 25.2511-2.

Example 2. Sale of spouse's life estate. The facts are the same as in *Example 1* except that during 1995, S sells S's interest in the property to D's children for $100,000. Pursuant to section 2519, S makes a gift of $200,000 ($300,000 less $100,000 value of the qualifying income interest in the property). S does not make a gift of the income interest under section 2511, because the consideration received for S's income interest is equal to the value of the income interest.

Example 3. Transfer of income interest in trust subject to partial election. D's will established a trust valued for estate tax purposes at $500,000, all of the income of which is payable annually to S for life. After S's death, the principal of the trust is to be distributed to D's children. Assume that only 50 percent of the trust was treated as qualified terminable interest property. During 1995, S makes a gift of all of S's interest in the trust to D's children at which time the fair market value of the trust is $400,000 and the fair market value of S's life income interest in the trust is $100,000. Pursuant to section 2519, S

makes a gift of $150,000 (the fair market value of the qualified terminable interest property, 50 percent of $400,000, less the $50,000 income interest in the qualified terminable interest property). S also makes a gift pursuant to section 2511 of $100,000 (i.e., the fair market value of S's life income interest).

Example 4. Transfer of a portion of income interest in trust subject to a partial election. The facts are the same as in *Example 3* except that S makes a gift of only 40 percent of S's interest in the trust. Pursuant to section 2519, S makes a gift of $150,000 (i.e., the fair market value of the qualified terminable interest property, 50 percent of $400,000, less the $50,000 value of S's qualified income interest in the qualified terminable interest property). S also makes a gift pursuant to section 2511 of $40,000 (i.e., the fair market value of 40 percent of S's life income interest). See also section 2702 for additional rules that may affect the value of the total amount of S's gift under section 2519 to take into account the fact that S's 30 percent retained income interest attributable to the qualifying income interest is valued at zero under that section, thereby increasing the value of S's section 2519 gift to $180,000. In addition, under § 25.2519-1(d), S's disposition of 40 percent of the income interest is deemed to be a transfer of a pro rata portion of the qualified terminable interest property. Thus, assuming no further lifetime dispositions by S, 30 percent (60 percent of 50 percent) of the trust property is included in S's gross estate under section 2036 and an adjustment is made to S's adjusted taxable gifts under section 2001(b)(1)(B). If S later disposes of all or a portion of the retained income interest, see § 25.2702-6.

Example 5. Transfer of a portion of spouse's interest in a trust from which corpus was previously distributed to the spouse. D's will established a trust valued for estate tax purposes at $500,000, all of the income of which is payable annually to S for life. The trustee is granted the discretion to distribute trust principal to S. All appointments of principal must be made from the portion of the trust subject to the section 2056(b)(7) election. After S's death, the principal of the trust is to be distributed to D's children. The executor makes the section 2056(b)(7) election with respect to 50 percent of the trust. In 1994, pursuant to the terms of D's will, the trustee distributed $50,000 of principal to S and charged the entire distribution to the qualified terminable interest portion of the trust. Immediately prior to the distribution, the value of the entire trust was $550,000 and the value of the qualified terminable interest portion was $275,000 (50 percent of $550,000). Provided S can establish the above facts, the qualified terminable interest portion of the trust immediately after the distribution is $225,000 or 45 percent of the value of the trust ($225,000/$500,000). In 1996, when the value of the trust is $400,000 and the value of S's income interest is $100,000, S makes a transfer of 40 percent of S's income interest. S's gift under section 2519 is $135,000; i.e., the fair market value of the qualified terminable interest property, 45 percent of $400,000 ($180,000), less the value of the income interest in the qualified terminable interest property, $45,000 (45 percent of $100,000). S also makes a gift under section 2511 of $40,000; i.e., the fair market value of 40 percent of S's income interest. S's disposition of 40 percent of the income interest is deemed to be a transfer under section 2519 of the entire 45 percent portion of the remainder subject to the section 2056(b)(7) election. Since S retained 60 percent of the income interest, 27 percent (60 percent of 45 percent) of the trust property is includible in S's gross estate under section 2036. See also section 2702 and *Example 4* as to the principles applicable in valuing S's gift under section 2702 and adjusted taxable gifts upon S's subsequent death.

Example 6. Transfer of Spousal Annuity Payable From Trust. D died prior to October 24, 1992. D's will established a trust valued for estate tax purposes at $500,000. The trust instrument required the trustee to pay an annuity to S of $20,000 a year for life. All the trust income other than the amounts paid to S as an annuity are to be accumulated in the trust and may not be distributed during S's lifetime to any person other than S. After S's death, the principal of the trust is to be distributed to D's children. Because D died prior to the effective date of section 1941 of the Energy Policy Act of 1992, S's annuity interest qualifies as a qualifying income interest for life. Under § 20.2056(b)-7(e) of this chapter, based on an ap-

plicable 10 percent interest rate, 40 percent of the property, or $200,000, is the value of the deductible interest. During 1996, S makes a gift of the annuity interest to D's children at which time the fair market value of the trust is $800,000 and the fair market value of S's annuity interest in the trust is $100,000. Pursuant to section 2519, S is treated as making a gift of $220,000 (the fair market value of the qualified terminable interest property, 40 percent of $800,000 ($320,000), less the $100,000 annuity interest in the qualified terminable interest property). S is also treated pursuant to section 2511 as making a gift of $100,000 (the fair market value of S's annuity interest). [Reg. § 25.2519-1.]

☐ [*T.D.* 8522, 2-28-94. *Amended by T.D. 9077,* 7-17-2003.]

[Reg. § 25.2519-2]

§ 25.2519-2. Effective date.—Except as specifically provided in § 25.2519-1(g), *Example 6,* the provisions of § 25.2519-1 are effective with respect to gifts made after March 1, 1994. With respect to gifts made on or before such date, the donee spouse of a section 2056(b)(7) or section 2523(f) transfer may rely on any reasonable interpretation of the statutory provisions. For these purposes, the provisions of § 25.2519-1 (as well as project LR-211-76, 1984-1 C.B., page 598, see § 601.601(d)(2)(ii)(*b*) of this chapter), are considered a reasonable interpretation of the statutory provisions. [Reg. § 25.2519-2.]

☐ [*T.D.* 8522, 2-28-94.]

DEDUCTIONS

[Reg. § 25.2522(a)-1]

§ 25.2522(a)-1. Charitable and similar gifts; citizens or residents.—(a) In determining the amount of taxable gifts for the "calendar period" (as defined in § 25.2502-1(c)(1)) there may be deducted, in the case of a donor who was a citizen or resident of the United States at the time the gifts were made, all gifts included in the "total amount of gifts" made by the donor during the calendar period (see section 2503 and the regulations thereunder) and made to or for the use of:

(1) The United States, any State, Territory, or any political subdivision thereof, or the District of Columbia, for exclusively public purposes.

(2) Any corporation, trust, community chest, fund, or foundation organized and operated exclusively for religious, charitable, scientific, literary, or educational purposes, including the encouragement of art and the prevention of cruelty to children or animals, if no part of the net earnings of the organization inures to the benefit of any private shareholder or individual, if it is not disqualified for tax exemption under section 501(c)(3) by reason of attempting to influ-

ence legislation, and if, in the case of gifts made after December 31, 1969, it does not participate in, or intervene in (including the publishing or distributing of statements), any political campaign on behalf of or in opposition to any candidate for public office.

(3) A fraternal society, order, or association, operating under the lodge system, provided the gifts are to be used by the society, order or association exclusively for one or more of the purposes set forth in subparagraph (2) of this paragraph.

(4) Any post or organization of war veterans or auxiliary unit or society thereof, if organized in the United States or any of its possessions, and if no part of its net earnings inures to the benefit of any private shareholder or individual.

The deduction is not limited to gifts for use within the United States or to gifts to or for the use of domestic corporations, trusts, community chests, funds, or foundations, or fraternal societies, orders, or associations operating under the lodge system. An organization will not be considered to meet the requirements of subparagraph (2) of this paragraph, or of paragraph (b)(2) or (3) of this section, if such organization engages in any activity which would cause it to be classified as an "action" organization under paragraph (c)(3) of § 1.501(c)(3)-1 of this chapter (Income Tax Regulations). For the deductions for charitable and similar gifts made by a nonresident who was not a citizen of the United States at the time the gifts were made, see § 25.2522(b)-1. See § 25.2522(c)-1 and § 25.2522(c)-2 for rules relating to the disallowance of deductions to trusts and organizations which engage in certain prohibited transactions or whose governing instruments do not contain certain specified requirements.

(b) The deduction under section 2522 is not allowed for a transfer to a corporation, trust, community chest, fund, or foundation unless the organization or trust meets the following four tests:

(1) It must be organized and operated exclusively for one or more of the specified purposes.

(2) It must not be disqualified for tax exemption under section 501(c)(3) by reason of attempting to influence legislation.

(3) In the case of gifts made after December 31, 1969, it must not participate in, or intervene in (including the publishing or distributing of statements), any political campaign on behalf of any candidate for public office.

(4) Its net earnings must not inure in whole or in part to the benefit of private shareholders or individuals other than as legitimate objects of the exempt purposes.

(c) In order to prove the right to the charitable, etc., deduction provided by section 2522, the donor must submit such data as may be requested by the Internal Revenue Service. As to the extent the deductions provided by this section are allowable, see section 2524. [Reg. § 25.2522(a)-1.]

☐ [*T.D.* 6334, 11-14-58. *Amended by T.D.* 7012, 5-14-69; *T.D.* 7238, 12-28-72; *T.D.* 7318, 7-10-74; *T.D.* 7910, 9-6-83 *and T.D.* 8308, 8-30-90.]

[Reg. § 25.2522(a)-2]

§ 25.2522(a)-2. Transfers not exclusively for charitable, etc., purposes in the case of gifts made before August 1, 1969.—(a) *Remainders and similar interests.*—If a trust is created or property is transferred for both a charitable and a private purpose, deduction may be taken of the value of the charitable beneficial interest only insofar as that interest is presently ascertainable, and hence severable from the noncharitable interest. The present value of a remainder or other deferred payment to be made for a charitable purpose is to be determined in accordance with the rules stated in § 25.2512-5. Thus, if money or property is placed in trust to pay the income to an individual during his life, or for a term of years, and then to pay the principal to a charitable organization, the present value of the remain-

der is deductible. If the interest involved is such that its value is to be determined by a special computation, see § 25.2512-5(d)(4). If the Commissioner does not furnish the factor, the claim for deduction must be supported by a full statement of the computation of the present value made in accordance with the principles set forth in the applicable paragraph of § 25.2512-5.

(b) *Transfer subject to a condition or a power.*—If, as of the date of the gift, a transfer for charitable purposes is dependent upon the performance of some act or the happening of a precedent event in order that it might become effective, no deduction is allowable unless the possibility that the charitable transfer will not become effective is so remote as to be negligible. If an estate or interest passes to or is vested in charity on the date of the gift and the estate or interest would be defeated by the performance of some act or the happening of some event, the occurrence of which appeared to have been highly improbable on the date of the gift, the deduction is allowable. If the donee or trustee is empowered to divert the property or fund, in whole or in part, to a use or purpose which would have rendered it, to the extent that it is subject to such power, not deductible had it been directly so given by the donor, the deduction will be limited to that portion of the property or fund which is exempt from the exercise of the power. The deduction is not allowed in the case of a transfer in trust conveying to charity a present interest in income if by reason of all the conditions and circumstances surrounding the transfer it appears that the charity may not receive the beneficial enjoyment of the interest. For example, assume that assets placed in trust by the donor consist of stock in a corporation, the fiscal policies of which are controlled by the donor and his family, that the trustees and remaindermen are likewise members of the donor's family, and that the governing instrument contains no adequate guarantee of the requisite income to the charitable organization. Under such circumstances, no deduction will be allowed. Similarly, if the trustees were not members of the donor's family but had no power to sell or otherwise dispose of closely held stock, or otherwise insure the requisite enjoyment of income to the charitable organization, no deduction will be allowed.

(c) *Effective date.*—This section applies only to gifts made before August 1, 1969. In the case of gifts made after July 31, 1969, see § 25.2522(c)-2. [Reg. § 25.2522(a)-2.]

☐ [*T.D.* 6334, 11-14-58. *Amended by T.D.* 7318, 7-10-74, *and T.D.* 8540, 6-9-94.]

[Reg. § 25.2522(b)-1]

§ 25.2522(b)-1. Charitable and similar gifts, nonresidents not citizens.—(a) The deduction for charitable and similar gifts in the case of a nonresident who was not a citizen of the United

States at the time he made the gifts is governed by the same rules as those applying to gifts by citizens or residents, subject, however, to the following exceptions:

(1) If the gifts are made to or for the use of a corporation, the corporation must be one created or organized under the laws of the United States or of any State or Territory thereof.

(2) If the gifts are made to or for the use of a trust, community chest, fund or foundation, or a fraternal society, order or association operating under the lodge system, the gifts must be for use within the United States exclusively for religious, charitable, scientific, literary or educational purposes, including encouragement of art and the prevention of cruelty to children or animals. [Reg. § 25.2522(b)-1.]

☐ [T.D. 6334, 11-14-58.]

[Reg. § 25.2522(c)-1]

§ 25.2522(c)-1. Disallowance of charitable, etc., deductions because of "prohibited transactions" in the case of gifts made before January 1, 1970.—(a) Sections 503(e) and 681(b)(5) provide that no deduction which would otherwise be allowable under section 2522 for a gift for religious, charitable, scientific, literary or educational purposes, including the encouragement of art and the prevention of cruelty to children or animals, is allowed if—

(1) The gift is made in trust and, for income tax purposes for the taxable year of the trust in which the gift is made, the deduction otherwise allowable to the trust under section 642(c) is limited by section 681(b)(1) by reason of the trust having engaged in a prohibited transaction described in section 681(b)(2); or

(2) The gift is made to any corporation, community chest, fund or foundation which, for its taxable year in which the gift is made, is not exempt from income tax under section 501(a) by reason of having engaged in a prohibited transaction described in section 503(c).

(b) For purposes of section 503(e) and section 681(b)(5), the term "gift" includes any gift, contribution, or transfer without adequate consideration.

(c) Regulations relating to the income tax contain the rules for the determination of the taxable year of the trust for which the deduction under section 642(c) is limited by section 681(b), and for the determination of the taxable year of the organization for which an exemption is denied under section 503(a). Generally, such taxable year is a taxable year subsequent to the taxable year during which the trust or organization has been notified by the Internal Revenue Service that it has engaged in a prohibited transaction. However, if the trust or organization during or prior to the taxable year entered into the prohibited transaction for the purpose of diverting its corpus or income from the charitable or other purposes by reason of which it is entitled to a

deduction or exemption, and the transaction involves a substantial part of such income or corpus, then the deduction of the trust under section 642(c) for such taxable year is limited by section 681(b), or the exemption of the organization for such taxable year is denied under section 503(a), whether or not the organization has previously received notification by the Internal Revenue Service that it has engaged in a prohibited transaction. In certain cases, the limitation of section 503 or 681 may be removed or the exemption may be reinstated for certain subsequent taxable years under the rules set forth in the income tax regulations under sections 503 and 681.

(d) In cases in which prior notification by the Internal Revenue Service is not required in order to limit the deduction of the trust under section 681(b), or to deny exemption of the organization under section 503, the deduction otherwise allowable under § 25.2522(a)-1 is not disallowed with respect to gifts made during the same taxable year of the trust or organization in which a prohibited transaction occurred, or in a prior taxable year, unless the donor or a member of his family was a party to the prohibited transaction. For purposes of the preceding sentence, the members of the donor's family include only his brothers and sisters (whether by whole or half blood), spouse, ancestors, and lineal descendants.

(e) This section applies only to gifts made before January 1, 1970. In the case of gifts made after December 31, 1969, see § 25.2522(c)-2. [Reg. § 25.2522(c)-1.]

☐ [T.D. 6334, 11-14-58. Amended by T.D. 7318, 7-10-74.]

[Reg. § 25.2522(c)-2]

§ 25.2522(c)-2. Disallowance of charitable, etc., deductions in the case of gifts made after December 31, 1969.—(a) *Organizations subject to section 507(c) tax.*—Section 508(d)(1) provides that, in the case of gifts made after December 31, 1969, a deduction which would otherwise be allowable under section 2522 for a gift to or for the use of an organization upon which the tax provided by section 507(c) has been imposed shall not be allowed if the gift is made by the donor after notification is made under section 507(a) or if the donor is a substantial contributor (as defined in section 507(d)(2)) who makes such gift in his taxable year (as defined in section 441) which includes the first day on which action is taken by such organization that culminates in the imposition of the tax under section 507(c) and any subsequent taxable year. This paragraph does not apply if the entire amount of the unpaid portion of the tax imposed by section 507(c) is abated under section 507(g) by the Commissioner or his delegate.

(b) *Taxable private foundations, section 4947 trusts, etc.*—Section 508(d)(2) provides that, in the case of gifts made after December 31, 1969, a deduction which would otherwise be allowable under section 2522 shall not be allowed if the gift is made to or for the use of—

(1) A private foundation or a trust described in section 4947(a)(2) in a taxable year of such organization for which such organization fails to meet the governing instrument requirements of section 508(e) (determined without regard to section 508(e)(2)(B) and (C)), or

(2) Any organization in a period for which it is not treated as an organization described in section 501(c)(3) by reason of its failure to give notification under section 508(a) of its status to the Commissioner.

For additional rules, see § 1.508-2(b)(1) of this chapter (Income Tax Regulations).

(c) *Foreign organizations with substantial support from foreign sources.*—Section 4948(c)(4) provides that, in the case of gifts made after December 31, 1969, a deduction which would otherwise be allowable under section 2522 for a gift to or for the use of a foreign organization which has received substantially all of its support (other than gross investment income) from sources without the United States shall not be allowed if the gift is made (1) after the date on which the Commissioner has published notice that he has notified such organization that it has engaged in a prohibited transaction or (2) in a taxable year of such organization for which it is not exempt from taxation under section 501(a) because it has engaged in a prohibited transaction after December 31, 1969. [Reg. § 25.2522(c)-2.]

☐ [*T.D.* 7318, 6-10-74.]

[Reg. § 25.2522(c)-3]

§ 25.2522(c)-3. Transfers not exclusively for charitable, etc., purposes in the case of gifts made after July 31, 1969.—(a) *Remainders and similar interests.*—If a trust is created or property is transferred for both a charitable and a private purpose, deduction may be taken of the value of the charitable beneficial interest only insofar as that interest is presently ascertainable, and hence severable from the noncharitable interest.

(b) *Transfers subject to a condition or a power.*—(1) If, as of the date of the gift, a transfer for charitable purposes is dependent upon the performance of some act or the happening of a precedent event in order that it might become effective, no deduction is allowable unless the possibility that the charitable transfer will not become effective is so remote as to be negligible. If an estate or interest has passed to, or is vested in, charity on the date of the gift and the estate or interest would be defeated by the performance of some act or the happening of some event, the possibility of occurrence of which appeared on such date to be so remote as to be negligible, the deduction is allowable. If the donee or trustee is empowered to divert the property or fund, in whole or in part, to a use or purpose which would have rendered it, to the extent that it is subject to such power, not deductible had it been directly so given by the donor, the deduction will be limited to that portion, if any, of the property or fund which is exempt from an exercise of the power.

(2) The application of this paragraph may be illustrated by the following examples:

Example (1). In 1965, A transfers certain property in trust in which charity is to receive the income for his life. The assets placed in trust by the donor consist of stock in a corporation the fiscal policies of which are controlled by the donor and his family. The trustees of the trust and the remainderman are members of the donor's family and the governing instrument contains no adequate guarantee of the requisite income to the charitable organization. Under such circumstances, no deduction will be allowed. Similarly, if the trustees are not members of the donor's family but have no power to sell or otherwise dispose of the closely held stock, or otherwise insure the requisite enjoyment of income to the charitable organization, no deduction will be allowed.

Example (2). C transfers a tract of land to a city government for as long as the land is used by the city for a public park. If on the date of gift the city does plan to use the land for a public park and the possibility that the city will not use the land for a public park is so remote as to be negligible, a deduction will be allowed.

(c) *Transfers of partial interests in property.*—(1) *Disallowance of deduction.*—(i) *In general.*—If a donor transfers an interest in property after July 31, 1969, for charitable purposes and an interest in the same property is retained by the donor, or is transferred or has been transferred for private purposes after such date (for less than an adequate and full consideration in money or money's worth), no deduction is allowed under section 2522 for the value of the interest which is transferred or has been transferred for charitable purposes unless the interest in property is a deductible interest described in subparagraph (2) of this paragraph. The principles that are used in applying section 2523 and the regulations thereunder shall apply for purposes of determining under this subparagraph whether an interest in property is retained by the donor, or is transferred or has been transferred by the donor. If, however, as of the date of the gift, a retention of an interest by a donor, or a transfer for a private purpose, is dependent upon the performance of some act or the happening of a precedent event in order that it may become effective, an interest in property will be considered retained by the donor, or transferred for a private purpose, unless the possibility of occurrence of such act or event is so remote as to be negligible. The application of this subparagraph may be illustrated by the following examples, in each of which it is assumed that the property interest which is transferred for private purposes is not transferred for an adequate and full consideration in money or money's worth:

Example (1). In 1973, H creates a trust which is to pay the income of the trust to W for her life, the reversionary interest in the trust being retained by H. In 1975, H gives the reversionary interest to charity, while W is still living. For purposes of this paragraph (c)(1)(i), interests in the same property have been transferred by H for charitable purposes and for private purposes.

Example (2). In 1973, H creates a trust which is to pay the income of the trust to W for her life and upon termination of the life estate to transfer the remainder to S. In 1975, S gives his remainder interest to charity, while W is still living. For purposes of this paragraph (c)(1)(i), interests in the same property have not been transferred by H or S for charitable purposes and for private purposes.

Example (3). H transfers Blackacre to A by gift, reserving the right to the rentals of Blackacre for a term of 20 years. After 4 years H transfers the right to the remaining rentals to charity. For purposes of this paragraph (c)(1)(i) the term "property" refers to Blackacre, and the right to rentals from Blackacre consists of an interest in Blackacre. An interest in Blackacre has been transferred by H for charitable purposes and for private purposes.

Example (4). H transfers property in trust for the benefit of A and a charity. An annuity of $5,000 a year is to be paid to charity for 20 years. Upon termination of the 20-year term the corpus is to be distributed to A if living. However, if A should die during the 20-year term, the corpus is to be distributed to charity upon termination of the term. An interest in property has been transferred by H for charitable purposes. In addition, an interest in the same property has been transferred by H for private purposes unless the possibility that A will survive the 20-year term is so remote as to be negligible.

Example (5). H transfers property in trust, under the terms of which an annuity of $5,000 a year is to be paid to charity for 20 years. Upon termination of the term, the corpus is to pass to such of A's children and their issue as A may appoint. However, if A should die during the 20-year term without exercising the power of appointment, the corpus is to be distributed to charity upon termination of the term. Since the possible appointees include private persons, an interest in the corpus of the trust is considered to have been transferred by H for private purposes.

(ii) *Works of art and copyright treated as separate properties.*—For purposes of paragraphs (c)(1)(i) and (c)(2) of this section, rules similar to the rules in § 20.2055-2(e)(1)(ii) shall apply in the case of transfers made after December 31, 1981.

(2) *Deductible interests.*—A deductible interest for purposes of subparagraph (i) of this paragraph is a charitable interest in property where—

(i) *Undivided portion of donor's entire interest.*—The charitable interest is an undivided portion, not in trust, of the donor's entire interest in property. An undivided portion of a donor's entire interest in property must consist of a fraction or percentage of each and every substantial interest or right owned by the donor in such property and must extend over the entire term of the donor's interest in such property and in other property into which such property is converted. For example, if the donor gave a life estate in an office building to his wife for her life and retained a reversionary interest in the office building, the gift by the donor of one-half of that reversionary interest to charity while his wife is still alive will not be considered the transfer of a deductible interest; because an interest in the same property has already passed from the donor for private purposes, the reversionary interest will not be considered the donor's entire interest in the property. If, on the other hand, the donor had been given a life estate in Blackacre for the life of his wife and the donor had no other interest in Blackacre on or before the time of gift, the gift by the donor of one-half of that life estate to charity would be considered the transfer of a deductible interest; because the life estate would be considered the donor's entire interest in the property, the gift would be of an undivided portion of such entire interest. An undivided portion of a donor's entire interest in property includes an interest in property whereby the charity is given the right, as a tenant in common with the donor, to possession, dominion, and control of the property for a portion of each year appropriate to its interest in such property. However, except as provided in paragraphs (c)(2)(ii), (iii), and (iv) of this section, for purposes of this subdivision a charitable contribution of an interest in property not in trust where the decedent transfers some specific rights to one party and transfers other substantial rights to another party will not be considered a contribution of an undivided portion of the decedent's entire interest in property. A gift of an open space easement in gross in perpetuity shall be considered a gift of an undivided portion of the donor's entire interest in property. A gift to charity made on or before December 17, 1980, of an open space easement in gross in perpetuity shall be considered the transfer to charity of an undivided portion of the donor's entire interest in property.

(ii) *Remainder interest in a personal residence.*—The charitable interest is an irrevocable remainder interest, not in trust, in a personal residence. Thus, for example, if the donor gives to charity a remainder interest in a personal residence and retains an estate in such property for life or a term of years the value of such remainder interest is deductible under section 2522. For purposes of this subdivision, the term "personal residence" means any property which is used by the donor as his personal residence even though it is not used as his principal residence. For example, a donor's vacation home may be a personal residence for purposes of this subdivision. The term "personal residence" also includes stock owned by the donor on the date of gift as a tenant-stockholder in a cooperative housing corporation (as those terms are defined in section 216(b)(1) and (2)) if the dwelling which the donor is entitled to occupy as such stockholder is used by him as his personal residence.

(iii) *Remainder interest in a farm.*—The charitable interest is an irrevocable remainder interest, not in trust, in a farm. Thus, for example, if the donor gives to charity a remainder interest in a farm and retains an estate in such property for life or a term of years, the value of such remainder interest is deductible under section 2522. For purposes of this subdivision, the term "farm" means any land used by the donor or his tenant for the production of crops, fruits, or other agricultural products or for the sustenance of livestock. The term "livestock" includes cattle, hogs, horses, mules, donkeys, sheep, goats, captive fur-bearing animals, chickens, turkeys, pigeons, and other poultry. A farm includes the improvements thereon.

(iv) *Qualified conservation contribution.*—The charitable interest is a qualified conservation contribution. For the definition of a qualified conservation contribution, see § 1.170A-14.

(v) *Charitable remainder trust and pooled income funds.*—The charitable interest is a remainder interest in a trust which is a charitable remainder annuity trust, as defined in section 664(d)(1) and § 1.664-2 of this chapter; a charitable remainder unitrust, as defined in section 664(d)(2) and (3) and § 1.664-3 of this chapter; or a pooled income fund, as defined in section 642(c)(5) and § 1.642(c)-5 of this chapter. The charitable organization to or for the use of which the remainder interest is transferred must meet the requirements of both section 2522(a) or (b) and section 642(c)(5)(A), section 664(d)(1)(C), or section 664(d)(2)(C), whichever applies. For example, the charitable organization to which the remainder interest in a charitable remainder annuity trust is transferred may not be a foreign corporation.

(vi) *Guaranteed annuity interest.*—*(a)* The charitable interest is a guaranteed annuity interest, whether or not such interest is in trust. For purposes of this paragraph (c)(2)(vi), the term "guaranteed annuity interest" means an irrevocable right pursuant to the instrument of transfer to receive a guaranteed annuity. A guaranteed annuity is an arrangement under which a determinable amount is paid periodically, but not less

often than annually, for a specified term of years or for the life or lives of certain individuals, each of whom must be living at the date of the gift and can be ascertained at such date. Only one or more of the following individuals may be used as measuring lives: the donor, the donor's spouse, and an individual who, with respect to all remainder beneficiaries (other than charitable organizations described in section 170, 2055, or 2522), is either a lineal ancestor or the spouse of a lineal ancestor of those beneficiaries. A trust will satisfy the requirement that all noncharitable remainder beneficiaries are lineal descendants of the individual who is the measuring life, or that individual's spouse, if there is less than a 15% probability that individuals who are not lineal descendants will receive any trust corpus. This probability must be computed, based on the current applicable Life Table contained in § 20.2031-7, at the time property is transferred to the trust taking into account the interests of all primary and contingent remainder beneficiaries who are living at that time. An interest payable for a specified term of years can qualify as a guaranteed annuity interest even if the governing instrument contains a savings clause intended to ensure compliance with a rule against perpetuities. The savings clause must utilize a period for vesting of 21 years after the deaths of measuring lives who are selected to maximize, rather than limit, the term of the trust. The rule in this paragraph that a charitable interest may be payable for the life or lives of only certain specified individuals does not apply in the case of a charitable guaranteed annuity interest payable under a charitable remainder trust described in section 664. An amount is determinable if the exact amount which must be paid under the conditions specified in the instrument of transfer can be ascertained as of the date of gift. For example, the amount to be paid may be a stated sum for a term of years, or for the life of the donor, at the expiration of which it may be changed by a specified amount, but it may not be redetermined by reference to a fluctuating index such as the cost of living index. In further illustration, the amount to be paid may be expressed as a fraction or percentage of the cost of living index on the date of gift.

(b) A charitable interest is a guaranteed annuity interest only if it is a guaranteed annuity interest in every respect. For example, if the charitable interest is the right to receive from a trust each year a payment equal to the lesser of a sum certain or a fixed percentage of the net fair market value of the trust assets, determined annually, such interest is not a guaranteed annuity interest.

(c) Where a charitable interest in the form of a guaranteed annuity interest is not in trust, the interest will be considered a guaranteed annuity interest only if it is to be paid by an insurance company or by an organization regularly engaged in issuing annuity contracts.

(d) Where a charitable interest in the form of a guaranteed annuity interest is in trust, the governing instrument of the trust may provide that income of the trust which is in excess of the amount required to pay the guaranteed annuity interest shall be paid to or for the use of a charity. Nevertheless, the amount of the deduction under section 2522 shall be limited to the fair market value of the guaranteed annuity interest as determined under paragraph (d)(2)(iv) of this section.

(e) Where a charitable interest in the form of a guaranteed annuity interest is in trust and the present value on the date of gift of all income interests for a charitable purpose exceeds 60 percent of the aggregate fair market value of all amounts in such trust (after the payment of liabilities), the charitable interest will not be considered a guaranteed annuity interest unless the governing instrument of the trust prohibits both the acquisition and the retention of assets which would give rise to a tax under section 4944 if the trustee had acquired such assets. The requirement in this *(e)* for a prohibition in the governing instrument against the retention of assets which would give rise to a tax under section 4944 if the trustee had acquired the assets shall not apply to a gift made on or before May 21, 1972.

(f) Where a charitable interest in the form of a guaranteed annuity interest is in trust, and the gift of such interest is made after May 21, 1972, the charitable interest generally is not a guaranteed annuity interest if any amount may be paid by the trust for a private purpose before the expiration of all the charitable annuity interests. There are two exceptions to this general rule. First, the charitable interest is a guaranteed annuity interest if the amount payable for a private purpose is in the form of a guaranteed annuity interest and the trust's governing instrument does not provide for any preference or priority in the payment of the private annuity as opposed to the charitable annuity. Second, the charitable interest is a guaranteed annuity interest if under the trust's governing instrument the amount that may be paid for a private purpose is payable only from a group of assets that are devoted exclusively to private purposes and to which section 4947(a)(2) is inapplicable by reason of section 4947(a)(2)(B). For purposes of this paragraph (c)(2)(vi)(*f*), an amount is not paid for a private purpose if it is paid for an adequate and full consideration in money or money's worth. See §53.4947-1(c) of this chapter for rules relating to the inapplicability of section 4947(a)(2) to segregated amounts in a split-interest trust.

(g) For rules relating to certain governing instrument requirements and to the imposition of certain excise taxes where the guaranteed annuity interest is in trust and for rules governing payment of private income interests by a split-interest trust, see section

4947(a)(2) and (b)(3)(A), and the regulations thereunder.

(vii) *Unitrust interest.*—(*a*) The charitable interest is a unitrust interest, whether or not such interest is in trust. For purposes of this paragraph (c)(2)(vii), the term "unitrust interest" means an irrevocable right pursuant to the instrument of transfer to receive payment, not less often than annually, of a fixed percentage of the net fair market value, determined annually, of the property which funds the unitrust interest. In computing the net fair market value of the property which funds the unitrust interest, all assets and liabilities shall be taken into account without regard to whether particular items are taken into account in determining the income from the property. The net fair market value of the property which funds the unitrust interest may be determined on any one date during the year or by taking the average of valuations made on more than one date during the year, provided that the same valuation date or dates and valuation methods are used each year. Where the charitable interest is a unitrust interest to be paid by a trust and the governing instrument of the trust does not specify the valuation date or dates, the trustee shall select such date or dates and shall indicate his selection on the first return on Form 1041 which the trust is required to file. Payments under a unitrust interest may be paid for a specified term of years or for the life or lives of certain individuals, each of whom must be living at the date of the gift and can be ascertained at such date. Only one or more of the following individuals may be used as measuring lives: the donor, the donor's spouse, and an individual who, with respect to all remainder beneficiaries (other than charitable organizations described in section 170, 2055, or 2522), is either a lineal ancestor or the spouse of a lineal ancestor of those beneficiaries. A trust will satisfy the requirement that all noncharitable remainder beneficiaries are lineal descendants of the individual who is the measuring life, or that individual's spouse, if there is less than a 15% probability that individuals who are not lineal descendants will receive any trust corpus. This probability must be computed, based on the current applicable Life Table contained in §20.2031-7, at the time property is transferred to the trust taking into account the interests of all primary and contingent remainder beneficiaries who are living at that time. An interest payable for a specified term of years can qualify as a unitrust interest even if the governing instrument contains a savings clause intended to ensure compliance with a rule against perpetuities. The savings clause must utilize a period for vesting of 21 years after the deaths of measuring lives who are selected to maximize, rather than limit, the term of the trust. The rule in this paragraph that a charitable interest may be payable for the life or lives of only certain specified individuals does not apply in the case of a charitable unitrust interest payable under a charitable remainder trust described in section 664.

(b) A charitable interest is a unitrust interest only if it is a unitrust interest in every respect. For example, if the charitable interest is the right to receive from a trust each year a payment equal to the lesser of a sum certain or a fixed percentage of the net fair market value of the trust assets, determined annually, such interest is not a unitrust interest.

(c) Where a charitable interest in the form of a unitrust interest is not in trust, the interest will be considered a unitrust interest only if it is to be paid by an insurance company or by an organization regularly engaged in issuing interests otherwise meeting the requirements of a unitrust interest.

(d) Where a charitable interest in the form of a unitrust interest is in trust, the governing instrument of the trust may provide that income of the trust which is in excess of the amount required to pay the unitrust interest shall be paid to or for the use of a charity. Nevertheless, the amount of the deduction under section 2522 shall be limited to the fair market value of the unitrust interest as determined under paragraph (d)(2)(v) of this section.

(e) Where a charitable interest in the form of a unitrust interest is in trust, the charitable interest generally is not a unitrust interest if any amount may be paid by the trust for a private purpose before the expiration of all the charitable unitrust interests. There are two exceptions to this general rule. First, the charitable interest is a unitrust interest if the amount payable for a private purpose is in the form of a unitrust interest and the trust's governing instrument does not provide for any preference or priority in the payment of the private unitrust interest as opposed to the charitable unitrust interest. Second, the charitable interest is a unitrust interest if under the trust's governing instrument the amount that may be paid for a private purpose is payable only from a group of assets that are devoted exclusively to private purposes and to which section 4947(a)(2) is inapplicable by reason of section 4947(a)(2)(B). For purposes of this paragraph (c)(2)(vii)(e), an amount is not paid for a private purpose if it is paid for an adequate and full consideration in money or money's worth. See § 53.4947-1(c) of this chapter for rules relating to the inapplicability of section 4947(a)(2) to segregated amounts in a split-interest trust.

(f) For rules relating to certain governing instrument requirements and to the imposition of certain excise taxes where the unitrust interest is in trust and for rules governing payment of private income interests by a split-interest trust, see sections 4947(a)(2) and (b)(3)(A), and the regulations thereunder.

(d) *Valuation of charitable interest.*—(1) *In general.*—The amount of the deduction in the case of a contribution of a partial interest in property to which this section applies is the fair market value of the partial interest on the date of gift. The fair market value of an annuity, life estate, term for years, remainder, reversion or unitrust interest is its present value.

(2) *Certain transfers after July 31, 1969.*—In the case of a transfer after July 31, 1969, of an interest described in paragraph (c)(2)(v), (vi), or (vii) of this section, the present value of such interest is to be determined under the following rules:

(i) The present value of a remainder interest in a charitable remainder annuity trust is to be determined under § 1.664-2(c) of this chapter (Income Tax Regulations).

(ii) The present value of a remainder interest in a charitable remainder unitrust is to be determined under § 1.664-4 of this chapter.

(iii) The present value of a remainder interest in a pooled income fund is to be determined under § 1.642(c)-6 of this chapter.

(iv) The present value of a guaranteed annuity interest described in paragraph (c)(2)(vi) of this section is to be determined under § 25.2512-5 except that, if the annuity is issued by a company regularly engaged in the sale of annuities, the present value is to be determined under § 25.2512-6. If by reason of all the conditions and circumstances surrounding a transfer of an income interest in property in trust it appears that the charity may not receive the beneficial enjoyment of the interest, a deduction will be allowed under section 2522 only for the minimum amount it is evident the charity will receive.

Example (1). In 1975, B transfers $20,000 in trust with the requirement that a designated charity be paid a guaranteed annuity interest (as defined in paragraph (c)(2)(vi) of this section) of $4,100 a year, payable annually at the end of each year for a period of 6 years and that the remainder be paid to his children. The fair market value of an annuity of $4,100 a year for a period of 6 years is $20,160.93 ($4,100 × 4.9173), as determined under § 25.2512-5A(c). The deduction with respect to the guaranteed annuity interest will be limited to $20,000, which is the minimum amount it is evident the charity will receive.

Example (2). In 1975, C transfers $40,000 in trust with the requirement that D, an individual, and X Charity be paid simultaneously guaranteed annuity interests (as defined in paragraph (c)(2)(vi) of this section) of $5,000 a year each, payable annually at the end of each year, for a period of 5 years and that the remainder be paid to C's children. The fair market value of two annuities of $5,000 each a year for a period of 5 years is $42,124 ([$5,000 × 4.2124] × 2), as determined under § 25.2512-5A(c). The trust instrument provides that in the event the trust fund is insufficient to pay both annuities in a given year, the trust fund will be evenly divided between the charitable and private annuitants. The deduction with respect to the charitable annuity will be limited to $20,000, which is the minimum amount it is evident the charity will receive.

Example (3). In 1975, D transfers $65,000 in trust with the requirement that a guaranteed annuity interest (as defined in paragraph (c)(2)(vi) of this section) of $5,000 a year, payable annually at the end of each year, be paid to Y Charity for a period of 10 years and that a guaranteed annuity interest (as defined in paragraph (c)(2)(vi) of this section) of $5,000 a year, payable annually at the end of each year, be paid to W, his wife, aged 62[,]for 10 years or until her prior death. The annuities are to be paid simultaneously, and the remainder is to be paid to D's children. The fair market value of the private annuity is $33,877 ($5,000 × 6.7754), as determined pursuant to §25.2512-5A(c) and by the use of factors involving one life and a term of years as published in Publication 723A (12-70). The fair market value of the charitable annuity is $36,800.50 ($5,000 × 7.3601), as determined under §25.2512-5A(c). It is not evident from the governing instrument of the trust or from local law that the trustee would be required to apportion the trust fund between the wife and charity in the event the fund were insufficient to pay both annuities in a given year. Accordingly, the deduction with respect to the charitable annuity will be limited to $31,123 ($65,000 less $33,877 [the value of the private annuity]), which is the minimum amount it is evident the charity will receive.

(v) The present value of a unitrust interest described in paragraph (c)(2)(vii) of this section is to be determined by subtracting the present value of all interests in the transferred property other than the unitrust interest from the fair market value of the transferred property.

(3) *Other transfers.*—The present value of an interest not described in paragraph (d)(2) of this section is to be determined under §25.2512-5.

(4) *Special computations.*—If the interest transferred is such that its present value is to be determined by a special computation, a request for a special factor, accompanied by a statement of the date of birth and sex of each individual the duration of whose life may affect the value of the interest, and by copies of the relevant instruments, may be submitted by the donor to the Commissioner who may, if conditions permit, supply the factor requested. If the Commissioner furnishes the factor, a copy of the letter supplying the factor must be attached to the tax return in which the deduction is claimed. If the Commissioner does not furnish the factor, the claim for deduction must be supported by a full statement of the computation of the present value made in accordance with the principles set forth in this paragraph.

(e) *Effective/applicability date.*—This section applies only to gifts made after July 31, 1969. In addition, the rule in paragraphs (c)(2)(vi)(a) and (c)(2)(vii)(a) of this section that guaranteed annuity interests or unitrust interests, respectively, may be payable for a specified term of years or for the life or lives of only certain individuals applies to transfers made on or after April 4, 2000. If a transfer is made on or after April 4, 2000, that uses an individual other than one permitted in paragraphs (c)(2)(vi)(a) and (c)(2)(vii)(a) of this section, the interest may be reformed into a lead interest payable for a specified term of years. The term of years is determined by taking the factor for valuing the annuity or unitrust interest for the named individual measuring life and identifying the term of years (rounded up to the next whole year) that corresponds to the equivalent term of years factor for an annuity or unitrust interest. For example, in the case of an annuity interest payable for the life of an individual age 40 at the time of the transfer on or after May 1, 2009 (the effective date of Table S), assuming an interest rate of 7.4 percent under section 7520, the annuity factor from column 1 of Table S(7.4), contained in IRS Publication 1457, Actuarial Valuations Version 3A, for the life of an individual age 40 is 12.1519 (1 − .10076 / .074). Based on Table B(7.4), contained in Publication 1457, "Actuarial Valuations Version 3A", the factor 12.1519 corresponds to a term of years between 32 and 33 years. Accordingly, the annuity interest must be reformed into an interest payable for a term of 33 years. A judicial reformation must be commenced prior to October 15th of the year following the year in which the transfer is made and must be completed within a reasonable time after it is commenced. A non-judicial reformation is permitted if effective under state law, provided it is completed by the date on which a judicial reformation must be commenced. In the alternative, if a court, in a proceeding that is commenced on or before July 5, 2001, declares any transfer, made on or after April 4, 2000, and on or before March 6, 2001, null and void ab initio, the Internal Revenue Service will treat such transfers in a manner similar to that described in section 2055(e)(3)(J). [Reg. §25.2522(c)-3.]

☐ [*T.D.* 7318, 7-10-74. *Amended by T.D.* 7340, 1-6-75; *T.D.* 7955, 5-10-84; *T.D.* 7957, 5-16-84; *T.D.* 8069, 1-13-86, *T.D.* 8540, 6-9-94; *T.D.* 8630, 12-12-95; *T.D.* 8923, 1-4-2001; *T.D.* 9068, 7-3-2003; *T.D.* 9448, 5-1-2009 *and T.D.* 9540, 8-9-2011.]

[Reg. §25.2522(c)-4]

§25.2522(c)-4. Disallowance of double deduction in the case of qualified terminable interest property.—No deduction is allowed under section 2522 for the transfer of an interest in property if a deduction is taken from the *total amount of gifts* with respect to that property by reason of section 2523(f). See §25.2523(h)-1. [Reg. §25.2522(c)-4.]

☐ [*T.D.* 8522, 2-28-94.]

[Reg. § 25.2522(d)-1]

§ 25.2522(d)-1. Additional cross references.— (a) See section 14 of the Wild and Scenic Rivers Act (Public Law 90-542, 82 Stat. 918) for provisions relating to the claim and allowance of the value of certain easements as a gift under section 2522.

(b) For treatment of gifts accepted by the Secretary of State or the Secretary of Commerce, for the purpose of organizing and holding an international conference to negotiate a Patent Corporation Treaty, as gifts to or for the use of the United States, see section 3 of Joint Resolution of December 24, 1969 (Public Law 91-160, 83 Stat. 443).

(c) For treatment of gifts accepted by the Secretary of the Department of Housing and Urban Development, for the purpose of aiding or facilitating the work of the Department, as gifts to or for the use of the United States, see section 7(k) of the Department of Housing and Urban Development Act (42 U. S. C. 3535), as added by section 905 of Public Law 91-609 (84 Stat. 1809).

(d) For treatment of certain property accepted by the Chairman of the Administrative Conference of the United States, for the purpose of aiding and facilitating the work of the Conference, as gifts to the United States, see 5 U. S. C. 575(c)(12), as added by section 1(b) of the Act of October 21, 1972 (Public Law 92-526, 86 Stat. 1048).

(e) For treatment of the Board for International Broadcasting as a corporation described in section 2522(a)(2), see section 7 of the Board for International Broadcasting Act of 1973 (Public Law 93-129, 87 Stat. 459). [Reg. § 25.2522(d)-1.]

☐ [T.D. 7318, 6-10-74.]

[Reg. § 25.2523(a)-1]

§ 25.2523(a)-1. Gift to spouse; in general.— (a) *In general.—*In determining the amount of taxable gifts for the calendar quarter (with respect to gifts made after December 31, 1970, and before January 1, 1982), or calendar year (with respect to gifts made before January 1, 1971, or after December 31, 1981), a donor may deduct the value of any property interest transferred by gift to a donee who at the time of the gift is the donor's spouse, except as limited by paragraphs (b) and (c) of this section. See § 25.2502-1(c)(1) for the definition of calendar quarter. This deduction is referred to as the *marital deduction.* In the case of gifts made prior to July 14, 1988, no marital deduction is allowed with respect to a gift if, at the time of the gift, the donor is a nonresident not a citizen of the United States. Further, in the case of gifts made on or after July 14, 1988, no marital deduction is allowed (regardless of the donor's citizenship or residence) for transfers to a spouse who is not a citizen of the United States at the time of the transfer. However, for certain special rules applicable in

the case of estate and gift tax treaties, see section 7815(d)(14) of Pub. L. 101-239. The donor must submit any evidence necessary to establish the donor's right to the marital deduction.

(b) *Deductible interests and nondeductible interests.—*(1) *In general.—*The property interests transferred by a donor to his spouse consist of either transfers with respect to which the marital deduction is authorized (as described in subparagraph (2) of this paragraph) or transfers with respect to which the marital deduction is not authorized (as described in subparagraph (3) of this paragraph). These transfers are referred to in this section and in § § 25.2523(b)-1 through 25.2523(f)-1 as *deductible interests* and *nondeductible interests,* respectively.

(2) *Deductible interest.—*A property interest transferred by a donor to his spouse is a *deductible interest* if it does not fall within either class of *nondeductible interests* described in subparagraph (3) of this paragraph.

(3) *Nondeductible interests.—*(i) A property interest transferred by a donor to his spouse which is a *terminable interest,* as defined in § 25.2523(b)-1, is a *nondeductible interest* to the extent specified in that section.

(ii) Any property interest transferred by a donor to the donor's spouse is a *nondeductible interest* to the extent it is not required to be included in a gift tax return for a calendar quarter (for gifts made after December 31, 1970, and before January 1, 1982) or calendar year (for gifts made before January 1, 1971, or after December 31, 1981).

(c) *Computation.—*(1) *In general.—*The amount of the marital deduction depends upon when the interspousal gifts are made, whether the gifts are terminable interests, whether the limitations of § 25.2523(f)-1A (relating to gifts of community property before January 1, 1982) are applicable, and whether § 25.2523(f)-1 (relating to the election with respect to life estates) is applicable, and (with respect to gifts made on or after July 14, 1988) whether the donee spouse is a citizen of the United States (see section 2523(i)).

(2) *Gifts prior to January 1, 1977.—*Generally, with respect to gifts made during a calendar quarter prior to January 1, 1977, the marital deduction allowable under section 2523 is 50 percent of the aggregate value of the deductible interests. See section 2524 for an additional limitation on the amount of the allowable deduction.

(3) *Gifts after December 31, 1976, and before January 1, 1982.—*Generally, with respect to gifts made during a calendar quarter beginning after December 31, 1976, and ending prior to January 1, 1982, the marital deduction allowable under section 2523 is computed as a percentage of the deductible interests in those gifts. If the aggre-

gate amount of deductions for such gifts is $100,000 or less, a deduction is allowed for 100 percent of the deductible interests. No deduction is allowed for otherwise deductible interests in an aggregate amount that exceeds $100,000 and is equal to or less than $200,000. For deductible interests in excess of $200,000, the deduction is limited to 50 percent of such deductible interests. If a donor remarries, the computations in this paragraph (c)(3) are made on the basis of aggregate gifts to all persons who at the time of the gifts are the donor's spouse. See section 2524 for an additional limitation on the amount of the allowable deduction.

(4) *Gifts after December 31, 1981.*—Generally, with respect to gifts made during a calendar year beginning after December 31, 1981 (other than gifts made on or after July 14, 1988, to a spouse who is not a United States citizen on the date of the transfer), the marital deduction allowable under section 2523 is 100 percent of the aggregate value of the deductible interests. See section 2524 for an additional limitation on the amount of the allowable deduction, and section 2523(i) regarding disallowance of the marital deduction for gifts to a spouse who is not a United States citizen.

(d) *Examples.*—The following examples (in which it is assumed that the donors have previously utilized any specific exemptions provided by section 2521 for gifts prior to January 1, 1977) illustrate the application of paragraph (c) of this section and the interrelationship of sections 2523 and 2503. Generally, the marital deduction is equal to one-half of the aggregate value of the "deductible interests." The following examples (in each of which it is assumed that the donor has previously utilized his entire $30,000 specific exemption provided by section 2521) illustrate the marital deduction computation and the interrelationship of sections 2503(b) and 2523(a):

Example 1. A donor made a transfer by gift of $6,000 cash to his spouse on December 25, 1971. The donor made no other transfers during 1971. The amount of the marital deduction for the fourth calendar quarter of 1971 is $3,000 (one-half of $6,000); the amount of the annual exclusion under §2503(b) is $3,000; and the amount of taxable gifts is zero ($6,000 – $3,000 (annual exclusion) – $3,000 (marital deduction)).

Example 2. A donor made transfers by gift to his spouse of $3,000 cash on January 1, 1971, and $3,000 cash on May 1, 1971. The donor made no other transfers during 1971. For the first calendar quarter of 1971 the marital deduction is zero because the amount excluded under section 2503(b) is $3,000, and the amount of taxable gifts is also zero. For the second calendar quarter of 1971 the marital deduction is $1,500 (one-half of $3,000), and the amount of taxable gifts is $1,500 ($3,000 – $1,500 (marital deduction)). Under section 2503(b) no amount of the second $3,000 gift may be excluded because the entire $3,000 an-

nual exclusion was applied against the gift made in the first calendar quarter of 1971.

Example 3. A donor made a transfer by gift to his spouse of $10,000 cash on April 1, 1972. The donor made no other transfers during 1972. For the second calendar quarter of 1972 the amount of the marital deduction is $5,000 (one-half of $10,000); the amount excluded under section 2503(b) is $3,000; the amount of taxable gifts is $2,000 ($10,000 – $3,000 (annual exclusion) – $5,000 (marital deduction)).

Example 4. A donor made transfers by gift to his spouse of $2,000 cash on January 1, 1971, $2,000 cash on April 5, 1971, and $10,000 cash on December 1, 1971. The donor made no other transfers during 1971. For the first calendar quarter of 1971 the marital deduction is zero because the amount excluded under section 2503(b) is $2,000, and the amount of taxable gifts is also zero. For the second calendar quarter of 1971 the marital deduction is $1,000 (one-half of $2,000) (see section 2524); the amount excluded under section 2503(b) is $1,000 because $2,000 of the $3,000 annual exclusion was applied against the gift made in the first calendar quarter of 1971; and the amount of taxable gifts is zero ($2,000 – $1,000 (annual exclusion) – $1,000 (marital deduction)). For the fourth calendar quarter of 1971, the marital deduction is $5,000 (one-half of $10,000); the amount excluded under section 2503(b) is zero because the entire $3,000 annual exclusion was applied against the gifts made in the first and second calendar quarters of 1971; and the amount of taxable gifts is $5,000 ($10,000 – $5,000 (marital deduction)).

Example 5. A donor made transfers by gift to his spouse of $2,000 cash on January 10, 1972, $2,000 cash on May 1, 1972, and a remainder interest valued at $16,000 on June 1, 1972. The donor made no other transfers during 1972. For the first calendar quarter of 1972, the marital deduction is zero because $2,000 is excluded under section 2503(b), and the amount of taxable gifts is also zero. For the second calendar quarter of 1972 the marital deduction is $9,000 (one-half of $16,000 plus one-half of $2,000); the amount excluded under section 2503(b) is $1,000 because $2,000 of the $3,000 annual exclusion was applied against the gift made in the first calendar quarter of 1971 [1972]; and the amount of taxable gifts is $8,000 ($18,000 – $1,000 (annual exclusion) – $9,000 (marital deduction)).

Example 6. A donor made transfers by gift to his spouse of $2,000 cash on January 1, 1972, a remainder interest valued at $16,000 on January 5, 1972, and $2,000 cash on April 30, 1972. The donor made no other transfers during 1972. For the first calendar quarter of 1972, the marital deduction is $9,000 (one-half of $16,000 plus one-half of $2,000); the amount excluded under section 2503(b) is $2,000; and the amount of taxable gifts is $7,000 ($18,000 – $2,000 (annual exclusion) – $9,000 (marital deduction)). For the second calendar quarter of 1972 the marital deduction is $1,000 (one-half of $2,000); the amount excluded under section 2503(b) is $1,000 because $2,000 of the $3,000 annual exclusion was applied against the gift of the present interest in the first calendar quarter of 1971 [1972]; and the amount of taxable gifts is zero ($2,000 – $1,000 (annual exclusion) – $1,000 (marital deduction)).

Example 7. A donor made a transfer by gift to his spouse of $12,000 cash on July 17, 1955. The donor made no other transfers during 1955. For the calendar year 1955 the amount of the marital deduction is $6,000 (one-half of $12,000); the amount excluded under section 2503(b) is $3,000; and the amount of taxable gifts is $3,000 ($12,000 – $3,000 (annual exclusion) – $6,000 (marital deduction)).

Example 8. A donor made a transfer by gift to the donor's spouse, a United States citizen, of $200,000 cash on January 1, 1995. The donor made no other transfers during 1995. For calendar year 1995, the amount excluded under section 2503(b) is $10,000; the marital deduction is $190,000; and the amount of taxable gifts is zero ($200,000 – $10,000 (annual exclusion) – $190,000 (marital deduction)).

(e) *Valuation.*—If the income from property is made payable to the donor or another individual for life or for a term of years, with remainder to the donor's spouse or to the estate of the donor's spouse, the marital deduction is computed (pursuant to § 25.2523(a)-1(c)) with respect to the present value of the remainder, determined under section 7520. The present value of the remainder (that is, its value as of the date of gift) is to be determined in accordance with the rules stated in § 25.2512-5 or, for certain periods, § 25.2512-5A. See the example in paragraph (d) of § 25.2512-5. If the remainder is such that its value is to be determined by a special computation, a request for a specific factor, accompanied by a statement of the dates of birth of each person, the duration of whose life may affect the value of the remainder, and by copies of the relevant instruments may be submitted by the donor to the Commissioner who, if conditions permit, may supply the factor requested. If the Commissioner does not furnish the factor, the claim for deduction must be supported by a full statement of the computation of the present value, made in accordance with the principles set forth in § 25.2512-5(d) or, for certain periods, § 25.2512-5A. [Reg. § 25.2523(a)-1.]

☐ [*T.D. 6334, 11-14-58. Amended by T.D. 7012, 5-14-69; T.D. 7238, 12-28-72; T.D. 7955, 5-10-84; T.D. 8522, 2-28-94 and T.D. 8540, 6-9-94.*]

[Reg. § 25.2523(b)-1]

§ 25.2523(b)-1. Life estate or other terminable interest.—(a) *In general.*—(1) The provisions of section 2523(b) generally disallow a marital deduction with respect to certain property interests (referred to generally as *terminable interests* and

defined in paragraph (a)(3) of this section) transferred to the donee spouse under the circumstances described in paragraph (a)(2) of this section, unless the transfer comes within the purview of one of the exceptions set forth in § 25.2523(d)-1 (relating to certain joint interests); § 25.2523(e)-1 (relating to certain life estates with powers of appointment); § 25.2523(f)-1 (relating to certain qualified terminable interest property); or § 25.2523(g)-1 (relating to certain qualified charitable remainder trusts).

(2) If a donor transfers a terminable interest in property to the donee spouse, the marital deduction is disallowed with respect to the transfer if the donor spouse also—

(i) Transferred an interest in the same property to another donee (see paragraph (b) of this section), or

(ii) Retained an interest in the same property in himself (see paragraph (c) of this section), or

(iii) Retained a power to appoint an interest in the same property (see paragraph (d) of this section).

Notwithstanding the preceding sentence, the marital deduction is disallowed under these circumstances only if the other donee, the donor, or the possible appointee, may, by reason of the transfer or retention, possess or enjoy any part of the property after the termination or failure of the interest therein transferred to the donee spouse.

(3) For purposes of this section, a distinction is to be drawn between "property," as such term is used in section 2523, and an "interest in property." The "property" referred to is the underlying property in which various interests exist; each such interest is not, for this purpose, to be considered as "property." A "terminable interest" in property is an interest which will terminate or fail on the lapse of time or on the occurrence or failure to occur of some contingency. Life estates, terms for years, annuities, patents, and copyrights are therefore terminable interests. However, a bond, note, or similar contractual obligation, the discharge of which would not have the effect of an annuity or term for years, is not a terminable interest.

(b) *Interest in property which another donee may possess or enjoy.*—(1) Section 2523(b) provides that no marital deduction shall be allowed with respect to the transfer to the donee spouse of a "terminable interest" in property, in case—

(i) The donor transferred (for less than an adequate and full consideration in money or money's worth) an interest in the same property to any person other than the donee spouse (or the estate of such spouse), and,

(ii) By reason of such transfer, such person (or his heirs or assigns) may possess or enjoy any part of such property after the termination or failure of the interest therein transferred to the donee spouse.

(2) In determining whether the donor transferred an interest in property to any person other than the donee spouse, it is immaterial whether the transfer to the person other than the donee spouse was made at the same time as the transfer to such spouse, or at any earlier time.

(3) Except as provided in § 25.2523(e)-1 or 25.2523(f)-1, if at the time of the transfer it is impossible to ascertain the particular person or persons who may receive a property interest transferred by the donor, such interest is considered as transferred to a person other than the donee spouse for the purpose of section 2523(b). This rule is particularly applicable in the case of the transfer of a property interest by the donor subject to a reserved power. See § 25.2511-2. Under this rule, any property interest over which the donor reserved a power to revest the beneficial title in himself, or over which the donor reserved the power to name new beneficiaries or to change the interests of the beneficiaries as between themselves, is for the purpose of section 2523(b), considered as transferred to a "person other than the donee spouse." The following examples, in which it is assumed that the donor did not make an election under sections 2523(f)(2)(C) and (f)(4), illustrate the application of the provisions of this paragraph (b)(3):

Example 1. If a donor transferred property in trust, naming his wife as the irrevocable income beneficiary for 10 years, and providing that, upon the expiration of that term, the corpus should be distributed among his wife and children in such proportions as the trustee should determine, the right to the corpus, for the purpose of the marital deduction, is considered as transferred to a "person other than the donee spouse."

Example 2. If, in the above example, the donor had provided that, upon the expiration of the 10-year term, the corpus was to be paid to his wife, but also reserved the power to revest such corpus in himself, the right to corpus, for the purpose of the marital deduction, is considered as transferred to a "person other than the donee spouse."

(4) The term "person other than the donee spouse" includes the possible unascertained takers of a property interest, as, for example, the members of a class to be ascertained in the future. As another example, assume that the donor created a power of appointment over a property interest, which does not come within the purview of § 25.2523(e)-1. In such a case, the term "person other than the donee spouse" refers to the possible appointees and takers in default (other than the spouse) of such property interest.

(5) An exercise or release at any time by the donor (either alone or in conjunction with any person) of a power to appoint an interest in property, even though not otherwise a transfer by him is considered as a transfer by him in determining, for the purpose of section 2523(b), whether he transferred an interest in such property to a person other than the donee spouse.

(6) The following examples illustrate the application of this paragraph. In each example, it is assumed that the donor made no election under sections 2523(f)(2)(C) and (f)(4) and that the property interest that the donor transferred to a person other than the donee spouse is not transferred for adequate and full consideration in money or money's worth:

Example 1. H (the donor) transferred real property to W (his wife) for life, with remainder to A and his heirs. No marital deduction may be taken with respect to the interest transferred to W, since it will terminate upon her death and A (or his heirs or assigns) will thereafter possess or enjoy the property.

Example 2. H transferred property for the benefit of W and A. The income was payable to W for life and upon her death the principal was to be distributed to A or his issue. However, if A should die without issue, leaving W surviving, the principal was then to be distributed to W. No marital deduction may be taken with respect to the interest transferred to W, since it will terminate in the event of her death if A or his issue survive, and A or his issue will thereafter possess or enjoy the property.

Example 3. H purchased for $100,000 a life annuity for W. If the annuity payments made during the life of W should be less than $100,000, further payments were to be made to A. No marital deduction may be taken with respect to the interest transferred to W, since A may possess or enjoy a part of the property following the termination of W's interest. If, however, the contract provided for no continuation of payments, and provided for no refund upon the death of W, or provided that any refund was to go to the estate of W, then a marital deduction may be taken with respect to the gift.

Example 4. H transferred property to A for life with remainder to W provided W survives A, but if W predeceases A, the property is to pass to B and his heirs. No marital deduction may be taken with respect to the interest transferred to W.

Example 5. H transferred real property to A, reserving the right to the rentals of the property for a term of 20 years. H later transferred the right to the remaining rentals to W. No marital deduction may be taken with respect to the interest since it will terminate upon the expiration of the balance of the 20-year term and A will thereafter possess or enjoy the property.

Example 6. H transferred a patent to W and A as tenants in common. In this case, the interest of W will terminate upon the expiration of the term of the patent, but possession and enjoyment of the property by A must necessarily cease at the same time. Therefore, since A's possession or enjoyment cannot outlast the termination of W's interest, the provisions of section 2523(b) do not disallow the marital deduction with respect to the interest.

(c) *Interest in property which the donor may possess or enjoy.*—(1) Section 2523(b) provides that no marital deduction is allowed with respect to the transfer to the donee spouse of a "terminable interest" in property, if—

(i) The donor retained in himself an interest in the same property, and

(ii) By reason of such retention, the donor (or his heirs or assigns) may possess or enjoy any part of the property after the termination or failure of the interest transferred to the donee spouse. However, as to a transfer to the donee spouse as sole joint tenant with the donor or as tenant by the entirety, see § 25.2523(d)-1.

(2) In general, the principles illustrated by the examples under paragraph (b) of this section are applicable in determining whether the marital deduction may be taken with respect to a property interest transferred to the donee spouse subject to the retention by the donor of an interest in the same property. The application of this paragraph may be further illustrated by the following example, in which it is assumed that the donor made no election under sections 2523(f)(2)(C) and (f)(4):

Example. The donor purchased three annuity contracts for the benefit of his wife and himself. The first contract provided for payments to the wife for life, with refund to the donor in case the aggregate payments made to the wife were less than the cost of the contract. The second contract provided for payments to the donor for life, and then to the wife for life if she survived the donor. The third contract provided for payments to the donor and his wife for their joint lives and then to the survivor of them for life. No marital deduction may be taken with respect to the gifts resulting from the purchases of the contracts since, in the case of each contract, the donor may possess or enjoy a part of the property after the termination or failure of the interest transferred to the wife.

(d) *Interest in property over which the donor retained a power to appoint.*—(1) Section 2523(b) provides that no marital deduction is allowed with respect to the transfer to the donee spouse of a "terminable interest" in property if—

(i) The donor had, immediately after the transfer, a power to appoint an interest in the same property, and

(ii) The donor's power was exercisable (either alone or in conjunction with any person) in such manner that the appointee may possess or enjoy any part of the property after the termination or failure of the interest transferred to the donee spouse.

(2) For the purposes of section 2523(b), the donor is to be considered as having, immediately after the transfer to the donee spouse, such a power to appoint even though the power cannot

be exercised until after the lapse of time, upon the occurrence of an event or contingency, or upon the failure of an event or contingency to occur. It is immaterial whether the power retained by the donor was a taxable power of appointment under section 2514.

(3) The principles illustrated by the examples under paragraph (b) of this section are generally applicable in determining whether the marital deduction may be taken with respect to a property interest transferred to the donee spouse subject to retention by the donor of a power to appoint an interest in the same property. The application of this paragraph may be further illustrated by the following example:

Example. The donor, having a power of appointment over certain property, appointed a life estate to his spouse. No marital deduction may be taken with respect to such transfer, since, if the retained power to appoint the remainder interest is exercised, the appointee thereunder may possess or enjoy the property after the termination or failure of the interest taken by the donee spouse. [Reg. § 25.2523(b)-1.]

☐ [*T.D.* 6334, 11-14-58. *Amended by T.D.* 8522, 2-28-94.]

[Reg. § 25.2523(c)-1]

§ 25.2523(c)-1. Interest in unidentified assets.—(a) Section 2523(c) provides that if an interest passing to a donee spouse may be satisfied out of a group of assets (or their proceeds) which include a particular asset that would be a nondeductible interest if it passed from the donor to his spouse, the value of the interest passing to the spouse is reduced, for the purpose of the marital deduction, by the value of the particular asset.

(b) In order for this section to apply, two circumstances must coexist, as follows:

(1) The property interest transferred to the donee spouse must be payable out of a group of assets. An example of a property interest payable out of a group of assets is a right to a share of the corpus of a trust upon its termination.

(2) The group of assets out of which the property interest is payable must include one or more particular assets which, if transferred by the donor to the donee spouse, would not qualify for the marital deduction. Therefore, section 2523(c) is not applicable merely because a group of assets includes a terminable interest, but would only be applicable if the terminable interest were nondeductible under the provisions of § 25.2523(b)-1.

(c) If both of the circumstances set forth in paragraph (b) of this section exist, only a portion of the property interest passing to the spouse is a deductible interest. The portion qualifying as a deductible interest is an amount equal to the excess, if any, of the value of the property interest passing to the spouse over the aggregate value of the asset (or assets) that if transferred to the spouse would not qualify for the marital deduction. See paragraph (c) of § 25.2523(a)-1 to determine the percentage of the deductible interest allowable as a marital deduction. The application of this section may be illustrated by the following example:

Example. H was absolute owner of a rental property and on July 1, 1950, transferred it to A by gift, reserving the income for a period of 20 years. On July 1, 1955, he created a trust to last for a period of 10 years. H was to receive the income from the trust and at the termination of the trust the trustee is to turn over to H's wife, W, property having a value of $100,000. The trustee has absolute discretion in deciding which properties in the corpus he shall turn over to W in satisfaction of the gift to her. The trustee received two items of property from H. Item (1) consisted of shares of corporate stock. Item (2) consisted of the right to receive the income from the rental property during the unexpired portion of the 20-year term. Assume that at the termination of the trust on July 1, 1965, the value of the right to the rental income from the then unexpired term of 5 years (item 2) will be $30,000. Since item (2) is a nondeductible interest and the trustee can turn it over to W in partial satisfaction of her gift, only $70,000 of the $100,000 receivable by her on July 1, 1965, will be considered as property with respect to which a marital deduction is allowable. The present value on July 1, 1955, of the right to receive $70,000 at the end of 10 years is $49,624.33 as determined under § 25.2512-5A(c). The value of the property qualifying for the marital deduction, therefore, is $49,624.33 and a marital deduction is allowed for one-half of that amount, or $24,812.17. [Reg. § 25.2523(c)-1.]

☐ [*T.D.* 6334, 11-14-58. *Amended by T.D.* 8522, 2-28-94 *and T.D.* 8540, 6-9-94.]

[Reg. § 25.2523(d)-1]

§ 25.2523(d)-1. Joint interests.—Section 2523(d) provides that if a property interest is transferred to the donee spouse as sole joint tenant with the donor or as a tenant by the entirety, the interest of the donor in the property which exists solely by reason of the possibility that the donor may survive the donee spouse, or that there may occur a severance of the tenancy, is not for the purposes of section 2523(b), to be considered as an interest retained by the donor in himself. Under this provision, the fact that the donor may, as surviving tenant, possess or enjoy the property after the termination of the interest transferred to the donee spouse does not preclude the allowance of the marital deduction with respect to the latter interest. Thus, if the donor purchased real property in the name of the donor and the donor's spouse as tenants by the entirety or as joint tenants with rights of survivorship, a marital deduction is allowable with respect to the value of the interest of the donee spouse in the property (subject to the limitations set forth in § 25.2523(a)-1). See paragraph (c) of § 25.2523(b)-1 and section 2524. [Reg. § 25.2523(d)-1.]

☐ [*T.D.* 6334, 11-14-58. *Amended by T.D.* 7238, 12-28-72 *and T.D.* 8522, 2-28-94.]

[Reg. § 25.2523(e)-1]

§ 25.2523(e)-1. Marital deduction; life estate with power of appointment in donee spouse.— (a) *In general.*—Section 2523(e) provides that if an interest in property is transferred by a donor to his spouse (whether or not in trust) and the spouse is entitled for life to all the income from the entire interest or all the income from a specific portion of the entire interest, with a power in her to appoint the entire interest or the specific portion, the interest transferred to her is a deductible interest, to the extent that it satisfies all five of the conditions set forth below (see paragraph (b) of this section if one or more of the conditions is satisfied as to only a portion of the interest):

(1) The donee spouse must be entitled for life to all of the income from the entire interest or a specific portion of the entire interest, or to a specific portion of all the income from the entire interest.

(2) The income payable to the donee spouse must be payable annually or at more frequent intervals.

(3) The donee spouse must have the power to appoint the entire interest or the specific portion to either herself or her estate.

(4) The power in the donee spouse must be exercisable by her alone and (whether exercisable by will or during life) must be exercisable in all events.

(5) The entire interest or the specific portion must not be subject to a power in any other person to appoint any part to any person other than the donee spouse.

(b) *Specific portion; deductible amount.*—If either the right to income or the power of appointment given to the donee spouse pertains only to a specific portion of a property interest, the portion of the interest which qualifies as a deductible interest is limited to the extent that the rights in the donee spouse meet all of the five conditions described in paragraph (a) of this section. While the rights over the income and the power must coexist as to the same interest in property, it is not necessary that the rights over the income or the power as to such interest be in the same proportion. However, if the rights over income meeting the required conditions set forth in paragraph (a)(1) and (2) of this section extend over a small share of the property interest than the share with respect to which the power of appointment requirements set forth in paragraph (a)(3) through (5) of this section are satisfied, the deductible interest is limited to the smaller share. Conversely, if a power of appointment meeting all the requirements extends to a smaller portion of the property interest than the portion over which the income rights pertain, the deductible interest cannot exceed the value of the portion to which such power of appointment applies. Thus, if the donor gives to the donee spouse the right to receive annually all of the income from a particular property interest and a power of appointment meeting the specifications prescribed in paragraph (a)(3) through (5) of this section as to only one-half of the property interest, then only one-half of the property interest is treated as a deductible interest. Correspondingly, if the income interest of the spouse satisfying the requirements extends to only one-fourth of the property interest and a testamentary power of appointment satisfying the requirements extends to all of the property interest, then only one-fourth of the interest in the spouse qualifies as a deductible interest. Further, if the donee spouse has no right to income from a specific portion of a property interest but a testamentary power of appointment which meets the necessary conditions over the entire interest, then none of the interest qualifies for the deduction. In addition, if, from the time of the transfer, the donee spouse has a power of appointment meeting all of the required conditions over three-fourths of the entire property interest and the prescribed income rights over the entire interest, but with a power in another person to appoint one-half of the entire interest, the value of the interest in the donee spouse over only one-half of the property interest will qualify as a deductible interest.

(c) *Meaning of specific portion.*—(1) *In general.*—Except as provided in paragraphs (c)(2) and (c)(3) of this section, a partial interest in property is not treated as a *specific portion* of the entire interest. In addition, any specific portion of an entire interest in property is nondeductible to the extent the specific portion is subject to invasion for the benefit of any person other than the donee spouse, except in the case of a deduction allowable under section 2523(e), relating to the exercise of a general power of appointment by the donee spouse.

(2) *Fraction or percentage share.*—Under section 2523(e), a partial interest in property is treated as a specific portion of the entire interest if the rights of the donee spouse in income, and the required rights as to the power described in §25.2523(e)-1(a), constitute a fractional or percentage share of the entire property interest, so that the donee spouse's interest reflects its proportionate share of the increase or decrease in the value of the entire property interest to which the income rights and the power relate. Thus, if the spouse's right to income and the spouse's power extend to a specified fraction or percentage of the property, or its equivalent, the interest is in a specific portion of the property. In accordance with paragraph (b) of this section, if the spouse has the right to receive the income from a specific portion of the trust property (after applying paragraph (c)(3) of this section) but has a power of appointment over a different specific portion of the property (after applying paragraph (c)(3) of this section), the marital deduction is limited to the lesser specific portion.

(3) *Special rule in the case of gifts made on or before October 24, 1992.*—In the case of gifts within the purview of the effective date rule contained in paragraph (c)(3)(iii) of this section:

(i) A specific sum payable annually, or at more frequent intervals, out of the property and its income that is not limited by the income of the property is treated as the right to receive the income from a specific portion of the property. The specific portion, for purposes of paragraph (c)(2) of this section, is the portion of the property that, assuming the interest rate generally applicable for the valuation of annuities at the time of the donor's gift, would produce income equal to such payments. However, a pecuniary amount payable annually to a donee spouse is not treated as a right to the income from a specific portion of trust property for purposes of this paragraph (c)(3)(i) if any person other than the donee spouse may receive, during the donee spouse's lifetime, any distribution of the property. To determine the applicable interest rate for valuing annuities, see sections 2512 and 7520 and the regulations under those sections.

(ii) The right to appoint a pecuniary amount out of a larger fund (or trust corpus) is considered the right to appoint a specific portion of such fund or trust in an amount equal to such pecuniary amount.

(iii) The rules contained in paragraphs(c)(3)(i) and (ii) of this section apply with respect to gifts made on or before October 24, 1992.

(4) *Local law.*—A partial interest in property is treated as a specific portion of the entire interest if it is shown that the donee spouse has rights under local law that are identical to those the donee spouse would have acquired had the partial interest been expressed in terms satisfying the requirements of paragraph (c)(2) of this section (or paragraph (c)(3) of this section if applicable).

(5) *Examples.*—The following examples illustrate the application of paragraphs (b) and (c) of this section, where D, the donor, transfers property to D's spouse, S:

Example 1. Spouse entitled to the lesser of an annuity or a fraction of trust income. Prior to October 24, 1992, D transferred in trust 500 identical shares of X Company stock, valued for gift tax purposes at $500,000. The trust provided that during the lifetime of D's spouse, S, the trustee is to pay annually to S the lesser of one-half of the trust income or $20,000. Any trust income not paid to S is to be accumulated in the trust and may not be distributed during S's lifetime. S has a testamentary general power of appointment over the entire trust principal. The applicable interest rate for valuing annuities as of the date of D's gift under section 7520 is 10 percent. For purposes of paragraphs (a) through (c) of this section, S is treated as receiving all of the income from the lesser of one-half of the stock ($250,000), or $200,000, the specific portion of the stock which, as determined in accordance with § 25.2523(e)-1(c)(3)(i) of this chapter, would produce annual income of $20,000 (20,000÷.10). Accordingly, the marital deduction is limited to $200,000 (200,000÷500,000 or $2/5$th of the value of the trust.)

Example 2. Spouse possesses power and income interest over different specific portions of trust. The facts are the same as in *Example 1* except that S's testamentary general power of appointment is exercisable over only $1/4$th of the trust principal. Consequently, under section 2523(e), the marital deduction is allowable only for the value of $1/4$th of the trust ($125,000); i.e., the lesser of the value of the portion with respect to which S is deemed to be entitled to all of the income ($2/5$th of the trust or $200,000), or the value of the portion with respect to which S possesses the requisite power of appointment ($1/4$th of the trust or $125,000).

Example 3. Power of appointment over shares of stock constitutes a power over a specific portion. D transferred 250 identical shares of Y company stock to a trust under the terms of which trust income is to be paid annually to S, during S's lifetime. S was given a testamentary general power of appointment over 100 shares of stock. The trust provides that if the trustee sells the Y company stock, S's general power of appointment is exercisable with respect to the sale proceeds or the property in which the proceeds are reinvested. Because the amount of property represented by a single share of stock would be altered if the corporation split its stock, issued stock dividends, made a distribution of capital, etc., a power to appoint 100 shares at the time of S's death is not necessarily a power to appoint the entire interest that the 100 shares represented on the date of D's gift. If it is shown that, under local law, S has a general power to appoint not only the 100 shares designated by D but also $100/250$ of any distributions by the corporation that are included in trust principal, the requirements of paragraph (c)(2) of this section are satisfied and S is treated as having a general power to appoint $100/250$ of the entire interest in the 250 shares. In that case, the marital deduction is limited to 40 percent of the trust principal. If local law does not give S that power, the 100 shares would not constitute a specific portion under § 25.2523(e)-1(c) (including § 25.2523(e)-1(c)(3)(ii)). The nature of the asset is such that a change in the capitalization of the corporation could cause an alteration in the original value represented by the shares at the time of the transfer and is thus not a specific portion of the trust.

(d) Definition of "entire interest".—Since a marital deduction is allowed for each qualifying separate interest in property transferred by the donor to the donee spouse, for purposes of paragraphs (a) and (b) of this section, each property interest with respect to which the donee spouse received some rights is considered separately in determining whether her rights extend to the entire interest or to a specific portion of the entire interest. A property interest which consists of several identical units of property (such as a block of 250 shares of stock, whether the ownership is evidenced by one or several certificates) is considered one property interest, unless certain of the units are to be segregated and accorded different treatment, in which case each segregated group of items is considered a separate property interest. The bequest of a specified sum of money constitutes the bequest of a separate property interest if immediately following the transfer and thenceforth it, and the investments made with it, must be so segregated or accounted for as to permit its identification as a separate item of property. The application of this paragraph may be illustrated by the following examples:

Example (1). The donor transferred to a trustee three adjoining farms, Blackacre, Whiteacre, and Greenacre. The trust instrument provided that during the lifetime of the donee spouse the trustee should pay her all of the income from the trust. Upon her death, all of Blackacre, a one-half interest in Whiteacre, and a one-third interest in Greenacre were to be distributed to the person or persons appointed by her in her will. The donee spouse is considered as being entitled to all of the income from the entire interest in Blackacre, all of the income from the entire interest in Whiteacre, and all of the income from the entire interest in Greenacre. She also is considered as having a power of appointment over the entire interest in Blackacre, over one-half of the entire interest in Whiteacre, and over one-third of the entire interest in Greenacre.

Example (2). The donor transferred $250,000 to C, as trustee. C is to invest the money and pay all of the income from the investments to W, the donor's spouse, annually. W was given a general power, exercisable by will, to appoint one-half of the corpus of the trust. Here, immediately following establishment of the trust, the $250,000 will be sufficiently segregated to permit its identification as a separate item, and the $250,000 will constitute an entire property interest. Therefore, W has a right to income and a power of appointment such that one-half of the entire interest is a deductible interest.

Example (3). The donor transferred 100 shares of Z Corporation stock to D, as trustee. W, the donor's spouse, is to receive all of the income of the trust annually and is given a general power, exercisable by will, to appoint out of the trust corpus the sum of $25,000. In this case the $25,000 is not, immediately following establishment of the trust, sufficiently segregated to permit its identification as a separate item of property in which the donee spouse has the entire interest. Therefore, the $25,000 does not constitute the entire interest in a property for the purpose of paragraphs (a) and (b) of this section.

(e) *Application of local law.*—In determining whether or not the conditions set forth in paragraph (a)(1) through (5) of this section are satisfied by the instrument of transfer, regard is to be had to the applicable provisions of the law of the jurisdiction under which the interest passes and, if the transfer is in trust, the applicable provisions of the law governing the administration of the trust. For example, silence of a trust instrument as to the frequency of payment will not be regarded as a failure to satisfy the condition set forth in paragraph (a)(2) of this section that income must be payable to the donee spouse annually or more frequently unless the applicable law permits payment to be made less frequently than annually. The principles outlined in this paragraph and paragraphs (f) and (g) of this section which are applied in determining whether transfers in trust meet such conditions are equally applicable in ascertaining whether, in the case of interests not in trust, the donee spouse has the equivalent in rights over income and over the property.

(f) *Right to income.*—(1) If an interest is transferred in trust, the donee spouse is "entitled for life to all of the income from the entire interest or a specific portion of the entire interest," for the purpose of the condition set forth in paragraph (a)(1) of this section, if the effect of the trust is to give her substantially that degree of beneficial enjoyment of the trust property during her life which the principles of the law of trusts accord to a person who is unqualifiedly designated as the life beneficiary of a trust. Such degree of enjoyment is given only if it was the donor's intention, as manifested by the terms of the trust instrument and the surrounding circumstances, that the trust should produce for the donee spouse during her life such an income, or that the spouse should have such use of the trust property as is consistent with the value of the trust corpus and with its preservation. The designation of the spouse as sole income beneficiary for life of the entire interest or a specific portion of the entire interest will be sufficient to qualify the trust unless the terms of the trust and the surrounding circumstances considered as a whole evidence an intention to deprive the spouse of the requisite degree of enjoyment. In determining whether a trust evidences that intention, the treatment required or permitted with respect to individual items must be considered in relation to the entire system provided for the administration of the trust. In addition, the spouse's interest shall meet the condition set forth in paragraph (a)(1) of this section if the spouse is entitled to income as defined or determined by applicable local law that provides for a reasonable apportionment between the income and remainder beneficiaries of the total return of the trust and that meets the requirements of §1.643(b)-1 of this chapter.

(2) If the over-all effect of a trust is to give to the donee spouse such enforceable rights as will preserve to her the requisite degree of enjoyment, it is immaterial whether that result is effected by rules specifically stated in the trust instrument, or, in their absence, by the rules for the management of the trust property and the allocation of receipts and expenditures supplied by the State law. For example, a provision in the trust instrument for amortization of bond premium by appropriate periodic charges to interest will not disqualify the interest transferred in trust even though there is no State law specifically authorizing amortization or there is a State law denying amortization which is applicable only in the absence of such a provision in the trust instrument.

(3) In the case of a trust, the rules to be applied by the trustee in allocation of receipts and expenses between income and corpus must be considered in relation to the nature and expected productivity of the assets transferred in trust, the nature and frequency of occurrence of the expected receipts, and any provisions as to change in the form of investments. If it is evident from the nature of the trust assets and the rules provided for management of the trust that the allocation to income of such receipts as rents, ordinary cash dividends and interest will give to the spouse the substantial enjoyment during life required by the statute, provisions that such receipts as stock dividends and proceeds from the conversion of trust assets shall be treated as corpus will not disqualify the interest transferred in trust. Similarly, provision for a depletion charge against income in the case of trust assets which are subject to depletion will not disqualify the interest transferred in trust, unless the effect is to deprive the spouse of the requisite beneficial enjoyment. The same principle is applicable in the case of depreciation, trustees' commissions, and other charges.

(4) Provisions granting administrative powers to the trustees will not have the effect of disqualifying an interest transferred in trust unless the grant of powers evidences the intention to deprive the donee spouse of the beneficial enjoyment required by the statute. Such an intention will not be considered to exist if the entire terms of the instrument are such that the local courts will impose reasonable limitations upon the exercise of the powers. Among the powers which if subject to reasonable limitations will not disqualify the interest transferred in trust are the power to determine the allocation or apportionment of receipts and disbursements between in-

come and corpus, the power to apply the income or corpus for the benefit of the spouse, and the power to retain the assets transferred to the trust. For example, a power to retain trust assets which consist substantially of unproductive property will not disqualify the interest if the applicable rules for the administration of the trust require, or permit the spouse to require, that the trustee either make the property productive or convert it within a reasonable time. Nor will such a power disqualify the interest if the applicable rules for administration of the trust require the trustee to use the degree of judgment and care in the exercise of the power which a prudent man would use if he were owner of the trust assets. Further, a power to retain a residence for the spouse or other property for the personal use of the spouse will not disqualify the interest transferred in trust.

(5) An interest transferred in trust will not satisfy the condition set forth in paragraph (a)(1) of this section that the donee spouse be entitled to all the income if the primary purpose of the trust is to safeguard property without providing the spouse with the required beneficial enjoyment. Such trusts include not only trusts which expressly provide for the accumulation of the income but also trusts which indirectly accomplish a similar purpose. For example, assume that the corpus of a trust consists substantially of property which is not likely to be income producing during the life of the donee spouse and that the spouse cannot compel the trustee to convert or otherwise deal with the property as described in subparagraph (4) of this paragraph. An interest transferred to such a trust will not qualify unless the applicable rules for the administration require, or permit the spouse to require, that the trustee provide the required beneficial enjoyment, such as by payments to the spouse out of other assets of the trust.

(6) If a trust may be terminated during the life of the donee spouse, under her exercise of a power of appointment or by distribution of the corpus to her, the interest transferred in trust satisfies the condition set forth in paragraph (a)(1) of this section (that the spouse be entitled to all the income) if she (i) is entitled to the income until the trust terminates, or (ii) has the right, exercisable in all events, to have the corpus distributed to her at any time during her life.

(7) An interest transferred in trust fails to satisfy the condition set forth in paragraph (a)(1) of this section, that the spouse be entitled to all the income, to the extent that the income is required to be accumulated in whole or in part or may be accumulated in the discretion of any person other than the donee spouse; to the extent that the consent of any person other than the donee spouse is required as a condition precedent to distribution of the income; or to the extent that any person other than the donee spouse has the power to alter the terms of the trust so as to deprive her of her right to the income. An interest transferred in trust will not fail to satisfy the condition that the spouse be entitled to all the income merely because its terms provide that the right of the donee spouse to the income shall not be subject to assignment, alienation, pledge, attachment or claims of creditors.

(8) In the case of an interest transferred in trust, the terms "entitled for life" and "payable annually or at more frequent intervals", as used in the conditions set forth in paragraph (a)(1) and (2) of this section, require that under the terms of the trust the income referred to must be currently (at least annually; see paragraph (e) of this section) distributable to the spouse or that she must have such command over the income that it is virtually hers. Thus, the conditions in paragraph (a)(1) and (2) of this section are satisfied in this respect if, under the terms of the trust instrument, the donee spouse has the right exercisable annually (or more frequently) to require distribution to herself of the trust income, and otherwise the trust income is to be accumulated and added to corpus. Similarly, as respects the income for the period between the last distribution date and the date of the spouse's death, it is sufficient if that income is subject to the spouse's power to appoint. Thus, if the trust instrument provides that income accrued or undistributed on the date of the spouse's death is to be disposed of as if it had been received after her death, and if the spouse has a power of appointment over the trust corpus, the power necessarily extends to the undistributed income.

(g) *Power of appointment in donee spouse.*— (1) The conditions set forth in paragraph (a)(3) and (4) of this section, that is, that the donee spouse must have a power of appointment exercisable in favor of herself or her estate and exercisable alone and in all events, are not met unless the power of the donee spouse to appoint the entire interest or a specific portion of it falls within one of the following categories:

(i) A power so to appoint fully exercisable in her own favor at any time during her life (as, for example, an unlimited power to invade); or

(ii) A power so to appoint exercisable in favor of her estate. Such a power, if exercisable during life, must be fully exercisable at any time during life, or, if exercisable by will, must be fully exercisable irrespective of the time of her death; or

(iii) A combination of the powers described under subdivisions (i) and (ii) of this subparagraph. For example, the donee spouse may, until she attains the age of 50 years, have a power to appoint to herself and thereafter have a power to appoint to her estate. However, the condition that the spouse's power must be exercisable in all events is not satisfied unless irrespective of when the donee spouse may die the entire interest or a specific portion of it will at the time of her death be subject to one power or the other.

(2) The power of the donee spouse must be a power to appoint the entire interest or a specific portion of it as unqualified owner (and free of the trust if a trust is involved, or free of the joint tenancy if a joint tenancy is involved) or to appoint the entire interest or a specific portion of it as a part of her estate (and free of the trust if a trust is involved), that is, in effect, to dispose of it to whomsoever she pleases. Thus, if the donor transferred property to a son and the donee spouse as joint tenants with right of survivorship and under local law the donee spouse has a power of severance exercisable without consent of the other joint tenant, and by exercising this power could acquire a one-half interest in the property as a tenant in common, her power of severance will satisfy the condition set forth in paragraph (a)(3) of this section that she have a power of appointment in favor of herself or her estate. However, if the donee spouse entered into a binding agreement with the donor to exercise the power only in favor of their issue, that condition is not met. An interest transferred in trust will not be regarded as failing to satisfy the condition merely because takers in default of the donee spouse's exercise of the power are designated by the donor. The donor may provide that, in default of exercise of the power, the trust shall continue for an additional period.

(3) A power is not considered to be a power exercisable by a donee spouse alone and in all events as required by paragraph (a)(4) of this section if the exercise of the power in the donee spouse to appoint the entire interest or a specific portion of it to herself or to her estate requires the joinder or consent of any other person. The power is not "exercisable in all events" if it can be terminated during the life of the donee spouse by any event other than her complete exercise or release of it. Further, a power is not "exercisable in all events" if it may be exercised for a limited purpose only. For example, a power which is not exercisable in the event of the spouse's remarriage is not exercisable in all events. Likewise, if there are any restrictions, either by the terms of the instrument or under applicable local law, on the exercise of a power to consume property (whether or not held in trust) for the benefit of the spouse, the power is not exercisable in all events. Thus, if a power of invasion is exercisable only for the spouse's support, or only for her limited use, the power is not exercisable in all events. In order for a power of invasion to be exercisable in all events, the donee spouse must have the unrestricted power exercisable at any time during her life to use all or any part of the property subject to the power, and to dispose of it in any manner, including the power to dispose of it by gift (whether or not she has power to dispose of it by will).

(4) If the power is in existence at all times following the transfer of the interest, limitations of a formal nature will not disqualify the interest. Examples of formal limitations on a power exercisable during life are requirements that an exercise must be in a particular form, that it must be filed with a trustee during the spouse's life, that reasonable notice must be given, or that reasonable intervals must elapse between successive partial exercises. Examples of formal limitations on a power exercisable by will are that it must be exercised by a will executed by the donee spouse after the making of the gift or that exercise must be by specific reference to the power.

(5) If the donee spouse has the requisite power to appoint to herself or her estate, it is immaterial that she also has one or more lesser powers. Thus, if she has a testamentary power to appoint to her estate, she may also have a limited power of withdrawal or of appointment during her life. Similarly, if she has an unlimited power of withdrawal, she may have a limited testamentary power.

(h) *Existence of a power in another.*—Paragraph (a)(5) of this section provides that a transfer described in paragraph (a) is nondeductible to the extent that the donor created a power in the trustee or in any other person to appoint a part of the interest to any person other than the donee spouse. However, only powers in other persons which are in opposition to that of the donee spouse will cause a portion of the interest to fail to satisfy the condition set forth in paragraph (a)(5) of this section. Thus, a power in a trustee to distribute corpus to or for the benefit of the donee spouse will not disqualify the trust. Similarly, a power to distribute corpus to the spouse for the support of minor children will not disqualify the trust if she is legally obligated to support such children. The application of this paragraph may be illustrated by the following examples:

Example (1). Assume that a donor created a trust, designating his spouse as income beneficiary for life with an unrestricted power in the spouse to appoint the corpus during her life. The donor further provided that in the event the donee spouse should die without having exercised the power, the trust should continue for the life of his son with a power in the son to appoint the corpus. Since the power in the son could become exercisable only after the death of the donee spouse, the interest is not regarded as failing to satisfy the condition set forth in paragraph (a)(5) of this section.

Example (2). Assume that the donor created a trust, designating his spouse as income beneficiary for life and as donee of a power to appoint by will the entire corpus. The donor further provided that the trustee could distribute 30 percent of the corpus to the donor's son when he reached the age of 35 years. Since the trustee has a power to appoint 30 percent of the entire interest for the benefit of a person other than the donee spouse, only 70 percent of the interest placed in trust satisfied the condition set forth in paragraph (a)(5) of this section. If, in this case, the donee spouse had a power, exercisable by her will, to appoint only one-half of the corpus as it was constituted at the time of her death, it should be noted that only 35 percent of the interest placed in the trust would satisfy the condition set forth in paragraph (a)(3) of this section. [Reg. § 25.2523(e)-1.]

☐ *[T.D. 6334, 11-14-58. Amended by T.D. 6542, 1-19-61; T.D. 8522, 2-28-94 and T.D. 9102, 12-30-2003.]*

[Reg. § 25.2523(f)-1A]

§ 25.2523(f)-1A. Special rule applicable to community property transferred prior to January 1, 1982.—(a) *In general.*—With respect to gifts made prior to January 1, 1982, the marital deduction is allowable with respect to any transfer by a donor to the donor's spouse only to the extent that the transfer is shown to represent a gift of property that was not, at the time of the gift, held as *community property*, as defined in paragraph (b) of this section.

(b) *Definition of "community property".*— (1) For the purpose of paragraph (a) of this section, the term "community property" is considered to include—

(i) Any property held by the donor and his spouse as community property under the law of any State, Territory, or possession of the United States, or of any foreign country, except property in which the donee spouse had at the time of the gift merely an expectant interest. The donee spouse is regarded as having, at any particular time, merely an expectant interest in property held at that time by the donor and herself as community property under the law of any State, Territory, or possession of the United States, or of any foreign country, if, in case such property were transferred by gift into the separate property of the donee spouse, the entire value of such property (and not merely one-half of it), would be treated as the amount of the gift.

(ii) Separate property acquired by the donor as a result of a "conversion," after December 31, 1941, of property held by him and the donee spouse as community property under the law of any State, Territory, or possession of the United States, or of any foreign country (except such property in which the donee spouse had at the time of the "conversion" merely an expectant interest), into their separate property, subject to the limitation with respect to value contained in subparagraph (5) of this paragraph.

(iii) Property acquired by the donor in exchange (by one exchange or a series of exchanges) for separate property resulting from such "conversion."

(2) The characteristics of property which acquired a noncommunity instead of a community status by reason of an agreement (whether antenuptial or postnuptial) are such that section

2523(f) classifies the property as community property of the donor and his spouse in the computation of the marital deduction. In distinguishing property which thus acquired a noncommunity status from property which acquired such a status solely by operation of the community property law, section 2523(f) refers to the former category of property as "separate property" acquired as a result of a "conversion" of "property held as such community property." As used in section 2523(f) the phrase "property held as such community property" is used to denote the body of property comprehended within the community property system; the expression "separate property" includes any noncommunity property, whether held in joint tenancy, tenancy by the entirety, tenancy in common, or otherwise; and the term "conversion" includes any transaction or agreement which transforms property from a community status into a noncommunity status.

(3) The separate property which section 2523(f) classifies as community property is not limited to that which was in existence at the time of the conversion. The following are illustrative of the scope of section 2523(f):

(i) A partition of community property between husband and wife, whereby a portion of the property became the separate property of each, is a conversion of community property.

(ii) A transfer of community property into some other form of coownership, such as a joint tenancy, is a conversion of the property.

(iii) An agreement (whether made before or after marriage) that future earnings and gains which would otherwise be community property shall be shared by the spouses as separate property effects a conversion of such earnings and gains.

(iv) A change in the form of ownership of property which causes future rentals, which would otherwise have been acquired as community property, to be acquired as separate property effects a conversion of the rentals.

(4) The rules of section 2523(f) are applicable, however, only if the conversion took place after December 31, 1941, and only to the extent stated in this section.

(5) If the value of the separate property acquired by the donor as a result of a conversion did not exceed the value of the separate property thus acquired by the donee spouse, the entire separate property thus acquired by the donor is to be considered, for the purposes of this section, as held by him and the donee spouse as community property. If the value (at the time of conversion) of the separate property so acquired by the donor exceeded the value (at that time) of the separate property so acquired by the donee spouse, only a part of the separate property so acquired by the donor (and only the same fractional part of property acquired by him in exchange for such separate property) is to be considered, for purposes of this section, as held

by him and the donee spouse as community property. The part of such separate property (or property acquired in exchange for it) which is considered as so held is the same proportion of it which the value (at the time of the conversion) of the separate property so acquired by the donee spouse is of the value (at the time) of the separate property so acquired by the donor. The following example illustrates the application of the provisions of this paragraph:

Example. During 1942 the donor and his spouse partitioned certain real property held by them under community property laws. The real property then had a value of $224,000. A portion of the property, then having a value of $160,000, was converted into the donor's separate property, and the remaining portion, then having a value of $64,000, was converted into his spouse's separate property. In 1955 the donor made a gift to his spouse of the property acquired by him as a result of the partition, which property then had a value of $200,000. The portion of the property transferred by gift which is considered as community property is

$$\frac{\$64,000 \text{ (value of property acquired by donee spouse)}}{\$160,000 \text{ (value of property acquired by donor spouse)}} \times \$200,000 = \$80,000$$

The marital deduction with respect to the gift is, therefore, limited to one-half of $120,000 (the difference between $200,000, the value of the gift, and $80,000, the portion of the gift considered to have been of "community property"). The marital deduction with respect to the gift is, therefore, $60,000. [Reg. § 25.2523(f)-1A.]

☐ [*T.D. 6334, 11-14-58. Redesignated and amended by T.D. 8522, 2-28-94.*]

[Reg. § 25.2523(f)-1]

§ 25.2523(f)-1. **Election with respect to life estate transferred to donee spouse.**—(a) *In general.*—(1) With respect to gifts made after December 31, 1981, subject to section 2523(i), a marital deduction is allowed under section 2523(a) for transfers of *qualified terminable interest property.* Qualified terminable interest property is terminable interest property described in section 2523(b)(1) that satisfies the requirements of section 2523(f)(2) and this section. Terminable interests that are described in section 2523(b)(2) cannot qualify as qualified terminable interest property. Thus, if the donor retains a power described in section 2523(b)(2) to appoint an interest in qualified terminable interest property, no deduction is allowable under section 2523(a) for the property.

(2) All of the property for which a deduction is allowed under this paragraph (a) is treated as passing to the donee spouse (for purposes of § 25.2523(a)-1), and no part of the property is treated as retained by the donor or as passing to any person other than the donee spouse (for purposes of § 25.2523(b)-1(b)).

(b) *Qualified terminable interest property.*—(1) *Definition.*—Section 2523(f)(2) provides the definition of *qualified terminable interest property.*

(2) *Meaning of property.*—For purposes of section 2523(f)(2), the term *property* generally means an *entire interest in property* (within the meaning of § 25.2523(e)-1(d)) or a *specific portion of the entire interest* (within the meaning of § 25.2523(e)-1(c)).

(3) *Property for which the election may be made.*—(i) *In general.*—The election may relate to all or any part of property that meets the requirements of section 2523(f)(2)(A) and (B), provided that any partial election must be made with respect to a fractional or percentage share of the property so that the elective portion reflects its proportionate share of the increase or decrease in the entire property for purposes of applying sections 2044 or 2519. Thus, if the interest of the donee spouse in a trust (or other property in which the spouse has a qualifying income interest) meets the requirements of this section, the election may be made under section 2523(f)(2)(C) with respect to a part of the trust (or other property) only if the election relates to a defined fraction or percentage of the entire trust (or other property) or specific portion thereof within the meaning of § 25.2523(e)-1(c). The fraction or percentage may be defined by formula.

(ii) *Division of trusts.*—If the interest of the donee spouse in a trust meets the requirements of this section, the trust may be divided into separate trusts to reflect a partial election that has been made, if authorized under the terms of the governing instrument or otherwise permissible under local law. A trust may be divided only if the fiduciary is required, either by applicable local law or by the express or implied provisions of the governing instrument, to divide the trust according to the fair market value of the assets of the trust at the time of the division. The division of the trusts must be done on a fractional or percentage basis to reflect the partial election. However, the separate trusts do not have to be funded with a pro rata portion of each asset held by the undivided trust.

(4) *Manner and time of making election.*—(i) An election under section 2523(f)(2)(C) (other than a deemed election with respect to a joint and survivor annuity as described in section 2523(f)(6)), is made on a gift tax return for the calendar year in which the interest is transferred. The return must be filed within the time prescribed by section 6075(b) (determined without regard to section 6019(a)(2)), including any extensions authorized under section 6075(b)(2) (re-

lating to an automatic extension of time for filing a gift tax return where the donor is granted an extension of time to file the income tax return).

(ii) If the election is made on a return for the calendar year that includes the date of death of the donor, the return (as prescribed by section 6075(b)(3)) must be filed no later than the time (including extensions) for filing the estate tax return. The election, once made, is irrevocable.

(c) *Qualifying income interest for life.*—(1) *In general.*—For purposes of this section, the term *qualifying income interest for life* is defined as provided in section 2056(b)(7)(B)(ii) and §20.2056(b)-7(d)(1).

(i) *Entitled for life to all the income.*—The principles outlined in §25.2523(e)-1(f) (relating to whether the spouse is entitled for life to all of the income from the entire interest or a specific portion of the entire interest) apply in determining whether the donee spouse is entitled for life to all the income from the property, regardless of whether the interest passing to the donee spouse is in trust. An income interest granted for a term of years, or a life estate subject to termination upon the occurrence of a specified event (e.g., divorce) is not a qualifying income interest for life.

(ii) *Income between last distribution date and date of spouse's death.*—An income interest does not fail to constitute a qualifying income interest for life solely because income for the period between the last distribution date and the date of the donee spouse's death is not required to be distributed to the estate of the donee spouse. See §20.2044-1 of this chapter relating to the inclusion of such undistributed income in the gross estate of the donee spouse.

(iii) *Pooled income funds.*—An income interest in a pooled income fund described in section 642(c)(5) constitutes a qualifying income interest for life for purposes of this section.

(iv) *Distribution of principal for the benefit of the donee spouse.*—An income interest does not fail to constitute a qualifying income interest for life solely because the trustee has a power to distribute principal to or for the benefit of the donee spouse. The fact that property distributed to a donee spouse may be transferred by the spouse to another person does not result in a failure to satisfy the requirement of section 2056(b)(7)(B)(ii)(II). However, if the governing instrument requires the donee spouse to transfer the distributed property to another person without full and adequate consideration in money or money's worth, the requirement of section 2056(b)(7)(B)(ii)(II) is not satisfied.

(2) *Immediate right to income.*—In order to constitute a qualifying income interest for life, the donee spouse must be granted the immediate right to receive the income from the property.

Thus, an income interest does not constitute a qualifying income interest for life if the donee spouse receives the right to trust income commencing at some time in the future, e.g., on the termination of a preceding life income interest of the donor spouse.

(3) *Annuities payable from trusts in the case of gifts made on or before October 24, 1992.*—(i) In the case of gifts made on or before October 24, 1992, a donee spouse's lifetime annuity interest payable from a trust or other group of assets passing from the donor is treated as a qualifying income interest for life for purposes of section 2523(f)(2)(B). The deductible interest, for purposes of §25.2523(a)-1(b), is the specific portion of the property that, assuming the applicable interest rate for valuing annuities at the time the annuity interest is transferred, would produce income equal to the minimum amount payable annually to the donee spouse. If, based on the applicable interest rate, the entire property from which the annuity may be satisfied is insufficient to produce income equal to the minimum annual payment, the value of the deductible interest is the entire value of the property. The value of the deductible interest may not exceed the value of the property from which the annuity is payable. If the annual payment may increase, the increased amount is not taken into account in valuing the deductible interest.

(ii) An annuity interest is not treated as a qualifying income interest for life for purposes of section 2523(f)(2)(B) if any person other than the donee spouse may receive during the donee spouse's lifetime, any distribution of the property or its income from which the annuity is payable.

(iii) To determine the applicable interest rate for valuing annuities, see sections 2512 and 7520 and the regulations under those sections.

(4) *Joint and survivor annuities.*—[Reserved]

(d) *Treatment of interest retained by the donor spouse.*—(1) *In general.*—Under section 2523(f)(5)(A), if a donor spouse retains an interest in qualified terminable interest property, any subsequent transfer by the donor spouse of the retained interest in the property is not treated as a transfer for gift tax purposes. Further, the retention of the interest until the donor spouse's death does not cause the property subject to the retained interest to be includible in the gross estate of the donor spouse.

(2) *Exception.*—Under section 2523(f)(5)(B), the rule contained in paragraph (d)(1) of this section does not apply to any property after the donee spouse is treated as having transferred the property under section 2519, or after the property is includible in the gross estate of the donee spouse under section 2044.

(e) *Application of local law.*—The provisions of local law are taken into account in determining whether or not the conditions of section 2523(f)(2)(A) and (B), and the conditions of paragraph (c) of this section, are satisfied. For example, silence of a trust instrument on the frequency of payment is not regarded as a failure to satisfy the requirement that the income must be payable to the donee spouse annually or more frequently unless applicable local law permits payments less frequently to the donee spouse.

(f) *Examples.*—The following examples illustrate the application of this section, where D, the donor, transfers property to D's spouse, S. Unless stated otherwise, it is assumed that S is not the trustee of any trust established for S's benefit:

Example 1. Life estate in residence. D transfers by gift a personal residence valued at $250,000 on the date of the gift to S and D's children, giving S the exclusive and unrestricted right to use the property (including the right to continue to occupy the property as a personal residence or rent the property and receive the income for her lifetime). After S's death, the property is to pass to D's children. Under applicable local law, S's consent is required for any sale of the property. If D elects to treat all of the transferred property as qualified terminable interest property, the deductible interest is $250,000, the value of the property for gift tax purposes.

Example 2. Power to make property productive. D transfers assets having a fair market value of $500,000 to a trust pursuant to which S is given the right exercisable annually to require distribution of all the trust income to S. No trust property may be distributed during S's lifetime to any person other than S. The assets used to fund the trust include both income producing assets and nonproductive assets. Applicable local law permits S to require that the trustee either make the trust property productive or sell the property and reinvest the proceeds in productive property within a reasonable time after the transfer. If D elects to treat the entire trust as qualified terminable interest property, the deductible interest is $500,000. If D elects to treat only 20 percent of the trust as qualified terminable interest property, the deductible interest is $100,000; i.e., 20 percent of $500,000.

Example 3. Power of distribution over fraction of trust income. The facts are the same as in *Example 2* except that S is given the power exercisable annually to require distribution to S of only 50 percent of the trust income for life. The remaining trust income may be accumulated or distributed among D's children and S in the trustee's discretion. The maximum amount that D may elect to treat as qualified terminable interest property is $250,000; i.e., the value of the trust for gift tax purposes ($500,000) multiplied by the percentage of the trust in which S has a qualifying income interest for life (50 percent). If D elects to treat only 20 percent of the portion of the trust in which S has a qualifying income interest as qualified terminable interest property,

the deductible interest is $50,000; i.e., 20 percent of $250,000.

Example 4. Power to distribute trust corpus to other beneficiaries. D transfers $500,000 to a trust providing that all the trust income is to be paid to D's spouse, S, during S's lifetime. The trustee is given the power to use annually $5,000 from the trust for the maintenance and support of S's minor child, C. Any such distribution does not necessarily relieve S of S's obligation to support and maintain C. S does not have a qualifying income interest for life in any portion of the trust because the gift fails to satisfy the condition in sections 2523(f)(3) and 2056(b)(7)(B)(ii)(II) that no person have a power, other than a power the exercise of which takes effect only at or after S's death, to appoint any part of the property to any person other than S. The trust would also be nondeductible under section 2523(f) if S, rather than the trustee, were given the power to appoint a portion of the principal to C. However, in the latter case, if S made a qualified disclaimer (within the meaning of section 2518) of the power to appoint to C, the trust could qualify for the marital deduction pursuant to section 2523(f), assuming that the power was personal to S and S's disclaimer terminates the power. Similarly, if C made a qualified disclaimer of the right to receive distributions from the trust, the trust would qualify under section 2523(f) assuming that C's disclaimer effectively negates the trustee's power under local law.

Example 5. Spouse's interest terminable on divorce. The facts are the same as in *Example 3* except that if S and D divorce, S's interest in the trust will pass to C. S's income interest is not a qualifying income interest for life because it is terminable upon S's divorce. Therefore, no portion of the trust is deductible under section 2523(f).

Example 6. Spouse's interest in trust in the form of an annuity. Prior to October 24, 1992, D established a trust funded with income producing property valued for gift tax purposes at $800,000. The trustee is required by the trust instrument to pay $40,000 a year to S for life. Any income in excess of the annuity amount is to be accumulated in the trust and may not be distributed during S's lifetime. S's lifetime annuity interest is treated as a qualifying income interest for life. If D elects to treat the entire portion of the trust in which S has a qualifying income interest as qualified terminable interest property, the value of the deductible interest is $400,000, because that amount would yield an income to S of $40,000 a year (assuming a 10 percent interest rate applies in valuing annuities at the time of the transfer).

Example 7. Value of spouse's annuity exceeds value of trust corpus. The facts are the same as in *Example 6*, except that the trustee is required to pay S $100,000 a year for S's life. If D elects to treat the entire portion of the trust in which S has a qualifying income interest for life as qualified terminable interest property, the value of the deductible interest is $800,000, which is the lesser of the entire value of the property ($800,000) or the amount of property that (assuming a 10 percent interest rate) would yield an income to S of $100,000 a year ($1,000,000).

Example 8. Transfer to pooled income fund. D transfers $200,000 on June 1, 1994, to a pooled income fund (described in section 642(c)(5)) designating S as the only life income beneficiary. If D elects to treat the entire $200,000 as qualified terminable interest property, the deductible interest is $200,000.

Example 9. Retention by donor spouse of income interest in property. On October 1, 1994, D transfers property to an irrevocable trust under the terms of which trust income is to be paid to D for life, then to S for life and, on S's death, the trust corpus is to be paid to D's children. Because S does not possess an immediate right to receive trust income, S's interest does not qualify as a qualifying income interest for life under section 2523(f)(2). Further, under section 2702(a)(2) and §25.2702-2(b), D is treated for gift tax purposes as making a gift with a value equal to the entire value of the property. If D dies in 1996 survived by S, the trust corpus will be includible in D's gross estate under section 2036. However, in computing D's estate tax liability, D's adjusted taxable gifts under section 2001(b)(1)(B) are adjusted to reflect the inclusion of the gifted property in D's gross estate. In addition, if S survives D, the trust property is eligible for treatment as qualified terminable interest property under section 2056(b)(7) in D's estate.

Example 10. Retention by donor spouse of income interest in property. On October 1, 1994, D transfers property to an irrevocable trust under the terms of which trust income is to be paid to S for life, then to D for life and, on D's death, the trust corpus is to be paid to D's children. D elects under section 2523(f) to treat the property as qualified terminable interest property. D dies in 1996, survived by S. S subsequently dies in 1998. Under §2523(f)-1(d)(1), because D elected to treat the transfer as qualified terminable interest property, no part of the trust corpus is includible in D's gross estate because of D's retained interest in the trust corpus. On S's subsequent death in 1998, the trust corpus is includible in S's gross estate under section 2044.

Example 11. Retention by donor spouse of income interest in property. The facts are the same as in *Example 10,* except that S dies in 1996 survived by D, who subsequently dies in 1998. Because D made an election under section 2523(f) with respect to the trust, on S's death the trust corpus is includible in S's gross estate under section 2044. Accordingly, under section 2044(c), S is treated as the transferor of the property for estate and gift tax purposes. Upon D's subsequent death in 1998, because the property was subject to inclusion in S's gross estate under section 2044, the exclusion rule in §25.2523(f)-1(d)(1) does not apply under §25.2523(f)-1(d)(2). However, because S is treated as the transferor of the property, the property is not subject to inclusion in D's gross estate under section 2036 or section 2038. If the executor of S's estate made a section 2056(b)(7) election with respect to the trust, the trust is includible in D's gross estate under section 2044 upon D's later death. [Reg. §25.2523(f)-1.]

☐ [*T.D.* 8522, 2-28-94.]

[Reg. §25.2523(g)-1]

§25.2523(g)-1. Special rule for charitable remainder trusts.—(a) *In general.*—(1) With respect to gifts made after December 31, 1981, subject to section 2523(i), if the donor's spouse is the only noncharitable beneficiary (other than the donor) of a charitable remainder annuity trust or charitable remainder unitrust described in section 664 (qualified charitable remainder trust), section 2523(b) does not apply to the interest in the trust transferred to the donee spouse. Thus, the value of the annuity or unitrust interest passing to the spouse qualifies for a marital deduction under section 2523(g) and the value of the remainder interest qualifies for a charitable deduction under section 2522.

(2) A marital deduction for the value of the donee spouse's annuity or unitrust interest in a qualified charitable remainder trust to which section 2523(g) applies is allowable only under section 2523(g). Therefore, if an interest in property qualifies for a marital deduction under section 2523(g), no election may be made with respect to the property under section 2523(f).

(3) The donee spouse's interest need not be an interest for life to qualify for a marital deduction under section 2523(g). However, for purposes of section 664, an annuity or unitrust interest payable to the spouse for a term of years cannot be payable for a term that exceeds 20 years or the trust does not qualify under section 2523(g).

(4) A deduction is allowed under section 2523(g) even if the transfer to the donee spouse is conditioned on the donee spouse's payment of state death taxes, if any, attributable to the qualified charitable remainder trust.

(5) For purposes of this section, the term *noncharitable beneficiary* means any beneficiary of the qualified charitable remainder trust other than an organization described in section 170(c).

(b) *Charitable remainder trusts where the donee spouse and the donor are not the only noncharitable beneficiaries.*—In the case of a charitable remainder trust where the donor and the donor's spouse are not the only noncharitable beneficiaries (for example, where the noncharitable interest is payable to the donor's spouse for life and then to another individual (other than the donor) for life), the qualification of the interest as qualified terminable interest property is determined solely under section 2523(f) and not under section 2523(g). Accordingly, if the transfer to the trust is made prior to October 24, 1992, the spousal annuity or unitrust interest may qualify under § 25.2523(f)-(1)(c)(3) as a qualifying income interest for life. [Reg. § 25.2523(g)-1.]

☐ [T.D. 8522, 2-28-94.]

[Reg. § 25.2523(h)-1]

§ 25.2523(h)-1. Denial of double deduction.— The value of an interest in property may not be deducted for Federal gift tax purposes more than once with respect to the same donor. For example, assume that D, a donor, transferred a life estate in a farm to D's spouse, S, with a remainder to charity and that D elects to treat the property as qualified terminable interest property. The entire value of the property is deductible under section 2523(f). No part of the value of the property qualifies for a charitable deduction under section 2522 for gift tax purposes. [Reg. § 25.2523(h)-1.]

☐ [T.D. 8522, 2-28-94.]

[Reg. § 25.2523(h)-2]

§ 25.2523(h)-2. Effective Dates.—Except as specifically provided, in § § 25.2523(e)-1(c)(3), 25.2523(f)-1(c)(3), and 25.2523(g)-1(b), the provisions of § § 25.2523(e)-1(c), 25.2523(f)-1, 25.2523(g)-1, and 25.2523(h)-1 are effective with respect to gifts made after March 1, 1994. With respect to gifts made on or before such date, donors may rely on any reasonable interpretation of the statutory provisions. For these purposes, the provisions of § § 25.2523(e)-1(c), 25.2523(f)-1, 25.2523(g)-1, and 25.2523(h)-1, (as well as project LR-211-76, 1984-1 C.B., page 598, see § 601.601(d)(2)(ii)(b) of this chapter), are considered a reasonable interpretation of the statutory provisions. In addition, the rule in the last sentence of § 25.2523(e)-1 (f)(1) regarding the determination of income under applicable local law applies to trusts for taxable years ending after January 2, 2004. [Reg. § 25.2523(h)-2.]

☐ [T.D. 8522, 2-28-94. Amended by T.D. 9102, 12-30-2003.]

[Reg. § 25.2523(i)-1]

§ 25.2523(i)-1. Disallowance of marital deduction when spouse is not a United States citizen.—(a) In general.—Subject to § 20.2056A-1(c) of this chapter, section 2523(i)(1) disallows the marital deduction if the spouse of the donor is not a citizen of the United States at the time of the gift. If the spouse of the donor is a citizen of the United States at the time of the gift, the gift tax marital deduction under section 2523(a) is allowed regardless of whether the donor is a citizen or resident of the United States at the time of the gift, subject to the otherwise applicable rules of section 2523.

(b) Exception for certain joint and survivor annuities.—Paragraph (a) does not apply to disallow the marital deduction with respect to any transfer resulting in the acquisition of rights by a noncitizen spouse under a joint and survivor annuity described in section 2523(f)(6).

(c) Increased annual exclusion.—(1) In general.—In the case of gifts made from a donor to the donor's spouse for which a marital deduction is not allowable under this section, if the gift otherwise qualifies for the gift tax annual exclusion under section 2503(b), the amount of the annual exclusion under section 2503(b) is $100,000 in lieu of $10,000. However, in the case of gifts made after June 29, 1989, in order for the increased annual exclusion to apply, the gift in excess of the otherwise applicable annual exclusion under section 2503(b) must be in a form that qualifies for the marital deduction but for the disallowance provision of section 2523(i)(1). See paragraph (d), Example 4, of this section.

(2) Status of donor.—The $100,000 annual exclusion for gifts to a noncitizen spouse is available regardless of the status of the donor. Accordingly, it is immaterial whether the donor is a citizen, resident or a nonresident not a citizen of the United States, as long as the spouse of the donor is not a citizen of the United States at the time of the gift and the conditions for allowance of the increased annual exclusion have been satisfied. See § 25.2503-2(f).

(d) Examples.—The principles outlined in this section are illustrated in the following examples. Assume in each of the examples that the donee, S, is D's spouse and is not a United States citizen at the time of the gift.

Example 1. Outright transfer of present interest. In 1995, D, a United States citizen, transfers to S, outright, 100 shares of X corporation stock valued for federal gift tax purposes at $130,000. The transfer is a gift of a present interest in property under section 2503(b). Additionally, the gift qualifies for the gift tax marital deduction except for the disallowance provision of section 2523(i)(1). Accordingly, $100,000 of the $130,000 gift is excluded from the total amount of gifts made during the calendar year by D for gift tax purposes.

Example 2. Transfer of survivor benefits. In 1995, D, a United States citizen, retires from employment in the United States and elects to receive a reduced retirement annuity in order to provide S with a survivor annuity upon D's death. The transfer of rights to S in the joint and survivor annuity is a gift by D for gift tax purposes. However, under paragraph (b) of this section, the gift qualifies for the gift tax marital deduction even though S is not a United States citizen.

Example 3. Transfer of present interest in trust property. In 1995, D, a resident alien, transfers property valued at $500,000 in trust to S, who is also a resident alien. The trust instrument provides that the trust income is payable to S at least quarterly and S has a testamentary general power to appoint the trust corpus. The transfer to S qualifies for the marital deduction under section 2523 but for the provisions of section 2523(i)(1). Because S has a life income interest in the trust, S has a present interest in a portion of the trust. Accordingly, D may exclude the present value of S's income interest (up to $100,000) from D's total 1995 calendar year gifts.

Example 4. Transfer of present interest in trust property. The facts are the same as in *Example 3*, except that S does not have a testamentary general power to appoint the trust corpus. Instead, D's child, C, has a remainder interest in the trust. If S were a United States citizen, the transfer would qualify for the gift tax marital deduction if a qualified terminable interest property election was made under section 2523(f)(4). However, because S is not a U.S. citizen, D may not make a qualified terminable interest property election. Accordingly, the gift does not qualify for the gift tax marital deduction but for the disallowance provision of section 2523(i)(1). The $100,000 annual exclusion under section 2523(i)(2) is not available with respect to D's transfer in trust and D may not exclude the present value of S's income interest in excess of $10,000 from D's total 1995 calendar year gifts.

Example 5. Spouse becomes citizen after transfer. D, a United States citizen, transfers a residence valued at $350,000 on December 20, 1995, to D's spouse, S, a resident alien. On January 31, 1996, S becomes a naturalized United States citizen. On D's federal gift tax return for 1995, D must include $250,000 as a gift ($350,000 transfer less $100,000 exclusion). Although S becomes a citizen in January, 1996, S is not a citizen of the United States at the time the transfer is made. Therefore, no gift tax marital deduction is allowable. However, the transfer does qualify for the $100,000 annual exclusion. [Reg. § 25.2523(i)-1.]

☐ [T.D. 8612, 8-21-95.]

[Reg. § 25.2523(i)-2]

§ 25.2523(i)-2. Treatment of spousal joint tenancy property where one spouse is not a United States citizen.—(a) *In general.*—In the case of a joint tenancy with right of survivorship between spouses, or a tenancy by the entirety, where the donee spouse is not a United States citizen, the gift tax treatment of the creation and termination of the tenancy (regardless of whether the donor is a citizen, resident or nonresident not a citizen of the United States at such time), is governed by the principles of sections 2515 and 2515A (as such sections were in effect before their repeal by the Economic Recovery Tax Act of 1981). However, in applying these principles, the donor spouse may not elect to treat the creation of a tenancy in real property as a gift, as provided in section 2515(c) (prior to its repeal by the Economic Recovery Tax Act of 1981, Pub. L. 97-34, 95 Stat. 172).

(b) *Tenancies by the entirety and joint tenancies in real property.*—(1) *Creation of the tenancy on or after July 14, 1988.*—Under the principles of section 2515 (without regard to section 2515(c)), the creation of a tenancy by the entirety (or joint tenancy) in real property (either by one spouse alone or by both spouses), and any additions to the value of the tenancy in the form of improvements, reductions in indebtedness thereon, or otherwise, is not deemed to be a transfer of property for purposes of the gift tax, regardless of the proportion of the consideration furnished by each spouse, but only if the creation of the tenancy would otherwise be a gift to the donee spouse who is not a citizen of the United States at the time of the gift.

(2) *Termination.*—(i) *Tenancies created after December 31, 1954 and before January 1, 1982 not subject to an election under section 2515(c), and tenancies created on or after July 14, 1988.*—When a tenancy to which this paragraph (b) applies is terminated on or after July 14, 1988, other than by reason of the death of a spouse, then, under the principles of section 2515, a spouse is deemed to have made a gift to the extent that the proportion of the total consideration furnished by the spouse, multiplied by the proceeds of the termination (whether in the form of cash, property, or interests in property), exceeds the value of the proceeds of termination received by the spouse. See section 2523(i), and § 25.2523(i)-1 and § 25.2503-2(f) as to certain of the tax consequences that may result upon termination of the tenancy. This paragraph (b)(2)(i) applies to tenancies created after December 31, 1954, and before January 1, 1982, not subject to an election under section 2515(c), and to tenancies created on or after July 14, 1988.

(ii) *Tenancies created after December 31, 1954 and before January 1, 1982 subject to an election under section 2515(c) and tenancies created after December 31, 1981 and before July 14, 1988.*—When a tenancy to which this paragraph (a) applies is terminated on or after July 14, 1988, other than by reason of the death of a spouse, then, under the principles of section 2515, a spouse is deemed to have made a gift to the extent that the proportion of the total consideration furnished by the spouse, multiplied by the proceeds of the termination (whether in the form of cash, property, or interests in property), exceeds the value of the proceeds of termination received by the spouse. See section 2523(i), and §§ 25.2523(i)-1 and 25.2503-2(f) as to certain of the tax consequences that may result upon termination of the tenancy. In the case of tenancies to which this paragraph applies, if the creation of the tenancy was treated as a gift to the noncitizen donee spouse under section 2515(c) (in the case of tenancies created prior to 1982) or section 2511 (in the case of tenancies created after December 31, 1981 and before July 14, 1988), then, upon termination of the tenancy, for purposes of applying the principles of section 2515 and the regulations thereunder, the amount treated as a gift on creation of the tenancy is treated as consideration originally belonging to the noncitizen spouse and never acquired by the noncitizen spouse from the donor spouse. This paragraph (b)(2)(ii) applies to tenancies created after December 31, 1954, and before January 1, 1982, subject to an election under section 2515(c), and to tenancies created after December 31, 1981, and before July 14, 1988.

(3) *Miscellaneous provisions.*—(i) *Tenancy by the entirety.*—For purposes of this section, *tenancy by the entirety* includes a joint tenancy between husband and wife with right of survivorship.

(ii) *No election to treat as gift.*—The regulations under section 2515 that relate to the election to treat the creation of a tenancy by the entirety as constituting a gift and the consequences of such an election upon termination of the tenancy (§§ 25.2515-2 and 25.2515-4) do not apply for purposes of section 2523(i)(3).

(4) *Examples.*—The application of this section may be illustrated by the following examples:

Example 1. In 1992, *A*, a United States citizen, furnished $200,000 and *A*'s spouse *B*, a resident alien, furnished $50,000 for the purchase and subsequent improvement of real property held by them as tenants by the entirety. The property is sold in 1998 for $300,000. *A* receives $225,000 and *B* receives $75,000 of the sales proceeds. The termination results in a gift of $15,000 by *A* to *B*, computed as follows:

$$\frac{\$200,000 \text{ (consideration furnished by } A)}{\$250,000 \text{ (total consideration furnished by both spouses)}} \times$$

$300,000 (proceeds of termination) = $240,000 (Proceeds of termination attributable to *A*.)

$240,000 – $225,000 (proceeds received by *A*) = $15,000 gift by *A* to *B*.

Example 2. In 1986, *A* purchased real property for $300,000 and took title in the names of *A* and *B*, *A*'s spouse, as joint tenants. Under section 2511 and § 25.2511-1(h)(1) of the regulations, *A* was treated as making a gift of one-half of the value of the property ($150,000) to *B*. In 1995, the real property is sold for $400,000 and *B* receives the entire proceeds of sale. For purposes of determining the amount of the gift on termination of the tenancy under the principles of section 2515 and the regulations thereunder, the amount treated as a gift to *B* on creation of the tenancy under section 2511 is treated as *B*'s contribution towards the purchase of the property. Accordingly, the termination of the tenancy results in a gift of $200,000 from *A* to *B* determined as follows:

$$\frac{\$150,000 \text{ (consideration furnished by } A)}{\$300,000 \text{ (total consideration deemed furnished by both spouses)}} \times$$

$400,000 (proceeds of termination) = $200,000 (Proceeds of termination attributable to *A*.)

$200,000 – 0 (proceeds received by *A*) = $200,000 gift by *A* to *B*.

(c) *Tenancies by the entirety in personal property where one spouse is not a United States citizen.*—(1) *In general.*—In the case of the creation (either by one spouse alone or by both spouses where at least one of the spouses is not a United States citizen) of a joint interest in personal property with right of survivorship, or additions to the value thereof in the form of improvements, reductions in the indebtedness thereof, or otherwise, the retained interest of each spouse, solely for purposes of determining whether there has been a gift by the donor to the spouse who is not a citizen of the United States at the time of the gift, is treated as one-half of the value of the joint interest. See section 2523(i) and §§ 25.2523(i)-1 and 25.2503-2(f) as to certain of the tax consequences that may result upon creation and termination of the tenancy.

(2) *Exception.*—The rule provided in paragraph (c)(1) of this section does not apply with respect to any joint interest in property if the fair market value of the interest in property (determined as if each spouse had a right to sever) cannot reasonably be ascertained except by reference to the life expectancy of one or both spouses. In these cases, actuarial principles may need to be resorted to in determining the gift tax consequences of the transaction. [Reg. § 25.2523(i)-2.]

☐ [*T.D.* 8612, 8-21-95.]

[Reg. § 25.2523(i)-3]

§ 25.2523(i)-3. **Effective date.**—The provisions of §§ 25.2523(i)-1 and 25.2523(i)-2 are effective in the case of gifts made after August 22, 1995. [Reg. § 25.2523(i)-3.]

☐ [*T.D.* 8612, 8-21-95.]

[Reg. § 25.2524-1]

§ 25.2524-1. **Extent of deductions.**—Under the provisions of section 2524, the charitable deduction provided for in section 2522 and the marital deduction provided for in section 2523 are allowable only to the extent that the gifts, with respect to which those deductions are authorized, are included in the "total amount of gifts" made during the "calendar period" (as defined in § 25.2502-1(c)(1)), computed as provided in section 2503 and § 25.2503-1 (i.e., the total gifts less exclusions). The following examples (in both of which it is assumed that the donor has previously utilized his entire $30,000 specific exemption provided by section 2521 which was in effect at the time) illustrate the application of the provisions of this section:

Example (1). A donor made transfers by gift to his spouse of $5,000 cash on January 1, 1971, and $1,000 cash on April 5, 1971. The donor made no other transfers during 1971. The first $3,000 of such gifts for the calendar year is excluded under the provisions of section 2503(b) in determining the "total amount of gifts" made during the first calendar quarter of 1971. The marital deduction for the first calendar quarter of $2,500 (one-half of $5,000) otherwise allowable is limited by section 2524 to $2,000. The amount of taxable gifts is zero ($5,000 – $3,000 (annual ex-

clusion) – $2,000 (marital deduction)). For the second calendar quarter of 1971, the marital deduction is $500 (one-half of $1,000); the amount excluded under section 2503(b) is zero because the entire $3,000 annual exclusion was applied against the gift in the first calendar quarter of 1971; and the amount of taxable gifts is $500 ($1,000 – $500 (marital deduction)).

Example (2). The only gifts made by a donor to his spouse during calendar year 1969 were a gift of $2,400 in May and a gift of $3,000 in August. The first $3,000 of such gifts is excluded under the provisions of section 2503(b) in determining the "total amount of gifts" made during the calendar year. The marital deduction for 1969 of $2,700 (one-half of $2,400 plus one-half of $3,000) otherwise allowable is limited by section 2524 to $2,400. The amount of taxable gifts is zero ($5,400 – $3,000 (annual exclusion) – $2,400 (marital deduction)). [Reg. § 25.2524-1.]

☐ *[T.D. 6334, 11-14-58. Amended by T.D. 7238, 12-28-72 and T.D. 7910, 9-6-83.]*

→ *Caution: Reg. § § 25.6001-1, 25.6011-1, 25.6019-1—25.6019-4, 25.6061-1, 25.6065-1, 25.6075-1— 25.6075-2, 25.6081-1, 25.6091-1—25.6091-2, 25.6151-1, 25.6161-1, 25.6165-1, 25.6321-1, 25.6323-1, 25.6324-1, 25.6601-1, 25.6905-1, and 25.7101-1, dealing with administration of the gift tax, are reproduced in Code section numerical order.*

Tax on Generation-Skipping Transfers

TAX IMPOSED

See p. 20,601 for regulations not amended to reflect law changes

[Reg. § 26.2600-1]

§ 26.2600-1. Table of contents.—*§ 26.2601-1. Effective dates.*

(d) Allocations after the transferor's death.

(1) Allocation by executor.

(2) Automatic allocation after death.

(e) Effective date.

§ 26.2641-1. *Applicable rate of tax.*

§ 26.2642-1. *Inclusion ratio.*

(a) In general.

(b) Numerator of applicable fraction.

(1) In general.

(2) GSTs occurring during an ETIP.

(c) Denominator of applicable fraction.

(1) In general.

(2) Zero denominator.

(3) Nontaxable gifts.

(d) Examples.

§ 26.2642-2. *Valuation.*

(a) Lifetime transfers.

(1) In general.

(2) Special rule for late allocations during life.

(b) Transfers at death.

(1) In general.

(2) Special rule for pecuniary payments.

(3) Special rule for residual transfers after payment of a pecuniary payment.

(4) Appropriate interest.

(c) Examples.

§ 26.2642-3. *Special rule for charitable lead annuity trusts.*

(a) In general.

(b) Adjusted GST exemption defined.

(c) Example.

§ 26.2642-4. *Redetermination of applicable fraction.*

(a) In general.

(1) Multiple transfers to a single trust.

(2) Consolidation of separate trusts.

(3) Property included in transferor's gross estate.

(4) Imposition of recapture tax under section 2032A.

(b) Examples.

§ 26.2642-5. *Finality of inclusion ratio.*

(a) Direct skips.

(b) Other GSTs.

§ 26.2642-6. *Qualified severance.*

(a) In general.

(b) Qualified severance defined.

(c) Effective date of qualified severance.

(d) Requirements for a qualified severance.

(e) Reporting a qualified severance.

(f) Time for making a qualified severance.

(g) Trusts that were irrevocable on September 25, 1985.

(1) In general.

(2) Trusts in receipt of a post-September 25, 1985, addition.

(h) Treatment of trusts resulting from a severance that is not a qualified severance.

(i) [Reserved]

(j) Examples.

(k) Effective date.

(1) In general.

(2) Transition rule.

§ 26.2651-1. *Generation assignment.*

(a) Special rule for persons with a deceased parent.

(1) In general.

(2) Special rules.

(3) Established or derived.

(4) Special rule in the case of additional contributions to a trust.

(b) Limited application to collateral heirs.

(c) Examples.

§ 26.2651-2. *Individual assigned to more than one generation.*

(a) In general.

(b) Exception.

(c) Special rules.

(1) Corresponding generation adjustment.

(2) Continued application of generation assignment.

(d) Example.

§ 26.2651-3. *Effective dates.*

(a) In general.

(b) Transition rule.

§ 26.2652-1. *Transferor defined; other definitions.*

(a) Transferor defined.

(1) In general.

(2) Transfers subject to Federal estate or gift tax.

(3) Special rule for certain QTIP trusts.

(4) Exercise of certain nongeneral powers of appointment.

(5) Split-gift transfers.

(6) Examples.

(b) Trust defined.

(1) In general.

(2) Examples.

(c) Trustee defined.

(d) Executor defined.

(e) Interest in trust.

§ 26.2652-2. *Special election for qualified terminable interest property.*

(a) In general.

(b) Time and manner of making election.

(c) Transitional rule.

(d) Examples.

§26.2653-1. *Taxation of multiple skips.*
(a) General rule.
(b) Examples.

§26.2654-1. *Certain trusts treated as separate trusts.*
(a) Single trust treated as separate trusts.
(1) Substantially separate and independent shares.
(2) Multiple transferors with respect to a single trust.
(3) Severance of a single trust.
(4) Allocation of exemption.
(5) Examples.
(b) Division of a trust included in the gross estate.
(1) In general.
(2) Special rule.
(3) Allocation of exemption.
(4) Example.
(c) Cross reference.

§26.2662-1. *Generation-skipping transfer tax return requirements.*
(a) In general.
(b) Form of return.
(1) Taxable distributions.
(2) Taxable terminations.
(3) Direct skip.
(c) Person liable for tax and required to make return.
(1) In general.
(2) Special rule for direct skips occurring at death with respect to property held in trust arrangements.
(3) Limitation on personal liability of trustee.
(4) Exceptions.
(d) Time and manner of filing return.
(1) In general.
(2) Exceptions.
(e) Place for filing returns.
(f) Lien on property.

§26.2663-1. *Recapture tax under section 2032A.*

§26.2663-2. *Application of chapter 13 to transfers by nonresidents not citizens of the United States.*
(a) In general.
(b) Transfers subject to Chapter 13.
(1) Direct skips.
(2) Taxable distributions and taxable terminations.
(c) Trusts funded in part with property subject to Chapter 13 and in part with property not subject to Chapter 13.
(1) In general.
(2) Nontax portion of the trust.
(3) Special rule with respect to estate tax inclusion period.
(d) Examples.

(e) Transitional rule for allocations for transfers made before December 27, 1995. [Reg. §26.2600-1.]

☐ *[T.D. 8644, 12-26-95. Amended by T.D. 8912, 12-19-2000; T.D. 9208, 6-28-2005; T.D. 9214, 7-15-2005; T.D. 9348, 8-1-2007 and T.D. 9421, 7-30-2008.]*

[Reg. §26.2601-1]

§26.2601-1. **Effective dates.**—(a) *Transfers subject to the generation-skipping transfer tax.*— (1) *In general.*—Except as otherwise provided in this section, the provisions of chapter 13 of the Internal Revenue Code of 1986 (Code) apply to any generation-skipping transfer (as defined in section 2611) made after October 22, 1986.

(2) *Certain transfers treated as if made after October 22, 1986.*—Solely for purposes of chapter 13, an inter vivos transfer is treated as if it were made on October 23, 1986, if it was—

(i) Subject to chapter 12 (regardless of whether a tax was actually incurred or paid); and

(ii) Made after September 25, 1985, but before October 23, 1986. For purposes of this paragraph, the value of the property transferred shall be the value of the property on the date the property was transferred.

(3) *Certain trust events treated as if occurring after October 22, 1986.*—For purposes of chapter 13, if an inter vivos transfer is made to a trust after September 25, 1985, but before October 23, 1986, any subsequent distribution from the trust or termination of an interest in the trust that occurred before October 23, 1986, is treated as occurring immediately after the deemed transfer on October 23, 1986. If more than one distribution or termination occurs with respect to a trust, the events are treated as if they occurred on October 23, 1986, in the same order as they occurred. See paragraph (b)(1)(iv)(B) of this section for rules determining the portion of distributions and terminations subject to tax under chapter 13. This paragraph (a)(3) does not apply to transfers to trusts not subject to chapter 13 by reason of the transition rules in paragraphs (b)(2) and (3) of this section. The provisions of this paragraph (a)(3) do not apply in determining the value of the property under chapter 13.

(4) *Example.*—The following example illustrates the principle that paragraph (a)(2) of this section is not applicable to transfers under a revocable trust that became irrevocable by reason of the transferor's death after September 25, 1985, but before October 23, 1986:

Example. T created a revocable trust on September 30, 1985, that became irrevocable when T died on October 10, 1986. Although the trust terminated in favor of a grandchild of T, the transfer to the grandchild is not treated as occurring on October 23, 1986, pursuant to paragraph (a)(2) of this section because it is not an inter vivos transfer subject to chapter 12. The transfer is not subject to chapter 13 because it is in the nature of a testamentary transfer that occurred prior to October 23, 1986.

(b) *Exceptions.*—(1) *Irrevocable trusts.*—(i) *In general.*—The provisions of chapter 13 do not apply to any generation-skipping transfer under a trust (as defined in section 2652(b)) that was irrevocable on September 25, 1985. The rule of the preceding sentence does not apply to a pro rata portion of any generation-skipping transfer under an irrevocable trust if additions are made to the trust after September 25, 1985. See paragraph (b)(1)(iv) of this section for rules for determining the portion of the trust that is subject to the provisions of chapter 13. Further, the rule in the first sentence of this paragraph (b)(1)(i) does not apply to a transfer of property pursuant to the exercise, release, or lapse of a general power of appointment that is treated as a taxable transfer under chapter 11 or chapter 12. The transfer is made by the person holding the power at the time the exercise, release, or lapse of the power becomes effective, and is not considered a transfer under a trust that was irrevocable on September 25, 1985. See paragraph (b)(1)(v)(B) of this section regarding the treatment of the release, exercise, or lapse of a power of appointment that will result in a constructive addition to a trust. See § 26.2652-1(a) for the definition of a transferor.

(ii) *Irrevocable trust defined.*—(A) *In general.*—Unless otherwise provided in either paragraph (b)(1)(ii)(B) or (C) of this section, any trust (as defined in section 2652(b)) in existence on September 25, 1985, is considered an irrevocable trust.

(B) *Property includible in the gross estate under section 2038.*—For purposes of this chapter a trust is not an irrevocable trust to the extent that, on September 25, 1985, the settlor held a power with respect to such trust that would have caused the value of the trust to be included in the settlor's gross estate for Federal estate tax purposes by reason of section 2038 (without regard to powers relinquished before September 25, 1985) if the settlor had died on September 25, 1985. A trust is considered subject to a power on September 25, 1985, even though the exercise of the power was subject to the precedent giving of notice, or even though the exercise could take effect only on the expiration of a stated period, whether or not on or before September 25, 1985, notice had been given or the power had been exercised. A trust is not considered subject to a power if the power is, by its terms, exercisable only on the occurrence of an event or contingency not subject to the settlor's control (other than the death of the settlor) and if the event or contingency had not in fact taken place on September 25, 1985.

(C) *Property includible in the gross estate under section 2042.*—A policy of insurance on an individual's life that is treated as a trust under section 2652(b) is not considered an irrevocable trust to the extent that, on September 25, 1985, the insured possessed any incident of ownership (as defined in § 20.2042-1(c) of this chapter, and without regard to any incidents of ownership relinquished before September 25, 1985), that would have caused the value of the trust, (i.e., the insurance proceeds) to be included in the insured's gross estate for Federal estate tax purposes by reason of section 2042, if the insured had died on September 25, 1985.

(D) *Examples.*—The following examples illustrate the application of this paragraph (b)(1):

Example 1. Section 2038 applicable. On September 25, 1985, T, the settlor of a trust that was created before September 25, 1985, held a testamentary power to add new beneficiaries to the trust. T held no other powers over any portion of the trust. The testamentary power held by T would have caused the trust to be included in T's gross estate under section 2038 if T had died on September 25, 1985. Therefore, the trust is not an irrevocable trust for purposes of this section.

Example 2. Section 2038 not applicable when power held by a person other than settlor. On September 25, 1985, S, the spouse of the settlor of a trust in existence on that date, had an annual right to withdraw a portion of the principal of the trust. The trust was otherwise irrevocable on that date. Because the power was not held by the settlor of the trust, it is not a power described in section 2038. Thus, the trust is considered an irrevocable trust for purposes of this section.

Example 3. Section 2038 not applicable. In 1984, T created a trust and retained the right to expand the class of remaindermen to include any of T's afterborn grandchildren. As of September 25, 1985, all of T's grandchildren were named remaindermen of the trust. Since the exercise of T's power was dependent on there being afterborn grandchildren who were not members of the class of remaindermen, a contingency that did not exist on September 25, 1985, the trust is not considered subject to the power on September 25, 1985, and is an irrevocable trust for purposes of this section. The result is not changed even if grandchildren are born after September 25, 1985, whether or not T exercises the power to expand the class of remaindermen.

Example 4. Section 2042 applicable. On September 25, 1985, T purchased an insurance policy on T's own life and designated child, C, and grandchild, GC, as the beneficiaries. T retained the power to obtain from the insurer a loan against the surrender value of the policy. T's insurance policy is a trust (as defined in section 2652(b)) for chapter 13 purposes. The trust is not considered an irrevocable trust because, on September 25, 1985, T possessed an incident of ownership that would have caused the value of the policy to be included in T's gross estate under section 2042 if T had died on that date.

Example 5. Trust partially irrevocable. In 1984, T created a trust naming T's grandchildren as the income and remainder beneficiaries. T retained the power to revoke the trust as to one-half of the principal at any time prior to T's death. T retained no other powers over the trust principal. T did not die before September 25, 1985, and did not exercise or release the power before that date. The half of the trust not subject to T's power to revoke is an irrevocable trust for purposes of this section.

(iii) *Trust containing qualified terminable interest property.*—(A) *In general.*—For purposes of chapter 13, a trust described in paragraph (b)(1)(ii) of this section that holds qualified terminable interest property by reason of an election under section 2056(b)(7) or section 2523(f) (made either on, before or after September 25, 1985) is treated in the same manner as if the decedent spouse or the donor spouse (as the case may be) had made an election under section 2652(a)(3). Thus, transfers from such trusts are not subject to chapter 13, and the decedent spouse or the donor spouse (as the case may be) is treated as the transferor of such property. The rule of this paragraph (b)(1)(iii) does not apply to that portion of the trust that is subject to chapter 13 by reason of an addition to the trust occurring after September 25, 1985. See § 26.2652-2(a) for rules where an election under section 2652(a)(3) is made. See § 26.2652-2(c) for rules where a portion of a trust is subject to an election under section 2652(a)(3).

(B) *Examples.*—The following examples illustrate the application of this paragraph (b)(1)(iii):

Example 1. QTIP election made after September 25, 1985. On March 28, 1985, T established a trust. The trust instrument provided that the trustee must distribute all income annually to T's spouse, S, during S's life. Upon S's death, the remainder is to be distributed to GC, the grandchild of T and S. On April 15, 1986, T elected under section 2523(f) to treat the property in the trust as qualified terminable interest property. On December 1, 1987, S died and soon thereafter the trust assets were distributed to GC. Because the trust was irrevocable on September 25, 1985, the transfer to GC is not subject to tax under chapter 13. T is treated as the transferor with respect to the transfer of the trust assets to GC in the same manner as if T had made an election under section 2652(a)(3) to reverse the effect of the section 2523(f) election for chapter 13 purposes.

Example 2. Section 2652(a)(3) election deemed to have been made. Assume the same facts as in *Example 1,* except the trust instrument provides that after S's death all income is to be paid annually to C, the child of T and S. Upon C's

death, the remainder is to be distributed to GC. C died on October 1, 1992, and soon thereafter the trust assets are distributed to GC. Because the trust was irrevocable on September 25, 1985, the termination of C's interest is not subject to chapter 13.

(iv) *Additions to irrevocable trusts.*—(A) *In general.*—If an addition is made after September 25, 1985, to an irrevocable trust which is excluded from chapter 13 by reason of paragraph (b)(1) of this section, a pro rata portion of subsequent distributions from (and terminations of interests in property held in) the trust is subject to the provisions of chapter 13. If an addition is made, the trust is thereafter deemed to consist of two portions, a portion not subject to chapter 13 (the non-chapter 13 portion) and a portion subject to chapter 13 (the chapter 13 portion), each with a separate inclusion ratio (as defined in section 2642(a)). The non-chapter 13 portion represents the value of the assets of the trust as it existed on September 25, 1985. The applicable fraction (as defined in section 2642(a)(2)) for the non-chapter 13 portion is deemed to be 1 and the inclusion ratio for such portion is 0. The chapter 13 portion of the trust represents the value of all additions made to the trust after September 25, 1985. The inclusion ratio for the chapter 13 portion is determined under section 2642. This paragraph (b)(1)(iv)(A) requires separate portions of one trust only for purposes of determining inclusion ratios. For purposes of chapter 13, a constructive addition under paragraph (b)(1)(v) of this section is treated as an addition. See paragraph (b)(4) of this section for exceptions to the additions rule of this paragraph (b)(1)(iv). See § 26.2654-1(a)(2) for rules treating additions to a trust by an individual other than the initial transferor as a separate trust for purposes of chapter 13.

(B) *Terminations of interests in and distributions from trusts.*—Where a termination or distribution described in section 2612 occurs with respect to a trust to which an addition has been made, the portion of such termination or distribution allocable to the chapter 13 portion is determined by reference to the allocation fraction, as defined in paragraph (b)(1)(iv)(C) of this section. In the case of a termination described in section 2612(a) with respect to a trust, the portion of such termination that is subject to chapter 13 is the product of the allocation fraction and the value of the trust (to the extent of the terminated interest therein). In the case of a distribution described in section 2612(b) from a trust, the portion of such distribution that is subject to chapter 13 is the product of the allocation fraction and the value of the property distributed.

(C) *Allocation fraction.*—(1) *In general.*—The allocation fraction allocates appreciation and accumulated income between the chapter 13 and non-chapter 13 portions of a trust. The numera-

Reg. § 26.2601-1(b)(1)(iv)(C)(1)

tor of the allocation fraction is the amount of the addition (valued as of the date the addition is made), determined without regard to whether any part of the transfer is subject to tax under chapter 11 or chapter 12, but reduced by the amount of any Federal or state estate or gift tax imposed and subsequently paid by the recipient trust with respect to the addition. The denominator of the allocation fraction is the total value of the entire trust immediately after the addition. For purposes of this paragraph (b)(1)(iv)(C), the total value of the entire trust is the fair market value of the property held in trust (determined under the rules of section 2031), reduced by any amount attributable to or paid by the trust and attributable to the transfer to the trust that is similar to an amount that would be allowable as a deduction under section 2053 if the addition had occurred at the death of the transferor, and further reduced by the same amount that the numerator was reduced to reflect Federal or state estate or gift tax incurred by and subsequently paid by the recipient trust with respect to the addition. Where there is more than one addition to principal after September 25, 1985, the portion of the trust subject to chapter 13 after each such addition is determined pursuant to a revised fraction. In each case, the numerator of the revised fraction is the sum of the value of the

chapter 13 portion of the trust immediately before the latest addition, and the amount of the latest addition. The denominator of the revised fraction is the total value of the entire trust immediately after the addition. If the transfer to the trust is a generation-skipping transfer, the numerator and denominator are reduced by the amount of the generation-skipping transfer tax, if any, that is imposed by chapter 13 on the transfer and actually recovered from the trust. The allocation fraction is rounded off to five decimal places (.00001).

(2) Examples.—The following examples illustrate the application of paragraph (b)(1)(iv) of this section. In each of the examples, assume that the recipient trust does not pay any Federal or state transfer tax by reason of the addition.

Example 1. Post September 25, 1985, addition to trust. (i) On August 16, 1980, T established an irrevocable trust. Under the trust instrument, the trustee is required to distribute the entire income annually to T's child, C, for life, then to T's grandchild, GC, for life. Upon GC's death, the remainder is to be paid to GC's issue. On October 1, 1986, when the total value of the entire trust is $400,000, T transfers $100,000 to the trust. The allocation fraction is computed as follows:

$$\frac{\text{Value of addition}}{\text{Total value of trust}} = \frac{\$100,000}{\$400,000 + \$100,000} = .2$$

(ii) Thus, immediately after the transfer, 20 percent of the value of future generation-skipping transfers under the trust will be subject to chapter 13.

Example 2. Effect of expenses. Assume the same facts as in *Example 1*, except immediately prior to the transfer on October 1, 1986, the fair market value of the individual assets in the trust totaled $400,000. Also, assume that the trust had accrued and unpaid debts, expenses, and taxes totaling $300,000. Assume further that the entire $300,000 represented amounts that would be deductible under section 2053 if the trust were includible in the transferor's gross estate. The numerator of the allocation fraction is $100,000

and the denominator of the allocation fraction is $200,000 (($400,000 - $300,000) + $100,000). Thus, the allocation fraction is .5 ($100,000/$200,000) and 50 percent of the value of future generation-skipping transfers will be subject to chapter 13.

Example 3. Multiple additions. (i) Assume the same facts as in *Example 1*, except on January 30, 1988, when the total value of the entire trust is $600,000, T transfers an additional $40,000 to the trust. Before the transfer, the value of the portion of the trust that was attributable to the prior addition was $120,000 ($600,000 x .2). The new allocation fraction is computed as follows:

$$\frac{\text{Total value of additions}}{\text{Total value of trust}} = \frac{\$120,000 + \$40,000}{\$600,000 + \$40,000} = \frac{\$160,000}{\$640,000} = .25$$

(ii) Thus, immediately after the transfer, 25 percent of the value of future generation-skipping transfers under the trust will be subject to chapter 13.

Example 4. Allocation fraction at time of generation-skipping transfer. Assume the same facts as in *Example 3*, except on March 1, 1989, when the value of the trust is $800,000, C dies. A generation-skipping transfer occurs at C's death because of the termination of C's life estate.

Therefore, $200,000 ($800,000 x .25) is subject to tax under chapter 13.

(v) Constructive additions.—(A) *Powers of Appointment.*—Except as provided in paragraph (b)(1)(v)(B) of this section, where any portion of a trust remains in the trust after the post-September 25, 1985, release, exercise, or lapse of a power of appointment over that portion of the trust, and the release, exercise, or lapse is treated to any extent as a taxable transfer under chapter 11

or chapter 12, the value of the entire portion of the trust subject to the power that was released, exercised, or lapsed is treated as if that portion had been withdrawn and immediately retransferred to the trust at the time of the release, exercise, or lapse. The creator of the power will be considered the transferor of the addition except to the extent that the release, exercise, or lapse of the power is treated as a taxable transfer under chapter 11 or chapter 12. See § 26.2652-1 for rules for determining the identity of the transferor of property for purposes of chapter 13.

(B) *Special rule for certain powers of appointment.*—The release, exercise, or lapse of a power of appointment (other than a general power of appointment as defined in § 2041(b)) is not treated as an addition to a trust if—

(1) Such power of appointment was created in an irrevocable trust that is not subject to chapter 13 under paragraph (b)(1) of this section; and

(2) In the case of an exercise, the power of appointment is not exercised in a manner that may postpone or suspend the vesting, absolute ownership or power of alienation of an interest in property for a period, measured from the date of creation of the trust, extending beyond any life in being at the date of creation of the trust plus a period of 21 years plus, if necessary, a reasonable period of gestation (the perpetuities period). For purposes of this paragraph (b)(1)(v)(B)(2), the exercise of a power of appointment that validly postpones or suspends the vesting, absolute ownership or power of alienation of an interest in property for a term of years that will not exceed 90 years (measured from the date of creation of the trust) will not be considered an exercise that postpones or suspends vesting, absolute ownership or the power of alienation beyond the perpetuities period. If a power is exercised by creating another power, it is deemed to be exercised to whatever extent the second power may be exercised.

(C) *Constructive addition if liability is not paid out of trust principal.*—Where a trust described in paragraph (b)(1) of this section is relieved of any liability properly payable out of the assets of such trust, the person or entity who actually satisfies the liability is considered to have made a constructive addition to the trust in an amount equal to the liability. The constructive addition occurs when the trust is relieved of liability (e.g., when the right of recovery is no longer enforceable). But see § 26.2652-1(a)(3) for rules involving the application of section 2207A in the case of an election under section 2652(a)(3).

(D) *Examples.*—The following examples illustrate the application of this paragraph (b)(1)(v):

Example 1. Lapse of a power of appointment. On June 19, 1980, T established an irrevo-

cable trust with a corpus of $500,000. The trust instrument provides that the trustee shall distribute the entire income from the trust annually to T's spouse, S, during S's life. At S's death, the remainder is to be distributed to T and S's grandchild, GC. T also gave S a general power of appointment over one-half of the trust assets. On December 21, 1989, when the value of the trust corpus is $1,500,000, S died without having exercised the general power of appointment. The value of one-half of the trust corpus, $750,000 ($1,500,000 x .5) is included in S's gross estate under section 2041(a) and is subject to tax under Chapter 11. Because the value of one-half of the trust corpus is subject to tax under Chapter 11 with respect to S's estate, S is treated as the transferor of that property for purposes of Chapter 13 (see section 2652(a)(1)(A)). For purposes of the generation-skipping transfer tax, the lapse of S's power of appointment is treated as if $750,000 ($1,500,000 x .5) had been distributed to S and then transferred back to the trust. Thus, S is considered to have added $750,000 ($1,500,000 x .5) to the trust at the date of S's death. Because this constructive addition occurred after September 25, 1985, 50 percent of the corpus of the trust became subject to Chapter 13 at S's death.

Example 2. Multiple actual additions. On June 19, 1980, T established an irrevocable trust with a principal of $500,000. The trust instrument provides that the trustee shall distribute the entire income from the trust annually to T's spouse, S, during S's life. At S's death, the remainder is to be distributed to GC, the grandchild of T and S. On October 1, 1985, when the trust assets were valued at $800,000, T added $200,000 to the trust. After the transfer on October 1, 1985, the allocation fraction was .2 ($200,000/$1,000,000). On December 21, 1989, when the value of the trust principal is $1,000,000, T adds $1,000,000 to the trust. After this addition, the new allocation fraction is 0.6 ($1,200,000/$2,000,000). The numerator of the fraction is the value of that portion of trust assets that were subject to chapter 13 immediately prior to the addition (by reason of the first addition), $200,000 (.2 x $1,000,000), plus the value of the second transfer, $1,000,000, which equals $1,200,000. The denominator of the fraction, $2,000,000, is the total value of the trust assets immediately after the second transfer. Thus, 60 percent of the principal of the trust becomes subject to chapter 13.

Example 3. Entire portion of trust subject to lapsed power is treated as an addition. On September 25, 1985, B possessed a general power of appointment over the assets of an irrevocable trust that had been created by T in 1980. Under the terms of the trust, B's power lapsed on July 20, 1987. For Federal gift tax purposes, B is treated as making a gift of ninety-five percent (100% - 5%) of the value of the principal (see section 2514). However, because the entire trust was subject to the power of appointment, 100

Reg. § 26.2601-1(b)(1)(v)(D)

percent (that portion of the trust subject to the power) of the assets of the trust are treated as a constructive addition. Thus, the entire amount of all generation-skipping transfers occurring pursuant to the trust instrument after July 20, 1987, are subject to chapter 13.

Example 4. Exercise of power of appointment in favor of another trust. On March 1, 1985, T established an irrevocable trust as defined in paragraph (b)(1)(ii) of this section. Under the terms of the trust instrument, the trustee is required to distribute the entire income annually to T's child, C, for life, then to T's grandchild, GC, for life. GC has the power to appoint any or all of the trust assets to Trust 2 which is an irrevocable trust (as defined in paragraph (b)(1)(ii) of this section) that was established on August 1, 1985. The terms of Trust 2's governing instrument provide that the trustee shall pay income to T's great grandchild, GGC, for life. Upon GGC's death, the remainder is to be paid to GGC's issue. GGC was alive on March 1, 1985, when Trust 1 was created. C died on April 1, 1986. On July 1, 1987, GC exercised the power of appointment. The exercise of GC's power does not subject future transfers from Trust 2 to tax under chapter 13 because the exercise of the power in favor of Trust 2 does not suspend the vesting, absolute ownership, or power of alienation of an interest in property for a period, measured from the date of creation of Trust 1, extending beyond the life of GGC (a beneficiary under Trust 2 who was in being at the date of creation of Trust 1) plus a period of 21 years. The result would be the same if Trust 2 had been created after the effective date of chapter 13.

Example 5. Exercise of power of appointment in favor of another trust. Assume the same facts as in *Example 4*, except that GGC was born on March 28, 1986. The valid exercise of GC's power in favor of Trust 2 causes the principal of Trust 1 to be subject to chapter 13, because GGC was not born until after the creation of Trust 1. Thus, such exercise may suspend the vesting, absolute ownership, or power of alienation of an interest in the trust principal for a period, measured from the date of creation of Trust 1, extending beyond the life of GGC (a beneficiary under Trust 2 who was not a life in being at the date of creation of Trust 1).

Example 6. Extension for the longer of two periods. Prior to the effective date of chapter 13, GP established an irrevocable trust under which the trust income was to be paid to GP's child, C, for life. C was given a testamentary power to appoint the remainder in further trust for the benefit of C's issue. In default of C's exercise of the power, the remainder was to pass to charity. C died on February 3, 1995, survived by a child who was alive when GP established the trust. C exercised the power in a manner that validly extends the trust in favor of C's issue until the later of May 15, 2064 (80 years from the date the trust was created), or the death of C's child plus

21 years. C's exercise of the power is a constructive addition to the trust because the exercise may extend the trust for a period longer than the permissible periods of either the life of C's child (a life in being at the creation of the trust) plus 21 years or a term not more than 90 years measured from the creation of the trust. On the other hand, if C's exercise of the power could extend the trust based only on the life of C's child plus 21 years or only for a term of 80 years from the creation of the trust (but not the later of the two periods) then the exercise of the power would not have been a constructive addition to the trust.

Example 7. Extension for the longer of two periods. The facts are the same as in *Example 6* except local law provides that the effect of C's exercise is to extend the term of the trust until May 15, 2064, whether or not C's child predeceases that date by more than 21 years. C's exercise is not a constructive addition to the trust because C exercised the power in a manner that cannot postpone or suspend vesting, absolute ownership, or power of alienation for a term of years that will exceed 90 years. The result would be the same if the effect of C's exercise is either to extend the term of the trust until 21 years after the death of C's child or to extend the term of the trust until the first to occur of May 15, 2064 or 21 years after the death of C's child.

(vi) *Appreciation and income.*—Except to the extent that the provisions of paragraphs (b)(1)(iv) and (v) of this section allocate subsequent appreciation and accumulated income between the original trust and additions thereto, appreciation in the value of the trust and undistributed income added thereto are not considered an addition to the principal of a trust.

(2) *Transition rule for wills or revocable trusts executed before October 22, 1986.*—(i) *In general.*—The provisions of chapter 13 do not apply to any generation-skipping transfer under a will or revocable trust executed before October 22, 1986, provided that—

(A) The document in existence on October 21, 1986, is not amended at any time after October 21, 1986, in any respect which results in the creation of, or an increase in the amount of, a generation-skipping transfer;

(B) In the case of a revocable trust, no addition is made to the revocable trust after October 21, 1986, that results in the creation of, or an increase in the amount of, a generation-skipping transfer; and

(C) The decedent dies before January 1, 1987.

(ii) *Revocable trust defined.*—For purposes of this section, the term *revocable trust* means any trust (as defined in section 2652(b)) except to the extent that, on October 22, 1986, the trust—

(A) Was an irrevocable trust described in paragraph (b)(1) of this section; or

(B) Would have been an irrevocable trust described in paragraph (b)(1) of this section had it not been created or become irrevocable after September 25, 1985, and before October 22, 1986.

(iii) *Will or revocable trust containing qualified terminable interest property.*—The rules contained in paragraph (b)(1)(iii) of this section apply to any will or revocable trust within the scope of the transition rule of this paragraph (b)(2).

(iv) *Amendments to will or revocable trust.*—For purposes of this paragraph (b)(2), an amendment to a will or a revocable trust in existence on October 21, 1986, is not considered to result in the creation of, or an increase in the amount of, a generation-skipping transfer where the amendment is—

(A) Basically administrative or clarifying in nature and only incidentally increases the amount transferred; or

(B) Designed to ensure that an existing bequest or transfer qualifies for the applicable marital or charitable deduction for estate, gift, or generation-skipping transfer tax purposes and only incidentally increases the amount transferred to a skip person or to a generation-skipping trust.

(v) *Creation of, or increase in the amount of, a GST.*—In determining whether a particular amendment to a will or revocable trust creates, or increases the amount of, a generation-skipping transfer for purposes of this paragraph (b)(2), the effect of the instrument(s) in existence on October 21, 1986, is measured against the effect of the instrument(s) in existence on the date of death of the decedent or on the date of any prior generation-skipping transfer. If the effect of an amendment cannot be immediately determined, it is deemed to create, or increase the amount of, a generation-skipping transfer until a determination can be made.

(vi) *Additions to revocable trusts.*—Any addition made after October 21, 1986, but before the death of the settlor, to a revocable trust subjects all subsequent generation-skipping transfers under the trust to the provisions of chapter 13. Any addition made to a revocable trust after the death of the settlor (if the settlor dies before January 1, 1987) is treated as an addition to an irrevocable trust. See paragraph (b)(1)(v) of this section for rules involving constructive additions to trusts. See paragraph (b)(1)(v)(B) of this section for rules providing that certain transfers to trusts are not treated as additions for purposes of this section.

(vii) *Examples.*—The following examples illustrate the application of paragraph (b)(2)(iv) of this section:

(A) *Facts applicable to Examples 1 through 5.*—In each of *Examples 1* through *5* assume that T executed a will prior to October 22, 1986, and that T dies on December 31, 1986.

Example 1. Administrative change. On November 1, 1986, T executes a codicil to T's will removing one of the co-executors named in the will. Although the codicil may have the effect of lowering administrative costs and thus increasing the amount transferred, it is considered administrative in nature and thus does not cause generation-skipping transfers under the will to be subject to chapter 13.

Example 2. Effect of amendment not immediately determinable. On November 1, 1986, T executes a codicil to T's will revoking a bequest of $100,000 to C, a non-skip person (as defined under section 2613(b)) and causing that amount to be added to a residuary trust held for a skip person. The amendment is deemed to increase the amount of a generation-skipping transfer and prevents any transfers under the will from qualifying under paragraph (b)(2)(i) of this section. If, however, C dies before T and under local law the property would have been added to the residue in any event because the bequest would have lapsed, the codicil is not considered an amendment that increases the amount of a generation-skipping transfer.

Example 3. Refund of tax paid because of amendment. T's will provided that an amount equal to the maximum allowable marital deduction would pass to T's spouse with the residue of the estate passing to a trust established for the benefit of skip persons. On October 23, 1986, the will is amended to provide that the marital share passing to T's spouse shall be the lesser of the maximum allowable marital deduction or the minimum amount that will result in no estate tax liability for T's estate. The amendment may increase the amount of a generation-skipping transfer. Therefore, any generation-skipping transfers under the will are subject to tax under chapter 13. If it becomes apparent that the amendment does not increase the amount of a generation-skipping transfer, a claim for refund may be filed with respect to any generation-skipping transfer tax that was paid within the period set forth in section 6511. For example, it would become apparent that the amendment did not result in an increase in the residue if it is subsequently determined that the maximum marital deduction and the minimum amount that will result in no estate tax liability are equal in amount.

Example 4. An amendment that increases a generation-skipping transfer causes complete loss of exempt status. T's will provided for the creation of two trusts for the benefit of skip persons. On November 1, 1986, T executed a codicil to the will specifically increasing the amount of a generation-skipping transfer under the will. All transfers made pursuant to the will or either of the trusts created thereunder are precluded from qualifying under the transition rule of paragraph (b)(2)(i) of this section and are subject to tax under chapter 13.

Example 5. Corrective action effective. Assume that T in *Example 4* later executes a second codicil deleting the increase to the generation-skipping transfer. Because the provision increasing a generation-skipping transfer does not become effective, it is not considered an amendment to a will in existence on October 22, 1986.

(B) *Facts applicable to Examples 6 through 8.*—T created a trust on September 30, 1985, in which T retained the power to revoke the transfer at any time prior to T's death. The trust provided that, upon the death of T, the income was to be paid to T's spouse, W, for life and then to A, B, and C, the children of T's sibling, S, in equal shares for life, with one-third of the principal to be distributed per stirpes to each child's surviving issue upon the death of the child. The trustee has the power to make discretionary distributions of trust principal to T's sibling, S.

Example 6. Amendment that affects only a person who is not a skip person. A became disabled, and T modified the trust on December 1, 1986, to increase A's share of the income. Since the amendment does not result in the creation of, or increase in the amount of, a generation-skipping transfer, transfers pursuant to the trust are not subject to chapter 13.

Example 7. Amendment that adds a skip person. Assume that T amends the trust to add T's grandchild, D, as an income beneficiary. The trust will be subject to the provisions of chapter 13 because the amendment creates a generation-skipping transfer.

Example 8. Refund of tax paid during interim period when effect of amendment is not determinable. Assume that T amends the trust to provide that the issue of S are to take a one-fourth share of the principal per stirpes upon S's death. Because the distribution to be made upon S's death may involve skip persons, the amendment is considered an amendment that creates or increases the amount of a generation-skipping transfer until a determination can be made. Accordingly, any distributions from (or terminations of interests in) such trust are subject to chapter 13 until it is determined that no skip person has been added to the trust. At that time, a claim for refund may be filed within the period set forth in section 6511 with respect to any generation-skipping transfer tax that was paid.

(3) *Transition rule in the case of mental incompetency.*—(i) *In general.*—If an individual was under a mental disability to change the disposition of his or her property continuously from October 22, 1986, until the date of his or her death, the provisions of chapter 13 do not apply to any generation-skipping transfer—

(A) Under a trust (as defined in section 2652(b)) to the extent such trust consists of prop-

erty, or the proceeds of property, the value of which was included in the gross estate of the individual (other than property transferred by or on behalf of the individual during the individual's life after October 22, 1986); or

(B) Which is a direct skip (other than a direct skip from a trust) that occurs by reason of the death of the individual.

(ii) *Mental disability defined.*—For purposes of this paragraph (b)(2), the term *mental disability* means mental incompetence to execute an instrument governing the disposition of the individual's property, whether or not there was an adjudication of incompetence and regardless of whether there has been an appointment of a guardian, fiduciary, or other person charged with either the care of the individual or the care of the individual's property.

(iii) *Decedent who has not been adjudged mentally incompetent.*—(A) If there has not been a court adjudication that the decedent was mentally incompetent on or before October 22, 1986, the executor must file, with Form 706, either—

(1) A certification from a qualified physician stating that the decedent was—

(i) mentally incompetent at all times on and after October 22, 1986; and

(ii) did not regain competence to modify or revoke the terms of the trust or will prior to his or her death; or

(2) Sufficient other evidence demonstrating that the decedent was mentally incompetent at all times on and after October 22, 1986, as well as a statement explaining why no certification is available from a physician; and

(3) Any judgement or decree relating to the decedent's incompetency that was made after October 22, 1986.

(B) Such items in paragraphs (b)(3)(iii)(A), (1), (2), and (3) of this section will be considered relevant, but not determinative, in establishing the decedent's state of competency.

(iv) *Decedent who has been adjudged mentally incompetent.*—If the decedent has been adjudged mentally incompetent on or before October 22, 1986, a copy of the judgment or decree, and any modification thereof, must be filed with the Form 706.

(v) *Rule applies even if another person has power to change trust terms.*—In the case of a transfer from a trust, this paragraph (b)(3) applies even though a person charged with the care of the decedent or the decedent's property has the power to revoke or modify the terms of the trust, provided that the power is not exercised after October 22, 1986, in a manner that creates, or increases the amount of, a generation-skipping transfer. See paragraph (b)(2)(iv) of this section for rules concerning amendments that create or increase the amount of a generation-skipping transfer.

(vi) *Example.*—The following example illustrates the application of paragraph (b)(3)(v) of this section:

Example. T was mentally incompetent on October 22, 1986, and remained so until death in 1993. Prior to becoming incompetent, T created a revocable generation-skipping trust that was includible in T's gross estate. Prior to October 22, 1986, the appropriate court issued an order under which P, who was thereby charged with the care of T's property, had the power to modify or revoke the revocable trust. Although P exercised the power after October 22, 1986, and while T was incompetent, the power was not exercised in a manner that created, or increased the amount of, a generation-skipping transfer. Thus, the existence and exercise of P's power did not cause the trust to lose its exempt status under paragraph (b)(3) of this section. The result would be the same if the court order was issued after October 22, 1986.

(4) *Retention of trust's exempt status in the case of modifications, etc.*—(i) *In general.*—This paragraph (b)(4) provides rules for determining when a modification, judicial construction, settlement agreement, or trustee action with respect to a trust that is exempt from the generation-skipping transfer tax under paragraph (b)(1), (2), or (3) of this section (hereinafter referred to as an exempt trust) will not cause the trust to lose its exempt status. In general, unless specifically provided otherwise, the rules contained in this paragraph are applicable only for purposes of determining whether an exempt trust retains its exempt status for generation-skipping transfer tax purposes. Thus (unless specifically noted), the rules do not apply in determining, for example, whether the transaction results in a gift subject to gift tax, or may cause the trust to be included in the gross estate of a beneficiary, or may result in the realization of gain for purposes of section 1001.

(A) *Discretionary powers.*—The distribution of trust principal from an exempt trust to a new trust or retention of trust principal in a continuing trust will not cause the new or continuing trust to be subject to the provisions of chapter 13, if—

(1) Either—

(i) The terms of the governing instrument of the exempt trust authorize distributions to the new trust or the retention of trust principal in a continuing trust, without the consent or approval of any beneficiary or court; or

(ii) at the time the exempt trust became irrevocable, state law authorized distributions to the new trust or retention of principal in the continuing trust, without the consent or approval of any beneficiary or court; and

(2) The terms of the governing instrument of the new or continuing trust do not extend the time for vesting of any beneficial interest in the trust in a manner that may postpone or suspend the vesting, absolute ownership, or power of alienation of an interest in property for a period, measured from the date the original trust became irrevocable, extending beyond any life in being at the date the original trust became irrevocable plus a period of 21 years, plus if necessary, a reasonable period of gestation. For purposes of this paragraph (b)(4)(i)(A), the exercise of a trustee's distributive power that validly postpones or suspends the vesting, absolute ownership, or power of alienation of an interest in property for a term of years that will not exceed 90 years (measured from the date the original trust became irrevocable) will not be considered an exercise that postpones or suspends vesting, absolute ownership, or the power of alienation beyond the perpetuities period. If a distributive power is exercised by creating another power, it is deemed to be exercised to whatever extent the second power may be exercised.

(B) *Settlement.*—A court-approved settlement of a bona fide issue regarding the administration of the trust or the construction of terms of the governing instrument will not cause an exempt trust to be subject to the provisions of chapter 13, if—

(1) The settlement is the product of arm's length negotiations; and

(2) The settlement is within the range of reasonable outcomes under the governing instrument and applicable state law addressing the issues resolved by the settlement. A settlement that results in a compromise between the positions of the litigating parties and reflects the parties' assessments of the relative strengths of their positions is a settlement that is within the range of reasonable outcomes.

(C) *Judicial construction.*—A judicial construction of a governing instrument to resolve an ambiguity in the terms of the instrument or to correct a scrivener's error will not cause an exempt trust to be subject to the provisions of chapter 13, if—

(1) The judicial action involves a bona fide issue; and

(2) The construction is consistent with applicable state law that would be applied by the highest court of the state.

(D) *Other changes.*—(1) A modification of the governing instrument of an exempt trust (including a trustee distribution, settlement, or construction that does not satisfy paragraph (b)(4)(i)(A), (B), or (C) of this section) by judicial reformation, or nonjudicial reformation that is valid under applicable state law, will not cause an exempt trust to be subject to the provisions of chapter 13, if the modification does not shift a beneficial interest in the trust to any beneficiary who occupies a lower generation (as defined in section 2651) than the person or persons who held the beneficial interest prior to the modification, and the modification does not extend the time for vesting of any beneficial interest in the trust beyond the period provided for in the original trust.

(2) For purposes of this section, a modification of an exempt trust will result in a shift in beneficial interest to a lower generation beneficiary if the modification can result in either an increase in the amount of a GST transfer or the creation of a new GST transfer. To determine whether a modification of an irrevocable trust will shift a beneficial interest in a trust to a beneficiary who occupies a lower generation, the effect of the instrument on the date of the modification is measured against the effect of the instrument in existence immediately before the modification. If the effect of the modification cannot be immediately determined, it is deemed to shift a beneficial interest in the trust to a beneficiary who occupies a lower generation (as defined in section 2651) than the person or persons who held the beneficial interest prior to the modification. A modification that is administrative in nature that only indirectly increases the amount transferred (for example, by lowering administrative costs or income taxes) will not be considered to shift a beneficial interest in the trust. In addition, administration of a trust in conformance with applicable local law that defines the term income as a unitrust amount (or permits a right to income to be satisfied by such an amount) or that permits the trustee to adjust between principal and income to fulfill the trustee's duty of impartiality between income and principal beneficiaries will not be considered to shift a beneficial interest in the trust, if applicable local law provides for a reasonable apportionment between the income and remainder beneficiaries of the total return of the trust and meets the requirements of § 1.643(b)-1 of this chapter.

(E) *Examples.*—The following examples illustrate the application of this paragraph (b)(4). In each example, assume that the trust established in 1980 was irrevocable for purposes of paragraph (b)(1)(ii) of this section and that there have been no additions to any trust after September 25, 1985. The examples are as follows:

Example 1. Trustee's power to distribute principal authorized under trust instrument. In 1980, Grantor established an irrevocable trust (Trust) for the benefit of Grantor's child, A, A's spouse, and A's issue. At the time Trust was established, A had two children, B and C. A corporate fiduciary was designated as trustee. Under the terms of Trust, the trustee has the discretion to distribute all or part of the trust income to one or more of the group consisting of A, A's spouse or A's issue. The trustee is also authorized to distribute all or part of the trust principal to one or more trusts for the benefit of A, A's spouse, or A's issue under terms specified by the trustee in the trustee's discretion. Any trust established under Trust, however, must terminate 21 years after the death of the last child of

A to die who was alive at the time Trust was executed. Trust will terminate on the death of A, at which time the remaining principal will be distributed to A's issue, per stirpes. In 2002, the trustee distributes part of Trust's principal to a new trust for the benefit of B and C and their issue. The new trust will terminate 21 years after the death of the survivor of B and C, at which time the trust principal will be distributed to the issue of B and C, per stirpes. The terms of the governing instrument of Trust authorize the trustee to make the distribution to a new trust without the consent or approval of any beneficiary or court. In addition, the terms of the governing instrument of the new trust do not extend the time for vesting of any beneficial interest in a manner that may postpone or suspend the vesting, absolute ownership or power of alienation of an interest in property for a period, measured from the date of creation of Trust, extending beyond any life in being at the date of creation of Trust plus a period of 21 years, plus if necessary, a reasonable period of gestation. Therefore, neither Trust nor the new trust will be subject to the provisions of chapter 13 of the Internal Revenue Code.

Example 2. Trustee's power to distribute principal pursuant to state statute. In 1980, Grantor established an irrevocable trust (Trust) for the benefit of Grantor's child, A, A's spouse, and A's issue. At the time Trust was established, A had two children, B and C. A corporate fiduciary was designated as trustee. Under the terms of Trust, the trustee has the discretion to distribute all or part of the trust income or principal to one or more of the group consisting of A, A's spouse or A's issue. Trust will terminate on the death of A, at which time, the trust principal will be distributed to A's issue, per stirpes. Under a state statute enacted after 1980 that is applicable to Trust, a trustee who has the absolute discretion under the terms of a testamentary instrument or irrevocable inter vivos trust agreement to invade the principal of a trust for the benefit of the income beneficiaries of the trust, may exercise the discretion by appointing so much or all of the principal of the trust in favor of a trustee of a trust under an instrument other than that under which the power to invade is created, or under the same instrument. The trustee may take the action either with consent of all the persons interested in the trust but without prior court approval, or with court approval, upon notice to all of the parties. The exercise of the discretion, however, must not reduce any fixed income interest of any income beneficiary of the trust and must be in favor of the beneficiaries of the trust. Under state law prior to the enactment of the state statute, the trustee did not have the authority to make distributions in trust. In 2002, the trustee distributes one-half of Trust's principal to a new trust that provides for the payment of trust income to A for life and further provides that, at A's death, one-half of the trust remainder will pass to B or

B's issue and one-half of the trust will pass to *C* or *C*'s issue. Because the state statute was enacted after Trust was created and requires the consent of all of the parties, the transaction constitutes a modification of Trust. However, the modification does not shift any beneficial interest in Trust to a beneficiary or beneficiaries who occupy a lower generation than the person or persons who held the beneficial interest prior to the modification. In addition, the modification does not extend the time for vesting of any beneficial interest in Trust beyond the period provided for in the original trust. The new trust will terminate at the same date provided under Trust. Therefore, neither Trust nor the new trust will be subject to the provisions of chapter 13 of the Internal Revenue Code.

Example 3. Construction of an ambiguous term in the instrument. In 1980, Grantor established an irrevocable trust for the benefit of Grantor's children, *A* and *B*, and their issue. The trust is to terminate on the death of the last to die of *A* and *B*, at which time the principal is to be distributed to their issue. However, the provision governing the termination of the trust is ambiguous regarding whether the trust principal is to be distributed per stirpes, only to the children of *A* and *B*, or per capita among the children, grandchildren, and more remote issue of *A* and *B*. In 2002, the trustee files a construction suit with the appropriate local court to resolve the ambiguity. The court issues an order construing the instrument to provide for per capita distributions to the children, grandchildren, and more remote issue of *A* and *B* living at the time the trust terminates. The court's construction resolves a bona fide issue regarding the proper interpretation of the instrument and is consistent with applicable state law as it would be interpreted by the highest court of the state. Therefore, the trust will not be subject to the provisions of chapter 13 of the Internal Revenue Code.

Example 4. Change in trust situs. In 1980, Grantor, who was domiciled in State *X*, executed an irrevocable trust for the benefit of Grantor's issue, naming a State *X* bank as trustee. Under the terms of the trust, the trust is to terminate, in all events, no later than 21 years after the death of the last to die of certain designated individuals living at the time the trust was executed. The provisions of the trust do not specify that any particular state law is to govern the administration and construction of the trust. In State *X*, the common law rule against perpetuities applies to trusts. In 2002, a State *Y* bank is named as sole trustee. The effect of changing trustees is that the situs of the trust changes to State *Y*, and the laws of State *Y* govern the administration and construction of the trust. State *Y* law contains no rule against perpetuities. In this case, however, in view of the terms of the trust instrument, the trust will terminate at the same time before and after the change in situs. Accordingly, the change in situs does not shift any beneficial interest in the trust to a beneficiary who occupies a lower generation (as defined in section 2651) than the person or persons who held the beneficial interest prior to the transfer. Furthermore, the change in situs does not extend the time for vesting of any beneficial interest in the trust beyond that provided for in the original trust. Therefore, the trust will not be subject to the provisions of chapter 13 of the Internal Revenue Code. If, in this example, as a result of the change in situs, State *Y* law governed such that the time for vesting was extended beyond the period prescribed under the terms of the original trust instrument, the trust would not retain exempt status.

Example 5. Division of a trust. In 1980, Grantor established an irrevocable trust for the benefit of his two children, *A* and *B*, and their issue. Under the terms of the trust, the trustee has the discretion to distribute income and principal to *A*, *B*, and their issue in such amounts as the trustee deems appropriate. On the death of the last to die of *A* and *B*, the trust principal is to be distributed to the living issue of *A* and *B*, per stirpes. In 2002, the appropriate local court approved the division of the trust into two equal trusts, one for the benefit of *A* and *A*'s issue and one for the benefit of *B* and *B*'s issue. The trust for *A* and *A*'s issue provides that the trustee has the discretion to distribute trust income and principal to *A* and *A*'s issue in such amounts as the trustee deems appropriate. On *A*'s death, the trust principal is to be distributed equally to *A*'s issue, per stirpes. If *A* dies with no living descendants, the principal will be added to the trust for *B* and *B*'s issue. The trust for *B* and *B*'s issue is identical (except for the beneficiaries), and terminates at *B*'s death at which time the trust principal is to be distributed equally to *B*'s issue, per stirpes. If *B* dies with no living descendants, principal will be added to the trust for *A* and *A*'s issue. The division of the trust into two trusts does not shift any beneficial interest in the trust to a beneficiary who occupies a lower generation (as defined in section 2651) than the person or persons who held the beneficial interest prior to the division. In addition, the division does not extend the time for vesting of any beneficial interest in the trust beyond the period provided for in the original trust. Therefore, the two partitioned trusts resulting from the division will not be subject to the provisions of chapter 13 of the Internal Revenue Code.

Example 6. Merger of two trusts. In 1980, Grantor established an irrevocable trust for Grantor's child and the child's issue. In 1983, Grantor's spouse also established a separate irrevocable trust for the benefit of the same child and issue. The terms of the spouse's trust and Grantor's trust are identical. In 2002, the appropriate local court approved the merger of the two trusts into one trust to save administrative costs and enhance the management of the investments. The merger of the two trusts does not shift any beneficial interest in the trust to a beneficiary who occupies a lower generation (as defined in section 2651) than the person or persons who held the beneficial interest prior to the merger. In addition, the merger does not extend the time for vesting of any beneficial interest in the trust beyond the period provided for in the original trust. Therefore, the trust that resulted from the merger will not be subject to the provisions of chapter 13 of the Internal Revenue Code.

Example 7. Modification that does not shift an interest to a lower generation. In 1980, Grantor established an irrevocable trust for the benefit of Grantor's grandchildren, *A*, *B*, and *C*. The trust provides that income is to be paid to *A*, *B*, and *C*, in equal shares for life. The trust further provides that, upon the death of the first grandchild to die, one-third of the principal is to be distributed to that grandchild's issue, per stirpes. Upon the death of the second grandchild to die, one-half of the remaining trust principal is to be distributed to that grandchild's issue, per stirpes, and upon the death of the last grandchild to die, the remaining principal is to be distributed to that grandchild's issue, per stirpes. In 2002, *A* became disabled. Subsequently, the trustee, with the consent of *B* and *C*, petitioned the appropriate local court and the court approved a modification of the trust that increased *A*'s share of trust income. The modification does not shift a beneficial interest to a lower generation beneficiary because the modification does not increase the amount of a GST transfer under the original trust or create the possibility that new GST transfers not contemplated in the original trust may be made. In this case, the modification will increase the amount payable to *A* who is a member of the same generation as *B* and *C*. In addition, the modification does not extend the time for vesting of any beneficial interest in the trust beyond the period provided for in the original trust. Therefore, the trust as modified will not be subject to the provisions of chapter 13 of the Internal Revenue Code. However, the modification increasing *A*'s share of trust income is a transfer by *B* and *C* to *A* for Federal gift tax purposes.

Example 8. Conversion of income interest into unitrust interest. In 1980, Grantor established an irrevocable trust under the terms of which trust income is payable to *A* for life and, upon *A*'s death, the remainder is to pass to *A*'s issue, per stirpes. In 2002, the appropriate local court approves a modification to the trust that converts *A*'s income interest into the right to receive the greater of the entire income of the trust or a fixed percentage of the trust assets valued annually (unitrust interest) to be paid each year to *A* for life. The modification does not result in a shift in beneficial interest to a beneficiary who occupies a lower generation (as defined in section 2651) than the person or persons who held the beneficial interest prior to the modification. In this case, the modification can only operate to

increase the amount distributable to A and decrease the amount distributable to *A*'s issue. In addition, the modification does not extend the time for vesting of any beneficial interest in the trust beyond the period provided for in the original trust. Therefore, the trust will not be subject to the provisions of chapter 13 of the Internal Revenue Code.

Example 9. Allocation of capital gain to income. In 1980, Grantor established an irrevocable trust under the terms of which trust income is payable to Grantor's child, *A*, for life, and upon *A*'s death, the remainder is to pass to *A*'s issue, per stirpes. Under applicable state law, unless the governing instrument provides otherwise, capital gain is allocated to principal. In 2002, the trust is modified to allow the trustee to allocate capital gain to the income. The modification does not shift any beneficial interest in the trust to a beneficiary who occupies a lower generation (as defined in section 2651) than the person or persons who held the beneficial interest prior to the modification. In this case, the modification can only have the effect of increasing the amount distributable to *A*, and decreasing the amount distributable to *A*'s issue. In addition, the modification does not extend the time for vesting of any beneficial interest in the trust beyond the period provided for in the original trust. Therefore, the trust will not be subject to the provisions of chapter 13 of the Internal Revenue Code.

Example 10. Administrative change to terms of a trust. In 1980, Grantor executed an irrevocable trust for the benefit of Grantor's issue, naming a bank and five other individuals as trustees. In 2002, the appropriate local court approves a modification of the trust that decreases the number of trustees which results in lower administrative costs. The modification pertains to the administration of the trust and does not shift a beneficial interest in the trust to any beneficiary who occupies a lower generation (as defined in section 2651) than the person or persons who held the beneficial interest prior to the modification. In addition, the modification does not extend the time for vesting of any beneficial interest in the trust beyond the period provided for in the original trust. Therefore, the trust will not be subject to the provisions of chapter 13 of the Internal Revenue Code.

Example 11. Conversion of income interest to unitrust interest under state statute. In 1980, Grantor, a resident of State X, established an irrevocable trust for the benefit of Grantor's child, A, and A's issue. The trust provides that trust income is payable to A for life and upon A's death the remainder is to pass to A's issue, per stirpes. In 2002, State X amends its income and principal statute to define income as a unitrust amount of 4% of the fair market value of the trust assets valued annually. For a trust established prior to 2002, the statute provides that the new definition of income will apply only if all the beneficiaries who have an interest in the trust consent to the change within two years after the effective date of the statute. The statute provides specific procedures to establish the consent of the beneficiaries. A and A's issue consent to the change in the definition of income within the time period, and in accordance with the procedures, prescribed by the state statute. The administration of the trust, in accordance with the state statute defining income to be a 4% unitrust amount, will not be considered to shift any beneficial interest in the trust. Therefore, the trust will not be subject to the provisions of chapter 13 of the Internal Revenue Code. Further, under these facts, no trust beneficiary will be treated as having made a gift for federal gift tax purposes, and neither the trust nor any trust beneficiary will be treated as having made a taxable exchange for federal income tax purposes. Similarly, the conclusions in this example would be the same if the beneficiaries' consent was not required, or, if the change in administration of the trust occurred because the situs of the trust was changed to State X from a state whose statute does not define income as a unitrust amount or if the situs was changed to such a state from State X.

Example 12. Equitable adjustments under state statute. The facts are the same as in *Example 11*, except that in 2002, State X amends its income and principal statute to permit the trustee to make adjustments between income and principal when the trustee invests and manages the trust assets under the state's prudent investor standard, the trust describes the amount that shall or must be distributed to a beneficiary by referring to the trust's income, and the trustee after applying the state statutory rules regarding allocation of receipts between income and principal is unable to administer the trust impartially. The provision permitting the trustees to make these adjustments is effective in 2002 for trusts created at any time. The trustee invests and manages the trust assets under the state's prudent investor standard, and pursuant to authorization in the state statute, the trustee allocates receipts between the income and principal accounts in a manner to ensure the impartial administration of the trust. The administration of the trust in accordance with the state statute will not be considered to shift any beneficial interest in the trust. Therefore, the trust will not be subject to the provisions of chapter 13 of the Internal Revenue Code. Further, under these facts, no trust beneficiary will be treated as having made a gift for federal gift tax purposes, and neither the trust nor any trust beneficiary will be treated as having made a taxable exchange for federal income tax purposes. Similarly, the conclusions in this example would be the same if the change in administration of the trust occurred because the situs of the trust was changed to State X from a state whose statute does not authorize the trustee to make adjustments between income and

principal or if the situs was changed to such a state from State X.

(ii) *Effective dates.*—The rules in this paragraph (b)(4) are generally applicable on and after December 20, 2000. However, the rule in the last sentence of paragraph (b)(4)(i)(D)(2) of this section and *Example 11* and *Example 12* in paragraph (b)(4)(i)(E) of this section regarding the administration of a trust and the determination of income in conformance with applicable state law applies to trusts for taxable years ending after January 2, 2004.

(5) *Exceptions to additions rule.*—(i) *In general.*—Any addition to a trust made pursuant to an instrument or arrangement covered by the transition rules in paragraph (b)(1), (2) or (3) of this section is not treated as an addition for purposes of this section. Moreover, any property transferred inter vivos to a trust is not treated as an addition if the same property would have been added to the trust pursuant to an instrument covered by the transition rules in paragraph (b)(2) or (3) of this section.

(ii) *Examples.*—The following examples illustrate the application of paragraph (b)(4)(i) of this section:

Example 1. Addition pursuant to terms of exempt instrument. On December 31, 1980, T created an irrevocable trust having a principal of $100,000. Under the terms of the trust, the principal was to be held for the benefit of T's grandchild, GC. Pursuant to the terms of T's will, a document entitled to relief under the transition rule of paragraph (b)(2) of this section, the residue of the estate was paid to the trust. Because the addition to the trust was paid pursuant to the terms of an instrument (T's will) that is not subject to the provisions of chapter 13 because of paragraph (b)(2) of this section, the payment to the trust is not considered an addition to the principal of the trust. Thus, distributions to or for the benefit of GC, are not subject to the provisions of chapter 13.

Example 2. Property transferred inter vivos that would have been transferred to the same trust by the transferor's will. T is the grantor of a trust that was irrevocable on September 25, 1985. T's will, which was executed before October 22, 1986, and not amended thereafter, provides that, upon T's death, the entire estate will pour over into T's trust. On October 1, 1985, T transfers $100,000 to the trust. While T's will would otherwise qualifies for relief under the transition rule in paragraph (b)(2) of this section, the transition rule is not applicable unless T dies prior to January 1, 1987. Thus, if T dies after December 31, 1986, the transfer is treated as an addition to the trust for purposes of any distribution made from the trust after the transfer to the trust on October 1, 1985. If T dies before January 1, 1987, the entire trust (as well as any distributions from or terminations of interests in the trust prior to T's death) is exempt, under paragraph (b)(2) of this section, from chapter 13 because the $100,000 would have been added to the trust under a will that would have qualified under paragraph (b)(2) of this section. In either case, for any generation-skipping transfers made after the transfer to the trust on October 1, 1985, but before T's death, the $100,000 is treated as an addition to the trust and a proportionate amount of the trust is subject to chapter 13.

Example 3. Pour over to a revocable trust. T and S are the settlors of separate revocable trusts with equal values. Both trusts were established for the benefit of skip persons (as defined in section 2613). S dies on December 1, 1985, and under the provisions of S's trust, the principal pours over into T's trust. If T dies before January 1, 1987, the entire trust is excluded under paragraph (b)(2) of this section from the operation of chapter 13. If T dies after December 31, 1986, the entire trust is subject to the generation-skipping transfer tax provisions because T's trust is not a trust described in paragraph (b)(1) or (2) of this section. In the latter case, the fact that S died before January 1, 1987, is irrelevant because the principal of S's trust was added to a trust that never qualified under the transition rules of paragraph (b)(1) or (2) of this section.

Example 4. Pour over to exempt trust. Assume the same facts as in *Example 3*, except upon the death of S on December 1, 1985, S's trust continues as an irrevocable trust and that the principal of T's trust is to be paid over upon T's death to S's trust. Again, if T dies before January 1, 1987, S's entire trust falls within the provisions of paragraph (b)(2) of this section. However, if T dies after December 31, 1986, the pour-over is considered an addition to the trust. Therefore, S's trust is not a trust excluded under paragraph (b)(2) of this section because an addition is made to the trust.

Example 5. Lapse of a general power of appointment. S, the spouse of the settlor of an irrevocable trust that was created in 1980, had, on September 25, 1985, a general power of appointment over the trust assets. The trust provides that should S fail to exercise the power of appointment the property is to remain in the trust. On October 21, 1986, S executed a will under which S failed to exercise the power of appointment. If S dies before January 1, 1987, without having exercised the power in a manner which results in the creation of, or increase in the amount of, a generation-skipping transfer (or amended the will in a manner that results in the creation of, or increase in the amount of, a generation-skipping transfer), transfers pursuant to the trust or the will are not subject to chapter 13 because the trust is an irrevocable trust and the will qualifies under paragraph (b)(2) of this section.

Example 6. Lapse of general power of appointment held by intestate decedent. Assume the same facts as in *Example 5*, except on October 22, 1986,

S did not have a will and that S dies after that date. Upon S's death, or upon the prior exercise or release of the power, the value of the entire trust is treated as having been distributed to S, and S is treated as having made an addition to the trust in the amount of the entire principal. Any distribution or termination pursuant to the trust occurring after S's death is subject to chapter 13. It is immaterial whether S's death occurs before January 1, 1987, since paragraph (b)(2) of this section is only applicable where a will or revocable trust was executed before October 22, 1986.

(c) *Additional effective dates.*—Except as otherwise provided, the regulations under §§ 26.2611-1, 26.2612-1, 26.2613-1, 26.2632-1, 26.2641-1, 26.2642-1, 26.2642-2, 26.2642-3, 26.2642-4, 26.2642-5, 26.2652-1, 26.2652-2, 26.2653-1, 26.2654-1, 26.2663-1, and 26.2663-2 are effective with respect to generation-skipping transfers as defined in § 26.2611-1 made on or after December 27, 1995. However, taxpayers may, at their option, rely on these regulations in the case of generation-skipping transfers made, and trusts that became irrevocable, after December 23, 1992, and before December 27, 1995. The last four sentences in paragraph (b)(1)(i) of this section are applicable on and after November 18, 1999. [Reg. § 26.2601-1.]

☐ [*T.D.* 8644, 12-26-95. *Amended by T.D.* 8912, 12-19-2000 (*corrected* 2-21-2001) *and T.D.* 9102, 12-30-2003.]

[Reg. § 26.2611-1]

§ 26.2611-1. Generation-skipping transfer defined.—A generation-skipping transfer (GST) is an event that is either a direct skip, a taxable distribution, or a taxable termination. See § 26.2612-1 for the definition of these terms. The determination as to whether an event is a GST is made by reference to the most recent transfer subject to the estate or gift tax. See § 26.2652-1(a)(2) for determining whether a transfer is subject to Federal estate or gift tax. [Reg. § 26.2611-1.]

☐ [*T.D.* 8644, 12-26-95.]

[Reg. § 26.2612-1]

§ 26.2612-1. Definitions.—(a) *Direct skip.*—A direct skip is a transfer to a skip person that is subject to Federal estate or gift tax. If property is transferred to a trust, the transfer is a direct skip only if the trust is a skip person. Only one direct skip occurs when a single transfer of property skips two or more generations. See paragraph (d) of this section for the definition of skip person. See § 26.2652-1(b) for the definition of trust. See § 26.2632-1(c)(4) for the time that a direct skip occurs if the transferred property is subject to an estate tax inclusion period.

(b) *Taxable termination.*—(1) *In general.*—Except as otherwise provided in this paragraph (b), a taxable termination is a termination (occurring for any reason) of an interest in trust unless—

(i) A transfer subject to Federal estate or gift tax occurs with respect to the property held in the trust at the time of the termination;

(ii) Immediately after the termination, a person who is not a skip person has an interest in the trust; or

(iii) At no time after the termination may a distribution, other than a distribution the probability of which occurring is so remote as to be negligible (including a distribution at the termination of the trust) be made from the trust to a skip person. For this purpose, the probability that a distribution will occur is so remote as to be negligible only if it can be ascertained by actuarial standards that there is less than a 5 percent probability that the distribution will occur.

(2) *Partial termination.*—If a distribution of a portion of trust property is made to a skip person by reason of a termination occurring on the death of a lineal descendant of the transferor, the termination is a taxable termination with respect to the distributed property.

(3) *Simultaneous terminations.*—A simultaneous termination of two or more interests creates only one taxable termination.

(c) *Taxable distribution.*—(1) *In general.*—A taxable distribution is a distribution of income or principal from a trust to a skip person unless the distribution is a taxable termination or a direct skip. If any portion of GST tax (including penalties and interest thereon) imposed on a distributee is paid from the distributing trust, the payment is an additional taxable distribution to the distributee. For purposes of chapter 13, the additional distribution is treated as having been made on the last day of the calendar year in which the original taxable distribution is made. If Federal estate or gift tax is imposed on any individual with respect to an interest in property held by a trust, the interest in property is treated as having been distributed to the individual to the extent that the value of the interest is subject to Federal estate or gift tax. See § 26.2652-1(a)(6) *Example 5*, regarding the treatment of the lapse of a power of appointment as a transfer to a trust.

(2) *Look-through rule not to apply.*—Solely for purposes of determining whether any transfer from a trust to another trust is a taxable distribution, the rules of section 2651(e)(2) do not apply. If the transferring trust and the recipient trust have the same transferor, see § 26.2642-4(a)(1) and (2) for rules for recomputing the applicable fraction of the recipient trust.

(d) *Skip person.*—A skip person is—

(1) An individual assigned to a generation more than one generation below that of the transferor (determined under the rules of section 2651); or

(2) A trust if—

(i) All interests in the trust are held by skip persons; or

(ii) No person holds an interest in the trust and no distributions, other than a distribution the probability of which occurring is so remote as to be negligible (including distributions at the termination of the trust), may be made after the transfer to a person other than a skip person. For this purpose, the probability that a distribution will occur is so remote as to be negligible only if it can be ascertained by actuarial standards that there is less than a 5 percent probability that the distribution will occur.

(e) *Interest in trust.*—(1) *In general.*—An interest in trust is an interest in property held in trust as defined in section 2652(c) and these regulations. An interest in trust exists if a person—

(i) Has a present right to receive trust principal or income;

(ii) Is a permissible current recipient of trust principal or income and is not described in section 2055(a); or

(iii) Is described in section 2055(a) and the trust is a charitable remainder annuity trust or unitrust (as defined in section 664(d)) or a pooled income fund (as defined in section 642(c)(5)).

(2) *Exceptions.*—(i) *Support obligations.*—In general, an individual has a present right to receive trust income or principal if trust income or principal may be used to satisfy the individual's support obligations. However, an individual does not have an interest in a trust merely because a support obligation of that individual may be satisfied by a distribution that is either within the discretion of a fiduciary or pursuant to provisions of local law substantially equivalent to the Uniform Gifts (Transfers) to Minors Act.

(ii) *Certain interests disregarded.*—An interest which is used primarily to postpone or avoid the GST tax is disregarded for purposes of chapter 13. An interest is considered as used primarily to postpone or avoid the GST tax if a significant purpose for the creation of the interest is to postpone or avoid the tax.

(3) *Disclaimers.*—An interest does not exist to the extent it is disclaimed pursuant to a disclaimer that constitutes a qualified disclaimer under section 2518.

(f) *Examples.*—The following examples illustrate the provisions of this section.

Example 1. Direct skip. T gratuitously conveys Blackacre to T's grandchild. Because the transfer is a transfer to a skip person of property subject to Federal gift tax, it is a direct skip.

Example 2. Direct skip of more than one generation. T gratuitously conveys Blackacre to T's great-grandchild. The transfer is a direct skip.

Only one GST tax is imposed on the direct skip although two generations are skipped by the transfer.

Example 3. Withdrawal power in trust. T transfers $50,000 to a new trust providing that trust income is to be paid to T's child, C, for life and, on C's death, the trust principal is to be paid to T's descendants. Under the terms of the trust, T grants four grandchildren the right to withdraw $10,000 from the trust for a 60 day period following the transfer. Since C, who is not a skip person, has an interest in the trust, the trust is not a skip person. T's transfer to the trust is not a direct skip.

Example 4. Taxable termination. T establishes an irrevocable trust under which the income is to be paid to T's child, C, for life. On the death of C, the trust principal is to be paid to T's grandchild, GC. Since C has an interest in the trust, the trust is not a skip person and the transfer to the trust is not a direct skip. If C dies survived by GC, a taxable termination occurs at C's death because C's interest in the trust terminates and thereafter the trust property is held by a skip person who occupies a lower generation than C.

Example 5. Direct skip of property held in trust. T establishes a testamentary trust under which the income is to be paid to T's surviving spouse, S, for life and the remainder is to be paid to a grandchild of T and S. T's executor elects to treat the trust as qualified terminable interest property under section 2056(b)(7). The transfer to the trust is not a direct skip because S, a person who is not a skip person, holds a present right to receive income from the trust. Upon S's death, the trust property is included in S's gross estate under section 2044 and passes directly to a skip person. The GST occurring at that time is a direct skip because it is a transfer subject to chapter 11. The fact that the interest created by T is terminated at S's death is immaterial because S becomes the transferor at the time of the transfer subject to chapter 11.

Example 6. Taxable termination. T establishes an irrevocable trust for the benefit of T's child, C, T's grandchild, GC, and T's great-grandchild, GGC. Under the terms of the trust, income and principal may be distributed to any or all of the living beneficiaries at the discretion of the trustee. Upon the death of the second beneficiary to die, the trust principal is to be paid to the survivor. C dies first. A taxable termination occurs at that time because, immediately after C's interest terminates, all interests in the trust are held by skip persons (GC and GGC).

Example 7. Taxable termination resulting from distribution. The facts are the same as in *Example 6*, except twenty years after C's death the trustee exercises its discretionary power and distributes the entire principal to GGC. The distribution results in a taxable termination because GC's interest in the trust terminates as a result of the distribution of the entire trust property to GGC, a skip person. The result would be the same if

the trustee retained sufficient funds to pay the GST tax due by reason of the taxable termination, as well as any expenses of winding up the trust.

Example 8. Simultaneous termination of interests of more than one beneficiary. T establishes an irrevocable trust for the benefit of T's child, C, T's grandchild, GC, and T's great-grandchild, GGC. Under the terms of the trust, income and principal may be distributed to any or all of the living beneficiaries at the discretion of the trustee. Upon the death of C, the trust property is to be distributed to GGC if then living. If C is survived by both GC and GGC, both C's and GC's interests in the trust will terminate on C's death. However, because both interests will terminate at the same time and as a result of one event, only one taxable termination occurs.

Example 9. Partial taxable termination. T creates an irrevocable trust providing that trust income is to be paid to T's children, A and B, in such proportions as the trustee determines for their joint lives. On the death of the first child to die, one-half of the trust principal is to be paid to T's then living grandchildren. The balance of the trust principal is to be paid to T's grandchildren on the death of the survivor of A and B. If A predeceases B, the distribution occurring on the termination of A's interest in the trust is a taxable termination and not a taxable distribution. It is a taxable termination because the distribution is a distribution of a portion of the trust that occurs as a result of the death of A, a lineal descendant of T. It is immaterial that a portion of the trust continues and that B, a person other than a skip person, thereafter holds an interest in the trust.

Example 10. Taxable distribution. T establishes an irrevocable trust under which the trust income is payable to T's child, C, for life. When T's grandchild, GC, attains 35 years of age, GC is to receive one-half of the principal. The remaining one-half of the principal is to be distributed to GC on C's death. Assume that C survives until GC attains age 35. When the trustee distributes one-half of the principal to GC on GC's 35th birthday, the distribution is a taxable distribution because it is a distribution to a skip person and is neither a taxable termination nor a direct skip.

Example 11. Exercise of withdrawal right as taxable distribution. The facts are the same as in *Example 10*, except GC holds a continuing right to withdraw trust principal and after one year GC withdraws $10,000. The withdrawal by GC is not a taxable termination because the withdrawal does not terminate C's interest in the trust. The withdrawal by GC is a taxable distribution to GC.

Example 12. Interest in trust. T establishes an irrevocable trust under which the income is to be paid to T's child, C, for life. On the death of C, the trust principal is to be paid to T's grandchild, GC. Because C has a present right to receive income from the trust, C has an interest in the trust. Because GC cannot currently receive distributions from the trust, GC does not have an interest in the trust.

Example 13. Support obligation. T establishes an irrevocable trust for the benefit of T's grandchild, GC. The trustee has discretion to distribute property for GC's support without regard to the duty or ability of GC's parent, C, to support GC. Because GC is a permissible current recipient of trust property, GC has an interest in the trust. C does not have an interest in the trust because the potential use of the trust property to satisfy C's support obligation is within the discretion of a fiduciary. C would be treated as having an interest in the trust if the trustee was required to distribute trust property for GC's support. [Reg. § 26.2612-1.]

☐ *[T.D. 8644, 12-26-95. Amended by T.D. 9214, 7-15-2005.]*

[Reg. § 26.2613-1]

§ 26.2613-1. Skip person.—For the definition of *skip person* see § 26.2612-1(d). [Reg. § 26.2613-1.]

☐ *[T.D. 8644, 12-26-95.]*

[Reg. § 26.2632-1]

§ 26.2632-1. Allocation of GST exemption.—(a) *General rule.*—Except as otherwise provided in this section, an individual or the individual's executor may allocate the individual's $1 million GST exemption at any time from the date of the transfer through the date for filing the individual's Federal estate tax return (including any extensions for filing that have been actually granted). If no estate tax return is required to be filed, the GST exemption may be allocated at any time through the date a Federal estate tax return would be due if a return were required to be filed (including any extensions actually granted). If property is held in trust, the allocation of GST exemption is made to the entire trust rather than to specific trust assets. If a transfer is a direct skip to a trust, the allocation of GST exemption to the transferred property is also treated as an allocation of GST exemption to the trust for purposes of future GSTs with respect to the trust by the same transferor.

(b) *Lifetime allocations.*—(1) *Automatic allocation to direct skips.*—(i) *In general.*—If a direct skip occurs during the transferor's lifetime, the transferor's GST exemption not previously allocated (unused GST exemption) is automatically allocated to the transferred property (but not in excess of the fair market value of the property on the date of the transfer). The transferor may prevent the automatic allocation of GST exemption by describing on a timely-filed United States Gift (and Generation-Skipping Transfer) Tax Return (Form 709) the transfer and the extent to which the automatic allocation is not to apply. In addition, a timely-filed Form 709 accompanied by payment of the GST tax (as shown on the return with respect to the direct skip) is sufficient to prevent an automatic allocation of GST exemption with respect to the transferred property. See paragraph (c)(4) of this section for special rules in the case of direct skips treated as occurring at the termination of an estate tax inclusion period.

(ii) *Time for filing Form 709.*—A Form 709 is timely filed if it is filed on or before the date required for reporting the transfer if it were a taxable gift (i.e., the date prescribed by section 6075(b), including any extensions to file actually granted (the due date)). Except as provided in paragraph (b)(1)(iii) of this section, the automatic allocation of GST exemption (or the election to prevent the allocation, if made) is irrevocable after the due date. An automatic allocation of GST exemption is effective as of the date of the transfer to which it relates. Except as provided above, a Form 709 need not be filed to report an automatic allocation.

(iii) *Transitional rule.*—An election to prevent an automatic allocation of GST exemption filed on or before January 26, 1996, becomes irrevocable on July 24, 1996.

(2) *Automatic allocation to indirect skips made after December 31, 2000.*—(i) *In general.*—An indirect skip is a transfer of property to a GST trust as defined in section 2632(c)(3)(B) provided that the transfer is subject to gift tax and does not qualify as a direct skip. In the case of an indirect skip made after December 31, 2000, to which section 2642(f) (relating to transfers subject to an estate tax inclusion period (ETIP)) does not apply, the transferor's unused GST exemption is automatically allocated to the property transferred (but not in excess of the fair market value of the property on the date of the transfer). The automatic allocation pursuant to this paragraph is effective whether or not a Form 709 is filed reporting the transfer, and is effective as of the date of the transfer to which it relates. An automatic allocation is irrevocable after the due date of the Form 709 for the calendar year in which the transfer is made. In the case of an indirect skip to which section 2642(f) does apply, the indirect skip is deemed to be made at the close of the ETIP and the GST exemption is deemed to be allocated at that time. In either case, except as otherwise provided in paragraph (b)(2)(ii) of this section, the automatic allocation of exemption applies even if an allocation of exemption is made to the indirect skip in accordance with section 2632(a).

(ii) *Prevention of automatic allocation.*—Except as otherwise provided in forms or other guidance published by the Service, the transferor may prevent the automatic allocation of GST exemption with regard to an indirect skip (including indirect skips to which section 2642(f) may apply) by making an election, as provided in paragraph (b)(2)(iii) of this section. Notwithstanding paragraph (b)(2)(iii)(B) of this section, the transferor may also prevent the automatic allocation of GST exemption with regard to an indirect skip by making an affirmative allocation of GST exemption on a Form 709 filed at any time on or before the due date for timely filing (within the meaning of paragraph (b)(1)(ii) of this section) of an amount that is less than (but not equal to) the value of the property transferred as reported on that return, in accordance with the provisions of paragraph (b)(4) of this section. See paragraph (b)(4)(iii) *Example 6* of this section. Any election out of the automatic allocation rules under this section has no effect on the application of the automatic allocation rules applicable after the transferor's death under section 2632(e) and paragraph (d) of this section.

(iii) *Election to have automatic allocation rules not apply.*—(A) *In general.*—A transferor may prevent the automatic allocation of GST exemption (elect out) with respect to any transfer or transfers constituting an indirect skip made to a trust or to one or more separate shares that are treated as separate trusts under §26.2654-1(a)(1) (collectively referred to hereinafter as a trust). In the case of a transfer treated under section 2513 as made one-half by the transferor and one-half by the transferor's spouse, each spouse shall be treated as a separate transferor who must satisfy separately the requirements of paragraph (b)(2)(iii)(B) to elect out with respect to the transfer. A transferor may elect out with respect to—

(1) One or more prior-year transfers subject to section 2642(f) (regarding ETIPs) made by the transferor to a specified trust or trusts;

(2) One or more (or all) current-year transfers made by the transferor to a specified trust or trusts;

(3) One or more (or all) future transfers made by the transferor to a specified trust or trusts;

(4) All future transfers made by the transferor to all trusts (whether or not in existence at the time of the election out); or

(5) Any combination of paragraphs (b)(2)(iii)(A)(1) through (4) of this section.

(B) *Manner of making an election out.*—Except as otherwise provided in forms or other guidance published by the IRS, an election out is made as described in this paragraph (b)(2)(iii)(B). To elect out, the transferor must attach a statement (election out statement) to a Form 709 filed within the time period provided in paragraph (b)(2)(iii)(C) of this section (whether or not any transfer was made in the calendar year for which the Form 709 was filed, and whether or not a Form 709 otherwise would be required to be filed for that year). See paragraph (b)(4)(iv) *Example 7* of this section. The election out statement must identify the trust (except for an election out under paragraph (b)(2)(iii)(A)(4) of this section), and specifically must provide that the transferor is electing out of the automatic allocation of GST exemption with respect to the described transfer or transfers. Prior-year transfers that are subject to section 2642(f), and to which the election out is to apply, must be specifically described or otherwise identified in the election out statement. Further, unless the election out is made for all transfers made to the trust in the current year and/or in all future years, the current-year transfers and/or future transfers to which the election out is to apply must be specifically described or otherwise identified in the election out statement.

(C) *Time for making an election out.*—To elect out, the Form 709 with the attached election out statement must be filed on or before the due date for timely filing (within the meaning of paragraph (b)(1)(ii) of this section) of the Form 709 for the calendar year in which—

(1) For a transfer subject to section 2642(f), the ETIP closes; or

(2) For all other elections out, the first transfer to be covered by the election out was made.

(D) *Effect of election out.*—An election out does not affect the automatic allocation of GST exemption to any transfer not covered by the election out statement. Except for elections out for transfers described in paragraph (b)(2)(iii)(A)(1) of this section that are specifically described in an election out statement, an election out does not apply to any prior-year transfer to a trust, including any transfer subject to an ETIP (even if the ETIP closes after the election is made). An election out does not prevent the transferor from allocating the transferor's available GST exemption to any transfer covered by the election out, either on a timely filed Form 709 reporting the transfer or at a later date in accordance with the provisions of paragraph (b)(4) of this section. An election out with respect to future transfers remains in effect unless and until terminated. Once an election out with respect to future transfers is made, a transferor need not file a Form 709 in future years solely to prevent the automatic allocation of the GST exemption to any future transfer covered by the election out.

(E) *Termination of election out.*—Except as otherwise provided in forms or other guidance published by the IRS, an election out may be terminated as described in this paragraph (b)(2)(iii)(E). Pursuant to this section, a transferor may terminate an election out made on a Form 709 for a prior year, to the extent that election out applied to future transfers or to a transfer subject to section 2642(f). To terminate an election out, the transferor must attach a statement (termination statement) to a Form 709 filed on or before the due date of the Form 709 for the calendar year in which is made the first transfer to which the election out is not to apply

Reg. §26.2632-1(b)(2)(iii)

(whether or not any transfer was made in the calendar year for which the Form 709 was filed, and whether or not a Form 709 otherwise would be required to be filed for that year). The termination statement must identify the trust (if applicable), describe the prior election out that is being terminated, specifically provide that the prior election out is being terminated, and either describe the extent to which the prior election out is being terminated or describe any current-year transfers to which the election out is not to apply. Consequently, the automatic allocation rules contained in section 2632(c)(1) will apply to any current-year transfer described on the termination statement and, except as otherwise provided in this paragraph, to all future transfers that otherwise would have been covered by the election out. The termination of an election out does not affect any transfer, or any election out, that is not described in the termination statement. The termination of an election out will not revoke the election out for any prior-year transfer, except for a prior-year transfer subject to section 2642(f) for which the election out is revoked on a timely filed Form 709 for the calendar year in which the ETIP closes or for any prior calendar year. The termination of an election out does not preclude the transferor from making another election out in the same or any subsequent year.

(3) *Election to treat trust as a GST trust.*— (i) *In general.*—A transferor may elect to treat any trust as a GST trust (GST trust election), without regard to whether the trust is subject to section 2642(f), with respect to—

(A) Any current-year transfer (or any or all current-year transfers) by the electing transferor to the trust;

(B) Any selected future transfers by the electing transferor to the trust;

(C) All future transfers by the electing transferor to the trust; or

(D) Any combination of paragraphs (b)(3)(i)(A) through (C) of this section.

(ii) *Time and Manner of making GST trust election.*—Except as otherwise provided in forms or other guidance published by the Internal Revenue Service, a GST trust election is made as described in this paragraph (b)(3)(ii). To make a GST trust election, the transferor must attach a statement (GST trust election statement) to a Form 709 filed on or before the due date for timely filing (within the meaning of paragraph (b)(1)(ii) of this section) of the Form 709 for the calendar year in which the first transfer to be covered by the GST trust election is made (whether or not any transfer was made in the calendar year for which the Form 709 was filed, and whether or not a Form 709 otherwise would be required to be filed for that year). The GST trust election statement must identify the trust, specifically describe or otherwise clearly identify the transfers to be covered by the election, and

specifically provide that the transferor is electing to have the trust treated as a GST trust with respect to the covered transfers.

(iii) *Effect of GST trust election.*—Except as otherwise provided in this paragraph, a GST trust election will cause all transfers made by the electing transferor to the trust that are subject to the election to be deemed to be made to a GST trust as defined in section 2632(c)(3)(B). Thus, the electing transferor's unused GST exemption may be allocated automatically to such transfers in accordance with paragraph (b)(2) of this section. A transferor may prevent the automatic allocation of GST exemption to future transfers to the trust either by terminating the GST trust election in accordance with paragraph (b)(3)(iv) of this section (in the case of trusts that would not otherwise be treated as GST trusts) or by electing out of the automatic allocation of GST exemption in accordance with paragraph (b)(2) of this section.

(iv) *Termination of GST trust election.*—Except as otherwise provided in forms or other guidance published by the Service, a GST trust election may be terminated as described in this paragraph (b)(3)(iv). A transferor may terminate a GST trust election made on a Form 709 for a prior year, to the extent that election applied to future transfers or to a transfer subject to section 2642(f). To terminate a GST trust election, the transferor must attach a statement (termination statement) to a Form 709 filed on or before the due date for timely filing (within the meaning of paragraph (b)(1)(ii) of this section) a Form 709 for the calendar year: in which is made the electing transferor's first transfer to which the GST trust election is not to apply; or that is the first calendar year for which the GST trust election is not to apply, even if no transfer is made to the trust during that year. The termination statement must identify the trust, describe the current-year transfer (if any), and provide that the prior GST trust election is terminated. Accordingly, if the trust otherwise does not satisfy the definition of a GST trust, the automatic allocation rules contained in section 2632(c)(1) will not apply to the described current-year transfer or to any future transfers made by the transferor to the trust, unless and until another election under this paragraph (b)(3) is made.

(4) *Allocation to other transfers.*—(i) *In general.*—An allocation of GST exemption to property transferred during the transferor's lifetime, other than in a direct skip, is made on Form 709. The allocation must clearly identify the trust to which the allocation is being made, the amount of GST exemption allocated to it, and if the allocation is late or if an inclusion ratio greater than zero is claimed, the value of the trust assets at the effective date of the allocation. See paragraph (b)(4)(ii) of this section. The allocation should also state the inclusion ratio of the trust after the

allocation. Except as otherwise provided in this paragraph, an allocation of GST exemption may be made by a formula; e.g., the allocation may be expressed in terms of the amount necessary to produce an inclusion ratio of zero. However, formula allocations made with respect to charitable lead annuity trusts are not valid except to the extent they are dependent on values as finally determined for Federal estate or gift tax purposes. With respect to a timely allocation, an allocation of GST exemption becomes irrevocable after the due date of the return. Except as provided in § 26.2642-3 (relating to charitable lead annuity trusts), an allocation of GST exemption to a trust is void to the extent the amount allocated exceeds the amount necessary to obtain an inclusion ratio of zero with respect to the trust. See § 26.2642-1 for the definition of inclusion ratio. An allocation is also void if the allocation is made with respect to a trust that has no GST potential with respect to the transferor making the allocation, at the time of the allocation. For this purpose, a trust has GST potential even if the possibility of a GST is so remote as to be negligible.

(ii) *Effective date of allocation.*—(A) *In general.*—(1) Except as otherwise provided, an allocation of GST exemption is effective as of the date of any transfer as to which the Form 709 on which it is made is a timely filed return (a timely allocation). If more than one timely allocation is made, the earlier allocation is modified only if the later allocation clearly identifies the transfer and the nature and extent of the modification. Except as provided in paragraph (d)(1) of this section, an allocation to a trust made on a Form 709 filed after the due date for reporting a transfer to the trust (a late allocation) is effective on the date the Form 709 is filed and is deemed to precede in point of time any taxable event occurring on such date. For purposes of this paragraph (b)(4)(ii), the Form 709 is deemed filed on the date it is postmarked to the Internal Revenue Service address as directed in forms or other guidance published by the Service. See § 26.2642-2 regarding the effect of a late allocation in determining the inclusion ratio, etc. See paragraph (c)(1) of this section regarding allocation of GST exemption to property subject to an estate tax inclusion period. If it is unclear whether an allocation of GST exemption on a Form 709 is a late or a timely allocation to a trust, the allocation is effective in the following order—

(i) To any transfer to the trust disclosed on the return as to which the return is a timely return;

(ii) As a late allocation; and

(iii) To any transfer to the trust not disclosed on the return as to which the return would be a timely return.

(2) A late allocation to a trust may be made on a Form 709 that is timely filed with

respect to another transfer. A late allocation is irrevocable when made.

(B) *Amount of allocation.*—If other transfers exist with respect to which GST exemption could be allocated under paragraphs (b)(4)(ii)(A)(1)(ii) and (iii), any GST exemption allocated under paragraph (b)(4)(ii)(A)(1)(i) of this section is allocated in an amount equal to the value of the transferred property as reported on the Form 709. Thus, if the GST exemption allocated on the Form 709 exceeds the value of the transfers reported on that return that have generation-skipping potential, the initial allocation under paragraph (b)(4)(ii)(A)(1)(i) of this section is in the amount of the value of those transfers as reported on that return. Any remaining amount of GST exemption allocated on that return is then allocated pursuant to paragraphs (b)(4)(ii)(A)(1)(ii) and (iii) of this section, notwithstanding any subsequent upward adjustment in value of the transfers reported on the return.

(iii) *Examples.*—The following examples illustrate the provisions of this paragraph (b):

Example 1. Modification of allocation of GST exemption. On December 1, 2003, T transfers $100,000 to an irrevocable GST trust described in section 2632(c)(3)(B). The transfer to the trust is not a direct skip. The date prescribed for filing the gift tax return reporting the taxable gift is April 15, 2004. On February 10, 2004, T files a Form 709 on which T properly elects out of the automatic allocation rules contained in section 2632(c)(1) with respect to the transfer in accordance with paragraph (b)(2)(iii) of this section, and allocates $50,000 of GST exemption to the trust. On April 13th of the same year, T files an additional Form 709 on which T confirms the election out of the automatic allocation rules contained in section 2632(c)(1) and allocates $100,000 of GST exemption to the trust in a manner that clearly indicates the intention to modify and supersede the prior allocation with respect to the 2003 transfer. The allocation made on the April 13 return supersedes the prior allocation because it is made on a timely-filed Form 709 that clearly identifies the trust and the nature and extent of the modification of GST exemption allocation. The allocation of $100,000 of GST exemption to the trust is effective as of December 1, 2003. The result would be the same if the amended Form 709 decreased the amount of the GST exemption allocated to the trust.

Example 2. Modification of allocation of GST exemption. The facts are the same as in *Example 1* except, on July 8, 2004, T files a Form 709 attempting to reduce the earlier allocation. The return filed on July 8, 2004, is not a timely filed return. The $100,000 GST exemption allocated to the trust, as amended on April 13, 2004, remains in effect because an allocation, once made, is irrevocable and may not be modified after the last date on which a timely filed Form 709 may be filed.

Example 3. Effective date of late allocation of GST exemption. On November 15, 2003, T transfers $100,000 to an irrevocable GST trust described in section 2632(c)(3)(B). The transfer to the trust is not a direct skip. The date prescribed for filing the gift tax return reporting the taxable gift is April 15, 2004. On February 10, 2004, T files a Form 709 on which T properly elects out of the automatic allocation rules contained in section 2632(c)(1) in accordance with paragraph (b)(2)(iii) of this section with respect to that transfer. On December 1, 2004, T files a Form 709 and allocates $50,000 to the trust. The allocation is effective as of December 1, 2004.

Example 4. Effective date of late allocation of GST exemption. T transfers $100,000 to an irrevocable GST trust on December 1, 2003, in a transfer that is not a direct skip. On April 15, 2004, T files a Form 709 on which T properly elects out of the automatic allocation rules contained in section 2632(c)(1) with respect to the entire transfer in accordance with paragraph (b)(2)(iii) of this section and T does not make an allocation of any GST exemption on the Form 709. On September 1, 2004, the trustee makes a taxable distribution from the trust to T's grandchild in the amount of $30,000. Immediately prior to the distribution, the value of the trust assets was $150,000. On the same date, T allocates GST exemption to the trust in the amount of $50,000. The allocation of GST exemption on the date of the transfer is treated as preceding in point of time the taxable distribution. At the time of the GST, the trust has an inclusion ratio of .6667 (1 - (50,000/150,000)).

Example 5. Automatic allocation to split-gift. On December 1, 2003, T transfers $50,000 to an irrevocable GST Trust described in section 2632(c)(3)(B). The transfer to the trust is not a direct skip. On April 30, 2004, T and T's spouse, S, each files an initial gift tax return for 2003, on which they consent, pursuant to section 2513, to have the gift treated as if one-half had been made by each. In spite of being made on a late-filed gift tax return for 2003, the election under section 2513 is valid because neither spouse had filed a timely gift tax return for that year. Previously, neither T nor S filed a timely gift tax return electing out of the automatic allocation rules contained in section 2632(c)(1). As a result of the election under section 2513, which is retroactive to the date of T's transfer, T and S are each treated as the transferor of one-half of the property transferred in the indirect skip. Thus, $25,000 of T's unused GST exemption and $25,000 of S's unused GST exemption is automatically allocated to the trust. Both allocations are effective on and after the date that T made the transfer. The result would be the same if T's transfer constituted a direct skip subject to the automatic allocation rules contained in section 2632(b).

Example 6. Partial allocation of GST exemption. On December 1, 2003, T transfers $100,000 to an irrevocable GST trust described in section 2632(c)(3)(B). The transfer to the trust is not a direct skip. The date prescribed for filing the gift tax return reporting the taxable gift is April 15, 2004. On February 10, 2004, T files a Form 709 on which T allocates $40,000 of GST exemption to the trust. By filing a timely Form 709 on which a partial allocation is made of $40,000, T effectively elected out of the automatic allocation rules for the remaining value of the transfer for which T did not allocate GST exemption.

(iv) *Example.*—The following example illustrates language that may be used in the statement required under paragraph (b)(2)(iii) of this section to elect out of the automatic allocation rules under various scenarios:

Example 1. On March 1, 2006, T transfers $100,000 to Trust B, a GST trust described in section 2632(c)(3)(B). Subsequently, on September 15, 2006, T transfers an additional $75,000 to Trust B. No other transfers are made to Trust B in 2006. T attaches an election out statement to a timely filed Form 709 for calendar year 2006. Except with regard to paragraph (v) of this *Example 1*, the election out statement identifies Trust B as required under paragraph (b)(2)(iii)(B) of this section, and contains the following alternative election statements:

(i) "T hereby elects that the automatic allocation rules will not apply to the $100,000 transferred to Trust B on March 1, 2006." The election out of the automatic allocation rules will be effective only for T's March 1, 2006, transfer and will not apply to T's $75,000 transfer made on September 15, 2006.

(ii) "T hereby elects that the automatic allocation rules will not apply to any transfers to Trust B in 2006." The election out of the automatic allocation rules will be effective for T's transfers to Trust B made on March 1, 2006, and September 15, 2006.

(iii) "T hereby elects that the automatic allocation rules will not apply to any transfers to Trust B made by T in 2006 or to any additional transfers T may make to Trust B in subsequent years." The election out of the automatic allocation rules will be effective for T's transfers to Trust B in 2006 and for all future transfers to be made by T to Trust B, unless and until T terminates the election out of the automatic allocation rules.

(iv) "T hereby elects that the automatic allocation rules will not apply to any transfers T has made or will make to Trust B in the years 2006 through 2008." The election out of the automatic allocation rules will be effective for T's transfers to Trust B in 2006 through 2008. T's transfers to Trust B after 2008 will be subject to the automatic allocation rules, unless T elects out of those rules for one or more years after 2008. T may terminate the election out of the automatic allocation rules for 2007, 2008, or both in accordance with the termination rules of paragraph (b)(2)(iii)(E) of this section. T may terminate the election out for one or more of the transfers made in 2006 only on a later but still timely filed Form 709 for calendar year 2006.

(v) "T hereby elects that the automatic allocation rules will not apply to any current or future transfer that T may make to any trust." The election out of the automatic allocation rules will be effective for all of T's transfers (current-year and future) to Trust B and to any and all other trusts (whether such trusts exist in 2006 or are created in a later year), unless and until T terminates the election out of the automatic allocation rules. T may terminate the election out with regard to one or more (or all) of the transfers covered by the election out in accordance with the termination rules of paragraph (b)(2)(iii)(E) of this section.

(c) *Special rules during an estate tax inclusion period.*—(1) *In general.*—(i) *Automatic allocations with respect to direct skips and indirect skips.*—A direct skip or an indirect skip that is subject to an estate tax inclusion period (ETIP) is deemed to have been made only at the close of the ETIP. The transferor may prevent the automatic allocation of GST exemption to a direct skip or an indirect skip by electing out of the automatic allocation rules at any time prior to the due date of the Form 709 for the calendar year in which the close of the ETIP occurs (whether or not any transfer was made in the calendar year for which the Form 709 was filed, and whether or not a Form 709 otherwise would be required to be filed for that year). See paragraph (b)(2)(i) of this section regarding the automatic allocation of GST exemption to an indirect skip subject to an ETIP.

(ii) *Other allocations.*—An affirmative allocation of GST exemption cannot be revoked, but becomes effective as of (and no earlier than) the date of the close of the ETIP with respect to the trust. If an allocation has not been made prior to the close of the ETIP, an allocation of exemption is effective as of the close of the ETIP during the transferor's lifetime if made by the due date for filing the Form 709 for the calendar year in which the close of the ETIP occurs (timely ETIP return). An allocation of exemption is effective in the case of the close of the ETIP by reason of the death of the transferor as provided in paragraph (d) of this section.

(iii) *Portion of trust subject to ETIP.*—If any part of a trust is subject to an ETIP, the entire trust is subject to the ETIP. See § 26.2642-1(b)(2) for rules determining the inclusion ratio applicable in the case of GSTs during an ETIP.

(2) *Estate tax inclusion period defined.*—(i) *In general.*—An ETIP is the period during which, should death occur, the value of transferred property would be includible (other than by reason of section 2035) in the gross estate of—

(A) The transferor; or

(B) The spouse of the transferor.

(ii) *Exceptions.*—(A) For purposes of paragraph (c)(2) of this section, the value of transferred property is not considered as being subject to inclusion in the gross estate of the transferor or the spouse of the transferor if the possibility that the property will be included is so remote as to be negligible. A possibility is so remote as to be negligible if it can be ascertained by actuarial standards that there is less than a 5 percent probability that the property will be included in the gross estate.

(B) For purposes of paragraph (c)(2) of this section, the value of transferred property is not considered as being subject to inclusion in the gross estate of the spouse of the transferor, if the spouse possesses with respect to any transfer to the trust, a right to withdraw no more than the greater of $5,000 or 5 percent of the trust corpus, and such withdrawal right terminates no later than 60 days after the transfer to the trust.

(C) The rules of this paragraph (c)(2) do not apply to qualified terminable interest property with respect to which the special election under § 26.2652-2 has been made.

(3) *Termination of an ETIP.*—An ETIP terminates on the first to occur of—

(i) The death of the transferor;

(ii) The time at which no portion of the property is includible in the transferor's gross estate (other than by reason of section 2035) or, in the case of an individual who is a transferor solely by reason of an election under section 2513, the time at which no portion would be includible in the gross estate of the individual's spouse (other than by reason of section 2035);

(iii) The time of a GST, but only with respect to the property involved in the GST; or

(iv) In the case of an ETIP arising by reason of an interest or power held by the transferor's spouse under subsection (c)(2)(i)(B) of this section, at the first to occur of—

(A) The death of the spouse; or

(B) The time at which no portion of the property would be includible in the spouse's gross estate (other than by reason of section 2035).

(4) *Treatment of direct skips.*—If property transferred to a skip person is subject to an ETIP, the direct skip is treated as occurring on the termination of the ETIP.

(5) *Examples.*—The following examples illustrate the rules of this section as they apply to the termination of an ETIP during the lifetime of the transferor. In each example assume that T transfers $100,000 to an irrevocable trust:

Example 1. Allocation of GST exemption during ETIP. The trust instrument provides that trust income is to be paid to T for 9 years or until T's prior death. The trust principal is to be paid to T's grandchild on the termination of T's income interest. If T dies within the 9-year period, the value of the trust principal is includible in T's gross estate under section 2036(a). Thus, the trust is subject to an ETIP. T files a timely Form 709 reporting the transfer and allocating $100,000 of GST exemption to the trust. The allocation of GST exemption to the trust is not effective until the termination of the ETIP.

Example 2. Effect of prior allocation on termination of ETIP. The facts are the same as in *Example 1*, except the trustee has the power to invade trust principal on behalf of T's grandchild, GC, during the term of T's income interest. In year 4, when the value of the trust is $200,000, the trustee distributes $15,000 to GC. The distribution is a taxable distribution. The ETIP with respect to the property distributed to GC terminates at the time of the taxable distribution. See paragraph (c)(3)(iii) of this section. Solely for purposes of determining the trust's inclusion ratio with respect to the taxable distribution, the prior $100,000 allocation of GST exemption (as well as any additional allocation made on a timely ETIP return) is effective immediately prior to the taxable distribution. See §26.2642-1(b)(2). The trust's inclusion ratio with respect to the taxable distribution is therefore .50 (1-(100,000/200,000)).

Example 3. Split-gift transfers subject to ETIP. The trust instrument provides that trust income is to be paid to T for 9 years or until T's prior death. The trust principal is to be paid to T's grandchild on the termination of T's income interest. T files a timely Form 709 reporting the transfer. T's spouse, S, consents to have the gift treated as made one-half by S under section 2513. Because S is treated as transferring one-half of the property to T's grandchild, S becomes the transferor of one-half of the trust for purposes of chapter 13. Because the value of the trust would be includible in T's gross estate if T died immediately after the transfer, S's transfer is subject to an ETIP. If S should die prior to the termination of the trust, S's executor may allocate S's GST exemption to the trust, but only to the portion of the trust for which S is treated as the transferor. However, the allocation does not become effective until the earlier of the expiration of T's income interest or T's death.

Example 4. Transfer of retained interest as ETIP termination. The trust instrument provides that trust income is to be paid to T for 9 years or until T's prior death. The trust principal is to be paid to T's grandchild on the termination of T's income interest. Four years after the initial transfer, T transfers the income interest to T's sibling. The ETIP with respect to the trust terminates on T's transfer of the income interest because, after the transfer, the trust property would not be includible in T's gross estate (other than by reason of section 2035) if T died at that time.

Example 5. Election out of automatic allocation of GST exemption for trust subject to an ETIP. On December 1, 2003, T transfers $100,000 to Trust A, an irrevocable GST trust described in section 2632(c)(3) that is subject to an estate tax inclusion period (ETIP). T made no other gifts in 2003. The ETIP terminates on December 31, 2008. T timely files a gift tax return (Form 709) reporting the gift on April 15, 2004. On May 15, 2006, T files a Form 709 on which T properly elects out of the automatic allocation rules contained in section 2632(c)(1) with respect to the December 1, 2003, transfer to Trust A in accordance with paragraph (b)(2)(iii) of this section. Because the indirect skip is not deemed to occur until December 31, 2008, T's election out of automatic GST allocation filed on May 15, 2006, is timely, and will be effective as of December 31, 2008 (unless revoked on a Form 709 filed on or before the date a Form 709 for calendar year 2008).

(d) *Allocations after the transferor's death.*— (1) *Allocation by executor.*—Except as otherwise provided in this paragraph (d), an allocation of a decedent's unused GST exemption by the executor of the decedent's estate is made on the appropriate United States Estate (and Generation-Skipping Transfer) Tax Return (Form 706 or Form 706NA) filed on or before the date prescribed for filing the return by section 6075(a) (including any extensions actually granted (the due date)). An allocation of GST exemption with respect to property included in the gross estate of a decedent is effective as of the date of death. A timely allocation of GST exemption by an executor with respect to a lifetime transfer of property that is not included in the transferor's gross estate is made on a Form 709. A late allocation of GST exemption by an executor, other than an allocation that is deemed to be made under section 2632(b)(1) or (c)(1), with respect to a lifetime transfer of property is made on Form 706, Form 706NA, or Form 709 (filed on or before the due date of the transferor's estate tax return) and applies as of the date the allocation is filed. An allocation of GST exemption to a trust (whether or not funded at the time the Form 706 or Form 706NA is filed) is effective if the notice of allocation clearly identifies the trust and the amount of the decedent's GST exemption allocated to the trust. An executor may allocate the decedent's GST exemption by use of a formula. For purposes of this section, an allocation is void if the allocation is made for a trust that has no GST potential with respect to the transferor for whom the allocation is being made, as of the date of the transferor's death. For this purpose, a trust has GST potential even if the possibility of a GST is so remote as to be negligible.

(2) *Automatic allocation after death.*—A decedent's unused GST exemption is automatically allocated on the due date for filing Form 706 or

Form 706NA to the extent not otherwise allocated by the decedent's executor on or before that date. The automatic allocation occurs whether or not a return is actually required to be filed. Unused GST exemption is allocated pro rata (subject to the rules of § 26.2642-2(b)), on the basis of the value of the property as finally determined for purposes of chapter 11 (chapter 11 value), first to direct skips treated as occurring at the transferor's death. The balance, if any, of unused GST exemption is allocated pro rata (subject to the rules of § 26.2642-2(b)) on the basis of the chapter 11 value of the nonexempt portion of the trust property (or in the case of trusts that are not included in the gross estate, on the basis of the date of death value of the trust) to trusts with respect to which a taxable termination may occur or from which a taxable distribution may be made. The automatic allocation of GST exemption is irrevocable, and an allocation made by the executor after the automatic allocation is made is ineffective. No automatic allocation of GST exemption is made to a trust that will have a new transferor with respect to the entire trust prior to the occurrence of any GST with respect to the trust. In addition, no automatic allocation of GST exemption is made to a trust if, during the nine month period ending immediately after the death of the transferor—

(i) No GST has occurred with respect to the trust; and

(ii) At the end of such period no future GST can occur with respect to the trust.

(e) *Effective dates.*—This section is applicable as provided in § 26.2601-1(c), with the following exceptions:

(1) Paragraphs (b)(2) and (b)(3), the third sentence of paragraph (b)(4)(i), the fourth sentence of paragraph (b)(4)(ii)(A)(1), paragraphs (b)(4)(iii) and (b)(4)(iv), and the fourth sentence of paragraph (d)(1) of this section, which will apply to elections made on or after July 13, 2004; and

(2) Paragraph (c)(1), and *Example 5* of paragraph (c)(5), which will apply to elections made on or after June 29, 2005. [Reg. § 26.2632-1.]

☐ [*T.D.* 8644, 12-26-95. *Amended by T.D.* 9208, 6-28-2005.]

[Reg. § 26.2641-1]

§ 26.2641-1. Applicable rate of tax.—The rate of tax applicable to any GST (applicable rate) is determined by multiplying the maximum Federal estate tax rate in effect at the time of the GST by the inclusion ratio (as defined in § 26.2642-1). For this purpose, the maximum Federal estate tax rate is the maximum rate set forth under section 2001(c) (without regard to section 2001(c)(2)). [Reg. § 26.2641-1.]

☐ [*T.D.* 8644, 12-26-95.]

[Reg. § 26.2642-1]

§ 26.2642-1. Inclusion ratio.—(a) *In general.*—Except as otherwise provided in this section, the inclusion ratio is determined by subtracting the applicable fraction (rounded to the nearest one-thousandth (.001)) from 1. In rounding the applicable fraction to the nearest one-thousandth, any amount that is midway between one one-thousandth and another one-thousandth is rounded up to the higher of those two amounts.

(b) *Numerator of applicable fraction.*—(1) *In general.*—Except as otherwise provided in this paragraph (b), and in § § 26.2642-3 (providing a special rule for charitable lead annuity trusts) and 26.2642-4 (providing rules for the redetermination of the applicable fraction), the numerator of the applicable fraction is the amount of GST exemption allocated to the trust (or to the transferred property in the case of a direct skip not in trust).

(2) *GSTs occurring during an ETIP.*—(i) *In general.*—For purposes of determining the inclusion ratio with respect to a taxable termination or a taxable distribution that occurs during an ETIP, the numerator of the applicable fraction is the sum of—

(A) The GST exemption previously allocated to the trust (including any allocation made to the trust prior to any taxable termination or distribution) reduced (but not below zero) by the nontax amount of any prior GSTs with respect to the trust; and

(B) Any GST exemption allocated to the trust on a timely ETIP return filed after the termination of the ETIP. See § 26.2632-1(c)(5) *Example 2.*

(ii) *Nontax amount of a prior GST.*—(1) The nontax amount of a prior GST with respect to the trust is the amount of the GST multiplied by the applicable fraction attributable to the trust at the time of the prior GST.

(2) For rules regarding the allocation of GST exemption to property during an ETIP, see § 26.2632-1(c).

(c) *Denominator of applicable fraction.*—(1) *In general.*—Except as otherwise provided in this paragraph (c) and in § § 26.2642-3 and 26.2642-4, the denominator of the applicable fraction is the value of the property transferred to the trust (or transferred in a direct skip not in trust) (as determined under § 26.2642-2) reduced by the sum of—

(i) Any Federal estate tax and any State death tax incurred by reason of the transfer that is chargeable to the trust and is actually recovered from the trust;

(ii) The amount of any charitable deduction allowed under section 2055, 2106, or 2522 with respect to the transfer; and

(iii) In the case of a direct skip, the value of the portion of the transfer that is a nontaxable gift. See paragraph (c)(3) of this section for the definition of nontaxable gift.

(2) *Zero denominator.*—If the denominator of the applicable fraction is zero, the inclusion ratio is zero.

(3) *Nontaxable gifts.*—Generally, for purposes of chapter 13, a transfer is a nontaxable gift to the extent the transfer is excluded from taxable gifts by reason of section 2503(b) (after application of section 2513) or section 2503(e). However, a transfer to a trust for the benefit of an individual is not a nontaxable gift for purposes of this section unless—

(i) Trust principal or income may, during the individual's lifetime, be distributed only to or for the benefit of the individual; and

(ii) The assets of the trust will be includible in the gross estate of the individual if the individual dies before the trust terminates.

(d) *Examples.*—The following examples illustrate the provisions of this section. See §26.2652-2(d) *Examples* 2 and 3 for illustrations of the computation of the inclusion ratio where the special (reverse QTIP) election may be applicable.

Example 1. Computation of the inclusion ratio. T transfers $100,000 to a newly-created irrevocable trust providing that income is to be accumulated for 10 years. At the end of 10 years, the accumulated income is to be distributed to T's child, C, and the trust principal is to be paid to T's grandchild. T allocates $40,000 of T's GST exemption to the trust on a timely-filed gift tax return. The applicable fraction with respect to the trust is .40 ($40,000 (the amount of GST exemption allocated to the trust) over $100,000 (the value of the property transferred to the trust)). The inclusion ratio is .60 (1 − .40). If the maximum Federal estate tax rate is 55 percent at the time of a GST, the rate of tax applicable to the transfer (applicable rate) will be .333 (55 percent (the maximum estate tax rate) x .60 (the inclusion ratio)).

Example 2. Gift entirely nontaxable. On December 1, 1996, T transfers $10,000 to an irrevocable trust for the benefit of T's grandchild, GC. GC possesses a right to withdraw any contributions to the trust such that the entire transfer qualifies for the annual exclusion under section 2503(b). Under the terms of the trust, the income is to be paid to GC for 10 years or until GC's prior death. Upon the expiration of GC's income interest, the trust principal is payable to GC or GC's estate. The transfer to the trust is a direct skip. T made no prior gifts to or for the benefit of GC during 1996. The entire $10,000 transfer is a nontaxable transfer. For purposes of computing the tax on the direct skip, the denominator of the applicable fraction is zero, and thus, the inclusion ratio is zero.

Example 3. Gift nontaxable in part. T transfers $12,000 to an irrevocable trust for the benefit of T's grandchild, GC. Under the terms of the trust, the income is to be paid to GC for 10 years or until GC's prior death. Upon the expiration of GC's income interest, the trust principal is payable to GC or GC's estate. Further, GC has the right to withdraw $10,000 of any contribution to the trust such that $10,000 of the transfer qualifies for the annual exclusion under section 2503(b). The amount of the nontaxable transfer is $10,000. Solely for purposes of computing the tax on the direct skip, T's transfer is divided into two portions. One portion is equal to the amount of the nontaxable transfer ($10,000) and has a zero inclusion ratio; the other portion is $2,000 ($12,000 - $10,000). With respect to the $2,000 portion, the denominator of the applicable fraction is $2,000. Assuming that T has sufficient GST exemption available, the numerator of the applicable fraction is $2,000 (unless T elects to have the automatic allocation provisions not apply). Thus, assuming T does not elect to have the automatic allocation not apply, the applicable fraction is one ($2,000/$2,000 = 1) and the inclusion ratio is zero (1 - 1 = 0).

Example 4. Gift nontaxable in part. Assume the same facts as in *Example 3*, except T files a timely Form 709 electing that the automatic allocation of GST exemption not apply to the $12,000 transferred in the direct skip. T's transfer is divided into two portions, a $10,000 portion with a zero inclusion ratio and a $2,000 portion with an applicable fraction of zero (0/$2,000 = 0) and an inclusion ratio of one (1 - 0 = 1). [Reg. §26.2642-1.]

☐ [*T.D.* 8644, 12-26-95.]

[Reg. §26.2642-2]

§26.2642-2. Valuation.—(a) *Lifetime transfers.*—(1) *In general.*—For purposes of determining the denominator of the applicable fraction, the value of property transferred during life is its fair market value on the effective date of the allocation of GST exemption. In the case of a timely allocation under §26.2632-1(b)(2)(ii), the denominator of the applicable fraction is the fair market value of the property as finally determined for purposes of chapter 12.

(2) *Special rule for late allocations during life.*— If a transferor makes a late allocation of GST exemption to a trust, the value of the property transferred to the trust is the fair market value of the trust assets determined on the effective date of the allocation of GST exemption. Except as otherwise provided in this paragraph (a)(2), if a transferor makes a late allocation of GST exemption to a trust, the transferor may, solely for purposes of determining the fair market value of the trust assets, elect to treat the allocation as having been made on the first day of the month during which the late allocation is made (valuation date). An election under this paragraph

(a)(2) is not effective with respect to a life insurance policy or a trust holding a life insurance policy, if the insured individual has died. An allocation subject to the election contained in this paragraph (a)(2) is not effective until it is actually filed with the Internal Revenue Service. The election is made by stating on the Form 709 on which the allocation is made—

(i) That the election is being made;

(ii) The applicable valuation date; and

(iii) The fair market value of the trust assets on the valuation date.

(b) *Transfers at death.*—(1) *In general.*—Except as provided in paragraphs (b)(2) and (3) of this section, in determining the denominator of the applicable fraction, the value of property included in the decedent's gross estate is its value for purposes of chapter 11. In the case of qualified real property with respect to which the election under section 2032A is made, the value of the property is the value determined under section 2032A provided the recapture agreement described in section 2032A(d)(2) filed with the Internal Revenue Service specifically provides for the signatories' consent to the imposition of, and personal liability for, additional GST tax in the event an additional estate tax is imposed under section 2032A(c). See § 26.2642-4(a)(4). If the recapture agreement does not contain these provisions, the value of qualified real property as to which the election under section 2032A is made is the fair market value of the property determined without regard to the provisions of section 2032A.

(2) *Special rule for pecuniary payments.*—(i) *In general.*—If a pecuniary payment is satisfied with cash, the denominator of the applicable fraction is the pecuniary amount. If property other than cash is used to satisfy a pecuniary payment, the denominator of the applicable fraction is the pecuniary amount only if payment must be made with property on the basis of the value of the property on—

(A) The date of distribution; or

(B) A date other than the date of distribution, but only if the pecuniary payment must be satisfied on a basis that fairly reflects net appreciation and depreciation (occurring between the valuation date and the date of distribution) in all of the assets from which the distribution could have been made.

(ii) *Other pecuniary amounts payable in kind.*—The denominator of the applicable fraction with respect to any property used to satisfy any other pecuniary payment payable in kind is the date of distribution value of the property.

(3) *Special rule for residual transfers after payment of a pecuniary payment.*—(i) *In general.*—Except as otherwise provided in this paragraph (b)(3), the denominator of the applicable fraction with respect to a residual transfer of property

after the satisfaction of a pecuniary payment is the estate tax value of the assets available to satisfy the pecuniary payment reduced, if the pecuniary payment carries appropriate interest (as defined in paragraph (b)(4) of this section), by the pecuniary amount. The denominator of the applicable fraction with respect to a residual transfer of property after the satisfaction of a pecuniary payment that does not carry appropriate interest is the estate tax value of the assets available to satisfy the pecuniary payment reduced by the present value of the pecuniary payment. For purposes of this paragraph (b)(3)(i), the present value of the pecuniary payment is determined by using—

(A) The interest rate applicable under section 7520 at the death of the transferor; and

(B) The period between the date of the transferor's death and the date the pecuniary amount is paid.

(ii) *Special rule for residual transfers after pecuniary payments payable in kind.*—The denominator of the applicable fraction with respect to any residual transfer after satisfaction of a pecuniary payment payable in kind is the date of distribution value of the property distributed in satisfaction of the residual transfer, unless the pecuniary payment must be satisfied on the basis of the value of the property on—

(A) The date of distribution; or

(B) A date other than the date of distribution, but only if the pecuniary payment must be satisfied on a basis that fairly reflects net appreciation and depreciation (occurring between the valuation date and the date of distribution) in all of the assets from which the distribution could have been made.

(4) *Appropriate interest.*—(i) *In general.*—For purposes of this section and § 26.2654-1 (relating to certain trusts treated as separate trusts), appropriate interest means that interest must be payable from the date of death of the transferor (or from the date specified under applicable State law requiring the payment of interest) to the date of payment at a rate—

(A) At least equal to—

(1) The statutory rate of interest, if any, applicable to pecuniary bequests under the law of the State whose law governs the administration of the estate or trust;

(2) If no such rate is indicated under applicable State law, 80 percent of the rate that is applicable under section 7520 at the death of the transferor; and

(B) Not in excess of the greater of—

(1) The statutory rate of interest, if any, applicable to pecuniary bequests under the law of the State whose law governs the administration of the trust; or

(2) 120 percent of the rate that is applicable under section 7520 at the death of the transferor.

(ii) *Pecuniary payments deemed to carry appropriate interest.*—For purposes of this paragraph (b)(4), if a pecuniary payment does not carry appropriate interest, the pecuniary payment is considered to carry appropriate interest to the extent—

(A) The entire payment is made or property is irrevocably set aside to satisfy the entire pecuniary payment within 15 months of the transferor's death; or

(B) The governing instrument or applicable local law specifically requires the executor or trustee to allocate to the pecuniary payment a pro rata share of the income earned by the fund from which the pecuniary payment is to be made between the date of death of the transferor and the date of payment. For purposes of paragraph (b)(4)(ii)(A) of this section, property is irrevocably set aside if it is segregated and held in a separate account pending distribution.

(c) *Examples.*—The following examples illustrate the provisions of this section:

Example 1. T transfers $100,000 to a newly-created irrevocable trust on December 15, 1996. The trust provides that income is to be paid to T's child for 10 years. At the end of the 10-year period, the trust principal is to be paid to T's grandchild. T does not allocate any GST exemption to the trust on the gift tax return reporting the transfer. On November 15, 1997, T files a Form 709 allocating $50,000 of GST exemption to the trust. Because the allocation was made on a late filed return, the value of the property transferred to the trust is determined on the date the allocation is filed (unless an election is made pursuant to paragraph (a)(2) of this section to value the trust property as of the first day of the month in which the allocation document is filed with the Internal Revenue Service). On November 15, 1997, the value of the trust property is $150,000. Effective as of November 15, 1997, the applicable fraction with respect to the trust is .333 ($50,000 (the amount of GST exemption allocated to the trust) over $150,000 (the value of the trust principal on the effective date of the GST exemption allocation)), and the inclusion ratio is .667 (1.0 - .333).

Example 2. The facts are the same as in *Example 1,* except the value of the trust property is $80,000 on November 15, 1997. The applicable fraction is .625 ($50,000 over $80,000) and the inclusion ratio is .375 (1.0 - .625).

Example 3. T transfers $100,000 to a newly-created irrevocable trust on December 15, 1996. The trust provides that income is to be paid to T's child for 10 years. At the end of the 10-year period, the trust principal is to be paid to T's grandchild. T does not allocate any GST exemption to the trust on the gift tax return reporting the transfer. On November 15, 1997, T files a Form 709 allocating $50,000 of GST exemption to the trust. T elects to value the trust principal on the first day of the month in which the allocation

is made pursuant to the election provided in paragraph (a)(2) of this section. Because the late allocation is made in November, the value of the trust is determined as of November 1, 1997. [Reg. § 26.2642-2.]

☐ [*T.D.* 8644, 12-26-95.]

[Reg. § 26.2642-3]

§ 26.2642-3. Special rule for charitable lead annuity trusts.—(a) *In general.*—In determining the applicable fraction with respect to a charitable lead annuity trust—

(1) The numerator is the adjusted generation-skipping transfer tax exemption (adjusted GST exemption); and

(2) The denominator is the value of all property in the trust immediately after the termination of the charitable lead annuity.

(b) *Adjusted GST exemption defined.*—The adjusted GST exemption is the amount of GST exemption allocated to the trust increased by an amount equal to the interest that would accrue if an amount equal to the allocated GST exemption were invested at the rate used to determine the amount of the estate or gift tax charitable deduction, compounded annually, for the actual period of the charitable lead annuity. If a late allocation is made to a charitable lead annuity trust, the adjusted GST exemption is the amount of GST exemption allocated to the trust increased by the interest that would accrue if invested at such rate for the period beginning on the date of the late allocation and extending for the balance of the actual period of the charitable lead annuity. The amount of GST exemption allocated to a charitable lead annuity trust is not reduced even though it is ultimately determined that the allocation of a lesser amount of GST exemption would have resulted in an inclusion ratio of zero. For purposes of chapter 13, a charitable lead annuity trust is any trust providing an interest in the form of a guaranteed annuity described in § 25.2522(c)-3(c)(2)(vi) of this chapter for which the transferor is allowed a charitable deduction for Federal estate or gift tax purposes.

(c) *Example.*—The following example illustrates the provisions of this section:

Example. T creates a charitable lead annuity trust for a 10-year term with the remainder payable to T's grandchild. T timely allocates an amount of GST exemption to the trust which T expects will ultimately result in a zero inclusion ratio. However, at the end of the charitable lead interest, because the property has not appreciated to the extent T anticipated, the numerator of the applicable fraction is greater than the denominator. The inclusion ratio for the trust is zero. No portion of the GST exemption allocated to the trust is restored to T or to T's estate. [Reg. § 26.2642-3.]

☐ [*T.D.* 8644, 12-26-95.]

[Reg. §26.2642-4]

§26.2642-4. Redetermination of applicable fraction.—(a) *In general.*—The applicable fraction for a trust is redetermined whenever additional exemption is allocated to the trust or when certain changes occur with respect to the principal of the trust. Except as otherwise provided in this paragraph(a), the numerator of the redetermined applicable fraction is the sum of the amount of GST exemption currently being allocated to the trust (if any) plus the value of the nontax portion of the trust, and the denominator of the redetermined applicable fraction is the value of the trust principal immediately after the event occurs. The nontax portion of a trust is determined by multiplying the value of the trust assets, determined immediately prior to the event, by the then applicable fraction.

(1) *Multiple transfers to a single trust.*—If property is added to an existing trust, the denominator of the redetermined applicable fraction is the value of the trust immediately after the addition reduced as provided in §26.2642-1(c).

(2) *Consolidation of separate trusts.*—If separate trusts created by one transferor are consolidated, a single applicable fraction for the consolidated trust is determined. The numerator of the redetermined applicable fraction is the sum of the nontax portions of each trust immediately prior to the consolidation.

(3) *Property included in transferor's gross estate.*—If the value of property held in a trust created by the transferor, with respect to which an allocation was made at a time that the trust was not subject to an ETIP, is included in the transferor's gross estate, the applicable fraction is redetermined if additional GST exemption is allocated to the property. The numerator of the redetermined applicable fraction is an amount equal to the nontax portion of the property immediately after the death of the transferor increased by the amount of GST exemption allocated by the executor of the transferor's estate to the trust. If additional GST exemption is not allocated to the trust, then, except as provided in this paragraph (a)(3), the applicable fraction immediately before death is not changed, if the trust was not subject to an ETIP at the time GST exemption was allocated to the trust. In any event, the denominator of the applicable fraction is reduced to reflect any federal or state, estate or inheritance taxes paid from the trust.

(4) *Imposition of recapture tax under section 2032A.*—(i) If an additional estate tax is imposed under section 2032A and if the section 2032A election was effective (under §26.2642-2(b)) for purposes of the GST tax, the applicable fraction with respect to the property is redetermined as of the date of death of the transferor. In making the redetermination, any available GST exemption not allocated at the death of the transferor (or at a prior recapture event) is automatically allocated to the property. The denominator of the applicable fraction is the fair market value of the property at the date of the transferor's death reduced as provided in §26.2642-1(c) and further reduced by the amount of the additional GST tax actually recovered from the trust.

(ii) The GST tax imposed with respect to any taxable termination, taxable distribution, or direct skip occurring prior to the recapture event is recomputed based on the applicable fraction as redetermined. Any additional GST tax as recomputed is due and payable on the date that is six months after the event that causes the imposition of the additional estate tax under section 2032A. The additional GST tax is remitted with Form 706-A and is reported by attaching a statement to Form 706-A showing the computation of the additional GST tax.

(iii) The applicable fraction, as redetermined under this section, is also used in determining any GST tax imposed with respect to GSTs occurring after the date of the recapture event.

(b) *Examples.*—The following examples illustrate the principles of this section:

Example 1. Allocation of additional exemption. T transfers $200,000 to an irrevocable trust which the income is payable to T's child, C, for life. Upon the termination of the trust, the remainder is payable to T's grandchild, GC. At a time when no ETIP exists with respect to the trust property, T makes a timely allocation of $100,000 of GST exemption, resulting in an inclusion ratio of .50. Subsequently, when the entire trust property is valued at $500,000, T allocates an additional $100,000 of T's unused GST exemption to the trust. The inclusion ratio of the trust is recomputed at that time. The numerator of the applicable fraction is $350,000 ($250,000 (the nontax portion as of the date of the allocation) plus $100,000 (the GST exemption currently being allocated)). The denominator is $500,000 (the date of allocation fair market value of the trust). The inclusion ratio is .30 (1 - .70).

Example 2. Multiple transfers to a trust, allocation both timely and late. On December 10, 1993, T transfers $10,000 to an irrevocable trust that does not satisfy the requirements of section 2642(c)(2). T makes identical transfers to the trust on December 10, 1994, 1995, 1996, and on January 15, 1997. Immediately after the transfer on January 15, 1997, the value of the trust principal is $40,000. On January 14, 1998, when the value of the trust principal is $50,000, T allocates $30,000 of GST exemption to the trust. T discloses the 1997 transfer on the Form 709 filed on January 14, 1998. Thus, T's allocation is a timely allocation with respect to the transfer in 1997, $10,000 of the allocation is effective as of the date of that transfer, and, on and after January 15, 1997, the inclusion ratio of the trust is .75 (1 – ($10,000/$40,000)). The balance of the allocation is a late allocation with respect to prior transfers to the trust and is effective as of January 14, 1998. In redetermining the inclusion ratio as of that date, the numerator of the redetermined applicable fraction is $32,500 ($12,500 (.25 x $50,000), the nontax portion of the trust on January 14, 1998) plus $20,000 (the amount of GST exemption allocated late to the trust). The denominator of the new applicable fraction is $50,000 (the value of the trust principal at the time of the late allocation).

Example 3. Excess allocation. (i) T creates an irrevocable trust for the benefit of T's child and grandchild in 1996 transferring $50,000 to the trust on the date of creation. T allocates no GST exemption to the trust on the Form 709 reporting the transfer. On July 1, 1997 (when the value of the trust property is $60,000), T transfers an additional $40,000 to the trust.

(ii) On April 15, 1998, when the value of the trust is $150,000, T files a Form 709 reporting the 1997 transfer and allocating $150,000 of GST exemption to the trust. The allocation is a timely allocation of $40,000 with respect to the 1997 transfer and is effective as of that date. Thus, the applicable fraction for the trust as of July 1, 1997 is .40 ($40,000/$100,000 ($40,000 + $60,000)).

(iii) The allocation is also a late allocation of $90,000, the amount necessary to attain a zero inclusion ratio on April 15, 1998, computed as follows: $60,000 (the nontax portion immediately prior to the allocation (.40 X $150,000)) plus $90,000 (the additional allocation necessary to produce a zero inclusion ratio based on a denominator of $150,000)/$150,000 equals one and, thus, an inclusion ratio of zero. The balance of the allocation, $20,000 ($150,000 less the timely allocation of $40,000 less the late allocation of $90,000) is void.

Example 4. Undisclosed transfer. (i) The facts are the same as in *Example 3*, except that on February 1, 1998 (when the value of the trust is $150,000), T transfers an additional $50,000 to the trust and the value of the entire trust corpus on April 15, 1998 is $220,000. The Form 709 filed on April 15, 1998 does not disclose the 1998 transfer. Under the rule in § 26.2632-1(b)(2)(ii), the allocation is effective first as a timely allocation to the 1997 transfer; second, as a late allocation to the trust as of April 15, 1998; and, finally as a timely allocation to the February 1, 1998 transfer. As of April 15, 1998, $55,000, a pro rata portion of the trust assets, is considered to be the property transferred to the trust on February 1, 1998 (($50,000/$200,000) X $220,000). The balance of the trust, $165,000, represents prior transfers to the trust.

(ii) As in *Example 3*, the allocation is a timely allocation as to the 1997 transfer (and the applicable fraction as of July 1, 1997 is .40) and a late

allocation as of 1998. The amount of the late allocation is $99,000, computed as follows: (.40 X $165,000 plus $99,000)/$165,000 = one.

(iii) The balance of the allocation, $11,000 ($150,000 less the timely allocation of $40,000 less the late allocation of $99,000) is a timely allocation as of February 1, 1998. The applicable fraction with respect to the trust, as of February 1, 1998, is .355, computed as follows: $60,000 (the nontax portion of the trust immediately prior to the February 1, 1998 transfer (.40 X $150,000)) plus $11,000 (the amount of the timely allocation to the 1998 transfer)/$200,000 (the value of the trust on February 1, 1998, after the transfer on that date) = $71,000/$200,000 = .355.

(iv) The applicable fraction with respect to the trust, as of April 15, 1998, is .805 computed as follows: $78,100 (the nontax portion immediately prior to the allocation (.355 X $220,000)) plus $99,000 (the amount of the late allocation)/$220,000 = $177,100/$220,000 = .805.

Example 5. Redetermination of inclusion ratio on ETIP termination. (i) T transfers $100,000 to an irrevocable trust. The trust instrument provides that trust income is to be paid to T for 9 years or until T's prior death. The trust principal is to be paid to T's grandchild, GC, on the termination of T's income interest. The trustee has the power to invade trust principal for the benefit of GC during the term of T's income interest. The trust is subject to an ETIP while T holds the retained income interest. T files a timely Form 709 reporting the transfer and allocates $100,000 of GST exemption to the trust. In year 4, when the value of the trust is $200,000, the trustee distributes $15,000 to GC. The distribution is a taxable distribution. Because of the existence of the ETIP, the inclusion ratio with respect to the taxable distribution is determined immediately prior to the occurrence of the GST. Thus, the inclusion ratio applicable to the year 4 GST is .50 (1 – ($100,000/$200,000)).

(ii) In year 5, when the value of the trust is again $200,000, the trustee distributes another $15,000 to GC. Because the trust is still subject to the ETIP in year 5, the inclusion ratio with respect to the year 5 GST is again computed immediately prior to the GST. In computing the new inclusion ratio, the numerator of the applicable fraction is reduced by the nontax portion of prior GSTs occurring during the ETIP. Thus, the numerator of the applicable fraction with respect to the GST in year 5 is $92,500 ($100,000 – (.50 X $15,000)) and the inclusion ratio applicable with respect to the GST in year 5 is .537 (1 – ($92,500/$200,000) = .463). Any additional GST exemption allocated on a timely ETIP return with respect to the GST in year 5 is effective immediately prior to the transfer. [Reg. § 26.2642-4.]

☐ [*T.D.* 8644, 12-26-95.]

[Reg. §26.2642-5]

§26.2642-5. Finality of inclusion ratio.—
(a) *Direct skips.*—The inclusion ratio applicable to a direct skip becomes final when no additional GST tax (including additional GST tax payable as a result of a cessation, etc. of qualified use under section 2032A(c)) may be assessed with respect to the direct skip.

(b) *Other GSTs.*—With respect to taxable distributions and taxable terminations, the inclusion ratio for a trust becomes final, on the later of—

(1) The expiration of the period for assessment with respect to the first GST tax return filed using that inclusion ratio (unless the trust is subject to an election under section 2032A in which case the applicable date under this subsection is the expiration of the period of assessment of any additional GST tax due as a result of a cessation, etc. of qualified use under section 2032A); or

(2) The expiration of the period for assessment of Federal estate tax with respect to the estate of the transferor. For purposes of this paragraph (b)(2), if an estate tax return is not required to be filed, the period for assessment is determined as if a return were required to be filed and as if the return were timely filed within the period prescribed by section 6075(a). [Reg. §26.2642-5.]

☐ [T.D. 8644, 12-26-95.]

[Reg. §26.2642-6]

§26.2642-6. Qualified severance.—(a) *In general.*—If a trust is divided in a qualified severance into two or more trusts, the separate trusts resulting from the severance will be treated as separate trusts for generation-skipping transfer (GST) tax purposes and the inclusion ratio of each new resulting trust may differ from the inclusion ratio of the original trust. Because the post-severance resulting trusts are treated as separate trusts for GST tax purposes, certain actions with respect to one resulting trust will generally have no GST tax impact with respect to the other resulting trust(s). For example, GST exemption allocated to one resulting trust will not impact on the inclusion ratio of the other resulting trust(s); a GST tax election made with respect to one resulting trust will not apply to the other resulting trust(s); the occurrence of a taxable distribution or termination with regard to a particular resulting trust will not have any GST tax impact on any other trust resulting from that severance. In general, the rules in this section are applicable only for purposes of the GST tax and are not applicable in determining, for example, whether the resulting trusts may file separate income tax returns or whether the severance may result in a gift subject to gift tax, may cause any trust to be included in the gross estate of a beneficiary, or may result in a realization of gain for purposes of section 1001. See §1.1001-1(h) of this chapter for rules relating to whether a qualified severance will constitute an exchange of property for other property differing materially either in kind or in extent.

(b) *Qualified severance defined.*—A qualified severance is a division of a trust (other than a division described in §26.2654-1(b)) into two or more separate trusts that meets each of the requirements in paragraph (d) of this section.

(c) *Effective date of qualified severance.*—A qualified severance is applicable as of the date of the severance, as defined in §26.2642-6(d)(3), and the resulting trusts are treated as separate trusts for GST tax purposes as of that date.

(d) *Requirements for a qualified severance.*—For purposes of this section, a qualified severance must satisfy each of the following requirements:

(1) The single trust is severed pursuant to the terms of the governing instrument, or pursuant to applicable local law.

(2) The severance is effective under local law.

(3) The date of severance is either the date selected by the trustee as of which the trust assets are to be valued in order to determine the funding of the resulting trusts, or the court-imposed date of funding in the case of an order of the local court with jurisdiction over the trust ordering the trustee to fund the resulting trusts on or as of a specific date. For a date to satisfy the definition in the preceding sentence, however, the funding must be commenced immediately upon, and funding must occur within a reasonable time (but in no event more than 90 days) after, the selected valuation date.

(4) The single trust (original trust) is severed on a fractional basis, such that each new trust (resulting trust) is funded with a fraction or percentage of the original trust, and the sum of those fractions or percentages is one or one hundred percent, respectively. For this purpose, the fraction or percentage may be determined by means of a formula (for example, that fraction of the trust the numerator of which is equal to the transferor's unused GST tax exemption, and the denominator of which is the fair market value of the original trust's assets on the date of severance). The severance of a trust based on a pecuniary amount does not satisfy this requirement. For example, the severance of a trust is not a qualified severance if the trust is divided into two trusts, with one trust to be funded with $1,500,000 and the other trust to be funded with the balance of the original trust's assets. With respect to the particular assets to be distributed to each separate trust resulting from the severance, each such trust may be funded with the appropriate fraction or percentage (pro rata portion) of each asset held by the original trust. Alternatively, the assets may be divided among the resulting trusts on a non-pro rata basis, based on the fair market value of the assets on the date

of severance. However, if a resulting trust is funded on a non-pro rata basis, each asset received by a resulting trust must be valued, solely for funding purposes, by multiplying the fair market value of the asset held in the original trust as of the date of severance by the fraction or percentage of that asset received by that resulting trust. Thus, the assets must be valued without taking into account any discount or premium arising from the severance, for example, any valuation discounts that might arise because the resulting trust receives less than the entire interest held by the original trust. See paragraph (j), *Example 6* of this section.

(5) The terms of the resulting trusts must provide, in the aggregate, for the same succession of interests of beneficiaries as are provided in the original trust. This requirement is satisfied if the beneficiaries of the separate resulting trusts and the interests of the beneficiaries with respect to the separate trusts, when the separate trusts are viewed collectively, are the same as the beneficiaries and their respective beneficial interests with respect to the original trust before severance. With respect to trusts from which discretionary distributions may be made to any one or more beneficiaries on a non-pro rata basis, this requirement is satisfied if—

(i) The terms of each of the resulting trusts are the same as the terms of the original trust (even though each permissible distributee of the original trust is not a beneficiary of all of the resulting trusts);

(ii) Each beneficiary's interest in the resulting trusts (collectively) equals the beneficiary's interest in the original trust, determined by the terms of the trust instrument or, if none, on a per-capita basis. For example, in the case of the severance of a discretionary trust established for the benefit of A, B, and C and their descendants with the remainder to be divided equally among those three families, this requirement is satisfied if the trust is divided into three separate trusts of equal value with one trust established for the benefit of A and A's descendants, one trust for the benefit of B and B's descendants, and one trust for the benefit of C and C's descendants;

(iii) The severance does not shift a beneficial interest in the trust to any beneficiary in a lower generation (as determined under section 2651) than the person or persons who held the beneficial interest in the original trust; and

(iv) The severance does not extend the time for the vesting of any beneficial interest in the trust beyond the period provided for in (or applicable to) the original trust.

(6) In the case of a qualified severance of a trust with an inclusion ratio as defined in § 26.2642-1 of either one or zero, each trust resulting from the severance will have an inclusion ratio equal to the inclusion ratio of the original trust.

(7)(i) In the case of a qualified severance occurring after GST tax exemption has been allo-

cated to the trust (whether by an affirmative allocation, a deemed allocation, or an automatic allocation pursuant to the rules contained in section 2632), if the trust has an inclusion ratio as defined in § 26.2642-1 that is greater than zero and less than one, then either paragraph (d)(7)(ii) or (iii) of this section must be satisfied.

(ii) The trust is severed initially into only two resulting trusts. One resulting trust must receive that fractional share of the total value of the original trust as of the date of severance that is equal to the applicable fraction, as defined in § 26.2642-1(b) and (c), used to determine the inclusion ratio of the original trust immediately before the severance. The other resulting trust must receive that fractional share of the total value of the original trust as of the date of severance that is equal to the excess of one over the fractional share described in the preceding sentence. The trust receiving the fractional share equal to the applicable fraction shall have an inclusion ratio of zero, and the other trust shall have an inclusion ratio of one. If the applicable fraction with respect to the original trust is .50, then, with respect to the two equal trusts resulting from the severance, the trustee may designate which of the resulting trusts will have an inclusion ratio of zero and which will have an inclusion ratio of one. Each separate trust resulting from the severance then may be further divided in accordance with the rules of this section. See paragraph (j), *Example 7*, of this section.

(iii) The trust is severed initially into more than two resulting trusts. One or more of the resulting trusts in the aggregate must receive that fractional share of the total value of the original trust as of the date of severance that is equal to the applicable fraction used to determine the inclusion ratio of the original trust immediately before the severance. The trust or trusts receiving such fractional share shall have an inclusion ratio of zero, and each of the other resulting trust or trusts shall have an inclusion ratio of one. (If, however, two or more of the resulting trusts each receives the fractional share of the total value of the original trust equal to the applicable fraction, the trustee may designate which of those resulting trusts will have an inclusion ratio of zero and which will have an inclusion ratio of one.) The resulting trust or trusts with an inclusion ratio of one must receive in the aggregate that fractional share of the total value of the original trust as of the date of severance that is equal to the excess of one over the fractional share described in the second sentence of this paragraph. See paragraph (j), *Example 9*, of this section.

(e) *Reporting a qualified severance.*—(1) *In general.*—A qualified severance is reported by filing Form 706-GS(T), "Generation-Skipping Transfer Tax Return for Terminations," (or such other form as may be provided from time to time by the Internal Revenue Service (IRS) for the pur-

Reg. § 26.2642-6(e)(1)

pose of reporting a qualified severance). Unless otherwise provided in the applicable form or instructions, the IRS requests that the filer write "Qualified Severance" at the top of the form and attach a Notice of Qualified Severance (Notice). The return and attached Notice should be filed by April 15th of the year immediately following the year during which the severance occurred or by the last day of the period covered by an extension of time, if an extension of time is granted, to file such form.

(2) *Information concerning the original trust.*— The Notice should provide, with respect to the original trust that was severed—

(i) The name of the transferor;

(ii) The name and date of creation of the original trust;

(iii) The tax identification number of the original trust; and

(iv) The inclusion ratio before the severance.

(3) *Information concerning each new trust.*— The Notice should provide, with respect to each of the resulting trusts created by the severance—

(i) The name and tax identification number of the trust;

(ii) The date of severance (within the meaning of paragraph (c) of this section);

(iii) The fraction of the total assets of the original trust received by the resulting trust;

(iv) Other details explaining the basis for the funding of the resulting trust (a fraction of the total fair market value of the assets on the date of severance, or a fraction of each asset); and

(v) The inclusion ratio.

(f) *Time for making a qualified severance.*—(1) A qualified severance of a trust may occur at any time prior to the termination of the trust. Thus, provided that the separate resulting trusts continue in existence after the severance, a qualified severance may occur either before or after—

(i) GST tax exemption has been allocated to the trust;

(ii) A taxable event has occurred with respect to the trust; or

(iii) An addition has been made to the trust.

(2) Because a qualified severance is effective as of the date of severance, a qualified severance has no effect on a taxable termination as defined in section 2612(a) or a taxable distribution as defined in section 2612(b) that occurred prior to the date of severance. A qualified severance shall be deemed to occur before a taxable termination or a taxable distribution that occurs by reason of the qualified severance. See paragraph (j) *Example 8* of this section.

(g) *Trusts that were irrevocable on September 25, 1985.*—(1) *In general.*—See § 26.2601-1(b)(4) for

rules regarding severances and other actions with respect to trusts that were irrevocable on September 25, 1985.

(2) *Trusts in receipt of a post-September 25, 1985, addition.*—A trust described in § 26.2601-1(b)(1)(iv)(A) that is deemed for GST tax purposes to consist of one separate share not subject to GST tax (the non-chapter 13 portion) with an inclusion ratio of zero, and one separate share subject to GST tax (the chapter 13 portion) with an inclusion ratio determined under section 2642, may be severed into two trusts in accordance with § 26.2654-1(a)(3). One resulting trust will hold the non-chapter 13 portion of the original trust (the non-chapter 13 trust) and will not be subject to GST tax, and the other resulting trust will hold the chapter 13 portion of the original trust (the chapter 13 trust) and will have the same inclusion ratio as the chapter 13 portion immediately prior to the severance. The chapter 13 trust may be further divided in a qualified severance in accordance with the rules of this section. The non-chapter 13 trust may be further divided in accordance with the rules of § 26.2601-1(b)(4).

(h) *Treatment of trusts resulting from a severance that is not a qualified severance.*—Trusts resulting from a severance (other than a severance recognized for GST tax purposes under § 26.2654-1) that does not meet the requirements of a qualified severance under paragraph (b) of this section will be treated, after the date of severance, as separate trusts for purposes of the GST tax, provided that the trusts resulting from such severance are recognized as separate trusts under applicable state law. The post-severance treatment of the resulting trusts as separate trusts for GST tax purposes generally permits the allocation of GST tax exemption, the making of various elections permitted for GST tax purposes, and the occurrence of a taxable distribution or termination with regard to a particular resulting trust, with no GST tax impact on any other trust resulting from that severance. Each trust resulting from a severance described in this paragraph (h), however, will have the same inclusion ratio immediately after the severance as that of the original trust immediately before the severance. (See § 26.2654-1 for the inclusion ratio of each trust resulting from a severance described in that section.) Further, any trust resulting from a nonqualified severance may be severed subsequently, pursuant to a qualified severance described in this § 26.2642-6.

(i) [Reserved].

(j) *Examples.*—The rules of this section are illustrated by the following examples:

Example 1. Succession of interests. T dies in 2006. T's will establishes a testamentary trust (Trust) providing that income is to be paid to T's sister, S, for her life. On S's death, one-half of the corpus is to be paid to T's child, C (or to C's estate if C fails to survive S), and one-half of the corpus is to be paid to T's grandchild, GC (or to GC's estate if GC fails to survive S). On the Form 706, "United States Estate (and Generation-Skipping Transfer) Tax Return," filed for T's estate, T's executor allocates all of T's available GST tax exemption to other transfers and trusts, such that Trust's inclusion ratio is 1. Subsequent to filing the Form 706 in 2007 and in accordance with applicable state law, the trustee divides Trust into two separate trusts, Trust 1 and Trust 2, with each trust receiving 50 percent of the value of the assets of the original trust as of the date of severance. Trust 1 provides that trust income is to be paid to S for life with remainder to C or C's estate, and Trust 2 provides that trust income is to be paid to S for life with remainder to GC or GC's estate. Because Trust 1 and Trust 2 provide for the same succession of interests in the aggregate as provided in the original trust, the severance constitutes a qualified severance, provided that all other requirements of section 2642(a)(3) and this section are satisfied.

Example 2. Succession of interests in discretionary trust. In 2006, T establishes Trust, an irrevocable trust providing that income may be paid from time to time in such amounts as the trustee deems advisable to any one or more members of the group consisting of T's children (A and B) and their respective descendants. In addition, the trustee may distribute corpus to any trust beneficiary in such amounts as the trustee deems advisable. On the death of the last to die of A and B, the trust is to terminate and the corpus is to be distributed in two equal shares, one share to the then-living descendants of each child, per stirpes. T elects, under section 2632(c)(5), to not have the automatic allocation rules contained in section 2632(c) apply with respect to T's transfers to Trust, and T does not otherwise allocate GST tax exemption with respect to Trust. As a result, Trust has an inclusion ratio of one. In 2008, the trustee of Trust, pursuant to applicable state law, divides Trust into two equal but separate trusts, Trust 1 and Trust 2, each of which has terms identical to the terms of Trust except for the identity of the beneficiaries. Trust 1 and Trust 2 each has an inclusion ratio of one. Trust 1 provides that income is to be paid in such amounts as the trustee deems advisable to A and A's descendants. In addition, the trustee may distribute corpus to any trust beneficiary in such amounts as the trustee deems advisable. On the death of A, Trust 1 is to terminate and the corpus is to be distributed to the then-living descendants of A, per stirpes, but, if A dies with no living descendants, the principal will be added to Trust 2. Trust 2 contains identical provisions, except that B and B's descendants are the trust beneficiaries and, if B dies with no living descendants, the principal will be added to Trust 1. Trust 1 and Trust 2 in the aggregate provide for the same beneficiaries and the same succession of interests as provided in Trust, and the sever-

ance does not shift any beneficial interest to a beneficiary who occupies a lower generation than the person or persons who held the beneficial interest in Trust. Accordingly, the severance constitutes a qualified severance, provided that all other requirements of section 2642(a)(3) and this section are satisfied.

Example 3. Severance based on actuarial value of beneficial interests. In 2004, T establishes Trust, an irrevocable trust providing that income is to be paid to T's child C during C's lifetime. Upon C's death, Trust is to terminate and the assets of Trust are to be paid to GC, C's child, if living, or, if GC is not then living, to GC's estate. T properly elects, under section 2632(c)(5), not to have the automatic allocation rules contained in section 2632(c) apply with respect to T's transfers to Trust, and T does not otherwise allocate GST tax exemption with respect to Trust. Thus, Trust has an inclusion ratio of one. In 2009, the trustee of Trust, pursuant to applicable state law, divides Trust into two separate trusts, Trust 1 for the benefit of C (and on C's death to C's estate), and Trust 2 for the benefit of GC (and on GC's death to GC's estate). The document severing Trust directs that Trust 1 is to be funded with an amount equal to the actuarial value of C's interest in Trust prior to the severance, determined under section 7520 of the Internal Revenue Code. Similarly, Trust 2 is to be funded with an amount equal to the actuarial value of GC's interest in Trust prior to the severance, determined under section 7520. Trust 1 and Trust 2 do not provide for the same succession of interests as provided under the terms of the original trust. Therefore, the severance is not a qualified severance. Furthermore, because the severance results in no non-skip person having an interest in Trust 2, Trust 2 constitutes a skip person under section 2613 and, therefore, the severance results in a taxable termination subject to GST tax.

Example 4. Severance of a trust with a 50% inclusion ratio. On September 1, 2006, T transfers $100,000 to a trust for the benefit of T's grandchild, GC. On a timely filed Form 709, "United States Gift (and Generation-Skipping Transfer) Tax Return," reporting the transfer, T allocates all of T's remaining GST tax exemption ($50,000) to the trust. As a result of the allocation, the applicable fraction with respect to the trust is .50 [$50,000 (the amount of GST tax exemption allocated to the trust) divided by $100,000 (the value of the property transferred to the trust)]. The inclusion ratio with respect to the trust is .50 [1 - .50]. In 2007, pursuant to authority granted under applicable state law, the trustee severs the trust into two trusts, Trust 1 and Trust 2, each of which is identical to the original trust and each of which receives a 50 percent fractional share of the total value of the original trust, valued as of the date of severance. Because the applicable fraction with respect to the original trust is .50 and the trust is severed into two equal trusts, the trustee may designate which resulting trust has an inclusion ratio of one, and which resulting trust has an inclusion ratio of zero. Accordingly, in the Notice of Qualified Severance reporting the severance, the trustee designates Trust 1 as having an inclusion ratio of zero, and Trust 2 as having an inclusion ratio of one. The severance constitutes a qualified severance, provided that all other requirements of section 2642(a)(3) and this section are satisfied.

Example 5. Funding of severed trusts on a non-pro rata basis. T's will establishes a testamentary trust (Trust) for the benefit of T's descendants, to be funded with T's stock in Corporation A and Corporation B, both publicly traded stocks. T dies on May 1, 2004, at which time the Corporation A stock included in T's gross estate has a fair market value of $100,000 and the stock of Corporation B included in T's gross estate has a fair market value of $200,000. On a timely filed Form 706, T's executor allocates all of T's remaining GST tax exemption ($270,000) to Trust. As a result of the allocation, the applicable fraction with respect to Trust is .90 [$270,000 (the amount of GST tax exemption allocated to the trust) divided by $300,000 (the value of the property transferred to the trust)]. The inclusion ratio with respect to Trust is .10 [1 - .90]. On August 1, 2008, in accordance with applicable local law, the trustee executes a document severing Trust into two trusts, Trust 1 and Trust 2, each of which is identical to Trust. The instrument designates August 3, 2008, as the date of severance (within the meaning of paragraph (d)(3) of this section). The terms of the instrument severing Trust provide that Trust 1 is to be funded on a non-pro rata basis with assets having a fair market value on the date of severance equal to 90% of the value of Trust's assets on that date, and Trust 2 is to be funded with assets having a fair market value on the date of severance equal to 10% of the value of Trust's assets on that date. On August 3, 2008, the value of the Trust assets totals $500,000, consisting of Corporation A stock worth $450,000 and Corporation B stock worth $50,000. On August 4, 2008, the trustee takes all action necessary to transfer all of the Corporation A stock to Trust 1 and to transfer all of the Corporation B stock to Trust 2. On August 6, 2008, the stock transfers are completed and the stock is received by the appropriate resulting trust. Accordingly, Trust 1 is funded with assets having a value equal to 90% of the value of Trust as of the date of severance, August 3, 2008, and Trust 2 is funded with assets having a value equal to 10% of the value of Trust as of the date of severance. Therefore, the severance constitutes a qualified severance, provided that all other requirements of section 2642(a)(3) and this section are satisfied. Trust 1 will have an inclusion ratio of zero and Trust 2 will have an inclusion ratio of one.

Example 6. Funding of severed trusts on a non-pro rata basis. (i) T's will establishes an irrevocable trust (Trust) for the benefit of T's descendants. As a result of the allocation of GST tax exemp-

tion, the applicable fraction with respect to Trust is .60 and Trust's inclusion ratio is .40 [1 - .60]. Pursuant to authority granted under applicable state law, on August 1, 2008, the trustee executes a document severing Trust into two trusts, Trust 1 and Trust 2, each of which is identical to Trust. The instrument of severance provides that the severance is intended to qualify as a qualified severance within the meaning of section 2642(a)(3) and designates August 3, 2008, as the date of severance (within the meaning of paragraph (d)(3) of this section). The instrument further provides that Trust 1 and Trust 2 are to be funded on a non-pro rata basis with Trust 1 funded with assets having a fair market value on the date of severance equal to 40% of the value of Trust's assets on that date and Trust 2 funded with assets having a fair market value equal to 60% of the value of Trust's assets on that date. The fair market value of the assets used to fund each trust is to be determined in compliance with the requirements of paragraph (d)(4) of this section.

(ii) On August 3, 2008, the fair market value of the Trust assets totals $4,000,000, consisting of 52% of the outstanding common stock in Company, a closelyheld corporation, valued at $3,000,000 and $1,000,000 in cash and marketable securities. Trustee proposes to divide the Company stock equally between Trust 1 and Trust 2, and thus transfer 26% of the Company stock to Trust 1 and 26% of the stock to Trust 2. In addition, the appropriate amount of cash and marketable securities will be distributed to each trust. In accordance with paragraph (d)(4) of this section, for funding purposes, the interest in the Company stock distributed to each trust is valued as a pro rata portion of the value of the 52% interest in Company held by Trust before severance, without taking into account, for example, any valuation discount that might otherwise apply in valuing the noncontrolling interest distributed to each resulting trust.

(iii) Accordingly, for funding purposes, each 26% interest in Company stock distributed to Trust 1 and Trust 2 is valued at $1,500,000 (.5 × $3,000,000). Therefore, Trust 1, which is to be funded with $1,600,000 (.40 × $4,000,000), receives $100,000 in cash and marketable securities valued as of August 3, 2008, in addition to the Company stock, and Trust 2, which is to be funded with $2,400,000 (.60 × $4,000,000), receives $900,000 in cash and marketable securities in addition to the Company stock. Therefore, the severance is a qualified severance, provided that all other requirements of section 2642(a)(3) and this section are satisfied.

Example 7. Statutory qualified severance. T dies on October 1, 2004. T's will establishes a testamentary trust (Trust) to be funded with $1,000,000. Trust income is to be paid to T's child, S, for S's life. The trustee may also distribute trust corpus from time to time, in equal or unequal shares, for the benefit of any one or more members of the group consisting of S and T's three grandchildren (GC1, GC2, and GC3). On S's death, Trust is to terminate and the assets are to be divided equally among GC1, GC2, and GC3 (or their respective then-living descendants, per stirpes). On a timely filed Form 706, T's executor allocates all of T's remaining GST tax exemption ($300,000) to Trust. As a result of the allocation, the applicable fraction with respect to the trust is .30 [$300,000 (the amount of GST tax exemption allocated to the trust) divided by $1,000,000 (the value of the property transferred to the trust)]. The inclusion ratio with respect to the trust is .70 [1 - .30]. On June 1, 2007, the trustee determines that it is in the best interest of the beneficiaries to sever Trust to provide a separate trust for each of T's three grandchildren and their respective families. The trustee severs Trust into two trusts, Trust 1 and Trust 2, each with terms and beneficiaries identical to Trust and thus each providing that trust income is to be paid to S for life, trust principal may be distributed for the benefit of any or all members of the group consisting of S and T's grandchildren, and, on S's death, the trust is to terminate and the assets are to be divided equally among GC1, GC2, and GC3 (or their respective then-living descendants, per stirpes). The instrument severing Trust provides that Trust 1 is to receive 30% of Trust's assets and Trust 2 is to receive 70% of Trust's assets. Further, each such trust is to be funded with a pro rata portion of each asset held in Trust. The trustee then severs Trust 1 into three equal trusts, Trust GC1, Trust GC2, and Trust GC3. Each trust is named for a grandchild of T and provides that trust income is to be paid to S for life, trust principal may be distributed for the benefit of S and T's grandchild for whom the trust is named, and, on S's death, the trust is to terminate and the trust proceeds distributed to the respective grandchild for whom the trust is named. If that grandchild has predeceased the termination date, the trust proceeds are to be distributed to that grandchild's then-living descendants, per stirpes, or, if none, then equally to the other two trusts resulting from the severance of Trust 1. Each such resulting trust is to be funded with a pro rata portion of each Trust 1 asset. The trustee also severs Trust 2 in a similar manner, into Trust GC1(2), Trust GC2(2), and Trust GC3(2). The severance of Trust into Trust 1 and Trust 2, the severance of Trust 1 into Trust GC1, Trust GC2, Trust GC3, and the severance of Trust 2 into Trust GC1(2), Trust GC2(2) and Trust GC3(2), constitute qualified severances, provided that all other requirements of section 2642(a)(3) and this section are satisfied with respect to each severance. Trust GC1, Trust GC2, Trust GC3 will each have an inclusion ratio of zero and Trust GC1(2), Trust GC2(2), and Trust GC3(2) will each have an inclusion ratio of one.

Example 8. Qualified severance deemed to precede a taxable termination. In 2004, T establishes an inter vivos irrevocable trust (Trust) for a term of 10

years providing that Trust income is to be paid annually in equal shares to T's child C and T's grandchild GC (the child of another then-living child of T). If either C or GC dies prior to the expiration of the 10-year term, the deceased beneficiary's share of Trust's income is to be paid to that beneficiary's then-living descendants, per stirpes, for the balance of the trust term. At the expiration of the 10-year trust term, the corpus is to be distributed equally to C and GC; if either C or GC is not then living, then such decedent's share is to be distributed instead to such decedent's then-living descendants, per stirpes. T allocates T's GST tax exemption to Trust such that Trust's applicable fraction is .50 and Trust's inclusion ratio is .50 [1-.50]. In 2006, pursuant to applicable state law, the trustee severs the trust into two equal trusts, Trust 1 and Trust 2. The instrument severing Trust provides that Trust 1 is to receive 50% of the Trust assets, and Trust 2 is to receive 50% of Trust's assets. Both resulting trusts are identical to Trust, except that each has different beneficiaries: C and C's descendants are designated as the beneficiaries of Trust 1, and GC and GC's descendants are designated as the beneficiaries of Trust 2. The severance constitutes a qualified severance, provided all other requirements of section 2642(a)(3) and this section are satisfied. Because the applicable fraction with respect to Trust is .50 and Trust was severed into two equal trusts, the trustee may designate which resulting trust has an inclusion ratio of one, and which has an inclusion ratio of zero. Accordingly, in the Notice of Qualified Severance reporting the severance, the trustee designates Trust 1 as having an inclusion ratio of one, and Trust 2 as having an inclusion ratio of zero. Because Trust 2 is a skip person under section 2613, the severance of Trust resulting in the distribution of 50% of Trust's corpus to Trust 2 would constitute a taxable termination or distribution (as described in section 2612(a)) of that 50% of Trust for GST tax purposes, but for the rule that a qualified severance is deemed to precede a taxable termination that is caused by the qualified severance. Thus, no GST tax will be due with regard to the creation and funding of Trust 2 because the inclusion ratio of Trust 2 is zero.

Example 9. Regulatory qualified severance. (i) In 2004, T establishes an inter vivos irrevocable trust (Trust) providing that trust income is to be paid annually in equal shares to T's children, A and B, for 10 years. Trust provides that the trustee has discretion to make additional distributions of principal to A and B during the 10-year term without adjustments to their shares of income or the trust remainder. If either (or both) dies prior to the expiration of the 10-year term, the deceased child's share of trust income is to be paid to the child's then living descendants, per stirpes, for the balance of the trust term. At the expiration of the 10-year term, the corpus is to be distributed equally to A and B; if A and B (or either or them) is not then living, then such decedent's share is to be distributed instead to such decedent's then living descendants, per stirpes. T allocates GST tax exemption to Trust such that Trust's applicable fraction is .25 and its inclusion ratio is .75.

(ii) In 2006, pursuant to applicable state law, the trustee severs the trust into three trusts: Trust 1, Trust 2, and Trust 3. The instrument severing Trust provides that Trust 1 is to receive 50% of Trust's assets, Trust 2 is to receive 25% of Trust's assets, and Trust 3 is to receive 25% of Trust's assets. All three resulting trusts are identical to Trust, except that each has different beneficiaries: A and A's issue are designated as the beneficiaries of Trust 1, and B and B's issue are designated as the beneficiaries of Trust 2 and Trust 3. The severance constitutes a qualified severance, provided that all other requirements of section 2642(a)(3) and this section are satisfied. Trust 1 will have an inclusion ratio of 1. Because both Trust 2 and Trust 3 have each received the fractional share of Trust's assets equal to Trust's applicable fraction of .25, trustee designates that Trust 2 will have an inclusion ratio of one and that Trust 3 will have an inclusion ratio of zero.

Example 10. Beneficiary's interest dependent on inclusion ratio. On August 8, 2006, T transfers $1,000,000 to Trust and timely allocates $400,000 of T's remaining GST tax exemption to Trust. As a result of the allocation, the applicable fraction with respect to Trust is .40 [$400,000 divided by $1,000,000]and Trust's inclusion ratio is .60 [1 - .40]. Trust provides that all income of Trust will be paid annually to C, T's child, for life. On C's death, the corpus is to pass in accordance with C's exercise of a testamentary limited power to appoint the corpus of Trust to C's lineal descendants. However, Trust provides that if, at the time of C's death, Trust's inclusion ratio is greater than zero, then C may also appoint that fraction of the trust corpus equal to the inclusion ratio to the creditors of C's estate. On May 3, 2008, pursuant to authority granted under applicable state law, the trustee severs Trust into two trusts. Trust 1 is funded with 40% of Trust's assets, and Trust 2 is funded with 60% of Trust's assets in accordance with the requirements of this section. Both Trust 1 and Trust 2 provide that all income of Trust will be paid annually to C during C's life. On C's death, Trust 1 corpus is to pass in accordance with C's exercise of a testamentary limited power to appoint the corpus to C's lineal descendants. Trust 2 is to pass in accordance with C's exercise of a testamentary power to appoint the corpus of Trust to C's lineal descendants and to the creditors of C's estate. The severance constitutes a qualified severance, provided that all other requirements of section 2642(a)(3) and this section are satisfied. No additional contribution or allocation of GST tax exemption is made to either Trust 1 or Trust 2 prior to C's death. Accordingly, the inclusion ratio with respect to Trust 1 is zero. The inclusion ratio with

respect to Trust 2 is one until C's death, at which time C will become the transferor of Trust 2 for GST tax purposes. (Some or all of C's GST tax exemption may be allocated to Trust 2 upon C's death.)

Example 11. Date of severance. Trust is an irrevocable trust that has both skip person and non-skip person beneficiaries. Trust holds two parcels of real estate, Property A and Property B, stock in Company X, a publicly traded company, and cash. On June 16, 2008, the local court with jurisdiction over Trust issues an order, pursuant to the trustee's petition authorized under state law, severing Trust into two resulting trusts of equal value, Trust 1 and Trust 2. The court order directs that Property A will be distributed to Trust 1 and Property B will be distributed to Trust 2, and that an appropriate amount of stock and cash will be distributed to each trust such that the total value of property distributed to each trust as of the date of severance will be equal. The court order does not mandate a particular date of funding. Trustee receives notice of the court order on June 24, and selects July 16, 2008, as the date of severance. On June 26, 2008, Trustee commences the process of transferring title to Property A and Property B to the appropriate resulting trust(s), which process is completed on July 8, 2008. Also on June 26, the Trustee hires a professional appraiser to value Property A and Property B as of the date of severance and receives the appraisal report on Friday, October 3, 2008. On Monday, October 6, 2008, Trustee commences the process of transferring to Trust 1 and Trust 2 the appropriate amount of Company X stock valued as of July 16, 2008, and that transfer (as well as the transfer of Trust's cash) is completed by October 9, 2008. Under the facts presented, the funding of Trust 1 and Trust 2 occurred within 90 days of the date of severance selected by the trustee, and within a reasonable time after the date of severance taking into account the nature of the assets involved and the need to obtain an appraisal. Accordingly, the date of severance for purposes of this section is July 16, 2008, the resulting trusts are to be funded based on the value of the original trust assets as of that date, and the severance is a qualified severance assuming that all other requirements of section 2642(a)(3) and this section are met. (However, if Trust had contained only marketable securities and cash, then in order to satisfy the reasonable time requirement, the stock transfer would have to have been commenced, and generally completed, immediately after the date of severance, and the cash distribution would have to have been made at the same time.)

Example 12. Other severance that does not meet the requirements of a qualified severance. (i) In 2004, T establishes an irrevocable inter vivos trust (Trust) providing that Trust income is to be paid to T's children, A and B, in equal shares for their joint lives. Upon the death of the first to die of A and B, all Trust income will be paid to the survivor of A and B. At the death of the survivor, the corpus is to be distributed in equal shares to T's grandchildren, W and X (with any then-deceased grandchild's share being paid in accordance with that grandchild's testamentary general power of appointment). W is A's child and X is B's child. T elects under section 2632(c)(5) not to have the automatic allocation rules contained in section 2632(c) apply with respect to T's transfers to Trust, but T allocates GST tax exemption to Trust resulting in Trust having an inclusion ratio of .30.

(ii) In 2009, the trustee of Trust, as permitted by applicable state law, divides Trust into two separate trusts, Trust 1 and Trust 2. Trust 1 provides that trust income is to be paid to A for life and, on A's death, the remainder is to be distributed to W (or pursuant to W's testamentary general power of appointment). Trust 2 provides that trust income is to be paid to B for life and, on B's death, the remainder is to be distributed to X (or pursuant to X's testamentary general power of appointment). Because Trust 1 and Trust 2 do not provide A and B with the contingent survivor income interests that were provided to A and B under the terms of Trust, Trust 1 and Trust 2 do not provide for the same succession of interests in the aggregate as provided by Trust. Therefore, the severance does not satisfy the requirements of this section and is not a qualified severance. Provided that Trust 1 and Trust 2 are recognized as separate trusts under applicable state law, Trust 1 and Trust 2 will be recognized as separate trusts for GST tax purposes pursuant to paragraph (h) of this section, prospectively from the date of the severance. However, Trust 1 and Trust 2 each have an inclusion ratio of .30 immediately after the severance, the same as the inclusion ratio of Trust prior to severance.

Example 13. Qualified severance following a nonqualified severance. Assume the same facts as in *Example 12*, except that, as of November 4, 2010, the trustee of Trust 1 severs Trust 1 into two trusts, Trust 3 and Trust 4, in accordance with applicable local law. The instrument severing Trust 1 provides that both resulting trusts have provisions identical to Trust 1. The terms of the instrument severing Trust 1 further provide that Trust 3 is to be funded on a pro rata basis with assets having a fair market value as of the date of severance equal to 70% of the value of Trust 1's assets on that date, and Trust 4 is to be funded with assets having a fair market value as of the date of severance equal to 30% of the value of Trust 1's assets on that date. The severance constitutes a qualified severance, provided that all other requirements of section 2642(a)(3) and this section are satisfied. Trust 3 will have an inclusion ratio of zero and Trust 4 will have an inclusion ratio of one.

(k) *Effective/applicability date.*—(1) *In general.*— Except as otherwise provided in this paragraph (k), this section applies to severances occurring on or after August 2, 2007. Paragraph (d)(7)(iii),

paragraph (h), and *Examples 9*, *12* and *13* of paragraph (j) of this section apply to severances occurring on or after September 2, 2008.

(2) *Transition rule.*—In the case of a qualified severance occurring after December 31, 2000, and before August 2, 2007, taxpayers may rely on any reasonable interpretation of section 2642(a)(3) as long as reasonable notice concerning the qualified severance and identification of the trusts involved has been given to the IRS. For this purpose, the proposed regulations (69 FR 51967) are treated as a reasonable interpretation of the statute. For purposes of the reporting provisions of § 26.2642-6(e), notice to the IRS should be mailed by the due date of the gift tax return (including extensions granted) for gifts made during the year in which the severance occurred. If no gift tax return is filed, notice to the IRS should be mailed by April 15th of the year immediately following the year during which the severance occurred. For severances occurring between December 31, 2000, and January 1, 2007, notification should be mailed to the IRS as soon as reasonably practicable after August 2, 2007, if sufficient notice has not already been given. [Reg. § 26.2642-6.]

☐ [*T.D.* 9348, 8-1-2007. *Amended by T.D.* 9421, 7-30-2008.]

[Reg. § 26.2651-1]

§ 26.2651-1. Generation assignment.— (a) *Special rule for persons with a deceased parent.*— (1) *In general.*—This paragraph (a) applies for purposes of determining whether a transfer to or for the benefit of an individual who is a descendant of a parent of the transferor (or the transferor's spouse or former spouse) is a generation-skipping transfer. If that individual's parent, who is a lineal descendant of the parent of the transferor (or the transferor's spouse or former spouse), is deceased at the time the transfer (from which an interest of such individual is established or derived) is subject to the tax imposed on the transferor by chapter 11 or 12 of the Internal Revenue Code, the individual is treated as if that individual were a member of the generation that is one generation below the lower of—

(i) The transferor's generation; or

(ii) The generation assignment of the individual's youngest living lineal ancestor who is also a descendant of the parent of the transferor (or the transferor's spouse or former spouse).

(2) *Special rules.*—(i) *Corresponding generation adjustment.*—If an individual's generation assignment is adjusted with respect to a transfer in accordance with paragraph (a)(1) of this section, a corresponding adjustment with respect to that transfer is made to the generation assignment of each—

(A) Spouse or former spouse of that individual;

(B) Descendant of that individual; and

(C) Spouse or former spouse of each descendant of that individual.

(ii) *Continued application of generation assignment.*—If a transfer to a trust would be a generation-skipping transfer but for paragraph (a)(1) of this section, any generation assignment determined under this paragraph (a) continues to apply in determining whether any subsequent distribution from (or termination of an interest in) the portion of the trust attributable to that transfer is a generation-skipping transfer.

(iii) *Ninety-day rule.*—For purposes of paragraph (a)(1) of this section, any individual who dies no later than 90 days after a transfer occurring by reason of the death of the transferor is treated as having predeceased the transferor.

(iv) *Local law.*—A living person is not treated as having predeceased the transferor solely by reason of a provision of applicable local law; e.g., an individual who disclaims is not treated as a predeceased parent solely because state law treats a disclaimant as having predeceased the transferor for purposes of determining the disposition of the disclaimed property.

(3) *Established or derived.*—For purposes of section 2651(e) and paragraph (a)(1) of this section, an individual's interest is established or derived at the time the transferor is subject to transfer tax on the property. See § 26.2652-1(a) for the definition of a transferor. If the same transferor, on more than one occasion, is subject to transfer tax imposed by either chapter 11 or 12 of the Internal Revenue Code on the property so transferred (whether the same property, reinvestments thereof, income thereon, or any or all of these), then the relevant time for determining whether paragraph (a)(1) of this section applies is the earliest time at which the transferor is subject to the tax imposed by either chapter 11 or 12 of the Internal Revenue Code. For purposes of section 2651(e) and paragraph (a)(1) of this section, the interest of a remainder beneficiary of a trust for which an election under section 2523(f) or section 2056(b)(7) (QTIP election) has been made will be deemed to have been established or derived, to the extent of the QTIP election, on the date as of which the value of the trust corpus is first subject to tax under section 2519 or section 2044. The preceding sentence does not apply to a trust, however, to the extent that an election under section 2652(a)(3) (reverse QTIP election) has been made for the trust because, to the extent of a reverse QTIP election, the spouse who established the trust will remain the transferor of the trust for generation-skipping transfer tax purposes.

(4) *Special rule in the case of additional contributions to a trust.*—If a transferor referred to in paragraph (a)(1) of this section contributes additional property to a trust that existed before the application of paragraph (a)(1), then the additional property is treated as being held in a separate trust for purposes of chapter 13 of the Internal Revenue Code. The provisions of § 26.2654-1(a)(2), regarding treatment as separate trusts, apply as if different transferors had contributed to the separate portions of the single trust. Additional subsequent contributions from that transferor will be added to the new share that is treated as a separate trust.

(b) *Limited application to collateral heirs.*—Paragraph (a) of this section does not apply in the case of a transfer to any individual who is not a lineal descendant of the transferor (or the transferor's spouse or former spouse) if the transferor has any living lineal descendant at the time of the transfer.

(c) *Examples.*—The following examples illustrate the provisions of this section:

Example 1. T establishes an irrevocable trust, Trust, providing that trust income is to be paid to T's grandchild, GC, for 5 years. At the end of the 5-year period or on GC's prior death, Trust is to terminate and the principal is to be distributed to GC if GC is living or to GC's children if GC has died. The transfer that occurred on the creation of the trust is subject to the tax imposed by chapter 12 of the Internal Revenue Code and, at the time of the transfer, T's child, C, who is a parent of GC, is deceased. GC is treated as a member of the generation that is one generation below T's generation. As a result, GC is not a skip person and Trust is not a skip person. Therefore, the transfer to Trust is not a direct skip. Similarly, distributions to GC during the term of Trust and at the termination of Trust will not be GSTs.

Example 2. On January 1, 2004, T transfers $100,000 to an irrevocable inter vivos trust that provides T with an annuity payable for four years or until T's prior death. The annuity satisfies the definition of a qualified interest under section 2702(b). When the trust terminates, the corpus is to be paid to T's grandchild, GC. The transfer is subject to the tax imposed by chapter 12 of the Internal Revenue Code and, at the time of the transfer, T's child, C, who is a parent of GC, is living. C dies in 2006. In this case, C was alive at the time the transfer by T was subject to the tax imposed by chapter 12 of the Internal Revenue Code. Therefore, section 2651(e) and paragraph (a)(1) of this section do not apply. When the trust subsequently terminates, the distribution to GC is a taxable termination that is subject to the GST tax to the extent the trust has an inclusion ratio greater than zero. See section 2642(a).

Example 3. T dies testate in 2002, survived by T's spouse, S, their children, C1 and C2, and C1's child, GC. Under the terms of T's will, a trust is established for the benefit of S and of T and S's descendants. Under the terms of the trust, all income is payable to S during S's lifetime and the trustee may distribute trust corpus for S's health, support and maintenance. At S's death, the corpus is to be distributed, outright, to C1 and C2. If either C1 or C2 has predeceased S, the deceased child's share of the corpus is to be distributed to that child's then-living descendants, per stirpes. The executor of T's estate makes the election under section 2056(b)(7) to treat the trust property as qualified terminable interest property (QTIP) but does not make the election under section 2652(a)(3) (reverse QTIP election). In 2003, C1 dies survived by S and GC. In 2004, S dies, and the trust terminates. The full fair market value of the trust is includible in S's gross estate under section 2044 and S becomes the transferor of the trust under section 2652(a)(1)(A). GC's interest is considered established or derived at S's death, and because C1 is deceased at that time, GC is treated as a member of the generation that is one generation below the generation of the transferor, S. As a result, GC is not a skip person and the transfer to GC is not a direct skip.

Example 4. The facts are the same as in *Example 3.* However, the executor of T's estate makes the election under section 2652(a)(3) (reverse QTIP election) for the entire trust. Therefore, T remains the transferor because, for purposes of chapter 13 of the Internal Revenue Code, the election to be treated as qualified terminable interest property is treated as if it had not been made. In this case, GC's interest is established or derived on T's death in 2002. Because C1 was living at the time of T's death, the predeceased parent rule under section 2651(e) does not apply, even though C1 was deceased at the time the transfer from S to GC was subject to the tax under chapter 11 of the Internal Revenue Code. When the trust terminates, the distribution to GC is a taxable termination that is subject to the GST tax to the extent the trust has an inclusion ratio greater than zero. See section 2642(a).

Example 5. T establishes an irrevocable trust providing that trust income is to be paid to T's grandniece, GN, for 5 years or until GN's prior death. At the end of the 5-year period or on GN's prior death, the trust is to terminate and the principal is to be distributed to GN if living, or if GN has died, to GN's then-living descendants, per stirpes. S is a sibling of T and the parent of N. N is the parent of GN. At the time of the transfer, T has no living lineal descendant, S is living, N is deceased, and the transfer is subject to the gift tax imposed by chapter 12 of the Internal Revenue Code. GN is treated as a member of the generation that is one generation below T's generation because S, GN's youngest living lineal ancestor who is also a descendant of T's parent, is in T's generation. As a result, GN is not a skip person and the transfer to the trust is not a direct skip. In addition, distributions to GN during the term of the trust and at the termination of the trust will not be GSTs.

Example 6. On January 1, 2004, T transfers $50,000 to a great-grandniece, GGN, who is the great-grandchild of B, a brother of T. At the time of the transfer, T has no living lineal descendants and B's grandchild, GN, who is a parent of GGN and a child of B's living child, N, is deceased. GGN will be treated as a member of the generation that is one generation below the lower of T's generation or the generation assignment of GGN's youngest living lineal ancestor who is also a descendant of the parent of the transferor. In this case, N is GGN's youngest living lineal ancestor who is also a descendant of the parent of T. Because N's generation assignment is lower than T's generation, GGN will be treated as a member of the generation that is one generation below N's generation assignment (i.e., GGN will be treated as a member of her parent's generation). As a result, GGN remains a skip person and the transfer to GGN is a direct skip.

Example 7. T has a child, C. C and C's spouse, S, have a 20-year-old child, GC. C dies and S subsequently marries S2. S2 legally adopts GC. T transfers $100,000 to GC. Under section 2651(b)(1), GC is assigned to the generation that is two generations below T. However, since GC's parent, C, is deceased at the time of the transfer, GC will be treated as a member of the generation that is one generation below T. As a result, GC is not a skip person and the transfer to GC is not a direct skip.

[Reg. § 26.2651-1.]

☐ [*T.D.* 9214, 7-15-2005.]

[Reg. § 26.2651-2]

§ 26.2651-2. Individual assigned to more than 1 generation.—(a) *In general.*—Except as provided in paragraph (b) or (c) of this section, an individual who would be assigned to more than 1 generation is assigned to the youngest of the generations to which that individual would be assigned.

(b) *Exception.*—Notwithstanding paragraph (a) of this section, an adopted individual (as defined in this paragraph) will be treated as a member of the generation that is one generation below the adoptive parent for purposes of determining whether a transfer to the adopted individual from the adoptive parent (or the spouse or former spouse of the adoptive parent, or a lineal descendant of a grandparent of the adoptive parent) is subject to chapter 13 of the Internal Revenue Code. For purposes of this paragraph (b), an adopted individual is an individual who is—

(1) Legally adopted by the adoptive parent;

(2) A descendant of a parent of the adoptive parent (or the spouse or former spouse of the adoptive parent);

(3) Under the age of 18 at the time of the adoption; and

(4) Not adopted primarily for the purpose of avoiding GST tax. The determination of whether an adoption is primarily for GST tax-avoidance purposes is made based upon all of the facts and circumstances. The most significant

factor is whether there is a bona fide parent/child relationship between the adoptive parent and the adopted individual, in which the adoptive parent has fully assumed all significant responsibilities for the care and raising of the adopted child. Other factors may include (but are not limited to), at the time of the adoption—

(i) The age of the adopted individual (for example, the younger the age of the adopted individual, or the age of the youngest of siblings who are all adopted together, the more likely the adoption will not be considered primarily for GST tax-avoidance purposes); and

(ii) The relationship between the adopted individual and the individual's parents (for example, objective evidence of the absence or incapacity of the parents may indicate that the adoption is not primarily for GST tax-avoidance purposes).

(c) *Special rules.*—(1) *Corresponding generation adjustment.*—If an individual's generation assignment is adjusted with respect to a transfer in accordance with paragraph (b) of this section, a corresponding adjustment with respect to that transfer is made to the generation assignment of each—

(i) Spouse or former spouse of that individual;

(ii) Descendant of that individual; and

(iii) Spouse or former spouse of each descendant of that individual.

(2) *Continued application of generation assignment.*—If a transfer to a trust would be a generation-skipping transfer but for paragraph (b) of this section, any generation assignment determined under paragraph (b) or (c) of this section continues to apply in determining whether any subsequent distribution from (or termination of an interest in) the portion of the trust attributable to that transfer is a generation-skipping transfer.

(d) *Example.*—The following example illustrates the provisions of this section:

Example. T has a child, C. C has a 20-year-old child, GC. T legally adopts GC and transfers $100,000 to GC. GC's generation assignment is determined by section 2651(b)(1) and GC is assigned to the generation that is two generations below T. In addition, because T has legally adopted GC, GC is generally treated as a child of T under state law. Under these circumstances, GC is an individual who is assigned to more than one generation and the exception in §26.2651-2(b) does not apply. Thus, the special rule under section 2651(f)(1) applies and GC is assigned to the generation that is two generations below T. GC remains a skip person with respect to T and the transfer to GC is a direct skip.

[Reg. §26.2651-2.]

☐ [*T.D.* 9214, 7-15-2005.]

[Reg. §26.2651-3]

§26.2651-3. Effective dates.—(a) *In general.*—The rules of §§26.2651-1 and 26.2651-2 are applicable for terminations, distributions, and transfers occurring on or after July 18, 2005.

(b) *Transition rule.*—In the case of transfers occurring after December 31, 1997, and before July 18, 2005, taxpayers may rely on any reasonable interpretation of section 2651(e). For this purpose, these final regulations, as well as the proposed regulations issued on September 3, 2004 (69 FR 53862), are treated as a reasonable interpretation of the statute. [Reg. §26.2651-3.]

☐ [*T.D.* 9214, 7-15-2005.]

[Reg. §26.2652-1]

§26.2652-1. Transferor defined; other definitions.—(a) *Transferor defined.*—(1) *In general.*—Except as otherwise provided in paragraph (a)(3) of this section, the individual with respect to whom property was most recently subject to Federal estate or gift tax is the transferor of that property for purposes of chapter 13. An individual is treated as transferring any property with respect to which the individual is the transferor. Thus, an individual may be a transferor even though there is no transfer of property under local law at the time the Federal estate or gift tax applies. For purposes of this paragraph, a surviving spouse is the transferor of a qualified domestic trust created by the deceased spouse that is included in the surviving spouse's gross estate, provided the trust is not subject to the election described in §26.2652-2 (reverse QTIP election). A surviving spouse is also the transferor of a qualified domestic trust created by the surviving spouse pursuant to section 2056(d)(2)(B).

(2) *Transfers subject to Federal estate or gift tax.*—For purposes of this chapter, a transfer is subject to Federal gift tax if a gift tax is imposed under section 2501(a) (without regard to exemptions, exclusions, deductions, and credits). A transfer is subject to Federal estate tax if the value of the property is includible in the decedent's gross estate as determined under section 2031 or section 2103.

(3) *Special rule for certain QTIP trusts.*—Solely for purposes of chapter 13, if a transferor of qualified terminable interest property (QTIP) elects under §26.2652-2(a) to treat the property as if the QTIP election had not been made (reverse QTIP election), the identity of the transferor of the property is determined without regard to the application of sections 2044, 2207A, and 2519.

(4) *Split-gift transfers.*—In the case of a transfer with respect to which the donor's spouse makes an election under section 2513 to treat the gift as made one-half by the spouse, the electing spouse is treated as the transferor of one-half of

the entire value of the property transferred by the donor, regardless of the interest the electing spouse is actually deemed to have transferred under section 2513. The donor is treated as the transferor of one-half of the value of the entire property. See § 26.2632-1(c)(5) *Example 3*, regarding allocation of GST exemption with respect to split-gift transfers subject to an ETIP.

(5) *Examples.*—The following examples illustrate the principles of this paragraph (a):

Example 1. Identity of transferor. T transfers $100,000 to a trust for the sole benefit of T's grandchild. The transfer is subject to Federal gift tax because a gift tax is imposed under section 2501(a) (without regard to exemptions, deductions, and credits). Thus, for purposes of chapter 13, T is the transferor of the $100,000. It is immaterial that a portion of the transfer is excluded from the total amount of T's taxable gift by reason of section 2503(b).

Example 2. Gift splitting and identity of transferor. The facts are the same as in *Example 1*, except T's spouse, S, consents under section 2513 to split the gift with T. For purposes of chapter 13, S and T are each treated as a transferor of $50,000 to the trust.

Example 3. Change of transferor on subsequent transfer tax event. T transfers $100,000 to a trust providing that all the net trust income is to be paid to T's spouse, S, for S's lifetime. T elects under section 2523(f) to treat the transfer as a transfer of qualified terminable interest property, and T does not make the reverse QTIP election under section 2652(a)(3). On S's death, the trust property is included in S's gross estate under section 2044. Thus, S becomes the transferor at the time of S's death.

Example 4. Effect of transfer of an interest in trust on identity of the transferor. T transfers $100,000 to a trust providing that all of the net income is to be paid to T's child, C, for C's lifetime. At C's death, the trust property is to be paid to T's grandchild. C transfers the income interest to X, an unrelated party, in a transfer that is a completed transfer for Federal gift tax purposes. Because C's transfer is a transfer of a term interest in the trust that does not affect the rights of other parties with respect to the trust property, T remains the transferor with respect to the trust.

Example 5. Effect of lapse of withdrawal right on identity of transferor. T transfers $10,000 to a new trust providing that the trust income is to be paid to T's child, C, for C's life and, on the death of C, the trust principal is to be paid to T's grandchild, GC. The trustee has discretion to distribute principal for GC's benefit during C's lifetime. C has a right to withdraw $10,000 from the trust for a 60-day period following the transfer. Thereafter, the power lapses. C does not exercise the withdrawal right. The transfer by T is subject to Federal gift tax because a gift tax is imposed under section 2501 (without regard to exemptions, deductions, and credits) and, thus,

T is treated as having transferred the entire $10,000 to the trust. On the lapse of the withdrawal right, C becomes a transferor to the extent C is treated as having made a completed transfer for purposes of chapter 12. Therefore, except to the extent that the amount with respect to which the power of withdrawal lapses exceeds the greater of $5,000 or 5% of the value of the trust property, T remains the transferor of the trust property for purposes of chapter 13.

Example 6. Effect of reverse QTIP election on identity of the transferor. T establishes a testamentary trust having a principal of $500,000. Under the terms of the trust, all trust income is payable to T's surviving spouse, S, during S's lifetime. T's executor makes an election to treat the trust property as qualified terminable interest property and also makes the reverse QTIP election. For purposes of chapter 13, T is the transferor with respect to the trust. On S's death, the then full fair market value of the trust is includible in S's gross estate under section 2044. However, because of the reverse QTIP election, S does not become the transferor with respect to the trust; T continues to be the transferor.

Example 7. Effect of reverse QTIP election on constructive additions. The facts are the same as in *Example 6*, except the inclusion of the QTIP trust in S's gross estate increased the Federal estate tax liability of S's estate by $200,000. The estate does not exercise the right of recovery from the trust granted under section 2207A. Under local law, the beneficiaries of S's residuary estate (which bears all estate taxes under the will) could compel the executor to exercise the right of recovery but do not do so. Solely for purposes of chapter 13, the beneficiaries of the residuary estate are not treated as having made an addition to the trust by reason of their failure to exercise their right of recovery. Because of the reverse QTIP election, for GST purposes, the trust property is not treated as includible in S's gross estate and, under those circumstances, no right of recovery exists.

Example 8. Effect of reverse QTIP election on constructive additions. S, the surviving spouse of T, dies testate. At the time of S's death, S was the beneficiary of a trust with respect to which T's executor made a QTIP election under section 2056(b)(7). Thus, the trust is includible in S's gross estate under section 2044. T's executor also made the reverse QTIP election with respect to the trust. S's will provides that all death taxes payable with respect to the trust are payable from S's residuary estate. Since the transferor of the property is determined without regard to section 2044 and section 2207A, S is not treated as making a constructive addition to the trust by reason of the tax apportionment clause in S's will.

Example 9. Split-gift transfers. T transfers $100,000 to an inter vivos trust that provides T with an annuity payable for ten years or until T's prior death. The annuity satisfies the definition of a qualified interest under section 2702(b).

When the trust terminates, the corpus is to be paid to T's grandchild, GC. T's spouse, S, consents under section 2513 to have the gift treated as made one-half by S. Under section 2513, only the actuarial value of the gift to GC is eligible to be treated as made one-half by S. However, because S is treated as the donor of one-half of the gift to GC, S becomes the transferor of one-half of the entire trust ($50,000) for purposes of Chapter 13.

(b) *Trust defined.*—(1) *In general.*—A trust includes any arrangement (other than an estate) that has substantially the same effect as a trust. Thus, for example, arrangements involving life estates and remainders, estates for years, and insurance and annuity contracts are trusts. Generally, a transfer as to which the identity of the transferee is contingent upon the occurrence of an event is a transfer in trust; however, a transfer of property included in the transferor's gross estate, as to which the identity of the transferee is contingent upon an event that must occur within 6 months of the transferor's death, is not considered a transfer in trust solely by reason of the existence of the contingency.

(2) *Examples.*—The following examples illustrate the provisions of this paragraph (b):

Example 1. Uniform gifts to minors transfers. T transfers cash to an account in the name of T's child, C, as custodian for C's child, GC (who is a minor), under a state statute substantially similar to the Uniform Gifts to Minors Act. For purposes of chapter 13, the transfer to the custodial account is treated as a transfer to a trust.

Example 2. Contingent transfers. T bequeaths $200,000 to T's child, C, provided that if C does not survive T by more than 6 months, the bequest is payable to T's grandchild, GC. C dies 4 months after T. The bequest is not a transfer in trust because the contingency that determines the recipient of the bequest must occur within 6 months of T's death. The bequest to GC is a direct skip.

Example 3. Contingent transfers. The facts are the same as in *Example 2*, except C must survive T by 18 months to take the bequest. The bequest is a transfer in trust for purposes of chapter 13, and the death of C is a taxable termination.

(c) *Trustee defined.*—The trustee of a trust is the person designated as trustee under local law or, if no such person is so designated, the person in actual or constructive possession of property held in trust.

(d) *Executor defined.*—For purposes of chapter 13, the executor is the executor or administrator of the decedent's estate. However, if no executor or administrator is appointed, qualified or acting within the United States, the executor is the fiduciary who is primarily responsible for payment of the decedent's debts and expenses. If there is no such executor, administrator or fiduciary, the executor is the person in actual or constructive possession of the largest portion of the value of the decedent's gross estate.

(e) *Interest in trust.*—See §26.2612-1(e) for the definition of *interest in trust*. [Reg. §26.2652-1.]

☐ [*T.D.* 8644, 12-26-95. *Amended by T.D.* 8720, 5-19-97.]

[Reg. §26.2652-2]

§26.2652-2. Special election for qualified terminable interest property.—(a) *In general.*—If an election is made to treat property as qualified terminable interest property (QTIP) under section 2523(f) or section 2056(b)(7), the person making the election may, for purposes of chapter 13, elect to treat the property as if the QTIP election had not been made (reverse QTIP election). An election under this section is irrevocable. An election under this section is not effective unless it is made with respect to all of the property in the trust to which the QTIP election applies. See, however, §26.2654-1(b)(1). Property that qualifies for a deduction under section 2056(b)(5) is not eligible for the election under this section.

(b) *Time and manner of making election.*—An election under this section is made on the return on which the QTIP election is made. If a protective QTIP election is made, no election under this section is effective unless a protective reverse QTIP election is also made.

(c) *Transitional rule.*—If a reverse QTIP election is made with respect to a trust prior to December 27, 1995, and GST exemption has been allocated to that trust, the transferor (or the transferor's executor) may elect to treat the trust as two separate trusts, one of which has a zero inclusion ratio by reason of the transferor's GST exemption previously allocated to the trust. The separate trust with the zero inclusion ratio consists of that fractional share of the value of the entire trust equal to the value of the nontax portion of the trust under §26.2642-4(a). The reverse QTIP election is treated as applying only to the trust with the zero inclusion ratio. An election under this paragraph (c) is made by attaching a statement to a copy of the return on which the reverse QTIP election was made under section 2652(a)(3). The statement must indicate that an election is being made to treat the trust as two separate trusts and must identify the values of the two separate trusts. The statement is to be filed in the same place in which the original return was filed and must be filed before June 24, 1996. A trust subject to the election described in this paragraph is treated as a trust that was created by two transferors. See §26.2654-1(a)(2) for special rules involving trusts with multiple transferors.

(d) *Examples.*—The following examples illustrate the provisions of this section:

Example 1. Special (reverse QTIP) election under section 2652(a)(3). T transfers $1,000,000 to a trust providing that all trust income is to be paid to T's spouse, S, for S's lifetime. On S's death, the trust principal is payable to GC, a grandchild of S and T. T elects to treat all of the transfer as a transfer of QTIP and also makes the reverse QTIP election for all of the property. Because of the reverse QTIP election, T continues to be treated as the transferor of the property after S's death for purposes of chapter 13. A taxable termination rather than a direct skip occurs on S's death.

Example 2. Election under transition rule. In 1994, T died leaving $4 million in trust for the benefit of T's surviving spouse, S. On January 16, 1995, T's executor filed T's Form 706 on which the executor elects to treat the entire trust as qualified terminable interest property. The executor also makes a reverse QTIP election. The reverse QTIP election is effective with respect to the entire trust even though T's executor could allocate only $1 million of GST exemption to the trust. T's executor may elect to treat the trust as two separate trusts, one having a value of 25% of the value of the single trust and an inclusion ratio of zero, but only if the election is made prior to June 24, 1996. If the executor makes the transitional election, the other separate trust, having a value of 75% of the value of the single trust and an inclusion ratio of one, is not treated as subject to the reverse QTIP election.

Example 3. Denominator of the applicable fraction of QTIP trust. T bequeaths $1,500,000 to a trust in which T's surviving spouse, S, receives an income interest for life. Upon the death of S, the property is to remain in trust for the benefit of C, the child of T and S. Upon C's death, the trust is to terminate and the trust property paid to the descendants of C. The bequest qualifies for the estate tax marital deduction under section 2056(b)(7) as QTIP. The executor does not make the reverse QTIP election under section 2652(a)(3). As a result, S becomes the transferor of the trust at S's death when the value of the property in the QTIP trust is included in S's gross estate under section 2044. For purposes of computing the applicable fraction with respect to the QTIP trust upon S's death, the denominator of the fraction is reduced by any Federal estate tax (whether imposed under section 2001, 2101 or 2056A(b)) and State death tax attributable to the trust property that is actually recovered from the trust. [Reg. § 26.2652-2.]

☐ [*T.D.* 8644, 12-26-95.]

[Reg. § 26.2653-1]

§ 26.2653-1. Taxation of multiple skips.—(a) *General rule.*—If property is held in trust im-

mediately after a GST, solely for purposes of determining whether future events involve a skip person, the transferor is thereafter deemed to occupy the generation immediately above the highest generation of any person holding an interest in the trust immediately after the transfer. If no person holds an interest in the trust immediately after the GST, the transferor is treated as occupying the generation above the highest generation of any person in existence at the time of the GST who then occupies the highest generation level of any person who may subsequently hold an interest in the trust. See § 26.2612-1(e) for rules determining when a person has an interest in property held in trust.

(b) *Examples.*—The following examples illustrate the provisions of this section:

Example 1. T transfers property to an irrevocable trust for the benefit of T's grandchild, GC, and great-grandchild, GGC. During GC's life, the trust income may be distributed to GC and GGC in the trustee's absolute discretion. At GC's death, the trust property passes to GGC. Both GC and GGC have an interest in the trust for purposes of chapter 13. The transfer by T to the trust is a direct skip, and the property is held in trust immediately after the transfer. After the direct skip, the transferor is treated as being one generation above GC, the highest generation individual having an interest in the trust. Therefore, GC is no longer a skip person and distributions to GC are not taxable distributions. However, because GGC occupies a generation that is two generations below the deemed generation of T, GGC is a skip person and distributions of trust income to GGC are taxable distributions.

Example 2. T transfers property to an irrevocable trust providing that the income is to be paid to T's child, C, for life. At C's death, the trust income is to be accumulated for 10 years and added to principal. At the end of the 10-year accumulation period, the trust income is to be paid to T's grandchild, GC, for life. Upon GC's death, the trust property is to be paid to T's great-grandchild, GGC, or to GGC's estate. A GST occurs at C's death. Immediately after C's death and during the 10-year accumulation period, no person has an interest in the trust within the meaning of section 2652(c) and § 26.2612-1(e) because no one can receive current distributions of income or principal. Immediately after C's death, T is treated as occupying the generation above the generation of GC (the trust beneficiary in existence at the time of the GST who then occupies the highest generation level of any person who may subsequently hold an interest in the trust). Thus, subsequent income distributions to GC are not taxable distributions. [Reg. § 26.2653-1.]

☐ [*T.D.* 8644, 12-26-95.]

[Reg. §26.2654-1]

§26.2654-1. Certain trusts treated as separate trusts.—(a) *Single trust treated as separate trusts.*—(1) *Substantially separate and independent shares.*—(i) *In general.*—If a single trust consists solely of substantially separate and independent shares for different beneficiaries, the share attributable to each beneficiary (or group of beneficiaries) is treated as a separate trust for purposes of Chapter 13. The phrase "substantially separate and independent shares" generally has the same meaning as provided in §1.663(c)-3. However, except as provided in paragraph (a)(1)(iii) of this section, a portion of a trust is not a separate share unless such share exists from and at all times after the creation of the trust. For purposes of this paragraph (a)(1), a trust is treated as created at the date of death of the grantor if the trust is includible in its entirety in the grantor's gross estate for Federal estate tax purposes. Further, except with respect to shares or trusts that are treated as separate trusts under local law, treatment of a single trust as separate trusts under this paragraph (a)(1) does not permit treatment of those portions as separate trusts for purposes of filing returns and payment of tax or for purposes of computing any other tax imposed under the Internal Revenue Code. Also, additions to, and distributions from, such trusts are allocated pro rata among the separate trusts, unless the governing instrument expressly provides otherwise. See §26.2642-6 and paragraph (b) of this section regarding the treatment, for purposes of Chapter 13, of separate trusts resulting from the discretionary severance of a single trust.

(ii) *Certain pecuniary amounts.*—For purposes of this section, if a person holds the current right to receive a mandatory (i.e., nondiscretionary and noncontingent) payment of a pecuniary amount at the death of the transferor from an inter vivos trust that is includible in the transferor's gross estate, or a testamentary trust, the pecuniary amount is a separate and independent share if—

(A) The trustee is required to pay appropriate interest (as defined in §26.2642-2(b)(4)(i) and (ii)) to the person; and

(B) If the pecuniary amount is payable in kind on the basis of value other than the date of distribution value of the assets, the trustee is required to allocate assets to the pecuniary payment in a manner that fairly reflects net appreciation or depreciation in the value of the assets in the fund available to pay the pecuniary amount measured from the valuation date to the date of payment.

(iii) *Mandatory severances.*—For purposes of this section, if the governing instrument of a trust requires the division or severance of a single trust into separate trusts upon the future occurrence of a particular event not within the discretion of the trustee or any other person, and if the trusts resulting from such a division or severance are recognized as separate trusts under applicable state law, then each resulting trust is treated as a separate trust for purposes of Chapter 13. For this purpose, the rules of paragraph (b)(1)(ii)(C) of this section apply with respect to the severance and funding of the trusts. Similarly, if the governing instrument requires the division of a single trust into separate shares under the circumstances described in this paragraph, each such share is treated as a separate trust for purposes of Chapter 13. The post-severance treatment of the resulting shares or trusts as separate trusts for GST tax purposes generally permits the allocation of GST tax exemption, the making of various elections permitted for GST tax purposes, and the occurrence of a taxable distribution or termination with regard to a particular resulting share or trust, with no GST tax impact on any other trust or share resulting from that severance. The treatment of a single trust as separate trusts under this paragraph (a)(1), however, does not permit treatment of those portions as separate trusts for purposes of filing returns and payment of tax or for purposes of computing any other tax imposed under the Internal Revenue Code, if those portions are not treated as separate trusts under local law. Also, additions to, and distributions from, such trusts are allocated pro rata among the separate trusts, unless the governing instrument expressly provides otherwise. Each separate share and each trust resulting from a mandatory division or severance described in this paragraph will have the same inclusion ratio immediately after the severance as that of the original trust immediately before the division or severance.

(2) *Multiple transferors with respect to single trust.*—(i) *In general.*—If there is more than one transferor with respect to a trust, the portions of the trust attributable to the different transferors are treated as separate trusts for purposes of chapter 13. Treatment of a single trust as separate trusts under this paragraph (a)(2) does not permit treatment of those portions as separate trusts for purposes of filing returns and payment of tax or for purposes of computing any other tax imposed under the Internal Revenue Code. Also, additions to, and distributions from, such trusts are allocated pro rata among the separate trusts unless otherwise expressly provided in the governing instrument.

(ii) *Addition by a transferor.*—If an individual makes an addition to a trust of which the individual is not the sole transferor, the portion of the single trust attributable to each separate trust is determined by multiplying the fair market value of the single trust immediately after the contribution by a fraction. The numerator of the fraction is the value of the separate trust immediately after the contribution. The denominator of the fraction is the fair market value of all the property in the single trust immediately after the transfer.

(3) *Severance of a single trust.*—A single trust treated as separate trusts under paragraphs (a)(1) or (2) of this section may be divided at any time into separate trusts to reflect that treatment. For this purpose, the rules of paragraph (b)(1)(ii)(C) of this section apply with respect to the severance and funding of the severed trusts.

(4) *Allocation of exemption.*—(i) *In general.*— With respect to a separate share treated as a separate trust under paragraph (a)(1) or (2) of this section, an individual's GST exemption is allocated to the separate trust. See §26.2632-1 for rules concerning the allocation of GST exemption.

(ii) *Automatic allocation to direct skips.*—If the transfer is a direct skip to a trust that occurs during the transferor's lifetime and is treated as a transfer to separate trusts under paragraphs (a)(1) or (a)(2) of this section, the transferor's GST exemption not previously allocated is automatically allocated on a pro rata basis among the separate trusts. The transferor may prevent an automatic allocation of GST exemption to a separate share of a single trust by describing on a timely-filed United States Gift (and Generation-Skipping Transfer) Tax Return (Form 709) the transfer and the extent to which the automatic allocation is not to apply to a particular share. See §26.2632-1(b) for rules for avoiding the automatic allocation of GST exemption.

(5) *Examples.*—The following examples illustrate the principles of this section (a):

Example 1. Separate shares as separate trusts. T transfers $100,000 to a trust under which income is to be paid in equal shares for 10 years to T's child, C, and T's grandchild, GC (or their respective estates). The trust does not permit distributions of principal during the term of the trust. At the end of the 10-year term, the trust principal is to be distributed to C and GC in equal shares. The shares of C and GC in the trust are separate and independent and, therefore, are treated as separate trusts. The result would not be the same if the trust permitted distributions of principal unless the distributions could only be made from a one-half separate share of the initial trust principal and the distributee's future rights with respect to the trust are correspondingly reduced. T may allocate part of T's GST exemption under section 2632(a) to the share held for the benefit of GC.

Example 2. Separate share rule inapplicable. The facts are the same as in *Example 1*, except the trustee holds the discretionary power to distribute the income in any proportion between C and GC during the last year of the trust. The shares of C and GC in the trust are not separate and independent shares throughout the entire term of the trust and, therefore, are not treated as separate trusts for purposes of chapter 13.

Example 3. Pecuniary payment as separate share. T creates a lifetime revocable trust providing that on T's death $500,000 is payable to T's spouse, S, with the balance of the principal to be held for the benefit of T's grandchildren. The value of the trust is includible in T's gross estate upon T's death. Under the terms of the trust, the payment to S is required to be made in cash, and under local law S is entitled to receive interest on the payment at an annual rate of 6 percent, commencing immediately upon T's death. For purposes of chapter 13, the trust is treated as created at T's death, and the $500,000 payable to S from the trust is treated as a separate share. The result would be the same if the payment to S could be satisfied using noncash assets at their value on the date of distribution. Further, the result would be the same if the decedent's probate estate poured over to the revocable trust on the decedent's death and was then distributed in accordance with the terms of the trust.

Example 4. Pecuniary payment not treated as separate share. The facts are the same as in *Example 3*, except the bequest to S is to be paid in noncash assets valued at their values as finally determined for Federal estate tax purposes. Neither the trust instrument nor local law requires that the assets distributed in satisfaction of the bequest fairly reflect net appreciation or depreciation in all the assets from which the bequest may be funded. S's $500,000 bequest is not treated as a separate share and the trust is treated as a single trust for purposes of chapter 13.

Example 5. Multiple transferors to single trust. A transfers $100,000 to an irrevocable generation-skipping trust; B simultaneously transfers $50,000 to the same trust. As of the time of the transfers, the single trust is treated as two trusts for purposes of chapter 13. Because A contributed 2/3 of the value of the initial corpus, 2/3 of the single trust principal is treated as a separate trust created by A. Similarly, because B contributed 1/3 of the value of the initial corpus, 1/3 of the single trust is treated as a separate trust created by B. A or B may allocate their GST exemption under section 2632(a) to the respective separate trusts.

Example 6. Additional contributions. A transfers $100,000 to an irrevocable generation-skipping trust; B simultaneously transfers $50,000 to the same trust. When the value of the single trust has increased to $180,000, A contributes an additional $60,000 to the trust. At the time of the additional contribution, the portion of the single trust attributable to each grantor's separate trust must be redetermined. The portion of the single trust attributable to A's separate trust immediately after the contribution is 3/4 (((2/3 x $180,000) + $60,000)/$240,000). The portion attributable to B's separate trust after A's addition is 1/4.

Example 7. Distributions from a separate share. The facts are the same as in *Example 6,* except that, after A's second contribution, $50,000 is distributed to a beneficiary of the trust. Absent a provision in the trust instrument that charges the distribution against the contribution of either A or B, 3/4 of the distribution is treated as made from the separate trust of which A is the transferor and 1/4 from the separate trust of which B is the transferor.

Example 8. Subsequent mandatory division into separate trusts. T creates an irrevocable trust that provides the trustee with the discretionary power to distribute income or corpus to T's children and grandchildren. The trust provides that, when T's youngest child reaches age 21, the trust will be divided into separate shares, one share for each child of T. The income from a respective child's share will be paid to the child during the child's life, with the remainder passing on the child's death to such child's children (grandchildren of T). The separate shares that come into existence when the youngest child reaches age 21 will be recognized as of that date as separate trusts for purposes of Chapter 13. The inclusion ratio of the separate trusts will be identical to the inclusion ratio of the trust before the severance. Any allocation of GST tax exemption to the trust after T's youngest child reaches age 21 may be made to any one or more of the separate shares. The result would be the same if the trust instrument provided that the trust was to be divided into separate trusts when T's youngest child reached age 21, provided that the severance and funding of the separate trusts meets the requirements of this section.

(b) *Division of a trust included in the gross estate.*—(1) *In general.*—The severance of a trust that is included in the transferor's gross estate (or created under the transferor's will) into two or more trusts is recognized for purposes of chapter 13 if—

(i) The trust is severed pursuant to a direction in the governing instrument providing that the trust is to be divided upon the death of the transferor; or

(ii) The governing instrument does not require or otherwise direct severance but the trust is severed pursuant to discretionary authority granted either under the governing instrument or under local law; and

(A) The terms of the new trusts provide in the aggregate for the same succession of interests and beneficiaries as are provided in the original trust;

(B) The severance occurs (or a reformation proceeding, if required, is commenced) prior to the date prescribed for filing the Federal estate tax return (including extensions actually granted) for the estate of the transferor; and

(C) Either—

(1) The new trusts are severed on a fractional basis. If severed on a fractional basis,

the separate trusts need not be funded with a pro rata portion of each asset held by the undivided trust. The trusts may be funded on a nonpro rata basis provided funding is based on either the fair market value of the assets on the date of funding or in a manner that fairly reflects the net appreciation or depreciation in the value of the assets measured from the valuation date to the date of funding; or

(2) If the severance is required (by the terms of the governing instrument) to be made on the basis of a pecuniary amount, the pecuniary payment is satisfied in a manner that would meet the requirements of paragraph (a)(1)(ii) of this section if it were paid to an individual.

(2) *Special rule.*—If a court order severing the trust has not been issued at the time the Federal estate tax return is filed, the executor must indicate on a statement attached to the return that a proceeding has been commenced to sever the trust and describe the manner in which the trust is proposed to be severed. A copy of the petition or other instrument used to commence the proceeding must also be attached to the return. If the governing instrument of a trust or local law authorizes the severance of the trust, a severance pursuant to that authorization is treated as meeting the requirement of paragraph (b)(1)(ii)(B) of this section if the executor indicates on the Federal estate tax return that separate trusts will be created (or funded) and clearly sets forth the manner in which the trust is to be severed and the separate trusts funded.

(3) *Allocation of exemption.*—An individual's GST exemption under §2632 may be allocated to the separate trusts created pursuant to this section at the discretion of the executor or trustee.

(4) *Examples.*—The following examples illustrate the provisions of this section (b):

Example 1. Severance of single trust. T's will establishes a testamentary trust providing that income is to be paid to T's spouse for life. At the spouse's death, one-half of the corpus is to be paid to T's child, C, or C's estate (if C fails to survive the spouse) and one-half of the corpus is to be paid to T's grandchild, GC, or GC's estate (if GC fails to survive the spouse). If the requirements of paragraph (b) of this section are otherwise satisfied, T's executor may divide the testamentary trust equally into two separate trusts, one trust providing an income interest to spouse for life with remainder to C, and the other trust with an income interest to spouse for life with remainder to GC. Furthermore, if the requirements of paragraph (b) of this section are satisfied, the executor or trustee may further divide the trust for the benefit of GC. GST exemption may be allocated to any of the divided trusts.

Example 2. Severance of revocable trust. T creates an inter vivos revocable trust providing that, at T's death and after payment of all taxes and administration expenses, the remaining corpus will be divided into two trusts. One trust, for the benefit of T's spouse, is to be funded with the smallest amount that, if qualifying for the marital deduction, will reduce the estate tax to zero. The other trust, for the benefit of T's descendants, is to be funded with the balance of the revocable trust corpus. The trust corpus is includible in T's gross estate. Each trust is recognized as a separate trust for purposes of chapter 13.

Example 3. Formula severance. T's will establishes a testamentary marital trust (Trust) that meets the requirements of qualified terminable interest property (QTIP) if an election under section 2056(b)(7) is made. Trust provides that all trust income is to be paid to T's spouse for life. On the spouse's death, the trust corpus is to be held in further trust for the benefit of T's then-living descendants. On T's date of death in January of 2004, T's unused GST tax exemption is $1,200,000, and T's will includes $200,000 of bequests to T's grandchildren. Prior to the due date for filing the Form 706, "United States Estate (and Generation-Skipping Transfer) Tax Return," for T's estate, T's executor, pursuant to applicable state law, divides Trust into two separate trusts, Trust 1 and Trust 2. Trust 1 is to be funded with that fraction of the Trust assets, the numerator of which is $1,000,000, and the denominator of which is the value of the Trust assets as finally determined for federal estate tax purposes. Trust 2 is to be funded with that fraction of the Trust assets, the numerator of which is the excess of the Trust assets over $1,000,000, and the denominator of which is the value of the Trust assets as finally determined for federal estate tax purposes. On the Form 706 filed for the estate, T's executor makes a QTIP election under section 2056(b)(7) with respect to Trust 1 and Trust 2 and a "reverse" QTIP election under section 2652(a)(3) with respect to Trust 1. Further, T's executor allocates $200,000 of T's available GST tax exemption to the bequests to T's grandchildren, and the balance of T's exemption ($1,000,000) to Trust 1. If the requirements of paragraph (b) of this section are otherwise satisfied, Trust 1 and Trust 2 are recognized as separate trusts for GST tax purposes. Accordingly, the "reverse" QTIP election and allocation of GST tax exemption with respect to Trust 1 are recognized and effective for generation-skipping transfer tax purposes.

(c) *Cross reference.*—For rules applicable to the qualified severance of trusts (whether or not includible in the transferor's gross estate), see § 26.2642-6.

(d) *Effective date.*—Paragraph (a)(1)(i), paragraph (a)(1)(iii), and *Example 8* of paragraph (a)(5) apply to severances occurring on or after September 2, 2008. [Reg. § 26.2654-1.]

☐ [*T.D.* 8644, 12-26-95. *Amended by T.D.* 9348, 8-1-2007 *and T.D.* 9421, 7-30-2008.]

ADMINISTRATION

[Reg. § 26.2662-1]

§ 26.2662-1. Generation-skipping transfer tax return requirements.—(a) *In general.*—Chapter 13 imposes a tax on generation-skipping transfers(as defined in section 2611). The requirements relating to the return of tax depend on the type of generation-skipping transfer involved. This section contains rules for filing the required tax return. Paragraph (c)(2) of this section provides special rules concerning the return requirements for generation-skipping transfers pursuant to certain trust arrangements (as defined in paragraph (c)(2)(ii) of this section), such as life insurance policies and annuities.

(b) *Form of return.*—(1) *Taxable distributions.*—Form 706GS(D) must be filed in accordance with its instructions for any taxable distribution (as defined in section 2612(b)). The trust involved in a transfer described in the preceding sentence must file Form 706GS(D-1) in accordance with its instructions. A copy of Form 706GS(D-1) shall be sent to each distributee.

(2) *Taxable terminations.*—Form 706GS(T) must be filed in accordance with its instructions for any taxable termination (as defined in section 2612(a)).

(3) *Direct skip.*—(i) *Inter vivos direct skips.*—Form 709 must be filed in accordance with its instructions for any direct skip (as defined in section 2612(c)) that is subject to chapter 12 and occurs during the life of the transferor.

(ii) *Direct skips occurring at death.*—(A) *In general.*—Form 706 or Form 706NA must be filed in accordance with its instructions for any direct skips (as defined in section 2612(c)) that are subject to chapter 11 and occur at the death of the decedent.

(B) *Direct skips payable from a trust.*—Schedule R-1 of Form 706 must be filed in accordance with its instructions for any direct skip from a trust if such direct skip is subject to chapter 11. See paragraph (c)(2) of this section for special rules relating to the person liable for tax and required to make the return under certain circumstances.

(c) *Person liable for tax and required to make return.*—(1) *In general.*—Except as otherwise provided in this section, the following person is liable for the tax imposed by section 2601 and must make the required tax return—

(i) The transferee in a taxable distribution (as defined in section 2612(b));

(ii) The trustee in the case of a taxable termination (as defined in section 2612(a));

(iii) The transferor (as defined in section 2652(a)(1)(B)) in the case of an inter vivos direct skip (as defined in section 2612(c));

(iv) The trustee in the case of a direct skip from a trust or with respect to property that continues to be held in trust; or

(v) The executor in the case of a direct skip (other than a direct skip described in paragraph (c)(1)(iv) of this section) if the transfer is subject to chapter 11. See paragraph (c)(2) of this section for special rules relating to direct skips to or from certain trust arrangements (as defined in paragraph (c)(2)(ii) of this section).

(2) *Special rule for direct skips occurring at death with respect to property held in trust arrangements.*—(i) *In general.*—In the case of certain property held in a trust arrangement (as defined in paragraph (c)(2)(ii) of this section) at the date of death of the transferor, the person who is required to make the return and who is liable for the tax imposed by chapter 13 is determined under paragraphs (c)(2)(iii) and (iv) of this section.

(ii) *Trust arrangement defined.*—For purposes of this section, the term *trust arrangement* includes any arrangement (other than an estate) which, although not an explicit trust, has the same effect as an explicit trust. For purposes of this section, the term "explicit trust" means a trust described in § 301.7701-4(a).

(iii) *Executor's liability in the case of transfers with respect to decedents dying on or after June 24, 1996, if the transfer is less than $250,000.*—In the case of a direct skip occurring at death, the executor of the decedent's estate is liable for the tax imposed on that direct skip by chapter 13 and is required to file Form 706 or Form 706NA (and not Schedule R-1 of Form 706) if, at the date of the decedent's death—

(A) The property involved in the direct skip is held in a trust arrangement; and

(B) The total value of the property involved in direct skips with respect to the trustee of that trust arrangement is less than $250,000.

(iv) *Executor's liability in the case of transfers with respect to decedents dying prior to June 24, 1996, if the transfer is less than $100,000.*—In the case of a direct skip occurring at death with respect to a decedent dying prior to June 24, 1996, the rule in paragraph (c)(2)(iii) of this section that imposes liability upon the executor applies only if the property involved in the direct skip with respect to the trustee of the trust arrangement, in the aggregate, is less than $100,000.

(v) *Executor's right of recovery.*—In cases where the rules of paragraphs (c)(2)(iii) and (iv) of this section impose liability for the generation-skipping transfer tax on the executor, the executor is entitled to recover from the trustee (if the property continues to be held in trust) or from the recipient of the property (in the case of a transfer from a trust), the generation-skipping transfer tax attributable to the transfer.

(vi) *Examples.*—The following examples illustrate the application of this paragraph (c)(2) with respect to decedents dying on or after June 24, 1996:

Example 1. Insurance proceeds less than $250,000. On August 1, 1997, T, the insured under an insurance policy, died. The proceeds ($200,000) were includible in T's gross estate for Federal estate tax purposes. T's grandchild, GC, was named the sole beneficiary of the policy. The insurance policy is treated as a trust under section 2652(b)(1), and the payment of the proceeds to GC is a transfer from a trust for purposes of chapter 13. Therefore, the payment of the proceeds to GC is a direct skip. Since the proceeds from the policy ($200,000) are less than $250,000, the executor is liable for the tax imposed by chapter 13 and is required to file Form 706.

Example 2. Aggregate insurance proceeds of $250,000 or more. Assume the same facts as in *Example 1*, except T is the insured under two insurance policies issued by the same insurance company. The proceeds ($150,000) from each policy are includible in T's gross estate for Federal estate tax purposes. T's grandchild, GC1, was named the sole beneficiary of Policy 1, and T's other grandchild, GC2, was named the sole beneficiary of Policy 2. GC1 and GC2 are skip persons (as defined in section 2613). Therefore, the payments of the proceeds are direct skips. Since the total value of the policies ($300,000) exceeds $250,000, the insurance company is liable for the tax imposed by chapter 13 and is required to file Schedule R-1 of Form 706.

Example 3. Insurance proceeds of $250,000 or more held by insurance company. On August 1, 1997, T, the insured under an insurance policy, dies. The policy provides that the insurance company shall make monthly payments of $750 to GC, T's grandchild, for life with the remainder payable to T's great grandchild, GGC. The face value of the policy is $300,000. Since the proceeds continue to be held by the insurance company (the trustee), the proceeds are treated as if they were transferred to a trust for purposes of chapter 13. The trust is a skip person (as defined in section 2613(a)(2)) and the transfer is a direct skip. Since the total value of the policy ($300,000) exceeds $250,000, the insurance company is liable for the tax imposed by chapter 13 and is required to file Schedule R-1 of Form 706.

Example 4. Insurance proceeds less than $250,000 held by insurance company. Assume the same facts as in *Example 3*, except the policy provides that the insurance company shall make monthly payments of $500 to GC and that the face value of the policy is $200,000. The transfer is a transfer to a trust for purposes of chapter 13. However, since the total value of the policy ($200,000) is less than $250,000, the executor is liable for the tax imposed by chapter 13 and is required to file Form 706.

Example 5. On August 1, 1997, A, the insured under a life insurance policy, dies. The insurance proceeds on A's life that are payable under policies issued by Company X are in the aggregate amount of $200,000 and are includible in A's gross estate. Because the proceeds are includible in A's gross estate, the generation-skipping transfer that occurs upon A's death, if any, will be a direct skip rather than a taxable distribution or a taxable termination. Accordingly, because the aggregate amount of insurance proceeds with respect to Company X is less than $250,000, Company X may pay the proceeds without regard to whether the beneficiary is a skip person in relation to the decedent-transferor.

(3) *Limitation on personal liability of trustee.*— Except as provided in paragraph (c)(3)(iii) of this section, a trustee is not personally liable for any increases in the tax imposed by section 2601 which is attributable to the fact that—

(i) A transfer is made to the trust during the life of the transferor for which a gift tax return is not filed; or

(ii) The inclusion ratio with respect to the trust, determined by reference to the transferor's gift tax return, is erroneous, the actual inclusion ratio being greater than the reported inclusion ratio.

(iii) This paragraph (c)(3) does not apply if the trustee has or is deemed to have knowledge of facts sufficient to reasonably conclude that a gift tax return was required to be filed or that the inclusion ratio is erroneous. A trustee is deemed to have knowledge of such facts if the trustee's agent, employee, partner, or co-trustee has knowledge of such facts.

(4) *Exceptions.*—(i) *Legal or mental incapacity.*—If a distributee is legally or mentally incapable of making a return, the return may be made for the distributee by the distributee's guardian or, if no guardian has been appointed, by a person charged with the care of the distributee's person or property.

(ii) *Returns made by fiduciaries.*—See section 6012(b) for a fiduciary's responsibilities regarding the returns of decedents, returns of persons under a disability, returns of estates and trusts, and returns made by joint fiduciaries.

(d) *Time and manner of filing return.*—(1) *In general.*—Forms 706, 706NA, 706GS(D), 706GS(D-1), 706GS(T), 709, and Schedule R-1 of Form 706 must be filed with the Internal Revenue Service office with which an estate or gift tax

return of the transferor must be filed. The return shall be filed—

(i) *Direct skip.*—In the case of a direct skip, on or before the date on which an estate or gift tax return is required to be filed with respect to the transfer (see section 6075(b)(3)); and

(ii) *Other transfers.*—In all other cases, on or before the 15th day of the 4th month after the close of the calendar year in which such transfer occurs. See paragraph (d)(2) of this section for an exception to this rule when an election is made under section 2624(c) to value property included in certain taxable terminations in accordance with section 2032.

(2) *Exception for alternative valuation of taxable termination.*—In the case of a taxable termination with respect to which an election is made under section 2624(c) to value property in accordance with section 2032, a Form 706GS(T) must be filed on or before the 15th day of the 4th month after the close of the calendar year in which the taxable termination occurred, or on or before the 10th month following the month in which the death that resulted in the taxable termination occurred, whichever is later.

(e) *Place for filing returns.*—See section 6091 for the place for filing any return, declaration, statement, or other document, or copies thereof, required by chapter 13.

(f) *Lien on property.*—The liens imposed under sections 6324, 6324A, and 6324B are applicable with respect to the tax imposed under chapter 13. Thus, a lien under section 6324 is imposed in the amount of the tax imposed by section 2601 on all property transferred in a generation-skipping transfer until the tax is fully paid or becomes uncollectible by reason of lapse of time. The lien attaches at the time of the generation-skipping transfer and is in addition to the lien for taxes under section 6321. [Reg. § 26.2662-1.]

☐ [T.D. 8644, 12-26-95.]

[Reg. § 26.2663-1]

§ 26.2663-1. Recapture tax under section 2032A.—See § 26.2642-4(a)(4) for rules relating to the recomputation of the applicable fraction and the imposition of additional GST tax, if additional estate tax is imposed under section 2032A. [Reg. § 26.2663-1.]

☐ [T.D. 8644, 12-26-95.]

[Reg. § 26.2663-2]

§ 26.2663-2. Application of chapter 13 to transfers by nonresidents not citizens of the United States.—(a) *In general.*—This section provides rules for applying chapter 13 of the Internal Revenue Code to transfers by a transferor who is a nonresident not a citizen of the United States (NRA transferor). For purposes of this section, an individual is a resident or citizen of the United States if that individual is a resident or citizen of the United States under the rules of chapter 11 or 12 of the Internal Revenue Code, as the case may be. Every NRA transferor is allowed a GST exemption of $1,000,000. See § 26.2632-1 regarding the allocation of the exemption.

(b) *Transfers subject to chapter 13.*—(1) *Direct skips.*—A transfer by a NRA transferor is a direct skip subject to chapter 13 only to the extent that the transfer is subject to the Federal estate or gift tax within the meaning of § 26.2652-1(a)(2). See § 26.2612-1(a) for the definition of *direct skip.*

(2) *Taxable distributions and taxable terminations.*—Chapter 13 applies to a taxable distribution or a taxable termination to the extent that the initial transfer of property to the trust by a NRA transferor, whether during life or at death, was subject to the Federal estate or gift tax within the meaning of § 26.2652-1(a)(2). See § 26.2612-1(b) for the definition of a *taxable termination* and § 26.2612-1(c) for the definition of a *taxable distribution.*

(c) *Trusts funded in part with property subject to chapter 13 and in part with property not subject to chapter 13.*—(1) *In general.*—If a single trust created by a NRA transferor is in part subject to chapter 13 under the rules of paragraph (b) of this section and in part not subject to chapter 13, the applicable fraction with respect to the trust is determined as of the date of the transfer, except as provided in paragraph (c)(3) of this section.

(i) *Numerator of applicable fraction.*—The numerator of the applicable fraction is the sum of the amount of GST exemption allocated to the trust (if any) plus the value of the nontax portion of the trust.

(ii) *Denominator of applicable fraction.*—The denominator of the applicable fraction is the value of the property transferred to the trust reduced as provided in § 26.2642-1(c).

(2) *Nontax portion of the trust.*—The nontax portion of a trust is a fraction, the numerator of which is the value of property not subject to chapter 13 determined as of the date of the initial completed transfer to the trust, and the denominator of which is the value of the entire trust. For example, T, a NRA transferor, transfers property that has a value of $1,000 to a generation-skipping trust. Of the property transferred to the trust, property having a value of $200 is subject to chapter 13 and property having a value of $800 is not subject to chapter 13. The nontax portion is .8 ($800 (the value of the property not subject to chapter 13) over $1,000 (the total value of the property transferred to the trust)).

(3) *Special rule with respect to the estate tax inclusion period.*—For purposes of this section, the provisions of § 26.2632-1(c), providing rules

applicable in the case of an estate tax inclusion period (ETIP), apply only if the property transferred by the NRA transferor is subsequently included in the transferor's gross estate. If the property is not subsequently included in the gross estate, then the nontax portion of the trust and the applicable fraction are determined as of the date of the initial transfer. If the property is subsequently included in the gross estate, then the nontax portion and the applicable fraction are determined as of the date of death.

(d) *Examples.*—The following examples illustrate the provisions of this section. In each example T, a NRA, is the transferor; C is T's child; and GC is C's child and a grandchild of T:

Example 1. Direct transfer to skip person. T transfers property to GC in a transfer that is subject to Federal gift tax under chapter 12 within the meaning of § 26.2652-1(a)(2). At the time of the transfer, C and GC are NRAs. T's transfer is subject to chapter 13 because the transfer is subject to gift tax under chapter 12.

Example 2. Transfers of both U.S. and foreign situs property. (i) T's will established a testamentary trust for the benefit of C and GC. The trust was funded with stock in a publicly traded U.S. corporation having a value on the date of T's death of $100,000, and property not situated in the United States (and therefore not subject to estate tax) having a value on the date of T's death of $400,000.

(ii) On a timely filed estate tax return (Form 706NA), the executor of T's estate allocates $50,000 of GST exemption under section 2632(a) to the trust. The numerator of the applicable fraction is $450,000, the sum of $50,000 (the amount of exemption allocated to the trust) plus $400,000 (the value of the nontax portion of the trust (4/5 x $500,000)). The denominator is $500,000. Hence, the applicable fraction with respect to the trust is .9 ($450,000/$500,000), and the inclusion ratio is .1 (1 - 9/10).

Example 3. Inter vivos transfer of U.S. and foreign situs property to a trust and a timely allocation of GST exemption. T establishes a trust providing that trust income is payable to T's child for life and the remainder is to be paid to T's grandchild. T transfers property to the trust that has a value of $100,000 and is subject to chapter 13. T also transfers property to the trust that has a value of $300,000 but is not subject to chapter 13. T allocates $100,000 of exemption to the trust on a timely filed United States Gift (and Generation-Skipping Transfer) Tax Return (Form 709). The applicable fraction with respect to the trust is 1, determined as follows: $300,000 (the value of the nontax portion of the trust) plus $100,000 (the exemption allocated to the trust)/$400,000 (the total value of the property transferred to the trust).

Example 4. Inter vivos transfer of U.S. and foreign situs property to a trust and a late allocation of GST exemption. (i) In 1996, T transfers $500,000 of property to an inter vivos trust the terms of which provide that income is payable to C, for life, with the remainder to GC. The property transferred to the trust consists of property subject to chapter 13 that has a value of $400,000 on the date of the transfer and property not subject to chapter 13 that has a value of $100,000. T does not allocate GST exemption to the trust. On the transfer date, the nontax portion of the trust is .2 ($100,000/$500,000) and the applicable fraction is also .2 determined as follows: $100,000 (the value of the nontax portion of the trust)/ $500,000 (the value of the property transferred to the trust).

(ii) In 1999, when the value of the trust is $800,000, T allocates $100,000 of GST exemption to the trust. The applicable fraction of the trust must be recomputed. The numerator of the applicable fraction is $260,000 ($100,000 (the amount of GST exemption allocated to the trust)) plus $160,000 (the value of the nontax portion of the trust as of the date of allocation (.2 x $800,000)). The denominator of the applicable fraction is $800,000. Accordingly, the applicable fraction with respect to the trust after the allocation is .325 ($260,000/$800,000) and the inclusion ratio is .675 (1 - .325).

Example 5. Taxable termination. The facts are the same as in *Example 4* except that, in 2006, when the value of the property is $1,200,000, C dies and the trust corpus is distributed to GC. The termination is a taxable termination. If no further GST exemption has been allocated to the trust, the applicable fraction remains .325 and the inclusion ratio remains .675.

Example 6. Estate Tax Inclusion Period. (i) T transferred property to an inter vivos trust the terms of which provided T with an annuity payable for 10 years or until T's prior death. The annuity satisfies the definition of a qualified interest under section 2702(b). The trust also provided that, at the end of the trust term, the remainder will pass to GC or GC's estate. The property transferred to the trust consisted of property subject to chapter 13 that has a value of $100,000 and property not subject to chapter 13 that has a value of $400,000. T allocated $100,000 of GST exemption to the trust. If T dies within the 10 year period, the value of the trust principal will be subject to inclusion in T's gross estate to the extent provided in sections 2103 and 2104(b). Accordingly, the ETIP rule under paragraph (c)(3) of this section applies.

(ii) In year 6 of the trust term, T died. At T's death, the trust corpus had a value of $800,000, and $500,000 was includible in T's gross estate as provided in sections 2103 and 2104(b). Thus, $500,000 of the trust corpus is subject to chapter 13 and $300,000 is not subject to chapter 13. The $100,000 GST exemption allocation is effective as of T's date of death. Also, the nontax portion of the trust and the applicable fraction are determined as of T's date of death. In this case, the nontax portion of the trust is .375, determined as follows: $300,000 (the value of the trust not subject to chapter 13)/$800,000 (the value of the trust). The numerator of the applicable fraction is $400,000, determined as follows: $100,000 (GST exemption previously allocated to the trust) plus $300,000 (the value of the nontax portion of the trust). The denominator of the applicable fraction is $800,000. Thus, the applicable fraction with respect to the trust is .50, unless additional exemption is allocated to the trust by T's executor or the automatic allocation rules of § 26.2632-1(d)(2) apply.

Example 7. The facts are the same as in *Example 6* except that T survives the termination date of T's retained annuity and the trust corpus is distributed to GC. Since the trust was not included in T's gross estate, the ETIP rules do not apply. Accordingly, the nontax portion of the trust and the applicable fraction are determined as of the date of the transfer to the trust. The nontax portion of the trust is .80 ($400,000/$500,000). The numerator of the applicable fraction is $500,000 determined as follows: $100,000 (GST exemption allocated to the trust) plus $400,000 (the value of the nontax portion of the trust). Accordingly, the applicable fraction is 1, and the inclusion ratio is zero.

(e) *Transitional rule for allocations for transfers made before December 27, 1995.*—If a NRA made a GST (inter vivos or testamentary) after December 23, 1992, and before December 27, 1995, that is subject to chapter 13 (within the meaning of § 26.2663-2), the NRA will be treated as having made a timely allocation of GST exemption to the transfer in a calendar year in the order prescribed in section 2632(c). Thus, a NRA's unused GST exemption will initially be treated as allocated to any direct skips made during the calendar year and then to any trusts with respect to which the NRA made transfers during the same calendar year and from which a taxable distribution or a taxable termination may occur. Allocations within the above categories are made in the order in which the transfers occur. Allocations among simultaneous transfers within the same category are made pursuant to the principles of section 2632(c)(2). This transitional allocation rule will not apply if the NRA transferor, or the executor of the NRA's estate, as the case may be, elected to have an automatic allocation of GST exemption not apply by describing on a timely-filed Form 709 for the year of the transfer, or a timely filed Form 706NA, the details of the transfer and the extent to which the allocation was not to apply. [Reg. § 26.2663-2.]

☐ [*T.D.* 8644, 12-26-95.]

Reg. § 26.2663-2(e)

Special Valuation Rules

See p. 20,601 for regulations not amended to reflect law changes

[Reg. § 25.2701-0]

§ 25.2701-0. Table of contents.—This section lists the major paragraphs contained in §§ 25.2701-1 through 25.2701-8.

(e) Computation of reduction if initial transfer is split under section 2513.

    (1) In general.

    (2) Transfers during joint lives.

    (3) Transfers at or after death of either spouse.

    (f) Examples.

    (g) Double taxation otherwise avoided.

    (h) Effective date.

§ 25.2701-6. *Indirect holding of interests.*

    (a) In general.

      (1) Attribution to individuals.

      (2) Corporations.

      (3) Partnerships.

      (4) Estates, trusts, and other entities.

      (5) Multiple attribution.

    (b) Examples.

§ 25.2701-7. *Separate interests.*

§ 25.2701-8. *Effective dates.*
[Reg. § 25.2701-0.]

☐ [*T.D.* 8395, 1-28-92. *Amended by T.D.* 8536, 5-4-94.]

[Reg. § 25.2701-1]

§ 25.2701-1. Special valuation rules in the case of transfers of certain interests in corporations and partnerships.—(a) *In general.*—(1) *Scope of section 2701.*—Section 2701 provides special valuation rules to determine the amount of the gift when an individual transfers an equity interest in a corporation or partnership to a member of the individual's family. For section 2701 to apply, the transferor or an applicable family member (as defined in paragraph (d)(2) of this section) must, immediately after the transfer, hold an applicable retained interest (a type of equity interest defined in § 25.2701-2(b)(1)). If certain subsequent payments with respect to the applicable retained interest do not conform to the assumptions used in valuing the interest at the time of the initial transfer, § 25.2701-4 provides a special rule to increase the individual's later taxable gifts or taxable estate. Section 25.2701-5 provides an adjustment to mitigate the effects of double taxation when an applicable retained interest is subsequently transferred.

    (2) *Effect of section 2701.*—If section 2701 applies to a transfer, the amount of the transferor's gift, if any, is determined using a subtraction method of valuation (described in § 25.2701-3). Under this method, the amount of the gift is determined by subtracting the value of any family-held applicable retained interests and other non-transferred equity interests from the aggregate value of family-held interests in the corporation or partnership (the "entity"). Generally, in determining the value of any applicable retained interest held by the transferor or an applicable family member—

    (i) Any put, call, or conversion right, any right to compel liquidation, or any similar right is valued at zero if the right is an "extraordinary payment right" (as defined in § 25.2701-2(b)(2));

    (ii) Any distribution right in a controlled entity (*e.g.,* a right to receive dividends) is valued at zero unless the right is a "qualified payment right" (as defined in § 25.2701-2(b)(6)); and

    (iii) Any other right (including a qualified payment right) is valued as if any right valued at zero did not exist but otherwise without regard to section 2701.

    (3) *Example.*—The following example illustrates rules of this paragraph (a).

    Example. A, an individual, holds all the outstanding stock of S Corporation. A exchanges A's shares in S for 100 shares of 10-percent cumulative preferred stock and 100 shares of voting common stock. A transfers the common stock to A's child. Section 2701 applies to the transfer because A has transferred an equity interest (the common stock) to a member of A's family, and immediately thereafter holds an applicable retained interest (the preferred stock). A's preferred stock is valued under the rules of section 2701. A's gift is determined under the subtraction method by subtracting the value of A's preferred stock from the value of A's interest in S immediately prior to the transfer.

    (b) *Transfers and other triggering events.*—(1) *Completed transfers.*—Section 2701 applies to determine the existence and amount of any gift, whether or not the transfer would otherwise be a taxable gift under chapter 12 of the Internal Revenue Code. For example, section 2701 applies to a transfer that would not otherwise be a gift under chapter 12 because it was a transfer for full and adequate consideration.

    (2) *Transactions treated as transfers.*—(i) *In general.*—Except as provided in paragraph (b)(3) of this section, for purposes of section 2701, transfer includes the following transactions:

    (A) A contribution to the capital of a new or existing entity;

    (B) A redemption, recapitalization, or other change in the capital structure of an entity (a "capital structure transaction"), if—

    (1) The transferor or an applicable family member receives an applicable retained interest in the capital structure transaction;

    (2) The transferor or an applicable family member holding an applicable retained interest before the capital structure transaction surrenders an equity interest that is junior to the applicable retained interest (a "subordinate interest") and receives property other than an applicable retained interest; or

    (3) The transferor or an applicable family member holding an applicable retained interest before the capital structure transaction surrenders an equity interest in the entity (other

than a subordinate interest) and the fair market value of the applicable retained interest is increased; or

(C) The termination of an indirect holding in an entity (as defined in §25.2701-6) (or a contribution to capital by an entity to the extent an individual indirectly holds an interest in the entity), if—

(1) The property is held in a trust as to which the indirect holder is treated as the owner under subchapter J of chapter 1 of the Internal Revenue Code; or

(2) If the termination (or contribution) is not treated as a transfer under paragraph (b)(2)(i)(C)(1) of this section, to the extent the value of the indirectly-held interest would have been included in the value of the indirect holder's gross estate for Federal estate tax purposes if the indirect holder died immediately prior to the termination.

(ii) *Multiple attribution.*—For purposes of paragraph (b)(2)(i)(C) of this section, if the transfer of an indirect holding in property is treated as a transfer with respect to more than one indirect holder, the transfer is attributed in the following order:

(A) First, to the indirect holder(s) who transferred the interest to the entity (without regard to section 2513);

(B) Second, to the indirect holder(s) possessing a presently exercisable power to designate the person who shall possess or enjoy the property;

(C) Third, to the indirect holder(s) presently entitled to receive the income from the interest;

(D) Fourth, to the indirect holder(s) specifically entitled to receive the interest at a future date; and

(E) Last, to any other indirect holder(s) proportionally.

(3) *Excluded transactions.*—For purposes of section 2701, a transfer does not include the following transactions:

(i) A capital structure transaction, if the transferor, each applicable family member, and each member of the transferor's family holds substantially the same interest after the transaction as that individual held before the transaction. For this purpose, common stock with nonlapsing voting rights and nonvoting common stock are interests that are substantially the same;

(ii) A shift of rights occurring upon the execution of a qualified disclaimer described in section 2518; and

(iii) A shift of rights occurring upon the release, exercise, or lapse of a power of appointment other than a general power of appointment described in section 2514, except to the extent the release, exercise, or lapse would otherwise be a transfer under chapter 12.

(c) *Circumstances in which section 2701 does not apply.*—To the extent provided, section 2701 does not apply in the following cases:

(1) *Marketable transferred interests.*—Section 2701 does not apply if there are readily available market quotations on an established securities market for the value of the transferred interests.

(2) *Marketable retained interests.*—Section 25.2701-2 does not apply to any applicable retained interest if there are readily available market quotations on an established securities market for the value of the applicable retained interests.

(3) *Interests of the same class.*—Section 2701 does not apply if the retained interest is of the same class of equity as the transferred interest or if the retained interest is of a class that is proportional to the class of the transferred interest. A class is the same class as is (or is proportional to the class of) the transferred interest if the rights are identical (or proportional) to the rights of the transferred interest, except for non-lapsing differences in voting rights (or, for a partnership, non-lapsing differences with respect to management and limitations on liability). For purposes of this section, non-lapsing provisions necessary to comply with partnership allocation requirements of the Internal Revenue Code (*e.g.*, section 704(b)) are non-lapsing differences with respect to limitations on liability. A right that lapses by reason of Federal or State law is treated as a non-lapsing right unless the Secretary determines, by regulation or by published revenue ruling, that it is necessary to treat such a right as a lapsing right to accomplish the purposes of section 2701. An interest in a partnership is not an interest in the same class as the transferred interest if the transferor or applicable family members have the right to alter the liability of the transferee.

(4) *Proportionate transfers.*—Section 2701 does not apply to a transfer by an individual to a member of the individual's family of equity interests to the extent the transfer by that individual results in a proportionate reduction of each class of equity interest held by the individual and all applicable family members in the aggregate immediately before the transfer. Thus, for example, section 2701 does not apply if P owns 50 percent of each class of equity interest in a corporation and transfers a portion of each class to P's child in a manner that reduces each interest held by P and any applicable family members, in the aggregate, by 10 percent even if the transfer does not proportionately reduce P's interest in each class. See §25.2701-6 regarding indirect holding of interests.

(d) *Family definitions.*—(1) *Member of the family.*—A member of the family is, with respect to any transferor—

(i) The transferor's spouse;

(ii) Any lineal descendant of the transferor or the transferor's spouse; and

(iii) The spouse of any such lineal descendant.

(2) *Applicable family member.*—An applicable family member is, with respect to any transferor—

(i) The transferor's spouse;

(ii) Any ancestor of the transferor or the transferor's spouse; and

(iii) The spouse of any such ancestor.

(3) *Relationship by adoption.*—For purposes of section 2701, any relationship by legal adoption is the same as a relationship by blood.

(e) *Examples.*—The following examples illustrate provisions of this section:

Example 1. P, an individual, holds all the outstanding stock of X Corporation. Assume the fair market value of P's interest in X immediately prior to the transfer is $1.5 million. X is recapitalized so that P holds 1,000 shares of $1,000 par value preferred stock bearing an annual cumulative dividend of $100 per share (the aggregate fair market value of which is assumed to be $1 million) and 1,000 shares of voting common stock. P transfers the common stock to P's child. Section 2701 applies to the transfer because P has transferred an equity interest (the common stock) to a member of P's family and immediately thereafter holds an applicable retained interest (the preferred stock). P's right to receive annual cumulative dividends is a qualified payment right and is valued for purposes of section 2701 at its fair market value of $1,000,000. The amount of P's gift, determined using the subtraction method of §25.2701-3, is $500,000 ($1,500,000 minus $1,000,000).

Example 2. The facts are the same as in *Example 1*, except that the preferred dividend right is noncumulative. Under §25.2701-2, P's preferred dividend right is valued at zero because it is a distribution right in a controlled entity, but is not a qualified payment right. All of P's other rights in the preferred stock are valued as if P's dividend right does not exist but otherwise without regard to section 2701. The amount of P's gift, determined using the subtraction method, is $1,500,000 ($1,500,000 minus $0). P may elect, however, to treat the dividend right as a qualified payment right as provided in §25.2701-2(c)(2). [Reg. §25.2701-1.]

☐ [*T.D. 8395, 1-28-92. Amended by T.D. 8536, 5-4-94.*]

[Reg. §25.2701-2]

§25.2701-2. Special valuation rules for applicable retained interests.—(a) *In general.*—In determining the amount of a gift under §25.2701-3, the value of any applicable retained interest (as defined in paragraph (b)(1) of this section) held by the transferor or by an applicable family member is determined using the rules of chapter 12, with the modifications prescribed by this section. See §25.2701-6 regarding the indirect holding of interests.

(1) *Valuing an extraordinary payment right.*—Any extraordinary payment right (as defined in paragraph (b)(2) of this section) is valued at zero.

(2) *Valuing a distribution right.*—Any distribution right (as defined in paragraph (b)(3) of this section) in a controlled entity is valued at zero, unless it is a qualified payment right (as defined in paragraph (b)(6) of this section). Controlled entity is defined in paragraph (b)(5) of this section.

(3) *Special rule for valuing a qualified payment right held in conjunction with an extraordinary payment right.*—If an applicable retained interest confers a qualified payment right and one or more extraordinary payment rights, the value of all these rights is determined by assuming that each extraordinary payment right is exercised in a manner that results in the lowest total value being determined for all the rights, using a consistent set of assumptions and giving due regard to the entity's net worth, prospective earning power, and other relevant factors (the "lower of" valuation rule). See §§20.2031-2(f) and 20.2031-3 for rules relating to the valuation of business interests generally.

(4) *Valuing other rights.*—Any other right (including a qualified payment right not subject to the prior paragraph) is valued as if any right valued at zero does not exist and as if any right valued under the lower of rule is exercised in a manner consistent with the assumptions of that rule but otherwise without regard to section 2701. Thus, if an applicable retained interest carries no rights that are valued at zero or under the lower of rule, the value of the interest for purposes of section 2701 is its fair market value.

(5) *Example.*—The following example illustrates rules of this paragraph (a).

Example. P, an individual, holds all 1,000 shares of X Corporation's $1,000 par value preferred stock bearing an annual cumulative dividend of $100 per share and holds all 1,000 shares of X's voting common stock. P has the right to put all the preferred stock to X at any time for $900,000. P transfers the common stock to P's child and immediately thereafter holds the preferred stock. Assume that at the time of the transfer, the fair market value of X is $1,500,000, and the fair market value of P's annual cumulative dividend right is $1,000,000. Because the preferred stock confers both an extraordinary payment right (the put right) and a qualified payment right (*i.e.*, the right to receive cumulative dividends), the lower of rule applies and the value of these rights is determined as if the put right will be exercised in a manner that results in the lowest total value being determined for the rights (in this case, by assuming that the put will be exercised immediately). The value of P's preferred stock is $900,000 (the lower of $1,000,000 or $900,000). The amount of the gift is $600,000 ($1,500,000 minus $900,000).

(b) *Definitions.*—(1) *Applicable retained interest.*—An applicable retained interest is any equity interest in a corporation or partnership with respect to which there is either—

(i) An extraordinary payment right (as defined in paragraph (b)(2) of this section), or

(ii) In the case of a controlled entity (as defined in paragraph (b)(5) of this section), a distribution right (as defined in paragraph (b)(3) of this section).

(2) *Extraordinary payment right.*—Except as provided in paragraph (b)(4) of this section, an extraordinary payment right is any put, call, or conversion right, any right to compel liquidation, or any similar right, the exercise or nonexercise of which affects the value of the transferred interest. A call right includes any warrant, option, or other right to acquire one or more equity interests.

(3) *Distribution right.*—A distribution right is the right to receive distributions with respect to an equity interest. A distribution right does not include—

(i) Any right to receive distributions with respect to an interest that is of the same class as, or a class that is subordinate to, the transferred interest;

(ii) Any extraordinary payment right; or

(iii) Any right described in paragraph (b)(4) of this section.

(4) *Rights that are not extraordinary payment rights or distribution rights.*—Mandatory payment rights, liquidation participation rights, rights to guaranteed payments of a fixed amount under section 707(c), and non-lapsing conversion rights are neither extraordinary payment rights nor distribution rights.

(i) *Mandatory payment right.*—A mandatory payment right is a right to receive a payment required to be made at a specific time for a specific amount. For example, a mandatory redemption right in preferred stock requiring that the stock be redeemed at its fixed par value on a date certain is a mandatory payment right and therefore not an extraordinary payment right or a distribution right. A right to receive a specific amount on the death of the holder is a mandatory payment right.

(ii) *Liquidation participation rights.*—A liquidation participation right is a right to participate in a liquidating distribution. If the transferor, members of the transferor's family, or applicable family members have the ability to compel liquidation, the liquidation participation

right is valued as if the ability to compel liquidation—

(A) Did not exist, or

(B) If the lower of rule applies, is exercised in a manner that is consistent with that rule.

(iii) *Right to a guaranteed payment of a fixed amount under section 707(c).*—The right to a guaranteed payment of a fixed amount under section 707(c) is the right to a guaranteed payment (within the meaning of section 707(c)) the amount of which is determined at a fixed rate (including a rate that bears a fixed relationship to a specified market interest rate). A payment that is contingent as to time or amount is not a guaranteed payment of a fixed amount.

(iv) *Non-lapsing conversion right.*—(A) *Corporations.*—A non-lapsing conversion right, in the case of a corporation, is a non-lapsing right to convert an equity interest in a corporation into a fixed number or a fixed percentage of shares of the same class as the transferred interest (or into an interest that would be of the same class but for non-lapsing differences in voting rights), that is subject to proportionate adjustments for changes in the equity ownership of the corporation and to adjustments similar to those provided in section 2701(d) for unpaid payments.

(B) *Partnerships.*—A non-lapsing conversion right, in the case of a partnership, is a non-lapsing right to convert an equity interest in a partnership into a specified interest (other than an interest represented by a fixed dollar amount) of the same class as the transferred interest (or into an interest that would be of the same class but for non-lapsing differences in management rights or limitations on liability) that is subject to proportionate adjustments for changes in the equity ownership of the partnership and to adjustments similar to those provided in section 2701(d) for unpaid payments.

(C) *Proportionate adjustments in equity ownership.*—For purposes of this paragraph (b)(4), an equity interest is subject to proportionate adjustments for changes in equity ownership if, in the case of a corporation, proportionate adjustments are required to be made for splits, combinations, reclassifications, and similar changes in capital stock, or, in the case of a partnership, the equity interest is protected from dilution resulting from changes in the partnership structure.

(D) *Adjustments for unpaid payments.*—For purposes of this paragraph (b)(4), an equity interest is subject to adjustments similar to those provided in section 2701(d) if it provides for—

(1) Cumulative payments;

(2) Compounding of any unpaid payments at the rate specified in § 25.2701-4(c)(2); and

Reg. § 25.2701-2(b)(1)

(3) Adjustment of the number or percentage of shares or the size of the interest into which it is convertible to take account of accumulated but unpaid payments.

(5) Controlled entity.—(i) *In general.*—For purposes of section 2701, a controlled entity is a corporation or partnership controlled, immediately before a transfer, by the transferor, applicable family members, and any lineal descendants of the parents of the transferor or the transferor's spouse. See § 25.2701-6 regarding indirect holding of interests.

(ii) *Corporations.*—(A) *In general.*—In the case of a corporation, control means the holding of at least 50 percent of the total voting power or total fair market value of the equity interests in the corporation.

(B) *Voting rights.*—Equity interests that carry no right to vote other than on liquidation, merger, or a similar event are not considered to have voting rights for purposes of this paragraph (b)(5)(ii). Generally, a voting right is considered held by an individual to the extent that the individual, either alone or in conjunction with any other person, is entitled to exercise (or direct the exercise of) the right. However, if an equity interest carrying voting rights is held in a fiduciary capacity, the voting rights are not considered held by the fiduciary, but instead are considered held by each beneficial owner of the interest and by each individual who is a permissible recipient of the income from the interest. A voting right does not include a right to vote that is subject to a contingency that has not occurred, other than a contingency that is within the control of the individual holding the right.

(iii) *Partnerships.*—In the case of any partnership, control means the holding of at least 50 percent of either the capital interest or the profits interest in the partnership. Any right to a guaranteed payment under section 707(c) of a fixed amount is disregarded in making this determination. In addition, in the case of a limited partnership, control means the holding of any equity interest as a general partner. See § 25.2701-2(b)(4)(iii) for the definition of a right to a guaranteed payment of a fixed amount under section 707(c).

(6) Qualified payment right.—(i) *In general.*— A qualified payment right is a right to receive qualified payments. A qualified payment is a distribution that is—

(A) A dividend payable on a periodic basis (at least annually) under any cumulative preferred stock, to the extent such dividend is determined at a fixed rate;

(B) Any other cumulative distribution payable on a periodic basis (at least annually) with respect to an equity interest, to the extent determined at a fixed rate or as a fixed amount; or

(C) Any distribution right for which an election has been made pursuant to paragraph (c)(2) of this section.

(ii) *Fixed rate.*—For purposes of this section, a payment rate that bears a fixed relationship to a specified market interest rate is a payment determined at a fixed rate.

(c) Qualified payment elections.—(1) *Election to treat a qualified payment right as other than a qualified payment right.*—Any transferor holding a qualified payment right may elect to treat all rights held by the transferor of the same class as rights that are not qualified payment rights. An election may be a partial election, in which case the election must be exercised with respect to a consistent portion of each payment right in the class as to which the election has been made.

(2) Election to treat other distribution rights as qualified payment rights.—Any individual may elect to treat a distribution right held by that individual in a controlled entity as a qualified payment right. An election may be a partial election, in which case the election must be exercised with respect to a consistent portion of each payment right in the class as to which the election has been made. An election under this paragraph (c)(2) will not cause the value of the applicable retained interest conferring the distribution right to exceed the fair market value of the applicable retained interest (determined without regard to section 2701). The election is effective only to the extent—

(i) Specified in the election, and

(ii) That the payments elected are permissible under the legal instrument giving rise to the right and are consistent with the legal right of the entity to make the payment.

(3) Elections irrevocable.—Any election under paragraph (c)(1) or (c)(2) of this section is revocable only with the consent of the Commissioner.

(4) Treatment of certain payments to applicable family members.—Any payment right described in paragraph (b)(6) of this section held by an applicable family member is treated as a payment right that is not a qualified payment right unless the applicable family member elects (pursuant to paragraph (c)(2) of this section) to treat the payment right as a qualified payment right. An election may be a partial election, in which case the election must be exercised with respect to a consistent portion of each payment right in the class as to which the election has been made.

(5) Time and manner of elections.—Any election under paragraph (c)(1) or (c)(2) of this section is made by attaching a statement to the Form 709, Federal Gift Tax Return, filed by the transferor on which the transfer is reported. An election filed after the time of the filing of the Form 709 reporting the transfer is not a valid election. An election filed as of March 28, 1992,

for transfers made prior to its publication is effective. The statement must—

(i) Set forth the name, address, and taxpayer identification number of the electing individual and of the transferor, if different;

(ii) If the electing individual is not the transferor filing the return, state the relationship between the individual and the transferor;

(iii) Specifically identify the transfer disclosed on the return to which the election applies;

(iv) Describe in detail the distribution right to which the election applies;

(v) State the provision of the regulation under which the election is being made; and

(vi) If the election is being made under paragraph (c)(2) of this section—

(A) State the amounts that the election assumes will be paid, and the times that the election assumes the payments will be made;

(B) Contain a statement, signed by the electing individual, in which the electing individual agrees that—

(1) If payments are not made as provided in the election, the individual's subsequent taxable gifts or taxable estate will, upon the occurrence of a taxable event (as defined in § 25.2701-4(b)), be increased by an amount determined under § 25.2701-4(c), and

(2) The individual will be personally liable for any increase in tax attributable thereto.

(d) *Examples.*—The following examples illustrate provisions of this section:

Example 1. On March 30, 1991, P transfers nonvoting common stock of X Corporation to P's child, while retaining $100 par value voting preferred stock bearing a cumulative annual dividend of $10. Immediately before the transfer, P held 100 percent of the stock. Because X is a controlled entity (within the meaning of paragraph (b)(5) of this section), P's dividend right is a distribution right that is subject to section 2701. See § 25.2701-2(b)(3). Because the distribution right is an annual cumulative dividend, it is a qualified payment right. See § 25.2701-2(b)(6).

Example 2. The facts are the same as in *Example 1*, except that the dividend right is non-cumulative. P's dividend right is a distribution right in a controlled entity, but is not a qualified payment right because the dividend is non-cumulative. Therefore, the non-cumulative dividend right is valued at zero under § 25.2701-2(a)(2). If the corporation were not a controlled entity, P's dividend right would be valued without regard to section 2701.

Example 3. The facts are the same as in *Example 1*. Because P holds sufficient voting power to compel liquidation of X, P's right to participate in liquidation is an extraordinary payment right under paragraph (b)(2) of this section. Because P holds an extraordinary payment right in conjunction with a qualified payment right (the

right to receive cumulative dividends), the lower of rule applies.

Example 4. The facts are the same as in *Example 1*, except that immediately before the transfer, P, applicable family members of P, and members of P's family, hold 60 percent of the voting rights in X. Assume that 80 percent of the vote is required to compel liquidation of any interest in X. P's right to participate in liquidation is not an extraordinary payment right under paragraph (b)(2) of this section, because P and P's family cannot compel liquidation of X. P's preferred stock is an applicable retained interest that carries no rights that are valued under the special valuation rules of section 2701. Thus, in applying the valuation method of § 25.2701-3, the value of P's preferred stock is its fair market value determined without regard to section 2701.

Example 5. L holds 10-percent non-cumulative preferred stock and common stock in a corporation that is a controlled entity. L transfers the common stock to L's child. L holds no extraordinary payment rights with respect to the preferred stock. L elects under paragraph (c)(2) of this section to treat the noncumulative dividend right as a qualified payment right consisting of the right to receive a cumulative annual dividend of 5 percent. Under § 25.2701-2(c)(2), the value of the distribution right pursuant to the election is the lesser of—

(A) The fair market value of the right to receive a cumulative 5-percent dividend from the corporation, giving due regard to the corporation's net worth, prospective earning power, and dividend-paying capacity; or

(B) The value of the distribution right determined without regard to section 2701 and without regard to the terms of the qualified payment election. [Reg. § 25.2701-2.]

☐ [*T.D.* 8395, 1-28-92.]

[Reg. § 25.2701-3]

§ 25.2701-3. Determination of amount of gift.—(a) *Overview.*—(1) *In general.*—The amount of the gift resulting from any transfer to which section 2701 applies is determined by a subtraction method of valuation. Under this method, the amount of the transfer is determined by subtracting the values of all family-held senior equity interests from the fair market value of all family-held interests in the entity determined immediately before the transfer. The values of the senior equity interests held by the transferor and applicable family members generally are determined under section 2701. Other family-held senior equity interests are valued at their fair market value. The balance is then appropriately allocated among the transferred interests and other family-held subordinate equity interests. Finally, certain discounts and other appropriate reductions are provided, but only to the extent permitted by this section.

(2) *Definitions.*—The following definitions apply for purposes of this section.

(i) *Family-held.*—Family-held means held (directly or indirectly) by an individual described in § 25.2701-2(b)(5)(i).

(ii) *Senior equity interest.*—Senior equity interest means an equity interest in the entity that carries a right to distributions of income or capital that is preferred as to the rights of the transferred interest.

(iii) *Subordinate equity interest.*— Subordinate equity interest means an equity interest in the entity as to which an applicable retained interest is a senior equity interest.

(b) *Valuation methodology.*—The following methodology is used to determine the amount of the gift when section 2701 applies.

(1) *Step 1—Valuation of family-held interests.*—(i) *In general.*—Except as provided in paragraph (b)(1)(ii) of this section[,] determine the fair market value of all family-held equity interests in the entity immediately after the transfer. The fair market value is determined by assuming that the interests are held by one individual, using a consistent set of assumptions.

(ii) *Special rule for contributions to capital.*— In the case of a contribution to capital, determine the fair market value of the contribution.

(2) *Step 2—Subtract the value of senior equity interests.*—*In general.*—If the amount determined in *Step 1* of paragraph (b)(1) of this section is not determined under the special rule for contributions to capital, from that value subtract the following amounts:

(A) An amount equal to the sum of the fair market value of all family-held senior equity interests, (other than applicable retained interests held by the transferor or applicable family members) and the fair market value of any family-held equity interests of the same class or a subordinate class to the transferred interests held by persons other than the transferor, members of the transferor's family, and applicable family members of the transferor. The fair market value of an interest is its pro rata share of the fair market value of all family-held senior equity interests of the same class (determined, immediately after the transfer, as is [if] all family-held senior equity interests were held by one individual); and

(B) The value of all applicable retained interests held by the transferor or applicable family members (other than an interest received as consideration for the transfer) determined under § 25.2701-2, taking into account the adjustment described in paragraph (b)(5) of this section.

(ii) *Special rule for contributions to capital.*— If the value determined in *Step 1* of paragraph

(b)(1) of this section is determined under the special rule for contributions to capital, subtract the value of any applicable retained interest received in exchange for the contribution to capital determined under § 25.2701-2.

(3) *Step 3—Allocate the remaining value among the transferred interests and other family-held subordinate equity interests.*—The value remaining after Step 2 is allocated among the transferred interests and other subordinate equity interests held by the transferor, applicable family members, and members of the transferor's family. If more than one class of family-held subordinate equity interest exists, the value remaining after Step 2 is allocated, beginning with the most senior class of subordinate equity interest, in the manner that would most fairly approximate their value if all rights valued under section 2701 at zero did not exist (or would be exercised in a manner consistent with the assumptions of the rule of § 25.2702-2(a)(4), if applicable). If there is no clearly appropriate method of allocating the remaining value pursuant to the preceding sentence, the remaining value (or the portion remaining after any partial allocation pursuant to the preceding sentence) is allocated to the interests in proportion to their fair market values determined without regard to section 2701.

(4) *Step 4—Determine the amount of the gift.*— (i) *In general.*—The amount allocated to the transferred interests in step 3 is reduced by the amounts determined under this paragraph (b)(4).

(ii) *Reduction for minority or similar discounts.*—Except as provided in § 25.2701-3(c), if the value of the transferred interest (determined without regard to section 2701) would be determined after application of a minority or similar discount with respect to the transferred interest, the amount of the gift determined under section 2701 is reduced by the excess, if any, of—

(A) A pro rata portion of the fair market value of the family-held interests of the same class (determined as if all voting rights conferred by family-held equity interests were held by one person who had no interest in the entity other than the family-held interests of the same class, but otherwise without regard to section 2701), over

(B) The value of the transferred interest (without regard to section 2701).

(iii) *Adjustment for transfers with a retained interest.*—If the value of the transferor's gift (determined without regard to section 2701) would be reduced under section 2702 to reflect the value of a retained interest, the value determined under section 2701 is reduced by the same amount.

(iv) *Reduction for consideration.*—The amount of the transfer (determined under section 2701) is reduced by the amount of consider-

Reg. § 25.2701-3(b)(4)(iv)

ation in money or money's worth received by the transferor, but not in excess of the amount of the gift (determined without regard to section 2701). The value of consideration received by the transferor in the form of an applicable retained interest in the entity is determined under section 2701 except that, in the case of a contribution to capital, the Step 4 value of such an interest is zero.

(5) *Adjustment in Step 2.*—(i) *In general.*—For purposes of paragraph (b)(2) of this section, if the percentage of any class of applicable retained interest held by the transferor and by applicable family members (including any interest received as consideration for the transfer) exceeds the family interest percentage, the excess is treated as a family-held interest that is not held by the transferor or an applicable family member.

(ii) *Family interest percentage.*—The family interest percentage is the highest ownership percentage (determined on the basis of relative fair market values) of family-held interests in—

(A) Any class of subordinate equity interest; or

(B) All subordinate equity interests, valued in the aggregate.

(c) *Minimum value rule.*—(1) *In general.*—If section 2701 applies to the transfer of an interest in an entity, the value of a junior equity interest is not less than its pro-rata portion of 10 percent of the sum of—

(i) The total value of all equity interests in the entity, and

(ii) The total amount of any indebtedness of the entity owed to the transferor and applicable family members.

(2) *Junior equity interest.*—For purposes of paragraph (c)(1) of this section, junior equity interest means common stock or, in the case of a partnership, any partnership interest under which the rights to income and capital are junior to the rights of all other classes of partnership interests. Common stock means the class or classes of stock that, under the facts and circumstances, are entitled to share in the reasonably anticipated residual growth in the entity.

(3) *Indebtedness.*—(i) *In general.*—For purposes of paragraph (c)(1) of this section, indebtedness owed to the transferor (or an applicable family member) does not include—

(A) Short-term indebtedness incurred with respect to the current conduct of the entity's trade or business (such as amounts payable for current services);

(B) Indebtedness owed to a third party solely because it is guaranteed by the transferor or an applicable family member; or

(C) Amounts permanently set aside in a qualified deferred compensation arrangement,

to the extent the amounts are unavailable for use by the entity.

(ii) *Leases.*—A lease of property is not indebtedness, without regard to the length of the lease term, if the lease payments represent full and adequate consideration for use of the property. Lease payments are considered full and adequate consideration if a good faith effort is made to determine the fair rental value under the lease and the terms of the lease conform to the value so determined. Arrearages with respect to a lease are indebtedness.

(d) *Examples.*—The application of the subtraction method described in this section is illustrated by the following examples:

Example 1. Corporation X has outstanding 1,000 shares of $1,000 par value voting preferred stock, each share of which carries a cumulative annual dividend of 8 percent and a right to put the stock to X for its par value at any time. In addition, there are outstanding 1,000 shares of non-voting common stock. A holds 600 shares of the preferred stock and 750 shares of the common stock. The balance of the preferred and common stock is held by B, a person unrelated to A. Because the preferred stock confers both a qualified payment right and an extraordinary payment right, A's rights are valued under the "lower of" rule of §25.2701-2(a)(3). Assume that A's rights in the preferred stock are valued at $800 per share under the "lower of" rule (taking account of A's voting rights). A transfers all of A's common stock to A's child. The method for determining the amount of A's gift is as follows—

Step 1: Assume the fair market value of all the family-held interests in X, taking account of A's control of the corporation, is determined to be $1 million.

Step 2: From the amount determined under Step 1, subtract $480,000 (600 shares × $800 (the section 2701 value of A's preferred stock, computed under the "lower of" rule of §25.2701-2(a)(3))).

Step 3: The result of Step 2 is a balance of $520,000. This amount is fully allocated to the 750 shares of family-held common stock.

Step 4: Because no consideration was furnished for the transfer, the adjustment under Step 4 is limited to the amount of any appropriate minority or similar discount. Before the application of Step 4 the amount of A's gift is $520,000.

Example 2. The facts are the same as in *Example 1,* except that prior to the transfer A holds only 50 percent of the common stock and B holds the remaining 50 percent. Assume that the fair market value of A's 600 shares of preferred stock is $600,000.

Step 1: Assume that the result of this step (determining the value of the family-held interest) is $980,000.

Step 2: From the amount determined under Step 1, subtract $500,000 ($400,000, the value of 500 shares of A's preferred stock determined under section 2701 plus $100,000, the fair market value of A's other 100 shares of preferred stock determined without regard to section 2701 pursuant to the valuation adjustment determined under paragraph (b)(5) of this section). The adjustment in Step 2 applies in this example because A's percentage ownership of the preferred stock (60 percent) exceeds the family interest percentage of the common stock (50 percent). Therefore, 100 shares of A's preferred stock are valued at fair market value, or $100,000 (100 × $1,000). The balance of A's preferred stock is valued under section 2701 at $400,000 (500 shares × $800). The value of A's preferred stock for purposes of section 2701 equals $500,000 ($100,000 plus $400,000).

Step 3: The result of Step 2 is $480,000 ($980,000 minus $500,000) which is allocated to the family-held common stock. Because A transferred all of the family-held subordinate equity interests, all of the value determined under Step 2 is allocated to the transferred shares.

Step 4: The adjustment under Step 4 is the same as in *Example 1*. Thus, the amount of the gift is $480,000.

Example 3. Corporation X has outstanding 1,000 shares of $1,000 par value non-voting preferred stock, each share of which carries a cumulative annual dividend of 8 percent and a right to put the stock to X for its par value at any time. In addition, there are outstanding 1,000 shares of voting common stock. A holds 600 shares of the preferred stock and 750 shares of 'the common stock. The balance of the preferred and common stock is held by B, a person unrelated to A. Assume further that steps one through three, as in *Example 1*, result in $520,000 being allocated to the family-held common stock and that A transfers only 75 shares of A's common stock. The transfer fragments A's voting interest. Under Step 4, an adjustment is appropriate to reflect the fragmentation of A's voting rights. The amount of the adjustment is the difference between 10 percent (75/750) of the fair market value of A's common shares and the fair market value of the transferred shares, each determined as if the holder thereof had no other interest in the corporation.

Example 4. On December 31, 1990, the capital structure of Y corporation consists of 1,000 shares of voting common stock held three-fourths by A and one-fourth by A's child, B. On January 15, 1991, A transfers 250 shares of common stock to Y in exchange for 300 shares of nonvoting, noncumulative 8% preferred stock with a section 2701 value of zero. Assume that the fair market value of Y is $1,000,000 at the time of the exchange and that the exchange by A is for full and adequate consideration in moneys' worth. However, for purposes of section 2701, if a subordinate equity interest is transferred in exchange for an applicable retained interest, consideration in the exchange is determined with reference to the section 2701 value of the senior interest. Thus, A is treated as transferring the common stock to the corporation for no consideration. Immediately after the transfer, B is treated as holding one-third (250/750) of the common stock and A is treated as holding two-thirds (500/750). The amount of the gift is determined as follows:

Step 1. Because Y is held exclusively by A and B, the Step 1 value is $1,000,000.

Step 2. The result of Step 2 is $1,000,000 ($1,000,000 – 0).

Step 3. The amount allocated to the transferred common stock is $250,000 (250/1,000 × $1,000,000). That amount is further allocated in proportion to the respective holdings of A and B in the common stock ($166,667 and $83,333, respectively).

Step 4. There is no Step 4 adjustment because the section 2701 value of the consideration received by A was zero and no minority discount would have been involved in the exchange. Thus, the amount of the gift is $83,333. If the section 2701 value of the applicable retained interests were $100,000, the Step 4 adjustment would have been a $33,333 reduction for consideration received ((250/750) × $100,000).

Example 5. The facts are the same as in *Example 4*, except that on January 6, 1992, when the fair market value of Y is still $1,000,000, A transfers A's remaining 500 shares of common stock to Y in exchange for 2500 shares of preferred stock. The second transfer is also for full and adequate consideration in money or money's worth. The result of Step 2 is the same—$1,000,000.

Step 3. The amount allocated to the common stock is $666,667 (500/750 × $1,000,000). Since A holds no common stock immediately after the transfer, A is treated as transferring the entire interest to the other shareholder (B). Thus, the amount of the gift is $666,667.

Step 4. There is no Step 4 adjustment because the section 2701 value of the consideration received by A was zero and no minority discount would have been involved in the exchange. Thus, the amount of the gift is the difference between $666,667 and the fair market value of B's shares immediately prior to the transfer to which section 2701 applied. [Reg. § 25.2701-3.]

☐ [*T.D. 8395, 1-28-92.*]

[Reg. § 25.2701-4]

§ 25.2701-4. Accumulated qualified payments.—(a) *In general.*—If a taxable event occurs with respect to any applicable retained interest conferring a distribution right that was previously valued as a qualified payment right (a "qualified payment interest"), the taxable estate or taxable gifts of the individual holding the interest are increased by the amount determined under paragraph(c) of this section.

(b) *Taxable event.*—(1) *In general.*—Except as otherwise provided in this section, taxable event means the transfer of a qualified payment interest, either during life or at death, by the individual in whose hands the interest was originally valued under section 2701 (the "interest holder") or by any individual treated pursuant to paragraph (b)(3) of this section in the same manner as the interest holder. Except as provided in paragraph (a)(2) of this section, any termination of an individual's rights with respect to a qualified payment interest is a taxable event. Thus, for example, if an individual is treated as indirectly holding a qualified payment interest held by a trust, a taxable event occurs on the earlier of—

(i) The termination of the individual's interest in the trust (whether by death or otherwise), or

(ii) The termination of the trust's interest in the qualified payment interest (whether by disposition or otherwise).

(2) *Exception.*—If, at the time of a termination of an individual's rights with respect to a qualified payment interest, the value of the property would be includible in the individual's gross estate for Federal estate tax purposes if the individual died immediately after the termination, a taxable transfer does not occur until the earlier of—

(i) The time the property would no longer be includible in the individual's gross estate (other than by reason of section 2035), or

(ii) The death of the individual.

(3) *Individual treated as interest holder.*—(i) *In general.*—If a taxable event involves the transfer of a qualified payment interest by the interest holder (or an individual treated as the interest holder) to an applicable family member of the individual who made the transfer to which section 2701 applied (other than the spouse of the individual transferring the qualified payment interest), the transferee applicable family member is treated in the same manner as the interest holder with respect to late or unpaid qualified payments first due after the taxable event. Thus, for example, if an interest holder transfers during life a qualified payment interest to an applicable family member, that transfer is a taxable event with respect to the interest holder whose taxable gifts are increased for the year of the transfer as provided in paragraph (c) of this section. The transferee is treated thereafter in the same manner as the interest holder with respect to late or unpaid qualified payments first due after the taxable event.

(ii) *Transfers to spouse.*—(A) *In general.*—If an interest holder (or an individual treated as the interest holder) transfers a qualified payment interest, the transfer is not a taxable event to the extent a marital deduction is allowed with respect to the transfer under sections 2056, 2106(a)(3), or 2523 or, in the case of a transfer

during the individual's lifetime, to the extent the spouse furnishes consideration for the transfer. If this exception applies, the transferee spouse is treated as if he or she were the holder of the interest from the date the transferor spouse acquired the interest. If the deduction for a transfer to a spouse is allowable under section 2056(b)(8) or 2523(g) (relating to charitable remainder trusts), the transferee spouse is treated as the holder of the entire interest passing to the trust.

(B) *Marital bequests.*—If the selection of property with which a marital bequest is funded is discretionary, a transfer of a qualified payment interest will not be considered a transfer to the surviving spouse unless—

(1) The marital bequest is funded with the qualified payment interest before the due date for filing the decedent's Federal estate tax return (including extensions actually granted) (the "due date"), or

(2) The executor—

(i) Files a statement with the return indicating the extent to which the marital bequest will be funded with the qualified payment interest, and

(ii) Before the date that is one year prior to the expiration of the period of limitations on assessment of the Federal estate tax, notifies the District Director having jurisdiction over the return of the extent to which the bequest was funded with the qualified payment interest (or the extent to which the qualified payment interest has been permanently set aside for that purpose).

(C) *Purchase by the surviving spouse.*—For purposes of this section, the purchase (before the date prescribed for filing the decedent's estate tax return, including extensions actually granted) by the surviving spouse (or a trust described in section 2056(b)(7)) of a qualified payment interest held (directly or indirectly) by the decedent immediately before death is considered a transfer with respect to which a deduction is allowable under section 2056 or section 2106(a)(3), but only to the extent that the deduction is allowed to the estate. For example, assume that A bequeaths $50,000 to A's surviving spouse, B, in a manner that qualifies for deduction under section 2056, and that subsequent to A's death B purchases a qualified payment interest from A's estate for $200,000, its fair market value. The economic effect of the transaction is the equivalent of a bequest by A to B of the qualified payment interest, one-fourth of which qualifies for the marital deduction. Therefore, for purposes of this section, one-fourth of the qualified payment interest purchased by B ($50,000 ÷ $200,000) is considered a transfer of an interest with respect to which a deduction is allowed under [section] 2056. If the purchase by the surviving spouse is not made before the due date of the decedent's return, the purchase of the qualified payment interest will not be considered a bequest for which a marital deduction is allowed unless the executor—

(1) Files a statement with the return indicating the qualified payment interests to be purchased by the surviving spouse (or a trust described in section 2056(b)(7)), and

(2) Before the date that is one year prior to the expiration of the period of limitations on assessment of the Federal estate tax, notifies the District Director having jurisdiction over the return that the purchase of the qualified payment interest has been made (or that the funds necessary to purchase the qualified payment interest have been permanently set aside for that purpose).

(c) *Amount of increase.*—(1) *In general.*—Except as limited by paragraph (c)(6) of this section, the amount of the increase to an individual's taxable estate or taxable gifts is the excess, if any, of—

(i) The sum of—

(A) The amount of qualified payments payable during the period beginning on the date of the transfer to which section 2701 applied (or, in the case of an individual treated as the interest holder, on the date the interest of the prior interest holder terminated) and ending on the date of the taxable event; and

(B) The earnings on those payments, determined hypothetically as if each payment were paid on its due date and reinvested as of that date at a yield equal to the appropriate discount rate (as defined below); over

(ii) The sum of—

(A) The amount of the qualified payments actually paid during the same period;

(B) The earnings on those payments, determined hypothetically as if each payment were reinvested as of the date actually paid at a yield equal to the appropriate discount rate; and

(C) To the extent required to prevent double inclusion, by an amount equal to the sum of—

(1) The portion of the fair market value of the qualified payment interest solely attributable to any right to receive unpaid qualified payments determined as of the date of the taxable event;

(2) The fair market value of any equity interest in the entity received by the individual in lieu of qualified payments and held by the individual at the taxable event; and

(3) The amount by which the individual's aggregate taxable gifts were increased by reason of the failure of the individual to enforce the right to receive qualified payments.

(2) *Due date of qualified payments.*—With respect to any qualified payment, the "due date" is that date specified in the governing instrument as the date on which payment is to be made. If no date is specified in the governing instrument, the due date is the last day of each calendar year.

(3) *Appropriate discount rate.*—The appropriate discount rate is the discount rate that was applied in determining the value of the qualified payment right at the time of the transfer to which section 2701 applied.

(4) *Application of payments.*—For purposes of this section, any payment of an unpaid qualified payment is applied in satisfaction of unpaid qualified payments beginning with the earliest unpaid qualified payment. Any payment in excess of the total of all unpaid qualified payments is treated as a prepayment of future qualified payments.

(5) *Payment.*—For purposes of this paragraph (c), the transfer of a debt obligation bearing compound interest from the due date of the payment at a rate not less than the appropriate discount rate is a qualified payment if the term of the obligation (including extensions) does not exceed four years from the date issued. A payment in the form of an equity interest in the entity is not a qualified payment. Any payment of a qualified payment made (or treated as made) either before or during the four-year period beginning on the due date of the payment but before the date of the taxable event is treated as having been made on the due date.

(6) *Limitation.*—(i) *In general.*—The amount of the increase to an individual's taxable estate or taxable gifts is limited to the applicable percentage of the excess, if any, of—

(A) The sum of—

(1) The fair market value of all outstanding equity interests in the entity that are subordinate to the applicable retained interest, determined as of the date of the taxable event without regard to any accrued liability attributable to unpaid qualified payments; and

(2) Any amounts expended by the entity to redeem or otherwise acquire any such subordinate interest during the period beginning on the date of the transfer to which section 2701 applied (or, in the case of an individual treated as an interest holder, on the date the interest of the prior interest holder terminated) and ending on the date of the taxable event (reduced by any amounts received on the resale or issuance of any such subordinate interest during the same period); over

(B) The fair market value of all outstanding equity interests in the entity that are subordinate to the applicable retained interest, determined as of the date of the transfer to which section 2701 applied (or, in the case of an individual treated as an interest holder, on the date the interest of the prior interest holder terminated).

(ii) *Computation of limitation.*—For purposes of computing the limitation applicable under this paragraph (c)(6), the aggregate fair market value of the subordinate interests in the entity are determined without regard to § 25.2701-3(c).

(iii) *Applicable percentage.*—The applicable percentage is determined by dividing the number of shares or units of the applicable retained interest held by the interest holder (or an individual treated as the interest holder) on the date of the taxable event by the total number of such shares or units outstanding on the same date. If an individual holds applicable retained interests in two or more classes of interests, the applicable percentage is equal to the largest applicable percentage determined with respect to any class. For example, if T retains 40 percent of the class A preferred and 60 percent of the class B preferred in a corporation, the applicable percentage with respect to T's holdings is 60 percent.

(d) *Taxpayer election.*—(1) *In general.*—An interest holder (or individual treated as an interest holder) may elect to treat as a taxable event the payment of an unpaid qualified payment occurring more than four years after its due date. Under this election, the increase under paragraph (c) of this section is determined only with respect to that payment and all previous payments for which an election was available but not made. Payments for which an election applies are treated as having been paid on their due dates for purposes of subsequent taxable events. The election is revocable only with the consent of the Commissioner.

(2) *Limitation not applicable.*—If a taxable event occurs by reason of an election described in paragraph (d)(1) of this section, the limitation described in paragraph (c)(6) of this section does not apply.

(3) *Time and manner of election.*—(i) *Timely-filed returns.*—The election may be made by attaching a statement to a Form 709, Federal Gift Tax Return, filed by the recipient of the qualified payment on a timely basis for the year in which the qualified payment is received. In that case, the taxable event is deemed to occur on the date the qualified payment is received.

(ii) *Election on late returns.*—The election may be made by attaching a statement to a Form 709, Federal Gift Tax Return, filed by the recipient of the qualified payment other than on a timely basis for the year in which the qualified payment is received. In that case, the taxable event is deemed to occur on the first day of the month immediately preceding the month in which the return is filed. If an election, other than an election on a timely return, is made after the death of the interest holder, the taxable event with respect to the decedent is deemed to occur on the later of—

(A) The date of the recipient's death, or

(B) The first day of the month immediately preceding the month in which the return is filed.

(iii) *Requirements of statement.*—The statement must—

(A) Provide the name, address, and taxpayer identification number of the electing individual and the interest holder, if different;

(B) Indicate that a taxable event election is being made under paragraph (d) of this section;

(C) Disclose the nature of the qualified payment right to which the election applies, including the due dates of the payments, the dates the payments were made, and the amounts of the payments;

(D) State the name of the transferor, the date of the transfer to which section 2701 applied, and the discount rate used in valuing the qualified payment right; and

(E) State the resulting amount of increase in taxable gifts.

(4) *Example.*—The following example illustrates the rules of this paragraph (d).

Example. A holds cumulative preferred stock that A retained in a transfer to which section 2701 applied. No dividends were paid in years 1 through 5 following the transfer. In year 6, A received a qualified payment that, pursuant to paragraph (c)(3) of this section, is considered to be in satisfaction of the unpaid qualified payment for year 1. No election was made to treat that payment as a taxable event. In year 7, A receives a qualified payment that, pursuant to paragraph (c)(4) of this section, is considered to be in satisfaction of the unpaid qualified payment for year 2. A elects to treat the payment in year 7 as a taxable event. The election increases A's taxable gifts in year 7 by the amount computed under paragraph (c) of this section with respect to the payments due in both year 1 and year 2. For purposes of any future taxable events, the payments with respect to years 1 and 2 are treated as having been made on their due dates. [Reg. § 25.2701-4.]

□ [*T.D.* 8395, 1-28-92.]

[Reg. § 25.2701-5]

§ 25.2701-5. **Adjustments to mitigate double taxation.**—(a) *Reduction of transfer tax base.*—(1) *In general.*—This section provides rules under which an individual (the initial transferor) making a transfer subject to section 2701 (the initial transfer) is entitled to reduce his or her taxable gifts or adjusted taxable gifts (the reduction). The amount of the reduction is determined under paragraph(b) of this section. See paragraph (e) of this section if section 2513 (split gifts) applied to the initial transfer.

(2) *Federal gift tax modification.*—If, during the lifetime of the initial transferor, the holder of a section 2701 interest (as defined in paragraph (a)(4) of this section) transfers the interest to or for the benefit of an individual other than the initial transferor or an applicable family member

of the initial transferor in a transfer subject to Federal estate or gift tax, the initial transferor may reduce the amount on which the initial transferor's tentative tax is computed under section 2502(a). The reduction is first applied on any gift tax return required to be filed for the calendar year in which the section 2701 interest is transferred; any excess reduction is carried forward and applied in each succeeding calendar year until the reduction is exhausted. The amount of the reduction that is used in a calendar year is the amount of the initial transferor's taxable gifts for that year. Any excess reduction remaining at the death of the initial transferor may be applied by the executor of the initial transferor's estate as provided under paragraph (a)(3) of this section. See paragraph (a)(4) of this section for the definition of a section 2701 interest. See § 25.2701-6 for rules relating to indirect ownership of equity interests transferred to trusts and other entities.

(3) *Federal estate tax modification.*—Except as otherwise provided in this paragraph (a)(3), in determining the Federal estate tax with respect to an initial transferor, the executor of the initial transferor's estate may reduce the amount on which the decedent's tentative tax is computed under section 2001(b) (or section 2101(b)) by the amount of the reduction (including any excess reduction carried forward under paragraph (a)(2) of this section). The amount of the reduction under this paragraph (a)(3) is limited to the amount that results in zero Federal estate tax with respect to the estate of the initial transferor.

(4) *Section 2701 interest.*—A section 2701 interest is an applicable retained interest that was valued using the special valuation rules of section 2701 at the time of the initial transfer. However, an interest is a section 2701 interest only to the extent the transfer of that interest effectively reduces the aggregate ownership of such class of interest by the initial transferor and applicable family members of the initial transferor below that held by such persons at the time of the initial transfer (or the remaining portion thereof).

(b) *Amount of reduction.*—Except as otherwise provided in paragraphs (c)(3)(iv) (pertaining to transfers of partial interests) and (e) (pertaining to initial split gifts) of this section, the amount of the reduction is the lesser of—

(1) The amount by which the initial transferor's taxable gifts were increased as a result of the application of section 2701 to the initial transfer; or

(2) The amount (determined under paragraph (c) of this section) duplicated in the transfer tax base at the time of the transfer of the section 2701 interest (the duplicated amount).

(c) *Duplicated amount.*—(1) *In general.*—The duplicated amount is the amount by which the transfer tax value of the section 2701 interest at

the time of the subsequent transfer exceeds the value of that interest determined under section 2701 at the time of the initial transfer. If, at the time of the initial transfer, the amount allocated to the transferred interest under § 25.2701-3(b)(3) (*Step 3* of the valuation methodology) is less than the entire amount available for allocation at that time, the duplicated amount is a fraction of the amount described in the preceding sentence. The numerator of the fraction is the amount allocated to the transferred interest at the time of the initial transfer (pursuant to § 25.2701-3(b)(3)) and the denominator of the fraction is the amount available for allocation at the time of the initial transfer (determined after application of § 25.2701-3(b)(2)).

(2) *Transfer tax value—in general.*—Except as provided in paragraph (c)(3) of this section, for purposes of paragraph (c)(1) of this section the transfer tax value of a section 2701 interest is the value of that interest as finally determined for Federal transfer tax purposes under chapter 11 or chapter 12, as the case may be (including the right to receive any distributions thereon (other than qualified payments)), reduced by the amount of any deduction allowed with respect to the section 2701 interest to the extent that the deduction would not have been allowed if the section 2701 interest were not included in the transferor's total amount of gifts for the calendar year or the transferor's gross estate, as the case may be. Rules similar to the rules of section 691(c)(2)(C) are applicable to determine the extent that a deduction would not be allowed if the section 2701 interest were not so included.

(3) *Special transfer tax value rules.*—(i) *Transfers for consideration.*—Except as provided in paragraph (c)(3)(iii) of this section, if, during the life of the initial transferor, a section 2701 interest is transferred to or for the benefit of an individual other than the initial transferor or an applicable family member of the initial transferor for consideration in money or money's worth, or in a transfer that is treated as a transfer for consideration in money or money's worth, the transfer of the section 2701 interest is deemed to occur at the death of the initial transferor. In this case, the estate of the initial transferor is entitled to a reduction in the same manner as if the initial transferor's gross estate included a section 2701 interest having a chapter 11 value equal to the amount of consideration in money or money's worth received in the exchange (determined as of the time of the exchange).

(ii) *Interests held by applicable family members at date of initial transferor's death.*—If a section 2701 interest in existence on the date of the initial transferor's death is held by an applicable family member and, therefore, is not included in the gross estate of the initial transferor, the section 2701 interest is deemed to be transferred at the death of the initial transferor to or for the benefit

Reg. § 25.2701-5(c)(3)(ii)

of an individual other than the initial transferor or an applicable family member of the initial transferor. In this case, the transfer tax value of that interest is the value that the executor of the initial transferor's estate can demonstrate would be determined under chapter 12 if the interest were transferred immediately prior to the death of the initial transferor.

(iii) *Nonrecognition transactions.*—If an individual exchanges a section 2701 interest in a nonrecognition transaction (within the meaning of section 7701(a)(45)), the exchange is not treated as a transfer of a section 2701 interest and the transfer tax value of that interest is determined as if the interest received in exchange is the section 2701 interest.

(iv) *Transfer of less than the entire section 2701 interest.*—If a transfer is a transfer of less than the entire section 2701 interest, the amount of the reduction under paragraph (a)(2) or (a)(3) of this section is reduced proportionately.

(v) *Multiple classes of section 2701 interest.*—For purposes of paragraph (b) of this section, if more than one class of section 2701 interest exists, the amount of the reduction is determined separately with respect to each such class.

(vi) *Multiple initial transfers.*—If an initial transferor has made more than one initial transfer, the amount of the reduction with respect to any section 2701 interest is the sum of the reductions computed under paragraph (b) of this section with respect to each such initial transfer.

(d) *Examples.*—The following examples illustrate the provisions of paragraphs (a) through (c) of this section.

Facts. (1) *In general.* (i) P, an individual, holds 1,500 shares of $1,000 par value preferred stock of X corporation (bearing an annual noncumulative dividend of $100 per share that may be put to X at any time for par value) and 1,000 shares of voting common stock of X. There is no other outstanding common stock of X.

(ii) On January 15, 1991, when the aggregate fair market value of the preferred stock is $1,500,000 and the aggregate fair market value of the common stock is $500,000, P transfers common stock to P's child. The fair market value of P's interest in X (common and preferred) immediately prior to the transfer is $2,000,000, and the section 2701 value of the preferred stock (the section 2701 interest) is zero. Neither P nor P's spouse, S, made gifts prior to 1991.

(2) *Additional facts applicable to Examples 1 through 3.* P's transfer consists of all 1,000 shares of P's common stock. With respect to the initial transfer, the amount remaining after Step 2 of the subtraction method of § 25.2701-3 is $2,000,000 ($2,000,000 minus zero), all of which is allocated to the transferred stock. P's aggre-

gate taxable gifts for 1991 (including the section 2701 transfer) equal $2,500,000.

(3) *Additional facts applicable to Examples 4 and 5.* P's initial transfer consists of one-half of P's common stock. With respect to the initial transfer in this case, only $1,000,000 (one-half of the amount remaining after Step 2 of the subtraction method of § 25.2701-3) is allocated to the transferred stock. P's aggregate taxable gifts for 1991 (the section 2701 transfer and P's other transfers) equal $2,500,000.

Example 1. Inter vivos transfer of entire section 2701 interest. (i) On October 1, 1994, at a time when the value of P's preferred stock is $1,400,000, P transfers all of the preferred stock to P's child. In computing P's 1994 gift tax, P, as the initial transferor, is entitled to reduce the amount on which P's tentative tax is computed under section 2502(a) by $1,400,000.

(ii) The amount of the reduction computed under paragraph (b) of this section is the lesser of $1,500,000 (the amount by which the initial transferor's taxable gifts were increased as a result of the application of section 2701 to the initial transfer) or $1,400,000 (the duplicated amount). The duplicated amount is 100 percent (the portion of the section 2701 interest subsequently transferred) times $1,400,000 (the amount by which the gift tax value of the preferred stock ($1,400,000 at the time of the subsequent transfer) exceeds zero (the section 2701 value of the preferred stock at the time of the initial transfer)).

(iii) The result would be the same if the preferred stock had been held by P's parent, GM, and GM had, on October 1, 1994, transferred the preferred stock to or for the benefit of an individual other than P or an applicable family member of P. In that case, in computing the tax on P's 1994 and subsequent transfers, P would be entitled to reduce the amount on which P's tentative tax is computed under section 2502(a) by $1,400,000. If the value of P's 1994 gifts is less than $1,400,000, P is entitled to claim the excess adjustment in computing the tax with respect to P's subsequent transfers.

Example 2. Transfer of section 2701 interest at death of initial transferor. (i) P continues to hold the preferred stock until P's death. The chapter 11 value of the preferred stock at the date of P's death is the same as the fair market value of the preferred stock at the time of the initial transfer. In computing the Federal estate tax with respect to P's estate, P's executor is entitled to a reduction of $1,500,000 under paragraph (a)(3) of this section.

(ii) The result would be the same if P had sold the preferred stock to any individual other than an applicable family member at a time when the value of the preferred stock was $1,500,000. In that case, the amount of the reduction is computed as if the preferred stock were included in P's gross estate at a fair market value equal to the sales price. If the value of P's taxable estate is less than $1,500,000, the amount of the adjustment available to P's executor is limited to the actual value of P's taxable estate.

(iii) The result would also be the same if the preferred stock had been held by P's parent, GM, and at the time of P's death, GM had not transferred the preferred stock.

Example 3. Transfer of after-acquired preferred stock. On September 1, 1992, P purchases 100 shares of X preferred stock from an unrelated party. On October 1, 1994, P transfers 100 shares of X preferred stock to P's child. In computing P's 1994 gift tax, P is not entitled to reduce the amount on which P's tentative tax is computed under section 2502(a) because the 1994 transfer does not reduce P's preferred stock holding below that held at the time of the initial transfer. See paragraph (a)(4) of this section.

Example 4. Inter vivos transfer of entire section 2701 interest. (i) On October 1, 1994, at a time when the value of P's preferred stock is $1,400,000, P transfers all of the preferred stock to P's child. In computing P's 1994 gift tax, P, as the initial transferor, is entitled to reduce the amount on which P's tentative tax is computed under section 2502(a) by $700,000.

(ii) The amount of the reduction computed under paragraph (b) of this section is the lesser of $750,000 (($1,500,000 × .5 ($1,000,000 over $2,000,000)) the amount by which the initial transferor's taxable gifts were increased as a result of the application of section 2701 to the initial transfer) or $700,000 (($1,400,000 × .5) the duplicated amount). The duplicated amount is 100 percent (the portion of the section 2701 interest subsequently transferred) times $700,000; e.g., one-half (the fraction representing the portion of the common stock transferred in the initial transfer ($1,000,000/$2,000,000)) of the amount by which the gift tax value of the preferred stock at the time of the subsequent transfer ($1,400,000) exceeds zero (the section 2701 value of the preferred stock at the time of the initial transfer).

Example 5. Subsequent transfer of less than the entire section 2701 interest. On October 1, 1994, at a time when the value of P's preferred stock is $1,400,000, P transfers only 250 of P's 1,000 shares of preferred stock to P's child. In this case, the amount of the reduction computed under paragraph (b) is $175,000 (one-fourth (250/1,000) of the amount of the reduction available if P had transferred all 1,000 shares of preferred stock.

(e) *Computation of reduction if initial transfer is split under section 2513.*—(1) *In general.*—If section 2513 applies to the initial transfer (a split initial transfer), the special rules of this paragraph (e) apply.

(2) *Transfers during joint lives.*—If there is a split initial transfer and the corresponding section 2701 interest is transferred during the joint lives of the donor and the consenting spouse, for purposes of determining the reduction under

paragraph (a)(2) of this section each spouse is treated as if the spouse was the initial transferor of one-half of the split initial transfer.

(3) *Transfers at or after death of either spouse.*— (i) *In general.*—If there is a split initial transfer and the corresponding section 2701 interest is transferred at or after the death of the first spouse to die, the reduction under paragraph (a)(2) or (a)(3) of this section is determined as if the donor spouse was the initial transferor of the entire initial transfer.

(ii) *Death of donor spouse.*—Except as provided in paragraph (e)(3)(iv) of this section, the executor of the estate of the donor spouse in a split initial transfer is entitled to compute the reduction as if the donor spouse was the initial transferor of the section 2701 interest otherwise attributable to the consenting spouse. In this case, if the consenting spouse survives the donor spouse—

(A) The consenting spouse's aggregate sum of taxable gifts used in computing each tentative tax under section 2502(a) (and, therefore, adjusted taxable gifts under section 2001(b)(1)(B) (or section 2101(b)(1)(B)) and the tax payable on the consenting spouse's prior taxable gifts under section 2001(b)(2) (or section 2101(b)(2))) is reduced to eliminate the remaining effect of the section 2701 interest; and

(B) Except with respect to any excess reduction carried forward under paragraph (a)(2) of this section, the consenting spouse ceases to be treated as the initial transferor of the section 2701 interest.

(iii) *Death of consenting spouse.*—If the consenting spouse predeceases the donor spouse, except for any excess reduction carried forward under paragraph (a)(2) of this section, the reduction with respect to any section 2701 interest in the split initial transfer is not available to the estate of the consenting spouse (regardless of whether the interest is included in the consenting spouse's gross estate). Similarly, if the consenting spouse predeceases the donor spouse, no reduction is available to the consenting spouse's adjusted taxable gifts under section 2001(b)(1)(B) (or section 2101(b)(1)(B)) or to the consenting spouse's gift tax payable under section 2001(b)(2) (or section 2101(b)(2)). See paragraph (a)(2) of this section for rules involving transfers by an applicable family member during the life of the initial transferor.

(iv) *Additional limitation on reduction.*—If the donor spouse (or the estate of the donor spouse) is treated under this paragraph (e) as the initial transferor of the section 2701 interest otherwise attributable to the consenting spouse, the amount of additional reduction determined under paragraph (b) of this section is the amount determined under that paragraph with respect to the consenting spouse. If a reduction was previously available to the consenting spouse under this paragraph (e), the amount determined under this paragraph (e)(3)(iv) with respect to the consenting spouse is determined as if the consenting spouse's taxable gifts in the split initial transfer had been increased only by that portion of the increase that corresponds to the remaining portion of the section 2701 interest. The amount of the additional reduction (i.e., the amount determined with respect to the consenting spouse) is limited to the amount that results in a reduction in the donor spouse's Federal transfer tax no greater than the amount of the increase in the consenting spouse's gift tax incurred by reason of the section 2701 interest (or the remaining portion thereof).

(f) *Examples.*—The following examples illustrate the provisions of paragraph (e) of this section. The examples assume the facts set out in this paragraph (f).

Facts. (1) In each example assume that P, an individual, holds 1,500 shares of $1,000 par value preferred stock of X corporation (bearing an annual noncumulative dividend of $100 per share that may be put to X at any time for par value) and 1,000 shares of voting common stock of X. There is no other outstanding stock of X. The annual exclusion under section 2503 is not allowable with respect to any gift.

(2) On January 15, 1991, when the aggregate fair market value of the preferred stock is $1,500,000 and the aggregate fair market value of the common stock is $500,000, P transfers all 1,000 shares of the common stock to P's child. Section 2701 applies to the initial transfer because P transferred an equity interest (the common stock) to a member of P's family and immediately thereafter held an applicable retained interest (the preferred stock). The fair market value of P's interest in X immediately prior to the transfer is $2,000,000 and the section 2701 value of the preferred stock (the section 2701 interest) is zero. With respect to the initial transfer, the amount remaining after Step 2 of the subtraction method of § 25.2701-3 was $2,000,000 ($2,000,000 minus zero), all of which is allocated to the transferred stock. P had made no gifts prior to 1991. The sum of P's aggregate taxable gifts for the calendar year 1991 (including the section 2701 transfer) is $2,500,000. P's spouse, S, made no gifts prior to 1991.

(3) P and S elected pursuant to section 2513 to treat one-half of their 1991 gifts as having been made by each spouse. Without the application of section 2701, P and S's aggregate gifts would have been $500,000 and each spouse would have paid no gift tax because of the application of the unified credit under section 2505. However, because of the application of section 2701, both P and S are each treated as the initial transferor of aggregate taxable gifts in the amount of $1,250,000 and, after the application of the unified credit under section 2505, each paid

$255,500 in gift tax with respect to their 1991 transfers. On October 1, 1994, at a time when the value of the preferred stock is the same as at the time of the initial transfer, P transfers the preferred stock (the section 2701 interest) to P's child.

Example 1. Inter vivos transfer of entire section 2701 interest. P transfers all of the preferred stock to P's child. P and S are each entitled to a reduction of $750,000 in computing their 1994 gift tax. P is entitled to the reduction because P subsequently transferred the one-half share of the section 2701 interest as to which P was the initial transferor to an individual who was not an applicable family member of P. S is entitled to the reduction because P, an applicable family member with respect to S, transferred the one-half share of the section 2701 interest as to which S was the initial transferor to an individual other than S or an applicable family member of S. S may claim the reduction against S's 1994 gifts. If S's 1994 taxable gifts are less than $750,000, S may claim the remaining amount of the reduction against S's next succeeding lifetime transfers.

Example 2. Inter vivos transfer of portion of section 2701 interest. P transfers one-fourth of the preferred stock to P's child. In this case, P and S are each entitled to a reduction of $187,500, the corresponding portion of the reduction otherwise available to each spouse (one-fourth of $750,000).

Example 3. Transfer at death of donor spouse. P, the donor spouse in the section 2513 election, dies on October 1, 1994, while holding all of the preferred stock. The executor of P's estate is entitled to a reduction in the computation of the tentative tax under section 2001(b). Since no reduction had been previously available with respect to the section 2701 interest, P's estate is entitled to a full reduction of $750,000 with respect to the one-half share of the preferred stock as to which P was the initial transferor. In addition, P's estate is entitled to an additional reduction of up to $750,000 for the remaining section 2701 interest as to which S was the initial transferor. The reduction for the consenting spouse's remaining section 2701 interest is limited to that amount that will produce a tax saving in P's Federal estate tax of $255,500, the amount of gift tax incurred by S by reason of the application of section 2701 to the split initial transfer.

Example 4. Transfer after death of donor spouse. The facts are the same as in *Example 3*, except that S acquires the preferred stock from P's estate and subsequently transfers the preferred stock to S's child. S is not entitled to a reduction because S ceased to be an initial transferor upon P's death (and S's prior taxable gifts were automatically adjusted at that time to the level that would have existed had the split initial transfer not been subject to section 2701).

Example 5. Death of donor spouse after inter vivos transfer. (i) P transfers one-fourth of the preferred stock to P's child. In this case, P and S are each entitled to a reduction of $187,500, the corresponding portion of the reduction otherwise available to each spouse (one-fourth of $750,000). S may claim the reduction against S's 1994 or subsequent transfers. P dies on November 1, 1994.

(ii) P's executor is entitled to include, in computing the reduction available to P's estate, the remaining reduction to which P is entitled and an additional amount of up to $562,500 ($750,000 minus $187,500, the amount of the remaining reduction attributable to the consenting spouse determined immediately prior to P's death). The amount of additional reduction available to P's estate cannot exceed the amount that will reduce P's estate tax by $178,625, the amount that S's 1991 gift tax would have been increased if the application of section 2701 had increased S's taxable gifts by only $562,500 ($750,000 – $187,500).

(g) *Double taxation otherwise avoided.*—No reduction is available under this section if—

(1) Double taxation is otherwise avoided in the computation of the estate tax under section 2001 (or section 2101); or

(2) A reduction was previously taken under the provisions of section 2701(e)(6) with respect to the same section 2701 interest and the same initial transfer.

(h) *Effective date.*—This section is effective for transfers of section 2701 interests after May 4, 1994. If the transfer of a section 2701 interest occurred on or before May 4, 1994, the initial transferor may rely on either this section, project PS-30-91 (1991-2 C.B. 1118, and 1992-1 C.B. 1239 (see § 601.601(d)(2)(ii)(*b*) of this chapter)) or any other reasonable interpretation of the statute. [Reg. § 25.2701-5.]

☐ *T.D. 8536, 5-4-94.*]

[Reg. § 25.2701-6]

§ 25.2701-6. Indirect holding of interests.— (a) *In general.*—(1) *Attribution to individuals.*— For purposes of section 2701, an individual is treated as holding an equity interest to the extent the interest is held indirectly through a corporation, partnership, estate, trust, or other entity. If an equity interest is treated as held by a particular individual in more than one capacity, the interest is treated as held by the individual in the manner that attributes the largest total ownership of the equity interest. An equity interest held by a lower-tier entity is attributed to higher-tier entities in accordance with the rules of this section. For example, if an individual is a 50-percent beneficiary of a trust that holds 50 percent of the preferred stock of a corporation, 25 percent of the preferred stock is considered held by the individual under these rules.

(2) *Corporations.*—A person is considered to hold an equity interest held by or for a corporation in the proportion that the fair market value

of the stock the person holds bears to the fair market value of all the stock in the corporation (determined as if each class of stock were held separately by one individual). This paragraph applies to any entity classified as a corporation or as an association taxable as a corporation for federal income tax purposes.

(3) *Partnerships.*—A person is considered to hold an equity interest held by or for a partnership in the proportion that the fair market value of the larger of the person's profits interest or capital interest in the partnership bears to the total fair market value of the corresponding profits interests or capital interests in the partnership, as the case may be (determined as if each class were held by one individual). This paragraph applies to any entity classified as a partnership for federal income tax purposes.

(4) *Estates, trusts and other entities.*—(i) *In general.*—A person is considered to hold an equity interest held by or for an estate or trust to the extent the person's beneficial interest therein may be satisfied by the equity interest held by the estate or trust, or the income or proceeds thereof, assuming the maximum exercise of discretion in favor of the person. A beneficiary of an estate or trust who cannot receive any distribution with respect to an equity interest held by the estate or trust, including the income therefrom or the proceeds from the disposition thereof, is not considered the holder of the equity interest. Thus, if stock held by a decedent's estate has been specifically bequeathed to one beneficiary and the residue of the estate has been bequeathed to other beneficiaries, the stock is considered held only by the beneficiary to whom it was specifically bequeathed. However, any person who may receive distributions from a trust is considered to hold an equity interest held by the trust if the distributions may be made from current or accumulated income from or the proceeds from the disposition of the equity interest, even though under the terms of the trust the interest can never be distributed to that person. This paragraph applies to any entity that is not classified as a corporation, an association taxable as a corporation, or a partnership for federal income tax purposes.

(ii) *Special rules.*—(A) Property is held by a decedent's estate if the property is subject to claims against the estate and expenses of administration.

(B) A person holds a beneficial interest in a trust or an estate so long as the person may receive distributions from the trust or the estate other than payments for full and adequate consideration.

(C) An individual holds an equity interest held by or for a trust if the individual is considered an owner of the trust (a "grantor trust") under subpart E, part 1, subchapter J of the Internal Revenue Code (relating to grantors and others treated as substantial owners). However, if an individual is treated as the owner of only a fractional share of a grantor trust because there are multiple grantors, the individual holds each equity interest held by the trust, except to the extent that the fair market value of the interest exceeds the fair market value of the fractional share.

(5) *Multiple attribution.*—(i) *Applicable retained interests.*—If this section attributes an applicable retained interest to more than one individual in a class consisting of the transferor and one or more applicable family members, the interest is attributed within that class in the following order—

(A) If the interest is held in a grantor trust, to the individual treated as the holder thereof;

(B) To the transferor;

(C) To the transferor's spouse; or

(D) To each applicable family member on a pro rata basis.

(ii) *Subordinate equity interests.*—If this section attributes a subordinate equity interest to more than one individual in a class consisting of the transferor, applicable family members, and members of the transferor's family, the interest is attributed within that class in the following order—

(A) To the transferee;

(B) To each member of the transferor's family on a pro rata basis;

(C) If the interest is held in a grantor trust, to the individual treated as the holder thereof;

(D) To the transferor;

(E) To the transferor's spouse; or

(F) To each applicable family member on a pro rata basis.

(b) *Examples.*—The following examples illustrate the provisions of this section:

Example 1. A, an individual, holds 25 percent by value of each class of stock of Y Corporation. Persons unrelated to A hold the remaining stock. Y holds 50 percent of the stock of Corporation X. Under paragraph (a)(2) of this section, Y's interests in X are attributed proportionately to the shareholders of Y. Accordingly, A is considered to hold a 12.5 percent (25 percent × 50 percent) interest in X.

Example 2. Z Bank's authorized capital consists of 100 shares of common stock and 100 shares of preferred stock. A holds 60 shares of each (common and preferred) and A's child, B, holds 40 shares of common stock. Z holds the balance of its own preferred stock, 30 shares as part of a common trust fund it maintains and 10 shares permanently set aside to satisfy a deferred obligation. For purposes of section 2701, A holds 60 shares of common stock and 66 shares of preferred stock in Z, 60 shares of each class directly

and 6 shares of preferred stock indirectly (60 percent of the 10 shares set aside to fund the deferred obligation).

Example 3. An irrevocable trust holds a 10-percent general partnership interest in Partnership Q. One-half of the trust income is required to be distributed to O Charity. The other one-half of the income is to be distributed to D during D's life and thereafter to E for such time as E survives D. D holds one-half of the trust's interest in Q by reason of D's present right to receive one-half of the trust's income, and E holds one-half of the trust's interest in Q by reason of E's future right to receive one-half of the trust's income. Nevertheless, no family member is treated as holding more than one-half of the trust's interest in Q because at no time will either D or E actually hold, in the aggregate, any right with respect to income or corpus greater than one-half.

Example 4. An irrevocable trust holds a 10-percent general partnership interest in partnership M. One-half of the trust income is to be paid to D for D's life. The remaining income may, in the trustee's discretion, be accumulated or paid to or for the benefit of a class that includes D's child F, in such amounts as the trustee determines. On the death of the survivor of D and F, the trust corpus is required to be distributed to O Charity. The trust's interest in M is held by the trust's beneficiaries to the extent that present and future income or corpus may be distributed to them. Accordingly, D holds one-half of the trust's interest in M because D is entitled to receive one-half of the trust income currently. F holds the entire value of the interest because F is a member of the class eligible to receive the entire trust income for such time as F survives D. See paragraph (a)(5) of this section for rules applicable in the case of multiple attribution.

Example 5. The facts are the same as in *Example 4*, except that all the income is required to be paid to O Charity for the trust's initial year. The result is the same as in *Example 4*. [Reg. §25.2701-6.]

☐ [*T.D.* 8395, 1-28-92.]

[Reg. §25.2701-7]

§25.2701-7. Separate interests.—The Secretary may, by regulation, revenue ruling, notice, or other document of general application, prescribe rules under which an applicable retained interest is treated as two or more separate interests for purposes of section 2701. In addition, the Commissioner may, by ruling issued to a taxpayer upon request, treat any applicable retained interest as two or more separate interests as may be necessary and appropriate to carry out the purposes of section 2701. [Reg. §25.2701-7.]

☐ [*T.D.* 8395, 1-28-92.]

[Reg. §25.2701-8]

§25.2701-8. Effective dates.—Sections 25.2701-1 through 25.2701-4 and §§25.2701-6 and 25.2701-7 are effective as of January 28, 1992. For transfers made prior to January 28, 1992, taxpayers may rely on any reasonable interpretation of the statutory provisions. For these purposes, the provisions of the proposed regulations and the final regulations are considered a reasonable interpretation of the statutory provisions. [Reg. § 25.2701-8.]

☐ [*T.D. 8395, 1-28-92.*]

[Reg. § 25.2702-0]

§ 25.2702-0. Table of contents.—This section lists the major paragraphs contained in §§ 25.2702-1 through 25.2702-7.

(b) Amount of reduction.

(1) In general.

(2) Treatment of annual exclusion.

(3) Overlap with section 2001.

(c) Examples.

§ 25.2702-7. Effective dates.
[Reg. § 25.2702-0.]

☐ [*T.D.* 8395, 1-28-92. *Amended by T.D.* 9181, 2-24-2005.]

[Reg. § 25.2702-1]

§ 25.2702-1. Special valuation rules in the case of transfers of interests in trust.—(a) *Scope of section 2702.*—Section 2702 provides special rules to determine the amount of the gift when an individual makes a transfer in trust to (or for the benefit of) a member of the individual's family and the individual or an applicable family member retains an interest in the trust. Section 25.2702-4 treats certain transfers of property as transfers in trust. Certain transfers, including transfers to a personal residence trust, are not subject to section 2702. See paragraph (c) of this section. Member of the family is defined in § 25.2702-2(a)(1). Applicable family member is defined in § 25.2701-1(d)(2).

(b) *Effect of section 2702.*—If section 2702 applies to a transfer, the value of any interest in the trust retained by the transferor or any applicable family member is determined under § 25.2702-2(b). The amount of the gift, if any, is then determined by subtracting the value of the interests retained by the transferor or any applicable family member from the value of the transferred property. If the retained interest is not a qualified interest (as defined in § 25.2702-3), the retained interest is generally valued at zero, and the amount of the gift is the entire value of the property.

(c) *Exceptions to section 2702.*—Section 2702 does not apply to the following transfers.

(1) *Incomplete gift.*—A transfer no portion of which would be treated as a completed gift without regard to any consideration received by the transferor. If a transfer is wholly incomplete as to an undivided fractional share of the property transferred (without regard to any consideration received by the transferor), for purposes of this paragraph the transfer is treated as incomplete as to that share.

(2) *Personal residence trust.*—A transfer in trust that meets the requirements of § 25.2702-5.

(3) *Charitable remainder trust.*—(i) For transfers made on or after May 19, 1997, a transfer to a pooled income fund described in section 642(c)(5); a transfer to a charitable remainder annuity trust described in section 664(d)(1); a transfer to a charitable remainder unitrust described in section 664(d)(2) if under the terms of the governing instrument the unitrust amount can be computed only under section 664(d)(2)(A); and a transfer to a charitable remainder unitrust if under the terms of the governing instrument the unitrust amount can be computed under section 664(d)(2) and (3) and either there are only two consecutive noncharitable beneficial interests and the transferor holds the second of the two interests, or the only permissible recipients of the unitrust amount are the transferor, the transferor's U.S. citizen spouse, or both the transferor and the transferor's U.S. citizen spouse.

(ii) For transfers made before May 19, 1997, a transfer in trust if the remainder interest in the trust qualifies for a deduction under section 2522.

(4) *Pooled income fund.*—A transfer of property to a pooled income fund (as defined in section 642(c)(5)).

(5) *Charitable lead trust.*—A transfer in trust if the only interest in the trust, other than the remainder interest or a qualified annuity or unitrust interest, is an interest that qualifies for deduction under section 2522.

(6) *Certain assignments of remainder interests.*—The assignment of a remainder interest if the only retained interest of the transferor or an applicable family member is as the permissible recipient of distributions of income in the sole discretion of an independent trustee (as defined in section 674(c)).

(7) *Certain property settlements.*—A transfer in trust if the transfer of an interest to a spouse is deemed to be for full and adequate consideration by reason of section 2516 (relating to certain property settlements) and the remaining interests in the trust are retained by the other spouse.

(8) *Transfer or assignment to a Qualified Domestic Trust.*—A transfer or assignment (as described in section 2056(d)(2)(B)) by a noncitizen surviving spouse of property to a Qualified Domestic Trust under the circumstances described in § 20.2056A-4(b) of this chapter, where the surviving spouse retains an interest in the transferred property that is not a qualified interest and the transfer is not described in section 2702(a)(3)(A)(ii) or 2702(c)(4). [Reg. § 25.2702-1.]

☐ [*T.D.* 8395, 1-28-92. *Amended by T.D.* 8612, 8-21-95 *and T.D.* 8791, 12-9-98.]

[Reg. § 25.2702-2]

§ 25.2702-2. Definitions and valuation rules.—(a) *Definitions.*—The following definitions apply for purposes of section 2702 and the regulations thereunder.

(1) *Member of the family.*—With respect to any individual, member of the family means the individual's spouse, any ancestor or lineal descendant of the individual or the individual's spouse, any brother or sister of the individual, and any spouse of the foregoing.

(2) *Transfer in trust.*—A transfer in trust includes a transfer to a new or existing trust and an assignment of an interest in an existing trust. Transfer in trust does not include—

(i) The exercise, release or lapse of a power of appointment over trust property that is not a transfer under chapter 12; or

(ii) The execution of a qualified disclaimer (as defined in section 2518).

(3) *Retained.*—Retained means held by the same individual both before and after the transfer in trust. In the case of the creation of a term interest, any interest in the property held by the transferor immediately after the transfer is treated as held both before and after the transfer.

(4) *Interest.*—An interest in trust includes a power with respect to a trust if the existence of the power would cause any portion of a transfer to be treated as an incomplete gift under chapter 12.

(5) *Holder.*—The holder is the person to whom the annuity or unitrust interest is payable during the fixed term of that interest. References to holder shall also include the estate of that person.

(6) *Qualified interest.*—Qualified interest means a qualified annuity interest, a qualified unitrust interest, or a qualified remainder interest. If a transferor retains a power to revoke a qualified annuity interest or qualified unitrust interest of the transferor's spouse, then the revocable qualified annuity or unitrust interest of the transferor's spouse is treated as a retained qualified interest of the transferor. In order for the transferor to be treated as having retained a qualified interest under the preceding sentence, the interest of the transferor's spouse (the successor holder) must be an interest that meets the requirements of a qualified annuity interest in accordance with § 25.2702-3(b) and (d), or a qualified unitrust interest in accordance with § 25.2702-3(c) and (d), but for the transferor's retained power to revoke the interest.

(7) *Qualified annuity interest.*—Qualified annuity interest means an interest that meets all the requirements of § 25.2702-3(b) and (d).

(8) *Qualified unitrust interest.*—Qualified unitrust interest means an interest that meets all the requirements of § 25.2702-3(c) and (d).

(9) *Qualified remainder interest.*—Qualified remainder interest means an interest that meets all the requirements of § 25.2702-3(f).

(10) *Governing instrument.*—Governing instrument means the instrument or instruments creating and governing the operation of the trust arrangement.

(b) *Valuation of retained interests.*—(1) *In general.*—Except as provided in paragraphs (b)(2)

and (c) of this section, the value of any interest retained by the transferor or an applicable family member is zero.

(2) *Qualified interest.*—The value[s] of a qualified annuity interest and a qualified remainder interest following a qualified annuity interest are determined under section 7520. The value[s] of a qualified unitrust interest and a qualified remainder interest following a qualified unitrust interest are determined as if they were interests described in section 664.

(c) *Valuation of a term interest in certain tangible property.*—(1) *In general.*—If section 2702 applies to a transfer in trust of tangible property described in paragraph (c)(2) of this section ("tangible property"), the value of a retained term interest (other than a qualified interest) is not determined under section 7520 but is the amount the transferor establishes as the amount a willing buyer would pay a willing seller for the interest, each having reasonable knowledge of the relevant facts and neither being under any compulsion to buy or sell. If the transferor cannot reasonably establish the value of the term interest pursuant to this paragraph (c)(1), the interest is valued at zero.

(2) *Tangible property subject to rule.*—(i) *In general.*—Except as provided in paragraph (c)(2)(ii) of this section, paragraph (c)(1) of this section applies only to tangible property—

(A) For which no deduction for depreciation or depletion would be allowable if the property were used in a trade or business or held for the production of income; and

(B) As to which the failure to exercise any rights under the term interest would not increase the value of the property passing at the end of the term interest.

(ii) *Exception for de minimis amounts of depreciable property.*—In determining whether property meets the requirements of this paragraph (c)(2) at the time of the transfer in trust, improvements that would otherwise cause the property not to qualify are ignored if the fair market value of the improvements, in the aggregate, do [sic] not exceed 5 percent of the fair market value of the entire property.

(3) *Evidence of value of property.*—The best evidence of the value of any term interest to which this paragraph (c) applies is actual sales or rentals that are comparable both as to the nature and character of the property and the duration of the term interest. Little weight is accorded appraisals in the absence of such evidence. Amounts determined under section 7520 are not evidence of what a willing buyer would pay a willing seller for the interest.

(4) *Conversion of property.*—(i) *In general.*—Except as provided in paragraph (c)(4)(iii) of this section, if a term interest in property is valued

under paragraph (c)(1) of this section, and during the term the property is converted into property a term interest in which would not qualify for valuation under paragraph (c)(1) of this section, the conversion is treated as a transfer for no consideration for purposes of chapter 12 of the value of the unexpired portion of the term interest.

(ii) *Value of unexpired portion of term interest.*—For purposes of paragraph (c)(4)(i) of this section, the value of the unexpired portion of a term interest is the amount that bears the same relation to the value of the term interest as of the date of conversion (determined under section 7520 using the rate in effect under section 7520 on the date of the original transfer and the fair market value of the property as of the date of the original transfer) as the value of the term interest as of the date of the original transfer (determined under paragraph (c)(1) of this section) bears to the value of the term interest as of the date of the original transfer (determined under section 7520).

(iii) *Conversion to qualified annuity interest.*—The conversion of tangible property previously valued under paragraph (c)(1) of this section into property a term interest in which would not qualify for valuation under paragraph (c)(1) of this section is not a transfer of the value of the unexpired portion of the term interest if the interest thereafter meets the requirements of a qualified annuity interest. The rules of § 25.2702-5(d)(8) (including governing instrument requirements) apply for purposes of determining the amount of the annuity payment required to be made and the determination of whether the interest meets the requirements of a qualified annuity interest.

(5) *Additions or improvements to property.*—(i) *Additions or improvements substantially affecting nature of property.*—If an addition or improvement is made to property a term interest in which was valued under paragraph (c)(1) of this section, and the addition or improvement affects the nature of the property to such an extent that the property would not be treated as property meeting the requirements of paragraph (c)(2) of this section if the property had included the addition or improvement at the time it was transferred, the entire property is deemed, for purposes of paragraph (c)(4) of this section, to convert (effective as of the date the addition or improvement is commenced) into property a term interest in which would not qualify for valuation under paragraph (c)(1) of this section.

(ii) *Other additions or improvements.*—If an addition or improvement is made to property, a term interest in which was valued under paragraph (c)(1) of this section, and the addition or improvement does not affect the nature of the property to such an extent that the property would not be treated as property meeting the

requirements of paragraph (c)(2) of this section if the property had included the addition or improvement at the time it was transferred, the addition or improvement is treated as an additional transfer (effective as of the date the addition or improvement is commenced) subject to § 25.2702-2(b)(1).

(d) *Examples.*—(1) The following examples illustrate the rules of § 25.2702-1 and § 25.2702-2. Each example assumes that all applicable requirements of those sections not specifically described in the example are met.

Example 1. A transfers property to an irrevocable trust, retaining the right to receive the income of the trust for 10 years. On the expiration of the 10-year term, the trust is to terminate and the trust corpus is to be paid to A's child. However, if A dies during the 10-year term, the entire trust corpus is to be paid to A's estate. Each retained interest is valued at zero because it is not a qualified interest. Thus, the amount of A's gift is the fair market value of the property transferred to the trust.

Example 2. A transfers property to an irrevocable trust, retaining a 10-year annuity interest that meets the requirements set forth in § 25.2702-3 for a qualified annuity interest. Upon expiration of the 10-year term, the trust is to terminate and the trust corpus is to be paid to A's child. The amount of A's gift is the fair market value of the property transferred to the trust less the value of the retained qualified annuity interest determined under section 7520.

Example 3. D transfers property to an irrevocable trust under which the income is payable to D's spouse for life. Upon the death of D's spouse, the trust is to terminate and the trust corpus is to be paid to D's child. D retains no interest in the trust. Although the spouse is an applicable family member of D under section 2702, the spouse has not retained an interest in the trust because the spouse did not hold the interest both before and after the transfer. Section 2702 does not apply because neither the transferor nor an applicable family member has retained an interest in the trust. The result is the same whether or not D elects to treat the transfer as a transfer of qualified terminable interest property under section 2056(b)(7).

Example 4. A transfers property to an irrevocable trust, under which the income is to be paid to A for life. Upon termination of the trust, the trust corpus is to be distributed to A's child. A also retains certain powers over principal that cause the transfer to be wholly incomplete for federal gift tax purposes. Section 2702 does not apply because no portion of the transfer would be treated as a completed gift.

Example 5. The facts are the same as in *Example 4,* except that the trust is divided into separate fractional shares and A's retained powers apply to only one of the shares. Section 2702 applies except with respect to the share of the trust as to which A's retained powers cause the transfer to be an incomplete gift.

(2) The following facts apply for *Examples 6 through 8*(examples illustrating § 25.2702-2(c)—tangible property exception):

Facts. A transfers a painting having a fair market value of $2,000,000 to A's child, B, retaining the use of the painting for 10 years. The painting does not possess an ascertainable useful life. Assume that the painting would not be depreciable if it were used in a trade or business or held for the production of income. Assume that the value of A's term interest, determined under section 7520, is $1,220,000, and that A establishes that a willing buyer of A's interest would pay $500,000 for the interest.

Example 6. A's term interest is not a qualified interest under § 25.2702-3. However, because of the nature of the property, A's failure to exercise A's rights with regard to the painting would not be expected to cause the value of the painting to be higher than it would otherwise be at the time it passes to B. Accordingly, A's interest is valued under § 25.2702-2(c)(1) at $500,000. The amount of A's gift is $1,500,000, the difference between the fair market value of the painting and the amount determined under § 25.2702-2(c)(1).

Example 7. Assume that the only evidence produced by A to establish the value of A's 10-year term interest is the amount paid by a museum for the right to use a comparable painting for 1 year. A asserts that the value of the 10-year term is 10 times the value of the 1-year term. A has not established the value of the 10-year term interest because a series of short-term rentals the aggregate duration of which equals the duration of the actual term interest does not establish what a willing buyer would pay a willing seller for the 10-year term interest. However, the value of the 10-year term interest is not less than the value of the 1-year term because it can be assumed that a willing buyer would pay no less for a 10-year term interest than a 1-year term interest.

Example 8. Assume that after 24 months A and B sell the painting for $2,000,000 and invest the proceeds in a portfolio of securities. A continues to hold an income interest in the securities for the duration of the 10-year term. Under § 25.2702-2(c)(4) the conversion of the painting into a type of property a term interest in which would not qualify for valuation under § 25.2702-2(c)(1) is treated as a transfer by A of the value of the unexpired portion of A's original term interest, unless the property is thereafter held in a trust meeting the requirements of a qualified annuity interest. Assume that the value of A's remaining term interest in $2,000,000 (determined under section 7520 using the section 7520 rate in effect on the date of the original transfer) is $1,060,000. The value of the unexpired portion of A's interest is $434,426, the amount that bears the same relation to $1,060,000 as $500,000 (the value of A's interest as of the date of the original transfer determined under paragraph (c)(1) of this section) bears to $1,220,000 (the value of A's interest as of the date of the original transfer determined under section 7520). [Reg. § 25.2702-2.]

☐ [*T.D.* 8395, 1-28-92. *Amended by T.D.* 9181, 2-24-2005.]

[Reg. § 25.2702-3]

§ 25.2702-3. Qualified interests.—(a) *In general.*—This section provides rules for determining if an interest is a qualified annuity interest, a qualified unitrust interest, or a qualified remainder interest.

(b) *Special rules for qualified annuity interests.*—An interest is a qualified annuity interest only if it meets the requirements of this paragraph and paragraph (d) of this section.

(1) *Payment of annuity amount.*—(i) *In general.*—A qualified annuity interest is an irrevocable right to receive a fixed amount. The annuity amount must be payable to (or for the benefit of) the holder of the annuity interest at least annually. A right of withdrawal, whether or not cumulative, is not a qualified annuity interest. Issuance of a note, other debt instrument, option, or other similar financial arrangement, directly or indirectly, in satisfaction of the annuity amount does not constitute payment of the annuity amount.

(ii) *Fixed amount.*—A fixed amount means—

(A) A stated dollar amount payable periodically, but not less frequently than annually, but only to the extent the amount does not exceed 120 percent of the stated dollar amount payable in the preceding year; or

(B) A fixed fraction or percentage of the initial fair market value of the property transferred to the trust, as finally determined for federal tax purposes, payable periodically but not less frequently than annually, but only to the extent the fraction or percentage does not exceed 120 percent of the fixed fraction or percentage payable in the preceding year.

(iii) *Income in excess of the annuity amount.*—An annuity interest does not fail to be a qualified annuity interest merely because the trust permits income in excess of the amount required to pay the annuity amount to be paid to or for the benefit of the holder of the qualified annuity interest. Nevertheless, the right to receive the excess income is not a qualified interest and is not taken into account in valuing the qualified annuity interest.

(2) *Incorrect valuations of trust property.*—If the annuity is stated in terms of a fraction or percentage of the initial fair market value of the trust property, the governing instrument must contain provisions meeting the requirements of

§ 1.664-2 (a) (1) (iii) of this chapter (relating to adjustments for any incorrect determination of the fair market value of the property in the trust).

(3) *Period for payment of annuity amount.*—The annuity amount may be payable based on either the anniversary date of the creation of the trust or the taxable year of the trust. In either situation, the annuity amount may be paid annually or more frequently, such as semi-annually, quarterly, or monthly. If the payment is made based on the anniversary date, proration of the annuity amount is required only if the last period during which the annuity is payable to the grantor is a period of less than 12 months. If the payment is made based on the taxable year, proration of the annuity amount is required for each short taxable year of the trust during the grantor's term. The prorated amount is the annual annuity amount multiplied by a fraction, the numerator of which is the number of days in the short period and the denominator of which is 365 (366 if February 29 is a day included in the numerator).

(4) *Payment of the annuity amount in certain circumstances.*—An annuity amount payable based on the anniversary date of the creation of the trust must be paid no later than 105 days after the anniversary date. An annuity amount payable based on the taxable year of the trust may be paid after the close of the taxable year, provided the payment is made no later than the date by which the trustee is required to file the Federal income tax return of the trust for the taxable year (without regard to extensions). If the trustee reports for the taxable year pursuant to § 1.671-4(b) of this chapter, the annuity payment must be made no later than the date by which the trustee would have been required to file the Federal income tax return of the trust for the taxable year (without regard to extensions) had the trustee reported pursuant to § 1.671-4(a) of this chapter.

(5) *Additional contributions prohibited.*—The governing instrument must prohibit additional contributions to the trust.

(c) *Special rules for qualified unitrust interests.*—An interest is a qualified unitrust interest only if it meets the requirements of this paragraph and paragraph (d) of this section.

(1) *Payment of unitrust amount.*—(i) *In general.*—A qualified unitrust interest is an irrevocable right to receive payment periodically, but not less frequently than annually, of a fixed percentage of the net fair market value of the trust assets, determined annually. For rules relating to computation of the net fair market value of the trust assets see § 25.2522(c)-3(c)(2)(vii). The unitrust amount must be payable to (or for the benefit of) the holder of the unitrust interest at least annually. A right of withdrawal, whether or not cumulative, is not a qualified unitrust interest. Issuance of a note, other debt instrument, option, or other similar financial arrangement, directly or indirectly, in satisfaction of the unitrust amount does not constitute payment of the unitrust amount.

(ii) *Fixed percentage.*—A fixed percentage is a fraction or percentage of the net fair market value of the trust assets, determined annually, payable periodically but not less frequently than annually, but only to the extent the fraction or percentage does not exceed 120 percent of the fixed fraction or percentage payable in the preceding year.

(iii) *Income in excess of unitrust amount.*—A unitrust interest does not fail to be a qualified unitrust interest merely because the trust permits income in excess of the amount required to pay the unitrust amount to be paid to or for the benefit of the holder of the qualified unitrust interest. Nevertheless, the right to receive the excess income is not a qualified interest and is not taken into account in valuing the qualified unitrust interest.

(2) *Incorrect valuations of trust property.*—The governing instrument must contain provisions meeting the requirements of § 1.664-3(a)(1)(iii) of this chapter (relating to the incorrect determination of the fair market value of the property in the trust).

(3) *Period for payment of unitrust amount.*—The unitrust amount may be payable based on either the anniversary date of the creation of the trust or the taxable year of the trust. In either situation, the unitrust amount may be paid annually or more frequently, such as semi-annually, quarterly, or monthly. If the payment is made based on the anniversary date, proration of the unitrust amount is required only if the last period during which the annuity is payable to the grantor is a period of less than 12 months. If the payment is made based on the taxable year, proration of the unitrust amount is required for each short taxable year of the trust during the grantor's term. The prorated amount is the annual unitrust amount multiplied by a fraction, the numerator of which is the number of days in the short period and the denominator of which is 365 (366 if February 29 is a day included in the numerator).

(4) *Payment of the unitrust amount in certain circumstances.*—A unitrust amount payable based on the anniversary date of the creation of the trust must be paid no later than 105 days after the anniversary date. A unitrust amount payable based on the taxable year of the trust may be paid after the close of the taxable year, provided the payment is made no later than the date by which the trustee is required to file the Federal income tax return of the trust for the taxable year (without regard to extensions). If the trustee reports for the taxable year pursuant to

§ 1.671-4(b) of this chapter, the unitrust payment must be made no later than the date by which the trustee would have been required to file the Federal income tax return of the trust for the taxable year (without regard to extensions) had the trustee reported pursuant to § 1.671-4(a) of this chapter.

(d) *Requirements applicable to qualified annuity interests and qualified unitrust interests.*—(1) *In general.*—To be a qualified annuity or unitrust interest, an interest must be a qualified annuity interest in every respect or a qualified unitrust interest in every respect. For example, if the interest consists of the right to receive each year a payment equal to the lesser of a fixed amount of the initial trust assets or a fixed percentage of the annual value of the trust assets, the interest is not a qualified interest. If, however, the interest consists of the right to receive each year a payment equal to the greater of a stated dollar amount or a fixed percentage of the initial trust assets or a fixed percentage of the annual value of the trust assets, the interest is a qualified interest that is valued at the greater of the two values. To be a qualified interest, the interest must meet the definition of and function exclusively as a qualified interest from the creation of the trust.

(2) *Contingencies.*—A holder's qualified interest must be payable in any event to or for the benefit of the holder for the fixed term of that interest. Thus, payment of the interest cannot be subject to any contingency other than either the survival of the holder until the commencement, or throughout the term, of that holder's interest, or, in the case of a revocable interest described in § 25.2702-2(a)(6), the transferor's right to revoke the qualified interest of that transferor's spouse.

(3) *Amounts payable to other persons.*—The governing instrument must prohibit distributions from the trust to or for the benefit of any person other than the holder of the qualified annuity or unitrust interest during the term of the qualified interest.

(4) *Term of the annuity or unitrust interest.*— The governing instrument must fix the term of the annuity or unitrust and the term of the interest must be fixed and ascertainable at the creation of the trust. The term must be for the life of the holder, for a specified term of years, or for the shorter (but not the longer) of those periods. Successive term interests for the benefit of the same individual are treated as the same term interest.

(5) *Commutation.*—The governing instrument must prohibit commutation (prepayment) of the interest of the holder.

(6) *Use of debt obligations to satisfy the annuity or unitrust payment obligation.*—(i) *In general.*—In the case of a trust created on or after September 20, 1999, the trust instrument must prohibit the

trustee from issuing a note, other debt instrument, option, or other similar financial arrangement in satisfaction of the annuity or unitrust payment obligation.

(ii) *Special rule in the case of a trust created prior to September 20, 1999.*—In the case of a trust created prior to September 20, 1999, the interest will be treated as a qualified interest under section 2702(b) if—

(A) Notes, other debt instruments, options, or similar financial arrangements are not issued after September 20, 1999, to satisfy the annuity or unitrust payment obligation; and

(B) Any notes or any other debt instruments that were issued to satisfy the annual payment obligation on or prior to September 20, 1999, are paid in full by December 31, 1999, and any option or similar financial arrangement issued to satisfy the annual payment obligation is terminated by December 31, 1999, such that the grantor receives cash or other trust assets in satisfaction of the payment obligation. For purposes of the preceding sentence, an option will be considered terminated only if the grantor receives cash or other trust assets equal in value to the greater of the required annuity or unitrust payment plus interest computed under section 7520 of the Internal Revenue Code, or the fair market value of the option.

(e) *Examples.*—The following examples illustrate the rules of paragraphs (b), (c), and (d) of this section. Each example assumes that all applicable requirements for a qualified interest are met unless otherwise specifically stated.

Example 1. A transfers property to an irrevocable trust, retaining the right to receive the greater of $10,000 or the trust income in each year for a term of 10 years. Upon expiration of the 10-year term, the trust is to terminate and the entire trust corpus is to be paid to A's child, provided that if A dies within the 10-year term the trust corpus is to be paid to A's estate. A's annual payment right is a qualified annuity interest to the extent of the right to receive $10,000 per year for 10 years or until A's prior death, and is valued under section 7520 without regard to the right to receive any income in excess of $10,000 per year. The contingent reversion is valued at zero. The amount of A's gift is the fair market value of the property transferred to the trust less the value of the qualified annuity interest.

Example 2. U transfers property to an irrevocable trust, retaining the right to receive $10,000 in each of years 1 through 3, $12,000 in each of years 4 through 6, and $15,000 in each of years 7 through 10. The interest is a qualified annuity interest to the extent of U's right to receive $10,000 per year in years 1 through 3, $12,000 in years 4 through 6, $14,400 in year 7, and $15,000 in years 8 through 10, because those amounts represent the lower of the amount actually payable each year or an amount that does not exceed

120 percent of the stated dollar amount for the preceding year.

Example 3. S transfers property to an irrevocable trust, retaining the right to receive $50,000 in each of years 1 through 3 and $10,000 in each of years 4 through 10. S's entire retained interest is a qualified annuity interest.

Example 4. R transfers property to an irrevocable trust retaining the right to receive annually an amount equal to the lesser of 8 percent of the initial fair market value of the trust property or the trust income for the year. R's annual payment right is not a qualified annuity interest to any extent because R does not have the irrevocable right to receive a fixed amount for each year of the term.

Example 5. A transfers property to an irrevocable trust, retaining the right to receive 5 percent of the net fair market value of the trust property, valued annually, for 10 years. If A dies within the 10-year term, the unitrust amount is to be paid to A's estate for the balance of the term. The interest of A (and A's estate) to receive the unitrust amount for the specified term of 10 years in all events is a qualified unitrust interest for a term of 10 years.

Example 6. The facts are the same as in *Example 5*, except that if A dies within the 10-year term the unitrust amount will be paid to A's estate for an additional 35 years. As in *Example 5*, the interest of A (and A's estate) to receive the unitrust amount for a specified term of 10 years in all events is a qualified unitrust interest for a term of 10 years. However, the right of A's estate to continue to receive the unitrust amount after the expiration of the 10-year term if A dies within that 10-year period is not fixed and ascertainable at the creation of the interest and is not a qualified unitrust interest.

Example 7. B transfers property to an irrevocable trust retaining the right to receive annually an amount equal to 8 percent of the initial fair market value of the trust property for 10 years. Upon expiration of the 10-year term, the trust is to terminate and the entire trust corpus is to be paid to B's child. The governing instrument provides that income in excess of the annuity amount may be paid to B's child in the trustee's discretion. B's interest is not a qualified annuity interest to any extent because a person other than the individual holding the term interest may receive distributions from the trust during the term.

Example 8. A transfers property to an irrevocable trust, retaining the right to receive an annuity equal to 6 percent of the initial net fair market value of the trust property for 10 years, or until A's prior death. At the expiration of the 10-year term, or on A's death prior to the expiration of the 10-year term, the annuity is to be paid to B, A's spouse, if then living, for 10 years or until B's prior death. A retains an inter vivos and testamentary power to revoke B's interest during the initial 10-year term. If not exercised by A during

the initial 10-year term (whether during A's life or on A's death), A's right to revoke B's interest will lapse upon either A's death during the 10-year term, or the expiration of A's 10-year term (assuming A survives the term). Upon expiration of B's interest (or on the expiration of A's interest if A revokes B's interest or if B predeceases A), the trust terminates and the trust corpus is payable to A's child. Because A has made a completed gift of the remainder interest, the transfer of property to the trust is not incomplete as to all interests in the property and section 2702 applies. A's annuity interest (A's right to receive the annuity for 10 years, or until A's prior death) is a retained interest that is a qualified annuity interest under paragraphs (b) and (d) of this section. In addition, because A has retained the power to revoke B's interest, B's interest is treated as an interest retained by A for purposes of section 2702. B's successive annuity interest otherwise satisfies the requirements for a qualified interest contained in paragraph (d) of this section, but for A's power to revoke. The term of B's interest is specified in the governing instrument and is fixed and ascertainable at the creation of the trust, and B's right to receive the annuity is contingent only on B's survival, and A's power to revoke. Following the expiration of A's interest, the annuity is to be paid for a 10-year term or for B's (the successor holder's) life, whichever is shorter. Accordingly, A is treated as retaining B's revocable qualified annuity interest pursuant to § 25.2702-2(a)(6). Because both A's interest and B's interest are treated as qualified interests retained by A, the value of the gift is the value of the property transferred to the trust less the value of both A's qualified interest and B's qualified interest (subject to A's power to revoke), each valued as a single-life annuity. If A survives the 10-year term without having revoked B's interest, then A's power to revoke lapses and A will make a completed gift to B at that time. Further, if A revokes B's interest prior to the commencement of that interest, A is treated as making an additional completed gift at that time to A's child. In either case, the amount of the gift would be the present value of B's interest determined under section 7520 and the applicable regulations, as of the date the revocation power lapses or the interest is revoked. See § 25.2511-2(f).

Example 9. (i) A transfers property to an irrevocable trust, retaining the right to receive 6 percent of the initial net fair market value of the trust property for 10 years, or until A's prior death. If A survives the 10-year term, the trust terminates and the trust corpus is payable to A's child. If A dies prior to the expiration of the 10-year term, the annuity is payable to B, A's spouse, if then living, for the balance of the 10-year term, or until B's prior death. A retains the right to revoke B's interest. Upon expiration of B's interest (or upon A's death if A revokes B's interest or if B predeceases A), the trust terminates and the trust corpus is payable to A's child. As is the case in *Example 8*, A's retained annuity interest (A's right to receive the annuity for 10 years, or until A's prior death) is a qualified annuity interest under paragraphs (b) and (d) of this section. However, B's interest does not meet the requirements of paragraph (d) of this section. The term of B's annuity is not fixed and ascertainable at the creation of the trust, because it is not payable for the life of B, a specified term of years, or for the shorter of those periods. Rather, B's annuity is payable for an unspecified period that will depend upon the number of years left in the original term after A's death. Further, B's annuity is payable only if A dies prior to the expiration of the 10-year term. Thus, payment of B's annuity is not dependent solely on B's survival, but rather is dependent on B's failure to survive.

(ii) Accordingly, the amount of the gift is the fair market value of the property transferred to the trust reduced by the value of A's qualified interest (A's right to receive the stated annuity for 10 years or until A's prior death). B's interest is not a qualified interest and is thus valued at zero under section 2702.

(f) *Qualified remainder interest.*—(1) *Requirements.*—An interest is a qualified remainder interest only if it meets all of the following requirements:

(i) It is a qualified remainder interest in every respect.

(ii) It meets the definition of and functions exclusively as a qualified interest from the creation of the interest.

(iii) It is non-contingent. For this purpose, an interest is non-contingent only if it is payable to the beneficiary or the beneficiary's estate in all events.

(iv) All interests in the trust, other than non-contingent remainder interests, are qualified annuity interests or qualified unitrust interests. Thus, an interest is a qualified remainder interest only if the governing instrument does not permit payment of income in excess of the annuity or unitrust amount to the holder of the qualified annuity or unitrust interest.

(2) *Remainder interest.*—Remainder interest is the right to receive all or a fractional share of the trust property on termination of all or a fractional share of the trust. Remainder interest includes a reversion. A transferor's right to receive an amount that is a stated or pecuniary amount is not a remainder interest. Thus, the right to receive the original value of the trust corpus (or a fractional share) is not a remainder interest.

(3) *Examples.*—The following examples illustrate rules of this paragraph (f). Each example assumes that all applicable requirements of a qualified interest are met unless otherwise specifically stated.

Example 1. A transfers property to an irrevocable trust. The income of the trust is payable to A's child for life. On the death of A's child, the trust is to terminate and the trust corpus is to be paid to A. A's remainder interest is not a qualified remainder interest because the interest of A's child is neither a qualified annuity interest nor a qualified unitrust interest.

Example 2. The facts are the same as in *Example 1*, except that A's child has the right to receive the greater of the income of the trust or $10,000 per year. A's remainder interest is not a qualified remainder interest because the right of A's child to receive income in excess of the annuity amount is not a qualified interest.

Example 3. A transfers property to an irrevocable trust. The trust provides a qualified annuity interest to A's child for 12 years. An amount equal to the initial value of the trust corpus is to be paid to A at the end of that period and the balance is to be paid to A's grandchild. A's interest is not a qualified remainder interest because the amount A is to receive is not a fractional share of the trust property.

Example 4. U transfers property to an irrevocable trust. The trust provides a qualified unitrust interest to U's child for 15 years, at which time the trust terminates and the trust corpus is paid to U or, if U is not then living, to U's child. Because U's remainder interest is contingent, it is not a qualified remainder interest. [Reg. § 25.2702-3.]

☐ [*T.D.* 8395, 1-28-92. *Amended by T.D.* 8536, 5-4-94; *T.D.* 8633, 12-20-95; *T.D.* 8899, 9-1-2000 (*corrected* 11-27-2000) *and T.D.* 9181, 2-24-2005.]

[Reg. § 25.2702-4]

§ 25.2702-4. Certain property treated as held in trust.—(a) *In general.*—For purposes of section 2702, a transfer of an interest in property with respect to which there are one or more term interests is treated as a transfer in trust. A term interest is one of a series of successive (as contrasted with concurrent) interests. Thus, a life interest in property or an interest in property for a term of years is a term interest. However, a term interest does not include a fee interest in property merely because it is held as a tenant in common, a tenant by the entireties, or a joint tenant with right of survivorship.

(b) *Leases.*—A leasehold interest in property is not a term interest to the extent the lease is for full and adequate consideration (without regard to section 2702). A lease will be considered for full and adequate consideration if, under all the facts and circumstances as of the time the lease is entered into or extended, a good faith effort is made to determine the fair rental value of the property and the terms of the lease conform to the value so determined.

(c) *Joint purchases.*—Solely for purposes of section 2702, if an individual acquires a term interest in property and, in the same transaction or series of transactions, one or more members of the individual's family acquire an interest in the same property, the individual acquiring the term interest is treated as acquiring the entire property so acquired, and transferring to each of those family members the interests acquired by that family member in exchange for any consideration paid by that family member. For purposes of this paragraph (c), the amount of the individual's gift will not exceed the amount of consideration furnished by that individual for all interests in the property.

(d) *Examples.*—The following examples illustrate rules of this section:

Example 1. A purchases a 20-year term interest in an apartment building and A's child purchases the remainder interest in the property. A and A's child each provide the portion of the purchase price equal to the value of their respective interests in the property determined under section 7520. Solely for purposes of section 2702, A is treated as acquiring the entire property and transferring the remainder interest to A's child in exchange for the portion of the purchase price provided by A's child. In determining the amount of A's gift, A's retained interest is valued at zero because it is not a qualified interest.

Example 2. K holds rental real estate valued at $100,000. K sells a remainder interest in the property to K's child, retaining the right to receive the income from the property for 20 years. Assume the purchase price paid by K's child for the remainder interest is equal to the value of the interest determined under section 7520. K's retained interest is not a qualified interest and is therefore valued at zero. K has made a gift in the amount of $100,000 less the consideration received from K's child.

Example 3. G and G's child each acquire a fifty percent undivided interest as tenants in common in an office building. The interests of G and G's child are not term interests to which section 2702 applies.

Example 4. B purchases a life estate in property from R, B's grandparent, for $100 and B's child purchases the remainder interest for $50. Assume that the value of the property is $300, the value of the life estate determined under section 7520 is $250 and the value of the remainder interest is $50. B is treated as acquiring the entire property and transferring the remainder interest to B's child. However, the amount of B's gift is $100, the amount of consideration ($100) furnished by B for B's interest.

Example 5. H and W enter into a written agreement relative to their marital and property rights that requires W to transfer property to an irrevocable trust, the terms of which provide that the income of the trust will be paid to H for 10 years. On the expiration of the 10-year term, the trust is to terminate and the trust corpus is to be paid to W. H and W divorce within two years after the

agreement is entered into. Pursuant to section 2516, the transfer to H would otherwise be deemed to be for full and adequate consideration. Section 2702 does not apply to the acquisition of the term interest by H because no member of H's family acquired an interest in the property in the same transaction or series of transactions. The result would not be the same if, on the termination of H's interest in the trust, the trust corpus were distributable to the children of H and W rather than W. [Reg. §25.2702-4.]

☐ [*T.D.* 8395, 1-28-92.]

[Reg. §25.2702-5]

§25.2702-5. Personal residence trusts.— (a)(1) *In general.*—Section 2702 does not apply to a transfer in trust meeting the requirements of this section. A transfer in trust meets the requirements of this section only if the trust is a personal residence trust (as defined in paragraph (b) of this section). A trust meeting the requirements of a qualified personal residence trust (as defined in paragraph (c) of this section) is treated as a personal residence trust. A trust of which the term holder is the grantor that otherwise meets the requirements of a personal residence trust (or a qualified personal residence trust) is not a personal residence trust (or a qualified personal residence trust) if, at the time of transfer, the term holder of the trust already holds term interests in two trusts that are personal residence trusts (or qualified personal residence trusts) of which the term holder was the grantor. For this purpose, trusts holding fractional interests in the same residence are treated as one trust.

(2) *Modification of trust.*—A trust that does not comply with one or more of the regulatory requirements under paragraph (b) or (c) of this section will, nonetheless, be treated as satisfying these requirements if the trust is modified, by judicial reformation (or nonjudicial reformation if effective under state law), to comply with the requirements. In the case of a trust created after December 31, 1996, the reformation must be commenced within 90 days after the due date (including extensions) for the filing of the gift tax return reporting the transfer of the residence under section 6075 and must be completed within a reasonable time after commencement. If the reformation is not completed by the due date (including extensions) for filing the gift tax return, the grantor or grantor's spouse must attach a statement to the gift tax return stating that the reformation has been commenced or will be commenced within the 90-day period. In the case of a trust created before January 1, 1997, the reformation must be commenced within 90 days after December 23, 1997, and must be completed within a reasonable time after commencement.

(b) *Personal residence trust.*—(1) *In general.*—A personal residence trust is a trust the governing instrument of which prohibits the trust from holding, for the original duration of the term interest, any asset other than one residence to be used or held for use as a personal residence of the term holder and qualified proceeds (as defined in paragraph (b)(3) of this section). A residence is held for use as a personal residence of the term holder so long as the residence is not occupied by any other person (other than the spouse or a dependent of the term holder) and is available at all times for use by the term holder as a personal residence. A trust does not meet the requirements of this section if, during the original duration of the term interest, the residence may be sold or otherwise transferred by the trust or may be used for a purpose other than as a personal residence of the term holder. In addition, the trust does not meet the requirements of this section unless the governing instrument prohibits the trust from selling or transferring the residence, directly or indirectly, to the grantor, the grantor's spouse, or an entity controlled by the grantor or the grantor's spouse, at any time after the original duration of the term interest during which the trust is a grantor trust. For purposes of the preceding sentence, a sale or transfer to another grantor trust of the grantor or the grantor's spouse is considered a sale or transfer to the grantor or the grantor's spouse; however, a distribution (for no consideration) upon or after the expiration of the original duration of the term interest to another grantor trust of the grantor or the grantor's spouse pursuant to the express terms of the trust will not be considered a sale or transfer to the grantor or the grantor's spouse if such other grantor trust prohibits the sale or transfer of the property to the grantor, the grantor's spouse, or an entity controlled by the grantor or the grantor's spouse. In the event the grantor dies prior to the expiration of the original duration of the term interest, this paragraph (b)(1) does not apply to the distribution (for no consideration) of the residence to any person (including the grantor's estate) pursuant to the express terms of the trust or pursuant to the exercise of a power retained by the grantor under the terms of the trust. Further, this paragraph (b)(1) does not apply to any outright distribution (for no consideration) of the residence to the grantor's spouse after the expiration of the original duration of the term interest pursuant to the express terms of the trust. For purposes of this paragraph (b)(1), a *grantor trust* is a trust treated as owned in whole or in part by the grantor or the grantor's spouse pursuant to sections 671 through 678, and *control* is defined in § 25.2701-2(b)(5)(ii) and (iii). Expenses of the trust whether or not attributable to trust principal may be paid directly by the term holder of the trust.

(2) *Personal residence.*—(i) *In general.*—For purposes of this paragraph (b), a personal residence of a term holder is either—

(A) The principal residence of the term holder (within the meaning of section 1034);

(B) One other residence of the term holder (within the meaning of section 280A(d)(1) but without regard to section 280A(d)(2)); or

(C) An undivided fractional interest in either.

(ii) *Additional property.*—A personal residence may include appurtenant structures used by the term holder for residential purposes and adjacent land not in excess of that which is reasonably appropriate for residential purposes (taking into account the residence's size and location). The fact that a residence is subject to a mortgage does not affect its status as a personal residence. The term personal residence does not include any personal property (*e.g.*, household furnishings).

(iii) *Use of residence.*—A residence is a personal residence only if its primary use is as a residence of the term holder when occupied by the term holder. The principal residence of the term holder will not fail to meet the requirements of the preceding sentence merely because a portion of the residence is used in an activity meeting the requirements of section 280A(c)(1) or (4) (relating to deductibility of expenses related to certain uses), provided that such use is secondary to use of the residence as a residence. A residence is not used primarily as a residence if it is used to provide transient lodging and substantial services are provided in connection with the provision of lodging (*e.g.* a hotel or a bed and breakfast). A residence is not a personal residence if, during any period not occupied by the term holder, its primary use is other than as a residence.

(iv) *Interests of spouses in the same residence.*—If spouses hold interests in the same residence (including community property interests), the spouses may transfer their interests in the residence (or a fractional portion of their interests in the residence) to the same personal residence trust, provided that the governing instrument prohibits any person other than one of the spouses from holding a term interest in the trust concurrently with the other spouse.

(3) *Qualified proceeds.*—Qualified proceeds means the proceeds payable as a result of damage to, or destruction or involuntary conversion (within the meaning of section 1033) of, the residence held by a personal residence trust, provided that the governing instrument requires that the proceeds (including any income thereon) be reinvested in a personal residence within two years from the date on which the proceeds are received.

(c) *Qualified personal residence trust.*—(1) *In general.*—A qualified personal residence trust is a trust meeting all the requirements of this paragraph (c). These requirements must be met by provisions in the governing instrument, and these governing instrument provisions must by their terms continue in effect during the existence of any term interest in the trust.

(2) *Personal residence.*—(i) *In general.*—For purposes of this paragraph (c), a personal residence of a term holder is either—

(A) The principal residence of the term holder (within the meaning of section 1034);

(B) One other residence of the term holder (within the meaning of section 280A(d)(1) but without regard to section 280A(d)(2)); or

(C) An undivided fractional interest in either.

(ii) *Additional property.*—A personal residence may include appurtenant structures used by the term holder for residential purposes and adjacent land not in excess of that which is reasonably appropriate for residential purposes (taking into account the residence's size and location). The fact that a residence is subject to a mortgage does not affect its status as a personal residence. The term personal residence does not include any personal property (*e.g.*, household furnishings).

(iii) *Use of residence.*—A residence is a personal residence only if its primary use is as a residence of the term holder when occupied by the term holder. The principal residence of the term holder will not fail to meet the requirements of the preceding sentence merely because a portion of the residence is used in an activity meeting the requirements of section 280A(c)(1) or (4) (relating to deductibility of expenses related to certain uses), provided that such use is secondary to use of the residence as a residence. A residence is not used primarily as a residence if it is used to provide transient lodging and substantial services are provided in connection with the provision of lodging (*e.g.* a hotel or a bed and breakfast). A residence is not a personal residence if, during any period not occupied by the term holder, its primary use is other than as a residence.

(iv) *Interests of spouses in the same residence.*—If spouses hold interests in the same residence (including community property interests), the spouses may transfer their interests in the residence (or a fractional portion of their interests in the residence) to the same qualified personal residence trust, provided that the governing instrument prohibits any person other than one of the spouses from holding a term interest in the trust concurrently with the other spouse.

(3) *Income of the trust.*—The governing instrument must require that any income of the trust be distributed to the term holder not less frequently than annually.

(4) *Distributions from the trust to other persons.*—The governing instrument must prohibit distributions of corpus to any beneficiary other than the transferor prior to the expiration of the retained term interest.

(5) *Assets of the trust.*—(i) *In general.*—Except as otherwise provided in paragraphs (c)(5)(ii) and (c)(8) of this section, the governing instrument must prohibit the trust from holding, for the entire term of the trust, any asset other than one residence to be used or held for use (within the meaning of paragraph (c)(7)(i) of this section) as a personal residence of the term holder (the "residence").

(ii) *Assets other than personal residence.*—Except as otherwise provided, the governing instrument may permit a qualified personal residence trust to hold the following assets (in addition to the residence) in the amounts and in the manner described in this paragraph (c)(5)(ii):

(A) *Additions of cash for payment of expenses, etc.*—(1) *Additions.*—The governing instrument may permit additions of cash to the trust, and may permit the trust to hold additions of cash in a separate account, in an amount which, when added to the cash already held in the account for such purposes, does not exceed the amount required:

(i) For payment of trust expenses (including mortgage payments) already incurred or reasonably expected to be paid by the trust within six months from the date the addition is made;

(ii) For improvements to the residence to be paid by the trust within six months from the date the addition is made; and

(iii) For purchase by the trust of the initial residence, within three months of the date the trust is created, provided that no addition may be made for this purpose, and the trust may not hold any such addition, unless the trustee has previously entered into a contract to purchase that residence; and

(iv) For purchase by the trust of a residence to replace another residence, within three months of the date the addition is made, provided that no addition may be made for this purpose, and the trust may not hold any such addition, unless the trustee has previously entered into a contract to purchase that residence.

(2) *Distributions of excess cash.*—If the governing instrument permits additions of cash to the trust pursuant to paragraph (c)(5)(ii)(A)(1) of this section, the governing instrument must require that the trustee determine, not less frequently than quarterly, the amounts held by the trust for payment of expenses in excess of the amounts permitted by that paragraph and must require that those amounts be distributed immediately thereafter to the term holder. In addition, the governing instrument must require, upon

termination of the term holder's interest in the trust, any amounts held by the trust for the purposes permitted by paragraph (c)(5)(ii)(A)(1) of this section that are not used to pay trust expenses due and payable on the date of termination (including expenses directly related to termination) be distributed outright to the term holder within 30 days of termination.

(B) *Improvements.*—The governing instrument may permit improvements to the residence to be added to the trust and may permit the trust to hold such improvements, provided that the residence, as improved, meets the requirements of a personal residence.

(C) *Sale proceeds.*—The governing instrument may permit the sale of the residence (except as set forth in paragraph (c)(9) of this section) and may permit the trust to hold proceeds from the sale of the residence, in a separate account.

(D) *Insurance and insurance proceeds.*—The governing instrument may permit the trust to hold one or more policies of insurance on the residence. In addition, the governing instrument may permit the trust to hold, in a separate account, proceeds of insurance payable to the trust as a result of damage to or destruction of the residence. For purposes of this paragraph, amounts (other than insurance proceeds payable to the trust as a result of damage to or destruction of the residence) received as a result of the involuntary conversion (within the meaning of section 1033) of the residence are treated as proceeds of insurance.

(6) *Commutation.*—The governing instrument must prohibit commutation (prepayment) of the term holder's interest.

(7) *Cessation of use as a personal residence.*—(i) *In general.*—The governing instrument must provide that a trust ceases to be a qualified personal residence trust if the residence ceases to be used or held for use as a personal residence of the term holder. A residence is held for use as a personal residence of the term holder so long as the residence is not occupied by any other person (other than the spouse or a dependent of the term holder) and is available at all times for use by the term holder as a personal residence. See §25.2702-5(c)(8) for rules governing disposition of assets of a trust as to which the trust has ceased to be a qualified personal residence trust.

(ii) *Sale of personal residence.*—The governing instrument must provide that the trust ceases to be a qualified personal residence trust upon sale of the residence if the governing instrument does not permit the trust to hold proceeds of sale of the residence pursuant to paragraph (c)(5)(ii)(C) of this section. If the governing instrument permits the trust to hold proceeds of sale pursuant to that paragraph, the

governing instrument must provide that the trust ceases to be a qualified personal residence trust with respect to all proceeds of sale held by the trust not later than the earlier of—

(A) The date that is two years after the date of sale;

(B) The termination of the term holder's interest in the trust; or

(C) The date on which a new residence is acquired by the trust.

(iii) *Damage to or destruction of personal residence.*—(A) *In general.*—The governing instrument must provide that, if damage or destruction renders the residence unusable as a residence, the trust ceases to be a qualified personal residence trust on the date that is two years after the date of damage or destruction (or the date of termination of the term holder's interest in the trust, if earlier) unless, prior to such date—

(1) Replacement of or repairs to the residence are completed; or

(2) A new residence is acquired by the trust.

(B) *Insurance proceeds.*—For purposes of this paragraph (C)(7)(iii), if the governing instrument permits the trust to hold proceeds of insurance received as a result of damage to or destruction of the residence pursuant to paragraph (c)(5)(ii)(D) of this section, the governing instrument must contain provisions similar to those required by paragraph (c)(7)(ii) of this section.

(8) *Disposition of trust assets on cessation as personal residence trust.*—(i) *In general.*—The governing instrument must provide that, within 30 days after the date on which the trust has ceased to be a qualified personal residence trust with respect to certain assets, either—

(A) The assets be distributed outright to the term holder;

(B) The assets be converted to and held for the balance of the term holder's term in a separate share of the trust meeting the requirements of a qualified annuity interest; or

(C) In the trustee's sole discretion, the trustee may elect to comply with either paragraph (C)(8)(i)(A) or (B) of this section pursuant to their terms.

(ii) *Requirements for conversion to a qualified annuity interest.*—(A) *Governing instrument requirements.*—For assets subject to this paragraph (c)(8) to be converted to and held as a qualified annuity interest, the governing instrument must contain all provisions required by §25.2702-3 with respect to a qualified annuity interest.

(B) *Effective date of annuity.*—The governing instrument must provide that the right of the term holder to receive the annuity amount begins on the date of sale of the residence, the date of damage to or destruction of the residence, or the date on which the residence ceases to be used or held for use as a personal residence, as the case may be ("the cessation date"). Notwithstanding the preceding sentence, the governing instrument may provide that the trustee may defer payment of any annuity amount otherwise payable after the cessation date until the date that is 30 days after the assets are converted to a qualified annuity interest under paragraph (c)(8)(i)(B) of this section ("the conversion date"); provided that any deferred payment must bear interest from the cessation date at a rate not less than the section 7520 rate in effect on the cessation date. The governing instrument may permit the trustee to reduce aggregate deferred annuity payments by the amount of income actually distributed by the trust to the term holder during the deferral period.

(C) *Determination of annuity amount.—* (1) *In general.—*The governing instrument must require that the annuity amount be no less than the amount determined under this paragraph (C).

(2) *Entire trust ceases to be a qualified personal residence trust.—*If, on the conversion date, the assets of the trust do not include a residence used or held for use as a personal residence, the annuity may not be less than an amount determined by dividing the lesser of the value of all interests retained by the term holder (as of the date of the original transfer or transfers) or the value of all the trust assets (as of the conversion date) by an annuity factor determined—

(i) For the original term of the term holder's interest; and

(ii) At the rate used in valuing the retained interest at the time of the original transfer.

(3) *Portion of trust continues as qualified personal residence trust.—*If, on the conversion date, the assets of the trust include a residence used or held for use as a personal residence, the annuity must not be less than the amount determined under paragraph (c)(8)(ii)(C)(2) of this section multiplied by a fraction. The numerator of the fraction is the excess of the fair market value of the trust assets on the conversion date over the fair market value of the assets as to which the trust continues as a qualified personal residence trust, and the denominator of the fraction is the fair market value of the trust assets on the conversion date.

(9) *Sale of residence to grantor, grantor's spouse, or entity controlled by grantor or grantor's spouse.—*The governing instrument must prohibit the trust from selling or transferring the residence, directly or indirectly, to the grantor, the grantor's spouse, or an entity controlled by the grantor or the grantor's spouse during the

retained term interest of the trust, or at any time after the retained term interest that the trust is a grantor trust. For purposes of the preceding sentence, a sale or transfer to another grantor trust of the grantor or the grantor's spouse is considered a sale or transfer to the grantor or the grantor's spouse; however, a distribution (for no consideration) upon or after the expiration of the retained term interest to another grantor trust of the grantor or the grantor's spouse pursuant to the express terms of the trust will not be considered a sale or transfer to the grantor or the grantor's spouse if such other grantor trust prohibits the sale or transfer of the property to the grantor, the grantor's spouse, or an entity controlled by the grantor or the grantor's spouse. In the event the grantor dies prior to the expiration of the retained term interest, this paragraph (c)(9) does not apply to the distribution (for no consideration) of the residence to any person (including the grantor's estate) pursuant to the express terms of the trust or pursuant to the exercise of a power retained by the grantor under the terms of the trust. Further, this paragraph (c)(9) does not apply to an outright distribution (for no consideration) of the residence to the grantor's spouse after the expiration of the retained trust term pursuant to the express terms of the trust. For purposes of this paragraph (c)(9), a *grantor trust* is a trust treated as owned in whole or in part by the grantor or the grantor's spouse pursuant to sections 671 through 678, and *control* is defined in § 25.2701-2(b)(5)(ii) and (iii).

(d) *Examples.—*The following examples illustrate rules of this section. Each example assumes that all applicable requirements of a personal residence trust (or qualified personal residence trust) are met unless otherwise stated.

Example 1. C maintains C's principal place of business in one room of C's principal residence. The room meets the requirements of section 280A(c)(1) for deductibility of expenses related to such use. The residence is a personal residence.

Example 2. L owns a vacation condominium that L rents out for six months of the year, but which is treated as L's residence under section 280A(d)(1) because L occupies it for at least 18 days per year. L provides no substantial services in connection with the rental of the condominium. L transfers the condominium to an irrevocable trust, the terms of which meet the requirements of a qualified personal residence trust. L retains the right to use the condominium during L's lifetime. The trust is a qualified personal residence trust.

Example 3. W owns a 200-acre farm. The farm includes a house, barns, equipment buildings, a silo, and enclosures for confinement of farm animals. W transfers the farm to an irrevocable trust, retaining the use of the farm for 20 years, with the remainder to W's child. The trust is not a personal residence trust because the farm includes assets not meeting the requirements of a personal residence.

Example 4. A transfers A's principal residence to an irrevocable trust, retaining the right to use the residence for a 20-year term. The governing instrument of the trust does not prohibit the trust from holding personal property. The trust is not a qualified personal residence trust.

Example 5. T transfers a personal residence to a trust that meets the requirements of a qualified personal residence trust, retaining a term interest in the trust for 10 years. During the period of T's retained term interest, T is forced for health reasons to move to a nursing home. T's spouse continues to occupy the residence. If the residence is available at all times for T's use as a residence during the term (without regard to T's ability to actually use the residence), the residence continues to be held for T's use and the trust does not cease to be a qualified personal residence trust. The residence would cease to be held for use as a personal residence of T if the trustee rented the residence to an unrelated party, because the residence would no longer be available for T's use at all times.

Example 6. T transfers T's personal residence to a trust that meets the requirements of a qualified personal residence trust, retaining the right to use the residence for 12 years. On the date the residence is transferred to the trust, the fair market value of the residence is $100,000. After 6 years, the trustee sells the residence, receiving net proceeds of $250,000, and invests the proceeds of sale in common stock. After an additional eighteen months, the common stock has paid $15,000 in dividends and has a fair market value of $260,000. On that date, the trustee purchases a new residence for $200,000. On the purchase of the new residence, the trust ceases to be a qualified personal residence trust with respect to any amount not reinvested in the new residence. The governing instrument of the trust provides that the trustee, in the trustee's sole discretion, may elect either to distribute the excess proceeds or to convert the proceeds into a qualified annuity interest. The trustee elects the latter option. The amount of the annuity is the amount of the annuity that would be payable if no portion of the sale proceeds had been reinvested in a personal residence multiplied by a fraction. The numerator of the fraction is $60,000 (the amount remaining after reinvestment) and the denominator of the fraction is $260,000 (the fair market value of the trust assets on the conversion date). The obligation to pay the annuity commences on the date of sale, but payment of the annuity that otherwise would have been payable during the period between the date of sale and the date on which the trust ceased to be a qualified personal residence trust with respect to the excess proceeds may be deferred until 30 days after the date on which the new residence is purchased. Any amount deferred must bear compound interest from the date the annuity is payable at the section 7520 rate in effect on the date of sale. The $15,000 of income distributed to the term holder during that period may be used to reduce the annuity amount payable with respect to that period if the governing instrument so provides and thus reduce the amount on which compound interest is computed. [Reg. § 25.2702-5.]

[*T.D.* 8395, 1-28-92. *Amended by T.D.* 8743, 12-22-97.]

[Reg. § 25.2702-6]

§ 25.2702-6. Reduction in taxable gifts.—
(a) *Transfers of retained interests in trust.*—(1) *Inter vivos transfers.*—If an individual subsequently transfers by gift an interest in trust previously valued (when held by that individual) under § 25.2702-2(b)(1) or (c), the individual is entitled to a reduction in aggregate taxable gifts. The amount of the reduction is determined under paragraph(b) of this section. Thus, for example, if an individual transferred property to an irrevocable trust, retaining an interest in the trust that was valued at zero under § 25.2702-2(b)(1), and the individual later transfers the retained interest by gift, the individual is entitled to a reduction in aggregate taxable gifts on the subsequent transfer. For purposes of this section, aggregate taxable gifts means the aggregate sum of the individual's taxable gifts for the calendar year determined under section 2502(a)(1).

(2) *Testamentary transfers.*—If either—

(i) A term interest in trust is included in an individual's gross estate solely by reason of section 2033, or

(ii) A remainder interest in trust is included in an individual's gross estate,

and the interest was previously valued (when held by that individual) under § 25.2702-2(b)(1) or (c), the individual's estate is entitled to a reduction in the individual's adjusted taxable gifts in computing the Federal estate tax payable under section 2001. The amount of the reduction is determined under paragraph (b) of this section.

(3) *Gift splitting on subsequent transfer.*—If an individual who is entitled to a reduction in aggregate taxable gifts (or adjusted taxable gifts) subsequently transfers the interest in a transfer treated as made one-half by the individual's spouse under section 2513, the individual may assign one-half of the amount of the reduction to the consenting spouse. The assignment must be attached to the Form 709 on which the consenting spouse reports the split gift.

(b) *Amount of reduction.*—(1) *In general.*—The amount of the reduction in aggregate taxable gifts (or adjusted taxable gifts) is the lesser of—

(i) The increase in the individual's taxable gifts resulting from the interest being valued at the time of the initial transfer under § 25.2702-2(b)(1) or (c); or

(ii) The increase in the individual's taxable gifts (or gross estate) resulting from the subsequent transfer of the interest.

(2) *Treatment of annual exclusion.*—For purposes of determining the amount under paragraph (b)(1)(ii) of this section, the exclusion under section 2503(b) applies first to transfers in that year other than the transfer of the interest previously valued under § 25.2702-2(b)(1) or (c).

(3) *Overlap with section 2001.*—Notwithstanding paragraph (b)(1) of this section, the amount of the reduction is reduced to the extent section 2001 would apply to reduce the amount of an individual's adjusted taxable gifts with respect to the same interest to which paragraph (b)(1) of this section would otherwise apply.

(c) *Examples.*—The rules of this section are illustrated by the following examples. The following facts apply for *Examples 1-4:*

Facts. In 1992, X transferred property to an irrevocable trust retaining the right to receive the trust income for life. On the death of X, the trust is to terminate and the trust corpus is to be paid to X's child, C. X's income interest had a value under section 7520 of $40,000 at the time of the transfer; however, because X's retained interest was not a qualified interest, it was valued at zero under § 25.2702-2(b)(1) for purposes of determining the amount of X's gift. X's taxable gifts in 1992 were therefore increased by $40,000. In 1993, X transfers the income interest to C for no consideration.

Example 1. Assume that the value under section 7520 of the income interest on the subsequent transfer to C is $30,000. If X makes no other gifts to C in 1993, X is entitled to a reduction in aggregate taxable gifts of $20,000, the lesser of the amount by which X's taxable gifts were increased as a result of the income interest being valued at zero on the initial transfer ($40,000) or the amount by which X's taxable gifts are increased as a result of the subsequent transfer of the income interest ($30,000 minus $10,000 annual exclusion).

Example 2. Assume that in 1993, 4 months after X transferred the income interest to C, X transferred $5,000 cash to C. In determining the increase in taxable gifts occurring on the subsequent transfer, the annual exclusion under section 2503(b) is first applied to the cash gift. X is entitled to a reduction in aggregate taxable gifts of $25,000, the lesser of the amount by which X's taxable gifts were increased as a result of the income interest being valued at zero on the initial transfer ($40,000) or the amount by which X's taxable gifts are increased as a result of the subsequent transfer of the income interest ($25,000 (($30,000 + $5,000) – $10,000 annual exclusion).

Example 3. Assume that the value under section 7520 of the income interest on the subsequent transfer to C is $55,000. X is entitled to reduce aggregate taxable gifts by $40,000, the lesser of the amount by which X's taxable gifts were increased as a result of the income interest being valued at zero on the initial transfer ($40,000) or the amount by which X's taxable gifts are increased as a result of the subsequent transfer of the income interest ($55,000 minus $10,000 annual exclusion = $45,000).

Example 4. Assume that X and X's spouse, S, split the subsequent gift to C. X is entitled to assign one-half the reduction to S. If the assignment is made, each is entitled to reduce aggregate taxable gifts by $17,500, the lesser of their portion of the increase in taxable gifts on the initial transfer by reason of the application of section 2702 ($20,000) and their portion of the increase in taxable gifts on the subsequent transfer of the retained interest ($27,500 – $10,000 annual exclusion).

Example 5. In 1992, A transfers property to an irrevocable trust, retaining the right to receive the trust income for 10 years. On the expiration of the 10-year term, the trust is to terminate and the trust corpus is to be paid to A's child, B. Assume that A's term interest has a value under section 7520 of $20,000 at the time of the transfer; however, because A's retained interest was not a qualified interest, it was valued at zero under § 25.2702-2(b)(1) for purposes of determining the amount of A's gift. Assume also that A and A's spouse, S, split the gift of the remainder interest under section 2513. In 1993, A transfers A's term interest to D, A's other child, for no consideration. A is entitled to reduce A's aggregate taxable gifts on the transfer. Assume that A and S also split the subsequent gift to D, and that A dies one month after making the subsequent transfer of the term interest and S dies six months later. The gift of the term interest is included in A's gross estate under section 2035(d)(2). To the extent S's taxable gifts are reduced pursuant to section 2001(e), S is entitled to no reduction in aggregate or adjusted taxable gifts under this section.

Example 6. T transfers property to an irrevocable trust retaining the power to direct the distribution of trust income for 10 years among T's descendants in whatever shares T deems appropriate. On the expiration of the 10-year period, the trust corpus is to be paid in equal shares to T's children. T's transfer of the remainder interest is a completed gift. Because T's retained interest is not a qualified interest, it is valued at zero under § 25.2702-2(b)(1) and the amount of T's gift is the fair market value of the property transferred to the trust. The distribution of income each year is not a transfer of a retained interest in trust. Therefore, T is not entitled to reduce aggregate taxable gifts as a result of the distributions of income from the trust.

Example 7. The facts are the same as in *Example 6,* except that after 3 years T exercises the right to direct the distribution of trust income by assigning the right to the income for the balance of the term to T's child, C. The exercise is a transfer of a retained interest in trust for purposes of this section. T is entitled to reduce aggregate taxable gifts by the lesser of the increase in taxable gifts resulting from the application of section 2702 to the initial transfer or the increase in taxable gifts resulting from the transfer of the retained interest in trust.

Example 8. In 1992, V purchases an income interest for 10 years in property in the same transaction or series of transactions in which G, V's child, purchases the remainder interest in the same property. V dies in 1997 still holding the term interest, the value of which is includible in V's gross estate under section 2033. V's estate would be entitled to a reduction in adjusted taxable gifts in the amount determined under paragraph (b) of this section. [Reg. § 25.2702-6.]

☐ [*T.D.* 8395, 1-28-92.]

[Reg. § 25.2702-7]

§ 25.2702-7. Effective dates.—Except as provided in this section, §§ 25.2702-1 through 25.2702-6 apply as of January 28, 1992. With respect to transfers to which section 2702 applied made prior to January 28, 1992, taxpayers may rely on any reasonable interpretation of the statutory provisions. For these purposes, the provisions of the proposed regulations and the final regulations are considered a reasonable interpretation of the statutory provisions. The fourth through eighth sentences of § 25.2702-5(b)(1) and § 25.2702-5(c)(9) apply with respect to trusts created after May 16, 1996. Section 25.2702-2(a)(5), the second and third sentences of § 25.2702-2(a)(6), § 25.2702-3(d)(2), the first two sentences of § 25.2702-3(d)(4), the last sentence of § 25.2702-3(e), *Example 5,* the last two sentences of § 25.2702-3(e), *Example 6,* and § 25.2702-3(e), *Examples 8* and *9,* apply for trusts created on or after July 26, 2004. However, the Internal Revenue Service will not challenge any prior application of the changes to *Examples 5* and *6* in § 25.2702-3(e). [Reg. § 25.2702-7.]

☐ [*T.D.* 8395, 1-28-92. *Amended by T.D.* 8743, 12-22-97 *and T.D.* 9181, 2-24-2005.]

[Reg. § 25.2703-1]

§ 25.2703-1. Property subject to restrictive arrangements.—(a) *Disregard of rights or restrictions.*—(1) *In general.*—For purposes of subtitle B (relating to estate, gift, and generation-skipping transfer taxes), the value of any property is determined without regard to any right or restriction relating to the property.

(2) *Right or restriction.*—For purposes of this section, right or restriction means—

(i) Any option, agreement, or other right to acquire or use the property at a price less than fair market value (determined without regard to the option, agreement, or right); or

(ii) Any restriction on the right to sell or use the property.

(3) *Agreements, etc., containing rights or restrictions.*—A right or restriction may be contained in a partnership agreement, articles of incorporation, corporate bylaws, a shareholders' agreement, or any other agreement. A right or restriction may be implicit in the capital structure of an entity.

(4) *Qualified easements.*—A perpetual restriction on the use of real property that qualified for a charitable deduction under either section 2522(d) or section 2055(f) of the Internal Revenue Code is not treated as a right or restriction.

(b) *Exceptions.*—(1) *In general.*—This section does not apply to any right or restriction satisfying the following three requirements—

(i) The right or restriction is a bona fide business arrangement;

(ii) The right or restriction is not a device to transfer property to the natural objects of the transferor's bounty for less than full and adequate consideration in money or money's worth; and

(iii) At the time the right or restriction is created, the terms of the right or restriction are comparable to similar arrangements entered into by persons in an arm's length transaction.

(2) *Separate requirements.*—Each of the three requirements described in paragraph (b)(1) of this section must be independently satisfied for a right or restriction to meet this exception. Thus, for example, the mere showing that a right or restriction is a bona fide business arrangement is not sufficient to establish that the right or restriction is not a device to transfer property for less than full and adequate consideration.

(3) *Exception for certain rights or restrictions.*—A right or restriction is considered to meet each of the three requirements described in paragraph (b)(1) of this section if more than 50 percent by value of the property subject to the right or restriction is owned directly or indirectly (within the meaning of § 25.2701-6) by individuals who are not members of the transferor's family. In order to meet this exception, the property owned by those individuals must be subject to the right or restriction to the same extent as the property owned by the transferor. For purposes of this section, members of the transferor's family include the persons described in § 25.2701-2(b)(5) and any other individual who is a natural object of the transferor's bounty. Any property held by a member of the transferor's family under the rules of § 25.2701-6 (without regard to § 25.2701-6(a)(5)) is treated as held only by a member of the transferor's family.

Reg. § 25.2703-1(b)(3)

(4) *Similar arrangement.*—(i) *In general.*—A right or restriction is treated as comparable to similar arrangements entered into by persons in an arm's length transaction if the right or restriction is one that could have been obtained in a fair bargain among unrelated parties in the same business dealing with each other at arm's length. A right or restriction is considered a fair bargain among unrelated parties in the same business if it conforms with the general practice of unrelated parties under negotiated agreements in the same business. This determination generally will entail consideration of such factors as the expected term of the agreement, the current fair market value of the property, anticipated changes in value during the term of the arrangement, and the adequacy of any consideration given in exchange for the rights granted.

(ii) *Evidence of general business practice.*—Evidence of general business practice is not met by showing isolated comparables. If more than one valuation method is commonly used in a business, a right or restriction does not fail to evidence general business practice merely because it uses only one of the recognized methods. It is not necessary that the terms of a right or restriction parallel the terms of any particular agreement. If comparables are difficult to find because the business is unique, comparables from similar businesses may be used.

(5) *Multiple rights or restrictions.*—If property is subject to more than one right or restriction described in paragraph (a)(2) of this section, the failure of a right or restriction to satisfy the requirements of paragraph (b)(1) of this section does not cause any other right or restriction to fail to satisfy those requirements if the right or restriction otherwise meets those requirements. Whether separate provisions are separate rights or restrictions, or are integral parts of a single right or restriction, depends on all the facts and circumstances.

(c) *Substantial modification of a right or restriction.*—(1) *In general.*—A right or restriction that is substantially modified is treated as a right or restriction created on the date of the modification. Any discretionary modification of a right or restriction, whether or not authorized by the terms of the agreement, that results in other than a *de minimis* change to the quality, value, or timing of the rights of any party with respect to property that is subject to the right or restriction is a substantial modification. If the terms of the right or restriction require periodic updating, the failure to update is presumed to substantially modify the right or restriction unless it can be shown that updating would not have resulted in a substantial modification. The addition of any family member as a party to a right or restriction (including by reason of a transfer of property that subjects the transferee family member to a right or restriction with respect to the transferred property) is considered a substantial modification unless the addition is mandatory under the terms of the right or restriction or the added family member is assigned to a generation (determined under the rules of section 2651 of the Internal Revenue Code) no lower than the lowest generation occupied by individuals already party to the right or restriction).

(2) *Exceptions.*—A substantial modification does not include—

(i) A modification required by the terms of a right or restriction;

(ii) A discretionary modification of an agreement conferring a right or restriction if the modification does not change the right or restriction;

(iii) A modification of a capitalization rate used with respect to a right or restriction if the rate is modified in a manner that bears a fixed relationship to a specified market interest rate; and

(iv) A modification that results in an option price that more closely approximates fair market value.

(d) *Examples.*—The following examples illustrate the provisions of this section:

Example 1. T dies in 1992 owning title to Blackacre. In 1991, T and T's child entered into a lease with respect to Blackacre. At the time the lease was entered into, the terms of the lease were not comparable to leases of similar property entered into among unrelated parties. The lease is a restriction on the use of the property that is disregarded in valuing the property for Federal estate tax purposes.

Example 2. T and T's child, C, each own 50 percent of the outstanding stock of X corporation. T and C enter into an agreement in 1987 providing for the disposition of stock held by the first to die at the time of death. The agreement also provides certain restrictions with respect to lifetime transfers. In 1992, as permitted (but not required) under the agreement, T transfers one-half of T's stock to T's spouse, S. S becomes a party to the agreement between T and C by reason of the transfer. The transfer is the addition of a family member to the right or restriction. However, it is not a substantial modification of the right or restriction because the added family member would be assigned to a generation under section 2651 of the Internal Revenue Code no lower than the generation occupied by C.

Example 3. The facts are the same as in *Example 2.* In 1993, the agreement is amended to reflect a change in the company's name and a change of address for the company's registered agent. These changes are not a substantial modification of the agreement conferring the right or restriction because the right or restriction has not changed. [Reg. § 25.2703-1.]

□ [*T.D.* 8395, 1-28-92.]

[Reg. § 25.2703-2]

§ 25.2703-2. Effective date.—Section 25.2703-1 applies to any right or restriction created or substantially modified after October 8, 1990, and is effective as of January 28, 1992. With respect to transfers occurring prior to January 28, 1992, and for purposes of determining whether an event occurring prior to January 28, 1992 constitutes a substantial modification, taxpayers may rely on any reasonable interpretation of the statutory provisions. For these purposes, the provisions of the proposed regulations and the final regulations are considered a reasonable interpretation of the statutory provisions. [Reg. § 25.2703-2.]

☐ [*T.D.* 8395, 1-28-92.]

[Reg. § 25.2704-1]

§ 25.2704-1. Lapse of certain rights.— (a) *Lapse treated as transfer.*—(1) *In general.*—The lapse of a voting right or a liquidation right in a corporation or partnership (an "entity") is a transfer by the individual directly or indirectly holding the right immediately prior to its lapse (the "holder") to the extent provided in paragraphs (b) and (c) of this section. This section applies only if the entity is controlled by the holder and members of the holder's family immediately before and after the lapse. The amount of the transfer is determined under paragraph (d) of this section. If the lapse of a voting right or a liquidation right occurs during the holder's lifetime, the lapse is a transfer by gift. If the lapse occurs at the holder's death, the lapse is a transfer includible in the holder's gross estate.

(2) *Definitions.*—The following definitions apply for purposes of this section.

(i) *Control.*—Control has the meaning given it in § 25.2701-2(b)(5).

(ii) *Member of the family.*—Member of the family has the meaning given it in § 25.2702-2(a)(1).

(iii) *Directly or indirectly held.*—An interest is directly or indirectly held only to the extent the value of the interest would have been includible in the gross estate of the individual if the individual had died immediately prior to the lapse.

(iv) *Voting right.*—Voting right means a right to vote with respect to any matter of the entity. In the case of a partnership, the right of a general partner to participate in partnership management is a voting right. The right to compel the entity to acquire all or a portion of the holder's equity interest in the entity by reason of aggregate voting power is treated as a liquidation right and is not treated as a voting right.

(v) *Liquidation right.*—Liquidation right means a right or ability to compel the entity to acquire all or a portion of the holder's equity interest in the entity, including by reason of aggregate voting power, whether or not its exercise would result in the complete liquidation of the entity.

(vi) *Subordinate.*—Subordinate has the meaning given it in § 25.2701-3(a)(2)(iii).

(3) *Certain temporary lapses.*—If a lapsed right may be restored only upon the occurrence of a future event not within the control of the holder or members of the holder's family, the lapse is deemed to occur at the time the lapse becomes permanent with respect to the holder, *i.e.* either by a transfer of the interest or otherwise.

(4) *Source of right or lapse.*—A voting right or a liquidation right may be conferred by and may lapse by reason of a State law, the corporate charter or bylaws, an agreement, or other means.

(b) *Lapse of voting right.*—A lapse of a voting right occurs at the time a presently exercisable voting right is restricted or eliminated.

(c) *Lapse of liquidation right.*—(1) *In general.*— A lapse of a liquidation right occurs at the time a presently exercisable liquidation right is restricted or eliminated. Except as otherwise provided, a transfer of an interest that results in the lapse of a liquidation right is not subject to this section if the rights with respect to the transferred interest are not restricted or eliminated. However, a transfer that results in the elimination of the transferor's right or ability to compel the entity to acquire an interest retained by the transferor that is subordinate to the transferred interest is a lapse of a liquidation right with respect to the subordinate interest.

(2) *Exceptions.*—Section 2704(a) does not apply to the lapse of a liquidation right under the following circumstances.

(i) *Family cannot obtain liquidation value.*— (A) *In general.*—Section 2704(a) does not apply to the lapse of a liquidation right to the extent the holder (or the holder's estate) and members of the holder's family cannot immediately after the lapse liquidate an interest that the holder held directly or indirectly and could have liquidated prior to the lapse.

(B) *Ability to liquidate.*—Whether an interest can be liquidated immediately after the lapse is determined under the State law generally applicable to the entity, as modified by the governing instruments of the entity, but without regard to any restriction described in section 2704(b). Thus, if, after any restriction described in section 2704(b) is disregarded, the remaining requirements for liquidation under the governing instruments are less restrictive than the State law that would apply in the absence of the governing instruments, the ability to liquidate is determined by reference to the governing instruments.

(ii) *Rights valued under section 2701.*—Section 2704(a) does not apply to the lapse of a liquidation right previously valued under section 2701 to the extent necessary to prevent double taxation (taking into account any adjustment available under § 25.2701-5).

(iii) *Certain changes in State law.*—Section 2704(a) does not apply to the lapse of a liquidation right that occurs solely by reason of a change in State law. For purposes of this paragraph, a change in the governing instrument of an entity is not a change in State law.

(d) *Amount of transfer.*—The amount of the transfer is the excess, if any, of—

(1) The value of all interests in the entity owned by the holder immediately before the lapse (determined immediately after the lapse as if the lapsed right was nonlapsing); over

(2) The value of the interests described in the preceding paragraph immediately after the lapse (determined as if all such interests were held by one individual).

(e) *Application to similar rights.*—[RESERVED]

(f) *Examples.*—The following examples illustrate the provisions of this section:

Example 1. Prior to D's death, D owned all the preferred stock of Corporation Y and D's children owned all the common stock. At that time, the preferred stock had 60 percent of the total voting power and the common stock had 40 percent. Under the corporate by-laws, the voting rights of the preferred stock terminated on D's death. The value of D's interest immediately prior to D's death (determined as if the voting rights were non-lapsing) was $100X. The value of that interest immediately after death would have been $90X if the voting rights had been non-lapsing. The decrease in value reflects the loss in value resulting from the death of D (whose involvement in Y was a key factor in Y's profitability). Section 2704(a) applies to the lapse of voting rights on D's death. D's gross estate includes an amount equal to the excess, if any, of $90X over the fair market value of the preferred stock determined after the lapse of the voting rights.

Example 2. Prior to D's death, D owned all the preferred stock of Corporation Y. The preferred stock and the common stock each carried 50 percent of the total voting power of Y. D's children owned 40 percent of the common stock and unrelated parties own the remaining 60 percent. Under the corporate by-laws, the voting rights of the preferred stock terminate on D's death. Section 2704(a) does not apply to the lapse of D's voting rights because members of D's family do not control Y after the lapse.

Example 3. The by-laws of Corporation Y provide that the voting rights of any transferred shares of the single outstanding class of stock are reduced to ½ vote per share after the transfer but are fully restored to the transferred shares after 5 years. D owned 60 percent of the shares prior to death and members of D's family owned the balance. On D's death, D's shares pass to D's children and the voting rights are reduced pursuant to the by-laws. Section 2704(a) applies to the lapse of D's voting rights. D's gross estate includes an amount equal to the excess, if any, of the fair market value of D's stock (determined immediately after D's death as though the voting rights had not been reduced and would not be reduced) over the stock's fair market value immediately after D's death.

Example 4. D owns 84 percent of the single outstanding class of stock of Corporation Y. The by-laws require at least 70 percent of the vote to liquidate Y. D gives one-half of D's stock in equal shares to D's three children (14 percent to each). Section 2704(a) does not apply to the loss of D's ability to liquidate Y, because the voting rights with respect to the corporation are not restricted or eliminated by reason of the transfer.

Example 5. D and D's two children, A and B, are partners in Partnership X. Each has a 3⅓ percent general partnership interest and a 30 percent limited partnership interest. Under State law, a general partner has the right to participate in partnership management. The partnership agreement provides that when a general partner withdraws or dies, X must redeem the general partnership interest for its liquidation value. Also, under the agreement any general partner can liquidate the partnership. A limited partner cannot liquidate the partnership and a limited partner's capital interest will be returned only when the partnership is liquidated. A deceased limited partner's interest continues as a limited partnership interest. D dies, leaving his limited partnership interest to D's spouse. Because of a general partner's right to dissolve the partnership, a limited partnership interest has a greater fair market value when held in conjunction with a general partnership interest than when held alone. Section 2704(a) applies to the lapse of D's liquidation right because after the lapse, members of D's family could liquidate D's limited partnership interest. D's gross estate includes an amount equal to the excess of the value of all D's interests in X immediately before D's death (determined immediately after D's death but as though the liquidation right had not lapsed and would not lapse) over the fair market value of all D's interests in X immediately after D's death.

Example 6. The facts are the same as in *Example 5*, except that under the partnership agreement D is the only general partner who holds a unilateral liquidation right. Assume further that the partnership agreement contains a restriction described in section 2704(b) that prevents D's family members from liquidating D's limited partnership interest immediately after D's death. Under State law, in the absence of the restriction in the partnership agreement, D's family members could liquidate the partnership. The restriction on the family's ability to liquidate is disregarded and the amount of D's gross estate is increased by reason of the lapse of D's liquidation right.

Example 7. D owns all the stock of Corporation X, consisting of 100 shares of non-voting preferred stock and 100 shares of voting common stock. Under the by-laws, X can only be liquidated with the consent of at least 80 percent of the voting shares. D transfers 30 shares of common stock to D's child. The transfer is not a lapse of a liquidation right with respect to the common stock because the voting rights that enabled D to liquidate prior to the transfer are not restricted or eliminated. The transfer is not a lapse of a liquidation right with respect to the retained preferred stock because the preferred stock is not subordinate to the transferred common stock.

Example 8. D owns all of the single class of stock of Corporation Y. D recapitalizes Y, exchanging D's common stock for voting common stock and non-voting, non-cumulative preferred stock. The preferred stock carries a right to put the stock for its par value at any time during the next 10 years. D transfers the common stock to D's grandchild in a transfer subject to section 2701. In determining the amount of D's gift under section 2701, D's retained put right is valued at zero. D's child, C, owns the preferred stock when the put right lapses. Section 2704(a) applies to the lapse, without regard to the application of section 2701, because the put right was not valued under section 2701 in the hands of C.

Example 9. A and A's two children are equal general and limited partners in Partnership Y. Under the partnership agreement, each general partner has a right to liquidate the partnership at any time. Under State law that would apply in the absence of contrary provisions in the partnership agreement, the death or incompetency of a general partner terminates the partnership. However, the partnership agreement provides that the partnership does not terminate on the incompetence or death of a general partner, but that an incompetent partner cannot exercise rights as a general partner during any period of incompetency. A partner's full rights as general partner are restored if the partner regains competency. A becomes incompetent. The lapse of A's voting right on becoming incompetent is not subject to section 2704(a) because it may be restored to A in the future. However, if A dies while incompetent, a lapse subject to section 2704(a) is deemed to occur at that time because the lapsed right cannot thereafter be restored to A. [Reg. § 25.2704-1.]

☐ [T.D. 8395, 1-28-92.]

[Reg. § 25.2704-2]

§ 25.2704-2. Transfers subject to applicable restrictions.—(a) *In general.*—If an interest in a corporation or partnership (an "entity") is transferred to or for the benefit of a member of the transferor's family, any applicable restriction is disregarded in valuing the transferred interest. This section applies only if the transferor and members of the transferor's family control the entity immediately before the transfer. For the definition of control, see § 25.2701-2(b)(5). For the definition of member of the family, see § 25.2702-2(a)(1).

(b) *Applicable restriction defined.*—An applicable restriction is a limitation on the ability to liquidate the entity (in whole or in part) that is more restrictive than the limitations that would apply under the State law generally applicable to the entity in the absence of the restriction. A restriction is an applicable restriction only to the extent that either the restriction by its terms will lapse at any time after the transfer, or the transferor (or the transferor's estate) and any members of the transferor's family can remove the restriction immediately after the transfer. Ability to remove the restriction is determined by reference to the State law that would apply but for a more restrictive rule in the governing instruments of the entity. See § 25.2704-1(c)(1)(B) for a discussion of the term "State law." An applicable restriction does not include a commercially reasonable restriction on liquidation imposed by an unrelated person providing capital to the entity for the entity's trade or business operations whether in the form of debt or equity. An unrelated person is any person whose relationship to the transferor, the transferee, or any member of the family of either is not described in section 267(b) of the Internal Revenue Code, provided that for purposes of this section the term "fiduciary of a trust" as used in section 267(b) does not include a bank as defined in section 581 of the Internal Revenue Code. A restriction imposed or required to be imposed by Federal or State law is not an applicable restriction. An option, right to use property, or agreement that is subject to section 2703 is not an applicable restriction.

(c) *Effect of disregarding an applicable restriction.*—If an applicable restriction is disregarded under this section, the transferred interest is valued as if the restriction does not exist and as if the rights of the transferor are determined under the State law that would apply but for the restriction. For example, an applicable restriction with respect to preferred stock will be disregarded in determining the amount of a transfer of common stock under section 2701.

(d) *Examples.*—The following examples illustrate the provisions of this section:

Example 1. D owns a 76 percent interest and each of D's children, A and B, owns a 12 percent interest in General Partnership X. The partnership agreement requires the consent of all the partners to liquidate the partnership. Under the State law that would apply in the absence of the restriction in the partnership agreement, the consent of partners owning 70 percent of the total partnership interests would be required to liquidate X. On D's death, D's partnership interest passes to D's child, C. The requirement that all the partners consent to liquidation is an applicable restriction. Because A, B and C (all members of D's family), acting together after the transfer, can remove the restriction on liquidation, D's interest is valued without regard to the restriction; *i.e.*, as though D's interest is sufficient to liquidate the partnership.

Example 2. D owns all the preferred stock in Corporation X. The preferred stock carries a right to liquidate X that cannot be exercised until 1999. D's children, A and B, own all the common stock of X. The common stock is the only voting stock. In 1994, D transfers the preferred stock to D's child, A. The restriction on D's right to liquidate is an applicable restriction that is disregarded. Therefore, the preferred stock is valued as though the right to liquidate were presently exercisable.

Example 3. D owns 60 percent of the stock of Corporation X. The corporate by-laws provide that the corporation cannot be liquidated for 10 years after which time liquidation requires approval by 60 percent of the voting interests. In the absence of the provision in the by-laws, State law would require approval by 80 percent of the voting interests to liquidate X. D transfers the stock to a trust for the benefit of D's child, A, during the 10-year period. The 10-year restriction is an applicable restriction and is disregarded. Therefore, the value of the stock is determined as if the transferred block could currently liquidate X.

Example 4. D and D's children, A and B, are partners in Limited Partnership Y. Each has a 3.33 percent general partnership interest and a 30 percent limited partnership interest. Any general partner has the right to liquidate the partnership at any time. As part of a loan agreement with a lender who is related to D, each of the partners agree that the partnership may not be liquidated without the lender's consent while any portion of the loan remains outstanding. During the term of the loan agreement, D transfers one-half of both D's partnership interests to each of A and B. Because the lender is a related party, the requirement that the lender consent to liquidation is an applicable restriction and the transfers of D's interests are valued as if such consent were not required.

Example 5. D owns 60 percent of the preferred and 70 percent of the common stock in Corporation X. The remaining stock is owned by individuals unrelated to D. The preferred stock carries a put right that cannot be exercised until 1999. In 1995, D transfers the common stock to D's child in a transfer that is subject to section 2701. The restriction on D's right to liquidate is an applicable restriction that is disregarded in determining the amount of the gift under section 2701. [Reg. §25.2704-2.]

  ☐ [*T.D.* 8395, 1-28-92.]

[Reg. §25.2704-3]

§25.2704-3. Effective date.—Section 25.2704-1 applies to lapses occurring after January 28, 1992, of rights created after October 8, 1990. Section 25.2704-2 applies to transfers occurring after January 28, 1992, of property subject to applicable restrictions created after October 8, 1990. In determining whether a voting right or a liquidation right has lapsed prior to that date, and for purposes of determining whether the lapse is subject to section 2704(a), taxpayers may rely on any reasonable interpretation of the statutory provisions. For transfers of interests occurring before January 28, 1992, taxpayers may rely on any reasonable interpretation of the statutory provisions in determining whether a restriction is an applicable restriction that must be disregarded in determining the value of the transferred interest. For these purposes, the provisions of the proposed regulations and the final regulations are considered a reasonable interpretation of the statutory provisions. [Reg. §25.2704-3.]

  ☐ [*T.D.* 8395, 1-28-92.]